20 Trinity Street Cambridge

heffers:
1876-1976

A BOOKSHOP FOR ALL SEASONS

All year round we send books all over the world.
We should like to sell *you* books in our centenary year.
Pay us a visit, or post your orders to

HEFFERS BOOKSHOP
20 Trinity Street, Cambridge, England

MONEY DOES GOOD AT GUY'S

The Endowment Fund of Guy's Hospital provides new buildings, refurbishes old ones, furnishes extra facilities for research projects, and makes it possible for doctors, nurses and other staff to have not only better working conditions, but better living conditions as well.

Guy's is a great and famous hospital. It's the people who work there who make it so. A legacy, a gift, or a covenant is the best way to thank them for the work they do. Please help us by showing this advertisement to your Clients.

For further details, write to:
The Clerk to the Special Trustees,
**The Endowment Fund of Guy's Hospital,
Guy's Hospital, London SE1 9RT.**

Registered Charity No. 251983

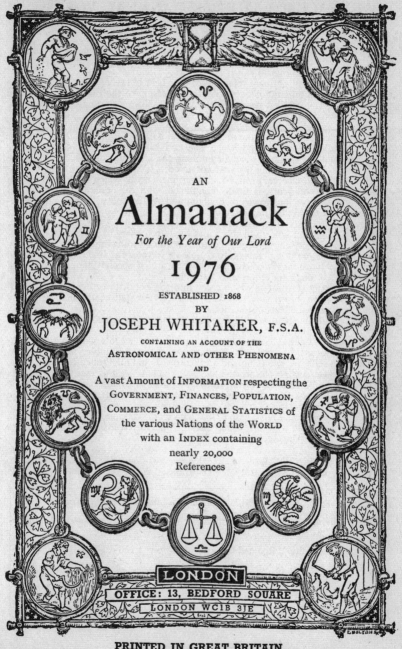

AN

Almanack

For the Year of Our Lord

1976

ESTABLISHED 1868

BY

JOSEPH WHITAKER, F.S.A.

CONTAINING AN ACCOUNT OF THE
ASTRONOMICAL AND OTHER PHENOMENA
AND
A vast Amount of INFORMATION respecting the
GOVERNMENT, FINANCES, POPULATION,
COMMERCE, and GENERAL STATISTICS of
the various Nations of the WORLD
with an INDEX containing
nearly 20,000
References

LONDON

OFFICE: 13, BEDFORD SQUARE
LONDON WC1B 3JE

PRINTED IN GREAT BRITAIN

PREFACE TO THE 108TH ANNUAL VOLUME
(1976)

In the 108th volume of " WHITAKER ", the Editor has again sought to combine the retention of the traditional and established contents of the Almanack with a number of features of topical value.

In June, in the first national referendum ever held in this country the electorate was asked to vote on Britain's continued membership of the European Economic Community. The detailed results of the voting, showing the massive affirmative vote, are given, area by area, in the Almanack.

Another precedent in British political history was the choice, for the first time, of a woman as leader of one of the major political parties. Mrs. Thatcher's election as the Conservative leader, and hence also as Leader of the Opposition, is duly chronicled, and her portrait is included among the illustrations. Changes made in Mr. Wilson's Ministry during the year are noted.

The record of the changes in the local government areas, which has been receiving attention for several years, is finally completed, with the declaration of city and borough status in various towns in England and Wales, and with the complete reorganization of the system in Scotland.

Topics of the Year comprise articles on the European Architectural Heritage Year, the U.S.-Soviet link-up in space and the tercentenary of the Royal Observatory. The two latter subjects are also commemorated by illustrations. Her Majesty the Queen is shown during her visit to the old Observatory at Greenwich during the course of the tercentenary celebrations, which are of special interest in view of " WHITAKER'S " long connection with astronomy.

The latest letter post rates, which came into force shortly before the Almanack went to press, are shown, and like many other of the statistical tables, unhappily reflect the continued effects of inflation.

A short article on the drama in England during the year has been added to the customary list of plays produced in London.

In the sports pages, a list of Olympic records is given in advance of the 1976 Olympic Games at Montreal. The section also covers a notable year for cricket, with two Test series between England and Australia, and the Prudential World Cup.

In the overseas section, the process has continued of recasting entirely the articles on a number of foreign countries, and the course of events has resulted in the inclusion for the first time of several newly independent states, notably among the former Portuguese colonies.

The Editor would once more wish to thank his world-wide circle of correspondents, official and unofficial, who have again been of the greatest assistance to him in the compilation of the Almanack.

13 BEDFORD SQUARE, W.C.1.   Telephone: 01-636 4748
    October, 1975   Telegrams: " Whitmanack, London, W.C.1. "

Note—" WHITAKER " for 1976 is published in three editions:

Library Edition, Leather Binding with 16 Coloured Maps, 1,220 pages—£4·75 *net*.
(SBN 85021 087 9)

Complete Edition, Red and Green Cloth Cover, 1,220 pages—£3·50 *net*.
(SBN 85021 085 2)

Shorter Edition, Orange Paper Cover, 692 pages—£1·60 *net*.
(SBN 85021 086 0)

© 1975   J. Whitaker & Sons, Ltd.

MADE AND PRINTED IN GREAT BRITAIN BY WILLIAM CLOWES & SONS, LIMITED
LONDON, BECCLES AND COLCHESTER

TABLE OF CONTENTS

And in "Complete Edition" and "Library Edition"

TAKE UP PELMANISM
For Courage and Clear-Thinking

The Grasshopper Mind

YOU know the people with "Grass-hopper Minds" as well as you know yourself. Their minds nibble at every thing and master nothing.

At home in the evening they tune in the radio or television—tire of it—then glance through a magazine—can't get interested. Finally, unable to concentrate on anything, they either go to the pictures or fall asleep in the chair. At their work they always take up the easiest job first, put it down when it gets hard and start something else. Jump from one thing to another all the time.

There are thousands of these people with "Grasshopper Minds" in the world. In fact they are the very people who do the world's most tiresome tasks—and get but a pittance for their work. They do the world's clerical work and the routine drudgery.

If you have a "Grasshopper Mind" you know that this is true. Even the blazing sun can't burn a hole in a piece of tissue-paper unless its rays are focused and concentrated on one spot! A mind that balks at sticking to one thing for more than a few minutes surely cannot be depended upon to get you anywhere in your years of life!

What Can You Do About It?

Take up Pelmanism now! A course of Pelmanism brings out the mind's latent powers and develops them to the highest point of efficiency. It develops strong, positive, vital qualities such as Optimism, Concentration, and Reliability, all qualities of the utmost value in any walk of life.

HOW TO LEARN LANGUAGES

The **Pelman Languages Institute** teaches **French, German, Spanish,** and **Italian** without translation. Write for particulars of the language that interests you, which will be sent to you free.

Pelman Languages Institute,
200 Tudor House, 9 Chiswick High Rd.,
London W4 2ND

What Pelmanism Does

Pelmanism enables you to overcome defects and failings. Amongst those most often met with are the following:

Inertia	Pessimism
Timidity	Forgetfulness
Indecision	Indefiniteness
Depression	Procrastination
Weakness of Will	Mind-Wandering

But Pelmanism does more than eliminate failings. It awakens dormant faculties. It develops powers you never thought you possessed. It strengthens mental attributes which are valuable in every career and every aspect of living. It develops:—

—Optimism	—Observation
—Perception	—Initiative
—Judgment	—Originality
—Self-Control	—Reliability
—Concentration	—Will-Power
—Mental Energy	—Personality
—Self-Confidence	—Resourcefulness
—Reliable Memory	—Presence of Mind

Pelmanists are not left to make the applications themselves. An experienced and sympathetic instructional staff shows them, in exact detail, how to apply the principles of Pelmanism to their own circumstances and aspirations. Thus every Pelman Course is an individual Course.

Remember—Everything you do is preceded by your attitude of mind

The general effect of the training is to induce an attitude of mind and a personal efficiency favourable to the happy management of life.

Send for the Free Book

Write to-day for a free copy of *"The Science of Success."* This will give you full details of the Course, which is private, individual to each Pelmanist, and carried out by correspondence, in your spare time, at moderate fees payable—if you like—by instalments.

PELMAN INSTITUTE
200 Tudor House
9 Chiswick High Rd.,
London W4 2ND
Established over 75 years

Pages 693–1220 are omitted from the Shorter Edition

APOSTLESHIP OF THE SEA

FOUNDED IN 1920 FOR SPIRITUAL AND MATERIAL CARE OF SEA-FARERS AND THEIR FAMILIES REGARDLESS OF RACE OR CREED

NATIONAL HEADQUARTERS:
      ANCHOR HOUSE, 81 BARKING ROAD, LONDON E16 4HB
      TEL: 01-476 6062

FORM OF BEQUEST

I GIVE AND BEQUEATH TO THE HON. TREASURER FOR THE TIME BEING OF THE APOSTLESHIP OF THE SEA (Episcopal Commission for England and Wales) ANCHOR HOUSE, LONDON E16 4HB

....

....£   :   FREE OF DUTY
TO BE PAYABLE PRIMARILY OUT OF MY PERSONAL ESTATE, AND I DECLARE THAT THE RECEIPT OF THE HON. TREASURER FOR THE TIME BEING SHALL BE A SUFFICIENT DISCHARGE FOR THE SAME.

CODICILS AS WELL AS WILLS MUST BEAR THE SIGNATURE OF TWO WITNESSES.

Pages 693–1220 are omitted from the Shorter Edition

The battle against pain...

ARTHRITIS RESEARCH

☐ **THE SAD SIX MILLION.**

One million people, including children, suffer from Rheumatoid Arthritis; and five million, including two out of every three people over 65, are handicapped by Osteoarthrosis. For them, pain is a daily experience and it can be so severe as to be barely tolerable.

☐ **HOW YOU CAN HELP.**

Please help us overcome all this pain and disability by contributing to the £1 million needed for research every year. We rely entirely on voluntary support in the form of covenants, donations and legacies. Forms of bequest and covenant are available from the Council at the address below.

THE ARTHRITIS AND RHEUMATISM COUNCIL FOR RESEARCH

IN GREAT BRITAIN AND THE COMMONWEALTH
(formerly Empire Rheumatism Council)

Patron: Her Royal Highness The Duchess of Kent
Chairman: The Rt Hon. the Lord Porritt, GCMG, GCVO, CBE, FRCP, FRCS

Faraday House, 8-10 Charing Cross Rd., London WC2 0HN

Pages 693–1220 *are omitted from the* Shorter Edition

Pages 693–1220 are omitted from the Shorter Edition

HELP
the
CENTRAL
CHURCH
FUND

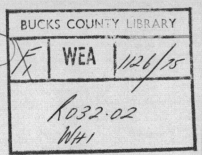
WITH A BEQUEST

As a faithful member of the Anglican Church you may want to leave a share of your estate in order to benefit the general purposes of the Church of England, after your lifetime.

You can best give effect to this desire by including in your Will a bequest to the Central Church Fund, expressed in the following suggested form of words:—

"I give and bequeath to the Central Board of Finance of the Church of England, whose registered office is at Church House, Dean's Yard, Westminster, London, SW1P 3NZ . . . . . per cent **of the residue of my estate** to be credited to the Central Church Fund and to be applied both as to capital and income to such ecclesiastical charitable purposes in the Church of England as the said Board shall in its absolute discretion decide, and I declare that the receipt of the Secretary for the time being of the said Board shall be sufficient discharge to my executors for the same."

Annual Report with Accounts and any further information available from The Secretary

THE CENTRAL BOARD OF FINANCE
OF THE CHURCH OF ENGLAND
Church House, Dean's Yard, Westminster, London SW1P 3NZ

Pages 693–1220 are omitted from the Shorter *Edition*

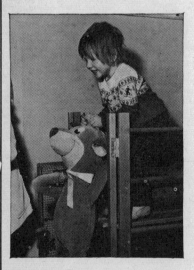

Pages 693–1220 *are omitted from the* Shorter Edition

Pages 693–1220 *are omitted from the* Shorter Edition

Pages 693–1220 *are omitted from the* Shorter Edition

Methodist Homes for the Aged

More and more generous people, wishing to give thanks for serenity and peace-of-mind in their later years, find fulfilment in remembering us in their Will. The legacies we receive make it possible for us to plan new Homes and to provide comfort and security for many who would otherwise be doomed to a lonely old-age. Please consult your legal or financial adviser or write to us for confidential advice about arranging a legacy or codicil.

WILL YOU BE *a friend in Deed!*

Secretary : Brian I. Callin M.A., B.Sc.
Pastoral Director : The Rev. Reginald W. Hopper B.D.
METHODIST HOMES FOR THE AGED
1 Central Buildings, Westminster, London, SW1H 9NS

Pages 693–1220 are omitted from the **Shorter Edition**

At one year old he was a bouncing baby

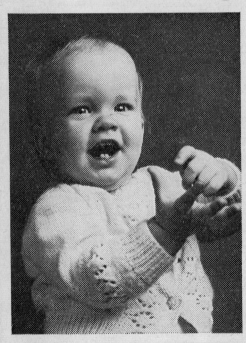

At 18 months he was toddling and a lovely, happy boy.

But gradually, heart-breakingly, his muscles began to fail until at 15 years of age he caught a chill, his respiratory system failed and he could no longer breathe.

THIS IS MUSCULAR DYSTROPHY. AS YET THERE IS NO CURE, AND WITHOUT CON-TINUOUS RESEARCH THERE NEVER WILL BE.

Please help the utterly helpless. Please tell your clients about us.

Muscular Dystrophy Group of Great Britain

Nattrass House, 35 Macaulay Road, SW4 0QP.   01-720 8055

Pages 693-1220 are omitted from the Shorter Edition

Pearson's Fresh Air Fund

Patron: HER MAJESTY THE QUEEN

Please help some of the thousands of needy or neglected children in Britain to be as happy as these.

£3 will ensure a week's holiday for a child in the country or at the seaside

PLEASE ALSO REMEMBER CHILDREN IN YOUR WILL

Donations to:

112 REGENCY STREET, LONDON, SW1P 4AX

Pages 693–1220 are omitted from the Shorter Edition

Going for a country walk is easy

For you. But not for Hilda.

Hilda, in a wheelchair for life, was a victim of Spina Bifida.

Queen Elizabeth's Foundation for the Disabled took over her rehabilitation in 1965, and gave her a resident job at their Dorincourt Workshops, handpainting tiles. There she met Sydney, also in a wheelchair, and almost completely deaf and dumb. She became his wife in 1970. Hilda and Syd now live in a flat in Great Bookham; he works at Dorincourt, Hilda now goes to work daily at a food research organisation.

Whatever it cost the Foundation was certainly money well spent, you'll say. The Foundation's four units help upwards of 1000 disabled men and women every year. And they don't do it by halves. They rehabilitate, train, re-educate. They provide residential workshops where the disabled can live and work in properly equipped surroundings. And they run a very special holiday and convalescent home.

Can you imagine how much all this costs? That is why we are asking you to send as much as you can . . . now. Every little helps – naturally a lot helps even more. Write it into your will. Mention it to your friends. Now. Please.

Queen Elizabeth's Training College • Banstead Place • Dorincourt Residential Sheltered Workshop · Lulworth Court Holiday and Convalescent Home.

Queen Elizabeth's Foundation for the Disabled

Leatherhead Court, (Room 19B), Leatherhead, Surrey.
Patron: Her Majesty Queen Elizabeth, The Queen Mother.

On average, people leave us £10,000 a month. This is why we feel entitled to ask for more.

We have some 250 patients of all ages, all suffering from illnesses which are as yet, incurable.

It costs us a great deal of money to run our Hospital and its residential annexe at Brighton. A lot of this comes from our patients (they all pay something), their sponsors, their relatives and our investments.

The balance must come from voluntary contributions. And that includes legacies.

This is why we feel privileged to ask you to consider leaving us some money.

Research.

We refuse to accept that disabled people cannot be helped or that illnesses at present incurable will not one day be cured.

For this reason we have made special provision for research in the Development Trust for the Young Disabled. Research to help the disabled everywhere. *Research that one day will cure the incurable.*

Today our own patients may be incurable, but they refuse just to sit around. We help them lead as full a life as possible, and with us, many make remarkable progress.

Our New Wing, which is being built for younger disabled patients, will have the sort of accommodation other, luckier, young people have.

And so, we are asking you to remember us in your will. Up to £100,000 left to a charity is free of tax. Your estate and our patients could both benefit. And your money would be used for a very *hopeful* cause.

Appeals Secretary:
Air Commodore D. F. Rixson, OBE., DFC., AFC.

**The Royal Hospital and Home for Incurables
(Putney and Brighton),
West Hill, Putney, London SW15 3SW.**

Pages 693–1220 are omitted from the Shorter Edition

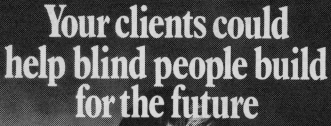

Your clients could help blind people build for the future

Every day, thirty two people go blind in this country.

Caring for them costs money – which most can ill-afford.

This means that the Royal National Institute for the Blind has to rely very heavily on charitable contributions.

Which is why we need legacies, especially of residue. Annual Deeds of Covenant are also welcome.

Our funds are spent on providing education, training, rehabilitation of the newly blind, residential care, and many other services – including research into the Prevention of blindness.

All legacies and donations will be gratefully acknowledged.

YOUR help in obtaining this essential financial assistance will be greatly appreciated.

ROYAL NATIONAL INSTITUTE FOR THE BLIND RNIB
224, Great Portland Street, London, W1N 6AA.
Registered in accordance with the National Assistance Act, 1948.

Pages 693–1220 *are omitted from the* Shorter Edition

Pages 693-1220 are omitted from the Shorter Edition

Pages 693–1220 are omitted from the Shorter Edition

Pages 693–1220 are omitted from the Shorter Edition

PEOPLE HAVE PROBLEMS,

and seamen aren't unique because they have problems too. But when you're away from home for nine months at a time, problems can sometimes snowball. And when they get too much to handle, that's where we come in. We can't give you case histories for obvious reasons, but our chaplains are experienced counsellors, and seamen come to us because they know we care. We care because we're Christians called to serve–do you care enough to help us?

The Missions to Seamen,
St. Michael Paternoster Royal,
College Hill, London EC4R 2RL

Pages 693–1220 are omitted from the Shorter Edition

Pages 693–1220 are omitted from the Shorter Edition

Pages 693–1220 are omitted from the Shorter Edition

Pages 693–1220 are omitted from the Shorter Edition

Pages 693–1220 are omitted from the **Shorter Edition**

Pages 693–1220 are omitted from the Shorter Edition

Pages 693-1220 are omitted from the Shorter Edition

Pages 693–1220 *are omitted from the* Shorter Edition

Pages 693–1220 *are omitted from the* Shorter Edition

Pages 693-1220 are omitted from the Shorter Edition

Pages 693–1220 are omitted from the Shorter Edition

Pages 693–1220 are omitted from the Shorter Edition

Pages 693–1220 are omitted from the Shorter Edition

Pages 693-1220 are omitted from the Shorter Edition

Pages 693–1220 are omitted from the **Shorter Edition**

Pages 693–1220 are omitted from the Shorter Edition

Pages 693–1220 are omitted from the Shorter Edition

Pages 693–1220 are omitted from the Shorter Edition

Pages 693–1220 are omitted from the Shorter Edition

Pages 693–1220 *are omitted from the* Shorter Edition

Pages 693–1220 are omitted from the Shorter Edition

Pages 693–1220 are omitted from the **Shorter Edition**

Pages 693–1220 are omitted from the **Shorter Edition**

Pages 693–1220 *are omitted from the* Shorter Edition

Pages 693–1220 are omitted from the Shorter Edition

Pages 693–1220 are omitted from the Shorter Edition

Pages 693–1220 are omitted from the Shorter Edition

OCCURRENCES DURING PRINTING

Home Affairs and Ireland. Sept. 17. Northern Ireland Constitutional Convention agreed that negotiations between Unionists and Nationalists should continue.

Sept. 19. Plessey Telecommunications announced immediate 2,000 redundancies because of cuts in Post Office orders for equipment.

Sept. 22. Provisional I.R.A. resumed widespread bombing; at least 12 bombs exploded in Ireland, injuring two policemen and causing widespread damage. In London three people were injured when a bomb exploded outside the Portman Hotel.

Sept. 23. Government announced cancellation of two guided missile projects—Hawker Siddeley Sub-Martel and B.A.C. Hawk-Swing—and said that similar missiles would be bought from U.S.A., France and Germany.

Newspaper Publishers Association offered rise of £6 a week to about 30,000 workers on national and London evening newspapers.

Sept. 24. Mr. Wilson announced number of steps to reduce incidence of unemployment, with special emphasis on providing work for school leavers.

Sept. 25. Bomb exploded outside public-house near Maidstone Barracks. There were only slight casualties, because a soldier saw the container before the bomb went off and gave the alarm.

Sept. 26. Local authorities agreed to pay rise for 500,000 manual workers of £6 a week, at estimated cost of £205,000,000 in full year.

Sept. 28. Ten T.A. soldiers on an exercise were drowned in River Trent near Newark.

First-class letter rate was increased from 7p to 8½p, and second-class rate from 5½ to 6½p; on Oct. 1 basic unit for ordinary telephone calls went up from 1·8p to 3p.

Sept. 29. Alderman L. R. Ring was elected Lord Mayor of London for 1975–76.

Sept. 30. At Labour Party Conference at Blackpool, Mr. Healey, Chancellor of the Exchequer, lost his place on National Executive Committee to Mr. Eric Heffer, who had been dismissed from the Government earlier in the year.

Alastair Steadman, a former R.A.F. bomber pilot, was sentenced to nine years' imprisonment for attempting to sell information to the U.S.S.R.

Oct. 1. The Lord Chief Justice refused application by the Attorney-General to prevent publication of political diaries and Cabinet memoirs of the late Richard Crossman.

Oct. 2. Mr. Malcolm Williamson was appointed Master of the Queen's Musick in succession to the late Sir Arthur Bliss.

Ten persons were killed and about 25 injured in a series of bombings and shootings in Northern Ireland.

Oct. 3. Bank of England increased its Minimum Lending Rate from 11 per cent. to 12 per cent.

Oct. 9. Bomb which exploded outside Green Park underground station killed one man and injured 18 other persons.

Oct. 13. At Horseferry Road Magistrates' Court, Westminster, committal proceedings began against John Thomas Stonehouse, Labour M.P. for Walsall, North, who faced 21 counts of forgery, fraud, theft and conspiracy, and his secretary, Mrs. Sheila Buckley, who faced five charges of theft and one of conspiracy.

A 30lb. bomb containing bolts, and with commercial gelignite produced in Eire, was defused outside a restaurant in Westminster used by M.P.s, three minutes before it was due to explode.

Mr. J. F. S. Cobb, Q.C., and Mr. R. L. A. Goff, Q.C., were appointed Judges of the High Court, Queen's Bench Division.

Overseas. Sept. 22. A shot was fired at President Ford as he left a San Francisco hotel; Sarah Jean Moore, a 45-year-old white woman, was arrested.

Sept. 25. Two British climbers, Dougal Haston and Douglas Scott, made first ascent of Everest by South-west face.

Oct. 9. Dr. Andrei Sakharov, the dissident Russian scientist, was awarded the 1975 Nobel Peace Prize.

Oct. 16. In Kenya, the Deputy Speaker and another active Government critic were arrested at gunpoint and detained, and President Kenyatta said that he would arrest all dissidents.

Obituary. Oct. 3. Guy Mollet, former French Prime Minister, aged 69.

Oct. 16. Vittorio Gui, distinguished Italian conductor, aged 90.

Oct. 17. Lord Holford, R.A., leading town planner, aged 68.

Oct. 19. Lesley Storm, playwright and novelist, aged 71.

Police Manpower in England and Wales

The Police Forces in England and Wales consist of the Metropolitan Police in London, for whom the Home Secretary is directly responsible, plus 42 locally administered, operationally independent forces (including the City of London). The Home Secretary, who is responsible for law and order, has certain powers of control and coordination of police forces. The office of Constable is an office of trust under the Crown and police officers are therefore not local authority servants or employees.

(Dec. 31)	Police			Civilians	Traffic Wardens	Cadets	Special Constables
	Men	Women	Total				
1970	90,127	3,621	93,748	26,060	5,043	4,124	32,813
1971	92,979	3,865	96,844	28,060	5,839	4,498	29,992
1972	95,494	4,187	99,681	29,316	6,356	4,630	27,440
1973	96,172	4,394	100,566	30,047	6,231	4,625	25,332
1974	97,319	4,767	102,086	32,971	5,943	5,130	24,178

The police of Scotland are administered by the Scottish Home and Health Department. On Dec. 31, 1974, there were 11,719 police in Scotland, including 532 women police. There were also 3,963 special constables (Men, 3,810; Women, 153).

On March 31, 1974, the Metropolitan Police had a total strength of 20,756, including 637 women; City Police, 794, including 25 women.

AVERAGE EARNINGS AND HOURS WORKED, 1968–1974

Year*	Manufacturing and certain other Industries.†				All Manufacturing Industries			
	Men (over 21)		Women (over 18)		Men		Women	
	Hours	Wages	Hours	Wages	Hours	Wages	Hours	Wages
		£		£		£		£
1968....................	46·4	23·00	38·3	11·30	45·8	23·62	38·2	11·31
1969....................	46·5	24·82	38·1	12·11	45·7	25·54	37·9	12·12
1970....................	45·7	28·05	37·9	13·99	44·9	28·91	37·7	13·98
1971....................	44·7	30·93	37·7	15·80	43·6	31·37	37·5	15·80
1972....................	45·0	35·82	37·9	18·30	44·1	36·20	37·7	18·34
1973....................	45·6	40·92	37·7	21·16	44·7	41·52	37·5	21·15
1974....................	45·1	48·63	37·4	27·01	44·0	49·12	37·2	27·05

* Average in October in each year.   † The other industries are mining and quarrying (except coal mining), construction, gas, electricity and water; transport and communications (except railways and London Transport); certain miscellaneous services and public administration.

RELATIVE RANK—SEA, LAND AND AIR

Officers of the Royal Navy, The Army, and The Royal Air Force rank with one another according to Seniority or Date of Appointment, as shown in the following table. Recognized abbreviations are shown in brackets. Comparable ranks in the Women's Royal Naval Service appear in *italics*. Commissioned ranks of the Women's Royal Army Corps are named as for the Army, the Director holding the rank of Brigadier. Commissioned ranks of the Women's Royal Air Force are named as for the R.A.F., the Director holding the rank of Air Commodore.

ROYAL NAVY	ARMY	ROYAL AIR FORCE
1. Admiral of the Fleet.	1. Field-Marshal (FM).	1. Marshal of the R.A.F.
2. Admiral.	2. General (Gen.).	2. Air Chief Marshal.
3. Vice Admiral (Vice-Adm.).	3. Lieutenant-General (Lt.-Gen.).	3. Air Marshal.
4. Rear-Admiral (Rear-Adm.).	4. Major-General (Maj.-Gen.).	4. Air Vice-Marshal.
5. Commodore (1st & 2nd Class) (Cdre.) (*Commandant*).	5. Brigadier (Brig.).	5. Air Commodore (Air Cdre.).
6. Captain (Capt.) (*Superintendent*) (*Supt.*).	6. Colonel (Col.).	6. Group Captain (Gp. Capt.).
7. Commander (Cdr.) (*Chief Officer*).	7. Lieutenant-Col. (Lt.-Col.).	7. Wing Commander (Wing Cdr.).
8. Lieutenant-Commander (Lt.-Cdr.) (*First Officer*).	8. Major (Maj.).	8. Squadron Leader (Sqn. Ldr.).
9. Lieutenant (Lt.) (*Second Officer*).	9. Captain (Capt.).	9. Flight-Lieutenant (Flt. Lt.).
10. Sub-Lieutenant (Sub-Lt.) (*Third Officer*).	10. Lieutenant (Lt.).	10. Flying Officer (F.O.).
11. Acting Sub-Lieutenant.	11. Second Lieutenant (2-Lt.).	11. Pilot Officer (P.O.).

Commissioned Officers of the Royal Marines rank at all times, when serving on shore, according to seniority, with Army Officers of the same titles. When serving afloat a Major, R.M., ranks with a Commander, R.N., a Captain, R.M., with 12 years' service from his First Commission ranks with a Lieutenant-Commander, R.N., and a Lieutenant, R.M., with four years' service ranks with a Lieutenant, R.N.

EXPECTATION OF LIFE

(English Life Table No. 12, 1960–62)

Expectation of life at under 1 year of age is: Males, 68·09 years; Females, 74·00 years.

Age	Male	Female	Age	Male	Female	Age	Male	Female	Age	Male	Female
1	68·80	74·43	26	44·89	50·11	51	21·84	26·69	76	6·66	8·27
2	67·90	73·52	27	43·93	49·14	52	21·02	25·81	77	6·28	7·77
3	66·97	72·58	28	42·98	48·17	53	20·21	24·95	78	5·92	7·28
4	66·02	71·62	29	42·02	47·20	54	19·42	24·09	79	5·57	6·83
5	65·06	70·66	30	41·06	46·23	55	18·65	23·24	80	5·25	6·39
6	64·09	69·69	31	40·11	45·26	56	17·89	22·39	81	4·94	5·98
7	63·13	68·71	32	39·16	44·30	57	17·16	21·56	82	4·66	5·60
8	62·16	67·73	33	38·21	43·34	58	16·44	20·73	83	4·39	5·24
9	61·18	66·75	34	37·26	42·38	59	15·74	19·91	84	4·14	4·90
10	60·21	65·77	35	36·31	41·42	60	15·06	19·11	85	3·90	4·58
11	59·23	64·79	36	35·37	40·47	61	14·40	18·31	86	3·68	4·29
12	58·25	63·80	37	34·43	39·52	62	13·76	17·53	87	3·48	4·01
13	57·28	62·82	38	33·49	38·57	63	13·14	16·76	88	3·30	3·76
14	56·30	61·83	39	32·55	37·63	64	12·54	16·00	89	3·13	3·53
15	55·33	60·85	40	31·62	36·69	65	11·95	15·26	90	2·97	3·32
16	54·36	59·87	41	30·70	35·75	66	11·39	14·53	91	2·83	3·12
17	53·40	58·89	42	29·77	34·82	67	10·84	13·81	92	2·70	2·94
18	52·45	57·91	43	28·86	33·90	68	10·31	13·12	93	2·58	2·78
19	51·51	56·93	44	27·95	32·98	69	9·79	12·44	94	2·47	2·63
20	50·57	55·95	45	27·05	32·06	70	9·29	11·78	95	2·38	2·49
21	49·63	54·98	46	26·15	31·15	71	8·81	11·14	96	2·29	2·37
22	48·69	54·00	47	25·27	30·25	72	8·35	10·52	97	2·21	2·26
23	47·74	53·03	48	24·40	29·35	73	7·90	9·93	98	2·14	2·16
24	46·80	52·06	49	23·53	28·46	74	7·47	9·35	99	2·07	2·07
25	45·84	51·08	50	22·68	27·57	75	7·05	8·80	100	2·00	1·99

Comparative Table

	Males				Females			
Age	England and Wales	England	Wales	Greater London	England and Wales	England	Wales	Greater London
0	68·1	68·2	66·8	68·7	74·0	74·1	73·2	75·0
10	60·2	60·3	59·2	60·6	65·8	65·9	65·1	66·6
20	50·6	50·7	49·6	51·0	56·0	56·0	55·3	56·7
30	41·1	41·2	40·2	41·4	46·2	46·3	45·6	47·0
40	31·6	31·7	30·8	32·0	36·7	36·8	36·1	37·5
50	22·7	22·7	21·9	23·0	27·6	27·6	27·1	28·3
60	15·1	15·1	14·5	15·2	19·1	19·2	18·7	19·8
70	9·3	9·3	8·9	9·4	11·8	11·8	11·4	12·3
80	5·2	5·3	5·1	5·4	6·4	6·4	6·2	6·8

EXPECTATION OF LIFE IN YEARS: VARIOUS COUNTRIES

	England and Wales 1965–67		Scotland 1968		Northern Ireland 1966–68		United States 1967		Austria 1968	
Age	Male	Female	Male	Female	Male	Female	Male	Female	Male	Female
0	68·7	74·9	66·9	73·0	68·1	73·4	67·0	74·2	66·7	73·5
1	69·1	75·1	67·5	73·3	69·0	74·1	67·7	74·6	67·6	74·1
5	65·4	71·3	63·8	69·5	65·2	70·3	63·9	70·9	63·9	70·4
10	60·5	66·4	58·9	64·7	60·4	65·4	59·1	66·0	59·1	65·5
15	55·6	61·5	54·1	59·7	55·5	60·5	54·2	61·1	54·2	60·7
20	50·9	56·6	49·3	54·8	50·7	55·6	49·6	56·3	49·6	55·8
30	41·4	46·9	39·8	45·0	41·2	45·8	40·5	46·7	40·3	46·1
40	31·9	37·3	30·5	35·6	31·8	36·3	31·4	37·3	31·2	36·6
50	23·0	28·2	21·8	26·6	22·9	27·2	23·1	28·4	22·6	27·4
60	15·3	19·8	14·5	18·5	15·3	18·8	16·0	20·2	14·9	18·9
70	9·5	12·4	9·0	11·4	9·5	11·6	10·4	13·0	9·2	11·5
75	7·3	9·4	6·9	8·5	7·3	8·8	8·3	10·0	6·9	8·5
80	5·5	6·9	5·3	6·2	5·3	6·5	6·4	7·3	5·2	6·1
85	4·0	5·0	3·8	4·2	3·9	4·6	4·7	5·0	3·9	4·4

FOREIGN EXCHANGE RATES

A. London Market Rates

Country	Denomination	1939 Average Rate to £ (approx.)	30 September, 1975 Middle Rates
Austria	*Schilling*	—	38·30
Belgium	*Franc*	26·49 *Belgas*	81·60†
Canada	*Dollar*	4·545	2·0950
Denmark	*Krone*	22·26	12·66¾
Finland	*Markka*	217¼	8·05½
France	*Franc*	176·10	9·22½
Germany (Federal Republic of)	*D. Mark*	—	5·40½
Greece	*Drachma*	545	70¼
Italy	*Lira*	85	1400½
Japan	*Yen*	1/2d‡	618½
Netherlands	*Florin*	8·34	5·56½
Netherlands Antilles	*Antillian Florin*	8·34	4·67½
Norway	*Krone*	19·45	11·62
Portugal	*Escudo*	110·07	55·77
Spain	*Peseta*	42·45	121·97†
Sweden	*Krona*	18·59	9·19
Switzerland	*Franc*	19·87	5·60½
U.S.A.	*Dollar*	4·485	2·0434½

B. Former Scheduled Territories

Country	Denomination	1939 Average Rate to £ (approx.)	30 September, 1975 Middle Rates
Australia	*Australian $*	A£1·2525	1·6240
Bahamas	*Bahamas $*	—	2·04
Barbados	*Barbados $*	—	4·1039
Belize	*Belize $*	—	3·97
Bermuda	*Bermuda $*	—	2·04342
Cyprus	*Cyprus $*	—	·803
Ghana	*Cedi*	—	2·36
Hong Kong	*Hong Kong $*	—	10·35¾
Iceland	*Krona*	—	336·15
India	*Rupee*	13·38	18·27½
Jamaica	*Jamaica $*	—	1·8560
Jordan	*Dinar*	PAR	·665
Kenya	*Shilling*	—	14·59
Kuwait	*Dinar*	—	·602½
Libya	*Dinar*	—	·613
Malawi	*Kwacha*	—	1·85
Malaysia	*Malaysia $*	8·571	5·28¾
Malta	*Maltese $*	—	·828
New Zealand	*New Zealand $*	£1·2425	1·9515
Nigeria	*Naira*	—	1·3898
Pakistan	*Rupee*	—	20·30
South Africa	*Rand*	S.A.£1	1·7765
Sri Lanka	*Rupee*	13·38 (Ceylon Rs.)	15·5688
Tanzania	*Shilling*	—	14·55
Trinidad	*Trinidad and Tobago $*	—	4·8195
Uganda	*Shilling*	—	14·51
Yemen	*Ryal*	—	9·50*
Zambia	*Kwacha*	—	1·3124

C. Other Rates

Country	Denomination	1939 Average Rate to £ (approx.)	30 September, 1975 Middle Rates
Algeria	*Dinar*	—	8·52½
Argentina	*Peso*	19	74·38†
Bolivia	*Bolivian Peso*	141·50	40·74
Brazil	*Cruzeiro*	82	17·33
Bulgaria	*Lev*	375	2·06†
Burma	*Kyat*	13·38	13·72*
Chile	*Escudo*	116½	13·05†
China	*Renmimbi*	4⅛	4·0571
Colombia	*Peso*	7·59	65·21
Costa Rica	*Colon*	25·16	17·8149
Cuba	*Peso*	4·386	1·69
Czechoslovakia	*Koruna*	—	12·30†
Ecuador	*Sucre*	66	50·75
Ethiopia	*Ethiopian $*	—	4·20
Germany (East)	*Ostmark*	—	5·40

* Selling rate.
† Indicates that other rates are obtainable, varying according to the nature of the transaction.
‡ One shilling and two pence.

Country	Denomination	1939 Average Rate to £ (approx.)	30 September, 1975 Middle Rates
Guatemala	Quetzal	4·386	2·0434½
Guinea	Sily	—	N/A
Haiti	Gourde	22·4	10·37½**
Honduras	Lempira	8⅜	4·10
Hungary	Forint	20¼	97·87†
Indonesia	Rupiah	—	830
Iran	Rial	80·50 (Persian)	141½
Iraq	Dinar	PAR	·601
Israel	Israel £	PAR	14·30*
Lebanon	Lebanese £	9·65	4·50
Malagasy	M G Franc	175 (F. Fr.)	461·05
Mexico	Peso	—	25·48½
Morocco	Dirham	176·10 (F. Fr.)	8·45
Nicaragua	Cordoba	24	14·33
Paraguay	Guarani	—	254½
Peru	Sol	24½	91·80*†
Philippines	Peso	—	N/A
Poland	Zloty	23½	40·56†
Romania	Leu	655	10·14†
Salvador, El	Colon	11·20	5·10
Saudi Arabia	Ryal	—	7·15
Sudan	Sudan £	97½ (per £100 London)	·71½
Syria	Syrian £	—	7·60*
Thailand	Baht	10·91	41·54
Tunisia	Tunisian Dinar	—	·860*
Turkey	Turkish Lira	—	32½
United Arab Republic (Egypt)	Egyptian £	97½ (per £100 London)	·841
Uruguay	New Peso	9	5·52
U.S.S.R.	Rouble	23·75	1·56*
Venezuela	Bolivar	14·15	8·74
Vietnam (South)	Piastre	—	N/A
Yugoslavia	New Yugoslav Dinar	197½ (Y.D.)	37·21
Zaire	Zaire	—	1·0225

* Selling rate.
** Approximate selling rate.
† Indicates that other rates are obtainable, varying according to the nature of the transaction.

BRITISH TRANSPORT DOCKS BOARD, 1974

Traffic

Traffic through the Board's ports in 1974 totalled 84,785,000 tonnes (1973, 89,742,000), consisting of ('000 tonnes): ores 11,374; timber, 1,686; coal, 5,661; petroleum 45,034; foodstuffs 4,032; manufactured goods and other commodities, 16,998. Net registered tonnage of shipping entering and leaving the ports in 1974 totalled 136,256,000 tons (1973, 137,026,000). Passengers in transit through the Board's ports in 1974 numbered 2,872,000 (1973, 2,884,000).

Finance.—Gross revenue totalled £64,082,000 (1973, £56,193,000) and working expenses £51,963,000 (1973, £44,497,000). Interest charges £7,018,000 (1973, £6,854,000); Surplus (after historic cost depreciation, £12,119,000 (1973, £11,696,000); Reserve for additional depreciation, £2,901,000 (1973, £1,972,000); Net surplus, 1974. £1,501,000 (1973, £3,293,000).

HISTORIC ATLANTIC PASSAGES

Year	Days	Ship	Tons	Year	Days	Ship	Tons
1862a	9	Scotia	3,871	1932c	4d. 15h. 56m.	Europa	51,656
1869a	8	City of Brussels	3,081	1933c	4d. 17h. 43m.	Bremen	51,650
1882a	7	Alaska	6,400	1934d	6h. 58m.	Emp. of Britain	42,348
1889a	6	City of Paris	10,669	1935f	4d. 3h. 2m.	Normandie	80,000
1894a	5⅓	Lucania	12,950	1936f	4d. 0h. 27m.	Queen Mary	81,237
1897b	6	Kaiser Wilhelm	14,349	1936g	3d. 23h. 57m.	Queen Mary	81,237
1903c	5½	Deutschland	16,502	1937f	3d. 23h. 2m.	Normandie	80,000
1909a	4d. 10h. 41m.	Mauretania	30,696	1938f	3d. 21h. 45m.	Queen Mary	81,237
1924e	5d. 1h. 49m.	Mauretania	30,696	1938g	3d. 20h. 42m.	Queen Mary	81,237
1929c	4d. 18h. 17m.	Bremen	51,650	1952f	3d. 12h. 12m.	United States	51,500
1930c	4d. 17h. 6m.	Europa	51,656	1952g	3d. 10h. 40m.	United States	51,500

a From Queenstown;   *b* from Southampton;   *c* from Cherbourg;   *d* Quebec to Cherbourg;   *e* to Cherbourg; *f* Bishop Rock to Ambrose Light (2,907 miles);   *g* Ambrose Light to Bishop Rock (2,938 miles).

ABBREVIATIONS IN COMMON USE

Ψ = Seaport.

A

A.A., Automobile Association; Anti-Aircraft.

A.A.A., Amateur Athletic Association.

A. and M., (Hymns) Ancient and Modern.

A.B., Able-bodied Seaman.

A.B.C., Alphabet (also Aerated Bread Company).

a.c., alternating current.

a/c., accounts.

A.C.A., *Associate* of Inst of Chartered Accountants (of England and Wales)

A.C.C.A.—of the Association of Certified Accountants.

A.C.I.S.—of the Chartered Institute of Secretaries and Administrators.

A.C.M.A.—of the Institute of Cost and Management Accountants.

A.D. (*Anno Domini*), In the year of our Lord.

A.D.C., Aide-de-Camp.

Ad lib. (*ad libitum*), At pleasure.

A.F.C., Air Force Cross.

A.F.M., Air Force Medal.

A.H. (*Anno Hegirae*), In the year of the Hejira.

A.I.A., *Associate* of the Institute of Actuaries.

A.I.B.—of Bankers.

A.I.C.S.—of Chartered Shipbrokers.

A.I.M.T.A.—of Munic. Treas. and Accountants.

A.I.Q.S.—of Quantity Surveyors.

A.K.C.—of King's College.

A.L. (*Anno Lucis*), in the year of Light.

A.L.A., *Associate* of the Library Association.

A.L.C.D.—of London College of Divinity.

A.M. (*Ante meridiem*), Before noon.

A.M. (*Anno mundi*), In the year of the world.

A.M.D.G. (*Ad majorem Dei Gloriam*), To the greater glory of God.

A.N.A.R.E., Australian National Antarctic Research Expeditions.

A.N.Z.A.C., Australian and New Zealand Army Corps.

A.O.C., Air Officer Commanding.

A.R.A., *Associate* of Royal Academy.

A.R.A.M.—of Royal Academy of Music.

A.R.B.S.—of the Royal Society of British Sculptors.

A.R.C.A.—of Royal Coll. of Art.

A.R.C.M.—of Royal College of Music.

A.R.C.O.—of Organists.

A.R.I.B.A.—of Royal Institute of British Architects.

A.R.I.C.—of Royal Institute of Chemistry.

A.R.I.C.S.—of Royal Institution of Chartered Surveyors.

A.R.P.S.—of Royal Photographic Society.

A.R.R.C.—of Royal Red Cross.

A.R.W.S.—of Royal Society of Painters in Water Colours.

A.S.V.A.—of Inc. Society of Valuers and Auctioneers.

A.S.A., Amateur Swimming Association.

A.S.D.I.C., Anti-Submarine Detector Indicator Committee.

A.S.L.I.B., Association of Special Libraries and Information Bureaux.

A.T.A., Air Transport Auxiliary.

A.T.C., Air Training Corps.

A.U.C. (*Ab urbe condita*). In the year from the foundation of Rome.

A.W.O.L., Absent Without Leave.

B

B.A., *Bachelor* of Arts.

B.Arch.—of Architecture.

B.Ch. (or Ch.B.)—of Surgery.

B.C.L.—of Civil Law.

B.Com.—of Commerce.

B.D.—of Divinity.

B.D.S. (or B.Ch.D.)—of Dental Surgery.

B.Ed.—of Education.

B.Eng.—of Engineering.

B.Litt.—of Literature *or* of Letters.

B.Pharm.—of Pharmacy.

B.Phil.—of Philosophy.

B.Sc.—of Science.

B.V.M.S.—of Veterinary Medicine and Surgery.

B.A.O.R., British Army of the Rhine.

B.B., Boy's Brigade.

B.B.C., British Broadcasting Corporation.

B.C., Before Christ.

B.D.A., British Dental Assocn.

B.E.A., British European Airways.

B.E.M., British Empire Medal.

B.M.A., British Medical Assocn.

B.N.C., Brasenose College (Oxon.).

B.O.A.C., British Overseas Airways.

B.R.C.S., British Red Cross Society.

B.S.T., British Standard Time.

Bt., Baronet.

B.Th.U., British Thermal Unit.

B.V.M., Blessed Virgin Mary.

C

C.—Conservative.

ca. (*circa*), about.

C.A., Chartered Accountant (*Scottish Institute*).

Cantab., Cambridge.

Cantuar., Canterbury.

C.B., Companion of the Bath.

C.B.E., Commander of Order of British Empire.

C.B.I., Confederation of British Industry.

c.c., cubic centimetres.

C.C., County Council.

C.C.F., Combined Cadet Force.

C.E., Civil Engineer.

C.E.N.T.O., Central Treaty Organization.

C.E.T., Central European Time.

C. of E., Church of England.

cf. (confer), Compare.

C.F., Chaplain to the Forces.

C.G.M., Conspicuous Gallantry Medal.

C.G.S., Centimetre - gramme - second (system).

C.H., Companion of Honour.

Ch. Ch., Christ Church.

C.I., Lady of Imperial Order of the Crown of India.

C.I., Channel Islands.

C.I.A., Central Intelligence Agency.

C.I.D., Criminal Investigation Department.

C.I.E., Companion, Order of Indian Empire.

C.I.F. (usually cif.), Cost, Insurance and Freight.

C.I.G.S., Chief of Imperial General staff.

C.-in-C., Commander-in-Chief.

C.I.O., Congress of Industrial Organizations (U.S.A.).

C.L.B., Church Lads' Brigade.

C.M.,(*Chirurgiae Magister*),Master of Surgery.

C.M.G., Companion, Order of St. Michael and St. George.

C.M.S., Church Missionary Society.

C.N.A.A., Council for National Academic Awards.

C.O., Commanding Officer.

C.O.D., Cash on delivery.

C.O.I.—Central Office of Information.

C.P.R.E.—Council for Protection of Rural England.

C.S.I., Companion, Order of Star of India.

C.T.C., Cyclists' Touring Club.

C.V.O., Commander, Royal Victorian Order.

cwt., Hundredweight.

D

D.B.E., Dame Commander of Order of British Empire.

d.c., direct current.

D.C., District of Columbia.

D.C.B., Dame Commander of the Order of the Bath.

D.C.L., *Doctor* of Civil Law.

D.D.—of Divinity.

D.D.S.—of Dental Surgery.

D.Litt.—of Letters, *or* of Literature.

D.Phil.—of Philosophy.

D.Sc.—of Science.

D.Th.—of Theology.

D.C.M., Distinguished Conduct Medal.

D.C.M.G.—Dame Commander, Order of St. Michael and St. George.

D.C.V.O.—Dame Commander of the Royal Victorian Order.

D.D.T., dichlorodiphenyltrichloroethane (insecticide).

del. (*delineavit*), He (she) drew it.

D.F.C., Distinguished Flying Cross.

D.F.M., Distinguished Flying Medal.

D.G. (*Dei gratia*), By the Grace of God.

D.I.C., *Diploma* of the Imperial College.

D.P.H.—in Public Health.

D.P.M.—in Psychological Medicine.

D.T.M.—in Tropical Medicine.

D.L., Deputy-Lieutenant.

D.N.B., Dictionary of National Biography.

Do. (ditto), The same. (Italian, *detto*.)

D.O.M., *Dominus Omnium Magister* (God the Master of All).

D.S.C., Distinguished Service Cross.

D.S.M., Do. Medal.

D.S.O., Companion of Distinguished Service Order.

D.V. (*Deo volente*), God willing.

dwt., Pennyweight.

E

E. and O.E., Errors and omissions excepted.

E.C., East Central District.

E.C.S.C., European Coal and Steel Community.

E.D., Efficiency Decoration.

E.E.C., European Economic Community.

E.F.T.A., European Free Trade Association.

e.g. (*exempli gratia*), for the sake of example.

E.M.A., European Monetary Agreement.

E.R., Elizabetha Regina, or Edwardus Rex.

E.R.D., Emergency Reserve Decoration.

etc. (*et cetera*). And the other things.

et seq. (*et sequentia*). And the following.

ex lib. (*ex libris*), from the books of.

F

F.A., Football Association.

F.B.A., *Fellow* of the British Academy.

F.C.A.—of Institute of Chartered Accountants (of England and Wales).

F.C.C.A.—of Association of Certified Accountants.

F.C.G.I.—of City and Guilds Institute.

F.C.I.A.—of Corporation of Insurance Agents.

F.C.I.B.—of Corporation of Insurance Brokers.

F.C.I.I.—of the Chartered Insurance Institute.

F.C.I.S.—of the Chartered Institute of Secretaries and Administrators.

F.C.I.T.—of the Chartered Institute of Transport.

F.C.M.A.—of the Institute of Cost and Management Accountants.

F.C.P.—of the College of Preceptors.

F.G.S.—of the Geological Society.

F.H.S.—of the Heraldry Society.

F.I.A.—of the Institute of Actuaries.

F.I.Arb.—of Arbitrators.

F.I.B.—of Bankers.

F.I.C.E.—of Institution of Civil Engineers.

F.I.C.S.—of Chartered Shipbrokers.

F.I.E.E.—of Electrical Engineers.

F.Inst.P.—of Physics.

F.I.Q.S.—of Quantity Surveyors.

F.J.I.—of Journalists.

F.L.A.—of Library Association.

F.L.S.—of the Linnean Society.

F.P.S.—of the Pharmaceutical Society.

F.R.A.I.—of Royal Anthropological Institute.

F.R.A.M.—of Royal Academy of Music.

F.R.A.S.—of the Royal Astronomical Society

F.R.Ae.S.—of Royal Aeronautical Society.

F.R.B.S.—of the Royal Society of British Sculptors.

F.R.C.M.—of the Royal College of Music.

F.R.C.O.—of Royal College of Organists.

F.R.C.O.G.—of Royal College of Obstetricians and Gynaecologists.

F.R.C.P., F.R.C.P.Ed., and F.R.C.P.I.—of the Royal College of Physicians of London, of Edinburgh, and in Ireland respectively.

F.R.C.P.S.G.—of the Royal Faculty of Physicians and Surgeons of Glasgow.

F.R.C.S.—of Royal College of Surgeons of England.

F.R.C.S.Ed., ditto of Edinburgh; F.R.C.S.I., of Ireland.

F.R.C.V.S.—of Royal College of Veterinary Surgeons.

F.R.G.S.—of the Royal Geographical Society.

F.R.H.S.—of the Royal Horticultural Society.

F.R.Hist.Soc., ditto Historical.

F.R.I.B.A.—of the Royal Institute of British Architects.

F.R.I.C.—of the Royal Institute of Chemistry.

F.R.I.C.S.—of the Royal Institution of Chartered Surveyors.

F.R.M.S.—of Royal Microscopical Society.

F.R. Met. S.—of Royal Meteorological Society.

F.R.N.S.—of Royal Numismatic Society.

F.R.P.S.—of Royal Photographic Society.

F.R.S.—of the Royal Society.

F.R.S.E., ditto of Edinburgh.

F.R.S.A.—of the Royal Society of Arts.

F.R.S.L.—Do. Literature.

F.S.A.—of the Society of Antiquaries.

F.S.S.—Do. Statistical Society.

F.S.V.A.—Do. Valuers and Auctioneers.

F.Z.S.—of the Zoological Society.

F.A.N.Y., First Aid Nursing Yeomanry.

F.A.O., Food and Agriculture Organization.

fcp., Foolscap.

F.D. (*Fidei Defensor*) Defender of the Faith.

Fec. (*fecit*), He did it (or made it).

F.H., Fire Hydrant.

F.I.D.O., Fog Investigation Dispersal Operations.

fl. (*floruit*), he, or she, flourished.

F.O., Flying Officer; Foreign Office.

FOB (*usually* f.o.b.), Free on board.

G

G.A.T.T., General Agreement on Tariffs and Trade.

G.B.E., Knight or Dame Grand Cross of British Empire.

G.C., George Cross.

G.C.B., Knight (or Dame) Grand Cross of the Bath.

G.C.I.E., Knight Grand Commander of Indian Empire.

G.C.M.G., Knight (or Dame) Grand Cross of St. Michael and St. George.

G.C.S.I., Knight Grand Commander of Star of India.

G.C.V.O., Knight or Dame Grand Cross of Royal Victorian Order.

G.H.Q., General Headquarters.

G.L.C., Greater London Council.

G.M., George Medal.

G.M.T., Greenwich Mean Time.

G.O.C., General Officer Commanding.

G.P.O., General Post Office.

G.R. (*Georgius Rex*), King George.

G.R.C.M., Graduate of the Royal College of Music.

G.R.S.M., Graduate of the Royal Schools of Music (Royal Academy and Royal College).

G.S.O., General Staff Officer.

H

H.A.C., Honble. Artillery Coy.

H.C.F., Highest Common Factor.

H.E., His Excellency; His Eminence.

H.E.H., His [Her] Exalted Highness.

H.H., His [Her] Highness.

H.I.H., His [Her] Imperial Highness.

H.I.M., His [Her] Imperial Majesty.

H.J.S., (*Hic jacet sepultus*), Here lies buried. *cf.* H.S.E.

H.M., His, or Her, Majesty.
H.M.A.S., Her Majesty's Australian Ship.
H.M.L., Her Majesty's Lieutenant.
H.M.S., Her Majesty's Ship.
H.M.S.O., Her Majesty's Stationery Office.
h.p., horse power.
H.Q., Headquarters.
H.R.H., His[Her]Royal Highness.
H.S.E. (*Hic sepultus est*), Here lies buried. *cf.* H.J.S.
H.S.H., His [Her] Serene Highness.

I

I.A., Indian Army.
Ibid. (*ibidem*), In the same place.
IBRD., Internat. Bank for Reconstruction and Development.
J.C.B.M., Inter-Continental ballistic missile.
I.C.S., Indian Civil Service.
Id. (*idem*), The same.
I.C.A.O., International Civil Aviation Organization.
i.d.c., Graduate of Imperial Defence College.
i.e. (*id est*), That is.
IFC, International Finance Corporation.
I.H.S. (*Iesus Hominum Salvator*), Jesus the Saviour of Mankind; originally, these were the Greek Capital letters, IHΣ.
I.L.O., International Labour Organization.
I.L.P., Independent Labour Party.
IMCO., Inter-Governmental Maritime Consultative Organization.
IMF, International Monetary Fund.
I.M.S., Indian Medical Service.
Incog. (*incognito*), Unknown.
In loc (*in loco*), In its place.
I.N.R.I. (*Iesus Nazarenus Rex Iudaeorum*), Jesus of Nazareth King of the Jews.
Inst. (instant), current month.
I.O.M., Isle of Man.
I.O.U., I owe you.
I.O.W., Isle of Wight.
I.P.F.A., Institute of Public Finance and Accountancy.
I.Q., Intelligence Quotient.
IRBM., Intermediate - range ballistic missile.
I.S.O., Imperial Service Order.
I.T.A., Independent Television Authority.
I.T.O., International Trade Organization.
I.T.U., International Telecommunication Union.

J

J,. Judge.
J.P., Justice of the Peace.

K

K.B.E. Knight Commander of Order of British Empire.
K.C.B.—Do. the Bath.
K.C.I.E.—Do. Indian Empire.
K.C.M.G.—Do. of St. Michael and St. George.
K.C.S.I—Do. the Star of India.

K.C.V.O.—Do. Royal Victorian Order.
K.G., Knight of the Garter.
k.o., knock out (boxing).
K.P., Knight of St. Patrick.
K.T., Knight of the Thistle.
Kt., Knight Bachelor.

L

L., Liberal.
Lab., Labour.
L.A.C., London Athletic Club; Leading Aircraftsman.
L.A.H., *Licentiate* of Apothecaries' Hall, Dublin.
L.C.P., Do. of College of Preceptors.
L.D.S., Do. in Dental Surgery.
L.M., Do. in Midwifery.
L.M.S.S.A. Do. in Medicine and Surgery, Soc. of Apothecaries.
L.R.A.M., Do. of Royal Acad. of Music.
L.R.C.P., Do. of the Roy. Coll. of Physicians.
L.R.C.P.Ed., ditto Edinburgh.
L.R.C.S.Ed.—of Roy. Coll. Surg., Edinburgh.
L.R.F.P.S.G., Do. of the Royal Faculty of Physicians and Surgeons of Glasgow.
L.S.A., Do. of Society of Apothecaries.
L.Th., Licenciate in Theology.
L.T.M., Do. of Tropical Medicine.
Lat., Latitude.
lb. (*libra*). Pound weight.
L.C.C., London County Council.
L.C.J., Lord Chief Justice.
L.C.M., Least Common Multiple.
Lit., Literary.
Litt.D., Doctor of Letters.
L.J., Lord Justice.
LL.B., Bachelor of Laws.
LL.D., Doctor of Laws.
LL.M., Master of Laws.
L.S. (*loco sigilli*), Place of the Seal.
L. s. d. (*Librae, solidi, denarii*). Pounds, shillings, pence.
L.T.A., Lawn Tennis Association.
Ltd., Limited Liability.
LXX., Septuagint.

M

M., Monsieur.
M.A., *Master* of Arts.
M.Ch.—of Surgery.
M.Ch.D.—of Dental Surgery.
M.S.—of Surgery.
M.Sc.—of Science.
M.Th.—of Theology.
M.B., Bachelor of Medicine.
M.D., Doctor of ditto.
M.B.E., *Member* of British Empire Order.
M.E.C.—of Executive Council.
M.I.Chem.E.—of Institution of Chemical Engineers.
M.I.C.E.—of Institution of Civil Engineers.
M.I.E.E.—of Institution of Electrical Engineers.
M.I.Mar.E.—of Institute of Marine Engineers.
M.I.Mech.E.—of Institution of Mechanical Engineers.
M.Inst.Met.—of Institute of Metals.

M.J.I.—of Journalists.
M.L.A., *Member* of Legislative Assembly.
M.L.C., ditto Council.
M.N., Merchant Navy.
M.P., Member of Parliament (also Military Police).
M.P.S. — of Pharmaceutical Society.
M.R.C.P.—of Royal College of Physicians.
M.R.C.S.—of Royal College of Surgeons.
M.R.C.V.S.—of Royal College of Veterinary Surgeons.
M.V.O.—of Royal Victorian Order.
M.C., Military Cross.
M.C.C., Marylebone Cricket Club.
M.F.H., Master of Fox Hounds.
Mgr., Monsignor.
Min. Plenip., Minister Plenipotentiary.
Mlle., Mademoiselle.
M.M., Military Medal (also MM., Messieurs).
Mme., Madame.
M.O.H., Medical Officer of Health.
m.p.h., Miles per hour.
MS., manuscript (pl. MSS.).
Mus. D.[B.J.] Doctor, [Bachelor], of Music.

N

N.A.A.F.I., Navy, Army and Air Force Institutes.
N.A.T.O., North Atlantic Treaty Organization.
N.B. (*Nota bene*). Note well; New Brunswick.
N.C.B., National Coal Board.
N.C.O., Non - commissioned Officer.
n.d., no date (of books).
N.D.P.S., National Data Processing Service.
Nem. con. (*Nemine contradicente*), No one contradicting.
N.F.U. — National Farmers' Union.
No. (*Numero*), Number.
N.P., Notary Public.
Non seq. (*non sequitur*), It does not follow.
N.R.A., National Rifle Association.
N.S., Nova Scotia.
N.S.P.C.C., National Society for the prevention of Cruelty to Children.
N.S.W., New South Wales.
N.T., New Testament.
N.U.J., *National Union of Journalists.*
N.U.R.—of Railwaymen.
N.U.S.—of Students.
N.W.P.[T.], Northwest Provinces [Territory].
N.Y., New York.
N.Z., New Zealand.

O

O.B.E., Officer of British Empire Order.
ob., or *obiit*. died.

O.C., Officer Commanding.

O.E.C.D., Organization for Economic Co-operation and Development.

O.E.D., Oxford English Dictionary.

O.H.M.S., On Her Majesty's Service.

O.M., Order of Merit (and member of).

O.P., Opposite Prompt side (of Theatre), Out of Print (of books).

op. cit. (*opere citato*), in the work cited.

O.S., Old Style.

O.S.B., Order of St. Benedict.

O.T., Old Testament.

O.U.D.S., Oxford University Dramatic Society.

Oxon., Oxford; Oxfordshire.

Oz., Ounce.

P

P.A., Press Association.

P.C., Privy Councillor.

P.E.N. (*Club*), Poets Essayists, Novelists.

p.f.c., Passed Flying College.

Ph.D., Doctor of Philosophy.

pinx(*it*), he (or she) painted it.

P.L.A., Port of London Authority.

P.M. (*post meridiem*), Afternoon (also *post mortem*).

P.M.G., Postmaster-General.

P.N.E.U., Parents' National Educational Union.

p.p., or per pro. (*per procurationem*)—by proxy.

Pro tem. (*pro tempore*), For the time being.

Prox. (*proximo*), Next Month.

P.S. (*Post scriptum*), Postscript.

p.s.c., Passed Staff College.

P.T., Physical Training.

P.T.O., Please turn over.

Q

Q.C., Queen's Counsel.

Q.e.d. (*quod erat demonstrandum*), which was to be proved.

Q.G.M., Queen's Gallantry Medal

Q.H.C., Honorary Chaplain to the Queen; Q.H.P., ditto Physician; Q.H S , ditto Surgeon; Q.H.D.S., ditto Dental Surgeon; Q.H.N.S., ditto Nursing Sister.

Q.M.G., Quartermaster-General.

Q.S., Quarter Sessions.

Q.S.O., Quasi-stellar object (quasar).

q.v. (*quod vide*), "which see".

R

R.A., *Royal* Artillery or Royal Academy (or Academician).

R.A.C.—Armoured Corps (also Royal Automobile Club).

R.A.D.C.—Army Dental Corps.

R.A.E.C.—Army Educational Corps.

R.Ae.S., Royal Aeronautical Society.

R.A.F.—Air Force.

R.A.M.—Academy of Music.

R.A.M.C. — Army Medical Corps.

R.A.N.—Australian Navy.

R.A.P.C.—Army Pay Corps.

R.A.O.C.—Army Ordnance Corps.

R.A.V.C.—Army Veterinary Corps.

R.B.A.—Society of British Artists.

R.B.S.—Society of British Sculptors.

R.C.N.—Canadian Navy.

R.C.N.C.—Corps of Naval Constructors.

R.C.T.—Corps of Transport.

R.D.—Naval Reserve Decoration.

R.E.—Engineers.

R.E.M.E.—Electrical and Mechanical do.

R.H.A.—Horse Artillery or—Hibernian Academy.

R.I.B.A.—Royal Institute of British Architects (also Member of the Institute).

R.M.—Marines.

R.M.A.—Military Academy.

R.M.S.—Mail Steamer.

R.N.—Navy; R.N.R. Naval Reserve; R.N.V.R., Naval Volunteer Reserve.

R.O.C.—Observer Corps.

R.O.I.—Institute of Oil Painters.

R.P.—Society of Portrait Painters.

R.P.C.—Pioneer Corps.

R.Sigs.—Signals.

R.S.A.—Scottish Academician.

R.S.P.C.A.—Society for the Prevention of Cruelty to Animals.

R.W.S.—Water Colour Society.

R.Y.S.—Yacht Squadron.

R.C., Roman Catholic.

R.D., Rural Dean; Refer to drawer (banking).

R.D.I., Designer for Industry of the Royal Society of Arts.

R.I.P. (*Requiescat in pace*), May he (she) rest in peace.

Ro. (*recto*), On the right-hand page. (*See* Vo.)

r.p.m., revolutions per minute.

R.R.C., Lady of Royal Red Cross.

R.S.V.P. (*Répondez s'il vous plaît*), Answer, if you please.

R.V., Revised Version (of Bible).

S

Sc.D., Doctor of Science.

S.E.A.T.O.—South East Asia Treaty Organization.

S.E.T., Selective Employment Tax.

S.H.A.P.E.—Supreme Headquarters, Allied Powers, Europe.

Sic, So written.

S.J., Society of Jesus.

S.O.S. ("Save Our Souls") Distress Signal.

s.p.(*sine prole*), Without issue.

S.P.C.K., Society for Promoting Christian Knowledge.

S.P.Q.R (*Senatus Populusque Romanus*), The Senate and People of Rome

S.R.N., State Registered Nurse.

S.S.A.F.A., Soldiers', Sailors', and Airmen's Families Assocn.

S.S.C., Solicitor in the Supreme Court (Scotland).

Stet, Let it stand.

S.T.P. (=D.D.), *Sacrae Theologiae Professor*.

T

T.A.N., Twilight all night.

t.b., Tuberculosis.

T.D., Territorial Decoration.

T.C.D., Trinity College, Dublin.

T.N.T., Trinitrotoluene (explosive).

Toc. H., Talbot House.

T.U.C., Trades Union Congress.

U

Ult. (*ultimo*), in the preceding month.

U.K., United Kingdom.

U.N.A.C., United Nations Appeal for Children.

U.N.E.S.C.O., United Nations Educational, Scientific and Cultural Organization.

U.N.O., United Nations Organization.

U.P.U., Universal Postal Union.

U.S.A. or U.S., United States of America.

U.S.C.L., United Society for Christian Literature.

U.S.S.R., Union of Soviet Socialist Republics.

V

v. (*versus*), Against.

V.A., Victoria and Albert Order or Vicar Apostolic.

V.A.D., Voluntary Aid Detachment.

V.A.T., Value Added Tax.

℣℃, Victoria Cross.

V.D., Vol. Officers' Decoration.

Ven., Venerable.

Verb. sap. (*Verbum sapienti satis est*), A word to the wise is enough.

V.I.P., Very Important Person.

Viz. (*videlicet*), Namely.

Vo. (*verso*), On the left-hand pagel (*See* Ro.)

V.R., Victoria Regina.

V.R.D.—Volunteer Reserve Decoration.

W

W.A.A.F., now W.R.A.F., Women's Auxiliary Air Force.

W.H.O., World Health Organization,

W.M.O. World Meteorological Organization.

W.O., Warrant Officer.

W.R.A.C., Women's Royal Army Corps.

W.R.A.F., Women's Royal Air Force.

W.R.N.S., Women's Royal Naval Service.

W.R.V.S., Women's Royal Voluntary Service.

W.S., Writer to the Signet.

Y

Y.M.C.A., Young Men's Christian Association.

Y.W.C.A., Young Women's do.

BEING BISSEXTILE OR LEAP YEAR

Golden Number	I	
Epact	29	
Dominical Letter	DC	
Solar Cycle	25	
Roman Indiction	14	
Julian Period (begins at noon)	6689	
Julian Day	2,442,779	
New Year's Day (Thursday)	Jan. 1	
Moslem New Year (1396)	,, 3	
Australia Day	,, 26	
Accession of Queen Elizabeth II	Feb. 6	
New Zealand Day	,, 6	
Septuagesima Sunday	,, 15	
Prince Andrew's Birthday (1960)	,, 19	
St. David's Day	Mar. 1	
Ash Wednesday	,, 3	
Prince Edward's Birthday (1964)	,, 10	
St. Patrick's Day	,, 17	
Good Friday	April 16	

Easter Day	Apr. 18	
Birthday of Queen Elizabeth II	,, 21	
St. George's Day	,, 23	
Ascension Day	May 27	
Whit Sunday	June 6	
Duke of Edinburgh's Birthday (1921)	,, 10	
Trinity Sunday	,, 13	
Queen's Official Birthday	,, 14	
Corpus Christi	,, 17	
Dominion Day, Canada (1867)	July 1	
The Queen Mother's Birthday (1900)	Aug. 4	
Princess Anne's Birthday (1950)	,, 15	
Jewish New Year (5737)	Sept. 25	
Remembrance Sunday	Nov. 14	
Prince of Wales's Birthday (1948)	,, 14	
St. Andrew's Day	,, 30	
Moslem New Year (1397)	Dec. 23	
Christmas Day (Saturday)	,, 25	

Spring Equinox.................... Sun enters Sign Aries........March 20d 12h
Summer Solstice.................. ,, ,, ,, Cancer....June 21d 06h } G.M.T.
Autumn Equinox.................. ,, ,, ,, Libra........Sept. 22d 22h
Winter Solstice................... ,, ,, ,, Capricornus..Dec. 21d 18h

CALENDAR FOR THE YEAR 1976

	January	April	July	October
Su.	— 4 11 18 25	— 4 11 18 25	— 4 11 18 25	— 3 10 17 24 31
M.	— 5 12 19 26	— 5 12 19 26	— 5 12 19 26	— 4 11 18 25 —
Tu.	— 6 13 20 27	— 6 13 20 27	— 6 13 20 27	— 5 12 19 26 —
W.	— 7 14 21 28	— 7 14 21 28	— 7 14 21 28	— 6 13 20 27 —
Th.	1 8 15 22 29	1 8 15 22 29	1 8 15 22 29	— 7 14 21 28 —
F.	2 9 16 23 30	2 9 16 23 30	2 9 16 23 30	1 8 15 22 29 —
S.	3 10 17 24 31	3 10 17 24 —	3 10 17 24 31	2 9 16 23 30 —
	February	May	August	November
Su.	1 8 15 22 29	— 9 16 23 30	1 8 15 22 29	— 7 14 21 28
M.	2 9 16 23 —	— 3 10 17 24 31	2 9 16 23 30	1 8 15 22 29
Tu.	3 10 17 24 —	— 4 11 18 25 —	3 10 17 24 31	— 9 16 23 30
W.	4 11 18 25 —	— 5 12 19 26 —	4 11 18 25 —	3 10 17 24 —
Th.	5 12 19 26 —	— 6 13 20 27 —	5 12 19 26 —	4 11 18 25 —
F.	6 13 20 27 —	— 7 14 21 28 —	6 13 20 27 —	5 12 19 26 —
S.	7 14 21 28 —	1 8 15 22 29 —	7 14 21 28 —	6 13 20 27 —
	March	June	September	December
Su.	— 7 14 21 28	— 6 13 20 27	— 5 12 19 26	— 5 12 19 26
M.	1 8 15 22 29	— 7 14 21 28	— 6 13 20 27	— 6 13 20 27
Tu.	2 9 16 23 30	1 8 15 22 29	— 7 14 21 28	— 7 14 21 28
W.	3 10 17 24 31	2 9 16 23 30	1 8 15 22 29	1 8 15 22 29
Th.	4 11 18 25 —	3 10 17 24 —	2 9 16 23 30	2 9 16 23 30
F.	5 12 19 26 —	4 11 18 25 —	3 10 17 24 —	3 10 17 24 31
S.	6 13 20 27 —	5 12 19 26 —	4 11 18 25 —	4 11 18 25 —

CALENDAR FOR THE YEAR 1977

	January	April	July	October
Su.	— 2 9 16 23 30	— 3 10 17 24	— 3 10 17 24 31	— 2 9 16 23 30
M.	— 3 10 17 24 31	— 4 11 18 25	— 4 11 18 25 —	— 3 10 17 24 31
Tu.	— 4 11 18 25 —	— 5 12 19 26	— 5 12 19 26 —	— 4 11 18 25 —
W.	— 5 12 19 26 —	— 6 13 20 27	— 6 13 20 27 —	— 5 12 19 26 —
Th.	— 6 13 20 27 —	— 7 14 21 28	— 7 14 21 28 —	— 6 13 20 27 —
F.	— 7 14 21 28 —	1 8 15 22 29	1 8 15 22 29 —	— 7 14 21 28 —
S.	1 8 15 22 29 —	2 9 16 23 30	2 9 16 23 30 —	1 8 15 22 29 —
	February	May	August	November
Su.	— 6 13 20 27	1 8 15 22 29	— 7 14 21 28	— 6 13 20 27
M.	— 7 14 21 28	2 9 16 23 30	1 8 15 22 29	— 7 14 21 28
Tu.	1 8 15 22 —	3 10 17 24 31	2 9 16 23 30	1 8 15 22 29
W.	2 9 16 23 —	4 11 18 25 —	3 10 17 24 31	2 9 16 23 30
Th.	3 10 17 24 —	5 12 19 26 —	4 11 18 25 —	3 10 17 24 —
F.	4 11 18 25 —	6 13 20 27 —	5 12 19 26 —	4 11 18 25 —
S.	5 12 19 26 —	7 14 21 28 —	6 13 20 27 —	5 12 19 26 —
	March	June	September	December
Su.	— 6 13 20 27	— 5 12 19 26	— 4 11 18 25	— 4 11 18 25
M.	— 7 14 21 28	— 6 13 20 27	— 5 12 19 26	— 5 12 19 26
Tu.	1 8 15 22 29	— 7 14 21 28	— 6 13 20 27	— 6 13 20 27
W.	2 9 16 23 30	1 8 15 22 29	— 7 14 21 28	— 7 14 21 28
Th.	3 10 17 24 31	2 9 16 23 30	1 8 15 22 29	1 8 15 22 29
F.	4 11 18 25 —	3 10 17 24 —	2 9 16 23 30	2 9 16 23 30
S.	5 12 19 26 —	4 11 18 25 —	3 10 17 24 —	3 10 17 24 31

Day of		
Month	**Week**	

Janus, god of the portal, facing two ways, past and future.

Sun's Longitude 300° ♒ 20ᵈ 22ʰ

1	Th.	**Circumcision.** A. H. Clough b. 1819
2	F.	James Wolfe b. 1727
3	S.	Josiah Wedgwood d. 1795
4	**☉.**	**2nd ☉. after Christmas.** T. S. Eliot d. 1965
5	M.	Catherine de Medici d. 1589 Konrad Adenauer b. 1876**
6	Tu.	**Epiphany.** Twelfth Day. Gustave Doré b. 1823
7	W.	Gerald Durrell b. 1925
8	Th.	Catherine of Aragon d. 1536. John Gregson d. 1975
9	F.	Napoleon III d. 1873 John Slater d. 1975
10	S.	Samuel Colt d. 1862. Col. Cody d. 1917
11	**☉.**	**1st ☉. after Epiphany.** Thomas Hardy d. 1928
12	M.	Jack London b. 1876** HILARY LAW SITTINGS
13	Tu.	James Joyce d. 1941 [BEGIN
14	W.	Edmund Halley d. 1742 Jean Ingres d. 1867
15	Th.	Emma, Lady Hamilton d. 1815 [d. 1942
16	F.	Edward Gibbon d. 1794 Sir Jeremiah Colman
17	S.	Anton Tchekov b. 1860. Earl Lloyd George b. 1863
18	**☉.**	**2nd ☉. after Epiphany.** Rudyard Kipling d. 1936
19	M.	Edgar Allan Poe b. 1809 Cézanne b. 1839
20	Tu.	George V d. 1936. John Ruskin d. 1900
21	W.	Louis XVI d. 1793. Lenin d. 1924
22	Th.	Queen Victoria d. 1901. André Ampère b. 1775
23	F.	Edouard Manet b. 1832 [d. 1965
24	S.	Frederick the Great b. 1712 Sir W. Churchill
25	**☉.**	**3rd ☉. Epiphany. Conversion of St. Paul.**
26	M.	AUSTRALIA DAY. Gen. Gordon d. 1885
27	Tu.	Mozart b. 1756. Verdi d. 1901
28	W.	Sir Francis Drake d. 1596. Dostoievski d. 1881
29	Th.	George III d. 1820. Delius b. 1862
30	F.	Charles I d. 1649. Edward Lear d. 1888
31	S.	Schubert b. 1797. Duke of Norfolk d. 1975

PHENOMENA

January 3ᵈ 06ʰ Mercury in conjunction with the Moon. Mercury 7° S.

4ᵈ 11ʰ Perihelion (147,000,000 kilometres).

7ᵈ 05ʰ Mercury at greatest eastern elongation (19°).

9ᵈ 12ʰ in conjunction with the Moon. Jupiter 4° S.

14ᵈ 03ʰ Mars in conjunction with the Moon. Mars 5° N.

17ᵈ 13ʰ Saturn in conjunction with the Moon. Saturn 5° N.

20ᵈ 11ʰ Saturn at opposition.

23ᵈ 06ʰ Mercury in inferior conjunction.

28ᵈ 08ʰ Venus in conjunction with the Moon. Venus 2° S.

CONSTELLATIONS

The following constellations are near the meridian at

	d	h		d	h
Dec. 1	24		Dec. 16	23	
Jan. 1	22		Jan. 16	21	
Feb. 1	20		Feb. 15	19	

Draco (below the Pole), Ursa Minor (below the Pole), Camelopardus, Perseus, Auriga, Taurus, Orion, Eridanus and Lepus.

MINIMA OF ALGOL

d	h	d	h
2	10	19	15
5	7	22	12
8	4	25	9
11	1	28	5
13	21	31	2
16	18		

PHASES OF THE MOON

		d	h	m
● New Moon		1	14	40
☽ First Quarter		9	12	40
○ Full Moon		17	04	47
☾ Last Quarter		23	23	04
● New Moon		31	06	20

		d	h
Apogee (404,410 kilometres)	8	17
Perigee (366,870 „)	20	13

Mean Longitude of Ascending Node on January 1, 229°.

MONTHLY NOTES

Jan. 1. New Year's Day. Bank Holiday in England, Wales, Northern Ireland and Scotland and in the Channel Islands.

2. Bank Holiday, Scotland.

3. Moslem New Year (A.H. 1396).

6. Dividends on Consols, etc., due.

25. Robert Burns born (1759).

26. Republic Day, India.

** Centenary.

Day	The Sun									Sidereal Time	Transit of First Point of Aries
	Right Ascension	Dec. —	Equation of Time	Rise		Transit	Set				
				52°	56°		52°	56°			
	h m s	° ′	m s	h m	h m	h m	h m	h m		h m s	h m s
1	18 42 10	23 05	− 3 02	8 08	8 32	12 03	15 58	15 35		6 39 09	17 18 01
2	18 46 36	23 01	− 3 30	8 08	8 32	12 04	15 59	15 36		6 43 05	17 14 05
3	18 51 00	22 55	− 3 59	8 08	8 31	12 04	16 00	15 37		6 47 02	17 10 09
4	18 55 25	22 50	− 4 27	8 08	8 31	12 05	16 01	15 39		6 50 58	17 06 13
5	18 59 49	22 44	− 4 54	8 08	8 31	12 05	16 03	15 40		6 54 55	17 02 17
6	19 04 13	22 37	− 5 21	8 08	8 30	12 06	16 04	15 41		6 58 51	16 58 21
7	19 08 36	22 30	− 5 48	8 07	8 30	12 06	16 05	15 43		7 02 48	16 54 25
8	19 12 59	22 23	− 6 14	8 07	8 29	12 06	16 06	15 44		7 06 45	16 50 29
9	19 17 21	22 15	− 6 40	8 06	8 28	12 07	16 08	15 46		7 10 41	16 46 33
10	19 21 43	22 07	− 7 05	8 06	8 28	12 07	16 09	15 47		7 14 38	16 42 38
11	19 26 04	21 58	− 7 30	8 05	8 27	12 08	16 10	15 49		7 18 34	16 38 42
12	19 30 24	21 49	− 7 54	8 05	8 26	12 08	16 12	15 51		7 22 31	16 34 46
13	19 34 44	21 39	− 8 17	8 04	8 25	12 08	16 13	15 52		7 26 27	16 30 50
14	19 39 04	21 29	− 8 40	8 03	8 24	12 09	16 15	15 54		7 30 24	16 26 54
15	19 43 22	21 19	− 9 02	8 03	8 23	12 09	16 16	15 56		7 34 20	16 22 58
16	19 47 40	21 08	− 9 23	8 02	8 22	12 10	16 18	15 58		7 38 17	16 19 02
17	19 51 58	20 57	− 9 44	8 01	8 21	12 10	16 19	16 00		7 42 14	16 15 06
18	19 56 14	20 45	−10 04	8 00	8 20	12 10	16 21	16 02		7 46 10	16 11 10
19	20 00 30	20 33	−10 24	7 59	8 18	12 11	16 23	16 03		7 50 07	16 07 14
20	20 04 46	20 21	−10 42	7 58	8 17	12 11	16 24	16 05		7 54 03	16 03 18
21	20 09 00	20 08	−11 00	7 57	8 15	12 11	16 26	16 07		7 58 00	15 59 23
22	20 13 14	19 55	−11 18	7 56	8 14	12 11	16 28	16 09		8 01 56	15 55 27
23	20 17 27	19 42	−11 34	7 55	8 13	12 12	16 29	16 11		8 05 53	15 51 31
24	20 21 39	19 28	−11 50	7 53	8 11	12 12	16 31	16 14		8 09 50	15 47 35
25	20 25 51	19 13	−12 05	7 52	8 10	12 12	16 33	16 16		8 13 46	15 43 39
26	20 30 02	18 59	−12 19	7 51	8 08	12 12	16 35	16 18		8 17 43	15 39 43
27	20 34 12	18 44	−12 33	7 49	8 06	12 13	16 37	16 20		8 21 39	15 35 47
28	20 38 21	18 29	−12 45	7 48	8 05	12 13	16 38	16 22		8 25 36	15 31 51
29	20 42 29	18 13	−12 57	7 47	8 03	12 13	16 40	16 24		8 29 32	15 27 55
30	20 46 37	17 57	−13 08	7 45	8 01	12 13	16 42	16 26		8 33 29	15 23 59
31	20 50 44	17 41	−13 18	7 44	7 59	12 13	16 44	16 28		8 37 25	15 20 03

At top of table: THE SUN   s.d. 16′·3

Duration of Civil (C), Nautical (N), and Astronomical (A), Twilight (in minutes)

Lat. °	Jan. 1			Jan. 11			Jan. 21			Jan. 31		
	C	N	A	C	N	A	C	N	A	C	N	A
52	41	84	125	40	82	123	38	80	120	37	78	117
56	47	96	141	45	93	138	43	90	134	41	87	130

ASTRONOMICAL NOTES

MERCURY is an evening star (magnitude −0·5 to +1·5) for the first part of the month, greatest eastern elongation occurring on the 7th. It is visible for a short while around the time of end of evening civil twilight, low in the south-western sky. For the last ten days of the month it is unsuitably placed for observation, inferior conjunction occurring on the 23rd.

VENUS is a magnificent morning star, magnitude −3·6, though the duration of its visibility in the S.E. sky before dawn shortens noticeably during the month. On the morning of the 28th the old crescent Moon passes 2° N. of the planet.

MARS is a brilliant evening star, its magnitude dropping during the month from −1·2 to −0·3. Mars is in the constellation of Taurus: the gibbous Moon passes 5° S. of it on the night of the 13th–14th.

JUPITER is a prominent evening star, magnitude −2·0, in the constellation of Pisces. On the early evening of the 9th the Moon, at First Quarter, will be seen passing about 5° above Jupiter.

SATURN is at opposition on the 20th, magnitude −0·1, and thus visible throughout the hours of darkness. Saturn is in the constellation of Cancer. The Full Moon passes 5° S. of the planet during the daylight hours of the 17th.

THE MOON

Day	R.A.	Dec.	Hor. Par.	Semi-diam.	Sun's Co-long.	P.A. of Bright Limb	Phase	Age	Rise 52°	Rise 56°	Transit	Set 52°	Set 56°
	h m	°	′	′	°	°		d	h m	h m	h m	h m	h m
1	18 09	−20·0	57·7	15·7	258	113	1	29·0	7 36	7 56	11 56	16 20	16 01
2	19 05	−18·4	57·1	15·6	270	222	0	0·4	8 16	8 33	12 49	17 28	17 12
3	19 59	−15·8	56·5	15·4	282	243	2	1·4	8 49	9 02	13 39	18 38	18 25
4	20 50	−12·5	55·9	15·2	294	245	6	2·4	9 15	9 25	14 26	19 46	19 38
5	21 39	− 8·7	55·3	15·1	306	245	12	3·4	9 38	9 44	15 11	20 54	20 49
6	22 25	− 4·6	54·8	14·9	319	245	19	4·4	9 59	10 01	15 54	21 59	21 59
7	23 10	− 0·4	54·5	14·8	331	245	27	5·4	10 19	10 18	16 36	23 04	23 07
8	23 55	+ 3·7	54·3	14·8	343	245	36	6·4	10 39	10 34	17 18	..	..
9	0 40	+ 7·7	54·2	14·8	355	247	45	7·4	11 00	10 52	18 00	0 09	0 15
10	1 25	+11·4	54·4	14·8	7	248	54	8·4	11 23	11 12	18 44	1 13	1 23
11	2 13	+14·7	54·7	14·9	19	251	64	9·4	11 50	11 36	19 31	2 17	2 31
12	3 02	+17·4	55·2	15·0	32	254	73	10·4	12 23	12 05	20 20	3 21	3 39
13	3 54	+19·3	55·8	15·2	44	257	81	11·4	13 04	12 44	21 11	4 24	4 43
14	4 48	+20·4	56·5	15·4	56	260	88	12·4	13 54	13 33	22 05	5 22	5 43
15	5 43	+20·4	57·2	15·6	68	263	94	13·4	14 53	14 33	23 00	6 14	6 34
16	6 40	+19·2	58·0	15·8	80	260	98	14·4	16 02	15 44	23 55	6 59	7 17
17	7 38	+16·9	58·6	16·0	92	219	100	15·4	17 17	17 03	..	7 37	7 52
18	8 35	+13·6	59·2	16·1	104	129	99	16·4	18 35	18 26	0 50	8 10	8 21
19	9 31	+ 9·4	59·6	16·2	117	120	96	17·4	19 55	19 51	1 44	8 38	8 45
20	10 25	+ 4·7	59·7	16·3	129	118	90	18·4	21 16	21 16	2 37	9 04	9 06
21	11 20	− 0·3	59·8	16·3	141	117	82	19·4	22 36	22 40	3 29	9 29	9 27
22	12 14	− 5·3	59·6	16·2	153	115	72	20·4	23 55	..	4 21	9 54	9 48
23	13 08	− 9·9	59·4	16·2	165	113	61	21·4	..	0 04	5 14	10 22	10 11
24	14 04	−14·0	59·0	16·1	177	110	50	22·4	1 13	1 26	6 07	10 53	10 39
25	15 00	−17·2	58·6	16·0	189	106	38	23·4	2 28	2 45	7 02	11 30	11 12
26	15 57	−19·3	58·2	15·9	202	102	28	24·4	3 37	3 57	7 57	12 15	11 54
27	16 55	−20·4	57·7	15·7	214	98	19	25·4	4 38	5 00	8 53	13 07	12 46
28	17 52	−20·2	57·3	15·6	226	95	11	26·4	5 31	5 51	9 48	14 08	13 48
29	18 48	−19·0	56·8	15·5	238	93	6	27·4	6 14	6 32	10 41	15 13	14 56
30	19 42	−16·7	56·3	15·3	250	97	2	28·4	6 49	7 03	11 31	16 21	16 07
31	20 33	−13·7	55·8	15·2	262	133	0	29·4	7 17	7 29	12 19	17 30	17 20

MERCURY ☿

Day	R.A.	Dec. −	Diam.	Phase	Transit	5° high W 52°	5° high W 56°	Day	R.A.	Dec. −	Diam.	Phase	Transit	
	h m	°	″		h m	h m	h m		h m	°	″		h m	
1	20 00	22·4	6	78	13 22	16 32	15 58	16	20 44	16·6	9	20	13 03	Mercury is
4	20 16	21·2	6	70	13 26	16 46	16 17	19	20 36	16·2	9	7	12 41	too close to
7	20 30	19·9	7	59	13 28	16 58	16 32	22	20 22	16·3	10	0	12 15	the Sun for
10	20 41	18·6	7	48	13 25	17 05	16 41	25	20 06	16·7	10	4	11 48	observation
13	20 46	17·5	8	33	13 17	17 05	16 43	28	19 52	17·3	10	8	11 23	
16	20 44	16·6	9	20	13 03	16 55	16 34	31	19 43	18·0	9	17	11 03	

VENUS ♀   MARS ♂

Day	R.A.	Dec. −	Diam.	Phase	5° high E 52°	5° high E 56°	Transit	Day	R.A.	Dec. +	Diam.	Phase	Transit	5° high W 52°	5° high W 56°
	h m	°	″		h m	h m	h m		h m	°	″		h m	h m	h m
1	15 51	17·9	15	73	5 29	5 52	9 12	1	5 04	26·0	15	98	22 20	6 16	6 38
6	16 15	19·2	15	75	5 43	6 09	9 17	6	4 59	25·9	15	98	21 55	5 53	6 13
11	16 41	20·3	15	76	5 57	6 24	9 23	11	4 55	25·8	14	97	21 32	5 30	5 52
16	17 06	21·2	14	78	6 10	6 40	9 29	16	4 53	25·7	13	96	21 11	5 07	5 29
21	17 32	21·8	14	79	6 22	6 53	9 35	21	4 52	25·7	13	95	20 51	4 45	5 07
26	17 59	22·2	14	81	6 31	7 03	9 41	26	4 53	25·6	12	94	20 32	4 24	4 46
31	18 25	22·3	13	82	6 38	7 11	9 48	31	4 55	25·6	11	93	20 15	4 06	4 28

SUNRISE AND SUNSET (G.M.T.)

Day	London a.m.	London p.m.	Bristol a.m.	Bristol p.m.	Birmingham a.m.	Birmingham p.m.	Manchester a.m.	Manchester p.m.	Newcastle a.m.	Newcastle p.m.	Glasgow a.m.	Glasgow p.m.	Belfast a.m.	Belfast p.m.
	h m	h m	h m	h m	h m	h m	h m	h m	h m	h m	h m	h m	h m	h m
1	8 06	4 01	8 16	4 11	8 18	4 02	8 26	3 59	8 32	3 47	8 48	3 53	8 48	4 07
2	8 06	4 02	8 16	4 12	8 18	4 03	8 25	4 00	8 31	3 48	8 48	3 54	8 47	4 08
3	8 06	4 03	8 16	4 13	8 18	4 04	8 25	4 01	8 31	3 49	8 47	3 55	8 47	4 09
4	8 06	4 04	8 16	4 14	8 18	4 06	8 25	4 03	8 31	3 51	8 47	3 57	8 47	4 11
5	8 06	4 05	8 15	4 16	8 18	4 07	8 25	4 04	8 31	3 52	8 47	3 58	8 47	4 12
6	8 06	4 06	8 15	4 17	8 17	4 08	8 24	4 05	8 30	3 53	8 46	3 59	8 46	4 13
7	8 05	4 07	8 15	4 18	8 17	4 10	8 24	4 07	8 30	3 55	8 46	4 01	8 46	4 15
8	8 05	4 09	8 15	4 19	8 16	4 11	8 23	4 08	8 29	3 56	8 45	4 02	8 45	4 16
9	8 04	4 10	8 14	4 21	8 16	4 12	8 23	4 09	8 28	3 58	8 44	4 04	8 44	4 18
10	8 04	4 11	8 14	4 22	8 15	4 14	8 22	4 11	8 28	3 59	8 44	4 05	8 44	4 19
11	8 03	4 12	8 13	4 23	8 14	4 15	8 21	4 12	8 27	4 01	8 43	4 07	8 43	4 21
12	8 03	4 14	8 13	4 25	8 14	4 17	8 21	4 14	8 26	4 03	8 42	4 09	8 42	4 23
13	8 02	4 15	8 12	4 26	8 13	4 18	8 20	4 15	8 25	4 04	8 41	4 10	8 41	4 24
14	8 01	4 17	8 11	4 28	8 13	4 20	8 19	4 17	8 24	4 06	8 40	4 12	8 40	4 26
15	8 01	4 18	8 11	4 29	8 12	4 21	8 19	4 18	8 23	4 08	8 39	4 14	8 39	4 28
16	8 00	4 20	8 10	4 30	8 11	4 23	8 18	4 20	8 22	4 09	8 38	4 16	8 38	4 29
17	7 59	4 21	8 09	4 32	8 10	4 24	8 17	4 21	8 21	4 11	8 37	4 18	8 37	4 31
18	7 58	4 23	8 08	4 33	8 09	4 26	8 16	4 23	8 20	4 13	8 36	4 20	8 36	4 33
19	7 57	4 25	8 07	4 35	8 08	4 28	8 15	4 25	8 19	4 15	8 34	4 21	8 35	4 35
20	7 56	4 26	8 06	4 37	8 07	4 29	8 14	4 27	8 18	4 17	8 33	4 23	8 34	4 37
21	7 55	4 28	8 05	4 38	8 06	4 31	8 13	4 28	8 16	4 18	8 31	4 25	8 33	4 38
22	7 54	4 30	8 04	4 40	8 05	4 33	8 11	4 30	8 15	4 20	8 30	4 27	8 31	4 40
23	7 53	4 31	8 03	4 41	8 04	4 34	8 10	4 32	8 14	4 22	8 29	4 29	8 30	4 42
24	7 51	4 33	8 01	4 43	8 02	4 36	8 09	4 34	8 12	4 25	8 27	4 32	8 29	4 44
25	7 50	4 35	8 00	4 45	8 01	4 38	8 07	4 36	8 11	4 27	8 26	4 34	8 27	4 46
26	7 49	4 37	7 59	4 47	8 00	4 40	8 06	4 38	8 09	4 29	8 24	4 36	8 26	4 48
27	7 47	4 39	7 57	4 49	7 58	4 42	8 04	4 40	8 07	4 31	8 22	4 38	8 24	4 50
28	7 46	4 40	7 56	4 50	7 57	4 43	8 03	4 42	8 06	4 33	8 21	4 40	8 23	4 52
29	7 45	4 42	7 55	4 52	7 56	4 45	8 01	4 44	8 04	4 35	8 19	4 42	8 21	4 54
30	7 43	4 44	7 53	4 54	7 54	4 47	8 00	4 46	8 03	4 37	8 17	4 44	8 19	4 56
31	7 42	4 46	7 52	4 56	7 53	4 49	7 58	4 48	8 01	4 39	8 15	4 46	8 17	4 58

JUPITER ♃   SATURN ♄

Day	R.A.	Dec. +	Transit	5° high W. 52°	5° high W. 56°	R.A.	Dec. +	Transit	5° high W. 52°	5° high W. 56°
	h m	°	h m	h m	h m	h m	°	h m	h m	h m
1	0 59	4·9	18 17	0 13	0 14	8 13	20·2	1 34	8 47	9 02
11	1 02	5·3	17 41	23 37	23 38	8 10	20·4	0 51	8 04	8 19
21	1 07	5·8	17 06	23 04	23 06	8 07	20·6	0 09	7 23	7 38
31	1 12	6·4	16 32	22 32	22 34	8 03	20·7	23 26	6 43	6 58

Equatorial diameter of Jupiter 40″ of Saturn 21″.   Diameters of Saturn's rings 46″ and 17″

URANUS ♅   NEPTUNE ♆

Day	R.A.	Dec. −	10° high E. 52°	10° high E. 56°	Transit	R.A.	Dec. −	Transit	
	h m	° ′	h m	h m	h m	h m	° ′	h m	
1	14 16·9	13 11	4 01	4 24	7 37	16 45·1	20 49	10 04	Neptune is
11	14 18·1	13 17	3 23	3 46	6 58	16 46·5	20 52	9 26	too close to
21	14 19·1	13 22	2 45	3 08	6 20	16 47·8	20 54	8 48	the Sun for
31	14 19·6	13 25	2 08	2 31	5 41	16 48·9	20 55	8 10	observation

Diameter 4″   Diameter 2″

Day OF		
Month	Week	

Februa, Roman festival
of Purification
Sun's Longitude 330° ♓ 19ᵈ 13ʰ

1	♒︎.	**4th ♒︎. after Epiphany.** Sir Stanley Matthews
2	M.	**Purification.** Candlemas [b. 1915
3	Tu.	Beau Nash d. 1762. George Crabbe d. 1832
4	W.	Thomas Carlyle d. 1881
5	Th.	J. B. Dunlop b. 1840. Sir Robert Peel b. 1788
6	F.	QUEEN's ACCESSION, 1952. Queen Anne b. 1665
7	S.	Sir Thomas More b. 1478. Charles Dickens b. 1812
8	♒︎.	**5th ♒︎. after Epiphany.** Jules Verne b. 1828
9	M.	Lord Darnley d. 1567. Marquess of Exeter b. 1905
10	Tu.	Harold Macmillan b. 1894. Lord Lister d. 1912
11	W.	Descartes d. 1650. Thomas Edison b. 1847
12	Th.	Charles Darwin b. 1809. Abraham Lincoln b. 1809
13	F.	Wagner d. 1883. Georges Simenon b. 1903
14	S.	VALENTINE's DAY. Sir P. G. Wodehouse d. 1975
15	♒︎.	**Septuagesima.** Gen. Lew Wallace d. 1905
16	M.	G. M. Trevelyan b. 1876**
17	Tu.	Heine d. 1856. Sir Donald Wolfit d. 1968
18	W.	Queen Mary I b. 1516. Paganini b. 1784
19	Th.	PRINCE ANDREW BORN, 1960. David Garrick [b. 1717
20	F.	Charles V b. 1500. Spinoza d. 1677
21	S.	Mary Shelley d. 1851. Gogol d. 1852
22	♒︎.	**Sexagesima.** Chopin b. 1810
23	M.	Samuel Pepys b. 1633. Keats d. 1821
24	Tu.	**St. Matthias.** Thomas Coutts d. 1822
25	W.	Princess Alice, Countess of Athlone b. 1883
26	Th.	Sir Christopher Wren d. 1723. Victor Hugo b. 1802
27	F.	John Evelyn d. 1706. Longfellow b. 1807
28	S.	Cyril Tourneur d. 1626. Henry James d. 1916
29	♒︎.	**Quinquagesima.** E. F. Benson d. 1940

PHENOMENA

February 6ᵈ 03ʰ Jupiter in conjunction with the Moon. Jupiter 4° S.
10ᵈ 16ʰ Mars in conjunction with the Moon. Mars 5° N.
13ᵈ 19ʰ Saturn in conjunction with the Moon. Saturn 5° N.
16ᵈ 15ʰ at Mercury greatest western elongation (26°).
27ᵈ 14ʰ Venus in conjunction with the Moon. Venus 6° S.
28ᵈ 00ʰ Mercury in conjunction with the Moon. Mercury 7° S.

CONSTELLATIONS

The following constellations are near the meridian at

d h	d h
Jan. 1 24	Jan. 16 23
Feb. 1 22	Feb. 15 21
Mar. 1 20	Mar. 16 19

Draco (below the Pole), Camelopardus, Auriga, Taurus, Gemini, Orion, Canis Minor, Monoceros, Lepus, Canis Major and Puppis (Argo).

MINIMA OF ALGOL

d h	d h
2 23	17 7
5 20	20 4
8 17	23 1
11 14	25 22
14 10	28 18

PHASES OF THE MOON

	d h m
☽ First Quarter	8 10 05
○ Full Moon	15 16 43
☾ Last Quarter	22 08 16
● New Moon	29 23 25

	d h
Apogee (405,100 kilometres)	5 13
Perigee (361,310 „)	17 10

Mean Longitude of Ascending Node on February 1, 228°.

MONTHLY NOTES

Feb. 1. Pheasant and partridge shooting ends.
4. Independence Commemoration Day, Sri Lanka.
6. National Day, New Zealand.

QUARTER DAYS (England, Wales and Northern Ireland)

Lady Day	March 25	*Michaelmas*	September 29
Midsummer	June 24	*Christmas*	December 25

SCOTTISH TERM DAYS

Candlemas	February 2	*Lammas*	August 1
Whitsunday	May 15	*Martinmas*	November 11

Removal Terms are May 28 and November 28.

** Centenary.

Day	Right Ascension	Dec. —	Equation of Time	Rise 52°	Rise 56°	Transit	Set 52°	Set 56°	Sidereal Time	Transit of First Point of Aries
	h m s	° ′	m s	h m	h m	h m	h m	h m	h m s	h m s
1	20 54 50	17 24	−13 28	7 42	7 58	12 14	16 46	16 30	8 41 22	15 16 08
2	20 58 55	17 07	−13 37	7 41	7 56	12 14	16 48	16 33	8 45 19	15 12 12
3	21 02 59	16 50	−13 44	7 39	7 54	12 14	16 49	16 35	8 49 15	15 08 16
4	21 07 03	16 33	−13 51	7 38	7 52	12 14	16 51	16 37	8 53 12	15 04 20
5	21 11 05	16 15	−13 57	7 36	7 50	12 14	16 53	16 39	8 57 08	15 00 24
6	21 15 07	15 57	−14 03	7 34	7 48	12 14	16 55	16 41	9 01 05	14 56 28
7	21 19 08	15 38	−14 07	7 33	7 46	12 14	16 57	16 44	9 05 01	14 52 32
8	21 23 09	15 20	−14 11	7 31	7 44	12 14	16 59	16 46	9 08 58	14 48 36
9	21 27 08	15 01	−14 14	7 29	7 42	12 14	17 01	16 48	9 12 54	14 44 40
10	21 31 07	14 42	−14 16	7 27	7 40	12 14	17 02	16 50	9 16 51	14 40 44
11	21 35 04	14 22	−14 17	7 25	7 37	12 14	17 04	16 52	9 20 47	14 36 48
12	21 39 01	14 03	−14 17	7 24	7 35	12 14	17 06	16 55	9 24 44	14 32 53
13	21 42 58	13 43	−14 17	7 22	7 33	12 14	17 08	16 57	9 28 41	14 28 57
14	21 46 53	13 23	−14 16	7 20	7 31	12 14	17 10	16 59	9 32 37	14 25 01
15	21 50 48	13 03	−14 14	7 18	7 29	12 14	17 12	17 01	9 36 34	14 21 05
16	21 54 42	12 42	−14 12	7 16	7 26	12 14	17 14	17 03	9 40 30	14 17 09
17	21 58 35	12 22	−14 08	7 14	7 24	12 14	17 15	17 05	9 44 27	14 13 13
18	22 02 27	12 01	−14 04	7 12	7 22	12 14	17 17	17 08	9 48 23	14 09 17
19	22 06 19	11 40	−14 00	7 10	7 19	12 14	17 19	17 10	9 52 20	14 05 21
20	22 10 10	11 18	−13 54	7 08	7 17	12 14	17 21	17 12	9 56 16	14 01 25
21	22 14 01	10 57	−13 48	7 06	7 15	12 14	17 23	17 14	10 00 13	13 57 29
22	22 17 51	10 35	−13 41	7 04	7 12	12 14	17 25	17 16	10 04 10	13 53 33
23	22 21 40	10 13	−13 34	7 02	7 10	13 14	17 27	17 19	10 08 06	13 49 38
24	22 25 29	9 52	−13 26	7 00	7 07	12 13	17 28	17 21	10 12 03	13 45 42
25	22 29 17	9 29	−13 18	6 58	7 05	12 13	17 30	17 23	10 15 59	13 41 46
26	22 33 04	9 07	−13 09	6 55	7 03	12 13	17 32	17 25	10 19 56	13 37 50
27	22 36 51	8 45	−12 59	6 53	7 00	12 13	17 34	17 27	10 23 52	13 33 54
28	22 40 37	8 22	−12 49	6 51	6 58	12 13	17 36	17 29	10 27 49	13 29 58
29	22 44 23	8 00	−12 38	6 49	6 55	12 13	17 38	17 31	10 31 45	13 26 02

THE SUN   s.d. 16′·2

Duration of Civil (C), Nautical (N), and Astronomical (A), Twilight (in minutes)

Lat. °	Feb. 1 C	N	A	Feb. 11 C	N	A	Feb. 21 C	N	A	Feb. 28 C	N	A
52	37	77	117	35	75	114	34	74	113	34	73	112
56	41	86	130	39	83	126	38	81	125	38	81	124

ASTRONOMICAL NOTES

MERCURY, although it attains its greatest western elongation on the 16th, is unsuitably placed for observation in these latitudes.

VENUS is a brilliant morning star, magnitude −3·4, but only visible in the south-eastern sky for a very short period of time before sunrise.

MARS is an evening star, but now noticeably fainter than when at opposition, its magnitude dropping to +0·5 by the end of February. The gibbous Moon will be seen near the planet on the evening of the 10th.

JUPITER is a prominent evening star, magnitude −1·8, in the constellation of Pisces. On the evening of the 5th the crescent Moon will be seen near the planet.

SATURN is a bright evening star, magnitude 0·0, and by the end of the month its retrograde motion has carried it back from Cancer to Gemini. On the evening of the 13th the gibbous Moon passes 5° S. of the planet.

ZODIACAL LIGHT. The evening cone may be observed in the western sky after the end of twilight from the 17th to the end of the month. This faint phenomenon is only visible under good conditions and in the absence of both moonlight and artificial lighting.

THE MOON

Day	R.A.	Dec.	Hor. Par.	Semi-diam.	Sun's Co-long.	P.A. of Bright Limb	Phase	Age	Rise 52°	Rise 56°	Transit	Set 52°	Set 56°
	h m	°	′	′	°	°		d	h m	h m	h m	h m	h m
1	21 22	−10·1	55·4	15·1	275	222	1	0·7	7 42	7 50	13 05	18 37	18 31
2	22 10	− 6·2	54·9	15·0	287	236	3	1·7	8 04	8 08	13 49	19 44	19 42
3	22 55	− 2·0	54·6	14·9	299	240	7	2·7	8 24	8 25	14 31	20 49	20 51
4	23 41	+ 2·1	54·3	14·8	311	242	13	3·7	8 44	8 41	15 13	21 54	21 59
5	0 25	+ 6·2	54·2	14·8	323	244	20	4·7	9 05	8 58	15 56	22 58	23 07
6	1 11	+10·0	54·1	14·8	336	247	28	5·7	9 27	9 17	16 39	..	..
7	1 57	+13·4	54·3	14·8	348	249	37	6·7	9 52	9 39	17 24	0 02	0 14
8	2 45	+16·2	54·6	14·9	0	253	46	7·7	10 22	10 06	18 10	1 05	1 21
9	3 35	+18·4	55·1	15·0	12	256	56	8·7	10 58	10 40	19 00	2 07	2 26
10	4 27	+19·9	55·8	15·2	24	260	65	9·7	11 42	11 22	19 51	3 06	3 26
11	5 21	+20·3	56·6	15·4	36	264	75	10·7	12 36	12 16	20 45	4 00	4 21
12	6 16	+19·7	57·4	15·6	49	268	83	11·7	13 39	13 20	21 39	4 49	5 08
13	7 13	+18·0	58·3	15·9	61	271	90	12·7	14 50	14 35	22 35	5 30	5 47
14	8 10	+15·1	59·2	16·1	73	271	96	13·7	16 08	15 56	23 30	6 06	6 19
15	9 07	+11·3	59·9	16·3	85	259	99	14·7	17 29	17 22	..	6 37	6 45
16	10 04	+ 6·7	60·4	16·5	97	160	100	15·7	18 51	18 49	0 24	7 05	7 09
17	11 00	+ 1·7	60·7	16·5	109	126	97	16·7	20 14	20 17	1 18	7 31	7 31
18	11 56	− 3·5	60·6	16·5	121	119	92	17·7	21 37	21 44	2 12	7 57	7 53
19	12 52	− 8·4	60·4	16·5	134	115	85	18·7	22 58	23 09	3 07	8 25	8 17
20	13 49	−12·7	59·9	16·3	146	111	75	19·7	..	..	4 02	8 56	8 44
21	14 47	−16·2	59·3	16·2	158	107	65	20·7	0 16	0 31	4 57	9 33	9 16
22	15 44	−18·7	58·6	16·0	170	103	54	21·7	1 28	1 47	5 54	10 15	9 56
23	16 42	−20·0	58·0	15·8	182	98	43	22·7	2 32	2 53	6 49	11 05	10 45
24	17 39	−20·1	57·3	15·6	194	93	32	23·7	3 27	3 48	7 44	12 03	11 42
25	18 35	−19·2	56·7	15·4	206	89	23	24·7	4 12	4 31	8 37	13 05	12 47
26	19 28	−17·2	56·1	15·3	219	86	15	25·7	4 49	5 05	9 27	14 11	13 56
27	20 20	−14·5	55·6	15·2	231	84	9	26·7	5 20	5 32	10 15	15 19	15 07
28	21 09	−11·1	55·2	15·0	243	85	4	27·7	5 46	5 55	11 01	16 26	16 18
29	21 56	− 7·4	54·8	14·9	255	94	1	28·7	6 09	6 14	11 45	17 32	17 28

MERCURY ☿

Day	R.A.	Dec. −	Diam.	Phase	Transit		Day	R.A.	Dec. −	Diam.	Phase	Transit	
	h m	°	″		h m			h m	°	″		h m	
1	19 41	18·2	9	21	10 57	Mercury is too close to the Sun for observation	16	20 09	19·7	7	59	10 29	Mercury is too close to the Sun for observation
4	19 39	18·8	9	30	10 44		19	20 23	19·5	7	64	10 31	
7	19 41	19·3	8	39	10 35		22	20 37	19·1	6	68	10 34	
10	19 48	19·6	8	47	10 31		25	20 53	18·5	6	72	10 38	
13	19 57	19·7	7	53	10 29		28	21 10	17·7	6	75	10 42	
16	20 09	19·7	7	59	10 29		31	21 27	16·7	6	78	10 48	

VENUS ♀

Day	R.A.	Dec. −	Diam.	Phase	5° high E 52°	5° high E 56°	Transit
	h m	°	″		h m	h m	h m
1	18 30	22·3	13	82	6 40	7 13	9 50
6	18 57	22·1	13	83	6 45	7 17	9 56
11	19 23	21·6	13	85	6 48	7 19	10 03
16	19 50	20·9	12	86	6 47	7 17	10 10
21	20 15	19·8	12	87	6 46	7 13	10 16
26	20 41	18·6	12	88	6 43	7 07	10 22
31	21 06	17·2	12	89	6 38	7 00	10 27

MARS ♂

Day	R.A.	Dec. +	Diam.	Phase	Transit	5° high W 52°	5° high W 56°
	h m	°	″		h m	h m	h m
1	4 56	25·6	11	93	20 11	4 02	4 24
6	4 59	25·6	11	92	19 55	3 45	4 07
11	5 04	25·7	10	92	19 40	3 30	3 52
16	5 09	25·7	10	91	19 26	3 16	3 38
21	5 15	25·8	9	91	19 13	3 04	3 26
26	5 23	25·8	9	90	19 01	2 51	3 13
31	5 30	25·8	8	90	18 49	2 39	3 01

SUNRISE AND SUNSET (G.M.T.)

Day	London a.m. h m	London p.m. h m	Bristol a.m. h m	Bristol p.m. h m	Birmingham a.m. h m	Birmingham p.m. h m	Manchester a.m. h m	Manchester p.m. h m	Newcastle a.m. h m	Newcastle p.m. h m	Glasgow a.m. h m	Glasgow p.m. h m	Belfast a.m. h m	Belfast p.m. h m
1	7 41	4 48	7 50	4 58	7 52	4 51	7 57	4 50	8 00	4 41	8 14	4 48	8 16	5 00
2	7 39	4 50	7 49	5 00	7 50	4 53	7 55	4 52	7 58	4 43	8 12	4 51	8 14	5 03
3	7 38	4 51	7 47	5 01	7 48	4 55	7 53	4 54	7 56	4 45	8 10	4 53	8 12	5 05
4	7 37	4 53	7 46	5 03	7 46	4 57	7 51	4 56	7 54	4 47	8 08	4 55	8 10	5 07
5	7 35	4 55	7 44	5 05	7 44	4 59	7 49	4 58	7 52	4 49	8 06	4 57	8 08	5 09
6	7 33	4 57	7 42	5 07	7 43	5 01	7 48	5 00	7 50	4 51	8 04	4 59	8 07	5 11
7	7 32	4 58	7 41	5 08	7 41	5 03	7 46	5 02	7 48	4 54	8 02	5 02	8 05	5 13
8	7 30	5 00	7 39	5 10	7 39	5 05	7 44	5 04	7 46	4 56	8 00	5 04	8 03	5 15
9	7 28	5 02	7 38	5 12	7 37	5 07	7 42	5 06	7 44	4 58	7 58	5 06	8 01	5 17
10	7 26	5 04	7 36	5 14	7 35	5 08	7 40	5 07	7 42	5 00	7 56	5 08	7 59	5 19
11	7 24	5 05	7 34	5 15	7 33	5 10	7 38	5 09	7 40	5 02	7 54	5 10	7 57	5 21
12	7 23	5 07	7 32	5 17	7 32	5 12	7 37	5 11	7 38	5 04	7 52	5 12	7 55	5 23
13	7 21	5 09	7 31	5 19	7 30	5 14	7 35	5 13	7 36	5 06	7 50	5 14	7 53	5 25
14	7 19	5 11	7 29	5 21	7 28	5 16	7 33	5 15	7 34	5 08	7 48	5 16	7 51	5 27
15	7 17	5 13	7 27	5 23	7 26	5 18	7 31	5 17	7 32	5 10	7 46	5 18	7 49	5 29
16	7 15	5 15	7 25	5 25	7 24	5 20	7 29	5 19	7 29	5 12	7 43	5 20	7 47	5 31
17	7 13	5 16	7 23	5 26	7 22	5 21	7 27	5 21	7 27	5 14	7 41	5 22	7 45	5 33
18	7 11	5 18	7 21	5 28	7 20	5 23	7 25	5 23	7 25	5 17	7 39	5 25	7 43	5 35
19	7 09	5 20	7 19	5 30	7 18	5 25	7 22	5 25	7 22	5 19	7 36	5 27	7 40	5 37
20	7 07	5 22	7 17	5 32	7 16	5 27	7 20	5 27	7 20	5 21	7 34	5 29	7 38	5 39
21	7 05	5 24	7 15	5 34	7 14	5 29	7 18	5 29	7 18	5 23	7 32	5 31	7 36	5 41
22	7 03	5 26	7 13	5 36	7 12	5 31	7 16	5 31	7 16	5 25	7 29	5 33	7 33	5 43
23	7 01	5 28	7 11	5 38	7 10	5 33	7 14	5 33	7 14	5 27	7 27	5 36	7 31	5 46
24	6 59	5 29	7 09	5 39	7 08	5 34	7 11	5 35	7 11	5 29	7 24	5 38	7 28	5 48
25	6 57	5 31	7 07	5 41	7 06	5 36	7 09	5 37	7 09	5 31	7 22	5 40	7 26	5 50
26	6 54	5 33	7 04	5 43	7 03	5 38	7 07	5 39	7 07	5 33	7 20	5 42	7 24	5 52
27	6 52	5 35	7 02	5 45	7 01	5 40	7 04	5 41	7 04	5 35	7 17	5 44	7 21	5 54
28	6 50	5 37	7 00	5 47	6 59	5 42	7 02	5 43	7 02	5 37	7 15	5 46	7 19	5 56
29	6 48	5 39	6 58	5 49	6 57	5 44	7 00	5 45	6 59	5 39	7 12	5 48	7 17	5 58

JUPITER ♃

Day	R.A. h m	Dec. + °	Transit h m	5° high W. 52° h m	5° high W. 56° h m
1	1 12	6·4	16 29	22 29	22 31
11	1 19	7·1	15 56	21 59	22 01
21	1 25	7·8	15 23	21 30	21 33
31	1 33	8·6	14 51	21 01	21 05

SATURN ♄

R.A. h m	Dec. + °	Transit h m	5° high W. 52° h m	5° high W. 56° h m
8 03	20·8	23 18	6 39	6 54
8 00	20·9	22 35	5 58	6 13
7 57	21·1	21 53	5 17	5 32
7 55	21·2	21 12	4 35	4 51

Equatorial diameter of Jupiter 36″; of Saturn 20″.   Diameters of Saturn's rings 46″ and 17″

URANUS ♅

Day	R.A. h m	Dec. − ° ′	10° high E. 52° h m	10° high E. 56° h m	Transit h m
1	14 19·7	13 25	2 04	2 27	5 37
11	14 19·9	13 25	1 25	1 48	4 58
21	14 19·7	13 24	0 45	1 08	4 19
31	14 19·2	13 22	0 06	0 29	3 39

NEPTUNE ♆

R.A. h m	Dec. − ° ′	10° high E. 52° h m	10° high E. 56° h m	Transit h m
16 49·0	20 55	5 36	6 23	8 06
16 49·9	20 56	4 57	5 45	7 28
16 50·6	20 57	4 18	5 06	6 49
16 51·0	20 57	3 40	4 27	6 10

Diameter 4″   Diameter 2″

Mars, Roman god of battle

Sun's Longitude 0° ♈ 20^d 12^h

Day of Month	Day of Week	
1	M.	ST. DAVID'S DAY. Lytton Strachey b. 1880
2	Tu.	Shrove Tuesday. Pius XII b. 1876**
3	W.	**Ash Wednesday.** Van Gogh b. 1853
4	Th.	R.N.L.I. founded 1824. Patrick Moore b. 1923
5	F.	James I d. 1625. Stalin d. 1953
6	S.	Louisa M. Alcott d. 1888. Adm. von Tirpitz d. 1930
7	**S.**	**1st S. in Lent.** Maurice Ravel b. 1875
8	M.	William III d. 1702. Kenneth Grahame b. 1859
9	Tu.	Amerigo Vespucci b. 1451. V. M. Molotov b. 1890
10	W.	PRINCE EDWARD BORN, 1964. Diaghilev b. 1872
11	Th.	Harold Wilson b. 1916. Sir Alexander Fleming [d. 1955
12	F.	John Bull d. 1628. Sun Yat Sen d. 1925
13	S.	Daniel Lambert b. 1770. Sir Frank Worrell d. 1967
14	**S.**	**2nd S. in Lent.** Karl Marx d. 1883
15	M.	Julius Caesar d. B.C. 44. Visct. Chandos b. 1893
16	Tu.	G. S. Ohm b. 1787. Aubrey Beardsley d. 1898
17	W.	ST. PATRICK'S DAY. Edmund Kean b. 1787
18	Th.	Rudolf Diesel b. 1858. Laurence Sterne d. 1768
19	F.	Sir Richard Burton b. 1821. David Livingstone [b. 1813
20	S.	Ibsen b. 1828. Sir Michael Redgrave b. 1908
21	**S.**	**3rd S. in Lent.** Aboukir 1801
22	M.	Nicholas Monsarrat b. 1910. Lord Stokes b. 1914
23	Tu.	Sir Muirhead Bone b. 1876**
24	W.	Queen Elizabeth I d. 1603. Queen Mary d. 1953
25	Th.	**Annunciation.** Lady Day. King Faisal d. 1975
26	F.	Beethoven d. 1827. Walt Whitman d. 1892
27	S.	James Callaghan b. 1912. Sir Arthur Bliss d. 1975
28	**S.**	**4th S. in Lent.** Rachmaninoff d. 1943
29	M.	Sir William Walton b. 1902. Joyce Cary d. 1957
30	Tu.	Goya b. 1746. Beau Brummell d. 1840
31	W.	John Donne d. 1631. Charlotte Brontë d. 1855

PHENOMENA

March 4^d 20^h Jupiter in conjunction with the Moon. Jupiter 3° S.

9^d 19^h Mars in conjunction with the Moon. Mars 6° N.

12^d 03^h Saturn in conjunction with the Moon Saturn 5° N.

20^d 12^h Vernal Equinox.

28^d 24^h Venus in conjunction with the Moon. Venus 6° S.

30^d 22^h Pluto at opposition.

CONSTELLATIONS

The following constellations are near the meridian at

	d	h		d	h
Feb.	1	24	Feb.	15	23
Mar.	1	22	Mar.	16	21
Apr.	1	20	Apr.	15	19

Cepheus (below the Pole), Camelopardus, Lynx, Gemini, Cancer, Leo, Canis Minor, Hydra, Monoceros, Canis Major and Puppis (Argo).

MINIMA OF ALGOL

d	h	d	h
2	15	19	20
5	12	22	17
8	9	25	14
11	6	28	11
14	3	31	7
16	23		

PHASES OF THE MOON

	d	h	m
☽ First Quarter......	9	04	38
○ Full Moon........	16	02	53
☾ Last Quarter......	22	18	54
● New Moon.......	30	17	08

	d	h
Apogee(406,000 kilometres)	4	04
Perigee(357,640 „)	16	19
Apogee(406,510 „)	31	10

Mean Longitude of Ascending Node on March 1, 226°.

Summer Time in 1976 (*see* p. 142).—Begins: March 21 at 2 a.m. G.M.T. Ends: October 24 at 2 a.m. G.M.T.

MONTHLY NOTES

Mar. 3. Lent begins (ends midnight April 17).
12. National Day, Mauritius.
17. Bank Holiday in Northern Ireland.
25. Lady Day. Quarter Day.
31. Financial Year 1975–76 ends.

** Centenary.

Day	THE SUN							Sidereal Time	Transit of First Point of Aries
	Right Ascension	Dec.	Equation of Time	Rise		Transit	Set		
				52°	56°		52°	56°		
	h m s	° ′	m s	h m	h m	h m	h m	h m	h m s	h m s
1	22 48 09	−7 37	−12 27	6 47	6 53	12 12	17 39	17 34	10 35 42	13 22 06
2	22 51 53	−7 14	−12 15	6 45	6 50	12 12	17 41	17 36	10 39 39	13 18 10
3	22 55 38	−6 51	−12 03	6 42	6 48	12 12	17 43	17 38	10 43 35	13 14 14
4	22 59 21	−6 28	−11 50	6 40	6 45	12 12	17 45	17 40	10 47 32	13 10 19
5	23 03 05	−6 05	−11 37	6 38	6 42	12 12	17 46	17 42	10 51 28	13 06 23
6	23 06 48	−5 42	−11 23	6 36	6 40	12 11	17 48	17 44	10 55 25	13 02 27
7	23 10 30	−5 19	−11 09	6 33	6 37	12 11	17 50	17 46	10 59 21	12 58 31
8	23 14 12	−4 55	−10 54	6 31	6 35	12 11	17 52	17 48	11 03 18	12 54 35
9	23 17 54	−4 32	−10 39	6 29	6 32	12 11	17 53	17 50	11 07 14	12 50 39
10	23 21 35	−4 08	−10 24	6 27	6 30	12 10	17 55	17 52	11 11 11	12 46 43
11	23 25 16	−3 45	−10 09	6 24	6 27	12 10	17 57	17 55	11 15 08	12 42 47
12	23 28 57	−3 21	− 9 53	6 22	6 24	12 10	17 59	17 57	11 19 04	12 38 51
13	23 32 37	−2 58	− 9 36	6 20	6 22	12 09	18 00	17 59	11 23 01	12 34 55
14	23 36 17	−2 34	− 9 20	6 17	6 19	12 09	18 02	18 01	11 26 57	12 30 59
15	23 39 57	−2 10	− 9 03	6 15	6 16	12 09	18 04	18 03	11 30 54	12 27 04
16	23 43 36	−1 47	− 8 46	6 13	6 14	12 09	18 06	18 05	11 34 50	12 23 08
17	23 47 15	−1 23	− 8 29	6 11	6 11	12 08	18 07	18 07	11 38 47	12 19 12
18	23 50 54	−0 59	− 8 11	6 08	6 09	12 08	18 09	18 09	11 42 43	12 15 16
19	23 54 33	−0 35	− 7 54	6 06	6 06	12 08	18 11	18 11	11 46 40	12 11 20
20	23 58 12	−0 12	− 7 36	6 04	6 03	12 07	18 13	18 13	11 50 36	12 07 24
21	0 01 51	+0 12	− 7 18	6 01	6 01	12 07	18 14	18 15	11 54 33	12 03 28
22	0 05 29	+0 36	− 7 00	5 59	5 58	12 07	18 16	18 17	11 58 30	11 59 32
23	0 09 08	+0 59	− 6 42	5 57	5 55	12 07	18 18	18 19	12 02 26	11 55 36
24	0 12 46	+1 23	− 6 24	5 54	5 53	12 06	18 20	18 21	12 06 23	11 51 40
25	0 16 25	+1 47	− 6 05	5 52	5 50	12 06	18 21	18 23	12 10 19	11 47 44
26	0 20 03	+2 10	− 5 47	5 50	5 48	12 06	18 23	18 25	12 14 16	11 43 49
27	0 23 41	+2 34	− 5 29	5 47	5 45	12 05	18 25	18 27	12 18 12	11 39 53
28	0 27 20	+2 57	− 5 11	5 45	5 42	12 05	18 26	18 29	12 22 09	11 35 57
29	0 30 58	+3 21	− 4 53	5 43	5 39	12 05	18 28	18 31	12 26 05	11 32 01
30	0 34 37	+3 44	− 4 35	5 41	5 37	12 04	18 30	18 34	12 30 02	11 28 05
31	0 38 15	+4 07	− 4 17	5 38	5 34	12 04	18 31	18 36	12 33 59	11 24 09

Duration of Civil (C), Nautical (N), and Astronomical (A), Twilight (in minutes)

Lat. °	Mar. 1			Mar. 11			Mar. 21			Mar. 31		
	C	N	A	C	N	A	C	N	A	C	N	A
52	34	73	112	34	73	113	34	74	116	34	76	120
56	38	81	124	37	80	124	37	82	129	38	84	136

ASTRONOMICAL NOTES

MERCURY is unsuitably placed for observation.

VENUS is a brilliant morning star at first, magnitude −3·3, but only visible low in the E.S.E. sky for a very short while before dawn. Gradually it becomes more and more difficult to observe and by the end of the month rises about the same time as the Sun.

MARS is an evening star, magnitude +0·8, passing from Taurus into Gemini in the middle of the month. On the evening of the 9th the Moon, at First Quarter, passes 6° S. of the planet.

JUPITER is an evening star, magnitude −1·7 but by the end of the month is too low in the western sky for observation after about 20h. On the evening of the 4th the crescent Moon passes 3° N. of the planet.

SATURN is a bright evening star, magnitude +0·2, almost stationary in the eastern part of Gemini, south of the Twins. On the morning of the 12th the gibbous Moon passes 5° S. of Saturn.

ZODIACAL LIGHT. The evening cone may be observed in the western sky after the end of twilight for the first two evenings of the month and again from the 17th onwards.

THE MOON

Day	R.A.	Dec.	Hor. Par.	Semi-diam.	Sun's Co-long.	P.A. of Bright Limb	Phase	Age	Rise 52°	Rise 56°	Transit	Set 52°	Set 56°
	h m	°	'	'	°	°		d	h m	h m	h m	h m	h m
1	22 42	− 3·3	54·5	14·9	267	161	0	0·0	6 30	6 32	12 28	18 37	18 37
2	23 27	+ 0·8	54·3	14·8	280	228	1	1·0	6 50	6 48	13 10	19 42	19 46
3	0 12	+ 4·9	54·1	14·7	292	239	4	2·0	7 11	7 06	13 53	20 46	20 53
4	0 57	+ 8·7	54·0	14·7	304	244	8	3·0	7 32	7 24	14 35	21 50	22 01
5	1 43	+12·2	54·0	14·7	316	248	14	4·0	7 57	7 45	15 19	22 53	23 07
6	2 31	+15·2	54·2	14·8	328	251	21	5·0	8 25	8 10	16 05	23 55	··
7	3 19	+17·6	54·5	14·9	341	255	29	6·0	8 58	8 40	16 52	··	0 12
8	4 10	+19·2	55·0	15·0	353	260	38	7·0	9 37	9 18	17 42	0 54	1 13
9	5 02	+20·0	55·6	15·2	5	264	48	8·0	10 25	10 05	18 33	1 49	2 09
10	5 55	+19·8	56·4	15·4	17	269	58	9·0	11 22	11 03	19 25	2 38	2 58
11	6 50	+18·6	57·3	15·6	29	273	68	10·0	12 28	12 11	20 19	3 22	3 39
12	7 46	+16·3	58·3	15·9	42	277	78	11·0	13 40	13 27	21 13	3 59	4 14
13	8 42	+13·0	59·2	16·1	54	280	86	12·0	14 58	14 48	22 07	4 32	4 43
14	9 38	+ 8·8	60·1	16·4	66	280	93	13·0	16 19	16 14	23 01	5 01	5 08
15	10 34	+ 4·0	60·8	16·6	78	276	98	14·0	17 42	17 42	23 56	5 29	5 31
16	11 31	− 1·1	61·2	16·7	90	227	100	15·0	19 07	19 12	··	5 56	5 54
17	12 29	− 6·3	61·3	16·7	102	126	99	16·0	20 31	20 41	0 52	6 24	6 17
18	13 27	−11·0	61·1	16·6	114	115	95	17·0	21 54	22 08	1 48	6 55	6 44
19	14 26	−14·9	60·6	16·5	127	109	88	18·0	23 11	23 29	2 46	7 30	7 15
20	15 26	−17·8	59·9	16·3	139	104	79	19·0	··	··	3 44	8 12	7 54
21	16 26	−19·5	59·0	16·1	151	98	69	20·0	0 21	0 41	4 42	9 01	8 41
22	17 25	−20·0	58·1	15·8	163	93	59	21·0	1 21	1 41	5 39	9 57	9 37
23	18 21	−19·3	57·3	15·6	175	88	48	22·0	2 10	2 29	6 33	10 59	10 41
24	19 16	−17·6	56·5	15·4	187	84	37	23·0	2 50	3 07	7 25	12 05	11 49
25	20 08	−15·0	55·8	15·2	200	80	28	24·0	3 23	3 36	8 13	13 11	12 59
26	20 57	−11·8	55·3	15·1	212	78	19	25·0	3 50	4 00	9 00	14 18	14 09
27	21 45	− 8·2	54·8	14·9	224	76	12	26·0	4 14	4 20	9 44	15 24	15 19
28	22 31	− 4·3	54·4	14·8	236	76	7	27·0	4 35	4 38	10 27	16 29	16 27
29	23 16	− 0·2	54·2	14·8	248	79	3	28·0	4 56	4 55	11 09	17 33	17 35
30	0 01	+ 3·8	54·0	14·7	261	90	1	29·0	5 16	5 12	11 51	18 37	18 43
31	0 46	+ 7·7	53·9	14·7	273	208	9	0·30	5 38	5 31	12 33	19 41	19 50

MERCURY ☿

Day	R.A.	Dec. −	Diam.	Phase	Transit		Day	R.A.	Dec. −	Diam.	Phase	Transit	
	h m	°	"		h m			h m	°	"		h m	
1	21 21	17·1	6	77	10 46	Mercury is too close to the Sun for observation	16	22 52	−9·6	5	90	11 18	Mercury is too close to the Sun for observation
4	21 38	16·0	6	80	10 52		19	23 11	−7·6	5	92	11 26	
7	21 56	14·7	5	83	10 58		22	23 31	−5·4	5	95	11 34	
10	22 14	13·2	5	85	11 04		25	23 51	−3·0	5	97	11 43	
13	22 33	11·5	5	88	11 11		28	0 12	−0·5	5	98	11 52	
16	22 52	9·6	5	90	11 18		31	0 34	+2·2	5	99	12 01	

VENUS ♀

Day	R.A.	Dec. −	Diam.	Phase	5° high E 52°	5° high E 56°	Transit
	h m	°	"		h m	h m	h m
1	21 01	17·5	12	89	6 39	7 01	10 26
6	21 26	15·8	12	90	6 33	6 53	10 31
11	21 50	14·0	11	90	6 26	6 43	10 36
16	22 14	12·0	11	91	6 18	6 32	10 40
21	22 38	9·9	11	92	6 09	6 21	10 44
26	23 01	7·7	11	93	6 00	6 10	10 47
31	23 24	5·4	11	94	5 51	5 58	10 51

MARS ♂

Day	R.A.	Dec. +	Diam.	Phase	Transit	5° high W 52°	5° high W 56°
	h m	°	"		h m	h m	h m
1	5 29	25·8	8	90	18 51	2 41	3 03
6	5 37	25·8	8	90	18 40	2 31	2 53
11	5 46	25·8	8	90	18 29	2 21	2 42
16	5 55	25·8	7	90	18 19	2 10	2 31
21	6 05	25·7	7	90	18 07	2 00	2 21
26	6 15	25·6	7	90	17 59	1 50	2 10
31	6 25	25·5	7	90	17 50	1 39	2 00

SUNRISE AND SUNSET (G.M.T.)

Day	London a.m. h m	London p.m. h m	Bristol a.m. h m	Bristol p.m. h m	Birmingham a.m. h m	Birmingham p.m. h m	Manchester a.m. h m	Manchester p.m. h m	Newcastle a.m. h m	Newcastle p.m. h m	Glasgow a.m. h m	Glasgow p.m. h m	Belfast a.m. h m	Belfast p.m. h m
1	6 46	5 40	6 56	5 50	6 55	5 46	6 58	5 47	6 57	5 42	7 10	5 51	7 15	6 00
2	6 44	5 42	6 54	5 52	6 52	5 47	6 55	5 48	6 54	5 43	7 07	5 53	7 12	6 01
3	6 42	5 44	6 51	5 54	6 50	5 49	6 53	5 50	6 52	5 45	7 05	5 55	7 10	6 03
4	6 40	5 46	6 49	5 56	6 47	5 51	6 50	5 52	6 49	5 47	7 02	5 57	7 07	6 05
5	6 38	5 47	6 47	5 57	6 45	5 53	6 48	5 54	6 47	5 49	6 59	5 59	7 05	6 07
6	6 36	5 49	6 45	5 59	6 43	5 55	6 46	5 56	6 45	5 51	6 57	6 01	7 03	6 09
7	6 33	5 50	6 43	6 00	6 40	5 57	6 43	5 58	6 42	5 53	6 54	6 03	7 00	6 11
8	6 31	5 52	6 41	6 02	6 38	5 59	6 41	6 00	6 40	5 55	6 52	6 05	6 58	6 13
9	6 29	5 54	6 39	6 04	6 36	6 00	6 39	6 01	6 37	5 57	6 49	6 07	6 55	6 15
10	6 27	5 55	6 36	6 05	6 34	6 02	6 37	6 03	6 35	5 59	6 47	6 09	6 53	6 17
11	6 24	5 57	6 34	6 07	6 31	6 04	6 34	6 05	6 32	6 02	6 44	6 12	6 50	6 20
12	6 22	5 59	6 32	6 09	6 29	6 06	6 32	6 07	6 29	6 04	6 41	6 14	6 47	6 22
13	6 20	6 00	6 30	6 10	6 27	6 07	6 30	6 09	6 27	6 06	6 39	6 16	6 45	6 24
14	6 17	6 02	6 27	6 12	6 24	6 09	6 27	6 11	6 24	6 08	6 36	6 18	6 42	6 26
15	6 15	6 04	6 25	6 14	6 22	6 11	6 25	6 12	6 22	6 09	6 33	6 20	6 40	6 27
16	6 13	6 06	6 23	6 16	6 20	6 13	6 22	6 14	6 19	6 11	6 31	6 22	6 37	6 29
17	6 11	6 07	6 21	6 17	6 18	6 14	6 20	6 16	6 16	6 13	6 28	6 24	6 35	6 31
18	6 08	6 09	6 18	6 19	6 15	6 16	6 17	6 17	6 14	6 15	6 26	6 26	6 32	6 33
19	6 06	6 11	6 16	6 21	6 13	6 18	6 15	6 20	6 12	6 17	6 23	6 28	6 30	6 35
20	6 04	6 13	6 14	6 23	6 11	6 20	6 12	6 22	6 09	6 19	6 20	6 30	6 27	6 37
21	6 01	6 14	6 11	6 24	6 08	6 21	6 10	6 24	6 07	6 21	6 18	6 32	6 25	6 39
22	5 59	6 16	6 09	6 26	6 06	6 23	6 07	6 26	6 04	6 23	6 15	6 34	6 22	6 41
23	5 57	6 18	6 07	6 28	6 04	6 25	6 05	6 27	6 02	6 24	6 12	6 36	6 20	6 42
24	5 54	6 20	6 04	6 30	6 01	6 27	6 03	6 29	6 00	6 26	6 10	6 38	6 18	6 44
25	5 52	6 21	6 02	6 31	5 59	6 28	6 00	6 31	5 57	6 28	6 07	6 40	6 15	6 46
26	5 50	6 23	6 00	6 33	5 57	6 30	5 58	6 33	5 55	6 30	6 05	6 42	6 13	6 48
27	5 47	6 25	5 57	6 34	5 54	6 32	5 55	6 35	5 52	6 32	6 02	6 44	6 10	6 50
28	5 45	6 26	5 55	6 36	5 52	6 33	5 53	6 36	5 49	6 34	5 59	6 46	6 07	6 52
29	5 43	6 28	5 53	6 38	5 50	6 35	5 51	6 38	5 46	6 36	5 56	6 48	6 04	6 54
30	5 41	6 30	5 51	6 39	5 48	6 37	5 49	6 40	5 44	6 38	5 54	6 51	6 02	6 57
31	5 39	6 31	5 49	6 41	5 45	6 38	5 46	6 41	5 41	6 40	5 51	6 53	5 59	6 58

JUPITER ♃ / SATURN ♄

Day	R.A. h m	Dec. + °	Transit h m	5° high W. 52° h m	5° high W. 56° h m	R.A. h m	Dec. + °	Transit h m	5° high W. 52° h m	5° high W. 56° h m
1	1 32	8·5	14 54	21 05	21 09	7 55	21·2	21 16	4 39	4 55
11	1 40	9·3	14 23	20 37	20 42	7 53	21·3	20 35	3 59	4 15
21	1 48	10·1	13 52	20 10	20 16	7 53	21·3	19 55	3 20	3 35
31	1 57	10·9	13 21	19 45	19 50	7 52	21·3	19 15	2 40	2 55

Equatorial diameter of Jupiter 34″; of Saturn 20″.   Diameters of Saturn's rings 44″ and 17″.

URANUS ⛢ / NEPTUNE ♆

Day	R.A. h m	Dec. − ° ′	5° high E. 52° h m	5° high E. 56° h m	Transit h m	R.A. h m	Dec. − ° ′	5° high E. 52° h m	5° high E. 56° h m	Transit h m
1	14 19·2	13 22	0 10	0 33	3 43	16 51·0	20 57	3 46	4 33	6 14
11	14 18·4	13 18	23 24	23 47	3 03	16 51·2	20 57	3 06	3 53	5 35
21	14 17·3	13 12	22 41	23 04	2 22	16 51·2	20 57	2 14	3 14	4 56
31	14 16·0	13 05	21 58	22 20	1 42	16 51·0	20 56	1 46	2 33	4 16

Diameter 4″   Diameter 2″

Month	Week		PHENOMENA
		Aperire, to open. Earth opens to receive seed. Sun's Longitude 30° ♉ 19ᵈ 23ʰ	

Aperire, to open. Earth opens to receive seed.
Sun's Longitude 30° ♉ 19ᵈ 23ʰ

1	Th.	Edgar Wallace b. 1875. R.A.F. formed 1918
2	F.	Emile Zola b. 1840. Georges Pompidou d. 1974
3	S.	Murillo d. 1682. Washington Irving b. 1783
4	☉.	5th ☉. in Lent. Sir Cuthbert Whitaker d. 1950
5	M.	John Wisden d. 1884. Gen. Chiang Kai-shek
6	Tu.	Raphael d. 1520. Badajoz 1812. [d. 1975
7	W.	Wordsworth b. 1770. P. T. Barnum d. 1891
8	Th.	F. W. Woolworth d. 1919. Picasso d. 1973
9	F.	Edward IV d. 1483. I. K. Brunel b. 1806
10	S.	Earl of Rochester b. 1647. Hazlitt b. 1778
11	☉.	6th ☉. in Lent. Palm Sunday
12	M.	Franklin D. Roosevelt d. 1945
13	Tu.	Edict of Nantes 1598. Vienna Captured 1945
14	W.	HILARY LAW SITTINGS END. Handel d. 1759
15	Th.	MAUNDY THURSDAY. Loss of *Titanic* 1912
16	F.	Good Friday. Sir Charles Chaplin b. 1889
17	S.	John Ford b. 1586. Ian Hay b. 1876**
18	☉.	Easter Day. Judge Jeffreys d. 1689
19	M.	Easter Monday. Byron d. 1824
20	Tu.	W. H. Davies b. 1871. Adolf Hitler b. 1889
21	W.	QUEEN ELIZABETH II BORN, 1926
22	Th.	Henry Fielding b. 1707. Yehudi Menuhin b. 1916
23	F.	ST. GEORGE'S DAY. Shakespeare b. 1564 d. 1616
24	S.	Anthony Trollope b. 1815
25	☉.	1st ☉. after Easter. St. Mark. ANZAC DAY
26	M.	Daniel Defoe d. 1730.
27	Tu.	EASTER LAW SITTINGS BEGIN. Magellan d. 1521
28	W.	Mutiny of the *Bounty*, 1789. Mussolini d. 1945
29	Th.	Jeremy Thorpe b. 1929
30	F.	Queen Juliana b. 1909. A. E. Housman d. 1936

PHENOMENA

April 1ᵈ 14ʰ Jupiter in conjunction with the Moon. Jupiter 2° S.
1ᵈ 18ʰ Mercury in superior conjunction.
7ᵈ 03ʰ Mars in conjunction with the Moon. Mars 7° N.
8ᵈ 12ʰ Saturn in conjunction with the Moon. Saturn 6° N.
12ᵈ 18ʰ Mercury in conjunction with Jupiter. Mercury 1°·9 N.
25ᵈ 05ʰ Uranus at opposition.
27ᵈ 20ʰ Jupiter in conjunction with the Sun.
28ᵈ 02ʰ Mercury at greatest eastern elongation (21°).
29ᵈ Annular eclipse of the Sun. See p. 148.

CONSTELLATIONS

The following constellations are near the meridian at

d	h		d	h
Mar. 1	24		Mar. 16	23
Apr. 1	22		Apr. 15	21
May 1	20		May 16	19

Cepheus (below the Pole), Cassiopeia (below the Pole), Ursa Major, Leo Minor, Leo, Sextant, Hydra and Crater.

MINIMA OF ALGOL

d	h	d	h
3	4	17	12
6	1	20	9
8	22	23	6
11	19	26	3
14	16	29	00

PHASES OF THE MOON

	d	h	m
☽ First Quarter	7	19	02
○ Full Moon	14	11	49
☾ Last Quarter	21	07	14
● New Moon	29	10	20

	d	h
Perigee (356,940 kilometres)	14	07
Apogee (406,400 ,,)	27	12

Mean Longitude of Ascending Node on April 1, 224°.

See note on *Summer Time*, p. 98.

MONTHLY NOTES

April 1. Refreshment House Licences to be renewed.

5. Income Tax Year (1975–76) ends.

15. First day of Passover.

16. Bank Holiday, Scotland.

17. Lent ends at midnight.

19. Bank and General Holiday, England, Wales and N. Ireland.

** Centenary.

Day	Right Ascension	Dec. +	Equation of Time	Rise 52°	Rise 56°	Transit	Set 52°	Set 56°	Sidereal Time	Transit of First Point of Aries
	h m s	° ′	m s	h m	h m	h m	h m	h m	h m s	h m s
1	0 41 54	4 30	− 3 59	5 36	5 32	12 04	18 33	18 38	12 37 55	11 20 13
2	0 45 33	4 54	− 3 41	5 34	5 29	12 04	18 35	18 40	12 41 52	11 16 17
3	0 49 12	5 17	− 3 23	5 31	5 26	12 03	18 37	18 42	12 45 48	11 12 21
4	0 52 51	5 40	− 3 06	5 29	5 24	12 03	18 38	18 44	12 49 45	11 08 25
5	0 56 30	6 02	− 2 49	5 27	5 21	12 03	18 40	18 46	12 53 41	11 04 30
6	1 00 09	6 25	− 2 31	5 24	5 19	12 02	18 42	18 48	12 57 38	11 00 34
7	1 03 49	6 48	− 2 14	5 22	5 16	12 02	18 43	18 50	13 01 34	10 56 38
8	1 07 28	7 10	− 1 57	5 20	5 13	12 02	18 45	18 52	13 05 31	10 52 42
9	1 11 08	7 33	− 1 41	5 18	5 11	12 02	18 47	18 54	13 09 28	10 48 46
10	1 14 48	7 55	− 1 24	5 15	5 08	12 01	18 49	18 56	13 13 24	10 44 50
11	1 18 29	8 17	− 1 08	5 13	5 06	12 01	18 50	18 58	13 17 21	10 40 54
12	1 22 10	8 39	− 0 52	5 11	5 03	12 01	18 52	19 00	13 21 17	10 36 58
13	1 25 51	9 01	− 0 37	5 09	5 00	12 01	18 54	19 02	13 25 14	10 33 02
14	1 29 32	9 22	− 0 22	5 06	4 58	12 00	18 55	19 04	13 29 10	10 29 06
15	1 33 13	9 44	− 0 07	5 04	4 55	12 00	18 57	19 06	13 33 07	10 25 10
16	1 36 55	10 05	+ 0 08	5 02	4 53	12 00	18 59	19 08	13 37 03	10 21 15
17	1 40 38	10 27	+ 0 22	5 00	4 50	12 00	19 00	19 10	13 41 00	10 17 19
18	1 44 20	10 48	+ 0 36	4 58	4 48	11 59	19 02	19 12	13 44 57	10 13 23
19	1 48 04	11 08	+ 0 49	4 56	4 45	11 59	19 04	19 14	13 48 53	10 09 27
20	1 51 47	11 29	+ 1 02	4 53	4 43	11 59	19 06	19 16	13 52 50	10 05 30
21	1 55 31	11 50	+ 1 15	4 51	4 40	11 59	19 07	19 18	13 56 46	10 01 35
22	1 59 16	12 10	+ 1 27	4 49	4 38	11 58	19 09	19 20	14 00 43	9 57 39
23	2 03 01	12 30	+ 1 39	4 47	4 36	11 58	19 11	19 22	14 04 39	9 53 43
24	2 06 46	12 50	+ 1 50	4 45	4 33	11 58	19 12	19 24	14 08 36	9 49 47
25	2 10 32	13 10	+ 2 00	4 43	4 31	11 58	19 14	19 26	14 12 32	9 45 51
26	2 14 18	13 29	+ 2 10	4 41	4 28	11 58	19 16	19 28	14 16 29	9 41 55
27	2 18 05	13 48	+ 2 20	4 39	4 26	11 58	19 17	19 30	14 20 26	9 38 00
28	2 21 53	14 07	+ 2 29	4 37	4 24	11 57	19 19	19 32	14 24 22	9 34 04
29	2 25 41	14 26	+ 2 38	4 35	4 21	11 57	19 21	19 34	14 28 19	9 30 08
30	2 29 29	14 45	+ 2 46	4 33	4 19	11 57	19 22	19 36	14 32 15	9 26 12

Duration of Civil (C), Nautical (N), and Astronomical (A), Twilight (in minutes)

Lat. °	Apr. 1 C	N	A	Apr. 11 C	N	A	Apr. 21 C	N	A	Apr. 30 C	N	A
52	34	76	121	35	79	128	37	84	138	39	89	152
56	38	85	137	40	90	148	42	96	167	44	105	200

ASTRONOMICAL NOTES

MERCURY is visible as an evening star (magnitude −1·5 to +0·7), except during the first ten days of the month. It may be located above the W.N.W. horizon around the time of end of evening civil twilight. Greatest eastern elongation occurs on the 28th and this is the most favourable evening apparition of the year for observers in the northern hemisphere. On the evening of the 12th Mercury passes 1°·9 N. of Jupiter which is then only very slightly brighter than Mars.

VENUS is too close to the Sun for observation.

MARS is an evening star, magnitude +1·2. Mars is in Gemini and a spectacular event occurs on the night of the 7th–8th when it occults the third magnitude star epsilon Geminorum, visible from part of the British Isles (see page 146 for details).

JUPITER is an evening star, magnitude −1·6, for the first two weeks of the month but thereafter is lost in the lengthening evening twilight. On the evening of the 1st the thin crescent Moon, only 2 days old, will be seen close to Jupiter.

SATURN is a bright evening star, magnitude +0·3, in the constellation of Gemini.

URANUS is at opposition on the 25th, in the eastern part of Virgo. It is barely visible to the naked-eye as its magnitude is +5·7, but it is easily located with only small optical aid. Telescopically it shows a slightly greenish disc 4″ in diameter.

ECLIPSE. An annular eclipse of the Sun occurs on the 29th, visible as a partial eclipse from the British Isles. See page 148 for details.

THE MOON

Day	R.A.	Dec.	Hor. Par.	Semi-diam.	Sun's Co-long.	P.A. of Bright Limb	Phase	Age	Rise 52°	Rise 56°	Transit	Set 52°	Set 56°
	h m	°	'	'	°	°		d	h m	h m	h m	h m	h m
1	1 31	+11.2	54.0	14.7	285	242	1	1.3	6 01	5 51	13 17	20 44	20 57
2	2 18	+14.4	54.1	14.7	297	250	5	2.3	6 28	6 14	14 02	21 46	22 02
3	3 07	+16.9	54.3	14.8	310	255	9	3.3	6 59	6 43	14 49	22 46	23 04
4	3 56	+18.7	54.6	14.9	322	260	16	4.3	7 37	7 18	15 37	23 42	..
5	4 47	+19.7	55.0	15.0	334	265	23	5.3	8 21	8 01	16 27	..	0 01
6	5 40	+19.8	55.6	15.1	346	269	32	6.3	9 14	8 54	17 18	0 32	0 52
7	6 33	+18.9	56.3	15.3	358	274	42	7.3	10 14	9 56	18 09	1 17	1 35
8	7 27	+17.0	57.1	15.6	11	278	52	8.3	11 21	11 06	19 01	1 55	2 11
9	8 21	+14.2	58.0	15.8	23	282	63	9.3	12 34	12 23	19 53	2 29	2 41
10	9 15	+10.5	58.9	16.1	35	285	73	10.3	13 51	13 44	20 46	2 59	3 07
11	10 10	+ 6.0	59.8	16.3	47	286	83	11.3	15 11	15 08	21 39	3 26	3 31
12	11 05	+ 1.2	60.6	16.5	59	287	91	12.3	16 33	16 35	22 33	3 53	3 53
13	12 02	− 3.9	61.1	16.7	71	285	97	13.3	17 57	18 04	23 29	4 20	4 16
14	13 00	− 8.8	61.4	16.7	84	275	100	14.3	19 22	19 34	..	4 50	4 41
15	13 59	−13.2	61.3	16.7	96	117	100	15.3	20 44	21 00	0 27	5 23	5 10
16	15 01	−16.6	60.9	16.6	108	105	97	16.3	22 01	22 20	1 27	6 03	5 46
17	16 02	−18.9	60.3	16.4	120	99	91	17.3	23 08	23 28	2 27	6 50	6 31
18	17 04	−19.8	59.4	16.2	132	93	83	18.3	..	..	3 27	7 46	7 25
19	18 03	−19.5	58.5	15.9	144	88	74	19.3	0 03	0 23	4 24	8 48	8 28
20	19 00	−18.0	57.5	15.7	157	83	64	20.3	0 48	1 05	5 18	9 54	9 37
21	19 54	−15.7	56.6	15.4	169	79	53	21.3	1 24	1 38	6 09	11 02	10 48
22	20 45	−12.6	55.8	15.2	181	75	43	22.3	1 53	2 04	6 57	12 09	11 59
23	21 33	− 9.0	55.2	15.0	193	73	33	23.3	2 18	2 26	7 42	13 16	13 09
24	22 19	− 5.2	54.7	14.9	205	72	24	24.3	2 41	2 45	8 25	14 21	14 18
25	23 05	− 1.2	54.3	14.8	218	71	17	25.3	3 01	3 02	9 08	15 25	15 26
26	23 49	+ 2.9	54.1	14.7	230	71	10	26.3	3 22	3 19	9 50	16 29	16 34
27	0 34	+ 6.7	54.0	14.7	242	72	5	27.3	3 43	3 37	10 32	17 33	17 41
28	1 20	+10.4	54.0	14.7	254	75	2	28.3	4 06	3 56	11 15	18 36	18 48
29	2 06	+13.6	54.1	14.7	267	80	0	29.3	4 31	4 19	12 00	19 39	19 54
30	2 54	+16.3	54.2	14.8	279	256	0	0.6	5 01	4 46	12 46	20 40	20 57

MERCURY ☿

Day	R.A.	Dec. +	Diam.	Phase	Transit		Day	R.A.	Dec. +	Diam.	Phase	Transit	5° high W 52°	5° high W 56°
	h m	°	"		h m			h m	°	"		h m	h m	h m
1	0 41	3.1	5	100	12 05	Mercury is	16	2 32	16.5	6	77	12 57	19 55	20 06
4	1 03	5.9	5	99	12 15	too close to	19	2 53	18.5	6	68	13 05	20 14	20 27
7	1 25	8.7	5	97	12 26	the Sun	22	3 11	20.2	7	57	13 12	20 29	20 44
10	1 48	11.5	5	92	12 37	for	25	3 28	21.5	7	47	13 16	20 40	20 57
13	2 11	14.1	6	86	12 47	observation	28	3 41	22.4	8	38	13 17	20 46	21 04
16	2 32	16.5	6	77	12 57		31	3 52	23.0	8	29	13 15	20 47	21 05

VENUS ♀

Day	R.A.	Dec.	Diam.	Phase	5° high E 52°	5° high E 56°	Transit
	h m	°	"		h m	h m	h m
1	23 29	−4.9	11	94	5 49	5 56	10 51
6	23 52	−2.5	11	95	5 39	5 44	10 54
11	0 14	−0.1	10	95	5 30	5 32	10 57
16	0 37	+2.3	10	96	5 20	5 21	11 00
21	1 00	+4.7	10	96	5 11	5 09	11 03
26	1 22	+7.1	10	97	5 02	4 58	11 06
31	1 45	+9.4	10	97	4 53	4 48	11 10

MARS ♂

Day	R.A.	Dec. +	Diam.	Phase	Transit	5° high W 52°	5° high W 56°
	h m	°	"		h m	h m	h m
1	6 27	25.4	7	90	17 48	1 37	1 58
6	6 38	25.2	6	90	17 39	1 26	1 47
11	6 49	25.0	6	90	17 30	1 16	1 36
16	7 00	24.7	6	90	17 22	1 05	1 25
21	7 11	24.4	6	91	17 13	0 55	1 14
26	7 23	24.0	6	91	17 05	0 44	1 03
31	7 34	23.5	6	91	16 57	0 33	0 51

SUNRISE AND SUNSET (G.M.T.)

Day	London a.m. h m	London p.m. h m	Bristol a.m. h m	Bristol p.m. h m	Birmingham a.m. h m	Birmingham p.m. h m	Manchester a.m. h m	Manchester p.m. h m	Newcastle a.m. h m	Newcastle p.m. h m	Glasgow a.m. h m	Glasgow p.m. h m	Belfast a.m. h m	Belfast p.m. h m
1	5 37	6 33	5 47	6 42	5 43	6 40	5 44	6 43	5 39	6 42	5 49	6 55	5 57	7 00
2	5 35	6 35	5 45	6 44	5 40	6 42	5 41	6 45	5 36	6 44	5 46	6 57	5 54	7 02
3	5 32	6 36	5 42	6 46	5 38	6 44	5 39	6 47	5 34	6 46	5 43	6 59	5 52	7 04
4	5 30	6 38	5 40	6 47	5 35	6 46	5 36	6 49	5 31	6 48	5 41	7 01	5 49	7 06
5	5 28	6 39	5 38	6 49	5 33	6 48	5 34	6 51	5 29	6 50	5 38	7 03	5 47	7 08
6	5 25	6 41	5 35	6 51	5 31	6 50	5 32	6 53	5 27	6 52	5 36	7 05	5 45	7 10
7	5 23	6 43	5 33	6 52	5 28	6 51	5 29	6 54	5 24	6 54	5 33	7 07	5 42	7 11
8	5 21	6 44	5 31	6 54	5 26	6 53	5 27	6 56	5 21	6 56	5 30	7 09	5 40	7 13
9	5 19	6 46	5 29	6 56	5 24	6 55	5 24	6 58	5 19	6 58	5 28	7 11	5 37	7 15
10	5 16	6 48	5 26	6 58	5 21	6 57	5 22	7 00	5 16	7 00	5 25	7 13	5 35	7 17
11	5 14	6 49	5 24	6 59	5 19	6 58	5 20	7 02	5 14	7 02	5 23	7 15	5 33	7 19
12	5 12	6 51	5 22	7 01	5 17	7 00	5 17	7 04	5 11	7 04	5 20	7 17	5 30	7 21
13	5 10	6 53	5 20	7 03	5 15	7 02	5 15	7 05	5 09	7 05	5 17	7 19	5 27	7 23
14	5 07	6 54	5 17	7 04	5 12	7 03	5 12	7 07	5 06	7 07	5 15	7 21	5 24	7 25
15	5 05	6 56	5 15	7 06	5 10	7 05	5 10	7 09	5 04	7 09	5 12	7 23	5 22	7 27
16	5 03	6 58	5 13	7 08	5 08	7 07	5 08	7 11	5 02	7 11	5 10	7 25	5 20	7 29
17	5 01	6 59	5 11	7 09	5 06	7 08	5 05	7 13	4 59	7 13	5 07	7 27	5 17	7 31
18	4 59	7 01	5 09	7 11	5 04	7 10	5 03	7 15	4 57	7 15	5 05	7 29	5 15	7 33
19	4 57	7 03	5 07	7 13	5 02	7 12	5 01	7 17	4 54	7 17	5 02	7 31	5 13	7 35
20	4 54	7 05	5 04	7 15	4 59	7 14	4 58	7 18	4 51	7 19	5 00	7 33	5 10	7 36
21	4 52	7 06	5 02	7 16	4 57	7 15	4 56	7 20	4 49	7 21	4 57	7 35	5 08	7 38
22	4 50	7 08	5 00	7 18	4 55	7 17	4 54	7 22	4 47	7 23	4 55	7 37	5 06	7 40
23	4 48	7 10	4 58	7 20	4 53	7 19	4 52	7 24	4 45	7 25	4 53	7 39	5 04	7 42
24	4 46	7 11	4 56	7 21	4 51	7 20	4 50	7 25	4 42	7 27	4 50	7 41	5 01	7 44
25	4 44	7 13	4 54	7 23	4 49	7 22	4 48	7 27	4 40	7 29	4 48	7 43	4 59	7 46
26	4 42	7 15	4 52	7 24	4 47	7 24	4 46	7 29	4 38	7 31	4 46	7 45	4 57	7 48
27	4 40	7 16	4 50	7 26	4 45	7 26	4 44	7 31	4 36	7 33	4 44	7 47	4 55	7 50
28	4 38	7 18	4 48	7 27	4 43	7 28	4 42	7 32	4 34	7 34	4 42	7 48	4 53	7 51
29	4 37	7 20	4 47	7 29	4 40	7 29	4 39	7 34	4 31	7 36	4 39	7 50	4 50	7 53
30	4 35	7 21	4 45	7 30	4 35	7 31	4 37	7 36	4 29	7 38	4 37	7 52	4 48	7 55

JUPITER ♃   SATURN ♄

Day	Jupiter R.A. h m	Jupiter Dec. + °	Jupiter Transit h m		Saturn R.A. h m	Saturn Dec. + °	Saturn Transit h m	Saturn 5° high W. 52° h m	Saturn 5° high W. 56° h m
1	1 58	11·0	13 18	Jupiter	7 52	21·3	19 11	2 36	2 51
11	2 07	11·8	12 48	is too close	7 53	21·3	18 33	1 58	2 13
21	2 16	12·6	12 18	to the Sun	7 55	21·2	17 55	1 19	1 35
31	2 25	13·4	11 48	for observation	7 57	21·2	17 18	0 41	0 57

Equatorial diameter of Jupiter 33″; of Saturn 19″   Diameters of Saturn's rings 42″ and 16″

URANUS ♅   NEPTUNE ♆

Day	Uranus R.A. h m	Uranus Dec. − ° ′	Uranus 5° high E. 52° h m	Uranus 5° high E. 56° h m	Uranus Transit h m	Neptune R.A. h m	Neptune Dec. − ° ′	Neptune 5° high E. 52° h m	Neptune 5° high E. 56° h m	Neptune Transit h m
1	14 15·9	13 04	21 54	22 16	1 38	16 50·9	20 56	1 42	2 29	4 12
11	14 14·3	12 57	21 14	21 36	0 57	16 50·5	20 55	1 02	1 49	3 33
21	14 12·7	12 48	20 33	20 55	0 16	16 49·8	20 53	0 22	1 09	2 53
31	14 11·1	12 40	19 52	20 14	23 31	16 49·0	20 52	23 38	0 29	2 12

Diameter 4″   Diameter 2″

DAY OF		
Month	**Week**	*Maia*, goddess of growth and increase. Sun's Longitude 60° II 20ᵈ 22ʰ

Maia, goddess of growth and increase.

Sun's Longitude 60° II 20^d 22^h

1	S.	**St. Philip and St. James.** Dryden d. 1700
2	**S.**	**2nd S. after Easter.** Leonardo da Vinci d. 1519
3	M.	Machiavelli b. 1469. R. d'Oyly Carte b. 1844
4	Tu.	Joseph Whitaker b. 1820. Sir Osbert Sitwell d. 1969
5	W.	Napoleon d. 1821. Metternich d. 1859
6	Th.	Edward VII d. 1910. Sigmund Freud b. 1856
7	F.	Tschaikovsky b. 1840. *Lusitania* torpedoed 1915
8	S.	J. S. Mill d. 1873. Flaubert d. 1880
9	**S.**	**3rd S. after Easter.** OFFICIAL END OF WAR
10	M.	Sir Thomas Lipton b. 1850 [IN EUROPE (1945)
11	Tu.	Fontenoy 1745. Irving Berlin b. 1888
12	W.	Edward Lear b. 1812. Florence Nightingale b. 1820
13	Th.	Sir Frank Brangwyn b. 1867. Gary Cooper d. 1961
14	F.	Strindberg d. 1912. Sir Rider Haggard d. 1925
15	S.	David O'Connell d. 1847
16	**S.**	**4th S. after Easter.** Albuera 1811
17	M.	Edward Jenner b. 1749. Talleyrand d. 1838
18	Tu.	George Meredith d. 1909. Dame Margot Fonteyn [b. 1919
19	W.	G. L. Jessop b. 1874. T. E. Lawrence d. 1935
20	Th.	Columbus d. 1506. Sir Max Beerbohm d. 1956
21	F.	Alexander Pope b. 1688. Elizabeth Fry b. 1780
22	S.	Sir Arthur Conan Doyle b. 1859. Lord Olivier b. 1907
23	**S.**	**5th S. after Easter.** ROGATION SUNDAY
24	M.	Queen Victoria b. 1819. H.M.S. *Hood* lost, 1941
25	Tu.	Ralph Waldo Emerson b. 1803
26	W.	Samuel Pepys d. 1703. Sir Matt Busby b. 1909
27	Th.	**Ascension Day.** Henry Kissinger b. 1923
28	F.	Duke of Windsor d. 1972. EASTER LAW SITTINGS
29	S.	Charles II b. 1630. G. K. Chesterton b. 1874 [END
30	**S.**	**S. after Ascension.** Joan of Arc d. 1431
31	M.	Heath Robinson b. 1872. Jutland 1916·

PHENOMENA

May 1^d 04^h Mercury in conjunction with the Moon. Mercury 4° N.

5^d 14^h Mars in conjunction with the Moon. Mars 7° N.

5^d 20^h Saturn in conjunction with the Moon. Saturn 6° N.

11^d 14^h Venus in conjunction with Jupiter. Venus 0°·2 S.

12^d 02^h Mars in conjunction with Saturn. Mars 1°·3 N.

13^d Partial eclipse of the Moon. See p. 148.

20^d 12^h Mercury in inferior conjunction.

27^d 04^h Jupiter in conjunction with the Moon. Jupiter 0°·8 S.

CONSTELLATIONS

The following constellations are near the meridian at

	d h		d h
Apr. 1	24	Apr. 15	23
May 1	22	May 16	21
June 1	20	June 15	19

Cephus (below the Pole), Cassiopeia (below the Pole), Ursa Minor, Ursa Major, Canes Venatici, Coma Berenices, Bootes, Leo, Virgo, Crater, Corvus, and Hydra.

ALGOL

ALGOL is inconveniently situated for observation during May.

PHASES OF THE MOON

		d	h	m
☽ First Quarter		7	05	17
○ Full Moon		13	20	04
☾ Last Quarter		20	21	22
● New Moon		29	01	47

		d	h
Perigee (359,180 kilometres)		12	17
Apogee (405,600 ,,)		25	00

Mean Longitude of Ascending Node on May 1, 223°.

See note on *Summer Time*, p. 98.

MONTHLY NOTES

May 3. Bank Holiday, Scotland.

10. Bank and General Holiday, Channel Islands.

15. Whitsunday (Scotland). Scottish Term Day.

17. Norway's National Day.

28. Removal Day, Scotland.

31. Bank and General Holiday, England, Wales and N. Ireland.

Day	Right Ascension	Dec. +	Equation of Time	Rise 52°	Rise 56°	Transit	Set 52°	Set 56°	Sidereal Time	Transit of First Point of Aries
	h m s	° ′	m s	h m	h m	h m	h m	h m	h m s	h m s
1	2 33 18	15 03	+ 2 54	4 31	4 17	11 57	19 24	19 38	14 36 12	9 22 16
2	2 37 08	15 21	+ 3 01	4 29	4 14	11 57	19 26	19 40	14 40 08	9 18 20
3	2 40 58	15 39	+ 3 07	4 27	4 12	11 57	19 27	19 42	14 44 05	9 14 24
4	2 44 48	15 56	+ 3 13	4 25	4 10	11 57	19 29	19 44	14 48 01	9 10 28
5	2 48 39	16 14	+ 3 19	4 24	4 08	11 57	19 31	19 46	14 51 58	9 06 32
6	2 52 31	16 31	+ 3 29	4 22	4 06	11 57	19 32	19 48	14 55 55	9 02 36
7	2 56 23	16 47	+ 3 28	4 20	4 04	11 56	19 34	19 50	14 59 51	8 58 40
8	3 00 16	17 04	+ 3 32	4 18	4 01	11 56	19 36	19 52	15 03 48	8 54 45
9	3 04 09	17 20	+ 3 35	4 16	3 59	11 56	19 37	19 54	15 07 44	8 50 49
10	3 08 03	17 36	+ 3 38	4 15	3 57	11 56	19 39	19 56	15 11 41	8 46 53
11	3 11 57	17 51	+ 3 40	4 13	3 55	11 56	19 40	19 58	15 15 37	8 42 57
12	3 15 52	18 07	+ 3 41	4 11	3 53	11 56	19 42	20 00	15 19 34	8 39 01
13	3 19 48	18 22	+ 3 42	4 10	3 51	11 56	19 44	20 02	15 23 30	8 35 05
14	3 23 44	18 36	+ 3 43	4 08	3 50	11 56	19 45	20 04	15 27 27	8 31 09
15	3 27 41	18 51	+ 3 43	4 06	3 48	11 56	19 47	20 06	15 31 23	8 27 13
16	3 31 38	19 05	+ 3 42	4 05	3 46	11 56	19 48	20 08	15 35 20	8 23 17
17	3 35 36	19 18	+ 3 41	4 03	3 44	11 56	19 50	20 09	15 39 17	8 19 21
18	3 39 34	19 32	+ 3 39	4 02	3 42	11 56	19 51	20 11	15 43 13	8 15 25
19	3 43 33	19 45	+ 3 36	4 01	3 40	11 56	19 53	20 13	15 47 10	8 11 30
20	3 47 33	19 58	+ 3 33	3 59	3 39	11 56	19 54	20 15	15 51 06	8 07 34
21	3 51 33	20 10	+ 3 30	3 58	3 37	11 57	19 56	20 17	15 55 03	8 03 38
22	3 55 33	20 22	+ 3 26	3 57	3 36	11 57	19 57	20 18	15 58 59	7 59 42
23	3 59 35	20 34	+ 3 21	3 55	3 34	11 57	19 58	20 20	16 02 56	7 55 46
24	4 03 36	20 45	+ 3 16	3 54	3 32	11 57	20 00	20 22	16 06 52	7 51 50
25	4 07 39	20 56	+ 3 10	3 53	3 31	11 57	20 01	20 23	16 10 49	7 47 54
26	4 11 41	21 07	+ 3 04	3 52	3 30	11 57	20 02	20 25	16 14 46	7 43 58
27	4 15 45	21 17	+ 2 57	3 51	3 28	11 57	20 04	20 27	16 18 42	7 40 02
28	4 19 48	21 27	+ 2 50	3 50	3 27	11 57	20 05	20 28	16 22 39	7 36 06
29	4 23 53	21 36	+ 2 43	3 49	3 26	11 57	20 06	20 30	16 26 35	7 32 10
30	4 27 57	21 45	+ 2 35	3 48	3 24	11 57	20 07	20 31	16 30 32	7 28 15
31	4 32 02	21 54	+ 2 26	3 47	3 23	11 58	20 09	20 32	16 34 28	7 24 19

THE SUN   s.d. 15′·8

Duration of Civil (C), Nautical (N), and Astronomical (A), Twilight (in minutes)

Lat. °	May 1 C	N	A	May 11 C	N	A	May 21 C	N	A	May 31 C	N	A
52	39	90	154	41	97	179	44	106	T.A.N.	46	116	T.A.N.
56	45	106	209	49	121	T.A.N.	53	143	T.A.N.	57	T.A.N.	T.A.N.

ASTRONOMICAL NOTES

MERCURY is visible as an evening star, magnitude +0·7 to +2·5, during the first half of the month, low above the W.N.W. horizon around the time of end of evening civil twilight. Thereafter it is unsuitably placed for observation, inferior conjunction occurring on the 20th.

VENUS is unsuitably placed for observation.

MARS is an evening star, magnitude +1·6. At the beginning of the month it will be seen in Gemini, passing south of Pollux, and then passing into Cancer. On the evening of the 28th Mars will be passing in front of the famous " Beehive " cluster, M.44 though it will not actually occult any of the brighter stars in it. On the early morning of the 12th Mars passes only 1°·3 north of Saturn.

JUPITER is unsuitably placed for observation.

SATURN is a bright evening star, magnitude +0·4, moving slowly from Gemini to Cancer during the month. On the evening of the 5th the crescent Moon, 6 days old, passes 6° south of Saturn. The Rings of Saturn are a beautiful sight even through small telescopes and are well seen in 1976, though no longer at their maximum width.

ECLIPSE. A partial eclipse of the Moon occurs on the 13th. See page 148 for details.

THE MOON

Day	R.A.	Dec.	Hor. Par.	Semi-diam.	Sun's Co-long.	P.A. of Bright Limb	Phase	Age	Rise 52°	Rise 56°	Transit	Set 52°	Set 56°
	h m	°	'	'	°	°		d	h m	h m	h m	h m	h m
1	3 44	+18.3	54.5	14.8	291	262	2	1.6	5 37	5 19	13 34	21 37	21 56
2	4 35	+19.5	54.8	14.9	303	266	6	2.6	6 19	6 00	14 24	22 29	22 49
3	5 27	+19.8	55.3	15.1	316	271	12	3.6	7 09	6 49	15 14	23 16	23 34
4	6 20	+19.2	55.8	15.2	328	275	19	4.6	8 07	7 48	16 05	23 56	..
5	7 13	+17.5	56.4	15.4	340	280	27	5.6	9 11	8 55	16 56	..	0 12
6	8 06	+15.0	57.0	15.5	352	283	37	6.6	10 20	10 07	17 46	0 30	0 44
7	8 59	+11.6	57.8	15.7	4	287	48	7.6	11 33	11 24	18 37	1 00	1 10
8	9 52	+ 7.5	58.6	16.0	17	289	59	8.6	12 49	12 44	19 28	1 27	1 33
9	10 45	+ 3.0	59.4	16.2	29	290	70	9.6	14 07	14 07	20 20	1 53	1 55
10	11 39	− 1.9	60.1	16.4	41	290	80	10.6	15 28	15 32	21 13	2 19	2 17
11	12 35	− 6.8	60.6	16.5	53	290	88	11.6	16 50	16 59	22 09	2 46	2 40
12	13 33	−11.3	61.0	16.6	65	288	95	12.6	18 13	18 27	23 07	3 17	3 06
13	14 33	−15.2	61.0	16.6	78	287	99	13.6	19 33	19 50	..	3 53	3 38
14	15 34	−18.0	60.8	16.6	90	76	100	14.6	20 46	21 06	0 07	4 36	4 18
15	16 37	−19.6	60.3	16.4	102	90	98	15.6	21 49	22 09	1 08	5 28	5 08
16	17 38	−19.8	59.5	16.2	114	86	93	16.6	22 40	22 59	2 08	6 29	6 09
17	18 38	−18.7	58.8	16.0	126	81	87	17.6	23 21	23 37	3 06	7 35	7 17
18	19 35	−16.6	57.7	15.7	138	77	78	18.6	23 54	..	4 00	8 45	8 30
19	20 28	−13.7	56.8	15.5	151	74	69	19.6	..	0 07	4 51	9 55	9 44
20	21 18	−10.2	56.0	15.2	163	71	59	20.6	0 22	0 30	5 38	11 03	10 56
21	22 06	− 6.3	55.3	15.1	175	70	49	21.6	0 45	0 50	6 23	12 10	12 06
22	22 52	− 2.3	54.7	14.9	187	69	39	22.6	1 07	1 08	7 05	13 15	13 15
23	23 37	+ 1.7	54.3	14.8	200	68	30	23.6	1 27	1 26	7 48	14 19	14 23
24	0 22	+ 5.7	54.1	14.7	212	69	22	24.6	1 48	1 43	8 30	15 23	15 30
25	1 07	+ 9.4	54.1	14.7	224	70	15	25.6	2 10	2 02	9 13	16 27	16 37
26	1 54	+12.8	54.1	14.7	236	71	9	26.6	2 35	2 23	9 57	17 30	17 44
27	2 41	+15.7	54.3	14.8	248	72	4	27.6	3 03	2 48	10 43	18 32	18 49
28	3 31	+17.9	54.6	14.9	261	71	1	28.6	3 37	3 19	11 31	19 31	19 50
29	4 22	+19.3	54.9	15.0	273	12	0	29.6	4 17	3 58	12 20	20 26	20 46
30	5 14	+19.9	55.3	15.1	285	282	1	0.9	5 05	4 45	13 11	21 15	21 34
31	6 07	+19.5	55.8	15.2	297	280	4	1.9	6 00	5 41	14 02	21 57	22 14

MERCURY ☿

Day	R.A.	Dec. +	Diam.	Phase	Transit	5° high W. 52°	5° high W. 56°	Day	R.A.	Dec. +	Diam.	Phase	Transit	
	h m	°	''		h m	h m	h m		h m	°	''		h m	
1	3 52	23.0	8	29	13 15	20 47	21 05	16	4 00	20.7	12	2	12 21	Mercury is
4	4 00	23.1	9	22	13 11	20 42	21 00	19	3 54	19.5	12	1	12 04	too close to
7	4 04	23.0	10	15	13 03	20 33	20 50	22	3 48	18.3	12	0	11 46	the Sun
10	4 05	22.5	11	9	12 52	20 18	20 34	25	3 42	17.2	12	2	11 28	for
13	4 04	21.7	11	5	12 38	19 58	20 14	28	3 37	16.3	12	5	11 12	observation
16	4 00	20.7	12	2	12 21	19 35	19 50	31	3 35	15.6	11	9	10 58	

VENUS ♀

Day	R.A.	Dec. +	Diam.	Phase	5° high E. 52°	5° high E. 56°	Transit
	h m	°	''		h m	h m	h m
1	1 45	9.4	10	97	4 53	4 48	11 10
6	2 09	11.7	10	98	4 45	4 39	11 13
11	2 32	13.8	10	98	4 38	4 30	11 17
16	2 56	15.8	10	99	4 32	4 22	11 22
21	3 21	17.6	10	99	4 27	4 16	11 26
26	3 46	19.2	10	99	4 23	4 11	11 32
31	4 11	20.6	10	100	4 21	4 06	11 38

MARS ♂

Day	R.A.	Dec. +	Diam.	Phase	Transit	5° high W. 52°	5° high W. 56°
	h m	°	''		h m	h m	h m
1	7 34	23.5	6	91	16 57	0 33	0 51
6	7 46	23.0	5	91	16 49	0 22	0 39
11	7 57	22.4	5	92	16 41	0 10	0 27
16	8 09	21.8	5	92	16 33	23 55	0 14
21	8 21	21.1	5	92	16 25	23 43	23 58
26	8 33	20.4	5	92	16 17	23 31	23 45
31	8 44	19.6	5	93	16 09	23 18	23 32

SUNRISE AND SUNSET (G.M.T.)

Day	London a.m. h m	London p.m. h m	Bristol a.m. h m	Bristol p.m. h m	Birmingham a.m. h m	Birmingham p.m. h m	Manchester a.m. h m	Manchester p.m. h m	Newcastle a.m. h m	Newcastle p.m. h m	Glasgow a.m. h m	Glasgow p.m. h m	Belfast a.m. h m	Belfast p.m. h m
1	4 33	7 23	4 43	7 32	4 36	7 33	4 35	7 38	4 27	7 40	4 35	7 54	4 46	7 57
2	4 31	7 24	4 41	7 34	4 34	7 35	4 33	7 40	4 24	7 42	4 32	7 56	4 44	7 59
3	4 29	7 26	4 39	7 35	4 32	7 36	4 31	7 42	4 22	7 44	4 30	7 58	4 42	8 01
4	4 27	7 27	4 37	7 37	4 30	7 38	4 29	7 43	4 20	7 46	4 28	8 00	4 40	8 02
5	4 26	7 29	4 36	7 39	4 29	7 40	4 27	7 45	4 18	7 48	4 26	8 02	4 38	8 04
6	4 24	7 30	4 34	7 40	4 27	7 41	4 25	7 47	4 16	7 50	4 24	8 04	4 36	8 06
7	4 22	7 32	4 32	7 42	4 25	7 43	4 23	7 49	4 14	7 52	4 22	8 06	4 34	8 08
8	4 20	7 34	4 30	7 44	4 23	7 45	4 21	7 50	4 12	7 53	4 19	8 08	4 31	8 10
9	4 18	7 35	4 28	7 45	4 21	7 46	4 19	7 52	4 10	7 55	4 17	8 10	4 29	8 12
10	4 17	7 37	4 27	7 47	4 20	7 48	4 17	7 54	4 08	7 57	4 15	8 12	4 27	8 14
11	4 15	7 38	4 25	7 48	4 18	7 49	4 16	7 56	4 06	7 59	4 13	8 14	4 26	8 16
12	4 13	7 40	4 23	7 50	4 16	7 51	4 14	7 58	4 04	8 01	4 11	8 16	4 24	8 18
13	4 12	7 42	4 22	7 52	4 15	7 53	4 12	7 59	4 02	8 03	4 09	8 18	4 22	8 19
14	4 10	7 43	4 20	7 53	4 13	7 54	4 10	8 01	4 01	8 05	4 08	8 20	4 20	8 21
15	4 08	7 45	4 18	7 55	4 11	7 56	4 09	8 03	3 59	8 07	4 06	8 22	4 19	8 23
16	4 07	7 46	4 17	7 56	4 10	7 57	4 07	8 04	3 57	8 08	4 04	8 24	4 17	8 24
17	4 05	7 48	4 16	7 58	4 08	7 59	4 05	8 06	3 55	8 10	4 02	8 25	4 15	8 26
18	4 04	7 49	4 14	7 59	4 07	8 00	4 04	8 07	3 54	8 12	4 00	8 27	4 14	8 28
19	4 03	7 51	4 13	8 01	4 06	8 02	4 03	8 09	3 52	8 13	3 58	8 29	4 12	8 29
20	4 01	7 52	4 12	8 02	4 04	8 03	4 01	8 10	3 51	8 15	3 57	8 31	4 11	8 31
21	4 00	7 54	4 11	8 04	4 03	8 05	4 00	8 12	3 49	8 17	3 55	8 33	4 09	8 33
22	3 59	7 55	4 10	8 05	4 02	8 06	3 59	8 13	3 48	8 18	3 54	8 34	4 08	8 34
23	3 57	7 56	4 08	8 06	4 00	8 07	3 57	8 14	3 46	8 20	3 52	8 36	4 06	8 36
24	3 56	7 58	4 07	8 08	3 59	8 09	3 56	8 16	3 44	8 22	3 50	8 38	4 04	8 38
25	3 55	7 59	4 06	8 09	3 58	8 10	3 55	8 17	3 43	8 23	3 49	8 39	4 03	8 39
26	3 54	8 00	4 05	8 10	3 57	8 11	3 54	8 19	3 42	8 25	3 48	8 41	4 02	8 41
27	3 53	8 02	4 04	8 11	3 55	8 13	3 52	8 20	3 40	8 26	3 46	8 43	4 00	8 42
28	3 52	8 03	4 03	8 12	3 54	8 15	3 51	8 22	3 39	8 28	3 45	8 44	3 59	8 44
29	3 51	8 04	4 02	8 14	3 53	8 16	3 50	8 23	3 38	8 29	3 44	8 46	3 58	8 45
30	3 51	8 05	4 01	8 15	3 52	8 17	3 49	8 24	3 37	8 30	3 42	8 47	3 57	8 46
31	3 50	8 07	4 00	8 16	3 51	8 18	3 48	8 26	3 36	8 32	3 41	8 48	3 56	8 48

JUPITER ♃   SATURN ♄

Day	R.A. h m	Dec. + °	Transit h m		R.A. h m	Dec. + °	Transit h m	5° high W. 52° h m	5° high W. 56° h m
1	2 25	13·4	11 48	Jupiter is	7 57	21·2	17 18	0 41	0 57
11	2 35	14·2	11 18	too close to	8 00	21·1	16 42	0 04	0 20
21	2 44	14·9	10 48	the Sun for	8 03	20·9	16 06	23 22	23 39
31	2 53	15·6	10 17	observation	8 07	20·7	15 30	22 47	23 02

Equatorial diameter of Jupiter 33"; of Saturn 18"   Diameters of Saturn's rings 40" and 15"

URANUS ⛢   NEPTUNE ♆

Day	R.A. h m	Dec. − ° '	Transit h m	5° high W. 52° h m	5° high W. 56° h m	R.A. h m	Dec. − ° '	5° high E. 52° h m	5° high E. 56° h m	Transit h m
1	14 11·1	12 40	23 31	3 18	2 56	16 49·0	20 52	23 38	0 29	2 12
11	14 09·5	12 32	22 50	2 38	2 16	16 48·0	20 50	22 57	23 43	1 32
21	14 08·0	12 24	22 09	1 58	1 36	16 46·9	20 48	22 16	23 02	0 52
31	14 06·7	12 17	21 29	1 18	0 57	16 45·8	20 46	21 35	22 21	0 11

Diameter 4"   Diameter 2"

Month	Week		

Junius, Roman *gens* (family).

Sun's Longitude 90° ♋ 21ᵈ 06ʰ

1	Tu.	Glorious First of June, 1794
2	W.	CORONATION DAY, 1953. Thomas Hardy b. 1840
3	Th.	George V. b. 1865. Georges Bizet d. 1875
4	F.	George III b. 1738. F. R. Spofforth d. 1926
5	S.	Adam Smith b. 1723. Stephen Crane d. 1900
6	☉.	Whit Sunday. Pentecost. "D" Day, 1944
7	M.	Robert the Bruce d. 1329. Gauguin b. 1848
8	Tu.	TRINITY LAW SITTINGS BEGIN. Millais b. 1829
9	W.	Charles Dickens d. 1870
10	Th.	DUKE OF EDINBURGH BORN, 1921
11	F.	St. Barnabas. Constable b. 1776**
12	S.	Charles Kingsley b. 1819. Earl of Avon b. 1897
13	☉.	Trinity Sunday. W. B. Yeats b. 1865
14	M.	Naseby 1645. J. L. Baird d. 1946
15	Tu.	Magna Carta 1215. Wat Tyler d. 1381
16	W.	Enoch Powell b. 1912. Lord Reith d. 1971
17	Th.	Edward I b. 1239. John Cowper Powys d. 1963
18	F.	Waterloo Day, 1815. D. R. Jardine d. 1958
19	S.	James I. b. 1566. W. R. Hammond b. 1903
20	☉.	1st Sunday after Trinity. William IV d. 1837
21	M.	Edward III d. 1377. Inigo Jones d. 1652
22	Tu.	Puccini b. 1858. Lord Hunt b. 1910
23	W.	Plassey 1757. Sir Leonard Hutton b. 1916
24	Th.	St. John Baptist. Bannockburn 1314
25	F.	Earl Mountbatten of Burma b. 1900
26	S.	George IV d. 1830. U.N. Charter, 1945
27	☉.	2nd ☉. after Trinity. Cherbourg captured 1944
28	M.	Victor Trumper d. 1915. Treaty of Versailles 1919
29	Tu.	St. Peter. Rubens b. 1577
30	W.	Elizabeth Barrett Browning d. 1861

PHENOMENA

June 2ᵈ 06ʰ Saturn in conjunction with the Moon. Saturn 6° N.

3ᵈ 01ʰ Neptune at opposition.

3ᵈ 02ʰ Mars in conjunction with the Moon. Mars 7° N.

15ᵈ 09ʰ Mercury at greatest western elongation (23°).

18ᵈ 04ʰ Venus in superior conjunction.

21ᵈ 06ʰ Summer Solstice.

23ᵈ 23ʰ Jupiter in conjunction with the Moon. Jupiter 0°·1 S.

25ᵈ 22ʰ Mercury in conjunction with the Moon. Mercury 1° N.

29ᵈ 18ʰ Saturn in conjunction with the Moon. Saturn 6° N.

CONSTELLATIONS

The following constellations are near the meridian at

	d h		d h
May 1	24	May 16	23
June 1	22	June 25	21
July 1	20	July 16	19

Cassiopeia (below the Pole), Ursa Minor, Draco, Ursa Major, Canes Venatici, Bootes, Corona, Serpens, Virgo and Libra.

ALGOL

ALGOL is inconveniently situated for observation during June.

PHASES OF THE MOON

	d	h	m
☽ First Quarter	5	12	20
○ Full Moon	12	04	15
☾ Last Quarter	19	13	15
● New Moon	27	14	50

	d	h
Perigee (363,550 kilometres)	9	19
Apogee (404,580 „)	21	17

Mean Longitude of Ascending Node on June 1, 221°.

See note on *Summer Time*, p. 98.

MONTHLY NOTES

June 4. Feast of Weeks.

5. Constitution Day, Denmark.

12. Queen's Official Birthday.

21. Longest day.

24. Midsummer Day.   Quarter Day.

** Centenary.

Day	Right Ascension	Dec. +	Equation of Time	Rise 52°	Rise 56°	Transit	Set 52°	Set 56°	Sidereal Time	Transit of First Point of Aries
	h m s	° '	m s	h m	h m	h m	h m	h m	h m s	h m s
1	4 36 08	22 02	+ 2 17	3 46	3 22	11 58	20 10	20 34	16 38 25	7 20 23
2	4 40 14	22 10	+ 2 08	3 45	3 21	11 58	20 11	20 35	16 42 22	7 16 27
3	4 44 20	22 18	+ 1 58	3 44	3 20	11 58	20 12	20 36	16 46 18	7 12 31
4	4 48 26	22 25	+ 1 48	3 44	3 19	11 58	20 13	20 38	16 50 15	7 08 35
5	4 52 33	22 32	+ 1 38	3 43	3 18	11 58	20 14	20 39	16 54 11	7 04 39
6	4 56 41	22 39	+ 1 27	3 42	3 17	11 59	20 15	20 40	16 58 08	7 00 43
7	5 00 48	22 45	+ 1 16	3 42	3 17	11 59	20 16	20 41	17 02 04	6 56 47
8	5 04 56	22 50	+ 1 05	3 41	3 16	11 59	20 17	20 42	17 06 01	6 52 51
9	5 09 04	22 55	+ 0 53	3 41	3 15	11 59	20 17	20 43	17 09 57	6 48 55
10	5 13 12	23 00	+ 0 42	3 40	3 15	11 59	20 18	20 44	17 13 54	6 45 00
11	5 17 21	23 05	+ 0 30	3 40	3 14	12 00	20 19	20 45	17 17 51	6 41 04
12	5 21 29	23 09	+ 0 18	3 40	3 14	12 00	20 20	20 46	17 21 47	6 37 08
13	5 25 38	23 12	+ 0 05	3 40	3 13	12 00	20 20	20 46	17 25 44	6 33 12
14	5 29 47	23 16	− 0 07	3 39	3 13	12 00	20 21	20 47	17 29 40	6 29 16
15	5 33 56	23 18	− 0 20	3 39	3 13	12 00	20 21	20 48	17 33 37	6 25 20
16	5 38 06	23 21	− 0 32	3 39	3 13	12 01	20 22	20 48	17 37 33	6 21 24
17	5 42 15	23 23	− 0 45	3 39	3 12	12 01	20 22	20 49	17 41 30	6 17 28
18	5 46 24	23 24	− 0 58	3 39	3 12	12 01	20 23	20 49	17 45 26	6 13 32
19	5 50 34	23 25	− 1 11	3 39	3 12	12 01	20 23	20 50	17 49 23	6 09 36
20	5 54 44	23 26	− 1 24	3 39	3 13	12 02	20 23	20 50	17 53 20	6 05 40
21	5 58 53	23 26	− 1 37	3 39	3 13	12 02	20 24	20 50	17 57 16	6 01 45
22	6 03 03	23 26	− 1 50	3 40	3 13	12 02	20 24	20 51	18 01 13	5 57 49
23	6 07 12	23 26	− 2 03	3 40	3 13	12 02	20 24	20 51	18 05 09	5 53 53
24	6 11 22	23 25	− 2 16	3 40	3 14	12 02	20 24	20 51	18 09 06	5 49 57
25	6 15 31	23 24	− 2 29	3 41	3 14	12 03	20 24	20 51	18 13 02	5 46 01
26	6 19 41	23 22	− 2 42	3 41	3 14	12 03	20 24	20 51	18 16 59	5 42 05
27	6 23 50	23 20	− 2 55	3 41	3 15	12 03	20 24	20 50	18 20 55	5 38 09
28	6 27 59	23 17	− 3 07	3 42	3 16	12 03	20 24	20 50	18 24 52	5 34 13
29	6 32 08	23 14	− 3 19	3 43	3 16	12 03	20 24	20 50	18 28 49	5 30 17
30	6 36 17	23 11	− 3 32	3 43	3 17	12 04	20 23	20 49	18 32 45	5 26 21

THE SUN s.d. 15'·8

Duration of Civil (C), Nautical (N), and Astronomical (A), Twilight (in minutes)

Lat. °	June 1 C	N	A	June 11 C	N	A	June 21 C	N	A	June 30 C	N	A
52	47	117	T.A.N.	48	125	T.A.N.	49	128	T.A.N.	49	125	T.A.N.
56	58	T.A.N.	T.A.N.	61	T.A.N.	T.A.N.	63	T.A.N.	T.A.N.	62	T.A.N.	T.A.N.

ASTRONOMICAL NOTES

MERCURY is at greatest western elongation on the 15th but the long duration of twilight makes observation impossible.

VENUS is at superior conjunction on the 18th and thus unsuitably placed for observation.

MARS is an evening star, magnitude + 1·8, and no longer a conspicuous object. By the end of the month it is not observable after 22ʰ. During the month Mars moves from Cancer into Leo.

JUPITER is unsuitably placed for observation at first but gradually becomes visible as a morning star, magnitude − 1·6, low on the eastern horizon before dawn, around the middle of the month. The old crescent Moon is near the planet on the morning of the 24th. Jupiter is in the constellation of Aries.

SATURN is an evening star, magnitude + 0·5 but gradually disappears from view in the long twilight during the second half of the month as it moves towards the Sun.

NEPTUNE is at opposition on the 3rd, in the constellation of Ophiuchus, about 6° N.E. of Antares. The angular diameter of Neptune is only 2½″ and its magnitude is + 7·7.

THE MOON

Day	R.A.	Dec.	Hor. Par.	Semi-diam.	Sun's Co-long.	P.A. of Bright Limb	Phase	Age	Rise 52°	Rise 56°	Tran-sit	Set 52°	Set 56°
	h m	°	′	′	°	°		d	h m	h m	h m	h m	h m
1	7 01	+18·1	56·2	15·3	310	283	9	2·9	7 03	6 46	14 53	22 33	22 48
2	7 54	+15·7	56·8	15·5	322	286	15	3·9	8 11	7 57	15 44	23 05	23 16
3	8 47	+12·5	57·3	15·6	334	289	24	4·9	9 22	9 12	16 34	23 32	23 40
4	9 39	+ 8·7	57·9	15·8	346	291	33	5·9	10 36	10 30	17 24	23 58	..
5	10 31	+ 4·3	58·5	15·9	359	292	44	6·9	11 51	11 50	18 14	..	0 01
6	11 23	− 0·4	59·0	16·1	11	293	56	7·9	13 09	13 12	19 05	0 22	0 22
7	12 17	− 5·2	59·6	16·2	23	292	67	8·9	14 28	14 35	19 57	0 48	0 43
8	13 12	− 9·7	60·0	16·3	35	291	77	9·9	15 48	15 59	20 52	1 16	1 07
9	14 09	−13·8	60·2	16·4	47	289	86	10·9	17 07	17 23	21 50	1 48	1 35
10	15 09	−17·0	60·3	16·4	60	287	93	11·9	18 23	18 42	22 50	2 26	2 10
11	16 10	−19·1	60·1	16·4	72	287	98	12·9	19 31	19 51	23 50	3 13	2 54
12	17 12	−19·9	59·8	16·3	84	327	100	13·9	20 28	20 48	..	4 09	3 48
13	18 13	−19·4	59·2	16·1	96	69	99	14·9	21 15	21 32	0 49	5 13	4 54
14	19 12	−17·7	58·4	15·9	108	73	95	15·9	21 52	22 07	1 46	6 23	6 06
15	20 08	−15·0	57·6	15·7	121	71	90	16·9	22 23	22 33	2 40	7 34	7 21
16	21 00	−11·7	56·8	15·5	133	69	83	17·9	22 49	22 55	3 29	8 45	8 36
17	21 50	− 7·8	56·0	15·3	145	68	74	18·9	23 11	23 15	4 16	9 54	9 49
18	22 37	− 3·8	55·3	15·1	157	67	65	19·9	23 32	23 32	5 01	11 01	10 59
19	23 23	+ 0·3	54·8	14·9	169	66	55	20·9	23 53	23 50	5 44	12 06	12 08
20	0 09	+ 4·4	54·4	14·8	182	67	46	21·9	..	..	6 26	13 11	13 16
21	0 54	+ 8·2	54·2	14·8	194	68	36	22·9	0 15	0 08	7 09	14 15	14 24
22	1 40	+11·7	54·2	14·8	206	69	28	23·9	0 38	0 28	7 53	15 18	15 31
23	2 27	+14·8	54·3	14·8	218	72	20	24·9	1 05	0 51	8 38	16 21	16 36
24	3 16	+17·2	54·6	14·9	231	74	13	25·9	1 36	1 20	9 25	17 21	17 39
25	4 06	+18·9	55·0	15·0	243	76	7	26·9	2 14	1 55	10 14	18 18	18 38
26	4 59	+19·8	55·4	15·1	255	76	3	27·9	2 59	2 39	11 04	19 10	19 30
27	5 52	+19·7	55·9	15·2	267	62	1	28·9	3 52	3 32	11 56	19 56	20 14
28	6 46	+18·6	55·5	15·4	280	318	0	0·4	4 53	4 35	12 48	20 35	20 51
29	7 40	+16·5	57·0	15·5	292	295	2	1·4	6 00	5 45	13 40	21 08	21 21
30	8 34	+13·5	57·5	15·7	304	293	6	2·4	7 11	7 00	14 31	21 38	21 46

MERCURY ☿

Day	R.A.	Dec. +	Diam.	Phase	Tran-sit		Day	R.A.	Dec. +	Diam.	Phase	Tran-sit
	h m	°	″		h m			h m	°	″		h m
1	3 34	15·4	11	10	10 54	Mercury is too close to the Sun for observation	16	4 02	17·2	8	38	10 25	Mercury is too close to the Sun for observation
4	3 35	15·2	10	15	10 43		19	4 15	18·2	7	45	10 26	
7	3 38	15·3	10	20	10 35		22	4 31	19·3	7	52	10 30	
10	3 44	15·7	9	26	10 29		25	4 48	20·4	7	60	10 36	
13	3 52	16·3	9	32	10 26		28	5 08	21·5	6	67	10 45	
16	4 02	17·2	8	38	10 25		31	5 30	22·4	6	76	10 56	

VENUS ♀

Day	R.A.	Dec. +	Diam.	Phase	Tran-sit	
	h m	°	″		h m	
1	4 17	20·9	10	100	11 39	Venus is too close to the Sun for observation
6	4 43	22·0	10	100	11 45	
11	5 09	22·9	10	100	11 52	
16	5 35	23·5	10	100	11 59	
21	6 02	23·8	10	100	12 06	
26	6 29	23·8	10	100	12 13	
31	6 56	23·6	10	100	12 20	

MARS ♂

Day	R.A.	Dec. +	Diam.	Phase	Tran-sit	5° high W 52°	5° high W 56°
	h m	°	″		h m	h m	h m
1	8 47	19·5	5	93	16 07	23 16	23 30
6	8 58	18·6	5	93	15 59	23 03	23 16
11	9 10	17·8	5	93	15 51	22 50	23 02
16	9 21	16·8	5	94	15 43	22 37	22 48
21	9 33	15·9	4	94	15 35	22 23	22 33
26	9 45	14·9	4	94	15 27	22 10	22 18
31	9 56	13·8	4	95	15 18	21 56	22 04

SUNRISE AND SUNSET (G.M.T.)

Day	London a.m. h m	London p.m. h m	Bristol a.m. h m	Bristol p.m. h m	Birmingham a.m. h m	Birmingham p.m. h m	Manchester a.m. h m	Manchester p.m. h m	Newcastle a.m. h m	Newcastle p.m. h m	Glasgow a.m. h m	Glasgow p.m. h m	Belfast a.m. h m	Belfast p.m. h m
1	3 49	8 08	3 59	8 17	3 50	8 20	3 47	8 27	3 35	8 33	3 40	8 50	3 55	8 49
2	3 48	8 09	3 58	8 18	3 49	8 21	3 46	8 28	3 34	8 34	3 39	8 51	3 54	8 50
3	3 47	8 10	3 57	8 19	3 48	8 22	3 45	8 29	3 33	8 35	3 38	8 52	3 53	8 51
4	3 47	8 11	3 57	8 20	3 48	8 23	3 44	8 30	3 32	8 37	3 37	8 54	3 52	8 52
5	3 46	8 12	3 56	8 21	3 47	8 24	3 44	8 31	3 31	8 38	3 36	8 55	3 52	8 53
6	3 45	8 12	3 55	8 22	3 46	8 25	3 43	8 32	3 30	8 39	3 35	8 56	3 51	8 54
7	3 45	8 13	3 55	8 23	3 46	8 26	3 42	8 33	3 30	8 40	3 35	8 57	3 50	8 55
8	3 44	8 14	3 54	8 24	3 45	8 27	3 42	8 34	3 29	8 41	3 34	8 58	3 50	8 56
9	3 44	8 15	3 54	8 24	3 45	8 27	3 41	8 35	3 28	8 42	3 33	8 59	3 49	8 57
10	3 43	8 16	3 53	8 25	3 44	8 28	3 41	8 36	3 28	8 43	3 33	9 00	3 49	8 58
11	3 43	8 16	3 53	8 26	3 44	8 29	3 40	8 37	3 27	8 44	3 32	9 01	3 48	8 59
12	3 43	8 17	3 53	8 27	3 44	8 30	3 40	8 38	3 27	8 45	3 32	9 02	3 48	9 00
13	3 43	8 17	3 53	8 27	3 44	8 30	3 39	8 38	3 26	8 45	3 31	9 02	3 47	9 00
14	3 42	8 18	3 52	8 28	3 43	8 31	3 39	8 39	3 26	8 46	3 31	9 03	3 47	9 01
15	3 42	8 19	3 52	8 28	3 43	8 31	3 39	8 40	3 26	8 47	3 31	9 04	3 47	9 02
16	3 42	8 19	3 52	8 29	3 43	8 32	3 39	8 40	3 26	8 47	3 31	9 04	3 47	9 02
17	3 42	8 19	3 52	8 29	3 43	8 32	3 39	8 41	3 26	8 48	3 30	9 05	3 47	9 03
18	3 42	8 20	3 52	8 30	3 43	8 33	3 39	8 41	3 26	8 48	3 30	9 05	3 47	9 03
19	3 42	8 20	3 52	8 30	3 43	8 33	3 39	8 41	3 26	8 48	3 30	9 06	3 47	9 03
20	3 42	8 20	3 52	8 30	3 43	8 33	3 39	8 42	3 26	8 49	3 31	9 06	3 47	9 04
21	3 42	8 21	3 52	8 31	3 43	8 34	3 39	8 42	3 26	8 49	3 31	9 06	3 47	9 04
22	3 43	8 21	3 53	8 31	3 44	8 34	3 39	8 42	3 26	8 49	3 31	9 07	3 47	9 04
23	3 43	8 21	3 53	8 31	3 44	8 34	3 39	8 42	3 26	8 49	3 31	9 07	3 47	9 04
24	3 43	8 21	3 53	8 31	3 44	8 34	3 40	8 42	3 27	8 49	3 32	9 07	3 48	9 04
25	3 44	8 21	3 54	8 31	3 45	8 34	3 40	8 42	3 27	8 49	3 32	9 07	3 48	9 04
26	3 44	8 21	3 54	8 31	3 45	8 34	3 41	8 42	3 28	8 49	3 32	9 07	3 49	9 04
27	3 44	8 21	3 54	8 31	3 45	8 34	3 41	8 42	3 28	8 49	3 33	9 06	3 49	9 04
28	3 45	8 21	3 55	8 31	3 46	8 34	3 42	8 42	3 29	8 49	3 34	9 06	3 50	9 04
29	3 46	8 21	3 56	8 31	3 47	8 34	3 42	8 42	3 29	8 49	3 34	9 06	3 50	9 04
30	3 46	8 21	3 56	8 30	3 47	8 33	3 43	8 41	3 30	8 48	3 35	9 05	3 51	9 03

JUPITER ♃

Day	R.A. h m	Dec. + o	5° high E. 52° h m	5° high E. 56° h m	Transit h m
1	2 54	15·6	3 27	3 17	10 14
11	3 03	16·3	2 53	2 43	9 44
21	3 12	16·8	2 19	2 08	9 13
31	3 20	17·4	1 45	1 33	8 42

SATURN ♄

R.A. h m	Dec. + o	Transit h m	5° high W. 52° h m	5° high W. 56° h m
8 07	20·7	15 27	22 43	22 58
8 12	20·5	14 52	22 07	22 22
8 16	20·2	14 17	21 32	21 47
8 21	20·0	13 43	20 58	21 13

Equatorial diameter of Jupiter 34"; of Saturn 17"   Diameters of Saturn's rings 38" and 14"

URANUS ♅

Day	R.A. h m	Dec. - o '	Transit h m	5° high W. 52° h m	5° high W. 56° h m
1	14 06·5	12 17	21 25	1 14	0 53
11	14 05·5	12 11	20 44	0 33	0 12
21	14 04·6	12 07	20 04	23 48	23 27
31	14 04·1	12 05	19 24	23 07	22 46

NEPTUNE ♆

R.A. h m	Dec. - o '	Transit h m	5° high W. 52° h m	5° high W. 56° h m
16 45·7	20 45	0 07	2 39	1 53
16 44·5	20 43	23 23	1 59	1 13
16 43·4	20 42	22 42	1 19	0 33
16 42·4	20 40	22 02	0 39	23 50

Diameter 4"   Diameter 2"

Day of Month	Week	♋ *Julius* Caesar, formerly *Quintilis*, 5th month (from March). Sun's Longitude 120° ♌ 22ᵈ 17ʰ
1	Th.	DOMINION DAY, CANADA. Gettysburg 1863
2	F.	Marston Moor, 1644. Lord Home b. 1903
3	S.	Viscount Scarsdale b. 1898. Earl Beauchamp b. 1903
4	☉.	3rd ☉. after Trinity. INDEPENDENCE DAY
5	M.	Georgette Heyer d. 1974 [U.S.A., 1776**
6	Tu.	Edward VI d. 1553. Sedgemoor 1685
7	W.	Edward I d. 1307. R. B. Sheridan d. 1816
8	Th.	Edward, "The Black Prince" d. 1376**
9	F.	Edward Heath b. 1916
10	S.	John Calvin b. 1509. Marcel Proust b. 1871
11	☉.	4th ☉. after Trinity. Oudenarde 1708
12	M.	Titus Oates d. 1705 H. D. Thoreau b. 1817
13	Tu.	John Clare b. 1793. Treaty of Berlin 1878
14	W.	FÊTE NATIONALE, France. Gerald Ford b. 1913
15	Th.	St. Swithin's Day. Rembrandt b. 1606
16	F.	Sir Joshua Reynolds b. 1723. Tsar Nicholas II
17	S.	Adam Smith d. 1790. Whistler d. 1903 [d. 1918
18	☉.	5th ☉. after Trinity. Dr. W. G. Grace b. 1848
19	M.	Degas b. 1834. A. J. Cronin b. 1896
20	Tu.	Sir Edmund Hillary b. 1919. Marconi d. 1937
21	W.	Ernest Hemingway b. 1898. First men on Moon,
22	Th.	St. Mary Magdalen. Falkirk 1298 [1969
23	F.	Gen. U. S. Grant d. 1885
24	S.	Simon Bolivar b. 1883. Lord Widgery b. 1911
25	☉.	6th ☉. after Trinity. St. James.
26	M.	G. B. Shaw b. 1856. Aldous Huxley b. 1894
27	Tu.	Killiecrankie 1689. Hilaire Belloc b. 1870
28	W.	J. S. Bach b. 1750. Selwyn Lloyd b. 1904
29	Th.	Mussolini b. 1883. van Gogh d. 1890
30	F.	Thomas Gray d. 1771. Henry Moore b. 1898
31	S.	TRINITY LAW SITTINGS END

PHENOMENA

July 1ᵈ 14ʰ Mars in conjunction with the Moon. Mars 6° N.

3ᵈ 04ʰ Aphelion (152,000,000 kilometres).

15ᵈ 15ʰ Mercury in superior conjunction.

21ᵈ 17ʰ Jupiter in conjunction with the Moon. Jupiter 0°·5 N.

24ᵈ 14ʰ Mercury in conjunction with Venus. Mercury 0°·4 N.

29ᵈ 14ʰ Saturn in conjunction with the Sun.

30ᵈ 02ʰ Mars in conjunction with the Moon. Mars 5° N.

CONSTELLATIONS

The following constellations are near the meridian at

	d h		d h
June 1	24	June 15	23
July 1	22	July 16	21
Aug. 1	20	Aug. 16	19

Ursa Minor, Draco, Corona, Hercules, Lyra, Serpens, Ophiuchus, Libra, Scorpius and Sagittarius.

MINIMA OF ALGOL

d	h	d	h
1	2	18	6
3	22	21	3
6	19	24	0
9	16	26	21
12	13	29	18
15	10		

PHASES OF THE MOON

		d	h	m
☽	First Quarter	4	17	28
○	Full Moon	11	13	09
☾	Last Quarter	19	06	29
●	New Moon	27	01	39

		d	h
Perigee (368,380 kilometres)		7	02
Apogee (404,060 ,,)		19	11

Mean Longitude of Ascending Node on July 1, 220°.

See note on *Summer Time*, p. 98.

MONTHLY NOTES

July 1. Special Sessions for Licences to deal in Game to be held this month.

3. Dog Days begin (end Aug. 15).

5. Dividends due. Tynwald Day, Isle of Man.

21. National Day, Belgium.

** Centenary.

| Day | THE SUN | | | | | | | | Sidereal Time | Transit of First Point of Aries |
| | Right Ascension | Dec. + | Equation of Time | Rise | | Transit | Set | | | |
				52°	56°		52°	56°		
	h m s	° ′	m s	h m	h m	h m	h m	h m	h m s	h m s
1	6 40 25	23 07	− 3 43	3 44	3 18	12 04	20 23	20 49	18 36 42	5 22 25
2	6 44 33	23 03	− 3 55	3 44	3 19	12 04	20 23	20 49	18 40 38	5 18 29
3	6 48 41	22 58	− 4 06	3 45	3 20	12 04	20 22	20 48	18 44 35	5 14 34
4	6 52 48	22 53	− 4 17	3 46	3 20	12 04	20 22	20 47	18 48 31	5 10 38
5	6 56 55	22 48	− 4 28	3 47	3 21	12 05	20 21	20 47	18 52 28	5 06 42
6	7 01 02	22 42	− 4 38	3 48	3 22	12 05	20 21	20 46	18 56 24	5 02 46
7	7 05 09	22 36	− 4 48	3 49	3 24	12 05	20 20	20 45	19 00 21	4 58 50
8	7 09 15	22 29	− 4 57	3 50	3 25	12 05	20 20	20 44	19 04 18	4 54 54
9	7 13 20	22 22	− 5 06	3 51	3 26	12 05	20 19	20 44	19 08 14	4 50 58
10	7 17 26	22 15	− 5 15	3 52	3 27	12 05	20 18	20 42	19 12 11	4 47 02
11	7 21 30	22 07	− 5 23	3 53	3 28	12 05	20 17	20 41	19 16 07	4 43 06
12	7 25 35	21 59	− 5 31	3 54	3 30	12 06	20 16	20 40	19 20 04	4 39 10
13	7 29 39	21 51	− 5 38	3 55	3 31	12 06	20 16	20 39	19 24 00	4 35 14
14	7 33 42	21 42	− 5 45	3 56	3 33	12 06	20 15	20 38	19 27 57	4 31 19
15	7 37 45	21 32	− 5 52	3 57	3 34	12 06	20 14	20 37	19 31 53	4 27 23
16	7 41 47	21 23	− 5 58	3 58	3 36	12 06	20 13	20 35	19 35 50	4 23 27
17	7 45 49	21 13	− 6 03	4 00	3 37	12 06	20 12	20 34	19 39 47	4 19 31
18	7 49 51	21 03	− 6 08	4 01	3 39	12 06	20 10	20 33	19 43 43	4 15 35
19	7 53 52	20 52	− 6 12	4 02	3 40	12 06	20 09	20 31	19 47 40	4 11 39
20	7 57 52	20 41	− 6 16	4 03	3 42	12 06	20 08	20 30	19 51 36	4 07 43
21	8 01 52	20 29	− 6 19	4 05	3 43	12 06	20 07	20 28	19 55 33	4 03 47
22	8 05 51	20 18	− 6 22	4 06	3 45	12 06	20 06	20 27	19 59 29	3 59 51
23	8 09 50	20 06	− 6 24	4 08	3 47	12 06	20 04	20 25	20 03 26	3 55 55
24	8 13 48	19 53	− 6 26	4 09	3 48	12 06	20 03	20 23	20 07 22	3 51 59
25	8 17 46	19 41	− 6 27	4 10	3 50	12 06	20 01	20 22	20 11 19	3 48 04
26	8 21 43	19 27	− 6 27	4 12	3 52	12 06	20 00	20 20	20 15 16	3 44 08
27	8 25 39	19 14	− 6 27	4 13	3 54	12 06	19 58	20 18	20 19 12	3 40 12
28	8 29 35	19 00	− 6 26	4 15	3 55	12 06	19 57	20 16	20 23 09	3 36 16
29	8 33 30	18 46	− 6 25	4 17	3 57	12 06	19 55	20 14	20 27 05	3 32 20
30	8 37 25	18 32	− 6 23	4 18	3 59	12 06	19 54	20 12	20 31 02	3 28 24
31	8 41 19	18 17	− 6 21	4 19	4 01	12 06	19 52	20 11	20 34 58	3 24 28

Duration of Civil (C), Nautical (N), and Astronomical (A), Twilight (in minutes)

| Lat. ° | July 1 | | | July 11 | | | July 21 | | | July 31 | | |
	C	N	A	C	N	A	C	N	A	C	N	A
52	48	124	T.A.N.	46	116	T.A.N.	44	107	T.A.N.	41	98	180
56	61	T.A.N.	T.A.N.	58	T.A.N.	T.A.N.	53	144	T.A.N.	49	122	T.A.N.

ASTRONOMICAL NOTES

MERCURY is at superior conjunction on the 15th and is thus unsuitably placed for observation.

VENUS is too close to the Sun for observation.

MARS is an evening star, magnitude + 1·9, at the beginning of the month but soon becomes too difficult to observe in the long evening twilight. On the evening of the 5th Mars will be seen within 1° of Regulus, Mars being above Regulus. Mars will not be visible again from these latitudes for the remainder of the year.

JUPITER is a bright morning star, magnitude − 1·8, in the constellation of Taurus. The old crescent Moon is near Jupiter on the mornings of the 21st and 22nd. During the second part of the month no planet is visible to the naked-eye in the night sky until Jupiter is located in the east, after midnight.

SATURN is in conjunction with the Sun on the 29th and thus unsuitably placed for observation.

TWILIGHT. Reference to the section just above these notes shows that astronomical twilight lasts all night for some time around the summer solstice, (i.e. in June & July) even in southern England. Under these conditions the sky never gets completely dark since the Sun is always less than 18° below the horizon.

THE MOON

Day	R.A.	Dec.	Hor. Par.	Semi-diam.	Sun's Co-long.	P.A. of Bright Limb	Phase	Age	Rise 52°	Rise 56°	Transit	Set 52°	Set 56°
	h m	°	′	′	°	°		d	h m	h m	h m	h m	h m
1	9 27	+ 9.8	57.9	15.8	316	294	13	3.4	8 25	8 18	15 21	22 04	22 09
2	10 19	+ 5.5	58.4	15.9	329	294	21	4.4	9 41	9 38	16 11	22 29	22 30
3	11 12	+ 0.8	58.7	16.0	341	295	31	5.4	10 57	10 58	17 02	22 54	22 51
4	12 04	− 3.9	59.0	16.1	353	294	42	6.4	12 15	12 20	17 53	23 20	23 13
5	12 58	− 8.5	59.3	16.2	5	292	53	7.4	13 32	13 42	18 46	23 50	23 38
6	13 54	−12.6	59.5	16.2	18	290	64	8.4	14 50	15 04	19 41	..	..
7	14 51	−16.0	59.5	16.2	30	287	75	9.4	16 05	16 23	20 38	0 24	0 09
8	15 50	−18.4	59.5	16.2	42	284	84	10.4	17 15	17 35	21 36	1 06	0 48
9	16 50	−19.7	59.3	16.2	54	281	92	11.4	18 16	18 36	22 35	1 56	1 36
10	17 50	−19.7	58.9	16.1	66	281	97	12.4	19 07	19 26	23 32	2 55	2 35
11	18 49	−18.5	58.4	15.9	79	297	99	13.4	19 48	20 04	..	4 02	3 44
12	19 46	−16.2	57.9	15.8	91	39	100	14.4	20 22	20 35	0 27	5 12	4 58
13	20 40	−13.1	57.2	15.6	103	60	97	15.4	20 50	20 59	1 19	6 24	6 13
14	21 32	− 9.5	56.5	15.4	115	63	93	16.4	21 15	21 20	2 08	7 35	7 27
15	22 21	− 5.4	55.8	15.2	127	64	87	17.4	21 37	21 38	2 54	8 44	8 40
16	23 08	− 1.3	55.2	15.1	139	64	79	18.4	21 58	21 56	3 38	9 51	9 51
17	23 54	+ 2.8	54.8	14.9	152	65	71	19.4	22 20	22 14	4 21	10 56	11 00
18	0 39	+ 6.8	54.4	14.8	164	66	62	20.4	22 42	22 34	5 04	12 01	12 08
19	1 25	+10.4	54.3	14.8	176	68	53	21.4	23 07	22 56	5 48	13 04	13 15
20	2 12	+13.6	54.3	14.8	188	70	43	22.4	23 36	23 21	6 32	14 07	14 21
21	3 00	+16.3	54.5	14.8	201	73	34	23.4	..	23 53	7 18	15 08	15 25
22	3 49	+18.3	54.8	14.9	213	77	25	24.4	0 11	..	8 06	16 07	16 26
23	4 41	+19.5	55.3	15.1	225	80	17	25.4	0 52	0 33	8 55	17 01	17 21
24	5 34	+19.7	55.8	15.2	237	83	10	26.4	1 41	1 22	9 47	17 49	18 08
25	6 28	+19.0	56.5	15.4	250	84	5	27.4	2 39	2 21	10 39	18 32	18 49
26	7 23	+17.3	57.2	15.6	262	79	2	28.4	3 45	3 28	11 32	19 08	19 22
27	8 17	+14.6	57.8	15.7	274	23	0	29.4	4 55	4 43	12 24	19 40	19 50
28	9 12	+11.0	58.3	15.9	286	309	1	0.9	6 10	6 01	13 16	20 08	20 14
29	10 05	+ 6.8	58.8	16.0	299	300	5	1.9	7 27	7 22	14 07	20 34	20 37
30	10 59	+ 2.2	59.1	16.1	311	298	11	2.9	8 45	8 44	14 59	21 00	20 58
31	11 52	− 2.6	59.3	16.2	323	296	19	3.9	10 03	10 07	15 50	21 26	21 20

MERCURY ☿

Day	R.A.	Dec. +	Diam.	Phase	Transit		Day	R.A.	Dec. +	Diam.	Phase	Transit	
	h m	°	″		h m			h m	°	″		h m	
1	5 30	22.4	6	76	10 56	Mercury is	16	7 45	22.8	5	100	12 12	Mercury is
4	5 55	23.2	6	85	11 09	too close to	19	8 12	21.8	5	98	12 27	too close to
7	6 21	23.7	5	90	11 23	the Sun	22	8 38	20.4	5	96	12 40	the Sun
10	6 49	23.8	5	96	11 39	for observation	25	9 02	18.8	5	93	12 53	for observation
13	7 17	23.5	5	98	11 56		28	9 25	16.9	5	90	13 03	
16	7 45	22.8	5	100	12 12		31	9 46	15.0	5	86	13 12	

VENUS ♀

Day	R.A.	Dec. +	Diam.	Phase	Transit	
	h m	°	″		h m	
1	6 56	23.6	10	100	12 20	Venus is
6	7 23	23.0	10	100	12 27	too close to
11	7 49	22.1	10	99	12 34	the Sun
16	8 15	21.0	10	99	12 40	for observation
21	8 41	19.7	10	99	12 46	
26	9 06	18.1	10	98	12 51	
31	9 30	16.3	10	98	12 56	

MARS ♂

Day	R.A.	Dec. +	Diam.	Phase	Transit	5° high W 52°	56°
	h m	°	″		h m	h m	h m
1	9 56	13.8	4	95	15 18	21 56	22 04
6	10 08	12.7	4	95	15 10	21 42	21 49
11	10 19	11.6	4	95	15 02	21 28	21 34
16	10 31	10.5	4	96	14 54	21 13	21 18
21	10 42	9.3	4	96	14 46	20 59	21 03
26	10 54	8.1	4	96	14 37	20 44	20 47
31	11 05	6.8	4	96	14 29	20 30	20 32

SUNRISE AND SUNSET (G.M.T.)

Day	London a.m. h m	London p.m. h m	Bristol a.m. h m	Bristol p.m. h m	Birmingham a.m. h m	Birmingham p.m. h m	Manchester a.m. h m	Manchester p.m. h m	Newcastle a.m. h m	Newcastle p.m. h m	Glasgow a.m. h m	Glasgow p.m. h m	Belfast a.m. h m	Belfast p.m. h m
1	3 47	8 21	3 57	8 30	3 48	8 33	3 44	8 41	3 31	8 48	3 36	9 05	3 52	9 03
2	3 47	8 20	3 57	8 30	3 48	8 33	3 44	8 41	3 32	8 48	3 37	9 05	3 52	9 03
3	3 48	8 20	3 58	8 29	3 49	8 32	3 45	8 40	3 33	8 47	3 38	9 04	3 53	9 02
4	3 49	8 19	3 59	8 29	3 50	8 32	3 46	8 40	3 33	8 46	3 38	9 03	3 54	9 02
5	3 50	8 19	4 00	8 28	3 51	8 31	3 47	8 39	3 34	8 46	3 39	9 03	3 55	9 01
6	3 51	8 18	4 01	8 28	3 52	8 31	3 48	8 39	3 35	8 45	3 40	9 02	3 56	9 01
7	3 52	8 18	4 02	8 27	3 53	8 30	3 49	8 38	3 37	8 44	3 42	9 01	3 57	9 00
8	3 53	8 17	4 03	8 27	3 54	8 30	3 50	8 37	3 38	8 43	3 43	9 00	3 58	8 59
9	3 54	8 17	4 04	8 26	3 55	8 29	3 51	8 36	3 39	8 43	3 44	9 00	3 59	8 58
10	3 55	8 16	4 05	8 25	3 56	8 28	3 52	8 35	3 40	8 41	3 45	8 58	4 00	8 57
11	3 56	8 15	4 06	8 24	3 57	8 27	3 53	8 35	3 41	8 41	3 46	8 57	4 01	8 57
12	3 57	8 14	4 07	8 24	3 58	8 26	3 55	8 34	3 43	8 40	3 48	8 56	4 03	8 56
13	3 58	8 14	4 08	8 23	3 59	8 26	3 56	8 33	3 44	8 39	3 49	8 55	4 04	8 55
14	3 59	8 13	4 09	8 22	4 00	8 25	3 57	8 32	3 45	8 38	3 51	8 54	4 05	8 54
15	4 00	8 12	4 10	8 21	4 01	8 24	3 58	8 31	3 46	8 37	3 52	8 53	4 06	8 53
16	4 01	8 11	4 11	8 20	4 03	8 22	4 00	8 29	3 48	8 35	3 54	8 51	4 08	8 51
17	4 02	8 10	4 13	8 19	4 04	8 21	4 01	8 28	3 49	8 34	3 55	8 50	4 09	8 50
18	4 03	8 08	4 14	8 18	4 05	8 20	4 02	8 27	3 51	8 33	3 57	8 49	4 11	8 49
19	4 04	8 07	4 15	8 17	4 07	8 19	4 04	8 26	3 52	8 31	3 58	8 47	4 12	8 47
20	4 06	8 06	4 16	8 16	4 08	8 17	4 05	8 24	3 54	8 30	4 00	8 46	4 14	8 46
21	4 07	8 05	4 18	8 15	4 10	8 16	4 07	8 23	3 55	8 28	4 01	8 44	4 15	8 44
22	4 08	8 04	4 19	8 14	4 11	8 15	4 08	8 22	3 57	8 27	4 03	8 43	4 17	8 43
23	4 10	8 02	4 20	8 12	4 13	8 13	4 10	8 20	3 59	8 25	4 05	8 41	4 19	8 41
24	4 11	8 01	4 22	8 11	4 14	8 12	4 11	8 19	4 00	8 23	4 06	8 39	4 20	8 39
25	4 12	7 59	4 23	8 09	4 15	8 10	4 12	8 17	4 02	8 22	4 08	8 38	4 22	8 38
26	4 14	7 58	4 24	8 08	4 17	8 09	4 14	8 16	4 04	8 20	4 10	8 36	4 24	8 36
27	4 15	7 56	4 26	8 06	4 18	8 07	4 15	8 14	4 05	8 19	4 12	8 34	4 25	8 35
28	4 17	7 55	4 27	8 05	4 20	8 06	4 17	8 13	4 07	8 17	4 13	8 32	4 27	8 33
29	4 19	7 53	4 29	8 03	4 22	8 04	4 19	8 11	4 09	8 15	4 15	8 30	4 29	8 31
30	4 20	7 52	4 30	8 02	4 23	8 03	4 20	8 10	4 10	8 13	4 17	8 28	4 30	8 30
31	4 21	7 50	4 31	8 00	4 24	8 01	4 22	8 08	4 12	8 12	4 19	8 27	4 32	8 28

JUPITER ♃   SATURN ♄

Day	R.A. h m	Dec. + °	5° high East 52° h m	5° high East 56° h m	Transit h m	R.A. h m	Dec. + °	Transit h m	
1	3 20	17·4	1 45	1 33	8 42	8 21	20·0	13 43	Saturn is
11	3 27	17·8	1 10	0 59	8 10	8 26	19·7	13 09	too close to
21	3 35	18·2	0 36	0 24	7 38	8 32	19·4	12 34	the Sun for
31	3 41	18·6	23 57	23 45	7 05	8 37	19·1	12 00	observation

Equatorial diameter of Jupiter 36″; of Saturn 17″.   Diameters of Saturn's rings 37″ and 13″

URANUS ♅   NEPTUNE ♆

Day	R.A. h m	Dec. − ° ′	Transit h m	5° high West 52° h m	5° high West 56° h m	R.A. h m	Dec. + ° ′	Transit h m	5° high West 52° h m	5° high West 56° h m
1	14 04·1	12 05	19 24	23 07	22 46	16 42·4	20 40	22 02	0 38	23 49
11	14 04·0	12 04	18 45	22 27	22 06	16 41·4	20 39	21 22	23 55	23 09
21	14 04·1	12 05	18 06	21 48	21 27	16 40·7	20 37	20 42	23 15	22 30
31	14 04·6	12 08	17 27	21 09	20 48	16 40·1	20 37	20 02	22 35	21 50

Diameter 4″   Diameter 2″

AUGUST XXXI DAYS [1976

118

DAY OF Month	Week	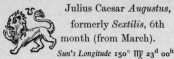 Julius Caesar *Augustus*, formerly *Sextilis*, 6th month (from March). Sun's Longitude 150° ♍ 23ᵈ 00ʰ
1	♌.	**7th ♌. after Trinity.** Queen Anne d. 1714
2	M.	Alexander Graham Bell d. 1922
3	Tu.	Rupert Brooke b. 1887. Joseph Conrad d. 1924
4	W.	QUEEN ELIZABETH THE QUEEN MOTHER b. 1900
5	Th.	Guy de Maupassant b. 1850
6	F.	**Transfiguration.** Tennyson b. 1809
7	S.	Earl Howe b. 1908
8	♌.	**8th ♌. after Trinity.** Visct. Cobham b. 1909
9	M.	Battle of Dupplin Moor 1332
10	Tu.	Herbert C. Hoover b. 1824. Treaty of Trianon 1921
11	W.	Cardinal Newman d. 1890
12	Th.	William Blake d. 1827
13	F.	Florence Nightingale d. 1910. H. G. Wells d. 1946
14	S.	John Galsworthy b. 1867
15	♌.	**9th ♌. after Trinity.** PRINCESS ANNE b. 1950
16	M.	Andrew Marvell d. 1678. Margaret Mitchell d. 1949
17	Tu.	Frederick the Great d. 1786. Balzac d. 1850
18	W.	W. H. Hudson d. 1922
19	Th.	James Watt d. 1819. Serge Diaghilev d. 1929
20	F.	Trotsky assassinated 1940
21	S.	PRINCESS MARGARET BORN, 1930
22	♌.	**10th ♌. after Trinity.** Richard III d. 1485
23	M.	Duke of Buckingham d. 1628
24	Tu.	**St. Bartholomew.** Graham Sutherland b. 1903
25	W.	David Hume d. 1776.** Paris Liberated, 1944
26	Th.	Sir Robert Walpole b. 1676.** Charles Lindbergh [d. 1974
27	F.	Titian d. 1576.** Sir Donald Bradman b. 1908
28	S.	Sir Edward Burne-Jones b. 1833
29	♌.	**11th ♌. after Trinity.** Jean Ingres b. 1780
30	M.	Lord Rutherford b. 1871
31	Tu.	John Bunyan d. 1688 Sir Bernard Lovell b. 1913.

PHENOMENA

August 18ᵈ 09ʰ Jupiter in conjunction with the Moon. Jupiter 1° N.

23ᵈ 23ʰ Saturn in conjunction with the Moon. Saturn 6° N.

26ᵈ 10ʰ Mercury at greatest eastern elongation (27°).

27ᵈ 00ʰ Venus in conjunction with the Moon. Venus 5° N.

27ᵈ 11ʰ Mercury in conjunction with the Moon. Mercury 0°·5 N.

27ᵈ 15ʰ Mars in conjunction with the Moon. Mars 4° N.

CONSTELLATIONS

The following constellations are near the meridian at

	d h		d h
July 1	24	July 16	23
Aug. 1	22	Aug. 16	21
Sept. 1	20	Sept. 15	19

Draco, Hercules, Lyra, Cygnus, Sagitta, Ophiuchus, Serpens, Aquila and Sagittarius.

MINIMA OF ALGOL

d	h	d	h
1	15	18	19
4	11	21	16
7	8	24	13
10	5	27	10
13	2	30	7
15	23		

PHASES OF THE MOON

		d	h	m
☽ First Quarter		2	22	07
○ Full Moon		9	23	44
☾ Last Quarter		18	00	13
● New Moon		25	11	01

		d	h
Perigee (369,110 kilometres)	1	04
Apogee (404,400 „)	16	06
Perigee (364,550 „)	28	02

Mean Longitude of Ascending Node on August 1, 218°.

See note on *Summer Time*, p. 98.

MONTHLY NOTES

Aug. 1. Lammas. Scottish Term Day.
2. Bank Holiday, Scotland.
5. Oyster season opens.
12. Grouse shooting begins.
26. First day of Ramadān.
30. Bank and General Holiday, England, Wales and N. Ireland.

** Centenary.

			THE SUN					s.d. 15'·8			Sidereal Time	Transit of First Point of Aries
Day	Right Ascension	Dec. +	Equation of Time	Rise		Transit	Set					
				52°	56°		52°	56°				
	h m s	° '	m s	h m	h m	h m	h m	h m	h m	h m s	h m s	
1	8 45 12	18 02	− 6 17	4 21	4 03	12 06	19 51	20 09		20 38 55	3 20 32	
2	8 49 05	17 47	− 6 14	4 22	4 05	12 06	19 49	20 07		20 42 51	3 16 36	
3	8 52 57	17 32	− 6 09	4 24	4 07	12 06	19 47	20 04		20 46 48	3 12 40	
4	8 56 48	17 16	− 6 04	4 25	4 08	12 06	19 45	20 02		20 50 45	3 08 44	
5	9 00 39	17 00	− 5 58	4 27	4 10	12 06	19 44	20 00		20 54 41	3 04 49	
6	9 04 30	16 44	− 5 52	4 29	4 12	12 06	19 42	19 58		20 58 38	3 00 53	
7	9 08 19	16 27	− 5 45	4 30	4 14	12 06	19 40	19 56		21 02 34	2 56 57	
8	9 12 08	16 10	− 5 38	4 32	4 16	12 06	19 38	19 54		21 06 31	2 53 01	
9	9 15 57	15 53	− 5 30	4 33	4 18	12 05	19 36	19 52		21 10 27	2 49 05	
10	9 19 45	15 36	− 5 21	4 35	4 20	12 05	19 34	19 49		21 14 24	2 45 09	
11	9 23 32	15 18	− 5 12	4 37	4 22	12 05	19 32	19 47		21 18 20	2 41 13	
12	9 27 19	15 00	− 5 02	4 38	4 24	12 05	19 30	19 45		21 22 17	2 37 17	
13	9 31 05	14 42	− 4 51	4 40	4 26	12 05	19 29	19 42		21 26 14	2 33 21	
14	9 34 50	14 24	− 4 40	4 42	4 28	12 05	19 27	19 40		21 30 10	2 29 25	
15	9 38 35	14 05	− 4 29	4 43	4 30	12 04	19 25	19 38		21 34 07	2 25 29	
16	9 42 20	13 46	− 4 17	4 45	4 32	12 04	19 23	19 35		21 38 03	2 21 34	
17	9 46 04	13 27	− 4 04	4 46	4 34	12 04	19 21	19 33		21 42 00	2 17 38	
18	9 49 48	13 08	− 3 51	4 48	4 36	12 04	19 18	19 31		21 45 56	2 13 42	
19	9 53 31	12 48	− 3 38	4 50	4 38	12 04	19 16	19 28		21 49 53	2 09 46	
20	9 57 13	12 29	− 3 24	4 51	4 40	12 03	19 14	19 26		21 53 49	2 05 50	
21	10 00 56	12 09	− 3 10	4 53	4 42	12 03	19 12	19 23		21 57 46	2 01 54	
22	10 04 37	11 49	− 2 55	4 55	4 44	12 03	19 10	19 21		22 01 43	1 57 58	
23	10 08 19	11 29	− 2 40	4 56	4 46	12 03	19 08	19 18		22 05 39	1 54 02	
24	10 11 59	11 08	− 2 24	4 58	4 47	12 02	19 06	19 16		22 09 36	1 50 06	
25	10 15 40	10 48	− 2 08	4 59	4 49	12 02	19 04	19 13		22 13 32	1 46 10	
26	10 19 20	10 27	− 1 51	5 01	4 51	12 02	19 01	19 11		22 17 29	1 42 14	
27	10 22 59	10 06	− 1 34	5 03	4 53	12 01	18 59	19 08		22 21 25	1 38 19	
28	10 26 39	9 45	− 1 17	5 04	4 55	12 01	18 57	19 06		22 25 22	1 34 23	
29	10 30 18	9 24	− 0 59	5 06	4 57	12 01	18 55	19 03		22 29 18	1 30 27	
30	10 33 56	9 02	− 0 41	5 08	4 59	12 01	18 53	19 01		22 33 15	1 26 31	
31	10 37 34	8 41	− 0 23	5 09	5 01	12 00	18 50	18 58		22 37 11	1 22 35	

Duration of Civil (C), Nautical (N), and Astronomical (A), Twilight (in minutes)

Lat. °	Aug. 1			Aug. 11			Aug. 21			Aug. 31		
	C	N	A	C	N	A	C	N	A	C	N	A
52	41	97	177	39	89	153	37	83	138	35	79	127
56	48	120	T.A.N.	45	106	205	42	96	166	40	89	147

ASTRONOMICAL NOTES

MERCURY is at greatest eastern elongation on the 26th but even so is unsuitably placed for observation.

VENUS becomes a brilliant evening star, magnitude − 3·3, at the beginning of the month, but is only visible for a very short while after sunset, low above the western horizon.

MARS is too close to the Sun for observation.

JUPITER is a prominent morning star, magnitude − 2·0. By the end of the month it is visible by 22ʰ, rising in the E.N.E. about 5° south of the Pleiades.

On the morning of the 18th, the Moon, at Last Quarter, will be seen approaching Jupiter.

SATURN is too close to the Sun for observation at first but during the second half of the month it gradually becomes a morning star, magnitude + 0·5. By the end of the month it is visible low in the eastern sky by about 03ʰ.

METEORS. The maximum of the famous Perseid meteor shower occurs during the night of the 11th–12th. Since Full Moon occurred only two days earlier strong moonlight will seriously interfere with observation.

THE MOON

Day	R.A.	Dec.	Hor. Par.	Semi-diam.	Sun's Co-long.	P.A. of Bright Limb	Phase	Age	Rise 52°	Rise 56°	Transit	Set 52°	Set 56°
	h m	°	′	′	°	°		d	h m	h m	h m	h m	h m
1	12 46	− 7·2	59·4	16·2	335	294	29	4·9	11 21	11 29	16 43	21 55	21 45
2	13 41	−11·5	59·4	16·2	347	291	39	5·9	12 39	12 51	17 37	22 27	22 14
3	14 38	−15·0	59·3	16·1	0	288	51	6·9	13 54	14 10	18 33	23 06	22 49
4	15 36	−17·7	59·0	16·1	12	284	62	7·9	15 04	15 23	19 30	23 52	23 33
5	16 34	−19·3	58·8	16·0	24	280	73	8·9	16 07	16 27	20 27	··	··
6	17 33	−19·7	58·4	15·9	36	276	82	9·9	17 00	17 20	21 23	0 47	0 27
7	18 32	−18·9	58·0	15·8	49	273	90	10·9	17 45	18 02	22 18	1 49	1 30
8	19 28	−17·0	57·6	15·7	61	272	95	11·9	18 21	18 35	23 10	2 56	2 40
9	20 22	−14·3	57·1	15·6	73	279	99	12·9	18 52	19 02	··	4 06	3 54
10	21 14	−10·9	56·5	15·4	85	344	100	13·9	19 18	19 24	0 00	5 17	5 08
11	22 04	− 7·0	56·0	15·3	97	49	99	14·9	19 41	19 44	0 47	6 26	6 21
12	22 52	− 2·9	55·6	15·1	109	58	96	15·9	20 03	20 02	1 32	7 34	7 33
13	23 38	+ 1·3	55·0	15·0	122	62	91	16·9	20 24	20 21	2 16	8 41	8 43
14	0 24	+ 5·3	54·6	14·9	134	64	85	17·9	20 47	20 40	2 59	9 46	9 52
15	1 10	+ 9·0	54·3	14·8	146	67	77	18·9	21 11	21 00	3 43	10 50	10 59
16	1 56	+12·4	54·2	14·8	158	69	69	19·9	21 38	21 25	4 26	11 53	12 05
17	2 44	+15·2	54·3	14·8	170	73	60	20·9	22 10	21 54	5 11	12 54	13 10
18	3 33	+17·4	54·5	14·8	183	76	50	21·9	22 48	22 29	5 58	13 53	14 11
19	4 23	+18·9	54·9	14·9	195	80	41	22·9	23 32	23 13	6 46	14 49	15 08
20	5 15	+19·6	55·4	15·1	207	84	31	23·9	··	··	7 36	15 39	15 59
21	6 08	+19·2	56·1	15·3	219	88	22	24·9	0 26	0 07	8 27	16 24	16 42
22	7 02	+17·9	56·8	15·5	232	91	14	25·9	1 27	1 09	9 20	17 04	17 19
23	7 56	+15·6	57·6	15·7	244	93	8	26·9	2 35	2 20	10 12	17 38	17 50
24	8 51	+12·4	58·4	15·9	256	92	3	27·9	3 48	3 38	11 05	18 08	18 16
25	9 46	+ 8·4	59·1	16·1	268	72	0	28·9	5 05	4 59	11 57	18 36	18 40
26	10 40	+ 3·9	59·7	16·3	281	322	1	0·5	6 24	6 22	12 50	19 03	19 03
27	11 35	− 0·9	60·0	16·4	293	302	3	1·5	7 44	7 47	13 43	19 30	19 25
28	12 31	− 5·7	60·1	16·4	305	296	9	2·5	9 05	9 12	14 37	19 58	19 50
29	13 27	−10·2	60·1	16·4	317	293	17	3·5	10 25	10 36	15 32	20 30	20 18
30	14 24	−14·0	59·8	16·3	329	289	26	4·5	11 42	11 57	16 28	21 08	20 52
31	15 23	−16·9	59·4	16·2	342	284	37	5·5	12 55	13 13	17 25	21 52	21 33

MERCURY ☿

Day	R.A.	Dec. +	Diam.	Phase	Transit		Day	R.A.	Dec.	Diam.	Phase	Transit	
	h m	°	″		h m			h m	°	″		h m	
1	9 53	14·3	5	85	13 15	Mercury is	16	11 17	+4·1	6	67	13 39	Mercury is
4	10 12	12·3	5	81	13 22	too close to	19	11 30	+2·1	6	63	13 41	too close to
7	10 30	10·2	6	78	13 28	the Sun	22	11 43	+0·3	7	60	13 41	the Sun
10	10 47	8·1	6	74	13 33	for	25	11 54	−1·5	7	55	13 40	for
13	11 02	6·1	6	71	13 37	observation	28	12 03	−3·1	7	50	13 37	observation
16	11 17	4·1	6	67	13 39		31	12 11	−4·4	8	45	13 33	

VENUS ♀

Day	R.A.	Dec. +	Diam.	Phase	Transit	5° high W 52°	5° high W 56°
	h m	°	″		h m	h m	h m
1	9 35	15·9	10	98	12 57	19 45	19 55
6	9 59	13·9	10	97	13 01	19 38	19 47
11	10 23	11·7	10	97	13 05	19 31	19 37
16	10 46	9·4	10	96	13 08	19 22	19 26
21	11 09	7·0	10	95	13 12	19 13	19 14
26	11 32	4·5	11	95	13 14	19 03	19 02
31	11 54	1·9	11	94	13 17	18 53	18 50

MARS ♂

Day	R.A.	Dec.	Diam.	Phase	Transit	
	h m	°	″		h m	
1	11 07	+6·6	4	96	14 27	Mars is
6	11 19	+5·3	4	97	14 19	too close to
11	11 30	+4·1	4	97	14 11	the Sun
16	11 42	+2·8	4	97	14 03	for
21	11 53	+1·5	4	98	13 55	observation
26	12 05	+0·1	4	98	13 47	
31	12 17	−1·2	4	98	13 39	

SUNRISE AND SUNSET (G.M.T.)

Day	London a.m. h m	London p.m. h m	Bristol a.m. h m	Bristol p.m. h m	Birmingham a.m. h m	Birmingham p.m. h m	Manchester a.m. h m	Manchester p.m. h m	Newcastle a.m. h m	Newcastle p.m. h m	Glasgow a.m. h m	Glasgow p.m. h m	Belfast a.m. h m	Belfast p.m. h m
1	4 23	7 49	4 33	7 59	4 26	8 00	4 23	8 06	4 14	8 10	4 21	8 25	4 33	8 26
2	4 24	7 47	4 34	7 57	4 27	7 58	4 25	8 04	4 16	8 08	4 23	8 23	4 35	8 24
3	4 26	7 45	4 36	7 55	4 29	7 56	4 27	8 02	4 18	8 05	4 25	8 20	4 37	8 22
4	4 27	7 43	4 37	7 53	4 30	7 54	4 28	8 00	4 19	8 03	4 26	8 18	4 38	8 20
5	4 29	7 42	4 39	7 52	4 32	7 53	4 30	7 59	4 21	8 02	4 28	8 16	4 40	8 18
6	4 31	7 40	4 41	7 50	4 34	7 51	4 32	7 57	4 23	8 00	4 30	8 14	4 42	8 16
7	4 32	7 38	4 42	7 48	4 35	7 49	4 34	7 55	4 25	7 58	4 32	8 12	4 44	8 14
8	4 34	7 37	4 44	7 46	4 37	7 47	4 35	7 53	4 26	7 56	4 34	8 10	4 46	8 12
9	4 35	7 35	4 45	7 44	4 38	7 45	4 37	7 51	4 28	7 54	4 36	8 08	4 48	8 10
10	4 37	7 33	4 47	7 42	4 40	7 43	4 39	7 48	4 30	7 51	4 38	8 05	4 50	8 07
11	4 39	7 31	4 49	7 40	4 42	7 41	4 41	7 46	4 32	7 49	4 40	8 03	4 52	8 05
12	4 40	7 29	4 50	7 39	4 44	7 39	4 43	7 44	4 34	7 47	4 42	8 01	4 54	8 03
13	4 42	7 28	4 52	7 37	4 46	7 37	4 45	7 42	4 36	7 44	4 44	7 58	4 55	8 01
14	4 43	7 26	4 53	7 35	4 47	7 35	4 46	7 40	4 38	7 42	4 46	7 56	4 57	7 59
15	4 45	7 24	4 55	7 33	4 49	7 33	4 48	7 38	4 40	7 40	4 48	7 54	4 59	7 57
16	4 46	7 22	4 56	7 31	4 51	7 31	4 50	7 36	4 42	7 38	4 50	7 52	5 01	7 55
17	4 48	7 20	4 58	7 29	4 52	7 29	4 51	7 34	4 43	7 36	4 51	7 50	5 02	7 53
18	4 49	7 17	4 59	7 27	4 54	7 26	4 53	7 31	4 45	7 33	4 53	7 48	5 04	7 50
19	4 51	7 15	5 01	7 25	4 56	7 24	4 55	7 29	4 47	7 31	4 55	7 45	5 06	7 48
20	4 52	7 13	5 02	7 23	4 57	7 22	4 56	7 27	4 49	7 29	4 57	7 43	5 08	7 46
21	4 54	7 11	5 04	7 21	4 59	7 20	4 58	7 25	4 51	7 26	4 59	7 40	5 10	7 43
22	4 56	7 09	5 06	7 19	5 01	7 18	5 00	7 23	4 53	7 24	5 01	7 38	5 11	7 41
23	4 57	7 07	5 07	7 17	5 02	7 16	5 01	7 21	4 55	7 21	5 03	7 35	5 13	7 39
24	4 59	7 05	5 09	7 15	5 04	7 14	5 03	7 19	4 56	7 19	5 04	7 33	5 15	7 37
25	5 00	7 03	5 10	7 13	5 05	7 12	5 05	7 16	4 58	7 16	5 06	7 30	5 17	7 34
26	5 02	7 00	5 12	7 10	5 07	7 09	5 07	7 14	5 00	7 14	5 08	7 28	5 19	7 32
27	5 04	6 58	5 14	7 08	5 09	7 07	5 08	7 12	5 02	7 12	5 10	7 25	5 20	7 29
28	5 05	6 56	5 15	7 06	5 10	7 05	5 10	7 09	5 04	7 09	5 12	7 23	5 22	7 27
29	5 07	6 54	5 17	7 04	5 12	7 03	5 12	7 07	5 06	7 07	5 14	7 20	5 24	7 24
30	5 09	6 52	5 19	7 02	5 14	7 01	5 14	7 04	5 08	7 04	5 16	7 18	5 26	7 22
31	5 10	6 49	5 20	6 59	5 15	6 58	5 15	7 02	5 09	7 02	5 18	7 15	5 28	7 19

JUPITER ♃   SATURN ♄

Day	R.A. h m	Dec. + °	5° high East 52° h m	5° high East 56° h m	Transit h m	R.A. h m	Dec. + °	5° high East 52° h m	5° high East 56° h m	Transit h m
1	3 42	18·6	23 54	23 41	7 02	8 38	19·1	4 50	4 37	11 57
11	3 47	18·9	23 18	23 05	6 28	8 43	18·7	4 18	4 05	11 23
21	3 51	19·1	22 42	22 28	5 53	8 48	18·4	3 46	3 33	10 49
31	3 55	19·2	22 05	21 51	5 17	8 53	18·1	3 13	3 01	10 14

Equatorial diameter of Jupiter 39″; of Saturn 17″. Diameters of Saturn's rings 37″ and 12″.

URANUS ♅   NEPTUNE ♆

Day	R.A. h m	Dec. − ° ′	Transit h m		R.A. h m	Dec. − ° ′	Transit h m	5° high West 52° h m	5° high West 56° h m
1	14 04·7	12 09	17 23	Uranus is	16 40·0	20 37	19 58	22 31	21 46
11	14 05·5	12 14	16 44	too close to	16 39·6	20 37	19 18	21 52	21 06
21	14 06·7	12 20	16 06	the Sun for	16 39·5	20 37	18 39	21 12	20 27
31	14 08·1	12 28	15 28	observation	16 39·5	20 37	17 59	20 33	19 47

Diameter 4″   Diameter 2″

SEPTEMBER XXX DAYS [1976

Day of		*Septem* (seven), 7th month of Roman (pre-Julian) Calendar. *Sun's Longitude* 180° ♎ 22ᵈ 22ʰ	
Month	Week		
1	W.	Jacques Cartier d. 1557. Louis XIV d. 1715	
2	Th.	Fire of London 1666. J. R. R. Tolkien d. 1973	
3	F.	Britain at War, 1939. Oliver Cromwell d. 1658	
4	S.	Grieg d. 1907. Albert Schweitzer d. 1965	
5	☖.	12th ☖. after Trinity. John Wisden b. 1826	
6	M.	Battle of the Marne 1914. Arthur Rackham d. 1939	
7	Tu.	Queen Elizabeth I b. 1533	
8	W.	Richard Strauss d. 1949	
9	Th.	Flodden 1513. F. R. Spofforth b. 1853	
10	F.	Treaty of St. Germain 1919	
11	S.	Malplaquet 1709. D. H. Lawrence b. 1885	
12	☖.	13th ☖. after Trinity. Sack of Drogheda 1649	
13	M.	Quebec 1759. Heath Robinson d. 1944	
14	Tu.	Dante d. 1321. Wellington d. 1852	
15	W.	Battle of Britain Day. I. K. Brunel d. 1859	
16	Th.	Fire of Moscow, 1812. Bonar Law b. 1858	
17	F.	James II d. 1701. Smollett d. 1771	
18	S.	Dr. Johnson b. 1709. Greta Garbo b. 1905	
19	☖.	14th ☖. after Trinity. William Golding b. 1911	
20	M.	Battle of the Alma, 1854. Sibelius d. 1957	
21	Tu.	St. Matthew. H. G. Wells b. 1866	
22	W.	Boulogne reoccupied 1944	
23	Th.	Wilkie Collins d. 1889. Sigmund Freud d. 1939	
24	F.	Horace Walpole b. 1717. Sir Alan Herbert b. 1890	
25	S.	William Faulkner b. 1897. Nikolai Poliakov d. 1974	
26	☖.	15th ☖. after Trinity. Pope Paul VI b. 1897	
27	M.	Edward II d. 1327. Degas d. 1917	
28	Tu.	Louis Pasteur d. 1895	
29	W.	St. Michael and All Angels. Nelson b. 1758	
30	Th.	Lord Raglan b. 1788. Calais reoccupied 1944	

PHENOMENA

September 6ᵈ 04ʰ Mercury in conjunction with Venus. Mercury 5° S.

10ᵈ 22ʰ Venus in conjunction with Mars. Venus 0°·4 N.

14ᵈ 19ʰ Jupiter in conjunction with the Moon. Jupiter 1° N.

20ᵈ 15ʰ Saturn in conjunction with the Moon. Saturn 6° N.

22ᵈ 01ʰ Mercury in inferior conjunction.

22ᵈ 22ʰ Autumnal Equinox.

25ᵈ 05ʰ Mars in conjunction with the Moon. Mars 2° N.

25ᵈ 18ʰ Venus in conjunction with the Moon. Venus 0°·7 N.

CONSTELLATIONS

The following constellations are near the meridian at

	d h		d h
Aug. 1	24	Aug. 16	23
Sept. 1	22	Sept. 15	21
Oct. 1	20	Oct. 16	19

Draco, Cepheus, Lyra, Cygnus, Vulpecula, Sagitta, Delphinus, Equuleus, Aquila, Aquarius and Capricornus.

MINIMA OF ALGOL

d	h	d	h
2	3	19	8
5	0	22	5
7	21	25	2
10	18	27	23
13	15	30	20
16	12		

PHASES OF THE MOON

		d	h	m
☽	First Quarter	1	03	35
○	Full Moon	8	12	52
☾	Last Quarter	16	17	20
●	New Moon	23	19	55
☽	First Quarter	30	11	12

	d	h
Apogee (405,330 kilometres)	12	23
Perigee (359,840 „)	25	03

Mean Longitude of Ascending Node on September 1, 216°.

See note on *Summer Time*, p. 98.

MONTHLY NOTES

Sept. 1. Partridge shooting begins.

25. Jewish New Year (A.M. 5737).

29. Michaelmas. Quarter day.

NATIONAL DAYS.—*Sept.* 1, Libya; 6, Swaziland; 7, Brazil; 9, Bulgaria; 15, Costa Rica, El Salvador, Honduras; 16, Mexico; 18, Chile; 30, Botswana.

Day	THE SUN s.d. 15'·9								Sidereal Time	Transit of First Point of Aries
	Right Ascension	Dec.	Equation of Time	Rise		Transit	Set			
				52°	56°		52°	56°		
	h m s	° '	m s	h m	h m	h m	h m	h m	h m s	h m s
1	10 41 12	+8 19	− 0 04	5 11	5 03	12 00	18 48	18 56	22 41 08	1 18 39
2	10 44 50	+7 57	+ 0 15	5 12	5 05	12 00	18 46	18 53	22 45 05	1 14 43
3	10 48 27	+7 35	+ 0 34	5 14	5 07	11 59	18 44	18 50	22 49 01	1 10 47
4	10 52 04	+7 13	+ 0 54	5 16	5 09	11 59	18 41	18 48	22 52 58	1 06 51
5	10 55 40	+6 51	+ 1 14	5 17	5 11	11 59	18 39	18 45	22 56 54	1 02 55
6	10 59 17	+6 29	+ 1 34	5 19	5 13	11 58	18 37	18 43	23 00 51	0 58 59
7	11 02 53	+6 06	+ 1 54	5 21	5 15	11 58	18 34	18 40	23 04 47	0 55 04
8	11 06 29	+5 44	+ 2 15	5 22	5 17	11 58	18 32	18 37	23 08 44	0 51 08
9	11 10 05	+5 21	+ 2 36	5 24	5 19	11 57	18 30	18 35	23 12 40	0 47 12
10	11 13 40	+4 59	+ 2 57	5 26	5 21	11 57	18 27	18 32	23 16 37	0 43 16
11	11 17 16	+4 36	+ 3 18	5 27	5 23	11 57	18 25	18 29	23 20 34	0 39 20
12	11 20 51	+4 13	+ 3 39	5 29	5 25	11 56	18 23	18 27	23 24 30	0 35 24
13	11 24 27	+3 50	+ 4 00	5 30	5 27	11 56	18 20	18 24	23 28 27	0 31 28
14	11 28 02	+3 27	+ 4 21	5 32	5 29	11 55	18 18	18 21	23 32 23	0 27 32
15	11 31 37	+3 04	+ 4 43	5 34	5 31	11 55	18 16	18 19	23 36 20	0 23 36
16	11 35 12	+2 41	+ 5 04	5 35	5 33	11 55	18 13	18 16	23 40 16	0 19 40
17	11 38 47	+2 18	+ 5 25	5 37	5 35	11 54	18 11	18 13	23 44 13	0 15 45
18	11 42 23	+1 54	+ 5 47	5 39	5 36	11 54	18 09	18 11	23 48 09	0 11 49
19	11 45 58	+1 31	+ 6 08	5 40	5 38	11 54	18 06	18 08	23 52 06	0 07 53
20	11 49 33	+1 08	+ 6 29	5 42	5 40	11 53	18 04	18 05	23 56 03	0 03 57
21	11 53 09	+0 45	+ 6 50	5 44	5 42	11 53	18 02	18 03	23 59 59	{ 0 00 01 / 23 56 05
22	11 56 44	+0 21	+ 7 12	5 45	5 44	11 53	17 59	18 00	0 03 56	23 52 09
23	12 00 20	−0 02	+ 7 33	5 47	5 46	11 52	17 57	17 57	0 07 52	23 48 13
24	12 03 55	−0 26	+ 7 53	5 48	5 48	11 52	17 55	17 55	0 11 49	23 44 17
25	12 07 31	−0 49	+ 8 14	5 50	5 50	11 52	17 52	17 52	0 15 45	23 40 21
26	12 11 07	−1 12	+ 8 35	5 52	5 52	11 51	17 50	17 49	0 19 42	23 36 25
27	12 14 43	−1 36	+ 8 55	5 54	5 54	11 51	17 48	17 47	0 23 38	23 32 30
28	12 18 20	−1 59	+ 9 15	5 55	5 56	11 51	17 46	17 44	0 27 35	23 28 34
29	12 21 56	−2 22	+ 9 35	5 57	5 58	11 50	17 44	17 42	0 31 32	23 24 38
30	12 25 33	−2 46	+ 9 55	5 58	6 00	11 50	17 41	17 39	0 35 28	23 20 42

Duration of Civil (C), Nautical (N), and Astronomical (A), Twilight (in minutes)

Lat. °	Sept. 1			Sept. 11			Sept. 21			Sept. 30		
	C	N	A	C	N	A	C	N	A	C	N	A
52	35	79	127	34	76	120	34	74	115	34	73	113
56	39	89	146	38	84	135	37	82	129	37	80	126

ASTRONOMICAL NOTES

MERCURY is at inferior conjunction on the 22nd and is thus unsuitably placed for observation except during the last few days of the month, when it may be glimpsed as a morning star, magnitude +1, low on the E.S.E. horizon at the beginning of morning civil twilight.

VENUS is a brilliant evening star, magnitude −3·3, but still only visible for a very short while after sunset low above the W.S.W. horizon. Although it is 8° farther from the Sun at the end of the month compared with the beginning, its rapid southward motion in declination compensates for this increase in elongation so that the time available for observation remains almost exactly the same throughout the month.

MARS is too close to the Sun for observation.

JUPITER is a brilliant morning star, magnitude − 2·2, almost stationary in Taurus, between the Pleiades and the Hyades. Just after rising on the evening of the 14th the gibbous Moon will be seen passing very close to the planet.

SATURN is a morning star, magnitude +0·6, moving slowly eastwards in the constellation of Cancer. By the end of the month it is visible low in the eastern sky by about 01ʰ 30ᵐ.

ZODIACAL LIGHT. The morning cone may be seen in the eastern sky before twilight commences from the 1st to the 6th and again from the 23rd onwards. This faint phenomenon may only be detected under good conditions and in the absence of both moonlight and artificial lighting.

THE MOON

Day	R.A.	Dec.	Hor. Par.	Semi-diam.	Sun's Co-long.	P.A. of Bright Limb	Phase	Age	Rise 52°	Rise 56°	Transit	Set 52°	Set 56°
	h m	°	′	′	°	°		d	h m	h m	h m	h m	h m
1	16 21	−18·8	58·9	16·1	354	279	48	6·5	14 00	14 20	18 22	22 44	22 24
2	17 20	−19·5	58·4	15·9	6	275	59	7·5	14 56	15 16	19 19	23 43	23 24
3	18 18	−19·0	57·9	15·8	18	270	70	8·5	15 43	16 01	20 13	..	..
4	19 14	−17·4	57·3	15·6	31	266	79	9·5	16 21	16 36	21 05	0 47	0 30
5	20 08	−15·0	56·8	15·5	43	264	87	10·5	16 53	17 05	21 55	1 55	1 41
6	21 00	−11·8	56·3	15·3	55	262	93	11·5	17 21	17 29	22 42	3 04	2 54
7	21 49	− 8·1	55·8	15·2	67	265	97	12·5	17 45	17 49	23 28	4 13	4 06
8	22 37	− 4·2	55·4	15·1	79	282	100	13·5	18 07	18 08	..	5 21	5 18
9	23 24	− 0·1	55·0	15·0	91	33	100	14·5	18 29	18 27	0 12	6 27	6 28
10	0 10	+ 3·9	54·6	14·9	104	58	98	15·5	18 51	18 45	0 55	7 33	7 37
11	0 56	+ 7·8	54·3	14·8	116	64	94	16·5	19 15	19 06	1 38	8 37	8 45
12	1 42	+11·2	54·2	14·8	128	68	89	17·5	19 41	19 29	2 22	9 40	9 52
13	2 29	+14·2	54·1	14·7	140	72	83	18·5	20 11	19 56	3 07	10 42	10 57
14	3 17	+16·6	54·2	14·8	152	76	75	19·5	20 46	20 28	3 52	11 42	11 59
15	4 07	+18·3	54·4	14·8	165	80	66	20·5	21 27	21 08	4 39	12 38	12 57
16	4 57	+19·2	54·8	14·9	177	84	57	21·5	22 16	21 56	5 28	13 30	13 49
17	5 49	+19·3	55·4	15·1	189	89	47	22·5	23 12	22 54	6 17	14 16	14 35
18	6 41	+18·4	56·1	15·3	201	93	37	23·5	..	23 59	7 08	14 57	15 13
19	7 35	+16·5	56·9	15·5	213	97	28	24·5	0 15	..	7 59	15 33	15 46
20	8 28	+13·7	57·8	15·7	226	100	19	25·5	1 25	1 12	8 51	16 05	16 15
21	9 23	+10·1	58·7	16·0	238	102	11	26·5	2 39	2 30	9 43	16 34	16 40
22	10 17	+ 5·8	59·6	16·2	250	101	5	27·5	3 56	3 52	10 36	17 01	17 03
23	11 12	+ 1·1	60·3	16·4	262	95	1	28·5	5 17	5 17	11 29	17 29	17 26
24	12 08	− 3·8	60·7	16·6	274	342	0	0·2	6 39	6 43	12 24	17 57	17 51
25	13 06	− 8·5	60·9	16·6	287	297	2	1·2	8 01	8 13	13 20	18 29	18 19
26	14 05	−12·7	60·8	16·6	299	290	7	2·2	9 23	9 36	14 18	19 06	18 51
27	15 04	−16·0	60·5	16·5	311	285	14	3·2	10 40	10 57	15 17	19 49	19 31
28	16 05	−18·2	59·9	16·3	323	279	23	4·2	11 50	12 09	16 16	20 39	20 20
29	17 05	−19·2	59·2	16·1	336	274	34	5·2	12 51	13 10	17 13	21 37	21 18
30	18 04	−19·0	58·4	15·9	348	269	45	6·2	13 41	13 59	18 09	22 41	22 23

MERCURY ☿

Day	R.A.	Dec. −	Diam.	Phase	Transit		Day	R.A.	Dec.	Diam.	Phase	Transit	
	h m	°	″		h m			h m	°	″		h m	
1	12 14	4·8	8	44	13 32	Mercury is too close to the Sun for observation	16	12 12	−5·7	10	9	12 29	Mercury is too close to the Sun for observation
4	12 19	5·9	8	37	13 25		19	12 03	−4·3	10	3	12 07	
7	12 22	6·6	9	31	13 15		22	11 53	−2·4	10	0	11 45	
10	12 22	6·8	9	23	13 03		25	11 43	−0·3	10	3	11 24	
13	12 19	6·6	10	15	12 48		28	11 36	+1·5	9	11	11 06	
16	12 12	5·7	10	9	12 29		31	11 35	+2·7	9	21	10 54	

VENUS ♀

Day	R.A.	Dec.	Diam.	Phase	Transit	5° high W 52°	5° high W 56°
	h m	°	″		h m	h m	h m
1	11 59	+1·4	11	94	13 18	18 50	18 48
6	12 21	−1·1	11	93	13 20	18 39	18 35
11	12 43	−3·7	11	92	13 23	18 28	18 22
16	13 06	−6·3	11	91	13 26	18 18	18 08
21	13 28	−8·8	11	90	13 29	18 07	17 55
26	13 51	−11·2	11	89	13 32	17 57	17 42
31	14 14	−13·5	12	88	13 35	17 46	17 29

MARS ♂

Day	R.A.	Dec. −	Diam.	Phase	Transit	
	h m	°	″		h m	
1	12 19	1·5	4	98	13 37	Mars is too close to the Sun for observation
6	12 31	2·8	4	98	13 29	
11	12 43	4·1	4	98	13 22	
16	12 55	5·4	4	99	13 14	
21	13 07	6·7	4	99	13 06	
26	13 20	8·0	4	99	12 59	
31	13 32	9·3	4	99	12 52	

SUNRISE AND SUNSET (G.M.T.)

Day	London a.m. h m	London p.m. h m	Bristol a.m. h m	Bristol p.m. h m	Birmingham a.m. h m	Birmingham p.m. h m	Manchester a.m. h m	Manchester p.m. h m	Newcastle a.m. h m	Newcastle p.m. h m	Glasgow a.m. h m	Glasgow p.m. h m	Belfast a.m. h m	Belfast p.m. h m
1	5 12	6 47	5 22	6 57	5 17	6 56	5 17	7 00	5 11	7 00	5 20	7 13	5 30	7 17
2	5 13	6 45	5 23	6 55	5 18	6 54	5 19	6 57	5 13	6 57	5 22	7 10	5 32	7 14
3	5 15	6 43	5 25	6 53	5 20	6 52	5 21	6 55	5 15	6 54	5 24	7 07	5 34	7 12
4	5 17	6 40	5 27	6 50	5 22	6 49	5 23	6 52	5 17	6 52	5 26	7 05	5 36	7 09
5	5 18	6 38	5 28	6 48	5 23	6 47	5 24	6 50	5 19	6 49	5 28	7 02	5 37	7 07
6	5 20	6 36	5 30	6 46	5 25	6 44	5 26	6 47	5 21	6 47	5 30	7 00	5 39	7 04
7	5 22	6 34	5 32	6 43	5 27	6 42	5 28	6 45	5 23	6 44	5 32	6 57	5 41	7 02
8	5 23	6 32	5 33	6 41	5 29	6 40	5 30	6 43	5 25	6 41	5 34	6 54	5 43	7 00
9	5 25	6 30	5 35	6 39	5 31	6 37	5 32	6 40	5 27	6 39	5 36	6 52	5 45	6 57
10	5 27	6 27	5 37	6 36	5 32	6 35	5 33	6 38	5 28	6 37	5 38	6 49	5 46	6 55
11	5 28	6 25	5 38	6 34	5 34	6 32	5 35	6 35	5 30	6 34	5 40	6 46	5 48	6 52
12	5 30	6 23	5 40	6 32	5 36	6 30	5 37	6 33	5 32	6 32	5 42	6 44	5 50	6 50
13	5 31	6 20	5 41	6 30	5 37	6 27	5 38	6 30	5 34	6 29	5 44	6 41	5 52	6 47
14	5 32	6 18	5 42	6 28	5 39	6 25	5 40	6 28	5 36	6 26	5 46	6 38	5 54	6 44
15	5 34	6 16	5 44	6 26	5 41	6 23	5 42	6 26	5 38	6 24	5 48	6 36	5 56	6 42
16	5 36	6 13	5 46	6 23	5 42	6 20	5 43	6 23	5 40	6 21	5 50	6 33	5 58	6 39
17	5 37	6 11	5 47	6 21	5 44	6 18	5 45	6 21	5 42	6 18	5 52	6 30	6 00	6 36
18	5 39	6 09	5 49	6 19	5 46	6 16	5 47	6 19	5 43	6 16	5 53	6 28	6 02	6 34
19	5 40	6 06	5 50	6 16	5 47	6 13	5 48	6 16	5 45	6 14	5 55	6 25	6 03	6 31
20	5 42	6 04	5 52	6 14	5 49	6 11	5 50	6 14	5 47	6 11	5 57	6 22	6 05	6 29
21	5 44	6 02	5 54	6 12	5 51	6 09	5 52	6 11	5 49	6 08	5 59	6 20	6 07	6 26
22	5 45	5 59	5 55	6 09	5 52	6 06	5 54	6 09	5 51	6 06	6 01	6 17	6 09	6 24
23	5 47	5 57	5 57	6 07	5 54	6 04	5 56	6 06	5 53	6 03	6 03	6 14	6 11	6 21
24	5 48	5 55	5 58	6 05	5 55	6 02	5 57	6 04	5 54	6 01	6 05	6 12	6 12	6 19
25	5 50	5 52	6 00	6 02	5 57	5 59	5 59	6 01	5 56	5 58	6 07	6 09	6 14	6 16
26	5 52	5 50	6 02	6 00	5 59	5 57	6 01	5 59	5 58	5 56	6 09	6 06	6 16	6 14
27	5 54	5 48	6 04	5 58	6 01	5 55	6 03	5 56	6 00	5 53	6 11	6 04	6 18	6 11
28	5 55	5 46	6 05	5 56	6 02	5 53	6 05	5 54	6 02	5 51	6 13	6 01	6 20	6 09
29	5 57	5 44	6 07	5 54	6 04	5 51	6 06	5 52	6 03	5 48	6 15	5 59	6 21	6 06
30	5 58	5 41	6 08	5 51	6 05	5 48	6 08	5 49	6 05	5 46	6 17	5 56	6 23	6 04

JUPITER ♃   SATURN ♄

Day	R.A. h m	Dec. + °	5° high East 52° h m	5° high East 56° h m	Transit h m	R.A. h m	Dec. + °	5° high East 52° h m	5° high East 56° h m	Transit h m
1	3 55	19·2	22 01	21 48	5 13	8 53	18·1	3 09	2 57	10 11
11	3 57	19·3	21 22	21 09	4 35	8 58	17·8	2 36	2 24	9 36
21	3 57	19·3	20 43	20 29	3 57	9 03	17·5	2 03	1 51	9 01
31	3 56	19·3	20 04	19 49	3 16	9 07	17·2	1 29	1 18	8 26

Equatorial diameter of Jupiter 43″; of Saturn 17″.   Diameters of Saturn's rings 38″ and 11″

URANUS ♅   NEPTUNE ♆

Day	R.A. h m	Dec. − ° ′	Transit h m		R.A. h m	Dec. − ° ′	Transit h m	5° high West 52° h m	5° high West 56° h m
1	14 08·3	12 29	15 25	Uranus is	16 39·6	20 38	17 55	20 29	19 43
11	14 10·0	12 38	14 47	too close to	16 39·9	20 39	17 17	19 50	19 04
21	14 11·9	12 48	14 10	the Sun for	16 40·4	20 40	16 38	19 11	18 26
31	14 14·1	13 00	13 33	observation	16 41·2	20 42	15 59	18 32	17 47

Diameter 4″   Diameter 2″

Month	Week	

Octo (eight), 8th month
of Roman (pre-Julian)
Calendar.

Sun's Longitude 210° ♏ 23ᵈ 07ʰ

1	F.	MICHAELMAS LAW SITTINGS BEGIN
2	S.	Graham Greene b. 1904. Paavo Nurmi d. 1973
3	♋.	**16th ♋. after Trinity.** William Morris d. 1896
4	M.	Rembrandt d. 1669. John Rennie d. 1821
5	Tu.	Offenbach d. 1880. R101 Disaster 1930
6	W.	Tennyson d. 1892. Leonard Cottrell d. 1974
7	Th.	Edgar Allan Poe d. 1849. Marie Lloyd d. 1922
8	F.	Henry Fielding d. 1754. Kathleen Ferrier d. 1953
9	S.	Alastair Sim b. 1900. Lord Hailsham b. 1907
10	♋.	**17th ♋. after Trinity.** Verdi b. 1813
11	M.	Camperdown 1797
12	Tu.	Edward VI b. 1537. Ramsay MacDonald b. 1866
13	W.	Mrs. Margaret Thatcher b. 1925
14	Th.	Hastings 1066. James II b. 1633
15	F.	Oscar Wilde b. 1856. Lord Snow b. 1905
16	S.	Marie Antoinette d. 1793. Eugene O'Neill b. 1888
17	♋.	**18th ♋. after Trinity.** Sir Philip Sidney d. 1586
18	M.	**St. Luke.** Thomas Edison d. 1931
19	Tu.	Swift d. 1745. Lord Rutherford d. 1937
20	W.	Sir Christopher Wren b. 1632
21	Th.	Trafalgar Day, 1805. Alfred Nobel b. 1833
22	F.	Sarah Bernhardt b. 1845
23	S.	Cézanne d. 1906. W. G. Grace d. 1915
24	♋.	**19th ♋. after Trinity.** David Oistrakh d. 1974
25	M.	Chaucer d. 1400. Agincourt 1415
26	Tu.	Hogarth d. 1764
27	W.	Theodore Roosevelt b. 1858
28	Th.	**St. Simon and St. Jude.** David Jones d. 1974
29	F.	Sir Walter Raleigh d. 1618. Edmund Halley b. 1656
30	S.	Dostoievski b. 1821. R. B. Sheridan b. 1632
31	♋.	**20th ♋. after Trinity.** Hallowmas Eve

PHENOMENA

October 4ᵈ 17ʰ Pluto in conjunction with the Sun.

7ᵈ 16ʰ Mercury at greatest western elongation (18°).

12ᵈ 01ʰ Jupiter in conjunction with the Moon. Jupiter 1° N.

18ᵈ 05ʰ Saturn in conjunction with the Moon. Saturn 6° N.

23ᵈ Total eclipse of the Sun. See p. 148.

25ᵈ 13ʰ Venus in conjunction with the Moon. Venus 4° S.

30ᵈ 19ʰ Uranus in conjunction with the Sun.

CONSTELLATIONS

The following constellations are near the meridian at

	d h		d h
Sept. 1	24	Sept. 15	23
Oct. 1	22	Oct. 16	21
Nov. 1	20	Nov. 15	19

Ursa Major (below the Pole), Cepheus, Cassiopeia, Cygnus, Lacerta, Andromeda, Pegasus, Capricornus, Aquarius and Piscis Austrinus.

MINIMA OF ALGOL

d	h	d	h
3	16	18	1
6	13	20	21
9	10	23	18
12	7	26	15
15	4	29	12

PHASES OF THE MOON

	d	h	m
○ Full Moon	8	04	55
☾ Last Quarter	16	08	59
● New Moon	23	05	10
☽ First Quarter	29	22	05

	d	h
Apogee (406,140 kilometres)	10	12
Perigee (357,160 ,,)	23	13

Mean Longitude of Ascending Node on October 1, 215°.

MONTHLY NOTES

Oct. 1. Pheasant shooting begins.

4. Day of Atonement (Yom Kippur).

9. First day of Tabernacles.

24. *Summer Time* ends at 2 a.m. G.M.T.

NATIONAL DAYS.—*Oct.* 1, China, Nigeria; 4, Lesotho; 9, Uganda; 24, Zambia; 26, Iran.

Day	Right Ascension	Dec. —	Equation of Time	Rise 52°	Rise 56°	Transit	Set 52°	Set 56°	Sidereal Time	Transit of First Point of Aries
	h m s	° '	m s	h m	h m	h m	h m	h m	h m s	h m s
1	12 29 10	3 09	+10 14	6 00	6 02	11 50	17 38	17 36	0 39 25	23 16 46
2	12 32 48	3 32	+10 34	6 02	6 04	11 49	17 36	17 34	0 43 21	23 12 50
3	12 36 25	3 55	+10 52	6 03	6 06	11 49	17 34	17 31	0 47 18	23 08 54
4	12 40 03	4 19	+11 11	6 05	6 08	11 49	17 31	17 28	0 51 14	23 04 58
5	12 43 41	4 42	+11 29	6 07	6 10	11 48	17 29	17 26	0 55 11	23 01 02
6	12 47 20	5 05	+11 47	6 08	6 12	11 48	17 27	17 23	0 59 07	22 57 06
7	12 50 59	5 28	+12 05	6 10	6 14	11 48	17 25	17 21	1 03 04	22 53 10
8	12 54 38	5 51	+12 22	6 12	6 16	11 47	17 22	17 18	1 07 00	22 49 15
9	12 58 18	6 14	+12 39	6 14	6 18	11 47	17 20	17 16	1 10 57	22 45 19
10	13 01 58	6 36	+12 55	6 15	6 20	11 47	17 18	17 13	1 14 54	22 41 23
11	13 05 39	6 59	+13 11	6 17	6 22	11 47	17 16	17 10	1 18 50	22 37 27
12	13 09 20	7 22	+13 26	6 19	6 24	11 46	17 13	17 08	1 22 47	22 33 31
13	13 13 02	7 44	+13 41	6 21	6 26	11 46	17 11	17 05	1 26 43	22 29 35
14	13 16 44	8 07	+13 55	6 22	6 28	11 46	17 09	17 03	1 30 40	22 25 39
15	13 20 27	8 29	+14 09	6 24	6 30	11 46	17 07	17 00	1 34 36	22 21 43
16	13 24 11	8 51	+14 22	6 26	6 32	11 46	17 05	16 58	1 38 33	22 17 47
17	13 27 55	9 13	+14 35	6 28	6 35	11 45	17 02	16 55	1 42 29	22 13 51
18	13 31 39	9 35	+14 47	6 29	6 37	11 45	17 00	16 53	1 46 26	22 09 56
19	13 35 25	9 57	+14 58	6 31	6 39	11 45	16 58	16 50	1 50 23	22 06 00
20	13 39 10	10 18	+15 09	6 33	6 41	11 45	16 56	16 48	1 54 19	22 02 04
21	13 42 57	10 40	+15 19	6 35	6 43	11 45	16 54	16 46	1 58 16	21 58 08
22	13 46 44	11 01	+15 28	6 36	6 45	11 44	16 52	16 43	2 02 12	21 54 12
23	13 50 32	11 22	+15 37	6 38	6 47	11 44	16 50	16 41	2 06 09	21 50 16
24	13 54 21	11 43	+15 45	6 40	6 49	11 44	16 48	16 38	2 10 05	21 46 20
25	13 58 10	12 04	+15 52	6 42	6 51	11 44	16 46	16 36	2 14 02	21 42 24
26	14 02 00	12 25	+15 58	6 43	6 53	11 44	16 44	16 34	2 17 58	21 38 28
27	14 05 51	12 45	+16 04	6 45	6 56	11 44	16 42	16 31	2 21 55	21 34 32
28	14 09 42	13 05	+16 09	6 47	6 58	11 44	16 40	16 29	2 25 52	21 30 36
29	14 13 34	13 25	+16 14	6 49	7 00	11 44	16 38	16 27	2 29 48	21 26 41
30	14 17 27	13 45	+16 17	6 50	7 02	11 44	16 36	16 25	2 33 45	21 22 45
31	14 21 21	14 05	+16 20	6 52	7 04	11 44	16 34	16 22	2 37 41	21 18 49

Duration of Civil (C), Nautical (N), and Astronomical (A), Twilight (in minutes)

Lat. °	Oct. 1 C	N	A	Oct. 11 C	N	A	Oct. 21 C	N	A	Oct. 31 C	N	A
52	34	73	113	34	73	112	34	74	113	36	75	114
56	37	80	125	37	80	124	38	81	124	40	83	126

ASTRONOMICAL NOTES

MERCURY is a morning star, magnitude +1·0 to −1·0, except for the last few days of the month. It may be located above the eastern horizon around the time of beginning of morning civil twilight. Greatest western elongation occurs on the 7th and this is the most favourable morning apparition of the year for observers in the northern hemisphere.

VENUS is a brilliant evening star, magnitude −3·4, and by the end of the month is visible for nearly an hour after sunset, low in the south-western sky. The new crescent moon will be seen near Venus on the evening of the 25th, while two evenings later Venus will be seen only a few degrees to the right of Antares.

MARS is too close to the Sun for observation.

JUPITER is a brilliant morning star, magnitude −2·4, and by the end of the month is visible in the east as early as 18h. On the night of the 11th–12th the gibbous Moon will be seen passing to the south of this planet.

SATURN is a bright morning star, magnitude +0·6, in the eastern part of the constellation of Cancer.

ECLIPSE. A total eclipse of the Sun occurs on the 23rd. See page 148 for details.

THE MOON

Day	R.A.	Dec.	Hor. Par.	Semi-diam.	Sun's Co-long.	P.A. of Bright Limb	Phase	Age	Rise 52°	Rise 56°	Transit	Set 52°	Set 56°
	h m	°	′	′	°	°		d	h m	h m	h m	h m	h m
1	19 01	−17·7	57·7	15·7	0	264	56	7·2	14 22	14 38	19 02	23 48	23 33
2	19 56	−15·5	57·0	15·5	12	261	66	8·2	14 56	15 08	19 52	..	..
3	20 48	−12·5	56·3	15·3	24	258	76	9·2	15 24	15 33	20 40	0 56	0 45
4	21 37	− 9·0	55·8	15·2	36	256	84	10·2	15 49	15 55	21 25	2 04	1 56
5	22 25	− 5·1	55·3	15·1	49	255	90	11·2	16 12	16 14	22 09	3 11	3 07
6	23 12	− 1·1	54·9	15·0	61	255	95	12·2	16 34	16 33	22 53	4 17	4 17
7	23 58	+ 2·9	54·5	14·9	73	258	99	13·2	16 56	16 51	23 36	5 22	5 26
8	0 43	+ 6·7	54·3	14·8	85	287	100	14·2	17 19	17 11	..	6 27	6 33
9	1 29	+10·3	54·1	14·7	97	63	99	15·2	17 44	17 33	0 19	7 30	7 40
10	2 16	+13·4	54·0	14·7	109	71	97	16·2	18 13	17 59	1 03	8 33	8 46
11	3 04	+15·9	54·0	14·7	122	76	93	17·2	18 46	18 29	1 49	9 33	9 49
12	3 53	+17·8	54·1	14·7	134	81	88	18·2	19 25	19 06	2 35	10 33	10 48
13	4 43	+18·9	54·3	14·8	146	85	81	19·2	20 10	19 51	3 23	11 23	11 42
14	5 33	+19·2	54·7	14·9	158	89	72	20·2	21 02	20 44	4 11	12 11	12 30
15	6 25	+18·6	55·2	15·1	170	94	64	21·2	22 01	21 45	5 00	12 53	13 10
16	7 17	+17·1	55·9	15·2	182	98	54	22·2	23 06	22 52	5 50	13 30	13 44
17	8 09	+14·7	56·7	15·5	195	102	44	23·2	..	..	6 40	14 02	14 14
18	9 01	+11·5	57·6	15·7	207	105	33	24·2	0 16	0 06	7 30	14 31	14 39
19	9 54	+ 7·6	58·6	16·0	219	107	23	25·2	1 30	1 23	8 21	14 59	15 03
20	10 48	+ 3·2	59·5	16·2	231	108	15	26·2	2 47	2 45	9 13	15 26	15 26
21	11 43	− 1·6	60·4	16·4	243	108	7	27·2	4 07	4 09	10 06	15 53	15 49
22	12 39	− 6·4	61·0	16·6	256	107	2	28·2	5 29	5 36	11 02	16 24	16 15
23	13 38	−10·9	61·3	16·7	268	99	0	29·2	6 53	7 04	12 00	16 58	16 46
24	14 39	−14·7	61·4	16·7	280	284	1	0·8	8 14	8 29	13 00	17 39	17 23
25	15 41	−17·4	61·0	16·6	292	279	5	1·8	9 31	9 49	14 01	18 28	18 09
26	16 43	−18·9	60·4	16·5	305	273	11	2·8	10 38	10 58	15 02	19 25	19 06
27	17 45	−19·2	59·7	16·3	317	268	20	3·8	11 35	11 54	16 01	20 29	20 11
28	18 45	−18·1	58·8	16·0	329	263	30	4·8	12 21	12 37	16 56	21 37	21 21
29	19 41	−16·1	57·8	15·8	341	259	40	5·8	12 58	13 11	17 48	22 47	22 34
30	20 35	−13·2	57·0	15·5	353	256	51	6·8	13 28	13 38	18 37	23 56	23 47
31	21 25	− 9·8	56·2	15·3	5	253	61	7·8	13 54	14 01	19 24	..	..

MERCURY ☿

Day	R.A.	Dec.	Diam.	Phase	5° high E 52°	5° high E 56°	Transit	Day	R.A.	Dec. −	Diam.	Phase	5° high E 52°	5° high E 56°	Transit
	h m	°	″		h m	h m	h m		h m	°	″		h m	h m	h m
1	11 35	+2·7	9	21	5 13	5 14	10 54	16	12 32	1·3	6	83	5 35	5 40	10 55
4	11 39	+3·2	8	35	5 03	5 04	10 47	19	12 50	3·3	5	89	5 51	5 58	11 01
7	11 47	+2·9	7	50	5 02	5 03	10 44	22	13 08	5·4	5	93	6 09	6 17	11 07
10	12 00	+1·9	6	62	5 06	5 08	10 45	25	13 27	7·5	5	96	6 27	6 37	11 14
13	12 15	+0·5	6	74	5 19	5 21	10 49	28	13 46	9·6	5	98	6 46	6 58	11 21
16	12 32	−1·3	6	83	5 35	5 40	10 55	31	14 04	11·6	5	99	7 05	7 19	11 28

VENUS ♀

Day	R.A.	Dec. −	Diam.	Phase	Transit	5° high W 52°	5° high W 56°
	h m	°	″		h m	h m	h m
1	14 14	13·5	12	88	13 35	17 46	17 29
6	14 38	15·7	12	87	13 39	17 36	17 16
11	15 02	17·7	12	86	13 34	17 27	17 03
16	15 27	19·5	12	85	13 49	17 19	16 52
21	15 52	21·2	13	84	13 54	17 12	16 41
26	16 17	22·6	13	83	13 00	17 07	16 32
31	16 43	23·7	13	81	14 06	17 03	16 24

MARS ♂

Day	R.A.	Dec. −	Diam.	Phase	Transit	
	h m	°	″		h m	
1	13 32	9·3	4	99	12 52	Mars is too close to the Sun for observation
6	13 45	10·6	4	99	12 45	
11	13 57	11·8	4	99	12 38	
16	14 11	13·0	4	100	12 31	
21	14 24	14·2	4	100	12 25	
26	14 37	15·3	4	100	12 19	
31	14 51	16·4	4	100	12 13	

SUNRISE AND SUNSET (G.M.T.)

Day	London a.m. h m	p.m. h m	Bristol a.m. h m	p.m. h m	Birmingham a.m. h m	p.m. h m	Manchester a.m. h m	p.m. h m	Newcastle a.m. h m	p.m. h m	Glasgow a.m. h m	p.m. h m	Belfast a.m. h m	p.m. h m
1	6 00	5 38	6 10	5 48	6 07	5 45	6 10	5 46	6 07	5 43	6 19	5 53	6 25	6 01
2	6 02	5 36	6 12	5 46	6 09	5 43	6 12	5 44	6 09	5 41	6 21	5 51	6 27	5 59
3	6 03	5 34	6 13	5 44	6 10	5 41	6 13	5 42	6 11	5 38	6 23	5 48	6 29	5 56
4	6 05	5 32	6 15	5 42	6 12	5 38	6 15	5 39	6 13	5 35	6 25	5 45	6 31	5 53
5	6 07	5 30	6 17	5 40	6 14	5 36	6 17	5 37	6 15	5 33	6 27	5 43	6 33	5 51
6	6 08	5 27	6 18	5 37	6 15	5 34	6 18	5 35	6 17	5 30	6 29	5 40	6 35	5 48
7	6 10	5 25	6 20	5 35	6 17	5 32	6 20	5 33	6 19	5 28	6 31	5 38	6 37	5 46
8	6 12	5 23	6 21	5 33	6 19	5 29	6 22	5 30	6 21	5 25	6 33	5 35	6 39	5 43
9	6 14	5 21	6 23	5 31	6 21	5 27	6 24	5 28	6 23	5 23	6 35	5 33	6 41	5 41
10	6 15	5 19	6 24	5 29	6 23	5 24	6 26	5 25	6 25	5 20	6 37	5 30	6 43	5 38
11	6 17	5 17	6 26	5 27	6 25	5 22	6 28	5 23	6 27	5 18	6 39	5 27	6 45	5 36
12	6 19	5 14	6 28	5 24	6 26	5 20	6 29	5 21	6 28	5 16	6 41	5 25	6 46	5 34
13	6 20	5 12	6 30	5 22	6 28	5 17	6 31	5 18	6 30	5 13	6 43	5 22	6 48	5 31
14	6 22	5 10	6 31	5 20	6 30	5 15	6 33	5 16	6 32	5 11	6 45	5 20	6 50	5 29
15	6 23	5 08	6 33	5 18	6 32	5 13	6 35	5 14	6 34	5 08	6 47	5 17	6 52	5 27
16	6 25	5 06	6 35	5 16	6 34	5 11	6 37	5 11	6 36	5 06	6 49	5 15	6 54	5 24
17	6 27	5 03	6 37	5 13	6 36	5 08	6 39	5 09	6 39	5 03	6 52	5 12	6 56	5 22
18	6 28	5 01	6 38	5 11	6 37	5 06	6 41	5 07	6 41	5 01	6 54	5 10	6 58	5 20
19	6 30	4 59	6 40	5 09	6 39	5 04	6 43	5 04	6 43	4 58	6 56	5 07	7 00	5 17
20	6 32	4 57	6 42	5 07	6 41	5 02	6 45	5 02	6 45	4 56	6 58	5 05	7 02	5 15
21	6 34	4 55	6 44	5 05	6 43	5 00	6 47	5 00	6 47	4 54	7 00	5 03	7 04	5 13
22	6 35	4 53	6 45	5 03	6 44	4 58	6 48	4 58	6 48	4 52	7 02	5 00	7 06	5 10
23	6 37	4 51	6 47	5 01	6 46	4 56	6 50	4 55	6 50	4 49	7 04	4 58	7 08	5 08
24	6 39	4 49	6 49	4 59	6 48	4 54	6 52	4 53	6 52	4 47	7 06	4 55	7 10	5 05
25	6 41	4 47	6 51	4 57	6 50	4 52	6 54	4 51	6 54	4 45	7 08	4 53	7 12	5 03
26	6 42	4 45	6 52	4 55	6 51	4 50	6 56	4 49	6 56	4 43	7 10	4 51	7 14	5 01
27	6 44	4 43	6 54	4 53	6 53	4 48	6 58	4 47	6 59	4 40	7 13	4 48	7 16	4 59
28	6 46	4 41	6 56	4 51	6 55	4 46	7 00	4 45	7 01	4 38	7 15	4 46	7 18	4 57
29	6 48	4 39	6 58	4 49	6 57	4 44	7 02	4 43	7 03	4 36	7 17	4 44	7 20	4 55
30	6 49	4 37	6 59	4 47	6 58	4 42	7 03	4 41	7 05	4 34	7 19	4 42	7 22	4 53
31	6 51	4 35	7 01	4 45	7 00	4 40	7 05	4 39	7 07	4 32	7 21	4 40	7 24	4 51

JUPITER ♃

Day	R.A. h m	Dec. + °	5° high East 52° h m	56° h m	Transit h m
1	3 56	19·3	20 04	19 49	3 16
11	3 54	19·1	19 23	19 09	2 35
21	3 51	18·9	18 42	18 28	1 52
31	3 46	18·7	18 00	17 47	1 08

SATURN ♄

Day	R.A. h m	Dec. + °	5° high East 52° h m	56° h m	Transit h m
1	9 07	17·2	1 29	1 18	8 26
11	9 10	17·0	0 55	0 44	7 50
21	9 13	16·8	0 19	0 09	7 14
31	9 15	16·7	23 39	23 29	6 37

Equatorial diameter of Jupiter 47″; of Saturn 18″   Diameters of Saturn's rings 40″ and 11″

URANUS ⛢

Day	R.A. h m	Dec. − ° ′	Transit h m	
1	14 14·1	130 0	13 33	Uranus is too
11	14 16·3	13 11	12 56	close to the
21	14 18·7	13 24	12 19	Sun for
31	14 21·1	13 36	11 42	observation

Diameter 4″

NEPTUNE ♆

Day	R.A. h m	Dec. − ° ′	Transit h m	
1	16 41·2	20 42	15 59	Neptune is
11	16 42·1	20 45	15 21	too close to
21	16 43·3	20 47	15 43	the Sun for
31	16 44·6	20 50	15 05	observation

Diameter 2″

NOVEMBER XXX DAYS

130   **[1976**

Novem (nine), 9th month
of Roman (pre-Julian)
Calendar.

Sun's Longitude 240° ♐ 22ᵈ 04ʰ

Month	Week	
1	M.	**All Saints.** Ezra Pound d. 1972
2	Tu.	All Souls' Day. Edward V b. 1470
3	W.	Baedeker b. 1801. Ludovic Kennedy b. 1919
4	Th.	Mendelssohn d. 1847. Wilfred Owen d. 1918
5	F.	Guy Fawkes Day (1605). Inkerman 1854
6	S.	Tschaikovsky d. 1893
7	**S.**	**21st S. after Trinity.** Eric Linklater d. 1974
8	M.	Milton d. 1674. Tolstoy d. 1910
9	Tu.	Edward VII b. 1841. Dylan Thomas d. 1953
10	W.	Catherine the Great d. 1796. Luther b. 1483
11	Th.	Armistice Day (1918)
12	F.	Mrs. Gaskell d. 1865. Baroness Orczy d. 1947
13	S.	Edward III b. 1312. Vittorio de Sica d. 1974
14	**S.**	**22nd S. after Trinity.** PRINCE OF WALES b. 1948
15	M.	Averell Harriman b. 1891. Sir Hugh Greene b. 1910
16	Tu.	Gustavus Adolphus d. 1632. Clark Gable d. 1960
17	W.	Mary I d. 1558. Erskine Childers d. 1974
18	Th.	Sir W. S. Gilbert b. 1836
19	F.	Charles I b. 1600. Schubert d. 1828
20	S.	QUEEN'S WEDDING DAY (1947)
21	**S.**	**23rd S. after Trinity.** Voltaire b. 1694
22	M.	George Eliot b. 1819. J. F. Kennedy d. 1963
23	Tu.	Perkin Warbeck d. 1499. Richard Hakluyt d. 1616
24	W.	John Knox d. 1572. Laurence Sterne b. 1713
25	Th.	Isaac Watts d. 1748. U Thant d. 1974
26	F.	William Cowper b. 1731. Cyril Connolly d. 1974
27	S.	Eugene O'Neill d. 1953
28	**S.**	**1st S. in Advent.** William Blake b. 1757
29	M.	Prince Rupert d. 1682
30	Tu.	**St. Andrew.** Mark Twain b. 1835

PHENOMENA

November 7ᵈ 09ʰ Mercury in superior conjunction.

8ᵈ 01ʰ Jupiter in conjunction with the Moon. Jupiter 1° N.

14ᵈ 15ʰ Saturn in conjunction with the Moon. Saturn 6° N.

18ᵈ 08ʰ Jupiter at opposition.

24ᵈ 13ʰ Venus in conjunction with the Moon. Venus 7° S.

25ᵈ 12ʰ Mars in conjunction with the Sun.

CONSTELLATIONS

The following constellations are near the meridian at

d h		d h
Oct. 1 24		Oct. 16 23
Nov. 1 22		Nov. 15 21
Dec. 1 20		Dec. 16 19

Ursa Major (below the Pole), Cepheus, Cassiopeia, Andromeda, Pegasus, Pisces, Aquarius and Cetus.

MINIMA OF ALGOL

d	h	d	h
1	9	18	13
4	5	21	10
7	2	24	7
9	23	27	4
12	20	30	1
15	17		

PHASES OF THE MOON

	d	h	m
○ Full Moon	6	23	15
☾ Last Quarter	14	22	39
● New Moon	21	15	11
☽ First Quarter	28	12	59

	d	h
Apogee (406,330 kilometres)	6	15
Perigee (357,490 ,,)	21	01

Mean Longitude of Ascending Node on November 1, 213°.

MONTHLY NOTES

Nov. 1. Hallowmas. Fox-hunting begins.

    11. Martinmas. Scottish Term Day.

    13. Lord Mayor's Day.

    14. Remembrance Sunday.

    28. Removal Day, Scotland.

NATIONAL DAYS.—*Nov.* 7, U.S.S.R.; 22, Lebanon; 28, Mauritania; 30, Barbados, Scotland (*see* above).

Day	Right Ascension	Dec. —	Equation of Time	Rise 52°	Rise 56°	Transit	Set 52°	Set 56°	Sidereal Time	Transit of First Point of Aries
	h m s	° '	m s	h m	h m	h m	h m	h m	h m s	h m s
1	14 25 15	14 24	+16 22	6 54	7 06	11 44	16 32	16 20	2 41 38	21 14 53
2	14 29 10	14 43	+16 24	6 56	7 08	11 44	16 30	16 18	2 45 34	21 10 57
3	14 33 07	15 02	+16 24	6 58	7 10	11 44	16 29	16 16	2 49 31	21 07 01
4	14 37 03	15 21	+16 24	7 00	7 13	11 44	16 27	16 14	2 53 27	21 03 05
5	14 41 01	15 39	+16 23	7 01	7 15	11 44	16 25	16 12	2 57 24	20 59 09
6	14 44 59	15 57	+16 21	7 03	7 17	11 44	16 23	16 10	3 01 21	20 55 13
7	14 48 59	16 15	+16 18	7 05	7 19	11 44	16 22	16 08	3 05 17	20 51 17
8	14 52 59	16 33	+16 15	7 07	7 21	11 44	16 20	16 06	3 09 14	20 47 21
9	14 57 00	16 50	+16 10	7 09	7 23	11 44	16 18	16 04	3 13 10	20 43 26
10	15 01 02	17 07	+16 05	7 10	7 25	11 44	16 17	16 02	3 17 07	20 39 30
11	15 05 04	17 24	+15 59	7 12	7 27	11 44	16 15	16 00	3 21 03	20 35 34
12	15 09 08	17 40	+15 52	7 14	7 30	11 44	16 14	15 58	3 25 00	20 31 38
13	15 13 12	17 56	+15 44	7 16	7 32	11 44	16 12	15 56	3 28 56	20 27 42
14	15 17 17	18 12	+15 35	7 18	7 34	11 44	16 11	15 55	3 32 53	20 23 46
15	15 21 24	18 28	+15 26	7 19	7 36	11 45	16 09	15 53	3 36 50	20 19 50
16	15 25 31	18 43	+15 15	7 21	7 38	11 45	16 08	15 51	3 40 46	20 15 54
17	15 29 38	18 58	+15 04	7 23	7 40	11 45	16 07	15 49	3 44 43	20 11 58
18	15 33 47	19 12	+14 52	7 25	7 42	11 45	16 05	15 48	3 48 39	20 08 02
19	15 37 57	19 26	+14 39	7 26	7 44	11 45	16 04	15 46	3 52 36	20 04 06
20	15 42 07	19 40	+14 25	7 28	7 46	11 46	16 03	15 45	3 56 32	20 00 11
21	15 46 18	19 54	+14 10	7 30	7 48	11 46	16 02	15 43	4 00 29	19 56 15
22	15 50 30	20 07	+13 55	7 31	7 50	11 46	16 00	15 42	4 04 25	19 52 19
23	15 54 43	20 19	+13 39	7 33	7 52	11 46	15 59	15 40	4 08 22	19 48 23
24	15 58 57	20 32	+13 22	7 35	7 54	11 47	15 58	15 39	4 12 19	19 44 27
25	16 03 11	20 44	+13 04	7 36	7 56	11 47	15 57	15 38	4 16 15	19 40 31
26	16 07 26	20 55	+12 45	7 38	7 57	11 47	15 56	15 37	4 20 12	19 36 35
27	16 11 42	21 07	+12 26	7 39	7 59	11 48	15 56	15 35	4 24 08	19 32 39
28	16 15 59	21 17	+12 06	7 41	8 01	11 48	15 55	15 34	4 28 05	19 28 43
29	16 20 16	21 28	+11 45	7 42	8 03	11 48	15 54	15 33	4 32 01	19 24 47
30	16 24 34	21 38	+11 24	7 44	8 05	11 49	15 53	15 32	4 35 58	19 20 51

THE SUN s.d. 16'·2

Duration of Civil (C), Nautical (N), and Astronomical (A), Twilight (in minutes)

Lat. °	Nov. 1 C	N	A	Nov. 11 C	N	A	Nov. 21 C	N	A	Nov. 30 C	N	A
52	36	75	115	37	78	117	38	80	120	39	82	123
56	40	84	127	41	87	130	43	90	134	45	93	137

ASTRONOMICAL NOTES

MERCURY is at superior conjunction on the 7th and thus is unsuitably placed for observation.

VENUS is a brilliant evening star, magnitude −3·5, visible above the south-western horizon after sunset. By the end of the month it sets about two hours after the Sun. The new crescent Moon is near on the evening of the 24th.

MARS is unsuitably placed for observation, conjunction occurring on the 25th.

JUPITER is at opposition on the 18th, magnitude −2·4, and thus visible throughout the hours of darkness. On the night of the 7th–8th the gibbous Moon passes south of the planet. The four Galilean satellites are readily observable with almost any small telescope or even good binoculars, provided they are held rigid. Details of the eclipses and shadow transits of these satellites are given on p. 150 for the convenience of observers with telescopes.

SATURN is a bright morning star, magnitude +0·5, and by the end of the month is visible in the east by 22h. Titan, Saturn's largest satellite, is of magnitude +8½, and thus visible in small telescopes.

THE MOON

Day	R.A.	Dec.	Hor. Par.	Semi- diam.	Sun's Co- long.	P.A. of Bright Limb	Phase	Age	Rise 52°	Rise 56°	Tran- sit	Set 52°	Set 56°
	h m	°	′	′	°	°		d	h m	h m	h m	h m	h m
1	22 14	− 6·0	55·5	15·1	18	251	71	8·8	14 17	14 20	20 08	1 03	0 58
2	23 00	− 2·1	55·0	15·0	30	250	79	9·8	14 39	14 39	20 51	2 09	2 08
3	23 46	+ 1·9	54·6	14·9	42	250	86	10·8	15 01	14 57	21 34	3 14	3 16
4	0 32	+ 5·8	54·3	14·8	54	250	92	11·8	15 24	15 17	22 17	4 18	4 24
5	1 18	+ 9·4	54·1	14·7	66	251	97	12·8	15 48	15 38	23 01	5 22	5 31
6	2 04	+12·6	54·0	14·7	78	250	99	13·8	16 15	16 02	23 46	6 25	6 37
7	2 52	+15·3	54·0	14·7	91	145	100	14·8	16 47	16 31	··	7 26	7 41
8	3 40	+17·4	54·0	14·7	103	87	99	15·8	17 24	17 06	0 32	8 24	8 42
9	4 30	+18·7	54·2	14·8	115	89	96	16·8	18 07	17 48	1 19	9 19	9 38
10	5 21	+19·2	54·5	14·8	127	92	92	17·8	18 57	18 38	2 08	10 09	10 28
11	6 12	+18·9	54·8	14·9	139	96	86	18·8	19 53	19 36	2 57	10 52	11 10
12	7 03	+17·6	55·3	15·1	151	100	78	19·8	20 55	20 40	3 46	11 30	11 46
13	7 54	+15·5	55·9	15·2	163	103	70	20·8	22 01	21 50	4 34	12 03	12 16
14	8 45	+12·6	56·6	15·4	176	106	60	21·8	23 11	23 03	5 23	12 33	12 42
15	9 36	+ 9·0	57·4	15·6	188	109	49	22·8	··	··	6 12	13 00	13 05
16	10 28	+ 4·9	58·2	15·9	200	110	39	23·8	0 24	0 20	7 01	13 26	13 27
17	11 20	+ 0·4	59·1	16·1	212	111	28	24·8	1 40	1 40	7 52	13 52	13 50
18	12 15	− 4·3	60·0	16·3	224	111	18	25·8	2 59	3 03	8 45	14 19	14 13
19	13 11	− 8·9	60·7	16·5	237	111	10	26·8	4 19	4 28	9 40	14 50	14 40
20	14 10	−13·0	61·2	16·7	249	110	4	27·8	5 41	5 55	10 38	15 27	15 13
21	15 11	−16·3	61·3	16·7	261	115	1	28·8	7 02	7 18	11 39	16 12	15 54
22	16 14	−18·4	61·2	16·7	273	252	0	0·4	8 16	8 35	12 42	17 06	16 46
23	17 18	−19·3	60·7	16·5	285	263	3	1·4	9 20	9 39	13 43	18 08	17 49
24	18 20	−18·8	60·0	16·3	298	261	8	2·4	10 13	10 31	14 43	19 17	19 00
25	19 20	−17·0	59·1	16·1	310	257	16	3·4	10 55	11 10	15 39	20 29	20 15
26	20 17	−14·4	58·1	15·8	322	254	25	4·4	11 29	11 41	16 31	21 41	21 30
27	21 10	−11·0	57·2	15·6	334	251	34	5·4	11 58	12 06	17 19	22 51	22 44
28	22 00	− 7·2	56·3	15·3	346	249	45	6·4	12 22	12 27	18 05	23 59	23 56
29	22 48	− 3·2	55·6	15·1	358	248	55	7·4	12 45	12 46	18 49	··	··
30	23 34	+ 0·8	55·0	15·0	11	248	64	8·4	13 07	13 04	19 32	1 05	1 05

MERCURY ☿

Day	R.A.	Dec. −	Diam.	Phase	Tran- sit		Day	R.A.	Dec. −	Diam.	Phase	Tran- sit	
	h m	°	″		h m			h m	°	″		h m	
1	14 11	12·3	5	99	11 30	Mercury is too close to the Sun for observation	16	15 45	20·7	5	99	12 06	Mercury is too close to the Sun for observation
4	14 29	14·2	5	100	11 37		19	16 05	22·0	5	98	12 13	
7	14 48	16·0	5	100	11 44		22	16 24	23·1	5	97	12 21	
10	15 07	17·7	5	100	11 51		25	16 44	24·0	5	96	12 29	
13	15 26	19·3	5	100	11 58		28	17 04	24·7	5	95	12 37	
16	15 45	20·7	5	99	12 06		31	17 24	25·3	5	93	12 46	

VENUS ♀   MARS ♂

Day	R.A.	Dec.	Diam.	Phase	Tran- sit	5° high W. 52°	5° high W. 56°	Day	R.A.	Dec.	Diam.	Phase	Tran- sit	
	h m	°	″		h m	h m	h m		h m	°	″		h m	
1	16 49	23·9	13	81	14 08	17 02	16 23	1	14 54	16·6	4	100	12 11	Mars is too close to the Sun for observation
6	17 15	24·7	14	80	14 14	17 03	16 20	6	15 08	17·6	4	100	12 06	
11	17 42	25·2	14	79	14 21	17 04	16 19	11	15 22	18·6	4	100	12 00	
16	18 08	25·4	14	77	14 28	17 10	16 23	16	15 36	19·5	4	100	11 55	
21	18 35	25·3	15	76	14 35	17 18	16 33	21	15 51	20·4	4	100	11 50	
26	19 01	24·9	15	74	14 42	17 29	16 46	26	16 06	21·1	4	100	11 45	
31	19 27	24·2	16	73	14 48	17 42	17 03	31	16 21	21·8	4	100	11 41	

SUNRISE AND SUNSET (G.M.T.)

Day	London		Bristol		Birmingham		Manchester		Newcastle		Glasgow		Belfast	
	a.m.	p.m.	a.m.	p.m.	a.m.	p.m.	a.m.	p.m.	a.m.	p.m.	a.m.	p.m.	a.m.	p.m.
	h m	h m	h m	h m	h m	h m	h m	h m	h m	h m	h m	h m	h m	h m
1	6 53	4 34	7 03	4 44	7 02	4 38	7 07	4 37	7 09	4 30	7 23	4 38	7 26	4 49
2	6 55	4 32	7 05	4 42	7 04	4 36	7 09	4 35	7 11	4 28	7 25	4 36	7 28	4 47
3	6 57	4 30	7 06	4 40	7 06	4 35	7 11	4 34	7 13	4 26	7 27	4 34	7 30	4 45
4	6 59	4 29	7 08	4 39	7 08	4 33	7 13	4 32	7 15	4 24	7 29	4 32	7 32	4 43
5	7 00	4 27	7 10	4 37	7 10	4 31	7 15	4 30	7 17	4 22	7 31	4 30	7 34	4 41
6	7 02	4 25	7 11	4 35	7 12	4 29	7 17	4 28	7 19	4 20	7 33	4 28	7 36	4 39
7	7 04	4 24	7 13	4 34	7 14	4 27	7 19	4 26	7 21	4 18	7 35	4 26	7 38	4 37
8	7 06	4 22	7 15	4 32	7 16	4 25	7 21	4 24	7 23	4 16	7 37	4 24	7 40	4 35
9	7 07	4 20	7 17	4 30	7 17	4 24	7 22	4 23	7 25	4 14	7 39	4 22	7 41	5 34
10	7 09	4 19	7 18	4 29	7 19	4 22	7 24	4 21	7 27	4 12	7 41	4 20	7 43	4 32
11	7 11	4 17	7 20	4 27	7 21	4 20	7 26	4 19	7 29	4 10	7 43	4 18	7 45	4 30
12	7 12	4 16	7 22	4 26	7 23	4 19	7 28	4 17	7 31	4 08	7 46	4 16	7 48	4 28
13	7 14	4 14	7 24	4 24	7 25	4 17	7 30	4 16	7 33	4 07	7 48	4 14	7 50	4 26
14	7 16	4 13	7 26	4 23	7 27	4 16	7 32	4 14	7 35	4 05	7 50	4 13	7 52	4 25
15	7 17	4 11	7 27	4 21	7 28	4 14	7 34	4 13	7 37	4 04	7 52	4 11	7 54	4 23
16	7 19	4 10	7 29	4 20	7 30	4 13	7 36	4 11	7 39	4 02	7 54	4 09	7 56	4 21
17	7 21	4 09	7 31	4 19	7 32	4 12	7 38	4 09	7 41	4 00	7 56	4 07	7 58	4 19
18	7 23	4 07	7 33	4 17	7 34	4 10	7 40	4 08	7 43	3 59	7 58	4 06	8 00	4 18
19	7 24	4 06	7 34	4 16	7 35	4 09	7 42	4 07	7 45	3 57	8 00	4 04	8 02	4 17
20	7 26	4 05	7 36	4 15	7 37	4 08	7 43	4 05	7 47	3 56	8 02	4 03	8 03	4 15
21	7 28	4 04	7 38	4 14	7 39	4 07	7 45	4 04	7 49	3 54	8 04	4 01	8 05	4 14
22	7 29	4 02	7 39	4 13	7 40	4 05	7 47	4 03	7 51	3 53	8 06	4 00	8 07	4 13
23	7 31	4 01	7 41	4 12	7 42	4 04	7 49	4 01	7 53	3 51	8 08	3 58	8 09	4 11
24	7 33	4 00	7 43	4 11	7 44	4 03	7 51	4 00	7 55	3 50	8 10	3 57	8 11	4 10
25	7 34	3 59	7 44	4 10	7 45	4 02	7 52	3 59	7 56	3 49	8 12	3 56	8 12	4 09
26	7 36	3 58	7 46	4 09	7 47	4 01	7 54	3 58	7 58	3 48	8 13	3 55	8 14	4 08
27	7 37	3 58	7 47	4 08	7 48	4 01	7 55	3 58	8 00	3 47	8 15	3 53	8 16	4 07
28	7 39	3 57	7 49	4 07	7 50	4 00	7 57	3 57	8 01	3 46	8 17	3 52	8 17	4 06
29	7 40	3 56	7 50	4 07	7 51	3 59	7 58	3 56	8 03	3 45	8 19	3 51	8 19	4 05
30	7 42	3 55	7 52	4 06	7 53	3 58	8 00	3 55	8 05	3 44	8 21	3 50	8 21	4 04

JUPITER ♃ — SATURN ♄

Day	Jupiter R.A.	Dec. +	Transit	5° high West 52°	5° high West 56°	Saturn R.A.	Dec. +	5° high East 52°	5° high East 56°	Transit
	h m	°	h m	h m	h m	h m	°	h m	h m	h m
1	3 46	18·7	1 04	8 08	8 21	9 16	16·6	23 36	23 25	6 33
11	3 40	18·4	0 19	7 20	7 33	9 17	16·6	22 58	22 47	5 55
21	3 35	18·1	23 30	6 34	6 46	9 18	16·5	22 20	22 09	5 17
31	3 29	17·8	22 45	5 49	6 01	9 18	16·5	21 41	21 30	4 38

Equatorial diameter of Jupiter 49″; of Saturn 19″ Diameters of Saturn's rings 42″ and 11″

URANUS ♅ — NEPTUNE ♆

Day	Uranus R.A.	Dec. −	Transit		Neptune R.A.	Dec. −	Transit	
	h m	° ′	h m		h m	° ′	h m	
1	14 21·4	13 37	11 38	Uranus is too close to the Sun for observation	16 44·7	20 50	14 01	Neptune is too close to the Sun for observation
11	14 23·8	13 49	11 01		16 46·1	20 53	13 23	
21	14 26·2	14 01	10 24		16 47·7	20 56	12 45	
31	14 28·5	14 12	9 47		16 49·2	20 59	12 07	

Diameter 4″ Diameter 2″

Day of		Decem (ten), 10th month of Roman (pre-Julian) Calendar.

Sun's Longitude 270° ♑ 21ᵈ 18ʰ

Month	Week	
1	W.	Henry I d. 1135. Queen Alexandra b. 1844
2	Th.	Austerlitz 1805. Marquis de Sade d. 1814
3	F.	Robert Louis Stevenson d. 1894
4	S.	Cardinal Richelieu d. 1652. Samuel Butler d. 1835
5	🅂.	**2nd 🅂. in Advent.** Claude Monet d. 1926
6	M.	Trollope d. 1882. Jefferson Davis d. 1889
7	Tu.	Pearl Harbour 1941
8	W.	De Quincey d. 1859. Herbert Spencer d. 1903
9	Th.	Milton b. 1608. Lord Butler b. 1902
10	F.	Alfred Nobel d. 1896. Pirandello d. 1936
11	S.	Accession of George VI 1936
12	🅂.	**3rd 🅂. in Advent.** Flaubert b. 1821
13	M.	Dr. Johnson d. 1784
14	Tu.	George VI b. 1895. Walter Lippmann d. 1974
15	W.	Jan Vermeer d. 1675. Rasputin d. 1916
16	Th.	Beethoven b. 1770. Jane Austen b. 1775
17	F.	Prince Rupert b. 1619. Simon Bolivar d. 1830
18	S.	Grimaldi b. 1779. Christopher Fry b. 1907
19	🅂.	**4th 🅂. in Advent.** J. M. W. Turner d. 1851
20	M.	Sir Robert Menzies b. 1894
21	Tu.	**St. Thomas.** MICHAELMAS LAW SITTINGS END
22	W.	George Eliot d. 1880. Richard Dimbleby d. 1965
23	Th.	Roger Ascham d. 1568. Sir Richard Arkwright
24	F.	Christmas Eve. M. C. Cowdrey b. 1932 [b. 1732
25	S.	**Christmas Day.** Sir Isaac Newton b. 1642
26	🅂.	**1st 🅂. after Christmas. St. Stephen.**
27	M.	**St. John.** Jack Benny d. 1974
28	Tu.	**Holy Innocents.** Maurice Ravel d. 1937
29	W.	W. E. Gladstone b. 1809. Christina Rosetti d. 1894
30	Th.	Rudyard Kipling b. 1865. Pablo Casals b. 1876**
31	F.	John Wycliffe d. 1384. Matisse b. 1869

PHENOMENA

December 5ᵈ 00ʰ Jupiter in conjunction with the Moon. Jupiter 0°·8 N.

5ᵈ 17ʰ Neptune in conjunction with the Sun.

11ᵈ 21ʰ Saturn in conjunction with the Moon. Saturn 6° N.

20ᵈ 10ʰ Mercury at greatest eastern elongation (20°).

21ᵈ 18ʰ Winter Solstice.

22ᵈ 15ʰ Mercury in conjunction with the Moon. Mercury 6° S.

24ᵈ 15ʰ Venus in conjunction with the Moon. Venus 7° S.

CONSTELLATIONS

The following constellations are near the meridian at

	d	h		d	h
Nov. 1	24		Nov. 15	23
Dec. 1	22		Dec. 16	21
Jan. 1	20		Jan. 16	19

Ursa Major (below the Pole), Ursa Minor (below the Pole), Cassiopeia, Andromeda, Perseus, Triangulum, Aries, Taurus, Cetus and Eridanus.

MINIMA OF ALGOL

d	h	d	h
2	22	20	2
5	18	22	23
8	15	25	20
11	12	28	17
14	9	31	14
17	6		

PHASES OF THE MOON

	d	h	m
○ Full Moon	6	18	15
☾ Last Quarter	14	10	14
● New Moon	21	02	08
☽ First Quarter	28	07	48

	d	h
Apogee (405,930 kilometres)	3	18
Perigee (360,960 ,,)	19	12
Apogee (405,100 ,,)	31	09

Mean Longitude of Ascending Node on December 1, 212°.

MONTHLY NOTES

Dec. 10. Grouse and Black Game Shooting ends.

15. Notices to owners and occupiers affected by private Bills in Parliament must be delivered.

21. Shortest day.

23. Moslem New Year (A.H. 1397).

25. Quarter day.

27. Bank Holiday, England, Wales and Northern Ireland.

31. Various licences expire.

** Centenary.

Day	Right Ascension	Dec. −	Equation of Time	Rise 52°	Rise 56°	Transit	Set 52°	Set 56°	Sidereal Time	Transit of First Point of Aries
	h m s	° ′	m s	h m	h m	h m	h m	h m	h m s	h m s
1	16 28 52	21 47	+ 11 02	7 45	8 06	11 49	15 52	15 31	4 39 54	19 16 56
2	16 33 11	21 56	+ 10 39	7 47	8 08	11 50	15 52	15 30	4 43 51	19 13 00
3	16 37 31	22 05	+ 10 16	7 48	8 10	11 50	15 51	15 30	4 47 48	19 09 04
4	16 41 52	22 14	+ 9 52	7 49	8 11	11 50	15 51	15 29	4 51 44	19 05 08
5	16 46 12	22 21	+ 9 28	7 51	8 13	11 51	15 50	15 28	4 55 41	19 01 12
6	16 50 34	22 29	+ 9 08	7 52	8 14	11 51	15 50	15 28	4 59 37	18 57 16
7	16 54 56	22 36	+ 8 38	7 53	8 16	11 52	15 49	15 27	5 03 34	18 53 20
8	16 59 18	22 42	+ 8 12	7 54	8 17	11 52	15 49	15 26	5 07 30	18 49 24
9	17 03 41	22 49	+ 7 45	7 56	8 18	11 52	15 49	15 26	5 11 27	18 45 28
10	17 08 05	22 54	+ 7 18	7 57	8 20	11 53	15 49	15 26	5 15 23	18 41 32
11	17 12 29	22 59	+ 6 51	7 58	8 21	11 53	15 49	15 25	5 19 20	18 37 36
12	17 16 53	23 04	+ 6 23	7 59	8 22	11 54	15 49	15 25	5 23 17	18 33 41
13	17 21 18	23 09	+ 5 55	8 00	8 23	11 54	15 49	15 25	5 27 13	18 29 45
14	17 25 43	23 12	+ 5 27	8 01	8 24	11 55	15 49	15 25	5 31 10	18 25 49
15	17 30 08	23 16	+ 4 58	8 02	8 25	11 55	15 49	15 25	5 35 06	18 21 53
16	17 34 34	23 19	+ 4 29	8 03	8 26	11 56	15 49	15 25	5 39 03	18 17 57
17	17 38 59	23 21	+ 4 00	8 03	8 27	11 56	15 49	15 25	5 42 59	18 14 01
18	17 43 25	23 23	+ 3 30	8 04	8 28	11 57	15 49	15 25	5 46 56	18 10 05
19	17 47 52	23 25	+ 3 01	8 05	8 29	11 57	15 50	15 26	5 50 52	18 06 09
20	17 52 18	23 26	+ 2 31	8 05	8 29	11 58	15 50	15 26	5 54 49	18 02 13
21	17 56 45	23 26	+ 2 01	8 06	8 30	11 58	15 50	15 27	5 58 46	17 58 17
22	18 01 11	23 26	+ 1 31	8 06	8 30	11 59	15 51	15 27	6 02 42	17 54 21
23	18 05 38	23 26	+ 1 01	8 07	8 31	11 59	15 51	15 28	6 06 39	17 50 25
24	18 10 04	23 25	+ 0 31	8 07	8 31	12 00	15 52	15 28	6 10 35	17 46 30
25	18 14 31	23 24	+ 0 01	8 08	8 31	12 00	15 53	15 29	6 14 32	17 42 34
26	18 18 57	23 22	− 0 29	8 08	8 32	12 01	15 53	15 30	6 18 28	17 38 38
27	18 23 23	23 20	− 0 58	8 08	8 32	12 01	15 54	15 30	6 22 25	17 34 42
28	18 27 49	23 17	− 1 28	8 08	8 32	12 02	15 55	15 31	6 26 21	17 30 46
29	18 32 15	23 14	− 1 57	8 08	8 32	12 02	15 56	15 32	6 30 18	17 26 50
30	18 36 41	23 10	− 2 26	8 08	8 32	12 03	15 57	15 33	6 34 15	17 22 54
31	18 41 06	23 06	− 2 55	8 08	8 32	12 03	15 58	15 34	6 38 11	17 18 58

Duration of Civil (C), Nautical (N), and Astronomical (A), Twilight (in minutes)

Lat. °	Dec. 1 C	N	A	Dec. 11 C	N	A	Dec. 21 C	N	A	Dec. 31 C	N	A
52	40	82	123	41	84	125	41	85	126	41	84	125
56	45	93	138	47	96	141	47	97	142	47	96	141

ASTRONOMICAL NOTES

MERCURY is at greatest eastern elongation on the 20th but as it is then 24° S. of the equator observation will not be easy. It may be glimpsed, magnitude 0, low above the S.W. horizon, around the time of ending of evening civil twilight, during the third week of the month.

VENUS is a magnificent evening star, magnitude −3·7, and by the end of the month visible for over three hours after sunset. The crescent Moon is near Venus on the evening of the 24th.

MARS is too close to the Sun for observation.

JUPITER is a brilliant evening star, magnitude −2·3. It is retrograding slowly and at the end of the month returns from Taurus into Aries. On the night of the 4th–5th the gibbous Moon passes south of the planet.

SATURN is a bright morning star, magnitude +0·3, moving very slowly westwards in the eastern part of Cancer. On the evening of the 11th the gibbous Moon passes 6° S. of the planet.

METEORS. The maximum of the famous Geminid meteor shower occurs during the night of 13th–14th. The Moon is at Last Quarter so that observations before midnight will not suffer interference from moonlight.

THE MOON

Day	R.A.	Dec.	Hor. Par.	Semi-diam.	Sun's Co-long.	P.A. of Bright Limb	Phase	Age	Rise 52°	Rise 56°	Transit	Set 52°	Set 56°
	h m	°	′	′	°	°		d	h m	h m	h m	h m	h m
1	0 20	+ 4·7	54·5	14·9	23	248	73	9·4	13 29	13 23	20 15	2 09	2 14
2	1 06	+ 8·4	54·2	14·8	35	249	81	10·4	13 52	13 43	20 59	3 13	3 21
3	1 52	+11·8	54·1	14·7	47	250	88	11·4	14 18	14 06	21 43	4 16	4 27
4	2 39	+14·7	54·0	14·7	59	251	93	12·4	14 48	14 33	22 29	5 18	5 32
5	3 27	+16·9	54·1	14·7	71	250	97	13·4	15 23	15 06	23 16	6 18	6 34
6	4 17	+18·5	54·3	14·8	83	242	99	14·4	16 04	15 45	··	7 14	7 33
7	5 08	+19·2	54·5	14·9	96	139	100	15·4	16 52	16 33	0 04	8 06	8 25
8	5 59	+19·1	54·8	14·9	108	107	98	16·4	17 47	17 29	0 54	8 52	9 11
9	6 51	+18·1	55·2	15·0	120	105	95	17·4	18 47	18 32	1 43	9 32	9 49
10	7 42	+16·2	55·6	15·2	132	107	90	18·4	19 52	19 40	2 32	10 07	10 21
11	8 34	+13·5	56·1	15·3	144	109	83	19·4	21 01	20 51	3 21	10 38	10 48
12	9 24	+10·1	56·7	15·4	156	111	75	20·4	22 11	22 06	4 09	11 05	11 12
13	10 15	+ 6·2	57·3	15·6	168	112	65	21·4	23 24	23 22	4 57	11 30	11 34
14	11 06	+ 1·8	58·0	15·8	181	113	55	22·4	··	··	5 46	11 55	11 55
15	11 57	− 2·7	58·7	16·0	193	113	44	23·4	0 39	0 41	6 36	12 21	12 17
16	12 51	− 7·1	59·4	16·2	205	112	33	24·4	1 56	2 02	7 28	12 49	12 41
17	13 47	−11·3	60·0	16·3	217	111	22	25·4	3 14	3 25	8 22	13 21	13 09
18	14 45	−14·9	60·5	16·5	229	108	13	26·4	4 33	4 48	9 20	14 00	13 44
19	15 46	−17·6	60·7	16·5	241	107	6	27·4	5 49	6 07	10 20	14 48	14 29
20	16 49	−19·0	60·7	16·5	254	109	2	28·4	6 58	7 18	11 22	15 45	15 25
21	17 52	−19·2	60·4	16·5	266	165	0	29·4	7 58	8 17	12 23	16 51	16 32
22	18 53	−18·0	59·9	16·3	278	244	1	0·9	8 47	9 03	13 22	18 03	17 47
23	19 53	−15·8	59·1	16·1	290	249	5	1·9	9 26	9 39	14 18	19 17	19 05
24	20 49	−12·6	58·3	15·9	302	248	11	2·9	9 58	10 08	15 10	20 30	20 22
25	21 42	− 8·9	57·4	15·6	315	247	19	3·9	10 25	10 31	15 58	21 41	21 37
26	22 32	− 4·8	56·5	15·4	327	246	28	4·9	10 49	10 52	16 44	22 50	22 49
27	23 20	− 0·7	55·7	15·2	339	246	37	5·9	11 12	11 11	17 28	23 56	23 59
28	0 06	+ 3·3	55·1	15·0	351	246	47	6·9	11 34	11 30	18 12	··	··
29	0 52	+ 7·2	54·6	14·9	3	247	56	7·9	11 57	11 50	18 55	1 01	1 07
30	1 38	+10·7	54·3	14·8	15	249	66	8·9	12 22	12 11	19 39	2 05	2 14
31	2 25	+13·7	54·1	14·8	28	251	74	9·9	12 50	12 36	20 24	3 07	3 20

MERCURY ☿

Day	R.A.	Dec. −	Diam.	Phase	Transit		Day	R.A.	Dec. −	Diam.	Phase	Transit	5° high W. 52°	5° high W. 56°
	h m	°	″		h m			h m	°	″		h m	h m	h m
1	17 24	25·3	5	93	12 46	Mercury is	16	19 00	24·8	6	74	13 22	16 09	15 27
4	17 44	25·6	5	91	12 54	too close to	19	19 16	24·1	6	66	13 25	16 20	15 41
7	18 04	25·7	5	88	13 02	the Sun	22	19 29	23·3	7	56	13 26	16 28	15 52
10	18 23	25·7	5	85	13 09	for observation	25	19 37	22·4	8	44	13 22	16 32	16 00
13	18 42	25·4	6	80	13 16		28	19 41	21·4	8	29	13 12	16 25	15 59
16	19 00	24·8	6	74	13 22		31	19 37	20·7	9	16	12 55	16 18	15 50

VENUS ♀

Day	R.A.	Dec. −	Diam.	Phase	Transit	5° high W. 52°	5° high W. 56°
	h m	°	″		h m	h m	h m
1	19 27	24·2	16	73	14 48	17 42	17 03
6	19 53	23·2	16	71	14 54	17 57	17 22
11	20 18	22·0	17	70	14 59	18 14	17 42
16	20 42	20·5	17	68	15 04	18 29	18 01
21	21 06	18·8	18	66	15 08	18 46	18 22
26	21 29	16·9	19	64	15 11	19 03	18 42
31	21 51	14·8	19	62	15 13	19 19	19 01

MARS ♂

Day	R.A.	Dec. −	Diam.	Phase	Transit	
	h m	°	″		h m	
1	16 21	21·8	4	100	11 41	Mars is
6	16 37	22·4	4	100	11 37	too close to
11	16 52	23·0	4	100	11 33	the Sun
16	17 08	23·4	4	100	11 29	for observation
21	17 24	23·7	4	100	11 25	
26	17 40	23·9	4	100	11 22	
31	17 57	24·0	4	100	11 18	

Day	SUNRISE AND SUNSET (G.M.T.)													
	London		Bristol		Birmingham		Manchester		Newcastle		Glasgow		Belfast	
	a.m.	p.m.	a.m.	p.m.	a.m.	p.m.	a.m.	p.m.	a.m.	p.m.	a.m.	p.m.	a.m.	p.m.
	h m	h m	h m	h m	h m	h m	h m	h m	h m	h m	h m	h m	h m	h m
1	7 43	3 54	7 53	4 05	7 54	3 57	8 01	3 54	8 06	3 43	8 22	3 49	8 22	4 03
2	7 45	3 54	7 55	4 05	7 56	3 57	8 03	3 54	8 08	3 42	8 24	3 48	8 24	4 02
3	7 46	3 53	7 56	4 04	7 57	3 56	8 04	3 53·	8 10	3 42	8 26	3 48	8 26	4 02
4	7 47	3 53	7 57	4 04	7 59	3 55	8 06	3 52	8 11	3 41	8 27	3 47	8 28	4 01
5	7 49	3 52	7 58	4 03	8 00	3 55	8 07	3 52	8 13	3 40	8 29	3 46	8 29	4 00
6	7 50	3 52	8 00	4 03	8 01	3 54	8 08	3 51	8 14	3 40	8 30	3 46	8 30	4 00
7	7 51	3 52	8 01	4 02	8 03	3 54	8 10	3 51	8 16	3 39	8 32	3 45	8 32	3 59
8	7 52	3 52	8 02	4 02	8 04	3 53	8 11	3 50	8 17	3 38	8 33	3 44	8 33	3 58
9	7 54	3 51	8 03	4 02	8 05	3 53	8 12	3 50	8 18	3 38	8 34	3 44	8 34	3 58
10	7 55	3 51	8 04	4 02	8 06	3 53	8 13	3 50	8 19	3 38	8 36	3 44	8 35	3 58
11	7 56	3 51	8 05	4 02	8 08	3 53	8 15	3 50	8 21	3 38	8 37	3 43	8 37	3 58
12	7 57	3 51	8 06	4 02	8 09	3 53	8 16	3 50	8 22	3 38	8 38	3 43	8 38	3 58
13	7 58	3 51	8 07	4 02	8 10	3 53	8 17	3 50	8 23	3 38	8 39	3 43	8 39	3 58
14	7 59	3 51	8 08	4 02	8 11	3 53	8 18	3 50	8 24	3 38	8 40	3 43	8 40	3 58
15	8 00	3 52	8 09	4 02	8 12	3 53	8 19	3 50	8 25	3 38	8 41	3 43	8 41	3 58
16	8 01	3 52	8 10	4 02	8 12	3 53	8 19	3 50	8 25	3 38	8 42	3 43	8 41	3 58
17	8 01	3 52	8 10	4 02	8 13	3 53	8 20	3 50	8 26	3 38	8 43	3 43	8 42	3 58
18	8 02	3 52	8 11	4 02	8 14	3 53	8 21	3 50	8 27	3 38	8 44	3 43	8 43	3 58
19	8 03	3 53	8 12	4 03	8 15	3 54	8 22	3 50	8 28	3 38	8 45	3 44	8 44	3 58
20	8 03	3 53	8 12	4 03	8 15	3 54	8 22	3 51	8 28	3 39	8 45	3 44	8 44	3 59
21	8 04	3 53	8 13	4 03	8 16	3 54	8 23	3 51	8 29	3 39	8 46	3 45	8 45	3 59
22	8 04	3 54	8 13	4 04	8 16	3 55	8 24	3 52	8 30	3 40	8 46	3 45	8 46	4 00
23	8 05	3 54	8 14	4 04	8 17	3 55	8 24	3 52	8 30	3 40	8 47	3 46	8 46	4 00
24	8 05	3 55	8 14	4 05	8 17	3 56	8 24	3 53	8 30	3 41	8 47	3 46	8 46	4 01
25	8 06	3 56	8 15	4 06	8 18	3 57	8 25	3 54	8 31	3 42	8 47	3 47	8 47	4 02
26	8 06	3 56	8 15	4 06	8 18	3 57	8 25	3 54	8 31	3 42	8 48	3 48	8 47	4 02
27	8 06	3 57	8 15	4 07	8 18	3 58	8 25	3 55	8 31	3 43	8 48	3 48	8 47	4 03
28	8 06	3 58	8 15	4 08	8 18	3 59	8 25	3 56	8 31	3 44	8 48	3 49	8 47	4 04
29	8 06	3 59	8 16	4 09	8 18	4 00	8 25	3 57	8 31	3 45	8 48	3 50	8 47	4 05
30	8 06	4 00	8 16	4 10	8 18	4 01	8 26	3 58	8 32	3 46	8 48	3 51	8 48	4 06
31	8 06	4 01	8 16	4 11	8 18	4 02	8 25	3 59	8 31	3 47	8 48	3 52	8 47	4 07

JUPITER ♃   SATURN ♄

Day	R.A.	Dec. +	Transit	5° high West		R.A.	Dec. +	5° high East		Transit
				52°	56°			52°	56°	
	h m	°	h m	h m	h m	h m	°	h m	h m	h m
1	3 29	17·8	22 45	5 49	6 01	9 18	16·5	21 41	21 30	4 38
11	3 25	17·6	22 01	5 04	5 15	9 18	16·6	21 00	20 49	3 58
21	3 21	17·3	21 18	4 20	4 31	9 16	16·7	20 18	20 07	3 17
31	3 18	17·2	20 36	3 37	3 48	9 14	16·9	19 36	19 25	2 36

Equatorial diameter of Jupiter 48″; of Saturn 20″   Diameters of Saturn's rings 44″ and 12″

URANUS ⛢   NEPTUNE ♆

Day	R.A.	Dec. −	5° high East		Transit	R.A.	Dec. −	Transit	
			52°	56°					
	h m	° ′	h m	h m	h m	h m	° ′	h m	
1	14 28·5	14 12	6 19	6 44	9 47	16 49·2	20 59	12 07	Neptune is
11	14 30·6	14 23	5 43	6 08	9 10	16 50·8	21 02	11 30	too close to
21	14 32·6	14 32	5 07	5 32	8 32	16 52·4	21 04	10 52	the Sun for
31	14 34·2	14 40	4 31	4 56	7 55	16 54·0	21 06	10 14	observation

Diameter 4″   Diameter 2″

INTRODUCTION TO ASTRONOMICAL SECTION

GENERAL

The astronomical data are given in a form suitable for those who practise naked-eye astronomy or use small telescopes. No attempt has been made to replace the *Astronomical Ephemeris* for professional astronomers. Positions of the heavenly bodies are given only to the degree of accuracy required by amateur astronomers for setting telescopes, or for plotting on celestial globes or star atlases. Where intermediate positions are required, linear interpolation may be employed.

All data are, unless otherwise stated, for 0^h G.M.T., or the midnight at the beginning of the day named.

(*See notes on British Summer Time, p. 142*).

Definitions of the terms used cannot be given in an ephemeris of this nature. They must be sought in astronomical literature and text-books. Probably the best source for the amateur is Norton's *Star Atlas* (Gall and Inglis, 15th edition, 1964; £1.05), which contains an excellent introduction to observational astronomy, and the finest series of star maps yet produced for showing stars visible to the naked eye. Certain more extended ephemerides are available in the British Astronomical Association Handbook, an annual very popular among amateur astronomers. (Secretary: Burlington House, Piccadilly, London, W.1.)

A special feature has been made of the times when the various heavenly bodies are visible in the British Isles. Since two columns, calculated for latitudes 52° and 56°, are devoted to risings and settings, the range 50° to 58° can be covered by interpolation and extrapolation. The times given in these columns are G.M.T.'s for the meridian of Greenwich. An observer west of this meridian must add his longitude (in time) and vice versa.

In accordance with the usual convention in astronomy, $+$ and $-$ indicate respectively north and south latitudes or declinations.

PAGE I OF EACH MONTH

The Zodiacal signs through which the Sun is passing during each month are illustrated. The date of transition from one sign to the next, to the nearest hour, is also given.

The FASTS AND FESTIVALS in black-letter type are those so given in the Prayer Book. The line immediately to the right of the Day of Week is shown heavy when the Law Courts are sitting in London.

Under the heading PHENOMENA will be found particulars of the more important conjunctions of the Sun, Moon and planets with each other, and also the dates of eclipses and other astronomical phenomena of special interest.

The CONSTELLATIONS listed each month are those that are near the meridian at the beginning of the month at 22^h local mean time. Allowance must be made for Summer Time if necessary. The fact that any star crosses the meridian 4^m earlier each night or 2^h earlier each month may be used, in conjunction with the lists given each month, to find what constellations are favourably placed at any moment. The table preceding the list of constellations may be extended indefinitely at the rate just quoted.

Times of MINIMA OF ALGOL are approximate times of the middle of the period of diminished light (*see* p. 153).

The Principal PHASES OF THE MOON are the G.M.T.'s when the difference between the longitude of the Moon and that of the Sun is 0°, 90°, 180° or 270°. The times of perigee and apogee are those when the Moon is nearest to, and farthest from, the Earth, respectively. The nodes or points of intersection of the Moon's orbit and the ecliptic make a complete retrograde circuit of the ecliptic in about 19 years. From a knowledge of the longitude of the ascending node and the inclination, whose value does not vary much from 5°, the path of the Moon among the stars may be plotted on a celestial globe or star atlas.

The MONTHLY NOTES are self-explanatory.

PAGE II OF EACH MONTH

The Sun's semi-diameter, in arc, is given once a month.

The right ascension given is that of the true Sun. The right ascension of the mean Sun is obtained by applying the equation of time, with the sign given, to the right ascension of the true Sun, or, more easily, by applying 12^h to the column Sidereal Time. The direction in which the equation of time has to be applied in different problems is a frequent source of confusion and error. Apparent Solar Time is equal to the Mean Solar Time plus the Equation of Time. For example at noon on Aug. 8 the Equation of Time is $-5^m 34^s$ and thus at 12^h Mean Time on that day the Apparent Time is $12^h - 5^m 34^s = 11^h 54^m 6^s$.

The Greenwich Sidereal Time at 0^h and the Transit of the First Point of Aries (which is really the mean time when the sidereal time is 0^h) are used for converting mean time to sidereal time and vice versa.

The G.M.T. of transit of the Sun at Greenwich may also be taken as the L.M.T. of transit in any longitude. It is independent of latitude. The G.M.T. of transit in any longitude is obtained by adding the longitude to the time given if west, and vice versa.

The legal importance of SUNRISE and SUNSET is that the Road Traffic Act, 1956, defines Lighting-up Time for vehicles as being from half an hour after sunset to half an hour before sunrise throughout the year. In all laws and regulations " sunset " refers to the local sunset, i.e. the time at which the Sun sets at the place in question. This common-sense interpretation has been upheld by legal tribunals. Thus the necessity for providing for different latitudes and longitudes, as already described, is evident.

The times of SUNRISE and SUNSET are those when the Sun's upper limb, as affected by refraction, is on the true horizon of an observer at sea-level. Assuming the mean refraction to be $34'$, and the Sun's semi-diameter to be $16'$, the time given is that when the true zenith distance of the Sun's centre is $90° + 34' + 16'$ or $90° 50'$, or, in other words, when the depression of the Sun's centre below the true horizon is 50'. The upper limb is then 34' below the true horizon, but is brought there by refraction. It is true, of course, that an observer on a ship might see the Sun for a minute or so longer, because of the dip of the horizon, while another viewing the sunset over hills or mountains would record an earlier time. Nevertheless, the moment when the true zenith distance of the Sun's centre is 90° 50' is a precise time dependent only on the latitude and longitude of the place, and independent of its altitude above sea-level, the contour of its horizon, the vagaries of refraction or the small seasonal change in the Sun's semi-diameter; this moment is suitable in every way as a definition of sunset (or sunrise) for all statutory purposes.

It is well known that light reaches us before sunrise and also continues to reach us for some time after sunset. The interval between darkness and sunrise or sunset and darkness is called twilight. Astronomically speaking, twilight is considered to begin or end when the Sun's centre is 18° below the horizon, as no light from the Sun can then reach the observer. As thus defined twilight may last several hours; in high latitudes at the solstices the depression of 18° is not reached, and twilight lasts from sunset to sunrise.

The need for some sub-division of twilight was met some years ago by dividing the gathering darkness into four steps.

(1) *Sunrise or Sunset*, defined as above.
(2) *Civil twilight*, which begins or ends when the Sun's centre is 6° below the horizon. This marks the time when operations requiring daylight may commence or must cease. In England it varies from about 30 to 60 minutes after sunset.
(3) *Nautical twilight*, which begins or ends when the Sun's centre is 12° below the horizon. This marks the time when it is, to all intents and purposes, completely dark.
(4) *Astronomical twilight*, which begins or ends when the Sun's centre is 18° below the horizon. This marks theoretical perfect darkness. It is not of practical importance, especially if nautical twilight is tabulated.

To assist observers the durations of civil, nautical and astronomical twilights are given at intervals of ten days. The beginning of a particular twilight is found by subtracting the duration from the time of sunrise, while the end is found by adding the duration to the time of sunset. Thus the beginning of astronomical twilight in latitude 52°, on the Greenwich meridian, on March 11 is found as $06^h 24^m - 113^m = 04^h 31^m$ and similarly the end of civil twilight as $17^h 57^m + 34^m = 18^h 31^m$.

The letters T.A.N. are printed when twilight lasts all night.

Lighting-up time is a crude attempt to approximate to civil twilight over the British Isles.

Under the heading ASTRONOMICAL NOTES will be found notes describing the position and visibility of all the planets and also of other phenomena; these are intended to guide naked-eye observers, or those using small telescopes.

PAGE III OF EACH MONTH

The Moon moves so rapidly among the stars that its position is given only to the degree of accuracy that permits linear interpolation. The right ascension and declination are geocentric, i.e. for an imaginary observer at the centre of the Earth. To an observer on the surface of the Earth the position is always different, as the altitude is always less on account of parallax which may reach 1°.

The lunar terminator is the line separating the bright from the dark part of the Moon's disk. Apart from irregularities of the lunar surface, the terminator is elliptical, because it is a circle seen in projection. It becomes the full circle forming the limb, or edge, of the Moon at New and Full Moon. The selenographic longitude of the terminator is measured from the mean centre of the visible disk, which may differ from the visible centre by as much as 8°, because of libration.

Instead of the longitude of the terminator the Sun's selenographic colongitude is tabulated. It is numerically equal to the selenographic longitude of the morning terminator, measured eastward from the mean centre of the disk. Thus its value is approximately 270° at New Moon, 360° at First Quarter, 90° at Full Moon and 180° at Last Quarter.

The Position Angle of the Bright Limb is the position angle of the midpoint of the illuminated limb, measured eastward from the north point on the disk. The column PHASE shows the percentage of the area of the Moon's disk illuminated; this is also the illuminated percentage of the diameter at right angles to the line of cusps. The terminator is a semi-ellipse whose major axis is the line of cusps, and whose semi-minor axis is determined by the tabulated percentage; from New Moon to Full Moon the east limb is dark, and vice versa.

The times given as moonrise and moonset are those when the upper limb of the Moon is on the horizon of an observer at sea-level. The Sun's horizontal parallax is about 9", and is negligible when considering sunrise and sunset, but that of the Moon averages about 57'. Hence the computed time represents the moment when the true zenith distance of the Moon is 90° 50' (as for the Sun) minus the horizontal parallax. The time required for the Sun or Moon to rise or set is about four minutes (except in high latitudes).

The tables have been constructed for the meridian of Greenwich, and for latitudes 52° and 56°. They give Greenwich Mean Time (G.M.T.) throughout the year. To obtain the G.M.T. of the phenomenon as seen from any other latitude and longitude, first interpolate or extrapolate for latitude by the usual rules of proportion. To the time thus found the longitude (expressed in time) is to be *added* if west (as it usually is in Great Britain) or *subtracted* if east. If the longitude is expressed in degrees and minutes of arc, it must be converted to time at the rate of $1° = 4^m$ and $15' = 1^m$.

The G.M.T. of transit of the Moon over the meridian of Greenwich is given: these times are independent of latitude, but must be corrected for longitude. For places in the British Isles it suffices to add the longitude if west, and vice versa. For more remote places a further correction is necessary because of the rapid movement of the Moon relative to the stars. The entire correction is conveniently determined by first finding the west longitude λ of the place. If the place is in west longitude, λ is the ordinary west longitude; if the place is in east longitude λ is the complement to 24^h (or $360°$) of the longitude, and will be greater than 12^h (or $180°$). The correction then consists of two positive portions, namely λ and the fraction $\lambda/24$ (or $\lambda°/360$) multiplied by the difference between consecutive transits. Thus for Sydney, N.S.W., the longitude is 10^h 05^m east, so $\lambda = 13^h$ 55^m and the fraction $\lambda/24$ is $0·58$. The transit on the local date 1976 Oct. 17 is found as follows:

	d	h	m
G.M.T. of transit at Greenwich....Oct.	16	05	50
λ................................		13	55
$0·58 \times (06^h \ 40^m - 05^h \ 50^m)$...........			29
G.M.T. of transit at Sydney........	16	20	14
Corr. to N.S.W. Standard Time....		10	00
Local standard time of transit.......	17	06	14

It is evident of course, that for any given place the quantities λ and the correction to local standard time may be combined permanently, being here 23^h 55^m.

Positions of Mercury are given for every third day, and those of Venus and Mars for every fifth day; they may be interpolated linearly. The column PHASE shows the illuminated percentage of the disk. In the case of the inner planets this approaches 100 at superior conjunction and 0 at inferior conjunction. When the phase is less than 50 the planet is crescent-shaped or horned; for greater phases it is gibbous. In the case of the exterior planet Mars, the phase approaches 100 at conjunction and opposition, and is a minimum at the quadratures.

Since the planets cannot be seen when on the horizon, the actual times of rising and setting are not given; instead, the time when the planet has an apparent altitude of 5° has been tabulated. The phenomenon tabulated is the one that occurs between sunset and sunrise; unimportant exceptions to this rule may occur because changes are not made during a month, except in the case of Mercury. The times given may be interpolated for latitude and corrected for longitude as in the case of the Sun and Moon.

The G.M.T. at which the planet transits the Greenwich meridian is also given. The times of transit are to be corrected to local meridians in the usual way, as already described.

PAGE IV OF EACH MONTH

The G.M.T.'s of Sunrise and Sunset may be used not only for these phenomena, but also for Lighting-up Times, which, under the Road Traffic Act, 1956, are from half an hour after sunset to half an hour before sunrise throughout the year.

The particulars for the four outer planets resemble those for the planets on Page III of each month, except that, under Uranus and Neptune, times when the planet is 10° high instead of 5° high are given; this is because of the inferior brightness of these planets. The polar diameter of Jupiter is about 3″ less than the equatorial diameter, while that of Saturn is about 2″ less. The diameters given for the rings of Saturn are those of the major axis (in the plane of the planet's equator) and the minor axis respectively. The former has a small seasonal change due to the slightly varying distance of the Earth from Saturn, but the latter varies from zero when the Earth passes through the ring plane every 15 years to its maximum opening half-way between these periods. The rings were completely closed on three occasions in 1966 and were open at their widest extent in the middle of 1973.

TIME

From the earliest ages, the natural division of time into recurring periods of day and night has provided the practical time scale for the everyday activities of mankind. Indeed, if any alternative means of time measurement is adopted, it must be capable of adjustment so as to remain in general agreement with the natural time scale defined by the diurnal rotation of the Earth on its axis. Ideally the rotation should be measured against a fixed frame of reference; in practice it must be measured against the background provided by the celestial bodies. If the Sun is chosen as the reference point, we obtain Apparent Solar Time, which is the time indicated by a sundial. It is not a uniform time, but is subject to variations which amount to as much as a quarter of an hour in each direction. Such wide variations cannot be tolerated in a practical time scale, and this has led to the concept of Mean Solar Time in which all the days are exactly the same length and equal to the average length of the Apparent Solar Day.

The positions of the stars in the sky are specified in relation to a fictitious reference point in the sky known as the First Point of Aries (or the Vernal Equinox). It is therefore convenient to adopt this same reference point when considering the rotation of the Earth against the background of the stars. The time scale so obtained is known as Apparent Sidereal Time.

Greenwich Mean Time

The daily rotation of the Earth on its axis causes the Sun and the other heavenly bodies to appear to cross the sky fron East to West. It is convenient to represent this relative motion as if the Sun really performed a daily circuit around a fixed Earth. Noon in Apparent Solar Time may then be defined as the time at which the Sun transits across the observer's meridian. In Mean Solar Time, noon is similarly defined by the meridian transit of a fictitious Mean Sun moving uniformly in the sky with the same average speed as the true Sun. Mean Solar Time observed on the meridian of the transit circle telescope of the Royal Observatory at Greenwich is called Greenwich Mean Time (G.M.T.) The mean solar day is divided into 24 hours and, for astronomical and other scientific purposes, these are numbered 0 to 23, commencing at midnight. Civil time is usually reckoned in two periods of 12 hours, designated a.m. (before noon) and p.m. (after noon).

Universal Time

Before 1925 January 1 G.M.T. was reckoned in 24 hours commencing at noon: since that date it has been reckoned from midnight. In view of the risk of confusion in the use of the designation G.M.T. before and after 1925, the International Astronomical Union recommended in 1928 that astronomers should, for the present, employ the term Universal Time, U.T. (or Welzeit, W.Z.) to denote G.M.T. measured from Greenwich Mean Midnight.

In precision work it has now become necessary to take account of small variations, hitherto negligible, in Universal Time. These arise from small irregularities in the rotation of the Earth. Observed astronomical time is designated U.T.o. Observed time corrected for the effects of the motion of the poles (giving rise to a " wandering " in longitude) is designated U.T.1. There is also a seasonal fluctuation in the rate of rotation of the Earth arising from meteorological causes, often called the annual fluctuation. U.T.1 corrected for this effect is designated U.T.2 and provides a time scale free from short-period fluctuations. It is still subject to small secular and irregular changes.

Apparent Solar Time

As has been mentioned, the time shown by a sundial is called Apparent Solar Time. It differs from Mean Solar Time by an amount known as the Equation of Time, which is the total effect of two causes which make the length of the apparent solar day non-uniform. One cause of variation is that the orbit of the Earth is not a circle, but an ellipse, having the Sun at one focus. As a consequence, the angular speed of the Earth in its orbit is not constant; it is greatest at the beginning of January when the Earth is nearest the Sun. The other cause is due to the obliquity of the ecliptic; the plane of the equator (which is at right-angles to the axis of rotation of the Earth) does not coincide with the ecliptic (the plane defined by the apparent annual motion of the Sun around the celestial sphere) but is inclined to it at an angle of $23° 27'$. As a result, the apparent solar day is shorter than average at the equinoxes and longer at the solstices. From the combined effects of the components due to obliquity and eccentricity, the equation of time reaches its maximum values in February (-14 mins.) and early November ($+16$ mins.). It has a zero value on four dates during the year, and it is only on these dates (approx. April 15, June 14, Sept. 1, and Dec. 25) that a sundial shows Mean Solar Time.

Sidereal Time

A sidereal day is the duration of a complete rotation of the Earth with reference to the First Point of Aries. The term sidereal (or " star ") time is perhaps a little misleading since the time scale so defined is not exactly the same as that which would be defined by successive transits of a selected star, as there is a small progressive motion between the stars and the First Point of Aries due to the precession of the Earth's axis. This makes the length

of the sidereal day shorter than the true period of rotation by $0·008$ seconds. Superimposed on this steady precessional motion are small oscillations called nutation, giving rise to fluctuations in apparent sidereal time amounting to as much as $1·2$ seconds. It is therefore customary to employ Mean Sidereal Time, from which these fluctuations have been removed. The conversion of G.M.T. to Greenwich sidereal time (G.S.T.) may be performed by adding the value of the G.S.T. at 0^h on the day in question (page II of each month) to the G.M.T. converted to sidereal time using the table on p. 146.

Example. To find the G.S.T. at August $8^d 02^h 41^m 11^s$ G.M.T.

				h m s
G.S.T. at 0^h	..	..	..	21 06 31
G.M.T. ..	..	..	..	2 41 11
Acceleration for 2^h	..	..	..	20
,, ,, $41^m 11^s$	..	..	7
Sum $=$ G.S.T.$=$ ..	..	..	..	23 48 09

If the observer is not on the Greenwich meridian then his longitude, measured positively westwards from Greenwich, must be subtracted from the G.S.T. to obtain Local Sidereal Time (L.S.T.). Thus, in the above example, an observer 5^h east of Greenwich, or 19^h west, would find his L.S.T. as $4^h 48^m 09^s$.

Ephemeris Time

In the study of the motions of the Sun, Moon and planets, observations taken over an extended period are used in the preparation of tables giving the apparent position of the body each day. A table of this sort is known as an ephemeris, and may be used in the comparison of current observations with tabulated positions. A detailed examination of the observations made over the past 300 years shows that the Sun, Moon and planets appear to depart from their predicted positions by amounts proportional to their mean motions. The only satisfactory explanation is that the time scale to which the observations were referred was not uniform as had been supposed. Since the time scale was based on the rotation of the Earth, it follows that this rotation is subject to irregularities. The fact that the discrepancies between the observed and ephemeris positions were proportional to the mean motions of the bodies made it possible to secure agreement by substituting a revised time scale and recomputing the ephemeris positions. The time scale which brings the ephemeris into agreement with the observations has been named Ephemeris Time (E.T.).

The new unit of time has been defined in terms of the apparent annual motion of the Sun. Thus the second is now defined in terms of the annual motion of the Earth in its orbit around the Sun ($1/31556925·9747$ of the Tropical Year for 1900 January 0 at 12^h. E.T.) instead of in terms of the diurnal rotation of the Earth on its axis ($1/86$ 400 of the Mean Solar Day). In many branches of scientific work other than astronomy there has been a demand for a unit of time that is invariable, and the second of Ephemeris time was adopted by the Comité International des Poids et Mésures in 1956. The length of the unit has been chosen to provide general agreement with U.T. throughout the 19th and 20th centuries. During 1976 the estimated difference E.T. − U.T. is 46 seconds. The precise determination of E.T. from astronomical observations is a lengthy process, as the accuracy with which a single observation of the Sun can be made is far less than that obtainable in, for instance, a comparison between clocks. It is therefore necessary to average the observations over an extended period. Largely on account of its faster motion, the position of the Moon may be observed with greater accuracy, and a close approximation to Ephemeris Time may be obtained by comparing observations of the Moon with its ephemeris position. Even in this case, however, the requisite standard of accuracy can only be achieved by averaging over a number of years.

Atomic Time

The fundamental standards of time and frequency must be defined in terms of a periodic motion adequately uniform, enduring and susceptible of measurement. This has led in the past to the adoption of standards based on the observed motions in the Solar System. Recent progress has made it possible to consider the use of other natural standards, such as atomic or molecular oscillations. The oscillations so far employed are not in fact continuous periodic motions such as the revolution of the electrons in their orbits around the nuclei. The continuous oscillations are generated in an electrical circuit, the frequency of which is then compared or brought into coincidence with the frequency characteristic of the absorption or emission by the atoms or molecules when they change between two selected energy levels. At the National Physical Laboratory regular comparisons have been made since the middle of 1955 between quartz clocks of high stability and a frequency defined by atoms of caesium. The standard has proved of great value in the precise calibration of frequencies and time intervals: it has also been possible to build up a scale of " atomic time " by using continuously-running quartz clocks calibrated in terms of the caesium frequency standard.

Radio Time Signals

The establishment of a uniform time system by the assessment of the performance of standard clocks in terms of astronomical observations is the work of a national observatory, and standard time is then made generally available by means of radio time signals. In the United Kingdom, the Royal Greenwich Observatory is responsible for the legal standard of time, and controls the " 6-pips " radio signals emitted by the British Broadcasting Corporation. Signals by land line from the Observatory correct the Post Office Speaking Clock, TIM.

For survey and scientific purposes in which the highest accuracy is required, special signals are transmitted from the Post Office Radio Station at Rugby. The International Signals, consisting of a five-minute series of pips, one-tenth of a second long, with the pips at the minutes lengthened for identification, are radiated at 02.54–03.00, 08.54–09.00, 14.54–15.00, 20.54–21.00 from GBR (16

kHz) and associated H.F. transmitters. The seconds pulses superposed on the MSF standard frequency transmissions, which consists of five cycles of a 1,000 c.p.s. tone, are derived from the same master control at the transmitting station, and are radiated for ten minutes in each quarter-hour on $2\frac{1}{2}$, 5, and 10 MHz for 24 hours per day, and continuously on 60 kHz. The carrier frequencies of all the MSF transmissions, and of GBR, are closely controlled, and measured regularly at the National Physical Laboratory in terms of the caesium atomic resonance.

The new Coordinated Universal Time (U.T.C.) system standard frequency emissions and radio time signals are broadcast on MSF, GBR, and by other national transmitters, eg. by WWV and WWVH in the U.S.A. in conformity with the International Atomic Time Scale in which the time intervals between pips correspond exactly to the seconds defined as follows: " The second is the duration of 9 192 631 770 periods of the radiation corresponding to the transition between the 2 hyperfine levels of the ground state of the caesium 133 atom."

As the rate of rotation of the Earth is variable the time signals will be adjusted by the introduction of a leap second when necessary in order that UTC shall not depart from UT by more than $0^s.9$. For convenience it has been decided to introduce leap seconds, when necessary, on the last second of a month preferably on 31 Dec. and/or 30 June. In the case of a positive leap second $23^h 59^m 60^s$ will be followed one second later by $0^h 00^m 00^s$ of the first day of the month. In the case of a negative leap second (required if the Earth were to have a sudden change of rate and begin to gain relative to UTC) $23^h 59^m 58^s$ will be followed one second later by $0^h 00^m 00^s$ of the first day of the month.

From 1972 Jan. 1 the six pips on the BBC have consisted of 5 short pips from second 55 to second 59 followed by one lengthened pip, the start of which indicates the exact minute.

SUMMER TIME

In the United Kingdom, Summer Time, one hour in advance of G.M.T. will be kept between 02^h G.M.T. on the day following the third Saturday in March and 02^h G.M.T. on the day following the fourth Saturday in October. Thus, in 1976, Summer Time will be in force between March 21 and October 24.

Variations from the standard time of some countries occurs during part of the year: they are decided annually and are usually referred to as Summer Time or Daylight Saving Time. These variations occur in:

British Commonwealth.—Parts of Australia; Bahamas; Canada; Channel Islands; Hong Kong; New Zealand.

Foreign Countries.—Albania; Argentina; Brazil; Chile; parts of China; Costa Rica; Cuba; Egypt; Formosa; Iceland; Italy; Macau; Malta; Morocco; Norway; Pescadores Is.; Poland; Sicily; Sudan; parts of U.S.A.; Syria; Tunisia; Turkey.

In the Dominican Republic, the Irish Republic, and Paraguay, the variation occurs in winter and is called Winter Time.

STANDARD TIME

In the year 1880 it was enacted by statute that the word " time ", when it occurred in any legal document relating to Great Britain, was to be interpreted, unless otherwise specifically stated, as the Mean Time of the Greenwich meridian.★ Since the year 1883 the system of Standard Time by Zones has been gradually accepted, and now almost throughout the world a Standard Time which differs from that of Greenwich by an integral number of hours, either fast or slow, is used.

The large territories of the United States, Canada and U.S.S.R. are divided into zones approximately $7\frac{1}{2}°$ on either side of central meridians. The important ones are given below; there are in addition zones from 5 to 13 hours fast in the U.S.S.R. centred at 60°E. to 180°E.

Fast on Greenwich Time

12 hrs. F...Fiji, Gilbert and Ellice Is., New Zealand, Marshall Is., Caroline Is. (east of 160° E.), New Hebrides.

$11\frac{1}{2}$,, F...Norfolk I., Nauru I.

11 ,, F...New Caledonia, Santa Cruz and Solomon Is., Truk, Ponape, Sakhalin.

10 ,, F...Victoria, N.S.W. (except Broken Hill Area), Queensland, Tasmania, British New Guinea, Admiralty Islds., Caroline Islds. (west of 160° E.), Australian Capital Territory, Mariana Islds.

$9\frac{1}{2}$,, F...South Australia, Northern Territory of Australia, N.S.W. (Broken Hill Area).

9 ,, F...Japan, Schouten Islds., Kurile Islds., Manchuria, Korea, West Irian (Indonesia).

$8\frac{1}{2}$,, F...Molucca Islds.

8 ,, F...China (coast), Hong Kong, Philippine Is., Macau, Timor, Western Australia, Sulawesi (Celebes), Kalimantan†, Formosa, Pescadores Islds., Malaysia, Vietnam (south).

$7\frac{1}{2}$,, F...Singapore.

7 ,, F...Sumatra, Java, Christmas I. (Indian Ocean), Thailand, Khmer Republic, Laos, Vietnam (north).

$6\frac{1}{2}$,, F...Burma, Cocos-Keeling Islds.

6 ,, F...Bangladesh.

$5\frac{1}{2}$,, F...India, Sri Lanka, Laccadive Islds., Andaman and Nicobar Islds.

5 ,, F...Chagos Archipelago, Pakistan.

4 ,, F...Mauritius, Seychelles, Réunion, U.S.S.R., 40° E. to 52° 30′ E.

$3\frac{1}{2}$,, F...Iran.

3 ,, F...U.S.S.R. west of 40° E., Iraq, Ethiopia, Yemen (Dem. Repub.), Socotra I., Somali Republic, Comoro Islds., Madagascar, Uganda, Kenya, Tanzania.

2 ,, F...Turkey, Greece, Bulgaria, Rumania, Finland, Israel, Jordan, U.A.R., Syria, Cyprus, Rhodesia, Malawi,

E. European   South Africa, Mozambique, Sudan, Burundi, Rwanda, Crete, Lebanon, Libya, Zambia, Botswana, Lesotho.

1 hr. F...Sweden, Norway, Denmark, Netherlands, Belgium, Germany, France, Luxemburg, Spain, Monaco, Balearic Islds., Poland, Austria.

Central-   Hungary, Switzerland, Italy, Czecho-
European   slovakia, Yugoslavia, Albania, Tunisia, Nigeria, Malta, Sicily, Central African Republic, Cameroon Republic, Zaire, Angola, Spitsbergen, Algeria, Dahomey, Corsica, Sardinia, Portugal, Niger, Irish Republic, Gibraltar.

Greenwich   The United Kingdom, Faroe, Chan-
Time   nel Is., Algeria, Morocco, Iceland, Mauritania, Sierra Leone, Ivory Coast, Ifni, Ghana, Principe I., St. Helena, Gambia, Canary Is., Ascension I., Tangier, São Tomé, Rio de Oro, Madeira, Mali, Senegal, Liberia.

Slow on Greenwich time

1 hr. S...Azores, Cape Verde Is., Guinea Bissau.

2 hrs. S...Fernando Noronha I., Scoresby Sound, South Georgia.

3 ,, S...Greenland (excluding Scoresby Sound and Thule), Eastern Brazil, Argentina, Uruguay, French Guiana.

$3\frac{1}{2}$,, S...Newfoundland, Dutch Guiana.

$3\frac{3}{4}$,, S...Guyana.

4 ,, S...Canada east of 68° W., Greenland (Thule Area), Puerto Rico, Lesser
Atlantic.   Antilles, Central Brazil, Falkland Islds., Paraguay, Bermuda, Bolivia, Chile, Curaçao I., Venezuela, Labrador.

5 hrs. S...Canada from 68° W. to 85° W. (north) or 90° W. (south), Eastern States of
Eastern.   U.S.A., Jamaica, Bahama Islds., Haiti, Peru, Panama, W. Brazil, Colombia, Cayman Is., Ecuador, Dominican Republic, Cuba, Nicaragua.

6 hrs. S...Central parts of U.S.A., Canada from 85° W. to 102°W., Costa Rica,
Central.   Salvador, Honduras, part of Mexico, Guatemala.

7 hrs. S...Canada from 102° W. to 120° W.,
Mountain.   Mountain States of U.S.A., part of Mexico.

8 hrs. S...Canada west of 120° W., Alaska,
Pacific.   (south-east coast), Western States of U.S.A., part of Mexico, Yukon (east of 138° W.).

9 hrs. S...Alaska 137° W. to 141° W., Yukon (west of 138° W.).

10 ,, S...Alaska from 141° W. to 161° W., Low Archipelago, Austral and Society Islds., Hawaii, Fanning I., Christmas Islds. (Pacific Ocean).

11 ,, S...Aleutian Islds., Alaska (west coast), Samoa, Midway Islds.

In the Tonga Islands the time $13h$ fast and in Chatham Is. $12h$ $45m$ fast on Greenwich is used, as the Date line is to the East of them.

THE DATE OR CALENDAR LINE

The line where the change of date occurs is a modification of the 180th meridian, and is drawn so as to include islands of any one group on the same side of the line, or for political reasons. It is indicated by joining up the following nine points:

Lat.	Long.	Lat.	Long.	Lat.	Long.
60° S.	180°	15° S.	$172\frac{1}{2}$° W.	53° N.	170° E.
51° S.	180°	5° S.	180°	$65\frac{1}{2}$° N.	160° W.
45° S.	$172\frac{1}{2}$° W.	48° N.	180°	75° N.	180°

★ Summer Time is the "legal" time during the period in which its use is ordained.   † Formerly Indonesian Borneo.

RISING AND SETTING TIMES

Table 1. Hour Angle

Dec.	Latitude and Declination of Opposite Signs						0°	Latitude and Declination of Same Signs					
	50°	45°	40°	30°	20°	10°	0°	10°	20°	30°	40°	45°	50°
°	h m	h m	h m	h m	h m	h m	h m	h m	h m	h m	h m	h m	h m
0	6 00	6 00	6 00	6 00	6 00	6 00	6 00	6 00	6 00	6 00	6 00	6 00	6 00
1	5 55	5 56	5 57	5 58	5 59	5 59	6 00	6 01	6 01	6 02	6 03	6 04	6 05
2	5 50	5 52	5 53	5 55	5 57	5 58	6 00	6 02	6 03	6 05	6 07	6 08	6 10
3	5 45	5 48	5 50	5 53	5 56	5 58	6 00	6 02	6 04	6 07	6 10	6 12	6 15
4	5 40	5 44	5 46	5 51	5 54	5 57	6 00	6 03	6 06	6 09	6 14	6 16	6 20
5	5 30	5 40	5 43	5 48	5 52	5 56	6 00	6 04	6 08	6 12	6 17	6 20	6 24
6	5 31	5 36	5 39	5 46	5 51	5 56	6 00	6 04	6 09	6 14	6 21	6 24	6 29
7	5 26	5 32	5 36	5 44	5 50	5 55	6 00	6 05	6 10	6 16	6 24	6 28	6 34
8	5 21	5 27	5 33	5 41	5 48	5 54	6 00	6 06	6 12	6 19	6 27	6 33	6 39
9	5 16	5 23	5 29	5 39	5 47	5 53	6 00	6 07	6 13	6 21	6 31	6 37	6 44
10	5 11	5 19	5 26	5 37	5 45	5 53	6 00	6 07	6 15	6 23	6 34	6 41	6 49
11	5 06	5 15	5 22	5 34	5 44	5 52	6 00	6 08	6 16	6 26	6 38	6 45	6 54
12	5 01	5 11	5 19	5 32	5 42	5 51	6 00	6 09	6 18	6 28	6 41	6 49	6 59
13	4 56	5 06	5 15	5 29	5 40	5 51	6 00	6 09	6 20	6 31	6 45	6 54	7 04
14	4 51	5 02	5 12	5 27	5 39	5 50	6 00	6 10	6 21	6 33	6 48	6 58	7 09
15	4 46	4 58	5 08	5 24	5 38	5 49	6 00	6 11	6 22	6 36	6 52	7 02	7 14
16	4 40	4 53	5 04	5 22	5 36	5 48	6 00	6 12	6 24	6 38	6 56	7 07	7 20
17	4 35	4 49	5 00	5 19	5 35	5 48	6 00	6 12	6 25	6 41	7 00	7 11	7 25
18	4 29	4 44	4 57	5 17	5 33	5 47	6 00	6 13	6 27	6 43	7 03	7 16	7 31
19	4 23	4 39	4 53	5 14	5 31	5 46	6 00	6 14	6 29	6 46	7 07	7 21	7 37
20	4 17	4 35	4 49	5 11	5 30	5 45	6 00	6 15	6 30	6 49	7 11	7 25	7 43
21	4 11	4 30	4 44	5 09	5 28	5 44	6 00	6 16	6 32	6 51	7 16	7 30	7 49
22	4 04	4 25	4 40	5 06	5 26	5 44	6 00	6 16	6 34	6 54	7 20	7 35	7 56
23	3 58	4 19	4 36	5 03	5 24	5 43	6 00	6 17	6 36	6 57	7 24	7 41	8 02
24	3 52	4 14	4 32	5 00	5 23	5 42	6 00	6 18	6 37	7 00	7 28	7 46	8 08
25	3 45	4 09	4 28	4 58	5 21	5 41	6 00	6 19	6 39	7 02	7 32	7 51	8 15
26	3 38	4 03	4 24	4 55	5 19	5 40	6 00	6 20	6 41	7 05	7 36	7 57	8 22
27	3 30	3 57	4 19	4 52	5 17	5 39	6 00	6 21	6 43	7 08	7 41	8 03	8 30
28	3 23	3 51	4 14	4 48	5 15	5 38	6 00	6 22	6 45	7 12	7 46	8 09	8 37
29	3 15	3 45	4 09	4 45	5 14	5 38	6 00	6 22	6 46	7 15	7 51	8 15	8 45

SUNRISE AND SUNSET

The local mean time of sunrise or sunset (as defined on page 138) may be found by determining the appropriate hour angle from the table above and applying it to the time of transit given in the ephemeris for each month. The hour angle is negative for sunrise and positive for sunset. A small correction to the hour angle, which always has the effect of increasing it numerically, is necessary to allow for the Sun's semi-diameter (16′) and for refraction (34′). This correction may be obtained from Table 2. The resulting local mean time may be converted into the standard time of the country by taking the difference between the longitude of the standard meridian of the country and that of the place, and adding it to the local mean time if the place is west of the standard meridian, and subtracting it if the place is east of the standard meridian.

Example.—Required the N.Z. Mean Time (12^h fast on G.M.T.) of sunset on May 24 at Auckland. The latitude is 36° 50′ south (or minus) and the longitude 11^h 39^m east. Taking the declination as +20°·7, we find

	h m
Tabular entry for 30° Lat. and Dec. 20°, opposite signs	+ 5 11
Proportional part for 6° 5′ of Lat	− 15
Proportional part for 0°·7 of Dec	− 3
Correction (Table 2)	+ 6
Hour angle	4 59
Sun transits	11 57
Longitudinal correction	+ 21
N.Z. Mean Time	17 17

Table 2. Correction for Refraction and Semi-Diameter

Latitude	Declination			
	0°	10°	20°	29°
°	m	m	m	m
0	4	4	4	5
20	4	4	5	5
30	5	5	5	6
40	5	6	6	7
50	6	6	7	9

MOONRISE AND MOONSET

It is possible to calculate the times of moonrise and moonset using Table 1 though the method is more complicated because the apparent motion of the Moon is much more rapid than that of the Sun.

Table 3. Longitude Correction

X A	40^m	45^m	50^m	55^m	60^m	65^m	70^m
h	m	m	m	m	m	m	m
1	2	2	2	2	3	3	3
2	3	4	4	5	5	5	6
3	5	6	6	7	8	8	9
4	7	8	8	9	10	11	12
5	8	9	10	11	13	14	15
6	10	11	13	14	15	16	18
7	12	13	15	16	18	19	20
8	13	15	17	18	20	22	23
9	15	17	19	21	23	24	26
10	17	19	21	23	25	27	29
11	18	21	23	25	28	30	32
12	20	23	25	28	30	33	35
13	22	24	27	30	33	35	38
14	23	26	29	32	35	38	41
15	25	28	31	34	38	41	44
16	27	30	33	37	40	43	47
17	28	32	35	39	43	46	50
18	30	34	38	41	45	49	53
19	32	36	40	44	48	51	55
20	33	38	42	46	50	54	58
21	35	39	44	48	53	57	61
22	37	41	46	50	55	60	64
23	38	43	48	53	58	62	67
24	40	45	50	55	60	65	70

Notation

φ = latitude of observer
λ = longitude of observer (measured positively towards the west)
T_{-1} = time of transit of Moon on previous day
T_0 = time of transit of Moon on day in question
T_1 = time of transit of Moon on following day
δ_0 = approximate declination of Moon
δ_R = declination of Moon at moonrise
δ_S = declination of Moon at moonset
h_0 = approximate hour angle of Moon
h_R = hour angle of Moon at moonrise
h_S = hour angle of moon at moonset
t_R = time of moonrise
t_S = time of moonset

The parallax of the Moon, about 57′, is near to the sum of the semi-diameter and refraction but has the opposite effect on these times. It is thus convenient to neglect all three quantities in the method outlined below.

METHOD

1. With arguments φ, δ_0 enter Table 1 on p. 144 to determine h_0 where h_0 is negative for moonrise and positive for moonset.

2. Form approximate times from
$$t_R = T_0 + \lambda + h_0$$
$$t_S = T_0 + \lambda + h_0$$

3. Determine δ_R, δ_S for times t_R, t_S respectively.

4. Re-enter Table 1 on p. 144 with—
   (a) arguments φ, δ_R to determine h_R
   (b) arguments φ, δ_S to determine h_S

5. Form $t_R = T_0 + \lambda + h_R + AX$
   $t_S = T_0 + \lambda + h_S + AX$

   where $A = (\lambda + h)$

   and $\begin{array}{l} X = (T_0 - T_{-1}) \quad \text{if } (\lambda + h) \text{ is negative} \\ X = (T_1 - T_0) \quad \text{if } (\lambda + h) \text{ is positive} \end{array}$

AX is the respondent in Table 3.

Example.—To find the times of moonrise and moonset at Vancouver ($\varphi = +49°$, $\lambda = +8^h 12^m$) on 1976 October 10. The starting data (from p. 128) are

$$\begin{array}{ll} & \text{h} \quad \text{m} \\ T_{-1} = & 0 \quad 19 \\ T_0 = & 1 \quad 03 \\ T_1 = & 1 \quad 49 \\ \delta = & +14° \end{array}$$

1. $h_0 = \quad 7^h 07^m$
2. Approximate values
$$\begin{aligned} t_R &= 10^d 01^h 03^m + 8^h 12^m + (-7^h 07^m) \\ &= 10^d 02^h 08^m \\ t_S &= 10^d 01^h 03^m + 8^h 12^m + (+7^h 07^m) \\ &= 10^d 16^h 22^m \\ \delta_R &= +13°·6 \\ \delta_S &= +15°·1 \\ h_R &= -7^h 05^m \\ h_S &= +7^h 12^m \\ t_R &= 10^d 01^h 03^m + 8^h 12^m - 7^h 05^m + 2^m \\ &= 10^d 02^h 12^m \\ t_S &= 10^d 01^h 03^m + 8^h 12^m + 7^h 12^m + 29^m \\ &= 10^d 16^h 56^m \end{aligned}$$

To get the L.M.T. of the phenomenon the longitude is subtracted from the G.M.T. thus
Moonrise $= 10^d 02^h 12^m - 8^h 12^m = 9^d 18^h 00^m$
Moonset $= 10^d 16^h 56^m - 8^h 12^m = 10^d 08^h 44^m$

ASTRONOMICAL CONSTANTS

Solar Parallax	8″·794	North Galactic Pole } R.A. $12^h 49^m$. (1950·0).	
Precession for the year 1976	50″·273	(I.A.U. *Standard*). } Dec. 27°·4 N.	
„ in R.A.	$3^s·074$	Solar Apex	R.A. $18^h 06^m$ Dec. +30°
„ in Declination	20″·040	Length of Year...Tropical	365·24220
Constant of Nutation	9″·21	(*In Mean*	Sidereal	365·25636
Constant of Aberration	20″·496	*Solar Days*	Anomalistic	365·25964
Mean Obliquity of Ecliptic (1976)	23° 26′ 33″		(*Perihelion to Perihelion*)
Moon's Equatorial Hor. Parallax	57′ 02″·70		Eclipse	346·6200
Velocity of Light in vacu *per sec.*	299792·5 km.			d h m s
Solar motion *per sec.*	20·0 km.	Length of Month New Moon to New	29 12 44 02·9
Equatorial radius of the Earth	6378·160 km.	(*Mean Values*)	Sidereal	27 07 43 11·5
Polar radius of the Earth	6356·775 km.		Anomalistic	27 13 18 33·2
			(*Perigee to Perigee*)

MEAN AND SIDEREAL TIME

Acceleration

h	m s	h	m s	m s	s
1	0 10	13	2 08	0 00	0
2	0 20	14	2 18	3 02	1
3	0 30	15	2 28	9 07	2
4	0 39	16	2 38	15 13	3
5	0 49	17	2 48	21 18	4
6	0 59	18	2 57	27 23	5
7	1 09	19	3 07	33 28	6
8	1 19	20	3 17	39 34	7
9	1 29	21	3 27	45 39	8
10	1 39	22	3 37	51 44	9
11	1 48	23	3 47	57 49	10
12	1 58	24	3 57	60 00	

Retardation

h	m s	h	m s	m s	s
1	0 10	13	2 08	0 00	0
2	0 20	14	2 18	3 03	1
3	0 29	15	2 27	9 09	2
4	0 39	16	2 37	15 15	3
5	0 49	17	2 47	21 21	4
6	0 59	18	2 57	27 28	5
7	1 09	19	3 07	33 34	6
8	1 19	20	3 17	39 40	7
9	1 28	21	3 26	45 46	8
10	1 38	22	3 36	51 53	9
11	1 48	23	3 46	57 59	10
12	1 58	24	3 56	60 00	

MEAN REFRACTION

Alt. Ref.		Alt. Ref.	
° '		° '	
1 20	21	4 30	10
1 30	20	5 06	9
1 41	19	5 50	8
1 52	18	6 44	7
2 05	17	7 54	6
2 19	16	9 27	5
2 35	15	11 39	4
2 52	14	15 00	3
3 12	13	20 42	2
3 34	12	26 17	1
4 00	11	90 00	0
4 30			

The length of a sidereal day in mean time is $23^h56^m04^s{\cdot}09$. Hence 1^h M.T. $= 1^h+9^s{\cdot}86$ S.T. and 1^h S.T. $= 1^h-9^s{\cdot}83$ M.T.

To convert an interval of mean time to the corresponding interval of sidereal time, enter the acceleration table with the given mean time (taking the hours and the minutes and seconds separately) and add the acceleration obtained for the given mean time. To convert an interval of sidereal time to the corresponding interval of mean time, take out the retardation for the given sidereal time and subtract.

The columns for the minutes and seconds of the argument are in the form known as Critical Tables. To use these tables, find in the appropriate left-hand column the two entries between which the given number of minutes and seconds lies; the quantity in the right-hand column between these two entries is the required acceleration or retardation. Thus the acceleration for 11^m26^s (which lies between the entries 9^m07^s and 15^m13^s) is 2^s. If the given number of minutes and seconds is a tabular entry, the required acceleration or retardation is the entry in the right-hand column *above* the given tabular entry; e.g. the retardation for 45^m46^s is 7^s.

Example.—Convert $14^h27^m35^s$ from S.T. to M.T.

	h	m	s
Given S.T.	14	27	35
Retardation for 14^h		2	18
Retardation for 27^m35^s			5
Corresponding M.T.	14	25	12

For further explanation, see p. 141.
The refraction table is also in the form of a critical table.

THE SUMMER TIME ACTS

In 1916 an Act ordained that during a defined period of that year the legal time for general purposes in Great Britain should be one hour in advance of Greenwich Mean Time. The practice was stabilized (until the war) by the *Summer Time Acts*, 1922 to 1925, which enacted that "For the purposes of this Act, the period of summer time shall be taken to be the period beginning at two o'clock, Greenwich Mean Time, in the morning of the day next following the third Saturday in April, or, if that day is Easter Day, the day next following the second Saturday in April and ending at two o'clock, Greenwich Mean Time, in the morning of the day next following the first Saturday in October."

During the Second World War the duration of Summer Time was extended and in the years 1941–45 and in 1947, Double Summer Time (2 hrs. in advance of Greenwich Mean Time) was in force. Summer Time was extended in each year from 1948 to 1952 and again in 1961–1964, by Order in Council.

The duration of Summer Time during the last few years is given in the following table.

1953 Apr. 19—Oct. 4	1961 Mar. 26—Oct. 29
1954 Apr. 11—Oct. 3	1962 Mar. 25—Oct. 28
1955 Apr. 17—Oct. 2	1963 Mar. 31—Oct. 27
1956 Apr. 22—Oct. 7	1964 Mar. 22—Oct. 25
1957 Apr. 14—Oct. 6	1965 Mar. 21—Oct. 2
1958 Apr. 20—Oct. 5	1966 Mar. 20—Oct. 2
1959 Apr. 19—Oct. 4	1967 Mar. 19—Oct. 29
1960 Apr. 10—Oct. 2	1968 Feb. 18—Oct. 27
1972 Mar. 19—Oct. 29	1973 Mar. 18—Oct. 28
1974 Mar. 17—Oct. 27	1975 Mar. 16—Oct. 26

(British Standard Time, also one hour ahead of G.M.T., was kept between 1968 Oct. 27–1971 Oct. 31.) In 1976 Summer Time will be in force from March 21 to October 24.

ASTRONOMERS ROYAL

John Flamsteed, first Astronomer Royal . 1675–1719	Sir George Biddell Airy 1835–1881
Edmund Halley 1720–1742	Sir William Henry Mahoney Christie ... 1881–1910
James Bradley 1742–1762	Sir Frank Watson Dyson 1910–1933
Nathaniel Bliss 1762–1762	Sir Harold Spencer Jones 1933–1955
Nevil Maskelyne 1765–1811	Sir Richard van der Riet Woolley 1955–1971
John Pond 1811–1835	Sir Martin Ryle 1972–

G.M.T.	Sat.	Phen.
d h m		

January

d	h	m		
2	21	32	III	Sh.I.
2	23	53	III	Sh.E.
4	21	05	II	Ec.D.
4	23	45	II	Ec.R.
5	20	58	I	Sh.I.
5	23	09	I	Sh.E.
6	18	29	II	Sh.E.
6	20	26	I	Ec.R.
7	17	38	I	Sh.E.
12	22	54	I	Sh.I.
13	18	02	III	Ec.R.
13	18	33	II	Sh.I.
13	21	05	II	Sh.E.
13	22	21	I	Ec.R.
14	17	23	I	Sh.I.
14	19	34	I	Sh.E.
20	19	42	III	Ec.D.
20	21	09	II	Sh.I.
20	22	03	III	Ec.R.
20	23	41	II	Sh.E.
21	19	19	I	Sh.I.
21	21	30	I	Sh.E.
22	18	22	II	Ec.R.
22	18	45	I	Sh.E.
28	21	16	I	Sh.I.
29	20	41	I	Ec.R.
29	21	01	II	Ec.R.
30	17	55	I	Sh.E.

February

d	h	m		
6	17	41	I	Sh.I.
6	19	51	I	Sh.E.
7	17	47	III	Sh.I.
7	18	11	II	Sh.E.
7	20	05	III	Sh.E.
13	19	37	I	Sh.E.
13	21	47	I	Sh.E.
14	18	15	II	Sh.I.
14	19	00	I	Ec.R.
14	20	47	II	Sh.E.
14	21	49	III	Sh.I.
20	21	33	I	Sh.I.
21	20	51	II	Sh.I.
21	20	55	I	Sh.E.
22	18	12	I	Sh.E.
23	18	18	II	Ec.R.
25	18	11	III	Ec.R.
29	20	08	I	Sh.E.

March

d	h	m		
1	20	57	II	Ec.R.
3	19	56	III	Ec.D.
7	19	53	I	Sh.I.
8	19	14	I	Ec.R.
15	21	10	I	Ec.R.
16	18	28	I	Sh.E.
17	20	30	II	Sh.E.
21	20	16	III	Ec.R.
23	20	24	I	Sh.E.

March

d	h	m		
24	20	33	II	Sh.I.
30	20	09	I	Sh.I.
31	19	28	I	Ec.R.

September

d	h	m		
6	03	01	I	Sh.I.
6	03	16	II	Ec.D.
6	04	25	III	Ec.D.
6	05	08	I	Sh.E.
7	00	13	I	Ec.D.
7	21	55	II	Sh.I.
7	23	37	I	Sh.E.
8	00	29	II	Sh.E.
13	04	54	I	Sh.I.
14	02	07	I	Ec.D.
14	23	23	I	Sh.I.
15	00	32	II	Sh.E.
15	01	30	I	Sh.E.
15	03	06	II	Sh.E.
16	21	37	II	Ec.R.
16	22	20	III	Sh.I.
17	00	29	III	Sh.E.
21	04	01	I	Ec.D.
22	01	16	I	Sh.I.
22	03	10	II	Sh.I.
22	03	24	I	Sh.E.
22	22	30	I	Ec.D.
23	21	41	II	Sh.I.
23	21	52	I	Sh.E.
24	02	20	III	Sh.I.
24	04	29	III	Sh.I.
29	03	10	I	Sh.I.
29	05	18	I	Sh.E.
30	00	24	I	Ec.D.
30	21	38	I	Sh.I.
30	23	46	I	Sh.E.

October

d	h	m		
1	00	15	II	Ec.D.
2	21	39	II	Sh.E.
4	20	25	III	Ec.D.
4	22	35	III	Ec.R.
6	05	03	I	Sh.I.
7	02	19	I	Ec.D.
7	23	31	I	Sh.E.
8	01	40	I	Sh.E.
8	02	49	II	Ec.D.
8	20	47	I	Ec.D.
9	20	08	I	Sh.E.
9	21	42	II	Sh.I.
10	00	16	II	Sh.E.
12	00	26	III	Ec.D.
12	02	36	III	Ec.R.
14	04	13	I	Ec.D.
15	01	25	I	Sh.I.
15	03	34	I	Sh.E.
15	05	24	II	Ec.D.
15	22	42	I	Ec.D.
16	19	54	I	Sh.I.

October

d	h	m		
16	22	02	I	Sh.E.
17	00	19	II	Sh.I.
17	02	53	II	Sh.E.
19	04	27	III	Ec.D.
21	06	08	I	Ec.D.
22	03	19	I	Sh.I.
22	05	28	I	Sh.E.
22	20	31	III	Sh.E.
23	00	36	I	Ec.D.
23	21	47	I	Sh.I.
23	23	56	I	Sh.E.
24	02	56	II	Ec.D.
24	05	30	II	Sh.E.
24	19	05	I	Ec.D.
25	21	16	II	Ec.D.
29	05	13	I	Sh.I.
29	22	20	III	Sh.E.
30	00	31	III	Sh.E.
30	02	31	I	Ec.D.
30	23	41	I	Sh.I.
31	01	51	I	Sh.E.
31	05	33	II	Sh.I.
31	21	00	I	Ec.D.

November

d	h	m		
1	18	10	I	Sh.I.
1	20	19	I	Sh.E.
1	23	51	II	Ec.D.
3	18	52	II	Sh.I.
3	21	26	II	Sh.E.
6	02	20	III	Sh.I.
6	04	26	I	Ec.D.
6	04	32	III	Sh.E.
7	01	35	I	Sh.I.
7	03	45	I	Sh.E.
7	22	55	I	Ec.D.
8	20	04	I	Sh.I.
8	22	13	I	Sh.E.
9	02	26	II	Ec.D.
9	17	23	I	Ec.D.
10	21	29	II	Sh.I.
11	00	03	II	Sh.E.
13	06	21	I	Ec.D.
13	06	21	III	Sh.I.
14	03	30	I	Sh.I.
14	05	39	I	Sh.E.
15	00	49	I	Ec.D.
15	21	58	I	Sh.I.
16	00	08	I	Sh.E.
16	05	01	II	Ec.D.
16	19	18	I	Ec.D.
16	20	29	III	Ec.D.
16	22	41	III	Ec.R.
17	18	37	I	Sh.E.
18	00	06	II	Sh.I.
18	02	40	II	Sh.E.
19	00	51	II	Ec.R.
21	05	24	I	Sh.I.
22	04	55	I	Ec.R.

November

d	h	m		
22	23	53	I	Sh.I.
23	02	03	I	Sh.E.
23	23	24	I	Ec.R.
24	02	42	III	Ec.R.
24	18	22	I	Sh.I.
24	20	31	I	Sh.E.
25	02	43	II	Sh.I.
25	05	16	II	Sh.E.
25	17	52	I	Ec.R.
26	23	27	II	Ec.R.
28	18	35	II	Sh.E.
30	01	48	I	Sh.I.
30	03	58	I	Sh.E.

December

d	h	m		
1	01	19	I	Ec.R.
1	20	16	I	Sh.I.
1	22	26	I	Sh.E.
2	19	47	I	Ec.R.
3	16	55	I	Sh.I.
4	02	03	II	Ec.R.
4	18	24	III	Sh.I.
4	20	37	III	Sh.E.
5	18	39	II	Sh.I.
5	21	11	II	Sh.E.
7	03	43	I	Sh.I.
8	03	14	I	Ec.R.
8	22	11	I	Sh.I.
9	00	21	I	Sh.E.
9	21	43	I	Ec.R.
10	18	50	I	Sh.I.
11	22	25	III	Sh.I.
12	00	38	III	Sh.E.
12	21	16	I	Sh.I.
12	23	48	II	Sh.E.
14	17	58	II	Ec.R.
16	00	06	I	Sh.I.
16	02	16	I	Sh.E.
16	23	38	I	Ec.R.
17	18	35	I	Sh.I.
17	20	45	I	Sh.E.
18	18	07	I	Ec.R.
19	02	26	III	Sh.I.
19	23	53	II	Sh.I.
20	02	25	II	Sh.E.
21	20	35	I	Ec.R.
22	18	49	III	Ec.R.
23	02	02	I	Sh.I.
24	01	43	I	Ec.R.
24	20	30	I	Sh.I.
24	22	40	I	Sh.E.
25	20	02	I	Ec.R.
26	17	09	I	Sh.E.
27	02	30	II	Sh.I.
28	23	13	II	Ec.R.
29	20	36	III	Ec.D.
29	22	51	III	Ec.R.
30	18	20	II	Sh.I.
31	22	26	I	Sh.I.

Jupiter's satellites transit across the disk from east to west, and pass behind the disk from west to east. The shadows that they cast also transit across the disk. With the exception at times of Satellite IV, the satellites also pass through the shadow of the planet, i.e. they are eclipsed. Just before opposition the satellite disappears in the shadow to the west of the planet, and reappears from occultation on the east limb. Immediately after opposition the satellite is occulted at the west limb, and reappears from eclipse to the east of the planet. At times approximately two to four months before and after opposition, both phases of eclipses of Satellite III may be seen. When Satellite IV is eclipsed, both phases may be seen.

The list of phenomena gives most of the eclipses and shadow transits visible in the British Isles under favourable conditions.

Ec. = Eclipse	R = Reappearance
Sh. = Shadow transit	I = Ingress
D = Disappearance	E = Egress

The times given in these predictions are strictly for the centre of the satellite. Observers will appreciate that as the satellite is of considerable size the immersion and emersion phases are not instantaneous. Even when the satellite enters or leaves the shadow along a radius of the shadow the phase can last for several minutes. With satellite IV grazing phenomena can occur so that the light from the satellite may fade and brighten again without a complete eclipse taking place.

CELESTIAL PHENOMENA FOR OBSERVATION IN 1976

ECLIPSES, 1976

There will be three eclipses during 1976, two of the Sun and one of the Moon. *Penumbral eclipses are not mentioned in this section as they are difficult to observe.*

1. An annular eclipse of the Sun on April 29, visible as a partial eclipse in the north-eastern part of South America, the north-eastern coast of North America, the Atlantic Ocean, Greenland, Europe (including the British Isles), Africa and Asia. The eclipse begins at $07^h 22^m$ and ends at $13^h 25^m$. The annular phase begins in the Atlantic Ocean and crosses north-western Africa, the Mediterranean Sea, Turkey, U.S.S.R. and ends in central China. As seen from London the partial eclipse begins at $09^h 01^m$ and ends at $11^h 29^m$; the middle of the eclipse occurs at $10^h 13^m$ when 41% of the Sun is obscured. The corresponding times for Edinburgh are $09^h 13^m$ to $11^h 21^m$; $10^h 16^m$ and 31%.

2. A partial eclipse of the Moon on May 13, visible from New Zealand, Australia, the Indian Ocean, Asia (except the north-east), Europe (except the north-west), Africa, the South Atlantic Ocean, Antarctica and the extreme north-eastern part of South America. The eclipse begins at $19^h 16^m$ and ends at $20^h 33^m$. At the time of maximum eclipse 0·13 of the Moon's diameter is obscured.

3. A total eclipse of the Sun on October 23. The path of totality extends from central Africa across the Indian Ocean and the southern coast of Australia, to the Tasman Sea. The partial phase is visible from Africa, the Indian Ocean, a small part of southern Asia, Indonesia, New Guinea, Australia New Zealand and Antarctica. The eclipse begins at $02^h 39^m$ and ends at $07^h 47^m$; the total phase begins at $03^h 36^m$ and ends at $06^h 50^m$. The maximum duration of totality is $4^m 37^s$.

OCCULTATION BY MARS

On April 8 Mars occults the 3^m star epsilon Geminorum, visible from the Pacific Ocean and western N. America in daylight and from eastern N. America, northern S. America, part of western Europe and north-west Africa, in darkness. The northern limit of the occultation crosses the British Isles and should provide an extremely interesting spectacle for observers, although the planet will only be about 10° above the horizon. If the prediction is absolutely accurate the northern limit can be drawn on a map by a straight line passing through Dublin and Cardiff and extended at either end if required. However a correction to the ephemeris of Mars of only $0''·1$ would move the track in latitude by about 2°·4 so that the actual limit could easily occur several hundred kilometres away from this predicted limit. From the British Isles the mid-time of the occultation will be $01^h 00^m$ while the duration will be less than 1 minute.

OCCULTATIONS OF STARS

The list on the opposite page includes most of the occultations visible under favourable conditions in the British Isles. No occultation is included unless the star is at least 10° above the horizon and the Sun sufficiently far below the horizon to permit the star to be seen with the naked eye or in a small telescope. The altitude limit is reduced from 10° to 2° for stars and planets brighter than magnitude 2·0 and such occultations are also predicted in daylight. The column Phase shows whether a disappearance (1) or reappearance (2) is to be observed. The column headed "El. of Moon" gives

the elongation of the Moon from the Sun, in degrees. The elongation increases from 0° at New Moon to 180° at Full Moon and on to 360° (or 0°) at New Moon again. Times and position angles (P), reckoned from the north point in the direction north, east, south, west, are given for Greenwich (Lat. 51° 30′, Long. 0°) and Edinburgh (Lat. 56° 00′, Long. 3° 12′ west). The coefficients a and b are the variations in the G.M.T. for each degree of longitude (positive to the west) and latitude (positive to the north) respectively: they enable approximate times (to within about 1^m generally) to be found for any point in the British Isles. If the point of observation is $\Delta\lambda$ degrees west and $\Delta\phi$ degrees north, the approximate time is found by adding $a.\Delta\lambda + b.\Delta\phi$ to the given G.M.T.

As an illustration the disappearance of Jupiter on May 27 at Liverpool will be found from both Greenwich and Edinburgh.

	Greenwich	Edinburgh
	°	°
Longitude................	0·0	+3·2
Long. of Liverpool........	+3·0	+3·0
$\Delta\lambda$......................	+3·0	−0·2
Latitude.................	+51·5	+56·0
Lat. of Liverpool........	+53·4	+53·4
$\Delta\phi$......................	+1·9	−2·6
	h m	h m
G.M.T..................	3 26·5	3 33·5
$a.\Delta\lambda$..................	+0·9	−0·1
$b.\Delta\phi$..................	+2·5	−3·6
	3 29·9	3 29·8

If the occultation is given for one station but not the other, the reason for the suppression is given by the following code.

N = star not occulted.

A = star's altitude less than 10° (2° for bright stars and planets).

S = Sun not sufficiently below the horizon.

G = occultation is of very short duration.

It will be noticed that in some cases the coefficients a and b are not given: this is because the occultation is so short that prediction for other places by means of these coefficients would not be reliable.

OCCULTATION OBSERVATIONS

Observations of the times of these occultations are made by both professional and amateur astronomers throughout the world. Such observations are later analysed at the Royal Greenwich Observatory to yield accurate positions of the Moon: this is one method of determining the difference between ephemeris time and universal time. Occultations of stars by the Moon occur almost instantaneously and many of the observations made by amateurs are obtained with the use of a stopwatch which is compared with a time signal immediately after the observation. Thus an accuracy of about one-fifth of a second is obtainable, though the observer's personal equation may amount to one-third or one-half of a second.

Date	Star	Mag.	Phase	El. of Moon	GREENWICH				EDINBURGH			
					G.M.T.	a	b	P	G.M.T.	a	b	P
				°	h m	m	m	°	h m	m	m	°
Jan. 9	222 B. Piscium.....	7·1	1	92	..	N	..	..	17 48·7	..	..	129
10	12 H. Arietis......	6·3	1	103	17 29·0	−1·3	+1·5	64	17 32·7	−1·0	+1·8	51
11	124 B. Arietis......	6·4	1	114	18 26·8	−1·3	+1·5	60	18 31·1	−1·0	+2·0	46
13	282 B. Tauri......	6·6	1	137	17 06·7	+0·3	+4·0	19	..	N	..	..
Feb. 5	B.D. +8° 158.....	6·8	1	62	19 31·3	−0·9	−1·0	76	19 24·8	−0·9	−0·6	62
6	B.D. +11° 248.....	7·1	1	74	22 19·1	−0·3	−0·9	65	22 14·5	−0·4	−0·7	53
8	26 B. Tauri......	6·4	1	97	23 45·7	−0·2	−1·7	95	23 37·7	−0·3	−1·5	86
9	234 B. Tauri......	6·0	1	108	23 29·2	..	..	163	23 09·7	−0·2	−3·5	143
10	ε Tauri...........	3·6	1	108	0 55·7	+0·1	−1·9	111	0 47·1	−0·1	−1·9	104
10	352 B. Tauri......	6·8	1	120	23 47·0	−0·4	−2·6	132	23 34·5	−0·5	−2·3	122
10	35 B. Tauri......	6·4	1	120	23 59·0	−0·8	−1·0	74	23 52·0	−0·9	−0·8	65
11	71 Orionis........	5·2	1	132	22 48·7	−1·2	−1·3	102	22 39·9	−1·2	−0·9	92
19	ψ Virginis........	4·9	2	227	..	N	..	..	0 00·9	−1·3	+2·8	236
Mar. 3	62 Piscium	6·1	1	31	19 09·1	−0·3	−2·7	114	18 57·6	−0·4	−2·0	98
3	δ Piscium.........	4·6	1	32	19 25·8	−0·3	−0·5	54	19 23·3	−0·3	−0·1	39
8	312 B. Tauri......	6·2	1	87	20 29·4	−1·2	−1·1	85	20 21·8	−1·2	−0·6	74
10	B.D.+18° 1040...	7·1	1	101	..	A	..	..	1 32·6	+0·4	−2·1	138
10	74 B. Geminorum	6·2	1	112	22 26·0	−1·3	−0·5	67	22 20·2	−1·4	−0·1	57
17	χ Virginis........	4·8	2	196	5 01·4	−0·5	−2·2	334	4 49·9	−0·5	−2·1	340
Apr. 7	λ Geminorum	3·6	1	92	19 57·3	..	..	177	19 37·2	−0·6	−3·2	158
10	14 Sextantis	6·3	1	132	22 00·7	−1·5	−0·6	89	21 54·1	−1·4	−0·3	82
11	19 Sextantis	5·9	1	133	1 35·9	−0·1	−2·3	153	1 25·5	−0·2	−2·1	149
17	β¹ Scorpii	2·9	2	217	0 38·7	−1·1	+0·5	290	0 37·8	−0·9	+0·6	294
17	β² Scorpii	5·1	2	217	0 38·7	−1·1	+0·4	291	0 37·7	−0·9	+0·5	295
May 3	19 B. Geminorum	6·2	1	51	21 02·1	−0·2	−1·3	78	20 55·4	−0·3	−1·3	72
3	B.D. +18° 1141...	6·8	1	51	..	A	..	..	22 04·8	+0·4	−2·2	144
27	Jupiter..........	−1·6	2	339	3 26·5	+0·3	+1·3	272	3 33·5	+0·3	+1·4	278
June 4	84 B. Sextantis...	6 6	1	83	21 47·0	−0·8	−1·2	69	..	S	..	..
6	78 B. Virginis....	6·5	1	109	22 50·1	−1·1	−0·5	49	22 44·8	..	..	41
7	50 Virginis.......	6·2	1	123	22 48·6	−1·3	−0·4	52	22 42·8	..	..	45
10	β¹ Scorpii	2·9	2	163	20 31·5	−1·2	+1·0	88	..	S	..	..
10	β¹ Scorpii	2·9	2	163	21 39·7	−1·2	+0·2	294	21 37·2	..	..	298
July 3	18 G. Virginis....	7·1	1	78	21 05·2	−0·6	−1·8	116	..	S	..	..
Aug. 1	α Virginis........	1·2	2	73	15 40·6	−1·3	+0·1	111	15 37·7	−1·1	+0·4	105
1	α Virginis........	1·2	2	73	16 53·5	−1·3	−0·6	296	16 47·5	−1·1	−0·4	300
31	υ Scorpii	4·3	1	84	19 42·0	−1·2	−0·9	81	19 34·8	−1·1	−0·7	76
Sept. 2	39 G. Sagittarii...	6·3	1	110	20 36·7	−1·2	+0·1	49	20 33·9	−1·0	+0·2	40
3	187 G. Sagittarii...	6·4	1	122	19 55·2	−1·7	−0·3	115	19 49·9	−1·4	+0·1	108
11	ε Piscium	4·4	1	206	3 00·7	−1·2	+0·9	44	3 02·9	−0·9	+1·6	27
11		4·4	2	206	4 13·1	−1·3	−1·3	272	4 01·3	−1·4	−2·0	289
16	ε Piscium	5·0	2	261	4 07·7	−1·3	+2·7	224	4 13·6	−1·2	+1·8	241
30	104 Tauri........	6·9	1	92	20 09·0	−0·8	+0·2	39	20 08·0	−0·6	+0·4	26
Oct. 13	B.D. −18° 5115...	4·7	2	240	22 07·3	0·0	+1·5	272	22 13·4	−0·1	+1·4	283
18	119 Tauri........	5·1	2	289	1 36·8	−0·3	+0·1	319	..	A	..	..
27	κ Cancri.........	6·5−7·3	1	60	18 35·1	−0·6	+0·1	37	..	A	..	..
29	B.D. −19° 5047...	3·2	2	85	17 29·6	−1·9	−0·3	291	17 22·9	−1·7	−0·2	301
Nov. 1	β² Capricorni.....	6·6	1	122	21 42·3	..	..	132	21 25·1	−1·8	−1·3	109
8	255 B. Aquarii....	4·2	1	199	19 33·3	−0·2	+1·4	98	19 39·8	−0·1	+1·6	89
8	δ³ Tauri..........	4·2	2	199	20 32·7	−0·2	+2·1	240	20 41·1	−0·3	+2·0	251
10	δ³ Tauri..........	4·7	2	213	..	S	..	..	6 07·0	−0·8	−1·3	260
12	119 Tauri........	3·6	1	236	..	S	..	..	6 32·8	−1·2	−0·7	73
27	λ Geminorum	6·8	1	79	..	N	..	..	18 33·7	−1·9	−1·0	120
Dec. 1	B.D. −9° 5854....	4·4	2	126	22 18·2	−1·0	+1·5	27	22 26·6	..	..	2
2	ε Piscium	7·0	1	136	20 13·0	−1·6	+0·7	82	20 12·6	−1·3	+1·1	69
2	300 B. Piscium....	5·9	1	137	23 02·0	−1·7	−2·9	122	22 47·7	−1·5	+1·4	102
30	54 Cati..........	7·1	1	117	19 55·8	−1·2	+2·2	32	20 05·7	..	..	10
	B.D. +12° 317....											

MEAN PLACES OF STARS, 1976·0

Name	Mag.	R.A.	Dec.	Spectrum
		h m	° '	
α Andromedæ *Alpheratz*.......	2·1	0 07·1	+28 57	Aop
β Cassiopeiæ *Caph*...........	2·4	0 07·9	+59 01	F5
γ Pegasi *Algenib*..............	2·9	0 12·0	+15 03	B2
α Phœnicis..................	2·4	0 25·1	−42 26	Ko
α Cassiopeiæ *Schedar*..........	2·3	0 39·1	+56 24	Ko
β Ceti *Diphda*................	2·2	0 42·4	−18 07	Ko
γ Cassiopeiæ★................	Var.	0 55·2	+60 35	Bop
β Andromedæ *Mirach*.........	2·4	1 08·4	+35 30	Mo
δ Cassiopeiæ..................	2·8	1 24·2	+60 07	A5
α Eridani *Achernar*...........	0·6	1 36·8	−57 22	B5
β Arietis *Sheratan*.............	2·7	1 53·3	+20 41	A5
γ Andromedæ *Almak*.........	2·3	2 02·4	+42 13	Ko
α Arietis *Hamal*..............	2·2	2 05·8	+23 21	K2
α Ursæ Minoris *Polaris*.......	2·1	2 08·3	+89 09	F8
β Persei *Algol*★..............	Var.	3 06·6	+40 52	B8
α Persei *Mirfak*..............	1·9	3 22·6	+49 47	F5
η Tauri *Alcyone*.............	3·0	3 46·1	+24 02	B5p
α Tauri *Aldebaran*...........	1·1	4 34·5	+16 28	K5
β Orionis *Rigel*.............	0·3	5 13·4	− 8 14	B8p
α Aurigæ *Capella*............	0·2	5 14·9	+45 59	Go
γ Orionis *Bellatrix*..........	1·7	5 23·8	+ 6 20	B2
β Tauri *Elnath*..............	1·8	5 24·8	+28 35	B8
δ Orionis....................	2·5	5 30·8	− 0 19	Bo
α Leporis...................	2·7	5 31·7	−17 50	Fo
ε Orionis...................	1·7	5 35·0	− 1 13	Bo
ζ Orionis...................	2·0	5 39·5	− 1 57	Bo
κ Orionis...................	2·2	5 46·6	− 9 41	Bo
α Orionis *Betelgeuse*★.........	Var.	5 53·9	+ 7 24	Mo
β Aurigæ *Menkalinan*.........	2·1	5 57·8	+44 57	Aop
β Canis Majoris *Mirzam*.......	2·0	6 21·6	−17 57	B1
α Carinæ *Canopus*...........	−0·9	6 23·4	−52 41	Fo
γ Geminorum *Alhena*.........	1·9	6 36·3	+16 25	Ao
α Canis Majoris *Sirius*........	−1·6	6 44·1	−16 41	Ao
ε Canis Majoris..............	1·6	6 57·7	−28 56	B1
δ Canis Majoris..............	2·0	7 07·4	−26 21	F8p
α Geminorum *Castor*.........	1·6	7 33·1	+31 57	Ao
α Canis Minoris *Procyon*.......	0·5	7 38·0	+ 5 17	F5
β Geminorum *Pollux*.........	1·2	7 43·8	+28 05	Ko
ζ Puppis....................	2·3	8 02·7	−39 56	Od
γ Velorum..................	1·9	8 08·8	−47 16	Oap
ε Carinæ...................	1·7	8 22·0	−59 26	Ko
δ Velorum..................	2·0	8 44·0	−54 37	Ao
λ Velorum *Suhail*...........	2·2	9 07·1	−43 20	K5
β Carinæ...................	1·8	9 12·9	−69 37	Ao
ι Carinæ...................	2·2	9 16·4	−59 10	Fo
α Hydræ *Alphard*...........	2·2	9 26·4	− 8 33	K2
α Leonis *Regulus*............	1·3	10 07·1	+12 05	B8
γ Leonis *Algeiba*...........	2·6	10 18·7	+19 58	Ko
β Ursæ Majoris *Merak*.......	2·4	11 00·4	+56 31	Ao
α Ursæ Majoris *Dubhe*.......	1·9	11 02·3	+61 53	Ko

★ γ Cassiopeiæ, 1975 mag. 2·4.   β Persei, mag. 2·2 to 3·5.
α Orionis, mag. 0·1 to 1·2.

The positions of heavenly bodies on the celestial sphere are defined by two co-ordinates, right ascension and declination, which are analogous to longitude and latitude on the surface of the Earth. If we imagine the plane of the terrestrial equator extended indefinitely, it will cut the celestial sphere in a great circle known as the celestial equator. Similarly the plane of the Earth's orbit, when extended, cuts in the ·great circle called the ecliptic. The two intersections of these circles are known as the First Point of Aries and the First Point of Libra. If from any star a perpendicular be drawn to the celestial equator, the length of this perpendicular is the star's declination. The arc, measured eastwards along the equator from the First Point of Aries to the foot of this perpendicular, is the right ascension. An alternative definition of right ascension is that it is the angle at the celestial pole (where the Earth's axis, if prolonged, would meet the sphere) between the great circles to the First Point of Aries and to the star.

The plane of the Earth's equator has a slow movement, so that our reference system for right ascension and declination is not fixed. The consequent alteration in these quantities from year to year is called precession. In right ascension it is an increase of 3^s a year for equatorial stars, and larger or smaller amounts for stars near the pole. In declination it varies between +20″ and −20″ according to the right ascension of the star.

A star or other body crosses the meridian when the sidereal time is equal to its right ascension. The altitude is then a maximum, and may be deduced by remembering that the altitude of the elevated pole is numerically equal to the latitude, while that of the equator at its intersection with the meridian is equal to the co-latitude, or complement of the latitude.

NAME	Mag	R.A.	Dec.	Spectrum
		h m	° '	
δ Leonis	2·6	11 12·8	+20 39	A3
β Leonis Denebola	2·2	11 47·8	+14 42	A2
γ Ursæ Majoris Phecda	2·5	11 52·6	+53 50	Ao
γ Corvi	2·8	12 14·6	−17 25	B8
α Crucis	1·0	12 25·3	−62 58	B1
γ Crucis	1·6	12 29·8	−56 59	M3
γ Centauri	2·4	12 40·2	−48 50	Ao
γ Virginis	2·9	12 40·4	− 1 19	Fo
β Crucis	1·5	12 46·3	−59 33	B1
ε Ursæ Majoris Alioth	1·7	12 53·0	+56 05	Aop
α Canum Venaticorum	2·9	12 54·9	+38 27	Aop
ζ Ursæ Majoris Mizar	2·4	13 23·0	+55 03	A2p
α Virginis Spica	1·2	13 23·9	−11 02	B2
η Ursæ Majoris Alkaid	1·9	13 46·6	+49 26	B3
β Centauri Hadar	0·9	14 02·1	−60 15	B1
θ Centauri	2·3	14 05·3	−36 15	Ko
α Bootis Arcturus	0·2	14 14·6	+19 18	Ko
α Centauri Rigil Kent	0·1	14 38·0	−60 44	Go
ε Bootis	2·7	14 43·9	+27 10	Ko
β Ursæ Minoris Kochab	2·2	14 50·8	+74 15	K5
α Coronæ Borealis Alphecca	2·3	15 33·7	+26 48	Ao
δ Scorpii	2·5	15 58·9	−22 33	Bo
β Scorpii	2·9	16 04·0	−19 44	B1
α Scorpii Antares	1·2	16 27·9	−26 23	Mo
α Trianguli Australis	1·9	16 46·1	−68 59	K2
ε Scorpii	2·4	16 48·6	−34 15	Ko
α Herculis*	Var.	17 13·6	+14 25	M3
λ Scorpii	1·7	17 32·0	−37 05	B2
α Ophiuchi Rasalhague	2·1	17 33·8	+12 35	A5
θ Scorpii	2·0	17 35·6	−42 59	Fo
κ Scorpii	2·5	17 40·8	−39 01	B2
γ Draconis	2·4	17 56·0	+51 29	K5
ε Sagittarii Kaus Australis	1·9	18 22·6	−34 24	Ao
α Lyræ Vega	0·1	18 36·1	+38 46	Ao
σ Sagittarii	2·1	18 53·8	−26 20	B3
β Cygni Albireo	3·2	19 29·8	+27 54	Ko
α Aquilæ Altair	0·9	19 49·6	+ 8 48	A5
β Capricorni	3·2	20 19·7	−14 52	Go
γ Cygni	2·3	20 21·4	+40 11	F8p
α Pavonis	2·1	20 23·8	−56 49	B3
α Cygni Deneb	1·3	20 40·6	+45 12	A2p
α Cephei Alderamin	2·6	21 18·0	+62 29	A5
ε Pegasi	2·5	21 43·0	+ 9 46	Ko
δ Capricorni	3·0	21 45·7	−16 14	A5
α Gruis	2·2	22 06·7	−47 05	B5
δ Cephei*	Var.	22 28·3	+58 18	*
β Gruis	2·2	22 41·2	−47 01	M3
α Piscis Austrini Fomalhaut	1·3	22 56·3	−29 45	A3
β Pegasi Scheat	2·6	23 02·6	+27 57	Mo
α Pegasi Markab	2·6	23 03·6	+15 05	Ao

*αHerculis, mag. 3·1 to 3·9.

δCephei, mag. 3·7 to 4·4, Spectrum F5 to Go

Thus in London (Lat. 51° 30′) the meridian altitude of *Sirius* is found as follows:

	°	′
Altitude of equator	38	30
Declination south	16	41
Difference	21	49

The altitude of *Capella* (Dec. +45° 59′) at lower transit is:

	°	′
Altitude of pole	51	30
Polar distance of star	44	01
Difference	7	29

The brightness of a heavenly body is denoted by its magnitude. Omitting the exceptionally bright stars *Sirius* and *Canopus*, the twenty brightest stars are of the first magnitude, while the faintest stars visible to the naked eye are of the sixth magnitude. The magnitude scale is a precise one, as a difference of five magnitudes represents a ratio of 100 to 1 in brightness, Typical second magnitude stars are *Polaris* and the stars in the Belt of Orion. The scale is most easily fixed in memory by comparing the stars with Norton's *Star Atlas* (see page 138). The stars *Sirius* and *Canopus* and the planets Venus and Jupiter are so bright that their magnitudes are expressed by negative numbers. A small telescope will show stars down to the ninth or tenth magnitude, while stars fainter than the twentieth magnitude may be photographed by long exposures with the largest telescopes.

Some of the astronomical information in this ALMANACK has been taken from the *Astronomical Ephemeris*, and is published here by arrangement with, and with the permission of, the Controller of H.M. Stationery Office.

THE STRUCTURE OF THE UNIVERSE

The Solar System, although occupying a volume of space large by terrestrial standards, is only a very tiny fraction of the whole Universe. The Sun itself is just one of the millions of stars which make up our Galaxy, and our Galaxy is just one of the millions of galaxies which are distributed through the visible Universe. All these stars and galaxies are in motion, many of them with enormous velocities; yet they are so remote that to the naked eye they present almost the same configurations for a period of many thousands of years, and even with telescopic aid the measurement of their motions is a delicate matter. The nearest star is about 250,000 times as far away as the Sun, the Great Galaxy in Andromeda, one of the few galaxies visible to the naked eye, is over 500,000 times as far away as the nearest star, and the largest telescopes can penetrate to a distance of at least 500 times that of the Andromeda Galaxy. It is convenient to express astronomical distances in terms of the time that light takes to accomplish the journey. Light travels at the rate of 300,000 kilometres a second; it takes $1\frac{1}{4}$ seconds to reach us from the Moon, our nearest neighbour in space; just over 8 minutes to reach us from the Sun; four years from the nearest star; two million years from the Andromeda Galaxy, and over 1000 million years from the most distant bodies yet photographed. We therefore talk about a star as being so many light years distant. Astronomers also use another unit of distance, the parsec. 1 parsec equals 3·26 light years.

THE STARS

The stars are classed according to their apparent brightness in magnitudes. A few of the brightest stars are brighter than the first magnitude. Stars as faint as the sixth magnitude can be seen by the naked eye. The 5 metre (200-inch) telescope, the world's largest, on Mount Palomar in California. can photograph stars of the 23rd magnitude, which is about 650 million times fainter than the first magnitude. This large range in the apparent brightness of the stars is due to a combination of two factors. The first of these is distance. According to a standard law of optics, the apparent brightness of any given luminous object is inversely proportional to the square of its distance away. Thus, if two similar stars are at distances one of which is 10 times the other, the more distant star will appear to be 100 times fainter than the nearer star. The second factor affecting the apparent brightness of a star is its real intrinsic brightness. There are many different kinds of stars; some are very large luminous objects, others are small and faint.

The distances of the stars can be determined in a variety of ways. The direct trigonometric method consists in measuring the minute difference of direction of the star as seen from opposite sides of the Earth's orbit; this is always done photographically. The distances of about 15,000 stars have been measured in this way, but the method has very little accuracy for distances greater than about 250 light years. For more distant stars, distances may be estimated from a study of their spectra. The distances of some double and variable stars can be found from their special characteristics. A star is said to be at a distance of one parsec if the radius of the Earth's orbit round the Sun subtends an angle of one second of arc at the star.

When the distance of any star has been determined and its apparent magnitude measured, the real intrinsic brightness of the star may be determined. As a convenient convention, astronomers adopt as the "absolute magnitude" of a star (or other object) that apparent magnitude which the star would have if it were moved from its real position to a distance of ten parsecs. Conversely, if the absolute magnitude of a star is known by spectroscopic or other methods, and its apparent magnitude is observed, its distance may be calculated.

STELLAR SPECTRA

A large number of stars have been examined spectroscopically, and it is found that their spectra fall, with very few exceptions, into a sequence of types, denoted by the letters O, B, A, F, G, K, M; the types merge imperceptibly one into the next. O and B stars, exemplified by the three stars which form *Orion's* belt, have spectra showing helium and hydrogen lines. A stars, like *Sirius*, are characterized by very strong hydrogen lines. F, G and K stars, like *Procyon*, our Sun, and *Arcturus*, respectively, have spectra showing large numbers of metallic lines, and hydrogen lines much weaker than in A stars. Finally, the M stars, like *Betelgeuse*, show very complex molecular spectra, chiefly of titanium oxide. This sequence of spectral types O to M is essentially a temperature sequence, the O stars being the hottest and the M stars the coolest. Approximate values of the surface temperatures of the stars are, a value for the middle of each type being quoted in degrees Centigrade: O, 30,000°; B, 18,000°; A, 10,000°; F, 7000°; G, 5500°; K, 4500°; M, 3000°. This sequence is also one of colour, the O stars being the bluest and the M stars the reddest. The colour of a star is capable of precise definition and measurement; there is a very close correlation between colour and surface temperature, and between colour and spectral type. The latter correlation is so good that for many astrophysical purposes colour measurements are used instead of spectral types.

When the spectral types (or colours) of a large number of stars are correlated with their absolute magnitudes, a surprising result emerges. The sequence O to M is one of decreasing absolute brightness. Approximate values of the absolute magnitudes of the stars are, a value for the middle of each type being quoted: O, −4; B, −2; A, +1; F, +3; G, +5; K, +7; M, +11. A graphical illustration of this relation between spectral type and absolute magnitude is known as the Hertz-sprung-Russell Diagram (or, when colours are used instead of spectral types, as a colour-magnitude diagram). The relationship represented by this diagram is one of the corner stones of modern astrophysics. The above series of stars of types O to M and absolute magnitude decreasing from − 4 to +11, or fainter, is known as the "main sequence", and a large proportion of all known stars are members of this sequence. A relatively small proportion of the stars of spectral types O to M do not belong to the main sequence. Closer examination of the spectra of these stars reveals slight differences between their spectra and ordinary stars of nominally the same type on the main sequence. These differences are sufficiently characteristic to enable the two types of stars to be segregated spectroscopically without independent knowledge of their absolute magnitudes. These stars are found to be brighter than the corresponding main sequence stars of the same types. Most of those of types G, K and M have absolute magnitudes about o; many of those types O to F and few of types G to M are still brighter, with absolute magnitudes ranging from −4 to −7. The exceptional brightness of these stars is believed to be due to their sizes: those with absolute magnitudes about o are called giants, those of −4 to −7 are called supergiants.

The sizes of the stars have been determined mostly by theoretical calculation. In very few cases direct determinations have been made by means of an interferometer, and sizes can also be inferred from observations of some eclipsing binary stars. The Sun is 1,392,000 kilometres in diameter. The main sequence is found to be a sequence of diminishing radii; an O star has a radius of about 20 times that of the Sun, while an average M star has a radius of one-third of the Sun. The giant stars of types G to M have radii between 10 and 100 times the Sun; supergiants have radii between 30 and 1000 times the Sun.

It is possible to determine the chemical composition of a star from a study of its spectrum. This has been done for main sequence stars and for giants and supergiants. All these stars appear to be of similar chemical composition, about 80 per cent by numbers of atoms being hydrogen, most of the remainder helium, heavier elements being less than one per cent of the total. All the differences between types O to M and main sequence, giant and supergiant stars can be accounted for by variations of surface temperature and of size (affecting the spectrum through the surface gravity).

A few stars cannot be classified according to the standard sequence O to M. Among these those classified as R and N stars show strong bands of carbon compounds instead of the titanium oxide of M stars, and the S stars show zirconium oxide instead of titanium oxide. A number of still less common types of stars show anomalous lines of strontium, barium, manganese, silicon, europium, lanthanum and other elements. The reasons for all these peculiarities are not known; it is probable that many of them are genuine differences from the standard chemical composition of the majority of the stars.

DOUBLE STARS

Many stars which appear single to the naked eye are found to be double in the telescope. These are frequently found to be in orbital motion round one another in periods varying from about one year to many thousands of years. Some binary stars are so close together that they cannot be seen separately even in large telescopes; their binary nature is revealed by the spectroscope. The varying motions of the stars in their orbits can be detected by the Doppler shifts of lines in their spectra. Some spectroscopic binaries, as they are called, are of special interest in that during their orbital motion the two components periodically eclipse each other, and the combined light of the two stars will vary. This happens when the Earth is nearly in the plane of the binary star orbits. Such binaries are called eclipsing variables, of which the best known is *Algol*, or β Persei.

VARIABLE STARS

We have already referred to the eclipsing variables, whose light variation is due to a geometrical cause. Some single stars vary in light. These include Cepheid variables, with periods of from a few hours up to about fifty days, long-period variables with periods of from a hundred to a thousand days, and numerous types of variable stars in which the periods and light fluctuations are entirely irregular. Many of these variations are attributed to pulsation of the stars by alternate expansion and contraction. The Cepheids are of particular interest because of the period-luminosity relation: the longer the period of a Cepheid the brighter is its mean absolute magnitude. An observation of the period of variation of the star immediately tells us its absolute magnitude and thence its distance.

Novæ are stars whose light increases by 10 to 15 magnitudes in a few days, and then fades gradually to normal brightness, reached a year or two later. The cause of the brightening is the sudden expansion of the star, but the reason for this is unknown. Supernovæ are stars whose brightness increases by up to 20 magnitudes; they are believed to be caused by the explosion of the whole star.

STAR CLUSTERS

Stars frequently occur in clusters; two types of clusters are known. The first, called open (or galactic) clusters, are groups of up to two or three hundred stars; the second, globular clusters, contain over one hundred thousand stars. The open clusters are found mainly in the neighbourhood of the Milky Way, the globular clusters avoid the Milky Way. Several open clusters are visible to the naked eye: the Pleiades, the Hyades and Praesepe are the best known of these. The colour-magnitude diagrams of open clusters are generally similar to those of nearby single stars; the most important difference is that when a cluster contains blue O and B stars it does not also contain red giant stars. The colour-magnitude diagrams of globular clusters are very similar among themselves, but differ greatly from the diagrams of galactic clusters and nearby stars. The main sequence does not exist in any globular cluster for stars of types O, B and A; red giants are present in all the clusters, and they range up to absolute magnitude −3. There is an additional sequence of stars with absolute magnitudes about o which is quite unlike any sequence in the diagrams for nearby stars.

INTERSTELLAR MATTER

The space between the stars is not empty; it contains a mixture of gas and dust which serves to dim the light of distant objects and tends to make them appear redder than normal. Very distant objects may be obscured completely if they lie in or near the plane of the Milky Way. The density of interstellar gas averages one atom in each cubic centimetre; this may be compared with a density 26 million million million times as great in ordinary air at normal pressure and temperature. As is the case for cosmic material in general, hydrogen predominates in interstellar gas. In addition to this widely distributed matter, there are denser clouds of gas and dust existing locally. These are frequently in evidence as dark clouds in front of a brighter stellar background. Some clouds have hot stars embedded, and the interstellar gas may then shine either by reflection of the starlight or it may be heated until it glows and emits its own characteristic light. Such dense glowing clouds are termed galactic nebulæ. Sometimes the cloud is more regular in shape and is excited by one star; such clouds are termed planetary nebulæ, and the Ring Nebula in Lyra is an excellent example of these objects. Planetary nebulæ are among the denser interstellar formations; their densities range up to 20,000 atoms per cubic centimetre. Hot stars can make ordinary interstellar gas glow even when the density is low; the spherical region of glowing gas surrounding a hot star is termed an ionized-hydrogen region. These regions are of particular interest for the study of the Galaxy and of extragalactic nebulæ because they are relatively bright and can be seen at large distances.

THE GALAXY

A cursory glance at the sky is sufficient to show that the fainter stars are concentrated towards the region of the Milky Way. This implies that the stars form a flattened system which extends farther in the direction of the Milky Way than it does at right angles to it. It is now known that this system called the Galaxy, is about 100,000 light years in diameter, and has a thickness of less than 5000 light years. The Milky Way is the centre plane of the system. We in the Solar System are situated at about 27,000 light years from the centre, and not far from the central plane. All the objects mentioned earlier, single and multiple stars, variable stars, novæ and supernovæ, galactic and globular clusters, interstellar gas, dust and galactic and planetary nebulæ, form part of the Galaxy. The distribution of these various objects in the Galaxy is not all alike. The hot O and B stars, galactic clusters and interstellar matter are closely concentrated towards the Milky Way plane, mostly lying within 300 light years on either side of the plane. The stars of types A to M tend to be less closely concentrated to the plane; globular clusters show hardly any concentration, forming a nearly spherical distribution stretching to over 30,000 light years from the plane. Most Cepheid variables with periods of more than a day are closely concentrated to the galactic plane; those with periods of less than a day have a distribution similar to that of globular clusters.

The Galaxy has a spiral structure similar to that of some external galaxies. This structure was first shown by studying the positions of O and B stars; these trace out spiral arms. Radio astronomers subsequently found that interstellar neutral hydrogen gas emits radio waves on 21 centimetres wavelength. Studies of this radio radiation have enabled the density and distribution of interstellar hydrogen to be determined. The hydrogen gas is found to be situated along the same spiral arms as the O and B stars. Indeed, there is a remarkably close correlation between O and B stars and interstellar matter.

Observations by both optical and radio methods have proved that the whole Galaxy is rotating about an axis through its centre perpendicular to the galactic plane. The period of rotation varies with distance from the centre, an average value being 200 million years. The total mass of the Galaxy is about 100 thousand million times the mass of the Sun.

STELLAR POPULATIONS

The two different types of colour-magnitude (or Hertzsprung-Russell) diagram mentioned above appear to apply not only to star clusters but to other objects in our Galaxy and in other galaxies. There seems little doubt that there are two fundamentally different types of stellar population: Population I has a colour-magnitude diagram similar to that of nearby stars and open clusters, Population II has a diagram similar to that for globular clusters. Population I includes both open clusters, longer-period Cepheid variables and supergiant stars, and is intimately associated with interstellar matter; it occurs prominently in the spiral structure of our Galaxy, and is generally concentrated towards the galactic plane. Population II includes the globular clusters, short-period Cepheids and other objects, tends to avoid the spiral structure of the Galaxy, has little or no interstellar dust associated with it, but may be associated with interstellar hydrogen gas, and is not concentrated towards the galactic plane. All the available evidence suggests that Population II stars are old objects, with ages averaging 5000 million years, while Population I stars are much younger, with ages in a few cases of only a few million years. Population II stars have lower content of metals relative to hydrogen than Population I stars.

EXTERNAL GALAXIES

Outside our own Galaxy there are large numbers of objects having a more or less hazy appearance on photographs. These are known as external galaxies. Some show a well-defined spiral structure, some are elliptical in form with no marked structural features, and some are irregular in form. The spiral galaxies consist of a central bulge surrounded by spiral arms embedded in a disk-shaped structure. The elliptical galaxies and the central bulges of the spiral galaxies are believed to be composed of stars of Population II. The spiral arms are composed of Population I and some Population II, together with large quantities of gas and dust. The presence of dust is evident because of the dark patches of absorption which are a feature of the photographs of spiral galaxies; the presence of hydrogen gas has been proved by the observation of regions of glowing gas and by the

NEBULAE, CLUSTERS AND GALAXIES

Designation	Name	Type	Mag.	R.A. (1950·0)		Dec.	Angular Size
				h	m	°	′ ′
N.G.C. 104.......	47 Tucanae.............	GC	4	0	22	−72·4	42 × 42
M.31............	Andromeda (Galaxy)......	G	4	0	40	+41·0	160 × 40
Nubecula Minor...	....	—	—	0	50	−73·9	(10 sq. deg.)
M.33............	....	G	7	1	31	+30·4	60 × 40
H. VI. 33, 34.....	Double Cluster............	OC	4	2	18	+56·9	2(36 × 36)
M.45............	Pleiades..................	OC	—	3	45	+23·9	90 × 60
	Hyades...................	OC	—	4	26	+15·8	180 × 180
Nubecula Major...	....	—	—	5	25	−69·3	(42 sq. deg.)
M.1.............	"Crab" nebula............	PN	10	5	32	+22·0	6 × 4
M.42............	"Great" nebula...........	N	6	5	33	− 5·4	66 × 60
N.G.C. 2070......	30 Doradus..............	OC+N	—	5	39	−69·1	—
M.44............	"Praesepe" or "Beehive"...	OC	4	8	37	+20·2	90 × 90
N.G.C. 3372......	η Carinae................	N	—	10	43	−59·4	80 × 80
N.G.C. 4755......	κ Crucis.................	OC	—	12	51	−60·1	10 × 10
	ω Centauri	GC	3	13	24	−47·1	45 × 45
M.3.............	....	GC	6	13	40	+28·6	19 × 19
M.13............	....	GC	6	16	40	+36·6	23 × 23
M.7.............	....	OC	5	17	51	−34·8	50 × 50
M.20............	"Trifid" nebula...........	N	8	17	59	−23·0	29 × 27
M.8.............	"Lagoon" nebula.........	N	5	18	01	−24·4	90 × 40
M.57............	"Ring" nebula...........	PN	9	18	52	+33·0	1 × 1
M.55............	....	GC	5	19	37	−31·0	15 × 15
M.27............	"Dumb-bell" nebula......	PN	8	19	57	+22·6	8 × 4

Types: N—Nebula.   PN—Planetary Nebula.   OC—Open Cluster.   GC—Globular Cluster.   G—Galaxy.

reception of radio waves on 21 centimetres wavelength. In a few of the nearer galaxies individual stars have been observed, and comparison with stars in our own Galaxy provides estimates of the distances and sizes of the galaxies. Many of them are found to be comparable with our own Galaxy—with diameters of 100,000 light years and masses 100 thousand million times the Sun. The two Magellanic Clouds are the nearest galaxies to our own, their distances being about 140,000 light years. The best known external galaxy is the Great Galaxy in Andromeda, at a distance of 2,000,000 light years; this spiral galaxy is believed to be similar to our own Galaxy in size and stellar content. External galaxies frequently occur in large clusters, each containing hundreds of galaxies. Many galaxies are in rotation in a manner similar to our own Galaxy and with comparable periods.

RADIO SOURCES

In addition to the 21 centimetre hydrogen radiation received from interstellar gas, radio noise is received on other wavelengths. Some of this originates in well-known objects; one important source of radio noise is the Crab Nebula, which is known to be the remains of the supernova of A.D. 1054. Some extragalactic nebulæ are also sources of radio noise, but many of the apparently isolated sources, "radio stars", do not seem to coincide with any visible stars or nebulæ. Recently several sources have been discovered which exhibit extremely regular variations in radio "brightness", with incredibly short periods (of the order of 1 second). These sources are now called "pulsars".

QUASARS

The observation of occultations of radio sources by the Moon has led to the accurate determination of the positions of these radio sources. Thus it has been possible to use large optical telescopes with small angular fields of view and high magnifications to photograph these positions. This has led to the discovery of a new type of object called a quasar (or quasi-stellar object or QSO). On a photographic plate such objects appear almost stellar, so they are not readily identified without the help of information from the radio astronomers. Spectroscopic examination of four of them shows that, like external galaxies, they have enormous velocities of recession. Such velocities imply great distances, yet no ordinary star (or even supergiant) would be detectable at even a fraction of these distances. The answer to the question ' what are quasars ? ' is not yet known with any certainty but the current explanation is that they are radio sources with the shape of a star but many millions of times larger, with unusually high ultra-violet radiation and sometimes with large red shifts. Already several dozen quasars are known.

COSMOLOGY

The large scale problems of the Universe are concerned with the motions and distribution of the extragalactic nebulæ through the observable region of space. It has been found that in spite of the tendency of galaxies to cluster together, on a still larger scale the galaxies are distributed remarkably uniformly. Observations have shown that distant galaxies have spectra showing " red-shifts ", which have been interpreted as Doppler shifts due to velocities of recession; all the distant galaxies appear to be moving away from us with velocities proportional to their distance. This suggests that the whole Universe is in expansion. One theory postulates a gigantic initial explosion some 5,000 million years ago. Another postulates a steady state, with continuous creation of matter producing new galaxies which eventually force the existing ones to continually increasing distances. Some recent observations suggest that the latter theory is no longer tenable.

THE SOLAR SYSTEM

The Sun is one of the millions of stars that make up the Universe. The energy that it radiates in the form of light and heat is maintained by nuclear reactions among the atoms in its interior. It is surrounded by an immense number of comparatively cold planets and comets, together with smaller particles that give rise to meteors and the zodiacal light.

The planets are solid bodies revolving about the Sun in elliptical orbits with the Sun at one focus, and at distances related to the periodic times in accordance with Kepler's third law: the squares of the periodic times vary as the cubes of the semi-major axes. All revolve in the same direction, the orbits being only slightly inclined to the plane of the ecliptic in which the Earth moves round the Sun. As seen from the Earth, therefore, the planets are always near the ecliptic, moving in general from west to east round the sky. Once in every such revolution the planet appears to become stationary and then retrograde, forming a looped path which is a consequence of the Earth's own orbital movement.

The nine major planets, of which the Earth is one, are of special interest, the five that are visible to the naked eye having been known from the earliest times. Six have satellites or moons revolving round them. These, like the planets themselves, are not self-luminous, but shine by the reflected light of the Sun. Notes on these bodies are given in the following pages. The thousands of minor planets that are also known, although of less interest to the observer, afford many problems to the mathematical astronomer. Comets are also members of the solar system; their orbits are inclined at all angles to the ecliptic, and are generally highly eccentric, reaching out to immense distances in space. The light of a comet is not due entirely to reflected sunlight, but partly to fluorescence caused by selective absorption of solar radiation. The return of a comet of short period may be predicted with some accuracy, but most comets appear quite unexpectedly. Meteoric dust appears to have a common origin with the comets, since some meteor showers have been shown to follow the orbits of certain comets.

THE SUN

The Sun is the ultimate source of most of the chemical energy available on the Earth. Hence the origin of that energy, which reaches the Earth in the form of light and heat from within the Sun, is of particular interest. The spectral distribution of the light from the Sun's surface indicates a temperature of about 5,700° C., but a relatively short distance inside the surface the temperature reaches 1,000,000° and deeper in the interior, near the centre, it is believed to be in the region of 14,000,000°. Now the constitution of the Sun is similar to that of the Earth, as shown by similarities in the chemical spectra of solar and terrestrial sources; but at these high temperatures the atoms become stripped of their outer layers of electrons. In this highly " ionized " state the substance of the Sun acts in much the same way as a " perfect gas "

does on the Earth, even though the density is high. Furthermore, the thermal velocities are sufficiently great for nuclear collisions to take place. Nuclear energy can be released in the Sun by a variety of collision-processes, in each of which the light atoms of hydrogen, by far the most abundant element, are ultimately combined into heavier atoms of helium. This energy, released almost entirely in the central regions, is transmitted by radiation and convection to the cooler outer layers of the Sun and thence to outer space, a very small proportion of it falling on the Earth. It is possible to infer with some certainty, by considering the Sun as a typical star, that this process has been going on for about three thousand million years and that it may be expected to continue similarly for perhaps a further ten thousand million years.

As viewed by projection through a low-power telescope the Sun presents various interesting features. Over most of its surface a fine mottling can be seen under good observing conditions. This " granulation " is visible evidence of a turbulent convective layer near the surface. Much more noticeable surface-markings called sunspots appear sporadically in the equatorial zones of the Sun and up to latitudes of 40°–50° north and south. These sunspots, which are sometimes visible to the naked eye, provide direct evidence of the rotation of the Sun on an axis which is inclined about 7° to the line joining the poles of the ecliptic. They also indicate that the Sun does not rotate as a solid body but somewhat faster in equatorial regions than at higher latitudes. Its mean sidereal rotation-period is about 25 days but the motion of the Earth in its orbit around the Sun results in an apparent rotation-period, as viewed from the Earth, of approximately 27 days. Associated with sunspots are bright regions called faculae but these can not be seen when the spot is near the centre of the disk.

Sunspots vary in size from small dark specks, barely visible in a telescope, but actually with an area of about a million square km., to large dark markings several thousand times as great. The largest spot ever measured (April 1947) covered 18,000 million square kilometres at its greatest, or approximately 0·7 per cent of the Sun's visible surface. Correspondingly, sunspots have lifetimes ranging from a few hours in the case of some of the smallest, to many weeks in the case of the most persistent spots, which are often regular in shape but not as a rule particularly large. The frequency of spots varies in a definite eleven-year cycle, though the number of spots may vary considerably in a haphazard way from week to week in a particular year. One of the observed properties of spots during the 11-year cycle is that high latitudes, north and south, are predominant towards the beginning of a cycle, while later on there is a gradual drift of the most densely occupied zones towards the equator. In addition, a strong magnetic-field is found to be associated with sunspots, as well as certain systematic drifts in the solar layers there. These and other observed properties, such as concern the detailed structure and movements of spots,

ELEMENTS OF THE SOLAR SYSTEM

Orb	Mean Distance from Sun		Sidereal Period	Synodic Period	Inclination of Orbit to Ecliptic	Diameter	Mass compared with Earth	Period of Rotation on Axis
	Radii of Earth's Orbit	Millions of kilometres						
			y d	Days	° ′	km.		d h m
Sun...........	...	...	...	...	...	1,392,000	333,434	25 09
Mercury........	0·39	58	88	116	7 00	4,840	0·04	59
Venus..........	0·72	108	225	584	3 24	12,100	0·83	244
Earth..........	1·00	150	1 0	...	...	12,756*eq.*	1·00	23 56
Mars..........	1·52	228	1 322	780	1 51	6,790	0·11	24 37
Jupiter.........	5·20	778	11 315	399	1 18	{143,200*eq.* / 134,700*p.*	318	{ 9 50 / 9 56
Saturn.........	9·54	1427	29 167	378	2 29	{119,300*eq.* / 107,700*p.*	95	{ 10 14 / 10 38
Uranus........	19·19	2870	84 6	370	0 46	47,100	15	10 49
Neptune.......	30·07	4497	164 288	367	1 46	51,000	17	15 48
Pluto..........	39·46	5950	247 255	367	17 09	5,900?	0·06?	6 09 17?

must be explained by any comprehensive physical theory of sunspots. At present no generally accepted theory exists, though it seems clear that the magnetic field of the spot inhibits convection in the turbulent layers near the Sun's surface and so produces local cooling.

The Table below gives dates of recent maxima and minima of the sunspot cycles. It will be seen that the intervals between successive maxima (or minima) vary considerably from the average value of 11·1 years.

Maxima		Minima	
1837·2	1907·0	1843·5	1913·6
1848·1	1917·6	1856·0	1923·6
1860·1	1928·4	1867·2	1933·8
1870·6	1937·4	1878·9	1944·2
1883·9	1947·5	1889·6	1954·3
1894·1	1957·9	1901·7	1964·7
	1968·9		

The 1957 sunspot maximum was unusual in its absence of giant spots, the intense activity being due to a very large number of smaller spots.

Other features of the Sun may be detected in light of wavelengths other than those of normal integrated visual light. With the light from the centre of strong spectral absorption lines such as Hα, the C-line of hydrogen, or the H and K lines of calcium, bright regions can almost always be seen around sunspots and these regions occasionally become exceptionally bright for periods of an hour, or thereabouts. This is the phenomenon of the " solar flare ", and its occurrence may be otherwise detected upon the Earth by immediate changes in propagation-conditions for long-distance radio-communication (changes in the ionosphere caused by a sudden increase in ionizing radiation) or, in the case of large flares, by the subsequent occurrence a day or two later, of a magnetic storm. A very few large flares have had associated with them, increases, occurring a few minutes later, of the high-energy cosmic-ray flux detected at the earth's surface.

Also visible in monochromatic wavelengths are the prominences, which extend outwards from the Sun's surface into its tenuous outer regions, called the corona. At the limb prominences appear as bright forms, often arched or branching, while against the Sun's disk they appear as dark filaments. The corona itself can normally only be observed in its brightest regions by using light from certain bright spectral lines in special instruments at a high altitude on the Earth. At lower altitudes, and in the outer corona at high altitudes, scattered sky-light is too great. However, when the Sun is obscured by the Moon at a total solar eclipse, the whole corona becomes easily seen. As well as the bright lines, it shows a weak continuous spectrum. It is also found that the corona has characteristically different appearances at sunspot maximum and sunspot minimum and that it frequently shows streamers extending outwards for several million kilometres. When observed with radio wave-lengths in the range 10 cm. to 5 m. the corona is normally detected, as well as short-lived emissions from disturbed regions around sunspots.

MERCURY

Mercury is the smallest planet and the nearest to the Sun. Because it moves in an orbit between the Sun and the Earth, it is never far west or east of the Sun. If east, it appears as an evening star; if west as a morning star. The extremes of these apparent excursions are known as Greatest Elongations; their times and extent, measured by the angular distance from the Sun, are given on the first page of each month under the heading PHENOMENA. The great ellipticity of the orbit of Mercury causes the amount of these elongations to vary from 18° to 28°. The planet is best placed for naked-eye observation some days before eastern elongation on spring evenings, or after western elongation on autumn mornings, though in Great Britain at these times its actual distance from the Sun is near its minimum.

In a telescope, Mercury shows phases to the Earth like the Moon, resembling it at first quarter when at eastern elongation, and at last quarter when at western elongation. The planet is exceedingly difficult to observe telescopically and is best scrutin-

THE SATELLITES

Name	Star Mag.	Mean distance from Primary	Sidereal Period of Revolution	Name	Star Mag.	Mean distance from Primary	Sidereal Period of Revolution
		km.	d h m			km.	d h m
Earth				*Saturn*			
Moon............	—	384,400	27 07 43	Janus............	14	159,000	17 58
				Mimas..........	12	186,000	22 37
Mars				Enceladus........	12	238,000	1 08 53
Phobos..........	11	9,400	7 39	Tethys..........	11	295,000	1 21 18
Deimos..........	12	23,500	1 06 18	Dione...........	11	378,000	2 17 41
Jupiter				Rhea...........	10	527,000	4 12 25
V. Unnamed....	13	181,000	11 57	Titan...........	8½	1,222,000	15 22 42
I. Io..........	5½	422,000	1 18 28	Hyperion.........	15	1,483,000	21 06 38
II. Europa.......	5½	671,000	3 13 14	Iapetus..........	11	3,560,000	79 07 56
III. Ganymede....	5	1,070,000	7 03 43	Phoebe..........	14	12,950,000	550
IV. Callisto......	6	1,883,000	16 16 32	*Uranus*			
XIII. Unnamed....	—	11,000,000	240	Miranda........	17	130,000	1 10 00
VI. „	15	11,480,000	251	Ariel............	14	192,000	2 12 29
X. „	19	11,720,000	254	Umbriel.........	14½	267,000	4 03 28
VII. „	18	11,740,000	260	Titania..........	14	438,000	8 16 56
XII. „	18	21,200,000	620	Oberon.........	14	586,000	13 11 07
XI. „	19	22,600,000	692	*Neptune*			
VIII. „	17	23,500,000	739	Triton..........	13½	355,000	5 21 03
IX. „	18½	23,600,000	745	Nereid..........	19½	5,562,000	359 10 00

ized with large apertures in full daylight. Recent radar observations, which are supported by theoretical investigations, give a rotation period of 59 days. Close-up photographs from space probes show that its surface has many craters.

VENUS

Venus, next from the Sun, has a diameter only about six hundred kilometres less than that of the Earth. Its apparent movement with regard to the Sun is similar to that of Mercury, but, owing to the greater size of its orbit, its elongations extend as far as 47°. Venus is the brightest planet and is several times brighter than any star; it can often be seen in full daylight with the naked eye.

Apart from the beauty of its phases, Venus is a disappointing object in the telescope, its extensive atmosphere being so highly reflective, owing to dense clouds, that its true surface can never be observed. Vague dusky shadings may be seen or imagined, but conspicuous markings are both rare and evanescent.

Photographs of Venus in violet light were taken by Kuiper in 1950 and 1954 with the 2-metre reflector of the McDonald Observatory in Texas, and show that the surface of the planet is banded, three or more dark and bright bands being noted lying in a direction perpendicular to the terminator. These bands have been attributed to zones of ascending and descending currents in the atmosphere of Venus. Assuming that the bands are parallel to the equator, Kuiper deduced the position of the pole of Venus at $3^h 32^m$, +81°, which is in Cepheus. The equator of Venus is therefore tilted at an angle of about 32° to its orbit. Recent radar observations have provided the unexpected value for the period of rotation given on p. 157.

The spectrum of the atmosphere above the reflecting layer reveals a considerable amount of carbon dioxide, but no oxygen; such might also be the conditions on the Earth, were it not for the constant absorption of carbon dioxide by vegetation and its replacement by oxygen. A remarkable feature of the upper atmosphere is the absence of all trace of water vapour. A Russian space probe has revealed that the lower layers are extremely dense.

MARS

Mars, the first planet whose orbit is exterior to that of the Earth, is a little larger than Mercury. Oppositions occur at intervals of about 2 years 2 months, but owing to the eccentricity of the orbit the opposition distance varies between 56 and 100 million kilometres. The most favourable approaches unfortunately take place when the planet is low in the sky for northern observers; but when, as in 1956, one occurs early in September the distance may be less than 65 million kilometres and the planet just north of the equator. It is only within two or three months of opposition that Mars is near enough for its surface to be successfully studied with a telescope; even at these times only the coarser details are likely to be recognized with instruments of less than 15 cm. aperture.

Except for Mercury, Mars is the only planet whose true surface we are able to see. This exhibits many well-defined markings, most of which are permanent, and from these the rotation period has been well determined; it is about 41½ minutes longer than that of the Earth. The axis of rotation is inclined at about 24° to the plane of the orbit. There are white spots at the poles which are deposited during the winter of each hemisphere and melt or evaporate during the summer. Recent observations by a spacecraft orbiting the planet indicate that these polar caps contain solid carbon dioxide. The major portion of the surface is of a featureless orange hue, which gives rise to the ruddy appearance of Mars. But there abound large areas, often with sharp boundaries, of a blue-grey colour. The latter were once thought to be seas but it is now known that there are no large sheets of open water, and some regard areas of vegetation as their most likely interpretation, especially as they undergo change of tint. It has been claimed that these changes follow the Martian seasons; but as 15 or 17 years must elapse between the times when we can study Mars under similar conditions, it cannot yet be confirmed that there are any changes of a truly seasonal character apart from the waxing and waning of the polar caps.

The controversy over the canal-like markings on Mars has ended with the successful close range photography of the surface by Mariner 4. The photographs show a surface covered with craters, but no " canals ".

Mars has an atmosphere which is considerably less dense than our own. The spectroscope has been unable to establish that it contains either oxygen or water vapour, which can therefore be present only in minute proportions. Recently, however, about the same amount of carbon dioxide has been detected as is found in our own atmosphere.

Mars has two faint satellites, Phobos and Deimos, which were discovered by Asaph Hall in 1877.

THE MINOR PLANETS

Moving in orbits which in general lie between those of Mars and Jupiter, are a large number of small bodies called minor planets or asteroids. It is estimated that at least 50,000 come within reach of present instruments. Scores of them are now found every year by photographing the sky. Their orbits are calculated as observations accrue, and when the results are reliable enough the new planets are given permanent numbers, and usually also names, by a central authority—now at the Cincinnati Observatory, U.S.A. At present there are over 1600 on the permanent list, and several dozen are likely to be added each year; and always there are many still under investigation. All are faint—none has ever been seen by an unaided eye except, just possibly, Vesta.

These celestial bodies are probably little more than masses of rock revolving round the Sun. The first four, found early in the 19th century, are also the largest. Recent radiometric measures of their diameters, in kilometres, are: Ceres 1000; Pallas 530; Juno 240; Vesta 530.

The periodic times of the revolutions about the Sun vary considerably around an average of $4\frac{1}{2}$ years, but interesting groups and gaps occur among the values for these times owing to disturbances of the orbits caused by the attraction on these bodies of the massive planet Jupiter. Although some of the orbits are nearly circular, others are very elongated ovals (ellipses); and though the inclinations of their planes to the ecliptic are mostly less than 20°, several exceed 30°, including Pallas 35°. The highest known, 43°, is that of Hidalgo. This planet has also the longest period, 14 years, and travels out as far as Saturn's orbit. On the other hand Icarus, discovered in 1949, comes within the orbit of Mercury, and three others Apollo, Adonis and Hermes, within that of Venus. Another, Eros, is of importance because in some circumstances it can be within 21 million kilometres of the Earth. This happened in 1931 when carefully planned photographic recording of the planet and the surrounding

stars enabled measurements of its distance to be made and hence a new value of the distance of the Sun from the Earth to be deduced.

Similarly, certain other minor planets with suitable orbits can be used for special purposes, as in the precise measurement of the equinox and equator, or in finding the masses of Mercury or Venus.

JUPITER

Jupiter, the largest planet, has a volume over 1000 times that of the Earth, but a density only one-quarter of ours. Its oblate shape is so marked, owing to its great size and rapid rotation, as to be obvious in quite small telescopes.

The characteristic surface features of Jupiter are bright zones separated by dusky belts, running practically parallel to the planet's equator. With telescopes of moderate size some of these may be resolved into finer detail, consisting of spots, wisps, streaks, etc., but the general banded appearance still remains. When the period of rotation is determined by timing objects such as these as they cross the planet's central meridian it is found that spots within about 10° of the equator indicate a period of approximately $9^h\ 50\frac{1}{2}^m$, while most of those in higher latitudes give periods between $9^h\ 55^m$ and $9^h\ 56^m$, the transition from the shorter to the longer being usually quite abrupt. When the rotation periods are examined in greater detail, it is found that the surface may be divided into many zones, each having a particular period characteristic of its latitude, but that the distribution in latitude of the various periods is quite haphazard. This differs from the Sun, whose rotation is also fastest at the equator, for whereas a definite formula connects the periods of solar spots with their latitude, no such law can be found for Jupiter. Actually the fastest moving spots are confined to a narrow strip in latitude about $+25°$; the last outbreak of such spots occurred in 1939.

Few Jovian markings have any degree of permanence, having generally lost their individuality after a few months. Two objects, however, form notable exceptions. The well-known " Bay " or " Hollow " in the South Equatorial Belt, which is so closely associated with the Great Red Spot, made famous in 1878–80 by its darkness and colour, is known to have existed from 1831 and the Red Spot itself may be identical with a similar object first depicted in the 17th century and followed for many years. The physical nature of the Red Spot is a mystery; its long duration suggests some connection with the solid surface, but the non-uniformity of its period of rotation seems to rule out this explanation. The other feature displaying considerable permanence is known as the South Tropical Disturbance, which has the same latitude as the Red Spot. Its rotation period is somewhat shorter than that of the latter; since its first detection in 1901 it has overtaken and passed the Red Spot eight times.

The spectroscope shows that Jupiter's atmosphere contains ammonia and considerable quantities of methane (marsh gas). The main constituents are unknown, but it is probable that hydrogen and helium abound and that the light clouds of the surface are due to minute droplets or crystals of ammonia, the surface temperature having been found by measurement to be of the order − 120° C., which is not far from the calculated value. It has been suggested that this atmosphere is very deep; but if so, the pressure at depths below 100 kilometres or so must be such as to give it the properties of a liquid rather than a gas. A recent theory is that it may be dense enough to support in flotation a light solid body at some depth below the surface, and that what we see as the Red Spot may be a manifestation in the atmosphere above it of thermal changes in such a solid.

Jupiter has four principal satellites—the first celestial objects discovered by telescope by Galileo. The two inner major satellites are about the size of our Moon, while the two outer are about as large as Mercury. A fifth, very much smaller and fainter and nearer to Jupiter, was discovered visually by Barnard in 1892; this satellite has the most rapid motion of any in the solar system. Eight other satellites have been discovered photographically but all are minute objects; the four outermost of these have retrograde motion and are so greatly disturbed by the solar attractions that their orbits are not even approximately elliptical.

Satellite I (Io) occulted a fifth magnitude star on 1971 May 14, and from the accurate photo-electric observations of this event its equatorial diameter has been determined as 3660±4 km. From a similar event in 1972 the diameter of Satellite III (Ganymede) was found to be 5,270 km.

Intense but irregular bursts of radio noise were detected at the Carnegie Institute at Washington in January 1955, on wavelengths of 13·5 and 10 metres; these signals were received only during the few minutes while Jupiter was crossing the aerial beam. Some evidence indicates that there is a connection between the positions of the satellite Io and these radio bursts.

SATURN

This planet is unique because of its encircling ring system, which makes it a very beautiful object in even a small telescope. There are two bright rings and an inner dusky one, which is transparent enough for the body of the planet to be seen through it. The dark line separating the two outer rings is known as Cassini's division in honour of its discoverer. The rings lie almost exactly in one plane, which is inclined at 27° to the planet's orbit and is sensibly that of its equator. It has been proved theoretically, and confirmed by spectroscopic observations, that the rings consist of a vast swarm of small individual particles, each pursuing its own orbit like a satellite around Saturn. The extreme thinness of the rings is illustrated every 15 years when the plane of the rings passes through the Earth; they then become almost completely invisible even in the greatest telescopes. Thus they cannot present when edgewise a width of more than a very few kilometres.

From the few spots that have been observed on Saturn's surface, the rotation period at the equator is about $10^h 15^m$, in higher latitudes $10^h 38^m$ has been found in the northern hemisphere and $10^h 37^m$ in the southern. There is thus some analogy with

Jupiter, but we are ignorant of the behaviour of intermediate zones.

The density of Saturn is less than three-quarters that of water; the oblateness is even more marked than is Jupiter's, the equatorial diameter exceeding the polar by about one part in nine. The general appearance of the disk is banded, but the dusky belts are fewer and wider than those on Jupiter and present less contrast with the brighter zones. The atmosphere is known to contain methane and ammonia.

Among the more interesting results obtained from measurements of infra-red absorption spectra with the 2-metre reflector of the McDonald Observatory in Texas are those of the constitution of Saturn's rings and the five inner satellites. The only substance which gives similar absorption bands to those observed would appear to be frost deposited on a material at very low temperatures. Estimates of the masses of Saturn's rings and of the five inner satellites show that their densities cannot be far from unity, and it is provisionally suggested that they are all composed of ice. Evaporation will be negligible at the low temperatures prevailing, and the small particles of which the ring is composed will suffer little or no loss.

Saturn has ten satellites, of which the largest, Titan, is easily seen with a small telescope. Titan is the largest satellite in the solar system, and the only one which shows definite evidence of possessing an atmosphere. The seven innermost satellites revolve nearly in the plane of the rings. When the rings are seen edgewise, these inner satellites may transit the planet or be eclipsed in the same manner as those of Jupiter. The faint outermost satellite, Phœbe, has a retrograde motion.

URANUS

This planet was discovered by William Herschel at Bath in 1781, and so has completed only two revolutions since its discovery. It is only just visible to the naked eye, but in a telescope is distinguishable by its disk, which is quite obvious, though less than 4″ in diameter, and by the different quality of its light. The two outer and brighter of its four main satellites were found by Herschel in 1787; the two inner by Lassell in 1851. Their movement is retrograde in a plane inclined 82° to the plane of the ecliptic. A fifth satellite was discovered by Kuiper in 1948. The period of rotation of Uranus has been determined spectroscopically to be 10 hours; the direction is the same as that of the satellites.

NEPTUNE

This planet is a telescopic object of about the 8th magnitude, presenting a disk of well over 2″ in diameter. A rotation period of 15·8 hours, inferred spectroscopically, is now generally accepted.

The planet was found in 1846 as a result of calculations made independently by J. C. Adams and Le Verrier, which gave the position of an unknown planet which was responsible for perturbations of the motion of Uranus. The planet was found near the indicated place by Galle of the Berlin Observatory. Neptune has two satellites, of which the inner, Triton, revolves about Neptune in a retrograde direction at a distance a little less than that of the Moon from the Earth.

The other satellite revolves in the normal direction in a period of about a year. Its orbit is remarkably eccentric, and the satellite's distance from Neptune varies from 1,300,000 to over 10 million kilometres.

PLUTO

The outermost planet of the solar system was discovered photographically at the Lowell Observatory in March 1930, as a result of a systematic search for a trans-Neptunian planet. The existence of such a planet had been suggested many years before, and although the predicted elements of the orbit differ in some respect from the facts, yet these predictions were undoubtedly responsible for the ultimate discovery. The planet was called Pluto, and would appear to be small, with a mass possibly much less than that of the Earth. It would also appear to be a poor reflector of the Sun's light, since it shines only as a star of the 14th–15th magnitude.

THE MOON

The Moon is the Earth's satellite, and although its motion is highly complicated, it may be considered to revolve about the Earth in an elliptical orbit inclined about 5° to the plane of the ecliptic. Owing to perturbations, the ellipse is continually varying in shape, and the whole orbit twists round in space so that the nodes, or points where the orbit intersects the ecliptic, move in a retrograde direction, making one complete revolution in 18·6 years.

The Moon, whose diameter is 3,476 kilometres, rotates in the same time that it revolves ($27^d\ 7^h\ 43^m$) so that the same face is always presented to the Earth. The tilt of its axis, and the variable speed in the orbit, cause it to undergo an apparent swaying motion called libration, which enables us, in the long run, to see rather more than an exact half of the lunar surface. In a telescope this surface shows many objects of great beauty and interest, the rugged ranges of mountains, the craters and plains forming an impressive picture of jet-black shadows and bright highlights. Recent photographs obtained from the successful *Ranger* series of lunar probes show craters as small as a metre in diameter. On 1969 July 21, the first men (Americans) landed on the Moon and returned with samples of lunar rock and dust for subsequent laboratory analysis.

The revolution of the Moon about the Earth with reference to the Sun takes rather longer than a sidereal revolution, so that the phases of the Moon repeat themselves in a period that varies slightly about a mean of 29½ days. Each month the Moon passes in front of all stars in its path. Such an *occultation* causes the light of the star to be extinguished instantly. This, together with the sharpness and intensity of the shadows on the Moon, indicates a complete lack of atmosphere. Eclipses occur at two " seasons " of the year, when the Moon is near one of its nodes and in line with the Earth and the Sun. A lunar eclipse takes place when the Full Moon passes through the Earth's shadow, and is visible over half the Earth at any one time. A solar eclipse takes place when the New Moon passes in front of the Sun, and is visible only from a rather small area of the Earth.

As a result of its eastward movement among the stars the Moon rises later each day by a variable amount that depends on the inclination of its apparent path to the observer's horizon. When this angle is small, the Moon rises at much the same time for several days in succession. Although this occurs each month, it is most noticeable in high latitudes at the Full Moon nearest to the Autumnal Equinox. This is the Harvest Moon.

THE AURORA BOREALIS (AND AUSTRALIS)

An aurora is the visible counterpart of a marked disturbance of the Earth's magnetic field (a " magnetic storm ") apparently due to the action of a stream of electrified particles shot earthward from localized regions of the Sun, such as that of a big sunspot. The glow of auroral patches, arches or streamers results from the action of this solar stream upon the constituent gases of the Earth's upper atmosphere. The usual height of the lower limit of the auroral luminescence is about 100 kilometres; upward, it may extend to 500 kilometres or higher. Aurorae are very frequent in the so-called auroral zones (magnetic latitude about 67°); they are most frequent for the Earth as a whole near sunspot maximum. Although the solar origin of great displays (e.g. 1938 January 25, and 1949 January 24–26), can be traced to particular sunspots with solar flares, many lesser auroral displays cannot be thus associated. However, their solar origin is evidenced by their tendency to recur at intervals of 27 days, the time required for the Sun to turn once on its axis with respect to the Earth.

THE ZODIACAL LIGHT

This faint phenomenon of the late evening or early morning sky can be seen only when the air is sufficiently clear, the sky quite dark, and the ecliptic making a fairly steep angle with the horizon. It then appears as a cone of faint light stretching up from the position of the Sun (below the horizon) in the direction of the ecliptic, with its apex anything from 60° to 110° from the Sun. In our latitudes it is best seen after sunset in spring and before sunrise in the autumn, when its brightest parts may appear brighter than the Galaxy.

Occasionally, under very good conditions, an extension of the Cone may be traced right round the ecliptic. This is known as the Zodiacal Band. The Gegenschein or " Counter-glow " may also be detected as a widening of the band at the antisolar point.

Recent work shows that the zodiacal cloud is a continuation of the Sun's corona, and that much of this fine dust must fall on the earth every day. The particles are much too small, however, to become visible (by incandescence) as they fall through the atmosphere, and there is evidence to show that they settle in the form of micrometeorites. These probably act as centres of condensation in the formation of rain.

METEORS

The scattered particles which move in streams about the Sun give rise to occasional showers of meteors (" shooting-stars ") or fireballs—bodies that differ only in size. They are visible in varying numbers every night, being sometimes so abundant as to be quite spectacular. Often on a particular date or dates, meteors radiate from the same part of the heavens every year. This is because a stream of particles more or less dense, is moving in an orbit that intersects that of the Earth. The orbits of some of these streams, Lyrids, Pons-Winneckeids, Perseids, Giacobinids, Leonids, are known to be closely similar to those of certain comets, but modern work on the measurement of meteor velocities by photographic and radar methods has given very different results for the other streams. Thus the Geminids and the November Taurids have been shown by Whipple (from photographic results) to have small but eccentric orbits, more like those of minor planets. The radar methods of studying meteors have the advantage of being equally useful in daylight, and unaffected by cloud. Besides making measurements of the major showers noted above, the radar technique has shown the presence of a number of extensive showers in daylight hours, particularly in the summer months. These also show the same type of small eccentric orbit as those determined by Whipple.

METEOR SHOWERS

Date	Radiant		Name
	R.A.	Dec.	
	°	°	
January 3.........	232	+52	Quadrantids
April 20-22.......	271	+33	Lyrids*
May 2-6..........	336	0	ηAquarids*
June 27-30........	213	+53	Pons-Winneckeids*
August 10-13.....	46	+58	Perseids
October 9........	262	+54	Giacobinids*
October 18-23....	96	+15	Orionids*
November 14-15..	152	+22	Leonids*
December 10-13...	112	+32	Geminids
December 22.....	217	+76	Bečvár's Stream*

* Not plentiful each year.

The real paths of a great number of meteors have been computed, and the average heights found to be about 110 kilometres at the beginning and about 75 kilometres at the end. The speeds vary from 15 to 80 km. per second. Fireballs, or very bright meteors, appear at all times of the year unexpectedly so that they are often imperfectly noted and computation of their flight is not practicable.

Fireballs would seem to have a different origin from the ordinary shooting star, and probably arise from the belt of minor planets. The largest fireballs, when not completely consumed, land on the earth as meteorites. The largest meteorite found weighs 30 tons, and considerable collections are to be seen in our museums. Very large falls were recorded in Siberia in 1908 and 1947, while craters (formed presumably by large meteorites) are found in Arizona, Ungava and elsewhere. A number of meteorites have been found at Barwell, Leicestershire, as the result of two exploding fireballs on 1965 December 24. At the other end of the scale are the micro-meteorites which are too small to become incandescent in the atmosphere and which drift slowly down to the earth's surface.

Above is a list of the nights when meteor showers may be expected, with the radiant points from which the meteors diverge. The dates given are those when the meteors are likely to be most abundant. In some cases, e.g. the Perseids, the apparition lasts beyond these limiting dates, and the position of the radiant, which changes from night to night, is given for the date of maximum.

COMETS

A comet is distinguished from other bodies in the solar system by its appearance: a hazy luminous patch moving in the sky, more or less round and usually brighter in the centre, sometimes with a star-like nucleus there; and from it not infrequently extends a tail which may, in bright comets, reach a length of as much as 150 million kilometres—a fine spectacle. Most comets are found accidentally and few observers search for these objects. One of the few is G. E. D. Alcock of Peterborough, Northants, who, after seaching unsuccessfully for six years, found two new comets in August, 1959, within the space of 5 days. Two naked-eye comets which appeared in 1957 (Comet Arend-Roland in April, and Comet Mrkos in August) aroused considerable interest.

Although generally large in volume, a comet is small in mass, probably less than one-millionth that of the Earth even in the largest comets—the centre being composed mainly of an aggregation of pieces of matter mostly of sizes between that of pebbles and fine dust, but probably containing also a solid core a few kilometres in diameter. According to a recent theory, the earthy material is held together by various " ices "—masses of frozen gases such as ammonia, carbon dioxide and methane —which, on approaching the Sun, begin to evaporate. The pressure of the Sun's radiation is great enough to repel these gases, together with fine dust, and thus form a tail. As the comet approaches the Sun, it grows brighter and as it recedes it grows fainter again, the tail now preceding it in its journey away from the Sun.

Most comets follow paths which are very elongated ovals (ellipses) and return to the Sun, if at all, only after hundreds or thousands of years. The arrival of such comets cannot therefore be predicted. A few dozen comets, however, mostly too faint ever to be seen with the unaided eye, move in smaller ellipses which are sufficiently accurately known to enable predictions to be made of their returns. The most famous and brightest of these periodic comets is Halley's comet whose spectacular appearances about every 75 years have been traced back over more than 2000 years— it is next due early in 1986. Two very faint comets are known which travel in nearly circular orbits and, on this account come within reach for photographic observation every year: Schwassmann-Wachmann (1), designated 1925 II, and Oterma. The former is of special interest, not only because its orbit is the only known one lying wholly between Jupiter and Saturn, but on account of the unexpected outbursts in brightness it occasionally manifests.

THE EARTH

The shape of the Earth is that of an oblate spheroid or solid of revolution whose meridian sections are ellipses not differing much from circles, whilst the sections at right angles are circles. The length of the equatorial axis is about 12,756 kilometres, and that of the polar axis 12,714 kilometres. The mean density of the Earth is 5·5 times that of water, although that of the surface layer is less. The Earth and Moon revolve about their common centre of gravity in a lunar month; this centre in turn revolves round the Sun in a plane known as the ecliptic, that passes through the Sun's centre. The Earth's equator is inclined to this plane at an angle of 23½°. This tilt is the cause of the seasons. In mid-latitudes, and when the Sun is high above the Equator, not only does the high noon altitude make the days longer, but the Sun's rays fall more directly on the Earth's surface; these effects combine to produce summer. In equatorial regions the noon altitude is large throughout the year, and there is little variation in the length of the day. In higher latitudes the noon altitude is lower, and the days in summer are appreciably longer than those in winter.

The average velocity of the Earth in its orbit is 30 kilometres a second. It makes a complete rotation on its axis in about 23^h 56^m of mean time, which is the sidereal day. Because of its annual revolution round the Sun, the rotation with respect to the Sun, or the solar day, is more than this by about four minutes (*see* p. 140). The extremity of the axis of rotation, or the North Pole of the Earth, is not rigidly fixed, but wanders over an area roughly 20 metres in diameter.

THE TIDES

The tides are caused by the attraction of the Moon for the waters of the Earth, while a similar but smaller effect is due to the Sun. Normally there are two high tides every day, about 12½ hours apart. They thus occur about 50 minutes later than those of the previous day, corresponding to the 24^h 50^m interval between consecutive meridian passages of the Moon. Briefly, a high tide occurs when the attraction on the water is greater than on the solid earth. On the other side of the Earth the water is farther from the Moon than the solid earth and thus is less strongly attracted to the Moon and a second high tide occurs at this point. The height of the tide varies considerably. The highest, called Spring Tides, always occur about the time of New or Full Moon, when the lunar and solar attractions act together. At Neap Tides, which occur about First and Last Quarter, the rise and fall is only about half as much as at Spring Tide.

The tidal flow of water across the Earth is greatly modified by the shape of the coastline and other geographical conditions. The complicated motion of the Moon, its changing position north or south of the equator, and its varying distance from the Earth, all add small variations; it is thus impossible to predict tides theoretically. Tide-tables for any place are always constructed from an analyis of past observations of times and heights. It is found that the height can be expressed as the sum of a series of periodic terms, which can be carried forward. (*See pages 170–184*.)

High water does not necessarily occur at the same time as the meridian passage of the Moon, nor do springs and neaps necessarily occur on the same day as the phases stated. Thus at London Bridge the tide is high when the Moon is somewhat west of the meridian, while Spring Tides occur about 2½ days after New or Full Moon.

The shape and depth of a channel or estuary very greatly modify the nature of the tides. At some places one of the daily tides becomes so small as to be negligible, while in other channels (e.g. Southampton Water) the high tides are doubled. The difference between high and low water, or range of the tide, may vary from a small amount, as in the land-locked Mediterranean, up to 13 metres in the Severn Estuary and 16 metres in the Bay of Fundy.

As the energy involved in this tidal flow is considerable, various schemes for harnessing tidal energy have been evolved. As a consequence of the friction caused by tidal flow, the Earth's period of rotation is increasing by about a thousandth of a second every century. Although very small at present, this effect was greater in the past, and has played a considerable part in the history of the Earth–Moon system.

High Water in the Thames, 1976
Occasions when a predicted height at London Bridge is 7·7 metres or more

January......19, 20	August.......27–29
February.....16–19	September....24–27
March.......16–20	October......23–26
April........14–17	

TERRESTRIAL MAGNETISM

The discovery that a piece of the commonly occurring iron ore, magnetite or lodestone, is subject to a directing force causing it to take up a definite direction when freed from other restraint seems to have been made in China during the first century A.D., if not somewhat earlier. Steel needles, magnetized by rubbing with a piece of lodestone and floated on water, were being used as navigational aids by Chinese sailors before A.D. 1000. From this primitive device the Mariner's compass subsequently developed. That the direction, though roughly north to south, is by no means accurately so, was also known to the Chinese before A.D. 1000.

William Gilbert, in 1600, demonstrated that in the proximity of the Earth magnetized needles behave much as if the Earth itself were a large magnetized sphere. It was soon found that the direction of the force in a particular locality slowly changed. Henry Gellibrand, observing near Greenwich in 1634, found the direction to be about 4° east of north, whereas there was undoubted evidence that in 1580 it had been about 11° east in the same neighbourhood. In 1722, Graham, the clockmaker, found that the direction oscillated slowly through a small angle every day. In the

British Isles the movement is eastwards till about 08h U.T., then rather quickly westwards till about 14h U.T., after which there is a gradual return eastwards. The amplitude may be as much as 15′ in the summer.

A magnetic compass points along the horizontal component of a magnetic line of force. These directions converge on the " magnetic dip-poles ". At these poles a freely suspended magnetized needle would become vertical. Not only do the positions of these poles change with time, but their exact location is ill-defined, particularly so in the case of the north dip-pole where the lines of force, on the north side of it, instead of converging radially, tend to bunch into a channel. Although it is therefore unrealistic to attempt to specify the locations of the dip-poles exactly, the present adopted positions are 76°·2 N., 100°·2 W. and 65°·8 S., 139°·5 E. The two magnetic dip-poles are thus not antipodal, the line joining them passing the centre of the Earth at a distance of about 1,100 kilometres. The distances of the magnetic dip-poles from the north and south geographic poles are about 1,600 and 2,700 kilometres respectively.

There is also a " magnetic equator ", at all points of which the vertical force is zero and a magnetized needle remains horizontal. This line runs between 2° and 10° north of the geographical equator in the eastern hemisphere, turns sharply south off the West African coast, and crosses South America through Brazil, Bolivia and Peru; it re-crosses the geographical equator in mid-Pacific.

Reference has already been made to secular changes in the Earth's field. The following table indicates the changes in magnetic declination (or variation of the compass). Similar, though much smaller, changes have occurred in " dip " or magnetic inclination. Secular changes differ throughout the world. Although the London observations strongly suggest a cycle of several hundred years, an exact repetition is unlikely.

London		Greenwich	
1580	11° 15′ E.	1850	22° 24′ W.
1622	5 56 E.	1900	16 29 W.
1665	1 22 W.	1925	13 10 W.
1730	13 00 W.	1950	9 07 W.
1773	21 09 W.	1972	6 56 W.

In order that up-to-date information on the variation of the compass may be available, many governments publish magnetic charts on which there are lines (called isogonic) passing through all places at which specified values of declination will be found at the date of the chart.

In the British Isles, isogonic lines now run approximately north-east to south-west. Though there are considerable local deviations due to geological causes, a rough value of magnetic declination may be obtained by assuming that at 50° N. on the meridian of Greenwich, the value in 1976 is 6° 26′ west and allowing an increase of 18′ for each degree of latitude northwards and one of 28′ for each degree of longitude westwards. For example, at 53° N., 5° W., declination will be about 6° 26′ +54′ +140′, i.e. 9° 40′ west. The average annual change at the present time is about 6′·5 decrease.

The number of magnetic observatories now approaches 200—widely scattered over the globe. In Great Britain three are maintained by the Government: at Hartland, North Devon, at Eskdalemuir in Dumfriesshire, Scotland, and at Lerwick, Shetland Islands, while a fourth is maintained by Stonyhurst College, Lancashire. Some recent annual mean values of the magnetic elements for Hartland are given below.

The normal worldwide terrestrial magnetic field corresponds approximately to that of a very strong small bar magnet near the centre of the Earth but with appreciable smooth spatial departures. The origin and slow secular change of the normal field is not yet fully understood but is generally ascribed to electric currents associated with fluid motions within the Earth's core. Superposed on the normal field are local and regional anomalies whose magnitudes may in places exceed that of the normal field; these are due to the influence of mineral deposits in the Earth's crust. A small proportion of the field is of external origin, mostly associated with electric currents in the ionosphere. The configuration of the external field and the ionization of the atmosphere depend on the incident particle and radiation flux. There are, therefore, short-term and non-periodic as well as diurnal, 27-day, seasonal and 11-year periodic changes in the magnetic field, dependent upon the position of the Sun and the degree of solar activity.

Year	Declina-tion West	Dip or Inclina-tion	Hori-zontal Force	Vertical Force
	° ′	° ′	oersted	oersted
1945	11 46	66 55	0·1843	0·4326
1950	11 06	66 54	0·1848	0·4334
1955	10 30	66 49	0·1859	0·4340
1960	9 59	66 44	0·1871	0·4350
1965	9 30	66 34	0·1887	0·4354
1970	9 06	66 26	0·1903	0·4364
1974	8 40	66 19	0·1917	0·4372

Magnetic Storms. Occasionally—sometimes with great suddenness—the Earth's magnetic field is subject for several hours to marked disturbance. In extreme cases, departures in field intensity as much as one tenth the normal value are experienced. In many instances, such disturbances are accompanied by widespread displays of aurorae, marked changes in the incidence of cosmic rays, an increase in the reception of ' noise ' from the Sun at radio frequencies together with rapid changes in the ionosphere and induced electric currents within the earth which adversely affect radio and telegraphic communications. The disturbances are generally ascribed to flux changes in the stream of neutral and ionized particles which emanates from the Sun and through which the Earth is continuously passing. Some of these changes are associated with visible eruptions on the Sun, usually in the region of sunspots. There is a marked tendency for disturbances to recur after intervals of about 27 days, the apparent period of rotation of the Sun on its axis, which is consistent with the sources being located on particular areas of the Sun.

ARTIFICIAL SATELLITES AND SPACE PROBES

The progress of rocket research during the last war led to the development by the Germans in 1944 of the V.2 rocket which, if fired vertically, attained a height of 180 km. Before the end of the decade the U.S. rocket engineers had increased this maximum height to 400 km by using a two-stage rocket, the first stage being a V.2 and the second a WAC Corporal. Plans for using multi-stage rockets to put artificial satellites into orbit around the earth during the International Geophysical Year (July 1957–December 1958) were announced by both the U.S. and the U.S.S.R. Such projects also called for an immense effort in establishing optical, radio, and radar tracking facilities around the world.

The historic event which heralded the Space Age occurred on 1957 October 4 when the U.S.S.R. successfully injected a " sputnik " into an orbit inclined at 65° to the earth's equator. One month later " Sputnik 2 " was also put into orbit, carrying a dog that survived the ascent trajectory and lived for several days orbiting the earth. The rate of satellite launching has increased since 1957 and by the end of 1960 the number of artificial satellites in orbit around the Earth exceeded the number of natural satellites known to be in the Solar System. All the satellites launched up to the end of 1960 have been sent up in the same direction as the rotation of the Earth, *i.e.*, eastwards. Thus they are able to start with the benefit of the Earth's rotational velocity at the particular launching site. This is why these satellites always appear to move in an easterly direction. However, the first satellite launching of 1961 (*Samos* 2) achieved a retrograde orbit.

Satellite Orbits

To consider the orbit of an artificial satellite it is best to imagine that one is looking at the Earth from a distant point in space. The Earth would then be seen to be rotating about its axis inside the orbit described by the rapidly revolving satellite. The inclination of a satellite orbit to the Earth's equator (which generally remains almost constant throughout the satellite's lifetime) gives at once the maximum range of latitudes over which the satellite passes. Thus a satellite whose orbit has an inclination of 53° will pass overhead all latitudes between S. 53° and N. 53°, but would never be seen in the zenith of any place nearer the poles than these latitudes. If we consider a particular place on the earth, whose latitude is less than the inclination of the satellite's orbit then the Earth's rotation carries this place under first the north-bound part of the orbit and then, later on, under the southbound position of the orbit, these two occurrences being always less than 12 hours apart for satellites moving in direct orbits (*i.e.* to the east). For satellites in retrograde orbits the words " north-bound " and " southbound " should be interchanged in the preceding statement. As the value of the latitude of the observer increases and approaches the value of the inclination of the orbit, so this interval gets shorter until (when the latitude

is equal to the inclination) only one overhead passage occurs each day.

Orbital Variations

The relatively simple picture described above is unfortunately complicated by the considerable variations in the shape, orientation and size of the orbit during a satellite's lifetime. The major variations are due to the Earth's oblateness and to air-drag. A third cause, radiation pressure from the Sun, is noticeable only on large satellites of extremely low density.

The oblate shape of the Earth—the equatorial diameter is 43 km longer than the polar diameter—has two marked effects on a satellite orbit. It causes a regression of the nodes, amounting to several degrees a day for close satellites. Thus from a point in space, the whole orbit is seen to twist around the Earth, making a complete turn of 360° within a few months. This regression, which may also be described as the rotation of the orbital plane around the Earth's axis, is in the opposite direction to the satellite's motion, *i.e.* the orbit of a satellite with a direct motion regresses to the west. The actual amount of the regression depends, first, on the inclination of the orbit to the equator, being greatest at low inclinations and zero for a true polar orbit (inclination 90°). It is also dependent on the distance of the satellite from the Earth, being greatest for small orbits. At the distance of the Moon the regression is only 19° *a year*.

The orbit of *Samos* 2 is extremely interesting from this point of view as its regression is to the east almost an identical rate with the movement of the Sun. Thus there is hardly any change in the area of visibility over a long period of time.

The other effect the Earth's oblateness has on a satellite orbit is to cause a rotation of the line of apsides (*i.e.* the line joining the perigee and apogee points of the orbit). The rate of the rotation is dependent on the inclination of the orbit, and also on the distance of the satellite, again being greater for close satellites than for more distant ones. The value of this rotation has its greatest positive value (*i.e.* it moves forward along the orbit in the same direction as the satellite) at the equator and becomes zero at an inclination of 63°·4. As the inclination moves from 63°·4 to 90° the value increases again numerically, but with the opposite sign, the motion of the line of apsides being backwards along the orbit.

Even at heights of several hundred kilometres there is still sufficient atmosphere to cause a retarding effect on satellites. Although air-drag will have most effect around the perigee point the actual result is to reduce the height of the apogee point with hardly any change in perigee height and thus to decrease the eccentricity of the orbit until, in the final stage of a satellite's life-time, the orbit is almost circular. Unfortunately the air density at perigee height is not constant. It alters as the perigee moves from daylight into darkness and from darkness into daylight, and also as the latitude of perigee changes

SATELLITE HEIGHTS AND VELOCITIES

Period		Height, kilometres	Velocity, km per hour	Period		Height, kilometres	Velocity, km per hour
h	m			h	m		
1	28	182	28,077	3	40	5,700	20,686
1	32	380	27,663	3	50	6,064	20,382
1	36	575	27,274	4	00	6,428	20,096
1	40	766	26,905	5	00	8,473	18,655
1	44	954	26,556	6	00	10,393	17,555
1	48	1,141	26,224	7	00	12,207	16,676
1	52	1,326	25,907	8	00	13,937	15,950
1	56	1,508	25,606	9	00	15,596	15,335
2	00	1,688	25,318	10	00	17,194	14,806
2	04	1,867	25,043	11	00	18,739	14,344
2	08	2,042	24,779	12	00	20,529	13,934
2	12	2,216	24,526	13	00	21,699	13,567
2	16	2,390	24,283	14	00	23,120	13,235
2	20	2,560	24,050	15	00	24,509	12,934
2	24	2,729	23,826	16	00	25,865	12,659
2	28	2,897	23,609	17	00	27,195	12,406
2	32	3,064	23,400	18	00	28,498	12,171
2	36	3,228	23,199	19	00	29,779	11,954
2	40	3,392	23,004	20	00	31,036	11,751
2	50	3,795	22,544	21	00	32,272	11,562
3	00	4,189	22,117	22	00	33,490	11,384
3	10	4,577	21,723	23	00	34,689	11,217
3	20	4,958	21,354	24	00	35,871	11,059
3	30	5,332	21,010				

due to the rotation of the line of apsides. There is already some evidence that the atmospheric density varies with the sunspot cycle. In addition unpredictable short-period variations in the output of solar radiation may also occur and these have the effect of increasing the air density at any given height. Thus the air-drag on a satellite is by no means a constant factor and this is the reason why it is not possible to forecast accurately the position of a satellite for any considerable period of time. There is also some retardation due to electrified particles but this effect may be included with the air-drag.

Radiation pressure from the Sun only has any appreciable effect on large satellites of extremely low density such as the 30 metre diameter balloon, *Echo* 1. For such satellites, however, this effect can be severe, and for heights greater than a few hundred kilometres, it can equal or even surpass that due to air-drag. The effect on the orbit is very much more complicated than that due to air-drag, and even the signs of the variations can change periodically with time. Thus it is possible for the eccentricity to increase rather than decrease, with an increase in apogee height and a decrease in perigee height.

For close artificial satellites the gravitational attractions of the Sun and Moon are many thousand times weaker than that of the Earth's equatorial bulge and need only be considered in an extremely precise analysis of observational material.

Height and Velocity

The mean height of a satellite above the Earth's surface, which is determined by its orbital velocity, is related to its period of revolution around the Earth as is shown by the table above.

As the orbit shrinks due to air-drag, both the mean height and the period decrease so that the retarding effect of air-drag actually causes the satellite to move faster, though in a smaller orbit.

Satellite Launchings, 1957–74

Many different types of orbit have been achieved though the vast majority have had a direct motion. The majority of the Russian satellite orbits have had inclinations of 65° or 49° and orbits entirely below 2000 kilometres in height. An important exception was Lunik 3 whose original inclination was 75° and initial apogee height 470,000 km. This satellite orbited the Moon on its first revolution, returning with the first photographs of the other side of the Moon, which were transmitted back to the Earth when near perigee.

The American satellites have been injected into orbits of various inclinations. The early Explorers and Vanguards are in orbits of inclination about 28–35° while near-polar orbits were achieved with the Discoverers. Other series of launchings such as the Transit, Tiros and Echo put satellites in orbits of intermediate inclinations. In contrast to the heavy, but short-lived, Russian satellites, a number of those launched by the U.S. have been very small and have been put in larger orbits which have given them considerably longer life-times.

One launching project caused great controversy amongst astronomers. This was the so-called "West Ford" project, involving the launching of a Midas satellite into a polar orbit, carrying a dispenser. The dispenser contains several hundred million small needles and these are released after the Midas has been successfully injected into a selected orbit. The needles form a belt around the Earth which is used as a reflector for radio signals. The first attempt (1961 α δ) failed but the second (1963–14) has been successful. [continued on p. 169

Designation	Satellite	Launch date	i	P	e	Perigee height (km)
1974-		1974	°	m		
16	Cosmos 636, rocket	March 20	65·0	89·9	0·015	168
17	Cosmos 637, launcher, launcher rocket	March 26	0·2	1426	0	35,600
18	Cosmos 638, rocket	April 3	51·8	89·4	0·009	186
19	Cosmos 639, rocket, capsule	April 4	81·3	88·5	0·002	188
20	? , capsule, capsule, rocket	April 10	94·5	88·4	0·007	148
21	Cosmos 640, rocket	April 11	81·3	88·8	0·002	201
22	Westar 1.	April 13	0	1436	0	35,786
23	Molniya 1AC, launcher rocket, launcher, rocket	April 20	62·9	737·6	0·741	624
24	Cosmos 641–648, rocket	April 23	74·0	114·6	0·006	1,389
25	Meteor 17, rocket	April 24	81·2	102·6	0·002	865
26	Molniya 2J, launcher rocket, launcher, rocket	April 26	62·9	737·0	0·742	600
27	Cosmos 649, rocket, capsule	April 29	62·8	89·3	0·009	181
28	Cosmos 650, rocket	April 29	74·0	113·5	0·002	1,369
29	Cosmos 651	May 15	65·0	89·6	0·001	250
30	Cosmos 652, rocket, capsule	May 15	51·8	89·6	0·013	173
31	Cosmos 653, rocket, capsule	May 15	62·8	89·3	0·007	192
32	Cosmos 654	May 17	65·0	89·6	0·001	248
33	SMS1	May 17	1·9	1340·4	0·038	32,345
34	Intercosmos 11, rocket	May 17	50·6	94·5	0·002	483
35	Cosmos 655, rocket	May 21	74·1	95·3	0·001	523
36	Cosmos 656, rocket	May 27	51·6	89·2	0·009	179
37	Luna 22, launcher rocket, launcher	May 29	(lunar probe)			
38	Cosmos 657, rocket	May 30	62·8	89·2	0·009	177
39	ATS6	May 30	0·8	1436·0	0	35,770
40	Explorer 52, rocket	June 3	89·8	3077·9	0·902	513
41	Cosmos 658, rocket	June 6	65·0	89·4	0·006	204
42	?	June 6	110·5	89·8	0·019	136
43	Cosmos 659, rocket, capsule	June 13	62·8	89·3	0·013	153
44	Cosmos 660, rocket	June 18	83·0	109·1	0·104	397
45	Cosmos 661, rocket	June 22	74·0	95·2	0·003	511
46	Salyut 3, rocket	June 24	51·6	89·1	0·003	213
47	Cosmos 662, rocket	June 26	70·9	95·5	0·039	271
48	Cosmos 663, rocket	June 27	82·9	104·9	0·002	972
49	Cosmos 664, rocket	June 29	72·8	89·7	0·010	191
50	Cosmos 665, launcher, rocket, launcher rocket	June 29	62·8	92·8	0·029	216
51	Soyuz 14*, rocket	July 3	51·6	88·5	0·002	195
52	Meteor 18, rocket	July 9	81·2	102·6	0·002	865
53	Cosmos 666, rocket, capsule	July 12	62·8	89·6	0·011	181
54	NTS-1, rocket	July 14	125·1	468·4	0·008	13,445
55	Aeros 2, rocket	July 16	97·4	95·6	0·047	224
56	Molniya 2K, launcher rocket, launcher, rocket	July 23	62·9	737·6	0·742	604
57	Cosmos 667, rocket, capsule	July 25	65·0	89·5	0·011	176
58	Cosmos 668, rocket	July 25	70·9	92·2	0·017	270
59	Cosmos 669, rocket, capsule	July 26	81·3	88·9	0·002	209
60	Molniya S1, launcher, launcher rocket, rocket	July 29	0·1	1439	0	35,850
61	Cosmos 670, rocket	August 6	50·6	89·5	0·006	211
62	Cosmos 671, rocket, capsule	August 7	62·8	89·8	0·012	182
63	? , rocket	August 9	98·9	101·8	0·005	806
64	Cosmos 672, rocket	August 12	51·8	88·6	0·002	195
65	?	August 14	110·5	89·9	0·020	135
66	Cosmos 673, rocket	August 16	81·2	97·2	0·002	607
67	Soyuz 15*, rocket	August 26	51·6	88·5	0·005	173
68	Cosmos 674, rocket	August 29	65·0	89·5	0·011	175
69	Cosmos 675, rocket	August 29	74·0	113·7	0·004	1,365
70	ANS1, rocket	August 30	98·0	99·1	0·064	258

ARTIFICIAL SATELLITES LAUNCHED IN 1974–75

Desig-nation	Satellite	Launch date	i	P	e	Perigee height (km)
			°	m		
1974-		**1974**				
71	Cosmos 676, rocket	September 11	74·0	101·0	0·001	796
72	Cosmos 677–684, rocket	September 19	74·0	114·5	0·004	1,399
73	Cosmos 685, rocket	September 20	65·0	89·4	0·006	205
74	Cosmos 686, rocket	September 26	71·0	92 2	0·016	273
75	Westar 2	October 10	0·0	1435·4	0	35,761
76	Cosmos 687, rocket	October 11	74·0	94·5	0·030	286
77	Ariel 5, rocket	October 15	2·9	95·0	0·003	504
78	Cosmos 688, rocket, capsule	October 18	62·8	89·8	0·013	179
79	Cosmos 689, rocket	October 18	82·9	105·1	0·002	981
80	Cosmos 690, rocket	October 22	62·8	90·3	0·011	215
81	Molniya 1AD, launcher rocket, launcher, rocket	October 24	62·8	736·4	0·740	656
82	Cosmos 691, rocket, capsule	October 25	65 0	89·5	0·012	173
83	Meteor 19, rocket	October 28	81·2	102·5	0·004	843
84	Luna 23, launcher, launcher rocket	October 28		(lunar	probe)	
85	? , rocket, capsule	October 29	96·7	88·9	0·008	162
86	Intercosmos 12, rocket	October 31	74·0	94·1	0·034	243
87	Cosmos 692, rocket, capsule	November 1	62·8	89·4	0·007	197
88	Cosmos 693, rocket, capsule	November 4	81·3	89·1	0·002	219
89	NOAA4, Oscar 7, Intasat 1	November 15	101·7	115·0	0·001	1,447
90	Cosmos 694, rocket, capsule	November 16	72·8	89·4	0·011	173
91	Cosmos 695, rocket	November 20	71·0	92·0	0·014	273
92	Molniya 3A, launcher rocket, launcher, rocket	November 21	62·8	737·3	0·741	628
93	Intelsat 4F, rocket	November 22	0·4	1436·2	0	35,781
94	Skynet 2B, rocket	November 23	2·3	1469·5	0·004	36,255
95	Cosmos 696, rocket	November 27	72·8	89·8	0·009	205
96	Soyuz 16★, rocket	December 2	51·8	89·2	0·008	184
97	Helios 1	December 10		(space	probe)	
98	Cosmos 697, rocket, capsule	December 13	62·8	90·2	0·016	174
99	Meteor 20, rocket	December 17	81·2	102·4	0·004	842
100	Cosmos 698, rocket	December 18	74·0	95·3	0·003	515
101	Symphonie 1	December 19	13·2	688·4	0·738	395
102	Molniya 2L, launcher rocket, launcher, rocket	December 21	62·9	736·8	0·740	659
103	Cosmos 699, rocket	December 24	65·0	89·8	0·023	114
104	Salyut 4, rocket	December 26	51·6	89·1	0·003	212
105	Cosmos 700, rocket	December 26	83·0	104·8	0·002	966
106	Cosmos 701, rocket	December 27	71·4	89·8	0·009	205
1975-		**1975**				
01	Soyuz 17★, rocket	January 10	51·6	88·8	0·005	185
02	Cosmos 702, rocket	January 17	71·3	89·7	0·008	205
03	Cosmos 703, rocket	January 21	82·0	102·1	0·091	197
04	Landsat 2	January 22	99·1	103·3	0·001	907
05	Cosmos 704, rocket, capsule	January 23	72·9	89·6	0·008	205
06	Cosmos 705, rocket	January 28	71·0	92·3	0·017	271
07	Cosmos 706, launcher rocket, launcher, rocket	January 30	62·8	719·5	0·737	623
08	Cosmos 707, rocket	February 5	74·0	95·1	0·003	501
09	Molniya 2M, launcher rocket, launcher, rocket	February 6	62·8	736·9	0·741	622
10	Starlette, rocket	February 6	49·8	104·5	0·023	807
11	SMS2	February 6	1·1	1456·4	0·012	35,680
12	Cosmos 708, rocket	February 12	69·2	113·6	0·003	1,369
13	Cosmos 709, rocket, capsule	February 12	62·8	89·4	0·010	181
14	SRATS, rocket	February 24	31·5	120·1	0·179	249
15	Cosmos 710, rocket	February 26	65·0	89·6	0·012	176

A third Anglo-American satellite, Ariel 3, was launched on May 5, 1967, and has been of great interest to visual observers. Sets of mirrors and highly reflective solar cells on its sides cause the observer to see a series of flashes and the observations are used to determine the direction of the axis of rotation of the satellite.

In order to monitor the Arab–Israeli war, and in particular the Egyptian battlefield, the Russians launched a number of Cosmos satellites in the first half of October 1973. The orbits were very carefully chosen to take the satellites, at low heights, directly over the battlefield during daylight.

Apart from their names, e.g. Cosmos 6 Rocket or Injun 3, the satellites are also classified according to their date of launch. Thus 1961 α refers to the launching of Samos 2. The next satellite launching was 1961 β and so on. A number following the Greek letter is intended to indicate the relative brightness of the satellites put in orbit. From the beginning of 1963 the Greek letters are replaced by numbers and the numbers by roman letters e.g. 1963–01A. In this table are given the designation and names of the main objects in orbit (in the order A, B, C . . . etc.), the launch date and some initial orbital data. These are the inclination to the equator (i), the nodal period of revolution (P), the eccentricity, e, and the perigee height. The names of those satellites which have already disintegrated in the Earth's atmosphere or returned to the Earth's surface are printed in *italics*. A satellite which carried a human being is indicated by an asterisk.

Since the last edition of *Whitaker's Almanack* the following satellites launched in the years 1964–74 have disintegrated in the Earth's atmosphere:—

1964-52A	1964-52B	1965-60B	1965-108A
1966-63A	1966-110B	1968-85D	1970-13A
1970-13D	1970-66A	1971-19A	1971-106A
1972-05A	1972-05C	1972-81E	1972-95A
1972-95F	1972-98A	1972-98D	1973-27B
1973-99B	1974-10A	1974-12A	

Observation of Satellites

The regression of the orbit around the Earth causes alternate periods of visibility and invisibility, though this is of little concern to the radio or radar observer. To the visual observer the following cycle of events normally occurs (though the cycle may start in any position): invisibility, morning observations before dawn, invisibility, evening observations after dusk, invisibility, morning observations before dawn, and so on. With reasonably high satellites and for observers in high latitudes around the summer solstice the evening observations follow the morning observations without interruption as sunlight passing over the polar regions can still illuminate satellites which are passing over temperate latitudes at local midnight. At the moment all satellites rely on sunlight to make them visible though a satellite with a flashing light has been suggested for a future launching. The observer must be in darkness or twilight in order to make any useful observations and the durations of twilight and the sunrise, sunset times given on page II of each month will be a useful guide.

Some of the satellites are visible to the naked eye and much interest has been aroused by the spectacle of a bright satellite disappearing into the Earth's shadow. The event is even more fascinating telescopically as the disappearance occurs gradually as the satellite traverses the Earth's penumbral shadow, and during the last few seconds before the eclipse is complete the satellite may change colour (under suitable atmospheric conditions) from yellow to red. This is because the last rays of sunlight are reflected through the denser layers of our atmosphere before striking the satellite.

Some satellites rotate about one or more axes so that a periodic variation in brightness is observed. This was particularly noticeable in several of the U.S.S.R. satellites.

Satellite research has already provided some interesting results. Among them may be mentioned a revised value of the Earth's oblateness. 1/298·2, and the discovery of the Van Allen radiation belts.

ROYAL OBSERVATORIES

Royal Greenwich Observatory
Herstmonceux, Sussex

The Royal Observatory was established at Greenwich in 1675 by Charles II for improving methods of navigation. Latterly the growth of London, with its smoke and bright lights, seriously hampered astronomical observations there, and it was decided in 1946 to move the telescopes to Herstmonceux Castle in Sussex. The removal was completed by 1958. The meridian of zero longitude still passes through the old site, which now houses the Department of Navigation and Astronomy of the National Maritime Museum.

At the Observatory astronomical measurements are made of the positions, motions and distances of the heavenly bodies, and of such physical characteristics as their luminosities, masses and temperatures. Two meridian instruments and six equatorially-mounted telescopes are devoted to this work, and the Isaac Newton telescope, a 2.5 metre reflector for the use of any qualified British astronomer, was completed in 1967. The Observatory is responsible for the time service of the United Kingdom and the time zones of the world are based on Greenwich Mean Time.

H.M. Nautical Almanac Office

The *Nautical Almanac* was first published for 1767 by the Board of Longitude. The Office is now a branch of the Royal Greenwich Observatory. Annual publications—Astronomical Ephemeris, Nautical Almanac, Air Almanac, Star Almanac.

Royal Observatory
Blackford Hill, Edinburgh 9

The Observatory, founded by the Astronomical Institution in 1818 on Calton Hill, was moved to its present site in 1896. Its work, which is closely linked with that of the Astronomy Department of Edinburgh University, is concerned with the physics of stars and interstellar matter and the structure and evolution of our galaxy and external galaxies. Observational data are secured with various telescopes in Edinburgh and in Monte Porzio, Italy, where the Observatory operates an outstation. The Observatory has specialized in the design and construction of advanced data processing equipment.

Astronomer Royal for Scotland and Regius Professor of Astronomy in the University of Edinburgh, Prof. V. C. Reddish O.B.E., Ph.D., D.Sc.

TIDAL CONSTANTS

THE TIME OF HIGH WATER *at the undermentioned Ports and Places may be* approximately *found by taking the appropriate Time of High Water at the* Standard Port *(as shown on pp. 172, 173, etc.) and adding thereto the quantities annexed. The columns headed " Springs " and " Neaps " show the height of the tide above datum for Mean High Water Springs and Mean High Water Neaps respectively.*

Tidal data is no longer available for a number of places which formerly appeared in the list below. These places (with the name of the substitute now recorded) are: *Air Point* (Mostyn Quay); *Ardrishaig* (East Loch Tarbert); *Arisaig* (Loch Moidart); *Ayr Pt., I.o.M.* (Peel); *Beachy Head* (Eastbourne); *Beaumaris* (Menai Bridge); *Brieile* (Scheveningen); *Broughty Ferry* (Newburgh); *Burryport* (Whiteford Lighthouse); *Caen* (Cayeux); *Caernarvon* (Llanddwyn Isld.); *Dumbarton* (Bowling); *Dumfries* (Port Carlisle); *Fareham* (Itchenor); *Fifeness* (Anstruther Easter); *Glasson Dock* (Tarn Pt.); *Gravesend* (Tilbury Dock); *Greenwich* (R. Albert Dock); *Hythe* (Totland Bay); *Lancaster* (Duddon Bar); *Lynmouth* (Porlock Bay); *Nash Pt.* (Chepstow); *Needles Pt.* (Freshwater Bay); *Neath* (Porthcawl); *Nore Lt.* (Chatham); *Port Harrington* (Heston Islet); *Portishead* (Avonmouth); *St. Agnes* (Coverack); *St. Mary's* (Sennen Cove); *Start Pt.* (Lulworth Cove); *Stockton* (Seaham); *Sutton Bridge* (Blacktoft); *Torbay* (Torquay); *Woolwich* (Hammersmith Br.); *Worms Head* (Ferryside); *Honfleur Harbour* (Duclair).

Port	Diff.	Springs	Neaps	Port	Diff.	Springs	Neaps
	h.m.	metres	metres		h.m.	metres	metres
Aberdeen..........*Leith*	−1 16	4·3	3·4	Coverack.........*Bristol*	−1 59	5·3	4·2
Aberdovey.....*Liverpool*	−3 16	4·8	3·8	*Cowes (West)...London*	−2 28	4·2	3·5
Aberystwyth...*Liverpool*	−3 34	4·8	3·7	Cromarty.........*Leith*	−2 51	4·2	3·4
Aldeburgh.......*London*	−3 6	2·8	2·7	Cromer............*Hull*	+0 37	5·3	4·2
Alderney..........*London*	+5 32	6·3	4·7	Dartmouth......*London*	+4 28	4·8	3·6
Alloa..............*Leith*	+0 46	5·6	4·2	Deal...............*London*	−2 27	6·1	5·0
Amlwch......*Liverpool*	−0 47	6·3	5·7	Devonport......*London*	+4 00	5·5	4·4
Anstruther Easter...*Leith*	−0 22	5·5	4·4	Dieppe...........*London*	−3 8	9·1	7·1
Antwerp........*London*	+1 20	5·4	4·5	Dingle Harbour.*Liverpool*	+5 30	3·5	2·6
Appledore.......*Bristol*	−1 24	7·5	5·2	Donegal Hbr...*Liverpool*	−5 26	3·6	2·7
Arbroath..........*Leith*	−0 30	5·0	4·1	Douglas.......*Liverpool*	−0 4	6·9	5·4
Ardrossan.......*Greenock*	−0 20	3·2	2·7	Dover...........*London*	−2 42	6·7	5·3
*Arundel..........*London*	−1 8	3·1	2·2	Duclair...........*London*	−0 42	7·8	6·4
Avonmouth......*Bristol*	0 0	13·2	10·0	Duddon Bar....*Liverpool*	+0 3	8·5	6·6
Ayr.............*Greenock*	−0 20	3·0	2·6	Dunbar............*Leith*	−0 8	5·2	4·2
Ballycotton......*Bristol*	−1 41	3·8	3·0	Dundalk (Sldr'sPt)..*L'pool*	+0 19	4·8	3·9
Banff.............*Leith*	−2 41	3·2	2·5	Dundee............*Leith*	+0 15	5·3	4·3
Bantry Harbour.*Liverpool*	+6 51	3·3	2·4	Dungeness......*London*	−2 56	8·0	6·3
Bardsey Island..*Liverpool*	−3 23	4·4	3·4	Dunkirk.........*London*	−1 57	6·8	4·7
Barmouth......*Liverpool*	−3 9	4·9	3·9	Eastbourne......*London*	−2 52	7·3	5·6
Barnstaple Bridge..*Bristol*	−1 7	4·1	1·4	East Loch Tarbert..*G'nock*	−0 5	3·2	2·8
Barrow........*Liverpool*	+0 15	9·2	7·1	Exmouth Dock...*London*	+4 50	4·0	2·8
Barry Island......*Bristol*	−0 25	11·6	8·9	Eyemouth.........*Leith*	−0 20	4·7	3·7
Belfast............*London*	−2 48	3·5	3·0	Falmouth........*London*	+3 30	5·3	4·2
Berwick...........*Leith*	−0 1	4·7	3·8	Ferryside.........*Bristol*	−1 00	6·7	4·5
Bideford.........*Bristol*	−1 24	5·9	3·6	Filey Bay.........*Leith*	+1 51	5·8	4·9
Blacktoft..........*Hull*	+0 24	5·6	3·3	Fishguard.....*Liverpool*	−4 9	4·7	3·4
Blakeney.........*Hull*	+0 31	3·1	2·1	Flushing......*London*	−0 37	4·7	3·9
Blyth.............*Leith*	+0 51	5·0	3·9	Folkestone.......*London*	−2 54	7·1	5·7
Boscastle.........*Bristol*	−1 39	7·3	5·6	Formby Pt......*Liverpool*	−0 21	9·0	7·3
Boulogne........*London*	−2 48	8·9	7·1	Fowey.........*London*	+3 48	5·4	4·3
Bowling.......*Greenock*	+0 24	4·0	3·4	Fraserburgh........*Leith*	−2 16	3·9	3·1
Brest............*London*	+2 25	7·4	5·8	†*Freshwater Bay.*London*	−4 33	2·6	2·3
Bridgewater Bar..*Bristol*	−0 22	4·6	1·9	Galway Bay.....*Liverpool*	−6 10	4·7	3·5
Bridlington........*Leith*	+2 4	6·0	4·7	Glasgow........*Greenock*	+0 27	4·8	4·0
Bridport.........*London*	+4 32	4·1	3·0	Goole............*Hull*	+1 12	5·6	3·6
Brighton.........*London*	−2 52	6·5	5·1	Granton Pier......*Leith*	0 0	5·6	4·5
Buckie............*Leith*	−2 54	3·6	3·0	Granville.........*London*	+4 32	12·8	9·5
Bude Haven.......*Bristol*	−1 34	7·7	5·8	Grimsby.........*Hull*	−0 26	7·0	5·6
Burntisland.......*Leith*	0 0	5·6	4·5	Hartlepool.........*Leith*	+0 59	5·1	4·0
Calais...........*London*	−2 25	6·9	5·6	Harwich.........*London*	−2 18	4·0	3·4
Campbeltown...*Greenock*	−0 32	3·0	2·5	Hastings.........*London*	−2 47	7·5	5·8
Cape Cornwall...*Bristol*	−2 26	6·0	4·3	Haverfordwest..*Liverpool*	−4 36	2·2	0·3
Cardiff............*Bristol*	−0 7	12·3	9·4	Havre, Le........*London*	−4 0	7·8	6·4
Cardigan......*Liverpool*	−4 7	4·7	3·5	Hestan Islet.....*Liverpool*	+0 25	8·3	6·3
Carmarthen Bar...*Bristol*	−0 39	2·6	0·4	Hilbre Island...*Liverpool*	−0 16	9·0	7·2
Cayeux...........*London*	−3 00	10·1	7·7	Holyhead......*Liverpool*	−0 54	5·7	4·5
Chatham (N.Lock)*London*	−1 4	6·0	4·9	Hook of Holland..*London*	+0 19	2·0	1·7
Chepstow........*Bristol*	+0 20	—	—	†*Hurst Point....*London*	−3 43	2·7	2·3
Cherbourg......*London*	−6 4	6·2	4·8	Ilfracombe........*Bristol*	−1 9	9·2	6·9
Chester.......*Liverpool*	+1 5	4·2	1·7	Inveraray.......*Greenock*	+0 11	3·3	3·0
Chichester Hbr...*London*	−2 30	4·9	3·0	Invergordon.......*Leith*	−2 41	4·3	3·3
†*Christchrch Hbr.*London*	−4 58	1·8	1·4	Ipswich.........*London*	−1 58	4·2	3·4
Cobh..........*Liverpool*	−5 59	3·7	2·8				

* Approximate figures only, owing to abnormality of tides in the area.

† 1st H.W. (Springs).

Port	Diff.	Springs	Neaps
	h.m.	metres	metres
Itchenor.........London	−2 21	5·1	4·0
Kinsale Harbour.Liverpool	−6 11	4·0	3·2
Kirkcudbright..Liverpool	+0 15	7·5	5·9
Kirkwall.........Leith	−4 11	2·6	1·9
Lamlash.......Greenock	−0 26	3·2	2·7
Lerwick Harbour...Leith	−3 46	1·8	1·3
Limerick.......Liverpool	−4 40	5·9	4·5
‡Littlehampton..London	−2 38	5·7	4·6
Lizard............Bristol	−2 14	5·3	4·2
Llanddwyn Islnd.Liverpool	−1 47	4·3	3·4
Llanelly Bar......Bristol	−0 52	5·8	5·8
Loch Long.....Greenock	−0 5	3·4	2·9
Loch Moidart...Greenock	+6 0	4·3	3·1
Londonderry....London	−5 41	2·5	1·8
Looe (East)......London	+3 50	5·4	4·2
Lossiemouth......Leith	−2 58	3·7	2·9
Lowestoft........London	−4 26	2·4	2·1
*Lulworth Cove..London	+4 55	2·3	1·5
Lundy Island....Bristol	−1 19	8·0	5·9
Lyme Regis.....London	+4 50	4·3	3·1
†*Lymington....London	−3 23	3·0	2·6
Lynn Road........Hull	+0 7		
Margate Pier.....London	−1 50	4·8	3·9
Maryport....Liverpool	+0 24	8·6	6·6
Menai Bridge...Liverpool	−0 25	7·4	5·8
Mevagissey.....London	+3 48	5·4	4·3
Middlesbrough.....Leith	+1 10	5·6	4·5
Milford Haven..Liverpool	−5 12	7·0	5·2
Minehead Pier.....Bristol	—	10·7	8·0
Montrose........Leith	−0 16	4·8	3·9
Morecambe.....Liverpool	+0 1	9·5	7·6
Mostyn Quay..Liverpool	−0 10	8·7	6·9
Newburgh.........Leith	+0 51	4·1	3·0
Newcastle on Tyne..Leith	+0 55	5·3	4·1
Newhaven........London	−2 57	6·6	5·2
Newport (Mon.)..Bristol	−0 10	12·1	9·0
Newquay........London	−1 59	6·9	5·4
New Quay (Card.).L'pool	−3 41	4·7	3·6
North Shields.....Leith	+0 52	5·0	3·9
North Sunderland...Leith	+0 6	4·8	3·7
Oban..........Greenock	+5 45	4·0	2·9
Orfordness......London	−2 51	2·8	2·7
Ostend..........London	−1 33	5·6	4·7
Padstow.........Bristol	−1 49	7·3	5·6
Peel (I.O.M.)...Liverpool	−0 2	5·3	4·2
Pembroke Dock.Liverpool	−5 5	7·0	5·2
Penzance......Bristol	−2 16	5·6	4·4
Peterhead.........Leith	−1 56	3·8	3·1
Plymouth B'water.London	+3 54	5·5	4·4
†*Poole(Entrance).London	−5 8	2·0	1·6
Porlock Bay......Bristol	−0 52	10·3	8·0
Portmadoc.....Liverpool	−3 8	5·1	4·0
Port Patrick..Liverpool	+0 22	3·8	3·0
Port Talbot......Bristol	−0 54	9·7	7·5
Porthcawl........Bristol	−0 49	9·9	7·5
Portland B'water..London	+5 5	2·1	1·4
Portsmouth......London	−2 28	4·7	3·8
Preston........Liverpool	0 0	5·4	3·5
Pwllheli.......Liverpool	−3 18	4·9	3·7
Ramsey(I.O.M.)Liverpool	+0 4	7·3	5·8
Ramsgate Harbour London	−2 22	4·9	3·8

Port	Diff.	Springs	Neaps
	h.m.	metres	metres
Ribble Lt. House.Liverpool	−0 4	—	—
Rosslare Hbr...Liverpool	−5 29	1·7	1·3
Rosyth...........Leith	+0 6	5·8	4·7
R.A. Dock.......London	−0 25	7·1	5·8
Ryde............London	−2 28	4·5	3·7
St. Helier.......London	+4 47	11·1	8·1
St. Ives........Bristol	−2 9	6·6	4·9
St. Malo.......London	+4 26	12·0	9·0
St. Peter Port....London	+4 53	9·0	6·7
Salcombe........London	+4 5	5·3	4·1
Saltash...........London	+4 9	5·6	4·4
Scarborough......Leith	+1 49	5·7	4·6
Scheveningen....London	+0 28	2·1	1·7
Scrabster........Leith	+6 07	5·0	3·7
Seaham..........Leith	+0 54	5·2	4·1
Selsey Bill......London	−2 33	5·3	4·4
Sennen Cove....Bristol	−2 26	6·1	4·8
Sharpness......Bristol	+0 42	9·3	5·8
Sheerness........London	−1 19	5·7	4·8
Shoreham Hbr....London	−2 45	6·2	5·0
Silloth.......Liverpool	+0 35	9·2	6·9
††Southampton..London	−2 55	4·5	3·7
Southend........London	−1 24	5·7	4·8
Southwold........London	−3 51	2·5	2·2
Spurn Head.....Hull	−0 34	6·8	5·4
Stirling..........Leith	−1 12	2·9	1·6
Stonehaven.......Leith	−1 6	4·5	3·6
Stornoway.....Liverpool	−4 17	4·3	3·2
Stranraer......Greenock	−0 20	3·0	2·5
Stromness........Leith	−5 22	3·1	2·3
Sunderland......Leith	+0 52	5·2	4·2
†*Swanage......London	−5 18	2·0	1·6
Swansea Bay.....Bristol	−0 43	9·6	7·3
Tarn Point.....Liverpool	+0 5	8·3	6·4
Tay River Bar....Leith	−0 18	5·2	4·2
Tees R. (Entrance)..Leith	−1 9	5·5	4·3
Teignmouth.....London	+4 32	4·8	3·6
Tenby.........Bristol	−1 3	8·4	6·3
Tilbury Docks....London	−0 59	6·5	5·4
Tobermory.....Liverpool	−5 14	4·5	3·4
Torquay.........London	+4 35	4·9	3·7
†*Totland Bay...London	−3 58	2·7	2·3
Troon...........Greenock	−0 20	3·1	2·6
Truro...........London	+3 38	5·3	4·2
‡Tynemouth.......Leith	+0 57	5·1	3·9
Ushant..........London	+2 20	7·5	5·8
Valentia Hbr...Liverpool	+5 28	3·5	2·7
Walton on Naze..London	−2 9	4·2	3·4
Waterford Hbr....L'pool	−5 46	4·2	3·4
Weston S. Mare...Bristol	−0 25	12·0	9·1
*Wexford......Liverpool	−5 6	1·7	1·4
Whitby.........Leith	+1 32	5·4	4·3
Whiteford Lt. Hse.Bristol	−0 55	8·7	6·7
Whitehaven....Liverpool	+0 2	8·2	6·3
Wick.........Leith	−3 23	3·4	2·7
Wisbech..........Hull	+0 10	7·4	5·5
Workington....Liverpool	+0 9	8·4	6·4
Worthing........London	−2 38	6·1	4·8
Yarmouth Roads...Lond	−5 1	2·4	2·0
††*Yarmth(I.O.W.).Lond	−3 33	3·1	2·5
Ymuiden........London	+1 13	2·1	1·7
Youghal.......Liverpool	−5 53	3·9	3·2

* Approximate figures only, owing to abnormality of tides in area.   † 1st H.W. (Springs)   †† 1st H.W.
— No data available   ‡ Entrance.

The Standard Ports referred to in the heading are given in italic.

EXAMPLE.—Required times of high water at Stranraer on January 10, 1976:—

(a) Morning Tide.
Appropriate time of high
  water at *Greenock*..... 0546 hrs. (*Jan.* 10)
Tidal difference......... − 0020 hrs

         H.W. at *Stranraer*... 0526 hrs.

(b) Afternoon Tide.
Appropriate time of high
  water at *Greenock*..... 1818 hrs. (*Jan.* 10).
Tidal difference......... − 0020 hrs.

         H.W. at *Stranraer*... 1798 hrs.

JANUARY, 1976

High Water at the undermentioned Places (G.M.T.*)—

Heights given as: † Datum of Predictions below/above for each place —
London Bridge 3·20 m below; Liverpool 4·93 m below; Avonmouth 6·50 m below; Hull (Saltend) 3·90 m below; Greenock 1·62 m below; Leith and Granton 2·90 m below; Dun Laoghaire 0·20 m above.

Day	DoW	LB Mn	Ht	LB Aft	Ht	Liv Mn	Ht	Liv Aft	Ht	Avon Mn	Ht	Avon Aft	Ht	Hull Mn	Ht	Hull Aft	Ht	Green Mn	Ht	Green Aft	Ht	Leith Mn	Ht	Leith Aft	Ht	DunL Mn	Ht	DunL Aft	Ht
1	Th	114	6·7	1338	6·8	1049	9·0	2315	9·2	653	13·0	1913	12·9	543	7·0	1758	7·3	159	3·6	1243	3·7	157	5·5	1418	5·5	1059	4·1	2333	3·9
2	F	159	6·8	1423	6·9	1133	9·0	2358	9·4	736	13·4	1956	13·1	632	7·1	1841	7·3	023	3·4	1325	3·8	246	5·6	15 2	5·6	1141	4·1	1223	4·2
3	S	240	6·9	15 4	7·1			1213	9·4	815	13·5	2033	13·1	716	7·1	1919	7·3	1 9	3·4	14 2	3·8	331	5·6	1544	5·5	016	3·9	1223	4·2
4	S	318	7·1	1543	7·1	039	9·1	1253	9·3	851	13·4	21 4	13·1	755	7·0	1954	7·1	154	3·4	1445	3·8	412	5·5	1624	5·5	057	3·8	13 6	4·1
5	M	355	7·1	1620	7·2	117	9·1	1331	9·1	928	13·1	2144	12·6	830	6·8	2026	7·1	234	3·4	1522	3·6	451	5·3	17 4	5·3	140	3·7	1349	4·1
6	Tu	428	7·0	1657	7·2	155	8·8	14 7	8·8	10 3	13·1	2217	12·6	9 4	6·8	2057	7·0	312	3·3	1559	3·6	528	5·1	1742	5·1	221	3·6	1429	3·9
7	W	5 2	6·9	1733	6·8	231	8·5	1445	8·5	1037	12·0	2248	11·6	938	6·4	2131	6·7	349	3·3	1639	3·4	5 8	4·9	1823	4·9	3 4	3·4	1513	3·7
8	Th	540	6·7	1814	6·6	310	8·1	1525	8·1	11 9	11·4	2320	11·0	1013	6·0	2205	6·5	425	3·3	1725	3·2	650	4·7	19 4	4·7	350	3·3	1556	3·6
9	F	622	6·4	19 2	6·3	353	7·5	1611	7·7	1143	10·8	2358	10·3	1057	5·9	2255	6·1	5 4	3·2	1818	3·1	735	4·5	1949	4·6	442	3·2	1647	3·4
10	S	714	6·1	1958	6·0	443	7·1	17 7	7·3			1225	10·1	1151	5·7	2357	5·8	546	3·1	1924	2·9	826	4·4	2041	4·5	542	3·1	1746	3·3
11	S	819	5·6	22 3	5·6	545	7·1	1813	7·2	048	9·8	1325	9·7			13 3	5·5	638	3·0	2038	3·0	925	4·4	2143	4·4	648	3·1	1856	3·3
12	M	925	5·5	23 3	5·6	657	7·1	1926	7·4	158	9·6	1441	9·8	237	5·7	1418	5·7	742	3·1	2238	3·1	1031	4·4	2356	4·6	748	3·3	20 0	3·3
13	Tu	1027	5·7	23 2	5·9	8 3	7·4	2031	7·6	316	9·9	1559	10·3	335	6·0	1519	6·0	851	3·1	2327	3·2			1142	4·7	840	3·4	2054	3·4
14	W	1127	5·9	2358	6·2	9 6	7·9	2125	8·1	428	10·7	17 5	11·2	343	6·0	1612	6·4	949	3·4	2327	3·2	036	4·7	1321	5·1	925	3·5	2141	3·6
15	Th	049	6·6	1312	6·7	949	8·4	2214	8·5	531	11·4	18 1	12·0	527	6·7	1657	6·7	1039	3·5	12 7	3·6	053	4·9	1321	5·1	10 5	3·6	23 5	3·7
16	F	135	6·9	1358	7·1	1032	8·9	2254	8·9	622	12·4	1851	12·7	620	6·7	1740	7·0	1124	3·5	1253	3·7	142	5·1	14 7	5·1	1046	4·0	2345	3·9
17	S	219	7·3	1442	7·5	1113	9·3	2337	9·2	7 7	13·5	1936	13·6	656	7·2	19 0	7·5	013	3·3	1338	3·9	2 6	5·4	1447	5·1	1124	4·2	12 5	4·2
18	S	3 0	7·5	1524	7·7	1155	9·6			749	13·5	2018	13·6	737	7·3	1941	7·6	1 0	3·3	1422	3·9	346	5·6	1526	5·7	028	4·0	1246	4·3
19	M	339	7·6	1607	7·7	020	9·4	1236	9·8	832	13·7	21 1	13·7	818	7·3	2020	7·7	145	3·3	15 3	4·0	427	5·7	1652	5·5	111	4·0	1332	4·3
20	Tu	419	7·5	1647	7·6	1 6	9·4	1319	9·8	915	13·8	2143	13·6	858	7·1	21 3	7·6	230	3·4	1553	3·8	511	5·5	1739	5·6	157	3·9	1418	4·2
21	W	459	7·4	1732	7·3	146	9·1	14 1	9·4	959	13·6	2225	13·2	941	7·0	2148	7·4	314	3·4	1638	3·8	557	5·4	1830	5·5	247	3·8	1510	4·1
22	Th	544	7·1	1821	6·9	231	9·1	1446	9·3	1040	13·1	23 5	12·5	1027	6·7	2238	7·0	356	3·3	1729	3·5	653	5·4	1923	5·4	342	3·6	16 7	4·0
23	F	635	6·8	1919	6·6	317	8·7	1535	8·8	1123	12·1	2349	11·4	1122	6·4	2339	6·6	437	3·3	1831	3·3	748	5·0	2022	5·0	443	3·6	1716	3·7
24	S	738	6·5	2026	6·3	411	8·3	1634	8·3			12 11	10·6			1229	6·1	520	3·3	1951	3·1	853	4·8	2130	4·9	556	3·5	1834	3·6
25	S	854	6·3	2141	6·3	514	7·9	1745	7·9	043	10·8	1315	10·6	059	6·3	1348	6·0	614	3·1	2120	3·0	11 21	4·9	2246	4·9	712	3·5	1951	3·6
26	M	1016	6·2	2258	6·3	630	7·8	19 9	7·9	157	10·4	1438	10·6	226	6·2	15 4	6·2	731	3·0	2230	3·1	12 21	5·0	2359	5·0	820	3·6	2058	3·6
27	Tu	1134	6·3			750	7·9	2029	8·1	325	10·4	16 5	10·6	342	6·4	16 7	6·5	9 5	3·0	2327	3·1			1226	5·1	919	3·8	2156	3·7
28	W	0 5	6·4	1236	6·5	858	8·3	2131	8·3	444	11·1	1717	11·4	445	6·6	17 1	6·8	1012	3·1	1226	3·1	059	5·2	1321	5·2	10 8	3·8	2244	3·7
29	Th	1 0	6·6	1327	6·7	952	8·7	2222	8·6	549	12·0	1814	12·1	549	6·8	1747	7·0	11 5	3·4	1321	3·2	151	5·3	1410	5·4	1053	4·0	2326	3·8
30	F	145	6·8	1411	6·9	1038	9·0	23 5	8·9	640	12·7	1859	12·5	621	7·0	1827	7·2	1150	3·5	1234	3·7	237	5·4	1451	5·5	1133	4·1	2326	3·8
31	S					1119	9·2	2343	8·9			1939	13·0					237	3·3	1234	3·7			1451	5·5			2326	3·8

* All times shown are Greenwich Mean Time.
† Difference of height in metres from Ordnance Datum (Newlyn).
‡ Difference of height in metres from Ordnance Datum (Ireland).

FEBRUARY, 1976

High Water at the undermentioned Places (G.M.T.*)—

Day of Month	Day of Week	LONDON BRIDGE Mn. h.m.	Ht. m.	Aft. h.m.	Ht. m.	LIVERPOOL Mn. h.m.	Ht. m.	Aft. h.m.	Ht. m.	AVONMOUTH Mn. h.m.	Ht. m.	Aft. h.m.	Ht. m.	HULL (Salend) Mn. h.m.	Ht. m.	Aft. h.m.	Ht. m.	GREENOCK Mn. h.m.	Ht. m.	Aft. h.m.	Ht. m.	LEITH AND GRANTON Mn. h.m.	Ht. m.	Aft. h.m.	Ht. m.	DUN LAOGHAIRE Mn. h.m.	Ht. m.	Aft. h.m.	Ht. m.
		† Datum of Predictions 3·20 m. below				† Datum of Predictions 4·93 m. below				† Datum of Predictions 6·50 m. below				† Datum of Predictions 3·90 m. below				† Datum of Predictions 1·62 m. below				† Datum of Predictions 2·90 m. below				‡ Datum of Predictions 0·20 m. above			
1	S	225	6·9	1449	7·1	1156		1231	9·3	757	13·4	2015	13·1	659	7·0	19 0	7·2	059	3·3	1314	3·7	317	5·5	1528	5·5	0 2	3·8	12 9	4·1
2	M	3 0	7·1	1524	7·3	020	8·9	1251	9·2	831	13·5	2048	13·3	733	7·0	1933	7·1	139	3·3	1352	3·7	352	5·4	16 1	5·5	037	3·7	1246	4·1
3	Tu	334	7·2	1557	7·3	054	8·7	13 5	9·0	9 2	13·5	2120	13·0	8 5	6·9	20 1	7·2	215	3·3	1426	3·7	425	5·3	1635	5·4	113	3·7	1322	4·0
4	W	4 4	7·2	1630	7·2	137	8·7	1337	9·0	937	13·0	2149	12·7	834	6·7	2030	6·9	248	3·3	1459	3·6	457	5·1	17 9	5·2	147	3·6	1357	3·9
5	Th	445	7·1	17 2	7·2	156	8·5	14 8	8·7	10 5	12·6	2213	12·2	9 2	6·7	2121	6·6	319	3·3	1530	3·5	531	4·9	1745	5·1	222	3·5	1433	3·7
6	F	511	6·9	1737	6·8	227	8·2	1440	8·3	1029	12·0	2236	11·6	935	6·5	2135	6·7	348	3·3	16 4	3·4	6 8	4·8	1822	4·8	3 0	3·4	1511	3·6
7	S	547	6·6	1817	6·5	3 0	7·9	1518	7·9	1053	11·2	2344	10·8	10 9	6·2	2214	6·3	421	3·3	1642	3·2	646	4·6	19 2	4·7	343	3·3	1554	3·4
8	S	629	6·0	19 4	6·0	343	7·5	16 7	7·5	1126	10·4			1052	5·8	23 6	6·0	459	3·2	1728	3·1	732	4·4	1950	4·5	435	3·2	1649	3·2
9	M	717	5·8	1954	5·7	439	7·2	1631	7·2	044	9·4	1330	9·4	1153	5·5			543	3·1	1822	3·0	826	4·3	2051	4·4	539	3·1	1759	3·1
10	Tu	816	5·4	2057	5·5	550	7·0	1951	7·1	211	9·5	15 7	9·8	155	5·5	1434	5·7	639	3·1	1932	3·0	936	4·3	2 4	4·4	652	3·1	1916	3·2
11	W	928	5·2	22 7	5·5	826	7·7	2057	7·9	345	10·2	1633	10·8	314	5·8	1538	6·1	749	3·0	21 3	3·0	1052	4·4	2324	4·6	853	3·5	2118	3·5
12	Th	1041	5·6	2319	6·1	10 8	8·3	2234	9·0	451	11·4	1738	11·9	416	6·2	1630	6·6	9 9	3·1	2216	3·0	029	4·8	1258	4·6	941	3·7	2218	3·7
13	F	1151	6·1			1052	9·4	2318	9·4	549	12·3	1828	12·8	5 8	6·6	1718	7·0	1013	3·3	23 10	3·2	122	5·1	1345	5·3	1023	3·9	2246	3·9
14	S	021	6·5	1249	6·8	1136	9·8			649	13·3	19 3	13·6	553	7·1	18 1	7·4	11 4	3·5	2310	3·2	2 6	5·5	1427	5·6	11 3	4·0	2326	4·0
15	S	113	6·9	1338	7·3	0 2	9·7	1218	10·1	734	13·9	20 3	14·0	717	7·6	1924	7·7	1152	3·7			246	5·7	15 7	5·8	1144	4·1		
16	M	158	7·4	1423	7·7	045	9·8	13 0	10·1	817	14·4	2046	14·1	757	7·6	20 5	7·9	045	3·5	13 9	3·8	325	5·8	1547	5·9	0 6	4·3	1228	4·4
17	Tu	240	7·7	15 5	7·9	127	9·7	1343	10·0	9 0	14·3	2127	14·0	837	7·5	2046	7·8	131	3·4	1326	3·9	4 5	5·8	1632	5·9	049	4·1	1311	4·4
18	W	321	7·8	1548	7·9	2 7	9·4	1423	9·8	942	14·0	22 7	13·5	9 6	7·5	2121	7·5	214	3·4	1410	4·0	451	5·7	1720	5·8	135	4·1	1359	4·3
19	Th	4 2	7·8	1630	7·7	254	8·9	1513	8·8	1022	13·3	2244	12·7	953	7·2	2220	7·1	255	3·5	1453	4·0	539	5·5	18 9	5·5	222	4·0	1450	4·2
20	F	444	7·6	1713	7·3	334	8·4	16 9	8·2	11 3	12·4	2324	11·7	1052	6·4	2319	6·5	334	3·5	1539	3·9	631	5·2	19 3	5·3	315	3·8	1547	3·9
21	S	529	7·3	18 0	6·9	446	8·0	1722	7·6	1147	11·3			1156	6·0			411	3·5	16 20	3·7	726	5·0	20 3	5·0	416	3·6	1655	3·5
22	S	618	6·8	1852	6·5	618	6·8	1852	7·4	015	10·7	1246	10·3	041	6·0	1320	5·8	453	3·4	17 8	3·5	829	4·8	2112	4·8	527	3·4	1816	3·5
23	M	717	6·4	1954	6·2	446	7·8	1954	7·8	110	10·0	1411	9·8	215	5·9	1444	5·9	540	3·2	18 5	3·4	945	4·6	2235	4·7	648	3·5	1940	3·4
24	Tu	829	6·1	21 4	6·0	845	8·0	2123	8·0	3 2	10·0	1549	10·2	334	6·4	1552	6·5	646	2·9	1923	2·9	8 4	3·5	2349	4·7	8 4	3·5	2050	3·5
25	W	950	6·0	2228	6·2	941	8·8	2210	8·4	430	10·8	17 0	11·4	434	6·4	1645	6·8	841	2·9	2115	2·9	945	4·6	2235	4·7	9 7	3·6	2148	3·6
26	Th	1115	6·2	2343	6·5	1025	8·8	2249	8·7	536	11·8	1842	12·5	520	6·7	1727	7·2	10 4	3·1	2229	3·0	050	5·0	1312	5·0	959	3·8	2233	3·7
27	F			1219	6·3	11 11	9·1	2334	8·8	624	12·6	1928	12·8	6 9	6·9	18 4	7·7	1055	3·3	2320	3·1	140	5·2	1356	5·3	1040	3·9	2310	3·7
28	S	039	6·9	13 5	7·1					7 2	13·0	1918	12·8					1138	3·4			222	5·3	1435	5·4	1117	4·0	2343	3·7
29	S	126	7·1	1351	7·1													0 1	3·2	1219	3·5								

* All times shown are Greenwich Mean Time.   † Difference of height in metres from Ordnance Datum (Newlyn).

‡ Difference of height in metres from Ordnance Datum (Ireland).

MARCH, 1976

High Water at the undermentioned Places (G.M.T.*)—

Day of month	Day of week	LONDON BRIDGE † Datum 3·20 m. below Mn. h.m.	Ht. m.	Aft. h.m.	Ht. m.	LIVERPOOL † Datum 4·93 m. below Mn. h.m.	Ht. m.	Aft. h.m.	Ht. m.	AVONMOUTH † Datum 6·50 m. below Mn. h.m.	Ht. m.	Aft. h.m.	Ht. m.	HULL (Saltend) † Datum 3·90 m. below Mn. h.m.	Ht. m.	Aft. h.m.	Ht. m.	GREENOCK † Datum 1·62 m. below Mn. h.m.	Ht. m.	Aft. h.m.	Ht. m.	LEITH AND GRANTON † Datum 2·90 m. below Mn. h.m.	Ht. m.	Aft. h.m.	Ht. m.	DUN LAOGHAIRE ‡ Datum 0·20 m. above Mn. h.m.	Ht. m.	Aft. h.m.	Ht. m.
1	M	2 4	7·1	1427	7·2	1135	9·2	2356	8·9	736	13·2	1952	13·0	635	7·0	1836	7·2	040	3·2	1257	3·6	257	5·3	15 6	5·4	1150	4·0	1222	4·0
2	Tu	239	7·2	15 1	7·3	026	8·9	1238	9·0	8 9	13·3	2024	13·1	716	7·1	19 6	7·2	115	3·2	1332	3·6	328	5·3	1536	5·4	013	3·7	1253	3·8
3	W	310	7·2	1531	7·3	056	8·8	13 7	9·1	842	13·3	2053	13·1	735	7·1	1935	7·2	149	3·3	14 3	3·6	357	5·3	16 5	5·4	043	3·7	1325	3·8
4	Th	338	7·1	1630	7·1	123	8·7	1335	8·8	912	13·1	2119	12·9	8 4	7·0	20 4	7·2	217	3·3	1433	3·5	426	5·2	1637	5·3	113	3·7	1359	3·7
5	F	4 9	7·1	1630	6·9	150	8·4	14 5	8·5	936	12·8	2142	12·4	830	6·9	2034	6·7	245	3·3	1459	3·4	458	5·0	1710	5·1	146	3·6	1436	3·6
6	S	441	6·9	17 4	6·6	220	8·1	1440	8·1	956	12·3	22 2	11·9	858	6·6	21 7	6·7	312	3·4	1530	3·3	530	4·8	1747	4·9	220	3·5	1518	3·4
7	S	516	6·7	1737	6·6	259	7·8	1526	7·7	1017	11·8	2226	11·2	929	6·4	2143	6·3	343	3·4	16 6	3·2	6 7	4·7	1826	4·8	3 0	3·4	16 0	3·3
8	M	554	6·3	1815	5·8	351	7·4	1629	7·3	1046	10·8	23 2	10·4	10 6	6·1	2230	5·9	419	3·3	1650	3·1	650	4·5	1913	4·5	347	3·3	1716	3·1
9	Tu	635	5·6	1857	5·5	5 2	7·2	1748	7·1	1130	10·0	2358	9·7	1057	5·7	2336	5·5	5 3	3·3	1740	3·0	742	4·4	2014	4·3	447	3·2	1837	3·1
10	W	724	5·5	1941	5·5	625	7·2	1914	7·3	124	9·5	1424	9·7	110	5·4	1342	5·6	555	3·1	1842	2·9	852	4·3	2130	4·3	6 0	3·2	1953	3·1
11	Th	834	5·5	2112	5·5	748	7·6	2027	7·9	3 5	10·1	16 1	10·7	240	5·7	1559	6·2	659	3·1	2019	2·9	1012	4·3	2251	4·4	716	3·3	2051	3·3
12	F	10 0	5·7	2238	6·0	852	8·3	2123	8·5	431	11·3	1713	12·0	346	6·2	1649	6·5	826	3·1	2155	3·0	1128	4·5	—	—	820	3·5	2139	3·5
13	S	1120	6·3	2350	6·5	943	9·5	22 9	9·6	535	12·5	1810	13·7	440	6·7	1736	7·0	945	3·3	2250	3·1	056	4·7	1320	5·0	912	3·7	2222	3·7
14	S	—	—	1224	6·9	1029	9·5	2254	9·9	628	13·4	1946	14·1	527	7·1	1821	7·5	1042	3·5	2336	3·2	141	5·4	14 3	5·3	958	4·0	23 2	3·9
15	M	046	7·1	1316	7·5	1113	9·9	2339	9·9	716	14·1	2029	14·3	611	7·5	19 3	7·8	1132	3·6	—	—	223	5·7	1443	5·9	1040	4·2	2343	4·1
16	Tu	134	7·5	14 4	7·8	1158	10·0	—	—	8 2	14·4	21 8	14·4	653	7·7	1945	8·0	022	3·3	1221	3·8	3 3	5·7	1525	6·0	1123	4·3	—	—
17	W	218	7·8	1444	7·9	022	10·0	1240	10·1	845	14·4	2146	13·6	813	7·7	2029	7·8	1 7	3·3	13 8	3·9	343	5·8	16 9	6·0	026	4·2	1251	4·4
18	Th	3 0	7·9	1610	7·9	1 8	9·9	1324	9·8	926	14·0	2224	12·7	853	7·7	2114	7·8	151	3·5	1353	3·8	430	5·8	1659	5·6	110	4·2	1340	4·4
19	F	342	7·7	1654	7·5	148	9·5	14 8	9·4	10 4	13·3	23 3	11·7	936	7·3	2214	7·5	230	3·6	1435	3·8	518	5·5	1751	5·3	159	4·1	1433	4·3
20	S	427	7·7	1740	7·3	232	8·9	1456	8·7	1044	12·5	2355	10·7	1044	6·9	23 4	6·3	3 8	3·6	1518	3·7	6 7	5·0	1945	4·9	253	3·9	1531	3·9
21	S	513	7·3	1740	6·9	322	8·5	1553	8·0	11 1	11·1	—	—	1125	6·0	—	—	346	3·6	1550	3·6	624	4·5	2054	4·6	352	3·7	1638	3·7
22	M	6 4	6·8	1828	6·4	423	7·9	17 4	7·5	1 3	10·0	1347	9·7	024	5·9	1248	5·7	426	3·5	1630	3·4	743	4·6	2215	4·8	5 3	3·5	1759	3·6
23	Tu	659	6·4	1923	6·0	539	7·5	1827	7·3	238	10·0	1524	9·7	155	5·7	1415	5·7	513	3·3	1746	3·1	848	4·6	2329	4·8	624	3·4	19 5	3·5
24	W	8 4	6·0	2007	5·9	7 8	7·5	1959	7·4	4 9	10·7	1641	10·9	311	5·9	1617	6·2	612	3·0	19 0	2·8	938	4·6	—	—	743	3·6	2034	3·5
25	Th	919	5·9	2149	5·8	824	7·8	21 3	8·0	514	11·6	1737	11·8	434	6·5	1734	6·8	8 2	2·9	21 2	2·7	1019	5·1	1250	5·0	848	3·6	2128	3·4
26	F	1047	6·1	2313	6·1	919	8·3	2148	8·6	636	12·3	1818	12·6	530	6·8	1734	6·9	941	3·0	2213	2·9	1 17	5·1	1333	5·2	938	3·7	2247	3·5
27	S	1153	6·6	—	—	10 1	8·6	2225	8·7	636	12·7	1852	12·6	6 4	6·9	1839	7·1	1034	3·1	2259	3·0	157	5·2	14 9	5·2	1019	3·8	2316	3·7
28	S	012	6·9	1243	7·0	1037	8·9	23 2	8·8	710	12·9	1924	12·6	6 4	6·9	1839	7·1	1115	3·3	2336	3·2	258	5·2	1439	5·3	1053	3·8	2316	3·7
29	M	140	6·9	1326	7·3	1113	9·1	2338	8·9	710	12·9	1924	12·8	635	7·1	19 6	7·1	1154	3·4	—	—	258	5·2	1439	5·3	1124	3·9	2344	3·7
30	Tu	140	7·1	14 2	7·3	1140	9·1	2358	8·9	—	—	—	—	—	—	—	—	012	3·1	1231	3·4	—	—	—	—	1154	3·8	—	—
31	W	213	7·2	1434	7·2	1140	9·1	2358	—	—	—	—	—	635	7·1	1839	7·1	045	3·2	13 5	3·4	—	—	—	—	—	—	—	—

All times shown are Greenwich Mean Time.   † Difference of height in metres from Ordnance Datum (Newlyn).   ‡ Difference of height in metres from Ordnance Datum (Ireland).

APRIL, 1976

High Water at the undermentioned places (G.M.T.*)—

Datum of Predictions: London Bridge † 3·20 m. below; Liverpool † 4·93 m. below; Avonmouth † 6·50 m. below; Hull (Salend) † 3·90 m. below; Greenock † 1·62 m. below; Leith and Granton † 2·90 m. below; Dun Laoghaire ‡ 0·20 m. above.

Day of Month	Day of Week	London Bridge				Liverpool				Avonmouth				Hull (Salend)				Greenock				Leith and Granton				Dun Laoghaire			
		Mn. h.m.	Ht. m.	Aft. h.m.	Ht. m.	Mn. h.m.	Ht. m.	Aft. h.m.	Ht. m.	Mn. h.m.	Ht. m.	Aft. h.m.	Ht. m.	Mn. h.m.	Ht. m.	Aft. h.m.	Ht. m.	Mn. h.m.	Ht. m.	Aft. h.m.	Ht. m.	Mn. h.m.	Ht. m.	Aft. h.m.	Ht. m.	Mn. h.m.	Ht. m.	Aft. h.m.	Ht. m.
1	Th	244	7·1	15 3	7·2	—	—	1211	8·9	816	13·0	2025	12·9	7 4	7·1	1910	7·1	115	3·2	1335	3·4	326	5·2	1537	5·3	012	3·7	1223	3·8
2	F	312	7·1	1531	7·1	026	8·9	1239	8·9	845	13·0	2051	12·9	733	7·0	1941	7·0	142	3·3	14 4	3·3	355	5·2	16 8	5·3	042	3·7	1256	3·7
3	S	342	7·0	16 0	7·0	054	8·7	13 7	8·5	910	12·8	2116	12·6	8 9	6·9	2012	6·9	2 8	3·3	1430	3·2	426	5·1	1643	5·2	113	3·6	1330	3·7
4	S	414	6·9	1633	6·9	121	8·6	1338	8·5	931	12·4	2136	12·2	829	6·8	2046	6·6	235	3·4	15 2	3·2	5 0	5·0	1720	5·0	149	3·6	14 8	3·6
5	M	449	6·7	17 5	6·7	152	8·4	1414	8·4	955	11·8	22 4	11·3	858	6·6	2122	6·3	3 8	3·4	1540	3·1	538	4·8	18 0	4·8	228	3·5	1453	3·4
6	Tu	526	6·5	1742	6·4	232	8·0	15 2	7·8	1025	11·1	2242	10·8	934	6·3	22 7	6·0	347	3·4	1623	3·1	619	4·6	1848	4·6	315	3·4	1545	3·3
7	W	6 7	6·2	1821	6·1	323	7·5	16 4	7·5	11 9	10·4	2337	10·2	1020	6·0	23 8	5·7	432	3·4	1712	3·0	712	4·5	1948	4·4	411	3·3	1647	3·2
8	Th	656	6·0	1914	5·9	431	7·5	1718	7·3	—	—	1218	9·9	1125	5·8	—	—	522	3·3	1812	2·9	8 0	4·4	21 0	4·4	518	3·3	18 3	3·2
9	F	8 2	5·9	2030	5·8	549	7·8	1840	7·5	056	10·0	1354	10·0	034	5·5	1253	5·7	622	3·1	1940	2·8	935	4·4	2218	4·5	635	3·5	1920	3·3
10	S	928	6·0	22 0	6·0	710	7·8	1954	8·0	232	10·4	1528	10·9	232	5·7	1418	6·0	745	3·1	2127	2·9	1050	4·6	2326	4·8	744	3·5	2023	3·5
11	S	1049	6·5	2318	6·6	819	8·3	2053	8·6	358	11·4	1641	11·9	312	6·2	1524	6·6	915	3·2	2222	3·1	1155	4·9	—	—	842	3·7	2114	3·7
12	M	1157	7·1	—	—	913	9·1	2143	9·6	5 5	12·5	1742	13·0	4 0	6·7	1620	7·1	1014	3·5	23 7	3·3	023	5·1	1249	5·3	931	4·0	2158	3·9
13	Tu	018	7·1	1252	7·5	10 2	9·4	2229	9·6	6 2	13·3	1836	13·6	459	7·3	1710	7·5	1111	3·6	2352	3·8	111	5·4	1334	5·6	1016	4·1	2239	4·1
14	W	112	7·4	1338	7·7	1049	9·8	2315	9·9	653	13·9	1924	14·0	544	7·5	1757	7·8	037	3·7	—	—	155	5·7	1417	5·9	11 0	4·3	2319	4·2
15	Th	155	7·6	1423	7·7	1135	10·0	—	—	743	14·1	20 8	14·2	628	7·7	1842	7·9	121	3·5	1247	3·8	236	5·8	15 3	6·0	1145	4·3	—	—
16	F	239	7·7	15 7	7·7	0 1	9·9	1222	9·6	828	14·1	2048	14·1	710	7·7	1928	7·9	2 3	3·6	1332	3·8	321	5·9	1550	5·8	0 2	4·2	1233	4·3
17	S	324	7·7	1550	7·5	046	9·8	13 6	9·6	9 9	13·8	2126	13·6	752	7·6	2013	7·7	242	3·7	1417	3·8	4 2	5·8	1641	5·6	049	4·1	1323	4·3
18	S	412	7·6	1635	7·3	129	9·5	1352	9·5	947	13·1	2203	12·6	833	7·3	21 1	7·3	320	3·7	15 0	3·7	458	5·6	1733	5·5	139	4·1	1414	4·2
19	M	459	7·3	1720	6·8	214	9·1	1442	8·6	1028	12·1	2248	11·8	917	6·9	2152	6·8	4 2	3·6	1544	3·5	550	5·3	1828	5·3	232	4·0	1514	3·8
20	Tu	549	6·9	18 7	6·4	3 5	8·5	1538	8·0	1112	11·2	2339	10·9	10 3	6·5	2249	6·2	446	3·4	1633	3·3	645	5·0	1925	4·9	331	3·8	1620	3·5
21	W	641	6·4	1855	6·1	4 3	8·0	1645	7·5	—	—	12 7	10·4	1058	6·1	2358	5·8	456	3·4	1727	3·1	745	4·7	2030	4·7	438	3·6	1738	3·4
22	Th	737	6·1	1952	5·8	513	7·6	18 4	7·3	044	10·3	1319	10·0	—	—	12 8	5·6	713	2·9	2022	2·7	853	4·6	2144	4·6	555	3·4	1858	3·4
23	F	843	6·0	21 3	5·8	632	7·7	1925	7·7	126	10·6	1444	10·7	117	5·6	1328	5·6	857	2·9	2140	2·8	10 8	4·5	2253	4·7	711	3·4	20 6	3·4
24	S	10 4	6·1	2231	6·0	747	7·7	2028	7·7	229	10·6	16 0	10·7	230	5·7	1440	5·8	958	3·0	2223	2·9	1118	4·6	2354	4·8	816	3·5	21 0	3·5
25	S	1119	6·5	2340	6·5	846	8·0	2116	8·3	435	11·3	1658	11·9	329	6·3	1536	6·1	1042	3·1	23 0	3·0	—	—	1214	4·8	9 7	3·6	2141	3·6
26	M	—	—	1212	6·9	930	8·3	2154	8·4	522	11·9	1740	12·2	416	6·3	1621	6·4	1121	3·2	2335	3·1	041	4·9	1259	4·9	949	3·7	2223	3·7
27	Tu	029	6·9	1257	7·2	10 7	8·6	2228	8·6	6 37	12·3	1852	12·4	455	6·5	17 1	6·6	1158	3·2	—	—	121	5·0	1333	5·1	1023	3·7	2245	3·7
28	W	112	7·0	1334	7·2	1041	8·7	23 0	8·7	713	12·4	1925	12·5	530	6·8	1737	6·8	0 8	3·1	1234	3·2	156	5·1	14 8	5·2	1055	3·7	2314	3·7
29	Th	147	7·1	14 6	7·1	1112	8·7	2331	8·8	747	12·6	1955	12·5	6 9	6·9	1812	6·9	039	3·2	13 6	3·2	227	5·2	1436	5·2	1126	3·7	2343	3·8
30	F	218	6·9	1434	7·0	1145	8·8	—	—					636	7·0	1848	6·9					256	5·3	1511	5·3	1157	3·7	—	—

* All times shown are Greenwich Mean Time.

† Difference of height in metres from Ordnance Datum (Newlyn).

‡ Difference of height in metres from Ordnance Datum (Ireland).

MAY, 1976

High Water at the undermentioned Places (G.M.T.*)—

Datum of Predictions († = metres below; ‡ = metres above):
London Bridge 3·20 m. below · Liverpool 4·93 m. below · Avonmouth 6·50 m. below · Hull (Salend) 3·90 m. below · Greenock 1·62 m. below · Leith and Granton 2·90 m. below · Dun Laoghaire 0·20 m. above

Day of Month	Day of Week	LONDON BRIDGE Mn h.m.	Ht	Aft h.m.	Ht	LIVERPOOL Mn h.m.	Ht	Aft h.m.	Ht	AVONMOUTH Mn h.m.	Ht	Aft h.m.	Ht	HULL (Salend) Mn h.m.	Ht	Aft h.m.	Ht	GREENOCK Mn h.m.	Ht	Aft h.m.	Ht	LEITH AND GRANTON Mn h.m.	Ht	Aft h.m.	Ht	DUN LAOGHAIRE Mn h.m.	Ht	Aft h.m.	Ht
1	S	247	6·9	15 4	7·0	0 0	8·8	1216	8·8	820	12·6	2025	12·7	7 6	7·0	1923	6·9	1 7	3·2	1337	3·1	327	5·2	1544	5·3	013	3·8	1230	3·7
2	S	318	6·9	1535	6·9	030	8·8	1247	8·7	849	12·6	2053	12·6	735	6·9	1957	6·8	135	3·4	14 6	3·1	4 1	5·1	1621	5·2	049	3·7	13 7	3·7
3	M	353	6·9	16 9	6·9	1 1	8·7	1322	8·5	916	12·4	2122	12·3	8 6	6·8	2033	6·6	2 5	3·4	1440	3·1	437	5·1	17 0	5·1	126	3·7	1349	3·5
4	Tu	428	6·8	1642	6·6	135	8·5	14 2	8·3	944	12·0	2156	11·5	837	6·7	2111	6·4	240	3·4	1521	3·1	516	4·9	1742	4·9	2 7	3·7	1435	3·5
5	W	5 6	6·7	1718	6·4	216	8·3	1449	8·0	1020	11·5	2237	11·4	915	6·5	2156	6·1	321	3·5	16 6	3·1	6 1	4·8	1831	4·6	253	3·6	1524	3·5
6	Th	549	6·6	1758	6·4	3 7	8·1	1547	7·7	1115	11·0	2330	11·0	10 2	6·3	2252	5·9	4 8	3·4	1656	3·0	652	4·7	1928	4·6	346	3·5	1625	3·3
7	F	638	6·4	1852	6·2	4 9	7·8	1656	7·6	—	—	12 8	10·6	11 5	6·1	—	—	458	3·4	1752	2·9	753	4·6	2032	4·5	449	3·5	1735	3·3
8	S	742	6·3	20 2	6·2	520	7·8	18 9	7·7	039	10·5	1328	10·5	0 4	5·8	1217	6·1	555	3·4	19 7	2·9	9 2	4·6	2142	4·6	559	3·5	1847	3·3
9	S	9 1	6·4	2128	6·3	634	8·0	1920	8·0	322	10·8	1452	11·4	124	5·9	1337	6·1	7 3	3·2	2047	2·9	1012	4·7	2249	4·8	8 1	3·6	1953	3·4
10	M	1020	6·7	2247	6·7	744	8·4	2022	8·6	430	11·4	16 6	11·9	236	6·0	1449	6·6	836	3·3	2148	3·0	1118	5·0	2348	5·1	9 5	3·9	2047	3·7
11	Tu	1130	7·1	2351	7·0	844	8·8	2115	9·0	532	12·0	1710	12·5	336	6·5	1550	7·0	942	3·3	2235	3·2	—	—	1214	5·3	955	3·9	2132	3·9
12	W	—	—	1228	7·3	937	9·2	22 5	9·4	723	12·9	18 8	13·2	430	7·0	1645	7·4	1038	3·5	2322	3·3	040	5·2	13 7	5·5	1042	4·1	2216	4·1
13	Th	048	7·2	1319	7·3	1026	9·5	2254	9·6	830	13·4	1946	13·7	519	7·3	1736	7·6	1130	3·5	—	—	127	5·6	1355	5·7	1128	4·1	2258	4·2
14	F	137	7·3	14 5	7·3	1117	9·6	2341	9·6	932	13·7	2028	13·8	6 5	7·5	1827	7·7	0 9	3·4	1223	3·6	214	5·7	1444	5·8	—	—	13 8	4·0
15	S	223	7·3	1449	7·3	—	—	1252	9·7	1012	13·8	2149	13·5	650	7·5	1915	7·7	054	3·5	1312	3·6	3 1	5·8	1534	5·9	120	4·1	14 1	3·9
16	S	310	7·4	1534	7·3	027	9·7	1339	9·4	1057	13·5	2233	13·2	734	7·4	20 4	7·4	138	3·6	1359	3·5	350	5·7	1625	5·7	214	4·2	1459	3·8
17	M	357	7·4	1617	7·3	113	9·4	1429	9·3	1146	13·2	2322	12·3	816	7·3	2051	7·3	220	3·7	1444	3·5	440	5·6	1716	5·5	310	4·0	1559	3·7
18	Tu	444	7·3	17 1	6·9	159	9·3	1520	8·7	—	—	1244	12·1	858	7·0	2139	6·7	3 1	3·7	1528	3·4	530	5·3	18 8	5·2	410	3·7	17 7	3·5
19	W	532	6·8	1744	6·3	248	8·7	16 4	8·1	018	12·8	1350	11·5	942	6·6	2228	6·3	343	3·6	1618	3·4	623	5·1	1958	4·7	517	3·5	1820	3·3
20	Th	618	6·6	1828	6·3	341	8·1	1724	7·8	122	12·3	1459	10·8	1030	6·3	2323	5·9	429	3·4	17 7	3·0	717	4·8	2059	4·6	628	3·4	1926	3·3
21	F	7 7	6·3	1919	6·1	441	7·8	1833	7·6	231	11·5	1559	10·5	1123	6·0	—	—	521	3·2	18 3	2·8	816	4·6	22 4	4·5	733	3·4	2020	3·4
22	S	8 5	6·1	2020	5·9	546	7·6	1952	7·7	336	10·8	1650	10·5	025	5·6	1229	5·8	626	2·9	1918	2·7	919	4·6	2356	4·7	827	3·4	21 4	3·4
23	S	912	6·0	2135	6·0	656	7·7	2116	8·0	429	11·4	1733	11·0	134	5·6	1340	5·7	754	2·8	2039	2·7	1025	4·6	—	—	912	3·5	2141	3·6
24	M	1030	6·3	2255	6·3	758	8·0	2154	8·2	516	11·6	1814	11·8	237	5·8	1444	5·8	9 6	2·8	2135	2·9	1125	4·8	23 5	5·0	951	3·5	2214	3·7
25	Tu	1134	6·6	—	—	849	8·2	2229	8·4	558	11·8	1854	12·0	331	6·0	1539	6·1	958	2·9	2218	3·0	—	—	1214	5·1	1025	3·6	2246	3·7
26	W	—	—	1222	6·8	931	8·4	23 3	8·5	638	12·2	1928	12·5	417	6·3	1626	6·4	1043	3·0	2255	3·0	040	4·8	1334	5·2	1058	3·6	2317	3·8
27	Th	039	6·7	13 3	6·9	1019	8·5	2338	8·7	719	12·4	20 3	12·6	457	6·6	17 9	6·6	1123	3·0	—	—	119	5·0	1413	5·1	1133	3·6	2351	3·8
28	F	117	6·7	1337	7·0	1045	8·7	—	—	754	12·4	2036	12·6	534	6·8	1750	6·8	0 3	3·2	12 2	3·1	155	5·1	1449	5·2	—	—	1209	3·6
29	S	151	6·7	14 8	6·8	1121	8·7	2352	8·7	829	12·6	20 3	12·6	610	6·9	1829	6·8	036	3·3	1237	3·0	230	5·2	1527	5·2	028	3·8	1249	3·6
30	S	223	6·8	1442	6·9	1157	8·7	—	—	754	12·4	20 3	12·6	643	6·9	19 9	6·8	1 9	3·3	1313	3·0	3 5	5·2	—	—	1 9	3·6	2351	3·6
31	M	300	6·8	1517	7·0	011	8·9	1233	8·7	829	12·6	2036	12·6	717	6·9	1947	6·8	1 9	3·3	1348	3·0	342	5·3	—	—	028	—	1249	3·6

* All times shown are Greenwich Mean Time.
† Difference of height in metres from Ordnance Datum (Newlyn).
‡ Difference of height in metres from Ordnance Datum (Ireland).

JUNE, 1976

High Water at the undermentioned Places (G.M.T.*)—

Day of Month	Day of Week	LONDON BRIDGE † 3·20 m. below				LIVERPOOL † 4·93 m. below				AVONMOUTH † 6·50 m. below				HULL (Salend) † 3·90 m. below				GREENOCK † 1·62 m. below				LEITH AND GRANTON † 2·90 m. below				DUN LAOGHAIRE ‡ 0·20 m. above			
		Mn. h.m.	Ht. m.	Aft. h.m.	Ht. m.	Mn. h.m.	Ht. m.	Aft. h.m.	Ht. m.	Mn. h.m.	Ht. m.	Aft. h.m.	Ht. m.	Mn. h.m.	Ht. m.	Aft. h.m.	Ht. m.	Mn. h.m.	Ht. m.	Aft. h.m.	Ht. m.	Mn. h.m.	Ht. m.	Aft. h.m.	Ht. m.	Mn. h.m.	Ht. m.	Aft. h.m.	Ht. m.
1	Tu	336	6·9	1552	6·9	047	8·9	1312	8·6	9 5	12·6	2113	12·5	751	6·9	2025	6·6	143	3·4	1427	3·0	419	5·2	1645	5·2	1 6	3·8	1332	3·6
2	W	414	7·0	1627	6·9	125	8·8	1353	8·5	940	12·4	2153	12·3	826	6·9	21 4	6·5	221	3·5	1511	3·0	5 0	5·2	1727	5·1	149	3·8	1417	3·6
3	Th	454	7·0	17 4	6·8	2 7	8·7	1440	8·1	1020	12·1	2237	12·0	9 5	6·8	2148	6·4	3 5	3·6	1555	3·1	546	5·1	1815	5·0	235	3·8	15 7	3·5
4	F	536	6·9	1744	6·7	255	8·5	1533	8·1	11 5	11·6	2325	11·6	950	6·7	2238	6·2	350	3·6	1635	3·0	636	5·0	19 7	4·8	324	3·7	16 1	3·4
5	S	624	6·8	1835	6·6	350	8·4	1633	8·0	1157	11·2	—	—	1045	6·5	2339	6·1	439	3·5	1735	3·0	731	4·8	20 1	4·7	421	3·7	17 6	3·4
6	S	723	6·6	1940	6·5	452	8·2	1738	8·0	023	11·1	13 1	11·0	1149	6·4	—	—	533	3·4	1837	2·9	831	4·6	21 7	4·6	525	3·6	1814	3·4
7	M	836	6·6	21 0	6·5	6 1	8·2	1847	8·1	130	11·1	1414	11·4	049	6·4	13 3	6·4	639	3·4	2012	2·9	937	4·5	2213	4·9	637	3·6	1922	3·5
8	Tu	953	6·8	2219	6·7	713	8·4	1953	8·4	246	11·7	1529	12·0	2 1	6·2	1418	6·6	758	3·2	2112	3·1	1045	5·0	2315	5·1	744	3·7	2011	3·8
9	W	11 5	6·9	2339	6·8	819	8·6	2053	8·6	358	12·3	1637	12·6	3 6	6·2	1527	6·9	911	3·2	22 2	3·1	1148	5·0	—	—	845	3·8	2111	3·8
10	Th	—	—	12 7	7·0	918	9·1	2146	9·1	5 5	13·1	1740	13·2	4 8	6·9	1627	7·1	1013	3·3	2258	3·3	014	5·2	1247	5·4	938	3·9	2159	4·0
11	F	031	6·8	13 2	7·0	1012	9·1	2237	9·1	6 8	13·3	1836	13·5	458	7·4	1723	7·3	1 8	3·3	1341	5·4	1 8	5·2	1341	5·3	1028	3·9	2243	4·1
12	S	124	6·8	1351	6·8	11 2	9·2	2325	9·2	7 3	13·1	1927	13·7	549	7·4	1817	7·3	157	5·6	1433	5·7	157	5·6	1433	5·5	1117	4·0	2328	4·1
13	S	212	6·9	1437	6·9	1152	9·2	—	—	752	13·2	2011	13·5	635	7·4	19 7	7·3	247	5·6	1522	5·7	247	5·6	1522	5·6	016	4·1	1256	3·9
14	M	258	7·1	1521	7·1	012	9·5	1238	9·1	836	13·0	2051	13·3	720	7·3	1954	7·2	335	5·6	16 1	5·6	335	5·6	16 1	5·6	1 4	4·1	1346	3·8
15	Tu	343	7·3	16 5	7·3	057	9·4	1325	9·4	916	13·0	2133	13·0	800	7·1	2039	7·0	423	5·5	1659	5·5	423	5·5	1659	5·5	154	4·1	1438	3·7
16	W	427	7·3	1648	7·2	142	9·4	1410	9·4	956	12·5	2215	12·5	840	7·1	2119	6·7	5 9	5·4	1745	5·5	5 9	5·4	1745	5·3	246	3·9	1531	3·5
17	Th	5 9	7·2	1730	6·8	225	9·2	1455	9·2	1037	12·1	2259	11·9	919	6·8	22 0	6·6	557	5·2	1832	4·9	557	5·2	1832	4·8	338	3·7	1626	3·4
18	F	551	6·8	1813	6·5	312	8·9	1543	8·9	1118	11·4	2344	11·3	10 0	6·6	2244	6·4	645	4·9	1920	4·6	645	4·9	1920	4·6	433	3·6	1728	3·2
19	S	635	6·5	1858	6·3	4 0	8·5	1636	8·5	031	10·8	1250	10·4	1041	6·3	2332	6·0	734	4·7	2012	4·6	734	4·7	2012	4·6	535	3·4	1833	3·1
20	S	726	6·3	1951	6·2	454	7·7	1732	7·7	124	10·3	1345	10·2	1132	6·0	—	—	826	4·5	21 7	4·5	826	4·5	21 7	4·5	638	3·3	1932	3·2
21	M	825	6·2	2057	6·2	555	7·5	1835	7·5	223	10·8	1448	10·3	031	5·6	1236	5·6	922	4·5	22 5	4·5	922	4·5	22 5	4·5	739	3·3	2020	3·2
22	Tu	931	6·2	2157	6·2	658	7·8	1939	7·5	325	10·8	1549	10·8	138	5·6	1348	5·8	1023	4·5	23 3	4·5	1023	4·5	23 3	4·7	831	3·3	21 2	3·4
23	W	1041	6·3	23 8	6·3	8 1	8·1	2033	7·8	424	11·1	1646	11·2	242	5·8	1456	6·2	1123	4·7	2356	4·7	1123	4·5	2356	4·8	915	3·4	2141	3·6
24	Th	1140	6·3	—	—	854	8·6	2120	8·2	518	11·2	1736	11·7	336	6·1	1555	6·4	1140	4·8	—	—	1216	4·8	—	—	955	3·5	2216	3·7
25	F	0 3	6·2	1227	6·2	939	8·1	22 1	8·4	6 6	12·1	1822	11·6	424	6·4	1645	6·6	043	4·8	13 4	4·8	043	4·8	13 4	4·8	1033	3·6	2253	3·8
26	S	045	6·3	13 6	6·3	1021	8·4	2239	8·6	651	12·5	19 3	12·4	5 6	6·8	1732	6·8	127	5·0	1350	5·0	127	5·0	1350	5·0	1110	3·6	2330	3·9
27	S	124	6·4	1348	6·4	1059	8·8	2317	8·9	734	12·7	1943	12·7	547	7·0	1815	7·0	2 8	5·1	1433	5·4	2 8	5·1	1433	5·2	1150	3·7	—	—
28	M	2 4	6·7	1427	6·7	1139	8·9	2355	9·1	813	12·7	2022	12·9	624	7·0	1856	7·2	247	5·3	1512	5·3	247	5·3	1512	5·3	0 8	3·9	1230	3·7
29	Tu	243	6·9	15 2	6·9	1218	9·1	—	—	854	12·9	21 5	13·0	7 2	7·1	1935	7·3	325	5·4	1550	5·4	325	5·4	1550	5·4	1230	3·7	—	—
30	W	322	7·1	1538	7·1	033	9·1	1259	9·1	930	13·0	2151	13·0	738	7·1	2015	6·9	128	3·5	1418	3·0	4 3	5·4	1629	5·4	047	4·0	1313	3·7

* All times shown are Greenwich Mean Time.

† Difference of height in metres from Ordnance Datum (Newlyn).

‡ Difference of height in metres from Ordnance Datum (Ireland).

JULY, 1976

High Water at the undermentioned Places (G.M.T.*)—

Datum corrections are given under each place name.

Day	Wk	LB Mn h.m	LB Ht	LB Aft h.m	LB Ht	Liv Mn h.m	Liv Ht	Liv Aft h.m	Liv Ht	Avon Mn h.m	Avon Ht	Avon Aft h.m	Avon Ht	Hull Mn h.m	Hull Ht	Hull Aft h.m	Hull Ht	Green Mn h.m	Green Ht	Green Aft h.m	Green Ht	Leith Mn h.m	Leith Ht	Leith Aft h.m	Leith Ht	DunL Mn h.m	DunL Ht	DunL Aft h.m	DunL Ht
1	Th	4 27	7·3	16 14	7·1	1 13	9·2	13 42	8·9	9 35	12·9	21 47	12·6	8 16	7·2	20 54	6·9	2 9	3·6	15 1	3·0	4 45	5·4	17 12	5·3	1 30	4·0	13 59	3·7
2	F	4 41	7·1	16 52	7·1	1 55	9·1	14 26	8·7	10 16	12·7	22 29	12·6	8 56	7·1	21 35	6·7	2 52	3·7	15 45	3·1	5 38	5·3	17 57	5·2	2 15	4·0	14 46	3·7
3	S	5 22	7·1	17 32	7·1	2 39	8·9	15 13	8·6	10 57	12·3	23 14	12·2	9 38	7·0	22 21	6·6	3 37	3·6	16 30	3·1	6 18	5·2	18 47	5·1	3 4	4·0	15 38	3·6
4	Su	6 3	6·9	18 19	6·8	3 29	8·7	16 3	8·3	11 41	11·7	—	—	10 27	6·9	23 13	6·4	4 23	3·6	17 14	3·1	7 12	5·1	19 41	4·9	3 57	3·9	16 38	3·6
5	M	7 3	6·7	19 19	6·6	4 26	8·4	17 7	8·1	0 2	11·7	12 34	11·1	11 25	6·7	—	—	5 13	3·4	18 6	3·0	8 8	5·0	20 40	4·9	5 0	3·7	17 43	3·5
6	Tu	8 11	6·6	20 33	6·5	5 32	8·2	18 15	8·1	1 2	11·1	13 41	10·8	0 13	6·4	12 36	6·5	6 2	3·1	19 17	2·9	9 11	4·9	21 45	4·9	6 11	3·6	18 54	3·6
7	W	9 25	6·6	21 53	6·5	6 46	8·1	19 27	8·1	2 15	10·9	14 58	10·9	1 31	6·4	13 57	6·5	7 25	3·1	20 40	3·0	10 20	4·9	22 54	4·9	7 25	3·6	19 58	3·6
8	Th	10 40	6·6	23 11	6·5	8 1	8·3	20 35	8·2	3 34	10·9	16 13	12·1	2 43	6·4	15 11	6·5	8 45	3·1	21 47	3·0	11 30	4·9	23 58	4·9	8 31	3·7	20 55	3·7
9	F	11 49	6·6	—	—	9 7	8·5	21 34	8·3	4 48	11·6	17 21	12·4	3 48	6·6	16 19	6·8	9 55	3·0	22 43	3·2	—	—	12 35	5·2	9 28	3·7	21 46	3·9
10	S	0 18	6·6	12 48	6·6	10 4	9·0	22 25	8·5	5 52	12·2	18 21	12·8	4 44	6·9	17 18	7·1	10 57	3·1	23 35	3·3	1 49	5·4	14 26	5·4	10 22	3·8	22 33	3·8
11	Su	1 14	6·6	13 38	6·6	10 53	9·1	23 13	9·0	6 49	12·7	19 11	13·3	5 36	7·1	18 10	7·2	11 55	3·1	—	—	2 37	5·5	15 13	5·5	11 10	3·8	23 19	4·1
12	M	2 4	6·7	14 22	6·7	11 40	9·3	23 57	9·1	7 37	13·1	19 55	13·5	6 22	7·3	18 57	7·2	0 22	3·5	12 46	3·2	3 20	5·6	15 57	5·6	11 57	3·8	—	—
13	Tu	2 47	6·9	15 3	6·9	—	—	12 23	9·4	8 19	13·1	20 35	13·5	7 17	7·3	19 40	7·2	1 7	3·7	13 34	3·2	4 4	5·5	16 39	5·5	0 4	4·1	12 40	3·8
14	W	3 28	7·1	15 41	7·1	0 39	9·4	13 5	9·3	8 57	12·8	21 15	12·9	7 42	7·3	20 18	7·2	1 50	3·7	14 17	3·2	4 46	5·4	17 19	5·4	0 49	4·1	13 25	3·7
15	Th	4 7	7·3	16 17	7·1	1 19	9·3	13 49	9·1	9 35	12·6	21 54	12·5	8 18	7·2	20 54	6·8	2 30	3·7	14 58	3·1	5 28	5·2	18 0	5·0	1 33	4·1	14 53	3·7
16	F	4 45	7·3	16 52	7·2	1 59	9·0	14 24	8·7	10 12	11·9	22 30	12·1	8 51	7·0	21 28	6·3	3 8	3·6	15 35	3·1	6 2	5·0	18 42	4·8	2 17	4·1	14 53	3·5
17	S	5 22	7·2	17 29	6·8	2 37	8·7	15 2	8·3	10 44	11·6	23 4	11·7	9 24	6·8	22 0	5·8	3 45	3·5	16 12	3·1	6 52	4·8	19 25	4·6	3 1	3·8	16 31	3·3
18	Su	6 0	6·9	18 10	6·7	3 17	8·3	15 43	7·9	11 15	11·6	23 38	11·0	10 0	6·6	22 30	5·8	4 23	3·3	16 49	2·9	7 37	4·6	20 11	4·4	3 47	3·8	17 27	3·2
19	M	6 45	6·5	18 59	6·3	3 57	7·9	16 28	7·5	11 50	10·6	—	—	10 42	6·2	23 30	5·8	5 5	3·1	17 30	2·8	8 25	4·5	21 6	4·4	4 38	3·4	18 30	3·2
20	Tu	7 37	6·2	19 58	6·0	4 53	7·5	17 28	7·3	0 9	10·3	12 34	10·0	11 39	5·9	—	—	5 54	2·9	18 17	2·8	9 23	4·4	22 6	4·4	5 35	3·3	19 30	3·2
21	W	8 39	5·9	21 11	5·7	5 56	7·3	18 36	7·3	1 9	9·8	13 35	9·7	0 35	5·8	12 52	5·7	6 54	2·7	19 16	2·9	10 30	4·4	23 11	4·5	6 41	3·2	20 23	3·4
22	Th	9 43	5·8	22 12	5·7	6 55	7·3	19 45	7·9	2 33	9·7	14 46	9·9	1 49	6·2	14 13	5·9	8 8	2·7	20 25	2·9	11 38	4·5	—	—	7 46	3·2	21 15	3·5
23	F	10 47	5·8	23 16	5·7	8 14	7·9	20 45	8·5	3 31	10·8	15 59	11·3	2 57	6·5	15 24	6·1	9 21	2·8	21 30	2·8	0 11	4·7	12 38	4·7	8 40	3·3	21 51	3·7
24	S	11 46	6·0	—	—	9 11	8·7	21 33	8·7	4 40	11·8	16 57	12·6	3 52	6·8	16 23	6·6	10 20	2·9	22 22	2·8	1 47	4·9	13 30	4·9	9 27	3·4	22 29	3·9
25	Su	0 11	6·0	12 35	6·3	9 57	9·0	22 15	9·0	5 39	12·2	17 57	12·6	4 40	6·5	17 12	6·8	11 56	2·9	23 51	3·3	2 28	5·3	14 16	5·2	10 9	3·6	23 15	3·9
26	M	0 57	6·3	13 20	6·6	10 40	9·2	22 57	9·2	6 29	12·6	18 43	13·1	5 23	6·9	17 57	7·0	0 33	3·4	12 39	3·3	3 7	5·6	15 32	5·6	10 50	3·7	23 47	4·0
27	Tu	1 41	6·8	14 2	7·0	11 20	9·3	23 36	9·3	7 14	13·1	19 26	13·1	6 4	7·0	18 38	7·1	1 17	3·5	13 23	3·3	3 45	5·6	16 11	5·6	11 28	3·8	—	—
28	W	2 23	7·1	14 42	7·3	0 17	9·5	12 3?	9·5	7 57	13·3	20 5	13·5	6 43	7·3	19 19	7·2	1 59	3·7	14 6	3·4	4 27	5·4	16 53	5·6	0 26	4·2	12 51	3·9
29	Th	3 4	7·5	15 21	7·5	0 57	9·6	13 25	9·6	8 39	13·4	20 52	13·5	7 21	7·6	19 57	7·2	2 41	3·7	14 48	3·2	5 12	5·6	17 38	5·4	1 8	4·2	13 35	3·9
30	F	3 45	7·6	15 59	7·5	1 39	9·6	14 2	9·6	9 23	13·4	21 36	13·2	8 1	7·6	20 36	7·1	3 25	3·5	14 48	3·1	5 55	5·6	16 53	5·4	1 54	4·2	13 35	3·9
31	S	4 24	7·5	16 37	7·4	2 19	9·5	14 42	9·5	10 10	13·2	22 18	13·1	8 40	7·5	21 15	7·1	2 41	3·7	15 30	3·2	5 12	5·4	17 38	5·4	1 54	4·2	14 21	3·9

* All times shown are Greenwich Mean Time.   † Difference in height in metres from Ordnance Datum (Newlyn).
‡ Difference of height in metres from Ordnance Datum (Ireland).

Datum of Predictions: London Bridge † 3·20 m. below; Liverpool † 4·93 m. below; Avonmouth † 6·50 m. below; Hull (Salend) † 3·90 m. below; Greenock † 1·62 m. below; Leith and Granton † 2·90 m. below; Dun Laoghaire ‡ 0·20 m. above.

AUGUST, 1976

High Water at the undermentioned Places (G.M.T.*)—

Day of Month	Day of Week	LONDON BRIDGE † Datum of Predictions 3·20 m. below Mn. h.m.	Ht. m.	Aft. h.m.	Ht. m.	LIVERPOOL † Datum of Predictions 4·93 m. below Mn. h.m.	Ht. m.	Aft. h.m.	Ht. m.	BRISTOL (Avonmouth) † Datum of Predictions 6·50 m. below Mn. h.m.	Ht. m.	Aft. h.m.	Ht. m.	HULL (Salend) † Datum of Predictions 3·90 m. below Mn. h.m.	Ht. m.	Aft. h.m.	Ht. m.	GREENOCK † Datum of Predictions 1·62 m. below Mn. h.m.	Ht. m.	Aft. h.m.	Ht. m.	LEITH AND GRANTON † Datum of Predictions 2·90 m. below Mn. h.m.	Ht. m.	Aft. h.m.	Ht. m.	DUN LAOGHAIRE ‡ Datum of Predictions 0·20 m. above Mn. h.m.	Ht. m.	Aft. h.m.	Ht. m.
1	S	5 6	7·3	1718	7·2	222	8·9	1451	8·9	1042	12·6	2258	12·5	922	7·4	2159	6·9	324	3·7	1610	3·2	6 1	5·5	1828	5·2	243	4·1	1513	3·8
2	M	550	7·8	18 4	6·9	3 8	9·3	1541	8·6	1122	11·9	2342	11·7	10 9	7·1	2248	6·6	4 8	3·7	1652	3·2	652	5·3	1921	5·1	336	4·0	1610	3·7
3	Tu	642	6·7	19 0	6·6	4 3	9·0	1640	8·2	—	—	12 9	11·7	11 5	6·8	2349	6·3	456	3·5	1739	3·2	747	5·1	2018	4·9	438	3·8	1716	3·6
4	W	744	6·4	2012	6·4	5 8	8·5	19 8	8·0	039	10·9	1315	10·5	—	—	1217	6·1	550	3·2	1839	2·9	851	4·9	2125	4·8	552	3·7	1830	3·5
5	Th	858	6·3	2132	6·3	628	8·1	2024	8·3	154	10·5	1438	10·4	1 4	6·1	1342	6·3	7 0	2·9	20 9	2·8	10 5	4·8	2240	4·8	711	3·6	1941	3·6
6	F	1016	6·3	2255	6·3	750	8·0	2124	8·3	321	10·5	16 2	10·4	225	6·2	15 5	6·4	829	2·9	2137	3·0	1123	4·9	2350	5·0	823	3·6	2045	3·7
7	S	1132	6·3	—	—	9 1	8·0	2215	8·7	441	11·4	1714	11·4	335	6·5	1614	6·9	953	2·9	2237	3·1	—	—	1231	5·1	925	3·7	2139	3·9
8	S	0 7	6·5	1234	6·5	957	8·3	2259	9·0	544	11·9	1812	12·7	433	6·8	1711	6·9	1056	3·0	2328	3·3	052	5·2	1329	5·3	10 8	3·8	2226	4·0
9	M	1 3	6·9	1324	6·6	1044	8·6	2339	9·4	637	12·9	1857	13·3	523	7·1	1758	7·1	1149	3·0	—	—	143	5·4	1419	5·5	1053	3·8	23 9	4·1
10	Tu	149	6·9	14 6	6·8	1125	9·0	—	—	721	12·9	1938	13·5	6 7	7·3	1841	7·1	014	3·4	1235	3·2	228	5·5	15 2	5·5	1144	3·9	2350	4·1
11	W	232	7·0	1444	7·0	—	—	124	9·1	759	13·1	2016	13·5	645	7·4	1917	7·2	056	3·5	1317	3·2	3 8	5·5	1540	5·5	029	4·1	1258	3·8
12	Th	313	7·3	1519	7·2	018	9·4	1240	9·3	835	13·1	2052	13·4	719	7·4	1951	7·1	136	3·6	1358	3·3	344	5·5	1615	5·4	1 7	4·1	1414	3·7
13	F	343	7·3	1553	7·3	054	9·3	1315	9·5	911	13·0	2127	13·1	751	7·3	2022	6·9	213	3·6	1434	3·3	420	5·4	1651	5·3	146	4·0	1453	4·0
14	S	417	7·2	1624	7·1	127	8·7	1348	9·5	942	12·7	2159	12·6	820	7·2	2053	6·8	247	3·5	15 5	3·2	456	5·3	1726	5·0	224	4·0	1536	4·0
15	S	449	7·0	1658	7·0	159	8·7	1453	9·0	1013	12·2	2225	12·0	850	7·0	2122	6·6	318	3·4	1537	3·2	533	5·1	18 3	4·7	3 3	3·7	1625	3·7
16	M	523	6·8	1736	6·7	233	8·0	1534	9·0	1033	11·5	2250	11·4	924	6·7	2156	6·3	351	3·3	16 9	3·1	612	4·9	1842	4·7	346	3·5	1724	3·5
17	Tu	553	6·8	1818	6·4	311	8·0	1627	8·7	1059	10·8	2321	10·4	10 2	6·7	2237	6·0	427	3·1	1646	3·0	652	4·7	1923	4·5	438	3·7	1834	3·3
18	W	648	6·2	19 7	5·9	359	7·5	1735	8·0	1135	10·1	—	—	1049	6·0	2332	5·7	510	2·9	1730	3·0	738	4·5	2013	4·4	545	3·5	1940	3·2
19	Th	740	5·8	20 8	5·5	5 0	7·5	1854	7·6	0 5	9·7	1231	9·5	1158	5·6	—	—	6 3	2·8	1821	2·9	835	4·3	2117	4·3	659	3·3	2035	3·4
20	F	843	5·5	2117	5·3	614	7·1	20 7	7·2	115	9·4	1349	9·4	049	5·5	1331	5·5	7 7	2·7	1925	2·9	947	4·3	2229	4·4	8 6	3·2	2122	3·6
21	S	952	5·5	2226	5·5	734	7·2	2114	7·6	244	9·5	1518	10·1	211	5·7	1454	5·7	835	2·8	2042	2·9	11 4	4·4	2339	4·6	9 0	3·4	22 3	3·8
22	S	—	—	2333	5·7	840	7·6	2151	8·0	4 7	10·5	1634	11·0	317	6·1	1556	6·1	955	2·8	2152	3·1	—	—	1212	4·6	945	3·7	2243	4·0
23	M	—	—	—	—	932	8·0	2313	8·9	513	11·6	1733	12·4	410	6·5	1647	6·6	1049	2·9	2245	3·2	037	4·8	13 7	4·9	1026	3·9	2331	4·1
24	Tu	029	6·4	1252	6·7	1016	8·9	2355	9·6	618	12·5	1824	12·9	457	7·0	1732	6·9	1134	3·0	—	—	124	5·1	1353	5·2	11 6	4·0	—	—
25	W	117	7·0	1337	7·2	1057	9·6	—	—	656	13·1	19 8	13·3	539	7·3	1814	7·3	017	3·5	1219	3·2	2 6	5·4	1433	5·5	1145	4·4	1226	4·1
26	Th	2 1	7·5	1419	7·6	1139	9·9	—	—	740	13·6	1953	13·8	7 0	7·8	1855	7·5	1 1	3·6	13 3	3·3	245	5·7	1510	5·7	0 2	4·4	13 8	4·1
27	F	243	7·8	1458	7·8	—	—	1221	9·9	824	13·8	2037	14·0	741	7·9	1934	7·6	146	3·7	1347	3·2	323	5·8	1549	5·8	046	4·4	1350	4·1
28	S	324	7·8	1538	7·7	037	9·9	13 3	9·9	9 5	13·8	2119	13·8	822	7·8	2013	7·5	228	3·8	1429	3·2	4 2	5·8	1632	5·6	132	4·4	1447	4·0
29	S	4 4	7·7	1619	7·7	118	9·8	1345	9·6	946	13·5	22 2	13·3	9 4	7·6	2053	7·2	310	3·6	15 8	3·4	452	5·6	1712	5·6	221	4·3	1545	3·8
30	M	447	7·4	17 2	7·2	2 2	9·2	1429	9·2	1023	12·8	2240	12·5	—	—	2135	7·0	—	—	1548	3·3	541	5·6	18 9	5·4	318	4·0	1447	4·1
31	Tu	532	7·0	1750	6·9	248	9·0	1518	8·7	1 3	11·5	2325	11·5	952	7·2	2223	6·7	353	3·7	1628	3·3	635	5·4	19 3	5·1	317	4·1	1545	3·8

* All times shown are Greenwich Mean Time.   † Difference of height in metres from Ordnance Datum (Newlyn).
‡ Difference of height in metres from Ordnance Datum (Ireland).

SEPTEMBER, 1976

High Water at the undermentioned Places (G.M.T.*)—

Day of Month	Day of Week	London Bridge † Datum of Predictions 3·20 m. below — Mn. h.m.	Ht. m.	Aft. h.m.	Ht. m.	Liverpool † Datum of Predictions 4·93 m. below — Mn. h.m.	Ht. m.	Aft. h.m.	Ht. m.	Avonmouth † Datum of Predictions 6·50 m. below — Mn. h.m.	Ht. m.	Aft. h.m.	Ht. m.	Hull (Salend) † Datum of Predictions 3·90 m. below — Mn. h.m.	Ht. m.	Aft. h.m.	Ht. m.	Greenock † Datum of Predictions 1·62 m. below — Mn. h.m.	Ht. m.	Aft. h.m.	Ht. m.	Leith and Granton † Datum of Predictions 2·90 m. below — Mn. h.m.	Ht. m.	Aft. h.m.	Ht. m.	Dun Laoghaire ‡ Datum of Predictions 0·20 m. above — Mn. h.m.	Ht. m.	Aft. h.m.	Ht. m.
1	W	621	6·6	1845	6·6	342	8·4	1617	8·2	1150	10·9	—	—	1048	6·8	2323	6·3	440	3·5	1714	3·2	732	5·1	2002	4·9	420	3·8	1050	3·7
2	Th	720	6·2	1954	6·2	450	7·9	1729	7·8	020	10·5	1257	10·2	—	—	1203	6·3	534	3·2	1810	3·0	839	4·8	2111	4·8	536	3·6	1809	3·6
3	F	830	6·0	2112	6·1	615	7·7	1854	7·8	139	9·9	1427	10·1	041	6·0	1335	6·1	641	2·9	1942	2·8	956	4·8	2230	4·8	701	3·6	1926	3·6
4	S	949	6·0	2237	6·2	745	7·7	2013	8·1	316	10·2	1559	10·8	208	6·1	1458	6·5	825	2·7	2129	3·1	1116	4·9	2344	4·9	817	3·3	2034	3·7
5	Su	1111	6·2	2350	6·5	855	8·5	2115	8·5	437	11·0	1708	11·4	319	6·4	1607	6·8	955	2·8	2231	3·1	—	—	1222	5·1	911	3·7	2130	3·9
6	M	—	—	1214	6·5	947	8·8	2212	8·9	537	11·9	1801	12·7	417	6·7	1657	7·0	1052	2·9	2317	3·3	043	5·1	1317	5·0	1008	3·8	2215	4·1
7	Tu	045	6·9	1314	6·9	1029	8·8	2242	9·1	624	12·6	1843	13·3	505	7·0	1739	7·2	1136	3·0	2359	3·4	131	5·4	1405	5·5	1050	3·9	2255	4·1
8	W	131	7·1	1345	7·1	1116	9·0	2318	9·3	703	12·9	1919	13·3	544	7·3	1817	7·2	—	—	1216	3·0	213	5·4	1444	5·5	1126	3·9	2331	4·1
9	Th	211	7·3	1423	7·2	1140	9·1	2352	9·1	738	13·0	1953	13·3	619	7·4	1849	7·2	036	3·4	1254	3·1	248	5·5	1517	5·5	1158	3·9	—	—
10	F	246	7·3	1456	7·3	—	—	1213	9·1	812	13·0	2029	13·3	650	7·4	1920	7·2	116	3·5	1330	3·1	320	5·5	1547	5·4	005	4·1	1229	3·9
11	S	318	7·3	1527	7·3	025	9·2	1243	9·0	843	13·0	2058	13·1	721	7·3	1949	7·1	151	3·5	1403	3·2	352	5·4	1619	5·3	039	4·1	1301	3·8
12	Su	348	7·2	1556	7·2	056	9·1	1312	8·8	912	12·8	2128	12·7	751	7·2	2018	7·0	221	3·4	1432	3·2	424	5·3	1653	5·1	111	4·0	1335	3·8
13	M	417	7·0	1628	7·0	125	8·8	1341	8·5	935	12·4	2150	12·2	820	7·1	2046	6·8	251	3·2	1500	3·3	459	5·1	1727	4·8	143	3·8	1410	3·7
14	Tu	449	6·9	1704	6·8	156	8·4	1410	8·2	956	11·9	2212	11·4	853	6·8	2115	6·5	321	3·2	1531	3·3	535	4·8	1803	4·8	224	3·7	1450	3·6
15	W	525	6·4	1742	6·4	230	8·1	1448	7·8	1020	11·3	2239	10·3	929	6·4	2152	6·2	355	3·1	1607	3·2	616	4·5	1844	4·6	306	3·5	1536	3·4
16	Th	603	6·2	1824	6·2	315	7·6	1539	7·5	1055	10·3	2320	9·9	1014	6·1	2238	5·9	436	3·0	1651	3·2	701	4·5	1932	4·4	356	3·4	1632	3·4
17	F	645	5·8	1913	5·8	416	7·2	1644	7·2	1146	9·7	—	—	1116	5·6	2347	5·6	524	2·9	1741	3·1	759	4·4	2035	4·3	459	3·3	1741	3·3
18	S	737	5·5	2016	5·5	531	7·0	1805	7·2	026	9·4	1304	9·4	—	—	1237	5·6	623	2·8	1840	3·0	911	4·3	2150	4·5	616	3·4	1854	3·6
19	Su	849	5·4	2136	5·4	658	7·3	1927	7·6	201	9·5	1440	9·9	117	5·7	1418	5·7	748	2·7	1956	3·0	1030	4·4	2304	4·5	732	3·6	1958	3·6
20	M	1013	5·6	2254	5·6	809	7·4	2031	8·1	336	10·6	1604	12·2	236	6·6	1524	6·6	1024	3·0	2219	3·3	1140	4·7	—	—	831	3·8	2050	3·8
21	Tu	1125	6·2	2358	6·2	949	8·4	2122	8·8	449	11·6	1709	13·1	335	7·1	1617	7·4	1153	3·1	2356	3·6	005	4·9	1237	5·0	1002	4·0	2216	4·3
22	W	—	—	1222	6·7	1032	9·5	2247	9·4	546	12·6	1800	13·8	426	7·5	1747	7·4	—	—	2308	3·5	056	5·2	1325	5·3	1040	4·2	2258	4·4
23	Th	050	7·3	1310	7·3	1115	9·8	2332	10·0	636	13·4	1850	14·1	511	7·8	1828	7·8	044	3·7	1321	3·3	140	5·5	1405	5·4	1119	4·3	2338	4·5
24	F	137	7·7	1354	7·7	1158	10·0	—	—	723	13·8	1936	14·2	554	8·0	1908	7·8	129	3·8	1404	3·4	220	5·8	1444	5·8	—	—	1243	4·3
25	S	220	7·9	1436	7·9	015	10·1	1241	10·0	807	14·1	2021	14·2	638	8·0	1948	7·7	212	3·8	1444	3·5	300	5·9	1525	5·9	023	4·5	1243	4·3
26	Su	301	7·9	1517	7·9	059	9·7	1325	9·7	848	14·0	2104	14·0	720	8·1	2029	7·7	254	3·8	1524	3·5	343	6·0	1609	5·9	110	4·4	1337	4·1
27	M	343	7·7	1600	7·7	143	9·5	1408	9·3	927	13·6	2144	13·3	804	7·9	2112	7·2	339	3·7	1606	3·5	432	5·9	1659	5·5	203	4·3	1422	4·1
28	Tu	427	7·4	1647	7·4	231	8·7	1458	8·7	1005	12·9	2224	12·4	849	7·7	2152	6·8	427	3·4	1653	3·3	523	5·7	1749	5·5	304	4·1	1521	4·0
29	W	513	7·5	1737	7·0	328	8·3	1557	8·2	1045	11·9	2310	11·3	938	7·2	2259	6·3	339	3·7	1606	3·5	618	5·4	1844	5·2	404	3·8	1629	3·8
30	Th	603	6·5	1834	6·5	—	—	1557	8·2	1136	10·9	—	—	1037	6·7	—	—	427	3·4	1653	3·3	718	5·1	1945	4·9	—	—	—	—

* All times shown are Greenwich Mean Time.   † Difference of height in metres from Ordnance Datum (Newlyn).

‡ Difference of height in metres from Ordnance Datum (Ireland).

OCTOBER, 1976

High Water at the undermentioned Places (G.M.T.)*—

Day of Month	Day of Week	LONDON BRIDGE † Datum of Predictions 3·20 m. below Mn. h.m.	Ht. m.	Aft. h.m.	Ht. m.	LIVERPOOL † Datum of Predictions 4·93 m. below Mn. h.m.	Ht. m.	Aft. h.m.	Ht. m.	AVONMOUTH † Datum of Predictions 6·50 m. below Mn. h.m.	Ht. m.	Aft. h.m.	Ht. m.	HULL (Saltend) † Datum of Predictions 3·90 m. below Mn. h.m.	Ht. m.	Aft. h.m.	Ht. m.	GREENOCK † Datum of Predictions 1·62 m. below Mn. h.m.	Ht. m.	Aft. h.m.	Ht. m.	LEITH AND GRANTON † Datum of Predictions 2·90 m. below Mn. h.m.	Ht. m.	Aft. h.m.	Ht. m.	DUN LAOGHAIRE ‡ Datum of Predictions 0·20 m. above Mn. h.m.	Ht. m.	Aft. h.m.	Ht. m.
1	F	659	6·1	1937	6·2	436	7·7	1710	7·8	0 6	10·4	1245	10·2	1151	6·2	—		521	3·1	1749	3·1	825	4·8	2055	4·8	521	3·6	1748	3·7
2	S	8 2	5·9	2049	6·0	6 1	7·7	1835	7·7	125	9·8	1415	10·0	015	6·0	1321	6·0	627	2·9	1914	2·9	942	4·8	2212	4·7	648	3·6	19 8	3·7
3	S	917	5·8	2210	5·8	731	8·0	1956	8·0	3 1	9·1	1547	9·8	142	6·0	1442	6·1	819	2·7	21 8	2·9	1059	4·9	2327	4·9	8 3	3·6	2016	3·8
4	M	1041	6·1	2325	6·5	839	8·4	2056	8·4	423	10·9	1655	11·8	257	6·2	1543	6·4	944	2·8	2216	3·1	—		12 4	5·0	9 2	3·7	2112	3·9
5	Tu	1149	6·6	—		929	8·8	2142	8·8	520	11·8	1743	12·6	353	6·6	1631	6·7	1033	3·0	2256	3·2	024	5·1	1256	5·2	951	3·9	2158	4·0
6	W	021	7·0	1239	7·0	10 9	9·0	2220	9·0	640	12·5	1820	13·0	438	6·9	1712	6·9	1112	3·1	2336	3·3	112	5·2	1341	5·3	1029	3·9	2235	4·1
7	Th	1 7	7·3	1321	7·3	1043	9·1	2254	9·1	713	12·8	1855	13·1	516	7·1	1747	7·1	1149	3·1	—		150	5·4	1418	5·4	112	4·0	23 7	4·1
8	F	147	7·4	1359	7·3	1114	9·2	2327	9·1	745	12·9	1928	13·1	551	7·2	1818	7·2	015	3·4	1223	3·2	223	5·4	1449	5·4	1159	4·0	2340	4·1
9	S	220	7·4	1432	7·3	1144	9·1	—		815	12·9	20 2	13·0	622	7·3	1849	7·2	051	3·4	1258	3·2	253	5·4	1520	5·4	0 9	4·0	1229	3·9
10	S	251	7·3	15 1	7·1	027	9·0	1215	9·0	841	12·8	21 1	12·7	653	7·3	1917	7·2	124	3·4	1329	3·2	323	5·4	1549	5·3	042	3·9	13 1	3·9
11	M	318	7·1	1529	7·1	056	8·8	1243	8·9	9 5	12·6	2126	12·3	726	7·2	1945	7·1	154	3·3	1357	3·3	354	5·3	1620	5·2	115	3·8	1336	3·8
12	Tu	346	7·0	16 2	7·0	126	8·5	1310	8·7	928	12·1	2146	11·7	757	7·0	2013	6·9	222	3·3	1424	3·4	429	5·2	1653	5·1	153	3·7	1415	3·7
13	W	419	6·9	1635	6·8	2 1	8·1	1417	8·4	954	11·5	2215	11·1	830	6·8	2043	6·7	253	3·2	1457	3·4	5 6	5·0	1730	4·9	236	3·6	15 0	3·6
14	Th	452	6·7	1713	6·6	2 4	7·7	16 7	7·7	1031	10·8	2255	10·4	9 7	6·5	2117	6·5	327	3·1	1535	3·4	545	4·8	1812	4·7	325	3·4	1553	3·5
15	F	527	6·4	1753	6·3	310	7·4	17 6	7·5	1121	10·2	2357	9·9	950	6·1	22 0	6·2	4 9	3·0	1619	3·3	633	4·6	19 1	4·4	426	3·4	1656	3·5
16	S	6 5	6·1	1838	6·0	344	7·4	1642	7·8	126	9·8	14 4	10·1	1047	5·8	23 1	6·0	457	3·0	17 8	3·3	730	4·5	20 1	4·4	539	3·5	1819	3·7
17	S	653	5·8	1935	5·8	456	7·2	1753	7·5	3 0	10·4	1539	11·0	—		1335	5·9	552	2·9	18 5	3·1	838	4·4	2112	4·4	655	3·6	20 7	3·9
18	M	758	5·7	2054	5·9	617	7·4	1842	7·8	416	11·5	1637	12·1	024	5·9	1447	6·1	7 4	2·8	1915	3·1	952	4·5	2224	4·6	8 0	3·6	2017	4·1
19	Tu	927	5·9	2232	6·2	731	7·8	1953	8·2	517	12·5	1735	13·1	157	6·6	1543	6·6	8 4	2·9	2020	3·4	11 2	4·7	2328	4·8	850	3·9	21 7	4·1
20	W	1047	6·4	2326	6·9	830	8·4	2048	8·8	612	13·3	1828	13·7	257	7·1	1633	7·2	953	3·0	2147	3·4	—		—		935	4·1	2152	4·3
21	Th	1150	7·0	—		919	9·4	2137	9·4	7 2	13·9	1919	14·1	352	7·6	1719	7·7	1038	3·1	2241	3·5	023	5·2	1252	5·2	1015	4·3	2235	4·4
22	F	1 4	7·5	1244	7·5	10 5	9·5	2223	9·8	747	14·1	20 5	14·2	442	7·9	18 2	8·0	1123	3·3	2330	3·6	110	5·5	1336	5·6	1055	4·4	2317	4·5
23	S	113	7·8	1330	7·7	1050	9·9	23 9	10·0	828	14·1	2047	13·9	529	8·0	1845	8·1	021	3·7	1253	3·6	153	5·8	1418	5·9	1137	4·4	—	
24	S	158	7·8	1411	7·9	1135	10·1	2357	10·0	9 7	13·7	2129	13·3	615	8·0	1927	8·0	1 9	3·8	1338	3·6	236	6·0	15 1	5·9	0 4	4·5	1222	4·4
25	M	242	7·7	1458	7·8	042	9·8	13 6	10·0	947	13·0	22 9	12·5	7 0	7·8	20 9	7·8	155	3·8	1420	3·7	324	6·0	1549	5·8	053	4·4	13 0	4·4
26	Tu	325	7·6	1545	7·8	129	9·4	1352	9·8	1032	12·2	2250	11·5	748	7·5	2053	7·3	239	3·7	15 2	3·7	412	5·9	1638	5·8	140	4·2	14 4	4·2
27	W	410	7·3	1634	7·5	218	8·9	1441	9·4	1123	11·2	2358	10·5	837	7·1	2139	6·9	325	3·6	1546	3·6	5 6	5·7	1732	5·5	245	4·0	15 7	4·1
28	Th	458	7·0	1725	7·1	314	8·3	1540	8·9	—		1228	10·3	928	6·7	2235	6·5	415	3·4	1634	3·5	6 1	5·5	1826	5·3	349	3·9	16 7	4·0
29	F	546	6·6	1818	6·6	314	8·3	1540	8·4	1 2	10·1	1348	10·3	1026	6·2	2343	6·1	5 7	3·2	1728	3·3	659	5·2	1925	5·0	349	3·9	1721	3·9
30	S	636	6·2	1914	6·3	420	7·7	1646	7·9	133	10·3	1348	10·3	1133	5·9	—		6 10	2·9	1842	3·0	8 5	4·9	2030	4·8	5 3	3·6	1721	3·8
31	S	733	5·9	20 0	6·1	537	7·4	—		1 2	10·1	1348	10·3	—		1250	5·9	—		—		915	4·8	2142	4·7	626	3·5	1840	3·7

* All times shown are Greenwich Mean Time.   † Difference of height in metres from Ordnance Datum (Newlyn).   ‡ Difference of height in metres from Ordnance Datum (Ireland).

NOVEMBER, 1976

High Water at the undermentioned Places (G.M.T.*)—

Day of Month	Day of Week	London Bridge — † Datum of Predictions 3·20 m. below				Liverpool — † Datum of Predictions 4·93 m. below				Avonmouth — † Datum of Predictions 6·50 m. below				Hull (Sælend) — † Datum of Predictions 3·90 m. below				Greenock — † Datum of Predictions 1·62 m. below				Leith and Granton — † Datum of Predictions 2·90 m. below				Dun Laoghaire — ‡ Datum of Predictions 0·20 m. above			
		Mn. h.m.	Ht. m.	Aft. h.m.	Ht. m.	Mn. h.m.	Ht. m.	Aft. h.m.	Ht. m.	Mn. h.m.	Ht. m.	Aft. h.m.	Ht. m.	Mn. h.m.	Ht. m.	Aft. h.m.	Ht. m.	Mn. h.m.	Ht. m.	Aft. h.m.	Ht. m.	Mn. h.m.	Ht. m.	Aft. h.m.	Ht. m.	Mn. h.m.	Ht. m.	Aft. h.m.	Ht. m.
1	M	837	5·9	2132	6·1	659	7·5	1922	7·8	227	10·1	1514	10·7	1 3	6·0	1406	6·0	744	2·8	2027	3·0	1027	4·8	2253	4·8	739	3·6	1950	3·8
2	Tu	959	6·0	2251	6·4	8 8	7·8	2024	8·1	347	10·7	1621	11·4	218	6·1	1508	6·2	911	2·9	2136	2·9	1131	4·9	2333	5·0	838	3·7	2047	3·8
3	W	1115	6·5	2350	6·9	859	8·4	2113	8·4	446	11·4	1710	12·0	317	6·3	1557	6·5	10 2	3·0	2224	3·2	—		1224	5·1	925	3·8	2131	3·9
4	Th	039	7·3	1258	7·0	940	8·5	2153	8·7	5 9	12·0	1749	12·4	4 6	6·5	1638	6·8	1040	3·1	2306	3·3	041	5·1	1309	5·2	10 2	3·9	2209	3·9
5	F	119	7·4	1334	7·3	1015	8·7	2227	8·8	6 9	12·3	1826	12·6	445	6·8	1715	7·0	1116	3·2	2345	3·3	120	5·1	1346	5·2	1035	3·9	2243	4·0
6	S	154	7·3	1406	7·4	1047	8·9	2301	8·9	643	12·5	1907	12·6	522	7·0	1749	7·1	1149	3·2	—		154	5·3	1419	5·3	11 5	4·0	2313	3·9
7	S	225	7·2	1436	7·6	1119	9·0	2333	8·9	727	12·7	2017	12·6	558	7·0	1821	7·2	023	3·3	1225	3·4	226	5·3	1450	5·3	1133	4·0	2344	3·9
8	M	253	7·1	1509	7·5	1148	9·0	—		8 9	12·7	2103	12·6	632	7·1	1850	7·2	056	3·3	1256	3·4	258	5·3	1522	5·3	—		12 2	4·0
9	Tu	322	7·0	1539	6·9	0 4	8·9	1228	9·0	842	12·6	2147	12·4	7 7	7·0	1920	7·1	128	3·3	1325	3·4	331	5·2	1553	5·3	016	3·8	1235	3·9
10	W	355	6·9	1614	6·9	035	8·7	1248	8·8	915	12·5	2203	12·1	741	6·9	1949	7·1	159	3·2	1354	3·4	4 6	5·1	1628	5·2	051	3·8	1310	3·8
11	Th	427	6·7	1651	6·8	1 7	8·5	1320	8·7	942	12·3	2243	11·6	818	6·7	2020	6·9	231	3·2	1423	3·5	443	5·0	17 5	5·1	130	3·7	1350	3·6
12	F	5 2	6·6	1730	6·6	144	8·3	1357	8·4	942	11·9	2243	11·6	854	6·5	2056	6·7	3 8	3·1	1449	3·5	525	5·0	1747	5·0	213	3·5	1435	3·5
13	S	540	6·4	1815	6·3	228	8·0	1444	8·2	1016	11·5	2337	11·1	938	6·2	2138	6·5	349	3·1	1525	3·5	6 0	4·8	1836	4·8	3 1	3·4	1524	3·4
14	S	625	6·4	1910	6·3	321	7·6	1540	7·9	11 6	11·0	—		1028	6·0	2231	6·3	4 6	3·1	1636	3·4	7 4	4·7	1931	4·7	357	3·4	1620	3·5
15	M	726	6·1	2022	6·3	424	7·6	1647	7·8	052	11·0	1325	10·5	1134	5·9	2342	6·3	525	3·0	1736	3·3	8 4	4·6	2031	4·7	5 3	3·4	1727	3·7
16	Tu	847	6·1	2143	6·6	536	7·6	1759	7·8	217	10·2	1447	10·5	—		1252	5·9	610	3·1	1836	3·3	912	4·6	2142	4·7	616	3·5	1838	3·7
17	W	1010	6·6	2255	7·0	649	7·6	19 1	8·1	336	10·5	16 5	10·8	1 2	6·2	1406	6·0	7 4	3·1	1943	3·4	1021	4·8	2248	4·9	725	3·6	1943	3·8
18	Th	1120	7·0	2358	7·3	753	8·4	2015	8·7	443	11·2	17 5	11·8	216	6·5	1508	6·3	8 6	3·2	2040	3·6	1122	5·0	2348	5·2	821	3·8	2040	4·0
19	F	—		1210	7·4	849	9·1	2111	9·4	543	11·8	1817	12·2	321	6·9	1603	6·7	912	3·4	2114	3·7	—		1217	5·2	9 9	4·1	2132	4·2
20	S	052	7·5	1310	7·6	941	9·4	22 2	9·5	638	12·2	1903	12·7	417	7·3	1652	7·1	10 2	3·6	2212	3·7	040	5·5	13 8	5·6	953	4·2	23 0	4·3
21	S	140	7·4	1358	7·6	1029	9·9	2252	9·8	740	12·7	1947	12·9	5 9	7·6	1739	7·4	1054	3·7	23 6	3·7	130	5·7	1355	5·8	1036	4·3	2348	4·3
22	M	225	7·4	1446	7·6	1117	9·9	2340	9·7	832	12·9	2031	13·0	558	7·7	1825	7·6	1141	3·7	2359	3·7	218	5·9	1442	5·9	1119	4·4	—	
23	Tu	310	7·3	1534	7·5	—		1253	9·8	932	13·0	2114	12·7	640	7·6	1910	7·7	—		1315	3·8	3 8	5·9	1530	5·9	039	4·2	1253	4·3
24	W	355	7·3	1621	7·5	028	9·6	1251	9·4	1016	12·7	2156	11·9	722	7·4	1954	7·6	050	3·7	14 0	3·8	357	5·9	1621	5·8	132	4·1	1347	4·1
25	Th	441	7·2	1708	7·0	116	9·1	1337	9·1	11 6	11·9	2241	11·2	8 0	7·2	2037	7·5	139	3·6	1444	3·7	450	5·7	1713	5·5	228	4·0	1443	4·2
26	F	526	6·8	1758	6·9	2 5	9·0	1426	8·9	1149	11·1	2330	11·1	841	7·0	2121	7·3	227	3·5	1529	3·8	544	5·5	18 5	5·1	329	3·7	1543	4·0
27	S	611	6·4	1848	6·5	257	8·4	1518	8·6	—		1215	11·1	924	6·7	2210	7·1	315	3·4	1615	3·7	637	5·2	1859	5·1	435	3·6	1649	3·8
28	S	7 0	6·1	1942	6·5	354	8·1	1615	8·3	027	11·1	13 4	10·7	10 9	6·3	2304	6·8	4 2	3·3	18 8	3·8	733	4·9	1958	4·9	549	3·5	18 2	3·7
29	M	758	6·0	2046	6·1	458	8·1	1720	8·1	132	10·7	1414	10·5	11 5	6·0	2304	6·3	450	3·1	1929	3·2	836	4·8	2059	4·7	7 1	3·5	1911	3·6
30	Tu	9 4	6·0	2156	6·2	6 9	8·0	1831	8·0	247	10·3	1524	10·3	0 8	6·0	1313	5·9	544	3·1	2020	3·6	942	4·7	22 5	4·7	8 9	3·5	2011	3·6

* All times shown are Greenwich Mean Time. † Difference of height in metres from Ordnance Datum (Newlyn).
‡ Difference of height in metres from Ordnance Datum (Ireland).

DECEMBER, 1976

High Water at the undermentioned Places (G.M.T.*)—

Each place gives **Mn.** (morning) and **Aft.** (afternoon) high water as *h.m.* and height in *m.*

Day of Month	Day of Week	London Bridge †3·20 m. below — Mn. (h.m. m.)	Aft. (h.m. m.)	Liverpool †4·93 m. below — Mn.	Aft.	Avonmouth †6·50 m. below — Mn.	Aft.	Hull (Saltend) †3·90 m. below — Mn.	Aft.	Greenock †1·62 m. below — Mn.	Aft.	Leith and Granton †2·90 m. below — Mn.	Aft.	Dun Laoghaire ‡0·20 m. above — Mn.	Aft.
1	W	9 8 6·0	22 2 6·3	7 18 7·5	19 39 7·8	2 44 10·3	15 23 10·7	1 20 5·9	14 19 5·9	8 12 2·9	20 47 3·0	10 47 4·7	23 8 4·8	8 2 3·5	20 10 3·7
2	Th	10 30 6·3	23 13 6·6	8 18 8·0	20 34 8·0	3 49 10·7	16 21 11·2	2 27 6·2	15 15 6·2	9 16 3·0	21 45 3·1	11 44 4·8	— —	8 51 3·6	21 0 3·7
3	F	11 36 6·6	— —	9 4 8·1	21 20 8·2	4 42 11·6	17 5 11·9	3 25 6·4	16 3 6·5	10 3 3·1	22 33 3·2	0 1 4·8	12 32 5·0	9 31 3·7	21 41 3·7
4	S	0 7 6·9	12 27 6·9	9 45 8·4	22 0 8·4	5 28 11·6	17 51 11·9	4 13 6·4	16 44 6·7	10 43 3·2	23 15 3·3	0 44 5·0	13 13 5·1	10 7 3·8	22 16 3·7
5	Su	0 50 7·1	13 7 6·9	10 22 8·6	22 35 8·6	6 9 12·0	18 30 12·3	4 57 6·6	17 20 6·9	11 19 3·3	23 55 3·4	1 24 5·1	13 49 5·2	10 39 3·9	22 50 3·8
6	M	1 27 7·0	13 42 6·9	10 55 8·8	23 11 8·7	6 46 12·3	19 8 12·5	5 37 6·8	17 57 7·1	11 54 3·4	— —	2 2 5·2	14 25 5·2	11 9 3·9	23 21 3·8
7	Tu	1 59 7·0	14 15 6·9	11 28 8·8	23 45 8·8	7 19 12·5	19 43 12·6	6 17 6·9	18 29 7·1	0 32 3·2	12 27 3·5	2 37 5·3	15 0 5·3	11 41 3·9	23 55 3·7
8	W	2 30 7·0	14 47 6·9	— —	12 0 8·9	7 52 12·7	20 16 12·6	6 55 6·9	19 3 7·1	1 7 3·2	12 59 3·5	3 13 5·3	15 37 5·3	— —	12 15 3·7
9	Th	3 8 7·0	15 22 7·0	0 20 8·8	12 33 9·0	8 25 12·6	20 49 12·5	7 33 6·9	19 35 7·1	1 41 3·2	13 32 3·5	3 49 5·3	16 10 5·3	0 32 3·7	12 55 3·7
10	F	3 38 7·0	15 59 7·0	0 54 8·7	13 6 8·8	8 59 12·5	21 23 12·3	8 17 6·8	20 14 6·8	2 17 3·1	14 8 3·6	4 26 5·3	16 47 5·3	1 11 3·7	13 30 3·7
11	S	4 12 6·9	16 35 7·0	1 32 8·6	13 45 8·8	9 34 12·5	21 59 12·3	8 47 6·6	20 44 6·5	2 55 3·1	14 50 3·7	5 5 5·2	17 28 5·3	1 53 3·7	14 33 3·6
12	Su	4 45 6·9	17 15 6·9	2 14 8·4	14 27 8·7	10 13 12·3	22 37 11·8	9 27 6·5	21 24 6·3	3 37 3·2	15 33 3·7	5 49 5·0	18 14 5·0	2 39 3·6	14 59 3·6
13	M	5 6 6·7	17 57 6·8	3 1 8·1	15 16 8·4	10 56 11·8	23 22 11·3	10 12 6·2	22 12 6·1	4 21 3·2	16 20 3·7	6 39 4·9	19 5 4·9	3 31 3·5	15 50 3·5
14	Tu	5 48 6·6	18 43 6·6	3 56 7·9	16 14 8·1	11 45 11·4	— —	11 6 6·2	23 11 6·1	5 11 3·2	17 11 3·6	7 34 4·8	20 2 4·8	4 31 3·5	16 52 3·5
15	W	6 5 6·5	19 43 6·5	4 58 7·9	17 19 8·0	0 10 10·8	12 47 10·9	0 21 6·4	12 15 6·4	6 11 3·2	18 10 3·6	8 34 4·8	21 4 4·9	5 38 3·5	18 2 3·5
16	Th	8 13 6·4	21 11 6·6	6 8 7·9	18 32 8·1	1 31 10·5	14 3 10·8	1 40 6·5	14 0 6·5	7 13 3·1	19 23 3·4	9 40 4·8	22 11 4·9	6 47 3·5	19 12 3·7
17	F	9 38 6·3	22 27 6·5	7 18 7·9	19 45 8·4	2 51 10·7	15 23 11·2	2 51 6·7	15 2 6·9	8 37 3·1	20 41 3·4	10 47 5·1	23 11 5·1	7 51 3·7	20 12 3·8
18	S	10 54 6·8	23 34 7·1	8 22 8·6	20 49 8·7	4 11 11·2	16 37 11·6	3 57 7·3	16 1 7·4	9 38 3·3	21 47 3·5	11 48 5·2	— —	8 47 3·8	21 12 3·8
19	Su	— —	12 57 7·1	9 20 9·0	21 46 9·1	5 16 12·0	17 42 12·6	4 57 7·4	16 57 7·6	10 31 3·4	22 46 3·6	0 18 5·3	12 45 5·4	9 35 4·0	21 52 4·1
20	M	0 34 7·2	13 48 7·5	10 13 9·4	22 39 9·4	6 10 13·1	18 41 13·2	5 51 7·5	17 47 7·6	11 13 3·6	23 46 3·6	1 13 5·5	13 38 5·6	10 21 4·2	22 52 4·3
21	Tu	1 26 7·0	14 36 7·5	11 3 9·7	23 29 9·4	7 9 13·7	19 32 13·6	6 43 7·5	18 34 7·6	11 48 3·7	— —	2 6 5·7	14 28 5·8	11 6 4·3	23 40 4·3
22	W	2 13 7·2	15 22 7·3	11 51 9·8	— —	7 55 14·0	20 16 13·7	7 33 7·5	19 21 7·6	0 21 3·6	12 12 3·8	2 57 5·8	15 17 5·7	11 52 4·1	— —
23	Th	2 57 7·0	16 5 7·1	0 16 9·4	12 36 9·6	8 35 14·0	20 58 13·5	8 19 7·3	20 23 7·2	1 7 3·6	13 36 3·8	3 46 5·8	16 5 5·7	0 29 4·1	12 40 4·0
24	F	3 41 7·0	16 52 7·0	1 3 9·3	13 21 9·6	9 17 13·6	21 39 13·1	9 3 7·2	21 3 7·2	3 1 3·5	15 14 3·8	4 33 5·7	16 52 5·5	1 18 3·9	13 30 3·9
25	S	4 23 6·8	17 34 6·7	1 48 9·0	14 6 9·3	10 4 13·1	22 20 12·5	9 43 6·7	21 42 6·6	3 44 3·4	16 41 3·6	5 20 5·5	17 40 5·5	2 8 3·9	14 21 3·7
26	Su	5 4 6·5	18 17 6·4	2 34 8·6	14 51 8·8	10 43 12·3	23 2 11·7	10 27 6·4	22 24 6·3	4 27 3·2	16 41 3·6	6 8 5·2	18 29 4·9	3 1 3·7	15 14 3·5
27	M	5 43 6·3	18 57 6·2	3 20 8·1	15 38 8·4	11 28 11·7	23 44 11·1	11 13 6·0	23 12 6·0	5 11 3·2	17 30 3·5	6 58 4·9	19 18 4·9	3 59 3·6	16 10 3·8
28	Tu	6 25 6·1	19 34 6·2	4 10 7·7	16 30 8·0	— —	12 13 11·2	— —	12 10 5·9	5 58 3·1	18 30 3·4	7 52 4·7	20 11 4·6	4 5 3·6	16 20 3·8
29	W	7 17 6·1	20 21 6·1	5 8 7·4	17 37 7·6	0 30 10·5	13 2 10·5	0 12 5·9	13 17 5·7	5 58 3·2	18 30 3·3	8 47 4·5	21 7 4·6	5 0 3·4	17 11 3·6
30	Th	8 20 6·0	21 11 6·2	6 11 7·4	18 37 7·5	1 24 10·1	14 3 10·1	0 59 5·9	14 3 5·7	6 57 3·1	19 44 3·0	9 50 4·5	22 8 4·5	7 15 3·3	19 26 3·3
31	F	9 34 6·0	22 20 6·2	7 20 7·3	19 44 7·5	2 30 10·1	15 11 10·1	1 27 5·7	14 25 5·8	8 10 3·0	20 56 3·0	10 52 4·6	23 12 4·6	8 10 3·4	20 23 3·4

* All times shown are Greenwich Mean Time.   † Difference of height in metres from Ordnance Datum (Newlyn).
‡ Difference of height in metres from Ordnance Datum (Ireland).

NOTES ON TIDAL PREDICTIONS

Changes in Chart Datum

During recent years the Department of the Hydrographer of the Navy has been carrying out a survey of tidal levels. On the conclusion of each section of the survey the Department is taking the opportunity to regularize the sequence of chart datums so that eventually chart datums throughout the British Isles will approximate to the Lowest Astronomical Tide, *i.e.* the lowest level which can be predicted to occur under average meteorological conditions and under any combination of astronomical conditions.

In some cases the changes in chart datum will be appreciable (perhaps as much as 1 metre) and the resulting predictions will appear to give heights of tide quite different from those of previous years. These changes do not imply that a physical change has taken place in tidal conditions.

It will be found that, where such datum changes have been made, the relationship between Ordnance Datum and the datum of the predictions will also have been altered. In order to compare the predictions for one year with those of another year for which the datum has been altered, it is necessary to refer both years to the same datum. Ordnance Datum (Newlyn) is a convenient datum to which tidal heights may thus be referred.

Example.—In 1972, at Folkstone, the highest predicted high water was 22·8 feet (= 6·9 metres) above chart datum; chart datum for that year was 10·06 feet (3·07 metres) below Ordnance Datum (Newlyn). In 1973 the highest predicted high water was 7·4 metres above chart datum, while chart datum for this year was altered to 3·75 metres below Ordnance Datum (Newlyn). To compare these two maximum predicted levels we must reduce both to Ordnance Datum (Newlyn) with the following results:—

$$1972 \quad 6·9–3·07 = 3·83 \text{ metres}$$
$$1973 \quad 7·4–3·75 = 3·65 \text{ metres}$$

Thus it will be seen that the highest prediction for 1973 is approximately 0·2 metres lower than for 1972.

Tidal predictions for London Bridge, Liverpool, Bristol, Hull and Leith are supplied by the Institute of Oceanographic Sciences, copyright reserved. Tidal predictions for Dún Laoghaire are based upon data supplied by the Institute of Oceanographic Sciences, copyright reserved. Tidal predictions for Greenock are Crown Copyright and have been supplied by the Institute of Oceanographic Sciences with the permission of the Controller of H.M. Stationery Office and the Hydrographer of the Navy.

Chronological Notes

TIME MEASURES

Kelvin (1883) estimated the age of the earth's crust at 20–400 million years. Study of radioactivity has since shown cooling to have been slower. Holmes and others gave 1,500–2,000 million years as the age of the oldest known rocks. Jeffreys suggests an age not exceeding 8,000 million years for the separate existence of the earth, which, probably with other related planets, separated from the sun after a star-collision. Very early rocks, almost without traces of fossils, are variously named in North America and Europe and account for a period down to about 5000 million years ago.

PALÆOZOIC (Old Animal Life) PERIODS include:—

Cambrian, Ordovician and Silurian rocks, all named from Wales (Cambria, Ordovices, Silures, the two latter ancient Celtic peoples). These rocks account for about 200 million years and there then followed a major phase of mountain-building, called *Caledonian* because studied early in Scotland, characterized by N.E.–S.W. lines of hills and valleys in several areas.

Devonian, including the Old Red Sandstone.

Carboniferous, including Mountain Limestone, Millstone Grit and Coal Measures.

These rocks account for about 100 million years and then there followed a major phase of mountain-building called *Hercyian* because widespread in W. Germany and adjacent areas. In Britain there are E.–W. lines of hills and valleys, and some N.–S.

MESOZOIC (Middle Forms of Life) PERIODS include:—

Permian rocks, widespread in Perm district, U.S.S.R. *Triassic*, including New Red Sandstone. *Jurassic*, important in the Jura Mts. *Cretaceous*, including the Greensands and the Chalk of England. In the Mesozoic, modern large land groups of animals, reptiles, birds and mammals first appear, but almost no modern genera or species of animals are known.

CAINOZOIC or CENOZOIC (Recent forms of Life) PERIODS include:—

Eocene. A few existing genera or species. *Oligocene.* A minority of existing forms. *Miocene.* Approach to a balance of existing and extinct forms. *Pliocene.* A majority of existing forms. *Pleistocene.* A very large majority of existing forms. *Holocene.* Existing forms only, save for a few exterminated by man. In the last 50 million years, from the Miocene through the Pliocene, the Alpine-Himalayan and the circum-Pacific phases of mountain building reached their climax.

During the Pleistocene period ice sheets repeatedly locked up masses of water as land ice, its weight depressed the land, but the locking up of water lowered sea-level by 100–200 metres. Milankovitch has worked out variations of radiation theoretically receivable from the sun and has reached conclusions not very markedly different as to dates from those of Penck who studied sediments, and both can fit into Deperet's scheme based on study of river terraces. Milankovitch gives 600,000 years for the Pleistocene.

Phases of the Pleistocene:—

(*a*) Early Glaciations (probably 2), Gunz glaciations of Penck's Alpine series. About 600 to 500 thousand years ago.

(*b*) An interglacial phase with high sea level, Milazzian terraces (of Deperet's series) around the Mediterranean. About 500,000 years ago.

(*c*) A second pair of Glaciations, the Mindel of Penck's series. About 500 to rather before 400 thousand years ago.

(*d*) A long interglacial phase with high sea level, but less high than during (*b*). Tyrrhenian terraces around the Mediterranean. From about 400 to about 200 thousand years ago.

(*e*) The penultimate series of glaciations (probably 3), the Riss of Penck's series. About 200 to 150 thousand years ago.

(*f*) An interglacial phase with fairly high sea level, less high than during (*d*). Monastirian terraces around the Mediterranean. From about 150 to about 120 thousand years ago.

(*g*) The ultimate series of glaciations (probably 3, preceded perhaps by a cool phase), the Wurm of Penck's series. From about 115 to rather more than 20 thousand years ago.

(*h*) The last glacial retreat merging into the Holocene period about 10,000 or 8,000 years ago.

MAN IN THE PLEISTOCENE

In the East African Miocene have been found by Hopwood and Leakey fragmentary remains of apes with possible human links in thigh bone characters.

In S. Africa at Taungs, Sterkfontein and Kroomdraai have been found remains of *Australopithecus*, *Plesianthropus* and *Paranthropus*, possibly linked with early man in limb characters and some features of skull and teeth though the brains are small and rather ape-like. The cave deposits in which they occur are supposed to be late Pliocene or early Pleistocene.

Java and Peking finds began with Dubois' discovery (1892) of an imperfect skull cap, some teeth and a possibly related femur indicating the erect posture. Later finds by von Koenigswald and by Weidenreich (1937–41) have emphasized the human relationship of the Java specimens, and also give evidence of gigantism (the name *Meganthropus* has been used). The specimens are usually given a Middle Pleistocene age. Oppenoorth (1932) discovered robust skulls and human Pleistocene bones on a terrace of the Solo river, Java. Twelve specimens from Chou Kou Tien near Peking studied by Black and Weidenreich and called *Sinanthropus* are broadly like the Java finds; the name *Pithecanthropus* had better be used for all.

A jaw from Mauer, Heidelberg, found 1902, and dated to the mid Pleistocene is very large but human in form. A skull cap from Neandertal near Düsseldorf, Germany, has been under discussion for 100 years. It and later found congeners belong to the onset of the 4th series of Glaciations (Penck's Wurm). The best preserved of these skulls is that of La Chapelle aux Saints (France) with very strong brow-ridges. Related skulls of rather earlier date from Steinheim, Ehringsdorf, Krapina and elsewhere are less specialized and more akin to modern man. Skulls from Sacco Pastore and Circeo in Italy are related to the Neandertal group.

Mt. Carmel has yielded to Professor Dorothy Garrod and Dr. McCown several mid- or late-Pleistocene specimens apparently related both to modern types and to the Neandertal group.

A skull from Galilee, and a skull from Kabwe (formerly Broken Hill), Zambia, are related to the Neandertal group.

Oakley has estimated the age of Pleistocene fossil bones from their fluorine content. The back part of a skull from Swanscombe, N. Kent, has in this way been dated to the mid Pleistocene. Its discoverer, Marston, has won widespread support for his view linking it with modern types.

Controversy over the Piltdown skull and jaw is ended. The skull was dated by Oakley's method as late Pleistocene, or later, so the old name *Eoanthropus* is inappropriate. The ape-like jaw was found to be modern and to have nothing to do with the skull.

With the last retreat of the ice sheets it seems that the Neandertal group, and probably the Pitecanthropus group, became extinct. Well-known specimens of man of modern type with diversity of form have been found at Combe Capelle, Cro-Magnon, Chancelade and elsewhere in the later Pleistocene in France and others in Czechoslovakia.

HUMAN CULTURAL STAGES

Until about 8 or 7 thousand years ago men lived by hunting and collecting. In the middle of the Pleistocene they already made finely shaped hand axes (Abbevillean and Acheulian) from stone cores by chipping off flakes, using flint, chert, obsidian, rhyolite, quartzite, etc. in many regions, and these cultures spread from Africa to Spain, France and Britain during some interglacial periods. Apparently the men hunted and made pitfalls for animals as Leakey has shown at Olorgesailie in Kenya, while women and children collected. Fire was used very early. In the continental interior of Eurasia rough stone flakes were long used rather than shaped stone cores and apparently in cold periods at any rate this culture spread west to Britain. In the later part of the Riss-Wurm interglacial, stone flakes became finer especially in regions where contact was made with makers of core-tools, and in some groups both cores and flakes were used.

With the last retreat of the ice-sheets stone flakes became the dominant tools, with diverse types suited to scraping, boring, sawing, etc.—Aurignacian, followed in France by Solutrian, in which long leaf-like flakes were treated as cores and shaped very skilfully by pressing off flakes. The Magdalenian stage next following used flakes but specialized in implements of bone, horn and ivory. In some areas the Aurignacian grades into the Magdalenian and this seems to be largely the case in parts of Britain. All the above cultures are often grouped as Palæolithic.

About 8 or 7 thousand years ago people in S.W. Asia began to cultivate cereals on river mud laid down by annual floods, thus keeping the soil fertile and allowing durable settlement with concomitant advances in mud brick construction, pot-making, stone grinding, which had begun earlier and gave an improved control of shape, carpentering, weaving and other inventions. In all this development the Nile valley was early concerned and its regular floods from summer rains in Abyssinia could be managed to give such an advantage that Egypt gained a unique primacy in early history. Domestication of animals was added very early to cultivation of crops, most probably as a source of milk, flesh, leather, sinews, etc. Neolithic Culture was thus characterized by stone axes shaped by grinding or rubbing, by cultivation, usually by domestic animals, often by durable settlements and a variety of arts and crafts.

Especially after the practice of castration of surplus male animals was introduced, domestic beasts were used for work, notably for pulling a modified hoe to scratch the drying surface of river-mud and so keep it from caking too hard. This is the early plough, valuable in lands where plant food in the soil is drawn up nearly to the surface as moisture rises and evaporates. Animals were also used as porters and tractors.

Heating stones in fires, probably for water-heating, led to the discovery of impure copper and the invention of bronze (standardized at about 10 per cent. tin and 90 per cent. copper) at the beginning of the Bronze Age in S.W. Asia and/or Egypt. By that time, about 5,000 years ago, cities and trade were developing and the basic arts were spreading to the Indus basin, the Mediterranean and the loess areas of Central Europe. Western Europe on the one hand and N. China on the other were affected somewhat later but more than 4,000 years ago; and China rapidly advanced to a high skill in pottery and bronze. Over 3,000 years ago in Anatolia the smelting of iron was developed, and it spread thence in the next centuries, beginning the Iron Age. Iron nails and tools made possible larger boats, houses, furniture and especially larger ploughs, working deeper into the earth and so suited to cooler lands, where plant food was often deep in the soil because evaporation was not very strong and rain might occur at every season. So the farmer needed to bring up the deeper layers to the surface in north-west Europe. With the spread of iron, especially about 2,000 to 1,000 years ago, northwest Europe emerged from its former low status and went ahead, still more after houses were improved with more privacy, chimneys and beds.

The evolution of culture in the Americas is much discussed. Early drifts of hunters viâ Alaska may have occurred in the late Pleistocene. Probably a good deal of Neolithic culture (stone implements, pottery, etc.) spread by the same route to America about or after 5,000 years ago but did not take Asiatic cereals or domestic animals. America also received contributions to its life by maritime routes especially following the North Pacific currents.

TIME MEASUREMENT AND CALENDARS

MEASUREMENTS OF TIME

Measurements of Time.—These are based on the time taken by the earth to rotate on its axis (*Day*); by the moon to revolve round the earth (*Month*); and by the earth to revolve round the sun (*Year*). From these, which are not commensurable, certain average or mean intervals have been adopted for ordinary use. Of these the first is the *Day*, which begins at midnight and is divided into 24 hours of 60 minutes, each of 60 seconds. The hours are counted from midnight up to 12 at noon (when the sun crosses the meridian), and these hours are designated A.M. (*ante meridiem*); and again from noon up to 12 at midnight, which hours are designated P.M. (*post meridiem*), except when the *Twenty-four Hour* reckoning is employed. The 24-hour reckoning ignores A.M. and P.M., and the hours are numbered 0 to 23 from midnight to midnight.

Colloquially the 24 hours are divided into *day* and *night*, day being the time while the sun is above the horizon (including the four stages of twilight defined on p. 139). Day is subdivided further into *morning*, the early part of daytime, ending at noon; *afternoon* from noon to 6 p.m. and *evening*, which may be said to extend from 6 p.m. until midnight. *Night*, the dark period between day and day, begins at the close of Astronomical Twilight (*see* p. 139) and extends beyond midnight to sunrise the next day.

The names of the *Days*—Sunday, Monday, Tuesday (Tiw = God of War), Wednesday (Woden or Odin), Thursday (Thor), Friday (Frig = wife of Odin), and Saturday are derived from Old English translations or adaptations of the Roman titles (Sol, Luna, Mars, Mercurius, Jupiter, Venus and Saturnius).

The *Week* is a period of 7 days.

The *Month* in the ordinary calendar is approximately the twelfth part of a year, but the lengths of the different months vary from 28 (or 29) days to 31.

The Year.—The *Equinoctial or Tropical Year* is the time that the earth takes to revolve round the sun from equinox to equinox, or 365·2422 mean solar days. The *Calendar Year* consists of 365 days, but a year the date of which is divisible by 4, without remainder, is called *bissextile* (see Roman Calendar) or *Leap Year* and consists of 366 days, one day being added to the month February, so that a date " leaps over " a day of the week. The last year of a century is not a leap year unless its number is divisible by 400 (*e.g.* the years 1800 and 1900 had only 365 days).

The Historical Year.—Before the year 1752, two Calendar systems were in use in England. The Civil or Legal Year began on March 25, while the Historical Year began on January 1. Thus the Civil or Legal date 1658 March 24, was the same day as 1659 March 24 Historical; and a date in that portion of the year is written as:

March 24 165$\frac{8}{9}$, the lower figure showing the Historical year.

The Masonic Year.—Two dates are quoted in warrants, dispensations etc., issued by the United Grand Lodge of England, those for the current year being expressed as *Anno Domini* 1976—*Anno Lucis* 5976. This *Year of Light* is based on the Book of Genesis I: 3, the 4000 year difference being derived from *Ussher's Notation*, published in 1654, which placed the Creation of the World in 4,000 B.C.

Regnal Years.—These are the years of a sovereign's reign, and each begins on the anniversary of his or her accession: *e.g.* Regnal year 24 of the present Queen began on Feb. 6, 1975. The system was used for dating Acts of Parliament until 1962. The *Summer Time Act* of 1925, for example, is quoted as 15 and 16 Geo. V. c. 64, because it became law in the session which extended over part of both of these regnal years. The regnal years of Edward VII began on January 22, which was the day of Queen Victoria's death in 1901, so that Acts passed in that reign are, in general, quoted with only one year number, but year 10 of the series ended on May 6, 1910, being the day on which King Edward died, and Acts of the Parliamentary Session 1910 are headed 10 Edw. VII. and 1 Geo. V.; Acts passed in 1936 were dated 1 Edw. VIII. and 1 Geo. VI.; Acts passed in 1952 were dated 16 Geo. VI. and 1 Elizabeth II. Since 1962 Acts of Parliament have been dated by the calendar year.

New Year's Day.—In England in the seventh century, and as late as the thirteenth, the year was reckoned from Christmas Day, but in the twelfth century the Anglican Church began the year with the Feast of The Annunciation of the Blessed Virgin (Lady Day) on March 25 and this practice was adopted generally in the fourteenth century. The Civil or Legal year in the British Dominions (excusive of Scotland), as opposed to the Historical, which already began on Jan. 1, began with " Lady Day " until 1751. But in and since 1752 the civil year has begun with Jan. 1. Certain dividends are still paid by the Bank of England on dates based on Old Style. The Income Tax year begins on April 6 (the New Style equivalent of March 25, Old Style) in accordance with Act of Parliament (39 Geo. III. 1798). New Year's Day in *Scotland* was changed from March 25 to Jan. 1 in 1600. On the Continent of Europe Jan. 1 was adopted as the first day of the year by Venice in 1522, Germany in 1544, Spain, Portugal, and the Roman Catholic Netherlands in 1556, Prussia, Denmark and Sweden in 1559, France 1564, Lorraine 1579, Protestant Netherlands 1583, Russia 1725, and Tuscany 1751.

The Longest Day.—The longest day measured from sunrise to sunset at any place is the day on which the Sun attains its greatest distance from the Equator, north or south, accordingly as the place is in the northern or southern hemisphere; in other words, it is the day of the Calendar on which a Solstice falls. If a Solstice falls on June 21 late in the day, by Greenwich Time, that day will be the longest of the year at Greenwich, though it may be by only a second of time or a fraction thereof, but it will be on June 22 (local date) in Japan, and therefore June 22 will be the longest day there and at places in Eastern longitudes.

But leaving this question of locality and confining consideration to Greenwich, the Solstices are events in the Tropical Year whose length is 365¼ days less about 11 minutes, and therefore, if a Solstice happens late on June 21 in one year, it will be nearly six hours later in the next, or early on June 22, and that will be the longest day. This delay of the Solstice is not permitted to continue because the extra day in Leap Year brings it back a day in the Calendar. For the remainder of this century the longest day will fall each year on June 21.

Because of the 11 minutes above mentioned the additional day in Leap Year brings the Solstice back too far by 44 minutes, and the time of the Solstice in the calendar is earlier as the century progresses. In the year 2000 the Summer Solstice reaches its earliest date for 100 years, i.e., June 21$^{\rm d}$ 02$^{\rm h}$.

To remedy this the last year of a century is in most cases not a Leap Year, and the omission of the extra day puts the date of the Solstice later by about six hours too much, compensation for which is made by making the fourth centennial year a Leap Year.

The Shortest Day.—Similar considerations apply to the shortest day of the year, or the day of the Winter Solstice. For the remainder of this century the shortest day will fall on Dec. 21 in two years of four and on Dec. 22 in the remaining two years. In the year 2000 the Winter Solstice reaches its earliest date, Dec. i.e., 21$^{\rm d}$ 13$^{\rm h}$. The difference due to locality also prevails in the same sense as for the longest day.

At Greenwich the Sun sets at its earliest by the clock about ten days before the shortest day, which is a circumstance that may require explanation. The daily change in the time of sunset is due in the first place to the Sun's movement southwards at this time of year, which diminishes the interval between the Sun's southing or Apparent noon, and its setting, and, secondly, because of the daily decrease of the Equation of Time subtractive from Apparent time, which causes the time of Apparent noon to be continuously later, day by day, and so in a measure counteracts the first effect. The rates of the resulting daily acceleration and retardation are not equal, nor are they uniform, but are such that their combinations causes the date of earliest sunset to be Dec. 12 or 13 at Greenwich. In more southerly latitudes the effect of the movement of the Sun is less, and the change in the time of sunset depends on that of the Equation of Time to a greater degree, and the date of earliest sunset is earlier than it is at Greenwich.

Lord Mayor's Day.—The Lord Mayor of London was previously elected on the Feast of St. Simon and St. Jude (Oct. 28), and from the time of Edward I, at least, was presented to the King or to the Barons of the Exchequer on the following day, except that day be a Sunday.

The day of election was altered to Oct. 16 in 1346, and after some further changes was fixed for Michaelmas Day in 1546, but the ceremonies of admittance and swearing-in of the Lord Mayor continued to take place on Oct. 28 and 29 respectively until 1751. In 1752, when Sept. 3 was reckoned as Sept. 14 at the reform of the Calendar, the Lord Mayor was continued in office until Nov. 8, the " New Style " equivalent of Oct. 28. The Lord Mayor is now presented to the Lord Chief Justice at the Royal Courts of Justice, on the second Saturday in November to make the final declaration of office, having been sworn in at Guildhall on the preceding day.

Dog Days.—The days about the heliacal rising of the Dog Star, noted from ancient times as the hottest and most unwholesome period of the year in the Northern Hemisphere. Their incidence has been variously calculated as depending on the Greater or Lesser Dog Star (Sirius or Procyon) and their duration has been reckoned as from 30 to 54 days. A generally accepted period is from July 3 to August 15.

Metonic (Lunar, or Minor) Cycle.—In the year 432 B.C. Meton, an Athenian astronomer, found that 235 Lunations are very nearly, though not exactly equal in duration to 19 Solar Years, and, hence, after 19 years the Phases of the Moon recur on the same days of the month (nearly). The dates of Full Moon in a cycle of nineteen years were inscribed in *figures of gold* on public monuments in Athens, and the number showing the position of a year in the Cycle is called the *Golden Number* of that year.

Solar (or Major) Cycle.—A period of twenty-eight years, in any corresponding year of which the days of the week recur on the same day of the month.

Julian Period.—Proposed by Joseph Scaliger in 1582. The period is 7980 Julian years, and its first year coincides with the year 4713 B.C. 7980 is the product of the number of years in the Solar Cycle, the Metonic Cycle and the cycle of the Roman Indication (28 × 19 × 15).

Roman Indication.—A period of fifteen years, instituted for fiscal purposes about A.D. 300.

Epact.—The age of the calendar Moon, diminished by one day, on January 1, in the ecclesiastical lunar calendar.

THE FOUR SEASONS

SPRING, the first season of the year, is defined astronomically to begin in the *Northern Hemisphere* at the Vernal Equinox when the Sun enters the sign Aries (i.e. about March 21) and crosses the Equator, thus causing day and night to be of equal length all over the world; and to terminate at the Summer Solstice. In *Great Britain*, Spring in popular parlance comprises the months of February, March and April; in *North America* the months of March, April and May. In the *Southern Hemisphere* Spring corresponds with Autumn in the Northern Hemisphere.

SUMMER, the second and warmest season, begins astronomically at the Summer Solstice when the Sun enters the sign of Cancer (about June 21). The Sun then attains its greatest northern declination and appears to stand still, the times of sunrise and sunset and the consequent length of the day showing no variation for several days together, before and after the Longest Day (June 21 or 22). Summer terminates at the Autumnal Equinox. In popular parlance Summer in *Great Britain* includes the months of May, June and August, Mid-summer Day being June 24. In *North America* the season includes the months of June, July and August.

AUTUMN, the third season, begins astronomically at the Autumnal Equinox (i.e., about September 21) when the Sun enters the sign Libra, the beginning of which sign is at the intersection of the Equator and the Ecliptic, the point in the sky where the Sun crosses from N. to S. of the Equator and causes the length of day and night to be equal all over the world. In *Great Britain* it is popularly held to include the months of September and October. A warm period sometimes occurs round about St. Luke's Day (Oct. 18) and is known as " St. Luke's Summer." In *North America*,

Autumn, or "The Fall," comprises September, October and November. Autumn ends at the Winter Solstice. In the *Southern Hemisphere* it corresponds with Spring of the Northern Hemisphere.

WINTER, the fourth and coldest season, begins astronomically at the Winter Solstice (*i.e.* about Dec. 21) when the Sun enters the sign Capricornus, and ends at the Vernal Equinox. In *Great Britain*

the season is popularly held to comprise the months of November, December and January, mid-winter being marked by the Shortest Day. A warm period sometimes occurs round about Martinmas (Nov.11) and is known as "St. Martin's Summer." In *North America* the season includes the months of December, January and February. In the *Southern Hemisphere* it corresponds with Summer of teh Northern Hemisphere.

THE CHRISTIAN CALENDAR

In the Christian chronological system the years are distinguished by cardinal numbers before or after the Incarnation, the period being denoted by the letters B.C. (Before Christ) or, more rarely, A.C. (*Ante Christum*), and A.D. (*Annus Domini*). The correlative dates of the epoch are the 4th year of the 194th Olympiad, the 753rd year from the Foundation of Rome, A.M. 3761 (Jewish Chronology), and the 4714th year of the Julian Period. This was introduced into Italy in the sixth century, and though first used in France in the seventh it was not universally established there until about the eighth century. It has been said that the system was introduced into England by St. Augustine (A.D. 596), but was probably not generally used until some centuries later. It was ordered to be used by the Bishops at the Council of Chelsea, A.D. 816. The actual date of the birth of Christ is somewhat uncertain. Dec. 25, 4 B.C., is supported by several lines of argument.

Old and New Style.—In the Julian Calendar all the centennial years were Leap Years, and for this reason towards the close of the sixteenth century there was a difference of 10 days between the tropical and calendar years; or, in other words, the equinox fell on March 11 of the Calendar, whereas at the time of the Council of Nicaea, A.D. 325, it had fallen on March 21. In 1582 Pope Gregory ordained that Oct. 5th should be called Oct. 15th, and that of the end-century years only the fourth should be a Leap Year (*see* p. 186). This change was adopted by Italy, France, Spain, and Portugal in 1582; by Prussia, the German Roman Catholic States, Switzerland, Holland, and Flanders on Jan. 1, 1583, Poland 1586, Hungary 1587, the German and Netherland Protestant States and Denmark 1700, Sweden (gradually) by the omission of eleven leap days, 1700–1740; Great Britain and her Dominions (including the North American Colonies) in 1752, by the omission of eleven days (Sept. 3 being reckoned as Sept. 14). This *Gregorian Calendar* was adopted by Japan in 1872, China in 1912, Bulgaria in 1915, Turkey and Soviet Russia in 1918, by Yugoslavia and Rumania in 1919, and by Greece in February, 1923. The Russian, Greek, Serbian and Rumanian Churches did not abandon the Julian Calendar until May, 1923, when the Gregorian, slightly modified, was adopted. The *difference* between the Old and New Styles was 11 days after 1752, 12 days after 1800, and has been 13 days since 1900. It happened that a change of the beginning of the year from March 25 to January 1 was made in England in 1752, the year in which the change from Julian to Gregorian Calendar was made, and for that reason the words Old and New Style have been used in a sense which is not strictly correct, but is nevertheless expressive.

The *Dominical Letter* is one of the letters A–G which are used to denote the Sundays in successive years. If the first day of the year is a Sunday the letter is A; if the second, B; the third, C; and so on. Leap year requires two letters, the first for Jan. 1–Feb. 29, the second for March 1–Dec. 31.

Epiphany.—The Feast of the Epiphany, commemorating the manifestation of the infant Jesus to the Gentiles, later became associated with the offering of gifts by the Magi. The day was of exceptional importance from the time of the Council of Nicaea (A.D. 325) as the primate of Alexandria was charged at every Epiphany Feast with the announcement in a letter to the Churches of the date of the forthcoming Easter. The day was of considerable importance in Britain as it influenced dates, ecclesiastical and lay, *e.g.* Plow Monday, when work was resumed in the fields, falls upon the Monday in the first full week after the Epiphany.

Lent.—The Teutonic word *Lent*, which denotes the Fast preceding Easter, originally meant no more than the Spring season; but from Anglo-Saxon times, at least, it has been used as the equivalent of the more significant Latin term *Quadragesima*, meaning the "Forty Days" or, more literally, the fortieth day. As early as the fifth century some of the Fathers of the Church put forward the view that the forty days Fast is of Apostolic origin, but this is not supported or believed by modern scholars; and it appears to some that it dates from the early years of the fourth century. There is some suggestion that the Fast was kept originally for only forty hours. *Ash Wednesday* is the first day of Lent, which ends at midnight before Easter Day.

Sexagesima and Septuagesima.—It has been suggested that the unmeaning application of the names *Sexagesima* and *Septuagesima* to the second and third Sundays before Lent was made by analogy with the names *Quadragesima* and *Quinquagesima*. Another less likely conjecture is that *Septuagesima* means the seventieth day before the Octave of Easter. It is not certain whether the name *Quinquagesima* is due to the fact that the Sunday in question is the fiftieth day before Easter (reckoned inclusive) or was simply formed on the analogy of *Quadragesima* (*New English Dictionary*).

Palm Sunday commemorates the triumphal entry of Our Lord into Jerusalem and is celebrated in Britain (when palm is not available) by branches of willow gathered for use in the decoration of churches on that day.

Maundy Thursday, the day before Good Friday, the name itself being a corruption of *dies mandati* (day of the mandate) when Christ washed the feet of the disciples and gave them the mandate to love one another.

Easter-Day is the first Sunday after the full moon which happens upon, or next after, the 21st day of March; and if the full moon happens upon a Sunday, Easter-Day is the Sunday after. This definition is contained in an Act of Parliament (24 Geo. II., cap. 23), and explanation is given in the preamble to the Act that the day of Full Moon depends on certain tables that have been prepared. These are the tables whose essential points are given in the early pages of the Book of Common Prayer. The Moon referred to is not the real Moon of the heavens, but a hypothetical Moon on whose "Full" the date of Easter depends, and the lunations of this "Calendar" Moon consist of twenty-nine and thirty days alternately with certain necessary modifications to make the date of its Full agree as nearly as possible with that of the real Moon, which is known as the *Paschal Full Moon.*

A Fixed Easter.—As at present ordained, Easter falls on one of 35 days—(March 22–April 25). On June 15, 1928, the House of Commons agreed to a motion for the third reading of the Bill that Easter Day shall, in the Calendar year next but one after the commencement of the Act and in all subsequent years, be *the first Sunday after the second Saturday in April.* Easter would thus fall between April 9 and 15, both inclusive—that is, on the second or third Sunday in April. A clause in the Bill provided that before it shall come into operation regard shall be had to any opinion expressed officially by the various Christian Churches. Efforts have been made recently by the World Council of Churches to secure a unanimous choice of date for Easter by its 239 member Churches. Press reports suggested the second Sunday in April as their most likely choice.

Holy Days and Saints Days were the normal factors in early times for settling the dates of future and recurrent appointments, *e.g.* the *Quarter Days* in England and Wales are the Feast of the Nativity, the Feast of the Annunciation, the Feast of St. John the Baptist and the Feast of St. Michael and All the Holy Angels, while *Term Days* in Scotland are Candlemas (Feast of the Purification), Whitsunday (a fixed date), Lammas (Loaf Mass) and Martinmas (St. Martin's Day). *Law Sittings* in England and Wales commence on the Feast of St. Hilary and the term which begins on Old Michaelmas Day ends on the feast of St. Thomas the Apostle.

The number of Saints commemorated in the Calendar of the Book of Common Prayer is 73, but (with the exception of All Saint's Day) "days" are appointed only for those whose names are mentioned in Scripture. *Red Letter Days* (*see also* p. 225) were Holy Days and Saints Days indicated in early ecclesiastical calendars by letters printed in red ink. The days to be distinguished in this way were finally approved at the Council of Nicaea, A.D. 325,

and special services are set apart for them in the Book of Common Prayer.

Rogation Days.—These are the Monday, Tuesday and Wednesday preceding Ascension Day, "Holy Thursday", and in the fifth century were ordered by the Church to be observed as Public Fasts with solemn processions and supplications. The processions were discontinued as religious observances at the Reformation, but survive in the ceremony known as "Beating the Parish Bounds".

Ember Days.—The Ember Days at the Four Seasons are the Wednesday, Friday and Saturday after (1) the First Sunday in Lent, (2) the Feast of Pentecost, (3) September 14, (4) December 13.

Whit Sunday.—It is generally said that this name is a variant of White Sunday, and was so called from the albs or white robes of the newly baptized. But other derivations have been suggested.

Trinity Sunday.—The Festival in honour of the Trinity is observed on the Sunday following Whit Sunday, and subsequent Sundays are reckoned in the Church of England as "after Trinity"; in the Roman Catholic Church Sundays are reckoned "after Pentecost".

Thomas Becket, called by his contemporaries Thomas of London (*born* 1118; *murdered* Dec. 29, 1170), was consecrated Archbishop of Canterbury on the Sunday after Whit Sunday and his first act was to ordain that the day of his consecration should be held as a new festival in honour of the Holy Trinity. The observance thus originated spread from Canterbury throughout the whole of Christendom.

Advent Sunday is the Sunday nearest to St. Andrew's Day, Nov. 30, which allows three Sundays between Advent and Christmas Day in all cases. The Sunday preceding Advent is the 27th after Trinity if Easter falls on one of the days, March 22–26 inclusive. It is the 22nd after Trinity when Easter Day is on April 24 or 25. If the date of Easter were determined as proposed (*see Fixed Easter*) there would generally be 24 Sundays after Trinity, the number being 25 only in the years when Easter fell on April 9. With a Fixed Easter there would never be a sixth Sunday after Epiphany. There would be a fifth Sunday when Easter Day fell on April 15 or April 14, the year being a leap year.

A TABLE OF THE MOVABLE FEASTS FOR 10 YEARS—1973–82

Year	Ash Wednesday	Easter	Ascension	Whit Sunday	Sundays after Trinity	Advent
1973.......	March 7	April 22	May 31	June 10	xxiii	Dec. 2
1974.......	Feb. 27	April 14	May 23	June 2	xxiv	Dec. 1
1975.......	Feb. 12	March 30	May 8	May 18	xxvi	Nov. 30
1976.......	March 3	April 18	May 27	June 6	xxiii	Nov. 28
1977.......	Feb. 23	April 10	May 19	May 29	xxiv	Nov. 27
1978.......	Feb. 8	March 26	May 4	May 14	xxvii	Dec. 3
1979.......	Feb. 28	April 15	May 24	June 3	xxiv	Dec. 2
1980.......	Feb. 19	April 6	May 15	May 25	xxv	Nov. 30
1981.......	Mar. 4	April 19	May 28	June 7	xxiii	Nov. 29
1982.......	Feb. 24	April 11	May 20	May 30	xxiv	Nov. 28

NOTES CONCERNING TABLE OF MOVABLE FEASTS

Ash Wednesday (first Day in *Lent*) can fall at earliest on February 4 and at latest on March 10.
Easter Day can fall at earliest on March 22 and at latest on April 25.
Ascension Day can fall at earliest on April 30 and at latest on June 3.
Whit Sunday can fall at earliest on May 10 and at latest on June 13.
Rogation Sunday is the Sunday next before *Holy Thursday* (Ascension Day).
Trinity Sunday is the Sunday next after *Whit Sunday*.
Corpus Christi falls on the Thursday next after *Trinity Sunday*.
There are not less than xxii and not more than xxvii *Sundays after Trinity*.
Advent Sunday is the Sunday nearest to November 30.

A TABLE OF EASTER DAYS AND SUNDAY LETTERS, 1500 TO 2000

		1500—1599	1600—1699	1700—1799	1800—1899	1900—2000		
d	Mar. 22	1573............	1668........	1761........	1818........	....	d	Mar. 22
e	,, 23	1505-16........	1600........	1788........	1845-56.......	1913........	e	,, 23
f	,, 24	....	1611-95.......	1706-99......	....	1940........	f	,, 24
g	,, 25	1543-54.......	1627-38-49.....	1722-33-44....	1883-94......	1951........	g	,, 25
A	,, 26	1559-70-81-92..	1654-65-76.....	1749-58-69-80.	1815-26-37....	1967-78-89....	A	,, 26
b	Mar. 27	1502-13-24-97..	1608-87-92....	1785-96......	1842-53-64....	1910-21-32....	b	Mar. 27
c	,, 28	1529-35-40.....	1619-24-30....	1703-14-25....	1869-75-80....	1937-48.......	c	,, 28
d	,, 29	1551-62........	1635-46-57....	1719-30-41-52.	1807-12-91....	1959-64-70....	d	,, 29
e	,, 30	1567-78-89.....	1651-62-73-84..	1746-55-66-77.	1823-34......	1902-75-86-97..	e	,, 30
f	,, 31	1510-21-32-83-94.	1605-16-78-89...	1700-71-82-93.	1839-50-61-72..	1907-18-29-91..	f	,, 31
g	April 1	1526-37-48.....	1621-32.......	1711-16......	1804-66-77-88..	1923-34-45-56..	g	April 1
A	,, 2	1553-64........	1643-48.......	1727-38-52(NS).	1809-20-93-99..	1961-72.......	A	,, 2
b	,, 3	1575-80-86.....	1659-70-81....	1743-63-68-74..	1825-31-36....	1904-83-88-94..	b	,, 3
c	,, 4	1507-18-91.....	1602-13-75-86-97.	1708-79-90....	1847-58......	1915-20-26-99..	c	,, 4
d	,, 5	1523-34-45-56..	1607-18-29-40...	1702-13-24-95..	1801-63-74-85-96.	1931-42-53....	d	,, 5
e	April 6	1539-50-61-72..	1634-45-56.....	1729-35-40-60..	1806-17-28-90..	1947-58-69-80...	e	April 6
f	,, 7	1504-77-88.....	1667-72.......	1751-65-76....	1822-33-44....	1901-12-85-96...	f	,, 7
g	,, 8	1509-15-20-99..	1604-10-83-94...	1705-87-92-98..	1849-55-60....	1917-28.......	g	,, 8
A	,, 9	1531-42........	1615-26-37-99...	1710-21-32....	1871-82......	1939-44-50.....	A	,, 9
b	,, 10	1547-58-69.....	1631-42-53-64...	1726-37-48-57..	1803-14-87-98..	1955-66-77.....	b	,, 10
c	April 11	1501-12-63-74-85-96	1658-69-80....	1762-73-84....	1809-30-41-52..	1909-71-82-93...	c	April 11
d	,, 12	1506-17-28.....	1601-12-91-96...	1789........	1846-57-68....	1903-14-25-36-98	d	,, 12
e	,, 13	1533-44........	1623-28.......	1707-18......	1800-73-79-84..	1941-52.......	e	,, 13
f	,, 14	1555-60-66.....	1639-50-61....	1723-34-45-54..	1805-11-16-95..	1963-68-74.....	f	,, 14
g	,, 15	1571-82-93.....	1655-66-77-88...	1750-59-70-81..	1827-38......	1900-06-79-90...	g	,, 15
A	April 16	1503-14-25-36-87-98	1609-20-82-93...	1704-75-86-97..	1843-54-65-76..	1911-22-33-95...	A	April 16
b	,, 17	1530-41-52.....	1625-36.......	1715-20......	1808-70-81-92..	1927-38-49-60...	b	,, 17
c	,, 18	1557-68........	1647-52.......	1731-42-56....	1802-13-24-97..	1954-65-76.....	c	,, 18
d	,, 19	1500-79-84-90..	1663-74-85....	1747-67-72-78..	1829-35-40....	1908-81-87-92...	d	,, 19
e	,, 20	1511-22-95.....	1606-17-79-90...	1701-12-83-94..	1851-62......	1919-24-30.....	e	,, 20
f	April 21	1527-38-49.....	1622-33-44....	1717-28......	1867-78-89....	1935-46-57.....	f	April 21
g	,, 22	1565-76........	1660........	1739-53-64....	1810-21-32....	1962-73-84.....	g	,, 22
A	,, 23	1508........	1671........		1848........	1905-16-2000....	A	,, 23
b	,, 24	1519........	1603-14-98....	1739-91......	1859........		b	,, 24
c	,, 25	1546........	1641........	1736........	1886........	1943........	c	,, 25

PUBLIC HOLIDAYS

BANK HOLIDAYS IN ENGLAND, WALES, NORTHERN IRELAND AND THE CHANNEL ISLANDS ARE (1976):— New Year's Day (January 1), Easter Monday (April 19), Spring Holiday (May 31), August Bank Holiday (August 30); and December 27; (1977) Jan. 1; April 11; May 30; Aug. 29; Dec. 26; Dec. 27.

Liberation Day (May 9) is a bank and public holiday in the Channel Islands.

Banks are also closed on Good Friday and Christmas Day and on all Saturdays.

The Stock Exchange is closed on Bank Holidays, Good Friday, Christmas Day and New Year's Day; and on Saturdays throughout the year.

Custom House and Docks, as Banks; with the Queen's Birthday (when decreed).

Excise and Stamp Offices, as Banks; with Whit Tuesday and Coronation Day, if and when decreed.

Law Offices.—Good Friday, Easter Monday and Tuesday, Spring Bank Holiday (see col. 1), Christmas Day, and first week-day after Christmas.

BANK HOLIDAYS IN SCOTLAND ARE (1976): New Year's Day (Jan. 1); Jan. 2; April 16, May 3; and August 2; (1977) Jan. 1 and 3; April 8; May 2; Aug. 1; and Dec. 26.

Banks in Scotland are also closed on Good Friday, Christmas Day and on Saturdays.

Scotland has special Term (Quarter) Days:— Candlemas, Feb. 2; Whitsunday, May 15 (Fixed date); Lammas, Aug. 1; and Martinmas, Nov. 11; the Removal Terms are May 28 and Nov. 28.

THE JEWISH CALENDAR

Origin.—The story in the Book of Genesis that the Flood began on the seventeenth day of the second month; that after the end of 150 days the waters were abated; and that on the seventeenth day of the seventh month the Ark rested on Mount Ararat, indicates a calendar of some kind and that the writers recognized 30 days as the length of a lunation. There is other mention of months by their original numbers in the Book of Genesis and in establishing the rite of the Passover Moses spoke of Abib as the month when the Israelites came out from Egypt and Abib was to be the first month of the year. In the first Book of Kings three month, are mentioned by name, Zif the second months Ethanim the seventh and Bul the eighth. but these are not names now in use. After the Dispersion, Jewish communities were left in considerable doubt as to the times of Fasts and Festivals, and this led to the formation of the Jewish Calendar as used to-day, which, it is said by some, was done in A.D. 358 by Rabbi Hillel II, a descendant of Gamaliel —though some assert that it did not happen until much later. This calendar is luni-solar, and is based on the lengths of the lunation and of the tropical year as found by Hipparchus (*Circ.* 120 B.C.) which differ little from those adopted at the present day. The year 5736 A.D. (1975–76) is the 17th year of the 302nd *Metonic* (Minor or Lunar) *Cycle* of 19 years and the 24th year of the 205th *Solar* (or Major) *Cycle* of 28 years since the Era of the Creation, which the Jews hold to have occurred at the time of the Autumnal Equinox in the year known in the Christian Calendar as 3760 B.C. (954 of the Julian Period) and the epoch or starting point of Jewish Chronology corresponds to Oct. 7, 3761 B.C. At the beginning of each Solar Cycle the *Teku ah* of Nisan (the vernal equinox) returns to the same day and to the same hour.

The hour is divided into 1080 *minims* and the month between one new moon and the next is reckoned as 29 days, 12 hours, 793 minims. The normal calendar year, called a Common Regular year, consists of 12 months of 30 days and 29 days alternately. Since 12 months such as these comprise only 354 days, in order that each of them shall not diverge greatly from an average place in the solar year, a thirteenth month is occasionally added after the fifth month of the Civil year (which commences on the first day of the month Tishri), or as the penultimate month of the Ecclesiastical (which commences on the first day of month Nisan), the years when this happens being called Embolismic. Of the 19 years that form a Metonic cycle, 7 are embolismic; they occur at places in the cycle indicated by the numbers 3, 6, 8, 11, 14, 17, 19, these places being chosen so that the accumulated excesses of the solar years should be as small as possible. The first of each month is called the day of New Moon, though it is not necessarily the day of astronomical New Moon, that being the day on which conjunction of Sun and Moon occurs, but there is generally a difference of a day or two. In practice, in a month which follows one of 30 days, the day preceding its first day is also observed as a day of New Moon. The dates in the Christian calendar of the first days of the months depend on that of the first of Tishri, which therefore controls the dates of fasts and festivals in the Jewish year. For certain ceremonial reasons connected with these, the first of Tishri must not

fall on a Sunday, Wednesday or Friday, and if this should happen as the result of the computation it is postponed to the next day in the Christian calendar. Also, if the New Moon of Tishri falls on any day of the week at noon or later than noon, then the following day is to be taken for the celebration of that New Moon and is Tishri 1, provided that it is not one of the forbidden days, in which case there is a further postponement of a day. These rules and others have been considered in detail, and finally a calendar scheme has been drawn up in which a Jewish year is of one of the following six types: Common Deficient (353 days), Common Regular (354 days), Common Abundant (355 days), Embolismic Deficient (383 days), Embolismic Regular (384 days), or Embolismic Abundant (385 days).

The Regular year has an alternation of 30 and 29 days. In an Abundant year, whether Common or Embolismic, Marcheshvan, the second month of the Civil year, has 30 days instead of 29; in Deficient years Kislev, the third month, has 29 instead of 30. The additional month in Embolismic years which is called Adar I., and precedes the month called Adar in Common years and Adar II., or Ve-Adar, in Embolismic, always has 30 days, but neither this, nor the other variations mentioned, is allowed to change the number of days in the other months which still follow the alternation of the normal twelve. In Embolismic years the month intercalated precedes Adar and usurps its name, but the usual Adar festivals are kept in Ve-Adar.

These are the main features of the Jewish Calendar which must be considered permanent, because as a Jewish law it cannot be altered except by a great Synhedrion.

The Jewish day begins between sunset and nightfall. The time used is that of the meridian of Jerusalem, which is 2h. 21m. in advance of Greenwich Mean Time. Rules for the beginning of Sabbaths and Festivals were laid down for the latitude of London in the eighteenth century and hours for nightfall are now fixed annually by the Chief Rabbi.

Jewish Calendar 5736–5738

Jewish Month			A.M. 5736			A.M. 5737			A.M. 5738	
Tishri	1	..	1975 September	6	..	1976 September 25	..	1977	September	13
Marcheshvan	1	..	October	6	..	October	25	..		October	13
Kislev	1	..	November	5	..	November 23	..		November	11
Tebet	1	..	December	5	..	December	22	..		December	11
Shebat	1	..	1976 January	3	..	1977 January	20	..	1978	January	9
Adar	1	..	February	2	..	February	19	..		February	8
Ve-Adar	1	..	March	3	..	..		..		March	10
Nisan	1	..	April	1	..	March	20	..		April	8
Iyar	1	..	May	1	..	April	19	..		May	8
Sivan	1	..	May	30	..	May	18	..		June	6
Tammuz	1	..	June	29	..	June	17	..		July	6
Ab	1	..	July	28	..	July	16	..		August	4
Elul	1	..	August	27	..	August	15	..		September	3

A.M. 5736 (known as 736 in the short system) is an Embolismic Abundant year of 13 months, 55 Sabbaths and 385 days. A.M. 5737 (737) is a Common Deficient year of 12 months, 51 Sabbaths and 353 days. A.M. 5738 (738) is an Embolismic Regular year of 13 months, 55 Sabbaths and 384 days.

Jewish Fasts and Festivals

Tishri	1	Rosh Hoshanah (New Year).	Tebet	10	Fast of Tebet.
,,	3	*Fast of Gedaliah.	Adar	13	§Fast of Esther.
,,	10	Yom Kippur (Day of Atonement).	,,	14	Purim.
,,	15–22	Succoth (Feast of Tabernacles).	,,	15	Shushan Purim.
,,	21	Hoshana Rabba.	Nisan	15–21	Passover.
,,	22	Solemn Assembly.	Sivan 6 and 7		Shavuot (Pentecost or Feast of Weeks).
,,	23	Rejoicing of the Law.	Tammuz	17	*Fast of Tammuz.
Kislev	25	Dedication of the Temple.	Ab	9	*Fast of Ab.

NOTES.—* If these dates fall on the Sabbath the Fast is kept on the following day.
§ This fast is observed on Adar 11 (or Ve-Adar 11 in Embolismic years) if Adar 13 falls on a Sabbath.

THE ROMAN CALENDAR

Roman historians adopted as an epoch the Foundation of Rome, which is believed to have happened in the year 753 B.C., and the ordinal number of the years in Roman reckoning is followed by the letters A.U.C. (*Ab Urbe Condita*), so that the year 1976 is 2729 A.U.C. (MMDCCXXIX). The Calendar that we know has developed from one established by Romulus, who is said to have used a year of 304 days divided into ten months, beginning with March, to which Numa added January and February, making the year consist of 12 months of 30 and 29 days alternately, with an additional day so that the total was 355. It is also said that Numa ordered an intercalary month of 22 or 23 days in alternate years, making 90 days in eight years, to be inserted after Feb. 23, but there is some doubt as to the origination and the details of the intercalation in the Roman Calendar, though it is certain that some scheme of this kind was inaugurated and not fully carried out, for in the year 46 B.C. Julius Cæsar, who was then Pontifex Maximus, found that the Calendar had been allowed to fall into some confusion. He therefore sought the help of the Egyptian astronomer Sosigenes, which led to the construction and adoption (45 B.C.) of the Julian Calendar, and, by a slight alteration, to the Gregorian now in use. The year 46 B.C. was made to consist of 445 days, and is called the *Year of Confusion*. In the Roman (Julian) Calendar the days of the month were counted backwards from three fixed points, or days, and an intervening day was said to be so many days *before* the next coming point, the first *and* last being counted. These three points were (1) the Kalends; (2) the Nones; and (3) the Ides. Their positions in the months and the method of counting from them will be seen in the table below. The year containing 366 days was called *bissextilis annus*, as it had a doubled sixth day (*bissextus dies*) before the March Kalends on Feb. 24—*ante diem sextum Kalendas Martias*, or VI Kal. Mart.

Present Days of the Month	March, May, July, October have thirty-one days	January, August, December have thirty-one days	April, June, September, November have thirty days	February has twenty-eight days, and in Leap Year twenty-nine
1	Kalendis.	Kalendis.	Kalendis.	Kalendis.
2	VI. ⎫	IV. ⎫ Ante	IV. ⎫ Ante	IV. ⎫ Ante
3	V. ⎪ Ante	III. ⎭ Nonas	III. ⎭ Nonas.	III. ⎭ Nonas.
4	IV. ⎬ Nonas.	Pridie Nonas.	Pridie Nonas.	Pridie Nonas.
5	III. ⎪	Nonis.	Nonis.	Nonis.
6	Pridie Nonas.	VIII. ⎫	VIII. ⎫	VIII. ⎫
7	Nonis.	VII. ⎪	VII. ⎪	VII. ⎪
8	VIII. ⎫	VI. ⎬ Ante	VI. ⎬ Ante	VI. ⎬ Ante
9	VII. ⎪	V. ⎭ Idus.	V. ⎭ Idus.	V. ⎭ Idus.
10	VI. ⎬ Ante	IV. ⎪	IV. ⎪	IV. ⎪
11	V. ⎭ Idus.	III. ⎭	III. ⎭	III. ⎭
12	IV. ⎪	Pridie Idus.	Pridie Idus.	Pridie Idus.
13	III. ⎭	Idibus.	Idibus.	Idibus.
14	Pridie Idus.	XIX. ⎫	XVIII. ⎫	XVI. ⎫
15	Idibus.	XVIII. ⎪	XVII. ⎪	XV. ⎪
16	XVII. ⎫	XVII. ⎪	XVI. ⎪	XIV. ⎪
17	XVI. ⎪	XVI. ⎪	XV. ⎪	XIII. ⎪
18	XV. ⎪	XV. ⎪	XIV. ⎪	XII. ⎪
19	XIV. ⎪	XIV. ⎪	XIII. ⎪	XI. ⎪
20	XIII. ⎬	XIII. ⎬	XII. ⎬	X. ⎬ Ante Kalendas Martias.
21	XII. ⎪	XII. ⎪	XI. ⎪	IX. ⎪
22	XI. ⎪	XI. ⎪	X. ⎪	VIII. ⎪
23	X. ⎪	X. ⎪	IX. ⎪	VII. ⎪
24	IX. ⎪	IX. ⎪	VIII. ⎪	VI. ⎪
25	VIII. ⎪	VIII. ⎪	VII. ⎪	V. ⎪
26	VII. ⎪	VII. ⎪	VI. ⎪	IV. ⎭
27	VI. ⎪	VI. ⎪	V. ⎪	III.
28	V. ⎪	V. ⎪	IV. ⎭	Pridie Kalendas Martias.
29	IV. ⎭	IV. ⎭	III.	
30	III.	III.	Pridie Kalendas (of the month following).	
31	Pridie Kalendas (of the month following).	Pridie Kalendas (of the month following).		

(Columns 2 and 3 are annotated: "Ante Kalendas (of the month following)." Column 4: "Ante Kalendas (of the month following).")

ROMAN NUMERALS

1.............I	9.........IX	17.......XVII	70.......LXX	600........DC
2............II	10.........X	18......XVIII	80.....LXXX	700....DCC
3...........III	11.......XI	19.......XIX	90.......XC	800....DCCC
4..........IV	12.......XII	20........XX	100.........C	900.......CM
5...........V	13.......XIII	30.......XXX	200........CC	1000........M
6..........VI	14.......XIV	40.........XL	300.......CCC	1500.......MD
7.........VII	15.......XV	50..........L	400.......CD	1900....MCM
8........VIII	16......XVI	60..........LX	500..........D	2000......MM

Other Examples: 43=XLIII; 66=LXVI; 98=XCVIII.
339=CCCXXXIX; 619=DCXIX; 988=CMLXXXVIII; 996=CMXCVI.
1674=MDCLXXIV; 1962=MCMLXII.
A bar placed over a numeral has the effect of multiplying the number by 1,000, *e.g.*:
6,000=V̄I; 16,000=X̄V̄I; 160,000=C̄L̄X; 666,000=D̄C̄L̄X̄V̄I.

THE MOSLEM CALENDAR

The basic date of the Moslem Calendar is the *Hejira*, or Flight of Muhammad from Mecca to Medina, the corresponding date of which is A.D. 622, July 16, in the Julian Calendar. Hejira years are used principally in Iran, Turkey, Arabia, Egypt, in certain parts of India and in Malaya. The system was adopted about A.D. 632, commencing from the first day of the month preceding the Hejira. The years are purely lunar and consist of 12 months containing in alternate sequence 30 or 29 days, with the intercalation of one day at the end of the 12th month at stated intervals in each cycle of 30 years, the object of the intercalation being to reconcile the date of the first of the month with the date of the actual New Moon. Some adherents still take the date of the evening of the first visibility of the crescent as that of the first of the month. In each cycle of 30 years 19 are common and contain 354 days and 11 are intercalary (355 days), the latter being called *kabishah*.

The mean length of the Hejira year is 354 days, 8 hours, 48 minutes and the period of mean lunation is 29 days, 12 hours, 44 minutes.

To ascertain if a Hejira year is common or *kabishah* divide it by 30; the quotient gives the number of completed cycles and the remainder shows the place of the year in the current cycle. If the remainder is 2, 5, 7, 10, 13, 16, 18, 21, 24, 26 or 29 the year is *kabishah* and consists of 355 days. Hejira year 1395 gives a quotient of 46 with remainder 15 and is a common year. A.H. 1396 (remainder 16) is *kabishah*. A.H. 1397 (remainder 17) is common.

Hejira Years 1395 and 1396

Name and Length of Month	A.H. 1395	A.H. 1396
Muharram (30)	1975 Jan. 14	1976 Jan. 3
Safar (29)	Feb. 13	Feb. 2
Rabia I (30)	Mar. 14	Mar. 2
Rabia II (29)	April 13	April 1
Jumâda I (30)	May 12	April 30
Jumâda II (29)	June 11	May 30
Rajab (30)	July 10	June 28
Shaabân (29)	Aug. 9	July 28
Ramadân (30)	Sept. 7	Aug. 26
Shawwâl (29)	Oct. 7	Sept. 25
Dhû 'l-Qa'da (30)	Nov. 5	Oct. 24
Dhû 'l-Hijja (29 or 30)	Dec. 5	Nov. 23

NOTE—A.H. 1397 (common year of 354 days) begins on December 23, 1976.

OTHER EPOCHS AND CALENDARS

China.—Until the year A.D. 1911 a Lunar Calendar was in force in China, but with the establishment of the Republic the Government adopted the Gregorian Calendar, and the new and old systems were used simultaneously by the people for several years. Since 1930 the publication and use of the old Calendar have been banned by the Government, and an official Chinese Calendar, corresponding with the European or Western system, is compiled, but the old Lunar Calendar is still in use to some extent in China. The old Chinese Calendar, with a cycle of 60 years, is still in use in Tibet, Hong Kong, Singapore, Malaysia and elsewhere in South-East Asia.

Ethiopia.—In the Coptic Calendar, which is used by part of the population of Egypt and Ethiopia, the year is made up of 12 months of 30 days each, followed, in general, by 5 complementary days. Every fourth year is an Intercalary or Leap year and in these years there are 6 complementary days.

The Intercalary year of the Coptic Calendar immediately precedes the Leap year of the Julian Calendar. The Era is that of Diocletian or the Martyrs, the origin of which is fixed at A.D. 284, Aug. 29 (Julian date).

Greece.—Ancient Greek chronology was reckoned in *Olympiads*, cycles of 4 years corresponding with the periodic Olympic Games held on the plain of Olympia in Elis once in 4 years, the intervening years being the first, second, etc., of the Olympiad which received the name of the victor at the Games. The first recorded Olympiad is that of Choroebus, 776 B.C.

India.—In addition to the Moslem reckoning there are six eras used in India. The principal astronomical system was the *Kaliyuga Era*, which appears to have been adopted in the fourth century A.D. It began on Feb. 18, 3102 B.C. The chronological system of Northern India, known as the *Vikrama Samvat Era*, prevalent in Western India, began on Feb. 23, 57 B.C. The year A.D. 1976 is, therefore, the year 2033 of the Vikrama Era.

The *Saka Era* of Southern India dating from March 3, A.D. 78, was declared the uniform national calendar of the Republic of India with effect from March 22, 1957, to be used concurrently with the Gregorian Calendar. As revised, the year of the new *Saka Era* begins at the spring equinox, with five successive months of 31 days and seven of 30 days in ordinary years; six months of each length in leap years. The year A.D. 1976 is 1898 of the revised *Saka Era*.

In the Hills, the *Saptarshi Era* dates from the moment when the Saptarshi, or saints, were translated and became the stars of the Great Bear in 3076 B.C.

The *Buddhists* reckoned from the death of Buddha in 543 B.C. (the actual date being 487 B.C.); and the epoch of the *Jains* was the death of Vardhamana, the founder of their faith, in 527 B.C.

Iran.—The chronology of Iran (Persia) is the Era of Hejira, which began on A.D. 622, July 16. The *Zoroastrian Calendar* was used in pre-Moslem days and is still employed by Zoroastrians in Iran and India (Parsees) with era beginning A.D. 632, June 16.

Japan.—The Japanese Calendar is the Gregorian, and is essentially the same as that in use by Western nations, the years, months and weeks being of the same length and beginning on the same days as those of the Western Calendar. The numeration of the years is different, for Japanese chronology is based on a system of epochs or periods, each of which begins at the accession of an Emperor or other important occurrence, the method being not unlike the former British system of Regnal years, but differing from it in the particular that each year of a period closes on Dec. 31. The Japanese scheme begins about A.D. 650 and the three latest epochs are defined by the reigns of Emperors, whose actual names are not necessarily used:—

Epoch Meiji	from 1868 Oct. 13 to 1912 July 31
„ Taishō	„ 1912 Aug. 1 to 1926 Dec. 25
„ Shōwa	„ 1926 Dec. 26

Hence the year Shōwa 51 begins 1976 Jan. 1. The months are not named. They are known as First Month, Second Month, etc., first month being the equivalent to January. The days of the week are Nichiyōbi (Sun-day), Getsuyōbi (Moon-day), Kayōbi (Fire-day), Suiyōbi (Water-day), Mokuyōbi (Wood-day), Kinyōbi (Metal-day), Doyōbi (Earth-day).

EASY REFERENCE CALENDAR

for any year between 1753 and 2000 together with the dates of Easter in each of those years
TO SELECT THE CORRECT CALENDAR FOR ANY YEAR consult the INDEX below

INDEX TO CALENDARS

1753	.. C									1959	.. I
1754	.. E	1795	.. I	1836	.. L*	1877	.. C	1918	.. E	1960	.. L*
1755	.. G	1796	.. L*	1837	.. A	1878	.. E	1919	.. G	1961	.. A
1756	.. J*	1797	.. A	1838	.. C	1879	.. G	1920	.. J*	1962	.. C
1757	.. M	1798	.. C	1839	.. E	1880	.. J*	1921	.. M	1963	.. E
1758	.. A	1799	.. E	1840	.. H*	1881	.. M	1922	.. A	1964	.. H*
1759	.. C	1800	.. G	1841	.. K	1882	.. A	1923	.. C	1965	.. K
1760	.. F*	1801	.. I	1842	.. M	1883	.. C	1924	.. F*	1966	.. M
1761	.. I	1802	.. K	1843	.. A	1884	.. F*	1925	.. I	1967	.. A
1762	.. K	1803	.. M	1844	.. D*	1885	.. I	1926	.. K	1968	.. D*
1763	.. M	1804	.. B*	1845	.. G	1886	.. K	1927	.. M	1969	.. G
1764	.. B*	1805	.. E	1846	.. I	1887	.. M	1928	.. B*	1970	.. I
1765	.. E	1806	.. G	1847	.. K	1888	.. B*	1929	.. E	1971	.. K
1766	.. G	1807	.. I	1848	.. N*	1889	.. E	1930	.. G	1972	.. N*
1767	.. I	1808	.. L*	1849	.. C	1890	.. G	1931	.. I	1973	.. C
1768	.. L*	1809	.. A	1850	.. E	1891	.. I	1932	.. L*	1974	.. E
1769	.. A	1810	.. C	1851	.. G	1892	.. L*	1933	.. A	1975	.. G
1770	.. C	1811	.. E	1852	.. J*	1893	.. A	1934	.. C	1976	.. J*
1771	.. E	1812	.. H*	1853	.. M	1894	.. C	1935	.. E	1977	.. M
1772	.. H*	1813	.. K	1854	.. A	1895	.. E	1936	.. H*	1978	.. A
1773	.. K	1814	.. M	1855	.. C	1896	.. H*	1937	.. K	1979	.. C
1774	.. M	1815	.. A	1856	.. F*	1897	.. K	1938	.. M	1980	.. F*
1775	.. A	1816	.. D*	1857	.. I	1898	.. M	1939	.. A	1981	.. I
1776	.. D*	1817	.. G	1858	.. K	1899	.. A	1940	.. D*	1982	.. K
1777	.. G	1818	.. I	1859	.. M	1900	.. C	1941	.. G	1983	.. M
1778	.. I	1819	.. K	1860	.. B*	1901	.. E	1942	.. I	1984	.. B*
1779	.. K	1820	.. N*	1861	.. E	1902	.. G	1943	.. K	1985	.. E
1780	.. N*	1821	.. C	1862	.. G	1903	.. I	1944	.. N*	1986	.. G
1781	.. C	1822	.. E	1863	.. I	1904	.. L*	1945	.. C	1987	.. I
1782	.. E	1823	.. G	1864	.. L*	1905	.. A	1946	.. E	1988	.. L*
1783	.. G	1824	.. J*	1865	.. A	1906	.. C	1947	.. G	1989	.. A
1784	.. J*	1825	.. M	1866	.. C	1907	.. E	1948	.. J*	1990	.. C
1785	.. M	1826	.. A	1867	.. E	1908	.. H*	1949	.. M	1991	.. E
1786	.. A	1827	.. C	1868	.. H*	1909	.. K	1950	.. A	1992	.. H*
1787	.. C	1828	.. F*	1869	.. K	1910	.. M	1951	.. C	1993	.. K
1788	.. F*	1829	.. I	1870	.. M	1911	.. A	1952	.. F*	1994	.. M
1789	.. I	1830	.. K	1871	.. A	1912	.. D*	1953	.. I	1995	.. A
1790	.. K	1831	.. M	1872	.. D*	1913	.. G	1954	.. K	1996	.. D*
1791	.. M	1832	.. B*	1873	.. G	1914	.. I	1955	.. M	1997	.. G
1792	.. B*	1833	.. E	1874	.. I	1915	.. K	1956	.. B*	1998	.. I
1793	.. E	1834	.. G	1875	.. K	1916	.. N*	1957	.. E	1999	.. K
1794	.. G	1835	.. I	1876	.. N*	1917	.. C	1958	.. G	2000	.. N*

* Leap Year

A

	January	May	September
Su.	.. 1 8 15 22 29	7 14 21 28	3 10 17 24
M.	.. 2 9 16 23 30	1 8 15 22 29	4 11 18 25
Tu.	.. 3 10 17 24 31	2 9 16 23 30	5 12 19 26
W.	.. 4 11 18 25	3 10 17 24 31	6 13 20 27
Th.	.. 5 12 19 26	4 11 18 25	7 14 21 28
F.	.. 6 13 20 27	5 12 19 26	1 8 15 22 29
S.	.. 7 14 21 28	6 13 20 27	2 9 16 23 30

	February	June	October
Su.	.. 5 12 19 26	4 11 18 25	1 8 15 22 29
M.	.. 6 13 20 27	5 12 19 26	2 9 16 23 30
Tu.	.. 7 14 21 28	6 13 20 27	3 10 17 24 31
W.	.. 1 8 15 22	7 14 21 28	4 11 18 25
Th.	.. 2 9 16 23	1 8 15 22 29	5 12 19 26
F.	.. 3 10 17 24	2 9 16 23 30	6 13 20 27
S.	.. 4 11 18 25	3 10 17 24	7 14 21 28

	March	July	November
Su.	.. 5 12 19 26	2 9 16 23 30	5 12 19 26
M.	.. 6 13 20 27	3 10 17 24 31	6 13 20 27
Tu.	.. 7 14 21 28	4 11 18 25	7 14 21 28
W.	.. 1 8 15 22 29	5 12 19 26	1 8 15 22 29
Th.	.. 2 9 16 23 30	6 13 20 27	2 9 16 23 30
F.	.. 3 10 17 24 31	7 14 21 28	3 10 17 24
S.	.. 4 11 18 25	1 8 15 22 29	4 11 18 25

	April	August	December
Su.	.. 2 9 16 23 30	6 13 20 27	3 10 17 24 31
M.	.. 3 10 17 24	7 14 21 28	4 11 18 25
Tu.	.. 4 11 18 25	1 8 15 22 29	5 12 19 26
W.	.. 5 12 19 26	2 9 16 23 30	6 13 20 27
Th.	.. 6 13 20 27	3 10 17 24 31	7 14 21 28
F.	.. 7 14 21 28	4 11 18 25	1 8 15 22 29
S.	.. 1 8 15 22 29	2 9 16 23 30	2 9 16 23 30

B (Leap year)

	January	May	September
Su.	.. 1 8 15 22 29	6 13 20 27	2 9 16 23 30
M.	.. 2 9 16 23 30	7 14 21 28	3 10 17 24
Tu.	.. 3 10 17 24 31	1 8 15 22 29	4 11 18 25
W.	.. 4 11 18 25	2 9 16 23 30	5 12 19 26
Th.	.. 5 12 19 26	3 10 17 24 31	6 13 20 27
F.	.. 6 13 20 27	4 11 18 25	7 14 21 28
S.	.. 7 14 21 28	5 12 19 26	1 8 15 22 29

	February	June	October
Su.	.. 5 12 19 26	3 10 17 24	7 14 21 28
M.	.. 6 13 20 27	4 11 18 25	1 8 15 22 29
Tu.	.. 7 14 21 28	5 12 19 26	2 9 16 23 30
W.	.. 1 8 15 22 29	6 13 20 27	3 10 17 24 31
Th.	.. 2 9 16 23	7 14 21 28	4 11 18 25
F.	.. 3 10 17 24	1 8 15 22 29	5 12 19 26
S.	.. 4 11 18 25	2 9 16 23 30	6 13 20 27

	March	July	November
Su.	.. 4 11 18 25	1 8 15 22 29	4 11 18 25
M.	.. 5 12 19 26	2 9 16 23 30	5 12 19 26
Tu.	.. 6 13 20 27	3 10 17 24 31	6 13 20 27
W.	.. 7 14 21 28	4 11 18 25	7 14 21 28
Th.	.. 1 8 15 22 29	5 12 19 26	1 8 15 22 29
F.	.. 2 9 16 23 30	6 13 20 27	2 9 16 23 30
S.	.. 3 10 17 24 31	7 14 21 28	3 10 17 24

	April	August	December
Su.	.. 1 8 15 22 29	5 12 19 26	2 9 16 23 30
M.	.. 2 9 16 23 30	6 13 20 27	3 10 17 24 31
Tu.	.. 3 10 17 24	7 14 21 28	4 11 18 25
W.	.. 4 11 18 25	1 8 15 22 29	5 12 19 26
Th.	.. 5 12 19 26	2 9 16 23 30	6 13 20 27
F.	.. 6 13 20 27	3 10 17 24 31	7 14 21 28
S.	.. 7 14 21 28	4 11 18 25	1 8 15 22 29

Easter Days

March 26.	1758	1769	1815	1826	1837	1967 1978
April 2.	1809	1893	1899	1961.		[1989.
April 9.	1871	1882	1939	1950.		
April 16.	1775	1786	1797	1843	1854	1865 1911
April 23.	1905.				[1922	1933 1995.

Easter Days

April 1.	1804	1888	1956.
April 8.	1792	1860	1928.
April 22.	1764	1832	1984.

C

	January			
Su. ..	7	14	21	28
M. .. 1	8	15	22	29
Tu. .. 2	9	16	23	30
W. .. 3	10	17	24	31
Th. .. 4	11	18	25
F. .. 5	12	19	26
S. .. 6	13	20	27

May
6 13 20 27
7 14 21 28
1 8 15 22 29
2 9 16 23 30
3 10 17 24 31
4 11 18 25
5 12 19 26

September
2 9 16 23 30
3 10 17 24
4 11 18 25
5 12 19 26
6 13 20 27
7 14 21 28
1 8 15 22 29

February
Su. .. 4 11 18 25
M. .. 5 12 19 26
Tu. .. 6 13 20 27
W. .. 7 14 21 28
Th. .. 1 8 15 22
F. .. 2 9 16 23
S. .. 3 10 17 24

June
3 10 17 24
4 11 18 25
5 12 19 26
6 13 20 27
7 14 21 28
1 8 15 22 29
2 9 16 23 30

October
7 14 21 28
1 8 15 22 29
2 9 16 23 30
3 10 17 24 31
4 11 18 25
5 12 19 26
6 13 20 27

March
Su. .. 4 11 18 25
M. .. 5 12 19 26
Tu. .. 6 13 20 27
W. .. 7 14 21 28
Th. .. 1 8 15 22 29
F. .. 2 9 16 23 30
S. .. 3 10 17 24 31

July
1 8 15 22 29
2 9 16 23 30
3 10 17 24 31
4 11 18 25
5 12 19 26
6 13 20 27
7 14 21 28

November
4 11 18 25
5 12 19 26
6 13 20 27
7 14 21 28
1 8 15 22 29
2 9 16 23 30
3 10 17 24

April
Su. .. 1 8 15 22 29
M. .. 2 9 16 23 30
Tu. .. 3 10 17 24
W. .. 4 11 18 25
Th. .. 5 12 19 26
F. .. 6 13 20 27
S. .. 7 14 21 28

August
5 12 19 26
6 13 20 27
7 14 21 28
1 8 15 22 29
2 9 16 23 30
3 10 17 24 31
4 11 18 25

December
2 9 16 23 30
3 10 17 24 31
4 11 18 25
5 12 19 26
6 13 20 27
7 14 21 28
1 8 15 22 29

Easter Days

March 25.	1883	1894	1951.			
April 1.	1866	1877	1923	1934	1945.	
April 8.	1787	1798	1849	1855	1917.	
April 15.	1759	1770	1781	1827	1838	1900	1906
	1979	1990.				
April 22.	1753	1810	1821	1962	1973.	

D (Leap year)

January
Su. .. 7 14 21 28
M. .. 1 8 15 22 29
Tu. .. 2 9 16 23 30
W. .. 3 10 17 24 31
Th. .. 4 11 18 25
F. .. 5 12 19 26
S. .. 6 13 20 27

May
5 12 19 26
6 13 20 27
7 14 21 28
1 8 15 22 29
2 9 16 23 30
3 10 17 24 31
4 11 18 25

September
1 8 15 22 29
2 9 16 23 30
3 10 17 24
4 11 18 25
5 12 19 26
6 13 20 27
7 14 21 28

February
Su. .. 4 11 18 25
M. .. 5 12 19 26
Tu. .. 6 13 20 27
W. .. 7 14 21 28
Th. .. 1 8 15 22 29
F. .. 2 9 16 23
S. .. 3 10 17 24

June
2 9 16 23 30
3 10 17 24
4 11 18 25
5 12 19 26
6 13 20 27
7 14 21 28
1 8 15 22 29

October
6 13 20 27
7 14 21 28
1 8 15 22 29
2 9 16 23 30
3 10 17 24 31
4 11 18 25
5 12 19 26

March
Su. .. 3 10 17 24 31
M. .. 4 11 18 25
Tu. .. 5 12 19 26
W. .. 6 13 20 27
Th. .. 7 14 21 28
F. .. 1 8 15 22 29
S. .. 2 9 16 23 30

July
7 14 21 28
1 8 15 22 29
2 9 16 23 30
3 10 17 24 31
4 11 18 25
5 12 19 26
6 13 20 27

November
3 10 17 24
4 11 18 25
5 12 19 26
6 13 20 27
7 14 21 28
1 8 15 22 29
2 9 16 23 30

April
Su. .. 7 14 21 28
M. .. 1 8 15 22 29
Tu. .. 2 9 16 23 30
W. .. 3 10 17 24
Th. .. 4 11 18 25
F. .. 5 12 19 26
S. .. 6 13 20 27

August
4 11 18 25
5 12 19 26
6 13 20 27
7 14 21 28
1 8 15 22 29
2 9 16 23 30
3 10 17 24 31

December
1 8 15 22 29
2 9 16 23 30
3 10 17 24 31
4 11 18 25
5 12 19 26
6 13 20 27
7 14 21 28

Easter Days

March 24.	1940.
March 31.	1872.
April 7.	1776	1844	1912	1996.
April 14.	1816	1968.

E

January
Su. .. 6 13 20 27
M. .. 7 14 21 28
Tu. .. 1 8 15 22 29
W. .. 2 9 16 23 30
Th. .. 3 10 17 24 31
F. .. 4 11 18 25
S. .. 5 12 19 26

May
5 12 19 26
6 13 20 27
7 14 21 28
1 8 15 22 29
2 9 16 23 30
3 10 17 24 31
4 11 18 25

September
1 8 15 22 29
2 9 16 23 30
3 10 17 24
4 11 18 25
5 12 19 26
6 13 20 27
7 14 21 28

February
Su. .. 3 10 17 24
M. .. 4 11 18 25
Tu. .. 5 12 19 26
W. .. 6 13 20 27
Th. .. 7 14 21 28
F. .. 1 8 15 22 29
S. .. 2 9 16 23

June
9 16 23 30
10 17 24
4 11 18 25
5 12 19 26
6 13 20 27
7 14 21 28
1 8 15 22 29

October
6 13 20 27
7 14 21 28
1 8 15 22 29
2 9 16 23 30
3 10 17 24 31
4 11 18 25
5 12 19 26

March
Su. .. 3 10 17 24 31
M. .. 4 11 18 25
Tu. .. 5 12 19 26
W. .. 6 13 20 27
Th. .. 7 14 21 28
F. .. 1 8 15 22 29
S. .. 2 9 16 23 30

July
7 14 21 28
1 8 15 22 29
2 9 16 23 30
3 10 17 24 31
4 11 18 25
5 12 19 26
6 13 20 27

November
3 10 17 24
4 11 18 25
5 12 19 26
6 13 20 27
7 14 21 28
1 8 15 22 29
2 9 16 23 30

April
Su. .. 7 14 21 28
M. .. 1 8 15 22 29
Tu. .. 2 9 16 23 30
W. .. 3 10 17 24
Th. .. 4 11 18 25
F. .. 5 12 19 26
S. .. 6 13 20 27

August
4 11 18 25
5 12 19 26
6 13 20 27
7 14 21 28
1 8 15 22 29
2 9 16 23 30
3 10 17 24 31

December
1 8 15 22 29
2 9 16 23 30
3 10 17 24 31
4 11 18 25
5 12 19 26
6 13 20 27
7 14 21 28

Easter Days

March 24.	1799.					
March 31.	1771	1782	1793	1839	1850	1861
April 7.	1765	1822	1833	1901	1985.	
April 14.	1754	1805	1811	1895	1963	1974.
April 21.	1867	1878	1889	1935	1946	1957.

F (Leap year)

January
Su. .. 6 13 20 27
M. .. 7 14 21 28
Tu. .. 1 8 15 22 29
W. .. 2 9 16 23 30
Th. .. 3 10 17 24 31
F. .. 4 11 18 25
S. .. 5 12 19 26

May
4 11 18 25
5 12 19 26
6 13 20 27
7 14 21 28
1 8 15 22 29
2 9 16 23 30
3 10 17 24 31

September
7 14 21 28
1 8 15 22 29
2 9 16 23 30
3 10 17 24
4 11 18 25
5 12 19 26
6 13 20 27

February
Su. .. 3 10 17 24
M. .. 4 11 18 25
Tu. .. 5 12 19 26
W. .. 6 13 20 27
Th. .. 7 14 21 28
F. .. 1 8 15 22 29
S. .. 2 9 16 23

June
1 8 15 22 29
2 9 16 23 30
3 10 17 24
4 11 18 25
5 12 19 26
6 13 20 27
7 14 21 28

October
5 12 19 26
6 13 20 27
7 14 21 28
1 8 15 22 29
2 9 16 23 30
3 10 17 24 31
4 11 18 25

March
Su. .. 2 9 16 23 30
M. .. 3 10 17 24 31
Tu. .. 4 11 18 25
W. .. 5 12 19 26
Th. .. 6 13 20 27
F. .. 7 14 21 28
S. .. 1 8 15 22 29

July
6 13 20 27
7 14 21 28
1 8 15 22 29
2 9 16 23 30
3 10 17 24 31
4 11 18 25
5 12 19 26

November
2 9 16 23 30
3 10 17 24 31
4 11 18 25
5 12 19 26
6 13 20 27
7 14 21 28
1 8 15 22 29

April
Su. .. 6 13 20 27
M. .. 7 14 21 28
Tu. .. 1 8 15 22 29
W. .. 2 9 16 23 30
Th. .. 3 10 17 24
F. .. 4 11 18 25
S. .. 5 12 19 26

August
3 10 17 24 31
4 11 18 25
5 12 19 26
6 13 20 27
7 14 21 28
1 8 15 22 29
2 9 16 23 30

December
7 14 21 28
1 8 15 22 29
2 9 16 23 30
3 10 17 24 31
4 11 18 25
5 12 19 26
6 13 20 27

Easter Days

March 23.	1788	1856.	
April 6.	1760	1828	1980.
April 13.	1884	1952.	
April 20.	1924.		

CALENDAR TABLES

G – J

G

	January	May	September
Su..	5 12 19 26	4 11 18 25	7 14 21 28
M..	6 13 20 27	5 12 19 26	1 8 15 22 29
Tu..	7 14 21 28	6 13 20 27	2 9 16 23 30
W..	1 8 15 22 29	7 14 21 28	3 10 17 24
Th..	2 9 16 23 30	1 8 15 22 29	4 11 18 25
F..	3 10 17 24 31	2 9 16 23 30	5 12 19 26
S..	4 11 18 25	3 10 17 24 31	6 13 20 27

	February	June	October
Su..	2 9 16 23	1 8 15 22 29	5 12 19 26
M..	3 10 17 24	2 9 16 23 30	6 13 20 27
Tu..	4 11 18 25	3 10 17 24	7 14 21 28
W..	5 12 19 26	4 11 18 25	1 8 15 22 29
Th..	6 13 20 27	5 12 19 26	2 9 16 23 30
F..	7 14 21 28	6 13 20 27	3 10 17 24 31
S..	1 8 15 22	7 14 21 28	4 11 18 25

	March	July	November
Su..	2 9 16 23 30	6 13 20 27	2 9 16 23 30
M..	3 10 17 24 31	7 14 21 28	3 10 17 24
Tu..	4 11 18 25	1 8 15 22 29	4 11 18 25
W..	5 12 19 26	2 9 16 23 30	5 12 19 26
Th..	6 13 20 27	3 10 17 24 31	6 13 20 27
F..	7 14 21 28	4 11 18 25	7 14 21 28
S..	1 8 15 22 29	5 12 19 26	1 8 15 22 29

	April	August	December
Su..	6 13 20 27	3 10 17 24 31	7 14 21 28
M..	7 14 21 28	4 11 18 25	1 8 15 22 29
Tu..	1 8 15 22 29	5 12 19 26	2 9 16 23 30
W..	2 9 16 23 30	6 13 20 27	3 10 17 24 31
Th..	3 10 17 24	7 14 21 28	4 11 18 25
F..	4 11 18 25	1 8 15 22 29	5 12 19 26
S..	5 12 19 26	2 9 16 23 30	6 13 20 27

Easter Days

March 23.	1845 1913.
March 30.	1755 1766 1777 1823 1834 1902 1975 1986 1997.
April 6.	1806 1817 1890 1947 1958 1969.
April 13.	1800 1873 1879 1941.
April 20.	1783 1794 1851 1862 1919 1930.

H (Leap year)

	January	May	September
Su..	5 12 19 26	3 10 17 24 31	6 13 20 27
M..	6 13 20 27	4 11 18 25	7 14 21 28
Tu..	7 14 21 28	5 12 19 26	1 8 15 22 29
W..	1 8 15 22 29	6 13 20 27	2 9 16 23 30
Th..	2 9 16 23 30	7 14 21 28	3 10 17 24
F..	3 10 17 24 31	1 8 15 22 29	4 11 18 25
S..	4 11 18 25	2 9 16 23 30	5 12 19 26

	February	June	October
Su..	2 9 16 23	7 14 21 28	4 11 18 25
M..	3 10 17 24	1 8 15 22 29	5 12 19 26
Tu..	4 11 18 25	2 9 16 23 30	6 13 20 27
W..	5 12 19 26	3 10 17 24	7 14 21 28
Th..	6 13 20 27	4 11 18 25	1 8 15 22 29
F..	7 14 21 28	5 12 19 26	2 9 16 23 30
S..	1 8 15 22 29	6 13 20 27	3 10 17 24 31

	March	July	November
Su..	1 8 15 22 29	5 12 19 26	1 8 15 22 29
M..	2 9 16 23 30	6 13 20 27	2 9 16 23 30
Tu..	3 10 17 24 31	7 14 21 28	3 10 17 24
W..	4 11 18 25	1 8 15 22 29	4 11 18 25
Th..	5 12 19 26	2 9 16 23 30	5 12 19 26
F..	6 13 20 27	3 10 17 24 31	6 13 20 27
S..	7 14 21 28	4 11 18 25	7 14 21 28

	April	August	December
Su..	5 12 19 26	2 9 16 23 30	6 13 20 27
M..	6 13 20 27	3 10 17 24 31	7 14 21 28
Tu..	7 14 21 28	4 11 18 25	1 8 15 22 29
W..	1 8 15 22 29	5 12 19 26	2 9 16 23 30
Th..	2 9 16 23 30	6 13 20 27	3 10 17 24 31
F..	3 10 17 24	7 14 21 28	4 11 18 25
S..	4 11 18 25	1 8 15 22 29	5 12 19 26

Easter Days

March 29.	1812 1964.
April 5.	1896.
April 12.	1868 1936.
April 19.	1772 1840 1908 1992.

I

	January	May	September
Su..	4 11 18 25	3 10 17 24 31	6 13 20 27
M..	5 12 19 26	4 11 18 25	7 14 21 28
Tu..	6 13 20 27	5 12 19 26	1 8 15 22 29
W..	7 14 21 28	6 13 20 27	2 9 16 23 30
Th..	1 8 15 22 29	7 14 21 28	3 10 17 24
F..	2 9 16 23 30	1 8 15 22 29	4 11 18 25
S..	3 10 17 24 31	2 9 16 23 30	5 12 19 26

	February	June	October
Su..	1 8 15 22	7 14 21 28	4 11 18 25
M..	2 9 16 23	1 8 15 22 29	5 12 19 26
Tu..	3 10 17 24	2 9 16 23 30	6 13 20 27
W..	4 11 18 25	3 10 17 24	7 14 21 28
Th..	5 12 19 26	4 11 18 25	1 8 15 22 29
F..	6 13 20 27	5 12 19 26	2 9 16 23 30
S..	7 14 21 28	6 13 20 27	3 10 17 24 31

	March	July	November
Su..	1 8 15 22 29	5 12 19 26	1 8 15 22 29
M..	2 9 16 23 30	6 13 20 27	2 9 16 23 30
Tu..	3 10 17 24 31	7 14 21 28	3 10 17 24
W..	4 11 18 25	1 8 15 22 29	4 11 18 25
Th..	5 12 19 26	2 9 16 23 30	5 12 19 26
F..	6 13 20 27	3 10 17 24 31	6 13 20 27
S..	7 14 21 28	4 11 18 25	7 14 21 28

	April	August	December
Su..	5 12 19 26	2 9 16 23 30	6 13 20 27
M..	6 13 20 27	3 10 17 24 31	7 14 21 28
Tu..	7 14 21 28	4 11 18 25	1 8 15 22 29
W..	1 8 15 22 29	5 12 19 26	2 9 16 23 30
Th..	2 9 16 23 30	6 13 20 27	3 10 17 24 31
F..	3 10 17 24	7 14 21 28	4 11 18 25
S..	4 11 18 25	1 8 15 22 29	5 12 19 26

Easter Days

March 22.	1761 1818.
March 29.	1807 1891 1959 1970.
April 5.	1795 1801 1863 1874 1885 1931 1942 1953.
April 12.	1789 1846 1857 1903 1914 1925 1998.
April 19.	1767 1778 1829 1835 1981 1987.

J (Leap year)

	January	May	September
Su..	4 11 18 25	2 9 16 23 30	5 12 19 26
M..	5 12 19 26	3 10 17 24 31	6 13 20 27
Tu..	6 13 20 27	4 11 18 25	7 14 21 28
W..	7 14 21 28	5 12 19 26	1 8 15 22 29
Th..	1 8 15 22 29	6 13 20 27	2 9 16 23 30
F..	2 9 16 23 30	7 14 21 28	3 10 17 24
S..	3 10 17 24 31	1 8 15 22 29	4 11 18 25

	February	June	October
Su..	1 8 15 22 29	6 13 20 27	3 10 17 24 31
M..	2 9 16 23	7 14 21 28	4 11 18 25
Tu..	3 10 17 24	1 8 15 22 29	5 12 19 26
W..	4 11 18 25	2 9 16 23 30	6 13 20 27
Th..	5 12 19 26	3 10 17 24	7 14 21 28
F..	6 13 20 27	4 11 18 25	1 8 15 22 29
S..	7 14 21 28	5 12 19 26	2 9 16 23 30

	March	July	November
Su..	7 14 21 28	4 11 18 25	7 14 21 28
M..	1 8 15 22 29	5 12 19 26	1 8 15 22 29
Tu..	2 9 16 23 30	6 13 20 27	2 9 16 23 30
W..	3 10 17 24 31	7 14 21 28	3 10 17 24
Th..	4 11 18 25	1 8 15 22 29	4 11 18 25
F..	5 12 19 26	2 9 16 23 30	5 12 19 26
S..	6 13 20 27	3 10 17 24 31	6 13 20 27

	April	August	December
Su..	4 11 18 25	1 8 15 22 29	5 12 19 26
M..	5 12 19 26	2 9 16 23 30	6 13 20 27
Tu..	6 13 20 27	3 10 17 24 31	7 14 21 28
W..	7 14 21 28	4 11 18 25	1 8 15 22 29
Th..	1 8 15 22 29	5 12 19 26	2 9 16 23 30
F..	2 9 16 23 30	6 13 20 27	3 10 17 24 31
S..	3 10 17 24	7 14 21 28	4 11 18 25

Easter Days

March 28.	1880 1948.
April 4.	1920.
April 11.	1784 1852.
April 18.	1756 1824 1976.

CALENDAR TABLES

K – N

K

	January	May	September
Su.	3 10 17 24 31	2 9 16 23 30	5 12 19 26
M.	4 11 18 25	3 10 17 24 31	6 13 20 27
Tu.	5 12 19 26	4 11 18 25	7 14 21 28
W.	6 13 20 27	5 12 19 26	1 8 15 22 29
Th.	7 14 21 28	6 13 20 27	2 9 16 23 30
F.	1 8 15 22 29	7 14 21 28	3 10 17 24
S.	2 9 16 23 30	1 8 15 22 29	4 11 18 25

	February	June	October
Su.	7 14 21 28	6 13 20 27	3 10 17 24 31
M.	1 8 15 22	7 14 21 28	4 11 18 25
Tu.	2 9 16 23	1 8 15 22 29	5 12 19 26
W.	3 10 17 24	2 9 16 23 30	6 13 20 27
Th.	4 11 18 25	3 10 17 24	7 14 21 28
F.	5 12 19 26	4 11 18 25	1 8 15 22 29
S.	6 13 20 27	5 12 19 26	2 9 16 23 30

	March	July	November
Su.	7 14 21 28	4 11 18 25	7 14 21 28
M.	1 8 15 22 29	5 12 19 26	1 8 15 22 29
Tu.	2 9 16 23 30	6 13 20 27	2 9 16 23 30
W.	3 10 17 24 31	7 14 21 28	3 10 17 24
Th.	4 11 18 25	1 8 15 22 29	4 11 18 25
F.	5 12 19 26	2 9 16 23 30	5 12 19 26
S.	6 13 20 27	3 10 17 24 31	6 13 20 27

	April	August	December
Su.	4 11 18 25	1 8 15 22 29	5 12 19 26
M.	5 12 19 26	2 9 16 23 30	6 13 20 27
Tu.	6 13 20 27	3 10 17 24 31	7 14 21 28
W.	7 14 21 28	4 11 18 25	1 8 15 22 29
Th.	1 8 15 22 29	5 12 19 26	2 9 16 23 30
F.	2 9 16 23 30	6 13 20 27	3 10 17 24 31
S.	3 10 17 24	7 14 21 28	4 11 18 25

Easter Days

March 28.	1869 1875 1937.
April 4.	1779 1790 1847 1858 1915 1926 1999.
April 11.	1762 1773 1819 1830 1841 1909 1971 1982 1993.
April 18.	1802 1813 1897 1954 1965.
April 25.	1886 1943.

L (Leap year)

	January	May	September
Su.	3 10 17 24 31	1 8 15 22 29	4 11 18 25
M.	4 11 18 25	2 9 16 23 30	5 12 19 26
Tu.	5 12 19 26	3 10 17 24 31	6 13 20 27
W.	6 13 20 27	4 11 18 25	7 14 21 28
Th.	7 14 21 28	5 12 19 26	1 8 15 22 29
F.	1 8 15 22 29	6 13 20 27	2 9 16 23 30
S.	2 9 16 23 30	7 14 21 28	3 10 17 24

	February	June	October
Su.	7 14 21 28	5 12 19 26	2 9 16 23 30
M.	1 8 15 22 29	6 13 20 27	3 10 17 24 31
Tu.	2 9 16 23	7 14 21 28	4 11 18 25
W.	3 10 17 24	1 8 15 22 29	5 12 19 26
Th.	4 11 18 25	2 9 16 23 30	6 13 20 27
F.	5 12 19 26	3 10 17 24	7 14 21 28
S.	6 13 20 27	4 11 18 25	1 8 15 22 29

	March	July	November
Su.	6 13 20 27	3 10 17 24 31	6 13 20 27
M.	7 14 21 28	4 11 18 25	7 14 21 28
Tu.	1 8 15 22 29	5 12 19 26	1 8 15 22 29
W.	2 9 16 23 30	6 13 20 27	2 9 16 23 30
Th.	3 10 17 24 31	7 14 21 28	3 10 17 24
F.	4 11 18 25	1 8 15 22 29	4 11 18 25
S.	5 12 19 26	2 9 16 23 30	5 12 19 26

	April	August	December
Su.	3 10 17 24	7 14 21 28	4 11 18 25
M.	4 11 18 25	1 8 15 22 29	5 12 19 26
Tu.	5 12 19 26	2 9 16 23 30	6 13 20 27
W.	6 13 20 27	3 10 17 24 31	7 14 21 28
Th.	7 14 21 28	4 11 18 25	1 8 15 22 29
F.	1 8 15 22 29	5 12 19 26	2 9 16 23 30
S.	2 9 16 23 30	6 13 20 27	3 10 17 24 31

Easter Days

March 27.	1796 1864 1932.
April 3.	1768 1836 1904 1988.
April 17.	1808 1892 1960.

M

	January	May	September
Su.	2 9 16 23 30	1 8 15 22 29	4 11 18 25
M.	3 10 17 24 31	2 9 16 23 30	5 12 19 26
Tu.	4 11 18 25	3 10 17 24 31	6 13 20 27
W.	5 12 19 26	4 11 18 25	7 14 21 28
Th.	6 13 20 27	5 12 19 26	1 8 15 22 29
F.	7 14 21 28	6 13 20 27	2 9 16 23 30
S.	1 8 15 22 29	7 14 21 28	3 10 17 24

	February	June	October
Su.	6 13 20 27	5 12 19 26	2 9 16 23 30
M.	7 14 21 28	6 13 20 27	3 10 17 24 31
Tu.	1 8 15 22	7 14 21 28	4 11 18 25
W.	2 9 16 23	1 8 15 22 29	5 12 19 26
Th.	3 10 17 24	2 9 16 23 30	6 13 20 27
F.	4 11 18 25	3 10 17 24	7 14 21 28
S.	5 12 19 26	4 11 18 25	1 8 15 22 29

	March	July	November
Su.	6 13 20 27	3 10 17 24 31	6 13 20 27
M.	7 14 21 28	4 11 18 25	7 14 21 28
Tu.	1 8 15 22 29	5 12 19 26	1 8 15 22 29
W.	2 9 16 23 30	6 13 20 27	2 9 16 23 30
Th.	3 10 17 24 31	7 14 21 28	3 10 17 24
F.	4 11 18 25	1 8 15 22 29	4 11 18 25
S.	5 12 19 26	2 9 16 23 30	5 12 19 26

	April	August	December
Su.	3 10 17 24	7 14 21 28	4 11 18 25
M.	4 11 18 25	1 8 15 22 29	5 12 19 26
Tu.	5 12 19 26	2 9 16 23 30	6 13 20 27
W.	6 13 20 27	3 10 17 24 31	7 14 21 28
Th.	7 14 21 28	4 11 18 25	1 8 15 22 29
F.	1 8 15 22 29	5 12 19 26	2 9 16 23 30
S.	2 9 16 23 30	6 13 20 27	3 10 17 24 31

Easter Days

March 27.	1785 1842 1853 1910 1921.
April 3.	1763 1774 1825 1831 1983 1994.
April 10.	1757 1803 1814 1887 1898 1955 1966
April 17.	1870 1881 1927 1938 1949.
April 24.	1791 1859. [1977.

N (Leap year)

	January	May	September
Su.	2 9 16 23 30	7 14 21 28	3 10 17 24
M.	3 10 17 24 31	1 8 15 22 29	4 11 18 25
Tu.	4 11 18 25	2 9 16 23 30	5 12 19 26
W.	5 12 19 26	3 10 17 24 31	6 13 20 27
Th.	6 13 20 27	4 11 18 25	7 14 21 28
F.	7 14 21 28	5 12 19 26	1 8 15 22 29
S.	1 8 15 22 29	6 13 20 27	2 9 16 23 30

	February	June	October
Su.	6 13 20 27	4 11 18 25	1 8 15 22 29
M.	7 14 21 28	5 12 19 26	2 9 16 23 30
Tu.	1 8 15 22	6 13 20 27	3 10 17 24 31
W.	2 9 16 23	7 14 21 28	4 11 18 25
Th.	3 10 17 24	1 8 15 22 29	5 12 19 26
F.	4 11 18 25	2 9 16 23 30	6 13 20 27
S.	5 12 19 26	3 10 17 24	7 14 21 28

	March	July	November
Su.	5 12 19 26	2 9 16 23 30	5 12 19 26
M.	6 13 20 27	3 10 17 24 31	6 13 20 27
Tu.	7 14 21 28	4 11 18 25	7 14 21 28
W.	1 8 15 22 29	5 12 19 26	1 8 15 22 29
Th.	2 9 16 23 30	6 13 20 27	2 9 16 23 30
F.	3 10 17 24 31	7 14 21 28	3 10 17 24
S.	4 11 18 25	1 8 15 22 29	4 11 18 25

	April	August	December
Su.	2 9 16 23 30	6 13 20 27	3 10 17 24 31
M.	3 10 17 24	7 14 21 28	4 11 18 25
Tu.	4 11 18 25	1 8 15 22 29	5 12 19 26
W.	5 12 19 26	2 9 16 23 30	6 13 20 27
Th.	6 13 20 27	3 10 17 24 31	7 14 21 28
F.	7 14 21 28	4 11 18 25	1 8 15 22 29
S.	1 8 15 22 29	5 12 19 26	2 9 16 23 30

Easter Days

March 26.	1780.
April 2.	1820 1972.
April 9.	1944.
April 16.	1876.
April 23.	1848 1916 2000.

The World

The *Superficial Area* of the Earth is estimated to be 196,836,000 square miles, of which 55,786,000 square miles are Land and 141,050,000 square miles Water. The *Diameter* of the Earth at the Equator is 7,926½ English miles, and at the Poles 7,900 English miles. The *Equatorial Circumference* is 24,901·8 English miles, divided into 360 Degrees of Longitude, each of 69·17 English (or 60 Geographical) miles; these Degrees are measured from the Meridian of Greenwich, and numbered East and West of that point to meet in the Antipodes at the 180th Degree. Distance North and South of the Equator is marked by Parallels of Latitude, which proceed from zero (at the Equator) to 90° at the Poles.

The velocity of a given point of the Earth's surface at the Equator exceeds 1,000 miles an hour (24,901·8 miles in 24 hours); the Earth's velocity in its orbit round the Sun is about 66,600 miles an hour (584,000,000 miles in 365¼ days). The Earth is distant from the Sun 93,000,000 miles, on the average.

AREA AND POPULATION

The total population of the world in June, 1972, was estimated by the *United Nations Statistical Office* at 3,782,000,000 compared with 3,003,000,000 in 1960 and 2,070,000,000 in 1930. Figures of areas in the following table are of land area and inland water, but exclude uninhabited polar regions and some uninhabited islands. Figures for Europe and Asia exclude U.S.S.R. which is shown separately. Figures for Oceania exclude Hawaii which is included with North America, being the 50th State of U.S.A.

Continent, etc.	Area		Estimated Population, 1971
	Sq. miles '000	Sq. km. '000	
Europe.......	1,903	4,929	466,000,000
Asia*........	10,661	27,611	2,104,000,000
U.S.S.R.....	8,649	22,402	245,000,000
Africa.......	11,683	30,258	354,000,000
America.....	16,241	42,063	522,000,000
Oceania.....	3,286	8,510	19,800,000
Total...	52,422	135,773	3,711,000,000

* Excludes U.S.S.R. (shown separately); includes European and Asiatic Turkey.

A United Nations report (*The Future Growth of World Population*) in 1958, pointed out that the population of the world had increased since the beginning of the 20th Century at an unprecedented rate: in 1850 it was estimated at 1,094,000,000 and in 1900 at 1,550,000,000, an increase of 42 per cent. in 50 years. By 1925 it had risen to 1,907,000,000—23 per cent. in 25 years—and by 1950 it had reached 2,500,000,000, an increase of 31 per cent. in 25 years. Levels of population and the trend in distribution of the population by continents as forecast for the years 1975 and 2000 were:—

Continent	1975		2000	
	Estimated Population	Per cent.	Estimated Population	Per cent.
Europe‡...	751	19·6	947	15·1
Asia*......	2,210	57·7	3,870	61·8
Africa.....	303	7·9	517	8·2
N. America.	240	6·3	312	5·0
Latin America†..	303	7·9	592	9·4
Oceania.....	21	0·5	29	0·5
World.....	3,828	100	6,267	100

[millions]

* Excluding U.S.S.R.   † Mexico and the remainder of America south of U.S.A.   ‡ Including U.S.S.R.

THE CONTINENTS

Europe (including European Russia) forms about one-fourteenth of the land surface of the globe. Its length from the North Cape, 71° 12′ N., to Cape Matapan, in the south of Greece, 36° 23′ N., is about 2,400 miles, and its breadth from Cape St. Vincent to the Urals is about 3,300 miles. The political boundary between Europe and Asia extends some distance beyond the Urals, to include the mining regions; in the south-east it follows the valley of the Manych, north of the Caucasus.

Asia (including Asiatic Russia) extends over nearly one-third of the land surface of the globe. The distance between its extreme longitudes, the west coast of Asia Minor (26° E.) and the East Cape (170° W.), is 6,000 miles. The extreme latitudes, Cape Chelyuskin (78° 30″ N.) and Cape Bulus (76 miles north of the Equator), are 5,350 miles apart. Asia is bounded by the ocean on all sides except the west. The Isthmus of Suez connects it with Africa. The land boundary between Europe and Asia is formed on the west mainly by the Ural Mountains and the Ural River. In the south-west the valley of the Manych, which stretches from the Caspian Sea to the mouth of the Don, is now taken as the line between the two continents, although the Caucasus was formerly considered as belonging to Europe. The islands of the archipelago which lie in the south-east between the continents of Asia and Australia may be divided into two groups by a line passing east of Timor, Timor Laut, the Kei Islands and the Moluccas.

Africa is about three times the area of Europe. Its extreme longitudes are 17° W. at Cape Verde and 51° 27′ 52″ E. at Ras Hafun. The extreme latitudes are Cape Blanco in 37° N. and Cape Agulhas in 35° S., at a distance of about 5,000 miles. It is surrounded by seas on all sides, except in the narrow isthmus through which is cut the Suez Canal, and may be considered as a great peninsula of the Eurasian continent.

North America, including Mexico, is a little less than twice the size of Europe. Its extreme longitudes extend from a little west of 170° W. to 52½° W. in the east of Newfoundland, and its extreme latitudes from about 80° N. lat. to 15° N. lat. in the south of Mexico. It is surrounded by seas on all sides except in the south, where it joins the Isthmian States of *Central America*, which have an area of about 200,000 square miles. The area of the *West Indies* is about 65,000 square miles, a little more than half that of the United Kingdom. They extend from about 27° N. latitude to 10° N. latitude.

South America is a little more than 1¾ times the size of Europe. The extreme longitudes are Cape Branco 35° W. and Punta Parina 81° W., and the extreme latitudes, Punta Gallinas, 12½° N. and Cape Horn 56° S. South America is surrounded by the ocean, except where it is joined to Central America by the narrow isthmus through which is cut the Panama Canal.

Oceania extends over an area 1½ times the size of Europe, from Australia (in the West) to the most easterly islands of Polynesia, and from New Zealand (in the south) to the Sandwich Islands (Hawaii) in the north.

The appended tables of area and population are based on such information as is immediately available. With regard to areas it will be realized that no complete survey of many countries has yet been either achieved or even undertaken and that consequently accurate area figures are not available. In addition, among the results of the war of 1939–1945 is a readjustment of boundaries which have not yet been definitely settled.

The populations given hereunder are derived from various sources; some have as their basis an authenticated census; some are official and some are unofficial estimates. In certain cases where later information becomes available during printing the new figures are given in the overseas sections of the ALMANACK. What has been said about the survey of many of the world's countries applies equally to the question of census.

AFRICA Ψ Seaport

COUNTRY	Area Sq. Miles	Population	Per Sq. Mile	Capital	Population of Capital
Afars and Issas Territory.	9,000	81,000	9	Ψ Djibouti............	62,000
Algeria...............	856,000	13,547,000	16	Ψ Algiers.............	943,000
Angola...............	488,000	5,673,046	12	Ψ St. Paul de Luanda...	346,763
Botswana.............	220,000	620,000	3	Gaborone..........	18,000
Burundi..............	10,700	3,475,000	325	Bujumbura........	70,000
Cameroon.............	183,000	5,836,000	32	Yaoundé..........	180,000
Cape Verde Islands...	1,516	272,071	179	Ψ Praia.............	6,000
Central African Republic	234,000	2,255,000	10	Bangui............	301,793
Chad.................	488,000	4,000,000	8	Ndjaména..........	126,000
Congo................	129,960	2,100,000	16	Brazzaville........	156,000
Dahomey.............	47,000	2,948,000	63	Ψ Porto Novo........	85,000
Egypt................	385,000	34,000,000	88	Cairo.............	8,143,000
Equatorial Guinea.....	11,000	286,000	26	Ψ Malabo...........	9,000
Ethiopia (Abyssinia).....	400,000	26,000,000	65	Addis Ababa........	912,000
Gabon...............	101,400	500,000	5	Ψ Libreville..........	31,000
Gambia..............	4,000	493,499	123	Ψ Banjul...........	39,476
Ghana...............	92,100	8,545,561	93	Ψ Accra............	851,614
Guinea...............	97,000	3,890,000	40	Ψ Conakry..........	120,000
Guinea Bissau	14,000	487,448	35	Ψ Bissau...........	6,000
Ivory Coast...........	127,000	5,400,000	42	Ψ Abidjan..........	600,000
Kenya...............	225,000	12,934,000	57	Nairobi...........	509,000
Lesotho..............	11,700	1,181,300	101	Maseru............	30,000
Liberia...............	43,000	1,481,524	34	Ψ Monrovia.........	201,600
Libya................	810,000	2,257,037	3	Ψ Tripoli...........	551,477
Madagascar...........	228,000	8,000,000	35	Tananarive........	400,000
Malawi..............	45,400	4,916,000	108	Lilongwe..........	87,000
Mali.................	465,000	4,929,000	11	Bamako...........	170,000
Mauritania...........	419,000	1,140,000	3	Nouakchott........	30,000
Mauritius, etc........	805	871,122	1,082	Ψ Port Louis.........	136,800
Morocco.............	180,000	15,379,259	85	Ψ Rabat...........	565,000
Mozambique..........	298,000	8,233,034	28	Ψ Lourenço Marques...	441,363
Niger................	459,000	4,030,000	9	Niamey...........	100,000
Nigeria..............	357,000	79,760,000	223	Ψ Lagos...........	1,000,000
Réunion.............	1,000	445,500	445	St. Denis..........	85,992
Rhodesia.............	151,000	5,780,000	40	Salisbury..........	503,000
Rwanda..............	10,169	3,500,000	344	Kigali.............	7,000
St. Helena...........	47	4,967	106	Ψ Jamestown........	1,475
Ascension.........	38	1,137	30	Ψ Georgetown.......	..
Tristan da Cunha.....	45	292	6	Ψ Edinburgh........	..
St. Tomé & Princípe...	372	73,811	198	Ψ São Tomé........	3,187
Senegal..............	78,000	3,800,000	49	Ψ Dakar...........	581,000
Seychelles............	125	52,650	421	Ψ Victoria..........	13,736
Sierra Leone..........	28,000	3,002,426	108	Ψ Freetown.........	274,000
Somalia..............	246,000	2,730,000	11	Ψ Mogadishu........	220,000
South Africa..........	472,000	21,282,000	45 {	Pretoria..........	561,703
				Ψ Cape Town........	1,096,597
S.W. Africa...........	318,000	746,328	2	Windhoek..........	60,000
Spanish Presidios:—					
Ceuta..............	5	67,187	..	..	..
Melilla.............	72	64,942	..		
Sahara..............	125,000	63,000	..	Villa Cisneros.......	250
Sudan...............	967,500	16,900,000	17	Khartoum..........	194,000
Swaziland............	6,700	465,000	69	Mbabane..........	20,700
Tanzania.............	363,000	13,968,000	38	Ψ Dar-es-Salaam......	306,000
Togo................	21,000	2,089,900	99	Lomé.............	214,200
Tunisia..............	63,380	5,409,000	85	Ψ Tunis...........	1,127,000
Uganda..............	91,000	10,400,000	114	Kampala..........	331,000
Upper Volta..........	100,000	5,514,000	55	Ouagadougou.......	125,000
Zaire................	905,000	21,637,000	24	Kinshasa..........	1,300,000
Zambia..............	291,000	4,054,000	14	Lusaka............	238,000

AMERICA

COUNTRY	Area Sq. Miles	Population	Per Sq. Mile	Capital	Population of Capital
North America					
Canada†	3,560,000	22,446,000	6	Ottawa	619,000
Alberta	249,000	1,714,000	7	Edmonton	448,530
British Columbia	359,000	2,395,000	7	Ψ Victoria	193,512
Manitoba	212,000	1,011,000	5	Winnipeg	552,500
New Brunswick	28,000	662,000	24	Ψ Fredericton	42,000
Newfoundland	143,000	542,000	4	Ψ St. John's	88,102
Nova Scotia	20,400	813,000	40	Ψ Halifax	225,000
Ontario	344,000	8,094,000	24	Toronto	2,628,043
Prince Edward Island	2,184	117,000	54	Ψ Charlottetown	18,500
Quebec	524,000	6,134,000	12	Ψ Quebec	187,500
Saskatchewan	220,000	912,000	4	Regina	147,000
Yukon Territory	205,000	19,000	..	Whitehorse	4,771
Northwest Territories	1,305,000	38,000	..	Yellowknife	7,000
Mexico	761,530	57,000,000	75	Mexico City	10,000,000
St. Pierre and Miquelon	93	5,000	54	Ψ St. Pierre	3,500
United States★	3,536,855	203,211,926	57	Washington, D.C.	2,861,123
Central America and the West Indies					
Anguilla	35	6,500	186	....	....
Antigua and Barbuda	170	66,000	388	Ψ St. John's	22,000
Bahamas	5,380	197,000	37	Ψ Nassau	112,000
Barbados	166	247,506	1,491	Ψ Bridgetown	18,789
Belize	8,900	122,000	14	Belmopan	3,500
Bermuda	21	53,000	2,574	Ψ Hamilton	3,000
Cayman Islands	100	10,652	107	Ψ George Town	3,000
Costa Rica	19,653	1,875,000	95	San José	215,441
Cuba	44,000	8,553,000	194	Ψ Havana	1,755,360
Dominica	290	70,302	243	Ψ Roseau	10,157
Dominican Republic	19,300	4,012,000	208	Ψ Santo Domingo	817,000
Grenada	133	105,000	789	Ψ St. George's	8,600
Guadeloupe	688	323,000	469	Ψ Pointe à Pitre	39,000
Guatemala	42,000	5,400,000	129	Guatemala	790,311
Haiti	10,700	4,768,000	446	Ψ Port au Prince	400,000
Honduras	43,000	2,646,828	61	Tegucigalpa	267,754
Jamaica	4,400	1,953,472	443	Ψ Kingston	572,653
Martinique	400	332,000	83	Ψ Fort de France	60,600
Montserrat	39	12,905	331	Ψ Plymouth	1,300
Netherlands Antilles	394	234,400	595	Ψ Willemstad	154,000
Nicaragua	57,000	2,400,000	42	Managua	400,000
Panama	31,900	1,428,082	45	Ψ Panama City	418,000
Panama Canal Zone	647	44,198	68	Ψ Balboa Heights	3,950
Puerto Rico	3,400	2,923,000	848	Ψ San Juan	851,247
St. Kitts-Nevis	101	48,000	475	Ψ Basseterre	17,000
St. Lucia	238	100,000	420	Ψ Castries	43,000
St. Vincent	150	92,000	613	Ψ Kingstown	23,000
El Salvador	7,700	3,863,793	500	San Salvador	620,000
Trinidad and Tobago	1,980	1,061,850	536	Ψ Port of Spain	100,000
Turks and Caicos Islds.	193	6,000	31	Ψ Grand Turk	2,339
Virgin Islands:—					
British	59	10,030	170	Ψ Road Town	2,129
U.S.	133	62,468	470	Ψ Charlotte Amalie	11,000
South America					
Argentina	1,080,000	23,360,000	22	Ψ Buenos Aires	8,774,529
Bolivia	415,000	4,658,000	11	La Paz	553,000
Brazil	3,289,000	108,000,000	33	Brasília	544,862
Chile	290,000	10,000,000	34	Santiago	4,000,000
Colombia	440,000	22,000,000	50	Bogotá	2,900,000
Ecuador	226,000	7,000,000	31	Quito	700,000
Falkland Islands	4,700	1,759	..	Ψ Stanley	1,079
Guiana, *French*	35,000	48,000	1	Ψ Cayenne	20,000
Guyana	83,000	714,233	9	Ψ Georgetown	168,000
Paraguay	157,000	2,395,614	15	Ψ Asunción	437,000
Peru	531,000	14,121,564	27	Lima	3,600,000
Surinam	54,000	480,000	9	Ψ Paramaribo	110,000
Uruguay	72,000	2,763,964	38	Ψ Montevideo	1,229,748
Venezuela	354,000	11,992,700	34	Caracas	2,183,935

★ The 50 States and Federal *District of Columbia* at the 1970 Census; for area and population of individual States *see* main article.   Ψ Seaport.   † For total areas (including freshwater), see p. 695.

ASIA

The expressions "The Near East," "The Middle East" and "The Far East" often appear in the Press of English-speaking countries, but have no definite boundaries. The following limits have been suggested:— *Near East* (Turkey to Iran) 25°–60° E. long., *Middle East* (Baluchistan to Burma) 60°–100° E. long., *Far East* (Thailand to Japan) 100°–160° E. long. Ψ Seaport.

COUNTRY	Area Sq. miles	Population	Per Sq. Mile	Capital	Population of Capital
Afghanistan	250,000	16,516,000	66	Kabul	500,000
Bahrain	231	216,000	935	Ψ Manama	89,608
Bangladesh	55,126	75,000,000	1,360	Dacca	1,300,000
Bhutan	18,000	1,010,000	56	Thimphu	..
Brunei	2,226	141,497	64	Ψ Bandar Seri Begawan	38,000
Burma	262,000	29,512,000	113	Ψ Rangoon	3,186,886
Cambodia	70,000	7,300,000	104	Ψ Phnom Penh	2,000,000
China	4,300,000	800,000,000	186	Peking	7,570,000
Formosa (Taiwan)	13,800	15,353,291	1,112	Taipei	1,921,736
Macau	5	248,316	..	Ψ Macau	157,175
Hong Kong	404	4,345,200	..	Ψ Victoria	767,000
India	1,262,000	547,949,809	434	Delhi	4,065,698
Indonesia	735,000	129,000,000	162	Ψ Jakarta	5,000,000
Iran (Persia)	628,000	28,448,000	45	Tehran	3,150,000
Iraq	172,000	9,498,362	55	Baghdad	2,696,000
Israel	8,000	3,230,000	404	Jerusalem	301,000
Japan	143,000	103,720,000	726	Tokyo	11,403,744
Jordan	37,700	2,660,000	71	Amman	615,000
Korea:—					
North Korea	48,000	14,500,000	302	Pyongyang	286,000
South Korea	38,500	33,459,000	869	Seoul	6,289,556
Kuwait	7,500	990,000	132	Ψ Kuwait	300,000
Laos	90,000	2,700,000	30	Vientiane	174,000
Lebanon	4,300	2,645,000	615	Ψ Beirut	600,000
Malaysia	128,000	10,434,000	82	Kuala Lumpur	770,000
Johore	7,330	1,274,000	174	Johore Bahru	..
Kedah	3,640	955,000	262	Alor Star	..
Kelantan	5,765	681,000	118	Koto Bahru	..
Malacca	640	404,000	631	Ψ Malacca	..
Negri Sembilan	2,570	479,000	186	Seremban	..
Pahang	13,900	503,000	36	Kuantan	..
Penang	400	777,000	1,942	Ψ George Town	234,930
Perak	8,100	1,563,000	193	Ipoh	125,776
Perlis	310	121,000	390	Kangar	..
Sabah	29,000	656,000	23	Kota Kinabalu	41,830
Sarawak	48,000	977,000	20	Ψ Kuching	63,491
Selangor	3,166	1,629,000	515	Kuala Lumpur	500,000
Trengganu	5,000	406,000	81	Kuala Trengganu	..
Maldive Islands	115	114,500	996	Ψ Malé	13,610
Mongolia (Outer)	600,000	1,300,000	2	Ulan Bator	195,300
Nepal	54,000	11,289,000	208	Katmandu	353,756
Oman	120,000	750,000	6	Ψ Muscat	7,650
Pakistan	310,403	64,892,000	209	Islamabad	235,000
Philippine Islds	115,000	42,517,330	370	Ψ Manila	1,438,252
Qatar	4,000	180,000	45	Doha	100,000
Saudi Arabia	927,000	7,200,000	8	Riyadh	450,000
Singapore	225	2,219,000	9,836	..	..
Sri Lanka	25,332	12,747,755	503	Ψ Colombo	563,705
Syria	71,000	6,294,000	89	Damascus	557,252
Thailand (Siam)	198,000	41,000,000	207	Ψ Bangkok	4,130,000
Timor, Eastern	7,329	610,541	83	Ψ Dili	7,000
Turkey in Asia.†	285,000	32,501,000	114	Ankara	1,440,779
United Arab Emirates	32,000	300,000	9	..	..
U.S.S.R. (Asia)					
R.S.F.S.R. (Asia)	4,887,000	*See* Europe			
Armenia (Hyastan)	11,000	2,728,000	241	Erevan	870,000
Azerbaidjan	33,000	5,514,000	165	Ψ Baku	1,383,000
Georgia	27,000	4,878,000	181	Tbilisi	1,006,000
Turkmenistan	188,000	2,430,000	13	Ashkhabad	289,000
Uzbekistan	157,000	13,289,000	84	Tashkent	1,595,000
Tadjikistan	54,000	3,283,000	61	Dushanbe	436,000
Kazakhstan	1,065,000	13,928,000	13	Alma Ata	837,000
Kirghizia	77,000	3,219,000	42	Frunze	486,000
Vietnam:—					
Northern Zone	63,000	23,780,375	377	Hanoi	1,378,335
Southern Zone	66,000	20,000,000	302	Ψ Saigon	3,000,000
Yemen	75,000	6,000,000	80	Sana'a	135,000
Yemen P.D.R.	180,000	1,598,275	9	Ψ Aden	250,000

† Total, incl. European parts: Area, 294,200 sq. miles; population, 35,666,549.

EUROPE AND THE MEDITERRANEAN

COUNTRY	Area Sq. Miles	Population	Per Sq. Mile	Capital	Population of Capital
Albania...............	10,700	2,377,600	222	Tirana...............	200,000
Andorra..............	180	25,000	139	Andorra La Vella.....	10,200
Austria...............	32,376	7,456,403	230	Vienna..............	1,614,841
Belgium..............	11,800	9,650,944	818	Brussels.............	1,075,000
Bulgaria..............	43,000	8,594,493	200	Sofia................	927,833
Cyprus...............	3,500	634,000	177	Nicosia..............	235,000
Czechoslovakia........	49,400	14,526,268	294	Prague..............	1,091,449
Denmark..............	17,000	5,054,909	297	Ѱ Copenhagen........	1,380,118
Finland..............	130,000	4,698,000	36	Ѱ Helsinki...........	526,896
France...............	213,000	52,346,000	246	Paris................	2,454,600
Germany:—					
Federal Republic of Germany‡..........	95,980	61,991,500	646	Bonn................	283,260
East Germany	41,768	16,979,600	407	East Berlin..........	1,088,827
Gibraltar..............	2	29,362	..	Ѱ Gibraltar...........	20,000
Greece...............	51,200	8,768,641	171	Athens..............	2,540,241
Hungary.............	36,000	10,448,000	290	Budapest............	2,049,132
Iceland...............	40,500	216,172	5	Ѱ Reykjavik..........	85,000
Irish Republic.........	26,600	2,978,248	112	Ѱ Dublin............	567,866
Italy.................	131,000	54,683,136	417	Rome...............	2,842,616
Liechtenstein...........	65	23,156	356	Vaduz..............	4,326
Luxemburg............	1,000	357,300	357	Luxemburg.........	78,300
Malta and Gozo.......	121	318,481	2,636	Ѱ Valletta...........	14,152
Monaco..............	⅔	24,500	..	Monaco.............	2,422
Netherlands..........	13,500	13,599,092	1,007 {	The Hague.......... Ѱ Amsterdam........	487,120 770,805
Norway..............	125,000	3,972,990	32	Ѱ Oslo..............	468,514
Poland...............	121,000	32,589,000	269	Warsaw.............	1,388,000
Portugal§.............	34,500	8,545,120	248	Ѱ Lisbon............	783,000
Rumania..............	91,600	20,827,525	227	Bucharest............	1,528,562
San Marino...........	23	19,000	826	San Marino..........	2,000
Spain................	197,000	34,032,801	173	Madrid..............	3,146,071
Sweden..............	173,000	8,177,000	47	Ѱ Stockholm.........	1,349,892
Switzerland...........	16,000	6,385,000	400	Berne..............	157,700
Turkey in Europe.....	9,200	3,166,000	344	Ankara.............	1,440,779
THE UNITED KINGDOM†.	93,026	55,521,534	597 }	Ѱ London............	7,379,014
England..............	50,053	45,870,062	916 }		
Wales..............	7,969	2,723,596	342	Ѱ Cardiff............	283,680
Scotland.............	29,798	5,227,706	171	ѰEdinburgh..........	448,682
Northern Ireland.....	5,206	1,536,065	295	Ѱ Belfast............	353,700
U.S.S.R. (Europe)......					
R.S.F.S.R.*.........	1,707,000	132,913,000	78	Moscow.............	7,368,000
Ukraine.............	252,000	48,521,000	192	Kiev...............	1,887,000
Belorussia...........	80,000	9,268,000	115	Minsk..............	1,082,000
Moldavia...........	14,000	3,764,000	270	Kishinev............	432,000
Estonia..............	17,400	1,418,000	81	Ѱ Tallinn............	392,000
Latvia..............	25,000	2,454,000	99	Ѱ Riga..............	776,000
Lithuania............	26,000	3,262,000	125	Vilnius.............	420,000
Vatican City State......	109 *acres*	1,000	..	Vatican City........	1,000
Yugoslavia............	99,000	21,500,000	217	Belgrade............	1,204,000

* Total population, Europe and Asia.   † *Land* areas are shown for U.K. and parts (*total* area of U.K., 94,216 sq. m.); populations at 1971 Census (prelim.) except Belfast.   ‡ Data include West Berlin. § Data include Madeira (314 sq. miles) and the Azores (922 sq. miles).   Ѱ Seaport.

THE SEVEN WONDERS OF THE WORLD

I. THE PYRAMIDS OF EGYPT.—From Gizeh (near Cairo) to a southern limit 60 miles distant. The oldest is that of Zoser, at Saggara, built about 2,700 B.C. The Great Pyramid of Cheops covers more than 12 acres and was originally 481 ft. in height and 756 × 756 ft. at the base.

II. THE HANGING GARDENS OF BABYLON.—Adjoining Nebuchadnezzar's palace, 60 miles south of Baghdad. Terraced gardens, ranging from 75 to 300 ft. above ground level, watered from storage tanks on the highest terrace.

III. THE TOMB OF MAUSOLUS.—At Halicarnassus, in Asia Minor. Built by the widowed Queen Artemisia about 350 B.C. The memorial originated the term mausoleum.

IV. THE TEMPLE OF DIANA AT EPHESUS.—Ionic temple erected about 350 B.C. in honour of the goddess and burned by the Goths in A.D. 262.

V. THE COLOSSUS OF RHODES.—A bronze statue of Apollo, set up about 280 B.C. According to legend it stood at the harbour entrance of the seaport of Rhodes.

VI. THE STATUE OF JUPITER OLYMPUS.—At Olympia in the plain of Ellis, constructed of marble inlaid with ivory and gold by the sculptor Phidias, about 430 B.C.

VII. THE PHAROS OF ALEXANDRIA.—A marble watch tower and lighthouse on the island of Pharos in the harbour of Alexandria.

OCEANIA

COUNTRY	Area Sq. Miles	Population	Per Sq. Mile	Capital	Population of Capital
Australia............	2,968,000	13,485,900	5	Canberra..........	187,600
New South Wales.....	309,000	4,798,000	16	Ψ Sydney............	2,850,630
Queensland..........	667,000	1,997,700	3	Ψ Brisbane...........	888,000
South Australia......	380,000	1,239,300	3	Adelaide..........	809,482
Tasmania...........	26,000	405,000	15	Ψ Hobart............	135,100
Victoria............	88,000	3,672,500	42	Ψ Melbourne........	2,394,117
Western Australia....	976,000	1,116,100	1	Perth.............	724,800
Northern Territory.....	520,000	69,700	..	Ψ Darwin...........	..
Norfolk Island.......	13	1,546	116	Ψ Kingston.........	..
British Solomon Is......	11,500	160,998	14	Ψ Honiara..........	11,191
Fiji..................	7,100	541,000	76	Ψ Suva.............	54,157
French Polynesia.....	2,500	109,000	44	Ψ Papeete..........	15,220
Gilbert and Ellice Is.....	283	54,000	150	Tarawa............	10,616
Guam................	209	105,000	502	Agaña.............	..
Mariana, Caroline and Marshall Islands†....	687	101,592	148	Saipan.............	..
Nauru...............	8	6,768	825	Ψ Nauru...........	..
New Caledonia........	7,200	98,000	14	Ψ Noumea.........	12,000
New Hebrides........	5,700	89,031	15	Ψ Vila.............	5,500
New Zealand.........	104,000	3,042,800	29	Ψ Wellington........	346,900
Cook Islands........}	200	{ 19,522	..	Avarua............	..
Niue...............}		{ 3,992	..	Alofi.............	956
Ross Dependency......	175,000	..	..	..	..
Papua New Guinea.....	178,000	2,724,740	15	Ψ Port Moresby.......	76,507
Samoa:—					
Eastern.............	76	28,000	368	Ψ Pago Pago.........	1,251
Western............	1,097	151,000	138	Ψ Apia.............	28,800
Tonga, etc............	270	92,360	342	Ψ Nuku'alofa.........	20,000

† Trust Territory of the Pacific Islands.   Ψ Seaport

OCEAN AREAS AND DEPTHS

The greatest known Ocean Depth (in the Pacific, off the Philippines, 36,198 feet) is not much greater than the greatest land height (in the Himalayas); but the mean depth of the Ocean floor exceeds 12,000 feet, while the mean height of the surface of the land area of the Earth above sea level is only 2,300 feet. The following table gives the areas of the principal oceans and seas, with the greatest known depth of each:—

Oceans

Name	Area of Basin (sq. miles)	Greatest Depth (feet)
Pacific.........	63,986,000	Mariana Trench, 36,198
Atlantic.......	31,530,000	Puerto Rico Trench, 27,498
Indian.........	28,350,000	Diamantina, 26,400
Arctic.........	5,541,600	 17,850

Seas

Name	Area of Basin (sq. miles)	Greatest Depth (feet)
Malay.........	3,137,000	Kei Trench, 21,342
Caribbean.....	1,770,170	Cayman, 23,000
Mediterranean..	1,145,000	Matapan, 14,435
Bering........	878,000	Buldir Trough, 13,422
Okhotsk.......	582,000	Kurile Trough, 11,154
East China.....	480,000	*about* 10,500
Hudson Bay....	472,000	*about* 1,500
Japan..........	405,000	*about* 10,200
Andaman......	305,000	*about* 11,000
North Sea.....	221,000	Skaggerak, 1,998
Red Sea.......	178,000	20° N., 7,254
Baltic.........	158,000	*about* 1,300

SOME FAMOUS TALL BUILDINGS

	Feet
Empire State, N.Y., U.S.A...............	1,472
Chrysler Building N.Y., U.S.A...........	1,046
Eiffel Tower, Paris (originally)...........	985
60 Wall Tower, N.Y., U.S.A...........	950
Bank of Manhattan, N.Y., U.S.A.........	927
Rockefeller Centre, N.Y., U.S.A.........	850
Woolworth's, N.Y., U.S.A..............	792
City Bank Farmers' Trust, 20 Exchange Place, N.Y., U.S.A.................	741
Toronto–Dominion Bank Tower, Toronto	740

	Feet
Metropolitan Life Building, Madison Avenue, N.Y., U.S.A..............	700
500 Fifth Avenue, N.Y., U.S.A.........	697
Chanin, Lexington Avenue and 42nd Street, N.Y., U.S.A.......................	680
Husky Tower, Calgary, Alberta..........	626
Post Office Tower, England..............	580
Pyramid of Cheops, Egypt..............	450
Salisbury Cathedral (Spire), England.......	440
St. Paul's Cathedral (Cross), England......	365

THE LARGEST CITIES OF THE WORLD

Ψ = Seaport	Population*	Ψ = Seaport	Population*
Ψ New York, U.S.A. (1970)	11,571,899	BUDAPEST, Hungary (1974)	2,049,132
TOKYO, Japan (1971)	11,403,744	Ψ Nagoya, Japan (1971)	2,037,952
Ψ Shanghai, China (1972)	10,820,000	Ψ Pusan, Korea (1973)	2,015,162
MEXICO CITY, Mexico (1974)	10,000,000	Guadalajara, Mexico (1974)	2,000,000
Ψ BUENOS AIRES, Argentina (1970)	8,774,529	Ψ Nanking, China (1975)	2,000,000
CAIRO, Egypt (1975)	8,143,000	Ψ PHNOM PENH, Cambodia (1973)	2,000,000
PEKING, China (1972)	7,570,000	Ψ Houston, U.S.A. (1970)	1,985,031
Ψ LONDON, England (1971)	7,379,014	TAIPEI, Formosa (1973)	1,921,736
MOSCOW, U.S.S.R. (1974)	7,368,000	Ψ Alexandria, Egypt (1969)	1,900,000
Ψ Los Angeles, U.S.A. (1970)	7,032,075	Kiev, U.S.S.R. (1974)	1,887,000
Ψ Chicago, U.S.A. (1970)	6,978,947	Ψ Newark, U.S.A. (1970)	1,856,556
SEOUL, Korea (1973)	6,289,556	Ψ Canton, China (1957)	1,840,000
São Paulo, Brazil (1970)	5,901,533	Minneapolis, U.S.A. (1970)	1,813,647
Ψ Bombay, India (1971)	5,850,000	Ψ HAVANA, Cuba (1970)	1,755,360
Ψ DJAKARTA, Indonesia (1974)	5,000,000	Ψ Hamburg, Germany (1973)	1,751,621
Ψ Philadelphia, U.S.A. (1970)	4,817,914	Ψ Barcelona, Spain (1969)	1,750,000
Ψ Rio de Janeiro, Brazil (1970)	4,296,782	Milan, Italy (1971)	1,724,819
Tientsin, China (1971)	4,280,000	VIENNA, Austria (1972)	1,614,841
Ψ Detroit, U.S.A. (1970)	4,199,931	Tashkent, U.S.S.R. (1975)	1,595,000
Ψ BANGKOK, Thailand (1974)	4,130,000	Dallas, U.S.A. (1970)	1,555,950
DELHI, India (1971)	4,065,698	Harbin, China (1957)	1,552,000
SANTIAGO, Chile (1972)	4,000,000	BUCHAREST, Rumania (1973)	1,528,562
Ψ Leningrad, U.S.S.R. (1974)	3,786,000	Ψ Lushun-Dairen, China (1957)	1,508,000
LIMA, Peru (1972)	3,600,000	Ψ Casablanca, Morocco (1971)	1,506,373
Ψ Karachi, Pakistan (1972)	3,469,000	ANKARA, Turkey (1970)	1,440,779
Ψ RANGOON, Burma (1973)	3,186,886	Johannesburg, South Africa (1970)	1,432,643
TEHRAN, Iran (1970)	3,150,000	Ψ Seattle, U.S.A. (1970)	1,421,869
MADRID, Spain (1970)	3,146,071	Anaheim, U.S.A. (1970)	1,420,386
Ψ Calcutta, India (1971)	3,141,180	Kyoto, Japan (1971)	1,415,880
Berlin, Germany (1973)	3,136,775	Milwaukee, U.S.A. (1970)	1,403,688
Ψ San Francisco, U.S.A. (1970)	3,109,519	Ψ MANILA, Philippines (1971)	1,399,583
Ψ SAIGON, S. Vietnam (1973)	3,000,000	Atlanta, U.S.A. (1970)	1,390,164
Ψ Osaka, Japan (1971)	2,980,409	WARSAW, Poland (1973)	1,388,000
WASHINGTON, U.S.A. (1970)	2,861,123	Cincinnati, U.S.A. (1970)	1,384,851
Ψ Sydney, Australia (1972)	2,850,630	Ψ Baku, U.S.S.R. (1975)	1,383,000
ROME, Italy (1971)	2,842,616	COPENHAGEN, Denmark (1972)	1,380,118
Ψ Montreal, Canada (1974)	2,828,795	HANOI, N. Vietnam (1974)	1,378,335
Ψ Boston, U.S.A. (1970)	2,753,700	Paterson, U.S.A. (1970)	1,358,794
BAGHDAD, Iraq (1970)	2,696,000	Ψ San Diego, U.S.A. (1970)	1,357,854
Ψ Toronto, Canada (1971)	2,628,043	Monterrey, Mexico (1974)	1,350,000
PARIS, France (1969)	2,590,000	Ψ STOCKHOLM, Sweden (1973)	1,349,892
ATHENS, Greece (1972)	2,540,000	Ψ Buffalo, U.S.A. (1970)	1,349,211
BOGOTA, Colombia (1970)	2,512,000	Munich, Germany (1973)	1,336,576
Ψ Madras, India (1971)	2,470,289	Kharkov, U.S.S.R. (1974)	1,330,000
Shenyang, China (1957)	2,411,000	Sian, China (1957)	1,310,000
Pittsburgh, U.S.A. (1970)	2,401,245	Dacca, Bangladesh (1974)	1,300,000
Ψ Melbourne, Australia (1971)	2,394,117	KINSHASA, Zaire (1971)	1,300,000
St. Louis, U.S.A. (1970)	2,363,017	Ψ Kobé, Japan (1971)	1,294,373
Ψ Istanbul, Turkey (1970)	2,312,751	Ψ Miami, U.S.A. (1970)	1,267,792
Ψ Yokohama, Japan (1971)	2,273,029	Gorky, U.S.S.R. (1974)	1,260,000
CARACAS, Venezuela (1971)	2,183,935	Ψ Naples, Italy (1971)	1,258,721
Lahore, Pakistan (1972)	2,148,000	Kansas City, U.S.A. (1970)	1,253,916
Wuhan, China (1957)	2,146,000	Hyderabad, India (1963)	1,251,119
Chungking, China (1957)	2,121,000	Novosibirsk, U.S.S.R. (1974)	1,243,000
Ψ SINGAPORE (1970)	2,074,507	Ψ Belo Horizonte, Brazil (1970)	1,232,708
Ψ Baltimore, U.S.A. (1970)	2,070,670	Denver, U.S.A. (1970)	1,227,529
Ψ Cleveland, U.S.A. (1970)	2,064,194	BELGRADE, Yugoslavia (1970)	1,204,000

* See paragraph 2, p. 199. U.S.A.—Populations of the largest cities are those of the standard metropolitan statistical areas at the Census of 1970.

THE CINQUE PORTS

As their name implies the Cinque Ports were originally 5 in number, Hastings, New Romney, Hythe, Dover and Sandwich. They were in existence before the Norman Conquest and were the Anglo-Saxon successors to the Roman system of coast defence organized from the Wash to Spithead to resist Saxon onslaughts. William the Conqueror reconstituted them and granted peculiar jurisdiction, most of which was abolished in 1855. Only jurisdiction in Admiralty still survives.

At some time after the Conquest the " antient towns " of Winchelsea and Rye were added with equal privileges. The other members of the Confederation, known as Limbs, are:—Lydd, Faversham, Folkestone, Deal, Tenterden, Margate and Ramsgate.

The Barons of the Cinque Ports have the ancient privilege of attending the Coronation Ceremony and are allotted special places in Westminster Abbey.

Lord Warden, Rt. Hon. Sir Robert Menzies, K.T., C.H., Q.C.

Judge, Court of Admiralty, Sir Henry Barnard.

Registrar, James A. Johnson, New Bridge House, Dover.

Lord Wardens since 1904

Marquess Curzon	1904
The Prince of Wales	1905
Earl Brassey	1908
Earl Beauchamp	1913
Marquess of Reading	1934
Marquess of Willingdon	1936
Sir Winston Churchill	1941
Sir Robert Menzies	1965

THE WORLD'S LAKES
The areas of some of these lakes are subject to seasonal variation.

Name	Country	Length (Miles)	Area (Sq. Miles)	Name	Country	Length (Miles)	Area (Sq. Miles)
Caspian Sea	Asia	680	170,000	Amadjuak	Baffin Land	75	4,000
Superior	North America	383	31,820	Onega	U.S.S.R.	145	3,800
Victoria Nyanza	Africa	200	26,200	Eyre	Australia	..	3,700
Aral	U.S.S.R.	265	24,400	Rudolf	Africa	185	3,500
Huron	North America	247	23,010	Titicaca	South America	120	3,200
Michigan	North America	321	22,400	Athabasca	Canada	100	3,058
Malawi	Africa	350	14,200	Nicaragua	Central America	195	3,000
Tanganyika	Africa	420	12,700	Gairdner	Australia	..	3,000
Great Bear	Canada	175	11,660	Van	Asia Minor	80	2,500
Baikal	U.S.S.R.	330	11,580	Reindeer	Canada	160	2,444
Great Slave	Canada	325	11,170	Torrens	Australia	130	2,400
Erie	North America	241	9,940	Koko-Nor	Tibet	68	2,300
Winnipeg	Canada	260	9,398	Issyk-Kul	U.S.S.R.	115	2,250
Maracaibo	South America	..	8,296	Vänern	Sweden	93	2,150
Ontario	North America	193	7,540	Winnipegosis	Canada	122	2,086
Balkhash	U.S.S.R.	323	7,050	Bangweolo	Africa	150	2,000
Ladoga	U.S.S.R.	125	7,000	Nipigon	Canada	70	1,870
Chad	Africa	..	6,000	Manitoba	Canada	191	1,817
Nettilling	Baffin Land	120	5,000				

VOLCANOES OF THE WORLD

Volcano	Locality	Height in Feet	Volcano	Locality	Height in Feet
Cotopaxi	Ecuador	19,344	Nyamuragira	Zaire	10,150
Kluchevskaya	U.S.S.R.	15,584	Villarica	Chile	9,325
Mount Wrangell	Alaska	14,000	Ruapehu	New Zealand	9,175
Mauna Loa	Hawaii	13,680	Paricutin	Mexico	9,100
Cameroun	Cameroun	13,350	Asama	Japan	8,340
Erebus	Antarctica	12,200	Ngauruhoe	New Zealand	7,515
Nyiragongo	Zaire	11,560	Hecla	Iceland	4,892
Iliamna	Aleutian Range, U.S.A.	11,000	Vesuvius	Italy	4,190
Etna	Sicily	10,958	Kilauea	Hawaii	4,090
Baker	Cascades	10,778	Stromboli	Lipari Islands, Italy	3,034
Chillan	Chile	10,500			

QUIESCENT

Volcano	Locality	Height	Volcano	Locality	Height
Llullaillaco	Chile	22,057	Tristan da Cunha	South Atlantic	6,700
Demavend	Iran	18,384	Pelée	Martinique, W. Indies	4,430
Pico de Teyde	Teneriffe	12,198	Tarawera	New Zealand	3,646
Semerou	Indonesia	12,060	Soufrière	St. Vincent Is., W.I.	3,000
Haleakala	Hawaii	10,022	Krakatoa	Sunda Strait	2,600
Tongariro	New Zealand	6,458			

BELIEVED EXTINCT

Name	Range	Height	Name	Range	Height
Aconcagua	Andes	22,834	Elbruz	Caucasus	18,480
Chimborazo	Ecuador	20,560	Popocatapetl	Mexico	17,887
Kilimanjaro	Tanzania	19,340	Karisimbi	Rwanda and Zaire	14,786
Antisana	Ecuador	18,713	Fujiyama	Japan	12,388
Citlaltepetl	Mexico	18,700			

THE HIGHEST MOUNTAINS
The following list contains some of the principal peaks of such ranges as the Himalayas and the Andes, and the highest mountains in other ranges.

Name	Range of Country	Height in Feet	Name	Range or Country	Height in Feet
EVEREST	Himalayas	29,028	Sajama	Andes	21,390
K 2	Karakoram	28,250	Chimborazo	Andes	20,560
Kanchenjunga	Himalayas	28,208	McKinley	Alaska	20,320
Makulu	Himalayas	27,824	Mount Logan	Yukon	19,850
Dhaulagiri	Himalayas	26,810	Cotopaxi	Andes	19,344
Nanga Parbat	Himalayas	26,660	Kilimanjaro	Tanzania	19,340
Annapurna	Himalayas	26,502	Antisana	Andes	18,713
Nanda Devi	Himalayas	25,645	Ciltlaltepetl	S. Madre	18,700
Kamet	Himalayas	25,447	Elbruz	Caucasus	18,480
Namcha Barwa	China	25,445	Demavend	Elburz	18,384
Minya Konka	China	24,900	Mount St. Elias	Alaska	18,008
Pik Kommunizma	Pamirs	24,590	Popocatapetl	S. Madre	17,887
Pik Pobedy	Tian Shan	24,406	Foraker	Alaska	17,395
Aconcagua	Andes	22,834	Mount Lucania	Yukon	17,150
Bonete	Andes	22,545	Tolima	Andes	17,109
Ojos del Salado	Andes	22,516	Kenya	Kenya	17,058
Huascaran	Andes	22,204	Ararat	Armenia	16,945
Llullaillaco	Andes	22,057	Vinson Massif	Antarctica	16,863

THE LONGEST RIVERS

River	Outflow	Length in Miles
Nile	Mediterranean	4,160
Amazon	Atlantic	4,050
Missouri-Mississippi– Red Rock	Gulf of Mexico	3,710
Yangtze	North Pacific	3,400
Yenisei	Arctic	3,300
Congo	Atlantic	3,000
Lena	Arctic	2,800
Mekong	China Sea	2,800
Obi	Arctic	2,700
Niger	Gulf of Guinea	2,600
Hwang-ho	North Pacific	2,600
Amur	,, ,,	2,500
Paraná	Atlantic	2,450
Volga	Caspian Sea	2,400
Mackenzie	Beaufort Sea	2,300
Yukon	Bering Sea	2,000
Arkansas	Mississippi	2,000
Madeira	Amazon	2,000
Colorado	Gulf of California	2,000
St. Lawrence	Gulf of St. Lawrence	1,800
Rio Grande del Norte	Gulf of Mexico	1,800
São Francisco	Atlantic	1,800
Salween	Gulf of Martaban	1,800
Danube	Black Sea	1,725
Euphrates	Persian Gulf	1,700
Indus	Arabian Sea	1,700
Brahmaputra	Bay of Bengal	1,680
Zambesi	Indian Ocean	1,633
Murray	Indian Ocean	1,609

Severn	Bristol Channel	220
Thames	North Sea (Thames Head to Nore)	215

SOME FAMOUS BRIDGES

Among the outstanding *suspension bridges* of the World are the Verrazano Narrows Bridge, New York (main span, 4,260 ft.); the Golden Gate Bridge, San Francisco (4,200 ft.); the Mackinac Bridge, Michigan (3,800 ft.); Bosporus, Turkey (3,523 ft.); George Washington Bridge, New York (3,500 ft.); the Ponte Salazar (Tagus Bridge), Portugal (3,323 ft.); Forth Road Bridge, Scotland (3,300 ft.); Severn Bridge, England and Wales (3,240 ft.); Tacoma Bridge, Washington, U.S.A. (2,800 ft.); Orinoco Bridge, Venezuela (2,336 ft.) and the Kanmon Bridge, Japan (2,336 ft.). Lengths shown above are all those of the main or longest span.

The Transbay Bridge (*suspension and cantilever*), crossing San Francisco Bay from Oaklands to San Francisco is 7½ miles long, with spans of 2,310 ft. each.

Among important *steel arch* bridges are the Bayonne Bridge, from New Jersey to Staten Island, U.S.A. (1,652 ft.); Sydney Harbour Bridge, Australia (1,650 ft.); the Runcorn-Widnes Bridge, England (1,082 ft.); and the Glen Canyon Bridge over the Colorado River, U.S.A. (1,028 ft.). Major *concrete trestle* bridges include the Lake Portchartain Causeway, U.S.A. of 2,170 spans extending 24 miles and the Oosterscheldebrug, Netherlands, 3⅛ miles long. Gladesville Bridge, Sydney, Australia, is a *concrete arch* bridge of 1,000 ft. span The Tay Road Bridge in Scotland is a *steel box girder* bridge supported on twin piers (42 spans), 7,365 ft. long.

The Chesapeake Bay Bridge–Tunnel (17·6 miles long) joining Cape Charles, Virginia, to Chesapeake Beach has 12·5 miles of *concrete trestle* bridge.

PRINCIPAL HEIGHTS ABOVE SEA LEVEL

	Feet
Europe: Alps—Mont Blanc	15,782
England: Scafell Pike	3,210
Wales: Snowdon	3,560
Scotland: Ben Nevis	4,406
Ireland: Carrantuohill	3,414
Asia: Everest	29,028
Africa: Kilimanjaro	19,340
North America: McKinley	20,320
South America: Aconcagua	22,834
Australia: Kosciusko	7,316
New Zealand: Cook	12,349
Oceania: Carstenz, Indonesia	16,500
Antarctica: Vinson Massif	16,863

THE LARGEST ISLANDS

Name of Island	Ocean	Area in Sq. miles
Greenland (Danish)	Arctic	827,300
New Guinea	Pacific	347,450
Borneo (various)	,,	307,000
Baffin Land (Canadian)	Arctic	231,000
Madagascar	Indian	228,000
Sumatra (Indonesian)	Indian	163,000
Great Britain	Atlantic	88,745
Honshū (Japanese)	Pacific	87,500
Sulawesi (Indonesian)	Indian	73,000
Prince Albert (Canadian)	Arctic	60,000
South Island, N.Z.	Pacific	58,500
Java (Indonesian)	Indian	48,400
North Island, N.Z.	Pacific	44,500
Cuba	Atlantic	44,000
Newfoundland (Canadian)	Atlantic	42,750
Luzon (Phillippines)	Pacific	41,000
Ellesmere (Canadian)	Arctic	41,000
Iceland	Atlantic	40,000
Mindanao (Philippines)	Pacific	37,000
Ireland	Atlantic	32,600

GREAT SHIP CANALS OF THE WORLD

Canal	Opened year	Length, miles	Depth, feet	Width,§ feet
Amsterdam (Netherlands)	1876	16½	23	88
Corinth (Greece)	1893	4	26·25	72
Elbe and Trave (Germany)	1900	41	10	72
Gota (Sweden)*	1832	115	10	47
Kiel (Germany)†	1895	61	45	150
Manchester (England)	1894	35·5	28–30	120
Panama (U.S.A.)	1914	50·5	45	300
Princess Juliana (Netherlands)	1935	20	16	52
Sault Ste. Marie (U.S.A.)	1855	1·6	22	100
Sault Ste. Marie (Canada)	1895	1·11	20·25	142
Suez (Egypt)	1869	100	34	197
Welland (Canada)‡	1887	26·75	25	200

* Reconstructed 1916.　† Reconstructed 1914.　‡ Reconstructed 1929-30.　§ At the bottom.

WATERFALLS OF THE WORLD

In order of height

Fall	Locality	Height in Feet
Angel Falls	Venezuela	3,212
Ribbon Fall	Yosemite, U.S.A.	1,612
Upper Yosemite	Yosemite, U.S.A.	(a) 1,430
Gavarnie	Pyrenees	1,385
Wollomombie	New South Wales	(b) 1,100
Staubbach	Switzerland	980
Seward	Peru	887
Vettisfoss	Norway	856
King Edward VIII	Guyana	840
Gersoppa	Mysore, India	(c) 830
Sutherland	New Zealand	(d) 815
Kaieteur (Köituök)	Guyana	741
Kalambo	Tanzania	(e) 704
Maletsunyane	Lesotho	630
Bridalveil	Yosemite, U.S.A.	620
Nevada	Yosemite, U.S.A.	594
Skjeggedalsfoss	Norway	525
Eas-Coul-Aulin	Scotland	(f) 511

In order of volume

Fall	Locality	Width in Yards
Khon Cataracts (1)	Indo-China	15,840
Guayra (2)	Brazil	5,300
Victoria (3)	Rhodesia—Zambia	1,760
Niagara (4)	Canada—U.S.A.	1,200

On the basis of annual flow the Guayra Falls in Brazil are the most spectacular, with a flow of 470,000 cubic feet per second (annual average).

NOTES.—(a) Out of a total fall of 2,565 ft.;
     (b) 1,700 ft.; (c) 960 ft.; (d) 1,904 ft.;
     (e) 3,000 ft; (f) 658 ft.

(1) Height, 50–70 ft.; (2) 90–130 ft.
(3) 236–354 ft.; (4) 158–175 ft.

LONGEST RAILWAY TUNNELS

E.R. = Eastern Region; L.M.R. = London Midland Region;
S.R. = Southern Region; W.R. = Western Region

United Kingdom

		Miles	Yards
Severn	W.R.	4	628
Totley	L.M.R.	3	950
Standedge	E.R.	3	66
Woodhead	L.M.R.	3	66
Sodbury	W.R.	2	924
Disley	L.M.R.	2	346
Bramhope	E.R.	2	241
Ffestiniog	L.M.R.	2	338
Cowburn	L.M.R.	2	182
Sevenoaks	S.R.	1	1693
Rhondda	W.R.	1	1683
Morley	E.R.	1	1609
Box	W.R.	1	1452
Catesby	L.M.R.	1	1240
Dove Holes	L.M.R.	1	1224
Littleborough (Summit)	L.M.R.	1	1125
Vict. Waterloo (Liverpool)	L.M.R.	1	946
Ponsbourne	E.R.	1	924
Polhill	S.R.	1	851
Queensbury	E.R.	1	741
Merthyr	W.R.	1	737
Kilsby	L.M.R.	1	666
Bleamoor	L.M.R.	1	869
Shepherd's Well	S.R.	1	609
Gildersome	E.R.	1	571
Strood	S.R.	1	569
Clayton	S.R.	1	499
Oxted	S.R.	1	501
Sydenham	S.R.	1	381
Drewton	E.R.	1	354

		Miles	Yards
Merstham New (Quarry)	S.R.	1	353
Wapping	L.M.R.	1	351
Mersey	Mersey	1	350
Greenock	Scottish Region	1	351
Bradway	E.R.	1	267
Slough	L.M.R.	1	255
Watford, New	L.M.R.	1	230
Caerphilly	W.R.	1	173
Llangyfelach	W.R.	1	192
Abbot's Cliff	S.R.	1	182
Corby	L.M.R.	1	166
Halton	L.M.R.	1	176
Wenvoe	W.R.	1	107
Sapperton	W.R.	1	100
Sharnbrook	L.M.R.	1	100

(The London Underground *Northern Line* between Morden and East Finchley by the City Branch serves 25 stations and uses tunnels totalling 17¼ miles in length).

The World

		Miles	Yards
Simplon	Switzerland-Italy	12	560
Apennine	Italy	11	880
St. Gotthard	Switzerland	9	550
Lötschberg	Switzerland	9	130
Mont Cenis	Italy	8	870
Cascade	United States	7	1410
Arlberg	Austria	6	650
Moffat	United States	6	200
Shimizu	Japan	6	70

DISTANCE OF THE HORIZON

The limit of distance to which one can see varies with the height of the spectator. The greatest distance at which an object on the surface of the sea, or of a level plain, can be seen by a person whose eyes are at a height of 5 feet from the same level is nearly 3 miles. At a height of 20 feet the range is increased to nearly 6 miles, and an approximate rule for finding the range of vision for small heights is to increase the square root of the number of feet that the eye is above the level surface by a third of itself, the result being the distance of the horizon in miles, but is slightly in excess of that in the table below, which is computed by a more precise formula. The table may be used conversely to show the distance of an object of given height that is just visible from a point in the surface of the earth or sea. Refraction is taken into account both in the approximate rule and in the Table.

At a height of	the range is	At a height of	the range is	At a height of	the range is
5ft.	2·9 miles	500 ft.	29·5 miles	4,000 ft.	83·3 miles
20 ,,	5·9 ,,	1,000 ,,	41·6 ,,	5,000 ,,	93·1 ,,
50 ,,	9·3 ,,	2,000 ,,	58·9 ,,	20,000 ,,	186·2 ,,
100 ,,	13·2 ,,	3,000 ,,	72·1 ,,		

RULERS OF FOREIGN COUNTRIES

Country	Ruler	Born	Acceded
Afghanistan........	Mohammad Daoud, *President*..............	1909	July 17, 1973
Algeria...........	Col. Houari Boumedienne, *President, Council of Revolution*.............................	..	June 19, 1965
Argentine.........	Maria Estela Péron, *President*................	1931	July 1, 1974
Austria...........	Dr. Rudolf Kirchschläger, *President*..........	1915	June 23, 1974
Bahrain..........	Khalifa Isa bin Sulman, *Emir*................	1932	Dec. 16, 1961
Belgium..........	Baudouin, *King*............................	Sept. 7, 1930	July 17, 1951
Bhutan...........	Jigme Singye Wangchuck, *King*.............	1955	July 24, 1972
Bolivia...........	Col. Hugo Banzer, *President*................	1928	Aug. 22, 1971
Brazil............	Gen. Ernesto Geisel, *President*..............	Aug. 3, 1908	Mar. 15, 1974
Bulgaria..........	Todor Zhivkov, *Chairman, Council of State*....	..	July 7, 1971
Burma...........	U Ne Win, *President*.......................	..	Mar. 2, 1962
Burundi..........	Col. Michel Micombero, *President*...........	1940	Nov. 28, 1966
Cambodia........	Prince Norodom Sihanouk, *Head of State*.....	1922	1975
Cameroun........	Ahmadou Ahidjo, *President*.................	..	May 5, 1960
Cent. African Rep..	Marshal Jean Bedel Bokassa, *President*.......	..	Jan. 1, 1966
Chad.............	Gen. Felix Malloum.........................	..	April 16, 1975
Chile.............	Gen. Augusto Pinochet (Ugarte), *President*....	Nov. 25, 1915	Sept. 11, 1973
Colombia.........	Dr. Alfonso López Michelsen, *President*.......	..	Aug. 7, 1974
Congo...........	Marien Ngouabi, *President*..................	..	Jan. 1, 1969
Costa Rica.......	Daniel Oduber Quirós, *President*............	1923	May 8, 1974
Cuba............	Dr. Osvaldo Dorticos Torrado, *President*......	..	July 17, 1959
Czechoslovakia....	Gustav Husak, *President*....................	Jan. 10, 1913	May 29, 1975
Dahomey.........	Lt.-Col. Mathieu Kerekou, *President*.........	..	Oct. 26, 1972
Denmark.........	Margrethe II, *Queen*.......................	April 16, 1940	Jan. 15, 1972
Dominican Republic	Joaquín Balaguer, *President*.................	Sept. 1, 1907	June 1, 1966
Ecuador..........	Brig.-Gen. Guillermo Rodriguez Laza, *President*	..	Feb. 15, 1972
Egypt............	Anwar El Sadat, *President*..................	..	Oct. 15, 1970
Equatorial Guinea..	Francisco Macias Nguema, *President*.........	1925	Oct. 12, 1968
Ethiopia..........	Brig.-Gen. Teferi Bante, *President of Provisional Military Council*........................	..	Nov. 28, 1974
Finland..........	Dr. U. K. Kekkonen, *President*..............	1900	Feb. 16, 1956
Formosa..........	Yen Chia-kan.............................	1905	Mar. 6, 1975
France...........	Valéry Giscard d'Estaing, *President*.........	Feb. 2, 1926	May 27, 1974
Gabon...........	Omar Bongo, *President*.....................	..	Dec. 1967
Germany (Fed. Rep.)	Walter Scheel, *Federal President*............	..	July 1, 1974
Germany (East).....	Willi Stoph, *Chairman, Council of State*.......	1914	Oct. 3, 1973
Greece...........	Constantine Tsatsos, *President*..............	1899	June 20, 1975
Guatemala........	Gen. Kjell Eugenio Laugerud Garciá, *President*..	..	July 1, 1974
Guinea...........	Ahmed Sékou Touré, *President*..............	..	Jan. 1961
Haiti.............	Jean Claude Duvalier, *President*.............	1951	April 21, 1971
Honduras.........	Col. Juan Melgar Castro, *Head of State*.......	..	April 22, 1975
Hungary..........	Pál Losonczi, *President*....................	..	April 1967
Iceland...........	Dr. Kristjan Eldjarn, *President*.............	1917	Aug. 1, 1968
Indonesia.........	Gen. Soeharto, *President*...................	June 9, 1921	Mar. 28, 1968
Iran..............	Shahpoor Mohammed Reza Pahlavi, *Shah*.....	Oct. 26, 1919	Sept. 16, 1941
Iraq..............	Ahmad Hasan al-Bakr, *President*............	..	July 17, 1968
Irish Republic......	Cearbhall O'Dálaigh, *President*..............	1911	Dec. 19, 1974
Israel............	Prof. Ephraim Katzir, *President*.............	1916	May 24, 1973
Italy.............	Giovanni Leone, *President*..................	1908	Dec. 24, 1971
Ivory Coast.......	Felix Houphouët-Boigny, *President*..........	..	Nov. 27, 1960
Japan............	Hirohito, *Emperor*........................	April 29, 1901	Dec. 25, 1926
Jordan...........	Hussein, *King*............................	Nov. 14, 1935	Aug. 11, 1952
Korea, South.....	Park, Chung Hee, *President*.................	..	Mar. 22, 1962
Kuwait...........	Sabah as-Salem as Sabah, *Amir*.............	1915	Nov. 24, 1965
Laos.............	Savang Vatthana, *King*.....................	1907	Nov. 1, 1959
Lebanon..........	Suleiman Franjieh, *President*................	..	Aug. 17, 1970
Liberia...........	William Richard Tolbert, *President*...........	1913	July 23, 1971
Libya............	Col. Muammar al-Qadhafi, *Chairman of Revolutionary Cmd. Council*.....................	..	Sept. 1, 1969
Liechtenstein.......	Franz Josef II., *Prince*.....................	Aug. 16, 1906	Aug. 25, 1938
Luxemburg........	Jean, *Grand Duke*.........................	Jan. 5, 1921	Nov. 1964
Madagascar.......	Capt. de F. Didier Ratsiraka, *Head of State*...	..	June 15, 1975
Maldives.........	Amir Ibrahim Nasir, *President*..............	..	..
Mali.............	Lt. Moussa Traore, *Chairman, Nat. Lib. Cttee*...	1937	Nov. 20, 1968
Mauritania........	Moktar Ould Daddah, *President*.............	..	Nov. 28, 1958
Mexico...........	Luis Echeverria (Alvarez), *President*..........	..	Dec. 1, 1970
Monaco..........	Rainier, *Prince*...........................	May 31, 1923	May 9, 1949
Mongolia (Outer)..	Yu Tsedenbal, *President*....................	..	..
Morocco..........	Hassan II, *King*...........................	July 9, 1929	Feb. 26, 1961
Mozambique......	Samora Machel, *President*..................	1934	June 25, 1975
Nepal............	Birendra Bir Bikram Shah Deva, *King*.......	1945	Jan. 31, 1972

RULERS OF FOREIGN COUNTRIES—continued

Country	Ruler	Born	Acceded
Netherlands	Juliana, *Queen*	April 30, 1909	Sept. 4, 1948
Nicaragua	Gen. Anastasio Somoza Debayle, *President*	..	Dec. 1, 1974
Niger	Lt.-Col. Seynie Kountché, *Head of State*	..	April 15, 1974
Norway	Olav V., *King*	July 2, 1903	Sept. 21, 1957
Oman	Qaboos bin Said, *Sultan*	..	July 23, 1970
Pakistan	Fazal Elahi Chaudhry, *President*	1905	Aug. 10, 1973
Panama	Demetrio Lakas, *President, Govt. Junta*	..	1969
Paraguay	Gen. Alfredo Stroessner, *President*	..	Aug. 15, 1954
Peru	Gen. Francisco Morales Bermudez, *President*	..	Aug. 29, 1975
Philippine Islands	Ferdinand Marcos, *President*	1917	Dec. 30, 1965
Poland	Henryk Jablonski, *Chairman of Council of State*	1909	Mar. 28, 1972
Portugal	Gen. Francisco de Costa Gomes, *President*	..	Oct. 1974
Qatar	Khalifa bin Hamad Al-Thani, *Amir*	..	Oct. 24, 1960
Rumania	Nicolae Ceausescu, *President*	1918	Dec. 9, 1967
Rwanda	Grégoire Kayibanda, *President*	1925	July 1, 1972
El Salvador	Col. Arturo Armando Molina, *President*	..	July 1, 1972
Saudi Arabia	Amir Khalid bin Abdul Aziz, *King*	1912	Mar. 25, 1975
Senegal	Leopold Senghor, *President*	..	Sept. 5, 1960
Somalia	Maj.Gen. Mohamed Siad Barre (*President, Revolutionary Council*	..	Oct. 21, 1969
South Africa	Johannes Jacobus Fouché, *President*	1898	April 10, 1968
Spain	General Francisco Franco Bahamonde, *Regent*	Dec. 4, 1892	Aug. 9, 1939
Sudan	Maj. Gen. Gaafar Mohamed El Nimeri (*President*)	..	May 25, 1969
Sweden	Carl XVI Gustaf, *King*	April 30, 1946	Sept. 19, 1973
Switzerland	Pierre Graber, *President*	1908	Jan. 1, 1975
Syria	Lt. Gen. Hafez al Assad, *President*	1930	Mar. 14, 1971
Thailand	Bhumibol Adulyadej, *King*	Dec. 5, 1927	June 9, 1946
Togo	General Gnassingbé Eyadéma, *President*	1937	April 14, 1967
Tunisia	Habib Bourguiba, *President*	..	July 25, 1957
Turkey	Fahri Korutürk, *President*	1903	April 6, 1973
UnitedArabEmirates	Shaikh Zaid bin Sultan Al Nahayyan, *President*	..	
United States	Gerald R. Ford, *President*	July 14, 1913	Aug. 9, 1974
Upper Volta	Gen. Sangoulé Lamizana, *President*	..	Feb. 1971
Uruguay	Juan Maria Bordaberry, *President*	1928	Dec. 6, 1971
U.S.S.R.	Nikolai V. Podgorny, *President*	1903	Dec. 9, 1965
Vatican City State	Paul VI, *Pope*	Sept. 26, 1897	June 21, 1963
Venezuela	Carlos Andrés Pérez, *President*	1922	Mar. 12, 1974
Vietnam, North	Ton Duc Thang, *President*	1889	Sept. 24, 1969
Yemen A.R.	Col. Ibrahim Mohammed al Hamdi	..	June 13, 1974
Yemen P.D.R.	Salim Rubi'a Ali (*Chairman, Presidential Council*)	..	
Yugoslavia	Josip Broz Tito, *President*	May 25, 1892	Jan. 14, 1953
Zaire	Gen. Mobutu Sese Seko, *President*	Oct. 30, 1930	Nov. 25, 1965

PRESIDENTS OF THE FRENCH REPUBLIC

	Acceded
Committee of Public Defence	Sept. 4, 1870
Louis Adolphe Thiers	Aug. 31, 1871
Maréchal MacMahon	May 24, 1873
Jules Grévy	Jan. 30, 1879
Sadi Carnot (assas.: June 14, 1894)	Dec. 3, 1887
Jean Casimir Périer	June 27, 1894
François Felix Faure	Jan. 17, 1895
Emile Loubet	Feb. 18, 1899
Armand Fallières	Jan. 18, 1906
Raymond Poincaré	Jan. 17, 1913
Paul Deschanel	Feb. 18, 1920
Alexandre Millerand	Sept. 20, 1920
Gaston Doumergue	June 13, 1924
Paul Doumer (assas.: May 7, 1932)	June 13, 1931
Albert Lebrun (deposed 1940)	May 10, 1932
Maréchal Pétain, " Vichy " nominee	July 11, 1940

[After the liberation of Paris, General Charles de Gaulle entered the capital and formed a provisional government on Sept. 10, 1944. This was regarded as a continuation of the *Third Republic*.] Acceded

Charles de Gaulle, *born* 1890	Sept. 10, 1944
Félix Gouin	Jan. 23, 1946
Georges Bidault, *born* 1899	June 2, 1946

[A new Constitution (*Fourth Republic*), adopted on Oct. 13, 1946, and amended in 1954, was in force until 1958.] Acceded

Vincent Auriol, *born* 1884	Jan. 16, 1947
René Coty, *born* 1882	Jan. 17, 1954

[The *Fifth French Republic* came into being on Oct. 5, 1958, after the approval of its constitution by a national referendum in September, 1958.]

Charles de Gaulle, *born* 1890	Jan. 8, 1959
Georges Pompidou, *born* 1911	June 20, 1969
Valéry Giscard d'Estaing, *born* 1926	May 27, 1974

POPES FROM 1800

Sovereign Pontiff	Family Name	Elected	Sovereign Pontiff	Family Name	Elected
Pius VII	Chiaramonti	1800	Pius XI	Ratti	1922
Leo XII	della Genga	1823	Pius XII	Pacelli	1939
Pius VIII	Castiglioni	1829	John XXIII	Roncalli	1958
Gregory XV	Cappellari	1831	Paul VI	Montini	1963
Pius IX	Mastai-Ferretti	1846			
Leo XIII	Pecci	1878			
Pius X	Sarto	1903			
Benedict XV	della Chiesa	1914			

Adrian IV (Nicholas Breakspear, the only Englishman elected Pope) was born at Langley, near St. Albans; elected Pope, on the death of Anastasius IV, 1154; died 1159.

ENGLISH KINGS AND QUEENS A.D. 827 TO 1603

Name	DYNASTY	MARRIED	Access.	Died	Age	Rgnd. Yrs.
	Saxons and Danes					
EGBERT	King of Wessex and all England		827	839	—	12
ETHELWULF	Son of Egbert		839	858	—	19
ETHELBALD	Son of Ethelwulf		858	860	—	2
ETHELBERT	Son of Ethelwulf		858	866	—	8
ETHELRED	Son of Ethelwulf		866	871	—	5
ALFRED THE GREAT	Son of Ethelwulf	Ealhswith of Gaini.	871	899	52	28
EDWARD THE ELDER	Son of Alfred the Great	1, Egwyn; 2, Elfled; 3, Eadgifu.	899	925	55	26
ATHELSTAN	Eldest son of Edward the Elder (by 1)		925	940	45	15
EDMUND	Third son of Edward the Elder (by 3)	1, Elgifu; 2, Ethelfled.	940	946	25	6
EDRED	Fourth son of Edward the Elder (by 3)		946	955	32	9
EDWY	Son of Edmund (by 1)		955	959	18	3
EDGAR	Second son of Edmund (by 1)	1, Ethelfled; 2, Elfthryth.	959	975	32	17
EDWARD THE MARTYR	Son of Edgar (by 1)		975	978	17	4
ETHELRED II	Younger son of Edgar (by 2)	1, Elfgifu; 2, Emma, dau. of Richard, Duke of Normandy.	978	1016	48	37
EDMUND IRONSIDE	Eldest son of Ethelred II (by 1)		1016	1016	27	0
CANUTE THE DANE	By conquest and election	1, Elfgifu of Deira; 2, Emma, widow of Ethelred II	1017	1035	40	18
HAROLD I	Son of Canute (by 1)		1035	1040	—	5
HARDICANUTE	Son of Canute (by 2)		1040	1042	24	2
EDWARD THE CONFESSOR	Son of Ethelred II (by 2)	Edith, dau. of Earl Godwin.	1042	1066	62	24
HAROLD II	Son of Earl Godwin		1066	1066	44	0
	The House of Normandy					
WILLIAM I	Obtained the Crown by Conquest	Matilda, dau. of Baldwin, Count of Flanders.	1066	1087	60	21
WILLIAM II	Third son of William I	(Died unmarried)	1087	1100	43	13
HENRY I	Youngest son of William I	1st Matilda, dau. of Malcolm Canmore, K. of Scotland; 2nd Adelicia, dau. of Godfrey, D. of Louvaine.	1100	1135	67	35
STEPHEN	Third son of Stephen, Count of Blois, by Adela, fourth dau. of William I.	Matilda, dau. of Eustace, Count of Boulogne.	1135	1154	50	19
	The House of Plantagenet					
HENRY II	Son of Geoffrey Plantagenet by Matilda, only dau. of Henry I; his grandmother, Matilda of Scotland, was a lineal descendant of Alfred and Egbert.	Eleanor, dau. of of Guienne and divorced Queen of Louis VII of France.	1154	1189	56	35
RICHARD I	Eldest surviving son of Henry II.	Berengaria, dau. of Sancho VI, K. of Navarre.	1189	1199	42	10
JOHN	Sixth and youngest son of Henry II.	1st Avisa, dau. of E. of Gloucester, divorced upon grounds of consanguinity; 2nd Isabella dau. of Aymer, Count of Angoulême.	1199	1216	50	17
HENRY III	Elder son of John.	Eleanor, dau. of Raymond, Count of Provence.	1216	1272	65	56
EDWARD I	Eldest surviving son of Henry III.	1st Eleanor, dau. of Ferdinand III, K. of Castile; 2nd Margaret, dau. of Philip III, the Hardy, K. of France.	1272	1307	68	35
EDWARD II	Eldest surviving son of Edward I.	Isabella, dau. of Philip IV, the Fair, K. of France	1307	1327	43	20

Name	DYNASTY	MARRIED	Access.	Died	Age	R.gnd.
EDWARD III..........	Eldest son of Edward II..............	Philippa, dau. of William, Count of Holland and Hainault.	1327	1377	65	Yrs. 50
RICHARD II..........	Son of the Black Prince, eldest son of Edward III	1st Anne, dau. of Emp. Charles IV; 2nd Isabel, dau. of Charles VI of France.	1377	dep. 1399 (d. 1400)	34	22
	The House of Lancaster					
HENRY IV...........	Son of John of Gaunt, 4th son of Edward III	1st Mary de Bohun, dau. of the E. of Hereford; 2nd Joanna of Navarre, widow of John de Montford, D. of Bretagne.	1399	1413	47	13
HENRY V............	Eldest son of Henry IV................	Katherine, dau. of Charles VI, K. of France....	1413	1422	34	9
HENRY VI...........	Only son of Henry V (died 1471)........	Margaret of Anjou, dau. of René, D. of Anjou.	1422	dep. 1461	49	39
	The House of York					
EDWARD IV.........	Son of Richard, grandson of Edmund, fifth son of Edward III; and of Anne, great-grand-daughter of Lionel, third son of Edward III.	Elizabeth Widvile (or Woodville), dau. of Sir Richard Widvile and widow of Sir John Grey of Groby.	1461	1483	41	22
EDWARD V..........	Eldest son of Edward IV..............	(Died unmarried)...................	1483	1483	13	75 days
RICHARD III........	Younger brother of Edward IV........	Anne, dau. of the E. of Warwick, and widow of Edward, Prince of Wales, s. of Henry VI	1483	1485	32	2
	The House of Tudor					
HENRY VII..........	Son of Edmund, eldest son of Owen Tudor, by Katherine, widow of Henry V; his mother, Margaret Beaufort, was great-grand-daughter of John of Gaunt.	Elizabeth, dau. of Edward IV............	1485	1509	53	24
HENRY VIII.........	Only surviving son of Henry VII........	1st Catherine of Aragon, widow of his elder brother Arthur, (divorced); 2nd Anne, dau. of Sir Thomas Boleyn, (beheaded); 3rd Jane, dau. of Sir John Seymour, (died in childbirth of a son, aft. Edward VI); 4th Anne sister of William, D. of Cleves, (divorced); 5th Catharine Howard, niece of the Duke of Norfolk, (beheaded); 6th Catherine, dau. of Sir Thomas Parr and widow of Edward Nevill, Lord Latimer.	1509	1547	56	38
EDWARD VI.........	Son of Henry VIII by Jane Seymour.....	(Died unmarried).................	1547	1553	16	6
JANE..............	Grand-daughter of Mary, younger sister of Henry VIII, (beheaded Feb. 12, 1554).	Lord Guildford Dudley..............	1553	1554	17	14 days
MARY I............	Daughter of Henry VIII by Katherine of Aragon.	Philip II of Spain................	1553	1558	43	5
ELIZABETH I........	Daughter of Henry VIII by Anne Boleyn..	(Died unmarried).................	1558	1603	69	44

BRITISH KINGS AND QUEENS FROM 1603

Name	DYNASTY	MARRIED	Access.	Died	Age	Rgnd. Yrs.
	The House of Stuart					
JAMES I (VI OF SCOT.)	Son of Mary, Queen of Scots, granddaughter of James IV and Margaret, daughter of Henry VII.	Anne, dau. of Frederick II of Denmark	1603	1625	59	22
CHARLES I	Only surviving son of James I	Henrietta-Maria, dau. of Henry IV of France	1625	Beh.1649	48	24
	Commonwealth declared May 19, 1649					
	Richard Cromwell, Lord Protector, 1658–9					
	Oliver Cromwell, Lord Protector, 1653–8					
CHARLES II	Eldest son of Charles I, (restored 1660)	The Infanta Catharine of Portugal, dau. of John IV and sister of Alphonso VI.	1649	1685	55	36
JAMES II (VII OF SCOT.)	Second son of Charles I (Interregnum, Dec. 11, 1688–Feb. 13, 1689)	1st Lady Anne Hyde, dau. of Edaward, E. of Clarendon, who died before James ascended the throne; 2nd Mary Beatrice Eleanor d'Este, dau. of Alphonso, D. of Modena.	1685	Dep.1688 Dec.1701	68	3
WILLIAM III and	Son of William Prince of Orange and grandson of Charles I.		1689	1702	51	13
MARY II	Eldest daughter of James II.		1702	1694	33	6
ANNE	Second daughter of James II.	Prince George of Denmark.	1702	1714	49	12
	The House of Hanover					
GEORGE I	Son of Elector of Hanover, by Sophia, daughter of Elizabeth, daughter of James I	Sophia Dorothea, dau. of George William, D. of Celle.	1714	1727	67	13
GEORGE II	Only son of George I.	Wilhelmina Caroline, dau. of John Frederick, Margrave of Brandenburg-Anspach.	1727	1760	77	33
GEORGE III	Grandson of George II.	Charlotte Sophia, dau. of Charles Lewis Frederick, D. of Mecklenburg-Strelitz.	1760	1820	81	59
GEORGE IV	Eldest son of George III, (Regent from February 5, 1811)	Caroline Amelia Elizabeth, dau. of Charles William Ferdinand, D. of Brunswick-Wolfenbuttel, by Augusta, eldest sister of George III.	1820	1830	67	10
WILLIAM IV	Third son of George III.	Amelia Adelaide Louisa Theresa Caroline, dau. of George Frederick Charles, D. of Saxe-Meiningen.	1830	1837	71	7
VICTORIA	Daughter of Edward, 4th son of George III.	Francis Albert Augustus Charles Emmanuel, D. of Saxe, Pr. of Saxe-Cobourg and Gotha.	1837	1901	81	63
	The House of Saxe-Coburg					
EDWARD VII	Eldest son of Victoria.	Princess Alexandra of Denmark.	1901	1910	68	9
	The House of Windsor					
GEORGE V	Surviving son of Edward VII.	H.S.H. Princess Victoria Mary of Teck.	1910	1936	70	25
EDWARD VIII	Eldest son of George V (abdicated 1936).	(Mrs. Wallis Warfield, June 3, 1937.)	1936	1972	77	325 days
GEORGE VI	Second son of George V	The Lady Elizabeth Angela Marguerite, dau. of 14th Earl of Strathmore and Kinghorne (HER MAJESTY QUEEN ELIZABETH THE QUEEN MOTHER).	1936	1952	56	15
ELIZABETH II	Elder daughter of George VI.	Philip, son of Prince Andrew of Greece (H.R.H. THE DUKE OF EDINBURGH).	1952	WHOM GOD PRESERVE.		

SCOTTISH KINGS AND QUEENS A.D. 1057 TO 1603

SOVEREIGN		MARRIED	Access.	Died
MALCOLM III (CANMORE)	Son of Duncan I	1st Ingibiorg, widow of Thorfinn, Earl of Orkney; 2nd Margaret, sister of Edgar the Atheling.	1057	1093
DONALD BAN	Brother of Malcolm Canmore		1093	—
DUNCAN II	Son of Malcolm Canmore, by first marriage		1094	1094
DONALD BAN	(Restored)		1094	1097
EDGAR	Son of Malcolm Canmore, by second marriage	Died unmarried	1097	1107
ALEXANDER I	Son of Malcolm Canmore	Sybilla, natural daughter of Henry I of England	1107	1124
DAVID I	Son of Malcolm Canmore	Matilda, daughter of Waltheof, Earl of Northumbria, widow of Simon, Earl of Northampton.	1124	1153
MALCOLM IV (THE MAIDEN)	Son of Henry, eldest son of David I	Died unmarried	1153	1165
WILLIAM I (THE LION)	Brother of Malcolm the Maiden	Ermengarde, daughter of Richard, Viscount of Beaumont.	1165	1214
ALEXANDER II	Son of William the Lion	1st Joanna, daughter of King John; 2nd Mary, daughter of Ingelram de Coucy (*Picardy*).	1214	1249
ALEXANDER III	Son of Alexander II, by second marriage	1st Margaret, daughter of Henry III of England; 2nd Joleta, daughter of the Count de Dreux.	1249	1286
MARGARET, MAID OF NORWAY	Daughter of Eric II of Norway, grand-daughter of Alexander III.	Died unmarried	1286	1290
JOHN BALIOL	Grandson of eldest daughter of David, Earl of Huntingdon, brother of William the Lion.		1292	1296
ROBERT I (BRUCE)	Great-grandson of 2nd daughter of David, Earl of Huntingdon, brother of William the Lion.	1st Isabella, daughter of Donald, Earl of Mar; 2nd Elizabeth de Burgh, sister of Earl of Ulster.	1306	1329
DAVID II	Son of Robert I, by second marriage	1st Joanna, daughter of Edward II of England; 2nd Margaret, widow of Sir John Logie (divorced, 1369).	1329	1371
ROBERT II (STEWART)	Son of Marjorie, daughter of Robert I by first marriage, and Walter the Steward.	1st Elizabeth, dau., of Sir Robert Mure (or More) of Rowallan; 2nd Euphemia, dau., of Hugh, Earl of Ross, widow of John, Earl of Moray.	1371	1390
ROBERT III	(John, Earl of Carrick) son of Robert II.	Annabella, daughter of Sir John Drummond of Stobhall, niece of Margaret Logie.	1390	1406
JAMES I	Son of Robert III	Jane Beaufort, daughter of John, Earl of Somerset, 4th son of John of Gaunt and grandson of Edward III of England.	1406	1437
JAMES II	Son of James I	Mary, daughter of Arnold, Duke of Gueldres.	1437	1460
JAMES III	Eldest son of James II	Margaret, daughter of Christian I of Denmark, Norway and Sweden.	1460	1488
JAMES IV	Eldest son of James III	Margaret Tudor, daughter of Henry VII.	1488	1513
JAMES V	Son of James IV	1st Madeleine, daughter of Francis I of France; 2nd Mary of Lorraine, daughter of Duc de Guise, widow of Duc de Longueville.	1513	1542
MARY	Daughter of James V, by second marriage	1st Francis, Dauphin of France; 2nd Henry, Lord Darnley; 3rd James, Earl of Bothwell.	1542	1587
JAMES VI (Ascended the Throne of England 1603)	Son of Mary, by second marriage	Anne, daughter of Frederick II of Denmark.	1567	1625

WELSH SOVEREIGNS AND PRINCES

WALES was ruled by Sovereign Princes from the " earliest times " until the death of Llywelyn in 1282. The first English Prince of Wales was the son of Edward I, and was born in Caernarvon town on April 25, 1284. According to a discredited legend, he was presented to the Welsh chieftains as their Prince, in fulfilment of a promise that they should have a Prince who " could not speak a word of English " and should be native born. This son, who afterwards became Edward II, was created " Prince of Wales and Earl of Chester " at the famous Lincoln Parliament on February 7, 1301. The title Prince of Wales is borne after individual conferment and is not inherited at birth; it was conferred on Prince Charles by Her Majesty the Queen on July 26, 1958. He was invested at Caernarvon on July 1, 1969.

INDEPENDENT PRINCES, A.D. 844 to 1282	
Rhodri the Great...................	844–878
Anarawd, son of Rhodri.............	878–916
Hywel Dda, the Good...............	916–950
Iago ab Idwal (or Ieuaf)..............	950–979
Hywel ab Ieuaf, the Bad.............	979–985
Cadwallon, his brother..............	985–986
Maredudd ab Owain ap Hywel Dda....	986–999
Cynan ap Hywel ab Ieuaf............	999–1008
Llewelyn ap Sitsyhlt................	1018–1023
Iago ab Idwal ap Meurig............	1023–1039
Gruffydd ap Llywelyn ap Seisyll......	1039–1063
Bleddyn ap Cynfyn..................	1063–1075
Trahaern ap Caradog................	1075–1081
Gruffydd ap Cynan ab Iago..........	1081–1137
Owain Gwynedd...................	1137–1170
Dafydd ab Owain Gwynedd.........	1170–1194
Llwelyn Fawr, the Great............	1194–1240
Dafydd ap Llywelyn................	1240–1246
Llywelyn ap Gruffyddap Llywelyn....	1246–1282

ENGLISH PRINCES, SINCE A.D. 1301	
Edward, b. 1284 (Edwd. II), cr. Pr. of Wales..	1301
Edward the Black Prince, s. of Edward III....	1343
Richard (Richard II), s. of the Black Prince...	1377
Henry of Monmouth (Henry V)............	1399
Edward of Westminster, son of Henry VI....	1454
Edward of Westminster (Edward V)........	1472
Edward, son of Richard III (d. 1484).........	1483
Arthur Tudor, son of Henry VII............	1489
Henry Tudor (Hen. VIII), s. of Henry VII.....	1503
Henry Stuart, son of James I (d. 1612)........	1610
Charles Stuart (Charles I), s. of James I.......	1616
Charles (Charles II), son of Charles I........	1630
James Francis Edward, " The Old Pretender " (d. 1766)........................	1688
George Augustus (Geo. II), s. of George I.....	1714
Frederick Lewis, s. of George II (d. 1751).....	1727
George William Frederick (George III)......	1751
George Augustus Frederick (George IV).....	1762
Albert Edward (Edward VII)..............	1841
George (George V)......................	1901
Edward (Edward VIII)....................	1910
Charles Philip Arthur George.............	1958

THE FAMILY OF QUEEN VICTORIA

QUEEN VICTORIA *was born* May 24, 1819; *succeeded* to the Throne June 20, 1837; *married* Feb. 10, 1840 Albert, PRINCE CONSORT (*born* Aug. 26, 1819, *died* Dec. 14, 1861); *died* Jan. 22, 1901. Her Majesty had issue:—

1. H.R.H. Princess Victoria (*Princess Royal*), born Nov. 21, 1840, married, 1858, Frederick, German Emperor; died Aug. 5, 1901, leaving issue:—

(1) H.I.M. William II., *German Emperor* 1888–1918, born Jan. 27, 1859, died June 4, 1941, having married Princess Augusta Victoria of Schleswig-Holstein-Sonderburg-Augustenburg (born 1858, died 1921), and secondly, Princess Hermine of Reuss (born 1887, died 1947). The late German Emperor's family:—

(a) The late Prince William (*Crown Prince* 1888–1918), born May 6, 1882, married Duchess Cecilia of Mecklenburg-Schwerin (who died May 6, 1954; died July 20, 1951. (The Crown Prince's children:—Prince Wilhelm, born July 4, 1906, died 1940; Prince Louis Ferdinand, born Nov. 9, 1907, married (1938) Grand Duchess Kira (died Sept. 8, 1967), daughter of Grand Duke Cyril of Russia (and has issue four sons and two daughters); Prince Hubertus, born Sept. 30 1909, died April 8, 1950; Prince Frederick George, born Dec. 19, 1911, died April 1966; Princess Alexandrine Irene, born April 7, 1915; Princess Cecilia, born Sept. 5, 1917.)

(b) The late Prince Eitel Frederick, born July 7, 1883, married Duchess Sophie of Oldenburg (marriage dissolved 1926); died Dec. 7, 1942.

(c) The late Prince Adalbert (born July 14, 1884, died Sept. 22, 1948), married Duchess Adelaide of Saxe-Meiningen. (Prince Adalbert's children:—Princess Victoria Marina, born Sept. 11, 1917; Prince William Victor, born Feb. 15, 1919.)

(d) The late Prince Augustus William, born Jan. 29, 1887, married Princess Alexandra of Schleswig-Glucksburg (marriage dissolved 1920); died March, 1949. (Prince Augustus's son is Prince Alexander, born Dec. 26, 1912.)

(e) The late Prince Oscar, born July 27, 1888, married Countess von Ruppin, died Jan. 27, 1958. (Prince Oscar's children:—Prince Oscar, born July 12, 1915, died 1939; Prince Burchard, born Jan. 8, 1917; Princess Herzeleida, born Dec. 25, 1918; Prince William, born Jan. 30, 1922.)

(f) The late Prince Joachim, born Dec. 17, 1890, married Princess Marie of Anhalt, died July 17, 1920 (leaving issue).

(g) Princess Victoria, born Sept. 13, 1892, married (1913) the then reigning Duke of Brunswick. (Princess Victoria's children:—Prince Ernest, born March 18, 1914, married Princess Ortrud von Glucksburg, 1951; Prince George, born March 25, 1915; Princess Frederica, born April 18, 1917, married Paul I., King of the Hellenes (*see* p. 215); Prince Christian Oskar, born Sept 1, 1919; Prince Welf Heinrich, born March 11, 1923, married Princess Alexandra of Ysemburg, 1960).

(2) The late Princess Charlotte, born July 24, 1860, married (1878) the late Duke of Saxe-Meiningen, died Oct. 1, 1919. (Princess Charlotte's daughter, Princess Feodora, born May 12, 1879, married (1898) the late Prince Henry XXX. of Reuss, died Aug. 26, 1945.)

(3) The late Prince Henry, born Aug. 14, 1862, married (1888) the late Princess Irene of Hesse, died April 20, 1929 (issue, Prince Waldemar, born March 20, 1889, died May 2, 1945; Prince Sigismund, born Nov. 27, 1896).

(4) The late Princess Victoria, born April 12, 1866, married firstly (1890) Prince Adolphus of Schaumburg-Lippe, secondly (1927) Alexander Zubkov, died Nov. 13, 1929.

(5) The late Princess Sophia, born June 14, 1870,

married (1889) the late Constantine, *King of the Hellenes*, died Jan. 13, 1932 leaving issue:—

(*a*) The late George II., *King of the Hellenes* 1922–24 and 1935–47, born July 7, 1890, married Princess Elisabeth of Roumania (marriage dissolved 1935); died April 1, 1947.

(*b*) The late Alexander, *King of the Hellenes* 1917–1920, born Aug. 1, 1893, married (1919) Aspasia Manos; died Oct. 25, 1920, leaving issue Princess Alexandra (born 1921) who married, March 20, 1944, King Petar II. of Yugoslavia.

(*c*) Princess Helena, born May 2, 1896, married (1921) late King Carol of Roumania, (marriage dissolved 1928), having issue, King Michael, G.C.V.O., born Oct. 25, 1921, married (1948) Princess Anne of Bourbon Parma, and has issue, Princess Marguerite, born March 26, 1949, Princess Helene, born Nov. 15, 1950, and Princess Irina, born Feb. 28, 1953.

(*d*) The late Paul (*Paul I., King of the Hellenes*), born Dec. 4, 1901, *acceded* April 1, 1947, married Jan. 9, 1938, Princess Frederica of Brunswick (*see p. 214*); and died Mar. 6, 1964, leaving issue Constantine (*Constantine XIII.*), born June 2, 1940, married, Sept. 18, 1964, H.R.H. Princess Anne-Marie of Denmark, and has issue; Sophia, born Nov. 2, 1938, married (1962) Don Juan Carlos, Prince of Spain, and has issue; and Irene, born May 11, 1942.

(*e*) Princess Eirene, born Feb. 13, 1904, married (1939) the Duke of Aosta, and has issue.

(*f*) Princess Catherine, born May 4, 1913, married (1947) Major R. C. A. Brandram and has issue.

(6) The late Princess Margarete, born April 22 1872, married (1839) the late Prince Frederick Charles of Hesse, died Jan. 21, 1954 (issue the late Prince Frederick William, born 1893, died 1916; the late Prince Maximilian, born 1894, died 1914; Prince Philipp, born 1896, married (1925) Princess Mafalda, daughter of King Victor Emmanuel III. of Italy (and has issue, Prince Maurice, born 1926, and Prince Henry, born 1927); Prince Wolfgang, born 1896; Prince Richard, born May 14, 1901).

2. H.M. KING EDWARD VII. (*see p. 216*).

3. H.R.H. Princess Alice, born April 25, 1843, married Prince Louis (afterwards reigning Grand Duke) of Hesse; died Dec. 14, 1878. Issue:—

(i) Victoria Alberta, born April 5, 1863, married Admiral of the Fleet the late Marquess of Milford Haven, died Sept. 24, 1950, leaving issue:—

(*a*) Alice (*H.R.H. Princess Andrew of Greece*), born Feb. 25, 1885, married Prince Andrew of Greece; died Dec. 5, 1969, leaving issue (*see p. 217*).

(*b*) Lady Louise Mountbatten (*Queen of Sweden*), born July 13, 1889; married Nov. 3, 1923, H.R.H. The Crown Prince of Sweden, now King Gustaf VI. Adolf (died Sept. 15, 1973); died March 7, 1965.

(*c*) George, Marquess of Milford Haven, G.C.V.O., born Nov. 6, 1892, Capt. R.N., married (1916) Countess Nadejda (died Jan. 22, 1963), daughter of late Grand Duke Michael of Russia; died April 8, 1938, leaving issue:—Lady Elizabeth, born 1917; David Michael, Marquess of Milford Haven, O.B.E., D.S.C., Lieutenant, R.N. ret.), born 1919, died April 14, 1970, leaving issue, George Ivar Louis, *Marquess of Milford Haven*, *b.* 1961; Lord Ivar Mountbatten, *b.* 1963.

(*d*) Louis, Admiral of the Fleet Earl Mountbatten of Burma, K.G., P.C., G.C.B., O.M., G.C.S.I., G.C.I.E., G.C.V.O., D.S.O., born June 25, 1900, Personal A.D.C. to the Queen, Governor of the Isle of Wight; married July 18, 1922, Edwina Cynthia Annette (died Feb. 20, 1960), daughter of Lord Mount Temple, and has issue two daughters, the lady Patricia (Lady Brabourne), born 1924 and the Lady Pamela Hicks, born 1929.

(ii) Elizabeth Fedorovna (*Grand Duchess Serius of Russia*), born Nov. 1, 1864; died July 1918.

(iii) Irene (*Princess Henry of Prussia*), born July 11, 1866, married the late Prince Henry of Prussia, and died Nov. 11, 1953 (*see p. 214*).

(iv) Ernest Ludwig, Grand Duke of Hesse, born Nov. 25, 1868, died Oct. 9, 1937, having married (1905) Princess Eleonore of Solms-Hohensolmslich, with issue (*a*) George, Grand Duke of Hesse, born Nov. 8, 1906, married Princess Cecilie of Greece and Denmark (*see p. 217*); *accidentally killed* (with mother, wife and two sons) Nov. 16, 1937; (*b*) Ludwig, Grand Duke of Hesse, born Nov. 20, 1908, married (Nov. 17, 1937) Margaret, daughter of 1st Lord Geddes; died May 30, 1968.

(v) Alix (*Tsaritsa of Russia*), born June 6, 1872, married (Nov. 25, 1894) the late Nicholas II. (*Tsar of All the Russias*), assassinated July 16, 1918, with the Tsar and their issue (Grand Duchess Olga; Grand Duchess Tatiana; Grand Duchess Marie; Grand Duchess Anastasia, and the Tsarevitch).

(vi) Mary, born May 24, 1874, died Nov. 15, 1878.

4. Admiral of the Fleet H.R.H. Prince Alfred, *Duke of Edinburgh*, born Aug. 6, 1844, married Jan. 2, 1874, Marie Alexandrovna (died Oct. 25, 1920), only daughter of Alexander II., Emperor of Russia; succeeded as *Duke of Saxe-Coburg and Gotha* Aug. 22, 1893; died July 30, 1900, leaving issue:—

(1) Alfred (*Prince of Saxe-Coburg*), born Oct. 15, 1874, died Feb. 6, 1899.

(2) Marie (*Queen of Roumania*), born Oct. 29, 1875, married (1893) the late King Ferdinand of Roumania; died July 18, 1938, having issue:—

(*a*) King Carol II. of Roumania, K.G., born Oct. 15, 1893, married (1921) Princess Helena of Greece (*see col. 1*), died April 4, 1953.

(*b*) Elisabeth (*Queen of the Hellenes*), born Oct. 11, 1894, married (1921) the late King George II of the Hellenes, died Nov. 15, 1956.

(*c*) Marie, born Jan. 8, 1900, married (1922) the late King Alexander of Yugoslavia, died June 22, 1961 (having issue:—Petar, King of Yugoslavia, born Sept. 6, 1923, married (1944) Princess Alexandra of Greece, died Nov. 5, 1970, leaving issue, Prince Alexander, born July 17, 1945; Prince Tomislav, born Jan. 19, 1928, married (1957) Princess Margarita of Baden (*see p. 217*) and has issue, Prince Nicholas, born 1958; Prince Andrej, born 1929, married 1956, Princess Christina of Hesse).

(*d*) H.R.H. Prince Nicolas, born Aug. 7, 1903.

(*e*) H.R.H. Princess Ileana, born Jan. 5, 1909; married 1st, Archduke Anton of Austria (having issue:—Stephen, born Aug. 15, 1932): 2nd, Dr. Stefan Issarescu.

(*f*) Prince Mircea, born Jan. 3, 1913, died 1916.

(3) Victoria, born Nov. 25, 1876, married (1894) Grand Duke of Hesse and (1905) the late Grand Duke Cyril of Russia; died March 2. 1936, having issue:—

(*a*) Marie, born Feb. 2, 1907, married (1925) Prince Friedrich Carl of Leiningen, died Oct. 27, 1951.

(*b*) Kira Cyrillovna, born May 22, 1909, married (1938) Prince Ludwig of Germany, died Sept. 8, 1967.

(*c*) Vladimir Cyrillovitch, born Aug. 17, 1917, married (1948) Princess Leonide Bagration-Moukhransky, and has issue, a daughter.

(4) Alexandra, born Sept. 1, 1878, married (1896) the late Prince of Hohenlohe Langenburg: died April 16, 1942, leaving issue:—

(*a*) Gottfried, born March 24, 1897, died May 11, 1960.

(*b*) Maria (*Princess Friedrich of Holstein-Glucksburg*), born Jan. 18, 1899; died Nov. 8, 1967.

(c) Princess Alexandra, born April 2, 1901; died Oct. 26, 1963.

(d) Princess Irma, born July 4, 1902.

(5) Princess Beatrice, born April 20, 1884, married 1909) Infante Alfonso Maria of Orleans, died July 13, 1966, leaving issue.

5. H.R.H. Princess Helena Augusta Victoria, born May 25, 1846, married July 5, 1866, General H.R.H. *Prince Christian of Schleswig-Holstein* (died Oct. 28, 1917); died June 9, 1923. Issue:—

(i) H.H. Prince Christian Victor, born April 14, 1867, died Oct. 29, 1900.

(ii) H.H. Prince Albert, born Feb. 26, 1869, died April 27, 1931.

(iii) H.H. Princess Helena Victoria, born May 3, 1870; died March 13, 1948.

(iv) H.H. Princess Marie Louise, born Aug. 12, 1872; died Dec. 8, 1956.

(v) H.H. Prince Harold, born May 12, died May 20, 1876.

6. H.R.H. Princess Louise, born March 18, 1848, married March 21, 1871, the Marquess of Lorne, afterwards the 9th Duke of Argyll K.G.; died Dec. 3, 1939, without issue.

7. Field Marshal H.R.H. Prince Arthur, *Duke of Connaught*, born May 1, 1850, married March 13, 1879, H.R.H. Princess Louisa of Prussia (died March 14, 1917); died Jan. 16, 1942. Issue:—

(i) H.R.H. Princess Margaret, born Jan. 15, 1882, married H.R.H. the Crown Prince of Sweden, now KING GUSTAF VI. ADOLF, K.G., G.C.B., G.C.V.O., died May 1, 1920, leaving issue:—

(a) Duke of Westerbotten, born April 22, 1906, married (1932) Princess Sybil of Saxe-Coburg-Gotha (who died Nov. 28 1972), died Jan. 26, 1947, leaving issue one son, now the Crown Prince of Sweden, and 4 daughters.

(b) Duke of Upland (Count Sigvard Bernadotte), born June 7, 1907.

(c) Princess Ingrid (*Queen Mother of Denmark*), born March 28, 1910, married (1935) the late King Frederick IX of Denmark, who died Jan. 14, 1972 and has issue 3 daughters.

(d) Duke of Halland, born Feb. 28, 1912.

(e) Duke of Dalecarlia, born Oct. 31, 1916.

(ii) Major-Gen. H.R.H. Prince Arthur, born

Jan. 13, 1883; married Oct. 15, 1913, H.H. the Duchess of Fife; died Sept. 12, 1938, leaving issue (see below).

(iii) H.R.H. Princess Patricia (*Lady Patricia Ramsay*) born March 17, 1886, married Feb. 27, 1919, Adm. Hon Sir Alexander Ramsay (who died Oct. 8, 1972), died Jan. 12, 1974, leaving issue Alexander Arthur Alfonso David, born Dec. 21, 1919.

8. H.R.H. Prince Leopold, *Duke of Albany*, born April 7, 1853, married Princess Helena of Waldeck (died Sept. 1, 1922); died March 28, 1884. Issue:—

(i) H.R.H. Princess Alice (*Countess of Athlone*), V.A., G.C.V.O., G.B.E., Commandant in Chief Women's Transport Service. Chancellor of the University of the West Indies, born Feb. 25, 1883, married Feb. 10, 1904, Maj.-Gen. the Earl of Athlone (who died Jan. 16, 1957), having issue—

(a) Lady May Helen Emma, born Jan. 23, 1906 married (1931) Sir Henry Abel-Smith, K.C.M.G., K.C.V.O., D.S.O., and has issue a son and 2 daughters.

(b) The late *Viscount Trematon*, born 1907, died April 15, 1928.

(ii) Charles Edward, *Duke of Saxe-Coburg-Gotha* (1900–1918), born July 19, 1884, married (1905) Princess Victoria of Schleswig-Holstein, died March 6, 1954, leaving surviving issue 2 sons and 2 daughters.

9. H.R.H. Princess Beatrice, born April 14, 1857, married July 23, 1885, H.R.H. Prince Henry of Battenberg (born Oct. 5, 1858, died Jan. 20, 1896); died Oct. 26, 1944, leaving issue:—

(i) Alexander, *Marquess of Carisbrooke*, born Nov. 23, 1886, married Lady Irene Denison (died July 15, 1956); died Feb. 23, 1960, leaving issue a daughter, Lady Iris Mountbatten, born Jan. 13, 1920.

(ii) Victoria Eugénie, V.A., born Oct. 24, 1887, married May 31, 1906. His late Majesty Alfonso XIII. (*King of Spain* 1886–1931; born 1886, died 1941), died April 15, 1969, leaving issue.

(iii) Major Lord Leopold Mountbatten, G.C.V.O., born May 21, 1889; died April 23, 1922.

(iv) Maurice, born Oct. 3, 1891; died of wounds received in action, Oct. 27, 1914.

THE FAMILY OF KING EDWARD VII

KING EDWARD VII., eldest son of Queen Victoria, *born* Nov. 9, 1841; *married* March 10, 1863, Her Royal Highness Princess Alexandra, eldest daughter of King Christian IX. of Denmark; *succeeded* to the Throne Jan. 22, 1901; *died* May 6, 1910. Issue:—

1. H.R.H. PRINCE ALBERT VICTOR, *Duke of Clarence and Avondale and Earl of Athlone*, born Jan. 8, 1864, died Jan. 14, 1892.

2. H.M. KING GEORGE V. (*see p. 217*). Assumed by Royal Proclamation (June 17, 1917 for his House and Family as well as for all descendants in the male line of Queen Victoria who are subjects of these Realms, the name of WINDSOR; died Jan. 20, 1936, having had issue (*see p. 217*).

3. H.R.H. LOUISE, *Princess Royal*, born Feb. 20, 1867; married July 27, 1889, 1st Duke of Fife (who died Jan. 29, 1912); died Jan. 4, 1931. Issue:—

(i) H.H. Princess Alexandra, Duchess of Fife (*H.R.H. Princess Arthur of Connaught*), born May 17, 1891; married Oct. 15, 1913, H.R.H. the late Prince Arthur; died Feb. 26, 1959. Issue:—

Alastair Arthur, Duke of Connaught, born Aug. 9, 1914; died April 26, 1943.

(ii) H.H. Princess Maud, born April 3, 1893;

married Nov. 12, 1923, 11th Earl of Southesk; died Dec. 14, 1945, leaving issue:—

The Duke of Fife, born Sept. 23, 1929; married (1956) Hon. Caroline Dewar (marriage dissolved, 1966) and has issue.

4. H.R.H. Princess VICTORIA, born July 6, 1868; died Dec. 3, 1935.

5. H.R.H. Princess MAUD, born Nov. 26, 1869; married July 22, 1896, Haakon VII., King of Norway, who died Sept. 21, 1957; died Nov. 20, 1938. Issue:—

H.M. Olav V., K.G., K.T., G.C.B., G.C.V.O., KING OF NORWAY, born July 2, 1903, *married* March 21, 1929, H.R.H. Princess Marthe of Sweden (who died April 5, 1954). Issue:—

(a) H.R.H. Princess Ragnhild, born June 9, 1930.

(b) H.R.H. Princess Astrid, born Feb. 12, 1932.

(c) H.R.H. Harald, Crown Prince of Norway, G.C.V.O., born Feb. 21, 1937.

THE FAMILY OF PRINCE ANDREW OF GREECE

Prince Andrew of Greece, *born* Feb. 2, 1882; *married* Princess Alice of Battenberg (*H.R.H. Princess Andrew of Greece*), who *died* Dec. 5, 1969 (*see p. 215*); *died* Dec. 2, 1944, having had issue:—

(1) Princess Margarita, *born* April 17, 1905, *married* Prince Gottfried of Hohenlohe-Langenburg (*see* p. 215), and has issue, Prince Kraft, *born* 1935, Princess Beatrix, *born* 1936, Prince George, *born* 1938, Prince Ruprecht and Prince Albrecht, *born* 1944

(2) Princess Theodora, *born* May 30, 1906, *married* Prince Berthold of Baden (who *died* Oct. 27, 1963), *died* Oct. 16, 1969, leaving issue, Princess Margarita, *born* 1932 (married, 1957, Prince Tomislav of Yugoslavia (see p. 215)), Prince Max, *born* 1933, Prince Louis, *born* 1937.

(3) Princess Cecilie, *born* June 22, 1911, *married* George, Grand Duke of Hesse, accidentally killed with husband and two sons, Nov. 16, 1937 (*see* p. 215).

(4) Princess Sophie, *born* June 26, 1914, *married* (i) Prince Christopher of Hesse (who died, 1944, leaving issue, Princess Christina, *born* 1933, Princess Dorothea, *born* 1934, Prince Charles, *born* 1937, Prince Rainer, *born* 1939, Princess Clarissa, born 1944); *married* (ii) Prince George of Hanover, and has further issue.

(5) Prince Philip (*H.R.H. the Prince Philip, Duke of Edinburgh*), *born* June 10, 1921 (*see* p. 218).

THE FAMILY OF KING GEORGE V

KING GEORGE V., second son of King Edward VII., *born* June 3, 1865; *married* July 6, 1893. Her Serene Highness Princess Victoria Mary Augusta Louise Olga Pauline Claudine Agnes (Queen Mary), *succeeded* to the throne May 6, 1910; *died* Jan. 20, 1936. Queen Mary died March 24, 1953. Issue:—

H.R.H. THE DUKE OF WINDSOR (EDWARD Albert Christian George Andrew Patrick David), K.G., K.T., K.P., G.C.B., G.C.S.I., G.C.M.G., G.C.I.E., G.C.V.O., G.B.E., I.S.O., M.C., F.R.S., Royal Victorian Chain, Admiral of the Fleet, Field Marshal, Marshal of the Royal Air Force, *born* June 23, 1894, *succeeded* to the Throne as KING EDWARD VIII., Jan. 20 1936; *abdicated* Dec. 11, 1936; *married* June 3, 1937, Mrs. Wallis Warfield (The Duchess of Windsor), *died* May 28, 1972.

H.M. KING GEORGE VI. (Albert Frederick Arthur George) *born* at York Cottage, Sandringham, Dec. 14, 1895; *married* April 26, 1923, to Lady Elizabeth Angela Marguerite (HER MAJESTY QUEEN ELIZABETH THE QUEEN MOTHER), daughter of the 14th Earl of Strathmore and Kinghorne, *succeeded* to the throne Dec. 11, 1936; *crowned* in Westminster Abbey, May 12, 1937; *died* Feb. 6, 1952, having had issue (*see* p. 218).

H.R.H. THE PRINCESS ROYAL (Victoria Alexandra Alice MARY), *born* April 25, 1897, *married* Feb. 28, 1922, the 6th Earl of Harewood (*born* Sept. 9, 1882; *died* May 24, 1947), died at Harewood House, Yorks., March 28, 1965, leaving ssue:—

   (1) George Henry Hubert Lascelles, *7th Earl of Harewood*, born Feb. 7, 1923; married, firstly, Sept. 29, 1949, Maria Donata (Marion), daughter of the late Erwin Stein (marriage dissolved 1967) (she married, March 14, 1973, Rt. Hon. Jeremy Thorpe), and has issue, David Henry George, *Viscount Lascelles*, *born* Oct. 21, 1950; James Edward, *born* Oct. 5, 1953, married, April 4, 1973, Fredericka Duhrrson; Robert Jeremy Hugh, born Feb. 14, 1955; secondly, July 31, 1967, Mrs. Patricia Elizabeth Tuckwell, and has issue, Mark Hubert, *born* July 5, 1964.

   (2) Gerald David Lascelles, *born* Aug. 21, 1924, *married* July 15, 1952, Miss Angela Dowding and has issue, Henry Ulick, *born* May 19, 1953.

H.R.H. THE DUKE OF GLOUCESTER (HENRY WILLIAM FREDERICK Albert), Duke of Gloucester, Earl of Ulster and Baron Culloden, *born* March 31, 1900, *married* Nov. 6, 1935, Lady Alice Montagu-Douglas-Scott, daughter of the 7th Duke of Buccleuch (H.R.H. Princess Alice, Duchess of Gloucester, C.I, G.C.V.O., G.B.E., Grand Cordon of Al Kamal, Colonel-in-Chief the Royal Hussars (Prince of Wales's Own), the King's Own Scottish Borderers, Deputy Colonel-in-Chief, Royal Anglian Regt., Air Chief Commandant W.R.A.F., *born* Dec. 25, 1901); *died* June 10, 1974. Issue; H.R.H. Prince William Henry Andrew Frederick, *born* Dec. 18, 1941; *accidentally killed* Aug. 28, 1972; H.R.H. Prince RICHARD Alexander Walter George, *Duke of Gloucester*, G.C.B., G.C.V.O., Colonel-in-Chief, Gloucestershire Regiment, Grand Prior of the Order of St. John of Jerusalem *born* Aug. 26, 1944, *married* July 8, 1972, Brigitte von Deurs and has issue, Alexander Patrick George Richard, Earl of Ulster, *born* Oct. 24, 1974.

H.R.H. THE DUKE OF KENT (George Edward Alexander Edmund), Duke of Kent, Earl of St. Andrews and Baron Downpatrick, *born* Dec. 20, 1902, *married* Nov. 29, 1934, H.R.H. Princess Marina of Greece and Denmark (*born* Nov. 30, O.S., 1906; *died* Aug. 27, 1968). *Killed on Active Service*, Aug. 25, 1942 leaving issue:—

   (1) H.R.H. Prince EDWARD George Nicholas Paul Patrick, *Duke of Kent*, G.C.M.G., G.C.V.O., *born* Oct. 9, 1935, Major The Royal Scots Greys, Personal A.D.C. to the Queen, Colonel, Scots Guards, Colonel-in-Chief, Royal Regiment of Fusiliers, *married* June 8, 1961, Katharine Lucy Mary, Controller Commandant, Women's Royal Army Corps, Hon. Major-General, Colonel-in-Chief Army Catering Corps, daughter of Sir William Worsley, Bt., and has issue, George Philip Nicholas, Earl of St. Andrews, *born* June 26, 1962; Helen Marina Lucy (Lady Helen Windsor), *born* April 28, 1964; Nicholas Charles Edward Jonathan (Lord Nicholas Windsor), *born* July 25, 1970. *Residences*—Anmer Hall, Norfolk; York House, St. James's Palace, S.W.1.

   (2) H.R.H. Princess ALEXANDRA Helen Elizabeth Olga Christabel, G.C.V.O., *born* Dec. 25, 1936, Colonel-in-Chief, 17th/21st Lancers, Deputy Colonel-in-Chief, The Light Infantry, Hon. Colonel North Irish Horse, Air Chief Commandant, Princess Mary's Royal Air Force Nursing Service, *married* April 24, 1963, Hon. Angus Ogilvy, son of the 12th Earl of Airlie, *born* Sept. 14, 1928. and his issue, James Robert Bruce, *born* Feb. 29, 1964 and Marina Victoria Alexandra, *born* July 31, 1966. *Residence of Princess Alexandra*—Kensington Palace, W.8.

   (3) H.R.H. Prince MICHAEL George Charles Franklin, *born* July 4, 1942, Captain, Royal Hussars.

H.R.H. PRINCE JOHN, *born* July 12, 1905; *died* Jan. 18, 1919.

The House of Windsor

Her Most Excellent Majesty ELIZABETH THE SECOND (Elizabeth Alexandra Mary of Windsor) by the Grace of God, of the United Kingdom of Great Britain and Northern Ireland and of Her other Realms and Territories Queen, Head of the Commonwealth, Defender of the Faith, Sovereign of the British Orders of Knighthood and Sovereign Head of the Order of St. John, Lord High Admiral of the United Kingdom, Colonel-in-Chief of The Life Guards, The Blues and Royals (Royal Horse Guards and 1st Dragoons), The Royal Scots Dragoon Guards (Carabiniers and Greys), 16th/5th The Queen's Royal Lancers, Royal Tank Regiment, Corps of Royal Engineers, Grenadier Guards, Coldstream Guards, Scots Guards, Irish Guards, Welsh Guards, The Royal Welch Fusiliers, The Queen's Lancashire Regiment, The Argyll and Sutherland Highlanders (Princess Louise's), The Royal Green Jackets, Royal Army Ordnance Corps, The Queen's Own Mercian Yeomanry, The Duke of Lancaster's Own Yeomanry, The Corps of Royal Canadian Engineers, The King's Own Calgary Regiment, Royal 22e Regiment, Governor-General's Foot Guards, The Canadian Grenadier Guards, Le Régiment de la Chaudière, Royal New Brunswick Regt., The 48th Highlanders of Canada, The Argyll and Sutherland Highlanders of Canada (Princess Louise's), The Royal Canadian Ordnance Corps, Royal Australian Engineers, Royal Australian Infantry Corps, Royal Australian Army Ordnance Corps, Royal Australian Army Nursing Corps, Royal New Zealand Engineers, Royal New Zealand Infantry Regiment, Malawi Rifles, Captain-General of the Royal Regiment of Artillery, The Honourable Artillery Comapny, Combined Cadet Force, Royal Canadian Artillery, Royal Regiment of Australian Artillery, Royal New Zealand Artillery, Royal New Zealand Armoured Corps, Air-Commodore-in-Chief, R. Aux.A.F., R.A.F. Regiment, Royal Observer Corps, Royal Canadian Air Force Auxiliary, Australian Citizen Air Force, Commandant-in-Chief, Royal Air Force College, Cranwell, Hon. Commissioner, Royal Canadian Mounted Police, Master of the Merchant Navy and Fishing Fleets, Head of the Civil Defence Corps, Head of the National Hospital Service Reserve.

Elder daughter of His late Majesty King George VI and of Her Majesty Queen Elizabeth the Queen Mother; *born* at 17 Bruton Street, London, W.1. April 21, 1926, *succeeded* to the throne February 6, 1952, *crowned* June 2, 1953; having *married*, November 20, 1947, in Westminster Abbey Philip, Duke of Edinburgh, Earl of Merioneth and Baron Greenwich (H.R.H. The Prince Philip, Duke of Edinburgh), K.G., P.C., K.T., O.M., G.B.E., Admiral of the Fleet, Field Marshal, Marshal of the Royal Air Force, Admiral of the Fleet, Royal Australian Navy, Field Marshal, Australian Military Forces, Marshal of the Royal Australian Air Force, Admiral of the Fleet, Royal New Zealand Navy, Captain General, Royal Marines, Colonel-in-Chief, The Queen's Royal Irish Hussars, The Duke of Edinburgh's Royal Regiment (Berkshire and Wiltshire), Queen's Own Highlanders (Seaforth and Camerons), Corps of Royal Electrical and Mechanical Engineers, Army Cadet Force, The Royal Canadian Regiment, The Seaforth Highlanders of Canada, The Cameron Highlanders of Ottawa, The Queen's Own Cameron Highlanders. Canada, The Royal Royal Canadian Army Cadets, The Royal Australian Electrical and Mechanical Engineers, The Australian Cadet Corps, Corps of Royal New Zealand Electrical and Mechanical Engineers, Colonel of Grenadier Guards, Hon. Colonel, Edinburgh and Heriot-Watt Universities Officers' Training Corps, The Trinidad and Tobago Regiment, Admiral, Sea Cadet Corps, Royal Canadian Sea Cadets, Air Commodore-in-Chief Air Training Corps, Royal Canadian Air Cadets, Master of the Corporation of Trinity House, Ranger of Windsor Park. *See* p. 217.

CHILDREN OF HER MAJESTY

H.R.H. THE PRINCE OF WALES (CHARLES Philip Arthur George), Prince of Wales and Earl of Chester, Duke of Cornwall and Duke of Rothesay, Earl of Carrick and Baron Renfrew Lord of the Isles and Great Steward of Scotland, K.G., Personal A.D.C. to the Queen, Great Master of the Order of the Bath, Lieutenant Royal Navy, Colonel-inChief The Royal Regiment of Wales (24th/41st Foot), Colonel Welsh Guards, Flight Lieutenant Royal Air Force, *born* November 14, 1948.

H.R.H. PRINCESS ANNE ELIZABETH ALICE LOUISE, G.C.V.O. Chief Commandant Women's Royal Naval Service, Colonel-in-Chief 14th/20th King's Hussars, The Worcestershire and Sherwood Foresters' Regiment, 8th Canadian Hussars (Princess Louise's), Commandant-in-Chief, Ambulance and Nursing Cadets, *born* August 15, 1950, *married* Nov. 14, 1973, Capt. Mark Anthony Peter Phillips, C.V.O., Queen's Dragoon Guards, Personal A.D.C. to the Queen.

H.R.H. PRINCE ANDREW ALBERT CHRISTIAN EDWARD, *born* Feb. 19, 1960.

H.R.H. PRINCE EDWARD ANTONY RICHARD LOUIS, *born* March 10, 1964.

MOTHER OF HER MAJESTY

H.M. QUEEN ELIZABETH THE QUEEN MOTHER (Elizabeth Angela Marguerite) (daughter of the 14th Earl of Strathmore and Kinghorne), Lady of the Garter, Lady of the Thistle, Order of the Crown of India, Grand Master of the Royal Victorian Order, Dame Grand Cross of the Order of the British Empire, Royal Victorian Chain, Doctor of Civil Law, Doctor of Literature, Colonel-in-Chief 1st the Queen's Dragoon Guards, The Queen's Own Hussars, 9th/12th Royal Lancers (Prince of Wales's), The King's Regiment, The Royal Anglian Regiment, The Light infantry, The Black Watch (Royal Highland Regiment), Royal Army Medical Corps, The Black Watch (Royal Highland Regiment) of Canada, The Toronto Scottish Regiment, The Royal Canadian Army Medical Corps, Royal Australian Army Medical Corps, Hon. Colonel The Royal Yeomanry, The London Scottish, University of London Officers' Training Corps, Commandant-in-Chiet R.A.F. Central Flying School, W.R.N.S., W.R.A.C., W.R.A.F., Air Chief Commandant, Women's Royal Australian Air Force, Patron St. Andrew's Ambulance Association, Commandant-in-Chief Nursing Corps and Divisions. *Born* August 4, 1900, *married* April 26, 1923, Prince Albert Frederick Arthur George of Windsor, Duke of York (*see* King GEORGE VI). *Residences.*—Clarence House, St. James's, S.W.1.; Castle of Mey, Caithness, Scotland.

SISTER OF HER MAJESTY

H.R.H. PRINCESS MARGARET ROSE (The Princess Margaret, Countess of Snowdon), C.I., G.C.V.O., Colonel-in-Chief, 15ht/19th the King's Royal Fusiliers (Princess Margaret's Own Glasgow and Ayrshire Regiment), Queen Alexandra's Royal Army Nursing Corps, Women's Royal Australian Army Corps, The Highland Fusiliers of Canada (Militia), The Princess Louise Fusiliers, Deputy

Colonel-in-Chief, The Royal Anglian Regiment, Commandant-in-Chief, St. John Ambulance Brigade Cadets, Grand President, St. John Ambulance Association and Brigade, Dame Grand Cross of the Order of St. John of Jerusalem, President of the Girl Guides Association; *born* Aug. 21, 1930; *married* May 6, 1960 Anthony Charles Robert Armstrong-Jones, G.C.V.O. (*born* March 7, 1930), son of the late Ronald Armstrong Jones, Q.C. and the Countess of Rosse, *created* Earl of Snowdon, 1961, Constable of Caernarvon Castle; and has issue, David Albert Charles, Viscount Linley, *born* Nov. 3, 1961; Sarah Frances Elizabeth (Lady Sarah Armstrong-Jones), *born* May 1, 1964.

Residence.—Kensington Palace, W.8.

ORDER OF SUCCESSION TO THE THRONE

The Queen's sons and daughter are in the order of succession to the throne, and after the Princess Margaret and her son and daughter, the Duke of Gloucester and his son; then the Duke of Kent, his sons and daughter, his brother and sister and her son and daughter, then the Earl of Harewood and his sons and the Hon. Gerald Lascelles and his son; then the Duke of Fife, son of the late Countess of Southesk, and his son and daughter; then King Olav of Norway and his children and granddaughter, the the children and grandchildren of the second daughter of the late Duke of Saxe-Coburg (his eldest daughter, the late Queen Marie of Roumania, having formally renounced on her marriage all possibility of claim to the the British Throne); then the children of the third daughter (the late Princess Alexandra of Hohenlohe-Langenburg); then the children of the eldest son of the late Princess Margaret of Connaught (Crown Princess of Sweden), her other sons and her daughter (Queen Ingrid of Denmark) and her children; then the son of the younger daughter of the first Duke of Connaught and Strathearn (Lady Patricia Ramsay); then the Princess Alice (Countess of Athlone) and her daughter and grandchildren.

Precedence in England

The Sovereign
The Prince Philip, Duke of Edinburgh.
The Prince of Wales, The Prince Andrew, The Prince Edward.
Archbishop of Canterbury.
Lord High Chancellor.
Archbishop of York.
The Prime Minister.
Lord President of the Council.
Speaker of the House of Commons.
Lord Privy Seal.
High Commissioners of Commonwealth Countries and Ambassadors of Foreign States.
Dukes, according to their Patents of Creation:
(1) Of England; (2) of Scotland; (3) of Great Britain; (4) of Ireland; (5) those created since the Union.
Ministers and Envoys.
Eldest sons of Dukes of Blood Royal.
Marquesses, in same order as Dukes.
Dukes' eldest Sons.
Earls, in same order as Dukes.
Younger sons of Dukes of Blood Royal.
Marquesses' eldest Sons.
Dukes' younger Sons.
Viscounts, in same order as Dukes.
Earls' eldest Sons.
Marquesses' younger Sons.
Bishops of London, Durham and Winchester.
All other English Bishops, according to their seniority of Consecration.
Secretaries of State, if of the degree of a Baron.
Barons, in same order as Dukes.
Treasurer of H.M.'s Household.
Comptroller of H.M.'s Household.
Vice-Chamberlain of H.M.'s Household.
Secretaries of State under the degree of Baron.

Viscounts' eldest Sons.
Earls' younger Sons.
Barons' eldest Sons.
Knights of the Garter if Commoners.
Privy Councillors if of no higher rank.
Chancellor of the Exchequer.
Chancellor of the Duchy of Lancaster.
Lord Chief Justice of England.
Master of the Rolls.
President of the Probate Court.
The Lords Justices of Appeal.
Judges of the High Court.
Vice-Chancellor of County Palatine of Lancaster.
Viscounts' younger Sons.
Barons' younger Sons.
Sons of Life Peers.
Baronets of either Kingdom, according to date of Patents.
Knights of the Thistle if Commoners.
Knights Grand Cross of the Bath.
Members of the Order of Merit.
Knights Grand Commanders of the Star of India.
Knights Grand Cross of St. Michael and St. George.
Knights Grand Commanders of the Indian Empire.
Knights Grand Cross of the Royal Victorian Order.
Knights Grand Cross of Order of the British Empire.
Companions of Honour.
Knights Commanders of the above Orders.
Knights Bachelor.
Official Referees of The Supreme Court.
Judges of County Courts and judges of the Mayor's and City of London Court.
Companions and Commanders *e.g.* C.B.; C.S.I.; C.M.G.; C.I.E.; C.V.O.; C.B.E.; D.S.O.; M.V.O. (4th); O.B.E.; I.S.O.
Eldest Sons of younger Sons of Peers.
Baronets' eldest Sons.

Eldest Sons of Knights in the same order as their Fathers.
M.V.O. (5th); M.B.E.
Younger Sons of the younger Sons of Peers.
Baronets' younger Sons.
Younger Sons of Knights in the same order as their Fathers.
Naval, Military, Air, and other Esquires by Office.

WOMEN

Women take the same rank as their husbands or as their eldest brothers; but the daughter of a Peer marrying a Commoner retains her title as Lady or Honourable. Daughters of Peers rank next immediately after the wives of their elder brothers, and before their younger brothers' wives. Daughters of Peers marrying Peers of lower degree take the same order of precedence as that of their husbands; thus the daughter of a Duke marrying a Baron becomes of the rank of Baroness only while her sisters married to commoners retain their rank and take precedence of the Baroness. Merely official rank on the husband's part does not give any similar precedence to the wife. For Dames Grand Cross, *see* pp. 300–301.

LOCAL PRECEDENCE

ENGLAND AND WALES.—No written code of county or city order of precedence has been promulgated, but in Counties the Lord Lieutenant stands first, and secondly (normally) the Sheriff, and therefore in Cities and Boroughs the Lord Lieutenant has social precedence over the Mayor; but at City or Borough functions the Lord Mayor or Mayor will preside. At Oxford and Cambridge the High Sheriff takes precedence of the Vice-Chancellor.

SCOTLAND.—*See* Index.

The Queen's Household

Lord Chamberlain, The Lord Maclean, P.C., K.T., G.C.V.O., K.B.E.
Lord Steward, The Duke of Northumberland, K.G., P.C., T.D., F.R.S.
Master of the Horse, The Duke of Beaufort, K.G., P.C., G.C.V.O.
Treasurer of the Household, W. Harrison, M.P.
Comptroller of the Household, J. Harper, M.P.
Vice-Chamberlain, J. Hamilton, M.P.
Administrative Adviser, Sir Basil Smallpeice, K.C.V.O.

Gold Sticks, Field-Marshal Sir Gerald Templer, K.G., G.C.B., G.C.M.G., K.B.E., D.S.O.; Admiral of the Fleet the Earl Mountbatten of Burma, K.G., P.C., G.C.B., O.M., G.C.S.I., G.C.I.E., G.C.V.O., D.S.O., A.D.C.
Vice-Admiral of the United Kingdom, Admiral Sir Deric Holland-Martin, G.C.B., D.S.O., D.S.C.
Rear-Admiral of the United Kingdom, Admiral Sir Nigel Henderson, G.B.E., K.C.B.
First and Principal Naval Aide-de-Camp, Admiral Sir Edward Ashmore, G.C.B., D.S.C.
Aides-de-Camp General, General Sir Peter Hunt, G.C.B., D.S.O., O.B.E.; General Sir Cecil Blacker, G.C.B., O.B.E., M.C.; General Sir William Jackson, G.B.E., K.C.B., M.C.; General Sir Harry Tuzo, G.C.B., O.B.E., M.C.
Air Aides-de-Camp, Air Chief Marshal Sir Lewis Hodges, K.C.B., C.B.E., D.S.O., D.F.C.; Air Chief Marshal Sir Andrew Humphrey, G.C.B., O.B.E., D.F.C., A.F.C.

Mistress of the Robes, The Duchess of Grafton, D.C.V.O.
Ladies of the Bedchamber, The Marchioness of Abergavenny, C.V.O.; The Countess of Airlie.
Women of the Bedchamber, Hon. Mary Morrison, C.V.O.; Mrs. John Dugdale, C.V.O.; Lady Susan Hussey, C.V.O.; Lady Abel Smith, C.V.O.
Extra Women of the Bedchamber, Hon. Mrs. Andrew Elphinstone, C.V.O.; Lady Rose Baring, D.C.V.O.

THE PRIVATE SECRETARY'S OFFICE
Buckingham Palace, S.W.1.
Private Secretary to the Queen, Lt.-Col. Rt. Hon. Sir Martin Charteris, K.C.B., K.C.V.O., O.B.E.
Deputy Private Secretary, P. B. C. Moore, C.B., C.M.G.
Assistant Private Secretary, W. F. P. Heseltine, C.V.O.
Defence Services Secretary, Air Vice-Marshal B. Stanbridge, C.B.E., M.V.O., A.F.C.
Press Secretary, R. Allison.
Assistant Press Secretaries, Mr. Michael Wall; R. E. Moore (*temp.*).
Chief Clerk, Miss Jean Taylor, M.V.O.
Secretary to the Private Secretary, A. C. Neal, M.V.O., B.E.M.
Clerks, Miss J. F. Munro, M.V.O.; Miss O. M. Short, M.V.O.; Miss A. M. Downes, M.V.O. (*Press*); Miss F. M. Simpson, M.V.O. (*Press*); Miss S. Reid; Miss C. Bailey; Miss M. Viney (*Press*); Miss D. Moore; Miss P. Keenan; Miss R. Macmillan; Miss J. Adams.

The Queen's Archives
Norman Tower, Windsor Castle.
Keeper of the Queen's Archives, Lt.-Col. Rt. Hon. Sir Martin Charteris, K.C.B., K.C.V.O., O.B.E.
Assistant Keeper, Sir Robert Mackworth-Young, K.C.V.O., F.S.A.
Registrar, Miss Jane Langton, M.V.O.
Assistant Registrars, Miss E. Cuthbert; Miss F. Dimond.
Historical Adviser, Sir John Wheeler-Bennett, G.C.V.O., C.M.G., O.B.E., F.B.A.

DEPARTMENT OF THE KEEPER OF THE PRIVY PURSE AND TREASURER TO THE QUEEN
Buckingham Palace, S.W.1.
Keeper of the Privy Purse and Treasurer to the Queen, Major Sir Rennie Maudslay, K.C.V.O., M.B.E.

Privy Purse Office
Assistant Keeper of the Privy Purse, Major S. G. B. Blewitt.
Chief Accountant, Edmund F. Grove, C.V.O.
Chief Clerk, D. Waters, M.V.O.
Accountant, M. Mortimore.
Clerks, Mrs. E. de Jong; Mrs. C. Kelly.

Land Agent, Sandringham, Julian Loyd, M.V.O.
Resident Factor, Balmoral, Col. W. G. McHardy, M.V.O., M.B.E., M.C.

Farm Manager, Royal Farms, Windsor, R. Reeks.
Consulting Engineers, J. Fraser (*Balmoral*); Sir Ralph Freeman, C.V.O., C.B.E. (*Sandringham*).

Treasurer's Office
Deputy Treasurer to the Queen, R. D. Wood, M.V.O., V.R.D.
Chief Accountant and Paymaster, Charles Warner. C.V.O.
Accountant, F. R. Mintram.
Establishment Officer, Peter Wright, M.V.O.

Royal Almonry
High Almoner, The Rt. Rev. the Lord Bishop of Rochester.
Hereditary Grand Almoner, The Marquess of Exeter, K.C.M.G.
Sub-Almoner, Rev. Canon J. S. D. Mansel, M.V.O., M.A., F.S.A.
Secretary, Peter Wright, M.V.O.

THE LORD CHAMBERLAIN'S OFFICE
St. James's Palace, S.W.1.
Comptroller, Lt.-Col. Sir Eric Penn, K.C.V.O., O.B.E., M.C.
Assistant Comptroller, Lt.-Col. J. F. D. Johnston, M.V.O., M.C.
Secretary, R. J. Hill, C.V.O., M.B.E.
Assistant Secretary, D. V. G. Buchanan, M.V.O.
Registrar, J. E. P. Titman, M.V.O.
State Invitation Assistant, P. D. Hartley.
Ceremonial Assistant, M. E. Bishop.
Clerks, I. D. Campbell; Mrs. G. Cousland, M.V.O.; Miss M. Greiner, M.V.O.; Miss J. Hoos; Miss S. Hay; Miss Z. McNeile; Miss V. Maynard; Miss E. Quartley-Mallett; Miss S. Wilson; Mrs. A. Wolfe.

Permanent Lords in Waiting, Brigadier The Lord Tryon, G.C.V.O., K.C.B., D.S.O.; The Lord Cobbold, K.G., G.C.V.O.
Lords in Waiting, The Earl of Westmorland, K.C.V.O.; The Lord Hamilton of Dalzell, M.C.; The Lord Jacques; The Lord Wells-Pestell; The Lord Winterbottom; The Lord Melchett; The Lord Lovell-Davis.
Gentlemen Ushers, H. L. Carron Greig, C.V.O.; Capt. Michael Nelville Tufnell, D.S.C., R.N.; Air Marshal Sir Maurice Heath, K.B.E., C.B.; Lt.-Cmdr. John Arundell Holdsworth, O.B.E., R.N.; Col. William Henry Gerard Leigh, M.V.O.; Vice-Admiral Sir Ronald Brockman, K.C.B., C.S.I., C.I.E., C.B.E.; Air Commodore the Hon. Peter Beckford Rutgers

Vanneck, C.B., O.B.E., A.F.C.; Lt.-Col. Sir Julian Tolver Paget, Bt.; Maj.-Gen. Sir James Bowes-Lyon, K.C.V.O., C.B., O.B.E., M.C.

Extra Gentlemen Ushers, Capt. Andrew Yates, M.V.O., R.N.; Major Thomas Harvey, C.V.O., D.S.O.; Brig. Charles Richard Britten, O.B.E., M.C.; Air Vice-Marshal Sir Ranald Reid, K.C.B., D.S.O., M.C.; Esmond Butler, C.V.O.; Sir Austin Strutt, K.C.V.O., C.B.; Capt. Philip Lloyd Neville, C.V.O., R.N.; Col. John Sidney North FitzGerald, C.V.O., M.B.E., M.C.; Maj.-Gen. Sir Cyril Harry Colquhoun, K.C.V.O., C.B., O.B.E.; Lt.-Col. Sir John Mandeville Hugo, K.C.V.O., O.B.E.; Sir John Mitchell Harvey Wilson, Bt., K.C.V.O.; Air Commodore John Wilkins Hubble, C.B.E., D.S.O., A.F.C.; General Sir Rodney Moore, G.C.V.O., K.C.B., C.B.E., D.S.O.

Gentleman Usher to the Sword of State, Admiral Sir Desmond Dreyer, G.C.B., C.B.E., D.S.C.

Gentleman Usher of the Black Rod, Admiral Sir Frank Twiss, K.C.B., D.S.C.

Serjeants at Arms, R. J. Hill, C.V.O., M.B.E.; C. G. R. Warner, C.V.O.

Constable & Governor of Windsor Castle, Marshal of the Royal Air Force the Lord Elworthy, G.C.B., C.B.E., D.S.O., M.V.O., D.F.C., A.F.C.

Keeper of the Jewel House, Tower of London, Maj.-Gen. W. D. M. Raeburn, C.B., D.S.O., M.B.E.

Adviser for the Queen's Pictures and Drawings, Professor Sir Anthony Frederick Blunt, K.C.V.O., F.S.A.

Surveyor of the Queen's Pictures, Sir Oliver Nicholas Millar, K.C.V.O., F.S.A., F.B.A.

Librarian, Sir Robert Mackworth-Young, K.C.V.O., F.S.A.

Librarian Emeritus, Sir Owen Morshead, G.C.V.O., K.C.B., D.S.O., M.C.

Curator of the Print Room, The Hon. Jane Low.

Adviser for the Queen's Works of Art, Sir Francis Watson, K.C.V.O., F.S.A.

Surveyor of the Queen's Works of Art, Geoffrey de Bellaigue, M.V.O., F.S.A.

Master of the Queen's Music (vacant).

Poet Laureate, Sir John Betjeman, C.B.E.

Bargemaster, H. A. Barry, M.V.O.

Keeper of the Swans, F. J. Turk.

Caretaker of St. James's Palace, H. C. Philips, M.B.E.

ASCOT OFFICE
St. James's Palace, S.W.1.

Her Majesty's Representative at Ascot, The Marquess of Abergavenny, K.G., O.B.E.

Secretary, Miss A. Ainscough, M.V.O.

ECCLESIASTICAL HOUSEHOLD
The College of Chaplains.

Clerk of the Closet, The Rt. Rev. R. P. Wilson, K.C.V.O., D.D.

Deputy Clerk of the Closet, Rev. Canon J. S. D. Mansel, M.V.O., M.A., F.S.A.

Chaplains to the Queen, Canon P. L. Gillingham, M.V.O., M.A.; Ven. J. F. Richardson, M.A.; Rev. H. D. Anderson, M.V.O., B.D.; Ven. E. J. G. Ward, M.V.O., M.A.; Canon D. H. Booth, M.B.E., M.A.; Rev. J. R. W. Stott, M.A.; Preb. S. A. Williams, M.A.; Canon H. C. Blackburne, M.A.; Rev. C. E. M. Roderick, M.A.; Canon C. H. G. Hopkins, M.A.; Canon W. Garlick, M.A., B.Sc.; Canon J. P. Pelloe, M.A.; Ven. B. Stratton, M.A.; Ven. L. W. Harland, M.B.E., M.A.; Rev. J. G. Downward, M.A.; Canon E. Saxon, B.A., B.D.; Canon R. S. O. Stevens, B.Sc., M.A.; Rev. P. T. Ashton, M.V.O., M.A.; Rev. A. H. H. Harbottle, M.A.; Canon G. H. G. Hewitt, M.A.; Canon E. M. Pilkington, M.A.; Canon G. R. Sansbury, M.A.; Ven. H. Johnson, M.A.; Ven. J. R. Youens, C.B., O.B.E., M.C.; Preb. D. M. Lynch, C.B.E., M.A.; Rev.

R. L. Roberts, C.V.O., M.A.; Canon L. L. Rees; Canon D. M. Paton, M.A.; Canon C. E. Young; Preb. D. W. C. Ford, B.D., M.Th.; Rev. E. Hughes, M.Th., Ph.D.; Rev. E. E. Staples, O.B.E.; Ven. R. B. Bradford, B.A.; Ven. F. N. Towndrow, M.A.; Rev. T. Barfett, M.A.

Extra Chaplains, Rev. M. F. Foxell, K.C.V.O., M.A.; Ven. A. S. Bean, M.B.E., M.A., D.D.; Rev. E. S. Abbott, K.C.V.O., M.A., D.D.

Chapels Royal

Dean of the Chapels Royal, The Bishop of London.

Sub-Dean of Chapels Royal, Rev. Canon J. S. D. Mansel, M.V.O., M.A., F.S.A.

Priests in Ordinary, Prof. the Rev. Canon G. R. Dunstan, M.A., D.D., F.S.A.; Rev. C. J. A. Hickling, M.A.; Rev. S. R. Cutt, M.A.

Organist, Choirmaster and Composer, T. R. W. Farrell, F.R.C.O., A.R.C.M.

Domestic Chaplain—Buckingham Palace, Rev. Canon J. S. D. Mansel, M.V.O., M.A., F.S.A.

Domestic Chaplain—Windsor Castle, The Dean of Windsor.

Domestic Chaplain—Sandringham, Rev. A. Glendining.

Chaplain—Royal Chapel, Windsor Great Park, Rev. A. H. H. Harbottle, M.A.

Chaplain—Hampton Court Palace, Rev. F. V. A. Boyse, M.A.

Chaplain—Tower of London, Rev. J. F. M. Llewellyn, M.A.

Organist and Choirmaster—Hampton Court Palace, Gordon Reynolds, A.R.C.M.

MEDICAL HOUSEHOLD

Physician, Head of the Medical Household, R. J. S. Bayliss, M.D., F.R.C.P.

Physicians, Miss M. G. Blackie, M.D.; J. C. Batten, M.D., F.R.C.P.

Physician-Paediatrician, P. R. Evans, C.B.E., M.Sc., M.D., Ch.B., F.R.C.P.

Serjeant Surgeon, H. E. Lockhart-Mummery, M.D., M.Chir., F.R.C.S., L.R.C.P.

Surgeon Oculist, S. J. H. Miller, M.D., F.R.C.S.

Surgeon Gynaecologist, G. D. Pinker, F.R.C.S.(Ed.), F.R.C.O.G.

Surgeon Dentist, N. A. Surridge, L.D.S., B.D.S., D.D.S.

Physician to the Household, A. M. Dawson, M.D., F.R.C.P.

Surgeon to the Household, J. L. Dawson, M.S., F.R.C.S.

Surgeon Oculist to the Household, P. J. Holmes-Sellors, B.M., B.Ch., F.R.C.S.

Apothecary to the Queen and to the Household, N. R. Southward, M.B., B.Chir., M.R.C.P.

Apothecary to the Household at Windsor, J. P. Clayton, M.V.O., M.B., B.Chir., M.R.C.S., L.R.C.P.

Apothecary to the Household at Sandringham, H. K. Ford, M.B., B.S., D.Obst., R.C.O.G., M.R.C.G.P.

Coroner of the Queen's Household, A. G. Davies, M.B., B.S., M.R.C.S., L.R.C.P.

Marshal of the Diplomatic Corps, Maj.-Gen. Hon. Sir Michael Fitzalan Howard, K.C.V.O., C.B., C.B.E., M.C.

Vice-Marshal, J. N. O. Curle, C.M.G., C.V.O.

CENTRAL CHANCERY
OF THE ORDERS OF KNIGHTHOOD
St. James's Palace, S.W.1

Secretary, Maj.-Gen. P. B. Gillett, C.B., C.V.O., O.B.E.

Chief Clerk, G. A. Harris, M.V.O., M.B.E.

Clerks, M. G. P. Kelly; J. McGurk; Miss A. A. Hamersley, M.V.O.; Mrs. E. Rogers, M.V.O.; Mrs. A. M. Hughes, M.V.O.; Mrs. H. Hill; Miss H. Speed.

The Honorable Corps of Gentlemen at Arms
St. James's Palace, S.W.1.

Captain, The Baroness Llewelyn-Davies of Hastoe, P.C.; *Lieutenant*, Col. K. E. Savill, D.S.O.; *Standard Bearer*, Col. H. N. Clowes, D.S.O., O.B.E.; *Clerk of the Cheque & Adjutant*, Lt.-Col. P. J. Clifton, D.S.O.; *Harbinger*, Lt.-Col., J. Chandos-Pole, O.B.E.

Gentlemen of the Corps

Brigadiers, Hon. R. G. Hamilton-Russell, D.S.O.; J. E. Swetenham, D.S.O.

Colonels, S. Enderby, D.S.O., M.C.; C. J. Kidston-Montgomerie, D.S.O., M.C.; P. F. I. Reid, O.B.E.; R. J. V. Crichton, M.C.; P. Pardoe; A. G. Way, M.C.

Lieutenant-Colonels, R. S. G. Perry, D.S.O.; Hon. M. G. Edwards, M.B.E.; Sir William Lowther, Bt., O.B.E.; H. A. Hope, O.B.E., M.C.; T. C. Sinclair, O.B.E., M.C.; N. H. R. Speke, M.C.; C. E. J. Eagles, R.M.; D. A. St. G. Laurie, O.B.E., M.C.; P. Hodgson; R. Steele, M.B.E.; W. S. P. Lithgow.

Majors, D. S. Allhusen; The Marquess of Donegall; Sir Richard Carne Rasch, Bt.; D. A. Jamieson, V.C.; J. D. Dillon, D.S.C., R.M.; The Lord Suffield, M.C.; T. St. Aubyn; J. E. Joicey, M.C.

The Queen's Bodyguard of the Yeoman of the Guard
St. James's Palace, S.W.1.

Captain, The Lord Strabolgi; *Lieutenant*, Lt.-Col. J. D. Hornung, O.B.E., M.C.; *Clerk of the Cheque and Adjutant*, Col. H. T. Brassey, O.B.E., M.C.; *Ensign*, Col. A. B. Pemberton, M.B.E.; *Exons.*, Capt. Sir Charles McGrigor, Bt.; Major B. M. H. Shand, M.C.

MASTER OF THE HOUSEHOLD'S DEPARTMENT
Board of Green Cloth.
Buckingham Palace, S.W.1.

Master of the Household, Vice-Admiral Sir Peter Ashmore, K.C.B., M.V.O., D.S.C.

Deputy Master of the Household (vacant).

Chief Clerk, G. H. Franklin, M.V.O.

Deputy Chief Clerk, A. Hancock.

Assistants to the Master of the Household, M. D. Tims, M.V.O.; R. Winship.

Senior Clerk, J. S. Cowdery.

Clerks, Miss A. Tyer; Miss S. Derry; Miss M. Bull; Miss J. Heard.

Superintendent, Windsor Castle, Major W. Nash M.B.E.

Palace Steward, J. Walton.

Chief Housekeeper, Miss V. Martin.

ROYAL MEWS DEPARTMENT
Buckingham Palace, S.W.1.

Crown Equerry, Lt.-Col. Sir John Mansel Miller, K.C.V.O., D.S.O., M.C.

Equerries, Major G. R. S. Broke; Capt. C. P. T. Fletcher (*temp.*).

Extra Equerries, Vice-Admiral Sir Conolly Abel-Smith, G.C.V.O., C.B.; Lt.-Col. the Lord Adeane, P.C., G.C.B., G.C.V.O.; Vice-Adm. Sir Peter Ashmore, K.C.B., M.V.O., D.S.C.; Cdr. Colin Buist, C.V.O., R.N.; Rear-Adm. the Earl Cairns, G.C.V.O., C.B.; Lt.-Col. Rt. Hon. Sir Martin Michael Charles Charteris, K.C.B., K.C.V.O., O.B.E.; Cdr. Sir Dudley Colles, K.C.B., K.C.V.O., O.B.E., R.N.; Vice-Adm. Sir Peter Dawnay, K.C.V.O., C.B., D.S.C.; Major Sir Geoffrey Eastwood, K.C.V.O.; C.B.E.; Air Vice-Marshal Sir Edward Fielden, G.C.V.O., C.B., D.F.C., A.F.C.; Sir Edward William

Spencer Ford, K.C.B., K.C.V.O.; Brigadier Walter Douglas Campbell Greenacre, C.B., D.S.O., M.V.O.; Brig. Sir Geoffrey Paul Hardy-Roberts, K.C.V.O., C.B., C.B.E.; Lt.-Col. John Frederick Dame Johnston, M.V.O., M.C.; Rt. Hon. Sir Alan Lascelles, G.C.B., G.C.V.O., C.M.G., M.C.; Major the Earl of Leicester, M.V.O.; Major Sir Rennie Maudslay, K.C.V.O., M.B.E.; Major Sir Mark Vane Milbank, Bt., K.C.V.O., M.C.; Air Commodore Dennis Mitchell, C.V.O., D.F.C., A.F.C.; Rear-Adm. Sir Patrick John Morgan, K.C.V.O., C.B., D.S.C.; Lt.-Col. Rirld Myddleton, M.V.O.; Lt.-Col. Sir Eric Charles William Mackenzie Penn, K.C.V.O., O.B.E., M.C.; Cdr. Sir Philip John Row, K.C.V.O., O.B.E., R.N.; Brig. Walter Morley Sale, C.V.O., O.B.E.; Maj.-Gen. Sir Arthur Guy Salisbury-Jones, G.C.V.O., C.M.G., C.B.E., M.C.; Group Capt. Peter Wooldridge Townsend, C.V.O., D.S.O., D.F.C.; Air Commodore Archie Little Winskill, C.V.O., C.B.E., D.F.C. (*Captain of the Queen's Flight*); Rear-Admiral R. J. Trowbridge.

Veterinary Surgeon, Peter Scott Dunn, M.R.C.V.S.

Supt. Royal Mews, Buckingham Palace, Major W. Phelps, M.B.E.

Comptroller of Stores, J. W. McNelly, M.V.O.

Chief Clerk, M. Carlisle.

HER MAJESTY'S HOUSEHOLD IN SCOTLAND

Hereditary Lord High Constable, The Countess of Erroll.

Hereditary Master of the Household, The Duke of Argyll.

Lyon King of Arms, Sir James Grant, K.C.V.O., W.S.

Hereditary Standard-Bearer, The Earl of Dundee, P.C.

Hereditary Keepers:—

Holyrood, The Duke of Hamilton and Brandon. Falkland. Maj. M. D. D. Crichton-Stuart, M.C. Stirling, The Earl of Mar and Kellie.

Keeper of Dumbarton Castle, Admiral Sir Angus Cunninghame Graham of Gartmore, K.B.E., C.B.

Governor of Edinburgh Castle, Lieut-Gen. D. W. Scott-Barrett, M.B.E., M.C.

Dean of the Order of the Thistle, The Very Rev. Prof. J. McIntyre, M.A., B.D., D.Litt., D.D.

Dean of the Chapel Royal, Very Rev. H. O. Douglas, C.B.E., M.A.

Chaplains in Ordinary, Rev. R. W. V. Selby Wright, C.V.O., T.D., D.D., F.R.S.A., F.S.A.(Scot.); Very Rev. H. C. Whitley, C.V.O., D.D., M.A., Ph.D.; Very Rev. W. R. Sanderson, D.D.; Rev. W. H. Rogan, D.D.; Rev. W. J. Morris, B.A., B.D., Ph.D.; Very Rev. G. T. H. Reid, M.C., M.A., D.D.; Rev. H. W. McP. Cant, M.A., B.D.; Rev. K. Macvicar, M.B.E., D.F.C., T.D., M.A.; Very Rev. Prof. J. McIntyre, M.A., B.D., D. Litt.

Extra Chaplains, Very Rev. J. A. Fraser, M.B.E., T.D., D.D.; Very Rev. the Lord MacLeod of Fuinary, M.C., D.D.; Very Rev. Prof. J. S. Stewart, D.D.; Rev. Prof. E. P. Dickie, M.C., D.D.; Very Rev. A. N. Davidson, D.D.; Rev. J. Lamb, C.V.O., D.D.; Rev. T. B. S. Thomson, M.C., T.D., D.D.; Very Rev. R. L. Small, C.B.E., D.D.

Domestic Chaplain Balmoral, Rev. T. J. T. Nicol, M.B.E., M.C., M.A., D.D.

Historiographer, J. D. Mackie, C.B.E., M.C., Ll.D.

Botanist, Harold R. Fletcher, Ph.D., D.Sc.

Painter and Limner, Stanley Cursiter, C.B.E., R.S.A., F.R.S.E., R.S.W.

Sculptor, Benno Schotz, R.S.A.

Astronomer, Prof. V. C. Reddish, B.Sc., Ph.D., D.Sc., F.R.S.E.

Physicians in Scotland, Prof. W. I. Card, M.D., F.R.C.P.; Prof. K. W. Donald, D.S.C., M.A.,

M.D., D.SC., F.R.C.P.E., F.R.C.P., F.R.S.E.; Prof. Sir
Ian Hill, C.B.E., T.D., M.D., Ch.B., F.R.S.E., F.R.C.P.
Extra Physicians in Scotland, Prof. Sir Stanley David-
son, M.D., F.R.C.P., F.R.S.E.; Prof. Sir Derrick
Dunlop, M.D., F.R.C.P., F.R.C.P.E., F.R.S.E.
Surgeons in Scotland, Prof. Sir John Bruce, C.B.E.,
T.D., F.R.C.S.Ed.; Prof. Sir Donald Macleod
Douglas, M.B.E., Ch.M., F.R.C.S.
Extra Surgeons in Scotland, George G. Bruce, M.D.,
Ch.B., M.B., F.R.C.S.Ed.; Prof. Sir Charles Illing-
worth, C.B.E., M.D., F.R.C.S.Ed.
Surgeon Oculist in Scotland, Prof. G. I. Scott, C.B.E.,
M.A., P.R.C.S.Ed., F.R.S.E.
Surgeon Dentist in Scotland, John Crawford Shiach,
F.D.S.
Surgeon Apothecary to the Household at Balmoral,
G. F. Lindsay, M.B., Ch.B.
*Surgeon Apothecary to the Household at Holyrood-
house*, D. G. Illingworth, M.D., F.R.C.P., Ch.B.

THE QUEEN'S BODYGUARD FOR SCOTLAND
The Royal Company of Archers.
Archers' Hall, Edinburgh.
Captain General and Gold Stick for Scotland, Col. the
Earl of Stair, C.V.O., M.B.E.
Captains, The Lord Elphinstone; Major Sir Hugh
Rose, Bt., T.D.; Major The Lord Home of the
Hirsel, K.T.; Brigadier The Lord Stratheden and
Campbell, C.B.E.
Lieutenants, The Duke of Buccleuch and Queens-
berry, V.R.D.; Admiral Sir Angus Cunninghame-
Graham, K.B.E., C.B.; Lt.-Col. Sir John Gilmour,
Bt., D.S.O., T.D., M.P.; Major Sir Alastair Blair,
K.C.V.O., T.D.
Ensigns, Col. The Lord Clydesmuir, K.T., C.B.,
M.B.E., T.D.; The Lord Maclean, P.C., K.T.,
G.C.V.O., K.B.E.; Major Sir Hew Hamilton-
Dalrymple, Bt., C.V.O. (*Adjutant*); Major The Earl
of Wemyss and March, K.T.
Brigadiers, The Earl of Airlie; Lt.-Gen. Sir William
Turner, K.B.E., C.B., D.S.O.; The Earl of Dal-
housie, K.T., G.B.E., M.C.; Capt. I. M. Tennant;
Maj.-Gen. The Earl Cathcart, C.B., D.S.O., M.C.;
Capt. N. E. F. Dalrymple-Hamilton, C.V.O.,
M.B.E., D.S.C., R.N.; The Marquess of Lothian;
Brigadier J. C. Monteith, M.C.; Col. the Hon.
John Warrender, O.B.E., M.C.; Commodore Sir
John Clerk of Penicuik, Bt., C.B.E., V.R.D., R.N.R.;
The Earl of Elgin and Kincardine; Col. G. R.
Simpson, D.S.O., T.D.; Major D. H. Butter, M.C.
Adjutant, Major Sir Hew Hamilton-Dalrymple, Bt.,
C.V.O.
Surgeon, Lt.-Col. D. N. Nicholson, T.D., M.B.,
F.R.C.P.E.
Chaplain, Very Rev. R. W. V. Selby Wright,
C.V.O., D.D., F.R.S.E.
President of the Council and Silver Stick for Scotland,
Col. the Lord Clydesmuir, K.T., C.B., M.B.E., T.D.
Vice-President, The Lord Elphinstone.
Secretary, Capt. G. W. Burnet.
Treasurer, Col. G. R. Simpson, D.S.O., T.D.

HOUSEHOLD OF THE PRINCE PHILIP, DUKE OF EDINBURGH
Private Secretary, Cdr. W. B. Willett, O.B.E.,
M.V.O., D.S.C., R.N.
Treasurer, Lord Rupert Nevill.
Equerry, Major H. Hugh-Smith.
Extra Equerry, J. B. V. Orr, C.V.O.
Temporary Equerries, Capt. I. M. Walden, M.B.E.,
R.M.; Capt. C. X. S. Fenwick.
Chief Clerk and Accountant, L. A. J. Treby, C.V.O.,
M.B.E., B.E.M.

HOUSEHOLD OF QUEEN ELIZABETH THE QUEEN MOTHER
Lord Chamberlain, Major the Earl of Dalhousie,
K.T., G.B.E., M.C.

Comptroller and Extra Equerry, Capt. Alastair S.
Aird, M.V.O.
Private Secretary and Equerry, Lt.-Col. Sir Martin
Gilliat, K.C.V.O., M.B.E.
Treasurer and Equerry, Major Sir Ralph Anstruther,
Bt., C.V.O., M.C.
Equerry, Major the Hon. Sir Francis Legh, K.C.V.O.
Press Secretary and Extra Equerry, Major Arthur
J. S. Griffin, C.V.O.
Extra Equerries, The Lord Sinclair, M.V.O.; Maj.
Raymond Seymour, M.V.O.; The Lord Adam
Gordon, K.C.V.O., M.B.E.
Equerry (Temp.), Capt. J. D. Miller.
Apothecary to the Household, Sir Ralph Southward,
K.C.V.O., M.B., Ch.B., F.R.C.P.
*Surgeon-Apothecary to the Household (Royal Lodge,
Windsor)*, J. P. Clayton, M.V.O., M.A., M.B., B.Chir.,
M.R.C.S., L.R.C.P.
Mistress of the Robes, The Duchess of Abercorn,
D.C.V.O.
Ladies of the Bedchamber, The Dowager Viscountess
Hambleden, D.C.V.O.; The Lady Grimthorpe.
Extra Ladies of the Bedchamber, The Dowager
Countess of Halifax, C.I., D.C.V.O.; The Dowager
Lady Harlech, D.C.V.O.; The Dowager Countess
of Scarbrough, D.C.V.O.
Women of the Bedchamber, The Lady Jean Rankin,
D.C.V.O.; The Hon. Mrs. John Mulholland,
D.C.V.O.; Ruth, Lady Fermoy, C.V.O., O.B.E.;
Mrs. Patrick Campbell-Preston.
Extra Women of the Bedchamber, The Lady Victoria
Wemyss, C.V.O.; The Hon. Mrs. Geoffrey
Bowlby, C.V.O.; The Lady Delia Peel, D.C.V.O.;
The Lady Katharine Seymour, D.C.V.O.; The
Lady Elizabeth Basset.
Clerk Comptroller, M. Blanch, M.V.O.
Chief Accountant, J. P. Kyle, M.V.O.
Clerks, Miss L. A. Gosling; Miss F. Fletcher.

HOUSEHOLD OF THE PRINCE OF WALES
Private Secretary and Equerry, Sqn.-Ldr. D. J.
Checketts, C.V.O.
Secretary, M. M. Colborne.
Equerry, Major V. P. W. Harmsworth.
Temporary Equerry, Capt. A. J. Davies.

HOUSEHOLD OF THE PRINCESS ANNE, MRS. MARK PHILLIPS
Private Secretary, Maj. B. J Herman, M.V.O., R.M.
Lady in Waiting, Miss Rowena Brassey, M.V.O.
Extra Ladies in Waiting, Mrs. Richard Carew Pole;
Miss Victoria Legge Bourke.
Secretary of H.R.H.'s Office, Mrs. David Hodgson.
Clerk, Miss P. J. Walters.

HOUSEHOLD OF THE PRINCESS MARGARET, COUNTESS OF SNOWDON
Treasurer, Major The Hon. Sir Francis Legh, K.C.V.O.
Private Secretary and Comptroller, The Lord Napier
and Ettrick.
Personal Secretary, Miss M. Murray Brown, M.V.O.
Lady in Waiting, The Hon. Davina Woodhouse.
Extra Ladies in Waiting, The Lady Elizabeth
Cavendish; Mrs. Alastair Aird; Mrs. Robin
Benson; The Lady Juliet Townsend; The Hon.
Mrs. Wills; Mrs. Jocelyn Stevens; The Lady
Anne Tennant; The Hon. Mrs. Whitehead.

THE DUKE AND DUCHESS OF GLOUCESTER'S HOUSEHOLD
Comptroller, Private Secretary and Equerry, Lt.-Col.
S. C. M. Bland, C.V.O.
Ladies in Waiting, Mrs. Michael Wigley; Miss Jen-
nifer Thomson.

PRINCESS ALICE, DUCHESS OF GLOUCESTER'S HOUSEHOLD
Comptroller, Private Secretary and Equerry, Lt.-Col. S. C. M. Bland, C.V.O.
Ladies in Waiting, Miss Jean Maxwell-Scott, C.V.O.; Miss Jane Egerton-Warburton *(temp.).*
Extra Ladies in Waiting, Miss Dorothy Meynell, C.V.O.; Mrs. Cedric Holland, C.V.O.; Miss Diana Harrison; The Hon. Jane Walsh.

THE DUKE AND DUCHESS OF KENT'S HOUSEHOLD
Treasurer, Sir Philip Hay, K.C.V.O., T.D.
Private Secretary, Lieut.-Cdr. Richard Buckley, C.V.O., R.N.
Ladies in Waiting, Mrs. Alan Henderson; Miss Jane Pugh.
Extra Lady in Waiting, Mrs. Peter Wilmot Sitwell.

HOUSEHOLD OF PRINCESS ALEXANDRA
Lady in Waiting, The Lady Mary Fitzalan-Howard, M.V.O.
Private Secretary and Extra Lady in Waiting, Miss Mona Mitchell.
Extra Ladies in Waiting, The Hon. Lady Rowley; The Lady Mary Colman; The Lady Caroline Waterhouse.
Extra Equerry, Maj. P. C. Clarke, C.V.O.

HONORARY PHYSICIANS TO THE QUEEN (CIVIL)
(Appointed for three years from Nov. 1, 1974)
T. T. Baird, *Chief Medical Officer, Northern Ireland Office*; R. T. Bevan, *Chief Medical Officer, Welsh Office*; D. H. D. Burbridge, O.B.E., *Senior Principal Medical Officer, Department of Health and Social Security*; D. E. Cullington, *Area Medical Officer, Berkshire Area Health Authority*; J. L. Gilloran, *Specialist in Community Medicine, Lothian Health Board*; C. W. Gordon, T.D., *Regional Medical Officer, West Midlands Regional Health Authority.*

THE QUEEN'S BIRTHDAY, 1976
The date for the observance of the Queen's Birthday in 1976 both at home and abroad will be Saturday, June 12.

ROYAL SALUTES
On the Anniversaries of the Birth, Accession and Coronation of the Sovereign a salute of 62 guns is fired on the wharf at the Tower of London. On extraordinary and triumphal occasions, such as on the occasion of the Sovereign opening,

proroguing or dissolving Parliament in Person, or when passing through London in procession, except when otherwise ordered, 41 guns only are fired.
On the occasion of the birth of a Royal infant, a salute of 41 guns is fired from the two Saluting Stations in London, *i.e.* Hyde Park and the Tower of London.
Constable of the Royal Palace and Fortress of London, Field-Marshal Sir Geoffrey Baker, G.C.B., C.M.G., C.B.E., M.C. (1975).
Lieutenant of the Tower of London, Lieut.-Gen. Sir Napier Crookenden, K.C.B., D.S.O., O.B.E.
Major, Resident Governor and Keeper of the Jewel House, Maj.-Gen. W. D. M. Raeburn, C.B., D.S.O., M.B.E.
Master Gunner of St. James's Park, Field-Marshal Sir Geoffrey Baker, G.C.B., C.M.G., C.B.E., M.C. (1970).
Master Gunner within the Tower, Col. G. E. Gilchrist, T.D.

THE ROYAL ARMS
QUARTERLY.—1st and 4th *gules,* three lions passant guardant in pale *or (England)*; 2nd *or,* a lion rampant within a double tressure flory counterflory *gules (Scotland)*; 3rd *azure,* a harp *or,* stringed *argent (Ireland)*; the whole encircled with the Garter.
SUPPORTERS.—*Dexter*: a lion rampant guardant *or,* imperially crowned. *Sinister*: a unicorn *argent,* armed crined and unguled *or,* gorged with a coronet composed of crosses patées and fleurs de lis, a chain affixed passing between the forelegs and reflexed over the back.
BADGES.—The red and white rose united *(England),* a thistle *(Scotland)*; a harp *or,* the strings *argent,* with a shamrock leaf *vert (Ireland)*; upon a mount *vert,* a dragon passant wings elevated *gules (Wales).*

THE UNION JACK
The national flag of the United Kingdom is the Union Flag, generally known as the Union Jack, the name deriving from the use of the Union Flag on the jack-staff of naval vessels. It is a combination of the cross of the patron saint of England, St. George *(cross gules in a field argent),* the cross of the patron saint of Scotland, St. Andrew *(saltire argent in a field azure)* and a cross similar to that of St. Patrick, patron saint of Ireland *(saltire gules in a field argent).* The Union Flag was first introduced in 1606 after the union of England and Scotland, the cross of St. Patrick being added in 1801.

ANNUITIES TO THE ROYAL FAMILY

The annuity payable to Her Majesty is known as the Civil List, and is payable out of the Consolidated Fund under the authority of a Civil List Act following the recommendation of a Parliamentary Select Committee. The amount of the Civil List was fixed in the Civil List Act 1952 at £475,000 and was increased from January 1, 1972, under the Civil List Act 1972 to £980,000, and in 1975 to £1,400,000.
The Civil List Acts also provide separate annuities payable from the Consolidated Fund to other members of the Royal Family. The amounts payable under the Acts of 1910, 1937, 1952 and 1972 are as follows:—

Queen Elizabeth The Queen Mother	£95,000
The Duke of Edinburgh	65,000
The Princess Anne	35,000
The Princess Margaret	35,000
Princess Alice, Duchess of Gloucester	20,000

In addition a sum of £60,000 a year is payable from the Consolidated Fund to the Royal Trustees (The Prime Minister, the Chancellor of the Exchequer and the Keeper of the Privy Purse) for contributions towards expenses incurred in undertaking Royal duties by other members of the Royal Family not in receipt of an annuity.

THE FLYING OF FLAGS

Days for hoisting the Union Flag on Government and Public Buildings (from 8 A.M. to sunset).

February 6 (1952).—Her Majesty's Accession.
February 19 (1960).—Birthday of Prince Andrew.
March 1.—St. David's Day (in Wales only).
March 10 (1964).—Birthday of Prince Edward.
April 21 (1926).—Birthday of Her Majesty the Queen.
April 23.—St. George's Day (in England only). Where a building has two or more flagstaffs the Cross of St. George may be flown in addition to the Union Jack but not in a superior position.
June 2 (1953).—Coronation Day.
June 10 (1921).—Birthday of the Duke of Edinburgh.
June 12.—Queen's Official Birthday, 1976.
Aug. 4 (1900).—Birthday of Her Majesty Queen Elizabeth the Queen Mother.
Aug. 15 (1950).—Birthday of the Princess Anne.
Aug. 21 (1930).—Birthday of the Princess Margaret.
Nov. 13.—Remembrance Sunday, 1976.
Nov. 14 (1948).—Birthday of the Prince of Wales.
Nov. 20 (1947).—Her Majesty's Wedding Day.
Nov. 30.—St. Andrew's Day (in Scotland only).

And on the occasion of the opening and closing of Parliament by the Queen, flags should be flown on public buildings in the Greater London area, whether or not Her Majesty performs the ceremony in person.

The only additions to the above list will be those notified to the Department of the Environment by Her Majesty's command and communicated by the Ministry to the other Departments. The list applies equally to Government and Public Buildings in London and elsewhere in the United Kingdom. In cases where it has been the practice to fly the Union Jack daily, *e.g.* on some Custom Houses, that practice may continue.

Flags will be flown at half-mast on the following occasions:—

(a) From the announcement of the death up to the funeral of the Sovereign, except on Proclamation Day, when they are hoisted right up from 11 a.m. to sunset.

(b) The funerals of members of the Royal Family, subject to special commands from Her Majesty in each case.

(c) The funerals of Foreign Rulers, subject to special commands from Her Majesty in each case.

(d) The funerals of Prime Ministers and ex-Prime Ministers of the United Kingdom.

(e) Other occasions by special command of Her Majesty.

On occasions when days for flying flags coincide with days for flying flags at half mast the following rules will be observed. Flags will be flown: (a) although a member of the Royal Family, or a near relative of the Royal Family, may be lying dead, unless special commands be received from Her Majesty to the contrary, and (b) although it may be the day of the funeral of a Foreign Ruler. If the body of a very distinguished subject is lying at a Government Office the flag may fly at half mast on that office until the body has left (provided it is a day on which the flag would fly) and then the flag is to be hoisted right up. On all other Public Buildings the flag will fly as usual.

The *Royal Standard* is only to be hoisted when the Queen is actually present in the building, and never when Her Majesty is passing in procession.

RED-LETTER DAYS

Scarlet Robes are worn by the Judges of the Queen's Bench Division on *Red-Letter Days* at the sittings of a Criminal Court or of the Court of Appeal (Criminal Divn.) and on all State Occasions.

RED-LETTER DAYS AND STATE OCCASIONS, 1976.		
Jan. 25. Conversion of St. Paul.	May 1. St. Philip and St. James.	Aug. 4. Birthday of Queen Elizabeth the Queen Mother.
Feb. 2. Purification.	,, 27. Ascension Day.	
,, 6. Queen's Accession.	June 2. Coronation Day.	Oct. 18. St. Luke.
,, 24. St. Matthias.	,, 10. Birthday of the Duke of Edinburgh.	,, 28. St. Simon and St. Jude.
,, 25. Annunciation.	,, 11. St. Barnabas.	Nov. 1. All Saints.
March 3. Ash Wednesday.	,, 12. Queen's Official Birthday (1976).	,, 6. Lord Mayor's Day.
Apr. 21. Queen's Birthday.	,, 24. St. John the Baptist.	,, 14. Birthday of the Prince of Wales.
,, 25. St. Mark	,, 29. St. Peter.	,, 30. St. Andrew.
	July 25. St. James.	Dec. 21. St. Thomas.

THE MILITARY KNIGHTS OF WINDSOR

Founded in 1348 after the Wars in France to assist English Knights, who, having been prisoners in the hands of the French, had become impoverished by the payments of heavy ransoms. They received a pension and quarters in Windsor Castle. Edward III founded the Order of the Garter later in the same year, incorporating the Knights of Windsor and the College of St. George into its foundation and raising the number of Knights to 26 to correspond with the number of the Knights of the Garter. Known later as the Alms Knights or Poor Knights of Windsor, their establishment was reduced under the will of King Henry VIII to 13 and Statutes were drawn up by Queen Elizabeth I.

In 1833 King William IV changed their designation to The Military Knights and granted them their present uniform which consists of a scarlet tail-coat with white cross sword-belt, crimson sash and cocked hat with plume. The badges are the Shield of St. George and the Star of the Order of the Garter. The Knights receive a small stipend in addition to their Army pensions and quarters in Windsor Castle. They take part in all ceremonies of the Noble Order of the Garter and attend Sunday morning service in St. George's Chapel as representatives of the Knights of the Garter.

Applications for appointment should be made to The Military Secretary, Ministry of Defence, Army Dept.

Governor, Maj.-Gen. Sir Edmund Hakewill Smith, K.C.V.O., C.B., C.B.E., M.C.
Military Knights, Lt.-Colonel R. F. Squibb, M.C.; Brigadier W. P. A. Robinson, M.C.; Major T. W. Garnett, M.B.E.; Brigadier A. A. Crook, D.S.O.; Lt.-Colonel R. J. L. Penfold; Lt.-Colonel L. W. Giles, O.B.E., M.C.; Colonel H. G. Duncombe, D.S.O.; Lt.-Colonel R. W. Dobbin, O.B.E.; Major H. Smith, M.B.E.; Lt.-Colonel A. R. Clark, M.C.; Lt.-Colonel C. A. Harvey; Lt.-Col. A. J. Spratley, M.B.E., M.M.

The Peerage

THE PEERAGE AND ITS DEGREES

The rules which govern the creation and succession of Peerages are extremely complicated. There were separate Peerages of England, of Scotland, and of Ireland, until the unions of the three countries: of England and Scotland, forming Great Britain, in 1707; and of Great Britain and Ireland, forming the United Kingdom, in 1801. Some Scottish Peers received additional Peerages of Great Britain or of the United Kingdom, since 1707; and some Irish Peers additional Peerages of the United Kingdom since 1801.

All Peers of England, Scotland, Great Britain, or the United Kingdom who are of full age and of British nationality are entitled to seats in the House of Lords. But Peers of Ireland who have no additional United Kingdom Peerage are not entitled to sit, although they are eligible for election to the House of Commons and to vote (if of voting age) in Parliamentary elections (which other Peers are not). The two Archbishops and 24 of the 41 diocesan Bishops of the Church of England also have seats in the House of Lords.

Certain ancient Peerages pass on death to the nearest heir, male or female, and several are now held by women who are thus Peeresses in their own Right. They are entitled to sit in the House of Lords if they are of full age and British nationality.

Since 1876 the Crown has conferred non-hereditary or Life Peerages in the degree of Baron on eminent judges to enable them to carry out the judicial function of the House of Lords. They are known as Law Lords. Under an Act passed in 1958 the Crown may confer Life Peerages on men and women giving them, in the degree of Baron or Baroness, seats in the House of Lords.

In 1963 an Act was passed enabling Peers to disclaim their Peerages for life: living Peers, within 12 months after the passing of the Act (July 31, 1963), future Peers within 12 months (one month if an M.P.) after the date of their succession, or of attaining their majority if later.

No fees for Dignities have been payable since 1937. No hereditary Peerages have been created since 1965.

PEERAGES EXTINCT SINCE THE LAST ISSUE

VISCOUNTCY.—Clifden (cr. 1781).
BARONIES.—Conesford (cr. 1955); Hailes (cr. 1957); Hurcourt (cr. 1950); Reid (cr. 1948) (Law Life Peerage); Salter (cr. 1953);

DISCLAIMER OF PEERAGES

The following peers have disclaimed their peerages under the Peerage Act, 1963: Earl of Durham; Earl of Home; Earl of Sandwich; Viscount Hailsham; Viscount Stansgate; Lord Altrincham; Lord Beaverbrook; Lord Fraser of Allander; Lord Monkswell; Lord Reith; Lord Sanderson of Ayot; Lord Silkin; Lord Southampton; Lord Archibald.

PEERS WHO ARE MINORS
(As at Jan. 1, 1976)

MARQUESS (1): Milford Haven (b. 1961).
EARLS (3): Craven (b. 1957); Hardwicke (b. 1971); Woolton (b. 1958).
BARONS (2): Fairfax of Cameron (b. 1956); Londesborough (b. 1959).

CONTRACTIONS AND SYMBOLS

Contractions and Symbols.—S. or I. appended to the date of creation denotes a *Scottish* or *Irish* title, the further addition of a ⋆ implies that the Peer in question holds also an *Imperial* title, which is specified (after the name) by its more definite description as *Engl.*, *Brit.*, or *U.K.* When both titles are alike, as in the case of Argyll, this star is appended to the conjoined date below, and it then denotes that such date is that of the imperial creation. The mark ° signifies that there is no " of " in the Marquessate or Earldom so designated; *b.* signifies born; *s.*, succeeded; *m.*, married; *w.*, widower or widow; *M.*, minor.

NUMBERS OF THE PEERAGE

	Hereditary	Minors	No Seat	Life or Term	In House of Lords
Royal Dukes.....................	4	—	—	—	4
Archbishops.....................	—	—	—	2	2
Dukes...........................	26	—	—	—	26
Marquesses......................	38	1	—	—	37
Earls...........................	199	3	21	—	175
Viscounts.......................	131	—	15	—	116
Bishops.........................	—	—	17	24	24
Barons (and Scots Lords)...........	487	2	36	16	465
Peeresses in own Right............	20	—	1	—	19
Life Peers (under 1958 Act)........	—	—	—	222	222
Life Peeresses (under 1958 Act).....	—	—	—	36	36
107 Totals...........	906	6	90	300	1,127

ROYAL DUKES

Style, His Royal Highness the Duke of ——.
Addressed as, Sir, or more formally, May it please your Royal Highness.

1947 *Edinburgh,* The Prince Philip, Duke of Edinburgh, K.G., P.C., K.T., O.M., G.B.E., *b.* 1921, *m.* (*see* pp. 217 and 218).

1337 *Cornwall,* Charles, Prince of Wales, Duke of Cornwall (*Scottish Duke, Rothesay,* 1398), K.G., *b.* 1948, (*see* p. 218).

1928 *Gloucester* (2nd), Richard, Duke of Gloucester, G.C.V.O., *b.* 1944, *s.* 1974, *m.* (see p. 217).

1934 *Kent* (2nd), Edward, Duke of Kent, G.C.M.G., G.C.V.O., *b.* 1935, *s.* 1942, *m.* (*see* p. 217).

ARCHBISHOPS

Style, The Most Rev. His Grace the Lord Archbishop of——.
Addressed as, My Lord Archbishop; or, Your Grace.

Trans.

1974   *Canterbury* (101st), Frederick Donald Coggan, P.C., D.D., *b.* 1909, *m.*
Consecrated Bishop of Bradford, 1956; *translated to York*, 1961.

1974   *York* (94th), Stuart Yarworth Blanch, P.C., M.A., *b.* 1918, *m.* Consecrated Bishop of Liverpool, 1966.

DUKES

Style, His Grace the Duke of——. *Addressed as*, My Lord Duke; or, Your Grace. The eldest sons of Dukes and Marquesses take, by courtesy, their father's second title. The other sons and the daughters are styled Lord Edward, Lady Caroline. etc.

Created.	Title, Order of Succession, Name, etc.	Eldest Son or Heir.
1868 I.*	*Abercorn* (4th), James Edward Hamilton (1st Brit. Marq., 1790, and 13th Scott. Earl, 1606 both Abercorn), *b.* 1904, *s.* 1953, *m.*	Marquess of Hamilton, *b.* 1934.
1701 S.	*Argyll*, Ian Campbell (12th Scottish and 5th U.K. Duke, Argyll),	Marquess of Lorne, *b.* 1968.
1892*	*b.* 1937, *s.* 1973, *m.*	
1703 S.	*Atholl* (10th), George Iain Murray, *b.* 1931, *s.* 1957.	Arthur S. P. M. *b.* 1899.
1682	*Beaufort* (10th), Henry Hugh Arthur FitzRoy Somerset, K.G., P.C., G.C.V.O., Royal Victorian Chain, *b.* 1900, *s.* 1924, *m.* (*Master of the Horse*).	David R. S., *b.* 1928.
1694	*Bedford* (13th), John Robert Russell, *b.* 1917, *s.* 1953, *m.*	Marquess of Tavistock, *b.* 1940.
1663 S.*	*Buccleuch* (9th) & (11th) *Queensbury* (1706), Walter Francis John Montagu-Douglas-Scott, V.R.D. (8th Engl. Earl, Doncaster, 1662), *b.* 1923, *s.* 1973, *m.*	Earl of Dalkeith, *b.* 1954.
1694	*Devonshire* (11th), Andrew Robert Buxton Cavendish, P.C., M.C., *b.* 1920, *s.* 1950, *m.*	Marquess of Hartington, *b.* 1944.
1900	*Fife* (3rd), James George Alexander Bannerman Carnegie, *b.* 1929, *s.* 1959. (*see p.* 216)	Earl of Macduff, *b.* 1961.
1675	*Grafton* (11th), Hugh Denis Charles FitzRoy, *b.* 1919, *s.* 1970, *m.*	Earl of Euston, *b.* 1947.
1643 S.*	*Hamilton* (15th), Angus Alan Douglas Douglas-Hamilton (*Premier Peer of Scotland*; 12th Brit. Duke, Brandon, 1711), *b.* 1938, *s.* 1973, *m.*	Lord James D.-H., M.P., *b.* 1942.
1766 I.*	*Leinster* (7th), Edward FitzGerald (*Premier Duke, Marquess and Earl of Ireland*; 7th Brit. Visct., Leinster, 1747), *b.* 1892, *s.* 1922, *m.*	Marquess of Kildare, *b.* 1914.
1719	*Manchester* (10th), Alexander George Francis Drogo Montagu, O.B.E., *b.* 1902, *s.* 1947, *m.*	Visct. Mandeville, *b.* 1929.
1702	*Marlborough* (11th), John George Vanderbilt Henry Spencer-Churchill, *b.* 1926, *s.* 1972, *m.*	Marquess of Blandford, *b.* 1955.
1707 S.*	*Montrose* (7th), James Angus Graham (5th Brit. Earl, Graham, 1722), *b.* 1907, *s.* 1954, *m.*	Marquess of Graham, *b.* 1935.
1756	*Newcastle* (under *Lyme*) (9th), Henry Edward Hugh Pelham-Clinton-Hope, O.B.E., *b.* 1907, *s.* 1941, *m.*	Edward C. Pelham-Clinton, *b.* 1920.
1483	*Norfolk* (17th), Miles Francis Fitzalan-Howard, C.B., C.B.E., M.C. (*Premier Duke and Earl*; 12th Eng. Baron Beaumont, 1309; 4th U.K. Baron Howard of Glossop, 1869), *b.* 1915, *s.* 1975, *m.* (*Earl Marshal*).	Earl of Arundel and Surrey, *b.* 1956.
1766	*Northumberland* (10th), Hugh Algernon Percy, K.G., P.C., T.D., F.R.S., *b.* 1914, *s.* 1940, *m.* (*Lord Steward*).	Earl Percy, *b.* 1953.
1716	*Portland* (7th), William Arthur Henry Cavendish-Bentinck, K.G., T.D., (3rd U.K. Baron, Bolsover, 1880) *b.* 1893, *s.* 1943, *m.*	Major Sir Ferdinand W. C.-B., K.B.E., C.M.G., *b.* 1888.
1675	*Richmond* (9th) & *Gordon* (4th, 1876), Frederick Charles Gordon-Lennox (9th Scott. Duke, Lennox. 1675), *b.* 1904, *s.* 1935, *m.*	Earl of March and Kinrara, *b.* 1929.
1707 S.*	*Roxburghe* (10th), Guy David Innes-Ker (5th U.K. Earl, Innes, 1837), *b.* 1954, *s.* 1974 (*Premier Baronet of Scotland*).	Lord Robert I.-K., *b.* 1959.
1703	*Rutland* (10th), Charles John Robert Manners, C.B.E., *b.* 1919, *s.* 1940, *m.*	Marquess of Granby, *b.* 1959.
1684	*St. Albans* (13th), Charles Frederick Aubrey de Vere Beauclerk, O.B.E., *b.* 1915, *s.* 1964, *m.*	Earl of Burford, *b.* 1939.
1547	*Somerset* (18th), Percy Hamilton Seymour, *b.* 1910, *s.* 1954, *m.*	Lord Seymour, *b.* 1952.
1833	*Sutherland* (6th), John Sutherland Egerton (5th U.K. Earl Ellesmere, 1846), *b.* 1915, *s.* 1963, *m.*	Cyril R. E., *b.* 1905.
1814	*Wellington* (8th), Arthur Valerian Wellesley, M.V.O., O.B.E., M.C. (9th Irish Earl, Mornington, 1760), *b.* 1915, *s.* 1972, *m.*	Marquess of Douro, *b.* 1945.
1874	*Westminster* (5th), Robert George Grosvenor, T.D., *b.* 1910, *s.* 1967, *m.*	Earl Grosvenor, *b.* 1951.

MARQUESSES

Style, The Most Hon. the Marquess of——. *Addressed as*, My Lord Marquess.
In titles marked ° the " of " is *not* used. For the style of Marquesses' sons and daughters, *see* under " DUKES," above.

1915   *Aberdeen and Temair* (5th), Archibald Victor Dudley Gordon, (11th Scott. Earl, Aberdeen, 1682), *b.* 1913, *s.* 1974.

Created.	Title, Order of Succession, Name, etc.	Eldest Son or Heir.
1876	Abergavenny (5th), John Henry Guy Larnach-Nevill, K.G., O.B.E., b. 1914, s. 1954, m.	Lord Rupert N., b. 1923.
1821	Ailesbury (8th), Michael Sidney Cedric Brudenell-Bruce, b. 1926, s. 1974, m.	Earl of Cardigan, b. 1952.
1831	Ailsa (7th), Archibald David Kennedy, O.B.E., (19th Scott. Earl, Cassillis, 1509), b. 1925, s. 1957, m.	Earl of Cassillis, b. 1956.
1815	Anglesey (7th), George Charles Henry Victor Paget, b. 1922, s. 1947, m.	Earl of Uxbridge, b. 1950.
1789	Bath (6th), Henry Frederick Thynne, E.D., b. 1905, s. 1946, m.	Viscount Weymouth, b. 1932.
1826	Bristol (6th), Victor Frederick Cochrane Hervey, b. 1915, s. 1960, m.	Earl Jermyn, b. 1954.
1796	Bute (6th), John Crichton-Stuart (11th Scott. Earl, Dumfries, 1633), b. 1933, s. 1956, m.	Earl of Dumfries, b. 1958.
1917	Cambridge (2nd), George Francis Hugh Cambridge, G.C.V.O., bi. 1895, s. 1927, m.	(None.)
1812	°Camden (5th), John Charles Henry Pratt, b. 1899, s. 1943, m.	Earl of Brecknock, b. 1930.
1815	Cholmondeley (6th), George Hugh Cholmondeley, M.C. (10th Irish Viscount, Cholmondeley, 1661), b. 1919, s. 1968, m. (Lord Great Chamberlain).	Earl of Rocksavage, b. 1960.
1816I.*	°Conyngham (7th), Frederick William Henry Francis Conyngham (7th U.K. Baron, Minster, U.K. 1821), b. 1924, s. 1974, m.	Earl of Mount Charles, b. 1951.
1791I.*	Donegall (7th), Dermot Richard Claude Chichester (7th Brit. Baron, Fisherwick, 1790, 6th Brit. Baron, Templemore, 1831), b. 1916, s. to Marquessate, 1975: to Templemore Barony, 1953, m.	Earl of Belfast, b. 1952.
1789I.*	Downshire (7th), Arthur Wills Percy Wellington Blundell Trumbull Sandys Hill (7th Brit. Earl, Hillsborough, 1772), b. 1894, s. 1918, m.	A. Robin I. H., b. 1929.
1888	Dufferin & Ava (5th), Sheridan Frederick Terence Hamilton-Temple-Blackwood (11th Irish Baron, Dufferin & Clandeboye, 1800), b. 1938, s. 1945, m.	(None to Marquessate), to Irish Barony, Sir Francis E. T. Blackwood, Bt., b. 1901.
1801I.*	Ely (8th) Charles John Tottenham (8th U.K. Baron, Loftus, 1801), b. 1913, s. 1969, m.	Viscount Loftus, b. 1943.
1801	Exeter (6th), David George Brownlow Cecil, K.C.M.G., b. 1905, s. 1956, m.	Lord Martin C., b. 1909.
1800I.*	Headfort (6th), Thomas Geoffrey Charles Michael Taylour (4th U.K. Baron, Kenlis, 1831), b. 1932, s. 1960, m.	Earl of Bective, b. 1959.
1793	Hertford (8th), Hugh Edward Conway Seymour (9th Irish Baron, Conway, 1712), b. 1930, s. 1940, m.	Earl of Yarmouth, b. 1958.
1599 S.*	Huntly (12th), Douglas Charles Lindsay Gordon (Premier Marquess of Scotland) (4th U.K. Baron, Meldrum, 1815), b. 1908, s. 1937.	Earl of Aboyne, b. 1944.
1784	Lansdowne (8th), George John Charles Mercer Nairne Petty-Fitzmaurice, P.C. (8th Irish Earl, Kerry, 1722), b. 1912, s. 1944, m.	Earl of Shelburne, b. 1941.
1902	Linlithgow (3rd), Charles William Frederick Hope, M.C. (10th Scott. Earl, Hopetoun, 1703), b. 1912, s. 1952, m.	Earl of Hopetoun, b. 1946.
1816I.*	Londonderry (9th), Alexander Charles Robert Vane-Tempest-Stewart (6th U.K. Earl, Vane, 1823), b. 1937, s. 1955, m.	Viscount Castlereagh, b. 1972.
1701 S.*	Lothian (12th), Peter Francis Walter Kerr (6th U.K. Baron, Kerr, 1821), b. 1922, s. 1940, m.	Earl of Ancram, b. 1945.
1917	Milford Haven (4th), George Ivar Louis Mountbatten, b. 1961, s. 1970, M.	Lord Ivar M, b. 1963.
1838	Normanby (4th), Oswald Constantine John Phipps, C.B.E. (8th Irish Baron, Mulgrave, 1767), b. 1912, s. 1932, m.	Earl of Mulgrave, b. 1954.
1812	Northampton (6th), William Bingham Compton, D.S.O., b. 1885, s. 1913, m.	Earl Compton, b. 1946.
1825 I.*	Ormonde (7th), James Hubert Theobald Charles Butler, M.B.E. (7th U.K. Baron, Ormonde, 1821), b. 1899, s. 1971, w.	(None to Marquessate), to Earldoms of Ormonde and Ossory, Viscount Mountgarret (see p. 236).
1682 S.	Queensberry (12th), David Harrington Angus Douglas, b. 1929, s. 1954, m.	Viscount Drumlanrig, b. 1967.
1926	Reading (3rd), Michael Alfred Rufus Isaacs, M.B.E., M.C., T.D., b. 1916, s. 1960, m.	Viscount Erleigh, b. 1942.
1789	Salisbury (6th), Robert Edward Peter Gascoyne-Cecil, b. 1916, s. 1972, m.	Viscount Cranborne, b. 1946.
1800 I.*	Sligo (10th), Denis Edward Browne (10th U.K. Baron, Monteagle, 1806), b. 1908, s. 1952, m.	Earl of Altamont, b. 1939.
1787	°Townshend (7th), George John Patrick Dominic Townshend, b. 1916, s. 1921, m.	Viscount Raynham, b. 1945.
1694 S.*	Tweeddale (12th), David George Montagu Hay, G.C. (3rd U.K. Baron, Tweeddale, 1881), b. 1921, s. 1967, m.	Earl of Gifford, b. 1947.
1789 I.*	Waterford (8th), John Hubert de la Poer Beresford (8th Brit. Baron, Tyrone, 1786), b. 1933, s. 1934, m.	Earl of Tyrone, b. 1958.
1936	Willingdon (2nd), Inigo Brassey Freeman-Thomas, b. 1899, s. 1941, m.	(None.)
1551	Winchester (18th), Nigel George Paulet (Premier Marquess of England), b. 1941, s. 1968, m.	Earl of Wiltshire, b. 1969.
1892	Zetland (3rd), Lawrence Aldred Mervyn Dundas (5th U.K Earl of Zetland, 1838, 6th Brit. Baron Dundas, 1794), b. 1908, s. 1961, m.	Earl of Ronaldshay, b. 1937.

EARLS

Style (*see also* note, p. 256). The Right Hon. the Earl of ——. *Addressed as*, My Lord. The eldest sons of Earls take, by courtesy, their father's second title, the younger sons being styled the Hon., *e.g.* the Hon. John ——, but the daughters Lady Elizabeth ——, etc. Where marked ° the " of " is not used.

Created.	Title, Order of Succession, Name, etc.	Eldest Son or Heir.
1639 S.	Airlie (13th), David George Coke Patrick Ogilvy, b. 1926, s. 1968, m.	Lord Ogilvy, b. 1958.
1696	Albemarle (9th), Walter Egerton George Lucian Keppel, M.C., b. 1882, s. 1942, m.	Viscount Bury, b. 1965.
1952	°Alexander of Tunis (2nd), Shane William Desmond Alexander, b. 1935, s. 1969, m.	Hon. Brian J. A., b. 1939.
1826	°Amherst (5th), Jeffery John Archer Armherst, M.C., b. 1896, s. 1927.	Hon. Humphrey W. A., b. 1903.
1892	Ancaster (3rd), Gilbert James Heathcote-Drummond-Willoughby, K.C.V.O., T.D. (26th E. Baron Willoughby de Eresby, 1313), b. 1907, s. 1951, w.	(To Earldom, none; to Barony, Lady Nancy H.-D.-W., b. 1934).
1789 I.	°Annesley (9th), Robert Annesley, b. 1900, s. 1957, m.	Viscount Glerawly, b. 1924.
1785 I.	Antrim (8th), Randal John Somerled McDonnell, K.B.E., b. 1911, s. 1932, m.	Viscount Dunluce, b. 1935.
1762 I.*	Arran (8th), Arthur Strange Kattendyke David Archibald Gore (4th U.K. Baron Sudley, 1884), b. 1910, s. 1958, m.	Viscount Sudley, b. 1938.
1955	°Attlee (2nd), Martin Richard Attlee, b. 1927, s. 1967, m.	Viscount Prestwood, b. 1956.
1961	°Avon (1st), (Robert) Anthony Eden, K.G., P.C., M.C., b. 1897, m.	Viscount Eden, O.B.E., T.D., b. 1930.
1714	Aylesford (11th), Charles Ian Finch-Knightley, b. 1918, s. 1958, m.	Lord Guernsey, b. 1947.
1937	°Baldwin of Bewdley (3rd), Arthur Windham Baldwin, b. 1904, s. 1958, m.	Viscount Corvedale, b. 1938.
1922	Balfour (4th) Gerald Arthur James Balfour, b. 1925, s. 1968, m.	Eustace A. G. B., b. 1921.
1800 I.	Bandon (5th), Percy Ronald Gardner Bernard, G.B.E., C.B., C.V.O., D.S.O., b. 1904, s. 1924, m.	Maj. Hon. Charles B. A. B., C.B.E., b. 1904 (Twin).
1772	°Bathurst (8th), Henry Allen John Bathurst, b. 1927, s. 1943, m.	Lord Apsley, b. 1961.
1919	°Beatty (3rd), David Beatty, b. 1946, s. 1972, m.	Viscount Borodale, b. 1973.
1815	°Beauchamp (8th), William Lygon, b. 1903, s. 1938, m.	Reginald A. L., b. 1904.
1797 I.	Belmore (8th), John Armar Lowry-Corry, b. 1951, s. 1960.	Frederick H. L.-C., b. 1926.
1739 I. ⎱ 1937* ⎰	Bessborough (2nd), Frederick Edward Neuflize Ponsonby, (10th Irish Earl Bessborough), b. 1913, s. 1956, m.	Arthur M. L. P., b. 1912 (to Irish Earldom only).
1922	Birkenhead (3rd), Frederick William Robin Smith, b. 1936, s. 1975.	(None.)
1815	Bradford (6th), Gerald Michael Orlando Bridgeman, T.D., b. 1911, s. 1957, m.	Viscount Newport, b. 1947.
1677 S.	Breadalbane and Holland (10th), John Romer Boreland Campbell, b. 1919, s. 1959.	(None).
1469 S.*	Buchan (16th), Donald Cardross Flower Erskine, (7th U.K. Baron Erskine), b. 1899, s. (to Barony), 1957, (to Earldom) 1960, m.	Lord Cardross, b. 1930.
1746	Buckinghamshire (9th), Vere Frederick Cecil Hobart-Hampden, b. 1901, s. 1963, m.	G. Miles H.-H., b. 1944.
1800	°Cadogan (7th), William Gerald Charles Cadogan, M.C., b. 1914, s. 1933, m.	Viscount Chelsea, b. 1937.
1878	°Cairns (5th), David Charles Cairns, G.C.V.O., C.B., b. 1909, s. 1946, m.	Viscount Garmoyle, b. 1939.
1543 S.	Caithness (20th), Malcolm Ian Sinclair, b. 1948, s. 1965, m.	Sir John R. N. B. S., Bt., b. 1928.
1800 I.	Caledon (6th), Denis James Alexander, b. 1920, s. 1968, m.	Viscount Alexander, b. 1955.
1661	Carlisle (12th), Charles James Ruthven Howard, M.C., b. 1923, s. 1963, m.	Viscount Morpeth, b. 1949.
1793	Carnarvon (6th), Henry George Alfred Marius Victor Francis Herbert, b. 1898, s. 1923.	Lord Porchester, b. 1924.
1748 I.*	Carrick (9th), Brian Stuart Theobald Somerset Caher Butler (3rd U.K. Baron, Butler, 1912), b. 1931, s. 1957, m.	Viscount Ikerrin, b. 1953.
1800 I.	°Castle Stewart (8th), Arthur Patrick Avondale Stuart, b. 1928, s. 1961, m.	Viscount Stuart, b. 1953.
1814	°Cathcart (6th), Alan Cathcart, C.B., D.S.O., M.C. (15th Scott. Baron, Cathcart), b. 1919, s. 1927, m.	Lord Greenock, b. 1952.
1647 I.	Cavan (12th), Michael Edward Oliver Lambart, T.D., b. 1911, s. 1950, m.	Roger C. L., b. 1944.
1827	°Cawdor (6th), Hugh John Vaughan Campbell, b. 1932, s. 1970, m.	Viscount Emlyn, b. 1962.
1801	Chichester (9th), John Nicholas Pelham, b. 1944, s. 1944.	Richard A. H. P., b. 1952.
1803 I.*	Clancarty (7th), Greville Sydney Rochfort Le Poer Trench (6th U.K. Visct. Clancarty, 1823), b. 1902, s. 1971, m.	Hon. William F. B. Le P. T., b. 1911.
1776 I.*	Clanwilliam (6th), John Charles Edmund Carson Meade (4th U.K. Baron Clanwilliam, 1828), b. 1914, s. 1953, m.	John H. M., b. 1919.

Created.	Title, Order of Succession, Name, etc.	Eldest Son or Heir.

1776   Clarendon (7th), George Frederick Laurence Villiers, b. 1933, s. 1955, m.   Hon. Nicholas V., b. 1916.

1620 I.*   Cork & Orrery (1660), Patrick Reginald Boyle (13th *Irish Earl* and 9th *Brit. Baron, Boyle of Marston*, 1711), b. 1910, s. 1967, m.   Hon. John W. B., D.S.C., b. 1916.

1850   Cottenham (8th), Kenelm Charles Everard Digby Pepys, b. 1948, s. 1968, m.   Charles D. L. P., b. 1909.

1762 I.*   Courtown (9th), James Patrick Montagu Burgoyne Stopford,O.B.E., T.D. (8th *Brit. Baron, Saltersford*, 1796), b. 1954, s. 1975.   Hon. Jeremy N. s. b. 1958.

1697   Coventry (11th), George William Coventry, b. 1934, s. 1940, m.   Viscount Deerhurst, b. 1957.

1857   °Cowley (6th), Richard Francis Wellesley, b. 1946, s. 1968, m.   Hon. Garret G. W., b. 1934.

1892   Cranbrook (4th), John David Gathorne-Hardy, C.B.E., b. 1900, s. 1915, m.   Lord Medway, b. 1933.

1801   Craven (7th), Thomas Robert Douglas Craven, b. 1957, s. 1965, M.   Hon. Simon G. C., b. 1961.

1398 S.*   Crawford (28th) *and Balcarres* (11th), David Alexander Robert Lindsay, K.T., G.B.E., (*Premier Earl on Union Roll and* 4th *U.K. Baron, Wigan*, 1826), b. 1900, s. 1940, m.   Lord Balniel, P.C., b. 1927. (*see* p. 250).

1861   Cromartie (4th), Roderick Grant Francis Mackenzie, M.C., b. 1904, s. 1962, m.   Viscount Tarbat, b. 1948.

1901   Cromer (3rd), George Rowland Stanley Baring, P.C., G.C.M.G., M.B.E., b. 1918, s. 1953, m.   Viscount Errington, b. 1946.

1633 S.*   Dalhousie (16th), Simon Ramsay, K.T., G.B.E., M.C. (4th *U.K. Baron, Ramsay*, 1875), b. 1914, s. 1950, m.   Lord Ramsay, b. 1946.

1725 I.*   Darnley (10th), Peter Stuart Bligh (19th *English Baron, Clifton of Leighton Bromswold*, 1608), b. 1915, s. 1955.   Hon. Adam I. S. B., b. 1941.

1711   Dartmouth (9th), Gerald Humphry Legge, b. 1924, s. 1962, m.   Viscount Lewisham, b. 1949.

1761   °De La Warr (9th), Herbrand Edward Dundonald Brassy Sackville, P.C., G.B.E., b. 1900, s. 1915, m.   Lord Buckhurst, b. 1921.

1622   Denbigh (11th) *and Desmond* (10th), William Rudolph Michael Feilding (10th *Irish Earl, Desmond*, 1622), b. 1943, s. 1966, m.   Viscount Feilding, b. 1970.

1485   Derby (18th), Edward John Stanley, M.C., b. 1918, s. 1948, m.   Hon. Richard S., b 1920.

1553   Devon (17th), Charles Christopher Courtenay, b. 1916, s. 1935, m.   Lord Courtenay, b. 1942.

1800 I.*   Donoughmore (7th), John Michael Henry Hely-Hutchinson, (7th *U.K. Visct. Hutchinson*, 1821), b. 1902, s. 1948, m.   Viscount Suirdale, b. 1927.

1661 I.*   Drogheda (11th), Charles Garrett Moore, K.G., K.B.E. (2nd *U.K Baron. Moore*, 1954), b. 1910, s. 1957, m.   Viscount Moore, b. 1937.

1837   Ducie (6th), Basil Howard Moreton, b. 1917, s. 1952, m.   Lord Moreton, b. 1951.

1860   Dudley (4th), William Humble David Ward, b. 1920, s. 1969, m.   Viscount Ednam, b. 1947.

1660 S.*   Dundee (11th), Henry James Scrymgeour-Wedderburn, P.C. (1st *U.K. Baron, Glassary*, 1954) b. 1902, s. 1924 (*claim admitted*, 1953), m. (*Hereditary Standard Bearer, Scotland*).   Lord Scrymgeour, b. 1949.

1669 S.   Dundonald (14th), Ian Douglas Leonard Cochrane, b. 1918, s. 1958, w.   Lord Cochrane, b. 1961.

1686 S.*   Dunmore (9th), John Alexander Murray (4th *U.K. Baron, Dunmore*, 1831), b. 1939, s. 1962, m.   Reginald A. M., b. 1911.

1822 I.   Dunraven and Mount Earl (7th), Thady Windham Thomas Wyndham-Quin, b. 1939, s. 1965, m.   Capt. Hon. Valentine M. W.-Q., R.N., b. 1890.

1837   Effingham (6th), Mowbray Henry Gordon Howard (16th *E. Baron, Howard of Effingham*, 1553), b. 1905, s. 1946, m.   David P. M. A. H., b. 1939.

1507 S. }   Eglinton (18th) & (9th) *Winton* (1600), Archibald George Montgomerie (6th *U.K. Earl Winton*, 1859), b. 1939, s. 1966, m.   Lord Montgomerie, b. 1966.
1859* }

1733 I.*   Egmont (11th), Frederick George Moore Perceval (9th *Brit. Baron, Lovel & Holland*, 1762), b. 1914, s. 1932, m.   Viscount Perceval, b. 1934.

1821   Eldon (4th), John Scott, G.C.V.O., b. 1899, s. 1926, w.   Viscount Encombe, b. 1937.

1633 S.*   Elgin (11th), & *Kincardine* (15th) (1647), Andrew Douglas Alexander Thomas Bruce, (4th *U.K. Baron, Elgin*, 1849), b. 1924, s. 1968, m.   Lord Bruce, b. 1961.

1789 I.*   Enniskillen (6th), David Lowry Cole, M.B.E., (4th *U.K. Baron, Grinstead*, 1815) b. 1918, s. 1963, m.   Viscount Cole, b. 1942.

1781 I.*   Erne (6th), Henry George Victor John Crichton (3rd *U.K. Baron, Fermanagh*, 1876), b. 1937, s. 1940, m.   Viscount Crichton, b. 1971.

1661   Essex (9th), Reginald George de Vere Capell, T.D., b. 1906, s. 1966, m.   Robert E. de V. C., b. 1920.

1711   °Ferrers (13th), Robert Washington Shirley, b. 1929, s. 1954, m.   Viscount Tamworth, b. 1952.

1628 I.*   Fingall (12th), Oliver James Horace Plunkett, M.C. (19th *I. Baron, Killeen*, 1449) (5th *U.K. Baron, Fingall*, 1831), b. 1896 s. 1929, m.   (None to Earldom or U.K. Barony), to Irish Barony Lord Dunsany (*see* p. 241).

1746*   °Fitzwilliam (8th) William Thomas George Wentworth-Fitzwilliam (10th *Irish Earl, Fitzwilliam*, 1716), b. 1904, s. 1952, m.   (None.)

Created.	Title, Order of Succession, Name, etc.	Eldest Son or Heir.
1789	°*Fortescue* (6th), Denzil George Fortescue, M.C., T.D., b. 1893, s. 1958, m.	Viscount Ebrington, b. 1922.
1841	*Gainsborough* (5th), Anthony Gerard Edward Noel, b. 1923, s. 1927, m.	Viscount Campden, b. 1950.
1623 S.*	*Galloway* (12th), Randolph Algernon Ronald Stewart (5th Brit. Baron, Stewart of Garlies, 1796), b. 1892, s. 1920, w.	Lord Garlies, b. 1928.
1703 S.*	*Glasgow* (9th), David William Maurice Boyle, C.B. D.S.C. (3rd U.K. Baron, Fairlie, 1897), b. 1910, s. 1963, m.	Viscount of Kelburn, b. 1939.
1806 I.*	*Gosford* (7th), Charles David Alexander John Sparrow Acheson (5th U.K. Baron, Worlingham, 1835), b. 1942, s. 1966.	Hon. Patrick B. V. M. A., b. 1915.
1945	*Gowrie* (2nd), Alexander Patrick Greysteel Hore-Ruthven (3rd U.K. Baron, Ruthven of Gowrie, 1919), b. 1939, s. 1955.	Viscount Ruthven of Canberra, b. 1964.
1684 I.*	*Granard* (9th), Arthur Patrick Hastings Forbes, A.F.C. (4th U.K. Baron, Granard, 1806), b. 1915, s. 1948, m. [m.	Hon. John F., b. 1920.
1833	°*Granville* (5th), Granville James Leveson-Gower, M.C., b. 1918, s. 1953.	Lord Leveson, b. 1959.
1806	°*Grey* (6th), Richard Fleming George Charles Grey, b. 1939, s. 1963, m.	Phillip K. G., b. 1940.
1752	*Guilford* (9th), Edward Francis North, b. 1933, s. 1949, m.	Lord North, b. 1971.
1619 S.	*Haddington* (12th), George Baillie-Hamilton, K.T., M.C., T.D., b. 1894, s. 1917, m.	Lord Binning, b. 1941.
1919	°*Haig* (2nd), George Alexander Eugene Douglas Haig, O.B.E. b. 1918, s. 1928, m.	Viscount Dawick, b. 1961.
1944	*Halifax* (2nd), Charles Ingram Courtenay Wood (4th U.K. Viscount, Halifax, 1866), b. 1912, s. 1959, m.	Lord Irwin, b. 1944.
1898	*Halsbury* (3rd), John Anthony Hardinge Giffard, F.R.S., b. 1908, s. 1943, m.	Viscount Tiverton, b. 1934.
1754	*Hardwicke* (10th), Joseph Philip Sebastian Yorke, b. 1971, s. 1974, M.	Richard C. J. Y., b. 1916.
1812	*Harewood* (7th), George Henry Hubert Lascelles, b. 1923, s. 1947, m. (See also p. 217.)	Viscount Lascelles, b. 1950.
1742	*Harrington* (11th), William Henry Leicester Stanhope (8th U.K. Viscount, Stanhope of Mahon, 1717), b. 1922, s. 1929, m.	Viscount Petersham, b. 1945.
1809	*Harrowby* (6th), Dudley Ryder, B. 1892, s. 1956, w.	Viscount Sandon, b. 1922.
1821	°*Howe* (6th), Edward Richard Assheton Curzon, C.B.E., b. 1908, s. 1964, m.	George C., b. 1898.
1529	*Huntingdon* (15th), Francis John Clarence Westenra Plantagenet Hastings, b. 1901, s. 1939, m.	David F. G. H., b. 1909.
1885	*Iddesleigh* (4th), Stafford Henry Northcote, b. 1932, s. 1970, m.	Viscount St. Cyres, b. 1957.
1750	*Ilchester* (9th), Maurice Vivian de Touffreville Fox-Strangways, b. 1920, s. 1970, m.	Hon. Raymond G. F.-S., b. 1921.
1929	*Inchcape* (3rd), Kenneth James William Mackay, b. 1917, s. 1939, m.	Viscount Glenapp, b. 1943.
1919	*Iveagh* (3rd), Arthur Francis Benjamin Guinness, b. 1937, s. 1967, m.	Viscount Elveden, b. 1969.
1925	*Jellicoe* (2nd), George Patrick John Rushworth Jellicoe, P.C., D.S.O., M.C., b. 1918, s. 1935, m.	Viscount Brocas, b. 1950.
1697	*Jersey* (9th), George Francis Child-Villiers (12th Irish Visct., Grandison, 1620), b. 1910, s. 1923, m.	Viscount Villiers, b. 1948.
1822 I.	*Kilmorey* (5th), Francis Jack Richard Patrick Needham, b. 1915, s. 1961, m.	Viscount Newry and Mourne, b. 1942.
1866	*Kimberley* (4th), John Wodehouse, b. 1924, s. 1941, m.	Lord Wodehouse, b. 1951.
1768 I.	*Kingston* (11th), Barclay Robert Edwin King-Tenison, b. 1943, s. 1948, m.	Viscount Kingsborough, b. 1969.
1633 S.*	*Kinnoull* (15th), Arthur William George Patrick Hay (9th Brit. Baron, Hay of Pedwardine, 1711), b. 1935, s. 1938, m.	Viscount Dupplin, b. 1962.
1602 S.	*Kintore* (12th), (James) Ian Baird (3rd U.K. Visct., Stonehaven, 1938), b. 1908, s. to Viscountcy, 1941, to Earldom, 1974, m.	Lord Inverurie, b. 1939.
1914	°*Kitchener of Khartoum* (3rd), Henry Herbert Kitchener, b. 1919, s. 1937.	Hon. Charles E. K., b. 1920.
1756 I.	*Lanesborough* (9th), Denis Anthony Brian Butler, b. 1918, s. 1959.	Cdr. Terence B. J. D. B., b. 1913.
1624 S.	*Lauderdale* (17th), Patrick Francis Maitland, b. 1911, s. 1968, m.	Viscount Maitland, b. 1937.
1837	*Leicester* (5th), Thomas William Edward Coke, M.V.O., b. 1908, s. 1949, m.	Anthony L. C., b. 1909.
1641 S.	*Leven* (14th) & (13th) *Melville* (1690), Alexander Robert Leslie-Melville, b. 1924, s. 1947, m.	Lord Balgonie, b. 1954.
1831	*Lichfield* (5th), Thomas Patrick John Anson, b. 1939, s. 1960, m.	Geoffrey R. A., b. 1929.
1803 I.*	*Limerick* (6th), Patrick Edmund Pery (6th U.K. Baron, Foxford, 1815), b. 1930, s. 1967, m.	Viscount Glentworth, b. 1963.
1633 S.	*Lindsay* (14th), William Tucker Lindesay-Bethune, b. 1901, s. 1943, m.	Viscount Garnock, b. 1926.
1626	*Lindsey* (14th) and *Abingdon* (9th) (1682), Richard Henry Rupert Bertie, b. 1931, s. 1963, m.	Lord Norreys, b. 1958.
1776 I.	*Lisburne* (8th), John David Malet Vaughan, b. 1918, s. 1965, m.	Viscount Vaughan, b. 1945.
1822 I.*	*Listowel* (3rd), William Francis Hare, P.C., G.C.M.G. (3rd U.K. Baron, Hare, 1869), b. 1906, s. 1931, m.	Viscount Ennismore, b. 1964.
1905	*Liverpool* (5th), Edward Peter Bertram Savile Foljambe, b. 1944, s. 1969, m.	Viscount Hawkesbury, b. 1972.

Created.	Title, Order of Succession, Name, etc.	Eldest Son or Heir.

1945 — °Lloyd George of Dwyfor (3rd), Owen Lloyd George, b. 1924, s. 1968, m. — Viscount Gwynedd, b. 1951.

1785 I.★ Longford (7th), Francis Aungier Pakenham, K.G., P.C. (6th U.K. Baron, Silchester, 1821; 1st U.K. Baron, Pakenham, 1945). b. 1905, s. 1961, m. — Lord Silchester, b. 1933.

1807 — Lonsdale (7th), James Hugh William Lowther, b. 1922, s. 1953, m. — Viscount Lowther, b. 1949.

1838 — Lovelace (5th), Peter Axel William Locke King (12th British Baron, King, 1725), b. 1951, s. 1964. — (None.)

1795 I.★ Lucan (7th), Richard John Bingham (3rd U.K. Baron, Bingham, 1934), b. 1934, s. 1964, m. — Lord Bingham, b. 1967.

1880 — Lytton (4th), Noel Anthony Scawen Lytton (17th English Baron, Wentworth, 1529), b. 1900, s. 1951, m. — Viscount Knebworth, b. 1950.

1721 — Macclesfield (9th), George Loveden William Henry Parker, b. 1888, s. 1896, w. — Viscount Parker, b. 1914.

1800 — Malmesbury (6th), William James Harris, T.D., b. 1907, s. 1950, m. — Viscount FitzHarris, b. 1946.

1776 & 1792 Mansfield and Mansfield (8th), William David Mungo James Murray (14th Scott. Visct., Stormont, 1621), b. 1930, s. 1971, m. — Viscount Stormont, b. 1956.

1565 S. — Mar (13th) & (14th) Kellie (1616), John Francis Hervey Erskine, b. 1921, s. 1955, m. — Lord Erskine, b. 1949.

1785 I. — Mayo (10th), Terence Patrick Bourke, b. 1929, s. 1962, m. — Lord Naas, b. 1953.

1627 I.★ Meath (14th), Anthony Windham Normand Brabazon (5th U.K. Baron, Chaworth, 1831), b. 1910, s. 1949, m. — Lord Ardee, b. 1941.

1766 I. — Mexborough (7th), John Raphael Wentworth Savile, b. 1906, s. 1945, m. — Viscount Pollington, b. 1931.

1920 — Midleton (2nd), George St. John Brodrick, M.C. (10th Irish Viscount, Midleton, 1717), b. 1888, s. 1942, m. — (None to Earldom), to Irish Viscountcy, Trevor L. B., b. 1903.

1813 — Minto (6th), Gilbert Edward George Lariston Garnet Elliot-Murray-Kynynmound, M.B.E., b. 1928, s. 1975, m. — Viscount Melgund, b. 1953.

1562 S.★ Moray (20th) Douglas John Moray Stuart (12th Brit. Baron, Stuart of Castle Stuart, 1796), b. 1928, s. 1974, m. — Lord Doune, b. 1966.

1815 — Morley (6th), John St. Aubyn Parker, b. 1923, s. 1962, m. — Visct. Boringdon, b. 1956.

1458 S. — Morton (21st), Sholto Charles John Hay Douglas, b. 1907, s. 1935. — John C. S. D., b. 1927.

1947 — °Mountbatten of Burma (1st), Louis Francis Albert Victor Nicholas Mountbatten, K G, P.C., G.C.B., O.M., G.C.S.I., G.C.I.E., G.C.V.O., D.S.O., b. 1900, w (Personal A.D.C. to the Queen), Admiral of the Fleet. (See also p. 215). — Baroness Brabourne, b. 1924. (see pp. 215 and 238).

1789 — Mount Edgcumbe (7th), Edward Piers Edgcumbe, b. 1903, s. 1965, m. — George A. V. E., b. 1907.

1831 — Munster (5th), Geoffrey William Richard Hugh FitzClarence, P.C., K.B.E., b. 1906, s. 1928, m. — Edward C. FitzC., b. 1899.

1805 — °Nelson (8th), George Joseph Horatio Nelson, b. 1905, s. 1972, m. — Peter J. H. N., b. 1941.

1827 I. — Norbury (6th), Noel Terence Graham-Toler, b. 1939, s. 1955, m. — Viscount Glandine, b. 1967.

1806 I.★ Normanton (6th), Shaun James Christian Welbore Ellis Agar (9th U.K. Baron, Mendip, 1791) (4th U.K. Baron, Somerton, 1873), b. 1945, s. 1967, m. — Hon. Mark S. A. A., b. 1948.

1647 S. — Northesk (13th), Robert Andrew Carnegie, b. 1926, s. 1975, m. — Lord Rosehill, b. 1954.

1801 — Onslow (7th), Michael William Coplestone Onslow, b. 1938, s. 1971, m. — Viscount Cranley, b. 1967.

1925 — Oxford & Asquith (2nd), Julian Edward George Asquith, K.C.M.G., b. 1916, s. 1928, m. — Viscount Asquith, b. 1952.

1929 — °Peel (3rd), William James Robert Peel (4th U.K. Viscount Peel, 1895), b. 1947, s. 1969, m. — Hon. Robert M. A. P., b. 1950.

1551 — Pembroke (17th) & (14th) Montgomery (1605), Henry George Charles Alexander Herbert, b. 1939, s. 1969, m. — Hon. David A. R. H., b. 1908.

1605 S. — Perth (17th), John David Drummond, P.C., b. 1907, s. 1951, m. — Viscount Strathallan, b. 1935.

1905 — Plymouth (3rd), Other Robert Ivor Windsor-Clive (15th English Baron, Windsor, 1529), b. 1923, s. 1943, m. — Viscount Windsor, b. 1951.

1785 I. — Portarlington (7th), George Lionel Yuill Seymour Dawson-Damer, b. 1938, s. 1959, m. — Viscount Carlow, b. 1965.

1743 — Portsmouth (9th), Gerard Vernon Wallop, b. 1898, s. 1943, m. — Viscount Lymington, b. 1923.

1804 — Powis (6th), Christian Victor Charles Herbert (7th Irish Baron, Clive, 1762), b. 1904, s. 1974. — George W. H., b. 1925.

1765 — Radnor (8th) Jacob Pleydell-Bouverie, b. 1927, s. 1968, m. — Viscount Folkestone, b. 1955.

1831 I.★ Ranfurly (6th), Thomas Daniel Knox, K.C.M.G. (7th U.K. Baron, Ranfurly, 1826), b. 1913, s. 1933, m. — Gerald F. N. K. b. 1929.

1771 I. — Roden (9th), Robert William Jocelyn, b. 1909, s. 1956, m. — Viscount Jocelyn. b. 1938.

1801 — Romney (6th), Charles Marsham, b. 1892, s. 1933, m. — Michael H. M., b. 1910.

1703 S.★ Rosebery (7th), Neil Archibald Primrose (3rd U.K. Earl of Midlothian, 1911), b. 1929, s. 1974, m. — Lord Dalmeny, b. 1967.

Created.	Title, Order of Succession, Name, etc.	Eldest Son or Heir.

1806 I. *Rosse* (6th), Laurence Michael Harvey Parsons, K.B.E., *b.* 1906, *s.* 1918, *m.* Lord Oxmantown, *b.* 1936.

1801 *Rosslyn* (6th), Anthony Hugh Francis Harry St. Clair-Erskine, *b.* 1917, *s.* 1939. Lord Loughborough, *b.* 1958.

1457 S. *Rothes* (21st), Ian Lionel Malcolm Leslie, *b.* 1932, *s.* 1975, *m.* Lord Leslie, *b.* 1958.

1861 °*Russell* (4th), John Conrad Russell, *b.* 1921, *s.* 1970. Hon. Conrad S. R. R., *b.* 1937.

1915 °*St. Aldwyn* (2nd), Michael John Hicks-Beach, P.C., K.B.E. T.D., *b.* 1912, *s.* 1916, *m.* Viscount Quenington, *b.* 1950.

1815 *St. Germans* (9th), Nicholas Richard Michael Eliot, *b.* 1914, *s.* 1960, *m.* Lord Eliot, *b.* 1941.

1690 *Scarborough* (12th), Richard Aldred Lumley, (13th *Irish Visct.*, *Lumley*, 1628), *b.* 1932, *s.* 1969, *m.* Viscount Lumley, *b.* 1973.

1701 S. *Seafield* (13th), Ian Derek Francis Ogilvie-Grant-Studley-Herbert, *b.* 1939, *s.* 1969, *m.* Visct. Reidhaven, *b.* 1963.

1882 *Selborne* (4th), John Roundell Palmer, *b.* 1940, *s.* 1971, *m.* Viscount Wolmer, *b.* 1971.

1646 S. *Selkirk* (7th) (George) Nigel Douglas-Hamilton, P.C., G.C.M.G., G.B.E., A.F.C., Q.C., *b.* 1906, *s.* 1940, *m.* The Master of Selkirk, *b.* 1939.

1672 *Shaftesbury* (10th), Anthony Ashley-Cooper, *b.* 1938, *s.* 1961, *m.* Hon. John P. H. N. A.-C., *b.* 1915.

1756 I.* *Shannon* (9th), Richard Bentinck Boyle (8th *Brit. Bn.*, *Carleton* 1786), *b.* 1924, *s.* 1963, *m.* Viscount Boyle, *b.* 1960.

1442 *Shrewsbury* (21st) *& Waterford* (I. 1446), John George Charles Henry Alton Alexander Chetwynd Chetwynd-Talbot (*Premier Earl of England and Ireland; Earl Talbot*, 1784), *b.* 1914, *s.* 1921, *m.* Viscount Ingestre, *b.* 1952.

1961 *Snowdon* (1st), Antony Charles Robert Armstrong-Jones, G.C.V.O., *b.* 1930, *m.* (*See also* p. 219.) Viscount Linley *b.* 1961 (*see* p. 219).

1880 °*Sondes* (5th), Henry George Herbert Milles-Lade, *b.* 1940, *s.* 1970. (None).

1633 S.* *Southesk* (11th), Charles Alexander Carnegie, K.C.V.O. (3rd *U.K. Baron, Balinhard*, 1869), *b.* 1893, *s.* 1941, *m.* The Duke of Fife, *b.* 1929 (*see* pp. 216 and 227).

1765 °*Spencer* (8th), Edward John Spencer, M.V.O., *b.* 1924, *s.* 1975. Viscount Althorp, *b.* 1964.

1703 S.* *Stair* (13th), John Aymer Dalrymple, C.V.O., M.B.E. (6th *U.K. Baron, Oxenfoord*, 1841), *b.* 1906, *s.* 1961, *m.* Viscount Dalrymple, *b.* 1961.

1628 *Stamford* (10th), Roger Grey, *b.* 1896, *s.* 1910. (None.)

1821 *Stradbroke* (4th), John Anthony Alexander Rous, *b.* 1903, *s.* 1947, *m.* Hon. Keith R., *b.* 1907.

1847 *Strafford* (7th), Robert Cecil Byng, *b.* 1904, *s.* 1951, *m.* Viscount Enfield, *b.* 1936.

1937 *Strathmore* (4th), Fergus Michael Claude Bowes-Lyon (17th *Scottish Earl, Strathmore & Kinghorne* 1606), *b.* 1928, *s.* 1972, *m.* Lord Glamis, *b.* 1957.

1603 *Suffolk* (21st) *& (14th) Berkshire* (1626), Michael John James George Robert Howard, *b.* 1935, *s.* 1941, *m.* Viscount Andover, *b.* 1974.

1955 *Swinton* (2nd), David Yarburgh Cunliffe-Lister, *b.* 1937, *s.* 1972, *m.* Hon. Nicholas J. C.-L., *b.* 1939.

1714 *Tankerville* (9th), Charles Augustus Grey Bennet, *b.* 1921, *s.* 1971, *m.* Lord Ossulston, *b.* 1956.

1822 °*Temple of Stowe* (7th), Ronald Stephen Brydges Temple-Gore-Langton, *b.* 1910, *s.* 1966. W. Grenville A. T.-G.-L., *b.* 1924.

1815 *Verulam* (7th), John Duncan Grimston (11th *Irish Visct.*, *Grimston*, 1719; 16th *Scott. Baron, Forrester of Corstorphine*, 1633), *b.* 1955, *s.* 1973. Lord Grimston of Westbury, *b.* 1897 (*see* p. 242).

1729 °*Waldegrave* (12th), Geoffrey Noel Waldegrave, K.G., T.D., *b.* 1905, *s.* 1936, *m.* Viscount Chewton, *b.* 1940.

1759 *Warwick & °Brooke* (1746), Charles Guy Fulke Greville (7th *Earl Brooke* and 7th *Earl of Warwick*), *b.* 1911, *s.* 1928, *m.* Lord Brooke, *b.* 1934.

1633 S.* *Wemyss* (12th) *& (8th) March* (1697), Francis David Charteris, K.T. (5th *U.K. Baron, Wemyss*, 1821), *b.* 1912, *s.* 1937, *m.* Lord Neidpath, *b.* 1948.

1621 I. *Westmeath* (13th), William Anthony Nugent, *b.* 1928, *s.* 1971, *m.* Lord Delvin, *b.* 1965.

1624 *Westmorland* (15th), David Anthony Thomas Fane, K.C.V.O., *b.* 1924, *s.* 1948, *m.* Lord Burghersh, *b.* 1951.

1876 *Wharncliffe* (4th), Alan James Montagu-Stuart-Wortley-Mackenzie, *b.* 1935, *s.* 1953, *m.* Alan R. Montagu-Stuart-Wortley, *b.* 1927.

1793 I. *Wicklow* (8th), William Cecil James Philip John Paul Forward-Howard, *b.* 1902, *s.* 1946, *m.* Cecil A. F.-H., *b.* 1909.

1801 *Wilton* (7th), Seymour William Arthur John Egerton, *b.* 1921, *s.* 1927, *m.* Lord Ebury, *b.* 1934 (*see* p. 241).

1628 *Winchilsea* (16th) *& (11th) Nottingham* (1681), Christopher Denys Stormont Finch-Hatton, *b.* 1936, *s.* 1950, *m.* Viscount Maidstone, *b.* 1967.

1766 I. °*Winterton* (7th), Robert Chad Turnour, *b.* 1915, *s.* 1962, *w.* N. Cecil T., D.F.M., C.D., *b.* 1919.

1956 *Woolton* (3rd), Simon Frederick Marquis, *b.* 1958, *s.* 1969, *M.* (None.)

1837 *Yarborough* (7th), John Edward Pelham, *b.* 1920, *s.* 1966, *m.* Lord Worsley, *b.* 1963.

1922 *Ypres* (3rd), John Richard Charles Lambart French, *b.* 1921, *s.* 1948, *m.* (None.)

VISCOUNTS

Style (*see also* note, p. 256), The Right Hon. the Viscount——. *Adressed as*, My Lord. The eldest sons of Viscounts and Barons have no distinctive title; they, as well as their brothers and sisters, are styled the Hon. Robert, Hon. Mary, &c.

Created.	*Title, Order of Succession, Name, etc.*	*Eldest Son or Heir.*
1945	*Addison* (2nd), Christopher Addison, *b.* 1904, *s.* 1951, *m.*	Hon. Michael *A.*, *b.* 1914.
1946	*Alanbrooke* (3rd), Alan Victor Harold Brooke, *b.* 1932, *s.* 1972.	(None).
1919	*Allenby* (2nd), Dudley Jaffray Hynman Allenby, *b.* 1903, *s.* 1936, *m.*	Hon. Michael *A.*, *b.* 1931.
1911	*Allendale* (3rd), Wentworth Hubert Charles Beaumont, *b.* 1922, *s.* 1956, *m.*	Hon. Wentworth P. I. *B.*, *b.* 1948.
1960	*Amory* (1st), Derick Heathcoat Amory, K.G., P.C., G.C.M.G., T.D., *s.* 1899.	(None.)
1642 S.	*Arbuthnott* (16th *Viscount of Arbuthnott*), John Campbell Arbuthnott, D.S.C., *b.* 1924, *s.* 1966, *m.*	Master of Arbuthnott, *b.* 1950.
1751 I.	*Ashbrook* (10th), Desmond Llowarch Edward Flower, M.B.E., *b.* 1905, *s.* 1936, *m.*	Hon. Michael *F.*, *b.* 1935.
1917	*Astor* (4th), William Waldorf Astor, *b.* 1951, *s.* 1966.	Hon. David *A.*, *b.* 1912.
1781 I.	*Bangor* (7th), Edward Henry Harold Ward, *b.* 1905, *s.* 1950.	Hon. William M. D. *W.*, *b.* 1948.
1720 I.*	*Barrington* (11th), Patrick William Daines Barrington (5th *U.K. Baron Shute*, 1880), *b.* 1908, *s.* 1960.	Hon. Rupert E. S. *B.*, D.S.O., *b.* 1877.
1925	*Bearsted* (3rd), Marcus Richard Samuel, T.D., *b.* 1909, *s.* 1948, *m.*	Hon. Peter *S.*, M.C., T.D., *b.* 1911.
1963	*Blakenham* (1st), John Hugh Hare, P.C., O.B.E., *b.* 1911, *m.*	Hon. Michael J. *H.*, *b.* 1938.
1935	*Bledisloe* (2nd), Benjamin Ludlow Bathurst, Q.C., *b.* 1899, *s.* 1958, *m.*	Hon. Christopher H. L. *B.*, *b.* 1934.
1712	*Bolingbroke & St. John* (7th), Kenneth Oliver Musgrave St. John, *b.* 1927, *s.* 1974, *m.*	Hon. Henry F. *St. J.*, *b.* 1957.
1960	*Boyd of Merton* (1st), Alan Tindal Lennox-Boyd, P.C., C.H., *b.* 1904, *m.*	Hon. Simon D. R. N. *L.-B.*, *b.* 1939.
1717 S*	*Boyne* (10th), Gustavus Michael George Hamilton-Russell (4th *U.K. Baron, Brancepeth*, 1866), *b.* 1931, *s.* 1942, *m.*	Hon. Michael G. S. *H.-R.*, *b.* 1965.
1929	*Brentford* (3rd), Lancelot William Joynson-Hicks, *b.* 1902, *s.* 1958, *m.*	Hon. Crispin W. *J.-H.*, *b.* 1933.
1929	*Bridgeman* (2nd), Robert Clive Bridgeman, K.B.E., C.B., D.S.O., M.C., *b.* 1896, *s.* 1935, *m.*	Robin J. O. *B.* *b.* 1930.
1868	*Bridport* (4th), Alexander Nelson Hood (7th *Duke of Brontë in Sicily* and 6th *Irish Baron, Bridport* 1794), *b.* 1948, *s.* 1969, *m.*	Hon. Peregrine A. N. *H.* *b.* 1974.
1952	*Brookeborough* (2nd), John Warden Brooke, P.C. (N.I.), *b.* 1922, *s.* 1973, *m.*	Hon. Alan H. *B.*, *b.* 1955.
1932	*Buckmaster* (3rd), Martin Stanley Buckmaster, *b.* 1921, *s.* 1974.	Hon. Colin J. *B.*, *b.* 1923.
1939	*Caldecote* (2nd), Robert Andrew Inskip, D.S.C., *b.* 1917, *s.* 1947, *m.*	Hon. Piers J. H. *I.*, *b.* 1947.
1941	*Camrose* (2nd), (John) Seymour Berry, T.D., *b.* 1909, *s.* 1954.	Lord Hartwell, M.B.E. T.D., *b.* 1911 (*see* p. 251.)
1954	*Chandos* (2nd), Antony Alfred Lyttelton, *b.* 1920, *s.* 1972, *m.*	Hon. Thomas O. *L.*, *b.* 1953.
1916	*Chaplin* (3rd), Anthony Freskyn Charles Hamby Chaplin, *b.* 1906, *s.* 1949, *m.*	(None.)
1665 I.	*Charlemont* (12th), Richard William St. George Caulfeild (16th *Irish Baron, Caulfeild of Charlemont*, 1620), *b.* 1887, *s.* 1971, *w.*	Charles W. *C.*, *b.* 1899.
1921	*Chelmsford* (3rd), Frederic Jan Thesiger, *b.* 1931, *s.* 1970, *m.*	Hon. Frederic C. P. *T.*, *b.* 1962.
1717 I.	*Chetwynd* (10th), Adam Richard John Casson Chetwynd, T.D., *b.* 1935, *s.* 1965, *m.*	Hon. Adam D. *C.*, *b.* 1969.
1911	*Chilston* (3rd), Eric Alexander Akers-Douglas, *b.* 1910, *s.* 1947, *w.*	Alastair G. *A.-D.*, *b.* 1946.
1902	*Churchill* (3rd), Victor George Spencer (5th *U.K. Baron Churchill*, 1815) *b.* 1934, *s.* 1973.	None to Viscountcy; to Barony, Richard H. R. *S. b.* 1926.
1718	*Cobham* (10th), Charles John Lyttelton, K.G., P.C., G.C.M.G., G.C.V.O. (7th *Irish Baron, Westcote*, 1766), *b.* 1909, *s.* 1949, *m.*	Hon. John W. L. *L.*, *b.* 1943.
1902	*Colville of Culross* (4th), John Mark Alexander Colville (13th *Scott. Baron, Colville of Culross*, 1604), *b.* 1933, *s.* 1945, *m.*	Master of Colville, *b.* 1959.
1827	*Combermere* (5th), Michael Wellington Stapleton-Cotton, *b.* 1929, *s.* 1969, *m.*	Hon. Thomas R. W. *S.-C.*, *b.* 1969.
1917	*Cowdray* (3rd), Weetman John Churchill Pearson (3rd *U.K. Baron, Cowdray*, 1910), *b.* 1910, *s.* 1933, *m.*	Hon. Michael *P.*, *b.* 1944.
1927	*Craigavon* (3rd), Janric Fraser Craig, *b.* 1944, *s.* 1974.	(None.)
1886	*Cross* (3rd), Assheton Henry Cross, *b.* 1920, *s.* 1932 *m.*	(None.)
1943	*Daventry* (2nd), Robert Oliver FitzRoy, *b.* 1893, *s.* 1962, *m.*	Hon. John M. *FitzRoy-Newdegate*, *b.* 1897.
1937	*Davidson* (2nd), John Andrew Davidson, *b.* 1928, *s.* 1970.	Hon. Malcolm W. M. *D.*, *b.* 1934.

Created.	Title, Order of Succession, Name, etc.	Eldest Son or Heir.
1956	*De L'Isle* (1st), William Philip Sidney, V.C., K.G., P.C., G.C.M.G., G.C.V.O., (6th *Baron De L'Isle and Dudley*, 1835), b. 1909, m.	Hon. Philip S., b. 1945.
1776 I.	*De Vesci* (6th), John Eustace Vesey (7th *Irish Baron, Knapton*, 1750), b. 1919, s. 1958, m.	Hon. Thomas E. V., b. 1955.
1917	*Devonport* (3rd), Terence Kearley, b. 1944, s. 1973, m.	
1964	*Dilhorne* (1st), Reginald Edward Manningham-Buller, P.C. (*Lord of Appeal*), b. 1905, m.	Hon. John M., M.-B., b. 1932.
1622 I.	*Dillon* (20th), Michael Eric Dillon, b. 1911, s. 1946, m.	Hon. Charles D., b 1945.
1785 I.	*Doneraile* (9th), Richard St. John St. Leger, b. 1923, s. 1957, m.	Hon. Richard A. St. L., b. 1946.
1680 I.*	*Downe* (11th), John Christian George Dawnay (4th *U.K. Baron, Dawnay*, 1897), b. 1935, s. 1965, m.	Hon. Richard D., b. 1967.
1959	*Dunrossil* (2nd), John William Morrison, b. 1926, s. 1961, m.	Hon. Andrew W. R. M., b. 1953.
1964	*Eccles* (1st), David McAdam Eccles, P.C., K.C.V.O., b. 1904, m.	Hon. John D. E., b. 1931.
1897	*Esher* (4th), Lionel Gordon Baliol Brett, C.B.E., b. 1913, s. 1963, m.	Hon. Christopher L. B. B., b. 1936.
1816	*Exmouth* (10th), Paul Edward Pellew, b. 1940, s. 1970, m.	Hon. Peter I. P., b. 1942.
1620 S.	*Falkland* (14th), Lucius Henry Plantagenet Cary (*Premier Scottish Viscount on the Roll*), b. 1905, s. 1961, m.	Master of Falkland, b. 1935.
1720	*Falmouth* (9th), George Hugh Boscawen (26th *Eng. Baron, Le Despencer*, 1264), b. 1919, s. 1962, m.	Hon. Evelyn A. H. B., b. 1955.
1918	*Furness* (2nd), William Anthony Furness, b. 1929, s. 1940.	(None.)
1720 I.*	*Gage* (6th), Henry Rainald Gage, K.C.V.O. (5th *Brit. Baron, Gage*, 1790), b. 1895, s. 1912, m.	Hon. George J. St. C. G., b. 1932.
1727 I.	*Galway* (10th,) William Arundell Monckton, b. 1894, s. 1971, w.	Edmund S. M., b. 1900.
1478 I.*	*Gormanston* (17th), Jenico Nicholas Dudley Preston (*Premier Viscount of Ireland; 5th U.K. Baron, Gormanston*, 1868), b. 1939, s. 1940.	Hon. Robert P., b. 1915.
1816 I.	*Gort* (8th), Colin Leopold Prendergast Vereker, b. 1916, s. 1975, m.	Hon. Foley R.S.P.V., b. 1951.
1900	*Goschen* (3rd), John Alexander Goschen, K.B.E., b. 1906, s. 1952. m.	Hon. Giles J. H. G., b. 1965.
1849	*Gough* (5th), Shane Hugh Maryon Gough, b. 1941, s. 1951.	(None.)
1937	*Greenwood* (2nd), David Henry Hamar Greenwood, b. 1914, s. 1948.	Hon. Michael G. H. G., b. 1923.
1946	*Hall* (2nd), (William George) Leonard Hall, b. 1913, s. 1965, w.	(None.)
1891	*Hambleden* (4th), William Herbert Smith, b. 1930, s. 1948, m.	Hon. William H. B., S., b. 1955.
1884	*Hampden* (5th), David Francis Brand, b. 1902, s. 1965, m.	Hon. Anthony D. B., b. 1937.
1936	*Hanworth* (2nd), David Bertram Pollock, b. 1916, s. 1936, m.	Hon. David P., b. 1946.
1791 I.	*Harberton* (9th), Henry Ralph Martyn Pomeroy, b. 1908, s. 1956.	Hon. Thomas De V. P., b. 1910.
1917	*Harcourt* (2nd), William Edward Harcourt, K.C.M.G., O.B.E., b. 1908, s. 1922, w.	(None.)
1846	*Hardinge* (4th), Caryl Nicholas Charles Hardinge, M.B.E., b. 1905, s. 1922, w.	Hon. H. Nicholas H., b. 1929.
1791 I.	*Hawarden* (8th), Robert Leslie Eustace Maude, b 1926, s. 1958, m.	Hon. Robert C. W. L., M., b. 1961.
1960	*Head* (1st), Antony Henry Head, P.C., G.C.M.G., C.B.E., M.C., b. 1906, m.	Hon. Richard A. H., b. 1937.
1550	*Hereford* (18th), Robert Milo Leicester Devereux (*Premier Viscount of England*), b. 1932, s. 1952, m.	Rupert M. D., b. 1907.
1842	*Hill* (8th), Antony Rowland Clegg-Hill, b. 1931, s. 1974, m.	Peter D.R.C. C.-H., b. 1945.
1796	*Hood* (6th), Samuel Hood, G.C.M.G. (6th *Irish Baron, Hood*, 1782), b. 1919, s. 1933.	Hon. Alexander L. H., b. 1914.
1956	*Ingleby* (2nd) Martin Raymond Peake, b. 1926, s. 1966, m.	(None.)
1945	*Kemsley* (2nd), (Geoffrey) Lionel Berry, b. 1909, s. 1968, m.	Hon. Denis G. B., T.D., b. 1911.
1911	*Knollys* (3rd) David Francis Dudley Knollys, b. 1931, s. 1966, m.	Hon. Patrick N. M. K., b. 1962.
1895	*Knutsford* (4th), Thurstan Holland-Hibbert, b. 1888, s. 1935, w.	Hon. Julian H.-H., C.B.E., b. 1920.
1945	*Lambert* (2nd), George Lambert, T.D., b. 1909, s. 1958, m.	Hon. Michael J. L., b. 1912.
1954	*Leathers* (2nd), Frederick Alan Leathers, b. 1908, s. 1965, m.	Hon. Christopher G. L., b. 1941.
1922	*Leverhulme* (3rd), Philip William Bryce Lever, T.D., b. 1915, s. 1949, w.	(None.) [1949.
1781 I.	*Lifford* (8th), Alan William Wingfield Hewitt, b. 1900, s. 1954, m.	Hon. Edward J. W. H., b.
1921	*Long* (4th), Richard Gerard Long, b. 1929, s. 1967, m.	Hon. James R. L., b. 1960.
1957	*Mackintosh of Halifax* (2nd), John Mackintosh, b. 1921, s. 1964, m.	Hon. J. Clive M., b. 1958.

Created	Title, Order of Succession, Name, etc.	Eldest Son or Heir
1955	*Malvern* (2nd), John Godfrey Huggins, *b.* 1922, *s.* 1971, *m.*	Hon. Ashley K. G. H., *b.* 1949.
1945	*Marchwood* (2nd), Peter George Penny, M.B.E., *b.* 1912, *s.* 1955, *m.*	Hon. David G. S. P., *b.* 1936.
1942	*Margesson* (2nd), Francis Vere Hampden Margesson, *b.* 1922, *s.* 1965, *m.*	Hon. Richard F. D. M., *b.* 1960.
1660 I.*	*Massereene* (13th) & (6th) *Ferrard* (1797), John Clotworthy Talbot Foster Whyte-Melville Skeffiington (6th *U.K. Baron,* Oriel, 1821), *b.* 1914, *s.* 1956, *m.*	Hon. John D. C. W. M. S., *b.* 1940.
1939	*Maugham* (2nd), Robert Cecil Romer Maugham, *b.* 1916, *s.* 1958.	(None.)
1802	*Melville* (9th), Robert David Ross Dundas, *b.* 1937, *s.* 1971.	Hugh McK. D., *b.* 1910.
1916	*Mersey* (3rd), Edward Clive Bingham, *b.* 1906, *s.* 1956, *m.*	Master of Nairne, *b.* 1934.
1962	*Mills* (2nd), Roger Clinton Mills, *b.* 1919, *s.* 1968, *m.*	Hon. Christopher P. R. M., *b.* 1956.
1716 I.	*Molesworth* (11th), Richard Gosset Molesworth, *b.* 1907, *s.* 1961, *m.*	Hon. Robert B. K. M., *b.* 1959.
1801 I.*	*Monck* (6th), Henry Wyndham Stanley Monck, O.B.E., (3rd *U.K. Baron, Monck,* 1866), *b.* 1905, *s.* 1927, *m.*	Hon. Charles S. M., *b.* 1953.
1957	*Monckton of Brenchley* (2nd), Gilbert Walter Riversdale Monckton, C.B., O.B.E., M.C., *b.* 1915, *s.* 1965, *m.*	Hon. Christopher W. M., *b.* 1952.
1935	*Monsell* (2nd), Henry Bolton Graham Eyres-Monsell, *b.* 1905, *s.* 1969.	(None.)
1946	*Montgomery of Alamein* (1st), Bernard Law Montgomery, K.G., G.C.B., D.S.O., Field Marshal, *b.* 1887, *w.*	Hon. David M., *b.* 1928.
1550 I.*	*Mountgarret* (17th), Richard Henry Piers Butler (4th *U.K. Baron, Mountgarret,* 1911), *b.* 1936, *s.* 1966, *m.*	Hon. Piers J. R. B., *b.* 1961.
1964	*Muirshiel* (1st), John Scott Maclay, P.C., K.T., C.H., C.M.G., *b.* 1905, *w.*	(None.)
1952	*Norwich* (2nd), John Julius Cooper, *b.* 1929, *s.* 1954, *m.*	Hon. Jason C. D. B. C., *b.* 1959.
1873	*Portman* (9th), Edward Henry Berkeley Portman, *b.* 1934, *s.* 1967, *m.*	Hon. Christopher E. B. P., *b.* 1958.
1743 I.*	*Powerscourt* (10th), Mervyn Niall Wingfield, (4th *U.K. Baron, Powerscourt,* 1885), *b.* 1935, *s.* 1973, *m.*	Hon. Mervyn A. W., *b.* 1963.
1962	*Radcliffe* (1st), Cyril John Radcliffe, P.C., G.B.E., *b.* 1899, *m.* (*Lord of Appeal,* retired).	(None.)
1900	*Ridley* (4th), Matthew White Ridley, T.D., *b.* 1925, *s.* 1964, *m.*	Hon. Matthew W. R., *b.* 1958.
1960	*Rochdale* (1st), John Durival Kemp, O.B.E., T.D. (2nd *U.K. Baron, Rochdale,* 1913), *b.* 1906, *s.* 1945, *m.*	Hon. St. John K., *b.* 1938.
1919	*Rothermere* (2nd), Edmond Cecil Harmsworth, *b.* 1898, *s.* 1940, *m.*	Hon. Vere H., *b.* 1925.
1937	*Runciman of Doxford* (2nd), Walter Leslie Runciman, O.B.E., A.F.C. (3rd. *U.K. Baron, Runciman,* 1933), *b.* 1900, *s.* 1949, *m.*	Hon. Walter G. R., *b.* 1934.
1918	*St. Davids* (2nd), Jestyn Reginald Austen Plantagenet Philipps (19th *English Baron, Strange of Knokin* 1299, 7th *English Baron, Hungerford,* 1926 *and De Moleyns,* 1945), *b.* 1917, *s.* 1938, *m.*	Hon. Colwyn P., *b.* 1939.
1801	*St. Vincent* (7th), Ronald George James Jervis, *b.* 1905, *s.* 1940, *m.*	Hon. Edward R. J. J., *b.* 1951.
1937	*Samuel* (2nd), Edwin Herbert Samuel C.M.G., *b.* 1898, *s.* 1963, *m.*	Hon. David H. S., Ph.D., *b.* 1922.
1911	*Scarsdale* (2nd), Richard Nathaniel Curzon, T.D. (6th *Brit. Baron, Scarsdale,* 1761), *b.* 1898, *s.* 1925, *m.*	Francis J. N. C., *b.* 1924.
1905	*Selby* (4th), Michael Guy John Gully, *b.* 1942, *s.* 1959, *m.*	Hon. Edward T. W. G., *b.* 1967.
1805	*Sidmouth* (6th), Raymond Anthony Addington, *b.* 1887, *s.* 1953, *m.*	Hon. John T. A., *b.* 1914.
1940	*Simon* (2nd), John Gilbert Simon, C.M.G., *b.* 1902, *s.* 1954, *m.*	Hon. Jan D. S., *b.* 1940.
1960	*Slim* (2nd), John Douglas Slim, O.B.E., *b.* 1927, *s.* 1970, *m.*	Hon. Mark W. R. S., *b.* 1960.
1954	*Soulbury* (2nd), James Herwald Ramsbotham, *b.* 1915, *s.* 1971, *w.*	Hon. Sir Peter E. R., K.C.M.G., *b.* 1919.
1776 I.	*Southwell* (7th), Pryers Anthony Joseph Southwell, *b.* 1930, *s.* 1960, *m.*	Hon. Richard A. P. S., *b.* 1956.
1959	*Stuart of Findhorn* (2nd), David Randolph Moray Stuart, *b.* 1924, *s.* 1971, *m.*	Hon. James D. S., *b.* 1948.
1806 I.	*Templetown* (5th), Henry Augustus George Mountjoy Heneage Upton, *b.* 1894, *s.* 1939, *m.*	(None.)
1957	*Tenby* (2nd), David Lloyd George, *b.* 1922, *s.* 1967.	Hon. William L. G., *b.* 1927.
1952	*Thurso* (2nd), Robin Macdonald Sinclair, *b.* 1922, *s.* 1970, *m.*	Hon. John A. S., *b.* 1953.
1721	*Torrington* (11th), Timothy Howard St. George Byng, *b.* 1943, *s.* 1961.	John L. B., M.C., *b.* 1919.
1936	*Trenchard* (2nd), Thomas Trenchard, M.C., *b.* 1923, *s.* 1956, *m.*	Hon. Hugh T., *b.* 1951.
1921	*Ullswater* (2nd), Nicholas James Christopher Lowther, *b.* 1942, *s.* 1949, *m.*	
1621 I.	*Valentia* (14th), Francis Dighton Annesley, M.C., *b.* 1888, *s.* 1951 (*claim established,* 1959), *m.*	Hon. Richard J. D. A., *b.* 1929.

Created.	Title, Order of Succession, Name, etc.	Eldest Son or Heir.
1960	*Ward of Witley* (1st), George Reginald Ward, P.C., *b.* 1907, *m.*	Hon. Anthony G. H. *W.*, *b.* 1943.
1964	*Watkinson* (1st), Harold Arthur Watkinson, P.C., C.H., *b.* 1910, *w.*	(None.)
1952	*Waverley* (2nd), David Alastair Pearson Anderson, *b.* 1911, *s.* 1958, *m.*	Hon. John D. F. *A.*, *b.* 1949.
1938	*Weir* (2nd), (James) Kenneth Weir, C.B.E., *b.* 1905, *s.* 1959, *m.*	Hon. William K. J. *W.*, *b.* 1933.
1918	*Wimborne* (3rd), Ivor Fox-Strangways Guest (4th *U.K. Baron, Wimborne*, 1880), *b.* 1939, *s.* 1967, *m.*	Hon. Ivor M.V.*G.*, *b.* 1968.
1923	*Younger of Leckie* (3rd), Edward George Younger, O.B.E., T.D., *b.* 1906, *s.* 1946, *m.*	Hon. George *Y.*, T.D., M.P. *b.* 1931

BISHOPS

Style, The Right Rev. the Lord Bishop of ——. *Addressed as*, My Lord.

Apptd.		
1973	*London* (115th), Gerald Alexander Ellison, P.C., D.D., *b.* 1910, *cons.* 1950, *trans.* 1955 and 1973, *m.*	
1973	*Durham* (91st), John Stapylton Habgood, M.A., Ph.D., *b.* 1927, *cons.* 1973, *m.*	
1974	*Winchester* (94th), John Vernon Taylor, M.A., *b.* 1914, *cons.* 1974, *m.*	
1975	*Bath and Wells* (74th), John Monier Bickersteth, M.A., *b.* 1921, *cons.* 1970, *trans.* 1975, *m.*	
1969	*Birmingham* (5th), Laurence Ambrose Brown, M.A., *b.* 1907, *cons.* 1960, *m.*	
1972	*Blackburn* (5th), Robert Arnold Schürhoff Martineau, M.A., *b.* 1913, *cons.* 1966, *m.*	
1972	*Bradford* (5th), Ross Sydney Hook, M.C., M.A., *b.* 1917, *cons.* 1965, *m.*	
	Bristol (vacant)	
1972	*Carlisle* (64th), Henry David Halsey, B.A., *b.* 1919, *cons.* 1968, *trans.* 1972, *m.*	
1971	*Chelmsford* (6th), Albert John Trillo, M.Th., B.D., F.K.C., *b.* 1915, *cons.* 1963, *trans.* 1968 and 1971, *m.*	
1974	*Chester* (38th), Hubert Victor Whitsey, M.A., *b.* 1916, *cons.* 1971, *trans.* 1974, *m.*	
1974	*Chichester* (99th), Eric Waldram Kemp, D.D., *b.* 1915, *m.*	
1956	*Coventry* (5th), Cuthbert Killick Norman Bardsley, C.B.E., D.D., *b.* 1907, *cons.* 1947 *m.*	
1969	*Derby* (4th), Cyril William Johnston Bowles, M.A., *b.* 1916, *cons.* 1969, *m.*	
1964	*Ely* (65th), Edward James Keymer Roberts, D.D., *b.* 1908, *cons.* 1956, *trans.* 1962 and 1964, *m.*	
1973	*Exeter* (68th), Eric Arthur John Mercer, B.A., *b.* 1917, *cons.* 1965, *m.*	
1975	*Gloucester* (37th) John Yates, M.A., *b.* 1925, *cons.* 1972, *trans.* 1975, *m.*	
1973	*Guildford* (6th), David Alan Brown, B.D., M.Th., B.A., *b.* 1922, *cons.* 1973, *m.*	
1973	*Hereford* (103rd), John Richard Gordon Eastaugh, *b.* 1920, *cons.* 1973, *m.*	
1953	*Leicester* (3rd), Ronald Ralph Williams, D.D., *b.* 1906, *cons.* 1953, *m.*	
1974	*Lichfield* (96th), Kenneth John Fraser Skelton, C.B.E., M.A., *b.* 1918, *cons.* 1962, *m.*	
1974	*Lincoln* (69th), Simon Wilton Phipps, M.C., M.A., *b.* 1921, *cons.* 1968, *trans.* 1974, *m.*	
1975	*Liverpool* (6th) David Stuart Sheppard, M.A., *b.* 1929, *cons.* 1969, *m.*	
1970	*Manchester* (8th), Patrick Campbell Rodger, M.A., *b.* 1920, *cons.* 1970, *m.*	
1972	*Newcastle* (9th), Ronald Oliver Bowlby, M.A., *b.* 1926, *cons.* 1972, *m.*	
1971	*Norwich* (69th), Maurice Arthur Ponsonby Wood, D.S.C., M.A., *b.* 1916, *cons.* 1971 *m.*	
1971	*Oxford* (39th), Kenneth John Woollcombe, M.A., *b.* 1924, *cons.* 1971, *m.*	
1972	*Peterborough* (35th), Douglas Russell Feaver, M.A., *b.* 1914, *cons.* 1972, *m.*	
1975	*Portsmouth* (6th), Archibald Ronald MacDonald Gordon, M.A., *b.* 1927, *cons.* 1975.	
1959	*Ripon* (9th), John Richard Humpidge Moorman, D.D., *b.* 1905, *cons.* 1959, *m.*	
1961	*Rochester* (104th), Richard David Say, D.D., *b.* 1914, *cons.* 1961, *m.*	
1970	*St. Albans* (7th), Robert Alexander Kennedy Runcie, M.C., M.A., *b.* 1921, *cons.* 1970, *m.*	
1966	*St. Edmundsbury & Ipswich* (6th), Leslie Wilfred Brown, C.B.E., D.D., *b.* 1912, *cons.* 1953, *m.*	
1973	*Salisbury* (75th), George Edmund Reindorp, D.D., *b.* 1911, *cons.* 1961, *trans.* 1973, *m.*	
1971	*Sheffield* (4th), William Gordon Fallows, M.A., *b.* 1913, *cons.* 1968, *m.*	
1966	*Sodar & Man* (77th), Vernon Sampson Nicholls, *b.* 1917, *cons.* 1974, *m.*	
1959	*Southwark* (6th), Arthur Mervyn Stockwood, D.D., *b.* 1913, *cons.* 1959.	
1970	*Southwell* (7th), John Denis Wakeling, M.C., M.A., *b.* 1918, *cons.* 1970, *m.*	
1973	*Truro* (11th), Graham Douglas Leonard, M.A., *b.* 1921, *cons.* 1964, *m.*	
1968	*Wakefield* (8th), Eric Treacy, M.B.E., *b.* 1907, *cons.* 1961, *m.*	
1971	*Worcester* (110th), Robert Wilmer Woods, K.C.V.O., M.A., *b.* 1914, *cons.* 1971, *m.*	

BARONS

Style (see *also* note, p. 256), The Right Hon. the Lord ——.
Addressed as, My Lord.

Created.	Title, Order of Succession, Name, etc	Eldest Son or Heir.
1911	*Aberconway* (3rd), Charles Melville McLaren, *b.* 1913, *s.* 1953, *m.*	Hon. Henry C. *McL.*, *b.* 1948.
1873	*Aberdare* (4th), Morys George Lyndhurst Bruce, P.C., *b.* 1919, *s.* 1957, *m.*	Hon. Alastair J. L. *B.*, *b.* 1947.
1835	*Abinger* (8th), James Richard Scarlett, *b.* 1914, *s.* 1943, *m.*	Hon. James H. *S.*, *b.* 1959.
1869	*Acton* (3rd), John Emerich Henry Lyon-Dalberg-Acton, C.M.G., M.B.E., *b.* 1907, *s.* 1924, *m.*	Hon. Richard *L.-D.-A.*, *b.* 1941.

Created.	Title, Order of Succession, Name, etc.	Eldest Son or Heir.
1887	*Addington* (5th), James Hubbard, b. 1930, s. 1971, m.	Hon. Dominic A. H., b. 1963.
1955	*Adrian* (1st), Edgar Douglas Adrian, O.M., M.D., F.R.S., b. 1889, w.	Hon. Richard H. A., b. 1927.
1921	*Ailwyn* (3rd), Eric William Edward Fellowes, C.B.E., b. 1887, s. 1936, m.	Hon. Carol A. F., T.D., b. 1896.
1907	*Airedale* (4th), Oliver James Vandeleur Kitson, b. 1915, s. 1958.	(None.)
1896	*Aldenham* (5th), and (3rd) *Hunsdon of Hunsdon* (1923), Antony Durant Gibbs, b. 1922, s. 1969, m.	Hon. Vicary T. G., b. 1948.
1962	*Aldington* (1st), Toby Austin Richard William Low, P.C., K.C.M.G., C.B.E., D.S.O., T.D., b. 1914, m.	Hon. Charles H. S. L., b. 1948.
1902	*Allerton* (3rd), George William Lawies Jackson, b. 1903, s. 1925. m.	Hon. Edward L. J., b. 1928.
1929	*Alvingham* (2nd), Robert Guy Eardley Yerburgh, O.B.E., b. 1926, s. 1955, m.	Hon. Robert R. G. Y., b. 1956.
1892	*Amherst of Hackney* (3rd), William Alexander Evering Cecil, C.B.E., b. 1912, s. 1919, m.	Hon. William C., b. 1940.
1929	*Amulree* (2nd), Basil William Sholto Mackenzie, M.D., b. 1900, s. 1942.	(None.)
1947	*Amwell* (2nd), Frederick Norman Montague, b. 1912, s. 1966, m.	Hon. Keith N. M., b. 1943.
1863	*Annaly* (5th), Luke Robert White, b. 1927, s. 1970.	Hon. Luke R. W., b. 1954.
1903	*Armstrong* (3rd), William Henry Cecil John Robin Watson-Armstrong, b. 1919, s. 1972, m.	(None.)
1885	*Ashbourne* (3rd), Edward Russell Gibson, C.B., D.S.O., b. 1901, s. 1942, m.	Hon. Edward B. G. G., b. 1933.
1835	*Ashburton* (6th), Alexander Francis St. Vincent Baring, K.G., K.C.V.O., b. 1898, s. 1938, m.	Hon. John F. H. B., b. 1928.
1892	*Ashcombe* (4th), Henry Edward Cubitt, b. 1924, s. 1962, m.	Alick J. A. C., b. 1927.
1911	*Ashton of Hyde* (2nd), Thomas Henry Raymond Ashton, b. 1901, s. 1933, m.	Hon. Thomas J. A., b. 1926.
1800 I.	*Ashtown* (5th), Dudley Oliver Trench, O.B.E., b. 1901, s. 1966, m.	Christopher O. T., b. 1931.
1956	*Astor of Hever* (2nd), Gavin Astor, b. 1918, s. 1971, m.	Hon. John J. A., b. 1946.
1780 I.⎫ 1793*⎭	*Auckland* (9th), Ian George Eden (9th *Brit. Baron, Auckland*), b. 1926, s. 1957, m.	Hon. Robert I. B. E., b. 1962.
1313	*Audley* (25th), Richard Michael Thomas Souter, b. 1914, s. 1973, m.	Three co-heiresses.
1900	*Avebury* (4th), Eric Reginald Lubbock, b. 1928, s. 1971, m.	Hon. Lyulph A. J. L., b. 1954.
1718 I.	*Aylmer* (10th), Kenneth Athalmer Aylmer, b. 1883, s. 1970, w.	Hugh Y. A., b. 1907.
1929	*Baden-Powell* (3rd), Robert Crause Baden-Powell, b. 1936, s. 1962. m.	Hon. David M. B.-P., b. 1940.
1780	*Bagot* (8th), Reginald Walter Bagot, b. 1897, s. 1973, m.	Heneage C. B., b. 1914.
1953	*Baillieu* (3rd), James William Latham Baillieu, b. 1950, s. 1973, m.	Hon. David C. L. B., 1952.
1607 S.	*Balfour of Burleigh* (8th), Robert Bruce, b. 1927, c. 1967, m.	Hon. Victoria B., b. 1973.
1945	*Balfour of Inchrye* (1st), Harold Harington Balfour, P.C., M.C., b. 1897, m.	Hon. Ian B., b. 1924.
1924	*Banbury of Southam* (2nd), Charles William Banbury, b. 1915, s. 1936.	Hon. Charles W. B., b. 1953.
1698	*Barnard* (11th), Harry John Neville Vane, T.D., b. 1923, s. 1964, m.	Hon. Henry F. C. V., b. 1959.
1922	*Barnby* (2nd), Francis Vernon Willey, C.M.G., C.B.E., M.V.O., T.D., b. 1884, s. 1929, m.	(None.)
1887	*Basing* (4th), George Lutley Sclater-Booth, T.D., b. 1903, s. 1969, m.	Hon. Neil L. S.-B., b. 1939.
1647 S.	*Belhaven & Stenton* (13th), Robert Anthony Carmichael Hamilton, b. 1927, s. 1961, m.	Master of Belhaven, b. 1953.
1848 I.	*Bellew* (5th), Edward Henry Bellew, M.B.E., b. 1889, s. 1935, w.	Hon. Bryan B., M.C., b. 1890
1856	*Belper* (4th), (Alexander) Ronald George Strutt, b. 1912, s. 1956.	Hon. Richard H. S., b. 1941.
1938	*Belstead* (2nd), John Julian Ganzoni, b. 1932, s. 1958.	(None.)
1922	*Bethell* (4th), Nicholas William Bethell, b. 1938, s. 1967.	Hon. James N. B., b. 1967.
1938	*Bicester* (3rd), Angus Edward Vivian Smith, b. 1932, s. 1968.	Hugh C. V. S., b. 1934.
1903	*Biddulph* (4th), Robert Michael Christian Biddulph, b. 1931, s. 1972, m.	Hon. Anthony N. C. B., b. 1959.
1938	*Birdwood* (3rd), Mark William Ogilvie Birdwood, b. 1938, s. 1962, m.	(None.)
1958	*Birkett* (2nd), Michael Birkett, b. 1929, s. 1962, w.	(None.)
1935	*Blackford* (3rd), Keith Alexander Henry Mason, D.F.C., b. 1923, s. 1972.	Hon. William K. M., b. 1962.
1907	*Blyth* (3rd), Ian Audley James Blyth, b. 1905, s. 1943, m.	Hon. Anthony B., b. 1931.
1797	*Bolton* (7th), Richard William Algar Orde-Powlett, b. 1929, s. 1963, m.	Hon. Harry A. N. O.-P. b. 1954.
1922	*Borwick* (4th), James Hugh Myles Borwick, M.C., b. 1917, s. 1961, m.	Hon. George S. B., b. 1922.
1761	*Boston* (9th), Gerald Howard Boteler Irby, M.B.E., b. 1897, s. 1972, m.	Hon. Timothy G. F. B. I., b. 1939.
1942	*Brabazon of Tara* (3rd), Ivon Anthony Moore-Brabazon, b. 1946, s. 1974, m.	(None.)
1880	*Brabourne* (7th), John Ulick Knatchbull, b. 1924, s. 1943, m.	Hon. Norton K., b. 1947.

Created.	Title, Order of Succession, Name, etc.	Eldest Son or Heir.
1925	*Bradbury* (2nd), John Bradbury, *b.* 1914, *s.* 1950, *m.*	Hon. John *B.*, *b.* 1940.
1962	*Brain* (2nd), Christopher Langdon Brain, *b.* 1926, *s.* 1966, *m.*	Hon. Michael C. *B.*, D.M., *b.* 1928.
1938	*Brassey of Apethorpe* (3rd), David Henry Brassey, T.D., *b.* 1932, *s.* 1967, *m.*	Hon. Edward *B.*, *b.* 1964.
1788	*Braybrooke* (9th), Henry Seymour Neville, *b.* 1897, *s.* 1943, *m.*	Hon. Robin *N.*, *b.* 1932.
1529	*Braye* (7th), Thomas Adrian Verney-Cave, *b.* 1902, *s.* 1952, *m.*	Hon. Penelope M. *V.-C.*, *b.* 1941.
1958	*Brecon* (1st), David Vivian Penrose Lewis, P.C., *b.* 1905, *m.*	(None.)
1957	*Bridges* (2nd), Thomas Edward Bridges, C.M.G., *b.* 1927, *s.* 1969, *m.*	Hon. Mark T. *B.*, *b.* 1954.
1945	*Broadbridge* (3rd), Peter Hewett Broadbridge, *b.* 1938, *s.* 1972, *m.*	Hon. Ralph G. C. *B.*, *b.* 1901.
1933	*Brocket* (3rd), Charles Ronald George Nall-Cain, *b.* 1952, *s.* 1967.	Hon. Richard P.C. *N.-C.*, *b.* 1953.
1860	*Brougham and Vaux* (5th), Michael John Brougham, *b.* 1938, *s.* 1967, *m.*	Hon. Charles *B.*, *b.* 1971.
1945	*Broughshane* (2nd), Patrick Owen Alexander Davison, *b.* 1903, *s.* 1953, *m.*	Hon. Alexander *D.*, *b.* 1936.
1776	*Brownlow* (6th), Peregrine Francis Adelbert Cust, *b.* 1899, *s.* 1927, *m.*	Hon. Edward *C.*, *b.* 1936.
1942	*Bruntisfield* (1st), Victor Alexander George Anthony Warrender, M.C., *b.* 1890, *m.*	Hon. John R. *W.*, O.B.E., M.C., T.D., *b.* 1921.
1950	*Burden* (2nd), Philip William Burden, *b.* 1916, *s.* 1970, *m.*	Hon. Andrew P. *B.*, *b.* 1959.
1529	*Burgh* (7th), Alexander Peter Willoughby Leith, *b.* 1935, *s.* 1959, *m.*	Hon. Alexander G. D. *L.*, *b.* 1958.
1903	*Burnham* (5th), William Edward Harry Lawson, *b.* 1920, *s.* 1963, *m.*	Hon. Hugh J. F. *L.*, *b.* 1931.
1897	*Burton* (3rd), Michael Evan Victor Baillie, *b.* 1924, *s.* 1962, *m.*	Hon. Evan *B.*, *b.* 1949.
1643	*Byron* (11th), Rupert Frederick George Byron, *b.* 1903, *s.* 1949, *m.*	Richard G. G. *B.*, D.S.O., *b.* 1899.
1937	*Cadman* (3rd), John Anthony Cadman, *b.* 1938, *s.* 1966.	Hon. James R. *C.*, *b.* 1944.
1796	*Calthorpe* (10th), Peter Waldo Somerset Gough-Calthorpe, *b.* 1927, *s.* 1945.	(None.)
1945	*Calverley* (3rd.), Charles Rodney Muff, *b.* 1946, *s.* 1971.	Hon. Peter R. *M.* *b.* 1953.
1383	*Camoys* (6th), (Ralph Robert Watts) Sherman Stonor, *b.* 1913, *s.* 1968, *m.*	Hon. Thomas C. G. *S.*, *b.* 1940.
1715 I.	*Carbery* (11th), Peter Ralfe Harrington Evans-Freke, *b.* 1920, *s.* 1970, *m.*	Hon. Michael P. *E.-F.*, *b.* 1942.
1834 I.⎱ 1838* ⎰	*Carew* (6th), William Francis Conolly-Carew, C.B.E. (6th *U.K.* Baron, Carew, 1838), *b.* 1905, *s.* 1927, *m.*	Hon. Patrick T. *C.-C.*, *b.* 1938.
1916	*Carnock* (3rd), Erskine Arthur Nicolson, D.S.O., *b.* 1884, *s.* 1952, *w.*	Hon. David H. A. *N.*, *b.* 1920.
1796 I.⎱ 1797* ⎰	*Carrington* (6th), Peter Alexander Rupert Carington, P.C., K.C.M.G., M.C. (6th *Brit.* Baron, Carrington, 1797), *b.* 1919, *s.* 1938, *m.*	Hon. Rupert F. J. *C.*, *b.* 1948.
1812 I.	*Castlemaine* (8th), Roland Thomas John Handcock, *b.* 1943, *s.* 1973, *m.*	Clifford F. *H.*, *b.* 1896.
1936	*Catto* (2nd), Stephen Gordon Catto, *b.* 1923, *s.* 1959, *m.*	Hon. Innes G. *C.*, *b.* 1950.
1918	*Cawley* (3rd), Frederick Lee Cawley, *b.* 1913, *s.* 1954, *m.*	Hon. John F. *C.*, *b.* 1946.
1937	*Chatfield* (2nd), Ernie David Lewis Chatfield, *b.* 1917, *s.* 1967, *m.*	(None.)
1858	*Chesham* (5th), John Charles Compton Cavendish, P.C., *b.* 1916, *s.* 1952, *m.*	Hon. Nicholas *C.*, *b.* 1941.
1945	*Chetwode* (2nd), Philip Chetwode, *b.* 1937, *s.* 1950, *m.*	Hon. Roger *C.*, *b.* 1968.
1945	*Chorley* (1st), Robert Samuel Theodore Chorley, Q.C., *b.* 1895, *m.*	Hon. Roger *C.*, *b.* 1930.
1858	*Churston* (4th), Richard Francis Roger Yarde-Buller, V.R.D., *b.* 1910, *s.* 1930, *m.*	Hon. John *Y.-B.*, *b.* 1934.
1946	*Citrine* (1st), Walter McLennan Citrine, P.C., G.B.E., *b.* 1887, *w.*	Hon. Norman *C.*, *b.* 1914.
1800 I.	*Clanmorris* (7th), John Michael Ward Bingham, *b.* 1908, *s.* 1960, *m.*	Hon. Simon J. W. *B.*, *b.* 1937.
1672	*Clifford of Chudleigh* (13th), Lewis Hugh Clifford, O.B.E., *b.* 1916, *s.* 1964, *m.*	Hon. Thomas H. *C.*, *b.* 1948.
1299	*Clinton* (22nd), Gerard Neville Mark Fane Trefusis, *b.* 1934, *title called out of abeyance* 1965, *m.*	Hon. Charles P. R. F. *T.*, *b.* 1962.
1955	*Clitheroe* (1st), Ralph Assheton, P.C., *b.* 1901, *m.*	Hon. Ralph J. *A.*, *b.* 1929.
1919	*Clwyd* (2nd), (John) Trevor Roberts, *b.* 1900, *s.* 1955, *m.*	Hon. J. Anthony *R.*, *b.* 1935.
1947	*Clydesmuir* (2nd), Ronald John Bisland Colville, K.T., C.B., M.B.E., T.D., *b.* 1917, *s.* 1954, *m.*	Hon. David R. *C.*, *b.* 1949.
1960	*Cobbold* (1st), Cameron Fromanteel Cobbold, K.G., P.C., G.C.V.O., *b.* 1904, *m.*	Hon. David A. F. *Lytton-Cobbold*, *b.* 1937.
1919	*Cochrane of Cults* (3rd), Thomas Charles Anthony Cochrane, *b.* 1922, *s.* 1968.	Hon. R. H. Vere *C.*, *b.* 1926.
1956	*Cohen of Birkenhead* (1st), Henry Cohen, C.H., M.D., D.SC., Ll.D., F.R.C.P., F.S.A., *b.* 1900.	(None.)
1954	*Coleraine* (1st), Richard Kidston Law, P.C., *b.* 1901, *m.*	Hon. J. Martin B. *L.*, *b.* 1931.

Created.	Title, Order of Succession, Name, etc.	Eldest Son or Heir.

1873   *Coleridge* (4th), Richard Duke Coleridge, K.B.E., b. 1905, s. 1955, m.   Hon. William D. C., b. 1937.

1946   *Colgrain* (3rd), David Colin Campbell, b. 1920, s. 1973, m.   Hon. Alastair C. L. C., b. 1951.

1917   *Colwyn* (3rd), (Ian) Anthony Hamilton-Smith, b. 1942, s. 1966, m.   Hon. Craig P. H.-S., b. 1968.

1956   *Colyton* (1st), Henry Lennox D'Aubigné Hopkinson, P.C., C.M.G., b. 1902, m.   Hon. Nicholas H. E. H., b. 1932.

1841   *Congleton* (8th), Christopher Patrick Parnell, b. 1930, s. 1967, m.   Hon. John P. C. P., b. 1959.

1927   *Cornwallis* (2nd), Wykeham Stanley Cornwallis, K.C.V.O., K.B.E., M.C., b. 1892, s. 1935, w.   Hon. Fiennes C., O.B.E., b. 1921.

1874   *Cottesloe* (4th), John Walgrave Halford Fremantle, G.B.E., T.D., b. 1900, s. 1956, m.   Hon. John T. F., b. 1927.

1914   *Cozens-Hardy* (4th), Herbert Arthur Cozens-Hardy, O.B.E., b. 1907, s. 1956.   (None.)

1929   *Craigmyle* (3rd), Thomas Donald Mackay Shaw, b. 1923, s. 1944, m.   Hon. Thomas C. S., b. 1960.

1899   *Cranworth* (3rd), Philip Bertram Gurdon, b. 1940, s. 1964, m.   Hon. Sacha W. R. G., b. 1970.

1959   *Crathorne* (1st), Thomas Lionel Dugdale, P.C., T.D., b. 1897, w.   Hon. Charles J. D., b. 1939.

1892   *Crawshaw* (4th), William Michael Clifton Brooks, b. 1933, s. 1946.   Hon. David B., b. 1934.

1940   *Croft* (2nd), Michael Henry Glendower Page Croft, b. 1916, s. 1947, w.   Hon. Bernard W. H. P. C., b. 1949.

1797 I.   *Crofton* (6th), Charles Edward Piers Crofton, b. 1949, s. 1974.   Hon. Guy P. G. C., b. 1951.

1375   *Cromwell* (6th), David Godfrey Bewicke-Copley, b. 1929, s. 1966, m.   Hon. Godfrey J. B.-C., b. 1960.

1947   *Crook* (1st), Reginald Douglas Crook, b. 1901, m.   Hon. Douglas C., b. 1926.

1971   *Cross of Chelsea*, (Arthur) Geoffrey (Neale) Cross, P.C., b. 1904, m. (*Lord of Appeal, retired*).   (Law Life Peerage.)

1920   *Cullen of Ashbourne* (2nd), Charles Borlase Marsham Cokayne, M.B.E., b. 1912, s. 1932, m.   Hon. Edmund C., b. 1916.

1914   *Cunliffe* (3rd), Roger Cunliffe, b. 1932, s. 1963, m.   Hon. Henry C., b. 1962.

1927   *Daresbury* (2nd), Edward Greenall, b. 1902, s. 1938, w.   Hon. Edward G. G., b. 1928.

1924   *Darling* (2nd), Robert Charles Henry Darling, b. 1919, s. 1936, m.   Hon. Robert D., b. 1944.

1946   *Darwen* (2nd), Cedric Percival Davies, b. 1915, s. 1950, m.   Hon. Roger M. D., b. 1938.

1923   *Daryngton* (2nd), Jocelyn Arthur Pike Pease, b. 1908, s. 1949.   (None.)

1932   *Davies* (3rd), David Davies, b. 1940, s. 1944, m.   Hon. Jonathan H. D., b. 1944.

1812 I.   *Decies* (6th), Arthur George Marcus Douglas de la Poer Beresford, b. 1915, s. 1944, m.   Hon. Marcus de la P.B., b. 1948.

1299   *De Clifford* (26th), Edward Southwell Russell, O.B.E., E.D., b. 1907, s. 1909, m.   Hon. John R., b. 1928.

1851   *De Freyne* (7th), Francis Arthur John French, b. 1927, s. 1935, m.   Hon. Fulke C. J. A. F., b. 1957.

1821   *Delamere* (4th), Thomas Pitt Hamilton Cholmondeley, b. 1900, s. 1931, m.   Hon. Hugh G. C., b. 1934.

1838   *De Mauley* (6th), Gerald John Ponsonby, b. 1921, s. 1962, m.   Hon. Thomas M. P., b. 1930.

1937   *Denham* (2nd), Bertram Stanley Mitford Bowyer, b. 1927, s. 1948, m.   Hon. Richard G. B., b. 1959.

1834   *Denman* (5th), Charles Spencer Denman, M.C., b. 1916, s. 1971, m.   Hon. Richard T. S. D., b. 1946.

1957   *Denning*, Alfred Thompson Denning, P.C., b. 1899, m. (*Master of the Rolls*).   (Law Life Peerage.)

1885   *Deramore* (6th), Richard Arthur de Yarburgh-Bateson, b. 1911, s. 1964, m.   (None.)

1887   *De Ramsey* (3rd), Ailwyn Edward Fellowes, K.B.E., T.D., b. 1910, s. 1925, m.   Hon. John A. F., b. 1942.

1881   *Derwent* (4th), Patrick Robin Gilbert Vanden-Bempde-Johnstone, C.B.E., b. 1901, s. 1949, m.   Hon. Robin V.-B.-J., M.V.O., b. 1930.

1831   *De Saumarez* (6th), James Victor Broke Saumarez, b. 1924, s. 1969, m.   Hon. Eric D. S., b. 1956.

1910   *De Villiers* (3rd), Arthur Percy De Villiers, b. 1911, s. 1934.   Hon. Alexander C. de V., b. 1940.

1961   *Devlin*, Patrick Arthur Devlin, P.C., F.B.A., b. 1905, m. (*Lord of Appeal retired*).   (Law Life Peerage.)

1930   *Dickinson* (2nd), Richard Clavering Hyett Dickinson, b. 1926, s. 1943, m.   Hon. Martin H. D., b. 1961.

1620 I. 1765*   *Digby* (12th), Edward Henry Kenelm Digby, (6th *Brit. Baron, Digby*), b. 1924, s. 1964, m.   Hon. Henry N. K. D., b. 1954.

1968   *Diplock*, (William John) Kenneth Diplock, P.C., b. 1907, m. (*Lord of Appeal*).   (Law Life Peerage.)

1615   *Dormer* (15th), Charles Walter James Dormer, b. 1903, s. 1922, m.   Hon. Joseph D., b. 1914.

1950   *Douglas of Barloch* (1st), Francis Campbell Ross Douglas, K.C.M.G., b. 1889, m.   (None.)

Created.	Title, Order of Succession, Name, etc.	Eldest Son or Heir.
1943	Dowding (2nd), Derek Hugh Tremenheere Dowding, b. 1919, s. 1970, m.	Hon. Piers H. T. D., b. 1948.
1963	Drumalbyn (1st), Niall Malcolm Stewart Macpherson, P.C., K.B.E., b. 1908, m.	(None.)
1929	Dulverton (2nd), (Frederick) Anthony Hamilton Wills, C.B.E., T.D., b. 1915, s. 1956, m.	Hon. Gilbert M. H. W., b. 1944.
1800 I.	Dunalley (6th), Henry Desmond Graham Prittie, b. 1912, s. 1948, m.	Hon. Henry P., b. 1948.
1324 I.	Dunboyne (28th), Patrick Theobald Tower Butler, b. 1917, s. 1945, m.	Hon. John F. B., b. 1951.
1802	Dunleath (4th), Charles Edward Henry John Mulholland, T.D., b. 1933, s. 1956, m.	Sir Michael H. M., Bt., b. 1915.
1439 I.	Dunsany (19th), Randal Arthur Henry Plunkett, b. 1906, s. 1957, m.	Hon. Edward P., b. 1939.
1780	Dynevor (9th), Richard Charles Uryan Rhys, b. 1935, s. 1962, m.	Hon. Hugo G. U. R., b. 1966.
1928	Ebbisham (2nd), Rowland Roberts Blades, T.D., b. 1912, s. 1953, m.	(None.)
1857	Ebury (6th), Francis Egerton Grosvenor, b. 1934, s. 1957, m.	Hon. Julian F. M. G., b. 1959.
1974	Edmund-Davies (Herbert) Edmund Edmund-Davies, P.C., b. 1906, m. (Lord of Appeal).	(Law Life Peerage).
1693 S.	Elibank (14th), Alan d'Ardis Erskine-Murray, b. 1923, s. 1973, m.	Master of Elibank, b. 1964.
1802	Ellenborough (8th), Richard Edward Cecil Law, b. 1926, s. 1945, m.	Hon. Rupert E. H. L., b. 1955.
1509 S.*	Elphinstone (17th), John Alexander Elphinstone (3rd U.K. Baron Elphinstone, 1885), b. 1914, s. 1955.	James A. E., b. 1953.
1934	Elton (2nd), Rodney Elton, T.D., b. 1930, s. 1973, m.	Hon. Edward P. E., b. 1966.
1964	Erroll of Hale (1st), Frederick James Erroll, P.C., T.D., b. 1914, m.	(None.)
1964	Erskine of Rerrick (1st), John Maxwell Erskine, G.B.E., b. 1893, m.	Hon. Iain M. E., b. 1926.
1932	Essendon (2nd), Brian Edmund Lewis, b. 1903, s. 1944, m.	(None.)
1627 S.	Fairfax of Cameron (14th), Nicholas John Albert Fairfax, b. 1956, s. 1964, M.	Hon. Hugh N. T. F., b. 1958.
1961	Fairhaven (3rd), Ailwyn Henry George Broughton, b. 1936, s. 1973, m.	Hon. James H. A. B., b. 1963.
1916	Faringdon (2nd), Alexander Gavin Henderson, b. 1902, s. 1934.	Charles M. H., b. 1937.
1756 I.	Farnham (12th), Barry Owen Somerset Maxwell, b. 1931, s. 1957, m.	Hon. Simon K. M., b. 1933.
1856 I.	Fermoy (5th), Edmund James Burke Roche, b. 1939, s. 1955, m.	Hon. Patrick M. R., b. 1967.
1826	Feversham (6th), Charles Anthony Peter Duncombe, b. 1945, s. 1963, m.	Hon. Jasper O. S. D., b. 1968.
1798 I.	ffrench (7th), Peter Martin Joseph Charles John ffrench, b. 1926, s. 1955, m.	Hon. Robuck J. P. C. M. ff., b. 1956.
1909	Fisher (3rd), John Vavasseur Fisher, D.S.C., b. 1921, s. 1955, m.	Hon. Patrick V. F., b. 1953.
1295	Fitzwalter (21st), Fitzwalter Brook Plumptre, b. 1914, called out of abeyance, 1953, m.	Hon. Julian B. P., b. 1952.
1776	Foley (8th), Adrian Gerald Foley, b. 1923, s. 1927, m.	Hon. Thomas H. F., b. 1961.
1445 S.	Forbes (22nd), Nigel Ivan Forbes, K.B.E. (Premier Baron of Scotland), b. 1918, s. 1953, m.	Master of Forbes, b. 1946.
1821	Forester (7th), Cecil George Wilfrid Weld-Forester, b. 1899, s. 1932, m.	Hon. G. C. Brooke W.-F., b. 1938.
1922	Forres (3rd), John Archibald Harford Williamson, b. 1922, s. 1954, m.	Hon. Alastair S. G. W., b. 1946.
1917	Forteviot (3rd), Henry Evelyn Alexander Dewar, M.B.E., b. 1906, s. 1947, m.	Hon. John J. E. D., b. 1938.
1946	Fraser of North Cape (1st), Bruce Austin Fraser, G.C.B., K.B.E., Admiral of the Fleet, b. 1888.	(None.)
1975	Fraser of Tullybelton, Walter Ian Reid Fraser, P.C., b. 1911, m. (Lord of Appeal).	(Law Life Peerage).
1951	Freyberg (2nd), Paul Richard Freyberg, O.B.E., M.C., b. 1923, s. 1963, m.	Hon. Valerian B. F., b. 1970.
1017	Gainford (3rd), Joseph Edward Pease, b. 1921, s. 1971, m.	Hon. George P., b. 1926.
1818 I.	Garvagh (5th), (Alexander Leopold Ivor) George Canning, b. 1920, s. 1956, m.	Hon. Spencer G. S. de R. C., b. 1953.
1942	Geddes (3rd), Euan Michael Ross Geddes, b. 1937, s. 1975, m.	James G. N. G., b. 1969.
1876	Gerard (4th), Robert William Frederick Alwyn Gerard, b. 1918, s. 1953.	Rupert C. F. G., M.B.E., b. 1916.
1824	Gifford (6th), Anthony Marice Gifford, b. 1940, s. 1961, m.	Hon. Thomas A. G., b. 1967.
1917	Gisborough (3rd), Thomas Richard John Long Chaloner, b. 1927, s. 1951, m.	Hon. Thomas P. L. C., b. 1961.
1960	Gladwyn (1st), (Hubert Miles) Gladwyn Jebb, G.C.M.G., G.C.V.O., C.B., b. 1900, m.	Hon. Miles A. J., b. 1930.
1899	Glanusk (4th), David Russell Bailey, b. 1917, s. 1948, m.	Hon. Christopher B., b. 1942.
1918	Glenarthur (3rd), Matthew Arthur, O.B.E., b. 1909, s. 1942, m.	Hon. Simon M. A., b. 1944.
1921	Glenavy (3rd), Patrick Gordon Campbell, b. 1913, s. 1963, m.	Hon. Michael C., b. 1924.
1911	Glenconner (2nd), Christopher Grey Tennant, b. 1899, s. 1920, m.	Hon. Colin T., b. 1926.

Created.	Title, Order of Succession, Name, etc.	Eldest Son or Heir.
1964	Glendevon (1st), John Adrian Hope, P.C., b. 1912, m.	Hon. Julian J. S. H., b. 1950.
1922	Glendyne (3rd), Robert Nivison, b. 1926, s. 1967, m.	Hon. John N., b. 1960.
1939	Glentoran (2nd), Daniel Stewart Thomas Bingham Dixon, P.C., (N.I.), K.B.E., b. 1912, s. 1950, m.	Hon. Thomas R. V. D., M.B.E., b. 1935.
1956	Godber (1st), Frederick Godber, b. 1888, m.	(None.)
1909	Gorell (4th), Timothy John Radcliffe Barnes, b. 1927, s. 1963, m.	Hon. Ronald A. H. B., b. 1931.
1953	Grantchester (1st), Alfred Jesse Suenson-Taylor, O.B.E., b. 1893, m.	Hon. Kenneth S.-T., Q.C., b. 1921.
1782	Grantley (7th), John Richard Brinsley Norton, M.C., b. 1923, s. 1954, m.	Hon. Richard W. B. N., b. 1956.
1794 I.	Graves (8th), Peter George Welleslay Graves, b. 1911, s. 1963, m.	Evelyn P. G., b. 1926.
1445 S.	Gray (22nd), Angus Diarmid Ian Campbell-Gray, b. 1931, s. 1946, m.	Master of Gray, b. 1964.
1950	Greenhill (2nd), Stanley Ernest Greenhill, M.D., b. 1917, s. 1967, m.	Hon. Malcolm G., b. 1924.
1927	Greenway (3rd), Charles Paul Greenway, b. 1917, s. 1963, m.	Hon. Ambrose C. D. G., b. 1941.
1902	Grenfell (2nd), Pascoe Christian Victor Francis Grenfell, C.B.E., b. 1905, s. 1925, m.	Hon. Julian G., b. 1935.
1944	Gretton (2nd), John Frederic Gretton, O.B.E., b. 1902, s. 1947, m.	Hon. John H. G., b. 1941.
1869	Greville (4th), Ronald Charles Fulke Greville, b. 1912, s. 1952.	(None.)
1955	Gridley (2nd), Arnold Hudson Gridley, b. 1906, s. 1965, m.	Hon. Richard D. A. G., b. 1956.
1964	Grimston of Westbury (1st), Robert Villiers Grimston, b. 1897, m.	Hon. Robert W. S. G., b. 1925.
1880	Grimthorpe (4th), Christopher John Beckett, O.B.E., b. 1915, s. 1963, m.	Hon. Edward J. B., b. 1954.
1961	Guest, Christopher William Graham Guest, P.C., b. 1901, m. (Lord of Appeal, retired).	(Law Life Peerage.)
1945	Hacking (3rd), Douglas David Hacking, b. 1938, s. 1971, m.	Hon. Douglas F. H., b. 1968.
1950	Haden-Guest (3rd), Richard Haden Haden-Guest, b. 1904, s. 1974, m.	Hon. Peter H. H.-G., b. 1913.
1886	Hamilton of Dalzell (3rd), John D'Henin Hamilton, M.C., b. 1911, s. 1952, m.	Hon. James L. H., b. 1938.
1874	Hampton (6th), Richard Humphrey Russell Pakington, b. 1925, s. 1974, m.	Hon. John H. A. P., b 1964.
1939	Hankey (2nd), Robert Maurice Alers Hankey, K.C.M.G., K.C.V.O., b. 1905, s. 1963, m.	Hon. Donald R. A. H., b. 1938.
1958	Harding of Petherton (1st), John Harding, G.C.B., C.B.E., D.S.O., M.C., Field Marshal, b. 1896, m.	Hon. John C. H., b. 1928.
1910	Hardinge of Penshurst (3rd), George Edward Charles Hardinge, b. 1921, s. 1960, m.	Hon. Julian A. H., b. 1945.
1877	Harlech (5th), (William) David Ormsby-Gore, P.C., K.C.M.G., b. 1918, s. 1964, m.	Hon. Francis D. O.-G., b. 1954.
1939	Harmsworth (2nd), Cecil Desmond Bernard Harmsworth, b. 1903, s. 1948, m.	Hon. Eric H., b. 1905.
1815	Harris (5th), George St. Vincent Harris, C.B.E., M.C., b. 1889, s. 1932, m.	Hon. George R. H., b. 1920.
1954	Harvey of Tasburgh (2nd), Peter Charles Oliver Harvey, b. 1921, s. 1968, m.	Hon. John W. H., b 1923.
1295	Hastings (22nd), Edward Delaval Henry Astley, b. 1912, s. 1956, m.	Hon. Delaval T. H. A., b. 1960.
1835	Hatherton (7th), Thomas Charles Tasman Littleton, T.D., b. 1907, s. 1973, m.	Edward C. L., b. 1950.
1776	Hawke (9th), Bladen Wilmer Hawke, b. 1901, s. 1939, m.	Hon. Theodore H., b. 1904.
1927	Hayter (3rd), George Charles Hayter Chubb, b. 1911, s. 1967, m.	Hon. George W. M. C., b. 1943.
1945	Hazlerigg (2nd), Arthur Grey Hazlerigg, M.C., b. 1910, s. 1949, w.	Hon. Arthur G. H., b. 1951.
1797 I.	Headley (7th), Charles Rowland Allanson-Winn, b. 1902, s. 1969, m.	Hon. John R. A.-W., b. 1934.
1943	Hemingford (2nd), Dennis George Ruddock Herbert, b. 1904, s. 1947, m.	Hon. Dennis H., b. 1934.
1906	Hemphill (5th), Peter Patrick Fitzroy Martyn Martyn-Hemphill, b. 1928, s. 1957, m.	Hon. Charles A. M. M.-H., b. 1954.
1945	Henderson (1st), William Watson Henderson, P.C., b. 1891.	(None.)
1799 I.*	Henley (7th), Michael Francis Eden (5th U.K. Baron, Northington, 1885), b. 1914, s. 1962, m.	Hon. Oliver M. R. E., b. 1953.
1800 I.*	Henniker (7th), John Ernest de Grey Henniker-Major (3rd U.K. Baron, Hartismere, 1866), b. 1883, s. 1956, w.	Hon. Sir John P. E. C. H.-M., K.C.M.G., C.V.O., M.C., b. 1916.
1886	Herschell (3rd), Rognvald Richard Farrer Herschell, b. 1923, s. 1929, m.	(None.)
1935	Hesketh (3rd), Thomas Alexander Fermor-Hesketh, b. 1950, s. 1955.	Hon. Robert F.-H., b. 1951.

Created.	Title, Order of Succession, Name, etc.	Eldest Son or Heir.
1828	*Heytesbury* (6th), Francis William Holmes à Court, *b.* 1931, *s.* 1971, *m.*	Hon. James W. H. à C., *b.* 1967.
1886	*Hillingdon* (4th), Charles Hedworth Mills, *b.* 1922, *s.* 1952, *m.*	Hon. Charles J. M., *b.* 1951.
1886	*Hindlip* (5th), Henry Richard Allsopp, *b.* 1912, *s.* 1966, *m.*	Hon. Charles H. A., *b.* 1940.
1950	*Hives* (2nd), John Warwick Hives, *b.* 1913, *s.* 1965, *m.*	Matthew H., *b.* 1971.
1960	*Hodson*, Francis Lord Charlton Hodson, P.C., M.C., *b.* 1895, *w.* (*Lord of Appeal, retired*).	(Law Life Peerage.)
1912	*Hollenden* (2nd), Geoffrey Hope Hope-Morley, *b.* 1885, *s.* 1929, *m.*	Gordon H. H.-M., *b.* 1914.
1897	*Holm Patrick* (3rd), James Hans Hamilton, *b.* 1928, *s.* 1942, *m.*	Hon. Hans J. D. H., *b.* 1955.
1933	*Horder* (2nd), Thomas Mervyn Horder, *b.* 1911, *s.* 1955.	(None.)
1797 I.	*Hotham* (8th), Henry Durand Hotham, *b.* 1940, *s.* 1967, *m.*	Hon. William B. H., *b.* 1972.
1881	*Hothfield* (4th), Thomas Sackville Tufton, *b.* 1916, *s.* 1961.	Lt.-Col. George W. A. T., T.D., *b.* 1904.
1597	*Howard de Walden* (9th), John Osmael Scott-Ellis (5th *U.K. Baron, Seaford*, 1826), *b.* 1912, *s.* 1946, *w.*	Co-heiresses. To U.K. Barony, W. F. *Ellis*, *b.* 1912.
1930	*Howard of Penrith* (2nd), Francis Philip Howard, *b.* 1905, *s.* 1939, *m.*	Hon. Philip H., *b.* 1945.
1960	*Howick of Glendale* (2nd), Charles Evelyn Baring, *b.* 1937, *s.* 1973, *m.*	Son, *b.* 1975.
1796 I.	*Huntingfield* (6th), Gerard Charles Arcedeckne Vanneck, *b.* 1915, *s.* 1969, *m.*	Hon. Joshua C. V., *b.* 1954.
1866	*Hylton* (5th), Raymond Hervey Jolliffe, *b.* 1932, *s.* 1967, *m.*	Hon. William H. M. J., *b.* 1967.
1933	*Iliffe* (2nd), Edward Langton Iliffe, *b.* 1908, *s.* 1960, *m.*	Robert P. R. I, *b.* 1944.
1543 I.	*Inchiquin* (17th), Phaedrig Lucius Ambrose O'Brien (*O'Brien of Thomond*), *b.* 1900, *s.* 1968, *m.*	Hon. Fionn M. O'B., *b.* 1903.
1962	*Inchyra* (1st), Frederick Robert Hoyer Millar, G.C.M.G., C.V.O., *b.* 1900, *m.*	Hon. Robert H., M. *b.* 1935.
1964	*Inglewood* (1st), William Morgan Fletcher-Vane, T.D., *b.* 1909, *m.*	Hon. W. Richard F.-V., *b.* 1951.
1946	*Inman* (1st), Philip Albert Inman, P.C., *b.* 1892, *m.*	(None.)
1919	*Inverforth* (2nd), Andrew Alexander Morton Weir, *b.* 1897, *s.* 1955, *m.*	Hon. A. C. Roy W., *b.* 1932.
1941	*Ironside* (2nd), Edmund Oslac Ironside, *b.* 1924, *s.* 1959, *m.*	Hon. Charles E.G.I., *b.* 1956.
1952	*Jeffreys* (2nd), Mark George Christopher Jeffreys, *b.* 1932, *s.* 1960, *m.*	Hon. Christopher H. M. J., *b.* 1957.
1924	*Jessel* (2nd), Edward Herbert Jessel, C.B.E., *b.* 1904, *s.* 1950, *m.*	(None.)
1906	*Joicey* (4th), Michael Edward Joicey, *b.* 1925, *s.* 1966, *m.*	Hon. James M. J., *b.* 1953.
1937	*Kenilworth* (3rd), John Tennant Davenport Siddeley, *b.* 1924, *s.* 1971, *m.*	Hon. John R. S., *b.* 1954.
1935	*Kennet* (2nd), Wayland Hilton Young, *b.* 1923, *s.* 1960, *m.*	Hon. William A. Y., *b.* 1957.
1776 I. ⎫ 1886* ⎭	*Kensington* (7th), William Edwardes (4th *U.K. Baron, Kensington*). *b.* 1904, *s.* 1938.	Hugh I. E., *b.* 1933.
1951	*Kenswood* (2nd), John Michael Howard Whitfield, *b.* 1930, *s.* 1963, *m.*	Hon. Michael C. W., *b.* 1955.
1788	*Kenyon* (5th), Lloyd Tyrell-Kenyon, C.B.E., *b.* 1917, *s.* 1927, *m.*	Hon. Lloyd T.-K., *b.* 1947.
1947	*Kershaw* (4th), Edward John Kershaw, *b.* 1936, *s.* 1962, *m.*	Hon. John C. E. K., *b.* 1971.
1943	*Keyes* (2nd), Roger George Bowlby Keyes, *b.* 1919, *s.* 1945, *m.*	Hon. Charles W. P. K., *b.* 1951.
1909	*Kilbracken* (3rd), John Raymond Godley, D.S.C., *b.* 1920, *s.* 1950.	Hon. Christopher J. G., *b.* 1945.
1971	*Kilbrandon*, Charles James Dalrymple Shaw, P.C., *b.* 1906, *m.* (*Lord of Appeal*).	(Law Life Peerage).
1900	*Killanin* (3rd), Michael Morris, M.B.E., T.D., *b.* 1914, *s.* 1927, *m.*	Hon. G. Redmond F. M., *b.* 1947.
1943	*Killearn* (2nd), Graham Curtis Lampson, *b.* 1919, *s.* 1964, *m.*	Hon. Victor M. G. A. L., *b.* 1941.
1789 I.	*Kilmaine* (6th), John Francis Archibald Browne, C.B.E., *b.* 1902, *s.* 1946, *m.*	Hon. John D. H. B., *b.* 1948.
1831	*Kilmarnock* (7th), Alastair Ivor Gilbert Boyd, *b.* 1927, *s.* 1975.	Hon. Robin J. B., *b.* 1941.
1941	*Kindersley* (2nd), Hugh Kenyon Molesworth Kindersley, C.B.E., M.C., *b.* 1899, *s.* 1954, *m.*	Hon. Robert H. M., K., *b.* 1929.
1223 I.	*Kingsale* (35th), John de Courcy (*Premier Baron of Ireland*), *b.* 1941, *s.* 1969.	Nevinson R. de C., *b.* 1920.
1682 S. ⎫ 1860* ⎭	*Kinnaird* (13th), Graham Charles Kinnaird (5th *U.K. Baron, Kinnaird*), *b.* 1912, *s.* 1972, *m.*	(None.)
1902	*Kinross* (3rd), John Patrick Douglas Balfour, *b.* 1904, *s.* 1939.	Hon. David A. B., O.B.E., T.D., *b.* 1906.
1951	*Kirkwood* (3rd), David Harvie Kirkwood, PH.D., *b.* 1931, *s.* 1970, *m.*	Hon. James S. K., *b.* 1937.

Created.	Title, Order of Succession, Name, etc.	Eldest Son or Heir.
1800 I.	*Langford* (9th), Geoffrey Alexander Rowley-Conway, O.B.E., *b.* 1912, *s.* 1953, *m.*	Hon. Owen G. *R.-C., b.* 1958.
1942	*Latham* (2nd), Dominic Charles Latham, *b.* 1954, *s.* 1970.	Hon. Anthony *L., b.* 1954.
1431	*Latymer* (7th), Thomas Burdett Money-Coutts, *b.* 1901, *s.* 1949, *m.*	Hon. Hugo N. *M.-C., b.* 1926.
1869	*Lawrence* (5th), David John Downer Lawrence, *b.* 1937, *s.* 1968.	(None.)
1947	*Layton* (2nd), Michael John Layton, *b.* 1912, *s.* 1966, *m.*	Hon. Geoffrey M. *L., b.* 1947.
1859	*Leconfield* (7th), John Max Henry Scawen Wyndham (2nd U.K. Baron, *Egremont*, 1963), *b.* 1948, *s.* 1972.	Hon. Harry H. P. *W., b.* 1957.
1839	*Leigh* (4th), Rupert William Dudley Leigh, *b.* 1908, *s.* 1938, *m.*	Hon. John P. *L., b.* 1935.
1962	*Leighton of St. Mellons* (2nd), (John) Leighton Seager, *b.* 1922, *s.* 1963, *m.*	Hon. Robert W. H. L. *S., b.* 1955.
1797	*Lilford* (7th), George Vernon Powys, *b.* 1931, *s.* 1949, *m.*	Robert C. L. *P., b.* 1930.
1945	*Lindsay of Birker* (2nd), Michael Francis Morris Lindsay, *b.* 1909, *s.* 1952, *m.*	Hon. James F. *L., b.* 1945.
1758 I.	*Lisle* (7th), John Nicholas Horace Lysaght, *b.* 1903, *s.* 1919, *m.*	Horace *L., b.* 1908.
1925	*Lloyd* (2nd), Alexander David Frederick Lloyd, M.B.E., *b.* 1912, *s.* 1941, *m.*	(None.)
1895	*Loch* (3rd), George Henry Compton Loch, *b.* 1916, *s.* 1942, *m.*	Hon. Spencer *L.*, M.C., *b.* 1920.
1850	*Londesborough* (9th), Richard John Denison, *b.* 1959, *s.* 1968, *M.*	(None.)
1541 I.	*Louth* (16th), Otway Michael James Oliver Plunkett, *b.* 1929, *s.* 1950, *m.*	Hon. Jonathan *O.P.,b* 1952.
1458 S. } 1837* }	*Lovat* (15th), Simon Christopher Joseph Fraser, D.S.O., M.C., T.D. (4th U.K. Baron, *Lovat*), *b.* 1911, *s.* 1933, *m.*	Master of Lovat, *b.* 1939.
1946	*Lucas of Chilworth* (2nd), Michael William George Lucas, *b.* 1926, *s.* 1967, *m.*	Hon. Simon W. *L., b.* 1957.
1929	*Luke* (2nd), Ian St. John Lawson-Johnston, *b.* 1905, *s.* 1943, *m.*	Hon. Arthur *L.-J., b.* 1933.
1839	*Lurgan* (4th), William George Edward Brownlow, *b.* 1902, *s.* 1937.	John D. C. *B.*, O.B.E., *b.* 1911.
1914	*Lyell* (3rd), Charles Lyell, *b.* 1939, *s.* 1943.	(None.)
1945	*Lyle of Westbourne* (2nd), Charles John Leonard Lyle, *b.* 1905, *s.* 1954, *m.*	(None.)
1859	*Lyveden* (5th), Sidney Munro Vernon, *b.* 1888, *s.* 1969, *m.*	Hon. Ronald C. *V., b.* 1915.
1959	*MacAndrew* (1st), Charles Glen MacAndrew, P.C., T.D., *b.* 1888, *m.*	Hon. Colin N. G. *MacA. b.* 1919.
1947	*MacDermott*, John Clarke MacDermott, P.C., M.C., *b.* 1896, *m.* (Lord Chief Justice of Northern Ireland, retired).	(Law Life Peerage.)
1776 I.	*Macdonald* (8th), Godfrey James Macdonald, *b.* 1947, *s.* 1970, *m.*	Hon. Alexander D. A. *M., b.* 1953.
1949	*Macdonald of Gwaenysgor* (2nd), Gordon Ramsay Macdonald, *b.* 1915, *s.* 1966, *m.*	Hon. Kenneth *M., b.* 1921.
1937	*McGowan* (3rd), Harry Duncan Cory McGowan, *b.* 1938, *s.* 1966, *m.*	Hon. Harry J. C. *Mc. G., b.* 1971.
1922	*Maclay* (3rd), Joseph Paton Maclay, *b.* 1942, *s.* 1969.	Hon. David M. *M., b.* 1944.
1955	*McNair* (2nd), (Clement) John McNair, *b.* 1915, *s.* 1975, *m.*	Hon. Duncan J. *McN., b.* 1947.
1951	*Macpherson of Drumochter* (2nd), James Gordon Macpherson, *b.* 1924, *s.* 1965, *w.*	Hon. Thomas I. *M., b.* 1948.
1937	*Mancroft* (2nd), Stormont Mancroft Samuel Mancroft, K.B.E., T.D., *b.* 1914, *s.* 1942, *m.*	Hon. Benjamin L. S. *M., b.* 1957.
1807	*Manners* (5th), John Robert Cecil Manners, *b.* 1923, *s.* 1972, *m.*	Hon. John H. R. *M., b.* 1956.
1922	*Manton* (3rd), Joseph Rupert Eric Robert Watson, *b.* 1924, *s.* 1968, *m.*	Hon. Miles R. M. *W., b.* 1958.
1908	*Marchamley* (3rd), John William Tattersall Whiteley, *b.* 1922, *s.* 1949, *m.*	Hon. William F. *W., b.* 1968.
1965	*Margadale* (1st), John Granville Morrison, T.D., *b.* 1906, *m.*	Hon. James I. *M.,* T.D., *b.* 1930.
1961	*Marks of Broughton* (2nd), Michael Marks, *b.* 1920, *s.* 1964.	Hon. Simon R. *M., b.* 1950.
1930	*Marley* (2nd), Godfrey Pelham Leigh Aman, *b.* 1913, *s.* 1952, *m.*	(None.)
1964	*Martonmere* (1st), (John) Roland Robinson, P.C., G.B.E., K.C.M.G., *b.* 1907, *m.*	Hon. Richard A. G. *R., b.* 1935.
1776 I.	*Massy* (9th), Hugh Hamon John Somerset Massy, *b.* 1921, *s.* 1958, *m.*	Hon. David H. S. *M., b.* 1947.
1935	*May* (3rd), Michael St. John May, *b.* 1931, *s.* 1950, *m.*	Hon. Jasper B. St. J. *M., b.* 1965.
1928	*Melchett* (4th), Peter Robert Henry Mond, *b.* 1948, *s.* 1973.	(None.)
1925	*Merrivale* (3rd), Jack Henry Edmond Duke, *b.* 1917, *s.* 1951, *m.*	Hon. Derek J. P. *D., b.* 1948.
1911	*Merthyr* (3rd), William Brereton Couchman Lewis, P.C., K.B.E., T.D., *b.* 1901, *s.* 1932, *m.*	Hon. Trevor O. *L., b.* 1935.

Created.	Title, Order of Succession, Name, etc.	Eldest Son or Heir.
1919	*Meston* (2nd), Dougall Meston, *b.* 1894, *s.* 1943, *m.*	Hon. James *M.*, *b.* 1950.
1838	*Methuen* (6th), Anthony John Methuen, *b.* 1925, *s.* 1975.	Hon. Robert A. H. *M.*, *b.* 1931.
1905	*Michelham* (2nd), Herman Alfred Stern, *b.* 1900, *s.* 1919, *w.*	Hon.Jack *Michelham*,*b.*1903.
1711	*Middleton* (12th), (Digby) Michael Godfrey John Willoughby, M.C., *b.* 1921, *s.* 1970, *m.*	Hon. Michael C. J. *W.*, *b.* 1948.
1939	*Milford* (2nd), Wogan Philipps, *b.* 1902, *s.* 1962, *m.*	Hon. Hugo J. L. *P.*, *b.* 1929.
1933	*Milne* (2nd), George Douglass Milne, *b.* 1909, *s.* 1948, *m.*	Hon. George *M.*, *b.* 1941.
1951	*Milner of Leeds* (2nd), Michael Milner, *b.* 1923, *s.* 1967, *m.*	Hon. Richard J. *M.*, *b.* 1959.
1947	*Milverton* (1st), Arthur Frederick Richards, G.C.M.G., *b.* 1885, *m.*	Rev. Hon. Fraser *R.*, *b.* 1930.
1873	*Moncreiff* (5th), Harry Robert Wellwood Moncreiff, *b.* 1915, *s.* 1942, *m.*	Hon. Rhoderick H. W. *M.*, *b.* 1954.
1884	*Monk Bretton* (3rd), John Charles Dodson, *b.* 1924, *s.* 1933, *m.*	Hon. Christopher M. *D.*, *b.* 1958.
1728	*Monson* (11th), John Monson, *b.* 1932, *s.* 1958, *m.*	Hon. Nicholas J. *M.*, *b.* 1955.
1885	*Montagu of Beaulieu* (3rd), Edward John Barrington Douglas-Scott-Montagu, *b.* 1926, *s.* 1929, *m.*	Hon. Ralph *D-S-M.*, *b.* 1961.
1839	*Monteagle of Brandon* (6th), Gerald Spring Rice, *b.* 1926, *s.* 1946, *m.*	Hon. Charles J.S. *R.*,*b.*1953.
1943	*Moran* (1st), Charles McMoran Wilson, M.C., M.D., *b.* 1882, *m.*	Hon. R. John M. *W.*, C.M.G., *b.* 1924.
1918	*Morris* (3rd), Michael David Morris, *b.* 1937, *s.* 1975.	Hon. Edward P. *M.*,*b.*1937.
1960	*Morris of Borth-y-Gest*, John William Morris, P.C., C.H., C.B.E., M.C., *b.* 1896. (*Lord of Appeal, retired*).	(Law Life Peerage).
1950	*Morris of Kenwood* (2nd), Philip Geoffry Morris, *b.* 1928, *s.* 1954, *m.*	Hon. Jonathan D. *M.b.* 1968.
1945	*Morrison* (2nd), Dennis Morrison, *b.* 1914, *s.* 1953, *m.*	(None.)
1831	*Mostyn* (5th), Roger Edward Lloyd Lloyd-Mostyn, M.C., *b.* 1920, *s.* 1965, *m.*	Hon. Llewellyn R. *L.-M.*, *b.* 1948.
1933	*Mottistone* (4th), David Peter Seely, *b.* 1920, *s.* 1966, *m.*	Hon. Peter J. P. *S.*, *b.* 1949.
1945	*Mountevans* (3rd), Edward Patrick Broke Evans, *b.* 1943, *s.* 1974.	Hon. Jeffrey de C. R. *E.*, *b.* 1948.
1283	*Mowbray* (26th), *Segrave* (27th) (1283), & *Stourton* (23rd) (1448), Charles Edward Stourton (*Premier Baron of England*), *b.* 1923, *s.* 1965, *m.*	Hon. Edward W. S. *S.*, *b.* 1953.
1932	*Moyne* (2nd), Bryan Walter Guinness, *b.* 1905, *s.* 1944, *m.*	Hon. Jonathan *G.*, *b.* 1930.
1929	*Moynihan* (3rd), Antony Patrick Andrew Cairnes Berkeley Moynihan, *b.* 1936, *s.* 1965, *m.*	Hon. Colin B. *M.*, *b.* 1955.
1781 I.	*Muskerry* (8th), Hastings Fitzmaurice Tilson Deane, *b.* 1907, *s.* 1966, *m.*	Hon. Robert F. *D.*, *b.* 1948.
1627 S.*	*Napier and Ettrick* (14th), Francis Nigel Napier (5th *U.K. Baron, Ettrick*, 1872), *b.* 1930, *s.* 1954, *m.*	Master of Napier, *b.* 1962.
1868	*Napier of Magdala* (5th), (Robert) John Napier, O.B.E., *b.* 1904, *s.* 1948, *m.*	Hon. Robert *N.*, *b.* 1940.
1940	*Nathan* (2nd), Roger Carol Michael Nathan, *b.* 1922, *s.* 1963, *m.*	Hon. Rupert H. B. *N.*, *b.* 1957.
1960	*Nelson of Stafford* (2nd), Henry George Nelson, *b.* 1917, *s.* 1962, *m.*	Hon. Henry R. G. *N.*, *b.* 1943.
1959	*Netherthorpe* (1st), James Turner, *b.* 1908, *m.*	Hon. James A. *T.*, *b.* 1936.
1946	*Newall* (2nd), Francis Storer Eaton Newall, *b.* 1930, *'s.* 1963, *m.*	Hon. Richard H. E. *N.*, *b.* 1961.
1776 I.	*Newborough* (7th), Robert Charles Michael Vaughan Wynn, D.S.C., *b.* 1917, *s.* 1965, *m.*	Hon. Robert V. *W.*, *b.* 1949.
1892	*Newton* (4th), Peter Richard Legh, *b.* 1915, *s.* 1960, *m.*	Hon. Richard T. *L.*, *b.* 1950.
1930	*Noel-Buxton* (and), Rufus Alexander Buxton, *b.* 1917, *s.* 1948, *m.*	Hon. Martin C. *Noel-Buxton*, *b.* 1940.
1957	*Norrie* (1st), (Charles) Willoughby (Moke) Norrie, G.C.M.G., G.C.V.O., C.B., D.S.O., M.C., *b.* 1893, *m.*	Hon. George W. M. *N.*, *b.* 1936.
1884	*Northbourne* (4th), Walter Ernest Christopher James, *b.* 1896, *s.* 1932, *m.*	Hon. Christopher G. W. *J.*, *b.* 1926.
1866	*Northbrook* (5th), Francis John Baring, *b.* 1915, *s.* 1947, *m.*	Hon. Francis T. *B.*, *b.* 1954.
1878	*Norton* (7th), John Arden Adderley, O.B.E., *b.* 1915, *s.* 1961, *m.*	Hon. James N. A. *A.*,*b.*1947.
1906	*Nunburnholme* (4th), Ben Charles Wilson, *b.* 1928, *s.* 1974, *m.*	Hon. Charles T. *W.*,*b.*1936.
1950	*Ogmore* (1st), David Rees Rees-Williams, P.C., T.D., *b.* 1903, *m.*	Hon. Gwilym *R.-W.*, *b.* 1931.
1870	*O'Hagan* (4th), Charles Towneley Strachey, *b.* 1945, *s.* 1961, *m.*	Hon. Richard T. *S.*, *b.* 1950.
1868	*O'Neil* (4th), Raymond Arthur Clanaboy O'Neill, T.D., *b.* 1933, *s.* 1944, *m.*	Hon. Shane S. *O'N.*, *b.* 1965.
1836 I.*	*Oranmore and Browne* (4th), Dominick Geoffrey Edward Browne (2nd *U.K. Baron Mereworth*, 1926), *b.* 1901, *s.* 1927, *m.*	Hon. Dominick G. T. *B.*, *b.* 1929.
1868	*Ormathwaite* (6th), John Arthur Charles Walsh, *b.* 1912, *s.* 1944.	(None.)

Created.	Title, Order of Succession, Name, etc.	Eldest Son or Heir.
1933	*Palmer* (3rd), Raymond Cecil Palmer, O.B.E., *b.* 1916, *s.* 1950, *m.*	Hon. Gordon W. N. P., O.B.E., T.D., *b.* 1918.
1914	*Parmoor* (2nd), Alfred Henry Seddon Cripps, *b.* 1882, *s.* 1941.	Hon. Frederick H. C., D.S.O., T.D., *b.* 1885.
1962	*Pearce*, Edward Holroyd Pearce, P.C., *b.* 1901, *m.* (*Lord of Appeal, retired*).	(Law Life Peerage.)
1965	*Pearson*, Colin Hargreaves Pearson, P.C., C.B.E., *b.* 1899, *m.* (*Lord of Appeal, retired.*).	(Law Life Peerage.)
1937	*Pender* (3rd), John Willoughby Denison-Pender, *b.* 1933, *s.* 1965, *m.*	Hon. Henry J. R. D.-P., *b.* 1968.
1866	*Penrhyn* (6th), Malcolm Frank Douglas-Pennant, D.S.O., M.B.E., *b.* 1908, *s.* 1967, *m.*	Hon. Nigel D.-P., *b.* 1909.
1909	*Pentland* (2nd), Henry John Sinclair, *b.* 1907, *s.* 1925, *m.*	(None.)
1603	*Petre* (17th), Joseph William Lionel Petre, *b.* 1914, *s.* 1915, *m.*	Hon. John P., *b.* 1942.
1918	*Phillimore* (3rd), Robert Godfrey Phillimore, *b.* 1939, *s.* 1947.	Hon. Claud P., *b.* 1911.
1945	*Piercy* (2nd), Nicholas Pelham Piercy, *b.* 1918, *s.* 1966, *m.*	Hon. James W. P., *b.* 1946.
1827	*Plunket* (8th), Robin Rathmore Plunket, *b.* 1925, *s.* 1975, *m.*	Hon. Shaun A. F. S. P., *b.* 1931.
1831	*Poltimore* (6th), Hugh de Burgh Warwick Bampfylde, *b.* 1888, *s.* 1967, *m.*	Mark C. B., *b.* 1957.
1690 S.	*Polwarth* (10th), Henry Alexander Hepburne-Scott, T.D., *b.* 1916, *s.* 1944, *m.*	Master of Polwarth, *b.* 1947.
1930	*Ponsonby of Shulbrede* (2nd), Matthew Henry Hubert Ponsonby, *b.* 1904, *s.* 1946, *m.*	Hon. Thomas A. P., *b.* 1930.
1958	*Poole* (1st), Oliver Brian Sanderson Poole, P.C., C.B.E., T.D., *b.* 1911, *m.*	Hon. David C. P., *b.* 1945.
1852	*Raglan* (5th), FitzRoy John Somerset, *b.* 1927, *s.* 1964, *m.*	Hon. Geoffrey S., *b.* 1932.
1932	*Rankeillour* (4th), Peter St. Thomas More Henry Hope, *b.* 1935, *s.* 1967.	Michael R. H., *b.* 1940.
1953	*Rathcavan* (1st), (Robert William) Hugh O'Neill, P.C., *b.* 1883, *w.*	Rt. Hon. Phelim R. H. O'N., *b.* 1909.
1916	*Rathcreedan* (and), Charles Patrick Norton, T.D., *b.* 1905, *s.* 1930, *m.*	Hon. Christopher J. N., *b.* 1949.
1868 I.	*Rathdonnell* (5th), Thomas Benjamin McClintock Bunbury, *b.* 1938, *s.* 1959, *m.*	Hon. William L. McC B., *b.* 1966.
1911	*Ravensdale* (3rd), Nicholas Mosley, M.C., *b.* 1923, *s.* 1966, *m.*	Hon. Shaun N. M., *b.* 1949.
1218	*Ravensworth* (8th), Arthur Waller Liddell, *b.* 1924, *s.* 1950, *m.*	Hon. Thomas A. H. L., *b.* 1954.
1821	*Rayleigh* (5th), John Arthur Strutt, *b.* 1908, *s.* 1947, *m.*	Hon. Charles S., *b.* 1910.
1937	*Rea* (2nd), Philip Russell Rea, P.C., O.B.E., *b.* 1900, *s.* 1948, *m.*	John N. R., M.D., *b.* 1928.
1628 S.	*Reay* (14th), Hugh William Mackay, *b.* 1937, *s.* 1963, *m.*	Master of Reay, *b.* 1965.
1902	*Redesdale* (5th), Clement Napier Bertram Freeman-Mitford, *b.* 1932, *s.* 1963, *m.*	Hon. Rupert B. F.-M., *b.* 1967.
1928	*Remnant* (3rd), James Wogan Remnant, *b.* 1930, *s.* 1967, *m.*	Hon. Philip J. R., *b.* 1954.
1806 I.	*Rendlesham* (8th), Charles Anthony Hugh Thellusson, *b.* 1915, *s.* 1943, *m.*	Hon. Charles W. B. T., *b.* 1954.
1933	*Rennell* (2nd), Francis James Rennell Rodd, K.B.E., C.B., *b.* 1895, *s.* 1941, *m.*	J. A. Tremayne R., *b.* 1935.
1964	*Renwick* (2nd), Harry Andrew Renwick, *b.* 1935, *s.* 1973, *m.*	Hon. Robert J. R., *b.* 1966.
1885	*Revelstoke* (4th), Rupert Baring, *b.* 1911, *s.* 1934.	Hon. John B., *b.* 1934.
1905	*Ritchie of Dundee* (3rd), John Kenneth Ritchie, P.C., *b.* 1902, *s.* 1948, *w.*	Hon. Colin R., *b.* 1908.
1935	*Riverdale* (2nd), Robert Arthur Balfour, *b.* 1901, *s.* 1957, *m.*	Hon. Mark R. B., *b.* 1927.
1961	*Robertson of Oakridge* (2nd), William Ronald Robertson, *b.* 1930, *s.* 1974, *m.*	
1938	*Roborough* (2nd), Massey Henry Edgcumbe Lopes, *b.* 1903, *s.* 1938, *m.*	Hon. Henry L., *b.* 1940.
1931	*Rochester* (2nd), Foster Charles Lowry Lamb, *b.* 1916, *s.* 1955, *m.*	Hon. David C. L., *b.* 1944.
1934	*Rockley* (2nd), Robert William Evelyn Cecil, *b.* 1901, *s.* 1941, *m.*	Hon. James H. C., *b.* 1934.
1782	*Rodney* (9th), John Francis Rodney, *b.* 1920, *s.* 1973, *m.*	Hon. George B. R., *b.* 1953.
1651 S.*	*Rollo* (13th), Eric John Stapylton Rollo 4th *U.K. Baron, Dunning,* 1869), *b.* 1915, *s.* 1947, *m.*	Master of Rollo, *b.* 1943.
1866	*Romilly* (4th), William Gaspard Guy Romilly, *b.* 1809, *s.* 1905, *m.*	(None.)
1959	*Rootes* (2nd), William Geoffrey Rootes, *b.* 1917, *s.* 1964, *m.*	Hon. Nicholas G. R., *b.* 1951.
1796 I. 1838* }	*Rossmore* (7th), William Warner Westenra (6th *U.K. Baron, Rossmore*), *b.* 1931, *s.* 1958.	(None.)
1939	*Rotherwick* (2nd), (Herbert) Robin Cayzer, *b.* 1912, *s.* 1958, *m.*	Hon. H. Robin C., *b.* 1954.
1885	*Rothschild* (3rd), Nathanial Mayer Victor Rothschild, G.B.E., G.M., F.R.S., *b.* 1910, *s.* 1937, *m.*	Hon. N. C. Jacob R., *b.* 1936.
1911	*Rowallan* (2nd), Thomas Godfrey Polson Corbett, K.T., K.B.E., M.C., T.D., *b.* 1895, *s.* 1933, *w.*	Hon. Arthur C., *b.* 1919.
1947	*Rugby* (2nd), Alan Loader Maffey, *b.* 1913, *s.* 1969, *m.*	Hon. John R. M., *b.* 1949.
1945	*Rusholme* (1st), Robert Alexander Palmer, *b.* 1890.	(None.)
1919	*Russell of Liverpool* (2nd), Edward Frederick Langley Russell, C.B.E., M.C., T.D., *b.* 1895, *s.* 1920, *m.*	Hon. Langley G. H. R., M.C., *b.* 1922.

Created.	Title, Order of Succession, Name, etc.	Eldest Son or Heir.
1876	*Sackville* (6th), Lionel Bertrand Sackville-West, *b.* 1913, *s.* 1965, *m.*	Hugh R. I. *S.-W.*, M.C., *b.* 1919.
1964	*St. Helens* (1st), Michael Henry Colin Hughes-Young, *b.* 1912, *w.*	Hon. Richard F. *H.-Y.*, *b.* 1945.
1559	*St. John of Bletso* (19th), John Moubray Russell St. John, *b.* 1917, *s.* 1934.	Andrew *B St. J.*, T.D., *b.* 1918.
1935	*St. Just* (2nd), Peter George Grenfell, *b.* 1922, *s.* 1941, *m.*	(None.)
1852	*St. Leonards* (4th), John Gerard Sugden, *b.* 1950, *s* 1972.	Edward C. S., *b.* 1902.
1887	*St. Levan* (3rd), Francis Cecil St. Aubyn, *b.* 1895, *s.* 1940, *m.*	Hon. John F. A. *St. A.*, D.S.C., *b.* 1919.
1885	*St. Oswald* (4th), Rowland Denys Guy Winn, M.C., *b.* 1916, *s.* 1957, *m.*	Hon. Derek E. A. *W.*, *b.* 1919.
1972	*Salmon*, Cyril Barnet Salmon, P.C., *b.* 1903, *m.* (*Lord of Appeal*).	(Law Life Peerage).
1445 S.	*Saltoun* (19th), Alexander Arthur Fraser. M.C., *b.* 1886, *s.* 1933, *m.*	Hon. Flora M. *Ramsay*, *b.* 1930.
1945	*Sandford* (2nd), Rev. John Cyril Edmondson, D.S.C., *b.* 1920, *s.* 1959, *m.*	Hon. James J. M. *E.*, *b.* 1949.
1871	*Sandhurst* (5th), (John Edward) Terence Mansfield, D.F.C., *b.* 1920, *s.* 1964, *m.*	Hon. Guy R. J. *M.*, *b.* 1949.
1802	*Sandys* (7th), Richard Michael Oliver Hill, *b.* 1931, *s.* 1961, *m.*	Marcus T. *H.*, *b.* 1931.
1888	*Savile* (3rd), George Halifax Lumley-Savile, *b.* 1919, *s.* 1931.	Hon. Henry L. T. *L.-S.*, *b.* 1923.
1447	*Saye and Sele* (21st), Nathaniel Thomas Allen Twisleton-Wykeham-Fiennes, *b.* 1920, *s.* 1968, *m.*	Hon. Richard I *T.-W.-F.*, *b.* 1959.
1932	*Selsdon* (3rd), Malcolm McEacharn Mitchell-Thomson, *b.* 1937, *s.* 1963, *m.*	Hon. Callum M. M. *M.-T.*, *b.* 1969.
1916	*Shaughnessy* (3rd), William Graham Shaughnessy, *b.* 1922, *s.* 1938, *m.*	Hon. Patrick J. *S.*, *b.* 1944.
1783 I. ⎱ 1839* ⎰	*Sheffield* (8th), Thomas Henry Oliver Stanley (8th *U.K. Baron, Stanley of Alderley and* 7th *U.K. Baron Eddisbury*, 1848), *b.* 1927, *s.* 1971, *m.*	Hon. Richard O. *S.*, *b.* 1956.
1946	*Shepherd* (2nd), Malcolm Newton Shepherd, P.C., *b.* 1918, *s.* 1934, *m.*	Hon. Graeme G.. *S*, *b.* 1949.
1784	*Sherborne* (7th), Charles Dutton, *b.* 1911, *s.* 1949, *m.*	Hon. George E. *D.*, *b.* 1912.
1964	*Sherfield* (1st), Roger Mellor Makins, G.C.B., G.C.M.G., *b.* 1904, *m.*	Hon. Christopher *M.*, *b.* 1942.
1902	*Shuttleworth* (4th), Charles Ughtred John Kay-Shuttleworth, M.C., *b.* 1917, *s.* 1942, *m.*	Hon. Charles G. N. *K.-S.*, *b.* 1948.
1963	*Silsoe* (1st), (Arthur) Malcolm Trustram Eve, G.B.E., M.C., T.D., Q.C., *b.* 1894, *m.*	Hon. David M. T. *E.*, Q.C., *b.* 1930.
1971	*Simon of Glaisdale*, Jocelyn Edward Salis Simon, P.C., *b.* 1911, *m.* (*Lord of Appeal*).	(Law Life Peerage.)
1947	*Simon of Wythenshawe* (2nd), Roger Simon, *b.* 1913, *s.* 1960, *m.*	Hon. Matthew *S.*, *b.* 1955.
1449 S.	*Sinclair* (17th), Charles Murray Kennedy St. Clair, M.V.O., *b.* 1914, *s.* 1957, *m.*	Master of Sinclair, *b.* 1968.
1957	*Sinclair of Cleeve* (1st), Robert John Sinclair, K.C.B., K.B.E., *b.* 1893, *m.*	Hon. John R. K. *S.*, O.B.E., *b.* 1919.
1919	*Sinha* (3rd), Sudhindro Prosannho Sinha, *b.* 1920, *s.* 1967, *m*	Hon. Sushanto *S. b.* 1953
1828	*Skelmersdale* (7th), Roger Bootle-Wilbraham, *b.* 1945, *s.* 1973, *m.*	
1916	*Somerleyton* (3rd), Savile William Francis Crossley, *b.* 1928, *s.* 1959, *m.*	Hon. Hugh F. S. *C.*, *b.* 1971.
1784	*Somers* (8th), John Patrick Somers Cocks, *b.* 1907, *s.* 1953, *m.*	Philip S. S. *C.*, *b.* 1948.
1917	*Southborough* (3rd), Francis John Hopwood, *b.* 1897, *s.* 1960, *m.*	Hon. Francis M. *H.*, *b.* 1922.
1959	*Spens* (2nd), William George Michael Spens, *b.* 1914, *s.* 1973, *m.*	Hon. Patrick M. R. *S.*, *b.* 1942.
1640	*Stafford* (14th), Basil Francis Nicholas Fitzherbert, *b.* 1926, *s.* 1941, *m.*	Hon. Francis M. W. *F.*, *b.* 1954.
1938	*Stamp* (3rd), Trevor Charles Stamp, M.D., *b.* 1907, *s.* 1941, *m.*	Hon. Trevor *S.*, M.D., *b.* 1935.
1918	*Strabolgi* (11th), David Montague de Burgh Kenworthy, *b.* 1914, *s.* 1953.	Rev. the Hon. Jonathan M. A. *K.*, *b.* 1916.
1954	*Strang* (1st), William Strang, G.C.B., G.C.M.G., M.B.E., *b.* 1893, *w.*	Hon. Colin *S.*, *b.* 1922.
1628	*Strange* (15th), John Drummond, *b.* 1900, *title called out of abeyance* 1964, *m.*	Three co-heiresses.
1955	*Strathalmond* (2nd), William Fraser, C.M.G., O.B.E., T.D., *b.* 1916, *s.* 1970, *w.*	Hon. William R. *F.*, *b.* 1947.
1936	*Strathcarron* (2nd), David William Anthony Blyth Macpherson, *b.* 1924, *s.* 1937, *w.*	Hon. Ian D. P. *M.*, *b.* 1949.
1955	*Strathclyde* (1st), Thomas Dunlop Galbraith, P.C., *b.* 1891, *m.*	Hon. Thomas G. D. *G.*, M.P., *b.* 1917.
1900	*Strathcona and Mount Royal* (4th), Donald Euan Palmer Howard, *b.* 1923, *s.* 1959, *m.*	Hon. Donald A. *H.*, *b.* 1961.
1836	*Stratheden & Campbell* (1841) (4th), Alastair Campbell, C.B.E., *b.* 1899, *s.* 1918, *m.*	Hon. Gavin *C.*, *b.* 1901.

Created.	Title, Order of Succession, Name, etc.	Eldest Son or Heir.
1884	*Strathspey* (5th), Donald Patrick Trevor Grant, *b.* 1912, *s.* 1948, *m.* 1941.	Hon. James P. G., *b.* 1943.
1838	*Sudeley* (7th), Nerlyn Charles Sainthill Hanbury-Tracy, *b.* 1939, *s.*	Claud E. F. *Hanbury-Tracy-Domville*, T.D., *b.* 1904
1786	*Suffield* (11th), Anthony Philip Harbord-Hamond, M.C., *b.* 1922, *s.* 1951, *m.*	Hon Charles A. A. *H.-H.* *b.* 1953.
1893	*Swansea* (4th), John Hussey Hamilton Vivian, *b.* 1925, *s.* 1934.	Hon. Richard A. H. *V.*, *b.* 1957.
1907	*Swaythling* (3rd), Stuart Albert Samuel Montagu, O.B.E., *b.* 1898, *s.* 1927, *m.*	Hon. David C. *M.*, *b.* 1928.
1919	*Swinfen* (2nd), Charles Swinfen Eady, *b.* 1904, *s.* 1919, *m.*	Hon. Roger M. *E.*, *b.* 1938.
1935	*Sysonby* (3rd), John Frederick Ponsonby, *b.* 1945, *s.* 1956.	(None.)
1831 I.	*Talbot of Malahide* (9th), Joseph Hubert George Talbot *b.* 1899, *s.* 1975, *m.*	Reginald J. R. *Arundell*, *b.* 1931.
1946	*Tedder* (2nd), John Michael Tedder, SC.D., PH.D., D.SC., *b.* 1926, *s.* 1967, *m.*	Hon. Robin J. *T.*, *b.* 1955.
1797 I.	*Teignmouth* (7th), Frederick Maxwell Aglionby Shore, D.S.C., *b.* 1920, *s.* 1964.	(None.)
1884	*Tennyson* (4th), Harold Christopher Tennyson, *b.* 1919, *s.* 1951.	Hon. Mark A. *T.*, D.S.C., *b.* 1920.
1918	*Terrington* (4th), (James Allen) David Woodhouse, *b.* 1915, *s.* 1961, *m.*	Hon. C. Montague *W.*, D.S.O., O.B.E., *b.* 1917.
1940	*Teviot* (2nd), Charles John Kerr, *b.* 1934, *s.* 1968, *m.*	Hon. Charles R. *K.*, *b.* 1971.
1616	*Teynham* (20th), John Christopher Ingham Roper-Curzon, *b.* 1928, *s.* 1972, *m.*	Hon. David J. H. I. *R.-C.*, *b.* 1965.
1964	*Thomson of Fleet* (1st), Roy Herbert Thomson, G.B.E., *b.* 1894, *w.*	Hon. Kenneth R. *T.*, *b.* 1923.
1792	*Thurlow* (8th), Francis Edward Hovell-Thurlow-Cumming-Bruce, K.C.M.G., *b.* 1912, *s.* 1971, *m.*	Hon. Roualeyn R. *H.-T.-C.-B.*, *b.* 1952.
1876	*Tollemache* (5th), Timothy John Edward Tollemache, *b.* 1939, *s.* 1975.	
1564 S.	*Torphichen* (15th), James Andrew Douglas Sandilands, *b.* 1946, *s.* 1975.	Bruce W. *s.*, *b.* 1921.
1947	*Trefgarne* (2nd), David Garro Trefgarne, *b.* 1941, *s.* 1960, *m.*	Hon. George G. *T.*, *b.* 1970.
1921	*Trevethin* (4th), *and Oaksey* (2nd), John Geoffrey Tristram Lawrence (2nd U.K. Baron, *Oaksey*, 1947), *b.* 1929, *s.* 1971, *m.*	Hon. Patrick J. T. *L.*, *b.* 1960.
1880	*Trevor* (4th), Charles Edwin Hill-Trevor, *b.* 1928, *s.* 1950, *m.*	Hon. Mark C. *H.-T.*, *b.* 1970.
1461 I.	*Trimlestown* (19th), Charles Aloysius Barnewall, *b.* 1899, *s.* 1937, *m.*	Hon. Anthony *B.*, *b.* 1928.
1940	*Tryon* (2nd), Charles George Vivian Tryon, P.C., G.C.V.O., K.C.B., D.S.O., *b.* 1906, *s.* 1940, *m.*	Hon. Anthony *T.*, *b.* 1940.
1950	*Tucker* (Frederick) James Tucker, P.C., *b.* 1888 (*Lord of Appeal, retired*), *w.*	(Law Life Peerage.)
1935	*Tweedsmuir* (2nd), John Norman Stuart Buchan, C.B.E., C.D., *b.* 1911, *s.* 1940, *m.*	Hon. William *B.*, *b.* 1916.
1523	*Vaux of Harrowden* (9th), Rev. Peter Hugh Gordon Gilbey, *b.* 1914, *s.* 1958.	Hon. John H. P. G. *b.* 1915.
1800 I.	*Ventry* (7th), Arthur Frederick Daubeney Olav Eveleigh-de-Moleyns, *b.* 1898, *s.* 1936.	Andrew W. *Daubeny-De M.*, *b.* 1943.
1762	*Vernon* (10th), John Lawrence Venables-Vernon, *b.* 1923, *s.* 1963, *m.*	Visct. Harcourt (*see p.* 235).
1922	*Vestey* (3rd), Samuel George Armstrong Vestey, *b.* 1941, *s.* 1954, *m.*	Hon. Mark W. *V.*, *b.* 1943.
1841	*Vivian* (5th), Anthony Crespigny Claude Vivian, *b.* 1906, *s.* 1940, *m.*	Hon. Nicholas *V.*, *b.* 1935.
1963	*Wakefield of Kendal* (1st), (William) Wavell Wakefield, *b.* 1898, *m.*	(None.)
1934	*Wakehurst* (3rd), (John) Christopher Loder, *b.* 1925, *s.* 1970, *m.*	Hon. Timothy W. *L.*, *b.* 1958.
1723	*Walpole* (9th), Robert Henry Montgomerie Walpole, *b.* 1913, *s.* 1931, *m.*	Hon. Robert H. *W.*, *b.* 1938.
1780	*Walsingham* (9th), John de Grey, M.C., *b.* 1925, *s.* 1965, *m.*	Hon. Robert *de G.*, *b.* 1969.
1936	*Wardington* (2nd), Christopher Henry Beaumont Pease, *b.* 1924, *s.* 1950, *m.*	Hon. William S. P., *b.* 1925.
1792 I.	*Waterpark* (7th), Frederick Caryll Phillip Cavendish, *b.* 1926, *s.* 1948, *m.*	Hon. Roderick A. *C.*, *b.* 1959.
1942	*Wedgwood* (4th), Piers Anthony Weymouth Wedgwood, *b.* 1954, *s.* 1970.	John *W.*, M.D., *b.* 1919.
1861	*Westbury* (5th), David Alan Bethell, M.C., *b.* 1922, *s.* 1961, *m.*	Hon. Richard N. *B.*, *b.* 1950.
1944	*Westwood* (2nd), William Westwood, *b.* 1907, *s.* 1953, *m.*	Hon. William G. *W.*, *b.* 1944.
1935	*Wigram* (2nd), (George) Neville (Clive) Wigram, M.C., *b.* 1915, *s.* 1960, *m.*	Hon. Andrew F. C. *W.*, *b.* 1949.
1964	*Wilberforce*, Richard Orme Wilberforce, P.C., C.M.G., O.B.E., *b.* 1907, *m.* (*Lord of Appeal.*)	(Law Life Peerage.)

Created.	Title, Order of Succession, Name, etc.	Eldest Son or Heir.
1491	*Willoughby de Broke* (20th), John Henry Peyto Verney, M.C., A.F.C., b. 1896, s. 1923, m.	Hon. Leopold D. V., b. 1938.
1946	*Wilson* (2nd), Patrick Maitland Wilson, b. 1915, s. 1964, m.	(None.)
1937	*Windlesham* (3rd), David James George Hennessy, P.C., b. 1932, s. 1962, m.	Hon. James R. H., b. 1968.
1951	*Wise* (2nd), John Clayton Wise, b. 1923, s. 1968, m.	Hon. Christopher J. C. W. b. 1948.
1869	*Wolverton* (5th), Nigel Reginald Victor Glyn, b. 1904, s. 1932.	Jeremy C. G., b. 1930.
1928	*Wraxall* (2nd), George Richard Lawley Gibbs, b. 1928, s. 1931.	Hon. Eustace H. B. G., b. 1929.
1915	*Wrenbury* (3rd), John Burton Buckley, b. 1927, s. 1940, m.	Hon. William E. B., b. 1966.
1838	*Wrottesley* (5th), Richard John Wrottesley, M.C., b. 1918, s. 1962, m.	Clifton H. L. de V. W., b. 1968.
1919	*Wyfold* (3rd), Hermon Robert Fleming Hermon-Hodge, b. 1915, s. 1942.	(None.)
1829	*Wynford* (8th), Robert Samuel Best, M.B.E., b. 1917, s. 1943, m.	Hon. John P. R. B., b. 1950.
1308	*Zouche* (18th), James Assheton Frankland, b. 1943, s. 1965.	Hon. Roger N. F., b. 1909.

Peeresses in Their Own Right

Peerages are occasionally granted immediately to ladies of distinction or the widows of distinguished men; but frequently the instances falling under this heading are the result of regular inheritance in lines which are open to females in default of males. A Peeress in her Own Right retains her title after marriage, and if her husband's rank is the superior she is designated by the two titles jointly, the inferior one last: her hereditary claim still holds good in spite of any marriage whether higher or lower. No rank held by a woman can confer any title or even precedence upon her husband but the rank of a Peeress in her Own Right is inherited by her eldest son (or perhaps daughter), to whomsoever she may have been married.

COUNTESSES IN THEIR OWN RIGHT.—*Style*, The Countess of ——
Addressed as, My Lady.

Created.	Title, Name, etc.	Eldest Son or Heir.
1643 S.	*Dysart*, Rosamund Greaves, b. 1914, s. 1975.	Lady Katherine Grant, b. 1918.
1452 S.	*Erroll*, Diana Denyse Hay (*Hereditary Lord High Constable and Knight Marischal of Scotland*), b. 1926, s. 1941, m.	Lord Hay, b. 1948.
1633 S.	*Loudoun*, Barbara Huddleston Abney-Hastings, b. 1919, s. 1960, m.	Lord Mauchline, b. 1942.
1404 S.	*Mar*, Margaret of Mar (*Premier Earldom of Scotland*), b. 1940, s. 1975, m.	The Mistress of Mar, b. 1963.
1660 S.	*Newburgh*, Maria Sofia Giuseppina Gravina di Ramacca (*Princess Giustiniani-Bandini*), b. 1889, s. 1941, w.	Prince Giulio Rospigliosi, b. 1907.
1235 S.	*Sutherland*, Elizabeth Millicent Sutherland, b. 1921, s. 1963, m.	Lord Strathnaver, b. 1947.

BARONESSES IN THEIR OWN RIGHT.—*Style*, The Baroness ——.
Addressed as, My Lady.

Created.	Title, Name, etc.	Eldest Son or Heir.
1421	*Berkeley*, Mary Lalle Foley-Berkeley, b. 1905, *title called out of abeyance*, 1967.	Hon. Cynthia E. Gueterbock, b. 1909.
1455	*Berners*, Vera Ruby Williams, b. 1901, s. 1950, m.	Two co-heiresses.
1307	*Dacre*, Rachel Leila Douglas-Home, b. 1929, *title called out of abeyance*, 1970, m.	Hon. James T. A. D.-H., b. 1952.
1332	*Darcy de Knayth*, Davina Marcia Ingrams, b. 1938, s. 1943, w.	Hon. Caspar D. I., b. 1962.
1264	*De Ros*, Georgiana Angela Maxwell, b. 1933, s. 1958, m. (*Premier Barony of England*).	Hon. Peter M., b. 1958.
1439	*Dudley*, Barbara Amy Felicity Wallace, b. 1907, s. 1972, w.	Hon. Jim A. H. W., b. 1930.
1489	*Herries*, Anne Elizabeth Fitzalan-Howard, b. 1938.	Lady Mary F.-H., b. 1940.
1602 S.	*Kinloss*, Beatrice Mary Grenville Freeman-Grenville, b. 1922, s. 1944, m.	Master of Kinloss, b. 1953.
1663	*Lucas of Crudwell* (*Scottish Baroness, Dingwall* 1609), Anne Rosemary Palmer, b. 1919, s. 1958, m.	Hon. Ralph M. P., b. 1951.
1681 S.	*Nairne*, Katherine Evelyn Constance Bigham (*Viscountess Mersey*), b. 1912, s 1944, m.	Master of Nairne, b. 1934.
1945	*Portal of Hungerford*, Rosemary Ann Portal, b. 1923, s. 1971.	Hon. Mavis E. A. P., b. 1926.
1651 S.	*Ruthven of Freeland*, Bridget Helen Monckton, C.B.E. (*Bridget, Viscountess Monckton of Brenchley*), b. 1896, s. 1956, w.	Earl of Carlisle, M.C., b. 1923 (*see p. 229*).
1489 S.	*Sempill*, Ann Moira Sempill, b. 1920, s. 1965, m.	Master of Sempill, b. 1949.

LIFE PEERS
Created under Life Peerages Act, 1958

BARONS

1972 *Adeane*, Michael Edward Adeane, P.C., G.C.B., G.C.V.O., Royal Victorian Chain, *b.* 1910, *m.*
1974 *Alexander of Potterhill*, William Picken Alexander, Ph.D., *b.* 1905, *m.*
1973 *Allan of Kilmahew*, Robert Alexander Allan, D.S.O., O.B.E., R.D., *b.* 1914, *m.*
1974 *Allen of Fallowfield*, Alfred Walter Henry Allen, C.B.E., *b.* 1914, *m.*
1961 *Alport*, Cuthbert James McCall Alport, P.C., T.D., *b.* 1912, *m.*
1965 *Annan*, Noel Gilroy Annan, O.B.E., *b.* 1916, *m.*
1970 *Ardwick*, John Cowburn Beavan, *b.* 1910, *m.*
1975 *Armstrong of Sanderstead*, William Armstrong, P.C., K.C.B., M.V.O., *b.* 1915, *m.*
1975 *Ashdown*, Arnold Silverstone, *b.* 1911, *m.*
1964 *Arwyn*, Arwyn Randall Arwyn, *b.* 1897, *m.*
1973 *Ashby*, Eric Ashby, D.SC., F.R.S., *b.* 1904, *m.*
1967 *Aylestone*, Herbert William Bowden, P.C., C.H., C.B.E., *b.* 1905, *m.*
1963 *Balerno*, Alick Drummond Buchanan-Smith, C.B.E., T.D., D.SC., F.R.S.E., *b.* 1898, *w.*
1972 *Ballantrae*, Bernard Edward Fergusson, K.T., G.C.M.G., G.C.V.O., D.S.O., O.B.E., *b.* 1911, *m.*
1975 *Balneil*, Robert Alexander Lindsay, P.C., *b.* 1927, *m.*
1975 *Banks*, Desmond Anderson Harvie Banks, C.B.E., *b,* 1918.
1975 *Barber*, Anthony Perrinott Lysberg Barber, P.C., T.D., *b.* 1920, *m.*
1975 *Barnetson*, William Denholm Barnetson, *b.* 1917, *m.*
1968 *Balogh*, Thomas Balogh, *b.* 1905.
1967 *Beaumont of Whitley*, Rev. Timothy Wentworth Beaumont, *b.* 1928, *m.*
1965 *Beeching*, Richard Beeching, Ph.D., *b.* 1913, *m.*
1969 *Bernstein*, Sidney Lewis Bernstein, *b.* 1899, *m.*
1964 *Beswick*, Frank Beswick, P.C., *b.* 1912.
1968 *Black*, William Rushton Black, *b.* 1893, *m.*
1971 *Blake*, Robert Norman William Blake, F.B.A., *b.* 1916, *m.*
1964 *Blyton*, William Reid Blyton, *b.* 1899, *m.*
1958 *Boothby*, Robert John Graham Boothby, K.B.E., *b.* 1900, *m.*
1964 *Bourne*, Geoffrey Kemp Bourne, G.C.B., K.B.E., C.M.G., *b.* 1902, *m.*
1964 *Bowden* Bertram Vivian Bowden Ph.D., *b,* 1910, *m.*
1972 *Boyd-Carpenter*, John Archibald Boyd-Carpenter, P.C., *b.* 1908, *m.*
1970 *Boyle of Handsworth*, Edward Charles Gurney Boyle, P.C., *b.* 1923.
1973 *Brayley*, John Desmond Brayley, M.C., *b.* 1917.
1975 *Briginshaw*, Richard William Briginshaw.
1965 *Brock*, Russell Claude Brock, F.R.C.S., *b.* 1903, *m.*
1964 *Brockway*, (Archibald) Fenner Brockway, *b.* 1888, *m.*
1966 *Brooke of Cumnor*, Henry Brooke, P.C., C.H., *b.* 1903, *m.*
1964 *Brown*, Wilfred Banks Duncan Brown, P.C., M.B.E., *b.* 1908, *m.*
1975 *Bruce of Donington*, Donald William Trevor Bruce, *b.* 1912, *m.*
1966 *Buckton*, Samuel Storey, *b.* 1896, *w.*
1970 *Burntwood*, Julian Ward Snow, *b.* 1910, *m.*
1965 *Butler of Saffron Walden*, Richard Austen Butler, K.G., P.C., C.H., *b.* 1902, *m.*
1964 *Byers*, (Charles) Frank Byers, P.C., O.B.E., *b.* 1915, *m.*
1965 *Caccia*, Harold Anthony Caccia, G.C.M.G., G.C.V.O., *b.* 1905, *m.*
1975 *Campbell of Croy*, Gordon Thomas Calthrop Campbell, P.C., M.C., *b.* 1921, *m.*
1966 *Campbell of Eskan*, John Middleton Campbell, *b.* 1912, *m.*
1964 *Caradon*, Hugh Mackintosh Foot, P.C., G.C.M.G., K.C.V.O., O.B.E., *b.* 1907, *m.*
1960 *Casey*, Richard Gardiner Casey, K.G., P.C., G.C.M.G., C.H., D.S.O., M.C., *b.* 1890, *m.*
1974 *Castle*, Edward Cyril Castle, *b.* 1907, *m.*
1964 *Chalfont*, Alun Arthur Gwynne Jones, P.C., O.B.E., M.C., *b.* 1919, *m.*
1962 *Champion*, Arthur Joseph Champion, P.C., *b.* 1897, *m.*
1963 *Chelmer*, Eric Cyril Boyd Edwards, M.C., T.D., *b.* 1914, *m.*
1974 *Chelwood*, Tufton Victor Hamilton Beamish, M.C., *b.* 1917, *m.*
1969 *Clark*, Kenneth Mackenzie Clark, C.H., K.C.B., F.B.A., *b.* 1903, *m.*
1965 *Cole*, George James Cole, G.B.E., *b.* 1906, *m.*
1964 *Collison*, Harold Francis Collison, C.B.E., *b.* 1909, *m.*
1966 *Cooper of Stockton Heath*, John Cooper, *b.* 1908.
1959 *Craigton*, Jack Nixon Browne, P.C., C.B.E., *b.* 1904.
1973 *Crowther-Hunt*, Norman Crowther Hunt, Ph.D., *b.* 1920, *m.*
1975 *Cudlipp*, Hugh Cudlipp, O.B.E., *b.* 1913, *m.*
1974 *Darling of Hillsborough*, George Darling, P.C., *b.* 1905, *m.*
1974 *Davies of Penrhys*, Gwilym Elfed Davis, *b.* 1913, *m.*
1970 *Davies of Leek*, Harold Davies, P.C., *b.* 1904, *m.*
1970 *Diamond*, John Diamond, P.C., *b.* 1907, *m.*
1967 *Donaldson of Kingsbridge*, John George Stuart Donaldson, O.B.E., *b.* 1907.
1967 *Douglass of Cleveland*, Harry Douglass, *b.* 1902, *m.*
1974 *Duncan-Sandys*, Ducan Edwin Duncan-Sandys, P.C., C.H., *b.* 1908, *m.*
1972 *Elworthy*, (Samuel) Charles Elworthy, G.C.B., C.B.E., D.S.O., M.V.O., D.F.C., A.F.C., *Marshal of the Royal Air Force, b.* 1911, *m.*
1974 *Elwyn-Jones*, Frederick Elwyn Elwyn-Jones, P.C., *b.* 1909, *m.* (*Lord High Chancellor*).
1967 *Evans of Hungershall*, Benjamin Ifor Evans, D.Lit., *b.* 1899, *m.*
1974 *Feather*, Victor Grayson Hardie Feather, C.B.E., *b.* 1908, *m.*
1958 *Ferrier*, Victor Ferrier Noel-Paton, E.D., *b.* 1900, *m.*

1974 *Fisher of Camden*, Samuel Fisher, *b.* 1905, *m.*
1970 *Fletcher*, Eric George Molyneux Fletcher, P.C., Ll.D., *b.* 1903, *m.*
1967 *Foot*, John Mackintosh Foot, *b.* 1909, *m.*
1962 *Franks*, Oliver Shewell Franks, P.C., G.C.M.G., K.C.B., C.B.E., F.B.A., *b.* 1905, *m.*
1974 *Fraser of Kilmorack*, (Richard) Michael Fraser, C.B.E., *b.* 1915, *m.*
1966 *Fulton*, John Scott Fulton, *b.* 1902, *m.*
1964 *Gardiner*, Gerald Austin Gardiner, P.C., C.H., *b.* 1900, *m.*
1969 *Garner*, (Joseph John) Saville Garner, G.C.M.G., *b.* 1908, *m.*
1967 *Garnsworthy*, Charles James Garnsworthy, O.B.E., *b.* 1907.
1958 *Geddes of Epsom*, Charles John Geddes, C.B.E., *b.* 1897, *m.*
1974 *Geoffrey-Lloyd*, Geoffrey William Geoffrey-Lloyd, P.C., *b.* 1902.
1970 *George-Brown*, George Alfred George-Brown, P.C., *b.* 1914, *m.*
1975 *Gibson*, (Richard) Patrick (Tallentyre) Gibson, *b.* 1916, *m.*
1974 *Glenkinglas*, Michael Antony Cristobal Noble, P.C., *b.* 1913, *m.*
1965 *Goodman*, Arnold Abraham Goodman, C.H., *b.* 1915.
1974 *Gordon-Walker*, Patrick Chrestien Gordon-Walker, P.C., C.H., *b.* 1907, *m.*
1969 *Gore-Booth*, Paul Henry Gore-Booth, G.C.M.G., K.C.V.O., *b.* 1909, *m.*
1974 *Goronwy-Roberts*, Goronwy Owen Goronwy-Roberts, P.C., *b.* 1913, *m.*
1967 *Granville of Eye*, Edgar Louis Granville, *b.* 1899, *m.*
1958 *Granville-West*, Daniel Granville West, *b.* 1904, *m.*
1975 *Greene of Harrow Weald*, Sidney Francis Greene, C.B.E., *b.* 1910, *m.*
1974 *Greenhill of Harrow*, Denis Arthur Greenhill, G.C.M.G., O.B.E., *b.* 1913, *m.*
1970 *Greenwood of Rossendale*, (Arthur William James) Anthony Greenwood, P.C., *b.* 1911, *m.*
1976 *Gregson*, John Gregson
1968 *Grey of Naunton*, Ralph Francis Alnwick Grey, G.C.M.G., G.C.V.O., O.B.E., *b.* 1910, *m.*
1970 *Hailsham of St. Marylebone*, Quintin McGarel Hogg, P.C., C.H., *b.* 1907, *m.*
1972 *Hale*, (Charles) Leslie Hale, *b.* 1902, *m.*
1970 *Hamnett*, Cyril Hamnett, *b.* 1906, *w.*
1975 *Harmar-Nicholls*, Harmar Harmar-Nicholls, *b.* 1912, *m.*
1974 *Harris of Greenwich*, John Henry Harris, *b.* 1930, *m.*
1968 *Hartwell*, (William) Michael Berry, M.B.E., T.D., *b.* 1911, *m.*
1971 *Harvey of Prestbury*, Arthur Vere Harvey, C.B.E., *b.* 1906, *m.*
1974 *Harvington*, Robert Grant Grant-Ferris, P.C., *b.* 1907, *m.*
1968 *Helsby*, Laurence Norman Helsby, G.C.B., K.B.E., *b.* 1908, *m.*
1972 *Hewlett*, (Thomas) Clyde Hewlett, C.B.E., *b.* 1923, *m.*
1967 *Heycock*, Llewellyn Heycock, C.B.E., *b.* 1905, *m.*
1963 *Hill of Luton*, Charles Hill, P.C., M.D., *b.* 1904, *m.*
1965 *Hilton of Upton*, Albert Victor Hilton, *b.* 1908, *m.*
1965 *Hinton of Bankside*, Christopher Hinton, K.B.E., F.R.S., *b.* 1901, *w.*
1967 *Hirshfield*, Desmond Barel Hirshfield, *b.* 1913, *m.*
1965 *Holford*, William Graham Holford, R.A., *b.* 1907, *m.*
1974 *Home of the Hirsel*, Alexander Frederick Douglas-Home, P.C., K.T., *b.* 1903, *m.*
1974 *Houghton of Sowerby*, (Arthur Leslie Noel) Douglas Houghton, P.C., C.H., *b.* 1898, *m.*
1970 *Hoy*, James Hutchison Hoy, P.C., *b.* 1909, *m.*
1961 *Hughes*, William Hughes, P.C., C.B.E., *b.* 1911, *m.*
1966 *Hunt*, (Henry Cecil) John Hunt, C.B.E., D.S.O., *b.* 1910, *m.*
1973 *Hunt of Fawley*, John Henderson Hunt, C.B.E., D.M., *b.* 1905, *m.*
1975 *Jacobson*, Sydney Jacobson, M.C., *b.* 1908, *m.*
1968 *Jacques*, John Henry Jacques, *b.* 1905, *m.*
1959 *James of Rusholme*, Eric John Francis James, *b.* 1909, *m.*
1970 *Janner*, Barnett Janner, *b.* 1892, *m.*
1965 *Kahn*, Richard Ferdinand Kahn, C.B.E., F.B.A., *b.* 1905.
1974 *Kaldor*, Nicholas Kaldor, F.B.A., *b.* 1908, *m.*
1970 *Kearton*, (Christopher) Frank Kearton, O.B.E., F.R.S., *b.* 1911, *m.*
1966 *Kilmany*, William John St. Clair Anstruther-Gray, P.C., M.C., *b.* 1905, *m.*
1965 *Kings Norton*, Harold Roxbee Cox, Ph.D., *b.* 1902, *m.*
1975 *Kirkhill*, John Farquharson Smith, *b.* 1930, *m.*
1974 *Kissin*, Harry Kissin, *b.* 1912, *m.*
1964 *Leatherland*, Charles Edward Leatherland, O.B.E., *b.* 1898.
1974 *Lee of Newton*, Frederick Lee, P.C., *b.* 1906, *m.*
1975 *Lever*, Leslie Maurice Lever, *b.* 1905, *m.*
1964 *Llewelyn-Davies*, Richard Llewelyn-Davies, *b.* 1912, *m.*
1965 *Lloyd of Hampstead*, Dennis Lloyd, Q.C., Ll.D., *b.* 1915, *m.*
1973 *Lloyd of Kilgerran*, Rhys Gerran Lloyd, C.B.E., Q.C., *b.* 1907, *m.*
1974 *Lovell-Davis*, Peter Lovell-Davis, *b.* 1924, *m.*
1975 *Lyons of Brighton*, Braham Jack Dennis Lyons.
1966 *McFadzean*, William Hunter McFadzean, *b.* 1903, *m.*
1974 *Mackie of Benshie*, George Yull Mackie, C.B.E., D.S.O., D.F.C., *b.* 1919, *m.*
1971 *Maclean*, Charles Hector Fitzroy Maclean, P.C., K.T., G.C.V.O., K.B.E., *b.* 1916, *m.* (*Lord Chamberlain*).
1967 *McLeavy*, Frank McLeavy, *b.* 1899, *m.*
1967 *MacLeod of Fuinary*, Very Rev. George Fielden MacLeod, M.C., D.D., *b.* 1895, *m.*
1966 *Maelor*, Thomas William Jones, *b.* 1898, *m.*
1967 *Mais*, Alan Raymond Mais, G.B.E., T.D., E.R.D., *b.* 1911, *m.*
1974 *Marples*, (Alfred) Ernest Marples, P.C., *b.* 1907, *m.*
1971 *Maybray-King*, Horace Maybray King, P.C., Ph.D., *b.* 1901, *m.*
1961 *Molson*, (Arthur) Hugh (Elsdale) Molson, P.C., *b.* 1903, *m.*

1967   *Morris of Grasmere*, Charles Richard Morris, K.C.M.G., *b.* 1898, *m.*
1971   *Moyola*, James Dawson Chichester-Clark, P.C. (N.I.), *b.* 1923, *m.*
1964   *Murray of Newhaven*, Keith Anderson Hope Murray, K.C.B., Ph.D., *b.* 1903.
1966   *Nugent of Guildford*, (George) Richard (Hodges) Nugent, P.C., *b.* 1907, *m.*
1973   *O'Brien of Lothbury*, Leslie Kenneth O'Brien, P.C., G.B.E., *b.* 1908, *m.*
1970   *Olivier*, Laurence Kerr Olivier, *b.* 1907, *m.*
1970   *O'Neill of the Maine*, Terence Marne O'Neill, P.C. (N.I.), *b.* 1914, *m.*
1971   *Orr-Ewing*, (Charles) Ian Orr-Ewing, O.B.E., *b.* 1912, *m.*
1975   *Paget of Northampton*, Reginald Thomas Paget, Q.C., *b.* 1908, *m.*
1974   *Pannell*, (Thomas) Charles Pannell, P.C., *b.* 1902, *m.*
1966   *Pargiter*, George Albert Pargiter, C.B.E., *b.* 1897, *m.*
1961   *Peddie*, James Mortimer Peddie, M.B.E., *b.* 1906, *m.*
1967   *Penney*, William George Penney, O.M., K.B.E., Ph.D., D.SC., F.R.S., *b.* 1909, *m.*
1968   *Pilkington*, William Henry (Harry) Pilkington, *b.* 1905, *m.*
1975   *Pitt of Hampstead*, David Thomas Pitt, *b.* 1913, *m.*
1967   *Platt*, Robert Platt, M.D., *b.* 1900, *m.*
1959   *Plowden*, Edwin Noel Plowden, K.C.B., K.B.E., *b.* 1907, *m.*
1975   *Plurenden*, Rudy Sternberg, *b.* 1917, *m.*
1966   *Popplewell*, Ernest Popplewell, C.B.E., *b.* 1899, *m.*
1973   *Porritt*, Arthur Espie Porritt, G.C.M.G., G.C.V.O., C.B.E., *b.* 1900, *m.*
1975   *Pritchard*, Derek Wilbraham Pritchard, *b.* 1910, *m.*
1974   *Ramsey of Canterbury*, Rt. Rev. Arthur Michael Ramsey, P.C., D.D., *b.* 1904, *m.*
1967   *Redcliffe-Maud*, John Primatt Redcliffe Maud, G.C.B., C.B.E., *b.* 1906, *m.*
1966   *Redmayne*, Martin Redmayne, P.C., D.S.O., T.D., *b.* 1910, *m.*
1970   *Reigate*, John Kenyon Vaughan-Morgan, P.C., *b.* 1905, *m.*
1964   *Rhodes*, Hervey Rhodes, K.G., P.C., D.F.C., *b.* 1895, *m.*
1970   *Rhyl*, (Evelyn) Nigel (Chetwoode) Birch, P.C., O.B.E., *b.* 1906, *m.*
1966   *Ritchie-Calder*, (Peter) Ritchie Calder, C.B.E., *b.* 1906, *m.*
1959   *Robbins*, Lionel Charles Robbins, C.H., C.B., F.B.A., *b.* 1898, *m.*
1961   *Robens of Woldingham*, Alfred Robens, P.C., *b.* 1910, *m.*
1969   *Roberthall*, Robert Lowe Roberthall, K.C.M.G., C.B., *b.* 1901, *m.*
1964   *Royle*, Charles Royle, *b.* 1896, *m.*
1975   *Ryder of Eaton Hastings*, Sydney Thomas (Don) Ryder, *b.* 1916, *m.*
1962   *Sainsbury*, Alan John Sainsbury, *b.* 1902, *m.*
1972   *Samuel of Wych Cross*, Harold Samuel, *b.* 1912, *m.*
1972   *Seebohm*, Frederic Seebohm, T.D., *b.* 1909, *m.*
1964   *Segal*, Samuel Segal, *b.* 1902, *m.*
1958   *Shackleton*, Edward Arthur Alexander Shackleton, K.G., P.C., O.B.E., *b.* 1911, *m.*
1959   *Shawcross*, Hartley William Shawcross, P.C., G.B.E., Q.C., *b.* 1902, *w.*
1970   *Shinwell*, Emanuel Shinwell, P.C., C.H., *b.* 1884, *m.*
1970   *Slater*, Joseph Slater, B.E.M., *b.* 1904, *m.*
1964   *Snow*, Charles Percy Snow, C.B.E., *b.* 1905, *m.*
1965   *Soper*, Rev. Donald Oliver Soper, Ph.D., *b.* 1903, *m.*
1969   *Stokes*, Donald Gresham Stokes, T.D., *b.* 1914, *m.*
1966   *Stow Hill*, Frank Soskice, P.C., Q.C., *b.* 1902, *m.*
1971   *Tanlaw*, Simon Brooke Mackay, *b.* 1934, *m.*
1958   *Taylor*, Stephen James Lake Taylor, M.D., *b.* 1910, *m.*
1968   *Taylor of Gryfe*, Thomas Johnston Taylor, *b.* 1912, *m.*
1966   *Taylor of Mansfield*, Harry Bernard Taylor, *b.* 1895, *m.*
1971   *Thomas*, (William) Miles (Webster) Thomas, D.F.C., *b.* 1897, *m.*
1967   *Thorneycroft*, (George Edward) Peter Thorneycroft, P.C., *b.* 1909, *m.*
1962   *Todd*, Alexander Robertus Todd, D.SC., D.PHIL., F.R.S., *b.* 1907, *m.*
1974   *Tranmire*, Robert Hugh Turton, P.C., K.B.E., M.C., *b.* 1903, *m.*
1974   *Trend*, Burke St. John Trend, P.C., G.C.B., C.V.O., *b.* 1914, *m.*
1968   *Trevelyan*, Humphrey Trevelyan, K.G., G.C.M.G., C.I.E., O.B.E., *b.* 1905, *m.*
1964   *Wade*, Donald William Wade, *b.* 1904, *m.*
1974   *Wallace of Coslany*, George Douglas Wallace, *b.* 1906, *m.*
1961   *Walston*, Henry David Leonard George Walston, *b.* 1912, *m.*
1972   *Watkins*, Tudor Elwyn Watkins, *b.* 1903, *m.*
1965   *Wells-Pestell*, Reginald Alfred Wells-Pestell, *b.* 1910, *m.*
1970   *Wheatley*, John Wheatley, P.C., *b.* 1908, *m.*
1971   *Widgery*, John Passmore Widgery, P.C., O.B.E., T.D., *b.* 1911, *m.* (*Lord Chief Justice of England*).
1967   *Wigg*, George Edward Cecil Wigg, P.C., *b.* 1900, *m.*
1974   *Wigoder*, Basil Thomas Wigoder, Q.C., *b.* 1921, *m.*
1962   *Williamson*, Thomas Williamson, C.B.E., *b.* 1897, *m.*
1964   *Willis*, Edward Henry Willis, *b.* 1918, *m.*
1969   *Wilson of Langside*, Henry Stephen Wilson, P.C., Q.C., *b.* 1916, *m.*
1975   *Wilson of Radcliffe*, Alfred Wilson, *b.* 1909, *m.*
1965   *Winterbottom*, Ian Winterbottom, *b.* 1913, *m.*
1974   *Wolfenden*, John Frederick Wolfenden, C.B.E., *b.* 1906, *m.*
1967   *Woolley*, Harold Woolley, C.B.E., *b.* 1905, *w.*
1964   *Wynne-Jones*, William Francis Kenrick Wynne-Jones, *b.* 1903, *w.*
1971   *Zuckerman*, Solly Zuckerman, O.M., K.C.B., F.R.S., M.D., D.SC., *b.* 1904, *m.*

BARONESSES

1970   *Bacon*, Alice Martha Bacon, P.C., C.B.E., *b.* 1911.
1967   *Birk*, Alma Birk, *b.* 1921, *m.*
1964   *Brooke of Ystradfellte*, Barbara Muriel Brooke, D.B.E., *b.* 1908, *m.*
1962   *Burton of Coventry*, Elaine Frances Burton, *b.* 1904.
1974   *Delacourt-Smith of Alteryn*, Margaret Rosalind Delacourt-Smith, *w.*
1972   *Elles*, Diana Elles, *m.*
1958   *Elliot of Harwood*, Katharine Elliot, D.B.E., *b.* 1903, *w.*
1964   *Emmet of Amberley*, Evelyn Violet Elizabeth Emmet, *b.* 1899, *w.*
1974   *Falkender*, Marcia Matilda Falkender, C.B.E., *b.* 1932.
1974   *Fisher of Rednal*, Doris Mary Gertrude Fisher, *b.* 1919, *m.*
1964   *Gaitskell*, Anna Dora Gaitskell, *w.*
1974   *Hornsby-Smith*, (Margaret) Patricia Hornsby-Smith, P.C., D.B.E., *b.* 1914.
1965   *Hylton-Foster*, Audrey Pellew Hylton-Foster, *b.* 1908, *w.*
1970   *Lee of Asheridge*, Janet Bevan, P.C., *b.* 1904, *w.*
1967   *Llewelyn-Davies of Hastoe*, Annie Patricia Llewelyn-Davies, P.C., *b.* 1915, *m.*
1971   *Macleod of Borve*, Evelyn Hester Macleod, *b.* 1915, *w.*
1970   *Masham of Ilton*, Susan Lilian Primrose Cunliffe-Lister, *b.* 1935, *m.* (Countess of Swinton).
1964   *Northchurch*, Frances Joan Davidson, D.B.E., (Dowager Viscountess Davidson), *b.* 1894, *w.*
1964   *Phillips*, Norah Mary Phillips, *b.* 1910, *w.*
1974   *Pike*, (Irene) Mervyn (Parnicott) Pike, *b.* 1918.
1974   *Robson of Kiddington*, Inga-Stina Robson, *b.* 1919, *m.*
1971   *Seear*, (Beatrice) Nancy Seear, *b.* 1913.
1967   *Serota*, Beatrice Serota, *b.* 1919, *m.*
1966   *Sharp*, Evelyn Adelaide Sharp, G.B.E., *b.* 1903.
1973   *Sharples*, Pamela Sharples, *w.*
1965   *Spencer-Churchill*, Clementine Ogilvy Spencer Churchill, G.B.E., *b.* 1885, *w.*
1974   *Stedman*, Phyllis Stedman, O.B.E., *b.* 1916, *m.*
1975   *Stewart of Alvechurch*, Mary Elizabeth Henderson Stewart, *m.*
1961   *Summerskill*, Edith Summerskill, P.C., C.H., *b.* 1901, *m.*
1970   *Tweedsmuir of Belhelvie*, Priscilla Jean Fortescue Buchan, P.C., *b.* 1915, *m.*
1975   *Vickers*, Joan Helen Vickers, D.B.E., *b.* 1907.
1975   *Ward of North Tyneside*, Irene Mary Bewick Ward, C.H., D.B.E., *b.* 1895.
1970   *White*, Eirene Lloyd White, *b.* 1909, *w.*
1958   *Wootton of Abinger*, Barbara Frances Wright, *b.* 1897, *w.*
1971   *Young*, Janet Mary Young, *b.* 1926, *m.*

Surnames of Peers and Peeresses differing from their Titles

Abney Hastings — Loudoun
Acheson—Gosford
Adderley—Norton
Addington—Sidmouth
Agar—Normanton
Akers Douglas—Chilston
Alexander—Alexander of Potterhill★
Alexander—Alexander of Tunis
Alexander—Caledon
Allan—Allan of Kilmahew★
Allen—Allen of Fallowfield★
Allanson Winn—Headley
Allsopp—Hindlip
Aman—Marley
Anderson—Waverley
Annesley—Valentia
Anson—Lichfield
Anstruther-Gray—Kilmany★
Armstrong—Armstrong of Sanderstead★
Armstrong Jones—Snowdon
Arthur—Glenarthur
Ashley Cooper—Shaftesbury
Ashton—Ashton of Hyde
Asquith—Oxford & A.
Assheton—Clitheroe
Astley—Hastings

Astor—Astor of Hever
Bailey—Glanusk
Baillie—Burton
Baillie Hamilton—Haddington
Baird—Kintore
Baldwin — Baldwin of Bewdley
Balfour—Kinross
Balfour—Riverdale
Balfour — Balfour of Inchrye
Bampfylde—Poltimore
Banbury — Banbury of Southam
Baring—Ashburton
Baring—Cromer
Baring—Howick of Glendale
Baring—Northbrook
Baring—Revelstoke
Barnes—Gorell
Barnewall—Trimlestown
Bathurst—Bledisloe
Beamish—Chelwood★
Beauclerk—St. Albans
Beaumont—Allendale
Beaumont—Beaumont of Whitley★
Beavan—Ardwick★
Beckett—Grimthorpe
Bennet—Tankerville
Beresford—Decies
Beresford—Waterford
Bernard—Bandon

Berry—Camrose
Berry—Hartwell★
Berry—Kemsley
Bertie—Lindsey
Best—Wynford
Bethell—Westbury
Bevan—Lee of Asheridge★
Bewicke Copley—Cromwell
Bigham—Mersey
Bigham—Nairne
Bingham—Clanmorris
Bingham—Lucan
Birch—Rhyl★
Blades—Ebbisham
Bligh—Darnley
Bootle Wilbraham — Skelmersdale
Boscawen—Falmouth
Bourke—Mayo
Bowden—Aylestone★
Bowes Lyon—Strathmore
Bowyer—Denham
Boyd—Kilmarnock
Boyle — Boyle of Handsworth★
Boyle—Cork and Orrery
Boyle—Glasgow
Boyle—Shannon
Brabazon—Meath
Brand—Hampden
Brassey — Brassey of Apethorpe
Brett—Esher
Bridgeman—Bradford

Brodrick—Midleton
Brooke—Alanbrooke
Brooke—Brooke of Cumnor★
Brooke—Brooke of Ystradfellte★
Brooke—Brookeborough
Brooks—Crawshaw
Brougham — Brougham and Vaux
Broughton—Fairhaven
Browne—Craigton★
Browne—Kilmaine
Browne — Oranmore and Browne
Browne—Sligo
Brownlow—Lurgan
Bruce—Aberdare
Bruce—Balfour of Burleigh
Bruce—Bruce of Donington★
Bruce — Elgin and Kincardine
Brudenell Bruce—Ailesbury
Buchan—Tweedsmuir
Buchan—Tweedsmuir of Belhelvie★
Buchanan-Smith — Balerno★
Buckley—Wrenbury
Burton—Burton of Coventry★
Butler—Butler of Saffron Walden★

★ Life Peer created under Life Peerages Act, 1958.

★ **Life Peer created under Life Peerages Act, 1958.**

Harvey—*Harvey of Prestbury*★
Harvey—*Harvey of Tasburgh*
Hastings—*Huntingdon*
Hay—*Erroll*
Hay—*Kinnoull*
Hay—*Tweeddale*
Heathcote Drummond Willoughby—*Ancaster*
Hely Hutchinson—*Donoughmore*
Henderson—*Faringdon*
Hennessy—*Windlesham*
Henniker Major—*Henniker*
Hepburne Scott — *Polwarth*
Herbert—*Carnarvon*
Herbert—*Hemingford*
Herbert—*Pembroke*
Herbert—*Powis*
Hermon Hodge—*Wyfold*
Hicks Beach—*St. Aldwyn*
Hervey—*Bristol*
Hewitt—*Lifford*
Hill—*Downshire*
Hill—*Hill of Luton*★
Hill—*Sandys*
Hill Trevor—*Trevor*
Hilton—*Hilton of Upton*★
Hinton—*Hinton of Bankside*★
Hobart Hampden—*Buckinghamshire*
Hogg—*Hailsham of St. Marylebone*★
Holland Hibbert—*Knutsford*
Holms à Court—*Heytesbury*
Hood—*Bridport*
Hope—*Glendevon*
Hope—*Linlithgow*
Hope—*Rankeillour*
Hope Morley—*Hollenden*
Hopkinson—*Colyton*
Hopwood — *Southborough*
Hore Ruthven—*Gowrie*
Houghton—*Houghton of Sowerby*★
Hovell Thurlow Cumming Bruce—*Thurlow*
Howard—*Carlisle*
Howard—*Effingham*
Howard—*Howard of Penrith*
Howard—*Strathcona*
Howard—*Suffolk and Berkshire*
Hoyer Millar—*Inchyra*
Hubbard—*Addington*
Huggins—*Malvern*
Hughes Young — *St. Helens*
Hunt—*Hunt of Fawley*★
Ingrams—*Darcy de Knayth*
Innes Ker—*Roxburghe*
Inskip—*Caldecote*
Irby—*Boston*
Isaacs—*Reading*
Jackson—*Allerton*
James—*James of Rusholme*★

James—*Northbourne*
Jebb—*Gladwyn*
Jervis—*St. Vincent*
Jocelyn—*Roden*
Jolliffe—*Hylton*
Jones—*Maelor*★
Joynson Hicks—*Brentford*
Kay Shuttleworth — *Shuttleworth*
Kearley—*Devonport*
Kemp—*Rochdale*
Kennedy—*Ailsa*
Kenworthy—*Strabolgi*
Keppel—*Albemarle*
Kerr—*Lothian*
Kerr—*Teviot*
King—*Lovelace*
King—*Maybray King*★
King Tenison—*Kingston*
Kitchener — *Kitchener of Khartoum*
Kitson—*Airedale*
Knatchbull—*Brabourne*
Knox—*Ranfurly*
Lamb—*Rochester*
Lambart—*Cavan*
Lampson—*Killearn*
Larnach Nevill—*Abergavenny*
Lascelles—*Harewood*
Law—*Coleraine*
Law—*Ellenborough*
Lawrence—*Trevethin and Oaksey*
Lawson—*Burnham*
Lawson Johnston—*Luke*
Lee—*Lee of Asheridge*★
Lee—*Lee of Newton*★
Le Poer Trench—*Clancarty*
Legge—*Dartmouth*
Legh—*Newton*
Leith—*Burgh*
Lennox Boyd—*Boyd of Merton*
Leslie—*Rothes*
Leslie Melville—*Leven*
Lever—*Leverhulme*
Leveson Gower—*Granville*
Lewis—*Brecon*
Lewis—*Essendon*
Lewis—*Merthyr*
Liddell—*Ravensworth*
Lindesay Bethune — *Lindsay*
Lindsay—*Balniel*★
Lindsay—*Crawford*
Lindsay — *Lindsay of Birker*
Littleton—*Hatherton*
Llewelyn-Davies—*Llewelyn-Davies of Hastoe*★
Lloyd—*Lloyd of Hampstead*★
Lloyd—*Lloyd of Kilgerran*★
Lloyd George—*Lloyd George of Dwyfor*
Lloyd George—*Tenby*
Lloyd Mostyn—*Mostyn*
Loder—*Wakehurst*
Lopes—*Roborough*

Low—*Aldington*
Lowry Corry—*Belmore*
Lowther—*Lonsdale*
Lowther—*Ullswater*
Lubbock—*Avebury*
Lucas—*Lucas of Chilworth*
Lumley—*Scarbrough*
Lumley Savile—*Savile*
Lygon—*Beauchamp*
Lyle—*Lyle of Westbourne*
Lyon Dalberg Acton—*Acton*
Lyons—*Lyons of Brighton*★
Lysaght—*Lisle*
Lyttelton—*Chandos*
Lyttelton — *Cobham (Viscountcy)*
McClintock Bunbury—*Rathdonnell*
Macdonald — *Macdonald of Gwaenysgor*
McDonnell—*Antrim*
Mackay—*Inchcape*
Mackay—*Reay*
Mackay—*Tanlaw*★
Mackenzie—*Amulree*
Mackie—*Mackie of Benshie*★
Mackintosh—*Mackintosh of Halifax*
McLaren—*Aberconway*
Macleod — *Macleod of Borve*★
MacLeod—*MacLeod of Fuinary*★
Maclay—*Muirshiel*
Macpherson—*Drumalbyn*
Macpherson — *Macpherson of Drumochter*
Macpherson—*Strathcarron*
Maffey—*Rugby*
Maitland—*Lauderdale*
Makins—*Sherfield*
Manners—*Rutland*
Manningham Buller—*Dilhorne*
Mansfield—*Sandhurst*
Marks—*Marks of Broughton*
Marquis—*Woolton*
Marsham—*Romney*
Martyn Hemphill — *Hemphill*
Mason—*Blackford*
Maud—*Redcliffe-Maud*★
Maude—*Hawarden*
Maxwell—*De Ros*
Maxwell—*Farnham*
Meade—*Clanwilliam*
Milles Lade—*Sondes*
Mills—*Hillingdon*
Milner—*Milner of Leeds*
Mitchell Thomson—*Selsdon*
Monckton—*Galway*
Monckton—*Monckton of Brenchley*
Monckton—*Ruthven of Freeland*
Mond—*Melchett*
Money-Coutts—*Latymer*
Montagu—*Manchester*
Montagu—*Swaythling*
Montagu Douglas Scott—*Buccleuch*

Montagu Stuart Wortley Mackenzie — *Wharncliffe*
Montague—*Amwell*
Montgomerie—*Eglinton*
Montgomery — *Montgomery of Alamein*
Moore—*Drogheda*
Moore Brabazon—*Brabazon of Tara*
Moreton—*Ducie*
Morris—*Killanin*
Morris — *Morris of Borth-y-Gest*
Morris—*Morris of Grasmere*★
Morris—*Morris of Kenwood*
Morrison—*Dunrossil*
Morrison—*Margadale*
Mosley—*Ravensdale*
Mountbatten—*Edinburgh*
Mountbatten — *Milford Haven*
Mountbatten — *Mountbatten of Burma*
Muff—*Calverley*
Mulholland—*Dunleath*
Murray—*Atholl*
Murray—*Dunmore*
Murray—*Mansfield and Mansfield*
Murray—*Murray of Newhaven*★
Nall Cain—*Brocket*
Napier — *Napier and Ettrick*
Napier — *Napier of Magdala*
Needham—*Kilmorey*
Nelson—*Nelson of Stafford*
Neville—*Braybrooke*
Nicolson—*Carnock*
Nivison—*Glendyne*
Noble—*Glenkinglas*★
Noel—*Gainsborough*
Noel Paton—*Ferrier*★
North—*Guilford*
Northcote—*Iddesleigh*
Norton—*Grantley*
Norton—*Rathcreedan*
Nugent — *Nugent of Guildford*★
Nugent—*Westmeath*
O'Brien—*Inchiquin*
O'Brien — *O'Brien of Lothbury*★
Ogilvy—*Airlie*
O'Neill—*O'Neill of the Maine*★
O'Neill—*Rathcavan*
Orde Powlett—*Bolton*
Ormsby Gore—*Harlech*
Paget—*Anglesey*
Paget—*Paget of Northampton*★
Pakenham—*Longford*
Pakington—*Hampton*
Palmer — *Lucas of Crudwell*
Palmer—*Rusholme*
Palmer—*Selborne*
Parker—*Macclesfield*
Parker—*Morley*

Parnell—*Congleton*
Parsons—*Rosse*
Paulet—*Winchester*
Peake—*Ingleby*
Pearson—*Cowdray*
Pease—*Daryngton*
Pease—*Gainford*
Pease—*Wardington*
Pelham—*Chichester*
Pelham—*Yarborough*
Pelham Clinton Hope— *Newcastle*
Pellew—*Exmouth*
Penny—*Marchwood*
Pepys—*Cottenham*
Perceval—*Egmont*
Percy—*Northumberland*
Pery—*Limerick*
Petty Fitzmaurice—*Lansdowne*
Philipps—*Milford*
Philipps—*St. Davids*
Phipps—*Normanby*
Pitt—*Pitt of Hampstead*★
Pleydell Bouverie—*Radnor*
Plumptre—*Fitzwalter*
Plunkett—*Dunsany*
Plunkett—*Fingall*
Plunkett—*Louth*
Pollock—*Hanworth*
Pomeroy—*Harberton*
Ponsonby—*Bessborough*
Ponsonby—*De Mauley*
Ponsonby—*P. of Shulbrede*
Ponsonby—*Sysonby*
Portal—*Portal of Hungerford*
Powys—*Lilford*
Pratt—*Camden*
Preston—*Gormanston*
Primrose—*Rosebery*
Prittie—*Dunalley*
Ramacca—*Newburgh*
Ramsay—*Dalhousie*
Ramsay—*Ramsey of Canterbury*★
Ramsbotham—*Soulbury*
Rees Williams—*Ogmore*
Rhys—*Dynevor*
Richards—*Milverton*
Ritchie—*Ritchie of Dundee* [*ingham*★
Robens—*Robens of Woldingham*★
Roberts—*Clwyd*
Robertson—*Robertson of Oakridge*
Robinson—*Martonmere*
Robson—*Robson of Kiddington*★
Roche—*Fermoy*
Rodd—*Rennell*
Roper Curzon—*Teynham*
Rous—*Stradbroke*
Rowley Conway—*Langford*

Runciman — *Runciman of Doxford*
Russell—*Bedford*
Russell—*De Clifford*
Russell—*R. of Liverpool*
Ryder—*Harrowby*
Ryder—*Ryder of Eaton Hastings*★
Sackville—*De La Warr*
Sackville West—*Sackville*
St. Aubyn—*St. Levan*
St. Clair—*Sinclair*
St. Clair Erskine—*Rosslyn*
St. John—*St. J. of Blesto*
St. John—*Bolingbroke and St. John*
St. Leger—*Doneraile*
Samuel—*Bearsted*
Samuel—*Samuel of Wych Cross*★
Sandilands—*Torphichen*
Saumarez—*De Saumarez*
Savile—*Mexborough*
Scarlett—*Abinger*
Sclater Booth—*Basing*
Scott—*Eldon* [*Walden*
Scott Ellis—*Howard de Scrymgeour Wedderburn—*Dundee*
Seager—*Leighton of St. Mellons*
Seely—*Mottistone*
Seymour—*Hertford*
Seymour—*Somerset*
Shaw—*Craigmyle*
Shaw—*Kilbrandon*
Shirley—*Ferrers*
Shore—*Teignmouth*
Siddeley—*Kenilworth*
Sidney—*De L'Isle*
Silverstone—*Ashdown*★
Simon—*Simon of Glaisdale*
Simon—*Simon of Wythenshawe*
Sinclair—*Caithness*
Sinclair—*Pentland*
Sinclair—*Sinclair of Cleeve*
Sinclair—*Thurso*
Skeffington—*Massereene*
Smith—*Bicester*
Smith—*Birkenhead*
Smith—*Colwyn*
Smith—*Hambleden*
Smith—*Kirkhill*★
Snow—*Burntwood*★
Somerset—*Beaufort*
Somerset—*Raglan*
Soskice—*Stow Hill*★
Souter—*Audley*
Spencer—*Churchill*
Spencer Churchill — *Marlborough*
Spring Rice—*Monteagle of Brandon*

Stanhope—*Harrington*
Stanley—*Derby*
Stanley—*Sheffield*
Stapleton Cotton—*Combermere*
Stern—*Michelham*
Sternberg—*Plurenden*
Stewart—*Galloway*
Stewart—*Stewart of Alvechurch*★
Stonor—*Camoys*
Stopford—*Courtown*
Storey—*Buckton*★
Stourton—*Mowbray*
Strachey—*O'Hagan*
Strutt—*Belper*
Strutt—*Rayleigh*
Stuart—*Castle Stewart*
Stuart—*Moray*
Stuart—*Stuart of Findhorn*
Studley Herbert — *Seafield*
Suenson Taylor—*Grantchester*
Sugden—*St. Leonards*
Talbot—*T. of Malahide*
Taylor—*Taylor of Gryfe*★
Taylor—*Taylor of Mansfield*
Taylour—*Headfort*
Temple Gore Langton— *Temple of Stowe*
Tennant—*Glenconner*
Thellusson—*Rendlesham*
Thesiger—*Chelmsford*
Thomson—*Thomson of Fleet*
Thynne—*Bath*
Tottenham—*Ely*
Trefusis—*Clinton*
Trench—*Ashtown*
Tufton—*Hothfield*
Turner—*Netherthorpe*
Turnour—*Winterton*
Turton—*Tranmire*★
Twisleton-Wykeham-Fiennes—*Saye and Sele*
Tyrell Kenyon—*Kenyon*
Upton—*Templetown*
Vanden Bempde Johnstone—*Derwent*
Vane—*Barnard*
Vane Tempest Stewart— *Londonderry*
Vanneck—*Huntingfield*
Vaughan—*Lisburne*
Vaughan Morgan — *Reigate*★
Vavasseur Fisher—*Fisher*
Venables Vernon—*Vernon*
Vereker—*Gort*
Verney—*Willoughby de Broke*
Verney Cave—*Braye*
Vernon—*Lyveden*

Vesey—*De Vesci*
Villiers—*Clarendon*
Vincent—*Wharton*
Vivian—*Swansea*
Wakefield—*Wakefield of Kendal*
Wallace—*Dudley (Barony)*
Wallace—*Wallace of Coslany*★
Wallop—*Portsmouth*
Walsh—*Ormathwaite*
Ward—*Bangor*
Ward—*Dudley (Earldom)*
Ward—*Ward of North Tyneside*★
Ward—*Ward of Witley*
Warrender—*Bruntisfield*
Watson—*Manton*
Watson Armstrong — *Armstrong*
Weir—*Inverforth*
Weld Forester—*Forester*
Wellesley—*Cowley*
Wellesley—*Wellington*
Wentworth Fitzwilliam —*Fitzwilliam*
West—*Granville-West*★
Westenra—*Rossmore*
White—*Annaly*
Whiteley—*Marchamley*
Whitfield—*Kenswood*
Willey—*Barnby*
Williams—*Berners*
Williams—★*Falkender*
Williamson—*Forres*
Willoughby—*Middleton*
Wills—*Dulverton*
Wilson—*Moran*
Wilson—*Nunburnholme*
Wilson—*Wilson of Langside*★
Wilson—*Wilson of Radcliffe*★
Windsor—*Cornwall*
Windsor—*Gloucester*
Windsor—*Kent*
Windsor Clive — *Plymouth*
Wingfield—*Powerscourt*
Winn—*St. Oswald*
Winn—*Headley*
Wodehouse—*Kimberley*
Wood—*Halifax*
Woodhouse—*Terrington*
Wright—*Wootton of Abinger*★
Wyndham—*Leconfield*
Wyndham Quin—*Dunraven*
Wynn—*Newborough*
Yarde Buller—*Churston*
Yerburgh—*Alvingham*
Yorke—*Hardwicke*
Young—*Kennet*
Younger—*Y. of Leckie*

★ Life Peer created under Life Peerages Act, 1958.

Courtesy Titles (*in actual existence in* 1976)

Holders of Courtesy Titles are addressed in the same manner as holders of substantive titles
From this list it will be seen that, for example, the " Marques of Blandford " is heir to the Dukedom of Marlborough, and " Viscount Althorp " to the Earldom of Spencer. Titles of second heirs are also given, and the Courtesy Title of the father of a second heir is indicated by ★; e.g., Earl of Burlington, eldest son of ★Marquess of Hartington.

In addition, the heir, and sometimes the second heir, to some Scottish peerages is usually styled " The Master of——"; *e.g., " The Master of Falkland " heir to Viscount Falkland; and " The Master of Lindsay " is eldest son of* ★Lord Balniel, *heir to the Earl of Crawford and Balcarres. Users of this style are not included here.*

Marquesses.

Blandford—*Marlborough*
Douro—*Wellington*
★Graham—*Montrose*
Granby—*Rutland*
★Hamilton—*Abercorn*
★Hartington—*Devonshire*
★Kildare—*Leinster*
Lorne—*Argyll*
★Tavistock—*Bedford*

Earls.

Aboyne—*Huntly*
Altamont—*Sligo*
Ancram—*Lothian*
Arundel and Surrey—*Norfolk*
Bective—*Headfort*
Belfast—*Donegall*
★Brecknock—*Camden*
★Burford—*St. Albans*
Burlington—★*Hartington*
Cardigan—*Ailesbury*
Cassillis—*Ailsa*
°Compton—*Northampton*
★Dalkeith—*Buccleuch*
Euston—*Grafton*
Gifford—*Tweeddale*
°Grosvenor—*Westminster*
°Hopetoun—*Linlithgow*
°Jermyn—*Bristol*
Macduff—*Fife*
★March and Kinrara—*Richmond*
★Mount Charles—*Conyngham*
Mulgrave—*Normanby*
Offaly—★*Kildare*
°Percy—*Northumberland*
Rocksavage — *Cholmondeley*
★Ronaldshay—*Zetland*
St. Andrews—*Kent*
★Shelburne—*Lansdowne*
Tyrone—*Waterford*
Ulster—*Gloucester*
Uxbridge—*Anglesey*
Wiltshire—*Winchester*
Yarmouth—*Hertford*

Viscounts.

Aithrie—★*Hopetoun*
Alexander—*Caledon*
Althorp—*Spencer*

Andover—*Suffolk and Berkshire*
Asquith—*Oxford & Asquith*
Bayham—★*Brecknock*
Boringdon—*Morley*
Borodale—*Beatty*
Boyle—*Shannon*
Brocas—*Jellicoe*
Bury—*Albemarle*
Calne and Calstone— ★*Shelburne*
Campden—*Gainsborough*
Carlow—*Portarlington*
Castlereagh—*Londonderry*
Chelsea—*Cadogan*
Chewton—*Waldegrave*
Cole—*Enniskillen*
Corvedale—*Baldwin of Bewdley*
Cranborne—*Salisbury*
Cranley—*Onslow*
Crichton—*Erne*
Darymple—*Stair*
Dawick—*Haig*
Deerhurst—*Coventry*
Drumlanrig — *Queensberry*
Dunluce—*Antrim*
Dupplin—*Kinnoull*
Ebrington—*Fortescue*
Eden—*Avon*
Ednam—*Dudley*
Elveden—*Iveagh*
Emlyn—*Cawdor*
Encombe—*Eldon*
Ennismore—*Listowel*
Enfield—*Strafford*
Erleigh—*Reading*
Errington—*Cromer*
Feilding—*Denbigh*
FitzHarris—*Malmesbury*
Folkestone—*Radnor*
Garmoyle—*Cairns*
Garnock—*Lindsay*
Glandine—*Norbury*
Glenapp—*Inchcape*
Glentworth—*Limerick*
Glerawly—*Annesley*
Gwynnedd—*Lloyd George of Dwyfor*
Hawkesbury—*Liverpool*
Ikerrin—*Carrick*

Ingestre—*Shrewsbury*
Jocelyn—*Roden*
Kelburn—*Glasgow*
Kingsborough—*Kingston*
Knebworth—*Lytton*
Lascelles—*Harewood*
Lewisham—*Dartmouth*
Linley—*Snowdon*
Loftus—*Ely*
Lowther—*Lonsdale*
Lumley—*Scarbrough*
Lymington—*Portsmouth*
Maidstone — *Winchilsea and Nottingham*
Maitland—*Lauderdale*
Mandeville—*Manchester*
Melgund—*Minto*
Moore—*Drogheda*
Morepeth—*Carlisle*
Newport—*Bradford*
Parker—*Macclesfield*
Perceval—*Egmont*
Petersham—*Harrington*
Pollington—*Mexborough*
Prestwood—*Attlee*
Quenington—*St. Aldwyn*
Raynham—*Townshend*
Reidhaven—*Seafield*
Ruthven of Canberra—*Gowrie*
St. Cyres—*Iddesleigh*
Sandon—*Harrowby*
Slane—★*Mount Charles*
Stormont—*Mansfield*
Strabane—★*Hamilton*
Strathallan—*Perth*
Stuart—*Castle Stewart*
Sudley—*Arran*
Suirdale—*Donoughmore*
Tamworth—*Ferrers*
Tarbat—*Cromartie*
Tiverton—*Halsbury*
Vaughan—*Lisburne*
Villiers—*Jersey*
Weymouth—*Bath*
Windsor—*Plymouth*
Wolmer—*Selborne*

Barons (Lord—)

Apsley—*Bathurst*
Ardee—*Meath*
Balgonie—*Leven & Melville*

Bingham—*Lucan*
Binning —*Haddington*
Brooke—*Warwick*
Bruce—*Elgin*
Buckhurst—*De La Warr*
Burghersh—*Westmorland*
Cardross—*Buchan*
Cochrane—*Dundonald*
Courtenay—*Devon*
Dalmeny—*Rosebery*
Delvin—*Westmeath*
Doune—*Moray*
Dundas—★*Ronaldshay*
Eliot—*St. Germans*
Erskine—*Mar & Kellie*
Fintrie—★*Graham*
Garlies—*Galloway*
Glamis—*Strathmore*
Greenock—*Cathcart*
Guernsey—*Aylesford*
Hay—*Erroll*
Howland—★*Tavistock*
Inverurie—*Kintore*
Irwin—*Halifax*
Leslie—*Rothes*
Leveson—*Granville*
Loughborough—*Rosslyn*
Mauchline—*Loudoun*
Medway—*Cranbrook*
Montgomerie—*Eglinton and Winton*
Moreton—*Ducie*
Naas—*Mayo* [March
Neidpath—*Wemyss & Norreys—*Lindley & Abingdon*
North—*Guilford*
Ogilvy—*Airlie*
Ossulston—*Tankerville*
Oxmantown—*Rosse*
Porchester—*Carnarvon*
Ramsay—*Dalhousie*
Rosehill—*Northesk*
Scrymgeour—*Dundee*
Settrington—★*March and Kinrara*
Seymour—*Somerset*
Silchester—*Longford*
Strathnaver—*Sutherland*
Vere of Hanworth— ★*Burford*
Wilmington—★*Compton*
Wodehouse—*Kimberley*
Worsley—*Yarborough*

THE PRIVY COUNCIL

The Privy Council consists of certain eminent persons whose names are given below. Members of the Cabinet must be Privy Counsellors, and they principally form the active Privy Council. The Council is summoned as such to act " with others " upon the demise of the Crown, and many matters are referred by the Sovereign to Committees of the Council, some of which are standing Committees, and others constituted to deal with particular cases, *e.g.*, the Judicial Committee.

Noble, *Cdr.* Sir Allan.....	1956	Rodgers, William Thomas	1975	Summerskill, Baroness....	1949
North, Sir Alfred.........	1966	Roskill, Sir Eustace.......	1971	Thatcher, Mrs. Margaret..	1970
Northumberland, Duke of	1973	Ross, William...........	1964	Thomas, George.........	1968
Nugent of Guildford, Lord.	1962	Rowling, Wallace.......	1974	Thomas, Peter..........	1964
Nutting, Sir Anthony, Bt.	1954	Russell, Sir Charles.......	1962	Thomson, George Morgan	1966
O'Brien of Lothbury, Lord	1970	Sachs, Sir Eric..........	1966	Thorneycroft, Lord......	1951
Ogmore, Lord............	1951	St. Aldwyn, Earl........	1959	Thorpe, Jeremy.........	1967
O'Malley, Brian.........	1975	Salmon, Lord............	1964	Tranmire, Lord..........	1955
Orme, Stanley.........	1974	Scarman, Sir Leslie.......	1973	Tredgold, Sir Robert.....	1957
Ormrod, Sir Roger......	1974	Selkirk, Earl of..........	1955	Trend, Lord.............	1972
Orr, Sir Alan............	1971	Sellers, Sir Frederic.......	1957	Tryon, Lord.............	1971
Page, Graham...........	1972	Shackleton, Lord........	1966	Tucker, Lord............	1945
Pannell, Lord............	1964	Shakespeare, Sir Geoffrey,		Turner, Sir Alexander....	1968
Pearce, Lord.............	1957	Bt...................	1945	Tweedsmuir of Belhelvie,	
Pearson, Lord...........	1961	Shaw, Sir Sebag	1975	Baroness..............	1974
Peart, Thomas Frederick.	1964	Shawcross, Lord.........	1946	Varley, Eric.............	1974
Pennycuick, Sir John.....	1974	Shearer, Hugh...........	1969	Walker, Peter...........	1970
Perth, Earl of...........	1957	Shepherd, Lord..........	1965	Wand, *Rt. Rev.* John	
Peyton, John...........	1970	Shinwell, Lord...........	1945	William Charles.......	1945
Pickthorn, Sir Kenneth, Bt.	1964	Shore, Peter.............	1967	Ward of Witley, Viscount	1957
Poole, Lord.............	1963	Short, Edward Watson		Watkinson, Viscount.....	1955
Powell, Enoch...........	1960	(*Lord President*)........	1964	Watt, David Gibson-.....	1974
Prentice, Reginald Ernest .	1966	Silkin, John.............	1966	Watt, Hugh.............	1974
Prior James.............	1970	Silkin, Samuel..........	1974	Welensky, Sir Roy.......	1960
Pym, Francis............	1970	Simon of Glaisdale, Lord .	1961	Wheatley, Lord..........	1947
Radcliffe, Viscount.......	1949	Slesser, Sir Henry.......	1929	Whitelaw, William.......	1967
Ramgoolam, Sir Seewoosa-		Smith, Sir Derek Walker-,		Widgery, Lord...........	1968
gur...................	1971	Bt...................	1957	Wigg, Lord.............	1964
Ramsden, James.........	1963	Smith, Sir Reginald Dor-		Wilberforce, Lord........	1964
Ramsey of Canterbury,		man-...................	1939	Wild, Sir Richard........	1966
Rt. Rev. Lord.........	1956	Smyth, Sir John, Bt.......	1962	Willey, Frederick Thomas	1964
Rathcavan, Lord.........	1937	Snedden, Billy Mackie...	1972	Williams, Eric...........	1964
Rawlinson, Sir Peter.....	1964	Soames, Sir Christopher ..	1958	Williams, Shirley........	1974
Rea, Lord..............	1962	Stable, Sir Wintringham	1965	Wills, Eustace George....	1967
Redmayne, Lord.........	1959	Stamp, Sir Blanshard......	1971	Willmer, Sir Henry Gordon	1958
Rees, Merlyn............	1974	Stephenson, Sir John	1971	Wilson, James Harold....	1947
Reigate, Lord............	1961	Stevenson, Sir Melford ...	1973	Wilson of Langside, Lord.	1967
Renton, Sir David........	1962	Stewart, Michael........	1964	Windeyer, Sir Victor.....	1963
Rhodes, Lord............	1969	Stodart, James Anthony...	1974	Windlesham, Lord........	1973
Rhyl, Lord..............	1955	Stonehouse, John Thomson	1968	Wood, Richard Frederick.	1959
Richmond, Sir Clifford...	1973	Stopford, *Rt. Rev.* Robert	1961	Woodburn, Arthur.......	1947
Rippon, Geoffrey........	1962	Stoot, Lord.............	1964	Woodcock, George.......	1967
Ritchie of Dundee, Lord..	1965	Stow Hill, Lord..........	1948	Woodhouse, Sir Arthur...	1974
Robens of Woldingham,		Strathclyde, Lord........	1953	Wylie, Lord.............	1970
Lord.................	1951	Strauss, George Russell ...	1947	York, Archbishop of.....	1974
Robinson, Kenneth......	1964			Younger, Sir Kenneth....	1951

Clerk of the Council, N. E. Leigh, C.V.O.　　　*Deputy Clerk of the Council*, C. E. S. Horsford.

THE PREFIX RIGHT HONOURABLE

" Right Honourable."—By long established custom, or courtesy, members of Her Majesty's Most Honourable Privy Council are entitled to be designated " The Right Honourable," but, in practice, this prefix is sometimes absorbed in other designations; for example, a Prince of the Blood admitted a Privy Councillor remains " His Royal Highness "; a Duke remains " His Grace "; a Marquess is still styled " Most Honourable ". The style of all other Peers, whether Privy Councillors or not, is " Right Honourable ", although it is more usual to describe them with the prefix " The ", omitting the more elaborate styles. A privy Councillor who is not a Peer should be addressed as the Right (or Rt.) Hon.——. A Peer below the rank of Marquess who is a Privy Councillor should be addressed as The Right (or Rt.) Hon. the Lord (or Earl or Viscount)——, P.C., or, less elaborately, The Lord (or Earl or Viscount)——P.C.

Orders of Chivalry

THE MOST NOBLE ORDER OF THE GARTER (1348)—K.G.

Ribbon, Garter Blue. *Motto*, Honi soit qui mal y pense (*Shame on him who thinks evil of it*).
The number of Knights Companions is limited to 24.

SOVEREIGN OF THE ORDER—THE QUEEN
Ladies of the Garter—H.M. QUEEN ELIZABETH THE QUEEN MOTHER, 1936.
H.M. THE QUEEN OF THE NETHERLANDS, 1958

ROYAL KNIGHTS
H.R.H. the Duke of Edinburgh, 1947.
H.R.H. The Prince of Wales, 1958.

EXTRA KNIGHTS
H.M. King Leopold III, 1935.

H.I.M. the Emperor of Ethiopia, 1954.
H.M. the King of Norway, 1959.
H.M. the King of the Belgians, 1963.
H.I.M the Emperor of Japan, 1971.

H.R.H. the Grand Duke of Luxembourg, 1972.
H.R.H. Prince Paul of Yugoslavia, 1939.

KNIGHTS COMPANIONS
The Duke of Beaufort, 1937.
The Earl Mountbatten of Burma, 1946.

The Viscount Montgomery of Alamein, 1946.
The Duke of Portland, 1948.
The Earl of Avon, 1954. [1959.
The Duke of Northumberland, Sir Gerald Templer, 1963.
The Viscount Cobham, 1964.
The Viscount Amory, 1968.
The Viscount De L'Isle, 1968.
The Lord Casey, 1969.
The Lord Ashburton, 1969.
The Lord Cobbold, 1970.

Sir Edmund Bacon, Bt., 1970.
Sir Cennydd Traherne, 1970.
The Earl of Longford, 1971.
The Earl Waldegrave, 1971.
The Lord Butler of Saffron Walden, 1971.
The Earl of Drogheda, 1972.
The Lord Rhodes, 1972.
The Marquess of Abergavenny, 1974.
The Lord Shackleton, 1974.

The Lord Trevelyan, 1974.
Prelate, The Bishop of Winchester.
Chancellor, The Viscount Cobham, K.G., P.C., G.C.M.G., G.C.V.O., T.D.
Register, The Dean of Windsor.
Garter King of Arms, Sir Anthony Richard Wagner, K.C.V.O.
Gentleman Usher of the Black Rod, Admiral Sir Frank Roddam Twiss, K.C.B., D.S.C.
Secretary, W. J. G. Verco, C.V.O.

THE MOST ANCIENT AND MOST NOBLE ORDER OF THE THISTLE—K.T.

Ribbon, Green. *Motto*, Nemo me impune lacessit (*No one provokes me with impunity*)
The number of Knights Companions is limited to 16.

SOVEREIGN OF THE ORDER—THE QUEEN
Lady of the Thistle—H.M. QUEEN ELIZABETH THE QUEEN MOTHER, 1937

ROYAL KNIGHT
H.R.H. the Duke of Edinburgh, 1952.
EXTRA KNIGHT
H.M. the King of Norway, 1962.
KNIGHTS COMPANIONS
The Earl of Haddington, 1951.
The Earl of Crawford and Balcarres, 1955.
The Lord Rowallan, 1957.
The Lord Home of the Hirsel, 1962.
Sir Robert Menzies, 1963.

Sir James Robertson, 1965.
The Earl of Wemyss and March, 1966.
The Lord Maclean, 1969.
Sir Richard O'Connor, 1971.
The Earl of Dalhousie, 1971.
The Lord Clydesmuir, 1973.
The Hon. Lord Birsay, 1973.
The Viscount Muirshiel, 1973.
Colonel Sir Donald Cameron of Lochiel, 1973.
The Lord Ballantrae, 1974.

Chancellor, The Lord Home of the Hirsel
Dean, The Very Rev. Prof. J. McIntyre, M.A., B.D., D.Litt. D.D.
Secretary and Lord Lyon King of Arms, Sir James Monteith Grant, K.C.V.O., W.S.
Usher of the Green Rod, Sir Reginald Graham of Larbert, Bt., V.C., O.B.E.

THE MOST HONOURABLE ORDER OF THE BATH (1725)

Ribbon, Crimson. *Motto*, Tria juncta in uno (*Three joined in one*). (Remodelled 1815, and enlarged many times since. The Order is divided into civil and military divisions.)

G.C.B. Mil.   G.C.B. Civ.   K.C.B. Mil.   K.C.B. Civ.   C.B. Mil.

THE SOVEREIGN; *Grand Master and First or Principal Knight Grand Cross*, H.R.H. The Prince of Wales, K.G., G.C.B.; *Dean of the Order*, The Dean of Westminster; *Bath King of Arms*, General Sir Richard Goodbody G.C.B., K.B.E., D.S.O.; *Registrar and Secretary*, Air Marshal Sir Anthony Selway, K.C.B., D.F.C.; *Genealogist*, C. M. J. F. Swan, Ph.D.; *Gentleman Usher of the Scarlet Rod*, Rear-Admiral C. D. Madden, C.B., C.B.E., M.V.O., D.S.C.; *Deputy Secretary*, The Secretary of the Central Chancery of the Orders of Knighthood; *Chancery*, Central Chancery of the Orders of Knighthood, St. James's Palace, S.W.1.—G.C.B., Knight (or Dame) Grand Cross; K.C.B., Knight Commander; D.C.B., Dame Commander; C.B., Companion. Women became eligible for the Order from Jan. 1, 1971.

THE ORDER OF MERIT (1902)—O.M. *Ribbon*, Blue and Crimson.

This Order is designed as a special distinction for eminent men and women—without conferring a kinghthood upon them. The Order is limited in numbers to 24, with the addition of foreign honorary members. Membership is of two kinds, Military and Civil, the badge of the former having crossed swords, and the latter oak leaves.
O.M.Mil. Membership is denoted by the suffix O.M., which follows the first class of the Order O.M.Civ. of the Bath and precedes the letters designating membership of the inferior classes of the Bath and all classes of the lesser Orders of Knighthood.

THE SOVEREIGN.
H.R.H. THE DUKE OF EDINBURGH (1968).

The Lord Adrian, 1942
Wilder Graves Penfield, 1953.
Sir (Frank) Macfarlane Burnet, 1958.
Graham Vivian Sutherland, 1960.
Sir Basil Urwin Spence, 1962.
Henry Spencer Moore, 1963.

Edward Benjamin Britten, 1965.
Dorothy Hodgkin, 1965.
The Earl Mountbatten of Burma, 1965.
Sir William Turner Walton, 1967.
Ben Nicholson, 1968.
The Lord Zuckerman, 1968.

Malcolm MacDonald, 1969.
The Lord Penney, 1969.
Dame Veronica Wedgwood, 1969.
Sir Isaiah Berlin, 1971.
Sir George Edwards, 1971.
Sir Alan Hodgkin, 1973.
Paul Adrian Maurice Dirac, 1973.

Secretary and Registrar (vacant).

Chancery, Central Chancery of the Orders of Knighthood, St. James's Palace, S.W.1.

THE MOST EXALTED ORDER OF THE STAR OF INDIA (1861)

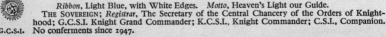

Ribbon, Light Blue, with White Edges. *Motto*, Heaven's Light our Guide.
THE SOVEREIGN; *Registrar*, The Secretary of the Central Chancery of the Orders of Knighthood; G.C.S.I. Knight Grand Commander; K.C.S.I., Knight Commander; C.S.I., Companion.
G.C.S.I. No conferments since 1947.

THE MOST DISTINGUISHED ORDER OF ST. MICHAEL AND ST. GEORGE (1818)

Ribbon Saxon Blue, with Scarlet centre. *Motto,* Auspicium melioris ævi (Token of a better age)
THE SOVEREIGN; *Grand Master,* H.R.H. The Duke of Kent, G.C.M.G., G.C.V.O., A.D.C.; *Prelate,*
The Bishop of Worcester; *Chancellor,* The Viscount De L'Isle, *V.C.,* K.G. P.C., G.C.M.G.,
G.C.V.O.; *Secretary,* Sir Michael Palliser, K.C.M.G.; *Registrar,* The Lord Gore-Booth, G.C.M.G.,
K.C.V.O.; *King of Arms,* Rt. Hon. Sir Morrice James, G.C.M.G., C.V.O., M.B.E.; *Gentleman Usher of the
Blue Rod,* Sir Anthony Abell, K.C.M.G.; *Dean,* The Dean of St. Paul's; *Deputy Secretary,* Maj.-Gen.
P. B. Gillet, C.B., C.V.O., O.B.E. *Chancery,* Central Chancery of the Orders of Knighthood,
St. James's Palace, S.W.1.—G.C.M.G., Knight (or Dame) Grand Cross; K.C.M.G., Knight
Commander; D.C.M.G., Dame Commander; C.M.G., Companion.

THE MOST EMINENT ORDER OF THE INDIAN EMPIRE (1868)

Ribbon, Imperial Purple. *Motto,* Imperatricis auspiciis (*Under the auspices of the Empress*).
THE SOVEREIGN; *Registrar,* The Secretary of the Central Chancery of the Orders of Knight-
G.C.I.E. hood; G.C.I.E., Knight Grand Commander; K.C.I.E., Knight Commander; C.I.E., Com-
panion. No conferments since 1947.

THE ROYAL VICTORIAN ORDER (1896)

Ribbon, Blue, with Red and White Edges. *Motto,* Victoria.
THE SOVEREIGN; *Grand Master,* H.M. Queen Elizabeth the Queen Mother; *Chan-
cellor,* The Lord Chamberlain; *Secretary,* The Keeper of the Privy Purse; *Registrar,* The
Secretary of the Central Chancery of the Orders of Knighthood; *Chaplain,* The Rev.
Canon C. E. Young. G.C.V.O., Knight or Dame Grand Cross; K.C.V.O., Knight
Commander; D.C.V.O., Dame Commander; C.V.O., Commander; M.V.O.,
Member, 4th or 5th Class.

THE ROYAL VICTORIAN CHAIN (1902)

Founded by King Edward VII, in 1902. It confers no precedence on its holders.
H.M. THE QUEEN
H.M. QUEEN ELIZABETH THE QUEEN MOTHER (1937).

The Duke of Beaufort (1953).	H.M. The King of Norway	The Lord Adeane (1972).
H.R.H. Prince Paul of Yugoslavia (1934).	(1955).	H.M. King Zahir Shah of Afghanistan (1972).
H.M. King Leopold III (1937).	H.M. The King of Thailand (1960).	Rt. Hon. Roland Michener (1973).
H.I.M. The Shahanshah of Iran (1948).	H.I.H. The Crown Prince of Ethiopia (1965).	The Right Rev. Lord Ramsey of Canterbury, (1974).
H.M. The Queen of the Nether-lands (1950).	H.M. The King of Jordan (1966).	H. M. The King of Nepal (1975).

THE MOST EXCELLENT ORDER OF THE BRITISH EMPIRE (1917)

Ribbon, Rose pink edged with pearl grey with vertical pearl stripe in centre (Military
Division); without vertical pearl stripe (Civil Division). *Motto,* For God and the Empire.
G.B.E. THE SOVEREIGN: *Grand Master,* H.R.H. the Prince Philip, Duke of Edinburgh, K.G., K.B.E.
P.C., K.T., O.M., G.B.E.; *Prelate,* The Bishop of London; *King of Arms,* Lieut.-Gen. Sir George Gordon Lennox,
K.B.E., C.B., C.V.O., D.S.O.; *Registrar,* The Secretary of the Central Chancery of the Orders of Knighthood;
Secretary, The Permanent Secretary to the Civil Service Department; *Dean,* The Dean of St. Paul's; *Gentle-
man Usher of the Purple Rod,* Sir Robert Bellinger, G.B.E.; *Chancery,* Central Chancery of the Order of
Knighthood, St. James's Palace, S.W.1. G.B.E., Knight or Dame Grand Cross; K.B.E. Knight Commander;
D.B.E., Dame Commander; C.B.E., Commander; O.B.E., Officer; M.B.E., Member. The Order was
divided into *Military* and *Civil* divisions in Dec. 1918.

ORDER OF THE COMPANIONS OF HONOUR (June 4, 1917)—C.H.

Ribbon, Carmine, with Gold Edges.
This Order consists of one Class only and carries with it no title. It ranks after the 1st Class of
the Order of the British Empire, *i.e.,* Knights and Dames Grand Cross (Mil. and Civ. Div.).
The number of awards is limited to 65 (excluding honorary members) and the Order is open to
both sexes. *Secretary and Registrar,* The Secretary of the Central Chancery of the Orders of Knighthood.

Ashley, Jack, 1975.	Cohen of Birkenhead, The Lord, 1974.	Houghton of Sowerby, the Lord, 1967.
Ashton, Sir Frederick, 1970.	Duncan-Sandys, The Lord, 1973.	Howells, Herbert Norman, 1972.
Aylestone, The Lord, 1975.	Gardiner, The Lord, 1975.	Kotelawala, Rt. Hon. Sir John, 1956.
Best, Charles Herbert, 1971.	Goodman, The Lord, 1972.	
Boult, Sir Adrian, 1969.	Gordon-Walker, The Lord, 1968.	Leach, Bernard Howell, 1973.
Boyd of Merton, The Viscount, 1960.	Gorton, Rt. Hon. John Gray, 1971.	Limerick, Angela, Countess of, 1974.
Britten, Edward Benjamin, 1953.	Greene, Graham, 1966.	Lloyd, Rt. Hon. Selwyn, 1962.
Brooke of Cumnor, The Lord, 1964.	Hailsham of St. Marylebone, The Lord, 1974.	McEwen, Rt. Hon. Sir John, 1969.
Bryant, Sir Arthur, 1967.	Hill, *Prof.* Archibald Vivian, 1946.	McMahon, Rt. Hon. William, 1972.
Butler of Saffron Walden, The Lord, 1954.	Holyoake, Rt. Hon. Sir Keith, 1963.	Marshall, Rt. Hon. Sir John Ross 1973.
Casey, The Lord, 1944.		
Cecil, Lord David Gascoyne, 1949.		Mayer, Sir Robert, 1973.
Clark, The Lord, 1959.		

Medawar, Sir Peter, 1972.
Menzies, Rt. Hon. Sir Robert, 1951.
Micklem, Rev. Nathaniel, 1974.
Moore, Henry Spencer, 1955.
Morris of Borth-y-Gest, The Lord 1975.
Muirshiel, The Viscount, 1962.
Perutz, *Prof.* Max Ferdinand, 1975.
Piper, John Egerton Christmas, 1972.
Payne, The Rev. Ernest Alexander, 1968.

Rahman, Tunku Abdul, 1960.
Richards, *Prof.* Ivor Armstrong, 1964.
Robbins, The Lord, 1968.
Shinwell, The Lord, 1965.
Smith, Arnold Cantwell, 1975.
Stewart, Rt. Hon. Michael, 1969.
Summerskill, The Baroness, 1966.
Thorndike, Dame Sybil, 1970.
Toynbee, *Prof.* Arnold Joseph, 1956.

Ward of North Tyneside, The Baroness, 1973.
Watkinson, The Viscount, 1962.
Wheeler, Sir Mortimer, 1967.
Whitelaw, Rt. Hon. William, 1974.
Williams, Rt. Hon. Eric, 1969.

Honorary Members, M. René Massigli, 1954; Lee Kuan Yew, 1970; Dr. Joseph Luns, 1971; M. Jean Monnet, 1972.

THE ROYAL VICTORIA AND ALBERT (for Ladies)—V.A.

Instituted in 1862, and enlarged in 1864, 1865, and 1880. Badge, a medallion of Queen Victoria and the Prince Consort, surmounted by a crown, which is attached to a bow of white moiré ribbon. The honour does not confer any rank or title upon the recipient.

FIRST CLASS

H.R.H. the Princess Alice, Countess of Athlone.

THE IMPERIAL ORDER OF THE CROWN OF INDIA (for Ladies)—C.I.

Instituted Dec. 31, 1877. Badge, the royal cipher in jewels within an oval, surmounted by an Heraldic Crown and attached to a bow of light blue watered ribbon, edged white. The honour does not confer any rank or title upon the recipient. No conferments have been made since 1947.

H.M. THE QUEEN, 1947.
H.M. Queen Elizabeth the Queen Mother, 1931.
H.R.H. the Princess Margaret, Countess of Snowdon, 1947.

H.R.H. the Princess Alice, Duchess of Gloucester, 1937.
Dorothy Evelyn Augusta, Dowager Countess of Halifax, 1926.
H.H. Maharani of Travancore, 1929.

Doreen Geraldine, Dowager Baroness Brabourne, 1937.
Eugenie Marie, Countess Wavell, 1943.

THE IMPERIAL SERVICE ORDER (1902)—I.S.O.

Ribbon, Crimson, with Blue Centre.

Appointment of Companion of this Order shall be open to those members of the Civil Services whose eligibility shall be determined by the grade held by such persons. The Order consists of the SOVEREIGN and Companions (not exclusively male) to a number not exceeding 1425 of whom 850 may belong to the Home Civil Services and 575 to Overseas Civil Services. *Secretary*, the Permanent Secretary to the Civil Service Department. *Registrar*, The Secretary of the Central Chancery of the Orders of Knighthood, 8 Buckingham Gate, S.W.1.

Baronets, Knights Grand Cross, Knights Grand Commanders Knights Commanders and Knights Bachelor

Badge of Baronets
of England, Great Britain, U.K.,
(and Ireland marked I.).

Badge of Baronets
of Scotland or Nova Scotia
(marked s.).

NOTES CONCERNING BARONETS

Clause II. of the Royal Warrant of February 8, 1910, ordains as follows:—" That no person whose name is not entered upon the Official Roll shall be received as a Baronet, or shall be addressed or mentioned by that title in any Civil or Military Commission, Letters Patent or other official document." When an obelisk (†) precedes a name it indicates that, *at the time of going to press*, the Baronet concerned has not been registered on the Official Roll of the Baronetage. The date of creation of the Baronetcy is given in parenthesis ( ).

Baronets are addressed as " Sir " (with Christian name) and in writing as " Sir Robert *A*—, Bt." Baronet's wives are addressed (formally) as " Your Ladyship " or " Lady *A*—," without any Christian name unless a daughter of a Duke, Marquess or Earl, in which case " The Lady Mary *A*—"; if daughter of a Viscount or Baron " The Hon. Lady *A*—."

NOTES CONCERNING KNIGHTS GRAND CROSS, ETC.

Knights Grand Cross, Knights Grand Commanders and Knights Commanders are addressed in the same manner as Baronets (*q.v.*), but in writing the appropriate initials (G.C.B., K.C.B., &c.) are appended to surname after "Bt." if they are also baronets or in place of "Bt." if they are not. Knights Bachelor are addressed as " Sir —— (first or Christian name) " and in writing as " Sir —— B—." The wife of a Knight Grand Cross, Knight Grand Commander, Knight Commander or Knight Bachelor is addressed as stated for the wife of a Baronet.

NOTES CONCERNING KNIGHTS BACHELOR

The Knights Bachelor do not constitute a Royal Order, but comprise the surviving representation of the ancient State Orders of Knighthood. The Register of Knights Bachelor, instituted by James I. in the 17th century, lapsed, and in 1908 a voluntary Association under the title of "The Society of Knights" (now "The Imperial Society of Knights Bachelor" by Royal command) was formed with the primary objects of continuing the various registers dating from 1257 and obtaining the uniform registration of every created Knight Bachelor. In 1926 a design for a badge to be worn by Knights Bachelor was approved and adopted, a miniature reproduction being shown above; in 1974 a neck badge and miniature were added. The Officers of the Society are:— *Knight Principal*, Sir Anthony Wagner, K.C.V.O., *Deputy Knight Principal*, Sir Gilbert Inglefield, G.B.E., T.D.; *Prelate*, The Bishop of London; *Hon. Registrar*, Sir John Weir Russell; *Hon. Treasurer*, Sir John Howard; *Registry and Library*, 21 Old Buildings, Lincoln's Inn, W.C.2.

BARONETAGE AND KNIGHTAGE
(Revised to Aug. 14, 1975)
Peers are not included in this list.

A full entry in *italic type* indicates that the recipient of a Knighthood died during the year in which the honour was conferred. The name is included for purposes of record.

Aarons, Sir Daniel Sidney, Kt., O.B.E., M.C.

Aarvold, *His Hon.* Sir Carl Douglas, Kt., O.B.E., T.D.

Abayomi, Sir Kofo Adekunle, Kt.

Abbott, *Very Rev.* Eric Symes, K.C.V.O., D.D.

Abbott, *Hon.* Sir Myles John, Kt.

Abdy, Sir Robert Henry Edward, Bt. (1850).

Abeles, Sir (Emil Herbert) Peter, Kt.

Abell, Sir Anthony Foster, K.C.M.G.

Abell, Sir George Edmond Brackenbury, K.C.I.E., O.B.E.

Abercromby, Sir Ian George, Bt. (s. 1636).

Abrahams, Sir Charles, K.C.V.O.

Ackner, *Hon.* Sir Desmond James Conrad, Kt.

Ackroyd, Sir John Robert Whyte, Bt. (1956).

Acland, *Capt.* Sir Hubert Guy Dyke, Bt., D.S.O., R.N. (1890).

Acland, Sir (Hugh) John (Dyke), K.B.E.

Acland, Sir Richard Thomas Dyke, Bt. (1644).

Acton, Sir Harold Mario Mitchell, Kt., C.B.E.

Acutt, Sir Keith Courtney, K.B.E.

Adair, *Maj.-Gen.* Sir Allan Henry Shafto, Bt., G.C.V.O., C.B., D.S.O., M.C. (1838).

Adam, *Hon.* Sir Alistair Duncan Grant, Kt.

Adam, *General* Sir Ronald Forbes, Bt., G.C.B., D.S.O., O.B.E. (1917).

Adams, Sir Maurice Edward, K.B.E.

Adams, Sir Philip George Doyne, K.C.M.G.

Adamson, Sir Kenneth Thomas, Kt., C.M.G.

Adcock, Sir Robert Henry, Kt., C.B.E.

Addis, Sir John Mansfield, K.C.M.G.

Addis, Sir William, K.B.E., C.M.G.

Addison, Sir William Wilkinson, Kt.

Adeane, *Col.* Sir Robert Philip Wyndham, Kt., O.B.E.

Ademola, *Rt. Hon.* Sir Adetokunbo Adegboyega, K.B.E.

Adermann, *Rt. Hon.* Sir Charles Frederick, K.B.E.

Adjaye, Sir Edward Otchere Asafu-, Kt.

Adrien, *Hon.* Sir Maurice Latour-, Kt.

Agnew, Sir Fulque Melville Gerald Noel, Bt. (s 1629).

Agnew, Sir Geoffrey William Gerald, Kt.

Agnew, Sir (John) Anthony Stuart, Bt. (1895).

Agnew, *Cdr.* Sir Peter Garnett, Bt. (1957).

Agnew, Sir (William) Godfrey, K.C.V.O., C.B.

Aiken, *Air Marshal* Sir John Alexander Carlisle, K.C.B.

Ainley, Sir (Alfred) John, Kt., M.C.

Ainscough, Sir Thomas Martland, Kt., C.B.E.

Ainsworth, Sir John Francis, Bt. (1917).

Aird, Sir (George) John, Bt. (1902).

Airey, *Lt.-Gen.* Sir Terence Sydney, K.C.M.G., C.B., C.B.E.

Aitchison, Sir Charles Walter de Lancey, Bt. (1938).

Aitken, Sir Arthur Percival Hay, Kt.

Aitken, Sir (John William) Maxwell, Bt., D.S.O., D.F.C. (1916).

Aitken, Sir Robert Stevenson, Kt., M.D., D.Phil.

Albert, Sir Alexis François, Kt., C.M.G., V.R.D.

Albu, Sir George, Bt. (1912).

Alderson, Sir Harold George, Kt., M.B.E.

Aldington, Sir Geoffrey William, K.B.E., C.M.G.

Alexander, Sir Alexander Sandor, Kt.

Alexander, Sir Charles Gundry, Bt. (1945).

Alexander, Sir Claud Hagart-, Bt. (1886).

Alexander, *Hon.* Sir Darnley Arthur Raymond, Kt., C.B.E.

Alexander, Sir Desmond William Lionel Cable, Bt. (1809).

Alexander, Sir Douglas Hamilton, Bt. (1921).

Alexander, Sir (John) Lindsay, Kt,

Alexander, Sir Norman Stanley. Kt., C.B.E.

Alford, Sir Robert Edmund, K.B.E., C.M.G.

Algie, *Hon.* Sir Ronald Macmillan, Kt.

Allan, Sir Henry Ralph Moreton Havelock-, Bt. (1858).

Allcroft, Sir Philip Magnus-, Bt., C.B.E. (1917).

Allen, Sir Donald Richard, Kt., O.B.E., M.C.

Allen, Sir Douglas Albert Vivian, G.C.B.

Allen, Sir Milton Pentonville, Kt., O.B.E.

Allen, Sir Peter Christopher, Kt.

Allen, Sir Philip, G.C.B.

Allen, Sir Richard Hugh Sedley, K.C.M.G.

Allen, *Prof.* Sir Roy George Douglas, Kt., C.B.E., D.Sc., F.B.A.

Allen, Sir (William) Denis, G.C.M.G., C.B.

Allen, Sir William Guildford, Kt., C.B.E.

Allen, Sir William Kenneth Gwynne, Kt.

Alleyne, *Capt.* Sir John Meynell, Bt., D.S.O., D.S.C., R.N. (1769).

Aluwihare, Sir Richard, K.C.M.G., C.B.E.

Amcotts, *Lt.-Col.* Sir Weston Cracroft-, Kt., M.C.

Ameer Ali, Sir Torick, Kt.

Ames, Sir Cyril Geraint, Kt.

Amies, *Prof.* Sir Arthur Barton Pilgrim, Kt., C.M.G.

Anderson, Sir Colin Skelton, K.B.E.

Anderson, Sir David Stirling, Kt. Ph.D.

Anderson, Sir Donald George, Kt., C.B.E.

Anderson, Sir Duncan Law, K.B.E., T.D.

Anderson, Sir Edward Arthur, Kt.

Anderson, Sir Gilmour Menzies, Kt., C.B.E.

Anderson, *Prof.* Sir (James) Norman (Dalrymple), Kt., O.B.E., Q.C., F.B.A.

Anderson, *General* Sir John D'Arcy, G.B.E., K.C.B., D.S.O.

Anderson, *Maj.-Gen.* Sir John Evelyn, K.B.E.

Anderson, Sir John Muir Kt. C.M.G.

Anderson, Sir Kenneth, K.B.E., C.B.

Anderson, Hon. Sir Kenneth McColl, K.B.E.

Anderson, Lt.-Gen. Sir Richard Neville, K.C.B., C.B.E., D.S.O.

Anderson, Prof. Sir William Ferguson, Kt., O.B.E.

Andrew, Rev. Sir (George) Herbert, K.C.M.G., C.B.

Andrewes, Sir Christopher Howard, Kt., M.D., F.R.S.

Andrews, Sir Edwin Arthur Chapman-, K.C.M.G., O.B.E.

Andrews, Rt. Hon. Sir John Lawson Ormrod, K.B.E.

Angas, Sir John Keith, Kt.

Ankole, The Omugabe of, Kt.

Annamunthodo, Prof. Sir Harry, Kt., F.R.C.S.

Ansell, Col. Sir Michael Picton, Kt., C.B.E., D.S.O.

Ansett, Sir Reginald Myles, K.B.E.

Anson, Rear-Admiral Sir Peter, Bt., C.B. (1831).

Ansorge, Sir Eric Cecil. Kt., C.S.I., C.I.E.

Anstey, Brig. Sir John, Kt., C.B.E., T.D.

Anstice, Vice-Adm. Sir Edmund Walter, K.C.B.

Anstruther, Sir Ralph Hugo, Bt. C.V.O., M.C. (s 1694).

Anstruther, Sir Windham Eric Francis Carmichael-, Bt. (s. 1700; G.B. 1798).

Anthony, Sir (Michael) Mobolaji Bank-, K.B.E.

Antico, Sir Tristan Venus, Kt.

Antrobus, Sir Philip Coutts, Bt. (1815).

Arbuthnot, Sir Hugh Fitzgerald, Bt. (1823).

Arbuthnot, Sir John Sinclair-Wemyss, Bt., M.B.E., T.D. (1964).

Archdale, Comdr. Sir Edward Folmer, Bt., D.S.C., R.N. (1928).

Archer, Sir Clyde Vernon Harcourt, Kt.

Archey, Sir Gilbert Edward, Kt., C.B.E.

Arkell, Capt. Sir (Thomas) Noel, Kt.

Armer, Sir (Isaac) Frederick, K.B.E., C.B., M.C.

Armitage, Sir Arthur Llewellyn, Kt.

Armitage, Sir Robert Perceval, K.C.M.G., M.B.E.

Armstrong, Sir Andrew St. Clare, Bt. (1841).

Armstrong, Sir Thomas Henry Wait, Kt., D.MUS.

Armytage, Capt. Sir (John) Lionel, Bt. (1738).

Arnold, Hon. Sir John Lewis, Kt.

Arnott, Sir John Robert Alexander, Bt. (1896).

Arnott, Prof. Sir (William) Melville, Kt., T.D., M.D.

Arrowsmith, Sir Edwin Porter, K.C.M.G.

Arthur, Sir Basil Malcolm, Bt. (1841).

Arthur, Sir Geoffrey George, K.C.M.G.

Arundell, Brig. Sir Robert Duncan Harris, K.C.M.G., O.B.E.

Arup, Sir Ove Nyquist, Kt., C.B.E.

Ashburnham, Sir Denny Reginald, Bt. (1661).

Ashenheim, Sir Neville Noel, Kt., C.B.E.

Ashmore, Admiral Sir Edward Beckwith, G.C.B., D.S.C.

Ashmore, Vice-Adm. Sir Peter William Beckwith, K.C.B., M.V.O., D.S.C.

Ashton, Sir (Arthur) Leigh (Bolland), Kt.

Ashton, Sir Frederick William Mallandaine, Kt., C.H., C.B.E.

Ashton, Sir Hubert, K.B.E., M.C.

Ashwin, Sir Bernard Carl, K.B.E., C.M.G.

Ashworth, Sir Herbert, Kt.

Ashworth, Hon. Sir John Percy, Kt., M.B.E.

Aske, Rev. Sir Conan, Bt. (1922).

Askin, Hon. Sir Robert William, G.C.M.G.

Astbury, Sir George, Kt.

Astley, Sir Francis Jacob Dugdale, Bt. (1821).

Aston, Hon. Sir William John, K.C.M.G.

Astwood, Lt.-Col. Sir Jeffrey Carlton, Kt., C.B.E., E.D.

Atkins, Prof. Sir Hedley John Barnard, K.B.E., D.M., F.R.C.S.

Atkinson, Rt. Hon. Sir Fenton, Kt.

Atkinson, Sir (John) Kenneth, Kt.

Atkinson, Maj.-Gen. Sir Leonard Henry, K.B.E.

Auchinleck, Field Marshal Sir Claude John Eyre, G.C.B., G.C.I.E., C.S.I., D.S.O., O.B.E.

Austin, Sir John (Byron Fraser), Bt. (1894).

Austin, Sir John Worroker, Kt.

Austin, Sir Thomas, K.C.I.E.

Auswild, Sir James Frederick John, Kt., C.B.E.

Ayer, Prof. Sir Alfred Jules, Kt., F.B.A.

Aykroyd, Sir William Miles, Bt., M.C. (1920).

Aykroyd, Sir Cecil William, Bt. (1929).

Aylmer, Sir Felix, Kt., O.B.E.

Aylmer, Sir Fenton Gerald, Bt. (I 1622).

Backhouse, Sir Jonathan Roger, Bt. (1901).

Bacon, Sir Edmund Castell, Bt. K.G., K.B.E., T.D. Premier Baronet of England (1611 and 1627).

Bacon, Sir Ranulph Robert Maunsell, Kt.

Baddeley, Sir John Beresford, Bt. (1922).

Bagge, Sir John Alfred Picton, Bt. (1867).

Bagnall, Hon. Sir William Arthur, Kt., M.B.E.

Bagrit, Sir Leon, Kt.

Bailey, Sir Derrick Thomas Louis, Bt., D.F.C. (1919).

Bailey, Sir Donald Coleman, Kt., O.B.E.

Bailey, Prof. Sir Harold Walter, Kt., D.Phil., F.B.A.

Baillie, Sir Gawaine George Hope, Bt. (1823).

Bairamian, Hon. Sir Vahe Robert, Kt.

Baird, Sir David Charles, Bt. (1809).

Baird, Prof. Sir Dugald, Kt., M.D.

Baird, Lt.-Gen. Sir James Parlane, K.B.E., M.D.

Baird, Sir James Richard Gardiner, Bt., M.C. (s. 1695).

Baker, Sir (Allan) Ivor, Kt., C.B.E.

Baker, Air Marshal Sir Brian Edmund, K.B.E., C.B., D.S.O., M.C., A.F.C.

Baker, Field-Marshal Sir Geoffrey Harding, G.C.B., C.M.G., C.B.E., M.C.

Baker, Rt. Hon. Sir George Gillespie, Kt., O.B.E.

Baker, Sir Humphrey Dodington Benedict Sherston-, Bt. (1796).

Baker, Prof. Sir John Fleetwood, Kt., O.B.E., Sc.D., F.R.S.

Baker, Air Chief Marshal Sir John Wakeling, G.B.E., K.C.B., M.C., D.F.C.

Baker, Sir Rowland, Kt., O.B.E.

Baker, Sir (Stanislaus) Josaph, Kt., C.B.

Balcon, Sir Michael, Kt.

Balfour, Sir John, G.C.M.G., G.B.E.

Balfour, Lt.-Gen. Sir Philip Maxwell, K.B.E., C.B., M.C.

Balfour, General Sir (Robert George) Victor FitzGeorge-, K.C.B., C.B.E., D.S.O., M.C.

Ball, Air Vice-Marshal Sir Benjamin, K.B.E., C.B.

Ball, Sir Nigel Gresley, Bt. (1911).

Balmer, Sir Joseph Reginald, Kt.

Bancroft, Sir Ian Powell, K.C.B.

Banks, Sir Maurice Alfred Lister, Kt.

Banner, Sir George Knowles Harmood-, Bt. (1924).

Bannerman, Lt.-Col. Sir Donald Arthur Gordon, Bt. (s 1682).

Bannister, Sir Roger Gilbert, Kt., D.M., F.R.C.P.

Banwell, Sir (George) Harold, Kt.

Barber, Sir Herbert William, Kt.

Barber, Lt.-Col. Sir William Francis, Bt., T.D. (1960).

Barclay, Sir Colville Herbert Sanford, Bt. (s 1668).

Barclay, Sir Roderick Edward, G.C.V.O., K.C.M.G.

Barford, Sir Leonard, Kt.

Baring, Sir Charles Christian, Bt. (1911).

Barker, Sir Alwyn Bowman, Kt., C.M.G.

Barker, Sir (Charles Frederic) James, Kt., M.B.E.

Barker, General Sir Evelyn Hugh, K.C.B., K.B.E., D.S.O., M.C.

Barker, Sir William, K.C.M.G., O.B.E.

Barlow, Sir Christopher Hilaro, Bt. (1803).

Barlow, Sir John Denman, Bt. (1907).

Barlow, Sir Robert, Kt.

Barlow, Sir Thomas Erasmus, Bt., D.S.C. (1902).

Barnard, Sir (Arthur) Thomas, Kt., C.B., O.B.E.

Barnard, *Capt.* Sir George Edward, Kt.

Barnard, Sir Henry William, Kt.

Barnes, Sir Denis Charles, K.C.B.

Barnes, Sir (Ernest) John (Ward), K.C.M.G., M.B.E.

Barnes, Sir William Lethbridge Gorell-, K.C.M.G., C.B.

Barnett, Sir Ben Lewis, K.B.E., C.B., M.C.

Barnett, *Air Chief Marshal* Sir Denis Hensley Fulton, G.C.B., C.B.E., D.F.C.

Barnett, Sir Oliver Charles, Kt., C.B.E., Q.C.

Barnewall, Sir Reginald Robert, Bt. (I 1623).

Barraclough, *Air Chief Marshal* Sir John, K.C.B., C.B.E., D.F.C., A.F.C.

Barraclough, *Brig.* Sir John Ashworth, Kt., C.M.G., D.S.O., O.B.E., M.C.

Barran, Sir David Haven, Kt.

Barran, Sir John Napoleon Ruthven, Bt. (1895)

Barratt, Sir Sydney, Kt.

Barrett, Sir Arthur George, Kt.

Barrie, Sir Walter, Kt.

Barrington, Sir Charles Bacon, Bt. (1831).

Barrington, Sir Kenneth Charles Peto, Kt.

Barritt, Sir David Thurlow, Kt.

Barron, Sir Donald James, Kt.

Barrow, Sir Richard John Uniacke, Bt. (1835).

Barry, Sir (Philip) Stuart Milner-, K.C.V.D., C.B., O.B.E.

Barry, Sir Rupert Rodney Francis Tress, Bt., M.B.E. (1809).

Bartlett, *Lt.-Col.* Sir Basil Hardington, Bt. (1913).

Barton, Sir Charles Newton, Kt., O.B.E., E.D.

Barton, *Prof.* Sir Derek Harold Richard, Kt., F.R.S., F.R.S.E.

Barttelot, Sir Brian Walter de Stopham, Bt. (1875).

Barwick, *Rt. Hon.* Sir Garfield Edward John, G.C.M.G.

Barwick, Sir Richard Llewellyn, Bt. (1912).

Bassett, Sir Walter Eric, K.B.E., M.C.

Basten, Sir Henry Bolton, Kt., C.M.G.

Bastyan, *Lt.-Gen.* Sir Edric Montague, K.C.M.G., K.C.V.O., K.B.E., C.B.

Bate, Sir William Edwin, Kt. O.B.E.

Bateman, Sir Cecil Joseph, K.B.E.

Bateman, Sir Charles Harold, K.C.M.G., M.C.

Bateman, Sir Geoffrey Hirst, Kt., F.R.C.S.

Bateman, Sir Ralph Merton, K.B.E.

Bates, Sir Alfred, Kt., M.C.

Bates, *Maj.-Gen.* Sir (Edward) John (Hunter), K.B.E., C.B., M.C.

Bates, Sir Geoffrey Voltelin, Bt., M.C. (1880).

Bates, Sir John David, Kt., C.B.E., V.R.D.

Bates, Sir (John) Dawson, Bt., (1937).

Bates, Sir (Julian) Darrell, Kt., C.M.G., C.V.O.

Batho, Sir Maurice Benjamin, Bt., (1928).

Bathurst, Sir Frederick Peter Methuen Hervey-, Bt. (1818).

Batsford, Sir Brian Caldwell Cook, Kt.

Batterbee, Sir Harry Fagg, G.C.M.G., K.C.V.O.

Batty, Sir William Bradshaw, Kt., T.D.

Baxter, *Prof.* Sir (John) Philip, K.B.E., C.M.G.

Bayly, *Vice-Adm.* Sir Patrick Uniacke, K.B.E., C.B., D.S.C.

Baynes, *Lt.-Col.* Sir Rory Malcolm Stuart, Bt. (1801).

Bazley, Sir Thomas Stafford, Bt. (1869).

Bazl-ul-lah, *Sahib Bahadur* K. B., Sir Muhammad, Kt., C.I.E., O.B.E.

Beadle, Sir Gerald Clayton, Kt., C.B.E.

Beadle, *Rt. Hon.* Sir (Thomas) Hugh (William), Kt., C.M.G., O.B.E.

Beale, *Hon.* Sir (Oliver) Howard, K.B.E., Q.C.

Beale, Sir William Francis, Kt., O.B.E.

Bean, Sir Edgar Layton, Kt., C.M.G.

Beaton, Sir Cecil Walter Hardy, Kt., C.B.E.

Beattie, *Hon.* Sir Alexander Craig, Kt.

Beauchamp, Sir Brograve Campbell, Bt. (1911).

Beauchamp, Sir Christopher Radstock Proctor-, Bt. (1745).

Beauchamp, Sir Douglas Clifford, Bt. (1918).

Beaumont, Sir George (Howland Francis), Bt. (1661).

Beaumont, Sir Richard Ashton, K.C.M.G., O.B.E.

Becher, Sir William Fane Wrixon, Bt., M.C. (1831).

Beck, Sir Edgar Charles, Kt., C.B.E.

Becker, Sir Jack Ellerton, Kt.

Beckett, *Capt.* Sir (Martyn) Gervase, Bt., M.C., (1921).

Bedingfeld, *Capt.* Sir Edmund George Felix Paston-, Bt. (1661).

Bednall, *Maj.-Gen.* Sir Peter, K.B.E., C.B., M.C.

Beecham, Sir Adrian Welles, Bt. (1914).

Beeley, Sir Harold, K.C.M.G., C.B.E.

Beetham, Sir Edward Betham, K.C.M.G., C.V.O., O.B.E.

Beevor, Sir Thomas Agnew, Bt. (1784).

Begg, *Admiral of the Fleet* Sir Varyl Cargill, G.C.B., D.S.O., D.S.C.

Behrens, Sir Leonard Frederick, Kt., C.B.E.

Beit, Sir Alfred Lane, Bt. (1924).

Beith, Sir John Greville Stanley, K.C.M.G.

Bell, Sir Arthur Capel Herbert, Kt.

Bell, Sir Gawain Westray, K.C.M.G., C.B.E.

Bell, Sir (George) Raymond, K.C.M.G., C.B.

Bell, Sir John Lowthian, Bt. (1885).

Bell, Sir William Hollin Dayrell Morrison-, Bt. (1905).

Bellew, Sir Arthur John Grattan-, Kt., C.M.G., Q.C.

Bellew, *Hon.* Sir George Rothe, K.C.B., K.C.V.O., F.S.A.

Bellew, Sir Henry Charles Gratton-, Bt. (1838).

Bellinger, Sir Robert Ian, G.B.E.

Bellingham, Sir Noel Peter Roger, Bt. (1796).

Bemrose, Sir (John) Maxwell, Kt.

Benn, *Capt.* Sir (Patrick Ion) Hamilton, Bt. (1920).

Benn, Sir John Andrews, Bt. (1914).

Bennett, Sir Arnold Lucas, Kt., Q.C.

Bennett, Sir Charles Mothi Te Arawaka, Kt., D.S.O.

Bennett, Sir Frederic Mackarness, Kt., M.P.

Bennett, Sir Hubert, Kt.

Bennett, Sir John Wheeler Wheeler-, G.C.V.O., C.M.G., O.B.E., F.B.A.

Bennett, Sir Ronald Wilfrid Murdoch, Bt. (1929).

Bennett, Sir Thomas Penberthy, K.B.E.

Bennett, Sir William Gordon, Kt.

Benson, Sir Arthur Edward Trevor, G.C.M.G.

Benson, *Rev.* Sir (Clarence) Irving, Kt., C.B.E.

Benson, Sir Henry Alexander, G.B.E.

Benstead, Sir John, Kt., C.B.E.

Benthall, Sir (Arthur) Paul, K.B.E.

Bentinck, *Maj.* Sir Ferdinand William Cavendish-, K.B.E., C.M.G.

Berar, H.H. the Prince of, G.C.I.E., G.B.E.

Berkeley, Sir Lennox Randal Francis, Kt., C.B.E.

Berlin, Sir Isaiah, Kt., O.M., C.B.E.

Bernard, Sir Dallas Gerald Mercer, Bt. (1954).

Berney, Sir Julian Reedham Stuart Bt., (1620).

Berrill, Sir Kenneth Ernest, K.C.B.

Berry, Sir (Henry) Vaughan, Kt.

Berryman, *General* Sir Frank Horton, K.C.V.O., C.B., C.B.E., D.S.O.

Berthoud, Sir Eric Alfred, K.C.M.G.

Bethune, Sir Alexander Maitland Sharp, Bt. (s 1683).

Betjeman, Sir John, Kt., C.B.E.

Bevan, Sir Martyn Evan Evans, Bt. (1958).

Bevan, *Rear-Adm.* Sir Richard Hugh Loraine, K.B.E., C.B., D.S.O., M.V.O.

Beverley, *Vice-Adm.* Sir (William) York (La Roche), K.B.E., C.B.

Bevir, Sir Anthony, K.C.V.O., C.B.E.

Bibby, *Maj.* Sir (Arthur) Harold, Bt., D.S.O. (1959).

Biddulph, Sir Francis Henry, Bt. (1664).

Biggart, *Prof.* Sir (John) Henry, Kt., C.B.E., D.SC., M.D., F.R.C.P.

Biggs, *Vice-Adm.* Sir Hilary Worthington, K.B.E., C.B., D.S.O.

Biggs, Sir Lionel William, Kt.

Bing, Sir Rudolf Franz Josef, K.B.E.

Bird, *Lt.-Gen.* Sir Clarence August, K.C.I.E., C.B., D.S.O.

Bird, Sir Cyril Pangbourne, Kt.

Bird, Sir Richard Geoffrey Chapman, Bt. (1922).

Bird, *Col.* Sir Richard Dawnay Martin-, Kt., C.B.E., T.D.

Birkin, Sir Charles Lloyd, Bt. (1905).

Birkmyre, Sir Henry, Bt. (1921).

Birley, Sir Robert, K.C.M.G., F.S.A.

Birsay, Lord, *see* Leslie, Sir Harald.

Bishop, Sir Frederick Arthur, Kt., C.B., C.V.O.

Bishop, Sir George Sidney, Kt., C.B., O.B.E.

Bishop, Sir Harold, Kt., C.B.E.

Bishop, *Instructor Rear-Adm.*, Sir William Alfred, K.B.E., C.B.

Bishop, *Maj.-Gen.* Sir William Henry Alexander, K.C.M.G., C.B., C.V.O., O.B.E.

Bishop, Sir William Poole, Kt., C.M.G.

Black, Sir Cyril Wilson, Kt.

Black, *Prof.* Sir Douglas Andrew Kilgour, Kt., M.D., F.R.C.P.

Black, Sir Harold, Kt.

Black, Sir Hermann David, Kt.

Black, *Prof.* Sir Misha, Kt., O.B.E.

Black, Sir Robert Andrew Stransham, Bt. (1922).

Black, Sir Robert Brown, G.C.M.G., O.B.E.

Blackall, Sir Henry William Butler, Kt., Q.C.

Blackburne, Sir Kenneth William, G.C.M.G., G.B.E.

Blacker, *General* Sir Cecil Hugh, G.C.B., O.B.E., M.C.

Blackett, Sir George William, Bt. (1673).

Blackwell, Sir Basil Henry, Kt.

Blackwood, Sir Francis Elliot Temple, Bt. (1819).

Blackwood, Sir Robert Rutherford, Kt.

Blagden, Sir John Ramsay, Kt., O.B.E., T.D.

Blair, *Maj.* Sir Alastair Campbell, K.C.V.O., T.D.

Blair, *Lt.-Gen.* Sir Chandos, K.C.V.O., O.B.E., M.C.

Blair, Sir James Hunter-, Bt. (1786).

Blake, Sir (Francis) Michael, Bt. (1907).

Blake, Sir Thomas Richard Valentine, Bt. (I 1622).

Blaker, Sir John, Bt. (1919).

Blakiston, Sir Arthur Norman Hunter, Bt. (1763).

Bland, Sir Henry Armand, Kt., C.B.E.

Blennerhassett, Sir Marmaduke Adrian Francis William, Bt. (1809).

Bligh, Sir Edward Clare, Kt.

Blois, Sir Charles Nicholas Gervase, Bt. (1686).

Blomefield, Sir Thomas Edward Peregrine, Bt. (1807).

Bloomfield, *Hon.* Sir John Stoughton, Kt., Q.C.

Blosse, Sir Richard Hely Lynch-, Bt. (1622).

Blount, Sir Edward Robert, Bt. (1642).

Blundell, Sir (Edward) Denis, G.C.M.G., G.C.V.O., K.B.E.

Blundell, Sir Michael, K.B.E.

Blunden, Sir William, Bt. (I 1766).

Blunt, *Prof.* Sir Anthony Frederick, K.C.V.O., F.B.A.

Blunt, Sir David Richard Reginald, Bt. (1720).

Blyde, Sir Henry Ernest, K.B.E.

Bodilly, *Hon.* Sir Jocelyn, Kt., V.R.D.

Boevey, Sir Thomas Michael Blake Crawley-, Bt. (1784).

Boileau, Sir Gilbert George Benson, Bt. (1838).

Boles, Sir Jeremy John Fortescue, Bt. (1922).

Bollers, *Hon.* Sir Harold Brodie Smith, Kt.

Bolte, *Hon.* Sir Henry Edward, G.C.M.G.

Bolton, Sir George Lewis French, G.C.M.G.

Bolton, Sir Ian Frederick Cheney, Bt., K.B.E. (1927).

Bonallack, Sir Richard Frank, Kt., C.B.E.

Bonar, Sir Herbert Vernon, Kt., C.B.E.

Bondi, *Prof.* Sir Hermann, K.C.B., F.R.S.

Bonham, *Maj.* Sir Antony Lionel Thomas, Bt. (1852).

Bonsor, Sir Bryan Cosmo, Bt., M.C., T.D. (1925).

Boord, Sir Richard William, Bt. (1896).

Booth, Sir Douglas Allen, Bt. (1916).

Booth, Sir Michael Savile Gore-, Bt. (I 1760).

Boothby, Sir Hugo Robert Brooke, Bt. (1660).

Boreel, Sir Francis David, Bt. (1645).

Boreham, *Hon.* Sir Leslie Kenneth Edward, Kt.

Bornu, The Waziri of, K.C.M.G., C.B.E.

Borthwick, Sir John Thomas, Bt. M.B.E. (1908).

Borwick, *Lt.-Col.* Sir Thomas Faulkner, Kt., C.I.E., D.S.O.

Bossom, *Maj. Hon.* Sir Clive, Bt. (1953).

Boswall, Sir Thomas Houstoun-, Bt. (1836).

Bottomley, Sir James Reginald Alfred, K.C.M.G.

Bouchier, *Air Vice-Marshal* Sir Cecil Arthur, K.B.E., C.B., D.F.C.

Boughey, Sir Richard James, Bt. (1798).

Boult, Sir Adrian Cedric, Kt., C.H., D.Mus.

Boulton, Sir Edward John, Bt. (1944).

Boulton, Sir Harold Hugh Christian, Bt. (1905).

Boulton, Sir William Whytehead, Kt., C.B.E., T.D.

Bourke, *Hon.* Sir Paget John, Kt.

Bourne, Sir Frederick Chalmers, K.C.S.I., C.I.E.

Boustead, *Col.* (Sir John Edmund) Hugh, K.B.E., C.M.G., D.S.O., M.C.

Bovenschen, Sir Frederick Carl, K.C.B., K.B.E.

Bowater, *Lt. Col.* Sir Ian Frank, G.B.E., D.S.O., T.D.

Bowater, Sir (John) Vansittart, Bt. (1914).

Bowater, Sir Noel Vansittart, Bt., G.B.E., M.C. (1939).

Bowden, Sir Frank, Bt. (1915).

Bowen, Sir Thomas Frederic Charles, Bt. (1921).

Bower, Sir John Dykes, Kt., C.V.O.

Bower, Sir Frank, Kt., C.B.E.

Bower, *Air Marshal* Sir Leslie William Clement, K.C.B., D.S.O., D.F.C.

Bower, *Lt.-Gen.* Sir Roger Herbert, K.C.B., K.B.E.

Bower, Sir (William) Guy Nott-, K.B.E., C.B.

Bowes, Sir (Harold) Leslie K.C.M.G., C.B.E.

Bowker, Sir (Reginald) James, G.B.E., K.C.M.G.

Bowlby, Sir Anthony Hugh Mostyn, Bt. (1923).

Bowman, Sir James, Bt., K.B.E. (1961).

Bowman, Sir John Paget, Bt. (1884).

Boxer, *Air Vice-Marshal* Sir Alan Hunter Cachemaille, K.C.V.O., C.B., D.S.O., D.F.C.

Boyce, Sir Robert Charles Leslie, Bt. (1916).

Boyd, Sir Alexander Walter, Bt. (1916).

Boyd, *Brig.* Sir John Smith Knox, Kt., O.B.E., M.D., F.R.S.

Boyes, Sir Brian Gerald Barratt-, K.B.E.

Boyle, *Marshal of the Royal Air Force* Sir Dermot Alexander, G.C.B., K.C.V.O., K.B.E., A.F.C.

Brabin, *Hon.* Sir Daniel James, Kt., M.C.

Bradbury, *Surgeon Vice-Adm.* Sir Eric Blackburn, K.B.E., C.B.

Bradford, Sir Edward Alexander Slade, Bt. (1902).

Bradlaw, *Prof.* Sir Robert Vivian, Kt., C.B.E.

Bradley, *Air Marshal* Sir John Stanley Travers, K.C.B., C.B.E.

Bradley, Sir Kenneth Granville, Kt., C.M.G.

Bradman, Sir Donald George, Kt.

Brain, Sir (Henry) Norman, K.B.E., C.M.G.

Brain, Sir Hugh Gerner, Kt., C.B.E., M.S.M.

Braine, Sir Bernard Richard, Kt., M.P.

Bramall, *Lt.-Gen.* Sir Edwin Noel Westby, K.C.B., O.B.E., M.C.

Bramall, Sir (Ernest) Ashley, Kt.

Brancker, *His Hon.* Sir (John Eustace) Theodore, Kt., Q.C.

Brand, *Hon.* Sir David, K.C.M.G.

Brand, Sir (William) Alfred, Kt., C.B.E.

Brandon, *Hon.* Sir Henry Vivian, Kt., M.C.

Branigan, Sir Patrick Francis, Kt., Q.C.

Branson, Col. Sir Douglas Stephenson, K.B.E., C.B., D.S.O., M.C., T.D.

Bray, *General* Sir Robert Napier Hubert Campbell, G.B.E., K.C.B., D.S.O.

Bray, Sir Theodore Charles, Kt., C.B.E.

Braynen, Sir Alvin Rudolph, Kt.

Brearley, Sir Norman, Kt., C.B.E., D.S.O., M.C., A.F.C.

Brebner, Sir Alexander, Kt., C.I.E.

Brechin, Sir (Herbert) Archbold, K.B.E.

Brett, *Hon.* Sir Lionel, Kt.

Brickwood, Sir Basil Graeme, Bt. (1927).

Bridge, *Rt. Hon.* Sir Nigel Cyprian, Kt.

Bridgeman, *Hon.* Sir Maurice Richard, K.B.E.

Bridges, *Hon.* Sir Phillip Rodney, Kt., C.M.G.

Briercliffe, Sir Rupert, Kt., C.M.G. O.B.E., M.D.

Briggs, Sir (Alfred) George (Ernest), Kt.

Briggs, *Hon.* Sir Francis Arthur, Kt.

Briggs, *Hon.* Sir Geoffrey Gould, Kt.

Brightman, *Hon.* Sir John Anson, Kt.

Brimelow, Sir Thomas, G.C.M.G., O.B.E.

Brinckman, *Col.* Sir Roderick Napoleon, Bt. D.S.O., M.C. (1831).

Brinton, *Maj.* Sir (Esme) Tatton (Cecil), Kt.

Brisco, Sir Donald Gilfrid, Bt. (1782).

Briscoe, Sir John Leigh Charlton, Bt., D.F.C. (1910).

Brise, Sir John Archibald Ruggles-, Bt., C.B., O.B.E., T.D. (1935).

Bristow, *Hon.* Sir Peter Henry Rowley, Kt.

Britton, Sir Edward Louis, Kt., C.B.E.

Broad, *Lt.-Gen.* Sir Charles Noel Frank, K.C.B., D.S.O.

Broadbent, Sir William Francis Bt. (1893).

Broadhurst, *Air Chief Marshal* Sir Harry, G.C.B., K.B.E., D.S.O., D.F.C., A.F.C.

Broadley, Sir Herbert, K.B.E.

Broadmead, Sir Philip Mainwaring, K.C.M.G., M.C.

Brocklebank, Sir Aubrey Thomas, Bt. (1885).

Brocklehurst, Sir John Ogilvy, Bt. (1903).

Brockman, *Vice-Adm.* Sir Ronald Vernon, K.C.B., C.S.I., C.I.E., C.B.E.

Brodie, Sir Benjamin David Ross, Bt. (1834).

Brodie, *Very Rev.* Sir Israel, K.B.E.

Brogan, *Lt.-Gen.* Sir Mervyn Francis, K.B.E., C.B.

Bromet, *Air Vice-Marshal* Sir Geoffrey Rhodes, K.B.E., C.B., D.S.O.

Bromhead, *Lt.-Col.* Sir Benjamin Denis Gonville, Bt., O.B.E. (1806).

Bromley, Sir Rupert Charles, Bt. (1757).

Bromley, Sir Thomas Eardley, K.C.M.G.

Brook, Sir Robin, Kt., C.M.G.

Brooke, *Maj.* Sir George Cecil Francis, Bt. (1903).

Brooke, *Maj.* Sir John Weston, Bt. (1919).

Brooke, Sir (Norman) Richard (Rowley), Kt., C.B.E.

Brooke, Sir Richard Christopher, Bt. (1662).

Brookes, Sir Raymond Percival, Kt.

Brooksbank, Sir (Edward) William, Bt. (1919).

Broom, *Air Marshal* Sir Ivor Gordon, K.C.B., C.B.E., D.S.O., D.F.C., A.F.C.

Brotherston, Sir John Howie Flint, Kt., M.D., F.R.S.E.

Broughton, Sir Alfred Davies Devonsher, Kt., M.P.

Broughton, *Air Marshal* Sir Charles, K.B.E., C.B.

Broughton, Sir Evelyn Delves, Bt. (1661).

Broun, Sir Lionel John Law, Bt. (s 1686).

Brown, Sir Allen Stanley, Kt., C.B.E.

Brown, Sir (Arthur James) Stephen, K.B.E.

Brown, *Lt.-Col.* Sir (Charles Frederick) Richmond, Bt. (1863).

Brown, Sir Charles James Officer, Kt., M.D.

Brown, Sir (Cyril) Maxwell (Palmer), K.C.B., C.M.G.

Brown, Sir David, Kt.

Brown, Sir Edward Joseph, Kt., M.B.E., M.P.

Brown, Sir (Frederick Herbert) Stanley, Kt., C.B.E.

Brown, Sir James Raitt, Kt.

Brown, Sir John Douglas Keith, Kt.

Brown, Sir John Gilbert Newton, Kt., C.B.E.

Brown, Sir Kenneth Alfred Leader, Kt.

Brown, *Air Vice-Marshal* Sir Leslie Oswald, K.C.B., C.B.E., D.S.C., A.F.C.

Brown, *Hon.* Sir Ralph Kilner, Kt., O.B.E., T.D.

Brown, Sir Raymond Frederick, Kt., O.B.E.

Brown, Sir Robert Crichton-, Kt., C.B.E.

Brown, *Hon.* Sir Stephen, Kt.

Brown, Sir Thomas, Kt.

Brown, *Air Commodore* Sir Vernon Sydney, Kt., C.B., O.B.E.

Brown, Sir William Brian Pigott-, Bt. (1903).

Browne, Sir (Edward) Humphrey, Kt., C.B.E.

Browne, *Rt. Hon.* Sir Patrick Reginald Evelyn, Kt., O.B.E., T.D.

Brownrigg, Sir Nicholas (Gawen), Bt. (1816).

Bruce, Sir Arthur Atkinson, K.B.E., M.C.

Bruce, Sir (Francis) Michael Ian, Bt. (s 1628).

Bruce, Sir Hervey James Hugh, Bt. (1804).

Bruce, *Hon.* Sir (James) Roualeyn Hovell-Thurlow-Cumming-, Kt.

Bruce, *Prof.* Sir John, Kt., C.B.E., T.D.

Brune, Sir Humphrey Ingelram Prideaux, K.B.E., C.M.G.

Brunner, Sir Felix John Morgan, Bt. (1895).

Brunton, Sir (Edward Francis) Lauder, Bt. (1908).

Bryan, Sir Andrew Meikle, Kt.

Bryan, Sir Paul Elmore Oliver, Kt., D.S.O., M.C., M.P.

Bryant, Sir Arthur Wynne Morgan, Kt., C.H., C.B.E.

Bryce, *Hon.* Sir (William) Gordon, Kt., C.B.E.

Buchan, Sir John, Kt., C.M.G.

Buchanan, Sir Charles Alexander James Leith-, Bt. (1775).

Buchanan, Sir Charles James, Bt. (1878).

Buchanan, *Prof.* Sir Colin Douglas, Kt., C.B.E.

Buchanan, Sir John Cecil Rankin, K.C.M.G., M.D.

Buchanan, *Maj.* Sir Reginald Narcissus Macdonald-, K.C.V.O., M.B.E., M.C.

Bucher, *General* Sir Roy, K.B.E., C.B., M.C.

Buckley, *Rt. Hon.* Sir Denys Burton, Kt., M.B.E.

Buckley, *Rear-Adm.* Sir Kenneth Robertson, K.B.E.

Budd, *Hon.* Sir Harry Vincent, Kt.

Bulkeley, Sir Richard Harry David Williams-, Bt. (1661).

Bull, Sir George, Bt. (1922).

Bullard, Sir Edward Crisp, Kt., Ph.D., Sc.D., F.R.S.

Bullard, Sir Reader William, K.C.B., K.C.M.G., C.I.E.

Bullock, Sir Alan Louis Charles, Kt., F.B.A.

Bullock, Sir Ernest, Kt., C.V.O. MUS.D.

Bullus, Sir Eric Edward, Kt.

Bulmer, Sir William Peter, Kt.

Bunbury, Sir (John) William Napier, Bt. (1681).

Bunbury, Sir (Richard David) Michael Richardson-, Bt. (I 1787).

Bunting, Sir (Edward) John, Kt., C.B.E.

Burbidge, Sir Herbert Dudley, Bt. (1916).

Burbury, Hon. Sir Stanley Charles, K.B.E.

Burder, Sir John Henry, Kt.

Burdett, Sir Savile Aylmer, Bt. (1665).

Burgess, Sir John Lawie, Kt., O.B.E., T.D.

Burgess, Sir Thomas Arthur Collier, Kt.

Burke, Sir Aubrey Francis, Kt. O.B.E.

Burke, Sir Thomas Stanley, Bt. (I 1797).

Burman, Sir (John) Charles, Kt.

Burman, Sir Stephen France, Kt., C.B.E.

Burne, Sir Lewis Charles, Kt., C.B.E., A.F.C.

Burnet, Sir (Frank) Macfarlane, O.M., K.B.E., M.D., F.R.S.

Burnett, Air Chief Marshal Sir Brian Kenyon, G.C.B., D.F.C., A.F.C.

Burnett, Maj. Sir David Humphery, Bt., M.B.E., T.D. (1913).

Burney, Sir Anthony George Bernard, Kt., O.B.E.

Burney, Sir Cecil Denniston, Bt. (1921).

Burns, Sir Alan Cuthbert, G.C.M.G.

Burns, Sir Charles Ritchie, K.B.E., M.D.

Burns, Sir John Crawford, Kt.

Burns, Sir Malcolm McRae, K.B.E.

Burns, Maj.-Gen. Sir (Walter Arthur) George, K.C.V.O., C.B., D.S.O., O.B.E., M.C.

Burrell, Vice-Adm. Sir Henry Mackay, K.B.E., C.B.

Burrell, Sir Walter Raymond, Bt., C.B.E., T.D. (1774).

Burrough, Admiral Sir Harold Martin, G.C.B., K.B.E., D.S.O.

Burrows, Sir Bernard Alexander Brocas, G.C.M.G.

Burrows, Sir (Robert) John (Formby), Kt.

Burton, Air Marshal Sir Harry, K.C.B., C.B.E., D.S.O.

Busby, Sir Matthew, Kt., C.B.E.

Bush, Admiral Sir John Fitzroy Duyland, G.C.B., D.S.C.

Busk, Sir Douglas Laird, K.C.M.G.

Bustamante, Rt. Hon. Sir (William) Alexander, Kt.

Butland, Sir Jack Richard, K.B.E.

Butler, General Sir Mervyn Andrew Haldane, K.C.B., C.B.E., D.S.O., M.C.

Butler, Hon. Sir Milo Boughton, G.C.M.G., G.C.V.O.

Butler, Sir (Reginald) Michael (Thomas), Bt. (1922).

Butler, Lt.-Col. Sir Thomas Pierce, Bt. C.V.O., D.S.O., O.B.E. (1628).

Butlin, Sir William Edmund, Kt., M.B.E.

Butt, Sir (Alfred) Kenneth Dudley, Bt. (1929).

Butterfield, Sir Harry Durham, Kt., C.B.E.

Butterfield, Prof. Sir Herbert, Kt., F.B.A.

Butterworth, Sir (George) Neville, Kt.

Buxton, Sir Thomas Fowell Victor, Bt. (1840).

Buzzard, Sir Anthony Farquhar, Bt. (1929).

Byass, Col. Sir Geoffrey Robert Sidney, Bt., T.D. (1926).

Byrne, Sir Clarence Askew, Kt., O.B.E., D.S.C.

Cader, Sir Hussein Hassanaly Abdool, Kt., C.B.E.

Cadwallader, Sir John, Kt.

Cadzow, Sir Norman James Kerr, Kt., V.R.D.

Caffyn, Brig. Sir Edward Roy, K.B.E., C.B., T.D.

Caffyn, Sir Sydney Morris, Kt., C.B.E.

Cahn, Sir Albert Jonas, Bt. (1934).

Cain, Sir Edward Thomas, Kt., C.B.E.

Caine, Sir Sydney, K.C.M.G.

Cairncross, Sir Alexander Kirkland, K.C.M.G.

Cairns, Rt. Hon. Sir David Arnold Scott, Kt.

Cairns, Sir Joseph Foster, Kt.

Cakobau, Ratu Sir George, G.C.M.G., O.B.E.

Caldicott, Hon. Sir John Moore, K.B.E., C.M.G.

Caldwell, Surgeon Vice-Adm. Sir Eric Dick, K.B.E., C.B.

Callaghan, Sir Allan Robert, Kt., C.M.G.

Callander, Lt.-Gen. Sir Colin Bishop, K.C.B., K.B.E., M.C,

Callard, Sir Eric John, Kt.

Calley, Sir Henry Algernon, Kt., D.S.O., D.F.C.

Calthorpe, Brig. Sir Richard Hamilton Anstruther-Gough-, Bt., C.B.E. (1929).

Cameron, Lt.-Gen. Sir Alexander Maurice, K.B.E., C.B., M.C.

Cameron of Lochiel, Sir Donald Hamish, K.T., C.V.O., T.D.

Cameron, Hon. Sir John, Kt., D.S.C., Q.C. (Lord Cameron).

Cameron, Air Marshal Sir Neil, K.C.B., C.B.E., D.S.O., D.F.C.

Camilleri, His Hon. Sir Luigi Antonio, Kt, Ll.D.

Campbell, Maj.-Gen. Sir (Alexander) Douglas, K.B.E., C.B., D.S.O., M.C.

†Campbell, Sir Bruce Colin Patrick, Bt. (s 1804).

Campbell, Sir Clifford Clarence, G.C.M.G., G.C.V.O.

Campbell, Sir Colin, Kt., O.B.E.

Campbell, Sir Colin Moffat, Bt., M.C. (s 1668).

Campbell, Prof. Sir David, Kt., M.C., M.D., Ll.D., F.R.S.E.

Campbell, Col. Sir Guy Theophilus Halswell, Bt., O.B.E., M.C. (1815).

Campbell, Maj.-Gen. Sir Hamish Manus, K.B.E., C.B.

Campbell, Vice-Adm. Sir Ian Murray Robertson, K.B.E., C.B., D.S.O.

Campbell, Sir Ian Vincent Hamilton, Bt., C.B. (1831).

Campbell, Sir Ilay Mark, Bt. (1808).

Campbell, Sir John Johnston, Kt., C.B., F.R.S.E.

Campbell, Sir Matthew, K.B.E., C.B., F.R.S.E.

Campbell, Sir Ralph Abercromby, Kt.

Campbell, Sir Robin Auchinbreck, Bt. (S. 1628).

Campbell, Rt. Hon. Sir Ronald Ian, G.C.M.G., C.B.

Campbell, Sir Thomas Cockburn-, Bt. (1821).

Campion, Sir Harry, Kt., C.B., C.B.E.

Cantley, Hon. Sir Joseph Donaldson, Kt., O.B.E.

Cantlie, Sir Keith, Kt., C.I.E.

Capper, Sir (William) Derrick, Kt.

Carberry, Sir John Edward Doston, Kt.

Carden, Lt.-Col. Sir Henry Christopher, Bt., O.B.E. (1887).

Carden, Sir John Craven, Bt. (I 1787).

Carew, Sir Thomas Palk, Bt. (1661).

Carlill, Vice-Adm. Sir Stephen Hope, K.B.E., C.B., D.S.O.

Carmichael, Sir David Peter William Gibson-Craig-, Bt. (s 1702 and 1831).

Carmichael, Sir John, K.B.E.

Carnac, Rev. Sir Thomas Nicholas Rivett-, Bt. (1836).

Carnwath, Sir Andrew Hunter, K.C.V.O.

Caröe, Sir (Einar) Athelstan (Gordon), Kt., C.B.E.

Caroe, Sir Olaf Kirkpatrick, K.C.S.I., K.C.I.E.

Carr, Sir (Frederick) Bernard, Kt., C.M.G.

Carr, Air Marshal Sir John Darcy Baker-, K.B.E., C.B., A.F.C.

Carr, Sir William Emsley, Kt.

Carreras, Lt.-Col. Sir James, Kt., M.B.E.

Carroll, Sir Alfred Thomas, K.B.E.

Carter, Sir (Arthur) Desmond Bonham-, Kt., T.D.

Carter, Sir Derrick Hunton, Kt., T.D.

Carter, Sir John, Kt., Q.C.

Carter, His Hon. Sir Walker Kelly, Kt., Q.C.

Carter, Sir William Oscar, Kt.

Cartland, Sir George Barrington, Kt., C.M.G.

Carver, Field-Marshal Sir (Richard) Michael (Power), G.C.B., C.B.E., D.S.O., M.C.

Cary, Sir (Arthur Lucius) Michael, K.C.B.

Cary, Sir Robert Archibald, Bt. (1955).

Cash, Sir Thomas James, K.B.E., C.B.

Cassel, Sir Harold Felix, Bt., Q.C. (1920).

Cassels, *Field Marshal* Sir (Archibald) James Halkett, G.C.B., K.B.E., D.S.O.

Cassidy, Sir Jack Evelyn, Kt.

Casson, Sir Hugh Maxwell, Kt., R.A., F.R.I.B.A.

Catherwood, Sir (Henry) Frederick (Ross), Kt.

Catlin, *Prof.* Sir George Edward Gordon, Kt., Ph.D.

Catling, Sir Richard Charles, Kt., C.M.G., O.B.E.

Caughey, Sir (Thomas) Herbert Clarke, K.B.E.

Caulfield, *Hon.* Sir Bernard, Kt.

Cave, Sir Charles Edward Coleridge, Bt. (1896).

Cave, Sir Robert Cave-Browne-, Bt. (1641).

Cawley, Sir Charles Mills, Kt., C.B.E., Ph.D.

Cayley, Sir Digby William David, Bt. (1661).

Cayzer, Sir James Arthur, Bt. (1904).

Cayzer, Sir (William) Nicholas, Bt. (1921).

Cazalet, *Vice-Adm.* Sir Peter Grenville Lyon, K.B.E., C.B., D.S.O., D.S.C.

Chacksfield, *Air Vice-Marshal* Sir Bernard Albert, K.B.E., C.B.

Chadwick, Sir Albert Edward, Kt., C.M.G., M.S.M.

Chadwick, Sir John Edward, K.C.M.G.

Chadwick, Sir Robert Burton Burton-, Bt. (1935).

Chain, *Prof.* Sir Ernest Boris, Kt., F.R.S., Ph.D., D.Phil.

Chalk, *Hon.* Sir Gordon William Wesley, K.B.E.

Chamberlain, Sir Henry Wilmot, Bt. (1828).

Chamberlain, *Hon.* Sir Reginald Roderic St. Clair, Kt.

Chambers, Sir (Stanley) Paul, K.B.E., C.B., C.I.E.

Champion, *Prof.* Sir Harry George, Kt., C.I.E., D.Sc.

Champion, *Rev.* Sir Reginald Stuart, K.C.M.G., O.B.E.

Champneys, *Capt.* Sir Weldon Dalrymple-, Bt., C.B. (1910).

Chance, Sir Roger James Ferguson, Bt., M.C. (1900).

Chance, Sir (William) Hugh (Stobart), Kt., C.B.E.

Chancellor, Sir Christopher John, Kt., C.M.G.

Chandler, *Hon.* Sir Gilbert Lawrence, K.B.E., C.M.G.

Chaplin, Sir Charles Spencer, K.B.E.

Chapman, Sir Robert Macgowan, Bt., C.B.E., T.D. (1958).

Chapman, *Air Chief Marshal* Sir Ronald Ivelaw-, G.C.B., K.B.E., D.F.C., A.F.C.

Chapman, *Hon.* Sir Stephen, Kt.

Charles, Sir John Pendrill, K.C.V.O., M.C.

Charles, Sir Noel Hughes Havelock, K.C.M.G., M.C. (1928).

Charley, Sir Philip Belmont, Kt.

Charlton, *Commodore* Sir William Arthur, Kt., D.S.C.

Charrington, Sir John, Kt.

Charteris, *Lt.-Col.* Rt. Hon. Sir Martin Michael Charles, K.C.B., K.C.V.O., O.B.E.

Chau, Sir Sik-nin, Kt., C.B.E.

Chaytor, Sir William Henry Clervaux, Bt. (1831).

Cheetham, Sir Nicolas John Alexander, K.C.M.G.

Chegwidden, Sir Thomas Sidney, Kt., C.B., C.V.O.

Cheshire, *Air Chief Marshal* Sir Walter Graeme, G.B.E., K.C.B.

Chester, Sir (Daniel) Norman, Kt., C.B.E.

Chesterman, Sir Clement Clapton, Kt., O.B.E.

Chesterman, Sir (Dudley) Ross, Kt., Ph.D.

Chesterton, Sir Oliver Sidney, Kt., M.C.

Chetwynd, Sir Arthur Ralph Talbot, Bt. (1795).

Cheyne, Sir Joseph Lister Watson, Bt. (1908).

Chichester, Sir (Edward) John, Bt. (1641).

Child, Sir (Coles John) Jeremy, Bt. (1919).

Chilton, *Air Marshal* Sir (Charles) Edward, K.B.E., C.B.

Chilton, *Brig.* Sir Frederick Oliver, Kt., C.B.E., D.S.O.

Chinoy, Sir Sultan Meherally, Kt.

Chisholm, Sir Henry, Kt., C.B.E.

Chitty, Sir Thomas Willes, Bt. (1924).

Cholmeley, Sir Montague John, Bt. (1896).

Christie, *Hon.* Sir Vernon Howard Colville, Kt.

Christie, Sir William, K.C.I.E., C.S.I., M.C.

Christie, Sir William, Kt., M.B.E.

Christison, *Gen.* Sir (Alexander Frank) Philip, Bt., G.B.E., C.B., D.S.O., M.C. (1871).

Christopher, Sir George Perrin, Kt.

Christophers, *Col.* Sir Samuel Rickard, Kt., C.I.E., O.B.E., F.R.S.

Christopherson, Sir Derman Guy, Kt., O.B.E., D.Phil., F.R.S.

Church, *Brig.* Sir Geoffrey Selby, Bt., C.B.E., M.C., T.D. (1901).

Cilento, Sir Raphael West, Kt., M.D.

Clague, *Col. Hon.* Sir (John) Douglas, Kt., C.B.E., M.C., T.D.

Clapham, Sir Michael John Sinclair, K.B.E.

Claringbull, Sir (Gordon) Frank, Kt., Ph.D.

Clark, Sir Andrew Edmund James, Bt., M.B.E., M.C., Q.C. (1883).

Clark, *Capt.* Sir George Anthony, Bt. (1917).

Clark, Sir George Norman, Kt., D.Litt.

Clark, Sir (Gordon) Colvin Lindesay, K.B.E., C.M.G., M.C.

Clark, Sir John Allen, Kt.

Clark, Sir John Stewart-, Bt. (1918).

Clark, Sir Robin Chichester-, Kt.

Clark, Sir Thomas, Bt. (1886).

Clark, Sir (Thomas) Fife, Kt., C.B.E.

Clarke, Sir (Charles Mansfield) Tobias, Bt. (1831).

Clarke, *Prof.* Sir Cyril Astley, K.B.E., M.D., Sc.D., F.R.S., F.R.C.P.

Clarke, Sir Ellis Emmanuel Innocent, G.C.M.G.

Clarke Sir Frederick Joseph, Kt.

Clarke, Sir (Henry) Ashley, G.C.M.G., G.C.V.O.

Clarke, Sir Henry Osmond Osmond-, K.C.V.O., C.B.E.

Clarke, Sir Percy Selwyn Selwyn-, K.B.E., C.M.G., M.C., M.D.

Clarke, Sir Rupert William John, Bt., M.B.E. (1882).

Clay, Sir Charles Travis, Kt., C.B.

Clay, Sir Henry Felix, Bt. (1841).

Clayden, *Rt. Hon.* Sir (Henry) John, Kt.

Claye, *Prof.* Sir Andrew Moynihan, Kt., M.D.

Clayson, Sir Eric Maurice, Kt.

Clayton, Sir Arthur Harold, Bt., D.S.C. (1732).

Clayton, *Air Marshal* Sir Gareth Thomas Butler, K.C.B., D.F.C.

Clayton, *Col. Hon.* Sir Hector Joseph Richard, Kt., E.D.

Clayton, *Prof.* Sir Stanley George, Kt., M.D.

Cleary, Sir Joseph Jackson, Kt.

Clee, Sir (Charles) Beaupré Bell, Kt., C.S.I., C.I.E.

Clegg, Sir Alexander Bradshaw, Kt.

Clegg, Sir Cuthbert Barwick, Kt.

Cleland, *Brig.* Sir Donald Mackinnon, Kt., C.B.E.

Clements, Sir John Selby, Kt., C.B.E.

Clerk, Sir John Dutton, Bt., C.B.E., V.R.D. (s 1679).

Clerke, Sir John Edward Longueville, Bt. (1660).

Clifford, Sir (Geoffrey) Miles, K.B.E., C.M.G., E.D.

Clifford, Sir Roger Charles Joseph Gerrard, Bt. (1887).

Clore, Sir Charles, Kt.

Clutterbuck, *Vice-Adm.* Sir David Granville, K.B.E., C.B.

Clutterbuck, Sir (Peter) Alexander, G.C.M.G., M.C.

Coate, *Maj.-Gen.* Sir Raymond Douglas, K.B.E., C.B.

Coates, Sir Albert Ernest, Kt., O.B.E., M.D.

Coates, Sir Ernest William, Kt., C.M.G.

Coates, Sir Frederick Gregory Lindsay, Bt. (1921).

Coates, Sir James Robert Edward Clive Milnes-, Bt. (1911).

Coats, Sir Alastair Francis Stuart, Bt. (1905).

Cochrane, Sir Desmond Oriel Alastair George Weston, Bt. (1903).

Cochrane, *Air Chief Marshal* Hon. Sir Ralph Alexander, G.B.E., K.C.B., A.F.C.

Cockburn, Sir John Elliot, Bt. (s 1671).

Cockburn, Sir Robert, K.B.E., C.B., Ph.D.

Cocker, Sir William Wiggins, Kt., O.B.E.

Cockerell, Sir Christopher Sydney, Kt., C.B.E., F.R.S.

Cockfield, Sir (Francis) Arthur, Kt.

Cockram, Sir John, Kt.

Cocks, Sir (Thomas George) Barnett, K.C.B., O.B.E.

Codrington, Sir Christopher William Gerald Henry, Bt. (1876).

Codrington, Sir William Alexander, Bt. (1721).

Coghill, *Capt.* Sir (Marmaduke Nevill) Patrick (Somerville), Bt. (1778).

Cohen, Sir Bernard Nathaniel Waley-, Bt. (1961).

Cohen, Sir Edward, Kt.

Cohen, Sir Jack, Kt., O.B.E.

Cohen, Sir John Edward, Kt.

Cohen, Sir Rex Arthur Louis, K.B.E.

Coldstream, Sir George Phillips, K.C.B., K.C.V.O., Q.C.

Coldstream, *Prof.* Sir William Menzies, Kt., C.B.E.

Cole, Sir David Lee, K.C.M.G., M.C.

Cole, Sir Noel, Kt.

Coles, Sir Arthur William, Kt.

Coles, Sir Edgar Barton, Kt.

Coles, Sir George James, Kt., C.B.E.

Coles, Sir Kenneth Frank, Kt.

Coles, *Air Marshal* Sir William Edward, K.B.E., C.B., D.S.O., D.F.C., A.F.C.

Colfox, Sir (William) John, Bt. (1939).

Colles, *Cmdr.* (S.) Sir (Ernest) Dudley, K.C.B., K.C.V.O., O.B.E., R.N.

Collett, Sir Ian Seymour, Bt. (1934).

Collett, Sir (Thomas) Kingsley, Kt., C.B.E.

Collier, *Air Vice-Marshal* Sir (Alfred) Conrad, K.C.B., C.B.E.

Collier, Sir Laurence, K.C.M.G.

Collingwood, *Lt.-Gen.* Sir (Richard) George, K.B.E., C.B., D.S.O.

Collins, Sir Charles Henry, Kt., C.M.G.

Collins, Sir David Charles, Kt., C.B.E.

Collins, Sir Geoffrey Abdy, Kt.

Collins, *Vice-Adm.* Sir John Augustine, K.B.E., C.B.

Collins, Sir William Alexander Roy, Kt., C.B.E.

Colman, Sir Michael Jeremiah, Bt. (1907).

Colquhoun, *Maj.-Gen.* Sir Cyril Harry, K.C.V.O., C.B., O.B.E.

Colquhoun of Luss, Sir Ivar Iain, Bt. (1786).

Colt, Sir Edward William Dutton Bt. (1694).

Colthurst, Sir Richard La Touche, Bt. (1744).

Colville, Sir (Henry) Cecil, Kt.

Colville, Sir John Rupert, Kt., C.B., C.V.O.

Combs, Sir Willis Ide, K.C.V.O., C.M.G.

Compston, *Vice-Adm.* Sir Peter Maxwell, K.C.B.

Compton, Sir Edmund Gerald, G.C.B., K.B.E.

Conant, Sir John Ernest Michael, Bt. (1954).

Connell, Sir Charles Gibson, Kt.

Connolly, Sir Willis Henry, Kt., C.B.E.

Conroy, Sir Diarmaid William, Kt., C.M.G., O.B.E., T.D., Q.C.

Constable, Sir Robert Frederick Strickland-, Bt. (1641).

Constantine, *Air Chief Marshal* Sir Hugh Alex, K.B.E., C.B., D.S.O.

Constantine, Sir Theodore, Kt., C.B.E., T.D.

Cook, Sir Francis Ferdinand Maurice, Bt. (1886).

Cook, Sir James Wilfred, Kt., D.Sc., Ph.D., F.R.S.

Cook, Sir William Richard Joseph, K.C.B., F.R.S.

Cooke, Sir Charles Arthur John, Bt. (1661).

Cooke, Sir John Fletcher-, Kt., C.M.G.

Cooke, Sir Leonard, Kt., O.B.E.

Cooke, *Hon.* Sir Samuel Burgess Ridgway, Kt.

Coop, Sir Maurice Fletcher, Kt.

Cooper, *Maj.* Sir Charles Eric Daniel, Bt. (1863).

Cooper, Sir Francis Ashmole, Bt., Ph.D. (1905).

Cooper, Sir Frank, K.C.B., C.M.G.

Cooper, *Hon.* Sir Gilbert Alexander, Kt., C.B.E., E.D.

Cooper, Sir (Harold) Stanford, Kt.

Cooper, Sir (Henry) Guy, Kt., M.C., D.C.M.

Cooper, Sir Patrick Graham Astley, Bt. (1821).

Cooper, *Prof.* Sir (William) Mansfield, Kt.

Coote, *Capt.* Sir Colin Reith, Kt., D.S.O.

Coote, *Rear-Adm.* (E.) Sir John Ralph, Bt., C.B., C.B.E., D.S.C., *Premier Baronet of Ireland* (I 1621).

Coppleson, Sir Lionel Wolfe, Kt.

Corah, Sir John Harold, Kt.

Corbet, Sir John Vincent, Bt., M.B.E. (1808).

Cordingley, *Air Vice-Marshal* Sir John Walter, K.C.B., K.C.V.O., C.B.E.

Corfield, Sir Conrad Laurence, K.C.I.E., C.S.I., M.C.

Corfield, *Rt. Hon.* Sir Frederick Vernon, Kt., Q.C.

Corley, Sir Kenneth Sholl Ferrand, Kt.

Cormack, Sir Magnus Cameron, K.B.E.

Cornwall, *General* Sir James Handyside Marshall-, K.C.B., C.B.E., D.S.O., M.C.

Corry, Sir James Perowne Ivo Myles, Bt. (1885).

Cory, Sir Clinton James Donald, Bt. (1919).

Coryton, *Air Chief Marshal* Sir (William) Alec, K.C.B., K.B.E., M.V.O., D.F.C.

Coslett, *Air Marshal* Sir (Thomas) Norman, K.C.B., O.B.E.

Costar, Sir Norman Edgar, K.C.M.G.

Cotter, *Lt.-Col.* Sir Delaval James Alfred, Bt., D.S.O. (I. 1763).

Cotterell, Sir Richard Charles Geers, Bt. C.B.E., T.D. (1805).

Cotton, Sir Charles Andrew, K.B.E.

Cotton, Sir John Richard, K.C.M.G., O.B.E.

Cottrell, Sir Alan Howard, Kt. Ph.D., F.R.S.

Cottrell, Sir Edward Baglietto, Kt., C.B.E.

Cotts, Sir (Robert) Crichton Mitchell, Bt. (1921).

Couchman, *Admiral* Sir Walter Thomas, K.C.B., C.V.O., D.S.O., O.B.E.

Coulson, Sir John Eltringham, K.C.M.G.

Couper, Sir Robert Nicholas Oliver, Bt. (1841).

Court, *Hon.* Sir Charles Walter Michael, Kt., O.B.E.

Courtenay, *Hon.* Sir (Woldrich) Harrison, Kt.

Courtenay, *Air Chief Marshal* Sir Christopher Lloyd, G.B.E., K.C.B., D.S.O.

Coutts, Sir Walter Fleming, G.C.M.G., M.B.E.

Covell, *Maj.-Gen.* Sir Gordon, C.I.E., M.D.

Cowan, Sir Christopher George Armstrong, Kt.

Cowley, *Lt.-Gen.* Sir John Guise, K.B.E., C.B.

Cowper, Sir Norman Lethbridge, Kt., C.B.E.

Cowperthwaite, Sir John James, K.B.E., C.M.G.

Cox, Sir Christopher William Machell, G.C.M.G.

Cox, Sir (Ernest) Gordon, K.B.E., T.D., D.Sc., F.R.S.

Cox, Sir Geoffrey Sandford, Kt., C.B.E.

Cox, Sir (George) Trenchard, Kt., C.B.E., F.S.A.

Cox, Sir John William, Kt., C.B.E.

Craddock, Sir (George) Beresford, Kt.

Craddock, *Lt.-Gen.* Sir Richard Walter, K.B.E., C.B., D.S.O.

Craig, Sir John Herbert McCutcheon, K.C.V.O., C.B.

Cramer, *Hon.* Sir John Oscar, Kt.

Crane, Sir Harry Walter Victor, Kt., O.B.E.

Craster, Sir John Montagu, Kt.

Craufurd, Sir Robert James, Bt. (1781).

Craven, *Air Marshal* Sir Robert Edward, K.B.E., C.B., D.F.C.

Crawford, Sir (Archibald James) Dirom, Kt.

Crawford, *Brig.* Sir Douglas Inglis, Kt., C.B., D.S.O., T.D.

Crawford, Sir Frederick, G.C.M.G., O.B.E.

Crawford, *Hon.* Sir George Hunter, Kt.

Crawford, Sir John Grenfell, Kt., C.B.E.

Crawford, Sir (Robert) Stewart, G.C.M.G., C.V.O.

Crawford, *Prof.* Sir Theodore, Kt.

Crawford, Sir (Walter) Ferguson, K.B.E., C.M.G.

Crawford, *Vice-Adm.* Sir William Godfrey, K.B.E., C.B., D.S.C.

Crawshaw, *Hon.* Sir (Edward) Daniel (Weston), Kt.

Crawshay, *Col.* Sir William Robert, Kt., D.S.O., E.R.D., T.D.

Creagh, *Maj.-Gen.* Sir (Kilner) Rupert Brazier-, K.B.E., C.B., D.S.O.

Creasy, Sir Gerald Hallen, K.C.M.G., K.C.V.O., O.B.E.

Creswell, Sir Michel Justin, K.C.M.G.

Creswick, Sir Alexander Reid, Kt.

Crichton, Sir Andrew James Maitland-Makgill-, Kt.

Crichton, *Hon.* Sir (John) Robertson (Dunn), Kt.

Crichton, Sir Robert, C.B.E.

Cripps, Sir Cyril Thomas, Kt., M.B.E.

Crisp, Sir (John) Peter, Bt. (1913).

Crisp, *Hon.* Sir Malcolm Peter, Kt.

Critchett, Sir Ian (George Lorraine), Bt. (1908).

Croft, Sir Bernard Hugh Denman, Bt. (1671).

Croft, Sir John William Graham, Bt. (1818).

Crofton, Sir (Hugh) Patrick Simon, Bt. (1801).

Crofton, Sir Malby Sturges, Bt. (1828).

Crookenden, *Lt.-Gen.* Sir Napier, K.C.B., D.S.O., O.B.E.

Croom, Sir John Halliday, Kt., T.D.

Croot, Sir (Horace) John, Kt., C.B.E.

Cross, *Prof.* Sir (Alfred) Rupert (Neale), Kt., F.B.A.

Cross, *Air Chief Marshal* Sir Kenneth Brian Boyd, K.C.B., C.B.E., D.S.O., D.F.C.

Crossland, Sir Leonard, Kt.

Crossley, Sir Christopher John, Bt. (1909).

Crosthwaite, Sir (Ponsonby) Moore, K.C.M.G.

Crowe, Sir Colin Tradescant, G.C.M.G.

Crowley, Sir Brian Hurtle, Kt., M.M.

Crowther, Sir William Edward Lodewyk Hamilton, Kt., C.B.E., D.S.O., V.D.

Crutchley, *Admiral* Sir Victor Alexander Charles, ♥℃, K.C.B., D.S.C.

Cumings, Sir Charles Cecil George, K.B.E.

Cumming, Sir Duncan Cameron, K.B.E., C.B.

Cumming, Sir Ronald Stuart, Kt., T.D.

Cumming, Sir William Gordon Gordon-, Bt. (1804).

Cunard, Sir Guy Alick, Bt. (1859).

Cuninghame, Sir John Christopher Foggo Montgomery-, Bt. (N.S. 1672).

Cuninghame, Sir William Alan Fairlie-, Bt., M.C. (S. 1630).

Cunliffe, Sir David Ellis, Bt. (1750).

Cunningham, *General* Sir Alan Gordon, G.C.M.G., K.C.B., D.S.O., M.C.

Cunningham, Sir Charles Craik G.C.B., K.B.E., C.V.O.

Cunningham, Sir Graham, K.B.E.

Cunningham, *Maj.-Gen.* Sir Hugh Patrick, K.B.E.

Cunningham, Sir Samuel Knox, Bt., Q.C., (1963).

Cunynghame, Sir (Henry) David St. Leger Brooke Selwyn, Bt. (S. 1702).

Curlewis, *His Hon.* Sir Adrian Herbert, Kt., C.V.O., C.B.E.

Curran, Sir Charles John, Kt.

Curran, *Rt. Hon.* Sir Lancelot Ernest, Kt.

Curran, Sir Samuel Crowe, Kt., D.SC., Ph.D., F.R.S., F.R.S.E.

Currie, Sir George Alexander, Kt.

Currie, Sir James, K.B.E., C.M.G.

Currie, Sir Walter Mordaunt Cyril, Bt. (1847).

Curtis, Sir Edward Leo, Kt.

Curtis, Sir Peter, Bt. (1802).

Cusack, *Hon.* Sir Ralph Vincent, Kt.

Cushion, *Air Vice-Marshal* Sir William Boston, K.B.E., C.B.

Cutforth, *Maj.-Gen.* Sir Lancelot Eric, K.B.E., C.B.

Cuthbert, *Vice-Adm.* Sir John Wilson, K.B.E., C.B.

Cuthbertson, Sir David Paton, Kt., C.B.E., M.D., D.SC.

Cutler, Sir (Arthur) Roden, V.C. K.C.M.G., K.C.V.O., C.B.E.

Cutler, Sir Charles Benjamin, K.B.E., E.D.

Dainton, *Prof.* Sir Frederick Sydney, Kt., Ph.D., SC., F.R.S.

Daldry, Sir Leonard Charles, K.B.E.

Dale, Sir William Leonard, K.C.M.G.

Dalling, Sir Thomas, Kt.

Dalrymple, Sir Hew Fleetwood Hamilton-, Bt. C.V.O. (S. 1697).

Dalton, *Maj.-Gen.* Sir Charles James George, Kt., C.B., C.B.E.

Dalton, *Vice-Adm.* Sir Norman Eric, K.C.B., O.B.E.

Daly, *Lt.-Gen.* Sir Thomas Joseph, K.B.E., C.B., D.S.O.

Dalyell, Sir Tam, Bt., M.P. (N.S. 1685).

Danckwerts, *Rt. Hon.* Sir Harold Otto, Kt.

Daniel, *Admiral* Sir Charles Saumarez, K.C.B., C.B.E., D.S.O.

Daniel, Sir Goronwy Hopkin, K.C.V.O., C.B., D.Phil.

Daniell, Sir Peter Averell, Kt., T.D.

Danks, Sir Alan John, K.B.E.

Dannatt, Sir Cecil, Kt., O.B.E., M.C.

Darell, Sir Jeffrey Lionel, Bt., M.C. (1795).

Dargie, Sir William Alexander, Kt., C.B.E.

Darling, Sir Frank Fraser, Kt.

Darling, Sir James Ralph, Kt., C.M.G., O.B.E.

Darling, *General* Sir Kenneth Thomas, G.B.E., K.C.B., D.S.O.

Darligton, *Inst. Rear-Adm.* Sir Charles Roy, K.B.E.

Darvall, Sir (Charles) Roger, Kt., C.B.E.

Dash, Sir Roydon Englefield Ashford, Kt., D.F.C.

Dashwood, Sir Francis John Vernon Hereward, Bt., *Premier Baronet of Great Britain* (1707).

Dashwood, Sir Richard James, Bt. (1684).

Davenport, *Lt.-Col* Sir Walter Henry Bromley-, Kt., T.D.

Davidson, *Hon.* Sir Charles William, K.B.E.

Davidson, *Prof.* Sir (Leybourne) Stanley (Patrick), Kt., M.D., F.R.S.E.

Davie, *Rev.* Sir Arthur Patrick Ferguson-, Bt. (1847).

Davie, Sir Paul Christopher, Kt.

Davies, Sir Alan Meredith Hudson, Kt., C.B.E.

Davies, *Hon.* Sir (Alfred William) Michael, Kt.

Davies, Sir David Henry, Kt.

Davies, Sir David Joseph, Kt.

Davies, *Rt. Hon.* Sir (William) Arthian, Kt.

Davis, Sir Charles Sigmund, Kt., C.B.

Davis, *Hon.* Sir Hughes, Kt.

Davis, Sir John Gilbert, Bt. (1946).

Davis, *Air Chief Marshal* Sir John Gilbert, G.C.B., O.B.E.

Davis, Sir John Henry Harris, Kt.

Davis, Sir Maurice Herbert, Kt., O.B.E.

Davis, Sir Rupert Charles Hart-, Kt.

Davis, *Admiral* Sir William Wellclose, G.C.B., D.S.O.

Dawnay, *Vice-Adm.* Sir Peter, K.C.V.O., C.B., D.S.C.

Dawson, *Cdr.* Sir Hugh Trevor, Bt., C.B.E., R.N. (1920).

†Dawson, Sir Lawrence Savile, Bt. (1929).

Dawson, *Air Chief Marshal* Sir Walter Lloyd, K.C.B., C.B.E., D.S.O.

Dawtry, Sir Alan Graham, Kt., C.B.E., T.D.

Deacon, Sir George Edward Raven, Kt., C.B.E., F.R.S., F.R.S.E.

Deakin, Sir (Frederick) William (Dampier), Kt., D.S.O.

Dean, Sir Arthur William Henry, Kt., C.I.E., M.C., E.D.

Dean, Sir John Norman, Kt.

Dean, Sir Maurice Joseph, K.C.B., K.C.M.G.

Dean, Sir Patrick Henry, G.C.M.G.

Debenham, Sir Gilbert Ridley, Bt. (1931).

De Bunsen, Sir Bernard, Kt., C.M.G.

de Freitas, *Rt. Hon.* Sir Geoffrey Stanley, K.C.M.G., M.P.

De Gale, Sir Leo Victor, K.C.M.G., C.B.E.

De Guingand, *Maj.-Gen.* Sir Francis W., K.B.E., C.B., D.S.O.

de Hoghton, Sir (Henry Philip) Anthony (Mary), Bt. (1611).

De la Bère, Sir Rupert, Bt., K.C.V.O. (1953).

Delacombe, *Maj.-Gen.* Sir Rohan, K.C.M.G., K.C.V.O., K.B.E., C.B., D.S.O.

de la Mare, Sir Arthur James, K.C.M.G., K.C.V.O.

De la Rue, Sir Eric Vincent, Bt. (1898).

De Lestang, Sir Marie Charles Emmanuel Clement Nageon, Kt.

Delfont, Sir Bernard, Kt.

De Lotbinière, *Lt.-Col.* Sir Edmond Joly, Kt.

Delve, Sir Frederick William, Kt., C.B.E.

de Montmorency, Sir Reginald D'Alton Lodge, Bt. (1 1631).

Denholm, Sir John Carmichael, Kt., C.B.E.

Denholm, *Col.* Sir William Lang, Kt., T.D.

Dening, Sir (Maberly) Esler, G.C.M.G., O.B.E.

Denning, *Vice-Adm.* Sir Norman Egbert, K.B.E., C.B.

Denning, *Lt.-Gen.* Sir Reginald Francis Stewart, K.C.V.O., K.B.E., C.B.

Denny, Sir Alistair Maurice Archibald, Bt. (1913).

Denny, Sir Anthony Coningham de Waltham, Bt. (1 1782).

Denny, Sir (Jonathan) Lionel (Percy), G.B.E., M.C.

de Normann, Sir Eric, K.B.E., C.B.

Dent, Sir Robert Annesley Wilkinson, Kt., C.B.

De Trafford, Sir Rudolph Edgar Francis, Bt., O.B.E. (1941).

Deverell, Sir Colville Montgomery, G.B.E., K.C.M.G., C.V.O.

Devitt, Sir Thomas Gordon, Bt. (1916).

Dewes, Sir Herbert John Salisbury, Kt., C.B.E.

Dewey, Sir Anthony Hugh, Bt. (1917).

D'Eyncourt, Sir (John) Jeremy (Eustace) Tennyson-, Bt. (1930).

De Zoysa, *Hon.* Sir Cyril, Kt.

de Zulueta, Sir Philip Francis, Kt.

Dhenin, *Air Marshal* Sir Geoffrey Howard, K.B.E., A.F.C., G.M., M.D.

Dhrangadhra, H.H. the Maharaja Raj Saheb of, K.C.I.E.

Dickens, *Air Commodore* Sir Louis Walter, Kt., D.F.C., A.F.C.

Dickinson, Sir Harold Herbert, Kt.

Dickson, *Marshal of the Royal Air Force* Sir William Forster, G.C.B., K.B.E., D.S.O., A.F.C.

Dilke, Sir John Fisher Wentworth, Bt. (1862).

Dill, Sir Nicholas Bayard, Kt., C.B.E.

Dillon, Sir Robert William Charlier, Bt. (1801).

Dimsdale, Sir John Holdsworth, Bt. (1902).

Dingle, Sir Philip Burrington, Kt., C.B.E.

Diver, *Hon.* Sir Leslie Charles, Kt.

Dixey, Sir Frank, K.C.M.G., O.B.E., D.Sc., F.R.S.

Dixie, Sir (Alexander Archibald Douglas) Wolstan, Bt. (1660).

Dixon, Sir Charles William, K.C.M.G., K.C.V.O., O.B.E.

Dixon, *Air Vice-Marshal* Sir (Francis Wilfred) Peter, K.B.E.

Dixon, Sir John, Bt. (1919).

Dobson, Sir Denis William, K.C.B., O.B.E., Q.C.

Dobson, *Lt. Gen.* Sir Patrick John Howard-, K.C.B.

Docker, Sir Bernard Dudley Frank, K.B.E.

Dodds, Sir Ralph Jordan, Bt. (1964).

Dods, *Prof.* Sir Lorimer Fenton, Kt., M.V.O.

Dodson, Sir Derek Sherborne Lindsell, K.C.M.G., M.C.

Dodsworth, Sir John Christopher Smith-, Bt. (1784).

Doig, Sir James Nimmo Crawford, Kt.

Doll, *Prof.* Sir (William) Richard (Shaboe), Kt., O.B.E., F.R.S., D.M., M.D., D.Sc.

Domville, Sir (Gerald) Guy, Bt. (1814).

Donald, *Air Marshal* Sir Grahame, K.C.B., D.F.C., A.F.C.

Donaldson, Sir Dawson, K.C.M.G.

Donaldson, *Hon.* Sir John Francis, Kt.

Donner, Sir Patrick William, Kt.

Dorman, *Maj.* Sir Charles Geoffrey, Bt., M.C. (1923).

Dorman, Sir Maurice Henry, G.C.M.G., G.C.V.O.

Dormer, Sir Cecil Francis Joseph, K.C.M.G., M.V.O.

Dos Santos, Sir Errol Lionel, Kt., C.B.E.

Dougherty, *Maj.-Gen.* Sir Ivan Noel, Kt., C.B.E., D.S.O., E.D.

Douglas, *Prof.* Sir Donald Macleod, Kt., M.B.E.

Douglas, Sir Sholto Courtenay Mackenzie, Bt., M.C. (1831).

Douglas, *Hon.* Sir William Randolph, Kt.

Dove, Sir Clifford Alfred, Kt., C.B.E., E.R.D.

Dow, Sir Hugh, G.C.I.E., K.C.S.I.

Down, *Lt-Gen.* Sir Ernest Edward, K.B.E., C.B.

Downer, *Hon.* Sir Alexander Russell, K.B.E.

Dowse, *Maj.-Gen.* Sir Maurice Brian, K.C.V.O., C.B., C.B.E.

Dowty, Sir George Herbert, Kt.

Doyle, *Capt.* Sir John Francis Reginald William Hastings, Bt. (1828).

D'Oyly, *Cdr.* Sir John Rochfort, Bt., R.N. (1663).

Drake, Sir (Arthur) Eric (Courtney), Kt., C.B.E.

Drake, Sir James, Kt., C.B.E.

Drew, Sir Arthur Charles Walter, K.C.B.

Drew, Sir Ferdinand Caire, Kt., C.M.G.

Drew, *Lt.-Gen.* Sir (William) Robert (Macfarlane), K.C.B., C.B.E., Q.H.P.

Dreyer, *Admiral* Sir Desmond Parry, G.C.B., C.B.E., D.S.C.

Dring, *Lt.-Col.* Sir Arthur John, K.B.E., C.I.E.

Driver, Sir Arthur John, Kt.

Drummond, *Lieut.-Gen.* Sir (William) Alexander (Duncan), K.B.E., C.B.

Drummond, Sir William Hugh Dudley Williams-, Bt. (1828).

Drury, Sir Alan Nigel, Kt., C.B.E., M.D., F.R.S.

Dryden, Sir John Stephen Gyles, Bt. (1733 and 1795).

Drysdale, Sir (George) Russell, Kt.

Duckworth, *Maj.* Sir Richard Dyce, Bt. (1909).

Du Cros, Sir Philip Harvey, Bt. (1916).

Dudding, Sir John Scarborough, Kt.

Duff, Sir Arthur Antony, K.C.M.G., C.V.O., D.S.O., D.S.C.

Duff, Sir (Charles) Michael (Robert Vivian), Bt. (1911).

Duffus, *Hon.* Sir Herbert George Holwell, Kt.

Duffus, *Hon.* Sir William Algernon Holwell, Kt.

Dugdale, Sir William Stratford, Bt., M.C. (1936).

du Heaume, Sir Francis Herbert, Kt., C.I.E., O.B.E.

Duke, Sir Charles Beresford, K.C.M.G., C.I.E., O.B.E.

Duke, *Maj.-Gen.* Sir Gerald William, K.B.E., C.B., D.S.O.

Dumas, Sir Russell John, K.B.E., C.M.G.

Dunbar, Sir Adrian Ivor, Bt., (S 1694).

Dunbar, Sir Archibald Ranulph, Bt. (S 1700).

Dunbar, Sir David Hope-, Bt. (S 1664).

Dunbar, Sir Drummond Cospatrick Ninian, Bt., M.G. (S 1698).

Dunbar, Sir John Greig, Kt.

Dunbar of Hempriggs, Dame Maureen Daisy Helen, Bt. (S 1706).

Duncan, Sir Arthur Bryce, Kt.

Duncan, Sir Val (John Norman Valette), Kt., O.B.E.

Duncombe, Sir Philip Digby Pauncefort-, Bt. (1859).

Dundas, Sir Robert Whyte Melville, Bt. (1821).

Dungarpur, H.H. the Maharawal of, G.C.I.E., K.C.S.I.

Dunham, *Prof.* Sir Kingsley Charles, Kt., Ph.D., F.R.S., F.R.S.E.

Dunk, Sir William Ernest, Kt., C.B.E.

Dunkley, Sir Herbert Francis, Kt.

Dunlop, *Prof.* Sir Derrick Melville, Kt., M.D.

Dunlop, Sir Ernest Edward, Kt., C.M.G., O.B.E.

Dunlop, Sir John Wallace, K.B.E.

Dunlop, Sir Thomas, Bt. (1916).

Dunlop, Sir William Norman Gough, Kt.

Dunn, *Lt.-Col.* Sir Francis Vivian, K.C.V.O., O.B.E.

Dunn, *Air Marshal* Sir Patrick Hunter, K.B.E., C.B., D.F.C.

Dunn, *Maj.* Sir Philip Gordon, Bt. (1921).

Dunn, *Hon.* Sir Robin Horace Walford, Kt., M.C.

Dunnett, Sir George Sangster, K.B.E., C.B.

Dunnett, Sir (Ludovic) James, G.C.B., C.M.G.

Dunning, Sir Simon William Patrick, Bt. (1930).

Dunphie, *Maj.-Gen.* Sir Charles Anderson Lane, Kt., C.B., C.B.E., D.S.O.

Duntze, Sir George Edwin Douglas, Bt., C.M.G. (1774).

Dupree, Sir Victor, Bt. (1921).

Dupuch, Sir (Alfred) Etienne (Jerome), Kt., O.B.E.

Durand, *Rev.* Sir (Henry Mortimer) Dickon, Bt. (1892).

Durlacher, Sir Esmond Otho, Kt.

Durlacher, *Admiral* Sir Laurence George, K.C.B., O.B.E., D.S.C.

Durrant, Sir William Henry Estridge, Bt. (1784).

Duthie, Sir William Smith, Kt., O.B.E.

Duveen, Sir Geoffrey, Kt., R.D.

Dyer, *Prof.* Sir (Henry) Peter (Francis) Swinnerton, Bt., F.R.S. (1678).

Dyke, Sir Derek William Hart, Bt. (1677).

Dyson, Sir Cyril Douglas, Kt.

Earle, *Air Chief Marshal* Sir Alfred, G.B.E., C.B.

Earle, Sir Hardman Alexander Mort, Bt. (1869).

East, Sir (Lewis) Ronald, Kt., C.B.E.

Eastick, *Brig.* Sir Thomas Charles, Kt., C.M.G., D.S.O., E.D.

Easton, *Admiral* Sir Ian, K.C.B., D.S.C.

Eastwood, Sir Eric, Kt., C.B.E., F.R.S.

Eastwood, *Maj.* Sir Geoffrey Hugh, K.C.V.O., C.B.E.

Eastwood, Sir John Bealby, Kt.

Easton, *Air Commodore* Sir James Alfred, K.C.M.G., C.B., C.B.E.

Eaton, *Vice-Adm.* Sir John Willson Musgrave, K.B.E., C.B., D.S.O., D.S.C.

Ebrahim, Sir (Mahomed) Currimbhoy, Bt. (1910).

Eccles, *Prof.* Sir John Carew, Kt., D.Phil., F.R.S.

Echlin, Sir Norman David Fenton, Bt. (I 1721).

Edden, *Vice-Adm.* Sir (William) Kaye, K.B.E., C.B.

Eddie, Sir George Brand, Kt., O.B.E.

Eden, *Rt. Hon.* Sir John Benedict, Bt., M.P. (1672 and 1776).

Edge, Sir Knowles, Bt. (1937).

Edmenson, Sir Walter Alexander, Kt., C.B.E.

Edmonstone, Sir Archibald Bruce Charles, Bt. (1774).

Edwards, *Lt.-Col.* Sir Bartle Mordaunt Marsham, Kt., C.V.O., M.C.

Edwards, Sir Christopher John Churchill, Bt. (1866).

Edwards, Sir George Robert, Kt., O.M., C.B.E., F.R.S.

Edwards, *Air Commodore* Sir Hughie Idwal, 𝒱𝒞, K.C.M.G., C.B., D.S.O., O.B.E., D.F.C.

Edwards, Sir John Arthur, Kt., C.B.E.

Edwards, Sir John Clive Leighton, Bt. (1921).

Edwards, *Prof.* Sir (John) Goronwy, Kt., D.Litt., F.B.A.

Edwards, Sir Martin Llewellyn, Kt.

Edwards, Sir Ronald Stanley, K.B.E.

Edwards, *Prof.* Sir Samuel Frederick, Kt., F.R.S.

Egerton, Sir (Philip) John (Caledon) Grey-, Bt. (1617).

Egerton, Sir Seymour John Louis, K.C.V.O.

Eggleston, *Hon.* Sir Richard Moulton, Kt.

Elder, Sir Stewart Duke-, G.C.V.O., M.D., F.R.S.

Eldridge, *Lt.-Gen.* Sir (William) John, K.B.E., C.B., D.S.O., M.C.

Eley, Sir Geoffrey Cecil Ryves, Kt., C.B.E.

Eliott, Sir Arthur Francis Augustus Boswell, Bt. (S 1666).

Elkins, Sir Anthony Joseph, Kt., C.B.E.

Elkins, *Vice-Adm.* Sir Robert Francis, K.C.B., C.V.O., O.B.E.

Elliot, Sir John Blumenfeld, Kt.

Elliott, Sir Hugh Francis Ivo, Bt., O.B.E. (1917).

Elliott, Sir Norman Randall, Kt., C.B.E.

Elliott, Sir (Robert) William, Kt., M.P.

Ellis, Sir (Bertram) Clough Williams-, Kt., C.B.E., M.C., F.R.I.B.A.

Ellis, Sir Charles Drummond, Kt., Ph.D., F.R.S.

Ellis, *Hon.* Sir Kevin, K.B.E.

Ellis, Sir Thomas Hobart, Kt.

Ellison, *Col.* Sir Ralph Harry Carr-, Kt., T.D.

Ellwood, *Air Marshal* Sir Aubrey Beauclerk, K.C.B., D.S.C.

Elmhirst, *Air Marshal* Sir Thomas Walker, K.B.E., C.B., A.F.C.

Elphinstone, Sir John, Bt. (S 1701).

Elphinstone, Sir Maurice Douglas Warburton, Bt., T.D. (1816).

Elstub, Sir St. John de Holt, Kt., C.B.E.

Elton, Sir Charles Abraham Grierson, Bt. (1717).

Elyan, Sir (Isadore) Victor, Kt.

Embry, *Air Chief Marshal* Sir Basil Edward, G.C.B., K.B.E., D.S.O., D.F.C., A.F.C.

Emery, Sir (James) Frederick, Kt.

Emmerson, Sir Harold Corti, G.C.B., K.C.V.O.

Empson, Sir Charles, K.C.M.G.

Empson, *Admiral* Sir (Leslie) Derek, G.B.E., K.C.B.

Emson, *Air Marshal* Sir Reginald Herbert, K.B.E., C.B., A.F.C.

Engholm, Sir Basil Charles, K.C.B.

Engineer, Sir Noshirwan Phirozshah, Kt.

Engledow, *Prof.* Sir Frank Leonard, Kt., C.M.G., F.R.S.

English, Sir Cyril Rupert, Kt.

Ennor, *Prof.* Sir Hugh (Arnold Hughes), Kt., C.B.E.

Entwistle, Sir (John Nuttall) Maxwell, Kt.

Errington, *Col.* Sir Geoffrey Frederick, Bt. (1963).

Erskine, Sir Derek Quicke, Kt.

Erskine, Sir (Robert) George, Kt., C.B.E.

Erskine, Sir (Thomas) David, Bt. (1821).

Esmonde, Sir Anthony Charles, Bt. (I 1629).

Esplen, Sir William Graham, Bt., (1921).

Eugster, *General* Sir Basil Oscar Paul, K.C.B., K.C.V.O., O.B.E., D.S.O., M.C.

Evans, Sir Anthony Adney, Bt. (1920).

Evans, Sir Arthur Trevor, Kt.

Evans, Sir Athol Donald, K.B.E.

Evans, Sir Bernard, Kt., D.S.O., E.D.

Evans, *Vice-Adm.* Sir Charles Leo Glandore, K.C.B., C.B.E., D.S.O., D.S.C.

Evans, Sir David Lewis, Kt., O.B.E., D.Litt.

Evans, Sir Francis Edward, G.B.E., K.C.M.G.

Evans, *Lt.-Gen.* Sir Geoffrey Charles, K.B.E., C.B., D.S.O.

Evans, Sir Geraint Llewellyn, Kt., C.B.E.

Evans, *Hon.* Sir Haydn Tudor, Kt.

Evans, Sir Ian William Gwynne-, Bt. (1913).

Evans, Sir (Robert) Charles, Kt.

Evans, Sir (Sidney) Harold, Bt., C.M.G., O.B.E. (1963).

Evans, Sir Trevor Maldwyn, Kt., C.B.E.

Evans, Sir (William) Vincent (John), K.C.M.G., M.B.E., Q.C.

Eveleigh, *Hon.* Sir Edward Walter, Kt., E.R.D.

Everard, *Maj.-Gen.* Sir Christopher Earle Welby-, K.B.E., C.B.

Everard, Sir Nugent Henry, Bt. (1911).

Everson, Sir Frederick Charles, K.C.M.G.

Every, Sir John Simon, Bt. (1641).

Evetts, *Lt.-Gen.* Sir John Fullerton, Kt., C.B., C.B.E., M.C.

Ewart, Sir (William) Ivan (Cecil), Bt., D.S.C. (1887).

Ewbank, *Maj.-Gen.* Sir Robert Withers, K.B.E., C.B., D.S.O.

Ewin, Sir (David) Ernest Thomas Floyd, Kt., O.B.E., M.V.O.

Ewing, *Prof.* Sir Alexander William Gordon, Kt., Ph.D.

Ewing *Vice-Adm.* Sir (Robert) Alastair, K.B.E., C.B., D.S.C.

Ewing, Sir Ronald Archibald Orr-, Bt. (1886).

Eyre, *Lt.-Col.* Sir Oliver Eyre Crosthwaite-, Kt.

Ezra, Sir Alwyn, Kt.

Ezra, Sir Derek, Kt., M.B.E.

Fadahunsi, Sir Joseph Odeleye, K.C.M.G.

Fagge, Sir John William Frederick, Bt. (1660).

Fairbairn, Sir (James) Brooke, Bt. (1869).

Fairbairn, Sir Robert Duncan, Kt.

Fairfax, Sir Vincent Charles, Kt., C.M.G.

Fairfax, Sir Warwick Oswald, Kt.

Fairhall, *Hon.* Sir Allen, K.B.E.

Falconer, *Lt.-Col.* Sir George Arthur, K.B.E., C.I.E.

Falconer, Sir James Fyfe, Kt., M.B.E.

Falk, Sir Roger Salis, Kt., O.B.E.

Falkiner, *Lt.-Col.* Sir Terence Edmond Patrick, Bt. (I 1778).

Falkner, Sir (Donald) Keith, Kt.

Falla, Sir Robert Alexander, K.B.E., C.M.G.

Falle, Sir Samuel, K.C.V.O., C.M.G., D.S.C.

Falshaw, Sir Donald, Kt.

Fanshawe, *Maj.-Gen.* Sir Evelyn Dalrymple, Kt., C.B., C.B.E.

Faridkot, *Col.* H.H. the Raja of, K.C.S.I.

Farmer, Sir Lovedin George Thomas, Kt.

Farquhar, *Lt.-Col.* Sir Peter (Walter), Bt., D.S.O. (1796).

Farquharson, Sir James Robbie, K.B.E.

Farrer, Sir (Walter) Leslie, K.C.V.O.

Farrington, *Maj.* Sir Henry Francis Colden, Bt. (1818).

Faulkner, Sir Eric Odin, Kt., M.B.E.

Faulkner, Sir Percy, K.B.E., C.B.

Faulks, *Hon.* Sir Neville Major Ginner, Kt., M.B.E., T.D.

Fawcus, Sir (Robert) Peter, K.B.E., C.M.G.

Fayrer, Sir Joseph Herbert Spens, Bt., D.S.C. (1896).

Feilden, *Maj.-Gen.* Sir Randle Guy, K.C.V.O., C.B., C.B.E.

Feilden, Sir William Morton Buller, Bt., M.C. (1846).

Feiling, Sir Keith Grahame, Kt., O.B.E., D.Litt.

Fell, *Vice-Adm.* Sir Michael Frampton, K.C.B., D.S.O., D.S.C.

Fellowes, Sir William Albemarle, K.C.V.O.

Fenner, Sir Claude Harry, K.B.E., C.M.G.

Fennessy, Sir Edward, Kt., C.B.E.

Fenton, *Col.* Sir William Charles, Kt., M.C.

Ferens, Sir Thomas Robinson, Kt., C.B.E.

Ferguson, *Lt.-Col.* Sir Neil Edward Johnson-, Bt., T.D. (1906).

Fergusson of Kilkerran, Sir Charles, Bt. (S. 1703).

Fergusson, Sir James Herbert Hamilton Colyer-, Bt. (1866).

Ferranti, Sir Vincent Ziani de, Kt., M.C.

Ferrier, Sir Harold Grant, Kt., C.M.G.

Festing, *Field Marshal* Sir Francis Wogan, G.C.B., K.B.E., D.S.O.

ffolkes, Sir Robert Francis Alexander, Bt. (1774).

fforde, Sir Arthur Frederic Brownlow, G.B.E.

Fidge, Sir (Harold) Roy, Kt.

Field, Sir John Osbaldiston, K.B.E., C.M.G.

Fielden, *Air Vice-Marshal* Sir Edward Hedley, G.C.V.O., C.B., D.F.C., A.F.C.

Fieldhouse, Sir Harold, K.B.E., C.B.

Fiennes, Sir John Saye Wingfield Twisleton-Wykeham-, K.C.B., Q.C.

Fiennes, Sir Maurice Alberic Twisleton-Wykeham-, Kt.

Fiennes, Sir Ranulph Twisleton-Wykeham-, Bt. (1916).

Figgers, *Col.* Sir John George, K.B.E., C.M.G.

Figgures, Sir Frank Edward, K.C.B., C.M.G.

Findlay, *Lt.-Col.* Sir Roland Lewis, Bt. (1925).

Finlay, Sir Graeme Bell, Bt., E.R.D. (1964).

Finniston, Sir (Harold) Montague, Kt., Ph.D., F.R.S.

Firth, *Prof.* Sir Raymond William, Kt., Ph.D., F.B.A.

Fisher, Sir George Read, Kt., C.M.G.

Fisher, *Hon.* Sir Henry Arthur Peers, Kt.

Fisher, Sir John, Kt.

Fisher, Sir Nigel Thomas Loveridge, Kt., M.C., M.P.

Fison, Sir (Frank Guy) Clavering, Kt.

Fison, Sir Richard Guy, Bt., D.S.C. (1905).

Fitts, Sir Clive Hamilton, Kt., M.D.

Fitzgerald, *Rev.* Sir Edward Thomas, Bt. (1903).

FitzGerald, Sir George Peter Maurice, Bt., M.C., *The Knight of Kerry* (1880).

Fitz-Gerald, Sir Patrick Herbert, Kt., O.B.E.

Fitzgerald, Sir William James, Kt., M.C., Q.C.

FitzHerbert, Sir John Richard Frederick, Bt. (1784).

Fitzmaurice, *Lt.-Col.* Sir Desmond FitzJohn, Kt., C.I.E.

Fitzmaurice, Sir Gerald Gray, G.C.M.G., Q.C.

Fitzpatrick, *General* Sir (Geoffrey Richard) Desmond, G.C.B., D.S.O., M.B.E., M.C.

Flanagan, Sir James Bernard, Kt., C.B.E.

Flavelle, Sir (Joseph) Ellsworth, Bt. (1917).

Flaxman, *Hon.* Sir Hubert James Marlowe, Kt., C.M.G.

Fleming, *Instr. Rear-Adm.* Sir John, K.B.E., D.S.C.

Flemming, Sir Gilbert Nicolson, K.C.B.

Fletcher, *Hon.* Sir Alan Roy, Kt.

Fletcher, Sir John Henry Lancelot Aubrey-, Bt. (1782).

Fletcher, *Hon.* Sir Patrick Bisset, K.B.E., C.M.G.

Fletcher, *Air Chief Marshal* Sir Peter Carteret, K.C.B., O.B.E., D.F.C., A.F.C.

Flett, Sir Martin Teall, K.C.B.

Flowers, *Prof.* Sir Brian Hilton, Kt., F.R.S.

Floyd, Sir Giles Henry Charles, Bt. (1816).

Follett, Sir David Henry, Kt., Ph.D.

Follows, Sir (Charles) Geoffry (Shield), Kt., C.M.G.

Fooks, Sir Raymond Hatherell, Kt., C.B.E.

Foot, *Rt. Hon.* Sir Dingle Mackintosh, Kt., Q.C.

Foots, Sir James William, Kt.

Forbes, *Hon.* Sir Alastair Granville, Kt.

Forbes, Sir Archibald Finlayson, G.B.E.

Forbes of Pitsligo, Sir Charles Edward Stuart-, Bt. (S 1626).

Forbes, Sir Douglas Stuart, Kt.

Forbes of Brux, *Hon.* Sir Ewan, Bt. (S 1630).

Forbes, *Hon.* Sir Hugh Henry Valentine, Kt.

Forbes, *Col.* Sir John Stewart, Bt., D.S.O. (1823).

Ford, *Capt.* Sir Aubrey St. Clair-, Bt., D.S.O., R.N. (1793).

Ford, *Prof.* Sir Edward, Kt., O.B.E., M.D.

Ford, *Maj,* Sir Edward William Spencer, K.C.B., K.C.V.O.

Ford, Sir Henry Russell, Bt. (1929).

Ford, *Prof.* Sir Hugh, Kt., F.R.S.

Ford, Sir Leslie Ewart, Kt., O.B.E.

Ford, *Maj.-Gen.* Sir Peter St. Clair-, K.B.E., C.B., D.S.O.

Ford, Sir Sidney William George, Kt., M.B.E.

Fordham, Sir (Alfred) Stanley, K.B.E., C.M.G.

Forrest, Sir James Alexander, Kt.

Forrest, *Rear Adm.* Sir Ronald Stephen, K.C.V.O.

Forsdyke, Sir (Edgar) John, K.C.B.

Forte, Sir Charles, Kt.

Forwood, Sir Dudley Richard, Bt. (1895).

Foster, Sir John Galway, K.B.E., Q.C.

Foster, Sir John Gregory, Bt. (1930).

Foster, *Hon.* Sir Peter Harry Batson Woodroffe, Kt., M.B.E., T.D.

Foster, Sir Robert Sidney, G.C.M.G., K.C.V.O.

Foulis, Sir Ian Primrose Liston-, Bt. (S 1634).

Fowke, Sir Frederick (Woollaston Rawdon), Bt. (1814).

Fowler, Sir Robert William Doughty, K.C.M.G.

Fox, Sir (Henry) Murray, G.B.E.

Fox, *Hon.* Sir Michael John, Kt.

Fox, Sir (Robert) David (John) Scott, K.C.M.G.

Fox, Sir Theodore Fortescue, Kt., M.D., Ll.D.

Foxell, *Rev.* Maurice Frederic, K.C.V.O.

France, Sir Arnold William, G.C.B.

Francis, Sir Frank Charlton, K.C.B., F.S.A.

Frank, Sir Robert John, Bt. (1920).

Frankel, Sir Otto Herzberg, Kt., D.SC., F.R.S.

Franklin, Sir Eric Alexander, Kt., C.B.E.

Fraser, Sir Basil Malcolm, Bt. (1921).

Fraser, Sir Bruce Donald, K.C.B.

Fraser, *General* Sir David William, K.C.B., O.B.E.

Fraser, Sir Douglas Were, Kt., I.S.O.

Fraser, *Air Marshal* Sir (Henry) Paterson, K.B.E., C.B., A.F.C.

Fraser, Sir Hugh, Bt. (1961).

Fraser, Sir Ian, Kt., D.S.O., O.B.E.

Fraser, Sir James David, Bt. (1943).

Fraser, Sir Keith Charles Adolphus, Bt. (1806).

Fraser, Sir Robert Brown, Kt., O.B.E.

Fraser, Sir (William) Robert, K.C.B., K.B.E.

Frederick, *Maj.* Sir Charles Boscawen, Bt. (1723).

Freeland, *Lt.-Gen.* Sir Ian Henry, G.B.E., K.C.B., D.S.O.

Freeman, Sir John Keith Noel, Bt. (1945).

Freeman, Sir (Nathaniel) Bernard, Kt., C.B.E.

Freeman, *Hon.* Sir Ralph, Kt., C.V.O., C.B.E.

Fressanges, *Air Marshal* Sir Francis Joseph, K.B.E., C.B.

Fretwell, Sir George Herbert, K.B.E., C.B.

Frew, *Air Vice-Marshal* Sir Matthew Brown, K.B.E., C.B., D.S.O., M.C., A.F.C.

Frewen, *Admiral* Sir John Byng, G.C.B.

Frith, *Brig.* Sir Eric Herbert Cokayne, Kt., C.B.E.

Frome, Sir Norman Frederick, Kt., C.I.E., D.F.C.

Fry, Sir John Nicholas Pease, Bt. (1894).

Fry, Sir Leslie Alfred Charles, K.C.M.G., O.B.E.

Fryars, Sir Robert Furness, Kt.

Fryberg, Sir Abraham, Kt., M.B.E.

Fuchs, Sir Vivian Ernest, Kt., Ph.D.

Fuller, *Hon.* Sir John Bryan Munro, Kt.

Fuller, *Maj.* Sir (John) Gerard (Henry Fleetwood), Bt. (1910).

Fung Ping-Fan, *Hon.* Sir Kenneth Kt., C.B.E.

Furlonge, Sir Geoffrey Warren, K.B.E., C.M.G.

Furness, Sir Stephen Roberts, Bt. (1913).

Gadsdon, Sir Lawrence Percival, Kt.

Gage, Sir Berkeley Everard Foley, K.C.M.G.

Gaggero, Sir George, Kt., O.B.E.

Gairdner, *General* Sir Charles Henry, G.B.E., K.C.M.G., K.C.V.O., C.B.

Gaitskell, Sir Arthur, Kt., C.M.G.

Gale, *General* Sir Richard Nelson, G.C.B., K.B.E., D.S.O., M.C.

Gallwey, Sir Philip Frankland-Payne-, Bt. (1812).

Galpern, Sir Myer, Kt., M.P.

Galpin, Sir Albert James, K.C.V.O., C.B.E.

Galsworthy, Sir Arthur Norman, K.C.M.G.

Galsworthy, Sir John Edgar, K.C.V.O., C.M.G.

Gamble, Sir David Arthur Josias, Bt. (1897).

Gamble, Sir (Frederick) Herbert K.B.E., C.M.G.

Ganilau, *Ratu* Sir Penaia Kanatabatu, K.B.E., C.M.G., C.V.O., D.S.O.

Gardener, Sir Alfred John, K.C.M.G., C.B.E.

Gardner, Sir Douglas Bruce Bruce-, Bt. (1945).

Gardner, Sir George William Hoggan, K.B.E., C.B.

Garner, Sir Harry Mason, K.B.E., C.B.

Garran, Sir (Isham) Peter, K.C.M.G.

Garrett, *Lt.-Gen.* Sir (Alwyn) Ragnar, K.B.E., C.B.

Garrett, Sir (Joseph) Hugh, K.C.I.E., C.S.I.

Garrett, *Hon.* Sir Raymond William, Kt., A.F.C.

Garrett, Sir William Herbert, Kt., M.B.E.

Garrow, Sir Nicholas, Kt., O.B.E.

Garthwaite, Sir William Francis Cuthbert, Bt., D.S.C. (1910).

Garvey, Sir Ronald Herbert, K.C.M.G., K.C.V.O., M.B.E.

Garvey, Sir Terence Willcocks, K.C.M.G.

Gascoigne, *Maj.-Gen.* Sir Julian Alvery, K.C.M.G., K.C.V.O., C.B., D.S.O.

Gass, Sir Michael David Irving, K.C.M.G.

Gasson, Sir Lionel Bell, Kt.

Gault, *Brig.* Sir James Frederick, K.C.M.G., M.V.O., O.B.E.

Geddes, Sir (Anthony) Reay (Mackay), K.B.E.

Gentry, *Maj.-Gen.* Sir William George, K.B.E., C.B., D.S.O.

George, Sir Arthur Thomas, Kt.

Georges, Sir (James) Olva, Kt., O.B.E.

Gerahty, Sir Charles Cyril, Kt., Q.C.

German, Sir Ronald Ernest, K.C.B., C.M.G.

Gethin, *Lt.-Col.* Sir Richard Patrick St. Lawrence, Bt. (I 1665).

Gibberd, Sir Frederick, Kt., C.B.E., R.A.

Gibbon, *General* Sir John Houghton, K.C.B., O.B.E.

Gibbons, Sir John Edward, Bt. (1752).

Gibbs, Sir Frank Stannard, K.B.E., C.M.G.

Gibbs, *Air Marshal* Sir Gerald Ernest, K.B.E., C.I.E., M.C.

Gibbs, *Rt. Hon.* Sir Harry Talbot, K.B.E.

Gibbs, *Rt. Hon.* Sir Humphrey Vicary, G.C.V.O., K.C.M.G., O.B.E.

Gibbs, *General* Sir Roland Christopher, K.C.B., C.B.E., D.S.O., M.C

Gibson, Sir Christopher Herbert, Bt. (1931).

Gibson, *Rev.* Sir David, Bt. (1926).

Gibson, *Vice-Adm.* Sir Donald Cameron Ernest Forbes, K.C.B., D.S.C.

Gibson, Sir Donald Edward Evelyn, Kt., C.B.E.

Gibson, Sir John Hinshelwood, Kt., C.B., T.D., Q.C.

Gibson, *Hon.* Sir Marcus George, Kt.

Gibson, Sir Ronald George, Kt., C.B.E., F.R.C.P.

Giddings, *Air Marshal* Sir (Kenneth Charles) Michael, K.C.B., O.B.E., D.F.C., A.F.C.

Gielgud, Sir (Arthur) John, Kt.

Gilbey, Sir (Walter) Derek, Bt. (1893).

Gilchrist, Sir Andrew Graham, K.C.M.G.

Giles, Sir Alexander Falconer, K.B.E., C.M.G.

Giles, Sir Henry Norman, Kt., O.B.E.

Gill, Sir Archibald Joseph, Kt.

Gillan, Sir (James) Angus, K.B.E., C.M.G.

Gillard, *Hon.* Sir Oliver James, Kt.

Gillett, Sir Edward Bailey, Kt.

Gillett, Sir (Sydney) Harold, Bt., M.C. (1959).

Gilliat, *Lt.-Col.* Sir Martin John, K.C.V.O., M.B.E.

Gillies, Sir Alexander, Kt.

Gilmour, Sir John Edward, Bt., D.S.O., T.D., M.P. (1897).

Gilmour, Sir John Little, Bt. (1926).

Gilroy, *His Eminence Cardinal* Norman Thomas, K.B.E.

Gladstone, Sir (Erskine) William Bt. (1846).

Gladstone, *Admiral* Sir Gerald Vaughan, G.B.E., K.C.B.

Glanville, Sir William Henry, Kt., C.B., C.B.E., D.SC., Ph.D., F.R.S.

Glass, Sir Leslie Charles, K.C.M.G.

Glen, Sir Alexander Richard, K.B.E., D.S.C.

Glenn, Sir Joseph Robert Archibald, Kt., O.B.E.

Glennie, *Admiral* Sir Irvine Gordon, K.C.B.

Glock, Sir William Frederick, Kt., C.B.E.

Glover, Sir Charles John, Kt.

Glover, *Col.* Sir Douglas, Kt., T.D.

Glover, Sir Gerald Alfred, Kt.

Glubb, *Lt.-Gen.* Sir John Bagot, K.C.B., C.M.G., D.S.O., O.B.E., M.C.

Gluckstein, Sir Louis Halle, G.B.E., T.D., Q.C.

Glyn, Sir Anthony Geoffrey Leo Simon, Bt. (1927).

Glyn, *Col.* Sir Richard Hamilton, Bt., O.B.E., T.D. (1759 and 1800).

Goad, Sir Edward Colin Viner, K.C.M.G.

Godber, Sir George Edward, G.C.B., D.M.

Goddard, *Air Marshal* Sir (Robert) Victor, K.C.B., C.B.E.

Godfrey, Sir Walter, K.B.E.

Godley, *Brig.* Sir Francis William Crewe Fetherston-, Kt., O.B.E.

Godwin, *Prof.* Sir Harry, Kt., F.R.S.

Goff, Sir Ernest (William) Davis-, Bt. (1905).

Goff, *Rt. Hon.* Sir Reginald William, Kt.

Goldman, Sir Samuel, K.C.B.

Goldsmid, Sir Henry Joseph d'Avigdor-, Bt., D.S.O., M.C. (1934).

Goldsmith, Sir Allen John Bridson, K.C.V.O., F.R.C.S.

Gombrich, *Prof.* Sir Ernst Hans Josef, Kt., C.B.E., Ph.D., F.B.A., F.S.A.

Gomes, Sir Stanley Eugene, Kt.

Gonzi, *Most Rev.* Monsignor Michael, K.B.E., D.D. (*Archbishop of Malta*).

Gooch, Sir Robert Douglas, Bt. (1866).

Gooch, *Col.* Sir Robert Eric Sherlock, Bt., K.C.V.O., D.S.O. (1746).

Goodale, Sir Ernest William, Kt., C.B.E., M.C.

Goodbody, *General* Sir Richard Wakefield, G.C.B., K.B.E., D.S.O.

Goode, Sir William Allmond Codrington, G.C.M.G.

Goodenough, Sir Richard Edmund, Bt. (1943).

Goodeve, Sir Charles Frederick, Kt., O.B.E., V.D., F.R.S.

Goodhart, Sir John Gordon, Bt. (1911).

Goodsell, Sir John William, Kt., C.M.G.

Goodson, *Lt.-Col.* Sir Alfred Lassam, Bt. (1922).

Goodwin, Sir Reginald Eustace, Kt., C.B.E.

Goodwin, *Lt.-Gen.* Sir Richard Elton, K.C.B., C.B.E., D.S.O.

Goold, Sir George Leonard, Bt. (1801).

Goonetilleke, Sir Oliver Ernest, G.C.M.G., K.C.V.O., K.B.E.

Gordon, Lord Adam Granville, K.C.V.O., M.B.E.

Gordon, Sir Andrew Cosmo Lewis Duff-, Bt. (1813).

Gordon, Sir Garnet Hamilton, Kt., C.B.E., Q.C.

Gordon, Sir John Charles, Bt. (S 1706).

Gordon, Sir Lionel Eldred Pottinger Smith-, Bt. (1838).

Gordon, *Hon.* Sir Sidney Samuel, Kt., C.B.E.

Gore, Sir Richard Ralph St. George, Bt. (I 1622).

Goring, Sir William Burton Nigel, Bt. (1627).

Goschen, Sir Edward Christian Bt., D.S.O. (1916).

Gosling, Sir Arthur Hulin, K.B.E., C.B., F.R.S.E.

Gothard, Sir Clifford Frederic, Kt., O.B.E.

Gotz, *Hon.* Sir (Frank) Léon (Aroho), K.C.V.O.

Gough, Sir Arthur Ernest, Kt.

Gould, Sir Ronald, Kt.

Gould, *Hon.* Sir Trevor Jack, Kt.

Goulding, *Hon.* Sir (Ernest) Irvine, Kt.

Goulding, Sir William Basil, Bt. (1904).

Gourlay, *General* Sir (Basil) Ian (Spencer), K.C.B., O.B.E., M.C., R.M.

Gowans, *Hon.* Sir (Urban) Gregory, Kt.

Gower, Sir (Herbert) Raymond, Kt., M.P.

Graaff, Sir de Villiers, Bt., M.B.E. (1911).

Grace, Sir John te Herekiekie, Kt., M.V.O.

Grace, Sir Raymond Eustace, Bt. (1795).

Grade, Sir Lew, Kt.

Graesser, *Col.* Sir Alastair Stewart Durward, Kt., D.S.O., O.B.E., M.C., T.D.

Graham, *Admiral* Sir Angus Edward Malise Bontine Cunninghame, K.B.E., C.B.

Graham, Sir (Frederick) Fergus, Bt., K.B.E., T.D. (1783).

Graham, Sir John Moodie, Bt. (1964).

Graham, *Hon.* Sir (John) Patrick, Kt.

Graham, Sir John Reginald Noble, Bt., ℣℄, O.B.E. (1906).

Graham, *Maj.-Gen.* Sir Miles William Arthur Peel, K.B.E., C.B., M.C.

Graham, Sir Montrose Stuart, Bt. (1629).

Graham, Sir Norman William, Kt., C.B.

Graham, Sir Richard Bellingham, Bt., O.B.E. (1662).

Grandy, *Marshal of the Royal Air Force* Sir John, G.C.B., K.B.E., D.S.O.

Grant, Sir Archibald, Bt. (S 1705).

Grant, *Maj.* Sir Ewan George Macpherson-, Bt. (1838).

Grant, Sir James Monteith, K.C.V.O.

Grant, Sir Kenneth Lindsay, Kt., O.B.E.

Grant, Sir Patrick Alexander Benedict, Bt. (S 1688).

Grantham, Sir Alexander William George Herder, G.C.M.G.

Grantham, *Admiral* Sir Guy, G.C.B., C.B.E., D.S.O.

Granville, Sir Keith, Kt., C.B.E.

Gray, *Prof.* Sir James, Kt., C.B.E., M.C., Sc.D., D.Sc., Ll.D., F.R.S.

Gray, Sir John Archibald Browne, Kt., Sc.D., F.R.S.

Gray, *Vice-Adm.* Sir John Michael Dudgeon, K.B.E., C.B.

Gray, Sir William, Bt. (1917).

Gray, Sir William Stevenson, Kt.

Grayson, Sir Ronald Henry Rudyard, Bt. (1922).

Greatbatch, Sir Bruce, Kt., K.C.V.O., C.M.G., M.B.E.

Greaves, Sir John Bewley, Kt., C.M.G., O.B.E.

Greaves, Sir (William) Walter, K.B.E.

Green, Sir (Edward) Stephen (Lycett), Bt., C.B.E. (1886).

Green, Sir George Edward, Kt.

Green, Sir John, Kt.

Green, *Lt.-Gen.* Sir (William) Wyndham, K.B.E., C.B., D.S.O., M.C.

Greenaway, Sir Derek Burdick, Bt., C.B.E. (1933).

Greenaway, Sir Thomas Moore, Kt.

Greene, Sir Hugh Carleton, K.C.M.G., O.B.E.

Greene, Sir (John) Brian Massy-, Kt.

Greenfield, Sir Cornelius Ewen Maclean, K.B.E., C.M.G.

Greenfield, Sir Harry, K.B.E., C.I.E.

Greenwell, Sir Peter McClinbock, Bt. (1906).

Greeson, *Surgeon Vice-Adm.* Sir Clarence Edward, K.B.E., C.B., Q.H.P.

Greeves, *Maj.-Gen.* Sir Stuart, K.B.E., C.B., D.S.O., M.C.

Gretton, *Vice-Adm.* Sir Peter William, K.C.B., D.S.O., O.B.E., D.S.C.

Grey, Sir Anthony Dysart, Bt. (1814).

Grey, Sir Paul Francis, K.C.M.G.

Grierson, Sir Richard Douglas, Bt. (S 1685).

Grieve, Sir (Herbert) Ronald (Robinson), Kt.

Grieve, *Prof.* Sir Robert, Kt.

Griffin, *Admiral* Sir Anthony Templer Frederick Griffith, G.C.B.

Griffin, Sir Charles David, Kt., C.B.E.

Griffin, Sir Elton Reginald, Kt., C.B.E.

Griffin, Sir Francis Frederick, C.B.E.

Griffin, Sir John Bowes, Kt., Q.C.

Griffiths, Sir Percival Joseph, K.B.E., C.I.E.

Griffiths, Sir Peter Norton-, Bt. (1922).

Griffiths, Sir Reginald Ernest, Kt.

Griffiths, *Hon.* Sir (William) Hugh, Kt., M.C.

Grime, Sir Harold Riley, Kt.

Groom, Sir Thomas Reginald, Kt.

Groom, *Air Marshal* Sir Victor Emmanuel, K.C.V.O., K.B.E., C.B., D.F.C.

Grotrian, Sir John (Appelbe) Brent, Bt. (1934).

Grounds, Sir Roy Burman, Kt.

Grove, Sir Walter Philip, Bt. (1874).

Grover, Sir Anthony Charles, Kt.

Groves, Sir Charles Barnard, Kt., C.B.E.

Grubb, Sir Kenneth George, K.C.M.G.

Grundy, *Air Marshal* Sir Edouard Michael Fitzfrederick, K.B.E., C.B.

Gubbins, *Maj.-Gen.* Sir Colin McVean, K.C.M.G., D.S.O., M.C.

Guest, *Air Marshal* Sir Charles Edward Neville, K.B.E., C.B.

Guinness, Sir Alec, Kt., C.B.E.

Guinness, Sir Kenelm Ernest Lee, Bt. (1867).

Guise, Sir John, K.B.E.

Guise, Sir John Grant, Bt. (1783).

Gull, Sir Michael Swinnerton Cameron, Bt. (1872).

Gunn, Sir William Archer, K.B.E., C.M.G.

Gunning, Sir Robert Charles, Bt. (1778).

Gunston, *Maj.* Sir Derrick Wellesley, Bt., M.C. (1938).

Gunter, Sir Ronald Vernon, Bt. (1901).

Gunther, Sir John Thomson, Kt., C.M.G., O.B.E.

Gutch, Sir John, K.C.M.G., O.B.E.

Guthrie, Sir Giles Connop McEacharn, Bt., O.B.E., D.S.C. (1936).

Guthrie, *Hon.* Sir Rutherford Campbell, Kt., C.M.G.

Guttmann, Sir Ludwig, Kt., C.B.E., M.D.

Hackett, *General* Sir John Winthrop, G.C.B., C.B.E., D.S.O., M.C.

Hackett, Sir Maurice Frederick, Kt., O.B.E.

Haddow, *Prof.* Sir Alexander, Kt., M.D., Ph.D., D.SC., F.R.S., F.R.S.E.

Haddow, Sir (Thomas) Douglas, K.C.B.

Hadley, Sir Leonard Albert, Kt.

Hadow, Sir Gordon, Kt., C.M.G., O.B.E.

Hadow, Sir Reginald Michael, K.C.M.G.

Haines, Sir Cyril Henry, K.B.E.

Hale, Sir Edward, K.B.E., C.B.

Haley, Sir William John, K.C.M.G.

Hall, Sir Arnold Alexander, Kt., F.R.S.

Hall, Sir Douglas Basil, K.C.M.G.

Hall, Sir (Frederick) John (Frank), Bt. (1923).

Hall, Sir John, Kt., O.B.E., M.P.

Hall, Sir John Bernard, Bt. (1919).

Hall, Sir John Hathorn, G.C.M.G., D.S.O., O.B.E., M.C.

Hall, Sir Neville Reynolds, Bt. (S 1687).

Hall, Sir Noel Frederick, Kt.

Hall, Sir Robert de Zouche, K.C.M.G.

Hall, *Brig.* Sir William Henry, Kt., C.B.E., D.S.O., E.D.

Hallett, *Vice-Adm.* Sir Cecil Charles Hughes-, K.C.B., C.B.E.

Halliday, Sir George Clifton, Kt.

Hallinan, Sir (Adrian) Lincoln, Kt.

Hallinan, Sir Charles Stuart, Kt., C.B.E.

Hallinan, Sir Eric, Kt.

Hallsworth, Sir Joseph, Kt.

Halsey, *Rev.* Sir John Walter Brooke, Bt. (1920).

Hambling, Sir (Herbert) Hugh, Bt. (1924).

Hamilton, Sir Charles William Feilden, Kt., O.B.E.

Hamilton, *Capt.* Lord Claud Nigel, G.C.V.O., C.M.G., D.S.O.

Hamilton, Sir Edward Sydney, Bt. (1776 and 1819).

Hamilton, *Admiral* Sir John Graham, G.B.E., C.B.

Hamilton, Sir Patrick George, Bt. (1937).

Hamilton, Sir (Robert Charles) Richard Caradoc, Bt. (S 1646).

Hamilton, *Capt.* Sir Robert William Stirling-, Bt., R.N. (S 1673).

Hammett, *Hon.* Sir Clifford James, Kt.

Hammick, Sir Stephen George, Bt. (1834).

Hampshire, Sir (George) Peter, K.C.M.G.

Hanbury, Sir John Capel, Kt., C.B.E.

Hancock, *Lt.-Col.* Sir Cyril Percy, K.C.I.E., O.B.E., M.C.

Hancock, Sir Patrick Francis, G.C.M.G.

Hancock, *Air Marshal* Sir Valston Eldridge, K.B.E., C.B., D.F.C.

Hancock, *Prof.* Sir (William) Keith, K.B.E., F.B.A.

Hanger, *Hon.* Sir Mostyn, K.B.E.

Hanham, Sir Michael William, Bt., D.F.C. (1667).

Hankinson, Sir Walter Crossfield, K.C.M.G., O.B.E., M.C.

Hanley, Sir Michael Bowen, K.C.B.

Hanmer, Sir (Griffin Wyndham) Edward, Bt. (1774).

Hannah, *Air Marshal* Sir Colin Thomas, K.C.M.G., K.B.E., C.B.

Hanson, Sir Anthony Leslie Oswald, Bt. (1887).

Hanson, Sir (Charles) John, Bt. (1918).

Hardie, Sir Charles Edgar Mathewes, Kt., C.B.E.

Harding, Sir Harold John Boyer, Kt.

Hardinge, Sir Robert, Bt. (1801).

Hardingham, Sir Robert Ernest, Kt., C.M.G., O.B.E.

Hardman, Sir Henry, K.C.B.

Hardman, *Air Chief Marshal* Sir (James) Donald (Innes), G.B.E., K.C.B., D.F.C.

Hardy, *Prof.* Sir Alister Clavering, Kt., D.SC., F.R.S.

Hardy, *General* Sir Campbell Richard, K.C.B., C.B.E., D.S.O., R.M.

Hardy, Sir Harry, Kt.

Hardy, Sir James Douglas, Kt., C.B.E.

Hardy, Sir Rupert John, Bt., (1876).

Hare, Sir Ralph Leigh, Bt. (1818).

Harford, Sir James Dundas, K.B.E., C.M.G.

Harford, Sir (John) Timothy, Bt. (1934).

Har Govind Misra, Sir, Kt., O.B.E.

Harington, *General* Sir Charles Henry Pepys, G.C.B., C.B.E., D.S.O., M.C.

Harland, *Air Marshal* Sir Reginald Edward Wynyard, K.B.E., C.B.

Harington, Sir Richard Dundas, Bt. (1611).

Harkness, Sir Douglas Alexander Earsman, K.B.E.

Harley, Sir Stanley Jaffa, Kt.

Harley, Sir Thomas Winlack, Kt., M.B.E., M.C.

Harman, Sir Cecil William Francis Stafford-King-, Bt. (1914).

Harman, Sir (Clement) James, G.B.E.

Harman, *Lt.-Gen.* Sir Jack Wentworth, K.C.B., O.B.E., M.C.

Harmer, Sir Frederic Evelyn, Kt., C.M.G.

Harmer, Sir (John) Dudley, Kt., (O.B.E.

Harmsworth, Sir (Arthur) Geoffrey (Annesley), Bt. (1918).

Harmsworth, Sir Hildebrand Alfred Beresford, Bt. (1922).

Harper, Sir Arthur Grant, K.C.V.O., C.B.E.

Harpham, Sir William, K.B.E., C.M.G.

Harris, *Marshal of the Royal Air Force* Sir Arthur Travers, Bt., G.C.B., O.B.E., A.F.C. (1953).

Harris, *Prof.* Sir Charles Herbert Stuart-, Kt., C.B.E., M.D.

Harris, Sir Charles Joseph William, K.B.E.

Harris, *Lt.-Gen.* Sir Frederick, K.B.E., C.B., M.C.

Harris, *Lt.-Gen.* Sir Ian Cecil, K.B.E., C.B., D.S.O.

Harris, *Maj.-Gen.* Sir Jack Alexander Sutherland-, K.C.V.O., C.B.

Harris, Sir Jack Wolfred Ashford, Bt. (1932).

Harris, Sir Percy Wyn, K.C.M.G., M.B.E.

Harris, Sir Ronald Montague Joseph, K.C.V.O., C.B.

Harris, Sir William Gordon, K.B.E., C.B.

Harris, Sir William Woolf, Kt., O.B.E.

Harrison, Sir Archibald Frederick, Kt., C.B.E.

Harrison, Sir (Bernard) Guy, Kt.

Harrison, Sir Cyril Ernest, Kt.

Harrison, Sir Geoffrey Wedgwood, G.C.M.G., K.C.V.O.

Harrison, Col. Sir (James) Harwood, Bt., T.D., M.P. (1961).

Harrison, Sir Robert Colin, Bt. (1922).

Harrod, Sir (Henry) Roy Forbes, Kt., F.B.A.

Hart, Sir Byrne, Kt., C.B.E., M.C.

Hart, Sir Francis Edmund Turton-, K.B.E.

Hart, Sir George Charles, K.B.E., B.E.M.

Hart, Sir William Ogden, Kt., C.M.G.

Hartley, *Air Marshal* Sir Christopher Harold, K.C.B., C.B.E., D.F.C., A.F.C.

Hartnett, Sir Laurence John, Kt., C.B.E.

Hartopp, Sir John Edmund Cradock-, Bt. (1796).

Hartwell, Sir Brodrick William Charles Elwin, Bt. (1805).

Hartwell, Sir Charles Herbert, Kt., C.M.G.

Harvey, Sir Richard Musgrave, Bt. (1933).

Haskard, Sir Cosmo Dugal Patrick Thomas, K.C.M.G., M.B.E.

Haslam, *Hon.* Sir Alec Leslie, Kt.

Hasluck, *Rt. Hon.* Sir Paul Meernaa Caedwalla, G.C.M.G., G.C.V.O.

Hassan, Sir Joshua Abraham, Kt., C.B.E., M.V.O., Q.C.

Hatty, Sir Cyril James, Kt.

Havelock, Sir Wilfred Bowen, Kt.

Havers, Cecil Robert, Kt.

Havers, *Air Vice-Marshal* Sir (Ephraim) William, K.B.E., C.B.

Havers, Sir (Robert) Michael (Oldfield), Kt., Q.C., M.P.

Hawker, Sir (Frank) Cyril, Kt.

Hawker, Sir Richard George, Kt.

Hawkey, Sir Roger Pryce, Bt. (1945).

Hawkins, *Admiral* Sir Geoffrey Alan Brooke, K.B.E., C.B., M.V.O., D.S.C.

Hawkins, Sir Humphry Villiers Caesar, Bt. (1778).

Hawkins, *Maj.* Sir Michael Babington Charles, K.C.V.O., M.B.E.

Hawkins, *Vice-Adm.* Sir Raymond Shayle, K.C.B.

Hawley, *Maj.* Sir David Henny, Bt. (1795).

Haworth, Sir (Arthur) Geoffrey, Bt. (1911).

Haworth, *Hon.* Sir William Crawford, Kt.

Hawthorne, *Prof.* Sir William Rede, Kt., C.B.E., Sc.D., F.R.S.

Hawton, Sir John Malcolm Kenneth, K.C.B.

Hay, Sir (Alan) Philip, K.C.V.O., T.D.

Hay, Sir Arthur Thomas Erroll, Bt., I.S.O. (S 1663).

Hay, Sir Frederick Baden-Powell, Bt. (S 1703).

Hay, Sir James Brian Dalrymple-, Bt. (1798).

Hay, *Lt.-Gen.* Sir Robert, K.C.I.E.

Hayday, Sir Frederick, Kt., C.B.E.

Hayes, Sir Claude James, K.C.M.G.

Hayes, *Vice-Adm.* Sir John Osler Chattock, K.C.B., O.B.E.

Hayman, Sir Peter Telford, K.C.M.G., C.V.O., M.B.E.

Haynes, Sir George Ernest, Kt., C.B.E.

Hayter, Sir William Goodenough, K.C.M.G.

Hayward, Sir Alfred, K.B.E.

Hayward, Sir Charles William, Kt., C.B.E.

Hayward, Sir Edward Waterfield, Kt.

Hayward, Sir Isaac James, Kt.

Hayward, Sir Richard Arthur, Kt., C.B.E.

Head, Sir Francis David Somerville, Bt. (1838).

Heald, *Rt. Hon.* Sir Lionel Frederick, Kt., Q.C.

Healey, *Maj.* Sir Edward Randal Chadwyck-, Bt., M.C. (1919).

Heap, Sir Desmond, Kt.

Heath, *Air Marshal* Sir Maurice Lionel, K.B.E., C.B.

Heathcote, Sir Michael Perryman, Bt. (1733).

Heaton, Sir Yvo Robert Henniker-, Bt. (1912).

Hedges, Sir John Francis, Kt., C.B.E.

Heinze, *Prof.* Sir Bernard Thomas, Kt., LL.D.

Hellings, *General* Sir Peter William Cradock, K.C.B., D.S.C., M.C., R.M.

Helpmann, Sir Robert Murray, Kt., C.B.E.

Henderson, Sir Guy Wilmot McLintock, Kt., Q.C.

Henderson, Sir James Thyne, K.B.E., C.M.G.

Henderson, Sir John, Kt.

Henderson, Sir (John) Nicholas, K.C.M.G.

Henderson, Sir Malcolm Siborne, K.C.M.G.

Henderson, Sir Neville Vicars, Kt., C.B.E.

Henderson, *Admiral* Sir Nigel Stuart, G.B.E., K.C.B.

Henderson, Sir Peter Gordon, K.C.B.

Hendy, Sir Philip, Kt.

Henig, Sir Mark, Kt.

Henley, Sir Douglas Owen, K.C.B.

Henley, *Rear-Adm.* Sir Joseph Charles Cameron, K.C.V.O., C.B.

Hennessy, Sir John Wyndham Pope-, Kt., C.B.E., F.B.A., F.S.A.

Hennessy, Sir Patrick, Kt.

Henniker, *Brig.* Sir Mark Chandos Auberton, Bt., C.B.E., D.S.O., M.C. (1813).

Henriques, *Hon.* Sir Cyril George Xavier, Kt.

Henry, *Hon.* Sir Albert Royle, K.B.E.

Harry, Sir Denis Aynsley, Kt., O.B.E., Q.C.

Henry, Sir James Holmes, Bt., C.M.G., M.C., T.D., Q.C. (1923).

Henry, *Hon.* Sir Trevor Ernest, Kt.

Henty, *Hon.* Sir Norman Henry Denham, K.B.E.

Hepburn, Sir Ninian Buchan Archibald John Buchan-, Bt. (1815).

Herbert, *Lt.-Gen.* Sir (Edwin) Otway, K.B.E., C.B., D.S.O.

Herchenroder, Sir (Marie Joseph Barnabe) Francis, Kt., Q.C.

Heron, Sir Conrad Frederick, K.C.B., O.B.E.

Herries, Sir Richard Alexander Robert Young-, Kt., O.B.E., M.C.

Herring, *Lt.-Gen. Hon.* Sir Edmund Francis, K.C.M.G., K.B.E., D.S.O., M.C., E.D., Q.C.

Hetherington, Sir Arthur Ford, Kt., D.S.C.

Heward, *Air Chief Marshal* Sir Anthony Williamson, K.C.B., O.B.E., D.F.C., A.F.C.

Hewetson, *General* Sir Reginald Hackett, G.C.B., C.B.E., D.S.O.

Hewett, Sir John George, Bt., M.C. (1813).

Hewitt, Sir (Cyrus) Lenox (Simson), Kt., O.B.E.

Hewitt, Sir Nicholas Charles Joseph, Bt. (1921).

Hewitt, Sir John Francis, K.C.V.O., C.B.E.

Hewitt, Sir Nicholas Charles Joseph, Bt. (1921).

Hewson, Sir (Joseph) Bushby, Kt.

Heyes, Sir Tasman Hudson Eastwood, Kt., C.B.E.

Heygate, Sir John Edward Nourse, Bt. (1831).

Heymanson, Sir (Sydney Henry) Randal, Kt., C.B.E.

Heywood, Sir Oliver Kerr, Bt. (1838).

Hezlet, *Vice-Adm.* Sir Arthur Richard, K.B.E., C.B., D.S.O., D.S.C.

Hickinbotham, Sir Tom, K.C.M.G., K.C.V.O., C.I.E., O.B.E.

Hickman, Sir (Alfred) Howard (Whitby), Bt. (1903).

Hicks, Sir (Cedric) Stanton, Kt., M.D., Ph.D.

Hicks, *Col.* Sir Denys Theodore, Kt., O.B.E., T.D.

Hicks, Sir Edwin William, Kt., C.B.E.

Hicks, *Prof.* Sir John Richard, Kt., F.B.A.

Higgs, Sir (John) Michael (Clifford), Kt.

Hildred, Sir William Percival, Kt., C.B., O.B.E.

Hildreth, *Maj.-Gen.* Sir (Harold) John (Crossley), K.B.E.

Hildyard, Sir David Henry Thoroton, K.C.M.G., D.F.C.

Hiley, *Hon.* Sir Thomas Alfred, K.B.E.

Hill, *Prof.* Sir Austin Bradford, Kt., C.B.E., Ph.D., D.Sc., F.R.S.

Hill, Sir (George) Cyril Rowley, Bt. (I 1779).

Hill, *Prof.* Sir Ian George Wilson, Kt., C.B.E., T.D., F.R.S.E.

Hill, Sir James, Bt. (1917).

Hill, Sir (James William) Francis, Kt., C.B.E.

Hill, *Prof.* Sir (John) Denis (Nelson), Kt.

Hill, Sir John McGregor, Kt., Ph.D.

Hill, Sir John Maxwell, Kt., C.B.E., D.F.C.

Hill, Sir Robert Erskine-, Bt. (1945).

Hillary, Sir Edmund, K.B.E.

Hilton, Sir Derek Percy, Kt., M.B.E.

Himsworth, Sir Harold Percival, K.C.B., M.D., F.R.S

Hinchliffe, Sir (Albert) Henry (Stanley), Kt.

Hinde, *Maj.-Gen.* Sir (William) Robert (Norris), K.B.E., C.B., D.S.O.

Hirsch, *Prof.* Sir Peter Bernhard, Kt., Ph.D., F.R.S.

Hirst, *Prof.* Sir Edmund Langley, Kt., C.B.E., Ph.D., F.R.S.

Hitchman, Sir (Edwin) Alan, K.C.B.

Hoare, Sir Frederick Alfred, Bt. (1962).

Hoare, Sir Peter Richard David, Bt. (1785).

Hoare, Sir Samuel, K.B.E., C.B.

Hoare, Sir Timothy Edward Charles, Bt. (1 1784).

Hobart, *Lt.-Cdr.* Sir Robert Hampden, Bt., R.N. (1914).

Hobhouse, Sir Charles Chisholm, Bt., T.D. (1812).

Hochoy, Sir Solomon, G.C.M.G., G.C.V.O., O.B.E.

Hodge, Sir John Rowland, Bt., M.B.E. (1921).

Hodge, Sir Julian Stephen Alfred, Kt.

Hodges, *Air Chief Marshal* Sir Lewis MacDonald, K.C.B., C.B.E., D.S.O., D.F.C.

Hodgkin, *Prof.* Sir Alan Lloyd, O.M., K.B.E., F.R.S., SC.D.

Hodgkinson, *Air Chief Marshal* Sir (William) Derek, K.C.B., C.B.E., D.F.C., A.F.C.

Hodson, Sir Michael Robin Adderley, Bt. (1 1789).

Hogan, Sir Michael Joseph Patrick, Kt., C.M.G.

Hogg, *Vice-Adm.* Sir Ian Leslie Trower, K.C.B., D.S.C.

Hogg, Sir John Nicholson, Kt., T.D.

Hogg, *Lieut.-Col.* Sir Kenneth Weir, Bt., O.B.E. (1846).

Hogg, Sir William Lindsay Lindsay-, Bt. (1905).

Holbrook, *Col.* Sir Claude Vivian, Kt., C.B.E.

Holcroft, Sir Reginald Culcheth, Bt. (1921).

Holden, Sir David Charles Beresford, K.B.E., C.B., E.R.D.

Holden, Sir Edward, Bt. (1893).

Holden, Sir George, Bt. (1919).

Holden, Sir James Robert, Kt.

Holden, *Hon.* Sir Michael Herbert Frank, Kt., C.B.E., E.D.

Holder, Sir John Eric Duncan, Bt. (1898).

Holder, *Air Marshal* Sir Paul Davie, K.B.E., C.B., D.S.O., D.F.C., Ph.D.

Holderness, Sir Richard William, Bt. (1920).

Holland, Sir Clifton Vaughan, Kt.

Holland, Sir Jim Sothern, Bt. (1917).

Hollings, *Hon.* Sir (Alfred) Kenneth, Kt., M.C.

Hollom, Sir Jasper Quintus, K.B.E.

Holmes, *Hon.* Sir (David) Ronald Kt., C.M.G., C.B.E., M.C., E.D.

Holmes, *Prof.* Sir Frank Wakefield Kt.

Holmes, Sir Maurice Andrew, Kt.

Holmes, *Maj.-Gen.* Sir Noel Galway, K.B.E., C.B., M.C.

Holmes, Sir Stanley, Kt.

Holmes, Sir Stephen Lewis, K.C.M.G., M.C.

Holt, Sir James Arthur, Kt.

Holt, Sir John Anthony Langford-, Kt., M.P.

Holyoake, *Rt. Hon.* Sir Keith Jacka, G.C.M.G., C.H.

Home, Sir David George, Bt. (S 1671).

Hone, Sir Brian William, Kt., O.B.E.

Hone, Sir Evelyn Denison, G.C.M.G., C.V.O., O.B.E.

Hone, *Maj.-Gen.* Sir (Herbert) Ralph, K.C.M.G., K.B.E., M.C., T.D., Q.C.

Honywood, *Col.* Sir William Wynne, Bt., M.C. (1660).

Hood, *Lt.-Gen.* Sir Alexander, G.B.E., K.C.B., K.C.V.O., M.B.E.

Hood, Sir Alexander William Fuller-Acland-, Bt. (1806).

Hood, Sir Harold Joseph, Bt., T.D. (1922).

Hood, *Col.* Sir Tom Fielden, K.B.E., C.B., T.D.

Hooker, Sir Leslie Joseph, Kt.

Hooker, Sir Stanley George, Kt., C.B.E., D.SC., D.Phil, F.R.S.

Hooper, Sir Stanley Robin Maurice, Bt. (1962).

Hooper, Sir Leonard James, K.C.M.G., C.B.E.

Hooper, Sir Robin William John, K.C.M.G., D.S.O., D.F.C.

Hope, Sir Archibald Philip, Bt., O.B.E., D.F.C. (S 1628).

Hope, Sir (Charles) Peter, K.C.M.G., T.D.

Hope, Sir James, Bt., M.M. (1932).

Hopkin, Sir (William Aylsham) Bryan, Kt., C.B.E.

Hopkins, *Admiral* Sir Frank Henry Edward, K.C.B., D.S.O., D.S.C.

Horlick, Sir John James Macdonald, Bt. (1914).

Hornby, Sir (Roger) Antony, Kt.

Horne, Sir Alan Edgar, Bt., M.C. (1929).

Hornbrook, Sir Manuel Richard, Kt., O.B.E.

Horobin, Sir Ian Macdonald, Kt.

Horrocks, *Lt.-Gen.* Sir Brian Gwynne, K.C.B., K.B.E., D.S.O., M.C.

Horsfall, Sir John Musgrave, Bt., M.C., T.D. (1909).

Horsley, *Air Marshal* Sir (Beresford) Peter (Torrington), K.C.B., C.B.E., M.V.O., A.F.C.

Hort, Sir James Fenton, Bt. (1767).

Hoskyns, Sir Benedict Leigh, Bt. (1676).

Hotchin, Sir Claude, Kt., O.B.E.

Houldsworth, Sir (Harold) Basil, Bt. (1956).

Houldsworth, Sir Reginald Douglas Henry, Bt., O.B.E., T.D. (1887).

House, *Maj.-Gen.* Sir David George, K.C.B., C.B.E., M.C.

How, Sir Friston Charles, Kt., C.B.

Howard, Sir Douglas Frederick, K.C.M.G., M.C.

Howard, Sir (Hamilton) Edward de Coucey, Bt., G.B.E. (1955).

Howard, Sir John Alfred Golding, Kt.

Howard, *Maj.-Gen.* Hon. Sir Michael Fitzalan-, K.C.V.O., C.B., C.B.E., M.C.

Howard, Sir Walter Stewart, Kt., M.B.E.

Howe, *Rt. Hon.* Sir (Richard Edward) Geoffrey, Kt., Q.C., M.P.

Howe, Sir Robert George, G.B.E., K.C.M.G.

Howe, Sir Ronald Martin, Kt., C.V.O., M.C.

Howie, Sir James William, Kt. M.D.

Hoyle, *Prof.* Sir Fred, Kt., F.R.S.

Hubble, *Prof.* Sir Douglas Vernon K.B.E., M.D.

Huddie, Sir David Patrick, Kt.

Hudleston, *Air Chief Marshal* Sir Edmund Cuthbert, G.C.B., C.B.E.

Hudson, Sir Edmund Peder, Kt., F.R.S.E.

Hudson, Sir William, K.B.E., F.R.S.

Hughes, Sir David Collingwood, Bt. (1773).

Hughes, *Air Marshal* Sir (Sidney Weetman) Rochford, K.C.B., C.B.E., A.F.C.

Hughes, Sir Trevor Denby Lloyd-, Kt.

Hugo, *Lt.-Col.* Sir John Mandeville, K.C.V.O., O.B.E.

Hull, Sir Hubert, Kt., C.B.E.

Hull, *Field Marshal* Sir Richard Amyatt, G.C.B., D.S.O.

Hulme, *Hon.* Sir Alan Shallcross, K.B.E.

Hulse, Sir (Hamilton) Westrow, Bt. (1739).

Hulton, Sir Edward George Warris, Kt.

Hulton, Sir Geoffrey Alan, Bt. (1905).

Hume, Sir Alan Blyth, Kt., C.B.

Humphrey, *Air Chief Marshal* Sir Andrew Henry, G.C.B., O.B.E., D.F.C., A.F.C.

Humphreys, Sir Olliver William, Kt., C.B.E.

Hunt, Sir David Wathen Stather, K.C.M.G., O.B.E.

Hunt, Sir John Joseph Benedict, K.C.B.

Hunt, Sir Joseph Anthony, Kt., M.B.E.

Hunt, *General* Sir Peter Mervyn, G.C.B., D.S.O., O.B.E.

Hunter, Sir (Ernest) John, Kt., C.B.E.

Hurley, Sir John Garling, Kt., C.B.E.

Hurley, Sir Wilfred Hugh, Kt.

Hurst, *His Hon.* Sir (James Henry) Donald, Kt.

Husband, Sir Henry Charles, Kt., C.B.E.

Hutchings, Sir Robert Howell, K.C.I.E., C.M.G.

Hutchinson, Sir Arthur Sydney, K.B.E., C.B., C.V.O.

Hutchinson, Sir Joseph Burtt, Kt., C.M.G., SC.D., F.R.S.

Hutchison, *Lt.-Cdr.* Sir (George) Ian Clark, Kt., R.N.

Hutchison, *Hon.* Sir James Douglas, Kt.

Hutchison, Sir James Riley Holt, Bt., D.S.O., T.D. (1956).

Hutchison, Sir Peter, Bt. (1939).

Hutchison, Sir (William) Kenneth, Kt., C.B.E., F.R.S.

Hutson, Sir Francis Challenor, Kt., C.B.E.

Hutt, Sir (Alexander McDonald) Bruce, K.B.E., C.M.G.

Hutton, Sir Leonard, Kt.

Hutton, Sir Noel Kilpatrick, K.C.B., Q.C.

Hutton, *Lt.-Gen.* Sir Thomas, G.C.I.E., C.B., M.C.

Huxley, *Prof.* Sir Andrew Fielding, Kt., F.R.S.

Huxley, Sir Leonard George Holden, K.B.E., D.PHIL., Ph.D.

Hyatali, *Hon.* Sir Isaac Emanuel, Kt.

Hynes, Sir Lincoln Carruthers, Kt., O.B.E.

Ibadan, The Olubadan of, Kt., O.B.E.

Ife, The Oni of, K.C.M.G., K.B.E.

Iggulden, Sir Douglas Percy, Kt., C.B.E., D.S.O., T.D.

Illingworth, *Prof.* Sir Charles Frederick William, Kt., C.B.E.

Ilott, Sir John Moody Albert, Kt.

Imrie, Sir John Dunlop, Kt., C.B.E.

Inch, Sir John Ritchie, Kt., C.V.O., C.B.E.

Indore, H.H. *ex*-Maharaja Holkar of, G.C.I.E.

Ingilby, Sir Thomas Colvin William, Bt. (1866).

Inglefield, Sir Gilbert Samuel, G.B.E., T.D.

Inglefield, *Col.* Sir John Frederick Crompton-, Kt., T.D.

Inglis, *Maj.-Gen.* Sir Drummond, K.B.E., C.B., M.C.

Inglis of Glencorse, Sir Roderick John, Bt. (S 1703).

Ingram, Sir Herbert, Bt. (1893).

Innes, Sir Charles Kenneth Gordon, Bt. (N.S. 1686).

Innes, Sir Walter James, Bt. (S 1628).

Inniss, *Hon.* Sir Clifford de Lisle, Kt.

Irish, Sir Ronald Arthur, Kt., O.B.E.

Ironmonger, Sir (Charles) Ronald, Kt.

Irvine, *Rt. Hon.* Sir Arthur James, Kt., Q.C., M.P.

Irving, *Rear-Adm.* Sir Edmund George, K.B.E., C.B.

Irwin, Sir James Campbell, Kt., O.B.E., E.D.

Isham, Sir Gyles, Bt. (1627).

Isitt, *Air Vice-Marshal* Sir Leonard Monk, K.B.E.

Issigonis, Sir Alec Arnold Constantine, Kt., C.B.E., F.R.S.

Ismay, Sir George, K.B.E., C.B.

Jack, *Hon.* Sir Alieu Sulayman, Kt.

Jack, Sir Daniel Thomson, Kt., C.B.E.

Jack, *Hon.* Sir Roy Emile, Kt.

Jackling, Sir Roger William, K.C.M.G.

Jackman, *Air Marshal* Sir (Harold) Douglas, K.B.E., C.B.

Jackson, Sir Donald Edward, Kt.

Jackson, *Col.* Sir Francis James Gidlow, Kt., M.C., T.D.

Jackson, Sir Geoffrey Holt Seymour, K.C.M.G.

Jackson, Sir George Christopher Mather-, Bt. (1869).

Jackson, Sir Hugh Nicolas, Bt. (1913).

Jackson, Sir John Montrésor, Bt. (1815).

Jackson, *Hon.* Sir Lawrence Walter, K.C.M.G.

Jackson, Sir Michael Roland, Bt. (1902).

Jackson, *Air Vice-Marshal* Sir Ralph Coburn, K.B.E., C.B.

Jackson, Sir Robert Gillman Allen, K.C.V.O., C.M.G., O.B.E.

Jackson, *General* Sir William Godfrey Fothergill, G.B.E., K.C.B., M.C.

Jacob, *Lt.-Gen.* Sir (Edward) Ian (Claud), G.B.E., C.B.

Jacobs, Sir Roland Ellis, Kt.

Jacobs, Sir Wilfred Ebenezer, Kt., O.B.E., Q.C.

Jaffray, Sir William Otho, Bt. (1892).

Jakeway, Sir (Francis) Derek, K.C.M.G., O.B.E.

James, *Wing-Cdr.* Sir Archibald William Henry, K.B.E., M.C.

James, *Rt. Hon.* Sir Arthur Evan, Kt.

James, Sir Gerard Bowes Kingston, Bt. (1823).

James, Sir John Hastings, K.C.V.O., C.B.

James, *Rt. Hon.* Sir (John) Morrice (Cairns), G.C.M.G., C.V.O., M.B.E.

Janes, Sir Herbert Charles, Kt.

Jansz, Sir Herbert Eric, Kt., C.M.G.

Janvrin, *Vice-Adm.* Sir (Hugh) Richard (Benest), K.C.B., D.S.C.

Jardine, *Maj.* Sir (Andrew) Rupert (John) Buchanan-, Bt., M.C. (1885).

Jardine, *Brig.* Sir Ian Liddell, Bt., O.B.E., M.C. (1916).

Jardine, Sir William Edward, Bt., O.B.E., T.D. (S 1672).

Jarrett, Sir Clifford George, K.B.E., C.B.

Jawara, *Hon.* Sir Dawda Kairaba, Kt.

Jayetileke, *Hon.* Sir Edward George Perera, Kt., Q.C.

Jeffcoate, *Prof.* Sir (Thomas) Norman (Arthur), Kt., F.R.C.S.

Jefferson, *Lt.-Col.* Sir John Alexander Dunnington-, Bt., D.S.O. (1958).

Jeffreys, *Prof.* Sir Harold, Kt., D.SC., F.R.S.

Jehanghir, Sir Hirjee Cowasjee, Bt. (1908).

Jejeebhoy, Sir Rustom, Bt. (1857).

Jenkin, Sir William Norman Prentice, Kt., C.S.I., C.I.E.

Jenkins, Sir Evan Meredith, G.C.I.E., K.C.S.I.

Jenkins, Sir (Thomas) Gilmour, K.C.B., K.B.E., M.C.

Jenkins, Sir William, Kt.

Jenkinson, Sir Anthony Banks, Bt. (1661).

Jenks, Sir Richard Atherley, Bt. (1932).

Jennings, Sir Albert Victor, Kt.

Jennings, Sir Raymond Winter Kt., Q.C.

Jenour, Sir (Arthur) Maynard (Chesterfield), Kt., T.D.

Jephcott, Sir Harry, Bt. (1962).

Jerram, *Rear-Adm.* (S.) Sir Rowland Christopher, K.B.E., D.S.O.

Jessel, Sir George, Bt., M.C. (1883).

Jessel, Sir Richard Hugh, Kt.

Joel, *Hon.* Sir Asher Alexander, K.B.E.

John, *Admiral of the Fleet* Sir Caspar, G.C.B.

John, Sir Rupert Godfrey, Kt.

Johnson, *Hon.* Sir David Powell Croom-, Kt., D.S.C., V.R.D.

Johnson, *Maj.-Gen.* Sir George Frederick, K.C.V.O., C.B., C.B.E., D.S.O.

Johnson, Sir Henry Cecil, K.B.E.

Johnson, Sir John Paley, Bt., M.B.E. (1755).

Johnson, Sir Ronald Ernest Charles, Kt., C.B.

Johnson, Sir Victor Philipse Hill, Bt. (1818).

Johnson, Sir William Clarence, Kt., C.M.G., C.B.E.

Johnston, Sir Alexander, G.C.B., K.B.E.

Johnston, Sir Charles Collier, Kt., T.D.

Johnston, Sir Charles Hepburn, G.C.M.G.

Johnston, Sir John Baines, K.C.M.G., K.C.V.O.

Johnston, Sir Thomas Alexander, Bt. (S 1626).

Johnstone, Sir Frederic Allan George, Bt. (S 1700).

Joint, Sir (Edgar) James, K.C.M.G., O.B.E.

Jolly, *General* Sir Alan, G.C.B., C.B.E., D.S.O.

Jones, *Maj.-Gen.* Sir (Arthur) Guy Salisbury-, G.C.V.O., C.M.G., C.B.E., M.C.

Jones, Sir Arthur Hope-, K.B.E., C.M.G.

Kolhapur, *Maj.* H.H. Maharaja of, G.C.S.I.

Kotalawala, *Col. Rt. Hon.* Sir John Lionel, C.H., K.B.E.

Krebs, *Prof.* Sir Hans Adolf, Kt., M.D., F.R.S.

Krusin, Sir Stanley Marks, Kt., C.B.

Kyle, *Air Chief Marshal* Sir Wallace Hart, G.C.B., C.B.E., D.S.O., D.F.C.

Labouchere, Sir George Peter, G.B.E., K.C.M.G.

Lacon, Sir George Vere Francis, Bt. (1818).

Lacy, Sir Hugh Maurice Pierce, Bt. (1921).

Laing, Sir (John) Maurice, Kt.

Laing, Sir John William, Kt., C.B.E.

Laing, Sir (William) Kirby, Kt.

Laithwaite, Sir (John) Gilbert, G.C.M.G., K.C.B., K.C.I.E., C.S.I.

Lake, Sir (Atwell) Graham, Bt. (1711).

Lakin, Sir Henry, Bt. (1909).

Lakshmanaswami Mudaliar, *Diwan Bahadur* Sir Arcot, Kt.

Lala Gujjar Mal, *Rai Bahadur* Sir, Kt.

Lamb, Sir Lionel Henry, K.C.M.G., O.B.E.

Lambart, Sir Oliver Francis, Bt. (1911).

Lambert, Sir Anthony Edward, K.C.M.G.

Lambert, Sir Edward Thomas, K.B.E., C.V.O.

†Lambert, Sir Greville Foley, Bt. (1711).

Lancaster, *Vice-Adm.* Sir John Strike, K.B.E., C.B.

Lancaster, Sir Osbert, Kt., C.B.E.

Lane, *Rt. Hon.* Sir Geoffrey Dawson, Kt., A.F.C.

Lang, *Lt.-Gen.* Sir Derek Boileau, K.C.B., D.S.O., M.C.

Lang, Sir John Gerald, G.C.B.

Langham, Sir James Michael, Bt. (1660).

Langker, Sir Erik, Kt., O.B.E.

Langman, Sir John Lyell, Bt. (1906).

Langrishe, Sir Hercules Ralph Hume, Bt. (I 1777).

Lapsley, *Air Marshal* Sir John Hugh, K.B.E., C.B., D.F.C., A.F.C.

Lapun, Sir Paul, Kt.

Larcom, Sir (Charles) Christopher Royden, Bt. (1868).

Larking, *Lt.-Col.* Sir (Charles) Gordon, Kt., C.B.E.

Lartigue, Sir Louis Cools-, Kt., O.B.E.

Lascelles, *Rt. Hon.* Sir Alan Frederick, G.C.B., G.C.V.O., C.M.G., M.C.

Lascelles, Sir Francis William, K.C.B., M.C.

Laskey, Sir Denis Seward, K.C.M.G., C.V.O.

Latey, *Hon.* Sir John Brinsmead, Kt., M.B.E.

Latham, Sir Joseph, Kt., C.B.E.

Latham, Sir Richard Thomas Paul, Bt. (1919).

Lathbury, *General* Sir Gerald William, G.C.B., D.S.O., M.B.E.

Latimer, Sir Courtenay Robert, Kt., C.B.E.

Lauder, *Maj.* Sir George Andrew Dick,- Bt. (S 1690).

Laurent, Sir Edgar, Kt., C.M.G., M.D.

Laurie, *Maj.-Gen.* Sir John Emilius, Bt., C.B.E., D.S.O. (1834).

Law, *Admiral* Sir Horace Rochfort, G.C.B., O.B.E., D.S.C.

Lawes, Sir John Claud Bennet, Bt. (1882).

Lawrence, Sir David Roland Walter, Bt. (1906).

Lawrence, Sir Frederick, Kt., O.B.E.

Lawrence, Sir John Waldemar, Bt., O.B.E. (1858).

Lawrence, Sir William, Bt. (1867).

Lawrence, Sir (William) Russell, Kt., Q.C.

Lawson, Sir Henry Brailsford, Kt., M.C.

Lawson, *Lt.-Col.* Sir John Charles Arthur Digby, Bt., D.S.O., M.C. (1900).

Lawson, *Hon.* Sir Neil, Kt.

Lawson, Sir William Howard, Bt. (1841).

Lawther, Sir William, Kt.

Lawton, *Rt. Hon.* Sir Frederick Horace, Kt.

Laycock, Sir Leslie Ernest, Kt., C.B.E.

Lea, Sir Frederick Meacham, Kt., C.B., C.B.E., D.S.C.

Lea, *Lt.-Gen.* Sir George Harris, K.C.B., D.S.O., M.B.E.

Lea, Sir Thomas Claude Harris, Bt. (1892).

Leach, *Prof.* Sir Edmund Ronald, Kt., Ph.D., F.B.A.

Leach, Sir Ronald George, Kt., C.B.E.

Leask, *Lt.-Gen.* Sir Henry Lowther Ewart Clark, K.C.B., D.S.O., O.B.E.

Leather, Sir Edwin Hartley Cameron, K.C.M.G., K.C.V.O.

Le Bailly, *Vice-Adm.* Sir Louis Edward Stewart Holland, K.B.E., C.B.

Le Cheminant, *Air Marshal* Sir Peter de Lacey, K.C.B., D.F.C.

Lechmere, Sir Berwick Hungerford, Bt. (1818).

Ledger, Sir Joseph Francis, Kt.

Ledwidge, Sir (William) Bernard (John), K.C.M.G.

Lee, Sir Arthur James, K.B.E., M.C.

Lee, *Air Chief Marshal* Sir David John Pryer, G.B.E., C.B.

Lee, Sir (George) Wilton, Kt.

Lee Hau Shik, *Col.* Sir, K.B.E.

Lee, Sir (Henry) Desmond (Pritchard), Kt.

Lee, *Col.* Sir William Allison, Kt., O.B.E., T.D.

Leeds, Sir George Graham Mortimer, Bt. (1812).

Lees, *Air Marshal* Sir (Ronald) Beresford, K.C.B., C.B.E., D.F.C.

Lees, Sir Thomas Edward, Bt. (1897).

Lees, Sir Thomas Harcourt Ivor, Bt. (1804).

Lees, Sir (William) Hereward Clare, Bt. (1937).

Leese, *Lt.-Gen.* Sir Oliver William Hargreaves, Bt., K.C.B., C.B.E., D.S.O. (1908).

Le Fleming, Sir William Kelland, Bt. (1705).

Le Gallais, *Hon.* Sir Richard Lyle, Kt.

Legard, Sir Thomas Digby, Bt. (1660).

Leggett, Sir Frederick William, K.B.E., C.B.

Legh, *Major* Hon. Sir Francis Michael, K.C.V.O.

Leigh, Sir John, Bt. (1918).

Leighton, Sir Michael John Bryan, Bt. (1693).

Leitch, Sir George, K.C.B., O.B.E.

Leith, Sir Andrew George Forbes-, Bt. (1923).

Le Marchant, Sir Denis, Bt. (1841).

Le Masurier, Sir Robert Hugh, Kt., D.S.C.

Lemon, Sir (Richard) Dawnay, Kt., C.B.E.

Lennard, *Lt.-Col.* Sir Stephen Arthur Hallam Farnaby, Bt. (1880).

Lennard, Sir Thomas Richard Fiennes Barrett-, Bt., O.B.E. (1801).

Lennox, *Rear Adm.* Sir Alexander Henry Charles, K.C.V.O., C.B., D.S.O.

Lennox, *Lt.-Gen.* Sir George Charles Gordon, K.B.E., C.B., C.V.O., D.S.O.

Leon, Sir John Ronald, Bt. (1911).

Le Quesne, Sir (Charles) Martin, K.C.M.G.

Leslie, Sir Harald Robert, K.T., C.B.E., T.D. (Lord Birsay).

Leslie, Sir John Norman Ide, Bt. (1876).

†Leslie, Sir Percy Theodore, Bt. (S 1625).

Lethbridge, *Capt.* Sir Hector Wroth, Bt. (1804).

Lever, Sir (Tresham) Christopher Arthur Lindsay, Bt. (1911).

Levinge, *Maj.* Sir Richard Vere Henry, Bt., M.B.E. (I 1704).

Levy, Sir (Enoch) Bruce, Kt., O.B.E.

Levy, Sir Ewart Maurice, Bt. (1913).

Lewando, Sir Jan Alfred, Kt., C.B.E.

Lewin, *Admiral* Sir Terence Thornton, K.C.B., M.V.O., D.S.C.

Lewis, Sir Allen Montgomery, Kt., Q.C.

Lewis, *Admiral* Sir Andrew Mackenzie, K.C.B.

Lewis, Sir Anthony Carey, Kt., C.B.E.

Lewis, *Brig.* Sir Clinton Gresham, Kt., O.B.E.

Lewis, Sir Edward Roberts, Kt.

Lewis, Sir Ian Malcolm, Kt.

Lewis, Sir (John) Duncan Orr-, Bt. (1920).

Lewis, Sir John Todd, Kt., O.B.E.

Lewis, Sir William Arthur, Kt.

Lewthwaite, Sir William Anthony, Bt. (1927).

Ley, Sir Gerald Gordon, Bt., T.D. (1905).

Leyland, Sir Vivyan Edward Naylor-, Bt. (1895).

Lidbury, Sir Charles, Kt.

Lidbury, Sir John Towersey, Kt.

Lidderdale, Sir David William Shuckburgh, K.C.B.

Liddle, Sir Donald Ross, Kt.

Lighthill, *Prof.* Sir (Michael) James, Kt., F.R.S.

Lighton, Sir Christopher Robert, Bt., M.B.E. (I 1791).

Liley, *Prof.* Sir Albert William, K.C.M.G.

Lim, Sir Han Hoe, Kt., C.B.E.

Lincoln, Sir Anthony Handley, K.C.M.G., C.V.O.

Lindley, Sir Arnold Lewis George, Kt.

Lindo, Sir (Henry) Laurence, G.C.M.G.

Lindon, Sir Leonard Charles Edward, Kt.

Lindop, Sir Norman, Kt.

Lindsay, Sir Ernest Daryl, Kt.

Lindsay, Sir Harvey Kincaid Stewart, Kt.

Lindsay, Sir Martin Alexander, Bt., C.B.E., D.S.O. (1962).

Lindsay, Sir William, Kt., C.B.E.

Lindsay, Sir William O'Brien, K.B.E.

Linfield, *Sir Arthur George*, K.C.V.O., C.B.E.

Linstead, Sir Hugh Nicholas, Kt., O.B.E.

Lintott, Sir Henry John Bevis, K.C.M.G.

Lister, Sir (Charles) Percy, Kt.

Lithgow, Sir William James, Bt., (1925).

Little, *Hon.* Sir Douglas Macfarlane, Kt.

Little, Sir (Rudolf) Alexander, K.C.B.

Littler, Sir Emile, Kt.

Livermore, Sir Harry, Kt.

Livingston, *Air Marshal* Sir Philip Clermont, K.B.E., C.B., A.F.C.

Llewellyn, Sir David Treharne, Kt.

Llewellyn, Sir (Frederick) John, K.C.M.G.

Llewellyn, *Lt.-Col.* Sir Rhys, Bt. (1922).

Llewellyn, *Col.* Sir (Robert) Godfrey, Bt., C.B., C.B.E., M.C., T.D. (1959).

Llewelyn, Sir Charles Michael Dillwyn-Venables-, Bt., M.V.O. (1890).

Lloyd, *Maj.* Sir (Ernest) Guy (Richard), Bt., D.S.O. (1960).

Lloyd, *Air Chief Marshal* Sir Hugh Pughe, G.B.E., K.C.B., M.C., D.F.C.

Lloyd, Sir (John) Peter (Daniel), Kt.

Lockhart, Sir Allan Robert Eliot, Kt., C.I.E.

Lockhart, Sir Muir Edward Sinclair-, Bt. (S 1636).

Lockhart, *General* Sir Rob (McGregor Macdonald), K.C.B., C.I.E., M.C.

Lockspeiser, Sir Ben, K.C.B., F.R.S.

Lockwood, Sir Joseph Flawith, Kt.

Loder, Sir Giles Rolls, Bt. (1887).

Lodge, Sir Thomas, Kt.

Loehnis, Sir Clive, K.C.M.G.

Loewen, *General* Sir Charles Falkland, G.C.B., K.B.E., D.S.O.

Logan, Sir Douglas William, Kt., D.Phil.

Lomax, Sir John Garnett, K.B.E., C.M.G., M.C.

Long, Sir Ronald, Kt.

Longden, Sir Gilbert James Morley, M.B.E.

Longland, Sir John Laurence, Kt.

Longley, Sir Norman, Kt., C.B.E.

Longworth, Sir Fred, Kt.

Looker, Sir Cecil Thomas, Kt.

Lord, Sir Ackland Archibald, Kt., O.B.E.

Loring, Sir (John) Nigel, K.C.V.O.

Lousada, Sir Anthony Baruh, Kt.

Lovell, *Prof.* Sir (Alfred Charles) Bernard, Kt., O.B.E., F.R.S.

Loveridge, Sir John Harry, Kt., C.B.E.

Low, Sir James Richard Morrison-, Bt. (1908).

Lowe, Sir David, Kt., C.B.E.

Lowe, *Air Marshal* Sir Douglas Charles, K.C.B., D.F.C., A.F.C.

Lowe, *Air Vice-Marshal* Sir Edgar Noel, K.B.E., C.B.

Lowe, Sir Francis Reginald Gordon, Bt. (1918).

Lowry, *Rt. Hon.* Sir Robert Lynd Erskine, Kt.

Lowson, Sir Denys Colquhoun Flowerdew, Bt. (1951).

Lowther, *Lt.-Col.* Sir (William) Guy, Bt., O.B.E. (1824).

Loyd, Sir Francis Alfred, K.C.M.G., O.B.E.

Lubbock, Sir Alan, Kt., F.S.A.

Lucas, *Maj.* Sir Jocelyn Morton, Bt., K.B.E., M.C. (1887).

Luce, Sir William Henry Tucker, G.B.E., K.C.M.G.

Luckhoo, *Hon.* Sir Joseph Alexander, Kt.

Luckhoo, Sir Lionel Alfred, K.C.M.G., C.B.E., Q.C.

Lucy, Sir Edmund John William Hugh Cameron-Ramsay-Fairfax-, Bt. (1836).

Luke, *Hon.* Sir Emile Fashole, K.B.E.

Luke, Sir Stephen Elliot Vyvyan, K.C.M.G.

Lumby, Sir Henry, Kt., C.B.E.

Lund, Sir Thomas George, Kt., C.B.E.

Lush, Sir Archibald James, Kt.

Lushington, Sir Henry Edmund Castleman, Bt. (1791).

Lusty, Sir Robert Frith, Kt.

Luyt, Sir Richard Edward, G.C.V.O., K.C.M.G., D.C.M.

Lydford, *Air Marshal* Sir Harold Thomas, K.B.E., C.B., A.F.C.

Lyle, Sir Gavin Archibald, Bt. (1929).

Lyle, Sir Ian Duff, Kt., D.S.C.

Lyon, *Maj.-Gen.* Sir (Francis) James (Cecil) Bowes-, K.C.V.O., C.B., O.B.E., M.C.

Lyons, Sir (Isidore) Jack, Kt., C.B.E.

Lyons, Sir James Reginald, Kt.

Lyons, Sir William, Kt.

McAdam, Sir Ian William James, Kt., O.B.E.

McAdden, Sir Stephen James, Kt., C.B.E., M.P.

McAllister, Sir Reginald Basil, Kt., C.M.G., C.V.O.

McAlpine, Sir Robert Edwin, Kt.

McAlpine, Sir Robin, Kt., C.B.E.

McAlpine, Sir Thomas George Bishop, Bt. (1918).

Macara, Sir (Charles) Douglas, Bt. (1911).

Macarthur, *Hon.* Sir Ian Hannay, Kt.

Macartney, Sir John Barrington, Bt. (I 1799).

Macaulay, Sir Hamilton, Kt., C.B.E.

McBride, *Rt. Hon.* Sir Philip Albert Martin, K.C.M.G.

McCall, Sir Charles Patrick Home, Kt., M.B.E., T.D.

McCall, *Admiral* Sir Henry William Urquhart, K.C.V.O., K.B.E., C.B., D.S.O.

MacCallum, Sir Peter, Kt., M.D.

McCance, Sir Andrew, Kt., D.Sc., F.R.S.

McCarthy, Sir Edwin, Kt., C.B.E.

McCarthy, *Rt. Hon.* Sir Thaddeus Pearcey, K.B.E.

McCauley, *Air Marshal* Sir John Patrick Joseph, K.B.E., C.B.

McCaw, *Hon.* Sir Kenneth Malcolm, Kt., Q.C.

McCombs, *Hon.* Sir Terence Henderson, Kt., O.B.E., E.D.

McConnell, *Cdr.* Sir Robert Melville Terence, Bt., V.R.D. (1900).

McCowan, Sir Hew Cargill, Bt. (1934).

McCutcheon, Sir Walter Osborn, Kt.

McDavid, Sir Edwin Frank, Kt., C.M.G., C.B.E.

MacDermot, Sir Dermot Francis, K.C.M.G., C.B.E.

McDermott, Sir (Lawrence) Emmet, K.B.E.

McDonald, Sir Alexander Fortes, Kt.

McDonald, *Air Chief Marshal* Sir Arthur William Baynes, K.C.B., A.F.C.

Macdonald, Sir Herbert George de Lome, K.B.E.

Macdonald of Sleat, Sir Ian Godfrey Bosville, Bt. (S 1625).

McDonald, Sir James, K.B.E.

McDonald, *Hon.* Sir John Gladstone Black, Kt.

Macdonald, Sir John Ronald Maxwell-, Bt. (S 1682 and S 1707).

Macdonald, Sir Peter George, Kt.

Macdonald, *Hon.* Sir Thomas Lachlan, K.C.M.G.

McDonald, *Hon.* Sir William John Farquhar, Kt.

MacDonald, *Air Chief Marshal* Sir William Laurence Mary, G.C.B., C.B.E., D.F.C.

MacDougall, Sir (George) Donald (Alastair), Kt., C.B.E., F.B.A.

McDowell, Sir Frank Schofield, Kt.

McDowell, Sir Henry McLorinan, K.B.E.

McEvoy, *Air Chief Marshal* Sir Theodore Newman, K.C.B., C.B.E.

McEwen, *Rt. Hon.* Sir John, G.C.M.G., C.H.

McEwen, Sir Robert Lindley, Bt. (1953).

McEwin, *Hon.* Sir (Alexander) Lyell, K.B.E.

McFadzean, Sir Francis Scott, Kt.

McFarland, Sir Basil (Alexander Talbot), Bt., C.B.E. (1914).

Macfarlane, Sir George Gray, Kt., C.B.

Macfarlane, Sir James Wright, Kt.

Macfarlane, Sir Robert Mafeking, K.C.M.G.

MacFarquhar, Sir Alexander, K.B.E., C.I.E.

McGeoch, *Vice-Adm.* Sir Ian Lachlan Mackay, K.C.B., D.S.O., D.S.C.

McGlashan, *Rear-Adm.* (E) Sir Alexander Davidson, K.B.E., C.B., D.S.O.

McGonigal, *Rt. Hon.* Sir Ambrose Joseph, Kt., M.C.

McGovern, Sir Patrick Silvesta, Kt., C.B.E.

McGrath, Sir Charles Gullan, Kt., O.B.E.

MacGregor, Sir Colin Malcolm, Kt.

Macgregor, Sir Edwin Robert, Bt. (1828).

McGregor, *Hon.* Sir George Innes, Kt.

MacGregor of MacGregor, Sir Gregor, Bt. (1795).

McGrigor, *Capt.* Sir Charles Edward, Bt. (1831).

McIlrath, Sir Martin, Kt.

McIlveen, *Brig.* Sir Arthur William, Kt., M.B.E.

McIntosh, Sir Alister Donald, K.C.M.G.

McIntosh, *Vice-Adm.* Sir Ian Stewart, K.B.E., C.B., D.S.O., D.S.C.

Macintosh, *Prof.* Sir Robert Reynolds, Kt., M.D.

McIntosh, Sir Ronald Robert Duncan, K.C.B.

Macintyre, Sir Donald, Kt., C.B.E.

McIntyre, Sir Laurence Rupert, Kt., C.B.E.

Mack, *Hon.* Sir William George Albert, K.B.E.

McKaig, *Admiral* Sir (John) Rae, K.C.B., C.B.E.

Mackay, Sir George Patrick Gordon, Kt., C.B.E.

Mackay, Sir James Mackerron, K.B.E., C.B.

McKay, Sir James Wilson, Kt.

McKay, Sir John Andrew, Kt., C.B.E.

Mackay, Sir William Calder, Kt., O.B.E., M.C.

McKee, *Air Marshal* Sir Andrew, K.C.B., C.B.E., D.S.O., D.F.C., A.F.C.

McKee, *His Hon.* Sir Dermot St. Oswald, Kt.

McKee, *Maj.* Sir William Cecil, Kt., E.R.D.

McKell, *Rt. Hon.* Sir William John, G.C.M.G., Q.C.

MacKenna, *Hon.* Sir Bernard Joseph Maxwell, Kt.

McKenzie, Sir Alexander, K.B.E.

Mackenzie, Sir Alexander Alwyne Brinton Muir-, Bt. (1805).

Mackenzie, Sir (Alexander George Anthony) Allan, Bt. (1890).

Mackenzie, *Vice-Adm.* Sir Hugh Stirling, K.C.B., D.S.O., D.S.C.

Mackenzie, Sir (Lewis) Roderick Kenneth, Bt. (s 1703).

Mackenzie, Sir Robert Evelyn, Bt. (s 1673).

Mackeson, Sir Rupert Henry, Bt. (1954).

McKie, Sir William Neil, Kt., M.V.O., D.Mus.

McKinney, Sir William, Kt., C.B.E.

MacKintosh, Sir Angus Mackay, K.C.V.O., C.M.G.

Mackintosh, *Capt.* Sir Kenneth Lachlan, K.C.V.O., R.N. (*ret.*).

McKissock, Sir Wylie, Kt., O.B.E., F.R.C.S.

Macklin, Sir Albert Sortain Romer, Kt.

Mackworth, *Cdr.* Sir David Arthur Geoffrey, Bt. (1776).

Maclaren, Sir Hamish Duncan, K.B.E., C.B., D.F.C.

Maclean, Sir Fitzroy Hew Royle, Bt., C.B.E. (1957).

McLean, Sir Francis Charles, Kt., C.B.E.

MacLean, *Vice-Adm.* Sir Hector Charles Donald, K.B.E., C.B., D.S.C.

McLean, *Lt.-Gen.* Sir Kenneth Graeme, K.C.B., K.B.E.

Maclean, Sir Robert Alexander, K.B.E.

McLeay, *Hon.* Sir John, K.C.M.G., M.M.

MacLehose, Sir (Crawford) Murray, K.C.M.G., M.B.E.

MacLennan, Sir Hector Ross, Kt., M.D.

Maclennan, Sir Ian Morrison Ross, K.C.M.G.

McLennan, Sir Ian Munro, K.B.E.

MacLennan, Sir Robert Laing, Kt., C.I.E.

McLeod, Sir Alan Cumbrae Rose, K.C.V.O.

McLeod, Sir Charles Henry, Bt. (1925).

MacLeod, Sir John, Kt., T.D.

McLeod, *General* Sir Roderick William, G.B.E., K.C.B.

McLintock, Sir William Traven, Bt. (1934).

Maclure, *Lt.-Col.* Sir John William Spencer, Bt., O.B.E. (1898).

McMahon, Sir (William) Patrick, Bt. (1817).

McMeekin, *Lt.-Gen.* Sir Terence Douglas Herbert, K.C.B., O.B.E.

McMichael, *Prof.* Sir John, Kt., M.D., F.R.S.

MacMillan, *General* Sir Gordon Holmes Alexander, K.C.B., K.C.V.O., C.B.E., D.S.O., M.C.

McMullin, *Hon.* Sir Alister Maxwell, K.C.M.G.

Macnab, *Brig.* Sir Geoffrey Alex Colin, K.C.M.G., C.B.

Macnaghten, Sir Patrick Alexander, Bt. (1836).

McNair, Sir William Lennox, Kt.

McNee, Sir John William, Kt., D.S.O., M.D., D.SC.

McNeice, Sir (Thomas) Percy (Fergus), Kt., C.M.G., O.B.E.

McNeil, Sir Hector, Kt., C.B.E.

McNicoll, *Vice-Adm.* Sir Alan Wedel Ramsay, K.B.E., C.B., G.M.

McPetrie, Sir James Carnegie, K.C.M.G., O.B.E.

Macready, Sir Nevil John Wilfrid, Bt. (1923).

McRobert, *Col.* Sir George Reid, Kt., C.I.E.

Macrory, Sir Patrick Arthur, Kt.

McShine, *Hon.* Sir Arthur Hugh, Kt.

MacTaggart, Sir Andrew McCormick, Kt.

Mactaggart, Sir Ian Auld, Bt. (1938).

MacTaggart, Sir William, Kt., R.A., R.S.A.

MacTier, Sir (Reginald) Stewart, Kt., C.B.E.

McTiernan, *Rt. Hon.* Sir Edward Aloysius, K.B.E.

McVeigh, *Rt. Hon.* Sir Herbert Andrew, Kt.

Madden, *Admiral* Sir Charles Edward, Bt., G.C.B. (1919).

Maddex, Sir George Henry, K.B.E.

Maddock, Sir Ieuan, Kt., C.B., O.B.E., F.R.S.

Maddocks, Sir Kenneth Phipson, K.C.M.G., K.C.V.O.

Maddox, Sir John Kempson, Kt., V.R.D., M.D.

Madgwick, Sir Robert Bowden, Kt., O.B.E.

Madhorao Genesh Deshpande *Rao Bahadur* Sir, K.B.E.

Magill, Sir Ivan Whiteside, K.C.V.O.

Maguire, *Air Marshal* Sir Harold John, K.C.B., D.S.O., O.B.E.

Mahon, Sir George Edward John, Bt. (1819).

Mahon, Sir Gerald MacMahon, Kt.

Maihar, The Maharaja of, K.C.I.E.

Maini, Sir Amar Nath, Kt., C.B.E.

Mais, *Hon.* Sir Robert Hugh, Bt.

Maitland, Sir Donald James Dundas, Kt., C.M.G., O.B.E.

Maitland, *Cdr.* Sir John Francis Whitaker, Kt.

Maitland, Sir Richard John, Bt. (1818).

Major, *Hon.* Sir John Patrick Edward Chandos Henniker-, K.C.M.G., C.V.O., M.C.

Makgill, *Maj.* Sir (John) Donald (Alexander Arthur), Bt. (s 1627).

Makins, Sir Paul Vivian, Bt. (1903).

Malcolm, Sir Michael Albert James, Bt. (s 1665).

Malet, *Col.* Sir Edward William St. Lo, Bt., O.B.E. (1791).

Mallabar, Sir John Frederick, Kt.

Mallaby, Sir (Howard) George (Charles), K.C.M.G., O.B.E.

Mallalieu, Sir (Edward) Lancelot, Kt.

Mallen, Sir Leonard Ross, Kt., O.B.E.

Mallet, Sir (William) Ivo, G.B.E., K.C.M.G.

Mallinson, *Col.* Sir Stuart Sidney, Kt., C.B.E., D.S.O., M.C.

Mallinson, Sir (William) Paul, Bt. (1935).

Mallowan, Sir Max Edgar Lucien, Kt., C.B.E., D.Lit., F.B.A., F.S.A.

Maltby, Sir Thomas Karran, Kt.

Mamo, Sir Anthony Joseph, Kt., O.B.E.

Mance, Sir Henry Stenhouse, Kt.

Mander, Sir Charles Marcus, Bt. (1911).

Mandi, *Col.* H.H. the Raja of, K.C.S.I.

Manifold, *Hon.* Sir (Thomas) Chester, K.B.E.

Manktelow, Sir (Arthur) Richard, K.B.E., C.B.

Mann, Sir Rupert Edward, Bt. (1905).

Manning, Sir George, Kt., C.M.G.

Manning, *Hon.* Sir James Kenneth, Kt.

Mansel, Sir Philip, Bt. (1622).

Mansergh, *Vice-Adm.* Sir (Cecil) Aubrey (Lawson), K.B.E., C.B., D.S.C.

Mansfield, *Hon.* Sir Alan James, K.C.M.G., K.C.V.O.

Mansfield, *Vice-Adm.* Sir (Edward) Gerard (Napier), K.B.E.

Mant, Sir Cecil George, Kt., C.B.E.

Manuwa, Sir Samuel Layinka Ayodeji, Kt., C.M.G., O.B.E.

Mara, *Rt. Hon. Ratu* Sir Kamisese Kapaiwa Tuimacilai, K.B.E.

Marchant, Sir Herbert Stanley, K.C.M.G., O.B.E.

Marett, Sir Robert Hugh Kirk, K.C.M.G., O.B.E.

Margai, *Hon.* Sir Albert Michael, Kt.

Margetson, *Maj.* Sir Philip Reginald, K.C.V.O., M.C.

Marjoribanks, Sir James Alexander Milne, K.C.M.G.

Mark, Sir Robert, Kt.

Markham, Sir Charles John, Bt. (1911).

Markham, Sir (Sydney) Frank, Kt.

Marks, Sir John Hedley Douglas, Kt., C.B.E.

Marling, *Lt.-Col.* Sir John Stanley Vincent, Bt., O.B.E. (1882).

Marnham, Sir Ralph, K.C.V.O.

Marr, Sir Leslie Lynn, Bt. (1919).

Marre, Sir Alan Samuel, K.C.B.

Marriott, *Maj.-Gen.* Sir John Charles Oakes, K.C.V.O., C.B., D.S.O., M.C.

Marriott, Sir Ralph George Cavendish Smith-, Bt. (1774).

Marriott, Sir Robert Ecklin, Kt., V.D.

Marsden, Sir John Denton, Bt., (1924).

Marshall, Sir Arthur Gregory George, Kt., O.B.E.

Marshall, Sir Douglas, Kt.

Marshall, Sir Frank Shaw, Kt.

Marshall, Sir Geoffrey, K.C.V.O., C.B.E., M.D.

Marshall, Sir Hugo Frank, K.B.E., C.M.G.

Marshall, Sir James, Kt.

Marshall, *Rt. Hon.* Sir John Ross, Kt., C.H.

Marshall, *Prof.* Sir (Oshley) Roy, Kt., C.B.E.

Marshall, Sir Robert Braithwaite, K.C.B., M.B.E.

Marshall, Sir Stirrat Andrew William Johnson-, Kt., C.B.E., F.R.I.B.A.

Martell, *Vice-Adm.* Sir Hugo Colenso, K.B.E., C.B.

Martin, Sir David Christie, Kt., C.B.E., Ph.D., F.R.S.E.

Martin, *Admiral* Sir Deric Holland-, G.C.B., D.S.O., D.S.C.

Martin, Sir George William, K.B.E.

Martin, *Air Marshal* Sir Harold Brownlow, K.C.B., D.S.O., D.F.C., A.F.C.

Martin, Sir James, Kt., C.B.E.

Martin, *Vice-Adm.* Sir John Edward Ludgate, K.C.B., D.S.C.

Martin, *Prof.* Sir (John) Leslie, Kt., Ph.D.

Martin, Sir John Miller, K.C.M.G., C.B., C.V.O.

Martin, *Prof.* Sir Leslie Harold, Kt., C.B.E.

Martin, *Hon,* Sir Norman (Angus), Kt.

Marwick, Sir Brian Allan, K.B.E., C.M.G.

Masefield, Sir Peter Gordon, Kt.

Mason, *Hon.* Sir Anthony Frank, K.C.B.

Mason, Sir Dan Hurdis, Kt., O.B.E., E.R.D.

Mason, *Vice-Adm.* (E) Sir Frank Trowbridge, K.C.B.

Mason, Sir Frederick Cecil, K.C.V.O., C.M.G.

Mason, Sir Paul, K.C.M.G., K.C.V.O.

Massey, Sir Arthur, Kt., C.B.E.

Massey, *Prof.* Sir Harrie Stewart Wilson, Kt., Ph.D., F.R.S.

Massiah, Sir (Hallum) Grey, K.B.E., M.D.

Masterman, Sir Christopher Hughes, Kt., C.S.I., C.I.E.

Masterman, Sir John Cecil, Kt., O.B.E.

Mather, Sir William Loris, Kt., O.B.E., M.C., T.D.

Matheson, *Major* Sir Torquhil Alexander, Bt. (1882).

Mathias, Sir Richard Hughes, Bt. (1917).

Mathys, Sir (Herbert) Reginald, Kt., T.D.

Matters, Sir (Reginald) Francis, Kt., V.R.D., M.D.

Matthews, Sir Bryan Harold Cabot, Kt., C.B.E., Sc.D., F.R.S.

Matthews, Sir (Harold Lancelot) Roy, Kt., C.B.E.

Matthews, Sir James Henry John, Kt.

Matthews, Sir Peter Alec, Kt.

Matthews, Sir Stanley, Kt., C.B.E.

Maudslay, *Major* Sir (James) Rennie, K.C.V.O., M.B.E.

Mavor, *Air Marshal* Sir Leslie Deane, K.C.B., A.F.C.

Mawby, Sir Maurice Alan Edgar, Kt., C.B.E.

Maxwell, Sir Aymer, Bt. (s 1681).

Maxwell, Sir Patrick Ivor Heron-, Bt. (s 1683).

Maxwell, Sir Robert Hugh, K.B.E.

May, *Hon.* Sir John Douglas, Kt.

May, *Surg. Vice-Adm.* Sir (Robert) Cyril, K.B.E., C.B., M.B.

Mayall, Sir (Alexander) Lees, K.C.V.O., C.M.G.

Mayer, Sir Robert, Kt., C.H.

Maynard, *Air Marshal* Sir Nigel Martin, K.C.B., C.B.E., D.F.C., A.F.C. [Kt.

Mbanefo, Sir Louis Nwachukwu, Mead, Sir Cecil, Kt.

Meade, Sir (Richard) Geoffrey (Austin), K.B.E., C.M.G., C.V.O.

Meagher, Sir Thomas, Kt.

Medawar, Sir Peter Brian, Kt., C.H., C.B.E., D.S.C., F.R.S.

Medlycott, Sir (James) Christopher, Bt. (1808).

Meech, Sir John Valentine, K.C.V.O.

Meere, Sir Francis Anthony, Kt., C.B.E.

Megarry, *Hon.* Sir Robert Edgar, Kt., F.B.A.

Megaw, *Rt. Hon.* Sir John, Kt., C.B.E., T.D.

Mellor, Sir John Serocold Paget, Bt. (1924).

Melville, Sir Eugene, K.C.M.G.

Melville, Sir Harry Work, K.C.B., Ph.D., D.Sc., F.R.S.

Melville, Sir Leslie Galfreid, K.B.E.

Melville, Sir Ronald Henry, K.C.B.

Mensforth, Sir Eric, Kt., C.B.E.

Menter, Sir James Woodham, Kt., Ph.D., Sc.D., F.R.S.

Menteth, Sir James Wallace Stuart-, Bt. (1838).

Menzies, Sir Laurence James, Kt.

Menzies, Sir Peter Thomson, Kt.

Menzies, *Rt. Hon.* Sir Robert Gordon, K.T., C.H., Q.C., F.R.S.

Meredith, *Air Vice-Marshal* Sir Charles Warburton, K.B.E., C.B., A.F.C.

Merton, *Air Chief Marshal* Sir Walter Hugh, G.B.E., K.C.B.

Messent, Sir Philip Santo, Kt.

Metcalfe, Sir Ralph Ismay, Kt.

Metcalfe, Sir Theophilus John, Bt. (1802).

Meyer, Sir Anthony John Charles, Bt., M.P. (1910).

Meyjes, Sir Richard Anthony, Kt.

Meyrick, *Lt.-Col.* Sir George David Elliott Tapps-Gervis-, Bt., M.C. (1791).

Meyrick, *Maj.* Sir Thomas Frederick, Bt. (1880).

Michaelis, *Brig. Hon.* Sir Archie, Kt.

Michelmore, Sir Walter Harold Strachan, Kt., M.B.E.

Michelmore, *Maj.-Gen.* Sir (William) Godwin, K.B.E., C.B., D.S.O., M.C., T.D.

Micklethwait, Sir Robert Gore, Kt., Q.C.

Middlemore, Sir William Hawkslow, Bt. (1919).

Middleton, Sir George Humphrey, K.C.M.G.

Middleton, Sir George Proctor, K.C.V.O.

Middleton, Sir Stephen Hugh, Bt. (1662).

Miers, *Rear-Adm.* Sir Anthony Cecil Capel, V C, K.B.E., C.B., D.S.O.

Milbank, *Maj.* Sir Mark Vane, Bt., K.C.V.O., M.C. (1882).

Milburn, Sir John Nigel, Bt. (1905).

†Mildmay, Sir Verus Arundell Maunder St. John-, Bt. (1772).

Miles, *Prof.* Sir (Arnold) Ashley, Kt., C.B.E., M.D., F.R.S.

Miles, Sir Bernard, Kt., C.B.E.

Miles, *Admiral* Sir Geoffrey John Audley, K.C.B., K.C.S.I.

Miles, Sir William Napier Maurice, Bt. (1859).

Millais, Sir Ralph Regnault, Bt. (1885).

Millar, Sir Oliver Nicholas, K.C.V.O., F.B.A.

Millard, Sir Guy Elwin, K.C.M.G., C.V.O.

Millbourn, Sir (Philip) Eric, Kt., C.M.G.

Miller, Sir Douglas Sinclair, K.C.V.O., C.B.E.

Miller, *Lt.-Gen.* Sir Euan Alfred Bews, K.C.B., K.B.E., D.S.O., M.C.

Miller, Sir (Ian) Douglas, Kt.

Miller, Sir James, G.B.E.

Miller, *Col.* Sir James MacBride, Kt., M.C., T.D.

Miller, Sir John Francis Compton, Kt., M.B.E., T.D.

Miller, Sir John Holmes, Bt. (1705).

Miller, *Lt.-Col.* Sir John Mansel, K.C.V.O., D.S.O., M.C.

Miller, Sir (Oswald) Bernard, Kt.

Miller, Sir Richard Hope, Kt.

Miller of Glenlee, Sir Frederick William Macdonald, Bt. (1788).

Milling, *Air Marshal* Sir Denis Crowley-, K.C.B., C.B.E., D.S.O., D.F.C.

Mills, *Vice-Adm.* Sir Charles Piercy, K.C.B., C.B.E., D.S.C.

Mills, Sir Peter Frederick Leighton, Bt. (1921).

Milman, Sir Dermot Lionel Kennedy, Bt. (1800).

Milmo, *Hon.* Sir Helenus Patrick Joseph, Kt.

Milner, Sir (George Edward) Mordaunt, Bt. (1717).

Milton, Sir Frank, Kt.

Milward, Sir Anthony Horace, Kt., C.B.E.

Minter, Sir Frederick Albert, G.C.V.O.

Mitchell, Sir Derek Jack, K.C.B., C.V.O.

Mitchell, Sir Godfrey Way, Kt.

Mitchell, Sir Hamilton, K.B.E.

Mitchell, *Col.* Sir Harold Paton, Bt. (1945).

Mitchell, *Prof.* Sir Mark Ledingham, Kt.

Mitchell, Sir (Seton) Steuart Crichton, K.B.E., C.B.

Mocatta, *Hon.* Sir Alan Abraham, Kt., O.B.E.

Mockett, Sir Vere, Kt., M.B.E.

Moffat, Sir John Smith, Kt., O.B.E.

Mogg, *General* Sir (Herbert) John, G.C.B., C.B.E., D.S.O.

Mohamed, Sir Abdool Razack, Kt.

Moir, Sir Ernest Ian Royds, Bt. (1916).

Molony, Sir Hugh Francis, Bt. (1925).

Molony, Sir Joseph Thomas, K.C.V.O., Q.C.

Monahan, Sir Robert Vincent, Kt.

Moncrieff, *Admiral* Sir Alan Kenneth Scott-, K.C.B., C.B.E., D.S.O.

Moncreiffe, Sir (Rupert) Iain (Kay), Bt. (s 1685).

Monnington, Sir Walter Thomas, Kt., P.R.A.

Monson, Sir (William Bonnar) Leslie, K.C.M.G., C.B.

Montgomery, Sir (Basil Henry) David, Bt. (1801).

Mookerjee, Sir Birendra Nath, Kt.

Moon, Sir Edward Penderel, Kt., O.B.E.

Moon, Sir John Arthur, Bt. (1887).

Moon, Sir (Peter) Wilfred Giles, Bt. (1855).

Moore, Sir Edward Stanton, Bt., O.B.E. (1923.)

Moore, Sir Harold (John de Courcy), Kt.

Moore, *Admiral* Sir Henry Ruthven, G.C.B., C.V.O., D.S.O.

Moore, *General* Sir (James Newton) Rodney, G.C.V.O., K.C.B., C.B.E., D.S.O.

Moore, Sir Norman Winfrid, Bt. (1919).

Moore, Sir William Samson, Bt. (1932).

Mootham, Sir Orby Howell, Kt.

Mordaunt, Sir Nigel John, Bt., M.B.E. (1611).

Mordecai, Sir John Stanley, Kt., C.M.G.

Morgan, Sir (Clifford) Naunton, Kt.

Morgan, Sir David John Hughes-Bt., C.B.E. (1925).

Morgan, *Hon.* Sir Edward James Ranembe, Kt.

Morgan, Sir Ernest Dunstan, K.B.E.

Morgan, Sir Morien Bedford, Kt., C.B., F.R.S.

Morgan, *Rear-Adm.* Sir Patrick John, K.C.V.O., C.B., D.S.C.

Morgan, *General* Sir William Duthie, G.C.B., D.S.O., M.C.

Morison, Sir Ronald Peter, Kt., Q.C.

Morland, Sir Oscar Charles, G.B.E., K.C.M.G.

Morley, Sir Godfrey William Rowland, Kt., O.B.E., T.D.

Morris, Sir Cedric Lockwood, Bt. (1806).

Morris, *Air Marshal* Sir Douglas Griffith, K.C.B., C.B.E., D.S.O., D.F.C.

Morris, Sir Geoffrey Newman-, Kt., E.D.

Morris, *Hon.* Sir Kenneth James, K.B.E., C.M.G.

Morris, *Air Marshal* Sir Leslie Dalton-, K.B.E., C.B.

Morris, *His Hon.* Sir Owen Temple Temple-, Kt., Q.C.

Morris, Sir Philip Robert, K.C.M.G., C.B.E.

Morris, *His Hon.* Sir William Gerard, Kt.

Morrison, Sir Nicholas Godfrey, K.C.B.

Morrow, Sir Arthur William, Kt., D.S.O., E.D.

Morrow, Sir Ian Thomas, Kt.

Morse, Sir Christopher Jeremy, K.C.M.G.

Morshead, Sir Owen Frederick, G.C.V.O., K.C.B., D.S.O., M.C.

Morton, Sir Brian, Kt.

Morton, Sir Ralph John, Kt., C.M.G., O.B.E., M.C.

Morton, Sir Stanley William Gibson, Kt.

Morton, Sir (William) Wilfred, K.C.B.

Moser, *Prof.* Sir Claus Adolf, K.C.B., C.B.E., F.B.A.

Moses, Sir Charles Joseph Alfred, Kt., C.B.E.

Mosley, Sir Oswald Ernald, Bt. (1781).

Moss, Sir Eric de Vere, Kt., C.I.E.

Moss, Sir John Herbert Theodore Edwards-, Bt. (1868).

Mostyn, Sir Jeremy John Antony, Bt. (1670).

Mott, Sir John Harmer, Bt. (1930).

Mott, *Prof.* Sir Nevill Francis, Kt., F.R.S.

Mount, Sir William Malcolm, Bt. (1921).

Mountain, Sir Brian Edward Stanley, Bt. (1922).

Mountford, Sir James Frederick, Kt., D.Litt.

Mowbray, Sir John Robert, Bt. (1880).

Mudie, Sir (Robert) Francis, K.C.S.I., K.C.I.E., O.B.E.

Muhamad Noor, *Khan Bahadur* Sir Khaja, Kt., C.B.E.

Muhammad Ahmad Sa'id Khan *Nawab* Sir, G.B.E., K.C.S.I., K.C.I.E.

Muir Sir David John, Kt., C.M.G.

Muir, Sir Edward Francis, K.C.B.

Muir, Sir John Harling, Bt. (1892).

Mulholland, Sir Michael Henry, Bt. (1945).

Mullens, Sir Harold Hill, Kt.

Mumford, Sir Albert Henry, K.B.E.

Munro, Sir Ian Talbot, Bt. (s. 1634).

Munro, Sir (Thomas) Torquil (Alfonso), Bt. (1825).

Murdoch, *Air Marshal* Sir Alister Murray, K.B.E., C.B.

Murphy, Sir Alexander Paterson, Kt.

Murphy, Sir Dermod Art Pelly, Kt., C.M.G., O.B.E.

Murphy, Sir (Oswald) Ellis (Joseph), Kt.

Murray, Sir Alan John Digby, Bt. (s 1628).

Murray, Sir Andrew Hunter Arbuthnot, Kt., O.B.E.

Murray, Sir (Francis) Ralph (Hay), K.C.M.G., C.B.

Murray, *General* Sir Horatius, G.C.B., K.B.E., D.S.O.

Murray, *Hon.* Sir John Murray, Kt.

Murray, Sir Kenneth, Kt.

Murray, Sir Rowland William Patrick, Bt. (s 1630).

Murray, Sir William Patrick Keith, Bt. (s 1673).

Murrie, Sir William Stuart, G.C.B., K.B.E.

Mursell, Sir Peter, Kt., M.B.E.

Musgrave, Sir Christopher Patrick Charles, Bt. (1611).

Musgrave, Sir (Frank) Cyril, K.C.B.

Musgrave, Sir Richard James, Bt. (I 1782).

Musker, Sir John, Kt.

Musson, *General* Sir Geoffrey Randolph Dixon, G.C.B., C.B.E., D.S.O.

Musto, Sir Arnold Albert, Kt., C.I.E.

Mya Bu, Sir, Kt.

Mynors, Sir Humphrey Charles Baskerville, Bt. (1964).

Mynors, *Prof.* Sir Roger Aubrey Baskerville, Kt., F.B.A.

Nairac, *Hon.* Sir André Laurence, Kt., C.B.E., Q.C.

Nairn, Sir (Michael) George, Bt. (1904).

Nairn, Sir Robert Arnold Spencer-, Bt. (1933).

Nairne, Sir Patrick Dalmahoy, K.C.B., M.C.

Nalder, *Hon.* Sir Crawford David, Kt.

Nall, *Lt.-Cdr.* Sir Michael Joseph, Bt., R.N.(1954).

Napier, *Hon.* Sir John Mellis, K.C.M.G.

Napier, Sir Joseph William Lennox, Bt., O.B.E. (1867).

Napier, Sir William Archibald, Bt. (s 1627).

Nathan, Sir Maurice Arnold, K.B.E.

Nayudu, *Sri Diwan Bahadur* Sir Madura Balasundram, Kt., C.I.E.

Neal, Sir Leonard Francis, Kt., C.B.E.

Neale, Sir Alan Derrett, K.C.B., M.B.E.

Neale, *Prof.* Sir John Ernest, Kt., F.B.A.

Neame, *Lt.-Gen.* Sir Philip, *VC*, K.B.E., C.B., D.S.O.

Neave, Sir Arundell Thomas Clifton, Bt. (1795).

Neden, Sir Wilfred John, Kt., C.B., C.B.E.

Neill, *Rt. Hon.* Sir Ivan, Kt.

Nelson, *Maj.-Gen.* Sir (Eustace) John (Blois), K.C.V.O., C.B., D.S.O., O.B.E., M.C.

Nelson, *Air Marshal* Sir (Sidney) Richard (Carlyle), K.C.B., O.B.E., M.D.

Nelson, *Maj.* Sir William Vernon Hope, Bt., O.B.E. (1912).

Nepean, *Lt.-Col.* Sir Evan Yorke, Bt. (1802).

Nevill, *Air Vice-Marshal* Sir Arthur de Terrotte, K.B.E., C.B.

Neville, *Lt.-Col.* Sir (James) Edmund (Henderson), Bt., M.C. (1927).

Neville, *Maj.-Gen.* Sir Robert Arthur Ross, K.C.M.G., C.B.E., R.M.

Newbold, Sir Charles Demorée, K.B.E., C.M.G., Q.C.

Newman, Sir Geoffrey Robert, Bt. (1836).

Newman, Sir Gerard Robert Henry Sigismund, Bt. (1912).

Newns, Sir (Alfred) Foley (Francis Polden), K.C.M.G., C.V.O.

Newton, Sir (Harry) Michael (Rex), Bt. (1900).

Newton, Sir Hubert, Kt.

Newton, Sir Kenneth Garner, Bt., O.B.E., T.D. (1924).

Newton, Sir (Leslie) Gordon, Kt.

Niall, Sir Horace Lionel Richard, Kt., C.B.E.

Nicholas, Sir Alfred James, Kt., C.B.E.

Nicholas, Sir Herbert Richard, Kt., O.B.E.

Nicholetts, *Air Marshal* Sir Gilbert Edward, K.B.E., C.B., A.F.C.

Nicholls, Sir Douglas Ralph, Kt., O.B.E.

Nichols, Sir Edward Henry, Kt., T.D.

Nicholson, Sir Arthur William, Kt., O.B.E.

Nicholson, *General* Sir Cameron Gordon Graham, G.C.B., K.B.E., D.S.O., M.C.

Nicholson, *Hon.* Sir David Eric, Kt.

Nicholson, Sir Godfrey, Bt. (1958).

Nicholson, Sir John Charles, Bt. (1859).

Nicholson, Sir John Norris, Bt., K.B.E., C.I.E. (1912).

Nicklin, *Hon.* Sir (George) Francis (Reuben), K.C.M.G., M.M.

Nicoll, Sir John Fearns, K.C.M.G.

Nicolson, Sir David Lancaster, Kt.

Nield, *Hon.* Sir Basil Edward, Kt., C.B.E., Q.C.

Nield, Sir William Alan, G.C.M.G., K.C.B.

Nightingale, Sir Charles Athelstan, Bt. (1628).

Nightingale, Sir John Cyprian, Kt., C.B.E., B.E.M., Q.P.M.

Nihill, *Hon.* Sir (John Harry) Barclay, K.B.E., M.C., Q.C.

Nimmo, *Hon.* Sir John Angus, Kt., C.B.E.

Nimmo, Sir Robert, Kt.

Niven, Sir (Cecil) Rex, Kt., C.M.G., M.C.

Nixon, Sir (Charles) Norman, Kt.

Nixon, *Maj.* Sir Christopher John Louis Joseph, Bt., M.C. (1906).

Noad, Sir Kenneth Beeson, Kt., M.D.

Noble, *Cmdr. Rt. Hon.* Sir Allan Herbert Percy, K.C.M.G., D.S.O., D.S.C., R.N.

Noble, Sir Andrew Napier, Bt., K.C.M.G. (1923).

Noble, *Col.* Sir Arthur, K.B.E., C.B., D.S.O., T.D.

Noble, Sir Marc Brunel, Bt. (1902).

Noble, Sir Peter Scott, Kt.

Noble, Sir (Thomas Alexander) Fraser, Kt., M.B.E.

Nock, Sir Norman Lindfield, Kt.

Nordmeyer, *Hon.* Sir Arnold Henry, K.C.M.G.

Norman, Sir Arthur Gordon, K.B.E., D.F.C.

Norman, Sir Charles, Kt., C.B.E.

Norman, Sir Edward James, Kt.

Norman, *Vice-Adm.* Sir (Horace) Geoffrey, K.C.V.O., C.B., C.B.E.

Norman, Sir Mark Annesley, Bt. (1915).

Norman, Sir Robert Wentworth, Kt.

Normand, Sir Charles William Blyth, Kt., C.I.E., D.SC.

Norrington, Sir Arthur Lionel Pugh, Kt.

Norris, Sir Alfred Henry, K.B.E.

Norris, *Vice-Adm.* Sir Charles Fred Wivell, K.B.E., C.B., D.S.O.

Norris, *Air Chief Marshal* Sir Christopher Neil Foxley-, G.C.B., D.S.O., O.B.E.

Norris, Sir Eric George, K.C.M.G.

Norris, *Maj.-Gen.* Sir Frank Kingsley, K.B.E., C.B., D.S.O., E.D.

North, *Rt. Hon.* Sir Alfred Kingsley, K.B.E.

North, Sir (William) Jonathan (Frederick), Bt. (1920).

Norton, Sir Clifford John, K.C.M.G., C.V.O.

Norton, *Admiral of the Fleet* Sir Peter John Hill-, G.C.B.

Norwood, Sir Walter Neville, Kt.

Nugent, Sir Hugh Charles, Bt. (I 1795).

Nugent, *Maj.* Sir Peter Walter James, Bt. (1831).

Nugent, Sir Robin George Colborne, Bt. (1806).

Nuttall, Sir Nicholas Keith Lillington, Bt. (1922).

Nutting, *Rt. Hon.* Sir (Harold) Anthony, Bt. (1903).

Nye, Sir Geoffrey Walter, K.C.M.G., O.B.E.

Oakeley, Sir (Edward) Atholl, Bt. (1790).

Oakes, Sir Christopher, Bt. (1939).

Oakshott, *Hon.* Sir Anthony Hendrie, Bt. (1959).

Oates, Sir Thomas, Kt., C.M.G., O.B.E.

Oatley, Sir Charles William, Kt., O.B.E., F.R.S.

O'Brien, Sir David Edmond, Bt. (1849).

O'Brien, *Admiral* Sir William Donough, K.C.B., D.S.C.

O'Bryan, *Hon.* Sir Norman, Kt.

O'Connell, Sir Bernard Thomas, Kt.

O'Connell, Sir Morgan Donal Conail, Bt. (1869).

O'Connor, *Lt.-Gen.* Sir Denis Stuart Scott, K.B.E., C.B.

O'Connor, Sir Kenneth Kennedy, K.B.E., M.C., Q.C.

O'Connor, *Hon,* Sir Patrick McCarthy, Kt.

O'Connor, *General* Sir Richard Nugent, K.T., G.C.B., D.S.O., M.C.

O'Dea, Sir Patrick Jerad, K.C.V.O.

Ogden, Sir Alwyne George Neville, K.B.E., C.M.G.

Ogden, Sir George Chester, Kt. C.B.E.

Ogg, Sir William Gammie, Kt.

Ogilvie, Sir Alec Drummond, Kt.

Ogilvy, Sir David John Wilfrid, Bt. (s 1626).

Ohlson, Sir Eric James, Bt. (1920).

Okeover, *Lieut.-Col.* Sir Ian Peter Andrew Monro Walker-, Bt., D.S.O., T.D. (1886).

Oliver, *Hon.* Sir Peter Raymond, Kt.

Oldfield, Sir Maurice, K.C.M.G., C.B.E.

Oldman, *Col.* Sir Hugh Richard Deare, K.B.E., M.C.

Oliphant, Sir Mark Laurence Elwin, K.B.E., F.R.S.

Oliver, Sir (Frederick) Ernest, Kt., C.B.E., T.D.

Oliver, *Admiral* Sir Geoffrey Nigel, G.B.E., K.C.B., D.S.O.

Oliver, *Lt.-Gen.* Sir William Pasfield, G.B.E., K.C.B., K.C.M.G.

O'Loghlen, Sir Coleman Michael, Bt. (1838).

Olver, Sir Stephen John Linley, K.B.E., C.M.G.

O'Neill, *Hon.* Sir Con Douglas Walter, G.C.M.G.

O'Neill, Sir (Matthew) John, Kt., C.B.E.

Onslow, *Maj.-Gen.* Sir Denzil Macarthur-, Kt., C.B.E., D.S.O., E.D.

Onslow, Sir John Roger Wilmot, Bt. (1797).

Onslow, *Admiral* Sir Richard George, K.C.B., D.S.O.

Oppenheim, Sir Alexander, Kt., O.B.E., D.S.C., F.R.S.E.

Oppenheim, Sir Duncan Morris, Kt.

Oppenheimer, Sir Michael Bernard Grenville, Bt. (1921).

Oppenheimer, Sir Philip Jack, Kt.

Opperman, *Hon.* Sir Hubert Ferdinand, Kt., O.B.E.

Orde, Sir Charles William, K.C.M.G.

Orde, Sir John Alexander Campbell-, Bt. (1790).

Organe, *Prof.* Sir Geoffrey Stephen William, Kt., M.D.

Ormerod, *Maj.* Sir Cyril Berkeley, K.B.E.

Ormond, Sir John Davies Wilder, Kt., B.E.M.

Ormrod, *Rt. Hon.* Sir Roger Fray Greenwood, Kt.

Orr, *Rt. Hon.* Sir Alan Stewart, Kt., O.B.E.

Ortcheson, Sir John, Kt., C.B.E.

Osborn, Sir Danvers Lionel Rouse, Bt. (1662).

Osborn, Sir Frederic James, Kt.

Osborne, Sir Basil, Kt., C.B.E.

Osborne, Sir Peter George, Bt. (I 1629).

Osman, Sir Abdul Raman Mahomed, G.C.M.G., C.B.E.

Osmond, Sir Douglas, Kt., C.B.E.

Outerbridge, *Col. Hon.* Sir Leonard Cecil, Kt., C.B.E., D.S.O.

Outram, Sir Alan James, Bt. (1859).

Overall, Sir John Wallace, Kt., C.B.E., M.C.

Overton, Sir Arnold Edersheim, K.C.B., K.C.M.G., M.C.

Owen, Sir Alfred George Beech, Kt., C.B.E.

Owen, Sir (Arthur) Douglas, K.B.E., C.B.

Owen, Sir Dudley Herbert Cunliffe-, Bt. (1920).

Owen, Sir Hugh Bernard Pilkington, Bt. (1813).

Owo, The Olowo of, Kt.

Packard, *Lieut.-Gen.* Sir (Charles) Douglas, K.B.E., C.B., D.S.O.

Padmore, Sir Thomas, G.C.B.

Pagan, *Brig.* Sir John Ernest, Kt., C.M.G., M.B.E., E.D.

Page, *Prof.* Sir Denys Lionel, Kt., F.B.A.

Page, Sir Harry Robertson, Kt.

Paget, Sir John Starr, Bt. (1886).

Paget, Sir Julian Tolver, Bt. (1871).

Pain, *Maj.-Gen.* Sir (Horace) Rollo (Squarey), K.C.B., M.C.

Pain, *Hon.* Sir Peter Richard, Kt.

Paley, *Maj.-Gen.* Sir (Alexander George) Victor, K.B.E., C.B., D.S.O.

Palliser, Sir (Arthur) Michael, K.C.M.G.

Palmer, Sir Charles Mark, Bt. (1886).

Palmer, Sir Geoffrey Christopher John, Bt. (1669).

Palmer, Sir John Edward Somerset, Bt. (1791).

Palmer, *Brig.* Sir Otho Leslie Prior-, Kt., D.S.O.

Panckridge, *Surgeon Vice-Adm.* Sir (William) Robert (Silvester), K.B.E., C.B.

Pape, *Hon.* Sir George Augustus, Kt.

Pararajasingam, Sir Sangarapillai, Kt.

Parham, *Admiral* Sir Frederick Robertson, G.B.E., K.C.B., D.S.O.

Paris, Sir Edward Talbot, Kt., C.B., D.SC.

Park, *Hon.* Sir Hugh Eames, Kt.

Parker, Sir (Arthur) Douglas Dodds-, Kt.]

Parker, Sir Douglas William Leigh, Kt., O.B.E.

Parker, Sir Harold, K.C.B., K.B.E., M.C.

Parker, Sir John Edward, Kt.

Parker, Sir Karl Theodore, Kt., C.B.E., Ph.D., F.B.A.

Parker, Sir Richard (William) Hyde, Bt. (1681).

Parker, Sir (Walter) Edmund, Kt., C.B.E.

Parker, *Vice-Adm.* Sir (Wilfred) John, K.B.E., C.B., D.S.C.

Parker, Sir (William) Alan, Bt. (1844).

Parkes, Sir Alan Sterling, Kt., C.B.E., Ph.D., D.SC., SC.D., F.R.S.

Parkes, Sir Basil Arthur, Kt., O.B.E.

Parkinson, Sir John, Kt., M.D.

Parkinson, Sir Kenneth Wade, Kt.

Parr, Sir Robert, K.B.E., C.M.G.

Parrott, Sir Cecil Cuthbert, K.C.M.G., O.B.E.

Parry, Sir (Frank) Hugh (Nigel), Kt., C.B E.

Parsons, Sir Anthony Derrick, K.C.M.G., M.V.O., M.C.

Parsons, Sir (John) Michael, Kt.

Parsons, Sir Maurice Henry, K.C.M.G.

Part, Sir Antony Alexander, Kt., G.C.B., M.B.E.

Partabgarh, H.H. the Maharawab of, K.C.S.I.

Partridge, Sir (Ernest) John, K.B.E.

Pasley, Sir Rodney Marshall Sabine, Bt. (1794).

Patch, *Air Chief Marshal* Sir Hubert Leonard, K.C.B., C.B.E.

Paterson, Sir (Alexander) Swinton, K.B.E., C.M.G.

Paterson, Sir George Mutlow, Kt., O.B.E., Q.C.

Paterson, Sir John Valentine Jardine, Kt.

Patna, Maharaja of, K.C.I.E.

Paton, *Prof.* Sir George Whitecross, Kt.

Paton, Sir Leonard Cecil, Kt., C.B.E., M.C.

Paton, *Capt.* Sir Stuart Henry, K.C.V.O., C.B.E., R.N. (*ret.*).

Paton, Sir (Thomas) Angus (Lyall), Kt., C.M.G., F.R.S.

Patron, Sir Joseph, Kt., O.B.E., M.C.

Patterson, Sir John Robert, K.B.E., C.M.G.

Pattinson, *Hon.* Sir Baden, K.D.E.

Paul, Sir John Warburton, G.C.M.G., O.B.E., M.C.

Paull, Sir Gilbert James, Kt.

Pavlides, Sir Paul George, Kt., C.B.E.

Payne, *Hon.* Sir Reginald Withers, Kt.

Payne, Sir Robert Frederick, Kt.

Peake, Sir Francis Harold, Kt.

Peake, Sir Harold, Kt.

Peard, *Rear-Adm.* Sir Kenyon Harry Terrell, K.B.E.

Pearman, *Hon.* Sir James Eugene, Kt., C.B.E.

Pearson, Sir Francis Fenwick, Bt., M.B.E. (1964).

Pearson, *Hon.* Sir Glen Gardner, Kt.

Pearson, Sir (James) Denning, Kt.

Pearson, Sir (James) Reginald, Kt., O.B.E.

Pearson, Sir Neville, Bt. (1916).

Pearson, *General* Sir Thomas Cecil Hook, K.C.B., C.B.E., D.S.O.

Pease, Sir (Alfred) Vincent, Bt. (1882).

Pease, Sir Richard Thorn, Bt. (1920).

Pechell, Sir Ronald Horace, Bt. (1797).

Peck, Sir Edward Heywood, G.C.M.G.

Peck, Sir John Howard, K.C.M.G.

Pedder, *Vice-Adm.* Sir Arthur Reid, K.B.E., C.B.

Pedler, Sir Frederick Johnson, Kt.

Peek, Sir Francis Henry Grenville, Bt. (1874).

Peek, *Vice-Adm.* Sir Richard Innes, K.B.E., C.B., D.S.C.

Peel, *Capt.* Sir (Francis Richard) Jonathan, Kt., C.B.E., M.C.

Peel, Sir John Harold, K.C.V.O.

Peel, Sir (William) John, Kt.

Peierls, Sir Rudolf Ernst, Kt., C.B.E., D.SC., D.Phil., F.R.S.

Peile, *Vice-Adm.* Sir Lancelot Arthur Babington, K.B.E., C.B., D.S.O., M.V.O.

Peirse, Sir Henry Grant de la Poer Beresford-, Bt. (1814).

Pelham, Sir (George) Clinton, K.B.E., C.M.G.

Pelly, Sir Harold Alwyne, Bt., M.C. (1840).

Pendred, *Air Marshal* Sir Lawrence Fleming, K.B.E., C.B., D.F.C.

Penn, *Lt.-Col.* Sir Eric Charles William Mackenzie, K.C.V.O., O.B.E., M.C.

Penny, Sir James Downing, K.C.I.E., C.S.I.

Pennycuick, *Rt. Hon.* Sir John, Kt.

Penrose, Sir Roland Algernon, Kt., C.B.E.

Penruddock, Sir Clement Frederick, Kt., C.B.E.

Peppiatt, Sir Kenneth Oswald, K.B.E., M.C.

Percival, Sir Anthony Edward, Kt., C.B.

Peren, *Prof.* Sir Geoffrey Sylvester, K.B.E.

Perkins, Sir (Albert) Edward, K.C.V.O.

Perkins, *Surgeon Vice-Adm.* Sir Derek Duncombe Steele-, K.C.B., K.C.V.O.

Perkins, Sir (Walter) Robert Dempster, Kt.

Perks, Sir (Robert) Malcolm Mewburn, Bt. (1908).

Perrin, Sir Michael Willcox, Kt., C.B.E.

Perring, Sir Ralph Edgar, Bt. (1963).

Perrott, Sir Donald Cyril Vincent, K.B.E.

Perry, Sir Walter Laing Macdonald, Kt., O.B.E., F.R.S.E.

Pestell, Sir John Richard, K.C.V.O.

Petch, Sir Louis, K.C.B.

Peters, *Admiral* Sir Arthur Malcolm, K.C.B., D.S.C.

Peters, *Prof.* Sir Rudolph Albert, Kt., M.C., F.R.S.

Peterson, Sir Arthur William, K.C.B., M.V.O.

Petit, Sir Dinshaw Manockjee, Bt. (1890).

Peto, *Brig.* Sir Christopher Henry Maxwell, Bt., D.S.O. (1927).

Peto, *Cdr.* Sir (Henry) Francis (Morton), Bt., R.N. (1855).

Petrie, Sir Charles Alexander, Bt., C.B.E. (1918).

Pettingel, Sir William Walter, Kt., C.B.E.

Pettit, Sir Daniel Eric Arthur, Kt.

Petty, *Hon.* Sir Horace Rostill, Kt.

Pevsner, *Prof.* Sir Nikolaus Bernhard Leon, Kt., C.B.E., Ph.D., F.B.A., F.S.A.

Phaltan, *Maj.* the Raja of, K.C.I.E.

Philip, Sir William Shearer, Kt., C.M.G., M.C.

Philips, *Prof.* Sir Cyril Henry, Kt.

Phillips, Sir Fred Albert, Kt., C.V.O.

Phillips, Sir Henry Ellis Isidore, Kt., C.M.G., M.B.E.

Phillips, Sir Horace, K.C.M.G.

Phillips, Sir John Grant, K.B.E.

Phillips, *Hon.* Sir (John) Raymond, Kt., M.C.

Phillips, Sir Leslie Walter, Kt., C.B.E.

Phillips, Sir Robin Francis, Bt. (1912).

Phillips, *Hon.* Sir Rowland Ricketts, Kt.

Phipps, *Rear-Adm.* Sir Peter, K.B.E., D.S.C., V.R.D.

Pickard, Sir Cyril Stanley, K.C.M.G.

Pickering, *Prof.* Sir George White, Kt., F.R.S.

Pickthorn, *Rt. Hon.* Sir Kenneth William Murray, Bt., Litt.D. (1959).

Pierre, Sir Joseph Henry, Kt.

Piers, Sir Charles Robert Fitzmaurice, Bt. (1 1661).

Pigot, *Brig.-Gen.* Sir Robert, Bt., D.S.O., M.C. (1764).

Pigott, *Maj.* Sir Berkeley, Bt. (1808).

Pike, Sir Philip Ernest Housden, Kt., Q.C.

Pike, Sir Theodore Ouseley, K.C.M.G.

Pike, *Marshal of the Royal Air Force* Sir Thomas Geoffrey, G.C.B., C.B.E., D.F.C.

Pike, *Lt.-Gen.* Sir William Gregory Huddleston, K.C.B., C.B.E., D.S.O.

Pilcher, Sir (Charlie) Dennis, Kt., C.B.E.

Pilcher, Sir John Arthur, G.C.M.G.

Pilditch, Sir Denys, Kt., C.I.E.

Pilditch, Sir Richard Edward, Bt. (1929).

Pile, *General* Sir Frederick Alfred, Bt., G.C.B., D.S.O., M.C. (1900).

Pile, Sir William Denis, K.C.B., M.B.E.

Pilkington, Sir Lionel Alexander Bethune, Kt.

Pilkington, *Capt.* Sir Richard Antony, K.B.E., M.C.

Pilkington, Sir Thomas Henry Milborne - Swinnerton-, Bt. (s 1635).

Pim, *Capt.* Sir Richard Pike, K.B.E., V.R.D., R.N.V.R.

Pinsent, Sir Roy, Bt. (1938).

Piper, *Air Marshal* Sir Thomas William, K.B.E., C.B., A.F.C.

Pippard, *Prof.* Sir (Alfred) Brian, Kt., F.R.S.

Pirbhai, Sir Eboo, Kt., O.B.E.

Pirie, *Air Chief Marshal* Sir George Clark, K.C.B., K.B.E., M.C., D.F.C.

Pitblado, Sir David Bruce, K.C.B., C.V.O.

Pitman, Sir Hubert Percival Lancaster, Kt., O.B.E.

Pitman, Sir (Isaac) James, K.B.E.

Pitts, Sir Cyril Alfred, Kt.

Pizey, *Admiral* Sir (Charles Thomas) Mark, G.B.E., C.B., D.S.O.

Plant, *Prof.* Sir Arnold, Kt.

Platt, Sir Harry, Bt., M.D. (1958).

Platt, *General* Sir William, G.B.E., K.C.B., D.S.O.

Playfair, Sir Edward Wilder, K.C.B.

Playford, *Hon.* Sir Thomas, G.C.M.G.

Pleass, Sir Clement John, K.C.M.G., K.C.V.O., K.B.E.

Plimmer, Sir Clifford Ulric, K.B.E.

Plimsoll, Sir James, Kt., C.B.E.

Plowman, *Hon.* Sir (John) Anthony, Kt.

Plumb, Sir (Charles) Henry, Kt.

Plummer, Sir (Arthur) Desmond (Herne), Kt., T.D.

Pochin, Sir Edward Eric, Kt., C.B.E., M.D., F.R.C.P.

Poett, *General* Sir (Joseph Howard) Nigel, K.C.B., D.S.O.

Pole, *Col.* Sir John Gawen Carew, Bt., D.S.O., T.D. (1628).

Pole, Sir Peter Van Notten-, Bt. (1791).

Pollard, Sir Charles Herbert, Kt., C.B.E.

Pollard, *Lt.-Gen.* Sir Reginald George, K.C.V.O., K.B.E., C.B., D.S.O.

Pollen, Sir John Michael Hungerford, Bt. (1795).

Pollock, Sir George, Kt., Q.C.

Pollock, Sir George Frederick, Bt. (1866).

Pollock, Sir George Seymour Montagu-, Bt. (1872).

Pollock, *Admiral of the Fleet* Sir Michael Patrick, G.C.B., M.V.O., D.S.C.

Pollock, Sir William Horace Montagu-, K.C.M.G.

Ponsonby, *Col.* Sir Charles Edward, Bt., T.D. (1956).

Poore, Sir Herbert Edward, Bt. (1795).

Pope, Sir George Reginald, Kt.

Pope, Sir Sidney Barton, Kt.

Popper, *Prof.* Sir Karl Raimund, Kt., Ph.D.

Porbandar, *Lt.-Col.* H.H. Maharaja of, K.C.S.I.

Portal, Sir Francis Spencer, Bt. (1901).

Portal, *Admiral* Sir Reginald Henry, K.C.B., D.S.C.

Porter, Sir Andrew Marshall Horsbrugh-, Bt., D.S.O. (1902).

Porter, *Prof.* Sir George, Kt., F.R.S., Ph.D., Sc.D.

Porter, *Air Marshal* Sir (Melvin) Kenneth (Drowley), K.C.B., C.B.E.

Porter, *Hon.* Sir Murray Victor, Kt.

Porter, *Rt. Hon.* Sir Robert Wilson, Kt., Q.C.

Pott, Sir Leslie, K.B.E.

Potter, Sir Henry Steven, K.C.M.G.

Potter, *Air Marshal* Sir Patrick Brunton Lee, K.B.E., M.D.

Potter, *Maj.-Gen.* Sir (Wilfrid) John, K.B.E., C.B.

Potter, Sir (William) Ian, Kt.

Pound, Sir Derek Allen, Bt. (1905).

Powell, Sir (Arnold Joseph) Philip, Kt., O.B.E., A.R.A., F.R.I.B.A.

Powell, *Maj.* Sir Richard George Douglas, Bt., M.C. (1897).

Powell, Sir Richard Royle, G.C.B., K.B.E., C.M.G.

Power, *Vice-Adm.* Sir Arthur Mackenzie, K.C.B., M.B.E.

Power, Sir John Patrick McLannahan, Bt. (1924).

Power, *Admiral* Sir Manley Laurence, K.C.B., C.B.E., D.S.O.

Powles, Sir Guy Richardson, K.B.E., C.M.G., E.D.

Powlett, *Vice-Adm.* Sir Peverill Barton Reibey Wallop William-, K.C.B., K.C.M.G., C.B.E., D.S.O.

Poynton, Sir (Arthur) Hilton, G.C.M.G.

Prain, Sir Ronald Lindsay, Kt., O.B.E.

Pratt, Sir (Edward) Bernard, Kt.

Prescott, Sir Mark, Bt. (1938).

Prescott, Sir Stanley Lewis, Kt., O.B.E.

Preston, Sir Kenneth Huson, Kt.

Preston, Sir Thomas Hildebrand, Bt., O.B.E. (1815).

Pretyman, Sir Walter Frederick, K.B.E.

Prevost, *Capt.* Sir George James Augustine, Bt. (1805).

Price, Sir (Archibald) Grenfell, Kt., C.M.G.

Price, Sir Charles Keith Napier Rugge-, Bt. (1804).

Price, Sir (Charles) Roy, K.C.M.G.

Price, Sir Frank Leslie, Kt.

Price, Sir Norman Charles, K.C.B.

Price, Sir Robert John Green-, Bt. (1874).

Price, Sir Rose Francis, Bt. (1815).

Prichard, Sir Montague Illtyd, Kt., C.B.E., M.C.

Prickett, *Air Chief Marshal* Sir Thomas Other, K.C.B., D.S.O., D.F.C.

Prideaux, Sir Humphrey Povah **Treverbian**, Kt., O.B.E.

Prideaux, Sir John Francis, Kt., O.B.E.

Pridie, Sir Eric Denholm, K.C.M.G., D.S.O., O.B.E.

Priestley, Sir Gerald William, K.C.I.E.

Primrose, Sir John Ure, Bt. (1903).

Pringle, *Air Marshal* Sir Charles Norman Seton, K.B.E.

Pringle, Sir Stuart Robert, Bt. (s 1683).

Pritchard, Sir Asa Hubert, Kt.

Pritchard, Sir Fred Eills, Kt., M.B.E.

Pritchard, Sir Neil, K.C.M.G.

Pritchett, Sir Victor Sawden, Kt., C.B.E.

Proby, *Maj.* Sir Richard George, Bt., M.C. (1952).

Proctor, Sir (George) Philip, K.B.E.

Proctor, Sir (Philip) Dennis, K.C.B.

Proud, Sir George, Kt.

Pryke, Sir David Dudley, Bt. (1926).

Puckey, Sir Walter Charles, Kt.

Pugh, Sir Idwal Vaughan, K.C.B.

Pugsley, *Prof.* Sir Alfred Grenville, Kt., O.B.E., D.S.C., F.R.S.

Pumphrey, Sir (John) Laurence, K.C.M.G.

Purchas, *Hon.* Sir Francis Brooks, Kt.

Purves, Sir Raymond Edgar, Kt., C.B.E.

Puttick, *Lt.-Gen.* Sir Edward, K.C.B., D.S.O.

Quartermaine, Sir Allan Stephen, Kt., C.B.E., M.C.

Quénet, Sir Vincent Ernest, Kt.

Quilter, Sir Anthony Raymond Leopold Cuthbert, Bt. (1897).

Raby, Sir Victor Harry, K.B.E., C.B., M.C.

Radcliffe, Sir Sebastian Everard, Bt., (1813).

Radclyffe, Sir Charles Edward Mott-, Kt.

Radzinowicz, *Prof.* Sir Leon, Kt., Ll.D.

Rae, Sir Alexander Montgomery Wilson, K.C.M.G., M.D.

Raeburn, Sir Edward Alfred, Bt. (1923).

Rahimtoola, Sir Fazil Ibrahim, Kt., C.I.E.

Raikes, Sir (Henry) Victor (Alpin MacKinnon), K.B.E.

Raisman, Sir (Abraham) Jeremy, G.C.M.G., G.C.I.E., K.C.S.I.

Rajapakse, Sir Lalita Abhaya, Kt., Q.C.

Ralli, Sir Godfrey Victor, Bt., T.D. (1912).

Ralphs, Sir (Frederick) Lincoln, Kt.

Ram Chandra Mardarai Deo, *Raja Bahadur*, Sir, Kt.

Ramgoolam, *Rt. Hon.* Sir Seewoosagur, Kt.

Rampton, Sir Jack Leslie, K.C.B.

Ramsay, *Maj.-Gen.* Sir Alan Hollick, Kt., C.B., C.B.E., D.S.O.

Ramsay, Sir Alexander William Burnett, Bt. (1806).

Ramsay, Sir Neis Alexander, Bt. (s 1666).

Ramsay, Sir Thomas Meek, Kt., C.M.G.

Ramsbotham, *Hon.* Sir Peter Edward, K.C.M.G.

Ramsden, Sir Geoffrey Charles Frescheville, Kt., C.I.E.

Ramsden, Sir (Geoffrey) William Pennington-, Bt. (1689).

Ramsey, Sir Alfred Ernest, Kt.

Ranasinha, Sir Arthur Godwin, Kt., C.M.G., C.B.E.

Randall, Sir Alec Walter George, K.C.M.G., O.B.E.

Randall, *Prof.* Sir John Turton, Kt., D.S.C., F.R.S.

Randall, Sir Richard John, Kt.

Rank, Sir Benjamin Keith, Kt., C.M.G.

Rankin, Sir Hugh (Charles Rhys), Bt. (1898).

Rankine, Sir John Dalziel, K.C.M.G., K.C.V.O.

Ransome, Sir Gordon Arthur, K.B.E.

Raper, *Vice-Adm.* Sir (Robert) George, K.C.B.

Rapp, Sir Thomas Cecil, K.B.E., C.M.G., M.C.

Rasch, *Maj.* Sir Richard Guy Carne, Bt. (1903).

Rashleigh, Sir Harry Evelyn Battie, Bt. (1831).

Ratteray, *Hon.* Sir George Oswald, Kt., C.B.E.

Rattigan, Sir Terence Mervyn, Kt., C.B.E.

Rawlinson, Sir Anthony Henry John, Bt. (1891).

Rawlinson, *Rt. Hon.* Sir Peter Anthony Grayson, Q.C., M.P.

Raymond, Sir Stanley Edward, Kt.

Rayne, Sir Max, Kt.

Rayner, Sir Derek George, Kt.

Rayner, *Brig.* Sir Ralph Herbert, Kt.

Read, *General* Sir (John) Antony (Jervis), G.C.B., C.B.E., D.S.O., M.C.

Read, *Lt.-Gen.* Sir John Hugh Sherlock, K.C.B., O.B.E.

Reade, Sir Clyde Nixon, Bt. (1661).

Readhead, Sir James Templeman, Bt. (1922).

Rebbeck, *Rear-Adm.* Sir (Leopold) Edward, K.B.E., C.B.

Reddish, Sir Halford Walter Lupton, Kt.

Redfearn, Sir Herbert, Kt.

Redfern, Sir (Arthur) Shuldham, K.C.V.O., C.M.G.

Redgrave, Sir Michael Scudamore, Kt., C.B.E.

Redman, *Lt.-Gen.* Sir Harold, K.C.B., C.B.E.

Redshaw, Sir Leonard, Kt., T.D.

Redwood, Sir Peter Boverton, Bt. (1911).

Reece, Sir Gerald, K.C.M.G., C.B.E.

Reece, Sir (Louis) Alan, Kt., C.M.G.

Reed, Sir Carol, Kt.

Reed, *Hon.* Sir Nigel Vernon, Kt. C.B.E.

Reed, Sir Reginald Charles, Kt., C.B.E.

Rees, *Hon.* Sir (Charles William) Stanley, Kt., T.D.

Reeve, *Hon.* Sir (Charles) Trevor, Kt.

Refshauge, *Maj.-Gen.* Sir William Dudley, Kt., C.B.E.

Reid, Sir Alexander James, Bt. (1897).

Reid, *Hon.* Sir George Oswald, Kt., Q.C.

Reid, *Air Vice-Marshal* Sir (George) Ranald Macfarlane, K.C.B., D.S.O., M.C.

Reid, Sir Hugh, Bt. (1922).

Reid, Sir John Thyne, Kt., C.M.G.

Reid, Sir Norman Robert, Kt.

Reid, Sir William, Kt., C.B.E., Ph.D.

Reilly, Sir (D'Arcy) Patrick, G.C.M.G., O.B.E.

Reilly, Sir Paul, Kt.

Reiss, Sir John Anthony Ewart, Kt., B.E.M.

Renals, Sir Stanley, Bt. (1895).

Rendel, Sir George William, K.C.M.G.

Rendall, Sir William, Kt.

Rennie, *Hon.* Sir Alfred Baillie, Kt.

Rennie, Sir Gilbert (McCall), G.B.E., K.C.M.G., M.C.

Rennie, Sir John Ogilvy, K.C.M.G.

Rennie, Sir John Shaw, G.C.M.G., O.B.E.

Renshaw, Sir (Charles) Stephen (Bine), Bt. (1903).

Renton, *Rt. Hon.* Sir David Lockhart-Mure, K.B.E., T.D., Q.C., M.P.

Renwick, Sir John, Kt.

Renwick, Sir Richard Eustace, Bt. (1921).

Reporter, Sir Shapoor Ardeshirji, K.B.E.

Reynolds, Sir David James, Bt. (1923).

Rhodes, Sir John Christopher Douglas, Bt. (1919).

Rich, Sir Almeric Frederic Conness, Bt. (1791).

Richards, *Hon.* Sir Edward Trenton, Kt., C.B.E.

Richards, Sir Gordon, Kt.

Richards, Sir James Maude, Kt., C.B.E.

Richardson, *General* Sir Charles Leslie, G.C.B., C.B.E., D.S.O.

Richardson, Sir Egerton Rudolf, Kt., C.M.G.

Richardson, Sir George Wigham, Bt. (1929).

Richardson, Sir (Horace) Frank, Kt.

Richardson, Sir (John) Eric, Kt.

Richardson, Sir (John) Henry (Swain), Kt.

Richardson, Sir John Samuel, Bt., M.V.O., M.D. (1963).

Richardson, Sir Leslie Lewis, Bt. (1924).

Richardson, Sir Ralph David, Kt.

Richardson, Sir Simon Alasdair Stewart-, Bt. (s 1630).

Richardson, Sir William Robert, Kt.

Riches, Sir Derek Martin Hurry, K.C.M.G.

Riches, Sir Eric William, Kt., M.C.

Riches, *General* Sir Ian Hurry, K.C.B., D.S.O.

Richmond, Sir Alan James, Kt.

Richmond, *Rt. Hon.* Sir Clifford Parris, Kt.

Richmond, Sir John Christopher Blake, K.C.M.G.

Richmond, Sir John Frederick, Bt. (1929).

Richmond, *Vice-Adm.* Sir Maxwell, K.B.E., C.B., D.S.O.

Richter, *Hon.* Sir Harold, Kt.

Rickett, Sir Denis Hubert Fletcher, K.C.M.G., C.B.

Ricketts, Sir Robert Cornwallis Gerald St. Leger, Bt. (1828).

Ricks, Sir John Plowman, Kt.

Riddell, Sir John Charles Buchanan-, Bt. (s 1628).

Ride, Sir Lindsay Tasman, Kt., C.B.E., E.D.

Ridley, Sir Sydney, Kt.

Rieger, Sir Clarence Oscar Ferrego, Kt., C.B.E.

Rigby, *Lt.-Col.* Sir (Hugh) John (Macbeth), Bt. (1920).

Rigby, *Hon.* Sir Ivo Charles Clayton, Kt.

Ringadoo, *Hon.* Sir Veerasamy, Kt.

Ripley, Sir Hugh, Bt. (1880).

Risson, *Maj.-Gen.* Sir Robert Joseph Henry, Kt., C.B., C.B.E., D.S.O., E.D.

Ritchie, Sir James Edward Thomson, Bt. (1918).

Ritchie, Sir (John) Douglas, Kt., M.C.

Ritchie, Sir John Neish, Kt., C.B.

Ritchie, *General* Sir Neil Methuen, G.B.E., K.C.B., D.S.O., M.C.

Ritson, Sir Edward Herbert, K.B.E., C.B.

Roberts, Sir Bryan Clieve, K.C.M.G., Q.C.

Roberts, *Hon.* Sir Denys Tudor Emil, K.B.E., Q.C.

Roberts, Sir Frank Kenyon, G.C.M.G., G.C.V.O.

Roberts, Sir Geoffrey Newland, Kt., C.B.E., A.F.C.

Roberts, *Brig.* Sir Geoffrey Paul Hardy-, K.C.V.O., C.B., C.B.E.

Roberts, Sir Gilbert, Kt., F.R.S.

Roberts, Sir Harold Charles West, Kt., C.B.E., M.C.

Roberts, Sir Leslie, Kt., C.B.E.

Roberts, *General* Sir Ouvry Lindfield, G.C.B., K.B.E., D.S.O.

Roberts, Sir Peter Geoffrey, Bt. (1919).

Roberts, *Col.* Sir Thomas Langdon Howland, Bt., C.B.E. (1809).

Roberts, Sir Walter St. Clair Howland, K.C.M.G., M.C.

Roberts, Sir William James Denby, Bt. (1909).

Robertson, *Prof.* Sir Alexander, Kt., C.B.E.

Robertson, Sir James Anderson, Kt., C.B.E.

Robertson, Sir James Wilson, K.T., G.C.M.G., G.C.V.O., K.B.E.

Robertson, *Prof.* Sir Rutherford Ness, Kt., C.M.G.

Robieson, Sir William Dunkeld, Kt., LL.D.

Robinson, Sir Albert Edward Phineas, Kt.

Robinson, Sir Dove Myer, Kt.

Robinson, *Prof.* Sir (Edward) Austin (Gossage), Kt., C.M.G., O.B.E., F.B.A.

Robinson, Sir Edward Stanley Gotch, Kt., C.B.E., F.S.A., F.B.A.

Robinson, *Hon.* Sir Ernest Stanley, Kt., C.B.E.

Robinson, Sir George Gilmour, Kt.

Robinson, Sir Harold Ernest, Kt.

Robinson, Sir John Beverley, Bt. (1854).

Robinson, Sir John Edgar, Kt.

Robinson, Sir John James Michael Laud, Bt. (1660).

Robinson, Sir Niall Bryan Lynch-, Bt., D.S.C. (1920).

Robinson, Sir (Wilfred Henry) Frederick, Bt. (1908).

Robson, *Prof.* Sir Hugh Norwood, Kt.

Robson, Sir Kenneth, Kt., C.B.E., M.D., F.R.C.P.

Robson, Sir Thomas Buston, Kt., M.B.E.

Robson, *Vice-Adm.* Sir (William) Geoffrey (Arthur), K.B.E., C.B., D.S.O., D.S.C.

Roche, Sir Standish O'Grady, Bt., D.S.O. (1838).

Rochfort, *Capt.* Sir Cecil Charles Boyd-, K.C.V.O.

Rodgers, Sir John Charles, Bt., M.P. (1964).

Rodrigues, Sir Alberto Maria, Kt., C.B.E., E.D.

Rogers, Sir Philip, G.C.B., C.M.G.

Rogers, Sir Philip James, Kt., C.B.E.

Roll, Sir Eric, K.C.M.G., C.B.

Roll, *Rev.* Sir James William Cecil, Bt. (1921).

Rootes, Sir Reginald Claud, Kt.

Ropner, *Col.* Sir Leonard, Bt., M.C., T.D. (1952).

Ropner, Sir Robert Desmond, Kt.

Ropner, Sir Robert Douglas, Bt. (1904).

Rose, Sir Alec Richard, Kt.

Rose, Sir Francis Cyril, Bt. (1872).

Rose, Sir Hugh, Bt., T.D. (1935).

Rose, Sir Julian Day, Bt. (1909).

Rose, Sir Philip (Humphrey Vivian), Bt. (1874).

Roseveare, Sir Martin Pearson, Kt.

Rosier, *Air Chief Marshal* Sir Frederick Ernest, G.C.B., C.B.E., D.S.O.

Roskill, Sir Ashton Wentworth, Kt., Q.C.

Roskill, *Rt. Hon.* Sir Eustace Wentworth, Kt.

Ross, Sir Alexander, Kt.

Ross, Sir Archibald David Manisty, K.C.M.G.

Ross, *Hon.* Sir Dudley Bruce, Kt.

Ross, *Prof.* Sir James Paterson, Bt., K.C.V.O. (1960).

Rosser, Sir Melvyn Wynne, Kt.

Rostron, Sir Frank, Kt., M.B.E.

Roth, *Prof.* Sir Martin, Kt., M.D., F.R.C.P.

Rothenstein, Sir John Knewstub Maurice, Kt., C.B.E., Ph.D.

Rous, Sir Stanley Ford, Kt., C.B.E.

Rouse, Sir Anthony Gerald Roderick, K.C.M.G., O.B.E.

Row, *Hon.* Sir John Alfred, Kt.

Row, *Cdr.*, Sir Philip John, K.C.V.O., O.B.E., R.N.

Rowe, Sir Michael Edward, Kt., C.B.E., Q.C.

Rowell, Sir (Herbert Babington) Robin, Kt., C.B.E., A.F.C.

Rowlands, *Air Marshal* Sir John Samuel, K.B.E., G.C.

Rowlands, *Surg.-Rear-Adm.* Sir (Richard) Alun, K.B.E., M.D.

Rowlandson, Sir (Stanley) Graham, Kt., M.B.E.

Rowley, Sir Charles Robert, Bt. (1836).

Rowley, Sir Joshua Francis, Bt. (1786).

Rowntree, Sir Norman Andrew Forster, Kt.

Roxburgh, *Vice-Adm.* Sir John Charles Young, K.C.B., C.B.E., D.S.O., D.S.C.

Roxburgh, Sir Ronald Francis, Kt.

Roy, Sir Asoka Kumar, Kt.

Royden, Sir John Ledward, Bt. (1905).

Royle, Sir Anthony Henry Fanshawe, K.C.M.G., M.P.

Royle, Sir Lancelot Carrington K.B.E.

Rucker, Sir Arthur Nevil, K.C.M.G., C.B., C.B.E.

Ruddle, *Lt.-Col.* Sir (George) Kenneth (Fordham), Kt., T.D.

Rugg, Sir (Edward) Percy, Kt.

Rumball, *Air Vice-Marshal* Sir (Campion) Aubrey, K.B.E.

Rumbold, Sir (Horace) Algernon (Fraser), K.C.M.G., C.I.E.

Rumbold, Sir (Horace) Anthony (Claude), Bt., K.C.M.G., K.C.V.O., C.B. (1779).

Runciman, *Hon.* Sir James Cochran Stevenson, Kt.

Rundall, Sir Francis Brian Anthony, G.C.M.G., O.B.E.

Rushton, Sir Reginald Fielding, Kt.

Russell, Sir Archibald Edward, Kt., C.B.E., F.R.S.

Russell, Sir Charles Ian, Bt. (1916).

Russell, *Rt. Hon.* Sir Charles Ritchie, Kt.

Russell, *Lt.-Gen.* Sir Dudley, K.B.E., C.B., D.S.O., M.C.

Russell, Sir (Edward) Lionel, Kt., C.B.E.

Russell, Sir Frederick Stratten, Kt., C.B.E., D.S.C., D.F.C., F.R.S.

Russell, Sir George Michael, Bt. (1812).

Russell, *Admiral* Hon. Sir Guy Herbrand Edward, G.B.E., K.C.B., D.S.O.

Russell, Sir John Weir, Kt.

Russell, Sir John Wriothsley, G.C.V.O., C.M.G.

Russell, Sir (Sydney) Gordon, Kt., C.B.E., M.C.

Russo, Sir Peter George, Kt., C.B.E.

Ryan, Sir Derek Gerald, Bt., (1919).

Rycroft, Sir (Richard) Newton, Bt. (1784).

Rydge, Sir Norman Bede, Kt., C.B.E.

Ryland, Sir (Albert) William (Cecil), Kt., C.B.

Ryle, *Prof.* Sir Martin, Kt., F.R.S.

Rymill, Sir Arthur Campbell, Kt.

Sachs, *Rt. Hon.* Sir Eric, Kt., M.B.E., T.D.

Sainsbury, Sir Robert James, Kt.

Saint, Sir (Sidney) John, Kt., C.M.G., O.B.E.

St. Aubyn, Sir John Molesworth-, Bt., C.B.E. (1689).

St. George, Sir Robert Alan, Bt. (1766).

St. Johnston, *Col.* Sir (Thomas) Eric, Kt., C.B.E.

Sakzewski, Sir Albert, Kt.

Salisbury, Sir Edward James, Kt., C.B.E., D.S.C., F.R.S.

Salmon, *Air Vice-Marshal* Sir (Cyril John) Roderic, K.B.E., C.B.

Salmon, Sir Julian, Kt., C.B.E.

Salmon, Sir Samuel Isidore, Kt.

Salt, Sir David Shirley, Bt. (1869).

Salt, Sir (Thomas) Michael John, Bt. (1899).

Samuel, Sir Jon Michael Glen, Bt. (1898).

Samuels, Sir Alexander, Kt., C.B.E.

Samuelson, Sir Francis Henry Bernard, Bt. (1884).

Sanders, Sir Harold George, Kt., Ph.D.

Sanderson, *Air Marshal* Sir (Alfred) Clifford, K.B.E., C.B., D.F.C.

Sanderson, Sir (Frank Philip) Bryan, Bt. (1920).

Sandford, Sir Folliott Herbert, K.B.E., C.M.G.

Sandover, Sir (Alfred) Eric, Kt., M.C.

Sarell, Sir Roderick Francis Gisbert, K.C.M.G., K.C.V.O.

Sargant, Sir (Henry) Edmund, Kt.

Sargent, Sir (Sidney) Donald, K.B.E., C.B.

Saunders, *Air Chief Marshal* Sir Hugh William Lumsden, G.C.B., K.B.E., M.C., D.F.C., M.M.

Saunders, *Hon.* Sir John Anthony Holt, Kt., C.B.E., D.S.O., M.C.

Saunders, *Prof.* Sir Owen Alfred, Kt., D.Sc., F.R.S.

Sauzier, Sir André Guy, Kt., C.B.E., E.D.

Savage, Sir Alfred William Lungley, K.C.M.G.

Savage, Sir (Edward) Graham, Kt., C.B.

Savill, Sir Eric Humphrey, K.C.V.O., C.B.E., M.C.

Savory, *Lt.-Gen.* Sir Reginald Arthur, K.C.I.E., C.B., D.S.O., M.C.

Savory, Sir Reginald Charles Frank, Kt., C.B.E.

Sayad Muhammad, *Nawab* Sir, Kt.

Sayer, *Vice-Adm.* Sir Guy Bourchier, K.B.E., C.B., D.S.C.

Sayers, *Prof.* Sir Edward George, Kt., C.M.G., M.D.

Sayers, Sir Frederick, Kt., C.I.E.

Scamp, Sir (Athelstan) Jack, Kt.

Scarlett, Sir Peter William Shelley Yorke, K.C.M.G., K.C.V.O.

Scarman, *Rt. Hon.* Sir Leslie George, Kt., O.B.E.

Scherger, *Air Chief Marshal* Sir Frederick Rudolph William, K.B.E., C.B., D.S.O., A.F.C.

Schon, Sir Frank, Kt.

Schultz, Sir (Joseph) Leopold, Kt., O.B.E.

Schuster, Sir (Felix) James Moncrieff, Bt., O.B.E. (1906).

Schuster, Sir George Ernest K.C.S.I., K.C.M.G., C.B.E., M.C.

Scicluna, Sir Hannibal Publius, Kt., M.B.E.

Scoones, *General* Sir Geoffry Allen Percival, K.C.B., K.B.E., C.S.I., D.S.O., M.C.

Scoones, *Maj.-Gen.* Sir Reginald Laurence, K.B.E., C.B., D.S.O.

Scopes, Sir Frederick, Kt.

Scopes, Sir Leonard Arthur, K.C.V.O., C.M.G., O.B.E.

Scott, Sir (Arleigh) Winston, G.C.M.G, G.C.V.O.

Scott, Sir (Arthur John) Guillum, Kt., T.D.

Scott, Sir (Charles) Hilary, Kt.

Scott, Sir David Aubrey, K.C.M.G.

Scott, Sir David John Montagu-Douglas-, K.C.M.G., O.B.E.

Scott, *Lt.-Col.* Sir Douglas Winchester, Bt. (1913).

Scott, Sir Edward Arthur Dolman. Bt. (1806).

Scott, Sir Eric, Kt., O.B.E.

Scott, Sir George Edward, Kt., C.B.E.

Scott, Sir (Henry) Maurice, Kt., C.B.E., D.F.C.

Scott, Sir Ian Dixon, K.C.M.G., K.C.V.O., C.I.E.

Scott, *Lt.-Col.* Sir James Walter, Bt. (1962).

Scott, Sir Michael Fergus Maxwell, Bt. (F 1642).

Scott, Sir Oliver Christopher Anderson, Bt. (1909).

Scott, Sir Peter Markham, Kt., C.B.E., D.S.C.

Scott, Sir Robert Heatlie, G.C.M.G., C.B.E.

Scott, Sir (Ronald) Bodley, G.C.V.O., D.M.

Scott, Sir Ronald Stewart, Kt.

Scott, Sir Terence Charles Stuart Morrison-, Kt., D.S.C., D.Sc.

Scott, Sir Walter, Bt. (1907).

Scott, Sir Walter, Kt., C.M.G.

Scott, *Maj.-Gen.* Sir William Arthur, K.C.M.G., C.B., C.B.E.

Scotter, *Lt.-Gen.* Sir William Norman Roy, K.C.B., O.B.E., A.F.C.

Scowen, *Prof.* Sir Eric Frank, Kt., M.D., D.Sc.

Scragg, *Air Vice-Marshal* Sir Colin, K.B.E., C.B., A.F.C.

Scrivenor, Sir Thomas Vaisey, Kt., C.M.G.

Seale, Sir John Henry, Bt. (1838).

Sebright, Sir Hugo Giles Edmund, Bt. (1626).

Seddon, Sir Herbert John, Kt., C.M.G., D.M.

Seel, Sir George Frederick, K.C.M.G.

Seely, Sir Victor Basil John, Bt. (1896).

Selby, Sir Kenneth, Kt.

Selleck, Sir Francis Palmer, K.B.E., M.C.

Sellers, Rt. Hon. Sir Frederic Aked, Kt., M.C.

Sellors, Sir Thomas Holmes, Kt., D.M.

Selway, Air Marshal Sir Anthony Dunkerton, K.C.B., D.F.C.

Senior, Sir Edward Walters, Kt., C.M.G.

Serpell, Sir David Radford, K.C.B., C.M.G., O.B.E.

Seton, Sir (Christopher) Bruce, Bt. (s 1663).

Seton, Sir Claud Ramsay Wilmot, Kt., M.C.

Seton, Sir Robert James, Bt. (s 1683).

Seward, Sir Eric John, K.B.E.

Seward, Sir Samuel Conrad, Kt., O.B.E.

Seymour, Sir Horace James, G.C.M.G., C.V.O.

Seymour, Cdr. Sir Michael Culme-, Bt., R.N. (1809).

Shakerley, Sir Geoffrey Adam, Bt. (1838).

Shakerley, Col. Sir Geoffrey Peter, Kt., C.B.E., M.C., T.D.

Shakespeare, Rt. Hon. Sir Geoffrey Hithersay, Bt. (1942).

Shankland, Sir Thomas Murray, Kt., C.M.G.

Sharp, Sir Edward Harold Wilfred, Bt. (1922).

Sharp, General Sir John Aubrey Taylor, K.C.B., M.C.

Sharp, Sir Milton Reginald, Bt. (1920).

Sharpe, Sir Reginald Taaffe, Kt., Q.C.

Shaw, Sir Bernard Vidal, Kt.

Shaw, Cdr. Sir John James Kenward Best-, Bt., R.N. (1665).

Shaw, Sir John Valentine Wistar, K.C.M.G.

Shaw, Sir Patrick, Kt., C.B.E.

Shaw, Sir Robert, Bt. (1821).

Shaw, Rt. Hon. Sir Sebag, Kt.

Shearman, Sir Harold Charles, Kt.

Sheehy, Hon. Sir Joseph Aloysius, K.B.E.

Sheffield, Sir Robert Arthur, Bt. (1755).

Sheldon, Sir Wilfrid Percy Henry, K.C.V.O.

Shelley, Brig. Sir John Frederick, Bt. (1611).

Shepheard, Sir Victor George, K.C.B.

Sheridan, Hon. Sir Dermot Joseph, Kt., C.M.G.

Sherlock, Sir Philip Manderson, Kt., C.B.E.

Sherman, Sir Louis, Kt., O.B.E.

Shields, Sir Neil Stanley, Kt., M.C.

Shiffner, Sir Henry David, Bt. (1818).

Shillington, Sir (Robert Edward) Graham, Kt., C.B.E.

Shires, Sir Frank, Kt.

Shirley, Air Vice-Marshal Sir Thomas Ulric Curzon, K.B.E., C.B.

Sholl, Hon. Sir Reginald Richard, Kt.

Shone, Sir Robert Minshull, Kt., C.B.E.

Shuckburgh, Sir (Charles Arthur) Evelyn, G.C.M.G., C.B.

Shuckburgh, Sir Charles Gerald Stewkley, Bt. (1660).

Sich, Sir Rupert Leigh, Kt., C.B.

Sidey, Air Marshal Sir Ernest Shaw, K.B.E., C.B., M.D.

Sie, Sir Banja Tejan-, G.C.M.G.

Sieff, Hon. Sir Marcus Joseph, Kt., O.B.E.

Sim, Sir (George) Alexander (Strachan), Kt.

Sim, Sir Wilfred Joseph, K.B.E., Q.C.

Simeon, Sir John Edmund Barrington, Bt. (1815).

Simmonds, Sir Oliver Edwin, Kt.

Simpson, General Sir Frank Ernest Wallace, G.B.E., K.C.B., D.S.O.

Simpson, Sir James Dyer, Kt.

Simpson, Sir (John) Cyril Finucane, Bt (1935).

Simpson, Sir John Roughton, Kt., C.B.

Sims, Sir Alfred John, K.C.B., O.B.E.

Sinclair, Sir George Evelyn, Kt., C.M.G., O.B.E., M.P.

Sinclair, Maj.-Gen. Sir John Alexander, K.C.M.G., C.B., O.B.E.

Sinclair, Sir John Rollo Norman Blair, Bt. (S 1704).

Sinclair, Air Vice-Marshal Sir Laurence Frank, K.C.B., G.C., C.B.E., D.S.O.

Sinclair, Sir Leonard, Kt.

Sinclair, Sir Ronald Ormiston, K.B.E.

Sinclair, Sir William, Kt., C.B.E.

Singhania, Sir Padampat, Kt.

Singhateh, Alhaj'i Sir Farimang, G.C.M.G.

Singleton, Sir Edward Henry Sibbald, Kt.

Sinker, Sir (Algernon) Paul K.C.M.G., C.B.

Sitwell, Sir Sacheverell, Bt. (1808).

Skelhorn, Sir Norman John, K.B.E., Q.C.

Skinner, Sir (Thomas) Keith (Hewitt), Bt. (1912).

Skipwith, Sir Patrick Alexander D'Estoteville, Bt. (1622).

Skyrme, Sir William Thomas Charles, K.C.V.O., C.B., C.B.E., T.D.

Slade, Sir Benjamin Julian Alfred, Bt. (1831).

Slater, Admiral Sir Robin (Leonard Francis) Durnford-, K.C.B.

Slattery, Rear-Adm. Sir Matthew Sausse, K.B.E., C.B.

Sleigh, Sir Hamilton Morton Howard, Kt.

Sleight, Sir John Frederick, Bt. (1920).

Slesser, Rt. Hon. Sir Henry, Kt.

Slessor, Marshal of the Royal Air Force Sir John Cotesworth, G.C.B., D.S.O., M.C.

Slimmings, Sir William Kenneth Macleod, Kt., C.B.E.

Small, Sir Andrew Bruce, Kt.

Smallpeice, Sir Basil, K.C.V.O.

Smallwood, Air Chief Marshal Sir Denis Graham, G.B.E. K.C.B., D.S.O., D.F.C.

Smeeton, Vice-Adm. Sir Richard Michael, K.C.B., M.B.E.

Smiley, Sir Hugh Houston, Bt. (1903).

Smirk, Prof. Sir Frederick Horace, K.B.E., M.D.

Smith, Sir Alexander Abel, Kt., T.D.

Smith, Sir Alexander Mair, Kt., Ph.D.

Smith, Sir (Alexander) Rowland, Kt.

Smith, Sir Allan Chalmers, Kt., M.C.

Smith, Lieut-Gen. Sir Arthur Francis, K.C.B., K.B.E., D.S.O., M.C.

Smith Sir Arthur Henry, Kt.

Smith, Sir Bryan Evers Sharwood-, K.C.M.G., K.C.V.O., K.B.E.

Smith, Sir Carl Victor, Kt., C.B.E.

Smith, Maj.-Gen. Sir Cecil Miller, K.B.E., C.B., M.C.

Smith, Sir Christopher .Sydney Winwood, Bt. (1809).

Smith, Rt. Hon. Sir Dereck Colclough Walker-, Bt., T.D., Q.C., M.P. (1960).

Smith, Maj.-Gen. Sir Edmund Hakewill, K.C.V.O., C.B., C.B.E., M.C.

Smith, Vice-Adm. Sir (Edward Michael) Conolly Abel, G.C.V.O., C.B.

Smith, Sir Edwin Rodney, K.B.E.

Smith, Sir (Frank) Ewart, Kt.

Smith, Vice-Adm. Sir Geoffrey Thistleton-, K.B.E., C.B., G.M.

Smith, Sir (George) Guy Bracewell, Bt., M.B.E. (1947).

Smith, Sir (Harold) Gengoult, Kt., V.D.

Smith, Col. Sir Henry Abe K.C.M.G., K.C.V.O., D.S.O.

Smith, Sir Henry Martin, Kt., C.B.E.

Smith, Sir Henry Thompson, K.B.E., C.B.

Smith, Sir Henry Wilson, K.C.B., K.B.E.

Smith, Sir Hubert Shirley-, Kt., C.B.E.

Smith, Sir John Hamilton-Spencer-, Bt. (1804).

Smith, Sir John Kenneth Newson-, Bt. (1944).

Smith, Sir Laurence Barton Grafftey-, K.C.M.G., K.B.E.

Smith, Sir Raymond Horace, K.B.E.

Smith, Col. Rt. Hon. Sir Reginald Hugh Dorman-, G.B.E.

Smith, Sir Richard Rathbone Vassar-, Bt., T.D. (1917).

Smith, Sir Thomas Gilbert, Bt. (1897).

Smith, *Vice-Adm.* Sir Victor Alfred Trumper, K.B.E., C.B., D.S.C.

Smith, Sir (William) Gordon, Bt., V.R.D. (1945).

Smith, Sir William Reardon Reardon-, Bt. (1920).

Smith, Sir (William) Reginald Verdon, Kt.

Smith, Sir (William) Richard Prince-, Bt. (1911).

Smithers, *Prof.* Sir David Waldron, Kt., M.D.

Smithers, Sir Peter Henry Berry Otway, Kt., V.R.D., D.Phil.

Smyth, *Brig. Rt. Hon.* Sir John George, Bt., *V̇C̣*, M.C. (1955).

Smyth, *Capt.* Sir Philip Weyland Bowyer-, Bt., R.N. (1661).

Smythe, Sir Reginald Harry, K.B.E.

Snelling, Sir Arthur Wendell, K.C.M.G., K.C.V.O.

Snelson, Sir Edward Alec Abbott, K.B.E.

Snow, Sir Frederick Sidney, Kt., C.B.E.

Soame, Sir Charles Burnett Buckworth-Herne-, Bt. (1697).

Soames, *Rt. Hon.* Sir (Arthur) Christopher (John), G.C.M.G., G.C.V.O., C.B.E.

Sobell, Sir Michael, Kt.

Sobers, Sir Garfield St. Auburn, Kt.

Sobha Singh, *Hon. Sardar Baha-dur* Sir Sardar, Kt., O.B.E.

Solomon, Sir David Arnold, Kt., M.B.E.

Somerset, Sir Henry Beaufort, Kt., C.B.E.

Somerville, Sir Robert, K.C.V.O.

Sopwith, Sir Charles Ronald, Kt.

Sopwith, Sir Thomas Octave Murdoch, Kt., C.B.E.

Sorsbir, Sir Malin, Kt., C.B.E.

South, Sir Arthur, Kt.

Southby, *Lt. Col.* Sir (Archibald) Richard (Charles), Bt., O.B.E. (1937).

Southern, Sir Richard William, Kt., F.B.A.

Southern, Sir Robert, Kt., C.B.E.

Southward, Sir Ralph, K.C.V.O., F.R.C.P.

Southwell, Sir (Charles Archibald) Philip, Kt., C.B.E., M.C.

Southworth, *Hon.* Sir Frederick, Kt.

Souyave, *Hon.* Sir (Louis) Georges, Kt.

Soysa, Sir Warusahennedige Abra-ham Bastian, Kt., C.B.E.

Spearman, Sir Alexander Bowyer, Bt. (1840).

Spearman, Sir Alexander (Cad-wallader) Mainwaring, Kt.

Speed, Sir Robert William Arney, Kt., C.B., Q.C.

Speelman, *Jonkheer* Sir Cornelis Jacob, Bt. (1686).

Speir, Sir Rupert Malise, Kt.

Spence, Sir Basil Urwin, Kt., O.M., O.B.E., T.D., R.A.

Spencer, Sir Kelvin Tallent, Kt., C.B.E., M.C.

Spencer, Sir Thomas George, Kt.

Spender, *Hon.* Sir Percy Claude, K.C.V.O., K.B.E., Q.C.

Spicer, *Hon.* Sir John Armstrong, Kt.

Spicer, Sir Peter James, Bt. (1906).

Spotswood, *Marshal of the Royal Air Force* Sir Denis Frank, G.C.B., C.B.E., D.S.O., D.F.C.

Springer, Sir Hugh Worrell, K.C.M.G., C.B.E.

Spry, *Brig.* Sir Charles Chambers Fowell, Kt., C.B.E., D.S.O.

Spry, Sir John Farley, Kt.

Spurling, *Hon.* Sir Arthur Dudley, Kt., C.B.E.

Stable, *Rt. Hon.* Sir Wintringham Norton, Kt., M.C.

Stack, *Air Marshal* Sir (Thomas Neville, K.C.B., C.V.O., C.B.E., A.F.C.

Stadler, Sir Sydney Martin, K.B.E.

Stainton, Sir Anthony Nathaniel, K.C.B., Q.C.

Stallard, Sir Peter Hyla Gawne, K.C.M.G., C.V.O., M.B.E.

Stallworthy, *Prof.* Sir John Arthur, Kt., F.R.C.S.

Stamer, Sir (Lovelace) Anthony, Bt. (1809).

Stamp, *Rt. Hon.* Sir (Edward) Blanshard, Kt.

Stainer, *Brig.* Sir Alexander Beville Gibbons, Bt., D.S.O., M.C. (1917).

Stanley, Sir Robert Christopher Stafford, K.B.E., C.M.G.

Stapledon, Sir Robert de Stapel-don, K.C.M.G., C.B.E.

Staples, Sir John Richard, Bt. (1. 1628).

Stapleton, Sir Miles Talbot, Bt. (1679).

Stark, Sir Andrew Alexander Steel K.C.M.G., C.V.O.

Starkey, *Lt.-Col.* Sir William Randle, Bt. (1935).

Starr, Sir Kenneth William, Kt., C.M.G., O.B.E., E.D.

Starritt, Sir James, K.C.V.O.

Stedman, Sir George Foster, K.B.E., C.B., M.C.

Steel, *Maj.* Sir (Fiennes) William Strang, Bt. (1938).

Steel, Sir James, Kt., C.B.E.

Steel, Sir (Joseph) Lincoln (Sped-ding), Kt.

Stenhouse, Sir Nicol, Kt.

Stening, *Col.* Sir George Grafton Lees, Kt., E.D.

Stephen, Sir Alastair Eward, Kt.

Stephen, Sir Andrew, Kt.

Stephen, Sir James Alexander, Bt. (1891).

Stephen, *Hon.* Sir Ninian Martin, K.C.B.

Stephens, Sir David, K.C.B., C.V.O.

Stephens, Sir (Leon) Edgar, Kt., C.B.E.

Stephenson, *Lt.-Col.* Sir (Henry) Francis (Blake), Bt., O.B.E., T.D. (1936).

Stephenson, *Rt. Hon.* Sir John Frederick Eustace, Kt.

Stephenson, Sir Percy, Kt.

Stephenson, Sir William Samuel, Kt., M.C., D.F.C.

Stevens, *Air Marshal* Sir Alick Charles, K.B.E., C.B.

Stevens, *Vice-Adm.* Sir John Fel-gate, K.B.E., C.B.

Stevens, Sir Roger Bentham, G.C.M.G.

Stevenson, *Rt. Hon.* Sir (Aubrey) Melford (Sted), Kt.

Stevenson, Sir Matthew, K.C.B., C.M.G.

Stevenson, Sir Ralph (Clarmont) Skrine, G.C.M.G.

Stevenson, Sir William Alfred, K.B.E.

Steward, Sir Harold MacDonald, Kt.

Steward, Sir William Arthur, Kt.

Stewart, Sir Bruce Fraser, Bt. (1920).

Stewart, Sir David Brodribb, Bt., T.D. (1960).

Stewart, Sir David James Hen-derson-, Bt. (1957).

Stewart, Sir Dugald Leslie Lorn, K.C.V.O., C.M.G.

Stewart, *Prof.* Sir (Frederick) Henry, Kt., Ph.D., F.R.S., F.R.S.E.

Stewart, Sir Herbert Kay, Kt., C.I.E.

Stewart, Sir Hugh Charlie God-fray, Bt. (1803).

Stewart, Sir Iain Maxwell, Kt.

Stewart, Sir James Watson, Bt. (1920).

Stewart, Sir Jocelyn Harry, Bt. (I 1623).

Stewart, Sir Michael Norman Francis, K.C.M.G., O.B.E.

Stewart, Sir Ronald Compton, Bt. (1937).

Stewart, *Lt.-Col.* Sir (Walter) Guy Shaw-, Bt., M.C. (S 1667).

Stirling, Sir Charles Norman, K.C.M.G., K.C.V.O.

Stoby, Sir Kenneth Sievewright, Kt.

Stockdale, Sir Edmund Villiers Minshull, Bt. (1960).

Stocker, *Hon.* Sir John Dexter, Kt., M.C., T.D.

Stockil, Sir Raymond Osbourne, K.B.E.

Stockwell, *General* Sir Hugh Charles G.C.B., K.B.E., D.S.O.

Stokes, Sir Harold Frederick, Kt., C.B.E.

Stone, Sir (John) Leonard, Kt., O.B.E., Q.C.

Stone, Sir Joseph Ellis, Kt.

†Stonhouse, Sir Philip Allan, Bt. (1628).

Stooke, Sir George Beresford-, K.C.M.G.

Stopford, *Rt. Rev.* Robert Wright, P.C., K.C.V.O., C.B.E., D.D.

Storrar, Sir John, Kt., C.B.E., M.C.

Stott, Sir Philip Sidney, Bt., (1920).

Stourton, Sir Ivo Herbert Evelyn Joseph, Kt., C.M.G., O.B.E.

Stout, Sir (Thomas) Duncan (Macgregor), Kt., C.B.E., D.S.O., E.D.

Stow, Sir Frederic Lawrence Philipson-, Bt. (1907).

Stow, Sir John Montague, G.C.M.G., K.C.V.O.

Stracey, Sir John Simon, Bt. (1818).

Strachan, Sir Andrew Henry, Kt., C.B.E.

Strachey, Sir Charles, Bt. (1801).

Strasser, Sir Paul, Kt.

Stratton, Sir (Francis) John, Kt., C.B.E.

Stratton, *Lt.-Gen.* Sir William Henry, K.C.B., C.V.O., C.B.E., D.S.O.

Streat, Sir (Edward) Raymond, K.B.E.

Streatfeild, Sir Geoffrey Hugh Benbow, Kt., M.C.

Strong, Sir Charles Lorz, K.C.V.O.

Strong, *Maj.-Gen.* Sir Kenneth William Dobson, K.B.E., C.B.

Strong, *Most Rev.* Philip Nigel Warrington, K.B.E., C.M.G., D.D.

Stronge, *Capt. Rt. Hon.* Sir (Charles) Norman (Lockhart), Bt., M.C. (1803).

Strutt, Sir (Henry) Austin, K.C.V.O., C.B.

Strutt, Sir Nigel Edward, Kt., T.D.

†Stuart, Sir Philip Luttrell, Bt. (1660).

Stubblefield, Sir (Cyril) James, Kt., D.SC., Ph.D., F.R.S.

Stucley, Sir Dennis Frederic Bankes, Bt. (1859).

Studd, Sir Peter Malden, G.B.E.

Studd, Sir Robert Kynaston, Bt. (1929).

Studdy, Sir Henry, Kt., C.B.E.

Studholme, Sir Henry Gray, Bt., C.V.O. (1956).

Style, *Lt. Cdr.* Sir Godfrey William, Kt., C.B.E., D.S.C., R.N.

Style, Sir William Montague, Bt. (1627).

Suffield, Sir (Henry John) Lester, Kt.

Sugden, *Maj.-Gen.* Sir Henry Haskins Clapham, K.B.E., C.B., D.S.O.

Sugerman, *Hon.* Sir Bernard, Kt.

Sullivan, Sir Richard Benjamin Magniac, Bt. (1804).

Summerfield, *Hon.* Sir John Crampton, Kt., C.B.E.

Summerhayes, Sir Christopher Henry, K.B.E., C.M.G.

Summers, Sir Felix Roland Bratten, Bt. (1952).

Summers, Sir (Gerard) Spencer, Kt.

Summers, Sir Richard Felix, Kt.

Summerscale, Sir John Percival, K.B.E.

Summerson, Sir John Newenham, Kt., C.B.E., F.B.A., F.S.A.

Summerville, Sir (William) Alan (Thompson), Kt., D.SC.

Sunderland, *Prof.* Sir Sydney, Kt., C.M.G., M.D.

Surridge, Sir (Ernest) Rex (Edward), Kt., C.M.G.

Sutherland, Sir Benjamin Ivan, Bt. (1921).

Sutherland, Sir (Frederick) Neil, Kt., C.B.E.

Sutherland, Sir Gordon Brims Black McIvor, Kt., F.R.S.

Suttie, Sir George Philip Grant-, Bt. (S 1702).

Sutton, Sir Frederick Walter, Kt., O.B.E.

Sutton, Sir (Oliver) Graham, Kt., C.B.E., D.SC., F.R.S.

Sutton, Sir Robert Lexington, Bt. (1772).

Sutton, Sir Stafford William Powell Foster-, K.B.E., C.M.G., Q.C.

Swallow, Sir William, Kt.

Swann, Sir. Anthony Charles Christopher, Bt., C.M.G., O.B.E., (1906).

Swann, *Prof.* Sir Michael Meredith, Kt., Ph.D., F.R.S., F.R.S.E.

Swanwick, *Hon.* Sir Graham Russell, Kt., M.B.E.

Swartz, *Hon.* Sir Reginald William Colin, K.B.E., E.D.

Swaziland, The Ngwenyama of, K.B.E.

Swiss, Sir Rodney Geoffrey, Kt., O.B.E.

Syers, Sir Cecil George Lewis, K.C.M.G., C.V.O.

Sykes, Sir (Benjamin) Hugh, Bt. (1921).

Sykes, Sir Charles, Kt., C.B.E., D.SC., Ph.D., F.R.S.

Sykes, Sir Francis Godfrey, Bt. (1781).

Sykes, Sir (Mark Tatton) Richard, Bt. (1783).

Syme, Sir Colin York, Kt.

Syme, *Prof.* Sir Ronald, Kt., F.B.A.

Symonds, *Air Vice-Marshal* Sir Charles, Putnam, K.B.E., C.B.

Symonette, Sir Roland Theodore, Kt.

Synge, Sir Robert Carson, Bt. (1801).

Tailyour, *General* Sir Norman Hastings, K.C.B., D.S.O., R.M.

Tait, Sir James Blair, Kt., Q.C.

Tait, Sir James Sharp, Kt., Ph.D.

Tait, Sir Peter, K.B.E.

Tait, *Air Vice-Marshal* Sir Victor Hubert, K.B.E., C.B.

Talbot, *Vice-Adm.* Sir (Arthur Allison) FitzRoy, K.B.E., C.B., D.S.O.

Talbot, *Hon.* Sir Hilary Gwynne, Kt.

Talbot, *Lt.-Gen.* Sir Norman Graham Guy, K.B.E., T.D.

Tallack, Sir Hugh Mackay, Kt.

Tancred, Sir Henry Lawson-, Bt. (1662).

Tang, Sir Shiu-Kin, Kt., C.B.E.

Tange, Sir Arthur Harold, Kt., C.B.E.

Tanner, Sir Edgar Stephen, Kt., C.B.E., E.D.

Tansley, Sir Eric Crawford, Kt., C.M.G.

Tapp, *Maj.-Gen.* Sir Nigel Prior Hanson, K.B.E., C.B., D.S.O.

Tarbat, Sir John Allan, Kt.

Tasker, Sir Theodore James, Kt., C.I.E., O.B.E.

Tate, *Lt.-Col.* Sir Henry, Bt. (1898).

Taylor, *Lt.-Gen.* Sir Allan Macnab, K.B.E., M.C.

Taylor, Sir Alvin Burton, Kt.

Taylor, Sir Charles Stuart, Kt., T.D.

Taylor, Sir (Eric) Stuart, Bt., O.B.E., M.D. (1917).

Taylor, Sir Frank, Kt.

Taylor, Sir George, Kt., D.SC., F.R.S., F.R.S.E.

Taylor, Sir James, Kt., M.B.E., D.SC.

Taylor, Sir John Aked, Kt., O.B.E., T.D.

Taylor, Sir Robert Mackinlay, Kt., C.B.E.

Tebbit, Sir Donald Claude, K.C.M.G.

Teeling, Sir (Luke) William Burke, Kt.

Teelock, Sir Leckraz, Kt., C.B.E.

Temple, *Maj.* Sir Richard Anthony Purbeck, Bt., M.C. (1876).

Templeman, *Hon.* Sir Sydney William, Kt., M.B.E.

Templer, *Field Marshal* Sir Gerald Walter Robert, K.G., G.C.B., G.C.M.G., K.B.E., D.S.O.

Tennant, Sir Mark Dalcour, K.C.M.G., C.B.

Tennant, Sir Peter Frank Dalrymple, Kt., C.M.G., O.B.E.

Tennyson, Sir Charles Bruce Locker, Kt., C.M.G.

Terrell, *Capt.* Sir Thomas Antonio Reginald, Kt.

Terry, *Maj.* Sir Edward Henry Bouhier Imbert-, Bt., M.C. (1917).

Tetley, Sir Herbert, K.B.E., C.B.

Tett, Sir Hugh Charles, Kt.

Tewson, Sir (Harold) Vincent, Kt., C.B.E., M.C.

Thesiger, *Hon.* Sir Gerald Alfred, Kt., M.B.E.

Thiess, Sir Leslie Charles, Kt., C.B.E.

Thomas, Sir Ben Bowen, Kt.

Thomas, Sir Frederick William, Kt.

Thomas, Sir (Godfrey) Michael (David) Bt. (1694).

Thomas, Sir (James William) Tudor, Kt., D.SC., M.D.

Thomas, *General* Sir (John) Noel, K.C.B., D.S.O., M.C.

Thomas, Sir Patrick Muirhead, Kt., D.S.O., T.D.

Thomas, Sir Robert Evan, Kt.

Thomas, Sir William James Cooper, Bt. (1929).

Thomas, Sir (William) Michael (Marsh), Bt. (1918).

Thompson, Sir Edward Hugh Dudley, Kt., M.B.E., T.D.

Thompson, Sir Edward Walter, Kt.

Thompson, *Lt.-Gen.* Sir Geoffrey Stuart, K.B.E., C.B., D.S.O.

Thompson, *Prof.* Sir Harold Warris, Kt., C.B.E., D.SC., F.R.S.

Thompson, Sir (Humphrey) Simon Mersey-, Bt. (1874).

Thompson, *Hon.* Sir John, Kt.

Thompson, Sir (John) Eric (Sidney) K.B.E., F.B.A.

Thompson, Sir (Joseph) Herbert, Kt., C.I.E.

Thompson, Sir Kenneth Pugh, Bt. (1963).

Thompson, Sir (Louis) Lionel (Harry), Kt., C.B.E.

Thompson, *Lt.-Col.* Sir Peile Beaumont, Bt., O.B.E. (1890).

Thompson, Sir Richard Hilton Marler, Bt. (1963).

Thompson, Sir Robert Grainger Ker, K.B.E., C.M.G., D.S.O., M.C.

Thompson, Sir (Thomas) Lionel Tennyson, Bt. (1806).

Thompson, *Lt.-Gen.* Sir Treffry Owen, K.C.S.I., C.B., C.B.E.

Thomson, Sir (Arthur) Landsborough, Kt., C.B., O.B.E., D.SC.

Thomson, *Prof.* Sir Arthur Peregrine, Kt., M.C., M.D.

Thomson, Sir Daniel, Kt., C.B., M.D., F.R.C.P.

Thomson, Sir (Frederick) Douglas, David, Bt. (1929).

Thomson, Sir George Paget, Kt., F.R.S.

Thomson, Sir Ivo Wilfrid Home, Bt. (1925).

Thomson, *Hon.* Sir James Beveridge, K.B.E.

Thomson, *Lt.-Col.* Sir John, K.B.E., T.D.

Thomson, Sir Ronald (Jordan), Kt.

Thorley, Sir Gerald Bowers, Kt., T.D.

Thorn, Sir Jules, Kt.

Thornley, Sir Colin Hardwick, K.C.M.G., C.V.O.

Thornton, Sir (Henry) Gerard, Kt., D.SC., F.R.S.

Thornton, *Lt.-Gen.* Sir Leonard Whitmore, K.C.B., C.B.E.

Thornton, Sir Peter Eustace, K.C.B.

Thornton, Sir Ronald George, Kt.

Thorold, Sir Anthony Henry, Bt., O.B.E., D.S.C. (1642).

Throckmorton, Sir Robert George Maxwell, Bt. (1642).

Thumboo Chetty, Sir Bernard, Kt., O.B.E.

Thuraisingham, Sir Ernest Emmanuel Clough, Kt., C.B.E.

Thwin, Sir U, Kt.

Tilney, Sir John Dudley Richard Tarleton, Kt., T.D., M.P.

Tippett, Sir Michael Kemp, Kt., C.B.E.

Titman, Sir George Alfred, Kt., C.B.E., M.V.O.

Titterton, *Prof.* Sir Ernest William, Kt., C.M.G.

Tivey, Sir John Proctor, Kt.

Tod, *Air Marshal* Sir John Hunter Hunter-, K.B.E., C.B.

Todd, Sir Geoffrey Sydney, K.C.V.O., O.B.E.

Todd, Sir Herbert John, Kt., C.I.E.

Tollemache, *Maj.-Gen.* Sir Humphry Thomas, Bt., C.B., C.B.E., R.M. (1793).

Tomkins, Sir Alfred George, Kt., C.B.E.

Tomkins, Sir Edward Emile, G.C.M.G., C.V.O.

Tomlinson, Sir Frank Stanley, K.C.M.G.

Tong, Sir Walter Wharton, Kt.

Toosey, *Brig.* Sir Philip John Denton, Kt., C.B.E., D.S.O., T.D.

Tooth, Sir Hugh Vere Huntly Duff Munro-Lucas-, Bt. (1920).

Tooth, *Hon.* Sir Seymour Douglas, Kt.

Toothill, Sir John Norman, Kt., C.B.E.

Tory, Sir Geofroy William, K.C.M.G.

Tottenham, Sir (George) Richard (Frederick), Kt., K.C.I.E., C.S.I.

Touche, Sir Norman George, Bt. (1920).

Touche, Sir Rodney Gordon, Bt. (1962).

Townley, Sir John Barton, Kt.

Townend, Sir Harry Douglas, Kt.

Townsend, *Prof.* Sir (Sydney) Lance, Kt., V.R.D., M.D., F.R.C.S.

Traherne, *Col.* Sir Cennydd George, K.G., T.D.

Travancore, *Maj.-Gen.* H.H. the Maharajah of, G.C.S.I., G.C.I.E.

Travers, Sir Thomas A'Beckett, Kt.

Treacher, *Admiral* Sir John Devereux, K.C.B.

Treatt, *Hon.* Sir Vernon Haddon, K.B.E., M.M., Q.C.

Tredgold, *Rt. Hon.* Sir Robert Clarkson, K.C.M.G., Q.C.

Trehane, Sir Walter Richard, Kt.

Trelawny, Sir John Barry Salusbury-, Bt. (1628).

Tremayne, *Air Marshal* Sir John Tremayne, K.C.B., C.B.E., D.S.O.

Trench, Sir David Clive Crosbie, G.C.M.G., M.C.

Trevaskis, Sir (Gerald) Kennedy (Nicholas), K.C.M.G.

Trevelyan, Sir George Lowthian, Bt. (1874).

Trevelyan, Sir Willoughby John, Bt. (1662).

Trewby, *Vice-Adm.* Sir (George Francis) Allan, K.C.B.

Trinder, Sir (Arnold) Charles, C.B.E.

Tritton, *Maj.* Sir Geoffrey Ernest, Bt., C.B.E. (1905).

Trivedi, Sir Chandulal Madhavlal, K.C.S.I., C.I.E., O.B.E.

Trollope, Sir Anthony Owen Clavering, Bt. (1642).

Troubridge, *Lt.-Cdr.* Sir Peter, Bt., R.N. (1799).

Troup, *Vice-Adm.* Sir John Anthony Rose, K.C.B., D.S.C.

Trout, Sir Herbert Leon, Kt.

Trowbridge, *Rear-Adm.* Sir Richard John, K.C.V.O.

Truscott, Sir Denis Henry, G.B.E.

Truscott, Sir George James Irving, Bt. (1909).

Trusted, Sir Harry Herbert, Kt., Q.C.

Tuck, Sir Bruce Adolph Reginald, Bt. (1910).

Tucker, Sir Henry James, K.B.E.

Tuckwell, Sir Edward George, K.C.V.O., F.R.C.S.

Tuite, *Maj.* Sir Dennis George, Harmsworth, Bt., M.B.E. (1622).

Tunbridge, *Prof.* Sir Ronald Ernest, Kt., O.B.E., M.D., F.R.C.P.

Tupper, Sir Charles, Hibbert, Bt. (1888).

Turbott, Sir Ian Graham, Kt., C.M.G., C.V.O.

Turing, Sir John Leslie, Bt., M.C. (S 1638).

Turnbull, Sir Francis Fearon, K.B.E., C.B., C.I.E.

Turnbull, Sir Richard Gordon, G.C.M.G.

Turnbull, Sir Winton George, Kt., C.B.E.

Turner, Sir Alan George, Kt., C.B.E.

Turner, *Rt. Hon.* Sir Alexander Kingcome, K.B.E.

Turner, *Admiral* Sir (Arthur) Francis, K.C.B., D.S.C.

Turner, Sir Cedric Oban, Kt., C.B.E.

Turner, *Eng. Vice-Adm.* Sir Frederick Richard Gordon, K.C.B., O.B.E.

Turner, Sir Harvey, Kt., C.B.E.

Turner, Sir Henry Samuel Edwin, Kt.

Turner, Sir Michael William, Kt., C.B.E.

Turner, *Prof.* Sir Ralph Lilley, Kt., M.C., F.B.A.

Turner, *Vice-Adm.* Sir Robert Ross, K.B.E., C.B., D.S.O.

Turner, Sir (Ronald) Mark (Cunliffe), Kt.

Turner, *Lt.-Gen.* Sir William Francis Robert, K.B.E., C.B., D.S.O.

Tuttle, *Air Marshal* Sir Geoffrey William, K.B.E., C.B., D.F.C.

Tuzo, *General* Sir Harry Craufurd, G.C.B., O.B.E., M.C.

Twiss, *Admiral* Sir Frank Roddam, K.C.B., D.S.C.

Tyler, *Maj.-Gen.* Sir Leslie Norman, K.B.E., C.B.

Tymms, Sir Frederick, K.C.I.E., M.C.

Tyndall, *Hon.* Sir Arthur, Kt., C.M.G.

Tyree, Sir Alfred William, Kt., O.B.E.

Tyrrell, Sir Murray Louis, K.C.V.O., C.B.E.

Tyrwhitt, Sir Reginald Thomas Newman, Bt. (1919).

Tyson, Sir John (Dawson), K.C.I.E., C.S.I., C.B.E.

Udoma, Sir Ethelbert Udo, Kt.

Uhr, Sir Clive Wentworth, Kt., C.B.E.

Unsworth, Hon. Sir Edgar Ignatius Godfrey, Kt., C.M.G.

Unwin, Sir Keith, K.B.E., C.M.G.

Upjohn, Sir William George Dismore, Kt., O.B.E., M.D.

Urquhart, Sir Andrew, K.C.M.G., M.B.E.

Urquhart, Sir Robert William, K.B.E., C.M.G.

Urton, Sir William Holmes Lister, Kt., M.B.E., T.D.

Usher, Sir Peter Lionel, Bt. (1899).

Vaghjee, Sir Harilall Ranchhordas, Kt.

Valentine, Sir Alexander Balmain Bruce, Kt.

Vallat, Sir Francis Aimé, K.C.M.G., Q.C.

Vanderfelt, Sir Robin Victor, K.B.E.

Vasey, Sir Ernest Albert, K.B.E., C.M.G.

Vaughan, Sir (George) Edgar, K.B.E.

Vavasour, *Cdr.* Sir Geoffrey William, Bt., D.S.C., R.N. (1828).

Venables, Sir Peter, Kt., Ph.D.

Verdin, *Lt.-Col.* Sir Richard Bertram, Kt., O.B.E., T.D.

Vereker, Sir (George) Gordon (Medlicott), K.C.M.G., M.C.

Verney, Sir John, Bt., M.C. (1946).

Verney, Sir Ralph Bruce, Bt., K.B.E. (1818).

Vernon, Sir James, Kt., C.B.E.

Vernon, Sir Nigel John Douglas, Bt. (1914).

Vesey, Sir (Nathaniel) Henry (Peniston), Kt., C.B.E.

Vestey, Sir (John) Derek, Bt. (1921).

Vick, Sir (Francis) Arthur, Kt., O.B.E., D.SC., Ph.D.

Vickers, Sir (Charles) Geoffrey, Kt., 𝒱𝒞.

Vickery, Sir Philip Crawford, Kt., C.I.E., O.B.E.

Victoria, Sir (Joseph Aloysius) Donatus, Kt., C.B.E.

Villiers, Sir Charles Hyde, Kt., M.C.

Villiers, *Vice-Adm.* Sir (John) Michael, K.C.B., O.B.E.

Vincent, Sir (Harold) Graham, K.C.M.G., C.B., C.V.O.

Vincent, Sir William Percy Maxwell, Bt. (1936).

Virtue, *Hon.* Sir John Evenden, K.B.E.

Vyse, *Lt.-Gen.* Sir Edward Dacre Howard-, K.B.E., C.B., M.C.

Vyvyan, Sir Richard Philip, Bt. (1645).

Wackett, Sir Lawrence James, Kt., D.F.C., A.F.C.

Waddell, Sir Alexander Nicol Anton, K.C.M.G., D.S.C.

Waddell, Sir James Henderson, Kt., C.B.

Wade, *Col.* Sir George Albert, Kt., M.C.

Wade, *Air Marshal* Sir Ruthven Lowry, K.C.B., D.F.C.

Wadham, *Prof.* Sir Samuel McMahon, Kt.

Wadley, Sir Douglas, Kt.

Wadsworth, Sir Sidney, Kt.

Waechter, Sir Harry Leonard D'Arcy, Bt. (1911).

Wagner, Sir Anthony Richard, K.C.V.O.

Wake, Sir Hereward, Bt., M.C. (1621).

Wakefield, Sir (Edward) Humphry (Tyrell), Bt. (1962).

Wakeley, Sir Cecil Pembrey Grey, Bt., K.B.E., C.B., D.SC. (1952).

Wakely, Sir Clifford Holland, K.B.E.

Wakeman, *Capt.* Sir Offley, Bt., C.B.E. (1828).

Waldock, *Prof.* Sir (Claud) Humphrey (Meredith), Kt., C.M.G., O.B.E., Q.C., D.C.L.

Walker, Sir Allan Grierson, Kt., Q.C.

Walker, Sir Baldwin Patrick, Bt. (1856).

Walker, Sir (Charles) Michael, K.C.M.G.

Walker, *Vice-Adm.* Sir (Charles) Peter (Graham), K.B.E., C.B., D.S.C.

Walker, Sir Edward Ronald, Kt., C.B.E.

Walker, *Air Chief Marshal* Sir (George) Augustus, G.C.B., C.B.E., D.S.O., D.F.C., A.F.C.

Walker, *Maj.* Sir George Ferdinand Forestier-, Bt. (1835).

Walker, *Admiral* Sir Harold Thomas Coulthard, K.C.B.

Walker, Sir (Horace) Alan, Kt.

Walker, *Maj.* Sir Hugh Ronald, Bt. (1906).

Walker, Sir Hugh Selby Norman-, K.C.M.G., O.B.E.

Walker, Sir James Graham, Kt., M.B.E.

Walker, Sir James Heron, Bt. (1868).

Walker, Sir John, K.C.M.G., O.B.E.

Walker, *General* Sir Walter Colyear, K.C.B., C.B.E., D.S.O.

Walker, Sir William Giles Newsom, Kt., T.D.

Walkley, Sir William Gaston, Kt., C.B.E.

Wall, Sir John Edward, Kt., O.B.E.

Wallace, *Hon.* Sir Gordon, Kt.

Wallace, Sir Martin Kelso, Kt.

Waller, *Hon.* Sir George Stanley, Kt., O.B.E.

Waller, Sir (John) Keith, Kt., C.B.E.

Waller, Sir John Stainer, Bt. (1815).

Waller, Sir Robert William, Bt. (I 1780).

Walley, Sir John, K.B.E., C.B.

Wallinger, Sir Geoffrey Arnold, G.B.E., K.C.M.G.

Wallis, Sir Barnes Neville, Kt., C.B.E., F.R.S.

Walmsley, *Air Marshal* Sir Hugh Sydney Porter, K.C.B., K.C.I.E., C.B.E., M.C., D.F.C.

Walsh, Sir David Philip, K.B.E., C.B.

Walsh, *Prof.* Sir John Patrick, K.B.E.

Walsham, *Rear-Adm.* Sir John Scarlett, Warren, Bt., C.B., O.B.E. (1831).

Walter, Sir Harold Edward, Kt.

Walters, Sir Roger Talbot, K.B.E., F.R.I.B.A.

Walton, *Brig.* Sir George Hands, K.B.E., C.B., T.D.

Walton, Sir John Robert, Kt.

Walton, *Hon.* Sir Raymond Henry, Kt.

Walton, Sir William Turner, Kt., O.M., MUS., DOC.

Wand, *Rt. Rev.* John William Charles, P.C., K.C.V.O., D.D.

Wanstall, *Hon.* Sir Charles Gray, Kt.

Warburg, Sir Siegmund George, Kt.

Ward, *General* Sir (Alfred) Dudley, G.C.B., K.B.E., D.S.O.

Ward, Sir Aubrey Ernest, Kt.

Ward, Sir John Guthrie, G.C.M.G.

Ward, Sir Joseph James Laffey, Bt. (1911).

Ward, *General* Sir Richard Erskine, K.C.B., D.S.O., M.C.

Ward, Sir Terence George, Kt., C.B.E.

Wardlaw, Sir Henry, Bt. (S 1631).

Wardle, Sir Thomas Edward Jewell, Kt.

Ware, Sir Henry Gabriel, K.C.B.

Waring, Sir Alfred Harold, Bt. (1935).

Waring, Sir Douglas Tremayne, Kt., C.B.E.

Wark, Sir Ian William, Kt., C.M.G., C.B.E., Ph.D., D.SC.

Warmington, *Lt.-Cdr.* Sir Marshall George Clitheroe, Bt., R.N. (1908).

Warner, Sir Edward Courtenay Henry, Bt. (1910).

Warner, Sir Edward Redston, K.C.M.G., O.B.E.

Warner, Sir Frederick Archibald, K.C.M.G.

Warner, Sir Frederick Edward, Kt.

Warner, Sir George Redston, K.C.V.O., C.M.G.

Warren, Sir (Harold) Brian (Seymour), Kt.

Warren, Sir Brian Charles Pennefather, Bt. (1784).

Warren, *Hon.* Sir Edward Emerton, K.C.M.G., K.B.E.

Wass, Sir Douglas William Gretton, K.C.B.

Waterhouse, Sir Ellis Kirkham, Kt., C.B.E.

Waterlow, Sir Christopher Rupert, Bt. (1873).

Waterlow, Sir Thomas Gordon, Bt., C.B.E. (1930).

Waterman, Sir Ewen McIntyre, Kt.

Waters, *Maj.* Sir Arnold Horace Santo, Kt., 𝒱𝒞., C.B.E., D.S.O., M.C.

Wates, Sir Ronald Wallace, Kt.

Watherston, Sir David Charles, K.B.E., C.M.G.

Watkins, *Hon.* Sir Tasker, Kt., 𝒱𝒞.

Watson, Sir (David) Ronald Milne-, Bt. (1937).

Watson, *Capt.* Sir Derrick William Inglefield Inglefield-, Bt., T.D. (1895).

Watson, Sir Francis John Bagot, K.C.V.O., F.B.A., F.S.A.

Watson, Sir James Andrew, Bt. (1866).

Watson, Sir Michael Milne-, Kt., C.B.E.

Watson, Sir Noel Duncan, K.C.M.G.

Watson, Sir Norman James, Bt. (1912).

Watson, *Vice-Adm.* Sir (Robert) Dymock, K.C.B., C.B.E.

Watson, Sir Stephen John, Kt., C.B.E., D.SC., F.R.S.E.

Watson, Sir William, Kt.

Watt, Sir Alan Stewart, Kt., C.B.E.

Watt, *Brig.* Sir George Steven Harvie-, Bt., T.D., Q.C. (1945).

Watt, *Surgeon Vice-Adm.* Sir James, K.B.E., F.R.C.S.

Wauchope, Sir Patrick George Don-, Bt. (S 1667).

Way, Sir Richard George Kitchener, K.C.B., C.B.E.

Wayne, *Prof.* Sir Edward Johnson, Kt., M.D., Ph.D.

Weatherhead, Sir Arthur Trenham, Kt., C.M.G.

Weaver, Sir Tobias Rushton, Kt., C.B.

Webb, *Lt.-Gen.* Sir Richard James Holden, K.B.E., C.B.

Webb, Sir Thomas Langley, Kt.

Webber, Sir William James Percival, Kt., C.B.E.

Webster, Sir Richard James, Kt., D.S.O.

Webster, Sir Robert Joseph, Kt., C.M.G., C.B.E., M.C.

Wedderburn, *Cdr.* Sir John Peter Ogilvy-, Bt., R.N. (1803).

Wedderspoon, Sir Thomas Adam, Kt.

Wedgwood, Sir John Hamilton, Bt., T.D. (1942).

Weeks, Sir Hugh Thomas, Kt., C.M.G.

Weidenfeld, Sir (Arthur) George, Kt.

Weinstock, Sir Arnold, Kt.

Weipers, *Prof.* Sir William Lee, Kt.

Welby, Sir Oliver Charles Earle, Bt. (1801).

Welch, *Lt.-Col.* Sir (George James) Cullum, Bt., O.B.E., M.C. (1957).

Weld, *Col.* Sir Joseph William, Kt., O.B.E., T.D.

Weldon, Sir Thomas Brian, Bt. (I. 1723).

Welensky, *Rt. Hon.* Sir Roy (Roland), K.C.M.G.

Wellings, Sir Jack Alfred, Kt., C.B.E.

Wellington, Sir (Reginald Everard) Lindsay, Kt., C.B.E.

Wells, Sir Charles Maltby, Bt. (1944).

West, *General* Sir Michael Montgomerie Alston Roberts, G.C.B., D.S.O.

Westall, *General* Sir John Chaddesley, K.C.B., C.B.E., R.M.

Westerman, Sir (Wilfred) Alan, Kt., C.B.E.

Weston, Sir Eric, Kt.

Weston, *Air Vice-Marshal* Sir John Gerard Willsley, K.B.E., C.B.

Wetherall, *Lt.-Gen.* Sir (Harry) Edward de Robillard, K.B.E., C.B., D.S.O., M.C.

Wheare, Sir Kenneth Clinton, Kt., C.M.G., F.B.A., D.Litt.

Wheatley, Sir (George) Andrew, Kt., C.B.E.

Wheeler, Sir Charles Reginald, K.B.E.

Wheeler, Sir Frederick Henry, Kt., C.B.E.

Wheeler, *Air Chief Marshal* Sir (Henry) Neil (George), G.C.B., C.B.E., D.S.O., D.F.C., A.F.C.

Wheeler, Sir John Hieron, Bt. (1920).

Wheeler, Sir (Robert Eric) Mortimer, Kt., C.H., C.I.E., M.C., F.R.S., F.B.A., F.S.A.

Wheler, *Capt.* Sir Trevor Wood, Bt. (1660).

Whishaw, Sir Charles Percival Law, Kt.

Whishaw, Sir Ralph, Kt., C.B.E.

Whitaker, *Maj.* Sir James Herbert Ingham, Bt. (1936).

White, *Hon.* Sir Alfred John, Kt.

White, *Brig.* Sir Bruce Gordon, K.B.E.

White, Sir Christopher Robert Meadows, Bt. (1937).

White, Sir Dennis Charles, K.B.E., C.M.G.

White, Sir Dick Goldsmith, K.C.M.G., K.B.E.

White, Sir (Eric Henry) Wyndham, K.C.M.G.

White, Sir Ernest Keith, Kt., C.B.E., M.C.

White, Sir Frederick William George, K.B.E., Ph.D., F.R.S.

White, Sir George Stanley Midelton, Bt. (1904).

White, Sir Harold Leslie, Kt., C.B.E.

White, *Wing-Cdr.* Sir Henry Arthur Dalrymple-, Bt., D.F.C. (1926).

White, *Surgeon Rear-Adm.* Sir Henry Ellis Yeo, K.C.V.O., O.B.E., M.D.

White, Sir John Woolmer, Bt. (1922).

White, Sir Thomas Astley Woollaston, Bt. (1802).

Whitehead, Sir Rowland John Rathbone, Bt. (1889).

Whiteley, Sir Hugo Baldwin Huntington-, Bt. (1918).

Whitford, *Hon.* Sir John Norman Keates, Kt.

Whitley, *Air Marshal* Sir John René, K.B.E., C.B., D.S.O., A.F.C.

Whitmore, Sir John Henry Douglas, Bt. (1954).

Whittaker, (Sir) Joseph Meredith, Kt., T.D.

Whitteridge, Sir Gordon Coligny, K.C.M.G., O.B.E.

Whittingham, *Air Marshal* Sir Harold Edward, K.C.B., K.B.E.

Whittle, *Air Commodore* Sir Frank, K.B.E., C.B.

Whyatt, Sir John, Kt., Q.C.

Wicks, *Hon.* Sir James, Kt.

Wien, *Hon.* Sir Philip, Kt.

Wigan, Sir Frederick Adair, Bt. (1898).

Wiggin, Sir John Henry, Bt., M.C. (1892).

Wigglesworth, *Prof.* Sir Vincent Brian, Kt., C.B.E., M.D., F.R.S.

Wigram, *Rev. Canon* Sir Clifford Woolmore, Bt. (1805).

Wilbraham, Sir Randle John Baker, Bt. (1776).

Wild, *Rt. Hon.* Sir (Herbert) Richard (Churton), K.C.M.G., E.D.

Wilkinson, Sir (David) Graham (Brook) Bt. (1941).

Wilkinson, *Prof.* Sir Denys Haigh, Kt., F.R.S.

Wilkinson, Sir Harold, Kt., C.M.G.

Wilkinson, Sir Peter Allix, K.C.M.G., D.S.O., O.B.E.

Wilkinson, Sir (Robert Frances) Martin, Kt.

Wilkinson, Sir Thomas Crowe Spenser-, Kt.

Willatt, Sir (Robert) Hugh, Kt.

Williams, Sir Alexander Thomas, K.C.M.G., M.B.E.

Williams, Sir Brandon Meredith Rhys-, Bt., M.P. (1918).

Williams, Sir Charles Henry Trelease, Kt., C.B.E.

Williams, *Admiral* Sir David, K.C.B.

Williams, Sir Edgar Trevor, Kt., C.B., C.B.E., D.S.O.

Williams, Sir Francis John Watkin, Bt., Q.C. (1798).

Williams, Sir Gwilym Tecwyn, Kt., C.B.E.

Williams, Sir Henry Morton Leech, Kt., M.B.E.

Williams, Sir John Francis, Kt.

Williams, Sir (John) Leslie, Kt., C.B.E.

Williams, *Capt.* Sir John Protheroe, Kt., C.M.G., O.B.E.

Williams, Sir Michael Sanigear, K.C.M.G.

Williams, Sir Osmond, Bt., M.C. (1909).

Williams, Sir Peter Watkin, Kt.

Williams, *Air Marshal* Sir Richard, K.B.E., C.B., D.S.O.

Williams, Sir Robert Ernest, Bt. (1866).

Williams, Sir (Robert) Philip (Nathaniel), Bt. (1915).

Williams, Sir Robin Philip, Bt. (1953).

Williams, Sir Rolf Dudley-, Bt. (1964).

Williams, Sir Roy Ellis Hume-, Bt. (1922).

Williams, Sir William Emrys, Kt., C.B.E.

Williams, *Lt.-Col.* Sir William Jones, K.C.V.O., O.B.E.

Williamson, Sir (Nicholas Frederick) Hedworth, Bt. (1642).

Willink, Sir Charles William, Bt. (1957).

Willis, *Admiral of the Fleet* Sir Algernon Usborne, G.C.B., K.B.E., D.S.O.

Willis, *Hon.* Sir Eric Archibald, K.B.E., C.M.G.

Willis, *Hon,* Sir John Ramsay, Kt.

Willison, *Lt.-Gen.* Sir David John, K.C.B., O.B.E., M.C.

Willison, Sir John Alexander, Kt., O.B.E.

Willmer, *Rt. Hon.* Sir (Henry) Gordon, Kt., O.B.E., T.D.

Willmott, Sir Maurice Gordon, Kt., M.C.

Willoughby, *Maj.-Gen.* Sir John Edward Francis, K.B.E., C.B.

Wills, *Lt.-Col.* Sir (Ernest) Edward de Winton, Bt. (1904).

Wells, Sir John Spencer, Kt.

Wills, Sir John Vernon, Bt. (1923).

Wills, *Brig.* Sir Kenneth Agnew, K.B.E., M.C., E.D.

Wilmot, Sir Henry Robert, Bt. (1759).

Wilmot, *Cdr.* Sir John Assheton Eardley-, Bt., M.V.O., D.S.C., R.N. (1821).

Wilson, Sir Alan Herries, Kt., F.R.S.

Wilson, *Lt.-Gen.* Sir (Alexander) James, K.B.E., M.C.

Wilson, Sir (Archibald) Duncan, G.C.M.G.

Wilson, Sir Arton, K.B.E., C.B.

Wilson, Sir Bertram, Kt.

Wilson, Sir Charles Haynes, Kt.

Wilson, Sir David, Bt. (1920).

Wilson, Sir Garnet Douglas, Kt.

Wilson, Sir Geoffrey Masterman, K.C.B., C.M.G.

Wilson, Sir George, K.B.E.

Wilson, *Prof.* Sir Graham Selby, Kt., M.D.

Wilson, Sir Hubert Guy Maryon, Bt. (1661).

Wilson, Sir John Foster, Kt., C.B.E.

Wilson, Sir John Martindale, K.C.B.

Wilson, Sir Keith Cameron, Kt.

Wilson, Sir Leonard, K.C.I.E.

Wilson, Sir (Leslie) Hugh, Kt., O.B.E.

Wilson, Sir Mathew Martin, Bt. (1874).

Wilson, Sir Michael Thomond, Kt., M.B.E.

Wilson, Sir Reginald Holmes, Kt.

Wilson, *Hon.* Sir Robert Christian, Kt., C.M.G.

Wilson, *Rt. Rev.* Roger Plumpton, K.C.V.O., D.D.

Wilson, Sir Roland, K.B.E.

Wilson, Sir Roy Mickel, Kt., Q.C.

Wilson, Sir Thomas Douglas, Bt., M.C. (1906).

Wilton, *Lt.-Gen.* Sir John Gordon Noel, K.B.E., C.B., D.S.O.

Windeyer, *Prof.* Sir Brian Wellingham, Kt.

Windeyer, *Rt. Hon.* Sir (William John) Victor, K.B.E., C.B., D.S.O., E.D.

Windham, *Hon.* Sir Ralph, Kt.

Wingate, *Col.* Sir Roland Evelyn Leslie, Bt., C.B., C.M.G., C.I.E., O.B.E. (1920).

Winneke, *Hon.* Sir Henry Arthur, K.C.M.G., O.B.E.

Winnifrith, Sir (Alfred) John (Digby), K.C.B.

Winnington, Sir Francis Salwey William, Bt. (1755).

Winterton, *Maj.-Gen.* Sir (Thomas) John (Willoughby), K.C.B., K.C.M.G., C.B.E.

Wise, Sir John Humphrey, K.C.M.G., C.B.E.

Wiseman, Sir John William, Bt. (1628).

Witt, Sir John Clermont, Kt.

Wodehouse, Sir Pelham Grenville, K.B.E.

Wolff, *Hon.* Sir Albert Asher, K.C.M.G.

Wolfson, Sir Isaac, Bt., F.R.S. (1962).

Wollen, Sir (Ernest) Russell (Storey), K.B.E.

Wolseley, Sir Charles Garnet Mark Richard, Bt. (1628).

Wolseley, Sir Garnet, Bt. (I 1745).

Wombwell, Sir (Frederick) Philip (Alfred William), Bt., M.B.E. (1778).

Womersley, Sir Peter John Walter, Bt. (1945).

Wontner, Sir Hugh Walter Kingwell, G.B.E., C.V.O.

Wood, Sir Anthony John Page, Bt. (1837).

Wood, Sir David Basil Hill-, Bt. (1921).

Wood, Sir George Ernest Francis, K.C.M.G., I.S.O.

Wood, Sir Henry Peart, Kt., C.B.E.

Wood, Sir Kenneth Millns, Kt.

Woodall, *Lt.-Gen.* Sir John Dane, K.C.M.G., K.B.E., C.B., M.C.

Woodhouse, *Rt. Hon.* Sir Arthur Owen, Kt., D.S.C.

Woodhouse, *Admiral* Sir Charles Henry Lawrence, K.C.B.

Woodroofe, Sir Ernest George, Kt., Ph.D.

Woodruff, *Prof.* Sir Michael Francis Addison, Kt., D.Sc.

Woods, *Most Rev.* Frank, K.B.E., D.D.

Woods, *Rt. Rev.* Robert Wilmer, K.C.V.O.

Woolf, Sir John, Kt.

Woolley, Sir Charles Campbell, G.B.E., K.C.M.G., M.C.

Woolley, Sir Richard van der Riet, Kt., O.B.E., F.R.S.

Worley, Sir Newnham Arthur, K.B.E., Q.C.

Worsley, *Lt.-Gen.* Sir John Francis, K.B.E., C.B., M.C.

Worsley, Sir (William) Marcus (John), Bt. (1838).

Wort, Sir Alfred William Ewart, Kt.

Worthington, *Air Vice Marshal* Sir Geoffrey Luis, K.B.E., C.B.

Wrangham, Sir Geoffrey Walter, Kt.

Wraxall, Sir Morville William Lascelles, Bt. (1813).

Wray, Sir Kenneth Owen Roberts-, G.C.M.G., Q.C.

Wrey, Sir (Castel) Richard Bourchier, Bt. (1628).

Wright, Sir Charles Seymour, K.C.B., O.B.E., M.C.

Wright, Sir Denis Arthur Hepworth, G.C.M.G.

Wright, Sir (John) Oliver, K.C.M.G., D.S.C.

Wright, Sir Michael Robert, G.C.M.G.

Wright, Sir Paul Hervé Giraud, K.C.M.G.

Wright, Sir Richard Michael Cory-, Bt. (1903).

Wright, *Admiral* Sir Royston Hollis, G.B.E., K.C.B., D.S.O.

Wrightson, Sir John Garmondsway, Bt. (1900).

Wrigley, Sir John Crompton, K.B.E., C.B.

Wrisberg, *Lt.-Gen.* Sir Frederick George, K.B.E., C.B.

Wyatt, *Vice-Adm.* Sir (Arthur) Guy (Norris), K.B.E., C.B.

Wykeham, *Air Marshal* Sir Peter Guy, K.C.B., D.S.O., O.B.E., D.F.C., A.F.C.

Wylie, Sir Campbell, Kt., E.D., Q.C.

Wyndham, Sir Harold Stanley, Kt., C.B.E.

Wynn, *Lt.-Col.* Sir Owen Watkin Williams-, Bt., C.B.E. (1688).

Yapp, Sir Stanley Graham, Kt.

Yarrow, Sir Eric Grant, Bt., M.B.E. (1916).

Yates, *Lt.-Gen.* Sir David Peel-, K.C.B., C.V.O., D.S.O., O.B.E.

Yates, Sir Thomas, Kt., C.B.E.

Yeabsley, Sir Richard Ernest, Kt., C.B.E.

Yeaman, Sir Ian David, Kt.

Yellowlees, Sir Henry, K.C.B.

Yonge, Sir (Charles) Maurice, Kt., C.B.E., D.S.C., F.R.S., F.R.S.E.

Yorston, Sir (Robert) Keith, Kt., C.B.E.

Youens, Sir Peter William, Kt., C.M.G., O.B.E.

Young, *Col.* Sir Arthur Edwin, K.B.E., C.M.G., C.V.O.

Young, *Prof.* Sir Frank George, Kt., D.SC., Ph.D., F.R.S.

Young, Sir George Samuel Knatchbull, Bt. (1813).

Young, *Hon.* Sir John McIntosh, K.C.M.G.

Young, Sir John William Roe, Bt. (1821).

Young, Sir Norman Smith, Kt.

Young, Sir Richard Dilworth, Kt.

Young, Sir Robert Christopher Mackworth-, K.C.V.O.

Young, Sir Stephen Stewart Templeton, Bt. (1945).

Young, Sir William, Kt., C.B.E.

Young, Sir William Neil, Bt. (1769).

Younger, *Maj.-Gen.* Sir John William, Bt., C.B.E. (1911).

Younger, *Rt. Hon.* Sir Kenneth Gilmour, K.B.E.

Younger, Sir William McEwan, Bt., D.S.O. (1964).

Baronetcies Extinct (Since last issue).—Blake of Langham (G.B., 1772); Dering (E., 1627); Duncan of Jordanstone (U.K., 1957); Kerr (U.K., 1957); Mappin (U.K., 1886); Verner (U.K., 1846).

Dames Grand Cross and Dames Commanders of the Order of the Bath, the Order of St. Michael and St. George, the Royal Victorian Order and the Order of the Brittish Empire

NOTE.—Dames Grand Cross (G.C.B., G.C.M.G., G.C.V.O. or G.B.E.) and Dames Commanders (D.C.B., D.C.M.G., D.C.V.O. or D.B.E.) are addressed in a manner similar to that of Knights Grand Cross or Knights Commanders, *e.g.* "Miss Florence Smith" after receiving the honour would be addressed as "Dame Florence", and in writing as "Dame Florence Smith, G. (or D.) C.B., G. (or D.) C.M.G., G. (or D.) C.V.O., or G. (or D.) B.E." Where such award is made to a lady already in enjoyment of a higher title the appropriate letters are appended to her name, *e.g.* "The Countess of —— G.C.V.O." Peeresses in their own right, and Life Peeresses, are not included in this list. Dames Grand Cross rank after wives of Baronets and before wives of Knights Grand Cross. Dames Commanders rank after the wives of Knights Grand Cross and before the wives of Knights Commanders.

Peeresses are not included in this list.

DAMES GRAND CROSS AND DAMES COMMANDERS

H.M. Queen Elizabeth The Queen Mother, K.G., K.T., C.I., G.M.V.O.

H.R.H. The Princess Margaret, Countess of Snowdon, C.I., G.C.V.O.

H.R.H. The Princess Alice, Duchess of Gloucester, G.C.B., C.I., G.C.V.O., G.B.E.

H.R.H. The Princess Alice, Countess of Athlone, V.A., G.C.V.O., G.B.E.

H.R.H. The Princess Alexandra of Kent, G.C.V.O.

H.R.H. The Princess Anne, G.C.V.O.

Abbot, Dame Elsie Myrtle, D.B.E.

Abercorn, The Duchess of, D.C.V.O.

Ackroyd, Dame (Dorothy) Elizabeth, D.B.E.

Albemarle, The Countess of, D.B.E.

Alexander of Tunis, Margaret Diane, Countess, G.B.E.

Anderson, Dame Judith, D.B.E.

Anderson, Dame Kitty, D.B.E., Ph.D.

Anderson, *Brig.* Hon. Dame Mary Mackenzie (Mrs. Pihl), D.B.E.

Angliss, Jacobena Victoria, Lady, D.B.E.

Ashby, Dame Margery Irene Corbett, D.B.E.

Ashcroft, Dame Peggy (Mrs. Hutchinson), D.B.E.

Ashworth, *Air Commandant* Dame Veronica Margaret, D.B.E., R.R.C.

Baden-Powell, Olave St. Clair, Baroness, G.B.E.

Baring, Lady Rose Gwendolen Louisa, D.C.V.O.

Barnes, Dame (Alice) Josephine (Mary Taylor) (Mrs. Warren), D.B.E., F.R.C.P., F.R.C.S.

Barnett, *Air Commandant* Dame (Mary) Henrietta, D.B.E.

Berry, Dame Alice Miriam, D.B.E.

Bishop, Dame (Margaret) Joyce, D.B.E.

Blaxland, Dame Helen Frances, D.B.E.

Bolte, Edith Lilian, Lady, D.B.E.

Bottomley, Dame Bessie Ellen, D.B.E.

Brecknock, The Countess of, D.B.E.

Brown, Dame Beryl Paston, D.B.E.

Bryans, Dame Anne Margaret, D.B.E.

Bryce, Dame Isabel Graham, D.B.E.

Buckley, Hon. Dame Ruth Burton, D.B.E.

Buttfield, Dame Nancy Eileen, D.B.E.

Buxton, Dame Rita Mary, D.B.E.

Bynoe, Dame Hilda Louisa, D.B.E.

Campbell, Dame Kate Isabel, D.B.E., M.D.

Carte, Dame Bridget D'Oyly, D.B.E.

Cartwright, Dame Mary Lucy, D.B.E., SC.D., D.Phil., F.R.S.

Cavan, Joan, Countess of, D.B.E.

Cayford, Dame Florence Evelyn, D.B.E.

Chick, Dame Harriette, D.B.E., D.SC.

Christie, Dame Agatha Mary Clarissa (Lady Mallowan), D.B.E.

Clode, Dame (Emma) Frances (Heather), D.B.E.

Cockayne, Dame Elizabeth, D.B.E.

Cole, Dame Margaret Isabel, D.B.E.

Coles, Mabel Irene, Lady, D.B.E.

Colvin, *Brig.* Dame Mary Katherine Rosamund, D.B.E., T.D.

Couchman, Dame Elizabeth May Ramsay, D.B.E.

Coulshed, *Brig.* Dame (Mary) Frances, D.B.E., T.D.

Courtneidge, Dame Cicely (Mrs. Hulbert), D.B.E.

Cox, Dame Marjorie Sophie, D.B.E.

Cozens, *Brig.* Dame (Florence) Barbara, D.B.E., R.R.C.

Cramer, Mary Terese, Lady, D.B.E.

Cripps, Isobel, Lady, G.B.E.

Crout, Dame Mabel, D.B.E.

Crowe, Dame Sylvia, D.B.E.

Daly, Dame Mary Dora, D.B.E.

Davies, *Commandant* Dame Jean (Mrs. Lancaster), D.B.E.

Daws, Dame Joyce Margaretta, D.B.E.

De La Warr, The Countess, D.B.E.

Denington, Dame Evelyn Joyce, D.B.E.

de Valois, Dame Ninette, D.B.E.

Devonshire, Mary Alice, Duchess of, G.C.V.O., C.B.E.

Doughty, Dame Adelaide Baillieu, D.B.E.

Doyle, *Air Commandant* Dame Jean Lena Annette Conan (Lady Bromet), D.B.E.

Drake, *Brig.* Dame Jean Elizabeth Rivett Rivett-, D.B.E.

Drummond, *Commandant* Dame (Edith) Margaret, D.B.E.

du Maurier, Dame Daphne (Lady Browning), D.B.E.

Elgin & Kincardine, The Countess of, D.B.E.

Evans, Dame Edith Mary (Mrs. Booth), D.B.E.

Evans, Lady Olwen Elizabeth Carey, D.B.E.

Farrer, Hon. Dame Frances Margaret, D.B.E.

Fell, Dame Honor Bridget, D.B.E., F.R.S.

Fonteyn, Dame Margot, D.B.E.

Frost, Dame Phyllis Irene, D.B.E.

Gardiner, Dame Helen Louisa, D.B.E., M.V.O.

Gardner, Dame Frances Violet (Mrs. Qvist), D.B.E.

Gardner, *Prof.* Dame Helen Louise, D.B.E.

Gibbs, Dame Anstice Rosa, D.C.V.O., C.B.E.

Gibbs, Molly Peel, Lady, D.B.E.

Giles, *Air Commandant* Dame Pauline, D.B.E., R.R.C.

Gillie, Dame (Katharine) Annis Calder (Mrs. Peter Smith), D.B.E.

Godwin, Dame (Beatrice) Anne, D.B.E.

Grafton, The Duchess of, D.C.V.O.

Green, Dame Mary Georgina, D.B.E.

Halifax, Dorothy, Countess of, C.I., D.C.V.O.

Hambleden, Patricia, Viscountess, D.C.V.O.

Hammond, Dame Joan Hood, D.B.E.

Hanbury, *Air Commandant* Dame Felicity Hyde, D.B.E.

Harlech, Beatrice, Baroness, D.C.V.O.

Harris, Dame (Muriel) Diana Reader-, D.B.E.

Heilbron, *Hon.* Dame Rose, D.B.E.

Herring, Mary, Lady, D.B.E.

Hill, *Air Commandant* Dame Felicity Barbara, D.B.E.

Hiller, Dame Wendy (Mrs. Gow), D.B.E.

Hillingdon, Edith Mary, Lady, D.B.E.

Holt, Dame Zara Kate, D.B.E.

Isaacs, Dame Albertha Madeline, D.B.E.

Jackson, Barbara, Lady, D.B.E.

Johnson, *Brig.* Dame (Cecilie) Monica, D.B.E., R.R.C.

Kelleher, *Brig.* Dame Joan Evelyn, D.B.E.

Kenyon, Dame Kathleen Mary, D.B.E., D.Lit.

Kettlewell, *Commandant* Dame Marion Mildred, D.B.E.

Kidd, Dame Margaret Henderson (Mrs. Macdonald), D.B.E., Q.C.

Kilroy, Dame Alix Hester Marie (Lady Meynell), D.B.E.

Kirk, Dame Lucy Ruth, D.B.E.

Lane, *Hon.* Dame Elizabeth Kathleen, D.B.E.

Leicester, The Countess of, D.C.V.O.

Limerick, Angela, Countess of, G.B.E., C.H.

Lister, Dame Unity Viola, D.B.E.

Lloyd, Dame Hilda Nora, D.B.E.

Loughlin, Dame Anne, D.B.E.

Lowrey, *Air Commandant* Dame Alice, D B.E., R.R.C.

Lynn, Dame Vera (Mrs. Lewis), D.B.E.

Lyons, Dame Enid Muriel, G.B.E.

Macknight, Dame Ella Annie Noble, D.B.E., M.D.

Macleod of Macleod, Dame Flora, D.B.E.

Macmillan, Hon. Dame Katharine, D.B.E.

Manning, Dame (Elizabeth) Leah, D.B.E.

Markova, Dame Alicia, D.B.E.

Marsh, Dame (Edith) Ngaio, D.B.E.

Menzies, Dame Pattie Maie, G.B.E.

Miles, Dame Margaret, D.B.E.

Millar, *Commandant* Dame (Evelyn Louisa) Elizabeth Hoyer-, D.B.E.

Miller, Dame Mabel Flora Hobart, D.B.E.

Morant, Dame Mary Maud (Sister Mary Regis), D.B.E.

Mulholland, *Hon.* Dame Olivia Vernon, D.C.V.O.

Murdoch, Elisabeth Joy, Lady, D.B.E.

Myer, Dame (Margery) Merlyn Baillieu, D.B.E.

Neagle, Dame Anna (Mrs. Wilcox), D.B.E.

Niccol, Dame Kathleen Agnes, D.B.E.

Ollerenshaw, Dame Kathleen Mary, D.B.E., D.Phil.

Peel, Lady Adelaide Margaret, D.C.V.O.

Pentland, Majorie Adeline, Baroness, D.B.E.

Pepys, Lady (Mary) Rachel, D.C.V.O.

Perham, Dame Margery Freda, D.C.M.G., C.B.E., D.Litt., F.B.A.

Plowden, The Lady, D.B.E.

Portland, The Duchess of, D.B.E.

Powell, Dame Muriel Betty, D.B.E.

Railton, *Brig.* Dame Mary, D.B.E.

Railton, Dame Ruth (Mrs. Cecil Harmsworth King), D.B.E.

Rambert, Dame Marie (Mrs. Ashley Dukes), D.B.E.

Rankin, Dame Annabelle Jane Mary, D.B.E.

Rankin, Lady Jean Margaret Florence, D.C.V.O.

Raven, Dame Kathleen Annie (Mrs. J. T. Ingram), D.B.E.

Rees, Dame Dorothy Mary, D.B.E.

Riddelsdell, Dame Mildred, D.C.B., C.B.E.

Ridley, Dame (Mildred) Betty, D.B.E.

Roberts, Dame Jean, D.B.E.

Robertson, *Commandant* Dame Nancy Margaret, D.B.E.

Robson, Dame Flora McKenzie, D.B.E.

Rosebery, The Countess of, D.B.E.

Salt, Dame Barbara, D.B.E.

Scarbrough, The Countess of, D.C.V.O.

Scott, Dame Catherine Campbell, D.B.E.

Seymour, Lady Katharine, D.C.V.O.

Shepherd, Dame Margaret Alice, D.B.E.

Smieton, Dame Mary Gullian, D.B.E.

Smith, Dame Enid Mary Russell Russell-, D.B.E.

Snagge, *Air Commandant* Dame Nancy Marion, D.B.E.

Stark, Dame Freya (Mrs. Perowne), D.B.E.

Stephens, *Air Commandant* Dame Anne, D.B.E.

Stevenson, Dame Hilda Mabel, D.B.E.

Stewart, Dame Muriel Acadia, D.B.E.

Strickland, Barbara, Lady, D.B.E.

Sutherland, Dame Lucy Stuart, D.B.E., D.Litt.

Tangney, Dame Dorothy Margaret, D.B.E.

Te Ata-I-Rangikaahu, Dame Ariki nui, D.B.E.

Tebbutt, Dame Grace, D.B.E.

Teyte, Dame Maggie (Mrs. Cottingham), D.B.E.

Thorndike, Dame Sybil (Lady Casson), C.H., D.B.E.

Turner, Dame Eva, D.B.E.

Turner, *Brig.* Dame Margot, D.B.E., R.R.C.

Tylecote, Dame Mabel, D.B.E.

Tyrwhitt, *Brigadier* Dame Mary Joan Caroline, D.B.E.

Van Praagh, Dame Margaret (Peggy), D.B.E.

Vaughan, Dame Janet Maria, (Mrs. Gourlay), D.B.E.

Wakehurst, Margaret, Lady, D.B.E.

Walker, Dame Susan Armour, D.B.E.

Wedgwood, Dame (Cicely) Veronica, O.M., D.B.E.

Wedgwood, Dame Ivy Evelyn, D.B.E.

Welsh, *Air Chief Commandant* Ruth Mary, Lady, D.B.E.

West, Dame Rebecca (Mrs. Andrews), D.B.E.

Whateley, *Chief Controller* Dame Leslie Violet, D.B.E.

Whyte, *Air Commandant* Dame Roberta Mary, D.B.E., R.R.C.

Williamson, *Air Commandant* Dame Alice Mary, D.B.E., R.R.C., Q.H.N.S.

Williamson, Dame (Elsie) Marjorie, D.B.E., Ph.D.

Winner, Dame Albertine Louise, D.B.E., M.D.

Woollcombe, Dame Jocelyn May, D.B.E.

Wormald, Dame Ethel May, D.B.E.

Yarwood, Dame Elizabeth Ann, D.B.E.

Younghusband, Dame Eileen Louise, D.B.E.

THE VICTORIA CROSS, VC
For Conspicuous Bravery.

The ribbon *is Crimson* for all Services (until 1918 it was *Blue* for Royal Navy).

Instituted on January 29, 1856, the Victoria Cross was awarded retrospectively to 1854, the first being held by Lieut. C. D. Lucas, R.N. for bravery in the Baltic Sea on June 21, 1854 (gazetted Feb. 24, 1857). The first 62 Crosses were presented by Queen Victoria in Hyde Park, London, on June 26, 1857.

The VC is worn before all other decorations, on the left breast, and consists of a cross-pattée of bronze, 1½ inches in diameter, with the Royal Crown surmounted by a lion in the centre, and beneath there is the inscription "For Valour." Holders of the VC receive a tax-free annuity of £100, irrespective of need or other conditions. In 1911, the right to receive the Cross was extended to Indian soldiers, and in 1920 a Royal Warrant extended the right to Matrons, Sisters and Nurses, and the Staff of the Nursing Services and other services pertaining to Hospitals and Nursing, and to Civilians of either sex regularly or temporarily under the orders, direction or supervision of the Naval, Military, or Air Forces of the Crown.

Surviving Recipients of the Victoria Cross

Agansing Rai, *Havildar* (Gurkha Rifles),*World War*.................................... 1944
Ali Haidar, *Sepoy* (Frontier Force Rifles), *World War*............................ 1945
Anderson, *Lt.-Col.* C. G. W., M.C.(Australian M.F.), *World War*....................... 1944
Annand, *Capt.* R. W. (Durham L.I.), *World War*.................................. 1940
Axford, *Corpl.* T. L., M.M.(A.I.F.), *Gt. War*.. 1918
Barrett, *Col.* John C. (R. Leic. R.), *Gt. War*.. 1918
Bassett, *Col.* Cyril R. G. (N.Z.), *Gt. War*... 1915
Bent, *R.-S.-M.* S. J. (East Lancs. R.), *Gt. War* 1914
Bhanbhagta Gurung, *Lance-Naik* (2nd Gurkha Rifles), *World War*...................... 1945
Bhandari Ram,*Lance-Naik*(Baluch R.), *World War*................................... 1944
Brereton, *C.-S.-M.* A. (Manitoba R.), *Gt. War*................................... 1918
Burton, *Corpl.* R. H. (Duke of Wellington's R.), *World War*...................... 1944
Campbell, *Brigadier* L. M., D.S.O., O.B.E., T.D. (A. & S. Highrs.), *World War*........... 1943
Carmichael, *Sergt.* J. (N. Staff. R.), *Gt. War*.. 1917
Carne, *Col.* J. P., D.S.O. (Glos. R.), *Korea*... 1951
Carroll, *Pte.* John (Aus. Inf.), *Gt. War*...... 1917
Cartwright, *Pte.* George (Aust.), *Gt. War*... 1918
Chapman, *Sergt.* E. T. (Monmouthshire R.), *World War*............................. 1945
Cheshire, *Group Capt.* G. L., D.S.O., D.F.C. (R.A.F.), *World War*.................... 1944
Cooper, *Lt.* E. (K.R.R.C.), *Gt. War*......... 1917
Cruickshank, *Fl. Lt.* J. A. (R.A.F.V.R.), *World War*............................. 1944
Crutchley, *Admiral* Sir Victor Alexander, K.C.B., D.S.C. (R.N.), *Gt. War*......... 1918
Currie, *Maj.* D. V., C.B.E. (S. Alberta R., Canada), *World War*................. 1944
Cutler, Sir A. R., K.C.M.G., K.C.V.O., C.B.E. (Australia), *World War*............. 1941
Davies, *Sergt.* J. (R. Welch Fus.), *Gt. War*.. 1916
Dean, *Col.* D. J., O.B.E. (R. W. Kent R.), *Gt. War*.............................. 1918
De L'Isle, *Maj.* The Viscount, K.G., P.C., G.C.M.G.,G.C.V.O.(Hon.W.P. Sidney)(Gren. Gds.), *World War*....................... 1944
Dinesen, *Lt.* T. (Royal Highlanders of Canada), *Gt. War*.................... 1918
Dresser, *Pte.* T. (Green Howards), *Gt. War*.. 1917
Eardley, *Sergt.* G. H., M.M. (K.S.L.I.), *World War*............................... 1944
Edwards, *Air Commodore* Sir Hughie, K.C.M.G., C.B., D.S.O., O.B.E., D.F.C. (R.A.F.), *World War*................................. 1941
Elliott,*Lt.*the Rev. K.(N.Z.M.F.),*World War* 1942
Ervine-Andrews, *Lt.-Col.* H. M. (E. Lancs. R.), *World War*...................... 1940
Foote, *Maj.-Gen.* H. R. B., C.B., D.S.O. (R. Tank R.), *World War*............. 1942
Foote, *Rev.* J. W. (Canada), *World War*... 1942
Fraser, *Cdr.* I. E., D.S.C.(R.N.R.), *World War* 1945
Ganju Lama, *Jemadar*, M.M. (Gurkha Rifles), *World War*............................ 1944
Gardner, *Capt.* P. J., M.C. (R.T.R.), *World War*................................... 1941
Geary, *Rev.* B. H., C.F.(E. Surr. R.), *Gt. War* 1915
Ghale, *Subedar* Gaje (Gurkha Rif.), *Wld. War* 1943
Gian Singh, *Jemadar* (Punjab R.), *World War*. 1945
Gordon, *W.O. II* J. H. (Australia), *World War* 1941
Gould, *Lt.* T. W. (R.N.), *World War*....... 1942
Gourley, *2nd Lt.* C.E., M.M. (R.F.A.), *Gt.*.................................... 1917

Graham, *Lt.-Col.* Sir Reginald, Bt., O.B.E. (M.G.C.), *Gt. War*..................... 1917
Gregg, *Brig.* Hon. Milton F., C.B.E., M.C. (Nova Scotia R.), *Gt. War*............. 1918
Grimshaw, *Lt.-Col.* John (Lanc. Fus.), *Gt. War*................................. 1915
Haine,*Lt.-Col.*R. L., M.C.(H.A.C.), *Gt. War* 1917
Hall, *Sergt.* Arthur (Australia), *Gt. War*..... 1918
Harvey, *Brig.* F. M. W., M.C. (Can. Inf.), *Gt. War*................................. 1917
Hinton, *Sergt.* J. D. (N.Z.M.F.), *World War*.. 1941
Holbrook, *Com.* N. D. (R.N.), *Gt. War*..... 1914
Hulme, *Sergt.* A. C. (N.Z.M.F.), *World War* 1941
Jackson, *W.O.* N.C. (R.A.F.V.R.), *Wld. War* 1944
James, *Brig.* Manley Angell, D.S.O., M.B.E., M.C. (Glouc. R.), *Gt. War*............. 1918
Jamieson, *Maj.* D. A. (R. Norfolk R.), *World War*............................ 1944
Jefferson, *L.-Corpl.* F. A. (Lancs. Fus.), *Wld. War*................................... 1944
Johnson, *Maj.-Gen.* Dudley G., C.B., D.S.O., M.C. (S. Wales B.), *Gt. War*......... 1918
Joynt, *Lt.-Col.* W. D. (Aust. I. F.), *Gt. War*.. 1918
Kamal Ram, *Havildar* (Punjab R.), *Wld. War* 1944
Kenna, *Pte.* E. (Australian M.F.), *Wld. War* 1945
Kenneally, *C.-Q.-M.-S.* J. P. (Irish Gds.), *World War*........................... 1943
Kenny, *Pte.* H. E. (Loyal R.) *Gt. War*...... 1916
Lachiman Gurung, *Rifleman* (Gurkha Rifles), *World War*......................... 1945
Laurent, *Lt.* H. J. (N.Z. Rif. Bgde.), *Gt. War* 1918
Learoyd, *Wing-Cmdr.* R. A. B. (R.A.F.), *World War*........................... 1940
Le Patourel, *Col.* H. W. (R. Hampshire R.), *World War*........................... 1942
Lewis, *Pte.* H. W. (Welch R.), *Gt. War*.... 1916
Luke, *Sergt.* F. (R.H.A.), *Gt. War*......... 1914
McNally, *Sergt.* William, M.M. (Green Howards), *Gt. War*................... 1918
Magennis, L/S J. J. (R.N.), *World War*..... 1945
Mahony, *Lt.-Col.* J. K. (Westminster R., Canada), *World War*............... 1944
Malleson, *Com.* W. St. A. (R.N.), *Gt. War*.. 1915
Martin, *Brig.* C. G., C.B.E., D.S.O. (R.E.), *Gt. War*................................. 1915
Merritt, *Lt.-Col.* C. C. I. (S. Saskatchewan R.), *World War*...................... 1942
Miers, *Rear-Adm.* Sir A. C. C., K.B.E., C.B., D.S.O. (R.N.), *World War*............. 1942
Mitchell, *Lt.-Col.* Coulson N., M.C. (Canad Engrs.), *Gt. War*.................. 1918
Moon, *Lt.* Rupert V. (Aust. Inf.), *Gt. War*.. 1917
Moyney, *Sergt.* John (Irish Gds.), *Gt. War*.. 1917
Myles, *Capt.* E. K., D.S.O. (Worc. R.), *Gt. War*................................. 1916
Namdeo Jadhao, *Havildar* (Mahratta L. I.), *World War*........................... 1945
Neame, *Lt.-Gen.* Sir Philip, K.B.E., C.B., D.S.O. (R.E.), *Gt. War*.................. 1914
Nicholls, *L.-Cpl.* H. (G. Gds.), *World War*.. 1940
Norton, *Capt.* G. R., M.M. (S.A.M.F.), *World War*................................... 1944
Parkash Singh, *Capt.* (Punjab R.), *World War* 1943
Payne, *W.O.* K. (Australian Army), *Vietnam* 1969
Pearkes, *Maj.-Gen.* Hon. George Randolph, C.B., D.S.O., M.C. (Can. Ind.), *Gt. War*..... 1917
Place, *Rear-Adm.* B. C. G., C.B., D.S.C.(R.N.), *World War*........................... 1943
Porteous, *Brig.* P.A. (R.A.), *World War*.... 1942
Rambahadur Limbu,*L/Corpl.*(Gurkha Rifles), *Sarawak*.............................. 1965
Rattey, *Sergt.* R. R. (Australia), *World War*. 1945
Reid, *Fl.-Lt.* W. (R.A.F.V.R.), *World War*. 1943

Roberts, *Maj.-Gen.* F. C., D.S.O., O.B.E., M.C. (Worc. R.), *Gt. War* 1918

Roberts, *Lt.-Com.* P. S. W., D.S.C. (R.N.), *World War* 1942

Rutherford, *Capt.* C. B., M.C., M.M. (Quebec R.), *Gt. War* 1918

Ryder, *Sergt.* Robert (Middx. R.), *Gt. War* 1916

Ryder, *Capt.* R. E. D. (R.N.), *World War* 1942

Simpson, *W.O.* R. S., D.C.M. (Australian Army), *Vietnam* 1969

Smith, *Sergt.* E. A. (Seaforth Highrs. of Canada), *World War* 1944

Smyth, *Brig.* Rt. Hon. Sir J. G., Bt., M.C., (Ludhiana Sikhs), *Gt. War* 1915

Smythe, *Lt.* Q. G. M. (S.A.M.F.), *Wld. War* 1942

Speakman, *Sergt.* W. (Black Watch), *Korea* .. 1951

Stannard, *Capt.* R. B., D.S.O., R.D. (R.N.R.), *World War* 1940

Starcevich, *Pte.* L. T. (Australia), *World War.* 1945

Steele, *Com.* G. C. (R.N.), *Gt. War* 1919

Steele, *Sergt.* T. (Seaforth H.), *Gt. War* 1917

Strachan, *Maj.* H., M.C. (Can. Cav.), *Gt. War* 1917

Tandey, *L/Corpl.* H., D.C.M., M.M. (W. Riding R.), *Gt. War* 1918

Tilston, *Col.* F. A. (Essex Scottish, Canada), *World War* 1945

Towers, *Pte.* James (Cameronians), *Gt. War.* 1918

Towner, *Maj.* Edgar Thomas, M.C. (Aust. M.G.C.), *Gt. War* 1918

Trent, *Group Capt.* L. H., D.F.C. (R.N.Z.A.F.), *World War* 1943

Triquet, *Brig.* P. (R. 22R. of Canada), *World War* 1943

Tulbahadur Pun, *W.O. I* (Gurkha Rifles), *World War* 1944

Umrao Singh, *Havildar* (I.A.), *World War* ... 1944

Upham, *Capt.* C. H. (and Bar, 1942), (N.Z.M.F.), *World War* 1941

Veale, *Corpl.* T. W. H. (Devon R.), *Gt. War* 1916

Vickers, *Capt.* Sir C. Geoffrey (Sherwood For.), *Gt. War* 1915

Waters, *Maj.* Sir Arnold, C.B.E., D.S.O., M.C. (R.E.), *Gt. War* 1918

Watkins, *Maj. Hon.* Sir Tasker (Welch R.), *World War* 1944

Welch, *Sgt.* J. (R. Berks. R.), *Gt. War* 1917

West, *Air Commodore* Ferdinand M. F., C.B.E., M.C. (R.A.F.), *Gt. War* 1918

Wilson, *Lt.-Col.* E. C. T. (E. Surrey R.), *World War* 1940

Wood, *Pte.* W. (R. Northd. Fus.), *Gt. War.* 1918

Wright, *C.S.M.* P. H. (Coldstream Gds.), *World War* 1943

Zengel, *Sergt.* Raphael L., M.M. (Saskatchewan R.), *Gt. War* 1918

THE GEORGE CROSS, G.C.—For Gallantry

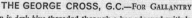

The ribbon is *dark blue* threaded through a bar adorned with laurel leaves.

INSTITUTED *September 24th,* 1940 (with amendments, *November 3rd,* 1942).

The George Cross is worn before all other decorations (except the VC on the left breast § and consists of a plain silver cross with four equal limbs, the cross having in the centre a circular medallion bearing a design showing St. George and the Dragon. The inscription "For Gallantry" appears round the medallion and in the angle of each limb of the cross is the Royal cypher "G VI" forming a circle concentric with the medallion. The reverse is plain and bears the name of the recipient and the date of the award. The cross is suspended by a ring from a bar adorned with laurel leaves on dark blue ribbon 1½ inches wide.

The cross is intended primarily for civilians and awards to the fighting services are confined to actions for which purely military honours are not normally granted. It is awarded only for acts of the greatest heroism or of the most conspicuous courage in circumstances of extreme danger. From April 1, 1965, holders of the Cross have received a tax-free annuity of £100.

§ When worn by a woman it may be worn on the left shoulder from a ribbon of the same width and colour fashioned into a bow.

Empire Gallantry Medal.—The Royal Warrant which ordained that the grant of the Empire Gallantry Medal should cease authorized holders of that medal to return it to the Central Chancery of the Orders of Knighthood and to receive in exchange the George Cross. A similar provision applied to posthumous awards of the Empire Gallantry Medal made after the outbreak of war in 1939.

In October 1971 all surviving holders of the Albert Medal and the Edward Medal exchanged those decorations for the George Cross.

THE DISTINGUISHED SERVICE ORDER (1886)—D.S.O.

Ribbon, Red, with Blue Edges.

Bestowed in recognition of especial services in action of commissioned officers in the Navy, Army and Royal Air Force and (1942) Mercantile Marine. The members are Companions only and rank immediately before the 4th Class of the Royal Victorian Order. A Bar may be awarded for any additional act of service.

PRINCIPAL DECORATIONS AND MEDALS (in order of Precedence)

Victoria Cross.—1856.—VC

George Cross.—1940.—G.C.

British Orders of Knighthood.

Royal Red Cross.—1883—R.R.C. (Class I.).—For ladies.

Distinguished Service Cross.—1914.—D.S.C.—In substitution for the Conspicuous Service Cross, 1901; is for officers of R.N. below the rank of Captain, and Warrant Officers.

Military Cross.—Dec. 1914.—M.C.—Awarded to Captains, Lieutenants, and Warrant Officers (Cl I. and II.) in the Army and Indian and Colonial Forces.

Distinguished Flying Cross.—1918.—D.F.C.—For bestowal upon Officers and Warrant Officers in the Royal Air Force

(and Fleet Air Arm from April 9, 1941) for acts of gallantry when flying in active operations against the enemy.

Air Force Cross.—1918.—A.F.C.— Instituted as preceding but for acts of courage or devotion to duty when flying, although not in active operations against the enemy (extended to Fleet Air Arm since April 9, 1941).

Royal Red Cross (Class II—A.R.R.C.).

Order of British India.

Kaisar-i-Hind Medal.

Order of St. John.

Albert Medal.—1866—A.M.—" For Gallantry in Saving

Life at Sea " or " on Land." (Holders receive £100 tax-free annuity).

Union of South Africa Queen's Medal for Bravery, in Gold.

Medal for Distinguished Conduct in the Field.—1854.—D.C.M.—Awarded to warrant officers, non-commissioned officers and men of the Army and R.A.F.

Conspicuous Gallantry Medal.—1874.—C.G.M.—Is bestowed upon warrant officers and men of the R.N. and since 1942 of Mercantile Marine and R.A.F.

The George Medal.—G.M.—Established by King George VI in 1940 is a recognition of acts of gallantry.

The Edward Medal.—1907.—In recognition of heroic acts by miners or quarrymen, or of others who have endangered their lives in rescuing those so employed. (Holders receive £100 tax-free annuity).

Royal West African Frontier Force Distinguished Conduct Medal.

King's African Rifles Distinguished Conduct Medal.

Union of South Africa Queen's Medal for Bravery in Silver.

Distinguished Service Medal.—1914.—D.S.M.—For chief petty officers, petty officers, men, and boys of all branches of the Royal Navy, and since 1942 of Mercantile Marine, to non-commissioned officers and men of the Royal Marines, and to all other persons holding corresponding positions in Her Majesty's Service afloat.

Military Medal.—1916.—M.M.—For warrant and non-commissioned officers and men and serving women.

Distinguished Flying Medal.—1918.—D.F.M.—and the Air Force Medal.—A.F.M.—For warrant and non-commissioned officers and men for equivalent services as for D.F.C. and A.F.C. (extended to Fleet Air Arm, April 9, 1941).

Constabulary Medal (Ireland).

Medal for Saving Life at Sea.

Colonial Police Medal for Gallantry.

Queen's Gallantry Medal—1974.

British Empire Medal.—B.E.M.—(formerly the Medal of the Order of the British Empire, for Meritorious Service; also includes the Medal of the Order awarded before Dec. 29, 1922).

Queen's Police (Q.P.M.) and Fire Services Medals for Distinguished Service, (Q.F.S.M.).

Queen's Medal for Chiefs.

War Medals and Stars (in order of date).

Polar Medals (in order of date).

Royal Victorian Medal (Gold, Silver and Bronze).

Imperial Service Medal.

Police Medals for Valuable Service.

Badge of Honour.

Jubilee, Coronation and Durbar Medals.

King George V, King George VI and Queen Elizabeth II Long and Faithful Service Medals.

Long Service and Good Conduct Medal.

Naval Long Service and Good Conduct Medal.

Medal for Meritorious Service.

Royal Marine Meritorious Service Medal.

Royal Air Force Meritorious Service Medal.

Royal Air Force Long Service and Good Conduct Medal.

Royal West African Frontier Force Long Service and Good Conduct Medal.

King's African Rifles Long Service and Good Conduct Medal.

Police and Fire Brigade Long Service and Good Conduct Medal.

Colonial Police and Fire Brigades Long Service Medal.

Colonial Prison Service Medal.

Army Emergency Reserve Decoration.—E.R.D.

Volunteer Officer's Decoration.—V.D.

Volunteer Long Service Medal.

Volunteer Officers' Decoration (for India and the Colonies).

Volunteer Long Service Medal (for India and the Colonies).

Colonial Auxiliary Forces Long Service Medal.

Medal for Good Shooting (Naval).

Militia Long Service Medal.

Imperial Yeomanry Long Service Medal.

Territorial Decoration.—1908.—T.D.

Efficiency Decoration.—E.D.

Territorial Efficiency Medal.

Efficiency Medal.

Special Reserve Long Service and Good Conduct Medal.

Decoration for Officers, Royal Navy Reserve.—1910.—R.D.

Decoration for Officers, R.N.V.R.—V.R.D.

Royal Naval Reserve Long Service and Good Conduct Medal.

R.N.V.R. Long Service and Good Conduct Medal.

Royal Naval Auxiliary Sick Berth Reserve Long Service and Good Conduct Medal.

Royal Fleet Reserve Long Service and Good Conduct Medal.

Royal Naval Wireless Auxiliary Reserve Long Service and Good Conduct Medal.

Air Efficiency Award.—1942.

The Queen's Medal.—(For Champion Shots in the Army T.A.V.R. and R.A.F.).

Cadet Forces Medal.—1950.

Coast Life Saving Corps Long Service Medal.—1911.

Special Constabulary Long Service Medal.

Royal Observer Corps Medal.

Civil Defence Long Service Medal.

Service Medal of the Order of St. John.

Badge of the Order of the League of Mercy.

Voluntary Medical Service Medal.—1932.

Women's Royal Voluntary Service Medal.

Colonial Special Constabulary Medal.

Foreign Orders, Decorations and Medals (in order of date).

THE ORDER OF ST. JOHN

The Most Venerable Order of the Hospital of St. John of Jerusalem

St. John's Gate, Clerkenwell, E.C.1

Grand Prior, H.R.H. The Duke of Gloucester, G.C.V.O.

The Order derives from the ancient Order of Knights Hospitaller founded in Jerusalem after the successful completion of the First Crusade in 1099. Vowed to the relief of sickness and distress without distinction of race, class or creed, the Knights maintained a Hospice for the care of the sick and were an important military body within the Kingdom of Jerusalem. After the loss of the Holy Land the Order became a Sovereign Body in Rhodes and later in Malta. In Britain its properties were sequestrated at the Dissolution of the Monasteries but a branch of the Order was revived in England after the Napoleonic Wars, and this was granted a Royal Charter by Queen Victoria in 1888 as a separate, British, Order of St. John. The Queen is the Sovereign Head and since 1888 the Grand Prior has been a member of the Royal Family. The Badge is a white eight-pointed cross, embellished in the four principal angles with a lion and a unicorn; the riband is of black watered silk. The work of the Order consists principally in the maintenance of two Foundations—The Ophthalmic Hospital in East Jerusalem (founded 1882) and The St. John Ambulance Association and Brigade, which is concerned with education in First Aid and kindred subjects and provides a body of trained and uniformed volunteers for attendance on the public where the rendering of First Aid may be required. This operates throughout the Commonwealth.

Lord Prior. The Lord Caccia, G.C.M.G., G.C.V.O. *Chancellor,* Sir Gilbert Inglefield, G.B.E., T.D.

The British Constitution

THE EXECUTIVE

The Crown (the Queen in Council) "makes peace and war, issues charters, increases the peerage, is the fountain of honour, of office, and of justice." The Sovereign entrusts the executive power to Ministers of the Crown, appointed on the advice of the accredited leader of the party in Parliament which enjoys, or can secure, a majority of votes in the House of Commons.

The Cabinet

The Cabinet has no corporate existence, but under the *Ministers of the Crown Act* (1937), provision was made for 17 Ministers of the first rank (Cabinet Ministers) and this number has been increased by later legislation. The *Ministers of the Crown (Parliamentary Secretaries) Act* (1960) laid down an aggregate limit of 33 Parliamentary Secretaries. Parts of these Acts were repealed by the *Ministers of the Crown Act* (1964) which varied the number of Parliamentary Secretaries (other than Treasury Secretaries) to 36.

The Prime Minister

The Prime Minister is appointed by the Sovereign. When a party is in opposition and its leadership becomes vacant it makes its free choice among the various personalities available; but if the party is in office, the Sovereign's choice may anticipate, and in a certain sense forestall, the decision of the party. In 1905 the office of Prime Minister, which had been in existence for nearly 200 years, was officially recognized and its holder was granted a place in the Table of Precedence.

The Leader of the Opposition

In 1937 the office of Leader of the Opposition was similarly recognized and a salary of £2,000 per annum was assigned to the post, thus following a practice which had prevailed in the Dominion of Canada since 1906. In 1957 the salary was increased to £3,000, in 1965 to £4,500, and in 1972 to £9,500. The present Leader of the Opposition is the Right Hon. Margaret Thatcher.

LEGISLATION

Legislation is initiated in the Houses of Parliament in the form of Bills. Public Bills are of two kinds, those introduced by the Government of the day, and those introduced by a private member. A Bill (except a Money Bill, which must originate in the House of Commons) can be introduced in either House and when presented receives its *First Reading*, after which it is printed and cirulated to members. The next stage is the *Second Reading*, in the debate on which the broad issues raised are discussed. If passed it reaches the *Committee Stage* and is referred to a Committee (of the whole House, Select, or Standing—*see* "Committees," p. 311). Bills of major importance are usually sent to a Committee of the whole House. In committee, a Bill is discussed clause by clause, and is returned to the House with or without amendment. A Private Bill, which is introduced to enable an individual or a body corporate to acquire or vary certain powers, is referred to a *Select Committee*, and if opposed, witnessess may be called and counsel heard by the Committee. The next step is the, *Report Stage*, when the Bill is accepted by the House, or sent back to the same, or sent back to another, Committee for further consideration. Finally the Bill receives its *Third Reading* (during which, in the House of Commons, only verbal amendments are permissible) and is sent to the other House. When a Bill has been passed by both Houses it becomes an *Act of Parliament*, on receiving the *Royal Assent*, which is signified by the Sovereign on the Throne, or by Commissioners (normally three Peers), in the Chamber of the House of Lords. The power to withhold assent (colloquially known as the *Royal Veto*) resides in the Sovereign, but has not been exercised in the United Kingdom since, 1707, in the reign of Queen Anne.

COUNCILLORS OF STATE

On every occasion that the Sovereign leaves the realm for distant parts of the Commonwealth or a foreign country, it is necessary to appoint Councillors of State under Letters Patent to carry out the chief functions of the Monarch, including the holding of Privy Councils and the signature of Acts passed by Parliament. The normal procedure is to appoint as Councillors three or four members of the Royal Family among those remaining in the United Kingdom. For instance, during the Queen's visit to Canada in 1967, the Councillors of State were the Prince of Wales, Queen Elizabeth the Queen Mother, Princess Margaret and the Duke of Gloucester.

In the event of the Sovereign on accession being under the age of eighteen years or at any time unavailable or incapacitated by infirmity of mind or body for the performance of the royal functions, provision is made for a Regency. Since the Prince of Wales attained the age of 18 in November 1966, the provisions of the Regency Act as to age no longer apply in the event of his accession to the throne.

SPEAKERS OF THE COMMONS SINCE 1660

PARLIAMENT OF ENGLAND

1660 Sir H. Grimston.	1685 Sir John Trevor.
1661 Sir E. Turner.	1688 H. Powle.
1673 Sir J. Charlton.	1694 Paul Foley.
1673 Edwd. Seymour.	1698 Sir T. Lyttelton.
1678 Sir Robt. Sawyer.	1700 Robert Harley
1679 Serjeant William Gregory.	(Earl of Oxford and Mortimer).
1680 W. Williams.	1702 John Smith.

PARLIAMENT OF GREAT BRITAIN

1708 Sir Richard Onslow (Lord Onslow).	1761 Sir John Cust.
	1770 Sir F. Norton.
1710 Wm. Bromley.	1780 C.W.Cornwall.
1713 Sir Th. Hanmer.	1788 Hon. W. Grenville
1715 Spencer Compton (Earl of Wilmington).	(Lord Grenville).
	1789 Henry Addington
	(Viscount Sidmouth).
1727 Arthur Onslow.	

PARLIAMENT OF UNITED KINGDOM

1801 Sir John Mitford (*Lord Redesdale*).
1802 Charles Abbot (*Lord Colchester*).
1817 Charles M. Sutton (*Viscount Canterbury*).
1835 James Abercromby (*Lord Dunfermline*).
1839 Charles Shaw-Lefevre (*Viscount Eversley*).
1857 J. Evelyn Denison (*Viscount Ossington*).
1872 Sir Henry Brand (*Viscount Hampden*).
1884 Arthur Wellesley Peel (*Viscount Peel*).
1895 William Court Gully (*Viscount Selby*).
1905 James W. Lowther (*Viscount Ullswater*).
1921 John Henry Whitley.
1928 Hon. Edward Algernon FitzRoy.
1943 Col. D. Clifton Brown (*Viscount Ruffside*).
1951 William Shepherd Morrison (*Viscount Dunrossil*).
1959 Sir Harry Hylton-Foster.
1965 Horace Maybray King, ph.D. (*Lord Maybray-King*).
1971 (John) Selwyn (Brooke) Lloyd.

THE HOUSES OF PARLIAMENT

Parliament emerged during the late thirteenth and early fourteenth centuries as a result of diverse forces including the general need for a superior court to deal with legal and administrative problems on a national basis, the financial needs of the Crown, ambition of the baronage to influence the King's government, and the King's desire to make his government more effective by involving in it all important sections of the community. The nucleus of early Parliaments were the officers of the King's household and the King's judges, who were joined by such ecclesiastical and lay magnates as the King might summon and occasionally by the knights of the shire, burgesses and proctors of the lower clergy. The Commons were summoned to all the Parliaments of Edward III and by the end of the reign a " House of Commons " was beginning to appear. The first known Speaker was elected in 1377. The House of Lords is the ultimate Court of Appeal for all Courts in Great Britain and Northern Ireland, except for criminal cases in Scotland. The Lords surrendered the ancient right of peers to be tried for treason or felony by their peers in 1948. Each House has the right to control its own internal proceedings and to commit for contempt.

The Commons claim exclusive control in respect of national taxation and expenditure and in respect of local rates and charges upon them. Bills such as the Finance Bill, which imposes taxation, and the Consolidated Fund Bills, which authorize expenditure, and are commonly known as Supply Bills, must begin in the Commons and have not been amended by the Lords in any respect in modern times. A bill of which the financial provisions are subsidiary may begin in the Lords; and the Commons may waive their rights in regard to Lords amendments affecting finance.

Normally a bill must be agreed to by both Houses before it receives the Royal Assent, but under the Parliament Acts, 1911 and 1949—(a) a bill which the Speaker has certified as a Money Bill, *i.e.* as concerned solely with national taxation, expenditure or borrowing, if not agreed to by the Lords within one month of its being sent to them, receives the Royal Assent and becomes law without their concurrence; (b) any other public bill (except one to extend the life of a Parliament) which has been passed by the Commons in two successive sessions and twice rejected by the Lords, receives the Royal Assent and becomes law, provided that one year has elapsed between its Second Reading in the first session and its Third Reading in the second session in the Commons.

The Parliament Act of 1911 also limited the duration of Parliament, if not previously dissolved, to 5 years. The term is reckoned from the date given on the writs for the new Parliament. During the War of 1914–18 the duration of Parliament was extended by successive Acts from 5 to 8 years, but a General Election was held before the end of the term finally prescribed and the Parliament which first met on Jan. 31, 1911, was dissolved on Nov. 25, 1918, fourteen days after the Armistice. At the outbreak of war in 1939 a similar course was followed and Parliament which first met on Nov. 26, 1935, was not dissolved until June 15, 1945.

Since 1803 reports of the proceedings of Parliament in open session have been published. From 1803–1888 these were known as *Hansard's Parliamentary Debates*, and in 1943 the word " Hansard " was restored to the title page. Copies are obtainable from H.M. Stationery Office and periodical issues are on sale throughout the country.

Payment of Members —Members of the House of Lords are unpaid. They are entitled to reimbursement of travelling expenses from their residence to the House in respect of regular attendance and repayment of expenses within a maximum of £8·50 for each day of such attendance.

Since 1911 Members of the House of Commons have received payments and travelling facilities. Their salary of £400 was increased to £600 in 1937, to £1,000 in 1947, to £1,750 in 1957, to £3,250 in 1964 and to £4,500 in January 1972; they are entitled to claim income tax relief on expenses incurred in the course of their Parliamentary duties. In October 1969 Members were allowed to claim up to £500 a year for secretarial expenses; the allowance was increased to £1,000 a year from January 1972, and to £1,750 a year from August 1, 1974. Also since January 1972, Members can claim reimbursement, within a limit of £750 a year (increased to £1,050 a year from August 1, 1974), for the additional cost of staying overnight away from their main residence while on Parliamentary business.★ The Members' Pension Act, 1965, introduced the first comprehensive pension scheme providing Members of Parliament and their dependants with a legal right to a pension. Under the Parliamentary and Other Pensions Act 1972 the pension scheme was modified to include provision for Ministers and other office holders. The pension scheme is funded by an Exchequer contribution of approximately three times the contribution of a participant which is 5 per cent. of salary per annum (currently 5 per cent. of £4,500 or £225 p.a.). Members receive pensions from age 65, or on ceasing to be a Member if later, provided they have served for 4 years or more. Pensions are based on one sixtieth of salary for each year of reckonable service. Members also continue to contribute £24 per annum and the Treasury up to £22,000 a year towards a Fund to provide annual or lump sum grants to ex-Members, their widows and children whose incomes are below certain limits. The income of the Fund in 1973–74 was £45,028 and expenditure on grants £34,577. The capital account stood in 1974 at £223,563.

★ For increases announced in the summer of 1975, *see* Parliamentary Summary.

THE HOUSE OF LORDS

The House of Lords consists of Lords Spiritual and Temporal. The Lords Spiritual are the two Archbishops, the Bishops of London, Durham and Winchester, and the 21 senior Bishops from the remaining English sees. The Lords Temporal are: Peers and Peeresses in their own right by descent of England, Scotland, Great Britain or the United Kingdom, hereditary peers of new creation, Lords of Appeal in Ordinary and retired Lords of Appeal in Ordinary (who are life peers), and Life Peers and Life Peeresses created under the Life Peerages Act, 1958. Under the Peerage Act, 1963, a person inheriting a peerage may within one year (or one month in the case of a Member of the House of Commons) disclaim the peerage for life. The subsequent descent of the peerage after his death is not affected.

THE HOUSE OF COMMONS

By the *Representation of the People Act* (1885) membership was increased from 658 (at which it had stood since 1801 through the *Act of Union with Ireland*) to 670, and by a similar Act (1918) it was increased to 707. By the *Government of Ireland Act* (1920) and the *Irish Free State Agreement Act* (1922) membership was decreased to 615. Irish representation being reduced from 105 to 13 members. By the *Representation of the People Act* of 1945 25 new constituencies were created, making the total 640; and by a similar Act of 1948 the total membership was reduced to 625. As the result of Orders in Council made in 1955 under the *House of Commons (Redistribution of Seats) Act*, 1949, the total membership was increased to 630 and under the same Act provision was made in 1970 for further increase to 635.

THE PALACE OF WESTMINSTER

An ordinance issued in the reign of Richard II stated that " Parliament shall be holden or kepid wheresoever it pleaseth the King " and at the present day the Sovereign summons parliament to meet and prescribes the time and place of meeting. The royal palace at Westminster, originally built by Edward the Confessor (Westminster Hall being added by William Rufus) was the normal place of Parliament from about 1340. St. Stephen's Chapel (first mentioned in the reign of John) was used from about 1550 for the meetings of the House of Commons, which had previously been held in the Chapter House or Refectory of Westminster Abbey. The House of Lords met in an apartment of the royal palace.

The disastrous fire of 1834 destroyed the whole palace, except Westminster Hall, and the present Houses of Parliament were erected on the site from the designs of Sir Charles Barry and Augustus Pugin, between the years 1840 and 1867, at a cost of £2,198,000.

The Chamber of the House of Commons was destroyed by enemy action in 1941 and the foundation stone of a new building, from the designs of Sir Giles Gilbert Scott, was laid by the Speaker on May 26, 1948. The new Chamber was used for the first time on Oct. 26, 1950.

The Victoria Tower of the House of Lords is 330 feet high and when Parliament is sitting the Union Jack flies from sunrise to sunset from its flagstaff. The clock tower of the House of Commons is 316 feet high and contains " Big Ben," the 13½-ton hour bell named after Sir Benjamin Hall, First Commissioner of Works when the original bell was cast in 1856. The dials of the clock are 23 feet in diameter, the hands being 9 feet and 14 feet long (including balance piece). The chimes and strike of " Big Ben " have achieved world-wide fame from broadcasting.

A light is displayed in the clock tower from sundown to sunrise during the hours the House is in session.

THE LORD CHANCELLOR

The Lord High Chancellor of Great Britain is (although not addressed as such) the Speaker of the House of Lords. Unlike the Speaker of the House of Commons, he takes part in debates and votes in divisions. He sits on one of the *Woolsacks*, couches covered with red cloth and stuffed with wool. If the Lord Chancellor wishes to address the House in any way except formally as Speaker, he leaves the Woolsack and steps towards its proper place as a peer, below the Royal Dukes.

PRIME MINISTER'S RESIDENCE

Number 10, Downing Street, S.W.1, is the official town residence of the Prime Minister, No. 11 of the Chancellor of the Exchequer and No. 12 is the office of the Government Whips. The street was named after Sir George Downing, Bt., soldier and diplomatist, who was M.P. for Morpeth from 1660 to 1684.

Chequers, a Tudor mansion in the Chilterns, about 3 miles from Princes Risborough, was presented together with a maintenance endowment by Lord and Lady Lee of Fareham in 1917 to serve, from Jan. 1, 1921, as a country residence for the Prime Minister of the day, the Chequers estate of 700 acres being added to the gift by Lord Lee in 1921. The mansion contains a famous collection of Cromwellian portraits and relics.

PRIME MINISTERS

Sir Robert Walpole, *Whig*, April 3, 1721.
Earl of Wilmington, *Whig*, Feb. 16, 1742.
Henry Pelham, *Whig*, Aug. 25, 1743.
Duke of Newcastle, *Whig*, May 18, 1754.
Duke of Devonshire, *Whig*, Nov. 16, 1756.
Duke of Newcastle, *Whig*, July 2, 1757.
Earl of Bute, *Tory*, May 28, 1762.
George Grenville, *Whig*, April 15, 1763.
Marquess of Rockingham, *Whig*, July 10, 1765.
Earl of Chatham, *Whig*, Aug. 2, 1766.
Duke of Grafton, *Whig*, Dec. 1767.
Lord North, *Tory*, Feb. 6, 1770.
Marquess of Rockingham, *Whig*, March 27, 1782.
Earl of Shelburne, *Whig*, July 13, 1782.
Duke of Portland, *Coalition*, April 4, 1783.
William Pitt, *Tory*, Dec. 7, 1783.
Henry Addington, *Tory*, March 21, 1801.
William Pitt, *Tory*, May 16, 1804.
Lord Grenville, *Whig*, Feb. 10, 1806.
Duke of Portland, *Tory*, March 31, 1807.
Spencer Perceval, *Tory*, Dec. 6, 1809.
Earl of Liverpool, *Tory*, June 16, 1812.
George Canning, *Tory*, April 30, 1827.
Viscount Goderich, *Tory*, Sept. 8, 1827.
Duke of Wellington, *Tory*, Jan. 26, 1828.
Earl Grey, *Whig*, Nov. 24, 1830.
Viscount Melbourne, *Whig*, July 13, 1834.
Sir Robert Peel, *Tory*, Dec. 26, 1834.
Viscount Melbourne, *Whig*, March 18, 1835.
Sir Robert Peel, *Tory*, Sept. 6, 1841.
Lord John Russell, *Whig*, July 6, 1846.
Earl of Derby, *Tory*, Feb. 28, 1852.
Earl of Aberdeen, *Peelite*, Dec. 28, 1852.
Viscount Palmerston, *Liberal*, Feb. 10, 1855.
Earl of Derby, *Conservative*, Feb. 25, 1858.
Viscount Palmerston, *Liberal*, June 18, 1859.
Earl Russell, *Liberal*, Nov. 6, 1865.
Earl of Derby, *Conservative*, July 6, 1866.
Benjamin Disraeli, *Conservative*, Feb. 27, 1868.
W. E. Gladstone, *Liberal*, Dec. 9, 1868.
Benjamin Disraeli, *Conservative*, Feb. 21, 1874.
W. E. Gladstone, *Liberal*, April 28, 1880.
Marquess of Salisbury, *Conservative*, June 24, 1885.
W. E. Gladstone, *Liberal*, Feb. 6, 1886.
Marquess of Salisbury, *Conservative*, Aug. 3, 1886.
W. E. Gladstone, *Liberal*, Aug. 18, 1892.
Earl of Rosebery, *Liberal*, March 3, 1894.
Marquess of Salisbury, *Conservative*, July 2, 1895.
A. J. Balfour, *Conservative*, July 12, 1902.
Sir H. Campbell-Bannerman, *Liberal*, Dec. 5, 1905.
H. H. Asquith, *Liberal*, April 8, 1908.
H. H. Asquith, *Coalition*, May 26, 1915.
D. Lloyd-George, *Coalition*, Dec. 7, 1916.
A. Bonar Law, *Conservative*, Oct. 23, 1922.
S. Baldwin, *Conservative*, May 22, 1923.
J. R. MacDonald, *Labour*, Jan. 22, 1924.
S. Baldwin, *Conservative*, Nov. 4, 1924.
J. R. MacDonald, *Labour*, June 8, 1929.
J. R. MacDonald, *Coalition*, Aug. 25, 1931.
S. Baldwin, *Coalition*, June 7, 1935.
N. Chamberlain, *Coalition*, May 28, 1937.
W. S. Churchill, *Coalition*, May 11, 1940.
W. S. Churchill, *Conservative*, May 23, 1945.
C. R. Attlee, *Labour*, July 26, 1945.
Sir W. S. Churchill, *Conservative*, Oct. 26, 1951.
Sir A. Eden, *Conservative*, April 6, 1955.
H. Macmillan, *Conservative*, Jan. 13, 1957.
Sir A. Douglas-Home, *Conservative*, Oct. 19, 1963.
J. H. Wilson, *Labour*, Oct. 16, 1964.
E. R. G. Heath, *Conservative*, June 19, 1970.
J. H. Wilson, *Labour*, March 4, 1974.

OFFICERS OF THE HOUSE OF LORDS

Speaker, The Rt. Hon. Frederick Elwyn-Jones, Lord Elwyn-Jones,(+ £17,500 as *Lord Chancellor*) £2,500
    Private Secretary to the Lord Chancellor, J. A. C. Watherston.
Lord Chairman of Committees, The Earl of Listowel, P.C., G.C.M.G.............................. £6,750
Deputy Principal Chairman of Committees, The Baroness Tweedsmuir of Belhelvie, P.C............ £5,500

Clerk of the Parliaments, Sir Peter Henderson, K.C.B.......................... £21,000
Clerk Assistant, J. E. Grey............... £15,000
Reading Clerk and Clerk of the Journals, J. C. Sainty......................... £12,410
Counsel to Lord Chairman of Committees, I. G. Talbot, C.B., Q.C................ £12,410
Second Counsel to Chairmen of Committees, Sir Charles Sopwith.................. £12,410
Principal Clerks, R. P. Cave, C.B., M.V.O. (*Judicial Office and Fourth Clerk at the Table*); E. D. Graham (*Private Bills and Committees*); M. F. Bond, O.B.E., F.S.A. (*Information Services and Clerk of the Records*)............................ £12,410
Chief Clerks, J. V. D. Webb; M. A. J. Wheeler-Booth; J. A. Vallance-White; J. M. Davies............... £9,060 to £11,410
Senior Clerks, P. D. G. Hayter (*seconded as Secretary to the Leader of the House and the Chief Whip*); C. A. J. Mitchell
    £6,090 to £7,860
Deputy Clerk of the Records, H. S. Cobb, F.S.A........................ £7,561 to £9,160

Assistant Clerk of the Records, D. J. Johnson
    £4,814 to £7,519
Accountant, E. W. Field........ £6,090 to £7,860
Assistant Accountant, R. A. Devin £5,310 to £6,310
Librarian, C. S. A. Dobson, F.S.A. £9,060 to £11,410
Asst. Librarian, R. H. V. C. Morgan
    £7,561 to £9,160
Examiners of Petitions for Private Bills, E. D. Graham; D. Scott.
Judicial Taxing Clerk, C. G. Osborne
    £5,310 to £6,310
Gentleman-Usher of the Black Rod and Serjeant-at-Arms, Admiral Sir Frank Twiss, K.C.B., D.S.C........................ £12,410
Yeoman Usher of the Black Rod and Deputy Serjeant-at-Arms, Grp.-Capt. R. M. B. Duke-Woolley, D.S.O., D.F.C.. £5,680 to £7,003
Staff Superintendent, Major D. M. Whyte, M.B.E.
Shorthand Writer, A. P. W. Brewin   *fees*
Editor, Official Report (Hansard), C. W. H. Blogg.............................. £8,910
Asst. do. C. R. Stanton................. £6,910

OFFICERS OF THE HOUSE OF COMMONS

Speaker, The Rt. Hon. (John) Selwyn (Brooke) Lloyd, C.H., C.B.E., T.D., Q.C., M.P. for Wirral... £13,000
Chairman of Ways and Means, The Rt. Hon. George Thomas, M.P. for Cardiff, West........... £6,750
First Deputy Chairman of Ways and Means, (Henry) Oscar Murton, O.B.E., T.D., M.P. for Poole.... £5,500
Second Deputy Chairman of Ways and Means, Sir Myer Galpern, M.P. for Glasgow, Shettleston.... £5,500

DEPT. OF THE CLERK OF THE HOUSE

Clerk of the House of Commons, Sir David Lidderdale, K.C.B.................... £18,675
Clerk Asst., R. D. Barlas, C.B., O.B.E..... £14,000
Second do., C. A. S. S. Gordon, C.B....... £12,410
Clerk of Committees, T. G. Odling, C.B... £14,000
Principal Clerks—
  Public Bills, A. A. Birley............. £12,410
  Journals, E. S. Taylor, Ph.D........... £12,410
  Services, M. H. Lawrence, C.M.G...... £12,410
  Expenditure Committee, F. G. Allen..... £12,410
  Overseas Office, K. A. Bradshaw (*acting*) £12,410
  Private Bills, D. Scott................ £11,660
  Standing Committees, R. S. Lankester... £11,660
  Select Committees, D. A. M. Pring, M.C. £11,410
Special Adviser (*Expenditure Committee*), C. Y. Carstairs, C.B., C.M.G. (*acting*).... £12,410
Deputy Principal Clerks, J. H. Willcox; C. A. James; H. M. Barclay; M. T. Ryle; C. J. Boulton; J. F. Sweetman, T.D.; D. W. Limon; J. R. Rose (*acting*); C. B. Winnifrith (*acting*); A. J. Hastings (*acting*); W. R. McKay (*acting*); D. J. Chapman (*acting*) .... £9,060 to £11,410
Senior Clerks, R. J. Willoughby; S. A. L. Panton; R. B. Sands; G. Cubie; M. R. Jack, Ph.D.; D. G. Millar; Mrs. J. Sharpe; Miss A. Milner-Barry; R. W. G. Wilson; W. A. Proctor; F. A. Cranmer; C. R. M. Ward; I. I. Milne, C.M.G., O.B.E. (*acting*); A. S. Martin, C.B.E. (*acting*) C. B. B. Heathcote-Smith, C.B.E. (*acting*); G. C. O. Key, O.B.E., D.F.C. (*acting*); P. A. Carter, C.M.G. (*acting*); P. D. Brittain (*acting*); E. James (*acting*); F. W. Clark (*acting*)......... £6,090 to £7,860
Examiners of Private Bills, E. D. Graham; D. Scott.
Taxing Officer, D. Scott.

DEPT. OF THE SPEAKER

Speaker's Secretary, Brig. N. E. V. Short, M.B.E., M.C.................. £6,090 to £7,860
Speaker's Counsel, Sir Robert Speed, C.B., Q.C.......................... £12,410
Second Speaker's Counsel, Sir Charles Davis, C.B.......................... £12,410
Chaplain to the Speaker, The Rev. Canon D. L. Edwards.
Editor, Official Report (Hansard), R. P. Dring................... £10,810 to £11,410
Deputy Editor, L. A. Giles.......... £8,660
Shorthand Writer, A. P. W. Brewin..........*fees*
Deliverer of the Vote, P. K. Marsden, O.B.E.
    £7,285 to £9,760
Deputy Deliverer of the Vote, G. R. Russell
    £5,310 to £6,535

DEPT. OF THE SERJEANT AT ARMS

Serjeant at Arms, Rear-Admiral Sir Alexander Gordon Lennox, K.C.V.O., C.B., D.S.O.......................... £12,410
Deputy do., Lt.-Col. P. F. Thorne, C.B.E.
    £9,060 to £11,410
Assistant do., Cdr. D. Swanston, D.S.O., D.S.C., R.N. (*ret.*)............. £7,860 to £9,060
Deputy Assistant do., Major G. V. S. Le Fanu..................... £6,535 to £7,860

DEPT. OF THE LIBRARY

Librarian, D. C. L. Holland, C.B........ £12,410
Deputy Librarian, D. Menhennet, D.Phil.
    £9,060 to £11,410
Assistant Librarians, D. J. T. Englefield; E. C. Thompson............. £9,060 to £10,208
Deputy Assistant Librarians, H. J. Palmer; G. F. Lock; M. A. Griffith-Jones; J. B. Poole, Ph.D.; Miss J. B. Tanfield; S. Z. Young.................. £7,561 to £9,160
Senior Library Clerks, Mrs. H. R. Coates; Miss P. J. Baines; Miss E. K. Andrews;

P. M. Hart; K. G. Cuninghame; Mrs.
B. L. Miller; Mrs. S. Hastings; Mrs.
J. M. Lourie; Mrs. F. Poole; Miss C. B.
Mann; Mrs. T. M. M. Medawar
£4,814 to £7,519

ADMINISTRATION DEPT.
Clerk Administrator, M. H. Lawrence,
C.M.G.

Accountant, F. J. Wilkin, O.B.E., D.F.M.
£9,060 to £11,410
Deputy Accountant, J. L. G. Dobson
£7,285 to £9,160
Assistant Accountants, A. J. Lewis; G. P.
Brown.................£5,310 to £7,035
Head of Establishments Section, H. McE.
Allen....................£9,060 to £10,810
Deputy Head of Establishments Section, D. J.
Mouat....................£5,310 to £6,310

NOTES ON PARLIAMENTARY PROCEDURE

WRITS FOR A NEW PARLIAMENT, ETC.— Writs for
a new Parliament are issued, on the Sovereign's
warrant, by the Lord Chancellor to Peers individually, but in the case of the Commons to the
returning officers of the various constituencies.
A Writ of Summons to the House of Lords, before
the time when baronies were created by Letters
Patent, is held (should the writ be good and the
Parliament legally summoned) to create a barony
for the recipient and his heirs. The oldest English
peerages, the baronies of De Ros and Mowbray,
are founded on writs of summons issued in 1264
and 1283 respectively. The right to sit in the
House of Lords is determined by the House.
A newly-created Peer may not sit or speak in the
House of Lords until he has been introduced by
two sponsors of his own degree in the Peerage.

VACANT SEATS.—When a vacancy occurs in the
House of Commons the Writ for a New Election
is generally moved, during a session of Parliament,
by the Chief Whip of the party to whom the
member whose seat has been vacated belonged.
If the House is in recess, the Speaker can issue a
writ, should two members certify to him that a
seat is vacant. He cannot, however, issue such a
writ if the seat has been vacated through the former
member's lunacy or his acceptance of the office of
Bailiff of the *Chiltern Hundreds*, or Steward of the
Manor of Northstead, a legal fiction which enables a
member to retire from the House, for it has long
been established that a member cannot, by his own
volition, relieve himself of the responsibilities to
his constituents which his membership involves.
Until 1926, however, it was necessary for a member
to retire from the House on accepting an office of
profit under the Crown, which, it may be noted,
subjected a private member who accepted ministerial office to the trouble and expense of seeking
re-election in his constituency. The Act of 1926,
which removed this necessity, retained the Chiltern
Hundreds and the Manor of Northstead as offices of
profit and thus perpetuated the fiction.

HOURS OF MEETING, ETC.—The House of Lords
normally meets during the Session at 2.30 p.m. on
Tuesday and Wednesday, and at 3 p.m. on Thursday. In the latter part of the Session, the House
usually sits also on Mondays at 2.30 p.m., and
occasionally on Fridays at 11 a.m. The House of
Commons meets on Monday, Tuesday, Wednesday
and Thursday at 2.30. and on Friday at 11. Morning sittings on Monday and Wednesday were held
from February–July, 1967 and occasionally during
1968 and 1969. *Strangers* are present during the debates of both Houses on sufferance, and may be excluded at any time; this applies equally to the *Press
Gallery*. Time has modified what was once
a rigid exclusion and strangers have in recent years
generally been admitted except during the secret
sessions of war time. The proceedings are opened
by Prayers in both Houses. The *Quorum* of the
House of Commons is forty members, including the
Speaker, and should a member point out to the
Speaker at any time fewer than forty members
are present, the division bells are rung, and if
forty members have not appeared within four

minutes, the House is said to be *Counted Out*, and
the sitting is adjourned. The *Quorum* of the Lords
is three.

PROROGATION AND DISSOLUTION.—A session of
Parliament is brought to an end by its Prorogation
to a certain date, while Parliament itself comes to
an end either by Dissolution by the Sovereign or
the expiration of the term of 5 years for which it
was elected (*see* p. 307).

ELECTION PETITIONS.—The right of a member of
the House of Commons to sit in Parliament can be
challenged by petition on several grounds, *e.g.*
ineligibility to sit owing to his bribery or corruption of the electors. Such petitions were
originally decided by the House itself, but as
party feeling was too much inclined to dictate the
decision, their trial was in 1868 referred to the High
Court of Justice.

STANDING ORDERS.—These are rules, which have
from time to time been established by both Houses
of Parliament, to regulate the conduct of business.
These orders are not irrevocable, and like the
Statutory Laws of England they can be easily
revised, amended or repealed. The custom and
precedents of Parliament, which dictate the bulk
of Parliamentary procedure, have acquired, in
seven centuries, prescriptive rights of obedience
as firmly seated as the Common Law. *Sessional
Orders* are applicable only to the session in which
they are passed.

GENERAL PROCEDURE.—There are differences in
the rules which govern the conduct of debates in
the house of Lords and in the House of Commons.
The Speaker in the Commons is responsible for the
preservation of order and discipline in the House,
but the only duty of the Lord Chancellor or the
presiding Peer is to put the question. A Peer
prefaces his remarks with " My Lords," whereas
a member of the House of Commons addresses
himself to Mr. Speaker. A member of the House of
Commons wishing to speak " rises in his place uncovered." When several members rise together the
one whom the Speaker calls to continue the debate is
described as *having caught the Speaker's eye*. In the
House of Lords in similar circumstances, the House
itself decides who shall speak. Broadly speaking, a
member may not, except in Committee, speak more
than once to a question except in explanation or reply, and this privilege is granted only to the mover
of a motion, or to the Minister or Member in charge
of a bill. A member may address the House from
notes but must not read his speech, a distinction
sometimes without a difference. In the Commons
members must not be mentioned by name; the proceedings of the other House and matters *sub judice*
must not be discussed; offensive words or epithets
must not be used; a member may not speak after a
question has been put, except on a point of order,
and then he must address the Speaker " *seated and
covered.*" He must bow to the Speaker on entering
and leaving the House.

QUESTION TIME.—After Prayers the first business
of importance in the House of Commons is
Question Time, which lasts from 2.45 until 3.30.

Two days' notice of questions must be given to the *Clerk of the House of Commons*, the senior official of the House, who presides over it in the brief interval between the first assembly of a new Parliament and the election of a Speaker, and whose counterpart in the House of Lords is the *Clerk of the Parliaments*. Members of the House may put an unlimited number of questions to Ministers, but not more than two demanding an oral answer may be made in any one day to the same Minister. Supplementary questions may be put either by the member asking the original question, or by other members, to obtain clarification of a Minister's answer. In the House of Lords up to four questions for oral answer may be asked on each sitting day.

COMMITTEES.—On the Assembly of a new Parliament, after the election of the Speaker, the House of Commons deals with the subject of Committees, which are of three kinds:—*Committees of the Whole House*, *Select Committees* (appointed for a specific purpose) and the *Standing Committees* which consider public bills and whose composition, though laid down by Standing Orders, is frequently modified by Sessional Orders. When a bill dealing *exclusively* with Scotland or with Wales and Monmouthshire is referred to a Standing Committee, in the first place all Scottish, and in the second, all Welsh members are automatically members thereof.

CLOSURE AND THE GUILLOTINE.—To prevent deliberate waste of Parliamentary time, a procedure known as the *Closure* (colloquially known as "The Gag") was brought into effect on Nov. 10, 1882. A motion may be made *that the question be now put*. If the Speaker decides that the rights of a minority are not being prejudiced and 100 members support the motion, it is put to the vote, and, if carried, the original motion is put to the House, without further debate. The *Guillotine* represents a more rigorous and systematic application of the Closure. Under this system, a bill proceeds in accordance with a rigid time table and discussion is limited to the time allotted to each group of clauses. If the number of amendments put down appears likely to require more time than has been allotted for their discussion, the Speaker selects those which he considers are most important. The guillotine was first put into use on June 17, 1887, after prolonged debates on the Crimes Bill.

THE PREVIOUS QUESTION.—When the House is disinclined to give a decision on a particular question it is possible to avoid the issue by moving the Previous Question, which is done by one of several motions, *e.g.* "That the Question be not now put" or "That the House do now proceed to the Orders of the Day."

MOTION FOR ADJOURNMENT.—Adjournment ends the sitting of either House and takes place either under the provisions of a Standing Order or through an *ad hoc* resolution. In the Commons a method of obtaining immediate discussion of a matter of urgency is by moving the adjournment for the purpose of discussing a specific and important matter that should have urgent consideration. A member may ask leave to make this motion by giving written notice to the Speaker after Question Time and if it obtains the support of 40 members and the Speaker considers the matter of sufficient importance, it is discussed at 7 p.m. on that day. A Committee of the Whole House cannot adjourn but its proceedings may be interrupted by a motion *That the Chairman report Progress*. This brings the Speaker back to the House and the Committee seeks permission to sit on a future date.

PRIVILEGES OF PARLIAMENT.—There are certain rights and jurisdictions peculiar to each House of Parliament, but privileges in their accepted meaning are common to both Houses. The right of imprisoning persons who commit what are in the opinion of the House breaches of privilege is beyond question, and such persons cannot be admitted to bail nor is any Court competent to investigate the causes of commitment. Each House is the sole and absolute judge of its own privileges and where law and privilege have seemed to clash a conflict of jurisdiction has arisen between Parliament and the Courts. Breaches of privilege may be described briefly as disobedience to the orders of either House; assaults or insults to Members or libels on them; and interference with the officers of the House in the carrying out of their duties. The House of Lords may imprison for a period, or may inflict a fine, but the House of Commons only commits generally and the commitment ceases on the prorogation of Parliament. The Bill of Rights established the principle that "freedom of speech and debates and proceedings in Parliament should not be impeached or questioned in any court or place out of parliament." Consequently the House itself is the only authority which can punish a member for intemperance in debate. Freedom from arrest was a much prized privilege, but it applied only to civil arrest for debt (now abolished) and arbitrary arrest by the Government; members are amenable to all other processes of the Law. Freedom from arrest, in the case of members of the House of Commons, applies to the forty days after the prorogation and the forty days before the next meeting of Parliament.

THE SPEAKER.—The *Speaker of the House of Commons* is the spokesman and president of the Chamber. He is elected by the House at the beginning of each Parliament. He was originally a partisan but throughout a century of development between Speaker Onslow (1728) and Speaker Shaw-Lefevre (1839), the theory of the non-partisan Speaker was perfected, and he now neither speaks in debates, nor votes in divisions, except when the voting is equal. His order in the precedence of the Kingdom is high, only the Prime Minister and the Lord President of the Council going before him. He takes precedence of all Peers, except the two Archbishops, and Speakers are almost invariably raised to the Peerage on vacating their office, though Speaker Whitley is believed to have declined the offer of a Viscountcy. The Speaker's most severe disciplinary measure against a member is to *Name* him. When a member has been named, *i.e.* contrary to the practice of the House called by surname and not addressed as the "Hon. Member for . . ." (his constituency), the Leader of the House moves that he "be suspended from the service of the House" for (in the case of a first offence) a period of a week. The period of suspension is increased, should the member offend again. Speaker Denison has left it on record that "The House is always kind and indulgent, but it expects its Speakers to be right. If he should be found tripping, his authority must soon be at an end." The Speaker's Deputy is the *Chairman of Committees*, officially the *Chairman of Ways and Means*, who presides in the absence of the Speaker and when the House has resolved itself into Committee by the passage of the motion *that the Speaker do now leave the Chair*. He, like the Speaker, is elected at the beginning of each Parliament, and when he is presiding as chairman of a committee neither speaks in debate nor votes except when the voting is equal). A *Deputy Chairman of Ways and Means* is also appointed, and several temporary chairmen, who frequently preside either over a Committee of the Whole House or over Standing Committees.

The Lord Chancellor is *Speaker of the House of Lords.* Being a member of the Government, he has none of the powers to maintain order that the Speaker of the House of Commons has. (These powers, in the Lords, are exercised by the House as a whole). A panel of Deputy Speakers is appointed by Royal Commission. The Chairman of Com-mittees is a salaried officer of the House who takes the chair in Committee of the Whole House and in some Select Committees. He is assisted by a panel of Deputy Chairmen, headed by the salaried Prin-cipal Deputy Chairman of Committees, who is also Chairman of the European Communities Com-mittee of the House.

GOVERNMENT BY PARTY

Before the reign of William and Mary the principal Officers of State were chosen by and were responsible to the Sovereign alone and not to Parliament or the nation at large. Such officers acted sometimes in concert with one another, but more often independently, and the fall of one did not, of necessity, involve that of others, although all were liable to be dismissed at any moment.

In 1693 the Earl of Sunderland recommended to William III the advisability of selecting a Ministry from the political party which enjoyed a majority in the House of Commons and the first united Minis-try was drawn in 1696 from the Whigs, to which party the King owed his throne, the principal mem-bers being Russell (the Admiral), Somers (the Ad-vocate), Lord Wharton and Charles Montague (afterwards Chancellor of the Exchequer). This group became known as the *Junto* and was regarded with suspicion as a novelty in the political life of the nation, being a small section meeting in secret apart from the main body of Ministers. It may be re-garded as the forerunner of the *Cabinet* and in course of time it led to the establishment of the principle of joint responsibility of Ministers, so that internal disagreement caused a change of *personnel* or res-ignation of the whole body of Ministers.

The accession of George I, who was unfamiliar with the English language, led to a disinclination on the part of the Sovereign to preside at meetings of his Ministers and caused the appearance of a *Prime Minister,* a position first acquired by Robert Walpole in 1721 and retained without interruption for 20 years and 326 days.

In 1828 the old party of the Whigs became known as *Liberals,* a name originally given to it by its opponents to imply laxity of principles, but gradually accepted by the party to indicate its claim to be pioneers and champions of political reform and progressive legislation. In 1861 a Liberal Registration Association was founded and Liberal Associations became widespread. As the outcome of a conference at Birmingham in 1877 a National Liberal Federation was formed, with headquarters in London. The Liberal Party was in power for long periods during the second half of the nineteenth century in spite of the set-back during the Home Rule crisis of 1886, which resulted in the secession of the Liberal Unionists, and for several years during the first quarter of the twentieth century, but after a further split into National and Independent Liberals it numbered only 59 in all after the General Election of 1929, with a further fall to 12 (excluding National Liberals) after the 1945 Election. The number is now 13.

Soon after the change from Whig to Liberal the Tory Party became known as *Conservative,* a name traditionally believed to have been invented by John Wilson Croker in 1830 and to have been generally adopted about the time of the passing of the Reform Act of 1832 to indicate that the preservation of national institutions was the leading principle of the party. After the Home Rule crisis of 1886 the dissentient Liberals entered into a compact with the Conservatives, under which the latter undertook not to contest their seats, but a separate *Liberal Unionist* organization was main-tained until 1912, when it was united with the Conservatives under the title of National Unionist Association of Conservative and Liberal Unionist Organizations, the members of which became known as *Unionists.*

The Labour Party.—Labour candidates for Par-liament made their first appearance at the General Election of 1892, when there were 27 standing as " Labour " or " Liberal-Labour." At the General Election of 1895 the number of successful candidates fell to 12, with a further fall to 11 at the election of 1900.

In 1900 the *Labour Representative Committee* was set up in order to establish a distinct Labour Group in Parliament, with its own whips, its own policy, and a readiness to co-operate with any party which might be engaged in promoting legislation in the direct interest of labour. In 1906 the L.R.C. became known as *The Labour Party.*

Parliamentary Whips

In order to secure the attendance of Members of a particular party in Parliament on all occasions, and particularly on the occasion of an important division, *Whips* (originally known as " Whippers-in ") are appointed for the purpose. The written appeal or circular letter issued by them is also known as a " whip," its urgency being denoted by the number of times it is underlined. Neglect to res-pond to a three-lined whip, headed " Most Im-portant," is tantamount to secession (at any rate temporarily) from the party. Whips are officially recognized by Parliament and are provided with office accommodation in both Houses. Government Whips receive salaries from public funds, the Par-liamentary (Patronage) Secretary to the Treasury (*Chief Whip in the Commons*) receiving £5,6;25 the Captain of the Gentlemen-at-Arms (*Chief Whip in the Lords*), the Captain of the Yeomen of the Guard (*Assistant do.*) and the first of the Junior Lords of the Treasury (*Deputy Chief Whip in the Commons*), each £3,000; the (Political) Lords in Waiting and the re-maining Junior Lords of the Treasury, each £2,000

The House of Lords

The *Government Whips* are: The Captain of the Honourable Corps of the Gentlemen at Arms (The Baroness Llewelyn-Davies of Hastoe), the Captain of the Queen's Bodyguard of the Yeo-men of the Guard (Lord Strabolgi) and the (Political) Lords in Waiting.

The *Conservative Whips* are: Earl St. Aldwyn (*Chief Whip*); Earl Cowley; Lord Denham; Lord Mowbray and Stourton; Lord Sandys; Lord Elton; Lord Lyell; Viscount Long.

The *Liberal Whip* is Lord Amulree.

The House of Commons

The *Government Whips* are: The Parliamentary (Patronage) Secretary to the Treasury (*Chief Whip*) and the Junior Lords of the Treasury. *Assistant Whips* are also usually appointed.

The *Conservative Whips* are: The Rt. Hon. H. E. Atkins (*Chief Whip*); B. B. Weatherill (*Deputy Chief Whip*); J. S. Thomas; Hon. Adam Butler; C. E. Parkinson; R. N. Luce; S. Le Marchant; M. H. A. Roberts; W. R. Benyon; F. J. Silvester; Hon. Anthony Berry; T. R. Fairgrieve.

The *Liberal Whip* is C. Smith.

(Formed March 1974; reconstructed June 1975)

THE CABINET

Prime Minister and First Lord of the Treasury, THE RT. HON. JAMES HAROLD WILSON, O.B.E., M.P., *born* March 11, 1916.

Secretary of State for Foreign and Commonwealth Affairs, The Rt. Hon. Leonard James Callaghan, M.P., *born* March 27, 1912.

Chancellor of the Exchequer, The Rt. Hon. Denis Winston Healey, M.P., *born* Aug. 30, 1917.

Lord High Chancellor, The Rt. Hon. Lord Elwyn-Jones, *born* Oct. 24, 1909.

Secretary of State for the Home Department, The Rt. Hon. Roy Harris Jenkins, M.P., *born* Nov. 11, 1920.

Secretary of State for Social Services, The Rt. Hon. Barbara Anne Castle, M.P., *born* Oct. 6, 1911.

Secretary of State for Defence, The Rt. Hon. Roy Mason, M.P., *born* April 18, 1924.

Secretary of State for Scotland, The Rt. Hon. William Ross, M.B.E., M.P., *born* April 7, 1911.

Secretary of State for Employment, The Rt. Hon Michael Mackintosh Foot, M.P., *born* July 23, 1913.

Secretary of State for Education and Science, The Rt. Hon. Frederick William Mulley, M.P., *born* July 3, 1918.

Secretary of State for Wales, The Rt. Hon. John Morris, M.P., *born* 1931.

Secretary of State for Trade, The Rt. Hon. Peter David Shore, M.P., *born* May 20, 1924.

Secretary of State for Industry, The Rt. Hon. Eric Graham Varley, M.P., *born* Aug. 11, 1932.

Secretary of State for the Environment, The Rt. Hon. Charles Anthony Raven Crosland, M.P., *b.* Aug. 29, 1918.

Secretary of State for Northern Ireland, The Rt. Hon. Merlyn Rees, M.P., *born* Dec. 18, 1920.

Secretary of State for Energy, The Rt. Hon. Anthony Neil Wedgwood Benn, M.P., *born* April 3, 1925.

Secretary of State for Prices and Consumer Protection, The Rt. Hon. Shirley Vivien Teresa Brittain Williams, M.P., *born* July 27, 1930.

Lord President of the Council and Leader of the House of Commons, The Rt. Hon. Edward Watson Short, M.P., *born* Dec. 17, 1912.

Lord Privy Seal and Leader of the House of Lords, The Rt. Hon. Lord Shepherd, *born* Sept. 27, 1918.

Chancellor of the Duchy of Lancaster, The Rt. Hon. Norman Harold Lever, *born* Jan. 15, 1914.

Minister of Agriculture and Fisheries, The Rt. Hon. Thomas Frederick Peart, M.P., *born* April 30, 1914.

Minister for Overseas Development, The Rt. Hon. Reginald Ernest Prentice, M.P., *born* July 16, 1923.

Parliamentary Secretary to the Treasury, The Rt. Hon. Robert Joseph Mellish, *born* 1913.

MINISTERS NOT IN THE CABINET

Minister for Housing and Construction, Reginald Yarnitz Freeson, M.P., *born* 1926.

Minister for Transport, John William Gilbert, Ph.D., M.P., *born* 1927.

Minister for Planning and Local Government, The Rt. Hon. John Ernest Silkin, M.P., *born* 1923.

Paymaster-General, The Rt. Hon. Edmund Emanuel Dell, M.P., *born* 1921.

Attorney-General, The Rt. Hon. Samuel Charles Silkin, Q.C., M.P., *born* 1918.

Lord Advocate. The Rt. Hon. Ronald King Murray, Q.C., M.P., *born* 1922.

Solicitor-General, Peter Kingsley Archer, Q.C., M.P., *born* 1926.

Solicitor-General for Scotland, John Herbert McCluskey, Q.C., *born* 1929.

Chief Secretary to the Treasury, The Rt. Hon. Joel Barnett, M.P., *born* 1922.

Financial Secretary to the Treasury, Robert Edward Sheldon, M.P., *born* 1923.

Ministers of State (Foreign and Commonwealth Office), The Rt. Hon. David Hedley Ennals, M.P., *born* 1922; The Rt. Hon. Roy Sydney George Hattersley, M.P., *born* 1932.

Ministers of State (Home Office), The Lord Harris of Greenwich, *b.* 1930; Alexander Ward Lyon, M.P., *b.* 1931.

Ministers of State (Scottish Office), The Rt. Hon. Bruce Millan, M.P., *born* 1927; The Lord Kirkhill, *born* 1930.

Minister of State (Health and Social Security), The Rt. Hon. Brian Kevin O'Malley, M.P., *born* 1930.

Minister of State (Employment), Albert Edward Booth, M.P., *born* 1938.

Minister of State (Defence), The Rt. Hon. William Thomas Rodgers, M.P., *born* 1928.

Ministers of State (Northern Ireland), The Rt. Hon. Stanley Orme, M.P., *born* 1923; Roland Dunstan Moyle, M.P., *born* 1928.

Minister of State (Agriculture and Fisheries), Edward Stanley Bishop, M.P., *born* 1920.

Minister of State (Treasury), (David John) Denzil Davies, *born* 1938.

Minister of State (Privy Council Office), Gerald Teasdale Fowler, M.P., *born* 1935.

Minister of State (Energy), The Rt. Hon. Lord Balogh, *born* 1905.

Minister of State (Environment), Denis Herbert Howell, M.P., *born* 1923 (*Sport*).

Ministers of State (Industry), The Rt. Hon. Lord Beswick, *born* 1912; (James) Gregor MacKenzie, M.P., *b.* 1916.

Minister of State (Prices and Consumer Protection), Alan John Williams, M.P., *born* 1930.

Minister of State (Health and Social Security), David Anthony Llewelyn Owen, *born*, 1938.

Minister of State (Civil Service Department), Charles Richard Morris, M.P., *born* 1926.

Minister of State (Education and Science), The Lord Crowther-Hunt, *born* 1920.

PARLIAMENTRY UNDER SECRETARIES, ETC.

Agriculture and Fisheries, G. S. Strang, M.P.

Civil Service Department, J. D. Grant, M.P.

Defence, F. A. Judd, M.P. (*Royal Navy*); R. C. Brown, M.P. (*Army*); B. T. John, M.P. (*Royal Air Force*).

Education and Science, H. G. Jenkins, M.P.; Miss J. Lestor, M.P.

Employment, J. D. Fraser, M.P.; H. Walker, M.P.

Energy, A. Eadie, M.P.; J. Smith, M.P.

Environment, N. G. Carmichael, M.P.; G. J. Oakes, M.P.; The Baroness Birk; E. Armstrong, M.P.

Foreign and Commonwealth Affairs, The Lord Goronwy-Roberts, P.C.; E. Rowlands, M.P.

Health and Social Security, M. H. Meacher, M.P. (*Social Security*); A. Morris, M.P. (*Disabled*).

Home, The Hon. Shirley Summerskill, M.P.

Industry, G. B. Kaufman, M.P.

Law Officers' Dept. A. Davidson, M.P.

Northern Ireland, The Lord Donaldson of Kingsbridge; J. D. Concannon, M.P.

Overseas Development, J. Grant, M.P.

Prices and Consumer Protection, R. A. R. MacLennan, M.P.

Privy Council Office, W. G. Price, M.P.

Scottish Office, H. D. Brown, M.P.; H. Ewing, M.P.

Trade, E. P. Deakins, M.P.; S. C. Davis, M.P.

Treasury, Junior Lords, D. R. Coleman, M.P.; J. A. Dunn, M.P.; T. Pendry, M.P.; M. F. L. Cocks, M.P.; J. D. Dormand, M.P.

Asst. Whips, T. M. Cox, M.P.; L. A. Pavitt, M.P.; E. G. Perry, M.P.; J. Ellis, M.P.; Miss B. Boothroyd, M.P.; Miss M. M. Jackson, M.P.; D. L. Stoddart, M.P.

Welsh Office, S. B. Jones, M.P.; T. A. Jones, M.P.

THE PRINCIPAL PARTIES IN PARLIAMENT (1929–1974)

General Election	Conservative	Liberal	Labour
1929	260	59	287
1931	471	72 (e)	65 (f)
1935	387	54 (g)	166 (h)
1945	189	25 (i)	396 (j)
1950	298 (k)	9	315 (l)
1951	320 (m)	6	296 (l)
1955	344 (m)	6	277 (n)
1959	365 (m)	6	258 (o)
1964	303 (m)	9	317
1966	253 (m)	12	363 (p)
1970	330 (q)	6	287 (r)
1974 (February)	296	14	301 (s)
1974 (October)	276	13	319 (b)

NOTES.—(a) Including 48 Non-Coalition Unionists. (b) Including 28 Non-Coalition Liberals. (c) Including 63 Non-Coalition Labour. d) Liberal National 59; Liberal 59. (e) Liberal National 35 (Simon); Liberal 33 (Samuel); 4 (Lloyd George). (f) National Labour 13 (Mac-Donald); Labour 52 (Henderson). (g) Liberal National 33; Liberal 21. (h) National Labour 8; Labour 154; I.L.P. 4. (i) Liberal National 13. Liberal 12. (j) Labour 393; I.L.P. 3. (k) Incl. Nat. Liberal. (l) Irish Nationalists (2) and Speaker make total of 625. (m) Including associates. (n) Sinn Fein (2) and Speaker make total of 630. (o) Independent (1) makes total of 630. (p) Republican Labour (1) makes total of 630. (q) Including Ulster Unionists. (r) Scottish Nationalist (1); Independent (5) and Speaker make total of 630. (s) United Ulster Unionist Council (11), Scottish Nationalists (7), Plaid Cymru (2); Social Democratic and Labour Party (1); Social Democrat (1); Independent Labour (1); and Speaker make total of 635. (t) Scottish Nationalists (11); United Ulster Unionist (10); Plaid Cymru (3); Social Democratic and Labour Party (1); Independent (1) and Speaker make a total of 635. Since the October 1974 election Conservatives have gained one seat (Woolwich, West) from Labour.

PARLIAMENTS SINCE 1852

Assembled	Dissolved	Duration yrs. m. d.	Assembled	Dissolved	Duration yrs. m. d.
	Victoria			*George V*	
1852 Nov. 4	1857 March 21	4 4 17	1911 Jan. 31	1918 Nov. 25	7 9 25
1857 April 30	1859 April 23	1 11 23	1919 Feb. 4	1922 Oct. 26	3 8 22
1859 May 31	1865 July 6	6 1 6	1922 Nov. 20	1923 Nov. 16	0 11 27
1866 Feb. 1	1868 Nov. 11	2 9 10	1924 Jan. 8	1924 Oct. 9	0 9 1
1868 Dec. 10	1874 Jan. 26	5 1 16	1924 Dec. 2	1929 May 10	4 5 7
1874 March 5	1880 March 25	6 0 20	1929 June 25	1931 Oct. 6	2 3 11
1880 April 29	1885 Nov. 18	5 6 20	1931 Nov. 3	1935 Oct. 25	3 11 22
1886 Jan. 12	1886 June 26	0 5 14		*George V, Edward VIII and George VI*	
1886 Aug. 5	1892 June 28	5 10 24	1935 Nov. 16	1945 June 15	9 6 25
1892 Aug. 4	1895 July 9	2 11 5		*George VI*	
1895 Aug. 12	1900 Sept. 25	5 1 14	1945 Aug. 1	1950 Feb. 3	4 6 3
			1950 March 1	1951 Oct. 5	1 7 4
	Victoria and Edward VII			*George VI and Elizabeth II*	
1900 Dec. 3	1906 Jan. 8	5 1 6	1951 Oct. 31	1955 May 6	3 6 6
				Elizabeth II	
			1955 June 9	1959 Sept. 18	4 3 9
	Edward VII		1959 Oct. 27	1964 Sept. 25	4 10 29
1906 Feb. 13	1910 Jan. 15	3 11 2	1964 Nov. 3	1966 March 10	1 4 7
			1966 April 21	1970 May 29	4 1 8
	Edward VII and George V		1970 July 2	1974 Feb. 8	3 7 6
1910 Feb. 15	1910 Nov. 28	0 9 13	1974 March 13	1974 Sept. 19	0 6 6
			1974 Oct. 29		

MAJORITIES IN THE HOUSE OF COMMONS
(Since the Reform Bill, 1832).

Year	Party	Majority	Year	Party	Majority
1833	Whig	307	1910 (Jan.)	Liberal	124
1835	Whig	107	1910 (Dec.)	Liberal	126
1837	Whig	51	1918	Coalition	263
1841	Conservative	81	1922	Conservative	79
1847	Whig	1	1923	No Majority.	
1852	Liberal	13	1924	Conservative	225
1857	Liberal	79	1929	No Majority.	
1859	Liberal	43	1931	National Government	425
1865	Liberal	67	1935	National Government	247
1868	Liberal	128	1945	Labour	146
1874	Conservative	46	1950	Labour	8
1880	Liberal	62	1951	Conservative	16
1885	Liberal (84) and Irish Nationalist (82).	166	1955	Conservative	59
1886	Unionist	114	1959	Conservative	100
1892	Liberal	40	1964	Labour	5
1895	Unionist	152	1966	Labour	99
1900	Unionist	134	1970	Conservative	31
1906	Liberal	356	1974 (Feb.)	No Majority.	
			1974 (Oct.)	Labour	5

FORFEITED DEPOSITS AT THE GENERAL ELECTION, 1974

Candidates at parliamentary elections who fail to obtain one-eighth of the total votes cast in their constituencies forfeit the deposit of £150 which all candidates must lodge.

Deposits forfeited at the 1974 October election totalled 453, 132 more than in Feb. 1974. Deposits were lost by 15 Labour candidates, 130 Liberals, 30 Conservatives, 29 Communists, 26 Plaid Cymru, 90 National Front and 133 others. In 1950 the previous record number of 443 deposits was lost.

VOTES CAST AT THE GENERAL ELECTIONS, 1959-74 AND AT BY-ELECTIONS SINCE 1964

General Election, 1959

Conservative and Associate	13,750,965
Labour	12,195,765
Liberal	1,661,262
Welsh Nationalist	77,571
Sinn Fein	63,915
Communist	30,897
Scottish Nationalist	21,738
Others	61,225
Total	27,863,338

General Election, 1964

Labour	12,205,581
Conservative and Associate	11,980,783
Liberal	3,101,103
Irish Republican	101,628
Welsh Nationalist	68,517
Scottish Nationalist	63,053
Communist	44,576
Others	90,908
Total	27,656,149

By-elections, 1964-66

At 13 by-elections between the General Elections of 1964 and 1966, the following votes were cast:—

Conservative	223,002
Labour	176,793
Liberal	83,832
Independent	2,659
Welsh Nationalist	1,551

General Election, 1966

Labour	13,064,951
Conservative and Associate	11,418,433
Liberal	2,327,533
Scottish Nationalist	128,474
Communist	62,112
Plaid Cymru	61,071
Others	201,032
Total	27,263,606

By-elections 1966-70

At 38 by-elections between the General Elections of 1966 and 1970, the following votes were cast:—

Conservative and Ulster Unionist	629,970

Labour	439,358
Liberal	126,301
Independent	57,527
Scottish Nationalist	40,737
Plaid Cymru	40,518
Communist	4,807

General Election, 1970

Conservative and Ulster Unionist	13,144,692
Labour	12,179,166
Liberal	2,117,638
Scottish Nationalist	306,796
Plaid Cymru	175,016
Communist	38,431
Others	383,068
Total	28,344,087

By-elections 1970-74

At 30 by-elections between the General Elections of 1970 and 1974, the following votes have been cast:—

Labour	415,798
Conservative	351,781
Liberal	156,744
Independent	53,673
Scottish Nationalist	36,204
Plaid Cymru	11,852
Communist	1,647

General Election, February 1974*

Conservative	11,868,906
Labour	11,639,243
Liberal	6,063,470
Scottish Nationalist	632,032
Plaid Cymru	171,634
Communist	32,741
Others	207,884

General Election, October, 1974*

Labour	11,456,597
Conservative	10,464,675
Liberal	5,346,800
Scottish Nationalist	839,628
Plaid Cymru	166,321
Others	195,065

* Excluding Northern Ireland

PARLIAMENTARY ASSOCIATIONS

COMMONWEALTH PARLIAMENTARY ASSOCIATION (1911)

The Commonwealth Parliamentary Association consists of 29 main branches in Parliaments of the self-governing countries of the Commonwealth and 26 auxiliary branches in countries or territories which are not yet self-governing. There are also branches in State and Provincial Legislatures, in Australia, Canada, India and Malaysia making a total of 100 branches. Commonwealth Parliamentary conferences and general meetings are held every year in different countries of the Commonwealth.

President, Dr. Hon. G. S. Dhillon (India).

Secretary-General, Sir Robin Vanderfelt, K.B.E., Houses of Parliament, S.W.1.

Secretary, *United Kingdom Branch*, P. G. Molloy, O.B.E., M.C., Westminster Hall, Houses of Parliament, S.W.1.

THE INTER-PARLIAMENTARY UNION

Place du Petit-Saconnex 1209, Geneva, Switzerland.

The Inter-Parliamentary Union has been in existence since 1889; originally started to popularize the idea of International Arbitration, it achieved its object very substantially in helping to create the Permanent Court of Arbitration by the First Hague Conference and to bring about the convocation of the Second Conference of The Hague. In 1945, the Union resumed work on all questions connected with peace and reconstruction, which have been studied under various aspects.

BRITISH GROUP.

Hon. Presidents, The Lord Chancellor; Mr. Speaker.

President, Rt. Hon. J. H. Wilson, O.B.E.

Vice-Presidents, The Lord Home of the Hursel, P.C., K.T., The Lord Butler of Saffron Walden. K.G., P.C., C.H.; The Rt. Hon. R. M. M. Stewart, C.H., M.P.; The Rt. Hon. E. R. G. Heath, M.B.E,, M.P.; The Rt. Hon. L. J. Callaghan, M.P.

Chairman, W. T. Williams, Q.C., M.P.

Secretary, Brigadier P. S. Ward, C.B.E.

ALPHABETICAL LIST OF MEMBERS OF THE HOUSE OF COMMONS
(Elected October 10, 1974)

For abbreviations, see page 9. The number before the name of each constituency is for easy reference and corresponds to the number of that constituency given on pp. 323–347.

	Maj.
*Abse, L. (*b.* 1917), *Lab.,* 470*Pontypool*	18,695
*Adley, R. J. (*b.* 1935), *C.,* 149*Christchurch and Lymington*	13,890
*Aitken, J. W. P. (*b.* 1942), *C.,* 569*Thanet, E.*	4,503
*Alison, M. J. H. (*b.* 1926), *C.,* 33*Barkston Ash*	9,941
*Allaun, F. J. (*b.* 1913), *Lab.,* 511*Salford, E.*	7,836
*Amery, Rt. Hon. J. (*b.* 1919), *C.,* 106 *Brighton, Pavilion*	7,417
*Anderson, Rt. Hon. Betty Harvie- (*b.* 1915), *C.,* 484*Renfrewshire, E.*	8,710
Anderson, D. (*b.* 1939), *Lab.,* 565*Swansea, E.*	20,721
*Archer, P. K. (*b.* 1926), *Lab.,* 596*Warley, W.*	14,857
*Armstrong, E. (*b.* 1915), *Lab.,* 207*Durham, N.W.*	18,756
Arnold, T. R. (*b.* 1947), *C.,* 299*Hazel Grove*	2,831
*Ashley, J. (*b.* 1927), *Lab.,* 551*Stoke, S.*	16,495
*Ashton, J. W. (*b.* 1933), *Lab.,* 39*Bassetlaw.*	12,169
*Atkins, Rt. Hon. H. E. (*b.* 1922), *C.,* 538 *Spelthorne*	5,948
*Atkins, R. H. (*b.* 1916), *Lab.* 475*Preston, N.*	1,784
*Atkinson, N. (*b.* 1923), *Lab.,* 579*Tottenham*	9,216
*Awdry, D.E. (*b.* 1924), *C.,* 145*Chippenham*	1,749
*Bagier, G. A. T. (*b.* 1924), *Lab.,* 558 *Sunderland, S.*	13,030
Bain, Mrs. M. A. (*b.* 1945), *Scot. Nat.,* 201 *Dunbartonshire, E.*	22
*Baker, K. W. (*b.* 1934), *C.,* 509*St. Marylebone*	6,503
*Banks, R. G. (*b.* 1937), *C.,* 290*Harrogate .*	13,314
*Barnett, Rt. Hon. J. (*b.* 1923), *Lab.,* 311 *Heywood and Royton*	7,899
*Barnett, N. G. (*b.* 1928), *Lab.,* 276*Greenwich*	9,906
*Bates, A. (*b.* 1944), *Lab.,* 45*Bebington and Ellesmere Port*	6,491
Bean, R. E. (*b.* 1935), *Lab.,* 491*Rochester and Chatham*	2,418
*Beith, A. J. (*b.* 1943), *L.,* 59*Berwick upon Tweed*	73
*Bell, R. M. (*b.* 1914), *C.,* 44*Beaconsfield* ..	10,626
*Benn, Rt. Hon. A. N. Wedgwood (*b.* 1925), *Lab.,* 110*Bristol, S.E.*	9,373
*Bennett, A. F. (*b.* 1929), *Lab.,* 546*Stockport, N.*	1,824
*Bennett, Sir F. M. (*b.* 1918), *C.,* 577*Torbay*	12,438
*Bennett, R. F. B. (*b.* 1911), *C.,* 234*Fareham*	4,448
*Benyon, W. R. (*b.* 1930), *C.,* 113*Buckingham*	2,918
*Berry, Hon. A. G. (*b.* 1925), *C.,* 534*Southgate*	14,922
*Bidwell, S. J. (*b.* 1917), *Lab.,* 529*Southall .*	9,983
*Biffen, W. J. (*b.* 1930), *C.,*454 *Oswestry.* .	8,414
*Bishop, E. S. (*b.* 1920), *Lab.,* 420*Newark .* .	5,771
*Blaker, P. A. R. (*b.* 1922), *C.,* 79*Blackpool, S.*	5,221
*Blenkinsop, A. (*b.* 1911), *Lab.,* 536*South Shields*	14,825
*Boardman, H. (*b.* 1907), *Lab.,* 367*Leigh .* .	14,635
*Body, R. (*b.* 1927), *C.,* 315*Holland with Boston*	8,684
*Booth, A E. (*b.* 1928), *Lab.,* 35*Barrow in Furness*	7,354
*Boothroyd, Miss B. (*b.* 1930), *Lab.,* 604 *West Bromwich, W.*	14,799
*Boscawen, Hon. R. T. (*b.* 1923), *C.,* 601 *Wells*	7,701

	Maj.
*Bottomley, Rt. Hon. A. G. (*b.* 1907), *Lab., Middlesbrough*	13,807
Bottomley, P. J. (*b.* 1944). *C.,* 625 *Woolwich, W.*	2,382
*Bowden, A. (*b.* 1930), *C.,* 105*Brighton, Kemptown*	2,605
*Bowman, Mrs. M. E. Kellett- (*b.* 1924), *C.,* 356*Lancaster*	1,421
*Boyden, H. J. (*b.* 1910), *Lab.,* 75*Bishop Auckland*	11,095
*Boyson, R. R. (*b.* 1925), *C.,* 97*Brent, N..*	7,312
*Bradford, Rev. R. J. (*b.* 1941), *U.U.U.,* 54*Belfast, S.*	18,401
*Bradley, T. G. (*b.* 1926), *Lab.,* 364*Leicester, E.*	3,811
*Braine, Sir B. R. (*b.* 1914), *C.,* 229*Essex, S.E.*	8,710
Bray, J. W. (*b.* 1930), *Lab.,* 416*Motherwell and Wishaw*	4,962
*Brittan, L. (*b.* 1939), *C.,* 152*Cleveland and Whitby*	1,528
Brotherton, M. L. (*b.* 1931), *C.,* 386*Louth*	2,880
*Broughton, Sir A. D. D. (*b.* 1902), *Lab.,* 41*Batley and Morley*	8,248
*Brown, Sir E. J. (*b.* 1913), *C.,* 40*Bath*	2,122
*Brown, H. D. (*b.* 1919), *Lab.,* 263*Provan..*	9,974
*Brown, R. C. (*b.* 1921), *Lab.,* 426*Newcastle, W.*	15,074
*Brown, R. W. (*b.* 1921), *Lab.,* 281*S. Hackney and Shoreditch.*	13,295
*Bryan, Sir P. E. O. (*b.* 1913), *C.,* 323 *Howden*	4,780
*Buchan, N. F. (*b.* 1922), *Lab.,* 485*Renfrewshire, E.*	5,300
*Buchanan, R. (*b.* 1912), *Lab.,* 266*Springburn*	8,395
*Buck, P. A. F. (*b.* 1928), *C.,* 155*Colchester*	5,500
*Budgen, N. W. (*b.* 1937), *C.,* 622*Wolverhampton, S.W.*	5,300
*Bulmer, J. E. (*b.* 1935), *C.,* 346*Kidderminster*	6,769
*Burden, F. F. A. (*b.* 1905), *C.,* 253*Gillingham*	3,996
*Butler, Hon. A. C. (*b.* 1931), *C.,* 87 *Bosworth*	302
*Butler, Mrs. J. S. (*b.* 1910), *Lab.,* 623*Wood Green*	8,211
*Callaghan, J. (*b.* 1927), *Lab.,* 408*Middleton and Prestwich*	3,714
*Callaghan, Rt. Hon. L. J. (*b.* 1912), *Lab.,* 127*Cardiff, S.E.*	10,718
*Campbell, I. (*b.* 1926), *Lab.,* 202*Dunbartonshire, W.*	1,814
Canavan, D. A. (*b.* 1942), *Lab.,* 545*Stirlingshire, W.*	367
*Cant, R. B. (*b.* 1915), *Lab.,* 549*Stoke, Central*	14,653
*Carlisle, M. (*b.* 1929), *C.,* 500*Runcorn*	5,468
*Carmichael, N. G. (*b.* 1921), *Lab.,* 260 *Kelvingrove*	4,118
*Carr, Rt. Hon. L. R. (*b.* 1916), *C.,* 133 *Carshalton*	3,698
*Carson, J. (*b.* 1930), *U.U.U.,* 53*Belfast, N.*	18,222
*Carter, R. J. (*b.* 1935), *Lab.,* 68*Northfield*	10,597
Cartwright, J. C. (*b.* 1933), *Lab.,* 624 *Woolwich, E.*	12,425
*Castle, Rt. Hon. Barbara (*b.* 1911), *Lab.,* 77*Blackburn*	7,652
*Chalker, Mrs. L. (*b.* 1942), *C.,* 589 *Wallasey*	1,970
*Channon, H. P. G. (*b.* 1935), *C.,* 533*Southend, W.*	7,071

	Maj.
*Pink, R. B. (b. 1912), C., 474Portsmouth, S.	8,071
Powell, Rt. Hon. J. E. (b. 1912), U.U.U., 195Down, S.	3,567
*Prentice, Rt. Hon. R. E. (b. 1923), Lab., 428Newham, N.E.	13,541
*Prescott, J. L. (b. 1938), Lab., 327Hull, E.	25,793
*Price, C. (b. 1932), Lab., 371Lewisham, W.	5,529
*Price, D. E. C. (b. 1924), C., 213Eastleigh.	7,815
*Price, W. G. (b. 1934), Lab., 498Rugby...	5,204
*Prior, Rt. Hon. J. M. L. (b. 1927), C., 387 Lowestoft.	2,062
*Pym, Rt. Hon. F. L. (b. 1922), C., 122 Cambridgeshire.	12,655
*Radice, G. H. (b. 1936), Lab., 142Chester-le-Street.	24,278
*Raison, T. H. F. (b. 1929), C., 25Aylesbury	8,973
*Rathbone, J. R. (b. 1933), C., 369Lewes..	13,847
*Rawlinson, Rt. Hon. Sir P. A. G. (b. 1919), C., 226Epsom and Ewell...	16,290
*Rees, Rt. Hon. M. (b. 1920), Lab., 360 Leeds, S.	15,265
*Rees, P. W. I. (b. 1926), C., 193Dover and Deal.	2,294
*Reid, G. N. (b. 1940), Scot. Nat., 544 Stirlingshire E., and Clackmannan.	7,341
*Renton, Rt. Hon. Sir D. L. M. (b. 1908), C., 329Huntingdonshire.	9,244
*Renton, R. T. (b. 1932), C., 562Mid Sussex.	11,997
*Richardson, Miss J. (b. 1923), Lab., 32 Barking.	16,290
*Ridley, Hon. N. (b. 1929), C., 150Cirencester and Tewkesbury.	10,160
*Ridsdale, J. E. (b. 1915), C., 295Harwich.	10,828
*Rifkind, M. L. (b. 1946), C., 220Pentlands	1,257
*Rippon, Rt. Hon. A. G. F. (b. 1924), C., 310Hexham.	4,641
*Roberts, A. (b. 1908), Lab., 437Normanton	14,633
*Roberts, G. E. (b. 1928), Lab., 123Cannock	12,222
*Roberts, I. W. P. (b. 1930), C., 158Conway	2,806
*Roberts, M. H. A. (b. 1927), C., 126 Cardiff, N.W.	4,333
*Robertson, J. (b. 1913), Lab., 458Paisley..	5,590
*Roderick, C. E. (b. 1927), Lab., 95Brecon and Radnor.	3,012
*Rodgers, G. (b. 1925), Lab., 148Chorley..	2,713
*Rodgers, Sir J. C., Bt. (b. 1906), C., 515 Sevenoaks.	11,605
*Rodgers, Rt. Hon. W. T. (b. 1928), Lab., 548Stockton.	14,474
*Rooker, J. W. (b. 1941), Lab., 69Perry Bar.	3,204
*Roper, J. F. H. (b. 1935), Lab., 236Farnworth.	14,695
*Rose, P. B. (b. 1935), Lab., 395Blackley...	7,119
*Ross, S. S. (b. 1926), L., 338Isle of Wight.	2,040
*Ross, Rt. Hon. W. (b. 1911), Lab., 347 Kilmarnock.	7,529
*Ross, W. (b. 1936), U.U.U., 384Londonderry.	9,020
*Rossi, H. A. L. (b. 1927), C., 319Hornsey	782
*Rost, P. L. (b. 1930), C., 181Derbyshire, S.E.	1,005
*Rowlands, E. (b. 1940), Lab., 406Merthyr Tydfil.	16,805
*Royle, Sir A. H. F. (b. 1927), C., 487 Richmond upon Thames.	4,215
Ryman, J. (b. 1931), Lab., 81Blyth.	78
*Sainsbury, Hon. T. A. D. (b. 1932), C., 322Hove.	14,876
*Sandelson, N. D. (b. 1923), Lab., 298Hayes and Harlington.	9,420
Scott, N. P. (b. 1933), C., 136Chelsea...	13,167

	Maj.
*Sedgemore, B. C. J. (b. 1937), Lab., 390 Luton, W.	6,439
*Selby, H. (b. 1914), Lab., 258Govan.	1,952
*Shaw, A. J. (b. 1909), Lab., 332Ilford, S...	1,749
*Shaw, J. G. D. (b. 1931), C., 477Pudsey..	4,581
*Shaw, M. N. (b. 1920), C., 514Scarborough	9,708
*Sheldon, R. E. (b. 1923), Lab., 24Ashton-under-Lyne.	10,72
*Shelton, W. J. M. (b. 1929), C., 553 Streatham.	2,867
Shepherd, C. R. (b. 1938), C., 305Hereford	1,112
*Shersby, J. M. (b. 1933), C., 586Uxbridge.	2,153
*Shore, Rt. Hon. P. D. (b. 1924), Lab., 542 Stepney and Poplar.	20,976
*Short, Rt. Hon. E. W. (b. 1912), Lab., 423 Newcastle, Central.	8,114
*Short, Mrs. R. (b. 1919), Lab., 620Wolverhampton, N.E.	14,653
*Silk, K. Kilroy- (b. 1942), Lab., 452Ormskirk.	8,851
*Silkin, Rt. Hon. J. E. (b. 1923), Lab., 177 Deptford.	13,034
*Silkin, Rt. Hon. S. C. (b. 1918), Lab., 198 Dulwich.	7,459
*Sillars, J. (b. 1937), Lab., 29Ayrshire, S...	14,478
*Silverman J. (b. 1905), Lab., 64Erdington..	8,777
*Silvester, F. J. (b. 1933), C., 400Withington	2,001
*Sims, R. E. (b. 1930), C., 147Chislehurst..	3,894
*Sinclair, Sir G. E. (b. 1912), C., 189 Dorking.	10,305
*Skeet, T. H. H. (b. 1918), C., 47Bedford..	4,088
*Skinner, D. E. (b. 1932), Lab., 83Bolsover.	21,066
*Small, W. W. (b. 1909), Lab., 257Garscadden.	7,626
*Smith, Hon. A. L. Buchanan- (b. 1932), C., 15North Angus and Mearns.	2,551
*Smith, C. (b. 1928), L., 490Rochdale.	2,753
*Smith, Rt. Hon. Sir D. C. Walker-. Bt. (b. 1910), C., 307Herts., E.	8,335
*Smith, D. G. (b. 1926), C., 598Warwick and Leamington.	8,245
*Smith, G. Johnson (b. 1924), C., 211East Grinstead.	9,280
*Smith, J. (b. 1938), Lab., 355Lanarkshire, N.	8,341
*Snape, P. C. (b. 1942), Lab., 603West Bromwich, E.	1,529
*Spearing, N. J. (b. 1930), Lab., 430Newham, S.	17,721
Speed, H. K. (b. 1934), C., 23Ashford....	6,025
*Spence, J. D. (b. 1920), C., 571Thirsk and Malton.	13,862
*Spicer, J. W. (b. 1925), C., 192Dorset, W.	8,685
*Spicer, W. M. H. (b. 1943), C., 627Worcs., S.	9,052
*Spriggs, L. (b. 1910), Lab., 507St. Helens.	22,066
*Sproat, I. M. (b. 1938), C., 4Aberdeen, S.	365
*Stainton, K. M. (b. 1921), C., 556Sudbury and Woodbridge.	12,063
*Stallard, A. W. (b. 1921), Lab., 510St. Pancras, N.	7,553
*Stanbrook, I. R. (b. 1924), C., 453 Orpington.	5,010
*Stanley, J. P. (b. 1942), C., 575Tonbridge and Malling.	8,609
*Steel, D. M. S. (b. 1938), L., 497Roxburgh, Selkirk and Peebles.	7,433
*Steen, A. D. (b. 1939), C., 381Wavertree..	2,755
*Stevas, N. A. F. St. John- (b. 1929), C., 135 Chelmsford.	4,002
*Stewart, B. H. I. H. (b. 1935), C., 313 Hitchin.	3,186
*Stewart, D. J. (b. 1920), Scot. Nat., 606 Western Isles.	5,232
*Stewart, Rt. Hon. R. M. M. (b. 1906), Lab., 246Fulham.	5,321
*Stoddart, D. L. (b. 1926), Lab., 567Swindon	10,270

THE HOUSE OF COMMONS BY CONSTITUENCIES, OCTOBER 1974

The figures following the name of the Constituency denote the total number of *Electors* in the Parliamentary Division at the General Election of October 1974.

ABBREVIATIONS.—*C.* = Conservative; *Comm.* = Communist; *N.I. Lab* = Northern Ireland Labour; *Ind.* = Independent; *L.* = Liberal; *Lab.* = Labour; *P.C.* = Plaid Cymru; *Scot. Nat.* = Scottish Nationalist; *S.D.L.P.* = Social Democratic and Labour Party; *Repub.* = Republican; *U.P.N.I.* = Unionist Party of Northern Ireland; *U.U.U.* = United Ulster Unionist.

An asterisk ★ denotes membership of the last House for the same division; † for a different division.

Aberavon
E. 64,687
1★*Rt. Hon. J. Morris,* Q.C., *Lab.*	29,683
N. K. Hammond, *C.*	7,931
Mrs. S. Cutts, *L.*	5,178
G. Thomas, *P.C.*	4,032
J. Bevan, *Ind.*	427
Lab. maj.	*21,752*
(Feb. '74, Lab. maj. 20,688)	

Aberdare
E. 48,380
2★*I. L. Evans, Lab.*	24,197
G. R. Owen, *P.C.*	8,133
B. G. C. Webb, *C.*	2,775
G. Hill, *L.*	2,118
A. T. M. Wilson, *Comm.*	1,028
Lab. maj.	*16,064*
(Feb. '74, Lab. maj. 11,832)	

Aberdeen
NORTH E. 65,230
3★*R. Hughes, Lab.*	23,130
J. A. McGugan, *Scot. Nat.*	13,509
P. Fraser, *C.*	5,125
F. McCallum, *L.*	3,700
Lab. maj.	*9,621*
(Feb. '74, Lab. maj. 11,856)	

SOUTH E. 68,241
4★*I. M. Sproat, C.*	18,475
R. Middleton, *Lab.*	18,110
A. Stronach, *Scot. Nat.*	10,481
A. A. Robbie, *L.*	5,018
C. maj.	*365*
(Feb. '74, C. maj. 3,558)	

Aberdeenshire
EAST E. 47,736
5★*D. Henderson, Scot. Nat.*	16,304
K. W. T. Raffan, *C.*	11,933
Mrs. S. B. Sissons, *Lab.*	3,173
A. Dow, *L.*	2,232
Scot. Nat. maj.	*4,371*
(Feb. '74, Scot. Nat. maj. 5,699)	

WEST E. 55,341
6★*T. R. Fairgrieve, C.*	15,111
D. C. P. Gracie, *L.*	12,643
N. Suttar, *Scot. Nat.*	9,409
C. W. Ellis, *Lab.*	5,185
C. maj.	*2,468*
(Feb. '74, C. maj. 1,640)	

Abertillery
E. 36,561
7★*J. Thomas, Lab.*	20,835
W. A. Richards, *P.C.*	2,480
Mrs. P. J. E. Larney, *C.*	2,364
H. W. Clark, *L.*	1,779
Lab. maj.	*18,355*
(Feb. '74, Lab. maj. 16,949)	

Abingdon
E. 90,451
8★*A. M. S. Neave,* D.S.O., O.B.E., M.C., T.D., *C.*	31,956
D. E. H Moriarty, *Lab.*	21,319
M. P. Fogarty, *L.*	15,239
C. maj.	*10,637*
(Feb. '74, C. maj. 13,743)	

Accrington
E. 50,820
9★*A. Davidson, Lab.*	19,838
J. McLaughlin, *C.*	13,618
W. I. Cooper, *L.*	5,704
D. Riley, *Nat. Front*	1,176
Lab. maj.	*6,220*
(Feb. '74, Lab. maj. 5,032)	

Acton
E. 56,689
10★*Sir G. S. K. Young, Bt., C*	17,669
G. A. Barnham, *Lab.*	16,861
M. R. Uziell-Hamilton, *L.*	4,569
C. maj.	*808*
(Feb. '74, C. maj. 1,451)	

Aldershot
E. 80,522
11★*J. M. G. Critchley, C.*	26,463
A. Burton, *L.*	16,104
Mrs. E. P. Sudworth, *Lab.*	14,936
A. Greenslade, *Nat. Front*	1,120
C. maj.	*10,359*
(Feb. '74, C. maj. 10,658)	

Aldridge-Brownhills
E. 61,731
12★*G. Edge, Lab.*	21,403
A. J. M. Teacher, *C.*	18,884
J. A. Crofton, *L.*	8,693
T. Keen, *Ind.*	210
Lab. maj.	*2,519*
(Feb. '74, Lab. maj. 366)	

Altrincham and Sale
E. 73,296
13 *W. F. Montgomery, C.*	23,910
E. Wood, *Lab.*	16,998
D. Blackburn, *L.*	14,980
C. maj.	*6,912*
(Feb. '74, C. maj. 8,696)	

Anglesey
E. 44,026
14★*Rt. Hon. C. Hughes, Lab.*	13,947
T. V. Lewis, *C.*	7,975
D. Iwan, *P.C.*	6,410
W. D. M. Ankers, *L.*	5,182
Lab. maj.	*5,972*
(Feb. '74, Lab. maj. 5,754)	

Angus North and Mearns
E. 37,604
15★*Hon. A. L. Buchanan-Smith, C.*	11,835
I. Murray, *Scot. Nat.*	9,284
J. M. S. McEwan, *Lab.*	3,344
M. Bruce, *L.*	2,700
C. maj.	*2,551*
(Feb. '74, C. maj. 7,451)	

Angus South
E. 52,275
16 *A. Welsh, Scot. Nat.*	17,073
★*J. Bruce-Gardyne, C.*	15,249
N. L. Geaughan, *Lab.*	4,103
H. Will, *L.*	2,529
Scot. Nat. maj.	*1,824*
(Feb. '74, C. maj. 5,343)	

Antrim
NORTH E. 103,737
17★*I. R. K. Paisley, U.U.U.*	43,186
H. Wilson, *Alliance*	8,689
Miss M. McAllister, *S.D.L.P.*	7,616
U.U.U. maj.	*34,497*
(Feb. '74, Prot. U. maj. 27,631)	

SOUTH E. 117,834
18★*J. H. Molyneaux, U.U.U.*	48,892
C. H. G. Kinahan, *Alliance*	10,460
P. J. Rowan, *S.D.L.P.*	9,061
U.U.U. maj.	*38,432*
(Feb. '74, U.U.U. maj. 35,644)	

Argyll
E. 41,814
19★*I. S. M. MacCormick, Scot. Nat.*	14,967
J. J. Mackay, *C.*	11,036
M. J. N. MacGregor, *Lab.*	4,103
Scot. Nat. maj.	*3,931*
(Feb. '74, Scot. Nat. maj. 3,288)	

Armagh
E. 91,060
20★*J. H. McCusker, U.U.U.*	37,518
S. Mallon, *S.D.L.P.*	19,855
M. McGurran, *Rep.*	5,138
U.U.U. maj.	*17,663*
(Feb. '74, U.U.U. maj. 15,104)	

Arundel
E. 83,464
21★*R. M. Marshall, C.*	34,215
J. R. Kingsbury, *L.*	15,404
M. E. Stedman, *Lab.*	11,286
C. maj.	*18,811*
(Feb. '74, C. maj. 19,943)	

Ashfield
E. 74,701
22*D. I. Marquand, Lab... 35,367
R. N. Kemm, C...... 12,452
H. C. Flint, L....... 7,959
Lab. maj......... *22,915*
(Feb. '74, Lab. maj. 21,788)

Ashford
E. 58,419
23 H. K. Speed, C...... 19,294
M. B. Jackson, Lab.... 13,269
C. G. Dennis, L...... 10,983
C. maj............ *6,025*
(Feb. '74, C. maj. 8,459)

Ashton-under-Lyne
E. 60,393
24*R. E. Sheldon, Lab.... 23,490
M. H. Litchfield, C.... 12,763
T. G. Jones, L....... 7,356
Lab. maj........... *10,727*
(Feb. '74, Lab. maj. 8,301)

Aylesbury
E. 67,729
25*T. H. F. Raison, C..... 23,565
R. Groves, Lab........ 14,592
M. J. Cook, L........ 12,219
C. maj............ *8,973*
(Feb. '74, C. maj. 11,183)

Ayr
E. 51,975
26*Hon. G. K. H. Younger,
T.D., C............ 17,487
R. S. Stewart, Lab..... 14,268
Miss E. Robinson, Scot.
Nat................ 6,902
M. Tosh, L........... 2,611
C. maj............ *3,219*
(Feb. '74, C. maj. 5,098)

Ayrshire
CENTRAL E. 59,273
27*D. Lambie, Lab....... 21,188
Miss M. Carse, C...... 11,633
L. Anderson, Scot. Nat. 11,533
J. Watts, L........... 2,640
Lab. maj............ *9,555*
(Feb. '74, Lab. maj. 6,277)

NORTH AND BUTE E. 49,071
28*J. A. Corrie, C....... 13,599
J. N. Carson, Lab..... 10,093
J. A. Murphy, Scot. Nat. 9,055
R. Stevenson, L....... 2,224
C. maj............ *3,506*
(Feb. '74, C. maj. 6,730)

SOUTH E. 51,330
29*J. Sillars, Lab....... 22,329
R. Mullin, Scot. Nat... 7,851
Mrs. J. Armstrong, C.. 7,402
R. Mabon, L......... 2,130
Lab. maj............ *14,478*
(Feb. '74, Lab. maj. 12,450)

Banbury
E. 67,530
30*H. N. Marten, C...... 24,210
A. C. Booth, Lab...... 18,019
D. Charlton, L........ 8,352
J. Barbour, Ind....... 547
C. maj............ *6,191*
(Feb. '74, C. maj. 6,878)

Banff
E. 31,992
31*I. H. Watt, Scot. Nat... 10,638
J. S. Gordon, C....... 8,787
C. Macleod, L........ 2,059
Mrs. A. W. M.
Porteous, Lab...... 1,700
Scot. Nat. maj....... *1,851*
(Feb. '74, Scot. Nat. maj. 2,785)

Barking
E. 50,039
32*Miss J. Richardson, Lab. 21,546
E. Forth, C.......... 5,256
M. F. Taylor, L....... 5,245
C. W. Bond, Nat. Front 1,661
Lab. maj............ *16,290*
(Feb. '74, Lab. maj. 14,834)

Barkston Ash
E. 83,803
33*M. J. H. Alison, C.... 30,498
J. H. Muir, Lab....... 20,557
D. R. O. Paige, L..... 12,483
C. maj............ *9,941*
(Feb. '74, C. maj. 13,197)

Barnsley
E. 76,572
34*Rt. Hon. R. Mason, Lab. 34,212
G. England, C........ 9,400
P. Tomlinson, L....... 8,753
Lab. maj............ *24,812*
(Feb. '74, Lab. maj. 24,626)

Barrow-in-Furness
E. 54,541
35*A. E. Booth, Lab...... 21,607
Lord Richard Cecil, C. 14,253
M. A. Benjamin, L..... 5,788
V. Moore, Ind........ 384
Lab. maj............ *7,354*
(Feb. '74, Lab. maj. 5,107)

Barry
E. 69,992
36*Sir H. R. Gower, C.... 23,360
J. E. Brooks, Lab..... 20,457
Miss J. Lloyd, L....... 8,764
Mrs. V. Wynne-Wil-
liams, P.C.......... 1,793
C. maj............ *2,903*
(Feb. '74, C. maj. 5,547)

Basildon
E. 91,416
37*E. Moonman, Lab..... 32,298
D. A. Atkinson, C..... 21,747
E. Fortune, L........ 12,816
R. Chaplin, Ind....... 599
Lab. maj............ *10,551*
(Feb. '74, Lab. maj. 10,667)

Basingstoke
E. 86,782
38*D. B. Mitchell, C...... 29,038
T. E. Hunt, Lab....... 22,826
N. A. L. Whitbread, L. 14,636
G. Goodall, Nat. Front. 763
C. maj............ *6,212*
(Feb. '74, C. maj. 7,797)

Bassetlaw
E. 71,724
39*J. W. Ashton, Lab..... 28,663
D. K. Harris, C....... 16,494
A. Wilkinson, L....... 7,821
A. Storkey, Ind....... 408
Lab. maj............ *12,169*
(Feb. '74, Lab. maj. 11,234)

Bath
E. 62,304
40*Sir E. J. Brown, M.B.E.,
C................. 18,470
†C. P. Mayhew, L..... 16,348
M. L. Bishop, Lab..... 14,011
J. Kemp, Ind......... 150
C. maj............ *2,122*
(Feb. '74, C. maj. 5,182)

Batley and Morley
E. 61,894
41*Sir A. D. D. Broughton,
Lab............... 21,179
G. N. A. Crone, C..... 12,931
I. H. Lester, L........ 8,928
Lab. maj............ *8,248*
(Feb. '74, Lab. maj. 7,091)

Battersea
NORTH E. 44,799
42*Rt. Hon. D. P. T. Jay,
Lab............... 17,161
S. J. C. Randall, C..... 6,019
C. R. Williams, L..... 3,048
R. Friend, Nat. Front.. 1,250
Miss C. Reakes, Ind.... 102
Lab. maj............ *11,142*
(Feb. '74, Lab. maj. 10,423)

SOUTH E. 46,724
43*E. G. Perry, Lab...... 14,284
W. T. O. Wallace, C.. 11,433
Mrs. J. Ware, L....... 4,021
T. Keen, Ind......... 170
Lab. maj............ *2,851*
(Feb. '74, Lab. maj. 1,653)

Beaconsfield
E. 68,541
44*R. M. Bell, Q.C., C.... 23,234
W. H. Eastwell, L..... 12,606
Mrs. M. Johnson, Lab.. 12,253
C. maj............ *10,628*
(Feb. '74, C. maj. 11,248)

Bebington and Ellesmere Port
E. 86,641
45*A. Bates, Lab........ 32,310
E. P. Cockeram, C.... 25,819
N. R. L. Thomas, L... 9,947
Lab. maj............ *6,491*
(Feb. '74, Lab. maj. 4,462)

Beckenham
E. 59,512
46*P. C. Goodhart, C..... 19,798
N. J. Sharp, Lab...... 11,140
G. D. Mitchell, L...... 10,578
C. maj............ *8,658*
(Feb. '74, C. maj. 10,155)

Bedford
E. 74,143
47*T. H. H. Skeet, C..... 24,834
B. S. Parkyn, Lab..... 20,746
J. C. Griffiths, L...... 11,360
C. maj............ *4,088*
(Feb. '74, C. maj. 6,221)

Bedfordshire
MID E. 75,171
48*S. L. E. Hastings, M.C.
C................. 26,885
Mrs. J. E. Crow, Lab... 17,559
P. W. Meyer, L....... 14,388
C. maj............ *9,326*
(Feb. '74, C. maj. 11,111)

SOUTH E. 64,329
49*W. D. Madel, C....... 20,794
R. A. Little, Lab..... 16,351
D. J. H. Penwarden, L. 13,194
C. maj............. 4,443
(Feb. '74, C. maj. 4,758)

Bedwellty
E. 50,183
50*N. G. Kinnock, Lab..... 27,418
P. L. Brooke, C....... 4,556
R. G. Morgan, L...... 3,621
D. Mogford, P.C..... 3,086
Lab. maj........... 22,862
(Feb. '74, Lab. maj. 21,637)

Beeston
E. 74,172
51*J. T. Lester, C........ 25,095
A. J. Gardner, Lab... 24,974
S. C. Reddish, L...... 9,658
C. maj............. 121
(Feb. '74, C. maj. 2,544)

Belfast
EAST E. 79,591
52*Rt. Hon. W. Craig,
U.U.U............ 31,594
P. J. McLachlan,
U.P.N.I........... 14,417
Rt. Hon. D. W. Bleak-
ley, N.I.Lab....... 7,415
U.U.U. maj........ 17,177
(Feb. '74, U.U.U. maj. 7,740)

NORTH E. 71,779
53*J. Carson, U.U.U...... 29,622
T. Donnelly, S.D.L.P.. 11,400
J. Ferguson, Alliance... 3,807
W. R. Boyd, N.I. Lab. 2,481
U.U.U. maj........ 18,222
(Feb. '74, U.U.U. maj. 8,776)

SOUTH E. 75,112
54*Rev. R. J. Bradford,
U.U.U............ 30,116
J. B. C. Glass, Alliance.. 11,715
S. R. McMaster, Ind. U. 4,982
B. J. Caraher, S.D.L.P. 2,390
J. E. Holmes, N.I. Lab. 1,643
U.U.U. maj........ 18,401
(Feb. '74, U.U.U. maj. 3,998)

WEST E. 66,279
55*G. Fitt, S.D.L.P..... 21,821
J. McQuade, U.U.U... 16,265
Mrs. K. O'Kane, Rep.. 3,547
S. M. Gibson, Ind...... 2,690
P. Kerins, Ind........ 203
S.D.L.P. maj........ 5,556
(Feb. '74, S.D.L.P. maj. 2,180)

Belper
E. 71,197
56*R. L. MacFarquhar, Lab. 27,365
S. D. Newall, C....... 21,681
J. J. Wates, L......... 9,017
Lab. maj........... 5,684
(Feb. '74, Lab. maj. 2,034)

Bermondsey
E. 55,254
57*Rt. Hon. R. J. Mellish,
Lab............... 22,875
H. E. Flight, C....... 4,294
J. Taylor, L.......... 2,520
G. Davey, Nat. Front.. 1,488
Lab. maj........... 18,581
(Feb. '74, Lab. maj. 18,721)

Berwick and East Lothian
E. 57,503
58 J. P. Mackintosh, Lab... 20,682
*M. A. F. J. Ancram
(Earl of Ancram), C. 17,942
R. Macleod, Scot. Nat. 6,323
C. F. Lawson, L....... 2,811
Lab. maj........... 2,740
(Feb. '74, C. maj. 540)

Berwick-on-Tweed
E. 41,861
59*A. J. Beith, L......... 14,684
C. A. E. Baker-Cress-
well, C........... 14,611
G. T. P. Spain, Lab.... 4,768
L. maj............. 73
(Feb. '74, L. maj. 443)

Bethnal Green and Bow
E. 53,763
60*I. Mikardo, Lab....... 19,649
T. D. Gates, L........ 3,700
C. P. Y. Murphy, C.... 2,995
W. E. Castleton, Nat.
Front.............. 2,172
Lab. maj........... 15,949
(Feb. '74, Lab. maj. 14,954)

Bexleyheath
E. 51,022
61*C. D. Townsend, C.... 17,399
J. Stanyer, Lab........ 15,412
W. E. H. Pickard, L... 6,882
C. maj............. 1,987
(Feb. '74, C. maj. 3,866)

Birkenhead
E. 60,400
62*E. E. Dell, Lab........ 21,748
E. Gearing, C......... 12,264
G. C. Lindsay, L...... 8,380
Lab. maj........... 9,484
(Feb. '74, Lab. maj. 6,994)

Birmingham
EDGBASTON E. 70,078
63*Mrs. J. C. J. Knight,
M.B.E., C......... 19,483
J. G. Hannah, Lab..... 17,073
P. Davies, L.......... 7,770
C. maj............. 2,410
(Feb. '74, C. maj. 5,920)

ERDINGTON E. 65,764
64*J. Silverman, Lab....... 22,160
J. Alden, C........... 13,383
Mrs. J. Mills, L....... 6,119
T. M. Finnegan, Nat.
Front.............. 1,413
Lab. maj........... 8,777
(Feb. '74, Lab. maj. 6,928)

HALL GREEN E. 67,043
65*R. E. Eyre, C......... 20,569
Mrs. T. J. Stewart, Lab. 17,945
I. G. Powney, L....... 8,532
C. maj............. 2,624
(Feb. '74, C. maj. 6,244)

HANDSWORTH E. 45,676
66*J. M. H. Lee, Lab...... 15,011
R. Tyler, C........... 11,115
D. I. Grant-Smith, L... 3,205
J. Finnegan, Nat. Front. 838
T. L. Keen, Ind....... 105
J. L. Hutchinson, Ind... 103
Lab. maj........... 3,896
(Feb. '74, Lab. maj. 1,623)

LADYWOOD E. 40,394
67*A. B. Walden, Lab..... 14,818
R. Lawn, C........... 5,079
K. G. Hardeman, L.... 3,086
Lab. maj........... 9,739
(Feb. '74, Lab. maj. 8,962)

NORTHFIELD E. 77,593
68*R. J. Carter, Lab....... 27,435
J. B. L. Cadbury, C.... 16,838
D. Hains, L.......... 7,851
Mrs. E. A. Davenport,
Ind............... 359
D. W. Robinson,
Comm.............. 180
Lab. maj........... 10,597
(Feb. '74, Lab. maj. 8,529)

PERRY BARR E. 52,509
69*J. W. Rooker, Lab..... 18,291
J. R. Kinsey, C........ 15,087
K. J. Hovers, L....... 4,231
R. J. Warren, Nat.
Front.............. 826
T. L. Keen, Ind....... 86
Lab. maj........... 3,204
(Feb. '74, Lab. maj. 2,023)

SELLY OAK E. 62,757
70 T. Litterick, Lab....... 17,320
*H. E. Gurden, C...... 16,994
R. A. Grant, L........ 7,850
Lab. maj........... 326
(Feb. '74, C. maj. 2,882)

SMALL HEATH E. 51,405
71*D. H. Howell, Lab..... 19,703
R. O'Connor, C...... 5,648
D. Caney, L.......... 4,260
Lab. maj........... 14,055
(Feb. '74, Lab. maj. 11,878)

SPARKBROOK E. 49,683
72*Rt. Hon. R. S. G. Hat-
tersley, Lab......... 17,476
D. J. Savage, C........ 8,955
C. Williams, L........ 2,920
J. Molloy, Ind........ 548
Lab. maj........... 8,521
(Feb. '74, Lab. maj. 7,405)

STECHFORD E. 62,516
73*Rt. Hon. R. H. Jenkins,
Lab............... 23,075
D. J. Wedgwood, C... 11,152
G. A. Gopsill, L....... 5,860
Lab. maj........... 11,923
(Feb. '74, Lab. maj. 10,232)

YARDLEY E. 59,052
74*S. Tierney, Lab........ 20,834
D. M. Coombs, C..... 16,664
J. Aldridge, L......... 4,518
H. Challendar, Nat.
Front.............. 1,034
T. L. Keen, Ind....... 111
Lab. maj........... 4,170
(Feb. '74, Lab. maj. 1,947)

Bishop Auckland
E. 72,581
75*H. J. Boyden, Lab...... 27,181
D. W. Etheridge, C.... 16,086
D. L. Cobbold, L...... 8,168
Lab. maj........... 11,095
(Feb. '74, Lab. maj. 7,875)

Blaby
E. 65,073
76*N. Lawson, C......... 25,405
M. F. Fox, Lab......... 13,244
D. Inman, L......... 12,290
C. maj............. 12,161
(Feb. '74, C. maj. 12,298)

Blackburn
E. 54,213
77*Rt. Hon. Barbara Castle,
Lab............... 20,344
I. D. McGaw, C....... 12,692
F. J. Beetham, L....... 4,741
J. K. Read, Nat. Front. 1,758
Lab. maj............. 7,652
(Feb. '74, Lab. maj. 6,300)

Blackpool
NORTH E. 59,743
78*N. A. Miscampbell, Q.C.,
C............... 19,662
I. J. Taylor, Lab....... 14,195
G. Mulholland, L....... 7,750
C. maj............. 5,467
(Feb. '74, C. maj. 8,154)

SOUTH E. 57,951
79*P. A. R. Blaker, C..... 18,188
M. Atkins, Lab....... 12,967
E. E. Wynne, L....... 9,327
C. maj............. 5,221
(Feb. '74, C. maj. 8,091)

Blaydon
E. 59,908
80*R. E. Woof, Lab....... 23,743
A. A. Craig, C....... 10,277
P. Barker, L....... 7,439
Lab. maj............. 13,466
(Feb. '74, Lab. maj. 11,574)

Blyth
E. 74,462
81 J. Ryman, Lab....... 20,308
*E. J. Milne, Ind. Lab.. 20,230
J. W. Shipley, L....... 8,177
B. Griffiths, C....... 6,590
Lab. maj............. 78
(Feb. '74, Ind. Lab. maj. 6,140)

Bodmin
E. 55,485
82 R. A. Hicks, C....... 20,756
*P. A. Tyler, L......... 20,091
P. C. Knight, Lab....... 4,814
C. maj............. 665
(Feb. '74, L. maj. 9)

Bolsover
E. 51,880
83*D. E. Skinner, Lab..... 27,275
C. L. Sternberg, C....... 6,209
M. Taylor, L....... 5,176
Lab. maj............. 21,066
(Feb. '74, Lab. maj. 21,313)

Bolton
EAST E. 60,177
84*D. W. Young, Lab..... 21,569
B. J. Heddle, C....... 17,504
T. J. Akeroyd, L....... 5,792
G. Booth, Nat. Front.. 1,106
H. Smith, Ind....... 149
Lab. maj............. 4,065
(Feb. '74, Lab. maj. 1,613)

WEST E. 50,782
85 Mrs. W. A. Taylor, Lab. 16,967
*R. S. Redmond, C..... 16,061
P. S. Linney, L....... 5,127
W. Roberts, Nat. Front 1,070
Lab. maj............. 906
(Feb. '74, C. maj. 603)

Bootle
E. 64,236
86*S. Mahon, Lab....... 27,633
J. F. Burrows, C..... 10,743
Mrs. H. Fjortoft, L..... 4,266
R. Morris, Comm....... 516
Lab. maj............. 16,890
(Feb. '74, Lab. maj. 14,935)

Bosworth
E. 83,820
87*Hon. A. C. Butler, C... 28,490
M. G. M. Sloman, Lab. 28,188
M. J. Galton, L....... 12,082
C. maj............. 302
(Feb. '74, C. maj. 1,687)

Bothwell
E. 59,357
88*J. Hamilton, Lab....... 22,086
J. McCool, Scot. Nat... 11,138
D. Roser, C....... 8,125
T. Grieve, L....... 4,057
Lab. maj............. 10,948
(Feb. '74, Lab. maj. 9,601)

Bournemouth
EAST E. 57,010
89*J. H. Cordle, C....... 20,790
G. H. Musgrave, L..... 10,129
D. E. Lock, Lab....... 8,422
M. J. Hayes, Nat. Front 828
C. maj............. 10,661
(Feb. '74, C. maj. 9,314)

WEST E. 61,211
90*Rt. Hon. Sir J. B. Eden,
Bt.,............... 21,294
L. F. Bennett, Lab..... 10,566
T. D. G. Richards, L.. 10,166
C. maj............. 10,728
(Feb. '74, C. maj. 10,818)

Bradford
NORTH E. 66,135
91*B. T. Ford, Lab....... 22,841
H. P. Thompson, C... 14,252
A. G. Lishman, L....... 9,475
Lab. maj............. 8,589
(Feb. '74, Lab. maj. 6,617)

SOUTH E. 73,272
92*T. W. Torney, Lab.... 25,219
G. C. Littlewood, C... 16,964
C. J. Cawood, L....... 10,306
Lab. maj............. 8,255
(Feb. '74, Lab. maj. 7,653)

WEST E. 62,684
93*E. Lyons, Q.C., Lab.... 21,133
J. A. D. Wilkinson, C. 16,192
S. Harris, L....... 5,884
H. Smith, Ind......... 339
Lab. maj............. 4,941
(Feb. '74, Lab. maj. 2,219)

Braintree
E. 65,538
94*A. H. Newton, C....... 20,559
J. K. Kyle, Lab....... 19,469
R. G. Holme, L....... 12,004
C. maj............. 1,090
(Feb. '74, C. maj. 2,001)

Brecon and Radnor
E. 54,300
95*C. E. Roderick, Lab..... 18,622
L. H. Davies, C....... 15,610
N. K. Thomas, L....... 7,682
D. N. Gittins, P.C..... 2,300
Lab. maj............. 3,012
(Feb. '74, Lab. maj. 2,277)

Brent
EAST E. 63,168
96*R. Y. Freeson, Lab..... 20,481
M. Knowles, C....... 11,554
P. O'Brien, L....... 4,416
N. Lyons, Nat. Front.. 1,096
J. Curran, Ind....... 382
Lab. maj............. 8,927
(Feb. '74, Lab. maj. 7,622)

NORTH E. 72,122
97*R. R. Boyson, C....... 24,853
T. J. C. Goudie, Lab... 17,541
F. Harrison, L....... 8,158
Mrs. J. Cattanach, Nat.
Front............... 1,297
C. maj............. 7,312
(Feb. '74, C. maj. 7,941)

SOUTH E. 61,244
98*L. A. Pavitt, Lab....... 21,611
M. Lennox-Boyd, C... 10,558
J.Q.G.H. Rappaport, L. 3,929
J. Harrison-Broadley,
Nat. Front......... 1,388
Lab. maj............. 11,053
(Feb. '74, Lab. maj. 10,624)

Brentford and Isleworth
E. 71,199
99*B. J. Hayhoe, C......... 22,527
P. J. Walker, Lab....... 22,295
R. Blundell, L....... 6,019
T. W. Benford, Nat.
Front............... 1,362
C. maj............. 232
(Feb. '74, C. maj. 726)

Brentwood and Ongar
E. 58,363
100*R. A. McCrindle, C... 21,136
H. E. Miller, Lab....... 13,190
L. R. Wernick, L....... 10,725
C. maj............. 7,946
(Feb. '74, C. maj. 9,093)

Bridgwater
E. 69,755
101*T. J. King, C....... 23,850
Mrs. A. Mitchell, Lab. 17,663
J. H. G. Wyatt, L..... 12,077
S. R. Harrad, Ind....... 288
C. maj............. 6,187
(Feb. '74, C. maj. 8,044)

Bridlington
E. 65,759
102*Rt. Hon. R. F. Wood,
C............... 21,901
J. M. S. Cherry, L..... 11,795
A. A. W. Dix, Lab... 9,946
F. Day, Nat. Front..... 987
C. maj............. 10,106
(Feb. '74, C. maj. 10,996)

Brigg and Scunthorpe
E. 90,159
103*J. Ellis, Lab......... 28,929
J. P. S. Riddell, C..... 22,187
J. F. Harris, L....... 12,452
Lab. maj............. 6,742
(Feb. '74, Lab. maj. 3,074)

Brighouse and Spenborough
E. 63,645
104*G. C. Jackson, *Lab*. . . 21,964
G. W. Proudfoot, *C*. . . 19,787
J. R. Smithson, *L*. 8,265
Lab. maj. 2,177
(Feb. '74, Lab. maj. 1,546)

Brighton
KEMPTOWN E. 65,443
105*A. Bowden, M.B.E., C. . 21,725
D. H. Hobden, *Lab*. . . 19,060
S. Osborne, *L*. 6,214
R. Beaumont, *Ind*. . . . 155
J. Buckle, *Ind*. 125
B. Ralfe, *Ind*. 47
C. maj. 2,665
(Feb. '74, C. maj. 4,020)
PAVILION E. 57,351
106*Rt. Hon. J. Amery, *C*. 19,041
G. W. Humphrey, *Lab*.11,624
Mrs. D. Venables, *L*. 8,648
C. maj. 7,417
(Feb. '74, C. maj. 10,618)

Bristol
NORTH EAST E. 51,970
107*A. M. F. Palmer, *Lab*. . 19,647
P. Hills, *C*. 11,056
W. Watts-Miller, *L*. . . 6,303
Lab. maj. 8,591
(Feb. '74, Lab. maj. 6,087)
NORTH WEST E. 66,381
108 R. R. Thomas, *Lab*. . . 22,156
*M. J. McLaren, *C*. . . . 21,523
E. David, *L*. 8,914
Lab. maj. 633
(Feb. '74, C. maj. 650)
SOUTH E. 61,040
109*M. F. L. Cocks, *Lab*. . . 25,108
R. J. Kelleway, *C*. . . . 10,124
D. Burrows, *L*. 6,289
P. H. Gannaway, *Nat.*
Front. 798
Lab. maj. 14,984
(Feb. '74, Lab. maj. 13,167)
SOUTH EAST E. 69,427
110*Rt. Hon. A. N. Wedg-
wood Benn, *Lab*. 25,978
J. P. Godwin, *C*. 16,605
R. Wardle, *L*. 8,987
R. J. Bale, *Nat. Front*. 775
R. Goding, *Ind*. 457
P. Rowe, *Ind*. 79
Lab. maj. 9,373
(Feb. '74, Lab. maj. 7,912)
WEST E. 60,447
111*R. G. Cooke, *C*. 18,555
R. G. R. Stacey, *L*. . . 11,598
J. Malos, *Lab*. 9,372
C. maj. 6,957
(Feb. '74, C. maj. 8,064)

Bromsgrove and Redditch
E. 87,849
112*H. D. Miller, *C*. 31,153
T. A. G. Davis, *Lab*. . . 29,085
P. Kelway, *L*. 9,679
C. maj. 2,068
(Feb. '74, C. maj. 3,589)

Buckingham
E. 79,077
113*W. R. Benyon, *C*. 26,597
I. R. Maxwell, *Lab*. . . 23,679
S. B. Crooks, *L*. 12,707
C. maj. 2,918
(Feb. '74, C. maj. 3,123)

Burnley
E. 52,930
114*D. Jones, B.E.M., *Lab*. . 21,642
A. Pickup, *C*. 9,766
S. P. Mews, *L*. 8,119
Lab. maj. 11,876
(Feb. '74, Lab. maj. 9,840)

Burton
E. 67,801
115*I. J. Lawrence, *C*. 23,496
D. R. Hill, *Lab*. 21,398
K. Stevens, *L*. 7,969
C. maj. 2,098
(Feb. '74, C. maj. 3,303)

Bury and Radcliffe
E. 77,798
116 F. R. White, *Lab*. 26,430
*M. M. Fidler, *C*. 25,988
A. Benson, *L*. 10,463
Lab. maj. 442
(Feb. '74, C. maj. 345)

Bury St. Edmunds
E. 87,321
117*E. W. Griffiths, *C*. . . . 32,179
J. K. Stephenson, *Lab*. 21,097
Mrs. S. M. Hobday, *L*. 10,631
C. maj. 11,082
(Feb. '74, C. maj, 13,253)

Caernarvon
E. 42,508
118*D. Wigley, P.C. 14,624
E. J. Sherrington, *Lab*. 11,730
R. L. Harvey, *C*. 4,325
D. Williams, *L*. 3,690
P.C. maj. 2,894
(Feb. '74, P.C. maj. 1,728)

Caerphilly
E. 56,462
119*A. T. Evans, *Lab*. 24,161
P. J. S. Williams, P.C. 10,452
D. R. Dover, *C*. 4,897
N. H. Lewis, *L*. 3,184
Lab. maj. 13,709
(Feb. '74, Lab. maj. 12,882)

Caithness and Sutherland
E. 28,837
120*R. A. R. MacLennan,
Lab. 7,941
E. A. C. Sutherland,
Scot. Nat. 5,381
M. R. Burnett, *Lab*. . . 4,949
A. McQuarrie, *C*. 4,240
Lab. maj. 2,560
(Feb. '74, Lab. maj. 2,352)

Cambridge
E. 75,947
121*D. W. S. S. Lane, *C*. . 21,790
J. P. Curran, *Lab*. . . . 19,017
M. W. B. O'Loughlin,
L. 11,129
C. J. Curry, *Ind*. 885
C. maj. 2,773
(Feb. '74, C. maj. 4,676)

Cambridgeshire
E. 84,434
122*Rt. Hon. F. L. Pym,
M.C., *C*. 30,508
M. P. Farley, *Lab*. . . 17,853
S. R. Jakobi, *L*. 15,841
C. maj. 12,655
(Feb. '74, C. maj. 13,812)

Cannock
E. 56,572
123*G. E. Roberts, *Lab*. . . . 23,887
E. G. Hill, *C*. 11,665
E. Freeman, *L*. 7,459
Lab. maj. 12,222
(Feb. '74, Lab. maj. 11,064)

Canterbury
E. 85,718
124*D. L. Crouch, *C*. 31,002
M. F. Fuller, *Lab*. 16,247
Mrs. S. E. Goulden, *L*. 13,898
K. R. McKilliam,
Nat. Front. 1,096
C. maj. 14,755
(Feb. '74, C. maj. 17,041)

Cardiff
NORTH E. 43,858
125*I. Grist, *C*. 13,480
J. Collins, *Lab*. 11,479
M. E. German, *L*. 5,728
P. Richards, P.C. 1,464
C. maj. 2001
(Feb. '74, C. maj. 3,853)
NORTH WEST E. 43,787
126*M. H. A. Roberts, *C*. . 15,652
C. A. Blewett, *Lab*. . . 11,319
H. J. O'Brien, *L*. 6,322
C. P. Palfrey, P.C. 1,278
C. maj. 4,333
(Feb. '74, C. maj. 6,013)
SOUTH EAST E. 57,299
127*Rt. Hon. L. J. Calla-
ghan, *Lab*. 21,074
S. Terlezki, *C*. 10,356
C. Bailey, *L*. 8,006
K. Bush, P.C. 983
B. C. D. Harris, *Ind*. . 75
Lab. maj. 10,718
(Feb. '74, Lab. maj. 7,146)
WEST E. 52,083
128*Rt. Hon. T. G. Thomas,
Lab. 18,153
W. F. N. Dunn, *C*. . . 11,481
R. M. James, *L*. 4,669
D. Hughes, P.C. 2,008
Lab. maj. 6,672
(Feb. '74, Lab. maj. 3,346)

Cardigan
E. 43,052
129*G. W. Howells, *L*. 14,612
D. E. Morgan, *Lab*. . . 12,202
C. G. Davies, P.C. 4,583
D. J. D. Williams C. . . 3,275
L. maj. 2,410
(Feb. '74, L. maj. 2,476)

Carlisle
E. 52,319
130*R. H. Lewis, *Lab*. 21,079
D. G. P. Bloomer, *C*. 14,825
F. Phillips, *L*. 5,306
Lab. maj. 6,254
(Feb. '74, Lab. maj. 4,980)

Carlton
E. 71,779
131*P. W. Holland, *C*. 24,638
D. Pettitt, *Lab*. 20,019
D. L. Lange, *L*. 9,859
C. Marriott, *Nat.*
Front. 1,273
C. maj. 4,619
(Feb. '74, C. maj. 7,158)

Carmarthen
E. 60,402
132 G. R. Evans, P.C..... 23,325
*G. G. Jones, Lab...... 19,685
D. R. Owen-Jones, L. 5,393
R. A. Hayward, C.... 2,962
E. B. Jones, Ind...... 342
P.C. maj.......... 3,640
(Feb. '74, Lab. maj. 3)

Carshalton
E. 66,856
133*Rt. Hon. L. R. Carr, C. 22,538
B. F. Atherton, Lab... 18,840
Mrs. H. M. G. Small-
bone, L........... 8,272
C. maj........... 3,698
(Feb. '74, C. maj. 5,690)

Cheadle
E. 65,558
134*T. Normanton, T.D., C. 25,863
C. F. Green, L...... 18,687
P. D. Castle, Lab..... 8,048
C. maj........... 7,176
(Feb. '74, C. maj. 6,224)

Chelmsford
E. 80,042
135*N. A. F. St. John-
Stevas, C.......... 26,334
S. G. Mole, L........ 22,332
J. T. Acklaw, Lab..... 14,711
C. maj........... 4,002
(Feb. '74, C. maj. 6,631)

Chelsea
E. 64,554
136 N. P. Scott, M.B.E., C. 19,674
G. A. Colerick, Lab... 6,507
N. L. Clarke, L....... 5,758
R. E. Byron, Ind..... 321
C. maj........... 13,167
(Feb. '74, C. maj. 15,308)

Cheltenham
E. 62,746
137 C. G. Irving, C....... 21,691
F. C. Rodger, L....... 13,237
F. C. Inglis, Lab...... 12,134
C. maj........... 8,454
(Feb. '74, C. maj. 5,912)

Chertsey and Walton
E. 67,527
138*G. E. Pattie, C....... 25,151
N. J. Brady, Lab...... 14,847
T. W. Robinson, L.... 9,194
H. J. Redgrave, Ind.. 424
C. maj........... 10,304
(Feb. '74, C. maj. 11,963)

Chesham and Amersham
E. 63,385
139*I. H. J. L. Gilmour, C.. 25,078
D. A. Stoddart, L..... 14,091
J. R. Poston, Lab..... 10,325
C. maj........... 10,987
(Feb. '74, C. maj. 10,416)

Chester
E. 69,605
140*Hon. P. H. Morrison,
C................ 23,095
J. Crawford, Lab..... 18,477
R. M. Green, L....... 10,907
C. maj........... 4,618
(Feb. '74, C. maj. 6,768)

Chesterfield
E. 71,210
141*Rt. Hon. E. G. Varley,
Lab.............. 30,953
J. D. Taylor, C....... 13,393
M. W. Brown, L..... 7,349
Lab. maj.......... 17,560
(Feb. '74, Lab. maj. 15,396)

Chester-le-Street
E. 68,570
142*G. H. Radice, Lab.... 33,511
D. McCourt, L...... 9,233
R. L. Ditchburn, C... 8,268
Lab. maj.......... 24,278
(Feb. '74, Lab. maj. 18,726)

Chichester
E. 69,768
143 R. A. Nelson, C...... 26,942
G. A. Jeffs, L........ 15,601
N. J. M. Smith, Lab.. 8,767
C. maj........... 11,341
(Feb. '74, C. maj. 11,413)

Chingford
E. 56,984
144*N. B. Tebbit, C....... 19,022
P. F. Tinnion, Lab.... 14,377
D. A. Nicholson, L... 8,438
C. maj........... 4,645
(Feb. '74, C. maj. 5,683)

Chippenham
E. 67,852
145*D. E. Awdry, T.D., C.. 22,721
R. E. J. Banks, L..... 20,972
J. Whiles, Lab........ 9,396
E. J. John, Ind........ 278
C. maj........... 1,749
(Feb. '74, C. maj. 3,092)

Chipping Barnet
E. 56,487
146*Rt. Hon. R. Maudling,
C................ 19,661
J. A. D. Mills, Lab.... 11,795
Miss N. M. Wyn-Ellis,
L.............. 8,884
R. Cole, Nat. Front . 1,207
C. maj........... 7,866
(Feb. '74, C. maj. 9,911)

Chislehurst
E. 53,699
147*R. E. Sims, C....... 18,926
A. H. MacDonald,
Lab.............. 15,032
J. M. Crowley, L..... 6,900
C. maj........... 3,894
(Feb. '74, C. maj. 5,493)

Chorley
E. 76,218
148*G. Rodgers, Lab....... 27,290
G. B. Porter, C....... 24,577
Mrs. N. Orrell, L.... 9,831
H. Smith, Ind........ 185
Lab. maj.......... 2,713
(Feb. '74, Lab. maj. 405)

Christchurch and Lymington
E. 55,299
149*R. J. Adley, C....... 23,728
J. Madeley, L........ 9,838
L. K. Hatts, Lab...... 7,759
C. maj........... 13,890
(Feb. '74, C. maj. 14,634)

Cirencester and Tewkesbury
E. 80,408
150*Hon. N. Ridley, C.... 28,930
R. G. Otter, L....... 18,770
J. R. Booth, Lab..... 13,973
C. maj........... 10,160
(Feb. '74, C. maj. 10,201)

City of London and Westminster South
E. 52,170
151*C. S. Tugendhat, C.... 14,350
P. J. Turner, Lab..... 8,589
T. G. Underwood, L. 4,122
D. Baxter, Nat. Front. 686
C. maj........... 5,761
(Feb. '74, C. maj. 8,247)

Cleveland and Whitby
E. 60,674
152*L. Brittan, C........ 19,973
B. J. Pimlott, Lab..... 18,445
G. G. Watson, L..... 7,795
C. maj........... 1,528
(Feb. '74, C. maj. 3,642)

Clitheroe
E. 52,086
153*A. D. Walder, E.R.D.,
C................ 19,643
B. W. McColgan, Lab. 12,775
C. W. Roberts, L..... 8,503
C. maj........... 6,868
(Feb. '74, C. maj. 8,528)

Coatbridge and Airdrie
E. 59,903
154*J. Dempsey, Lab...... 23,034
D. R. M. Hill, Scot.
Nat............ 12,466
J. Love, C........... 7,683
A. Smith, L......... 1,446
Lab. maj.......... 10,568
(Feb. '74, Lab. maj. 11,783)

Colchester
E. 81,836
155*P. A. F. Buck, Q.C., C.. 27,693
D. Whytock, Lab..... 22,193
D. Christian, L....... 12,421
C. maj........... 5,500
(Feb. '74, C. maj. 6,862)

Colne Valley
E. 60,774
156*R. S. Wainwright, L... 21,997
D. G. Clark, Lab..... 20,331
K. E. Davy, C....... 7,337
L. maj........... 1,666
(Feb. '74, L. maj. 719)

Consett
E. 590,14
157*D. J. Watkins, Lab.... 27,123
M. Lycett, C......... 7,677
J. Gillinder, L....... 5,695
Lab. maj.......... 19,446
(Feb. '74, Lab. maj. 18,343)

Conway
E. 51,730
158*I. W. P. Roberts, C... 15,614
Rev. D. B. Rees, Lab. 12,808
D. T. Jones, L....... 6,344
M. Farmer P.C....... 4,668
C. maj........... 2,806
(Feb '74, C. maj. 4,549)

Cornwall North
E. 51,779
159*J. W. Pardoe, L....... 21,368
G. A. Neale, C........ 17,512
R. Tremlett, Lab.... 2,663
R. J. Bridgwater, Ind.. 148
L. maj............ 3,856
(Feb. '74, L. maj. 8,729)

Coventry
NORTH EAST E. 63,605
160*G. M. Park, Lab...... 26,489
I. Clarke, C.......... 10,520
R. Dredge, L........ 6,846
A. Wilkins, Ind...... 352
J. Hosey, Comm...... 309
Lab. maj............ 15,969
(Feb. '74, Lab. maj. 15,427)
NORTH WEST E. 49,247
161*M. Edelman, Lab...... 19,205
Hon. J. B. Guinness,
C................. 11,717
Mrs. P. Newnham, L. 5,798
Mrs. A. L. Whittaker,
Ind............... 313
Lab. maj............ 7,488
(Feb. '74, Lab. maj. 6,658)
SOUTH EAST E. 50,818
162*W. Wilson, Lab...... 20,771
C. Hannington, C... 8,640
D. Woodcock, L..... 4,952
Lab. maj............ 12,131
(Feb. '74, Lab. maj. 10,751)
SOUTH WEST E. 67,841
163*Mrs. A. Wise, Lab.... 23,225
J. R. Jeffrey, C...... 21,107
N. B. Chapple, L..... 8,579
R. Rickard, Nat. Front 822
T. L. Keen, Ind...... 144
Lab. maj............ 2,118
(Feb. '74, Lab. maj. 513)

Crewe
E. 59,227
164*Hon. Mrs. G. P. Dun-
woody, Lab........ 21,534
J. G. Park, C........ 14,279
E. Richardson, L..... 7,559
Lab. maj............ 7,255
(Feb. '74, Lab. maj. 5,123)

Crosby
E. 78,605
165*Rt. Hon. R. G. Page,
M.B.E., C........ 29,764
Miss M. J. Hignett,
Lab.............. 17,589
A. Hill, L.......... 10,429
C. maj............ 12,175
(Feb. '74, C. maj. 15,570)

Croydon
CENTRAL E. 66,746
166*J. E. M. Moore, C.... 20,390
D. Winnick, Lab.... 20,226
I. H. Maxwell, L..... 7,834
C. maj............ 164
(Feb. '74, C. maj. 1,314)
NORTH EAST E. 58,306
167*B. B. Weatherill, C.... 17,938
D. H. Simpson, Lab.. 15,787
P. T. Streeter, L..... 7,228
W. Stringer, Ind...... 451
C. maj............ 2,151
(Feb. '74, C. maj. 3,820)

NORTH WEST E. 55,176
168*R. G. Taylor, C....... 16,035
S. J. Boden, Lab...... 14,556
W. H. Pitt, L........ 6,563
P. Holland, Nat. Front. 1,049
C. maj............ 1,479
(Feb. '74, C. maj. 3,071)

SOUTH E. 60,090
169*W. G. Clark, C...... 25,703
D. Nunneley, L..... 11,514
D. W. Keene, Lab.... 7,203
C. maj............ 14,189
(Feb. '74, C. maj. 15,867)

Dagenham
E. 70,004
170*J. Parker, C.B.E., Lab... 29,678
A. G. Hamilton, C... 7,684
G. Poole, L......... 7,564
G. C. Wake, Comm... 569
Lab. maj............ 21,994
(Feb. '74, Lab. maj. 23,490)

Darlington
E. 62,955
171*E. J. Fletcher, Lab. ... 21,334
B. H. Hord, C....... 17,620
P. Freitag, L........ 7,882
Lab. maj............ 3,714
(Feb. '74, Lab. maj. 2,069)

Dartford
E. 57,038
172*Rt. Hon. S. Irving, Lab. 20,817
G. F. J. Bright, C..... 15,331
G. Dunk, L.......... 6,606
R. H. Aldous, Nat.
Front............. 939
Lab. maj............ 5,486
(Feb. '74, Lab. maj. 3,654)

Darwen
E. 70,611
173*C. Fletcher-Cooke, Q.C.,
C................. 23,577
D. N. Campbell-
Savours, Lab....... 17,926
A. Cooper, L........ 12,572
C. maj............ 5,651
(Feb. '74, C. maj. 9,310)

Daventry
E. 83,253
174*A. A. Jones, C........ 29,801
D. Forwood, Lab..... 20,739
D. Cassidy, L........ 13,640
C. maj............ 9,062
(Feb. '74, C. maj. 9,749)

Dearne Valley
E. 63,265
175*E. Wainwright, Lab... 33,315
Lord Irwin, C........ 6,046
P. Hargreaves, L...... 5,588
Lab. maj............ 27,269
(Feb. '74, Lab. maj. 26,854)

Denbigh
E. 63,506
176*W. G. O. Morgan,
Q.C., C.......... 18,751
D. L. Williams, L.... 14,200
P. P. Flynn, Lab...... 9,824
I. W. Jones, P.C..... 5,754
C. maj............ 4,551
(Feb. '74, C. maj. 6,015)

Deptford
E. 61,210
177*Rt. Hon. J. E. Silkin,
Lab.............. 21,145
C. H. Cross, C...... 8,111
M. M. Steele, L...... 4,931
R. Edmonds, Nat.
Front............. 1,731
Lab. maj............ 13,034
(Feb. '74, Lab. maj. 11,629)

Derby
NORTH E. 82,697
178*P. Whitehead, Lab..... 26,960
D. J. Penfold, C...... 22,767
M. D. Peel, L........ 10,595
H. Smith, Ind........ 242
Lab. maj............ 4,193
(Feb. '74, Lab. maj. 1,293)
SOUTH E. 74,342
179*W. H. Johnson, Lab.... 26,342
A. J. Bussell, C...... 17,010
R. Palmer, L........ 7,520
A. S. Ashby, Ind..... 793
Lab. maj............ 9,332
(Feb. '74, Lab. maj. 7,143)

Derbyshire
NORTH EAST E. 68,869
180*T. H. Swain, Lab..... 25,234
J. C. Ramsden, C.... 14,997
C. Cook, L.......... 10,336
Lab. maj............ 10,237
(Feb. '74, Lab. maj. 7,282)
SOUTH EAST E. 53,739
181*P. L. Rost, C........ 18,856
R. J. Madeley, Lab... 17,851
H. Warschauer, L..... 6,404
C. maj............ 1,005
(Feb. '74, C. maj. 3,035)
WEST E. 49,142
182*J. S. R. Scott-Hopkins,
C................. 18,468
P. M. Worboys, L..... 10,622
D. A. Townsend, Lab. 9,456
C. maj............ 7,846
(Feb. '74, C. maj. 8,460)

Devizes
E. 77,793
183*Hon. C. A. Morrison,
C................. 24,842
V. E. Finlayson, Lab.. 17,821
J. B. Ainslie, L....... 15,851
C. maj............ 7,021
(Feb. '74, C. maj. 9,898)

Devon
NORTH E. 73,598
184*Rt. Hon. J. J. Thorpe,
L................. 28,209
A. Speller, C........ 21,488
Mrs. A. J. Golant, Lab. 8,356
F. Hansford-Miller,
Ind............... 568
L. maj............ 6,721
(Feb. '74, L. maj. 11,072)
WEST E. 57,431
185*P. M. Mills, C........ 22,594
M. A. Pinney, L...... 16,665
J. B. H. Duffin, Lab... 5,899
C. maj............ 5,929
(Feb. '74, C. maj. 5,268)

Dewsbury
E. 61,508
186*D. Ginsburg, Lab...... 20,378
Mrs. M. Wood, C.... 13,477
A. Allsop, L........ 10,991
Lab. maj............ 6,901
(Feb. '74, Lab. maj. 5,412)

Doncaster
E. 59,464
187*H. Walker, Lab...... 22,177
T. Wilkinson, C..... 14,747
W. J. Davison, L..... 6,336
Lab. maj........... 7,430
(Feb. '74, Lab. maj. 5,476)

Don Valley
E. 88,777
188*R. Kelley, Lab........ 41,187
P. J. Le Bosquet, C.... 13,767
E. Simpson, L........ 10,161
Lab. maj........... 27,420
(Feb. '74, Lab. maj. 27,945)

Dorking
E. 58,955
189*Sir G. E. Sinclair,
C.M.G., O.B.E., C.... 22,403
G. S. A. Andrews, L.. 12,098
Miss J. Chapman, Lab. 9,714
C. maj........... 10,305
(Feb. '74, C. maj. 10,313)

Dorset
NORTH E. 71,325
190*D. P. James, M.B.E.,
D.S.C., C.......... 28,891
P. G. Watkins, Lab.... 20,350
T. G. Jones, Lab...... 7,245
C. maj........... 8,541
(Feb. '74, C. maj. 6,883)
SOUTH E. 70,416
191*E. M. King, C........ 24,351
A. Chedzoy, Lab..... 17,652
C. Sandy, L.......... 11,075
C. maj........... 6,699
(Feb. '74, C. maj. 8,615)
WEST E. 53,569
192*J. W. Spicer, C...... 20,517
R. M. Angus, L....... 11,832
P. J. Dawe, Lab...... 9,350
C. maj........... 8,685
(Feb. '74, C. maj. 7,451)

Dover and Deal
E. 74,704
193*P. W. I. Rees, Q.C., C.. 25,647
L. J. A. Bishop, Lab.... 23,353
R. S. Young, L....... 9,767
C. maj........... 2,294
(Feb. '74, C. maj. 4,850)

Down
NORTH E. 93,604
194*J. A. Kilfedder, U.U.U. 40,996
K. Jones, Alliance..... 9,973
Maj. W. Brownlow,
U.P.N.I......... 6,037
U.U.U. maj......... 31,023
(Feb. '74, U.U.U. maj. 16,226)
SOUTH E. 91,354
195 Rt. Hon. J. E. Powell,
M.B.E., U.U.U...... 33,614
S. Hollywood,
S.D.L.P........... 30,047
G. O'Hanlon, Rep..... 2,327
D. Vipond, Ind...... 152
U.U.U. maj......... 3,567
(Feb. '74, U.U.U. maj. 5,602)

Dudley
EAST E. 60,381
196*J. W. Gilbert, Lab..... 23,621
J. M. Taylor, C..... 11,430
G. Hopkins, L........ 5,003
C. Knott, Nat. Front.. 1,171
Lab. maj........... 12,191
(Feb. '74, Lab. maj. 11,622)

WEST E. 74,746
197*C. B. Phipps, Lab..... 28,740
L. E. Smith, C....... 20,215
A. Martin, L......... 7,259
Lab. maj........... 8,525
(Feb. '74, Lab. maj. 4,669)

Dulwich
E. 67,542
198*Rt. Hon. S. C. Silkin,
Q.C., Lab.......... 21,790
E. Morley, C....... 14,331
W. H. Pearson, L.... 7,866
Lab. maj........... 7,459
(Feb. '74, Lab. maj. 5,341)

Dumfries
E. 61,856
199*H. S. P. Monro, C.... 18,386
J. F. Wheatley, Lab... 12,558
L. A. B. Whitley, Scot.
Nat........... 12,542
A. Sinclair, L....... 3,961
C. maj........... 5,828
(Feb. '74, C. maj. 8,968)

Dunbartonshire
CENTRAL E. 49,357
200*H. McCartney, Lab.... 15,837
A. C. W. Aitken, Scot.
Nat........... 11,452
M. W. Hirst, C....... 6,792
J. Reid, Comm...... 3,417
J. E. Cameron, L.... 1,895
Lab. maj........... 4,385
(Feb. 74, Lab. maj. 6,664)
EAST E. 61,788
201 Mrs. M. A. Bain, Scot.
Nat........... 15,551
*J. S. B. Henderson, C.. 15,529
E. F.McGarry, Lab.... 15,122
J. A. Thompson, L.... 3,636
Scot. Nat. maj...... 22
(Feb. '74, Scot. Nat. maj. 3,676)
WEST E. 51,943
202*I. Campbell, Lab...... 15,511
A. Murray, Scot. Nat. 13,697
R. R. MacDonald, C. 9,421
J. D. Murricane, L.... 2,029
Lab. maj........... 1,814
(Feb. '74, Lab. maj. 2,609)

Dundee
EAST E. 63,152
203*R. G. Wilson, Scot.
Nat........... 22,120
G. Machin, Lab...... 15,137
W. L. Walker, C.... 7,784
C. Brodie, L......... 1,302
Scot. Nat. maj...... 6,983
(Feb. '74, Scot. Nat. maj. 2,966)
WEST E. 63,916
204*P. M. Doig, Lab...... 19,480
J. Fairlie, Scot. Nat... 16,678
C. G. Findlay, C..... 8,769
R. Hewett, L........ 2,195
H. McLevy, Comm... 381
Lab. maj........... 2,802
(Feb. '74, Lab. maj. 6,448)

Dunfermline
E. 60,679
205*A. Hunter, Lab....... 18,470
Miss A. C. Cameron,
Scot. Nat........ 13,179
K. MacLeod, C..... 10,611
M. D. H. Valentine, L.. 3,800
Lab. maj........... 5,291
(Feb. '74, Lab. maj. 4,410)

Durham
E. 74,711
206*W. M. Hughes, Lab... 31,305
D. L. Conway, C..... 13,189
P. A. J. Heesom, L.... 9,011
Lab. maj........... 18,116
(Feb. '74, Lab. maj. 15,203)

Durham North West
E. 61,283
207*E. Armstrong, Lab..... 27,953
M. J. B. Cookson, C. 9,197
J. K. Forster, L....... 6,418
Lab. maj........... 18,756
(Feb. '74, Lab. maj. 17,461)

Ealing North
E. 73,898
208*W. J. Molloy, Lab.... 24,574
G. K. Dickens, C..... 21,652
C. S. Phillips, L...... 8,351
Lab. maj........... 2,922
(Feb. '74, Lab. maj. 2,448)

Easington
E. 63,815
209*J. D. Dormand, Lab... 28,984
J. S. Smailes, C....... 8,047
N. J. Scaggs, L....... 7,005
Lab. maj........... 20,937
(Feb. '74, Lab. maj. 20,530)

Eastbourne
E. 74,697
210*I. R. E. Gow, C...... 30,442
G. H. Millar, L....... 14,417
L. Caine, Lab........ 10,830
C. maj........... 16,025
(Feb. '74, C. maj. 7,475)

East Grinstead
E. 55,602
211*G. Johnson Smith, C... 22,035
P. Hayden, L....... 12,755
D. W. J. Blake, Lab... 6,648
C. maj........... 9,280
(Feb. '74, C. maj. 8,577)

East Kilbride
E. 65,799
212*M. S. Miller, Lab..... 21,810
G. S. Murray, Scot.
Nat............ 19,106
G. W. Parvin, C..... 8,513
D. Miller, L........ 2,644
Lab. maj........... 2,704
(Feb. '74, Lab. maj. 7,968)

Eastleigh
E. 75,826
213*D. E. C. Price, C...... 26,869
E. A. Presman, Lab.... 19,054
G. D. Johnson, L..... 13,832
C. maj........... 7,815
(Feb. '74, C. maj. 10,110)

Ebbw Vale
E. 37,640
214*Rt. Hon. M. M. Foot,
Lab............ 21,226
A. Donaldson, L..... 3,167
J. P. Evans, C....... 2,153
G. ap Robert, P.C.... 2,101
Lab. maj........... 18,059
(Feb. '74, Lab. maj. 15,664)

Eccles
E. 57,549
215*L. Carter-Jones, Lab... 22,328
R. J. Dunn, C......... 13,062
Mrs. A. M. Collier, L.   6,170
T. E. Keenan, Comm.   348
Lab. maj........... 9,266
(Feb. '74, Lab. maj. 7,786)

Edinburgh
CENTRAL E. 40,956
216*R. F. Cook, Lab..... 11,129
P. Jones, C.......... 7,176
A. W. S. Rae, Scot.
Nat................ 6,866
C. B. H. Scott, L..... 2,463
Lab. maj........... 3,953
(Feb. '74, Lab. maj. 961)

EAST E. 57,460
217*G. S. Strang, Lab..... 19,669
G. C. MacDougall,
Scot. Nat........... 11,213
A. M. Hogg, C...... 10,111
G. N. Dalzell, L...... 2,578
Mrs. I. Swann, Comm.   213
Lab. maj........... 8,456
(Feb. '74, Lab. maj. 5,549)

LEITH E. 39,407
218*Rt. Hon. R. K. Murray,
Q.C., Lab........ 11,708
W. R. V. Percy, C..... 8,263
R. Scott, Scot. Nat.   7,688
A. J. H. Squair, L..... 1,836
Lab. maj........... 3,445
(Feb. '74, Lab. maj. 721)

NORTH E. 47,215
219*A. M. Fletcher, C...... 12,856
M. J. O'Neill, Lab..... 8,465
J. Lynch, Scot. Nat.   7,681
M. MacDonald, L...... 3,677
C. maj............. 4,391
(Feb. '74, C. maj. 7,013)

PENTLANDS E. 54,955
220*M. L. Rifkind, C...... 14,083
G. Foulkes, Lab...... 12,826
J.   Hutchison,   Scot.
Nat................ 10,189
S. P. Ross-Smith, L.   4,411
C. maj............. 1,257
(Feb. '74, C. maj. 4,602)

SOUTH E. 56,154
221*A. M. C. Hutchison, C. 14,962
Mrs. C. Haddow, Lab. 11,736
R.   J.   Shirley,   Scot.
Nat................ 9,034
N. L. Gordon, L...... 5,921
C. maj............. 3,226
(Feb. '74, C. maj. 6,381)

WEST E. 52,569
222 Lord James Douglas-
Hamilton, C...... 15,354
W. J. Taylor, Lab.... 10,152
Mrs. C. M. Moore,
Scot. Nat........... 8,135
D. C. E. Gorrie, L...... 6,606
C. maj............. 5,202
(Feb. '74, C. maj. 8,477)

Edmonton
E. 65,476
223*T. E. Graham, Lab..... 20,229
J. Attwood, C....... 13,401
J. Dawnay, L........ 5,699
D. J. Bruce, Nat. Front 1,895
Lab. maj........... 6,828
(Feb. '74, Lab. maj. 5,723)

Enfield North
E. 67,818
224*B. Davies, Lab....... 20,880
C. de H. Parkinson, C. 16,087
Mrs. S. Curtis, L..... 9,526
R. Burton, Nat. Front 1,330
Lab. maj........... 4,793
(Feb. '74, Lab. maj. 3,416)

Epping Forest
E. 64,055
225*J. A. Biggs-Davison, C. 22,392
S. J. Palfreman, Lab... 15,618
D. F. J. Wood, L..... 8,952
C. maj............. 6,774
(Feb. '74, C. maj. 8,167)

Epsom and Ewell
E. 80,597
226*Rt. Hon. Sir P. A. G.
Rawlinson, Q.C., C.. 32,109
D. J. H. Griffiths, L.... 15,819
N. J. Kearney, Lab.... 11,471
C. maj............. 16,290
(Feb. '74, C. maj. 16,924)

Erith and Crayford
E. 60,595
227*A. J. Wellbeloved, Lab.. 22,670
M. MacDonald, C.... 14,203
T. Hibbert, L........ 7,423
Lab. maj........... 8,467
(Feb. '74, Lab. maj. 7,081)

Esher
E. 47,572
228*D. C. M. Mather, C.... 19,741
C. Welchman, L...... 8,881
A. G. Hudson, Lab.... 6,729
C. maj............. 10,860
(Feb. '74, C. maj. 10,715)

Essex South East
E. 76,013
229*Sir B. R. Braine, C...... 27,348
D. B. Jones, Lab...... 18,638
A. Morris, L......... 10,049
C. maj............. 8,710
(Feb. '74, C. maj. 9,265)

Eton and Slough
E. 63,813
230*Miss J. Lestor, Lab.... 22,238
S. Dolland, C........ 14,575
P. Goldenberg, L...... 8,213
A. P. Coniam, Nat.
Front............. 1,241
J. Renton, Ind........ 120
Lab. maj........... 7,663
(Feb. '74, Lab. maj. 6,891)

Exeter
E. 67,184
231*J. G. Hannam, C....... 21,970
F. K. Taylor, Lab..... 19,622
D. J. Morrish, L...... 12,342
C. maj............. 2,348
(Feb. '74, C. maj. 5,076)

Eye
E. 65,710
232*Sir J. H. Harrison, Bt.,
T.D., C............ 22,387
D. Robinson, L...... 14,530
R. Bushby, Lab...... 13,948
C. maj............. 7,857
(Feb. '74, C. maj. 7,675)

Falmouth and Camborne
E. 66,921
233*W. D. Mudd, C....... 23,950
M. G. Dalling, Lab... 18,094
E. Sara, L........... 6,428
A. G. S. T. Davey, Ind.
L................ 2,246
C. maj............. 5,856
(Feb. '74, C. maj. 4,264)

Fareham
E. 57,330
234*R. F. B. Bennett, V.R.D.,
C................ 19,053
P. Smith, L......... 14,605
B. R. Townsend, Lab. 8,153
W. P. Boulden, Ind... 1,727
R. M. Doughty, Nat.
Front............. 617
C. maj............. 4,448
(Feb. '74, C. maj. 7,877)

Farnham
E. 62,738
235*Rt. Hon. M. V. Mac-
millan, C......... 23,885
P. Davies, L........ 15,626
Miss H. C. Hodge,
Lab............... 8,305
C. maj............. 8,259
(Feb. '74, C. maj. 6,462)

Farnworth
E. 70,565
236*J. F. H. Roper, Lab.... 28,184
R. H. Shepherd, C.... 13,489
Mrs. M. P. Rothwell,
L................. 11,059
Lab. maj........... 14,695
(Feb. '74, Lab. maj. 12,637)

Faversham
E. 76,000
237*R. D. Moate, C....... 25,087
M. Freedman, Lab.... 22,210
P. J. Morgan, L...... 10,979
C. maj............. 2,877
(Feb. '74, C. maj. 5,407)

Feltham and Heston
E. 78,983
238*R. W. Kerr, Lab...... 26,611
R. P. Ground, C...... 17,464
J. A. Quinn, L....... 7,554
Mrs. J. M. Reid, Nat.
Front............. 1,984
Lab. maj........... 9,147
(Feb. '74, Lab. maj. 8,055)

Fermanagh and S. Tyrone
E. 71,343
239 M. F. Maguire, Ind.... 32,795
*Rt. Hon. H. W. West,
U.U.U.......... 30,285
A. J. Evans, Ind...... 185
Ind. maj........... 2,510
(Feb. '74, U.U.U. maj. 10,629)

Fife
CENTRAL E. 58,402
240*W. W. Hamilton, Lab. 22,400
D.   V.   Livingstone,
Scot. Nat........... 14,414
P. Clarke, C......... 5,308
A. Maxwell, Comm... 1,040
Lab. maj........... 7,986
(Feb. '74, Lab. maj. 14,094)

EAST E. 56,453
241*Sir J. E. Gilmour, Bt.,
D.S.O., T.D., C..... 16,116
J. Braid, Scot. Nat. ... 13,202
Mrs. H. Liddell, Lab.. 7,040
D. Docherty, L...... 5,247
C. maj........... 2,914
(Feb. '74, C. maj. 12,579)

Finchley
E. 53,933
242*Rt. Hon. Mrs. M. H.
Thatcher, C........ 16,498
M. J. O'Connor, Lab. 12,587
L. S. Brass, L....... 7,384
Mrs. J. Godfrey, Nat.
Front............ 993
C. maj........... 3,911
(Feb. '74, C. maj. 5,978)

Flint
EAST E. 69,273
243*S. B. Jones, Lab..... 27,002
M. J. A. Penston, C. 17,416
R. Fairley, L........ 8,986
F. Evans, P.C....... 1,779
Lab. maj......... 9,586
(Feb. '74, Lab. maj. 8,852)
WEST E. 64,302
244*Sir A. J. C. Meyer, Bt.,
C............ 20,054
N. B. Harries, Lab... 15,234
P. J. Brighton, L..... 10,881
N. Taylor, P.C...... 2,306
C. maj........... 4,820
(Feb. '74, C. maj. 7,142)

Folkestone and Hythe
E. 64,714
245*A. P. Costain, C..... 20,930
B. W. Budd, Q.C., L... 12,488
M. J. S. Butler, Lab... 11,639
H. Button, Ind...... 265
C. maj........... 8,442
(Feb. '74, C. maj. 8,510)

Fulham
E. 58,303
246*Rt. Hon. R. M. M.
Stewart, C.H., Lab... 20,616
M. Stevens, C....... 15,295
G. A. Dowden, L..... 4,577
J. Cordrey, Nat. Front. 855
Lab. maj......... 5,321
(Feb. '74, Lab. maj. 3,549)

Fylde
NORTH E. 74,799
247*W. Clegg, C........ 29,661
H. J. Berkeley, Lab... 12,522
A. Perry, L......... 11,254
C. maj........... 17,139
(Feb. '74, C. maj. 19,658)
SOUTH E. 90,861
248*E. L. Gardner, Q.C., C.. 37,193
A. Lawson, L........ 14,527
T. A. Dillon, Lab..... 13,724
C. maj........... 22,666
(Feb. '74, C. maj. 25,379)

Gainsborough
E. 61,749
249*M. R. Kimball, C..... 19,163
R. B. Blackmore, L... 15,195
T. J. Lansbury, Lab... 11,797
C. maj........... 3,968
(Feb. '74, C. maj. 6,210)

Galloway
E. 39,407
250 G. H. Thompson, Scot.
Nat............ 12,242
K. A. Ross, C....... 12,212
D. R. Hannay, L..... 3,181
T. G. Fulton, Lab.... 2,742
Scot. Nat. maj..... 30
(Feb. '74, C. maj. 4,008)

Gateshead
EAST E. 63,496
251*B. Conlan, Lab...... 27,620
R. A. Ryder, C...... 10,021
K. A. Buckingham, L. 6,998
Lab. maj......... 17,599
(Feb. '74, Lab. maj. 15,299)
WEST E. 30,768
252*J. R. Horam, Lab.... 13,859
P. Brown, C........ 4,432
Mrs. K. Stoddart, L... 1,909
Lab. maj......... 9,427
(Feb. '74, Lab. maj. 8,467)

Gillingham
E. 62,099
253*F. F. A. Burden, C. ... 19,042
H. G. N. Clother, Lab. 15,046
T. Jones, L......... 12,131
S. Campbell, Nat.
Front............ 922
C. maj........... 3,996
(Feb. '74, C. maj. 5,882)

Glasgow
CATHCART E. 49,826
254*E. M. Taylor, C..... 16,301
Mrs. J. E. Carnegie,
Lab............ 14,544
A. Ewing, Scot. Nat... 6,292
H. Wills, L......... 1,058
C. maj........... 1,757
(Feb. '74, C. maj. 2,095)
CENTRAL E. 25,516
255*T. M. McMillan, Lab.. 9,231
B. Nugent, Scot. Nat.. 2,790
N. Woolfson, C...... 1,880
E. Bennett, L....... 605
Lab. maj......... 6,441
(Feb. '74, Lab. maj. 5,965)
CRAIGTON E. 44,333
256*B. Millan, Lab....... 16,952
R. G. Houston, Scot.
Nat............ 8,171
G. F. Belton, C...... 6,734
R. McIntyre, L...... 1,728
Lab. maj......... 8,781
(Feb. '74, Lab. maj. 7,238)
GARSCADDEN E. 54,700
257*W. W. Small, Lab.... 19,737
K. S. Bovey, Scot. Nat. 12,111
J. Corbett, C........ 5,004
M. R. Kibby, L...... 1,915
Lab. maj......... 7,626
(Feb. '74, Lab. maj. 11,264)
GOVAN E. 32,094
258*H. Selby, Lab....... 11,392
Mrs. M. MacDonald,
Scot. Nat....... 9,440
Miss M. Todd, C..... 1,623
E. Mason, L........ 444
M. A. Brooks, Nat.
Front............ 86
T. Clyde, Ind....... 27
Lab. maj......... 1,952
(Feb. '74, Lab. maj. 543)

HILLHEAD E. 41,726
259*Hon. T. G. D. Gal-
braith, C......... 11,203
D. Welsh, Lab...... 8,507
G. Borthwick, Scot.
Nat............ 6,897
A. Rennie, L........ 3,596
C. maj........... 2,696
(Feb. '74, C. maj. 6,381)

KELVINGROVE E. 42,654
260*N. G. Carmichael, Lab. 11,567
J. G. Rennie, C...... 7,448
C. D. Calman, Scot.
Nat............ 6,274
S. Glasgow, L....... 1,735
Lab. maj......... 4,119
(Feb. '74, Lab. maj. 2,398)

MARYHILL E. 51,545
261*J. M. Craigen, Lab.... 19,589
A. McIntosh, Scot.
Nat............ 10,171
J. S. Younger, C..... 3,160
Mrs. E. Attwooll, L.. 1,063
Lab. maj......... 9,418
(Feb. '74, Lab. maj. 11,383)

POLLOK E. 59,451
262*J. White, Lab........ 18,695
G. Malone, C....... 11,604
D. P. Macquarrie,
Scot. Nat....... 10,441
M. C. Todd, L....... 2,274
Lab. maj......... 7,091
(Feb. '74, Lab. maj. 3,406)

PROVAN E. 54,975
263*H. D. Brown, Lab.... 20,602
R. Edwards, Scot. Nat. 10,628
R. McKay, C........ 3,448
J. Jackson, Comm.... 503
Lab. maj......... 9,974
(Feb. '74, Lab. maj. 15,787)

QUEENS PARK E. 38,776
264*F. P. McElhone, Lab... 14,574
D. G. MacKellar, Scot.
Nat............ 5,660
I. D. Mackinnon, C... 4,421
Miss M. Aitchison, L. 966
J. R. Kay, Comm.... 354
Lab. maj......... 8,914
(Feb. '74, Lab. maj. 8,366)

SHETTLESTON E. 38,324
265*Sir M. Galpern, Lab. .. 13,391
R. Hamilton, Scot.
Nat............ 7,042
J. Cran, C......... 3,543
R. J. Brodie, L....... 690
Lab. maj......... 6,349
(Feb. '74, Lab. maj. 7,736)

SPRINGBURN E. 48,066
266*R. Buchanan, Lab..... 17,444
W. J. Morton, Scot.
Nat............ 9,049
S. Taylor, Lab....... 4,245
T. Marshall, L....... 865
N. McLellan, Comm... 352
Lab. maj......... 8,395
(Feb. '74, Lab. maj. 10,395)

Gloucester
E. 62,503
267*Mrs. S. Oppenheim, C. 22,664
Mrs. A. C. Roberts,
Lab............ 19,136
D. G. Halford, L..... 7,357
C. maj........... 3,528
(Feb. '74, C. maj. 4,837)

Gloucestershire

SOUTH E. 79,439
268*J. Cope, C........... 26,581
Miss O. A. McDonald,
  Lab.............. 22,235
D. C. Short, L....... 14,412
  C. maj........... 4,346
  (Feb. '74, C. maj. 6,459)

WEST E. 67,255
269 J. T. Watkinson, Lab. . 22,481
P. Marland, C......... 22,072
A. I. MacGregor, L... 9,353
  Lab. maj........... 409
  (Feb. '74, Lab. maj. 1,624)

Goole

E. 64,631
270*E. I. Marshall, Ph.D.,
  Lab.............. 26,804
N. P. Kemp, C...... 12,707
J. T. Clarkson, L..... 5,285
  Lab. maj........ 14,097
  (Feb. '74, Lab. maj. 13,225)

Gosport

E. 48,871
271*P. J. Viggers, C........ 17,487
P. M. Tebbutt, Lab.... 10,621
P. D. Clark, L........ 8,701
  C. maj........... 6,866
  (Feb. '74, C. maj. 7,228)

Gower

E. 56,867
272*I. Davies, Lab........ 25,067
D. F. R. George, C... 8,863
R. Owen, L......... 5,453
M. Powell, P.C...... 4,369
  Lab. maj........ 16,204
  (Feb. '74, Lab. maj. 15,076)

Grantham

E. 78,404
273*Rt. Hon. J. B. Godber,
  C.............. 27,738
Mrs. S. M. Smedley,
  Lab.............. 19,708
W. T. Bailey, L....... 10,752
  C. maj........... 8,030
  (Feb. '74, C. maj. 11,343)

Gravesend

E. 87,269
274*J. F. Ovenden, Lab.... 29,569
R. F. Needham, C.... 27,264
L. Cartier, L......... 10,244
J. D. Turner, Nat.
  Front.............. 1,304
T. L. Keen, Ind....... 239
  Lab. maj........... 2,305
  (Feb. '74, Lab. maj. 1,582)

Greenock and Port Glasgow

E. 62,126
275*J. D. Mabon, Lab..... 21,279
J. K. Wright, Scot.
  Nat.............. 9,324
W. M. Campbell, L.. 8,580
A. Foote, C......... 4,969
  Lab. maj........ 11,955
  (Feb. '74, Lab. maj. 11,776)

Greenwich

E. 52,847
276*N. G. Barnett, Lab.... 19,155
Mrs. S. M. T. Harold,
  C.............. 9,249
A. J. D. Wilson, L.... 5,838
D. Green, Ind....... 254
  Lab. maj........... 9,906
  (Feb. '74, Lab. maj. 8,870)

Grimsby

E. 66,302
277*Rt. Hon. C. A. R.
  Crosland, Lab....... 21,657
K. C. Brown, C...... 14,675
D. M. Rigby, L...... 9,487
J. McElrea, Ind...... 166
  Lab. maj........... 6,982
  (Feb. '74, Lab. maj. 5,671)

Guildford

E. 72,302
278*D. A. R. Howell, C.... 25,564
C. J. Fox, L......... 14,660
R. W. Harris, Lab... 11,727
  C. maj........... 10,904
  (Feb. '74, C. maj. 9,891)

Hackney

CENTRAL E. 48,524
279*S. C. Davis, Lab...... 17,650
K. S. Lightwood, C.. 4,797
Mrs. M. G. Snow. L. 3,174
  Lab. maj........... 12,853
  (Feb. '74, Lab. maj. 12,403)

NORTH AND STOKE NEWINGTON
E. 52,870
280*D. Weitzman, Q.C.,
  Lab.............. 16,525
A. J.Wylson, C...... 5,972
S. J. Lyons, L........ 3,796
H. C. Lord, Nat. Front. 1,044
M. Goldman, Comm.. 418
M. Van der Poorten,
  Ind.............. 159
  Lab. maj........... 10,553
  (Feb. '74, Lab. maj. 9,334)

SOUTH AND SHOREDITCH
E. 49,540
281*R. W. Brown, Lab.... 17,333
K. H. Proctor, C..... 4,038
C. Bone, L......... 3,173
R. May, Nat. Front... 2,544
  Lab. maj........... 13,295
  (Feb. '74, Lab. maj. 12,018)

Halesowen and Stourbridge

E. 82,189
282*J. H. R. Stokes, C.... 24,387
D. Turner, Lab...... 23,537
L. T. Eden, L........ 14,672
  C. maj........... 850
  (Feb. '74, C. maj. 4,049)

Halifax

E. 63,562
283*Hon. Shirley Summerskill,
  Lab.............. 20,976
S. R. Lyons, C...... 16,798
A. Clegg, L......... 8,693
R. S. Pearson, Ind... 919
  Lab. maj........... 4,178
  (Feb. '74, Lab. maj. 3,003)

Haltemprice

E. 76,257
284*P. H. B. Wall, M.C.,
  V.R.D., C......... 28,206
R.Walker, L........ 16,545
L. Cross, Lab....... 12,362
  C. maj........... 11,661
  (Feb. '74, C. maj. 11,824)

Hamilton

E. 50,346
285*A. Wilson, Lab....... 18,487
I. C. H. Macdonald,
  Scot. Nat........... 15,155
G. Warner, C....... 3,682
J. M. Calder, L....... 1,559
  Lab. maj........... 3,332
  (Feb. '74, Lab. maj. 6,378)

Hammersmith North

E. 52,371
286*F. Tomney, Lab....... 18,061
R. G. Beckett, C..... 9,939
S. H. J. A. Knott, L... 5,200
J. P. McFadden, Ind... 633
  Lab. maj........... 8,122
  (Feb. '74, Lab. maj. 7,041)

Hampstead

E. 64,085
287*G. Finsberg, M.B.E., C. 18,139
A. J. Clarke, Lab..... 16,414
R. H. Longland, L.... 5,566
Mrs. M. Maguire, Ind. 146
R. O. Critchfield, Ind. 118
C. Rao, Ind. 31
  C. maj........... 1,725
  (Feb. '74, C. maj. 2,257)

Harborough

E. 65,855
288*J. A. Farr, C......... 25,776
N. G. Reynolds, L... 12,567
R. L. W. Briant, Lab. 11,934
  C. maj........... 13,209
  (Feb. '74, C. maj. 12,473)

Harlow

E. 62,964
289*A. S. Newens, Lab.... 24,961
J. E. Smith, C....... 11,510
B. E. Goldstone, L.... 10,869
  Lab. maj........... 13,451
  (Feb. '74, Lab. maj. 12,534)

Harrogate

E. 64,759
290*R. G. Banks, C....... 24,583
I. de C. Bayley, L.... 11,269
B. H. Seal, Lab...... 8,047
A. H. W. Brons, Nat.
  Front.............. 1,030
C. Margolis, Ind...... 719
  C. maj........... 13,314
  (Feb. '74, C. maj. 11,789)

Harrow

CENTRAL E. 45,260
291*J. A. Grant, C....... 14,356
D. M. Offenbach, Lab. 12,288
R. S. Montgomerie, L. 5,566
C. Byrne, Nat. Front.. 813
  C. maj........... 2,068
  (Feb. '74, C. maj. 2,917)

EAST E. 49,315
292*H. J. M. Dykes, C.... 17,073
R.W. Lewis, Lab..... 13,595
J. McDonnell, L...... 6,268
  C. maj........... 3,478
  (Feb. '74, C. maj. 4,493)

WEST E. 56,641
293*A. J. Page, C......... 21,924
M. P. Reynolds, Lab.. 10,342
R. E. Bell, L......... 9,903
  C. maj........... 11,582
  (Feb. '74, C. maj. 11,869)

Hartlepool
E. 65,345
294*E. L. Leadbitter, Lab... 24,440
N. H. Freeman, C.... 16,546
L. Tostevin, L........ 6,314
Lab. maj........... 7,894
(Feb. '74, Lab. maj. 4,288)

Harwich
E. 88,710
295*J. E. Ridsdale, C....... 29,963
J. B. Fryer, Lab...... 19,135
T. O. Kellock, Q.C., L. 15,048
C. maj........... 10,828
(Feb. '74, C. maj. 12,463)

Hastings
E. 57,023
296*K. R. Warren, C..... 18,337
M. J. Foster, Lab..... 13,685
A. Leggett, L........ 8,793
C. maj........... 4,652
(Feb. '74, C. maj. 7,083)

Havant and Waterloo
E. 75,472
297*I. S. Lloyd, C........ 24,880
S. Brewin, L........ 16,148
T. King, Lab........ 14,615
C. maj........... 8,732
(Feb. '74, C. maj. 9,188)

Hayes and Harlington
E. 55,960
298*N. D. Sandelson, Lab. 20,291
N. R. Balfour, C..... 10,871
C. Lyon, L.......... 6,336
J. S. Fairhurst, Nat.
Front............ 1,189
R. Bull, Ind....... 198
Lab. maj........... 9,420
(Feb. '74, Lab. maj. 10,048)

Hazel Grove
E. 67,648
299 T. R. Arnold, C....... 25,012
*M. P. Winstanley, L.. 22,181
A. Roberts, Lab...... 8,527
C. maj........... 2,831
(Feb. '74, L. maj. 1,998)

Hemel Hempstead
E. 83,795
300 R. Corbett, Lab....... 29,223
*J. H. Allason, O.B.E., C. 28,738
Miss C. A. M. Baron,
L.............. 10,497
Lab. maj........... 485
(Feb. '74, C. maj. 187)

Hemsworth
E. 69,810
301*A. Woodall, Lab...... 37,467
P. Carvis, C........ 5,895
R. F. Taylor, L...... 5,607
Lab. maj........... 31,572
(Feb. '74, Lab. maj. 34,941)

Hendon
NORTH E. 50,762
302*J. M. Gorst, C. 16,299
J. S. Champion, Lab.. 14,549
I. Senior, L.......... 5,822
C. maj........... 1,750
(Feb. '74, C. maj. 2,612)

SOUTH E. 51,889
303*Rt. Hon. P. J. M.
Thomas, Q.C., C.... 16,866
R. M. Hadley, Lab... 11,903
M. D. Colne, L...... 7,404
C. maj........... 4,963
(Feb. '74, C. maj. 6,597)

Henley
E. 62,475
304*M. R. D. Heseltine, C. 22,504
S. R. C. Evans, L..... 12,288
I. M. Haig, Lab...... 11,141
C. maj........... 10,216
(Feb. '74, C. maj. 8,900)

Hereford
E. 57,830
305 C. R. Shepherd, C.... 17,060
C. B. T. Nash, L..... 15,948
M. K. Prendergast,
Lab.............. 10,820
C. maj........... 1,112
(Feb. '74, C. maj. 3,438)

Hertford and Stevenage
E. 82,218
306*Rt. Hon. Shirley
Williams, Lab..... 29,548
V. W. H. Bendall, C.. 20,502
T. N. Willis, L....... 11,419
K. Taylor, Nat. Front. 1,232
Lab. maj........... 9,046
(Feb. '74, Lab. maj. 8,176)

Hertfordshire
E. 88,848
EAST E. 88,848
307*Rt. Hon. Sir. D. C.
Walker-Smith, Bt.,
T.D., Q.C., C....... 29,334
M. M. Keir, Lab..... 20,999
P. C. Clark, L....... 15,446
C. maj........... 8,335
(Feb. '74, C. maj. 11,358)

SOUTH E. 64,666
308*C. E. Parkinson, C.... 21,018
A. Dubs, Lab...... 18,790
J. D. O. Henchley, L. 9,393
C. maj........... 2,228
(Feb. '74, C. maj. 3,086)

SOUTH WEST E. 75,992
309*G. H. Dodsworth, C... 24,939
A. L. C. Cohen, Lab.. 19,098
J. E. S. Jarrett, L...... 14,470
C. maj........... 5,841
(Feb. '74, C. maj. 8,098)

Hexham
E. 65,088
310*Rt. Hon. A. G. F.
Rippon, Q.C., C..... 21,352
E. Wade, Lab....... 16,711
R. Cairncross, L...... 10,991
C. maj........... 4,641
(Feb. '74, C. maj. 7,930)

Heywood and Royton
E. 77,705
311*Rt. Hon. J. Barnett,Lab. 27,206
P. Morgan, C........ 19,307
V. N. Bingham, L..... 12,969
Lab. maj........... 7,899
(Feb. '74, Lab. maj. 7,162)

High Peak
E. 57,095
312*S. Le Marchant, C.... 19,043
D. Bookbinder, Lab... 17,041
C.Walmsley, L....... 9,875
C. maj........... 2,002
(Feb. '74, C. maj. 2,275)

Hitchin
E. 72,815
313*B. H. I. H. Stewart, C.. 25,842
Miss A. Mallalieu, Lab. 22,656
E. Dix, L........... 9,454
C. maj........... 3,186
(Feb. '74, C. maj. 4,018)

Holborn and St. Pancras South
E. 39,171
314*Mrs. L. M. Jeger, Lab. 11,790
R. F. J. Parsons, C.... 6,349
F. M. J. Lee, L....... 2,938
Lab. maj........... 5,441
(Feb. '74, Lab. maj. 4,191)

Holland with Boston
E. 80,454
315*R. Body, C........ 28,145
M. D. Cornish, Lab... 19,461
G. R. Stephenson, L.. 10,476
C. maj........... 8,684
(Feb. '74, C. maj. 12,381)

Honiton
E. 73,070
316*P. F. H. Emery, C.... 29,720
V. T. Howell, L....... 16,500
R. L. Spiller, Lab..... 9,048
C. maj........... 13,220
(Feb. '74, C. maj. 14,123)

Horncastle
E. 49,627
317*P. H. B. Tapsell, C.... 16,750
M. J. C. Starky, L..... 11,506
K. Bratton, Lab...... 6,849
C. maj........... 5,244
(Feb. '74, C. maj. 6,789)

Hornchurch
E. 60,423
318*A. L. Williams, Lab... 21,336
R. C. Squire, C...... 14,535
B. G. McCarthy, L.... 7,284
B. Percy-Davis, Ind... 797
Lab. maj........... 6,801
(Feb. '74, Lab. maj. 6,196)

Hornsey
E. 58,278
319*H. A. L. Rossi, C..... 17,226
I. H. Kuczynski, Lab.. 16,444
P. Smulian, L........ 5,283
Mrs. J. Stubbs, Nat.
Front.............. 973
C. maj........... 782
(Feb. '74, C. maj. 2,208)

Horsham and Crawley
E. 90,944
320*P. M. Hordern, C..... 29,867
M. A. Oakeshott, Lab. 26,168
Mrs. P. Greenwood, L. 13,848
A. Brewer, Nat. Front 1,101
C. maj........... 3,699
(Feb. '74, C. maj. 6,774)

Houghton-le-Spring
E. 59,995
321*T. W. Urwin, Lab.... 29,699
W. Robson, L....... 9,298
R. C. Ritchie, C...... 4,399
Lab. maj........... 20,401
(Feb. '74 Lab. maj. 23,963)

Hove
E. 73,034
322*Hon. T. A. D. Sains-
bury, C........... 27,345
J. M. Walsh, L....... 12,469
L. E. Hamilton, Lab... 11,179
C. maj........... 14,876
(Feb. '74, C. maj. 11,509)

Howden
E. 57,512
323*Sir P. E. O. Bryan, D.S.O., M.C., C..... 19,583
S. C. Haywood, L... 14,803
F. H. V. Lewis, Lab... 7,271
   C. maj............ 4,780
   (Feb. '74, C. maj. 6,211)

Huddersfield
EAST E. 53,515
324*J. P. W. Mallalieu, Lab. 19,522
A. F. J. Povey, C..... 11,108
G. M. Lee, L.......... 7,326
J. Robertshaw, Nat. Front............. 764
   Lab. maj........... 8,414
   (Feb. '74, Lab. maj. 7,304)

WEST E. 53,510
325*K. Lomas, Lab........ 16,882
J. M. Stansfield, C..... 15,518
Mrs. K. J. L. Hasler, L. 7,503
D. Ford, Nat. Front... 760
H. Smith, Ind........ 136
   Lab. maj........... 1,364
   (Feb. '74, Lab. maj. 630)

Hull
CENTRAL E. 63,278
326*J. K. McNamara, Lab... 22,417
P. W. J. Carver, C... 12,596
N. W. Turner, L...... 7,810
   Lab. maj........... 9,821
   (Feb. '74, Lab. maj. 7,619)
EAST E. 81,624
327*J. L. Prescott, Lab..... 34,190
S. Dorrell, C......... 10,397
J. Adamson, L........ 10,196
   Lab. maj........... 23,793
   (Feb. '74, Lab. maj. 23,593)
WEST E. 57,592
328*J. Johnson, Lab........ 20,393
C. M. K. Taylor, C.... 10,272
A. Michell, L........ 6,508
   Lab. maj........... 10,121
   (Feb. '74, Lab. maj. 7,931)

Huntingdonshire
E. 79,724
329*Rt. Hon. Sir D. L. M. Renton, K.B.E., T.D., Q.C., C............. 26,989
A. G. Dowson, Lab... 17,745
D. G. Rowe, L..... 15,152
   C. maj............ 9,244
   (Feb. '74, C. maj. 10,002)

Huyton
E. 73,485
330*Rt. Hon. J. H. Wilson, O.B.E., Lab......... 31,750
W. Peters, C........ 15,517
M. P. Braham, L...... 4,956
   Lab. maj........... 16,233
   (Feb. '74, Lab. maj. 15,305)

Ilford
NORTH E. 65,195
331 Mrs. M. Miller, Lab... 20,621
*T. L. Iremonger, C... 19,843
G. L. P. Wilson, L..... 8,080
   Lab. maj........... 778
   (Feb. '74, C. maj. 285)
SOUTH E. 56,257
332*A. J. Shaw, Lab....... 17,538
N. Thorne, C........ 15,789
Miss E. Yates, L...... 5,734
T. L. Keen, Ind....... 169
   Lab. maj........... 1,749
   (Feb. '74, Lab. maj. 1,143)

Ilkeston
E. 74,980
333*L. R. Fletcher, Lab.... 31,153
A. N. R. Hamilton, C. 15,295
G. F. Pool, L........ 9,671
   Lab. maj........... 15,858
   (Feb. '74, Lab. maj. 14,180)

Ince
E. 77,113
334*M. T. F. McGuire, Lab..............35,453
J. R. Dyson, C....... 11,923
J. Gibb, L............ 8,436
   Lab. maj........... 23,530
   (Feb. '74, Lab. maj. 22,759)

Inverness
E. 57,527
335*D. R. Johnston, L..... 13,128
D. G. Barr, Scot. Nat.. 11,994
R. E. Henderson, C... 8,922
J. W. L. Cumming, Lab.............. 6,332
U. Bell, Ind.......... 155
   L. maj............. 1,134
   (Feb. '74, L. maj. 5,223)

Ipswich
E. 87,675
336 K. T. Weetch, Lab.... 31,566
*E. D. D. Money, C... 29,833
R. B. Salt, L........ 8,295
   Lab. maj........... 1,733
   (Feb. '74, C. maj. 259)

Isle of Ely
E. 68,491
337*C. R. Freud, L....... 22,040
I. T. Stuttaford, C.... 19,355
M. B. Ferris, Lab...... 11,420
   L. maj............. 2,685
   (Feb. '74, L. maj. 8,347)

Isle of Wight
E. 85,897
338*S. S. Ross, L......... 29,697
J. D. Fishburn, C.... 27,657
L. D. Brooke, Lab.... 8,562
   L. maj............ 2,040
   (Feb. '74, L. maj. 7,766)

Islington
CENTRAL E. 45,347
339*J. D. Grant, Lab...... 14,689
C. Stanbrook, C..... 5,296
P. W. Murphy, L..... 3,786
R. Score, Nat. Front.. 1,335
   Lab. maj........... 9,393
   (Feb. '74, Lab. maj. 8,691)
NORTH E. 41,390
340*M. J. O'Halloran, Lab. 12,973
Marquess Douro, C... 6,155
M. W. S. Davenport, L................. 2,736
D. Fallon, Ind....... 558
   Lab. maj........... 6,818
   (Feb. '74, Lab. maj. 6,628)
SOUTH AND FINSBURY E. 42,251
341*G. Cunningham, Lab... 14,544
Miss P. Hodgson, C... 4,951
R. G. Adams, L...... 3,661
Mrs. M. Betteridge, Comm........... 512
   Lab. maj........... 9,593
   (Feb. '74, Lab. maj. 8,591)

Jarrow
E. 54,735
342*Rt.Hon. E. Fernyhough, Lab............. 24,558
Mrs. B. Bolam, C.... 8,707
L. Ormston, L....... 5,818
   Lab. maj........... 15,851
   (Feb. '74, Lab. maj. 13,892)

Keighley
E. 51,741
343*G. R. Cryer, Lab..... 19,569
C. J. H. Taylor, C.... 16,488
Miss M. Holmstedt, L. 5,839
G. Wright, Nat. Front. 859
C. W. Deakin, Ind.... 179
   Lab maj........... 3,081
   (Feb. '74, Lab. maj. 878)

Kensington
E. 61,105
344*Sir B. M. Rhys-Williams, Bt., C... 15,562
J. V. Tilley, Lab..... 13,645
R. Cohen, L......... 5,236
   C. maj............ 1,917
   (Feb. '74, C. maj. 5,132)

Kettering
E. 85,802
345*Rt. Hon. Sir G. S. de Freitas, K.C.M.G., Lab. 30,970
G. D. Reed, C....... 19,800
A. J. W. Haigh, L..... 12,038
   Lab. maj........... 11,170
   (Feb. '74, Lab. maj. 9,787)

Kidderminster
E. 78,965
346*J. E. Bulmer, C....... 25,602
R. H. Jones, Lab...... 18,833
A. J. Batchelor, L..... 14,733
   C. maj............ 6,769
   (Feb. '74, C. maj. 8,685)

Kilmarnock
E. 60,380
347*Rt. Hon. W. Ross, M.B.E., Lab......... 22,184
A. MacInnes, Scot. Nat 14,655
W. Adams, C........ 9,203
K. Purcell, L........ 2,508
   Lab. maj........... 7,529
   (Feb. '74, Lab. maj. 9,727)

Kingston on Thames
E. 59,251
348*N. S. H. Lamont, C... 20,680
A. Quicke, Lab....... 12,266
S. J. E. Wells, L...... 9,580
   C. maj............ 8,414
   (Feb. '74, C. maj. 10,307)

Kingswood
E. 55,967
349*T. W. Walker, Lab... 20,703
D. F. J. Hunt, C...... 18,137
J. H. Aspinwall, L..... 8,216
   Lab. maj........... 2,566
   (Feb. '74, Lab. maj. 1,641)

Kinross and West Perthshire
E. 35,237
350 N. H. Fairbairn, Q.C., C............. 11,034
D.Cameron, Scot. Nat. 10,981
D. A. Barrie, L....... 2,427
D. G. Skene, Lab..... 2,028
   C. maj............ 53
   (Feb. '74, C. maj. 8,082)

Kirkcaldy
E. 60,824
351*H. P. H. Gourlay, *Lab.*.. 20,688
 R. T. Knox, *Scot. Nat.* 14,587
 R. B. Jones, *C.*....... 7,539
 F. Young, *L.*......... 2,788
 Lab. maj......... 6,101
 (Feb. '74, Lab. maj. 9,382)

Knutsford
E. 55,238
352*Rt. Hon. J. E. H.
 Davies, M.B.E., *C.*... 21,636
 B. M. Lomax, *L.*..... 11,210
 D. L. Swain, *Lab.*.... 9,565
 C. maj........... 10,426
 (Feb. '74, C. maj. 11,090)

Lambeth Central
E. 48,722
353*M. Lipton, C.B.E., *Lab.*.. 15,381
 N. Lyell, *C.*......... 6,704
 P. Easton, *L.*........ 3,211
 S. Smart, *Ind.* 233
 P. Bratton, *Ind.*..... 88
 Lab. maj......... 8,677
 (Feb. '74, Lab. maj. 7,369)

Lanark
E. 48,408
354*Rt. Hon. *Judith Hart,*
 Lab................ 14,948
 T. McAlpine, *Scot.*
 Nat.............. 14,250
 A. Bell, *C.*......... 9,222
 F. McDermid, *L.*..... 1,374
 Lab. maj......... 698
 (Feb. '74, Lab. maj. 2,100)

Lanarkshire North
E. 54,147
355*J. Smith, *Lab.*....... 19,902
 Mrs. P. Watt, *Scot.*
 Nat.............. 11,561
 J. Crichton, *C.*...... 9,665
 A. P. Brodie, *L.*..... 1,899
 Lab. maj......... 8,341
 (Feb. '74, Lab. maj. 6,784)

Lancaster
E. 49,643
356*Mrs. M. E. Kellett-
 Bowman, C........ 16,540
 D. Owen, *Lab.*...... 15,119
 M. Mumford, *L.*..... 7,161
 C. maj........... 1,421
 (Feb. '74, C. maj. 2,469)

Leeds
EAST E. 67,736
357*Rt. Hon. D. W. Healey,
 M.B.E., *Lab.*........ 24,745
 J. W. Dawson, *C.*.... 12,434
 S. Marsh, *L.*........ 6,970
 Mrs. N. Russell, *Ind.*.. 327
 Lab. maj......... 12,311
 (Feb. '74, Lab. maj. 10,514)
NORTH EAST E. 58,968
358*Rt. Hon. *Sir* K. S.
 Joseph, Bt., C...... 18,749
 W. J. Gunnell, *Lab.*.. 13,121
 C. J. Greenfield, *L.*... 6,737
 C. maj........... 5,628
 (Feb. '74, C. maj. 7,260)
NORTH WEST E. 65,062
359*Sir D. Kaberry, Bt, T.D.
 C................. 19,243
 L. G. K. Fenwick, *Lab.* 15,216
 D. Rolfe, *L.*........ 8,663
 C. maj........... 4,027
 (Feb. '74, Lab. maj. 6,671)

SOUTH E. 52,709
360*Rt. Hon. M. Rees, *Lab.* 21,653
 T. N. M. Stow, *C.*... 6,388
 J. Adams, *L.*........ 5,563
 Lab. maj......... 15,265
 (Feb. '74, Lab. maj. 11,860)
SOUTH EAST E. 49,797
361*S. Cohen, *Lab.*....... 17,160
 Mrs. M. Sexton, *C.*.. 6,144
 Miss M. G. Clay, *L.*.. 4,429
 W. H. Innes, *Comm.* . 317
 Lab. maj......... 11,016
 (Feb. '74, Lab. maj. 9,454)
WEST E. 60,402
362*J. J. Dean, *Lab.*..... 20,669
 M. J. Meadowcroft, *L.* 13,062
 R. D. Hall, *C.*....... 7,907
 Lab. maj......... 7,607
 (Feb. '74, Lab. maj. 3,985)

Leek
E. 83,930
363*D. L. Knox, *C.*...... 30,796
 B. Whittam, *Lab.*.... 26,472
 M. Holden, *L.*...... 8,615
 C. maj........... 4,324
 (Feb. '74, C. maj. 5,732)

Leicester
EAST E. 63,899
364*T. G. Bradley, *Lab.*... 20,688
 K. G. Reeves, *C.*..... 16,877
 W. Capstick, *L.*..... 5,668
 A. Reed-Herbert, *Nat.*
 Front............. 2,967
 Lab. maj......... 3,811
 (Feb. '74, Lab. maj. 1,413)
SOUTH E. 72,558
365 J. Marshall, *Lab.*...... 21,588
 *T. G. Boardman, *C.*... 20,455
 H. Young, *L.*....... 5,709
 A. R. Cartwright, *Nat.*
 Front............. 2,072
 G. H. Rousseau, *Ind.*.. 136
 Lab. maj......... 1,133
 (Feb. '74, C. maj. 1,766)
WEST E. 64,650
366*Hon. G. E. Janner, Q.C.,
 Lab................ 23,406
 A. Simpson, *C.*...... 13,446
 J. Windram, *L.*...... 5,135
 W. J. Newcombe,
 Nat. Front........ 2,253
 Lab. maj......... 9,960
 (Feb. '74, Lab. maj. 8,652)

Leigh
E. 65,053
367*H. Boardman, *Lab.*.... 27,036
 Mrs. M. Williams, *C.* 12,401
 R. D. Pemberton, *L.*.. 8,640
 Lab. maj......... 14,635
 (Feb. '74, Lab. maj. 13,647)

Leominster
E. 44,055
368*P. Temple-Morris, *C.*... 15,741
 R. J. Pincham, *L.*.... 15,162
 S. Allen, *Lab.*....... 3,264
 C. maj........... 579
 (Feb. '74, C. maj. 1,619)

Lewes
E. 72,060
369*J. R. Rathbone, *C.*.... 27,588
 G. Hook, *L.*........ 13,741
 J. F. Little, *Lab.*..... 11,857
 C. maj........... 13,847
 (Feb. '74, C. maj. 14,257)

Lewisham
EAST E. 69,540
370*Hon. R. D. Moyle, *Lab.* 24,350
 D. Mahony, *C.*...... 15,398
 M. A. Minter, *L.*.... 8,069
 Lab. maj......... 6,306)
 (Feb. '74, Lab. maj. 6,306)
WEST E. 62,435
371*C. Price, *Lab.*........ 21,102
 Miss M. Marshall, *C.*.. 15,573
 J. D. Eagle, *L.*...... 5,952
 P. Williams, *Nat. Front* 1,114
 Lab. maj......... 5,529
 (Feb. '74, Lab. maj. 2,402)

Leyton
E. 64,341
372*B. Magee, *Lab.*....... 22,130
 B. S. Dare, *C.*....... 10,617
 R. Scott, *L.*........ 5,408
 Mrs. S. M. Bothwell,
 Nat. Front........ 2,168
 Lab. maj......... 11,513
 (Feb. '74, Lab. maj. 9,937)

Lichfield and Tamworth
E. 89,752
373 B. J. Grocott, *Lab.*.... 29,872
 *Maj.-Gen. J. A. d'Avig-
 dor-Goldsmid,
 C.B., O.B.E., M.C., *C.*.. 29,541
 P. Rule, *L.*......... 10,714
 Lab. maj......... 331
 (Feb. '74, C. maj. 1,807)

Lincoln
E. 53,022
374 Miss M. M. *Jackson,*
 Lab................ 14,698
 *D. Taverne, Q.C. *Soc.*
 Dem.............. 13,714
 P. M. Moran, *C.*..... 11,223
 Lab. maj......... 984
 (Feb. '74, Soc. Dem. maj. 1,293)

Liverpool
EDGE HILL E. 40,970
375*Rt. Hon. *Sir* A. J.
 Irvine, Q.C., *Lab.*... 13,023
 D. Alton, *L.*........ 6,852
 S. N. Perry, *C.*...... 5,208
 Lab. maj......... 6,171
 (Feb. '74, Lab. maj. 5,750)
GARSTON E. 81,030
376*E. Loyden, *Lab.*...... 27,857
 D. C. Stanley, *C.*.... 24,557
 G. H. Black, *L.*..... 5,865
 Lab. maj......... 3,300
 (Feb. '74, Lab. maj. 681)
KIRKDALE E. 45,344
377*J. A. Dunn, *Lab.*..... 17,686
 M. J. Jones, *C.*...... 8,205
 M. J. Storey, *L.*..... 2,908
 Lab. maj......... 9,481
 (Feb. '74, Lab. maj. 6,525)
SCOTLAND EXCHANGE E. 35,146
378*R. Parry, *Lab.*....... 15,154
 P. Rankin, *C.*....... 2,234
 Mrs. P. Crockett, *L.*.. 944
 R. O'Hara, *Comm.*... 556
 Lab. maj......... 12,920
 (Feb. '74, Lab. maj. 12,332)
TOXTETH E. 45,883
379*R. Crawshaw, O.B.E.,
 Lab................ 15,312
 H. L. J. Malins, *C.*... 8,062
 D. L. Mahon, *L.*.... 3,176
 J. Dillon, *Ind.*...... 365
 Lab. maj......... 7,250
 (Feb. '74, Lab. maj. 5,557)

WALTON E. 51,967
380*E. S. Heffer, Lab...... 20,568
R. Gould, C......... 10,706
J. R. Watton, L...... 4,221
Lab. maj.......... 9,862
(Feb. '74, Lab. maj. 8,216)

WAVERTREE E. 59,720
381*A. D. Steen, C....... 18,971
R. E. Morris, Lab.... 16,216
W. A. Limont, L...... 6,193
C. maj........... 2,755
(Feb. '74, C. maj. 5,275)

WEST DERBY E. 58,890
382*E. Ogden, Lab....... 23,964
J. W. Last, C........ 11,445
R. Ousby, L......... 4,215
Lab. maj........ 12,519
(Feb. '74, Lab. maj. 9,973)

Llanelli
E. 64,495
383*D. J. D. Davies, Lab.. 29,474
M. M. Gimblett, L.... 7,173
R. Williams, P.C..... 6,797
G. D. J. Richards, C.. 6,141
Lab. maj.......... 22,301
(Feb. '74, Lab. maj. 21,445)

Londonderry
E. 93,141
384*W. Ross, U.U.U..... 35,138
J. Hume, S.D.L.P.... 26,118
M. Montgomery, Rep. 2,530
R. Foster, Ind..... 846
U.U.U. maj........ 9,020
(Feb. '74, U.U.U. maj. 9,390)

Loughborough
E. 70,244
385*J. D. Cronin, Lab..... 22,869
R. M. Yorke, Q.C., C. 20,521
M. Bennett, L........ 10,409
K. Sanders, Nat. Front. 1,215
H. Smith, Ind........ 125
Lab. maj........... 2,348
(Feb. '74, Lab. maj. 697)

Louth
E. 70,498
386 M. L. Brotherton, C... 19,819
J. C. L. Sellick, L..... 16,939
R. Mitchell, Lab...... 14,747
C. maj........... 2,880
(Feb. '74, C. maj. 9,718)

Lowestoft
E. 76,936
387*Rt. Hon. J. M. L. Prior,
C................. 25,510
D. A. Baker, Lab..... 23,448
P. J. Hancock, L...... 11,165
C. maj........... 2,062
(Feb. '74, C. maj. 3,604)

Ludlow
E. 48,626
388*J. E. More, C......... 17,124
E. Robinson, L........ 10,888
J. Marek, Lab........ 8,353
C. maj........... 6,236
(Feb. '74, C. maj. 7,987)

Luton
EAST E. 53,549
389*I. M. Clemitson, Lab.. 17,877
A. Johnston, C....... 14,200
E. J. Fisher, L........ 6,947
L. Byrne, Ind........ 299
Lab. maj.......... 3,677
(Feb. '74, Lab. maj. 1,425)

WEST E. 58,272
390*B. C. J. Sedgemore, Lab. 20,402
R. J. Atkins, C....... 13,963
M. J. Dolling, L...... 9,289
Lab. maj.......... 6,439
(Feb. '74, Lab. maj. 5,042)

Macclesfield
E. 80,150
391*N. R. Winterton, C... 31,685
K. W. Little, Lab..... 18,592
A. J. Berry, L........ 12,764
C. maj........... 13,093
(Feb. '74, C. maj. 14,286)

Maidstone
E. 88,130
392*J. J. Wells, C....... 28,852
E. J. Burnett, L....... 18,581
K. M. Graham, Lab... 17,828
C. maj........... 10,271
(Feb. '74, C. maj. 7,656)

Maldon
E. 61,725
393*J. Wakeham, C....... 20,485
A. J. Shaw, Lab...... 14,098
J. R. C. Beale, L..... 12,473
C. maj........... 6,387
(Feb. '74, C. maj. 7,222)

Manchester
ARDWICK E. 47,937
394*G. B. Kaufman, Lab... 15,632
R. H. Hargreaves, C. 8,849
G. Wilmott, L....... 3,675
Lab. maj.......... 6,783
(Feb. '74, Lab. maj. 4,895)

BLACKLEY E. 54,860
395*P. B. Rose, Lab...... 19,720
A. S. Lea, C........ 12,601
D. Jackson, L....... 5,517
H. Andrews, Nat.
Front.............. 914
Lab. maj.......... 7,119
(Feb. '74, Lab. maj. 5,506)

CENTRAL E. 39,857
396*Rt. Hon. N. H. Lever,
Lab............... 14,753
R. Jackson, C........ 4,142
P. Coleman, L....... 2,382
Lab. maj.......... 10,611
(Feb. '74 Lab. maj. 10,004)

GORTON E. 55,955
397*K. Marks, Lab........ 21,287
S. H. Waley-Cohen,
C................ 12,423
A. Cottam, L........ 5,984
Lab. maj.......... 8,864
(Feb. '74, Lab. maj. 8,976)

MOSS SIDE E. 51,444
398*F. Hatton, Lab........ 15,212
J. R. L. Lee, C....... 11,101
W. J. L. Wallace, L... 5,686
N. Boyle, Ind........ 238
H. Smith, Ind........ 96
Lab. maj.......... 4,111
(Feb. '74, Lab. maj. 2,392)

OPENSHAW E. 42,554
399*C. R. Morris, Lab..... 16,109
G. Green, C........ 7,596
A. R. Wood, L....... 3,980
P. Widdall, Comm... 300
Lab. maj.......... 8,513
(Feb. '74, Lab. maj. 7,457)

WITHINGTON E. 58,200
400*F. J. Silvester, C...... 16,937
P. J. Hildrew, Lab.... 14,936
Mrs. A. B. Davies, L.. 7,555
C. maj........... 2,001
(Feb. '74, C. maj. 4,413)

WYTHENSHAWE E. 65,123
401*A. R. Morris, Lab.... 26,448
Mrs. J. D. W. Hill, C. 12,269
R. N. Scott, L....... 6,071
Lab. maj.......... 14,179
(Feb. '74, Lab. maj. 12,438)

Mansfield
E. 69,555
402*J. D. Concannon, Lab.. 28,964
J. R. Wood, C....... 11,685
D. J. Chambers, L.... 9,358
F. C. Westacott,
Comm............ 448
Lab. maj.......... 17,279
(Feb. '74, Lab. maj. 16,142)

Melton
E. 82,139
403*M. A. Latham, C..... 30,943
D. J. Knaggs, Lab..... 16,747
J. B. Pick, L........ 15,567
C. maj........... 14,196
(Feb. '74, C. maj. 12,749)

Meriden
E. 97,364
404*J. E. Tomlinson, Lab... 34,641
C. F. Horne, C....... 25,675
D. G. Minnis, L...... 12,992
Lab. maj.......... 8,966
(Feb. '74, Lab. maj. 4,485)

Merioneth
E. 26,728
405*D. E. Thomas, P.C..... 9,543
W. H. Edwards, Lab.. 6,951
R. O. Jones, L....... 3,454
R. R. Owen, C...... 2,509
P.C. maj........... 2,592
(Feb. '74, P.C. maj. 588)

Merthyr Tydfil
E. 39,714
406*E. Rowlands, Lab..... 21,260
E. Roberts, P.C..... 4,455
L. J. Walters, C...... 1,300
D. Bettall-Higgins, L. 1,300
T. Roberts, Comm.... 509
Lab. maj.......... 16,805
(Feb. '74, Lab. maj. 13,150)

Middlesbrough
E. 60,259
407*Rt. Hon. A. G. Bot-
tomley, O.B.E., Lab.. 22,791
E. Leigh, C........ 8,984
C. Wood, L......... 5,080
Lab. maj.......... 13,807
(Feb. '74, Lab. maj. 13,409)

Middleton and Prestwich
E. 76,737
408*J. Callaghan, Lab..... 26,639
A. D'A. Fearn, C..... 22,925
J. Clarney, L........ 8,340
H. Smith, Ind........ 234
Lab. maj.......... 3,714
(Feb. '74, Lab. maj. 517)

Midlothian
E. 89,191
409*A. Eadie, B.E.M., Lab... 28,652
J. G. McKinlay, Scot.
Nat.............. 24,568
A. Ballantyne, C...... 11,046
P. Wheeler, L........ 4,793
Lab. maj........... 4,084
(Feb. '74, Lab. maj. 11,742)

Mitcham and Morden
E. 65,398
410*B. L. H. Douglas-Mann,
Lab.............. 22,384
D. Samuel, C........ 16,193
M. Simpson, L....... 7,429
S. E. French, Comm.. 281
Miss G. Giddins, Ind.. 106
W. G. Boaks, Ind..... 68
Lab. maj........... 6,191
(Feb. '74, Lab. maj. 3,225)

Monmouth
E. 74,838
411*J. S. Thomas, C..... 25,460
R. O. Faulkner, Lab.. 23,118
D. M. Hando, L...... 10,076
T. Brimmacombe,
P.C............. 839
C. maj........... 2,342
(Feb. '74, C. maj. 4,562)

Montgomery
E. 33,583
412*H. E. Hooson, Q.C., L. 11,280
W. R. C. Williams-
Wynne, C........ 7,421
P. W. Harries, Lab... 5,031
A. P. Jones, P.C..... 2,440
L. maj........... 3,859
(Feb. '74, L. maj. 4,651)

Moray and Nairn
E. 41,194
413*Mrs. W. M. Ewing,
Scot. Nat......... 12,667
A. Pollock, C....... 12,300
E. G. Smith, Lab..... 2,985
K. Schellenberg, L.... 2,814
Scot. Nat. maj....... 367
(Feb '74, Scot. Nat. maj. 1,817)

Morecambe and Lonsdale
E. 68,473
414*A. G. F. Hall-Davis, C. 24,877
E. Garbutt, Lab....... 12,633
A. R. D. Stuttard, L.. 12,404
C. maj........... 12,244
(Feb. '74, C. maj. 14,756)

Morpeth
E. 48,518
415*G. Grant, Lab....... 22,696
D. M. Curry, C...... 8,009
B. Rogers, L......... 4,866
Lab. maj........... 14,687
(Feb. '74, Lab. maj. 13,034)

Motherwell and Wishaw
E. 51,506
416 J. W. Bray, Lab...... 17,319
J. MacKay, Scot. Nat.. 12,357
G. Rae, C.......... 7,069
D. P. Young, L..... 1,126
J. W. Sneddon, Comm. 946
Lab. maj........... 4,962
(Feb. '74, Lab. maj. 6,313)

Nantwich
E. 61,196
417*J. H. Cockcroft, C..... 20,395
A. E. Bailey, Lab..... 17,021
Mrs. H. Glidewell, L. 9,209
C. maj............ 3,374
(Feb. '74, C. maj. 5,168)

Neath
E. 52,257
418*D. R. Coleman, Lab... 25,028
H. G. Evans, P.C..... 7,305
M. J. Harris, C....... 4,641
D. Owen, L........ 3,759
Lab. maj........... 17,723
(Feb. '74, Lab. maj. 16,593)

Nelson and Colne
E. 48,356
419 E. D. H. Hoyle, Lab.. 17,505
*D. C. Waddington,
Q.C., C........... 16,836
A. R. Greaves, L..... 4,850
Lab. maj........... 669
(Feb. '74, C. maj. 177)

Newark
E. 71,346
420*E. S. Bishop, Lab...... 26,598
D. H. Cargill, C...... 20,827
I. G. M. Jones, L..... 8,116
Lab. maj........... 5,771
(Feb. '74, Lab. maj. 4,497)

Newbury
E. 72,587
421*R. M. C. McNair-
Wilson, C........ 23,499
D. S. C. Clouston, L. 22,477
Mrs. C. A. Fletcher,
Lab.............. 9,390
C. maj........... 1,022
(Feb. '74, C. maj. 1,201)

Newcastle-under-Lyme
E. 72,781
422*J. Golding, Lab....... 28,154
N. C. Bonsor, C...... 20,784
R. C. M. Fyson, L... 7,604
S. Rowe, Ind........ 256
Lab. maj........... 7,370
(Feb. '74, Lab. maj. 5,648)

Newcastle-upon-Tyne
CENTRAL E. 25,156
423*Rt. Hon. E. W. Short,
Lab.............. 10,546
Mrs. S. Faith, C...... 2,432
A. Ellis, L.......... 1,716
Lab. maj........... 8,114
(Feb. '74, Lab. maj. 8,002)

EAST E. 45,651
424 M. S. Thomas, Lab.... 17,312
M. A. Hill, C....... 11,063
T. Symonds, L....... 4,391
Lab. maj........... 6,249
(Feb. '74, Lab. maj. 6,092)

NORTH E. 40,238
425*Sir R. W. Elliott, C.... 11,217
A. L. Banks, Lab..... 10,748
D. J. Herd, L........ 4,189
C. maj............ 469
(Feb. '74, C. maj. 2,980)

WEST E. 76,966
426*R. C. Brown, Lab.... 30,057
R. M. Stewart, C..... 14,983
R. H. B. Devereux, L. 7,945
Lab. maj........... 15,074
(Feb. '74, Lab. maj. 11,396)

New Forest
E. 78,109
427*P. M. E. D. McNair-
Wilson, C........ 28,778
A. J. Hayes, L....... 15,355
P. J. Brushett, Lab... 13,825
C. maj........... 13,423
(Feb. '74, C. maj. 11,382)

Newham
NORTH EAST E. 65,975
428*Rt. Hon. R. E. Prentice,
Lab.............. 22,205
T. J. Stroud, C....... 8,664
L. H. Cohen, L...... 4,880
J. Newham, Nat. Front 2,715
Miss V. Redgrave, Ind. 572
Lab. maj........... 13,541
(Feb. '74, Lab. maj. 13,331)

NORTH WEST E. 53,489
429*A. W. J. Lewis, Lab... 18,388
Mrs. R. Brown, C... 5,007
A. Hetherington, L... 4,201
Lab. maj........... 13,381
(Feb. '74, Lab. maj. 12,548)

SOUTH E. 57,695
430*N. J. Spearing, Lab... 21,332
I. W. I. Shipley, L.... 3,611
A. D. C. Gemmill, C. 3,440
E. O. Bayly, Nat. Front 2,412
Lab. maj........... 17,721
(May '74, by-election, Lab. maj.
7,459)
(Feb. '74, Lab. maj. 18,583)

Newport
E. 75,061
431*R. J. Hughes, Lab..... 30,069
G. A. L. Price, C..... 16,253
J. H. Morgan, L...... 9,207
G. Lee. P.C......... 1,216
Lab. maj........... 13,816
(Feb. '74, Lab. maj. 11,382)

Newton
E. 95,268
432*J. Evans, Lab......... 38,956
R. M. Baldwin, C.... 22,484
W. N. Leather, L..... 11,738
Lab. maj........... 16,472
(Feb. '74, Lab. maj. 14,770)

Norfolk
NORTH E. 90,526
433*R. F. Howell, C....... 33,312
Rev. D. M. Mason,
Lab.............. 22,191
R. G. Moore, L...... 13,776
C. maj........... 11,121
(Feb. '74, C. maj. 14,290)

NORTH WEST E. 79,743
434*C. Brocklebank-Fowler,
C.............. 27,513
R. L. Williams, Lab.. 26,170
R. A. Walker, L...... 8,862
C. maj........... 1,343
(Feb. '74, C. maj. 803)

SOUTH E. 90,810
435*J. R. R. MacGregor,
O.B.E., C........ 31,478
H. Gray, Lab........ 22,713
M. J. Scott, L....... 14,687
C. C. Fairhead, Ind... 317
C. maj........... 8,765
(Feb. '74, C. maj. 11,019)

SOUTH WEST E. 53,719
436*P. L. Hawkins, T.D., C. 19,778
H. Toch, Lab........ 14,850
B. Baxter, L........ 6,658
C. maj........... 4,928
(Feb. '74, C. maj. 6,043)

Normanton
E. 58,936
437*A Roberts, Lab........ 24,372
J. Makin, C........... 9,739
W. K. Whitaker, L... 7,384
Lab. maj............ 14,633
(Feb. '74, Lab. maj. 15,174)

Northampton
NORTH E. 49,030
438*Mrs. M. M. Colquhoun,
Lab.............. 16,314
R. Tracey, C........ 14,776
R. B. Baker, L....... 6,160
Lab. maj............ 1,538
(Feb. '74, Lab. maj. 1,033)

SOUTH E. 44,343
439*M. W. L. Morris, C.... 14,393
J. Dilks, Lab......... 14,252
R. F. Miller, L....... 4,842
C. maj............ 141
(Feb. '74, C. maj. 179)

Northwich
E. 52,626
440*A. R. Goodlad, C..... 18,663
P. A. Kent, Lab...... 14,053
D. Reaper, L........ 8,645
C. maj............ 4,610
(Feb. '74, C. maj. 6,293)

Norwich
NORTH E, 45,079
441*Rt. Hon. D. H. Ennals,
Lab.............. 17,958
T. P. C. Doe, C...... 8,754
E. M. Wheeler, L.... 5,378
Lab. maj............ 9,204
(Feb. '74, Lab. maj. 7,294)

SOUTH E. 44,862
442*J. L. Garrett, Lab...... 16,590
Miss M. Tomison, C. 13,185
P. G. Smith, L....... 5,429
Lab. maj............ 3,405
(Feb. '74, Lab. maj. 652)

Norwood
E. 52,893
443*J. D. Fraser, Lab...... 16,449
Miss D. B. Hancock,
C.............. 11,678
E. Hawthorne, L..... 4,377
M. J. Greatbanks, Ind. 223
Lab. maj............ 4,771
(Feb. '74, Lab. maj. 4,022)

Nottingham
EAST E. 53,786
444*J. J. Dunnett, Lab...... 16,530
S. M. Swerling, C.... 10,574
E. J. Rowan, L....... 4,442
D. W. Peetz, Ind.... 736
Lab. maj............ 5,956
(Feb. '74, Lab. maj. 3,978)

NORTH E. 76,490
445*W. C. Whitlock, Lab.. 24,694
M. F. Spungin, C.... 17,853
M. Crew-Gee, L.... 7,470
D. Caine, Nat. Front.. 792
J. H. Peck, Comm.... 525
Lab. maj............ 6,841
(Feb. '74, Lab. maj. 4,445)

WEST E. 77,711
446*M. English, Lab....... 27,373
P. R. C. Lloyd, C.... 18,108
A. Johnson, L....... 9,598
Lab. maj............ 9,265
(Feb. '74, Lab. maj. 5,797)

Nuneaton
E. 77,892
447*L. J. Huckfield, Lab.... 32,308
R. Freeman, C....... 14,547
N. Hawkins, L....... 10,729
Lab. maj............ 17,761
(Feb. '74, Lab. maj. 17,493)

Ogmore
E. 67,927
448*W. E. Padley, Lab..... 30,453
R. K. Jones, C....... 8,249
Mrs. J. T. Gibbs, L.. 8,203
D. I. Jones, P.C...... 4,290
Lab. maj............ 22,204
(Feb. '74, Lab. maj. 17,553)

Oldham
EAST E. 50,737
449*J. A. Lamond, Lab..... 19,054
L. McGrandle, C..... 10,917
C. G. Hilyer, L...... 6,142
Lab. maj............ 8,137
(Feb. '74, Lab. maj. 6,302)

WEST E. 48,062
450*M. H. Meacher, Lab.. 18,444
D. A. Trippier, C..... 10,407
K. Stocks, L........ 5,838
Lab. maj............ 8,037
(Feb. '74, Lab. maj. 6,305)

Orkney and Shetland
E. 26,289
451*Rt. Hon. J. Grimond,
T.D., L........... 9,877
H. N. Firth, Scot. Nat. 3,025
R. Fraser, C........ 2,495
W. J. G. Wills, Lab... 2,175
L. maj............ 6,852
(Feb. '74, L. maj. 7,305)

Ormskirk
E. 96,593
452*R. Kilroy-Silk, Lab.. . 35,392
B. M. Keefe, C...... 26,541
D. Parry, L......... 8,387
Lab. maj............ 8,851
(Feb. '74, Lab. maj. 7,803)

Orpington
E. 65,686
453*I. R. Stanbrook, C.... 24,394
Lady Avebury, L..... 19,384
Mrs. C. Spillane, Lab. 8,121
C. maj............ 5,010
(Feb. '74, C. maj. 3,664)

Oswestry
E. 56,429
454*W. J. Biffen, C....... 19,165
J. Bishton, Lab....... 10,751
D. J. Evans, L........ 10,623
C. maj............ 8,414
(Feb. '74, C. maj. 7,010)

Oxford
E. 77,270
455 D. E. T. Luard, Lab... 23,359
*Hon. C. M. Wood-
house, D.S.O., O.B.E.,
C.............. 22,323
Mrs. M. S. Butler, L... 8,374
I. H. M. Anderson,
Nat. Front......... 572
Mrs. B. O. Smith, Ind. 64
Lab. maj............ 1,036
(Feb. '74, C. maj. 821)

Oxon, Mid
E. 59,697
456*Hon. D. R. Hurd, C.B.E.
C.............. 20,944
M. J. Saunders, Lab... 13,641
Miss M. E. Burton, L. 11,006
C. maj............ 7,303
(Feb. '74, C. maj. 7,973)

Paddington
E. 58,499
457*A. C. Latham, Lab.... 17,155
G. M. Wolfson, C.... 14,844
N. J. S. Lewis, L...... 3,742
C. D. Wertheim, Ind. 192
S. Allman, Ind...... 135
Lab. maj............ 2,311
(Feb. '74, Lab. maj. 872)

Paisley
E. 66,659
458*J. Robertson, Lab...... 21,368
D. R. Rollo, Scot. Nat. 15,778
I. Robertson, C....... 7,440
D. Thompson, L...... 3,116
Lab. maj............ 5,590
(Feb. '74, Lab. maj. 8,897)

Peckham
E. 63,349
459*H. G. Lamborn, Lab... 24,587
N. B. Baker, C...... 5,760
S. W. F. Saltmarsh, L. 3,971
Lab. maj............ 18,827
(Feb. '74, Lab. maj. 18,071)

Pembroke
E. 72,053
460*R. N. Edwards, C..... 23,190
G. S. D. Parry, Lab... 22,418
P. E. C. Jones, L...... 9,116
R. B. Davies, P.C.... 2,580
C. maj............ 772
(Feb. '74, C. maj. 1,479)

Penistone
E. 67,060
461*J. J. Mendelson, Lab... 27,146
G. C. W. Harris, C... 12,011
D. Chadwick, L...... 10,900
Lab. maj............ 15,135
(Feb. '74, Lab. maj. 13,713)

Penrith and the Border
E. 55,602
462*Rt. Hon. W. S. I.
Whitelaw, C.H., M.C.,
C.............. 23,547
J. N. D. Weedall, Lab. 9,791
J. G. Pease, L........ 7,215
C. maj............ 13,756
(Feb. '74, C. maj. 17,338)

Perth and East Perthshire
E. 57,646
463 G. D. Crawford, Scot.
Nat.............. 17,337
*I. MacArthur, C...... 16,544
J. White, Lab........ 5,805
R. Duncan, L....... 2,851
Scot. Nat. maj...... 793
(Feb. '74, C. maj. 8,975)

Peterborough
E. 63,044
464 M. J. Ward, Lab...... 21,820
*Sir H. Nicholls, Bt., C. 19,972
P. J. Boizot, L........ 7,302
Lab. maj............ 1,848
(Feb. '74, C. maj. 22)

Petersfield
E. 74,260

465 M. J. Mates, C...... 28,689
T. W. Slack, L...... 19,702
J. M. Bloom, Lab.. 8,301
P. H. H. Bishop, Ind.. 117
C. maj............ 8,987
(Feb. '74, C. maj. 9,580)

Plymouth
DEVONPORT E. 50,105

466*D. A. L. Owen, Lab... 17,398
Dame Joan Vickers,
D.B.E., C......... 15,139
N. E. Westbrook, L.. 3,953
J. N. Hill, Ind....... 312
Lab. maj......... 2,259
(Feb. '74, Lab. maj. 437)

DRAKE E. 55,556

467*Miss J. E. Fookes, C... 17,287
B. W. Fletcher, Lab.. 17,253
Miss M. E. Castle, L.. 7,354
C. maj............ 34
(Feb. '74, C. maj. 2,611)

SUTTON E. 61,007

468*Hon. A. K. M. Clark,
C.............. 20,457
J. G. Priestley, Lab.. 15,269
S. G. Banks, L....... 10,131
C. maj............ 5,188
(Feb. '74, C. maj. 8,104)

Pontefract and Castleford
E. 60,288

469*J. Harper, Lab....... 30,208
I. R. Bloomer, C..... 6,966
S. F. Galloway, L..... 5,259
T. Parsons, Ind...... 457
Lab. maj......... 23,242
(Feb. '74, Lab. maj. 23,804)

Pontypool
E. 55,112

470*L. Abse, Lab........ 25,381
R. J. Moreland, C..... 6,686
E. A. R. Mathias, L.. 5,744
R. D. Tanner, P.C.... 2,223
Lab. maj......... 18,695
(Feb. '74, Lab. maj. 17,465)

Pontypridd
E. 70,200

471*B. T. John, Lab....... 29,302
I. A. S. Jones, C...... 10,528
Mrs. M. G. Murphy,
L.............. 8,050
R. A. Kemp, P.C.... 3,917
Lab. maj......... 18,774
(Feb. '74, Lab. maj. 16,622)

Poole
E. 83,403

472*H. O. Murton, O.B.E.,
T.D., C........... 28,982
G. M. Goode, L..... 17,557
G. W. Hobbs, Lab.... 16,262
C. maj............ 11,425
(Feb. '74, C. maj. 10,068)

Portsmouth
NORTH E. 69,089

473*F. A. Judd, Lab....... 24,352
J. Ward, C.......... 23,007
Mrs. E. Brooks, L.... 5,208
T. L. Keen, Ind...... 527
Lab. maj......... 1,345
(Feb. '74, Lab. maj. 320)

SOUTH E. 70,773

474*R. B. Pink, C.B.E.,
V.R.D., C........ 23,379
A. M. Halmos, Lab... 15,308
M. Tribe, L......... 9,807
A. D. Rifkin, Ind.... 612
C. maj............ 8,071
(Feb. '74, C. maj. 10,982)

Preston
NORTH E. 51,369

475*R. H. Atkins, Lab..... 18,044
Miss M. Holt, C..... 16,260
G. Payne, L......... 4,948
H. Smith, Ind....... 138
Lab. maj......... 1,784
(Feb. '74, Lab. maj. 255)

SOUTH E. 51,522

476*S. G. Thorne, Lab..... 18,449
A. Green, C.B.E., C... 14,700
R. P. Marshall, L.... 5,456
E. Harrison, Nat. Front 663
H. Smith, Ind........ 87
Lab. maj......... 3,749
(Feb. '74, Lab. maj. 1,887)

Pudsey
E. 65,354

477*J. G. D. Shaw, C..... 20,180
S. J. Cooksey, L...... 15,599
K. Targett, Lab....... 15,293
C. maj............ 4,581
(Feb. '74, C. maj. 3,739)

Putney
E. 66,515

478*H. G. Jenkins, Lab... 21,611
G. A. Wade, C....... 18,836
A. C. Slade, L....... 7,159
T. L. Keen, Ind....... 125
Lab. maj......... 2,775
(Feb. '74, Lab. maj. 1,439)

Ravensbourne
E. 48,541

479*J. L. Hunt, C....... 18,318
D. E. A. Crowe, L.... 9,813
C. Howes, Lab....... 7,204
I. Stevens, Nat. Front. 574
C. maj............ 8,505
(Feb. '74, C. maj. 8,897)

Reading
E. 64,484

480*R. A. B. Durant, C.... 18,734
Miss M. J. Denby,
Lab............. 18,266
K. E. V. Watts, L.... 9,064
P. Baker, Nat. Front.. 594
C. maj............ 468
(Feb. '74, C. maj. 2,369)

SOUTH E. 69,124

481*G. F. Vaughan, C..... 21,959
P. R. Burall, L....... 15,293
L. Silverman, Lab..... 14,375
C. maj............ 6,666
(Feb. '74, C. maj. 5,359)

Redcar
E. 62,365

482*J. Tinn, Lab.......... 23,204
R. Hall, C.......... 12,774
N. Clark, L......... 7,101
Lab. maj......... 10,430
(Feb. '74, Lab. maj. 9,254)

Reigate
E. 72,745

483*G. A. Gardiner, C..... 27,769
M. G. Ormerod, Lab.. 14,185
A. C. Bryan, L....... 12,554
M. Taggart, Ind...... 266
C. maj............ 13,584
(Feb. '74, C. maj. 14,060)

Renfrewshire
EAST E. 61,811

484*Rt. Hon. Betty Harvie
Anderson, O.B.E., T.D.,
C.............. 19,847
I. Jenkins, Scot. Nat... 11,137
C. J. Roberts, Lab.... 9,997
W. G. A. Craig, L.... 7,015
C. maj............ 8,710
(Feb. '74, C. maj. 15,486)

WEST E. 67,078

485*N. F. Buchan, Lab..... 20,674
C. D. Cameron, Scot.
Nat.............. 15,374
J. Ross-Harper, C.... 14,399
D. O. Brown, L...... 3,271
Lab. maj......... 5,300
(Feb. '74, Lab. maj. 2,668)

Rhondda
E. 65,787

486*T. A. Jones, Lab..... 38,654
D. Morgan, P.C...... 4,173
P. Leyshon, C........ 3,739
D. J. Austin, L....... 2,142
A. True, Comm...... 1,404
Lab. maj......... 34,481
(Feb. '74, Lab. maj. 30,141)

Richmond (Surrey)
E. 53,821

487*Sir A. H. F. Royle,
K.C.M.G., C........ 17,450
A. J. Watson, L...... 13,235
R. G. Marshall-
Andrews, Lab...... 8,714
E. A. Russell, Nat.
Front............. 1,000
C. maj............ 4,215
(Feb. '74, C. maj. 3,827)

Richmond (Yorks.)
E. 62,002

488*Sir T. P. G. Kitson, C. 23,156
Mrs. P. Waudby, L... 9,528
I. A. Wilkie, Lab...... 8,025
C. maj............ 13,628
(Feb. '74, C. maj. 15,267)

Ripon
E. 50,172

489*K. Hampson, C....... 20,636
D. Austick, L........ 13,632
S. P. Meyer, Lab..... 5,330
C. maj............ 7,004
(Feb. '74, C. maj. 4,335)

Rochdale
E. 67,029

490*C. Smith, M.B.E., L.... 20,092
J. Connell, Lab....... 17,339
R. Young, C........ 7,740
M. W. Sellors, Nat.
Front............. 1,927
L. maj............ 2,753
(Feb. '74, L. maj. 8,899)

Rochester and Chatham
E. 79,799
491	R. E. Bean, *Lab.*	25,467
	Mrs. P. E. Fenner, C.	23,049
	Mrs. M. Black, L.	9,035
	G. Hazelden, *Nat.*	
	Front	1,150
	Lab. maj.	2,418
	(Feb. '74, C. maj. 843)	

Romford
E. 55,337
492	*M. J. Neubert, C.*	17,164
	D. R. O'Flynn, *Lab.*	14,513
	T. E. Hurlstone, C.	7,663
	L. C. H. Sampson, *Ind.*	200
	C. maj.	2,651
	(Feb. '74, C. maj. 3,073)	

Ross and Cromarty
E. 29,411
493	*J. H. N. Gray, C.*	7,954
	W. McRae, *Scot. Nat.*	7,291
	B. D. H. Wilson, *Lab.*	3,440
	T. Glen, L.	1,747
	C. maj.	663
	(Feb. '74, C. maj. 2,871)	

Rossendale
E. 50,463
494	M. A. Noble, *Lab.*	16,156
	R. W. T. Bray, C.	15,953
	J. A. Hamilton, L.	8,693
	Lab. maj.	203
	(Feb. '74, C. maj. 797)	

Rotherham
E. 61,209
495	*Rt. Hon. B. K. O'Malley, Lab.*	25,874
	R. A. Hambro, C.	8,840
	V. Bottomley, L.	5,350
	Lab. maj.	17,034
	(Feb. '74, Lab. maj. 16,734)	

Rother Valley
E. 91,963
496	*P. Hardy, Lab.*	44,670
	G. P. A. Waller, C.	11,893
	Rev. G. Reid, L.	9,828
	Lab. maj.	32,777
	(Feb. '74, Lab. maj. 33,474)	

Roxburgh, Selkirk and Peebles
E. 57,824
497	*D. M. S. Steel, L.*	20,006
	Mrs. C. M. Anderson, C.	12,573
	A. Edmonds, *Scot. Nat.*	9,178
	D. A. Graham, *Lab.*	4,076
	L. maj.	7,433
	(Feb. '74, L. maj. 9,017)	

Rugby
E. 59,590
498	*W. G. Price, Lab.*	22,926
	A. R. Marlow, C.	17,722
	A. Butcher, L.	6,775
	A. S. Frost, *Ind.*	137
	Lab. maj.	5,204
	(Feb. '74, Lab. maj. 6,154)	

Ruislip–Northwood
E. 54,119
499	*F. P. Crowder, Q.C., C.*	20,779
	D. A. G. Race, *Lab.*	10,490
	Miss J. M. Arram, L.	8,621
	Mrs. W. Hobday, *Ind.*	458
	C. maj.	10,289
	(Feb. '74, C. maj. 11,421)	

Runcorn
E. 69,929
500	*M. Carlisle, Q.C., C.*	25,047
	A. J. Eccles, *Lab.*	19,579
	Rev. D. Sanders, L.	9,188
	N. Dobson, *Ind.*	464
	C. maj.	5,468
	(Feb. '74, C. maj. 7,268)	

Rushcliffe
E. 63,976
501	*K. H. Clarke, C.*	27,074
	Mrs. V. Bell, *Lab.*	12,131
	J. E. Hamilton, L.	10,300
	C. maj.	14,943
	(Feb. '74, C. maj. 17,709)	

Rutherglen
E. 48,824
502	*J. G. Mackenzie, Lab.*	17,088
	I. O. Bayne, *Scot. Nat.*	9,732
	J. Thomson, C.	9,248
	R. E. Brown, L.	2,424
	Lab. maj.	7,356
	(Feb. '74, Lab. maj. 4,153)	

Rutland and Stamford
E. 54,656
503	*K. Lewis, C.*	19,101
	M. R. C. Withers, *Lab.*	12,111
	D. C. Howie, L.	10,131
	C. maj.	6,990
	(Feb. '74, C. maj. 8,885)	

Rye
E. 72,261
504	*B. G. Irvine, C.*	30,511
	D. R. S. Moore, L.	14,828
	D. W. Threlfall, *Lab.*	8,303
	C. maj.	15,683
	(Feb. '74, C. maj. 16,135)	

Saffron Walden
E. 62,397
505	*P. M. Kirk, C.*	21,291
	F. P. D. Moore, L.	14,770
	H. Green, *Lab.*	12,652
	C. maj.	6,521
	(Feb. '74, C. maj. 7,545)	

St. Albans
E. 69,693
506	*V. H. Goodhew, C.*	24,436
	E. Hudson, *Lab.*	15,301
	A. C. Shaw, L.	14,614
	C. maj.	9,135
	(Feb. '74, C. maj. 8,421)	

St. Helens
E. 76,067
507	*L. Spriggs, Lab.*	32,620
	K. J. Bridgeman, C.	10,554
	A. E. Lycett, L.	7,689
	Lab. maj.	22,066
	(Feb. '74, Lab. maj. 21,716)	

St. Ives
E. 51,440
508	*J. W. F. Nott, C.*	17,198
	G. E. T. Tonkin, L.	11,330
	B. M. Tidy, *Lab.*	9,388
	C. maj.	5,868
	(Feb. '74, C. maj. 5,425)	

St. Marylebone
E. 43,633
509	*K. W. Baker, C.*	13,660
	Mrs. P. J. Moberly, *Lab.*	7,157
	B. Silver, L.	4,067
	C. maj.	6,503
	(Feb. '74, C. maj. 8,717)	

St. Pancras North
E. 41,629
510	*A. W. Stallard, Lab.*	14,155
	J. R. Major, C.	6,602
	P. J. W. Medlicott, L.	3,428
	Lab. maj.	7,553
	(Feb. '74, Lab. maj. 6,835)	

Salford
EAST E. 40,144
511	*F. J. Allaun, Lab.*	14,276
	S. Latimer, C.	6,440
	A. F. Bell, L.	3,160
	Lab. maj.	7,836
	(Feb. '74, Lab. maj. 6,931)	

WEST E. 45,833
512	*Rt. Hon. S. Orme, Lab.*	17,112
	J. N. L. Tillett, C.	8,540
	A. E. Arstall, L.	4,237
	Lab. maj.	8,572
	(Feb. '74, Lab. maj. 6,462)	

Salisbury
E. 62,817
513	*M. A. Hamilton, C.*	20,478
	J. F. Lakeman, L.	16,298
	C. J. Connor, *Lab.*	10,140
	C. maj.	4,180
	(Feb. '74, C. maj. 6,217)	

Scarborough
E. 58,553
514	*M. N. Shaw, C.*	19,831
	M. J. L. Brook, L.	10,123
	D. J. Taylor-Goodby, *Lab.*	9,923
	C. maj.	9,708
	(Feb. '74, C. maj. 5,107)	

Sevenoaks
E. 74,969
515	*Sir J. C. Rodgers, Bt., C.*	26,670
	J. Scanlan. *Lab.*	15,065
	R. F. Webster, L.	15,024
	C. maj.	11,605
	(Feb. '74, C. maj. 13,713)	

Sheffield
ATTERCLIFFE E. 63,917
516	*A. E. P. Duffy, Lab.*	29,601
	Miss P. M. Santhouse, C.	8,043
	G. P. Broadhead, L.	5,282
	Lab. maj.	21,558
	(Feb. '74, Lab. maj. 21,176)	

BRIGHTSIDE E. 54,095
517	*Miss V. J. Maynard, Lab.*	18,108
	E. Griffiths, Ind. Lab.	10,182
	R. E. Walker, C.	4,905
	W. T. W. Blades, L.	3,271
	Lab. maj.	7,926
	(Feb. '74, Lab. maj. 20,567)	

HALLAM E. 77,400
518	*J. H. Osborn, C.*	26,083
	C. J. C. Betts, *Lab.*	15,419
	M. A. K. Johnson, L.	11,724
	C. maj.	10,664
	(Feb. '74, C. maj. 12,913)	

HEELEY E. 65,244
519	*F. O. Hooley, Lab.*	24,728
	A. E. Page, C.	15,322
	R. J. Fairfax, L.	7,151
	P. Revell, *Nat. Front*	723
	Lab. maj.	9,406
	(Feb. '74, Lab. maj. 6,585)	

HILLSBOROUGH E. 52,032
520*M. H. Flannery, Lab... 21,026
   R. B. Williamson, C. 8,718
   R. C. Osner, L........ 4,912
   Lab. maj........... 12,308
   (Feb. '74, Lab. maj. 11,280)

PARK E. 67,425
521*Rt. Hon. F. W. Mulley,
   Lab............... 30,057
   F. R. Butler, L....... 6,093
   R. Trench, C........ 5,539
   G. Ashberry, Comm... 403
   Lab. maj.......... 23,964
   (Feb. '74, Lab. maj. 22,677)

Shipley
E. 52,006
522*J. M. Fox, C....... 18,518
   Rev. M. J. Wedge-
   worth, Lab........ 15,482
   G. G. Roberts, L...... 8,094
   C. maj........... 3,036
   (Feb. '74, C. maj. 4,155)

Shoreham
E. 68,498
523*R. N. Luce, C....... 26,170
   P. F. Bartram, L..... 14,797
   Q. Barry, Lab....... 10,200
   C. maj........... 11,373
   (Feb. '74, C. maj. 9,758)

Shrewsbury
E. 60,228
524*Sir J. A. Langford-Holt,
   C............... 19,064
   W. Marsh, L........ 13,642
   D. W. Woodvine, Lab. 11,504
   C. maj........... 5,422
   (Feb. '74, C. maj. 6,181)

Sidcup
E. 49,564
525*Rt. Hon. E. R. G.
   Heath, M.B.E., C.... 18,991
   W. J. Jennings, Lab.. 11,448
   I. R. P. Josephs, L.... 6,954
   D. H. Jones, Ind...... 174
   M. J. Norton, Ind.... 61
   C. maj........... 7,543
   (Feb. '74, C. maj. 9,698)

Skipton
E. 52,562
526*G. B. Drayson, T.D., C. 17,822
   Mrs. K. C. Brooks, L. 17,232
   C. G. Burks, Lab..... 8,109
   C. maj........... 590
   (Feb. '74, C. maj. 2,116)

Solihull
E. 79,992
527*W. P. Grieve, Q.C., C. 31,707
   J. A. Windmill, L..... 15,848
   D. McShane, Lab..... 12,640
   C. maj........... 15,859
   (Feb. '74, C. maj. 17,363)

Somerset North
E. 89,056
528*A. P. Dean, C....... 32,146
   H. R. White, Lab.... 22,671
   Mrs. J. M. Bourne, L. 16,428
   J. K. Polling, Ind..... 387
   C. maj........... 9,475
   (Feb. '74, C. maj. 12,155)

Southall
E. 70,832
529*S. J. Bidwell, Lab..... 24,218
   R. C. Patten, C...... 14,235
   C. I. M. Arnold, L.... 6,557
   Lab. maj........... 9,983
   (Feb. '74, Lab. maj. 8,812)

Southampton
ITCHEN E. 82,009
530*R. C. Mitchell, Lab... 28,168
   P. T. James, C....... 20,373
   J. Cherryson, L...... 9,071
   Lab. maj........... 7,795
   (Feb. '74, Lab. maj. 5,590)

TEST E. 73,895
531 B. C. Gould, Lab.... 22,780
   *S. J. A. Hill, C....... 22,250
   J. R. Wallis, L....... 8,994
   Lab. maj........... 530
   (Feb. '74, C. maj. 1,403)

Southend
EAST E. 57,295
532*Sir S. J. McAdden,
   C.B.E., C.......... 18,083
   Mrs. S. K. Ward, Lab. 13,480
   J. W. J. Curry, L..... 7,856
   C. maj........... 4,603
   (Feb. '74, C. maj. 4,952)

WEST E. 67,438
533*H. P. G. Channon, C. 23,480
   W. Greaves, L....... 16,409
   A. N. Wright, Lab.... 9,451
   C. maj........... 7,071
   (Feb. '74, C. maj. 5,155)

Southgate
E. 70,935
534*Hon. A. G. Berry, C... 25,888
   J. P. Sheppard, Lab... 10,966
   G. J. Bridge, L....... 9,922
   B. W. Pell, Nat. Front 1,255
   C. maj........... 14,922
   (Feb. '74, C. maj. 14,454)

Southport
E. 66,109
535*W. I. Percival, Q.C., C. 23,014
   R. C. Fearn, L....... 17,387
   I. G. James, Lab..... 8,323
   C. maj........... 5,627
   (Feb. '74, C. maj. 3,882)

South Shields
E. 72,584
536*A. Blenkinsop, Lab.... 26,492
   N. S. Smith, C....... 11,667
   L. Garbutt, L....... 8,106
   W. Owen, Nat. Front. 711
   Lab. maj........... 14,825
   (Feb. '74, Lab. maj. 11,986)

Sowerby
E. 48,747
537*M. O. F. Madden,
   Lab............... 14,971
   D. Thompson, C..... 14,325
   D. T. Shutt, L....... 9,136
   H. Smith, Ind........ 157
   Lab. maj........... 646
   (Feb. '74, Lab. maj. 115)

Spelthorne
E. 69,411
538*Rt. Hon. H. E. Atkins,
   C............... 23,125
   C. H. Dodwell, Lab.. 17,177
   P. E. Winner, L...... 10,212
   J. Clifton, Nat. Front. 1,180
   C. maj........... 5,948
   (Feb. '74, C. maj. 8,059)

Stafford and Stone
E. 78,817
539*Rt. Hon. H. C. P. J.
   Fraser, M.B.E., C.... 27,173
   T. E. Cowlishaw, Lab. 20,845
   H. S. Martin, L...... 11,491
   D. E. Sutch, Ind...... 351
   C. maj........... 6,328
   (Feb. '74, C. maj. 8,983)

Staffordshire South West
E. 61,042
540*P. T. Cormack, C..... 22,604
   I. K. Wymer, Lab.... 15,065
   A. Lambert, L....... 8,355
   C. maj........... 7,539
   (Feb. '74, C. maj. 9,758)

Stalybridge and Hyde
E. 66,389
541*T. Pendry, Lab....... 25,161
   S. Burgoyne, C...... 15,404
   D. F. Burden, L...... 7,725
   G. Tetler, Ind....... 318
   Lab. maj........... 9,757
   (Feb. '74, Lab. maj. 8,068)

Stepney and Poplar
E. 60,458
542*Rt. Hon. P. D. Shore,
   Lab............... 24,159
   H. Greenway, C..... 3,183
   Mrs. F. W. Alexander,
   L............... 3,181
   K. Halpin, Comm..... 617
   Lab. maj........... 20,976
   (Feb. '74, Lab. maj. 23,330)

Stirling, Falkirk and
Grangemouth
E. 64,362
543*H. Ewing, Lab........ 22,090
   Dr. R. D. McIntyre,
   Scot. Nat....... 20,324
   G. A. Campbell, C... 7,186
   J. Angles, L........ 1,477
   Lab. maj........... 1,766
   (Feb. '74, Lab. maj. 3,849)

Stirlingshire
EAST AND CLACKMANNAN
E. 62,693
544*G. N. Reid, Scot. Nat. 25,998
   R. G. Douglas, Lab... 18,657
   T. N. A. Begg, C..... 5,269
   D. Shields, L......... 1,268
   Scot. Nat. maj. 7,341
   (Feb. '74, Scot. Nat. maj. 3,610)

WEST E. 52,989
545 D. A. Canavan, Lab.... 16,698
   Mrs. J. T. Jones, Scot.
   Nat........... 16,331
   D. W. Mitchell, C.... 7,875
   I. MacFarlane, L...... 1,865
   Lab. maj........... 367
   (Feb. '74, Lab. maj. 4,844)

Stockport
NORTH E. 52,842
546*A. F. Bennett, Lab..... 17,979
   I. W. Owen, C...... 16,155
   P. J. Arnold, L....... 7,085
   Lab. maj........... 1,824
   (Feb. '74, Lab. maj. 203)

SOUTH E. 47,795
547*M. Orbach*, Lab....... 16,281
Viscount Lewisham,
   C................. 12,061
C. J. Carter, *L*....... 7,160
   Lab. maj.......... 4,220
   (Feb. '74, Lab. maj. 3,098)

Stockton
E. 85,519
548*W. T. Rodgers*, Lab... 32,962
B. S. Mawhinney, *C*.. 18,488
Mrs. N. Long, *L*..... 6,906
Mrs. V. Fletcher, *Ind*.. 750
   Lab. maj.......... 14,474
   (Feb. '74, Lab. maj. 12,371)

Stoke-on-Trent
CENTRAL E. 61,217
549*R. B. Cant*, Lab....... 24,146
W. Williams, *C*...... 9,493
A. Thomas, *L*........ 6,313
   Lab. maj.......... 14,653
   (Feb. '74, Lab. maj. 11,748)
NORTH E. 59,899
550*J. S. Forrester*, Lab.... 25,264
J. W. D. Davies, *C*... 10,192
M. Smith, *L*......... 6,239
   Lab. maj.......... 15,072
   (Feb. '74, Lab. maj. 12,459)
SOUTH E. 72,629
551*J. Ashley*, C.H., Lab.. 30,699
J. S. Heath, *C*...... 14,204
Mrs. E. Johnson, *L*... 5,278
   Lab. maj.......... 16,495
   (Feb. '74, Lab. maj. 15,669)

Stratford-on-Avon
E. 71,895
552*A. E. U. Maude*, T.D.,
   C................. 27,123
M. J. W.Wright, *L*... 14,555
D. V. Hunt, *Lab*...... 11,551
   C. maj............ 12,568
   (Feb. '74, C. maj. 13,221)

Streatham
E. 56,453
553*W. J. M. Shelton*, C... 16,515
Mrs. J. Gaffin, *Lab*... 13,648
R. G. O. Silver, *L*..... 4,987
T. Lamb, *Nat. Front* . 817
Mrs. T. Moore, *Ind*... 210
   C. maj............ 2,867
   (Feb. '74, C. maj. 4,475)

Stretford
E. 68,766
554*W. S. Churchill*, C.... 22,114
P. N. Scott, *Lab*...... 20,877
D. I. Wrigley, *L*...... 9,629
   C. maj............ 1,237
   (Feb. '74, C. maj. 3,989)

Stroud
E. 69,398
555*J. A. Kershaw*, M.C., C. 24,406
W. H. Maddocks, *Lab.* 17,352
Mrs. S. A. Ritchie, *L.* 13,756
J. S. Churchill, *Ind*.... 241
   C. maj............ 7,054
   (Feb. '74, C. maj. 8,471)

Sudbury and Woodbridge
E. 84,286
556*K. M. Stainton*, C..... 30,049
R. E. Russell, *Lab*.... 17,986
N. S. Lewis, *L*....... 15,206
   C. maj............ 12,063
   (Feb. '74, C. maj. 13,701)

Sunderland
NORTH E. 75,577
557*Rt. Hon. F. T. Willey*,
   Lab................. 29,618
J. D. S. Brown, *C*.... 13,947
J. A. Lennox, *L*...... 7,077
   Lab. maj.......... 15,671
   (Feb. '74, Lab. maj. 11,400)
SOUTH E. 76,479
558*G. A. T. Bagier*, Lab.. 28,623
Sir J. C. Buchanan-
   Riddell, Bt., *C*.... 15,593
W. J. Nicholson, *L*... 7,828
   Lab. maj.......... 13,030
   (Feb. '74, Lab. maj. 8,596)

Surbiton
E. 46,073
559*Sir N. T. L. Fisher*,
   M.C., *C*........... 15,330
A. S. Mackinlay, *Lab.* 9,309
D. A. S. Brooke, *L*... 8,931
   C. maj............ 6,021
   (Feb. '74, C. maj. 6,500)

Surrey
EAST E. 55,673
560*Rt. Hon. Sir R. E. G.
   Howe*, Q.C., *C*.... 22,227
K. S. Vaus, *L*....... 12,382
D. L. Allonby, *Lab.*.. 7,797
   C. maj............ 9,845
   (Feb. '74, C. maj. 8,019)
NORTH WEST E. 68,928
561*W. M. J. Grylls*, C... 25,524
P. F. Whiteley, *Lab*... 11,943
L. E. Sims, *L*........ 11,356
   C. maj............ 13,581
   (Feb. '74, C. maj. 14,949)

Sussex, Mid
E. 61,074
562*R. T. Renton*, C...... 25,126
R. A. Symes-
   Schutzman, *L*...... 13,129
Miss M. R. Fraser,
   Lab................. 8,404
   C. maj............ 11,997
   (Feb. '74, C. maj. 12,155)

Sutton and Cheam
E. 60,559
563*D. N. MacFarlane*, C.. 22,156
G. N. Tope, *L*....... 16,995
J. K. Rhodes, *Lab*.... 7,118
Dr. Una Kroll, *Ind*... 298
   C. maj............ 5,161
   (Feb. '74, C. maj. 1,719)

Sutton Coldfield
E. 60,491
564*P. N. Fowler*, C...... 25,729
Sir J. A. Watson, Bt.,
   L................. 12,373
G. W. Wells, *Lab*.... 6,955
   C. maj............ 13,356
   (Feb. '74, C. maj. 13,426)

Swansea
EAST E. 58,780
565 *D. Anderson*, Lab..... 26,735
D. J. Mercer, *C*...... 6,014
R. H. Anstey, *L*...... 5,173
J. G. Ball, *P.C*...... 3,978
   Lab. maj.......... 20,721
   (Feb. '74, Lab. maj. 19,687)

WEST E. 65,225
566*A. J. Williams*, Lab.... 22,565
A. P. Thomas, *C*..... 17,729
B. E. Keal, *L*........ 6,842
G. ap Gwent, *P.C*.... 1,778
   Lab. maj.......... 4,836
   (Feb. '74, Lab. maj. 3,338)

Swindon
E. 62,900
567*D. L. Stoddart*, Lab.... 24,124
J. N. Gripper, *C*...... 13,854
R. Hubbard, *L*....... 8,349
Mrs. K. B. Blakeney,
   Ind................. 206
   Lab. maj.......... 10,270
   (Feb. '74, Lab. maj. 8,709)

Taunton
E. 63,654
568*Rt. Hon. E. D. L. du
   Cann*, C........... 22,542
B. J. Sheerman, *Lab*... 15,721
M. E. Mann, *L*....... 11,984
L. D. Bradford, *Ind*... 283
   C. maj............ 6,821
   (Feb. '74, C. maj. 8,440)

Thanet
EAST E. 47,941
569*J. W. P. Aitken*, C.... 15,813
Mrs. S. M. Bartlett,
   Lab................. 11,310
C. Hogarth, *L*....... 6,472
K. Munson, *Nat. Front* 708
   C. maj............ 4,503
   (Feb. '74, C. maj. 6,597)
WEST E. 43,901
570*W. R. Rees-Davies*,
   Q.C., *C*........... 13,763
C. J. Smith, *Lab*..... 8,655
I. G. Tiltman, *L*...... 7,935
   C. maj............ 5,108
   (Feb. '74, C. maj. 7,660)

Thirsk and Malton
E. 63,856
571*J. D. Spence*, C........ 24,779
R. Kent, *L*.......... 10,917
R. K. Illingworth,
   Lab................. 10,842
   C. maj............ 13,862
   (Feb. '74, C. maj. 14,408)

Thornaby
E. 62,330
572*I. W. Wrigglesworth*,
   Lab................. 22,130
J. H. V. Sutcliffe, *C*... 17,482
R. F. Tennant, *L*..... 5,442
   Lab. maj.......... 4,648
   (Feb. '74, Lab. maj. 1,718)

Thurrock
E. 89,448
573*H. J. Delargy*, Lab.... 34,066
P. W. C. Lomax, *C*.. 14,986
A. Charlton, *L*....... 12,255
   Lab. maj.......... 19,080
   (Feb. '74, Lab. maj. 18,518)

Tiverton
E. 69,884
574*R. J. Maxwell-
   Hyslop*, C.......... 25,265
F. J. Suter, *L*....... 19,911
M. Phillips, *Lab*..... 8,946
   C. maj............ 5,354
   (Feb. '74, C. maj. 5,541)

Tonbridge and Malling
E. 65,589
575*J. P. Stanley, C...... 23,188
Mrs. P. Knight, Lab... 14,579
M. J. B. Vann, L..... 11,767
C. maj............ 8,609
(Feb. '74, C. maj. 10,108)

Tooting
E. 53,793
576*T. M. Cox, Lab...... 18,530
A. C. Elliot, C....... 10,675
R. F. J. Heron, L..... 4,644
R. E. Lewis, Comm... 268
Lab. maj........... 7,855
(Feb. '74, Lab. maj. 6,108)

Torbay
E. 85,575
577*Sir F. M. Bennett, C... 30,208
J. M. Goss, L........ 17,770
J. R. W. Tench, Lab.. 14,441
C. maj........... 12,438
(Feb. '74, C. maj. 12,408)

Totnes
E. 80,715
578*R. L. Mawby, C...... 27,987
A. H. Rogers, Lab.... 21,586
Mrs. S. M. Spence,
Lab............... 12,366
C. maj........... 6,401
(Feb. '74, C. maj. 9,643)

Tottenham
E. 47,530
579*N. Atkinson, Lab...... 15,708
P. Lilley, C......... 6,492
Miss K. Alexander, L. 2,288
R. W. Painter, Nat.
Front............ 2,211
Lab. maj........... 9,216
(Feb. '74, Lab. maj. 9,126)

Truro
E. 71,992
580 D. C. Penhaligon, L... 22,549
*P. J. S. Dixon, C...... 22,085
A. F. Long, Lab...... 11,606
J. C. A. Whetter, Ind. 384
L. maj............. 464
(Feb. '74, C. maj. 2,561)

Tunbridge Wells
E. 69,138
581*P. B. B. Mayhew, Q.C.,
C............... 24,829
D. C. Owens, L..... 12,802
R. C. Blackwell, Lab. 12,499
C. maj........... 12,027
(Feb. '74, C. maj. 11,028)

Twickenham
E. 72,210
582*T. F. H. Jessel, C..... 24,959
Mrs. M. Cunningham,
Lab............ 15,452
S. E. Kramer, L...... 13,021
W. Burgess, Ind...... 287
C. maj........... 9,507
(Feb. '74, C. maj. 11,503)

Tynemouth
E. 76,449
583*N. G. Trotter, C..... 24,510
J. E. Miller, Lab..... 21,389
R. S. Turner, L...... 10,895
C. maj........... 3,121
(Feb. '74, C. maj. 6,387)

Ulster, Mid
E. 81,689
584*J. Dunlop, U.U.U..... 30,552
I. A. Cooper, S.D.L.P. 25,885
F. Donnelly, Rep..... 8,091
U.U.U. maj....... 4,667
(Feb. '74, U.U.U. maj. 6,632)

Upminster
E. 64,429
585*J. W. Loveridge, C.... 20,966
J. E. D. Whysall, Lab. 20,272
A. Merton, L........ 7,844
C. maj........... 694
(Feb. '74, C. maj. 1,008)

Uxbridge
E. 59,746
586*J. M. Shersby, C...... 19,969
G. E. Pringle, Lab.... 17,816
J. S. Pincham, L...... 7,081
C. maj........... 2,153
(Feb. '74, C. maj. 2,415)

Vauxhall
E. 46,502
587*Rt. Hon. G. R. Strauss,
Lab.............. 15,493
V. J. MacColl, C..... 5,727
E. F. Cousins, L...... 3,300
Lab. maj........... 9,766
(Feb. '74, Lab. maj. 8,641)

Wakefield
E. 66,535
588*W. Harrison, Lab..... 25,616
E. J. L. Koops, C..... 12,810
A. Fussey, L........ 8,304
Lab. maj........... 12,806
(Feb. '74, Lab. maj. 11,418)

Wallasey
E. 70,095
589*Mrs. L. Chalker, C.... 23,499
G. McNamara, Lab... 21,529
P. E. Tyrer, L....... 7,643
J. Fishwick, Nat. Front 787
C. maj............ 1,970
(Feb. '74, C. maj. 2,492)

Wallsend
E. 90,300
590*W. E. Garrett, Lab.... 37,180
Miss J. F. Chambers,
C............... 15,911
P. Hampton, L....... 10,453
K. Flynn, Ind....... 435
Lab. maj........... 21,269
(Feb. '74, Lab. maj. 17,247)

Walsall
NORTH E. 71,525
591*Rt. Hon. J. T. Stone-
house, Lab........ 28,340
R. G. Hodgson, C.... 12,455
W. Gill, L......... 6,377
J. Richards, Comm... 465
Lab. maj........... 15,885
(Feb. '74, Lab. maj. 14,704)
SOUTH E. 59,241
592*B. T. George, Lab..... 20,917
H. Smith, O.B.E., C... 16,255
G. F. A. Hooper, L... 5,031
J. C. Parker, Nat.
Front............ 1,226
T. L. Keen, Ind....... 150
Lab. maj........... 4,662
(Feb. '74, Lab. maj. 1,580)

Walthamstow
E. 52,280
593*E. P. Deakins, Lab.... 19,088
D. Arnold, C........ 8,424
M. P. O'Flanagan, L.. 5,199
R. Adde, Nat. Front.. 1,911
Lab. maj........... 10,664
(Feb. '74, Lab. maj. 8,734)

Wanstead and Woodford
E. 58,378
594*Rt. Hon. C. P. F.
Jenkin, C.......... 21,209
R. Darlington, Lab... 10,369
D. J. Gilby, L....... 8,272
C. maj............ 10,840
(Feb. '74, C. maj. 11,901)

Warley
EAST E. 57,530
595*A. M. W. Faulds, Lab. 21,065
P. Holliday, C....... 12,888
R. Smith, L......... 4,664
Lab. maj........... 8,177
(Feb. '74, Lab. maj. 7,571)
WEST E. 61,274
596*P. K. Archer, Q.C., Lab. 24,761
R. Evans, C......... 9,904
D. Owen, L......... 6,363
Lab. maj........... 14,857
(Feb. '74, Lab. maj. 14,624)

Warrington
E. 46,549
597*W. T. Williams, Q.C.,
Lab............... 19,882
J. W. Hayton, C..... 7,621
F. J. Deakin, L...... 4,158
Lab. maj........... 12,261
(Feb. '74, Lab. maj. 11,106)

Warwick and Leamington
E. 78,666
598*D. G. Smith, C....... 27,721
J. W. England, Lab... 19,476
T. A. Jones, L....... 11,625
C. maj............ 8,245
(Feb. '74, C. maj. 11,293)

Watford
E. 56,010
599*R. H. Tuck, Lab...... 19,177
T. W. A. Garel-Jones,
C............... 15,220
D. A. Jacobs, L...... 8,243
J. E. Wotherspoon,
Nat. Front......... 671
Lab. maj........... 3,957
(Feb. '74, Lab. maj. 2,795)

Wellingborough
E. 85,288
600*P. D. Fry, C......... 29,078
J. H. Mann, Lab...... 27,320
Mrs. P. Jessel, L...... 11,500
C. maj............ 1,758
(Feb. '74, C. maj. 2,270)

Wells
E. 69,658
601*Hon. R. T. Boscawen,
M.C., C........... 23,979
A. A. S. Butt-Philip,
L................. 16,278
G. Mortimer, Lab..... 13,909
Miss P. Howard, Ind.. 778
C. maj............ 7,701
(Feb. '74, C. maj. 7,785)

Welwyn and Hatfield
E. 67,149
602 Mrs. H. V. H. Hayman,
Lab............. 23,339
*Rt. Hon. Lord
Balniel, C......... 22,819
P. H. Robinson, L.... 8,418
Lab. maj.......... 520
(Feb. '74, Lab. maj. 1,415)

West Bromwich
EAST E. 58,400
603*P. C. Snape, Lab..... 19,942
D. Mellor, C........ 12,413
J. P. T. Hunt, L....... 5,442
G. Bowen, Nat. Front 1,692
Lab. maj.......... 7,529
(Feb. '74, Lab. maj. 5,209)
WEST E. 59,749
604*Miss B. Boothroyd, Lab. 23,336
J. N. W. Bridges-
Adams, C......... 8,537
D. J. Corney, L..... 3,619
R. Churms, Nat. Front 2,022
Lab. maj.......... 14,799
(Feb. '74, Lab. maj. 13,431)

Westbury
E. 73,592
605*D. M. Walters, M.B.E.,
C................. 24,172
A. W. G. Court, L... 18,129
A. J. Smith, Lab..... 15,613
C. maj............ 6,043
(Feb. '74, C. maj. 8,419)

Western Isles
E. 22,477
606*D. J. Stewart, Scot.
Nat............. 8,758
Mrs. M. Doig, Lab.... 3,526
N. K. Wilson, C...... 1,180
N. MacMillan, L..... 789
Scot. Nat. maj....... 5,232
(Feb. '74, Scot. Nat. maj. 7,200)

Westhoughton
E. 72,055
607*R. W. Stott, Lab..... 30,373
B. H. Tetlow, C..... 16,798
R. S. Hale, L....... 8,926
Lab. maj.......... 13,575
(Feb. '74, Lab. maj. 12,665)

West Lothian
E. 77,526
608*T. Dalyell, Lab....... 27,687
W. C. Wolfe, Scot.
Nat............. 24,997
A. H. Lester, C...... 6,086
H. MacAulay, L..... 2,083
C. Bett, Comm....... 247
Lab. maj.......... 2,690
(Feb. '74, Lab. maj. 6,422)

Westmorland
E. 55,880
609*T. M. Jopling, C...... 20,559
B. N. Wates, L....... 12,844
M. Taylor, Lab..... 7,028
C. maj............ 7,715
(Feb. '74, C. maj. 6,534)

Weston-super-Mare
E. 84,988
610*A. W. Wiggin, C...... 31,028
R. S. Miller, L....... 18,169
P. H. Owen, Lab..... 14,057
E. P. Iszatt, Ind...... 296
C. maj............ 12,859
(Feb. '74, C. maj. 13,601)

Whitehaven
E. 50,964
611*J. A. Cunningham, Lab. 21,832
P. B. Vose, C......... 11,899
M. Gilbert, L....... 5,563
Lab. maj.......... 9,933
(Feb. '74, Lab. maj. 7,362)

Widnes
E. 75,141
612*G. J. Oakes, Lab...... 31,532
A. H. K. Maynard, C. 14,661
A. Turner, L......... 7,067
Lab. maj.......... 16,871
(Feb. '74, Lab. maj. 16,499)

Wigan
E. 56,915
613*E. A. Fitch, Lab....... 27,692
P. M. Beard, C....... 8,865
J. Campbell, L 5,548
Lab. maj.......... 18,827
(Feb. '74, Lab. maj. 18,202)

Wimbledon
E. 70,726
614*Sir R. M. O. Havers,
Q.C., C............. 23,615
K. Bill, Lab.......... 14,909
K. N. Searby, L....... 10,133
C. maj............ 8,706
(Feb. '74, C. maj. 12,213)

Winchester
E. 82,790
615*Rear Adm. M. C. M.
Giles, D.S.O., O.B.E.,
G.M., C............. 27,671
J. W. Matthew, L..... 18,451
W. H. Allchin, Lab... 16,153
C. maj............ 9,220
(Feb. '74, C. maj. 10,504)

Windsor and Maidenhead
E. 79,703
616*A. J. Glyn, E.R.D., C.. 28,013
M. D. Golder, Lab.... 15,172
G. H. Kahan, L...... 14,022
C. maj............ 12,841
(Feb. '74, C. maj. 14,995)

Wirral
E. 93,135
617*Rt. Hon. J. S. B. Lloyd,
C.H., C.B.E., T.D.,
Q.C., The Speaker... 35,705
P. R. Thomas, Lab... 22,217
M. R. D. Gayford, L. 12,345
The Speaker's maj... 13,488
(Feb. '74, The Speaker's maj. 15,847)

Woking
E. 67,916
618*C. G. D. Onslow, C.. 22,804
P. Wade, L......... 14,069
J. W. Tattersall, Lab.. 11,737
R. Vaughan-Smith,
Nat. Front....... 921
C. maj............ 8,735
(Feb. '74, C. maj. 7,583)

Wokingham
E. 84,598
619*W. R. van Straubenzee,
M.B.E., C........... 24,009
R. W. Crew, Lab..... 16,304
T. Blyth, L.......... 15,329
C. maj............ 7,705
(Feb. '74, C. maj. 10,432)

Wolverhampton
NORTH EAST E. 69,513
620*Mrs. R. Short, Lab.... 25,788
P. W. Hawksley, C... 11,135
J. F. Porter, L........ 7,156
A. D. C. Webber, Nat.
Front............. 1,928
Lab. maj.......... 14,653
(Feb. '74, Lab. maj. 12,617)
SOUTH EAST E. 55,382
621*R. J. Edwards, Lab.... 21,466
Mrs. E. J. Holt, C.... 9,768
B. Norcott, L........ 3,636
G. Oldland, Nat. Front 1,703
Lab. maj.......... 11,698
(Feb. '74, Lab. maj. 10,905)
SOUTH WEST E. 64,075
622*N. W. Budgen, C.... 20,854
I. E. Geffen, Lab..... 15,554
J. Wernick, L........ 9,215
G. A. Cooper, Nat.
Front............. 1,573
C. maj............ 5,300
(Feb. '74, C. maj. 6,901)

Wood Green
E. 52,019
623*Mrs. J. S. Butler, Lab.. 16,605
T. Benyon, C........ 8,394
M. J. Walton, L....... 4,782
K. Squires, Nat. Front. 2,603
Lab. maj.......... 8,211
(Feb. '74, Lab. maj. 7,644)

Woolwich
EAST E. 50,998
624 J. C. Cartwright, Lab.. 19,812
B. H. Watson, C..... 7,387
D. J. Woodhead, L.... 4,638
M. Skeggs, Nat. Front 1,000
Lab. maj.......... 12,425
(Feb. '74, Lab. maj. 11,977)
WEST E. 56,368
625*W. Hamling, Lab..... 19,614
P. J. Bottomley, C.... 16,073
J. P. Johnson, L....... 5,962
Lab. maj.......... 3,541

(By-election, June 26, 1975)

P. J. Bottomley, C.... 17,280
J. Stanyer, Lab...... 14,898
Mrs. S. M. Hobday, L. 1,884
Mrs. R. Robinson,
Nat. Front....... 856
R. Mallone, Ind...... 218
F. Hansford-Miller,
Ind.............. 140
R. Simmerson, Ind... 104
P. Bishop, Ind....... 41
C. maj............ 2,382
(Feb. '74, Lab. maj. 2,436)

Worcester
E. 74,844
626*Rt. Hon. P. E. Walker,
M.B.E., C.......... 25,183
Rev. W. B. Morgan,
Lab.............. 20,194
Mrs. D. Elliott, L..... 9,888
C. maj............ 4,989
(Feb. '74, C. maj. 7,467)

Worcestershire South
E. 73,695
627*W. M. H. Spicer, C... 26,790
J. P. Birch, L........ 17,738
S. J. Randall, Lab..... 10,838
C. maj............ 9,052
(Feb. '74, C. maj. 7,165)

Workington
E. 53,114
628*Rt. Hon. T. F. Peart,
  Lab............... 22,539
  R. L. Page, C........ 12,988
  Mrs. J. Burns, L...... 4,728
  Lab. maj........... 9,551
  (Feb. '74, Lab. maj. 7,770)

Worthing
E. 72,594
629*T. L. Higgins, C...... 30,036
  M. H. C. Foley, L.... 12,691
  M. W. J. Neves, Lab.. 8,890
  C. maj........... 17,345
  (Feb. '74, C. maj. 18,930)

Wrekin, The
E. 82,659
630*G. T. Fowler, Lab..... 30,385
  P. Banks, C........ 23,547
  W. Dewsnip, L...... 8,442
  Lab. maj........... 6,838
  (Feb. '74, Lab. maj. 6,521)

Wrexham
E. 76,106
631*R. T. Ellis, Lab..... 28,885
  D. M. Thomas, L.... 12,519
  J. L. Pritchard, C.... 12,251
  H. W. Roberts, P.C.. 2,859
  Lab. maj........... 16,366
  (Feb. '74, Lab. maj. 13,083)

Wycombe
E. 78,832
632*Sir J. Hall, O.B.E., T.D.,
  C............... 27,131
  W. F. Back, Lab...... 18,052
  M. T. James, L...... 11,333
  D. H. Smith, Nat.
    Front............. 2,049
  C. maj........... 9,079
  (Feb. '74, C. maj. 10,699)

Yarmouth
E. 70,802
633*A. Fell, C........... 22,573
  Mrs. P. L. Hollis, Lab. 20,313
  P. R. Coleby, L...... 9,250
  C. maj........... 2,260
  (Feb. '74, C. maj. 4,937)

Yeovil
E. 75,159
634*Rt. Hon. J. W. W.
    Peyton, C......... 24,709
  M. T. McVicar, Lab.. 17,330
  G. F. Taylor, L...... 17,298
  J. E. Tippett, Ind.... 332
  C. maj........... 7,379
  (Feb. '74, C. maj. 7,490)

York
E. 77,172
635*A. W. Lyon, Lab...... 26,983
  J. G. B. Watson, C... 23,294
  Miss E. Graham, L.... 7,370
  H. Smith, Ind........ 304
  H. L. Stratton, Ind.... 171
  Lab. maj........... 3,689
  (Feb. '74, Lab. maj. 831)

SMALL MAJORITIES
The smallest majorities at the election of October 1974 were as follows:

Mrs. M. A. Bain (*Scot. Nat.*), Dunbartonshire East............... 22
G. H. Thompson (*Scot. Nat.*), Galloway.... 30
Miss J. E. Fookes (*C.*), Plymouth, Drake.... 34
N. H. Fairbairn (*C.*), Kinross and West Perthshire............... 53
A. J. Beith (*L.*), Berwick on Tweed....... 73
J. Ryman (*Lab.*), Blyth.................. 78
J. T. Lester (*C.*), Beeston 121
M. W. L. Morris (*C.*), Northampton, South 141
J. E. M. Moore (*C.*), Croydon, Central...... 164
M. A. Noble (*Lab.*), Rossendale.......... 203
B. J. Hayhoe (*C.*), Brentford and Chiswick.. 232

Hon. A. C. Butler (*C.*), Bosworth.......... 302
T. Litterick (*Lab.*), Selly Oak............. 326
B. J. Grocott (*Lab.*), Litchfield and Tamworth 331
I. M. Sproat (*C.*), Aberdeen, South........ 365
D. A. Canavan (*Lab.*), Stirlingshire, West... 367
Mrs. W. M. Ewing (*Scot. Nat.*), Moray and Nairn............... 367
J. T. Watkinson (*Lab.*), Gloucestershire, West. 409
F. R. White (*Lab.*), Bury and Radcliffe...... 442
D. C. Penhaligon (*L.*), Truro.............. 464
R. R. B. Durant (*C.*), Reading North....... 468
Sir R. W. Elliott (*C.*), Newcastle, North.... 469
R. Corbett (*Lab.*), Hemel Hempstead....... 485

WOMEN MEMBERS OF PARLIAMENT
Six new Women Members of Parliament were elected in October 1974. Five were Labour Candidates (Miss M. M. Jackson, Lincoln; Mrs. H. V. H. Hayman, Welwyn and Hatfield; Miss V. J. Maynard, Sheffield, Brightside; Mrs. M. Miller, Ilford, North; Mrs. W. A. Taylor, Bolton, West). The sixth was a Scottish Nationalist, Mrs. M. A. Bain, Dunbartonshire, E.

VOTING RESULTS, OCTOBER 1974

M.P.s	Electorate	Total votes and Turnout	Party Votes, Percentages and Members					
			C.	Lab.	L.	Comm.	Plaid Cymru Scot. Nat.	Others
ENGLAND 516	33,351,228	24,174,726 72·5%	9,410,026 38·9% 252	9,685,147 40·1% 255	4,878,568 20·2% 8	7,032 — —	— — —	193,953 0·8% 1
SCOTLAND 71	3,578,498	2,687,466 75·1%	668,677 24·9% 16	988,538 36·8% 41	206,834 7·7% 3	7,453 0·3% —	815,851 30·3% 11	113 — —
WALES 36	2,008,744	1,537,798 76·5%	367,248 23·9% 8	761,447 49·1% 23	238,997 15·5% 2	2,941 0·2% —	166,321 10·8% 3	844 — —
N. IRELAND 12	1,036,523	702,094 67·7%	— — —	11,539 1·6% —	— — —	— — —	— — —	690,555 98·3% 12
U. KINGDOM 635	39,974,993	29,102,084 72·8%	10,445,951 35·9% 276	11,446,671 39·3% 319	5,234,399 18·3% 13	17,426 — —	982,172 3·4% 14	885,465 3·0% 13

PARLIAMENTARY SUMMARY, LORDS AND COMMONS, 1974–75

THE QUEEN'S SPEECH.—A record 26 bills—as a minimum—was outlined in the Royal Speech in the House of Lords on October 29, 1974, when the Queen opened the first session of the new Parliament elected in October.

In her speech setting out the Labour Government's legislative proposals, the Queen said:

" My Government will give their full support to international efforts to solve the world-wide problem of inflation and will play a full part in international discussions to solve the problems created by higher oil prices. They will continue the policy of strengthening the United Nations, its agencies and other international institutions dedicated to the peaceful settlements of disputes, the promotion of human rights, the rule of law and the improvement of the quality of life. In the effort needed to deal with world problems, they attach high importance to the Commonwealth association.

" My Government will energetically continue their renegotiation of the terms of the United Kingdom's membership of the European Economic Community. Within twelve months the British people will be given the opportunity to decide whether, in the light of the outcome of the negotiations, this country should retain its membership.

" My Government will continue to give full support to the maintenance of the North Atlantic Alliance. They will regard the North Atlantic Treaty Organisation as an instrument of *détente* as well as of defence. In consultation with their allies and in the light of a searching review of our defence commitments and forces they will ensure the maintenance of a modern and effective defence system while reducing its cost as a proportion of our national resources.

" My Ministers will continue to work for a political solution in Northern Ireland. The proposed Constitutional Convention will provide a means by which those elected to it can consider what provision for the government of Northern Ireland is likely to command the most widespread acceptance throughout the community; any solution must, if it is to work, provide for some form of genuine power-sharing and participation by both communities in the direction of affairs in Northern Ireland. My Ministers will continue to act decisively against terrorism and lawlessness. They attach particular importance to co-operation with the Government of the Republic of Ireland in the field of security and in other matters of mutual interest.

" At home, my Government, in view of the gravity of the economic situation, will as its most urgent task seek the fulfilment of the social contract as an essential element in its strategy for curbing inflation, reducing the balance of payments deficit, encouraging industrial investment, maintaining employment, particularly in the older industrial areas, and promoting social and economic justice.

" The use of subsidies to keep down prices of certain foods will be continued. Further measures for the protection of consumers will be brought forward.

" My Ministers will pursue their aim of achieving a fair redistribution of income and wealth. A measure will be brought before you for the introduction of a tax on capital transfers. My Ministers will propose the establishment of a Select Committee to examine the form which a wealth tax might take.

" Measures will be placed before you to amend the Trade Union and Labour Relations Act 1974; and to establish the Conciliation and Arbitration Service on a statutory basis and to protect and improve working conditions generally. Proposals will be brought forward to tackle the abuses of the lump as a step towards creating a stable workforce in the construction industry. My Ministers will publish proposals to ensure comprehensive safeguards for employment in the docks.

" My Government attach major importance to a general improvement in social security benefits in the interests of social justice. Measures will be introduced to increase existing social security benefits, including family allowances; to make additional provision for the disabled; to pay a Christmas bonus; and to set up a new earnings-related pension scheme.

" My Government's education policy will continue to give priority to areas of greatest need and to children with special difficulties. Particular attention will be given to the development of a fully comprehensive system of secondary education and to nursery education. A Bill will be introduced to provide public lending rights for authors.

" My Ministers will energetically pursue their policies for encouraging local authorities and housing associations to provide more homes to rent and to develop their programmes for improving existing homes, particularly in the areas of greatest stress. They will take action to secure a stable and adequate flow of mortgages. Bills will be laid before you to reform the law relating to rents and housing subsidies in England and Wales and in Scotland.

" Legislation will be introduced to enable land required for development to be taken into community ownership and to tax realisations of development value.

" Legislation will be introduced to regulate further the development of off-shore petroleum, to establish a British National Oil Corporation with rights to participate in this development; to ensure that the community receives a fair share of the profits; and to provide for the acquisition of oil sites in Scotland.

" My Ministers wish to encourage industrial investment and expansion within vigorous and profitable public and private sectors of industry. For this purpose, legislation will be introduced to provide for the establishment of planning agreements and a National Enterprise Board; and to enable the shipbuilding and aircraft industries to be taken into public ownership.

" Legislation will be introduced to provide additional protection for policyholders of insurance companies, and for people booking overseas holidays and travel who suffer loss as a result of the failure of travel organisers.

" My Government will urgently prepare for the implementation of the decision to set up directly elected assemblies in Scotland and Wales.

" Legislation will be brought before you with the aim of ending sex discrimination.

" A Bill will be introduced to reform the law relating to the adoption, guardianship and fostering of children.

" An early opportunity will be given for you to consider whether your proceedings should be broadcast."

After the normal party skirmishings over the Government's plans in the first four days of debate in the Commons, the fifth day—November 4—produced the first division of the new Parliament with a Government majority of 14 on an Opposition amendment regretting nationalisation and certain other proposals.

In the closing period of debate speeches from both

front benches were drowned at times by continuous interruptions from both sides of the packed chamber. The Energy Secretary (Mr. Eric Varley) said that the Petroleum Bill, setting up the British National Oil Corporation, would be brought forward in a matter of weeks. Meanwhile three Government ministers would be embarking on negotiations to obtain public participation in existing licences.

Earlier the Industry Secretary (Mr. Anthony Wedgwood Benn) warned industries due for nationalisation that any transactions between now and vesting day must be carried out "in good faith " or they might be reversed. No company would be penalised for "normal action taken in good faith in the course of business ". But his nationalisation legislation would contain a provision enabling any transaction entered into up to vesting day to be reversed if it was considered disadvantageous to the new undertaking. Those provisions applied from July 1974 to shipbuilding, ship-repairing and marine engineering and from that day for the aircraft industry. The industries' commercial contracts would remain binding. Shareholders and long-term debenture holders would be compensated.

The Opposition's amendment, moved by the Conservative spokesman on trade (Mr. Michael Heseltine) regretted " the disastrous proposals for the nationalisation of the aircraft, shipbuilding and off-shore oil industries, the establishment of a National Enterprise Board and the imposition of planning agreements which will lead to bureaucratic interference, further loss of confidence, damage to investment and rising unemployment ". Mr. Patrick Jenkin, winding up for the Opposition, accused Labour of " dressing up the same dreary, wholly doctrinaire ideas in trendy modern gear so beloved by the Industry Secretary, Mr. Benn ". Mr. Jenkin warned that it was more than possible that the National Union of Mineworkers was once again on a collision course with the Government.

Replying, Mr. Varley said that oil was as good an investment for the Government as for the oil companies. The cost of the initial investment would be considerable but the rate of return would be very, very good indeed. The Conservative's amendment showed the total irrelevance of the Tory Party as it " drifted unrealistically out of the mainstream of British political life." It was now a rump and a fringe party.

On November 5, the sixth and last day of the debate, an Opposition amendment regretting that the Queen's speech " in no way measures up to the perils facing the country, and that its doctrinaire proposals will divide rather than unite the nation " was defeated by 310 votes to 268, a Government majority of 42. Liberals forced a second division on the motion to approve Labour's programme. The Government had a majority of 294—voting 308 to 14 against, only Liberal MPs voting with support from 3 Tories and an Ulster Unionist.

Moving the Opposition amendment, the Shadow Environment spokesman (Mrs. Margaret Thatcher) said: " The general impression of the Speech is that the Government thinks the financial weather is that of a warm spring day instead of the bleak blizzard we face". If the Chancellor's target of only a 10 per cent. growth in prices by the end of 1975 was to be achieved, wages could not grow at more than 20 per cent. in 1974, 17 per cent. in 1975 and 14 per cent. to 15 per cent. in 1976.

The country was faced perhaps with a supreme test of its democratic institutions, the Employment Secretary (Mr. Michael Foot) said. Perhaps it was the supreme test of the century, " not of the same kind but comparable in degree to 1940 or 1917 ". The country must save itself, and the next two or three years would be of momentous character in seeking that aim. The Government had no intention of bringing in a freeze or statutory control of incomes.

PENSIONS.—On November 6, M.P.'s gave a second reading without a division to the Bill to finance new higher retirement pensions, after an Opposition amendment was defeated by 291 to 274. The keynote of the Opposition's attack was the effect of increased contributions on self-employed people and on married women and widows who had chosen not to pay insurance contributions.

The Opposition Social Services spokesman (Sir Geoffrey Howe) said that the burden of increases to be borne by the self-employed—over one million of them—was so unjustified as to be harsh and vindictive.

Moving the Second Reading, Mr. Brian O'Malley, Minister of State, Social Services, said that without the change there would not be enough money in the Fund to pay the £10 and £16 pensions brought in on July 22, let alone enough to put any increases into effect.

THE NOVEMBER BUDGET.—Unusually there was a full-scale Budget on November 12, and in introducing this the Chancellor of the Exchequer (Mr. Denis Healey) saw it as helping to lay the foundation of a comprehensive strategy for dealing with Britain's economic problems over the next four years.

Britain entered 1974 in a worse condition than nearly all her partners in the industrial world. His job in March was to stop the rot, and he claimed to have succeeded at least in this. Level of total output recovered almost to that of a year ago, personal consumption recovered in the third quarter and investment rose strongly in the first half of the year, and unemployment was increasing more slowly than was generally expected.

Our balance of payments problem was a formidable one, but it was reasonable to hope that our external deficit on current account in the year would be distinctly below the generally predicted figure of £4,000 million. The Chancellor foresaw no difficulty in financing the current account deficit, but that did not mean borrowing indefinitely on anything like the present scale. " I am determined that the balance of payments shall show a continuing and sustained improvement, and this will be a crucial objective of my strategy for the economy over the next four years," he remarked.

On inflation, Mr. Healey said that it was impossible to count on a fall in food prices expected a few months ago, and that the most important single influence on inflation would be the rate at which earnings rose. If settlements were not confined to what was needed to cover the increase in the cost of living, but rose beyond the limits set by the T.U.C., the Government would be compelled to take action to curtail demand. The effect on the financial position of the company sector would be bound to lead to unemployment.

Turning to his medium term objectives, the Chancellor said: " There is no cause for complacency, but North Sea oil makes our prospects better than most of our competitors in one key respect. A first objective must be to shift resources into exports and investment. A great majority cannot expect any increase in living standards in the next few years. The Government has set itself the target of limiting the growth in public expenditure over

the next four years to an average rate of 2¾ per cent.
a year in demand terms. The second objective is
to mount a national campaign against waste, and
above all to adjust national behaviour to the enormous increases in the cost of energy. In particular,
the aim must be the elimination of subsidies to the
use of energy through artificial nationalised industry prices. We must change the pattern of our
private and public spending to take account of
other immense changes in world prices. In the
coming year the key to victory lies in adherence to
the guidelines for collective bargaining laid down
by the T.U.C. The third objective must be for
Government to manage monetary policy so as to
restrain inflationary pressures."

The Chancellor said that an immediate threat to
employment was posed by the impact of inflation
on the company sector. Inflation had made the
operation of price controls far more severe than
was originally intended. There were firms whose
failure to make profits was no fault of the system.
The Government would make further funds available selectively under the Industry Act for such
special cases. He would also consider accelerated
public purchasing where a firm faced purely
temporary lack of demand. At present there were
special problems facing firms which made equipment for space heating. Hire purchase controls
would be relaxed. The new terms would be a
minimum down payment of 10 per cent. and a
maximum repayment period of 5 years. It was not
right to abolish the Price Code in present circumstances, but there was room for some changes. The
present 50 per cent. rate of productivity deduction
would be reduced to 20 per cent. for firms with an
average proportion of labour costs, with a new
sliding scale to relate the amount of deduction to
the proportion of labour costs incurred by specific
firms. He announced new relief for investment
(companies would be permitted to recoup in increased prices over a year up to 17½ per cent. of the
cost of their investment programmes for that year)
and new proposals to clarify and improve safeguards
in cases where profit margins had been reduced well
below April 1973 levels.

There would be no cut in the corporation tax,
but he was persuaded that industry needed a substantial immediate improvement of its liquidity
through the deferment of tax on that part of the
profit which corresponded to the abnormal increase
in the value of stock and work in progress. Companies would have the right to reduce the closing
value of stock and work in progress for accounting
periods ending in 1973–74 by the amount by which
the increase in the book value of stocks exceeded
10 per cent. of trading profits. In other words, the
maximum profit represented by the increase in the
value of stocks on which tax would be payable this
year would be limited to 10 per cent. of the trading
profit. There would be an increase from 40 per
cent. to 50 per cent. of initial allowance given for
industrial buildings, the effect of Price Code
changes would increase profitability by some
£800,000,000 in 1975, and the effect of corporate
tax changes would improve liquidity by nearly
£800,000,000 during the winter.

The Chancellor said that revenue support for
nationalised industries was running at over
£1,000,000,000 a year. He had set it as his objective to phase out these subsidies completely as
fast as possible, but he could not then anticipate
specific measures which would be needed.

Next came proposals for an initial allowance for
expenditure on insulation of industrial buildings to
be increased from 40 per cent. to 100 per cent.; a
new rate of VAT on petrol " as a means of dis-
couraging its wasteful use " with 25 per cent. VAT
as from the following Monday on petrol but not
DERV or liquefied petroleum gas; an Oil
Taxation Bill to impose new tax on profits of oil
companies from the Continental Shelf; a review
of all public expenditure programmes so that the
increase in public expenditure did not exceed 2¾
per cent. a year in demand terms on average over
the next four years, with a statement on defence
expenditure within the next few weeks.

The Chancellor declared: " Discussions with
local authorities on the level of rates and rate support
grant are now in progress. Some increase in the
rates is inevitable. It will probably be substantial
but it can be kept within bounds."

The main features of new social security measures
were: next uprating of pensions to be brought
forward to April 1975; a proposed increase in
weekly benefits for pensions and other long-term
benefits of £1·60 and £2·50 to £11·60 and
£18·50 for the single and married rates respectively,
with effect from April; short-term benefits to
increase by £1·20, single and £2 married to
£9·80 and £15·90 respectively; a total of
£925,000,000 to be distributed. Family allowances would be increased to £1·50 a week from
April 1975, at a cost of £205,000,000 in 1975/6.

On investment income surcharge, Mr. Healey
said that the starting point was to be reduced from
£2,000 to £1,000 and £1,500 for the over 65s.
There would be a new tax allowance (age allowance) to replace age exemption limits with higher
tax allowances for all over 65 of £950 (single) and
£1,425 (married) for 1975–76, except where the
total income exceeded £3,000. Above £3,000,
the allowance would be reduced by £2 for every
£3 of excess. The cost would be £220,000,000 in
1975–76, and £285,000,000 in a full year. The
blind allowance would be increased from £130 to
£180 for 1975–76.

On tax reform, the Chancellor stated a capital
transfer tax would replace estate duty on deaths
after the Finance Bill had received Royal Assent
and on gifts made on or after March 26, 1974.
Some rates would apply for estate duty chargeable
on deaths on or after that day—as would exemptions for transfer between husband and wife and
withdrawal of special reliefs for agricultural land,
business assets and woodlands. It was expected
that the new tax would in the long term produce a
higher yield than the existing estate duty, although
in the early years, it would be lower—some
£15,000,000 less in 1974–75, and some £25,000,000
less in 1975–76. Proposals for a wealth tax were to
be considered by a Select Committee, and a separate
bill was to be introduced during the Session, for a
development land tax. Relief lost by trade unions
not registered under the Industrial Relations Act
1971 was to be restored for the period from April
6, 1972 to the commencement of the Trade Union
and Labour Relations Act 1974.

The Opposition Leader (Mr. Heath), opening the
debate on the Budget statement, accused the
Chancellor of reversing policies which he had
adopted for electoral purposes and charged the
Government with putting up prices. Mr. Healey
had said that earnings under the social contract had
got to do no more than keep pace with the cost of
living, but the Chancellor was mistaken if he
thought this would keep the rate of inflation down
to 10 per cent. It would be much more like 20 per
cent. and the significance for this country would be
enormous. Mr. Heath added that if earnings did
not keep within that range, the only alternative
was to cut back demand and create unemployment.
The Chancellor had not told the truth of what was

going on. He saw nothing in the Chancellor's measures which in the long term would solve the basic problems of industry and finance, nor was there anything in the budget to encourage private savings.

The Government's new package deal of an extra £1,125,000,000 in Social Security benefits shared by 15,000,000 people was announced in detail in the Commons on November 13 by Social Services Secretary (Mrs. Barbara Castle). Mrs. Castle said that the Environment Secretary had authorised her to say that he proposed, after consulting his advisory committee, to make increases in the needs allowance for rent and rate rebates and rent allowances.

The Opposition Shadow spokesman on social services (Sir Geoffrey Howe) welcomed " Mrs. Castle's conversion to the need for more frequent upratings of benefits while inflation persists at its present scale ". The linking of long-term benefit rates with rises in national average earnings was confirmed in the Bill as a requirement for the future.

M.P.s then continued to debate the Budget statement and were told that oil companies had been invited to begin negotiations on Government participation in the offshore oil industry. The Paymaster General (Mr. Edmund Dell) made clear that the Government was anxious not to deter further private investment. The new Petroleum Revenue Tax to be set out in proposed legislation the following week " must leave oil companies with an adequate return on their capital and sufficient incentive to continue with the difficult and hazardous work in the North Sea ". Mr. Dell said that the tax was designed to ensure that a proper share of the profits came to the community as a whole. The Government " take " would have four components —existing royalties, corporation tax, the new petroleum revenue tax, and the proceeds of freely-negotiated direct state participation.

Mr. Dell also announced help for people building their own homes. VAT payments made from that day on purchase of materials for do-it-yourself housebuilding projects would be repayable by Customs and Excise after the houses were completed.

The Shadow Chancellor (Mr. Robert Carr) declared: " Mr. Healey has put industry in an economic kidney machine and saved its life for this winter and next year. But he has created a kidney machine economy. Industry is not cured and will have to come back for repeated treatment because the Chancellor has withheld the necessary remedy." The cause of Britiain's crisis was simple—they were living beyond their means. It was a half-truth budget because it was still not giving the people the warning they must have if they were to respond. It was only waging a phoney war against inflation.

The Prices Minister (Mrs. Shirley Williams) said that the Government accepted the case for a reduction in the productivity deduction under which a percentage of a firm's increased productivity must be passed to the consumer, adding: " We must however keep a productivity deduction, because it prevents firms from passing on labour costs in prices, and discourages excessive salary and wage settlements."

The Liberal Leader (Mr. Jeremy Thorpe) said that the Government would have to become committed to a tax on inflation if it was to contain inflation. It was important to have guaranteed minimum earnings and he hoped that the Government would use negative income tax as a positive way of attacking poverty.

On November 14, the third and last day of the Budget debate, Mr. Harold Lever (Chancellor of the Duchy of Lancaster) who said that " storm clouds of a slump are gathering all over the advanced industrial nations of the world " told the Commons that Britain would only survive if she maintained her credit abroad strong enough to borrow the billions of pounds required to fuel industry and feed our people. Britain had " an astronomical balance of payments deficit " not made any easier because her neighbours shared similar astronomical deficits. There was no hope for measures passed in the House " if a world slump of massive proportions falls upon them. It could only be avoided if the level of international co-operation was swiftly and massively improved. "

The Opposition spokesman on financial matters and public expenditure (Mrs. Margaret Thatcher) said that to eliminate the deficits of the nationalised industries would involve very substantial increases in prices of electricity, rail fares and Post Office charges. No relief from capital transfer tax had been provided for small businesses. If none was forthcoming that would end the life of the small family business.

Winding up, the Chancellor of the Exchequer said that gas prices were to go up " in the New Year " and some other nationalised industry charges were likely to rise before the pensions increase in April, and domestic electricity charges would also go up because of the increase in fuel charges already occurring. Mr. Healey said that the increases had yet to be demanded by the industries themselves and then would be subject to the agreement of the Price Commission. But, he warned, " these increases will be substantial ". However, the Government regarded it as its obligation under the social contract to help those worse off to cope with the consequences of these increases.

The Government had a majority of 258 on the first of the divisions on the budget. Nationalists and Liberals pressed a division against the increased VAT on petrol, but the proposal was carried by 302 votes to 44. On a second division, forced by Conservatives, the Government's majority dropped to 27. Voting was 306 to 279 in favour of the proposal to reduce the level of investment income on which tax was payable. In the third and final division, the Government had a majority of 38 on its proposal to repay trade unions £10,000,000 tax relief, voting being 306 to 268 in its favour.

THE CHURCH OF ENGLAND.—Meanwhile in the House of Lords on November 14, the Archbishop of Canterbury (Dr. Michael Ramsey) on his last day in office and his 70th birthday, introduced a Church measure of some controversy, the Church of England (Worship and Doctrine) Measure, which was designed to give the Church control over its own doctrine and its forms of worship. It contained a proviso that the Book of Common Prayer must be always available as a form of worship. Dr. Ramsey stressed that the measure was not one for disestablishment of the Church of England, nor a step towards separating the Church from the Crown. The powers of the 1965 Measure allowing new forms of service would expire around 1980. Was it possible or desirable to revert to the position in which the only services possessing lawful authority would be the 1662 Prayer Book? The Measure was the Church's attempt to find a solution. The Measure provided that the General Synod would have for indefinite periods the power to sanction alternative forms of service. It gave the General Synod considerably more power in the control of worship and doctrine. But to conserve both the Church's doctrinal identity, and the place of the Book of Common Prayer and the rights of the laity, there were important provisos built into the Measure. The Leader of the House (Lord Shepherd) said that the Government's position was one of benevolent neutrality; he did not propose to raise any objections. Lord Beaumont of Whitley said that Liberals believed that the Church should have freedom to control its own constitutional and democratic position. The Church of England had gone to very considerable lengths to build up a democratic system of Government. Earl Waldegrave greatly feared that if extreme care was not taken they would find the Book of Common Prayer might be on the way out. In a maiden speech, the Bishop of Durham said that the passing of this measure would not unleash new reforming zeal, but would enable the Church of England to know that its worship was its own, freely chosen by its leaders and elected representatives and that was the only way in which people of integrity could worship. Opposing the measure, Baroness Berkeley said that Christians needed a stable church to cling to—not a Church which appeared to be set on a course of change for change's sake. The Earl of Onslow, who believed that the measure was " disestablishment by the back door ", quoted verses from the Authorised Version and the New English Bible, comparing the beauty of the language in the Authorised Version with the ugliness of the new version. The Measure was approved without a division.

EDUCATION.—The Education Secretary (Mr. Prentice) warned M.P.s in the Commons on November 15, that the education service would face an era of austerity over the next few years, but this would not mean a period of standstill. It would present a challenge to the government, local education authorities, and the teaching profession, to use ingenuity to find ways towards efficiency. He was moving the second reading of the Education Bill, covering England and Wales, which provided for an extension of mandatory grants-in-aid for higher national diploma education of £700,000 in a full year, a new system of State grants to students costing £100,000 in a full year at seven residential colleges, and help to aided schools costing £1,500,000 in a full year.

The Opposition Education spokesman (Mr. Norman St. John-Stevas) said teachers' status had declined and he welcomed any effort to give them interim relief. A conference should be called of parents, teachers, religious and social workers to analyse the problems of religious education.

Mr. Ernest Armstrong (Under Secretary, Education and Science) announced that the Government would be making provision for students to have two mandatory awards when they went on from the Diploma of Higher Education or the Higher National Diploma to a degree, although the second award was likely to be limited in duration. The Bill received an unopposed second reading.

RATES.—The Government had a majority of 49 on November 20, at the end of a debate on rates, voting on a technical motion to adjourn the House being 313 to 264. The Shadow Environment Secretary (Mr. Paul Channon) said that if projected rates increases next year were as large as predicted there was a grave danger of a complete breakdown. There was a strong case for transferring more expenditure from local to central government, including more of the cost of police and fire services.

The Environment Secretary (Mr. Anthony Crosland) said that the last Conservative Government had responded to the growing revolt among ratepayers with all the sense of urgency of an ageing

snail. If the Layfield inquiry came up with a viable alternative to rates, " no one will be more delighted than I ". But the Government was not prepared to be stampeded into solutions.

Winding up for the Government, the Minister for Planning and Local Government (Mr. John Silkin) said the suggestion to remove teachers' salaries from the rates to the Exchequer was an idea that required some thought and analysis. They ought to be satisfied that it could be done without fatally damaging the independence of local authorities.

THE I.R.A.—After having given a preliminary statement on November 22, to a crowded and angry Chamber on the previous night's bomb explosions in Birmingham, the Home Secretary (Mr. Roy Jenkins) made a detailed one on November 25, in which he announced that the I.R.A. was to be banned and so was its " uniform ". He outlined the Government's plans, which he called draconian powers to prevent " acts of terrorism with respect to Northern Ireland and to deal with such terrorists ". The Bill would give him power to proscribe organisations " which appeared to him to be concerned in terrorism or in promoting or encouraging it with respect to affairs in Northern Ireland". It would specify the I.R.A. at least " but additional proscriptions which may well be necessary will be made by order ". The Bill provided for its provisions to expire after six months, but they might be continued for a further six months. Mr. Jenkins said that it would be an offence to wear clothing or armbands which were plainly I.R.A. insignia—and be an offence to carry banners in support of the I.R.A. There would be powers to make exclusion orders to keep people suspected of terrorism out of Britain, and to expel such people already here. These orders might also be made against a person who had knowingly harboured anyone against whom an exclusion order had been made. There would be powers of arrest without warrant where a police officer reasonably expected a person to be concerned with terrorism. Identity cards would not be introduced at present but the Home Secretary promised to keep the possibility under review. The Bill also gave police powers to exercise a security control over all passengers entering and leaving Britain on journeys to or from Ireland. Mr. Jenkins said: " These powers are draconian. In combination they are unprecedented in peacetime." He was seeking urgent discussions with the Government of the Irish Republic to consider their part in counter-terrorist operations.

The Shadow Home Secretary (Sir Keith Joseph) and the Opposition Leader (Mr. Heath) promised to help the Bill through Parliament as quickly as possible. Dealing with the question of the death penalty for terrorism, Mr. Jenkins said, in reply to questions, that he had no doubt the matter would and should be debated. But M.P.s would not wish to deal with this matter as part of these measures, which must pass with the greatest speed that week.

Both Houses settled down to some protracted discussions on November 28, on all stages of the Prevention of Terrorism (Temporary Provisions) Bill, which was being rushed through in the wake of the Birmingham I.R.A. bombings. The Lords, having concluded their consideration in the late evening, were warned that M.P.s would be occupied throughout the night and adjourned their sitting to next morning. In the Commons at 10 p.m., the Bill was given a second reading without a vote, and the House went into Committee for the marathon line-by-line examination. Argument over the broad principles became submerged in a welter of speeches concerned with details of the Bill's drafting.

Mr. Jenkins was supported by the Northern Ireland Secretary (Mr. Merlyn Rees) and the Attorney General (Mr. S. C. Silkin) in answering misgivings which at times came almost entirely from Labour backbenchers, but predictable objections were heard from Ulster Unionist M.P.s led by Mr. Enoch Powell. He and his colleagues had tabled a succession of amendments criticising elements in the legislation which seemed to them to allow Ulster to become a " dumping ground " for would-be terrorists from the rest of the U.K. The first division came when a Labour back bench proposal to provide an appeal tribunal for people subject to an exclusion order was rejected by 218 votes to 51. When M.P.s debated the part of the Bill dealing with the powers of the Home Secretary to approve the extension of the period of detention beyond 48 hours after arrest, Mr. George Cunningham (Lab., Islington S. and Finsbury) sought an assurance that this decision would be taken by the Home Secretary or a Home Office Minister, and not a departmental official. Mr. Jenkins confirmed that the decision would be taken by the Home Secretary, or if he was away, another Home Office minister. A new clause dealing with appeal against an exclusion order was defeated by 193 votes to 61. The new clause moved by Mr. John Prescott (Lab., Hull E) would have established a tribunal, independent of the police, to review allegations of abuse made by people who had been detained under the Bill's powers of arrest and detention. The only substantive change in the Bill came on the Report stage. The Home Secretary agreed to delete from the legislation the section which made possession of a document addressed to an individual as a member of a proscribed organisation, evidence of membership of that organisation. Mr. Jenkins' concession followed protests by Labour backbenchers and a few Tories. At long last the Report stage was completed and the Bill was given an unopposed Third Reading without any further debate, the Commons having spent a total of 16 hours 53 minutes considering the measure. It was sent to the Lords at 9 a.m. to receive the Royal Assent.

DEFENCE POLICY.—The Government was to save a total of £4,700,000,000 on defence expenditure over the next 10 years, the Defence Secretary (Mr. Roy Mason) told the Commons on December 3. The proposals would mean: (1) reducing manpower by about 35,000 servicemen and by about 30,000 directly employed civilians; (2) reductions in the planned defence programme likely to reduce employment in defence industries by 10,000 over the period 1978–79; and (3) a saving of £300,000,000 in 1975–76, about £500,000,000 a year by 1978–79 and some £750,000,000 a year by 1983–84.

In his lengthy statement, Mr. Mason said that his proposals were designed for the circumstances they must expect over the next 10 years and would provide for a modern and effective defence structure which would make a significant contribution to establishing their economic health and thus to strengthening NATO. The Government had decided to reduce defence expenditure as a proportion of the Gross National Product from its present level of 5½ per cent. to 4½ per cent. over the ensuing ten years. Describing the general principles followed in the review, he said: "NATO is the first linchpin of British security and will remain the first charge on the resources available for defence. We shall also maintain the effectiveness of our Polaris force." The Defence Secretary declared: " We intend to enter into negotiations with

the South African Government with a view to terminating the Simonstown Agreement." He told M.P.s that the reductions in the planned defence programme were likely to reduce employment in the defence industries " by only some 10,000 or 4 per cent. over the period up to 1978–79 " but " there will be problems in certain areas and for certain firms ". The Shadow Defence Secretary (Mr. Peter Walker) said that this was no time to announce such cuts when the Warsaw Pact countries had 50 per cent. more men under arms than NATO, were spending an increasing amount on research, and Britain had considerable internal security problems. The Government staved off two attacks on its defence cuts policy on December 12. A Conservative amendment which suggested that the cuts would " imperil the nation's security " was rejected by 316 votes to 256. A second challenge—from Labour's left-wing—was defeated by 241 votes to 58.

The Defence Secretary said that the economic reality was not the only essential behind Britain's defence review. "I have also had in the front of my mind the other reality—the continued threat to Western security caused by the massive and growing military power of the Warsaw Pact countries ", he remarked. He had been asking the House to approve his review which cut defence spending from 5½ per cent. to 4½ per cent. of gross national product. Left-Wing Labour backbenchers had earlier described the defence cuts as " phoney ". Several had claimed that they did not match the Labour Manifesto pledges to make real arms cuts, and they made clear that they would not hesitate to force a vote.

BRITISH LEYLAND.—Mr. Anthony Wedgwood Benn (Industry Secretary) told the Commons on December 6, that the Government planned a measure of public ownership of British Leyland. He said: " Discussions have been taking place with the Company regarding both its short-term requirements for working capital and its long-term investment programme. Because of the Company's position in the economy as a leading exporter and its importance to employment directly and indirectly through the many firms dependent on it, the Government is informing the Company's bankers that the approval of Parliament will be sought for the guarantee of the working capital requirement over and above existing facilities. This will enable the Company's existing requirements to continue to be met without interruption. As to the request for further support, the Government also intend to introduce longer term arrangements including a measure of public ownership. The Government proposes to appoint a high-level team led by Sir Don Ryder to advise on the Company's situation and prospects."

ENERGY SAVING.—Compulsory heating limits in many buildings and lower speed limits, except on motorways, were announced by the Energy Secretary (Mr. Eric Varley) in the Commons on December 9. Presenting his package of energy-saving measures, Mr. Varley said that speed limits on all single carriageway roads would be reduced to 50 m.p.h. and on dual carriageways—other than motorways—to 60 m.ph. Motorway speed limits would be unchanged at 70 m.p.h. Maximum heating levels in buildings except homes would be 20 degrees centigrade (68 Fahrenheit) with limited exemptions to protect the young, the old, the sick, the disabled and certain types of material and equipment. Mr. Varley also appealed for maximum voluntary savings in private households. The use of electricity for external display and advertising was to be restricted during daylight hours in the New Year, but floodlighting would not be banned. Standards of thermal insulation in new dwellings were to be approximately doubled. These proposals were an interim package which would be extended and reinforced in future. A loan scheme would be introduced to provide finance for energy saving investment in industry, the Government making available £5,000,000 a year. The Government would use its powers to ensure that the next round of oil price increases would hit motor spirit more heavily than oil products. Measures aimed at eventual savings of about £20,000,000 a year were to be introduced in respect of government buildings, including defence establishments. Government was opening urgent discussions with local authorities and others to see what savings they could make. No precise estimate could be made of the savings which the package of proposals might achieve, but if 10 per cent. of consumption could be saved, it would be a major contribution to the nation's wellbeing and future. The Shadow Energy Minister (Mr. Patrick Jenkin) promised the full support of the Opposition for all sensible measures in the national interest to save energy.

CAPITAL PUNISHMENT.—By a majority of 152, M.P.s on December 11, rejected on a free vote, a move to bring back the death penalty for terrorism. Voting was 369 to 217 against a call by Mrs. Jill Knight (C., Edgbaston) for legislation to impose the death penalty for acts of terrorism causing death. This had been moved as an amendment to a motion by Mr. Brian Walden (Lab., Ladywood) which recognised that a reappraisal of established attitudes was needed, but expressed the belief that a reintroduction of the death penalty would neither deter terrorists, nor increase the safety of the public. Mr. Walden's motion was approved without a division. The Home Secretary (Mr. Roy Jenkins) urged the House to support Mr. Walden's motion, and warned that if Mrs. Knight's amendment were successful it would not be regarded as a defeat or deterrent by the I.R.A. but a victory. The Home Secretary said that there was no prospect of amnesties for those who had committed cold-blooded and indiscriminate murder or maiming in this country. " I do not recognise political excuses for crimes of that order. Those who have received long sentences should serve them, whatever political settlement there may be." During the debate, M.P.s expressed the view that capital punishment might be an " attraction " to the terrorist and that there was a threat from the creation of martyrs. It was also suggested that hostages might be taken where terrorists were under sentence of death and that young people, who would not be liable to the death penalty, might be induced to carry out acts of terrorism. There was also some concern that " lynchings " might occur if the Government did not respond to what some felt to be the mood of the country, and brought back the death penalty. The Shadow Home Secretary (Sir Keith Joseph) explained he was giving his own personal views and not speaking as a member of the Opposition front bench. He had been against capital punishment for murder for a long time because most murders were unpremeditated. " This is still my position but terrorism is quite different. Every action is premeditated, so for today my abolitionist views do not apply." Moving her amendment, Mrs. Knight stressed that they were discussing the death penalty, and not hanging, for terrorist killings and not other murders. She did not believe the method of execution should be hanging. She

had received 8,000 letters and signatures from people all over the United Kingdom who demanded the death penalty for terrorist killing and only 15 expressing the opposite view.

The next day (December 12), the Lord Chief Justice (Lord Widgery) advocated in the Lords a return to capital punishment for really serious premeditated murders. He was speaking during a debate on a motion calling attention to capital punishment as a means of combating terrorism. In a maiden speech in his new office as Archbishop of Canterbury (Dr. Donald Coggan) opposed the death penalty. He said: " The satisfaction of human wrath by taking of human lives is an unworthy method of procedure. Panic should not be allowed to move rational men. All too easily, revenge can prove counter-productive." The Lord Chancellor (Lord Elwyn-Jones) said that putting a captive terrorist to death would further inflame the situation in Northern Ireland. There was the possibility that they might hang the wrong man.

Moving the motion, Lord Hunt, said that he not only believed that the "spectre of the rope " was unlikely to deter terrorists but his own experience was that it would fan the fires of the cause for which they were prepared to die as heroes. The former Lord Chancellor, Lord Hailsham, said that in the light of the Commons decision the Lords were arguing an academic point. He believed there was nothing which could exercise a more powerful influence in the mind of potential criminals than the death penalty.

NORTHERN IRELAND.—The Northern Ireland Secretary (Mr. Merlyn Rees) said in the Commons on January 14, 1975, that if there were a genuine and sustained end of violence he would progressively release detainees. Once he was satisfied that violence had come to a permanent end he would be prepared to speed up the rate of releases with a view to releasing all detainees. Meantime he would be prepared to grant short home leaves for people who remained in detention and would also consider how released detainees could be resettled. Mr. Rees also said that he would not act precipitately. Any early releases must be carefully judged in relation to whether a cessation of violence was genuine and sustained.

The Opposition Leader (Mr. Heath) said that Mr. Rees's dilemma was how to make progress without creating a situation in which the Provisional I.R.A. could reform, regroup and restrengthen. He asked for an undertaking that the Minister was not having negotiations with the I.R.A. Mr. Rees replied that there would be no negotiations with the I.R.A., but he wanted to make sure " that our view does get to the I.R.A. at second hand and that we get their view as well ". Replying to Mr. Gerry Fitt (S.D.L.P., Belfast W.) who expressed " deep, sincere and heartfelt disappointment " that steps had not been taken to bring detention to an end, Mr. Rees said that if there were a sustained cessation of violence his aim was to release all detainees. " But we must proceed carefully and cautiously."

THE AIRCRAFT INDUSTRY.—A furious row broke out in the Commons on January 15, after the Industry Secretary (Mr. Anthony Wedgwood Benn) had announced plans to bring the aircraft industry into public ownership. The companies he named were: British Aircraft Corporation, Hawker Siddeley and Hawker Siddeley Dynamics. They were those whose turnover in accounts of the last financial year ending October 29, 1974, together with subsidiaries, were more than £20,000,000. The row, in which the Opposition

Leader (Mr. Edward Heath) joined, was over a claim by Mr. Benn that the last Conservative Government had bankrupted Rolls-Royce, " the jewel of the British aero-engine industry ". Mr. Benn was replying to a comment by an Opposition spokesman (Mr. Michael Heseltine), who accused Mr. Benn's department of being a " major aggravator " of the economic and industrial crisis facing the country. Mr. Heseltine suggested that Mr. Benn was making statements which he knew to be totally untrue, but Mr. Benn repeated the allegation that the Conservatives had first bankrupted and then nationalised Rolls-Royce. Mr. Heath intervened angrily as the noise continued: " This matter arose because Mr. Benn in particular constantly makes statements in this Chamber which everybody knows bear no resemblance to the truth ". As the row continued the Speaker urged that both questions and statements should be less provocative. Mr. Heath said that Rolls Royce had gone into liquidation because it could not carry out the terms of a contract negotiated during Mr. Benn's period as Minister and under his personal persuasion. " To put the whole of the aircraft industry in a similar position will have similar disastrous consequences." Conservatives would oppose Mr. Benn's measures by all Parliamentary procedures under their control. Mr. Benn persisted that it was clear that Rolls Royce need never have gone into bankruptcy at all. In his statement, Mr. Benn had said that a new Aircraft Corporation was to be established and a Bill to bring the aircraft industry into public ownership would be introduced in good time for passage during the current Parliamentary session. He said: " We propose to vest in a new Aircraft Corporation the shares of any company in Great Britain which carries on the business of developing or manufacturing complete aircraft or guided weapons (but not including helicopters) whose turnover as shown in the accounts of its last financial year ending before October 29, 1974, together with that of its subsidiaries, exceeds £20,000,000." He said: " The powers of the Secretary of State will be the minimum needed to secure Government influences over the main strategies of the Corporation and to protect the public investment in it. We intend to provide that the powers and duties of the Corporation and the powers of the Secretary of State may be capable of amendment. This will introduce an important new element of flexibility into the statutory arrangements governing relations with a nationalised industry."

THE CHANNEL TUNNEL.—The Government had a majority of 76 in the Commons on January 20, in support of its decision to drop the Channel Tunnel project. Voting was 294 to 218 on a procedural motion at the end of an emergency debate which had been called for earlier in the day by Mr. Eric Ogden (Lab., Liverpool West Derby). Mr. Ogden was one of several Labour critics of the decision, which was announced earlier by Mr. Anthony Crosland, Environment Secretary. Mr. Crosland said that he was more of a tunneller than many of his colleagues and greatly regretted that the project should end in this way. He could not in all conscience advise the House to accept the terms which the companies had put forward. " I reluctantly advise the House that the present project is dead." Mr. Crosland also denied allegations that the decision was a concession to anti-marketeers. This was not a political but an economic decision. Opening the debate, Mr. Ogden said that the tunnel was as important for Britain as any stretch of motorway had ever been. Winding up for the Opposition, the Shadow Leader of the House (Mr.

John Peyton) said that the Government stumbled into this decision with a mixture of relief and irresponsibility. It appeared that the Government was deliberately engaging in a manoeuvre to make the companies the scapegoat for their own scruffy conduct.

THE COMMON MARKET REFERENDUM.—The Prime Minister confirmed to the Commons on January 23, that the Government had decided that the decision over Britain's continued membership of the Common Market should be taken by referendum. Provided the outcome of renegotiation was known in time, the Government intended to hold the referendum before the summer holidays, in practice not later than the end of June. " If, when the time comes, members of the Government including members of the Cabinet do not feel able to accept the Government's recommendation, whatever it may be, they will, once the recommendation has been announced, be free to support and speak in favour of a different conclusion in the referendum campaign ", he added.

The Opposition Leader (Mr. Edward Heath) said that the Prime Minister had announced a "major constitutional innovation and asked him to confirm that the referendum "if it takes place will be advisory and consultative and cannot be binding on M.P.s ". Mr. Wilson declared: " As far as this Government is concerned, we shall accept the verdict of the referendum ". Mr. Wilson told Mr. Jeremy Thorpe, the Liberal Leader: " It will be our recommendation that the choice put to the British people will be 'in or out' 'Yes or No'. A straight question."

Mr. Enoch Powell (U.U.U., Down S.) said that he assumed that a bare majority in the referendum was unlikely to be regarded as indicating fullhearted consent of the British people, which the leaders of both main parties regarded as an essential condition of continued British membership. Mr. Wilson said that he had found that people tended to be satisfied with a bare majority if it went their way, but not if it went against them. When the statement was repeated in the Lords, Lord Hailsham, acting Leader of the Opposition, said: " I regret this decision to proceed by referendum rather than by a general election. The referendum is incompatible with Government responsibility and collective responsibility, and supplants responsible constitutional government by demagogy." Lord Byers, Liberal Leader, deplored the introduction of the referendum into the British constitution. The Leader of the Lords (Lord Shepherd) replied that there had been two general elections in 1974, in both of which the Labour Party had made clear that it would consult the people if it formed the Government.

EARNINGS RULE FOR PENSIONERS.—The Government was defeated in the Commons on January 29, on a bid to stop a relaxation of the earnings rule applying to pensioners who carried on working. Their attempt to delete from the Social Security Benefits Bill a provision, written in by M.P.s at the Committee Stage, that allowable income be increased over three years from £13 a week to £50 was rejected by 280 votes to 265, a majority of 15. But the Government had a majority of 35 when they sought to remove clauses which would have ended the earnings rule altogether by April 1980. Voting was 293 to 258. A number of Labour backbenchers had indicated their intention to vote against the Government. Ministers from both the Health and Social Security Department and the Treasury had promised action on the problem later. But they failed to stop the revolt of nine Labour M.P.s which, with the votes of Conservatives, Liberals, Nationalists and Ulster Unionists, was enough to retain the Committee decision. Having achieved their object of relaxing the rule, the Labour rebels returned to the fold to defeat the proposed ending of the rule by 1980. The Opposition Leader (Mr. Edward Heath) demanded: " We want a firm declaration from the Chancellor that he is no longer going to screw down the faces of those who are retired, but will accept the decision of this House and give them a better standard of life in their old age."

The Chancellor of the Exchequer (Mr. Dennis Healey), amid backbench uproar, said: " I shall ensure that the necessary revenue is raised from those best able to provide it and I put Mr. Heath on his honour to support any measures which I shall introduce to that end."

PRICES BILL.—The Commons on January 30, gave the Prices Bill a second reading with a majority for the Government of 220, voting being 270 to 50. This was after an official Opposition amendment to reject the Bill had been defeated by 281 to 214. The amendment claimed that indiscriminate food subsidies had proved an extravagant way of helping the needy and created distortions and shortages. Subsidies also concealed inflation, rather than dealt with inflation, it claimed. The measure raised the financial ceiling for the subsidies on milk, butter, bread, cheese, flour and tea from the existing £700,000,000 to £1,200,000,000 with power to increase it to £1,700,000,000 by Order. The Prices and Consumer Protection Secretary (Mrs. Shirley Williams) moving the second reading, said that the Bill would enable the subsidies to be continued in 1975–76. But it remained the Government's intention eventually to run down the programme. The timing of the run-down would depend on the introduction of further long-term social benefits to assist the less well-off. The Opposition Consumer Affairs spokesman (Mr. Timothy Raison) said that Parliament was now talking about the possibility of spending an additional £1,000,000,000 of public money, £500,000,000 in the current financial year and a further £500,000,000 from April 1976. The Tories believed that the time had come for a planned run down in food subsidies.

DEVOLUTION.—If devolution was to work between Scotland, Wales and the U.K., there would have to be continuous consultation and co-operation, said Mr. Edward Short, Leader of the Commons, on February 3. In a general two-day debate on devolution, Mr. Short said that that called for more than goodwill. It also called for efficient administrative machinery to make co-operation work. Mr. Short said that it was too soon to give a firm indication of the Government's timetable, although he hoped the Bill would be ready by the end of the year. He went on: " While we are giving priority to the establishment of the Welsh and Scottish assemblies, we must also consider the question of devolution in the United Kingdom context. The assemblies must meet the aspirations of Scotland and Wales for a closer involvement in the running of their own affairs, but must not threaten the unity of the United Kingdom. We must retain to the U.K. government and to Parliament, the functions essential to the sovereignty of Parliament and the overall management of the U.K. economy." The Government was committed to preserving the unity of the United Kingdom. It was looking forward to the beginning of a new relationship between Scotland, Wales and the central government, but it was not looking back to the position before the Act of Union of 1707. The Shadow Devolution Minister (Mr. William Whitelaw) pointed out that whatever was said about Scotland and Wales must inevitably have a bearing on the future size of Northern Ireland representation in the Commons. Equally the North of England would be watching very carefully to see whether what was regarded as " preferential treatment " now afforded to Scotland was to be extended still further. " We on the Conservative benches stand unequivocally by the unity of the United Kingdom under a sovereign parliament here at Westminister. In our judgment the necessary political will for separation does not exist." Mr. Whitelaw continued: " We have taken upon ourselves the reform of a constitution which has grown up over centuries and served the United Kingdom well. The penalty for failure will be very great. There would be further disillusionment and increased demands for further separation, leading almost inevitably to the break-up of the United Kingdom as we know it." Mr. Grimond (L., Orkney and Shetland) said that the system of government in the U.K. was too centralised, too rigid, too bureaucratic and too remote. It had stifled and distorted Scotland's development and drawn off its most talented sons and daughters. Self-government would allow the nation to contribute more to Britain, Europe and the world, but he thought that defence, foreign affairs and major matters of planning and economic decisions, which must be on a wider basis, must remain in London. Mr. Donald Stewart (Scot. Nat., Western Isles) said that his Party accepted that no country could be totally isolated. But in the Commons there was some recognition of the desire of the Scottish people to resume control of their own affairs. Mr. William Craig (U.U.U., Belfast E.) said that the eventual form of constitution of the United Kingdom would be very close to the federal system. If this was not the approach, the bonds of unity would be weakened. Mr. Gwynfor Evans (Plaid Cymru, Carmarthen) said that the British State had not served, succoured or strengthened the Welsh nation. " In Wales, the role of the State has not been a subordinate one of servant, but a dominant one of master." Nothing could be more obvious than that the people of Wales would have a chance of a much fuller life in a self-governing country.

The Scottish Secretary (Mr. William Ross) reaffirmed, on February 4, that the Government accepted the principle that Wales and Scotland needed to have " meaningful " assemblies. But he said that the Government did not think the House wanted to endanger the political and economic integrity of the United Kingdom. The Welsh Secretary (Mr. John Morris) said that he did not believe that in Wales there was any significant demand for separatism or even federalism. Mr. Peter Thomas (Shadow Welsh Secretary) said that the question of constitutional change was an in-group subject in Wales. He did not believe that most of the Welsh people were greatly interested in having an assembly. Mr. Emlyn Hooson (L., Montgomery) said that devolution for Scotland and Wales was as much a major constitutional matter as the Common Market, and remarked: " If it is right to have a referendum on one it is equally right to have it on the other ". In his reply, Mr. Ross said that the national identity of Scotland did not require the establishment of a nation state to preserve it. The Government was not taking up the devolution theme to appease the nationalists.

THE STEEL INDUSTRY.—The phasing of redundancies in the steel industry could introduce a new dimension into redundancy problems in the public sector of industry, said the Industry Secretary (Mr. Anthony Wedgwood Benn) in a Commons statement on February 4. He announced that the Government had accepted the conclusions in the report of his Minister of State (Lord Beswick) on the British Steel Corporation's proposed plant closures published earlier the same day. He recalled that the review would preserve about 13,500 jobs for two to four years or more by deferring closures at Cardiff, Shotton and Hartlepool. About 800 jobs at Shelton would be saved permanently and the future of steelmaking at Shotton was left for future consideration. Nothing announced that day would pre-empt decisions still to be taken of the B.S.C.'s proposals for Scotland or other cases still under review. The Opposition Industry spokesman (Mr. Michael Heseltine) said that Mr. Benn's claim that 13,500 jobs would be saved for between two and four years would cost the B.S.C. at least £120,000,000. The Liberal Employment spokesman (Mr. Cyril Smith) said that the statement put off closures rather than cancelled them. Mr. Benn agreed that some of the results of the review had been deferment but this was important because it gave time to create new jobs.

THE LEADERSHIP OF THE OPPOSITION.—There was a surprising, graceful and touching episode in the Commons on February 6, when the Prime Minister (Mr. Wilson) used part of his Question Time to pay tribute to Mr. Edward Heath, lately deposed leader of the Opposition. Mr. Heath was not in the Chamber when Mr. Wilson said that the House would not wish to leave the " events of this week ", the Opposition's election of their leader under a new voting system from which Mr. Heath withdrew after coming second to Mrs. Thatcher in the first ballot, without referring to the departure from his accustomed place of Mr. Heath. M.P.s murmured approval of this departure from procedure as Mr. Wilson continued: " While it has not escaped the notice of the House and the country, that over the years, Mr. Heath and I have had our differences, those differences have been political, representing a deep divergence of political philosophies. They have not been personal." Mr. Heath had made a most notable contribution to the work of the House. He added: " I can recall many acts of individual consideration and kindness, going far beyond the normal exchanges and activities of Parliamentary life in our democracy. In whatever field his talents and experience may be deployed, and in his continuing membership of this House, which we welcome, I know the whole House will wish him well."

THE ROYAL HOUSEHOLD.—The newly-elected Tory Leader (Mrs. Margaret Thatcher) had her baptism at the Despatch Box on February 12, during exchanges on the proposals to increase the Civil List to cover Royal Household expenses. After Mrs. Thatcher had supported the extra provision, the Prime Minister, speaking for his colleagues, congratulated her on her " outstanding " election success. He added: " I wish you happiness and enjoyment in a life which you know you can expect to be exciting but sometimes arduous and difficult." There was laughter when Mr. Wilson added: " From a study of your speeches I have formed the impression there may well be a deep gulf between us on our respective political philosophies." Mrs. Thatcher agreed that they might

have some hard things to say to each other at the Despatch Box, but added: " I hope we will be able to keep the mutual respect of keen antagonists." The Liberal Leader, Mr. Jeremy Thorpe, congratulated Mrs. Thatcher on becoming the first lady leader in the House. The Prime Minister had previously announced an increase of £420,000 in the Civil List allowances for the Queen's staff and said: " The pay increases are within the T.U.C. guidelines." Mr. Wilson said that Civil List expenditure did not represent any increase in real expenditure and the Royal trustees had reported that every effort had been made to secure economies in administration of the Royal Household. By the end of 1975, salaries and wages might be expected to have increased by something like 70 per cent. over the three years from 1972. The increased provision was required to meet increases in wages and salaries of existing members, officials and staff of the Royal Household. The Queen had intimated that she thought it right for her to make a further contribution from her own resources towards the increased cash requirement for the Civil List this year and had offered £150,000 for 1975, which the Government had accepted and which would reduce the actual net call on the Exchequer by that amount to £270,000. Mrs. Margaret Thatcher welcomed the statement and said that proper provision should continue to be made for the Royal Household in the performance of its official functions. It was their most precious asset. The Liberal Leader (Mr. Thorpe) said: " Inflation inevitably hits any head of state in whatever system it is operated; the present system is not only psychologically unfair but totally misleading."

THE INDUSTRY BILL.—The Industry Secretary (Mr. Anthony Wedgwood Benn) described his Industry Bill in the Commons on February 7, as the end of a chapter in our industrial history. The industrial system to which the Conservatives adhered had failed them, he said. He was moving the Second Reading of the measure, which proposed to set up the controversial National Enterprise Board and give powers to extend public ownership into profitable areas of manufacturing industry. Among its other provisions, the Bill empowered the Secretary of State to compel companies to disclose information about present and future activities of their U.K. undertakings. Mr. Benn said that there had been a catastrophic fall in investment when the Conservatives were in power. If the market economy could not or would not give them the investment they needed they must do it directly. The verdtic of the Opposition spokesman (Mr. Michael Heseltine) was that bureaucracy, which always fed on itself, would multiply. The Bill was a weary combination of old-fashioned nationalisation. It was a damaging erosion of the privacy within which every government and company must operate. Mr. Heseltine, speaking of the determination of " the left-wing architects of this particular measure " said that the Government would have power to direct companies to obey its political will and the power to force companies into planning agreements. The Bill represented a cataclysmic decline in the possibilities of the success for British free enterprise, and the Conservatives would repeal it. The Liberal spokesman on industry (Mr. Richard Wainwright) said the real danger was that the largest farmyard of lame ducks ever known would be assembled under the presidency of the N.E.B. A former Director General of the C.B.I. and former Trade and Industry Secretary, Mr. John Davies (C., Knutsford) said that Mr. Benn might imagine himself the guardian of industry, but industry itself had no confidence in the Minister. He remarked: " He is regarded as the scourge of industry and always has been. He is regarded as a menace and a danger to industry." At the end of the two-day debate on the Bill on February 18, it received a second reading with a majority of 14, voting being 313 to 299. The final stages of the debate took place amidst mounting noise and interruptions from both sides. Earlier the Paymaster General (Mr. Edmund Dell) said that provided the principle of greater disclosure was maintained, the Government was ready to listen to and consider constructive criticism and alternative proposals for safeguarding information of vital importance to a firm. The Opposition Industry spokesman (Mr. Eldon Griffiths) said that the Bill was one of a series of measures designed to impose a Socialist state. It was the most concentrated, most destructive and most class-conscious attack on the remains of private enterprise and on capital and property ownership that the country had ever seen. The Liberal spokesman (Mr. Cyril Smith) said that the real reason for the lack of investment in industry over the years had been constant government interference with and dabbling in industry. The Bill was ill-conceived and rotten.

BROADCASTING OF PARLIAMENT.—The Commons decided on February 24, by 354 votes to 182, on a four-week experimental radio broadcast of their proceedings. But by a majority of 12 (275 to 263) they rejected a three-week experimental televising of the House. Both were free votes. The Parliamentary Secretary, Privy Council Office (Mr. William Price) said that broadcasting the proceedings would lead to more open government. He commented: " We have to accept that rows in this Chamber make good television; that bad behaviour will not be suppressed to save us embarrassment." The question was whether television would be even more damaging than the written word and whether Parliament was prepared to pay that price. Supporting experiments with both radio and television, Mr. Edward du Cann (C., Taunton), Chairman of the 1922 Committee, said that he was astonished that M.P.s were still talking about the matter 15 years after it had first been raised. The Father of the House, Mr. George Strauss (Lab., Vauxhall) however, said that he did not want either committees or the Chamber televised. Cameras would be bound to pick out, and editors would select, portions of speeches which were dramatic, enlivening and sensational. Also opposing televising the House, Mr. John Mendelson (Lab., Penistone) said that a dangerous proposition had been growing up that nothing important could be done unless it was instantly televised. The Shadow Leader of the House (Mr. John Peyton) said that every M.P. ought to be ready to run the risk of appearing idiotic and silly, and on balance it would be wise and right for them to allow the experiment. Mr. Ronald Bell (C., Beaconsfield) said that television and broadcasting were under an iron discipline to hold the attention of their viewers—" they must be piquant and they must be light and I do not want to see the proceedings of Parliament fall into that category ". Mr. James Craigen (Lab., Maryhill) thought that if Parliament was televised " we would run the risk of being dictated to by a cathode ray tube ". Mr. Colin Jackson (Lab., Brighouse and Spenborough) said that the British people were missing history every day because the workings of Parliament were shrouded and kept from public view. Mr. Cranley Onslow (C., Woking) said: " Let them bring in the television cameras and show us—warts and all ".

DIRECT GRANT SCHOOLS.—Direct grant grammar schools were to be phased out from September 1976, the Education Secretary (Mr. Prentice) told the Commons on March 11. He said " The time has come to implement the pledge in the Labour Party Election Manifesto to stop the present system of direct grant schools. Grants to schools which are unwilling to enter the maintained school system or which it is not practicable to absorb into the system will be phased out, starting in September 1976. Arrangements to safeguard the interests of pupils already in the schools will be made. Meanwhile I do not propose to make any change in the level of the grant ".

The Shadow Education Secretary (Mr. Norman St. John-Stevas) said that Mr. Prentice's statement would be regarded by the educational world as " an unprecedented step of educational vandalism ". He reaffirmed the Opposition's pledge to re-open the direct grant school list; schools would be restored on a basis which would make it impossible for them to be destroyed again by Ministers.

REFERENDUM PROPOSALS AND THE E.E.C.—The Government won the vote on the Common Market Referendum on March 11, with a majority of 50 at the end of more than seven hours debate on the White Paper containing the referendum proposals. Voting on a formal motion was 312 to 262. The Leader of the House (Mr. Edward Short) who said that the Conservative Government's handling of the European issue had not matched up to its previous promises, disagreed with the view that a referendum was alien to the principles and practices of Parliamentary democracy. The referendum could not be held without Parliamentary approval, nor, if the decision was to leave the Community, could it be made effective without further legislation. The Leader of the Opposition (Mrs. Thatcher) said that a precedent could be set requiring that every piece of legislation would need full-hearted consent. Used by the present Government, in the form proposed, the referendum was a tactical device to get over a split in their own party. The Government could not be properly accountable to Parliament unless it acknowledged a collective responsibility in matters of main policy. The Liberal Leader (Mr. Jeremy Thorpe) said that it seemed that the Labour Government could not agree, and so they were to have a referendum at the people's expense. The Prime Minister on March 18, announced in the Commons that the Government had decided to recommend that Britain should stay in the E.E.C. The announcement, greeted with silence by a large proportion of Labour M.P.s, received resounding approval from the Opposition and Liberal benches. Mr. Wilson made his statement to a crowded House. As the Prime Minister disclosed details of the renegotiations which had led to the decision in favour of recommending that Britain should stay in the Market, he made the following points: Economic and Monetary Union—" There is no prospect of our coming under pressure, to agree to an arrangement threatening the level of employment in Britain "; proposals in the Industry Bill for a National Enterprise Board and planning agreements were in no way incompatible with the Treaty of Rome; potential problems over steel prices could be resolved by close contact between Government and the Steel Board while possible difficulties about mergers could also be solved. " There is nothing which precludes us from extending nationalisation of the present private sector in steel, or even total nationalisation of the industry."

Contrary to the situation four years earlier, the

problem of V.A.T. harmonisation was no longer a real threat. Mr. Wilson: " To sum up, I believe that our renegotiation objectives have been substantially, though not completely, achieved." The Leader of the Opposition (Mrs. Thatcher) welcomed Mr. Wilson's statement, saying that it " has not been necessary to change one single clause in the basic treaties to carry out these negotiations ". The Liberal Leader (Mr. Jeremy Thorpe) also welcomed the Prime Minister's statement, and congratulated him, amid laughter, " for the consistency he has always shown on European matters ". After the statement had been repeated in the Lords, the Leader of the Opposition (Lord Carrington) said that the outcome had been desirable and congratulated the Government. For the Liberals Lord Gladwyn said that the decision was very welcome to his party. Lord Shinwell (Lab.) said that the terms renegotiated were totally unacceptable, completely inconsistent with repeated declarations, and a betrayal of decisions made by prominent members of the Government. Lord Harmar-Nicholls (C.) called the statement " a bucket of camouflage ". The renegotiations and forthcoming referendum were a cynical manoeuvre which was a betrayal of their Parliamentary system. Lord Bruce of Donington (Lab.) said there were many who would do their best to ensure that the sovereignty of the British people was restored to where it properly belonged—the Palace of Westminster. The Leader of the Lords (Lord Shepherd) did not believe that remaining in the E.E.C. in any way weakened the sovereignty of Parliament.

AID FOR OPPOSITION PARTIES.—The Commons agreed by a majority of 95 votes on March 20, to give financial aid to opposition political parties, following-up the undertaking given in the Queen's Speech. Voting was 142 to 47 on a Government motion which set out the main proposals as a payment of £500 for each seat won by the party, plus £1 for every 200 votes cast for it at the last General Election, with a maximum payment of £150,000. It also provided that a party must have had at least two members elected, or one member elected and at least 150,000 votes cast for the party. The House rejected, by 159 votes to 47 an amendment by Mr. Arthur Lewis (Lab., Newham N.W.) that the proposals should be deferred until after the next General Election. Mr. Short acknowledged that it was becoming increasingly difficult for opposition parties to keep up with those who were backed by the resources of Government, either in the research or administration fields. " I believe that a healthy and lively opposition is an essential part of democracy ", he remarked.

THE COMMON MARKET AGAIN.—On April 9 the Commons approved the Government's recommendation to continue British membership of the Common Market by 396 votes to 170. The decision, on a free vote, came at the end of a three-day debate which had seen, during its final stages, an impressive debut on the back benches by the former Opposition Leader (Mr. Edward Heath) and the defiance by the Minister of State, Industry (Mr. Eric Heffer) of Mr. Wilson's ruling ordering ministers to toe the party line in the Chamber, if not outside.

Another prominent anti-marketeer, Mr. Enoch Powell, was involved in an exchange with Mr. Heath as to whether " full-hearted consent " had been given by the British people to the country's membership of the E.E.C. The last round-up of the debate had begun with a speech from the

Agriculture Minister (Mr. Peart), who warned that it would be foolish to suppose that any of Britain's traditional food suppliers would be willing to gear themselves primarily to meeting their needs if they left the E.E.C., especially at the expense of other outlets where they could get a higher return. Mr. Heath said that sovereignty was not something to be hoarded, sterile, and barren, carefully protected in a greatcoat with its collar turned up. It was something for them as custodians to use in the interests of their own country. To go it alone would mean a loss of their political influence, trade and jobs, and a massive loss of investment, said Mr. Heath. Mr. Eric Heffer's speech had been awaited with interest by M.P.s from the time he had entered the Chamber and taken a place on the backbenches before the debate began. After several attempts to speak, he finally caught the Speaker's eye, and passionately argued against the Common Market, stating that he believed that the guidelines on the Market were as unacceptable as the guidelines on the question of ministerial discussion in the House. Mr. William Hamilton (Lab., Fife Central) attacked dissident ministers who were still prepared to remain members of the Government and declared that if they felt strongly about it they should resign.

The final stages of the debate were noisy, with shouting in a full Chamber. Winding up, the Shadow Foreign Secretary (Mr. Maudling) said that the referendum would damage the status of Parliament and he did not think the constitutional implications had been thought out fully. Replying, the Foreign Secretary (Mr. Callaghan) did not believe the economics of a mixed economy could be effectively challenged by the Commission or anyone else. Some Labour M.P.s jeered when Mr. Callaghan explained why he had changed his mind over membership in the last 12 months, but Mr. Callaghan hit back: " I say to those who jeer that the ounce of practice I have had is worth a ton of their theory."

Not only a majority of Labour M.P.s—145 altogether—but seven Cabinet Ministers and more than 20 other Ministers of middle and junior rank, including whips, voted against their own Government's recommendation. Eight Conservative M.P.s supported the anti-marketeers along with 11 Nationalists and six Ulster Unionists. Twelve Liberals voted with the Government and their other M.P. did not vote.

The date of the referendum on Britain's continued membership of the Common Market was Thursday, June 5, the Leader of the House (Mr. Edward Short) announced in the Commons on April 10 when he moved the second reading of the Referendum Bill.

Mr. Short said that he had tabled amendments to make special arrangements for servicemen overseas and wives to vote in person at their units, but that it was administratively not possible for other British people working abroad to vote. This announcement provoked angry interruptions from Tory backbenchers, but Mr. Short said that the problems involved would be " insoluble ". Mr. John Peyton, Opposition spokesman on House of Commons affairs, called the Referendum Bill " a wretched little measure " and said Conservatives regarded the measure as a trivial one and the whole idea of a referendum as " damaging to our country, damaging to Parliament and damaging to the Labour Party ". The Liberal Chief Whip (Mr. David Steel) said the referendum was " a delusion on the public ". The whole exercise was a £9 million fraud on the British people. Mr. Douglas Henderson (SNP, Aberdeenshire E.) applauded the Government's decision to give the people an opportunity to make a decision one way or the other on this constitutional change. The Opposition Law spokesman (Sir Michael Havers) said that if a referendum had to be held all Britons qualified to vote should be allowed to do so, and that must include those who were overseas. The Minister of State, Privy Council Office (Mr. Gerald Fowler) said the Government accepted that the decision not to include British citizens resident abroad in the vote was disappointing for those people. The Bill was given a second reading by 312 votes to 248.

THE APRIL BUDGET.—The Chancellor of the Exchequer (Mr. Healey) presented another Budget on April 15, and its main points were: "Now that the consequences of the oil crisis can be seen more clearly they provide a formidable setting for British economic policy in the next few years. The increase in the price of oil combined with increases in the price of food and raw materials have inflicted a heavy blow on the nation's real income. Oil imports last year cost about £2,900,000,000 more than the year before and we were left with a current balance of payments deficit of £3,800,000,000 —equivalent to more than 5 per cent. of our G.N.P. The second consequence of the oil crisis concerns the impact of inflation. Higher world prices were the major cause of inflation for most of last year. But for the last six months or so the main cause of rising prices in Britain has been the scale of wage and salary increases, which were far in excess of what could be justified by the increases in prices and could not possibly be offset by improvements in productivity. One of the more damaging effects of continuing inflation at nearly 20 per cent. will be on our international competitiveness. The Government has honoured its side of the Social Contract and many in the trade union movement have worked hard to apply the T.U.C. guidelines but the general rate of pay increases has been well above the rise in the cost of living. Pay has recently been running about 8 or 9 per cent. ahead of prices. Unless, however, the voluntary policy achieves stricter adherence to guidelines laid down by the trade unions of their own free will, the consequence can only be rising unemployment, cuts in public expenditure, lower living standards for the country as a whole and growing tension throughout society. It would be unwise to stimulate a further growth in home consumption now. The July and November measures should ensure that our levels of unemployment remain lower than those in other countries affected by the world recession. The main purpose of my Budget today will be to ensure that our economy can take full advantage of the strong recovery in world trade we can expect next year. The strategy must be to achieve a very substantial improvement in our current account deficit in the next two years and eliminate it entirely as rapidly as possible thereafter. Our overseas deficit must be removed—and the world must know it will be removed."

To avoid the wasteful disruption and extra costs always involved in short-term cuts in expenditure programmes, the Chancellor had decided to rely on higher taxation in the current year, with the reduction in public expenditure taking place in 1976–77.

The Chancellor intended the growth in money supply to be contained at a level which did not fuel inflation and the credit available to be concentrated on the essential needs of the economy.

The Chancellor said: " In our present situation the most important single object of economic

policy must be to improve the performance of our manufacturing industry."

One of the most persistent problems was the shortage of skilled manpower in key industries and key areas. In consultation with the Secretary of State for Employment an additional £20,000,000 in 1975–76 and £30,000,000 in 1976–77 would be allocated to the Manpower Services Commission to strengthen training programmes.

The Secretary of State would also be introducing an amendment to the Employment Protection Bill to provide enabling powers for a Temporary Employment Subsidy. If required this would enable special payments to be made to firms for a limited period if they were prepared to defer redundancies.

As regards the private sector, full use would be made of powers of selective assistance under the Industry Act to prime the pump for viable investment projects. In addition further schemes would be introduced designed to assist certain industries as a whole to modernise and rationalise. Preliminary discussion on a scheme for the ferrous foundry industry were being held with the Economic Development Committee; £100,000,000 would be allocated for these two purposes. To help with exports, the E.C.G.D. would provide facilities to guarantee loans for pre-shipment finance on large-scale projects. Also the scope of the investment relief in the Price Code would be extended to cover investment for exporting and the rate of the investment relief would be increased from 17½ per cent. to 20 per cent. and extended to cover commercial vehicles.

They were just as concerned to get the best use of resources in agriculture as in industry, and the Minister of Agriculture was about to publish a White Paper which concluded that the future levels of world prices would call for a continuing increase in the output of our own agriculture over the next five years.

The planned level of expenditure in 1976–77 would be reduced by over £1,100,000,000 at present prices or £900,000,000 at 1974 Survey Prices. The Defence Budget would be cut by £110,000,000—about 3 per cent. In civil programmes, current expenditure on goods and services, including manpower, would be reduced by 1½ per cent. and capital expenditure by 10 per cent., with certain exceptions, e.g., general practitioner service or provision of essential school places. Reductions would save about £125,000,000 on current expenditure and about £280,000,000 on capital expenditure.

There would be no reduction in the building of new council houses, but a saving of £50,000,000 from other capital expenditure in the housing programme. Subsidies on nationalised industries prices would come down from £550,000,000 in 1974–75 to about £70,000,000 in the current year, and were likely to be phased out completely by April 1976.

Food subsidies in 1976–77 would be reduced by £150,000,000 and housing subsidies by £65,000,000.

Nationalised industries investment programmes were to produce savings of £100,000,000 and the overseas aid programme would be reduced by £20,000,000 (spaced over two years). There would be no mid-term census.

Beyond 1976–77 there would be at best only very restricted room for growth in public expenditure. Nonetheless, the Government was fully conscious of the needs of families with children, and the child benefit scheme already announced would be introduced in April 1977— the earliest date by which it was administratively practicable. As an interim scheme, family allowances at the new rate of £1·50 per week would be extended to the first children of single parent families from April 1976.

The Chancellor said there would be no new general reliefs for the company sector in the current year; the rate of Corporation Tax would remain at 52 per cent.; rates for small companies, cooperatives and building societies were also to remain the same; there would be no advance Corporation Tax supplement during the year; stock relief (introduced in the Autumn Budget) would be continued and extended to unincorporated businesses and companies which did not previously qualify. Relief for those not benefiting in the autumn would be for two years, with additional relief to compensate for the wait.

The Finance Bill would include a provision preventing oil companies from offsetting against profits losses from transactions at artificial prices in overseas oil.

Of the Value Added Tax, the Chancellor said that the 25 per cent. rate on petrol would be applied to a wider range of goods, e.g. (a) most domestic electrical appliances, other than cookers, space heaters and fitted water heaters; (b) radios, TVs, hi-fi, etc.; (c) boats, aircraft and caravans, other than those currently zero-rated; (d) cameras, binoculars, furs and jewellery. The additional yield would be £325,000,000 in a full year.

The VAT regulator would be amended to provide for 25 per cent. variation in rate, rather than 20 per cent. No relief from VAT in any other sectors was possible " at a time when I am looking for such sacrifices in other fields ".

On Revenue Duties, Mr. Healey stated that the effective burden of taxation on those goods had been going down, and it was time for further increases in the circumstances. Beer would go up by 2p a pint on average; spirits by 64p on a standard bottle of whisky or gin; wine by 24p a standard bottle; tobacco by between 5½p and 10p for a packet of cigarettes depending on size and type—the average would be 7p. Additional full year yields would be £185,000,000 from beer, £60,000,000 from spirits, £80,000,000 from wine and British wine and £275,000,000 from tobacco plus £25,000,000 consequential VAT from these goods.

Regarding changes in duty structure, the customs duties on beer, wine and spirits would be split into protective and revenue elements. Other items were: betting and pool betting, no change; bingo, doubled to 5 per cent. with effect from September 29, 1975; gaming licence duty, restructure of duty and increase of rates; gaming machines, reduction in duty on second and subsequent machines, but " take " to be charged with VAT. An additional £12,000,000 in a full year would come from gaming and bingo. Hydrocarbon oil duty, no change in petrol or oil prices. No two-tier pricing for petrol. The total additional yield from Customs taxation would be £965,000,000 in a full year. Vehicle Excise Duty: annual rate on cars up from £25 to £40, with the 60 per cent. increase to apply to motor-bicycles and three-wheelers—an additional yield of £209,000,000 in a full year. Rates for commercial vehicles would increase by a third—with a minimum rate for general goods vehicles of £40. Hackney carriages would go up from £12 to £20. Additional yield £61,000,000 and additional yield for all Vehicle Excise Duties £270,000,000.

All indirect tax measures would lead to an increase in the Retail Price Index of about 2¾ per cent. in the ensuing three months or so, and the chancellor remarked: "None of these increases

touch essential goods but they are all necessary because as a nation we are at present living beyond our means. For this reason attempts to offset them, or any other tax measures, through pay increases would be wrong, damaging, and in the end self-defeating."

There would be legislation to end " bed and breakfast " arrangements (whereby companies get relief for losses on shares which they have no real intention of parting with) and " double banking " whereby wealthy taxpayers obtain relief for a capital loss on gilts held for more than twelve months). The Chancellor was not yet persuaded that indexation for capital gains tax was necessary, but he would review the incidence of the tax. Relief for working farmers, small businessmen and owners of historic houses would be on broadly the same lines as concessions for Capital Transfer Tax.

Mr. Healey announced measures to increase the fairness of the tax system. These were: (a) The PAYE system to apply to office workers and other staff engaged through agencies. (b) The benefit enjoyed by an employee from employers' medical insurance schemes would be taxable. (c) New legislation on remuneration by voucher—but with no change in the luncheon voucher concession. (d) New measures to deal with the " Lump "—" only subcontractors who could satisfy the Revenue that they had genuine businesses and would meet their future tax liabilities in full would be entitled to be paid gross. (e) Issues of stock dividends would be charged to tax. (f) Interest would be paid on repayments of tax delayed beyond 5 April in the year following the year of assessment; this would also apply to repayments of Corporation Tax.

The Chancellor also announced that the earnings ceiling for national insurance contributions would be increased from April 1976 by up to £8 a week more than it would otherwise have been, in order to pay for the relaxation in the earnings rule for pensioners recently voted by the House against the Government's recommendation.

The single allowance would go up from £625 to £675; and the married allowance from £865 to £955. The cost would be £546,000,000 in a full year, and it would take 400,000 people out of tax. The additional personal allowance for a single parent with family would be increased from £180 to £280.

Referring to income tax rates, the Chancellor said: " I made it clear in my Budget Speech last November that if wages rose above the level laid down in the guidelines of the T.U.C. I would find it necessary to raise taxation in order to remove the excess demand involved. The increase I am about to announce can be regarded as an anti-inflation surcharge." The basic and higher rates of income tax would go up by 2 percentage points (except for the top rate). The additional revenue yield would be £771,000,000 in a full year. The combination of the measures he had announced would reduce the public sector borrowing requirement by about £1,200,000,000 in the current year.

The Chancellor's principal conclusions were: that 1975 should be a better year for balance of payments; the deficit should be at least a billion pounds lower than in 1974. The non-oil deficit on the current account would have turned into surplus. Prices would continue to increase. For some months yet they must expect high figures for the Retail Price Index compared with twelve months previously. But the rate of increase in the month on month index should begin to fall by the middle of the year, with the possibility of an annual increase of 12–16 per cent. between June and

December provided there was no acceleration in wage and salary increases.

In 1975/6 the borrowing requirement was expected to be about £9 billion. By 1976–77 the borrowing requirement should be significantly lower The situation would be even better if exports increased to the extent that output and employment at home could return to full employment conditions.

Income tax changes would benefit particularly low income taxpayers. Altogether nine million taxpayers, or 35 per cent. of the total, would pay less tax as a result of the Budget; that figure included families with two children up to around average earnings.

Unemployment was difficult to forecast; it could be almost 1 million, or 4 per cent., by the end of the year and Budget measures might be responsible for about 20,000 of these. Mr. Healey said: " This is part of the price we have to pay for inflation at current levels. But in 1976, as world trade begins to grow vigorously again, I would expect to see a reversal of this trend set in."

Opening the debate, Mrs. Thatcher said that the budget was the " strongest brew I have seen a Chancellor do. I have never listened to a budget which puts so much extra tax on the British people at one go. It is a typical Socialist budget; equal shares of misery for all." If Mr. Healey had not increased public expenditure so much, the rate of inflation would not be so high.

A four-day debate ensued, during which the Liberal leader (Mr. Jeremy Thorpe) said that public sector borrowing had been carried on to a reckless degree and he described the Chancellor's anti-inflation surcharge as " an inflation incentive scheme" because it would hit everyone. He renewed his call for a statutory prices and incomes policy.

The Government had majorities ranging from 9 to 275 in a series of votes at the end of the budget debate on April 2. The Tories put their main strength behind their move to ensure that the Capital Transfer Tax and Estate Duty could be debated and amended when the Finance Bill, which followed the budget proposals, came before the Commons. But their amendment was defeated by 287 to 278, a Government majority of 9. The Scottish Nationalists forced a division on the formal motion on which the budget debate had taken place, and were in effect voting against the budget as a whole. The Government motion was carried by 286 to 11; Government majority of 275. Three days were spent on the remaining stages of the Referendum Bill which was given a Third Reading on April 24 by 180 votes to 41; Government majority of 139.

THE REFERENDUM PLANS.—On April 22, a backbench move to give referendum votes to Britons working and living abroad was rebuffed by a Government majority of 40. An amendment, sponsored by Labour M.P.s, which would have paved the way for the provision of voting facilities for British passport holders abroad was defeated by 251 votes to 211. The mover, Mr. Roderick MacFarquhar (Lab., Belper), said that the referendum was a unique occasion; therefore there should be a unique extension of the franchise for British citizens living abroad.

After a two-day debate the Lords approved, by a majority of 241 on April 22, the Government's recommendation that Britain should stay in the E.E.C. Voting was 261–20 in favour of the motion. An amendment moved by Lord Wigg (Ind.), a former Labour cabinet minister, to reject the Government recommendation was defeated by 242 votes (263–21). The holding of a referendum

was bitterly attacked by the former Labour Foreign Secretary, Lord George-Brown. The previous day, and despite a warning from the Leader of the Commons (Mr. Edward Short) that referendum results announced on a regional basis would lead to differences and bitterness, M.P.s decided on a free vote that county regional voting should be declared. They carried by 270 votes to 153 an amendment by Mr. Roderick MacFarquhar that the result would show the numbers voting each way in counties of England and Wales; Greater London; Isles of Scilly; regions and island areas in Scotland, and in Northern Ireland.

Most of the debate centred on a Liberal amendment that the count should be held on constituency level, but this was defeated by 264 votes to 131 Next day, the Leader of the House agreed to make changes in the Bill in the Lords so that votes could be counted at county and regional level. On May 6 the Lords gave an unopposed Third Reading and passed the Referendum Bill.

BRITISH LEYLAND.—The Prime Minister, Mr. Harold Wilson, told M.P.s on April 24 that the U.K. must remain in the world league as far as a British-owned automobile industry was concerned. He was making a statement announcing the Government's acceptance of the Ryder Report on British Leyland, which was published that afternoon. Mr. Wilson, who outlined the details of the report, which included a new structure of joint management and union councils, committees, and conferences said: " We are giving British Leyland the opportunity through massive investment to overcome weaknesses of the past and play a full part as leader in the world markets."

Mr. Wilson said that the Company was not bankrupt, but if the Government had not given help there would have been no alternative to liquidation or the appointment of a receiver, and added: " The Government agree with the proposal that they should offer to buy out existing shareholders and underwrite a new rights issue. In this way the shareholders will be given a fair choice between selling their shares at 10p each, or retaining them and, if they wish, taking an additional stake in the Company at the same price. The Government also accept that they may be required to provide £500,000,000 of extra capital to British Leyland between 1976–78 if none is available from other sources; the question of funds beyond that date will be a matter for later consideration. In return for this massive investment of public money, the Government intend that they should have a majority shareholding in the reconstructed Company." Meanwhile, British Leyland would need further working capital. The House would be asked to approve an Order seeking authority for an increase of up to £50,000,000 in the guarantees already approved." Mr. Wilson said that following the initial injection of equity capital in 1975 the release of further stages of Government funding would be determined in the light of the contribution being made to the improvements in the performance of British Leyland by better industrial relations and higher productivity. Vast amounts of public money were involved, representing one of the greatest single investments in manufacturing industry which any British Government had ever contemplated. On this decision a million jobs were at stake. Mr. Wilson said that the Government was injecting about £1,400,000,000, and clearly that could not be on the basis of being a tuppenny-ha'penny minority shareholder.

The former Leader of the Opposition (Mr. Heath)

declared; " This is one of the gravest statements affecting our national affairs which has ever been made to the Commons."

In the Lords, the Leader of the Opposition (Lord Carrington) said it was difficult to judge exactly what the Government had committed itself to.

The Liberal Leader (Lord Byers) said that his first reaction was that the amount of public money to be put at risk was " quite frightening. It is almost as though we were starting to print motorcars."

The Government had a majority of 21 on May 21 for the second reading of the British Leyland Bill, which allowed up to £265,000,000 to be spent on acquiring shares in the Company. Mr. James Prior said that Mr. Benn was allowing the workers to think that if their strikes bankrupted the Company he would take over. The Bill received its second reading by 282 to 261. Moving the second reading, Mr. Benn said that bankruptcy for British Leyland would have been totally irresponsible. Hundreds and thousands of Midlands firms depended on British Leyland.

CONTROL OF OIL RESOURCES.—On April 30, the Energy Secretary (Mr. Eric Varley) moved the Second Reading of the Petroleum and Submarine Pipelines Bill to set up the British National Oil Corporation, and declared that it was one of the most important ever brought before Parliament and was intended to ensure that the British people exercised their due rights over their oil in a proper and mutually acceptable relationship with the oil companies. It was not a view shared by the Opposition Energy spokesman (Mr. Patrick Jenkin) who said that it was a total disaster and conferred powers on the Government which were vast and arbitrary. Money was going to be siphoned off to huge, wild, socialist schemes. It had a guarded welcome from the Scottish Nationalists. Mr. Gordon Wilson (S.N.P., Dundee E.) said that they would vote for its second reading, but warned that unless there were substantial amendments in Committee, particularly on the principle of Scottish control of oil resources, the Nationalists might well have to reconsider their vote on Third Reading. The Bill received a second reading by 286 to 258.

DEFENCE DEBATE.—A left-wing attempt to reject the Government's Defence Estimates was defeated in the Commons at the end of a two-day debate on May 7 by 489 to 57. Then the Government motion endorsing the defence review was approved by 291 votes to 251. Earlier the Defence Under Secretary, R.A.F. (Mr. Brynmor John), had said that all sides accepted that defence could not be considered in isolation from the country's economic health, but it was also difficult to understand those M.P.s who automatically described all defence expenditure as wasteful, and who supposed that the country's defence would look after itself if the money was spent instead on hospitals and comprehensive schools. The final Opposition speaker (Mr. Cranley Onslow) accused the Government of having done a fairly efficient demolition job with the Defence White Paper, which however had been destroyed even before the debate by the Secretary of State's further round of unplanned arbitrary cuts, taking £110,000,000 from the Defence Budget.

REFERENDUM RESULT.—Monday, June 9, was an historic occasion for the Commons on its return after the Whitsun Recess and the national referendum campaign and vote on the U.K.'s continued membership of the Common Market. First, the

Prime Minister announced the result of the previous Thursday's vote in favour of staying-in the E.E.C. Second, it was the start of a four-week experiment to broadcast live on radio for the first time the proceedings of the House.

In his statement, Mr. Wilson declared: " What has impressed all of us has been not only the high turn-out and the clear and unmistakable nature of the decision, but also the consistent pattern of positive voting over almost every county and region of the U.K. I hope this House and the country as a whole will follow the lead which the Government intend to give in placing past divisions behind us, and in working together to play a full and constructive part in all Community policies and activities." The Prime Minister said that it followed from the decision to remain in the Community that the U.K. should be fully represented in all the Community's institutions. A recommendation that the House should be fully represented in the European Assembly would be made to the Parliamentary Labour party. Mrs. Thatcher joined with Mr. Wilson in rejoicing over " this excellent result which confirms the earlier Parliamentary decision ". The Prime Minister should regard it as vital to take the necessary steps to restore British confidence and deal with their economic problems. Mr. Wilson replied that for the first time throughout those many years of controversy they had had the full-hearted consent of the whole British people.

GOVERNMENT ECONOMIC POLICY.—Mr. Healey announced, to a surprised and crowded House of Commons on July 1, that the Government would have to legislate to enforce a 10 per cent. wages and dividends limit if agreement was not reached to satisfy their targets for reducing inflation. The Government would much prefer to proceed on the basis of a voluntary policy agreed with the C.B.I. and T.U.C., but a voluntary policy would not be acceptable to the Government unless it satisfied the targets it had set for reducing inflation and included convincing arrangements for ensuring compliance. The Government would announce its decision in a White Paper the next week. Mr. Healey stated: " The Government is determined to bring the rate of domestic inflation down to 10 per cent. by the end of the next pay round and to single figures by the end of 1976. This means the increase in wages and salaries during the next pay round cannot exceed 10 per cent. The same limit is being set for dividends." The Chancellor explained that the Government had already reached an advanced stage in preparing measures which were fair and just; they would ensure that all sections of the community shared the burden fairly. The measures would deal with the central problem of compliance and they would take action through the Price Code to encourage compliance by private employers. Sir Geoffrey Howe, Opposition spokesman on Treasury and economic affairs, welcomed the fact that the Government had at last begun to grapple with the nation's economic problems; this statement was also a confession of its failure during the past 16 months of deception and incompetence, but he was gravely disquieted that there was no reference to the abandonment of further plans for nationlisation or the extent of public spending. Mr. Eric Heffer (Lab., Walton, Liverpool) said that there was a clear indication that the Government was steadily moving towards a statutory incomes policy which was contrary to the election pledges they gave. Mr. John Pardoe, the Liberal spokesman, pledged support for the policy but said that to reduce pay increases to 10 per cent. would involve a substantial decrease in the standard of living of them all and it was absolutely impossible to achieve such a reduction by voluntary means.

INDUSTRY BILL.—M.P.s gave the controversial Industry Bill a third reading by 289–276 votes (Government majority of 13) on July 3 when the Industry Secretary (Mr. Varley) said that its aim was to help to bring about the solution to the problems which had held back the regeneration of industry. Investment per worker had been well below that of competing nations and this problem had to be tackled. Planning agreements could change the direction of industry and were the key to industrial progress. Mr. Heseltine, Opposition spokesman on industry, declared that underlining the Bill was a determination that power now spread widely throughout Britain in the industrial world should be gradually eroded and transferred to the State. It was an irrelevant and expensive Bill at a time when unemployment was rising, investment slumping, and the country was in one of the worst economic crises since the war. When this Bill was debated in the Lords on second reading on July 10, Viscount Watkinson, president-elect of the C.B.I., said that the Government had introduced a sordid li.tle measure, the purpose of which was to hand industry over lock, stock, and barrel to the State. Free enterprise still provided nearly all the exports with which this country paid its way in the world. Lord Beswick, Minister of State, Industry, said that the Bill was intended to help industry and all who worked in it; it sought to improve efficiency and aimed to create an economic climate in which all industries could more readily develop. The Bill received an unopposed second reading.

MR. WILSON'S ECONOMIC STATEMENT.—On July 11, ten days after the Chancellor of the Exchequer made a statement on the attack on inflation, Mr. Wilson honoured Mr. Healey's undertaking that by the end of the week the Government would make a further announcement about the recent consultations with the T.U.C. and C.B.I., setting out its judgment as to whether a voluntary policy, which was both viable and effective, had been reached. The Prime Minister stated: " The Government have decided to accept an overriding limit of £6 per week for pay settlements during the next pay round, a figure consistent with the aim of reducing the rate of inflation to 10 per cent. by the late summer of next year. Our policy is based on consent and willing co-operation within our democracy. We reject, for the reasons I have so frequently stated, the idea of statutory policies based on criminal sanctions against workers. In the White Paper (published that day), we have set out the Government's proposals, directed to strengthening the fight against inflation right along the line, covering both the public and the private sectors. The Government have decided that the cut-off for the increase of up to £6 should be £8,500. It is a requirement of the new proposals that no settlement can be approved within twelve months of the previous settlement. While the Government accepts the proposal for a flat rate limit of £6, this is not an entitlement; it is a maximum. It will have to be negotiated by established collective bargaining procedures, and it is not a requirement on employers who simply cannot afford to pay it.

" The Government are concerned that unions or groups of workers who make a settlement early in the pay round should legitimately be able to demand protection against the action of other groups who, on past experience, might prejudice their position by negotiating considerably bigger settlements later in the round. We intend to ensure observance of the new pay policy by employing the full battery of weapons available.

" As employer, the Government will ensure that all settlements in respect of its employees in the Civil Service, the National Health Service, and the Armed Forces comply with the pay limit. It will call on all other public sector employers to do the same. As paymaster and treasurer, on behalf of the taxpayer, for publicly owned industries and services, the Government will use all its powers to see that settlements are made within the pay limit. It will ensure that the money available is strictly controlled, and that none is available for the payment of incomes over the agreed limit. This means that for the nationalised industries and services, no money will be made available for excess settlements, whether by subsidies, whether by permission to borrow, or by loading excess cost on the public by increased prices or charges. There will be a strict limit on expenditure. Those seeking to negotiate settlements above the agreed limits must face the certain consequence that there will be an inescapable cutback in the current expenditure of the board or corporation concerned, directly affecting employment in that industry.

" There must be no less stringent control in respect of local authorities' spending. In this as in other areas, legislation will be necessary to supplement and strengthen the policy we have worked out with industry. The Bill will be introduced next week. So far as local authorities are concerned legislation will be brought before Parliament to enable the Government to restrict payment of Rate Support Grant to individual local authorities so that no grant is forthcoming in respect of any part of a settlement made in breach of the pay limit. Moreover, unless there is a tighter restriction on the numbers of staff employed, the Government will further have to restrict the scale of provision of grants. In addition, if this proves necessary, as a further sanction, the Government will be prepared to use its powers to control local authority borrowing, including access to the capital market, to reduce the capital programmes of individual local authorities to offset any excess expenditure on pay settlements.

" In the private sector, the Government will use all its powers against any breach of the pay limit. The Bill will relieve employers of any contractual obligations which would otherwise compel them to increase pay by more than the limit.

" In the field of price control, the Bill will ensure that where an employer breaks the pay limit, not only the excess, but the whole pay increase will be disallowed for the approval of price increases. This sanction will also be applied to nationalised industry prices. From now on, the Government will not give discretionary assistance under the Industry Act to companies which have broken the pay limit.

" The Government believe that these measures are necessary to secure compliance by all employers with the policy I have stated, but if our faith in the agreed policy is disappointed, if there are any who seek to abuse a system based on consensus and consent, or to cheat by any means, the Government will not hesitate to apply legal powers of compulsion against the employers concerned, to ensure compliance. We must have these powers in reserve. Legislation has therefore already been prepared, for introduction if need be, which, when applied to particular cases, would make it illegal for the employer to exceed the pay limit. If the pay limit is endangered the Government will ask Parliament to approve this legislation forthwith.

" In present circumstances a general price freeze

is not realistic and would simply depress investment and aggravate the unemployment problem. But the Government's policy on prices, in addition to acting as a sanction against recalcitrant employers, is also designed to provide the necessary assurance to employees, required to justify the flat rate pay limit.

" The Government will therefore continue the present strict prices control enforced under the Price Code. We shall introduce legislation to extend the control powers beyond March 31, 1976, when they would expire. As the pay limit comes into full effect, the Government intend to ensure that the rate of price increase for a range of goods of special, strategic importance in the family expenditure will be held to about the 10 per cent. target. The C.B.I. and the Retail Consortium are prepared to enter into immediate discussions with the Government to achieve this price limitation programme.

" To assist with the cost of living during this period, and particularly to protect the living standards of lower income families and pensioners, the Government has also decided to delay the phasing out of food subsidies which was announced in the last Budget. This will involve an expenditure of an additional £70,000,000 during 1976/77. Local authority rents were frozen by the Government between March 1974 and March 1975, but increases are now in the pipeline because of pay increases and other inflationary influences. For 1976/77 the Government propose to limit rent increases so that rents do not rise faster than prices generally. This will mean that on average rent increases next spring will be of the order of 60p. a week rather than £1 a week or more. For this purpose the Government will provide an extra £80,000,000. The Government will introduce the temporary employment subsidy (to assist firms in areas of high unemployment) at the earliest possible moment. However, this subsidy will not be available to companies who exceed the pay limits. We shall also take special temporary measures to encourage the training and employment of school leavers and other young people in industry.

Mrs. Thatcher said that one reason for these measures was the Government's disastrous policies over the past 16 months. In a state of 25 per cent. inflation, they all might have to accept policies which they would otherwise find intolerable. The Opposition's main strategy was to reduce inflation and they welcomed the Government's conversion to that aim. The Liberal leader (Mr. Thorpe) said that the country would welcome the acceptance that they could not go on as they had and that new policies, backed by law, were necessary. Mr. Sydney Bidwell (Lab., Southall) declared that the Government had embarked upon a dangerous and perilous course, and there were other undisguised criticisms from Labour M.P.s on the Left wing of the Party. The White Paper, *The Attack on Inflation*, contained the Government's proposals, was debated for two days on July 21 and 22, and there was plenty of verbal hard-hitting from all sides. At the finish, the Shadow Cabinet advised Conservative M.P.s to abstain from voting on the motion to approve the White Paper, but Left wing Labour M.P.s forced a division, being defeated, however, by 262–54 votes; Government majority of 208. Previously, a Conservative amendment supporting the Government's " belated commitment " to anti-inflation measures but condemning its failure to reduce public spending and its persistence with nationalisation legislation was defeated by 327–269; Government majority of 58. There were rowdy scenes at the end of the debate during which the Employment Secretary (Mr. Foot) confirmed that

he might resign from the Cabinet if the Government introduced the reserve bill containing back-up statutory powers for their wage-pegging policy. At one stage Mr. Heath, former Opposition leader, spoke in support of the White Paper incomes policy, describing it as " unequivocally " crucial for the country. The Chancellor of the Exchequer declared that Parliament would be asked to approve reserve legislation forthwith if the £6 wage limit was threatened, and Mrs. Thatcher's view was that while the Opposition agreed with Mr. Healey's immediate objective of reducing inflation, she doubted if his policy would do the job. Mr. Thorpe considered that despite very real reservations the White Paper must be given a chance to succeed.

PARLIAMENTARY SALARIES.—On July 16 the Leader of the House (Mr. Edward Short), in a statement on Parliamentary salaries, said that the Top Salaries Review Body under Lord Boyle's chairmanship had recommended that the salary of an M.P. should be increased from £4,500 to £8,000 a year, an increase of 78 per cent. At present the amount of Members' salary payable to ministers was £3,000 and the review body had recommended this element should be increased to £5,000 a year. The review body recommended against any form of link between M.P.s' salaries and any other salary scale or index, but proposed instead a two-yearly review. The Government had decided that the Boyle recommendations on allowances should be implemented in full from June 13. These increased secretarial allowance from £1,750 to £3,200 a year, raised additional costs allowance from £1,050 to £1,350 a year, and the London supplement from £228 to £340 a year, with car mileage allowance up from 7·7p to 10·2p a mile plus more free travel vouchers, from 10 to 15 a year, to Westminster for an M.P.'s wife or husband. The Government accepted that a increase in M.P.s' pay was clearly justified, but at a time when it had announced anti-inflation measures, it could not support a recommendation for a 78 per cent. increase; therefore they proposed that M.P.s' salaries should be increased by £1,250 instead of the £3,500 recommended, giving a new salary of £5,750 implemented from June 13 last. Pension rights, however, should not be prejudiced, and that proposed arrangements which would allow M.P.s' pensions to be based on the figure of £8,000 recommended by the review body. There would be no increase in the amount of the Parliamentary salary drawn by Cabinet ministers. Ministers outside the Cabinet would receive an increase of £700 compared with the £2,000 recommended. The Shadow Leader of the House (Mr. Peyton) said that the Government could hardly expect to be congratulated on their handling of the affair. Mr. Ashton (Lab., Bassetlaw) declared that the Government had ratted on an independent arbitration award; Mr. Ogden (Lab., Liverpool, W. Derby) described the " miserable " recommendation of the Cabinet as pandering only to the prejudice and ignorance of the uninformed; Mr. Andrew Faulds (Lab., Warley E.) said that it was a typical piece of " Wilsonian legerdemain " which would lead to greater abuse; Mr. Winterton (C., Macclesfield) called the recommendations of the Cabinet an insult and a kick in the teeth to backbenchers; and this was the general theme of M.P.s' comments.

On July 22, immediately after approving the Government's White Paper on the attack on inflation, M.P.s staged a lengthy and at times confused debate on their own proposed salary increases, and this ended in a dramatic vote at about 3 a.m. on July 23, when they carried by one vote a Labour back-bencher's amendment accepting in principle that their pay should be linked to " a point on the scale paid to an assistant secretary in the public service not later than three months after the next General Election ". The amendment added that meantime M.P.s should receive pay increases of at least the size given to assistant secretaries. The voting was 128-127 on a free vote. Assistant secretaries' salary at the time was between £8,600 and £11,000 a year. Another move by other Labour M.P.s to restrict the increase of M.P.s' pay to £6 a week in support of the new pay limit was defeated by 197–37 votes, a majority of 160, and Government motions to approve the immediate salary increase to £5,750 and the improved allowances were carried without a division.

A £2 a day increase for peers backdated to June 13 was announced in the Lords on July 24 when Lord Shepherd, Leader of the House, said the Government proposed that their daily attendance allowance should be raised from £11·50p to £13·50p. Lord Aberdare, deputy Opposition leader, said that the country received very good value from the peers in the amount of work they did, and he knew that a number of them had been out of pocket attending the House.

THE £6 LIMIT.—On July 25, the Commons completed in a marathon all-night session the committee stage of the Remuneration, Charges and Grants Bill which enabled the Government to act in support of the £6 wage limit under its attack on inflation proposals. It was the second longest post-war sitting, lasting 26 hours 26 minutes, discussion on the committee stage details of the measure having begun the previous afternoon. Consequently, Government business arranged for July 25 to discuss E.E.C. agriculture and fisheries policy automatically lapsed. The Government did not lose a single division although its majority once fell to one vote, the principal critics of the Bill being Labour Left wingers. After an all-night sitting on the report stage of the Bill on July 29/30, it was given an unopposed third reading shortly after 5 a.m. on July 30, the Employment Secretary stating

that if a 25 per cent. rate of inflation continued, all the other propositions in the Labour Manifesto would be swept away in an inflationary flood.

END OF THE SESSION.—There were furious exchanges in the Commons on July 30 after the Trade Secretary (Mr. Shore) announced that the Government rejected the criticisms of the then Industry Secretary (Mr. Benn) by the Ombudsman and the inspectors appointed to make an inquiry into the collapse of Court Line, the holidays firm, in 1974. The Government, he said, respected the criticisms that Mr. Benn's statements that Government intervention had stabilised the situation over Court Line holidays were liable to mislead the public, but they considered then and still believed that the statements made were right in the difficult circumstances at the time. The Opposition demanded that Mr. Benn should make an apology, but without avail, and on August 6 the issue was sifted in a half-day's debate on the Government's handling of the affair, especially Mr. Benn's part in it. But at the close the formal motion on which the discussion arose was won by the Government by 180–156 votes; a majority of 24. Mr. Benn accepted full personal responsibility for all the decisions taken by the Government in 1974, for the statements he made in the House, and for his relations with his civil servants.

On July 31, Mr. Benn was again the focal point of the Opposition's attack when the Industry Secretary (Mr. Varley) and Mr. Benn's successor, reported that the Government would not make further funds available to Norton Villiers Triumph, the motorcycle firm. Mr. Heseltine, Opposition spokesman on industry, alleged that in 1974 Mr. Benn had told employees at N.V.T.works at Small Heath that the Government were fully committed to securing the future of the British motor-cycle industry and, declaring that there had been a major ministerial blunder, called for a full public inquiry so that those responsible could be held publicly accountable. Mr. Varley, however, rounded on the Tory critics of Mr. Benn, whom he supported against all Opposition accusations.

PUBLIC ACTS OF PARLIAMENT 1974-75

This list of Public Acts commences with 39 Public Acts which received the Royal Assent before September 1974. Those Public Acts which follow received the Royal Assent after August 1974. The date stated after each Act is the date on which it came into operation.

SLAUGHTERHOUSES ACT 1974 (April 1, 1974) consolidates certain enactments relating to slaughterhouses and knackers' yards and the slaughter of animals.

HORTICULTURE (SPECIAL PAYMENTS) ACT 1974 (February 8, 1974) authorises payments of moneys provided by Parliament to assist certain commercial growers of horticultural produce, the growing of which has become uneconomic as a result of the United Kingdom's membership of the EEC.

CHARLWOOD AND HORLEY ACT 1974 (February 8, 1974) transfers part of the new parishes of Charlwood and Horley to the new county of Surrey, and for connected purposes.

RABIES ACT 1974 (May 23, 1974) makes further provision for the prevention and control of rabies, and for connected purposes. *Inter alia* the Act extends the powers to deal with an outbreak of rabies outside quarantine and brings in extra provisions relating to the control of importation of animals which may carry rabies.

LORD HIGH COMMISSIONER (CHURCH OF SCOTLAND) ACT 1974 (June 27, 1974) provides that the allowance payable to Her Majesty's High Commissioner to the General Assembly of the Church of Scotland is to be of such amount as the Secretary of State with the concurrence of the Treasury may think fit.

DUMPING AT SEA ACT 1974 (June 27, 1974) controls dumping at sea. The Act ratifies the Convention for the Prevention of Marine Pollution by Dumping from Ships and Aircraft concluded at Oslo in February 1972 and the Convention on the Prevention of Marine Pollution by Dumping of Wastes and Other Matter concluded at London in December 1972.

MINISTERS OF THE CROWN ACT 1974 (June 27, 1974) amends the Ministerial and Other Salaries Act 1972 and other provisions about Ministers of the Crown.

STATUTE LAW (REPEALS) ACT 1974 (June 27, 1974) promotes the reform of the statute law by the repeal of certain enactments (in whole or in part) which are no longer of practical utility.

JURIES ACT 1974 (August 9, 1974) consolidates certain enactments relating to juries, jurors and jury service with corrections and improvements made under the Consolidation of Enactments (Procedure) Act 1949.

PRICES ACT 1974 (July 9, 1974) authorises the payment of food subsidies, enables the Secretary of State to regulate the price of food and other goods; and for connected purposes.

LORD CHANCELLOR (TENURE OF OFFICE AND DISCHARGE OF ECCLESIASTICAL FUNCTIONS) ACT 1974 (July 9, 1974) enables Roman Catholics to hold the office of Lord Chancellor and provides for the exercise of ecclesiastical functions during any tenure of such office by a Roman Catholic.

SOLICITORS (AMENDMENT) ACT 1974 (various dates) allows non-British subjects to practise as solicitors, amends the Solicitors Acts 1957 to 1965, extends the powers of the Law Society and provides for other connected matters.

EDUCATION (MENTALLY HANDICAPPED CHILDREN) (SCOTLAND) ACT 1974 (day or days to be appointed) puts the law of Scotland with regard to the education of mentally handicapped children into the same position as the rest of the U.K.

NORTHERN IRELAND ACT 1974 (July 17, 1974) provides for the dissolution of the existing Northern Ireland Assembly and its prorogation until dissolution and makes temporary provision for the government of Northern Ireland; and for various other connected matters.

PARKS REGULATION (AMENDMENT) ACT 1974 (July 17, 1974) amends the Act of 1872.

FINANCE ACT 1974 (July 31, 1974) grants certain duties, alters others and amends the law relating to the National Debt and Public Revenue. *Inter alia* the Act brings in a new tax on Development Gains from land.

APPROPRIATION (No. 2) ACT 1974 (July 31, 1974) applies certain sums out of the Consolidated Fund to the service of the years ending on March 31, 1973 and 1975; appropriates the supplies granted in this Session of Parliament and repeals certain Consolidated Fund and Appropriation Acts.

TOWN AND COUNTRY AMENITIES ACT 1974 (sections 8 and 9 on a day to be appointed, the rest on August 31, 1974).

NORTHERN IRELAND (YOUNG PERSONS) ACT 1974 (July 31, 1974) makes temporary provision for the holding in custody of young persons charged with certain offences in Northern Ireland.

PAKISTAN ACT 1974 (July 31, 1974) amends the Act of 1973 so as to extend the voting rights of certain persons who, by virtue of that Act, ceased to be British subjects.

CARRIAGE OF PASSENGERS BY ROAD ACT 1974 (day to be appointed) gives effect to a Convention on the Contract for the International Carriage of Passengers and Luggage by Road, and for connected purposes.

MINES (WORKING FACILITIES AND SUPPORT) ACT 1974 (July 31, 1974) amends the 1966 Act.

HEALTH AND SAFETY AT WORK, ETC. ACT 1974 (various dates) implements the basic recommendations of the Robens Committee on Safety and Health at Work 1970–72 (Cmnd. 5034) by making various provisions for securing the health, safety and welfare of persons at work, for protecting others against risks to health or safety in connection with the activities of persons at work; amends the law relating to building regulations and the Building (Scotland) Act 1959; and for connected purposes.

LAND TENURE REFORM (SCOTLAND) ACT 1974 (September 1, 1974) provides for the prohibition of new feuduties and other periodical payments from land; for the right to redeem feuduties and other perpetual payments on a term day; for the redemption by law of feuduties and other such payments on transfer of land; for limitations on the residential use of property subject to long lease and other rights of occupancy; for the variation of heritable securities in the event of residential use of the security subjects; for the abolition of the right to create leasehold casualties; for the recognition of interposed leases; and for various other related matters.

CONSUMER CREDIT ACT 1974 (various dates) establishes for the protection of consumers a new system, administered by the Director General of Fair Trading, of licensing and other control of traders concerned with the provision of credit, or the supply of goods on hire or hire-purchase, and their transactions, in place of the present enactments regulating moneylenders, pawnbrokers and hire-purchase traders and their transactions; and for related matters.

CONTROL OF POLLUTION ACT 1974 (various dates) makes further provision with respect to waste disposal, water pollution, noise, atmospheric pollution and public health, and for connected purposes.

POLICING OF AIRPORTS ACT 1974 (July 31, 1974 makes provision for enabling the policing of any airport designated for that purpose to be undertaken by the police force for the area in which it is wholly or mainly situated; and for connected purposes.

INDEPENDENT BROADCASTING AUTHORITY (No. 2) ACT 1974 (July 31, 1974) extends to July 31, 1979, the date until which the IBA are to provide television and local sound broadcasting services.

MERCHANT SHIPPING ACT 1974 (various dates) makes further provision concerning oil pollution by ships and related matters, gives power to protect shipping and trading interests against foreign action concerning or affecting carriage of goods by sea; and makes various other connected provisions.

HOUSING ACT 1974 (various dates) extends the functions of the Housing Corporation and provides for the registration of, and the giving of financial assistance to, certain housing associations; and makes various other provisions, for example, with respect to clearance areas and improvement grants.

HOUSING (SCOTLAND) ACT 1974 (various dates) makes provision for improvement grants and housing action areas, extends local authorities powers to make advances for the purpose of increasing housing accommodation and provides for connected purposes.

FRIENDLY SOCIETIES ACT 1974 (various dates) consolidates the Friendly Societies Acts 1896 to 1971 and certain other enactments relating to the societies to which those Acts apply with amendments to give effect to recommendations of the Law Commission and the Scottish Law Commission.

SOLICITORS ACT 1974 (May 1, 1975) consolidates the Solicitors Acts 1957 to 1974 and certain other enactments relating to solicitors.

RAILWAYS ACT 1974 (sections 1, 2 and 3 (7) on January 1, 1975, the rest on July 31, 1974) amends the law relating to the British Railways Board, provides for the performance by the Secretary of State of functions in relation to the Board under certain regulations of the Council of the European Communities relating to transport; and for connected purposes.

INSURANCE COMPANIES ACT 1974 (subject to section 89, on August 31, 1974) consolidates, with certain exceptions, the provisions of the Insurance Companies Acts 1958 to 1973.

ROAD TRAFFIC ACT 1974 (various dates) makes further provision with respect to road traffic and operators' licences, and for connected purposes. For example, it provides that vehicle owners as well as drivers may become liable for fixed penalty offences and excess charges, and makes it an offence to park a motor vehicle on the footway or verge of an urban highway.

RENT ACT 1974 (August 14, 1974) amends the Rent Act 1968 and the Rent (Scotland) Act 1971 and the provisions of Part II of the Housing Finance Act 1972 and of the Housing (Financial Provisions) (Scotland) Act 1972 relating to rent allowances, and for connected purposes. In particular the Act brings most residential furnished tenancies into the full protection of the Rent Acts.

TRADE UNION AND LABOUR RELATIONS ACT 1974 (part on July 31, 1974, the rest on September 16, 1974) repeals the Industrial Relations Act 1971; makes provision with respect to the law relating to trade unions, employers' associations, workers and employers, including the law relating to unfair dismissal, and with respect to the jurisdiction and procedure of industrial tribunals; and for connected purposes.

REHABILITATION OF OFFENDERS ACT 1974 (no later than July 1, 1975) rehabilitates offenders who have not been reconvicted of any serious offence for periods of years; penalises the unauthorised disclosure of their previous convictions; amends the law of defamation; and for connected purposes.

PENSIONERS' PAYMENTS ACT 1974 (November 14, 1974) provides for tax-free lump sum payments to pensioners and for purposes connected therewith. (The £10 " Christmas " payment).

NATIONAL THEATRE ACT 1974 (November 29, 1974) removes the limits imposed by the National Theatre Act 1949 on the contributions which may be made under that Act towards the cost of erecting and equipping a national theatre.

PREVENTION OF TERRORISM (TEMPORARY PROVISIONS) ACT 1974 (November 29, 1974) proscribes organisations concerned in terrorism and gives power to exclude certain persons from Great Britain or the U.K. in order to prevent acts of terrorism, and for connected purposes.

CONSOLIDATED FUND (No. 4) ACT 1974 (December 12, 1974) applies a sum out of the Consolidated Fund to the service of the year ending on March 31, 1975.

SOCIAL SECURITY AMENDMENT ACT 1974 (various dates) amends the Social Security Act 1973 as to the rate or amount of contributions; and makes various other provisions for connected matters.

CONSOLIDATED FUND ACT 1975 (January 30, 1975) applies certain sums out of the Consolidated Fund to the service of the years ending on March 31, 1975 and 1976.

EDUCATION ACT 1975 (various dates) makes further provision with respect to local education authority awards and grants; enables the Secretary of State to bestow awards on students in respect of their attendance at adult education colleges; and increases the proportion of the expenditure incurred in the maintenance or provision of aided and special agreement schools that can be met by contributions or grants from the Secretary of State.

ARBITRATION ACT 1975 (day to be appointed) gives effect to the New York Convention on the Recognition and Enforcement of Foreign Arbitral Awards.

BIOLOGICAL STANDARDS ACT 1975 (day to be appointed) provides for the establishment of the National Biological Standards Board having functions relating to the establishment of standards for, the provision of standard preparations of, and the testing of biological substances; and for connected purposes.

GENERAL RATE ACT 1975 (February 25, 1975) provides for the postponement till April 1, 1980, of the coming into force of new valuation lists under Part V of the General Rate Act 1967.

HOUSING RENTS AND SUBSIDIES ACT 1975 (part on February 25, 1975, the rest on March 11, 1975) repeals those provisions of the Housing Finance Act 1972 relating to the fixing of public sector rents; introduces new housing subsidies for local authorities and new town corporations and abolishes certain existing subsidies; makes certain housing associations eligible for housing association grant and revenue deficit grant under the Housing Act 1974; makes other minor amendments to housing enactments; and for connected purposes.

FINANCE ACT 1975 (March 13, 1975) grants certain duties, alters others, and amends the law relating to the National Debt and the Public Revenue. In particular, this Act abolishes estate duty and brings in a new tax on gifts made by a person both during his life and on his death called Capital Transfer Tax.

OFFSHORE PETROLEUM DEVELOPMENT (SCOTLAND) ACT 1975 (March 13, 1975) provides for the acquisition by the Secretary of State of land in Scotland for purposes relating to exploration for and exploitation of offshore petroleum; enables the Secretary of State to carry out works and facilitate operations for those purposes; and provides for connected purposes.

SUPPLY POWERS ACT 1975 (April 13, 1975) consolidates the outstanding provisions of the Ministry of Supply Act 1939 and enactments and instruments amending those provisions, with amendments to give effect to recommendations of the Law Commission and the Scottish Law Commission.

STATUTE LAW (REPEALS) ACT 1975 (March 13, 1975) provides for the repeal, in accordance with recommendations of the Law Commission and the Scottish Law Commission, of certain enactments which are no longer of practical utility, and makes other provision in connection with those repeals.

SOCIAL SECURITY BENEFITS ACT 1975 (various dates) provides further with respect to basic scheme benefits and benefits in respect of industrial injuries and diseases; increases family allowances; amends the Supplementary Benefit Act 1966; and for connected purposes.

CONSOLIDATED FUND (No. 2) ACT 1975 (March 20, 1975) applies certain sums out of the Consolidated Fund to the service of the years ending on March 31, 1974 and 1975.

UNSOLICITED GOODS AND SERVICES (AMENDMENT) ACT 1975 (various dates) amends the Unsolicited Goods and Services Act 1971 and enables the Secretary of State to make regulations with respect to the contents and form of notes of agreement, invoices and similar documents and provides for conviction on indictment in relation to an offence under section 3 (2) of the said Act; and for connected matters.

SOCIAL SECURITY ACT 1975 (subject to section 3 (5) of the Social Security (Consequential Provisions) Act 1975, on April 6, 1975) consolidates for England, Wales and Scotland so much of the Social Security Act 1973 as establishes a basic scheme of contributions and benefits, together with the National Insurance (Industrial Injuries) Acts 1965 to 1974 and other enactments relating to social security.

SOCIAL SECURITY (NORTHERN IRELAND) ACT 1975 (subject to section 3 (5) of the Social Security (Consequential Provisions) Act 1975, on April 6, 1975) consolidates for Northern Ireland so much of the Social Security Act 1973 as establishes a basic scheme of contributions and benefits, together with the National Insurance (Industrial Injuries) Measures Northern Ireland) 1966 to 1974 and other enactments relating to social security.

INDUSTRIAL INJURIES AND DISEASES (OLD CASES) ACT 1975 (subject to section 3 (5) of the Social Security (Consequential Provisions) Act 1975, on April 6, 1975) consolidates the Industrial Injuries and Diseases (Old Cases) Acts 1967 to 1974 and related enactments.

INDUSTRIAL INJURIES AND DISEASES (NORTHERN IRELAND OLD CASES) ACT 1975 (subject to section 3 (5) of the Social Security (Consequential Provisions) Act 1975 on April 6, 1975) consolidates the Workmen's Compensation (Supplementation) Measures (Northern Ireland) 1966 to 1974 and related enactments.

SOCIAL SECURITY (CONSEQUENTIAL PROVISIONS) ACT 1975 (subject to section 3 (5), on April 6, 1975) makes provision consequential on, and in connection with, the four immediately preceding Acts.

EXPORT GUARANTEES AMENDMENT ACT 1975 (March 27, 1975) makes further provision in connection with the powers and duties of the Secretary of State under the Export Guarantees Acts 1968 and 1970.

DISTRICT COURTS (SCOTLAND) ACT 1975 (with certain exceptions, May 16, 1975) abolishes the existing inferior courts and establishes district courts, makes provision as to the appointment and removal of JP's and their clerks and provides for connected purposes.

CRIMINAL PROCEDURE (SCOTLAND) ACT 1975 (various dates) consolidates certain enactments relating to criminal procedure in Scotland.

OIL TAXATION ACT 1975 (May 8, 1975) imposes a new tax (Petroleum Revenue Tax) on profits from substances won or capable of being won under the authority of licences granted under the Petroleum (Production) Act 1934 or the Petroleum (Production) Act (Northern Ireland) 1964; makes amendments to income tax and corporation tax law in connection with such substances or with petroleum companies; and for connected purposes.

RESERVOIRS ACT 1975 (day or days to be appointed) makes further provision against escapes of water from large reservoirs or from lakes or lochs artificially created or enlarged.

HOUSE OF COMMONS DISQUALIFICATION ACT 1975 (May 8, 1975) consolidates certain enactments relating to disqualification for membership of the House of Commons.

NORTHERN IRELAND ASSEMBLY DISQUALIFICATION ACT 1975 (May 8, 1975) consolidates certain enactments relating to disqualification for membership of the Northern Ireland Assembly.

MINISTERS OF THE CROWN ACT 1975 (May 8, 1975) consolidates the enactments relating to the redistribution of functions between Ministers of the Crown, the alteration of the style and title of such Ministers and certain other provisions about such Ministers.

MINISTERIAL AND OTHER SALARIES ACT 1975 (May 8, 1975) consolidates the enactments relating to the salaries of Ministers and Opposition Leaders and Chief Whips and to other matters connected therewith.

HOUSING RENTS AND SUBSIDIES (SCOTLAND) ACT 1975 (May 16, 1975) brings in a new system of rents for public sector housing and makes other provisions with respect to public sector housing; makes certain housing associations eligible for housing association grant and revenue deficit grant; places further controls on private sector housing as to, for example, rent increases; and provides for various other connected matters.

MENTAL HEALTH (AMENDMENT) ACT 1975 (day to be appointed) strengthens the Mental Health Act 1959 to enable potentially dangerous patients to be detained in institutions.

LOCAL GOVERNMENT (SCOTLAND) ACT 1975 (various dates) makes further provision as respects local government finance in Scotland; restricts certain grants under the Transport Act 1968; provides for the appointment and the functions of a Commissioner for Local Administration for the investigation of administrative action taken by or on behalf of local and other authorities; and for connected purposes.

MALTA REPUBLIC ACT 1975 (May 8, 1975) makes provision as to the operation of the law in relation to Malta as a republic within the Commonwealth.

PRICES ACT 1975 (May 8, 1975) amends the Prices Act 1974.

REFERENDUM ACT 1975 (May 8, 1975) provides for the holding of a referendum on the U.K.'s membership of the EEC.

EVIDENCE (PROCEEDINGS IN OTHER JURISDICTIONS) ACT 1975 (day to be appointed) makes new provision for enabling the High Court, the Court of Session and the High Court of Justice in Northern Ireland to assist in obtaining evidence required for the purposes of proceedings in other jurisdictions; and extends their powers to issue process effective throughout the U.K. for securing the attendance of witnesses; and for connected purposes.

FARRIERS (REGISTRATION) ACT 1975 (various dates) prevents and avoids suffering by and cruelty to horses arising from the shoeing of horses by unskilled persons by promoting the proper shoeing of horses, the training of farriers and shoeing smiths' establishing a Farriers Registration Council and prohibiting the shoeing of horses by unqualified persons; and for connected purposes.

AIR TRAVEL RESERVE FUND ACT 1975 (May 22, 1975) provides for the establishment of a fund from which payments may be made in certain cases in respect of losses or liabilities incurred by customers of air travel organisers when the latter are unable to meet their financial commitments in respect of certain descriptions of travel contracts, and establishes an agency to run the fund; provides for contributions to be made and for loans by the Secretary of State and for purposes connected therewith.

NURSING HOMES ACT 1975 (day to be appointed) consolidates various enactments relating to nursing homes.

EXPORT GUARANTEES ACT 1975 (August 3, 1975) consolidates the Acts of 1968 to 1975.

DISEASES OF ANIMALS ACT 1975 (days to be appointed) makes further provision for preventing the introduction or spreading through imports into Great Britain of diseases of animals and poultry; and for connected purposes.

The following list of Public Acts also received the Royal Assent before September, 1975.

INDUSTRIAL AND PROVIDENT SOCIETIES ACT 1975 (August 3, 1975) raises the limits from £1,000 to £5,000 on the interest in the shares in a society registered under the Act of 1965 which any one member may hold and authorises the further alteration of that limit from time to time.

INTERNATIONAL ROAD HAULAGE PERMITS ACT 1975 (September 1, 1975) makes further provision with respect to the forgery, carriage and production of licences, permits, authorisations and other documents relating to the international carriage of goods by road; and for connected purposes.

LITIGANTS IN PERSON (COSTS AND EXPENSES) ACT 1975 (days to be appointed) makes further provision as to the costs or expenses recoverable by litigants in person in civil proceedings.

MOBILE HOMES ACT 1975 (October 1, 1975) amends the law in respect of mobile homes and residential caravan sites; and for connected purposes.

SAFETY OF SPORTS GROUNDS ACT 1975 (day or days to be appointed) makes provision for safety at sports stadia and other sports grounds.

PUBLIC SERVICE VEHICLE (ARREST OF OFFENDERS) ACT 1975 (August 1, 1975) authorises the arrest without warrant of certain persons suspected of contravening regulations about the conduct of passengers in public service vehicles.

HEARING AID COUNCIL (EXTENSION) ACT 1975.
NEW TOWNS ACT 1975.
BRITISH LEYLAND ACT 1975.
APPROPRIATION ACT 1975.
FINANCE No. 2 ACT 1975.
CONSERVATION OF WILD CREATURES AND WILD PLANTS ACT 1975.
GUARD DOGS ACT 1975.
SALMON AND FRESHWATER FISHERIES ACT 1975.
LIMITATION ACT 1975.
STATUTORY CORPORATIONS (FINANCIAL PROVISIONS) ACT 1975.
COAL INDUSTRY ACT 1975.
REMUNERATION, CHARGES AND GRANTS ACT 1975.
LOTTERIES ACT 1975.
CRIMINAL JURISDICTION ACT 1975.
SOCIAL SECURITY PENSIONS ACT 1975.
CHILD BENEFIT ACT 1975.
NORTHERN IRELAND (EMERGENCY PROVISIONS) AMENDMENT ACT 1975.

Government and Public Offices

NOTE—The salaries shown are in most cases those actually received. In certain instances, however, the National Scale without corresponding London weighting is given.

MINISTRY OF AGRICULTURE, FISHERIES AND FOOD
Whitehall Place, London, S.W.1†
[01–839 7711]

The Ministry of Agriculture, Fisheries and Food is responsible in England and Wales for administering government policy for agriculture, horticulture and fishing industries. In association with the Intervention Board for Agricultural Produce and the other Agricultural Departments in the United Kingdom it is responsible for the administration of the EEC common agricultural and fisheries policy and for various national support schemes. It also administers schemes for the control and eradication of animal and plant diseases and the improvement and drainage of agricultural land. The Ministry sponsors the food and drink manufacturing industries and distribution trades. It is concerned with the quality of food, food compositional standards, hygiene and labelling and advertising. It acts as agent for the Department of Prices and Consumer Protection in administering and operating food subsidies. It has certain responsibilities for ensuring public health standards in the manufacture, preparation and distribution of basic foods. Some functions relating to agriculture and fisheries in Wales and Gwent are the joint responsibility of the Minister and the Secretary of State for Wales, and some of the Ministry's responsibilities for animal health extend to Scotland. The Ministry maintains relations with overseas countries and participates in some activities of certain international organizations concerned with agriculture, fisheries and food. The Ministry is also responsible for the Royal Botanic Gardens, Kew.
†Unless otherwise stated, this is the main address of Divisions of the Ministry.

Salary List
Minister	£13,000
Minister of State	£ 7,500
Parliamentary Secretary	£ 5,500
Permanent Secretary	£18,675
Second Permanent Secretary	£17,175
Deputy Secretary	£14,000
Under Secretary	£12,000
Assistant Secretary	£ 8,650 to £11,000
Senior Principal	£ 7,750 to £ 9,350
Principal	£ 5,680 to £ 7,450
Senior Executive Officer	£ 4,900 to £ 5,900
(HEO-A)	£ 3,900 to £ 4,700
Assistant Solicitor	£ 9,033 to £11,000
Chief Scientific Officer	£10,950
Deputy Chief Scientific Officer	£ 8,100 to £ 9,440
Senior Principal Scientific Officer	£ 8,650 to £ 9,798
Chief Statistician	£ 8,650 to £11,000
Chief Engineer	£10,240

Minister, THE RT. HON. (THOMAS) FREDERICK PEART, M.P.
  Private Secretary (Principal), D. F. Roberts.
  Assistant Private Secretary (HEO-A), P. Elliott.
  Parliamentary Private Secretary, G. Grant, M.P.
Minister of State, EDWARD STANLEY BISHOP, M.P.
  Private Secretary, Mrs. A. M. Blackburn.
Parliamentary Secretary, Dr. G. S. Strang, M.P.
  Private Secretary, F. J. H. Scollen.
Parliamentary Clerk (Senior Executive Officer), A. P. Woodhouse, T.D.
Permanent Secretary, Sir Alan Neale, K.C.B., M.B.E.
  Private Secretary, P. M. Boyling.
Second Permanent Secretary, Sir Frederick Kearns, K.C.B., M.C.
  Private Secretary, H. B. Brown.
ESTABLISHMENT DEPARTMENT
Director of Establishments (Under Secretary), J. G Kelsey.

Personnel Division I
Victory House, 30–34 Kingsway, W.C.2
[01–405 4310]
Assistant Secretary, I. P. M. Macdonald
Personnel Division II
Victory House, 30–34 Kingsway, W.C.2
[01–405 4310]
Assistant Secretary, P. Pooley.
Staff Training Branch,
Government Buildings, Tolcarne Drive, Pinner, Middlesex
[01–868 7161]
Principal, A. W. Bunn, I.S.O.
Office Services Division★
Assistant Secretary, H. W. Foot.

Welfare Branch
Victory House, 30–34 Kingsway, W.C.2
[01–405 4310]
Chief Welfare Officer (Senior Executive Officer), Miss D. C. Dixson.

FINANCE DEPARTMENT
Principal Finance Officer (Under Secretary), J. M. Grant.
Finance Division I★
Assistant Secretary, Mrs. H. I. Pinkerton.
Finance Division II★
Assistant Secretary, T. A. Ivey.
Appropriation Accounts and Data Processing Division
Government Buildings, 98–122 Epsom Road, Guildford, Surrey
[0483 68121]
Assistant Secretary, D. Kimber.
Audit and Costings Division
29 Bressenden Place, S.W.1
[01–828 4366]
Assistant Secretary, S. T. K. Hester.
INFORMATION DIVISION
Chief Information Officer-A (Assistant Secretary), L. E. E. Jeanes.
Chief Press Officer, T. J. B. Dawes.
Chief Librarian, F. C. Hirst.

LEGAL DEPARTMENT
55 Whitehall, S.W.1
[01–839 7711]
Legal Adviser and Solicitor (Deputy Secretary), G. F. Aronson.
Principal Assistant Solicitors (Under Secretaries), R. W. Brown; H. R. Reade.
Legal Division A
Assistant Solicitor, G. R. J. Robertson.
Legal Division B
Assistant Solicitor, L. Neville.
Legal Division C
Assistant Solicitor, A. E. Munir.
Legal Division D
Assistant Solicitor, D. B. McGilligan.
Legal Division E
Assistant Solicitor, H. G. Roberts.
Legal Division F
Assistant Solicitor, F. A. Richards.
Legal Division G
Assistant Solicitor, A. Hall-Brown.

MANAGEMENT SERVICES
Under Secretary, Miss I. O. H. Lepper.
Management Services Division I
Victory House, 30–34 Kingsway, W.C.2
[01–405 4310]
Assistant Secretary, G. Seymour.
Management Services Division II★
Assistant Secretary, A. J. Smith.
CHIEF SCIENTIST'S GROUP
Chief Scientist (Deputy Secretary), H. C. Pereira F.R.S.

★ At Great Westminster House, Horseferry Road. S.W.1 [01–216 6311].

Chief Scientific Adviser, Food, and Deputy Chief
Scientist, G. A. H. Elton (Under Secretary).
Deputy Chief Scientist (Chief Scientific Officer),
W. F. Raymond.

RESEARCH AND DEVELOPMENT
REQUIREMENTS DIVISION★
Assistant Secretary, M. M. A. Gray.
FOOD SCIENCE DIVISION
Deputy Chief Scientific Officer, A. W. Hubbard.
ROYAL BOTANIC GARDENS, KEW
Kew, Richmond, Surrey
[01-940 1171]
Director (Under Secretary), J. Heslop-Harrison, F.R.S.
F.R.S.E.
Deputy Director (Deputy Chief Scientific Officer),
J. P. M. Brenan.

EUROPEAN ECONOMIC COMMUNITY
Under Secretary, A. K. H. Atkinson.
European Economic Community Division I
Assistant Secretary, J. W. Hepburn.
European Economic Community Division II
Assistant Secretary, D. H. Griffiths.

EXTERNAL RELATIONS,
AND TROPICAL FOODS
Under Secretary, J. H. V. Davies.
External Relations Division I
Assistant Secretary, J. C. Edwards.
External Relations Division II
Assistant Secretary, J. A. Anderson.
Tropical Foods Division
[01-828 4366]
29 Bressenden Place, S.W.1
Assistant Secretary, M. Madden.

AGRICULTURE
Deputy Secretary, B. D. Hayes.
GENERAL AGRICULTURAL POLICY
Under Secretary, D. F. Williamson.
General Agricultural Policy Division I
Assistant Secretary, C. R. Cann.
General Agricultural Policy Division II
49/53 Parliament Street, S.W.1
[01-930-4300]
Assistant Secretary, E. H. Doling.

CEREALS AND SUGAR
Under Secretary, M. E. Johnston.
Cereals Division
49/53 Parliament Street, S.W.1
[01-930 4300]
Assistant Secretary, T. R. M. Sewell.
Under Secretary, J. E. Dixon.
Sugar Division
Assistant Secretary, A. V. Vickery.

MEAT, POULTRY AND EGGS
Under Secretary (vacant).
Pigs and Poultry Products
Assistant Secretary, R. W. Holmwood.
Beef Division
Assistant Secretary, J. H. Holroyd.
Sheep and Livestock Subsidies Division
Assistant Secretary, D. R. Dow.

MILK, POTATOES AND
AGRICULTURAL MARKETING
Under Secretary, D. H. Andrews, C.B.E.
Milk and Milk Products Division
Assistant Secretary, J. Stopforth.
Marketing Policy and Potatoes Division★
Assistant Secretary, (vacant)

FISHERIES AND FOOD
Deputy Secretary, J. R. Moss, C.B.
FISHERIES DEPARTMENT★
Fisheries Secretary (Under Secretary), J. Graham.
Fisheries Division I
Assistant Secretary, W. R. Small.
Fisheries Division II
Assistant Secretary, K. W. Wilkes.
★ At Great Westminster House, Horseferry Road,
S.W.1 [01-216 6311].

Fisheries Division III
Assistant Secretary, G. P. Jupe.
Sea Fisheries Inspectorate
Chief Inspector, P. G. Jeffery £9,350
Fisheries Research
Director of Fisheries Research (Chief Scientific Officer),
A. J. Lee, D.S.C.
Deputy Directors of Fisheries Research (Deputy Chief
Scientific Officers), D. H. Cushing; A. Preston.
Sea Fisheries Research Laboratory
Pakefield Road, Lowestoft, Suffolk
[0502 4251]
Sea Fisheries Radiobiological Laboratory
Hamilton Dock, Lowestoft, Suffolk
[0502 4381]
Sea Fisheries Laboratory
Remembrance Avenue, Burnham-on-Crouch,
Essex
[0621 782658]
Sea Fisheries Experiment Station
Castle Bank, Conwy, Gwynedd
[Conwy 2419]
Salmon and Freshwater Fisheries
Laboratory
Whitehall Place, S.W.1
[01-839 7711]
Chief Salmon and Freshwater Fisheries Officer (Senior
Principal Scientific Officer), I. R. H. Allan.
Fish Diseases Laboratory
The Nothe, Weymouth, Dorset
[03057 72137]
Officer-in-charge (Senior Principal Scientific Officer),
J. P. Stevenson.
Torry Research Station
P.O. Box 31, 135 Abbey Road,
Aberdeen
[0224 76711]
Director (Deputy Chief Scientific Officer), G. H. O.
Burgess, F.R.S.E.
Humber Laboratory
Wassand Street, Hull
[0482 27879]
Officer-in-charge (Senior Principal Scientific Officer),
J. R. Burt.

FOOD POLICY
Under Secretary, W. E. Mason.
Food and Drink Industries Division I
Assistant Secretary, J. R. Catford.
Food and Drink Industries Division II
Assistant Secretary, E. S. Virgo.
Food Policy Division
Assistant Secretary, D. Evans.
Planning Unit
Assistant Secretary, A. V. Vickery.
FOOD STANDARDS AND SUBSIDIES
Under Secretary, R. F. Giles.
Food Standards Division★
Assistant Secretary, H. M. Goodall.
Food Subsidies Division
Assistant Secretary, R. E. Melville.
HORTICULTURE
Under Secretary, G. R. Woodward.
Horticulture Division I★
Assistant Secretary, N. J. P. Hutchison.
Horticulture Division II★
Assistant Secretary, V. T. Humphreys.
Emergencies, Fertilisers and
Feedingstuffs Standards Division
Assistant Secretary, L. G. Hanson.

LAND AND SERVICES
Deputy Secretary, E. W. Maude, C.B.
LAND
Under Secretary, M. E. Johnston.
Land Improvement Division★
Assistant Secretary, J. S. W. Henshaw.
Land Use and Tenure Division★
Assistant Secretary, H. J. B. Rice.
★At Great Westminster House, Horseferry Road,
S.W.1 [01-216 6311]

Land Drainage and Water Supply Division★
Assistant Secretary, A. F. Longworth.

POLLUTION, SEEDS, SAFETY AND LABOUR
Under Secretary, J. B. Foxlee.

Environmental Pollution, Pesticides and Infestation Control Division★
Assistant Secretary, D. W. M. Herbert.

Plant Variety Rights Office and Seeds Division
Huntingdon Road, Cambridge
[0223 76381]
Assistant Secretary and Controller, H. A. S. Doughty.

Agricultural Safety, Training and Wages Division

83–91 Victoria Street, S.W.1
[01-216 6311]
Assistant Secretary, O. A. Robertson.

Farm Safety Inspectorate
St. Stephen's House, S.W.1
[01-839 4266]
Director, J. C. Weeks.

ANIMAL HEALTH
Under Secretary, C. H. Shillito.

Animal Health Division I
Government Buildings, Hook Rise South,
Tolworth, Surbiton, Surrey
[01-337 6611]
Assistant Secretary, Mrs. E. A. Attridge.

Animal Health Division II
Government Buildings, Garrison Lane,
Chessington, Surrey
[Chessington 7828661]
Assistant Secretary, H. Pease.

Animal Health Division III
Government Buildings, Hook Rise South,
Tolworth, Surbiton, Surrey
[01-337 6611]
Assistant Secretary, W. T. Barker.

Animal Health Division IV
Government Buildings, Hook Rise South,
Tolworth, Surbiton, Surrey
[01-337 6611]
Assistant Secretary, K. A. Bird.

ECONOMICS AND STATISTICS
Director of Economics and Statistics (Under Secretary),
L. Napolitan, C.B.

Economics Division I
Senior Principal Agricultural Economist, J. A. Evans
£8,650 to £11,000

Economics Division II
Senior Principal Agricultural Economist, C. W. Capstick, C.M.G. . . . . £8,650 to £11,000

Economics Division III
49–53 Parliament Street, S.W.1
Senior Principal Agricultural Economist, G. Sharp
£8,650 to £11,000

Statistics Division I★
Chief Statistician, Miss J. R. Weatherburn.

Statistics Division II
Government Buildings, Tolcarne Drive,
Pinner, Middlesex
[01-868 7161]
Government Buildings, 98–122 Epsom Road,
Guildford, Surrey
[0483 68121]
Whitehall Place, S.W.1
[01-839 7711]
Chief Statistician, A. H. J. Baines.

★ At Great Westminster House, Horseferry Road,
S.W.1 [01-216 6311].

Food Economics Unit
Senior Principal Agricultural Economist, A. P. Power
£8,650 to £11,000

REGIONAL ORGANIZATION
Deputy Secretary, E. W. Maude, C.B.

Eastern Region
Block C, Government Buildings,
Brooklands Avenue, Cambridge
[0223 58911]
Chief Regional Officer, T. W. Nicol
£8,650 to £11,000

East Midland Region
Block 2, Government Buildings, Chalfont Drive,
Nottingham
[0602 292251]
Chief Regional Officer, B. J. Marshall
£8,650 to £11,000

Northern Region
Government Buildings, Kenton Bar,
Newcastle-upon-Tyne
[0632 869811]
Chief Regional Officer, F. H. Goodwin
£8,650 to £11,000

South Eastern Region
Block A, Government Offices,
Coley Park, Reading
[0734 581222]
Chief Regional Officer, R. M. Loosmore
£8,650 to £11,000

South Western Region
Block 3, Government Bldgs., Burghill Road,
Westbury-on-Trym, Bristol
[0272 622851]
Chief Regional Officer, K. Harrison Jones
£8,650 to £11,000

West Midland Region
Woodthorne, Wolverhampton
[0902 754190]
Chief Regional Officer, E. G. Griffiths
£8,650 to £11,000

Yorkshire/Lancashire Region
Block 2, Government Buildings,
Lawnswood, Leeds
[0532 674411]
Chief Regional Officer, J. A. Brown
£8,650 to £11,000

WELSH DEPARTMENT
Plas Crug, Aberystwyth, Dyfed
[0970 3162]
Welsh Secretary (Under Secretary), W. R. Smith, C.B.
Assistant Secretary (Policy), J. Medway.
Assistant Secretary (Administration), A. W. Bridges.
Senior A. D. A. S. Officer, R. W. Soden, T.D.

AGRICULTURAL DEVELOPMENT AND ADVISORY SERVICE (A.D.A.S.)
Director General (Deputy Secretary), Dr. K. Dexter.
Deputy Director General, E. S. Carter £13,460

AGRICULTURE★
Chief Agricultural Officer (Under Secretary), A. J. Davies.
Senior Agricultural Officer, M. Barker £11,000
Senior Horticultural Officer, R. Gardiner . . . £11,000
Superintending Horticultural Marketing Inspector,
A. F. Gardner . . . . £7,750 to £9,350

SCIENCE★
Chief Science Specialist, H. C. Gough £11,000

LAND DRAINAGE SERVICE★
Chief Engineer (Directing Grade), G. Cole.

LANDS★
Chief Surveyor (Under Secretary), R. G. A. Lofthouse.

Pest Infestation Control Laboratory
London Road, Slough, Berks.
[75 34626]

★ At Great Westminster House, Horseferry Road,
S.W.1 [01-216 6311].

Director (Chief Scientific Officer), F. H. Jacob.
Deputy Director (Deputy Chief Scientific Officer), J. A. Freeman, O.B.E.

PLANT PATHOLOGY LABORATORY AND PLANT HEALTH AND SEEDS INSPECTORATE
Hatching Green, Harpenden, Herts.
[0582 75241/46]
Director (Deputy Chief Scientific Officer), (vacant).
    Great Westminster House,
    Horseferry Road, S.W.1
    [01-216 6311]
Superintending Plant Health and Seeds Inspector, J. P. Cleary......................£7,750 to £9,350

VETERINARY
Government Buildings, Hook Rise South, Tolworth, Surbiton, Surrey
[01-337 6611]
Chief Veterinary Officer, A. C. L. Brown...£13,460
Deputy Chief Veterinary Officer (Under Secretary), A. J. Stevens.
    Central Veterinary Laboratory, New Haw,
    Weybridge, Surrey
    [91 41111]
Deputy Chief Veterinary Officer and Director of Veterinary Laboratories (Under Secretary), A. B. Paterson.
    Lasswade Veterinary Laboratory, Eskgrove,
    Lasswade, Midlothian.
    [031-663 6525]
    Cattle Breeding Centre, Shinfield, Reading,
    Berks.
    [0734 883157]

INTELLIGENCE AND TRAINING DIVISION★
Head of Division, B. Peart.
SPECIAL PROJECTS DIVISION★
Head of Division, J. J. North.
ADMINISTRATION
Under Secretary, J. H. Perrin.
AGRICULTURAL AND ADVICE DIVISION★
Assistant Secretary, Miss M. Hooley.

ADVISORY COUNCIL FOR AGRICULTURE AND HORTICULTURE IN ENGLAND AND WALES
Whitehall Place, S.W.1
[01-216 7333]
Chairman, Sir Nigel Strutt, T.D.
Vice-Chairman, E. S. Dobb, C.B., T.D.
Members, Sir Richard Boughey, Bt.; Prof. D. K. Britton; The Lord Collison, C.B.E.; H. A. Fell; Sir Emrys Jones; Prof. I. A. M. Lucas; D. H. Phillips, D.F.C.; Sir Gwilym Williams, C.B.E.
Secretary, S. Hampson.

AGRICULTURAL RESEARCH COUNCIL
160 Great Portland Street, W.1
The Agricultural Research Council was incorporated by Royal Charter on July 23, 1931. The *Science and Technology Act*, 1965, transferred responsibility for the Research Council to the Secretary of State for Education and Science and a new Charter received Royal approval in 1967. The Council is charged with the organization and development of agricultural and food research and may, in particular, establish or develop institutions or departments of institutions and make grants for investigation and research relating to the advance of agriculture. The Council is financed jointly from the Parliamentary vote of the Department of Education and Science and the Ministry of Agriculture, Fisheries and Food.
Council, The Hon. J. J. Astor, M.B.E. (*Chairman*); W. A. Biggar, O.B.E., M.C.; Prof. P. W. Brian, C.B.E., Ph.D., Sc.D., F.R.S.; A. C. L. Brown; E. S. Dobb, C.B., T.D.; W. W. Gauld; E. M. W. Griffith; Prof. J. L. Harley, D.Phil., F.R.S.; Prof. H. Harris, D.Phil., F.R.S.; Prof. D. L. Hughes, Ph.D.; J. D.

★ At Great Westminster House, Horseferry, Road S.W.1 [01-216 6311].

Hutchison, C.B.E., M.C., T.D., D.SC., F.R.S.; Prof. Sir Bernard Katz, M.D., Ph.D., D.SC., F.R.S.; C. Mackay; Prof. J. Mandelstam, M.C., Ph.D., F.R.S.; J. S. Martin; Prof. K. S. Mather, C.B.E., Ph.D., D.SC., F.R.S.; E. W. Maude, C.B.; Prof. A. Neuberger, C.B.E., M.D., Ph.D., F.R.S.; H. C. Pereira, Ph.D., D.SC., F.R.S.; The Earl of Selborne; The Visct. Trenchard, M.C.; Prof. A. R. Ubbelohde, C.B.E., D.SC., F.R.S.
Secretary, W. M. Henderson, D.Sc.
Chief Scientific Officer, G. W. Cooke, Ph.D., F.R.S.
Under Secretary, G. M. P. Myers.
Assistant Secretaries, F. V. Bird, O.B.E.; F. J. S. Culley; E. Lester.
Scientific Advisers to the Secretary, K. N. Burns; J. K. R. Gasser; J. V. Lake, Ph.D.; R. Scarisbrick, Ph.D.; K. L. Robinson, D.SC.; G. C. Stevenson; H. Fore, Ph.D.; A. J. Pritchard, Ph.D.; D. C. Corbett.
Planning Section, T. L. V. Ulbricht, Ph.D., D.SC.; W. S. Wise.
Clerk to the Council, L. S. Porter, O.B.E.
Information Officer, J. A. Cole-Morgan.
For the Research Institutes under the control of the Council, *see* Index.

EXECUTIVE COUNCIL OF THE COMMONWEALTH AGRICULTURAL BUREAUX
Farnham House, Farnham Royal, Slough, Bucks.
[Farnham Common: 2281]
The Commonwealth Agricultural Bureaux, founded in 1929, consist of four Institutes and ten Bureaux, under the control of an Executive Council, comprising representatives of the Commonwealth countries which contribute to its funds. Each Institute and Bureau is concerned with its own particular branch of agricultural science and acts as a clearing house for the dissemination of information of value to research workers throughout the world. They deal respectively with entomology, mycology, helminthology and nematology, biological control, agricultural economics, animal breeding and genetics, animal health, nutrition, dairy science and technology, forestry, horticulture and plantation crops, pastures and field crops, plant breeding and genetics, and soils and fertilizers. The information is published in journals which have a monthly circulation of 30,000 in 150 countries. The abstract journals are produced by computer-assisted processes, and the whole data base is being consolidated and made available in machine-readable form. Review articles, books, maps, monographs and annotated bibliographies on particular subjects are also issued.
Chairman, T. N. Tandon (*India*).
Vice-Chairman, J. W. Greenwood (*Canada*).
Secretary, E. A. Runacres.

Institutes
Commonwealth Institute of Entomology, 56 Queen's Gate, S.W.7. *Director*, A. H. Parker, Ph.D. (*acting*).
Commonwealth Mycological Institute, Ferry Lane, Kew, Surrey. *Director*, A. Johnston.
Commonwealth Institute of Biological Control, Gordon Street, Curepe, Trinidad. *Director*, F. J. Simmonds, Ph.D., D.SC.
Commonwealth Institute of Helminthology, The White House, 103 St. Peter's Street, St. Albans, Herts.— *Director*, Miss S. M. Willmott, Ph.D.

Bureaux
Agricultural Economics, Dartington House, Little Clarendon Street, Oxford.—*Director*, J. O. Jones.
Animal Breeding and Genetics, Animal Breeding Research Organization, The King's Buildings, West Mains Road, Edinburgh 9, Scotland.— *Director*, J. D. Turton.
Animal Health, Central Veterinary Laboratory, New Haw, Weybridge, Surrey.—*Director*, R. Mack (*acting*).
Dairy Science and Technology, National Institute for Research in Dairying, Shinfield, Reading. —*Director*, E. J. Mann.

Forestry, Commonwealth Forestry Institute, South Parks Road, Oxford.—*Director*, P. G. Beak, M.B.E.

Horticulture and Plantation Crops, East Malling Research Station, nr. Maidstone, Kent.— *Director*, G. E. Tidbury.

Nutrition, Rowett Research Institute, Bucksburn, Aberdeen, Scotland.—*Director*, Miss D. L. Duncan, Ph.D.

Pastures and Field Crops, Hurley, nr. Maidenhead, Berks.—*Director*, P. J. Boyle.

Plant Breeding and Genetics, Department of Applied Biology, Downing Street, Cambridge.—*Director*, R. H. Richens, Ph.D.

Soils, Rothamsted Experimental Station, Harpenden, Herts.—*Director*, B. Butters (*acting*).

COLLEGE OF ARMS OR HERALDS COLLEGE

Queen Victoria Street, E.C.4
[01-248 2762]

The College of Arms is open daily from 10-4 (Saturdays, 10-1, by appointment) when an Officer of Arms is in attendance to deal with enquiries by the public, though such enquiries may also be directed to any of the Officers of Arms, either personally or by letter.

There are 13 officers of the College, 3 Kings of Arms, 6 Heralds and 4 Pursuivants, who specialize in genealogical and heraldic work for their respective clients. The College possesses the finest records on these subjects in the world. It is the official repository of the Arms and pedigrees of English, Northern Irish, and Commonwealth families and their descendants, and its records include official copies of the records of Ulster King of Arms, the originals of which remain in Dublin.

Arms have been and still are granted by Letters Patent from the Kings of Arms under Authority delegated to them by the Sovereign, such authority having been expressly conferred on them since at least the fifteenth century. A right to Arms can only be established by the registration in the official records of the College of Arms of a pedigree showing direct male line descent from an ancestor already appearing therein as being entitled to Arms, or by making application to the College of Arms for a Grant of Arms.

Earl Marshal, His Grace the Duke of Norfolk, C.B., C.B.E., M.C.

Kings of Arms

Garter, Sir Anthony Richard Wagner, K.C.V.O., D.Litt., F.S.A.

Clarenceux, John Riddell Bromhead Walker, M.V.O. M.C.

Norroy and Ulster, Walter John George Verco, C.V.O. (*Earl Marshal's Secretary*).

Heralds

Windsor, Alexander Colin Cole, F.S.A.

Richmond (*and Registrar*), John Philip Brooke Brooke-Little, M.V.O. F.S.A.

Somerset, Rodney Onslow Dennys, M.V.O., O.B.E., F.S.A.

York, Conrad Marshall John Fisher Swan, Ph.D.

Lancaster, Francis Sedley Andrus.

Chester (vacant).

Pursuivants

Portcullis, Michael Maclagan, F.S.A.

Rouge Croix, David Hubert Boothby Chesshyre.

Rouge Dragon, Theobald David Mathew.

Bluemantle, Peter Llewellyn Gwynn-Jones.

COURT OF THE LORD LYON

H.M. New Register House, Edinburgh
[031-556 7255]

The Scottish Court of Chivalry, including the genealogical jurisdiction of the *Ri-Sennachie* of Scotland's Celtic Kings, adjudicates rights to arms and administration of *The Scottish Public Register of All Arms and Bearings* (under *1672*

cap. 47) and *Public Register of All Genealogies*. The Lord Lyon presides and judicially establishes rights to existing arms or succession to Chiefship, or for cadets with scientific "differences" showing position in clan or family. Pedigrees are also established by decrees of Lyon Court, and by Letters Patent. As *Royal Commissioner in Armory*, he grants Patents of Arms (which constitute the grantee and heirs noble in the Noblesse of Scotland) to "virtuous and well-deserving" Scotsmen, and petitioners (personal or corporate) in Her Majesty's overseas realms of Scottish connection, and issues birthbrieves. In Scots Law, Arms are protected by Statute; their usurpation is punishable, and the Registration Fees of Honour on patents and matriculations are payable to H.M. Exchequer.

Lord Lyon King of Arms, Sir James Monteith Grant, K.C.V.O., W.S., F.S.A. *Scot.*

Heralds

Rothesay, Lt.-Col. Harold Andrew Balvaird Lawson, C.V.O.

Albany, Sir Iain Moncreiffe of that Ilk, Bt., Ph.D., Advocate.

Marchmont, Malcolm Rognvald Innes of Edingight, W.S., F.S.A. *Scot.*

Pursuivants

Unicorn, John Inglis Drever Pottinger.

Ormond, Major David Maitland Maitland-Titterton T.D., F.S.A. *Scot.*

Carrick, John A. Spens, R.D.

Lyon Clerk and Keeper of Records, Malcolm Rognvald Innes of Edingight, W.S., F.S.A. *Scot.*

Procurator-Fiscal, Ivor Reginald Guild, W.S.

Herald Painter, Mrs. M. J. Murray.

Macer, Thomas C. Gray.

ART GALLERIES, ETC.

ROYAL FINE ART COMMISSION

2 Carlton Gardens, S.W.1
[01-930 3935]

Appointed in May, 1924, "to enquire into such questions of public amenity or of artistic importance as may be referred to them from time to time by any of our Departments of State, and to report thereon to such Department; and, furthermore, to give advice on similar questions when so requested by public or quasi-public bodies, where it appears to the said Commission that their assistance would be advantageous." In August, 1933, a Royal Warrant extended the Terms of Reference of the Commission—" so that it shall also be open to the said Commission, if they so desire, to call the attention of any of Our Departments of State, or of the appropriate public or quasi-public bodies, to any project or development which in the opinion of the said Commission may appear to affect amenities of a national or public character "; in May, 1946, a Royal Warrant further extended the Terms of Reference of the Commission as follows:—

We Do give and grant unto you, or any three or more of you, full power to call before you such persons as you shall judge likely to afford you any information upon the subject of this Our Commission; and also to call for, have access to and examine all such books, documents, registers and records as may afford you the fullest information on the subject, and to inquire of and concerning the premises by all other lawful ways and means whatsoever: We Do authorize and empower you, or any three or more of you, to visit and personally inspect such places as you may deem it expedient so to inspect for the more effectual carrying out of the purposes aforesaid:

Chairman, Sir Colin Anderson, K.B.E.

Commissioners, The Countess of Airlie; Sir Hugh Casson, R.A., F.R.I.B.A.; Miss E. Chesterton; A. W. Cox, C.B E., F R I.B.A.; P. M. Dowson, C.B.E.; S Ralph Freeman, C.V.O., C.B.E.; Mark Girou A. J. Gordon, C.B.E.; The Duke of Grafto

Lord James of Rusholme; Prof. Bernard Meadows; David Piper, C.B.E., F.S.A.; John Piper, C.H.; Sir Philip Powell, O.B.E., A.R.A., F.R.I.B.A.; E. F. Ward, C.B.E.; W. Whitfield; Sir Hugh Wilson, O.B.E., P.P.R.I.B.A.

Secretary, Prof. F. Fielden, F.R.I.B.A.

ROYAL FINE ART COMMISSION FOR SCOTLAND
22 Melville Street,
Edinburgh 3
[031-225 5434]

Commissioners, The Lord Johnston, T.D. (*Chairman*); J. A. Coia, C.B.E., R.S.A., F.R.I.B.A.; N. Johnston, R.S.A., F.R.I.B.A.; C. L. Matthew, F.R.I.B.A.; Prof. Sir Robert Matthew, C.B.E., A.R.S.A., P.P.R.I.B.A.; Prof. F. N. Morcos-Asäad, Ph.D.; R. Philipson, P.R.S.A.; A. Reiach, O.B.E., A.R.S.A., F.R.I.B.A.; Prof. A. Thompson, Ph.D., F.R.S.A.; Mrs. Murray Usher of Cally; H. A. Wheeler, O.B.E., R.S.A.

Secretary, J. T. Bannatyne, M.B.E., R.S.A.(scot.).

NATIONAL GALLERY
Trafalgar Square, W.C.2
[01-839 3321]

Hours of opening.—Weekdays 10 to 6 (June–Sept. Tuesdays and Thursdays 10 to 9), Sundays 2 to 6. Closed on Good Friday, Christmas Eve, Christmas Day, Boxing Day and New Year's Day.

The National Gallery is the result of a Parliamentary grant of £60,000 in 1824 for the purchase and exhibition of the Angerstein collection of pictures. The present site was first occupied in 1838 and enlarged and improved at various times throughout the years. A substantial extension to the north of the building with a public entrance in Orange Street was opened in 1975. Expenses for 1974–75 were estimated at £825,000.

TRUSTEES
Prof. J. Hale, F.S.A. (*Chairman*); John Piper; Dame Veronica Wedgwood, O.M., D.B.E.; Miss Mary Woodall, C.B.E., D.Litt., F.S.A.; Sir Gordon Sutherland, F.R.S.; Prof. M. Froy; The Lord Poole, P.C., C.B.E., T.D.; H. Hodgkin; Prof. B. Yamey, C.B.E.; Sir Isaiah Berlin, O.M., C.B.E., F.B.A.; Mrs. Heather Brigstocke.

OFFICERS
Director, M. V. Levey, M.V.O. £12,410
Keeper, C. H. M. Gould. . . . . . £9,060 to £10,208
Deputy Keepers, A. Braham; A. Smith
£7,561 to £9,160
Scientific Adviser to the Trustees, R. H. G. Thompson
£9,060 to £10,208
Chief Restorer, A. W. Lucas, O.B.E.
£9,060 to £10,208
Building and Security, G. Fox. . . . £6,090 to £7,860
Finance and Establishments, R. H. Mitchem
£5,300 to £6,300

NATIONAL PORTRAIT GALLERY
St. Martin's Place, Charing Cross Road, W.C.2
[01-930 8511]

Open Monday to Friday 10 to 5. Saturday 10 to 6. Sunday 2 to 6.

The first grant was made in 1856 to form a gallery of the portraits of the most eminent persons in British history, the collections being successively housed in Great George Street, Westminster, in South Kensington, and in Bethnal Green. The present building was opened in 1896, £80,000 being contributed to its cost by¹ Mr. W. H. Alexander; an extension erected at the expense of Lord Duveen was opened in 1933.

Chairman, The Lord Kenyon, C.B.E., F.S.A.

Trustees, The Lord President of the Council; The President of the Royal Academy of Arts; Prof. Lawrence Gowing, C.B.E.; The Duke of Grafton, F.S.A.; Prof. J. H. Plumb, Ph.D., Litt.D., F.B.A., F.S.A.; A. D. Powell, C.B.E.; Prof. Dame Helen Gardner, D.B.E., F.B.A.; Sir Christopher Cockerell, C.B.E., F.R.S.; The Countess of Longford, C.B.E.; Sir Philip Magnus-Allcroft, Bt., C.B.E.; Rev. Prof. J. McManners; J. P. Ehrman, F.B.A., F.S.A.; The

Viscount Cobham, K.G., P.C., G.C.M.G., G.C.V.O.; Sir Oliver Millar, K.C.V.O., F.S.A., F.B.A.; Sir Anthony Wagner, K.C.V.O., F.S.A.

Director, Keeper, and Secretary, J. J. Hayes, Ph.D., F.S.A. £7,988
Deputy Keeper, R. L. Ormond. . £3,331 to £5,458
Assistant Keepers, C. J. Ford; J. F. Kerslake, F.S.A.; R. W. Gibson; M. Rogers. . . £3,331 to £5,458

TATE GALLERY
Millbank, S.W.1
[01-828 1212]

Hours of opening.—Weekdays 10 to 6. Sundays 2 to 6. Closed on New Year's Day, Good Friday, Christmas Eve, Christmas Day and Boxing Day.

The Tate Gallery comprises two national art collections: (a) British painting, from the 16th century to the present day, including works by Turner, Blake, Constable and the Pre-Raphaelites; (b) Modern Foreign Painting, from the Impressionists, and Modern Sculpture, British and foreign. There is an almost continuous programme of temporary exhibitions within the field of the collection. The Gallery was opened in 1897, the cost of erection (£80,000) being defrayed by Sir Henry Tate, who also contributed the nucleus of the present collection. The Turner Wing, built at the expense of Sir Joseph Duveen was opened in 1920. Lord Duveen defrayed the cost of galleries to contain the collection of modern foreign painting, completed in 1926, and a new sculpture hall, completed in 1937. Expenses for 1975–76 are estimated at £1,714,000

Director, Sir Norman Reid. £12,000
Trustees, Sir Alan Bullock, F.B.A. (*Chairman*). S. D. Ferranti; F. L. T. Graham-Harrison C.B.; The Lord Harlech, P.C., K.C.M.G.; H. Hodgkin; P. Huxley; N MacDermot, C.B.E., Q.C.; C. St.; Wilson, F.R.I.B.A.

Keeper of the British Collection, M. R. F. Butlin
£8,650 to £9,798
Keeper of the Modern Collection, R. E. Alley
£8,650 to £9,798
Keeper of Exhibitions and Education, M. G. Compton
£8,650 to £9,798
Keeper of Conservation, The Viscount Dunluce
£8,650 to £9,798
Keeper and Assistant Director, Mrs. J. Jeffreys
£8,650 to £9,798
Deputy Keepers, R. E. Morphet; L. A. Parris
£7,151 to £8,750
Assistant Keepers (Class I), Miss E. Koslovska-Einberg; T. Measham; Miss R. Rattenbury; Miss A. Seymour; R. Parkinson; D. Brown; Mrs. P. Gilmour. . . . . £4,404 to £7,109
Establishment Officer, P. G. O'Donohoe
£4,900 to £5,900

WALLACE COLLECTION
Hertford House, Manchester Square, W.1
[01-935 0687]

Admission free. Open on weekdays 10 a.m. to 5 p.m.; Sundays 2 p.m. to 5 p.m. Closed on Good Friday, and December 24–26.

The Wallace Collection was bequeathed to the nation by the widow of Sir Richard Wallace, Bt., K.C.B., M.P., on her death in 1897, and Hertford House was subsequently acquired by the Government. The collection includes pictures, drawings and miniatures, French furniture, sculpture, bronzes porcelain, armour and miscellaneous *objets d'art*. The total net expenses were estimated at £250,000 in 1975–76.

Director, T. W. I. Hodgkinson, C.B.E. £9,798
Assistant Directors, R. A. Cecil; A. V. B. Norman, F.S.A. . . . . £4,404 to £7,109

NATIONAL GALLERIES OF SCOTLAND
Edinburgh
[031-556 8921]

Comprising:—
National Gallery of Scotland, The Mound, Edinburgh.
Scottish National Portrait Gallery, Queen Street, Edinburgh.

Scottish National Gallery of Modern Art, Inverleith
House, Royal Botanic Garden, Edinburgh.
Director of the National Galleries of Scotland, T. H.
Scrutton, C.B.E........................£8,850
Keeper, National Gallery, C. E. Thompson
£5,501 to £6,700
Assistant Keeper, National Gallery, H. N. A. Brig-
stocke....................£3,331 to £5,458
Keeper of Prints and Drawings, K. K. Andrews
£5,501 to £6,700
Keeper, Scottish National Portrait Gallery, Robert E.
Hutchison................£5,501 to £6,700
Assistant Keepers, Scottish National Portrait Gallery,
D. Thomson, Ph.D.; Rosalind K. Marshall, Ph.D.
£3,331 to £5,458
Keeper, Scottish National Gallery of Modern Art,
W. D. Hall................£5,501 to £6,700
Secretary, Accountant and Establishment Officer, Miss
R. J. Johnston..............£3,756 to £4,542

(For other British Art Galleries, *see* Index.)

UNITED KINGDOM ATOMIC ENERGY AUTHORITY
11 Charles II Street, S.W.1
[01–930 6262]
Established by the *Atomic Energy Authority Act,*
1954, the Authority took over, on August 1, 1954,
the control of atomic energy research and development. The Minister of Trade and Industry is
responsible to Parliament for general atomic energy
policy and for money provided for the Authority.
Chairman, Sir John Hill, Ph.D............£19,600
Deputy Chairman, F. J. Doggett, C.B.....£15,600
Members (Full-time), R. V. Moore, G.C., C.B.E.;
A. M. Allen; Dr. W. Marshall, C.B.E., F.R.S.
each £10,100 to £14,000
(Part-time) The Lord Kearton, O.B.E., F.R.S.;
Sir Leslie Williams, C.B.E.; Prof. Sir Brian
Flowers, F.R.S.; W. B. S. Walker; Dr. N. L.
Franklin, O.B.E.; *each* £1,000; R. A. Peddie
(unpaid).
Secretary, A. M. Allen.

BRITISH AIRPORTS AUTHORITY
2 Buckingham Gate, S.W.1.
Set up under the *Airports Authority Act,* 1965, the
Authority owns and manages seven major airports—
Heathrow, Gatwick, Stansted, Glasgow, Prestwick,
Edinburgh and Aberdeen.
Chairman, N. G. Foulkes.......*(part-time)* £9,000
Chief Executive, N. G. Payne, O.B.E.

BRITISH AIRWAYS
Airways Terminal, Victoria, S.W.1
[01–828 6822]
Established in 1972 by the Civil Aviation Act of
1971 to control all the activities of B.E.A. and
B.O.A.C. The group now trades under the name
of British Airways. It has seven operating divis-
ions: British Airways European Division, British
Airways Overseas Division, British Airways
Regional Division, British Airways Helicopters,
British Airways Associated Companies, British
Airways Engine Overhaul and International
Aeradio. A British Airways Travel division has
been set up to handle selling in the United Kingdom
for the operating divisions and British Airways
Cargo U.K. has been established to control cargo
handling at 18 airports in the United Kingdom.
Since April, 1974, B.E.A. and B.O.A.C. have been
dissolved. The British Airways Group have about
200 aircraft, total assets of over £500 millions and
annual revenues of nearly £500 millions.
Chairman, Sir Frank McFadzean £23,330
Deputy Chairman and Managing Director, H. E.
Marking, C.B.E., M.C.
Deputy Managing Directors, S. F. Wheatcroft,
O.B.E.; J. R. Stainton, C.B.E.
Secretary, B. Wood.

BRITISH BROADCASTING CORPORATION
Broadcasting House, W.1
[01–580 4468]
The BBC was incorporated under Royal
Charter as successor to the British Broadcasting

Company, Ltd., whose licence expired Dec. 31,
1926. Its present Charter came into force July 30,
1964, for 12 years. In 1974 it was announced that it
would be extended for a further three years to July
1979. The Chairman, Vice-Chairman and other
Governors are appointed by the Crown. The BBC
is financed by revenue from receiving licences for
the Home services and by a Grant in Aid from
Parliament for the External services. The total number of television licences in force in March 1975
was 17,700,815, of which 10,120,493 were for
monochrome receivers and 7,580,322 for colour
receivers.
Chairman, Sir Michael Swann, F.R.S. £10,000
Vice-Chairman, The Hon. Mark Bonham Carter
£2,000
Governors, Lady Avonside, O.B.E. *(Scotland)* £2,000;
Dr. G. T. Hughes *(Wales),* £2,000; W. O'Hara
(N. Ireland); The Lord Allan of Kilmahew, D.S.O.,
O.B.E., R.D.; R. B. Fuller, C.B.E.; A. W. C.
Morgan; G. Howard; The Lord Feather, C.B.E.;
The Lord Greenhill of Harrow, G.C.M.G., O.B.E.;
Mrs. Stella Clarke..............*(each)* £1,000
Director-General, Sir Charles Curran.
Managing Directors, I. Trethowan *(Television);*
P. H. Newby, C.B.E. *(Radio);* G. E. H. Mansell
(External Broadcasting).
Directors, S. Redmond, *(Engineering);* Hon. K. H. L.
Lamb *(Public Affairs);* M. O. Tinniswood *(Per-
sonnel);* H. P. Hughes *(Finance);* D. Muggeridge
(Programmes, Radio); A. D. G. Milne *(Programmes,
Television).*
Deputy Director of Engineering, D. E. Todd.
General Manager, Publications, J. G. Holmes.
Legal Adviser, R. J. Marshall.
Chief Assistant to Director-General, P. H. Scott.
Chief Secretary, C. D. Shaw.
Controller, Information Services, G. T. M. de M.
Morgan, M.C.
Head of Publicity, H. G. Campey, O.B.E.
Assistant Secretary and Head of Secretariat, J. A.
Norris.

Controllers of Regional Offices
English Regions, J. F. Grist, Broadcasting Centre,
Pebble Mill Road, Birmingham.
Scotland, H. A. Hetherington, Broadcasting House,
Queen Margaret Drive, Glasgow, W.2.
Wales, O. Edwards, Broadcasting House, Llandiff,
Cardiff.
Northern Ireland, R. T. L. Francis, Broadcasting
House, 25–27 Ormeau Avenue, Belfast.

BRITISH RAILWAYS BOARD
222 Marylebone Road, N.W.1
[01–262 3232]
Chairman, Rt. Hon. R. W. Marsh.......£23,100
Deputy Chairman, J. M. W. Bosworth, C.B.E.
£19,100
Full-time Members, H. L. Farrimond; D. Fowler;
R. L. E. Lawrence, C.B.E., E.R.D.; D. McKenna,
C.B.E.; varying sums between £12,600 and
£17,600.
Part-time Members, Sir Frederick Hayday, C.B.E.;
Dr. S. Jones, C.B.E.; Sir Alistair Pilkington; Sir
David Serpell, K.C.B., C.M.G., O.B.E.; The Lord
Taylor of Gryfe; H. A. Walker
from £1,000 to £3,000
Chief Secretary and Legal Adviser, E. Harding.

BRITISH STEEL CORPORATION
33 Grosvenor Place, S.W.1
[01–235 1212]
The British Steel Corporation was established
under the Iron and Steel Act 1967 which vested in
the Corporation the shares of the fourteen major
steel companies. The Corporation's main duty is
to supply such iron and steel products as it thinks
fit in sufficient quantity and at such prices as will
meet reasonable demand.
Chairman, Sir Montague Finniston, F.R.S... £27,750
Deputy Chairmen, M. Littman, Q.C.; P. A. Matthews.
Members (full-time), The Lord Layton; L. R. P.
Pugh, C.B.E.; R. Scholey; R. Smith, C.B.E.
Deputy Chairmen and full-time members in
salary range £16,000 to £22,500.

Members (part-time), G. R. Chetwynd, C.B.E.;
W. D. Griffiths; Sir Melvyn Rosser; A. Silberston; Sir Matthew Stevenson, K.C.B., C.M.G.;
Hon. W. K. J. Weir . . . . . *from* £1,000 to £4,000
Secretary, R. W. Roseveare.

BRITISH TOURIST AUTHORITY
Queen's House, 64 St. James's Street, S.W.1
[01–629 9191]

Under the Development of Tourism Act, 1969, four co-equal statutory Tourist Boards were established: the British Tourist Authority, the English Tourist Board, the Scottish Tourist Board and the Wales Tourist Board. Each is financed mainly by direct grant-in-aid from Government and is an independent statutory body. The British Tourist Authority has specific responsibility for promoting tourism to Great Britain from overseas. It also has a general responsibility for tourism within Great Britain as a whole.
Chairman, Sir Alexander Glen, K.B.E., D.S.C.
Director General, L. J. Lickorish, C.B.E.

BRITISH TRANSPORT DOCKS BOARD
Melbury House, Melbury Terrace, N.W.1
[01–4866 621]
Constituted under the *Transport Act*, 1962. The Board owns and operates 19 active ports.
Chairman, Sir Humphrey Browne, C.B.E.
(part-time) £10,283
Vice-Chairman, C. R. Cory . . . . (part-time) £3,136
Members, S. Johnson, C.B.E. (*Managing Director*) (£13,182); J. H. Collier-Wright, C.B.E. (*Deputy Managing Director*) (£11,932); D. A. Stringer, O.B.E.; A. J. Tomsett, O.B.E. (*each* £11,182); C. W. Lowthian, C.B.E.; D. F. Martin-Jenkins, T.D. (*part-time*) (*each* £1,000).
Secretary, J. K. Stuart.

BRITISH WATERWAYS BOARD
Melbury House, Melbury Terrace, N.W.1
[01–262 6711]
Chairman, Sir Frank Price (*part-time*) £6,665
Vice-Chairman, The Lord Feather, C.B.E. (*part-time*)
£2,307
Members (all part-time), The Rt. Hon. Sir Frederick Corfield, Q.C.; B. C. Gillinson; I. Harrington; D. R. Hunter, C.B.E., M.C., T.D.; The Baroness White (*each* £1,000).
General Manager, D. G. McCance.
Secretary, T. T. Luckcuck.

CABINET OFFICE
Whitehall, S.W.1
[01–930 5422]
Chancellor of the Duchy of Lancaster, THE RT. HON. HAROLD LEVER, M.P.
Secretary of the Cabinet, Sir John Hunt, K.C.B.
£20,175
Second Permanent Secretary, J. Garlick, C.B.; Sir G. R. Denman, C.B., C.M.G. £17,175
Deputy Secretaries, P. Benner, C.B.; T. F. Brenchley, C.M.G.; J. A. Hamilton, C.B., M.B.E.; Sir Leonard Hooper, K.C.M.G., C.B.E.; D. L. Pearson; R. Press, C.B., C.B.E., Ph.D. £14,000
Under Secretaries, D. Bayley; J. D. Bryars; P. Cradock, C.M.G.; G. E. Gammie; J. W. Gibson; A. D. Gordon-Brown; J. A. Marshall; M. E. Quinlan; J. S. Scott-Whyte; E. J. G. Smith; W. O. Ulrich £12,000
Assistant Secretaries, J. L. Bantock; R. L. Baxter; D. Cunningham; J. S. Elliott, O.B.E.; M. B. Green; Mrs. A. K. Jackson; R. G. S. Johnston; J. M. Mackintosh, C.M.G.; A. M. Macpherson; J. M. Moss; D. A. Nicholls; J. A. Patterson; Miss R. D. Pease; J. Peters; R. A. Stead; N. Summers; D. C. Thomas; W. R. Tomkys; M. W. Townley; C. R. Walker; Miss K. Whalley; B. O. White; C. Wilson; G. S. Wishart (*Establishment Officer*) . . . . £6,700 to £8,850
Senior Principal, Dr. D. C. Wilson
£6,000 to £7,050
Senior Principal Scientific Officers, D. J. Beckley;

Dr. D. W. Braben; Dr. J. Swaffield; Dr. P. T. Warren
£6,750 to £7,750
Deputy Establishment Officer, H. L. Theobald, O.B.E.
£5,680 to £7,450
Chief Clerk and Departmental Record Officer, R. W. Smith . . . . £5,680 to £7,450
Central Policy Review Staff, Head, Sir Kenneth Berrill, K.C.B. £18,675
Deputy Secretary, C. R. Ross, C.B. £14,000
Under Secretary, W. J. L. Plowden. £12,000
Assistant Secretaries, J. M. Crawley; M. I. Goulding; J. R. S. Guinness; Dr. M. J. Harte; P. B. Rogers; A. B. Urwick; D. E. Young
£6,700 to £8,850
Senior Economic Adviser, H. C. G. Hawkins.
Special Appointments, Dr. M. Hart; Dr. D. G. B. Horne; M. Mire; Miss K. M. H. Mortimer.
Central Statistical Office:
Director and Head of the Government Statistical Service, Prof. Sir Claus Moser, K.C.B., C.B.E., F.B.A. £17,175
Deputy Secretary, A. J. Boreham, C.B. £14,000
Under Secretaries, O. Nankivell; T. S. Pilling A. A. Sorrell; J. W. S. Walton £12,000
Chief Statisticians, G. A. Dean; R. W. Green; J. Hibbert; P. B. Kenny; M. J. G. M. Lockyer; Mrs. M. Nissel; R. M. Norton; P. J. Stibbard; E. J. Thompson; W. B. Wakefield
£6,700 to £8,850
Deputy Chief Scientific Officer, Dr. J. B. Harding
£8,100 to £9,440
Historical Section:
C. J. Child, O.B.E. (*Departmental Records Adviser*)
£6,700 to £8,850

CABLE AND WIRELESS LIMITED
Head Office—Mercury House, Theobald's Road, W.C.1
[01–242 4433]
Chairman, H. G. Lillicrap (*part-time*) £8,920
Managing Director A. A. Willett £12,600
Directors, W. H. Davies; P. A. McCunn; R. A. Rice; R. W. Cannon . . . . . . £9,100 to £10,100 J. Hodgson (*unpaid*).
Secretary, A. Cooke.

CHARITY COMMISSION
Ryder Street, St. James's, S.W.1
[01–214 6000]
Graeme House, Derby Square, Liverpool
[051–27 3191]
Central Register of Charities,
St. Albans House, Haymarket, S.W.1
[01–227 3190]
The Charity Commission was constituted under Act of Parliament in 1853 and reconstituted under the Charities Act, 1900, with the general function of promoting the effective use of charitable monies and a duty to keep a register of charities in England and Wales. The Official Custodian for Charities holds investments for charities and remits the income, free of income tax, to trustees.
Chief Commissioner, T. C. Green, C.B. £13,230
Commissioners, T. Keith; C. A. H. Parsons; T. Fitzgerald. £12,000
Deputy Commissioners, M. B. Tripp; C. A. Weston, D.F.C., G.M.; Miss A. M. E. Jacobsen; F. W. Trinder; B. T. Dixon; R. W. Groves
£9,033 to £11,000
Asst. Commissioners, M. A. Rao; Miss B. K. Searle; J. Farquharson; J. F. Claricoat; Miss B. R. Heitzmann; G. S. Goodchild; M. G. Sayer; B. B. Davies; D. P. F. Giles; A. B. Rabagliati; G. J. Morgan; Mrs. J. F. R. Quint; H. K. Udvadia
£5,443 to £8,750
Secretary and Asst. Commissioner, R. S. Morgan
£8,650 to £11,000
Principals, R. Booth (*Asst. Commissioner*); Miss E. M. M. Thornton(*Asst. Commissioner*); S. H. Way; W. P. Richards . . . . £5,680 to £7,450
Official Custodian for Charities, L. A. Jimenez
£7,750 to £9,350

Deputy Official Custodian, G. C. Robertson
       £5,680 to £7,450
Establishment Officer, Miss C. M. Ciark
       £5,680 to £7,450
Deputy Establishment Officer, J. Macmillan
       £4,900 to £5,900
Senior Executive Officers, D. McNaught; Miss S. M.
St. C. Smith; J. Samuels; J. Q. Nichols; Mrs. J.E.
Smith; R. J. Crick; K. C. Norman; J. P. Beacall
       £4,900 to £5,900

CHURCH COMMISSIONERS
1 Millbank, Westminster, S.W.1
[01-930 5444]

The Church Commissioners were established on
April 1, 1948, by the amalgamation of *Queen Anne's
Bounty* (established 1704) and the *Ecclesiastical
Commissioners* (established 1836). The Commissioners have three main tasks:—
   (1) the management of their capital assets so that
they may earn income;
   (2) the proper distribution of that income; and
   (3) the discharge of a large number of administrative duties conferred on them by Acts of Parliament and Measures of the General Synod (former
Church Assembly).

The Commissioners' income for the year ended
March 31, 1975, was derived from the following
sources:—

Stock exchange investments	£14,848,073
Land and property	11,986,104
Mortgages and loans	4,260,967
Money received for particular beneficiaries	3,015,525
	£34,110,669

This income was used as follows:—

Clergy stipends and pensions	£25,640,468
Clergy houses (maintenance, out-goings, provision and improvements)	3,439,498
Other church property	672,056
Added to capital to improve future income	882,189
Professional fees	185,056
Administrative costs of Commissioners' office	2,094,789
Administrative costs of Church of England Pensions Board and Advisory Board for Redundant Churches	209,959
For allocation after April 1, 1975	986,654
	£34,110,669

Constitution
The 2 Archbishops, the 41 diocesan Bishops,
5 deans, 10 other clerks and 10 laymen appointed
by the General Synod; 4 laymen nominated
by the Queen; 4 persons nominated by the
Archbishop of Canterbury; The Lord Chancellor;
The Lord President of the Council; the First Lord
of the Treasury; The Chancellor of the Exchequer;
The Secretary of State for the Home Dept.; The
Speaker of the House of Commons; The Lord
Chief Justice; The Master of the Rolls; The
Attorney-General; The Solicitor-General; The
Lord Mayor and two Aldermen of the City of
London; The Lord Mayor of York and one
representative from each of the Universities of
Oxford and Cambridge.
   Church Estates Commissioners:—
First, Sir Ronald Harris, K.C.V.O., C.B.
Second, T. W. Walker, M.P.
Third, Dame Betty Ridley, D.B.E.
Secretary, S. P. Osmond, C.B.
Deputy Secretary, L. D. Walker, O.B.E.
Financial Secretary, H. M. G. Pryor.
Investments Secretary, A. I. McDonald.
Estates Secretary, J. E. Shelley.

Assistant Secretaries, D. I. Archer *(Accountant)*; K. A. L.
Argent *(Pastoral)*; P. Locke *(Stipends)*; R. K.
Pears, D.F.C. *(Houses)*; D. G. Ward *(Redundant
Churches)*.
See Houses Officer, P. T. Rafferty.
Deputy Investments Secretary, I. D. Adam.
Deputy Accountant and Trust Officer, G. C. Baines.
Principals, J. R. Beard; J. M. Davies; D. J. Day;
D. N. Goodwin; W. J. Pennel; T. M. Robinson;
E. W. Turner.
Senior Executive Officers, A. W. Atkins; Mrs. B. A.
Bartlett; T. Batchelor; C. P. Canton; J. Chees-
man; G. Duckworth; M. D. Elengorn; A. R.
Gibson; S. E. Gray; W. R. Herbert; D. W. H.
Lewis; L. C. Marshall; G. A. Modell; F. R.
Neale; F. A. Norman; G. A. Pincott; J. C. A.
Radley; E. J. Robinson; Miss W. M. Rossiter;
M. J. Symon; N. M. Waring.

Legal Department
Official Solicitor, R. H. Rogers.
Deputy Solicitor, J. W. Cook.
Assistant Solicitor, P. Leslie.
Senior Legal Assistants, A. J. L. Campbell; B. G. Hall;
B. J. T. Hanson; R. A. G. Lees; R. D. C. Murray.

Architects's Department
Official Architect, H. A. Scarth.
Deputy Architect, V. A. Brown.

Surveyor's Department
Official Surveyor, J. M. N. Barnes.
Deputy Surveyor, R. N. May.

Agents
Messrs. Clutton, 5 Great College Street, West-
minster, S.W.1; Messrs. Smiths Gore, Dean's
Court, Minster Precincts, Peterborough; Messrs.
Chesterton & Sons, 116 Kensington High
Street, W.8.

CIVIL AVIATION AUTHORITY
129 Kingsway, W.C.2
[01-404 6922]

The Civil Aviation Authority is a statutory body
established by the *Civil Aviation Act* 1971, responsible for economic, technical and safety regulation, and for the operation of the National Air
Traffic Services. It is the government's adviser on
civil aviation matters, including airport planning;
and it is responsible for general aviation, civil
aviation statistics, research, consumer interest, and
the running of the Scottish Highlands and Islands
airports.
Chairman, The Lord Boyd-Carpenter, P.C.
Deputy Chairman, R. R. Goodison, C.B.
Secretary, A. W. G. Kean.

CIVIL SERVICE DEPARTMENT
Whitehall, S.W.1 (01-839 7733)

The Civil Service Department is under the
control of the Prime Minister as Minister for the
Civil Service, with responsibility for the day-to-day
work of the Department delegated to the Lord
Privy Seal. The Permanent Secretary is also the
official head of the Home Civil Service. The Department's primary functions are recruitment and
selection for permanent appointments; the pay and
management of the Civil Service and the co-
ordination of government policy on pay and pensions throughout the public sector. It also has
central responsibility for personnel management,
including recruitment planning and policy, training
and career management; manpower requirements
and the development and dissemination of adminis-
trtive and managerial techniques including computing, and is concerned with the organization of
the machinery of government.
The Prime Minister.
The Lord Privy Seal.
Minister of State in the Civil Service Department,
   CHARLES RICHARD MORRIS, M.P. £7,500
Parliamentary Secretary, J. D. Grant, M.P. £5,500
*Head of the Home Civil Service and Permanent
Secretary to the Civil Service Department,* Sir
Douglas Allen, G.C.B. £20,175

Second Permanent Secretary, (vacant).
Ceremonial Officer, Sir Stuart Milner-Barry, K.C.V.O.,
C.B., O.B.E. . . . . £8,650 to £11,000
Deputy Secretaries, F. G. Burrett, C.B.; Dr. F. H.
Allen, C.B. (*also First Civil Service Commissioner*);
E. Grebenik; J. E. Herbecq; J. M. Moore, C.B.,
D.S.C. £15,000

Central Group
Under Secretary, B. M. Thimont (*Establishment Officer
and Principal Finance Officer*) £12,000

Central Division
Assistant Secretary, B. T. Gilmore
£8,650 to £11,000

Information
Head of Division, S. T. Cursley . . £8,650 to £11,000
Information Adviser to Civil Service Commission, J. T.
Hughes, O.B.E. . . . . £8,650 to £11,000

Personnel Services
Senior Principal, A. T. Wisbey . . £7,750 to £9,350

Finance
Senior Principal, R. D. H. Baker (*Finance Officer*)
£7,750 to £9,350

Office Services
Senior Principal, W. J. Derbyshire, I.S.O.
£7,750 to £9,350

Chessington Computer Centre
Senior Principal, J. J. Raftery, O.B.E.
£7,750 to £9,350

Behavioural Sciences Research Division
Director, Dr. E. Anstey . . . . £8,100 to £9,440

Recruitment and Selection
First Commissioner, Dr. F. H. Allen £14,000
Commissioners (Under Secretaries), D. G. Daymond;
G. R. R. East; K. A. G. Murray (*Director of Civil
Service Selection Board*) £12,000

General Recruitment Divisions
Assistant Secretary, E. J. Morgan
£8,650 to £11,000

Science and Technology Divisions
Deputy Chief Scientific Officer, C. F. Watkinson
£8,100 to £9,440

Civil Service Selection Board
Director, K. A. G. Murray £12,000
Deputy Director, J. A. Howard £8,650 to £11,000

Management Services
Under Secretary, R. W. L. Wilding £12,000
General: Assistant Secretary, N. E. A. Moore
£8,650 to £11,000
Special Assignments: Assistant Secretaries, R. N.
Burton; C. Priestley; S. D. Walker
£8,650 to £11,000
Operational Research: Chief Scientific Officer, E. K. G.
James £10,950
Accountancy: Assistant Secretary, E. Walker
£8,650 to £11,000

Manpower
Under Secretary, (vacant) £12,000
Assistant Secretaries, J. E. Pestell; D. T. West; G. H.
Wollen . . . . £8,650 to £11,000

Machinery of Government
Under Secretary, W. F. Mumford £12,000
Assistant Secretaries, B. C. Bishop; J. B. Pearce
£8,650 to £11,000

Pay
Under Secretary, K. C. Lawrance £12,000
Assistant Secretaries, W. E. Dowling; F. N. Swales;
B. Traynor; R. W. Williams
£8,650 to £11,000

Statistics
Under Secretary, A. R. Smith £12,000
Chief Statisticians, R. F. A. Hopes; D. B. Manwaring
£8,650 to £11,000
Assistant Secretary, C. P. H. Marks
£8,650 to £11,000

Superannuation and Home and Overseas Allowances
Under Secretary, S. D. Light £12,000
Assistant Secretaries, P. F. Clifton; K. H. McNeill
£8,650 to £11,000

Personnel Management
Under Secretaries, C. Bamfield; A. M. Fraser, T.D.
£12,000

Assistant Secretaries, A. Duke; T. A. A. Hart; A. C.
Hughes; G. T. Morgan; P. L. Towers
£8,650 to £11,000

Central Computer Agency
Director, W. R. Atkinson £12,000
Assistant Secretaries, R. D. Aylward; Brig. R. H.
Borthwick; D. Eldridge; P. Hearson; R. E.
Pysden . . . . £8,650 to £11,000
Deputy Chief Scientific Officer, G. H. Perry
£8,100 to £9,440
Assistant Director Engineer, R. O. Bennett
£8,650 to £9,798

Civil Service Catering Organization
Chief Executive, H. A. Guest £12,000
Director of Personnel and Administration, D. A. J.
Tratner . . . . £7,750 to £9,350

Medical Advisory Service
Medical Adviser, Sir Daniel Thomson, C.B., M.D.,
F.R.C.P. £13,230
Principal Medical Officer, W. F. Townsend-Coles,
M.D., F.R.C.P. £10,240

Civil Service College
Principal Civil Service College, E. Grebenik . £14,000
Deputy Principal, Mrs. M. B. Sloman £12,000
Secretary, P. A. Smith . . . . £7,750 to £9,350
Assistant Secretary (Head of Edinburgh Centre), K. J.
Shanahan . . . . £8,650 to £11,000
Directors of Programmes, Mrs. A. C. Ellis; A. W.
Wyatt . . . . £8,650 to £11,000
Directors of Studies, H. W. Parris; S. Rosenbaum;
C. S. Smith; K. J. Wigley . £8,650 to £11,000
Director of Specialised Training, W. S. Ryan
£8,650 to £11,000

COMMONWEALTH DEVELOPMENT CORPORATION
33 Hill Street, W.1
[01–629 8484]

The Corporation was formerly known as the
Colonial Development Corporation. The change
of name was effected by the Commonwealth
Development Act, 1963, which also restored the
Corporation's full powers of operation in all
those countries which had achieved independence
within the Commonwealth since 1948. The Overseas Resources Development Act, 1969, empowered
the Corporation, with Ministerial approval, to
engage in operations in any developing country in
or out of the Commonwealth. The Corporation
is authorized to borrow up to £225,000,000 on
long or medium term and £10,000,000 on short
term.
Chairman (part-time), Sir Eric Griffith-Jones, K.B.E.,
C.M.G., Q.C.
Deputy Chairman (part-time), The Lord Grey of
Naunton, G.C.M.G., G.C.V.O., O.B.E.
Members (part-time), W. J. M. Borthwick, D.S.C;
The Lord Campbell of Eskan; J. M. Clay;
J. K. Dick, C.B.E.; A. E. Oram; The Lord
Greenwood of Rossendale, P.C.; Sir Bryan Hopkin,
C.B.E.; J. M. H. Millington-Drake; G. F. Smith,
C.B.E.; The Lord Walston.
General Manager, P. Meinertzhagen, C.M.G.

COMMONWEALTH OFFICE
see **FOREIGN AND COMMONWEALTH OFFICE**

COMMONWEALTH SECRETARIAT
Marlborough House,
Pall Mall, S.W.1
[01–839 3411]
Secretary-General, S. S. Ramphal.

COUNTRYSIDE COMMISSION
John Dower House, Crescent Place,
Cheltenham, Glos.
[0242 21381]
The Countryside Commission was set up under
the Countryside Act, 1968. It has absorbed the
National Parks Commission, taking over the duties

of that body under the National Parks and Access to the Countryside Act, 1949, and having in addition a wider range of advisory and executive functions relating to the whole of the countryside and coast. Members of the Commission are appointed by the Secretary of State for the Environment and the Secretary of State for Wales acting jointly.

Chairman, J. S. Cripps, C.B.E. £5,400
Deputy Chairman, R. A. E. Herbert £2,750
Members, T. J. A. Colman; J. Cousins; J. Disley; Mrs. E. M. C. Foulkes; B. F. Hubbard; J. Kegie, O.B.E.; Hon. Trevor Lewis; Miss J. V. Lipson; Prof. O. R. McGregor; Mrs. J. Riley . . . . *unpaid*
Director, R. J. S. Hookway £12,000
Assistant Director (*Executive*), R. G. Brown
£8,650 to £11,000
Assistant Director (*Advisory*), J. M. Davidson
£8,650 to £9,798
Secretary, O. M. Davies . . . . £7,750 to £9,350
Principal Information Officer, B. Sluman
£5,680 to £7,450

Office for Wales
8 Broad Street, Newtown, Powys
[0686 26799]
Chairman, The Hon. Trevor Lewis £2,750
Principal Officer, J. N. G. Davies
£5,680 to £7,450

COUNTRYSIDE COMMISSION FOR SCOTLAND
Battleby, Redgorton, Perth
[0738 27921]

Established under the Countryside (Scotland) Act, 1967, with functions for the provision, development and improvement of facilities for the enjoyment of the Scottish countryside, and for the conservation and enhancement of the natural beauty and amenity thereof.

Chairman, Mrs. Jean Balfour.
Vice-Chairman, A. B. Campbell.
Commissioners, Mrs. M. Barclay; The Marquess of Bute; Major A. J. Cameron; Rear-Adm. D. A. Dunbar-Naismith, C.B., D.S.C.; Dr.W.J.Eggeling, C.B.E., F.R.S.E.; D. N. Lowe, O.B.E.; D. McColl; W. H. Murray, O.B.E.; B. K. Parnell; D. Ross.
Director, J. Foster.
Deputy Director, T. Huxley.
Asst. Directors. D. Aldridge (*Conservation Education*); J. R. Turner (*Planning*).

COVENT GARDEN MARKET AUTHORITY
Market Towers, New Covent Garden Market, 1 Nine Elms Lane, S.W.8
[01-720 2211]

The Covent Garden Market Authority is constituted under the Covent Garden Market Acts, 1961 to 1969, the members being appointed by the Ministry of Agriculture, Fisheries and Food. The Authority owns a 68-acre site comprising a fruit and vegetable market, a flower market and an administration building. The Authority is empowered to borrow capital up to £45,000,000.
Chairman, Sir Henry Hardman, K.C.B.
Members, G. A. H. Cadbury; Sir Samuel Goldman, K.C.B.; P. J. Hunt; P. A. Land; W. J. Tudor; Hon. Andrew Turner.
General Manager, C. M. G. Allen.
Assistant General Manager, L. T. G. Sully, C.B.E.
Secretary, C. H. Bates.

CROWN AGENTS FOR OVERSEA GOVERNMENTS AND ADMINISTRATIONS
4 Millbank, S.W.1
[01-222 7730]

The Crown Agents are the officially appointed business and financial agents of a large number of Governments and public authorities. These include independent Governments such as Bahrain, Brunei,

Cyprus, Jamaica, Jordan, Kenya, Malaysia, Mauritius, Nigeria, Sierra Leone, Singapore, Sri Lanka, Tanzania, Tonga, Trinidad and Tobago, Uganda, Western Samoa, and Zambia and all the territories overseas under British administration or trusteeship. Other authorities for whom they act include the United Nations, many railway, transport, broadcasting, telecommunications and electrical undertakings, port commissioners, universities, currency boards and local government authorities, in addition to many development and research bodies. The office is not a Department of the British Government. It is self-supporting, its funds being derived from fees charged to its principals from whom instructions are received direct. The Crown Agents do not act for private individuals or commercial concerns.

The work of the Crown Agents' office includes the purchase, inspection, shipment and insurance of engineering plant and equipment and of stores of all kinds; the design of engineering structures; the issue and management of loans and the investment of funds; the payment of salaries to officers on leave; the engagement of staff for certain overseas Government appointments; the booking of passages for Government officers and their families; and many other functions.

Chairman, J. G. Cuckney.

CROWN ESTATE COMMISSIONERS
13/15 Carlton House Terrace, S.W.1
[01-839 2211]
Mount Lane, Bracknell, Berks.
[0344 20321]

THE CROWN ESTATE (formerly The Crown Lands).—The Land Revenues of the Crown in *England and Wales* have been collected on the public account since 1760, when George III surrendered them and received a fixed annual payment or *Civil List.* At the time of the surrender the gross revenues amounted to about £89,000 and the net return to about £11,000.

In the year ended March 31, 1975, the total Receipts by the Commissioners were £9,500,000. The Expenditure was £3,450,000. The sum of £5,450,000 was paid to the Exchequer in 1974–75 as *Surplus Revenue*, being a net sum from which no deductions have been made for administration.

The Land Revenues in *Ireland* have been carried to the Consolidated Fund since 1820; from April 1, 1923, as regards Southern Ireland, they have been collected and administered by the Irish Free State (Republic of Ireland).

The Land Revenues in *Scotland* were transferred to the Commissioners in 1833.

First Commissioner and Chairman (*part-time*), The Earl of Perth, P.C.
Second Commissioner (*and Secretary*), W. A. Wood, C.B. £14,000
Commissioners (*part-time*), The Lord Allen of Fallowfield, C.B.E.; R. B. Caws; Sir Oliver Chesterton; M.C.; G. D. Lillingston; Capt. I. M. Tennant; The Lord Walston.
Deputy Commissioner, P. S. Bolshaw
£8,650 to £11,000
Assistant Commissioner and Clerk to the Board, J. Griffiths . . . . £7,750 to £9,350
Crown Estate Surveyor, E. J. Shaw
£8,650 to £9,798
Deputy Crown Estate Surveyor, A. R. Roper
£6,280 to £7,450
Establishment Officer, E. F. Richards
£5,680 to £7,450
Crown Estate Receiver for Scotland, D. T. Hunt
£5,680 to £7,450
Accountant and Receiver-General, A. Barker
£4,900 to £5,900
Senior Executive Officers, S. A. Allwood; D. W. Broughton; G. R. Clark; J. L. Isom; Miss J. Phillips; C. R. Smith; J. Stumbke
£4,900 to £5,900

Legal Advisor and Solicitor, J. G. Allan, C.B.E.
£12,000
Senior Legal Assistants, M. A. Jaffe; J. B. Postgate
£6,625 to £8,750
Civil Engineer (Marine Survey), J. G. Edwards,
M.B.E. .... £6,468 to £8,833
Solicitor, Scotland, D. F. Stewart.

Windsor Estate
Surveyor and Deputy Ranger, A. R. Wiseman.

BOARD OF CUSTOMS AND EXCISE
King's Beam House, Mark Lane, E.C.3
[01–626 1515]
Commissioners of Customs were first appointed
in 1671 and housed by the King in London, the
present "Long Room" in the Custom House,
Lower Thames Street, E.C.3, replacing that built
by Charles II and rebuilt after destruction by fire in
1718 and 1814. The Excise Department was
formerly under the Inland Revenue Department,
and was amalgamated with the Customs Department on April 1, 1909.

The Board
Chairman, R. W. Radford, C.B., M.B.E.... £18,675
Private Sec., Miss D. E. Barratt.
Deputy Chairmen, J. M. Woolf, C.B.; A. J. Phelps
£14,000
Commissioners, H. E. Christopherson; C. T. Cross;
C. Freedman; L. D. Hawken; Mrs. D. C. L.
Johnstone, C.B.E.; E. A. Knight; B. H. Knox;
J. C.Leeming; H. Tenant. £12,000

Headquarters Offices
Assistant Secretaries, A. S. Ball; J. Barber; M. K.
Barford; W. A. Bassett; A. R. Beach; O. A.
Brown, M.M., B.E.M.; D. L. Bryars; J. Clary; Miss
D. R. A. Cooper; R. Coote; J. E. Donald; G.
Duncan; J. D. Farmer; R. A. Fowkes; N. E.
Godfrey; E. N. Griffiths; R. E. Grimstead;
B. Halliwell; W. J. Haswell; R. Hopwood; S. J.
House; G. F. Howell; P. Jefferson-Smith; M. G.
Jeremiah; A. Jones; H. C. Kenway, T.D.; C. S.
Killingley; G. G. Lawrance; M. M. McLaren;
J. Midgley; T. R. Moore, M.M.; R. J. Petch; W.
A. R. Phillips; K. C. Piper; G. Porter; L. J. Shew,
I.S.O.; Mrs, V. P. M. Strachan; K. Taylor; J. H.
Tee; J. E. Tipton, D.F.C.; J. E. Turnbull; G. H.
Tyson; F. Veasey; S. D. Walker; A. Watson;
H. J. Webb; C. J. Wilcox... £8,650 to £11,000
Chief Information Officer, M. Nockles
£7,750 to £9,350
Chief Statistician, B. F. Middleton
£8,650 to £11,000

V.A.T. Central Unit
Alexander House, 21 Victoria Avenue,
Southend-on-Sea, Essex
[Southend: 48944]
Controller, D. G. Pitt........ £8,650 to £11,000
Deputy Controllers, C. A. Pilgrim; G. M. A. Smith
£7,750 to £9,350

Solicitor's Office
Solicitor, G. Krikorian, C.B............. £14,000
Principal Assistant Solicitors, G. F. Gloak; R. K. F.
Hutchings......................... £12,000
Assistant Solicitors, R. G. R. Cross; V. S. Eaton;
P. J. C. Ellis; W. L. Fearnehough, T.D.; J. A. D.
Heal; W. S. Hill; A. J. Jeddere-Fisher; V. E.
Jenvey; R. G. C. King; W. Rawlinson; P. J.
Sutton; Miss E. S. Thomas; F. Townley
£9,033 to £11,000

Accountant and Comptroller-General's Office
Accountant and Comptroller-General, G. G. Leighton
Boyce............................. £12,000
Deputy Accountant-General, R. S. Graddon
£8,650 to £11,000

Statistical Office
Controller, R. Ash............ £8,650 to £11,000

Investigation Division
14 New Fetter Lane, E.C.4
[01–353 6500]
Chief Investigation Officer, D. A. Jordan
£8,650 to £11,000

Collectors of Customs and Excise
England and Wales
Birmingham: F. Humphreys.
Brighton: N. Brazil.
Bristol: W. H. Leach.
Chester: J. A. H. Bracken.
Douglas: (Collector–Surveyor), J. R. Leighton (c).
Dover: R. Colling.
Harwich: S. Cooper.
Hull: F. W. Jones.
Leeds: J. E. Tate.
Liverpool: W. J. Campbell, M.B.E. (b).
London Airports: J. F. Blunt (b).
London Central: C. W. Watson.
London North: D. C. Restorick.
London Port: B. M. Field.
London South: D. S. Frampton.
London West: J. E. Ruberry.
Manchester: R. L. Mitchell.
Newcastle: H. Peart.
Northampton: G. B. Diamond.
Nottingham: J. Hoile.
Plymouth: T. R. Barber, O.B.E.
Preston: R. V. J. Neeves.
Reading: A. H. Barrett.
Southampton: J. Hall.
South Wales and the Borders: J. R. Allsopp.
Scotland
Aberdeen: W. Welch.
Edinburgh: W. Surtees.
Glasgow: W. F. Egerton.
Greenock: J. K. Lawson.
Northern Ireland
Belfast: R. F. Mountjoy.
Salaries:
All £8,650 to £11,000 except (a) £10,950; (b)
£9,860; (c) £4,900 to £5,900.

MINISTRY OF DEFENCE
See Armed Forces Section.

DEVELOPMENT COMMISSION
11 Cowley Street, S.W.1
[01–930 7134]
Chairman, W. D. Chapman.
Other Commissioners, G. N. Bowman-Shaw; The
Marquess of Bute; B. Davies; J. P. R. Glyn,
C.B.E.; Sir Jack Longland; W. B. Swan, C.B.E.,
T.D.; Dr. R. C. Tress, C.B.E.
Secretary, K. J. Reeves (acting) £8,650 to £11,000

THE DUCHY OF CORNWALL
10 Buckingham Gate, S.W.1
[Telephone: 01–834 7346]
The Duchy of Cornwall was instituted by
Edward III in 1337 for the support of his eldest
son, Edward, the Black Prince, and since that
date the eldest son of the Sovereign has succeeded
to the Dukedom by inheritance.

The Council
The Earl Waldegrave, K.G., T.D. (*Lord Warden of the
Stannaries*); The Hon. John Baring (*Receiver
General*); The Lord Clinton; Major Sir Rennie
Maudslay, K.C.V.O., M.B.E.; The Lord Franks,
P.C., G.C.M.G., K.C.B., C.B.E., F.B.A.; A. J. L. Lloyd,
Q.C. (*Attorney-General to the Prince of Wales*);
F. J. Williams; F. A. Gray (*Secretary*).

Other Offices of the Duchy of Cornwall
Auditor, J. H. Bowman.
Solicitor, J. F. Burrell.
Asst. Secretary, M. R. E. Ruffer, M.V.O., T.D.
Deputy Receiver, G. A. Briggs.
Sheriff (1975–76), Lt.-Col. J. A. Molesworth St.
Aubyn, M.B.E.

THE DUCHY OF LANCASTER
Lancaster Place, Strand, W.C.2
[01–836 8277]
The estates and jurisdiction known as the Duchy
and County Palatine of Lancaster have been

attached to the Crown since 1399, when John of Gaunt's son came to the throne as Henry IV. As the Lancaster inheritance it goes back to 1265. Edward III erected Lancashire into a County Palatine in 1351.

Chancellor of the Duchy of Lancaster, THE RT. HON. HAROLD LEVER. M.P. £9,750
Private Secretary, H. G. Walsh.
Attorney-General and Attorney and Serjeant within the County Palatine of Lancaster, C. J. Slade, Q.C.
Receiver-General, Major Sir Rennie Maudslay, K.C.V.O., M.B.E.
Vice-Chancellor, His Hon. A. J. Blackett-Ord.
Clerk of the Council and Keeper of Records, E. R. Wheeler, C.V.O., M.B.E.
Solicitor, H. G. Southern.
Asst. Solicitor, K. E. P. J. Harding.
Chief Clerk, P. C. Clarke, C.V.O.

DEPARTMENT OF EDUCATION AND SCIENCE
Elizabeth House, York Road, S.E.1
[01–928 9222]

The Government Department of Education was, until the establishment of a separate office, a Committee of the Privy Council appointed in 1839 to supervise the distribution of certain grants which had been made by Parliament since 1834. The Act of 1899 established the Board of Education, with a President and Parliamentary Secretary, and created a Consultative Committee. The Education Act of 1944 established the Ministry of Education. In April 1964 the office of the Minister of Science was combined with the Ministry to form the Department of Education and Science. The cost of administration for the financial year 1975–76 was estimated at £12,543,000.

Secretary of State for Education and Science, THE RT. HON. FREDERICK WILLIAM MULLEY, M.P.
£13,000
Private Sec., C. Booth.
Minister of State, THE LORD CROWTHER-HUNT
£9,500
Minister for the Arts, H. G. Jenkins, M.P. . . . £5,500
Parliamentary Under Secretary of State, Miss J. Lestor, M.P. £5,500
Permanent Secretary, Sir William Pile, K.C.B., M.B.E.
£18,675
Deputy Secretaries, J. A. Hudson, C.B.; A. Thompson; E. H. Simpson; C. W. Wright, C.B.; G. E. Dudman, C.B. (*Legal Adviser*); Miss S. J. Browne (*Senior Chief Inspector*) £14,000
Secretary for Welsh Education (*Under-Secretary*), L. Jones £12,000
Under Secretary for Finance and Accountant General, J. D. Brierley £12,000
Under Secretaries, G. F. Cockerill; K. G. Forecast (*Director of Statistics*); H. A. Harding, C.M.G.; N. T. Hardyman; F. A. Harper, M.B.E. (*Director of Establishments*); Miss W. P. Harte; H. Jordan; J. L. H. Kitchin (*Chief Architect*); D. E. Lloyd Jones, M.C.; W. K. Reid; J. A. Richards; G. J. Spence; R. Toomey £12,000

Architects and Building Branch
Assistant Secretary, D. W. Tanner
£8,650 to £11,000
Principals, D. M. Forrester; M. McBride; G. H. Osborne; D. R. Pollard . . . . £5,680 to £7,450
Directing Architects, K. E. Foster; J. D. Kay; D. L. Medd, O.B.E. £11,000
Superintending Architects, R. Clynes; W. A. Fletcher; D. H. Griffin; M. S. Hacker; G. E. Hughes; R. L. Thompson . . . . £8,650 to £9,798
Superintending Quantity Surveyor, R. C. King
£8,650 to £9,798
Superintending Engineer (*Mechanical and Electrical*), L. E. J. Piper . . . . £8,650 to £9,798
Principal Architects, R. W. U. Alcock; G. W. Ballard; J. N. Boon; A. J. Branton; J. S. B. Coatman; A. G. Davidson; Miss C. G. Edwards; R. L. Fitzwilliam; S. C. Halbritter; L. J. P. Halstead, O.B.E.; F. Jackson; D. S. Nightingale; S. J. Parker; D. H. W. Poole; T. W. Prosser; O. M. Stepan
£6,280 to £7,450

Principal Quantity Surveyors, G. C. Battersby; P. F. Bottle; D. W. Carden; B. A. Staples; B. G. Whitehouse . . . . £6,280 to £7,450
Principal Engineer (*Mechanical and Electrical*), A. Grimshaw . . . . £6,280 to £7,450
Architects, Grade I, Miss P. H. Baker; Miss E. A. Berkson; R. A. Beswick; J. R. C. Brooke; A. M. Cutler; Mrs. E. R. Fraser; J. C. Greves; H. F. Kendall; Mrs. K. M. S. Livingston; P. Marriott; R. R. Oak; R. D. Post; K. F. Routledge; J. J. Wilson . . . . £4,720 to £5,930
Quantity Surveyors, Grade I, R. B. Boosey; E. E. N. Fry; M. J. Lawton; J. L. S. Sinclair; W. H. Smith
£4,720 to £5,930
Senior Executive Officers, G. A. Dinmore; G. L. Emmett . . . . £4,900 to £5,900

Arts and Libraries Branch
38, Belgrave Square, S.W.1
[01–235 4801]
Assistant Secretaries, C. Graham; H. C. Rackham
£8,650 to £11,000
Principals, Miss O. R. Arnold; P. F. Curran; W. Gamble; D. R. Jones; Miss M. Nicholls
£5,680 to £7,450
Library Advisers, E. M. Broome; A. C. Jones; P. H. Sewell, O.B.E. . . . . £5,680 to £7,450
Senior Executive Officer, G. W. Dickerson
£4,900 to £5,900

Establishments and Organization Branch
Assistant Secretaries, J. V. Cowen; Miss J. M. Grinham. . . . . £8,650 to £11,000
Senior Principals, D. J. Brazier, D.S.M.; W. G. Easeman, T.D. . . . . £7,750 to £9,350
Principals, C. G. Benjamin; R. Bromley; J. E. Clegg; Miss D. C. Fordham; E. R. Gibbs; E. B. Granshaw; F. Sussex; N. E. Worcester
£5,680 to £7,450
Senior Executive Officers, Miss J. Y. Alexander; F. W. Beale; Miss P.I. Cartwright; C. J. Corner; G. H. Evans; V. H. Froggett; Miss T. Gale; D. C. Hobbs; G. A. C. Jones; A. J. Kirk; Miss M. J. Smith; R. F. Smith; I. J. Wade £4,900 to £5,900

Information and Library
Information Department
Chief Information Officer, Miss J. Price
£8,650 to £11,000
Principal Information Officers, A. G. Campbell; J. G. Millwood; T. J. Perks . . . . £5,680 to £7,450
Senior Information Officers, M. H. L. Clemans; H. L. Cook; Mrs. S. M. Ellingford; B. H. Hill; Miss D. M. Long; Mrs. P. A. O'Brien; I. M. Paterson . . . . £4,900 to £5,900
Library
Librarian, Miss D. M. Jepson . . . . . £4,900 to £5,900

Finance Branch
Deputy Accountant General (*Assistant Secretary*), N. B. W. Thompson . . . . £8,650 to £11,000
Director of External Services, T. A. J. Warlow, C.B.E.
£8,650 to £11,000
Assistant Director, V. J. Delany . £7,605 to £9,379
Senior Economic Adviser, B. E. Rodmell
£8,650 to £11,000
Senior Principals, D. H. Grattidge.; E. Ll. Evans
£7,750 to £9,350
Principals, G. R. E. Stewart; D. F. H. Taylor; A. W. Thompson . . . . £5,680 to £7,450
Economic Advisers, J. M. Bateson; S. T. Cook
£5,680 to £7,450
Senior Executive Officers, J. A. E. Blackburn; E. B. Robson; R. J. Taylor
£4,900 to £5,900

Higher and Further Education Branch I
Assistant Secretaries, R. E. Duff; M. L. Herzig; D. F. E. King. . . . . £8,650 to £11,000
Principals, W. J. Archibald; Mrs. C. M. Chattaway; W. H. Miller; R. C. Pulford
£5,680 to £7,450
Senior Executive Officers, P. A. Clarke; Miss B. S. Gilbert; L. A. Hendry; A. A. J. Howling; F. C. Street; R. S. Young . . . . £4,900 to £5,900

Senior Catering Adviser, Miss F. M. Cowell
£5,680 to £7,450

Higher and Further Education Branch II
Assistant Secretaries, R. H. Bird; A. E. D. Chamier;
R. H. Stone.............£8,650 to £11,000
Principals, G. J. Aylett; R. Carpenter, D.S.C.; Miss
V. D. M. Chapman; K. R. Coppinger; Miss M.
d'Armenia; G. Dickson; Mrs. Z. M. Dovey;
E. W. Grogan; S. R. C. Jones; R. Klein
£5,680 to £7,450

Higher and Further Education Branch III
Assistant Secretaries, D. G. Libby; H. G. M. Peters
£8,650 to £11,000
Staff Inspector, G. R. A. Titcomb........£10,508
Senior Principal, K. W. Morris. .£7,750 to £9,350
Principals, M. M. Capey; R. W. Chattaway; L. G.
Cook; E. R. Gibbs; W. J. Huntingford; A.
H. Prosser; S. M. Smith....£5,680 to £7,450
Senior Executive Officers, K. L. H. English; J. D.
Searle....................£4,900 to £5,900

Higher and Further Education Branch IV
Assistant Secretaries, L. J. Melhuish; D. F. Robinson;
J. H. Thompson........£8,650 to £11,000
Senior Principal Scientific Officer, H. J. Norton
£8,650 to £9,798
Principals, K. E. G. Barber; Miss M. d'Armenia;
G. Etheridge; D. S. Timms; J. C. Walne
£5,680 to £7,450
Principal Scientific Officers, S. F. Denning; G. R.
Field; F. P. Verdon........£5,514 to £7,205
Senior Executive Officers, C. H. Boxall; J. K. Bush-
nell; G. E. Huggins; F. M. Scott; J. Walmesley;
G. M. Weaver..............£4,900 to £5,900

Legal Branch
Assistant Legal Adviser, S. Williams
£9,033 to £11,000
Senior Legal Assistant, Mrs. P. E. Durkin
£6,625 to £8,750
Senior Executive Officers, Miss M. J. Bryant; Miss
V. D. Steer...............£4,900 to £5,900

Pensions Branch
Mowden Hall, Staindrop Road,
Darlington, Co. Durham
[Darlington: 60155]
Assistant Secretary, S. B. Hallett. .£8,650 to £11,000
Principals, K. H. R. Maynard, O.B.E.; R. K. Usher
£5,680 to £7,450
Senior Executive Officers, Miss M. D. Bishop;
R. K. Bradley; A. Chaffer; Miss B. Hyman;
J. F. Price.................£4,900 to £5,900

Planning and Programmes
Assistant Secretary, E. C. Appleyard
£8,650 to £11,000
Principals, M. B. Baker; D. McLaughlin
£5,680 to £7,450

Schools Branch I
Assistant Secretaries, A. S. Gann; M. W. Hodges;
E. E. H. Jenkins...........£8,650 to £11,000
Senior Principal, J. R. Middleton
£7,750 to £9,350
Principals, Miss J. D. Dawson; Miss V. G. Ford;
E. B. Granshaw; G. F. Hawker; J. I. Lang-
try; Miss B. O. Naylor; Miss S. L. Scales; D. V.
Stafford; W. J. Stewart; N. D. Wolf; A. G. B.
Woollard ....£5,680 to £7,450
Senior Executive Officer, J. K. Sawtell
£4,900 to £5,900

Schools Branch II
Assistant Secretaries, J. I. Jones; P. S. Litton; Mrs. D.
M. White............£8,650 to £11,000
Staff Inspector, B. W. Kay............£10,508
Principals, D. H. Griffiths; R. D. Horne; J. A.
Reeve; H. C. Riddett....£5,680 to £7,450
Senior Executive Officer, H. G. Rutherford
£4,900 to £5,900
Senior Catering Adviser, Miss M. J. Warrington
£5,680 to £7,450
Catering Advisers, Mrs. M. I. Graham; Mrs. H. J. E.
Robertson.................£4,900 to £5,900

Schools Branch III
Assistant Secretaries, H. O. Dovey; B. C. Peatey;
M. A. Walker..............£8,650 to £11,000
Principals, J. G. Bagley; B. L. Baish; D. L. Corder,
O.B.E.; Miss M. S. Hardwick; J. C. Hedger; Miss
N. E. Jones; M. Moss; M. J. F. Rabarts; M. J. G.
Smith.....................£5,680 to £7,450
Senior Executive Officers, Miss J. Reynolds; Mrs. C.
K. Saville; G. J. Sheppard....£4,900 to £5,900

Science Branch
Assistant Secretaries, D. E. Morgan; J. A. G. Banks
(*Sec. Council for Scientific Policy*)
£8,650 to £11,000
Senior Principal Scientific Officer, A. V. Cohen
£8,650 to £9,798
Principals, Miss H. F. Graham; J. C. R. Hudson;
R. E. Judd; M. D. Phipps....£5,680 to £7,450
Senior Executive Officer, Mrs. M. E. Granshaw
£4,900 to £5,900

Statistics Branch
Assistant Secretary, W. H. G. Harvey
£8,650 to £11,000
Senior Principal, F. C. Heward. .£7,750 to £9,350
Chief Statisticians, Mrs. C. M. Firth; G. M. Goat-
man.....................£8,650 to £11,000
Principals, R. Griffiths; P. Ramsden; S. G. Reed;
L. C. Smith; L. R. F. Wiggins
£5,680 to £7,450
Statisticians, C. J. Bellis; A. R. Hammond; Mrs. S.
Keith; N. Lescure; B. O. Longman; C. A. Mc-
Intyre; Mrs. A. E. Mellor; J. R. Watkins; M.
Wilson....................£5,680 to £7,450
Senior Research Officer, D. J. Hodges
£5,680 to £7,450
Senior Executive Officers, Miss M. A. Bellamy; J. A.
C. Cooke; K. Coombs; R. S. Evans; T. H. Hunt;
Miss D. M. Lane; Miss D. E. Lorenz; R. C.
Martin; J. Melbourne; D. G. Smith; C. J. Wood;
R. Woodward..............£4,900 to £5,900

Teachers Branch (Supply Salaries and Qualification)
Assistant Secretaries, S. J. Barker, D.S.C.; I. R. M
Thom..........£8,650 to £11,000
Senior Principal, H. G. Jenkins. .£7,750 to £9,350
Principals, M. A. Barry, E.R.D.; Miss N. Bartman;
J. Blatcher; G. L. Macey; R. W. J. Mitchell
£5,680 to £7,450
Senior Executive Officers, K. T. V. Humberstone; B.
Lowe; H. V. Pines..........£4,900 to £5,900

Welsh Education Office
Assistant Secretary, R. Dellar.. .£8,650 to £11,000
Principal, D. M. Basey.........£5,680 to £7,450

H.M. Inspectorate (England)
Chief Inspectors, A. D. Collop; A. G. J. Luffman,
O.B.E.; Miss M. J. Marshall; E. J. Sidebottom;
N. Thomas........................£11,440
Divisional Inspectors, M. J. Beaver; J. K. Brierley;
P. M. Burns; J. Dalglish; H. J. Edwards; F. Makin;
F. C. Ruffet.........................£10,508
Staff Inspectors, M. F. Bird; N. Booth; Miss K. M. P.
Burton; P. D. Dudley; M. Edmundson; G. W.
Elsmore; J. R. Fish; T. J. Fletcher; W. S. Fowler;
H. E. Gardiner; R. P. Greenwood; D. Hilton;
E. Houghton; H. C. H. Jones; H. R. Jones;
B. W. Kay; D. G. Lambert; J. E. Lavender;
Eric Lord; Miss E. McDougall; Miss E. McKaig;
J. Maitland-Edwards; D. T. E. Marjoram; H. E.
S. Marks; G. W. Milburn; R. F. Mildon; J. H.
Mundy; W. H. Parry; Mrs. P. Perry; P. Phillips;
Miss E. G. Pollard; Miss M. Rayment; C. W.
Rowland; P. Samuel; E. Sims; J. G. Slater; J. L.
Smedley; G. Snowball; L. Speak; M. E. Sprinks;
L. A. Stockdale; E. W. Sudale; D. F. Symes; G.
R. A. Titcomb; Miss K. M. Tobin; D. G. Toose;
R. A. Wake; W. M. White; E. Whiteley; A.
Wigglesworth; M. R. Wigram; C. L. Williams;
R. C. Williams; P. G. Willmore.....£10,508
H.M. Inspectors, Miss K. Addison; O. P. Alexander;
T. W. F. Allan; D. J. Allen; T. I. Ambrose; H.
M. Archer; P. T. Armistead; A. Arnison; R.
Arnold; B. C. Arthur; Miss P. M. Ash; A. Ash-

brook; Miss J. L. Atkin; D. Baillie; R. C. Baker; D. Bamber; Miss C. H. Barker; A. M. Barnes; G. Barratt; D. A. Barton Wood; A. Bell; Mrs. J. Bell; G. Benfield; T. H. Bennetts; Miss P. Biggs; S. G. L. Bignell; D. B. F. Billimore; Miss G. M. Bishop; R. W. Blake; E. J. Bolton, T.D.; Mrs. J. W. Bonnard; P. R. Booth; Miss J. M. Bosdêt; Mrs. B. K. Bottomley; D. M. W. Boulton; R. J. Brake; R. S. Breckon; W. H. Briggs; E. F. H. Brittain; J. Broadbent; Miss M. I. Brogden; P. Brown; D. G. Buckland; T. A. Burdett; K. R. Burford; J. M. Burgess; P. J. Burn; Miss A. Burns; J. W. Butler; I. B. Butterworth; P. Cadenhead; Mrs. D. M. Caffery; Miss M. E. Caistor; W. F. Campbell; C. B. Carr; T. Carroll; Mrs. E. Cave; R. B. Chalmers; M. G. C. Channon; B. A. Chaplin; Miss J. Chreseson; J. T. G. Chugg; Miss G. D. Clark; A. G. Clegg; Miss M. I. Clough; E. W. Clubb; E. C. Cordell; Miss M. Corlett; G. Cranmer; J. Creedy; Miss S. Crisp; J. D. Dale; Mrs. R. D. Dale; R. Daniels; D. M. Davies; Miss I. E. Davies; J. A. Davies; D.F.C.; N. Davis; Miss M. B. Davison; J. E. B. Dawson, M.B.E.; J. R. Deans; Mrs. E. V. de Bray; D. A. Denegri; T. Dickinson; Mrs. G. Dolden; J. A. S. Dossett; R. C. Dove; F. J. Downs; S. R. G. Downs; W. Drabble; K. T. Elsdon; D. W. Emery; P. Enticknap; J. M. Evans; Miss V. J. Evans; J. A. Everson; J. H. Fairhurst; E. Fanthorpe; V. A. Farthing; Miss P. E. Fassom; J. Featherstone; Miss R. R. Feldmeier; B. P. Fitzgerald; D. Flanagan; P. H. Forrest; R. C. Fox; J. P. A. Frain; Miss J. M. Francis; W. H. Francis; J. A. Fuller; Mrs. M. Gaskell; B. Gay; G. D. Gibbs; A. Gibson; M. D. Gill; C. R. Gillings; M. S. Girling; D. J. Gold; Mrs. K. W. Gosling; J. G. Goulding; Miss S. Gracey; J. Graham; W. Graham; Miss S.E. Grant; F. H. Green; V. Green; J. W. Gregory; N. M. Griffiths; R. M. Griffiths; L. S. Grimsdale; P. C. Haeffner; Miss D. Haigh; B. J. Hall; W. G. Hamfleet; J. Hampson; B. R. Harris; M. Hart; K. N. Hastings; B. W. V. Hawes; F. W. Hawkins; B. P. Hayes; G. M. Hearnshaw; R. A. S. Hennessey; P. M. Hesketh; R. Hiley; Miss A. A. Hill; Miss B. E. Hill; J. A. Hill; M. W. Himsworth; D. Hollingsworth; Mrs. M. I. Holmes; T. Howarth; Miss A. M. Hughes; R. A. J. Hughes; J. B. Hurn; W. E. Husband; J. B. Huskins; K. B. Hutton; A. J. Hymans; E. S. Ingledew; A. R. Ivatts; K. M. Jack; L. Jackson; K. Jary; W. F. J. Jeff; T.D.; R. A. Jeffery; J. C. Jennings; D. W. John; W. T. John; Miss S. H. Johns; Miss D. M. Jones; H. Jones; J. L. Kay; Miss V. M. Keating; Miss M. Kellett; L. P. Kelly; R. A. Kelly; F. R. Kitchen; J. Kitching; Miss A. A. Knowles; Miss M. Knox-Johnston; G. N. E. Lageard; B. M. Lane; E. H. Leaton; A. J. Legge; J. P. Leigh; D. F. Lewis; D. J. Lewis; Miss M. K. Lightowler; Miss B. M. Lockwood; Mrs. R. Lockwood; A. G. Loosemore; W. G. Lowe; G.A. Lucas, T.D.; D.W. McAllister; F. McDonald; Mrs. J. E. McDonald; J. McGinn; Mrs. J. C. McGinty; Miss J. L. Maltby; W. J. A. Mann; D. J. Marjoram; Miss R. J. Marlor; P. F. Marlow; Mrs. G. D. Marshall; T. W. Martin; C. H. Maude; J. H. Mayhew; Miss B. E. Megson; T. P. Melia; T. G. Melling; A. R. H. Monk; J. O'C. Morgan; D. A. Morris; Miss N. R. Mulcahy; R. W. Mycock; H. Myers; Miss P. W. Myers; G. J. Neal; G. F. Neesham; R. Nicholls; P. M. Nixon; C. A. Norman; E. Norris; J. P. O'Connor; Miss K. M. O'Leary; P. J. Oliver; Miss M. Osborn; J. Ounsted; A. Owen; I. P. Owen; Miss P. Park; K. Parker; J. B. Parnaby; Mrs. B. Parr, O.B.E.; F. Parrott; C. P. Parsons; E. H. Parsons; Miss J. Paterson; Mrs. R. W. Peacocke; G. T. Peaker; Miss I. Perlmutter; K. Pinder; B. J. Pitchers; P. B. Pitman; Miss S. A. Polak; Miss E. M. Potts; D. R. Prestwich; H. A. Price; R. M. Prideaux; B. H. Proctor; Miss R. C. Ramirez; P. B. Rattenbury; Miss B. E. Rawlins; D. Raymond; D. Ll. Rees; Mrs. B. Rees-Davies; J. Reynolds; J. D. Richards; C. D. Roberts; J. R. Roberts; I. A. Robertson, D.F.C.; C. M. Robinson; N. H. Roche; G. R.

Romans; A. J. Rose; R. Roundhill; C. K. Rowland; D. H. Rutt; I. P. Salisbury; M. V. Salter; K. J. Sargent; Miss H. M. Sebestyen; C. H. Selby; E. L. Sewell; D. R. Shannon; D. T. V. Sharman; B. E. Shaw; J. R. Shirtcliff; T. A. G. Silk; P. J. Silvester; R. H. D. Sinclair; P. Singh; P. F. Smart; P. R. Smith; R. T. Smith; W. H. Snowdon; Mrs. M. H. Somers; D. E. Soulsby; J. F. Spencer; M. E. Sprakes; J. W. Steel; Mrs. E. M. Stenton; J. W. Stephens; L. W. Stewart, T.D.; R. W. Stockdale; H. C. Story; R. Summersby; Miss J. Sumner Smith; F. Sutcliffe; E. F. A. Suttle; G. H. Swinden; D. W. Sylvester; C. J. Symonds; B. Taylor; Miss P. M. M. Taylor; W. W. Taylor; J. D. Thomas; R. V. Thomas; Miss A. D. Thompson; W. H. Thomson, D.S.C.; J. E. Trickey; G. E. Trodd; T. N. Tunnard; A. F. Turberfield; M. J. Tyerman; J. R. Ungoed-Thomas; D. G. Vallis; G. W. Verow; W. H. Wainwright; A. Walmsley; Miss P. Walters; R. E. Ward; R. K. Warren; E. R. Wastnedge; R. G. Watson; D. H. Watts; Miss O. C. Weilenbeck; D. J. Wells; P. E. Weston; J. B. Whinnerah; C. G. White; Miss S. Whitworth; J. B. Wilcock; I. G. E. Wilding; A. J. Wiles; J. Wilkinson; G. M. Willan, D.F.C.; D. G. Williams; H. G. Williams; Miss D. E. Wiseman; D. C. Wollman; Miss M. S. Wood; J. T. Woodend; E. H. Wright; J. L. Wright; M. Wylie; F. P. Young; T. R. Young . . . . £6,625 to £9,415

H.M. Inspectorate Support Services

Senior Executive Officer, N. J. Bennett
     £4,900 to £5,900

H.M. Inspectorate (Wales)

Chief Inspector, E. O. Davies £11,440
Staff Inspectors, T. I. Davies, C.B.E.; Miss E. C. Edwards; G. L. Jones; I. R. Lloyd; P. E. Owen; C. Reid; T. H. Thomas; P. C. Webb . . £10,508
H.M. Inspectors, S. J. Adams; Miss M. Anthony; G. Bowen; Miss E. M. Davies, O.B.E.; H. W. Davies; T. R. Edwards; G. Evans; K. M. Evans; L. M. Evans; N. B. Evans; J. Garrett, O.B.E.; Mrs. K. P. Godfrey; A. Higgins; Miss J. E. Hughes; G. E. Humphreys; E. H. Hutton; R. L. James; W. R. Jenkins; T. W. John; D. B. Jones; G. D. Jones; L. Jones; O. E. Jones; R. E. Jones; I. M. Lewis; Miss N. O. Lloyd-Jones; R. A. Lowe; J. K. Millington; J. Nicholas; Miss P. A. Nicholas; T. G. Prosser; Miss D. Sellick; M. W. Stone; D. A. Thomas; Glyndwr Thomas; P. Thomas; W. E. Thomas; G. Warren; Miss E. N. Williams; M. J. F. Wynn . . . . £6,625 to £9,415

ELECTRICITY AUTHORITIES

THE ELECTRICITY COUNCIL
30 Millbank, S.W.1

Chairman, Sir Peter Menzies £22,750
Deputy Chairmen, R. F. Richardson, C.B.E. (£18,750); Sir Alan Wilson, F.R.S. (*part-time*)
     £2,000

Members, L. F. Robson; H. C. Spear
     (*each*) £12,250 to £17,750
Members from the Central Electricity Generating Board, A. E. Hawkins; F. E. Bonner, C.B.E.
Secretary, B. C. O. Murphy.

CENTRAL ELECTRICITY GENERATING BOARD
Sudbury House, 15 Newgate Street, E.C.1
[01-248 1202]

Chairman, A. E. Hawkins £21,100
Deputy Chairman, F. E. Bonner £18,000
Members, R. A. Peddie; D. R. R. Fair, O.B.E.
each £13,600
Part-time Members, A. G. Derbyshire, F.R.I.B.A.; The Lord Kearton, O.B.E., F.R.S.; P. A. Lingard, D.F.C.; A. G. Frame . . . . *each* £1,000
Secretary and Solicitor, A. L. Wright.

ELECTRICITY BOARDS
The 12 Area Electricity Boards
(The Chairmen of Area Boards receive a salary of £12,250 to £17,250).

London, 46 New Broad Street, E.C.2. *Chairman*, O. Francis, C.B. *Sec.*, D. G. Rees.

South Eastern, Queen's Gardens, Hove, 3, Sussex. *Chairman*, T. Rutherford. *Sec.*, D. A. Green.

Southern, Southern Electricity House, Littlewick Green, Maidenhead, Berks. *Chairman*, A. W. Bunch. *Sec.*, C. M. de L. Byrde, M.B.E.

South Western, Electricity House, Colston Avenue, Bristol 1. *Chairman*, G. England. *Sec.*, S. G. Marshall.

Eastern, P.O. Box 40, Wherstead, Ipswich, Suffolk. *Chairman*, H. D. B. Wood, C.B.E. *Sec.*, W. L. M. French.

East Midlands, P.O. Box 4, North P.D.O., 398 Coppice Road, Arnold, Nottingham. *Chairman*, P. A. Lingard. *Sec.*, T. F. C. Walker.

Midlands, Mucklow Hill, Halesowen, West Midlands. *Chairman*, G. T. Shepherd. *Sec.* P. Cuthill.

South Wales, St. Mellons, Cardiff. *Chairman*, W. E. Richardson. *Sec.*, R. G. Williams.

Merseyside and North Wales, Sealand Road, Chester. *Chairman*, D. G. Dodds. *Sec.*, M. M. Parker.

Yorkshire, Scarcraft, Leeds. *Chairman*, E. S. Booth, C.B.E. *Sec.*, E. K. Richmond, T.D.

North Eastern, Carliol House, Newcastle upon Tyne 1. *Chairman*, A. H. Norris. *Sec.*, J. Millar.

North Western, Cheetwood Road, Manchester 8. *Chairman*, R. Mallet. *Sec.*, G. H. Richardson.

NORTH OF SCOTLAND HYDRO-ELECTRIC BOARD

16 Rothesay Terrace, Edinburgh 3

[031-225 1361]

Chairman, Sir Douglas Haddow, K.C.B. (*part-time*)
£8,125
Deputy Chairman and Chief Executive, K. R. Vernon.
Members (*part-time*), D. D. S. Craib, C.B.E. (*Chairman of Consultative Council*) (£2,100); F. L. Tombs (*unpaid*); Col. H. A. C. Mackenzie, O.B.E., M.C., T.D.; A. Wallace; S. L. Henderson; W. Kemp, M.B.E.; I. S. Campbell............each £1,000
Secretary and Solicitor, D. A. S. MacLaren.

SOUTH OF SCOTLAND ELECTRICITY BOARD

Inverlair Avenue, Glasgow

[041-637 7177]

Chairman, F. L. Tombs................£16,600
Deputy-Chairman, D. R. Berridge.......£13,100
Part-time Members, W. D. Coats; W. G. P. Fraser; J. Kane, O.B.E.; E. McCulloch; C. H. Martineau (*Chairman of Consultative Council* (£2,100); W. Ure, M.B.E. (£1,000); Sir Douglas Haddow, K.C.B., F.R.S.E. (*unpaid*).
Secretary, D. M. McGrouther.

DEPARTMENT OF EMPLOYMENT

8 St. James's Square. S.W.1

[01-214 6000]

The Department of Employment is responsible for Government policies affecting the working life of the country's population and the needs of potential workers.

These policies include the promotion of good industrial relations, pay, measures to deal with unemployment and redundancy and regional employment problems.

The Department is also responsible for producing and publishing a wide range of statistics, including the figures for retail prices, earnings, employment and unemployment and industrial disputes.

Many of the Department's executive functions and services have been transferred to a number of new bodies, operating independently, but reporting to the Secretary of State for Employment.

Secretary of State for Employment, THE RT. HON. MICHAEL MACKINTOSH FOOT, M.P......£13,000
Private Secretary, D. W. Brown.
Assistant Private Secretaries, R. Dykes; Miss K. M. Hegarty.

Parliamentary Private Secretary, N. G. Kinnock, M.P.

Minister of State, ALBERT EDWARD BOOTH, M.P.
£7,500
Under-Secretaries of State, J. D. Fraser, M.P.; H. Walker, M.P......................£5,500
Permanent Secretary, Sir Conrad Heron, K.C.B., O.B.E.
£18,675
Deputy Secretaries, K. Barnes, C.B.; J. H. Locke; A. R. Thatcher, C.B.; D. J. Derx, C.B.... £14,000
Solicitor, F. D. Lawton, C.B...............£14,000

Industrial Relations

Under Secretaries, J. L. Edwards; D. B. Smith
£12,000
Assistant Secretaries, A. F. Hatfull; D. J. Hodgkins; G. W. Robertson.........£8,650 to £11,000
Chief Conciliation Officer (vacant).
£8,650 to £11,000

Incomes Division

Under Secretaries, G. A. Brand; A. W. Brown
£12,000
Assistant Secretaries, D. R. Bower; A. Burridge; R. J. Dawe, O.B.E.........£8,650 to £11,000
Chief Wages Inspector, I. Prost... £7,750 to £9,350
Secretary of Wages Councils, Miss Y. M. Simmons
£5,680 to £7,450

Economic Policy (Manpower) Division

Under Secretary, C. A. Larsen............£12,000
Assistant Secretaries, Mrs. J. M. Collingridge; A. B. Moore; E. Norcross........£8,650 to £11,000
H. M. Inspector of Schools, E. Lord
£6,625 to £9,415

Manpower General
Under Secretary, Mrs. D. M. Kent........£12,000
Assistant Secretaries, N. Covington; Miss M. E. Green; J. C. Healey; D. J. Sullivan; B. D. Winkett..................£8,650 to £11,000

Overseas Division

Under-Secretary, A. M. Morgan, C.M.G.... £12,000
Assistant Secretary, Miss B. Green
£8,650 to £11,000

Research and Planning Division

Under Secretary, N. S. Forward..........£12,000
Assistant Secretary, H. A. Simons
£8,650 to £11,000
Chief Psychologist, G. Jessup.......£8,650 to £11,000
Senior Economic Adviser, J. Dixon
£8,650 to £11,000

Establishments Division

Director of Establishments, A. F. A. Sutherland
£12,000
Assistant Secretaries, L. J. Goss, C.B.E.; G. A. E. Laming, O.B.E.; L. G. Morgan, O.B.E.
£8,650 to £11,000
Director of Information, K. D. McDowall.. £11,670
Deputy Director of Information, J. H. Mackenzie
£7,750 to £9,350
Chief Inspector, E. W. Fawcett.. £7,750 to £9,350

Finance Division

Accountant-General, E. A. Ferguson.......£12,000
Director of Accounts and Audit, S. H. N. Hinton
£9,650 to £11,000
Assistant Accountant General, G. S. Day
£7,750 to £9,350
Regional Finance Officers, F. O. Lewis (*Wales and South Western*); T. R. Muncie* (*Midlands*); T. H. G. Symons (*South East*) (£5,680 to £7,450); F. Collier* (*North Western*); Mrs. H. D. Bradley (*Scotland*); W. H. Robinson* (*Yorkshire and Humberside and Northern*).. £4,976 to £6,159
(* = temporary)

Solicitor's Division

Solicitor, F. D. Lawton, C.B..............£14,000
Principal Assistant Solicitor, D. E. Belham, C.B.
£12,000
Assistant Solicitors, J. B. H. Billam, D.F.C.; D. Bowdon-Dan; D. M. D. D. Grazebrook; G. E. McClelland...............£8,650 to £11,000

Senior Legal Assistants, H. T. Morgan, O.B.E.; C. N. Langellier; Miss V. W. Rice-Pyle; K. Halil; R. Mollart; M. Harris; H. R. L. Purse; Miss G. S. Johnson; Miss B. R. Heitzman
£6,625 to £8,750

Statistics Division
Director of Statistics, A. R. Thatcher......£14,000
Deputy Director, A. G. Carruthers........£12,000
Assistant Secretary, Miss M. A. Barkess
£8,650 to £11,000
Chief Statisticians, F. G. Forsyth; R. E. Fry; R. Turner................£8,650 to £11,000

Regional Offices
Northern Region
Regional Director, R. M. Walker
£8,650 to £11,000
Deputy Regional Director, A. R. Hill
£7,750 to £9,350

Yorkshire and Humberside Region
Regional Director, A. A. G. McNaughton
£8,650 to £11,000
Deputy Regional Director, S. Duncalf
£7,750 to £9,350

South East Region
Regional Director, J. H. Devey, O.B.E......£11,670
Deputy Regional Directors, G. C. Breden; E. Reeves
£7,750 to £9,350

South West Region
Regional Director, W. D. Scott..£8,650 to £11,000
Wales
Director, A. E. L. Winter......£8,650 to £11,000

Midland Region
Regional Director, M. J. Porter. £8,650 to £11,000
Deputy Regional Director, E. H. Thomas
£7,750 to £9,350

North West Region
Regional Director, D. A. Savage £8,650 to £11,000
Deputy Regional Director, L. R. Frost
£7,750 to £9,350

Scotland
Director, A. Y. W. Cowie............£11,670
Deputy Director, A. P. D. Ross..£7,750 to £9,350

INDEPENDENT OFFICES

The Industrial Tribunals
See under Law Courts and Offices

Industrial Arbitration Board
Created by the Industrial Courts Act 1919
1 The Abbey Garden, Great College Street, SW1
[01–930 4571]
President, Sir Roy Wilson, Q.C.........£13,280
Secretary, O. Killick...........£4,976 to £6,159

Office of the Umpire
6 Grosvenor Gardens, S.W.1
[01–730 9236]
Independent statutory authority—appointed by the Crown to decide appeals under Reinstatement in Civil Employment Act and National Service Acts.
Umpire, D. W. E. Neligan, O.B.E............*fees*

DEPARTMENT OF ENERGY
Thames House, South,
Millbank, S.W.1 (unless otherwise stated)
[01–211 3000]
The Department of Energy is responsible for the Government's relationship with the National Coal Board, the Electricity Council and the Central Electricity Generating Board, the British Gas Corporation and the United Kingdom Atomic Energy Authority. It is the sponsoring Department for the nuclear construction industry and the oil industry and is responsible for the Government's policy in respect of the resources of the North Sea. Through the Offshore Supplies Office, it is responsible for assisting in the development in the U.K. of an industrial capability to provide supplies to the oil industry in its offshore activities.
Secretary of State for Energy, THE RT. HON ANTHONY WEDGWOOD BENN, M.P...............£13,000
Private Secretary, R. A. Custis.

Parliamentary Private Secretary, J. W. Ashton, M.P.
Assistant Private Secretaries, A. Proctor; Miss E. Morton; Miss C. N. Jones.
Minister of State for Energy, THE LORD BALOGH
£9,500
Private Secretary, B. D. Emmett.
Assistant Private Secretary, Miss S. McMaster.
Parliamentary Under-Secretaries of State, A. Eadie, B.E.M., M.P.; J. Smith, M.P...............£5,500
Permanent Under Secretary of State, Sir Jack Rampton, K.C.B...............£17,175
Private Secretary, Mrs. M. C. S. Aitchison.
Deputy Secretaries, P. le Cheminant; J. G. Liverman, C.B., O.B.E.; B. G. Tucker, O.B.E.; L. Williams, C.B...............£14,000
Chief Scientist, Dr. W. Marshall.
Chief Economic Adviser, F. J. Atkinson,
Director of Information, B. Ingham.
Parliamentary Clerk, P. E. R. Cohen.

Establishment Division
Principal Establishment Officer (Under Secretary), I. T. Manley...............£12,000
Assistant Secretaries, J. H. Thomas; D. E. R. Scarr
£8,650 to £11,000
Senior Principal, A. D. Hampson.. £7,750 to £9,350

Electricity Division
Under Secretary, T. P. Jones............£12,000
Assistant Secretaries, D. I. Morphet; Miss J. A.M. Oliver; J. Whaley; B. Hampton
£8,650 to £11,000
Chief Electrical Engineering Inspector, A. T. Baldock

Coal Division
Under Secretary, J. R. Cross, C.M.G.......£12,000
Assistant Secretaries, C. N. Tebay; G. W. Thyme
£8,650 to £11,000

Atomic Energy Division
Under Secretary, C. Herzig...............£12,000
Assistant Secretaries, W. C. F. Butler; W. E. Fitzsimmons...............£8,650 to £11,000
Senior Principal, J. L. Cohen.... £7,750 to £9,350

Energy Technology Division
Under Secretary, L. H. Leighton £12,000
Deputy Chief Scientific Officers, D. C. Gore; Dr. R. G. Skipper...............£8,650 to £11,000

Energy and Conservation Policy Division
Under Secretary, G. G. Campbell.........£12,000
Assistant Secretaries, Miss S. M. Cohen; R. H. Ellingworth; W. K Pryke; R. Wakefield
£8,650 to £11,000

Economics and Statistics Division
Under Secretary, T. A. Kennedy.........£12,000
Chief Statisticians, B. D. Cullen; F. W. Hutber; W. N. T. Roberts.........£8,650 to £11,000
Senior Economic Adviser, N. J. Cunningham

Community and International Policy Division
Under Secretary, Miss G. Brown.........£12,000
Assistant Secretaries, P. T. Harding; E. J. Lindley; A. R. M. Watts, O.B.E......£8,650 to £11,000

Oil Policy (Home) Division
Under Secretary, R. H. Wilmott, C.M.G. .. £12,000
Assistant Secretaries, L. F. Barclay; Mrs. D. E. F. Carter; C. L. Jones.........£8,650 to £11,000
Senior Principal, D. W. Hills.... £6,280 to £9,350

Gas Division
Under Secretary, J. A. Roberts...........£12,000
Assistant Secretaries, S. W. Fremantle; S. W. T. Mitchelmore...............£8,650 to £9,350

Gas Standards Branch
Government Buildings, Saffron Road, Wigston, Leicester
[Wigston: 5354]
Controller, G. R. Boreham.

Petroleum Production Division
Under Secretary, G. F. Kear...............£12,000
Assistant Secretaries, J. A. Molyneux; A. R. D. Murray...............£8,650 to £11,000
Petroleum Specialist I, H. R. George.

Offshore Supplies Office
Headquarters Office:
249 West George St., Glasgow
[041-221 8777]
Under Secretaries, A. Blackshaw; J. P. Gibson
£12,000
Assistant Secretaries, J. E. W. d'Ancona; T. B. Buyers; A. Wilson; Dr. J. E. P. Miles
£8,650 to £11,000
London Office
Assistant Secretary, P. J. Walker
£8,650 to £11,000
Assistant Director, S. C. Bridges.

Corporate Planning and Finance Division
Under Secretary, S. W. Spain............£12,000
Assistant Secretaries, P. S. Ross; M. E. Micklewright; M. H. Cadman; R. J. Priddle£8,650 to £11,000

Continental Shelf Policy Division
Under Secretary, C. E. H. Tuck..........£12,000
Assistant Secretaries, G. Corti; G. W. Monger; M. Z. Wasilewski...............£8,650 to £11,000

DEPARTMENT OF THE ENVIRONMENT
2 Marsham Street, S.W.1
[01-212 3434]
The Department of the Environment is responsible for the range of functions affecting the physical environment. These include housing, construction, transport, planning and local government. The Department is also concerned with the co-ordination of work on the prevention of environmental pollution, with special responsibility for clean air and anti-noise functions, and for research into roads, buildings, hydraulics, water pollution, fire prevention and use of timber. The Property Services Agency is an integral part of the Department responsible for government property management services, building construction, maintenance and supplies.
Secretary of State for the Environment, THE RT. HON. (CHARLES) ANTHONY (RAVEN) CROSLAND M.P................................£13,000
Private Secretary, T. M. Heiser.
Special Assistant, D. Lipsey.
Parliamentary Private Secretary, P. Hardy, M.P.
Minister for Planning and Local Government, THE RT. HON. JOHN ERNEST SILKIN., M.P.
£9,500
Private Secretary, K. E. C. Sorenson.
Special Assistant, Mrs. A. Carlton.
Parliamentary Private Secretary, N. G. Barnett, M.P.
Minister for Transport, JOHN WILLIAM GILBERT, Ph.D., M.P................................£9,500
Private Secretary, D. A. R. Peel.
Parliamentary Private Secretary, G. M. Park, M.P.
Minister for Housing and Construction, REGINALD FREESON, M.P......................£9,500
Private Secretary, G. N. Benden
Parliamentary Private Secretary, A. W. Stallard, M.P.
Minister of State, DENIS HERBERT HOWELL, M.P.
£7,500
Private Secretary, J. J. Rendell.
Parliamentary Under-Secretaries of State:—
G. J. Oakes, M.P.; N. G. Carmichael, M.P.; The Baroness Birk; E. Armstrong, M.P........£5,500
Permanent Secretary, Sir Ian Bancroft, K.C.B. £18,675
Private Secretary, Mrs. M. MacDonald.
Second Permanent Secretaries, Sir Idwal Pugh, K.C.B.; Sir Robert Marshall, K.C.B., M.B.E......£17,175
Private Secretaries (to Sir Idwal Pugh), W. Sutherland; *(to Sir Robert Marshall),* G. D. Rowe.
Chief Executive, Property Services Agency, W. R. Cox, C.B................................£17,175
Private Secretary, P. J. J. Britton.
Industrial Adviser on Construction, R. W. Evans.

PLANNING
Deputy Secretary and Chief Planner, W. Burns, C.B., C.B.E................................£14,000

Development Plans and Regional Strategies
Under Secretary, Mrs. J. Toohey........£12,000

Assistant Secretaries, R. A. Isaacson; G. M. Wedd
£8,650 to £11,000
Assistant Chief Planners, A. Buchanan; Miss K. B. Pailing; R. T. White................£11,000

Planning Land Use Policy
Under Secretary, Mrs. J. Bridgeman......£12,000
Assistant Secretaries, J. H. H. Baxter; A. G. Lyall; B. S. Quilter; J. P. G. Rowcliffe
Director "B", T. O'Toole...........£11,000

Planning Urban and Passenger Transport
Under Secretary, G. W. Mosely..........£12,000
Assistant Secretaries, G. Hopkinson; M. W. Jackson; R. Lloyd-Thomas; J. T. Williams
£8,650 to £11,000

Local Transportation and Roads
Under Secretary, D. Bishop, M.C..........£12,000
Assistant Secretaries, Miss A. R. Head; D. T. Routh
£8,650 to £11,000
Deputy Chief Scientific Officer, R. Spence
£8,100 to £9,440
Assistant Chief Engineer, D. Greenwood....£11,000

Urban Affairs and Commercial Property
Under Secretary, J. Palmer...............£12,000
Assistant Secretaries, E. W. Bryant; S. T. Garrish; M. L. Woods.............£8,650 to £11,000
Assistant Chief Planner, J. Peake........£11,000
Chief Estate Officer, P. G. Burnett........£11,000

Leisure Experiments
Under Secretary, Miss W. M. Fox........£12,000

Planning Intelligence
Duputy Chief Planner, D. E. Johnson......£10,240

PLANNING AND LOCAL GOVERNMENT
Deputy Secretary, C. P. Scott-Malden, C.B.. £14,000

Regional and Minerals
Under Secretary, J. Crocker...............£12,000
Assistant Secretaries, L. M. Dunston; O. H. Lawn; R. T. Scowen...............£8,650 to £11,000

Sport and Countryside
Under Secretary, A. Leavett...............£12,000
Assistant Secretaries, J. E. Morton; D. O'Connell; J. B. W. Robins; D. A. S. Sharp
£8,650 to £11,000

Local Government
Under Secretary, C. J. Pearce, C.B.........£12,000
Assistant Secretaries, E. S. Foster; R. C. Lawrance; D. C. Milefanti.............£8,650 to £11,000

New Towns
Under Secretary, J. A. L. Barber..........£12,000
Assistant Secretaries, A. Flexman; J. C. H. Marlow; H. W. Pryce..............£8,650 to £11,000

PLANNING SOUTH-EAST ENGLAND
Deputy Secretary, T. H. Shearer, C.B......£14,000

South-Eastern Region
Regional Director, J. Lane..............£12,000
Assistant Chief Planner (Airports Policy), S. W. Smith..............................£11,000
Regional Controllers:
Planning, L. Mann.......£8,650 to £11,000
Housing, N. Hamilton......£8,650 to £11,000
Roads and Transportation, G. H. Oversby-Powell
£8,650 to £11,000

Eastern Region
Regional Director, A. G. Powell..........£12,000
Regional Controllers:
Planning, N. Digney.......£8,650 to £11,000
Housing, J. R. Fells........£8,650 to £11,000
Roads and Transportation, N. Dean
£8,650 to £11,000

Planning London
Under Secretary, J. A. L. Gunn.........£12,000
Assistant Secretary, P. L. Daniel. £8,650 to £11,000
Assistant Chief Planner, M. Richardson....£11,000
Assistant Chief Engineer, G. E. Rowland...£11,000

Channel Tunnel Unit
Superintending Engineer, H. B. Gould
£8,850 to £9,798

Ancient Monuments and Historic Buildings
Under Secretary, V. D. Lipman............£12,000
Assistant Secretaries, C. F. R. Barclay, C.M.G.;
R. Ditchfield; H. L. Warburton
£8,650 to £11,000
Assistant Director, J. C. Ellis........£11,000

ENVIRONMENTAL PROTECTION AND WATER ENGINEERING
Deputy Secretary and Chief Water Engineer, T. P. Hughes, C.B.....................£14,000

Water
Under Secretary, J. R. Niven........£12,000
Assistant Secretaries, R. Dorrington; R. J. Green;
W. C. Knox.............£8,650 to £11,000

Noise, Clean Air and Wastes
Under Secretary, H. L. Jenkyns..........£12,000
Assistant Secretaries, W. J. S. Batho; Miss E. P. Kruse..................£8,650 to £11,000

Central Unit on Environmental Pollution
Under Secretary, A. J. Fairclough.........£12,000
Assistant Secretaries, G. D. Crane; T. W. Hall
£8,650 to £11,000

Water Engineering
Directors, O. Gibb; A. W. Kenny; D. C. Musgrave;
S. F. White.....................£11,440
Assistant Directors, R. Best; H. Cronshaw; T. A. Dick; L. E. Ellis; A. J. Herlihy; D. H. Newsome; R. E. Smith; J. Sumner, O.B.E.; L. E. Taylor; R. J. White.....................£11,000

TRANSPORT INDUSTRIES
Deputy Secretary, T. L. Beagley, C.B.......£14,000

Ports
Under Secretary, J. E. Sanderson........£12,000
Assistant Secretaries, D. G. Fagan; J. M. Hope
£8,650 to £11,000

Railways
Under Secretary, W. J. Sharp...........£12,000
Assistant Secretaries, M. S. Albu; K. Peter
£8,650 to £11,000
Chief Inspecting Officer, Lt.-Col. I. K. A. McNaughton.....................£11,440

International Transport and Nationalized Industries (General)
Under Secretary, E. S. Ainley...........£12,000
Assistant Secretaries, J. A. Dole; J. Peeler
£8,650 to £11,000

Freight
Under Secretary, S. M. A. Banister.......£12,000
Assistant Secretaries, R. J. E. Dawson; G. Flanagan
£8,650 to £11,000

Traffic Area Offices
Chairmen of Traffic Commissioners and Licensing Authorities
East Midlands (Nottingham), C. M. Sheridan, C.M.G.
Eastern (Cambridge), H. E. Robson.
Metropolitan (Acton), A. S. Robertson.
Northern (Newcastle upon Tyne), J. A. T. Hanlon.
North West (Manchester) (vacant).
Scotland, A. B. Birnie.
South East (Eastbourne), Maj.-Gen. A. F. J. Elmslie, C.B., C.B.E.
West Midlands (Birmingham), A. A. Crabtree.
Western (Bristol), Maj.-Gen. Sir John Potter, K.B.E., C.B.
Yorkshire (Leeds), R. S. Thornton.
South Wales (Cardiff), R. R. Jackson. (each) £11,000

HIGHWAYS
Director General, J. A. Jukes, C.B.........£14,000
Deputy Director General, M. Milne.......£13,230

Construction Units
Under Secretary, R. J. Bridle............£12,000
Assistant Secretary, R. M. Denny
£8,650 to £11,000
Assistant Chief Engineer, W. H. Farrow...£11,000

Road Construction Units
Eastern (Bedford)
Director, J. Tiplady.....................£11,440
North East (Harrogate)
Director, J. A. Mackenzie.............£11,440
North West (Preston)
Director, D. F. Dean.................£11,440
Midland (Leamington Spa)
Director, A. N. Brant.................£11,440
South East (Dorking)
Director, B. F. Edbrooke.............£11,440
South West (Taunton)
Director, P. G. Lyth.................£11,440

Highways Engineering
Chief Highway Engineer, J. S. Berry......£13,230
Deputy Chief Highway Engineers, J. Ford, G.M.;
H. Williams.....................£11,440
Assistant Chief Engineers, B. M. Cobbe, O.B.E.;
K. L. Duncan; P. Elliott; J. R. Lake; K. Sriskandan.....................£11,000

Highways Programming, Contracts and Lands
Under Secretary, F. J. Ward.............£12,000
Assistant Secretaries, D. J. Chapman; G. Cockerham;
L. E. Henderson..........£8,650 to £11,000
Senior Economic Adviser, G. A. C. Searle
£8,650 to £11,000

Highways Planning and Management
Under Secretary, G. D. Spearing........£12,000
Assistant Secretary, K. P. Leary. £8,650 to £11,000
Assistant Chief Engineers, J. L. Hammond; R. P. Sleep.....................£11,000

Road Safety
Under Secretary, H. F. Ellis-Rees........£12,000
Assistant Secretaries, V. G. Curtis; N. S. Despicht;
A. B. Saunders; P. A. Waller
£8,650 to £11,000

Vehicle Engineering and Inspection
Chief Mechanical Engineer, J. W. Furness..£11,440
Assistant Chief Engineers, G. Donald; C. C. Toyne
£11,000

HOUSING AND CONSTRUCTION INDUSTRIES
Deputy Secretary, P. E. Lazarus, C.B.......£14,000

Housing "A"
Under Secretary, K. T. Barnett..........£12,000
Assistant Secretaries, P. F. Owen; A. G. Semple
£8,650 to £11,000

Housing "B"
Under Secretary, J. E. Hannigan..........£12,000
Assistant Secretaries, F. W. Girling; W. P. Jackson;
D. C. Pickup; R. J. A. Sharp £8,650 to £11,000

Housing "C"
Under Secretary, S. W. Gilbert..........£12,000
Assistant Secretaries, H. W. Marshall; P. W. Rumble.............£8,650 to £11,000
Director " B ", A. D. H. Embling........£11,000

Housing "D"
Under Secretary, T. L. Jones..........£12,000
Assistant Secretaries, D. J. Crouch; K. F. J. Ennals;
G. J. Skinner.............£8,650 to £11,000
Director " B ", I. C. MacPherson........£11,000

Housing Development
Director, Miss P. R. Tindale.........£12,000
Assistant Directors, D. T. I. G. Davies; A. G. Rayner.....................£11,000

Construction Industry Overseas
Under Secretary, J. H. Burgess...........£12,000
Assistant Secretary, D. P. Walley
£8,650 to £11,000

Construction Industry Home
Under Secretary, P. N. Gerosa............£12,000
Assistant Secretaries, R. J. A. Sharp; B. Taylor
£8,650 to £11,000

RESEARCH
Director General of Research, D. J. Lyons, C.B.
£14,000

Research Requirements
Director, W. J. Reiners................£12,000
Deputy Chief Scientific Officers, G. Charlesworth; F. Gale; A. J. M. Hitchcock; A. F. E. Wise
£8,100 to £9,440

Research Management
Deputy Chief Scientific Officer (vacant)
£8,100 to £9,440

Systems Analysis Research Unit
Deputy Chief Scientific Officer, P. C. Roberts
£8,100 to £9,440

Secretariat
Assistant Secretary, W. Deakin..£8,650 to £11,000

Building Research Establishment
Director, J. B. Dick....................£13,230
Deputy Director, M. E. Burt.............£11,670
Deputy Chief Scientific Officers, P. L. Bakke; S. C. C. Bate; D. F. Cornelius; E. J. Gibson; R. E. Jeanes; G. R. Nice; W. H. Ward; R. H. Wood
£8,100 to £9,440

Hydraulics Research Station
Director, R. C. H. Russell..............£10,950

Transport and Road Research Laboratory
Director, A. Silverleaf.................£13,230
Deputy Director, L. B. Mullett...........£10,950
Assistant Director, W. A. Lewis..£8,100 to £9,440
Deputy Chief Scientific Officers, J. W. Fitchie; L. J. Griffin; A. P. Goode; G. Margason; J. H. Nicholas; H. Taylor; F. V. Webster
£8,100 to £9,440

PROPERTY SERVICES AGENCY
Chief Executive, W. R. Cox, C.B........£17,175

Secretariat and Planning Unit
Assistant Secretary, P. Critchley £8,650 to £11,000

DEPUTY CHIEF EXECUTIVE I
Deputy Secretary, A. Sylvester-Evans, C.B..£14,000

Civil Accommodation
Director, J. Delafons...................£12,000
Assistant Secretaries, W. H. Alexander; D. W. Cain; J. R. Coates..............£8,650 to £11,000
Assistant Directors, M. J. Baggott; A. W. Loten
£11,000

Estate Surveying Services
Director, A. R. J. Baldwin..............£12,000
Deputy Director, J. P. Hatfield..........£11,440
Assistant Directors, D. L. Bowyer; B. E. Hodgson; N. P. Lawrence; P. E. Rayner........£11,000

Estate Management Overseas
Director, B. Roberts....................£11,670

DEPUTY CHIEF EXECUTIVE II
Deputy Secretary, E. H. A. Stretton, C.B...£14,000

Scottish Services
Director, G. M. Patrick, C.M.G., D.S.C......£12,000
Assistant Secretary, M. D. King..£8,650 to £11,000
Assistant Director, R. W. Leeper.........£11,000

Home Regional Services
Director, A. J. Isaac...................£12,000
Assistant Secretaries, J. C. Goldsmith; S. J. Vincent
£8,650 to £11,000
Director "B ", L. E. Atkins..............£11,000

Property Services Agency Regions (Home)
Regional Works Directors:
London, A. MacInnes..................£12,000
Eastern, H. J. Giles....................£11,320
Midland, N. P. Walsh..................£11,320
North East, J. F. Hill, O.B.E., T.D........£11,320
North West, S. J. Heritage.............£11,320
South East, J. M. Rex, T.D.............£11,320
South West, F. S. Butler...............£11,320
Southern, M. J. Hislop................£11,320
Central Office for Wales, M. M. Davis..£11,320

Establishments, Property Services Agency
Principal Establishment Officer, P. D. Davies. £12,000
Assistant Secretaries, F. C. Argent; J. W. S. Dempster; P. S. Draper; Miss J. M. Foster.
£8,650 to £11,000

Finance, Property Services Agency
Principal Finance Officer, G. May.........£12,000
Assistant Secretary, B. Strong...£8,650 to £11,000
Comptroller of Accounts, P. H. Elsley
£8,650 to £11,000

Contracts
Director, I. C. Fletcher.................£11,670
Assistant Secretaries, R. F. Halse; J. H. Lewis
£8,650 to £11,000
Director Accountant, P. L. Jones. £8,650 to £11,000

DEPUTY CHIEF EXECUTIVE III
Deputy Secretary, H. P. Johnston.........£14,000

Defence Services I
Director, E. Vickers....................£12,000
Assistant Secretaries, P. C. Aggleton; D. Wright
£8,650 to £11,000
Directors "B ", K. W. Dando; G. T. Richards
£11,000

Defence Services II
Director, F. R. Martin..................£12,000
Assistant Secretaries, P. J. M. Butter; R. G. Clubley
£8,650 to £11,000
Directors "B ", J. I. Dawson; G. V. Rose; G. F. Woodward..........................£11,000

Post Office Services
Director, I. T. Lawman.................£12,000
Assistant Secretary, J. M. Entwistle
£8,650 to £11,000
Director "B ", A. Levy.................£11,000

DIRECTOR GENERAL OF DESIGN SERVICES
Deputy Secretary, W. D. Lacey, C.B.E.....£14,000

Building Development
Director, W. I. Appleton................£12,000
Directors "B ", M. F. Chaplin; B. G. Skeates
£11,000

Civil Engineering Development
Director, F. Walley....................£12,000
Assistant Director, D. F. Evans..........£11,000

Engineering Services Development
Director, A. C. Gronhaug...............£12,000
Assistant Directors, H. Dixon; E. G. Mallalieu
£11,000

Quantity Surveying Development
Director, K. Linsdell...................£12,000
Assistant Directors, D. W. Azzaro; R. Neil..£11,000

SUPPLIES
Controller, H. Leadbeater...............£12,000
Assistant Controllers, L. A. Baldwin; D. Castle; A. E. Davies; F. J. Garvey; A. D. Ormond
£8,650 to £11,000

CENTRAL SERVICES
AUDIT INSPECTORATE
Chief Inspector of Audit, S. V. Collins, C.B...£12,000
Deputy Chief Inspector, L. Tovell.........£11,440

PLANNING INSPECTORATE
Director, C. F. Allen...................£12,000
Deputy Directors, W. Orbell, M.B.E.; R. F. F. Williams, G.M............£8,650 to £11,000

LEGAL
Solicitor and Legal Adviser, K. A. T. Davey, C.B.
£14,000
Principal Assistant Solicitors, J. S. Ryan; H. Woodhouse, C.B...........................£12,000

RESOURCE ALLOCATION AND CENTRAL ECONOMIC SERVICES
Director General, Economics and Resources, H. J. D. Cole..............................£14,000

Central Policy Planning Unit
Assistant Secretary, A. H. Pollington
£8,650 to £11,000

Economics, Housing, Urban and Environment
Director, D. J. Ovens..................£12,000
Senior Economic Advisers, A. J. Harrison; A. E. Holmans; Mrs. J. M. Marquand
£8,650 to £11,000

Economics, Transport
Director, E. H. M. Price................£12,000
Senior Economic Advisers, D. F. Hagger; G. A. C. Searle; J. K. Welsby.....£8,650 to £11,000

Statistics
Director, G. Penrice..................£12,000
Chief Statisticians, B. J. Billington; B. J. Buckingham; Miss G. P. Ford; P. S. MacCormack; H. Palca; J. A. Rushbrook; F. D. Sando; W. H. Stott....................£8,650 to £11,000

FINANCE

Finance, Housing, Transport Industries and Central Services
Principal Finance Officer, A. J. Rosenfeld...£12,000
Assistant Secretaries, D. J. Burr; D. J. Lyness
£8,650 to £11,000

Local Government Finance Policy
Principal Finance Officer, T. H. Caulcott...£12,000
Assistant Secretaries, H. H. Browne; G. H. Chipperfield; T. R. Hornsby; A. A. Pelling
£8,650 to £11,000
Senior Economic Adviser, P. R. Smethurst
£8,650 to £11,000

Local Authority Expenditure
Principal Finance Officer, A. G. Rayner....£12,000
Assistant Secretaries, G. D. Miles; C. D. Packett; C. E. Seward.............£8,650 to £11,000

ESTABLISHMENT AND MANAGEMENT SERVICES
Director General, Organization and Establishments, G. C. Wardale, C.B.................£14,000

Organization and Development
Assistant Secretary (vacant)

Senior Staff Management
Under Secretary, N. H. Calvert..........£12,000
Assistant Secretaries, Miss I. M. Davis; L. R. Mustill, C.B.E........................£8,650 to £11,000

Personnel, Manpower and Training
Under Secretary, A. R. Atherton.........£12,000
Assistant Secretaries, G. T. Bright; D. Holmes; F. G. Rickard; J. G. Thompson....£8,650 to £11,000
Deputy Chief Scientific Officer, D. J. Wiblin
£8,100 to £9,440

Management Services
Under Secretary, M. Mendoza...........£12,000
Assistant Secretaries, R. C. Geall; D. W. Royle; C. K. Spinks.............£8,650 to £11,000
Chief Librarian, W. Pearson, M.B.E.
£5,680 to £7,450

Information
Director, N. Taylor....................£12,000
Deputy Director, P. G. Broderick
£8,650 to £11,000

Driver and Vehicle Licensing
Under Secretary, W. Dawson...........£12,000
Assistant Secretaries, J. A. Fowles; N. H. Kelly; F. Kendall...................£8,650 to £11,000

REGIONAL OFFICES
West Midlands (Birmingham)
Regional Director and Economic Planning Board Chairman, Miss S. W. Fogarty............£12,000
Regional Controllers, R. D. Law; W. W. Morris; G. J. Shoebridge...........£8,650 to £11,000

Yorkshire and Humberside (Leeds)
Regional Director and Economic Planning Board Chairman, R. G. Wilson, M.B.E............£12,000
Regional Controllers, K. C. Westhorpe; P. I. Wolf
£8,650 to £11,000

North West (Manchester)
Regional Director and Economic Planning Board Chairman, W. R. Corrie...................£12,000
Regional Controllers, D. M. Beaton; P. W. Peck; J. Stobart.................£8,650 to £11,000

Northern (Newcastle upon Tyne)
Regional Director and Economic Planning Board Chairman, D. J. King.....................£12,000
Regional Controllers, S. D. Olley; R. Williams
£8,650 to £11,000

South West (Bristol)
Regional Director and Economic Planning Board Chairman, P. R. Sheaf.....................£12,000
Regional Controllers, S. H. Godsell; A. W. Wright
£8,650 to £11,000

East Midlands (Nottingham)
Regional Director and Economic Planning Board Chairman, A. E. A. Brain..................£12,000
Regional Controllers, J. M. Hawksworth; G. Stockley...................£8,650 to £11,000

South East
Regional Director and Economic Planning Board Chairman, J. Lane........................£12,000
Regional Controllers, N. Hamilton; L. Mann; G. H. Oversby-Powell...........£8,650 to £11,000

Eastern
Regional Director, A. G. Powell..........£12,000
Regional Controller and Economic Planning Board Chairman for East Anglia, N. Digney
£8,650 to £11,000
Regional Controllers, N. Dean; J. R. Fells
£8,650 to £11,000

EXCHEQUER AND AUDIT DEPARTMENT
Audit House, Victoria Embankment, E.C.4
[01-353-8901]

This is the Department of the Comptroller and Auditor General, an office created by the Act 29 & 30 Vict. *c.* 39 (1866) to replace, with extended powers, the separate offices of Comptroller General of the Receipt and Issue of the Exchequer and of the Commissioners for Auditing the Public Accounts. This officer is appointed by Letters Patent under the Great Seal, and is irremovable except upon an address from the two Houses of Parliament. In his capacity of Comptroller General of the Receipt and Issue of the Exchequer, he authorizes all issues from the Consolidated and National Loans Funds after satisfying himself that Parliament has given authority for them. He examines the accounts of the Consolidated and National Loans Funds and makes an annual report on them to Parliament. In his capacity of Auditor General of Public Accounts, he is charged with the duty of examining on behalf of the House of Commons the accounts of expenditure out of funds provided by Parliament, the accounts of the receipt of revenue, and generally all other public accounts, including the accounts of Government stores and of trading services conducted by Government Departments. The results of this examination of those accounts are reported to the House of Commons. He is also the auditor by agreement of the accounts of many bodies, generally in receipt of public moneys, and of certain international organizations; he reports, when required to do so, to the governing bodies concerned.
Comptroller and Auditor General, Sir David Pitblado, K.C.B., C.V.O.................£18,675
Secretary, J. F. T. Cheetham.............£13,230
Deputy Secretary, P. R. Billett..........£11,670
Director of Establishments and Accounts, F. T. Womack
Directors of Audit, D. V. Boyd; R. C. Hooper; G. P. Morrell; J. French; D. F. Smith; R. A. Best; F. W. Eele; R. Stewart; R. Thomas
£8,650 to £11,000

Deputy Directors of Audit, T. N. Finch; P. G. Spary; H. R. Francis; S. L. Teasdale, O.B.E.; J. C. McDowell; M. F. Hughes; H. Solomon; F. J. E. Blanks; D. K. Clark; G. N. Debenham; P. M. Jefford; H. D. Myland; G. W. Garside; J. A. Collens; C. J. Stacey; P. J. C. Keemer; D. A. Dewar; D. T. Lipscombe; D. G. Lusmore; A. S. Woodward; P. J. Beck......£7,750 to £9,350

EXPORT CREDITS GUARANTEE DEPARTMENT

P.O. Box 272, Aldermanbury House,
Aldermanbury, E.C.2
[01-606-6699

The Export Credits Guarantee Department is responsible to the Secretary of State for Trade. The export Guarantees Act, 1975, enables E.G.C.D. to encourage U.K. exports by making available export credit insurance to British firms engaged in selling overseas, to guarantee repayment to British banks providing finance for export credit and, in clearly defined circumstances, to refinance a proportion of banks' medium and long-term export credit advances. Guarantees under Section 1 of the 1975 Act are given after consultation with an Advisory Council of businessmen.

The Overseas Investment and Export Guarantees Act 1972 empowers E.C.G.D. to insure British private investment overseas against political risks, such as war, expropriation and restrictions on remittances.

Export Guarantees Advisory Council

Chairman, Sir Michael Wilson, M.B.E.
Deputy Chairman, J. A. R. Staniforth, C.B.E.
Other Members, Hon. Robin D. Campbell; D. W. Hardy; E. Kaye, C.B.E.; Hon. Hugo Kindersley; R. A. S. Lane, M.C.; Sir Peter Matthews; J. N. S. Ridgers; J. R. Steele.

Investment Insurance Advisory Committee

Chairman, Sir Michael Wilson, M.B.E.
Members, Sir George Bishop, C.B., C.B.E.; R. J. Blair, O.B.E.; G. V. K. Burton, C.B.E.; E. J. Symons.

Officers

Secretary, K. Taylor, C.B................£14,000
Under Secretaries, K. W. Cotterill; T. Gill; D. C. Smith........................£12,000
Assistant Secretaries, M. S. Bremner; V. I. Chapman; J. A. Dyer; L. Elmes; R. A. Freeman (*Finance Officer*); M. W. Gentle; W. H. Johnson, D.F.C., D.F.M.; R. T. Kemp; E. G. Lowton; E. Panton; M. G. Stephens; E. T. Walton (*Establishment Officer*)...................£8,650 to £11,000
Senior Principals, L. M. Broad; J. A. Crossen; J. Cunningham; Mrs. E. Davidson; J. H. Hall; K. C. Harrison; R. C. Jack; E. J. Jackson; F. C. Mann; R. K. Pearson; J. G. Sorbie; G. A. Stay; D. H. Twyford; V. E. Young
£7,750 to £9,350
Principal Information Officer, C. F. A. Salaman
£5,680 to £7,650
Principals, A. E. J. Berry; G. C. Bird; G. Blackburn; J. Bolsover; A. J. Bray; G. E. J. Breach; G. Bromley; F. Chapman; J. W. Coggins; T. H. Collinson; A. J. Croft; H. C. Cunningham; B. J. Davison; A. Dawson; T. W. Denyer; K. Dixey; P. C. B. Duncan; J. E. Elliott; A. C. Elston; G. W. Ethall; P. A. F. Field; R. D. Foister; W. Ford; A. P. Fowell; C. Foxall; D. H. J. Furbank; C. W. Gentry; D. A. Green; L. M. Haines; D. G. Hake; L. Halligan; L. C. Harmer; G. A. Harvey; P. Henley; N. J. A. Hooker; R. H. K. Hughes; K, F. Jackson; D. M. Jaffray; I. Jennings; F. Jones; H. K. Jones; J. Lake; F. H. Light; G. J. A. Link; J. R. Llewelyn; K. G. Lockwood; R. L. F. Martin; R. C. Milsted; R. A. Napier-Andrews; B. Oattes; J. W. Pannell; W. J. C. Pinnell; P. G. Plows; A. C. Polti; R. A. Ranson; E. A. F. Rides; A. J. Saunders; J. K. Sedman; D. W. Shannon; B. M. Sidwell, T.D.; A. J. Somerville; H. L. H. Stevens, M.B.E.; C. R. Stickland; F. W. Vernau; J. F. Vose; R. Wild; F. Wilmot; T. D. Wright; J. R. G. Wythers, B.E.M.............................£6,680 to £7,450

Statistician, M. J. Le Good......£5,680 to £7,450
Chief Accountant, A. J. Gooch...£5,680 to £7,450
Senior Executive Officers, H. E. Allen; J. S. Anderson; P. Armstrong; C. F. Bailey; J. V. Baker; A. W. Balcombe; H. R. Barber; T. L. Barry; J. A. H. Bayliss; A. E. Beedle; Miss D. Bell; A. B. Bennett; R. Bennett; B. Blades; C. M. Bossom; Miss D. E. Brandel; A. J. Brander; F. Burge; A. R. Burrows; J. D. Cameron; J. C. Cawthron; L. D. N. Charman; Miss B. K. Cleaver; J. G. M. Cochrane; P. G. Coles; J. A. Collin; D. R. Coombe; Miss P. Currin; R. A. Dew; B. J. Duffield; Miss I. E. Dunlop; C. L. W. Durning; R. X. Fear; L. C. Ford; G. M. Foster; J. M. Foster; R. R. Fryatt; J. F. Gaynor; A. R. J. Gibbs; R. E. Gove; C. Haddy; P. Handovsky; C. W. Hanny; H. Harris; S. B. Harris; Miss V. M. Harvey; T. W. Hawes; J. Hawkins; Miss O. K. R. Hender; H. E. Higgs; W. F. G. Hills; W. F. Hinshelwood; R. C. Hirschfield; R. Holloway; Miss B. M. Howard; K. I. Humphrey; Miss S. J. Hunt; V. D. Hunt; R. E. Johnson; A. L. Jolley; G. G. Jones; L. Jones; R. Jones; G. Keegan; N. A. Lambert; R. W. Lane; B. H. Lewis; Mrs. M. J. Linter; M. L. Long; E. S. Lowe; W. A. Mann; K. A. Marshall; Miss R. M. Martin; G. Milan; P. A. Neal; C. C. Ostle; E. R. Packer; A. E. Paice; E. J. Perkin; O. H. Pettafor; R. A. Phelps; R. J. Pomeroy; C. F. Proctor; C. G. Purdy; H. J. Quilter; R. F. Reville; Miss J. A. Roffey; S. Rosenthal; F. Rossington; H. Ryden; T. Sanderson; R. W. Smeatham; W. E. Smith; R. M. Sutton; L. J. Syrett; D. P. Taylor; R. J. Thomas; Miss E. Thornhill; C. M. Thorogood; D. L. Townley; J. A. Walsh; H. Watson; D. S. Webb; R. S. Wheaton; R. A. Wilson; D. E. Wiltshire; R. J. Wise; C. R. Wright; G. A. Young
£4,900 to £5,900
Senior Information Officer, J. W. Pilbeam
£4,900 to £5,900

Regional Offices

Belfast: River House, High Street, Belfast (Belfast 31743); *Birmingham:* Colmore Centre, 115 Colmore Row, Birmingham (021-233-1771); *Bristol:* Robinson Building, 1 Redcliff Street, Bristol 1 (Bristol 299971); *Cambridge:* 72–80 Hills Road, Cambridge (Cambridge 68801/7); *Central London:* Waverley House, 7–12 Noel Street, W.1 (01-437-2292); *Glasgow:* Fleming House, 134 Renfrew Street, Glasgow (041-322 8707); *Leeds:* West Riding House, 67 Albion Street, Leeds (Leeds 450631); *London (North):* 593–599 High Road, Tottenham, N.17 (01-808-4570); *London (South):* 320 Purley Way, Croydon (01-686-9921); *Manchester:* Elisabeth House, St. Peter's Square, Manchester (061-228 3621).

FOREIGN AND COMMONWEALTH OFFICE

On the recommendations of the Committee on Representational Services Overseas appointed by the Prime Minister under the Chairmanship of Lord Plowden in 1962, H.M. Diplomatic Service was created on Jan. 1, 1965, by the amalgamation of the Foreign Service, the Commonwealth Service, and the Trade Commission Service, and is now responsible for the manning of the overseas posts of these three former services. On Aug. 1, 1966, the Colonial Office was merged into the Commonwealth Relations Office to form the Commonwealth Office. The Foreign Office and Commonwealth Office combined on Oct. 1, 1968.

In November 1970 overseas development became the ultimate responsibility of the Secretary of State for Foreign and Commonwealth Affairs, although it remained in the day-to-day charge of the Minister for Overseas Development, except for the period from March 1974 to June 1975 when the Ministry of Overseas Development reverted to its independent status.

Downing Street, S.W.1
[01-930-8440, 01-930-2323]

Secretary of State, THE RT. HON. JAMES CALLAGHAN,
M.P. £13,000
Private Secretary, S. J. Barrett
£9,040 to £11,410
Assistant Private Secretaries, R. N. Dales; J. D. F.
Holt; P. Weston. . . . . £6,090 to £7,860
Political Adviser, T. McNally . . £6,700 to £7,110
Parliamentary Private Secretary, J. A. Cunningham,
Ph.D., M.P.
Social Secretary, Miss G. A. Cogdon.
Ministers of State, THE RT. HON. DAVID HEDLEY
ENNALS, M.P.; THE RT. HON. ROY SYDNEY
GEORGE HATTERSLEY, M.P. £9,500
Parliamentary Under Secretaries of State, The Lord
Goronwy-Roberts, P.C.; E. Rowlands, M.P.
£5,500
Parliamentary Under Secretary of State and Head of the
Diplomatic Service, Sir Michael Palliser, K.C.M.G.
£18,675
Private Secretary, J. O. Kerr.
Deputy Under Secretaries, A. H. Campbell, C.M.G.;
H. A. H. Cortazzi, C.M.G.; Sir Antony Duff,
K.C.M.G., C.V.O., D.S.O., D.S.C., E. N. Larmour
C.M.G., N. Statham, C.M.G.; C.V.O.; R. A. Sykes,
C.M.G.; Sir Donald Tebbit, K.C.M.G. (Chief
Clerk) £14,000
Assistant Under Secretaries, N. Aspin, C.M.G.; M. D.
Butler, C.M.G.; R. W. H. Boulay, C.M.G., C.V.O.
(Vice Marshal of the Diplomatic Corps); R. H. G.
Edmonds, C.M.G., M.B.E.; R. S. Faber; O. G.
Forster, M.V.O. (Deputy Chief Clerk); D. F. Haw-
ley, C.M.G., M.B.E.; J. P. Hayes (Chief Economic
Adviser); R. A. Hibbert, C.M.G.; P. H. Laurence,
M.C. (Chief Inspector); P. J. E. Male, C.M.G., M.C.;
J. C. M. Mason; K.R.C. Pridham (Director of
Communications); R. S. Scrivener, C.M.G.; H. S.
Stanley, C.M.G.; J. A. Thomson, C.M.G.; M. S.
Weir, C.M.G.; A. J. Wilton, C.M.G., M.C. £12,410
Inspectors, E. J. Anglin; G. L. Bullard; H. C. Byatt;
C. McLean, M.B.E.; J. A. Pugh, O.B.E.
£9,660 to £11,410
Commercial Inspectors, P. McKearney; G. L. Sim-
mons, M.V.O. . . . . £9,660 to £11,410
Legal Adviser, Sir Vincent Evans, K.C.M.G., M.B.E.,
Q.C. £15,000
Second Legal Adviser, I. M. Sinclair, C.M.G. . £14,000
Deputy Legal Advisers, D. G. Gordon-Smith, C.M.G.;
A. R. Rushford, C.M.G. £12,410
Legal Counsellors, D. H. Anderson; R. K. Batstone;
F. D. Berman; F. Burrows; Mrs. E. M. Denza;
P. R. N. Fifoot; J. R. Freeland, C.M.G.
£9,443 to £11,410
Historical Adviser, R. d'O. Butler, C.M.G. . . £6,846
Senior Economic Advisers, Miss P. I. J. Harvey;
A. Smith.
Overseas Labour Adviser, G. Foggon, C.M.G., O.B.E.
£11,360
Overseas Police Adviser, M. J. Macoun, C.M.G., O.B.E.,
Q.P.M. . . . . £9,060 to £10,208

*Signals Department (Government Communications
Headquarters)*
Priors Road, Cheltenham, Gloucestershire
[0242–21491]
Director, A. W. Bonsall, C.B.E. £15,000
Principal Establishment Officer, J. A. F. Somerville,
C.B.E. £12,000

Heads of Departments

(£9,060 to £11,410 Assistant Heads of Dept.,
£6,090 to £7,860; except where stated)
Accommodation and Services Dept., K. C. Thom;
Assts., R. W. Hopcroft; R. S. Ford.
Arms Control and Disarmament Dept., J. C. Edmonds,
C.V.O.; Assts., Miss B. Richards; D. Thomas;
M. J. Wilmshurst.
Caribbean Dept., M. P. Preston; Asst., F. S. E.
Trew.
Central and Southern African Dept., H. M. S. Reid;
Assts., A. Ibbott; M. Reith.
Claims Dept., D. F. Burdon; Asst., J. Lee, D.F.C.
Commonwealth Co-ordination Dept., Mrs. M. B.
Chitty; Asst., J. C. E. Hyde.

Communications Administration Dept., N. Walton
O.B.E.; Asst., W. F. Walker.
Communications Engineering Dept., H. S. Rowe,
M.B.E.; Deputy Head of Dept., B. V. Harris.
Communications Operations Dept., J. W. Hutson,
Deputy Heads of Dept., W. J. Mundy; I. S. Zetter.
Communications Planning Staff, A. Routledge; Asst.,
B. B. Bushell.
Communications Technical Services Dept., R. G.
Holden; Assts., J. P. Allen; R. W. Read.
Consular Dept., O. R.JBlair; Assts., D. E. H. Hel-
lings, M.B.E.; T. T. Gaffy, O.B.E.
Cultural Exchange Dept., C. F. Hill; Asst., W. T.
Hull, M.B.E.
Cultural Relations Dept., J. A. L. Morgan; Asst.,
T. E. J. Mound.
Defence Dept., W. J. A. Wilberforce; Asst., A. J.
Hunter.
East African Dept., E. K. Ewans; Asst., R. A.
Neilson, M.V.O.
Eastern European and Soviet Dept., B. G. Cartledge.
Energy Dept., S. L. Egerton; Assts., H. D. A. C.
Miers; M. J. Wilmshurst.
European Integration (External) Dept., R. Q. Braith-
waite; Asst., H. J. Arbuthnott.
European Integration (Internal) Dept., M. J. E.
Fretwell, C.M.G.; Assts., Miss J. J. D'A. Collings;
T. J. B. George.
Far Eastern Dept., W. Bentley; Asst., D. M. March,
O.B.E.
Finance Dept., G. W. Jewkes; Assts., R. J. Bray;
R. F. Muston; T. W. Sharp.
Financial Relations Dept., S. J. G. Cambridge;
Assts., E. T. Davies; D. M. Kerr, O.B.E.
Gibraltar and General Dept., E. G. Lewis, C.M.G.,
O.B.E.
Guidance and Information Policy Dept., Miss A. M.
Warburton, C.V.O.; Deputy Head of Dept., P. R.
Metcalfe; Assts., R. E. Jones; M. Kendall, M.V.O.
Hong Kong and Indian Ocean Dept., P. L. O.'Keeffe,
C.V.O.; Asst., D. K. Timms.
India Office Library and Records: Director, Miss J. C.
Lancaster, F.S.A.; Deputy Librarian, R. G. C.
Desmond; Deputy Archivist, M. I. Moir.
Library: Assistant Keepers, Miss O. M. Lloyd; Mrs.
M. Archer; R. J. Bingle, D.Phil.; M. J. C.
O'Keefe; Mrs. U. Sims-Williams; Mrs. U.
Tripathi; Records: Assistant Keepers, A. J. Farring-
ton; Mrs. V. C. Weston; Mrs. P. J. Tuson.
Information Administration Depts., C. G. Mays; Asst.,
R. G. Tallboys, M.B.E.
Information Research Dept., T. C. Barker; Deputy
Head of Department and Assistant, J. G. McMinnies,
O.B.E.; Assts., P. Joy, O.B.E.; Mrs. J. M. O'Connor-
Howe.
Latin American Dept., H. M. Carless; Asst., A. J.
Collins, O.B.E.
Library and Records Dept., B. Cheeseman, O.B.E.;
Assts., Miss E. C. Blayney; H. G. F. Harcombe.
Marine and Transport Dept., B. Hitch; Asst., M. W.
Atkinson, M.B.E.
Middle East Dept., Hon. I. T. M. Lucas; Asst., T. J.
Clark.
Migration and Visa Dept., H. E. Rigney; Assts.,
F. C. Hensby, O.B.E.; J. H. Mallett, M.M.
Nationality and Treaty Dept., J. S. Dixon, O.B.E.;
Assts., Miss T. M. Cullis; G. T. Winters.
Near East and North Africa Dept., A. B. Urwick;
Asst., F. B. Wheeler.
News Dept., T. D. McCaffrey; Deputy Head, Miss
E. M. Booker, O.B.E.; Asst., J. Bourgoin, O.B.E.
North America Dept., D. M. D. Thomas; Asst.,
G. N. Smith.
Pacific Dependent Territories Dept., E. A. W. Bullock;
Asst., R. S. Pettitt.
Permanent Under Secretary's Dept., J. M. Edes;
Deputy Head, D. Tonkin; Asst., P. H. C. Eyers,
M.V.O.
Personnel Operations Dept., R. E. Parsons; Deputy
Head, H. B. Walker; Assts., R. J. Carrick, M.V.O.;
G. A. Fletcher; J. B. Weymes, O.B.E.
Personnel Policy Dept., P. H. Moberly; Asst., R. A.
Neilson, M.V.O.
Personnel Services Dept., J. S. Whitehead; Assts.,

D. L. Benest; A. S. Donkin; B. T. Holmes.

Planning Staff, R. S. Faber.

Protocol and Conference Dept., R. W. H. du Boulay, C.M.G., C.V.O. (*H.M. Vice-Marshal of the Diplomatic Corps*); S. W. F. Martin; G. G. Collins (*Assistant Marshals of the Diplomatic Corps*). £6,090 to £7,860. *Asst.*, Miss S. M. Strachan, O.B.E.

Republic of Ireland Dept., G. W. Harding, C.V.O.; *Asst.*, J. D. N. Hartland-Swann.

Research Dept., E. E. Orchard, C.B.E. (*Director*).

Rhodesia Dept., P. M. Caver; *Asst.*, P. J. Barlow.

Science and Technology Dept., J. Mellon; *Asst.*, P. R. Fearn.

Security Dept., C. J. Howells; *Assts.*, A. E. Furness; K. Kirby, O.B.E.

South Asian Dept., R. J. O'Neill; *Asst.*, C. H. Seaward.

South-East Asian Dept., C. W. Squire, M.V.O.; *Asst.*, A. K. Goldsmith.

Southern-European Dept., A. C. Goodison, C.M.G.; *Assts.*, R. H. Baker; M. C. S. Weston.

South-West Pacific Dept., L. Bevan; *Asst.*, P. G. de Courcy-Ireland.

Trade Relations and Exports Dept., J. C. Cloake; *Assts.*, B. W. Gordon, O.B.E.; P. J. L. Popplewell.

Training Dept. Head of Dept. and Director of Language Centre, C. A. Thompson; *Assts.*, H. Gilmartin; C. W. M. Wilson.

United Nations Dept., P. M. Maxey; *Asst. and Deputy Head*, M. L. Tait, M.V.O.; *Asst.*, J. H. Symons.

West African Dept., M. E. Heath; *Asst.*, D. W. R. Lewis.

West Indian and Atlantic Dept., P. C. Duff; *Asst.*, J. M. Willson.

Western European Dept., A. D. S. Goodall; *Assts.*, D. Beattie, A. C. McCarthy.

Passport Office

Clive House, Petty France, S.W.1
[01-222-8010]

Chief Passport Officer, M. G. Dixon, O.B.E.
£8,650 to £11,000

Deputy Chief Passport Officer, R. P. B. Cave, O.B.E.
£7,750 to £9,350

Liverpool Office

India Buildings, Water Street, Liverpool 2
[051-227-3461]

Officer in Charge, Miss V. M. Brady
£5,680 to £7,450

Glasgow Office

Empire House, 131 West Nile Street, Glasgow, C.1
[041-332-0271]

Officer in Charge, J. T. Robertson
£5,680 to £7,450

Newport Office

Olympia House, Upper Dock Street, Newport, Gwent
[0633-52431]

Officer in Charge, Mrs. T. M. Godfrey
£5,680 to £7,450

Peterborough Office

55 Westfield Road, Peterborough
[0733-263636]

Officer in Charge, R. W. Dennis. £5,480 to £7,450

Belfast Agency

30 Victoria Street, Belfast 1
[OBE-2-32371]

Officer in Charge, Mrs. M. T. Haughey.

Corps of Queen's Messengers

Superintendent of the Queen's Messenger Service, Capt. J. G. Canning.

Queen's Diplomatic Service Messengers, R. A. Perryman; T. D. Nettleton; Wing-Cdr. J. C. Norris, D.F.C.; Col. J. H. Wakefield; Lt.-Col. A. F. Rowe; Lt.-Col. R. K. Constantine; Lt.-Col. C. F. V. Bagot, O.B.E.; Lt.-Col. J. M. B. Poyntz, O.B.E.; Maj. M. P. D. Cruickshank; Sq.-Ldr. A. P. Hollick; A. P. H. Lousada; Wing-Cdr. T. Stevenson, A.F.C.; Sq.-Ldr. S. G. R. White; Wing-Cdr. J. M. Morgan, D.F.C.; Capt. D. V. Walmesley; Maj. W. R. A. Catcheside; J. H. Kidner; R. C. H. Risley; J. O. Hollis; Flt.-Lt. P. C. Stevens, D.F.C.; Lt.-Col. B. A. A. Plummer; Maj. P. Sherston-Baker, M.C.; Maj. C. M. Tuffill; Maj. J. K. Nairne; Lt.-Col. B. A. Hannaford; F. N. Cory-Wright; Group Capt. S. P. Coulson, D.S.O., D.F.C.; Sqn.-Ldr. L. V. Davies, D.F.M.; E. W. J. Eyers; Maj. A. W. Gay; J. A. Golding, C.V.O.; Maj. L. A. Smeeton, M.M.; Maj. K. H. M. O'Kelly; Lt.-Col. H. Forwood; Maj. D. B. Metcalfe; Lt.-Col. C. R. Simms-Reeve; Wing-Cdr. K. Smith, D.F.C.; R. J. Angel; Sqn.-Ldr. L. C. Bazalgette; Maj. C. T. H. Campbell; Maj. G. M. Benson; Lt.-Cdr. B. R. Bezance; Maj. M. J. Fuller; G. F. Miller; Maj. A. M. Farmer; Lt.-Col. B. C. F. Arkle, M.B.E.; Lt.-Col. E. M. T. Crump; J. W. Hannah, M.B.E.; P. L. Burkinshaw, O.B.E.; Maj. L. M. Phillips; Maj. P. T. Dunn; Wing-Cdr. R. A. Nash; Capt. D. F. A. Bloom, G.M.

India Office Library and Records

Orbit House, 197 Blackfriars Road, S.E.1

The Record Office has the custody of the archives of the East India Company (1600–1858), the Board of Control (1784–1858), the India Office (1858–1947) and the Burma Office (1937–1947).

Director, Miss J. C. Lancaster, F.S.A.

FORESTRY COMMISSION

231 Corstorphine Road, Edinburgh
[031-334-0303]

The Forestry Commissioners are charged with the general duty of promoting the interests of forestry, the development of afforestation, the production and supply of timber and the maintenance of reserves of growing trees in Great Britain. Including the former Crown Woods, transferred to it in 1924, the Commission has acquired about 3,000,000 acres of land (75 per cent. being plantable), of which 1,998,599 acres are under plantations. Under various grant schemes, financial assistance is given to private owners and local authorities in respect of approved works of afforestation.

Chairman, The Lord Taylor of Gryfe (*part-time*)
£6,200

Director-General and Deputy Chairman, J. A. Dickson, C.B. £14,000

Head of Forest and Estate Management, G. G. Stewart
£12,000

Head of Administration and Finance, P. Nicholls
£12,000

Head of Harvesting and Marketing, G. D. Holmes
£12,000

Senior Officer, *Wales* (Churchill House, Cardiff), J. W. L. Zehetmayr. £11,000

NATIONAL FREIGHT CORPORATION

Argosy House, 215 Great Portland Street, W.1
[01-636-8688]

The National Freight Corporation is a statutory corporation set up under the Transport Act, 1968, to provide integrated road and rail freight services in Great Britain and in so doing to make the maximum economic use of rail, with due regard to the needs of the person for whom the goods are being carried, and the requirements of the goods themselves. On January 1, 1969, it inherited the securities, rights and liabilities of the Road Haulage and Shipping Subsidiaries of the Transport Holding Company. It also acquired from the British Railways Board, National Carriers Ltd. and a 51 per cent. interest in Freightliners Ltd. (formerly the "Sundries" and "Freightliner" Divisions respectively of the Railways Board).

Chairman, Sir Daniel Pettit. £19,863

Members, Prof. R. J. Ball; Sir Sidney Greene, C.B.E.; F. S. Law (£2,000); R. L. E. Lawrence, O.B.E., E.R.D.; D. G. MacDonald; D. D. Sieff; R. O. C.

Swayne, M.C.; C. H. Urwin; L. G. Whyte, C.B.E.
each (part-time) £1,000
Vice-Chairman, Executive Board, V. G. Paige.
Chief Secretary and Legal Adviser, P. A. Mayo.

FREIGHT INTEGRATION COUNCIL
2 Marsham Street, S.W.1
[01-212-8168]
Chairman, Sir Anthony Burney, O.B.E.
Members, The Lord Greene of Harrow Weald, C.B.E.; A. H. Kitson; Col. F. T. Davies; J. A. McMullen, O.B.E.; Rt. Hon. R. W. Marsh; Sir Daniel Pettit.
Secretary, J. S. Buchanan.

REGISTRY OF FRIENDLY SOCIETIES (CENTRAL OFFICE) AND OFFICE OF THE INDUSTRIAL ASSURANCE COMMISSIONER
17 North Audley Street, W.1
[01-629-7001]

A Barrister was appointed in 1828 to certify the Rules of Savings Banks, and in 1829 to certify those of Friendly Societies. In 1846 he was constituted Registrar of Friendly Societies. By the Friendly Societies Act, 1875, the Central Office of the Registry of Friendly Societies was created consisting of the Chief Registrar and the Assistant Registrars for England. It exercises numerous and important functions under the Friendly Societies Acts, the Industrial and Provident Societies Acts, the Building Societies Acts, the Trustee Savings Banks and National Savings Bank Acts, the Loan Societies Act, the Shop Clubs Acts and the Superannuation and other Trust Funds (Validation) Act. Under the Industrial Assurance Acts and the Insurance Companies Acts, the Chief Registrar is charged with various powers and duties in relation to Industrial Assurance Companies and Collecting Societies, and in that capacity is styled the Industrial Assurance Commissioner.
Chief Registrar and Industrial Assurance Commissioner, K. Brading, C.B., M.B.E. £13,230
Private Sec., Mrs. W. Hughes.
Asst. Registrar and Deputy Head of Department, A. Vollmar. £11,440
Asst. Registrar, J. E. Gower, O.B.E., M.C.
£9,033 to £11,000
Executive Registrar and Establishment Officer, J. A. Walter. .... £7,750 to £9,350
Senior Legal Assistants, M. J. Pearce; A. Wilson
£6,625 to £8,750
Legal Assistant, C. B. E. White.
£3,424 to £6,125
Registration Branch (Head), J. W. D. Goss, £5,680 to £7,450; *(Asst. Head)* I. D. Christie
£4,900 to £5,900
Returns and Statistics Branch (Head), E. S. Burgess, £5,680 to £5,450; *(Asst. Head)* R. L. Devlin
£4,900 to £5,900
Establishment and Records Branch (Head), L. G. Hill
£4,900 to £5,900
Investigations Branch (Head), R. E. Kilbey
£4,900 to £5,900
Disputes Branch (Head), M. F. G. Howell
£4,900 to £5,900
Registry of Friendly Societies, Scotland
19 Heriot Row Edinburgh, 3
[031-556-4371]
Assistant Registrar, J. Craig, O.B.E., W.S.

GAMING BOARD FOR GREAT BRITAIN
Berkshire House, 168-173 High Holborn, W.C.1
[01-240-0821]

Established on October 25, 1968, to maintain a broad oversight of developments in gaming in Great Britain, to check prospective gaming licensees management and staff, and to advise the Home Secretary on making regulations which may be needed for the further control of gaming.
Chairman, Sir Stanley Raymond.
Members, Sir Ranulph Bacon; Sir Philip Allen, K.C.B.; R. T. M. McPhail; Hon. R. O. Stanley; Sir James Starritt, C.V.O.
Secretary, W. J. Stephens.

BRITISH GAS CORPORATION
59 Bryanston Street W1.
[01-723-7030]
Chairman, Sir Arthur Hetherington, D.S.C.
(plus allowances £1,000) £20,000
Deputy Chairman, D. E. Rooke, C.B.E.
(plus allowances £500) £16,000
Members (full-time), J. A. Buckley, C.B.E.; C. E. Mills; G. F. I. Roberts; J. H. Smith; R. L. Worsfold; *(part-time),* P. G. Badham, C.B.E.; D. Beavis; G. E. Cooper; P. E. Gallaher, C.B.E.; J. King, O.B.E.; The Lord Ryder of Eaton Hastings; Sir Ernest Woodroofe, Ph.D.
Secretary, W. Burnstone.

THE GOVERNMENT ACTUARY
Steel House, Tothill Street, S.W.1
[01-273-3000]
Government Actuary, E. A. Johnston, C.B. . . £17,000
Under-Secretaries (Directing Actuaries), L. V. Martin; G. G. Newton; C. M. Stewart. £12,410
Principal Actuaries, C. L. Connon; J. L. Field; R. T. Foster; R. C. Gilder; D. H. Loades; J. R. Watts
£9,060 to £11,410
Actuaries, D. G. Ballantine; A. H. Gould; C. A. Harris; A. P. Pavelin; M. A. Pickford; D. F. Renn. .... £7,560 to £9,760

THE GOVERNMENT CHEMIST
See under DEPARTMENT OF TRADE AND INDUSTRY

GOVERNMENT HOSPITALITY FUND
2 Carlton Gardens, S.W.1
[01-214-6000]
Instituted in 1908 for the purpose of organizing official hospitality on a regular basis, with a view to the promotion of international goodwill.
Minister in Charge, C. R. Morris, M.P.
Secretary, W. J. M. Paterson, C.M.G.

GOVERNMENT SOCIAL SURVEY DEPARTMENT
See OFFICE OF POPULATION CENSUSES AND SURVEYS.

DEPARTMENT OF HEALTH AND SOCIAL SECURITY
Alexander Fleming House, Elephant and Castle, S.E.1
[01-407-5522]

The Department of Health and Social Security was created on November 1, 1968, from the Ministry of Health and Ministry of Social Security. The new Department performs the functions of the two former Ministries.

The Department is responsible for the administration of the National Health Service in England and for the personal social services run by local authorities in England for children, the elderly, infirm, handicapped and other persons in need. It has functions relating to food hygiene and welfare foods. The Department is also concerned with the medical and surgical treatment of war pensioners in England, the Channel Isles, Isle of Man or living in the Irish Republic, and is responsible for the ambulance and first aid services in emergency, under the Civil Defence Act, 1948. The Department represents the United Kingdom on the World Health Organization of the United Nations. Responsibility for the administration of the Health Services in Wales was transferred to the Welsh Office on April 1, 1969. The Department is responsible for the social security services in England, Scotland and Wales. These services comprise schemes for war pensions, national insurance, family allowances and supplementary benefits. Within the Department, the Supplementary Benefits Commission is responsible, subject to regulations made by the Secretary of State for Social Services, for guiding the scheme of supplementary benefits.
Secretary of State for Social Services, THE RT. HON. MRS. BARBARA ANNE CASTLE, M.P. £13,000
Private Secretary, N. R. Warner
£8,650 to £11,000

Assistant Private Secretaries, T. F. Crawley; Miss K. Higgs.
Parliamentary Private Secretary, J. Ashley, M.P.
Ministers of State, THE RT. HON. BRIAN KEVIN O'MALLEY, M.P. (*Social Security*); DAVID ANTHONY LLEWELLYN OWEN, M.P. (*Health*)......£7,500
Parliamentary Under Secretaries of State, M. H. Meacher, M.P. (*Social Security*); A. Morris, M.P. (*Disablement*).
Chairman, Supplementary Benefits Commission, Prof. D. V. Donnison.....................£7,180
Deputy Chairman, Mrs. C. M. Carmichael..£2,000
Members, K. J. Griffin, O.B.E.; S. C. Hamburger, C.B.E.; Prof. D. C. Marsh; Mrs. B. N. Rodgers; M. R. F. Simson, O.B.E.
Permanent Secretary, Sir Patrick Nairne, K.C.B., M.C.
£18,675

Private Secretary, W. Healey.
Second Permanent Secretary, L. Errington, C.B.
£17,175
Private Secretary, G. A. Points.
Deputy Secretaries, J. A. Atkinson, D.F.C.; C. L. Bourton; A. J. Collier; M. M. V. Custance, C.B.; R. Gedling, C.B.; N. Jordan-Moss, C.B., C.M.G.; G. B. Otton.......................£14,000
Chief Medical Officer, Sir Henry Yellowlees, K.C.B.
£17,175
Librarian, Miss A. M. C. Kahn..£5,680 to £7,650
Establishment and Personnel Division I
Director of Establishments and Personnel (Departmental)
Under Secretary, R. S. Swift...........£12,000
Assistant Secretaries, Miss J. A. Bates; H. T. Elsworth; R. Graham, D.S.O
£8,650 to £11,000
Establishment and Personnel Division II
Director of Establishments and Personnel (Headquarters)
Under Secretary, R. S. Matthews......£12,000
Assistant Secretaries, G. A. Hart; E. L. Wallis
£8,650 to £11,000
Regional Directorate
Under Secretary, E. L. Trew...........£12,000
Assistant Secretaries, E. Caines; J. H. C. Nightingall; E. T. Randall; R. Toulmin..£8,650 to £11,000
Insurance Division L
Under Secretary, A. J. G. Crocker, C.B.....£12,000
Assistant Secretaries, Mrs. A. E. Bowtell; D. W. Polley; D. C. Ward.........£8,650 to £11,000
Statistics and Research Division
Director of Statistics and Research, W. Rudoe, C.B.
£12,000
Assistant Secretary, M. E. H. Platt
£8,650 to £11,000
Chief Statisticians, J. B. Dearman; K. M. Francis, O.B.E.; D. S. S. Hutton, O.B.E.; J. A. Rowntree; F. E. Whitehead...........£8,650 to £11,000
International Relations Division
Under Secretary, F. B. Hindmarsh........£12,000
Assistant Secretaries, A. L. Parrott; L. G. Refell; D. White.................£8,650 to £11,000
Information Division
Director of Information, A. P. G. Brown...£10,950
Deputy Directors and Chief Information Officers, J. M. Bolitho; I. M. Gillis.........£7,750 to £11,000
Economic Advisers Office
Chief Economic Adviser, Prof. J. L. Nicholson
£12,000
Senior Economic Advisers, G. J. Mungeam; J. D. Pole; R. Van Slooten...........£8,650 to £11,000
Solicitors Division
Solicitor, M. W. M. Osmond...........£14,000
Principal Assistant Solicitors, H. Knorpel; R. F. N. Thoyts; R. N. Williams...........£12,000
Office of the Chief Insurance Officer
Chief Insurance Officer, J. C. Hobbs
£8,650 to £11,000
Deputy Chief Insurance Officer, E. F. Hannam
£7,750 to £9,350
Insurance Division A
Under Secretary, R. Windsor, C.B.....£12,000
Assistant Secretaries, F. K. Forrester, M.B.E.; I. G. Gilbert; T. C. Naylor......£8,650 to £11,000

Insurance Division B
Under Secretary, C. M. Regan..........£12,000
Assistant Secretaries, E. D. McGinnis; H. S. McPherson; R. D. F. Whitelaw..£8,650 to £11,000
Insurance Division C
Under Secretary, S. B. Kibbey..........£12,000
Assistant Secretaries, T. A. Howell; J. D. H. Long; J. M. Nicholson; M. J. A. Partridge
£8,650 to £11,000
Insurance Division D
Under Secretary, P. R. Oglesby..........£12,000
Assistant Secretary, B. J. Ellis...£8,650 to £11,000
Insurance Division K
Under Secretary, E. W. Whittemore, M.M..£12,000
Assistant Secretaries, R. Dronfield; T. S. Heppell
£8,650 to £11,000

Registrar of Non-Participating Employments
Registrar, J. D. Hiscocks........£5,680 to £7,450
Deputy Registrar, H. J. Childs...£4,900 to £5,900
Supplementary Benefits—Division 1
Under Secretary, T. C. Stephens.........£12,000
Assistant Secretaries, Miss J. I. Barnes; A. C. Palmer
£8,650 to £11,000
Supplementary Benefits—Division II
Under Secretary, H. Archer, D.F.C........£12,000
Assistant Secretaries, J. S. Campbell-Dick; G. W. Woodman.................£8,650 to £11,000
Accountant General (Finance Division)
[Social Security]
Accountant General (Social Security), D. Overend, C.B...........................£12,000
Assistant Secretaries, B. Bridges; L. J. Hayward; J. L. Oxlade; J. H. Ward........£8,650 to £11,000
Accountant General Division [Health]
Under Secretary for Finance and Accountant General (Health), R. G. Radford..............£12,000
Assistant Secretaries, Mrs. G. T. Banks; S. Bayfield; B. H. Betts; H. W. Seabourn; K. A. Sidford; C. G. Taylor..............£8,650 to £11,000
Medical Divisions (Health)
Deputy Chief Medical Officers, H. M. Archibald, M.B.E.; F. D. Beddard, C.B.; J. J. A. Reid, C.B.; R. M. Shaw, C.B....................£14,000
Senior Principal Medical Officers, D. H. D. Burbidge, O.B.E.; D.A.Cahal; T.E.A.Carr; F.A.Fairweather; Gillian Ford; T. J. Geffen; J. E. McA. Glancy; A. B. Harrington; E. L. Harris; J. L. Kilgour; Elizabeth C. Shore; Esther E. Simpson; J. M. G. Wilson.......................£12,000
Consultant Advisor, Prof. I. D. P. Wootton.
Chief Scientific Officer, J. C. A. Raison.
Principal Medical Officers, J. Brothwood; P. S. Elias; N. J. B. Evans; J. A. Holgate; J. L. Hunt; W. H. Inman; W. Lees, C.B.E.; A. E. Martin; D. S. McKenzie; Eileen M. Ring; A. T. Roden; W. Wintersgill; D. R. G. Wynne Griffith..£10,240

N.H.S. PERSONNEL DIVISIONS
Division P1
Under Secretary, T. E. Nodder..........£12,000
Assistant Secretaries, Miss J. M. Firth; W. F. Lake; D. de Peyer; W. O. Roberts; S. Smith
£8,650 to £11,000
Division P2
Under Secretary, P. G. Perry..........£12,000
Assistant Secretaries, G. P. Goodale; V. J. Harley; A. J. Merifield; B. M. Street..£8,650 to £11,000
Division P3
Under Secretary, R. B. Hodgetts........£12,000
Assistant Secretaries, J. B. Brown; R. B. Mayoh; Mrs. M. A. J. Pearson; S. I. Smith; Miss G. M. Walker.................£8,650 to £11,000
Division P4
Under Secretary, E. B. S. Alton, M.B.E., M.C.£12,000

Assistant Secretaries, M. W. Draper; W. F. Farrant;
Miss I. M. James, O.B.E......£8,650 to £11,000

Supply Division
Controller of Supply, F. J. Aldridge.......£12,000
Directors of Supply, S. M. Davies, C.M.G.; N. Hollens; G. E. John; W. Scott-Moncrieff
£8,650 to £11,000
Director of Scientific and Technical Services, P. M. Harms.

Socially Handicapped Division
Under Secretary, J. T. Woodlock.........£12,000
Assistant Secretaries, G. M. Bebb; R. Cattran; Mrs. P. A. Lee; Mrs. V. J. M. Poole
£8,650 to £11,000

Mental Health Division
Under Secretary, K. Moyes.............£12,000
Assistant Secretaries, J. R. Brough; C. Emerson; P. H. Williamson.........£8,650 to £11,000

Regional and Planning Division I
Under Secretary, J. C. C. Smith.........£12,000
Assistant Secretaries, C. Graham; F. D. K. Williams; J. Wormald...............£8,650 to £11,000

Regional and Planning Division 2
Under Secretary, R. Beltram............£12,000
Assistant Secretaries, R. L. Briggs; L. Devine; J. Hallowell................£8,650 to £11,000

Central Planning and Services Division
Under Secretary (vacant)...............£12,000
Assistant Secretaries, N. E. Clarke; T. R. H. Luce; A. G. MacDonald.........£8,650 to £11,000

Computers and Research Division
Under Secretary, J. P. Cashman.........£12,000
Assistant Secretaries, J. W. E. Clutterbuck; W. T. Hartland; B. R. Rayner....£8,650 to £11,000

Children's Division
Under Secretary, J. W. Stacpoole.........£12,000
Assistant Secretaries, A. C. Clarke; P. V. Foster; A. E. Taggart............£8,650 to £11,000

Local Authority—Social Services Division 2
Under Secretary, G. B. Hulme...........£12,000
Assistant Secretaries, R. A. Birch; R. S. King
£8,650 to £11,000

Social Work Service
Director of Social Work Service, Miss J. D. Cooper, C.B..................£12,000
Deputy Director of Social Work Service, Miss A. M. Sheridan.................£9,860
Assistant Directors, Mrs. B. J. Kahan; Mrs. D. Ottley
£6,700 to £8,850
Principal Social Work Service Officers, Miss I. Bergman; Miss G. Browne-Williamson; Miss P. E. Harwood; Miss A. L. Howard; Miss P. P. Thayer; Miss J. M. Vann....£6,000 to £7,750

Medicines and Environmental Health Division
Under Secretary, A. G. Beard...........£12,000
Assistant Secretaries, J. B. Sharp; R. E. Tringham; R. F. Tyas................£8,650 to £11,000

Superannuation Division
Under Secretary, A. G. Beard...........£12,000
Assistant Secretary, K. Shuttleworth
£8,650 to £11,000

Health Service—Division 1
Under Secretary, N. M. Hale...........£12,000
Assistant Secretaries, P. J. Fletcher; E. L. Mayston; C. H. Wilson.............£8,650 to £11,000

Health Service—Division 2
Under Secretary, L. H. Brandes.........£12,000
Assistant Secretaries, R. P. S. Hughes; N. Illingworth; E. L. McMillan, C.B.E., A.F.C.
£8,650 to £11,000

Health Service—Division 3
Under Secretary, K. J. Moyes, M.B.E......£12,000

Assistant Secretary, J. B. Cornish.£8,650 to £11,000

Hospital Building Division
Under Secretary, D. Somerville, C.B......£12,000
Assistant Secretaries, W. J. Littlewood; M. Nelson; W. D. Paget; L. A. R. Smith; E. L. Wallis
£8,650 to £11,000

Catering and Dietetics Branch
Chief Officer on Catering and Dietetics, A. R. Horton
£7,074 to £8,250
Deputy Chief Officer, Mrs. J. W. Ryalls
£5,600 to £6,981

Domestic Services Management Branch
Chief Officer, I. W. Little, M.B.E. £7,750 to £9,350

Architectural Division
Chief Architect, R. H. Goodman.........£12,000
Assistant Chief Architects, M. J. Bench; C. Davies; M. A. Meager......................£11,000

Surveying Division
Chief Surveyor, B. E. Drake.
Assistant Chief Surveyors, R. T. V. Amery; A. P. R. Pell-Hiley.........................£11,000
Superintending Surveyors, N. G. M. Barton; W. V. F. Buckle; K. W. Hudson; D. A. Turner.

Engineering Division
Chief Engineer, J. Bolton...............£12,000
Assistant Chief Engineers, M. Drury, O.B.E.; G. S. Gillard; R. Manser; T. R. Nicholls.....£11,000

Medical Division (Social Security)
Chief Medical Adviser, Dr. J. A. G. Carmichael.
Deputy Chief Medical Adviser, G. O. Mayne.
Principal Medical Officers, R. T. Fletcher, M.B.E.; M. R. Hayes; R. M. McGowan; E. G. Wright, O.B.E.

Dental Division
Chief Dental Officer, G. D. Gibb.........£12,000
Deputy Chief Dental Officer, G. B. Roberts.
Senior Dental Officers, H. A. Dixey; I. C. S. Fraser; H. M. Hughes; V. D. Lees; R. Middleton; W. N. McNiven; J. Rodgers, D.F.M.; J. H. Whittle.

Nursing Division
Chief Nursing Officer, Miss P. M. Friend, C.B.E.
£12,000
Deputy Chief Nursing Officer, Miss A. M. Lamb; O.B.E.; Miss D. M. White, O.B.E.; Miss J. G. Whitehead........................£9,818

Pharmaceutical Division
Chief Pharmacist, T. D. Whittet.......£10,950
Deputy Chief Pharmacists, E. Fawcitt, I.S.O.; A. G. Fishburn...........£8,650 to £9,798
Pharmacists, Superintending Grade, R. Baker; S. F. Hall.................£8,650 to £9,798
Pharmacists, Senior Grade, J. M. Calderwood; H. Glynn; W. P. Jones; D. S. Nunn; J. H. Oakley; W. G. W. Price; G. Sykes; J. A. Wandless.............£6,280 to £7,450
Senior Principal Scientific Officers, C. A. Johnson; G. R. Kitteringham.........£8,650 to £9,798

Blackpool Central Office
Controller, K. Shuttleworth....£8,650 to £11,000

Newcastle upon Tyne Central Office
Controller, C. K. Whitaker..............£12,000

Scotland
Argyll House, 3 Lady Lawson Street, Edinburgh
Controller, J. C. Moy £11,670

Wales
Government Buildings, Gabalfa, Cardiff.
Controller, R. K. Meatyard....£8,650 to £11,000

Regional Organisation [England]
Northern, Arden House, Regent Farm Road, Gosforth, Newcastle upon Tyne. *Regional Controller,* S. Watson, D.F.C.

Yorkshire and Humberside, Government Buildings, Otley Road, Lawnswood, Leeds. *Regional Controller,* J. M. Tones.

East Midlands and East Anglia, Block 1, Government Buildings, Chalfont Drive, Nottingham. *Regional Controller,* R. A. E. Tow.

London North, Olympic House, Olympic Way, Wembley, Middx. *Regional Controller,* S. H. Bate.

London South, Sutherland House, 29–37 Brighton Road, Sutton, Surrey. *Regional Controller,* B. C. James.

London West, Grosvenor House, Basing View, Basingstoke, Hants. *Regional Controller,* L. C. H. Stadames.

South Western, Government Buildings, Flowers Hill, Bristol. *Regional Controller,* J. C. Lewis.

West Midlands, Cumberland House, 200 Broad Street, Birmingham 15. *Regional Controller,* W. R. Denaro, C.B.E.

North Western (Manchester), Albert Bridge House East, Bridge Street, Manchester. *Regional Controller,* G. Collins.

North Western (Merseyside), St. Martin's House, Stanley Precinct, Bootle. *Regional Controller,* F. Hill, O.B.E.

NATIONAL INSURANCE ADVISORY COMMITTEE
10 John Adam Street, W.C.2
[01-217-4109]

The National Insurance Advisory Committee is constituted under the Social Security Act 1975 to give advice and assistance to the Secretary of State in connection with the discharge of his (or her) functions under the Act, and to perform any other duties allotted to it under the Act. These other duties include the consideration of preliminary drafts of regulations to be made under the Social Security Act, and of representations received thereon. When the regulations are laid before Parliament, the Committee's Report on the preliminary draft is laid with them, together with a statement by the Secretary of State showing what amendments to the preliminary draft have been made, what effect has been given to the Committee's recommendations, and, if effect has not been given to any recommendation, the reasons for not adopting it. The Secretary of State may also refer to the Committee for consideration and advice any questions relating to the operation of the Act (including questions as to the advisability of amending it).

Chairman, Prof. D. S. Lees.

Members, R. J. Donaldson, O.B.E.; Prof. J. A. Faris; G. Harry; P. R. A. Jacques; P. M. Madders; H. K. Mitchell; Miss A. M. Patrick.

Secretary, K. Edwards.

INDUSTRIAL INJURIES ADVISORY COUNCIL
Keysign House, 421–429 Oxford Street, W.1.
[01-499-3400]

The Industrial Injuries Advisory Council is a statutory body under the Social Security Act, 1975, which considers and advises the Secretary of State for Social Services on Regulations and other questions, as the Secretary of State thinks fit, relating to industrial injuries benefit or its administration.

Chairman, Prof. D. S. Lees.

Members, Prof. T. Anderson, C.B.E.; Dr. P. L. Bidstrup; R. J. Donaldson O.B.E.; R. G. Hitchcock; P. R. A. Jacques; Prof. C. R. Lowe; J. L. I. McQuitty, Q.C.; T. Parry, O.B.E.; Mrs. C. M. Patterson, O.B.E.; D. M. Rea; I. G. Reid; S. J. Stanbrook; Dr. Alice M. Stewart; Dr. J. Watkins-Pitchford, C.B.

Secretary, D. M. Wooley.

NATIONAL INSURANCE AND INDUSTRIAL INJURIES JOINT AUTHORITIES
10 John Adam Street, W.C.2
[01-217-3000]

Members, The Secretary of State for Social Services; the Minister of Health and Social Services for Northern Ireland.

Deputies for the Secretary of State for Social Services, Sir Patrick Nairne, K.C.B., M.C., F. B. Hindmarsh; for the Minister of Health and Social Services for Northern Ireland, N. Dugdale; C. G. Oakes.

Joint Financial Advisers, E. A. Johnston; D. Overend, C.B.; D. W. Lowry.

Secretary, D. S. Beaumont.

PNEUMOCONIOSIS, BYSSINOSIS AND MISCELLANEOUS DISEASES BENEFIT SCHEME (1966) AND WORKMEN'S COMPENSATION (SUPPLEMENTATION) SCHEME (1966)
Norcross, Blackpool, Lancs.
[Blackpool: 52311]

Chairman, D. M. Campbell, Q.C.

Deputy Chairman, Sir Lionel Brett.

Members, D. W. Boydell; A. J. Collins; A. J. Lewis, G. H. Lowthian, C.B.E.; W. Malt; T. C. Naylor.

Secretary, H. V. Hutson.

OFFICE OF THE CHIEF INSURANCE OFFICER FOR NATIONAL INSURANCE
Penderel House, 287 High Holborn, W.C.1
[01-242-9020]

Chief Insurance Officer, J. C. Hobbs.

Deputy Chief Insurance Officer, E. F. Hannam.

OFFICE OF THE REGISTRAR OF NON-PARTICIPATING EMPLOYMENTS
Apex Tower, High Street,
New Malden, Surrey
[01-942-8949]

Registrar, J. D. Hiscocks.

Deputy Registrar, H. J. Childs.

NATIONAL HEALTH SERVICE REGIONAL HOSPITAL BOARDS

England and Wales are divided into 15 hospital regions, each with its own Hospital Board which administers the hospital and specialist services in the area. The Hospital Boards do not, however, administer Teaching Hospitals, which have their own Boards of Governors.

The Chairmen and members of Hospital Boards and Boards of Governors are appointed by the Secretary of State in accordance with the third schedule to the National Health Service Act, 1946.

As from April 1, 1974, the Regional Hospital Boards will cease to exist and their functions will be taken over by new health authorities set up under the National Health Service Reorganization Act, 1973.

Areas

Northern, Benfield Road, Walker Gate, Newcastle upon Tyne 6. *Chairman,* Col. W. A. Lee, O.B.E., T.D. *Secretary,* R. Dobbin, O.B.E.

Yorkshire, Park Parade, Harrogate, Yorks. *Chairman,* Sir Leslie Laycock, C.B.E. *Secretary,* W. Bowring.

Trent, Fulwood House, Old Fulwood Road, Sheffield, 10. *Chairman,* S. P. King, O.B.E. *Secretary,* W. M. Naylor.

East Anglia, Union Lane, Chesterton, Cambridge. *Chairman,* Sir Stephen Lycett Green, Bt., C.B.E. *Secretary,* T. W. Kidman.

North West Thames, 40 Eastbourne Terrace, W.2. *Chairman,* Sir Maurice Hackett, O.B.E. *Secretary,* G. H. Weston.

North East Thames, 40 Eastbourne Terrace, W.2. *Chairman,* Sir Graham Rowlandson, M.B.E. *Secretary,* L. C. Phipps, O.B.E.

South East Thames, Randolph House, 46–48 Wellesley Road, Croydon. *Chairman,* J. C. Donne. *Secretary,* H. N. Lamb.

South West Thames, 40 Eastbourne Terrace, W.2. *Chairman,* Sir Desmond Bonham-Carter, T.D. *Secretary,* M. W. Southern.

Oxford, Old Road, Headington, Oxford. *Chairman,* D. Woodrow. *Secretary,* D. Norton.

South Western, 27 Tyndalls Park Road, Bristol 8. *Chairman,* Sir John English, M.B.E. *Secretary,* H. W. White, O.B.E.

West Midlands, Arthur Thomson House, 146–150. Hagley Road, Birmingham 16. *Chairman,* D. A. Perris, M.B.E. *Secretary,* F. S. Adams, O.B.E.

North Western, Gateway House, Piccadilly South, Manchester 1. *Chairman,* T. Hourigan, C.B.E. *Secretary,* E. Pethybridge.

Mersey, Wilberforce House, The Strand, Liverpool 2. *Chairman,* Sir David Solomon, M.B.E. *Secretary,* J. D. Shepherd.

Wessex, Highcroft, Romsey Road, Winchester, Hants. *Chairman,* Col. Sir Joseph Weld, O.B.E., T.D. *Secretary,* J. T. Shaw.

SCOTTISH HOME AND HEALTH DEPARTMENT
and
NATIONAL HEALTH SERVICE, SCOTLAND
See Scottish Office

HERRING INDUSTRY BOARD
10 Young Street, Edinburgh 2
[031-225-2515]

Chairman and Chief Executive, W. J. Lyon Dean, O.B.E. *(part-time)* £5,575 *in respect of this and other appointments in White Fish Authority.*

Members, E. H. M. Clutterbuck; Admiral Sir Deric Holland-Martin, G.C.B., D.S.O., D.S.C. *(part-time)* £1,000

HIGHLANDS AND ISLANDS DEVELOPMENT BOARD
Bridge House, Bank Street, Inverness.

The Board, a grant-aided body, responsible to the Secretary of State for Scotland, has two broad objectives. These are (1) to assist the people of the Highlands and Islands to improve their economic and social conditions; (2) to enable the Highlands and Islands to play a more effective part in the economic and social development of the nation. To this end the Board will concert, promote, assist or undertake measures for the economic and social development of the seven Highland counties. *Secretary,* R. A. Fasken.

HISTORIC BUILDINGS COUNCILS

Under the *Historic Buildings and Ancient Monuments Act,* 1953, as since amended, these councils advise the Secretary of State for the Environment and the Secretaries of State for Scotland and Wales on the exercise of the powers contained in the Act to make grants and loans towards the repair or maintenance of buildings of outstanding historic or architectural interest, their contents and adjoining land, and, where necessary, to acquire such buildings or to assist the National Trusts or local authorities to acquire them.

Also under the *Town and Country Planning (Amendment) Act* 1972, to advise the Secretaries of State on their powers to make grants or loans towards the cost incurred in the promotion, preservation or enhancement of the character or appearance of outstanding conservation areas. In 1975–76 £2,250,000 is available for repair grants in England, £107,500 in Wales and £225,000 in Scotland. In addition, the amounts available for conservation grants are £1,250,000 in England, £50,000 in Wales and £100,000 in Scotland, where there is a further allocation of £100,000 for the Edinburgh New Town Conservation Area.

England
25 Savile Row, W.1

Chairman, Mrs. Jennifer Jenkins.

Members, J. H. Benson, F.R.I.B.A.; J. M. Brandon-Jones; Miss Elizabeth Chesterton; H. M. Colvin, C.B.E., F.B.A.; R. G. Cooke, M.P.; J. Cornforth; Dr. J. M. Crook; T. E. N. Driberg; The Duke of Grafton, F.S.A.; The Lord Holford, R.A., F.R.I.B.A.; E. Hollamby, O.B.E., F.R.I.B.A.; D. W. Insall, F.R.I.B.A.; J. Parker, C.B.E., M.P.; Sir Nikolaus Pevsner, C.B.E., Ph.D., F.B.A., F.S.A.; J. Smith, C.B.E.; Miss Dorothy Stroud, M.B.E.; Sir John Summerson, C.B.E., F.S.A., F.B.A.; A. A. Wood.

Secretary, I. M. Glennie.

Wales
Welsh Office, St. David's House, Wood Street, Cardiff

Chairman, Maj. H. J. Lloyd-Johnes, O.B.E., T.D., F.S.A.

Members, The Marquess of Anglesey, F.S.A.; W. H. Edwards; J. Eynon, F.R.I.B.A., F.S.A.; J. D. K. Lloyd, O.B.E., F.S.A.; Prof. Glanmor Williams, D.Litt.; The Earl Lloyd George of Dwyfor.

Secretary, W. G. M. Jones.

Scotland
Argyle House, Edinburgh.

Chairman, The Lord Stratheden and Campbell, C.B.E.

Members, Rt. Hon. Betty Harvie Anderson, O.B.E., T.D., M.P.; R. G. Cant; The Lady Mary Cumming, O.B.E.; J. D. Dunbar Nasmith; J. F. A. Gibson, T.D.; W. A. P. Jack, F.R.I.B.A.; C. E. Jauncey, Q.C.; J. Liddell, M.B.E.; Rt. Hon. A. Woodburn.

Secretary, H. J. Graham.

HISTORICAL MANUSCRIPTS COMMISSION
See Record Office

ROYAL COMMISSION ON HISTORICAL MONUMENTS [ENGLAND]
Fortress House, 23 Savile Row, W.1
[01-734-6010]

The Royal Commission on Historical Monuments (England) was appointed in 1908 to survey and publish in inventory form an account of every building, earthwork or stone construction up to the year 1714. A new Royal Warrant in 1943 abolished the date limit and the Commissioners then set themselves a limit of 1850, but with discretion to record later buildings of outstanding significance The Commission has published up to present date inventories covering in whole or in part eleven counties, four cities, Roman York and Roman London. It is a purely recording body and though the Commissioners may recommend that certain. structures should be preserved, they have no power to implement their recommendations. The Commission is also responsible for the direction of the National Monuments Record, created in 1964, which includest he National Buildings Record begun in 1941, of which the Commissioners are the managing trustees.

Chairman, The Lord Adeane, P.C., G.C.B., G.C.V.O.

Commissioners, C. A. Ralegh Radford, D.Litt., F.B.A., F.S.A.; H. M. Colvin, C.B.E., F.S.A.; A. J. Taylor, C.B.E., F.S.A.; Prof. W. F. Grimes, C.B.E., D.Litt., F.S.A.; Prof. S. S. Frere, F.S.A.; Prof. M. W. Barley, F.S.A.; Prof. R. J. C. Atkinson, F.S.A.; Prof. H. C. Darby, O.B.E., Litt.D., F.B.A.; Sir John Betjeman, C.B.E.; Prof. G. Zarnecki, C.B.E., F.B.A., F.S.A.; H. M. Taylor, C.B.E., T.D., F.S.A.; Prof. J. K. S. St. Joseph, O.B.E., Ph.D., F.S.A.; A. R. Dufty, C.B.E., F.S.A.; P. Ashbee, F.S.A., and the Lords Lieutenant of the counties at the time of survey.

Secretary, R. W. McDowall, O.B.E., F.S.A.

ROYAL COMMISSION ON ANCIENT AND HISTORICAL MONUMENTS IN WALES
Edleston House, Queens Road, Aberystwyth
[Aberystwyth: 4381]

The Commission was appointed in 1908 to make an inventory of the Ancient and Historical Monuments in Wales and Monmouthshire. The Commission now includes the National Monuments Record for Wales.

Chairman, Prof. W. F. Grimes, C.B.E., F.B.A., F.S.A.
Commissioners, Prof. R. J. C. Atkinson, F.S.A.; Prof. I. Ll. Foster, F.S.A.; Prof. E. M. Jope, F.S.A.; D. M. Rees, O.B.E., F.S.A.; H. N. Savory, D.Phil., F.S.A.; A. J. Taylor, C.B.E., F.S.A.; Prof. Dewi-Prys Thomas; Prof. Glanmor Williams, Litt. D.; Prof. J. G. Williams; R. B. Wood-Jones, D.Phil., F.S.A.
Secretary, P. Smith, F.S.A.

ROYAL COMMISSION ON ANCIENT AND HISTORICAL MONUMENTS OF SCOTLAND

54 Melville Street, Edinburgh 3
[031-225-5994]

The Commission was appointed in 1908 to make an inventory of the Ancient and Historical Monuments of Scotland from the earliest times to 1707, and to specify those that seem most worthy of preservation. The terms of reference were extended by Royal Warrant dated Jan. 1, 1948, to cover the period since 1707 at the Commissioners' discretion. The National Monument Records of Scotland, a branch of the Commission housed in the same premises, contains an extensive collection of photographs, drawings and printed books relating to Scottish architecture, which may be consulted by members of the public.
Chairman, The Earl of Wemyss and March, K.T.
Commissioners, Prof. S. Piggott, C.B.E., F.B.A., F.S.A., F.R.S.E.; Prof. K. H. Jackson, F.B.A.; Prof. G. Donaldson, Ph.D.; P. J. Nuttgens, Ph.D., R.I.B.A.; Prof. A. A. M. Duncan; J. D. Dunbar-Nasmith, R.I.B.A.; Prof. Rosemary Cramp, F.S.A., F.S.A.Scot.
Secretary, K. A. Steer, Ph.D., F.S.A., F.R.S.E.

ANCIENT MONUMENTS BOARDS
England

Fortress House, 23 Savile Row, W.1.
Chairman, Sir Edward, Muir, K.C.B., F.S.A.
Members, Prof. E. Birley, M.B.E., F.B.A., F.S.A.; R. L. S. Bruce-Mitford, F.S.A.; Prof. J. G. D. Clark, C.B.E., Sc.D., Ph.D., F.B.A., F.S.A.; Prof. Rosemary Cramp, F.S.A., F.S.A.Scot.; B. M. Feilden, O.B.E., F.R.I.B.A., F.S.A.; Sir David Follett, Ph.D.; Prof. S. S. Frere, F.B.A., F.S.A.; B. J. Greenhill, C.M.G., F.S.A.; Prof. W. F. Grimes, C.B.E., D.Litt., F.S.A.; R. W. McDowall, O.B.E., F.S.A.; J. N. L. Myres, C.B.E., F.B.A., P.P.S.A.; Prof. A. C. Renfrew, F.S.A., F.S.A.Scot.; Prof. J. K. S. St. Joseph, O.B.E., Ph.D., F.S.A.; Marshall Sisson, C.V.O., C.B.E., R.A., F.R.I.B.A., F.S.A.; A. J. Taylor, C.B.E., F.B.A., P.S.A.
Secretary, J. S. M. Vinter, M.C.

Wales

Government Buildings, St. Agnes Road, Gabalfa, Cardiff
Chairman, J. D. K. Lloyd, O.B.E., F.S.A.
Members, Miss I. E. Anthony, Ph.D., F.S.A.; Prof. R. J. C. Atkinson, F.S.A.; Prof. W. F. Grimes, C.B.E., D.Litt., F.S.A.; C. N. Johns, F.S.A.; E. D. Jones, F.S.A., F.S.A.; L. Jones; Mrs. H. Ramage; D. M. Rees, O.B.E., F.S.A.; H. N. Savory, D.Phil., F.S.A.; P. Smith, F.S.A.; A. J. Taylor, C.B.E., F.S.A.

Scotland

Argyle House, Edinburgh 3
Chairman, Sir Alan Hume, C.B.
Members, Prof. L. Alcock, F.S.A., F.S.A.Scot.; J. D. Dunbar-Nasmith; G. Jobey, D.S.O., F.S.A.; Prof. S. G. E. Lythe, F.S.A.Scot.; B. R. S. Megaw, F.R.S.E., F.S.A., F.S.A.Scot.; R. M. Orr; Prof. Anne S. Robertson, D.Litt., F.S.A., F.S.A.Scot.; G. G. Simpson, Ph.D., F.S.A., F.S.A.Scot.; K. A. Steer, Ph.D., F.R.S.E., F.S.A. F.S.A.Scot.; R. B. K. Stevenson, F.S.A., F.S.A.Scot.; Prof. E. L. G. Stones, Ph.D., F.S.A.; A. S. Taylor, C.B.E., D.Litt., F.B.A., P.S.A.
Secretary, A. M. Thomson.

HOME OFFICE
Whitehall, S.W.1
[01-213-3000]

The Home Office deals with such internal affairs in England and Wales as are not assigned to other Departments. The Home Secretary is the channel of communication between the Crown and the subjects of the realm, and between the U.K. Government and the Governments of the Channel Islands and the Isle of Man. He exercises certain prerogative powers of the Crown of which the most important are the prerogative of mercy and the maintenance of the Queen's Peace. He is also concerned with the administration of justice; criminal law; the treatment of offenders; probation; the prison service; public morals and safety; the police, fire and civil defence services; immigration and nationality; community relations and community and urban programmes; legislative and constitutional aspects of broadcasting; regulation of the use of radio. Other subjects dealt with include firearms, drugs, poisons, vivisection, liquor licensing, cremations and burials, betting and gaming, addresses and petitions to the Queen and ceremonial and formal business connected with honours.

Secretary of State for the Home Department, THE RT. HON. ROY JENKINS, M.P. £13,000
  Private Secretary, G. H. Phillips.
  Assistant Private Secretaries, C. Farrington; W. J. A. Innes.
  Parliamentary Private Secretary, I. W. Wrigglesworth, M.P.
  Parliamentary Clerk, S. W. Bennett.
Ministers of State, ALEXANDER LYON, M.P. £7,500; THE LORD HARRIS OF GREENWICH.
Parliamentary Under-Secretary of State, Dr. Shirley Summerskill, M.P. £5,500
  Correspondence Clerk, G. E. Dunkley (SEO)
    £4,900 to £5,900
Permanent Under Secretary of State, Sir Arthur Peterson,, K.C.B., M.V.O. . . . £17,175 to £20,175
Deputy Under Secretaries of State, B. C. Cubbon, C.B.; N. F. Cairncross, C.B.; E. D. Wright, C.B. (*Director-General of the Prison Service*); R. T. Armstrong, C.B., C.V.O.; Dr. O. Simpson . . . £14,000
Chief Medical Officer, Sir Henry Yellowlees, K.C.B.

Broadcasting Department
Waterloo Bridge, House, Waterloo Road, S.E.1
[01-275-3000]
Assistant Under-Secretary of State, J. Dromgoole
    £12,000
Assistant Secretaries, A. O. Carter; N. M. Johnson
    £8,650 to £11,000
Principals, J. P. Jarvis; Miss S. Muir; R. W. Story, D.F.C.; Mrs. M. A. G. Veal, C. J. Walters
    £5,680 to £7,450
Senior Executive Officers, E. T. Dole; Mrs. J. W. Harvey . . . . £4,900 to £5,900

Community Programmes Department
Horseferry House, Dean Ryle Street, S.W.1
[01-211-3000]
Assistant Under-Secretary of State, T. A. Critchley
    £12,000
Assistant Secretaries, Miss M. A. Clayton; R. J. Fries; G. P. Renton . . . . £8,650 to £11,000
Principals, P. Done; B. R. Gange; Miss B. M. Latimer; Mrs. D. M. Saldji; G. K. Sandiford; R. R. G. Watts . . . . £5,680 to £7,450
Senior Executive Officer, T. N. Gerrish
    £4,900 to £5,900

Criminal Policy Department
Assistant Under-Secretary of State, M. J. Moriarty
    £12,000
Assistant Secretaries, J. A. Chilcot; Miss E. M. Chadwell; C. J. Train . . . . . . £8,650 to £11,000
Principals, P. E. Bolton; F. Carter; J. C. Davey; J. C. Hindley; Miss K. A. O'Neill, O.B.E.; J. G. Pilling; Q. J. Thomas; D. Roberts; N. R. Varney; Mrs. P. D. White . . . . £5,680 to £7,450
Senior Executive Officer, Mrs. R. M. Mitev
    £4,900 to £5,900

Criminal Justice Department
Assistant Under-Secretary of State, D. H. J. Hilary
    £12,000
Assistant Secretaries, E. R. Cowlyn; R. L. Jones; C. H. Prior . . . . £8,650 to £11,000

Senior Principal, N. F. Law..... £7,750 to £9,350
Principals, B. O. Bubbear; P. C. Edwards; Miss H.
E. Forbes; B. F. Jones; G. T. L. Hubert; F. H.
Keens; A. Marshall; Miss M. Norman; A. R.
Rawsthorne; E. A. Slater; D. B. Staines; A.
Sutton..................... £5,680 to £7,450
Senior Executive Officers, Miss P. L. Boxall; Miss
J. E. Clarke; P. A. Drury; G. Greenall; S. D.
Holdershaw; Mrs. S. Murray; W. F. Whiteing
£4,900 to £5,900

Fire Department
Horseferry House, Dean Ryle Street, S.W.1
[01–211–3000]
Assistant Under-Secretary of State, R. F. D. Shuffrey
£12,000
Assistant Secretaries, J. McIntyre, C.B.E.; H. V. H.
Marks; G. T. Rudd; D. R. Sands
£8,650 to £11,000
Principals, D. R. Dewick; D. S. J. Evans; W. J. A.
Innes; R. O. Lane, D.F.C.; G. T. Newton; D.
Polley; J. G. Quarrell; C. L. Scoble; E. Soden
£5,680 to £7,450
Principal Scientific Officers, P. L. Parsons; Dr. E. F.
Pearson..................... £5,514 to £7,205
Senior Executive Officers, Miss G. V. Cooksley;
N. C. L. Hackney; R. J. Peate; Mrs. B. Sim-
monds; W. H. Simons...... £4,900 to £5,900

Fire Service Inspectorate
Chief Inspector, K. L. Holland, C.B.E...... £11,618
Inspectors (Grade I), C. Bidgood, O.B.E.; A. Bloom-
field; L. O. Clarke, O.B.E.; E. T. Hayward, O.B.E.;
N. F. Richards, M.B.E.; A. H. Warren, O.B.E.;
P. S. Wilson-Dickson, O.B.E.. £8,999 to £9,682
Inspectors (Grade II), S. C. Baker; J. Bingley; W. J.
Carvin; F. W. Harbridge, M.B.E.; P. G. Robin-
son; H. J. Shayle............ £6,749 to £7,262
Engineering Inspector, F. C. A. Shirling, O.B.E.
£6,630 to £7,800
Water Inspector, R. M. Simpson
£5,030 to £6,240

Fire Service Staff College
Wotton House, Abinger Common, Dorking,
Surrey
Commandant, S. F. Crook, O.B.E.
£8,999 to £9,682

Fire Service Technical College
Moreton-in-Marsh, Gloucestershire
Commandant, D. Blacktop, O.B.E.
£8,999 to £9,682
Senior Executive Officer, C. J. Titchener
£4,900 to £5,900

General Department
Assistant Under-Secretary of State, K. P. Witney
£12,000
Assistant Secretaries, Capt. N. F. Carrington, D.S.C.,
R.N.(ret.); J. E. Hayzelden; E. N. Kent; W. J.
Stephens................... £8,650 to £11,000
Principals, M. J. Addison; M. K. Brenchley; Miss M.
D. Cook; J. V. Dance; T. S. Fookes; J. L. God-
dard; E. C. Huggett; D. S. McCutcheon; W.
Middlemass; E. J. Sermon; Miss A. Turner
£5,680 to £7,450
Senior Executive Officers, J. W. Clark; Mrs. Mc-
Farlane; Miss M. V. Wakefield-Richmond; Miss
C. Soret................... £4,900 to £5,900

Immigration and Nationality Department
Lunar House, Wellesley Road, Croydon, Surrey
[01–686–0333]
Assistant Under-Secretary of State, A. J. E. Brennan
£12,000
Assistant Secretaries, A. E. Corben; W. M. Lee; N.
S. Ross; P. L. Taylor....... £8,650 to £11,000
Senior Principals, J. Hamilton; Miss M. E. Millson;
R. M. Whitfield............ £7,750 to £9,350
Principals, S. J. Gregory; J. A. Ingman; J. E. Johnson;
R. A. McDowell; D. G. McMurray; A. Parkin-
son; R. K. Prescott; R. B. Prosser; J. D. Webb;
R. S. Weekes; J. V. Wingfield; M. Youngs
£5,680 to £7,450
Senior Executive Officers, P. D. Brown; Miss G.
Cobbler; W. G. Feakins; E. A. Gray; D. W.

Greenhalgh; B. Hunter; R. W. B. Hurley; R.
B. Ingham; B. J. Jordan; E. J. Kings; Miss B.
Korman; K. L. McDonald; W. R. Mann; Mrs.
N. Needler; K. Osborne; P. M. Pawsey; F. G.
Pegg; R. S. Pepper; A. M. Pickersgill; J. Pitty;
A. R. Ralf; K. E. R. Rogers; Mrs. H. M. Searle;
T. J. Tuffield; D. J. H. Walker; J. L. Ward; D. A.
Wrigley................... £3,756 to £4,542

Immigration Service
Chief Inspector, H. J. G. Richards
£8,650 to £11,000
Deputy Chief Inspectors, R. J. Lemon; R. E. Smith
£7,750 to £9,350
Assistant Chief Inspectors, A. A. Holton; J. A. Lomas;
H. J. Pickering; P. J. Saunders; R. G. Smith;
C. F. Woodiss............. £5,680 to £7,450
Inspectors, F. W. Flemen; C. B. Manchip; A. A.
Stevens................... £5,045 to £5,900

Legal Adviser's Branch
Legal Adviser, Sir Kenneth Jones, C.B.E.... £14,000
Principal Assistant Legal Advisers, P. Harvey; J. D.
Semken, M.C................ £12,000
Assistant Legal Advisers, A. H. Hammond; J.
Nursaw; J. Pakenham-Walsh; Miss B. R. Pugh;
T. H. Williams; H. W. Wollaston
£9,033 to £11,000
Senior Legal Assistants, J. R. O'Meara; T. H.
Williams; A. W. D. Wilson
£6,625 to £8,750

Personnel and Administration
Home Office, Whitehall, S.W.1
[01–213 3000]
Kingsgate House, Victoria Street, S.W.1
[01–828 7722]
Portland House, Stag Place, S.W.1
[01–828 9848]
Tintagel House, Albert Embankment, S.E.1
[01–230 1212]
Tolworth Tower, Surbiton, Surrey
[01–399 5191]
Whittington House, Alfred Place, W.C.1
[01–637 2355]
Deputy Under-Secretary of State (Principal Establish-
ment Officer), B. C. Cubbon, C.B...... £14,000
Assistant Under-Secretaries of State, D. A. Peach
(Principal Finance Officer); D. A. C. Morrison
(Personnel); R. R. Pittam (Organization and
Management Services)........ £12,000
Director of Information Services, D. Grant... £10,950
Assistant Secretaries, J. H. J. Beck; D. E. R. Faulkner;
R. J. P. Hayes; P. A. McIlvenna, M.B.E.; R. W.
Mott; G. P. Pratt; Miss N. Peppard; E. A.
Sedgley; R. W. G. Smith; V. H. Wallis
£8,650 to £11,000
Senior Principals, S. R. Cameron; T. J. Kempton;
B. Morgan; M. G. Thompson; J. R. Troop
£7,750 to £9,350
Senior Economic Adviser, G. J. Wasserman
£8,650 to £11,000
Chief Information Officers, P. L. Marshall; W. J.
Rawles.
Principals, J. A. Atfield; H. H. Bland; K. J. Bradley;
M. A. Christian; D. L. Cole; Miss J. M. F.
Cousins; A. F. Davies; M. E. Dewberry; J. T.
Dungan; R. F. Elliott; B. H. Ford; D. J. Hard-
wick; J. Hay; R. M. Hoare; D. J. Hollis; P. W.
Jamieson; I. D. King; J. D. Lodder; R. Marsden;
L. G. Martin; R. G. Oram; H. G. Pearson; A. G.
Pridmore; J. K. Richards; J. Roy; Mrs. M. R.
Ryan; L. A. Scudder; F. Stewart; C. H. Taylor;
I. R. Thomas; G. W. Waring; F. J. A. Warne; M.
L. Winspear; R.E. Wiscombe. £5,680 to £7,450
Head of Work Study, A. D. Jackson
£5,680 to £7,450
Principal Information Officers, J. L. Elgar; M. A. S.
Garrod; J. Parker.......... £5,680 to £7,450
Principal Scientific Officer, Dr. J. A. Harwood
£5,514 to £7,205
Senior Executive Officers, C. Archer; J. Barsby;
C. H. Basson; A. Best; D. R. Birleson; H.
Blackbourn; J. Blythin; F. J. Brown; J. W.

Burgess; M. F. Butters; A. E. Coleshill; R. G.
W. Cooke; A. F. Davies; V. B. Dixon; J. D.
Forster; D. W. French; G. Gibson; H. W. Gillies,
M.B.E.; C. M. Greening; Miss G. M. Griffith; G.E.
Guy; J. A. Hart; J. T. Horrocks; D. V. Horsley;
G. Hoyle; Mrs. E. J. Hughes; W. A. Jones; G.
C. Jones-Evans; D. P. King; R. C. Morris; D.
Mullaruy; M. J. Murphy; Miss B. Niehorster;
Miss L. Noble; K. R. North; F. Parker; L. J.
Parsons; J. Plumridge; K. M. F. Quinfaba; D. J.
Ridout; Miss S. K. Rooney; G. A. Rouse; H.
Stead; Miss M. Symon; E. M. Twine; J. Walsh;
R. Waye; E. J. White; Mrs. M. Wilder; N. F.
Willder....................£4,900 to £5,900
Senior Information Officers, R. E. Hill; Mrs. S. M. L.
May; G. H. Moores; A. C. Tilbury; B. R. Willis
£4,900 to £5,900
Senior Librarian, D. B. Gibson.. £4,900 to £5,900

Home Office Unit for Educational Methods
Fire Service Technical College,
Moreton-in-Marsh, Gloucestershire
Head of Unit, J. F. Barton......£5,356 to £6,010

Police Department
Horseferry House, Dean Ryle Street, S.W.1
[01-211-3000]
Assistant Under-Secretaries of State, A. S. Baker,
O.B.E., D.F.C.; J. B. Howard, C.B.; W. N. Hyde;
R. A. James, M.C.....................£12,000
Controller, Forensic Science Service, E. G. Davies
Assistant Secretaries, G. L. Angel; G. H. Baker,
D.S.C.; W. J. Bohan; J. F. D. Buttery; G. W. A.
Duguid; D. Heaton; Miss G. M. B. Owen; T. C.
Platt...................£8,650 to £11,000
Principals, D. J. Belfall; S. W. Boys-Smith; M. J.
Butcher; W. J. Carney; J. M. Clift; Miss W. M.
Goode; J. F. Halliday; R. A. Harrington; Miss
M. Hornsby, O.B.E.; E. Hutchings; D. McQueen;
G. C. Maxted; C. E. Mellish; N. L. Morgan; J. A.
Pemberton; Mrs. J. Reisz; J. F. Roger; A. W.
Scaplehorn; P. M. Scott; H. S. Seaford; Miss P. J.
Stacey; R. M. Whalley; F. J. Woodland; R. C.
Yeates...................£5,680 to £7,450
Senior Executive Officers, J. L. Baker; D. A. Birks;
J. W. Clark; K. A. Day; J. L. Durward; J. Wake
£4,900 to £5,900
Assistant Chief Training Officer, Lt.-Col. G. W.
Laverick...................£5,159 to £5,939
H.M. Chief Inspector of Constabulary, J. Haughton,
C.B.E., Q.P.M.....................£11,186
H.M. Inspectors, C. Cooksley, C.B.E., Q.P.M.; R. G.
Fenwick, C.B.E.; N. Galbraith, C.B.E.; S. E. Peck,
C.B.E., B.E.M.; G. Twist...............£10,114
Assistant Inspector of Constabulary, Miss J. S. S. Law,
O.B.E.....................£6,315 to £6,747

Police Scientific Development Branch
Director, G. Phillips.....................£9,440
Deputy Director, A. T. Burrows, M.B.E., E.R.D.
£8,650 to £9,798
Principal Scientific Officers, Dr. A. Ganson; Dr. R. A.
Hinder; A. Holt; F. A. V. Jenkins; Dr. B. S.
Luetchford; M. E. Moncaster; Dr. D. M. S. Peace
£5,514 to £7,205

Police National Computer Unit
Romney House, Marsham Street, S.W.1
[01-212-7676]
Assistant Secretary, J. R. Cubberley
£8,650 to £11,000
Senior Principals, D. Menzies; K. Parks; E. Todd;
R. G. Urquhart...................£7,250 to £9,350
Principals, G. F. Atherton; A. Bailey; M. A. Button;
J. Clarke; W. Clements; G. M. Cole; D. Dunkin;
T. Egan; R. Gregory; R. Oliver; R. Grover; D.
Quarmby; E. E. Quinney; H. Randall; T. G.
Roberts; R. V. Wallace.....£5,680 to £7,950
Principal Scientific Officers, J. R. Lowe; R. T.
Robinson; J. Watts.....£5,514 to £7,205
Senior Executive Officers, R. Ayres; V. Banham;
D. Blackwood; J. Cane; C. A. Carter; D.
Chapman; W. S. Cowie; H. A. C. Cowley; P. A.
Davies; C. Dean; G. Dorow; L. Edgar; S. Frean;
K. Gadsdon; D. H. Gannon; F. Goodsell; D.
Grant; R. Harwood; J. Henderson; L. Hunt; D.

Lovering; J. McLaren; D. C. Moulton; B.
Pullin; R. Richie; T. Roberts; A. Rouse; C.
Saunders; M. Scandritt; R. Shelvey; K. M.
Shewry; M. Slavin; R. Smiches; P. J. A. Somer-
ville; B. G. Stocking; Mrs. C. A. Sullivan;
J. Truscorr; T. W. Wrighton..£4,900 to £5,900
Senior Communications Officers, W. Dorward; J. H.
Kitsell; J. N. Warley; A. Watts

Joint ADP Unit
Tintagel House, Albert Embankment, S.E.1
[01-230 1212]
Assistant Secretary, M. D. Hutton
£8,650 to £11,000
Senior Principals, H. Eccles; R. V. Robinson; K. E.
Salmon.....................£7,750 to £9,350
Principals, T. Clark; T. S. Diaper; F. R. Hayhurst;
A. F. G. Hitchman; P. G. V. Pike; D. W.
Punshon; J. Richards; J. Smedley
£5,680 to £7,450
Senior Executive Officers, C. A. Allison; M. J.
Bloomfield; T. G. Cronin; B. J. Flaherty; A. Hall;
A. C. Jenkins; D. G. Jones; Mrs. J. Morgan; D.
J. Moss; C. Muid; K. Pleant; H. D. Poulson; D.
S. Roberts; B. Rollins; A. Silver; S. D. Walsh;
H. Warland; J. Waud; R. C. Weller; F. H.
Wormley.....................£4,900 to £5,900

Directorate of Telecommunications
60 Rochester Row, S.W.1
[01-828-9848]
Director of Telecommunications, W. P. Nicol
£11,000
Deputy Directors, J. N. Hallet; R. M. Hughes; N.
Morley; P. H. L. Trodden.....£8,650 to £9,798
Principals, D. E. N. Boon; S. Klein
£5,680 to £7,450
Senior Executive Officers, F. J. Atkins; A. O. Cam-
brook; R. F. J. Heath; K. F. Templar
£4,900 to £5,900
Chief Wireless Engineers, H. L. Collins; E. W.
Crompton; R. E. Fudge; W. R. Harris; J. J. E.
Lebutt; J. C. Lucas; G. J. Mewett; D. S. Oldnall;
P. P. H. Smith; R. S. Stoodley; J. P. Titheradge;
H. Woodmansey.....................£6,280 to £7,450

Police College
Bramshill House, Basingstoke, Hampshire
[Hartley Witney 2931]
Commandant, J. F. Walker, Q.P.M.
Deputy Commandant, J. C. J. Maskell.
Dean of Academic Studies, I. A. Watt
£6,421 to £7,143
Principal, P. Leyshon.....£5,680 to £7,450

Home Defence College
The Hawkhills, Easingwold, Yorks.
Principal, Air Marshal Sir Leslie Mavor, K.C.B.
A.F.C.....................£9,033

*Home Office H.Q. Warning and Monitoring
Organization*
Horsefair, Banbury, Oxon.
[Banbury 56151]
Director, V. G. Barry, D.F.C.....£7,750 to £9,350
Deputy Directors, R. F. Cooke; G. A. Potter
£5,680 to £7,450

Prison Department
89 Eccleston Square, S.W.1
[01-828-9843]
Director-General of the Prison Service, E. D. Wright,
C.B.....................£14,000
Assistant Under-Secretaries of State, M. S. Gale, M.C
(*Controller, Operational Administration*); D. G.
Hewlings, D.F.C., A.F.C. (*Controller, Planning and
Development*); T. G. Weiler (*Controller, Personnel
and Services*).....................£12,000.
Chief Inspector of the Prison Service, G. W. Fowler
£11,670
Director of Prison Medical Services, I. G. W. Picker-
ing, V.R.D., M.D.....................£12,000
Assistant Secretaries, P. Beedle; K. H. Dawson; R.
M. Morris; S. G. Norris; A. P. Wilson
£8,650 to £11,000
Assistant Controllers, W. A. Brister; E. A. Town-
drow.....................£11,000

Assistant Director of Prison Medical Services, Dr.
J. H. Orr............................£11,440
Senior Principals, V. G. Gotts; F. C. Millward
£7,750 to £9,350
Governors I, S. E. Henderson Smith; D. W.
Higman; C. P. Honey; R. A. B. A. Howden;
Maj. P. L. James; Miss O. Parry........£9,424
Principals, P. R. Burleigh; P. Canovan; C. S.
Cullerne-Brown; P. A. Chadwell; E. W. Durn-
dell; Mrs. B. Fair; R. G. Ferguson; W. O.
Fortune; E. W. A. Fryer; A. K. Guymer; G. E.
Hart; A. H. Hewins; J. B. Irving; B. Johnson;
Miss C. L. Jones; J. E. A. Mumford; Miss M.
Peck; Maj. L. Snowden, M.B.E.; J. F. Theobald;
A. H. Turner; D. F. Turnham; G. P. Willmets;
D. A. R. Wood....................£7,450
Governors II, G. J. Dadds; I. M. Dunbar; R. L. D.
Skrine........................£7,083 to £8,066
Director of Psychological Services, G. R. Twiselton
£8,650 to £9,798
Chief Education Officer, A. S. Baxendale
£7,750 to £9,350
Police Advisers, Cdr. D. Neesham; Det. Chief Supt.
S. J. Moore; Det. Chief Insp. D. C. Price.
Chaplain General, Rev. Canon L. L. Rees..£4,966
Governors III, N. Berry; D. C. Leach; E. Martin; F.
B. O'Friel; A. G. Pearson; J. F. Richardson; H. L.
Spencer; G. Walker............£5,690 to £6,717
Senior Executive Officers, L. G. Ball; C. Barlow;
C. A. Bartley; F. M. Clark; T. P. R. Crompton;
J. Finn; G. P. Gee; J. A. Gibbs; J. B. Harvey;
R. E. P. A. Hughes; R. James; R. C. Latham;
G. Rendell; J. Simpson; D. L. Smith; B. J. Valen-
tine; M. Wann; R. J. White; F. Wilkinson
£4,900 to £5,900
Organizer of Physical Education, I. T. Copeland
£5,680 to £7,450

Directorate of Industries and Supply
Tolworth Tower, Tolworth, Surbiton, Surrey
[01-399-5491]
Director, K. J. Neale, O.B.E.
Planning and Services Manager, S. Barraclough
£8,650 to £11,000
Commercial Manager, I. E. Scarlett.
Chief Farms and Garden Manager, P. D. Stevens
£8,650 to £9,798
Production Services Manager, P. F. Hewett
£5,680 to £7,450
Personnel Manager, D. F. Scagell.
Planning Manager, D. J. Wilkes.
Senior Farms and Gardens Officers, A. Donkin; C.
E. Marshall; D. A. Norman
£6,280 to £7,450
Catering Manager, P. Stephenson
£5,080 to £7,400
Chief Architect's Branch and Directorate of Works
St. Vincent House, 30 Orange Street, W.C.2
[01-930-8499]
Chief Architect and Director of Works, J. E. H. D.
Cairns........................£10,240
Deputy Chief Architect and Deputy Director of Works,
A. Ball..........................£11,000
Superintending Architects, R. H. Clare; N. E. Hill;
G. E. F. Slatter............£8,650 to £9,798
Superintending Engineer, T. R. Jones
£8,650 to £9,798
Superintending Quantity Surveyor, K. F. J. Kenward
£8,650 to £9,798
Principal Professional and Technology Officers, H. G. S.
Banks; M. J. Bridgford; M. A. Brooks; J. A.
Burrell; B. D. Charlson; G. W. Chrisp; J. H.
Cooper; H. J. Davies; P. W. H. Davis; R. D.
Evernden; R. A. Greaves; R. W. T. Haines; D.
W. Harris; A. F. Lane; L. O. Lee; L. E. Luck; R.
F. W. Malthouse; C. A. G. Poole; B. R. Redd; R.
J. Scott; J. E. Sheldon; B. A. Stickley; V. A. C.
Trigwell; P. A. G. Walker.....£6,280 to £7,450
Senior Executive Officer, J. V. Dyer
£4,900 to £5,900

Supply and Transport Branch
Crown House, 52 Elizabeth Street,
Corby, Northants.
[Corby 2101]

Director, P. R. Wall..........£7,750 to £9,350
Senior Executive Officers, S. E. Ilett; J. W. Little; L.
Moore....................£4,900 to £5,900

Regional Offices
Birmingham
Regional Director, M. D. McLeod.......£11,000
Deputy Regional Directors, W. B. Gibbs *(Adminis-
tration)* (£5,680 to £7,450); A. W. Driscoll *(Op-
erations)*; J. L. Rham *(Young Adult Offenders)*
£7,083 to £8,066
Bristol
Regional Director, D. W. Fisher.......£11,000
Deputy Regional Directors, G. C. Woods *(Adminis-
tration)* (£5,680 to £7,450); B. A. Marchant
(Operations); J. S. McCarthy *(Young Adult
Offenders)*..............£7,083 to £8,066
Manchester
Regional Director, L. J. F. Wheeler......£11,000
Deputy Regional Directors, D. L. Tacey *(Administra-
tion)* (£5,680 to £7,450); R. M. Dauncey;
Lt.-Cdr. S. E. Hawkins *(Operations)*; J. D. U.
Lewis *(Young Adult Offenders)*. £7,083 to £8,066
Tolworth
Regional Director, K. Gibson..........£11,000
Deputy Regional Directors, R. W. Hampton
(Administration) (£5,680 to £7,450); E. S. Nash;
L. A. Portch *(Operations)*; D. A. Brown *(Young
Adult Offenders)*..........£7,083 to £8,066

PRISONS
Governors
Acklington, Northumberland, R. Cooper
£5,690 to £6,717
Albany, I.O.W., T. R. Carnegie..........£9,424
Appleton Thorn, Lancs., M. Langdon
£5,690 to £6,717
Ashwell, Leics., P. O. E. Randell. £7,083 to £8,066
Askham Grange, Yorks., Miss S. F. McCormick
£5,690 to £6,717
Aylesbury, D. A. Guild........£7,083 to £8,066
Bedford, D. O'C. Grubb......£5,690 to £6,717
Birmingham, W. Perrie................£9,424
Blundeston, Suffolk, J. E. Simmons
£7,083 to £8,066
Bristol, A. B. Hughes.........£7,083 to £8,066
Brixton, S.W.2., B. D. Wigginton........£9,424
Camp Hill, I.O.W., D. A. Ward. £7,083 to £8,066
Canterbury, J. H. Absalom......£7,083 to £8,066
Cardiff, G. E. Griffiths.......£7,083 to £8,066
Channings Wood, Devon, R. Clarke
£5,690 to £6,717
Chelmsford, M. F. G. Selby.....£7,083 to £8,066
Coldingley, Surrey, J. A. Green..£7,083 to £8,066
Dartmoor, C. B. Heald.......£5,690 to £6,717
Dorchester, S. Brumby........£5,690 to £6,717
Durham, I. W. F. Steinhausen..........£9,424
Exeter, J. W. N. Brown.......£7,083 to £8,066
Ford, Sussex, R. K. Lawson....£7,083 to £8,066
Gartree, Leics., J. K. Beaumont..£7,083 to £8,066
Gloucester, A. H. Rayfield......£5,690 to £6,717
Grendon and Spring Hill, Bucks., Dr. R. L. Jiller
(Medical Superintendent)...........£11,440
Haverigg, Cumbria, W. E. Cowper-Johnson
£7,083 to £8,066
Holloway, N.7, Dr. M. P. Bull..£7,083 to £8,066
Hull, A. C. Kearns..........£7,083 to £8,066
Kingston, Portsmouth, E. R. E. Skelton
£5,690 to £6,717
Kirkham, Lancs., N. Clay......£7,083 to £8,066
Lancaster, R. Fall...........£5,690 to £6,717
Leeds, B. A. Emes.................£9,424
Leicester, N. F. Low.........£7,083 to £8,066
Lewes, C. T. Pratt...........£7,083 to £8,066
Leyhill, Glos., D. Atkinson.....£7,083 to £8,066
Lincoln, S. Mitchell..........£7,083 to £8,066
Liverpool, D. T. Cross................£9,424
Long Lartin, Worcs., J. Williams........£9,424
Maidstone, P. Timms........£7,083 to £8,066
Manchester, A. R. Moreton.............£9,424
Moor Court, Staffs., Miss O. J. Prichard-Carr
£5,690 to £6,717
Northallerton, H. Parr.......£5,690 to £6,717
Northeye, Sussex, R. Croxford..£5,690 to £6,717
Norwich, M. J. Brown........£7,083 to £8,066

Nottingham, P. L. Harrap....... £5,690 to £6,717
Oxford, M. D. Jenkins......... £5,690 to £6,717
Parkhurst, I.O.W., M. Bryan............ £9,424
Pentonville, P. A. M. Heald.............. £9,424
Preston, R. E. Adams....... £7,083 to £8,066
Ranby Camp, J. R. Sandy...... £5,690 to £6,717
Reading, R. A. Richards....... £5,690 to £6,717
Shepton Mallet, G. J. Burford... £5,690 to £6,717
Shrewsbury, D. St. L. Simon.... £5,690 to £6,717
Stafford, G. Lister....................... £9,424
Standford Hill, E. R. Cooper..... £7,083 to £8,066
Styal, Cheshire, Miss M. Morgan £7,083 to £8,066
Sudbury, W. S. Smith, D.S.C.... £7,083 to £8,066
Swansea, L. Lewis............ £5,690 to £6,717
Swinfen Hall, Staffs., G. W. Axe

£5,690 to £6,717
Thorp Arch, Yorks, E. Sumner.... £5,690 to £6,717
The Verne, Dorset, E. A. Esquilant

£7,083 to £8,066
Wakefield, Maj. M. Oldfield, M.C., E.R.D....£9,424
Wakefield Staff College, W. J. Booth...... £9,424
Wandsworth, S.W.18, R. S. Llewellyn...... £9,424
Winchester, F. M. Liesching..... £7,083 to £8,066
Wormwood Scrubs, W.12, N. C. Honey.... £9,424]

BORSTALS
Governors
Bullwood Hall, Essex, Miss J. A. M. Kinsley

£5,690 to £6,717
Deerbolt, R. J. T. Nash........ £5,690 to £6,717
Dover, E. A. Stratford......... £7,083 to £8,066
East Sutton Park, Kent, Miss M. Farmery

£5,690 to £6,717
Everthorpe, Humberside, P. R. D. Meech

£7,083 to £8,066
Feltham, Middlx., E. V. H. Williams

£7,083 to £8,066
Finnamore Wood, Bucks., M. P. Goodall

£4,673 to £5,340
Gaynes Hall, Cambs, W. J. Cooper, M.B.E.

£5,690 to £6,717
Glen Parva, (vacant)........... £5,690 to £6,717
Guys Marsh, Dorset, A. J. Webley

£5,690 to £6,717
Hatfield, Yorks., E. Owens...... £5,690 to £6,717
Hewell Grange, Worcs., W. R. Booth, R.D.

£5,690 to £6,717
Hindley, Lancs, F. S. Richardson. £5,690 to £6,717
Hollesley Bay Colony, Suffolk, A. F. H. Arnold

£7,083 to £8,066
Huntercombe, Oxon., J. H. M. Anderson

£5,690 to £6,717
Lowdham Grange, Notts., F. M. Mitchell

£7,083
Morton Hall, Lincs., D. E. Preston, M.B.E.

£5,690 to £6,717
Onley, Warwicks., L. C. Oxford £7,083 to £8,066
Pollington, Humberside, R. R. Tilt

£4,673 to £5,340
Portland, Dorset, D. F. Dennis... £7,083 to £8,066
Rochester, S. A. Bester......... £7,083 to £8,066
Stoke Heath, Salop, W. B. Ritson

£7,083 to £8,066
Usk, Gwent, D. F. Campbell.... £5,690 to £6,717
Wellingborough, J. W. Green..... £7,083 to £8,066
Wetherby, Yorks., G. W. A. Ellington

£5,690 to £6,717

REMAND CENTRES
Governors
Ashford, Middx., R. A. Attrill... £7,083 to £8,066
Brockhill, Worcs., R. Sharp..... £5,690 to £6,717
Latchmere House, Surrey, L. C. Davies

£4,673 to £5,340
Low Newton, Co. Durham, D. Whitehead

£4,673 to £5,340
Pucklechurch, Bristol, A. A. Fyfe. £5,690 to £6,717
Risley, Cheshire, R. F. Owens........ £9,424
Thorp Arch, Yorks., Maj. D. W. S. Martin

£4,673 to £5,340

DETENTION CENTRES
Wardens
Aldington, Kent, J. L. Smith.... £5,690 to £6,717
Blantyre House, Kent, C. J. Knight, D.S.M.

£5,690 to £6,717

Buckley Hall, Lancs., R. M. Parfitt

£5,690 to £6,717
Campsfield House, Oxford, H. Jones

£4,673 to £5,340
Eastwood Park, Glos., E. K. Wheeler

£4,763 to £5,340
Erlestoke House, Wilts., Capt. P. E. Marshall, V.R.D.

£5,690 to £6,717
Foston Hall, Derby, W. L. Thom £4,673 to £5,340
Haslar, Hants., A. R. Parsons... £5,690 to £6,717
Kirklevington, Cleveland, D. A. Marsden

£4,673 to £5,340
Medomsley, Co. Durham, J. M. Reid

£5,690 to £6,717
New Hall, Yorks., W. A. Martin £5,690 to £6,717
North Sea Camp, Lincs., B. E. N. Lyte

£5,690 to £6,717
Send, Surrey, R. Green......... £5,690 to £6,717
Werrington House, Staffs., P. L. Pye

£5,690 to £6,717
Whatton, Notts., C. B. Cogman. £5,690 to £6,717

Probation and After-Care Department
Romney House, Marsham Street, S.W.1
[01-212-7676]
Assistant Under-Secretary of State, A. W. Glanville

£12,000
Assistant Secretaries, G. I. de Deney; G. Emerson;
M. E. Head................ £8,650 to £11,000
Adviser in After Care, A. Hague, R.D....... £10,321
Principals, N. W. R. Baker; Miss R. E. Henn;
B. Lockett; J. A. Peacock; Miss P. M. Strong;
R. J. H. West; Miss M. L. O. Williams, M.B.E.;
W. J. Wright.............. £5,680 to £7,450
Senior Executive Officers, Miss R. M. Glen; Miss
J. M. Jeffrey; S. R. Mann; B. G. Meilton; Mrs.
M. E. W. Pusovnik; K. W. Rowe; P. G.
Spurgeon; A. Wakefield..... £4,900 to £5,900
Chief Probation Inspector, M. H. Hogan.... £11,000
Deputy Chief Probation Inspectors, R. W. Spiers;
R. S. Taylor........................ £9,861
Superintending Inspectors, G. C Orton; Miss M. D.
Samuels; C. T. Swann........ £7,750 to £9,350
Senior Inspector, D. F. Duchemin

£7,750 to £9,350
Inspectors, J. D. Benwell; R. A. Betteridge; Miss
R. E. Chant; G. W. Childs; I. A. Cooper; G. E.
Davies; R. O. Davies; J. J. Dowd; Miss A. M.
Farrer; W. A. Griffiths; M. J. Hensman; Mrs. M.
H. Johnson; P. G. Parker; K. G. W. Parris; D. N.
Rogers; F. N. Stephens; Miss F. M. Stone; Miss
S. J. G. Vidal; J. D. Wigzell.. £5,680 to £7,600
Drugs Branch
Chief Inspector, C. G. Jeffery.... £7,450 to £9,350
Deputy Chief Inspector, H. B. Spear

£5,680 to £7,450
Principals, R. Kendall; D. G. Turner

£5,680 to £7,450
Senior Executive Officer, H. R. Emery

£4,900 to £5,900
Cruelty to Animal Acts Inspectorate
Chief Inspector, D. J. Rankin, Ph.D....... £10,240
Superintending Inspectors, Group Capt. J. R. Cellars,
A.F.C.; R. L. Macpherson, M.B.E....... £11,000
Inspectors, Mrs. R. M. Collister, M.D.; C. B. Hart;
M. G. Jackson-Smyth; H. L. Jenkins, M.D.;
J. D. Laws; R. Mitchell; M. A. Richards; C. E.
Stuart; W. D. Tavernor; A. G. Warren

£6,987 to £9,662

Radio Regulatory Department
Waterloo Bridge House, Waterloo Rd., S.E.1
[01-275-3000]
Assistant-Under-Secretary of State, H. A. Daniels

£12,000
Assistant Secretary, D. E. Baptiste

£8,650 to £11,000
Director, T. Kilvington, O.B.E........... £11,000
Senior Principal, A. A. Mead.... £7,750 to £9,350
Deputy Directors, W. H. Bellchambers; R. A.
Dilworth................. £8,650 to £9,798
Principals, E. R. Emery; P. W. F. Fryer; W. Gold-
smith.................... £5,680 to £7,450
Senior Executive Officers, T. F. H. Howarth; Miss
B. R. West; J. West, M.B.E.. £4,900 to £5,900

Statistical Department
Tolworth Tower, Tolworth, Surrey
[01-399-5191]
Assistant Under-Secretary of State, Miss S. V. Cunliffe
£12,000
Chief Statisticians, Dr. C. M. Glennie; J. N. Lithgow;
J. R. Williams.............£8,650 to £11,000
Statisticians, C. J. C. Brown; P. Chandler; L. David-
off; J. Doyle; D. E. Edwards; A. S. Greenhorn;
Mrs. E. Oatham; Dr. F. O'Hara; S. M. Speller;
B. H. Ward.............£5,680 to £7,450
Senior Executive Officers, P. W. Brand; T. Chapman;
J. D. Fuller; L. C. Green.....£4,900 to £5,900

Research Unit
Romney House, Marsham Street, S.W.1
[01-212-7676]
Head of Unit, I. J. Croft......£8,650 to £11,000
Senior Research Officers, Miss E. K. C. Banks, ph.d.;
R. J. Baxter, ph.d.; R. V. G. Clarke, ph.d.; A. F.
C. Crook; P. J. Didcott (*Edinburgh*); M. S.
Folkard, ph.d. (*Manchester*); K. H. Heal; T. F.
Marshall; Miss J. W. Mott; K. G. Pease, ph.d.
(*Manchester*); Miss M. J. Shaw; D. E. Smith
(*Manchester*)............£5,680 to £7,450
Principals, W. W. Abson, Miss W. M. Goode,
C.B.E.....................£5,680 to £7,450
Senior Executive Officer, T. F. Corbett
£4,900 to £5,900

Special Duties on Equal Opportunities for Women

Whitehall, S.W.1
[01-213-3000]
Assistant Under-Secretary of State, J. T. A. Howard-
Drake...........................£12,000
Assistant Secretary, Mrs. S. Littler, £8,650 to £11,000
Senior Principal, F. B. Warner.. £7,750 to £9,350

Equal Opportunities Commission Planning Unit
20 Grosvenor Hill W.1
[01-629-8233]
Assistant Secretary, C. M. J. Hess
£8,650 to £11,000

Scientific Advisory Branch

Horseferry House, Dean Ryle Street, S.W.1
[01-211-3000]
Director, J. K. S. Clayton (*acting*)
Principal Scientific Officers, J. C. Cotterill; Mrs.
J. M. Hogg; J. R. Lowe; J. A. Miles; Miss P.
M. Morgan; P. L. Parsons; F. H. Pavry; A. D.
Perryman; J. E. Simes; J. Thompson; F. H. Ven-
ables; A. M. Wintern.......£5,514 to £7,205

Women's Royal Voluntary Service
17 Old Park Lane, W.1
[01-499-6040]
Chairman, Lady Pike.
Chief Administrator (*Regions*), Miss E. Hyatt.

HORSERACE TOTALISATOR BOARD

Tote House, 8–12 New Bridge Street, E.C.4.
[01-353-1066]
Established by the Betting and Gaming Act, 1960,
as successor in title to the Racecourse Betting
Control Board established by the Racecourse
Betting Act, 1928.
Its function is to operate totalisators on approved
racecourses in Great Britain, and it also provides off-
course cash and credit offices. Under the Horse-
race Totalisator and Betting Levy Board Act, 1972,
it is now further empowered to offer bets at starting
price (or other bets at fixed odds) on any sporting
event.
Chairman, The Lord Mancroft, K.B.E., T.D... £8,000
Deputy Chairman, Sir Leonard Barford.
Members, R. A. Withers; K. Winckles, M.B.E.;
Sir Henry D'Avigdor-Goldsmid, Bt., D.S.A., M.C.;
R. E. Sangster; G. H. C. Ardron, M.B.E., Ph.D.
(*Director-General*).

INDEPENDENT BROADCASTING AUTHORITY

70 Brompton Road, S.W.3
[01-584-7011]
The Authority was created in July 1954 as the
Independent Television Authority. In July 1972
it was renamed the Independent Broadcasting
Authority and its functions extended to cover the
provision of independent local radio. The Chairman and Members of the Authority are appointed
by Ministers responsible for broadcasting matters.
The eleven members of the Authority constitute
the body which has the statutory task of providing
the independent broadcasting services in television
and radio. This task includes both the provision
of the transmitting facilities and the general supervision of programmes and advertising. In both
media, the Authority is required to obtain its
normal programme supply from programme companies operating under contract to the Authority.
Fifteen television programme companies hold contracts to provide programmes in the 14 independent
television regions of Britain (two companies share
the contract for London—one on weekdays, the
other at weekends). They are financed by selling
advertising time. The contractors pay a rental to
the Authority to meet the I.B.A.'s own requirements, and an additional rental, which is calculated
in relation to their profits, to the Exchequer to
recognize their use of frequencies which are public
assets. Under the terms of the Independent Broadcasting Act 1973, the I.B.A. has set up 19 independent local radio stations.
Chairman, The Lady Plowden, D.B.E......£10,000
Deputy Chairman, C. Bland...............£2,000
Members, W. C. Anderson, C.B.E.; Dr. T. F. Carbery
(*Scotland*); The Baroness Macleod of Borve;
W. J. Blease (*Northern Ireland*); A. W. Page;
Prof. J. Ring; Mrs. M. Warnock; T. G. Davies;
C.B.E.; The Baroness Stedman, O.B.E.....£1,000
Director-General, B. W. M. Young.
Deputy Directors General, B. C. Sendall, C.B.E.
(*Programme Services*); A. W. Pragnell, O.B.E.,
D.F.C.(*Administrative Services*).
Director of Engineering, H. Steele.
Director of Internal Finance, R. D. Downham.
Director of External Finance, A. Brook.
Head of Information, B. C. L. Keelan.
Head of Programme Services, D. Glencross.
Head of Advertising Control, P. B. Woodhouse.
Director of Radio, J. B. Thompson.
Secretary, B. Rook.
Regional Officers, F. W. L. G. Bath (*Midlands*);
J. Blair-Scott (*South England*); W. A. C. Colling-
wood, O.B.E. (*South-West England, Channel
Islands*); R. Cordin (*Yorkshire*); L. J. Evans, O.B.E.
(*Wales and the West*); A. D. Fleck (*Northern
Ireland*); J. N. R. Hallett, M.B.E. (*East of England*);
J. E. Harrison (*North-West England*); J. Lindsay
(*Scotland*); R. J. F. Lorimer (*North-East England,
the Borders and the Isle of Man*.).

DEPARTMENT OF INDUSTRY

1 Victoria Street, S.W.1
[01-215 7877]
The Department of Industry is responsible for
general industrial policy, national and regional.
In particular it is responsible for the sponsorship
of individual industries; technical services to industry; and industrial development and finance.
The aerospace industries come within its responsibilities, and industrial research and development,
including supervision of the industrial research
establishments of the former Department of Trade
and Industry. It is also departmentally responsible
for the Post Office Corporation. Attached to the
Department of Industry are the regional offices of
the former Department of Trade and Industry.
These will also serve the Department of Trade and
the Department of Prices and Consumer Protection.

SALARY LIST

Secretary of State......................£13,000
Ministers of State......................£9,500
Parliamentary Under Secretary of State......£5,500
Permanent Secretary....................£18,675
Secretary (Industry)...................£17,175
Deputy Secretary.......................£14,000
Under Secretary........................£12,000
Assistant Secretary............£8,650 to £11,000
Chief Statistician.............£8,650 to £11,000
Senior Economic Adviser.......£8,650 to £11,000
Director Engineer.......................£11,000
Senior Principal...............£7,750 to £9,350
Principal.....................£5,680 to £7,450
The Solicitor..........................£14,000
Under Secretary (Legal)................£12,000
Assistant Solicitor...........£9,033 to £11,000
Senior Director of Accountants.........£11,670
Director of Accountants........£8,650 to £11,000
Chief Scientific Officer...............£10,950
Deputy Chief Scientific Officer...£8,330 to £9,440
Chief Information Officer (A)...£8,650 to £11,000
(B).....£7,750 to £9,350

Research Establishments
Director, National Physical Laboratory......£14,000
Director, National Engineering Laboratory...£13,230
Government Chemist.....................£12,000
Director, Warren Spring Laboratory........£12,000
Director, Computer Aided Design Centre.....£9,440

Secretary of State for Industry, THE RT. HON.
ERIC GRAHAM VARLEY, M.P.
Principal Private Secretary, R. Williams.
Parliamentary Private Secretary, R. W. Stott, M.P.
Special Adviser, K. J. Griffin.
Ministers of State, THE LORD BESWICK, P.C.;
GREGOR MACKENZIE, M.P.
Private Secretaries, (to Lord Beswick), Mrs. E.
Akenhead; (to Mr. Mackenzie), R. Nicklen.
Parliamentary Under Secretary of State for Industry,
G. B. Kaufman, M.P.
Secretary, Department of Industry, Sir Antony Part,
G.C.B., M.B.E.
Private Secretary, N. R. Thornton.
Secretary (Industry), P. W. Carey, C.B.
Private Secretary, D. E. Love.
Deputy Secretaries, L. S. Berman, C.B. (Director of
Statistics); R. H. W. Bullock, C.B.; D. le B. Jones,
C.B.; M. J. Kerry (The Solicitor); D. A. Lovelock,
C.B. (Principal Establishment and Finance Officer);
Sir Ieuan Maddock, C.B., O.B.E., F.R.S (Chief Scien-
tist); G. D. W. Odgers; Professor A. T. Peacock,
D.S.C. (Chief Economic Adviser); R. F. Prosser,
C.B., M.C. A. K. Rawlinson; P. W. Ridley, C.B.E.
Parliamentary Clerk (Principal), Miss P. Davey
Industrial Advisers, S. Baker (Co-ordinator); B.
Nicholls.

AEROSPACE
Air Division
Monsanto House, 10–18 Victoria Street, S.W.1
[01-215 7877]
Under Secretary, A. Warrington.
Assistant Secretaries, D. R. Ford; D. J. Gerhard;
R. Jardine; R. Mountfield.
Deputy Chief Scientific Officer, K. W. Smith

Space and Air Research Division
Monsanto House, 10–18 Victoria Street, S.W.1
[01-215 7877]
Under Secretary, H. G. R. Robinson, O.B.E.
Deputy Chief Scientific Officers, D. Cavanagh; R. A.
Jeffs.

Concorde Division
Monsanto House, 10–18 Victoria Street, S.W.1
[01-215 7877]
Under Secretary, K. G. Binning.
Assistant Secretary, J. M. Healey.
Deputy Chief Scientific Officer, J. D. Hayhurst, O.B.E.

RESEARCH AND DEVELOPMENT
Research and Development Requirements Division
Abell House, John Islip Street, S.W.1
[01-211 3000]
Under Secretary, B. W. Oakley.
Assistant Secretary, C. B. Nixon.
Deputy Chief Scientific Officers, Dr. A. B. Hammond;
P. H. Stephenson.

Research and Development Contractors Division
Abell House, John Islip Street, S.W.1
Under Secretary, J. W. Nichols.
Deputy Chief Scientific Officers, E. Barlow-Wright;
R. J. F. Franklin; C. G. Giles, O.B.E.

National Physical Laboratory
Teddington, Middlesex
[01-977 3222]
Director, Dr. J. V. Dunworth, C.B., C.B.E.

Laboratory of the Government Chemist
Cornwall House, Stamford Street, S.E.1
[01-928 7900]
Government Chemist, Dr. H. Egan.

National Engineering Laboratory
East Kilbride, Glasgow
[East Kilbride: 20222]
Director (Chief Scientific Officer), D. H. Mallinson

Warren Spring Laboratory
Gunnels Wood Road, Stevenage, Herts.
[Stevenage: 3388]
Director, A. J. Robinson.

Computor Aided Design Centre
Madingley Road, Cambridge
[Cambridge: 63125]
Director, A. I. Llewelyn, O.B.E

THE SOLICITOR
Solicitor's Department
Kingsgate House, 66–74 Victoria Street, S.W.1
[01-215 7877]
The Solicitor, M. J. Kerry.
Under Secretaries (Legal), W. C. Beckett; J. B. Evans;
T. D. Salmon; J. A. Trapnell
Assistant Solicitors, D. A. Grant, M.C.; H. S. A. Hart;
R. Higgins; A. D. Howlett; K. A. M. Johnson;
J. McElheran; D. E. Moore; T. J. G. Pratt; G.
Preston; C. B. Robson; Mrs. F. A. Scarborough;
G. A. Shewell; W. Walford-White; L. V.
Wellard.

ECONOMICS AND STATISTICS
Economics and Statistics Division 1
1 Victoria Street, S.W.1
[01-215 7877]
Under Secretary, D. R. H. Sawers.
Senior Economic Advisers, M. S. Bradbury; M. J.
Fores; N. K. A. Gardner; R. S. Howard.

Economics and Statistics Division 4
Under Secretary, R. O. Goss.
Chief Statistician, M. L. M. Neifield
Senior Economic Advisers, H. Christie; P. J. Goate.

Economics and Statistics Division 5
Under Secretary, T. S. Pilling.
Chief Statisticians, P. D. Dworkin; B. A. Waine-
wright.
Senior Economic Advisers, D. R. Coates; G. P.
Jefferies.

Economics and Statistics Division 6
Under Secretary, Miss R. J. Maurice.
Chief Statisticians, Mrs. J. G. Cox; M. J. M. Erritt;
P. H. Richardson.

Economics and Statistics Division 3

Dean Bradley House, 52 Horseferry Road,
[01-212 7676]
Under Secretary, P. M. Rees
Chief Statisticians, A. Crystal; J. R. Howe; J. D. Wells; W. A. Wessell
Senior Economic Adviser, D. A. W. Broyd

Business Statistics Office

Cardiff Road, Newport, Gwent
[Newport: 56111]
Under Secretary, M. C. Fessey
Assistant Secretary   J. A. Tiffin
Chief Statisticians, J. M. Simmonds; Dr. R. H. S. Phillips; Dr. B. Mitchell
Senior Principal, R. W. Makepeace

ESTABLISHMENT

Establishment Senior Staff Management Division
1 Victoria Street, S.W.1
[01-215 7877]
Under Secretary, G. Parker, C.B.
Assistant Secretary, J. L. Clark.

Establishment Personnel Division
Under Secretary, E. J. D. Warne.
Assistant Secretaries, K. L. Blake; J. S. H. White.
Norman Shaw South Building,
Victoria Embankment, S.W.1
[01-839 7799]
Assistant Secretary, F. A. Carter

Establishment Management Services and Manpower Division
1 Victoria Street, S.W.1
[01-215 7877]
Under Secretary, G. C. Lowe
Assistant Secretary, H. A. Dawson.
Sanctuary Bldgs., 16-200 Great Smith Street
[01-215 7877]
Assistant Secretaries, D. G. Church, O.B.E.; R. L. Davies

Establishment General Services Division
1 Victoria Street, S.W.1
[01-215 7877]
Under Secretary, J. Fish
Assistant Secretaries, N. E. Ablett; F. T. Jones

FINANCE AND ACCOUNTS

Finance and Economic Appraisal Division
Abell House, John Islip Street, S.W.1
[01-211 3000]
Under Secretary, H. Scholes
Assistant Secretaries, K. W. N. George; D. W. Hellings; Miss E. P. Marston

Accounts Branch
24-26 Newport Road, Cardiff
[Cardiff 42611]
Senior Principal (Director of Accounts), J. G. P. Cater

Internal Audit
Chapter St. House, Chapter Street, S.W.1
[01-834 7032]
Senior Principal (Head of Internal Audit), D. L. Gatland

Programme Analysis Unit
Grimesdyke House, Chilton, Didcot, Berks.
[Abingdon: 4141]
Deputy Chief Scientific Officer (Director of Unit), Dr. P. M. S. Jones

Accountancy Services Division
Hillgate House, 26 Old Bailey, E.C.4
[01-248 5757]
Senior Director, H. A. Parfitt, C.B.E.
Directors, N. A. Atley; W. H. Cunningham

INDUSTRIAL AND COMMERCIAL POLICY

Industrial and Commercial Policy Division
1 Victoria Street, S.W.1
[01-215 7877]
Under Secretary, Miss A. E. Mueller.
Assistant Secretaries, A. F. Toms; S. W. Treadgold; W. B. Willott; J. A. Woolmer.

INFORMATION

Information Division
1 Victoria Street, S.W.1.
[01-215 7877]
Head of Information Division, R. J. J. Tuite, M.B.E.
Chief Information Officers, D. S. Evans; R. Mayes

Gaywood House, Great Peter Street, S.W.1
[01-212 7676]
Chief Information Officer, D. M. Edwards

REGIONAL DEVELOPMENT

Regional Industrial Development Division
Millbank Tower, Millbank, S.W.1
[01-211 3000]
Under Secretary, M. H. M. Reid.
Assistant Secretaries, D. Eagers; D. Steel

Regional Industrial Finance Division
Millbank Tower, Millbank, S.W.1
[01-211 3000]
Under Secretary A. J. Lippitt.
Assistant Secretaries, J. L. Judd; V. F. Lane; A. B. Powell, C.M.G.; A. C. Russell.

Regional Development Grants Division
Millbank Tower, Millbank, S.W.1
[01-211 3000]
Under Secretary, J. E. Barnes
Assistant Secretaries, S. J. Irwin; N. E. Nolan

Small Firms Division
Abell House, John Islip Street, S.W.1
[01-211 3000]
Under Secretary, J. E. Barnes
Assistant Secretary, J. E. Cammell.

Industrial Planning Division
Millbank Tower, Millbank, S.W.1
[01-211 3000]
Under Secretary, R. E. Dearing.
Assistant Secretaries, J. A. Battersby; C. J. Farrow; N. N. Walmsley.

REGIONAL ORGANISATION

Northern Regional Office
Wellbar House, Gallowgate, Newcastle upon Tyne
[Newcastle upon Tyne: 27575]
Regional Director (Under Secretary), R. L. Sutton
Regional Industrial Director (Under Secretary), H. T. Hill

North West Regional Office
Sunley Bldg., Piccadilly Plaza, Manchester
[061-236 2171]
Regional Director (Under Secretary), N. S. Belam
Regional Industrial Director (Under Secretary), A. W. Ward

Yorkshire and Humberside Regional Office
Priestley House, Park Row, Leeds
[Leeds: 443171]
Regional Director (Under Secretary), J. H. McEnery
Regional Industrial Director (Under Secretary), A. R. M. Graham

West Midlands Regional Office
Ladywood House, Stephenson Street, Birmingham
[021-632 4111]
Regional Director (Deputy Chief Scientific Officer), J. K. L. Thompson, M.B.E., T.D.

East Midlands Regional Office
Cranbrook House, Cranbrook Street, Nottingham
[Nottingham: 46121]
Regional Director (Assistant Secretary), N. Lott

South West Regional Office
The Pithay, Bristol
[Bristol: 291071]
Regional Director (Assistant Secretary), R. C.
McVickers.

South West Industrial Development Office
Phoenix House, Notte Street, Plymouth
[Plymouth: 21891]
*Regional Industrial Director (Assistant Secretary) (part
time),* C. E. Cannell
Eastern Regional Office
Cromwell House, Dean Stanley Street, S.W.1
[01–212 7676]
Regional Director (Assistant Secretary), B. Feinstein
London and South Eastern Regional Office
Cromwell House, Dean Stanley Street, S.W.1
[01–212 7676]
Regional Director (Assistant Secretary), A. C. Coging
Industrial Development Unit
Millbank Tower, Millbank, S.W.1
[01–211 3000]
Director, G. D. W. Odgers
Deputy Directors, D. Eastmond; M. G. M. Haines;
I. F. Halliday; R. L. Hamilton.
Secretariat and General Policy:
Assistant Secretary, C. B. Benjamin
Iron and Steel Division
Thames House South, Millbank, S.W.1
[01–211 3000]
Under Secretary, S. J. Gross, C.M.G.
Assistant Secretaries, J. D. Henes; J. H. Pownall;
R. A. Rowe.
Deputy Chief Scientific Officer, R. L. Long.

GENERAL INDUSTRIAL DEVELOPMENT
Paper, Timber and Miscellaneous Manufacturers Branch
Millbank Tower, Millbank, S.W.1
[01–211 3000]
Under Secretary, J. E. Barnes
Assistant Secretary, F. A. Neal

Special Industry Problems Adviser, A. J. Gray.

Chemicals and Textiles Division
Millbank Tower, Millbank, S.W.1
[01–211–3000]
Under Secretary (vacant).
Assistant Secretaries, D. M. Dell; D. M. J. Gwinnell;
Miss L. Lowne.

Special Industry Problems Adviser, A. J. Gray.
Shipbuilding Policy Division
Millbank Tower, Millbank, S.W.1
[01–211 3000]
Under Secretary, E. V. Marchant.
Assistant Secretaries, J. Darragh; H. J. Gummer;
A. McDonald
Deputy Chief Scientific Officer, D. Neville-Jones
**Minerals, Metals, Electrical Engineering,
Process Plant and Industrial Technologies
Division**
Millbank Tower, Millbank, S.W.1
[01–211 3000]
Under Secretary, D. C. Clark.
Assistant Secretaries, J. F. Gwynn; M. D. C. Johnson.
Directing Engineer, A. J. Havelock.
**Machine Tools and
Mechanical Engineering Division**
Abell House, John Islip Street, S.W.1
[01–211 3000]
Under Secretary, D. N. Byrne.
Assistant Secretary, C. M. Drukker.
Deputy Chief Scientific Officer, R. Gill
Vehicle Division
Abell House, John Islip Street, S.W.1
[01–211–3000]
Under Secretary, W. R. G. Bell.
Assistant Secretaries, P. J. Cooper; A. J. Suich.
Computers, Systems and Electronics Division
Dean Bradley House, 52 Horseferry Road, S.W.1
[01–212 7676]
Under Secretary, M. P. Lam
Assistant Secretaries, M. P. Gillings; B. Murray

Deputy Chief Scientific Officers, D. Harrison; J. H.
Major
Posts and Telecommunications Division
Waterloo Bridge House, Waterloo Road, S.E.1
[01–275 3000]
Under Secretary, D. G. C. Lawrence, O.B.E.
Assistant Secretaries, J. E. M. Beale; J. C. Y. de
Pauley.; Miss S. P. M. Fisher; T. U. Meyer.

CENTRAL OFFICE OF INFORMATION
Hercules Road, S.E.1
[01–928–2345]
The Central Office of Information is a common
service department which produces information and
publicity material, and supplies publicity services,
for other Government departments which require
them. In the United Kingdom it conducts Government display press, television and poster advertising
(except for the National Savings Committee), produces and distributes booklets, leaflets, films, television material, exhibitions, photographs and other
visual material; and distributes departmental press
notices. For the overseas departments it supplies
British Information posts overseas with press, radio
and television material, booklets, magazines,
reference services, films, exhibitions, photographs,
display and reading room material; manages
schemes for promoting the overseas sale of British
newspapers and periodicals; arranges tours in
the United Kingdom for official visitors from
overseas. Administrative responsibility for the
Central Office of Information rests with Civil
Service Department Ministers, while the ministers
whose departments it serves are responsible for the
policy expressed in its work.
Director-General, H. L. James............ £13,640
Private Secretary, Mrs. M. L. Evans.
Controllers, R. A. Fleming (*Home*); D. F. Kerr,
C.V.O., O.B.E. (*Overseas*)............... £12,080
Assistant Controllers, P. W. Probert (*Home*); K. W.
Sutton, O.B.E. (*Overseas*)......£8,160 to £9,760
Head of Research, N. H. Phillips. £8,160 to £9,760
Principal Information Officer, Miss G. R. Hembry
£6,090 to £7,860
Senior Information Officers, Mrs. E. J. Belcher; C. A.
Cross....................... £5,310 to £6,310
Advertising Division
Director, O. G. Thetford...... £9,060 to £11,410
Chief Information Officer, B. C. Davies
£8,160 to £9,760
Principal Information Officers, D. G. Marsh; Miss
V. E. Thorne, O.B.E......... £6,090 to £7,860
Senior Information Officers, M. J. C. Brodie; B. F. C.
Crampin; J. C. Danckwerts; A. H. C. Royou;
J. C. Segrue; G. W. Tavender. £5,310 to £6,310
Senior Executive Officer, E.A. Davis. £5,310 to £6,310
Establishment and Organization Division
Atlantic House, Holborn Viaduct, E.C.1.
[01–248–5744]
Director, A. Youngs (*Establishment Officer*)
£9,060 to £11,410
Senior Principal, W. F. Garnett.. £8,160 to £9,760
Principals, E. Bridger; M. Collins; A. H. Robinson
£6,090 to £7,860
Senior Executive Officers, Miss G. E. A. Bargus;
W. J. Colwill; D. Drake; S. G. Kerr; I. L. Mar-
getts; D. P. Morgan; J. G. Rowbotham; M.
Rowland; R. F. Stapley; K. R. Stephens
£5,310 to £6,310
Exhibitions Division
St. Christopher House Annexe,
Sumner Street, S.E.1
[01–928–2371]
Director, E. R. I. Allan, O.B.E... £9,060 to £11,410
Principal Information Officers, P. R. Daniell; R. J.
Reeves; B. H. Reynolds..... £6,090 to £7,860
Senior Information Officers, M. W. Chitty; J. J.
Darnell; M. D. Dyer; A. D. Estill; R. C. Fuliford;
R. S. Harper; I. E. Lain; P. J. London; C. B.
Seymour; R. J.Vallance; J. B. Yearsley
£5,310 to £6,310
Senior Executive Officer, J. F. Hinds. £5,310 to £6,310

Films and Television Division
Director, Miss D. V. F. Cockburn
£9,060 to £11,410
Chief Information Officer, A. C. White
£8,160 to £9,760
Principal Information Officers, Sir John Barran, Bt.;
Mrs. R. Brownrigg; R. J. Hall; J. A. Leys; A.
W. Thomson . . . . £6,090 to £7,860
Principal, Miss J. M. Reid . . . . £6,090 to £7,860
Senior Information Officers, D. S. Andrews; P. S.
Brawn; P. W. Coldham; L. S. Dawes; M. J.
Draper; R. A. P. Duval; L. F. Eaton; Miss
S. L. Y. Eley; W. J. G. Evans; J. B. Frankfort;
B. V. Gillman; J. Harris; F. G. Hermges; Miss
D. C. Hermon; Miss A. B. I. James; P. G. Jones;
Miss E. V. Moynihan; Miss F. Nelson; R. V.
Prime; Mrs. M. G. Reynolds; R. W. Salmon;
Miss R. Serlin; Miss H. P. Standage; Mrs. A. A.
Unsworth; G. A. Woodford . £5,310 to £6,310

Finance and Accounts Division
Director, D. J. Etheridge . . . . £9,060 to £11,410
Finance Branch
Principal, G. W. M. Pearson . . . . £6,090 to £7,860
Senior Executive Officers, R. W. Clarke; D. C.
Marquet; E. W. Whyman . . . £5,310 to £6,310
Accounts Branch
Sutherland House, Brighton Road,
Sutton, Surrey
[01-642-6022]
Principal, R. K. Evans. . . . . £5,940 to £7,710
Senior Executive Officer, Miss K. R. Walker
£5,160 to £6,160

Overseas Press and Radio Division
Director, H. J. Watters . . . . £9,060 to £11,410
Chief Information Officer, J. K. Holroyd
£8,160 to £9,760
Principal Information Officers, J. Ensoll; Miss M. M.
Foster; R. C. Herbert; K. G. Hicks; D. W.
James; R. J. Macdonald; D. J. Payton-Smith;
F. R. Pickering, M.B.E.; D. A. Smith; G. L.
Stickland; E. Turnbull . . . . . . £6,090 to £7,860
Senior Information Officers, Mrs. A. A. Beattie;
J. D. Beaumont; N. H. Browne; R. J. Chalk;
R. E. Collins; M. A. David; R. M. Douglas;
G. L. Duffus; J. E. Everett; M. S. C. Fare; B. C.
Freestone; R. Gair; O. Henry; J. E. Horton;
F. R. Mackenzie; H. R. Mander; J. H. Neil;
M. J. Quan; R. W. Tindall; Miss P. J. Tyler;
P. D. Wallace; J. F. Webb; Mrs. C. A. Whelan;
F. Wilson; Miss M. L. Yardley
£5,310 to £6,310
Senior Executive Officer, P. Abbott
£5,310 to £6,310

Photographs Division
Director, R. E. Hicks, O.B.E. . . . . £8,160 to £9,760
Principal Information Officer, J. A. Bond
£6,090 to £7,860
Senior Information Officers, D. J. Cooper; Miss H. R.
Dunt; D. F. Eddleston; S. I. Robertson; D. A.
Whyte . . . . £5,310 to £6,310
Senior Executive Officer, A. H. Kemp
£5,310 to £6,310

Publications and Design Services Division
Director, E. R. Kelly . . . . £9,060 to £11,410
Chief Information Officer, A. E. Bevens
£8,160 to £9,760
Principal Information Officers, J. L. Bishop; C. H.
Bourchier; F. V. Ellis; D. A. Loxley; D. N.
Steward . . . . £6,090 to £7,860
Senior Information Officers, T. A. Benger; R. W.
Brand; R. Doughty; H. Edwards; A. E. Gatland;
M. Jacobson; H. P. Jolowicz; Miss B. M.
Kirby; Miss M. E. J. Orna; G. R. Parsons; C. A.
Patchett; Miss J. Penfold; D. M. Robarts; R. T.
Ronan; E. H. Sired; S. A. H. Surman
£5,310 to £6,310
Senior Executive Officer, K. F. G. Fogwill
£5,310 to £6,310

Reference Division
Director, E. G. Farmer . . . . £8,160 to £9,760
Principal Information Officers, Mrs. J. Bonnor;
H. Witheford . . . . £6,090 to £7,860

Senior Information Officers, Dr. T. Kempinski;
J. F. Langley; Mrs. D. L. Long (part-time);
S. C. Lyle-Smythe; C. E. F. Manning; Mrs. S.
Saunders; Miss E. D. Skinner . £5,310 to £6,310
Senior Executive Officer, R. Widdup
£5,310 to £6,310

Tours and Distribution Division
Director, N. Bicknell . . . . £8,160 to £9,760
Principal Information Officer, J. B. Crompton
£6,090 to £7,860
Senior Information Officers, Miss B. M. E. Breden;
L. K. Carley; D. J. T. Cooke; C. J. Davies;
C. M. Hull; M. H. Pelly . . . . £5,310 to £6,310
Senior Executive Officers, G. W. S. Gilbert; D. Ross
£5,310 to £6,310

News Distribution Service
Duty Officer, T. P. Blakiston.

Regional Offices
Northern—Andrews House, Gallowgate,
Newcastle upon Tyne
Chief Regional Officer, H. G. Roberts
£7,750 to £9,350
Senior Information Officer, L. W. Mandy, M.B.E.
£4,900 to £5,900

Yorkshire and Humberside—City House,
New Station Street, Leeds
Chief Regional Officer, T. Cooban
£7,750 to £9,350
Senior Information Officers, P. M. Craven; C. E.
Dove . . . . £4,900 to £5,900

East Midland—Cranbrook House,
Cranbrook Street, Nottingham
Chief Regional Officer, P. J. Brazier
£7,750 to £9,350
Senior Information Officers, A. Waller; P. D. Yorke
£4,900 to £5,900

Eastern—Block D, Government Buildings,
Brooklands Avenue, Cambridge
Chief Regional Officer, A. A. McLoughlin
£7,750 to £9,350
Senior Information Officers, O. J. B. Prince-White;
D. C. Robinson . . . . £4,900 to £5,900

London and South Eastern—
St. Christopher House Annexe,
Sumner Street, S.E.1
Chief Regional Officer, R. Dean, O.B.E.
£8,160 to £9,760
Senior Information Officers, A. J. Goodson; S. T.
Sharpe . . . . £5,310 to £6,310
Southern—Market Place House, Reading
Chief Regional Officer, A. S. Poole
£5,680 to £7,450
Senior Information Officers, T. G. S. Crawford; J. R.
Wood . . . . £4,900 to £5,900
South Western—The Pithay, Bristol, 1
Chief Regional Officer, W. J. D. Irving, M.V.O.
£5,680 to £7,450
Senior Information Officer, J. W. Coe
£4,900 to £5,900
West Midland—Five Ways House,
Islington Row Middle Way, Birmingham 15
Chief Regional Officer, D. C. Boyd
£7,750 to £9,350
Senior Information Officer, A. Thompson
£4,900 to £5,900
North Western—Sunley Building,
Piccadily Plaza, Manchester
Chief Regional Officer, H. V. Tillotson, M.V.O.
£7,750 to £9,350
Senior Information Officers, H. Booth; J. Bradbury;
R. C. Stockdale . . . . £4,900 to £5,900

BOARD OF INLAND REVENUE
Somerset House, W.C.2
[01-438 6622]
The Board of Inland Revenue was constituted
under the Inland Revenue Board Act, 1849, by the
consolidation of the Board of Excise and the Board
of Stamps and Taxes. In 1909 the administration
of excise duties was transferred to the Board of
Customs. The Board of Inland Revenue is

responsible for the management and collection of income tax, surtax, profits tax, capital gains tax, corporation tax, estate duty, capital transfer tax, stamp duties and other direct taxes, and for the valuation of freehold and leasehold property for Inland Revenue taxation, for certain purposes on behalf of other Government Departments and public authorities and, in England and Wales, for local authority rating. The Board is also responsible for the management and collection of tithe redemption annuities. Salaries and expenses of the Board for 1973–74 were estimated at £154,300,000.

The Board
Chairman, Sir Norman Price, K.C.B. £18,675
Private Secretary, Mrs. C. B. Hubbard.
Deputy Chairmen, J. M. Green; A. H. Dalton.
Deputy Secretaries, E. V. Symons, C.B.; E. V. Adams
. . . . £14,000
Other Members, J. H. Gracey; A. J. G. Isaac; W. H. B. Johnson; Mrs. A. H. Smallwood; J. D. Taylor-Thompson; J. Webb; Miss G. Wolters. £12,000

Establishments Division
Personnel Group
Director of Personnel, J. Webb. £12,000
Assistant Secretaries, E. J. King; E. McGivern; F. W. Newcombe; W. M. Stewart
. . . . £8,650 to £11,000
Principals, J. D. Benson; S. Brown; A. H. Francome; R. S. Hayward (*Chief Welfare Officer*); M. A. Johns; R. F. Knight; A. McCormack; J. Macleod; W. J. Maddren; R. F. Madson; L. W. Matthews; R. J. F. Phillips; J. Tudor
. . . . £5,680 to £7,450
Senior Executive Officers, L. Clabbon; J. Eastman; M. Geraghty; D. E. Gray; D. H. Hawkes; E. C. Hawkes; E. M. Hayes; D. J. Hughes; M. J. Lee; L. Pears; Miss M. E. Ray; H. A. W. Rumbelow; W. D. Shearer; G. H. Smith; H. C. Sykes; T. J. Tupper. . . . . £4,900 to £5,900

Manpower and Organization Group
Director of Manpower and Organization, J. D. Taylor-Thompson. £12,000
Assistant Secretaries, C. L. Deller; D. Y. Pitts; J. B. Shepherd. . . . . £8,650 to £11,000
Senior Principal, J. W. Waters. . . £7,750 to £9,350
Principals, D. J. Critchley; R. J. Hedge; B. R. Spooner; W. G. Westlake. . £5,680 to £7,450

Management Services (A.D.P.†)
Senior Principal, R. E. M. Kirkman
. . . . £7,750 to £9,350
Principals, H. R. Brockwell; H. R. Game; G. I. Harding; M. Richardson; W. J. Willis
. . . . £5,680 to £7,450
Senior Executive Officers, N. Duffield; D. J. Gray; A. R. J. Green; D. Morley; M. E. Perry; G. T. Ripley; D. Selwood; D. W. Shepherd; A. G. Wakeford; O. F. Weald; R. J. Wheeler
. . . . £4,900 to £5,900

Management Services (General)
15 Adam Street, W.C.2
Senior Management Services Officers (Principals), R. O. Connolly; K. Pryce; E. F. Smith; J. Turnbull; A. O. Wilson, M.B.E. . . £5,680 to £7,450
Management Services Officers (Senior Executive Officers), J. P. M. Anderson; W. J. Andrews; J. W. Bamford; P. E. P. Berry; R. Brooks; T. A. Cooper; D. J. Curtis; S. C. Finn; Miss M. I. Gaines; Miss H. Hegarty; Miss V. M. Hunn; T. A. Lawson; R. H. Parker; F. B. Rennie; A. H. Shepherd; R. A. Yates. £4,900 to £5,900

†Automatic Data Processing.
M & O Planning Units
Assistant Secretary, G. D. Wroe. . £8,650 to £11,000
Senior Principal, S. E. S. Whitby
. . . . £7,750 to £9,350
Principals, G. Allcock; J. D. J. Bonfield; Miss M. V. Gifford; H. E. R. Greatorex; T. Hudson; P. C. Menhennett; D. V. Roberts; N. C. Smith
. . . . £5,680 to £7,450

Senior Executive Officers, E. F. Bianchi; Mrs. E. B. Brinkman; Mrs. S. D. Carmichael; J. N. Elsden; D. C. Faucherand; M. D. Holgate; B. D. Kent; P. McMahon; R. F. Moore; T. P. O'Brien; I. J. Parsons; G. F. Raney; F. P. Sturges; Mrs. J. D. M. Tournoff; P. Webber
. . . . £4,900 to £5,900

Office Services Group
Somerset House, W.C.2
Controller of Office Services (Senior Principal), D. B. Willis. . . . . £7,750 to £9,350
Principals, J. B. Clifton; N. Cumming; D. B. Duff (*Accommodation Officer*). . . . . . £5,680 to £7,450
Senior Executive Officers, J. E. F. Banks; V. C. Bowmer; A. L. Cowden, M.B.E.; D. Currie; B. H. Durham; F. W. Duxberry; R. J. Ewens; R. J. Lloyd; J. C. Richards; J. Stuart; A. Swarbrick; P. Taylor, M.B.E.; J. F. C. Tompkins; L. Winder. . . . . £4,900 to £5,900

Stamps and Taxes Division
Assistant Secretaries, R. F. Bailey; A. M. W. Battishill; L. J. H. Beighton; R. J. Bitton; R. A. Blythe; G. Briddon; M. H. Collins; C. W. Corlett; D. G. Draper; F. B. Harrison; P. G. Heard; D. Hopkins; D. J. Lawday; P. Lewis; R. I. McConnachie; M. McDonald; B. Pollard; F. I. Robertson; I. R. Spence; B. J. Thomas; N. Wainwright. . . . . £8,650 to £11,000
Senior Economic Adviser, E. B. Butler
. . . . £8,650 to £11,000
Principals, C. N. Atkin; J. B. Berry; G. Britton; J. P. B. Bryce; M. J. R. Coppack; M. J. G. Elliott; G. A. Elmer; P. W. Fawcett; C. G. Field; R. A. Forth; R. C. Fullbrook; A. B. Gardner; A. C. Gray; I. P. Gunn; S. G. Hammond; P. Harrison; Miss P. Hart; G. B. N. Hartog; W. G. Johns; G. M. Kirby, I.S.O.; G. L. Laufer; J. P. O. Lewis (*Press Officer*); R. G. Lusk; S. C. T. Matheson; A. G. Morgan; N. C. Munro; B. O'Connor; E. F. Palmer; D. E. Pipe; W. Reith; T. F. H. Richter; B. R. Spooner; M. Swann; J. Tennant; H. B. Thompson; D. Ward; E. A. Winstanley; I. A. Young. . . . . £5,680 to £7,450
Senior Executive Officers, A. G. Cumbers; Mrs. E. C. Robertson; M. K. Robins; J. Rodway
. . . . £4,900 to £5,900

Statistics Division
Somerset House, W.C.2
Director, S. F. James. £12,000
Chief Statisticians, A. T. Dunn; Dr. J. R. L. Schneider
. . . . £8,650 to £11,000
Assistant Secretary, E. A. Rapsey
. . . . £8,650 to £11,000
Statisticians, A. C. Clare; A. G. Ganguly; W. Gonzalez; S. D. Kingaby; R. V. S. Quinn; U. M. Rizki. . . . . £5,680 to £7,450
Principals, R. F. Bruford; W. G. Meadows; E. B. Paterson; A. G. Solly. . . . . . . £5,680 to £7,450

Assessments Division
Barington Road, Worthing, Sussex
Controller, C. E. Howick. . . . . . £7,750 to £9,350
Principals, C. G. Baseley; R. J. Doylend; R. Heeley; D. R. Laver. . . . . £5,680 to £7,450

Office of the Controller of Stamps
Bush House, South-West Wing, Strand, W.C.2
and Barrington Road, Worthing, Sussex
Controller, A. A. E. E. Ettinghausen, O.B.E. . . £9,524
Principals, J. A. Cargill; G. O. Hughes
. . . . £5,680 to £7,450

Director of Stamping
Avon House, 275 Borough High Street, S.E.1
Director, J. Green, I.S.O. . . . . . . £5,680 to £7,450

Estate Duty Office
Minford House, Rockley Road,
West Kensington, W.14
Controllers of Death Duties, W. J. G. Allen. . £12,000
Deputy Controllers of Death Duties, K. W. Chetwood; P. H. Fletcher; E. J. Mann. £11,000
Asst. Controllers of Death Duties, H. Booth, M.B.E.; J. F. Daykin; R. D. J. Dean; B. E. Glaze; R. R. Greenfield; R. K. Johns, I.S.O.; J. F. Johnson; P. H. Moss; P. B. Smallwood; J. B. Wells. £9,278
Senior Principal, R. Ellis. . . . . . . £7,750 to £9,350

Chief Examiners, J. D. Armour; W. J. Atkinson; R. M. Balsillie; J. A. Banks; A. L. Barton; R. A. Beare; G. A. Beasley; R. G. Bigmore; J. W. Bogle; J. Bugden; E. C. Burden; A. Cherns; D. D. Chitty; Miss M. Clark; J. G. Colebrook, M.B.E.; S. Collingwood; J. F. Cunningham; G. F. Dawe; B. W. Eyre; T. D. Flavin; A. W. George; H. J. Hall; J. Hillas; R. Horrex; C. D. Hughes; H. Hughes; F. Irwin; A. S. Johnson; B. T. Jones, M.B.E.; R. T. Kablean; G. J. Kennard; J. G. Kingsley; K. S. Lake; K. J. Lees; F. W. Leigh; P. Marshall; S. Noden; E. W. J. Panting; A. R. Payne; J. Pearce; E. G. Peel; C. M. Phillips; D. F. Reading; E. Redhead; E. O. Rice; W. H. Rundle; D. H. Salloway; F. E. Spurrell; R. A. Suckling; G. Thompson; J. Thorndycraft; F. H. Thornton; R. F. J. Thornton; P. Vernon, O.B.E.; F. Wood............£5,680 to £7,599
Principals, G. N. Alpe; J. H. Critch; N. J. Powell; J. Steele..................£5,680 to £7,450
Senior Executive Officer, W. Hardman, M.B.E.
£4,900 to £5,900

Solicitor's Office
Somerset House, W.C.2

Solicitor, E. G. R. Moses, C.B.............£11,100
Principal Assistant Solicitors, R. S. Boyd; J. S. Clarke, M.C.; J. W. Weston..........£9,000
Assistant Solicitors, A. L. L. Alexander; Mrs. A. Boyd; P. Carter; J. C. Doggett; J. F. Easton; M. C. Furey; P. D. Hall; D. M. Hatton; E. O. Jackson; H. G. Kingston; R. K. Miller; A. K. Tavaré.................£7,050 to £8,850
Senior Legal Assistants, C. J. C. Baron; J. G. H. Bates; D. S. Blair; R. T. Brand; K. O. Butterfield; B. R. D. Clarke; B. E. Cleave; T. P. J. Cockin; M. J. Cotton; A. S. Croxson; Miss M. A. Flitton; B. V. Godden; A. J. Gunz; J. F. W. Hinson; J. D. H. Johnston; Miss A. Joslin; D. MacDonagh; A. A. MacKeith; R. L. M. Parsey; N. R. Phillips; Mrs. E. K. Picard; P. L. Ridd; F. H. Sims; B. J. Walker; R. S. Waterson; A. Wheaten; J. T. Woodhouse; M. Woods..................£4,976 to £6,700
Principal, I. P. Dunkley.......£5,680 to £7,450
Senior Executive Officers, D. A. Gibb; O. D. Leanaghan.................£4,900 to £5,900

Superannuation Funds Office
Apex House, High Street, New Malden, Surrey

Controller, R. C. Tebboth.....£8,050 to £11,000
Assistant Controllers, P. Beever; Miss D. Bickmore; H. H. Jago; W. T. Lyons....£7,750 to £9,350
Principals, J. N. Gosling; J. G. Hull; L. A. Palmer; K. J. Style; B. S. Taylor; R. A. White
£5,680 to £7,450

Surtax Office
Lynwood Road, Thames Ditton, Surrey
Companies Division
Government Buildings, Garrison Lane, Chessington, Surrey
Office of the Inspector of Foreign Dividends
New Malden House, Blagdon Road, New Malden, Surrey

Controller of Surtax and Inspector of Foreign Dividends, D. S. Kirtley.........£8,650 to £11,000
Assistant Controllers of Surtax, W. J. Hunt; G. E. P. Matthews; J. Richardson; R. A. J. Webber
£7,750 to £9,350
Assistant Inspector of Foreign Dividends, N. W. Sydee
£7,750 to £9,350
Principals, H. Booth; S. J. C. Boucher; H. C. Buck; A. Campbell; R. Carrington; A. W. Coates; W. H. Day; H. Elsworth; H. B. Every; B. E. Greville; D. A. Hebbert; L. S. Jowsey; B. Lyons; Miss J. Madgwick; W. J. Moore; J. Sinfield; C. A. Thorpe; E. V. Wigglesworth
£5,680 to £7,450

Tithe Redemption Office
Barrington Road, Worthing, Sussex

Controller, D. H. Pooley.......£7,750 to £9,350

Accountant and Comptroller-General's Office
Bush House, South-West Wing, Strand, W.C.2
Accountant and Comptroller-Gen., F. H. Brooman
£12,000

Deputy Accountants and Comptrollers General, J. F. Hill; J. B. Sweeting; G. B. Walker, I.S.O.
£8,650 to £11,000
Assistant Accountants and Comptrollers-General, S. G. Ash, M.B.E.; L. C. Gilbertson; G. R. Lister; E. E. Wheeler..............£7,750 to £9,350

General Accounting and Collection of Taxes Division
Principal Collectors, F. E. Bance; J. A. Bolton; P. D. Connell; J. L. Cridge; F. C. Cullington; V. G. Ellen, I.S.O.; K. L. Fickling; D. C. Geddes; N. W. Griffiths; H. G. Grimshaw; J. G. C. Hopkins; G. Hull; W. A. Impey; G. D. Jenkins; E. G. Lewin; W. J. Millan; A. J. Morrison; R. A. Newberry; P. R. Newbury; B. H. Reynolds; W. H. J. Sharp, I.S.O.; A. L. Smith, I.S.O........................£5,680 to £7,450

Audit Division
Principal Collectors, W. Donaldson; G. Edmiston; A. B. D. Mason............£5,680 to £7,450

Office of the Chief Inspector of Taxes
Somerset House, W.C.2

Deputy Secretaries, E. V. Adams; E. V. Symons, C.B.
£14,000
Deputy Chief Inspectors, J. F. Boyd; R. W. Rae
£12,000
Under Secretaries, E. W. Boyles; D. H. Moorcraft; K. C. Southall.....................£12,000
Senior Principal Inspectors, C. W. Adam; G. L. Ayres, C.B.E.; N. E. Beck; J. T. Cannon; O. P. Davies; R. E. Dean; W. M. Dermit; F. S. Dodd; A. Gill; N. B. Hall; N. Hannah; R. A. Hogg; D. A. Jones; R. Kingsbury; R. E. Kirby; J. E. Lawrence; P. L. O'Leary; W. A. Perry; R. D. Rawson, M.B.E.; L. F. Robins; A. B. Scott, V.R.D.; J. A. Stephenson; L. S. Stratford; P. R. Sweetman, C.B.E.; I. R. E. Symons; F. J. Taylor-Gooby; I. D. Thomson; T. J. Thomson; P. Tillson; T. W. M. Tuite; P. Tyrer; J. K. Ward; W. P. A. Winton; A. S. Wray £11,440
Principal Inspectors (at Head Office), J. N. Allen; F .W. Bailey, O.B.E.; E. Ball; J. F. S. Banks; A. C. Batchelor; T. Bingham; A. D. M. Brown; R. W. Burgess; R. T. W. Butter; F. Carr; T. M. Ditchfield; E. Dowsland; C. D. Edwards; R. M. Elliss; G. R. Evans; A. Fleming; G. Galey; G. D. Hackston; H. C. Hart; P. Housden; P. Hudson; H. Innocent; P. B. G. Jones; A. G. King; G. E. Lane; J. Livesey; E. U. Miller; R. C. Murgatroyd; D. M. Portsmouth; W. S. Rankin; H. T. Reed; J. H. Roberts; T. Scott; R. J. Smith; D. H. Stanton; A. I. J. Steadman; G. E. Stoker; R. W. Storr; K. H. Sturtevant; J. P. Tomlinson; E. Walker; H. A. White.......£8,650 to £11,000
Senior Inspectors (at Head Office), A. G. Andrews; J. Barrie; E. S. Bew; M. F. Bickerton; D. W. Bond; K. R. Brown; A. R. Brunsdon; P. W. Burton; B. S. Caley; J. S. Chapman; K. H. Colmer; P. H. Dennis; F. W. F. Dobby; W. R. Drabble; E. Earnshaw; R. J. Fairlie; J. T. Fleming; T. C. Forsyth; A. Frost; M. J. Frost; J. P. G. Fysh; S. Gale; R. E. German; K. S. Goddard; A. Gordon; D. Haine; M. J. S. Harlock; H. O. Heather; R. Highnam; S. J. Hill; P. W. Johnstone; Miss E. M. Lacy; G. O. Lawton; S. R. Lock; E. J. McDonald; H. A. MacKinlay; I. A. MacLean; E. G. Markey; C. P. Melluish; Miss P. Millen; D. G. F. Money; R. H. Moore; H. R. J. Morris; J. A. Murphy; D. Myall; D. Newman; H. M. Newton; W. J. Northover; G. W. Orrell; R. N. Page; E. N. Parsons; E. Pattison; P. G. Perry; L. C. Phelps; J. H. W. Phillips; E. Pye; R. F. Ratcliff, I.S.O.; R. T. W. Roberts; J. F. A. Robertson; R. J. Scoble; F. H. Shea; R. W. C. Shepherd; Miss D. M. Sirett; A. M. Slater; J. W. Sutcliffe; L. G. Taylor; J. P. Thacker; J. E. Thompstone; D. W. Van Arkadie; R. E. Venn; P. W. Warrington; C. Watt; A. A. West; L. A. White; W. D. Widdup; D. Wilde; C. W. Willoughby; R. Wills; S. J. Wood
£6,980 to £9,350
Senior Principal Inspector (Scotland), I. D. Thomson.

Principal Inspectors (*Scotland*), J. Rankin; G. B. Small....................£8,650 to £11,000
Senior Inspector (*Scotland*), H. Morrell
£6,980 to £9,300
Principal Inspector (*Northern Ireland*), L. N. Mathers, O.B.E. ....£8,650 to £11,000
Principal Accountants, A. E. Allchurch; E. Lawson
£5,891 to £7,367
Chief Accountants, T. B. Carr; W. B. Cundy; J. M. Fulton; B. W. Gow; R. Halsall; W. E. Haslam; J. L. Henderson; C. U. Mack; F. R. Marshall; G. A. Reed; W. H. Simon; E. J. T. Smales; R. J. Ward; N. J. Wykes; A. B. Yewdall
£5,680 to £7,450

Valuation Office
New Court, Carey Street, W.C.2
Chief Valuer, M. I. Prevett, C.B., C.B.E. . . . £14,000
Deputy Chief Valuers, R. A. Garner; C. H. Tinsley
£12,000
Assistant Chief Valuers, E. A. Bullock; J. A. Christopher; J. J. Claringbull; M. Clark; J. B. Hyne; J. H. Martin; W. G. M. Williams...... £11,320
Superintending Valuers (*at Head Office*), J. V. C. Anthony, O.B.E.; N. I. Behr; P. J. Borrett; W. S. Culwick; A. C. Dolby-Jones; R. G. Edwards; T. A. Gerrard; R. D. E. Gilbard; T. L. Mason; J. S. Preston, T.D.; R. J. Schumacher
£9,798 to £10,563
First Class Valuers (*at Head Office*), L. W. Carr; G. Crawshaw; J. L. Flann; G. D. Francis; M. C. Fuller-Hall, O.B.E.; J. E. Hayes; D. O. Hodgon; S. H. Keith; D. R. Morrogh; J. F. Parker; T. H. Pursey; G. F. G. Russell; A. K. L. Ryde; G. S. A. Squire; J. P. Stevens; R. S. Stubbs; P. H. Sutton; W. Thomas; K. C. Walter, O.B.E.
£8,382 to £9,497
Senior Principal, D. McCluskey.. £7,750 to £9,350
Principals, G. E. Cole; W. C. Hughes
£5,680 to £7,450
Senior Executive Officers, L. N. Fletcher; F. E. Fokinther; A. H. Haggart; D. E. McKewan; T. R. Peckham; J. D. Scott; S. E. Watt
£4,900 to £5,900

INLAND REVENUE (SCOTLAND)
Controller of Stamps and Taxes
16 Waterloo Place, Edinburgh
Controller (*Principal*), D. M. Watson, I.S.O.
£5,680 to £7,450

Estate Duty Office
47 Robb's Loan, Edinburgh
Registrar of Death Duties, I. W. Grant.... £11,000
Deputy Registrar of Death Duties, J. W. Grant
£9,278
Chief Examiners, Miss M. M. M. Armstrong; I. S. Beveridge; P. G. Bruce; J. B. Donald; G. T. Graham, D.S.C.; F. F. King; J. B. M. McKean; A. M. McPake; J. A. Taylor.. £5,680 to £7,599

Solicitor's Office
16 Waterloo Place, Edinburgh 1
Solicitor, J. K. W. Dunn................ £9,440
Senior Legal Assistants, W. W. C. Pollock; T. H. Scott..................... £4,976 to £6,700

Valuation Office, Scotland
43 Rose Street, Edinburgh 2
Chief Valuer for Scotland, J. Beggs........ £11,440
Assistant Chief Valuers, W. L. Chesser, M.C., T.D.; J. Gilchrist............... £9,798 to £10,563
First Class Valuers (*at Head Office*), T. C. Grieve; A. Harvey; W. B. McGarva; A. Nimmo
£8,382 to £9,497

SPECIAL COMMISSIONERS OF INCOME TAX
Turnstile House, High Holborn, W.C.1
[01-438 6622]
The Special Commissioners are an independent body applied by the Treasury to hear appeals concerning income tax, surtax, corporation tax, capital gains tax, capital transfer tax and petroleum revenue tax.
Presiding Special Commissioner, R. A. Furtado, C.B.
£12,540

Special Commissioners, W. E. Bradley; J. B. Hodgson; B. James; J. G. Lewis; H. H. Monroe, Q.C.; H. G. Watson..................... £10,240
Clerk to Special Commissioners of Income Tax, C. H. Windeatt, I.S.O....... £5,680 to £7,450

INTERVENTION BOARD FOR AGRICULTURAL PRODUCE
Steel House, Tothill Street, S.W.1
[01-222 3391]
Fountain House, 2 West Mall, Reading
[Reading: 583636]
The Board was formed as a Government Department on November 22, 1972, and is responsible under the Agricultural Ministers for the implementation within the United Kingdom of the guarantee functions of the Common Agricultural Policy of the European Economic Community. Policy matters are the responsibility of the Agricultural Ministers of the United Kingdom.
Chairman: A. F. Shaw.
Chief Executive (*Under Secretary*), A. Savage*
£12,000

SECRETARIAT
Secretary and Information Officer (*Senior Executive Officer*), J. A. Colmer*...... £4,900 to £5,000

ESTABLISHMENTS BRANCH
Establishments Officer (*Principal*), G. R. Holloway
£5,680 to £7,450
Senior Executive Officers, J. Bird; D. A. Maddock
£4,900 to £5,900

FINANCE AND AUDIT DIVISION
Finance Officer (*Assistant Secretary*), H. R. Neilson
£8,650 to £11,000

Finance Branch
Principal, J. Owen............. £5,680 to £7,450
Senior Executive Officers, E. J. Kennedy; R. H. Ebsworth................ £4,900 to £5,900

Audit Branch
Chief Accountant, W. McLaren... £5,680 to £7,450
Senior Accountant, G. Thomas.. £4,900 to £5,000

INTERNAL MARKET DIVISION
Assistant Secretary, J. N. Jotcham
£8,650 to £11,000
Senior Principal, J. A. Bamford.. £7,750 to £9,350
Principals, J. N. Diserens; J. O. Macarthur; W. Thomson................ £5,680 to £7,450
Commodity Specialists, J. I. Payne; D. G. Griffiths
£5,680 to £7,450
Senior Executive Officers, D. L. Underwood; N. P. J. Rowe; D. H. Potter........ £4,900 to £5,900

IMPORT AND EXPORT DIVISION
Senior Principal, D. Salton...... £7,750 to £9,350
Principals, J. F. Robinson, O.B.E.; E. Prince
£5,680 to £7,450
Senior Executive Officers, A. D. Williams; F. Harrison; P. E. Robinson; R. W. Roughley
£4,900 to £5,900

UNITED KINGDOM SEEDS EXECUTIVE
Prof. O. G. Williams (*Chairman*),* J. Cormack; H. A. S. Doughty; T. P. Gibson; J. Gray, O.B.E.; T.D.; Prof. J. D. Ivins; J. D. Palmer; A. F. Shaw.
Secretary, J. A. Colmer (S.E.O.)
* At Steel House.

H.M. LAND REGISTRY
Lincoln's Inn Fields, W.C.2
[01-405 3488]
The registration of title to land was first introduced in England and Wales by the Land Registry Act, 1862. Many changes have been made to the original system by subsequent legislation and H.M. Land Registry operates today under the Land Registration Acts, 1925 to 1971. The object of registering title to land is for dealings with it to be made more simple and economical. This is achieved by maintaining a register of land owners whose title is guaranteed by the State and by providing simple forms for the transfer, mortgage

and other dealings with real property. Under the Land Registration Act 1966, the voluntary first registration of land in non-compulsory areas was severely curtailed in order to facilitate an accelerated programme for the extension of the compulsory system to cover all the built-up areas of the country within a few years. The intention is that registration of title shall ultimately be universal throughout England and Wales. Nevertheless, a great deal of land was formerly registered voluntarily in non-compulsory areas and it is still possible to register building estates, upon certain conditions, throughout the country. A great deal of land in non-compulsory areas is therefore already registered. H.M. Land Registry is administered under the Lord Chancellor by the Chief Land Registrar and the work is decentralized to a number of regional offices. The Chief Land Registrar is also responsible for the Land Charges Department and the Agricultural Credits Department.

Headquarters Office
Chief Land Registrar, R. B. Roper £14,000
Deputy Chief Land Registrar, A. G. W. James
         £12,000
Chief Assistant (Establishment Officer), K. E. Aris
         £11,320
Land Registrar, C. N. T. Waterer £9,033 to £11,000
Assistant Land Registrars, Mrs. A. B. Macfarlane;
   P. A. Meehan . . . . £6,625 to £8,750
Assistant Secretaries, H. R. Goose (Controller North);
   B. M. White (Controller South) £8,650 to £11,000
Senior Principal (Management Services), J. L. Memory
         £7,750 to £9,350
Principals, T. Chipperfield; G. H. Fisher; P. Gittings, I.S.O.; B. E. Kitching; J. J. Manthorpe;
E. F. Martin; J. B. Plail; P. F. Taylor
         £5,680 to £7,450

Establishment and Accounts
Deputy Establishment Officer, A. M. Wallace
         £5,750 to £9,350
Chief Accountant, K. Batey . . . . . . £5,680 to £7,450
Finance Officer, J. H. Haynes . . . . £5,680 to £7,450

Croydon District Land Registry
Sunley House, Bedford Park, Croydon
[01–686 8833]
District Land Registrar, S. Jacey . £9,033 to £11,000
Land Registrar, U. Davidson . . . £9,033 to £11,000
Assistant Land Registrars, A. E. Farwell; R. G.
   Glenister . . . . £6,625 to £8,750
Area Manager, A. W. Pardey . . £7,750 to £9,350

Durham District Land Registry
Aykley Heads, Durham
[Durham 61361]
District Land Registrar, Miss M. M. F. G. Walker
         £9,033 to £11,000
Assistant Land Registrars, P. H. Curnow; J. L. Hinchliffe; E. J. Pryer; H. M. Taylor
         £6,625 to £8,750
Area Manager, D. R. H. Grigg . . £5,680 to £7,450

Gloucester District Land Registry
Twyver House, Bruton Way,
Gloucester
[Gloucester: 28666]
District Land Registrar, C. W. K. Donaldson
         £9,033 to £11,000
Assistant Land Registrars, D. M. J. Moss; F. Quickfall;
   A. E. H. Sladen . . . . £6,625 to £8,750
Area Manager, H. J. Wiles . . . . £7,750 to £9,350

Harrow District Land Registry
Lyon House, Harrow, Middlesex
[01–427 8811]
District Land Registrar, A. O. Viney
         £9,033 to £11,000
Assistant Land Registrars, Miss J. E. Bagshaw; A. D.
   Dewar; Miss A. M. Phillips
         £6,625 to £8,750
Area Manager, A. G. Caudle . . £7,750 to £9,350

Lytham District Land Registry
Birkenhead House, Lytham St. Annes, Lancs.
[Lytham: 7541]

District Land Registrar, R. E. Shorrocks
         £9,033 to £11,000
Assistant Land Registrars, J. F. Bamber; B. E. Berry;
   K. L. Charles; J. B. Duckworth; F. G. D. Emler;
   L. D. Jefferies; Mrs. D. C. Palmer; J. B. Rhodes
         £6,625 to £8,760
Area Manager, P. J. Dix . . . . £7,750 to £9,350

Nottingham District Land Registry
Chalfont Drive, Nottingham
[Nottingham: 291111]
District Land Registrar, D. L. Groom
         £9,033 to £11,000
Assistant Land Registrars, F. G. Adamson; Miss C.
   M. Bannister; J. A. Hicks; N. U. A. Hogg
         £6,625 to £8,750
Area Manager, R. Palmer . . . . . . £7,750 to £9,350

Plymouth District Land Registry
Railway Offices, North Road, Plymouth, Devon
[Plymouth 69381]
District Land Registrar, W. D. Hosking
         £9,033 to £11,000
Assistant Land Registrars, E. G. Thomas; C. J. West
         £6,625 to £8,750
Area Manager, E. W. Hannam . . £5,680 to £7,450

Land Charges and Agricultural Credit
Department,
Burrington Way, Plymouth
[Plymouth: 779 831]
Superintendent of Land Charges, D. I. Whyte
         £4,360 to £5,775
Head of Computer Services Division, R. B. Parker
         £7,750 to £9,350
Principal, A. A. Restorick . . . . . . £5,680 to £7,450

Stevenage District Land Registry
Brickdale House, Danestrete, Stevenage, Herts.
[Stevenage: 4488]
District Land Registrar, G. A. Weddell
         £9,033 to £11,000
Assistant Land Registrars, M. H. Baines; W. W.
   Budden; H. S. Early; D. M. T. Mullett
         £6,625 to £8,750
Area Manager, A. C. Forrester . . £7,750 to £9,350

Swansea District Land Registry
37, The Kingsway, Swansea, Glam.
[Swansea 50971]
District Land Registrar, A. P. Roberts
         £9,033 to £11,000
Assistant Land Registrar, J. L. Inskip
         £6,625 to £8,750
Area Manager, H. Walker . . . . . £5,680 to £7,450

Tunbridge Wells District Land Registry
Curtis House, Tunbridge Wells, Kent
[Tunbridge Wells 26141]
District Land Registrar, D. P. Chivers
         £9,033 to £11,000
Land Registrar, P. Kendall . . . £9,033 to £11,000
Assistant Land Registrars, J. S. R. Bevington;
   R. H. Ellis; A. Gould; D. G. Thomas;
         £6,625 to £8,750
Area Manager, J. C. Eames, M.B.E. £7,750 to £9,350

LAW OFFICERS' DEPARTMENT
Attorney-General's Chambers,
Royal Courts of Justice, W.C.1.
The Law Officers of the Crown for England and Wales (the Attorney-General and the Solicitor-General) represent the Crown in courts of justice, advise Government departments and represent them in court. The Attorney-General has also certain administrative functions, including supervision of the Director of Public Prosecutions.
Attorney-General, THE RT. HON. SAMUEL CHARLES
   SILKIN, Q.C., M.P. £14,500
Parliamentary Private Secretary, D. Anderson, M.P.
Solicitor-General, PETER KINGSLEY ARCHER, Q.C.,
   M.P. £11,000
Parliamentary Private Secretary, J. W. Rooker, M.P.
Parliamentary Secretary, A. Davidson, M.P. £5,500
Legal Secretary, T. C. Hetherington, C.B.E., T.D.
         £14,000
Asst. Legal Sec., M. G. de Winton, C.B.E., M.C.
         £12,000

LIBRARIES

THE BRITISH LIBRARY
Store Street, W.C.1
[01-636 0755]

The British Library was established on July 1, 1973, under the British Library Act, 1972, to provide, on a national scale, comprehensive reference, lending, bibliographic and other services based on its vast collections of books, manuscripts maps, music, periodicals and other material.

The Library was created by bringing together under a management Board a number of national organizations to form three main Divisions. The Reference Division comprises the former library departments of the British Museum including the Newspaper Library at Colindale and Science Reference Library. The Lending Division comprises the former National Lending Library for Science and Technology and the former National Central Library. The Bibliographic Services Division incorporates the British National Bibliography and the (former British Museum) Copyright Receipt Office. There is also a Research and Development Department, and a Central Administration.

The Reference Division contains more than 9,000,000 printed books, about 80,000 Western and 35,000 Oriental manuscripts, and outstanding collections of newspapers, official papers, papyri, charters, seals, maps, music and postage stamps. Admission to the reading rooms for research is by ticket only. The Science Reference Library is the principal public reference library in the United Kingdom for contemporary literature of science and technology, and here no reader's ticket is necessary.

The Lending Division in Yorkshire operates a rapid postal loan or photocopy service for organizations and currently receives about 2,500,000 requests a year. Individuals should apply through their local libraries. The stock contains some 2,350,000 volumes of books and periodicals, about 1,500,000 documents in microfilm, and large quantities of semi-published materials such as reports, translations and theses.

BOARD MEMBERS
Chairman, The Viscount Eccles, P.C., K.C.V.O.
Deputy Chairman and Chief Executive, H. T. Hookway.
Directors General, Reference Division, D. T. Richnell, C.B.E.; Bibliographic Services Division, R. E. Coward; Lending Division, M. B. Line.
Part-time Members, The Lord Adeane, P.C., G.C.B., G.C.V.O. (*appointed by Her Majesty The Queen*); J. W. Barrett, C.B.E.; Sir John Brown, C.B.E.; Mrs. Alison Munro, C.B.E.; A. E. Ritchie; J. S. Watson; Prof. Glanmor Williams; A. Wilson.

CENTRAL ADMINISTRATION
Secretary to the Board and Head of Central Administration, E. Martindale.

REFERENCE DIVISION
Reference Division, Gt. Russell St., London, W.C.1
[01-636 1544]
Science Reference Library
25 Southampton Buildings, London, W.C.2
[01-405 8721]
and
10 Porchester Gardens, London, W.2
[01-405 8721]
Newspaper Library, Colindale Avenue, N.W.9
[01-205 6039]
Keepers, Department of Printed Books, J. L. Wood; R. J. Fulford.
Keeper, Department of Manuscripts, D. P. Waley.
Keeper, Department of Oriental Manuscripts and Printed Books, G. E. Marrison.
Director of Science Reference Library, M. W. Hill.
LENDING DIVISION
Boston Spa, Wetherby, Yorks.
[0937 843434]
Executive Director, K. Barr.

BIBLIOGRAPHIC SERVICES DIVISION
Store Street, W.C.1
[01-636 0755]
Director of Copyright and English Language Services, J. Downing.
RESEARCH AND DEVELOPMENT DEPARTMENT
Elizabeth House, York Road, S.E.1
[01-928 9222]
Director, J. C. Gray.

PRESS AND PUBLIC RELATIONS SECTION
Store Street, W.C.1
[01-636 0755]

NATIONAL LIBRARY OF SCOTLAND
George IV Bridge, Edinburgh
[01-226 4531]

Open free. Reading Room, weekdays, 9.30 a.m. to 8.30 p.m. Saturdays 9.30 to 1. Map Room, weekdays, 9.30 to 5 p.m.; Saturdays, 9.30 to 1. Exhibition, weekdays, 9.30 a.m. to 5 p.m. Saturdays, 9.30 to 1; Sundays, 2 to 5. During Edinburgh International Festival open till 8.30 p.m. on weekdays. (Sundays, 2 to 5.)

The Library, which had been founded as the Advocates' Library in 1682, became the National Library of Scotland by Act of Parliament in 1925. It continues to share the rights conferred by successive Copyright Acts since 1710. Its collections of printed books and MSS., augmented by purchase and gift, are very large and it has an unrivalled Scottish collection. The present building was opened by H.M. the Queen in 1956.

The Reading Room is for reference and research which cannot conveniently be pursued elsewhere. Admission is by ticket issued to an approved applicant.

Chairman of the Trustees, M. F. Strachan, M.B.E.
Librarian and Secretary to the Trustees, E. F. D. Roberts, Ph.D. £11,000
Secretary of the Library, M. A. Pegg, Ph.D.
£7,151 to £8,750
Assistant Keepers, First Class, M. A. Begg; A. M. Marchbank, Ph.D. .... £4,404 to £7,100
Keepers of Printed Books, J. R. Seaton £8,650 to £9,749); W. H. Brown, E.R.D.; A. M. Cain, Ph.D.; R. Donaldson, Ph.D. ... £7,151 to £8,750
Assistant Keepers, First Class, T. A. F. Cherry; Alison A. Harvey Wood; Alexia F. Howe; W. A. Kelly; I. D. McGowan; J. B. McKeeman; Ann Matheson; J. Morris; Margaret Wilkes
£4,404 to £7,109
Senior Research Assistants, Margaret E. Cramb; Ruth I. Hope; Christine E. G. Wright
£4,185 to £5,778
Keepers of Manuscripts, J. S. Ritchie; T. I. Rae, Ph.D.
£7,151 to £8,750
Assistant Keepers, First Class, A. S. Bell; P. M. Cadell; I. C. Cunningham; B. G. Hutton; I. F. MacIver; S. M. Simpson; Elspeth D. Yeo
£4,404 to £7,109

THE NATIONAL LIBRARY OF WALES
LLYFRGELL GENEDLAETHOL CYMRU
Aberystwyth

Readers' room open on weekdays, 9.30 a.m. to 6 p.m. (Saturdays, 5 p.m.); closed on Sundays. Admission by Reader's Ticket.

Founded by Royal Charter, 1907, and maintained by annual grant from the Treasury. One of the six libraries entitled to most privileges under Copyright Act. Contains nearly 2,000,000 printed books, 30,000 manuscripts, 3,500,000 deeds and documents, and numerous maps, prints and drawings. Specializes in manuscripts and books relating to Wales and the Celtic peoples. Repository for pre-1858 Welsh probate records. Approved by the Master of the Rolls as a repository for manorial records and tithe documents, and by the Lord Chancellor for certain legal records. Bureau of the Regional Libraries Scheme for Wales.
Librarian, D. Jenkins.

LOCAL GOVERNMENT. *See* DEPARTMENT OF THE ENVIRONMENT

LONDON TRANSPORT EXECUTIVE
55 Broadway, S.W.1
[01-222 5600]

The Greater London Council is responsible for the overall policy and financial control of London Transport, but the Executive is wholly responsible for the day-to-day management and operation.

Chairman, The Rt. Hon. Kenneth Robinson
       £19,600
Deputy Chairman and Chief Executive, R. Bennett
       £15,600
Managing Director (Railways), R. M. Robbins
       £14,100
Members, J. G. Glendinning, O.B.E.; W. W. Maxwell; D. A. Quarmby; J. C. F. Cameron (*each* £12,000); S. J. Barton; L. W. Robson; Sir Peter Masefield (*part-time*).............*each* £1,000
Secretary, P. E. Garbutt, M.B.E.

LORD ADVOCATE'S DEPARTMENT
Fielden House, 10 Great College Street,
Westminster, S.W.1

The Law Officers for Scotland are the Lord Advocate and the Solicitor-General for Scotland. The Lord Advocate's Department is responsible for drafting Scottish legislation, for providing legal advice to other departments on Scottish questions and for assistance to the Law Officers for Scotland in certain of their legal duties.

Lord Advocate, The Rt. Hon. Ronald King Murray, Q.C., M.P.............................. £11,000
Solicitor-General for Scotland, J. H. McCluskey, Q.C.
       £7,750
Legal Secretary and First Parliamentary Draftsman, G. I. Mitchell, C.B., Q.C. £14,000
Deputy Legal Secretary and Parliamentary Draftsman, J. M. Moran.......................... £12,000
Asst. Legal Secs. and Parlty. Draftsmen, N. J. Adamson; A. C. B. Reid; J. F. Wallace
       £9,798 to £11,440
Junior Legal Secs. and Parlty. Draftsmen, G. M. Clark; J. C. McCluskie............ £6,625 to £8,750

LORD GREAT CHAMBERLAIN'S OFFICE
House of Lords, S.W.1
[01-219 3100]

The Lord Great Chamberlain is a Great Officer of State, the office being hereditary since the grant of Henry I to the family of De Vere, Earls of Oxford.

Lord Great Chamberlain, The Marquess of Cholmondeley, M.C.
Secretary to the Lord Great Chamberlain, Admiral Sir Frank Twiss, K.C.B., D.S.C.
Clerks to the Lord Great Chamberlain, Lady Elizabeth Montgomerie; Miss G. Holland.

LORD PRIVY SEAL
House of Lords

Lord Privy Seal and Leader of the House of Lords, THE LORD SHEPHERD, P.C.
Private Secretary, N. B. J. Gurney.

OFFICE OF MANPOWER ECONOMICS
22 Kingsway, W.C.2
[01-405 5944]

The Office of Manpower Economics was set up in 1970 and the first Director was appointed in 1971. It is an independent non-statutory organization which is responsible for providing a common secretariat for three review bodies which advise on sectors of public service pay for which no negotiating machinery is appropriate: these are the Top Salaries Review Body which covers the Higher Judiciary, the Chairmen and members of the nationalized industry Boards, the senior grades of the Higher Civil Service and senior officers of the armed forces; the Armed Forces Pay Review Body, which advises on the pay and allowances of all ranks up to and including Brigadier; and the Review Body on Doctors' and Dentists' Remuneration, which advises on the remuneration of doctors and dentists in the National Health Service. It also provides the secretariat for the Post Office Arbitration Tribunal and other *ad hoc* arbitrations, and for courts of inquiry.

Director, Miss J. F. H. Orr.
Chief Statistician, R. F. Burch.

MANPOWER SERVICES COMMISSION
Stratton House, Stratton Street, Piccadilly,
London, W.1
[01-409 0491]

The Manpower Services Commission was established under the Employment and Training Act 1973, and administers the employment and training services previously provided by the Department of Employment, through two executive arms; the Employment Service Agency and the Training Services Agency. The Commission also advises the Government on manpower policies, and comprises representatives of employers, unions, local government and education. The Commission's chief functions are to help people train for and obtain jobs which satisfy their aspirations and abilities, and to help employers find suitable workers.

Chairman, Sir Denis Barnes, K.C.B....... £21,000
Deputy Chairman, D. A. C. Dewdney, C.B.E.
Members, M. O. Bury, O.B.E.; D. J. Docherty; K. Graham, O.B.E.; R. L. Helmore; D. McGarvey, C.B.E.; V. G. Paige; C. H. Urwin; Mrs. E. A. Yates, C.B.E.;
Secretary, J. H. Galbraith.............. £12,000
Director of Manpower, Intelligence and Planning, G. Reid.............................. £12,000
Finance Officer, I. M. Miller.... £8,650 to £11,000
Director of Information, A. P. Dignum

MEDICAL RESEARCH COUNCIL
20 Park Crescent, W.1
[01-636 5422]

The Council, formerly the Medical Research Committee established in 1913 under the National Health Insurance Act, was incorporated under its present title by Royal Charter on April 1, 1920; a revised charter was issued in 1966. It is responsible to the Secretary of State for Education and Science.

The Council's constitution enables it to pursue an independent policy for the advancement of knowledge in the medical sciences and to initiate and encourage research both in this country and abroad: it is advised by four Research Boards, an Environmental Medicine (Research Policy) Committee and a number of expert Committees covering particular fields. The Council supports research by employing its own scientific staff in the National Institute for Medical Research, the Clinical Research Centre, the National Institute for Biological Standards and Control, and other research establishments (listed below); by financing projects in university and other departments through various schemes of research grants; and by the award of fellowships and scholarships for training in research methods. The Council is supported by a Parliamentary grant-in-aid but is also in a position to receive funds from private sources.

Members, The Duke of Northumberland, K.G., P.C., T.D., F.R.S. (*Chairman*); Sir John Gray, SC.D., F.R.S. (*Secretary*); Prof. I. R. C. Batchelor; Sir Douglas Black, M.D.; Sir John Brotherston, M.D., F.R.S.E.; J. P. Bull, C.B.E., M.D.; A. S. V. Burgen, M.D., F.R.S.; Prof. S. Cohen, M.D., Ph.D.; D. G. Davey, O.B.E., Ph.D.; Prof. A. C. Dornhorst, M.D.; The Earl of Halsbury, F.R.S.; Helen Muir, M.A., D.Phil; Prof. D. C. Phillips, Ph.D., F.R.S.; G. F. Vaughan, M.P.; Prof. J. N. Walton, T.D., M.D., D.SC.; Prof. R. B. Welbourn, M.D., F.R.C.S.; Prof. T. P Whitehead, Ph.D.; H. Yellowlees, C.B.
Second Secretary, S. G. Owen, M.D.
Administrative Secretary, J. G. Duncan.

Tropical Medicine Research Board
Development Administration)
Chairman, Prof. S. Cohen, M.D., Ph.D.

Neurobiology and Mental Health Board
Chairman, Prof. I. R. C. Batchelor, F.R.S.E.

Physiological Systems and Disorders Board
Chairman, Prof. A. C. Dornhorst, M.D.

Cell Biology and Disorders Board
Chairman, Prof. D. C. Phillips, Ph.D., F.R.S.

Environmental Medicine (Research Policy) Committee
Chairman, J. P. Bull, C.B.E., M.D.

HEADQUARTERS OFFICE
Senior Principal Medical Officer, R. C. Norton.

Research Programmes Division A
Principal Medical Officer, Katherine Lévy.
Senior Medical Officers, M. J. Fisher; D. M. G. Murphy.
Medical Officers, June R. Hill; Margaret M. Macpherson; Soraja Ramaswamy.
Principal Scientific Officers, Bronwen Loder, D.Phil.; T. Vickers, Ph.D.

Research Programmes Division B
Principal Medical Officer, Sheila Howarth.
Senior Medical Officers, H. W. Bunjé, M.D.; P. J. Chapman; Barbara Rashbass.
Medical Officers, Enid Bennett; Joan Box; Helen N. Duke, Ph.D.; D. Sturrock.
Principal Scientific Officers, Clare Gichard; M. B. Kemp, Ph.D.

Commissioned Research Group
Senior Principal Medical Officer, R. C. Norton.
Principal Scientific Officer, Victoria Harrison, D.Phil.

Secretariat and Universities Division
Head of Division, C. A. Kirkman.
Secretariat, J. H. Morris.
Universities, J. S. Gordon.

Administrative Division
Head of Division, J. G. Duncan.
Assistant Secretaries, A. E. Turner; F. Rushton; D. Noble.

Establishment and Management Services
Head of Section, J. E. A. Hay.

National Institute for Medical Research
Mill Hill, N.W.7
[01–959 3666]
Director, A. S. V. Burgen, M.D., F.R.S.

Clinical Research Centre
Watford Road, Harrow, Middlesex
[01–864 5311]
Director, G. M. Bull, M.D.

National Institute for Biological Standards and Control
Holly Hill, Hampstead, N.W.3
[01–436 2232]
Director, Prof. D. G. Evans, C.B.E., D.SC., Ph.D., F.R.S.

Research Units
Abnormal Haemoglobin Unit, University Dept. of Biochemistry, Addenbrooke's Hospital, Cambridge. *Hon. Director*, Prof. H. Lehmann, Ph.D., SC.D., F.R.S.
Air Pollution Unit, St. Bartholomew's Hospital Medical College, Charterhouse Square, E.C.1. *Director*, Prof. P. J. Lawther, D.SC.
Applied Psychology Unit, 15 Chaucer Road, Cambridge. *Director*, A. D. Baddeley, Ph.D.
Biochemical Parasitology Unit, Molteno Institute, Downing Street, Cambridge. *Director*, B. A. Newton, Ph.D.
Blood Group Reference Laboratory, Gatliff Road, S.W.1. *Director*, K. L. G. Goldsmith, Ph.D.
Blood Group Unit, Lister Institute of Preventive Medicine, Chelsea Bridge Road, S.W.1. *Director*, Ruth Sanger, Ph.D., F.R.S.
Blood Pressure Unit, Western Infirmary, Glasgow. *Director*, A. F. Lever.

Brain Metabolism Unit, Dept. of Pharmacology, The University, 1 George Square, Edinburgh. *Director*, G. W. Ashcroft, D.SC.
Cell Biophysics Unit, Dept. of Biophysics, University of London, King's College, 26–29 Drury Lane, W.C.2. *Hon. Director*, Prof. M. H. F. Wilkins, C.B.E., Ph.D., F.R.S.
Cell Mutation Unit, University of Sussex, Falmer, Brighton. *Director*, Prof. B. A. Bridges, Ph.D.
Cellular Immunology Unit, Sir William Dunn School of Pathology, Oxford. *Director*, Prof. J. L. Gowans, C.B.E., D.Phil., F.R.S.
Clinical and Population Cytogenetics Unit, Western General Hospital, Crewe Road, Edinburgh. *Director*, Prof. H. J. Evans, Ph.D., F.R.S.E.
Clinical Genetics Unit, Institute of Child Health, 30 Guilford Street, W.C.1. *Director*, C. O. Carter, D.M.
Clinical Pharmacology Unit, University Department of Clinical Pharmacology, Radcliffe Infirmary, Oxford. *Hon. Director*, Prof. D. G. Grahame-Smith, Ph.D., F.R.C.P.
Clinical Psychiatry Unit, Graylingwell Hospital, Chichester, Sussex. *Director*, P. Sainsbury, M.D.
Cyclotron Unit, Hammersmith Hospital, Ducane Road, W.12. *Director*, D. D. Vonberg.
Demyelinating Diseases Unit, Newcastle General Hospital, Westgate Road, Newcastle-upon-Tyne. *Director*, H. M. Wisniewski, M.D., Ph.D.
Dental Unit, Dental School, Lower Maudlin Street, Bristol. *Hon. Director*, Prof. A. I. Darling, C.B.E., D.D.SC.
Dental Epidemiology Unit, The London Hospital Medical College, Turner Street, E.1. *Hon. Director*, Prof. G. L. Slack, C.B.E., T.D., D.D.S.
Unit on the Development and Integration of Behaviour, Subdept. of Animal Behaviour, Madingley, Cambridge. *Hon. Director*, Prof. R. A. Hinde, SC.D., D.Phil., F.R.S.
Developmental Neurobiology Unit, M.R.C. Laboratories, Woodmansterne Road, Carshalton, Surrey. *Director*, R. Balazs, Dr.Med., Dr.Phil.
Developmental Psychology Unit, Drayton House, Gordon Street, W.C.1. *Director*, N. O'Connor, Ph.D.
Dunn Nutrition Unit, Milton Road, Cambridge. *Director*, R. G. Whitehead, Ph.D.
Unit for the Study of Environmental Factors in Mental and Physical Illness, London School of Economics and Political Science, 20 Hanway Place, W.1. *Director*, J. W. B. Douglas.
Environmental Physiology Unit, London School of Hygiene and Tropical Medicine, Keppel Street, W.C.1. *Director*, Prof. J. S. Weiner, D.SC.
Epidemiology and Medical Care Unit, Northwick Park Hospital, Harrow, Middx. *Director*, T. W. Meade.
Epidemiology Unit (Jamaica), University of the West Indies, Mona, Kingston, Jamaica. *Director*, G. R. Serjeant, M.D.
Epidemiology Unit (South Wales), 4 Richmond Road, Cardiff. *Director*, P. C. Elwood, M.D.
Medical Research Council Laboratories, Gambia, Fajara, P.O. Box 273, Banjul, Gambia, W. Africa. *Director*, R. S. Bray, Ph.D., D.SC.
Unit for Epidemiological Studies in Psychiatry, University of Psychiatry, Royal Edinburgh Hospital, Morningside Park, Edinburgh. *Director*, N. B. Kreitman, M.D.
Experimental Haematology Unit, St. Mary's Hospital Medical School, W.2. *Director*, Prof. P. L. Mollison, M.D., F.R.S.
Unit on the Experimental Pathology of Skin, Medical School, The University, Birmingham. *Director*, C. N. D. Cruickshank, M.D.
Gastroenterology Unit, Central Middlesex Hospital Park Royal, N.W.10. *Director*, E. N. Rowlands, M.D.
Hearing and Balance Unit, Institute of Neurology, National Hospital, Queen Square, W.C.1. *Director*, J. D. Hood, D.SC.
Human Biochemical Genetics Unit, Galton Laboratory University College, Wolfson House, 4 Stephen-

son Way, N.W.1. *Hon. Director,* Prof. H. Harris, M.D., F.R.S.

Immunochemistry Unit, University Department of Biochemistry, South Parks Road, Oxford. *Hon. Director,* Prof. R. R. Porter, Ph.D., F.R.S.

Industrial Injuries and Burns Unit, Birmingham Accident Hospital, Bath Row, Birmingham 15. *Director,* J. P. Bull, C.B.E., M.D.

Laboratory Animals Centre, M.R.C. Laboratories, Woodmansterne Road, Carshalton, Surrey. *Director,* J. Bleby.

Unit for Laboratory Studies of Tuberculosis, Royal Postgraduate Medical School, Ducane Road, W.12. *Director,* Prof. D. A. Mitchison.

Leukaemia Unit, Royal Postgraduate Medical School, Ducane Road, W.12. *Hon. Director,* D. A. G. Galton, M.D.

Lipid Metabolism Unit, Hammersmith Hospital, Ducane Road, W.12. *Director,* N. B. Myant, D.M.

Mammalian Development Unit, University College London, Wolfson House, 4 Stephenson Way, N.W.1. *Director,* Anne McLaren, D.Phil., F.R.S.

Mammalian Genome Unit, University of Edinburgh, Dept. of Zoology, West Mains Road, Edinburgh. *Director,* Prof. P. M. B. Walker, Ph.D.

Mammalian Genome Unit, University of Edinburgh, Dept. of Zoology, West Mains Road, Edinburgh. *Director,* Prof. P. M. B. Walker, Ph.D.

Medical Sociology Unit, Centre for Social Studies, Westburn Road, Aberdeen. *Director,* Prof. R. Illsley, Ph.D.

Unit for Metabolic Studies in Psychiatry, University Dept. of Psychiatry, Middlewood Hospital, P.O. Box 134, Sheffield. *Hon. Director,* Prof. F. A. Jenner, Ph.D.

Microbial Systematics Unit, Adrian Building, University of Leicester. *Director,* Prof. P. H. A. Sneath, M.D.

Mineral Metabolism Unit, The General Infirmary, Great George Street, Leeds. *Director,* Prof. B.E. C. Nordin, M.D., D.Sc.

Laboratory of Molecular Biology, University Postgraduate Medical School, Hills Road, Cambridge. *Chairman of Governing Board,* M. F. Perutz, C.H., C.B.E., Ph.D., F.R.S.

Unit on Neural Mechanisms of Behaviour, 3 Malet Place, W.C.1. *Director,* I. S. Russell, Ph.D.

Neurochemical Pharmacology Unit, University Dept. Hills Road, Cambridge. *Director,* L. L. Iversen, Ph.D.

Neurological Prostheses Unit, Institute of Psychiatry, De Crespigny Park, Denmark Hill, S.E.5. *Director,* Prof. G. S. Brindley, M.D., F.R.S.

Neuropharmacology Unit, The Medical School, Birmingham 15. *Hon. Director,* Prof. P. B. Bradley, D.Sc.

Unit for Physical Aids for the Disabled, Princess Margaret Rose Orthopædic Hospital, Fairmile, head, Edinburgh. *Hon. Director,* Prof. D. C, Simpson, M.B.E., Ph.D., F.R.S.E.

Pneumoconiosis Unit, Llandough Hospital, Penarth, Glam. *Director,* J. C. Gilson, C.B.E.

Radiobiology Unit, Harwell, Didcot, Oxon. *Director,* R. H. Mole.

Reproduction and Growth Unit, Princess Mary Maternity Hospital, Newcastle-upon-Tyne, *Director,* Prof. A. M. Thomson.

Reproductive Biology Unit, Dept. of Obstetrics and Gynaecology, 39 Chalmers Street, Edinburgh. *Director,* R. V. Short, Sc.D., F.R.S.

Rheumatism Unit, Canadian Red Cross Memorial Hospital, Taplow, Maidenhead, Berks. *Director,* Prof. E. G. L. Bywaters.

Social and Applied Psychology Unit, Dept. of Psychology, University of Sheffield. *Director,* P. B. Warr, Ph.D.

Social Medicine Unit, London School of Hygiene, and Tropical Medicine, Keppel Street, W.C.1. *Hon. Director,* Prof. J. N. Morris, C.B.E., M.D., D.Sc.

Social Psychiatry Unit, Institute of Psychiatry, De Crespigny Park, Denmark Hill, S.E.5. *Director,* Prof. J. K. Wing, M.D., Ph.D.

Statistical Research and Services Unit, University College, Hospital Medical School, 115 Gower Street, W.C.1. *Director,* I. Sutherland, D.Phil.

Toxicology Unit, M.R.C. Laboratories, Woodmansterne Road, Carshalton. *Director,* J. M. Barnes, C.B.E.

Tuberculosis and Chest Diseases Unit, Brompton Hospital, Fulham Road, S.W.3. *Director,* W. Fox, C.M.G., M.D.

Virology Unit, Institute of Virology, Church Street, Glasgow. *Hon. Director,* Prof. J. H. Subak-Sharpe, Ph.D., F.R.S.E.

Vision Unit, School of Biological Sciences, University of Sussex, Falmer, Brighton. *Director,* Prof. H. J. A. Dartnall, D.Sc.

METRICATION BOARD
22 Kingsway, W.C.2
[01-242 6828]

Chairman, The Lord Orr-Ewing, O.B.E.
Deputy Chairman, The Baroness White.
Members, M. A. Abrams, Ph.D.; B. N. Baxter, Ph.D.; Miss F. K. College; E. Cust; D. H. Darbishire; J. C. Dewar; J. M. Ferguson; D. Hobman; P. J. L. Homan (*Director*); Miss D. D. Hyams, O.B.E.; D. M. Landau; Prof. M. L. McGlashan; H. P. Scanlon; Mrs. A. Stanley; Mrs. J. Upward.
Secretary, A. B. Clarke.

THE ROYAL MINT
Llantrisant, nr. Pontyclun,
Mid-Glamorgan
[0443-222111]

Master Works and Warden, The Chancellor of the Exchequer (*ex officio*).
Deputy Master and Comptroller, J. R. Christie*.
Secretary and Establishment Officer, R. F. Liggins
       £7,750 to £9,350
Director of Marketing and Sales, A. J. Dowling, O.B.E., D.F.C.* .... £8,650 to £11,000
Director of Production, R. A. Yates £11,000
Chemist and Assayer, E. G. V. Newman, O.B.E.*
       £8,650 to £9,798
Superintendent, E. J. Howlett ... £8,650 to £9,798
Principals, F. Cornell*; D. C. Snell (*Finance Officer*);
   A. Forster .... £5,680 to £7,450
Principal Professional and Technology Officers, E. M. Phillips; R. W. Gravenor ... £6,280 to £7,450
Principal Scientific Officer, I. Hepburn (*Quality Manager*)................. £5,514 to £7,205
Chief Engraver, E. Sewell ...... £5,871 to £6,463

   * Stationed at Royal Mint, Tower Hill, E.C.3 [01-488-3424].

MONOPOLIES AND MERGERS COMMISSION
New Court, 48 Carey Street, W.C.2
[01-405 9722]

The Commission was established under the Monopolies and Restrictive Practices (Inquiry and Control) Act 1948 as the Monopolies and Restrictive Practices Commission and was reconstituted on subsequent occasions. It became the Monopolies and Mergers Commission when the Fair Trading Act, 1973, came into operation on November 1, 1973. The Commission has the duty of investigating and reporting on questions referred to it in accordance with the Act with respect to (*a*) the existence or possible existence of monopoly situations not registrable under the Restrictive Trade Practices Act, 1956, as extended by the 1973 Act, and relating to the supply of goods or services to the United Kingdom or part of the United Kingdom or to the supply of goods for export; (*b*) the transfer of a newspaper or newspaper's assets; (*c*) the creation or possible creation of a merger situation qualifying for investigation within the meaning of the Act.

In monopoly references (except those "limited to the facts ") and in merger references it is the duty of the Commission to report on the effect of the facts which they find in the public interest and to consider and, if they think fit, to recommend the action to be taken to remedy or prevent adverse effects. In addition the Fair Trading Act, 1973, provides for references to the Commission on the general effect on the public interest of specified monopoly or other uncompetitive practices and of restrictive labour practices.

Chairman, J. G. Le Quesne.............. £16,350
Deputy Chairmen, Sir Alexander Johnston, G.C.B., K.B.E. (part time) (£6,480); E. L. Richards, C.B.E. M.C., T.D. (part-time) £6,480
Members, G. F. Ashford, O.B.E.; R. G. Aspray; Prof. T. Barna, C.B.E., Ph.D.; D. E. Bernard; Sir Max Brown, K.C.B., C.M.G.; Sir Roger Falk, O.B.E.; J. Gratwick; Lady Laura Hall; F. E. Jones, M.B.E., Ph.D., D.SC., F.R.S.; T. P. Lyons; R. G. Opie; C. T. H. Plant, C.B.E. L. Robertson, C.B.E.; S. A. Robinson; J. S. Sadler; Miss R. Stephen, M.B.E.; Prof. H. Street, F.B.A.; Prof. B. S. Yamey, each £2,300

Secretary, Miss Y. Lovat-Williams.

MUSEUMS

STANDING COMMISSION ON MUSEUMS AND GALLERIES
2 Carlton Gardens, S.W.1
[01-930 0095]
First appointed Feb. 11, 1931. The functions of the Commission are:—(1) To advise generally on questions relevant to the most effective development of the National Institutions as a whole and on any specific questions which may be referred to them from time to time; (2) to promote co-operation between the National Institutions themselves and between the National and Provincial Institutions; (3) to stimulate the generosity and direct the efforts of those who aspire to become public benefactors.
Chairman, The Earl of Rosse, K.B.E., F.S.A.
Members, Sir Trenchard Cox, C.B.E., F.R.S.A., F.S.A.; The Earl of Crawford and Balcarres, K.T., G.B.E.; Sir Arthur Drew, K.C.B.; Prof. I. Ll. Foster, F.S.A.; The Earl of Halsbury, F.R.S.; S. C. Mason, C.B.E.; Sir Terence Morrison-Scott, D.S.C., D.Sc.; Sir John Pilcher, K.C.M.G.; The Earl of Plymouth; P. F. Scott; F. J. Stott, O.B.E.; Sir Duncan Wilson, G.C.M.G.
Secretary, Mrs. B. Granger-Taylor.

THE BRITISH MUSEUM
Great Russell Street, W.C.1
[01-636 1555]
Antiquities Department: Egyptian, Prehistoric and Romano-British, Greek and Roman, Mediæval and Later; Oriental, Western Asiatic; also, Coins and Medals, Prints and Drawing, Ethnography. Main entrance, Great Russell Street, W.C.1; North entrance, Montague Place, W.C.1. Open weekdays (including Bank Holidays) 10 to 5 and Sundays 2.30 to 6. Closed on Good Friday, Christmas Eve, Christmas Day, Boxing Day and New Year's Day. The ethnographical collections are displayed in The Museum of Mankind at 6 Burlington Gardens, W.1. Opening times as above.
The British Museum may be said to date from 1753, when Parliament granted funds to purchase the collections of Sir Hans Sloane and the Harleian manuscripts, and for their proper housing and maintenance. The building (Montague House) was opened in 1759. The present buildings were erected between 1823 and the present day, and the original collection has increased to its present dimensions by gifts and purchases. The administrative expenses were estimated at £4,065,000 in 1975–76, and were met by a vote under " Museums, Galleries and the Arts ", Class IX of the Civil Estimates. The constitution of the British Museum was revised under the terms of the British Museum Act, 1963.

Under the provisions of the British Library Act 1972 and the British Library Act (Appointed Day) Order 1973, the Library Departments of the British Museum were transferred on July 1, 1973, from the responsibility of the Trustees of the British Museum to that of the British Library Board and became part of the British Library.

BOARD OF TRUSTEES
Appointed by the Sovereign: H.R.H. The Duke of Gloucester. Appointed by the Prime Minister: (Chairman) The Lord Trevelyan, K.G., G.C.M.G., C.I.E., O.B.E (Chairman); The Lord Annan, O.B.E.; Prof. Sir Misha Black, O.B.E.; The Viscount Boyd of Merton, P.C., C.H.; The Lord Boyle of Handsworth, P.C.; Sir Arthur Drew, K.C.B.; The Earl of Drogheda, K.G., K.B.E.; The Lord Fletcher, P.C., LL.D.; Prof. Sir Ernst Gombrich, C.B.E., Ph.D., F.B.A., F.S.A.; Prof. L. C. B. Gower, M.B.E., F.B.A.; E. T. Hall, D.Phil.; C. D. Hamilton, D.S.O.; The Lord Holford, R.A., F.R.I.B.A.; Simon Hornby; Sir Richard Thompson, Bt,; The Lord Trend, P.C., G.C.B., G.C.V.O.
Nominated by the Royal Society, Royal Academy, British Academy and Society of Antiquaries of London: Sir John Kendrew, C.B.E. (Royal Society); Miss Elizabeth Frink, C.B.E., A.R.A. (Royal Academy); Sir Max Mallowan, C.B.E., D.Litt., F.B.A., F.S.A. (British Academy); Prof. J. G. D. Clark, C.B.E., SC.D., F.B.A. (Society of Antiquaries).
Appointed by the Trustees of the British Museum: The Lord Ashby, D.Sc., F.R.S.; The Lord Clark, C.H., K.C.B., F.B.A.; Dame Kathleen Kenyon, D.B.E., D.Litt., L.H.D., F.B.A., F.S.A.; Sir Edmund Leach, Ph.D., F.B.A.

OFFICERS
Director, Sir John Pope-Hennessy, C.B.E... £14,480
Deputy Director, Maysie F. Webb
.... £10,180 to £11,000
Secretary, G. B. Morris......... £7,151 to £8,750
Assistant Secretary, Barbara J. Youngman
.... £4,404 to £7,109
Administrative Assistant, Jean M. Rankine
.... £4,404 to £7,109
Head of Public Services, S. P. Cooper
.... £8,650 to £9,798
Assistant Keeper, Information Services, Marilyn R. Luscombe................. £4,404 to £7,109
Education Officer, (vacant) ...... £7,151 to £8,750
Design Officer, Margaret Hall, O.B.E.
.... £4,404 to £7,109
Senior Principal, C. W. Berry... £7,750 to £9,350
Principals, J. F. W. Ryde; R. A. J. French
.... £5,680 to £7,450
Senior Executive Officers, G. E. Cooper; F. T. Jones: D. A. Thomas.............. £4,900 to £5,900
Guide Lecturer, K. P. Whitehorn
.... £4,185 to £5,778
Keeper of Prints and Drawings, J. A. G. Gere
.... £8,650 to £9,798
Deputy Keepers, P. H. Hulton; J. K. Rowlands
.... £7,151 to £8,750
Assistant Keepers, Frances A. Carey; J. A. R. Wilton; N. J. L. Turner............. £4,404 to £7,109
Keeper of Coins and Medals, G. K. Jenkins
.... £8,650 to £9,798
Deputy Keepers, R. A. G. Carson; J. P. C. Kent
.... £7,151 to £8,750
Assistant Keepers, M. G. Powell-Jones; Marion M. Archibald; N. M. Lowick; M. J. Price
.... £4,404 to £7,109
Keeper of Egyptian Antiquities, T. G. H. James
.... £8,650 to £9,798
Assistant Keeper, W. V. Davies.. £4,404 to £7,109
Keeper of Western Antiquities, E. Sollberger
.... £8,650 to £9,798
Deputy Keeper, T. C. Mitchell.. £7,151 to £9,798
Assistant Keepers, J. E. Curtis; C. B. F. Walker
.... £4,404 to £7,109
Keeper of Greek and Roman Antiquities, D. E. L. Haynes.................. £8,650 to £9,798
Deputy Keeper, R. A. Higgins.. £7,151 to £8,750
Assistant Keepers, Ann Birchall; B. F. Cook
.... £4,404 to £7,109

Keeper of Mediæval and Later Antiquities, N. M.
Stratford.................. £8,650 to £9,798
Deputy Keeper, G. H. Tait...... £7,151 to £8,750
Assistant Keepers, J. Cherry; Leslie E. Webster;
R. M. Camber; R. Marks; D. Kidd
£4,404 to £7,109
Keeper of Prehistoric and Romano-British Antiquities,
I. H. Longworth............. £8,650 to £9,798
Deputy Keepers, K. S. Painter; G. de G. Sieveking
£7,151 to £8,750
Assistant Keepers, I. M. Stead; I. A. Kinnes
£4,404 to £7,109
Keeper of Oriental Antiquities, D. E. Barrett
£8,650 to £9,798
Deputy Keeper, R. H. Pinder-Wilson
£7,151 to £8,750
Assistant Keepers, W. Zwalf; L. R. H. Smith;
Jessica M. Rawson; R. Whitfield
£4,404 to £7,109
Keeper of Ethnography, M. D. McLeod
£8,650 to £9,798
Deputy Keepers, B. A. L. Cranstone; J. W. Picton
£7,151 to £8,750
Assistant Keepers, Elizabeth M. Carmichael; Sheila
G. Weir; Dorota Starzecka... £4,404 to £7,109
Keeper of Research Laboratory, M. Tite
£8,650 to £9,798
Principal Scientific Officers, A. D. Baynes-Cope;
W. A. Oddy............... £5,514 to £7,205
Keeper of Conservation, H. Barker
£8,650 to £9,798

THE BRITISH MUSEUM (NATURAL HISTORY)
Cromwell Road S.W.7
[01–589 6323]
Open free on week-days (except New Year's
Day, Good Friday, Christmas Eve, Christmas Day
and Boxing Day) 10 to 6, and on Sundays from
2.30 to 6.
The Natural History Museum originates from
the natural history departments of the British
Museum, Bloomsbury. During the 19th century
the natural history collections grew so extensively
that it became necessary to find new quarters for
them and in 1881 they were moved to South
Kensington. The British Museum Act, 1963, made
the Natural History Museum completely independent with its own body of Trustees. The Zoological
Museum, Tring, bequeathed by the second Lord
Rothschild, has formed part of the Museum since
1938. Research workers are admitted to the
libraries and study collections by Student's Ticket,
applications for which should be made in writing
to the Director. There are lectures for visitors at
3 p.m. on week-days and lecturers are also available
at other times for special parties by arrangement
with the Department of Public Services.
The administrative expenses were estimated at
£2,765,000 in 1975–76.

Board of Trustees

Director, Sir Frank Claringbull, Ph.D...... £12,000
Deputy Director, R. H. Hedley, D.sc.
£10,590 to £11,600
Secretary, A. P. Coleman (*Establishment Officer*)
£8,160 to £9,760
Office Manager, B. Johnston..... £6,090 to £7,860
Librarian, M. J. Rowlands..... £9,060 to £10,208

Department of Public Services
Head, R. S. Miles, D.sc...... £9,060 to £10,208
Education Officer, F. H. Brightman
£5,924 to £7,615
Exhibition Development Officer, W. R. Hamilton,
Ph.D..................... £5,924 to £7,615
Exhibition Production Officer, M, G. Belcher
£6,090 to £7,860

Department of Zoology
Keeper, J. G. Sheals, Ph.D...... £10,590 to £11,600
Deputy Keepers, G. B. Corbet, Ph.D.; J. F. Peake
£9,060 to £10,208
Senior Principal Scientific Officers, P. H. Greenwood,
D.sc.; C. A. Wright, D.sc.... £9,060 to £10,208
Principal Scientific Officers, Miss A. M. Clark;
Miss P. L. Cook; C. R. Curds, Ph.D.; J. D.
George, Ph.D.; Miss A. G. C. Grandison; R. J.
Lincoln, Ph.D.; S. Prudhoe; P. E. Purves, Ph.D.;
R. W. Sims; J. D. Taylor, Ph.D.; P. J. P. White-
head...................... £5,924 to £7,615

Sub-Department of Ornithology
Park Street, Tring, Herts.
[Tring: 4181]
Senior Principal Scientific Officer, D. W. Snow,
D.Phil. (*Head*)............... £8,650 to £9,798
Principal Scientific Officers, P. J. K. Burton, Ph.D.;
I. C. J. Galbraith; R. P. D. Goodwin
£5,514 to £7,205

Department of Entomology
Keeper, P. Freeman, D.sc..... £10,590 to £11,600
Deputy Keepers, L. A. Mound; D. R. Ragge, Ph.D
£9,060 to £10,208
Senior Principal Scientific Officers, R. W. Crosskey,
D.sc.; V. F. Eastop, D.sc.; P. F. Mattingly, D.sc.
£9,060 to £10,208
Principal Scientific Officers, D. S. Fletcher; P. M.
Hammond; W. J. Knight, Ph.D.; I. W. B. Nye,
Ph.D.; R. D. Pope; K. S. O. Sattler, Ph.D.
F. G. A. M. Smit; K. G. V. Smith; R. I. Vane-
Wright; Miss C. M. F. von Hayek; A. Watson;
P. E. S. Whalley............. £5,924 to £7,615

Department of Palaeontology
Keeper, H. W. Ball, Ph.D...... £9,060 to £10,208
Deputy Keepers, C. G. Adams, Ph.D.; G. F. Elliot,
D.sc...................... £9,060 to £10,208
Senior Principle Scientific Officer, C. Patterson, Ph.D.
£9,060 to £10,208
Principal Scientific Officers, R. H. Bate, Ph.D.;
C. H. C. Brunton, Ph.D.; A. J. Charig, Ph.D.;
L. R. M. Cocks, D.Phil.; A. W. Gentry, D.Phil.;
M. K. Howarth, Ph.D.; R. P. S. Jefferies, Ph.D.;
C. P. Nuttall; J. M. Pettitt, Ph.D.; J. A. Sutcliffe,
Ph.D.................... £5,924 to £7,615

Sub-Department of Physical Anthropology
Principal Scientific Officer, D. Tills
£5,924 to £7,615

Department of Mineralogy
Keeper, A. C. Bishop, Ph.D..... £9,060 to £10,208
Deputy Keeper, D. R. C. Kempe, D.Phil.
£9,060 to £10,208
Principal Scientific Officers, R. J. Davis, D.Phil.;
P. G. Embrey; R. Hutchison, Ph.D.; A. A. Moss,
Ph.D.; A. R. Woolley, Ph.D.... £5,924 to £7,615

Department of Botany
Keeper, R. Ross............. £10,590 to £11,600
Deputy Keeper, J. F. M. Cannon
£9,060 to £10,208
Senior Principal Scientific Officer, W. T. Stearn, D.sc.
£9,060 to £10,208
Principal Scientific Officers, A. Eddy; P. W. James;
A. C. Jermy; J. Lewis; J. H. Price; N. K. B.
Robson, Ph.D............... £5,924 to £7,615

Department of Central Services
Head, R. H. Hedley, D.sc. (*Deputy Director*)
£10,590 to £11,600
Biometrics, M. Hills, Ph.D...... £5,924 to £7,615
Electronic Data Processing, D. B. Williams, Ph.D.
£5,924 to £7,615
Electron Microscope Unit, C. G. Ogden
£4,595 to £6,188

MUSEUM OF LONDON

This London Museum and the Guildhall Museum formally amalgamated on June 1, 1975. The Museum is controlled by a Board of Governors, appointed (6 each) by the Government, the Corporation of London and the Greater London Council. It is due to open in a new building at the corner of London Wall and Aldersgate Street in the City at the end of 1976. The exhibition will illustrate the history of London from prehistoric times to the present day. The former Guildhall Museum closed in 1974, and the former London Museum closed on May 31, 1975.

Chairman of Board of Governors, The Viscount Harcourt, K.C.M.G., O.B.E.
Director, T. A. Hume, F.S.A.

THE SCIENCE MUSEUM
South Kensington, S.W.7
[01-589 6371]

Open on weekdays 10 to 6; Sundays 2.30 to 6. Closed on Good Friday, Christmas Eve, Christmas Day, Boxing Day and New Year's Day.
For Science Museum Library, see below.
The Science Museum, which is the National Museum of Science and Industry, was instituted in 1853 under the Science and Art Department as a part of the South Kensington Museum, and opened in 1857; to it were added in 1883 the Collections of the Patent Museum. In 1909 the administration of the Science Collections was separated from that of the Art Collections, which were transferred to the Victoria and Albert Museum. The Collections in the Science Museum illustrate the development of science and engineering and related industries.
The administrative expenses of the Museum and Library were estimated at £2,001,000 for 1975–76.

Director and Secretary, Miss Margaret Weston
£12,000
Museum Superintendent, V. C. Clark
£6,090 to £7,860

Department of Physics
Keeper, V. K. Chew..........£9,060 to £10,208
Deputy Keepers, A. B. Sahiar; D. Vaughan
£5,252 to £7,957

Department of Chemistry
Keeper, F. Greenaway........£9,060 to £10,208
Deputy Keeper (vacant)........£5,252 to £7,957
Assistant Keepers (First Class), D. A. Robinson; R. G. W. Anderson.........£4,814 to £7,519

Department of Electrical Engineering and Communications
Keeper, L. R. Day...........£9,060 to £10,208
Deputy Keepers, B. P. Bowers; W. K. E. Geddes
£5,252 to £7,957

Department of Transport
Keeper, G. W. B. Lacey.......£9,060 to £10,208
Deputy Keeper, W. J. Tuck.....£5,252 to £7,957
Assistant Keepers (First Class), B. W. Bathe; Mrs. L. A. West; P. D. Stephens..£4,814 to £7,519

Department of Mechanical and Civil Engineering and Circulation
Keeper, W. Winton..........£9,060 to £10,208
Deputy Keeper, R. J. Law.......£5,252 to £7,957
Assistant Keepers (First Class), A. K. Corry; A. E. Butcher; G. C. Snead.......£4,814 to £7,519

Department of Astronomy, Mathematics and the Earth Sciences
Keeper, J. Wartnaby.........£9,060 to £10,208
Assistant Keepers, E. J. S. Becklake; Miss J. M. Pugh; J. C. Robinson.............£4,814 to £7,519

Department of Museum Services
Keeper I, D. B. Thomas.......£9,060 to £10,208
Keepers II, M. R. Preston; J. T. Van Riemsdijk
£7,560 to £9,160
Assistant Keeper (First Class), A. L. Rowles
£4,814 to £7,519

Library
SCIENCE MUSEUM LIBRARY, South Kensington, S.W.7.—A national library especially devoted to pure and applied science, 417,000 volumes, 10,800 periodicals and transactions of learned societies, about 5,300 current. Bibliographies supplied.—Open on weekdays 10 to 5.30. Closed on Sundays and Bank Holiday weekends. Photocopying, microfilm and microfiche service.
Keeper, J. A. Chaldecott......£9,060 to £10,208
Deputy Keeper, Miss H. J. Parker £5,252 to £7,957
Assistant Keepers (First Class), Miss H. D. Phippen; H. Woolfe.................£4,814 to £7,519

THE VICTORIA AND ALBERT MUSEUM
South Kensington, S.W.7
[01-589 6371]

Hours 10 to 6 (weekdays and Bank Holidays); Sundays, 2.30 to 6. Closed Good Friday, Christmas Eve, Christmas Day, Boxing Day and New Year's Day. The National Art Library is open on weekdays from 10 to 5.45 and the Print Room from 10 to 4.35. A museum of all branches of fine and applied art, under the Department of Education and Science, it descends direct from the Museum of Manufactures (later called Museum of Ornamental Art), opened in Marlborough House in 1852. The Museum was moved in 1857 to become part of the collective South Kensington Museum. It was renamed the Victoria and Albert Museum in 1899. The branch museum at Bethnal Green was opened in 1872 and the building is the most important surviving example of the type of glass and iron construction used by Paxton for the Great Exhibition of 1851. The Victoria and Albert Museum also administers the Wellington Museum (Apsley House), Ham House, Richmond, Osterley Park, Middlesex, and the Theatre Museum, due to open shortly. Administrative expenses of the Museum were estimated at £3,229,000 for 1975–76.

Director and Secretary, R. C. Strong, PH.D., F.S.A.
£12,000
Assistant to the Director, J. F. Physick (*Secretary to Advisory Council*)...........£7,151 to £8,750

Department of Architecture and Sculpture
Keeper, J. G. Beckwith........£8,650 to £9,798
Deputy Keeper, C. H. F. Avery. £4,404 to £7,109†
Assistant Keeper I, A. F. Radcliffe
£4,404 to £7,109

Department of Ceramics
Keeper, R. J. Charleston.......£8,650 to £9,798
Deputy Keeper, J. V. G. Mallet..£4,404 to £7,109†
Assistant Keeper I, D. M. Archer. £4,404 to £7,109

Department of Circulation
Keeper, H. G. Wakefield.......£8,650 to £9,798
Deputy Keeper, C. Hogben....£4,404 to £7,109†
Assistant Keepers, I, Mrs. B. J. Morris; M. Haworth-Booth.....................£4,404 to £7,109

Library
Keeper, J. P. Harthan.........£8,650 to £9,798
Deputy Keeper, R. W. Lightbown
£4,404 to £7,109†
Assistant Keepers I, R. C. Kenedy; A. P. Burton
£4,404 to £7,109

Department of Metalwork
Keeper, C. Blair...............£8,650 to £9,798
Deputy Keeper, Mrs. S. J. Bury..£4,404 to £7,109†
Assistant Keeper, J. K. D. Cooper. £4,404 to £7,109

Department of Prints and Drawings and Paintings
Keeper, C. M. Kauffmann......£8,650 to £9,798
Deputy Keepers, J. H. Mayne; P. W. Ward-Jackson
£4,404 to £7,109†
Assistant Keeper I, J. Murdoch.. £4,404 to £7,109†

Department of Museum Services
Keeper, J. F. Physick...........£7,151 to £8,750
Deputy Keeper (Publications Production), T. M. MacRobert...............£4,404 to £7,109†
Assistant Keeper I, I. Heal.......£4,404 to £7,109

Education Services
Keeper, Mrs. M. Mainstone..... £7,151 to £8,750

Department of Textiles
Keeper, D. King.............. £8,650 to £9,798
Deputy Keeper, Miss N. K. A. Rothstein
£4,404 to £7,109†

Department of Furniture and Woodwork
Keeper, P. K. Thornton........ £8,650 to £9,798
Deputy Keeper, S. S. Jervis.... £4,404 to £7,109†

Oriental Department
Keeper, J. C. Irwin............ £8,650 to £9,798
Indian Section
Deputy Keeper, R. W. Skelton. £4,404 to £7,109†
Assistant Keeper I, J. J. Lowry... £4,404 to £7,109
Far Eastern Section
Keeper, J. G. Ayers............ £7,151 to £8,750
Assistant Keeper I, E. G. Capon.. £4,404 to £7,109

Department of Conservation
Keeper, N. S. Brommelle...... £8,650 to £9,798

Secretariat
Museum Superintendent, R. Burgess, M.B.E.
£5,680 to £7,450

Theatre Museum
Curator, A. Schouvaloff........ £7,151 to £8,750
† Plus *Allce.* £438.

BETHNAL GREEN MUSEUM
The Museum of Childhood
Cambridge Heath Road, Bethnal Green, E.2.
A branch of the Victoria and Albert Museum, opened in 1872. Toys, dolls, dolls' houses, model theatres, children's books and costume. Also items connected with local history, and, temporarily, wedding dresses, continental 19th century furniture, Japanese armour and sculptures by Rodin.
Officer-in-charge, Miss E. M. Aslin
£7,561 to £9,160

THE COMMONWEALTH INSTITUTE
Kensington High Street, W.8
[01–602 3252]
The management of the Institute is vested in a Board of Governors of which Sir David Hunt, K.C.M.G., O.B.E. is the Chairman. Membership of the Board consists of the High Commissions in London of the Commonwealth Governments and of representatives of Commonwealth, educational, cultural and commercial interests as appointed by the Minister.
Exhibition Galleries open weekdays, 10 a.m. to 5.30 p.m.; Sundays, 2.30 p.m. to 6 p.m. Admission free. Cinema. Closed Good Fridays, Christmas Eve, Christmas Day, Boxing Day and New Year's Day.
Director, J. K. Thompson, C.M.G........ £11,410
Deputy Director, F. Lightfoot, M.B.E........ £8,932
Chief Education Officer, J. F. Callander
£6,090 to £7,800
Establishment and Finance Officer, S. A. Christy
£6,090 to £7,860
Chief Exhibition Officer, C. W. Tosdevin
£6,090 to £7,860
Curator, Art Gallery, D. G. Bowen, F.R.S.A.
£5,310 to £6,310
Librarian, M. J. Foster........ £5,310 to £6,310
Senior Education Officers, A. J. Spicer, O.B.E.; C. K. Kumar.................. £5,310 to £6,310
Theatre Manager, L. Black...... £4,310 to £5,110
Publicity Officer, M. G. Evans... £4,310 to £5,110

IMPERIAL WAR MUSEUM
Lambeth Road, S.E.1
[01–735 8922]
Open daily (except Good Friday, Christmas Eve, Christmas Day, Boxing Day and New Year's Day) 10 a.m.–6 p.m. Reference Depts. open Monday–Friday (except on public holidays), 10 a.m.–5 p.m.
The Museum, which was founded in 1917 and established by Act of Parliament in 1920, illustrates and records all aspects of the two world wars and other military operations involving Britain and the Commonwealth since 1914. It was opened in its present home, formerly Bethlem Hospital or Bedlam, in 1936. Its extensive collections include aircraft, armoured fighting vehicles, artillery, uniforms, models, orders and decorations, badges and insignia, works of art, posters, photographs, films, books, documents and sound recordings.
The Museum provides regular programmes of films and talks for visiting parties from schools, colleges and the armed services. General administrative expenses of the Museum 1975–1976, £856,000.
Director, A. N. Frankland, D.F.C., D.Phil., F.S.A.
£11,410
Deputy Director, C. H. Roads, Ph.D.
£9,060 to £10,208
Assistant Director and Keeper of Department of Art (Deputy Keeper), J. C. Darracott
£7,561 to £9,160
Deputy Keepers, G. T. C. Coultass; C. Dowling, D.Phil.; P. J. Simkins........ £7,561 to £9,160
Assistant Keepers (First Class), G. M. Bayliss, Ph.D.; R. W. K. Crawford; D. G. Lance; D. J. Penn; R. W. A. Suddaby......... £4,814 to £7,519
Secretary (Assistant Keeper, First Class), J. J. Chadwick...................... £4,814 to £7,519
Establishment and Finance Officer (Senior Executive Officer), J. F. Golding..... £5,310 to £6,310

NATIONAL MARITIME MUSEUM
Greenwich, S.E.10
[01–858 4422]
Open weekdays 10 till 6 (Mon.–Fri. in winter, 10–5); Sundays 2.30 to 6. Closed on Good Friday, Christmas Eve, Christmas Day, Boxing Day and New Year's Day.
Reading Room open on weekdays 10 to 5; tickets of admission on written applications to the Director.
The National Maritime Museum was established by Act of Parliament in 1934, for the illustration of the maritime history, archæology and art of Great Britain. The Museum is in two groups of buildings, in Greenwich Park, the Main Buildings, centred round the Queen's House (built by Inigo Jones, 1617–35) and the Old Royal Observatory, including the Wren Flamsteed House, to the south. The collections include paintings; actual craft and ship-models; ships' lines; prints and drawings; maps, atlases and charts; navigational and astronomical instruments; uniforms and relics; books and MSS. The amount for salaries and expenses, including a Grant-in-Aid, was estimated at £681,000 for 1974–75.
Director and Accounting Officer, B. J. Greenhill, C.M.G.
£11,670
Deputy Director, D. W. Waters
£8,650 to £9,798
Secretary (Principal), Capt. T. L. Martin, R.N.
£5,680 to £7,450
Keeper, B. T. Carter.......... £8,650 to £9,798
Deputy Keepers, P. G. W. Annis; Dr. A. P. McGowan; J. Munday; D. V. Proctor
£7,151 to £8,750
Assistant Keepers (First Class), E. H. H. Archibald; H. D. Howse, M.B.E., D.S.C.; J. F. McGrail; A. W. H. Pearsall; H. H. Preston; Dr. M. W. B. Sanderson; Mrs. A. M. Shirley; A. N. Stimson; Dr. R. J. B. Knight; C. C. W. Terrell; J. A. H. Lees, O.B.E.; N. E. Upham... £4,404 to £7,109
Restorer I, W. W. Percival-Prescott
£4,404 to £7,109

(For other Museums in England—*see* Index)

THE NATIONAL MUSEUM OF WALES
AMGUEDDEA GENEDLAETHOL CYMRU
Cardiff
Open on weekdays, 10 a.m. to 5 p.m. (April to Sept., 10 a.m. to 6 p.m.). Sundays 2.30 to 5 p.m. Bank Holidays and Tuesdays following, 10 a.m. to 6 p.m. Closed on Christmas Eve, Christmas Day,

Boxing Day, New Year's Day and Good Friday.

Founded by Royal Charter, 1907, and maintained principally by annual grant from the Government and partly by Museum rate from the Cardiff City Council. The collections consist of: (Geology), Collections of geological specimens (rocks, minerals and fossils) from all parts of Wales with comparative material from other regions. Relief maps, models and photographs illustrating the structure and scenery of Wales. (Botany), the Welsh National Herbarium, illustrating especially the flora of Wales and comprising the Griffith, D. A. Jones, Vachell, Salter, Shoolbred, Wheldon and other herbaria, and display collections illustrating general and forest botany and the ecology of Welsh plants. (Zoology), Collections of skins, British mammals and birds, eggs of British birds, extensive entomological collections, Melvill-Tomlin collection of molluscs, spirit collections, chiefly of Welsh interest. (Archæology), Welsh prehistoric. Roman and mediæval antiquities, casts of pre-Norman monuments of Wales, important numismatic collection. (Industry), The history and development of industry in Wales, illustrated by models, dioramas, original objects and machines. (Art), The works of Richard Wilson, Augustus John, O.M., and Sir Frank Brangwyn, are well represented; the Gwendoline and Margaret Davies Bequests of works of the 19th-century French School, the British School and Old Masters, Pyke Thompson collection of watercolour drawings, and a general collection of paintings in oil; sculpture, including many works by Sir W. Goscombe John, R.A., Swansea and Nantgarw porcelain, the De Winton collection of Continental porcelain and the Jackson collection of silver, etc.

President, A. B. Oldfield-Davies, C.B.E.
Vice-President, Col. Sir William Crawshay, D.S.O., E.R.D., T.D.
Director, G. O. Jones, Ph.D., D.Sc.
Secretary, D. W. Dykes, F.S.A.
Keepers (Geology), D. A. Bassett, Ph.D.; (Botany), S. G. Harrison; (Zoology), J. A. Bateman; (Archæology), H. N. Savory, D.Phil., F.S.A.; (Industry), D. Morgan Rees, F.S.A.; (Art), R. L. Charles, M.C.

Welsh Folk Museum
Amgueddfa Werin Cymru
St. Fagans

The museum is situated 4 miles west of Cardiff. Open weekdays 10 a.m. to 7 p.m.; July and August 10 a.m. to 6 p.m., April, May, June, Sept. 10 a.m. to 5 p.m. October to March (admission 10p). Open Sundays 12.30 p.m. to 7 p.m., April to September 2.30 to 5 p.m., Oct. to March. Closed on Christmas Eve, Christmas Day, Boxing Day and New Year's Day. The museum was made possible by the gift of St. Fagans Castle and its Grounds by the Earl of Plymouth in 1946. The rooms of the Castle contain period furniture; the gardens are maintained. A woollen factory from Brecknockshire, a tannery from Radnorshire, a 16th-century barn from Flintshire, four farmhouses, an 18th-century cockpit from Denbigh, a turnpike house, a cottage, a smithy and an 18th-century chapel have been re-erected and other typical Welsh buildings are being re-erected in an area adjoining the Castle to picture the Welsh way of life and to show the rural crafts of the past. The new museum building contains galleries of Material Culture, Costume, Agriculture and Agricultural Vehicles.
Curator, T. M. Owen, F.S.A.
Keepers (Material Culture), J. G. Jenkins, F.S.A.; (Oral Traditions and Dialects), V. H. Phillips.

Legionary Museum of Caerleon
Caerleon, Gwent.

Open on weekdays (May-September), 9.30 a.m. to 7 p.m., (March, April and Oct.) 9.30 a.m. to 5.30 p.m. (Nov.-Feb.), 9.30 a.m. to 4 p.m. Sundays from 2 p.m. Closed on Christmas Eve, Christmas Day, Boxing Day and New Year's Day. Admission Free.

Contains material found on the site of the Roman fortress of Isca and its suburbs.

Turner House Art Gallery
Penarth, N. Cardiff

Open weekdays, 11 a.m.-12.45 p.m. and 2 p.m. to 5 p.m. Sundays, 2 p.m. to 5 p.m. Closed Mondays, except Bank Holidays, and on Christmas Eve, Christmas Day, Boxing Day, New Year's Day and Good Friday.

North Wales Quarrying Museum,
Llanberis, Gwynedd

Open weekdays and Sundays, 9.30-7, Easter to September. Admission 10p. Waterwheel, foundry, smithy, fitting shops, slate-sawing tables and dressing machines, items from quarry hospital, office furniture, etc.

Segontium Roman Fort Museum,
Beddgelert Road, Caernarvon, Gwynedd

Open weekdays at 9.30, Sundays at 2. Closes at 7 from May to September, at 5.30 in March, April and October, at 4 from November to February. Admission 5p. On the site of the fort, in the guardianship of the Department of the Environment. Contains mostly material excavated there.

ROYAL SCOTTISH MUSEUM
Chambers Street, Edinburgh
[031-225 7534]

Open, Mon.-Sat., 10 a.m. to 5 p.m.; and Sun., 2 to 5 p.m.
Director, N. Tebble, D.Sc. £11,000
Keeper, Department of Art and Archæology, R. Oddy
£7,151 to £8,750
Keeper, Department of Technology, A. G. Thomson, Ph.D. . . . . £7,151 to £8,750
Keeper, Department of Natural History, A. S. Clarke, Ph.D. . . . . £7,151 to £8,750
Keeper, Department of Geology, C. D. Waterston, Ph.D. . . . . £7,151 to £8,750
Assistant Keepers (First Class), M. C. Baker; H. O. A. F. Fernandez; Mrs. D. Idiens; A. Livingstone, Ph.D.; I. H. J. Lyster; Mrs. P. C. Macdonald, Ph.D.; H.G.Macpherson, Ph.D.; M. J. Moore; E. C. Pelham-Clinton; Miss J. M. Scarce; A. D. Simpson; G. Smaldon, Ph.D.; J. D. Storer; Miss N. E. A. Tarrant; Miss M. S. Thomson
£4,404 to £7,109

NATIONAL MUSEUM OF ANTIQUITIES OF SCOTLAND
Queen Street, Edinburgh, 2
[031-556-8921]

Founded in 1781 by the Society of Antiquaries of Scotland, and transferred to the Nation in 1858. Open free. Weekdays, 10 a.m. to 5 p.m.; Sundays, 2-5 p.m.
Keeper, R. B. K. Stevenson. £10,282
Deputy Keepers, S. Maxwell; A. Fenton.
Assistant Keeper, Miss J. Close-Brooks.
Principal Scientific Officer, Dr. H. McKerrell.

NATIONAL BUS COMPANY
25 New Street Square, E.C.4
[01-583 9177]

The National Bus Company is a statutory body under the provisions of the Transport Act, 1968. It controls more than 50 operating companies covering almost every part of England and Wales outside London and the municipal undertakings. The N.B.C. bus and coach fleets total about 20,000 vehicles and it employs a staff of about 68,000.
Chairman, F. A. S. Wood . . . . . (part-time) £8,825
Members (part-time), A. P. de Boer; The Lord Cooper of Stockton Heath; W. F. Higgins; I. S. Irwin; A. E. Orchard-Lisle, C.B.E. (each £1,000).
Chief Executive, S. J. B. Skyrme.

NATIONAL COAL BOARD
Hobart House, Grosvenor Place, S.W.1
[01-235 2020]

The National Coal Board was constituted in 1946. It took over the mines on January 1, 1947.

Chairman, Sir Derek Ezra, M.B.E......... £23,100
Deputy Chairman, N. Siddall, C.B.E...... £19,100
Members, D. M. Clement, C.B.E.; D. Davies, O.B.E.;
L. Grainger; L. J. Mills; W. L. Miron, C.B.E.,
T.D.; G.C. Shephard...... £12,600 to £17,600
Part-time Members, R. F. Richardson, C.B.E.; P. H.
Robinson; J. A. Wellings, C.B.E......... £1,000
Secretary, D. G. Brandrick.

NATIONAL DEBT OFFICE
and Office for Payment of Government
Life Annuities
Royex House, Aldermanbury Square, E.C.2
*Secretary of the National Debt Commissioners and
Comptroller-General*, I. de L. Radice, C.B.
£12,000
Asst. Comptroller, F. D. Ashby, O.B.E.
£7,750 to £9,350
Chief Executive Officer, S. J. Payne
£5,680 to £7,450
Senior Executive Officers, W. G. Stevens; G. F. W.
Berry; L. A. S. Swift; E.T. Taylor
£4,900 to £5,900
Brokers, Messrs. Mullens & Co.......... £2,000

NATIONAL DOCK LABOUR BOARD
22–26 Albert Embankment, S.E.1
The National Dock Labour Board administers
the scheme for giving permanent employment to
dock workers under the *Dock Workers (Regulation of
Employment) (Amendment) Scheme, 1967*.
Chairman, P. G. H. Lewison.
General Manager and Secretary, J. H. C. Pape.

NATIONAL ECONOMIC DEVELOPMENT
OFFICE
Millbank Tower, Millbank, S.W.1
[01–834 3811]
Council
Government Members, The Chancellor of the
Exchequer (*Chairman*); the Secretaries of State
for Employment, Energy, Prices and Consumer
Production, Industry, and Trade, and the Chan-
cellor of the Duchy of Lancaster. *Management
Members*: W. O. Campbell Adamson; R. M.
Bateman; Sir Michael Clapham, K.B.E.; R. E. B.
Lloyd; The Lord Netherthorpe; Sir John Part-
ridge, K.B.E. *Trade Union Members*: A. W. Allen,
C.B.E.; D. Basnett; Sir Sidney Greene, C.B.E.;
J. L. Jones, M.B.E.; L. Murray, O.B.E.; H. Scanlon.
Nationalized Industries: Sir Montague Finniston,
F.R.S.; Rt. Hon. R. W. Marsh. *Independent
Member*, Sir Eric Roll, K.C.M.G., C.B. *National
Economic Development Office*,Sir Ronald McIntosh,
K.C.B. (*Director-General*).

Secretary, C. C. Lucas.
Industrial Director, K. W. Cook.
Industrial Advisers and Assistant Industrial Directors,
J. R. S. Homan; P. W. H. Roffey; P. F. D.
Wallis; H. R. Windle.
Economic Director, M. Panic.

NATIONAL GALLERIES
See ART GALLERIES

NATIONAL HEALTH SERVICE
See HEALTH SERVICE
(under Ministry of Health)

OFFICE OF THE NATIONAL
INSURANCE COMMISSIONER
6 Grosvenor Gardens, S.W.1
[01–730 9236]
23 Melville Street, Edinburgh 3
[031–225 2201]
Portcullis House, 21 Cowbridge Road East, Cardiff
[0222 388531, Ext. 395]
The Commissioner is the final Statutory
Authority to decide claims under the Family
Allowances Acts and the Social Security Acts.

Chief Commissioner, R. J. A. Temple, C.B.E., Q.C.
Commissioners, H. A. Shewan, C.B., O.B.E., Q.C.(*Edin-
burgh*); D. W. E. Neligan, O.B.E.; D. Reith, Q.C.
(*Edinburgh*); H. B. Magnus, Q.C.; J. S. Watson,
M.B.E., Q.C.; R. S. Lazarus, Q.C.; E. R. Bowen,
Q.C. (*Cardiff*); J. G. Monroe.
Secretary, A. J. Macklin, M.B.E.
Senior Legal Assistants, Mrs. C. R. Corbett; Mrs.
M. V. Steel.
Legal Assistant, D. E. Buckley.

NATIONAL PORTS COUNCIL
Commonwealth House, 1–19 New Oxford St.,
W.C.1
Chairman, E. P. Chappell.
Deputy Chairman, J. L. Jones, M.B.E.
Members, J. Morris Gifford, C.B.E. (*Director General*);
F. O. P. Brann; J. F. Denholm, C.B.E.; P. G. H.
Lewison; Sir William Lithgow, Bt.; Sir Daniel
Pettit; L. T. J. Reynolds, M.B.E.
Joint Secretaries, R. C. Livesey (*Asst.-Director
General*); K. A. Heathcote.

NATIONAL RESEARCH DEVELOPMENT
CORPORATION
Kingsgate House, 66–74 Victoria Street, S.W.1
[01–828 3400]
The National Research Development Corporation operates under the Development of Inventions
Act 1967. Its function is to secure, " where the
public interest so requires ", the development and
exploitation of inventions derived from publicly
supported research and from other sources. The
Corporation provides firms with the opportunity
to take up, under licence, inventions arising from
public research. It also offers financial assistance
towards the development of technically new products. These may be based on a firm's own ideas
or on inventions which it has acquired from the
Corporation or from other sources.
Chairman, Sir Frank Schon.
Managing Director, W. Makinson.
Head of Public Relations, B. S. W. Mann.

DEPARTMENT FOR NATIONAL SAVINGS
Blythe Road, W.14
[01–603 2000]
The Department for National Savings was
established as a Government Department when the
former Post Office Savings Department became
separated from the Post Office on October 1, 1969.
At the same time the civil service staff supporting
the National Savings Committees for England and
Wales and for Scotland, were integrated with
the Department, so that its scope was extended to
cover the promotion as well as the operation of
National Savings. The Department operates the
National Savings Bank and maintains the records of
holdings of National Savings Certificates, Save As
You Earn contracts, Premium Savings Bonds,
British Savings Bonds (and their forerunners
Defence and National Development Bonds) and
Government stock on the National Savings Stock
Register.
Director of Savings, J. Littlewood, C.B..... £15,000
Deputy Directors, P. E. Plummer (Controller (Na-
tional Savings Bank)); Miss B. K. Billot. £12,000
Assistant Directors, J. Higson; S. A. Ingham
£8,650 to £11,000
Establishment Officer, C. W. Hand
£8,650 to £11,000
Finance Officer, R. H. Dryden. £8,650 to £11,000
Controllers, G. W. Mantle, O.B.E.; H. R. West,
O.B.E.; J. P. Wilde, O.B.E.; J. W. King, O.B.E.
(*Publicity*)................. £8,650 to £11,000
Senior Principals, J. A. Cuthbertson; A. Green
£7,750 to £9,350
Principals, M. Marshall; B. C. Smith, M.B.E.; S. J.
Allison; M. Morris, I.S.O.; D. M. Jones; J. R.
Acland; C. M. Roberts; C. F. H. Taylor; Miss
J. M. J. Wedge; R. J. F. Lindsay; C. L. Dann;
T. Wilson; Miss C. N. Lall, M.B.E.; J. Stamp;
R. S. Robinson; G. R. Wilson; A. Hirst; L. B.

Clark, M.B.E.; J. W. Richardson; S. W. Shepherd;
B. White; J. G. Booth; T. I. McMahon; J.
Crooks; G. E. Long; I. T. Standen; A. W.
Hasmall; I. B. Arkinstall; C. J. Paul; R. S. Watts;
R. H. Lee.................£5,680 to £7,450
Principal Information Officers, P. G. Hutchings;
P. N. S. Hickman-Robertson. £5,680 to £7,450

THE NATIONAL SAVINGS COMMITTEE
Alexandra House, Kingsway, W.C.2
[01–836–1599]
President and Chairman, Sir John Anstey, C.B.E., T.D.
Vice-President, Sir Athelstan Caröe, C.B.E.
Vice-Chairmen, General Sir Geoffrey Musson, G.C.B.,
C.B.E., D.S.O.; L. Murray, O.B.E.; J. Archbold,
O.B.E.; Mrs. E. Perkins, C.B.E.

OFFICERS
Secretary, K. T. Pinch.........£8,650 to £11,000
Deputy Secretary, J. C. Timms, O.B.E.
£7,750 to £9,350
Principals, A. F. Brown; S. Burke; K. G. Burton;
A. W. W. Fairley; M. Falder; K. J. Griffin;
R. J. Heathorn; F. E. Mack; K. Nicholas;
R. Rees, M.B.E.; J. K. Roberts; R. T. Rowland;
G. Thomas.................£5,080 to £7,450

NATIONAL SAVINGS COMMITTEE FOR SCOTLAND
22 Melville Street, Edinburgh
[031–225 5486]
President, The Hon. Lord Birsay, K.T., C.B.E., T.D.
Chairman, The Earl of Elgin and Kincardine.
Vice-Chairmen, D. M. McIntosh, C.B.E., F.R.S.E.;
R. M. Addison.
Secretary, A. K. Grant.........£7,750 to £9,350
Deputy Secretary, Mrs. J. W. A. Reaper, M.B.E.
£5,680 to £7,450

NATURAL ENVIRONMENT RESEARCH COUNCIL
Alhambra House, 27–33 Charing Cross Road, W.C.2
[01–930 9232]
The Natural Environment Research Council
was established by Royal Charter on June 1, 1965,
under the Science and Technology Act, 1965, to
encourage, plan and conduct research in those
sciences, both physical and biological, which relate
to man's natural environment.
   The Council carries out research and training
through its own institutes and grant-aided institutes, and by grants, fellowships and post-graduate
awards to universities and other institutions of
higher education.
Chairman, Sir Peter Kent, F.R.S.
Secretary, R. J. H. Beverton, C.B.E., F.R.S.

Institute of Geological Sciences
Exhibition Road, South Kensington, S.W.7
[01–589 3444]
The Geological Museum, Exhibition Road, South
Kensington, S.W.7. Open weekdays, 10 to 6;
Sundays 2.30 to 6. Closed on Good Friday,
Christmas Eve, Christmas Day and Boxing Day.
Director, A. W. Woodland, C.B.E., Ph.D.

Institute of Oceanographic Science
Wormley Laboratory, Godalming, Surrey
[042879 2122]
Director, Prof. H. Charnock.
   Bidston Observatory, Birkenhead
[051–052 2396]
   Taunton Laboratory, Crossway, Taunton
[0823 82691]

Institute for Marine Environmental Research
67–69 Citadel Road, Plymouth
[0752 20681]
Director, R. S. Glover.

Institute of Marine Biochemistry
St. Fittick's Road, Torry, Aberdeen
[0224 57195]
Director, P. T. Grant, Ph.D.

Institute of Hydrology
Maclean Building, Crowmarsh Gifford,
Wallingford, Oxon.
[04913 2265]
Director, J. S. G. McCulloch, Ph.D.
Culture Centre of Algae and Protozoa
36 Storeys Way,
Cambridge
[0223 61378]
Director, E. A. George.
Institute of Terrestrial Ecology
68 Hills Road, Cambridge
[0223–69745]
Director, M. W. Holdgate, Ph.D.
Research Stations: Merlewood, Monks Wood;
Furzebrook; Colney; Edinburgh (Bush and Hope
Terrace); Banchory (Hill of Brathens and Black-
hall); Bangor.
Unit of Invertebrate Virology
5 South Parks Road, Oxford
[0865–52081]
Director, T. W. Tinsley, Ph.D.
British Antarctic Survey
2 All Saints Passage, Cambridge
[0223 61188]
Director, R. M. Laws, Ph.D.
Research Vessel Base
No. 1 Dock, Barry, East Glamorgan
[04462 77451]
Director, Capt. D. M. H. Stobie, D.S.C., R.N.(ret.).
Experimental Cartography Unit
6A Cromwell Place, S.W.7
[01–589 0026]
Director, D. P. Bickmore.

NATURE CONSERVANCY COUNCIL
19–20 Belgrave Square, S.W.1
[01–235 3241]
Establishes, maintains and manages National
Nature Reserves, advises generally on nature
conservation, gives advice to the Government on
nature conservation policies and on how other
policies may affect nature conservation, and sup-
ports, commissions and undertakes relevant re-
search.
Chairman, Sir David Serpell, K.C.B., C.M.G., O.B.E.
Director, R. E. Boote, C.V.O.
Territorial Headquarters:
England: 1/2 Cambridge Gate, Regent's Park,
N.W.1.
[01–935 5533]
   Director, Dr. M. Gane.
Scotland: 12 Hope Terrace, Edinburgh.
[031–447 4784]
   Director, Dr. J. Morton Boyd.
Wales: Penrhos Road, Bangor, Gwynedd.
[Bangor 2201]
   Director, Dr. T. Pritchard.

NORTHERN IRELAND OFFICE
Great George Street, S.W.1
[01–930 4300]
Stormont Castle, Belfast
[Belfast: 63011]
The Secretary of State for Northern Ireland in
the Cabinet is responsible for Government administration in Northern Ireland. The Northern Ireland
Act 1974 made temporary arrangements for the
government of Northern Ireland, exercised through
the Secretary of State, and also provided for the
holding of a Constitutional Convention to consider
what provision for the government of Northern
Ireland would be likely to command the most
widespread acceptance throughout the community
there.
Secretary of State for Northern Ireland, THE RT. HON.
MERLYN REES, M.P.................£13,000
Private Secretary, K. J. Jordan.
Assistant Private Secretaries, A. R. Williams; D.
Chesterton*.
Special Adviser, R. Darlington
Parliamentary Private Secretary, Dr. E. I. Marshall,
M.P.
Parliamentary Clerk, Miss A. F. Brown.

Ministers of State, ROLAND DUNSTAN MOYLE, M.P.;
THE RT. HON. STANLEY ORME, M.P..... £7,500
Parliamentary Under Secretaries of State, The Lord
Donaldson; J. D. Concannon, M.P....... £5,500
Permanent Secretary, Sir Frank Cooper, K.C.B., C.M.G.
£18,675
Permanent Secretary (NICS), M. K. Harris★, £13,250
Deputy Secretaries, P. T. E. England★; J. D. W.
Janes, C.B.................................. £14,000
Deputy Secretaries (NICS), J. V. Morrison★; J. H.
Parkes★ £12,230
Under Secretaries, J. B. Bourn★; J. H. G. Leahy★;
D. H. Payne★; W. J. Smith; D. J. Trevelyan;
J. F. Waterfield (*Principal Establishment and
Finance Officer*).................... £12,000
Senior Assistant Secretaries (NICS), C. F. Darling★;
D. Gilliland★; W. G. Robinson★....... £11,610
Assistant Secretaries, J. N. Allan★; S. S. Bampton;
E. N. Barry★; I. M. Burns; P. W. J. Buxton★;
T. A. Cromey★; W. I. Davies★; A. F. Dowling,
M.V.O., M.B.E., T.D.; F. B. Hall★; S. C. Jackson★;
J. K. Lawrence★; A. R. Marsh★; D. K. Middle-
ton★; A. E. Mullin★; P. E. Pickering; J. J. Scott★;
R. G. Smartt★; R. S. Sterling★; B. M. Webster★;
A. P. D. Westhead★; D. J. Wyatt★
£8,650 to £11,000
Chief Information Officer, R. J. Seaman
£8,650 to £11,000
★ Located in Northern Ireland.

ORDNANCE SURVEY
Romsey Road, Maybush, Southampton
[Southampton 775555]
Director-General, Maj.-Gen. B. St.G. Irwin, C.B.
£12,000
Directors:
Field Survey, Brig. G. A. Hardy
Map Publication. A. G. Dalgleish...... £11,000
Establishment and Finance, W. L. W. Isdale
£8,650 to £11,000
Deputy Directors:
Field Survey, B. E. Furmston.. £8,650 to £9,798
Planning and Development Col. R. N. Atkey.
Map Production, Col. W. N. Morris, M.C.
Establishments, W. Rayer..... £7,750 to £9,350
Publications, Miss B. D. Drewitt. £7,750 to £9,350
Assistant Directors:
Geodetic Services, Lt.-Col. M. R. Richards.
Topographic Surveys, Lt.-Col. H. G. W. Crawford.
Cartography, P. MacMaster.. £7,584 to £8,345
Reproduction, A. C. Marles .... £7,584 to £8,345
Training and Information, D. T. Arnott
£7,584 to £8,345
Research and Development J. F. Bell
£7,584 to £8,345
Computer, K. Nolan......... £5,680 to £7,450
Publications, J. Chapman.... £5,680 to £7,450
Personnel, A. St. J. Perkins.... £5,680 to £7,450
Office Services, F. Judd, B.E.M. £5,680 to £7,450
Finance, J. A. Everett .... £5,680 to £7,450
Management Services, D. L. Dowds
£5,680 to £7,450

MINISTRY OF OVERSEAS
DEVELOPMENT
Eland House, Stag Place, S.W.1
[01–834 2377]
The Ministry of Overseas Development deals
with British development assistance to overseas
countries. This includes both capital aid on con-
cessional terms and technical assistance (mainly in
the form of specialist staff abroad and training
facilities in the United Kingdom), whether provided
directly to developing countries or through the
various multilateral and organizations, including the
United Nations and its specialized agencies.
Minister for Overseas Development, THE RT. HON.
REGINALD ERNEST PRENTICE, M.P........ £13,000
Private Secretary, R. G. M. Manning.
Parliamentary Private Secretary, M. J. Ward, M.P.
Parliamentary Secretary, J. D. Grant, M.P.... £5,500
Private Secretary, J. C. Machin.
Permanent Secretary, R. B. M. King, C.B., M.C.
£18,675

Private Secretary, Miss V. M. Read.
Deputy Secretaries, W. A. C. Mathieson, C.B., C.M.G.,
M.B.E.; R. S. Porter, C.B., O.B.E.; D. Williams,
C.V.O............................ £14,000
Under Secretaries, R. H. Belcher, C.M.G.; E. C. Burr;
A. G. Hurrell; Dr. J. L. Kilgour; D. J. Kirkness;
E. N. Larmour, C.M.G.; M. P. J. Lynch; L. C. J.
Martin; A. R. Melville, C.M.G.; M. G. Smith;
J. E. C. Thornton, O.B.E.; J. K. Wright.. £12,000
Economic Planning Staff
Director General of Economic Planning, R. S. Porter,
C.B., O.B.E............................ £14,000
Deputy Director General of Economic Planning, J. K.
Wright........................... £12,000
Director, International Economics Division, Dr. J. M.
Healey............................ £11,440
Director, Geographical Division, G A. Bridger
£11,440
Director, Statistics Division, K. V. Henderson
£11,440
Senior Economic Advisers, R. M. Ainscow; Dr. B. E.
Cracknell; N. B. Hudson; J. B. Wilmshurst
£8,650 to £11,000
Economic Advisers, A. D. Adamson; G. A. Beattie;
G. A. C. Houston; B. R. Ireton; Miss J. M. Lewis;
J. A. Peat; J. T. Roberts; C. H. Smee; H. B.
Wenban-Smith; C. J. B. White; J. T. Win-
penny........................... £5,680 to £7,450
Chief Statisticians, R. M. Allen; D. C. Upton
£8,650 to £11,000
Statisticians, T. L. F. Devis; S. J. Webster
£5,680 to £7,450
Information Department
Chief Information Officer, R. T. G. Miles
£8,650 to £11,000
Principal Information Officers, J. W. T. Cooper; Mrs.
N. Good.................... £5,680 to £7,450
Senior Information Officers, G. V. T. Church; K. J.
Hanford; Mrs H. Dean...... £4,900 to £5,900
Heads of Development Division
Caribbean (*Bridgetown*), Sir Bruce Greatbatch,
K.C.V.O., C.M.G., M.B.E.; *Middle East Develop-
ment Division* (*Beirut*), J. C. Rowley; *East Africa
Development Division* (*Nairobi*), J. C. Edwards;
South-East Asia Development Division (*Bangkok*),
M. B. Hudson; *Southern Africa Development
Division* (*Blantyre*) W. T. A. Cox
£8,650 to £11,000

Assistant Secretaries, K. G. Ashton; R. L. Baxter;
R. A. Browning; J. L. F. Buist; M. L. Cahill;
R. F. R. Deare; A. J. A. Douglas, C.M.G., O.B.E.;
P. C. Duff; F. P. Dunnill; M. de N. Ensor, O.B.E.;
I. H. Harris; J. W. Howard; C. R. O. Jones;
D. M. Kitching; A. A. W. Landymore, C.B.E.;
P. S. McLean, O.B.E.; W. D. Maniece; L. W.
Norwood; K. O. H. Osborne; A. J. Peckham;
C. R. A. Rae; J. E. Rednall; A. K. Russell; D. F.
Smith; G. W. Thom, O.B.E.; A. M. Turner;
J. E. Whitelegg; Miss E. M. Young
£8,650 to £11,000
Senior Principals, K. G. Fry; J. H. D. Gambold;
G. C. Lawrence, C.M.G., O.B.E.; L. V. Martin,
O.B.E.; W. D. J Morgan; J. L. West
£7,750 to £9,350
Principals, M. D. Allen; Miss A. M. Archbold;
B. D. Barber; E. T. Barnes; Miss P. M. D.
Baxter; E. A. Bennett; W. T. Birrell; J. M. B.
Blair-Fish; H. H. Bracken, C.B.E.; S. A. Bunce;
J. A. Burgess, O.B.E.; P. J. Burton; D. G. Camps;
D. E. B. Carr; R. O. Carter; Miss R. M. B.
Chevallier; D. J. Church; B. Cook; A. D.
Cooper; L. E. Dawes; F. W. Essex, C.M.G.;
J. A. L. Faint; A. S. Fair; M. J. Fairlie, O.B.E.;
C. R. V. Farran; F. W. Foreman; D. S. Foster;
P. D. M. Freeman; K. W. G. Frost; Hon. D. C.
Geddes; C. T. Gerard; D. E. Glason; D. W.
Goodman, M.B.E.; R. M. Graham-Harrison;
C. M. H. Harrison; W. Hobman; F. J. Holloway;
H. Holmes; M. H. Jay; P. H. Johnston, C.M.G.;
B. T. Jordan; J. V. Kerby; R. O. Kiernan;
K. D. Law; A. N. MacCleary; M. C. McCulloch;
Miss M. P. Maguire; R. G. M. Manning; B. A.

Mitchell; H. A. Moisley; S. J. Moore; K. H. R.
Mundy; I. T. Nance; D. G. Osborne; K. P.
O'Sullivan; P. G. Ottewill, G.M., A.F.C.; M. F.
Page, C.B.E.; M. A. Pattison; S. C. Pennock;
R. G. Pettit; M. Prescott; R. M. Prideaux; R. S.
Ridgwell; A. G. Ridley, M.V.O.; G. F. Roberts;
A. K. Robertson; Mrs. M. C. Rosser; D. Sands-
Smith; E. Scott; P. L. J. Scott; J. M. Scoular;
A. G. Simpson; F. E. Sitch; J. A. B. Smith; D. L.
Stanton; G. F. H. Stapley; I. F. Stickels; A. H.
Tansley; A. M. Trick; J. M. M. Vereker; R. J.
Walsgrove; A. F. Watkins; S. Wellington;
D. M. Whitecross; G. A. Williams; T. J. Wil-
shire; K. J. Windsor, O.B.E.; K. A. F. Woolver-
ton; R. W. Wootton; T. D. Wright, M.V.O.
                                £5,680 to £7,450
Appointments Officer, Sir George Duntze, Bt., C.M.G.
                                £5,680 to £6,953
Senior Executive Officers, J. A. Anning; A. D.
Appleby; Miss J. W. Balls, M.B.E.; E. H. Becraft;
D. H. Braun; E. A. Byron, M.B.E.; P. H. Charters;
Miss D. W. Cherry; T. W. Church; G. H.
Clark; B. B. Davies; E. Eames; K. C. Elkins;
C. E. Eyles; Miss M. Fairlie, M.B.E.; H. J. Finch;
D. I. Fletcher; C. F. G. Foss; J. R. Gilbert;
C. T. R. Gordon; Miss P. Grosvenor; J. R.
Hards; A. H. Harrison; N. E. Hoult; Miss S. P.
Hurn; Miss G. V. Jackson; I. N. Jenkins; Mrs.
B. M. Kelly; Miss M. J. Kinchington, M.B.E.;
L. A. Lampard; P. S. Lindsey; B. W. Lister; L. J.
McCarthy; J. M. McDonough; V. J. McGee;
C. A. Maher; E. Martin; E. M. Minns; Miss D.
Nicholls; Miss P. M. North; Miss L. H. R.
Roberts; Miss E. F. Saracco; P. J. Shaw; G. H.
Sinclair; B. A. Thorpe; W. J. C. Tomlinson;
Miss E. M. Ware; P. J. Watson; H. C. Williams;
P. M. Wilson . . . . £4,900 to £5,900

Advisory and Specialist Staff

Chief Education Adviser, J. E. C. Thornton, O.B.E.
                                £12,000
Education Advisers, P. Collister; W. A. Dodd;
Dr. I. Griffiths; Dr. R. B. Ingle
                                £8,650 to £9,798
Education Adviser (Technical), Dr. O. G. Pickard,
C.B.E. . . . . £8,650 to £9,798
Principal Engineering Adviser, B. M. U. Bennell
                                £8,100 to £9,440
Engineering Adviser, B. G. Little. £8,650 to £9,798
Architectural Adviser, M. V. S. Smith
                                £8,650 to £9,798
Overseas Labour Adviser, C. Foggon, C.M.G., O.B.E.
(*See also Foreign & Commonwealth Office*)
Employment Adviser, F. J. Glynn, O.B.E. £7,500
Chief Medical Adviser, Dr. J. L. Kilgour (*See also
Department of Health & Social Security*)
Medical Advisers, Dr. W. J. M. Evans, C.B.E.; Dr.
J. A. B. Nicholson, M.B.E. £11,000
Nursing Adviser (part-time), Miss B. G. Schofield,
O.B.E. £3,752
Chief Natural Resources Adviser, A. R. Melville,
C.M.G. £12,000
Deputy Chief Natural Resources Adviser, J. Wyatt-
Smith . . . . £8,100 to £9,440
Principal Agricultural Adviser, D. C. P. Evans
                                £8,100 to £9,440
Agricultural Advisers, A. W. Peers, O.B.E.; P. Tuley,
M.B.E.; P. R. Weare . . . . £8,650 to £9,798
Assistant Agricultural Advisers, K. Wilson-Jones;
J. B. Warren . . . . £5,514 to £7,205
Agricultural Economics and Management Adviser, P. W.
Stutley, O.B.E. . . . . £8,650 to £9,798
Agricultural Research Adviser, Dr. R. K. Cunning-
ham . . . . £8,100 to £9,440
Assistant Agricultural Research Adviser, R. W. Smith
                                £5,514 to £7,205
Principal Animal Health Adviser, A. L. C. Thorne,
C.B.E. . . . . £8,100 to £9,440
Animal Health Adviser, J. Davie . £8,650 to £9,798
Co-operatives Adviser, B. J. Youngjohns
                                £8,650 to £9,798
Environmental Co-ordination Adviser, Dr D. W. Hall
                                £8,650 to £9,798

Principal Fisheries Adviser, Dr D. N. F. Hall
                                £8,100 to £9,400
Fisheries Adviser, J. Stoneman. . . . £8,650 to £9,798
Principal Forestry Adviser, J. Wyatt Smith
                                £8,100 to £9,400
Forestry Adviser, D. F. Davidson, O.B.E.
                                £8,650 to £9,798
Land Tenure Adviser, J. C. D. Lawrance, O.B.E.
                                £8,650 to £9,798
Physical (Land Use) Planning Adviser, G. H. Franklin
                                £8,650 to £9,798
Police Training Adviser, M. J. ⎫
Macoun, C.M.G., O.B.E., Q.P.M. ⎪ *See also Foreign
Deputy Police Training Adviser, ⎬ *and Common-
L. A. Hicks, Q.P.M.   ⎪ wealth Office.*
                            ⎭
Adviser on Social Development, A. R. G. Prosser,
C.M.G., M.B.E. . . . . £8,650 to £9,798

Centre for Overseas Pest Research
College House, Wrights Lane, W.8
[01–937 8191]
Director, P. T. Haskell, C.M.G., Ph.D. £11,670

Technical Education and Training
Organisation for Overseas Countries
Grosvenor Gardens House,
35–37 Grosvenor Gardens, S.W.1
[01–834 3665]
Director-General, W. L. Bell, C.M.G., M.B.E. £9,440

Directorate of Overseas (Geodetic and
Topogaraphic) Surveys
Kingstown Road, Tolworth, Surbiton, Surrey
[01–377 8661]
Director, D. E. Warren, C.M.G. . . . £8,100 to £9,440

Inter-University Council for Higher
Education Overseas
90–91 Tottenham Court Road, W.1
[01–580 6572]
Director, R. C. Griffiths £12,000

Land Resources Division
Tolworth Tower, Surbiton, Surrey
[01–399 5281]
Director, A. J. Smyth . . . . £8,100 to £9,440

Overseas Services Resettlement Bureau
Eland House, Stag Place, S.W.1
[01–834 2377]
Director and Head of Bureau, Sir Edwin Arrowsmith,
K.C.M.G. . . . . £7,150 to £7,450

Population Bureau
29 Bressenden Place, S.W.1
[01–828 4366]
Director and Head of Bureau (vacant).

Tropical Products Institute
56–62 Gray's Inn Road, W.C.1
[01–242 5412]
Director, P. C. Spensley, D.Phil. £11,670

OFFICE OF THE PARLIAMENTARY
COMMISSIONER AND HEALTH
SERVICE COMMISSIONER
Church House, Great Smith Street, S.W.1
[01–212 7676]

The Parliamentary Commissioner for Administration is responsible for investigating complaints
referred to him by Members of the House of
Commons from members of the public who claim
to have sustained injustice in consequence of maladministration in connection with administrative
action taken by or on behalf of Government Departments. Certain types of action by Departments
are excluded from investigation. Actions taken
by other public bodies (such as local authorities,
the police, the Post Office and nationalised industries) are outside the Commissioner's scope.

The Health Service Commissioners for England,
for Scotland and for Wales are responsible for
investigating complaints against National Health
Service authorities that are not dealt with by those
authorities to the satisfaction of the complainant.
Complaints can be referred direct by the member of
the public who claims to have sustained injustice
or hardship in consequence of the failure in a service

provided by a relevant body, failure of that body to provide a service or in consequence of any other action by that body. Certain types of action are excluded, in particular, action taken solely in consequence of the exercise of clinical judgment. The three offices are initially held by the Parliamentary Commissioner.

Parliamentary Commissioner and Health Service Commissioner, Sir Alan Marre, K.C.B..... £21,000
Secretaries, H. B. McK.Johnston; J. L. C. Scarlett, C.B.E............................ £12,000
Directors, R. J. S. Bryant; Miss M. F. Gracey; Miss J. Horsham; T. W. Jones, O.B.E.; D. G. Plaister, O.B.E. (*Establishment Officer*); H. T. Sowden; A. Thompson..... £8,650 to £11,000
Principals, J. R. Abbott; J. P. Carey; F. D. Chessel; A. Davies; W. D. George; M. J. Goodson; K. H. Green; D. M. P. Jones; J. A. Mahoney; D. F. J. Mills; R. A. Pocock; W. Thain; J. Wallbank; B. W. White....£5,680 to £7,450

PARLIAMENTARY COUNSEL
36 Whitehall, S.W.1 [01-930 1234]
First Counsel, Sir Anthony Stainton, K.C.B., Q.C. £21,000
Second Counsel, H. P. Rowe, C.B.; T. R. F. Skemp, C.B........................... £17,000
Counsel, G. J. Carter; G. J. J. Engle; P. Graham; F. B. Humphrey, C.B.; C. H. de Waal; D. Rippengal..................... up to £15,000

PAROLE BOARD
Romney House, Marsham Street, S.W.1 [01-212 6009]
The Board was constituted under section 59 of the Criminal Justice Act, 1967 and the Members were appointed on November 7, 1967.

The function of the Board is to advise the Secretary of State for the Home Department with respect to: (1) Release on licence under section 60 (i) or 61 and recall under section 62 of the Criminal Justice Act, 1967 of persons whose cases have been referred to the Board by the Secretary of State; (2) The conditions of such licences, and the variation and cancellation of such conditions; and (3) any other matter so referred which is connected with release on licence or recall of persons to whom section 60 or 61 of the Act applies.
Chairman, Sir Louis Petch, K.C.B.
Vice-Chairman, The Hon. Mr. Justice Cusack.
Members, Dr. D. Anton-Stephens; G. W. Appleyard, O.B.E.; Miss E. E. Barnard; His Hon. C. Beaumont; J. Bliss, Q.P.M.; A. E. Bottoms, Ph.D.; S. G. Clarke, C.B.E.; Mrs. P. M. David; A. R. Davis, C.B.E.; Dr. J. E. Duffield; S. R. Elliott; A. Falla, M.D.; L. Frayne; His Hon. B. H. Gerrard; The Hon. Mr. Justice Griffiths, M.C.; Sir Richard Hayward, C.B.E.; K. Hollingsworth; P. W. Hopson; Miss J. K. Lawrence; R. M. Lee; I. P. Llewellyn-Jones; D. M. Lowson; Mrs. A. Morris; J. D. Mortimer, Ph.D.; P. L. Osborne; M. A. Partridge, D.M.; P. W. Paskell, O.B.E.; The Hon. Mr. Justice Phillips; His Hon. J. Ross, Q.C.; Dr. M. R. P. Williams, C.B.E.; A. Yates, Q.P.M.
Secretary, H. L. J. Gonsalves.... £6,990 to £7,860

PATENT OFFICE
(and Industrial Property and Copyright Department,
Department of Trade and Industry)
25 Southampton Buildings, W.C.2 [01-405 8721]
Sale Branch: Orpington, Kent
The duties of the Department consist in the administration of the Patent Acts, the Registered Designs Act and the Trade Marks Act and in dealing with questions relating to the Copyright Acts. The Department also provides information service about patent specifications published during the last 50 years. In 1974 the Office sealed 35,883 patents and registered 4,016 designs and 10,626 trade marks.
Comptroller-General, E. Armitage, C.B...... £13,230
Assistant Comptrollers, J. D. Fergusson (£11,670); R. Bowen; I. J. G. Davis.............. £11,440

Superintending Examiners, J. E. Mirams; K. M. Smith; D. G. Gay; H. W. Brace; N. W. P. Wallace; R. E. Branton; G. O. Byfleet; K. J. Kearley; A. L. Pheasey; F. C. Strachan; D. L. T. Cadman £11,190
Principal Examiners, O. O. Thorp; E. A. McMillan; A. E. Bishop; W. J. Cluff; R. E. Dalley; C. W. Smith; J. A. Watkinson; T. H. Mobbs; G. A. C. Ashcroft; M. D. Moore; K. F. Sloman; H. F. Viney; James Harrison; A. H. W. Kennard; A. G. Edwards; D. C. Snow; J. C. Keeping; J. R. Mends; W. Anderton; D. J. H. Day; D. S. G. Collins; D. A. Cowlett; J. G. Clark; B. P. Scanlan; H. C. Bailey; A. K. Jones; J. K. Sigournay; L. F. Oliver; A. F. C. Miller; R. E. Bridges; C. W. Hackett; F. E. Wastell; C. G. Harrison; V. S. Dodd; A. G. Lilleker; N. A. Robertson; D. C. L. Blake; D. F. Carter; G. E. K. Askew; R. H. P. Barber; L. L. Bow; N. B. Dean; K. P. Jessop; N. G. Tarnofsky; R. M. Bennett; C. S. Richenberg; M. Fox; J. F. Elliott; P. E. Taylor; A. J. F. Chadwick; C. I. C. Byrne; V. Tarnofsky; J. Mather; K. E. Butterworth; M. G. Currell; R. G. Williams; J. B. Partridge; L. J. Hedge; D. Spencer; P. G. Cruickshank; J. G. Bennett; J. S. Lea-Wilson; D. O. Westrop; S. A. Goodchild £9,415 to £10,180
Assistant Registrar, Trade Marks, R. L. Moorby £7,750 to £9,350
Senior Principals, A. R. Summers; A. J. Mills, I.S.O. £8,650 to £11,000
Senior Examiner, Information Retrieval Services, P. A. Higham.............. £6,125 to £8,750

Manchester Office
Baskerville House, Browncross Street, Salford [061-832 9571]
Keeper, F. J. McDougal................. £4,890

PAYMASTER GENERAL
H.M. Treasury, Parliament Street, S.W.1 [01-930 1234]
Paymaster General, THE RT. HON. EDMUND DELL, M.P................................ £9,500
Private Secretary, J. S. Beastall.

Paymaster General's Office
Russell Way, Crawley, West Sussex [Crawley 27833]
The Paymaster General's Office was formed by the consolidation in 1835 of various separate pay departments then existing, some of which dated back at least to the Restoration of 1660. Its function is that of paying agent for Government Departments, other than the Revenue Departments. Most of its payments are made through banks, to whose accounts the necessary transfers are made at the Bank of England. The payment of many types of public service pensions is an important feature of its work. The expenses of the office were estimated at £3,093,000 for 1975-76.
Assistant Paymaster General, F. J. Clay, O.B.E. £8,650 to £11,000
Dep. Asst. Paymaster Gen., D. M. Wheble, O.B.E. £7,750 to £9,350
Senior Principal, N. C. Norfolk, I.S.O. £7,750 to £9,350
Principals, L. A. Andrews; R. A. Heavens, M.B.E.; A. Lawrence; H. T. Reading; E. F. Webster, M.B.E...................... £5,680 to £7,450
Senior Executive Officers, D. R. Alexander; J. K. Bell; O. J. Breeden; S. W. Cole; D. J. P. Dutton; T. R. George; E. D. Hatswell; A. Jones; H. C. Leng; A. J. McClatchey; D. N. McNee; I. J. Pells; R. F. Russen, B.E.M.; K. Sullens; G. Thomas; G. F. Tidy; P. R. Tight; G. T. Wheway £4,900 to £5,900

POLITICAL HONOURS SCRUTINY COMMITTEE
Civil Service Department, Standard House, Northumberland Avenue, W.C.2 [01-839 7733]
Chairman, The Lord Crathorne, P.C., T.D.

Members, The Lord Rea, P.C., O.B.E.; The Baroness Summerskill, P.C., C.H.
Secretary, Sir Stuart Milner-Barry, K.C.V.O., C.B., O.B.E.

OFFICE OF POPULATION CENSUSES AND SURVEYS
St. Catherine's House, W.C.2
[01–242 0262]

The Office of Population Censuses and Surveys was created by a merger in May 1970 of the General Register Office and the Government Social Survey Department. The Registrar General controls the local registration service in England and Wales in the exercise of its registration and marriage duties. Copies of the original registrations of births, stillbirths, marriages and deaths are kept in London. A register of adopted children is held at Titchfield. Central indexes are compiled quarterly and certified copies of entries may be obtained on payment of certain fees. Since 1841 the Registrar General has been responsible for taking the census of population. He also prepares and publishes a wide range of statistics and appropriate commentary relating to population, fertility, births, still-births, marriages, deaths and cause of death, infectious diseases, sickness and injuries. The Registrar General also maintains, at Southport, a central register of persons on doctors' lists, for the purposes of the National Health Service.

Hours of public access, Mon.–Fri., 8.30 a.m.–4.30 p.m.

Director and Registrar General, G. Paine, C.B., D.F.C.
£14,000
Deputy Director, P. Redfern............£12,000
Deputy Registrar General, F. A. Rooke-Matthews
£8,650 to £11,000
Assistant Secretaries, S. Witzenfeld, I.S.O. (*Establishment Officer*); P. H. Kenney..£8,650 to £11,000
Chief Statisticians, A. M. Adelstein (*Medical*), £12,000; N. H. W. Davis (*Population*); D. Newman (*Census*); Miss J. H. Thompson (*Population*)
£8,650 to £11,000
Senior Statisticians (*Medical*), P. M. Lambert; Mrs. J. A. C. Weatherall............£11,000
Head of Social Survey Division, C. G. Thomas
£8,650 to £11,000
Adviser on Survey Research, L. Moss
(+ *allce.*) £8,650 to £11,000
Senior Principals, G. F. P. Boston; T. E. Broughton; A. A. Cushion; Miss A. B. Graham; J. P. Hisley; J. R. Jeffery; T. M. Jenkins (*Deputy Establishment Officer*)..............£7,750 to £9,350
Chief Social Survey Officers, P. G. Gray; W. F. F. Kemsley; Miss R. Morton-Williams
£7,750 to £9,350
Statisticians, M. I. A. Bulmer; L. Bulusu; R. A. Campbell; J. Craig; M. Milner; D. L. Pearce; Miss L. V. Roberts; J. B. Werner.
£5,680 to £7,400
Principals, B. S. T. Alcock; G. P. Barnes; R. H. Birch; N. W. Brown; P. J. Cook; G. A. Fielden; R. K. Freeman; A. L. Gay; E. Graver; F. J. Harvey; K. R. Hedderly; I. Hutchinson; C. F. James; E. T. Jones; G. P. Knight; M. L. Pennington; T. A. Russell; R. P. Thorby; Miss M. M. Turvey; T. B. West; T. O. Youlten
£5,680 to £7,450
Principal Social Survey Officers, Mrs. P. E. Astbury; Miss J. Atkinson; R. Barnes; R. M. Blunden; Miss A. I. Harris; Mrs. E. A. Hunt; S. R. Parker; A. J. Pearce; R. K. Thomas; Miss J. E. Todd
£5,680 to £7,400
Senior Research Officers, R. J. Beacham; C. J. Denham; S. M. Farid; G. P. Hawes
£5,680 to £7,400
Senior Survey Officers, N. Bateson; F. Birch; Mrs. M. R. Bone; M. J. Bradley; S. M. Brown; Mrs. M. L. Durant; E. S. Finch; Mrs. E. M. Goddard; Miss J. A. Higgins; I. B. Knight; Mrs. M. Mansfield; Miss E. M. McCrossan; Mrs. C. M. Pillay; Mrs. I. Rauta; Miss J. Ritchie; K. K. Sillitoe; Mrs. A. C. Thomas; S. R. Turner; P. K. Wingfield-Digby............£4,900 to £5,900

Senior Executive Officers, A. G. Ammon; T. Anderson; N. E. Auckland; E. Barton; G. Benson; D. E. Birch; Mrs. F. R. Bowker; T. B. Bryson; R. J. Carpenter; A. M. Clark; D. H. Cleverly; R. J. Deacon; J. Denton; G. P. S. Fitterer; H. D. Gee; F. B. Gentle; P. H. Gibson; I. M. Golds; J. E. Good; R. P. Hackett, M.B.E.; S. A. Haskell; P. Howell; J. J. Huttly; F. G. Johnson; G. J. A. Johnson; T. Johnson; A. F. Jones; J. H. Kempf; Miss J. D. Kennaway; B. G. Little; J. H. Lloyd; Miss R. M. Loy; R. McLeod; J. A. McNiven, M.B.E.; M. E. M. Mumford; L. Nelson; R. M. Nicholls; D. L. Nix; Miss D. M. Pace; N. L. Perryman; Mrs. M. J. Porter; J. A. Rampton; J. V. Ribbins; C. F. Savage; A. A. Sellar; P. Shepherd; E. E. Simpson; G. W. Smith; K. J. Stalker; D. Stewart; D. F. Stobart; Mrs. D. M. Stobart; S. C. Stracey; D. Taylor; H. D. Terry; A. W. Tester; Miss M. C. C. Tyler; P. A. Wake; J. R. Watkins; R. D. Whymark; C. A. Wileman; D. W. Williams; W. Williams; S. E. Wright
£4,900 to £5,900
Research Officer, Mrs. C. Hakim. £4,404 to £5,433

PORT OF LONDON AUTHORITY
Head Office, World Trade Centre, E.1
[01–476 6900]

The Port of London Act, 1968, consolidated and brought up to date the Port of London legislation.

Under the Harbour Revision Order, 1967, the Board was reduced to no fewer than 15 and not more than 16 members as from October 1, 1967. The members are appointed by the Secretary of State for the Environment after consultation with interested organizations as follows: National Ports Council (2 members). The Chamber of Shipping of the United Kingdom and the London General Shipowners' Society (3). The London Chamber of Commerce and the British Shippers' Council (3). The London Wharfingers' Association (1). The Association of Master Lightermen and Barge Owners in London (1). The Greater London Council (1). The Corporation of the City of London (1). The Corporation of Trinity House (1). Persons representative of organized labour (2). The sixteenth member is the Director-General who is co-opted by the Board.

The working of the Port for the year ended Dec. 31, 1974, showed a profit of £553,000.
Chairman, The Lord Adlington, P.C., K.C.M.G. C.B.E., D.S.O., T.D.
Vice-Chairman, Sir Andrew Crichton.

Board of Management
Director-General, J. Lunch, V.R.D.
Deputy Director-General, W. Bowey.
Assistant Directors-General, N. N. B. Ordman; A. M. Cameron; J. D. Presland.
Director of Real Estate and Legal Adviser, I. Hughes.
Director of Manpower, J. H. Gabony.
Director of Marine Services, Capt. P. Leighton.
Director of Tilbury, J. N. Black.
Director of Upper Docks, J. McNab.

THE POST OFFICE
23 Howland Street, W.1
[01–631 2345]

Crown services for the carriage of Government despatches were set up about 1516. The conveyance of public correspondence began in 1635 and the mail service was made a Parliamentary responsibility with the setting up of a Post Office in 1657. Telegraphs came under the Post Office control in 1870 and the Post Office Telephone Service began in 1880. The National Data Processing Service, the Post Office's commercial computer bureau, was set up in 1967. The Giro service of the Post Office began in 1968. The Post Office ceased to be a Government Department on October 1, 1969, following the Post Office Act 1969. On that date the office of Postmaster General was abolished and responsibility for the running of the postal, telecommunications, giro, remittance and data processing services was transferred to the new public authority called the Post Office. The Chairman and members of the Post Office Board are appointed by the Secretary of State but responsibility for the running of the Post Office as a whole rests with the Board in its corporate capacity.

Post Office Board

Chairman, Sir William Ryland, C.B...... £23,100
Deputy Chairman and Managing Director, Tele-communications, Sir Edward Fennessy, C.B.E.
£19,100
Managing Director, Posts, A. Currall, C.B., C.M.G.
Member for Technology, Prof. J. H. H. Merriman, C.B., O.B.E.
Member for Personnel and Industrial Relations, K. M. Young.
Managing Director, Giro and Data Processing, A. E. Singer.
Member for Finance and Corporate Planning, M. Elderfield.
Salary range of Members ...... £12,600 to £17,600

PRICE COMMISSION
Neville House, Page Street, S.W.1
[01-222 8020]
The Commission is responsible for the application of the Price Code, including the " vetting " of submissions for price increases, investigation and enforcement work and the monitoring of fresh food retail prices.
Chairman, Sir Arthur Cockfield.
Deputy Chairman, K. A. Noble, C.B.E.
Secretary, C. D. E. Keeling.
Members, Miss S. P. Black; Prof. D. C. Hague; Miss M. E. Head, O.B.E.; A. W. Howitt; F. B. Kitchen; B. I. Petch.

DEPARTMENT OF PRICES AND CONSUMER PROTECTION
1 Victoria Street, S.W.1
(unless otherwise stated) [01-215 7877]
The Department of Prices and Consumer Protection sponsors the consumer interest. Its responsibilities cover policy on prices and price control (including the administration of consumer subsidies on food), monopolies, mergers and restrictive practices, consumer protection, consumer credit and standards, weights and measures (including metrication).

SALARY LIST

Secretary of State £13,000
Minister of State £7,500
Parliamentary Under Secretary of State £5,500
Permanent Secretary £18,675
Deputy Secretary £14,000
Under Secretary £12,000
Assistant Secretary .... £8,650 to £11,000
Principal .... £5,680 to £7,450
Chief Information Officer (A) .... £8,650 to £11,000
Director Engineer £11,000
Secretary of State for Prices and Consumer Protection, THE RT. HON. MRS. SHIRLEY WILLIAMS, M.P.
Private Secretary, G. E. Rees
Parliamentary Private Secretary, R. C. Mitchell, M.P.
Special Advisers, J. Lyttle; Dr. J. Mitchell.
Minister of State for Prices and Consumer Protection, ALAN JOHN WILLIAMS, M.P.
Private Secretary, J. D. M. Rhodes.
Parliamentary Under Secretary of State, R. A. R. Maclennan, M.P.
Permanent Secretary, K. H. Clucas, C.B.
Private Secretary, M. G. Mecham.
Deputy Secretaries, J. C. Burgh, C.B.; W. P. Shovelton, C.M.G.
Personnel and General Co-ordinator (Assistant Secretary), Miss J. Blow
Head of Information Division (CIO (A)), Miss S. Jefferies.
Parliamentary Clerk (Principal), Miss P. A. Davey.

Consumer Credit Branch
Assistant Secretary, D. G. Hyde.

Prices Policy Division 1
Under Secretary, W. Nicoll, C.M.G.
Assistant Secretaries, Miss E. M. Llewellyn-Smith; J. H. M. Solomon.

Prices Policy Division 2
Under Secretary, Mrs. J. M. Archer.
Assistant Secretaries, G. J. Hill; A. J. Lane; J. G. Morris.

Fair Trading Division
Under Secretary, C. E. Coffin.
Assistant Secretaries, M. B. Casey; A. Dunning; A. J. Nieduszynski; G. Stapleton.

Standards, Weights and Measures Division
Abell House, John Islip Street, S.W.1
[01-211 3000]
Under Secretary, Dr. E. N. Eden.
Assistant Secretary, A. Fortnam.
Deputy Chief Scientific Officer, E. E. Williams, O.B.E.
26 Chapter Street, S.W.1
[01-834 7032]
Director Engineer, J. D. Platt.

PRIVY COUNCIL OFFICE
Whitehall, S.W.1
Lord President of the Council (and Leader of the House of Commons), RT. HON. EDWARD WATSON SHORT, M.P......................... £13,000
Private Secretary, C. H. Saville.
Assistant Private Secretary, Miss J. E. Wheeler.
Parliamentary Private Secretary, Dr. M. S. Miller, M.P.
Minister of State, GERALD TEASDALE FOWLER, M.P.
£9,500
Clerk to the Council, N.E. Leigh, C.V.O..... £12,000
Deputy Clerk to the Council, C. E. S. Horsford
£8,650 to £11,000
Senior Clerk, A. W. Kimberley.. £5,276 to £6,509

PUBLIC HEALTH LABORATORY SERVICE
Headquarters Office:
Lower Entrance, Colindale Hospital,
Colindale Avenue, N.W.9
[01-205 1295]
The Service was originally set up in 1939 as an emergency service to augment the existing public health resources of England and Wales in combating outbreaks of infectious diseases such as might arise from enemy action or abnormal conditions in time of war. In 1945 the Government decided to retain the Service on a permanent footing, and statutory authority for doing so was included in the National Health Service Act, 1946, the Minister of Health being empowered to provide a Bacteriological Service in England and Wales for the control of the spread of infectious diseases. The Service was administered by the Medical Research Council, as agents of the Ministry of Health until August 1, 1961, when, under the provision of the Public Health Laboratory Service Act, 1969, a new Public Health Laboratory Service Board was established as a statutory body capable of acting in its own right as agent for the Department of Health and Social Security.
Members of the Board: C. E. G. Smith, C.B., M.D. (Chairman): F. A. Adams, C.B.; H. M. Archibald; W. G. Harding; Prof. K. McCarthy, M.D.; Prof. D. D. Reid, M.D.; Prof. R. A. Shooter, M.D.; C. C. Stevens, O.B.E.; G. I. Watson, O.B.E., M.D.
Director, Prof. R. E. O. Williams, M.D.
Deputy Directors, J. C. Kelsey, M.D.; J. E. M. Whitehead, M.D.
Secretary, J. D. Whittaker, C.B.E.

CENTRAL PUBLIC HEALTH LABORATORY,
LONDON, N.W.9
Director, S. P. Lapage

REFERENCE LABORATORIES
(With name of Director)
Cross-Infection Reference (incorporating Streptococcus and Staphylococcus Reference) M. T. Parker. M.D.

Disinfection Reference, J. C. Kelsey, M.D.,
Enteric Reference, Prof. E. S. Anderson, M.D., F.R.S.
Leptospirosis Reference L. H. Turner, M.B.E., M.D.
Mycological Reference (London School of Hygiene and Tropical Medicine), D. W. R. Mackenzie, Ph.D.
Mycoplasma Reference, B. E. Andrews.
Salmonella and Shigella Reference, B. Rowe.
Tuberculosis Reference, University Hospital of Wales, Cardiff. J. Marks, M.D.
Venereal Diseases Reference, London Hospital, E.1. A. E. Wilkinson (*part-time*).
Virus Reference, Mrs. M. S. Pereira, M.D.

SPECIAL LABORATORIES
(*With name of Director*)
Bacterial Metabolism Research Laboratory, M. J. Hill
Computer Trials, S. P. Lapage.
Epidemiology Research Laboratory, T. M. Pollock.
Food Hygiene, Miss B. C. Hobbs, D.SC.
National Collection of Type Cultures, S. P. Lapage.
Quality Control, P. B. Crone, M.D.
Standards Laboratory for Serological Reagents, Mrs. C. M. P. Bradstreet.

CONSTITUENT PUBLIC HEALTH LABORATORIES
(*With name of Director*)
Bath, P. G. Mann, M.D.; *Birmingham*, J. G. P. Hutchinson, M.D.; *Brighton*, B. T. Thom; *Bristol*, H. R. Cayton; *Cambridge*, G. R. E. Naylor, M.D.; *Cardiff*, C. H. L. Howells, M.D.; *Carlisle*, D. G. Davies, M.D.; *Carmarthen*, H. D. S. Morgan; *Chelmsford*, R. Pilsworth, M.D.; *Chester*, Miss P. M. Poole, M.D.; *Conway*, A. J. Kingsley Smith; *Coventry*, Mrs. E. J. Finnie, M.D.; *Derby*, (vacant); *Dorchester*, G. H. Tee, PH.D.; *Epsom*, D. R. Gamble; *Exeter*, B. Moore, M.D.; *Gloucester*, A. E. Wright, T.D., M.D.; *Guildford*, Miss J. M. Davies, M.D.; *Hereford*, D. R. Christie; *Hull*, J. H. McCoy; *Ipswich*, P. K. Fraser, M.D.; *Leeds*, G. L. Gibson, M.D.; *Leicester*, N. S. Mair; *Lincoln*, J. G. Wallace; *Liverpool*, G. C. Turner, M.D.; *London*, C. E. D. Taylor, M.D. (*Central Middlesex Hospital*); C. Dulake (*Dulwich Hospital*); D. G. Fleck, M.D. (*St. George's Hospital, Tooting Grove*); B. Chattopadhay (*Whipps Cross Hospital*); *Luton*, A. T. Willis, M.D.; *Maidstone*, A. L. Furniss, M.D.; *Manchester*, D. M. Jones, M.D.; *Newcastle*, J. H. Hale, O.B.E., M.D.; *Newport*, R. D. Gray, M.D.; *Norwich*, W. Shepherd; *Nottingham*, E. R. Mitchell; *Oxford*, J. O'H. Tobin; *Peterborough*, E. J. G. Glencross; *Plymouth*, P. D. Meers, M.D.; *Poole*, W. L. Hooper; *Portsmouth*, D. J. H. Payne; *Preston*, L. Robertson; *Reading*, J. V. Dadswell; *Salisbury*, P. J. Wormald, M.D.; *Sheffield*, B. W. Barton; *Shrewsbury*, G. A. Morris, M.D.; *Southampton*, A. M. R. Mackenzie; *Southend*, J. A. Rycroft; *Stoke-on-Trent*, P. Cavanagh, M.D.; *Swansea*, W. Kwantes; *Taunton*, J. V. S. Pether; *Truro*, G. I. Barrow, M.D.; *Watford*, B. R. Eaton; *Wolverhampton*, I. A. Harper (*Hon.*); *Worcester*, R. J. Henderson, M.D. (*part-time*).

PUBLIC RECORD OFFICE
See RECORD OFFICES

PUBLIC TRUSTEE OFFICE
Sardinia Street, Kingsway, W.C.2
[01–405 4300]
Public Trustee, A. A. Creamer £13,990
Assistant Public Trustee, J. Radford £12,410
Chief Administrative Officers, J. A. Boland; D. A. Wakeford; R. O. A. Wertheim
£9,443 to £11,410
Acceptance Officer, R. A. Cunningham
£6,090 to £7,860
Officer in Charge of Legality of Investments, S. B. Ince
£7,035 to £9,160
Senior Legal Assistants, J. G. Allen; R. C. Annis; V. J. Burt; A. P. Carlton-Smith; J. S. Chapman; A. J. Dawes; S. J. Dunn; T. R. Herzog; H. K. Mackinder; J. B. Measures; A. G. Prideaux; J. C. Rowe; F. Wheatley . . . . . . £7,035 to £9,160

Establishment Officer, L. A. Widden, O.B.E.
£8,160 to £9,760
Deputy Establishment Officer, G. Davison
£5,310 to £6,310
Training Officer, G. A. Mars . . . . £4,310 to £5,110
Chief Accountant, R. R. Smith . . £8,160 to £9,760
Asst. Chief Accountants, F. A. Boocock; J. E. Duffy; R. L. Mew . . . . £6,090 to £7,860
Accountants, T. L. Avery; A. S. Baker; R. J. Beal; M. J. Blyth; L. J. Cobley; D. M. Cox; J. A. Matson . . . . £5,310 to £6,310
Income Tax Officer, R. V. Walsh . £5,310 to £6,310
Chief Investment Manager, F. A. Beecham
£8,160 to £9,760
Senior Investment Managers, I. L. Brydon; A. L. Childs; K. Stilliard . . . . £6,090 to £7,860
Investment Managers, R. J. M. Gibson; T. H. Nicholls . . . . £5,310 to £6,310
Securities Officer, A. R. Smith . . £5,310 to £6,310
Chief Property Adviser, S. Vidler, O.B.E.
£6,690 to £7,860
Senior Property Advisers, D. E. Fewings; R. Myers
£5,130 to £6,340

PUBLIC WORKS LOAN BOARD
Royex House, Aldermanbury Square, E.C.2
[01–606 7321]
The Board is an independent statutory body, consisting of 12 unpaid Commissioners appointed by the Crown to hold office for 4 years; 3 Commissioners retire each year and may be re-appointed.
The functions of the Commissioners, derived chiefly from the Public Works Loans Act, 1875, and the National Loans Act, 1968, are to consider applications for loans by Local Authorities and other prescribed bodies, and when loans are approved, to collect the repayments.
Funds for loans are authorised from time to time by Parliament and are drawn from the National Loans Fund. Rates of interest on the Board's loans and fees to cover management expenses are fixed by the Treasury.
During the year ended March 31, 1975, estimated gross issues from the National Loans Fund for advance by the Public Works Loan Board amounted to £1,625,000,000.
Chairman, Sir Bernard Waley-Cohen, Bt . . . . *unpaid*
Deputy Chairman, F. Haywood, C.B.E. . . . . . . *unpaid*
Other Commissioners, W. Bowdell, C.B.E.; J. E. A. R. Guinness; W. R. Harman, M.B.E.; Miss D. J. Hope-Wallace, C.B.E.; R. H. Moores; R. Partington; T. N. Ritchie, T.D.; Dr. C. H. Stout; S. F. Tongue; C. G. Vaughan-Lee, D.S.C . . . . . . *unpaid*
Secretary, I. de L. Radice, C.B. (*Secretary to National Debt Commissioners—q.v.*).
Asst. Secretary and Establishment Officer, H. W. Darvill, O.B.E. . . . . £7,750 to £9,350
Senior Executive Officers, T. S. Kirk; W. H. Clarke; I. H. Peattie . . . . £4,900 to £5,900

RACE RELATIONS BOARD
5 Lower Belgrave Street, S.W.1
[01–730 6291]
Chairman, Sir Geoffrey Wilson, K.C.B., C.M.G.
£8,500
Members, Mrs. E. Christie; Mrs. S. Denman; L. Freedman; M. R. Malik; Miss A. Patrick; Miss S. Roberts; T. S. Roberts; W. Simpson; Mota Singh; Sir Roy Wilson, Q.C £1,000
Chief Officer, T. Connelly.

RECORD OFFICES, ETC.
THE PUBLIC RECORD OFFICE
Chancery Lane, W.C.2
[01–405 0741]
National Records since the Norman Conquest brought together from Courts of Law and Government Departments. Search rooms open daily to holders of readers' tickets from 9.30 to 5; Saturdays, 9.30 to 1. The Museum (open Monday to Friday, 1 to 4 p.m., and to organized parties at other times by arrangement) contains *Domesday Book* (2 vols.),

made by order of William the Conqueror in 1085, and *Domesday Chest*; the *Gunpowder Plot* papers (1605); bull of Pope Clement VIII, confirming Henry VIII as *Fidei Defensor* (1524); the Log Book of H.M.S. *Victory* at Trafalgar (1805); and many other documents of national interest.

Keeper of Public Records, J. R. Ede.........£12,410
Deputy Keeper, A. W. Mabbs...£6,528 to £10,208
Records Administration Officer, E. W. Denham
£9,060 to £10,208
Establishment Officer, J. A. Gavin. £6,090 to £7,860
Principal Assistant Keepers, Miss P. M. Barnes; L. Bell; Miss D. H. Gifford; R. F. Hunnisett; A. A. H. Knightbridge; M. Roper; E. K. Timings...................£7,561 to £9,160
Assistant Keepers, First Class, P. A. Brand; C. D. Chalmers; N. G. Cox; N. E. Evans; Mrs. J. M. Hoare; C. J. Kitching; Mrs. A. N. Nicol; P. A. Penfold; J. L. Walford......£4,814 to £7,519
Senior Inspecting Officer, J. G. Wickham
£6,090 to £7,860
Inspecting Officers, D. Ashton; A. W. Bance; J. D. Cantwell; B. S. Freeman; P. F. McCaffrey; A. J. W. McDonald; N. D. Robertson
£5,310 to £6,310
Senior Executive Officer, L. G. Seed
£5,310 to £6,310

ADVISORY COUNCIL ON PUBLIC RECORDS

Public Record Office, Chancery Lane, W.C.2
Created by the Public Records Act, 1958, to advise the Lord Chancellor, as minister responsible for public records, on matters concerning public records in general and, in particular, on those aspects of the work of the Public Record Office which affect members of the public who make use of its facilities.
Chairman, The Master of the Rolls.
Members, The Rt. Hon. Lord Justice Buckley, M.B.E.; Sir Alan Bullock, F.B.A.; Prof. A. G. Dickens, C.M.G., F.B.A.; M. Edelman, M.P.; P. C. Goodhart, M.P.; Prof. M. Gowing; Prof. J. C. Holt; Prof. P. N. S. Mansergh, O.B.E.; G. D. Squibb, Q.C.; The Lord Teviot; The Lord Trend, G.C.B., C.V.O.; Prof. Glanmor Williams; Prof. C. H. Wilson, F.B.A.
Secretary, P. A. Brand.

HOUSE OF LORDS RECORD OFFICE
House of Lords, S.W.1
[01–219 3074]
Since 1497, the records of Parliament have been kept within the Palace of Westminister. They are in the custody of the Clerk of the Parliaments, who in 1946 established a record department to supervise their preservation and their production to students. The Search Room of this office is open to the public throughout the year, Mondays to Fridays inclusive from 9.30 a.m. to 5.30 p.m. The records preserved number some 3,000,000 documents, and include Acts of Parliament from 1497, Journals of the House of Lords from 1510. Minutes and Committee proceedings from 1610, and Papers laid before Parliament from 1531. Amongst the records are the Petition of Right, the Death Warrant of Charles I, the Declaration of Breda and the Bill of Rights. The House of Lords Record Office also has charge of the Journals of the House of Commons (from 1547), and other surviving records of the Commons (from 1572), which include plans and annexed documents relating to Private Bill legislation from 1818. Among other documents are the records of the Lord Great Chamberlain, the political papers of certain members of the two Houses (including those papers previously preserved in the Beaverbrook Library), and documents relating to Parliament acquired on behalf of the nation. All the manuscripts and other records are preserved in the Victoria Tower of the Houses of Parliament.
Clerk of the Records and Principal Clerk, Information Services, M. F. Bond, O.B.E., F.S.A......£12,410
Deputy Clerk of the Records, H. S. Cobb, F.S.A.
£7,561 to £9,160

Assistant Clerk of the Records, D. J. Johnson
£4,814 to £7,519

ROYAL COMMISSION ON HISTORICAL MANUSCRIPTS
Quality House, Quality Court, Chancery Lane, W.C.2
[01–242 1198]
The Historical Manuscripts Commission was first appointed by Royal Warrant in 1869, and was empowered to make enquiry into the place of deposit of collections of manuscripts and papers of historical interest and with the consent of the owners to publish their contents. The Commission was reconstituted by Royal Warrant in 1959, with wider terms of reference, including the preservation of records and assistance to other bodies working in the same field. The Master of the Rolls, who is the Chairman of the Commission, exercises through it his responsibility under the Law of Property (Amendment) Act 1924, and the Tithe Act, 1936, for manorial and tithe documents. The Commission has published over 200 volumes of printed reports upon manuscripts of historical import and compiles the *National Register of Archives*, which now contains over 19,000 typed reports upon privately-owned records, with extensive indexes, and may be consulted by historical researchers. The Commission undertakes to advise owners upon the preservation and use of their manuscripts and records.
Chairman, The Master of the Rolls.
Commissioners, Prof. Sir J. G. Edwards, D.Litt, F.B.A., F.S.A.; Prof. G. R. Potter, Ph.D., F.S.A.; Dame Veronica Wedgwood, O.M., D.B.E., Litt.D.; Sir David L. Evans, O.B.E., D.Litt.; The Very Rev. S. J. A. Evans, C.B.E., F.S.A.; Sir John Summerson, C.B.E., F.B.A., F.S.A.; Sir Edgar Stephens, C.B.E., F.S.A.; Sir Robert Somerville, K.C.V.O., F.S.A.; Prof. J. C. Beckett; The Lord Kenyon, C.B.E., F.S.A.; The Lord Fletcher, P.C. LlD., F.S.A.; Prof. A. Goodwin; The Hon. Nicholas Ridley, M.P.; The Duke of Northumberland, K.G., F.R.S.; J. P. W. Ehrman, F.B.A., F.S.A.; The Earl of Wemyss and March, K.T.; The Lord Blake, F.B.A.; Prof. S. F. C. Milsom, F.B.A.
Secretary, G. R. C. Davis, D.Phil., F.S.A.
Assistant Secretary, H. M. G. Baillie, M.B.E., F.S.A.

SCOTTISH RECORD OFFICE
H.M. General Register House, Edinburgh 1
[031–5566 585]
The Scottish Record Office has a continuous history from the 13th century. Its present home, the General Register House, was founded in 1774 and built to designs by Robert Adam, later modified by Robert Reid. Here are preserved, in accordance with the Treaty of Union, the older public records of Scotland and many collections of local and church records and family muniments. Search Rooms open daily from 9 to 4.45; Saturdays, 9 to 12.30 (Historical Search Room only). Certain groups of records, mainly the more modern records of courts and government departments and the plans collection, are preserved in the Scottish Record Office's auxiliary repository at the West Register House in Charlotte Square—the former St. George's Church which was designed by Robert Reid. The West Register House Search Room opens daily from 9 to 4.45 (Mondays to Fridays). Permanent and special exhibitions of documents are mounted in the Museum at the West Register House, which is open to the public on weekdays during Search Room hours. The National Register of Archives (Scotland), which is a branch of the Scottish Record Office, is based in the West Register House.
Keeper of the Records of Scotland, J. Imrie.

DEPARTMENT OF THE REGISTERS OF SCOTLAND
Register House, Edinburgh
[031–556 2561]
The Registers of Scotland consist of:—
(1) General Register of Sasines; (2) Register of

Deeds in the Books of Council and Session;
(3) Register of Protests; (4) Register of English
and Irish Judgments; (5) Register of Service of
Heirs; (6) Register of the Great Seal; (7) Register
of the Quarter Seal; (8) Register of the Prince's
Seal; (9) Register of Crown Grants; (10) Register
of Sheriffs' Commissions; (11) Register of the
Cachet Seal; (12) Register of Inhibitions and
Adjudications; (13) Register of Entails; (14)
Register of Hornings.

The largest of these is the General Register of
Sasines, which forms the chief security in Scotland
of the rights of land and other heritable (or real)
property.

Keeper of the Registers of Scotland, D. Williamson
£8,650 to £11,850
Deputy Keeper, J. D. Robertson . . £7,750 to £9,350
Assistant Keepers, A. Farquharson; W. S. Morwood;
W. S. Penman; W. Russell; J. F. Stewart
£5,620 to £7,450
Accountant, J. Carmichael . . . . . . £5,324 to £6,324
Senior Examiners, J. W. Barron; G. I. Fraser; W. G.
Lobban; J. D. Morton; T. M. Nichol; J. Spence;
J. Robertson; D. Sharp; J. Shaw; P. G. Skea;
A. A. Snowdon . . . . £4,900 to £5,900

CORPORATION OF LONDON RECORDS OFFICE
Guildhall, E.C.2
[01-606 3030]
Contains the municipal archives of the City of
London which are regarded as the most complete
collection of ancient municipal records in existence.
Includes charters of William the Conqueror,
Henry II, and later Kings and Queens to 1957;
ancient custumals: Liber Horn, Dunthorne,
Custurmarum, Ordinacionum, Memorandorum
and Albus, Liber de Antiquis Legibus, and collections of Statutes; continuous series of judicial
rolls and books from 1252 and Council minutes
from 1275; records of the Old Bailey and Guildhall Sessions from 1603, and financial records from
the 16th century, together with the records of
London Bridge from the 12th century and numerous subsidiary series and miscellanea of historical
interest. A Guide was published in 1951. Readers' Room open Monday to Friday, 9.30 A.M. to
5 P.M.; Saturday, by appointment only.
Keeper of the City Records, The Town Clerk.
Deputy Keeper, Miss B. R. Masters.
Assistant Keeper, J. R. Sewell.

ROYAL COMMISSION FOR THE EXHIBITION OF 1851
1 Lowther Gardens, Exhibition Road, S.W.7
[01-589 3665]
Incorporated by Supplemental Charter as a
permanent Commission after winding up the
affairs of the Great Exhibition of 1851. It has for
its object the promotion of scientific and artistic
education by means of funds derived from its
Kensington Estate, purchased with the surplus left
over from the Great Exhibition.
President, H.R.H. The Duke of Edinburgh, K.G.,
P.C., K.T., O.M., G.B.E.
Chairman Board of Management, Marshal of the
Royal Air Force Lord Elworthy, G.C.B., C.B.E.,
D.S.O., M.V.O., D.F.C., A.F.C.
Secretary to Commissioners, C. A. H. James.

SCIENCE RESEARCH COUNCIL
State House, High Holborn, W.C.1
[01-242 1262]
Chairman, Prof. Sir Samuel Edwards, F.R.S.
Members of the Council, Prof. Sir Hermann Bondi,
K.C.B., F.R.S.; Prof. W. E. Burcham, F.R.S.; Prof.
H. G. Callan, F.R.S.; Prof. H. Elliot, F.R.S.; J. M.
Ferguson; J. H. Horlock; A. T. James,
Ph.D.; A. J. Kennedy; Sir Norman Lindop; D. J.
Lyons, F.R.S., C.B.; Sir Ieuan Maddock, C.B.,
C.B.E., F.R.S.; Prof. R. Mason, F.R.S.; R. W.
Pringle, O.B.E., Ph.D.; Prof. D. W. N. Stibbs.
Secretary, R. St. J. Walker, C.B.E.

SCOTTISH OFFICE
Dover House, Whitehall, S.W.1
[01-930 6151]
Secretary of State for Scotland, THE RT. HON.
WILLIAM ROSS, M.B.E., M.P. £13,000
Private Secretary, P. Mackay.
Assistant Private Secretaries, A. J. Bree; M. J.
Hunter.
Parliamentary Private Secretary, J. M. Craigen, M.P.
Ministers of State, THE LORD KIRKHILL (*Develop-
ment and E.E.C.*); THE RT. HON. BRUCE MILLAN,
M.P. (*Economic Planning and Oil*) £7,500
Parliamentary Under Secretaries of State, H. D. Brown,
M.P. (*Agriculture and Housing*), H. Ewing, M.P.
(*Devolution and Home Affairs*) £5,500
Permanent Under Secretary of State, Sir Nicholas
Morrison, K.C.B. £18,675
Private Secretary, D. J. Crawley.
Assistant Under-Secretary of State, I. M. Wilson
£12,000
Liaison Staff:
Assistant Secretary, A. M. Stephens, O.B.E.
£8,650 to £11,000
Principals, C. T. Hole; G. A. M. McIntosh
£5,680 to £7,450
Senior Executive Officer, G. A. D. Philip
£4,900 to £5,900
Deputy Director, Scottish Information Office, J.
Woodrow . . . . £7,750 to £9,350
Parliamentary Clerk, Miss W. M. Doonan.

New St. Andrew's House, St. James's Centre,
Edinburgh
[031-556 8400]
MANAGEMENT GROUP SUPPORT STAFF
Principal, J. M. Currie . . . . £5,680 to £7,400

CENTRAL SERVICES
Deputy Secretary (Central Services), W. K. Fraser
£14,000

Devolution Division
Under Secretary, J. M. Ross £12,000
Assistant Secretary, A. H. Bishop
£8,650 to £11,000
Principal, H. H. Mills. . . . . £5,680 to £7,450
Senior Executive Officer, E. S. Wall £4,900 to £5,900

Personnel Division
Under Secretary, J. A. Ford, M.C. (*Principal Estab-
lishment Officer*) £12,000
Assistant Secretary, J. Inglis . . . . £8,650 to £11,000
Senior Principals, D. H. Bayes; J. R. Gordon; J.
Smith . . . . £7,750 to £9,350
Principals, I. M. L. Batts; I. F. Hunter; A. New-
bigging; D. B. D. Petrie; R. S. Reid; D. C.
Thompson; Miss B. S. Thomson; R. J. T. S.
Walker . . . . £5,680 to £7,450
Senior Executive Officers, T. Chalmers; P. Charles;
J. S. Cornwall; A. C. Darby; Miss M. M.
Douglas; J. R. M. Flucker; G. H. Fox; D. W.
Garland; P. McLaren; C. Moir; D. M. Rowland;
Miss N. C. Telfer, M.V.O.; G. Thompson; T. J.
H. Wishart; J. Wood . . . . £4,900 to £5,900

Management Services Division
Under Secretary, J. S. Gibson £12,000
Assistant Secretary (vacant) . . . . . . £8,650 to £11,000
Senior Principal, R. Barrie. . . . . . £7,780 to £9,350
Principals, R. W. Alexander; W. G. Dalgleish; J. S.
Dick; Miss M. B. Farquhar; Miss I. W. Inglis;
N. MacLeod; J. Pettigrew. . . £5,680 to £7,450
Senior Executive Officers, A. T. Boyle; E. D. Ewing;
T. G. Gas; J. R. Grant; A. Johnston; J. McGhee;
D. Murie; T. Naysmith; W. B. Ritchie; T. M.
Thomson; G. W. Tucker. . . . £4,900 to £5,900
Librarian, H. A. Colquhoun . . . . £4,900 to £5,900
Computer Service
Broomhouse Drive, Edinburgh 11
[031-443 4040]
Manager (Assistant Secretary), J. S. Robertson
£8,650 to £11,000
Deputy Manager (Senior Principal), J. S. Wheeler
£7,750 to £9,350

Principals, J. Duffy; F. Ibbotson. £5,680 to £7,450
Senior Executive Officers, H. J. Boatwright; J. R. Brown; J. B. Currie; W. Davidson; A. R. Donaldson; I. W. Goodwin; C. B. Knox; R. T. McGeorge; H. Mackay; A. B. Patton; G. A. Paul; C. F. Weaver......... £4,900 to £5,900

Finance Division
Under-Secretary, R. A. Dingwall-Smith... £12,000
Assistant Secretaries, I. R. Duncan, O.B.E.; W. A. M. Good; R. R. Hillhouse; D. G. Mackay; A. H. M. Mitchell.............. £8,650 to £11,000
Senior Principals, F. B. Drysdale; I. Nicholson; I. S. Scott........ £7,750 to £9,350

Principals, A. J. Crawford; P. W. Daley; R. Earle; E. E. Hancock; G. Hardie; T. E. Hartland; D. K. C. Jeffrey; J. F. Kerr; R. W. MacIntosh; P. McKinlay; T. M. MacNair; T. J. Muirhead; D. M. W. Napier; G. Paterson; J. F. Reid; A. D. Robertson; R. C. Sinclair; G. G. Stewart; A. Walker; Miss E. M. Wilson
£5,620 to £7,450
Chief Accountants, R. G. Carter; T. C. Hill; J. W. Troman; R. Turnbull...... £5,620 to £7,450
Senior Executive Officers, W. Anness; J. A. Boyd; J. Brown; D. Cook; L. P. S. Dunbar; A. B. Forrest; G. L. Kerr; W. A. Lamberton; D. A. McNiven; J. Mann; D. A. Mayer; J. F. Munro; T. A. Murray; A. Naismith; W. Pilmer; R. R. Ross; J. R. Sinclair; J. T. Skinner; W. T. Tait; B. P. Underwood; G. P. Walker; T. Winwick
£4,900 to £5,900

Solicitor's Office
(For the Scottish Departments and certain U.K. services including H.M. Treasury, in Scotland).
Solicitor, R. W. Deans................. £14,000
Deputy Solicitor, A. G. Brand, M.B.E.... £12,000
Assistant Solicitors, *J. B. Allan; H. D. Glover; J. L. Jamieson; R. A. Lawrie; A. A. McMillan; E. S. Robertson; *A. J. Sim; *A. J. F. Tannock, M.C.; J. E. Taylor; Miss M. Y. Walker; C. J. Workman, T.D.......... £9,033 to £11,000
    * Seconded to Scottish Law Commission

Scottish Information Office
(for the Scottish Departments and certain U.K. services)
Director, C. MacGregor, M.B.E.. £8,650 to £11,000

Statistical Services
Chief Statistician, W. J. Fearnley
£8,650 to £11,000

Inquiry Reporters
44 York Place, Edinburgh 1
[031-556 9191]
Chief Reporter, A. J. Hunt, O.B.E......... £12,000
Deputy Chief Reporter, A. G. Bell
£9,798 to £11,000

DEPARTMENT OF AGRICULTURE AND FISHERIES FOR SCOTLAND
Chester House, 500 Gorgie Road, Edinburgh
[031-443 4020]
Dover House, Whitehall, London, S.W.1
[01-930 6151]
Secretary, J. I. Smith, C.B............... £14,000
Fisheries Secretary, E. L. Gillett......... £12,000
Under Secretaries, W. W. Gauld; N. J. Steele
£12,000
Assistant Secretaries, A. T. Brooke; J. Cormack; B. Gordon; Miss I. F. Haddow; L. P. Hamilton; D. A. Leitch; A. I. Macdonald; H. G. Robertson; Miss J. L. Ross; S. H. Wright
£8,650 to £11,000
Principals, J. Blaikie; T. M. Brown; Miss E. A. Buglass; J. Cruickshank, D. J. Davidson; Miss M. I. Davis; W. Dinnie; J. W. Dougal; E. W. Ferguson; D. A. Flett; P. Gowans; J. N. Johnston; G. G. Lyall; J. I. Macbeath; A. Macdonald; A. J. Monk; Miss E. V. Ramsay; D. Stott; T. G. Strong, I.S.O.; D. C. Todd; B. G. S. Ward; C. Wilkinson.............. £5,680 to £7,450
Senior Executive Officers, H. W. Bradford; W. M. Bremner; D. R. Dickson; G. B. Downie; P. G.

Glynn; Miss A. M. Hamilton; J. L. Helm; J. G. Henderson; G. P. S. Macarthur; K. W. McKay; Miss G. B. Mackie; J. A. M. McLeod; W. Malcolm; Miss I. H. Rose; Miss M. F. M. Roy; T. Spence; A. G. Templeman; M. T. A. Vance; D. Watson................. £4,900 to £5,900
Chief Agricultural Officer, C. Mackay..... £12,000
Deputy Chief Agricultural Officer, A. H. Boggan
£11,000
Divisional Agricultural Officers, D. C. Collie; A. Edwards; R. Macdonald; I. L. Mackenzie
£8,650 to £9,798
Chief Agricultural Economist, J. M. Dunn, D.Phil.
£8,650 to £11,000
Chief Fatstock Officer, A. Scott, O.B.E.
£5,680 to £7,450
Chief Food and Dairy Officer, M. E. M. Anderson
£6,466 to £8,075
Chief Surveyor, J. G. Cullen...... £8,650 to £9,798
Scientific Adviser, J. G. Brotherston
£8,650 to £9,798
Technical Development Officer, G. S. Lawrie
£8,650 to £9,798

Royal Botanic Garden
Inverleith Row, Edinburgh 3
[031-552 7171]
Regius Keeper, D. M. Henderson, F.R.S.E.
£10,180 to £11,190
Assistant Keeper, J. Cullen, Ph.D.. £8,650 to £9,798
Senior Principal Scientific Officer, B. L. Burtt, F.R.S.E.
£8,650 to £9,798

Agricultural Scientific Services
East Craigs, Corstorphine, Edinburgh 12
[031-334 3361]
Director, J. M. Todd........ £10,180 to £11,190
Deputy Director, D. C. Graham, Ph.D.
£8,650 to £9,798
Assistant Director, R. D. Seaton
£8,650 to £9,798

Fisheries Research Services
Marine Laboratory, P.O. Box 101,
Victoria Road, Torry, Aberdeen
[0224 29944]
Director of Fishing Research and Controller of Fisheries Research and Development (U.K.), B. B. Parrish, F.R.S.E................... £11,670
Deputy Director, J. H. Steele, D.Sc., F.R.S.E.
£10,180 to £11,190
Senior Principal Scientific Officers, J. J. Foster; A. D. McIntyre, D.Sc., F.R.S.E.; A Saville; T. H. Simpson, Ph.D., F.R.S.E.; H. J. Thomas, Ph.D., F.R.S.E.
£8,650 to £9,798
Freshwater Fisheries Laboratory,
Faskally, Pitlochry, Perthshire
[0796 2060]
Senior Principal Scientific Officer, A. V. Holden, F.R.S.E..................... £8,650 to £9,798

Sea Fisheries Inspectorate
Chief Inspector of Sea Fisheries, A. Oag...... £9,350
Inspector of Salmon and Freshwater Fisheries, S. D. Sedgwick................. £5,687 to £7,205
Marine Superintendent, Captain F. C. Chisholm
£7,341 to £7,636

Crofters Commission
4/6 Castle Wynd, Inverness
[0463 37231]
Chairman, J. S. Grant, C.B.E............. £9,000
Members (part-time), N. A. MacAskill (£5,767); R. H. W. Bruce, C.B.E.; A. Fraser, Ph.D.; J. MacDonald; G. McIver, O.B.E.; J. M. Macmillan, O.B.E.................... £2,883
Secretary and Solicitor (vacant). £8,650 to £11,000
Assistant Secretary, D. F. Campbell
£5,680 to £7,450
Chief Technical Officer, W. Macfarlane
£6,280 to £7,450

Red Deer Commission
Knowsley, 82 Fairfield Road, Inverness
[0463 31751]
Chairman, I. Miller............... £4,325
Secretary, J. Dooner........... £4,900 to £5,900

SCOTTISH DEVELOPMENT DEPARTMENT
New St. Andrew's House, St. James's Centre, Edinburgh
[031–556 8400]
Dover House, Whitehall, London, S.W.1
[01–930 6151]

Secretary, K. Newis, C.B., C.V.O......... £14,000
Under Secretaries, R. D. M. Bell, C.B.; R. D. Cramond; J. B. Fleming; P. C. Rendle. £12,000
Assistant Secretaries, S. C. Aldridge; F. Dawson; C. Gilbraith; G. F. Hendry; H. F. G. Kelly; J. Kerr; J. F. Laing; T. L. Lister; J. B. More; M.H. Orde, O.B.E.; A. W. Russell; W. W. Scott; J. W. Sinclair............. £8,650 to £11,000
Principals, N. G. Campbell; D. J. Essery; L. J. Fotheringham; A. Gow; Miss E. J. Graham; H. J. Graham; I. G. F. Gray; J. Hamill; A. Heyworth; J. M. Howieson; C. K. Lambie; J. Loudfoot; K. Mackay; A. S. Neilson; M. H. Orde, O.B.E.; S. G. Patterson; R. Patton; B. V. Philp; T. Rarity; W. M. Robertson; R. E. S. Robinson; G. Robson; Mrs. F. J. Ross; N. J. Shanks; D. Stevenson; A. M. Thomson; J. Watson; R. G. B. Wilkie...£5,680 to £7,450
Director, Road Safety Advisory Unit, Lt.-Col. D. Birrell..................... £5,680 to £7,450
Senior Executive Officers, M. A. Duffy; J. F. Fraser; M. A. Grant; J. M. Haynes; J. C. Henderson; W.E. Irvine; Miss M.M. Jamieson; T. Johnston; J. B. Jolly; P. Kemp; G. P. McConnell; H. Maclean; A. R. Menzies; Miss M. N. Mowat; L. S. Nash; A. W. Russell; R. S. Stewart; J. Thompson; S. J. B. Walker; H. Young
£4,900 to £5,900

Professional Staff
Chief Engineer, J. W. Shiell............. £12,000
Deputy Chief Engineer, S. C. Agnew...... £11,000
Assistant Chief Engineers, P. Martin; J. G. Munro; E. H. Nicoll; J. Storry; A. Wotherspoon
£8,650 to £9,798
Chief Architect, B. P. Beckett........ £12,000
Deputy Chief Architect, D. I. Black...... £11,000
Superintending Architects, A. R. H. Bott; Miss M. J. Blanco White, O.B.E.; J. H. Fullarton; R. W. Naismith; R. I. Watson; P. E. White; D. E. Whitham................. £8,650 to £9,798
Chief Planning Officer, W. D. C. Lyddon... £12,000
Deputy Chief Planning Officers, H. Irving; R. G. H. Turnbull..................... £11,000
Regional Planning Officers, W. Amcotts; P. D. McGovern, Ph.D.; A. MacKenzie; G. R. Sloman
£8,650 to £9,798
Chief Research Officer, Miss B. D. Baker, O.B.E. ..
£8,650 to £9,798
Senior Principal Research Officers, C. P. A. Levein, Ph.D.; C. C. Macdonald....£7,750 to £9,350
Chief Quantity Surveyor, A. Y. Hamilton.. £11,000
Deputy Chief Quantity Surveyor, A. Duncan
£8,650 to £9,798
Superintending Quantity Surveyors, R. R. Armour; D. J. Campbell........... £8,650 to £9,798
Chief Road Engineer, G. F. Norris........ £12,000
Deputy Chief Road Engineer, D. P. Gray... £11,000
Assistant Chief Road Engineer, L. Clements £11,000
Superintending Engineers, D. M. Fisher; J. R. A. Griffith; E. G. Miller....... £8,650 to £9,798
H.M. Chief Industrial Pollution Inspector, E. A. B. Birse, O.B.E., Ph.D................. £11,000
Chief Estates Officer, P. H. Miller £8,650 to £9,798

SCOTTISH ECONOMIC PLANNING DEPARTMENT
New St. Andrew's House, St. James's Centre, Edinburgh
[031–556 8400]
Dover House, Whitehall, S.W.1
[01–930 6151]

Secretary, T. R. H. Godden, C.B........ £14,000
Under Secretary (Regional Development) and Chief Economic Adviser, R. G. L. McCrone, Ph.D.
£12,000

Under Secretaries, W. I. McIndoe; A. L. Rennie
£12,000
Assistant Secretaries, R. F. Butler; D. Connelly; J. Glendinning, M.B.E.; G. S. Murray; J. A. Scott, M.V.O.; G. R. Wilson...... £8,650 to £11,000
Senior Economic Adviser, G. L. Reid
£8,650 to £11,000
Senior Principal, J. J. Hunter, D.F.C.
£7,750 to £9,350
Principals, G. B. Baird; C. Barbour; J. A. Cowell, O.B.E.; Mrs. K. S. Gillender; F. A. Hamilton; R. M. Laidlaw; Miss E. A. Mackay; J. R. McKechnie; R. P. C. Macnab; J. G. Middlemiss; A. M. Russell; M. R. Wilson
£5,680 to £7,450
Senior Executive Officers, J. T. Brown; W. R. McKie; A. Maclean; D. Reid; R. N. Shaw
£4,900 to £5,900

Industrial Development Division
314 St. Vincent Street, Glasgow
[041–248 2855]
Under Secretaries, A. G. Manzie; W. B. Kirkpatrick (*Industrial Director*).................. £12,000
Assistant Secretary, R. Burns... £8,650 to £11,000
Senior Principals, T. M. Baird; J. E. Milne; R. J. Pounce.................. £7,750 to £9,350
Principals, H. J. Henson; G. W. H. Kelly; A. D. M. Malcolm; L. C. Roberts...... £5,680 to £7,450
Senior Executive Officers, L. J. Baston; Miss B. O'Callaghan; W. F. Robertson; D. L. Ross; J. Scullion; G. H. Smith; G. M. Thomson; J. S. Whitehouse............. £4,900 to £5,900

SCOTTISH EDUCATION DEPARTMENT
New St. Andrew's House, St. James's Centre, Edinburgh
[031–556 8400]
Dover House, Whitehall, London, S.W.1
[01–930 6151]

Secretary, J. M. Fearn............. £14,000
Under Secretaries, J. B. Hume; W. Hutchison; J. M. Robertson, M.V.O................... £12,000
Assistant Secretaries, Miss P. A. Cox; G. M. Fair; J. J. Farrell; B. J. Fiddes; A. K. Forbes (*H.M. Chief Inspector of Schools*); I. D. Hamilton; J. Kidd; J. F. McClellan; H. Robertson, M.B.E.
£8,650 to £11,000
Senior Principals, A. W. Brodie; A. J. C. Mitchell
£7,750 to £9,350
Principals, G. E. Brewerton; J. A. Clare; Mrs. E. C. G. Craghill; E. C. Davison; T. Drummond; T. B. Haig; A. W. M. Heggie; S. R. Hook; L. Jobson; J. M. Lawson; Miss M, Maclean; J. S. B. Martin; Mrs. N. S. Munro; R. Naylor; N. C. L. Shipman; R. E. Smith; Mrs. G. M. Stewart; Miss W. J. Strongman; W. Weir; A. C. Wilson
£5,680 to £7,450
Senior Executive Officers, G. H. J. Bell; T. Blacklock; W. A. Bruce; D. A. Christie; Miss W. S. Duguid; Miss M. E. Graham; Miss E. B. Hewitt; H. M. McGilvray; W. E. M. Maxwell; D. M. Porter; G. T. Reed; W. H. Stein; B. V. Surridge; G. H. Walker; I. M. Watt; N. Wood
£4,900 to £5,900

H.M. Inspectors of Schools
Senior Chief Inspector, J. F. McGarrity.... £12,000
Depute Senior Chief Inspectors, A. D. Chirnside; J. A. Ferguson.................. £11,440
Chief Inspectors, W. K. Ferguson; D. S. Graham; R. S. Johnston; S. E. McClelland, Ph.D.; J. G. Morris; W. R. Ritchie; H. F. Smith; E. F. Thompkins; J. H. Thomson; Miss H. J. S. Sandison; T. F. Williamson.......... £11,000
Inspectors, M. T. J. Axford; W. T. Beveridge; W. F. L. Bigwood; J. Boyes; Miss C. L. Boyle; T. Brown; E. D. Brunjes; J. Bryce; J. W. Burdin; Miss C. S. Cameron; Miss G. C. Campbell; D. G. Carter; L. Clark; C. Cleall; G. A. B. Craig; M. Q. Cramb; A. H. B. Davidson; D. W. Duncan; A. H. Ferguson; A. W. Finlayson; B. Fryer; T. N. Gallacher; A. R. Gallon; A. B. Giovanazzi; G. P. D. Gordon; Mrs. M. A. S. Grant; J. Hay;

Miss M. J. Hay; J. Howgego; J. Inglis; R. D.
Jackson; A. W. Jeffrey; E. S. Kelly; J. Kiely;
D. G. Kirkpatrick; I. Lawson; J. C. Leitch; R. E.
Lygo; M. McAllan; J. McAlpine; D. McCalman;
J. F. MacDonald; G. M. McGavin; Miss M. C.
McKellar; H. M. MacLaren; M. Macleod; D. R.
McNicoll; A. A. McPherson; A. J. Macpherson;
H. L. Martin; A. C. T. Mascarenhas; W. M.
Mein; A. Milne; S. Milne, Ph.D.; H. Morris;
Miss W. Morrison; Miss E. R. Mowat; G. S.
Mutch; R. H. Nelson; B. Nickerson, Ph.D.; W.
Nicol; A. Nisbet; J. Nisbet; D. A. Osler; I. P.
Pascoe; L. Pendleton; D. S. Petrie; J. Picken; Mrs.
J. G. Pillans; Miss A. H. M. Prain; R. B. Prescott;
A. M. Rankin; T. A. Rankin; J. C. Rankine;
D. Reid; W. M. Roach; I. D. S. Robertson;
J. N. Robertson; A. L. Robson; M. Roebuck;
M. G. Scott; G. M. Sinclair, Ph.D.; S. T. S.
Skillen; J. A. Sloggie; A. L. Small; H. Smith;
A. M. Steele; W. P. Stewart; Miss E. M. W.
Thomson; S. Thornton, Ph.D.; H. Walker; G.
Wallis; R. F. Webster; D. M. Whyte; J. G. L.
Wright; D. B. Young; R. W. J. Young, Ph.D.
£6,625 to £9,415

Social Work Services Group
St. Andrew's House, Edinburgh
[031-556 8501]

The Social Work Services Group, which is
attached to the Scottish Education Department,
administers the provisions of the Social Work
(Scotland) Act, 1968.

Under-Secretary, J. A. F. Reid............£12,000
Assistant Secretaries, R. J. W. Clark; F. H. Cowley;
G. J. Murray; A. M. Thomson
£8,650 to £11,000
Principals, D. A. Bennet; R. J. Edie; Mrs. E. M. A.
McGregor; G. G. McHaffie; K. B. T. Mackenzie;
J. P. Wallace..............£5,680 to £7,450
Senior Executive Officers, J. Graham; J. C. McLean;
A. C. Thompson; R. W. Williamson
£4,900 to £5,900
Chief Adviser on Social Work in Scotland, Miss B.
Jones...........................£11,520
Deputy Chief Advisers on Social Work in Scotland,
D. Colvin; Miss M. M. McInnes
£8,650 to £11,000
Senior Advisers on Social Work in Scotland, A. C.
Adams; Miss D. M. Boardman; W. M. Chal-
loner; Miss B. E. Drake; J. Gallagher; Miss C. P.
Kerr; R. Percival; Miss P. M. Hammond; W. J.
McCollam................£8,250 to £9,798

SCOTTISH HOME AND HEALTH
DEPARTMENT
New St. Andrew's House, St. James's Centre,
Edinburgh
[031-556 8400]
Dover House, Whitehall, London,
S.W.1
[01-930 6151]

Secretary, R. P. Fraser, C.B..............£14,000
Under Secretaries, D. J. Cowperthwaite; E. U. E.
Elliott-Binns; J. A. M. Mitchell, C.V.O., M.C.;
I. L. Sharp.......................£12,000
Assistant Secretaries, J. E. Fraser; J. Keeley; W. P.
Lawrie; Miss M. K. Macdonald; T. H. McLean;
H. McNamara; Miss M. A. McPherson; A. T. F.
Ogilvie; J. Oliver, O.B.E.; J. D. Penman; G.
Robertson; N. E. Sharp; V. C. Stewart; J. E.
Stewart; J. E. Tinkler; J. Walker; W. A. P.
Weatherston............£8,650 to £11,000
Senior Principals, G. Aithie; J. Leithead
£7,750 to £9,350
Principals, R. C. Allan, M.V.O.; D. C. Anderson;
R. M. Bell; J. Borthwick; Miss M. H. B. Brown;
R. D. M. Calder; D. H. Collier; T. Collinson;
J. N. Davison; A. C. Easson; H. C. Fraser; J. P.
Fraser; T. B. Hamilton; J. J. Haughney; W. W.
Howitt; J. Linn; D. G. McCulloch; A. Mac-
donald; W. M. McIntyre; I. J. Mackenzie; I. A.
Macpherson; Miss L. R. Maddock; W. R.
Miller; K. W. Moore; R. Mowat; G. N. Munro;
G. Murray; E. C. Reavley; E. Redmond; G. H.

Rigg; F. H. Roberts; J. Rodger; D. D. Rose;
G. Scott; W. J. A. Scott; A. Simmen; N. W.
Smith; J. A. Sutherland; J. Taylor; A. Walker
£5,680 to £7,450
Senior Executive Officers, N. Archer; Miss M. R. M.
Bald; M. Bunney; J. S. Burnett; N. F. Butler;
D. M. Ferguson; P. G. Glynn; I. K. Kennedy;
S. M. Liddle; W. Liddle; J. S. C. Little; J. Mc-
Callum; W. H. McCulloch; Miss M. Macdonald,
M.B.E.; N. S. McIntyre; G. Mason; T. Melville;
R. Nurse; G. Pearson; A. W. Rhind; R. N.
Roberts; D. A. Robertson; J. S. Ross; R. M.
Russell; J. L. Sime; G. Simmons; Miss K. J.
Sinclair; Miss A. C. C. Smart; A. Stephenson;
W. H. Stewart; Miss M. B. M. Talbot; B. A. F.
Vincent; I. T. Wallace; J. T. Watt; T. W.
Wilson; Miss M. J. Yeats; J. C. Young
£4,900 to £5,900

Medical Services
Chief Medical Officer, Sir John Brotherston, M.D.,
F.R.S.E..........................£14,000
Deputy Chief Medical Officers, I. S. Macdonald;
J. Smith, O.B.E., T.D., Q.H.P.........£12,000
Principal Medical Officers, M. Ashley-Miller; J. H.
Grant; J. H. Henderson; W. K. Henderson; J. K.
Hunter, O.B.E.; I. M. Macgregor; D. M. Pend-
reigh; G. A. Scott; W. T. Thom, O.B.E.
£11,440
Senior Medical Officers, A. E. Bell; Margaret Bell;
J. T. Boyd; F. B. Davidson; W. Forbes; J. W.
Gibb; R. M. Gordon; K. T. Gruer; L. F. Howitt;
D. W. A. McCreadie; A. D. McIntyre; N.
McNeil; H. Miller; A. T. B. Moir; J. A. Morton;
J. S. Patterson; R. A. W. Ratcliff; G. W. Simp-
son; D. J. Sloan; D. E. Walker; J. Watson
£11,000
Medical Officers, P. W. Brooks; D. C. Drummond;
G. I. Forbes; Iole L'E. K. McLean; R. M.
Melville, O.B.E.; W. M. Prentice; J. L. Tester,
O.B.E.; Elizabeth M. Whiteside; H. W. Woolner;
A. B. Young................£6,987 to £9,562
Regional Medical Officers, I. G. Conn; J. A. Fergus-
son; T. E. S. Fergusson; J. H. Leckie; J. W.
Logan, D.S.O.; A. C. McBlane; J. B. Morris; D.
N. B. Morrison; C. Murrary; R. C. Nimmo-
Smith; W. M. Reid; P. I. T. Walker
£6,987 to £9,562
Chief Scientist, Prof. Sir Andrew Kay, F.R.S.E.
Chief Dental Officer, J. L. Trainer........£11,200
Senior Dental Officer, A. Pacitti..........£11,000
Dental Officers, R. A. Morrison; A. B. Potts;
A. Boyd................£6,987 to £9,562
Chief Nursing Officer, Dame Muriel Powell, D.B.E.
£10,865
Chief Pharmacist, R. Higson....£8,650 to £9,798
Senior Principal Scientific Officer, W. F. Gunn
£8,650 to £9,798

Miscellaneous Appointments
H.M. Chief Inspector of Constabulary for Scotland,
D. Gray, O.B.E.....................£10,650
H.M. Inspector of Constabulary, Q. C. Wilson, O.B.E.
£10,114
Commandant, Scottish Police College, Col. R. C.
Robertson-Macleod, D.S.O., M.C., T.D....£8,633
H.M. Inspector of Fire Services, J. Jackson, O.B.E.
£6,738 to £7,540
Commandant, Scottish Fire Service Training School,
J. Hartill..................£4,900 to £5,900
Secretary, Scottish Health Service Planning Council,
T. D. Hunter.

Prisons Division
Broomhouse Drive, Edinburgh 11
[031-443 4040]
Director of Scottish Prison Service, J. Scrimgeour
£11,670
Assistant Secretary (Controller, Operations), J. Oliver,
C.B.E...................£8,650 to £11,000
Assistant Secretary (Controller, Administration), J.
Keeley.................£8,650 to £11,000
Senior Principal (Personnel), G. Aithie
£7,750 to £9,350
Principal (Controller, Industries and Supplies), T.
Collinson.................£5,680 to £7,450

Inspector of Scottish Prison Service, J. H. Frisby
£9,424
Assistant Inspector of Scottish Prison Service, D. Mac-
Iver........................£5,690 to £6,717
Governor Seconded to Headquarters, A. C. Meikle
£7,083 to £8,044

Prison Governors

Aberdeen, G. B. Duncan........£5,690 to £6,717
Castle Huntly Borstal Institution, J. Drummond
£5,690 to £6,717
Cornton Vale, Lady Martha Bruce, O.B.E., T.D.
£7,083 to £8,066
Dumfries Young Offenders Institution, T. McLaughlan
£5,690 to £6,717
Edinburgh, A. Gallacher........£7,083 to £8,066
Edinburgh Young Offenders Institution, T. Binnie
£5,690 to £6,717
Glasgow (Barlinnie), R. F. Hendry........£9,424
Glasgow (Barlinnie Young Offenders Institution), W.
G. Walker................£5,690 to £6,717
Glasgow (Barlinnie Special Unit), G. W. Jackson
£4,673 to £5,340
Glenochil Detention Centre, W. McVey
£5,690 to £6,717
Greenock, J. P. Dow...........£4,673 to £5,340
Inverness, T. A. M. Davidson...£5,690 to £6,717
Longriggend Remand Institution, D. Robertson
£5,690 to £6,717
Low Moss, W. Gordon........£5,690 to £6,717
Noranside Borstal Institution, A. J. Smith
£5,690 to £6,717
Penninghame, J. S. Bertram....£4,673 to £5,340
Perth, G. N. S. Neave........£7,083 to £8,066
Perth (Friarton Young Offenders Institution), R. M.
McLeod...................£4,673 to £5,340
Peterhead, W. Gardner £9,424
Polmont Borstal Institution, C. W. Hills
£7,083 to £8,066
Scottish Prison Governors Institution, G. Dingwall
£5,690 to £6,717

Mental Welfare Commission for Scotland
22 Melville Street, Edinburgh, 3
Commissioners, The Hon. Lord McDonald, M.C.
(*Chairman*); Prof. W. M. Millar, C.B.E., M.D.;
Lt.-Col. R. C. M. Monteith, M.C., T.D.; J. F. A.
Gibson, T.D.; H. F. Smith; Miss M. Megan
Browne, O.B.E.; Mrs. N. H. Mansbridge; M. M.
Whittet, O.B.E..........................£330
Medical Commissioners, Anne N. M. Brittain;
J. M. Loughran.....................£11,000
Medical Officers, Elizabeth M. Whiteside; Iole L'E.
K. Maclean; H. W. Woolner £6,987 to £9,562
Secretary, Miss M. McDonald, M.B.E.
£4,900 to £5,900
*Counsel to the Secretary of State for Scotland under
Private Legislation Procedure (Scotland) Act,* 1936
India Buildings, Victoria Street, Edinburgh 1).
Senior Counsel, G. S. Douglas, Q.C.
Junior Counsel, P. K. Vandore

NATIONAL HEALTH SERVICE, SCOTLAND
Health Boards
Argyll and Clyde, Gilmour House, Paisley. *Chair-
man,* W. P. Blyth, T.D. *Secretary,* W. G. Ayling.
Ayrshire and Arran, P.O. Box 13, Ayr. *Chairman,*
J. Lockhart. *Secretary,* R. A. McCrorie.
Borders, Huntlyburn, Melrose, Roxburghshire.
Chairman, J. Gibb. *Secretary,* A. G. Welstead.
Dumfries and Galloway, Charnwood Road, Dum-
fries. *Chairman,* J. Wyllie-Irving, T.D. *Secretary,*
E. Errington.
Fife, 7 Comely Park, Dunfermline. *Chairman,* J.
Crawford. *Secretary,* R. Mitchell.
Forth Valley, 33 Spittal Street, Stirling. *Chairman,*
J. A. Macreadie. *Secretary,* J. Wallace, M.B.E.
Grampian, 1–5 Albyn Place, Aberdeen. *Chairman,*
W. S. Crosby. *Secretary,* J. Wallace, M.B.E.
Greater Glasgow, 351 Sauchiehall Street, Glasgow.
Chairman, S. Stevenson. *Secretary,* R. D. R.
Gardner.
Highland, Reay House, 17 Old Edinburgh Road,
Inverness. *Chairman,* R. Wallace, C.B.E. *Secre-
tary,* R. R. W. Stewart.

Lanarkshire, Board Office, Hartwood, Shotts,
Lanarkshire. *Chairman,* A. R. Miller, C.B.E.
Secretary, G. G. Savage.
Lothian, 11 Drumsheugh Gardens, Edinburgh.
Chairman, Mrs. R. T. Nealon. *Secretary,* W. L.
Douglass.
Orkney, Balfour Hospital, New Scapa Road,
Kirkwall, Orkney. *Chairman,* S. P. Robertson,
M.B.E. *Secretary,* F. G. Cusiter.
Shetland, 44 Commercial Street, Lerwick. *Chair-
man,* R. Adair. *Secretary,* C. F. Fletcher.
Tayside, P.O. Box 75, Vernonholme, Riverside
Drive, Dundee. *Chairman,* D. K. Thomson,
C.B.E., T.D. *Secretary,* J. K. Johnston, O.B.E.
Western Isles, Health Board Offices, Lewis Hospital,
Stornoway, Isle of Lewis. *Chairman,* R. Stewart.
Secretary, J. Paterson.

Common Services Agency
17 Rothesay Terrace, Edinburgh.
Secretary, A. McPhee. *Treasurer,* J. W. Morrison.

GENERAL REGISTER OFFICE (Scotland)
New Register House, Edinburgh 1
[031–556 3952]
Registrar General, W. Baird.............£11,670
Deputy Registrar General, R. Macleod
£8,650 to £11,000
Chief Statistician, H. B. Lawson. £8,650 to £11,000
Statisticians, R. A. De Mellow; B. N. Downie;
J. Travers..................£6,300 to £7,988
Principals, D. J. Baird; G. F. Baird; J. Boyd; A. R.
Clark; I. G. Dewar; J. A. Hamilton; A. R. Irons
£5,080 to £7,450
Senior Executive Officers, A. W. Auld; D. Banna-
tynne; I. G. Bowie; J. Bush; H. G. Cottrell;
A. Lister; J. C. Duncan; J. B. Lyall; J. M. Nicol;
J. Paterson; R. R. Taylor; Mrs. J. B. Walker;
H. A. Waugh; R. T. Wilson. . £4,900 to £5,900

SOCIAL SCIENCE RESEARCH COUNCIL
1 Temple Avenue, E.C.4
[01–353 5252]
The S.S.R.C. was set up by Royal Charter in
1965 for the promotion of social science research. The
Council carries out its role by awarding grants for
research projects, through its postgraduate training,
bursary and bursary and fellowship schemes, and
through its research units. In addition the Council
provides advice and disseminates knowledge on the
social sciences. A list of publications is available
from the S.S.R.C. Information Section.
Chairman, D. Robinson.
Secretary, C. S. Smith.

HER MAJESTY'S STATIONERY OFFICE
Atlantic House, Holborn Viaduct, E.C.1
[01–248 9876]
Sovereign House, Botolph Street, Norwich
[0603 22211]
Bookshops in London:—
*Retail.—*49 High Holborn, W.C.1.
*Wholesale and post orders.—*P.O. Box 569, S.E.1.
H. M. Stationery Office was established in 1786
and is the British Government's central organization for the supply of printing, binding, office
supplies and office machinery of all kinds, and published books and periodicals for the Public Service
at home and abroad; it also undertakes duplicating
and distributing for government departments. The
Stationery Office is the publisher for the government, and has bookshops for the sale of government
publications in London, Edinburgh, Cardiff,
Manchester, Bristol, Birmingham and Belfast;
leading booksellers in the larger towns act as agents;
and there are wholesale departments in London,
Edinburgh and Belfast from which booksellers
may obtain supplies. It is also the agent for the
sale of publications of the United Nations and its
specialized agencies and for certain other international organizations. The Controller of the
Stationery Office is under Letters Patent the *Queen's
Printer of the Acts of Parliament* and in him is vested the
Copyright in all British Government documents.

Government publications are of a wide and varied range and over 7,500 publications are produced each year. They include *London Gazette*, which has been issued since 1665, and *Hansard*, the verbatim report of the proceedings in both Houses of Parliament, available on the morning following the debate. The Stationery Office has in stock some 90,000 titles and its subscriptions and standing order lists contain about 150,000 addresses. The annual sales total about 37,000,000 copies.

The aggregate net estimate for the department for 1975–76 was £73,335,000 (an increase of £18,150,000 on the same estimate for 1974–75).

Generally the department obtains its supplies from commercial sources by competitive tender. For printing and binding, however, the Stationery Office has its own printing works and binderies which produce about one-third of the total requirement, including telephone directories, pension allowance books, national savings certificates and stamps, postal orders, premium bonds. National Insurance stamps, road fund licences, and television licences.

The staff employed on April 1, 1975, was 7,183, including 1,633 in warehouses and 2,285 at printing works: the total space occupied was 2,925,760 square feet, including 1,005,000 sq. ft. for warehouse space and 1,081,000 sq. ft. for the printing works.

Controller, H. Glover.................£14,000
  Executive Assistant, P. R. C. Gainsborough.
  Personal Secretary, Mrs. M. A. Hawkins.
Assistant Controllers, J. P. Turner, C.B.E.; J. J. Cherns; R. T. Walker........................£11,670
Head of Printing Services, D. E. Masson, O.B.E.
              £8,650 to £11,000
Head of Finance, D. C. Dashfield, O.B.E., M.V.O.
              £8,650 to £11,000
Head of Publishing, F. E. Davey. £8,650 to £11,000
Director of Supply, C. W. Blundell, O.B.E.
              £8,650 to £11,000
Directors of Works, G. D. Macaulay; K. A. Allen
              £8,650 to £11,000
Adviser of Typography, Ruari McLean, C.B.E.

Accounts

Chief Accountants, M. C. Holgate; C. G. Wood; R. T. Wykes...............£5,680 to £7,450
Senior Accountants, R. W. Chapman; D. T. Cooke; R. M. Glenn; B. J. Jackson; B. F. Perry; D. Silver; K. H. Staff.........£4,900 to £5,900
Accountancy Executive, J. A. Wills
              £5,310 to £6,310

Personnel Services Division

Director, R. H. Chisholm......£7,750 to £9,350
Deputy Directors, A. M. Foote; T. S. Harris, M.B.E.; F. J. Wilson...............£5,680 to £7,450
Assistant Directors, J. R. Allen; M. J. Cuming; E. L. Franklin; F. G. Gibbs; H. B. Jackson; G. G. Robbie; J. R. Wilson . £4,900 to £5,900
Chief Welfare Officer, J. L. A. G. Jones
              £4,900 to £5,900

Finance Division

Director, H. V. Roe, O.B.E......£7,750 to £9,350
Deputy Directors, P. W. Buckerfield; P. Jefford
              £5,680 to £7,450
Assistant Directors, W. H. Burberry; G. F. C. Clarke; Miss F. V. Page; B. Wilson; E. J. Woods
              £4,900 to £5,900
Chief Examiner, Printers' & Binders' Accounts, B. W. P. Downing...........£4,900 to £5,900

Industrial Relations Division

Director, R. C. Beever.........£8,160 to £9,760
Deputy Director, D. D. Hinnigan. £5,680 to £7,450
Assistant Director, R. E. Wooldridge
              £4,900 to £5,900

Management Services

Director, D. J. Balls............£5,860 to £7,450
Accountable Management, D. W. Ray
              £5,680 to £7,450
Assistant Directors, F. R. Payne; K. J. Rhodes, M.B.E.; J. W. Rowe; C. N. Southgate
              £4,900 to £5,900

Chief Work Study Officer, D. S. Henshall
              £4,900 to £5,900
Project Co-ordinator, R. E. H. Mills
              £4,900 to £5,900

Print Procurement Division

Director, E. J. Deller...........£7,750 to £9,350
Deputy Director (Norwich), J. H. Hynes, O.B.E.
              £5,680 to £7,450
Deputy Director (London), A. S. Powis, I.S.O.
              £5,680 to £7,450
Assistant Directors, K. E. Hutchings, B.E.M.; T. H. Kearsley; J. N. Palmer.......£4,900 to £5,900

Publishing Group

Director of Publishing, H. W. Leader
              £7,750 to £9,350
Director of Publications Distribution, J. P. Morgan
              £7,750 to £9,350
Director of Publication Marketing, D. G. R. Perry
              £9,760
Director of Graphic Design, J. Westwood
              £5,680 to £7,450
Deputy Directors, R. Brearley; E. S. Brooks; J. Carpenter; A. J. Woolway... £5,680 to £7,450
Assistant Directors, R. C. Barnard; G. C. Beard; E. Beaumont; L. C. de Brunner; G. E. Finch; Mrs. K. P. D. Griffiths; L. B. Mills; J. F. Saville
              £4,900 to £5,900

Reprographic Centre

Director, G. B. Furn..........£7,750 to £9,350
Assistant Director, A. Mackenzie. £4,900 to £5,900
Manager, E. B. McKendrick.... £5,680 to £7,450
Production Manager, J. W. Brunton
              £4,900 to £5,900
Administration Manager, F. J. Meads
              £4,900 to £5,900
Co-ordinator of Government Reprographic Services, A. W. Martyn...........£5,680 to £7,450
Deputy Co-ordinator, G. J. York. £4,900 to £5,900
Assistant Co-ordinators, J. S. Nash; J. A. Owen
              £4,900 to £5,900

Supply Division

Deputy Directors, A. E. J. Brunwin; S. A. Cowie; B. C. E. Lee; R. F. Norris; W. S. Porter
              £5,680 to £7,450
Assistant Directors, F. E. Ashman; E. G. N. Calver; J. Doherty; A. A. Gummett; C. E. Harrold; C. G. Lloyd; S. A. Munns; D. A. Prutton; D. N. Roberts; R. A. Youl... £4,900 to £5,900
Manager, Office Machinery Technical Service, D. W. Farquhar..................£4,720 to £5,930

Technical Services Division

Director, W. D. Bissett.........£7,750 to £9,350
Assistant Directors, E. J. Cletheroe; T. J. Soutar; H. S. Todd................£4,900 to £5,900
Head of Laboratory, S. M. Goldfarb
              £6,280 to £7,450
Deputy Heads of Laboratory, F. E. Arnold; W. J. R. Howell; J. O. P. Jones.......£4,720 to £5,930

Works Division

Head of Works Administration, K. P. Sandford
              £5,680 to £7,450
Head of Works Production & Finance, S. R. Hays
              £5,680 to £7,450
Head of Works Reorganizaion, A. A. Smith
              £5,680 to £7,450
Assistant Directors, A. R. Affolter; J. H. Payne
              £4,900 to £5,900
Senior Works Managers, C. J. Errington, I.S.O.; D. G. Forbes; W. N. Frost; R. H. Gowen
              £5,680 to £7,450
Works Managers, R. A. De Cleyn; C. J. Newman; E. J. Smith; E. Warburton, M.B.E.
              £4,900 to £5,900
Deputy Senior Works Managers, A. J. B. Baptie; F. J. Beesley; A. S. Brown; R. M. Gair; A. J. Latham; A. R. Ling; K. J. Lowe; F. L. Pymm; R. S. Roberts.............£4,900 to £5,900
Head of Works Engineering Services, R. Miller
              £6,280 to £7,450
Deputy Head of Works Engineering Services, C. F. Croisdale..................£4,720 to £5,930

REGIONAL OFFICES AND BOOKSHOPS

Scotland
Government Buildings, Bankhead Avenue, Edinburgh
Bookshop: 13a Castle Street, Edinburgh
Director, G. L. Birch........£5,680 to £7,450
Deputy Director, G. S. McGowan
£4,900 to £5,900

Northern Ireland
Chichester Street, Belfast
Retail and Trade Bookshop, Chichester Street, Belfast
Director, F. A. G. Lonon.......£5,680 to £7,450

Manchester
Broadway, Chadderton, Lancs.
Bookshop: Brazennose House, Brazennose Street, Manchester
Director, R. A. Dunn..........£5,680 to £7,450
Deputy Director, Miss E. M. Coyle
£4,900 to £5,900
Assistant Directors, M. D. Lynn; C. E. S. Robbs
£4,900 to £5,900

Western
Ashton Vale Road, Bristol
Bookshops: 258 Broad Street, Birmingham; Southey House, Wine Street, Bristol; 41 The Hayes, Cardiff.
Director, R. O. Stonehouse, O.B.E.
£5,680 to £7,450

STATUTE LAW COMMITTEE
House of Lords, S.W.1
President, The Lord Chancellor.
Vice-Chairman, Mr. Justice Cooke.
Members, The Attorney-General; the Lord Advocate; I. B. Bancroft, C.B.; Sir Dennis Dobson, K.C.B., O.B.E., Q.C.; C. Fletcher Cooke, Q.C., M.P.; H. Glover; Sir Michael Havers, Q.C., M.P.; P. G. Henderson; The Hon. Lord Hunter; Sir James Jones, K.C.B.; The Lord Kilbrandon; Sir David Lidderdale, K.C.B.; Rt. Hon. Sir Robert Lowry; G. I. Mitchell, C.B.; Sir Nicholas Morrison, K.C.B.; Sir Arthur Peterson, K.C.B., M.V.O.; H. W. Pritchard, C.B.E.; The Lord Simon of Glaisdale, P.C.; Sir Robert Speed, C.B., Q.C.; Sir Anthony Stainton, K.C.B.; T. G. Talbot, C.B., Q.C.; Sir Henry Ware, K.C.B.; The Lord Wilberforce, P.C., C.M.G., O.B.E.; W. T. Williams, Q.C., M.P.
Secretary, J. M. Davies.

Statutory Publications Office
12 Buckingham Gate
Editor, P. J. A. Smith.........£9,443 to £11,410
Assistant Editors, S. G. G. Edgar, C.B.E.; R. N. Ogle
£7,035 to £9,160

SUGAR BOARD
52 Mark Lane, E.C.3
[01-480 6221]
The Sugar Board was constituted under the Sugar Act, 1956, on October 15, 1956. The Board buys the sugar which the United Kingdom has contracted to buy under the Commonwealth Sugar Agreement up to the end of 1974 at prices negotiated triennially by the Government and resells the sugar commercially at world prices. To meet the difference between the two prices, the Treaty of Accession to the E.E.C. provides for the Board to levy a charge on the importation of the sugar if the world prices are lower than the negotiated prices, or to pay a subvention in the reverse position if world prices exceed them.
Chairman, R. G. R. Wall, C.B..........£10,750
Vice-Chairman, Sir Leonard Cooke, O.B.E... £4,125
Members (part-time), P. G. Smith, C.B.E.; N. Vinson; Sir John Wall, O.B.E.................£1,000
General Manager, A. V. Parsons, M.B.E.
Secretary and Finance Officer, E. G. Pearson

THAMES WATER AUTHORITY
New River Head, Rosebery Avenue, E.C.1
[01-278 2300]

The Thames Water Authority is one of ten Regional Water Authorities set up in England and Wales by the Water Act, 1973. On April 1, 1974, it assumed control over the entire water cycle throughout its 5,000 sq. mile area. It is responsible for all water functions, including water resources, water supply, sewerage and sewage disposal, pollution control, fisheries, river and reservoir amenities and recreational facilities.
Chairman, P. B. Black.
Chief Executive, A. Morrison.

NATIONAL THEATRE BOARD
10a Aquinas Street, S.E.1
[01-928 2033]
Appointed by the Minister with special responsibility for the Arts.
Chairman, Sir Max Rayne.
Members, A. R. M. Carr; H.W. Cutler; A. Francis, O.B.E.; I. Harrington, O.B.E.; H. W. Hinds; Sir Ronald Leach, C.B.E.; V. Mishcon; J. C. Mortimer, Q.C.; The Lord O'Brien of Lothbury, P.C., G.B.E.; H. H. Sebag-Montefiore; Prof. T. J. B. Spencer.
Director of National Theatre, Peter Hall, C.B.E.
Secretary, D. Gosling.

DEPARTMENT OF TRADE
1 Victoria Street, S.W.1
[01-215 7877]
The Department of Trade is responsible for commercial policy and relations with overseas countries; the promotion of United Kingdom commercial interests overseas and the administration of United Kingdom protective tariffs. Under the direction of the British Overseas Trade Board it is responsible for export services and promotions, overseas finance and planning. The Department is responsible for the legal framework for the regulation of industrial and commercial enterprises: company law, patent, trade mark and copyright matters, the insolvency service and the insurance industry. It is also responsible for marine safety and sponsors the shipping and civil aviation industries, tourism and the hotel and travel industries; the newspaper, printing and publishing industries; the film industry and the distributive and service trades.

SALARY LIST
Secretary of State....................£13,000
Parliamentary Under Secretaries of State......£5,500
Permanent Secretary.................£18,675
Deputy Secretary.....................£14,000
Under Secretary......................£12,000
Assistant Secretary............£8,650 to £11,000
Senior Principal.............£7,750 to £9,350
Principal.................£5,680 to £7,450
Controller, Export Licensing Branch........£7,450
Chief Information Officer (A).....£8,650 to £11,000
Inspector General of the Insolvency Service..£12,000
Deputy Inspectors General.............£11,320
Inspector of Companies................£11,320
Accidents Investigation Branch:
  Chief Inspector of Accidents..........£10,950
  Deputy Chief Inspector of Accidents
£8,650 to £11,000
Marine Survey Service:
  Surveyor General....................£8,950
  Chief Nautical Surveyor ⎫
  Engineer Surveyor in Chief ⎬.........£8,850
  Chief Ship Surveyor ⎭
Secretary of State for Trade and President of the Board of Trade, THE RT. HON. PETER DAVID SHORE, M.P.
Principal Private Secretary, A. C. Hutton.
Parliamentary Private Secretary, B. C. Gould, M.P.
Parliamentary Under Secretaries of State, E. P. Deakins, M.P. (Trade); S. C. Davis, M.P. (Companies, Aviation and Shipping)
Secretary, Department of Trade, Sir Peter Thornton, K.C.B.
Private Secretary, A. J. Hunt.
Deputy Secretaries, P. A. R. Brown; R. W. Gray; D. F. Hubback, C.B.; P. S. Preston, C.B.
Parliamentary Clerk (Principal), Miss P. A. Davey.

TRADE
Commercial Relations and Exports
Division 1
[01-215 7877]
Under Secretary, S. Abramson
Assistant Secretaries, P. Gent; J. B. Ingram; E. Wright

Division 2
Under Secretary, W. M. Knighton
Assistant Secretaries, Mrs. E. C. Jones; M. G. Petter; M. J. Treble

Division 3
Under Secretary, D. N. Royce
Assistant Secretaries, J. R. Hack; A. H. K. Slater

Division 4
Under Secretary, L. Lightman
Assistant Secretaries, C. W. Roberts; Miss M. Z. Terry

Division 5
Under Secretary, J. Caines
Assistant Secretaries, P. M. S. Corley; R. E. Gamble, O.B.E.

Export Development Division
[01-215 7877]
Under Secretary, R. N. Royce
Assistant Secretaries, Miss B. M. Eyles; J. S. Norman

Europe, Industry and Technology Division
[01-215 7877]
Under Secretary, Miss K. E. Boyes
Assistant Secretaries, P. E. Dougherty; C. L. Silver

General Division
Kingsgate House, 66–74 Victoria Street, S.W.1
[01-215 7877]
Under Secretary, J. R. Steele
Assistant Secretaries, G. A. Barry; P. G. M. Clark; F. R. Mingay

Export Licensing Branch
Sanctuary Bldgs., 16–20 Gt. Smith Street, S.W.1
[01-215 7877]
Controller, D. A. Whitby

British Overseas Trade Board
1 Victoria Street, S.W.1
[01-215 7877]
Chairman, Sir Frederick Catherwood
Members, The Lord Briginshaw; J. W. Buckley, C.B.E.; R. H. W. Bullock, C.B.; G. R. Denman, C.B., C.M.G.; Sir Derek Ezra, M.B.E.; H.R.H. The Duke of Kent, G.C.M.G., G.C.V.O.; Sir Cyril Kleinwort; Sir Jan Lewando, C.B.E.; The Earl of Limerick; Sir Donald Maitland, C.M.G., O.B.E.; Sir Peter Matthews; J. H. Neill, C.B.E., T.D.; The Lord Shackleton, K.G., O.B.E.; K. Taylor, C.B.; J. Whitehorn, C.M.G.
Chief Executive, J. S. Rooke, C.M.G., O.B.E.

Hillgate House, 26 Old Bailey, E.C.4
[01-248 5757]
Special Adviser on Japanese Market, J. I. McGhie
Overseas Project Group
1 Victoria Street, S.W.1
[01-215 7877]
Assistant Secretary, P. G. F. Bryant

Export Services and Promotions Division
Export House, 50 Ludgate Hill, E.C.4
[01-248 5757]
Under Secretary, W. K. Ward
Assistant Secretaries, D. P. Dick; V. F. Kimber; W. T. Pearce, C.M.G.; A. R. Titchener
Senior Principal, G. McMahon

INDUSTRIAL PROPERTY, INSURANCE COMPANY LAW AND INSOLVENCY
Patent Office and Industrial Property and Copyright Department
25 Southampton Buildings, W.C.2
[01-405 8721]
Comptroller General of Patents, Designs and Trade Marks, E. Armitage, C.B.
Assistant Comptrollers, R. Bowen; I. J. G. Davis; J. D. Fergusson

Assistant Registrar of Trade Marks (Assistant Secretary), R. L. Moorby.
Senior Principal, A. J. Mills, I.S.O.

Insurance Division
Sanctuary Bldgs., 16–20 Gt. Smith Street, S.W.1
[01-215 7877]
Under Secretary, M. S. Morris
Assistant Secretaries, G. C. Dick; R. F. Fenn; N. E. Robbins; D. Simpson

Companies Division
Sanctuary Bldgs., 16–20 Gt. Smith Street, S.W.1
[01-215 7877]
Under Secretary, R. C. M. Cooper
Assistant Secretaries, L. S. Davis, O.B.E.; J. W. Preston
Companies House, 55–71 City Road, E.C.1
[01-253 9393]
Registrar of Companies and Registrar of Business Names (Assistant Secretary), R. W. Westley
2–14 Bunhill Row, E.C.1
[01-606 4071]
Companies Investigation Branch, Inspector of Companies, H. C. Gill

The Insolvency Service
2–14 Bunhill Row, E.C.1
[01-606 4071]
Inspector General of the Insolvency Service, C. A. Taylor
Deputy Inspectors General, J. B. Clemetson; E. G. Harper

SHIPPING AND CIVIL AVIATION
Accidents Investigation Branch
Shell Mex House, Strand, W.C.2
[01-217 3000]
Chief Inspector of Accidents, W. H. Tench
Deputy Chief Inspector of Accidents, G. M. Kelly
Civil Aviation Division 1
Shell Mex House, Strand, W.C.2
[01-217 3000]
Under Secretary, P. G. Hudson
Assistant Secretaries, R. H. F. Croft; G. R. Sunderland
Civil Aviation Safety Advisor, J. R. Neill.
Civil Aviation Division 2
Shell Mex House, Strand, W.C.2
[01-217 3000]
Under Secretary, G. T. Rogers
Assistant Secretaries, A. P. Gardner; O. I. Green; O. H. Kemmis; J. Sumner
Civil Aviation Division 3
The Adelphi, John Adam Street, W.C.2
[01-217 3000]
Under Secretary, S. D. Wilks
Assistant Secretaries, J. R. Gildea; N. F. Ledsome; G. R. Smith

Shipping Policy Division
The Adelphi, John Adam Street, W.C.2
[01-217 3000]
Under Secretary, G. Lanchin
Assistant Secretaries, E. Y. Bannard; J. K. T. Frost; K. W. McQueen, O.B.E.

Marine Division
Sunley House, 90–93 High Holborn, W.C.1
[01-405 6911]
Under Secretary, J. N. Archer
Assistant Secretaries, S. N. Burbridge; E. R. Hargreaves; M. J. Service; L. F. Standen
Surveyor General, D. MacIver Robinson, O.B.E.
Chief Nautical Surveyor, Capt. J. A. Hampton
Engineering Surveyor in Chief, G. Victory
Chief Ship Surveyor, N. Bell

Printing, Publishing, Services and Distribution Division
Cleland House, Page Street, S.W.1
[01-834 2255]
Under Secretary, Miss M. J. Lackey, O.B.E... £9,000
Assistant Secretaries, H. F. Heinemann; N. E. Pulvermacher

TRAINING SERVICES AGENCY
162–168 Regent Street, W.1
[01-214-600]

Chief Executive, J. S. Cassels.............£12,000
Deputy Chief Executives, D. G. Storer (*Training Opportunities*); F. C. Hayes (*Industry*)...£10,950
Director of Training, Dr. R. M. Johnson....£9,860
Director of Planning and Intelligence, G. Holland
£8,650 to £11,000
Director of Corporate Services, L. R. Levy
£8,650 to £11,000
Director of Marketing Services, A. P. Dignum
£7,750 to £9,350
Director of Training Opportunities Services, D. W. J. Orchard.................£8,650 to £11,000
Director of Training Opportunities Operations, J. R. Shipway.................£8,650 to £11,000
Director of Training Opportunities Development, M. W. Smart.................£8,650 to £11,000

THE TREASURY
Parliament Street, S.W.1
[01–930–1234]

The Office of the Lord High Treasurer has been continuously in commission for well over 200 years. The Lord High Commissioners of H.M. Treasury consist of the First Lord of the Treasury (who is also the Prime Minister), the Chancellor of the Exchequer and five Junior Lords. This Board of Commissioners is assisted at present by the Paymaster General, Chief Secretary, a Parliamentary Secretary who is the Chief Whip, a Financial Secretary and Minister of State (who are also members of the Government) and by the Permanent Secretary. The Prime Minister and First Lord is not primarily concerned in the day-to-day aspects of Treasury business. The Parliamentary Secretary and the Junior Lords are Government Whips in the House of Commons. The management of the Treasury devolves upon the Chancellor of the Exchequer and, under him, the Paymaster General, Chief Secretary, the Financial Secretary and the Minister of State. The Paymaster General deals mainly with E.E.C. affairs and the Chief Secretary is responsible for the control of public expenditure. The Financial Secretary discharges the traditional responsibility of the Treasury for the largely formal procedure for the voting of funds by Parliament. All Treasury Ministers are concerned in tax matters.

Prime Minister and First Lord of the Treasury, THE RT. HON. (JAMES) HAROLD WILSON, O.B.E., F.R.S., M.P........................£20,000
Principal Private Secretary, K. R. Stowe.
Private Secretaries, P. R. H. Wright (*Overseas Affairs*): F. E. R. Butler (*Home Affairs*); N. W. Stuart (*Parliamentary Affairs*); P. Wood (*Home Affairs*).
Senior Policy Adviser to Prime Minister, B. Donoughue.
Assistant Private Secretaries, Miss D. R. Edmunds, M.B.E.; Miss J. C. Parsons, M.B.E.; Miss J. M. Porter, M.B.E.; Miss S. F. Wright, M.B.E.
Secretary for Appointments, C. V. Peterson.
Personal and Political Secretary, The Baroness Falkender, C.B.E.
Parliamentary Private Secretary, K. Marks, M.P.
Chief Press Secretary, J. T. W. Haines.....£12,000
Press Secretaries, Mrs. J. Hewlett-Davies (*Press Relations*); G. E. Moggridge. (*Co-ordination*).
Senior Information Officer, Miss J. Denham.
Political Office, A. Murray.

Lord Commissioners of the Treasury
The Prime Minister (*First Lord*); The Chancellor of the Exchequer.

Junior Lords of the Treasury
D. R. Coleman, M.P.; J. A. Dunn, M.P.; M. F. L. Cocks, M.P.; T. Pendry, M.P.; J. D. Dormand, M.P...........................*each* £4,000

Chancellor of the Exchequer, THE RT. HON. DENIS WINSTON HEALEY, M.B.E., M.P....£13,000
Principal Private Secretary, C. W. France.
Private Secretaries, S. A. Robson; R. K. Hinkley.
Assistant Private Secretary, Mrs. M. Connolly, M.B.E.

Special Assistant, A. Ham.............£5,500
Parliamentary Clerk, B. O. Dyer.
Parliamentary Private Secretary, H. G. Lamborn, M.P.
Paymaster General, THE RT. HON. EDMUND DELL, M.P........................£9,500
Private Secretary, S. C. T. Matheson.
Assistant Private Secretary, D. M. Nooney.
Chief Secretary to the Treasury, THE RT. HON. JOEL BARNETT, M.P........................£9,500
Private Secretary, M. C. Scholar.
Assistant Private Secretary, P. E. Denison.
Parliamentary Private Secretary, W. M. Hughes, Ph.D., M.P.
Parliamentary Secretary to the Treasury and Deputy Leader of the House of Commons, THE RT. HON. ROBERT JOSEPH MELLISH, M.P........£9,500
Private Secretary, A. H. Warren, C.B.E.
Financial Secretary, ROBERT EDWARD SHELDON, M.P........................£9,500
Private Secretary, M. Brown.
Minister of State, (DAVID JOHN) DENZIL DAVIES. M.P........................£9,500.
Private Secretary, M. L. Williams.
Assistant Whips, Miss B. Boothroyd, M.P.; T. M. Cox, M.P.; J. Ellis, M.P.; Miss M. M. Jackson, M.P.; L. A. Pavitt, M.P.; E. G. Perry, M.P.; D. L. Stoddart, M.P......................*each* £4,000
Permanent Secretary, Sir Douglas Wass, K.C.B.
£20,175
Private Secretary, M. T. Folger.
Second Permanent Secretaries, Sir Douglas Henley, K.C.B.; A. Lord, C.B.; Sir Derek Mitchell, K.C.B., C.V.O.............................£17,175
Head of Government Economic Service and Chief Economic Adviser to the Treasury, Sir Bryan Hopkin, C.B.E......................£15,350
Deputy-Chief Economic Adviser, M. V. Posner.
Deputy Secretaries, L. Airey; P. R. Baldwin, C.B.; F. R. Barratt, C.B.; K. E. Couzens; C. W. Fogarty, C.B.; F. Jones, C.B.E.; L. Pliatzky, C.B.
£14,000

Civil Public Sector
General Expenditure:
  Under Secretary, J. Anson.........£12,000
  Assistant Secretaries, B. C. Brown (*Chief Statistician*); A. R. H. Glover..£8,650 to £11,000
Home and General:
  Under Secretary, H. A. Copeman.......£12,000
  Assistant Secretary, P. B. Kent
£8,650 to £11,000
Management Accounting and Purchasing Policy:
  Assistant Secretary, E. P. Kemp
£8,650 to £11,000
Treasury Officer of Accounts and Public Purchasing:
  Under Secretary, D. McKean...........£12,000
Public Enterprises:
  Under Secretary, P. J. Harrop.........£12,000
  Assistant Secretaries, P. Mountfield; Mrs. R. E. J. Gilmore; D. J. L. Moore .£8,650 to £11,000
Social Services:
  Under Secretary, Miss J. M. Forsyth......£12,000
  Assistant Secretaries, N. J. Monck; M. Phillips; C. H. A. Judd...........£8,650 to £11,000
Agriculture, Trade and Employment:
  Under Secretary, W. S. Ryrie.........£12,000
  Assistant Secretaries, W. J. E. Norton; G. W. Wilson; J. W. Whitaker..
£8,650 to £11,000

Environment and Public Service:
  Under Secretary, P. Cousins.........£12,000
  Assistant Secretaries, R. Jones; P. H. Halsey, M.V.O.; M. S. Buckley...........£8,650 to £11,000
Public Sector Economical Unit:
  Under Secretary (*Economics*), I. C. R. Byatt
£12,000
  Senior Economic Advisers, G. P. Smith; J. R. Shepherd...............£8,650 to £11,000

Defence (Policy and Material)
Under Secretary, M. G. F. Hall...........£12,000
Assistant Secretary, J. E. Hansford
£8,650 to £11,000

Economic Management

European Co-ordination, Economic Briefing, Industrial Policy:
Under Secretary, A. M. Bailey £12,000

Industrial Policy:
Assistant Secretaries (European Co-ordination), J. T. Caff; G. R. Ashford . . . . . £8,650 to £11,000
Senior Economic Adviser, J. F. Smith
£8,650 to £11,000

Economic Assessment:
Under Secretaries (Economics), Miss M. P. Brown; H. H. Liesner £12,000
Senior Economic Advisers, D. Todd; Mrs. V. H. Stamler . . . . £8,650 to £11,000

Fiscal Policy:
Under Secretary, A. H. Lovell £12,000
Assistant Secretaries, A. J. Wiggins; M. S. Levitt; B. T. Houghton . . . . £8,650 to £11,000

Prices and Incomes Policy:
Under Secretary, P. J. Kitcatt £12,000
Assistant Secretary, W. L. St. Clair
£8,650 to £11,000
Chief Information Officer (A), H. M. Griffiths
£8,650 to £11,000

Home Finance:
Under Secretary, G. S. Downey £12,000
Under Secretary (Economics), F. Cassell . . £12,000
Assistant Secretaries, H. S. Lee; J. M. Bridgeman; J. B. Unwin . . . . £8,650 to £11,000

Overseas Finance

Under Secretary (Economics), J. G. Littler . . . £12,000

International Monetary:
Assistant Secretaries, C. H. W. Hodges; R. G. Lavelle . . . . £8,650 to £11,000

Reserves:
Under Secretary, Mrs M. E. Hedley-Miller
£12,000
Assistant Secretaries, D. A. Walker; A. J. C. Edwards . . . . £8,650 to £11,000

Development:
Under Secretary, M. Widdup £12,000
Assistant Secretaries, T. U. Burgner; J. F. Slater, C.M.G.; Miss J. Kelley . . . . £8,650 to £11,000

Establishment and Organization Branch

Under Secretary (Establishment Officer), R. L. Sharp
£12,000
Assistant Secretary (Deputy Establishment Officer), D. C. Lee, C.B.E. . . . . £8,650 to £11,000
Senior Economic Adviser, P. G. Davies
£8,650 to £11,000

Information Division

Head of Division (Assistant Secretary), P. V. Dixon
£6,300 to £8,338
Deputy Head (Chief Information Officer (B)), E. C. Crosfield

Treasury Representatives in U.S.A.

Economic Minister, Financial Adviser and Head of U.K. Treasury and Supply Delegation, W. S. Ryrie.
Assistant Secretary, H. M. Griffiths.

Rating of Government Property

Jameson House, 69 Notting Hill Gate, W.11
[01–229 9841]
Treasury Valuer, W. W. Brown £11,320
Deputy Treasury Valuer, P. J. Dahlhoff £9,748
Inspector of Rates, R. C. Robin £8,650

Queen's and Lord Treasurer's Remembrancer

See Scottish Law Courts and Offices.

THE TREASURY SOLICITOR

Department of H.M. Procurator-General and Treasury Solicitor
Matthew Parker Street, S.W.1
[01–930–7363 and 1124]
Procurator-General and Treasury Solicitor, B. B. Hall, C.B., M.C., T.D. £21,000
Deputy Treasury Solicitor, T. C. Hetherington, C.B.E.
£15,000

Advisory Division

Under Secretary (Legal), J. C. Hooton, C.M.G., M.B.E.
£12,410
Assistant Solicitors, D. L. Davies; O.B.E.; G. A. Hosker; A. D. Osborne . . . . £9,443 to £11,410
Senior Legal Assistants, R. Armitage; Miss W. G. Beer; J. E. Collins; R. P. Ellis; J. M. Gibson; E. W. Wills . . . . £7,035 to £9,160

Litigation Divisions

Under Secretaries (Legal), J. B. Bailey; R. K. Price; F. B. Stone £12,410
Assistant Solicitors, W. H. Godwin; J. A. Hornsby, T.D.; N. D. Ing; M. E. Mead; R. D. Munrow; A. J. Murray; G. S. Payne; Miss V. M. Peto; G. F. Sills; D. A. Watson; J. H. Wilkinson
£9,443 to £11,410
Senior Legal Assistants, N. L. Braund; A. Bridge; M. J. C. Haines; I. Hood; Mrs. D. J. Jones; G. H. Kirby-Smith; A. D. Lawton, C. G. Leonard; Mrs. A. D. B. McFee; E. G. Mosely; R. N. Ricks; A. B. Sandal; M. B. Sturdy
£7,035 to £9,160
Principals, A. Deane; E. J. King; F. L. Parker, I.S.O.; E. J. Pratt; G. Roberts . . . . . £6,090 to £7,860

Queen's Proctor Division

Queen's Proctor, B. B. Hall, C.B., M.C., T.D.
Assistant Queen's Proctor, G. S. Payne
£9,443 to £11,410

Conveyancing Division

Under Secretary (Legal), G. V. Freeman £12,410
Assistant Solicitors, R. W. Corbett; E. B. D. Eastham; R. B. Gardner; J. Holdron; J. C. Leck; N. J. Orchard; J. B. Sweetman
£9,443 to £11,410
Senior Legal Assistants, D. E. T. Bevan; E. K. Bridges; R. W. M. Cooper; M. R. M. Davis; R. W. Dyer; Mrs. A. M. I. Frankl; D. J. C. Garnett; Miss G. Gilder; D. H. Godkin; J. B. Howe; J. E. H. Jones; W. S. Karran; I. T. Lewis; A. P. Millar; P. Noble; G. E. Papes; D. F. Pascho; D. A. J. Simpson; P. M. Sprott; Mrs. J. M. Stone; S. A. Tobin; R. M. C. Venables; J. Wyer . . . . £7,035 to £9,160
Principals, A. N. Applegate; T. W. Brigden; B. A. J. Brockwell; B. A. Brown; L. H. Pountney
£6,090 to £7,860

Accounts, Costs and Establishments Division

Legal Personnel Officer, A. L. M. Chitty
£9,443 to £11,410
Establishment Officer, G. J. Judge . £6,090 to £7,860
Chief Accountant, B. C. Shephard
£6,090 to £7,860
Head of Costs Branch, A. M. Niven
£6,090 to £7,860

Bona Vacantia Division

35 Old Queen Street, S.W.1
[01–930–7363 and 1124]
Assistant Solicitor, J. D. Harries-Jones
£9443 to £11,410
Senior Legal Assistant, C. R. Crockett
£7,035 to £9,160
Principal, R. A. Roberts . . . . £6,090 to £7,860

Claims Commission Branch, Army Department

Queen Anne's Chamber, 41 Tothill Street, S.W.1
[01–218–9000]
Senior Legal Assistants, N. D. Knowles; H. Parke
£7,035 to £9,160

Department of Energy Branch

Kingsgate House, 66–74 Victoria Street, S.W. 1
[01–211–3000]
Legal Adviser (Under Secretary (Legal)), P. G. Ashcroft £12,410
Assistant Solicitors, A. W. Baker; G. B. Claydon; J. E. Coleman . . . . £9,443 to £11,410
Senior Legal Assistants, D. H. Ingham; D. R. M. Long; M. L. Saunders . . . . . . £7,035 to £9,160

COUNCIL ON TRIBUNALS
6 Spring Gardens, Cockspur Street, S.W.1
[01–930–8691]

The Council on Tribunals, with its Scottish Committee, was constituted in 1958 under the provisions of the *Tribunals and Inquiries Act* of that year to act as an advisory body in the field of administrative tribunals and statutory inquiries. It now operates under the Tribunals and Inquiries Act, 1971.

Its principal functions are (a) to keep under review the constitution and working of the various tribunals which have been placed under its general supervision by the Act; (b) to report on particular matters relating to any tribunal which may be referred to it by the Lord Chancellor and the Lord Advocate; and (c) to report on matters relating to statutory inquiries which may be similarly referred to it or which the Council may determine to be of special importance. In addition, the Council must be consulted both about rules of procedure for statutory inquiries and before rules are made for any of the tribunals under its general supervision, and it may make general recommendations about appointments to membership of such tribunals. The numerous tribunals which have been placed under the Council's supervision are concerned with a wide variety of matters varying from agriculture and road traffic to independent schools and pensions. They include the main National Health Service and National Insurance Tribunals, together with such tribunals as the Civil Aviation Authority, Industrial Tribunals, the Land Tribunal, the Mental Health Review Tribunals, Local Valuation Courts, Rent Tribunals, Rent Assessment Committees and the Transport Tribunal. There is power in the 1971 Act to extend the Council's jurisdiction to additional classes of tribunals and inquiries or hearings.

The Scottish Committee of the Council considers Scottish tribunals and matters relating only to Scotland.

The Members of the Council are appointed by the Lord Chancellor and the Lord Advocate. The Scottish Committee is composed partly of members of the Council designated by the Lord Advocate and partly of other persons appointed by him. The Parliamentary Commissioner for Administration is *ex officio* a member both of the Council and of the Scottish Committee.

The Council submits an annual report on its proceedings and those of the Scottish Committee to the Lord Chancellor and the Lord Advocate, which must be laid before Parliament.

Chairman, The Lord Tweedsmuir, C.B.E., C.D.
Members, Mrs. E. Bayliss; Prof. K. M. Bell; C. R. Dale; Mrs. C. Davis, O.B.E.; Lady Fulton; Sir Desmond Heap; D. C.-H. Hirst, Q.C.; J. Macdonald; The Lord Mancroft, K.B.E., T.D.; Sir Alan Marre, K.C.B.(*Parliamentary Commissioner for Administration*); C. Moseley; Sir William Murrie, G.C.B., K.B.E.; J. M. Turner, O.B.E.; R. K. Will, W.S.; D. G. T. Williams.
Secretary, W. S. Carter, C.M.G., C.V.O.

Scottish Committee
22 Melville Street, Edinburgh 3
[031–225–3236]

Chairman, R. K. Will, W.S.
Members, J. Macdonald; Sir Alan Marre, K.C.B. (*Parliamentary Commissioner for Administration*); Mrs. B. Leburn, M.B.E.; J. A. Matheson; R. Moore, C.B.E.; D. M. Ross, Q.C.; J. M. Turner, O.B.E.
Secretary, R. Walker.

CORPORATION OF TRINITY HOUSE
Trinity House, Tower Hill, E.C.3
[01–480–6601]

Trinity House, the first General Lighthouse and Pilotage Authority in the Kingdom, was a body of importance when Henry VIII granted the institution its first charter in 1514. The Corporation is the general lighthouse authority for England and Wales, the Channel Islands and Gibraltar, with certain statutory jurisdiction over aids to navigation maintained by local harbour authorities, etc., and by the General Lighthouse Authorities for Scotland and Ireland. It is also responsible for dealing with wrecks dangerous to navigation, except those occurring within port limits or wrecks of H.M. ships. The Lighthouse Service, including those of Scotland and Ireland, is maintained out of the General Lighthouse Fund which is provided from light dues levied on ships using the ports of the United Kingdom and Eire. The Corporation is also the principal pilotage authority in the United Kingdom and is responsible for London and 40 other districts. Certain charitable trusts are administered by the Corporation for the relief of aged or distressed mariners and their dependants. The affairs of the Corporation are managed by a Board of ten active Elder Brethren and the Secretary, assisted by Administrative, engineering and marine staff. The active Elder Brethren also act as nautical assessors in marine causes in the Admiralty Division of the High Court of Justice.

Elder Brethren
Master, H.R.H. the Duke of Edinburgh, K.G.
Deputy Master, Captain D. S. Tibbits, D.S.C., R.N.(*ret.*). *Elder Brethren,* H.R.H. The Prince of Wales, K.G.; Commodore T. L. Owen, O.B.E., R.D., R.N.R.(*ret.*); Capt. G. C. H. Noakes, R.D., R.N.R.(*ret.*); Admiral of the Fleet the Earl Mountbatten of Burma, K.G., P.C., G.C.B., O.M., G.C.S.I., G.C.I.E., G.C.V.O., D.S.O.; Capt. D. Dunn; Capt. G. P. McCraith; Capt. R. J. Galpin, R.D., R.N.R. (*ret.*); The Earl of Avon, K.G., P.C., M.C.; Capt. Sir George Barnard; Capt. R. N. Mayo, C.B.E.; Capt. D. A. G. Dickens; Capt. J. E. Bury; Capt. J. A. N. Bezant, D.S.C., R.D., R.N.R. (*ret.*); Capt. D. J. Cloke; The Rt. Hon. J. H. Wilson, O.B.E., M.P.; Capt. M. B. Wingate; The Rt. Hon. E. R. G. Heath, M.B.E., M.P.; Capt. I. R. C. Saunders; The Visct. Runciman of Doxford, O.B.E., A.F.C.; Capt. P. F. Mason; Capt. T. Woodfield; The Lord Simon of Glaisdale, P.C.; Sir Eric Drake, C.B.E.; Admiral Sir Terence Lewin, K.C.B., M.V.O., D.S.C.; Commodore D. T. Smith.

Officers
Secretary, L. N. Potter.
Deputy Secretary, S. W. Heesom.
Engineer-in-Chief, I. C. Clingan.
Principal, Lights Department, D. C. Henry.
Chief Accountant, A. Snook.
Chief, Administration Department, N. F. Matthews.
Establishment Officer, G. Warnes.
Surveyor of Shipping, W. R. Foley.
Principal, Pilotage Department, H. E. Oliver.
Principal, Corporate Department, V. G. Stamp.
Press Officer, J. Manning.

COMMISSIONERS OF NORTHERN LIGHTHOUSES
84 George Street, Edinburgh.
[031–226–7051]

The Commissioners of Northern Lighthouses are the General Lighthouse Authority for Scotland and the Isle of Man. The present Board owes its origin to an Act of Parliament passed in 1786 which authorized the erection of 4 lighthouses; 19 Commissioners were appointed to carry out the Act. At the present time the Commissioners operate under the Merchant Shipping Act, 1894 and are 23 in number.

The Commissioners control 61 Major manned Lighthouses, 1 manned Lightvessel, 26 Major unmanned Lighthouses, 87 Minor Lights and many Lighted and Unlighted Buoys. They have a fleet of 3 Motor Vessels.

Commissioners
The Lord Advocate, the Solicitor General, the Lord Provosts of Edinburgh, Glasgow and Aberdeen; the Provost of Inverness; the Chairman of Argyll & Bute; the Sheriffs-Principal of North Strathclyde; Tayside, Central & Fife; Grampian, Highlands & Islands; South Strathclyde, Dumfries

& Galloway; Lothians & Borders; and Glasgow & Strathkelvin; W. A. Robertson, D.S.C.; J. P. H. Mackay, Q.C.; W. D. H. Gregson, C.B.E.; T. Macgill.

Officers:

General Manager, W. Alastair Robertson, D.S.C.
Engineer-in-Chief, P. H. Hyslop, D.S.C.
Secretary, J. Robson.

CLYDE PORT AUTHORITY
16 Robertson Street, Glasgow
Chairman, A. G. McCrae, C.B.E.
Managing Director, J. P. Davidson.
Secretary and Solicitor, J. B. Maxwell.

UNIVERSITY GRANTS COMMITTEE
14 Park Crescent, W.1
[01–636–7799]
The Committee was appointed by the Chancellor of the Exchequer in July, 1919, and its present terms of reference are as follows:
" To inquire into the financial needs of university education in Great Britain; to advise the Government as to the application of any grants made by Parliament towards meeting them; to collect, examine, and make available information relating to university education throughout the United Kingdom; and to assist, in consultation with the universities and other bodies concerned, the preparation and execution of such plans for the development of the universities as may from time to time be required in order to ensure that they are fully adequate to national needs."
Chairman, Sir Frederick Dainton, F.R.S.... £17,175
Other Members, Prof. R. J. C. Atkinson; Sir Donald Barron; Prof. A. J. Brown, C.B.E., D.Phil., F.B.A.; D. P. J. Browning; Prof. Violet R. Cane; Prof. K. M. Clayton; Prof. W. H. Cockroft; Prof. J. Cruickshank; Prof. T. W. Goodwin, C.B.E., F.R.S.; Prof. J. C. Gunn; Miss M. Hulme; Prof. N. C. Hunt, C.B.E., Ph.D. J. Munn; Sir Alex Smith; Prof. P. G. Stein, Ph.D., F.B.A.; Prof. Barbara M. H. Strang; Prof. Sir Charles Stuart-Harris, C.B.E., M.D.; Prof. B. C. L. Weedon, C.B.E., F.R.S.; Prof. J. C. West.
Secretary, J. P. Carswell................ £14,000
Under Secretary, E. H. St. G. Moss...... £12,000
Assist. Secretaries, L. P. Angell; A. P. J. Edwards; Miss M. L. Senior; N. P. Thomas
£8,650 to £11,000
Principals, Mrs. E. W. Cahan; C. A. Clark; A. Eaves(*Statistician*); P. J. Fallon; K. C. Humphrey; A. C. Locke............... £5,680 to £7,450
Directing Architect, W. R. C. Cleary..... £11,000
Superintending Quantity Surveyor, I. H. Keates
£8,650 to £9,798

VALUE ADDED TAX TRIBUNALS
Value added tax tribunals for England and Wales have been established in London, Cardiff, Birmingham, Leeds and Manchester, and value added tax tribunals for Scotland and Northern Ireland in Edinburgh and Belfast respectively. A person dissatisfied with a decision of the Commissioners of Customs and Excise relating to certain aspects of value added tax may appeal to a tribunal.
The tribunals are entirely independent of the Commissioners. They are under the supervision of the Council on Tribunals and are intended to determine disputes concerning value added tax speedily and with a minimum of formality, and to assist in obtaining uniformity in the application of the tax throughout the United Kingdom.

17 North Audley Street, W.1
[01–629–5542]
President, The Hon. K. B. Suenson-Taylor, Q.C.
Registrar (*Senior Principal*), R. J. Powell, I.S.O.

Tribunal Centres
London: 17 North Audley Street, W.1
[01–629–5542]
Chairman, N. P. M. Elles.
Edinburgh: 44 Palmerston Place, Edinburgh
[031–226–3551]
Vice-President, Scotland, D. Y. Abbey.

Belfast: Midland Hotel, Whitla Street, Belfast
[Belfast 749214]
Manchester: Warwickgate House, Warwick Road, Old Trafford, Manchester [061–872–6471]
Chairman, P. A. Ferns, T.D.

COMMONWEALTH WAR GRAVES COMMISSION
2 Marlow Road, Maidenhead, Berkshire
[Maidenhead: 34221]
The Commonwealth War Graves Commission (formerly Imperial War Graves Commission) was founded by Royal Charter in 1917. It is responsible for the commemoration of 1,695,000 members of the forces of the Commonwealth who fell in the two world wars. More than one million graves are maintained in 23,589 burial grounds throughout the world. Nearly three-quarters of a million men and women who have no known grave or who were cremated are commemorated by name on memorials built by the Commission.
The funds of the Commission are derived from the seven Governments participating in its work—The United Kingdom, Canada, Australia, New Zealand, South Africa, India and Pakistan.
President, H.R.H. The Duke of Kent, G.C.M.G., G.C.V.O.
Chairman: The Secretary of State for Defence.
Vice-Chairman, General Sir Noel Thomas, K.C.B., D.S.O., M.C.
Members, The Minister for Housing and Construction; The High Commissioners for Canada, the Commonwealth of Australia, New Zealand, and India; the Ambassadors for the Republics of South Africa and Pakistan; Sir Robert Black, G.C.M.G., O.B.E.; Miss Joan Woodgate, C.B.E., R.R.C.; Sir John Winnifrith, K.C.B.; Admiral Sir Frank Twiss, K.C.B., D.S.C.; E. L. Gardner, Q.C., M.P.; The Lord Wallace of Coslany; Air Chief Marshal Sir John Barraclough, K.C.B., C.B.E., D.F.C., A.F.C.
Director-General, A. K. Pallot, C.M.G.
Assistant Directors-General, A. S. Laing, M.V.O. (*Secretariat*); J. Saynor (*Administration*).
Legal Adviser and Solicitor, P. R. Matthew.
Director of External Relations, P. H. M. Swan.
Director of Works, W. H. Dukes.
Director of Horticulture, W. F. W. Harding, O.B.E.
Director of Information Services, S. G. Campbell, M.C.
Establishment Officer, H. Westland.
Chief Finance Officer, P. J. Cook.
Honorary Artistic Adviser, Professor The Lord Holford, R.A., F.R.I.B.A.
Hon. Consulting Engineer, P. A. Scott.
Hon. Botanical Adviser, Sir George Taylor, D.Sc., F.R.S., F.R.S.E.

Imperial War Graves Endowment Fund
Trustees, E. M. P. Welman; Sir John Hogg, T.D.; General Sir Noel Thomas, K.C.B., D.S.O., M.C.
Hon. Secretary to the Trustees, W. J. Chalmers, C.B., C.B.E.

WELSH OFFICE
Gwydyr House, Whitehall, S.W.1
[01–930–3151]
Secretary of State, THE RT. HON. JOHN MORRIS, Q.C., M.P.................... £13,000
Private Secretary, J. W. Lloyd.
Parliamentary Private Secretary, I. L. Evans, M.P
Parliamentary Under-Secretaries of State, S. B. Jones, M.P.; T. A. Jones, M.P.................. £5,500
Private Secretaries, D. A. Rees; D. H. Jones.
Permanent Secretary, H. W. Evans, C.B...... £18,675
Deputy Secretary, O. H. Morris, C.M.G..... £14,000
Assistant Secretary, S. T. Charles £8,650 to £11,000
Principal, J. Taffinder....... £5,680 to £7,480

Cathays Park, Cardiff
[0222–28066]
Under Secretaries, J. A. Annaud; R. T. Bevan; J. H. Clement; I. Davey; I. S. Dewar; D. A. R. Hall; P. B. Hunt; D. G. Jones; L. Jones; R. A. Lloyd-Jones; A. Owen, M.C.......... £12,000
Assistant Secretaries, J. A. Annand; M. E. Bevan;

B. H. Evans; W. J. Griffiths; R. Hall-Williams;
L. H. Hayward; P. J. Hosegood; H. E. O.
Hughes, C.B.E.; R. W. Jarman; D. W. Jones;
R. H. Jones, C.V.O.; J. E. King; L. M. Lloyd,
M.B.E.; R. A. Owen; R. D. Potter; L. Pritchard;
O. Rees; D. J. Tallis; H. K. Trimmell; E. K.
Williams................£8,650 to £11,000

Assistant Secretary (Finance Officer), W. B. Jones
£8,650 to £11,000

Senior Principals, M. G. Evans; J. C. Lewis; P. E.
Loveluck; L. R. Rogers; D. A. Sullivan; D. M.
Timlin....................£7,750 to £9,350

Principals, R. M. Abel; S. K. Bateman; H. R.
Bollington; J. E. Booker, O.B.E.; F. E. Brewer;
J. H. Brown; J. L. Caddy; J. A. Chadwick;
W. L. Chapman; M. Cohen; G. C. G. Craig; J. F.
Craig; I. B. Cullis; J. I. Davies; J. N. G. Davies;
G. G. Elliott; G. T. Evans; Mrs. M. Evans;
Mrs. S. G. Evans; P. Finnison; J. S. Gill; L. L.
Ginn; W. J. Griffiths; S. H. Handley, M.B.E.;
C. W. Harris; F. Hind; Mrs. E. O. James; G. M.
Jenkins; A. H. H. Jones; L. Kane; H. E. Leonard,
O.B.E.; J. W. Lloyd; D. T. Marshall; G. H. Miles;
B. S. Millwood; D. Morgan, O.B.E.; J. A.
Morgan; G. H. Nowell, M.B.E.; J. C. Price;
J. Rhys; T. Roberts; H. I. W. Sparkes;
B. Taffinder; Miss E. E. J. Thomas; A. R. A.
Tredget; W. A. Vinall; A. Whitaker; P. J. E.
Wilcox; A. D. Williams....£5,680 to £7,450

Head of Road Safety Unit, G. G. Gates, M.B.E.
£3,635 to £4,908

Architectural Staff

Chief Architect, G. J. Kelly..............£11,000

Architects (Senior Grade), H. O. M. Coleman; J. R.
Coward; J. T. Darch; C. Eyres; S. C. Halbritter;
G. N. Harding; E. T. Williams
£6,280 to £7,450

Quantity Surveyors (Senior Grade), R. Broad;
T. A. Campden; K. G. G. Cosslett; I. Smith
£6,280 to £7,450

Engineering Staff

Chief Engineer, H. Cronshaw...........£11,000

Superintending Engineers, G. M. Jones; A. S. R.
Mutch....................£8,650 to £9,798

Engineering Inspector, W. D. A. Waters
£6,468 to £8,833

Engineers (Senior Grade), L. G. Edwards; J. Jarvis;
C. A. Jenkins; H. Ruttley; J. E. Saunders
£6,280 to £7,450

Engineering Staff (Roads)

Director of Highways, D. A. R. Hall......£12,000

Superintendent Engineers, J. E. Morgan; A. Orme
£8,650 to £9,798

Senior Engineers, P. I. Adams; P. C. Dunstan;
J. G. Evans; M. Griffin; J. A. L. Harries; B. J. W.
Martin; W. H. Prosser; E. G. Whitcutt
£6,280 to £7,450

Senior Quantity Surveyor, D. G. Minas
£6,280 to £7,450

Health Staff

Chief Medical Officer, R. T. Bevan, M.D....£12,000

Principal Medical Officers, P. Alwyn-Smith; W. C.
D. Lovett, O.B.E....................£11,440

Senior Medical Officers, A. G. Jones; R. B. Morley-
Davies; J. N. M. Parry; Miss F. M. Richards
£11,000

Chief Nursing Officer, Miss E. A. Bell......£9,818

Medical Officers, D. J. W. Anderson; R. Buntwal;
R. F. Doyle; E. J. S. Evans; G. M. Evans; A. J. R.
Hudson, V.R.D.; J. N. P. Hughes; D. F. Lewis;
G. J. Moses; H. A. Mullen, T.D.; L. J. Powell;
T. T. Westhead; P. R. E. Williams
£6,987 to £9,562

Chief Dental Officer, D. R. Edwards......£11,000

Dental Officers, A. Cobb; G. Morris; T. A.
Williams..................£6,987 to £9,562

Principal Nursing Officers, E. E. Beckerton; Miss I.
John..................................£8,638

Nursing Officers, Miss E. G. Bennett; Miss M. Coker;
Miss P. D. Jones; Miss M. D. Wells; Miss J. P.
White..................£6,968 to £7,761

Scientific Adviser, R. A. Saunders £8,650 to £9,798

Pharmaceutical Adviser, D. L. Thomas
£8,650 to £9,798

Planning Staff

Chief Planner, J. A. Colley..............£11,000

Senior Research Officers, D. T. M. Davies; A. S.
Dredge; C. G. Parry........£5,680 to £7,450

Senior Planning Officers, G. Fairhurst; I. N. Jones;
J. O. Pryce; C. W. W. Smart; B. G. Taylor;
Miss M. P. Thomas.........£6,280 to £7,450

Senior Estate Officer, G. K. Hoad..£6,280 to £7,450

Principal Scientific Officers, J. C. Finnigan; J. N. M.
Firth....................£5,514 to £7,205

Senior Housing and Planning Inspectors, M. R. Mul-
lins, M.B.E.; L. G. H. Pannell; E. M. Roberts;
J. W. Tester................£7,093 to £8,650

Legal Staff

Legal Adviser, G. Davies.......£9,033 to £11,000

Assistant Solicitors, A. J. Beale; D. G. Lambert
£9,033 to £11,000

Senior Legal Assistants, J. D. H. Evans; P. J. Murrin;
A. J. Watkins..............£6,625 to £8,750

Information Staff

Director, Information Division, J. E. B. Evans
£8,650 to £11,000

Social Work Service

Chief Social Work Service Officer, E. Glithero
£8,650 to £11,000

Principal Social Work Service Officers, R. L. Jones;
Miss Z. E. Williams........£8,250 to £9,798

Social Work Service Officers, W. F. Brien; Miss W.
O. M. Copleston; G. H. Davies; D. G. Evans;
Mrs. B. M. Johnson; Miss J. C. M. Jones; J. F.
Mooney; Mrs. C. Owens; L. Pugh; G. W. Smith
£5,680 to £7,750

Senior Economic Adviser, O. T. Hooker
£8,650 to £11,000

Chief Statistician, D. A. Jones..£8,650 to £11,000

WHITE FISH AUTHORITY

10 Young Street, Edinburgh 2
[031-225-2515]

Chairman, C. I. Meek, C.M.G............£5,625

Deputy-Chairman, Sir Matthew Campbell, K.B.E.,
C.B., F.R.S.E. *(part-time)*.

Members (part-time), Dr. W. J. L. Dean, O.B.E.;
E. H. M. Clutterbuck, O.B.E.; K. L. Hall, C.B.E.;
Admiral Sir Deric Holland-Martin, G.C.B., D.S.O.,
D.S.C.; Miss J. Stewart.

Chief Executive, C. I. Meek, C.M.G.

Secretary, J. R. D. Murray.

COMMISSIONS, ETC.

COMMUNITY RELATIONS COMMISSION

15–16 Bedford Street, W.C.2
[01–836–3545]

Established on November 26, 1968, under the
Race Relations Act, 1968, to help people of
different races and cultures to live and work together in harmony.

Chairman, Hon. Mark Bonham Carter.

Deputy Chairmen, The Very Rev. A. Jowett, C.B.E.;
The Lord Pitt of Hampstead.

Members, The Lord Campbell of Eskan; P. C.
Chitnis; Mrs. P. Crabbe, O.B.E.; C. Plant, O.B.E.;
A. F. A. Sayeed; The Baroness Serota; Mrs.
R. L. Wolff; P. L. B. Woodroffe.

FOREIGN COMPENSATION COMMISSION

Alexandra House, Kingsway, W.C.2

The Commission was set up by the *Foreign Compensation Act*, 1950, to distribute funds paid by
foreign governments as compensation for expropriated British property and other losses sustained
by British nationals. The *Foreign Compensation
Act*, 1962, provided, *inter alia*, for the payment out
of moneys provided by Parliament of additional

compensation in respect of claims arising in connection with certain events in Egypt. The Foreign Compensation Act, 1969, provided, *inter alia*, for the payment by the Board of Trade to the Commission for distribution of moneys held by the Custodian of Enemy Property being former property of a Baltic State or ceded territory. The Commission has completed the final distribution of the funds contributed by Yugoslavia, Czechoslovakia, Bulgaria, Poland, Rumania and Hungary, and the moneys received from the Board of Trade in respect of claims under the U.S.S.R. Distribution Order. The Commission has registered certain British claims in Czechoslovakia and also in the Baltic States and territories annexed by the Soviet Union. The £27,500,000 compensation paid by the Government of the United Arab Republic under the financial agreement of Feb. 28, 1959, has been fully distributed. The Foreign Compensation (Egypt) Order in respect of British-owned property affected by Egyptian measures of nationalization between 1960 and 1964 came into operation on Feb. 1, 1972, and the Commission is engaged in determining claims thereunder. The Foreign Compensation (German Democratic Republic) (Registration) Order 1975 which came into operation on May 7, 1975, enables certain claims relating to property in the German Democratic Republic and Berlin (East) owned by United Kingdom nationals or relating to debts owed by persons resident in the German Democratic Republic and Berlin (East) to United Kingdom nationals to be registered with, and reported upon by, the Commission.
Chairman, Sir Ralph Windham.
Commissioners, Sir James Henry, Bt., C.M.G., M.C., T.D.; Sir Daniel Crawshaw.
Legal Officer, J. R. Whimster.
Secretary and Chief Examiner, Miss H. M. Walsh, O.B.E.
Registrar, T. W. Leopard.

ROYAL COMMISSION ON ENVIRONMENTAL POLLUTION

Church House, Great Smith Street, S.W.1
[01-212 8620]

Set up on Feb. 20, 1970, " to advise on matters, both national and international, concerning the pollution of the environment; on the adequacy of research in this field; and the future possibilities of danger to the environment."
Chairman, Sir Brian Flowers, F.R.S.
Members, The Marchioness of Anglesey; D.W. Bowett; Prof. T. J. Chandler; F. J. Chapple; J. G. Collingwood; T. O. Conran; Prof. E. J. Denton, C.B.E., F.R.S.; Sir Richard Doll, O.B.E., F.R.S.; Prof. P. J. Lindop; Prof. J. M. Mitchison; Prof. R. E. Nicholl; Prof. T. R. E. Southwood; P. P. Streeten; Sir Ralph Verney, K.B.E.; Sir Frederick Warner; The Baroness White.
Secretary, L. F. Rutterford.

ROYAL COMMISSION ON STANDARDS OF CONDUCT IN PUBLIC LIFE

20 Grosvenor Hill, W.1.
[01-629 6183]

Set up on December 6, 1974, "to inquire into standards of conduct in central and local government and other public bodies in the United Kingdom in relation to the problems of conflict of interest and the risk of corruption involving favourable treatment from a public body: and to make recommendations as to the further safeguards which may be required to ensure the highest standard of probity in public life."
Chairman, The Lord Salmon, P.C.
Members, The Lord Houghton of Sowerby, P.C.,

C.H.; The Rt. Hon. Margaret M. Herbison; The Lord Avebury; The Lord Orr-Ewing, O.B.E.; The Lord Cudlipp, O.B.E.; Sir Philip Allen, G.C.B.; Sir Henry Jones, G.B.E.; Sir Leslie Williams, C.B.E.; Sir Melvyn Rosser; B. S. Kellett; Mrs. Muriel Ward-Jackson.
Secretary, A. J. Langdon.

ROYAL COMMISSION ON CIVIL LIABILITY AND COMPENSATION FOR PERSONAL INJURY

GKN House, 22 Kingsway, W.C.2

Appointed on March 19, 1973, " to consider to what extent, in what circumstances and by what means compensation should be payable in respect of death or personal injury (including antenatal injury) suffered by any person—(a) in the course of employment; (b) through the use of a motor vehicle or other means of transport; (c) through the manufacture, supply or use of goods or services; (d) on premises belonging to or occupied by another; or (e) otherwise through the act or omission of another where compensation under the present law is recoverable only on proof of fault or under the rules of strict liability, having regard to the cost and other implications of the arrangements for the recovery of compensation, whether by way of compulsory insurance or otherwise."
Chairman, The Lord Pearson, P.C., C.B.E.
Members, Sir Philip Allen, G.C.B.; W. C. Anderson, C.B.E.; Mrs. M. Brooke; The Hon. Lord Cameron, D.S.C.; Prof. R. B. Duthie, F.R.C.S.; R. A. MacCrindle, Q.C.; N. S. Marsh, Q.C.; D. A. Marshall; Prof. A. R. Prest, Ph.D.; A. E. Sansom; Prof. R. S. F. Schilling, C.B.E., M.D., D.S.C., F.R.C.P.; R. S. Skerman, C.B.E.; Miss O. Stevenson; James Stewart, W.S.; A. W. Ure, R.D.
Secretary, Mrs. M. E. Parsons.

ROYAL COMMISSION ON THE DISTRIBUTION OF INCOME AND WEALTH

Neville House, Page Street, S.W.1.
[01-222 8020]

The Commission enquires into and reports on such matters concerning the distribution of personal incomes, both earned and unearned, and wealth, as may be referred to it by the Government.
Chairman, The Lord Diamond, P.C.
Members, Sir Neville Butterworth; R. A. Cox; G. Doughty; Prof. J. Greve; D. Lea; L. Murphy, Prof. E. H. Phelps-Brown, M.B.E.; Mrs. D. E. C. Wedderburn.
Secretary, I. F. Hudson.

ROYAL COMMISSION ON THE PRESS

Standard Hse., 27 Northumberland Ave., W.C.2
[01-839 2855/8]

Set up on May 2, 1974, " to enquire into the factors affecting the maintenance of the independence, diversity and editorial standards of newspapers and periodicals, and the public's freedom of choice, of newspapers and periodicals, nationally, regionally and locally, with particular reference to—(a) the economics of newspaper and periodical publishing and distribution; (b) the interaction of the newspaper and periodical interests held by the companies concerned with their other interests and holdings, within and outside the communications industry; (c) management and labour practices and relations in the newspaper and periodical industry; (d) conditions and security of employment in the newspaper and periodical industry; (e) the distribution and concentration of ownership of the newspaper and periodical industry, and the adequacy of existing law in relation thereto; (*f*) the responsibilities, constitution and functioning of the Press Council; and to make recommendations."

Chairman, Prof. O. R. McGregor.
Members, Mrs. E. Anderson; D. Basnett; G. S. Bishop; R. R. E. Chorley; G. Goodman; Prof. L. C. B. Gower; M. Horsman; The Lord Hunt, C.B.E., D.S.O.; P. Johnson; J. E. Jones, O.B.E.; I. Richardson; Miss E. Roberts, O.B.E.; Z. A. Silberston.
Secretary, P. McQuail.

CRIMINAL INJURIES COMPENSATION BOARD
10–12 Russell Square, W.C.1
[01-636-2812]

The Board was constituted in 1964 to administer the Government scheme for the compensation of victims of crimes of violence, which came into operation on August 1, 1964.
Chairman, His Hon. Sir Walker Carter, Q.C.
Members, D. A. Barker, Q.C.; I. J. Black, Q.C.; Sir William Carter; J. Law, Q.C.; Miss J. Littlewood; D. G. A. Lowe, Q.C.; Sir Ronald Morison, Q.C.; M. Ogden, Q.C.; D. B. Weir, Q.C.
Secretary, D. H. Harrison.

THE BRITISH COUNCIL
10 Spring Gardens, S.W.1

The British Council was established in 1934. Its Royal Charter (1940) defines its aims as the promotion of a wider knowledge of Britain and English abroad, and the development of closer cultural relations with other countries. Most of its funds are provided by Parliament: the gross budget for 1975–76 is £30,000,000, and it administers a further sum, estimated for 1974–75 at £19,100,000, as agent for Government Departments and international organizations.
Chairman, The Lord Ballantrae, G.C.M.G., G.C.V.O., D.S.O., O.B.E.
Director-General, Sir John Llewellyn, K.C.M.G., Ph.D., D.SC.

THE NATIONAL TRUST
40–42 Queen Anne's Gate, Westminster, S.W.1
[01-930 0211]

The National Trust was founded in 1895 by Miss Octavia Hill, Sir Robert Hunter and Canon Rawnsley, their object being to preserve as much as possible the history and beauty of their country for its people. It became an organization incorporated by Act of Parliament (1907) to ensure the preservation of lands and buildings of historic interest or natural beauty for public access and benefit. It is independent of the State and relies on the voluntary support of private individuals for working funds. As a charity, however, it is allowed certain tax exemptions.

The Trust is now the largest private landowner in the country and third overall only to the Crown and the Forestry Commission. It protects nearly 500,000 acres, much of it superb hill country in the Lake District, Snowdonia, the Peak District and other National Parks. The Trust also owns and opens to the public some 200 country houses and gardens, and preserves villages, nature reserves, archæological sites and many farms.

In 1965 the Trust launched a campaign to acquire as much as possible of the most beautiful stretches of coastline which were under threat from development. The Trust now protects 355 miles of coastline, the first target of £2,000,000 was reached in November 1973, and the appeal continues.

The Trust has now nearly 500,000 members paying an annual subscription and about 100,000 new members are joining each year. Rents, admission fees, legacies and gifts are other important sources of support and income.

The policy of the Trust is determined by the governing body, the Council. Half of its members are appointed by national institutions, such as the British Museum, the National Gallery, the Ramblers' Association and the Royal Horticultural Society; the other half are elected by Trust members at the Annual General Meeting. The Council appoints the Executive Committee, which in turn has established Regional Committees responsible for the management of the Trust's properties.

THE NATIONAL TRUST FOR SCOTLAND
5 Charlotte Square, Edinburgh 2

The National Trust for Scotland was founded in 1931, and its objects are similar to those of the National Trust. Like that organization, it is incorporated by Act of Parliament, is dependent for finance upon legacies, donations and the subscriptions of its members, is recognized as a charity for tax exemption purposes, and enjoys certain privileges under various Finance Acts regarding death duties.

The Trust administers about 80 major properties covering over 82,000 acres. Great houses in its care include:— The Binns, West Lothian; Brodick Castle, Isle of Arran; Crathes Castle, Kincardineshire; Culzean Castle, Ayrshire; Falkland Palace, Fife; Hill of Tarvit and Kellie Castle, Fife, and Leith Hall and Craigievar Castle, Aberdeenshire.

In the Trust's care are also several noteworthy gardens. Some are associated with the great houses, others are:— Inverewe, in Wester Ross; the re-created 17th century garden of Pitmedden in Aberdeenshire; and Threave in Kirkcudbrightshire, where a School of Practical Gardening is run; and Branklyn Gardens, Perth.

Among the mountainous country owned by the Trust is the Pass of Glencoe and the mountain group " The Five Sisters of Kintail " and the estate of Torridon in Wester Ross.

Islands in the Trust's care include the St. Kilda group, and Fair Isle. At Bannockburn, Killiecrankie, Glenfinnan and Culloden, the Trust owns sites associated with Scottish history.

Among smaller properties are houses associated with famous Scots:— the birthplaces of Barrie in Kirriemuir, Carlyle in Ecclefechan, and Hugh Miller in Cromarty; and Burns' Bachelors' Club, Tarbolton and Souter Johnnie's House, Kirkoswald in Ayrshire.

At Culross in Fife, and at Dunkeld, Perthshire, the restoration of attractive groups of houses led to the creation of a special fund under which such properties are brought, restored and sold. Under this scheme over 100 properties in the coastal burghs of East Fife and elsewhere have been and are being restored. This operation was one of the four pilot projects in the United Kingdom selected for special allocation during European Architectural Heritage Year, 1975.

THE PILGRIM TRUST
Fielden House, Little College Street, S.W.1

Trustees, The Lord Harlech, P.C., K.C.M.G. (*Chairman*); The Lord Franks, P.C., G.C.M.G., K.C.B., C.B.E.; The Earl of Crawford and Balcarres, K.T., G.B.E.; W. F. Oakeshott; The Hon. Sir Henry Fisher; The Lord Boyle of Handsworth, P.C.; David Piper, C.B.E.; The Rt. Hon. R. H. Jenkins, M.P.
Secretary, Sir Edward Ford, K.C.B., K.C.V.O.

The Pilgrim Trust was founded in 1930 by the late Edward S. Harkness of New York, who placed in the hands of British trustees £2,000,000 for the benefit of Great Britain. Since then the Trust has been able to make substantial grants for the repair of ancient buildings, the preservation of the countryside, the support of learned societies, the preservation of historical records, the purchase of works of art and the assistance of social welfare schemes.

Since its foundation the Trust has made grants amounting to over £7,800,000 and in 1974 the Trustees voted sums totalling £365,000. These grants were made under the following three heads:—Preservation, £165,000, Art and Learning, £130,000, Social Welfare, £70,000.

Among grants and loans voted in 1974 were £50,000 to the Canterbury Cathedral Appeal; £10,000 to the Ely Cathedral Appeal; £10,000 to Romsey Abbey; £10,000 to the York Civic Trust for the restoration of Peasholme House; £5,000 to the Boston Preservation Trust for repairs to six 18th-century cottages in Spain Court, Boston, Lincs.; £10,000 to the Royal Society's Development Appeal; £7,500 to the Archaeological Research Laboratory, Oxford for research in archaeomagnetism; £10,000 to the Whitworth Art Gallery towards the acquisition of seven sketchbooks of J. R. Cozens; £5,000 to the British Library towards purchase of a notebook of poems by Robert Sidney (1563–1626); £2,500 for new stage-lighting at the Coliseum Theatre, Oldham; £5,000 for improvements to the Theatre and Arts Centre at Coleg Harlech; £5,000 to the Invalid Children's Aid Association for a home for aphasic children in Nottinghamshire; £3,000 to St. Christopher's Hospice, London; £3,000 to Prisoners' Wives Service; and £2,500 to the Keskidee Trust for premises in West Islington.

BRITISH STANDARDS INSTITUTION
British Standards House, 2 Park Street, W.1

The British Standards Institution is the recognized authority in the U.K. for the preparation and publication of national standards for industrial and consumer products. The Institution originated in 1901, when the Institutions of Civil, Mechanical and Electrical Engineers, together with the Iron and Steel Institute and the Institution of Naval Architects, formed a joint Engineering Standards Committee—which subsequently became the British Engineering Standards Association. A Royal Charter was granted in 1929 and with the extension of the scope of the organization to include the building, chemical and textile industries its title was later changed to " British Standards Institution ".

The Institution, in consultation with the interests concerned, now prepares standards relating to nearly every sector of the nation's industry and trade. There are over 7,000 British Standards covering specifications of quality, construction dimensions, performance or safety; methods of test and analysis; glossaries of terms; and codes of practice. About 500 new and revised British Standards are published each year.

The Institution represents the U.K. in the International Organization for Standardization (ISO), the International Electrotechnical Commission (IEC) and other international bodies concerned with harmonizing standards.

British Standards are issued for voluntary adoption though in a number of cases compliance with a British Standard is required by legislation. The Institution operates certification schemes under which industrial and consumer products are certified as complying with the relevant British Standard and manufacturers satisfying the requirements of such schemes may use the Institution's registered certification mark (known as the " Kitemark "). Other testing and certification services, together with information services, are available to industry, including help in meeting technical requirements in export markets.

The Institution is financed by voluntary subscriptions, an annual Government grant, the sale of its publications and fees for testing and certification. There are more than 16,000 subscribing members of B.S.I., including public authorities, trade and technical bodies, professional institutions, manufacturers, distributors and large scale purchasers.

Chairman of the Executive Board, Prof. Sir Frederick Warner.
Director General, G. B. R. Feilden, C.B.E., F.R.S.

HOUSING CORPORATION
Sloane Square House, S.W.1
[01–730–9991]

Set up on Sept. 1, 1964 to promote the growth of housing societies and through them, to stimulate the building of new houses and flats for letting at fair rents or co-ownership. Up to £750,000,000 is being made available for this purpose by the Government to the Corporation.

Chairman, The Lord Goodman, C.H.
Deputy Chairman, The Lord Greenwood of Rossendale, P.C.
Members, Rev. P. Byrne; J. R. Coward, O.B.E.; Mrs. P. Crabbe, O.B.E.; J. Kegie, O.B.E.; D. Llewellyn; J. R. Madge (*Chief Executive*); Sir Stanley Morton; D. Mumford; K. Ryden, M.C.; W. L. Taylor; L. E. Waddilove, O.B.E.
Secretary, R. Vipond, D.F.C.

DESIGN COUNCIL
28 Haymarket, S.W.1
[01–839–8000]

The Council, originally set up in 1944 as the Council of Industrial Design, is sponsored by the Department of Industry to promote the improvement of design in the products of British industry. Its name was changed in 1972 to reflect its increasing activity in the field of engineering design.

The Council's services to industry are based on teams of engineering field officers and industrial officers who visit companies throughout the United Kingdom to diagnose engineering design problems and to discuss and advise on design policy. The Council's Record of Engineering Design Expertise provides information about consultants, companies, universities and research organizations able to advise companies on engineering design problems and the Council's Designer Selection Service can recommend selected industrial designers for specific jobs.

The Council maintains permanent exhibitions of independently selected British goods from Design Index and its Design Centres in London's Haymarket and at 72 St. Vincent Street, Glasgow. Thematic exhibitions are also mounted at the Design Centres and at the Council's smaller Welsh Office in Cardiff. Design Index, the Council's unique photographic and sample record of about 10,000 current British products selected for their good design, can also be consulted at the Design Centres.

Other services include annual award schemes for consumer and engineering goods; training courses and conferences for retail staff, manufacturers and managers; publications, including the monthly magazines *Design* and *Engineering*; a slide loan library; and press and information services. *Crafts* magazine is published bi-monthly by the Council as part of its services to the Crafts Advisory Committee.

Chairman, The Viscount Caldecote, D.S.C.

Chairman of Scottish Committee, Sir Robert Fairbairn.
Director, Sir Paul Reilly.
Chief Executive, Scottish Committee, R. G. Clark.

SPORTS COUNCIL
70 Brompton Road, S.W.3
[01-589 3411]

The Sports Council received its Royal Charter on April 1, 1972, formally recognizing it as an independent body, with the primary aims of promoting sport and recreation in Great Britain and of fostering the provision of facilities. For this purpose the Sports Council receives an annual grant-in-aid from the Department of the Environment.

Chairman, Sir Robin Brook, C.M.G., O.B.E.

Vice-Chairman, J. I. Disley.

Members, B. P. Atha,; H. Baxter; N. R. Collins; N. Croucher; T. Glyn Davies, C.B.E.; Mrs. M. A. Glen Haig, M.B.E.; A. Hardaker, O.B.E.; P. Heatley, C.B.E.; J. W. T. Hill; L. E. Liddell, E.R.D., T.D.; Lt.-Col. H. M. Llewellyn, C.B.E.; P. B. Lucas, D.S.O., D.F.C.; E. Major, M.B.E.; A. J. M. Miller, D.S.C., V.R.D.; K. K. Mitchell; D. D. Molyneux; Lord Rupert Nevill; A. Pascoe, M.B.E.; Miss M. Peters; Prof. H. B. Rodgers; W. J. Slater; R. J. W. Struthers, M.B.E.; Lieut.-Gen. Sir James Wilson, K.B.E., M.C.

Director, W. Winterbottom, C.B.E.

Administrator, J. F. Coghlan, M.B.E., T.D.

THE BANK OF ENGLAND
Threadneedle Street, E.C.2.

The Bank of England was incorporated in 1694 under Royal Charter. It is the banker of the Government on whose behalf it manages the Note Issue, and also manages the National Debt and administers the Exchange Control regulations. As central reserve bank of the country, the Bank keeps the accounts of British banks, who maintain with it a proportion of their cash resources, and of most overseas central banks; but it has gradually withdrawn from new commercial business.

Governor, Gordon William Humphreys Richardson, M.B.E. (*1978).
Deputy Governor, Jasper Quintus Hollom (*1980).
Directors, George Adrian Hayhurst Cadbury (*1978); John Martin Clay (*1979); Jack Gale Wilmot Davies, O.B.E. (*1976); Leopold David de Rothschild (*1979); John Christopher Roderick Dow (*1977); Sir Val Duncan, O.B.E. (*1977); John Standish Fforde (*1978); The Lord Greene of Harrow Weald C.B.E. (*1978); Hector Laing (*1979); Sir (John) Maurice Laing (*1976);

Christopher William McMahon (*1977); The Lord Nelson of Stafford (*1979); Sir Alastair (Lionel Alexander Bethune) Pilkington, F.R.S. (*1976); The Lord Robens of Woldingham, P.C. (*1978); Sir Eric Roll, K.C.M.G., C.B. (*1977); The Hon. William Kenneth James Weir (*1976).
* Date of Retirement.

Chief Cashier, J. B. Page.
Chief Accountant, R. C. Balfour, M.B.E.
Chief of the Overseas Dept., R. P. Fenton, C.M.G.
Chief of the Economic Intelligence Dept., M. J. Thornton, M.C.
Secretary, P. A. S. Taylor.
Chief of Establishments, K. J. S. Andrews, M.B.E.
Chief of Exchange Control, E. B. Bennett, D.S.C.
Chief of Management Services, G. L. L. de Marbray.
General Manager, Printing Works, M. J. S. Cubbage, M.B.E.
Advisers to the Governors, G. Blunden; W. P. Cooke; R. C. H. Hallett (*1975); Sir Henry Benson, G.B.E.; J. A. Kirbyshire.

THE LONDON CLEARING BANKS

COMMITTEE OF LONDON CLEARING BANKERS
(1821), 10 Lombard Street, E.C.3

The Committee consists of the Chairmen of the six Clearing Banks (Barclays, Coutts, Lloyds, Midland, National Westminster, and Williams & Glyn's) and meets regularly to discuss matters of common interest. It is the body through which the Bank of England communicates official policy to the banks and through which the banks may present their views to the Bank of England and the Treasury.

Secretary-General, P. J. Nicholson.
Deputy Secretaries, M. N. Karmel; G. B. Scrine; J. H. Buxton.

BANKERS' AUTOMATED CLEARING SERVICES, LTD.
3 De Havilland Road, Edgware, Middlesex

Bankers' Automated Clearing Services is a company wholly owned by the London Clearing Banks. Its function is to receive money transfers recorded on magnetic tape and to distribute them to the appropriate bank. Nearly all standing orders in Great Britain are interchanged through BACS as is a substantial volume of direct debits originated by non-banking organizations for payments of rates, insurance premiums and hire purchase payments. Credits are also received on magnetic tape, mainly for payment of salaries and pensions.

Managing Director, D. J. Pyne.

BANKERS' CLEARING HOUSE
10 Lombard Street, E.C.3

This is the organization through which the Clearing Banks and the Bank of England exchange cheques drawn on each other and settle their indebtedness to one another. The clearing system came into being in London during the second half of the eighteenth century, and has served as a pattern for the Clearing Houses that have been established since throughout the world.

To obtain payment for any cheque received from a customer for his credit, a banker must present it for payment to the bank on which it is drawn, and the Bankers' Clearing House affords a quick and efficient means of doing this. On an average day 3,500,000 cheques with a total value of £6,500 million, are exchanged and paid for by the six Clearing Banks and the Bank of England on behalf of their branches throughout England and Wales which number over 10,000.

At present two cheque clearings are operated each business day. The Town Clearing, which takes place from 2.30 p.m. until 3.50 p.m., enables cheques of £5,000 and over to be cleared the same day, provided that such cheques are drawn on, and paid into, a Town Clearing branch. There are over ninety branches of the Clearing Banks so designated within a half-mile radius of the Clearing House.

The General Clearing, which takes place each morning, handles all cheques, drawn on branches of the member banks, which cannot be passed through the Town Clearing or cleared under local arrangements. Since April, 1960, a Credit Clearing has been operated through which the member banks exchange credit items in respect of monetary transfers between their customers. The daily average for this Clearing, including work passed through the Bankers' Automated Clearing Service, is 1,000,000 items with a total value of £128 million.

At the end of the day each member bank works out the net balance resulting from its transactions in that day's Town Clearing, the previous day's General Clearing and Credit Clearing, and such differences as need to be adjusted. This net balance is either credited to or deducted from the bank's own account at the Bank of England.

Chief Inspector, K. L. Tibbatts.

Deputy Inspector, S. C. Veal.

BRITISH BANKERS' ASSOCIATION
10 Lombard Street, E.C.3.

The Association provides a means of communication and consultation for the commercial banking industry in this country. Membership is restricted to institutions accepted as banks or discount houses by the Bank of England—over 300. The Association is a member of the E.E.C. Banking Federation.

Secretary-General, R. K. C. Giddings, M.C.

PRINCIPAL BANKS OPERATING IN THE BRITISH COMMONWEALTH

* *Clearing Bankers.*   ‡ *Army Agents.*

London Banking Hours are 9.30 a.m. to 3.30 p.m. (Saturdays, *closed*). In addition, most branches open on one evening a week from 4.30 p.m. to 6.00 p.m. *Scotland.*—Banking hours in Scotland are: Mon.-Wed., 9.30-12.30; 1.30-3.30; Thursday, 9.30-12.30; 1.30-3.30; 4.30-6 p.m.; Fri. 9.30-3.30; Saturday, *Closed.*

ALEXANDERS DISCOUNT CO., LTD. (1810), 24 Lombard St., E.C.3.—Capital, paid up, £5,005,362. Published Reserves, £3,611,689. Deposits, etc. (31 Dec. 1974) £406,664,394.

ALLIED IRISH BANKS LTD. (1966 by alliance of Munster and Leinster, Provincial and Royal Banks).Lansdowne House, Ballsbridge, Dublin, 4. London Agents, Barclays Bank Ltd., Midland Bank, National Westminster Bank. (31.3.75) Capital issued, £11,088,000; Share Premium and Reserves £54,025,000. Total Assets £1,223,120,000. Current Deposit and other accounts £1,139,424,000. Advances to Customers and other accounts, less provisions, £499,667,000.

ALLEN HARVEY & ROSS LIMITED (1888), 45 Cornhill. (1975), Issued Capital, £1,864,000; Reserves, £1,936,000; Deposit, etc., £150,431,000.

THE AMERICAN EXPRESS INTERNATIONAL BANKING CORPORATION. The Subsidiary of American Express Co., New York (1868), 65 Broadway, *New York,* U.S.A.; 52 Cannon Street, E.C.4.— Capital, $31,000,000 (Shares fully paid).

ANGLO-PORTUGUESE BANK, LTD. (1929), 7 Bishopsgate, E.C.2.—Capital, £10,000,000. Issued and fully paid, £7,500,000; Share Premium Account, £2,250,000; Reserves £5,000,000; Deposits, 31/1/75, £72,207,725.

AUSTRALIA AND NEW ZEALAND BANKING GROUP LIMITED, *Registered Office,* 71 Cornhill, E.C.3.— Capital Authorized, £50,000,000; issued and paid up, £36,720,000; Reserves, £79,370,000; Total assets, £3,661,119,000 (at 30/9/74).

AUSTRALIA AND NEW ZEALAND SAVINGS BANK LIMITED, *Head Office,* 351 Collins Street, *Melbourne;* Capital Authorized, $A14,000,000; Issued and Paid up, $A5,000,000; Reserve Fund at 30/9/74, $A21,200,000. Total Assets at 30/9/74, $A1,155,659.

A.N.Z. SAVINGS BANK (NEW ZEALAND) LIMITED, *Regd. Office,* 196 Featherston Street, *Wellington,* New Zealand. Capital Authorized, Issued and Paid up, $NZ500,000; Deposits, etc., at 30/9/74, $NZ114,383,000; Reserve Fund, $NZ2,100,000; Total Assets at 30/9/74, $NZ117,420,000.

BANCO DE BILBAO (1857), *Bilbao,* Spain (Bilbao House, 36 New Broad Street, E.C.2.; 40 King Street, W.C.2.; 74 Commercial Street, E.1.; 32 Cranbourn Street, W.C.2; 3 Sloane Street, S.W.1, New Covent Garden Market, S.W.8; 28-29 High Street, Southampton.—Capital subscribed and paid-up, Pesetas 9,413,040,500; Reserve Fund, Pesetas 11,513,492,331. Deposits, etc., Pesetas 324,592,037,338. (Over 500 Branches in Spain, France, United Kingdom and New York.) Representative offices in Milan and Frankfurt.

BANGKOK BANK LTD. (1941), *Bangkok,* Thailand (59-67 Gresham Street, E.C.2).—(31/12/74)

Capital issued and paid-up, Baht 1,000,000,000; Reserves, Baht 1,293,900,000; Undivided Profit, Baht 100,876,627; Deposits, etc., Baht 35,469,820,218.

BANKERS TRUST COMPANY, 280 Park Avenue, *New York* 10017(9.Queen Victoria Street, E.C.4 and 32-34 Grosvenor Square, W.1).—Capital stock (par value $0.10 per share), $105,120,000.

BANK LEUMI (U.K.) LTD. formerly Anglo-Israel Bank Ltd.), 4-7 Woodstock Street W.1. —Capital: Authorized, £2,500,000 (31/12/74); Issued and fully paid, £2,000,000, ordinary shares £1 each; Reserves £2,000,000 (31/12/74).

BANK OF ADELAIDE (1865), *Adelaide,* South Australia (11 Leadenhall St., E.C.3). Capital, Authorized $A50,000,000; issued $A25,203,750 (Shares in units of $A1 each, fully paid); Reserve Fund, $A20,048,218. (141 Offices.)

BANK OF AMERICA NATIONAL TRUST AND SAVINGS ASSOCIATION (1904), *San Francisco, California, U.S.A.* (27-29 Walbrook, E.C.4 and 29 Davies Street, W.1.)—Capital Funds, $1,913,572,000; Total Deposits, $51,192,118,000. Over 1,000 branches in California and over 100 foreign branches plus representative offices, subsidiaries and/or affiliates in 80 countries.

BANK OF BERMUDA, LTD. (1889), *Hamilton,* Bermuda (*London Agents,* Bank of Bermuda (Europe, Ltd.))—Capital paid up BD$3,600,000; Reserves, BD$8,997,393; Resources 31/12/74. BD$508,382,888; Dividend, 1974, BD$0·68 per share.

BANK OF N. T. BUTTERFIELD & SON, LTD., *Hamilton,* Bermuda. Established 1858. (*Representative Office,* Reliance House, 123/7 Cannon Street, E.C.4.) Capital fully paid, BD$2,400,000. Reserves and Undivided Profits 31/12/72, BD$6,331,815. Total Resources, BD$253,088,477.

BANK OF ENGLAND. *See* p. 446.

BANK OF INDIA (1906), *Bombay* (Kent House, 11-16 Telegraph Street, E.C.2).—Capital paid up, Rs. 4,05,00,000. Reserve Fund, Rs. 9,70,16,000 (860 Branches).

BANK OF IRELAND (1783), Lower Baggot Street, *Dublin* (*London Agents,* Bank of England; Lloyds Bank Ltd.; Coutts & Co.; Brown, Shipley & Co. Ltd.).—Capital (Authorized), £30,000,000; (Issued and Fully Paid), £20,446,590. Reserves, £57,992,000. Deposit, current and other accounts, £1,167,683,000. Dividend (31/3/75) 24P per £1 of Capital Stock.

BANK OF LONDON AND MONTREAL, LTD. (1958), P.O. Box N 1262, Nassau, Bahama Islands. A member of the Lloyds Bank Group. Capital (Authorized), $Bah. 30,000,000; (Paid up), $Bah. 21,450,000. (18 Branches and Agencies).

BANK OF LONDON & SOUTH AMERICA, LTD. (1862), 40-66 Queen Victoria Street, E.C.4.—*See* LLOYDS BANK INTERNATIONAL LTD.

BANK OF MONTREAL (1817), *Montreal,* Canada (47 Threadneedle St., E.C.2, and 9 Waterloo Place, S.W.1).—Capital, authorized, $100,000,000; fully paid $68,343,750. Rest, $344,000,000;

Deposits, 31/10/74, $16,088,761,601; Dividend, 1974, 96 cents per share. (Over 1,225 Branches and Agencies).

BANK OF NEW SOUTH WALES (1817) AND BANK OF NEW SOUTH WALES SAVINGS BANK LTD. (1955), Head Office, *Sydney*, N.S.W. (29 Threadneedle St., E.C.2, 9–15 Sackville Street, W.1. and 14 Kingsway, W.C.2).—At 30/9/73: Capital, authorized and pai. up, $A107,500,000; Reserve Fund, $A88,498,000; Aggregate Assets, $A6,608,464,000; Dividend, 1973, 13½ p.c. (1,289 Branches and Agencies.)

BANK OF NEW ZEALAND, Incorporated in New Zealand in 1861. (1 Queen Victoria St., E.C.4.) 31/3/74: Capital Authorized and Paid up, NZ $16,500,000; Reserves, NZ $45,970,000; Deposits, NZ $1,109,300,000; Total Assets, NZ $1,269,921,000 (422 Branches and Agencies in New Zealand; also Branches in Melbourne, Sydney, Fiji and London and Representative Offices in Tokyo and Singapore).

BANK OF NOVA SCOTIA (1832). *Halifax*, N.S.; Executive Offices, *Toronto*, Ontario, Canada (Regional Office, 19/23 Knightsbridge, S.W.1.)— Capital, Authorized, $50,000,000; Paid-up $37,000,000 ($C2 Shares); Reserve Fund, $364,692,617; Total Assets, $13,462,476,000 (at Oct. 31, 1974); (1,000 Branches and Representative Offices in 39 countries.)

BANK OF SCOTLAND (1695), The Mound, *Edinburgh*; (30 Bishopsgate, E.C.2; 16/18 Piccadilly, W.1.; 57–60 Haymarket, S.W.1; 332 Oxford Street, W.1. and 140 Kensington High Street, W.8).— Capital £32,250,000; Reserve Fund and Balance carried forward, £56,159,000. Deposits and Credit Balances, 28/2/74, £1,040,696,000. (593 Branches and Sub-Branches.)

BANK OF VALLETTA LTD. (1974), 45 Republic Street, Valletta, *Malta*. (Merger of National Bank of Malta, Ltd. (1946), Sciclunas Bank (1830) and Tagliaferro Bank Ltd. (1812)). Authorized capital, £6,000,000. Paid up £3,000,000. Branches: 27 in Malta and Gozo.

BANQUE BELGE LTD. (1934), 16 St. Helen's Place E.C.3.—Capital Authorized: £8,000,000, in Ordinary shares of £1 each, all issued, of which half are fully paid and half 50p paid.

BANQUE CANADIENNE NATIONALE, *Montreal*, Canada (Bank of Hochelaga and Banque Nationale amalgamated).—Capital (issued), $14,000,000; Reserve $88,000,000; Assets, $4,126,000,000. (480 Offices in Canada.)

BANQUE NATIONALE DE PARIS LTD. (formerly British and French Bank Ltd.), *Head Office:* (temp.) Plantation House, 10–15 Mincing Lane, E.C.3. Authorized Share Capital, £20,000,000; Issued and fully paid share capital, £5,000,000 (Subsidiary of the BANQUE NATIONALE DE PARIS.)

BARCLAYS BANK LIMITED (1896), *Head Office*, 54 Lombard St., E.C.3; *City Office*, 170 Fenchurch Street, E.C.3.—Capital Authorized, £275,000,000. Capital Issued £194,661,953; Reserves, £360,652,000; Deposits, £6,165,496,000. Dividend, 1974: Ord. Stock 12·5763 p.c., Staff stock, 20 p.c. Over 3,000 branches in England and Wales. Subsidiary Companies: BARCLAYS BANK U.K. MANAGEMENT LTD.; BARCLAYS BANK FINANCE COMPANY (JERSEY) LTD.; BARCLAYS FINANCE COMPANY (GUERNSEY) LTD.; BARCLAYS FINANCE COMPANY (ISLE OF MAN) LTD. International Division: BARCLAYS BANK INTERNATIONAL LTD.; BARCLAYS NATIONAL BANK LTD.; BARCLAYS BANK OF NIGERIA LTD.; BARCLAYS BANK OF CALIFORNIA; BARCLAYS DISCOUNT BANK LTD.; BARCLAYS BANK OF UGANDA LTD.; BARCLAYS BANK OF ZAMBIA LTD.; BARCLAYS BANK S.A.; BARCLAYS BANK OF GHANA LTD.; BARCLAYS BANK OF NEW YORK; SOCIÉTÉ BANCAIRE BARCLAYS (SUISSE) S.A.; BARCLAYS BANK OF SIERRA

LEONE LTD.; BARCLAYS BANK S.Z.A.R.L.; BARCLAYS OVERSEAS DEVELOPMENT CORPORATION LTD.; BARCLAYS NATIONAL MERCHANT BANK LTD.; BARCLAYS FINANCE CORPORATION OF JAMAICA LTD.; BARCLAYS FINANCE CORPORATION (BAHAMAS) LTD.; BARCLAYS FINANCE CORPORATION OF BARBADOS LTD.; BARCLAYS BANK OF TRINIDAD AND TOBAGO LTD.; BARCLAYS FINANCE CORPORATION OF TRINIDAD AND TOBAGO LTD.; BARCLAYS FINANCE CORPORATION (MALTA) LTD.; BARCLAYS FINANCE CORPORATION (CYPRUS) LTD.; BARCLAYS FINANCE CORPORATION OF THE LEEWARD AND WINDWARD ISLANDS LTD.; BARCLAYS FINANCE CORPORATION OF THE CAYMAN ISLANDS LTD.; INVESTMENT BANK OF MALTA LTD.; BARCLAYS INSURANCE BROKERS SOUTH AFRICA LTD.; BARCLAYS AUSTRALIA LTD.; BANCA BARCLAYS CASTELLINI S.p.A.; BARCLAYS KOL AND COMPANY N.V.; INTERCREDIT S.A. Financial Services Division; BARCLAY'S BANK OF SWAZILAND; BARCLAYS CANADA LTD.; BANCO POPULAR ANTILANO N.V.; BARCLAYS BANK (LONDON INTERNATIONAL) LTD.; BARCLAYS BANK TRUST COMPANY LTD.; BARCLAYS UNICORN LTD.; BARCLAYS UNICORN INTERNATIONAL (ISLE OF MAN) LTD.; BARCLAYS LIFE ASSURANCE COMPANY LTD.; DILLON WALKER AND COMPANY LTD.; BARCLAYTRUST CHANNEL ISLANDS LTD.; BARCLAYTRUST ISLE OF MAN LTD.; BARCLAYTRUST INTERNATIONAL LTD.; BARCLAYTRUST INTERNATIONAL (BERMUDA) LTD.; BARCLAY UNICORN INTERNATIONAL (CHANNEL ISLANDS) LTD.; BARCLAYTRUST PROPERTY MANAGEMENT LTD.; BARCLAYS EXPORT AND FINANCE COMPANY LTD.; BARCLAYS INSURANCE SERVICES COMPANY LTD. Associated Companies: BANK SCOTLAND; SOCIÉTÉ FINANCIERE EUROPÉENNE—S.F.E. LUXEMBOURG BANQUE DE LA SOCIÉTÉ FINANCIERE EUROPÉENNE; MERCANTILE CREDIT COMPANY LTD.; YORKSHIRE BANK LTD.; BANQUE DE BRUXELLES S.A.; BARIC COMPUTING SERVICES LTD.; BANCO DEL DESARROLLO ECONOMICO ESPANOL; TOZER KEMSLEY & MILLBOURN (HOLDINGS) LTD.; ANGLO-ROMANIAN BANK LTD.; INTERNATIONAL ENERGY BANK LTD.

BARCLAYS BANK INTERNATIONAL LTD, 54 Lombard St., E.C.3.—Authorized Capital, £130,000,000; Issued Capital, £130,000,000; Reserves, £139,456,000; Deposits, 31/3/75, £6,463,004,000. (1,708 Branches, Sub-Branches, and Agencies.)

BARING BROTHERS & CO., LTD. (1763), 88 Leadenhall Street, E.C.3, and Liverpool.—Capital, Authorized, issued and fully paid, £5,550,000; Reserve, £9,000,000; Deposits, 31/12/74, £213,584,678.

BRANDTS, LTD. (1805), 36 Fenchurch Street, E.C.3.— Capital Authorized, £10,000,000; Issued and Fully Paid, £7,500,000.

BRITISH BANK FOR FOREIGN TRADE, LTD. (1911), 1 Crown Court, Cheapside, E.C.2.—Subscribed Capital, £700,000; 7,000,000 Shares of 10p each fully paid.

BRITISH BANK OF COMMERCE LTD. (1936), 4 West Regent Street, Glasgow.—Capital, fully-paid, £5,559,654; Ultimate holding company—National and Grindlays Holdings Ltd.

THE BRITISH BANK OF THE MIDDLE EAST (1889), 20 Abchurch Lane, E.C.4.— Capital; authorized £15,000,000; issued and fully paid, (£1 shares): 16/12/74; Revenue Reserves, £15,528,929; Deposits, £679,033,489; Dividend, 1974, £0·24 per share.

BROWN, SHIPLEY & CO. LTD. (1810), Founders Court, Lothbury, E.C.2.—Capital, Authorized and Issued, £4,500,000; Reserves £2,907,000; Deposits, £109,159,000.

BUNGE & CO., LIMITED (1905), Bunge House, St. Mary Axe, E.C.3.—Capital subscribed and paid up £1,000,000. Reserves, £10,574,000 (1973).

CANADIAN IMPERIAL BANK OF COMMERCE (1961). *Toronto*, Ontario, Canada (2 Lombard St., E.C.3). —Capital Authorized $125,000,000 (62,500,000 shares of $2); Paid up $69,680,000. Rest Account, $415,000,000; Total Assets, 31/10/73 $16,101,666,056; Dividend 1973, 48 p.c. (Over 1,600 Branches in Canada and elsewhere.)

CATER RYDER & CO. LTD. (1960), 1 King William Street, E.C.4.—Capital authorized, £6,000,000; issued and fully paid, £5,469,000. Reserve £2,500,000. Deposits, etc., 30/4/75, £302,526,468; Dividend 1974–5, 22 p.c.

CENTRAL BANK OF INDIA (1911), *Bombay*. 31/12/74: Paid-up capital (wholly owned by Central Government of India), Rs.4,75,14,600; Reserve Fund and other reserves, Rs.10,37,91,070; Deposit and other accounts, Rs.10,26 77,46,700. (1,220 branches, etc.)

CHARTERED BANK (1853), 10 Clements Lane, E.C.4. —Capital, Authorized, £15,000,000 (divided into 15,000,000 shares of £1 each); Issued and converted into stock, £9,680,000; Reserves, £59,928,000; Deposits, 31/12/73, £1,182,220. (194 Branches.)

CHARTERHOUSE JAPHET LIMITED (1880), 1 Paternoster Row, E.C.4.—Capital, authorized and paid-up, £6,000,000.

THE CHASE MANHATTAN BANK, *N.A. New York*, *U.S.A.* (Woolgate House, Coleman Street, E.C.2, 1 Mount Street. W.1, and 29 Sloane Street, S.W.1. —Capital, $536,275,170; Surplus, $708,997,162; Undivided Profits, $384,894,497; Total Deposits $29,818,496,976. (223 Branches in New York and affiliated Branches and associated Banks in over 80 overseas countries).

CLIVE DISCOUNT COMPANY, LTD. (1946), 1 Royal Exchange Avenue, E.C.3.—Capital, Authorized, issued and fully paid, £4,100,000.

CLYDESDALE BANK, LTD (1838), St. Vincent Place, *Glasgow*. (*Edinburgh*, Chief Office, 29 George St.), Chief London Office, 30 Lombard St., E.C.3. *Affiliated to* Midland Bank, Ltd.—Authorized Capital, £10,419,000; Paid-up Capital, £6,419,000; Reserve Fund, £37,160,000; Deposits, 31/12/74, £594,203,000. (367 Branches.)

COMMERCIAL BANK OF AUSTRALIA, LTD. (1866), Collins St., *Melbourne* (12 Old Jewry, E.C.).— Paid-up Capital; $A35,895,928 ($A20 Preference, fully paid; $A1 Ordinary, fully paid); Deposits, etc., 30/6/73, $A1,359,093,000; Reserve Funds $A23,300,000. (758 Branches and Agencies.)

COMMERCIAL BANK OF THE NEAR EAST, LTD. (1922) Bankside House, 107–112 Leadenhall Street, E.C.3.—Capital, fully paid, £200,000; Reserve Fund £1,050,000. Deposits, 31/12/74, £36,064,535.

COMMERCIAL BANKING CO., OF SYDNEY, LTD. (1834), 343 George St., *Sydney*, N.S.W. (27–32 Old Jewry, E.C.2).—Authorized Capital, $A50,000,000 (Shares of $A1 each); Issued and paid-up $A32,091,806 ($A1 shares); Reserve Fund, $A28,200,000. (606 Branches in Australia.)

COMMONWEALTH SAVINGS BANK OF AUSTRALIA *Sydney*, N.S.W. (8 Old Jewry, E.C.2. and 48 Aldwych, W.C.2.) Owned and guaranteed by the Australian Government. Deposits, etc., 30/6/74, $A4,341,328,355; Reserve Fund $A53,168,016. (7,776 Branches and Agencies.)

COMMONWEALTH TRADING BANK OF AUSTRALIA (1953), *Sydney*, N.S.W. (8 Old Jewry, E.C.2;

Australia House, Strand, W.C.2).—Owned and guaranteed by the Australian Government. 30/6/74: Deposits, etc., $A3,313,631,431; Reserve Fund, $A28,934,078. (1,223 Branches and Agencies.)

CONTINENTAL ILLINOIS NATIONAL BANK AND TRUST COMPANY OF CHICAGO, *Chicago*., Ill., U.S.A. (58–60 Moorgate, E.C.2 and 47 Berkeley Square, W.1).—31/12/74. Capital Stock, $200,000,000; Surplus $485,000,000; Undivided Profits, $93,506,000; Reserves $200,781,000. (29 Branches, etc.)

CO-OPERATIVE BANK LTD. (1872), New Century House, *Manchester* (and 16 Rood Lane, E.C.3).— Capital, paid up, £8,000,000. (43 Branches.)

COPLEYS BANK, LTD. (1916), Ludgate House, 107–11 Fleet Street, E.C.4.—Capital authorized, £2,500,000; paid up, £1,000,000.

★COUTTS & CO. (1692), 440 Strand, W.C.2; Temporary Head Office during rebuilding, 1 Suffolk St., S.W.1); Strand Office (temporary 59 Strand, W.C.2); 15 Lombard St., E.C.3; 1 Old Park Lane, W.1.; 16 Cavendish Square, W.1; 1 Cadogan Place, Sloane St., S.W.1.; 10 Mount St., W.1.; 188 Fleet St., E.C.4; Royex House, Aldermanbury Square, E.C.2; and 15 High St., Eton, Windsor.—Capital issued and paid up, £1,000,000; Reserves, £10,262,000; Deposits, etc. 31/12/74, £574,317,000. (A subsidiary of National Westminster Bank, Ltd.) *Main Subsidiary*: COUTTS FINANCE CO.

CREDIT LYONNAIS (1863), 19 Boulevard des Italiens, *Paris* (40 Lombard St., E.C.3.; 18 Regent St., S.W.1; 19 Old Brompton Road, S.W.7).— Capital, Frs. 480,000,000; Reserve Fund, Frs. 641,000,000. (2,400 Branches throughout the world.)

DISCOUNT BANK (OVERSEAS) LTD., 63–66 Hatton Garden, E.C.1; 89 Duke Street, W.1.

EASTERN BANK LTD. A member of the Standard and Chartered Banking Group Ltd.

FIRST NATIONAL CITY BANK OF NEW YORK (1812), 399 Park Avenue, *New York* 10022 (Citibank House, 336 Strand, W.C.2., 34 Moorgate, E.C.2., and 17 Bruton St., Berkeley Sq., W.1). 31/12/74: Capital $638,191,000; 4 p.c. Convertible Capital; Notes $22,482,000; Deposits, $44,989,342, Surplus, Undivided Profits and unallocated Reserve for Contingencies, $1,545,604,000. (243 Branches in New York, 250 Branches in 103 countries, overseas.

FLEMING (ROBERT) & CO. LTD. (1932), 8 Crosby Square, E.C.3.

ANTHONY GIBBS HOLDINGS LTD. (1808), 23 Blomfield St., E.C.2.

GILLETT BROTHERS DISCOUNT CO., LTD. (1867), 65 Cornhill, E.C.3. Issued Capital, £2,296,066; Deposits, 1975, £153,664,927. Dividend, 1975, 6.7 p.c.

★‡GLYN, MILLS & CO. (1753), incorporating CHILD & CO. and HOLT & CO., *See* WILLIAMS AND GLYNS BANK LIMITED.

GRINDLAYS BANK LIMITED, P.O. Box 280, 23 Fenchurch Street, E.C.3.—(31/12/74) Capital authorized, £20,000,000; Issued and paid up £13,410,000 (Shares of £1 each); Advances £954,200,000; Deposits £1,514,400,000 (over 130 offices).

GUINNESS MAHON & CO. LTD. (1836), 32 St. Mary at Hill, E.C.3.

GUINNESS & MAHON LTD. (1836), 17 College Green, *Dublin* 2 (a member of the Guinness Peat Group).

HAMBROS BANK, LTD. (1839). *Head Office*, 41 Bishopsgate, E.C.2; *West End Office*, 67 Pall

Mall, S.W.1; *Holborn Office*, 1 Charterhouse St., E.C.1.—Authorized Capital, £13,000,000. Banking Group Consolidated figures: Reserve, £29,705,000; Deposits, 31/3/75, £743,141,000. Hambros Bank Ltd. is a wholly-owned subsidiary of Hambros Ltd., the dividend of which for 1974-75 was 71p on £10 shares (£2·50 paid) and 7·1p on 25p fully-paid shares; 4·2p on £1 " A " shares.

HARRODS (KNIGHTSBRIDGE) LIMITED, (1889), 87-135 Brompton Rd., S.W.1.

HELBERT, WAGG & CO., LTD. *See* J. HENRY SCHRODER WAGG & CO. LIMITED.

HILL SAMUEL GROUP LTD. (1831), 100 Wood Street, E.C.2.—(31/3/75): Capital, authorized £17,500,000; Issued, £14,633,000 (shares of 25p each); Reserves, £45,002,000; Current Deposit and other accounts, £616,323,000; Dividend, 1974-75. 3·5563p per share net.

C. HOARE & CO. (1672), 37 Fleet St., E.C.4, and Aldford House, Park Lane, W.1.—Capital and Reserve Fund, £1,000,000; Deposits, 4/4/75, £56,724,050.

HONGKONG AND SHANGHAI BANKING CORPORA-TION (1865), 1 Queen's Road Central, *Hong Kong* (9 Gracechurch St., E.C.3).—Capital, authorized, $H750,000,000; Issued and fully paid $HK694,129,945 ($HK 2·50 Shares); Reserve Funds, $HK963,457,268; Deposits, etc., 31/12/74, $HK19,933,646,323.

INTERNATIONAL WESTMINSTER BANK LTD. (as from 1/1/73). Previously Westminster Foreign Bank Ltd. (1913), 41 Lothbury, E.C.2.

IONIAN BANK, LTD. (1839), 64 Coleman Street, E.C.2.—Capital, Authorized, £2,500,000; Issued and fully paid £1,925,000; Reserve Fund, £932,443; Deposits, £14,505,656.

ISLE OF MAN BANK LTD. (1865). (A Member Bank of the National Westminster Group), *Douglas, I.O.M.* (*London Agents*, National Westminster Bank Ltd.).—Issued Capital, £2,000,000 in 2,000,000 shares of £1 each, fully paid, con-verted into stock; Reserve Fund £4,797,188; Deposits, 31/12/74, £49,641,398. (20 Branches.)

S. JAPHET & CO. LTD., *see* CHARTERHOUSE JAPHET LIMITED.

LEOPOLD JOSEPH & SONS LTD. (1919), 31 Gresham Street, E.C.2.—Capital, authorized, £5,000,000; Issued and paid up, £3,892,956.

JESSEL, TOYNBEE & CO. LTD. (1922), 30 Cornhill, E.C.3.—Capital authorized, £3,000,000; paid up, £1,625,000.

KEYSER ULLMANN LIMITED (1966). Amalgamation of Ullmann & Co. Ltd. (1932) and A. Keyser & Co. Ltd. (Estd. 1868, Inc. 1946). *Regd. Office*. 25 Milk Street, E.C.2.

KING AND SHAXSON, LTD. (1866), 52 Cornhill E.C.3. Capital authorized £3,000,000; issued and fully paid, £2,600,000; General Reserve, £1,600,000.

KLEINWORT, BENSON LIMITED (1830), 20 Fenchurch St., E.C.3. Total Assets, £1,072,325,000. De-posits, etc., £804,478,000.

LAZARD BROTHERS & CO. LTD. (1870), 21 Moor-fields, E.C.2. Capital authorized and paid up, £10,125,000.

*‡LLOYDS BANK, LIMITED (1865), *Head Office*, 71 Lombard St., E.C.3; *Branches Stock Office*, 111 Old Broad Street, E.C.2; *Overseas Department*, 6 Eastcheap, E.C.3; *Trust Division*, 34 Thread-needle Street, E.C.2. *Principal London Offices:*— City Office, 72 Lombard Street, E.C.3; 39 Threadneedle Street, E.C.2.; 6 Pall Mall, S.W.1 (Cox's & King's Branch); 16 St. James' Street, S.W.1; Law Courts, 222 Strand, W.C.2.— Capital authorized, £150,000,000; issued,

£129,766,000; Reserves, £361,723,000; Cur-rent Deposit and Other Accounts, 31/12/74: £3,982,886,000; Dividend 1974, first interim 2·95p per share, second interim 0·215p per share and final 3·7668p per share. 2,425 offices.

The LLOYDS BANK GROUP, in addition to LLOYDS BANK LIMITED, comprises LLOYDS BANK INTERNATIONAL LIMITED, LLOYDS ASSOCIATED BANKING COMPANY LIMITED, LEWIS'S BANK LIMITED, THE NATIONAL BANK OF NEW ZEALAND LIMITED, EXPORTERS' REFINANCE CORPORATION LIMITED, LLOYDS ASSOCIATED AIR LEASING LIMI-TED, LLOYDS BANK TRUST COMPANY (CHANNEL ISLANDS) LIMITED, LLOYDS BANK PROPERTY COMPANY LIMITED, LLOYDS BANK UNIT TRUST MANAGERS LIMITED, LLOYDS FIRST WESTERN CORPORATION AND LLOYDS LEASING LIMITED. LLOYDS BANK LIMITED is closely associated with NATIONAL AND COMMERCIAL BANKING GROUP LIMITED, GRINDLAYS HOLDINGS LIMITED, YORK-SHIRE BANK LIMITED, LLOYDS & SCOTTISH LIMITED, FINANCE FOR INDUSTRY LIMITED, THE JOINT CREDIT CARD COMPANY LIMITED.

LLOYDS BANK INTERNATIONAL LIMITED (1971), 40-66 Queen Victoria Street, E.C.4.—Author-ized Capital, £75,000,000; Paid-up Capital, £39,801,919. Wholly owns Bank of London & South America Limited, Lloyds Bank Inter-national (France) Limited, Bank of London & Montreal Limited, Lloyds Bank International (Belgium) S.A. and Lloyds Bank (Cannes) S.A.

MANUFACTURERS HANOVER TRUST COMPANY (1961), *New York*, U.S.A. (7 Princes Street, E.C.2 and 88 Brook Street, W.1).—Capital stock $210,000,000; Surplus $440,000,000.

MARTINS BANK LTD. (1838). Merged 15/12/69 with BARCLAYS BANK LIMITED, *q.v.*

MERCANTILE BANK LTD. (1853), 1 Queen's Road Central, *Hong Kong* (15 Gracechurch Street, E.C.3).—Issued Capital, £2,940,000 (2,940,000 Ordinary Shares, £1 each fully paid); Reserve Fund, £6,400,000; Deposits, £98,842,758. Share capital acquired in 1959 by Hongkong and Shanghai Banking Corporation.

*MIDLAND BANK, LTD. (1836), *Head Office*, Poultry, E.C.2; *Principal City Branches*, Poultry and Princes St., E.C.2; 5 Threadneedle St., E.C.2; *Overseas Branch*, 60 Gracechurch Street, E.C.3.—Auth-orized Capital, £150,000,000; Issued Capital, £132,473,941 (Shares of £1 each, fully paid); Reserve Fund, £276,877,000; Deposits, 31/12/74, £6,995,394,000; Dividend, 1974, 10·75563p per share. (Group operates through 3,635 branches and offices in British Isles and Republic of Ireland, and 149 overseas.) *Affiliations:* CLYDES-DALE BANK LTD., CLYDESDALE BANK FINANCE CORPORATION LTD., CLYDESDALE BANK INSUR-ANCE SERVICES LTD., MIDLAND BANK TRUST COMPANY LTD., MIDLAND BANK TRUST COMPANY (CHANNEL ISLANDS) LTD., MIDLAND BANK FINANCE CORPORATION LTD., FORWARD TRUST LTD., FORWARD LEASING LTD., MIDLAND BANK TRUST CORPORATION (JERSEY) LTD., MIDLAND BANK TRUST CORPORATION (GUERNSEY) LTD., MIDLAND BANK INSURANCE SERVICES LTD., NOR-THERN BANK LTD., NORTHERN BANK DEVELOP-MENT CORPORATION LTD., NORTHERN BANK FINANCE CORPORATION LTD., NORTHERN BANK EXECUTOR AND TRUSTEE COMPANY LTD., NORTHERN BANK TRUSTEE COMPANY LTD., SCOTTISH COMPUTER SERVICES LTD., MIDLAND MONTAGU LEASING LTD., GRIFFIN FACTORS LTD., SOUTHERN MARINE & AVIATION UNDERWRITERS INC., SAMUEL MONTAGU & CO. LTD. (*incorpor-ating* DRAYTON), SAMUEL MONTAGU (M.B.F.C.)

LTD., MIDLAND MONTAGU INDUSTRIAL FINANCE LTD., BLAND PAYNE (U.K.) LTD., GUYERZELLER ZURMONT BANK AG, COOK INTERNATIONAL LTD.

MIDLAND BANK TRUST CO. LTD. (1909), *Head Office*, 6 Threadneedle Street, E.C.2. *Affiliated to* Midland Bank Ltd. Subscribed Capital, £1,000,000; Paid-up Capital, £1,000,000 (200,000 shares of £5 fully paid); Reserve Fund, £1,000,000 (39 Offices).

SAMUEL MONTAGU & CO. LTD. (1853), (*incorporating* Drayton), 114 Old Broad Street, E.C.2. Capital, authorized and paid up, £40,000,000; Reserves, £12,326,000; Loan Capital, £9,224,000; Current Deposits, etc., £878,646,000 (31/12/74).

MONTREAL CITY AND DISTRICT SAVINGS BANK (1846), *Montreal*, Canada (*London Agents*, Bank of Montreal).—Capital (paid up), $2,000,000; Reserve Fund $22,500,000. (87 Branches in Montreal and District.)

MORGAN GRENFELL & CO. LIMITED (1838), 23 Great Winchester St., E.C.2.; Private limited Coy. (1934).—Authorized Capital, £10,000,000; issued and fully paid, £10,000,000.

MORGAN GUARANTY TRUST COMPANY OF NEW YORK (1959), 23 Wall Street, *New York*, U.S.A. (33 Lombard Street, E.C.3 and 31 Berkeley Sq., W.1).—Capital, $228,085,000 (9,123,400 shares —$25 par); Surplus Fund, $336,500,000.

NATIONAL AND COMMERCIAL BANKING GROUP LIMITED. Registered Office: 36 St. Andrew Square, *Edinburgh*. *London Office*, 3 Bishopsgate, E.C.2.—(30/9/74): Capital authorized. £60,000,000; issued, £57,090,000; Reserves, £161,544,000; Customers' current and deposit accounts, £2,611,972,000. Ordinary dividend; interim 0·935p per share; final 1·0732p per share. (Approximately 1,000 offices.) Owns (*inter alia*) all capital of THE ROYAL BANK OF SCOTLAND LIMITED and WILLIAMS & GLYN'S BANK LIMITED.

NATIONAL BANK OF AUSTRALASIA, LTD., THE (1858), Collins St., *Melbourne* 3001 (6–8 Tokenhouse Yard, E.C.2, Australia House, Strand, W.C.2 and 11 Albemarle Street, W.1.—Capital, paid up A$57,488,000; Reserve Fund, $A53,694,800; Deposits, 30/9/74, $A2,275,981,000. Dividend, 1974; 13·5 p.c. (939 Branches and Agencies in Australia.) The NATIONAL BANK SAVINGS BANK LIMITED (Collins Street, Melbourne) a wholly owned subsidiary of The National Bank of Australasia Limited was incorporated on May 16, 1962, with Capital, authorized, $A20,000,000; paid-up, $A8,000,000.

NATIONAL BANK OF NEW ZEALAND, LTD. (1872), 8 Moorgate, E.C.2.—Capital (Authorized, £6,000,000), Issued and fully-paid, £3,500,000; Reserve Fund, £3,840,206. (205 Branches and Agencies.)

NATIONAL DISCOUNT CO., LTD. Merged on June 16, 1970, with GERRARD & REID, LTD., under the name of GERRARD & NATIONAL DISCOUNT CO. LTD.

*NATIONAL WESTMINSTER BANK LIMITED, Head Office: 41 Lothbury, E.C.2. Est. 1968 to merge the businesses of National Provincial, Westminster and District Banks: Balance sheet at 31/12/74 showed Capital, Authorized, £265,000,000; Issued £197,364,161; Reserves, £625,183,000; Total Assets, £9,026,855,000. Deposit, Current and other accounts, £8,078,269,000. Dividend 1974, 11·96013p. (Over 3,300 branches.) Principal subsidiary companies: CENTRE-FILE LTD.; COUNTY BANK LTD.; COUTTS & CO. (*q.v.*); CREDIT FACTORING INTERNATIONAL LTD.; ISLE OF MAN BANK LTD.; LOMBARD NORTH CENTRAL LTD. and its subsidiaries; NATIONAL WESTMINSTER BANK FINANCE

(C.I.) LTD.; NATIONAL WESTMINSTER GUERNSEY TRUST CO. LTD.; NATIONAL WESTMINSTER INSURANCE SERVICES LTD.; NATIONAL WESTMINSTER JERSEY TRUST CO. LTD.; NATIONAL WESTMINSTER UNIT TRUST MANAGERS LTD.; ULSTER BANK LTD. and its subsidiaries; INTERNATIONAL WESTMINSTER BANK LTD., EUROCOM DATA (HOLDINGS) LTD., NATIONAL WESTMINSTER (HONG KONG) LTD.

NETHERLANDS BANK OF SOUTH AFRICA LIMITED, *Head Office*, Johannesburg, S. Africa (37 Lombard Street, E.C.3; 71 Haymarket, S.W.1).—Capital, issued and fully paid, R12,555,625 (shares of R1 each); Reserves, R20,038,000. Current, deposit and other accounts, 30/9/70, R484,141,000. Dividend, 1969–70, 16½ p.c.

NORTHERN BANK LTD. (1824), *Belfast* (*Affiliated with* Midland Bank Ltd.).—Capital, £6,000,000, (£1 Shares); Capital paid up, £6,000,000; Reserve Fund, £22,011,000; Deposits, 31/12/74, £312,639,000; Dividend, interim dividend of 7p per share on 16/9/74 and final dividend for the year of 7p per share on 2/4/75 (165 Branches and 97 Sub-branches).

OTTOMAN BANK (1863),Bankakar Caddesi, Karakoy, *Istanbul*, Turkey (23 Fenchurch Street, E.C.3), —Capital, £10,000,000 (£20 Shares, £10 paid), Statutory Reserve, £1,250,000.

PROVINCIAL BANK OF CANADA (1900) (BANQUE PROVINCIALE DU CANADA), 221 St. James St. *Montreal*.—Capital $11,700,000 ($2 Shares, fully paid); Reserve Fund, $45,000,000; Deposits, 30/4/74 $2,190,151,125. Regular dividend, 1973, 41·5 p.c.; Special, nil. (284 Branches and 34 Agencies.)

GERALD QUIN, COPE & CO. LTD. (1892), 52–54 Gracechurch Street, E.C.3.

RELIANCE BANK, LTD. (1900), 101 Queen Victoria St., E.C.4.—Capital, £60,000; Reserve Fund, £484,499; Deposits, 31/3/75, £6,763,244.

RESERVE BANK OF NEW ZEALAND (1934), *Wellington*, N.Z. Branches at *Christchurch* and *Auckland*, N.Z. (*London Agents*, Bank of England). Owned by the New Zealand Government.—Reserve Funds, $NZ24,048,829; Total Assets, 31/3/75, $NZ.1,099,032,243.

N. M. ROTHSCHILD & SONS LTD. (1804), New Court, St. Swithin's Lane, E.C.4.—Capital issued and paid up £10,000,000.

ROYAL BANK OF CANADA (1869), *Montreal* (6 Lothbury, E.C.2, and 2 Cockspur St., S.W.1), —Capital, $100,000,000 ($2 Shares); Paid-up: $66,528,000; Rest Account, $448,500,000; Undivided Profits, $1,758,385; Assets, $21,669,879,818; Deposits, 31/10/74, $19,441,372,513; Dividend, 1974, $1·10 per share (1,470 Branches).

ROYAL BANK OF SCOTLAND LIMITED. *Registered Office:* 42 St. Andrew Square, Edinburgh. (30/9/74).—Capital, authorized and issued, £37,500,000; Reserves, £59,396,000; Deposit and current accounts, £1,177,030,000. Approximately 590 Branches in Scotland and in London. Owns all capital of NATIONAL COMMERCIAL & GLYNS LIMITED, ROYAL BANK DEVELOPMENT LIMITED, ROYAL BANK LEASING COMPANY and LOGANAIR LIMITED. Also owns 41·1 p.c. of the capital of LLOYDS & SCOTTISH LIMITED. A member of the NATIONAL AND COMMERCIAL BANKING GROUP LTD.

DAVID SASSOON AND CO., LIMITED (1860), 57–60 Haymarket, S.W.1.—Capital authorized, £5,000,000; Paid up, £2,000,000.

J. HENRY SCHRODER WAGG & CO. LIMITED (1804), 120 Cheapside, E.C.2.—Capital, Authorized, £10,000,000; issued and paid up, £10,000,000.

SINGER AND FRIEDLANDER LTD. (1907), 20 Cannon Street, E.C.4. A member of the C. T. Bowring & Co. Ltd. Group.—Authorized Capital, £10,000,000 (Ordinary Shares of £1 each). Issued and fully paid, £7,000,000 (ordinary shares of £1 each).

SLATER, WALKER, LIMITED, 30 St. Paul's Churchyard, E.C.4. Capital Authorized, £10,000,000; issued and fully paid up, £10,000,000. Reserve, £7,873,171; Deposits, £211,013,433 (31/12/74).

SMITH ST. AUBYN & CO. LTD. (1801), White Lion Court, Cornhill, E.C.3.—Capital authorized, £2,500,000; Issued, £2,070,000; Deposits and Contingency Reserve, £7,421,604.

SOCIÉTÉ GÉNÉRALE (1864), 29 Boulevard Haussmann, *Paris* (105-108 Old Broad St., E.C.2 and 28-32 Fountain Street, Manchester).—Subscribed Capital authorized, issued and paid up, *Francs* 400,000,000. Reserve Funds, *Francs* 400,000,000. (2,400 Branches.)

STANDARD BANK, LTD., THE (1862), 10 Clements Lane, E.C.4.—Authorized Capital, £40,000,000; Issued Capital, £26,808,075; Reserves, £57,021,000. Over 1,300 offices.) A member of THE STANDARD AND CHARTERED BANKING GROUP LIMITED.

STATE BANK OF INDIA (1955), *Bombay, Calcutta, Madras, New Delhi, Ahmedabad, Hyderabad, Kanpur, Bhopal* and *Patna*. (Clements House, Gresham Street, E.C.2; 10/12 Clifford Street, W.1; King's House, The Green, Southall.)—Capital, Authorized, *Rs.* 20,00,00,000; Paid up, *Rs.* 5,62,50,000; Reserve, *Rs.* 45,82,75,052.

GEORGE STEUART & CO. LTD., *Colombo*, Sri Lanka (*London Correspondents*, Coutts & Co.).

SWISS BANK CORPORATION (1872), *Basle* (99 Gresham Street, E.C.2).—Capital and Reserves, *Swiss Francs* 1,971,381,800 (31/12/74); Dividend, 1974, 16 p.c. (156 Branches, etc.).

TORONTO-DOMINION BANK, *Toronto*, Ontario, Canada (an amalgamation (1955) of The Bank of Toronto (1856) and The Dominion Bank (1871)) (St. Helens, 1 Undershaft, E.C.3. Regional Office Europe and Africa, 62 Cornhill, E.C.3. and 103 Mount Street, W.1.)—Capital (paid-up), $36,988,002; Rest Account, $300,000,000; Un-

divided Profits, $1,901,310. (885 Branches in Canada.)

ULSTER BANK, LTD. (1836), *Head Office*, Waring St., *Belfast*. (A member of the National Westminster Group).—Capital, £3,000,000 (£1 Shares); Issued and fully paid, £2,250,000; Reserve Fund, £13,624,000; Share Premium Account, £250,000; Deposits, 31/12/74, £369,720,000; Dividend, 1974, 14 p.c. (140 Offices and 98 Sub-Offices.)

UNION BANK OF INDIA LTD. (1919), 66–80 Bombay Sanachar Marg, *Bombay* 400 023. Acquired July 18, 1969 by the Government of India. Capital: paid-up. *Rs.* 12,500,000; Deposits, 31/12/74 *Rs.* 3,962,502,000. (644 branches.)

UNION DISCOUNT COMPANY OF LONDON, LTD. (1885), 78/80 Cornhill, E.C.3.—Capital Issued, £7,500,000 in units of £1 each fully paid; Reserves and carry forward, £4,509,666; Deposits, provisions and other liabilities £646,475,236; Dividend, 1974, 16·08 p.c.

UNITED COMMERCIAL BANK, 10 Brabourne Road, *Calcutta* (wholly owned by the Govt. of India). —Capital, paid-up *Rs.* 2,80,00,000 Reserves *Rs.* 6,00,00,000. (739 Branches.)

WALLACE BROTHERS BANK LTD. (1963); 4 Crosby Square, E.C.3. Issued Capital, £9,000,000. Combines the businesses of Wallace Bros. & Co. Ltd. (1837) and E. D. Sassoon Banking Co. Ltd. (1930).

WARBURG (S. G.) & CO. LTD. (Incorporating Seligman Brothers), 30 Gresham Street, E.C.2. —Capital, authorized, £20,000,000; issued and paid-up, £18,255,000.

★WILLIAMS & GLYNS BANK, LTD., *Registered Office*, 20 Birchin Lane, E.C.3. Established to merge the businesses of WILLIAMS DEACON'S, GLYN, MILLS and NATIONAL BANKS. Capital authorized and issued, £33,750,000; Reserves, £64,156,000; Deposit and current accounts, £1,464,000,000. (320 branches in England and Wales.)

YORKSHIRE BANK LIMITED (1911), 2 Infirmary Street, *Leeds* (56–58 Cheapside, E.C.2). Capital, £12 000,000 (Capital, paid up £12,000,000, £1 Shares fully paid); Reserves, £20,988,638; Deposits, 31/12/74, £266,509,340, (180 branches.)

PREMIUM SAVINGS BONDS

One of the most popular forms of saving in the United Kingdom is through Premium Savings Bonds. These bonds are a United Kingdom Government security and were first introduced on November 1, 1956. Instead of earning interest, however, each bond offers to its holder the chance of winning a money prize in a prize draw. Bonds are issued in values ranging from £2 to £500 and each £1 buys one bond unit, which has one chance in the prize draw.

Prizes are paid from a fund formed by the interest, at present 5½ per cent. *per annum*, on each bond eligible for the draw. A bond becomes eligible for the draw three clear calendar months following the month of purchase and goes into every subsequent draw whether or not it has won a prize until the end of the month in which it is repaid. Bonds belonging to a deceased bondholder will remain eligible for all Prize Draws held

in the month of death and in the following 12 calendar months, provided they have not been repaid earlier. They will then become ineligible for all further draws. These terms also apply to bonds purchased before August 1, 1960 (Series "A"). Prizes range in value from £5,000 to £25, a single prize of £75,000 and a second prize of £25,000 each month, one of £50,000 and 25 of £1,000 each week, the winning numbers being selected by the electronic random number indicator equipment—usually called "ERNIE". Winning numbers are printed monthly in the *London Gazette*.

It is estimated that by the end of June, 1975, bonds to the value of £1,871,889,693 had been sold. Of these £793,881,786 had been cashed, leaving £1,078,007,907 still invested. After the draws in July, 1975, 11,989,008 prizes, totalling £470,923,900 had been distributed since the inception of the Premium Savings Bond Scheme.

NATIONAL SAVINGS CERTIFICATES

The amount, including accrued interest, remaining to the credit of investors in National Savings Certificates on March 31, 1975, was approximately £2,534,082,000. In 1974–75, £311,658,206 was subscribed and £353,226,467 (excluding interest) was repaid.
Note.—Certificates of the current Fourteenth Issue may be purchased in denominations of 1, 2, 3, 4, 5, 10, 20, 50, 100, 200 and 500 units.

Issue and Maximum Holding	Unit Cost s. d.	Value After Years	Value After £ p	Interest Per Unit
1st (1916–22)........	15 6	}52	}3·40	After 52 years, $\frac{5}{12}$p per completed month★.
2nd (1922–23)........	16 0			
3rd (1923–32) and Conversion (1932)	16 0	43	2·70	After 43 years, $\frac{5}{12}$p per completed month★.
4th (1932–33)........	16 0	42	2·36$\frac{5}{8}$	After 42 years, 1$\frac{A}{4}$p per completed 3 months★.
5th (1933–35)........	16 0	40	2·24$\frac{1}{2}$	After 40 years, 1$\frac{A}{4}$p per completed 3 months★.
6th (1935–39)........	15 0	36	2·05	After 36 years, 1$\frac{1}{4}$p per completed 3 months★.
7th (1939–47)........ (Maximum holding, 1st–7th Combined, 500 units)	15 0	27	1·62$\frac{1}{2}$	After 27 years, 1$\frac{1}{2}$p per completed 3 months plus 2$\frac{1}{2}$p bonus at end of 29th year.
		29	1·75	During 30th year, 2$\frac{A}{8}$p per completed 4 months.
		30	1·81$\frac{1}{2}$	After 30 years, 2$\frac{1}{2}$p per completed 4 months plus bonus of 1$\frac{1}{2}$p at end of 35th year.
		35	2·20	During 36th year, 4p per completed 4 months.
		38	2·65	During 37th year, 5p per completed 4 months. During 38th year, 6p per completed 4 months†.
£1 (1943–47)......... (250)	£1	28	1·57$\frac{1}{2}$	After 28 years, 1$\frac{1}{2}$p per completed 4 months plus 5p bonus at end of 29th year; 2$\frac{1}{2}$p per completed 4 months in 30th year.
		30	1·73	After 30 years, 2$\frac{1}{2}$p per completed 4 months plus 4$\frac{1}{2}$p bonus at end of 33rd year.
		33	2·00	After 33 years, 4$\frac{1}{2}$p per completed 4 months plus a bonus of 1p at end of 35th year†.
		35	2·28	
8th (1947–51)........ (1,000)	10 0	24	1·02$\frac{1}{2}$	During 25th year, 1$\frac{3}{8}$p per completed 4 months.
		25	1·07$\frac{1}{2}$	After 25th year, 1$\frac{1}{2}$p per completed 4 months plus 4$\frac{1}{2}$p bonus at end of 29th year.
		29	1·30	During 30th year, 2$\frac{1}{2}$p per completed 4 months.
		31	1·48	During 31st year, 3$\frac{1}{2}$p per completed 4 months†.
9th (1951–56)........ (1,400)	15 0	19	1·40	After 19th year, 1$\frac{5}{8}$p per completed 4 months plus 2$\frac{1}{2}$p bonus at end of 22nd year.
		22	1·57$\frac{1}{2}$	After 22nd year, 2p per completed 4 months plus 4$\frac{1}{2}$p bonus at end of 25th year.
		25	1·80	After 25th year, 4p per completed 4 months plus 1p bonus at end of 27th year.
		27	2·05	
10th (1956–63)....... (1,200)	15 0	12	1·18$\frac{3}{4}$	After 12 years, 1$\frac{1}{2}$p per completed 4 months plus 2$\frac{1}{2}$p bonus at end of 15th year.
		15	1·32$\frac{1}{2}$	During 16th year, 1$\frac{3}{8}$p per completed 4 months.
		16	1·37$\frac{1}{2}$	After 16th year, 2p per completed 4 months plus a 4$\frac{1}{2}$p bonus at end of 19th year.
		19	1·60	During 20th year, 3$\frac{1}{2}$p per completed 4 months.
		21	1·83	During 21st year 4p per completed 4 months plus $\frac{1}{2}$p bonus at year-end†.
11th (1963–66)....... (600)	£1	9	1·40	After 9 years, 1$\frac{5}{8}$p per completed 4 months plus 5p bonus at end of 12th year.
		12	1·60	During 13th year, 3$\frac{1}{2}$p per completed 4 months.
		14	1·83	During 14th year 4p per completed 4 months plus $\frac{1}{2}$p bonus at year-end†.
12th (1966–70)....... (1,500)	£1	5	1·25	After 5 years, 1$\frac{1}{2}$p per completed 4 months plus 7p bonus at end of 9th year.
		9	1·50	During 10th year, 3p per completed 4 months.
		11	1·71	During 11th year 4p per completed 4 months†.
Decimal (1970–74).... (1,500)	£1	4	1·25	After 1 year, 3p is added; during 2nd year, 1$\frac{1}{2}$p per completed 4 months; during 3rd year, 2$\frac{1}{2}$p per completed 4 months; during 4th, year 3p per completed 4 months plus 1p bonus at year-end.
		6	1·43	During 5th year, 2$\frac{1}{2}$p per completed 4 months; during 6th year 3$\frac{1}{2}$p per completed 4 months†.
Fourteenth (1974–)... (1,000)	£1	4	1·34	After 1 year, 6p is added; during 2nd year, 2$\frac{1}{2}$p per completed 4 months; during 3rd year, 3p per completed 4 months; during 4th year, 3$\frac{1}{2}$p per completed 4 months plus 1p bonus at year-end†.

May be held from date of issue: ★ until further notice; † as announced by the Treasury.

In June, 1975, the Government introduced Index-linked National Savings Certificates costing £10 each. They are available only to men aged 65 and over and women of 60 and over, up to a maximum of £500 per person. These certificates have a life of five years and, if held to maturity, will attract a tax-free bonus of 4 per cent. of the purchase price in addition to any increase due to the upward movement of the Retail Price Index. If the certificate is encashed before maturity but after one year, repayment will include any increase due to movement in the RPI, but no bonus will be payable.

BRITISH SAVINGS BONDS

9½% British Savings Bonds (1st Issue) are a guaranteed state security. They cost £5 each and may be held up to a maximum of £10,000. Bonds acquired by inheritance do not count towards this limit. They may be held by individuals solely or jointly; by trustees; by charitable, friendly and provident societies; by clubs and funds; by corporate bodies generally. Interest is earned at the rate of 9½% a year, provided they are held for a minimum period of 6 months. The interest which is payable half yearly is taxable but tax is not deducted at source. The value of British Savings Bonds remains constant and they may be encashed at par on one month's notice. They will be redeemable at the rate of £103 for £100 of Bonds on the next interest date after 5 years have passed from the purchase date. The £3 capital bonus is exempt from United Kingdom Tax. British Savings Bonds may be bought at any Post Office transacting Savings Bank business, Trustee Savings and other Banks.

GOVERNMENT STOCKS AND BONDS

Government Stocks and Bonds on the National Savings Stock Register can be bought and sold at low rates of commission through the Department for National Savings, Bonds and Stock Office, Lytham St. Annes, Lancashire, or a Trustee Savings Bank. Prices are those current on the Stock Exchange at the time of the transaction. Application forms and information leaflets with a list of the Stocks and Bonds are available at Post Offices transacting Savings Bank business and at Trustee Savings Banks. The amount standing to the credit of holders in the Department for National Savings section of the National Savings Stock Register as at March 31, 1975 was £856,134,000.

SAVE AS YOU EARN

The " Save As You Earn " Service was brought into operation on October 1, 1969. A Second Issue was introduced on July 1, 1974, and a Third Issue (" Index-linked ") was brought in on July 1, 1975. Any individual aged 16 or over may participate by making regular monthly payments with a minimum of £4 and a maximum of £20.

Savings may be contributed by deductions from pay, by standing order on a bank or National Giro or by cash payments at most post offices. At the end of five years, the repayment value will be the total contributions plus any increase due to the monthly linking of contributions to the Retail Price Index. Completed savings which are not withdrawn will qualify for further index-linking and a bonus equal to two monthly contributions at the end of seven years.

Indexation applies only to completed savings contracts. Savers who wish to stop payments will be able to withdraw the total sum saved, but there cannot be partial withdrawals. Tax-free compound interest will be paid at the rate of 6 per cent. per annum on amounts withdrawn after the first but before the end of the fifth year, or where the contributions cease but the savings are left invested for the remainder of the five years.

By the end of June, 1975, 296,785 live SAYE contracts remained registered with the Department for National Savings, with a total monthly commitment to save of £2,303,102. The total payments received since October 1, 1969, amounted to £129,363,822.

SAVINGS BANKS

National Savings Bank.—On December 31, 1974, there were approximately 21,000,000 active accounts with the sum of £1,515,178,438 due to depositors in Ordinary accounts and £572,225,083 in Investment accounts. Interest on National Savings Bank Ordinary deposits is allowed at 4 per cent. per annum. A higher rate of interest is paid on deposits in National Savings Bank Investment accounts (the current rate can be ascertained at any Savings Bank Post Office). A depositor may have more than one account in either series. The total balance in the Ordinary account is subject to a limit of £10,000 with certain exceptions; there is no upper limit on the balance that may be held in an Investment account.

On December 31, 1974, the average amount held in Ordinary accounts was £72·66; in Investment accounts, approximately £694.

Trustee Savings Banks were started in the early years of the 19th century by public-spirited men who recognized the importance of individual thrift to the well-being of the community.

On Nov. 20, 1974, there were 14,058,134 active accounts in the Trustee Savings Banks. The total assets of the Banks amounted to £4,037,983,476 which comprised £3 517,791,122 due to depositors in the Ordinary, Current and Special Investment Departments, £374,667,255 Stocks and Bonds held for depositors, £72,177,217 in respect of Save As You Earn contributions and £73,347,877 representing the accumulated surplus of the individual Trustee Savings Banks throughout the country. Information about these banks and their offices, can be obtained from the *Trustee Savings Banks Association Ltd.*, P.O. Box 99, 3 Gracechurch Street, E.C.3. *Chairman*, Sir Athelstan Caröe, C.B.E. *Chief General Manager*, T. Bryans, M.B.E.

Law Courts and Offices

LAW SITTINGS (1976)—*Hilary*, Jan. 12 to April 14; *Easter*, April 27 to May 28; *Trinity*, June 8 to July 31
Michaelmas, Oct. 1 to Dec. 21.

THE JUDICIAL COMMITTEE

The Judicial Committee of the Privy Council consists of the Lord Chancellor, Lord President, ex-Lords President, the Lords of Appeal in Ordinary (*see* below) and such other members of the Privy Council as shall from time to time hold or have held " high judicial office." Among the last are included Viscount Radcliffe, Lord MacDermott, Lord Tucker, Lord Morris of Borth-y-Gest, Lord Hodson, Lord Guest, Lord Pearce, Lord Devlin, Lord Gardiner, Lord Pearson, Lord Hailsham of St. Marylebone, and certain judges from the Commonwealth.

Office—Downing Street, S.W.1.
Registrar of the Privy Council, E. R. Mills.
Chief Clerk (Judicial), J. K. Dixon.

THE HOUSE OF LORDS

The Supreme Judicial Authority for Great Britain and Northern Ireland is the House of Lords, which is the ultimate Court of Appeal from all the Courts in Great Britain and Northern Ireland (except criminal courts in Scotland).

The Lord High Chancellor—
The Rt. Hon. the Lord Elwyn-Jones (*born* 1909, *apptd.* 1974), (£17,500 as Judge and £2,500 as Speaker of the House of Lords) £20,000.

Lords of Appeal in Ordinary (each £21,175)

	Apptd.
Rt. Hon. Lord Wilberforce, C.M.G., O.B.E., *born* 1907	1964
Rt. Hon. Lord Diplock, *born* 1907	1968
Rt. Hon. Viscount Dilhorne, *born* 1905	1969
Rt. Hon. Lord Simon of Glaisdale, *born* 1911	1971
Rt. Hon. Lord Kilbrandon, *born* 1906	1971
Rt. Hon. Lord Salmon, *born* 1903	1972
Rt. Hon. Lord Edmund-Davies, *born* 1906	1974
Rt. Hon. Lord Fraser of Tullybelton, *born* 1911	1975
Rt. Hon. Lord Russell of Killowen, *born* 1908	1975

Registrar: The Clerk of the Parliaments, Sir Peter Henderson, K.C.B.

SUPREME COURT OF JUDICATURE
COURT OF APPEAL

Ex officio Judges.—The Lord High Chancellor, the Lord Chief Justice of England, the Master of the Rolls, and the President of the Family Division.

The Master of the Rolls (£21,175)
The Rt. Hon. Lord Denning (*born* 1899, *apptd.* 1962).
Secretary, Miss P. B. Bergin; *Clerk,* R. S. Chesney, B.E.M.

Lords Justices of Appeal (each £19,425)

	Apptd.
Rt. Hon. Sir John Megaw, C.B.E., T.D., *born* 1909	1969
Rt. Hon. Sir Denys Burton Buckley, M.B.E., *born* 1906	1970
Rt. Hon. Sir David Arnold Scott Cairns, *born* 1902	1970
Rt. Hon. Sir (Edward) Blanshard Stamp, *born* 1905	1971
Rt. Hon. Sir John Frederick Eustace Stephenson, *born* 1910	1971
Rt. Hon. Sir Alan Stewart Orr, O.B.E., *born* 1911	1971

Rt. Hon. Sir Eustace Wentworth Roskill, *born* 1911	1971
Rt. Hon. Sir Frederick Horace Lawton, *born* 1911	1972
Rt. Hon. Sir Leslie George Scarman, O.B.E., *born* 1911	1973
Rt. Hon. Sir Arthur Evan James, *born* 1916	1973
Rt. Hon. Sir Roger Fray Greenwood Ormrod, *born* 1911	1974
Rt. Hon. Sir Patrick Reginald Evelyn Browne, O.B.E., T.D., *born* 1907	1974
Rt. Hon. Sir Geoffrey Dawson Lane, A.F.C., *born* 1918	1974
Rt. Hon. Sir Reginald William Goff, *born* 1907	1975
Rt. Hon. Sir Nigel Cyprian Bridge, *born* 1917	1975
Rt. Hon. Sir Sebag Shaw, *born* 1906	1975

HIGH COURT OF JUSTICE
Chancery Division
President, The Lord High Chancellor

Judges (each £18,675)

	Apptd.
Hon. Sir (John) Anthony Plowman, *born* 1905 (*Vice-Chancellor*)	1961
Hon. Sir Robert Edgar Megarry, *born* 1910	1967
Hon. Sir (John) Patrick Graham, *born* 1906	1969
Hon. Sir Peter Harry Batson Woodroffe Foster, M.B.E., T.D., *born* 1912	1969
Hon. Sir John Norman Keates Whitford, *born* 1913	1970
Hon. Sir John Anson Brightman, *born* 1911	1970
Hon. Sir (Ernest) Irvine Goulding, *born* 1910	1971
Hon. Sir Sydney William Templeman, M.B.E., *born* 1920	1972
Hon. Sir Raymond Henry Walton, *born* 1915	1973
Hon. Sir Peter Raymond Oliver, *born* 1921	1974
Hon. Sir Michael John Fox, *born* 1921	1975

Queen's Bench Division
The Lord Chief Justice of England (£19,100)
The Rt. Hon. The LORD WIDGERY, O.B.E., T.D. (*born* 1911, *apptd.* 1971)
Secretary, S. E. S. Bollon; *Clerk,* A. E. Shelton.

Judges (each £18,675)

	Apptd.
Rt. Hon. Sir (Aubrey) Melford (Steed) Stevenson, *born* 1902	1957
Hon. Sir Gerald Alfred Thesiger, M.B.E., *born* 1902	1958
Hon. Sir Basil Edward Nield, C.B.E., *born* 1903	1960
Hon. Sir Bernard Joseph Maxwell MacKenna, *born*, 1905	1961
Hon. Sir Alan Abraham Mocatta, O.B.E., *born* 1907	1961
Hon. Sir John Thompson, *born* 1907	1961
Hon. Sir Helenus Patrick Joseph Milmo, *born* 1908	1964
Hon. Sir Joseph Donaldson Cantley, O.B.E., *born* 1910	1965
Hon. Sir George Stanley Waller, O.B.E., *born* 1911	1965
Hon. Sir Hugh Eames Park, *born* 1910	1965
Hon. Sir Ralph Vincent Cusack, *born* 1916	1966
Hon. Sir Stephen Chapman, *born* 1907	1966
Hon. Sir John Ramsay Willis, *born* 1908	1966
Hon. Sir Graham Russell Swanwick, M.B.E., *born* 1906	1966

Hon. Sir Patrick MacCarthy O'Connor, *born 1914*............................ 1966
Hon. Sir John Francis Donaldson, *born 1920* 1966
Hon. Sir (John) Robertson (Dunn) Crichton, *born 1912*............................ 1967
Hon. Sir Samuel Burgess Ridgway Cooke, *born 1912*............................ 1967
Hon. Sir Bernard Caulfield, *born 1914*..... 1968
Hon. Sir Hilary Gwynne Talbot, *born 1912* 1968
Hon. Sir Edward Walter Eveleigh, E.R.D., *born 1917*............................ 1968
Hon. Sir William Lloyd Mars-Jones, M.B.E., *born 1915*............................ 1969
Hon. Sir Ralph Kilner Brown, O.B.E., T.D., *born 1909*............................ 1970
Hon. Sir Phillip Wien, *born 1913*.......... 1970
Hon. Sir Peter Henry Rowley Bristow, *born 1913*............................ 1970
Hon. Sir Hugh Harry Valentine Forbes, *born 1917*............................ 1970
Hon. Sir Desmond James Conrad Ackner, *born 1920*............................ 1971
Hon. Sir William Hugh Griffiths, M.C., *born 1923*............................ 1971
Hon. Sir Robert Hugh Mais, *born 1907*.... 1971
Hon. Sir Neil Lawson, *born 1908*.......... 1971
Hon. Sir David Powell Croom-Johnson, D.S.C., V.R.D., *born 1914*............ 1971
Hon. Sir Tasker Watkins, V.C., *born 1918* 1971
Hon. Sir (John) Raymond Phillips, M.C., *born 1915*............................ 1971
Hon. Sir Leslie Kenneth Edward Boreham, *born 1918*............................ 1972
Hon. Sir John Douglas May, *born 1923*.... 1972
Hon. Sir Michael Robert Emanuel Kerr, *born 1921*............................ 1972
Hon. Sir (Alfred William) Michael Davies, *born 1921*............................ 1973
Hon. Sir John Dexter Stocker, M.C., T.D., *born 1918*............................ 1973
Hon. Sir Kenneth George Illtyd Jones, *born 1921*............................ 1974
Hon. Sir Peter Richard Pain, *born 1913*.... 1975
Hon. Sir Kenneth Graham Jupp, M.C. *born 1917*............................ 1975

Court of Appeal (Criminal Division)
Judges, The Lord Chief Justice of England, The Master of the Rolls, Lord Justices of Appeal and all the Judges of the Queen's Bench Division.

Family Division
President (£20,175)
Rt. Hon. Sir George Gillespie Baker, O.B.E. (*born* 1910, *apptd.* 1971).
Sec., Mrs. H. M. Keegan; *Clerk*, B. H. Erhard.
Judges (each £18,675)— Apptd.
Hon. Sir Charles William Stanley Rees, T.D., *born 1907*............................ 1962
Hon. Sir Reginald Withers Payne, *born 1904* 1962
Hon. Sir Neville Major Ginner Faulks, M.B.E., T.D., *born 1908*...................... 1963
Hon Sir (James) Roualeyn Hovell-Thurlow-Cumming-Bruce, *born 1912*............ 1964
Hon. Sir John Brinsmead Latey, M.B.E., *born 1914*............................ 1965
Hon. Dame Elizabeth Kathleen Lane, D.B.E., *born 1905*............................ 1965
Hon. Sir Henry Vivian Brandon, M.C., *born 1920*............................ 1966
Hon. Sir Robin Horace Walford Dunn, M.C., *born 1918*...................... 1969
Hon. Sir William Arthur Bagnall, M.B.E., *born 1917*............................ 1970

Hon. Sir (Alfred) Kenneth Hollings, M.C., *born 1918*............................ 1971
Hon. Sir John Lewis Arnold, *born 1915*.... 1972
Hon. Sir (Charles) Trevor Reeve, *born 1915*. 1973
Hon. Sir Francis Brooks Purchas, *born 1919*. 1974
Hon. Sir Haydn Tudor Evans, *born 1920*... 1974
Hon. Dame Rose Heilbron, D.B.E., *born 1914* 1974
Hon. Sir Stephen Brown, *born 1924*....... 1975

Judge Advocate of the Fleet, W. M. Howard, Q.C.
Queen's Proctor, Sir Henry Ware, K.C.B.

LORD CHANCELLOR'S OFFICE
House of Lords, S.W.1
[01-219-3000]
Permanent Secretary and Clerk of the Crown, Sir Denis Dobson, K.C.B., O.B.E., Q.C............£18,675
Private Secretary to the Lord Chancellor, J. A. C. Watherston................£6,625 to £8,750
Private Secretary to Permanent Secretary, Miss D. Dalgliesh, M.B.E.............£3,900 to £4,700
Deputy Secretaries, H. Boggis-Rolfe, C.B., C.B.E.; J. W. Bourne, C.B....................£14,000
Secretary of Commissions, Sir Thomas Skyrme, K.C.V.O., C.B., C.B.E., T.D..............£12,000
Under Secretaries, K. M. H. Newman; R. H. Widdows...........................£12,000
Deputy Secretary of Commissions, Sir Bryan Roberts, K.C.M.G.................£9,033 to £11,000
Assistant Solicitors, R. C. L. Gregory, C.B.E.; A. D. M. Oulton; D. S. Gordon; J. L. Heritage; T. S. Legg.....................£9,033 to £11,000
Senior Legal Assistants, M. C. Blair; W. H. Elliot; M. D. Huebner.............£6,625 to £8,750
Legal Assistants, Mrs. V. C. Bell; Miss M. McLellan; P. M. Harris.............£3,424 to £6,125
Assistant Secretaries of Commissions, D. J. Williams; E. R. Horsman, O.B.E.; R. F. N. Anderson, O.B.E., M.C.................£5,680 to £7,450
Secretary for Ecclesiastical Patronage, C. V. Peterson.
Assistant Secretary for Ecclesiastical Patronage, Col. W. A. Salmon, O.B.E........£5,259 to £6,793
Crown Office
Clerk of the Crown, Sir Denis Dobson, K.C.B., O.B.E., Q.C.
Deputy Clerk of the Crown, H. Boggis-Rolfe, C.B., C.B.E.
Clerk of the Chamber, Miss D. M. P. Malley, M.B.E.....................£4,900 to £5,900

Court Business Branch
67 Tufton Street, S.W.1
[01-212 7676]
Assistant Solicitor, A. M. F. Webb, C.M.G. £9,033 to £11,000
Senior Legal Assistants, D. R. Wells; W. B. Scott, C.B.E.; D. H. O. Owen......£6,625 to £8,750

Establishments and Finance Division
Romney House, Marsham Street, S.W.1
[01-212 7676]
Principal Establishment Officer, J. A. Bergin £12,000
Assistant Secretaries, Miss J. M. Brewster; D. B. Frudd; J. A. C. Kelsey; M. D. Hobkirk £8,650 to £11,000

SUPREME COURT OFFICES, ETC.
Conveyancing Counsel of the Supreme Court
V. G. H. Hallett; J. Monckton; P. W. E. Taylor.

Examiners of the Court
(Empowered to take Examination of Witnesses in all Divisions of the High Court)
M. F. Meredith-Hardy; M. E. M. Brooke; R. Walker; K. S. Lewis; M. R. M. Nunns.

Official Referees of the Supreme Court
His Honour Norman Grantham Lewis Richards, O.B.E., Q.C.; His Honour William Walter Stabb, Q.C.; His Honour Edgar Stuart Fay, Q.C.

Official Solicitor's Department
48–49 Chancery Lane, W.C.2
Official Solicitor to the Supreme Court, N. H. Turner
£12,000
Asst. Do., T. W. Swift ...... £9,033 to £11,000
Assistant Solicitor, R. S. Dhondy
£9,033 to £11,000
Senior Legal Assts., H. D. S. Venables; D. C. Relf; W. H. McBryde; H. J. Baker £6,625 to £8,750
Legal Assistant, Mrs. C. L. Hastings
£3,424 to £6,125
Chief Clerk, J. A. P. Morris ..... £5,680 to £7,450
Principal Clerks, B. C. Harris; R. F. Dunn; J. A. Dawson .... £5,680 to £7,450

Supreme Court Pay Office
Royal Courts of Justice, W.C.2
Accountant General, Sir Denis Dobson, K.C.B., O.B.E., Q.C.
Chief Accountant, F. W. Hathaway
£5,680 to £7,450
Senior Executive Officers, W. P. Coult; E. D. Fagg; T. C. Weidner; B. Williams .. £4,900 to £5,900

Central Office of the Supreme Court
Royal Courts of Justice, W.C.2
Senior Master of the Supreme Court (Q.B.D.), and Queen's Remembrancer, I. H. Jacob £12,500
Masters of the Supreme Court (Q.B.D.), I. H. Jacob; J. Ritchie, M.B.E.; J. B. Elton; J. R. Bickford-Smith; S. J. Waldman; I. S. Warren; C. W. S. Lubbock; P. B. Creightmore £11,000
Chief Clerk (Central Office), J. F. Mason
£5,680 to £7,450
Chief Clerk to the Q.B. Judges in Chambers, N. Sims
£5,680 to £7,450

Action Department*
Head Clerk, F. Simpson .... £5,348 to £5,900
Filing Department*
Head Clerk, W. N. Last .... £5,348 to £5,900
Masters' Secretary's Department and Queen's Remembrancer's Department*
Chief Clerk (Secretary to the Masters), F. Simmons
£5,348 to £5,900
Crown Office and Associates' Dept.
Head Clerk (Crown Office), F. Hearn
£5,348 to £5,900
Chief Associate, B. M. Spicer .... £5,348 to £5,900
Criminal Appeals Office
(Royal Courts of Justice, W.C.2)
Registrar, D. R. Thompson, C.B. £12,500
Assistant Registrars, W. H. Greenwood; M. W. Palmer; P. J. Morrish .... £6,625 to £8,750
Deputy Assistant Registrars, P. C. Kratz; E. G. Blandford, C.B.E.; G. Hoffman
£6,625 to £8,750
Senior Legal Assistants, Mrs. B. M. Hindley; E. M. Kotwal; C. Jones .... £6,625 to £8,750
Head Clerk, A. F. P. Ottway .... £5,348 to £5,900
Courts-Martial Appeals Office
(Royal Courts of Justice, W.C.2)
Registrar, D. R. Thompson £12,500
Assistant Registrar, W. H. Greenwood
£3,659 to £5,754
* Office hours, 10 to 4.30; (1 Aug. to 31 Aug., 10 to 2.30.) Saturdays, closed.

Supreme Court Taxing Office
Chief Master, Graham John Graham-Green, T.D.
£12,500
Masters of the Supreme Court, Leonard Humphrey Razzall; Edwin James Thomas Matthews, T.D.; Frederic Thomas Horne; Michael Arthur Clews; Frederic George Berkeley; A. J. Wright; Charles Roger Nicholas Martyn £11,000

Chief Clerk, D. Hutchings ...... £5,680 to £7,450
Principal Clerks, A. G. Warren; G. H. R. Scales; J. Price; R. W. E. Ranger; E. M. Guest; C. R. Blinks; G. P. Tandy; D. C. Dennis; A. J. Burroughs; P. J. Moran .... £5,348 to £5,900

CHANCERY DIVISION
Chancery Judges' Chambers
Royal Courts of Justice, W.C.2
Chief Master (attached to all the Judges), Robert Edward Ball, M.B.E. £12,500
Chief Clerk, C. L. R. Dalley .... £5,680 to £7,450
GROUP A
At Chambers.—*Masters of the Supreme Court, A to F.* Marshal Butler Cholmondeley Clarke; *G to N,* Robert Edward Ball, M.B.E.; *O to Z,* Edmund Rawlings Heward £11,000
GROUP B
At Chambers.—*Masters of the Supreme Court, A to F,* Peter Athol Taylor; *G to N,* John Michael Dyson; *O to Z,* Richard Chamberlain, T.D. £11,000
Principal Clerks, C. A. C. Partridge; D. F. J. Emery; W. E. Loveday; D. F. James; A. T. D. Higgs; A. T. Cole; K. A. B. Nias; P. J. Angel
£5,348 to £5,900

Chancery Registrars' Office
Royal Courts of Justice, W.C.2
Chief Registrar, C. M. Kidd £11,000
Registrars, P. Halliday; H. J. Wilson; D. G. Leach; M. S. Edwards; H. W. Nichols; A. W. Hancock
£9,744
Senior Assistant Registrars, R. S. Stevens; R. F. Russell; D. G. Pullen; J. T. Glover
£6,140 to £8,110
Assistant Registrars, W. R. Heeler; C. I. R. Williams .... £3,659 to £5,754
Chief Clerk and Secretary to Chief Registrar, C. L. R. Dalley.

Companies Court
Thomas More Building,
Royal Courts of Justice, W.C.2
Judges, The Hon. Mr. Justice Oliver; The Hon. Mr. Justice Megarry; The Hon. Mr. Justice Brightman; The Hon. Mr. Justice Templeman.
Registrar, G. F. Deerbergh
Principal, A. A. Clipstone ...... £5,680 to £7,450
Senior Executive Officer, H. H. Stringer
£5,348 to £5,900
Senior Official Receiver, Companies Department, J. B. Clemetson.

Bankruptcy (High Court) Department
Thomas More Building, Royal
Courts of Justice, Strand, W.C.2.
Judges, The Hon. Mr. Justice Goff; The Hon. Mr. Justice Foster; The Hon. Mr. Justice Goulding; The Hon. Mr. Justice Walton.
Chief Registrar, G. M. Parbury £12,500
Registrar, R. H. Hunt £11,000
Official Receivers' Department
Senior Official Receiver, J. B. Clemetson.
Official Receivers, I. Tye; D. A. Thorne.
Assistant do., R. B. Wood; A. B. Ford; C. G. Churcher; T. J. White; K. V. Whiting; A. D. Davenport.

FAMILY DIVISION
PRINCIPAL REGISTRY
Somerset House, W.C.2
Senior Registrar, D. A. Newton £12,500
Registrars, R. L. Bayne-Powell; W. D. S. Caird; D. R. L. Holloway; L. I. Stranger-Jones; C. Kenworthy; B. Garland; Mrs. A. E. O. Butler-Sloss; B. P. Tickle; C. F. Turner; T. G. Guest; D. H. Colgate £11,000

Secretary, W. J. Pickering, I.S.O.; £5,680 to £7,450
Establishment Officer, Miss J. J. Learmonth
£5,680 to £7,450
Clerk of the Rules and Orders (Royal Courts of Justice), W. G. Mason . . . . . . £5,680 to £7,450
Principal, B. W. Campbell . . . . . . £5,680 to £7,450
Senior Executive Officers, Miss K. W. Simes; R. S. G. Norman; Miss I. L. Murray; Mrs. P. M. Fern; Mrs. I. L. L. Brooker; L. T. Hyder; G. A. Wood; W. I. Martyn; G. A. Goodwin; E. W. Morris; R. Conn . . . . £4,900 to £5,900

DISTRICT PROBATE REGISTRIES
Birmingham, F. R. E. Jones.
Brighton and Maidstone, E. E. Hosking.
Bristol, Exeter and Bodmin, T. B. Williams.
Ipswich, Norwich and Peterborough, R. C. Robinson.
Leeds, Hull and York, H. Wilkinson.
Liverpool and Lancaster, G. Wentworth.
Llandaff, Bangor and Carmathen, A. Crawshaw.
Manchester, G. A. Terian.
Newcastle, Carlisle and Middlesbrough, J. D. Drayson.
Nottingham, Leicester and Lincoln, C. S. Fisher.
Oxford and Gloucester, Miss M. L. Farmborough.
Sheffield, Chester and Stoke on Trent, H. W. Jackson.
Winchester, F. G. Diddams.

Admiralty Registry and Marshal's Office
Royal Courts of Justice, W.C.2
Registrar, J. D. H. Rochford £11,000
Marshal and Chief Clerk, P. V. Gray
£5,680 to £7,450

COURT OF PROTECTION
25 Store Street, W.C.1
Master, J. A. Armstrong, O.B.E., T.D.
Chief Clerk, G. R. Isard.

OFFICE OF THE LORD CHANCELLOR'S VISITORS
Staffordshire House, Store Street, W.C.1
Legal Visitor, I. G. H. Campbell, T.D., Q.C. . £11,250
Medical Visitors, A. B. Monro, M.D., Ph.D., F.R.C.P.; M. Cuthbert; J. Harper £11,250

RESTRICTIVE PRACTICES COURT
Royal Courts of Justice, W.C.2
Judicial Members, Mr. Justice Mocatta (President); Mr. Justice Cumming-Bruce; Mr. Justice Bagnall; Mr. Justice Gibson; Lord Kissen.
Lay Members, P. A. Delafield; A. I. Mackenzie; N. C. Pearson, O.B.E., T.D.; W. R. Booth; N. L. Salmon; P. G. Walker.
Clerk of the Court, Mr. Registrar Dearbergh.

LAW COMMISSION
England and Wales
Conquest House, 37–38 John Street,
Theobalds Road, W.C.1
Set up on June 16, 1965, under the Law Commissions Act, 1965, to make proposals to the Government for the examination of the Law and for its revision where it is unsuited for modern requirements, obscure, or otherwise unsatisfactory. It recommends to the Lord Chancellor programmes for the examination of different branches of the law and suggests whether the examination should be carried out by the Commission itself or by some other body. The Commission is also responsible for the preparation of Consolidation and Statute Law Revision Bills.
Chairman, The Hon. Mr. Justice Cooke.
Members, A. L. Diamond; S. B. Edell; W. D. T. Hodgson, Q.C.; N. S. Marsh, Q.C.
Secretary, J. M. Cartwright Sharp.

CIRCUIT JUDGES
(each £13,000)

Midland and Oxford Circuit
W. A. L. Allardice; B. D. Bush; R. M. A. Chetwynd-Talbot; W. N. Davison; A. R. M. Ellis; C. H. Gage; H. J. Garrard; G. Green; M. K. Harrison-Hall; T. R. Heald; C. G. Heron; R. H. Hutchinson; J. E. M. Irvine; J. G. Jones; J. T. C. Lee; E. Daly Lewis; D. T. Lloyd; J. R. Macgregor; G. K. Mynett, Q.C.; P. C. Northcote; J. Perrett; J. Ross, Q.C.; W. A. Sime, M.B.E., Q.C.; H. A. Skinner, Q.C.; G. F. I. Sunderland; R. J. Toyn; W. R. Wickham; J. Brooke Willis.

Northern Circuit
J. L. Addleshaw; D. P. Bailey; R. M. Bingham, T.D., Q.C.; A. J. Blackett-Ord (Vice Chancellor, County Palatine of Lancaster); J. Booth; R. J. H. Collinson; T. A. Cunliffe; P. Curtis; J. W. Da Cunha; J. M. Davies, Q.C.; K. W. Dewhurst; A. A. Edmondson; D. G. F. Franks; B. H. Gerrard; F. P. R. Hinchliffe, Q.C.; W. H. W. Jalland; J. E. Jones; P. C. S. Kershaw; K. K. F. Lawton; R. R. Leech; R. Lyons, Q.C. (Recorder of Liverpool); Sir William Morris (Recorder of Manchester); F. J. Nance; W. H. Openshaw; F. D. Paterson; T. H. Pigot, Q.C.; A. M. Prestt, Q.C.; J. W. Stansfield; E. Steel; R. Wood; J. Zigmond.

North Eastern Circuit
H. C. Beaumont, M.B.E.; H. G. Bennett, Q.C.; C. D. Chapman, Q.C.; Myrella Cohen, Q.C.; J. A. Cotton; C. R. Dean, Q.C.; D. S. Forrester-Paton, Q.C.; S. S. Gill; M. Gosnay; H. G. Hall; G. H. Hartley; V. R. Hurwitz; J. R. Johnson; G. Milner; T. R. Nevin, T.D.; H. S. Pears; P. Stanley Price, Q.C.; J. H. E. Randolph; H. C. Scott, Q.C.; A. G. Sharp, M.B.E., Q.C.; R. P. Smith, Q.C.; L. B. Stephen; H. G. Suddards; J. D. Walker; L. Wilkes.

South Eastern Circuit
J. S. R. Abdela, T.D., Q.C.; M. J. Anwyl-Davies, Q.C.; M. V. Argyle, M.C., Q.C.; A. P. Babington; J. A. Baker; R. A. Barr; R. I. S. Bax, Q.C.; E. G. H. Beresford; P. M. Blomefield; J. Bolland; B. R. Braithwaite; H. T. Buckee, D.S.O.; J. H. Buzzard; C. V. Callman; F. H. Cassels, T.D.; B. R. Clapham; E. Clarke, Q.C.; R. G. Clover, T.D., Q.C.; J. F. Coplestone-Boughey; P. J. Corcoran; M. E. F. Corley; P. H. Counsell; P. V. Crocker; C. J. Cunliffe; N. H. Curtis-Raleigh; T. Dewar; R. G. Dow; The Lord Dunboyne; C. H. Duveen, M.B.E., Q.C.; T. K. Edie; H. Elam; J. H. Ellison, V.R.D.; R. M. H. Everett, Q.C.; E. S. Fay, Q.C.; I. B. Fife, M.C., T.D.; A. L. Figgis; I. Finestein, Q.C.; B. Finlay, Q.C.; R.H. Forrest, Q.C.; R. G. Freeman; A. G. Friend; E. B. Gibbens, Q.C.; F. E. H. G. Gibbens; B. J. Gillis, Q.C.; J. H. Gower, Q.C.; D. A. Grant, D.S.O., Q.C.; H. B. Grant; S. H. Granville-Smith, O.B.E.; P. B. Greenwood; J. A. Grieves, Q.C.; J. M. G. Griffith-Jones, M.C. (Common Serjeant); Jean Graham Hall; R. E. Hammerton; A. H. Head; M. R. Hickman; D. E. Hill-Smith, V.R.D.; V. G. Hines, Q.C.; J. B. Hobson; A. E. Holdsworth, Q.C.; F. Honig; W. H. Hughes; T. C. Humphreys, Q.C.; A. D. Karmel, Q.C.; W. Kee; M. A. B. King-Hamilton, Q.C.; J. F. Kingham; C. Lawson, Q.C.; P. H. Layton; C. G. Lea, M.C.; J. C. B. W. Leonard; N. Lermon, Q.C.; G. F. Leslie; B. Lewis; P. E. Lewis; A. C. L. Lewisohn; A. Lipfriend; J. C. Llewellyn; I. B. Lloyd, Q.C.; A. Lonsdale; G. D. Lovegrove, Q.C.; R. D. Lymbery, Q.C.; D. L. McDonnell, O.B.E.; F. D. L. McIntyre, Q.C.; N. N. McKinnon, Q.C.; O. S. Macleay; J. L. E. MacManus, T.D., Q.C.; M. J. P. Macnair; J. F. Marnan, M.B.E., Q.C.; G. F. P. Mason, Q.C.; J. H. E. Mendl; J. W. Miskin, Q.C. (Recorder of London); E. F. Monier-Williams; G.

R. F. Morris, Q.C.; S. A. Morton, T.D.; J. D. F. Moylan; J. I. Murchie; S. H. Noakes; Suzanne F. Norwood; C. R. Oddie; S. O. Olson; R. B. C. Parnall; D. E. Peck; J. C. Perks, M.C., T.D.; F. H. L. Petre; A. J. Phelan; J. R. Pickering; D. C. L. Potter; R. D. Ranking; R. G. Rees; E. B. B. Richards; G. N. L. Richards, O.B.E., Q.C.; H. S. L. Rigg, Q.C.; Deborah M. Rowland; K. W. Rubin; H. S. J. Ruttle; J. H. A. Scarlett; N. W. M. Sellers, V.R.D.; G. G. Slack; E. D. Smith; M. B. Smith; A. P. Solomon; W. W. Stabb, Q.C.; D. J. Stinson; E. Stockdale; F. A. Stockdale; J. S. Streeter; J. H. A. Stucley, D.S.C.; W. D. M. Sumner, O.B.E., Q.C.; E.D. Sutcliffe, Q.C.; D. A. Thomas, M.B.E.; A. S. Trapnell; L. J. Verney, T.D.; R. W. Vick; D. E. Waddilove, M.B.E.; B. J. Wakley, M.B.E.; M. E. Ward; D. S. West-Russell; F. J. White; D. H. Wild; J. E. Williams; R. B. Willis, T.D.; W. G. Wingate, Q.C.; B. S. Wingate-Saul; E. E. Youds.

Wales and Chester Circuit

J. G. Burrell, Q.C.; R. R. D. G. David, Q.C.; D. Meurig Evans; W. N. Francis; B. F. Griffiths, Q.C.; Rowe Harding; P. Hopkin Morgan, Q.C.; J. D. Seys Llewellyn; D. T. Lloyd-Jones, V.R.D.; D. Morgan-Hughes; C. N. Pitchford; D. W. Powell; J. C. Rutter; E. P. Wallis-Jones.

Western Circuit

G. B. Best; N. J. L. Brodrick, Q.C.; A. C. Bulger; R. C. Chope; P. H. F. Clarke; T. Elder-Jones; G. A. Forrest; A. C. Goodall, M.C.; I. S. Hill, Q.C.; W. H. E. James; M. G. King; C. M. Lavington, M.B.E.; A. M. Lee, D.S.C., Q.C.; Sir Ian Lewis; H. E. L. McCreery, Q.C.; G. G. Macdonald; E. B. McLellan; D. E. T. Pennant; M. G. Polson, Q.C.; H. S. Russell; J. G. K. Sheldon; K. C. L. Smithies; R. Stock, Q.C.; D. H. W. Vowden, Q.C.; K. M. Willcock, Q.C.

CENTRAL CRIMINAL COURT
Old Bailey, E.C.4

Judges,

The Lord Mayor,	Judges of the High Court,
The Aldermen of the City	The Recorder of London, The Common Serjeant of London.

Additional Judges of the Central Criminal Court appointed under the City of London (Courts) Act 1964, Circuit Judges, Recorders, Magistrates in the case of Appeals and Committals for sentence.

Courts Administrator, Leslie Balfour Boyd.

Secondary and Under-Sheriff, Ralph Mordaunt Snagge, M.B.E., T.D., 78 Cranmer Court, S.W.3.

COURTS SERVICE

First-tier centres deal with both civil and criminal cases and are served by High Court and Circuit Judges. Second-tier centres deal with criminal cases only but are served by both High Court and Circuit Judges. Third-tier centres deal with criminal cases only and are served only by Circuit Judges.

Midland and Oxford Circuit

First-tier—Birmingham, Lincoln, Nottingham, Stafford, Warwick. Second-tier—Leicester, Northampton, Oxford, Shrewsbury, Worcester. Third-tier—Coventry, Derby, Dudley, Grimsby, Hereford, Huntingdon, Stoke-on-Trent, Walsall, Warley, West Bromwich, Wolverhampton.

Circuit Administrator, C. W. Pratley, 2 Newton Street, Birmingham £12,000

Deputy Circuit Administrator, T. A. F. Lawler.

Courts Administrators, Birmingham Group, F. Cox; Northampton Group, C. A. Green; Nottingham Group, B. G. R. Barrett; Stafford Group, F. H. Yendle.

North Eastern Circuit

First-tier—Leeds, Newcastle upon Tyne, Sheffield, Teesside. Second-tier—York. Third-tier Beverley, Bradford, Doncaster, Durham, Huddersfield, Kingston-upon-Hull, Wakefield.

Circuit Administrator, T. A. Whittington, National Westminster House, 4th Floor, 29 Bond Street, Leeds..............................£12,000

Deputy Circuit Administrator, B. Cooke.

Courts Administrators, Leeds Group, H. L. Flower; Newcastle upon Tyne Group, M. McKenzie; Sheffield Group, C. A. White.

Northern Circuit

First-tier—Carlisle, Liverpool, Manchester (Courts of Justice), Preston. Third-tier—Barrow-in-Furness, Birkenhead, Burnley, Kendal, Lancaster, Manchester (Minshull Street).

Circuit Administrator, C. R. Seaton, Aldine House, West Riverside, New Bailey Street, Salford.
£12,000

Deputy Circuit Administrator, E. T. Connolly.

Courts Administrators, Manchester Group, C. W. Wood; Liverpool Group, Miss M. L. Williams; Preston Group, G. Davies.

South Eastern Circuit

First-tier—London, Norwich. Second-tier—Chelmsford, Ipswich, Lewes, London, Central Criminal Court (q.v.), Maidstone, Reading, St. Albans. Third-tier—Aylesbury, Bedford, Brighton, Bury St. Edmunds, Cambridge, Canterbury, Chichester, Gravesend, Guildford, King's Lynn, Kingston-on-Thames, Southend, Croydon, Surbiton.

Middlesex Guildhall, S.W.1. *Administrator,* F. H. B. Clough; Newington Causeway, S.E.1. *Administrator,* R. Grobler; Snaresbrook, The Courthouse, Hollybush Hill, Snaresbrook, E.11. *Administrator,* L. Eley.

Circuit Administrator, P. D. Robinson, Thanet House, 231/2 Strand, W.C.2..........£13,230

Deputy Circuit Administrator, G. M. O. Briegel.

Courts Administrators, Chelmsford Group, K. A. Henderson; Maidstone Group, J. E. Greenwood; Norwich Group, F. G. Fuller; Kingston Group, A. G. Keats.

Wales and Chester Circuit

First-tier—Caernarvon, Cardiff, Chester, Mold, Swansea. Second-tier—Carmarthen, Newport, Welshpool. Third-tier—Dolgellau, Haverfordwest, Knutsford, Merthyr Tydfil.

Circuit Administrator, A. Howe, Churchill House, Churchill Way, Cardiff £12,000

Deputy Circuit Administrator, L. R. Beckett.

Courts Administrators, Cardiff Group, L. A. Gay; Chester Group, S. W. L. James; Swansea Group, E. H. Thomas.

Western Circuit

First-tier—Bodmin, Bristol, Exeter, Winchester. Second-tier—Dorchester, Gloucester, Plymouth. Third-tier—Barnstaple, Bournemouth/Poole, Devizes, Newport (I.O.W.), Portsmouth, Salisbury, Southampton, Swindon, Taunton.

Circuit Administrator, I. E. Ashworth, Bridge House, Clifton, Bristol......................£12,000

Deputy Circuit Administrator, B. H. Sayer.

Courts Administrators, Bristol Group, T. A. F. Lawler; Exeter Group, R. A. J. Barker; Winchester Group, J. K. W. Phipps.

RECORDERS

J. D. Alliott, Q.C.; B. J. Appleby, Q.C.; H. W. J. ap Robert; J. F. A. Archer, Q.C.; J. R. Arthur, D.F.C.; P. Ashworth, Q.C.; T. G. F. Atkinson; P. Back, Q.C.; G. Baker, Q.C.; J. B. Baker, Q.C.; P. M. Baker, Q.C.; D. A. Barker, Q.C.; D. Barker; J. M. A. Barker; F. W. I. Barnes; A. R. Barrowclough, Q.C.; P. M. Beard; C. O. M. Bedingfield, T.D.; A. R. A. Beldam, Q.C.; A. W. Bell; P. Bennett, Q.C.; R. H. Bernstein, D.F.C., Q.C.; G. J. Black, D.S.O., D.F.C.; I. J. Black, Q.C.; N. R. Blaker, Q.C.; F. A. Blennerhassett, Q.C.; J. F. Blythe, T.D.; A. S. Booth, Q.C.; J. N. W. Bridges-Adams; D. D. Brown; J. W. A. Butler-Sloss; N. M. Butter; A. C. Caffin; D. C. Calcutt, Q.C.; K. B. Campbell, Q.C.; G. A. Carman, Q.C.; B. R. O. Carter; Sir Harold Cassel, Bt., Q.C.; B. H. Cato; P. Chadd, Q.C.; M. L. M. Chavasse, Q.C.; B. W. Chedlow, Q.C.; F. L. Clark, Q.C.; J. D. Clarke; D. J. Clarkson, Q.C.; C. M. Clothier, Q.C.; J. F. S. Cobb, Q.C.; J. N. Coffey; G. J. K. Coles; Patricia Coles, Q.C.; J. M. Collins, Q.C.; J. P. Comyn, Q.C.; R. K. Cooke, O.B.E.; A. G. W. Coulthard; D. M. Cowley, Q.C.; A. E. Cox; B. R. E. Cox, Q.C.; J. A. Cox; P. J. Cox, D.S.C., Q.C.; J. Crabtree; P. J. Crawford; C. J. Crespi; M. A. L. Cripps, C.B.E., D.S.O., T.D., Q.C.; G. H. Crispin, Q.C.; F. P. Crowder, Q.C., M.P.; R. H. Curtis; G. W. Davey; I. T. R. Davidson; A. T. Davies, Q.C.; L. J. Davies Q.C.; W. L. M. Davies, Q.C.; C. F. Dehn, Q.C.; W. E. Denny, Q.C.; A. C. H. de Piro, Q.C.; T. M. Dillon, Q.C.; J. M. Dodson; F. M. Drake, D.F.C., Q.C.; D. P. Draycott, Q.C.; G. A. Draycott; J. M. Drinkwater, Q.C.; B. R. Duckworth; M. Dyer.

T. M. Eastham, Q.C.; J. B. S. Edwards; Q. T. Edwards, Q.C.; A. H. M. Evans, Q.C.; J. F. Evans, Q.C.; J. K. Q. Evans; T. M. Evans, Q.C.; P. Fallon, Q.C.; D. H. Farquharson, Q.C.; B. A. Farrer; P. R. Faulks, M.C.; M. H. Feeny; J. D. A. Fennell, Q.C.; D. B. B. Fenwick; T. G. Field-Fisher, T.D., Q.C.; W. A. B. Forbes, Q.C.; W. G. Fordham, Q.C.; J. R. B. Fox-Andrews, Q.C.; C. J. S. French, Q.C.; R. H. K. Frisby, Q.C.; B. J. F. Galpin; E. L. Gardner, Q.C., M.P.; P. N. Garland, Q.C.; L. Gassman; M. Gibbon, Q.C.; R. B. Gibson, Q.C.; R. L. A. Goff, Q.C.; P. W. Goldstone; R. N. Gooderson; K. F. Goodfellow, Q.C.; M. B. Goodman; J. K. Gore; J. P. Gorman, Q.C.; H. G. A. Gosling; G. Gray, Q.C.; R. I. Gray, Q.C.; W. P. Grieve, Q.C., M.P.; I. O. Griffiths, Q.C.; J. C. Griffiths, Q.C.; L. Griffiths; H. Hague; J. A. S. Hall, D.F.C., Q.C.; Sir Lincoln Hallinan; A. W. Hamilton, Q.C.; G. M. Hamilton, T.D.; R. G. Hamilton; J. A. T. Hanlon; R. J. Hardy; Rosina S. A. Hare; R. D. Harman, Q.C.; J. P. Harris, D.S.C., Q.C.; R. J. S. Harvey, Q.C.; C. L. Hawser, Q.C.; J. B. R. Hazan, Q.C.; D. Herrod, Q.C.; H. Hewitt; B. J. Higgs, Q.C.; W. D. T. Hodgson, Q.C.; D. A. Hollis, V.R.D., Q.C.; H. E. Hooson, Q.C., M.P.; A. C. W. Hordern; R. Houlker, Q.C.; W. M. Howard, Q.C.; D. W. Howells; J. Hugill; G. W. Humphries; A. E. Hutchinson; J. N. Hutchinson, Q.C.; G. B. Hutton; B. A. Hytner, Q.C.; C. F. Ingle; J. H. Inskip, Q.C.; N. F. Irvine, Q.C.; F. C. Irwin, Q.C.; R. Ives; I. H. M. Jones, Q.C.; T. G. Jones; E. F. Jowitt, Q.C.; D. Karmel, C.B.E., Q.C.; D. N. Keating, Q.C.; T. O. Kellock, Q.C.; R. D. L. Kelly, M.C.; M. E. I. Kempster, Q.C.; I. A. Kennedy, Q.C.; P. J. M. Kennedy, Q.C.; H. A. Kershaw; R. I. Kidwell, Q.C.

H. L. Lachs; G. F. B. Laughland; E. H. Laughton-Scott, Q.C.; A. C. Lauriston, Q.C.; R. B. Lauriston; L. D. Lawton, Q.C.; C. N. Lees; A. P. Leggatt, Q.C.; H. J. Leonard, Q.C.; J. G. Le Quesne, Q.C.; J. M. Lever; E. ap G. Lewis, Q.C.; Gwynedd M. Lewis; T. E. I. Lewis-Bowen; A. L. J. Lincoln, Q.C.; F. A. Lincoln, Q.C.; V. J. Lissack; I. P. Llewellyn-Jones;

J. Lloyd-Eley, Q.C.; J. H. Lord; R. J. Lowry, Q.C.; E. Lyons, Q.C., M.P.; A. J. D. McCowan, Q.C.; I. C. R. McCullough, Q.C.; A. C. Macdonald; G. A. Mac-Donald; D. B. McNeill, Q.C.; W. A. MacPherson, T.D., Q.C.; J. R. Main, Q.C.; J. G. Marriage, Q.C.; M. J. W. Marsh, M.C., T.D.; O. S. Martin, Q.C.; P. W. Medd, O.B.E., Q.C.; K. S. W. Mellor, Q.C.; A. L. Mildon, Q.C.; Sir Joseph Molony, K.C.V.O., Q.C.; D. G. Morgan; W. G. O. Morgan, Q.C., M.P.; M. Morland, Q.C.; A. J. H. Morrison; J. B. Mortimer, Q.C.; H. C. Muscroft; M. J. Mustill, Q.C.; A. L. Myerson, Q.C.; A. S. Myerson, Q.C.; B. T. Neill, Q.C.; J. H. R. Newey, Q.C.; R. M. H. Noble; E. M. Ogden, Q.C.; H. H. Ognall, Q.C.; B. R. Oliver; D. A. Orde; P. H. Otton, Q.C.; J. A. D. Owen, Q.C.; P. L. W. Owen, T.D., Q.C.; Helen Paling; R. H. S. Palmer; M. C. Parker, Q.C.; T. I. Payne; The Hon. R. B. H. Pearce, Q.C.; I. Percival, Q.C., M.P.; R. A. Percy; A. Phillips, O.B.E.; D. A. Phillips; J. Pickles; O. B. Popplewell, Q.C.; F. M. Potter; F. H. Potts, Q.C.; H. C. Pownall; M. J. Pratt; A. J. Price; E. J. Prosser.

A. Rankin, Q.C.; A. D. Rawley; L. F. Read, Q.C.; H. C. Rigby, D.F.C.; H. E. P. Roberts, Q.C.; J. H. Robson; J. W. Rogers, Q.C.; R. G. Rougier, Q.C.; T. P. Russell, Q.C.; P. J. M. Ryan; C. Salmon, Q.C.; D. M. Savill, Q.C.; B. C. Sheen, Q.C.; M. D. Sherrard, Q.C.; L. S. Shields, Q.C.; G. J. Shindler, Q.C.; J. K. E. Slack, T.D.; P. M. J. Slot; G. Slynn, Q.C.; F. B. Smedley; D. A. L. Smout, Q.C.; Jean Southworth, Q.C.; J. A. C. Spokes, Q.C.; R. O. C. Stable, Q.C.; S. A. Stamler, Q.C.; C. S. T. J. T. Staughton, Q.C.; J. Stephenson; N. F. Stogdon; R. A. R. Stroyan, Q.C.; M. Stuart-Smith, Q.C.; C. S. Stuart-White; J. G. St. G. Syms, Q.C.; H. C. Tayler; I. R. Taylor, Q.C.; J. B. Taylor, M.B.E., T.D.; K. J. Taylor; P. M. Taylor, Q.C.; E. S. Temple, M.B.E., Q.C.; K. J. Tetley; D. O. Thomas, Q.C.; Rt. Hon. P. J. M. Thomas, Q.C., M.P.; S. B. Thomas, Q.C.; R. N. Titheridge, Q.C.; H. J. M. Tucker, Q.C.; R. H. Tucker, Q.C.; M. J. Turner, Q.C.; A. R. Tyrrell; M. T. B. Underhill, Q.C.; A. R. Vandermeer; A. O. R. Vick; D. C. Waddington, Q.C.; D. St. J. R. Wagstaff; A. F. Waley, V.R.D., Q.C.; M. Walker; P. H. C. Walker; B. Walsh; M. B. Ward; R. L. Ward, Q.C.; J. R. Warde; R. G. Waterhouse, Q.C.; V. B. Watts; C. D. G. P. Waud; I. S. Webster; P. A. Webster; P. E. Webster, Q.C.; P. Weitzman, Q.C.; W. T. Wells, Q.C.; C. H. Whitby, Q.C.; G. G. A. Whitehead, D.F.C.; F. Whitworth, Q.C.; The Lord Wigoder, Q.C.; G. W. Willett; D. B. Williams, T.D., Q.C.; H. G. Williams;. W. T. Williams, Q.C., M.P.; J. G. Wilmers, Q.C.; H. Wilson; J. Woodcock, T.D.; H. K. Woolf; N. G. Wootton; G. N. Worthington; J. M. Wright, Q.C.; O. Wrightson; R. Wyeth; R. M. Yorke, Q.C.

METROPOLITAN STIPENDIARY MAGISTRATES

Bow Street, Covent Garden, W.C.2

Chief Metropolitan Stipendiary Magistrate, Kenneth James Priestley Barraclough, C.B.E., T.D.

£13,000

Magistrates, Evelyn Charles Sackville Russell; William Edward Charles Robins; Christopher John Bourke.................(each) £11,750
Chief Clerks, R. Hines; Mrs. J. M. Ferley..£8,970 to £9,735 or £10,005

Camberwell Green, D'Eynsford Road, S.E.5

Magistrates, Maurice Juniper Guymer; Edgar Leonard Bradley; Ralph Hamilton Lownie (*one vacancy*).................(each) £11,750
Senior Chief Clerk, I. Fowler............£10,005
Chief Clerk, W. Johnston......£8,970 to £9,735

Clerkenwell, Kings Cross Road, W.C.1

Magistrates, John Dennis Purcell; Mark Romer
(one vacancy)....................(each) £11,750
Senior Chief Clerk, D. V. Wainwright.... £10,005
Chief Clerk, J. Patron......... £8,970 to £9,735
    Greenwich, Blackheath Road, S.E.10
Magistrates, David Prys Jones; John William
Cheeseman....................(each) £11,750
Senior Chief Clerk, G. Crankshaw....... £10,005
    Woolwich, Market Street, S.E.18
Magistrates (as Greenwich).
Chief Clerk, G. Edwards....... £8,970 to £9,735

    Highbury Corner, Holloway Road, N.7
Magistrates, Tobias Springer; Ian Graeme McLean;
David Armand Hopkin.........(each) £11,750
Senior Chief Clerk, A. L. Gooch......... £10,005
Chief Clerk, P. W. Johnson..... £8,970 to £9,735
    Horseferry Road, Horseferry Road, S.W.1
Magistrates, Kenneth Douglas Evelyn Herbert
Harington; David Fairbairn; Roderick Jessel
Romain....................(each) £11,750
Senior Chief Clerk, P. J. Calnan......... £10,005
Chief Clerk, R. Harbord....... £8,970 to £9,735
Chief Clerk (Licensing), L. G. Bowerman
                £8,970 to £9,735
    Marlborough Street,
    Great Marlborough Street, W.1
Magistrates, St. John Bernard Vyvyan Harmsworth,
Neil Martin McElligott.........(each) £11,750
Chief Clerk, E. L. Yabsley...... £8,970 to £9,735
    Marylebone, 181 Marylebone Road, N.W.1
Magistrates, Rupert Rawden Smith; Edmond
Geoffrey MacDermott; Peter Walter Goldstone;
Ronald Knox Mawer.........(each) £11,750
Senior Chief Clerk, C. A. Reston........ £10,005
    Old Street, E.C.1
Magistrates, Kenneth John Heastey Nichols; James
Hobson Jobling..............(each) £11,750
Chief Clerk, K. Anderson.... £8,970 to £9,735
    South Western, Lavender Hill, S.W.11
Magistrates, Donaldson Loudoun; Charles Richard
Beddington; Albert William Clark
               (each) £11,750
Senior Chief Clerk, C. E. Hollingdale..... £10,005
Chief Clerk, J. S. Pulford....... £8,970 to £9,735
    Thames, Aylward Street, E.1
Magistrates, Peter Duncan Fanner; Ronald David
Bartle..........................(each) £11,750
Senior Chief Clerk, J. A. Bradbury....... £10,005
Chief Clerk, J. D. Heywood.... £8,970 to £9,735
    Tower Bridge, Tooley Street, S.E.1
Magistrates, Nigel Francis Maltby Robinson;
Richard Kenneth Cooke, O.B.E....(each) £11,750
Chief Clerk, J. P. S. Walker.... £8,970 to £9,735
    Wells Street, 59/65 Wells Street, W.1
Magistrates, Christopher Besley; Edward James
Branson; Mrs. Audrey Mary Frisby; Geoffrey
Lindsay James Noel.............(each) £11,750
Senior Chief Clerk, G. D. Shaw.......... £9,227
Chief Clerk, Miss I. Snatt................ £8,920
    West London, Southcombe Street, W.14
Magistrates, Mrs. Nina Lowry; Eric Crowther
               (each) £11,750
Senior Chief Clerk, K. Edwards.......... £10,005

Unattached Magistrates, Peter Gilmour Noto Badge;
Brian John Canham............(each) £11,750

*Principal Chief Clerk & Clerk to the Committee of
Magistrates* (office: 3rd Floor, North West Wing,
Bush House, Aldwych, W.C.2), A. V. E. J.
Mindham........................£11,472
Chief Clerk (Training), S. G. Clixby......£10,059
    Juvenile Courts, 185 Marylebone Road, N.W.1
Senior Chief Clerk, Miss P. M. Austin.... £10,197
Chief Clerk, J. J. Senior........ £8,920 to £9,927

STIPENDIARY MAGISTRATES

Birmingham, John Frederick Milward (1951).
Cardiff, Hywel Wyn Jones ap Robert (1972).
Kingston upon Hull, Ian Robertson Boyd (1972).
Leeds, Francis David Lindley Loy (1972).
Liverpool, Leslie Mervyn Pugh (1965).
Manchester, John Bamber (1965).
Merthyr Tydfil, David Powys Rowland (1961).
Mid Glamorgan, David Alan Phillips.
Salford, (vacant).
South Yorkshire, John Alfred Henham (1975).
Wolverhampton, Howard William Maitland Coley
(1961).

CITY OF LONDON JUSTICE ROOMS
MANSION HOUSE JUSTICE ROOM.
Chief Magistrate, The Lord Mayor.
Chief Clerk, J. H. Tratt....................£8,412
Deputy Chief Clerk, C. F. Grimwood.....£6,309
GUILDHALL JUSTICE ROOM
Chief Clerk, A. G. J. Chandler, O.B.E......£8,412
Deputy Chief Clerk, F. A. Treeby.........£6,309

DIRECTOR OF PUBLIC PROSECUTIONS
12 Buckingham Gate, S.W.1
Director, Sir Norman Skelhorn, K.B.E., Q.C.
Deputy Director, M. J. Jardine.
Assistant Directors, J. M. Evelyn; P. R. Barnes.
Assistant Solicitors, O. Nugent, C.B.; P. M. J.
Palmes; J. Wood; A. G. Flavell; J. E. Leck; T. J.
Taylor; K. Dowling; J. M. Walker.

OFFICE OF THE JUDGE ADVOCATE
GENERAL OF THE FORCES
*(Lord Chancellors Establishment; Joint Service for the
Army and the Royal Air Force)*
6 Spring Gardens, Cockspur Street, S.W.1
Judge Advocate General, F. H. Dean....£14,000
Vice Judge Advocate General, J. G. Morgan-Owen,
M.B.E.....................................£12,160
Assistant Judge Advocates General, B. R. Allen;
J. Stuart-Smith; G. Ll. Chapman; C. G. Gould;
J. E. Pullinger; G. E. Empson; G. R. Canner;
F. L. Daly................. £9,943 to £11,410
Deputy Judge Advocates, E. G. Moelwyn-Hughes;
A. P. Pitts; S. B. Spence..... £7,035 to £9,160

METROPOLITAN POLICE OFFICE
New Scotland Yard, Broadway, S.W.1
[01-230 1212]
Commissioner, Sir Robert Mark, Q.P.M....£18,675
Deputy Commissioner, C. P. J. Woods, C.B.E.
                £14,646
Receiver, R. J. Guppy, C.B............£13,420
"A" Department
Administration and Operations
Assistant Commissioner, R. J. Mastel, C.B.E. £13,290
Deputy Assistant Commissioners, W. H. Gibson;
J. Kelland, Q.P.M...........£9,777 to £10,884
Principal, W. T. Davis .... £5,680 to £7,450
Commanders, W. W. R. Fleming; L. Garrett, Q.P.M.;
K. G. Hannam; P. Marshall; E. T. Matthews;
R. C. Steventon............£8,733 to £9,165
Senior Executive Officers, D. W. Brown; N. W. H.
Fairfax; D. L. Gomez; C. R. A. Messenger; B. A.
Phillips....................£4,900 to £5,900
Metropolitan Special Constabulary, Chief Commandant,
A. A. Hammond.

"B" Department
Traffic
Assistant Commissioner, P. B. Kavanagh, Q.P.M.
                £13,290
Deputy Assistant Commissioners, H. Hodgson; D.
Powis......................£9,777 to £10,884
Senior Principal, R. V. Clark....£7,750 to £9,350
Principals, G. W. Barns, M.B.E.; P. A. Barwood;
S. H. Carter; J. C. Cutts, O.B.E.; P. I. May;
G. H. T. Shrimpton, C.B.E., T.D.
              £5,680 to £7,450

Commanders, R. A. C. Barker; G. E. H. Maggs,
Q.P.M.; J. Toogood.........£8,733 to £9,165
Senior Executive Officers, R. S. Ainsworth; A. J.
Chatwin; E. C. Cox; D. Giddings; P. J. Groom;
J. S. Johnstone; M. E. B. Keller; C. A. A.
Roberts; K. J. Tetley; K. H. Varney
£4,900 to £5,900

"C" Department
Criminal Investigation
Assistant Commissioner, J. S. Wilson, O.B.E.
£13,290
Deputy Assistant Commissioners, R. H. Anning,
Q.P.M.; E. R. Bond, Q.P.M.; J. W. D. Crane;
V. S. Gilbert ....£9,777 to £10,884
Principal, J. A. Crutchlow......£5,680 to £7,450
Commanders, R. L. J. Ashby; R. A. Davis; D. C.
Dilley, Q.P.M.; R. Habershon, M.B.E.; G. T. C.
Lambourne; J. A. Lock, Q.P.M.; J. Morrison; K. G.
Pendered; M. D. Rodger, Q.P.M.; P. A. Saunders;
H. D. Walton, Q.P.M.........£8,733 to £9,165
Senior Executive Officers, K. Jones; R. D. Mearns;
M. J. Pratt.................£4,900 to £5,900

Metropolitan Police Laboratory
Director, R. L. Williams.....£10,180 to £11,430
Deputy Director, T. H. Jones....£8,650 to £9,798
Senior Principal Scientific Officers, B. J. Culliford;
Miss M. Pereira............£8,650 to £9,798
Principal Scientific Officers, R. R. Berrett; Mrs. S. J.
Butcher; K. Chaperlin; B. E. Connett; D.
Cousins; D. M. Ellen; C. F. M. Fryd; N. A.
Fuller; J. V. Jackson; Mrs. S. M. Keating;
C. J. O. Lee; Mrs. F. R. Lewington; L. Morse;
D. Neylan; B. H. Parkin; D. Rudram; R. A.
Stedman; B. B. Wheals; M. J. Whitehouse
£5,514 to £7,205

"D" Department
Personnel and Training
Assistant Commissioner, H. J. E. Hunt, O.B.E. £13,290
Deputy Assistant Commissioners, P. V. Collier, O.B.E.,
Q.P.M.; J. A. Dellow........£9,777 to £10,884
Principals, R. G. Giddings; H. E. W. Hodson;
F. C. B. Varney, O.B.E.........£5,680 to £7,450
Commanders, N. Baxter; F. E. Chalkley; S. Leckey;
G. D. McLean; Miss K. D. Skillern.
£8,733 to £9,165
Senior Executive Officers, O. A. Collier; J. H.
Mailing; C. E. D. Reeves; R. C. Vivian
£4,900 to £5,900
Welfare Officer, Capt. A. H. Little, C.B.E., R.N. (ret.)
£4,900 to £5,900
Director of Catering, Col. R. R. Owens, O.B.E.
£7,750 to £9,350
Deputy Director, A. F. Taylor... £6,625 to £7,450

Metropolitan Police Cadet Corps
Commander, N. Baxter.........£8,733 to £9,165
Director of Academic Studies, K. H. Patterson, V.R.D.
£4,900 to £6,875

Medical and Dental Branch
Chief Surgeon, R. W. Nevin, T.D.
Consulting Physician and Deputy to Chief Surgeon, Sir
John Richardson, Bt., M.V.O.
Medical Officer, E. C. A. Bott.
Dental Officer, Group Capt. H. V. Jessop.

Inspectorate
Deputy Assistant Commissioners, W. H. Brown,
Q.P.M.; S. Coates; J. H. Crisp; J. H. Gerrard,
O.B.E., M.C., Q.P.M...........£9,777 to £10,884
Commanders, J. T. R. Barnett; E. O. Howells,
Q.P.M.; R. D. Saunders; A. S. Wickstead Q.P.M.
£8,733 to £9,165

Management Services
Director, R. A. Root.........£8,650 to £11,000

Senior Principal Scientific Officer and Deputy Director,
N. E. Hand.................£8,650 to £9,798
Principal, R. J. Whyman.......£5,680 to £7,450
Chief Work Study Officer, J. E. Holbrow
£5,680 to £7,450
Principal Psychologist, J. H. Jones-Lloyd
£5,680 to £7,450
Principal Scientific Officer, R. P. du Parcq
£5,514 to £7,205
Senior Executive Officers, J. E. Geater; Mrs. C.
Macleod...................£4,900 to £5,900
Senior Work Study Officers, R. C. Bright; A. Kasler
£4,900 to £5,900

DIRECTORATE OF ADMINISTRATION AND FINANCE
Deputy Receiver, G. S. Downes.........£11,670

"E" Department
Establishments and Secretariat
Secretary, D. Meyler, D.S.C.... £8,650 to £11,000
Senior Principals, G. E. Stonely; J. W. Syms
£7,750 to £9,350
Principals, F. A. W. Pilborough; J. E. Tubb
£5,680 to £7,450
Senior Executive Officers, Miss B. Arnold; T. J. Beer;
M. Ferry, T.D.; A. Hartley; A. J. Henderson;
J. E. G. King; G. C. Nockles; M. W. Simmons;
R. W. Smith; B. W. Smyth; A. M. J. Williams
£4,900 to £5,900
General Registry
Senior Executive Officer, E. G. Harvey
£4,900 to £5,900

"F" Department
Finance
Director of Finance, B. G. David. £8,650 to £11,000
Deputy Directors of Finance, J. L. Davies; C. N. Hill
£7,750 to £9,350
Assistant Directors of Finance, R. W. Barker; M.
Brothers; R. F. Gridley......£5,680 to £7,450
Senior Executive Officers, J. G. Day; Miss S. M.
Goater; B. J. B. Rawlings; N. A. E. Rex; J. A.
Starling; J. C. H. Taylor; G. H. E. Velvick
£4,900 to £5,900

"G" Department
Administration
Director of Administration, P. J. G. Buckley
£8,650 to £11,000
Deputy Directors of Administration, R. H. Beaver,
O.B.E.; L. Joughin, M.C.; M. Lee
£7,750 to £9,350
Principals, N. N. I. Batten; D. F. F. Hannaford;
R. B. Jones; M. W. Maidment; A. Morley, M.B.E.
£5,680 to £7,450
Statistical Adviser, G. C. Reed.... £5,680 to £7,450
Senior Executive Officers, E. R. Bright; D. H. Burr;
D. M. Davis; P. Emmerson, T.D.; A. Fearon;
I. M. Fernie; C. E. Ford; J. R. Hamilton; J. R.
S. Hurworth; H. D. Moore; R. P. Sargent;
R. F. Spain; D. Wilson........£4,900 to £5,900
Controller of Printing and Reprographic Services, H. T.
Hudson, M.B.E..............£5,680 to £7,450

Chief Architect and Surveyor's Department
Chief Architect and Surveyor, M. L. Belchamber
£11,000
Deputy Chief Architect and Surveyor, G. B. Vint
£8,650 to £9,798
Assistant Chief Architect, C. A. Legerton
£8,650 to £9,798
Assistant Chief Surveyors, D. N. Fogden (Estates);
H. R. Ewence, O.B.E. (Building)
£8,650 to £9,798
Senior Architects, D. E. Chapman; C. G. Liardet:
A. E. Matcham; I. G. Mowat; P. Silsby
£6,280 to £7,450

Senior Surveyors, A. H. Bailey; J. W. Burton; J. A. Chipchase; L. Hibbs; R. E. Winchester
£6,280 to £7,450
Senior Public Health Engineers, M. Randall; F. A. Rowbotham . . . . £6,280 to £7,450

Chief Engineer's Department

Chief Engineer, B. France £11,000
Deputy Chief Engineers, D. Hale; D. E. Mosley; Col. J. E. Owen . . . . £8,650 to £9,798
Principal Professional and Technology Officers, E. Blade; C. W. Cornock; D. E. Keech; L. F. Squibb; F. H. G. Taylor; J. M. Wardle; P. J. Wright
£6,280 to £7,450
Senior Engineer, I. O. Levy . . . . . £6,280 to £7,450

"S" Department
Solicitors

Solicitor, E. O. Lane, C.B.E., D.F.C., A.F.C. . . £13,840
Deputy Solicitor, R. E. T. Birch £12,000
Assistant Solicitors, G. E. Clark; J. B. Egan; R. L. Kiley; R. G. Mays; D. M. O'Shea; W. H. S. Relton; A. H. Simpson; J. M. Tuff; D. W. Warran; C. N. Winston . . . . £9,033 to £11,000
Senior Legal Assistants, R. P. Coupland; R. W. Davies; H. J. Drake; W. S. Frost; I. G. F. Graham; H. B. Hargrave; S. M. Howard; Miss P. M. Long; J. R. McCann; R. E. Marsh; J. O'Keeffe; C. S. Porteous; P. A. Shawdon; R. M. D. Thorne; R. B. Vince; N. M. Weston; M. H. Wilmot . . . . £6,625 to £8,750
Legal Assistants, Miss J. M. Craig; Miss D. Crebbin; G. R. Edwards; P. R. Essex; A. M. P. Falk; G. Gibb; P. S. K. Haddock; Miss F. M. Hegarty; Miss A. M. Hewett; J. R. P. Hyde; Miss S. M. James; A. G. Mainds; J. P. McCooey; Miss A. M. Martin; S. A. O'Doherty; Miss J. M. Perrigo; Miss P. J. Phipps; R. N. Short; R. C. Wheeler; H. A. Youngerwood . . . . £3,424 to £6,125
Senior Principal Legal Executive, W. McCrorie
£7,750 to £9,350
Principal Legal Executives, W. E. Ball; C. W. White; E. Worboys . . . . £5,680 to £7,450
Senior Legal Executive Officers, A. Astill; J. Clarke; G. Davies; J. Niblett; P. Stenning; K. Stokes; B. Tickner . . . . £4,900 to £5,900

"P" Department
Public Relations

Public Relations Officer, G. D. Gregory, O.B.E., D.S.C.
£8,650 to £11,000
Deputy Public Relations Officer, J. S. Courtney
£7,750 to £9,350
Head of News Branch, E. Wright
£5,680 to £7,450
Head of Publicity Branch, J. H. V. Bradley
£5,680 to £7,450
Senior Information Officers, E. Davis; M. C. Johnson; J. L. Miller; R. A. A. Moore; J. C. Stern
£4,900 to £5,900
Senior Executive Officers, C. J. Boorman; M. G. Down, M.B.E.; T. Gibson; A. J. James
£4,900 to £5,900

General Secretary of the Association of Chief Police Officers of England, Wales and Northern Ireland, F. W. C. Pennington, O.B.E., Q.P.M.
£6,625 to £7,450

CITY OF LONDON POLICE
26 Old Jewry, E.C.2

Commissioner, C. J. Page, Q.P.M. £14,445
Assistant Commissioner, W. H. Stapleton, Q.P.M.
£10,218 to £11,043
Commander, P. Coppack (Operations)
£8,532 to £8,964
Chief Superintendents, W. Burley (Administration); G. Lee (Traffic and Communications); K. Short

(" B " Divn); J. Stimson (" C " Divn.); A. Francis (" D " Divn.); S. Smith (C.I.D.); K. Taylor (C.I.D.); B. Rowland (Sec. of Superintendents' Association of England & Wales & Northern Ireland) . . . . £7,538 to £8,135

City of London Special Constabulary
Commandant, Major S. Holmes, T.D.
Chief Staff Officer, J. Oakley.

INDUSTRIAL AND OTHER TRIBUNALS
The Industrial Tribunals
Established under the Industrial Training Act 1964.

Central Office (England and Wales)
93 Ebury Bridge Road, S.W.1

President, E. A. Seeley £13,500
Chairman, Rt. Hon. Sir John Clayden £11,750
Secretary, G. R. Fisher . . . . . . £5,680 to £7,450
Central Office (Scotland)
St. Andrews House, 141 West Nile Street, Glasgow
President, I. MacDonald £13,250
Chairman, T. W. Strachan £11,750
Secretary, B. M. Sheridan . . . . . . £4,976 to £6,159

Compensation (Defence) Act 1939
SHIPPING CLAIMS TRIBUNAL
President, The Rt. Hon. Sir Gordon Willmer, O.B.E., T.D.

Lands Tribunal
5 Chancery Lane, W.C.2
[01-831-6611]
President, D. G. H. Frank, Q.C.
Members, J. R. Laird, T.D.; R. C. Walmsley; J. S. Daniel, Q.C.; J. H. Emlyn Jones, M.B.E.; E. C. Strathon; J. D. Russell-Davis; V. G. Wellings, Q.C.; W. H. Rees.
Registrar, J. H. Ayers.

Patents and Registered Designs Appeal Tribunal
Room 169, Royal Courts of Justice, W.C.2
Judges, The Hon. Mr. Justice Graham; The Hon. Mr. Justice Whitford.
Registrar, W. E. Loveday.

Performing Right Tribunal
Room 105, 25 Southampton Buildings, W.C.2
Chairman, H. E. Francis, Q.C.
Members, Sir William Slimmings, C.B.E.; Mrs. K. E. Spitz; P. G. Walker; D. Perkins.
Secretary, A. Holt.

Transport Tribunal
Watergate House, 15 York Buildings
Adelphi, W.C.2
President, G. D. Squibb, Q.C.
Registrar and Secretary, Miss P. E. Kennedy.

Board of Referees Income Tax Act, 1952
Room 745, Royal Courts of Justice, W.C.2
Registrar, F. H. Cowper.

Parliamentary and Local Government Election Petitions Office
Room 120, Royal Courts of Justice, W.C.2
Prescribed Officer, I. H. Jacob.
Clerk, F. Simmons.

Pensions Appeal Tribunals
Staffordshire House, Store St., W.C.1
President, Hon. Sir Alastair Forbes.
Secretary, C. J. Smitten, M.B.E.

Benefices Act, 1898
Room 120, Royal Courts of Justice, W.C.2
Registrar of the Court, Master J. R. Bickford Smith.

Immigration Appeals
Head Office, Thanet House,
231 Strand, W.C.2
Chief Adjudicator, J. Bennett.
Immigration Appeals Tribunal
President, Sir Derek Hilton, M.B.E.
Vice-President, P. N. Dalton.
Secretary to the Appellate Authorities, R. R. Rowe.

SCOTTISH LAW COURTS AND OFFICES, PARLIAMENT SQUARE, EDINBURGH

COURT OF SESSION (Established 1532).
Lord President, Lord Emslie (Rt. Hon. George Carlyle Emslie, M.B.E.)

INNER HOUSE.—*First Division*.

The Lord President, Lord Emslie, Rt. Hon. George Carlyle Emslie, M.B.E.........	£20,425
Lord Cameron, Sir John Cameron, D.S.C...	16,675
Lord Johnston, Douglas Harold Johnston, T.D...................................	16,675
Lord Avonside, Rt. Hon. Ian Hamilton Shearer...............................	16,675
Lord Kincraig, Robert Smith Johnston...	16,675
Lord Maxwell, Peter Maxwell..........	16,675
Lord McDonald, Robert Howat McDonald, M.C..................................	16,675
Lord Wylie, Rt. Hon. Norman Russell Wylie, V.R.D..........................	16,675
Lord Stewart, Ewan Stewart, M.C.......	16,675

Second Division

Lord Justice Clerk, Lord Wheatley, Rt. Hon.

John Wheatley.......................	£19,300
Lord Kissen, Manuel Kissen.............	16,675
Lord Hunter, John Oswald Mair Hunter (*Seconded to Scottish Law Commission*)...	16,675
Lord Leechman, James Leechman........	16,675

OUTER HOUSE

Lord Thomson, Alexander Thomson....	£16,675
Lord Robertson, Ian Macdonald Robertson, M.B.E., T.D.........................	16,675
Lord Stott, Rt. Hon. George Gordon Stott	16,675
Lord Dunpark, Alastair McPherson Johnston, T.D......................	16,675
Lord Keith, Henry Shanks Keith........	16,675
Lord Grieve, William Robertson Grieve..	16,675
Lord Brand, David William Robert Brand	16,675

Principal Clerk of Session and Clerk of Justiciary, O. J. Brown.............. £8,650 to £11,000
Deputy Principal Clerk, George H. Robertson
£5,680 to £7,450
Keeper of the Rolls, George MacDonald, O.B.E.
£4,900 to £5,900
Depute Clerks, Inner House, H. G. Manson; E. Smith.................... £4,900 to £5,900
Depute Clerks, Outer House, D. Scott; J. Watson; A. S. Rodger; P. Whitten; H. C. Macpherson; A. Wylie; R. Sibbald; V. A. Woods; A. Brown; H. S. Foley; W. Gillon...... £4,900 to £5,900
Deputy Principal Clerk of Justiciary, W. Howard.................... £5,680 to £7,450
Deputies and Assistants, G. Paton; J. F. McNish; A. A. Brown...... £4,900 to £5,900

NOTE.—The word "Lord" prefixed to the names of Judges of the Court of Session, or to titles different from their names, is strictly an official honour and may be compared with the terms "Hon. Mr. Justice" and "Lord Chief Justice" in England.

Lord Advocate's Department
See Index
Crown Office,
9 Parliament Square, Edinburgh
Crown Agent, W. G. Chalmers, M.C...... £13,230
Deputy Crown Agent, A. V. Sheehan
£9,780 to £11,000
Senior Legal Assistants, F. J. Keane; J. D. Allan; K. Valentine.................. £6,625 to £8,750
Legal Assistant, Miss I. McGillivray
£3,424 to £6,125

Exchequer Office
102 George Street, Edinburgh
Queen's and Lord Treasurer's Remembrancer, J. B. I. McTavish, O.B.E..... £9,033 to £10,180
Chief Clerk, D. E. D. Robertson
£5,680 to £7,450
Senior Executive Officers, A. J. Ware; S. P. Frater (*Temporary*)...... £4,900 to £5,900

Companies Registration Office
102 George Street, Edinburgh
Registrar (and Keeper, Edinburgh Gazette Office), J. B. I. McTavish, O.B.E.

Sheriff Court of Chancery
Sheriff Court, Lawnmarket, Edinburgh
Sheriff of Chancery, W. J. Bryden, C.B.E., Q.C.
Sheriff Clerk of Chancery, W. D. McInnes.

H.M. Commissary Office,
16 North Bank Street, Edinburgh
Commissary Clerk, W. D. McInnes.
Deputy do., A. D. Stevenson.

Crown Estate Commissioners
11 Charlotte Square, Edinburgh
Crown Estate Receiver, D. T. Hunt.

SCOTTISH LAND COURT
1 Grosvenor Crescent, Edinburgh
Members, The Hon. Lord Birsay, K.T., C.B.E., T.D. (*Chairman*); D. W. Cunningham; John McVicar; A. Gillespie.
Principal Clerk, T. MacD. Wilson.
Depute Clerks of Court and Senior Legal Assessors, S. Forrest; D. H. Cameron.
Deputy Clerks of Court and Legal Assessors, J. G. Riddoch; K. H. R. Graham.
Clerk of Accounts and Establishment, R. Landels.

SCOTTISH LAW COMMISSION
Old College, South Bridge, Edinburgh
[031-667-3437/8]
Chairman, The Hon. Lord Hunter.
Commissioners, Prof. T. B. Smith, Q.C., Ll.D., F.B.A.; A. E. Anton, C.B.E. (*full-time*); R. B. Jack (*part-time*).
Secretary, J. B. Allan.
Asst. Secretary, A. J. Sim.
Chief Clerk, Miss M. H. McNeilage.

STIPENDIARY MAGISTRATES (GLASGOW)
Court Chambers
Central, Thomas Joseph McLauchlan (1966).
Marine, Martin S. Morrow (1972).
Govan, Robert Mitchell (1975).

SHERIFFS PRINCIPAL, SHERIFFS, SHERIFF CLERKS AND PROCURATORS FISCAL OF COUNTIES IN SCOTLAND

SHERIFFDOM AND SHERIFF PRINCIPAL	SHERIFFS	SHERIFF CLERKS	PROCURATORS FISCAL
Grampian, Highland and Islands.— G. S. Gimson, Q.C., 11 Royal Circus, Edinburgh.	*Aberdeen, Stonehaven,* M. J. A. Rose, D.F.C.; A. M. G. Russell, Q.C.	J. B. Blair....... A. Oliver.......	M. T. MacNeill. M. MacPhail.
	Banff and Peterhead, T. M. Croan (*also Aberdeen*).	C. Gordon......	W. A. Brown.
	Elgin, M. Layden (*also Nairn*)...	T. Fyffe.........	J. T. MacDougall.
	Wick, Inverness, E. Stewart.....	W. J. Burns..... B. J. Young.....	G. E. Scott. A. M. Skinner.
	Stornoway and Lochmaddy, Fort William, Portree, Nairn, D. A. Donald; S. Scott Robinson, M.B.E., T.D. (*except Nairn*).		C. S. MacKenzie. W. A. H. Merry. D. Macmillan.
	Kirkwall, Lerwick, A. A. MacDonald.	J. M. Lynn...... Mrs. C. F. Johnson	A. W. Wright. A. J. Cluness.
	Dingwall and Tain, Dornoch, Captain W. R. M. Murdoch, C.B.E., D.S.C., V.R.D., R.N.R. (*ret.*).	D. D. Mackay ... D. MacDonald ...	T. F. Aitchison. J. D. McNaughton.
Tayside, Central and Fife.— R. R. Taylor, Ph.D., Q.C., 51 Northumberland Street, Edinburgh.	*Arbroath, Forfar,* S. O. Kermack (*also Perth*).	D. M. Cameron.. R. G. Davis.....	A. L. Ingram. A. L. Ingram.
	Dundee, J. B. W. Christie; G. L. Fox.	J. A. C. Weir....	C. G. Hogg.
	Perth, H. F. Ford............	A. A. Steele.....	R. L. J. Miln.
	Falkirk, R. R. Kerr...........	R. D. S. Mercer..	D. B. MacFarlane.
	Stirling, Alloa, W. C. Henderson	D. Waddell...... K. McKenzie.....	I. Dean. G. H. Summerfield.
	Cupar, J. C. McInnes..........	P. G. Corcoran..	E. H. Galt.
	Dunfermline, G. I. W. Shiach...	J. S. Douglas.....	J. H. Douglas.
	Kirkcaldy, J. Allan...........	J. G. C. Bone...	E. G. Smith.
Lothian and Borders.— W. J. Bryden, C.B.E., Q.C., Sheriff Principal's Chambers, Sheriff Court House, Lawnmarket, Edinburgh.	*Edinburgh, Peebles,* V. D. B. Skae (*except Peebles*); J. A. Smith (*except Peebles*); N. MacVicar (*except Peebles*); J. A. Dick, M.C., Q.C. (*except Peebles*); Miss I. L. Sinclair, Q.C. (*also Selkirk*); K. W. B. Middleton (*also Haddington, not Peebles*); R. D. Ireland, Q.C.* (*Director, Scottish Courts Administration*); C. R. Macarthur, Q.C.*; J. L. M. Mitchell.*	W. D. McInnes..	N. Milne. E. Laverock.
	Linlithgow, W. T. Hook.......	R. W. M. Hall...	D. R. Smith.
	Haddington, K. W. B. Middleton (*also Edinburgh*).	J. Cumming.....	R. W. McConachie.
	Jedburgh, Duns, Selkirk, J. V. Paterson (*except Selkirk*); Miss I. L. Sinclair, Q.C. (*except Jedburgh and Duns*).	Mrs.E.S.P.Smart.	C. B. Allan. J. C. Whitelaw. C. B. Allan.
Glasgow and Strathkelvin.— The Lord Wilson of Langside, P.C., Q.C., Sheriff Principal's Chambers, Sheriff Court House, 149 Ingram Street, Glasgow.	*Glasgow,* F. Middleton; J. Bayne; S. E. Bell; C. H. Johnston; Q.C.; W. O. Pattullo; J. I. Smith; P. G. B. McNeill; J. M. Paterson; N. D. MacLeod; A. C. Horsfall; J. J. Maguire; A. A. Bell, Q.C.; I. D. MacPhail; J. S. Mowat.	D. McMillan.....	H. Herron.
North Strathclyde.— F. W. F. O'Brien, Q.C., 12 Boswall Road, Edinburgh.	*Dunoon, Campbeltown, Oban, Rothesay,* D. J. McDiarmid (*except Dunoon and Rothesay*); H. Lyons (*except Oban and Campbeltown–but also Paisley*).	J. McGhie.......	W. D. Stewart. D. MacNeill. G. H. Pagan. Miss C. McNaughton.
	Dumbarton, J. C. M. Jardine; M. Stone; B. Kearney.*	J. R. Cowie	J. M. Tudhope.
	Paisley, A. K. F. Hunter; H. R. MacLean; R. A. Inglis; H. Lyons (*also Dunoon and Rothesay*).	A. McDougall ...	J. Skeen.
	Greenock, J. B. Patrick........	A. P. McPherson.	W. Macnab.
	Kilmarnock, R. N. Levitt, O.B.E., T.D.	R. R. Dale......	J. L. McLeod.

SHERIFFDOM AND SHERIFF PRINCIPAL	SHERIFFS	SHERIFF CLERK	PROCURATORS FISCAL
South Strathclyde, Dumfries and Galloway.— R. Reid, Q.C., 33 Regent Terrace, Edinburgh.	Hamilton, I. A. Dickson; P. Thomson; N. E. D. Thomson.	J. Davidson......	D. B. Copeland.
	Lanark, M. G. Gillies, T.D., Q.C. (also Glasgow).	J. A. Watson.....	T. J. Cochrane.
	Ayr, G. S. Reid; D. M. K. Grant (also Kilmarnock).	J. Shaw.........	R. J. Cruickshank.
	Stranraer, Kirkcudbright, N. J. G. Ramsay.	J. M. Ross....... M. Hardy	R. F. Gibb. W. M. Morton.
	Dumfries, C. G. B. Nicholson...	W. B. Davidson..	I. G. Pirie.
	Airdrie, A. R. McIlwraith; A. L. Stewart.	J. H. Thomson...	J. Farrell.

* Floating Sheriff

BRITISH FORCES BROADCASTING SERVICE

King's Buildings, Dean Stanley Street, London S.W.1

The Service came into existence during the early part of the Second World War to entertain, inform and to maintain the morale of the Serviceman in the field. No exact date can be given for the inception of the Service because, in answer to the need, special broadcasting for the Services overseas began in many different places almost simultaneously during 1942. The first mobile transmitters were provided by the then War Office in 1943 and these were sent with specially selected staff to North Africa. From 1943 onwards a whole network of Forces Broadcasting Stations grew up covering the Mediterranean area, the Persian Gulf, India and Germany. After the war the Service continued to entertain and inform Servicemen wherever they might be stationed overseas and the network was extended to the Far East.

In 1960 the War Office called on the help of the BBC to reorganize B.F.B.S. and as a result, a Head Office was created in London and a Director was appointed. The Head Office now produces between 30 and 35 hours a week of programmes featuring leading personalities in sport, music and entertainment. Special regard is paid to Service information and interest and these programmes are recorded, dubbed and flown out to the B.F.B.S. stations abroad, also to H.M. ships and submarines in many parts of the world, and for the benefit of unaccompanied personnel serving in such places as Gan. The number of these stations has diminished in recent years with the withdrawal of British Forces

overseas. Much of their output is produced locally and the task of these stations is to reflect the life of the Serviceman and his family in their surroundings overseas, drawing them in to take part in quizzes, discussions, interviews, etc. Through the programmes produced in Head Office and by relays of BBC news and current affairs the B.F.B.S. stations overseas create for the Serviceman a strong link with home, and keep abreast of the changes that are going on while he is away.

A live British television service combining programmes from all three channels in the U.K. is being planned for the British Forces in West Germany. All the main concentrations of personnel and their families should be served by B.F.B.S. TELEVISION within the next two or three years.

The C.S.E. section of B.F.B.S. organizes live entertainment shows and every year about 40 shows are sent over to Northern Ireland and Commands overseas. Many of the great names in the entertainment world have entertained the Services in this way.

B.F.B.S. is organized to serve all three Services. Its staff are all civilian, professional broadcasters and engineers, and many of the household names of radio and television at home have had their initial training through Forces broadcasting. The Service is administered by the Army on behalf of the other two Services and is financed from the Treasury through the Ministry of Defence.

Director, I. J. Woolf.

THE ARMED FORCES

MINISTRY OF DEFENCE
Main Building, Whitehall, S.W.1.
[01-930 7022]
Secretary of State for Defence, THE RT. HON. ROY MASON, M.P........................£13,000
Private Secretary, J. F. Mayne.
Assistant Private Secretaries, N. H. Nicholls; D. B. Omand; D. Spalding; M. G. Dunmore; E. E. Rowlands.
Minister of State for Defence, THE RT. HON. WILLIAM THOMAS RODGERS, M.P................£9,500
Private Secretary, C. T. Sandars.
Assistant Private Secretaries, Miss J. M. Bennett; P. S. Gray.
Parliamentary Private Secretary, R. T. Ellis, M.P.
Parliamentary Under Secretary of State for Defence for the Royal Navy, F. A. Judd, M.P.........£5,500
Parliamentary Under Secretary of State for Defence for the Army, R. C. Brown, M.P...........£5,500
Parliamentary Under Secretary of State for Defence for the Royal Air Force, B. T. John, M.P.....£5,500

Chief of Defence Staff, Field-Marshal Sir Michael Carver, G.C.B., C.B.E., D.S.O., M.C.
Chief of the Naval Staff and First Sea Lord, Admiral Sir Edward Ashmore, G.C.B., D.S.C., A.D.C.
Chief of the General Staff, General Sir Peter Hunt, G.C.B., D.S.O., O.B.E., A.D.C. (*Gen.*).
Chief of the Air Staff, Air Chief Marshal Sir Andrew Humphrey, G.C.B., O.B.E., D.F.C., A.F.C., A.D.C.

Permanent Under Secretary of State, Sir Michael Cary, K.C.B................................£18,675
Private Secretary, M. J. V. Bell.
Second Permanent Under Secretary of State (Administration), W. Geraghty, C.B £17,175
Vice Chief of Defence Staff, Vice-Admiral H. C. Leech.
Director-General of Intelligence (Ministry of Defence), Lt.-Gen. Sir David Willison, K.C.B., O.B.E., M.C. £14,100
Deputy Chief of the Defence Staff (Intelligence), Air Marshal R. G. Wakeford, M.V.O., O.B.E., A.F.C.

Deputy Chief of Defence Staff (Operational Requirements), Air Marshal Sir Michael Giddings, K.C.B., O.B.E, D.F.C., A.F.C.

Chief of Personnel and Logistics, General Sir Richard Ward, K.C.B., D.S.O., M.C.

Assist. Chief of Personnel and Logistics, Rear-Admiral F. W. Hearn.

Assistant Chiefs of Defence Staff, Rear-Admiral C. Rusby, M.V.O. (Operations); Air Vice-Marshal J. Gingell, C.B.E. (Policy); Air Vice-Marshal S. M. Davidson, C.B.E. (Signals).

Chief of Naval Personnel and Second Sea Lord, Admiral Sir David Williams, K.C.B.

Chief of Fleet Support, Vice-Admiral P. White, C.B.E.

Vice-Chief of Naval Staff, Vice-Admiral R. D. Lygo.

Chief Scientist (Royal Navy), B. W. Lythall, C.B.
.................................£14,000

Adjutant-General, General Sir Cecil Blacker, G.C.B., O.B.E., M.C., A.D.C. (Gen.)

Quartermaster-General, General Sir William Jackson, K.C.B., O.B.E., M.C., A.D.C. (Gen.)

Vice-Chief of the General Staff, Lieutenant General Sir William Scotter, K.C.B., O.B.E., M.C.

Chief Scientist (Army), Dr. W. H. Penley, C.B., C.B.E.
.................................£14,000

Air Member for Personnel, Air Marshal Sir Neil Cameron, K.C.B., C.B.E., D.S.O., D.F.C.

Air Member for Supply and Organization, Air Chief Marshal Sir Anthony Heward, K.C.B., O.B.E., D.F.C., A.F.C.

Vice-Chief of the Air Staff, Air Marshal Sir Ruthven Wade, K.C.B., D.F.C.

Chief Scientist (Royal Air Force), W. J. Charnley, C.B.
.................................£14,000

Defence Services Secretary, Air Vice-Marshal B. G. T. Stanbridge, C.B.E., M.V.O., A.F.C.

Naval Secretary, Rear-Admiral J. M. Forbes.

Military Secretary, Lt.-Gen. Sir Patrick Howard-Dobson, K.C.B.

Air Secretary, Air Chief Marshal Sir Derek Hodgkinson, K.C.B., C.B.E., D.F.C., A.F.C.

Chief Scientific Adviser, Prof. Sir Hermann Bondi, K.C.B., F.R.S. £18,675

Director-General of Supply Co-ordination, Maj.-Gen. J. T. Stanyer, C.B.E £12,000

Director, Women's Royal Naval Service, Commandant Mary I. Talbot, C.B., HON.A.D.C.

Director, Women's Royal Army Corps, Brig. Eileen J. Nolan, HON.A.D.C.

Director, Women's Royal Air Force, Air Commodore Molly G. Allott, C.B., HON.A.D.C.

Chaplain of the Fleet, The Ven. B. A. O'Ferrall, Q.H.C.

Chaplain-General to the Forces, The Ven. P. Mallett, Q.H.C.

Chaplain-in-Chief, R.A.F., The Ven. J. H. Wilson, Q.H.C.

Matron-in-Chief, Queen Alexandra's Royal Naval Nursing Service, Miss C. F. J. Cooke, C.B.E., R.R.C., Q.H.N.S.

Matron-in-Chief (Army) and Director of Army Nursing Services, Brig. Helen Cattanach, R.R.C., Q.H.N.S.

Matron-in-Chief, Princess Mary's R.A.F. Nursing Service, Air Commandant Barbara M. Ducat-Amos, C.B., R.R.C., Q.H.N.S.

Chief Executive, Royal Dockyards, H. R. P. Chatten, C.B. £14,000

Commandant, Royal College of Defence Studies, Air Chief Marshal Sir John Barraclough, K.C.B., C.B.E., D.F.C., A.F.C.

Deputy Under Secretaries of State,
(Royal Navy), D. R. J. Stephen (Civilian Manage-

ment); E. Broadbent, C.B., C.M.G.

(Army), R. C. Kent, C.B. (Policy and Programmes); A. P. Hockaday, C.B., C.M.G.

(Air) P. J. Hudson (Finance and Budget); E. G. Gass, C.B., O.B.E. (Personnel and Logistics); R. Haynes, C.B...............(each) £14,000

Director of Dockyard Manpower and Productivity, J. C. Allen.........................£12,000

Director of Dockyard Production and Support, Rear-Admiral M. H. Griffin, C.B.

Deputy Chief Adviser (Projects and Nuclear), V. H. B. Macklen, C.B......................£14,000

Assistant Chief Scientific Advisers, J. E. Twinn (Projects); Dr. I. J. Shaw, O.B.E. (Studies); Dr. F. H. Panton, M.B.E. (Nuclear) £12,000

Assistant Under Secretaries of State, R. J. Andrew (General Staff); H. C. Budden (Supply (Air)); G. F. Carpenter, E.R.D. (Civilian Management (General)) T. Cullen (Operational Requirements); B. M. Day (Civilian Management (Administrators)); H. L. Emmett (Civilian Management (B)); G. E. Emery (Director-General of Defence Accounts); D. M. Evans (Programmes and Budget); K. E. Glover (Statistics); G. T. Glue (Director-Gen., Supplies and Transport (Naval)); A. A. Golds (Royal College of Defence Studies); J. S. Goldsmith (Fleet Support); A. D. Harvey (Organization (Air)); F. C. Herd (Personnel (Defence Secretariat)); C. A. Whitmore (Defence Staff); A. R. M. Jaffray (Naval Staff); T. C. G. James, C.M.G. (Air Staff); J. A. Millson (Logistics); J. H. Nelson (Personnel (Air)); J. M. Parkin (Adjutant Gen./Quartermaster Gen. (Army Dept.)); A. A. Pritchard (Naval Personnel); J. L. Sabatini (Management Services); J. H. Taylor (Central Finance); W. I. Tupman (Director General of Internal Audit)...................£12,000

General Managers of H.M. Dockyards, F. P. Skinner (Chatham); Capt. J. Wright, D.S.C., R.N. (ret.) (Devonport); W. R. Seward (Portsmouth); K. H. W. Thomas (Rosyth)...........£12,000

Deputy Chief Scientist (Royal Navy), Dr. J. Tunstead..............................£12,000

Deputy Chief Scientist (Army), Dr. E. R. R. Holmberg..............................£12,000

Deputy Chief Scientist (R.A.F.), E. Benn...£12,000

Director, Defence Operational Analysis Establishment, Dr. A. Stratton.....................£12,000

Procurement Executive

Chief Executive, E. C. Cornford, C.B.....£18,675

Private Secretary, J. S. Bosomworth

Deputy Under-Secretary of State (Policy), G. H. Green £14,000

Head of Defence Sales, Sir Lester Suffield..£15,100

Deputies to Head of Defence Sales, R. Anderson, C.M.G. (Assistant Under Secretary) (£12,000) and Air Vice-Marshal C. W. Coulthard, C.B., A.F.C.

Assistant Under Secretaries, T. Cullen (Operational Requirements); G. C. B. Dodds (International and Industrial Policy)...................£12,000

Director-General Defence Contracts, E. F. Hedger, O.B.E............................£12,000

Deputy Under-Secretary of State (Administration), K. T. Nash........................£14,000

Director-General Quality Assurance, P. Corner £12,000

Assistant Under Secretaries, J. G. Ashcroft (Management Services); E. W. Sarginson (Personnel); P. H. M. Brightling (Finance)..............£12,000

Master-General of the Ordnance, General Sir John Gibbon, K.C.B., O.B.E.

Deputy Master-General of the Ordnance, Maj.-Gen. G. Burch

Deputy Controller Guided Weapons and Electronics (Army), (vacant)...................£13,230

Assistant Under Secretary (Ordnance), N. Craig
£12,000

Director-General Fighting Vehicles and Engineer Equipment, Maj.-Gen. A. M. L. Hogge.

Director-General Weapons (Army), Maj.-Gen. D. E. Isles, O.B.E.

Managing Director Royal Ordnance Factories, S. C. Bacon, C.B..........................£14,100

Directors-General, Ordnance Factories, R. J. MacDonald (*Production*); J. S. W. Henderson (*Procurement and Admin.*); G. Smith (*Finance*); W. Meakin (*Weapons and Fighting Vehicles*).........£12,000

Controller of the Navy, Admiral Sir Anthony Griffin, G.C.B.

Assistant Controller, Rear-Admiral G. W. Bridle, M.B.E.

Assistant Under Secretary (Material) (Naval), M. G. Power............................£12,000

Director-General Ships, R. J. Daniel, O.B.E.

Deputy Director-General Ships, Rear-Admiral L. D. Dymoke, C.B.

Director of Research, Ships and Scientific Adviser to Director General Ships, F. S. Burt......£12,000

Director of Naval Ship Production, Rear-Admiral P. R. Marrack.

Director of Warships Design, N. Hancock..£14,160

Deputy Directors, R. Hawkes (*Design Constructive " A "*); J. C. Lawrence (*Design Constructive " B "*); F. W. Butler (*Design Electrical*); F. E. Hutchins (*Engineering Electrical*); L. J. Brooks (*Engineering Constructive*)........................£12,000

Director of Engineering (Ships), E. W. Satchell.

Director-General Weapons (Navy), Vice-Admiral P. A. Watson, M.V.O.

Director of Surface Weapons Projects (Navy), Commodore L. S. Bryson

Director Underwater Weapons Projects (Naval), S. E. Shapcott...........................£12,000

Director Weapons (Production), J. I. G. Evans £12,000

Deputy Controller Polaris, Rear-Admiral W. D. S. Scott, C.B.

Director Project Team Submarines (Polaris), L. G. Bell
£13,230

Deputy Director of Submarines (Polaris), L. J. Rydill
£12,000

Controller Aircraft, Air Marshal Sir Douglas Lowe, K.C.B., D.F.C., A.F.C.

Deputy Under-Secretary of State (Air Systems) (P.E.) A. R. M. Jaffray........................£14,000

Vice-Controller Aircraft, L. F. Nicholson, C.B £13,230

Deputy Controllers, Dr. W. Stewart (*Aircraft " A "*) (£13,230); Rear-Admiral T. R. Cruddas, C.B. (*Aircraft "B"*); Air Vice-Marshal A. P. Dick, C.B.E., A.F.C. (*Aircraft " C "*); H. W. Pout, O.B.E. (*Aircraft " D "*)........................£13,230

Director-General, Strategic Electronic Systems, Dr D. G. Kiely........................£12,000

Director-General, Air Electronic Systems, J. Alvey
£12,000

Assistant Under Secretary (Aircraft), J. L. Roberts
£12,000

Director-General of Equipment, F. O'Hara..£12,000

Director-General Multi-Role Combat Aircraft, I. H. Johnston...........................£12,000

Director-General Engines (PE), I. M. Davidson
£12,000

Director-General Performance and Cost Analysis, D. J. Harper...........................£12,000

Controller Research and Development Establishments and Research, Sir George Macfarlane, C.B.
£15,100

Deputy Controller " A " R & D Estabs. and Research and Chief Scientists (Royal Navy), B. W. Lythall C.B..............................£14,000

Director-General Establishments, Resources and Programmes " A ", Dr. D. H. Parkinson...£12,000

Director-General Research (Electronics), Dr. M. H. Oliver..............................£12,000

Deputy Controller " B " R & D Estabs. and Research and Chief Scientist (Army), Dr. W. H. Penley, C.B., C.B.E..........................£14,000

Director-General Establishments, Resources and Programmes " B ", W. B. H. Lord........£13,230

Director-General Research Weapons, P. R. Wallis
£12,000

Deputy Controller " C " R & D Estabs. and Research and Chief Scientist, (R.A.F.,) W. J. Charnley, C.B.
£14,000

Director-General Establishments, Resources Programmes " C ", J. F. Barnes...........£12,000

Director-General Research, Aircraft, Dr. J. Seddon
£12,000

Assistant Under-Secretary (R & D Estabs. and Research Administration), V. H. E. Cole....£12,000

Research Establishments

Director, Admiralty Surface Weapons Establishment, J. Alvey £13,230

Director, Admiralty Underwater Weapons Establishment, I. L. Davies..................£13,230

Director, Admiralty Research Laboratory, A. B. Mitchell...........................£12,000

Director, Chemical Defence Establishment, Dr. R. G. H. Watson............................£12,000

Director, Micro-Biological Research Establishment, Prof. R. J. C. Harris......................£12,000

Director, Military Vehicles and Engineering Establishment, D. Cardwell, C.B...........£12,000

Director, National Gas Turbine Establishment, T. H. Kerr..............................£12,000

Director, Royal Aircraft Establishment, R. P. Probert, C.B............................£14,000

Director, Royal Armament Research and Development Establishment, F. H. East.............£13,230

Director, Royal Radar Establishment, R. J. Lees
£13,230

Director, Services Electronics Research Laboratory G. P. Wright £11,390

Meteorological Office

London Road, Bracknell, Berks.
[Bracknell: 20242]

The Meteorological Office is the State Meteorological Service. It forms part of the Ministry of Defence, the Director General being ultimately responsible to the Secretary of State for Defence.

Except for the common services provided by other government departments as part of their normal functions, the cost of the Meteorological Office is borne by Defence Votes.

Of the expenditure chargeable to Defence Votes about £9,800,000 represents expenditure associated with staff and £8,200,000 on stores, communications and miscellaneous services. About £4,100,000 is recovered from outside bodies in respect of special services rendered, sales of meteorological equipment, etc.

Director General, B. J. Mason, C.B., D.SC., F.R.S.
£14,000

Director of Research, J. S. Sawyer, F.R.S.....£12,000

Director of Services, J. K. Bannon, I.S.O. £12,000

THE ROYAL NAVY

THE QUEEN

Admirals of the Fleet

The Lord Fraser of North Cape, G.C.B., K.B.E., *born* Feb. 5, 1888..........................Oct. 22, 1948

Sir Algernon U. Willis, G.C.B., K.B.E., D.S.O., *born* May 17, 1889.......................March 20, 1949

H.R.H. the Prince Philip, Duke of Edinburgh, K.G., P.C., K.T., O.M., G.B.E., *born* June 10, 1921...Jan. 15, 1953

The Earl Mountbatten of Burma, K.G., P.C., G.C.B., O.M., G.C.S.I., G.C.I.E., G.C.V.O., D.S.O., *born* June 25, 1900...Oct. 22, 1956

Sir Caspar John, G.C.B., *born* March 22, 1903...May 23, 1962

Sir Varyl C. Begg, G.C.B., D.S.O., D.S.C., *born* Oct. 1, 1908..............................Aug. 12, 1968

Sir Peter Hill-Norton, G.C.B., *born* Feb. 8, 1915...March 12, 1971

Sir Michael Pollock, G.C.B., M.V.O., D.S.C., *born* Oct. 19, 1916..........................March 1, 1974

Admirals

Sir Edward Ashmore, G.C.B., D.S.C. (*Chief of Naval Staff and First Sea Lord*) (*First and Principal Naval Aide-de-Camp*).

Sir Anthony Griffin, G.C.B. (*Controller of the Navy*).

Sir Derek Empson, G.B.E., K.C.B.

Sir Terence Lewin, K.C.B., M.V.O., D.S.C. (*C.-in-C., Naval Home Command*).

Sir Rae McKaig, K.C.B., C.B.E.

Sir David Williams, K.C.B. (*Chief of Naval Personnel and Second Sea Lord*).

Sir John Treacher, K.C.B. (*C.-in-C., Fleet, Allied C.-in-C., Channel and C.-in-C., Eastern Atlantic Area*).

Sir Ian Easton, K.C.B., D.S.C.

Vice-Admirals

Sir James Watt, Q.H.S. (*Medical Director-General*).

Sir John Troup, K.C.B., D.S.C. (*Flag Officer, Scotland and North Ireland, Commander, Northern Sub-Area Eastern Atlantic and Commander Nore Sub-Area Channel*).

J. E. Pope (*Chief of Staff to Commander, Allied Naval Forces, Southern Europe*).

I. G. Raikes, C.B.E., D.S.C. (*Flag Officer, Submarines*).

P. White, C.B.E. (*Chief of Fleet Support*).

P. A. Watson, M.V.O. (*Director-General Weapons (Naval)*).

H. C. Leach (*Vice-Chief of the Defence Staff*).

P. M. Austin (*Flag Officer, Naval Air Command*).

J. G. Jungius (*Deputy Allied Commander, Atlantic*).

A. G. Tait, D.S.C. (*Flag Officer, Plymouth, Port Admiral Devonport, Commander Sub-Area Eastern Atlantic and Commander Plymouth Sub-Area Channel*).

R. D. Lygo (*Vice-Chief of Naval Staff*).

A. S. Morton (*Flag Officer, First Flotilla*).

Rear-Admirals

R. J. Trowbridge.

L. D. Dymoke, C.B. (*Deputy Director-General (Ships)*).

G. P. D. Hall, C.B., D.S.C.

G. C. Mitchell, C.B.

W. D. S. Scott, C.B. (*Deputy Controller, Polaris*).

M. H. Griffin, C.B. (*Director of Dockyard Production and Support*).

H. W. E. Hollins (*Admiral Commanding Reserves*).

T. R. Cruddas, C.B. (*Deputy Controller of Aircraft (B)*).

J. H. F. Eberle (*Flag Officer, Carriers and Amphibious Ships*).

A. G. Watson, C.B. (*Assistant Chief of Naval Staff (Operational Requirements)*).

B. B. Mungo, C.B.

J. O. Roberts (*Chief of Staff to C.-in-C., Fleet*).

D. G. Satow (*Chief Staff Officer (Engineering) to C.-in-C. Fleet*).

H. Gardner (*Senior Naval Member, Ordance Board*).

D. A. Loram, M.V.O. (*Commandant National Defence College*).

P. E. C. Berger, M.V.O., D.S.C.

R. P. Clayton

L. R. B. Davies (*European Representative, Supreme Allied Commander, Atlantic*).

F. W. Hearn (*Assistant Chief of Personnel and Logistics*).

S. F. Berthon (*Flag Officer, Medway and Port Admiral, Chatham*).

R. A. Harcus.

A. D. Cassidi (*Director General Naval Manpower and Training*).

A. R. Rawbone, A.F.C. (*Deputy Assistant Chief of Staff (Operations), Supreme Allied Command, Europe*).

W. N. Ash, M.V.O. (*Director of Service Intelligence*).

P. R. Marrack (*Director of Naval Ship Production*).

R. D. Macdonald, C.B.E. (*Chief of Staff to C.-in-C., Naval Home Command*).

A. J. Monk, C.B.E. (*Flag Officer, Naval Air Command*)

D. Hepworth.

S. R. Sandford (*Flag Officer and Port Admiral, Gibraltar*).

D. W. Bazalgette (*Admiral President, Royal Naval College Greenwich*).

C. Rusby, M.V.O. (*Assistant Chief of Defence Staff (Operations)*).

A. E. Cadman, C.B., O.B.E., Q.H.D.S. (*Director of Naval Dental Services*).

J. M. Forbes (*Naval Secretary*).

T. B. Homan (*Director-General Naval Personnel Services*).

J. D. E. Fieldhouse (*Flag Officer, Second Flotilla*).

G. W. Bridle, M.B.E. (*Assistant Controller of the Navy*).

K. G. Ager (*Flag Officer, Admiralty Interview Board*).

C. R. P. C. Branson (*Assistant Chief of Naval Staff (Operations)*).

J. S. A. Rawlings, O.B.E., Q.H.P. (*Medical Officer-in-Charge, Institute of Naval Medicine*).

J. A. Bell (*Director of Naval Education Service*).

P. D. G. Pugh, O.B.E., Q.H.S. (*Medical Officer-in-Charge, R.N.H., Haslar*).

D. W. Haslam, O.B.E. (*Hydrographer of the Navy*).

O. N. A. Cecil (*Flag Officer, Malta*).

J. R. S. Gerard-Pearse (*Flag Officer, Sea Training*).

E. J. W. Flower (*Flag Officer and Port Admiral, Portsmouth*).

R. W. Halliday, D.S.C. (*Commander British Navy Staff, Washington*).

H. P. Janion (*Flag Officer, Royal Yachts*).

H. R. Mallows, Q.H.P. (*Medical Officer-in-Charge, R.N.H., Plymouth*).

J. S. C. Lea (*Assistant Chief of Fleet Support*).

M. L. Stacey (*Assistant Chief of Naval Staff (Policy)*).

W. T. Pillar (*Port Admiral, Rosyth*).

A. J. Cooke (*Senior Naval Member, Royal College of Defence Studies*).

HER MAJESTY'S FLEET

Type/Class	Operational, preparing for service or engaged on trials and training	Reserve or undergoing long refit, conversion, etc.
Aircraft Carrier................	Ark Royal	
Commando Ships..............	Hermes, Bulwark	
Submarines....................	(24)	(8)
Polaris Submarines............	Repulse, Renown	Revenge, Resolution
Fleet Submarines..............	Valiant, Warspite, Courageous, Swiftsure, Sovereign	Dreadnought, Churchill, Conqueror
OBERON Class................	Onyx, Otus, Opossum, Ocelot, Onslaught, Odin, Otter, Osiris, Oracle, Orpheus, Oberon	Opportune, Olympus
PORPOISE Class................	Finwhale, Rorqual, Narwhal, Cachalot, Walrus	Sea Lion, Porpoise
Assault Ships..................	Fearless, Intrepid	
Cruisers......................	Blake, Tiger	
Guided-Missile Destroyers	(10)	
County Class................	Norfolk, Kent, Hampshire, Devonshire, Antrim, Fife, Glamorgan, London	
Type 82.....................	Bristol	
Type 42.....................	Sheffield	
General Purpose Frigates	(32)	(6)
LEANDER Class..............	Leander, Ajax, Galatea, Minerva, Argonaut, Juno, Danae, Andromeda, Charybdis, Jupiter, Hermione, Bacchante, Scylla, Achilles, Diomede, Apollo, Ariadne, Penelope, Naiad, Euryalus	Aurora, Arethusa, Cleopatra, Phobe, Sirius, Dido
Type 21.....................	Amazon, Antelope,★ Ambuscade,★ Arrow★	
Tribal Class.................	Ashanti, Gurkha, Mohawk, Nubian, Eskimo, Tartar, Zulu	
MERMAID Class..............	Mermaid	
Anti-Aircraft Frigates		
Type 41.....................	Leopard	Lynx, Jaguar
Aircraft Direction Frigates	(3)	
Type 61.....................	Chichester, Salisbury, Llandaff	Lincoln
Anti-Submarine Frigates........	(14)	
	Rothesay, Yarmouth, Plymouth, Londonderry, Lowestoft, Berwick, Falmouth, Brighton, Rhyl, Eastbourne, Torquay	
Type 14.....................	Exmouth, Hardy, Dundas	Keppel
Mine Countermeasure Forces	(40)	(3)
Coastal Minesweepers/Mine-hunters....................	(34)	
Inshore Minesweepers.........	(6)	
Fleet Maintenance Ships.......		Triumph, Berry Head
Submarine Depot Ship..........	Forth	
MCM Support Ship............	Abdiel	
Diving Trials Ship............	Reclaim	
Trials Ship	Matapan	
Coastal Patrol Vessels..........	(5)	
Fast Training/Patrol Boats......	(5)	
Seaward Defence Boats........	Droxford, Dee	
Royal Yacht/Hospital Ship......	Britannia	
Ice Patrol Ship................	Endurance	
Survey Ships/Vessels...........	(13)	
Submarine Tender..............	Wakeful	
Offshore Patrol Vessels..........	Jura, Reward	

★Under construction on March 31, 1975, and planned to enter Service during the year.

ROYAL MARINES

The Corps of Royal Marines, about 8,000 strong, first formed in 1664, is part of the Royal Navy and provides Britain's sea soldiers, in particular a commando brigade Headquarters and four commandos, of which one is serving in Malta and one specializes in mountain and arctic warfare. They also serve at sea in H.M. Ships and provide landing craft crews, special boat sections (frogmen) and other detachments for amphibious operations. The Royal Marines Band Section provides bands for the Royal Navy and Royal Marines.

The Royal Marines Reserve of about 1,000 volunteers consists of five main centres at London, Bristol, Liverpool, Newcastle and Glasgow.

Commander-General, Royal Marines, Lieut.-General P. J. F. Whiteley, O.B.E.

Major-Generals, P. J. Ovens, O.B.E., M.C. (*Chief of Staff*); E. G. D. Pound, C.B. (*Commando Forces*); D. C. Alexander (*Training Group*).

THE ARMY

THE QUEEN

Field Marshals

The Viscount Montgomery of Alamein, K.G., G.C.B., D.S.O., *born* Nov. 17, 1887..........Sept. 1, 1944

Sir Claude J. E. Auchinleck, G.C.B., G.C.I.E., C.S.I., D.S.O., O.B.E., Col. 1 Punjab R. and Indian Grenadiers, *born* June 21, 1884.....................................June 1, 1946

H.R.H. the Prince Philip, Duke of Edinburgh, K.G., P.C., K.T., O.M., G.B.E., Field-Marshal, Australian Military Forces, Col.-in-Chief, Q.R.I.H., D.E.R.R., Q. O. Hldrs., Corps of Royal Electrical and Mechanical Engineers, A.C.F., Col. W. G., *born* June 10, 1921......Jan. 15, 1953

The Lord Harding of Petherton, G.C.B., C.B.E., D.S.O., M.C., *born* Feb. 10, 1896........July 21, 1953

Sir Gerald W. R. Templer, K.G., G.C.B., G.C.M.G., K.B.E., D.S.O., Col. R. H. G./D., *born* Sept. 11, 1898...Nov. 27, 1956

Sir Francis W. Festing, G.C.B., K.B.E., D.S.O., *born* Aug. 28, 1902........................Sept. 1, 1960

Sir Richard A. Hull, G.C.B., D.S.O., *born* May 7, 1907....................................Feb. 8, 1965

Sir A. James H. Cassels, G.C.B., K.B.E., D.S.O., *born* Feb. 28, 1907........................Feb. 29, 1968

Sir Geoffrey H. Baker, G.C.B., C.M.G., C.B.E., M.C., Col. Comdt. R.A. and R.H.A. (*Constable of the Royal Palace and Fortress of London*) (*Master Gunner, St. James's Park*), *born* June 20, 1912
March 31, 1971

Sir Michael Carver, G.C.B., C.B.E., D.S.O., M.C., Col. Comdt, R.A.C. and R.E.M.E. (*Chief of Defence Staff*), *born* April 24, 1915..July 18, 1973

Generals

Sir John Mogg, G.C.B., C.B.E., D.S.O. (*Deputy to SACEUR*).

Sir Peter Hunt, G.C.B., D.S.O., O.B.E., A.D.C. (*Gen.*), (*Chief of the General Staff*).

Sir Cecil Blacker, G.C.B., O.B.E., M.C., A.D.C.(*Gen.*), Col. 5 Innis. D.G., Col. Comdt. R.M.P. and A.P.T.C. (*Adjutant-General*).

Sir Richard Ward, K.C.B., D.S.O., M.C., Col. Comdt. R.T.R. (*Chief of Personnel and Logistics*).

Sir William Jackson, G.B.E., K.C.B., M.C.,A.D.C.(*Gen.*), Col. Gurkha Engrs, Col. Comdt. R.E. and R.A.O.C. (*Quartermaster-General*).

Sir Harry Tuzo, G.C.B., O.B.E., M.C., A.D.C. (*Gen.*) Col. Comdt. R.A. (*C.-in-C., B.A.O.R.*).

Sir John Gibbon, K.C.B., O.B.E. (*Master General of the Ordnance*)

Sir Roland Gibbs, K.C.B., C.B.E., D.S.O., M.C., Col. Comdt. 2 R.G.J. and Para. Regt. (*C.-in-C., United Kingdom Land Forces*).

Sir John Sharp, K.C.B., M.C., Col. Comdt. R.H.A., R.A. and R.A.E.C. (*C.-in-C., Allied Forces, Northern Europe*).

Sir David Fraser, K.C.B., O.B.E. (*U.K. Military Representative, H.Q., N.A.T.O.*).

Lieutenant-Generals

Sir Frank King, K.C.B., M.B.E., Col. Comdt., A.A.C.

Sir Allan Taylor, K.B.E., M.C., Col. Comdt, R.T.R. (*Deputy C.-in-C., U.K. Land Forces*).

Sir Jack Harman, K.C.B., O.B.E., M.C. (*G.O.C.1 (British) Corps*).

Sir James Baird, K.B.E., M.D., Q.H.P. (*Director-General, Army Medical Services*).

Sir Edwin Bramall, K.C.B., O.B.E., M.C., Col. Comdt. 3 R.G.J. (*Commander, British Forces Hong Kong*).

Sir Patrick Howard-Dobson, K.C.B. (*Military Secretary*).

Sir James Wilson, K.B.E., M.C., Deputy Col. (Lancs.) Royal Regt. of Fusiliers Col. Comdt. Queen's Div. (*G.O.C., South-East District*).

Sir William Scotter, K.C.B., O.B.E., M.C. (*Vice-Chief of the General Staff*).

D. W. Scott-Barrett, M.B.E., M.C. (*G.O.C., Scotland and Governor of Edinburgh Castle*).

Sir David House, C.B.E., M.C., Col. Comdt. The Light Div. (*G.O.C., and Director of Operations, Northern Ireland*).

Sir Rollo Pain, K.C.B., M.C., Col. Comdt., M.P.S.C. (*Head of British Defence Staff and Defence Attaché, Washington*).

Major-Generals

J. McGhie, M.D., Q.H.P. (*Director of Army Psychiatry*).

J. M. Strawson, C.B., O.B.E. (*Chief of Staff, U.K. Land Forces*).

T. A. Richardson, M.B.E. (*Defence and Military Adviser, India*).

A. H. Farrar-Hockley, D.S.O., M.B.E. M.C. (*Director of Combat Development (Army)*).

J. Irvine, O.B.E., M.D., Q.H.S.

G. de E. Collin, C.B., M.C. (*G.O.C., North East District*).

V. H. J. Carpenter, C.B., M.B.E. (*Director of Movements*).

R. E. Worsley, O.B.E. (*Vice Quartermaster-General*).

R. C. Ford, C.B., C.B.E. (*Commandant, Royal Military Academy, Sandhurst*).

A. J. Archer, O.B.E. (*Director of Army Staff Duties*).

H. E. Roper.

Sir Hugh Cunningham, K.B.E. (*Assistant Chief of General Staff (Operational Requirements)*).

R. W. T. Britten, M.C. (*G.O.C., West Midland District*).

J. M. W. Badcock, M.B.E., Col. Comdt., R. Signals (*Head of British Defence Liaison Staff and Defence Attaché, Canberra*).

W. G. H. Beach, O.B.E., M.C. (*Commandant, Staff College, Camberley*).

J. M. Brockbank, C.B.E., M.C. (*Vice-Adjutant-General*).

H. D. G. Butler, C.B. (*Chief of Staff, Contingency Planning, SHAPE*).

D. A. D. J. Bethell (*President, Regular Commissions Board*).

W. F. Cooper, C.B.E., M.C. (*Deputy Quartermaster-General*).

D. J. St. M. Tabor, M.C. (*G.O.C., Eastern District*).

Sir John Younger, Bt., C.B.E. (*Director, Management and Support Intelligence*).

K. Hall, O.B.E., (*Director of Army Education*).

C. W. B. Purdon, C.B.E., M.C. (*G.O.C., Near East Land Forces*).

P. R. Leuchars, C.B.E., Col.R.W.F. (*G.O.C., Wales*).

T. M. Creasey, C.B., O.B.E. (*Director of Infantry*).

P. J. M. Pellereau (*President, Ordnance Board*).

M. E. Tickell, C.B.E., M.C. (*Commandant, Royal Military College of Science*).

E. L. O. Hood, Q.H.P.

J. E. Miller, M.C., Q.H.S.

V. Metcalfe (*Commander, Support Group, R.E.M.E.*).

N. H. Speller (*Director of Ordnance Services*).

J. C. Robertson (*Director, Army Legal Services*).

R. S. N. Mans, C.B.E., Dep. Col., Queens (*Minister, Military Assistance Officer*).

P. Blunt, M.B.E., G.M. (*Transport Officer-in-Chief*).

J. G. R. Allen (*Director, Royal Armoured Corps*).

R. Lyon, O.B.E. (*G.O.C., South-West District*).

J. M. Gow, Col. Comdt. Int. Corps (*Director of Army Training*).

P. B. Tillard, C.B.E. (*Chief of Staff, B.A.O.R.*).

P. J. H. Leng, C.B., M.B.E., M.C. (*Director of Military Operations*).

P. B. Foster, M.C. (*Major-Gen. Royal Artillery, B.A.O.R.*).

P. Hudson, C.B.E. (*Chief of Staff to C.-in-C., Allied Forces, Northern Europe*).

E. M. Mackay, C.B.E. (*Chief Engineer, B.A.O.R.*).

G. Burch (*Deputy Master-General of the Ordnances*).

P. J. N. Ward, C.B.E. (*G.O.C. London District and Commander, Household Division*).

J. W. Stanier, M.B.E. (*G.O.C., No. 1 Div..*).

O. McC. Roome, C.B.E. (*Chief Joint Services Liaison Organization, B.A.O.R.*).

W. D. Mangham (*G.O.C., No. 2 Division*).

R. L. C. Dixon, M.C. (*Director of Army Air Corps*).

A. P. Dignan, M.B.E., Q.H.S. (*Director of Army Surgery and Consultant Surgeon to the Army*).

K. G. Galloway, O.B.E., Q.H.D.S. (*Director of Army Dental Services*).

J. Kelsey, C.B.E. (*Director of Military Survey*).

J. H. Page, O.B.E., M.C. (*Director of Personal Services*).

R. M. Carnegie, O.B.E. (*G.O.C., No. 3 Division*).

G. L. C. Cooper, M.C.

P. C. Shapland, M.B.E. (*Director, Volunteers, Territorials and Cadets*).

C. E. Eberhardie, M.B.E., M.C. *Assistant Chief of Staff (Intelligence) SHAPE*).

P. A. M. Tighe, M.B.E. (*Signal Officer in Chief*).

H. S. R. Watson, C.B.E. (*Senior Army Member, Royal College of Defence Studies*).

R. W. L. McAlister, O.B.E. (*Deputy Commander Land Forces, Hong Kong*).

G. H. Mills, O.B.E. (*Director of Manning (Army)*).

A. J. H. Foster (*Engineer-in-Chief*).

K. J. McQueen (*G.O.C., North-West District*).

H. Macdonald-Smith (*Director Electrical and Mechanical Engineering*).

D. B. Wood (*Director of Army Quartering*).

H. S. Gavourin, M.B.E., Q.H.S. (*Commandant, Royal Army Medical College*).

R. P. Bradshaw (*Director of Medical Services, B.A.O.R.*).

W. O'Brien, O.B.E., M.D., Q.H.P. (*Director of Army Medicine*).

A. M. L. Hogge (*Director-General, Fighting Vehicles and Engineering Equipment*).

K. Perkins, M.B.E., D.F.C. (*Commander, Sultan's Armed Forces*).

D. G. Milne (*Deputy Director, Army Medical Services*).

S. E. Large (*Director of Medical Services, U.K. Land Forces*).

D. T. Young (*Commander, Land Forces, N. Ireland*).

K. Saunders, O.B.E. (*Paymaster-in-Chief*).

D. E. Isles (*Director-General, Weapons (Army)*).

H. E. M. L. Garrett, C.B.E. (*i/c Administration, U.K. Land Forces*).

R. M. F. Redgrave (*G.O.C. Berlin (British Sector)*).

H. A. J. Sturge (*Chief Signals Officer, B.A.O.R.*).

P. J. O'B. Minogue (*Commander, Base Organisation, R.A.O.C.*).

T. L. Moroney (*Director, Royal Artillery*).

CONSTITUTION OF THE BRITISH ARMY

The Regular Forces include the following Arms, Branches and Corps. Soldiers' Records Offices are shown at the end of each group; the records of officers are maintained at the Ministry of Defence.

Household Cavalry.—The Life Guards; The Blues and Royals (Royal Horse Guards and 1st Dragoons). *Records*, Horse Guards, London, S.W.1.

Royal Armoured Corps.—Cavalry Regiments: 1st The Queen's Dragoon Guards; The Royal Scots Dragoon Guards (Carabiniers and Greys); 4th/7th Royal Dragoon Guards; 5th Royal Inniskilling Dragoon Guards; The Queen's Own Hussars; The Queen's Royal Irish Hussars; 9th/12th Royal Lancers (Prince of Wales's); The Royal Hussars (Prince of Wales's Own), 13/18th Royal Hussars (Queen Mary's Own); 14th/20th King's Hussars; 15th/19th The King's Royal Hussars; 16/5th The Queen's Royal Lancers; 17th/21st Lancers; Royal Tank Regiment comprising four regular regiments. *Records*, Friern Barnet Lane, Whetstone, N.20.

Artillery.—The Royal Regiment of Artillery. *Records*, Foots Cray, Sidcup, Kent.

Engineers.—The Corps of Royal Engineers. *Records*, Ditchling Road, Brighton.

Signals.—The Royal Corps of Signals. *Records*, Balmore House, Caversham, Reading.

Infantry.—The Brigades/Regiments of Infantry of the Line have now been reformed into Divisions as follows:—

The Guard's Division—Grenadier, Coldstream, Scots, Irish and Welsh Guards. Divisional HQ: HQ Household Division, Horse Guards, S.W.1. *Depot*: Pirbright Camp, Brookwood, Surrey. *Records*: Each Regiment of Foot Guards has its own Record Office. Grenadier Guards and Scots Guards at 4 Bloomsbury Court, W.C.1; Coldstream, Irish and Welsh Guards at King's Buildings, Dean Stanley Street, S.W.1.

The Scottish Division—The Royal Scots (The Royal Regiment); The Royal Highland Fusiliers (Princess Margaret's Own Glasgow and Ayrshire Regiment); The King's Own Scottish Borderers; The Black Watch (Royal Highland Regiment); Queen's Own Highlanders (Seaforth and Camerons); The Gordon Highlanders; The Argyll and Sutherland Highlanders (Princess Louise's). *Divisional HQ*, The Castle, Edinburgh. *Depots*, Scottish Divisional Depôts, Glencorse, Milton Bridge,

Midlothian and Gordon Barracks, Bridge of Don, Aberdeen. *Records*, Cavalry Barracks, Fulford, York.

The Queen's Division—The Queen's Regiment, The Royal Regiment of Fusiliers, The Royal Anglian Regiment. *Divisional HQ*, Bassingbourn Barracks, Royston, Herts. *Depôt*, Bassingbourn Barracks, Royston, Herts. *Records*, Higher Barracks, Exeter, Devon.

The King's Division—The King's Own Royal Border Regiment, The King's Regiment; The Prince of Wales's Own Regiment of Yorkshire; The Green Howards (Alexandra, Princess of Wales's Own Yorkshire Regiment); The Royal Irish Rangers (27th (Inniskilling) 83rd and 87th); The Queen's Lancashire Regiment; The Duke of Wellington's Regiment (West Riding). *Divisional HQ*, Imphal Barracks, York. *Depôts*, The King's Division Depôt (Lancashire) Fulwood Barracks, Preston, Lancs. The King's Division Depôt (Yorkshire), Queen Elizabeth Barracks, Strensall, Yorks. The King's Division Depôt (Royal Irish Rangers), St. Patrick's Barracks, Ballymena, Northern Ireland. *Records*, Cavalry Barracks, Fulford, York.

The Prince of Wales's Division—The Devonshire and Dorset Regiment; The Cheshire Regiment; The Royal Welch Fusiliers, The Royal Regiment of Wales; The Gloucestershire Regiment; The Worcestershire and Sherwood Foresters Regiment (29th/45th Foot); The Royal Hampshire Regiment; The Staffordshire Regiment (The Prince of Wales's); The Duke of Edinburgh's Royal Regiment (Berkshire and Wiltshire). *Divisional HQ*, Whittington Barracks, Lichfield, Staffs. *Depôts*, Wessex Depôt, The Prince of Wales's Division, Wyvern Barracks, Exeter, Devon; Mercian Depôt, The Prince of Wales's Division, Whittington Barracks, Lichfield, Staffs; Welsh Depôt, The Prince of Wales's Division, Cwrt-y-Gollen, Crickhowell, Breconshire. *Records*, Cavalry Barracks, Fulford, York.

The Light Division—The Light Infantry; The Royal Green Jackets, Divisional H.Q., Peninsula Barracks, Winchester, Hants. *Depôts*, The Light Infantry Depôt, Sir John Moore Barracks, Copthorne, Shrewsbury, Salop. The Rifle Depôt, Peninsula Barracks, Winchester, Hants. *Records*, Higher Barracks, Exeter.

The Parachute Regiment—*Depot*, Browning Barracks, Aldershot, Hants. *Records*, Higher Barracks, Exeter.

The Brigade of Gurkhas—2nd King Edward VII's Own Gurkha Rifles (The Sirmoor Rifles); 6th Queen Elizabeth's Own Gurkha Rifles; 7th Duke of Ednbiurgh's Own Gurkha Rifles; 10th Princess Mary's Own Gurkha Rifles, Gurkha Engineers, Gurkha Signals, Gurkha Transport Regt. *Brigade HQ*, Victoria Barracks, Hong Kong. *Depot*, Training Depôt, Brigade of Gurkhas, Sek Kong (South), Hong Kong, B.F.P.O. 1. *Records*, The Brigade of Gurkha Record Office, Hong Kong, B.F.P.O. 1.

The Special Air Service Regiment—*Regimental HQ*, Duke of York's Headquarters, Sloane Square, S.W.3. *Depôt*, Bradbury Lines, Hereford. *Records*, Higher Barracks, Exeter, Devon.

Royal Corps of Transport, Army Catering Corps. *Records*, Ore Place, Hastings.

Royal Army Medical Corps, Royal Army Dental Corps, Queen Alexandra's Royal Army Nursing Corps, and Women's Royal Army Corps. *Records*, Lower Barracks, Winchester.

Royal Army Ordnance Corps, Royal Electrical and Mechanical Engineers. *Records*, Glen Parva Barracks, Saffron Road, South Wigston, Leicester.

Small Arms School Corps. *Records*, Higher Barracks, Exeter.

General Service Corps. *Records*, Cavalry Barracks, Fulford Road, York.

Army Air Corps, Royal Military Police, Royal Army Pay Corps, Royal Army Veterinary Corps, Royal Army Educational Corps, Royal Pioneer Corps, Intelligence Corps, and other ancillary corps not listed above. *Records*, Higher Barracks, Exeter, Devon.

———

The Territorial and Army Volunteer Reserve (TAVR) came into being on April 1, 1967, replacing the Army Emergency Reserve and the Territorial Army. Its main function is to reinforce the Regular Army in times of national emergency.

The Establishment is approximately 74,000 and the TAVR is designed to provide a reserve of highly trained and well equipped units and individuals.

THE ROYAL AIR FORCE
THE QUEEN
Marshals of the Royal Air Force

Sir Arthur T. Harris, Bt., G.C.B., O.B.E., A.F.C., *born April* 13, 1892..........................Jan. 1, 1946

Sir John C. Slessor, G.C.B., D.S.O., M.C., *born June* 3, 1897..................................June 8, 1950

H.R.H. the Prince Philip, Duke of Edinburgh, K.G., P.C., K.T., O.M., G.B.E. (*Air Commodore-in-Chief, Air Training Corps, Marshal of the R.A.A.F.*) *born June* 10, 1921....................Jan. 15, 1953

Sir William F. Dickson, G.C.B., K.B.E., D.S.O., A.F.C., *born Sept.* 24, 1898...................June 1, 1954

Sir Dermot A. Boyle, G.C.B., K.C.V.O., K.B.E., A.F.C., *born Oct.* 2, 1904......................Jan. 1, 1958

Sir Thomas G. Pike, G.C.B., C.B.E., D.F.C., *born June* 29, 1906.............................April 6, 1962

The Lord Elworthy, G.C.B., C.B.E., D.S.O., M.V.O., D.F.C., A.F.C. (*Governor and Constable of Windsor Castle*), *born March* 23, 1911...April 1, 1967

Sir John Grandy, G.C.B , K.B.E., D.S.O., *born Feb.* 8, 1913 (*Governor and Commander-in-Chief, Gibraltar*)..April 1, 1971

Sir Denis Spotswood, G.C.B., C.B.E., D.S.O., D.F.C., *born Sept.* 26, 1916..................March 31, 1974

Air Chief Marshals		
	Sir Neil Wheeler, G.C.B., C.B.E., D.S.O., D.F.C., A.F.C.	Sir Derek Hodgkinson, K.C.B., C.B.E., D.F.C., A.F.C. (*Air Secretary*).
Sir Andrew Humphrey, G.C.B., O.B.E., D.F.C., A.F.C., A.D.C. (*Chief of Air Staff*).	Sir Denis Smallwood, G.B.E., K.C.B., D.S.O., D.F.C. (*C.-in-C., U.K. Air Forces*).	Sir Anthony Heward, K.C.B., O.B.E., D.F.C., A.F.C. (*Air Member for Supply and Organization*).
Sir Lewis Hodges, K.C.B., C.B.E., D.S.O., D.F.C., A.D.C. (*Deputy C.-in-C., Allied Forces, Central Europe*).	Sir John Barraclough, K.C.B., C.B.E., D.F.C., A.F.C. (*Commandant, Royal College of Defence Studies*).	**Air Marshals** Sir Neville Stack, K.C.B., C.V.O., C.B.E., A.F.C., (*A.O.C.-in-C., Training Command*).

Sir Peter Le Cheminant, K.C.B., D.F.C.

Sir Nigel Maynard, K.C.B., C.B.E., D.F.C., A.F.C. (*C.-in-C., R.A.F., Germany*).

Sir John Aiken, K.C.B. (*A.O.C.-in-C., Near East Air Force*).

Sir Douglas Lowe, K.C.B., D.F.C., A.F.C. (*Controller of Aircraft*).

Sir Charles Pringle, K.B.E. (*Controller of Engineering and Supply*).

Sir Ruthven Wade, K.C.B., D.F.C. (*Vice-Chief of Air Staff*).

Sir Michael Giddings, K.C.B., O.B.E., D.F.C., A.F.C. (*Deputy Chief of Defence Staff (Operational Requirements*)).

Sir Reginald Harland, K.B.E., C.B. (*A.O.C.-in-C., Support Command*).

Sir Geoffrey Dhenin, K.B.E., A.F.C., G.M., Q.H.P. (*Director-General of Medical Services*).

Sir Neil Cameron, K.C.B., C.B.E., D.S.O., D.F.C. (*Air Member for Personnel*).

Sir Ivor Broom, K.C.B., C.B.E., D.S.O., D.F.C., A.F.C. (*Controller, National Air Traffic Services*).

A. H. W. Ball, C.B., D.S.O., D.F.C. (*U.K. Representative, Permanent Military Deputies Group, CENTO*).

R. G. Wakeford, M.V.O., O.B.E., A.F.C. (*Deputy Chief of the Defence Staff (Intelligence*)).

M. J. Beetham, C.B.E., D.F.C., A.F.C. (*Deputy C.-in-C., Strike Command*).

Air Vice-Marshals

A. McK. S. Steedman, C.B., C.B.E., D.F.C. (*Director General of Organisation*).

J. C. T. Downey, C.B., D.F.C., A.F.C.

D. G. Evans, C.B.E. (*A.O.C., No. 1 Group*).

H. Durkin, C.B. (*Director-General of Engineering and Supply Management, Ministry of Defence*).

R. J. A. Morris, C.B., Q.H.S. (*P.M.O., Strike Command*).

A. Sidney-Wilmot, O.B.E. (*Director of Legal Services*).

F. B. Sowrey, C.B., O.B.E., A.F.C. (*Director-General of R.A.F. Training*).

R. W. G. Freer, C.B.E. (*A.O.C., No. 18 Group*).

P. J. O'Connor, O.B.E., Q.H.P. (*Consultant Advisor, Central Medical Establishment*).

R. D. Roe, C.B., A.F.C. (*S.A.S.O., Near East Air Force*).

F. R. L. Mellersh, D.F.C. (*Air Officer, Flying and Officer Training, Training Command*).

C. W. Coulthard, C.B., A.F.C. (*Military Deputy to Head of Defence Sales*).

A. Griffiths, C.B., A.F.C. (*Commandant-General, R.A.F. Regiment*).

A. D. Button, O.B.E. (*Director of Educational Services*).

F. S. Hazlewood, C.B., C.B.E., A.F.C. (*Commandant, Joint Warfare Establishment*).

A. C. Davies, C.B., C.B.E. (*Deputy Chief of Staff (Operations and Intelligence) NATO H.Q.*).

R. D. Austen-Smith, C.B., D.F.C.

P. G. K. Williamson, C.B.E., D.F.C. (*A.O.C., No. 38 Group*).

W. J. Stacey, C.B.E.

J. M. Nicholls, C.B.E., D.F.C., A.F.C. (*Assitant Chief of the Air Staff (Policy*)).

G. H. Ford, C.B. (*Air Officer Engineering, Strike Command*).

J. N. Stacey, C.B., C.B.E., D.S.O., D.F.C. (*A.O.A., Support Command*).

D. J. Furner, C.B.E., D.F.C., A.F.C. *Assistant Air Secretary*).

W. E. Colahan, C.B.E., D.F.C. (*A.O.C. and Commandant, Cranwell*).

P. I. Lagesen, C.B., D.F.C., A.F.C. (*A.O.C., No. 1 Group*).

N. E. Hoad, C.V.O., C.B.E., A.F.C. (*A.O.C., No. 46 Group*).

C. M. Gibbs, C.B.E., D.F.C. (*Director-General of Personnel Services (R.A.F.*)).

J. Gingell, C.B.E. (*Assistant Chief of Defence Staff (Policy*)).

P. D. G. Terry, C.B., A.F.C. (*Assistant Chief of Staff (Plans and Policy), SHAPE*).

J. I. R. Bowring, C.B.E. (*Air Officer Engineering and Supply Support Command*).

G. E. Thirlwall (*Air Officer Ground Training Command*).

H. C. Southgate, C.B.E. (*Director-General of Supply Policy and Plans*).

D. F. G. Macleod, Q.H.D.S.

J. J. McNair, Q.H.P. (*P.M.O., Support Command*).

G. C. Lamb, C.B.E., A.F.C. (*Chief of Staff, No. 18 Group*).

B. G. Lock, C.B.E., A.F.C. (*Commander, North Maritime Air Region and Air Officer Scotland and Northern Ireland*).

D. L. Attlee, M.V.O. (*A.O.A., Training Command*).

K. A. Williamson, A.F.C. (*Commandant, R.A.F. College, Bracknell*).

S. M. Davidson, C.B.E. (*Assistant Chief of Defence Staff (Signals*)).

G. C. Cairns, C.B.E., A.F.C. (*Assistant Chief of Air Staff (Operational Requirements*)).

W. Harrison, C.B.E., A.F.C.(*A.O.C., No. 11 Group*).

C. G. Maughan, C.B.E., A.F.C. (*S.A.S.O., Strike Command*).

D. B. Craig, O.B.E. (*Assistant Chief of the Air Staff (Operations*)).

P. M. S. Hedgeland, O.B.E. (*Vice-President, Ordnance Board*).

B. G. T. Stanbridge C.B.E., M.V.O., A.F.C. (*Defence Services Secretary*).

A. D. Dick, O.B.E. A.F.C. (*Deputy Controller of Aircraft C*).

THE UNION JACK SERVICES CLUBS

Patron-in-Chief: Her Majesty the Queen.

President: Major-Gen. Sir Julian Gascoigne, K.C.M.G., K.C.V.O., C.B., D.S.O.

Comptroller: Col. C. A. la T. Leatham.

Club Secretary: L. F. Moulton.

THE UNION JACK CLUB

Sandell Street, S. E.1

[Tel.: 01–928 6401]

The Union Jack Club has recently been rebuilt and the new premises stand on the site of the old building. It provides residential accommodation for service and ex-service men and women and their families. All serving men and women below commissioned rank are members. Ex-service membership is by election. Honorary membership is extended to the Forces of other nations visiting the United Kingdom.

The new premises provides the most modern standards of accommodation with 417 single bedrooms and 55 double bedrooms for families. The facilities include restaurant, bars, a full range of public rooms including billiards, a sauna bath and launderette. A new feature of the Union Jack Club is a separate conference area with a maximum capacity of 200 persons for meetings, or 120 for Regimental or Association dinners.

The original Union Jack Club was erected by public subscription as a National Memorial to those who had fallen in the South African War and other campaigns and was opened in 1907 by King Edward VII.

SERVICE SALARIES AND PENSIONS

The following military salaries became effective on April 1, 1975, replacing those introduced one year earlier. Cost of living supplements have been subsumed into the new rates. The fourth Report of the Review Body on Armed Forces Pay, on whose recommendation these rates are based, was concerned with ranks up to and including that of Brigadier, whilst the salaries of Major-Generals (or equivalent rank) and above were reviewed separately. Since 1970 the determining factor of the Review Body's recommendations has been the relation of forces' salaries to civilian earnings by job evaluation. On this occasion their recommendations were made following the ending in July 1974 of the Government's statutory pay controls. The Review Body also recommended the undermentioned salaries for the Women's Services. These rates reflect equal pay for equal work and conditions, but because the X-factor for women is lower than that for men, women's total emoluments approximate to 95.45 per cent. of the rates for men.

ROYAL NAVY AND ROYAL MARINES
Normal Rates

Rank (and equivalent rank, R.M.)	Pay Daily	Pay Annual
	£	£
Midshipman	4·68	1,708
After 1 year in the rank	6·25	2,281
Sub-Lieutenant	7·33	2,675
After 2 years in the rank	9·11	3,325
After 3 years in the rank	9·83	3,588
Lieutenant R.N.	11·29	4,121
After 1 year in the rank	11·59	4,230
After 2 years in the rank	11·89	4,340
After 3 years in the rank	12·19	4,449
After 4 years in the rank	12·49	4,559
After 5 years in the rank	12·79	4,668
After 6 years in the rank	13·09	4,778
Lieutenant R.M.	9·11	3,325
After 1 year in the rank	11·29	4,121
After 2 years in the rank	11·59	4,230
After 3 years in the rank	11·89	4,340
After 4 years in the rank	12·19	4,449
After 5 years in the rank	12·49	4,559
After 6 years in the rank	12·79	4,668
After 7 years in the rank	13·09	4,778
Lieutenant-Commander/Captain R.M.	13·98	5,103
After 1 year in the rank	14·32	5,227
After 3 years in the rank	14·66	5,351
After 4 years in the rank	15·00	5,475
After 5 years in the rank	15·34	5,599
After 6 years in the rank	15·68	5,723
After 7 years in the rank	16·02	5,847
After 8 years in the rank	16·36	5,971
	16·70	6,096
Commander R.N./Major R.M.	18·47	6,742
After 2 years in the rank or with 19 years' service	18·96	6,920
After 4 years in the rank or with 21 years' service	19·45	7,099
After 6 years in the rank or with 23 years' service	19·94	7,278
After 8 years in the rank or with 25 years' service	20·43	7,457
Captain R.N./Lieutenant-Colonel R.M.	22·38	8,169
After 2 years in the rank	22·97	8,384
After 4 years in the rank	23·56	8,599
Captain R.N. with 6 years' seniority/Colonel R.M.	27·40	10,001
Rear-Admiral/Major-General R.M.	32·87	11,998
Vice-Admiral/Lieutenant-General R.M.	38·35	13,998
Admiral/General R.M.	49·11	17,925
Admiral of the Fleet	53·90	19,674

ARMY
Normal Rates

Rank	Pay Daily	Pay Annual
	£	£
Second-Lieutenant	7·33	2,675
Lieutenant	9·11	3,325
After 1 year in the rank	9·35	3,413
After 2 years in the rank	9·59	3,500
After 3 years in the rank	9·83	3,588
After 4 years in the rank	10·07	3,676
Captain	11·29	4,121
After 1 year in the rank	11·59	4,230
After 2 years in the rank	11·89	4,340
After 3 years in the rank	12·19	4,449
After 4 years in the rank	12·49	4,559
After 5 years in the rank	12·79	4,668
After 6 years in the rank	13·09	4,778
Major	13·98	5,103
After 1 year in the rank	14·32	5,227
After 2 years in the rank	14·66	5,351
After 3 years in the rank	15·00	5,475
After 4 years in the rank	15·34	5,599
After 5 years in the rank	15·68	5,723
After 6 years in the rank	16·02	5,847
After 7 years in the rank	16·36	5,971
After 8 years in the rank	16·70	6,096
Lieutenant-Colonel—Special List	18·61	6,793
Lieutenant-Colonel	18·47	6,742
After 2 years in the rank or with 19 years' service	18·96	6,920
After 4 years in the rank or with 21 years' service	19·45	7,099
After 6 years in the rank or with 23 years' service	19·94	7,278
After 8 years in the rank or with 25 years' service	20·43	7,457
Colonel	22·38	8,169
After 2 years in the rank	22·97	8,384
After 4 years in the rank	23·56	8,599
After 6 years in the rank	24·15	8,815
After 8 years in the rank	24·74	9,030
Brigadier	27·40	10,001
Major-General	32·87	11,998
Lieutenant-General	38·35	13,998
General	49·11	17,925
Field-Marshal	53·90	19,674

ROYAL AIR FORCE
Normal Rates

Rank *In this rank	Daily	Annual	Rank *In this rank	Daily	Annual
	£	£		£	£
Acting Pilot Officer.............	6·25	2,281	Squadron Leader—*contd.*		
After 6 months* (aircrew officers			After 7 years*...............	16·36	5,971
only)......................	6·42	2,343	After 8 years*...............	16·70	6,096
Pilot Officer....................	7·33	2,675	Wing Commander.............	18·47	6,742
Flying Officer..................	9·11	3,325	After 2 years* or 19 years'		
After 1 year*...............	9·35	3,413	commissioned service........	18·96	6,920
After 2 years*...............	9·59	3,500	After 4 years* or 21 years'		
After 3 years*...............	9·83	3,588	commissioned service........	19·45	7,099
After 4 years*...............	10·07	3,676	After 6 years* or 23 years'		
Flight Lieutenant................	11·29	4,121	commissioned service........	19·94	7,278
After 1 year*...............	11·59	4,230	After 8 years* or 25 years'		
After 2 years*...............	11·89	4,340	commissioned service........	20·43	7,457
After 3 years*...............	12·19	4,449	Group Captain.................	22·38	8,169
After 4 years*...............	12·49	4,559	After 2 years*...............	22·97	8,384
After 5 years*...............	12·79	4,668	After 4 years*...............	23·56	8,599
After 6 years*...............	13·09	4,778	After 6 years*...............	24·15	8,815
Squadron Leader................	13·98	5,103	After 8 years*...............	24·74	9,030
After 1 year*...............	14·32	5,227	Air Commodore................	27·40	10,001
After 2 years*...............	14·66	5,351	Air Vice Marshal.............	32·87	11,998
After 3 years*...............	15·00	5,475	Air Marshal..................	38·35	13,998
After 4 years*...............	15·34	5,599	Air Chief Marshal.............	49·11	17,925
After 5 years*...............	15·68	5,723	Marshal of the Royal Air Force...	53·90	19,674
After 6 years*...............	16·02	5,847			

ALL SERVICES
Rates for Officers promoted from the ranks

Years of commissioned service	Years of Service in the Ranks					
	Less than 12 years		12 years but less than 15 years		15 years or more	
	Daily	Annual	Daily	Annual	Daily	Annual
	£	£	£	£	£	£
On appointment...............	11·89	4,340	12·49	4,559	13·09	4,778
After 1 year................	12·19	4,449	12·79	4,668	13·31	4,858
After 2 years...............	12·49	4,559	13·09	4,778	13·53	4,938
After 3 years...............	12·79	4,668	13·31	4,858	13·75	5,109
After 4 years...............	13·09	4,778	13·53	4,938	13·97	5,099
After 5 years...............	13·31	4,858	13·75	5,019	14·19	5,179
After 6 years...............	13·53	4,938	13·97	5,099	14·41	5,260
After 8 years...............	13·75	5,019	14·19	5,179	14·63	5,340
After 10 years...............	13·97	5,099	14·41	5,260	—	—
After 12 years...............	14·19	5,179	14·63	5,340	—	—
After 14 years...............	14·41	5,260	—	—	—	—
After 16 years...............	14·63	5,340	—	—	—	—

ROYAL NAVY SEAMAN BRANCH
Daily Rates

Rating/Rank	Less than 6 years Scale A			6 years but less than 9 years Scale B			9 years or more Scale C		
Scale	III	II	I	III	II	I	III	II	I
	£	£	£	£	£	£	£	£	£
Ordinary Rating..................	—	4·68	5·11	—	4·98	5·41	—	5·43	5·86
Able Rating......................	5·63	6·09	6·49	5·93	6·39	6·79	6·38	6·84	7·24
Leading Rating...................	—	7·52	8·03	—	7·82	8·33	—	8·26	8·78
Petty Officer.....................	—	8·70	8·86	—	9·00	9·16	—	9·45	9·61
Chief Petty Officer (incl. Artisans)....	—	9·63	9·81	—	9·93	10·11	—	10·38	10·56
Fleet Chief Petty Officer.............	—	—	10·82	—	—	11·12	—	—	11·57

ARTIFICERS AND MECHANICIANS

Daily Rates

Rating	less than 6 years	6 years but less than 9 years	9 years or more
	Scale A	Scale B	Scale C
	£	£	£
Mechanician 5th Class (Able Rating)....................	6·49	6·79	7·24
Artificer 3rd Class (Leading Rating)................... }	7·52	7·82	8·27
Mechanician Acting 4th Class (Acting Leading Rating).... }			
Mechanician 4th Class (Leading Rating).................	8·03	8·33	8·78
Mechanician 3rd Class (Petty Officer).................. }	8·92	9·22	9·67
Artificer Acting 2nd Class (Acting Petty Officer).......... }			
Petty Officer 2nd Class..............................	9·36	9·66	10·11
Chief Petty Officer 1st Class.........................	10·38	10·68	11·13
After 2 years................................	10·71	11·01	11·46
After 4 years................................	10·82	11·12	11·57
After 6 years................................	10·90	11·20	11·65
Chief Artificer/Mechanician..........................	11·22	11·52	11·97
Fleet Chief Petty Officer.............................	11·54	11·84	12·29

ARMY

Other Ranks

Daily Rates

Rank		Scale A*			Scale B*			Scale C*		
	Band	1	2	3	1	2	3	1	2	3
		£	£	£	£	£	£	£	£	£
Private Class IV............		4·68	—	—	4·98	—	—	5·43	—	—
Class III............		5·08	5·63	—	5·38	5·93	—	5·83	6·38	—
Class II............		5·40	5·95	—	5·70	6·25	—	6·15	6·70	—
Class I............		5·74	6·29	6·90	6·04	6·59	7·20	6·49	7·04	7·65
Lance Corporal Class III....		5·74	6·29	—	6·04	6·59	—	6·49	7·04	—
Class II.....		6·10	6·65	—	6·40	6·95	—	6·85	7·40	—
Class I.....		6·49	7·04	7·65	6·79	7·34	7·95	7·24	7·79	8·40
Corporal Class II............		6·97	7·52	—	7·27	7·82	—	7·72	8·27	—
Class I............		7·48	8·03	8·64	7·78	8·33	8·94	8·23	8·78	9·39

Rank		Scale A*				Scale B*				Scale C*			
	Band	4	5	6	7	4	5	6	7	4	5	6	7
		£	£	£	£	£	£	£	£	£	£	£	£
Sergeant.....................		8·10	8·70	9·36	—	8·40	9·00	9·66	—	8·85	9·45	10·11	—
Staff Sergeant...............		8·56	9·16	9·82	10·54	8·86	9·46	10·12	10·84	9·31	9·91	10·57	11·29
Warrant Officer Class II....		9·05	9·65	10·31	11·03	9·35	9·95	10·61	11·33	9·80	10·40	11·06	11·78
Class I....		9·56	10·16	10·82	11·54	9·86	10·46	11·12	11·84	10·31	10·91	11·57	12·29

* SCALES.—A = less than 6 years; B = 6 years but less than 9 years; C = 9 years or more.

LENGTH OF SERVICE INCREMENTS

R.N., R.M., Q.A.R.N.N.S. and W.R.N.S.	No. of years' Service				ARMY, Q.A.R.A.N.C. and W.R.A.C.	No. of Years' Service				
Rating/Rank	9	12	16	22	Rank	9	12	15	18	22
	£	£	£	£		£	£	£	£	£
Able/Marine 1st Class.......	0·20	0·30	—	—	Private..........	0·20	0·30	0·30	0·30	0·30
Leading/Corporal (R.M.)....	0·20	0·30	—	—	Lance-Corporal..	0·20	0·30	0·30	0·30	0·30
P.O./Sergeant (R.M.).....	0·25	0·35	0·55	—	Corporal........	0·20	0·30	0·35	0·35	0·35
C.P.O./Colour Sergeant.....	0·30	0·50	0·60	—	Sergeant........	0·25	0·35	0·45	0·55	0·55
Warrant Officer Class II (R.M.)	0·30	0·50	0·65	0·80	Staff-Sergeant....	0·25	0·35	0·45	0·60	0·60
Fleet C.P.O./Warrant Officer Class I (R.M.)...........	0·30	0·50	0·65	0·85	Warrant Officer Class II.........	0·25	0·35	0·45	0·60	0·70
					Warrant Officer Class I.........	0·25	0·35	0·45	0·60	0·85

ROYAL AIR FORCE

Rank					Rank			
AIRCREW (i) Pilots, Navigators, Air Electronics Operators and Air Engineers (A)	A*	B*	C*	AIRCREW (ii) Air Signallers, Air Engineers and Air Loadmasters	A*	B*	C*
		£	£	£		£	£	£
Sergeant...................		9·36	9·66	10·11	Sergeant...................	8·70	9·00	9·45
Flight Sergeant.............		10·82	11·12	11·57	Flight Sergeant.............	10·10	10·40	10·85
Master Aircrew.............		11·54	11·84	12·29	Master Aircrew.............	10·82	11·12	11·57

* SCALES.—A = less than 6 years; B = 6 years but less than 9 years; C = 9 years or more.

AIRMEN (Ground Trades)

Rank	Band	Less than 6 years Scale A			6 years but less than 9 years—Scale B			9 years or more Scale C		
		1	2	3	1	2	3	1	2	3
		£	£	£	£	£	£	£	£	£
Aircraftman		4·68	4·68	4·68	4·98	4·98	4·98	5·43	5·43	5·43
Leading Aircraftman		5·08	5·63	6·24	5·38	5·93	6·54	5·83	6·38	6·99
Senior Aircraftman		5·74	6·29	6·90	6·04	6·59	7·20	6·49	7·04	7·65
Junior Technician		6·49	7·04	7·65	6·79	7·34	7·95	7·24	7·79	8·40
Corporal		7·39	7·94	8·64	7·69	8·24	8·94	8·14	8·69	9·39

Rank	Band	4	5	6	7	4	5	6	7	4	5	6	7
		£	£	£	£	£	£	£	£	£	£	£	£
Sergeant		8·10	8·70	9·36	—	8·40	9·00	9·66	—	8·85	9·45	10·11	—
Chief Technician		8·41	9·01	9·67	—	8·71	9·31	9·97	—	9·16	9·76	10·42	—
Flight Sergeant		8·73	9·33	10·10	10·82	9·03	9·63	10·40	11·12	9·48	10·08	10·85	11·57
Warrant Officer		9·56	10·16	10·82	11·54	9·86	10·46	11·12	11·84	10·31	10·91	11·57	12·29

LENGTH OF SERVICE INCREMENTS

R.A.F. P.M.R.A.F.N.S. (N.C.E.) and W.R.A.F. Rank	No. of Years' Service				
	9	12	15	18	22
	£	£	£	£	£
Leading Aircraftman, Senior Aircraftman and Junior Technician	0·20	0·30	0·30	0·30	0·30
Corporal	0·20	0·30	0·35	0·35	0·35
Sergeant	0·25	0·35	0·45	0·55	0·55
Chief Technician	0·25	0·35	0·45	0·60	0·60
Flight Sergeant	0·25	0·35	0·45	0·60	0·60
Warrant Officer	0·25	0·35	0·45	0·60	0·85

Officers of W.R.N.S.

Rank	Daily	Annual
	£	£
Probationary 3rd Officer	7·00	2,555
3rd Officer	7·57	2,763
After 2 years in the rank	8·70	3,176
After 3 years in the rank	8·92	3,256
After 4 years in the rank	9·15	3,340
After 5 years in the rank	9·38	3,424
After 6 years in the rank	9·61	3,508
2nd Officer	10·78	3,935
After 1 year in the rank	11·06	4,037
After 2 years in the rank	11·35	4,143
After 3 years in the rank	11·64	4,249
After 4 years in the rank	11·92	4,351
After 5 years in the rank	12·21	4,457
After 6 years in the rank	12·49	4,559
1st Officer	13·34	4,869
After 1 year in the rank	13·67	4,990
After 2 years in the rank	13·99	5,106
After 3 years in the rank	14·32	5,227
After 4 years in the rank	14·64	5,344
After 5 years in the rank	14·97	5,464
After 6 years in the rank	15·29	5,581
After 7 years in the rank	15·62	5,701
After 8 years in the rank	15·94	5,818
Chief Officer	17·63	6,435
After 2 years in the rank or 19 years' service	18·10	6,607
After 4 years in the rank or 21 years' service	18·57	6,778
After 6 years in the rank or 23 years' service	19·05	6,953

W.R.N.S.—*continued*

Rank	Daily	Annual
	£	£
After 8 years in the rank or 25 years' service	19·54	7,132
Superintendent	21·70	7,921
After 2 years in the rank	22·29	8,136
After 4 years in the rank	22·88	8,351
After 6 years in the rank	23·47	8,567
After 8 years in the rank	24·06	8,782
Director W.R.N.S.	26·99	9,851

Officers of W.R.A.C., and non-nursing officers of Q.A.R.A.N.C.

Rank	Daily	Annual
	£	£
Second-Lieutenant	7·00	2,555
Lieutenant	8·70	3,176
After 1 year in the rank	8·92	3,256
After 2 years in the rank	9·15	3,340
After 3 years in the rank	9·38	3,424
After 4 years in the rank	9·61	3,508
Captain	10·78	3,935
After 1 year in the rank	11·06	4,037
After 2 years in the rank	11·35	4,143
After 3 years in the rank	11·64	4,249
After 4 years in the rank	11·92	4,351
After 5 years in the rank	12·21	4,457
After 6 years in the rank	12·49	4,559
Major	13·34	4,869
After 1 year in the rank	13·67	4,990
After 2 years in the rank	13·99	5,106
After 3 years in the rank	14·32	5,227
After 4 years in the rank	14·64	5,344
After 5 years in the rank	14·97	5,464
After 6 years in the rank	15·29	5,581
After 7 years in the rank	15·62	5,701
After 8 years in the rank	15·94	5,818
Lieutenant Colonel	17·63	6,435
With 19 years' service or after 2 years in the rank	18·10	6,607
With 21 years' service or after 4 years in the rank	18·57	6,778
With 23 years' service or after 6 years in the rank	19·05	6,953
With 25 years' service or after 8 years in the rank	19·54	7,132
Colonel	21·70	7,921
After 2 years in the rank	22·29	8,136
After 4 years in the rank	22·88	8,351
After 6 years in the rank	23·47	8,567
After 8 years in the rank	24·06	8,782
Brigadier	26·99	9,851

Officers of W.R.A.F.

Rank	Daily £	Annual £
Acting Pilot Officer	5·97	2,179
Pilot Officer	7·00	2,555
Flying Officer	8·70	3,176
After 1 year in the rank	8·92	3,256
After 2 years in the rank	9·15	3,340
After 3 years in the rank	9·38	3,424
After 4 years in the rank	9·61	3,508
Flight Lieutenant	10·28	3,935
After 1 year in the rank	11·06	4,037
After 2 years in the rank	11·35	4,143
After 3 years in the rank	11·64	4,249
After 4 years in the rank	11·92	4,351
After 5 years in the rank	12·21	4,457
After 6 years in the rank	12·49	4,559
Squadron Leader	13·34	4,869
After 1 year in the rank	13·67	4,990
After 2 years in the rank	13·99	5,106
After 3 years in the rank	14·32	5,227
After 4 years in the rank	14·64	5,344
After 5 years in the rank	14·97	5,464
After 6 years in the rank	15·29	5,581
After 7 years in the rank	15·62	5,701
After 8 years in the rank	15·94	5,818
Wing Commander	17·63	6,435
After 2 years* or 19 years' commissioned service	18·10	6,607
After 4 years* or 21 years' commissioned service	18·57	6,778
After 6 years* or 23 years' commissioned service	19·05	6,953
After 8 years* or 25 years' commissioned service	19·54	7,132

Officers of W.R.A.F.—*contd.*

Rank	Daily £	Annual £
Group Captain	21·70	7,921
After 2 years*	22·29	8,136
After 4 years*	22·88	8,351
After 6 years*	23·47	8,567
After 8 years*	24·06	8,782
Air Commodore	26·99	9,851

* In the rank.

W.R.N.S. Ratings

Rating	Scale	Band 1 £	Band 2 £	Band 3 £
Wren (Ordinary)	under 17½	3·38	3·38	3·38
	at 17½	4·47	4·47	4·47
Wren (Able)	III	4·83	5·36	5·94
	II	5·27	5·80	6·38
	I	5·65	6·18	6·76
Leading Wren	II	6·64	7·17	7·75
	I	7·12	7·65	8·23

Rating	Scale	Band 4 £	Band 5 £	Band 6 £	Band 7 £
P.O. Wren	II	7·64	8·21	8·84	9·53
	I	7·80	8·37	9·00	9·69
Chief Wren	II	8·21	8·78	9·41	10·10
	I	8·43	9·00	9·63	10·32
Fleet Chief Wren	I	9·11	9·68	10·31	11·00

W.R.A.C.

Rank	Band	Less than 6 years — Scale A 1 £	2 £	3 £	6 years but less than 9 years — Scale B 1 £	2 £	3 £	9 years or more — Scale C 1 £	2 £	3 £
Private Class IV under 17½		3·38	—	—	—	—	—	—	—	—
Class IV		4·47	—	—	4·77	—	—	5·22	—	—
Class III		4·83	5·36	—	5·13	5·66	—	5·58	6·11	—
Class II		5·14	5·67	—	5·44	5·97	—	5·89	6·42	—
Class I		5·46	5·99	6·57	5·76	6·29	6·87	6·21	6·74	7·32
Lance Corporal Class III		5·46	5·99	—	5·76	6·29	—	6·21	6·74	—
Class II		5·80	6·33	—	6·10	6·63	—	6·55	7·08	—
Class I		6·18	6·71	7·29	6·48	7·01	7·59	6·93	7·46	8·04
Corporal Class II		6·64	7·17	—	6·94	7·47	—	7·39	7·92	—
Class I		7·12	7·65	8·23	7·42	7·95	8·53	7·87	8·40	8·98

Rank	Band	4 £	5 £	6 £	7 £	4 £	5 £	6 £	7 £	4 £	5 £	6 £	7 £
Sergeant		7·72	8·29	8·92	—	8·02	8·59	9·22	—	8·47	9·04	9·67	—
Staff Sergeant		8·16	8·73	9·36	10·05	8·46	9·03	9·66	10·35	8·91	9·48	10·11	10·80
Warrant Officer Class II		8·62	9·19	9·82	10·51	8·92	9·49	10·12	10·81	9·37	9·94	10·57	11·26
Class I		9·11	9·68	10·31	11·00	9·41	9·98	10·61	11·30	9·86	10·43	11·06	11·75

Sergeants and above whose employment classification is Class II and Corporals whose employment classification is Class III shall be paid £0·12 or £0·06 a day respectively less than the rates shown.

W.R.A.F. AIRWOMEN

Rank	Less than 6 years Scale A			6 years but less than 9 years Scale B			9 years or more Scale C		
Band	1	2	3	1	2	3	1	2	3
	£	£	£	£	£	£	£	£	£
Aircraftwoman under 17½	3·38	—	—	—	—	—	—	—	—
17½ and above	4·47	4·47	4·47	—	—	—	—	—	—
Leading Aircraftwoman	4·83	5·36	5·94	5·13	5·66	6·24	5·58	6·11	6·69
Senior Aircraftwoman	5·46	5·99	6·57	5·76	6·29	6·87	6·21	6·74	7·32
Junior Technician	6·18	6·71	7·29	6·48	7·01	7·59	6·93	7·46	8·04
Corporal	7·04	7·57	8·23	7·34	7·87	8·53	7·79	8·32	8·98
Band	4	5	6	7	4	5	6	7	4	5	6	7

Rank	4	5	6	7	4	5	6	7	4	5	6	7
	£	£	£	£	£	£	£	£	£	£	£	£
Sergeant	7·72	8·29	8·92	—	8·02	8·59	9·22	—	8·47	9·04	9·67	—
Chief Technician	8·02	8·59	9·22	—	8·32	8·89	9·52	—	8·77	9·34	9·97	—
Flight Sergeant	8·32	8·89	9·63	10·32	8·62	9·19	9·93	10·62	9·07	9·64	10·38	11·07
Warrant Officer	9·11	9·68	10·31	11·00	9·41	9·98	10·61	11·30	9·86	10·43	11·06	11·75

Q.A.R.N.N.S., Q.A.R.A.N.C., P.M.R.A.F.N.S.

Rank	Daily	Annual
	£	£
Nursing Sister/Lieutenant/Flying Officer	8·70	3,176
After 1 year in the rank	8·92	3,256
After 2 years in the rank	9·15	3,340
After 3 years in the rank	9·38	3,424
After 4 years in the rank	9·61	3,508
Senior Nursing Sister/Captain/Flight Officer	10·78	3,935
After 1 year in the rank	11·06	4,037
After 2 years in the rank	11·35	4,143
After 3 years in the rank	11·64	4,249
After 4 years in the rank	11·92	4,351
After 5 years in the arnk	12·21	4,457
After 6 years in the rank	12·49	4,559
Superintending Sister/Major/Squadron Officer	13·34	4,869
After 1 year in the rank	13·67	4,990
After 2 years in the rank	13·99	5,106
After 3 years in the rank	14·32	5,227
After 4 years in the rank	14·64	5,344
After 5 years in the rank	14·97	5,464
After 6 years in the rank	15·29	5,581
After 7 years in the rank	15·62	5,701
After 8 years in the rank	15·94	5,818
Matron/Lieutenant-Colonel/Wing Officer	17·63	6,435
After 2 years* or with 19 years' service	18·10	6,607
After 4 years* or with 21 years' service	18·57	6,778
After 6 years* or with 23 years' service	19·05	6,953
After 8 years* or with 25 years' service	19·54	7,132
Principal Matron/Colonel/Group Officer	21·70	7,921
After 2 years in the rank	22·29	8,136
After 4 years in the rank	22·88	8,351
After 6 years in the rank	23·47	8,567
After 8 years in the rank	24·06	8,782
Matron-in-Chief/Brigadier/Air Commandant	26·99	9,851

* In this rank

CHAPLAINS (R.N., R.A.F.)

Rank	Daily	Annual
	£	£
Chaplain		
On entry	11·29	4,121
After 2 years	11·60	4,234
After 4 years	11·91	4,347
After 6 years	13·24	4,833
After 8 years	13·60	4,964
After 10 years	13·98	5,103
After 12 years	14·31	5,223
After 14 years	16·72	6,103
After 16 years	17·07	6,231
After 18 years	17·43	6,362
After 20 years	19·09	6,968
After 22 years	19·45	7,099
After 26 years	20·29	7,406
Principal Chaplain	22·38	8,169
Chaplain of the Fleet	} 27·40	10,001
Chaplain-in-Chief, R.A.F.		

CHARGES FOR SINGLE QUARTERS

Rank	Weekly	Annual
	£	£
Standard Accommodation		
Young servicemen receiving less than the minimum adult rate (i.e. Private IV rate)	1·54	80·30
Corporal and below	2·03	105·85
Warrant Officer and Senior N.C.O.	3·92	204·40
Captain and below	5·53	288·35
Major	6·79	354·05
Lieutenant Colonel and above	7·56	394·20
Senior Officers occupying single rooms		
Major	5·74	299·30
Lieutenant Colonel and above	6·23	324·85
Sub-Standard Accommodation		
Young servicemen receiving less than the minimum adult rate (i.e. Private IV rate)	1·05	54·75
Corporal and below	1·33	69·35
Warrant Officer and Senior N.C.O.	2·59	135·05
Captain and below	3·71	193·45
Major	4·55	237·25
Lieutenant Colonel and above	5·04	262·80

SERVICE RETIREMENT BENEFITS, ETC.
RETIREMENT BENEFITS (MEN)
Officers—All Services

NOTE—A major change in the Armed Forces pension arrangements was made in 1975 with the introduction, from April 1, of "preserved" pensions to comply with the appropriate provisions of the Social Security Act 1973. Those who leave the Forces having served at least five years after the age of 21, but not long enough to qualify for the appropriate immediate pension, now qualify for a preserved pension and terminal grant both of which are payable at age 60. The tax-free resettlement grants shown below are payable on release to those who qualify for a preserved pension and who have completed 9 years service from age 21 (officers) or 12 years from age 18 (other ranks).

No. years' reckonable service completed	Captain (incl. Q.M.), Lieut.(R.N.), Flt. Lt.*	Major (incl. Q.M.), Lt. Cmdr., Sqn. Leader	Lt.-Col., Commander, Wing Commander	Lt.-Col., (Q.M.)	Colonel, Capt.(R.N.), Group Captain	Brigadier, Capt.(R.N.), (after 6 yrs), Air Cdore.	Maj.-Gen, Rear Adm., Air Vice-Marshal	Lt.-General, Vice-Adm., Air Marshal	General, Admiral, Air Chief Marshal
	£ a year	£ a year	£ a year	£ a year	£ a year	£ a year	£ a year	£ a year	£ a year
16	1,362	1,596	1,972	1,778	—	—	—	—	—
17	1,415	1,672	2,063	1,854	—	—	—	—	—
18	1,468	1,747	2,155	1,929	2,610	—	—	—	—
19	1 521	1,823	2,246	2,005	2,721	—	—	—	—
20	1,574	1,898	2,338	2,080	2,831	—	—	—	—
21	1,627	1,974	2,429	2,156	2,942	—	—	—	—
22	1,680	2,050	2,520	2,232	3,053	3,517	—	—	—
23	1,733	2,125	2,612	2,307	3,163	3,628	—	—	—
24	1,786	2,201	2,703	2,383	3,274	3,739	4,487	—	—
25	1,840	2,276	2,795	2,458	3,384	3,850	4,620	—	—
26	1,893	2,352	2,886	2,534	3,495	3,961	4,754	—	—
27	1,946	2,428	2,977	2,610	3,606	4,072	4,887	6,108	—
28	1,999	2,503	3,069	2,685	3,716	4,183	5,020	6,275	—
29	2,052	2,579	3,160	2,761	3,827	4,294	5,154	6,441	—
30	2,105	2,655	3,251	2,837	3,938	4,406	5,287	6,608	9,252
31	2,158	2,730	3,343	2,912	4,048	4,517	5,420	6,775	9,485
32	2,211	2,806	3,434	2,988	4,159	4,628	5,553	6,942	9,719
33	2,264	2,881	3,526	3,063	4,269	4,739	5,687	7,108	9,952
34	2,317	2,957	3,617	3,139	4,380	4,850	5,820	7,275	10,185

* And below

NOTES: Admirals of the Fleet, Field Marshals, Marshals of the Royal Air Force receive half-pay of £11,500. Rates are subject to deduction for voluntary retirement in certain circumstances. Terminal grants are three times the rate of retired pay.

OFFICERS' GRATUITIES (All Services): Rate of gratuity for an officer retiring before becoming eligible for retired pay:
For the first 10 years qualifying service........ £3,075
For each further year's qualifying service...... £615
Standard rate of short service gratuity for each year of service............................. £465

Ratings, Soldiers and Airmen—Basic Rates of Pension

No. of years' reckonable service completed	Below Corporal, Able Rating, Aircraftman	Corporal, Leading Rating, Corporal (R.A.F.)	Sergeant, Petty Officer, Sergeant (R.A.F.)	Staff-Sgt., Chief Petty Officer, Flight Sergeant	Warrant Officer Class II	W.O. Class I, Warrant Officer (R.A.F.) (or commissioned Officer)
	£ a year	£ a year	£ a year	£ a year	£ a year	£ a year
22	853	1,061	1,162	1,286	1,316	1,414
23	883	1,098	1,203	1,331	1,363	1,466
24	912	1,135	1,243	1,376	1,410	1,519
25	942	1,172	1,284	1,421	1,457	1,571
26	972	1,209	1,324	1,466	1,505	1,623
27	1,002	1,246	1,365	1,511	1,552	1,676
28	1,031	1,283	1,405	1,556	1,599	1,728
29	1 061	1,320	1,446	1,601	1,646	1,780
30	1,091	1,357	1,486	1,645	1,693	1,833
31	1,121	1,394	1,527	1,690	1,740	1,885
32	1,150	1,431	1,567	1,735	1,787	1,937
33	1,180	1,468	1,608	1,780	1,834	1,990
34	1,210	1,505	1,648	1,825	1,882	2,042
35	1 240	1,542	1,689	1,870	1,929	2,094
36	1,269	1,579	1,729	1,915	1,976	2,147
37	1,299	1,616	1,770	1,960	2,023	2,199

RETIREMENT BENEFITS (WOMEN)

OFFICERS' RETIRED PAY.—Captain/2nd Offr. W.R.N.S./Flt. Lt. 16–34 years' reckonable service, £1,301 to £2,213 per annum; Major/1st Officer W.R.N.S./Sqn. Ldr. 16–34 years', £1,524 to £2,824, Lt. Colonel/Chief Officer W.R.N.S./Wing Cdr. 16–34 years', £1,883 to £3,454, Colonel/Suptd. W.R.N.S./Group Captain, 18–34 years', £2,532 to £4,249; Brigadier/Comdt. W.R.N.S. (Supt. after 6 years in rank)/Air Commodore, 22–34 years', £3,464 to £4,777.

OTHER RANKS.—After 22 to 37 years' reckonable service: below Corporal/WREN/Aircraftwoman £815— £1,241 per annum; Corporal/Leading WREN/Corporal (W.R.A.F.), £1,013–£1,543; Sergeant/P.O. WREN/Sergeant (W.R.A.F.), £1,110–£1,690; Staff Sgt./Chief WREN/Flight Sergeant, £1,228–£1,872; Warrant Officer Class II, £1,257–£1,932, Warrant Officer Class I/Fleet Chief WREN/Warrant Officer (W.R.A.F.), £1,350–£2,100.

Terminal Grants are three times the rate of retired pay.

RESETTLEMENT GRANTS.—Officers: Men, £1,593; Women, £1,521. Other ranks: Men, £1,105; Women £1,055.

The Church of England

Province of Canterbury

CANTERBURY. £9,420
101st *Archbishop and Primate of All England*, Rt. Hon. and Most Rev. Frederick Donald Coggan, D.D. (Lambeth Palace, S.E.1), *cons.* 1956, 1961 and 1975. [Signs Donald Cantuar:]..1975
Assistant Bishop, Rt. Rev. Kenneth Charles Harman Warner, D.D. (*cons.* 1947).........1962

Bishops Suffragan (£3,650)
Dover, Rt. Rev. Anthony Paul Tremlett, M.A. (Upway, St. Martin's Hill, Canterbury)...1964
Croydon, Rt. Rev. John Taylor Hughes, C.B.E., M.A. (209 Turnpike Lane, East Croydon)...1956
Maidstone, Rt. Rev. Geoffrey Lewis Tiarks, M.A. (Bishop's House, Egerton, Ashford)...1969

Dean (£3,650)
Very Rev. Ian Hugh White-Thomson, M.A...1963

Canons Residentiary (£2,200)
T. E. Prichard, M.A.1968	A. M. Allchin.....1973
J. Robinson, M.Th.,	Archd. Pawley....1972
B.D...........1968	

Organist, Allan Wicks, M.A., F.R.C.O.......1961

Archdeacons
Canterbury, Ven. B. C. Pawley, M.A.........1972
Croydon, The Bishop of Croydon...........1968
Maidstone, Ven. N. K. Nye, A.K.C..........1972
Beneficed Clergy, 224; *Curates*, &c., 76
Vicar-General of Province and Diocese, Sir Harold Kent, G.C.B.
Commissary of Diocese, J. H. F. Newey, Q.C., M.A., LL.B.........................1971
Registrar of the Province and Archbishop's Legal Sec., D. M. M. Carey, M.A., 1 The Sanctuary, S.W.1.
Registrar of the Diocese of Canterbury, D. M. M. Carey, M.A., 9 The Precincts, Canterbury.

LONDON. £6,520
115th *Bishop*, Rt. Rev. and Rt. Hon. Gerald Alexander Ellison, D.D., *cons.* 1950, *trs.* 1955 and 1973 (19 Cowley Street, S.W.1.) [Signs Gerald Londin:].........................1973

Bishops Suffragan
Kensington, Rt. Rev. Ronald Cedric Osbourne Goodchild, M.A. (19 Campden Hill Square, W.8)...................................1964
Willesden, Rt. Rev. Geoffrey Hewlett Thompson, M.A. (173 Willesden Lane, Brondesbury, N.W.6)...............................1974
Stepney, Rt. Rev. Ernest Urban Trevor Huddleston, M.A. (400 Commercial Road, E.1.) (*cons.* 1962)...................1968
Edmonton, Rt. Rev. William John Westwood, B.A. (167 Friern Barnet Lane, Whetstone, N.20)..................................1975
Fulham (for North and Central Europe), Rt. Rev. John Richard Satterthwaite, B.A. (19 Brunswick Gardens, W.8.)...................1970
Assistant Bishops, Rt. Rev. Cecil John Patterson, C.M.G., C.B.E., D.D. (*cons.* 1942), 1969; Rt. Rev. Mark Allin Hodson, B.A. (*cons.* 1956)..1973

Dean of St. Paul's (£3,170)
Very Rev. Martin Gloster Sullivan, M.A., The Deanery, Dean's Court, E.C.4...........1967

Canons Residentiary (each £2,045)
L. J. Collins, M.A...1948	D. Webster, M.A.,
Archd. Wood-	1969
house.........1968	H. Wilson, M.A...1973

Organist, C. H. Dearnley, M.A., B.Mus., F.R.C.O.1968
Receiver of St. Paul's, Sir Ernest Floyd Ewin, O.B.E., M.V.O., M.A.

Archdeacons
London, Ven. S. M. F. Woodhouse, M.A.....1967
Middlesex, Ven. J. N. Perry, B.A............1975
Hampstead, Ven. F. Pickering, M.A..........1974
Hackney, Ven. G. B. Timms, M.A............1971
Northolt, Ven. R. Southwell, A.K.C..........1970
Beneficed Clergy, 515; *Curates*, &c., 460
Chancellor and Commissary of the Dean and Chapter G. H. Newsom, Q.C., M.A..............1971
Registrar, D. W. Faull, 1 The Sanctuary, S.W.1.1969
Chapter Clerk, R. M. Hollis.

Westminster. £3,170
The Collegiate Church of St. Peter—(A Royal Peculiar)
Dean, Very Rev. Edward Frederick Carpenter, M.A., B.D., Ph.D., F.K.C....................1974

Canons Residentiary (£2,045)
D. L. Edwards, M.A.	Rt. Rev. E. G.
(*Sub-Dean*).....1970	Knapp-Fisher,
J. A. Baker, M.A.,	M.A............1975
B.Litt..........1973	

Archdeacon (vacant)
Chapter Clerk, Registrar, and Receiver General, W. R. J. Pullen, M.V.O., LL.B..........1959
Precentor, Rev. E. R. G. Job, M.A...........1974
Organist, D. A. Guest, C.V.O., M.A., Mus.B., F.R.C.M., F.R.C.O...................1963
Legal Secretary, C. L. Hodgetts, LL.B.........1973

WINCHESTER. £4,530
94th *Bishop*, Rt. Rev. John Vernon Taylor, M.A. (Wolvesey, Winchester) [Signs John Winton:]...................................1974

Bishops Suffragan
Southampton, Rt. Rev. John Kingsmill Cavell, M.A. (Shepherds, Shepherds Lane, Compton, Winchester)...........................1972
Basingstoke, Rt. Rev. Colin Clement Walter James, M.A. (11 The Close, Winchester)....1973

Dean (£3,170)
Very Rev. Michael Staffurth Stancliffe, M.A...1969

Dean of Jersey, Very Rev. Thomas Ashworth Goss, M.A..........................1971
Dean of Guernsey, Very Rev. Frederick Walter Cogman, A.K.C., B.D..................1966

Canons Residentiary (£2,045)
E. A. Amand de	A. G. Wedderspoon,
dieta, D.D.......1962	M.A., B.D........1970
F. Bussby, M.B.E.,	Bp. of Basingstoke.1973
M.A., M.Litt., B.D.1967	

Organist, Martin Neary, M.A., F.R.C.O.......1972

Archdeacons
Winchester, Ven. E. D. Cartwright, M.A......1973
Basingstoke, Ven. G. G. Finch, M.A..........1971
Beneficed Clergy, 247; *Curates*, &c., 61
Chancellor, Prof. A. Phillips, O.B.E., M.A., Ph.D.1964
Registrar and Legal Secretary, R. C. White, M.A..1975

BATH AND WELLS. £3,985
74th *Bishop*, Rt. Rev. John Monier Bickersteth, M.A. *cons.* 1970. (The Palace, Wells) Signs John Bath: et Well:].....................1975

Bishop Suffragan
Taunton, Rt. Rev. Francis Horner West, M.A. (The Old Rectory, Dinder, Wells)........1962

Dean (£3,170)
Very Rev. Patrick Reynolds Mitchell, M.A....1973
Canons Residentiary of Wells (£2,045)
P. M. Martin, M.A.1970	A. L. Birbeck, M.A. 1974
Archd. Haynes....1974	D. R. Vicary, M.A.1975

Organist, A. Crossland.....................1970

Archdeacons

Bath, Ven. J. E. Burgess, B.D................1975
Taunton, Ven. A. Hopley.................1971
Wells, Ven. P. Haynes, M.A..............1974
Beneficed Clergy, 290; Curates, &c., 50.
Chancellor, G. H. Newsom, Q.C............1970
Registrar, Sec. & Chapt. Clerk, C. W. Harris, Wells.

BIRMINGHAM. £3,985
5th Bishop, Rt. Rev. Laurence Ambrose Brown, M.A. (*cons.* 1960, *trans.* 1969) (Bishop's Croft, Harborne, Birmingham 17) [Signs Laurence Birmingham]...............1969

Bishop Suffragan
Aston, Rt. Rev. Mark Green, M.C., M.A. (5 Greenhill Road, Wylde Green, Sutton Coldfield) 1972

Provost
Very Rev. Basil Stanley Moss, M.A.........1972

Archdeacons
Aston, Ven. F. F. G. Warman, M.A..........1965
Birmingham, Ven. G. Hollis, M.A..........1974
Beneficed Clergy, 165; Curates, &c., 76
Organist, D. M. Bruce-Payne, B.MUS., F.R.C.O., A.R.C.M...................................1974
Chancellor, F. J. Aglionby..................1970
Registrar and Legal Secretary, R. L. Ekin, B.A. (85 Cornwall Street, Birmingham 3).

BRISTOL. £3,985
53rd Bishop Rt. Rev. Ernest John Tinsley, M.A., B.D. (Bishop's House, Clifton Hill, Bristol [Signs John Bristol]................1975

Bishop Suffragan
Malmesbury, Rt. Rev. Frederick Stephen Temple, M.A. (Morwena, Mill Lane, Swindon)..............................1973

Dean
Very Rev. Alfred Hounsell Dammers, M.A.....1973

Canons Residentiary
E. M. Pilkington, | C. H. Shells, M.A..1973
M.A...........1967 | P. E. Coleman,
              | LL.B., A.K.C....1971
Organist, Clifford Harker, B.MUS., F.R.C.O., A.R.C.M....................................1949

Archdeacons
Bristol, Ven. L. A. Williams, M.A..........1967
Swindon, Ven. J. S. Maples, M.A...........1974
Beneficed Clergy, 138; Curates, &c., 68
Chancellor, D. C. Calcutt, Ll.B., MUS.B.......1971
Registrar and Sec., T. R. Urquhart.........1972

CHELMSFORD. £3,985
6th Bishop, Rt. Rev. Albert John Trillo, F.K.C., B.D., M.Th. (*cons.* 1963) (Bishopscourt, Chelmsford) [Signs John Chelmsford].....1971

Bishops Suffragan
Colchester, Rt. Rev. Roderic Norman Coote, D.D. (Bishop's House, 32 Inglis Road, Colchester) (*cons.* 1951)..................1966
Barking, Rt. Rev. Albert James Adams, B.A. (670 High Road, Buckhurst Hill).........1975
Bradwell, Rt. Rev. John Gibbs, B.A., B.D. (23 Tabors Avenue, Great Baddow, Chelmsford)1973
Provost, Very Rev. Hilary Martin Connop Price, M.A.................................1967
Organist, J. W. Jordan, M.A., MUS.B., F.R.C.O..1966

Archdeacons
Southend, Ven. P. S. G. Bridges............1972
West Ham, Ven. J. B. Taylor, M.A..........1975
Colchester, Ven. C. D. Bond, A.K.C.........1972
Beneficed Clergy, 498; Curates, &c., 142
Chancellor, Miss S. M. Cameron, M.A........1970
Diocesan Registrar, D. W. Faull, 1 The Sanctuary, S.W.1...........................1963

CHICHESTER. £3,985
99th Bishop, Rt. Rev. Eric Waldram Kemp, D.D. (The Palace, Chichester) [Signs Eric Cicestr:]................................1974

Bishops Suffragan
Lewes, Rt. Rev. James Herbert Lloyd Morrell, F.K.C. (83 Davigdor Road, Hove).........1959
Horsham, Rt. Rev. Ivor Colin Docker, M.A. (The Old Rectory, Worth, nr. Crawley)...1975
Assistant Bishops, Rt. Rev. Richard Ambrose Reeves, M.A. (*cons.* 1949)................1966
Rt. Rev. Albert Kenneth Craig, M.A., D.Phil. (*cons.* 1970).............................1974

Dean
Very Rev. John Walter Atherton Hussey, M.A.1955

Canons Residentiary
A. K. Walker, B.Sc., | R. T. Greenacre,
Ph.D........1971 | M.A..........1975
Organist, J. A. Birch, M.A., F.R.C.O..........1958

Archdeacons
Chichester, Ven. R. M. S. Eyre M.A.........1975
Horsham, Ven. F. G. Kerr-Dineen, M.A......1975
Lewes and Hastings, Ven. M. L. Godden, M.A.1975
Beneficed Clergy, 309; Curates, &c., 126
Chancellor, B. T. Buckle, M.A..............1960
Legal Secretary to the Bishop, and Diocesan Registrar, C. L. Hodgetts, LL.B.

COVENTRY. £3,985
5th Bishop, Rt. Rev. Cuthbert Killick Norman Bardsley, C.B.E., D.D. (The Bishop's House, 23 Davenport Road, Coventry.) [Signs Cuthbert Coventry.].....................1956
Assistant Bishop, Rt. Rev. John David McKie, M.A. (*cons.* 1946)......................1960
Provost, Very Rev. Harold Claude Noel Williams, B.A...............................1958
Organist, R. G. Weddle, M.A., F.R.C.O.......1972

Canons Residentiary
J. W. Poole, M.A...1963 | K. E. Wright, B.A.,
G. P. A. Spink....1970 | B.SC...........1974
P. A. Berry, M.A...1973 |

Archdeacons
Coventry, Ven. E. A. Buchan, B.A...........1965
Warwick, Ven. E. Taylor, A.K.C............1974
Beneficed Clergy, 165, Curates, &c., 42
Chancellor, His Hon. Conolly Hugh Gage, M.A.1948
Registrar, S. L. Penn, Coventry.............1957

DERBY. £4,285
4th Bishop, Rt. Rev. Cyril William Johnston Bowles, M.A. (Bishop's House, Turnditch, Derby) [Signs Cyril Derby.].............1969

Bishop Suffragan
Repton, Rt. Rev. William Warren Hunt, M.A. (Underwood, Baslow Road, Bakewell)....1965
Assistant Bishop, Rt. Rev. Thomas Richards Parfitt, M.A. (*cons.* 1952)................1962
Provost, Very Rev. Ronald Alfred Beddoes, M.A....................................1953

Canons Residentiary
P. W. Miller.....1966 | D. P. Wilcox, M.A..1972

Archdeacons
Chesterfield, Ven. T. W. I. Cleasby, M.A......1963
Derby, Ven. R. S. Dell, M.A.................1973
Organist, W. M. Ross, MUS. BAC., F.R.C.O......1958
Beneficed Clergy, 201; Curates, &c., 29
Chancellor, J. A. D. Owen, Q.C., M.A..........1973
Registrar, J. R. S. Grimwood-Taylor, Derby.

ELY. £3,985
65th Bishop, Rt. Rev. Edward James Keymer Roberts, D.D. (*cons.* 1956, *trans.* 1962 *and* 1964) (The Bishop's House, Ely) [Edward Elien:]..1964

Bishop Suffragan

Huntingdon, Rt. Rev. Eric St. Quintin Wall, M.A. (Whitgift House, Ely)..............1972

Dean (£3,170)

Very Rev. Michael Sausmarez Carey, M.A.....1970

Canons Residentiary (each £2,045)

G. Youell, M.A.....1970 | B. of Huntingdon.1972
G. C. Stead, M.A.....1971 | A. J. Morcom, M.A.1974
Organist, A. W. Wills, Mus. Doc., F.R.C.O.....1959

Archdeacons

Ely, Ven. J. S. Long, M.A....................1970
Wisbech, Ven. B. G. B. Fox, M.C............1965
Huntingdon, Ven. D. N. de L. Young, M.A....1975
Beneficed Clergy, 250; *Curates, &c.*, 85
Chancellor, Rev. K. G. Routledge, Ll.B., M.A..1973
Registrar, J. B. Green, M.A.
Legal Secretary, D. M. Moir Carey, M.A., 1 The Sanctuary, S.W.1.

EXETER. £3,000

68th Bishop, Rt. Rev. Eric Arthur John Mercer (cons. 1965) (The Palace, Exeter) [Signs Eric Exon:]...................................1973

Bishops Suffragan

Crediton, Rt. Rev. Philip John Pasterfield, M.A. (The Close, Exeter)....................1974
Plymouth, Rt. Rev. Richard Fox Cartwright, M.A., D.D. (Bishop's Lodge, Yeoland Lane, Yelverton)................................1972
Assistant Bishops, Rt. Rev. John Armstrong, C.B., O.B.E. (cons. 1963); Rt. Rev. Charles Robert Claxton, D.D. (cons. 1946); Rt. Rev. John Maurice Key, D.D. (cons. 1947); Rt. Rev. Wilfrid Arthur Edmund Westall, D.D. (cons. 1954).

Dean (£2,400)

Very Rev. Clifford Thomas Chapman, Ph.D., B.A., B.D., M.Th., A.K.C.................1973

Canons Residentiary

Archd. Newhouse.1966 | F. G. Rice........1970
Archd. Ward......1970 | J. A. Thurmer, M.A.1973
Organist, L. Nethsingha, M.A., F.R.C.O........1972
Chapter Clerk, J. F. Eden, M.A.............1966

Archdeacons

Barnstaple, Ven. R. G. Herniman, B.A.......1970
Totnes, Ven. R. J. D. Newhouse, M.A........1966
Plymouth, Ven. F. A. J. Matthews, M.A......1962
Exeter, Ven. A. F. Ward, B.A...............1970
Beneficed Clergy, 323; *Curates, &c.*, 88
Chancellor, D. Calcutt, M.A., Ll.B., Mus.B.....1971
Registrar and Secretary, J. F. G. Michelmore, 18 Cathedral Yard, Exeter.

GLOUCESTER. £3,985

37th Bishop, Rt. Rev. John Yates, M.A. (cons. 1972) (Palace House, Gloucester) [Signs John Gloucestr:]........................1975

Bishop Suffragan

Tewkesbury, Rt. Rev. Thomas Carlyle Joseph Robert Hamish Deakin, M.A. (Green Acre, Hempsted, Gloucester)..................1973

Dean (£3,170)

Very Rev. Alfred Gilbert Goddard Thurlow M.A., F.S.A...............................1972

Canons Residentiary (£2,045)

W. T. Wardle, | A. J. Holloway,
M.A...........1948 | B.D., M.Th........1974
W. R. Houghton, | D. C. St. V. Welander,
M.A...........1968 | B.D.............1975
Archd. Evans, M.A.1969 |
Organist, J. D. Sanders, M.A., Mus.B., F.R.C.O., A.R.C.M..................................1967

Archdeacons

Gloucester, Ven. W. T. Wardle M.A.........1948
Cheltenham, Ven. T. E. Evans, M.A..........1975

Beneficed Clergy, 228; *Curates, &c.*, 49
Chancellor & Vicar-Gen., Rev. E. Garth Moore, M.A...1957
Registrar, H. A. Gibson, 34 Brunswick Road, Gloucester.
Legal Sec., D. M. Moir Carey, M.A., 1 The Sanctuary, Westminster, S.W.1.
Diocesan Sec., J. H. Martin, Church House, College Green, Gloucester.

GUILDFORD. £3,985

6th Bishop, Rt. Rev. David Alan Brown, B.D., M.Th., B.A. (Willow Grange, Stringer's Common, Guildford) [Signs David Guildford]..1973

Bishop Suffragan

Dorking, Rt. Rev. Kenneth Dawson Evans, M.A. (13 Pilgrim's Way, Guildford)........1968
Assistant Bishop, Rt. Rev. St. John Surridge Pike, D.D. (cons. 1958)...................1963
Dean, Very Rev. Antony Cyprian Bridge....1968

Canons Residentiary

L. E. Tanner, M.A..1971 F. S. Telfer, M.A...1973
R. W. Gibbin, M.A.1973
Organist, P. Moore............................1974

Archdeacons

Surrey, Ven. J. M. Evans, M.A..............1968
Dorking, Ven. W. H. S. Purcell, M.A.........1968
Beneficed Clergy, 153; *Curates, &c.*, 73
Chancellor, M. B. Goodman, M.A.
Legal Sec., R. M. Hollis, M.A.
Registrar of Diocese, R. M. Hollis, M.A.
Registrar of the Archdeaconries, R. M. Hollis, M.A.

HEREFORD. £3,985

102nd Bishop, Rt. Rev. John Richard Gordon Eastaugh, B.A. (The Palace, Hereford) [Signs John Hereford]........................1973
Assistant Bishop, Rt. Rev. William Arthur Partridge, B.A. (cons. 1953)...............1963

Dean (£3,170)

Very Rev. Norman Stanley Rathbone, M.A...1968

Canons Residentiary (£2,045)

J. M. Irvine, M.A....1965 | C. A. Shaw, M.A...1975
Archd. Lewis.....1970 |
Organist, Roy Massey, B.Mus., F.R.C.O.......1974

Archdeacons

Hereford, Ven. J. W. Lewis, M.A............1970
Ludlow, Ven. A. H. Woodhouse, D.S.C., M.A..1970
Beneficed Clergy, 226; *Curates, &c.*, 27
Chancellor, Rev. K. J. T. Elphinstone.......1952
Registrar, Philip Gwynne James, 5 St. Peter Street, Hereford.

LEICESTER. £3,985

3rd Bishop, Rt. Rev. Ronald Ralph Williams, D.D. (Bishop's Lodge, Leicester.) [Signs Ronald Leicester]........................1953
Assistant Bishops, Rt. Rev. James Lawrence Cecil Horstead, C.M.G., C.B.E., D.D. (cons. 1936)..................................1961
Rt. Rev. John Ernest Llewellyn Mort, C.B.E., M.A. (cons. 1952)......................1972
Rt. Rev. Thomas Samuel Garrett, M.A. (cons. 1971)................................1975
Provost, Very Rev. John Chester Hughes, M.A..1963

Canons Residentiary

D. W. Gundry, Bp. Mort.........1970
B.D., M.Th.......1963
Organist, Peter White, M.A., Mus.B., F.R.C.O....1968

Archdeacons

Leicester, Ven. R. B. Cole.................1963
Loughborough, Ven. H. Lockley, Ph.D.........1963
Beneficed Clergy, 220; *Curates, &c.*, 45
Chancellor, R. A. Forrester, C.V.O., M.A......1953
Registrars, R. J. Moore and G. K. J. Moore, 5 Bowling Green Street, Leicester.

LICHFIELD. £3,985

96th Bishop, Rt. Rev. Kenneth John Fraser Skelton, C.B.E., M.A. (cons. 1967) (Bishop's House, The Close, Lichfield) [Signs Kenneth Lichfield].................................1974

Bishops Suffragan

Shrewsbury, Rt. Rev. Francis William Cocks, C.B., M.A. (Athlone, London Road, Shrewsbury)..................................1970

Stafford, Rt. Rev. John Waine, B.A. (St. Thomas' Lodge, Radford Rise, Stafford)...1975

Dean (£3,170)

Rt. Rev. George Edward Holderness, M.A.....1969

Canons Residentiary (each £2,045)

D. K. Robertson, B.A.............1960	D. A. Hodges, M.A. 1965
	Archd. Ninis......1974

Organist, R. G. Greening, M.A., B.Mus., F.R.C.O..1959

Archdeacons

Stafford, Ven. R. B. Ninis, M.A..............1974
Salop, Ven. S. D. Austerberry..............1959
Stoke on Trent, Ven. C. W. Borrett, M.A.....1971
Beneficed Clergy, 424; Curates, &c., 122
Chancellor, His Hon. C. H. Gage..............1954
Diocesan Registrar and Bishop's Sec., M. B. S. Exham.

LINCOLN. £3,985

69th Bishop, Rt. Rev. Simon Wilton Phipps, M.C., M.A. (cons. 1968, trans. 1974) (Bishop's House, Eastgate, Lincoln). [Signs Simon Lincoln:]...............................1974

Bishops Suffragan

Grimsby, Rt. Rev. Gerald Fitzmaurice Colin, M.A. (21 Westgate, Louth)............1966

Grantham, Rt. Rev. Dennis Gascoyne Hawker, M.A. (Fairacre, Barrowby High Road, Grantham)............................1972

Assistant Bishops, Rt. Rev. Anthony Otter, M.A. (cons. 1949)........................1965
Rt. Rev. Kenneth Healey, M.A. (cons. 1958)...1965
Rt. Rev. George William Clarkson, M.A. (cons. 1954)........................1968

Dean (£3,170)

Very Rev. the Hon. Oliver William Twisleton-Wykeham-Fiennes, M.A..................1968

Canons Residentiary (£2,045)

P. B. G. Binnall, M.A., F.S.A......1962	V. A. de Waal, M.A. 1969
D. C. Rutter, M.A....1965	Archd. Dudman...1971

Organist, Philip Marshall, Mus.Doc., F.R.C.O..1966

Archdeacons

Stow, Ven. D. Scott, M.A..................1975
Lincoln, Ven. A. C. Smith, V.R.D., M.A........1960
Lindsey, Ven. R. W. Dudman, B.A.........1971
Beneficed Clergy, 350; Curates, &c., 110
Chancellor, M. B. Goodman, M.A..........1971
Registrar, H. J. J. Griffith, 2 Bank Street, Lincoln.

NORWICH. £3,985

69th Bishop (and 110th of East Anglia, Rt. Rev. Maurice Arthur Ponsonby Wood, D.S.C., M.A. (The Bishop's House, Norwich) [Signs Maurice Norvic]......................1971

Bishops Suffragan

Lynn, Rt. Rev. William Aubrey Aitken, M.A. (Elsing, Dereham)......................1973

Thetford, Rt. Rev. Eric William Bradley Cordingly, M.B.E. (The Rectory, Caistor St. Edmunds, Norwich)....................1963

Dean

Very Rev. Alan Brunskill Webster, M.A., B.D..1970

Canons Residentiary

H. Drury, B.A...1973	F. Colquhoun, M.A.1973
	P. Bradshaw, M.A..1974

Organist, M. B. Nicholas, M.A., F.R.C.O......1971

Archdeacons

Norfolk, The Bishop of Thetford............1962
Norwich, Ven. T. Dudley-Smith, M.A.......1973
Lynn, The Bishop of Lynn................1973
Beneficed Clergy, 302; Curates, &c., 30
Chancellor, His Hon. J. H. Ellison, V.R.D., M.A..1955
Registrar and Sec., B. O. L. Prior, T.D.

OXFORD. £3,985

39th Bishop, Rt. Rev. Kenneth John Woollcombe, M.A. (Bishop's House, Cuddesdon, Oxford) [Signs Kenneth Oxon]...........1971

Bishops Suffragan

Buckingham, Rt. Rev. Simon Hedley Burrows, M.A. (Sheridan, Grimms Hill, Great Missenden)..............................1974

Dorchester, Rt. Rev. Peter Knight Walker, M.A. (Christ Church, Oxford)................1972

Reading, Rt. Rev. Eric Wild, M.A. (The Well House, Upper Basildon, Reading)........1972

Assistant Bishops, Rt. Rev. David Goodwin Loveday, M.A. (cons. 1957)............1971
Rt. Rev. Eric Henry Knell, M.A. (cons. 1955)..1972

Dean of Christ Church (£3,170)

Very Rev. Henry Chadwick, D.D............1969

Canons Residentiary

Archd. Witton-Davies......1956	J. Macquarrie, D.Lit. 1969
W. R. F. Browning, M.A., B.D. (Canon of the Cathedral Church) 1965	M. F. Wiles, M.A...1970 Bp. of Dorchester.1972 P. R. Baelz, M.A...1972 J. McManners, M.A. 1972

Organist, S. Preston M.A., B.Mus............1970

Archdeacons

Oxford, Ven. C. Witton-Davies, M.A........1956
Berks., Ven. W. R. Birt...................1973
Bucks., Ven. D. I. T. Eastman, M.A., M.A......1970
Beneficed Clergy, 367; Curates, &c., 104
Chancellor, P. T. S. Boydell..............1958
Registrar and Legal Sec., F. E. Robson........1969

Windsor.

(*The Queen's Free Chapel of St. George within Her Castle of Windsor—A Royal Peculiar*)

Dean, Rt. Rev. William Launcelot Scott Fleming, D.D., M.S., F.R.S.E............1971

Canons Residentiary

G. B. Bentley, M.A.1957	S. E. Verney, M.A..1970
J. A. Fisher, M.A....1958	A. O. Dyson, B.D., M.A., D.Phil.....1974

Organist, C. J. Robinson, M.A., B.Mus., F.R.C.O..1974
Chapter Clerk, H. G. M. Bass, C.M.G., M.A.

PETERBOROUGH. £3,985

35th Bishop, Rt. Rev. Douglas Russell Feaver, M.A. (The Palace, Peterborough) [Signs Douglas Petriburg].....................1972

Assistant Bishops, Rt. Rev. Archibald Rollo Graham-Campbell, C.B.E., M.A. (cons. 1948)...........................1965
Rt. Rev. Guy Marshall, M.B.E., A.K.C. (cons. 1967).............................1974
Rt. Rev. Alan Francis Bright Rogers, M.A. (cons. 1959).........................1975

Dean (£3,120)

Very Rev. Richard Shuttleworth Wingfield-Digby, M.A........................1966

Canons Residentiary (each £2,045)

Archd. Towndrow1966	P. H. Cecil, B.D.,
A. S. Gribble, M.A..1967	A.K.C...........1971

Master of the Music, W. S. Vann, D.Mus., F.R.C.O.............................1953

Archdeacons

Northampton, Ven. B. R. Marsh, B.A........1964
Oakham, Ven. F. N. Towndrow, M.A.........1967
Beneficed Clergy, 250; Curates, &c., 30
Chancellor, T. R. Fitzwalter Butler, O.B.E.....1962
Registrar, R. Hemmingray, 37 Priestgate, Peterborough.

PORTSMOUTH. £3,985

6th Bishop, Rt. Rev. Archibald Ronald Mac-
donald Gordon, M.A. (Bishopswood, Fare-
ham, Hants.) [Signs Ronald Portsmouth]...1975
Assistant Bishop, Rt. Rev. Laurence Henry
Woolmer, M.A. (*cons.* 1949))..............1968
Provost, Very Rev. Michael John Nott, B.D.,
A.K.C..1972
Organist, C. Gower, M.A., F.R.C.O.

Canons Residentiary

T. C. Heritage, M.A............1964	N. H. Crowder, M.A...........1975
F. C. Carpenter, M.A............1968	

Archdeacons

Portsmouth, Ven. C. Prior, C.B., M.A.........1969
I. of Wight, Ven. R. V. Scruby, M.A..........1965
    Beneficed Clergy, 119; *Curates, &c.,* 62
Chancellor, B. T. Buckle, M.A................1971
Registrar and Legal Sec., T. B. Birkett, 132 High
Street, Portsmouth........................1957

ROCHESTER. £3,985

104th Bishop, Rt. Rev. Richard David Say, D.D.
(Bishopscourt, Rochester), [Signs David
Roffen:]......................................1961

Bishop Suffragan

Tonbridge, Rt. Rev. Philip Harold Ernest
Goodrich, M.A. (Bishop's Lodge, St. Bo-
tolph's Road, Sevenoaks)..................1973
Assistant Bishop, Rt. Rev. John Keith Russell,
M.A. (*cons.* 1955)...........................1965

Dean (£3,170)

Rt. Rev. Stanley Woodley Betts, C.B.E., M.A..1966

Canons Residentiary

P. A. Welsby, M.A., Ph.D..........1966	Archd. Stewart-Smith..........1969
	M. J. Baddeley, M.A...........1974

Organist, R. J. Ashfield, D.Mus., F.R.C.O......1956

Archdeacons

Tonbridge, Ven. E. E. Maples Earle, M.A.....1952
Bromley, Ven. H. W. Cragg, M.A............1969
Rochester, Ven. D. C. Stewart-Smith, M.A....1969
    Beneficed Clergy, 220; *Curates, &c.,* 124
Chancellor, M. B. Goodman, M.A............1971
Registrar, O. R. Woodfield (1955), Rochester.
Sec. D. W. Faull, 1 The Sanctuary, S.W.1....1963

ST. ALBANS. £3,985

7th Bishop, Rt. Rev. Robert Alexander Kennedy Runcie, M.C., M.A. (Abbey Gate House,
St. Albans) [Signs Robert St. Albans]......1970

Bishops Suffragan

Bedford, Rt. Rev. John Tyrell Holmes Hare,
M.A. (168 Kimbolton Road, Bedford)......1968
Hertford, Rt. Rev. Peter Mumford, M.A. (Hert-
ford House, Abbey Mill Lane, St. Albans)..1974

Dean (£3,170)

Very Rev. Peter Clement Moore, M.A., D.Phil..1973
Organist, P. Hurford, M.A., Mus.B., F.R.C.O.,
A.R.C.M......................................1958

Archdeacons

St. Albans, Ven. D. J. Farmbrough, M.A......1974
Bedford, Ven. R. S. Brown, M.A.............1973
    Beneficed Clergy, 265; *Curates, &c.,* 154
Chancellor, G. H. Newsom, Q.C., M.A........1958
Joint Registrars and Legal Secs., D. W. Faull
(1963) and P. F. B. Beesley (1969), 1 The
Sanctuary, S.W.1.

ST. EDMUNDSBURY AND IPSWICH. £4,285

6th Bishop, Rt. Rev. Leslie Wilfrid Brown,
C.B.E., D.D. (Bishop's House, Ipswich), *cons.*
1953, *trans.* 1966 [Signs Leslie St. Edm. &
Ipswich]......................................1966

Bishop Suffragan

Dunwich, Rt. Rev. David Rokeby Maddock,
M.A. (Old Newton House, Stowmarket)...1967
Provost, Very Rev. John Albert Henry Wad-
dington, M.B.E., T.D. M.A..................1958,

Canons Residentiary

C. Rhodes, M.A....1964   D. A. Payne, M.A..1973

Archdeacons

Ipswich, Ven. C. G. Hooper, M.A...........1963
Suffolk, Ven. D. J. Smith..................1975
Sudbury, Ven. K. Child, B.A................1970
Organist, T. F. H. Oxley, M.A., B.Mus., F.R.C.O. 1957
    Beneficed Clergy, 245; *Curates, &c.,* 25
Chancellor, J. C. C. Blofeld, M.A...........1974
Registrar, J. D. Mitson, M.A., LL.B. 22-28
Museum Street, Ipswich.

SALISBURY. £3,985

75th Bishop, Rt. Rev. George Edmund Rein-
dorp, D.D. (South Canonry, The Close,
Salisbury) (*cons.* 1961, *trans.* 1973) [Signs
George Sarum]..............................1973

Bishops Suffragan

Sherborne, Rt. Rev. Victor Joseph Pike, C.B.
C.B.E., D.D. (69 The Close, Salisbury)......1960
Ramsbury, Rt. Rev. John Robert Geoffrey
Neale, A.K.C. (Chittoe Vicarage, Bromham,
Chippenham)................................1974

Dean (£3,170)

Very Rev. William Fenton Morley, M.A., B.D..1971

Canons Residentiary (£2,045)

Arch. Wingfield-Digby........1968	I. G. D. Dunlop, M.A., F.S.A......1972
	C. Moxon, M.A.......1975

Organist, R. G. Seal, M.A., F.R.C.O..........1968

Archdeacons

Wilts, The Bishop of Ramsbury............1975
Dorset, Ven. R. L. Sharp, M.A..............1975
Sherborne, Ven. E. J. G. Ward, M.V.O., M.A...1967
Sarum, Ven. S. B. Wingfield-Digby, M.B.E.,
M.A...1968
    Beneficed Clergy, 305; *Curates, &c.,* 54
Chancellor of the Diocese, His Hon. J. H. Ellison,
M.A...1955
Registrar and Legal Secretary, Alan M. Barker,
B.A., Bishop's Walk, The Close, Salisbury.

SOUTHWARK. £3,985

6th Bishop, Rt. Rev. Arthur Mervyn Stock-
wood, D.D. (Bishop's House, 38 Tooting Bec
Gardens, S.W.16) [Signs Mervyn South-
wark].......................................1959
Assistant Bishop, Rt. Rev. John Arthur Thomas
Robinson, M.A., Ph.D., D.D. (*cons.* 1959)..1969

Bishops Suffragan

Kingston on Thames, Rt. Rev. Hugh William
Montefiore, M.A., B.D. (23 Bellevue Road,
Wandsworth Common, S.W.17)...........1970
Woolwich, Rt. Rev. Michael Eric Marshall,
M.A...1975
Provost, Very Rev. Harold Edward Frankham.1970

Canons Residentiary

D. M. Tasker, B.A..1961	I. G. Smith-Camer-on, B.A..........1972
P. H. Penwarden, M.A...........1971	P. A. Delaney, A.K.C...........1973

Organist, E. H. Warrell, A.R.C.O., A.R.C.M....1968

Archdeacons

Southwark, Ven. M. H. D. Whinney, M.A.....1973
Lewisham, Ven. I. G. Davies, B.A., B.D........1972
Kingston, Ven. P. D. Robb, M.A.............1953
Wandsworth, Ven. P. B. Coombs, M.A........1975
    Beneficed Clergy, 315; *Curates, &c.,* 338
Chancellor, Rev. E. Garth Moore, M.A........1948
Secretary and Registrar, D. W. Faull, 1 The
Sanctuary, S.W.1...........................1963

TRURO. £3,985

11th Bishop, Rt. Rev. Graham Douglas Leonard, M.A., D.D. (Lis Escop, Truro) (cons. 1964, trans. 1973) [Signs Graham Truron:]..1973

Bishop Suffragan

St. Germans, Rt. Rev. Cecil Richard Rutt, C.B.E., M.A., D.Litt. (32 Falmouth Road, Truro) (cons. 1966)......................1974

Dean

Very Rev. Henry Morgan Lloyd, D.S.O., O.B.E., M.A...............................1960

Canons Residentiary

Archd. Young....1965 | M. S. F. Thornton,
R. P. H. Buck, | M.A., S.T.D.......1975
A.K.C..........1974 |

Organist, J. Winter........................1971

Archdeacons

Cornwall, Ven. P. C. Young, B.Litt., M.A.....1965
Bodmin, Ven. C. J. E. Meyer, M.A............1969
Beneficed Clergy, 170; *Curates*, &c., 23

Chancellor, P. T. S. Boydell, Q.C...........1957
Registrar and Secretary, R. W. Money, 2 Princes Street, Truro.

WORCESTER. £3,985.

110th Bishop, Rt. Rev. Robert Wilmer Woods, K.C.V.O., M.A. (The Bishop's House, Hartlebury Castle, Kidderminster) [Signs Robin Worcester]..........................1970

Assistant Bishop, Rt. Rev. David Howard Nicholas Allenby, M.A. (cons. 1962)........1968

Bishop Suffragan

Dudley, Rt. Rev. Michael Ashley Mann (Elmbridge Vicarage, Droitwich).

Dean (£3,170)

Very Rev. Thomas George Adames Baker, M.A...............................1975

Canons Residentiary (£2,045)

G. C. B. Davies, | E. S. Turnball, M.A.1971
D.D..........1963 | Archd. Williams...1975
W. E. Purcell, M.A.1966 |

Organist, D. Hunt, MUS.D., F.R.C.O...........1975

Archdeacons

Dudley (vacant)
Worcester, Ven. J. C. Williams, B.A..........1975
Beneficed Clergy, 130; *Curates*, &c., 83

Chancellor, P. T. S. Boydell Q.C............1959
Registrar, Rev. J. A. Dale, Diocesan Registry, Worcester.

Province of York

YORK. £7,070

94th Archbishop and Primate of England Most Rev. and Rt. Hon. Stuart Yarworth Blanch, M.A., cons. 1966, trans. 1974 (Bishopthorpe, York) [Signs Stuart Ebor:]..............1974

Assistant Bishops, Rt. Rev. George Eyles Irwin Cockin, B.A. (cons. 1959)..............1969
Rt. Rev. Douglas Noel Sargent, M.A. (cons. 1962)..........................1972

Bishops Suffragan

Selby, Rt. Rev. Morris Henry St. John Maddocks, M.A. (Tollgarth, Tadcaster Road, Dringhouses, York)..................1972

Whitby (vacant)

Hull, Rt. Rev. Hubert Lawrence Higgs, M.A. (Hullen House, Woodfield Lane, Hessle)....1965

Dean (£3,170)

Very Rev. Ronald Claude Dudley Jasper, D.D.1975

Canons Residentiary (£2,045)

R. E. Cant, M.A...1957 | J. P. Burbridge,
| M.A...........1966

Organist, Francis Jackson, MUS.D., F.R.C.O.....1946

Archdeacons

York, Ven. L. C. Stanbridge, M.A...........1972
East Riding, Ven. D. G. Snelgrove, M.A.......1970

Cleveland, Ven. J. E. Southgate, B.A........1974
Beneficed Clergy, 297; *Curates*, &c., 76

Official Principal and Auditor of the Chancery Court, Sir Harold Kent, G.C.B.

Chancellor of the Diocese, Rev. K. J. T. Elphinstone, M.A..........................1971

Vicar-General of the Province and Official Principal of the Consistory Court, Rev. K. J. T. Elphinstone, M.A.

Registrar and Secretary, G. P. Knowles, M.A., LL.B............................1968

DURHAM. £5,635

91st Bishop, Rt. Rev. John Stapylton Habgood, M.A., Ph.D. (Auckland Castle, Bishop Auckland) [Signs John Dunelm]..............1973

Bishop Suffragan

Jarrow, Rt. Rev. Alexander Kenneth Hamilton, M.A. (Melkridge House, Gilesgate, Durham).........................1965

Dean (£3,170)

Very Rev. Eric William Heaton, M.A........1974

Canons Residentiary (£2,045)

D. R. Jones, M.A...1964 | S. W. Sykes, M.A...1974
Archd. Perry.....1970 | R. L. Coppin, M.A.1974
C. H. G. Hopkins, | Archd. Marchant..1974
B.A...........1970 |

Organist, R. Lloyd, MUS.B., F.R.C.O..........1974

Archdeacons

Durham, Ven. M. C. Perry, M.A............1970
Auckland, Ven. G. J. C. Marchant, B.A.......1974
Beneficed Clergy, 235; *Curates*, &c., 89

Chancellor, Rev. E. Garth Moore, M.A........1954
Registrar and Legal Secretary (vacant).

BLACKBURN. £3,985

5th Bishop, Rt. Rev. Robert Arnold Schurhoff Martineau, M.A., cons. 1966, trans. 1972 (Bishop's House, Blackburn) [Signs Robert Blackburn]........................1972

Bishops Suffragan

Lancaster Rt. Rev. Dennis Fountain Page, M.A. (Winmarleigh Vicarage, nr. Preston)......1975
Burnley, Rt. Rev. Richard Charles Challinor Watson, M.A. (Palace House, Burnley).....1970

Assistant Bishop, Rt. Rev. Anthony Leigh Egerton Hoskyns-Abrahall (cons. 1955).....1975

Provost, Very Rev. Lawrence Jackson, A.K.C...1973

Canons Residentiary

T. A. Rockley, B.A.1964 | G. A. Williams,
| M.A...........1965
| P.C. Ruffle, B.D..1974

Archdeacons

Lancaster, Ven. G. Gower-Jones, M.A........1966
Blackburn, Ven. C. W. D. Carroll, M.A.......1973
Organist, J. Bertalot, M.A., F.R.C.O., A.R.C.M...1964
Beneficed Clergy, 240; *Curates*, &c., 54

Chancellor, R. A. Forrester, M.A............1949
Registrar, Leslie Ranson, LL.B.............1954

BRADFORD. £3,985

5th Bishop, Rt. Rev. Ross Sydney Hook, M.C., M.A. (Bishopscroft, Ashwell Road, Heaton, Bradford), cons. 1965, trans. 1972 [Signs Ross Bradford]..........................1972

Provost, Very Rev. William Hugh Alan Cooper, M.A..........................1962

Canons Residentiary

J. W. Towell, M.A.1967 | F. P. Sargeant, B.A..1973
Organist, K. V. Rhodes, B.Mus., F.R.C.O......1964

Archdeacons

Bradford, Ven. W. Johnston, M.A............1965
Craven, Ven. M. Kaye, M.A.................1972
Beneficed Clergy, 123; *Curates*, &c., 23

Chancellor, J. F. S. Cobb, Q.C.............1972
Registrar and Secretary, H. Firth, Martins Bank Chambers, Tyrrel Street, Bradford.

CARLISLE. £3,985

64th Bishop, Rt. Rev. Henry David Halsey, B.A.
(Rose Castle, Dalston, Carlisle), *cons.* 1968.
[Signs David Carliol]....................1972

Bishop Suffragan

Penrith, Rt. Rev. William Edward Augustus
Pugh, M.A.................................1970

Dean (£3,170)

Very Rev. John Howard Churchill, M.A.....1973

Canons Residentiary (£2,045)

Archd. Bradford..1966 | R. M. Wadding-
A. H. Attwell, | ton, M.A.........1972
M.A., M.Th.....1972 |

Organist, R. A. Seivewright, M.A., A.R.C.O....1960

Archdeacons

Carlisle, Ven. R. B. Bradford, B.A..........1971
West Cumberland, Ven. A. G. Hardie, M.A.....1971
Westmorland and Furness, Ven. W. F. Ewbank,
M.A., B.D................................1971

Beneficed Clergy, 229

Chancellor, His Hon. D. J. Stinson, M.A.......1971
Registrar and Sec., I. S. Sutcliffe, M.A., LL.B.,
Carlisle.................................1964

CHESTER. £3,985

38th Bishop, Rt. Rev. Hubert Victor Whitsey,
M.A. (Bishop's House, Chester) (*cons.* 1971)
[Signs Victor Cestr:]....................1973

Bishop Suffragan

Stockport, Rt. Rev. Rupert Gordon Strutt, B.D.
(Bishop's Lodge, Macclesfield Road, Alderley
Edge)...................................1965
Birkenhead, Rt. Rev. Ronald Brown, B.A.
(Trafford House, Queen's Park, Chester)...1974

Dean (£3,170)

Very Rev. George William Outram Addleshaw, M.A., B.D., F.S.A..................1963

Canons Residentiary (£2,045)

R. Simpson, M.V.O., | J. S. Lawton, M.A.,
M.A............1974 | B.D., D.Phil.....1975
K. M. Maltby, M.A., | K. M. Whittam,
B.D............1974 | M.A...........1975

Organist, R. A. Fisher, M.A., F.R.C.O..........1967

Archdeacons

Chester, Ven. H. L. Williams, B.A...........1975
Macclesfield, Ven. F. H. House, O.B.E., M.A....1967

Beneficed Clergy, 290; *Curates*, &c., 78

Chancellor, Rev. K. J. T. Elphinstone, M.A....1950
Legal Secretaries, Gamon & Co., 2 White Friars,
Chester.

LIVERPOOL. £3,985

6th Bishop, Rt. Rev. David Stuart Sheppard,
M.A. (*cons.* 1969) (Bishop's Lodge, Woolton
Park, Liverpool) [Signs David Liverpool]..1975

Bishop Suffragan

Warrington (vacant)
Asst. Bishop, Rt. Rev. William Scott Baker,
M.A. (*cons.* 1943)......................1968

Dean (£3,170)

Very Rev. Edward Henry Patey, M.A........1964

Canons Residentiary

C. B. Naylor, M.A..1956 | Archd. Corbett....1971
L. F. Hopkins, | G. Bates..........1973
M.A., B.D.......1964 |

Organist, Noel Rawsthorne, F.R.C.O..........1955

Archdeacons

Liverpool, Ven. C. E. Corbett, M.A..........1971
Warrington, Ven. J. A. Lawton, M.A..........1970

Beneficed Clergy, 227; *Curates*, &c., 103

Chancellor, His Hon. E. Steel, LL.B...........1957
Registrar, R. H. Arden, 1 Hanover Street,
Liverpool 1.

MANCHESTER. £4,285

8th Bishop, Rt. Rev. Patrick Campbell Rodger,
M.A. (Bishopscourt, Bury New Road, Manchester 7), [Signs Patrick Manchester].......1970

Bishops Suffragan

Hulme, Rt. Rev. David George Galliford, M.A.1975

Middleton, Rt. Rev. Edward Raplh Wickham,
B.D. (1 Portland Road, Eccles, Manchester)..1959
Assistant Bishop, Rt. Rev. Richard Patrick
Crosland Hanson, D.D. (*cons.* 1970)........1974
Dean (£3,170) Very Rev. Alfred Jowett, C.B.E.,
M.A....................................1964

Canons Residentiary (£2,045)

M. M. Hennell | Archd. Ballard....1972
M.A...........1970 | A. C. Hall, M.A....1974
G. O. Morgan, |
B.SC...........1971 |

Organist, D. E. Cantrell, M.A., B.MUS., F.R.C.O..1961

Archdeacons

Manchester, Ven. A. H. Ballard, M.A..........1972
Rochdale, Ven. H. O. Fielding, M.A..........1972

Beneficed Clergy, 300; *Curates*, &c., 120

Chancellor, His Hon. E. Steel, LL.B..........1971
Registrar and Bishop's Secretary, J. Maloney, 90
Deansgate, Manchester...................1972

NEWCASTLE. £3,985

9th Bishop, Rt. Rev. Ronald Oliver Bowlby,
M.A. (The Bishop's House, 29 Moor Road,
South, Newcastle upon Tyne 3) [Signs
Ronald Newcastle:].....................1973
Assistant Bishops, Rt. Rev. John Alexander
Ramsbotham, D.D. (*cons.* 1950) (1968); Rt.
Rev. Anthony George Weaver Hunter (*cons.*
1968)...................................1975
Provost, Very Rev. Conrad Clifton Wolters,
M.A....................................1962

Canons Residentiary

Archd. Unwin....1963 | D. E. F. Ogden,
A. Wilson, M.A....1964 | B.A...........1966
| R. G. Cornwell,
| M.A...........1968

Organist, Russell A. Missin, F.R.C.O..... ...1967

Archdeacons

Northumberland, Ven. C. P. Unwin, T.D., M.A..1963
Lindisfarne, Ven. M. H. Bates M.A..........1970

Beneficed Clergy, 151; *Curates*, &c., 55

Chancellor, His Hon. A. J. Blackett-Ord, M.A..1971
Registrar and Sec., R. R. V. Nicholson, 46
Grainger Street, Newcastle upon Tyne.

RIPON. £3,985

9th Bishop, Rt. Rev. John Richard Humpidge
Moorman, D.D., Litt.D. (Bishop Mount,
Ripon.) [Signs John Ripon]..............1959

Bishop Suffragan

Knaresborough, Rt. Rev. Ralph Emmerson,
B.D., A.K.C. (76 Leadhall Lane, Harrogate)...1972

Dean (£3,170)

Very Rev. Frederick Edwin Le Grice, M.A....1968

Canons Residentiary (each £2,045)

J. G. B. Ashworth, | W. Dillam........1973
M.A...........1965 |

Organist, Ronald Perrin, F.R.C.O.............1966

Archdeacons

Leeds, Ven. A. C. Page, M.A................1969
Richmond, Ven. J. W. Turnbull, B.A..........1962

Beneficed Clergy, 172; *Curates*, &c., 58

Chancellor, J. B. Mortimer, Q.C., M.A........1971
Registrar and Secretary, J. R. Balmforth, M.A.,
Phoenix House, South Parade, Leeds.

SHEFFIELD. £4,585

4th Bishop, Rt. Rev. William Gordon Fallows,
M.A. (Bishopscroft, Snaithing Lane, Sheffield
10) (*cons.* 1968) [Signs Gordon Sheffield]....1971

Bishop Suffragan

Doncaster, Rt. Rev. Stuart Hetley Price, M.A.
(344 Grimesthorpe Road, Sheffield 4)......1972
Provost, Very Rev. Wilfred Frank Curtis,
A.K.C..................................1974

Archdeacons

Sheffield, Ven. H. Johnson, M.A.............1963
Doncaster, Ven. E. J. G. Rogers, B.A..........1967
Organist, G. Matthews, B.MUS., F.R.C.O........1967

Beneficed Clergy, 161; Curates, &c., 112
Chancellor, G. B. Graham, Q.C. 1971
Registrar and Legal Sec., V. H. Sandford, M.A.,
30 Bank Street, Sheffield.

SODOR AND MAN. £3,985
77th Bishop, Rt. Rev. Vernon Sampson
Nicholls, M.A. (The Bishop's House, 8 Co-
burg Road, Ramsey, Isle of Man) [Signs
Vernon Sodor and Man] 1974
Archdeacon, Ven. E. B. Glass, M.A. 1964
Beneficed Clergy, 27; Curates, &c., 14
Vicar-General and Registrar, P. W. S. Farrant,
24 Athol Street, Douglas.
Assistant Secretary, C. Curphey.

SOUTHWELL. £3,525
7th Bishop, Rt. Rev. John Denis Wakeling,
M.C., M.A. (Bishop's Manor, Southwell)
[Signs Denis Southwell] 1970
Bishop Suffragan
Sherwood, Rt. Rev. Harold Richard Darby,
B.A. 1975
Asst. Bishop, Rt. Rev. Bernard Markham, B.A.
(cons. 1962) 1972
Provost, Very Rev. John Francis Isaac Pratt,
M.A. 1970
Canons Residentiary
E. E. Roberts ......1969 | C. S. Bayes, B.A. 1970
H. A. Kirton, M.A. ..1970 |
Organist, K. B. Beard, M.A., MUS.B., F.R.C.O. 1959
Archdeacons
Newark, Ven. B. W. Woodhams, B.A. 1965
Nottingham, Ven. M. R. W. Brown, M.A. 1960

Beneficed Clergy, 170; Curates, &c., 45
Chancellor, B. T. Buckle, M.A. 1959
Registrar, P. H. Mellors, M.A., Ll.B. 1970

WAKEFIELD. £3,985
8th Bishop, Rt. Rev. Eric Treacy, M.B.E.
Bishop's Lodge, Woodthorpe, Wakefield)
(cons. 1961) [Signs Eric Wakefield] 1968
Bishop Suffragan
Pontefract, Rt. Rev. Thomas Richard Hare,
M.A. (306 Barnsley Road, Wakefield) 1971
Asst. Bishops, Rt. Rev. Kenneth Graham
Bevan *(cons.* 1940) 1968
Rt. Rev. Victor George Shearburn, M.A.
(cons. 1955) 1967
Provost, Very Rev. John Field Lister, M.A. 1971
Archdeacons
Pontefract, Ven. E. C. Henderson, B.D. 1968
Halifax, Ven. J. R. Alford, M.A. 1972
Organist, J. L. Bielby, M.A., MUS.B., F.R.C.O. 1971
Beneficed Clergy, 212; Curates, &c., 44
Chancellor, G. B. Graham, Q.C., Ll.B. 1959
Registrar and Sec., C. E. Coles, M.A., Burton
Street, Wakefield 1963
———
The General Synod of the Church of England,
Church House, Dean's Yard, S.W.1.—*Presidents,*
The Archbishop of Canterbury; The Archbishop of
York; *Sec.-Gen.,* W. D. Pattinson. THE HOUSE
OF BISHOPS.—*Chairman,* The Archbishop of Can-
terbury; *Vice-Chairman,* The Archbishop of York.
Chairmen of the House of Clergy and House of
Laity were due to be elected by the new Synod in
Nov. 1975.

THE CHURCH IN WALES

BANGOR. £3,970
78th Bishop and 7th Archbishop of Wales, Most
Rev. Gwilym Owen Williams, D.D., *b.* 1913
(Ty'r Esgob, Bangor, Gwynedd), *cons.* 1957,
elected Archbishop of Wales, 1971.

LLANDAFF. £4,385
99th Bishop, Rt. Rev. Eryl Stephen Thomas,
M.A., *b.* 1910 (Llys Esgob, The Cathedral
Green, Llandaff, Cardiff), *cons.* 1968, *trans.*
1971 1971

MONMOUTH. £4,385
6th Bishop of Monmouth, Rt. Rev. Derrick
Greenslade Childs, B.A., *b.* 1918 (Bishopstow,
Stow Hill, Newport, Gwent) 1972

ST. ASAPH. £4,385
73rd Bishop, Rt. Rev. Harold John Charles,
M.A., *b.* 1914 (The Palace, St. Asaph) 1971

ST. DAVID'S. £4,385
123rd Bishop, Rt. Rev. Eric Matthias Roberts,
M.A., *b.* 1914 (Llys Esgob, Abergwili, Carmarthen) 1971

SWANSEA AND BRECON. £3,970
5th Bishop, Rt. Rev. John James Absalom
Thomas, D.D., *b.* 1908 (Ely Tower, Brecon). 1958

BISHOPS ABROAD

CANADA
Primate
The Most Rev. Edward Walter Scott 1971
Sees.   Apptd. Clgy.

Province of Canada
The Most Rev. Archbishop
Nova Scotia, William Wallace Davis, *b.*
1908 *(cons.* 1958), *Archbishop and Metro-
politan* 1971   123
The Rt. Rev. Bishops
Fredericton, H. L. Nutter, *b.* 1923 1971   180
Montreal, R. K. Maguire, *b.* 1923 1963   113
Newfoundland, R. L. Seaborn, *b.* 1911
(cons. 1958) 1966   94
Bp. Suff., G. S. Legge, *b.* 1912 1968
Nova Scotia (see above).
Bp. Suff., G. F. Arnold, *b.* 1914 1967
Quebec, T. J. Matthews, *b.* 1907 1971   50

Province of Rupert's Land
The Most Rev. Archbishop
Qu' Appelle, George Frederic Clarence
Jackson, *b.* 1907 *(Archbishop and Metro-
politan)* 1970 1960   63
The Rt. Rev. Bishop
Arctic, J. R. Sperry 1974   24
Athabasca, F. H. W. Crabb 1975   19
Brandon, J. F. S. Conlin 1975   36

Sees   *The Rt. Rev. Bishops*   Apptd. Clgy.
Calgary, M. L. Goodman, *b.* 1917 1967   61
Edmonton, W. G. Burch, *b.* 1911 *(cons.*
1960) 1960   49
Keewatin, H. J. P. Allan 1974   19
Rupert's Land, B. Valentine, *b.* 1927 *(cons.*
1969) 1970   63
Saskatchewan, H. V. R. Short, *b.* 1914 ...1970   30
Saskatoon, D. A. Ford, *b.* 1917 1970   28
Mackenzie Episcopal Dist., J. R. Sperry *(Epis-
copal Administrator)* 1974

Province of Ontario
The Most Rev. Archbishop
Moosonee, James Augustus Watton, *b.*
1915 *(cons.* 1963), *Archbishop and Metro-
politan* 1974   29
The Rt. Rev. Bishops
Algoma, F. F. Nock, *b.* 1916 1975   79
Huron, T. D. B. Ragg, *b.* 1919 1974   216
Moosonee (see above)
Bp. Suff. (James Bay), N. R. Clarke.
Niagara, J. C. Bothwell *(cons.* 1971) 1973   148
Ontario, H. G. Hill 1975   61
Ottawa, W. J. Robinson, *b.* 1916 1970   85
Toronto, L. S. Garnsworthy *b.* 1922 *(cons.*
1968) 1973   327
Bp. Suff., A. A. Read.

Sees	Apptd. Clgy.

Province of British Columbia
The Rt. Rev. Bishops
British Columbia, F. R. Gartrell, b. 1914.1970   55
Caledonia, D. W. Hambridge, b. 1927....1969   19
Cariboo (vacant).   14
Kootenay, R. E. F. Berry.............1971   31
New Westminster, T. D. Somerville, b.
  1915 (cons. 1969)...................1971   85
Yukon, J. T. Frame, b. 1934 (Acting Metro-
  politan)............................1968   12

AUSTRALIA
Primate of Australia
The Most Rev. Frank Woods, K.B.E.,
Archbishop of Melbourne, b. 1907, cons.
1952, trs. 1957. Elected Primate of
Australia, 1971.

Province of New South Wales
Archbishop and Metropolitan
Sydney, The Most Rev. Marcus Lawrence
  Loane, b. 1911 (cons. 1958)......1966   302
  Bps. Coadj., A. J. Dain, b. 1912 (1965);
  J. R. Reid, b. 1929 (1972); D. W. B.
  Robinson, b. 1922 (1973); K. H. Short,
  b. 1927 (1975); E. D. Cameron, b. 1926
  (1975)

The Rt. Rev. Bishops
Armidale, R. C. Kerle, b. 1915 (cons. 1956)1965   43
Bathurst, E. K. Leslie, O.B.E., b. 1911....1958   43
Canberra and Goulburn, C. A. Warren, b.
  1924 (cons. 1965)...................1971   63
Grafton, D. N. Shearman, b. 1926 (cons.
  1963)..............................1973   41
Newcastle, I. W. A. Shevill, b. 1917 (cons.
  1953)..............................1973   85
Riverina, B. R. Hunter, b. 1927........1971   35

Province of Victoria
Archbishop and Metropolitan
Melbourne (see above).   319
  Bps. Coadj., R. W. Dann, b. 1914
  (1969); J. A. Grant, b. 1931 (1970);
  G. B. Muston (b. 1927)..........1971
The Rt. Rev. Bishops
Ballarat (vacant)   60
Bendigo (vacant)   31
Gippsland (vacant)   37
St. Arnaud, A. E. Winter, b. 1903......1951   26
Wangaratta, K. Rayner, b. 1929......1969   34

Province of Queensland
Archbishop and Metropolitan
Brisbane, The Most Rev. Felix Raymond
  Arnott, b. 1911 (cons 1963)........1970
  Bp. Coadj., R. E. Wicks, b. 1921.....1973
The Rt. Rev. Bishops
Carpentaria, H. T. U. Jamieson........1974   14
New Guinea, G. D. Hand, b. 1918 (cons.
  1950)..............................1963   16
  Asst. Bps., G. Ambo (1960); B.S.
  Meredith, b. 1927 (1967); H. T. A.
  Kendall, b. 1905 (1968).
N. Queensland, H. J. Lewis, b. 1926......1971   30
Northern Territory, K. B. Mason. b. 1927.1968
Rockhampton, J. B. R. Grindrod, b. 1919
  (cons. 1966)........................1971

Province of Western Australia
Archbishop and Metropolitan
Perth, The Most Rev. Geoffrey Tre-
  mayne Sambell, b. 1914 (cons. 1962)..1969   125
  Asst. Bps., T. B. Macdonald, O.B.E.
  (1964); D. W. Bryant, D.F.C. (1967);
  A. C. Holland (1970).
The Rt. Rev. Bishops
Bunbury R. G. Hawkins, b. 1911........1957   34
  Coadj. Bp. W S. Bastian...........1968
N.W. Australia, H. A. J. Witt, b. 1920..1965   13

Sees	Apptd. Clgy.

Province of South Australia
Archbishop and Metropolitan
The Rt. Rev. Bishops
Adelaide, The Most Rev. Keith Rayner,
  b. 1929 (cons. 1969)...............1975   126
Murray, R. G. Porter, b. 1924........1970
Willochra, S. B. Rosier, b. 1928 (cons.
  1967)..............................1970   19
Extra-Provincial Diocese
Tasmania, R. E. Davies, b. 1913 (cons.
  1960)..............................1963   78

PROVINCE OF NEW ZEALAND
Archbishop and Primate
Waikato, The Most Rev. Allen Howard
  Johnston, b. 1912, cons. 1953, trans.
  1969..............................1972   62
  Asst. Bp., S. N. Spence (cons. 1970)....1972
The Rt. Rev. Bishops
Auckland, E. A. Gowing b. 1913........1960   164
  Asst. Bp., G. R. Monteith, b. 1904....1965
Christchurch, W. A. Pyatt, b. 1916......1966   118
Dunedin, W. W. Robinson, b. 1919......1969   42
Nelson, P. E. Sutton, b. 1923..........1965   35
Polynesia, J. L. Bryce, b. 1935..........1975   24
  Bp. Suff. (Nuku' alofa), F. T. Halapua,
  b. 1910............................1967
Waiapu, P. A. Reeves, b. 1932........1971   49
  Bp. Suff. (Aotearoa), M. A. Bennett, b.
  1916..............................1968
Wellington, E. K. Norman, b. 1916......1973   133
  Asst. Bp , G. M. McKenzie, O.B.E......1962
PROVINCE OF MELANESIA
Archbishop
Central Melanesia (vacant)
The Rt. Rev. Bishops
Malaita, L. Alufurai, cons..............1963
New Hebrides, D. A. Rawcliffe, O.B.E....1974
Ysabel, D. Tuti.......................1963
PROVINCE OF SOUTH AFRICA
Archbishop and Metropolitan
Cape Town, The Most Rev. Bill Bendy-
  she Burnett, b. 1917 (cons. 1957)......1974   141
  Bps. Suff., S. W. Wade, b. 1909 (1970);
  G. A. Swartz, b. 1928..............1972
The Rt. Rev. Bishops
Bloemfontein, F. A. Amoore, b. 1913....1967
Damaraland, C. O'B. Winter, b. 1928...1968   23
  Bp. Suff., R. Wood, b. 1920..........1973
George, P. H. F. Barron, b. 1911 (cons.
  1964)..............................1966   26
Grahamstown K. C. Oram, b. 1919......1974
Johannesburg, T. J. Bavin, b. 1935......1974   140
  Bp. Suff., J. S. Carter, b. 1921........1968
Kimberley & Kuruman, P. W. Wheeldon,
  O.B.E., b. 1913 (cons. 1954)..........1967
Lebombo, D. P. Cabral, b. 1924 (cons.
  1967)..............................1968
Lesotho, J. A. Arrowsmith Maund,
  b. 1909............................1950   36
  Bp. Suff., F. Makhetha, b. 1916......1967
Natal, P. W. R. Russell, b. 1919 (cons.
  1966)..............................1974
  Bp. Suff., K. B. Hallowes, b. 1913....1969
Port Elizabeth, B. R. Evans, b. 1929....1974
Pretoria (vacant)   48
  Bp. Suff. M. Nye, b. 1909..........1973
St. Helena, A. K. Giggall, b. 1914......1973   4
St. John's, J. L. Schuster, b. 1912......1956   106
  Bp. Suff., E. A. Sobukwe, b. 1908....1969
Swaziland (vacant)
Zululand (vacant)   65
PROVINCE OF THE WEST INDIES
Archbishop of West Indies
Guyana, The Most Rev. Alan John
  Knight, C.M.G., Archbp. & Metropolitan,
  b. 1902 (cons. 1937)................1950   42

Sees	Apptd. Clgy.
Bp. Suff. (*Stabroek*), P. E. R. Elder, *b.* 1923	1966

The Rt. Rev. Bishops

Antigua, O. U. Lindsay, *b.* 1928	1970	28
Barbados, D. W. Gomez, *b.* 1937	1972	59
Belize, E. A. Sylvester	1972	9
Jamaica (vacant)		
Bps. Suff. (*Kingston*), J. T. Clark (1966); (*Mandeville*), H. D. Edmondson (1972); (*Montego Bay*), M. W. de Souza (1973)		
Nassau and the Bahamas, M. H. Eldon (*cons.* 1971)	1972	30
Trinidad, C. O. Abdulah	1970	40
Windward Isles, E. C. M. Woodroffe, C.B.E., *b.* 1918	1969	22

PROVINCE OF WEST AFRICA
Archbishop

Sierra Leone, The Most Rev. Moses Nathanael Christopher Omobiala Scott, C.B.E., *b.* 1911 (*cons.* 1961) elected Archbp. of West Africa 1969 35

The Rt. Rev. Bishops

Aba, H. A. I. Afonya (*cons.* 1957)	1972	32
Accra, I. S. M. LeMaire (*cons.* 1963)	1968	50
Asst. Bp., K. A. Nelson	1966	
Benin, A. Iwe	1962	80
Ekiti, J. A. Adetiloye	1970	77
Enugu, G. N. Otubelu, *b.* 1927	1969	30
Gambia and Rio Pongas, J. R. Elisee	1972	6
Ibadan, T. O. Olufosoye, *b.* 1918 (*cons.* 1965)	1970	94
Ilesha, J. A. I. Falope	1974	
Kumasi, J. B. Arthur (*cons.* 1966)	1973	17
Kwara, H. Haruna	1974	
Lagos, F. O. Segun (*cons.* 1970)	1975	124
Asst. Bp., J. S. Adeniyi	1970	
The Niger, J. A. Onyemelukwe	1975	80
Niger Delta, Y. A. Fubara	1971	35
Northern Nigeria, T. E. Ogbonyomi	1975	49
Ondo, E. O. Idowu	1971	81
Owerri, B. C. Nwankiti (*cons.* 1968)	1969	82

PROVINCE OF CENTRAL AFRICA
Archbishop

Southern Malawi, The Most Rev. Donald Seymour Arden, *b.* 1916 (*cons.* 1961)..1971

The Rt. Rev. Bishops

Botswana, C. S. Mallory, *b.* 1936	1972
Central Zambia, J. Cunningham, *b.* 1922.1971	
Lake Malawi, J. Mtekateka, *b.* 1903 (*cons.* 1965)	1971
Lusaka, F. Mataka, *b.* 1909 (*cons.* 1964)..1970	
Mashonaland, J. P. Burrough, M.B.E., *b.* 1916	1968
Asst. Bp., P. A. Murindagomo, *b.* 1925.1973	
Matabeleland, S. M. Wood, *b.* 1919	1971
Northern Zambia, J. Mabula, *b.* 1922	1971

PROVINCE OF KENYA
Archbishop

Nairobi, The Most Rev. Festo Habakkuk Olang' (*cons.* 1955) 1970 27
Asst. Bp. C. Nzano 1975

The Rt. Rev. Bishops

Maseno North, J. Mundia	1970	
Maseno South, H. Okullu	1974	
Mombasa, P. Mwang'ombe	1964	27
Mount Kenya, O. Kariuki (*cons.* 1955)..1961		44
Asst. Bp., E. Ngaruiya	1972	
Nakuru, N. Langford-Smith (*cons.* 1960).1961		42
Asst. Bp., M. Kuria	1970	

PROVINCE OF TANZANIA
Archbishop

Dar es Salaam, The Most Rev. John Sepeku, *b.* 1907 (*cons.* 1963) 1965

Sees	Apptd.

The Rt. Rev. Bishops

Central Tanganyika, Y. Madinda, *b.* 1926 (*cons.* 1964)	1971
Masai, H. G. Chisonga	1968
Morogoro, G. Chitemo	1965
Ruvuma, M. Ngahyoma	1971
South West Tanganyika, J. Mlele (*cons.* 1965)	1974
Asst. Bp., J. Rusibamayila, *b.* 1925	1973
Victoria Nyanza, M. L. Wiggins (*cons.* 1959)	1963
Western Tanganyika, M. Kahurananga, *b.* 1921 (*cons.* 1962)	1969
Zanzibar and Tanga, J. Jumaa	1968

PROVINCE OF UGANDA, RWANDA, BURUNDI AND BOGA-ZAIRE
Archbishop

Kampala, The Most Rev. Janani Luwum (*cons.* 1969) 1974

The Rt. Rev. Bishops

Ankole, A. Betungura	1970
Boga-Zaire, P. B. Ridsdale	1972
Bukedi, Y. Okoth	1972
Bunyoro, Y. Ruhindi	1972
Burundi, Y. Nkunzumwami (*cons.* 1965).1966	
Busoga, C. Bamwoze	1972
Kigezi, F. Kivengere	1972
Madi and West Nile, S. G. Wani (*cons.* 1964)	1969
Mbale, E. K. Masaba, M.B.E.	1964
Namirembe, D. K. Nsubuga (*cons.* 1964).1965	
Northern Uganda, B. Ogwal	1974
Ruwenzori, Y. Rwakaikara (*cons.* 1967)..1972	
Rwanda, A. Sebununguri (*cons.* 1965)...1966	
Soroti, A. Maraka	1965
West Buganda, C. Senyonjo	1974

PROVINCE OF THE INDIAN OCEAN
Archbishop

Mauritius, The Most Rev. Ernest Edwin Curtis, *b.* 1906 (*cons.* 1966) 1973

The Rt. Rev. Bishops

Antananarivo (vacant)	
Diego Suarez, G. Josoa (*cons.* 1957) 1969	
Seychelles, G. C. Briggs	1973
Tamatave (vacant)	

PROVINCE OF SOUTH AMERICA
The Rt. Rev. Bishops

Argentina and E. S. America with Falkland Is., R. S. Cutts	1975
Chile, Bolivia and Peru, G. E. D. Pytches, *b.* 1931 (*cons.* 1971)	1975
Asst. Bps. C. F. Bazley (1969); J. W. H. Flagg	1969
Northern Argentina, P. B. Harris, *b.* 1934.1973	
Asst. Bp., D. Leake	1969
Paraguay, D. Milmine	1973

UNDER THE ARCHBISHOP OF CANTERBURY
The Rt. Rev. Bishops

Bermuda (vacant)	
Gibraltar, J. R. Satterthwaite, *b.* 1925...1970	
Asst. Bps., E. M. H. Capper, O.B.E. (*cons.* 1967) (1972); H. Isherwood, M.V.O., O.B.E.	1974
Hong Kong, J. H. Baker, *b.* 1910	1966
Kuching, B. Temengong	1968
Pusan, W. Choi	1974
Sabah, Chhoa Heng Sze	1971
Seoul, P. Lee	1965
Singapore, Chiu Ban It	1966
Sudan, E. J. Ngaiamu (*cons.* 1963)	1974
Asst. Bps., Y. K. Dotiro (1963); B. T. Shukai (1970); B. W. Yugusuk (1970).	

Taejon,. M. Pae.....................1974
West Malaysia, J. G. Savarimuthu *(cons.* 1958)........................1973

THE ARCHBISHOPRIC IN JERUSALEM
Vicar General, Rt. Rev. Robert Wright Stopford, P.C., K.C.V.O., C.B.E...............1974

Jerusalem, Coadj. Bp., F. I. Haddad..........1974
    Asst. Bps., A. K. Cragg (1970); L. J. Ashton (1974)
Jordan, Lebanon and Syria, N. A. Cuba'in.....1958
    Coadj. Bp., F. I. Haddad...............1974
    Asst. Bp., A. Aql.....................1974
Iran, H. B. Dehqani-Tafti................1961
Egypt, I. Musaad.......................1974

CHURCH OF ENGLAND ARCHBISHOPS AND BISHOPS WHO HAVE RESIGNED THEIR SEES OR SUFFRAGAN BISHOPRICS

	Cons.	Res.
G. F. Allen, *b.* 1902; *Derby*	1947	1968
D. H. N. Allenby, *b.* 1909; *Kuching*	1962	1969
S. F. Allison, *b.* 1907; *Winchester*	1951	1974
G. Appleton, *b.* 1902; *Jerusalem*	1961	1974
J. Armstrong, *b.* 1905; *Bermuda*	1963	1968
M. Armstrong, *b.* 1906; *Jarrow*	1958	1964
R. G. Arthur, *b.* 1909; *Grafton*	1956	1973
H. E. Ashdown, *b.* 1904; *Newcastle*	1957	1972
W. S. Baker, *b.* 1902; *Zanzibar*	1943	1968
W. F. Barfoot, *b.* 1893; *Rupertsland*	1941	1958
F. R. Barry, *b.* 1890; *Southwell*	1941	1963
L. J. Beecher, *b.* 1906; *Nairobi*	1950	1970
S. W. Betts, *b.* 1912; *Maidstone*	1956	1966
K. G. Bevan, *b.* 1898; *E. Szechwan*	1940	1950
C. L. P. Bishop, *b.* 1908; *Malmesbury*	1962	1973
T. Bloomer, *b.* 1895; *Carlisle*	1946	1966
P. J. Brazier, *b.* 1903; *Ruanda-Urundi*	1951	1964
S. C. Bulley, *b.* 1907; *Carlisle*	1959	1972
H. J. Buxton, *b.* 1880; *Gibraltar*	1933	1947
E. M. H. Capper, *b.* 1905; *St. Helena*	1967	1972
H. J. Carpenter, *b.* 1901; *Oxford*	1955	1970
P. Carrington, *b.* 1892; *Quebec*	1935	1960
T. H. Cashmore, *b.* 1892; *Dunwich*	1955	1967
S. G. Caulton, *b.* 1895; *Melanesia*	1947	1953
W. F. P. Chadwick, *b.* 1905; *Barking*	1959	1975
L. M. Charles-Edwards, *b.* 1902; *Worcester*	1956	1970
G. W. Clarkson, *b.* 1897; *Pontefract*	1954	1961
C. R. Claxton, *b.* 1903; *Blackburn*	1964	1971
K. J. Clements, *b.* 1905; *Canberra and Goulburn*	1949	1971
R. G. Clitherow, *b.* 1919; *Stafford*	1958	1974
G. E. I. Cockin, *b.* 1908; *Owerri*	1959	1969
W. R. Coleman, *b.* 1917; *Kootenay*	1961	1968
N. E. Cornwall, *b.* 1903; *Borneo*	1949	1963
G. F. Cranswick, *b.* 1894; *Tasmania*	1944	1966
W. H. H. Crump, *b.* 1903; *Saskatchewan*	1960	1971
J. H. Cruse, *b.* 1908; *Knaresborough*	1965	1972
B. M. Dale, *b.* 1905; *Jamaica*	1950	1955
J. C. S. Daly, *b.* 1903; *Taejon*	1935	1967
R. S. Dean, *b.* 1915; *Cariboo*	1957	1973
J. H. Dickinson, *b.* 1901; *Melanesia*	1930	1937
C. Eastaugh, *b.* 1897; *Peterborough*	1949	1972
E. L. Evans, *b.* 1904; *Barbados*	1957	1972
W. L. S. Fleming, *b.* 1906; *Norwich*	1949	1971
D. A. Garnsey, *b.* 1909; *Gippsland*	1959	1974
G. V. Gerard, *b.* 1898; *Waiapu*	1938	1944
W. P. Gilpin, *b.* 1902; *Kingston upon Thames*	1952	1970
H. R. Gough, *b.* 1905; *Sydney*	1948	1966
G. P. Gower, *b.* 1899; *New Westminister*	1951	1971
A. R. Graham-Campbell, *b.* 1903; *Colombo*	1948	1964
E. M. Gresford-Jones, *b.* 1901; *St. Albans*	1942	1969
W. A. Hardie, *b.* 1904; *Ballarat*	1960	1974
M. H. Harland, *b.* 1896; *Durham*	1942	1960
K. Healey, *b.* 1899; *Grimsby*	1958	1965
E. B. Henderson, *b.* 1910; *Bath and Wells*	1955	1975
M. A. Hodson, *b.* 1907; *Hereford*	1956	1973
G. E. Holderness, *b.* 1913; *Burnley*	1955	1969
F. T. Horan, *b.* 1905; *Tewkesbury*	1960	1973
J. L. C. Horstead, *b.* 1898; *Sierra Leone*	1936	1961
A. L. E. Hoskyns-Abrahall, *b.* 1903; *Lancaster*	1955	1974

	Cons.	Res.
J. A. G. Housden, *b.* 1904; *Newcastle, N.S.W.*	1958	1972
K. W. Howell, *b.* 1909; *Chile, Bolivia and Peru*	1963	1971
W. J. Hughes, *b.* 1894; *Trinidad*	1944	1970
T. G. V. Inman, *b.* 1904; *Natal*	1951	1974
A. G. W. Hunter, *b.* 1916; *Swaziland*	1968	1975
L. S. Hunter, *b.* 1890; *Sheffield*	1939	1962
F. M. E. Jackson, *b.* 1902; *Trinidad*	1946	1949
J. M. Key, *b.* 1905; *Truro*	1947	1973
E. G. Knapp-Fisher, *b.* 1915; *Pretoria*	1960	1975
E. H. Knell, *b.* 1903; *Reading*	1955	1972
D. R. Knowles, *b.* 1898; *Antigua*	1953	1969
K. E. N. Lamplugh, *b.* 1901; *Southampton*	1951	1971
B. Lasbrey, *b.* 1881; *Niger*	1922	1945
W. Q. Lash, *b.* 1904; *Bombay*	1947	1961
W. S. Llewellyn, *b.* 1907; *Lynn*	1963	1972
T. Longworth, *b.* 1891; *Hereford*	1939	1961
D. G. Loveday, *b.* 1896; *Dorchester*	1957	1971
F. E. Lunt, *b.* 1900; *Stepney*	1957	1968
A. C. MacInnes, *b.* 1901; *Jerusalem*	1953	1968
B. Markham, *b.* 1907; *Nassau*	1962	1972
H. H. Marsh, *b.* 1899; *Yukon*	1962	1968
C. A. Martin, *b.* 1895; *Liverpool*	1944	1965
S. J. Matthews, *b.* 1900; *Carpentaria*	1960	1968
J. A. Meaden; *Newfoundland*	1956	1965
R. H. Moberly, *b.* 1884; *Stepney*	1936	1952
R. W. H. Moline, *b.* 1889; *Perth*	1947	1962
E. R. Morgan, *b* 1888; *Truro*	1943	1959
A H. Morris, *b.* 1898; *St. E. and Ipswich*	1949	1965
J. E. L. Mort, *b.* 1915; *N. Nigeria*	1952	1969
R. C. Mortimer, *b.* 1902; *Exeter*	1949	1973
S. C. Neill, *b.* 1901; *Tinnevelly*	1939	1945
A. Otter, *b.* 1896; *Grantham*	1949	1965
T. R. Parfitt, *b.* 1911; *Madagascar*	1952	1961
C. G. St. M. Parker, *b.* 1900; *Bradford*	1953	1971
W. A. Parker, *b.* 1897; *Shrewsbury*	1959	1969
C. J. Patterson, *b.* 1908; *Niger*	1942	1969
J. H. L. Phillips, *b.* 1910; *Portsmouth*	1960	1975
S. C. Pickard, *b.* 1910; *Lebombo*	1958	1968
H. G. Pigott, *b.* 1894; *Windward Islands*	1962	1969
St. J. S. Pike, *b.* 1900; *Gambia*	1958	1963
J. R. W. Poole-Hughes, *b.* 1916; *S.W. Tanganyika*	1962	1974
D. B. Porter, *b.* 1906; *Aston*	1962	1972
J. A. Ramsbotham, *b.* 1906; *Wakefield*	1940	1967
K. V. Ramsey, *b.* 1909; *Hulme*	1953	1975
A. S. Reeve, *b.* 1907; *Lichfield*	1953	1974
R. A. Reeves, *b.* 1899; *Johannesburg*	1949	1961
R. E. Richards, *b.* 1908; *Bendigo*	1957	1974
K. Riches, *b.* 1908; *Lincoln*	1952	1974
C. J. G. Robinson, *b.* 1903; *Bombay*	1947	1970
J. A. T. Robinson, *b.* 1919; *Woolwich*	1959	1969
A. F. B. Rogers, *b.* 1907; *Edmonton*	1959	1975
J. K. Russell, *b.* 1916; *N. Uganda*	1955	1964
C. R. Rutt, *b.* 1925; *Taejon*	1967	1975
W. G. Sanderson, *b.* 1905; *Plymouth*	1962	1972
C. K. Sansbury, *b.* 1905; *Singapore*	1961	1966
D. N. Sargent, *b.* 1907; *Selby*	1962	1971
G. D. Savage, *b.* 1915; *Southwell*	1960	1970
V. G. Shearburn, *b.* 1901; *Rangoon*	1955	1966
G. Sinker, *b.* 1900; *Nagpur*	1949	1954
G. B. Snell, *b.* 1907; *Toronto*	1956	1972
G. D'O. Snow, *b.* 1903; *Whitby*	1961	1971

	Cons.	Res.
R. W. Stannard, b. 1895; Woolwich...	1947	1959
A. Stanway, b. 1908; Cent. Tanganyika.	1951	1971
R. W. Stopford, b. 1901; London.......	1955	1973
L. E. Stradling, b. 1908; Johannesburg ..	1945	1974
C. E. Storrs, b. 1889; Grafton..........	1946	1955
C. E. Stuart, b. 1893; Uganda..........	1932	1952
R. S. Taylor, b. 1909; Cape Town.....	1941	1974
W. J. Thompson, b. 1885; Iran........	1935	1960
F. O. Thorne, b. 1892; Nyasaland.....	1936	1961
O. S. Tomkins, b. 1908; Bristol.......	1959	1975
G. F. Townley, b. 1891; Hull..........	1957	1965
E. J. Trapp, b. 1910; Bermuda........	1947	1975
C. J. Tucker, b. 1911; Argentina......	1965	1975
L. C. Usher-Wilson, b. 1903; Mbale...	1936	1961

	Cons.	Res.
I. C. Vockler, b. 1924; Polynesia......	1959	1968
B. N. Y. Vaughan, b. 1917; Honduras..	1961	1971
J. W. C. Wand, b. 1885; London.......	1934	1954
A. K. Warren, b. 1900; Christchurch....	1951	1966
R. H. Waterman, b. 1897; Nova Scotia.	1948	1963
W. L. M. Way, b. 1905; Masai.......	1952	1959
J. Wellington, b. 1890; Shantung......	1940	1950
G. A. West, b. 1893; Rangoon........	1935	1954
W. A. E. Westall, b. 1900; Credition..	1954	1974
R. B. White, b. 1896; Tonbridge......	1959	1967
F. R. Willis, b. 1900; Delhi..........	1951	1966
D. J. Wilson, b. 1903; Trinidad.......	1938	1956
R. P. Wilson, b. 1905; Chichester.....	1959	1974
L. H. Woolmer, b. 1906; Lahore......	1949	1968

ECCLESIASTICAL COURTS

Judge, The Rt. Worshipful Sir Harold Kent, G.C.B., Q.C.

[Judge of the Provincial Courts of Canterbury and York under " The Ecclesiastical Jurisdiction Measure, 1963."]

Court of Arches

Registry 1 The Sanctuary, Westminster, S.W.1

Dean, The Rt. Worshipful Sir Harold Kent, G.C.B., Q.C.

Registrar, D. M. M. Carey.

Court of Faculties

[Registry and Office for Marriage Licences (Special and Ordinary). Appointment of Notaries Public, &c., 1, The Sanctuary, Westminster, S.W.1. Office hours, 10 to 4; Saturdays, 10 to 12]

Master, The Rt. Worshipful Sir Harold Kent, G.C.B., Q.C.

Registrar, D. M. M. Carey.

Vicar General's Office

for granting Marriage Licences for Churches in the Province of Canterbury, and COURT OF PECULIARS, 1 The Sanctuary Westminster, S.W.1. Office hours, 10 to 4; Saturdays, Christmas Day, and Bank Holidays.

Vicar General & Chancellor, Sir Harold Kent, G.C.B., Q.C.

Registrar D. M. M. Carey.

Apparitor General, M. Saunders.

OFFICE OF THE VICAR GENERAL OF THE PROVINCE OF YORK.

Vicar General & Chancellor The Worshipful Kenneth John Tristran Elphinstone.

Registrar, G. P. Knowles.

Chancery Court of York

Auditor, Sir Harold Kent, G.C.B., Q.C.

Registrar G. P. Knowles.

THE CHURCH OF SCOTLAND

Church Office, 121 George Street, Edinburgh 2.

THE CHURCH OF SCOTLAND is Presbyterian in constitution, and is governed by Kirk Sessions, Presbyteries, Synods, and the General Assembly, which consists of both clerical and lay representatives from each of the Presbyteries. It is presided over by a Moderator (chosen annually by the Assembly) to whom Her Majesty the Queen has granted precedence in Scotland, during his term of office, next after the Lord Chancellor of Great Britain. The Sovereign, if not present in person, is represented by a Lord High Commissioner, who is appointed each year by the Crown. The country, for Church purposes, is divided into 12 Synods and 46 Presbyteries, and there are about 2,000 ministers and licentiates engaged in ministerial and other work. The figures at Dec. 31, 1974, were:—

Congregations, 1,993: total membership 1,061,706. In 21 Overseas Mission fields there are 184 European missionaries (and in addition many missionaries' wives, most of whom are doing mission work in the various fields).

LORD HIGH COMMISSIONER (1975). Sir Hector Mac-Lennan, M.D.

MODERATOR OF THE ASSEMBLY (1975–76), Right Rev. J. G. Matheson, D.D.

Principal Clerk, Rev. D. F. M. Macdonald, M.A., Ll.B.

Depute Clerk, Rev. A. G. McGilvray, M.A., B.D.

Procurator, C. K. Davidson. Q.C.

Law Agent and Solicitor of the Church, R. A. Paterson M.A. LL.B.

Parliamentary Solicitor Colin McCulloch (London).

General Treasurer, W. G. P. Colledge C.A.

The Presbyterian Church in Ireland.—The largest of the Presbyterian churches in Ireland consists of 22 presbyteries, 432 ministers, 562 congregations, with 135,743 communicants, 127,979 families and 6,846 Sabbath-school teachers. During the 12 months ended Dec. 31, 1974, the branch

contributed by congregational effort £472,145 for religious, charitable, and missionary purposes. The total income for the period raised by congregations for all purposes was £3,740,568—*General Sec.,* Rev. A. J. Weir, M.Sc., D.D. Church House, Belfast, 1.

UNITED REFORMED CHURCH

The United Reformed Church was formed by the union of the Congregational Church in England and Wales and the Presbyterian Church in England on October 5, 1972. It is divided into 12 Provinces, each with a Provincial Moderator, and 65 Districts. 187,408 members, and 1,837 ministers. It carries out its overseas work through the Council for World Mission (Congregational and Reformed).

Its ministers are trained at five recognized colleges.

General Sec.: Rev. A. I. Macarthur, M.A., M.Litt., Church House, 86 Tavistock Place, W.C.1.

Those members of the Congregational Church who did not join the United Reformed Church comprise the Congregational Federation. *Sec.,* J. B. Wilcox, 12 Canal Street, Nottingham.

THE EPISCOPAL CHURCH IN SCOTLAND

Sees.	THE RT. REV. BISHOPS.	Cons.	Clgy.	Stipd.
Aberdeen and Orkney, Ian Forbes				
Begg, D.D., *b.* 1909		1972..20	£*2,138	
Argyll and the Isles, Richard				
Knyvet Wimbush, M.A., *b.*				
1909(*Most Rev. Primus*, 1973).1963..12			*2.562	
Brechin, Lawrence Edward Lus-				
combe, *b.* 1925		1975.24	£*1,744	
Edinburgh (vacant)		77	*2,600	

Sees.	THE RT. REV. BISHOPS.	Cons.	Clgy.	Stipd.
Glasgow and Galloway, Frederick				
Goldie M.A., *b.* 1914		1974..64	*2,650	
Moray, Ross and Caithness,				
George Minshull Sessford,				
M.A., *b.* 1918		1970..20	£*2,507	
St. Andrews, Dunkeld and				
Dunblane, Michael Geoffrey				
Hare-Duke, M.A., *b.* 1925...1969..34			£*2,206	

★ With residence.

Registrar of the Episcopal Synod, I. R. Guild, w.s., 16 Charlotte Square, Edinburgh, 2.
Churches, Mission Stations, &c., 348. Clergy, 251; Communicants, 45.692

THE CHURCH OF IRELAND

Sees	ARCHBISHOPS		Appointed	Clergy
Armagh★	Most Rev. George Otto Simms, Ph.D., D.D., *b.* 1910 (*cons.* 1952)		1969	60
Dublin	Most Rev. Alan Alexander Buchanan, M.A., D.D., *b.* 1907 (*cons.* 1958)		1970	89
	BISHOPS			
Meath	(vacant)			18
Cashel & Waterford	Rt. Rev. John Ward Armstrong, B.D., *b.* 1915		1969	14
Clogher	Rt. Rev. Robert William Heavener, M.A., *b.* 1905		1973	37
Connor	Rt. Rev. Arthur Hamilton Butler, M.B.E., D.D., *b.* 1912 (*cons.* 1958)		1970	118
Cork, Cloyne & Ross	Rt. Rev. Richard Gordon Perdue, D.D., *b.* 1910 (*cons.* 1958)		1957	35
Derry & Raphoe	Rt. Rev. Robert Henry Alexander Eames, ll.B., Ph.D., *b.* 1937		1975	66
Down & Dromore	Rt. Rev. George Alderson Quin, M.A., *b.* 1914ö		1970	114
Killaloe	Rt. Rev. Edwin Owen, M.A., *b.* 1910		1972	14
Kilmore, Elphin &				
Ardagh	Rt. Rev. Edward Francis Butler Moore, Ph.D., D.D., *b.* 1906		1958	31
Limerick & Ardfert	Rt. Rev. Donald Arthur Richard Caird, B.D., *b.* 1925		1970	14
Ossory, Ferns &				
Leighlin	Rt. Rev. Henry Robert McAdoo, Ph.D., D.D., *b.* 1916		1962	43
Tuam	Rt. Rev. John Coote Duggan, B.D., *b.* 1918		1970	12

*Primate.

ST. PATRICK'S NATIONAL CATHEDRAL, DUBLIN. Dean and Ordinary, Very Rev. V. G. B. Griffin, ph.D., B.A.

Chief Officer and Secretary to the REPRESENTATIVE CHURCH BODY, J. G. Briggs, Church of Ireland House, Church Avenue, Rathmines, Dublin 6.

THE METHODIST CHURCH

The Methodist Church is governed primarily by the Conference, secondarily by the District Synods (held in the autumn and the spring), consisting of all the ministers and of selected laymen in each district, over which a chairman is appointed by the Conference; and thirdly by circuit quarterly meeting of the ministers and lay officers of each circuit. The authority of both Synods and Quarterly Meetings is subordinate to the Conference, which has the supreme legislative and judicial power in Methodism.

President of the Conference (July 1975–76), Rev. A. R. George, M.A., B.D.

Vice-President of the Conference (July 1975–76), W. A. Cockell.

Secretary of the Conference, Rev. K. G. Greet, D.D., 1 Central Buildings, Westminster, S.W.1.

President Designate (1976–77), Rev. C. M. Morris, B.A.

Vice-President Designate (1976–77), C. J. Bennett.

Statistics.—In 1975 in association with the Conference in Great Britain there were 3,865 Ministers, 16,962 Local Preachers, 557,249 Members in 734 Circuits. Statistics are published triennially.

The World Methodist Council, founded 1881, re-organized 1951, associates Methodism throughout the world in 82 countries.

The Methodist Church was founded in 1739 by the two brothers Wesley and rapidly spread throughout the British Isles and to America before 1770. The Methodist Church in Great Britain was united in 1932 by the fusion of the Wesleyan Methodist Church which was the original section, the Primitive Methodist Church, which arose through the evangelists Hugh Bourne and William Clowes in 1810, and the United Methodist Church, itself a fusion in 1907 of the Methodist New Connexion which dated from 1797, the Bible Christian Methodist Church, which dated from 1815 and the United Methodist Free Churches which originated in controversies in 1828 and 1849. The United Methodist Church of America was formed by a union of United Methodist denominations with the United Evangelical Brethren.

METHODIST CHURCH IN IRELAND
The Methodist Church in Ireland has 232 Ministers, 285 Lay Preachers, 24,469 Adult and 17,125 Junior Members.
President (1975–76), Rev. H. W. Plunkett.
Secretary, Rev. H. Sloan, 3 Upper Malone Road, Belfast, 9.

THE UNITED CHURCH OF CANADA
The United Church of Canada is the result of the union (1925) of Methodist, Presbyterian and Congregational Churches in Canada. Subsequently several other communions have become part of the Church. *Moderator*, Rt. Rev. W. K. Howard, B.A., D.D. *Sec. of General Council*, Rev. D. G. Ray, D.F.C., B.A., D.D., The United Church House, 85 St. Clair E., Toronto.

INDEPENDENT METHODISTS
Independent Methodists.—This body is Congregational in its organization, with an unpaid Ministry. Its first Conference was held in 1805. In 1975 there were in Great Britain 189 Ministers, 5,367 Members, 132 Chapels and 4,984 Sunday scholars, *Secretary*, D. S. Downing, 45 Mountfields Drive. Loughborough, Leics.

WESLEYAN REFORM UNION

This Union is Methodist in doctrine, Congregational in government, with, if any church desires it, a paid ministry. It is the remnant of the original Reformers expelled from Wesleyan Methodism in 1849. The adherents are mainly in the Midland and Northern counties. In 1974 there were in

Great Britain 22 Ministers, 237 Lay Preachers, 4,523 Members, 152 Chapels and 4,932 Sunday scholars.—*President* (1975–76), Rev. R. Graves, Bradford. *General Secretary and Connexional Editor*, Rev. D. A. Morris, Wesleyan Reform Church House, 123 Queen Street, Sheffield 1.

THE PRESBYTERIAN CHURCH OF WALES

The PRESBYTERIAN OR CALVINISTIC METHODIST CHURCH OF WALES is the only Church of purely Welsh origin, and embraces a very large section of the Welsh-speaking population. Its form of government is Presbyterian, and it is a constituent of the World Alliance of Reformed Churches. It is also a member of the British Council of Churches and the World Council of Churches.

In 1973 the body numbered—chapels and other buildings, 1,235; ministers in pastoral charge, 290; elders, 5,971; communicants 99,288; Sunday scholars 38,097. Contributions for various religious purposes (including the ministry), £1,437,080.

The *Eastern Association* which includes nine of the English Presbyteries, was formed in 1947.
Moderator of General Assembly (1975–76), Rev. J. H. Hughes, B.A., Pontypridd.
Moderator of Associations (1975–76) *South Wales*, Rev. H. O. John, Fishguard; *North Wales*, Rev. G. Owen, B.A., B.D., Old Colwyn; *The East*, L. I. H. Owen, M.A., B.Sc., Llandrindod.
Chief Secretary, Rev. G. Evans, B.A., 9 Camden Road, Brecon.

The BAPTISTS have over 33,000,000 members in all countries. In Britain they are for the most part grouped in associations of churches, and the majority of these belong to the Baptist Union, which was formed in 1812–13. In the British Isles there were, in 1974, 1,572 pastors and deaconesses. The members numbered 187,144, young people (14–20), 36,304, juveniles (under 14) 144,329. *President of the Baptist Union of Great Britain and Ireland*

(1975–76), Rev. S. A. Turl. *Secretary*, Rev. D. S. Russell. *Office*, 4 Southampton Row, W.C.1.

THE JEWS

It is estimated that about 410,000 Jews are resident in the British Isles, some 280,000 being domiciled in Greater London.

The *Board of Deputies of British Jews*, established in 1760, is the representative body of British Jewry and is recognized by H.M. Government. The basis of representation is mainly synagogal, but secular organizations are also represented. It is a deliberative body and its objects are to watch over the interests of British Jewry, to protect Jews against any disability which they may suffer by reason of their creed and to take such action as may be conducive to their welfare.
President, The Lord Fisher of Camden.
Secretary, A. J. Marks. (Woburn House, Upper Woburn Place, W.C.1).
CHIEF RABBI—The Very Rev. I. Jakobovits, Ph.D.
Executive Director, M. Davis. *Office*, Adler House, Tavistock Square, W.C.1.

The *Beth Din* (Court of Judgment) is a rabbinic body consisting of *Dayanim* (Assessors) and the Chief Rabbi, who is President of the Court. The Court arbitrates when requested in cases between Jew and Jew and gives decisions on religious questions. The decisions are based on Jewish Law and practice and do not conflict with the law of the land. The *Beth Din* also deals with matters concerning dietary laws and marriages and divorces, according to Jewish Law.
Dayanim, L. Grossnass; Dr. M. Lew; M. Swift.
Clerk to the Court, Marcus Carr, Adler House, Tavistock Square, W.C.1.

OTHER RELIGIOUS DENOMINATIONS

The General Assembly of Unitarian and Free Christian Churches has about 176 ministers, 272 chapels and other places of worship in Great Britain and Ireland. *Gen. Sec.*, Rev. B. L. Golland, Essex Hall, Essex Street, W.C.2.

The Salvation Army, first known as the Christian Mission, was founded by William Booth, in the East End of London in 1865. In 1878 it took its present name and adopted a quasi-military method of government. Since then it has become established in over 80 countries of the world. The head of the denomination, known as the General, is elected by a High Council, consisting of all active Commissioners and Territorial Commanders who have held the rank of Colonel for at least two years. In 1974 there were in Great Britain, 1,033 Corps (Churches) and 2,054 Officers engaged in evangelistic and social work. The latest statistics for the world (1974) are 16,268 Corps and 24,861 Officers. *General*, Clarence D. Wiseman.
International Headquarters:—101 Queen Victoria Street, E.C.4.

The Society of Friends (Quakers) consists of 20,242 members in Great Britain, and has 436 places of worship (*Recording Clerk*, Arthur J. White).
The total number in the world is about 192,500

(119,000 are in U.S.A. and Canada). *Central Office* (*Great Britain*), Friends House, Euston Road N.W.1, (*Ireland*), 6 Eustace Street, Dublin.

The First Church of Christ, Scientist, in Boston, Massachusetts, U.S.A. (District Manager, Committees on Publication for Great Britain and Ireland, 108 Palace Gardens Terrace, W.8), has about 300 branch churches and societies in Great Britain and Ireland.

The Moravian Church, 5 Muswell Hill, N.10, has in the U.K. 40 congregations and preaching stations, with 3,500 communicants.

The Free Church of England (otherwise called The Reformed Episcopal Church) has 33 churches in England. *Gen. Sec.*, Rev. A. Ward, 65 Elmfield Avenue, Teddington, Middlesex.

The Seventh Day Adventists (*Hdqrs.*, Stanborough Park, Watford, Herts.), have 142 organized churches, 41 companies and 12,522 members in the British Isles.

At Woking, Surrey, is the Shah Jehan Mosque for Moslems, the first in Great Britain, built in 1889. There are also Mosques at Southfields, S.W.18, Commercial Road, E.1, Birmingham, Manchester, Cardiff, Newcastle-upon-Tyne, South Shields, Coventry and Glasgow.

THE ROMAN CATHOLIC CHURCH

HIS HOLINESS POPE PAUL VI (Giovanni Battista Montini), Roman Pontiff, *born* in Concesio, Italy, September 26, 1897; *ordained priest* May 29, 1920; nominated *Archbishop of Milan*, November 1, 1954; *Cardinal*, December 15, 1958; *elected Pope* June 21, 1963; *crowned* June 30, 1963.

THE SACRED COLLEGE OF CARDINALS, when complete, consisted of six Cardinal Bishops, fifty Cardinal Priests and fourteen Cardinal Deacons. This number was fixed by Pope Sixtus V in 1586. Pope John XXIII created 52 new Cardinals. The present Pope created 27 new Cardinals on Feb. 22, 1965, 27 on June 26, 1967, 33 on Apr. 28, 1969, and a further 30 on March 5. 1973. In July 1975 there were 124 Cardinals. The Cardinals are advisers and assistants of the Sovereign Pontiff and form the supreme council or Senate of the Church. On the death of the Pope they elect his successor. The assembly of the Cardinals at the Vatican for the election of a new Pope is known as the Conclave in which, in complete seclusion, the Cardinals elect by secret ballot; a two-thirds majority is necessary before the vote can be accepted as final. When a Cardinal receives the necessary votes the Dean of the Sacred College formally asks him if he will accept election and the name by which he wishes to be known. On his acceptance of the office the Conclave is dissolved and the First Cardinal Deacon announces the election to the assembled crowd in St. Peter's Square. On the first Sunday or Holyday following the election the new Pope is crowned with the tiara, the triple crown, the symbol of his supreme spiritual authority. A new pontificate is dated from the coronation.

FORMS OF ADDRESS: *Cardinal*, " His Eminence Cardinal . . . " (if an Archbishop, " His Eminence the Cardinal Archbishop of . . ."); *Archbishop* " The Most Rev. Archbishop of . . ."; *Bishop*, " The Rt. Rev. the Bishop of . . ."

ENGLAND AND WALES

Apostolic Delegate to Gt. Britain and Gibraltar, The Most Rev. Bruno Heim.

The Most Revd. Archbishops CONS. CLERGY★

Westminster, H.E. Cardinal John Heenan (1963)	1951	971
Auxil., Basil Christopher Butler	1966	
Auxil., Victor Guazzelli	1970	
Auxil., Gerald Mahon	1970	
Birmingham, George Dwyer (1966)	1959	592
Auxil., Joseph Cleary	1966	
Auxil., Anthony Emery	1968	
Cardiff, John A. Murphy (1961)	1948	188
Auxil., Daniel Mullins	1970	
Liverpool, Andrew Beck (1964)	1948	661
Auxil., Augustine Harris	1966	
Auxil., Joseph Gray	1969	
Southwark, Cyril Cowderoy	1949	578
Auxil., Charles Henderson	1972	

The Rt. Revd. Bishops

Arundel and Brighton, Michael Bowen (1971)	1970	357
Brentwood, Patrick Casey (1970)	1966	239
Clifton, Mervyn Alexander (1975)	1972	278
Hexham and Newcastle, Hugh Lindsay (1975)	1970	373
Lancaster Brian C. Foley	1962	289
Auxil., Thomas Pearson	1949	
Leeds, Gordon Wheeler	1964	405
Auxil. Gerald Moverley	1968	
Menevia (Wales), Langton Fox (1972)	1965	180
Middlesbrough, John McClean	1967	247
Northampton, Charles Grant	1961	278
Auxil., Alan Clark	1969	
Nottingham, James McGuinness (1975)	1972	318
Plymouth, Cyril Restieaux	1955	200
Portsmouth, Derek Worlock	1965	347
Salford, Thomas Holland, D.S.C. (1964)	1961	591
Auxil., Geoffrey Burke	1967	
Shrewsbury, William Eric Grasar	1962	287
Auxil., John Brewer	1972	

SCOTLAND

The Most Revd. Archbishops

St. Andrews & Edinburgh, H.E. Cardinal Gordon Gray	1951	232
Auxil., James Monaghan	1970	
Glasgow, Thomas Winning (1974)	1972	375

The Rt. Revd. Bishops

Aberdeen, Michael Foylan	1965	78
Argyle & Isles, Colin MacPherson	1969	33
Dunkeld, William Hart	1955	73
Galloway, Joseph McGee	1952	80

		CONS. CLERGY.
Motherwell, Francis Thompson	1965	187
Paisley, Stephen McGill (1969)	1960	99

NORTHERN IRELAND†

The Most Revd. Archbishop

Armagh, H.E. Cardinal William Conway (1963)	1958	278
Auxil., Francis Lenny	1974	

The Rt. Revd. Bishops

Clogher, Patrick Mulligan	1969	140
Derry, Edward Daly	1974	151
Down & Connor, William Philbin	1962	328
Dromore, Eugene O'Doherty	1944	74
Kilmore, Francis McKernan	1972	126

BRITISH COMMONWEALTH

Europe

The Most Revd. Archbishop CONS.

Malta, Michael Gonzi, K.B.E.(1943)		1924

The Rt. Revd. Bishops

Gozo, Nicola Cauchi (1972)		1967
Gibraltar, Edward Rapallo		1973

America

Pro-Nuncio to Canada, Most Rev. Guido Del Mestri (*Archbishop of Tuscamia*).

The Most Revd. Archbishops CONS.

Edmonton, Joseph MacNeill (1973)	1969
Grouard-McLennan, Henri Legare	1972
Halifax, James Martin Hayes (1967)	1965
Kingston, Joseph L. Wilhelm (1967)	1963
Moncton, Donat Chiasson	1972
Montreal, Paul Gregoire	1968
Ottawa, Joseph A. Plourde (1967)	1964
Port of Spain, Anthony Pantin	1967
Quebec, H.E. Cardinal Maurice L. Roy, O.B.E. (1947)	1946
Regina, Michael C. O'Neill	1948
Rimouski, Giles Ouelett (1972)	1968
St. Boniface, Antony Hacault (1974)	1964
St. John's, Newfoundland, Patrick Skinner (1951)	1950
Sherbrooke, John Fortier (1968)	1962
Toronto, Philip F. Pocock (1971)	1951
Vancouver, B.C., James F. Carney (1969)	1966
Winnipeg, H.E. Cardinal George Flahiff (1961)	1961
Winnipeg (*Byzantine Rite*), Maxim Hermaniuk (1956)	1951

★ In addition there are 71 priests serving as regular chaplains in H.M. Forces. The Right Rev, Gerard Tickle, *Bp.* of *Bela*, was appointed Bishop-in-Ordinary to H.M. Forces in 1963.

† There is one hierarchy for the whole of Ireland. Several of the Dioceses listed above have territory partly in the Republic of Ireland and partly in Northern Ireland.

CONS.

The Rt. Revd. Bishops

Alexandria, Eugene Larocque	1974
Amos, Gaston Hains (1969)	1964
Antigonish, William Power	1960
Bathurst in Canada, Edgar Godin	1969
Belize, Robert Hodapp	1968
Calgary, Paul J. O'Byrne	1968
Castries, B.W.I., Patrick Webster (1974)	1969
Charlottetown, Francis John Spence	1970
Chicoutimi, Mario Paré	1956
Churchill-Baie d'Hudson, Omer Robidoux	1970
Edmundston, Fernand Lacroix	1970
Edmonton (Byzantine Rite), Nicholas Savaryn (1943)	1956
Gaspé, Bertrand Blanchet	1973
Georgetown, Benedict Singh	1972
Grand Falls-Harbour Grace, Alphonsus Penney	1972
Gravelbourg, Noel Delaquis	1974
Hamilton, Paul, F. Reding	1973
Hamilton in Bermuda (vacant)	
Hauterive (vacant)	
Hearst, Roger A. Despati	1973
Hull, Adolphe E. Proulx (1973)	1967
Joilette, René Audet (1968)	1963
Kamloops, B.C., Adam Exner	1974
Keewatin-Le Pas, Paul Dumouchel	1955
Kingston (Jamaica), Samuel Carter (1970)	1966
Labrador-Schefferville, Peter A. Sutton (1974)	1974
London, Gerald Carter (1964)	1962
MacKenzie—Fort Smith, Paul Piché (1967)	1959
Mont Laurier, Joseph Ouellette (1957)	1965
Montego Bay, Edgerton Clarke	1967
Moosonee, Jules Leguerriere (1967)	1964
Nassau (Bahamas), Leonard Hagarty (1960)	1950
Nelson, Wilfrid Doyle	1958
Nicolet, Joseph Martin	1950
Pembroke, Joseph Windle	1971
Peterboro', Anthony Marrocco (1968)	1956
Prince Albert, Lawrence Morin (1959)	1955
Prince George, Fergus J. O'Grady	1956
Roseau (Dominica), Arnold Boghaert	1957
Rouyn-Noranda, Jean-Guy Hamelin	1974
St. Anne de la Pocatière, Charles Lévesque (1968)	1969
St. Catharines, Thomas J. McCarthy (1958)	1955
St. George's, N.F., Richard McGrath	1970
St. George's (Grenada), Sidney Charles	1974
St. Hyacinthe, Albert Sanschagrin	1967
St. Jean de Ouebec, Gerard Coderre (1955)	1951
St. Jerome, Bernard Hubert	1971
St. John, New Brunswick, Canada, Arthur J. Gilbert	1974
St. Paul in Alberta, Raymond Roy	1972
Saskatoon, James P. Mahoney	1967
Saskatoon (Byzantine Rite), Andrew Roborecki (1956)	1948
Sault Ste Marie, Alexander Carter (1958)	1957
Thunder Bay, Norman Gallagher	1970
Timmins, Jacques Landriault	1971
Toronto (Byzantine Rite), Isidore Borecky (1956)	1948
Trois Rivières, Georges L. Pelletier (1947)	1943
Valleyfield, Guy Belanger	1969
Victoria, B.C., Remi De Roo	1962
Whitehorse, Hubert O'Connor	1971
Yarmouth, Austin Burke	1968

Africa

EAST AFRICA: Pro-Nuncio to Uganda, Most Rev. Luigi Bellotti; Pro-Nuncio to Malawi and Zambia, Most Rev. Luciano Angeloni; Pro-Nuncio to Kenya, Most Rev. Pierluigi Satorelli; Pro-Nuncio to Tanzania, Franco Brambilla.

WEST CENTRAL AFRICA: Most Rev. Amelio Poggio.

WEST AFRICA: Most Rev. John Mariani.

CONS.

The Most Revd. Archbishops

Blantyre, James Chiona (1967)	1965
Cape Coast, John Kodwo Amissah (1960)	1957
Dar-es-Salaam, H.E. Cardinal Laurence Rugambwa (1969)	1952
Freetown and Bo, Thomas Brosnahan	1953
Kaduna, John McCarthy (1959)	1954
Kampala, Emmanuel Nsubuga 1967)	1966
Kasama, Elias Mutale (1973)	1971
Lagos, Anthony Okogie (1973)	1971
Lusaka, Emmanuel Milingo	1969
Nairobi, H.E. Cardinal Maurice Otunga	1971
Onitsha, Francis Aringe (1967)	1965
Salisbury, Francis Markall	1956
Tabora, Mark Mihayo	1960

The Rt. Revd. Bishops

Abakaliki, Thomas McGettrick (1973)	1955
Accra, Dominic Kodwo Andoh	1971
Arua, Angelo Tarantino	1959
Arusha, Denis Durning	1963
Bafia, Andrea Loucheur	1968
Bathurst in Gambia, Michael Molony, C.B.E.	1959
Benin City, Patrick Ebosele Ekpu	1973
Buea, Pius Awa (1973)	1971
Bukoba, Nestor Timanywa	1974
Bulawayo, Ernest Karlen (1974)	1968
Calabar, Brian Usanga (1970)	1969
Chikwawa, Franz Vroemen, S.M.M.	1965
Chipata, Medardo Mazombwe	1970
Dedza, Cornelius Citsulo (1959)	1957
Dodoma, Matthias Isuja	1972
Ekiti, Michael Fagun (1972)	1971
Eldoret, Joseph Njenga	1970
Enugu, Godfrey Okoye (1970)	1961
Fort Portal, Serapio Magambo (1972)	1967
Gaborone, Urban Murphy, C.P.	1966
Gulu, Cipriano Kihangire (1969)	1963
Gweio, Louis Haene (1955)	1950
Hoima, Edward Baharagate	1969
Ibadan, Felix Job (1974)	1971
Ijebu-Ode. Antonio Sansusi	1969
Ikot Ekpene, Dominic Ekandem (1954)	1963
Ilorin, William Mahony	1969
Iringa Mario Mgulunde	1970
Issele-Uku, Anthony Gbuji	1973
Jinja, Joseph Williigers	1967
Jos, Gabrielle Ganaka (1974)	1973
Kabale, Barnabas Halem' Imana	1969
Kenema, Joseph Ganda	1970
Keta, Antony Konings	1954
Kigoma, Alphonse Nsabi	1969
Kisii, Tiberio Mugendi	1969
Kisumu, John de Reeper (1965)	1964
Kitui, William Dunne	1964
Kumasi, Peter Sarpong	1970
Lilongwe, Patrick Kalilombe	1972
Lira, Caesar Asili (1968)	1969
Livingstone, Phelim O'Shea (1959)	1950
Lodwar, John Mahon (Pref.-Ap.)	
Lokoja, Alexis Makozi	1972
Machakos, Urbanus Kioko	1973
Mahenge, Patrick Iteka	1973
Maiduguri, Timothy Cotter, O.S.A.	1966
Makeni, Augusto Azzolini	1962
Makurdi, Donald Murray, C.S.Sp	1968
Mansa, James Spaitia	1974
Mangochi, Allesandro Assolar	1974
Marsabit. Charles Cavellera	1964
Masaka, Adrian Ddungu	1962
Mbala, Adolf Furstenberg (1968)	1959
Mbarara, John Kakubi	1969
Mbeya, James Sangu	1966
Mbulu, Basil Hhando	1971
Meru. Laurence Bessone	1954
Minna, Christopher Abba	1973

CONS.

Mombasa, Eugene Butler	1957
Monze, James Corboy	1962
Morogoro, Adrian MKoba	1967
Moroto, Sisto Mazzildi (1967)	1966
Moshi, Joseph Sipendi	1967
Mtwara, Maurus Libaba	1973
Musoma, John Rudin	1957
Mwanza, Renatus Lwamosa Butibubage (1966)	1960
Mzuzu, Jean Jobidon	1961
Nachingwea, Bernard Cotey	1963
Nakuru, Raphael Ndingi	1971
Navrongo, Rudolph Akanlu	1973
Ndola, Nicola Agnozzi O.F.M. Conv. (1966)	1962
Nyeri, *Kenya*, Caesar Gatimu (1964)	1961
Ngong, Colin Davies (*Pref.-Ap.*)	
Njombe, Raymond Mwanyika	1971
Ogoja, Joseph Ukpo (1973)	1971
Ondo, William Field	1958
Oweri, Mark Unegbu	1970
Oyo, Julius Adelakun	1973
Port Harcourt, Edmund Fitzgibbon (*Adm. Ap.*)	
Port Louis, Jean Margéot	1969
Port Victoria, Gervais Aeby (*Adm. Ap.*)	
Qacha's Nek, Joseph des Rosiers, O.M.I. (1951)	1948
Rulenge, Christopher Mwoleka	1969
Same, Henry Winkelmolen (*Pref.-Ap.*).	
Sekondi-Takoradi, Amihere Essuah (1969)	1962
Shinyanga, Edward McGurkin	1956
Singida, Bernard Mabula	1972
Sokoto, Michael Dempsey, O.P.	1967
Solwezi Severiano Potani (*Pref.-Ap.*)	
Songea, James Komba (1969)	1962
Sumbawanga, Charles Msakila (1970)	1958
Sunyani, James Kwadwo Owusu	1973
Tamale (vacant)	
Tanga, Maura Komba	1970
Tororo, James Odongo	1969
Umtali, Daniel Lamont	1957
Umuahia, Antony Nwedo, O.B.E.	1959
Wa, Peter P. Dery	1960
Wankie, Ignatius Vega	1963
Warri, Luca Nwaezeapu	1964
Yola, Patrick Sheehan	1970
Zanzibar and Pemba, Adrian Mkoba (*Ap. Admin.*) (1969)	1967
Zomba, Matthias Chimole	1970

Asia

Pro-Nuncio to India, Most Rev. John Gordon	1969
Pro-Nuncio to Bangladesh, Most Rev. Edward Cassidy	1973
Apostolic Delegate to Sri Lanka, Most Rev. Carlo Curis	1969

The Most Revd. Archbishops

Agra, Domenic Athaide	1956
Bangalore, Packiam Arokiaswamy	1971
Bhopal, Eugene D'Souza (1963)	1951
Bombay, H.E. Cardinal Valerian Gracias (1950)	1946
Calcutta, Lorenzo Picachy	1969
Changanacherry, Anthony Padlyara (1970)	1955
Colombo, H.E. Cardinal Thomas Cooray (1947)	1946
Dacca, Theotonius Ganguly (1968)	1960
Delhi, Angelo Fernandes (1967)	1959
Ernakulam, H.E. Cardinal Joseph Parecattil (1956)	1953
Gauhati-Shillong, Alberto D'Rosario (1969)	1964
Hyderabad, Saminini Arulappa	1972
Madhurai, Justin Diraviam	1967
Madras and Mylapore, Rayappa Arulappa	1965
Malaca-Johore, James Chan	1973
Nagpur (vacant)	
Pondicherry, Venmani Selvanather (1973)	1949
Ranchi, Pio, Kerketta (1961)	1961

CONS.

Trivandrum (*Syro-Malankara Rite*), Gregorios Thangalathil (1955)	1953
Verapoly, Joseph Kelanthara	1971
The Rt. Revd. Bishops	
Ahmedabad, Charles Gomez	1974
Ajmer and Jaipur, Leo D'Mello	1949
Allahabad Alfred Ferrandez (1970)	1967
Alleppey, Michael Arattukulam	1954
Amravati, Joseph A. Rosario	1955
Balasone, Jacob Vadakevetil (*Pref. Ap.*)	
Badulla, Leo Nanayakkara (1972)	1959
Banaras, Patrick D'Souza	1970
Baroda, Ignatius de Souza	1966
Belgaum, Ignazio Lobo	1968
Bellary, Ambrose Yednapally, O.F.M.	1964
Berhampur, Thomas Thiruthalil	1974
Bhagalpur, Urban McGarry	1965
Bijnor (*Malabar Rite*), Graziona Mundadan	1972
Calicut, Aldo Patroni	1948
Chanda, Paul Palathuruthy	1968
Chikmagalur, Alphonse Matthias	1964
Chilaw, Frank M. Fernando (1972)	1965
Chittagong, Joachim Rozario	1968
Cochin, Alexander Edezhath	1952
Coimbatore, Manuel Visuvasam	1972
Cuttack-Bhubaneswar, Henry D'Souza	1973
Cyprus, Elias Farah	1954
Daltonganj, George Saupin	1971
Darjeeling, Enrico Benjamin	1962
Dibrugarh, Robert Kerketta	1970
Dinajpur, Michael Rozario	1968
Dumka, Leone Tigga	1962
Galle, Antonio De Sacrum (1965)	1963
Guntar (vacant)	
Hong Kong, John Baptist Wu	1975
Indore, George Marian Anathil	1973
Jabalpur, Leonard de Souza (1966)	1964
Jaffna, Jacob Deogupillai (1972)	1967
Jagdalpur (*Malabar Rite*), Paul Jeera Kath	1972
Jalpaiguri, James Toppa	1971
Jameshedpur, Joseph Rodericks	1970
Jhansi, Bapist Mudartha (1967)	1963
Jullundar, Symphorian Keeprath	1972
Kandy, Paul Perera	1973
Kashmir and Jammu, John Boerkamp(*Pref. Ap.*)	
Khulna, Michael D'Rozario	1970
Kohima-Imphal, Abraham Alamgrimattathil	1973
Kota Kinabalu, Peter Chung Wan Ting	1972
Kothamangalam, Matthew Potanamuzhi	1956
Kottar, Marianus Arokiasamy	1970
Kottayam, Kuriakose Kunnacherry (1947)	1968
Krishnagar, Matteo Baroi	1973
Kuala Lumpur, Dominic Vendargon	1955
Kuching, Charles Reiterer, V.A. (1968)	1967
Kumbakonam, Paul Arulswami	1955
Kurnool, Joseph Rayappa	1967
Lucknow, Cecil D'Sa	1972
Mananthavady, Jacob Toomkuzhy	1973
Mangalore, Basil D'Souza	1965
Meerut, Patrick Nair	1974
Miri, Anthony Galvin, V.A.	1960
Multan, Ernest Boland, O.P.	1966
Mysore, Matthias Fernandes	1964
Nellore, Pudhota Chinniah Balasamy	1974
Ootacamund, James Aruldas	1974
Palai, Sebastian Vayalil	1950
Palayamkottai, Sava Iruthayara	1973
Palghat, Joseph Irimpen	1974
Patna, Augustine Wildermuth	1947
Penang, Gregorio Yong Sooi Nghean	1968
Poona, William Gomes (1967)	1961
Quilon, Jerome Fernandez	1937
Raigarh-Ambikapur, Francis Ekka	1971
Raipur, John Weidner (*Ap. Admin.*)	
Sagar, Clemens Thottunkai	1968

CONS.

Salem, Michael Duraisamy............	1974
Sambalpur, Raphael Cheenath..........	1974
Satna, Abraham Mattam (1968)........	1974
Silchar, Denzil de Souza...............	1969
Simla and Chandigarh, Gilbert Rego......	1971
Tanjore, Arokiaswami R. Sundaram	1953
Tellicherry, Sebastian Valloppilly.........	1956
Tezpur, Joseph Mittathani..............	1969
Tiruchirapally, James Fernando (1970).....	1953
Tiruvalla, Cheriyan Polachirakal (1955)....	1954
Trichur, Joseph Kundukulam............	1970
Trincomalee, Leo Anthony (1974)........	1968
Trivandrum (*Latin Rite*), Peter Pereira (1966).	1955
Tura, Oreste Marengo (*Ap. Admin.*)	
Tuticorin, Mathal Ambrose............	1972
Ujjain, John Perumattam	1968
Varanasi, Patrick D'Souza............	1970
Vellore, Royappan Anthonimuthu........	1971
Vijayapuram, Cornelius Elanjikal.........	1971
Vijayavada, Joseph S. Thumma..........	1971
Visakhapatnam, Ignatio Gopu (1966).......	1962
Warangal, Alfonso Beretta (1951)	1953

Australia

Pro-Nuncio to Australia, Papua and New Guinea, Most Rev. Gino Paro........... 1969

The Most Revd. Archbishops

Adelaide, James Gleeson (1971).........	1957
Brisbane, Francis Robert Rush (1973)......	1961
Canberra-Goulburn, Thomas Cahill, C.B.E. (1967).................................	1949
Hobart, Guilford Young (1955).........	1948
Melbourne, Thomas Francis Little (1974)....	1973
Perth, Lancelot Goody (1969)...........	1954
Sydney, H.E. Cardinal James Freeman (1971).	1957

The Rt. Revd. Bishops

Armidale, Henry Kennedy...............	1971
Australia (*Byzantine Rite*), John Prasko.....	1958
Ballarat, Ronald Mulkaearns (1971)........	1968
Bathurst, Albert Thomas...............	1963
Broome, John Jobst (1966)...............	1959
Bunbury Myles McKeon (1969)............	1962
Cairns, John Ahern Torple..............	1967
Darwin, John O'Loughlin................	1949
Geraldton, Francis Thomas.............	1962
Lismore, John Satterthwaite (1971)	1969
Maitland, John Toohey (1956)............	1948
Port Pirie, Bryan Gallagher..............	1952

CONS.

Rockhampton, Bernard Wallace...........	1974
Sale, Arthur Francis Fox (1968)...........	1957
Sandhurst, Bernard Stewart (1950)........	1947
Toowoomba, William Brennan...........	1953
Townsville, Anthony Faulkner...........	1967
Wagga-Wagga, Francis Patrick Carroll (1968)	1967
Wilcannia-Forbes, Douglas J. Warren (1967).	1964
Wollongong (vacant)	

New Zealand

Pro-Nuncio to New Zealand and the Pacific Islands, Most Rev. Angelo Acerbi (1974).

The Most Revd. Archbishop

Wellington, Reginald John Delargey (1974)..	1958

The Rt. Revd. Bishops

Auckland, John Mackey................	1974
Christchurch, Brian Patrick Ashby........	1964
Dunedin, John Kavanagh (1957)...........	1949
Rarotonga, John Rodgers (1973)...........	1954

Oceania

The Most Revd. Archbishops

Madang, Adolf Noser (1966)...........	1947
Port Moresby, Virgil Copas (1966)..........	1960
Rabaul, John Hohne (1966)..............	1963
Suva, George Pearce (1957)..............	1956
Tonga and Niue Islands, Patrick Punou-Ki-Hihifo Finau..........................	1972

The Rt. Revd. Bishops

Aitape, Kevin Rowell....................	1969
Apia, Pio Taofinu'u	1956
Bereina, Virgil Copas (*Ap. Admin.*)	
Bougainville, Gregory Singkai............	1974
Daru, Gerard Deschamps................	1966
Gizo, John Crawford (1966).............	1960
Goroka, John Cahill....................	1969
Honiara, Daniel Stuyvemberg (1966).......	1957
Kavieng, Alfred Stemper (1966)...........	1957
Lae, Enrico van Lieshout.................	1966
Mendi, Firmin Schmitt...................	1966
Mount Hagen, George Bernarding (1966)...	1960
Port Vila, Louis Julliard (1966)............	1962
Sideia, Desmond Moore..................	1970
Taiohae, Herve-Marie Le Cleac'h (*Apost. Admin.*)..........................	
Tarawa, Pierre Guichet (1966)............	1961
Vanimo, Pascal Sweeney.................	1966
Wewak, Leo Arkfield (1966).............	1948

LONDON CATHEDRALS, CHURCHES, ETC.

ST. PAUL'S CATHEDRAL, CITY OF LONDON, E.C.4 (1675–1710), cost £747,660. The cross on the dome is 365 ft. above the ground level, the inner cupola 218 ft. above the floor. "Great Paul," in S.W. tower weighs 17 tons. Organ by Father Smith (enlarged by Willis) in case carved by Grinling Gibbons (who also carved the choir stalls). The choir and high altar were restored in 1958 after war damage and the North Transept in 1962. The American War Memorial Chapel was consecrated in November, 1958. The Chapel of the Most Excellent Order of the British Empire in the Crypt of the Cathedral was dedicated on May 20, 1960. Nave and transepts free; Fees to the following parts (on weekdays only, 10.45 a.m. to 3.15 p.m. and—during Summer Time only—4.45 p.m. to 6 p.m.); Crypt, 15p; library, whispering gallery, stone gallery and ball, 20p: total 35p. Service on Sundays at 8, *10.30 and *3.15. Weekdays at 8, *10, *4.

WESTMINSTER ABBEY, S.W.1. (built A.D. 1050–1760).—Open on weekdays 8 a.m. to 6 p.m. (8 p.m., Weds.). Admission to Royal Chapels by fee of 30p. (children 5p) (weekdays) except on Wednesdays from 6 p.m. to 8 p.m. (open free). Transepts and Nave open on Sundays only between services.

Holy Communion at 8; matins at 10.30; Holy Communion at 11.40. Evensong at 3. Evening service with Sermon at 6.30; Daily—Holy Communion at 8 a.m; Westminster School Service at 9 a.m. (term-time only); matins 9.20 a.m. (choral Tuesdays and Fridays); evensong (choral), 5.0 p.m. (said on Wednesdays) (Saturday, 3 p.m.). Chapel of Henry VII Chapter House and Cloisters; King Edward the Confessor's shrine, A.D. 1269, tombs of kings and queens (Edward I, Edward III, Henry V, Mary Queen of Scots, Queen Elizabeth I), and many other monuments and objects of interest, including the grave of "An Unknown Warrior" and St. George's Chapel at the W. end of Nave and Poets' Corner. The Coronation Chair encloses the "Stone of Scone" brought from Scotland by Edward I in 1927.

SOUTHWARK CATHEDRAL, south side of the Thames, near London Bridge, S.E.1.—Mainly 13th century, but the nave is largely rebuilt. Open 7.30 a.m. to 6.30 p.m., free. Sunday services, Holy Communion, 9 and 11 a.m., Choral Evensong, 4 p.m. Weekdays: Mondays, Holy Communion, 5.30 p.m., Tuesdays, Wednesdays and Thursdays, Holy Communion, 8 a.m., Thursdays, Holy Communion, 5.30 p.m., Fridays, Holy Communion, 1.10 p.m., Saturdays, Holy Communion, 12 noon.

Evensong, Tuesdays 6 p.m. (sung), Wednesdays 5.30 p.m. (said), Fridays 5.30 p.m. (sung). The tomb of John Gower (1330–1408) is between the Bunyan and Chaucer memorial windows, in the N. aisle; Shakespeare effigy backed by view of Southwark and Globe Theatre in S. aisle; the altar screen (erected 1520) has been restored; the tomb of Bishop Andrews (died 1626) is near screen. The Early English Lady Chapel (behind the choir), restored 1930, is the scene of the Consistory Courts of the reign of Mary (Gardiner and Bonner); and is still used for this purpose. John Harvard, after whom Harvard University is named was baptized here in 1607.

TEMPLE CHURCH, The Temple, E.C.4.—The nave formed one of five remaining round churches in England, the others being at Cambridge, Northampton, Little Maplestead (Essex), and Ludlow Castle. Rebuilding of the church was completed in 1958. Sunday morning services, open to the public, 11.15 a.m., except in August and September. *Master of the Temple,* Very Rev. R. L. P. Milburn, M.A. *Reader,* Rev. W.D. Kennedy-Bell, M.A.

Church of Scotland
CROWN COURT CHURCH, Russell Street, Covent Garden, W.C.2.—Sundays, 11.15 and 6.30. *Minister,* Rev. J. M. Scott, M.A., B.D., F.S.A.Scot.
ST. COLUMBA'S, Pont Street, S.W.1. Sundays, 11 and 6.30. *Minister,* Rev. J. F. McLuskey, M.C., D.D.

United Reformed
CITY TEMPLE, Holborn Viaduct E.C.1.—Sundays 11 and 6.30. *Minister* (vacant).
WESTMINSTER CHAPEL, Buckingham Gate, S.W.1. —Sundays, 11 and 6.30. *Minister,* (vacant).

Methodist
CENTRAL HALL, Westminster, S.W.1.—Sunday Services, 11 a.m. and 6.30 p.m. *Minister,* Rev. M. Barnett, M.A., B.D., Ph.D.
KINGSWAY METHODIST CHURCH, Kingsway, W.C.2.—Sundays at 10, 11, and 6.30, *Minister,* Rev. the Lord Soper, M.A., Ph.D.

Baptist
BLOOMSBURY CENTRAL BAPTIST CHURCH, Junction of Shaftesbury Avenue and New Oxford Street, W.C.2.—Sundays, 11 and 6.30. *Minister,* Rev. H. Howard Williams, Ph.D.

Society of Friends
FRIENDS' HOUSE, Euston Road, N.W.1.

Roman Catholic
WESTMINSTER CATHEDRAL, Ashley Place, Westminster, S.W.1. (close to Victoria Station), built 1895–1903 from the designs of J. F. Bentley (the campanile is 283 feet high—open to public by lift, 15p).—*Sundays.* Masses, 7, 8, 9, 10.30 (High), 12 noon, 5.30 p.m. and 7 p.m.; Solemn Vespers and Benediction, 3.30. *Weekdays.* Masses, 7, 7.30, 8, 8.30, 9, 10.30 (High), 12.30 and 6 p.m. Morning Office, 10.5, Vespers and Benediction, 5 p.m. *Holy days of obligation.* Low Masses, 7, 7.30, 8, 8.30, 9, 10.30 (High), 11.50, 12.30, 6 and 8 p.m. Cathedral open 6.45 a.m. to 8 p.m.
THE ORATORY, Brompton, S.W.7.—*Sundays:* Masses, 6.15, 7, 8, 9, 10, 11; (High Mass); 12.30 4.30, 7; Vespers and Benediction, 3.30. *Weekdays:* Masses, 7, 7.30, 8, 10; 12.30, 6 p.m. (no 12.30 on Sats.). Service Thurs. 8 p.m. *Holy days:* Masses 6.15, 7, 8, 9, 10, 11, 12.15, 1.15 and 8 p.m.; 6 p.m. (High Mass). On the eve, Vespers and Benediction, 5.30 p.m.

PATRON SAINTS

St. George, Patron Saint of England.—St. George is believed to have been born in Cappadocia, of Christian parents, in the latter part of the 3rd century and to have served with distinction as a soldier under the Emperor Diocletian, including a visit to England on a military mission. When the persecution of Christians was ordered, St. George sought a personal interview to remonstrate with the Emperor and after a profession of faith resigned his military commission. Arrest and torture followed and he was martyred at Nicomedia on April 23, 303, a day ordered to kept in remembrance as a national festival by the Council of Oxford in 1222, although it was not until the reign of Edward III that he was made patron saint of England. His connection with a dragon seems to date from the close of the 6th century and to be due to the transfer of his remains from Nicomedia to Lydda, close to the scene of the legendary exploit of Perseus in rescuing Andromeda and slaying the sea monster, credit for which became attached to the Christian martyr.

St. David, Patron Saint of Wales.—St. David is believed to have been born near the beginning and to have died towards the end of the 6th century. St. David was an eloquent preacher and became Primate of South Wales while Bishop of Caerleon on Usk, but he afterwards moved the seat of the Primacy from Caerleon to Menevia, now St. David's.

At the request of Henry I he was canonized in the early part of the 12th century and became the tutelary saint of Wales, his annual festival being observed on March 1.

St. Andrew, Patron Saint of Scotland.—St. Andrew, one of the Christian Apostles and brother of Simon Peter was born at Bethsaida on the Lake of Galilee and lived at Capernaum. He preached the Gospel in Asia Minor and in Scythia along the shores of the Black Sea and became the patron saint of Russia. It is believed that he suffered crucifixion at Patras in Achaea, on a *crux decussata* (now known as St. Andrew's Cross) and that his relics were removed from Patras to Constantinople and thence to St. Andrews, probably in the 8th century, since which time he has been the patron saint of Scotland. The festival of St. Andrew is held on November 30, a church festival indicated in the calendar by red letters.

St. Patrick, Patron Saint of Ireland.—St. Patrick was born in England about 389 and was carried off to Ireland as a slave about sixteen years later, escaping to Gaul at the age of 22. He was ordained deacon and afterwards and having been consecrated Bishop in 432 was despatched to Wicklow to reorganize the Christian communities in Ireland. He founded the see of Armagh and introduced Latin into Ireland as the language of the Church. He died in 461 and his festival is celebrated on March 17.

EDUCATION DIRECTORY

THE UNIVERSITY OF OXFORD

FULL TERMS, 1976

Hilary, Jan. 8 to March 3
Trinity, April 5 to June 19
Michaelmas, Oct. 10 to Dec. 4

NUMBER OF UNDERGRADUATES IN RESIDENCE
Michaelmas Term, 1974, 8,011

UNIVERSITY OFFICES, &c.

	Elect.
Chancellor, Rt. Hon. Harold Macmillan, Balliol	1960
High Steward, The Lord Wilberforce, P.C., C.M.G., O.B.E., M.A., All Souls	1967
Vice-Chancellor, H. J. Habakkuk, M.A. Principal of Jesus	1973
Proctors, B. E. F. Fender, M.A., Ph.D., St. Catherine's; R. P. Martineau, M.A., Ph.D., Wadham	1975
Assessor, H. Shukman, Ph.D., St. Anthony's	1975
Assessor of the Chancellor's Court, Sir Humphrey Waldock, C.M.G., O.B.E., Q.C., D.C.L., All Souls	1947
Public Orator, J. G. Griffith, M.A., Jesus	1973
Bodley's Librarian, R. Shackleton, M.A., D.Litt., Brasenose	1966
Keeper of Archives, T. H. Aston, M.A., Corpus Christi	1969
Director of the Ashmolean Museum, D. T. Piper, M.A., Worcester	1973
Keeper of the Dept. of Western Art, K. J. Garlick, M.A., Balliol	1968
Keeper of Dept. of Antiquities, H. J. Case, M.A., Balliol	1973
Keeper of Dept. of Eastern Art, J. C. Harle, M.A., D.Phil., Christ Church	1967
Keeper of Heberden Coin Room (vacant)	
Curator of the Museum of History of Science, F. R. Maddison, M.A., Linacre	1965
Registrar of the University, G. K. Caston, B.A., Merton	1972
Deputy Registrars, A. L. Fleet, M.A., Pembroke (Administration); A. J. Dorey, M.A., D.Phil., Linacre (General)	1973
Establishment Officer, D. W. Roberts, M.A. (Pembroke)	1975
Senior Assistant Registrars, C. H. Paterson, M.A., Corpus (1971); Mrs. E. R. M. Brain, M.A., Linacre (1969); A. Ostler, B.C.L., M.A., Queen's (1970); P. Garnham, M.A., Worcester	1973
Information Officer, E. E. Sabben-Clare, M.A., New College	1970
Assistant Registrars, R. A. Malyn, M.A., St. Peter's (1961); H. P. Ruglys, M.A., Hertford (1966); G. P. Collyer, M.A., St. Catherine's (1966); P. S. Crane, M.A., Jesus (1966); J. P. W. Roper, M.A., Lincoln (1967); Miss M. E. Grinyer, M.A., St. Hilda's (1968); Miss A. M. Barr (1969); J. D. Brown (1971); I. M. Herrman, D.Phil., St. Catherine's (1970); M. J. Stanley, M.A., St. Catherine's (1973); A. P. Weale, M.A. University	1973
Secretary of Faculties, H. W. Deane, M.A.	1971
Secretary to the Curators of the University Chest, W. T. Horsley, M.A., Hertford	1972
Chief Accountant, H. Barrett, M.A., Balliol	1961
Head of Data Processing and Management Services, R. W. Ewart	1973
Registrar of the Chancellor's Court, F. R. Williamson, M.A., Pembroke	1964
University Counsel, F. H. B. W. Layfield, M.A., Corpus	1971
Clerk of the Schools, G. A. Barnes	1971
Land Agent to the University, J. R. Mills, M.A., Wolfson	1961
Surveyor to the University, J. Lankester, M.A., St. Catherine's	1956
Director, Department of Educational Studies, H. G. Judge, M.A., B.N.C.	1973

SECRETARY TO DELEGATES OF:—
Examination of Schools, A. R. Davis, M.A., St. John's.
Local Exams., J. R. Cummings, B.Litt., M.A., B.N.C.
Science Area, G. E. S. Turner, M.A., St. Catherine's.
University Press, G. B. Richardson, M.A., St. John's.

SECRETARY OF:—
Accommodation Committee, A. W. Davies, M.A., Magdalen.
Committee for Appointments, T. Snow, M.A., New College.
The Rhodes Trustees, Sir Edgar Williams, C.B., C.B.E., D.S.O., M.A., Balliol.

HEBDOMADAL COUNCIL

Ex-Officio Members, the Chancellor; the Vice-Chancellor; Warden of Merton (Vice-Chancellor Elect); Prof. J. H. Burnett, M.A., D.Phil., St. John's (Vice Chairman of the General Board); the Proctors; the Assessor.

Elected by Congregation—
The Provost of Oriel; the Provost of Queen's; the Dean of Christ Church; the Principal of Linacre; the Principal of St. Hilda's; the Principal of St. Anne's; the Rector of Exeter; The Master of St. Catherine's; Sir Edgar Williams, C.B., C.B.E., D.S.O., M.A.; M. G. Brock, M.A.; R. P. H. Gasser, M.A., D.Phil.; M. Shock, M.A.; Miss E. A. O. Whiteman, M.A., D.Phil.; Prof. Sir Denys Wilkinson, M.A., F.R.S., A. H. Cooke, M.A., D.Phil.; Prof. R. J. Elliott, M.A., D.Phil.; Prof. Sir Richard Doll, D.M.; Prof. J. K. B. M. Nicholas, M.A.

Oxford Colleges and Halls
(With dates of foundation)

All Souls (1438), J. H. A. Sparrow, M.A., Warden (1952).
Balliol (1263), J. E. C. Hill, M.A., D.Litt., Master (1965).
Brasenose (1509) Prof. H. L. A. Hart, M.A., Principal (1973).
Christ Church (1546), Very Rev. H. Chadwick, D.D., Dean (1969).
Corpus Christi (1517), (vacant) President.
Exeter (1314), W. G. Barr, M.A., Rector (1972).
Hertford (1874), G. J. Warnock, M.A., Principal (1972).
Jesus (1571), H. J. Habakkuk, M.A., Principal (1967).
Keble (1868), Rev. D. E. Nineham, B.D., M.A., Warden (1969).
Linacre (1962), J. B. Bamborough, M.A., Principal (1962).
Lincoln (1427), The Lord Trend, P.C., G.C.B., C.V.O., M.A., Rector (1973).
Magdalen (1458), J. H. E. Griffiths, O.B.E., M.A., D.Phil., President (1968).
Merton (1264), R. E. Richards, M.A., D.Phil., D.Sc., Warden (1969).
New College (1379), Sir William Hayter, K.C.M.G., M.A., Warden (1958).
Nuffield (1937), Sir Norman Chester, M.A., Warden (1954).
Oriel (1326), K. C. Turpin, M.A., B.Litt., Provost (1957).

Pembroke (1624), Sir Geoffrey Arthur, K.C.M.G., Master (1974).

Queen's (1340), The Lord Blake, M.A., *Provost* (1969).

St. Antony's (1950), A. R. M. Carr, M.A., *Warden* (1968).

St. Catherine's (1962), Sir Alan Bullock, M.A., D.Litt., *Master* (1962).

St. Cross (1965), W. E. van Heyningen, M.A., Ph.D., D.Sc., *Master* (1965).

St. Edmund Hall (1270), Rev. Canon J. N. D. Kelly, D.D., *Principal* (1951).

St. John's (1555), Sir Richard Southern, M.A. *President* (1969).

St. Peter's (1929) Sir Alec Cairncross, K.C.M.G., *Master Trinity* (1554), A. G. Ogston, M.A., D.Sc., F.R.S., President (1970).

University (1249), The Lord Redcliffe-Maud, G.C.B., C.B.E., *Master* (1963).

Wadham (1612), S. N. Hampshire, M.A., *Warden* (1970).

Wolfson (1965), The Hon. Sir Henry Fisher, M.A., *President* (1975).

Worcester (1714), The Lord Franks, P.C., G.C.M.G., K.C.B., C.B.E., M.A., *Provost* (1962).

Campion Hall, Rev. B. Winterborn, M.A. *Master* (1972).

St. Benet's Hall, Rev. C. L. J. Forbes, M.A., *Master* (1964).

Mansfield (1886), Rev. G. B. Caird, D.Phil., D.D., *Principal* (1970).

Regent's Park, Rev. B. R. White, M.A., D.Phil., *Principal* (1972).

Greyfriars Hall, Very Rev. C. J. Reel, B.Litt., M.A., *Warden* (1972).

_____

Lady Margaret Hall (1878), Mrs. E. M. Chilver, M.A. *Principal* (1971).

St. Anne's (1952) (Originally *Society of Oxford Home-Students* (1879)), Mrs. N. K. Trenaman, M.A., *Principal* (1966).

St. Hilda's (1893), Mrs. M. L. S. Bennett, M.A., *Principal* (1965).

St. Hugh's (1886), Miss M. R. Trickett, M.A., *Principal* (1973).

Somerville (1879), Mrs. B. Craig, M.A., *Principal* (1967).

UNIVERSITY PROFESSORS

	Elect.
American History (Harmsworth), J. P. Greene, M.A., Queen's	1975
American History and Institutions (Rhodes), H. G. Nicholas, M.A., New College	1969
Anatomy (Lee's), C. G. Phillips, D.M., F.R.S.	1975
Anaesthetics (Nuffield), A. C. Smith, M.A., Pemb	1965
Anglo-Saxon (vacant)	
Anthropology, Social, M. Freedman, M.A., All Souls	1970
Arabic (Laudian), A. F. L. Beeston, M.A., D.Phil., St. John's	1955
Archæology of the Roman Empire, S. S. Frere, M.A., All Souls	1966
Archæology, Classical (Lincoln), C. M. Robertson, M.A., Linc.	1961
Archæology, European, B. W. Cunliffe, M.A., D.Phil., Keble	1972
Armenian Studies (Gulbenkian), C. J. F. Dowsett, M.A., D.Phil., Pembroke	1965
Astronomy (Savilian), D. E. Blackwell, M.A., New Coll.	1960
Biochemistry (Whitley), R. R. Porter, M.A., F.R.S., Trinity	1967
Biomathematics (vacant)	
Botany (Sherardian), F. R. Whatley, M.A., F.R.S., Magdalen	1971

	Elect.
Byzantine and Modern Greek Lang. and Lit. (Bywater and Sotheby), C. Mango, M.A., Exeter	1973
Celtic, I. Ll. Foster, M.A., Jesus	1947
Chemical Crystallography (Royal Society's Wolfson Research Professor), Mrs. D. M. Hodgkin, O.M., D.Sc., M.A., F.R.S., Somerville	1960
Chemical Microbiology (Iveagh), J. Mandelstam, M.A., Linacre	1966
Chemical Pathology, E. P. Abraham, C.B.E., M.A., D.Phil., F.R.S., Lincoln	1964
Chemistry, Inorganic (vacant)	
Chemistry (Lee's), J. S. Rowlinson, M.A., D.Phil., F.R.S., Exeter	1974
Chemistry (Waynflete), Sir Ewart Jones, M.A., F.R.S., Magd.	1955
Chinese, P. van der Loon, M.A., University	1972
Civil Law (Regius), A. M. Honoré, D.C.L., All Souls	1971
Clinical Biochemistry, P. J. Randle, M.A., D.Phil., M.D.	1975
Clinical Neurology, W. B. Matthews, D.M., St. Edmund Hall	1970
Clinical Pharmacology, D. G. Grahame-Smith, M.A., Corpus	1971
Comparative Philology, Mrs. A. E. Davies, M.A., Somerville	1971
Comparative Slavonic Philology, R. Auty, M.A., Brasenose	1965
Divinity (Regius), Rev. Canon M. F. Wiles, D.D., Ch. Ch.	1970
Divinity (Lady Margaret), Rev. Canon J. Macquarrie, M.A., Ch. Ch.	1970
Eastern Religions and Ethics (Spalding), (vacant)	
Ecclesiastical History (Regius), Rev. Canon J. McManners, M.A., Ch. Ch.	1972
Economic History (Chichele), P. Mathias, M.A., All Souls	1968
Economics, Applied, J. A. C. Brown, M.A., Merton	1970
Economics, J. A. Mirrlees, M.A., Nuffield	1968
Economics of Underdeveloped Countries, I. M. D. Little, M.A., D.Phil., Nuffield	1971
Egyptology (vacant)	
Engineering, H. Motz, M.A., St. John's	1972
Engineering Science, D. W. Holder, M.A., F.R.S., B.N.C.	1961
Engineering (Stewarts and Lloyds), W. S. Hemp, M.A., Keble	1965
English Language, E. J. Dobson, M.A., D.Phil., Jesus	1961
English Language and Literature (Merton), N. Davis, M.B.E., M.A., Merton	1959
English Literature (Merton), J. Carey, M.A., D.Phil.	1975
English Literature (Goldsmiths'), R. Ellmann, M.A., New Coll.	1970
English Literature (Thomas Warton), J. O. Bayley, M.A., St. Catherine's	1974
Exegesis (Ireland), Rev. G. D. Kilpatrick, D.D., Queen's	1949
Experimental Philosophy (Lee's), B. Bleaney, C.B.E., M.A., D.Phil., F.R.S., Wadham	1957
Fine Art (Slade), M. Girouard, M.A., All Souls	1975
Forest Science, J. L. Harley, M.A., D.Phil., F.R.S., St. John's	1969
French (Foch), J. Scherer, M.A., All Souls	1973
French Literature, I. D. MacFarlane, M.A.	1971
Genetics, W. F. Bodmer, M.A., F.R.S., Keble.	1970
Geography, J. Gottmann, M.A., Hertford	1968
Geography (Mackinder), J. W. House, M.A., St. Peter's	1974

Elect.

Geology, E. A. Vincent, M.A., *University*.... 1966

Geometry (Savilian), I. M. James, M.A., D.Phil., F.R.S., *St. John's*............... 1970

George Eastman Visiting, J. Pappenheimer, M.A............................... 1975

German, P. F. Ganz, M.A., *St. Edmund Hall*.. 1972

German Language and Literature (Taylor), S. S. Prawer, M.A., D.Litt., *Queen's*........... 1969

Government and Public Administration (Gladstone), S. E. Finer, M.A., *All Souls*........ 1957

Greek (Regius), P. H. J. Lloyd-Jones, M.A., *Ch. Ch.*.............................. 1960

Hebrew (Regius), W. D. McHardy, M.A., D.Phil., *St. John's*...................... 1960

History, Ancient (Camden), P. A. Brunt, M.A., *Brasenose*............................ 1970

History, Ancient (Wykeham), A. Andrewes, M.A., *New Coll.*....................... 1953

History of Art, F. J. H. Haskell, M.A., *Trinity* 1967

History of the British Commonwealth (Beit), R. E. Robinson, M.A., *Balliol*........... 1971

History of Latin America, D. C. M. Platt, M.A., D.Phil., *St. Antony's*.............. 1973

History of Philosophy, J. L. Ackrill, M.A., *B.N.C.*.............................. 1966

History of Science, Mrs. M. M. Gowing, M.A. 1973

History of War (Chichele), N. H. Gibbs, M.A., D.Phil., *All Souls*..................... 1953

International Relations (Montague Burton), Hon. A. F. Buchan, C.B.E., M.A., *Balliol*... 1972

Interpretation of Holy Scripture, Rev. H. F. D. Sparks, D.D., F.B.A., *Oriel*............. 1952

Italian (Serena), C. Grayson, M.A., *Magdalen* 1958

Jurisprudence, R. M. Dworkin, M.A., *University*............................... 1969

Latin (Corpus), R. G. M. Nisbet, M.A., *Corpus* 1970

Law (Comparative), J. K. B. M. Nicholas, M.A., *Brasenose*..................... 1971

Law (English), H. W. R. Wade, Q.C., D.C.L., *St. John's*........................... 1961

Law (English) (Vinerian), Sir Rupert Cross, D.C.L., F.B.A., *All Souls*............... 1964

Logic (Wykeham), Sir Alfred Ayer, M.A., F.B.A., *New Coll.*..................... 1959

Mathematical Logic, D. S. Scott, M.A., *Merton* 1972

Mathematics, J. F. C. Kingman, M.A., D.Sc., F.R.S., *St. Cross*....................... 1969

Mathematics (Rouse Ball), R. Penrose, M.A., F.R.S., *Wadham*..................... 1973

Mathematics (Theory of Plasma), L. C. Woods, M.A., D.Phil., D.Sc., *Balliol*.............. 1970

Medicine (Regius), Sir Richard Doll, O.B.E., D.M., M.D., D.Sc., F.R.C.P., F.R.S., *Christ Church*............................... 1969

Medicine, Cardiovascular (Field Marshal Alexander), P. Sleight, D.M., *Exeter*....... 1973

Medicine, Clinical (Nuffield), D. J. Weatherall, M.D., F.R.C.P., *Magd.*..................... 1974

Medicine, Social and Community, M. P. Vessey, M.A., *St. Cross*................. 1974

Metallurgy (Wolfson), Sir Peter Hirsch, M.A., D.Phil., F.R.S., *St. Edmund Hall*........ 1966

Metallurgy, Physical, J. W. Christian, M.A., D.Phil., *St. Edmund Hall*.............. 1967

Metaphysical Philosophy (Wayneflete), P. F. Strawson, M.A., *Magd.*.................. 1968

Modern History (Chichele), J. M. Wallace-Hadrill, M.A., D.Litt., *All Souls*.......... 1974

Modern History (Regius), H. R. Trevor-Roper, M.A., *Oriel*.................... 1957

Modern History, R. C. Cobb, M.A., *Worcester* 1973

Molecular Biophysics, D. C. Phillips, M.A., *Corpus Christi*........................ 1966

Elect.

Moral and Pastoral Thelogy (Regius), Rev. Canon P. R. Baelz, M.A., *Christ Church*.. 1975

Moral Philosophy (White's), R. M. Hare, M.A., *Corpus Christi*..................... 1966

Morbid Anatomy, J. O'D. McGee, M.A., M.D. 1975

Music, D. M. Arnold, M.A., *Wadham*....... 1975

Natural Philosophy (Sedleian), A. E. Green, M.A., D.Sc., *Queen's*.................. 1968

Numerical Analysis (and Director of Computing Laboratory), L. Fox, M.A., D.Phil., D.Sc., *Balliol*............................. 1964

Nuclear Structure, K. W. Allen, M.A., *Balliol* 1963

Obstetrics and Gynæcology (Nuffield), A. C. Turnbull, M.D., M.A., *Queen's*......... 1973

Orthopædic Surgery (Nuffield), R. B. Duthie, M.A., *Worcester*..................... 1966

Paediatrics, J. P. M. Tizard, B.M., M.A., *Jesus*. 1972

Pathology, H. Harris, M.A., D.Phil., F.R.S., *Lincoln*............................. 1963

Pathology (Royal Society's), J. L. Gowans, M.A., D.Phil., *St. Catherine's*.......... 1962

Pharmacology, W. D. M. Paton, C.B.E., D.M., F.R.S., *New Coll.*................... 1959

Philosophy of the Christian Religion (Nolloth), B. G. Mitchell, M.A., *Oriel*............ 1967

Physics (Wykeham), R. J. Elliott, M.A., D.Phil., *New College*................. 1974

Physics, Elementary Particle, D. H. Perkins, M.A., F.R.S........................ 1965

Physics, Experimental, Sir Denys Wilkinson, M.A., F.R.S., *Ch. Ch.*................. 1959

Physics, Theoretical (Royal Society's), R. H. Dalitz, M.A., *All Souls*.................. 1963

Physiology (Wayneflete), D. Whitteridge, B.SC., D.M., F.R.S., *Magd.*................. 1968

Poetry, J. B. Wain, M.A..................... 1973

Political Economy (Drummond), (vacant)

Psychiatry (Handley), M. G. Gelder, D.M., *Merton*............................ 1969

Psychology, L. Weiskrantz, M.A., *Magdalen*.. 1967

Psychology (Watts), J. S. Bruner, M.A., *Wolfson*........................... 1972

Public International Law (Chichele), D. P. O'Connell, M.A., *All Souls*............ 1972

Pure Mathematics (Wayneflete), G. Higman, M.A., D.Phil., F.R.S., *Magdalen*........ 1960

Race Relations (Rhodes), K. Kirkwood, M.A., *St. Ant*............................ 1954

Romance Languages, S. Ullmann, M.A., *Trinity* 1968

Rural Economy (Sibthorpian), J. H. Burnett, M.A., D.Phil., *St. John's*............. 1970

Russian, J. L. I. Fennell, M.A., *New Coll*.... 1966

Russian and Balkan History, D. Obolensky, M.A., *Ch. Ch.*..................... 1961

Sanskrit (Boden), T. Burrow, M.A., F.B.A., *Balliol*............................ 1944

Social and Political Theory (Chichele) (vacant)

Spanish Studies (King Alfonso XIII), P. E. Russell, M.A., *Exeter*.................. 1953

Surgery (Nuffield), P. J. Morris, M.A., F.R.C.S., *Balliol*............................ 1974

Zoology (Entomology) (Hope), G. C. Varley, M.A., *Jesus*...................... 1948

Zoology (Linacre), J. W. S. Pringle, M.B.E., M.A., D.SC., F.R.S., *Merton*............... 1961

THE UNIVERSITY OF CAMBRIDGE

FULL TERMS, 1976

Lent, Jan. 13 to Mar. 12; Easter, Apr. 20 to June 11, Michaelmas, Oct. 5 to Dec. 3

NUMBER OF UNDERGRADUATES IN RESIDENCE
1974–75: Men, 7,181; Women, 1,711

Chancellor, The Lord Adrian, O.M., M.D., F.R.S., *Trin*............................ 1967

Elect.

Vice-Chancellor, Miss A. R. Murray, M.A.,
D.Phil., *President of New Hall*   1975
High Steward, The Lord Devlin, P.C., M.A.,
F.B.A., *Chr.*   1966
Deputy High Steward, Rt. Hon. J. S. B. Lloyd,
C.H., C.B.E., Q.C., M.P., M.A., *Magd.*   1971
Commissary, The Lord Morris of Borth-y-
Gest, P.C., C.B.E., M.C., Q.C., *Tr. H.*   1968
Orator, F. H. Stubbings, M.A., Ph.D.   1974
†*Registrary,* R. E. Macpherson, M.A., *King's*   1969
†*Deputy Registrary,* R. F. Holmes, M.A.,
Darw.   1972
Librarian, E. B. Ceadel, M.A., *Corp.*   1967
Treasurer, T. C. Gardner, C.B.E., M.A., *Wolfs.*   1969
Deputy Treasurer, A. B. Shone, M.A., *Selw.*.   1969
Secretary General of the Faculties, A. D. I.
Nicol, M.A., Ph.D., *Fitzw.*   1972
Deputy Secretary General of the Faculties,
L. M. Harvey, M.A., *Chur.*   1963
Esquire Bedells, P. T. Sinker, M.A., *Cla.*   1960
P. C. Melville, M.A., *Selw.*   1968
Proctors, P. N. Brooks, M.A., Ph.D., *Down*;
P. J. Wheatley, Ph.D., *Qu.* (for 1975–6)
Organist, G. H. Guest, M.A., Mus.B., *Joh.*   1974
Director, Dept. of Applied Economics, Hon.
W. A. H. Godley, M.A., *King's*   1970
Director of the Fitzwilliam Museum, Prof. A.
M.Jaffé, M.A., *King's.*   1973
Director of the Museum of Zoology, K. A.
Joysey, M.A., *Fitzw.*   1970
Director, University Computing Service, D. F.
Hartley, M.A., Ph.D., *Darw.*   1970
*Director in Industrial Co-operation, Wolfson
Cambridge Industrial Unit,* D. B. Welbourn,
M.A., *Selw.*   1971
*Curator of the Museum of Archaeology and
Ethnology,* P. W. Gathercole, M.A., *Pet.*   1970
Curator of the Museum of Classical Archæology,
Prof. R. M. Cook, M.A., *Cla.*   1962
Curators of the Sedgwick Museum of Geology,
C. L. Forbes, M.A., Ph.D., *Cla.*   1967
R. B. Rickards, M.A., *Emm.*   1968
*Curator of the Whipple Museum of the History
of Science,* D. Bryden, B.Sc., M.A., *Caius.*.   1970
Director of the Botanic Garden, S. M. Walters,
M.A., Ph.D., *King's.*   1973
Representative on General Medical Council,
W. S. Lewin, M.A., *Darw.*   1971

SECRETARY TO:—

Local Examinations Syndicate, F. Wild, M.A.,
Ph.D., *Down.*   1972
Board of Extra-mural Studies, J. M. Y. Andrew,
M.A., *Cath.,* Madingley Hall.   1967
Highest Grade Schools Examination Syndicate,
H. F. King, M.A., M.SC., *Emm.,* 10 Trump-
ington Street.   1969
Appointments Board, W. P. Kirkman, M.A.,
Wolfs., 6 Chaucer Road   1968
Women's Appointments Board, Miss J. F.
Holgate, M.A., *Newn.,* 6 Chaucer Road . .   1966
University Press, G. A. Cass, M.A., *Jes.*   1972

COUNCIL OF THE SENATE
(*Secretary,* The Registrary)
Ex officio Members, The Chancellor; Vice-Chan-
cellor.
Heads of Colleges, The Master of *Jesus;* The Master
of *Fitzwilliam;* The President of *Queen's.*

† Correspondence for the *Registrary* and *Deputy
Registrary* should be sent to the *University Registry,*
The Old Schools, Cambridge.

Professors and Readers, Prof. A. D. Buckingham,
Ph.D., *Pemb.;* Prof. M. B. Hesse, M.A., Ph.D., F.B.A.,
Wolfs.; Miss P. M. Deane, M.A., *Newn.;* Prof.
H. P. F. Swinnerton-Dyer, M.A., F.R.S., *Cath.*
Elected as Members of the Regent House, Mrs. C. U.
Bertram, Ph.D., *L.Cav.;* S. G. Fleet, M.A., Ph.D.,
Down; C. B. Goodhart, M.A., Ph.D., *Cai.;* C. M.
P. Johnson, M.A., Ph.D., *Joh.;* J. S. Morrison, M.A.,
Wolfs.; P. O'Higgins, M.A., Ph.D., *Chr.,* G. A.
Reid, M.A., Ph.D., *Joh.;* J. F. Q. Switzer, M.A.,
Sid.

Cambridge Colleges
(*With dates of foundation*)

Christ's (1505), The Lord Todd, M.A., F.R.S., *Master*
(1963).
Churchill (1960), (men and women) Prof. Sir
William Hawthorne, C.B.E., M.A., F.R.S., *Master*
(1968).
Clare (1326) (men and women), R. C. O. Matthews,
M.A., F.B.A. *Master* (1975).
Clare Hall (1966) (men and women), Prof. R. W.
K. Honeycombe, Ph.D., *President* (1973).
Corpus Christi (1352), Sir Duncan Wilson, G.C.M.G.,
Master (1971).
Darwin (1964) (men and women), Prof. Sir Frank
Young, M.A., F.R.S. *Master* (1964).
Downing (1800), Sir Morien Morgan, C.B., M.A.,
F.R.S., *Master* (1972).
Emmanuel (1584), Sir Gordon Sutherland, SC.D.,
F.R.S., *Master* (1964).
Fitzwilliam (1966), E. Miller, M.A., *Master* (1971).
Gonville & Caius (1348), N. J. T. M. Needham,
SC.D., F.R.S., *Master* (1966).
Jesus (1496), Sir Alan Cottrell, M.A., Ph.D., F.R.S.
Master 1974.
King's (1441) (men and women), E. R. Leach, M.A.,
Ph.D., *Provost* (1966).
Magdalene (1542), W. Hamilton, M.A., *Master* (1966).
Pembroke (1347), W. A. Camps, M.A., *Master* (1970).
Peterhouse (1284), Prof. J. G. D. Clark, C.B.E.,
SC.D., F.B.A., *Master* (1973).
Queens' (1448), D. W. Bowett, M.A., Ll.B., Ph.D.,
President (1970).
St. Catherine's (1473), Prof. H. P. F. Swinnerton-
Dyer, M.A., F.R.S., *Master* (1973).
St. Edmund's House (1896), Very Rev. Canon G. D.
Sweeney, M.A., *Master* (1964).
St. John's (1511), Prof. P. N. S. Mansergh, O.B.E.,
Litt.D., *Master* (1969).
Selwyn (1882) (men and women from Oct. 1976),
Rev. Prof. W. O. Chadwick, D.D., F.B.A., *Master*
(1956).
Sidney Sussex (1596) (men and women from Oct.
1976), Prof. J. W. Linnett, Ph.D., F.R.S., *Master*
(1970).
Trinity (1546), The Lord Butler of Saffron Walden,
K.G., P.C., C.H., M.A., *Master* (1965).
Trinity Hall (1350), T. M. Sugden, SC.D., F.R.S.,
Master (1976).
Wolfson (1965), J. S. Morrison, M.A., *President*
(1966).

COLLEGES FOR WOMEN

Girton (1869), Miss M. C. Bradbrook, Litt.D.,
Mistress (1968).
New Hall (1954), Miss A. R. Murray, M.A., D.Phil.,
President.
Newnham (1871), Mrs. J. Floud, B.SC. (Econ.),
M.A., *Principal* (1972).

APPROVED SOCIETIES

Hughes Hall (*formerly Cambridge T.C.*) (1885),
(for post-graduate students and candidates for
B.Ed.), Sir Desmond Lee, M.A., *President* (1974).

Lucy Cavendish Collegiate Society (1965) (for women research students and mature undergraduates), Mrs. C. K. Bertram, M.A., Ph.D., *President* (1970).

UNIVERSITY PROFESSORS   Elect.

Aerial Photographic Studies, J. K. S. St. Joseph, M.A., Ph.D., *Selw* 1973
Aeronautical Engineering (Francis Mond), W. A. Mair, C.B.E., M.A., *Down* 1952
Agriculture (Drapers), J. W. L. Beament, SC.D., F.R.S., *Qu* 1969
American History and Institutions (Pitt), R. N. Fogel (for 1975–76).
Anatomy, R. J. Harrison, M.D., F.R.S., *Down*. 1968
Ancient History, M. I. Finley, M.A., *Jes*...... 1970
Ancient Philosophy (Laurence), G. E. L. Owen, M.A., B.Phil., F.B.A., *King's*............ 1973
Anglo-Saxon (Elrington and Bosworth), P. A. M. Clemoes, Ph.D., *Emm*............ 1969
Animal Embryology (Charles Darwin), C. R. Austin, M.A., *Fitzw*.................. 1967
Applied Mathematics, G. K. Batchelor, Ph.D., F.R.S., *Trin*........................ 1964
Applied Thermodynamics (Hopkinson and Imperial Chemical Industries), Sir William Hawthorne, C.B.E., M.A., SC.D., F.R.S., *Chur*. 1951
Arabic (Sir T. Adam's), R. B. Serjeant, Ph.D., *Trin*.............................. 1970
Archæology (Disney), G. E. Daniel, Litt.D., F.S.A., *Joh*........................... 1974
Architecture, C. A. St. J. Wilson, M.A., F.R.I.B.A., *Chur* 1975
Astronomy and Experimental Philosophy (Plumian), M. J. Rees, M.A., Ph.D., *King's*. 1973
Astronomy and Geometry (Lowndean), J. F. Adams, M.A., Ph.D., F.R.S., *Trin* 1970
Astrophysics, D. Lynden-Bell, M.A., Ph.D., *Cla*. 1972
Biochemistry (Sir William Dunn), H. L. Kornberg, M.A., D.SC., Ph.D., F.R.S., *Chr*....... 1975
Biology (Quick), R. R. A. Coombs, SC.D., F.R.S., *Corp*........................... 1966
Biophysics (John Humphrey Plummer), Sir Alan Hodgkin, O.M., K.B.E., SC.D., F.R.S., *Trin*. 1970
Botany, P. W. Brian, SC.D., F.R.S., *Qu*..... 1968
Cellular Pathology, K. C. Dixon, M.D., *King's* 1973
Chemical Engineering, J. F. Davidson, SC.D., *Trin*.............................. 1975
Chemical Engineering (Shell), P. V. Danckwerts, G.C., M.B.E., M.A., F.R.S., *Pemb*..... 1959
Chemical Microbiology, E. F. Gale, SC.D., F.R.S., *Joh*........................... 1960
Chemistry (1968), A. D. Buckingham, Ph.D., *Pemb*.............................. 1969
Chemistry (1970), J. Lewis, M.A., F.R.S., *Sid*.. 1970
Chinese, D. C. Twitchett, M.A., Ph.D., *Cath* 1968
Civil Law (Regius), P. G. Stein, M.A., Ll.B., *Qu*................................. 1968
Classical Archæology (Laurence), R. M. Cook, M.A., *Cla*........................... 1962
Clinical Biochemistry, H. Lehmann, SC.D., *Chr*. 1967
Clinical Oncology (Career Research Campaign), N. M. Bleehen, M.A., B.SC., B.M., B.Ch 1975
Comparative Philology, W. S. Allen, M.A., Ph.D., *Trin*........................ 1955
Comparative Physiology, J. A. Ramsay, M.B.E., M.A., Ph.D., F.R.S., *Qu*............... 1969
Computer Technology, M. V. Wilkes, M.A., Ph.D., F.R.S., *Joh*.................... 1965
Criminology (Wolfson), N. D. Walker, M.A., Ph.D., D.Litt., *King's*................. 1973
Divinity (Ely), Rev. G. C. Stead, M.A., *King's* 1971
,,   (Lady Margaret's), Rev. C. F. D. Moule, M.A., F.B.A., *Cla*.......... 1951
,,   (Norris-Hulse), D. M. MacKinnon, M.A., *Corp*...................... 1960

    Elect.

Divinity (Regius), Rev. Canon G. W. H. Lampe, M.C., D.D., *Cai*................. 1971
Drama, R. H. Williams, Litt.D., *Jes*........ 1974
Ecclesiastical History (Dixie), Rev. E. G. Rupp, D.D., F.B.A., *Emm*.............. 1968
Economic History, D. C. Coleman, B.SC., Ph.D. 1971
Economics (1970), F. H. Hahn, M.A., *Chur*.... 1972
Economics (1965), R. R. Neild, M.A., *Trin*.... 1971
Economics. and Statistics, D. G. Champernowne, M.A., *Trin*..................... 1970
Education, P. H. Hirst, M.A., *Wolfs*.......... 1971
Egyptology (Herbert Thompson), Rev. J. M. Plumley, M.A., *Selw*................. 1957
Electrical Engineering, P. S. Brandon, M.A., *Jes*.................................. 1971
Engineering, A. H. W. Beck, M.A., *Corp.* (1966); M. F. Ashby, M.A., Ph.D., *Cl. H.* (1973); A. G. J. MacFarlane, Ph.D., D.SC., *Selw* (1974); A. N. Schofield, M.A., Ph.D., *Chur.* (1974); J. Heyman, M.A., Ph.D., *Pet.* (1971); (Rank) J. E. Ffowcs-Williams, M.A., *Emm*................................ 1972
English, Miss M. C. Bradbrook, Litt.D., *Girton* (1966); C. B. Ricks, M.A., B.Litt., *Chr*................................. 1975
English Constitutional History, G. R. Elton, Litt.D., F.B.A., *Cla*................... 1967
English Law (Rouse Ball), G. Ll. Williams, Q.C., Ll.D., F.B.A., *Jes*.............. 1968
English Literature (King Edward VII), J. F. Kermode, M.A., *King's*.............. 1974
Experimental Psychology, O. L. Zangwill, M.A., *King's*....................... 1952
Finance and Accounting (P. D. Leake), J. R. N. Stone, C.B.E., SC.D., F.B.A., *King's*..... 1955
Fine Art (Slade), W. Watson, M.A., F.B.A., *Cai.* (for 1975–76).
French, Miss A. A. B. Fairlie, Ph.D., *Girton* (1972); R. A. Leigh, Litt.D., *Trin.*; Mrs. O. M. H. L. de Mourgues, L.H.D., *Girton* 1975
French (Drapers), Ll. J. Austin, M.A., F.B.A., *Jes*................................. 1967
French Literature, J. B. M. Barrère, M.A., *Joh*. 1954
Genetics (Arthur Balfour), J. M. Thoday, SC.D., F.R.S., *Emm*...................... 1959
Geography, H. C. Darby, O.B.E., Litt.D., F.B.A., *King's* (1966); R. J. Chorley, SC.D., *Sid*... 1974
Geology (Woodwardian), H. B. Whittington, M.A., F.R.S., *Sid*.................... 1966
Geophysics, J. A. Jacobs, M.A., Ph.D., D.SC..... 1974
German (Schröder), L. W. Forster, M.A., *Selw*. 1961
Greek (Regius), G. S. Kirk, Litt.D., *Tr. H*... 1973
Hæmatological Medicine (Leukaemia Research Fund), F. G. J. Hayhoe, M.D., *Darw*...... 1968
Hebrew (Regius), Rev. J. A. Emerton, D.D., *Joh*................................. 1968
Histology, C. C. D. Shute, M.D., *Chr*........ 1969
History of International Relations, F. H. Hinsley, O.B.E., M.A., *Joh*............. 1969
History of the British Commonwealth (Smuts), E. T. Stokes, M.A., Ph.D., *Cath*........ 1970
History of Western Art, A. M. Jaffé, M.A., *King's*............................... 1973
Imperial and Naval History (Vere Harmsworth), J. A. Gallagher, M.A., *Trin*..... 1970
Industrial Relations (Montague Burton), H. A. F. Turner, M.A., *Chur*............... 1964
International Law, C. Parry, Ll.D., *Down*.... 1969
International Law (Whewell), R. Y. Jennings, Q.C., M.A., Ll.B., *Jes*............... 1955
Italian, U. Limentani, M.A., *Magd*.......... 1962
Land Economy, D. R. Denman, M.A., *Pemb*.. 1968
Latin (Kennedy), E. J. Kenney, M.A., F.B.A., *Pet*................................. 1974

Elect.

Latin-American Studies (Simón Bolívar), I. Bernal (for 1975–76).

Law, K. Lipstein, Ph.D., Cla 1973

Laws of England (Downing), G. H. Jones, Ll.D., Trin 1975

Legal Science (Arthur Goodhart), O. Kahn-Freund, M.A., Ll.M., Dr.Jur., Tr. H. (for 1975–6).

Mathematical Physics, J. C. Polkinghorne, M.A., Ph.D., F.R.S., Trin 1968

Mathematical Statistics, D. G. Kendall, M.A., F.R.S., Chur 1962

Mathematics, H. P. F. Swinnerton-Dyer, M.A., F.R.S., Cath 1971

Mathematics (Lucasian), Sir James Lighthill, B.A., F.R.S., F.B.A., Trin 1969

Mathematics (Rouse Ball), J. G. Thompson, M.A., Chur 1971

Mathematics for Operational Research (Churchill), P. Whittle, M.A., Chur 1967

Mechanics, W. Johnson, B.Sc., B.Sc.Tech., D.Sc., Fitzw 1975

Mechanics of Solids, R. Hill, Sc.D., Cai 1972

Medicine, I. H. Mills, M.D., Chur 1963

Medieval and Renaissance English, J. A. W. Bennett, M.A., Magd 1964

Medieval History, W. Ullmann, Litt.D., Trin. 1972

Membrane Physiology, I. M. Glynn, M.D., Trin 1975

Metallurgy (Goldsmiths'), R. W. K. Honey-combe, Ph.D., Tr. H 1966

Mineralogy and Petrology, W. A. Deer, Ph.D., F.R.S., Tr. H 1961

Modern English, J. Holloway, Litt.D., Qu 1972

Modern History, C. H. Wilson, M.A., F.B.A., Jes 1963

Modern History (Regius), Rev. W. O. Chad-wick, D.D., F.B.A., Selw 1968

Modern Languages, D. H. Green, M.A., Trin. 1966

Music, R. K. Orr, Mus.D., Joh 1965

Natural Philosophy (Jacksonian), A. H. Cook, Sc.D., Corp 1972

Numismatics, P. Grierson, Litt.D., F.B.A., Cai. 1971

Organic Chemistry (1702), R. A. Raphael, M.A., Chur 1972

Organic Chemistry (1969), A. R. Battersby, M.A., F.R.S., Cath 1969

Palaeoecology, R. G. West, Sc.D., Cla 1975

Pathology, P. Wildy, M.A., M.B., B.Chir., Cai. 1975

Pharmacology (Sheild), G. V. R. Born, D.Phil., F.R.S., Cai 1973

Philosophy, Miss G. E. M. Anscombe, M.A., New H 1970

Philosophy (Knightbridge), B. A. O. Williams, M.A., King's 1967

Philosophy of Science, Miss M. B. Hesse, M.A., Ph.D., F.B.A., Wolfs 1975

Physic (Regius), J. S. Mitchell, C.B.E., M.D., F.R.S., Joh 1957

Physical Chemistry, J. W. Linnett, Ph.D., F.R.S., Sid 1965

Physics, D. Shoenberg, B.A., Ph.D., Cai. (1973); D. Tabor, Sc.D., Cai. (1973); B. D. Josephson, M.A., Ph.D., Trin 1974

Physics (Cavendish), A. B. Pippard, F.R.S., Cl. H 1971

Physics (John Humphrey Plummer), S. F. Ed-wards, M.A., Ph.D., Cai 1972

Physiology, R. D. Keynes, Sc.D., Chur 1973

Physiology of Reproduction (Mary Marshall and Arthur Walton), T. R. R. Mann, C.B.E., Sc.D., F.R.S., Trinity Hall 1967

Plant Biochemistry, D. H. Northcote, Sc.D., Joh 1972

Elect.

Political Economy, W. B. Reddaway, M.A., Cla 1969

Political Science, W. B. Gallie, M.A., Pet 1967

Pure Mathematics, A. Baker, M.A., Ph.D., Trin. 1974

Pure Mathematics (Sadleirian), J. W. S. Cassels, Ph.D., F.R.S., Trin 1967

Radio Astronomy, Sir Martin Ryle, M.A., F.R.S., Trin 1959

Radio Astronomy (1971), A. Hewish, M.A., Ph.D., F.R.S., Chur 1971

Sanskrit, J. Brough, M.A., F.B.A., Joh 1967

Slavonic Studies, L. R. Lewitter, M.A., Ph.D., Christ's 1968

Social Anthropology, E. R. Leach, M.A., King's 1972

Social Anthropology (William Wyse), J. R. Goody, Sc.D., Joh 1973

Sociology, J. A. Barnes, D.S.C., M.A., Chur . . . 1969

Spanish, C. C. Smith, M.A., Ph.D., Cath 1975

Surgery, R. Y. Calne, M.A., F.R.S., F.R.C.S., Tr. H 1965

Theoretical Astronomy, R. A. Lyttelton, M.A., Ph.D., F.R.S., Joh 1969

Veterinary Clinical Studies, A. T. Phillipson, M.A., Ph.D., Chur 1963

Zoology, T. Weis-Fogh, M.A., Christ's 1966

THE UNIVERSITY OF DURHAM

(Founded 1832; re-organized 1908, 1937 and 1963)
Old Shire Hall, Durham

Undergraduates (1974–75), 3,962

Chancellor, Rt. Hon. Malcolm J. MacDonald, P.C., O.M., M.A.

Vice-Chancellor and Warden, Sir Derman Christo-pherson, O.B.E., D.Phil., F.R.S.

Pro-Vice-Chancellor, Prof. W. K. R. Musgrave, Ph.D., D.Sc.

Second Pro-Vice-Chancellor, Prof. J. L. Brooks, M.A.

Registrar and Secretary, I. E. Graham, M.A.

Professor of Education, G. R. Batho, M.A.

Director of Institute of Education, J. J. Grant, C.B.E., M.A., Ed.B.

Colleges

University, D. W. MacDowell, M.A., D.Phil., F.S.A., Master.

Hatfield, T. Whitworth, M.A., D.Phil., Master.

Grey, S. Holgate, M.A., Ph.D., Master.

Van Mildert, P. W. Kent, M.A., Ph.D., D.Phil., D.Sc. D.Litt., Master.

Collingwood, P. C. Bayley, M.A., Master.

St. Chad's, Rev. J. C. Fenton, M.A., B.D., Principal.

St. John's, Rev. J. C. P. Cockerton, M.A., Principal.

St. Mary's, Miss F. I. Calvert, M.A., Principal.

St. Aidan's, Miss I. Hindmarsh, M.A., Principal.

Trevelyan, Joan Constance Bernard, M.A., B.D., Principal.

St. Hild and St. Bede, J. V. Armitage, B.Sc., Ph.D., Principal.

*Neville's Cross, R. G. Emmett, B.Sc. (Econ.), M.A., Ph.D., Principal.

St. Cuthbert's Society, Prof. J. L. Brooks, M.A., Principal.

The Graduate Society, Prof. W. B. Fisher, B.A., Doc. D'Univ., Principal.

Ushaw, Rt. Rev. Mgr. P. Loftus, B.C.L., President.
* Hall of Residence.

THE UNIVERSITY OF LONDON, 1836

Senate House, W.C.1

Internal Students (1973–74), 40,198, External Students, 32,174.

Visitor, H.M. the Queen in Council.

Chancellor, H.M. Queen Elizabeth the Queen Mother.

Vice-Chancellor, Prof. Sir Cyril Philips, M.A., Ph.D.

Chairman of the Court, Rt. Hon. Sir Leslie Scarman, O.B.E., M.A.

Chairman of Convocation, Prof. J. P. Quilliam, M.Sc., D.Sc., F.R.C.P.

Principal, F. M. G. Willson, B.A. (Admin.), M.A., D.Phil. (1975).

THE COURT

Ex Officio, The Chancellor, The Vice-Chancellor, The Chairman of Convocation.

Appointed by the Senate, Prof. F. R. Crane, LL.B.; F. Hartley, C.B.E., Ph.D.; Sir Harry Melville, K.C.B., F.R.S.; Prof. N. F. Morris, M.D.; Prof. Sir Cyril Philips, M.A., Ph.D.; B. Thwaites, M.A., Ph.D., Sir Bernard Waley-Cohen, Bt., M.A.; *By Her Majesty in Council*, Sir Michael Clapham, M.B.E., M.A.; P. Parker, M.V.O., M.A.; The Lord Shawcross, G.B.E., P.C., Q.C.; *By the I.L.E.A.*, Sir Reginald Goodwin, C.B.E.; Sir Desmond Plummer, T.D.; *Home Counties and Outer London Boroughs Member*, T. I. Smith, O.B.E., M.A.; *Co-opted Member*, Rt. Hon. A. G. F. Rippon, Q.C., M.A., M.P.

THE SENATE

Ex-Officio, The Chancellor, The Vice-Chancellor, The Chairman of Convocation, The Principal.

Heads of the following Schools—University College, King's College, Bedford College, Birkbeck College, Imperial College of Science and Technology, London School of Economics and Political Science, Queen Mary College, Royal Holloway College, School of Oriental and African Studies, Westfield College. *Appointed by Convocation*— *(Arts)* H. A. L. Cockerell, O.B.E.; A. H. Chaplin; Miss M. C. Grobel; D. D. A. Leslie; H. B. A. Wise; *(Economics)*, J. B. Bonham; *(Engineering)* J. Gratwick; Dr. N. A. White; *(Laws)*, Mrs. M. C. Hoare; *(Medicine)*; Dr. A. J. M. Reese; N. A. Thorne; *(Music)*, C. P. J. Steinitz; *(Science)*, Mrs. M. F. Church; J. S. Cook; M. V. Hoare; W. C. Peck; J. H. Pryor; *(Theology)*, Rev. Dr. G. Huelin. *Appointed by the Faculties*—*(Arts)*, Prof. J. P. Collas; Prof. A. G. Dickens; Prof. R. Quirk; Prof. F. M. L. Thompson; *(Economics)*, Prof. H. C. Edey; *(Engineering)*, Prof. H. Billett; Prof. A. D. Young, O.B.E.; *(Laws)*, Prof. F. R. Crane; *(Medicine)*, Prof. J. N. Hunt; Prof. M. D. Milne; Prof. N. F. Morris; Prof. J. G. Murray; *(Music)*, Prof. I. W. A. Spink; *(Science)*, Prof. R. Howie; Prof. W. C. Price; Prof. A. J. B. Robertson; Prof. W. F. Widdas; *(Theology)*, Rev. Prof. P. R. Ackroyd. *Appointed by General Medical Schools*, Dr. J. C. Houston; Dr. Frances V. Gardner. *By King's College Theological Dept.*, Rev. Canon S. H. Evans. *By University College*, Sir Bernard Waley-Cohen, Bt. *Director of British Post-Graduate Medical Federation*, Prof. G. Smart, *Co-opted Members*, Dr. H. S. Darling, C.B.E.; Dr. K. G. Denbigh; Dr. F. Hartley; Prof. Sir Brian Windeyer.

Principal Officers

Clerk of the Court, J. R. Stewart, C.B.E., M.A.

Clerk of the Senate, H. F. Patterson, M.A. (*acting*)

Registrar, P. F. Vowles, M.A.

Secretary to University Entrance and School Examinations Council, A. R. Stephenson, M.A.

Secretary for External Students, R. J. L. Feil, B.Sc. (Econ.).

Director of Central Library Services, K. Garside, M.A.

Director, Careers Advisory Service, E. H. K. Dibden, B.Sc., M.A.

Secretary to the Athlone Press, A. M. Wood, M.Sc., M.A.

University Institutes

Courtland Institute of Art, 20 Portman Square, W.1., Prof. P. E. Lasko, B.A., F.S.A., *Dir.*

Institute of Advanced Legal Studies, 25 Russell Square, W.C.1, Prof. Sir Norman Anderson, O.B.E., Q.C., M.A., F.B.A., *Dir.*

Institute of Archæology, 31–34 Gordon Square, W.C.1, Prof. J. D. Evans, M.A., Ph.D., F.S.A., *Dir.*

Institute of Classical Studies, 31–34 Gordon Square, W.C.1, Prof. E. W. Handley, M.A., F.B.A., *Dir.*

Institute of Commonwealth Studies, 27 Russell Square, W.C.1, Prof. W. H. Morris-Jones, B.Sc.(Econ.), *Dir.*

Institute of Education, Maler Street, W.C.1, W. Taylor, B.Sc. (Econ.), Ph.D., M.A., *Dir.*

Institute of Germanic Studies, 29 Russell Square, W.C.1, Prof. C. V. Bock, M.A., Dr.Phil., *Hon. Dir.*

Institute of Historical Research, Senate House, W.C.1 Prof. A. G. Dickens, M.A., D.Litt., F.B.A., F.S.A., *Dir.*

Institute of Latin American Studies, 31 Tavistock Square, W.C.1, Prof. J. Lynch, M.A., Ph.D., *Dir.*

British Institute in Paris, 6 Rue de la Sorbonne, Paris Ve., Prof. F. H. Scarfe, O.B.E., M.A., M.Litt., *Dir.*

School of Slavonic and E. European Studies, University of London, Senate House, W.C.1, G. H. Bolsover, C.B.E., M.A., Ph.D., *Dir.*

Institute of United States Studies, 31 Tavistock Square, W.C.1, Prof. E. Wright, M.A., *Dir.*

Warburg Institute, Woburn Square, W.C.1, Prof. Sir Ernst Gombrich, C.B.E., Ph.D., F.B.A., F.S.A., *Dir.*

Schools of the University*

Bedford College, Inner Circle, Regent's Park, N.W.1, J. N. Black, M.A., D.Phil., D.Sc., F.R.S.E., *Principal* (1971).

Birkbeck College, Malet Street, W.C.1, R. C. Tress, C.B.E., B.Sc.(Econ.), D.Sc., *Master* (1968).

Chelsea College, Manresa Road, S.W.3, D. J. E. Ingram M.A., D.Phil., D.Sc., *Principal* (1973).

Imperial College of Science and Technology, Prince Consort Road, S.W.7, Sir Brian Flowers, M.A., M.Sc., D.Sc., F.R.S., *Rector* (1973).

King's College, Strand, W.C.2, Sir Richard Way, K.C.B., C.B.E., *Principal* (1975).

London School of Economics and Political Science, Houghton Street, Aldwych, W.C.2, Prof. R. Dahrendorf, Ph.D., Dr.Phil., *Director* (1974).

Queen Elizabeth College, Campden Hill Road, W.8, K. G. Denbigh, D.Sc., F.R.S., *Principal* (1966).

Queen Mary College, Mile End Road, E.1, Sir Harry Melville, K.C.B., Ph.D., D.Sc., F.R.S., *Principal* (1967).

Royal Holloway College, Egham Hill, Egham, Surrey, L. H. Butler, M.A., D.Phil., *Principal* (1973).

School of Oriental and African Studies, University of London, W.C.1., Prof. Sir Cyril Philips, M.A., Ph.D., Dir. (1958).

School of Pharmacy, Brunswick Square, W.C.1, F. Hartley, C.B.E., B.Sc., Ph.D., *Dean* (1962).

University College, Gower Street, W.C.1, The Lord Annan, O.B.E., M.A., *Provost* (1966).

Westfield College, Kidderpore Avenue, Hampstead, N.W.3, B. Thwaites, M.A., Ph.D., *Principal* (1966).

Wye College, Wye nr. Ashford, Kent, H. S. Darling, C.B.E., B.Sc., M.Agric., Ph.D., D.Sc. (1968).

King's College Theological Department, Rev. Canon S. H. Evans, M.A., B.D., *Dean* (1956).

New College, 527 Finchley Road, N.W.3, Rev. C. S. Duthie, M.A., D.D., *Principal* (1964).

Heythrop College, 11 Cavendish Square, W.1, Rev. W. F. Maher, S.J., S.T.L., *Principal* (1971).

Lister Institute of Preventive Medicine, Chelsea Bridge Road, S.W.1, Prof. W. J. T. Morgan, C.B.E., Ph.D., D.Sc., F.R.S., *Director* (1973).

* For Medical Schools, Training Colleges and Veterinary Colleges, *see under* Professional Education.

THE UNIVERSITY OF MANCHESTER
Oxford Road, Manchester
(Founded 1851; re-organized 1880 and 1903).
Full-time Students (1974–75), *Men,* 9,165; *Women* 4,087.
Chancellor, The Duke of Devonshire, P.C., M.C. (1965).
Vice-Chancellor, Prof. Sir Arthur Armitage, M.A. (1970).
Registrar, V. Knowles, M.A. (1951).

MANCHESTER INSTITUTE OF SCIENCE
AND TECHNOLOGY (1824)
Sackville Street, Manchester
Full-time Students (1974–75), (*Men*) 2,981; (*Women*) 434.
Principal, The Lord Bowden, M.A., Ph.D. (1964).
Secretary and Registrar, D. H. McWilliam, B.A.

THE UNIVERSITY OF NEWCASTLE
(Founded 1852; re-organized 1908, 1937 and 1963)
Newcastle upon Tyne.
Students (1974–75), 6,316.
Chancellor, The Duke of Northumberland, K.G., T.D., F.R.S. (1963).
Vice-Chancellor, H. Miller, M.D., F.R.C.P.
Pro-Vice-Chancellors, Prof. J. R. O'Callaghan, B.E., M.Sc.; Prof. E. S. Page, M.A., Ph.D., B.Sc.
Registrar, E. M. Bettenson, M.A.

THE UNIVERSITY OF BIRMINGHAM
Birmingham 15
Full-time Students (1974–75), 7,633.
Chancellor, Sir Peter Scott, C.B.E., D.S.C., M.A.
Vice-Chancellor and Principal, R. B. Hunter, M.B.E., F.R.C.P. (1968).
Secretary, H. Harris, B.Sc.(Econ.), Ll.B.
Registrar, W. R. G. Lewis, B.A.

THE UNIVERSITY OF LIVERPOOL, 1903
Liverpool
Students (1975), 7,826.
Chancellor, Sir Kenneth Wheare, C.M.G., F.B.A.
Vice-Chancellor, T. C. Thomas, M.A. (1970).
Treasurer, B. L. Rathbone.
Registrar, H. H. Burchnall, M.A. (1962).

THE UNIVERSITY OF LEEDS, 1904
Full-time Students (1975), 9,536.
Chancellor, H.R.H. the Duchess of Kent (1966).
Vice-Chancellor, The Lord Boyle of Handsworth, P.C., M.A., (1970).
Registrar, J. MacGregor, B.A., M.Ed., Ph.D. (1971).
Bursar, E. Williamson, T.D., B.Sc.(Econ.) (1965).

THE UNIVERSITY OF SHEFFIELD, 1905
Sheffield
Full-time Students (1974–75)—Men, 4,428; Women, 2,219.
Chancellor, The Lord Butler of Saffron Walden, K.G., P.C., C.H., M.A. (1959).
Vice-Chancellor, Prof. G. D. Sims, M.Sc., Ph.D. (1974).
Registrar and Secretary, A. M. Currie, B.A., B.Litt. (1965).

THE UNIVERSITY OF BRISTOL, 1909
Full-time Students (1974)—Men, 3,918; Women 2,411.
Chancellor, Prof. Dorothy Hodgkin, O.M., M.A., Ph.D., D.Sc., Sc.D., F.R.C.P., F.R.S. (1971).
Vice-Chancellor, A. W. Merrison, B.Sc., Ph.D., F.R.S. (1967).
Director of Administration, D. G. H. Cannon, M.A. (1973).
Registrar, E. C. Wright, M.A. (1973).

THE UNIVERSITY OF READING, 1926
Whiteknights, Reading
Number of Students (1974), 5,137.

Chancellor, The Lord Sherfield, G.C.B., G.C.M.G. (1970).
Vice-Chancellor, H. R. Pitt, Ph.D., F.R.S. (1964).
Registrar, J. F. Johnson, B.A. (1955).

THE UNIVERSITY OF NOTTINGHAM, 1948
University Park, Nottingham
Chancellor, Sir Francis Hill, C.B.E., M.A., Ll.M. (1972).
Vice-Chancellor (vacant).
Registrar, A. Plumb, M.A. (1958).

THE UNIVERSITY OF SOUTHAMPTON, 1952
Students (1974–75), *Men,* 3,363; *Women,* 1,688.
Chancellor, Sir Eric Roll, K.C.M.G., C.B., Ph.D. (1974).
Vice-Chancellor, L. C. B. Gower, Ll.M., F.B.A. (1971).
Secretary and Registrar, R. M. Urquhart, O.B.E., M.A. (1966).
Academic Registrar, D. A. Schofield, M.A. (1969).

THE UNIVERSITY OF HULL, 1954
Full-time Students (1974–75)—*Men,* 2,251; *Women,* 1,717.
Chancellor, The Lord Cohen of Birkenhead, C.H., M.D., F.R.C.P. (1970).
Vice-Chancellor, Prof. S. R. Dennison, C.B.E., M.A. (1972).
Registrar, F. T. Mattison, M.A., Ll.B.

THE UNIVERSITY OF EXETER, 1955
Full-time Students (1974–75), 3,750.
Chancellor, The Viscount Amory, K.G., P.C., G.C.M.G., T.D., M.A.
Vice-Chancellor, H. Kay, M.A., Ph.D.
Academic Registrar and Secretary, K. T. Nash, M.A.

THE UNIVERSITY OF LEICESTER, 1957
Full-time Students (1974–75), 3,775.
Chancellor, Prof. Sir Alan Hodgkin, K.B.E., O.M., F.R.S. (1971).
Vice-Chancellor, Sir Fraser Noble, M.B.E., M.A. (1962).
Registrar, M. A. Baatz, M.A. (1973).

THE UNIVERSITY OF SUSSEX, 1961
Brighton
Full-time Students (1974–75), 3,979.
Chancellor, The Lord Shawcross, P.C., Q.C.
Vice-Chancellor, Prof. A. Briggs, B.Sc.(Econ.), M.A.
Registrar and Secretary, G. Lockwood, B.Sc.(Econ.).

THE UNIVERSITY OF KEELE, 1962
Keele, Staffordshire.
Undergraduates (1974–75), 2,316.
Chancellor, H.R.H. the Princess Margaret, Countess of Snowdon, C.I., G.C.V.O. (1962).
Vice-Chancellor, Prof. W. A. C. Stewart, M.A., Ph.D.
Registrar, J. F. N. Hodgkinson, M.A.

THE UNIVERSITY OF EAST ANGLIA, 1963
Earlham Hall, Norwich
Students (1974–75), 3,400.
Chancellor, The Lord Franks, P.C., G.C.M.G., K.C.B., C.B.E., M.A., F.B.A. (1965).
Vice-Chancellor, F. Thistlethwaite, M.A.
Registrar and Secretary, G. A. Chadwick, B.Sc.

THE UNIVERSITY OF YORK, 1963
Heslington, York
Undergraduates (1974), 2,300.
Chancellor, The Lord Clark, C.H., K.C.B., F.B.A. (1969).
Pro-Chancellors, R. S. Butterfield, O.B.E., M.C.; A. S. Rymer, O.B.E.
Vice-Chancellor, G. M. Carstairs, M.A., M.D., D.P.M., F.R.C.P. Ed.
Registrar, J. P. West-Taylor, M.A.

THE UNIVERSITY OF LANCASTER, 1964
Bailrigg, Lancaster
Undergraduates (1975–76), 3,250.
Chancellor, H.R.H. the Princess Alexandra, G.C.V.O.
Vice-Chancellor, C. F. Carter, M.A., D.Econ.Sc., F.B.A.
Secretary, A. S. Jeffreys, B.A., B.Litt.

THE UNIVERSITY OF ESSEX, 1964
Wivenhoe Park, Colchester
Students (1975–76), 2,200.
Chancellor, The Lord Butler of Saffron Walden, K.G., P.C., C.H., M.A.
Pro-Chancellors, Col. Sir John Ruggles-Brise, Bt., C.B., O.B.E., T.D.; J. F. Crittall, M.A.
Vice-Chancellor, A. E. Sloman, M.A., D.Phil.
Registrar, G. E. Chandler, B.A.

THE UNIVERSITY OF WARWICK, 1965
Coventry, Warwickshire
Students (1974–75), 3,375.
Chancellor, The Viscount Radcliffe, P.C., G.B.E.
Pro-Chancellor, Sir Stanley Harley, B.Sc.,
Vice-Chancellor, J. B. Butterworth, M.A.,
Secretary and Registrar, A. Rowe-Evans, B.A.

UNIVERSITY OF KENT AT CANTERBURY, 1965
Canterbury, Kent
Students (1975–76), 2,800.
Chancellor, Rt. Hon. J. Grimond, T.D., M.P. (1970).
Vice-Chancellor, G. Templeman, M.A., Ph.D., F.S.A.
Registrar, E. Fox, M.A.

LOUGHBOROUGH UNIVERSITY OF TECHNOLOGY, 1966
Students (1974–75), 3.735.
Chancellor, The Lord Pilkington.
Vice-Chancellor, C. C. Butler, PhD., F.R.S.
Registrar, F. L. Roberts, B.A.

THE UNIVERSITY OF ASTON IN BIRMINGHAM, 1966
Gosta Green, Birmingham 4
Full-time Students (1974–75), 4,054.
Chancellor, The Lord Nelson of Stafford, M.A.
Vice-Chancellor, J. A. Pope, D.Sc., Ph.D.
Secretary, P. R. Tebbit, B.A.
Registrar, K. N. Houghton, M.A.

THE CITY UNIVERSITY 1966
St. John Street, E.C.1
Students (1974–75), 2,400.
Chancellor, The Lord Mayor of London.
Vice-Chancellor, E. W. Parkes, Sc.D.
Registrar, L. A. Fairbairn, B.Sc., Ph.D.

BRUNEL UNIVERSITY, 1966
Uxbridge, Middlesex
Students (1974–75), 3,700.
Chancellor, The Earl of Halsbury, F.R.S.
Vice-Chancellor, S. L. Bragg.
Academic Registrar, E. R. Chandler.

UNIVERSITY OF BATH, 1966
Claverton Down, Bath, Som.
Undergraduates (1974–75), 2,824.
Chancellor, The Lord Hinton of Bankside, K.B.E., M.A., F.R.S.
Vice-Chancellor, L. Rotherham, C.B.E., D.SC., F.R.S.
Registrar, G. S. Horner, M.A.

UNIVERSITY OF BRADFORD, 1966
Undergraduates (1974–75), *Men*, 2,253; *Women*, 915.
Chancellor, Rt. Hon. J. H. Wilson, O.B.E., M.P., M.A., F.R.S.
Vice-Chancellor and Principal, E. G. Edwards, Ph.D., B.Sc.
Registrar, I. M. Sanderson, M.B.E., B.Sc.

UNIVERSITY OF SURREY, 1966
Guildford, Surrey
Undergraduates (1974–75), 2,247.
Chancellor, The Lord Robens of Woldingham, P.C.
Vice-Chancellor, A. Kelly, Sc.D., F.R.S.
Academic Registrar, G. Haigh, Ph.D.

UNIVERSITY OF SALFORD, 1967
Undergraduates (1974–75), 3,261.
Chancellor, H.R.H. the Prince Philip, Duke of Edinburgh, K.G., P.C., K.T.
Vice-Chancellor, J. H. Horlock, M.A., Ph.D.
Registrar, S. R. Bosworth, B.A.

ROYAL COLLEGE OF ART, 1837
Kensington Gore, S.W.7
Under Royal Charter (1967) the Royal College of Art grants the degrees of Doctor, Doctor of Philosophy, Master of Arts and Master of Design (RCA).
Students (1975), 568 (all postgraduate).
Provost, Sir Colin Anderson, K.B.E.
Rector and Vice-Provost, The Viscount Esher, C.B.E., M.A.
Registrar, B. Cooper, B.A.

CRANFIELD INSTITUTE OF TECHNOLOGY 1969
Cranfield, Bedford
Under Royal Charter (1969) the Cranfield Institute of Technology grants the degrees of Doctor and Master in applied science, engineering, technology and management.
Students (1974), 575 (all postgraduate); 2,500 short course.
Chancellor, The Lord Kings Norton, Ph.D., D.I.C., D.Sc.
Vice-Chancellor, A. H. Chilver, D.Sc., Ph.D., M.A.
Secretary, Air Vice-Marshal P. C. Cleaver, C.B., C.B.E., M.Sc.

THE OPEN UNIVERSITY (1969)
Walton Hall, Milton Keynes, Bucks.
Students (1975), 50,000.
Tuition by correspondence linked with special radio and television programmes, summer schools and a locally-based tutorial and counselling service. Under Royal Charter the University awards degrees of B.A., B.Phil., M.Phil., Ph.D., D.Sc. and D.Litt. There are six faculties—arts, educational studies, mathematics, science, social sciences and technology.
Chancellor, The Lord Gardiner, P.C.
Vice-Chancellor, Sir Walter Perry, O.B.E., M.D., D.Sc.
Secretary, A. Christodoulou, M.A.
Deputy Secretary and Registrar, D. J. Clinch, B.A.

UNIVERSITY COLLEGE AT BUCKINGHAM
Buckingham
First undergraduate admissions, Feb. 1976.
Chairman of Council, Sir Sydney Caine, K.C.M.G.
Principal, Prof. M. Beloff, M.A., F.B.A.
Registrar and Secretary, L. Wilson, M.A.

THE UNIVERSITY OF WALES, 1893
University Registry, Cardiff
Chancellor, H.R.H. the Prince Philip, Duke of Edinburgh, K.G., P.C., K.T., (1948).
Pro-Chancellor, The Lord Edmund-Davies, P.C. (1974).
Vice-Chancellor, A. F. Trotman-Dickenson, D.Sc. (1975).
Registrar, J. Gareth Thomas, M.A. (1962).
COLLEGES
(with number of undergraduates, 1974–75)
Aberystwyth (2,895).—*Princ.*, Sir Goronwy Daniel, K.C.V.O., C.B., D.Phil. (1969).
Bangor, N. Wales (2,673).—*Princ.*, Sir Charles Evans, M.A., D.Sc., F.R.C.S. (1958).

Cardiff, Institute of Science and Technology (2,386).—
  Princ., A. F. Trotman-Dickenson, M.A., Ph.D.,
  D.SC. (1968).
Cardiff, National School of Medicine (544).—*Provost*,
  J. P. D. Mounsey, M.A., M.D., F.R.C.P. (1969).
Cardiff (University College) (4,085).—*Princ.* C. W. L.
  Bevan, C.B.E., D.SC. (1966).
Lampeter (St. David's College) (471).—*Princ.* Rev.
  Canon J. R. Lloyd Thomas, M.A. (1953).
Swansea (3,187).—*Princ.* R. W. Steel, M.A. (1974).

SCOTLAND

UNIVERSITY OF ST. ANDREWS, 1411
Students (1974–75), *Men*, 1,807; *Women*, 1,477.
Chancellor, Brigadier The Lord Ballantrae, G.C.M.G.,
  G.C.V.O., D.S.O., O.B.E. (1975).
Principal and Vice-Chancellor, J. S. Watson, M.A.,
  D.Litt., F.R.S.E. (1966).
Registrar and Secretary, D. M. Devine, M.A., Ll.B.
  (1972).

UNIVERSITY OF GLASGOW, 1451
Gilmorehill, Glasgow
Students (1974–75), *Men*, 6,106; *Women*, 3,901.
Chancellor, Sir Alec Cairncross, K.C.M.G., F.B.A.
Vice-Chancellor, Sir Charles Wilson, M.A. (1961).
Secretary to the University Court and Registrar,
  J. McCargon, M.A.

UNIVERSITY OF ABERDEEN, 1495
Undergraduates (1975), 4,883.
Chancellor, The Lord Polwarth, T.D.
Principal, E. M. Wright, M.A., D.Phil., D.SC., F.R.S.E.
  (1962).
Vice-Principal, Prof. R. C. Cross, C.B.E., M.A.
Secretary, T. B. Skinner, M.A.

UNIVERSITY OF EDINBURGH, 1583
Old College, South Bridge, Edinburgh 8
Students (1974–75), 11,204.
Chancellor, H.R.H. the Prince Philip, Duke of
  Edinburgh, K.G., P.C., K.T. (1952).
Vice-Chancellor and Principal, Prof. Sir Hugh
  Robson, M.B., Ch.B., F.R.C.P., F.R.C.P.E.
Secretary, C. H. Stewart, O.B.E., M.A., Ll.B. (1948).

UNIVERSITY OF STRATHCLYDE, 1964
George Street, Glasgow
Full-time Students (1974–75), 5,873.
Chancellor, The Lord Todd, D.SC., D.Phil., F.R.S.
Principal, Sir Samuel Curran, M.A., Ph.D., D.SC.,
  F.R.S. (1964).
Registrar, D. W. J. Morrell, M.A., Ll.B. (1973).

HERIOT-WATT UNIVERSITY, 1966
Edinburgh
Students (1974–75), 2,607.
Chancellor, The Lord Home of the Hirsel, K.T., P.C.
  (1966).
Principal and Vice-Chancellor, G. M. Burnett, Ph.D.,
  D.SC., F.R.S.E. (1974).
Secretary, D. I. Cameron, B.L. (1966).

UNIVERSITY OF DUNDEE, 1967
Full-time Students (1974–75), 2,711.
Chancellor, H.M. Queen Elizabeth the Queen
  Mother.
Principal and Vice-Chancellor, J. Drever, M.A., F.R.S.E.
Secretary, R. Seaton, M.A., Ll.B.

UNIVERSITY OF STIRLING, 1967
Undergraduates (1974–75), 1,919.
Chancellor, The Lord Robbins, C.H., C.B., M.A.,
  B.SC. (Econ.), F.B.A. (1967).
Vice-Chancellor, W. A. Cramond, O.B.E., M.D.,
  (1975).
Secretary, R. G. Bomont, B.SC. (Econ.) (1973).

NORTHERN IRELAND

THE QUEEN'S UNIVERSITY OF BELFAST, 1908
Full-time Students (1974–75), 5,471.
Chancellor, The Lord Ashby, M.A., D.SC., F.R.S
  (1970).
President and Vice-Chancellor, Sir Arthur Vick, O.B.E.,
  B.SC., Ph.D., D.SC. (1966).
Secretary, G. R. Cowie, M.A., Ll.B. (1948).
Secretary to the Academic Council, D. G. Neill, M.A.
  (1966).

NEW UNIVERSITY OF ULSTER, 1965
Coleraine, Co. Londonderry
(First students admitted, 1968)
Undergraduates (1974–75), 1,467.
Chancellor, The Duke of Abercorn.
Vice-Chancellor, N. A. Burges, M.SC., Ph.D. (1966).
Registrar and Secretary, W. T. Ewing, M.A., Ll.B.
  (1966).

THE ASSOCIATION OF COMMONWEALTH UNIVERSITIES
36 Gordon Square, W.C.1
The Association holds quinquennial Congresses
of the Universities of the Commonwealth and
other meetings in the intervening years, publishes
the *Commonwealth Universities Yearbook*, etc., acts
as a general information centre on universities in
U.K. and other Commonwealth countries and provides an advisory service for the filling of university
teaching staff appointments overseas. It also supplies the secretariat for the Commonwealth
Scholarship Commission in the United Kingdom,
for the Marshall Aid Commemoration Commission
and for the Kennedy Memorial Trust.
Secretary-General, Sir Hugh Springer, K.C.M.G.,
  C.B.E., M.A.

REPUBLIC OF IRELAND

UNIVERSITY OF DUBLIN TRINITY COLLEGE, 1591
Undergraduates (1974–75), 4,772 (including post-
  graduates).
Chancellor, F. H. Boland (1964).
Provost, F. S. L. Lyons, M.A., Ph.D. (1974).
Registrar, A. Clarke, M.A., Ph.D. (1974).

NATIONAL UNIVERSITY OF IRELAND, DUBLIN, 1908
49 Merrion Square, Dublin 2
Chancellor, Eamon de Valéra (1921).
Vice-Chancellor, T. Murphy, M.D.
Registrar, J. Bourke, Ph.D., M.Comm.

CONSTITUENT COLLEGES
Univ. Coll., Dublin, T. Murphy, M.D. (1972).
Univ. Coll., Cork, M. D. McCarthy, M.A., Ph.D.,
  D.SC., *President* (1967).
Univ. Coll., Galway, M. O. Tnúthail, D.SC., *President*
  (1960).

RECOGNIZED COLLEGE
St. Patrick's Coll. Maynooth, Right Rev. Mgr.
  Tomás O' Fiaich, M.A., *President* (1974).

COUNCIL FOR NATIONAL ACADEMIC AWARDS
344–354 Gray's Inn Road, W.C.1
Established in 1964 with powers to award degrees
and other academic distinctions, comparable in
standard with awards granted and conferred by
universities to students in polytechnics and other
institutions of higher education in the United
Kingdom which do not have the power to award
their own degrees. The Council awards degrees
and honours degrees of B.A., B.Ed. and B.SC. and has

higher and research degrees and doctorates. On Sept. 1, 1974, the Council assumed responsibility for the work formerly undertaken by the National Council for Diplomas in Art and Design.
President, H.R.H. the Duke of Edinburgh, K.G., K.T.
Chairman, Sir Michael Clapham, K.B.E., M.A.
Chief Officer, E. Kerr, B.SC., Ph.D.

POLYTECHNICS

CITY OF BIRMINGHAM POLYTECHNIC, Perry Barr, Birmingham.—*Dir.*, S. W. Smethurst.
BRIGHTON POLYTECHNIC, Moulsecoomb, Brighton. —*Dir.*, G. R. Hall.
BRISTOL POLYTECHNIC, Coldharbour Lane, Bristol. —*Dir.*, Dr. W. Birch.
GLAMORGAN POLYTECHNIC, Llantwit Road, Treforest, Pontypridd, Glamorgan.—*Princ.*, D. W. F. James, Ph.D.
HATFIELD POLYTECHNIC, Hatfield, Herts.—*Dir.*, Sir Norman Lindop.
HUDDERSFIELD POLYTECHNIC, Queensgate, Huddersfield.—*Rector*, K. J. Durrands.
KINGSTON POLYTECHNIC, Penrhyn Road, Kingston upon Thames.—*Dir.*, L. E. Lawley, Ph.D.
LANCHESTER POLYTECHNIC, Priory Street, Coventry. —*Dir.*, K. Legg, Ph.D.
LEEDS POLYTECHNIC, Calverley Street, Leeds.— *Dir.*, P. J. Nuttgens, Ph.D.
LEICESTER POLYTECHNIC, P.O. Box 143, Leicester. —*Dir.*, D. Bethel.
LIVERPOOL POLYTECHNIC, Richmond House, 1 Rumford Place, Liverpool.—*Rector*, G. Bulmer.
LONDON:
 CITY OF LONDON POLYTECHNIC, 117–119 Houndsditch, E.C.3.—*Prov.*, A. Suddaby, Ph.D.
 NORTH-EAST LONDON POLYTECHNIC, Romford Road, E.15.—*Dir.*, G. S. Brosan, T.D., Ph.D.
 POLYTECHNIC OF CENTRAL LONDON, 309 Regent Street, W.1.—*Dir.*, C. Adamson, D.SC.
 POLYTECHNIC OF NORTH LONDON, Holloway Road, N.7.—*Dir.*, T. G. Miller, T.D.
 POLYTECHNIC OF THE SOUTH BANK, Borough Road, S.E.1.—*Dir.*, V. Pereira Mendoza.
 THAMES POLYTECHNIC, Wellington Street, S.E.18, —*Dir.*, D. E. R. Godfrey, Ph.D.
MANCHESTER POLYTECHNIC, Lower Ormond Street, All Saints, Manchester.—*Dir.*, Sir Alex Smith, Ph.D.
NEWCASTLE UPON TYNE POLYTECHNIC, Ellison Building Ellison Place, Newcastle upon Tyne.— *Dir.*, G. S. Bosworth, C.B.E.
NORTH STAFFORDSHIRE POLYTECHNIC, Beaconside, Stafford.—*Dir.*, J. F. Dickenson, Ph.D.
OXFORD POLYTECHNIC, Gipsy Lane, Headington, Oxford.—*Dir.*, B. B. Lloyd, D.SC.
PLYMOUTH POLYTECHNIC, Drake Circus, Plymouth.—*Dir.*, R. F. M. Robbins, Ph.D.
PORTSMOUTH POLYTECHNIC, Ravelin House, Museum Road, Portsmouth.—*Pres.*, W. Davey.
SHEFFIELD POLYTECHNIC, Pond Street, Sheffield.— *Principal*, Rev. G. Tolley, Ph.D.
SUNDERLAND POLYTECHNIC, Chester Road, Sunderland.—*Rector*, M. Hutton, Ph.D.
TEESIDE POLYTECHNIC, Borough Road, Middlesbrough, Cleveland.—*Dir.*, J. Houghton, Ph.D.
TRENT POLYTECHNIC, Burton Street, Nottingham. —*Dir.*, R. Hedley.
THE POLYTECHNIC—WOLVERHAMPTON, Wulfruna Street, Wolverhampton.—*Dir.*, R. Scott.
 Two further Polytechnics remain to be established, a proposed polytechnic in central Lancashire based on the Harris College, Preston and part of the work of Blackburn College of Technology and Design; and The Middlesex Polytechnic based on

Enfield College of Technology, Hendon College of Technology and Hornsey College of Art.
 In addition to these colleges, there are 7,968 Evening Institutes and similar types of establishment providing a wide variety of non-vocational classes for adults.

EDUCATIONAL TRUSTS

BOEKE TRUST, care of Messrs. Cadbury Schweppes Ltd., Bournville, Birmingham. (Applications by individuals for financial assistance not considered.) —*Sec.*, G. O. Jones.
CARNEGIE TRUST FOR THE UNIVERSITIES OF SCOTLAND, The Merchants Hall, Hanover Street, Edinburgh.—*Sec. and Treasurer*, A. E. Ritchie.
CASSEL EDUCATIONAL TRUST, 21 Hassocks Road, Hurstpierpoint, Sussex.—*Sec.*, D. Hardman.
DARTINGTON HALL TRUST, Totnes, Devon.— *Chairman*, M. A. Ash.
EDUCATION SERVICES, 19 Norham Road, Oxford.— *Hon. Sec.*, Mrs. R. W. Bellerby.
GILCHRIST EDUCATIONAL TRUST, 1 York Street, W.1.—*Sec.*, Miss S. Salmon.
HARKNESS FELLOWSHIPS OF THE COMMONWEALTH FUND OF NEW YORK, Harkness House, 38 Upper Brook Street, W.1.
KING GEORGE'S JUBILEE TRUST, 39 Victoria Street, S.W.1.—*Sec.* Maj. Sir Michael Hawkins, K.C.V.O., M.B.E.
LEVERHULME TRUST FUND (1925), 15–19 New Fetter Lane, E.C.4.—Annual income, about £1,500,000. Awards to institutions, at home and overseas, mainly in the form of fellowships, studentships and scholarships for research and education. Awards to individuals are also made on the recommendation of a Research Awards Advisory Committee under six specific schemes. *Dir.*, The Lord Holford.
LORD KITCHENER NATIONAL MEMORIAL FUND, Barn Meadow, Great Warley, Brentwood, Essex. —*Sec.*, C. R. Allison. Awards annually for university courses 30 to 40 scholarships, established to reward long and distinguished service, and especially war service, in H.M. Armed Forces. Competition is open to (*a*) sons of members or exmembers (men or women) of the British Navy, Army or Air Force, aged over 17 and under 20 on 1st January of year competing, and (*b*) male applicants aged under 30, who have done regular or national service. *No awards are made in respect of post-graduate studies.* Application forms, available after Nov. 1, are returnable by Jan. 31.
MITCHELL CITY OF LONDON CHARITY AND EDUCATIONAL FOUNDATION, Bedford Chambers, Covent Garden, W.C.2.—*Clerk*, A. E. L. Cox.
ELIZABETH NUFFIELD EDUCATIONAL FUND (1956). Nuffield Lodge, Regent's Park, N.W.1.—*Sec.*, Miss D. Dutton.
ROYAL COMMISSION FOR THE EXHIBITION OF 1851, 1 Lowther Gardens, Exhibition Road, S.W.7.— *Sec.*, C. A. H. James.
SIR RICHARD STAPLEY EDUCATIONAL TRUST, 121 Gloucester Place, Portman Square, W.1.—*Sec.*, R. Groves.
CITY PAROCHIAL FOUNDATION (TRUSTEES OF THE LONDON PAROCHIAL CHARITIES) 10 Fleet Street, E.C.4. Gross income 1974, £810,391. Grants made for the maintenance of City Churches and for the welfare of the poorer classes of the Metropolitan Police District of London and the City of London.
THOMAS WALL TRUST, 1 York Street, W.1. *Sec.*, Miss B. S. Salmon.
WINSTON CHURCHILL MEMORIAL TRUST (Churchill

Fellowships).—15 Queen's Gate Terrace, S.W.7.
—*Dir.-Gen.*, Maj.-Gen. H. A. Lascelles, C.B.,
C.B.E., D.S.O.

LOCAL EDUCATION AUTHORITIES
English and Welsh Counties

AVON, Avon House North, St James Barton,
Bristol.—*Chief Education Officer*, D. Williams.
BEDFORDSHIRE, County Hall, Bedford.—*Chief
Education Officer*, D. P. J. Browning.
BERKSHIRE, Kennet House, 80/82 Kings Road,
Reading.—*Director*, R. J. Hornsby.
BUCKINGHAMSHIRE, County Offices, Aylesbury.—
Chief Education Officer, R. P. Harding.
CAMBRIDGESHIRE, Shire Hall, Cambridge.—*Chief
Education Officer*, I. G. Cunningham.
CHESHIRE, County Hall, Chester.—*Director*, J.
R. G. Tomlinson.
CLEVELAND, Woodlands Road, Middlesbrough.—
Director, A. D. Jackson.
CLWYD, Shire Hall, Mold.—*Director*, J. H. Davies.
CORNWALL, County Hall, Truro.—*Secretary*, K.
Cruise.
CUMBRIA, 5 Portland Square, Carlisle.—*Director*,
P. C. Boulter.
DERBYSHIRE, County Offices, Matlock.—*Director*,
C. Phillips.
DEVON, County Hall, Exeter.—*Chief Education
Officer*, J. G. Owen.
DORSET, County Hall, Dorchester.—*Director*, R. D.
Price.
DURHAM, County Hall, Durham.—*Director*, D. H.
Curry.
DYFED, County Hall, Carmarthen.—*Director*, H. D.
Thomas.
ESSEX, Threadneedle House, Market Road, Chelms-
ford.—*Chief Education Officer*, J. A. Springett.
GLOUCESTERSHIRE, Shire Hall, Gloucester.—*Chief
Education Officer*, C. P. Milroy.
GWENT, County Hall, Newport.—*Director*, T. M.
Morgan.
GWYNEDD, Castle Street, Caernarfon.—*Director*,
T. Ellis.
HAMPSHIRE, The Castle, Winchester.—*County
Education Officer*, J. H. Aldman, M.C.
HEREFORD and WORCESTER, Castle Street, Worces-
ter.—*Director*, M. J. Gifford.
HERTFORDSHIRE, County Hall, Hertford.—*County
Education Officer*, D. Fisher.
HUMBERSIDE, County Hall, Beverley.—*Director*, J.
Bower.
ISLE OF WIGHT, County Hall, Newport.—*Director*,
R. O. Burton.
KENT, Springfield, Maidstone.—*County Education
Officer*, W. H. Petty.
LANCASHIRE, County Hall, Preston.—*Chief Educa-
tion Officer*, J .C. D. Rainbow.
LEICESTERSHIRE, County Hall, Glenfield, Leicester.
—*Director*, A. N. Fairbairn, M.C.
LINCOLNSHIRE, County Offices, Lincoln.—*County
Education Officer*, G. V. Cooke.
MID GLAMORGAN, County Hall, Cathays Park,
Cardiff.—*Director*, J. L. Brace.
NORFOLK, County Hall, Norwich.—*Chief Education
Officer*, D. Coatesworth.
NORTHAMPTONSHIRE, Northampton House, Wel-
lington Street, Northampton.—*Chief Education
Officer*, M. J. Henley.
NORTHUMBERLAND, Eldon House, Regent Centre,
Gosforth, Newcastle upon Tyne.—*Director*, M. H.
Trollope.
NOTTINGHAMSHIRE, County Hall, West Bridgford.
—*Director*, J. A. Stone.

OXFORDSHIRE, County Offices, New Road, Ox-
ford.—*Unit Education Officer*, J. Garne.
POWYS, County Hall, Llandrindod Wells.—*Director*,
R. W. Bevan.
SHROPSHIRE, Shirehall, Shrewsbury.—*County Educa-
tion Officer*, J. Boyers.
SOMERSET, County Hall, Taunton.—*Chief Education
Officer*, B. Taylor.
SOUTH GLAMORGAN, County Offices, Kingsway,
Cardiff.—*Director*, F. J. Adams.
STAFFORDSHIRE, Tipping Street, Stafford and Earl
Street, Stafford.—*Director*, A. Riley.
SUFFOLK, County Hall, Ipswich.—*Chief Education
Officer*, F. J. Hill.
SURREY, Penrhyn Road, Kingston upon Thames.—
Chief Education Officer, J. W. Henry.
SUSSEX (East), County Hall, Lewes.—*Chief Educa-
tion Officer*, J. Rendel-Jones.
SUSSEX (West), County Hall, Chichester.—*Director*,
G. R. Potter.
WARWICKSHIRE, 22 Northgate Street, Warwick.—
County Education Officer.—M. L. Ridger.
WEST GLAMORGAN, Princess House, Princes Way,
Swansea.—*Director*, J. Beale.
WILTSHIRE, County Hall, Trowbridge.—*Chief
Education Officer*, J. F. Everett, M.B.E., T.D.
WORCESTERSHIRE, Castle Street, Worcester.—
County Education Officer, J. C. Brooke.
YORKSHIRE (North), County Hall, Northallerton.—
Director, E. E. L. Owens, PH.D.

London

INNER LONDON EDUCATION AUTHORITY.—*Education
Officer*, E. W. H. Briault, PH.D.

Education Officers

BARKING, Town Hall.—J. L. Haseldon.
BARNET, Town Hall, Friern Barnet, N.11.—J.
Dawkins.
BEXLEY, Town Hall, Crayford.—P. Green.
BRENT, Chesterfield House, Park Lane, Wembley.—
Miss G. M. Rickus.
BROMLEY, Sunnymead, Bromley Lane, Chislehurst.
—D. R. Barraclough.
CROYDON, Taberner House, Park Lane.—K. J.
Revell.
EALING, 81 Uxbridge Road, W.5.—R. J. Hartles.
ENFIELD, P.O. Box 56, Civic Centre, Enfield.—M.
Healey.
HARINGEY, Somerset Road, Tottenham, N.17.—
A. G. Groves.
HARROW, Civic Centre, Harrow.—*Director*, M.
Johnson.
HAVERING, Mercury House, Mercury Gardens,
Romford, Essex.—D. H. Wilcockson.
HILLINGDON, Belmont House, 38 Market Square,
Uxbridge, Middx.—*Director*, A. H. R. Calder-
wood.
HOUNSLOW, 88 Lampton Road.—*Director*, P. J.
Lee.
KINGSTON UPON THAMES, Tolworth Tower, Sur-
biton, Surrey.—W. F. E. Gibbs.
MERTON, Station House, London Road, Morden,
Surrey.—R. Greenwood.
NEWHAM, 29 The Broadway, Stratford, E.15.—
J. S. Wilkie, PH.D.
REDBRIDGE, Lynton House, High Road, Ilford,
Essex.—J. E. Fordham.
RICHMOND UPON THAMES, Regal House, Twicken-
ham, Middx.—D. Naismith.
SUTTON, The Grove, Carshalton, Surrey.—C.
Melville.
WALTHAM FOREST, Municipal Offices, High Road,
Leyton, E.10.—E. A. Hartley.

Metropolitan District Councils

BIRMINGHAM, Margaret Street, Birmingham 3.—*Chief Education Officer*, K. Brooksbank, D.S.C.

BOLTON, Victoria House, Civic Centre.—*Chief Education Officer*, P. Waddington.

BRADFORD, Provincial House, Bradford.—*Director*, W. R. Knight.

BURY, Athenaeum House, Market Street.—*Director*, M. Gray.

CALDERDALE.—Alexandra Buildings, King Edward Street, Halifax.—*Chief Education Officer*, A. Pickavance.

COVENTRY, Council Offices, Earl Street.—*Director*, R. Aitken.

DONCASTER, Princegate.—*Chief Education Officer*, M. J. Pass.

GATESHEAD, Prince Consort Road.—*Director*, Miss M. A. Sproat.

KIRKLEES, Oldgate House, Huddersfield.—*Director*, E. T. Butcher.

KNOWSLEY, Civic Buildings, Archway Road, Huyton.—*Director*, J. W. Davies.

LEEDS, Municipal Buildings, Calverley Street.—*Director*, R. S. Johnson.

LIVERPOOL, 14 Sir Thomas Street.—*Education Officer*, K. A. Antcliffe.

MANCHESTER, Cumberland House, Crown Square.—*Chief Education Officer*, D. A. Fiske.

NEWCASTLE UPON TYNE, Civic Centre, Barras Bridge.—*Director*, J. F. Chadderton.

NORTH TYNESIDE, The Chase, North Shields.—*Director*, J. F. Partington.

OLDHAM, Chadderton Town Hall.—*Director*, G. R. Pritchett.

ROCHDALE, Municipal Offices, Middleton.—*Chief Education Officer*, A. N. Naylor.

ROTHERHAM, Municipal Offices, Howard Street, —*Director*, L. G. Taylor.

ST. HELENS, Century House, Hardshaw Street.—*Director*, W. H. Cubitt.

SALFORD, Chapel Street.—*Director*, J. A. Barnes.

SANDWELL, Highfields, High Street, West Bromwich.—*Director*, G. A. Brinson.

SEFTON, Burlington House, Crosby, Liverpool 22.—*Director*, K. Robinson.

SHEFFIELD, Leopold Street.—*Director*, G. M. A. Harrison.

SOLIHULL, The Council House.—*Director*, D. B. Love.

SOUTH TYNESIDE, Town Hall, Jarrow.—*Director*, K. Stringer.

STOCKPORT, Town Hall.—*Director*, B. L. Harmon.

SUNDERLAND, Town Hall.—*Director*, J. Bridge, G.C., G.M.

TAMESIDE, Town Hall, Dukinfield.—*Director*, G. Mayall.

TRAFFORD, Town Hall, Sale.—*Director*, D. J. Hatfield.

WAKEFIELD, Bond Street.—*Director*, R. Eyles.

WALSALL, Civic Offices, Darwall Street, Walsall.—*Director*, R. D. Nixon.

WIGAN, Civic Centre.—*Director*, K. Crawford.

WIRRAL, Cleveland Street, Birkenhead.—*Director*, R. E. Price.

WOLVERHAMPTON, St. John's Square.—*Director*, D. Grayson.

Channel Islands, etc.

JERSEY, P.O. Box 142, Highlands, St. Saviour.—*Director*, J. S. Rodhouse.

GUERNSEY, La Couperderle, St. Peter Port.—*Director*, M. D. Hutchings.

ISLE OF MAN, Strand Street, Douglas.—*Director*, F. Bickerstaff.

ISLES OF SCILLY, Town Hall, St. Mary's.—*Chief Executive*, R. Phillips.

Regional and Islands Councils

BORDERS, County Offices, Newtown St. Boswells.—Director, J. McLean.

CENTRAL, Viewforth, Stirling.—*Director*, I. Collie.

DUMFRIES AND GALLOWAY, Council Offices, Dumfries.—*Director*, J. K. Purves.

FIFE, Wemyssfield, Kirkcaldy.—*Director*, I. S. Flett.

GRAMPIAN, Woodhill House, Ashgrove Road West, Aberdeen.—*Director*, J. A. D. Michie.

HIGHLAND, Regional Buildings, Glenurquhart Road, Inverness.—*Director*, R. MacDonald.

LOTHIAN, 40 Torphichen Street, Edinburgh.—*Director*, W. D. C. Semple.

ORKNEY, County Offices, Kirkwall, Orkney.

SHETLAND, Brentham Place, Harbour Street, Lerwick.—*Director*, R. A. B. Barnes.

STRATHCLYDE, 25 Bothwell Street, Glasgow.—*Director*, E. Miller.

TAYSIDE, 14 City Square, Dundee.—*Director*, D. G. Robertson.

WESTERN ISLES, L. C. Hostel, Stornoway, Isle of Lewis.—*Director*, A. Macleod.

Northern Ireland

Education and Library Boards

BELFAST, Board Headquarters, 40 Academy Street, Belfast 1.—*Chief Officer*, W. C. H. Eakin.

NORTH-EASTERN, Education Office, County Hall, Galgorm Road, Ballymena, Co. Antrim.—*Chief Officer*, R. J. Dickson, PH.D.

SOUTH-EASTERN, 18 Windsor Avenue, Belfast 9.—*Chief Officer*, F. H. Ebbitt.

SOUTHERN, 3 Charlemont Place, The Mall, Armagh. —*Chief Officer*, W. J. Dickson.

WESTERN, Headquarters Offices, Omagh, Co. Tyrone.—*Chief Officer*, M. H. F. Murphy.

ADULT EDUCATION

Adult Education is carried on in the United Kingdom by universities and university colleges (pp. 501–510), local education authorities (pp. 512–513) and by a wide variety of voluntary organizations.

The Universities Council for Adult Education, consisting of one representative from each university, was constituted in 1946 for interchange of ideas and formulation of common policy on extra-mural education.—*Hon. Secretary*, N. A. Jepson, B.A., PH.D. Department of Adult Education, The University, Leeds.

The National Institute of Adult Education (England and Wales), 35 Queen Anne Street, W.1 (*Sec.*, A. K. Stock), and the Scottish Institute of Adult Education, 57 Melville Street, Edinburgh (*Sec.*, F. J. Taylor), exist to provide a means of consultation and co-operation between the various forces in adult education.

UNIVERSITY DEPARTMENTS OF EXTRA-MURAL STUDIES AND ADULT EDUCATION

OXFORD, Department for External Studies, Rewley House, Wellington Square, Oxford.—*Dir.*, F. W. Jessup, C.B.E.

CAMBRIDGE, Board of Extra-Mural Studies, Madingley Hall, Madingley, Cambridge.—*Dir.*, J. M. Y. Andrew.

DURHAM, Department of Extra-Mural Studies, 32 Old Elvet, Durham.—*Dir.*, J. F. Dixon.

LONDON, Department of Extra-Mural Studies, University of London, 7 Ridgmount Street, W.C.1. —*Dir.*, W. Burmeister.

BIRMINGHAM, Department of Extra-Mural Studies, P.O. Box 363, University of Birmingham, Birmingham, 15.—*Dir.*, A. M. Parker.

BRISTOL, Department of Extra-Mural Studies, The University, Bristol.—*Dir.*, Prof. G. Cunliffe.

EXETER, Department of Extra-Mural Studies, The University, Exeter.—*Head*, Prof. T. F. Daveney.

HULL, Department of Adult Education, the University, Hull.—*Dir.*, Prof. B. Jennings.

KEELE, Department of Adult Education, The University, Keele, Staffs.—*Dir.*, Dr. R. F. Dyson (*acting*).

LEEDS, Department of Adult Education and Extra-Mural Studies, The University, Leeds, 2.—*Head of Dept.*, Prof. N. A. Jepson.

LEICESTER, Department of Adult Education, The University, Leicester.—*Head of Dept.*, Prof. H. A. Jones, C.B.E.

LIVERPOOL, Institute of Extension Studies, 1 Abercromby Square, Liverpool.—*Dir.*, Prof. E. Rhodes.

MANCHESTER, Department of Extra-Mural Studies, The University, Manchester, 13.—*Dir.*, Prof. E. G. Weddell.

NEWCASTLE, Department of Adult Education, The University, Newcastle upon Tyne.—*Dir.* E. W. Hughes.

NOTTINGHAM, Department of Adult Education, 14–22 Shakespeare Street, Nottingham.—*Dir.* Prof. M. D. Stephens.

READING, The University, Whiteknights, Reading. *Registrar*, J. F. Johnson.

SHEFFIELD, Department of Extra-Mural Studies, The University, Sheffield.—*Dir.* Prof. G. W. Roderick.

SOUTHAMPTON, Department of Adult Education, University of Southampton.—*Dir.*, P. E. Fordham.

WALES, The University Extension Board, University Registry, Cathays Park, Cardiff.—*Sec.*, J. Gareth Thomas.

ABERYSTWYTH, University College, Aberystwyth. —*Dir.* (Vacant).

BANGOR, University College, Bangor.—*Dir.*, Prof. A. Llywelyn-Williams.

CARDIFF, University College Cardiff, Department of Extra-Mural Studies, 38–40 Park Place, Cathays Park, Cardiff.—*Dir.* J. S. Davies.

SWANSEA, University College Swansea.—*Dir.*, I. M. Williams.

ABERDEEN, Department of Adult Education and Extra-Mural Studies, The University, Aberdeen. —*Dir.*, K. A. Wood.

DUNDEE, Department of Extra-Mural Education, The University, Dundee.—*Dir.*, A. G. Robertson.

EDINBURGH, Department of Educational Studies, 11 Buccleuch Place, Edinburgh.—*Dir. of Extra-Mural Studies*, B. C. Skinner (*acting*).

GLASGOW, Department of Extra-Mural and Adult Education, 57–9 Oakfield Avenue, Glasgow —*Dir.*, N. Dees.

ST. ANDREWS, Department of Adult Education and Extra-Mural Studies, University of St. Andrews, 3 St. Mary's Place.—*Dir.* J. C. Geddes.

BELFAST, Queen's University, Department of Extra-Mural Studies and Adult Education.—*Dir.* E. C. Read.

RESIDENTIAL COLLEGES FOR ADULT EDUCATION
(Offering courses for a year or longer)

England

CLIFF COLLEGE, Calver, Sheffield. Residential Methodist Lay Training College open to all denominations (Men and Women).—*Principal*, Rev. H. A. G. Belben.

CO-OPERATIVE COLLEGE, Stanford Hall, Loughborough, Leics. (Men and Women).—*Principal*, R. L. Marshall, O.B.E.

FIRCROFT COLLEGE, Selly Oak, Birmingham 29 (Men) (50).—*Principal*, A. J. Corfield.

HILLCROFT RESIDENTIAL COLLEGE FOR WOMEN, Surbiton, Surrey (75).—*Principal*, Mrs. J. Cockerill.

PLATER COLLEGE, Headington, Oxford (Men and Women).—*Principal*, J. R. Kirwan.

RUSKIN COLLEGE, Oxford (Men and Women) (180). *Principal*, H. D. Hughes.

WOODBROOKE, 1046 Bristol Road, Selly Oak, Birmingham 29. Quaker centre for religious, social and international studies (Men and Women). Shorter Courses also available.— *Warden*, E. S. Tucker.

Wales

COLEG HARLECH, Harlech, Merioneth (Men and Women) (135).—*Warden*, I. W. Hughes.

Scotland

NEWBATTLE ABBEY COLLEGE, Dalkeith, Midlothian (Men and Women).—*Warden*, A. D. Reid.

Residential Colleges
(Offering Shorter Courses)

ATTINGHAM ADULT COLLEGE, Attingham Park, nr. Shrewsbury (Shropshire Adult College).— *Warden*, G. S. G. Toms.

AVONCRAFT RESIDENTIAL COLLEGE FOR SHORT-TERM ADULT EDUCATION COURSES, Stoke Prior, nr. Bromsgrove, Worcs.—*Principal*, B. G. Foord.

BELSTEAD HOUSE, nr. Ipswich, Suffolk.—*Warden*, D. C. Barbanell.

BURTON MANOR, Burton, Wirral, Cheshire.— *Principal*.—A. Kingsbury.

DENMAN COLLEGE, Marcham, Abingdon, Oxon. (N.F.W.I.).—*Warden*, Miss H. Anderson.

DILLINGTON HOUSE, Ilminster, Somerset.—*Director*, J. Pick.

DUNFORD HOUSE, Midhurst, Sussex (Y.M.C.A. Adult Education and Training Centre).—*Principal*, Rev. P. G. Hayman.

GRANTLEY HALL, Ripon, Yorks.—*Warden*, Dr. H. C. Strick.

HOLLY RYDE COLLEGE (Manchester University Extra-Mural Dept.), 56–64 Palatine Road, West Didsbury, Manchester 20.—*Warden*, F. W. Chandler.

HORNCASTLE RESIDENTIAL COLLEGE, Horncastle, Lincs.—*Warden*, B. Jenkins.

HUNTERCOMBE MANOR, Taplow, Maidenhead, Berks. (Buckinghamshire Education Cttee.).— *Warden*, G. F. Thomas.

KNUSTON HALL, Irchester, Wellingborough, Northants.—*Principal*, Miss E. Smith.

MISSENDEN ABBEY, Great Missenden, Bucks.— *Warden*, P. F. Hebden.

MOOR PARK COLLEGE, Farnham, Surrey.—*Warden*, J. F. Powell.

ROFFEY PARK INSTITUTE, Management College, Horsham, Sussex.—*Director*, W. J. Giles.

URCHFONT MANOR, Devizes, Wilts.—*Warden*, A. T. C. Slee, PH.D.

WEDGWOOD MEMORIAL COLLEGE, Barlaston, nr. Stoke-on-Trent.—*Warden*, D. Goodman.

WESTHAM HOUSE, Barford, nr. Warwick.— *Principal*, F. Owen, O.B.E., T.D.

PRINCIPAL UNIVERSITY SETTLEMENTS AND ADULT EDUCATION CENTRES

BERNHARD BARON ST. GEORGE'S JEWISH SETTLEMENT, 192 Hanbury Street, E.1.—*Sec.*, Mrs. I. Marks.

BIRMINGHAM SETTLEMENT, 318 Summer Lane, Birmingham; Residential Centre, 3 Tower Street, Birmingham.—*Warden and Dir.*, P. D. Houghton.

BOSTON, Department of Adult Education, University of Nottingham, Pilgrim College.—*Warden and Residential Tutor*, A. Champion.

BRADFORD, LEEDS UNIVERSITY ADULT EDUCATION CENTRE, 10 Mornington Villas, Manningham Lane, Bradford 8. (Dept. of Adult Education and Extra-Mural Studies, University of Leeds.)—*Warden*, R. K. S. Taylor.

BRISTOL, The Folk House, 40 Park Street.—*Warden*, R. Cann.

BRISTOL (University Settlement, Bristol Community Association), 43 Ducie Road, Bristol.—*Director*, M. Sykes.

CAMBRIDGE HOUSE AND TALBOT, 131–139 Camberwell Road and 48 Addington Square, S.E.5—*Head*, Rev. P. Libby.

CITY LITERARY CENTRE for adult studies, Stukeley Street, Drury Lane, W.C.2.—*Principal*, R. J. South, Ph.D.

DOCKLAND SETTLEMENTS, branches at Isle of Dogs, E.14; Bristol; Rotherhithe, S.E.16; Dagenham, Essex; Stratford, E.15 (2 branches); Hainault Estate, Chigwell, Essex; School of Adventure, Ross-shire; Guest House, Herne Bay, Kent—*Gen. Sec.*, R. W. Logan-Hunt, 164 Romford Road, Stratford, E.15.

EDINBURGH UNIVERSITY SETTLEMENT, Student Centre, Bristol Street, Edinburgh.—*Dir.*, J. R. Waddington; *Adult Education Centre*, Kirk o' Field College, Wilkie House, Guthrie Street, Edinburgh, 1.—*Sec.*, Miss E. Wood.

GOLDSMITHS' COLLEGE, New Cross, S.E.14.—*Principal, Dept. of Adult Studies*, P. A. Baynes.

LEICESTER UNIVERSITY Centre, Vaughan College, St. Nicholas Circle.—*Warden*, D. J. Rice.

LIVERPOOL UNIVERSITY SETTLEMENT, Nile Street.—*Director*, J. P. Warren.

LOUGHBOROUGH, Quest House, Loughborough Technical College, Radmoor.—*Warden*, D. H. Bodger, Dept. of Adult Education, University of Nottingham.

MIDDLESBOROUGH: NEWPORT SETTLEMENT YOUTH AND COMMUNITY CENTRE, 130–132 Newport Road, Middlesbrough.—*Warden*, A. Thompson.

MIDDLESBROUGH: UNIVERSITY ADULT EDUCATION CENTRE, 37 Harrow Road, Middlesbrough (Department of Adult Education and Extra-mural Studies, University of Leeds.)—*Warden*, J. W. Saunders.

MANSFIELD HOUSE, Fairbairn Hall, E.13.—*Warden*, Rev. Canon E. A. Shipman.

ROBERT BROWNING SETTLEMENT, Browning Street, Walworth, S.E.17.—*Warden*, Rev. H. Rathbone Dunnico.

ROLAND HOUSE SCOUT CENTRE, 29 Stepney Green, E.1.—*Warden*, H. L. Ransome.

ST. MARGARET'S HOUSE SETTLEMENT, 21 Old Ford Road, Bethnal Green, E.2.—*Warden*, R. Delafield.

SPENNYMOOR SETTLEMENT, King Street, Spennymoor, Co. Durham.

TOYNBEE HALL, THE UNIVERSITIES' SETTLEMENT IN EAST LONDON, 28 Commercial Street, Whitechapel, E.1.—*Warden*, A. Locke.

WORKING MEN'S COLLEGE, Crowndale Road, N.W.1.—*Principal*, L. P. Thompson-McCausland, C.M.G.; *Warden*, W. J. Evans.

YORK EDUCATIONAL SETTLEMENT, 128 Holgate Hill. —*Wardens*, A. J. Peacock; M. Peacock.

PROFESSIONAL EDUCATION

NOTE.—References to university courses in the sections following cover *first* degrees; the considerable facilities available at universities for postgraduate study or research are not treated.

ACCOUNTANCY

(*See also* Business Management and Administration).

Degrees in *Accounting* or *Accountancy* are granted by the Universities of Birmingham, Exeter, Glasgow, Kent, Strathclyde. At several other universities one of these subjects can be combined with e.g. Financial Administration, Finance or Economics.

Courses leading to degrees in *Accounting* granted by the Council for National Academic Awards are provided by City of Birmingham Polytechnic, Bristol Polytechnic (*Accounting and Finance*), City of London Polytechnic, Glasgow College of Technology, Leeds Polytechnic, Liverpool Polytechnic, Manchester Polytechnic, Middlesex Polytechnic (*Accounting and Finance*), North East London Polytechnic (*Finance with Accounting*), Polytechnic of North London, Portsmouth Polytechnic, Trent Polytechnic (*Accountancy and Finance*).

Professional Bodies.—The main bodies granting membership on examination after a period of practical work are:

INSTITUTE OF CHARTERED ACCOUNTANTS IN ENGLAND AND WALES, Chartered Accountants' Hall, Moorgate Place, E.C.2.

INSTITUTE OF CHARTERED ACCOUNTANTS OF SCOTLAND, 27 Queen Street, Edinburgh, 2, and 218 St. Vincent Street, Glasgow, C.2.

ASSOCIATION OF CERTIFIED ACCOUNTANTS, 22 Bedford Square, W.C.1.

CHARTERED INSTITUTE OF PUBLIC FINANCE AND ACCOUNTANCY, 1 Buckingham Place, S.W.1.

INSTITUTE OF COST AND MANAGEMENT ACCOUNTANTS, 63 Portland Place, W.1.

ACTUARIAL SCIENCE

Degrees in *Actuarial Science* are granted by the City University and in *Actuarial Mathematics* by Heriot-Watt University.

Two professional organizations grant qualifications after examination:

INSTITUTE OF ACTUARIES, Staple Inn Hall, High Holborn, W.C.1.

FACULTY OF ACTUARIES IN SCOTLAND, *Hall and Library*, 23 St. Andrew Square, Edinburgh.

AERONAUTICS

and Aeronautical Engineering

Degrees in *Aeronautical Engineering* are granted by the Universities of Bath, Belfast, Bristol, Cambridge (*Aeronautics*), the City University, the Universities of Glasgow, London (Imperial College of Science and Technology; Queen Mary College), Loughborough (*Aeronautical Engineering and Design*), Manchester, Salford (*Aeronautical Engineering Science*) and (*Aeronautics and Astronautics*), Southampton; and in *Air Transport Engineering* by the City University. Courses leading to degrees in *Aeronautical Engineering* granted by the Council for National Academic Awards are provided by Hatfield Polytechnic and Kingston Polytechnic.

COLLEGE OF AERONAUTICAL AND AUTOMOBILE ENGINEERING, Shoreham Aerodrome, Sussex.

COLLEGE OF AIR TRAINING, Hamble, Southampton.

AGRICULTURE

Degrees in *Agriculture* or *Agricultural Science(s)* are granted by the Universities of Aberdeen, Belfast, Edinburgh, Glasgow, Leeds, London (Wye College), Newcastle upon Tyne, Nottingham, Oxford (*Agricultural and Forest Sciences*), Reading and Wales (University Colleges of Aberystwyth and Bangor); and in *Horticulture* by Bath, London (Wye College), Nottingham, Reading and Strathclyde.

Other schools of agriculture are:

ABERDEEN (North of Scotland College of Agriculture, 581 King Street—*Sec.*, H. Munro, M.A.

CIRENCESTER, Royal Agricultural College.—*Principal*, Sir Emrys Jones, B.SC.

EDINBURGH SCHOOL OF AGRICULTURE, THE, West Mains Road, Edinburgh, 9.—*Principal*, Prof. N. F. Robertson, B.SC., PH.D.

HARPER ADAMS AGRICULTURAL COLLEGE, Newport, Salop—*Principal*, R. Kenney. B.SC.

SEALE-HAYNE AGRICULTURAL COLLEGE, Newton Abbot, S. Devon.—*Principal*, G. J. Dowrick, B.SC., PH.D.

SHUTTLEWORTH AGRICULTURAL COLLEGE, Old Warden Park, Biggleswade, Bedfordshire.—*Principal*, J. E. Scott, B.SC., M.S.

WEST OF SCOTLAND AGRICULTURAL COLLEGE, Auchincruive, Ayr.—*Principal*, Prof. J. S. Hall, B.SC.

There are in addition over twenty country Agricultural Institutes giving a one-year course.

ARBITRATION

THE INSTITUTE OF ARBITRATORS, 16 Park Crescent, W.1, conducts examinations and maintains a Register of Fellows and Associates, and a panel of arbitrators.—*Sec.*, B. W. Vigrass, O.B.E., V.R.D.

ARCHÆOLOGY

Degrees in Archæology (sometimes in combination with another subject) are granted by the Universities of Belfast, Birmingham, Bradford, Bristol, Cambridge, Durham, Edinburgh, Exeter, Glasgow, Lancaster, Leeds, Leicester, Liverpool, London (Institute of Archæology, Bedford, King's and University Colleges; also School of Oriental and African Studies for *Archæology of China* and *of South or South-East Asia*), Manchester, Nottingham, Reading, Sheffield, Southampton, Wales (University Colleges of Bangor and Cardiff).

ARCHITECTURE

The Board of Education of THE ROYAL INSTITUTE OF BRITISH ARCHITECTS, 66 Portland Place, W.1, sets standards and guides the whole system of architectural education throughout the United Kingdom. Courses at the following Schools are recognized by the R.I.B.A. They are visited regularly by the R.I.B.A. Visiting Board to ensure that they meet the minimum standards for exemption from the R.I.B.A.'s own examinations.

UNIVERSITY SCHOOLS

(Subject to exceptions noted below, courses are full-time for five years, leading to a degree or diploma; number of students and name of Head of School or Department of Architecture are included.)

BATH: University School of Architecture and Building Engineering, Claverton Down (104).—K. W. Smithies (6-yr. composite sandwich course in architecture).

BELFAST: Queen's University (151).—Prof. W. J. Kidd.

BRISTOL: University Dept. of Architecture (200).—Prof. I. Smith.

CAMBRIDGE: Department of Architecture (190).—Prof. C. St. J. Wilson.

CARDIFF: The Welsh School of Architecture, University of Wales, Institute of Science and Technology (219).—Prof. D-P. Thomas.

DUNDEE: School of Architecture, University of Dundee: Duncan of Jordanstone College of Art, Perth Road (185).—J. Paul.

EDINBURGH: University of Edinburgh, Dept. of Architecture (150).—Prof. G. B. Oddie.

—Heriot-Watt University (joint course with Edinburgh College of Art), Lauriston Place (200).—Prof. R. Cowan.

GLASGOW: University of Strathclyde, Dept. of Architecture and Building Science— Prof. T. A. Markus; Prof. F. N. Morcos-Asaad; Prof. T. W. Maver.

LIVERPOOL: University of Liverpool School of Architecture (220).—Prof. J. N. Tarn.

LONDON: University College London (190).—*Bartlett Professor of Architecture*, N. Watson.

MANCHESTER: University of Manchester School of Architecture (196).—Prof. N. McKinnell.

NEWCASTLE UPON TYNE: University School of Architecture (180).—Prof. M. Danby (*acting*).

NOTTINGHAM: University Dept. of Architecture (170) Prof. C. Riley.

SHEFFIELD: University Dept. of Architecture (200).—Prof. K. H. Murta; Prof. D. Gosling.

NON-UNIVERSITY SCHOOLS

(Subject to the exceptions listed below, courses are full-time and lead to a diploma. Number of students and name of Head of School are shown.)

ABERDEEN: Scott Sutherland School of Architecture, Robert Gordon's Institute of Technology (200).—S. Wilkinson (C.N.A.A. degree (*hons.*)).

BIRMINGHAM: School of Architecture, Corporation Street (200).—A. J. Howrie (five-year sandwich course).

BRIGHTON: School of Architecture, Brighton Polytechnic, Grand Parade (156).—J. P. Lomax, PH.D.

CANTERBURY: School of Architecture, Canterbury College of Art, New Dover Road (161).—A. Wade.

GLASGOW: The Mackintosh School of Architecture, Glasgow University and Glasgow School of Art, 167 Renfrew Street* (307).—Prof. A. MacMillan.

HULL: School of Architecture, Regional College of Art, Brunswick Avenue (92).—M. S. Robinson (*acting*); M. R. Lloyd (*Consultant Head*)

KINGSTON UPON THAMES: Polytechnic School of Architecture, Knight's Park (230).—D. Berry.

LEEDS: Department of Architectural Studies, Leeds Polytechnic, 43A Woodhouse Lane (210).—J. M. Jenkins.

LEICESTER: Polytechnic School of Architecture, P.O. Box 143, Oxford Street (232).—R. Howrie, M.B.E.

LONDON: Architectural Association School of Architecture, 36 Bedford Square, W.C.1. (620).—A. Boyarsky.

Department of Architecture, Polytechnic of the South Bank, Wandsworth Road, S.W.8. (121).—A. Reed.

Depts. of Architecture, Surveying and Social and Environmental Planning, Civil Engineering Building, Polytechnic of Central London, 35 Marylebone Road, N.W.1.

Dept. of Environmental Design, Polytechnic of North London, Holloway, N.7 (186).—M. Quantrill (C.N.A.A. degree).

Thames Polytechnic, School of Architecture, Vencourt House, King Street, W.6. (255)—Dr. J. Paul.

MANCHESTER: Polytechnic School of Architecture Dept. of Environmental Design, Cavendish Street (6-yr. composite course) (150).—M. H. Darke.

OXFORD: Polytechnic School of Architecture, Gypsy Lane (280).—R. Cave.

PORTSMOUTH: Polytechnic School of Architecture, King Henry I Street (198).—G. H. Broadbent.

ART

Degrees in *Art* or *History of Art* (sometimes in combination with another subject) are granted by the Universities of Aberdeen, Bristol, Cambridge, East Anglia, Edinburgh, Essex, Exeter, Glasgow, Leeds, London (Courtauld Institute of Art; Birkbeck, University and Westfield Colleges), Manchester, Newcastle upon Tyne, Nottingham, Reading, St. Andrews, Sussex, Wales (University College,

Aberystwyth) and Warwick. The degrees in *Art*, granted by the Royal College of Art are higher degrees.

Courses leading to degrees in *Art and Design* granted by the Council for National Academic Awards are provided by more than 40 colleges, schools of art and polytechnics.

LONDON.—Royal Academy Schools of Painting and Sculpture, Burlington Gardens, W.1. (65).— *Keeper*, Peter Greenham, R.A.; *Secretary*, S. C. Hutchison; *Curator*, W. Woodington: *Registrar*, K. J. Tanner.

LONDON.—The Slade School of Fine Art, University College, W.C.1. provides courses in Drawing, Painting and Sculpture, Etching, Engraving, Lithography, Silk Screen Printing and Stage Design. Facilities available for the Study of Film.—*Slade Professor*, Sir William Coldstream, C.B.E.; *Sec.*, I. E. T. Jenkin, M.A.

LONDON.—Royal Drawing Society, 17 Carlton House Terrace, S.W.1.—*Pres.*, J. Mills, F.S.A.; *Sec.*, D. Flanders.

LONDON.—Royal College of Art, *see* p. 509.

OXFORD, The Ruskin School of Drawing and Fine Art, at 74 High Street, Oxford (90 students).— *Principal*, P. Morsberger (Ruskin Master of Drawing). Courses in Drawing, Painting and Printmaking. The University awards a Certificate in Fine Art.

GLASGOW, School of Art, 167 Renfrew Street.— *Chairman*, R. W. Begg; *Director*, H. J. Barnes, C.B.E.; *Sec. & Treas.*, F. W. Kean.

ASTRONOMY

Degrees in *Astronomy* are granted by the Universities of Glasgow, Leicester (*Mathematics with Astronomy*), London (University College), Newcastle upon Tyne (*Astronomy and Astrophysics*), St. Andrews and Sussex (*Physics with Astronomy*); and in *Astrophysics* by the Universities of Edinburgh, Leeds (*Physics with Astrophysics*), Leicester (*Physics with Astrophysics*), London (Queen Elizabeth College—*Physics and Astrophysics*; Queen Mary College) Newcastle upon Tyne (*Astronomy and Astrophysics*), and the University of Wales (University College, Aberystwyth (*Physics with Planetary and Space Physics*).

BANKING

Degrees with specialization in *Banking and Finance* are granted by the Universities of Birmingham and Wales (Institute of Science and Technology), the City University (*International Banking and Finance*) and Loughborough University of Technology.

Professional organizations granting qualifications after examination:—

THE INSTITUTE OF BANKERS, 10 Lombard Street, E.C.3.

THE INSTITUTE OF BANKERS IN SCOTLAND, 20 Rutland Square, Edinburgh.

BIOLOGY, CHEMISTRY, PHYSICS

Degrees are granted by Universities and by the Council for National Academic Awards. Many technical College courses lead to diplomas, certificates or associateships. Professional qualifications are awarded by:—

THE INSTITUTE OF BIOLOGY, 41 Queen's Gate, S.W.7.—*Gen. Sec.*, D. J. B. Copp.

THE INSTITUTE OF PHYSICS, 47 Belgrave Square, S.W.1.

THE ROYAL INSTITUTE OF CHEMISTRY, 30 Russell Square, W.C.1.—*President*, Prof. C. Kemball, F.R.S.; *Sec.* and *Registrar*, R. E. Parker, Ph.D.

BREWING

DEGREES in Brewing are granted by Heriot-Watt University.

BUILDING

(*See also* Estate Management and Surveying)

Degrees in *Building*, *Building Engineering* or *Building Technology* are granted by the following Universities: Aston in Birmingham (also *Building Economics and Quantity Surveying*), Bath, Brunel, Heriot-Watt (also *Building Economics and Quantity Surveying*), Liverpool, London (University College; *Architecture, Planning, Building and Environmental Studies*), Manchester (Manchester Institute of Science and Technology), Reading (*Quantity Surveying*), and Salford (also *Quantity Surveying and Construction Economics*). Courses leading to degrees in Building granted by the Council for National Academic Awards are provided by Brighton Polytechnic (*Building Technology and Management*), Polytechnic of Central London, Lanchester Polytechnic, Leeds Polytechnic, Sheffield Polytechnic (*Construction*), the Polytechnic of the South Bank, and Trent Polytechnic.

Ordinary and Higher National Certificates and Diplomas in Building are awarded by the Department of Education and Science and the Scottish Education Department following appropriate courses at Polytechnics or Technical Colleges.

Examinations are conducted by:—

THE INSTITUTE OF BUILDING, Englemere, King's Ride, Ascot, Berks.

THE INSTITUTE OF CLERKS OF WORKS OF GREAT BRITAIN, 6 Highbury Corner, N.5.—*Sec.* A. P. Macnamara.

THE INSTITUTION OF MUNICIPAL ENGINEERS, 25 Eccleston Square, S.W.1 (Building Control Officers' Ordinary and Higher Certificates).

BUSINESS, MANAGEMENT AND ADMINISTRATION

Degrees in *Business Studies* are granted by the Universities of Bath (*Business Administration*), Belfast (*Business Administration*), Bradford (also *Operations Management*), Brunel with the Administrative Staff College, Henley (*Management Studies*), Heriot-Watt (*Business Organization*), Salford (*Business Operation and Control*), Sheffield, Stirling, Strathclyde (*Marketing and Operational Research*), Wales (University College, Aberystwith) (*Economics and Business*), Wales (Institute of Science and Technology) (*Business Administration*); in *Administration* by the Universities of Aston in Birmingham (*Administrative Science*; also *Managerial and Administrative Studies*) and Strathclyde; in *Management Sciences/Studies* by the City University (*Systems and Management*), Loughborough University of Technology, and the Universities of Kent at Canterbury (also *Public Administration and Management*), Lancaster (*Management Sciences—Economics* or *Financial Control* or *Operational Research*), Leeds (*Textile Management*; *Management Studies—Operational Research*), Manchester (Institute of Science and Technology; also *Textile Economics and Management*) Wales (Cardiff University College), and Warwick; and in *Commerce* by the following universities: Birmingham, Edinburgh and Liverpool. These subjects also form part of degree courses in other universities.

Courses leading to degrees in *Business Studies* granted by the Council for National Academic Awards are provided by City of Birmingham Polytechnic, Brighton Polytechnic, Bristol Polytechnic, City of London Polytechnic, Dundee Institute of Art and Technology, Ealing Technical College, Glamorgan Polytechnic, Glasgow College of Technology, Hatfield Polytechnic, Huddersfield Polytechnic, Kingston Polytechnic, Lanchester Polytechnic, Leeds Polytechnic, City of Leicester

Polytechnic, Liverpool Polytechnic, Manchester Polytechnic, Middlesex Polytechnic (also *European Business Administration*), Napier College of Commerce and Technology, Newcastle upon Tyne Polytechnic, North East London Polytechnic, N. Staffordshire Polytechnic, Oxford Polytechnic, Plymouth Polytechnic, Polytechnic of Central London, Portsmouth Polytechnic, Preston Polytechnic, Robert Gordon's Institute of Technology, Sheffield Polytechnic, Polytechnic of the South Bank, Teeside Polytechnic, Thames Polytechnic, Trent Polytechnic, Ulster Polytechnic, and Wolverhampton Polytechnic.

The Thames Polytechnic also provides courses for the C.N.A.A. degree in *International Marketing*; Huddersfield Polytechnic courses for C.N.A.A. degrees in *Marketing (Engineering) or (Chemicals)* and *Textile Marketing*; and City of Leicester, Manchester, Sheffield, Teeside and Trent Polytechnics and Glasgow College of Technology courses for C.N.A.A. degrees in *Public Administration*.

Professional bodies conducting training and/or examinations in Administration and Management include:

ROYAL INSTITUTE OF PUBLIC ADMINISTRATION, Hamilton House, Mabledon Place, W.C.1.
THE INSTITUTE OF HEALTH SERVICE ADMINISTRATORS 75 Portland Place, W.1.
THE INSTITUTE OF PERSONNEL MANAGEMENT, Central House, Upper Woburn Place, W.C.1.
INSTITUTION OF WORKS MANAGERS, 45 Cardiff Road, Luton, Beds.
INSTITUTE OF HOUSING MANAGERS, Victoria House, Southampton Row, W.C.1.
INSTITUTE OF ADMINISTRATIVE MANAGEMENT, 205 High Street, Beckenham, Kent.

ADMINISTRATIVE STAFF COLLEGE, Greenlands, Henley-on-Thames, Oxon.—*Princ.*, Prof. T. Kempner (1972).
LONDON GRADUATE SCHOOL OF BUSINESS STUDIES, Sussex Place, Regent's Park, N.W.1.—*Princ.*, Prof. R. Ball.
MANCHESTER BUSINESS SCHOOL, Booth Street West, Manchester.—*Dir.*, Prof. W. G. McClelland.
Courses of advanced training in most branches of commerce, including preparation for examinations of the recognized professional organizations as well as for the National Certificates in Business Studies are available at the Polytechnics and other institutions listed by cities on p. 511.

Throughout the country commercial education at a lower level is provided at *Evening Institutes*, particulars of which may be obtained from the Local Education Authority.

There are also numbers of well-established private schools awarding certificates which are widely accepted.

Institutions awarding Professional Qualifications in Commerce:—

A. GENERAL
THE ROYAL SOCIETY OF ARTS EXAMINATIONS BOARD, 18 Adam Street, Adelphi, W.C.2.
THE LONDON CHAMBER OF COMMERCE AND INDUSTRY, Marlowe House, Station Road, Sidcup, Kent.
THE SCOTTISH BUSINESS EDUCATION COUNCIL, 22 Great King Street, Edinburgh 3.
THE EAST MIDLAND EDUCATIONAL UNION, Robins Wood House, Robins Wood Road, Apsley, Nottingham.
THE NORTHERN COUNTIES TECHNICAL EXAMINATIONS COUNCIL, 5 Grosvenor Villas, Grosvenor Road, Newcastle upon Tyne, 2.
THE UNION OF EDUCATIONAL INSTITUTIONS, Norfolk House, Smallbrook Queensway, Birmingham 5.

THE UNION OF LANCASHIRE AND CHESHIRE INSTITUTES, 36 Granby Row, Manchester 1.
THE YORKSHIRE AND HUMBERSIDE COUNCIL FOR FURTHER EDUCATION, Bowling Green Terrace, Leeds.
WELSH JOINT EDUCATION COMMITTEE, 245 Western Avenue, Cardiff.

B. SPECIALIZED
THE INSTITUTE OF CHARTERED SECRETARIES AND ADMINISTRATORS, 16 Park Crescent, W.1.
THE FACULTY OF SECRETARIES, 51 Tormead Road, Guildford, Surrey.
THE INSTITUTE OF EXPORT, World Trade Centre, E.1.
THE INSTITUTE OF CHARTERED SHIPBROKERS, 25 Bury Street, E.C.3.
INSTITUTE OF MARKETING, Moor Hall, Cookham, Maidenhead, Berks.
THE CHARTERED INSTITUTE OF TRANSPORT, 80 Portland Place, W.1.
THE ADVERTISING ASSOCIATION, Abford House, 15 Wilton Road, S.W.1.
INSTITUTE OF PRACTITIONERS IN ADVERTISING, 44 Belgrave Square, S.W.1.
INSTITUTE OF PURCHASING AND SUPPLY, York House, Westminster Bridge Road, S.E.1.
INSTITUTE OF PERSONNEL MANAGEMENT, Central House, Upper Woburn Place, W.C.1.

COMPUTER SCIENCE

Degrees in *Computer/Computing Science(s)/Computing* are granted by Brunel, City, Heriot-Watt and Loughborough Universities and by the Universities of Aberdeen, Belfast, Bradford, Cambridge, East Anglia, Edinburgh, Essex, Glasgow, Keele, Kent (also *Computers and Cybernetics*), Lancaster, Leeds (*Computational Science and Data Processing*), Liverpool, London (Imperial, Queen Mary, University and Westfield Colleges; London School of Economics and Political Science), Loughborough (also *Data Processing*), Manchester (also Institute of Science and Technology: *Computation*), Newcastle upon Tyne, Reading, Salford (*Electronic Computer Systems*), St. Andrews (*Computational Science*), Stirling, Strathclyde, Sussex, Wales (University College, Aberystwyth; University College, Cardiff: *Computer Systems*; University College, Swansea: *Computer Technology*), and Warwick. These subjects also form part of degree courses, often as Mathematics/Statistics and Computer Science, at many other universities and colleges.

Courses leading to degrees in *Computer Science* granted by the Council for National Academic Awards are provided by Brighton Polytechnic, City of London Polytechnic (*Statistics and Computing*), Glamorgan Polytechnic, Hatfield Polytechnic, Kingston Polytechnic, Lanchester Polytechnic, Leeds Polytechnic (*Operational Research with Computing*), City of Leicester Polytechnic, Liverpool Polytechnic ((*Applied*) *Statistics and Computing*), Polytechnic of North London (*Statistics and Computing*), North Staffordshire Polytechnic, Paisley College of Technology (*Computing with Operational Research*), Portsmouth Polytechnic, Sheffield Polytechnic, Teesside Polytechnic (also *Computer Technology*), Thames Polytechnic, Ulster Polytechnic, and Wolverhampton Polytechnic; in *Computer and Control Systems* by Lanchester Polytechnic; and in *Mathematics and Computer Science/Computing* by Glamorgan Polytechnic, Polytechnic of North London, Oxford Polytechnic and the Polytechnic of the South Bank.

DANCING

THE ROYAL ACADEMY OF DANCING (incorporated by Royal Charter), 48 Vicarage Crescent, S.W.11. Three years' teachers' course and professional and children's examinations.—*Gen. Sec.*, P. E. Starr.

THE ROYAL BALLET SCHOOL, 155 Talgarth Road, W.14. and White Lodge, Richmond Park.—*Director*, M. Wood.
IMPERIAL SOCIETY OF TEACHERS OF DANCING (1904), 70 Gloucester Place, W.1.—*Gen. Sec.*, P. J. Pearson.

DEFENCE
Royal Naval Colleges
ROYAL NAVAL COLLEGE
Greenwich, S.E.10.
Admiral President, Rear-Admiral D. W. Bazalgette.
Captain of the College, Capt. R. E. Wilson, C.B.E., D.F.C., R.N.
Dean of the College, Instructor Capt. W. A. Waddell, O.B.E., R.N.
Director, R.N. War College, Capt. P. I. F. Beeson, M.V.O., R.N.
Director, R.N. Staff College, Capt. T. G. Briggs, R.N.

INSTITUTE OF NAVAL MEDICINE
Alverstoke, Hants.
Medical Officer in Charge and Dean of Naval Medicine, Surgeon Rear Adm. J. S. P. Rawlins, O.B.E.

BRITANNIA ROYAL NAVAL COLLEGE
Dartmouth
Captain, Capt. M. A. Higgs, R.N.
Commander, Cdr. S. D. S. Bailey, R.N.
Dir. of Studies, H. G. Stewart, M.B.E., M.A.
ROYAL NAVAL ENGINEERING COLLEGE moved to Manadon, Plymouth 1962 (founded 1880 at Devonport). Trains R.N. and R.N. Engineering Service Officers as well as officers of Foreign and Commonwealth Navies for CNAA BSc degree in Mechanical and Electrical Engineering etc.
Captain, Capt. R. G. Baylis, O.B.E.
Dean, Capt. H. E. Morgan.
Commander, Cdr. A. Wheatley.
Dir. of Naval Engineering, Cdr. D. J. F. Atkins.
Dir. of Electrical Engineering, Cdr. R. G. Emmons.
Dir. of Mechanical Engineering, Capt. J. E. Franklin.

Military Colleges
STAFF COLLEGE, CAMBERLEY
Officers who graduate at the college have the letters *p.s.c.* after their names in Service Lists.
Commandant, Maj.-Gen. J. W. Stanier, M.B.E.
Deputy Commandant, Brig. D. K. Neville.

ROYAL MILITARY ACADEMY
SANDHURST
Camberley, Surrey.
The Royal Military Academy, Woolwich, founded in 1741, and the Royal Military College, Sandhurst, founded in 1799, were amalgamated in 1947 under the above title.
Mons Officer Cadet School, Aldershot, opened in 1942 for the training of short service officers, also became part of RMA Sandhurst in 1972.
Commandant, Maj.-Gen. R. C. Ford, C.B., C.B.E.
ROYAL MILITARY COLLEGE OF SCIENCE
Shrivenham, nr. Swindon, Wilts.
The College was founded at Woolwich in 1864 and transferred to Shrivenham in 1946. Officer (and a few civilian) students are prepared for degrees in Applied Science and Engineering of the Council for National Academic Awards; Staff Officers for the Home and Commonwealth armies take postgraduate courses in science and technology and officers of the three Services take more advanced courses.
Commandant, Maj.-Gen. M. E. Tickell, C.B.E.
Dean, F. J. M. Farley, SC.D., Ph.D., F.R.S.
Registrar, H. E. Davies.

ARMOUR SCHOOL
R.A.C. CENTRE
Bovington Camp, nr. Wareham, Dorset.

Commanding Officer and Chief Instructor, Col. B. C. Greenwood.

WELBECK COLLEGE
Worksop, Notts.
Headmaster, M. J. Maloney.
Bursar, Col. R. Mathews.

INSTITUTE OF ARMY EDUCATION
Court Road, S.E.9 (90)
Commandant, Col. W. C. J. Naylor, D.S.C.

Royal Air Force Colleges
ROYAL AIR FORCE STAFF COLLEGE
Bracknell, Berks.
Commandant, Air Vice-Marshal, K. A. Williamson, A.F.C.

ROYAL AIR FORCE COLLEGE
Cranwell
Founded in 1920, the College provides permanent officers for the General Duties, Engineer, Supply, Secretarial and R.A.F. Regiment Branches of the Royal Air Force. It also provides initial specialist training for all officers of the Engineering Supply and Secretarial branches, and advanced training in tactics, operations, navigation and systems engineering for officers of the General Duties and Engineer branches.
Air Officer Commanding and Commandant, Air Vice-Marshall W. E. Colahan, C.B.E., D.F.C.

ROYAL AIR FORCE SCHOOL OF EDUCATION
Newton, Nottingham
Commanding Officer, Gp. Capt. G. Fithen.

DENTISTRY
Degrees in Dentistry are granted by the Universities of Belfast, Birmingham, Bristol, Dundee, Edinburgh, Glasgow, Leeds, Liverpool, London (Guy's Hospital Dental School, King's College Hospital Medical School, London Hospital Medical College, Royal Dental Hospital School of Dental Surgery, University College Hospital Medical School), Manchester, Newcastle upon Tyne, Sheffield, Wales (University College, Cardiff, and Welsh National School of Medicine).
Any person is entitled to be registered in the Dentists Register if he holds the degree or diploma in dental surgery of a University in the United Kingdom or Republic of Ireland or the diploma of any of the Licensing Authorities (The Royal College of Surgeons of England, of Edinburgh and in Ireland, and the Royal College of Physicians and Surgeons of Glasgow).

DIETETICS
Courses leading to *degrees* in *Dietetics* granted by the Council for National Academic Awards are provided by Leeds Polytechnic and Robert Gordon's Institute of Technology (*Nutrition and Dietetics*). The professional association is the British Dietetic Association, Daimler House, 305 Paradise Street, Birmingham. Membership is open to dietitians holding a recognized qualification who may also become State Registered Dietitians through the Council for Professions Supplementary to Medicine (*q.v.*),

DRAMA
Degrees in Drama are granted by the Universities of Birmingham, Bristol, Exeter, Hull and Manchester. Drama also forms part of degree courses in other universities.
The chief training institutions in Drama are:—
GUILDHALL SCHOOL OF MUSIC AND DRAMA (*see* p. 526).
ROYAL ACADEMY OF DRAMATIC ART (founded by Sir Herbert Beerbohm Tree, 1904), 62–64 Gower Street, W.C.1.—*Principal*, H. P. Cruttwell.

BRITISH THEATRE ASSOCIATION (formerly BRITISH DRAMA LEAGUE), 9 Fitzroy Square, W.1.

CENTRAL SCHOOL OF SPEECH AND DRAMA, Embassy Theatre, Swiss Cottage, N.W.3.

ROSE BRUFORD COLLEGE OF SPEECH AND DRAMA, Lamorbey Park, Sidcup, Kent.—*Principal,* J. N. Benedetti.

ENGINEERING

Degrees in *General Engineering* or *Engineering Science* are granted by the Universities of Aberdeen, Cambridge, Durham, Edinburgh, Exeter, Lancaster, Leicester, Loughborough, Oxford, Reading, Surrey, and Warwick. Courses leading to degrees in *Engineering* granted by the Council for National Academic Awards are provided by Kingston Polytechnic, Lanchester Polytechnic, Manchester Polytechnic (*Engineering Technology*), Middlesex Polytechnic, Oxford Polytechnic, Paisley College of Technology (*Engineering with Marketing*), Sheffield Polytechnic, Sunderland Polytechnic, and Thames Polytechnic; also by the Royal Military College of Science. The fifteen member institutions of The Council of Engineering Institutes, 2 Little Smith Street, S.W.1, are the principal qualifying Societies (*see below*).

Aeronautical Engineering

See main heading:
AERONAUTICS AND AERONAUTICAL ENGINEERING

Agricultural Engineering

Degrees are granted by the University of Newcastle upon Tyne. Courses leading to degrees granted by the Council for National Academic Awards are provided by National College of Agricultural Engineering, Silsoe, Beds.

Chemical Engineering

Degrees are granted by the Universities of Aston in Birmingham, Bath, Belfast, Birmingham, Bradford, Cambridge, Edinburgh, Exeter, Heriot-Watt, Leeds, London (Imperial College of Science and Technology; University College), Loughborough, Manchester (Manchester Institute of Science and Technology), Newcastle upon Tyne, Nottingham, Salford, Sheffield, Strathclyde, Surrey, Wales (University College, Swansea). Courses leading to degrees granted by the Council for National Academic Awards are provided by Glamorgan Polytechnic, North East London Polytechnic, the Polytechnic of the South Bank, and Teesside Polytechnic.

Civil, Electrical & Mechanical Engineering

Degrees in *Civil, Electrical and Mechanical Engineering* are granted by Aberdeen, Aston in Birmingham, Bath (*E. & M. & Structural*), Belfast, Birmingham, Bradford, Bristol, Brunel (*E. & M.*), Cambridge, City, Dundee, Edinburgh, Glasgow, Heriot-Watt, Lancaster, Leeds, Liverpool, London (Imperial College of Science and Technology, King's College, Queen Mary College, University College), Loughborough, Manchester, *also* Manchester Institute of Science and Technology, Newcastle upon Tyne, Nottingham, Reading (*E. & M.*), Salford, Sheffield, Southampton, Strathclyde, Surrey, Sussex (*E. & M. & Structural*), Wales (University Colleges of Cardiff and Swansea; Institute of Science and Technology, Cardiff; University College, Bangor (*E.*).

Some 30 polytechnics or colleges of technology provide courses (in one or more of civil, electrical and mechanical engineering) leading to degrees granted by the Council for National Academic Awards.

Electronic Engineering & Electronics

Degrees in *Electronic Engineering* or *Electronics* or *Electrical and Electronic Engineering* are granted by the following universities; Bath, Belfast, Birmingham, Bradford, Bristol, City, Dundee, Edinburgh, Essex, Glasgow, Heriot-Watt, Hull, Keele, Kent at Canterbury, Leeds, Liverpool, London (Chelsea College, King's, Queen Mary and University Colleges), Loughborough, Manchester (*also* Manchester Institute of Science and Technology), Newcastle upon Tyne, Nottingham, Salford, Sheffield, Southampton, Strathclyde, Surrey, Sussex, Wales (University Colleges of Bangor and Cardiff; Institute of Science and Technology).

Courses leading to degrees in *Electronic Engineering* or in *Electrical and Electronic Engineering*, granted by the Council for National Academic Awards are provided by more than 20 polytechnics or colleges of technology.

Marine Engineering and Naval Architecture

Degrees in *Marine Engineering* and *Naval Architecture and Shipbuilding* are granted by the University of Newcastle upon Tyne; in *Naval Architecture and Ocean Engineering* by the University of London (University College); in *Naval Architecture* by Glasgow and Strathclyde; in *Ship Science* by the University of Southampton and in *Maritime Technology* by the University of Wales (Institute of Science and Technology).

Offshore Engineering

Degrees are granted by Heriot-Watt University.

Production Engineering

Degrees are granted by the following Universities: Aston in Birmingham, Bath, Birmingham, Brunel, City (*Manufacturing Engineering*), Liverpool (*Industrial Engineering*), Loughborough, Nottingham, Salford, Strathclyde and Wales (University College, Swansea: *Industrial Engineering*; Institute of Science and Technology). Courses leading to degrees granted by the Council for National Academic Awards are provided by City of Birmingham Polytechnic (*Industrial Engineering*), Dundee Institute of Art and Technology (*Industrial Engineering*), Hatfield Polytechnic (*Industrial Engineering*), Lanchester Polytechnic, Leeds Polytechnic and Trent Polytechnic.

Structural Engineering

Degrees are granted by the Universities of Bath, Bradford (*Civil and Structural Engineering*), Cambridge (*Structural and Civil Engineering*), Heriot-Watt, London (University College: *Civil, Structural and Environmental Engineering*), Sheffield (*Civil and Structural Engineering*), Sussex, and Wales (University College, Cardiff (*Civil and Structural Engineering*)). Courses leading to degrees granted by the Council for National Academic Awards are provided by the Polytechnic of the South Bank.

Qualifying Engineering Institutions

ROYAL AERONAUTICAL SOCIETY, 4 Hamilton Place, W.1.

INSTITUTE OF FUEL, 18 Devonshire Street, W.1.

INSTITUTION OF CHEMICAL ENGINEERS, 15 Belgrave Square, S.W.1.

INSTITUTION OF CIVIL ENGINEERS, Great George Street, S.W.1.

INSTITUTION OF ELECTRICAL ENGINEERS, Savoy Place, W.C.2.

INSTITUTION OF ELECTRONIC AND RADIO ENGINEERS, 8/9 Bedford Square, W.C.1.

INSTITUTION OF GAS ENGINEERS, 17 Grosvenor Crescent, S.W.1.

INSTITUTE OF MARINE ENGINEERS, 76 Mark Lane, E.C.3.

INSTITUTION OF MECHANICAL ENGINEERS, 1 Birdcage Walk, S.W.1.

INSTITUTION OF MINING ENGINEERS, Hobart House, Grosvenor Place, S.W.1.

INSTITUTION OF MINING AND METALLURGY, 44 Portland Place, W.1.

INSTITUTION OF MUNICIPAL ENGINEERS, 25 Eccleston Square, S.W.1.

INSTITUTION OF PRODUCTION ENGINEERS, 66 Little Ealing Lane, W.5.

INSTITUTION OF STRUCTURAL ENGINEERS, 11 Upper Belgrave Street, S.W.1.

ROYAL INSTITUTION OF NAVAL ARCHITECTS, 10 Upper Belgrave Street, S.W.1.

ESTATE MANAGEMENT AND SURVEYING

Degrees are granted by the Universities of Aberdeen (*Land Economy*), Cambridge (*Land Economy*) and Reading (*Estate Management*).

Degrees in *Surveying* and another subject are granted by the University of Newcastle upon Tyne, in *Quantity Surveying* by the University of Reading, and in *Quantity Surveying and Construction Economics* by the University of Salford. Courses leading to degrees granted by the Council for National Academic Awards are provided by the following: in *General Practice Surveying* by Newcastle upon Tyne Polytechnic; in *Land Surveying Sciences* by North East London Polytechnic; in *Building Surveying* by City of Leicester Polytechnic and Thames Polytechnic; in *Quantity Surveying* by Bristol Polytechnic, Polytechnic of Central London, Glamorgan Polytechnic, Glasgow College of Technology with Glasgow College of Building and Printing, Leeds Polytechnic, Liverpool Polytechnic, Newcastle upon Tyne Polytechnic, Portsmouth Polytechnic, Robert Gordon's Institute of Technology, Polytechnic of the South Bank, Thames Polytechnic and Trent Polytechnic; in *Housing Studies* by Sheffield Polytechnic; in *Estate Management* with courses at City of Leicester Polytechnic, Polytechnic of the South Bank and Thames Polytechnic; in *Land Economics* with courses at Paisley College of Technology; in *Urban Estate Management* at Glamorgan and Liverpool Polytechnics, in *Urban Estate Surveying* by Trent Polytechnic; in *Urban Land Economics* by Sheffield Polytechnic; in *Urban Land Administration* by Portsmouth Polytechnic; and in *Valuation and Estate Management* by Bristol Polytechnic.

Qualifying professional bodies include:

THE INCORPORATED SOCIETY OF VALUERS AND AUCTIONEERS, 3 Cadogan Gate, S.W.1.

RATING AND VALUATION ASSOCIATION, 115 Ebury Street, S.W.1.

THE INCORPORATED ASSOCIATION OF ARCHITECTS AND SURVEYORS, 29 Belgrave Square, S.W.1.

THE ROYAL INSTITUTE OF BRITISH ARCHITECTS, 66 Portland Place, W.1.

THE ROYAL INSTITUTION OF CHARTERED SURVEYORS, 12 Great George Street, S.W.1.

THE INSTITUTE OF QUANTITY SURVEYORS, 98 Gloucester Place, W.1.

THE FACULTY OF ARCHITECTS AND SURVEYORS, with which is incorporated the Institute of Registered Architects, 68 Gloucester Place, W.1.

FISHERY SCIENCE

Degrees in *Wildlife and Fisheries Management* are granted by the University of Edinburgh.

Courses leading to degrees in Fishery Science granted by the Council for National Academic Awards are provided by Plymouth Polytechnic.

FOOD AND NUTRITION SCIENCE

(*See also* Dietetics, Home Economics and Hotelkeeping)

Degrees in *Food Science* are granted by the Universities of Belfast, Leeds, London (Queen Elizabeth College: *Food and Management Science*), Loughborough (*Food Processing Technology*), Nottingham, Reading (also *Food Technology*), and Strathclyde; and in *Nutrition* by the Universities of London (Queen Elizabeth College), Nottingham and Surrey.

Courses leading to degrees in *Food Science* granted by the Council for National Academic Awards are provided by the Polytechnic of the South Bank; and in *Nutrition and Dietetics* by Robert Gordon's Institute of Technology.

Scientific and professional bodies include:

NUTRITION SOCIETY, Chandos House, 2 Queen Anne Street, W.1.

FORESTRY

Degrees in Forestry are granted by the Universities of Aberdeen, Edinburgh, Oxford (*Agricultural and Forest Sciences*), and (also *Wood Science*) Wales (University College, Bangor).

Professional Organizations

THE COMMONWEALTH FORESTRY ASSOCIATION, Royal Commonwealth Society, Northumberland Avenue, W.C.2.

THE ROYAL FORESTRY SOCIETY OF ENGLAND, WALES AND NORTHERN IRELAND, 102 High Street, Tring, Herts.

THE ROYAL SCOTTISH FORESTRY SOCIETY, 26 Rutland Square, Edinburgh.

THE INSTITUTE OF FORESTERS OF GREAT BRITAIN, 6 Rutland Square, Edinburgh.

FUEL AND ENERGY STUDIES

Degrees in *Fuel and Combustion Science* and in *Fuel and Energy Engineering* are granted by the University of Leeds; in *Petroleum Engineering* by London (Imperial College of Science and Technology); in *Natural Gas Engineering* by the University of Salford; in *Energy Studies* by the Universities of Sheffield and Wales (University College, Swansea); and in *Fuel Technology* by the University of Sheffield.

Courses leading to certificates and qualification by professional bodies are available at many Technical Colleges.

The principal professional bodies are:—

THE INSTITUTION OF GAS ENGINEERS, 17 Grosvenor Crescent, S.W.1.

THE INSTITUTE OF FUEL, 18 Devonshire Street, Portland Place, W.1.

THE INSTITUTE OF PETROLEUM, 61 New Cavendish Street, W.1.

GEOLOGY

Degrees in *Geology* or *Applied Geology* are granted by the Universities of Aberdeen, Aston in Birmingham, Belfast, Birmingham, Bristol, Cambridge, Dundee, Durham, East Anglia, Edinburgh, Exeter (*also Physical Geology*), Glasgow, Hull, Keele, Leeds, Leicester, Liverpool, London (Bedford College, Birbeck College, Chelsea College, Imperial College of Science and Technology, King's College, Queen Mary College, University College), Manchester, Newcastle upon Tyne, Nottingham, Oxford, Reading, St. Andrews, Sheffield, Southampton, Strathclyde (*Applied Geology*), Wales (University Colleges at Aberystwyth, Cardiff and Swansea). Courses leading to external degrees in *Geology* of the University of London are provided by Derby College of Art and Technology.

Courses leading to degrees in *Geology* granted by the Council for National Academic Awards are provided by Kingston Polytechnic; in *Geology and Environment* by Oxford Polytechnic; and in *Engineering Geology* by Portsmouth Polytechnic.

HOME ECONOMICS AND CATERING

(*See also* DIETETICS, FOOD, HOTELKEEPING and INSTITUTIONAL MANAGEMENT).

Degrees are granted by the Universities of Strathclyde (*Hotel and Catering Managment*) and Surrey (*Home Economics*; and *Hotel and Catering Administration*).

Courses leading to degrees in *Catering Studies* granted by the Council for National Academic Awards are provided by Huddersfield and Sheffield Polytechnics.

In addition to Colleges listed below, the Colleges of Education marked with an asterisk on pp. 529–31 offer specialist courses in Home Economics:

BATH (Coll. of Higher Education, Sion Hill Place).

CARDIFF (Llandaff College of Education (Home Economics)).

EDINBURGH, Queen Margaret College, Clerwood Terrace.

LEEDS POLYTECHNIC, Department of Educational Studies.

LEICESTER (Coll. of Education (Home Economics Dept.), Knighton Fields).

LIVERPOOL (F. L. Calder College of Education, Dowsefield Lane).

LONDON (Battersea Coll. of Education, Manor House, 58 North Side, Clapham Common, S.W.4, and Manresa House, Holybourne Avenue, S.W.15.).

SEAFORD, Sussex (Seaford Coll. of Education, Cricketfield Road).

SHREWSBURY (Radbrook College).

HOTELKEEPING

Degrees are granted by the Universities of Strathclyde (*Hotel and Catering Management*) and Surrey (*Hotel and Catering Administration*).

Courses leading to degrees in *Catering Studies* granted by the Council for National Academic Awards are granted by Huddersfield and Sheffield Polytechnics.

Three-year courses leading to a Higher National Diploma in Hotelkeeping and Catering are available at the following centres:—Barnet (Hendon Coll. of Technology); Birmingham Coll. of Food and Domestic Arts; Blackpool College of Technology and Art; Bournemouth College of Technology; Brighton Polytechnic; S. Devon Technical College; Ealing Technical College; N. Gloucestershire Technical College; Huddersfield Polytechnic; Westminster Technical College; Manchester (Hollings College); Oxford Polytechnic; and in Wales at Llandrillo Technical College.

Two-year full-time courses leading to an Ordinary National Diploma are available at all the above centres and at 48 other colleges in England and Wales.

Details of the diploma conditions are obtainable from H.M. Stationery Office. (*See also* DOMESTIC SCIENCE AND CATERING).

INSTITUTIONAL MANAGEMENT

Three-year sandwich courses leading to a Higher National Diploma in Institutional Management are available at the following centres in England and Wales:

CARDIFF.—Llandaff College of Education and Home Economics.

GLOUCESTER.—Gloucestershire College of Education.

LEEDS.—Leeds Polytechnic.

LONDON.—Polytechnic of North London.

MANCHESTER.—Elizabeth Gaskell College of Education.

NEWCASTLE UPON TYNE.—Newcastle College of Further Education.

OXFORD.—Oxford Polytechnic.

SHEFFIELD.—Sheffield Polytechnic.

SHREWSBURY.—Radbrook College.

Two-year full-time courses leading to an Ordinary National Diploma are available at the Birmingham, Leeds, Manchester and Newcastle centres mentioned above and at 28 other centres in England and Wales.

Qualifying professional bodies in the two subjects above are:

HOTEL, CATERING AND INSTITUTIONAL MANAGEMENT ASSOCIATION, 191 Trinity Road, S.W.17.

INSURANCE

Organizations conducting examinations and awarding diplomas:—

THE CHARTERED INSURANCE INSTITUTE, 20 Aldermanbury, E.C.2.

THE ASSOCIATION OF AVERAGE ADJUSTERS, 3–6 Bury Court, St. Mary Axe, E.C.3.

THE CHARTERED INSTITUTE OF LOSS ADJUSTERS, Manfield House, 376 Strand, W.C.2.

JOURNALISM

Courses for trainee newspaper journalists are available at 10 centres. One-year full-time courses are available for selected students leaving school. Particulars of all these courses are available from the Director of the National Council for Training of Journalists, Harp House, 179 High Street, Epping, Essex.

Short courses for experienced journalists are also arranged by the National Council. For periodical journalists courses are offered at a London College through N.C.T.J. enrolment including a one-year full-time course for school leavers.

LANGUAGES

Degrees in a very wide range of languages (including Oriental and African languages) are granted by universities. Degrees in *Linguistics* are awarded by the Universities of East Anglia, Hull, Lancaster, London (School of Oriental and African Studies and University College), Reading (also *Linguistics and Language Pathology*) and Wales (University College, Bangor), in *Language* by the University of York, and in *Languages* (*Interpreting and Translating*) by Heriot-Watt University. These subjects also form part of degree courses at many other universities.

Courses leading to degrees in various *Languages* granted by the Council for National Academic Awards are provided by Bristol Polytechnic, Cambridgeshire College of Arts and Technology, Polytechnic of Central London, Ealing Technical College, Lanchester Polytechnic, Leeds Polytechnic, Liverpool Polytechnic, Manchester Polytechnic, Newcastle upon Tyne Polytechnic, Polytechnic of North London, Portsmouth Polytechnic, Polytechnic of the South Bank and Wolverhampton Polytechnic.

LAW

Degrees in Law are granted by the Universities of Aberdeen, Belfast, Birmingham, Bristol, Brunel, Cambridge, Dundee, Durham, East Anglia (provisional), Edinburgh, Exeter, Glasgow, Hull, Keele, Kent at Canterbury, Leeds, Leicester, Liverpool, London (King's College; London School of Economics and Political Science; Queen Mary College; School of Oriental and African Studies; University College), Manchester, Newcastle upon Tyne, Nottingham, Oxford, Reading, Sheffield, Southampton, Strathclyde, Sussex, Wales (University Colleges at Aberystwyth and Cardiff, Institute of Science and Technology) and Warwick.

Courses leading to external degrees in Law of the University of London are provided by Mid-Essex Technical College.

Courses leading to degrees in Law granted by the Council for National Academic Awards are provided by City of Birmingham Polytechnic, Bristol Polytechnic, Polytechnic of Central London, City of London Polytechnic (*Business Law*), Ealing Technical College, Kingston Polytechnic, Lanchester Polytechnic (*Business Law*), Leeds Polytechnic, City of Leicester Polytechnic, Liverpool Polytechnic, Manchester Polytechnic, Mid-Essex Technical College and School of Art, Middlesex Polytechnic, Newcastle upon Tyne Polytechnic, Polytechnic of North London, North East London Polytechnic, North Staffordshire Polytechnic, Preston Polytechnic, Polytechnic of the South Bank, Trent Polytechnic and Wolverhampton Polytechnic.

Qualifications for Barrister are obtainable only at one of the Inns of Court or Faculty of Advocates; for Solicitor, from the Law Society or its equivalent in Scotland or Ireland.

THE INNS OF COURT

THE SENATE OF THE INNS OF COURT AND THE BAR

11 South Square, Gray's Inn, W.C.1.

The governing body of the Barristers' branch of the legal profession, established in 1974 assuming the functions of the former Senate of the Four Inns of Court and the former General Council of the Bar.

President, The Hon. Mr Justice Templeman M.B.E.
Chairman, The Rt. Hon. Sir Peter Rawlinson, Q.C., M.P.
Vice-Chairman, P. E. Webster, Q.C.
Treasurer, H. H. Monroe, Q.C.
Secretary, Sir Arthur Power, K.C.B. M.B.E.

THE INNER TEMPLE, E.C.4
Treasurer (1975) The Viscount Dilhorne, P.C.
Sub-Treasurer, Cdr. R. S. Flynn, R.N.
Deputy Sub-Treasurer, Miss J. Morris.

THE MIDDLE TEMPLE, E.C.4
Treasurer (1975) The Hon. Mr. Justice Cumming-Bruce
Under-Treasurer, Capt. J. B. Morison, R.N. (*ret.*).
Asst. Under-Treasurer, H. W. Challoner.

LINCOLN'S INN, W.C.2
Treasurer (1975) His Hon. Judge Gillis, Q.C.
Master of the Library, The Lord Hailsham of St. Marleybone, P.C.
Under-Treasurer and Steward, Col. E. R. Bridges, O.B.E., R.M.
Deputy do., F. C. Coales.

GRAY'S INN, W.C.1
Treasurer (till Dec. 31, 1975) Prof. C. J. Hamson, Q.C.
Master of Library, Rt. Hon. Sir Frederic Sellers, M.C.
Under-Treasurer, Oswald Terry.
Deputy do., C. R. G. Hughes.

COUNCIL OF LEGAL EDUCATION

(4 Gray's Inn Place, W.C.1.)

Established by the four Inns of Court to superintend the Education and Examination of Students for the English Bar.

Chairman, Rt. Hon. Lord Justice Scarman.
Vice-Chairmen, R. L. A. Goff, Q.C.; His Hon. Judge Monier-Williams.
Chairman, Board of Studies, R. L. A. Goff, Q.C.
Chairman of the Finance Committee, His Hon. Judge Monier-Williams
Inns of Court School of Law, Dean of Faculty, C. A. Morrison.
Sub-Dean, E. Tenenbaum.

FACULTY OF ADVOCATES

(Advocates' Library, Edinburgh)

Application for admission as an Advocate of the Scottish Bar is made by Petition to the Court of Session. The candidate is remitted for examination to the Faculty of Advocates. Enquiries should be addressed to The Clerk of Faculty.

Dean of Faculty, D. M. Ross, Q.C.
Vice-Dean, J. P. H. Mackay, Q.C.
Treasurer, D. A. O. Edward, Q.C.
Clerk of Faculty, J. M. Pinkerton.
Keeper of the Library, C. K. Davidson, Q.C.
Agent, P. J. Oliphant.

NORTHERN IRELAND

Admission to the Bar of Northern Ireland is controlled by the Honourable Society of the Inn of Court of Northern Ireland (established Jan. 11, 1926), Royal Courts of Justice, Belfast.

Treasurer, Rt. Hon. Sir Robert Lowry, Lord Chief Justice.
Under-Treasurer and Librarian, J. A. L. McLean, Q.C.

THE LAW SOCIETY

(113 Chancery Lane, W.C.2)

The Society controls the education and examination of articled clerks, and the admission of solicitors in England and Wales. Number of members, 25,000.

President of the Society (1975–76), E. N. Liggins.
Vice-President (1975–76), D. Napley.
Secretary-General, J. L. Bowron.
Secretaries, J. F. Warren (*Education and Training*); P. A. Leach (*Future of the Profession*); J. R. Bonham (*Non-Contentious Business*); A. F. Seton Pollock (*Legal Aid*); P. G. W. Simes (*Professional Purposes*); G. P. Sanctuary (*Professional and Public Relations*); J. A. Nicholson (*Finance and Administration*); M. T. Sennett (*Contentious Business*).

THE COLLEGE OF LAW (incorporating The Law Society's School of Law), Braboeuf Manor, St. Catherine's, Guildford, Surrey (and at 33–35 Lancaster Gate, W.2, 27 Chancery Lane, W.C.2, and Christleton Hall, Chester), provides courses for The Law Society, Bar and London, ll.b. examinations.

LAW SOCIETY OF SCOTLAND

Law Society's Hall, 26–27 Drumsheugh Gardens, Edinburgh

The Society comprises all practising solicitors in Scotland. It controls the examination of legal apprentices and the admission of solicitors in Scotland and acts as registrar of solicitors under the Solicitors (Scotland) Acts, 1933 to 1965.

The Law Society of Scotland administers the Legal Aid and Advice Scheme set up under the Legal Aid and Advice (Scotland) Acts, 1967 and 1972.

LIBRARIANSHIP AND ARCHIVE ADMINISTRATION

Degrees are granted by the University of Belfast (*Library and Information Studies*), Loughborough University of Technology (*Library Studies* and *Information Science*), and the University of Wales (Aberystwyth) (*Librarianship*) (jointly with the College of Librarianship, Wales), and by the University of Strathclyde (*Librarianship* with another subject).

Courses leading to degrees in *Librarianship* granted by the Council for National Academic Awards are provided by Birmingham Polytechnic, Leeds Polytechnic, Liverpool Polytechnic, Manchester Polytechnic (*Library Studies*). The Polytechnic of North London, Newcastle upon Tyne Polytechnic and Robert Gordon's Institute of Technology; in *Librarianship with Modern Languages* by Brighton Polytechnic; and in *Information Science* by Leeds Polytechnic.

The Library Association, 7 Ridgmount Street, W.C.1, maintains the professional register of Chartered Librarians (Fellows and Associates), for which examinations are held twice yearly.

Schools of Librarianship conducting full-time courses of instruction in preparation for the examinations of the Library Association: Robert Gordon's Institute of Technology, Aberdeen; College of Librarianship, Wales, Llanbadarn, Aberystwyth; Birmingham Polytechnic, Birmingham 4; Brighton Polytechnic, Brighton 7; Ealing Technical College, W.5; Leeds Polytechnic; Polytechnic of North London, N.W.5; Loughborough Technical College, Leics.; Manchester Polytechnic; The Polytechnic, Education Precinct, St. Mary's Place, Newcastle upon Tyne.

MATHEMATICS

Degrees in *Mathematics* and/or *Applied Mathematics* are granted by all universities. Courses leading to external degrees in *Mathematics* of the University of London are provided by Derby College of Art and Technology.

Courses leading to degrees in *Mathematics* granted by the Council for National Academic Awards are provided by Brighton Polytechnic, Bristol Polytechnic, Glamorgan Polytechnic (also *Mathematics and Computer Science*), Hatfield Polytechnic, Kingston Polytechnic, Lanchester Polytechnic, City of Leicester Polytechnic, Manchester Polytechnic, Middlesex Polytechnic (*Mathematics for Business*), Newcastle upon Tyne Polytechnic, North East London Polytechnic, Polytechnic of North London (*Mathematics and Computing*), North Staffordshire Polytechnic (also *Mathematical Analysis for Business*), Oxford Polytechnic (*Mathematics and Computer Science/Computing*), Portsmouth Polytechnic, Polytechnic of the South Bank (*Mathematics and Computing*), Robert Gordon's Institute of Technology, Southampton College of Technology, Teesside Polytechnic, Thames Polytechnic and Wolverhampton Polytechnic.

MEDICINE

Degrees in *Medicine* and *Surgery* are granted by the Universities of Aberdeen, Belfast, Birmingham, Bristol, Cambridge, Dundee, Edinburgh, Glasgow, Leeds, Leicester, Liverpool, London (*see* Teaching Hospitals, *below*), Manchester, Newcastle upon Tyne, Nottingham, Oxford, Sheffield, Southampton, Wales (University College, Cardiff, and Welsh National School of Medicine).

MEDICAL SCHOOLS OF TEACHING HOSPITALS IN LONDON

Under the National Health Service (Designation of Teaching Hospitals) Order, 1957, and subsequent amendments, the following were designated Teaching Hospitals for the *University of London*.

CHARING CROSS HOSPITAL, Fulham Palace Road, W.6.

GUY'S HOSPITAL, St. Thomas Street, S.E.1.— Medical School, *Dean* J. C. Houston, M.D., F.R.C.P.; *Dean of Dental Studies*, Prof. R. D. Emslie. *Secretary*, D. G. Bompas, C.M.G.

KING'S COLLEGE HOSPITAL, Denmark Hill, S.E.5.

THE LONDON HOSPITAL, Whitechapel, E.1.— Medical College and Dental School, Turner Street, E.1. *Dean* J. R. Ellis, M.B.E., M.A., M.D., F.R.C.P. *Dean of Dental Studies*, Prof. G. R. Seward. *Secretary*, H. P. Laird.

THE MIDDLESEX HOSPITAL, Mortimer Street, W.1.—Medical School. *Dean*, D. Ranger, F.R.C.S. *Secretary*, G. Clark.

ROYAL DENTAL HOSPITAL OF LONDON, Leicester Square, W.C.2.—School of Dental Surgery: *Dean*, Prof. G. L. Howe, T.D. *Secretary*, E. G. Smith.

ROYAL FREE HOSPITAL, Pond Street, Hampstead, N.W.3.—School of Medicine, Hunter Street, W.C.1. *Dean*, B. B. MacGillivray. *Secretary*, Mrs. S. C. S. Robinson.

ST. BARTHOLOMEW'S HOSPITAL, West Smithfield, E.C.1. Medical College. *Dean*, Prof. R. A. Shooter. *Secretary*, C. E. Morris.

ST. GEORGE'S HOSPITAL, Hyde Park Corner, S.W.1. Medical School. *Dean*, R. D. Lowe, PH.D. *Secretary*, E. Fairhurst.

ST. MARY'S HOSPITAL, Norfolk Place, W.2. Medical School. *Dean*, C. H. Edwards, F.R.C.P. *Secretary*, J. E. Stevenson.

ST. THOMAS' HOSPITAL, S.E.1.—Medical School. Albert Embankment, S.E.1. *Dean*, Dr. W. D. Wylie. *Secretary*, V. H. Warren.

UNIVERSITY COLLEGE HOSPITAL, Gower Street, W.C.1.—Medical School. University Street, W.C.1. *Dean*, T. A. J. Prankerd, M.D., F.R.C.P.; *Secretary*, D. H. Lloyd Morgan.

WESTMINSTER HOSPITAL, Dean Ryle Street, S.W.1. Medical School, *Dean*, Dr. J. B. Wyman, M.B.E. *Secretary*, Capt. A. D. Robin, D.S.C., R.N. (*ret*.).

POSTGRADUATE MEDICAL SCHOOLS OF THE UNIVERSITY OF LONDON

London School of Hygiene and Tropical Medicine, Keppel Street, W.C.1. C.E. Gordon Smith, C.B., *Dean*.

ROYAL POSTGRADUATE MEDICAL SCHOOL, Du Cane Road, Shepherd's Bush, W.12. M. Godfrey, M.B., F.R.C.P., *Dean*.

British Postgraduate Medical Federation (University of London), 33 Millman Street, W.C.1. G.A. Smart, B.SC., M.D., F.R.C.P., *Director*. Comprises:—

INSTITUTE OF BASIC MEDICAL SCIENCES, Royal College of Surgeons, Lincoln's Inn Fields, W.C.2. H. Hanley, M.D., F.R.C.S., *Dean*.

INSTITUTE OF CANCER RESEARCH, Fulham Road, S.W.3. Prof. T. Symington, M.D. *Director*.

CARDIO-THORACIC INSTITUTE, Fulham Road, S.W.3.

INSTITUTE OF CHILD HEALTH, 30 Guildford Street, W.C.1. Prof. J. A. Dudgeon, M.C., T.D., M.A., M.D., F.R.C.Path., *Dean*.

INSTITUTE OF DENTAL SURGERY, Eastman Dental Hospital, Gray's Inn Road, W.C.1. Prof. I. R. H. Kramer, M.D.S., F.D.S.F.F.D, F.R.C.Path., *Dean*.

INSTITUTE OF DERMATOLOGY, St. John's Hospital for Diseases of the Skin, Lisle Street, W.C.2. R. H. Meara, M.A., M.B., B.Chir., F.R.C.P.

INSTITUTE OF LARYNGOLOGY AND OTOLOGY, Royal National Throat, Nose and Ear Hospital, 330–336 Gray's Inn Road, W.C.1. R. F. McNab Jones, M.B., B.S., F.R.C.S., *Dean*.

INSTITUTE OF NEUROLOGY, National Hospital, Queen Square, W.C.1. P. C. Gautier-Smith, M.D., F.R.C.P., *Dean*.

INSTITUTE OF OBSTETRICS AND GYNÆCOLOGY, Chelsea Hospital for Women, Dovehouse Street, S.W.3. R. B. K. Rickford, M.D., F.R.C.S., F.R.C.O.G., *Dean*.

INSTITUTE OF OPHTHALMOLOGY, Judd Street, W.C.1. J. Gloster, M.D. PH.D, *Dean*.

INSTITUTE OF ORTHOPÆDICS, Royal National Orthopædic Hospital, 234 Great Portland Street, W.1. P. D. Byers, B.SC., PH.D, M.D., M.R.C.Path., *Dean*

INSTITUTE OF PSYCHIATRY, De Crespigny Park, Denmark Hill, S.E.5. J. L. T. Birley, B.A., B.M., M.R.C.P., M.R.C.Psych. *Dean*.

INSTITUTE OF UROLOGY, 172 Shaftesbury Avenue, W.C.2. D. Innes Williams, M.D., M.Chir., F.R.C.S., *Dean*.

ROYAL ARMY MEDICAL COLLEGE, Millbank, S.W.1. —*Commandant and Postgraduate Dean*, Maj.-Gen. H. S. Gavourin, M.B.E.

LIVERPOOL SCHOOL OF TROPICAL MEDICINE, Pembroke Place, Liverpool 3.—*Dean*, Prof. W. Peters.

Licensing Corporations granting Diplomas

THE ROYAL COLLEGE OF PHYSICIANS OF LONDON AND THE ROYAL COLLEGE OF SURGEONS OF ENGLAND, Examining Board in England, Examination Hall, Queen Square, W.C.1.

THE SOCIETY OF APOTHECARIES, Black Friars Lane, E.C.4.

ROYAL COLLEGE OF OBSTETRICIANS AND GYNÆCOLOGISTS, 27 Sussex Place, Regent's Park, N.W.1.

THE ROYAL COLLEGE OF PHYSICIANS AND THE ROYAL COLLEGE OF SURGEONS, Edinburgh.

THE ROYAL COLLEGE OF PHYSICIANS AND SURGEONS OF GLASGOW, 242 St. Vincent Street, Glasgow.

THE SCOTTISH TRIPLE QUALIFICATION BOARD, 18 Nicolson Street, Edinburgh and 242 St. Vincent Street, Glasgow.

PROFESSIONS SUPPLEMENTARY TO MEDICINE

The standard of professional education in chiropody, dietetics, medical laboratory technology, occupational therapy, orthoptics, physiotherapy, radiography and remedial gymnastics is the responsibility of eight professional boards, which also publish an annual register of qualified practitioners. The work of the Boards is co-ordinated and supervised by The Council for Professions Supplementary to Medicine (York House, Wesminster Bridge Road, S.E.1).

CHIROPODY

Professional qualifications are granted by the Society of Chiropodists, 8 Wimpole Street, W.1, to students who have passed the qualifying examinations after attending a course of fulltime training for three years at one of the eight recognized schools in England and Wales and two in Scotland. Qualifications granted by the Society are approved by the Chiropodists Board for the purpose of State Registration, which is a condition of employment within the National Health Service.

DIETETICS

(*See* main heading, p. 519)

MEDICAL LABORATORY TECHNOLOGY

Courses at higher and further education establishments and training in medical laboratories are approved for progress to the professional examinations and qualifications of the Institute of Medical Laboratory Technology, 12 Queen Anne Street, W.1.

OCCUPATIONAL THERAPY

Professional qualifications are awarded after examination by the British Association of Occupational Therapists, 20 Rede Place, Bayswater, W.2. which recognizes 14 training schools in England, Wales, Scotland, N. Ireland and Eire.

ORTHOPTICS

Orthoptists undertake the diagnosis and treatment of all types of squint and other anomalies of binocular vision, under the direction of an ophthalmic surgeon or a recognized ophthalmic medical practitioner. The training and maintenance of professional standards are the responsibility of the Orthoptists Board of the Council for the Professions Supplementary to Medicine. The examining and qualifying body is the British Orthoptic Council. Training consists of a three-year course at one of 10 approved Orthoptic Schools in England and Wales and 1 in Scotland.

The Professional Association is the British Orthoptic Society. The registered office of the Council and Society is at the Manchester Royal Eye Hospital, Oxford Road, Manchester.

(*See also* under Optics.)

PHYSIOTHERAPY

Examinations leading to qualification are conducted by the Chartered Society of Physiotherapy, 14 Bedford Row, W.C.1. Full-time 3-yr. courses are available at 39 recognized schools in Great Britain.

RADIOGRAPHY AND RADIOTHERAPY

Examinations leading to qualification are conducted by The Society of Radiographers, 14 Upper Wimpole Street, W.1.

There are recognized training centres in radiography and radiotherapy at many cities and towns in England and Wales, Scotland and Northern Ireland.

In London courses are available at the London Teaching Hospitals listed on p. 524; and at Hammersmith, Lambeth and Royal Northern Hospitals, at Bromley, Oldchurch County Hospital, Romford, Essex and Woolwich.

REMEDIAL GYMNASTICS

Examinations leading to qualification are conducted by the Society of Remedial Gymnasts, c/o Northampton Town F.C., County Ground, Abington, Northampton. The recognized training centres are the School of Remedial Gymnastics and Recreational Therapy, Pinderfields Hospital, Wakefield, Yorks and the Welsh School of Remedial Gymnastics and Recreational Therapy, University Hospital of Wales, Heath Park, Cardiff.

METALLURGY

Degrees in *Metallurgy* and/or *Metallurgical Engineering* are granted by the following universities: Aston in Birmingham, Birmingham, Brunel, Cambridge, Leeds, Liverpool, London (Imperial College of Science and Technology), Loughborough, Manchester, *also* Manchester Institute of Science and Technology, Newcastle upon Tyne, Nottingham, Oxford, Salford, Sheffield, Strathclyde, Surrey, Wales (University Colleges at Cardiff and Swansea).

Courses leading to degrees in *Metallurgy/Metallurgy and Materials* granted by the Council for National Academic Awards are provided by the City of London Polytechnic, and Sheffield Polytechnic.

THE INSTITUTION OF METALLURGISTS, Northway House, High Road, Whetstone, N.20, is a qualifying body.

METEOROLOGY

Degrees in Meteorology are granted by the University of Reading.

MINING AND MINING ENGINEERING

Degrees in *Mining* or *Mining Engineering* are granted by the following universities: Birmingham (*Minerals Engineering*), Leeds, London (Imperial College of Science and Technology), Newcastle upon Tyne, Nottingham, Strathclyde, Wales (University College, Cardiff: *Mineral Exploitation*).

Courses leading to degrees in *Mining Engineering* granted by the Council for National Academic Awards are provided by North Staffordshire Polytechnic and Camborne School of Mines. Courses of study in preparation for certificates of competence in Mining and Mining Engineering awarded by the Board for Mining Examinations and the Institution of Mining Engineers are available at these universities together with most Technical Colleges in mining districts.

Miscellaneous Authorities

MINING QUALIFICATIONS BOARD, Health and Safety Executive, Thames House South, Millbank, S.W.1.

THE INSTITUTION OF MINING ENGINEERS, Hobart House, Grosvenor Place, S.W.1.

COUNCIL OF ENGINEERING INSTITUTIONS, 2 Little Smith Street, S.W.1.

MUSIC

Degrees in Music are granted by the Universities of Aberdeen, Belfast, Birmingham, Bristol, Cambridge, City, Durham, East Anglia, Edinburgh, Exeter, Glasgow, Hull, Lancaster, Leeds, Liverpool, London (King's College, Royal Holloway College; *also* Goldsmiths' College, Royal Academy of Music, Royal College of Music, and Trinity College of Music), Manchester, Newcastle upon Tyne, Nottingham, Oxford, Reading, Sheffield, Southampton, Surrey, Sussex, Wales University Colleges at Aberystwyth, Bangor and Cardiff), and York. Courses leading to degrees in Music granted by the Council for National Academic Awards are provided by Dartington College of Arts, Huddersfield Polytechnic and North East Essex Technical College.

ASSOCIATED BOARD OF THE ROYAL SCHOOLS OF MUSIC, 14 Bedford Square, W.C.1.
Conducts the local examinations in music and speech for the four Royal Schools of Music—the Royal Academy of Music and the Royal College of Music in London, the Royal Northern College of Music, Manchester and the Royal Scottish Academy of Music and Drama, Glasgow.
Secretary, P. Cranmer, M.A. B.Mus., F.R.C.O., F.R.N.C.M.

ROYAL ACADEMY OF MUSIC (1822)
Marylebone Road, N.W.1
A complete training is offered to students of both sexes intending to take up music as a profession. There is a wide range of concert and opera opportunities for performers. The G.R.S.M. Diploma confers graduate status. The L.R.A.M. Diploma is open to external candidates.
Principal, Sir Anthony Lewis, C.B.E., M.A., MUS.B., F.R.C.M.
Administrator, G. J. C. Hambling, D.S.C.
Warden, N. Cox, B.Mus., F.R.A.M.

ROYAL COLLEGE OF MUSIC (1883)
Prince Consort Road, South Kensington, S.W.7
A.R.C.M., and G.R.S.M. awarded by examination. No. of Students 700.
Director, David Willcocks, C.B.E., M.C., F.R.C.M.
Registrar, M. G. Matthews, F.R.C.M., L.R.A.M., A.R.C.O.
Bursar, Maj. D. A. Imlay.

GUILDHALL SCHOOL OF MUSIC AND DRAMA (1880)
John Carpenter Street, E.C.4
Full-time and part-time courses in Music, Speech and Drama. Awards Diplomas of Graduate (G.G.S.M.), Associate (A.G.S.M.) and Licentiate (L.G.S.M.). The Diploma of Graduateship (G.G.S.M.) confers graduate addition to salary.
Principal, A. Percival, C.B.E., Mus.B.
Director of Drama, P. A. Bucknell.
Director of Music, L. East, M.Mus.
Gen. Administrator, J. Isard.

TRINITY COLLEGE OF MUSIC (1872)
Mandeville Place, W.1
Complete training in music for teachers and performers. Courses lead to the university degree of B.Mus., the Graduate Diploma in Music (approved for Graduate equivalent status), the Teacher's Diploma in Music and the Performer's Diploma in Music.
Principal, M. Foggin, C.B.E., F.R.A.M.
Dir. of Studies, C. Cork, B.Mus.
Dir. of Examinations, E. Heberden, M.A.

LONDON COLLEGE OF MUSIC
Great Marlborough Street, W.1
Comprehensive full-time musical training for performers and teachers. Graduate and School Music Courses recognised by the Dept. of Education and Science and Burnham Committee.
Director, W. S. Lloyd-Webber, D.Mus., F.R.C.M., F.R.C.O.
Secretary, K. R. Beard.

ROYAL COLLEGE OF ORGANISTS (1864)
Kensington Gore, S.W.7
For the promotion of the highest standard in organ playing and choir-training. Awards Diplomas of Associateship (A.R.C.O.) and Fellowship (F.R.C.O.); and choir-training (CHM).
Hon. Sec., Sir John Dykes Bower, C.V.O., M.A., D.MUS.

BIRMINGHAM SCHOOL OF MUSIC
Paradise Circus, Birmingham 3
Head, L. Carus, L.R.A.M.

TONIC SOLFA ASSOCIATION
108 High Street, Battersea, S.W.11
International examining body maintaining the Tonic Solfa College (1863) and the Curwen Institute (1975)

ROYAL SCHOOL OF CHURCH MUSIC
Addington Palace, Croydon, Surrey
Founded (1927) for the advancement of good music in the Church
Director, L. Dakers, B.Mus., F.R.A.M.
Secretary, V. E. Waterhouse.

ROYAL NORTHERN COLLEGE OF MUSIC
124 Oxford Road, Manchester
Principal, J. Manduell, F.R.A.M.

ROYAL MILITARY SCHOOL OF MUSIC
Kneller Hall, Twickenham (42)
Commandant, Col. R. G. Style.
Director of Music and Chief Instructor, Lt.-Col. T. Le M. Sharpe, M.B.E.

ROYAL MARINES SCHOOL OF MUSIC
Deal, Kent
Commandant, Col. J. D. Shallow, M.C. (1976).
Principal Director of Music, Royal Marines, Lt.-Col. P. J. Neville, M.V.O., F.R.A.M., R.M. (Eleven Bands in Commission in 1974).

ROYAL SCOTTISH ACADEMY OF MUSIC AND DRAMA
St. George's Place, Glasgow, 2 (900)
Curriculum provides for all branches of study necessary for entry into the professions of music and drama. Special Diploma Courses for those who wish to teach music and drama in schools.
Principal, K. Barritt, D.MUS., F.R.A.M., F.R.C.O.

NAUTICAL STUDIES

The University of Wales grants a degree in *Maritime Technology*, *Maritime Commerce*, *Maritime Geography* (courses at Institute of Science and Technology) and the University of Southampton grants a degree in *Nautical Studies*. Courses leading to degrees in *Nautical Studies* granted by the Council for National Academic Awards are provided by Liverpool Polytechnic, Plymouth Polytechnic (also *Fishery Science*) and Sunderland Polytechnic; and in *Maritime Studies* by City of London Polytechnic.

Merchant Navy Training Schools

For Officers
MERCHANT NAVY COLLEGE, Greenhithe, Kent.—*Principal*, Capt. E. K. Ballard.

SOUTHAMPTON SCHOOL OF NAVIGATION, WARSASH, SOUTHAMPTON
Director, Capt. C. R. Phelan.
For Seamen
INDEFATIGABLE AND NATIONAL SEA TRAINING SCHOOL FOR BOYS (Direct Grant Nautical School (Residential)), Plas Llanfair, Llanfairpwll, Anglesey (140); Capt. W. Wade; *Sec.*, R. N. Hatfield, Room 22, Oriel Chambers, 14 Water Street, Liverpool, 2.
NATIONAL SEA TRAINING SCHOOL, Denton, Gravesend, Kent. *Princ.*, Capt. P. H. Adlam; *Secretary*, M. H. S. Salter, 146–150 Minories, E.C.3.

NURSING

Courses leading to *degrees* are provided by the following universities: Brunel (B. Tech. Sociology and Psychology, Mental Nursing option), Edinburgh (B.Sc. (Social Science) with Nursing, Liverpool (B.Sc., S.R.N.—Life Sciences with Nursing), London (Nursing/B.Sc. Social Science and Administration—Bedford College/Middlesex Hospital), Manchester (B.Nurs.), Southampton (B.Sc. Sociology and Social Administration, Health Visiting option), Surrey, B.Sc. Human Biology with Nursing option), Ulster, Wales (Welsh National School of Medicine) (B.N.)
Courses leading to degrees in *Nursing* granted by the Council for National Academic Awards are provided by Dundee Institute of Art and Technology, Leeds Polytechnic, Newcastle upon Tyne Polytechnic and Polytechnic of the South Bank.
Three-year courses for State Registration in general, sick children's mental and mental deficiency nursing. Two-year course for State enrolment. Training schools in many parts of Great Britain.

THE ROYAL COLLEGE OF NURSING
THE UNITED KINGDOM
Henrietta Place, W.1
The Royal College of Nursing provides education at post-registration level in hospital, occupational health and community health fields. Advanced courses are held in preparation for senior posts in administration and teaching and also preparatory courses.
Director of Education, Miss J. B. Rule.

CENTRAL MIDWIVES BOARD
39 Harrington Gardens, S.W.7
Chairman, Miss M. I. Farrer, O.B.E.
Secretary, R. J. Fenney, C.B.E., B.A. (Admin.).

CENTRAL MIDWIVES BOARD
for Scotland
24 Dublin Street, Edinburgh 1
Chairman, G. D. Matthew, M.D., F.R.C.O.G., F.R.C.S.E.
Secretary, Miss D. S. Young, M.A.

OPTICS

Degrees in *Ophthalmic Optics* are granted by the following Universities: Aston in Birmingham, Bradford, City (also *Visual Science*), Manchester (Manchester Institute of Science and Technology), and Wales (Institute of Science and Technology). Courses leading to degrees in *Ophthalmic Optics* granted by the Council for National Academic Awards are provided by the Glasgow College of Technology.
Examining bodies granting qualifications as an ophthalmic or dispensing optician:—
THE BRITISH OPTICAL ASSOCIATION, 65 Brook Street, W.1.
THE WORSHIPFUL COMPANY OF SPECTACLE MAKERS, Apothecaries Hall, Black Friars Lane, E.C.4.

THE ASSOCIATION OF DISPENSING OPTICIANS, 22 Nottingham Place, W.1 (training institution; qualification as dispensing optician).
THE SCOTTISH ASSOCIATION OF OPTICIANS, 116 Blythswood Street, Glasgow, C.2 (qualification as ophthalmic optician).

OSTEOPATHY

LONDON COLLEGE OF OSTEOPATHY, 24–25 Dorset Square, N.W.1.

PATENT AGENCY

The Register of Patent Agents is kept, under the authority of the Department of Trade by the Chartered institute of Patent Agents. Qualification is by examination; Intermediate and Final Examinations are held each year. Details can be obtained from the Institute.
CHARTERED INSTITUTE OF PATENT AGENTS, Staple Inn Buildings, W.C.1.—*Sec. and Registrar*, P. E. Lincroft, M.B.E.

PHARMACY

Degrees in Pharmacy are granted by the Universities of Aston in Birmingham, Bath, Belfast, Bradford, Heriot-Watt, London (Chelsea College and the School of Pharmacy), Manchester, Nottingham, Strathclyde, Wales (Institute of Science and Technology).
Courses leading to degrees in Pharmacy granted by the Council for National Academic Awards are provided by Brighton Polytechnic, City of Leicester Polytechnic, Liverpool Polytechnic, Portsmouth Polytechnic, Robert Gordon's Institute of Technology, and Sunderland Polytechnic.
Further information may be obtained from The Registrar, The Pharmaceutical Society of Great Britain, 17 Bloomsbury Square, W.C.1.

PHOTOGRAPHY

Courses leading to *Degrees* in *Photographic Arts* and in *Photographic Sciences* granted by the Council for National Academic Awards are provided by the Polytechnic of Central London.
INSTITUTE OF INCORPORATED PHOTOGRAPHERS (1901) (*formerly* BRITISH PHOTOGRAPHERS), Amwell End, Ware, Herts.—*Gen. Sec.*, E. I. N. Waughray.
Professional qualifying examinations in Commercial and Industrial, Scientific and Technical, Medical, Portrait, Illustrative, Advertising and Editorial Photography, for Associateships; general vocational examinations in photography leading to Licentiateships. Fellowships awarded for distinguished ability and experience in one or more branches of photography or photographic technology.

PHYSICAL EDUCATION

At the University of Birmingham *Physical Education* can be taken for a degree in combination with another subject. Loughborough University of Technology awards a degree for which courses are provided at Loughborough College of Education.
Physical Education also forms part of the course at many colleges leading to a B.Ed. granted by the Council for National Academic Awards.

Training Colleges
M.=For Men; *W.*=For Women
BEDFORD (College of Physical Education, Lansdowne Road, Bedford). *W.* (430).—*Principal*, Mrs. P. A. Bowen-West.
BIRMINGHAM UNIVERSITY. *M. & W.* (110).—*Director*, W. J. Slater.
CANTERBURY (Nonington College of Physical Education, Dover). *M. & W.* (450).—*Principal*, S. Beaumont.

CHESTER (Chester College) *see* p. 529.

DARTFORD, Kent (Dartford College of Education), *see* p. 529.

EASTBOURNE (Chelsea College of Physical Education, Denton Road). *W.* (520).—*Principal*, Miss A. J. Bambra.

EDINBURGH (Dunfermline College of Physical Education, Cramond). *W.* (600). *Principal*, Miss M. P. Abbott.

EXETER (St. Luke's College). *See* p. 529.

LIVERPOOL (I. M. Marsh College of Physical Education, Barkhill Road, Liverpool, 17), Liverpool Education Committee. *W.* (470).—*Principal*, Miss M. I. Jamieson.

LONDON (I.L.E.A. Coll. of Physical Education, 16 Paddington Street, W.1). Courses for serving teachers only. *M.* & *W.*—*Principal* Miss J. McLaren.

LOUGHBOROUGH, Leics. (Loughborough T.C.). *See* p. 530.

MADELEY, Staffs. (Madeley College), *see* p. 530.

SUTTON COLDFIELD, Warwickshire (Anstey Dept. of Physical Education, Chester Road). (City of Birmingham Polytechnic). *W.* (150).

WENTWORTH WOODHOUSE, Yorks. (Lady Mabel College of Education), *see* p. 532.

YORK (St. John's College). *M.* & *W.*—*see* p. 531.

PRINTING

Degrees in *Typography and Graphic Communication* are awarded by the University of Reading.

Courses leading to *Degrees* in *Printing Technology* granted by the Council for National Academic Awards are provided by Watford College of Technology.

Courses in technical and general, design and administrative aspects of printing are available at technical colleges throughout the United Kingdom. Details can be obtained from the Institute of Printing and the British Federation of Master Printers (*see below*).

In addition to the examining and organizing bodies listed below, examinations are held by various independent regional examining boards in further education.

INSTITUTE OF PRINTING (1961), 10–11 Bedford Row, W.C.1.

JOINT COMMITTEE (AND SCOTTISH JOINT COMMITTEE) FOR NATIONAL CERTIFICATES IN PRINTING.

BRITISH PRINTING INDUSTRIES FEDERATION, 11 Bedford Row, W.C.1.

PSYCHIATRIC SOCIAL WORK

The main patterns of training are: (1) a degree or diploma in social studies (*see below*) followed by some social work experience and a one-year post-credential course at a university in psychiatric social work; or (2) a degree in a subject other than social studies, followed by a postgraduate social studies course and, after some social work experience, by a professional course in psychiatric social work; or (3) a degree in a subject other than social studies followed by an 18-month or two-year postgraduate course combining social studies and social work; or (4) a 4-year degree course in combined studies and social work.

SOCIAL WORK

Degrees in *Social Studies* or in *Social Sciences* are granted by most universities. Courses leading to degrees in *Social Science* or *Social Sciences or Sociology* granted by the Council for National Academic Awards are provided by almost 30 polytechnics and colleges.

The following are among the associations awarding professional qualifications and/or providing training:—

THE BRITISH ASSOCIATION OF SOCIAL WORKERS, 16 Kent Street, Birmingham, 5.

MIND (THE NATIONAL ASSOCIATION FOR MENTAL HEALTH), 22 Harley Street, W.1.—*Dir.*, A. Smythe.

THE INSTITUTE OF HOUSING MANAGERS, Victoria House, Southampton Row, W.C.1.—*Sec.*, H. Key.

JOSEPHINE BUTLER HOUSE, 34 Alexandra Drive, Liverpool, 17.

SPEECH THERAPY
(see also "Languages ")

Degrees in *Speech* are awarded by the University of Newcastle upon Tyne, in *Speech Pathology and Therapy* by the University of Manchester and in *Speech Pathology and Therapeutics* (with courses at Jordanhill College of Education) by the University of Glasgow.

The Directory of qualified Speech Therapists is published by the College of Speech Therapists, 47 St. John's Wood High Street, N.W.8. Courses leading to the Diploma of Licentiateship of The College of Speech Therapists are available at:

THE CENTRAL SCHOOL OF SPEECH AND DRAMA (Department of Speech Therapy), Embassy Theatre, Swiss Cottage, N.W.3.

CITY OF BIRMINGHAM POLYTECHNIC SCHOOL OF SPEECH THERAPY, Perry Bar, Birmingham.

ELIZABETH GASKELL COLLEGE OF EDUCATION, Hathersage Road, Manchester, 13.

LEEDS POLYTECHNIC, School of Speech Therapy, Calverley Street, Leeds 1.

THE EDINBURGH SCHOOL OF SPEECH THERAPY, 7 Buccleuch Place, Edinburgh 8.

ABERDEEN SCHOOL OF SPEECH THERAPY, Robert Gordon's Institute of Technology, St. Andrew's Street, Aberdeen.

CARDIFF SCHOOL OF SPEECH THERAPY, Llandaff College of Technology, Western Avenue, Cardiff.

CITY OF LEICESTER COLLEGE OF EDUCATION, Dept. of Speech Pathology and Therapeutics, Scraptoft, Leicester.

NATIONAL HOSPITALS COLLEGE OF SPEECH-SCIENCES, 59 Portland Place, W.1.

SCHOOL FOR THE STUDY OF DISORDERS OF HUMAN COMMUNICATION, 86 Blackfriars Road, S.E.1.

SPORTS SCIENCE

Courses in Sports Science leading to degrees granted by the Council for National Academic Awards are provided by Liverpool Polytechnic.

SURVEYING, *see* ESTATE MANAGEMENT AND SURVEYING

TEACHING

Degrees in *Education* (B.Ed.) are granted by many universities (to selected students training to become teachers at colleges of education associated with the Universities usually through their Institutes or Schools of Education). Graduates in other subjects may take at many universities a one-year course leading to a postgraduate diploma or certificate in education.

Courses leading to the degree of B.Ed. granted by the Council for National Academic Awards are provided by some 30 colleges of education.

COLLEGES OF EDUCATION

(With number of students and name of Principal, Colleges marked* below offer specialist courses in

Home Economics; for Colleges of Physical Education, *see* p. 527-28.)
M.=For Men; *W.*=For Women; L.E.A.=Local Education Authority; C. of E.=Church of England; R.C.=Roman Catholic.

ABERDEEN (Aberdeen College, Hilton Place). *M. & W.* (1,600).—J. Scotland, C.B.E.

ABINGDON, Oxon. (Culham College). C. of E. *M. & W.* (570).—J. F. Wyatt.

ALNWICK (Alnwick College). L.E.A. *W.* Mature Course (2-yr. and 3-yr.) *M. & W.* (400).—Miss L. K. Hollamby.

AMBLESIDE, Cumbria (Charlotte Mason College). *M. & W.* (325).—S. W. Percival.

AYR (Craigie College of Education). *M. & W.* (900).—P. C. McNaught.

BANGOR, Gwynedd (St. Mary's College, Bangor), Church in Wales. *W.* (300).—F. E. Clegg.

,, *(Normal College, Bangor). L.E.A. North Wales Counties Joint Education Committee *M. & W.* (850).—J. A. Davies.

BARNSLEY, Yorks. (Wentworth Castle College). L.E.A. *M. & W.* (300).—J. G. Minton, Ph.D.

BARRY, S. Wales (Glamorgan Polytechnic). L.E.A. *M. & W.* (600).—C. Roberts.

BATH, Avon (College of Higher Education: Newton Park and Sion Hill). L.E.A. *M. & W.* (1,050).—N. P. Payne.

BEDFORD (Bedford College, Polhill Avenue, Bedford), L.E.A. *M. & W.* (660).—Miss P. B. Dempster.

BINGLEY, YORKS. L.E.A. *M. & W.* (750).—W. R. Stirling.

BIRMINGHAM (Bordesley Dept. (Teacher Training), City of Birmingham Polytechnic). L.E.A. *W.* (Day College) (350).—Mrs. R. M. D. Roe.

,, (City of Birmingham College). L.E.A. *M. & W.* (950).—R. H. Durham.

,, (Newman College, Bartley Green). R.C. *M. & W.* (720).—S. Quinlan.

,, (St. Peter's College, Saltley). C. of E. *M. & W.* (650).—Rev. C. Buckmaster.

,, (Westhill College, Selly Oak). Free Church. *M. & W.* (530).—A. G. Bamford.

BISHOP'S STORTFORD, Herts. (Hockerill College). *M. & W.* (490). C. of E.—Miss J. A. Hall.

BOGNOR REGIS, Sussex (Bognor Regis College, Upper Bognor Road). L.E.A. *M. & W.* (750).—J. P. Parry.

BOLTON (Bolton College of Education (Technical), Chadwick Street). L.E.A. *M. & W.* (550).—*Director*, V. J. Sparrow.

BRADFORD COLLEGE (Margaret McMillan School of Education). L.E.A. *M. & W.* (700).—E. Robinson.

BRENTWOOD, Essex (Brentwood College, Sawyers Hall Lane). L.E.A. *M. & W.* (700).—C. Crane.

BRIGHTON (Brighton College, Falmer). L.E.A. *M. & W.* (1,200).—E. C. Ryman.

BRISTOL (The College of St. Matthias, Fishponds). C. of E. *M. & W.* (801).—R. A. Adcock (from Sept. 1976 part of Bristol Polytechnic Faculty of Education).

,, (Redland College, Redland Hill). L.E.A. *M. & W.* (840).—J. W. P. Taylor.

BROMSGROVE, Worcs. (Shenstone New College, Burcot Lane). L.E.A. *M. & W.* (850).—D. Brailsford.

CAERLEON (Gwent College). L.E.A. *M. & W.* (700).—M. I. Harris.

CAMBRIDGE (Homerton College). *W.* (730).—Miss A. C. Shrubsole.

CANTERBURY (Christ Church College). C. of E. *M. & W.* (650).—Rev. F. Mason.

CARDIFF (City of Cardiff College, Cyncoed). *M. & W.* (950).—L. G. Bewsher.

CARMARTHEN (Trinity College). Church in Wales. *Bilingual. M. & W.* (650).—K. M. J. Jones.

CHALFONT ST. GILES, Bucks. (Newland Park College). L.E.A. *M. & W.* (530).—A. M. D. I. Oakeshott.

CHELTENHAM, Glos. (St. Mary's College). *W.* (600). C. of E.—Miss G. M. Owen, Ph.D.

,, (St. Paul's College). *M.* (580). C. of E.—G. D. Barnes.

CHESTER (Chester College). *M. & W.* (900). C. of E.—M. V. J. Seaborne.

CHICHESTER, Sussex (Bishop Otter College). *M. & W.* (700). C. of E.—G. P. McGregor.

CHORLEY, Lancs. (Chorley College, Union Street). L.E.A. *M. & W.* (1,100).—L. Kenworthy.

CLACTON-ON-SEA, Essex* St. Osyth's College, Marine Parade). L.E.A. *M. & W.* (520).—J. Bucknall, Ph.D.

COVENTRY, Warwicks (Coventry College). L.E.A. *M. & W.* (1,250).—Miss J. D. Browne, C.B.E.

CREWE (Crewe and Alsager College of Education). L.E.A. *M. & W.* (2,400).—Miss B. P. R. Ward.

DARLINGTON (Darlington College). Voluntary. *M. & W.* (435).—J. A. Huitson.

,, (Middleton St. George College). L.E.A. *M. & W.* (680).—E. L. Black.

DARTFORD, Kent (Dartford College of Education) (L.E.A.). *M. & W.* (610).—*Principal*, Mrs. M. J. Chamberlain.

DERBY (Bishop Lonsdale College, Western Road, Mickleover). *M. & W.* (800). C. of E.—N. Evans.

DONCASTER (Doncaster College, High Melton), L.E.A. *M. & W.* (700).—D. C. A. Bradshaw.

,, (Scawsby College), L.E.A. *M. & W.* (360).—J. Straffen.

DUDLEY, West Midlands (Dudley College, Castle View). L.E.A. *M. & W.* (1,000).—D. Broadhurst.

DUNDEE (Dundee College, Gardyne Road). *M. & W.* (1,250).

DURHAM (Neville's Cross College). L.E.A. *M. & W.* (605).—R. Emmett.

,, (St. Hild and St. Bede), *M. & W.* (1,000). C. of E.—J. V. Armitage.

EASTBOURNE, Sussex (Eastbourne College, Darley Road). L.E.A. *M. & W.* (630).—Miss T. S. Hichens.

EDINBURGH (Craiglockhart College). R.C. *M. & W.* (450).—Sister Sheila Hayes.

,, (Moray House College). *M. & W.* (2,900). T. Ruthven.

ENFIELD, Middlesex Polytechnic, Faculty of Education, Trent Park, Cockfosters. L.E.A. *M. & W.* (1,200).—*Dean*, Dr. A. D. Grady.

EXETER (St. Luke's College). *M. & W.* (1,150). C. of E.—J. C. Dancy.

EXMOUTH, Devon (Rolle College). L.E.A. *M. & W.* (860).—F. C. A. Cammaerts.

FALKIRK, Stirlingshire (Callendar Park College). *M. & W.* (550).—C. E. Brown.

GLASGOW (Jordanhill College). *M. & W.* (3,450).—T. R. Bone, Ph.D.

,, (Notre Dame College, Bearsden). R.C. *M. & W.* (1,400).

GLOUCESTER* (Gloucestershire College). L.E.A. *M. & W.* (500).—J. H. Hunter.

HAMILTON (Hamilton College, Bothwell Road). *M. & W.* (900).—G. Paton.

HEREFORD (County College). L.E.A. *M. & W.* (650).—Miss M. E. Hipwell.

HERTFORD (Balls Park College). L.E.A. *M.* & *W.* (640).—P. E. Sangster.

HUDDERSFIELD (Polytechnic, Dept. of Education).

ILKLEY, Yorks.* (Ilkley College). L.E.A. *M.* & *W.* (530).—Miss B. M. Mayer.

KINGSTON ON THAMES, Surrey (Gipsy Hill College, Kenry House, Kingston Hill). L.E.A. *M.* & *W.* (785).—Miss F. D. Batstone.

KINGSTON UPON HULL (Endsleigh College). R.C. *M.* & *W.* (585).—Sister Joan McNamara.

,, (Kingston upon Hull College, Cottingham Road). L.E.A. *M.* & *W.* (900).—Dr. C. Bibby.

LANCASTER (St. Martin's College). C. of E. *M.* & *W.* (750).—H. M. Pollard, ph.D.

LEEDS (City of Leeds and Carnegie College, Beckett Park). L.E.A. *M.* & *W.* (1,400).—L. Connell, ph.D.

,, (James Graham College, Chapel Lane, Farnley). L.E.A. *M.* & *W.* (Day students only) (420).—Miss J. Harland.

,, (Trinity College). R.C. *W.* (720).—Sister Augusta Maria; *and* (All Saints' College). R.C. *M.*—A. M. Kean.

LEICESTER (City of Leicester College, Scraptoft). L.E.A. *M.* & *W.* (1,000).—B. A. Fisher, ph.D.

LINCOLN (Bishop Grosseteste College). *M.* & *W.* (660). C. of E.—L. G. Marsh.

LIVERPOOL (City of Liverpool, C. F. Mott College, Prescot). L.E.A. *M.* & *W.* (1,200).—B. S. Cane.

,, (S. Katharine's College). *M.* & *W.* (800). C. of E.—G. L. Barnard, ph.D.

,, (Notre Dame College, Mount Pleasant). *M.* & *W.* (750). R.C.—Miss K. M. Hughes.

LONDON (Avery Hill College, Eltham, S.E.9). L.E.A. *M.* & *W.* (1,200; Annexe, 300).—Mrs. K. E. Jones.

,, (Battersea College, 58 North Side, Clapham Common, S.W.4) (630).

,, (Borough Road College, Isleworth, Middx.). *M.* & *W.* (900).—K. E. Priestley.

,, *(College of All Saints, N.17). C. of E. *M.* & *W.* (630).—P. G. Hampton.

,, The Polytechnic of North London, Prince of Wales Road, N.W.5. L.E.A. *M.* & *W.* (360). Day College.—S. Jones.

,, (Philippa Fawcett College, Leigham Court Road, S.W.16). L.E.A. *M.* & *W.* (640). —Mrs. R. O. Brown.

,, *(Digby Stuart College, Roehampton, S.W. 15). *M.* & *W.* (840). R.C.—Sister D. Bell.

,, (Froebel Institute College, Grove House, Roehampton Lane, S.W.15). *M.* & *W.* (640).—M. Morgan.

,, (Furzedown College, Welham Road, S.W.17). L.E.A. *M.* & *W.* (760).—Miss M. E. Garvie.

,, (Garnett College (Technical), Downshire House, Roehampton Lane, S.W.15). L.E.A. *M.* & *W.* (1,500).—E. J. Brent, ph.D.

,, (Goldsmiths' College, Dept. of Arts, Science and Educ., New Cross, S.E.14). London Univ. *M.* & *W.* (1,900).—Dr. R. Hoggart.

,, (Maria Assumpta College, 23 Kensington Square, W.8). *M.* & *W.* (350). R.C.—Sister Augustine Mary.

,, (Maria Grey College, 300 St. Margaret's Road, Twickenham). L.E.A. *M.* & *W.* (994).—Mrs. K. M. Saunders.

,, (Rachel McMillan College, Deptford, S.E.8). *M.* & *W.* (600).—Miss E. M. Puddephat.

,, (St. Gabriel's College, Cormont Road, Camberwell, S.E.5). *M.* & *W.* (300). C. of E.—Miss E. Blackburn.

,, (St. Mary's College, Strawberry Hill, Twickenham). *M.* & *W.* (1,200). R.C.—Very Rev. T. P. Cashin.

,, (Shoreditch College, Cooper's Hill, Englefield Green, Surrey). L.E.A. *M.* & *W.* (700). —J. N. Smith.

,, (Sidney Webb School of Educ., Polytechnic of Central London, 9–12 Barrett Street, W.1). L.E.A. *M.* & *W.* (450).—Miss R. Beresford.

,, (Southlands College, 65 Wimbledon Parkside, S.W.19). *M.* & *W.* (795). Methodist.—Miss M. P. Callard.

,, (Stockwell College, Bromley, Kent). L.E.A. *M.* & *W.* (900).—Miss R. F. Carr.

,, (Whitelands College, West Hill, Putney, S.W.15). C. of E. *M.* & *W.* (750).—R. F. Knight.

LOUGHBOROUGH, Leics. (Loughborough College). L.E.A. *M.* & *W.* (1,050).—J. E. Kane, ph.D.

MADELEY, Staffs. *(College, Madeley, nr. Crewe). L.E.A. *M.* & *W.* (1,150).—K. B. Thompson.

MANCHESTER (Manchester College, Long Millgate). L.E.A. *M.* & *W.* (900).—Miss M. A. Mycock.

,, (Didsbury College, Wilmslow Road, Didsbury). *M.* & *W.* (1,450).—F. Gorner.

,, *(Elizabeth Gaskell College). L.E.A. *M.* & *W.* (900).—P. R. Long.

,, (Sedgley Park College, Prestwich). *M.* & *W.* (500). R.C.—Sister Barbara Hughes.

MATLOCK, Derbyshire. L.E.A. *M.* & *W.* (700). —R. Clayton.

MIDDLETON, Manchester (De la Salle College). *M.* (900). R.C.—The Rev. Brother Augustine.

MILTON KEYNES., Bucks. L.E.A. *M.* & *W.* (400).—K. W. S. Garwood, ph.D.

NEWCASTLE UPON TYNE (Newcastle Polytechnic Faculty of Education). L.E.A. *M.* & *W.* (620).—G. Bosworth.

,, *(Northern Counties College, Coach Lane). L.E.A. *M.* & *W.* (960).—P. T. Underdown, ph.D.

,, (St. Mary's College). *M.* & *W.* (800). R.C. —Sister P. M. G. Wilson.

NORTHUMBERLAND (Northumberland College, Ponteland). L.E.A. *M.* & *W.* (960).—Miss E. M. Churchill.

NORWICH (Keswick Hall). *M.* & *W.* (700). C. of E.—W. Etherington.

NOTTINGHAM (Mary Ward College, Keyworth). R.C. *M.* & *W.*—Miss C. M. Wilkinson.

ORMSKIRK, Lancs. (Edge Hill College, St. Helens Road). L.E.A. *M.* & *W.* (1,300).—P. K. C. Millins.

OXFORD (Westminster College, North Hinksey). *M.* & *W.* (650). Methodist.—D. W. Crompton. (*See also* WHEATLEY).

PLYMOUTH, Devon (College of S. Mark and S. John, Derriford Road). C. of E. *M.* & *W.* (700).—J. E. Anderson.

PORTSMOUTH (Faculty of Educ., Portsmouth Polytechnic). *M.* & *W.* (830).—Mrs. D. J. Williams.

POULTON-LE-FYLDE, Nr. Blackpool, Lancs. (Preston Polytechnic, School of Education). L.E.A. *M.* & *W.* (550).—R. H. Eaton.

READING, Berks. (Bulmershe College). L.E.A. *M.* & *W.* (1,250).—J. F. Porter.

RETFORD, Notts. (Eaton Hall College). L.E.A. *M.* & *W.* (600).—E. R. Morgan.

RUGBY, Warwicks. (St. Paul's College, Newbold Revel, Stretton-under-Fosse). *W.* (520). R.C. —Sister Christina.

SALISBURY, Wilts. (College of Sarum St. Michael). C. of E. *W.* (440).—C. J. R. Wilson.

SCARBOROUGH, Yorks. (North Riding College). L.E.A. *M. & W.* (400).—F. W. Wright.

SHEFFIELD (Sheffield City College, Collegiate Crescent). *M. & W.* (1,100).—H. J. Peake, PH.D.
  „ *(Totley-Thornbridge College, Totley). L.E.A. M. & W.* (1,000).—P. G. Spinks.

SOUTHAMPTON (La Sainte Union College, The Avenue). *M. & W.* (736). R.C.—Sister Imelda Marie.

SUNDERLAND (Faculty of Education, Sunderland Polytechnic). L.E.A. *M. & W.* (1,100).—*Dean*, H. Webster.

SWANSEA (Swansea College, Townhill Road, Cockett). L.E.A. *M. & W.* (715).—Miss M. R. Smith.

WAKEFIELD, Yorks. (Bretton Hall College). L.E.A. *M. & W.* (740).—A. S. Davies.

WARRINGTON, Cheshire (Padgate College, Fearnhead). L.E.A. *M. & W.* (800).—J. R. Williams.

WATFORD, Herts. (Wall Hall College, Aldenham). L.E.A. *M. & W.* (700).—Miss A. K. Davies.

WENTWORTH WOODHOUSE, Yorks. (Lady Mabel College of Education). *M. & W.* (425).—J. Foster.

WEST WICKHAM, Kent (Coloma Coll., Wickham Court). *M. & W.* (550). R.C.—Sister Mary More.

WEYMOUTH, Dorset. (Weymouth College, Cranford Avenue; Annexe at Poole). L.E.A. *M. & W.* (1,000).—Miss N. M. O'Sullivan.

WHEATLEY, Oxon. (Lady Spencer-Churchill College). L.E.A. *W.* Graduates (*M. & W.*), (560).—Lady Linstead, D.Phil.

WINCHESTER, Hants. (King Alfred's College). *M. & W.* (1,016). C. of E.—M. Rose.

WOLVERHAMPTON (Day College, Walsall Street). L.E.A. *M. & W.* (400).—Miss J. Garrett.
  „ (Technical Teachers' College, Compton Road West). L.E.A. *M. & W.* (450).—(vacant).

WORCESTER* (Worcester College, Henwick Grove). L.E.A. *M. & W.* (1,250).—E. G. Peirson, C.B.E.

WREXHAM (Cartrefle College). L.E.A. *M. & W.* (750).—H. I. Evans.

YORK (College of Ripon and York St. John). *M. & W.* C. of E. (950 at York; 550 at Ripon)—J. V. Barnett.

For Teachers of the Deaf

DEPARTMENT OF AUDIOLOGY AND EDUCATION OF THE DEAF, Manchester University. *M. & W.* (120).—*Head of Dept.*, Prof. I. G. Taylor, M.D.

COURSE FOR TEACHERS OF THE DEAF, Lady Spencer-Churchill College, Wheatley, Oxon. *M. & W.* —(40). *Princ.*, Lady Linstead, D.Phil.

For Teachers of the Blind

THE COLLEGE OF THE TEACHERS OF THE BLIND *Hon. Registrar*, B. Hechle, Royal School for the Blind, Church Road North, Wavertree, Liverpool 15. Award certificates after examination to blind pianoforte tuners, school teachers and craft instructors of the blind (700).

Courses of training are also available at:
THE NORTH REGIONAL ASSOCIATION FOR THE BLIND. *M. & W.* Headingley Castle, 72 Headingley Lane, Leeds.

TECHNICAL EDUCATION

Degrees in one or more technologies are awarded by almost all universities; and many polytechnics and colleges of technology provide courses leading to degrees granted by the Council for National Academic Awards. Details are given under individual subject headings.

(*See also:* AERONAUTICS; BUILDING; COMPUTER SCIENCE; ENGINEERING; FUEL TECHNOLOGY; MINING; OPTICS; PATENT AGENCY; PRINTING AND TEXTILES.)

CITY AND GUILDS OF LONDON INSTITUTE
76 Portland Place, W.1

Chairman, D. E. Woodbine Parish, C.B.E.
Director General, Sir Cyril English.
Secretary, B. B. Phillips.

Regional Advisory Councils

Set up in 1947 (i) to bring education and industry together to find out the needs of young workers and advise on the provision required, and (ii) to secure reasonable economy of provision. They also have certain responsibilities in connection with the procedure for the approval by the Department of Education and Science of advanced courses, and issue handbooks, etc., giving, for the guidance of students and teachers, information about the facilities available within a region or district for various types of training (*e.g.* electrical engineering, textiles, building and chemistry). There are ten Regional Advisory Councils in England and Wales:—

REGION 1 (LONDON AND HOME COUNTIES).—Regional Advisory Council for Technological Education, Tavistock House South, Tavistock Square, W.C.1.

REGION 2 (SOUTHERN).—Regional Council for Further Education, 9 Bath Road, Reading.

3 (SOUTH-WEST).—Regional Council for Further Education, 37–38 Fore Street, Taunton.

4 (WEST MIDLANDS).—Advisory Council for Further Education, Pitman Buildings, 161 Corporation Street, Birmingham, 4.

5 (EAST MIDLANDS).—Regional Advisory Council for the Organization of Further Education, Robins Wood House, Robins Wood Road, Aspley, Nottingham.

6 (EAST ANGLIAN).—Regional Advisory Council for Further Education, County Hall, Martineau Lane, Norwich.

7 (YORKSHIRE AND HUMBERSIDE).—Council for Further Education, Bowling Green Terrace, Green Terrace, Leeds 11.

8 (NORTH-WESTERN).—Regional Advisory Council for Further Education, 36 Granby Row, Manchester, 1.

9 (NORTHERN).—Advisory Council for Further Education, 5 Grosvenor Villas, Grosvenor Road, Newcastle upon Tyne, 2.

10 (WALES).—Welsh Joint Education Committee, 245 Western Avenue, Cardiff.

For Polytechnics, etc., see p. 511

Scottish Technical Colleges

Technical education is available at approximately 100 day-course schools and colleges in Scotland, including those which specialize in a particular subject. The following are among those recognized by the Scottish Education Department as " central institutions" (colleges for higher technical learning); other Scottish central institutions appear under Agriculture, Art, Domestic Science and Music.

ABERDEEN: ROBERT GORDON'S INSTITUTE OF TECHNOLOGY, Aberdeen.—*Director*, P. Clarke, PH.D.

DUNDEE COLLEGE OF TECHNOLOGY, Bell Street, Dundee.—*Princ.*, H. G. Cuming, PH.D.

GALASHIELS: SCOTTISH COLLEGE OF TEXTILES, Galashiels, Selkirkshire.—*Princ.*, J. G. Martindale, PH.D.

LEITH NAUTICAL COLLEGE, 59 Commercial Street, Leith, Edinburgh.—*Princ.*, E. T. Morgan.

PAISLEY COLLEGE OF TECHNOLOGY, High Street, Paisley.—*Princ.*, T. M. Howie.

Northern Ireland

BELFAST (College of Technology).—*Princ.*, W. F. K. Kerr, PH.D.

LONDONDERRY (Technical and Teacher Training Coll.).—*Princ.*, T. Williams.

Industrial Training Boards

Established under the Industrial Training Act, 1964.

AGRICULTURAL, HORTICULTURAL AND FORESTRY, Bourne House, 32–34 Beckenham Road, Beckenham, Kent.—*Dir.*, R. S. Butler.

CARPET, Evelyn House, 32 Alderley Road, Wilmslow, Cheshire.—*Sec.*, D. Borthwick.

CERAMICS, GLASS AND MINERAL PRODUCTS, Bovis House, Northolt Road, Harrow, Middx.—*Sec.*, H. B. Chubb, O.B.E.

CHEMICAL AND ALLIED PRODUCTS, Staines House, 158–162 High Street, Staines, Middx.—*Sec.*, G. Plant.

CLOTHING AND ALLIED PRODUCTS, Tower House, Merrion Way, Leeds.—*Chief Exec. Officer*, K. F. Swinfen.

CONSTRUCTION, Radnor House, London Road, Norbury, S.W.16.—*Sec.*, G. R. Gardner.

DISTRIBUTIVE INDUSTRY, MacLaren House, Talbot Road, Stretford, Manchester.—*Sec.*, H. A. Whitehead, M.B.E.

ENGINEERING, 54 Clarendon Road, Watford, Herts. *Sec.*, H. M. Lang.

FOOD, DRINK AND TOBACCO, Leon House, High Street, Croydon.—*Sec.*, J. T. Newton.

FOOTWEAR, LEATHER AND FUR SKIN, Maney Building, 29 Birmingham Road, Sutton Coldfield, West Midlands.—*Sec.*, C. J. Bailey.

FOUNDRY INDUSTRY TRAINING COMMITTEE, 50–54 Charlotte Street, W.1.—*Sec.*, L. A. Rice.

FURNITURE AND TIMBER, 31 Octagon Parade, High Wycombe, Bucks.—*Secretaries*, P. J. D. Nesbitt-Hawes (*Training*); H. A. d'Avray (*Administration*).

HOTEL AND CATERING, Ramsey House, Central Square, Wembley, Middx.—*Sec.*, H. A. Lax.

IRON AND STEEL, 4 Little Essex Street, W.C.2. —*Dir.*, R. Duncan.

KNITTING, LACE AND NET, 4 Hamilton Road, Nottingham.—*Sec.*, A B. Ross.

MAN-MADE FIBRES PRODUCING, 3 Pond Place, S.W.3.—*Chief Officer*, E. Lord, O.B.E.

PAPER AND PAPER PRODUCTS, Star House, Potters Bar, Herts.—*Sec.*, O. T. P. Carne, M.B.E.

PETROLEUM, York House, Empire Way, Wembley, Middx.—*Sec.*, J. A. Bey.

PRINTING AND PUBLISHING, Merit House, Edgware Road, Colindale, N.W.9.—*Sec.*, G. F. Reid.

ROAD TRANSPORT, Capitol House, Empire Way, Wembley, Middx.—*Dir. Gen.*, T. E. Tindall.

RUBBER AND PLASTICS PROCESSING, Brent House, 950 Great West Road, Brentford, Middx.—*Sec.* S. K. Hardy.

SHIPBUILDING, Raeburn House, Northolt Road, South Harrow, Middx.—*Sec.*, D. O. Savill.

WOOL, JUTE and FLAX, Butterfield House, Otley Road, Baildon, Shipley, W. Yorks.—*Sec.*, F. Bingham.

LOCAL GOVERNMENT TRAINING BOARD, 8 The Arndale Centre, Luton, Beds.—*Dir.*, D. Lofts.

Industrial Training Foundation

18 Thurloe Place, S.W.7

Formed in 1964 with the support of the Ministry of Labour (now Department of Employment and Productivity) and the Department of Education and Science to assist in implementing the Industrial Training Act, 1964.

It provides a service for all industries and all categories of employees through its six regional offices. A Training Officer and Advisory Service assists individual firms in the development of training programmes and makes available the part-time services of qualified training officers. This service also provides assistance in maintaining training records required by Industrial Training Boards and advice on dealing with questionnaires and grant claims.

The main activities of the ITF are: assessment of training needs; provision of training for apprentices, operators, supervisors, instructors and salesmen. There is a personal tutorial service for management. The Foundation operates training schemes to the requirements of individual firms or on a group basis.

A further activity of the ITF under its training officer service is the operation of the Engineering Industries Group Apprenticeship Scheme (EIGA) formed in 1953, which serves 1,000 firms throughout the country and provides 3,000 training places.

TEXTILES

Degrees in *Textiles* or *Fibre Science* are awarded by the Universities of Bradford, Leeds, Manchester (Manchester Institute of Science and Technology), Strathclyde. Courses leading to degrees in *Textile Marketing* granted by the Council for National Academic Awards are provided by Huddersfield Polytechnic; and in *Textile Technology* by the City of Leicester Polytechnic.

THE TEXTILE INSTITUTE, 10 Blackfriars Street, Manchester.—*Gen. Sec.*, J. T. Wenham.

THEOLOGY

Degrees in *Theology* or *Divinity* are granted by the Universities of Aberdeen, Belfast, Birmingham, Bristol, Cambridge, Durham, Edinburgh, Exeter, Glasgow, Hull, Kent at Canterbury, Leeds, London (Heythrop and King's Colleges), Manchester, Nottingham, Oxford, St. Andrew's, Southampton and Wales (Bangor, Cardiff, and St. David's University Colleges); in *Biblical Studies* by the Universities of Manchester, Sheffield and Wales (Bangor and Cardiff University Colleges); and in *Religious Studies* by the Universities of Aberdeen, Cambridge (*Theological and Religious Studies*), Edinburgh, Lancaster, Leeds (*Theology and Religious Studies*), London (King's College), Manchester, Newcastle upon Tyne, Stirling, Sussex and Wales (University College, Cardiff).

Courses leading to degrees in *Theology* granted by the Council for National Academic Awards are provided by the London Bible College and Spurgeon's College.

Theological Colleges

Church of England and Church in Wales

BANGOR (University Anglican Chaplaincy) (Church Hostel) (28).—*Warden*, Rev. G. Hopley.

BIRMINGHAM (Queen's Coll., Somerset Road, Edgbaston) (75).—*Princ.*, Rev. A. P. Bird (Ecumenical College).

BRISTOL. Trinity College (110).—*Princ.*, Rev. J. A. Motyer.

CAMBRIDGE (Ridley Hall) (47).—*Princ.*, Rev. K. N. Sutton.

,, (Westcott House, Jesus Lane) (45).—*Princ.*, Rev. M. Santer.

CANTERBURY (St. Augustine's College—King's College London) (60).—*Warden*, Rev. A. E. Harvey.

CHICHESTER (50).—*Princ.*, Rev. R. J. Halliburton, PH.D.

CUDDESDON, Oxon. (Ripon College) (54).—*Princ.*, Rev. J. L. Houlden.

DURHAM. *See* University of Durham—St. Chad's; St. John's.

LAMPETER (St. David's College) *see* University of Wales.

LINCOLN (Theological College) (65).—*Warden*, Rev. Canon A. A. K. Graham.

LLANDAFF, Cardiff (St. Michael's) (57).—*Warden*, Rev. Chancellor O. G. Rees.

LONDON (King's College, W.C.2).—*See* University of London.

MIRFIELD (College of the Resurrection) (50).—*Princ.*, Rev. B. Green.

NOTTINGHAM (St. John's College, Bramcote)—*Princ.*, Rev. R. E. Nixon.

OAK HILL (Southgate, N.14) (72).—*Princ.*, Rev. D. H. Wheaton, M.A., B.D.

OXFORD (St. Stephen's House) (55).—*Princ.*, Rev. D. M. Hope, D.Phil.

,, (Wycliffe Hall) (60).—*Princ.*, Rev. J. P. Hickinbotham.

SALISBURY AND WELLS (100).—*Princ.*, Rev. R. J. A. Askew.

Church of Scotland

ABERDEEN (Christ's Coll.).—*Master*, Rev. Prof. J. S. McEwen, D.D.

EDINBURGH (New Coll., Faculty of Divinity, Univ. of Edinburgh) (196).—*Princ.*, Rev. D. W. D. Shaw.

GLASGOW (Trinity Coll.) (70).—*Princ.*, Rev. Prof. A. D. Galloway, Ph.D.

ST. ANDREWS (College of St. Mary, University of St. Andrews).

Scottish Episcopal Church

EDINBURGH (24).—*Princ.*, Rev. Canon A. I. M. Haggart, Ll.D.

Presbyterian

BELFAST (Presbyterian Coll.).—*Princ.*, Very Rev. J. L. M. Haire, D.D.

CAMBRIDGE (Westminster Coll.) (36).—*Princ.*, Rev. A. G. MacLeod.

Presbyterian Church of Wales

ABERYSTWYTH (United Theological Coll.) (31).—*Princ.*, Rev. Prof. S. I. Enoch.

Methodist

BELFAST (Edgehill Coll.) (25).—*Princ.*, Rev. V. Parkin.

BRISTOL (Wesley Coll., Westbury-on-Trym) (58).—*Princ.*, Dr. J. A. Newton.

CAMBRIDGE (Wesley House) (20).—*Princ.*, Rev. M. J. Skinner.

RICHMOND.—*See* University of London.

United Reform

BANGOR (Bala-Bangor Independent Coll.)—*Princ.*, R. T. Jones, D.Phil., D.D.

CAMBRIDGE (Cheshunt College, with Westminster College, Madingley Road, Cambridge).—*Pres.*, Rev. J. E. Newport.

EDINBURGH (Scottish Congregational College, 9 Rosebery Crescent (10).—*Princ.*, Rev. J. Wood.

MANCHESTER (Congregational College) (36).—*Princ.*, Rev. E. Jones, Ph.D.

OXFORD (Mansfield College) (91).—*Princ.*, Rev. G. B. Caird, D.Phil., D.D., F.B.A.

SWANSEA (29).—*Princ.*, Prof. W. T. Pennar Davies, Ph.D.

Roman Catholic
(Colleges for the Diocesan Clergy)

ABERYSTWYTH (St. Mary's College (for late vocations, secular and regular) (30).—*Prior*, Very Rev. D. C. Flanagan, O. Carm.

ALLEN HALL, 28 Beaufort Street, Chelsea, S.W.3.—*Rector*, Rt. Rev. Mgr. J. O'Brien.

GLASGOW (St. Peter's Coll., Cardross, Dunbartonshire) (33).—*Rector*, Very Rev. J. McMahon.

OSCOTT COLL., Sutton Coldfield, West Midlands (110).—*Rector*, Rt. Rev. Mgr. F. G. Thomas.

OSTERLEY, Middlesex (Campion House, 112 Thornbury Road) (165).—*Superior*, Rev. J. R. Brooks, S.J.

UPHOLLAND, Skelmersdale, Lancs. (now the Upholland Northern Institute for Adult Christian Education).—*Rector*, Rt. Rev. Mgr. W. Dalton.

USHAW (Durham) (180).—*Pres.*, Rt. Rev. Mgr. P. Loftus.

WONERSH, Guildford (St. John's) (114).—*Rector*, Rt. Rev. J. P. McConnon.

Baptist

BANGOR (North Wales Baptist Coll.) (22).—*Princ.*, Rev. D. E. Morgan.

BRISTOL (40).—*Pres.*, Rev. Dr. W. M. S. West.

CARDIFF (S. Wales Baptist Coll.) (16).—*Princ.*, D. G. Davies.

GLASGOW (The Baptist Theological College of Scotland, 31 Oakfield Avenue, Glasgow, W.2) (19).—*Princ.*, Rev., R. E. O. White.

LONDON (Spurgeon's Coll., South Norwood Hill, S.E.25) (62).—*Princ.*, Rev. R. Brown, Ph.D.

MANCHESTER (Northern Baptist College, Brighton Grove, Rusholme) affiliated to Manchester Univ.) (65).—*Princ.*, Rev. M. H. Taylor.

OXFORD (Regent's Park College) (48).—*Princ.*, Rev. B. R. White, D.Phil.

Unitarian

MANCHESTER (Unitarian College, Victoria Park) (14).—*Princ.*, Rev. A. J. Long.

Interdenominational—Unitarian

OXFORD (Manchester Coll.).—*Princ.*, Rev. B. Findlow.

Jewish

JEWS' COLLEGE, 67 Montagu Place, W.1.—*Princ.*, Rabbi N. L. Rabinovitch, Ph.D.

LEO BAECK COLLEGE, 33 Seymour Place, W.1.—*Rabbinic Director*, Rabbi Dr. A. H. Friedlander.

TOWN AND COUNTRY PLANNING

Degrees are granted by Heriot-Watt University (*Town Planning*), and by the Universities of Dundee (*Town and Regional Planning*), London (University College: *Architecture, Planning, Building and Environmental Studies*), Manchester (*Town and Country Planning*), Newcastle upon Tyne (*Town and Country Planning*), Reading (*Scientific Bases of Planning*), and Wales (Institute of Science and Technology: *Town Planning Studies*). Courses leading to degrees in *Town Planning* granted by the Council for National Academic Awards are provided by City of Birmingham Polytechnic and Polytechnic of the South Bank; in *Town and Country Planning* by Glasgow School of Art, Liverpool Polytechnic and Trent Polytechnic; and in *Urban and Regional Planning* by Lanchester Polytechnic and Oxford Polytechnic.

The ROYAL TOWN PLANNING INSTITUTE, 26 Portland Place, W.1, conducts examinations in town planning.

VETERINARY STUDIES

Degrees in *Veterinary Science/Medicine and Surgery* are granted by the Universities of Bristol, Cambridge, Edinburgh, Glasgow, Liverpool and London (Royal Veterinary College).

PUBLIC SCHOOLS

The Association of Governing Bodies of Public Schools (G.B.A.) includes schools in membership of the Headmasters' Conference (with a few exceptions) together with the following schools:—

Ackworth, Pontefract, Yorks.
Adams' Grammar Sch., Newport, Salop.
Austin Friars Sch., Carlisle.
Avonhurst School, Bristol.
Bearwood College, Wokingham.
Belmont Abbey Sch., Hereford.
Bentham Grammar Sch., Bentham, Lancs.
Bethany School, Goudhurst, Kent.
†Canon Slade Gr. Sch., Bolton.
Carmel College, Wallingford.
Cokethorpe School, Witney.
Colston's Boys' Sch., Bristol.
Dollar Academy, Clackmannan.
Duke of York's R.M. Sch., Dover.
Dundee High School.
Frensham Heights, Rowledge, Surrey.
Friends' Sch., Great Ayton, N. Yorks.
Friends' Sch., Saffron Walden.
Friends' School, Wigton, Cumberland.
Grenville Coll., Bideford, Devon.
Keil School, Dumbarton.
King's School, Gloucester.
Langley School, Norwich.
Lindisfarne College, Wrexham.
Millfield School, Somerset.
Milton Abbey School, Blandford Forum, Dorset.
Morrison's Academy, Crieff.

Newcastle High Sch., Staffs.
Oswestry School, Salop.
Pangbourne College, Berks.
Pierrepoint School, Frensham, Surrey.
Rannoch School, Perthshire.
Reading Blue Coat School, Caversham, Berks.
Redrice Sch., nr. Andover, Hants.
Rishworth Sch., nr. Halifax, Yorks.
Royal Lancaster Grammar School.
Royal Wolverhampton School.
Ruthin School, Denbighshire.
Ryde School, Isle of Wight.
St. Augustine's Coll., Ramsgate, Kent.
St. Bede's Coll., Manchester.
St. Boniface's Coll., Plymouth.
St. Brendan's Coll., Bristol.
St. John's Coll., Southsea, Hants.
Scarborough College.
Seaford College, Petworth, Sussex.
Shebbear Coll., Beaworthy, Devon.
Shiplake Coll., Henley, Oxon.
†Sidcot Sch., Winscombe, Som.
Truro Cathedral School.
Wakefield Grammar School.
†Wells Cathedral School.
Woodbridge School, Suffolk.

† Co-educational School.

HEADMASTERS' CONFERENCE SCHOOLS

THE HEADMASTERS' CONFERENCE—*Chairman* (1975), Rev. N. P. Barry, O.S.B. (Ampleforth); *Principal Sec.*, E. J. Dorrell, 29 Gordon Square, W.C.1; *Deputy Sec.*, B. C. Harvey. The annual meetings are, as a rule, held at the end of September.

In considering applications for election to membership the Committee will have regard to the scheme or other instrument under which the school is administered (taking particularly into consideration the degree of independence enjoyed by the Headmaster and the Governing Body; the number of boys over thirteen years of age in the school; the number of boys in proportion to the size of the school who are in the sixth form, *i.e.* engaged on studies at the Advanced Level of the General Certificate of Education.

Name of School	F'ded.	No. of Boys	Annual Fees D=Day Boys	Headmaster (With date of Appointment)
England and Wales				
Abbotsholme, Uttoxeter, Staffs	1889	240†	£1,485....D£990	S. D. Snell (1967)
Abingdon, Berks	1256	630	£1,140....D£480	M. St. J. Parker (1975)
Aldenham, Elstree, Herts	1597	365	£1,488...D£894	P. W. Boorman (1974)
Alleyn's School, Dulwich, S.E.22	1619	800	........D£660	J. L. Fanner (1967)
Allhallows, Rousdon, Dorset	1534	301†	£1,284...D£744	D. J. Mathewson (1974)
Ampleforth College (R.C.), York	1802	730	£1,350.........	Rev. N. P. Barry, O.S.B. (1964)
Archbishop Holgate's Grammar, York	1546	800	£490.......Dnil	D. A. Frith (1959)
Ardingly Coll., Hayward's Heath, Sussex*	1858	350	£1,485.........	C. H. Bulteel, M.C. (1962)
Arnold School, Blackpool	1870	775	£870....D£444	A. J. C. Cochrane (1974)
Ashville College, Harrogate	1877	425	£891....D£420	G. R. Southam (1958)
Bablake, Coventry	1344	860	....D£336	E. H. Burrough, T.D. (1962)
Bancroft's, Woodford Green, Essex	1737	600	£591....D£480	I. M. Richardson (1965)
Barnard Castle, Co. Durham	1883	500	....D£...	S. D. Woods (1965)
Bedales, Petersfield, Hants	1893	340†	£1,500...D£900	C. P. Nobes (1974)
Bedford School	1552	1000	£1,293...D£711	C. I. M. Jones (1975)
Bedford Modern School	1834	942	£934....D£445	B. H. Kemball-Cook (1965)
Berkhamsted, Herts	1544	730	£1,449...D£759	J. L. Spencer, T.D. (1972)
Birkenhead, Cheshire	1860	740	£987....D£406	J. A. Gwilliam (1963)
Bishop's Stortford College, Herts	1868	530	£1,395..D£1,020	G. C. Greetham (1971)
Bloxham School, Banbury, Oxon.*	1860	350	£1,140...D£879	D. R. G. Seymour (1965)
Blundell's, Tiverton	1604	410	£1,398...D£768	A. C. S. Gimson, M.B.E., M.C.
Bolton	1524	851	....D£396	C. D. A. Baggley (1966) [(1971)
Bootham, York	1823	280	£....D£...	J. H. Gray (1972)
Bradfield College, Berks	1850	460	£1,485....D£990	A. O. H. Quick (1971)
Bradford Grammar, Yorks	1662	1115	....D£408	D. A. G. Smith (1974)
Brentwood School, Essex	1557	920	£1,062....D£498	R. Sale (1966)
Brighton College, Sussex	1845	425	£1,425-£1,470 D£975	W. S. Blackshaw (1971)
Brislington School, Bristol	1956	1839†	...........Dnil	J. S. Hellier (1955)
Bristol Cathedral School	1542	410	........D£486	D. J. Jewell (1970)
Bristol Grammar School	1532	1000	........D£516	J. R. Avery (1975)
Bromsgrove, Worcs	1688	550	£1,359...D£999	Rev. J. N. F. Earle (1971)
Bryanston School, Blandford	1928	495	£1,690..D£1,126	Rev. D. I. S. Jones (1974)
Bury Grammar, Lancs	1726	720	....D£312	W. J. H. Robson (1969)
Canford, Wimborne, Dorset	1923	480	£1,530..D£1,020	I. A. Wallace (1961)
Caterham, Surrey	1811	570	£993....D£465	S. R. Smith (1974)
Charterhouse, Godalming	1611	680†	£1,575..D£1,107	B. Rees (1973)
Cheadle Hulme	1855	1000†	£969....D£390	D. R. Wilcox (1974)
Cheltenham College	1841	440	£1,500...D£960	D. Ashcroft, T.D. (1959)
Chigwell, Essex	1629	460	£1,230...D£837	B. J. Wilson (1971)
Christ College, Brecon	1541	270	£950....D£700	J. B. Cook, Ph.D. (1973)
Christ's Hospital, Horsham	1553	830	(various).........	D. H. Newsome (1970)
City of London, E.C.4	1442	780	........D£840	J. A. Boyes (1965)
Claysmore, Iwerne Minster, Blandford	1896	225†	£1,245...D£830	R. McIsaac (1966)
Clifton College, Bristol	1862	690	£1,491....D£894	S. M. Andrews (1975)
Cranleigh, Surrey	1863	520†	£1,761..D£1,227	M. van Hasselt (1970)
Culford School, Bury St. Edmunds	1881	710†	£1,224...D£567	D. Robson (1971)
Dame Allan's Sch., Newcastle on Tyne	1705	440	....D£453	F. Wilkinson (1970)
Dauntsey's, Devizes	1543	520	£1,155...D£414	G. E. King-Reynolds (1969)
Dean Close, Cheltenham	1884	380†	£1,065..D£1,065	C. G. Turner (1968)
Denstone College, Uttoxeter, Staffs.*	1873	320	£1,500.........	D. Maland (1969)
Douai (R.C.), Woolhampton	1615	260	£1,170.........	Rev. P.W. Sollom, O.S.B., Ph.D.
Dover College, Kent	1871	375†	£1,410..D£1,050	D. R. Cope (1973) [(1975)
Downside (R.C.), Stratton-on-the-Fosse, Somerset	1606	555	£1,350...D£675	Dom R. Appleby (1975)
Dulwich College, S.E.21	1619	1420	£1,380...D£780	D. A. Emms (1975)
Durham	1414	290	£1,473...D£954	M. W. Vallance (1972)

† Pupils.   * a Woodard Corporation School.

Name of School	F'ded.	No. of Boys	Annual Fees D = Day Boys	Headmaster (With date of Appointment)
Eastbourne College, Sussex............	1867	470	£1,295....D£923	S. J. B. Langdale (1973)
Ellesmere College, Salop★............	1884	350	£1,525....D£990	D. J. Skipper (1969)
Eltham College, S.E.9................	1842	580	£1,128...D£471	C. Porteous (1959)
Epsom College, Surrey...............	1855	590	£1,473....D£981	O. J. T. Rowe (1970)
Eton College, Windsor...............	1440	1200	£1,575........	M. W. McCrum (1970)
Exeter, Devon......................	1633	530	£990......D£450	R. M. Hone (1966)
Felsted, Dunmow, Essex..............	1564	462†	£1,350...D£855	A. F. Eggleston O.B.E. (1968)
Forest School, Snaresbrook, E.17......	1834	623	£1,134...D£807	D. A. Foxall (1960)
Framlingham College, Suffolk........	1864	400	£1,194....D£669	L. I. Rimmer (1971)
Giggleswick, Settle, Yorks...........	1512	247	£1,470....D£870	R. A. C. Meredith (1970)
Gresham's, Holt, Norfolk............	1555	470†	£1,500....D£963	L. Bruce-Lockhart (1955)
Haberdashers' Aske's, Elstree, Herts.....	1690	1260	£1,158....D£564	B. H. McGowan (1973)
Haileybury, Herts....................	1862	595†	£1,530..D£1,056	D. M. Summerscale (1976)
Harrow, Middlesex..................	1571	734	£1,270....D£635	B. M. S. Hoban (1971)
Hereford, Cathedral School..........	1381	390†	£909......D£414	B. B. Sutton (1975)
Highgate, N. 6......................	1565	700	£1,416..D£762	R. C. Giles (1974)
Hulme Grammar School, Oldham......	1611	730	........D£318	S. W. Johnson (1965)
Hurstpierpoint College, Sussex★.......	1849	366	£1,200...D£999	R. N. P. Griffiths (1964)
Hymers College, Hull...............	1889	525	........D£402	J. Ashurst (1971)
Ipswich, Suffolk....................	1400	550	£1,197–£1,281 D£762–801	J. M. Blatchly, Ph.H. (1972)
John Lyon School, Harrow...........	1876	450	........D£200	G. V. Surtees (1968)
Kelly College, Tavistock.............	1877	300	£1,398....D£900	D. W. Ball, M.B.E. (1972)
Kent College, Canterbury............	1885	489	£973....D£490	D. E. Norfolk (1960)
Kimbolton, Cambs..................	1600	540	£1,050...D£495	D. W. Donaldson (1973)
King Edward VII School, Lytham......	1908	650	........D£324	C. J. Lipscomb (1968)
King Edward's, Bath, Avon..........	1552	660	........D£426	B. H. Holbeche, C.B.E. (1962)
King Edward's, Birmingham..........	1552	700	........D£420	F. G. R. Fisher (1974)
King Edward's, Witley, Surrey........	1553	430	£786...........	J. T. Hansford (1969)
King Henry VIII, Coventry..........	1545	870	........D£336	R. Cooke (1974)
King's College, Taunton★............	1522	580	£1,521..D£1,014	J. M. Batten (1969)
King's College Sch., Wimbledon, S.W.19	1829	582	£1,200...D£810	C. C. B. Wightwick (1975)
King's School, Bruton...............	1519	285	£1,332....D£867	G. H. G. Doggart (1972)
King's School, Canterbury...........	598	700†	£1,392...D£930	Rev. P. Pilkington (1975)
King's School, Chester..............	1541	570	........D£450	A. R. Munday (1964)
King's School, Ely.................	970	640	£1,428....D£807	H. Ward (1970)
King's School, Macclesfield..........	1552	1250	........D£483	A. H. Cooper (1966)
King's School, Rochester............	604	504	£1,413....D£735	R. A. Ford (1975)
King's School, Worcester............	1541	681	£1,140....D£468	D. M. Annett (1959)
Kingston Grammar, Surrey..........	1561	560	........D£378	J. A. Strover (1970)
Kingswood School, Bath............	1748	435†	£1,308....D£864	L. J. Campbell (1970)
Lancaster, Royal G. S...............	1467	....	........Dnil	A. M. Joyce (1972)
Lancing College, Sussex★............	1848	480†	£1,440....D£900	I. D. S. Beer (1969)
Latymer Upper, Hammersmith, W.6....	1624	1100	........D£540	M. L. R. Isaac (1971)
Leeds Gr. Sch., Leeds 6.............	1552	1200	........D£442	(vacant)
Leighton Park Sch., Reading.........	1890	310	£1,341....D£894	W. H. Spray (1971)
The Leys School, Cambridge.........	1875	415	£1,500........	B. T. Bellis (1975)
Liverpool College, Liverpool 18......	1840	710	£1,044....D£654	M. F. Robins (1970)
Llandovery College.................	1848	262	£1,025....D£660	R. G. Jones (1968)
Lord Wandsworth Coll., Long Sutton, Hants............................	1912	388	£1,320....D£954	C. A. N. Henderson (1968)
Loughborough Grammar............	1495	820	£1,020....D£405	J. S. Millward (1973)
Magdalen College School, Oxford.....	1478	510	£1,077...D£465	W. B. Cook (1970)
Malvern College, Worcester.........	1865	595	£1,515..D£1,065	M. J. W. Rogers (1971)
Manchester Grammar School........	1515	1440	........D£402	P. G. Mason, M.B.E. (1962)
Manchester, Wm. Hulme's Gr........	1881	800	........D£426	P. A. Filleul (1974)
(Sir Roger) Manwood's Sch., Sandwich, Kent..................	1563	420	£645........Dnil	J. F. Spalding (1960)
Marlborough Coll., Wilts...........	1843	873	£1,635..........	R. W. Ellis (1972)
Merchant Taylor's, Crosby..........	1620	800	£846....D£327	Rev. H. M. Luft (1964)
Merchant Taylor's, Northwood.......	1561	660	£1,185...D£840	F. Davey (1974)
Mill Hill, N.W.7...................	1807	480	£1,479...D£990	A. F. Elliott (1974)
Monkton Combe, Bath..............	1868	303	£1,146....D£774	R. J. Knight (1968)
Monmouth.........................	1614	480	£996....D£501	R. F. Glover, T.D. (1959)
Mount St. Mary's Coll., Spinkhill, Derbyshire (R.C.).................	1842	300	£1,077...D£732	Rev. A. A. Nye, S.J. (1968)
Newcastle on Tyne (Royal Gr. Sch.)....	1545	1000	........D£564	A. S. Cox (1972)
Newport High School...............	1896	1800†	........Dnil	D. P. M. Michael, C.B.E. (1960)
Norwich School....................	1250	652	£978....D£417	P. G. Stibbe (1975)

† Pupils.　　★ a Woodard Corporation School.

Name of School	F'ded	No. of Boys	Annual Fees D=Day Boys	Headmaster (With date of Appointment)
Nottingham High School	1513	968	......D £504	D. T. Witcombe, Ph.D. (1970)
Oakham, Leics	1584	900†	£1,470....D £825	J. D. Buchanan, M.B.E. (1958)
The Oratory (R.C.), Woodcote, Reading	1859	315	£1,197....D £822	A. J. Snow (1972)
Oundle, Peterborough, Northants	1556	740	£1,392........	B. M. W. Trapnell, Ph.D. (1968)
Perse Sch., Cambridge	1615	570	£874.....D £433	A. E. Melville (1969)
Plymouth College	1877	640	£1,074...D £570	R. H. Merrett (1975)
Pocklington Sch., York	1514	611	£933.....D £402	G. L. Willatt (1966)
Portsmouth Gr. School	1732	750	......D £396	D. M. Richards (1975)
Prior Park Coll. (R.C.), Bath	1830	280	£1,260.........	Rev. M. P. Power (1972)
Queen Elizabeth's Gr., Blackburn	1567	940	......D £432	D. J. Coulson (1965)
Queen Elizabeth Gr. Sch., Wakefield	1591	730	£756.....D £426	J. G. Parker (1975)
Queen Elizabeth's Hospital, Bristol	1590	420	£981.....D £516	H. G. Edwards, M.B.E. (1968)
Queen Mary's Gr., Walsall, Staffs	1554	630	..........Dnil	S. L. Darby (1955)
Queen's College, Taunton, Som	1843	431	£1,197...D £762	M. Robinson (1974)
Radley Coll., Abingdon	1847	528	£1,380.......	D. R. W. Silk (Warden) (1968)
Ratcliffe Coll., (R.C.), Leicester	1847	297	£1,350.......	Rev. A. J. Baxter (1973)
Reed's, Cobham, Surrey	1813	350	£1,344...D £897	R. N. Exton (1964)
Rendcomb Coll., Cirencester, Glos	1920	241†	£1,170.......	R. M. A. Medill (1971)
Repton School, Derby	1557	485	£1,515..D £1,095	J. F. Gammell, M.C. (1968)
Rossall, Fleetwood, Lancs	1844	560	£1,440...D £972	J. Sharp, D.Phil. (1973)
Royal Masonic School, Bushey	1798	420	£1,260...D £750	A. F. Vyvyan-Robertson (1972)
Rugby, Warwickshire	1567	725	£1,386...D £633	J. S. Woodhouse (1967)
Rydal, Colwyn Bay, Clwyd	1885	285†	£1,260...D £675	P. F. Watkinson (1968)
St. Albans, Herts	1570	675	......D £453	F. I. Kilvington (1964)
St. Bees, Cumbria	1583	270	£1,470...D £849	G. W. Lees (1963)
St. Benedict's, Ealing, W.5 (R.C.)	1902	600	......D £375	Rev. G. G. Brown, O.S.B. (1969)
St. Dunstan's, Catford, S.E.6	1888	920	......D £555	B. D. Dance (1973)
St. Edmund's, Canterbury	1749	410	£1,257...D £921	F. R. Rawes, M.B.E. (1964)
St. Edmund's Coll. (R.C.), Ware, Herts	1568	500	£1,300...D £770	Rev. M. G. Garvey (1968)
St. Edward's, Oxford	1863	515	£1,500..D £1,125	C. H. Christie (1971)
St. George's Coll., Weybridge, (R.C.)	1869	580	£1,089...D £714	Rev. B. P. Murtough (1949)
St. John's, Leatherhead	1851	406	£1,281....D £954	E. J. Hartwell (1970)
St. Lawrence Coll., Ramsgate	1879	380	£1,500..D £1,014	P. H. Harris (1969)
St. Paul's, Lonsdale Rd., Barnes, S.W.13	1509	680	£1,449...D £984	J. W. Hele (1973)
St. Peter's, York	627	408	£1,488....D £834	P. D. R. Gardiner (1967)
Sedbergh, Yorks	1525	450	£1,485...D £990	P. J. Attenborough (1975)
Sevenoaks School, Kent	1418	831	£1,350....D £843	A. R. Tammadge (1971)
Sherborne, Dorset	1550	632	£1,500..D £1,125	R. D. Macnaghten (1974)
Shrewsbury School	1552	636	£1,500...D £882	W. E. K. Anderson (1975)
Silcoates School, Wakefield, Yorks	1820	367	£900.....D £600	R. J. M. Evans, Ph.D. (1960)
Solihull, Warwicks	1560	970	£1,227...D £687	G. D. Slaughter (1973)
Stamford, Lincs	1532	830	£1,020....D £423	H. A. Staveley (1968)
Stockport Gr. Sch	1487	700	......D £400	F. W. Scott (1962)
Stonyhurst Coll. (R.C.), nr. Whalley, Lancs	1594	513	£1,404...D £702	Rev. M. J. F. Bossy, S.J. (1972)
Stowe, Bucks	1923	648†	£1,680..D £1,176	R. Q. Drayson, D.S.C. (1964)
Sutton Valence, Kent	1576	360	£1,488...D £993	M. R. Ricketts (1967)
Taunton, Somerset	1847	600†	£1,399...D £928	N. S. Roberts (1970)
Tettenhall College, Staffs	1863	385	£1,095...D £678	W. J. Dale (1968)
Tonbridge, Kent	1553	600	£1,314...D £909	C. H. D. Everett (1975)
Trent College, Long Eaton, Derbyshire	1868	500	£1,400...D £915	A. J. Maltby (1968)
Trinity School, Croydon	1596	750	......D £537	R. J. Wilson (1972)
Truro, Cornwall	1880	848	£1,095...D £510	D. W. Burrell (1959)
(Sir William) Turner's Sch., Redcar Cleveland	1692	700	£395........Dnil	S. G. Barker (1953)
University Coll. Sch., Frognal, N.W.3	1830	500	......D £759	W. A. Barker (1975)
Uppingham, Leics	1584	630	£1,450.......	C. MacDonald (1975)
Warwick	914	955	£1,053–1,092 D £519-552	P. W. Martin, T.D. (1962)
Watford Gr. Sch	....	....	..........Dnil	L. K. Turner (1963)
Wellingborough, Northants	1595	260	£1,368...D £743	G. Garrett (1973)
Wellington Coll., Crowthorne, Berks	1856	720†	£1,314....D £876	Hon. F. F. Fisher, M.C. (1966)
Wellington Sch., Somerset	1841	536†	£915....D £387	J. MacG. K. Kendall-Carpenter (1973)
West Buckland Sch., Barnstaple	1858	400	£1,038...D £510	Rev. G. Ridding (1968)
Westminster, Dean's Yard, S.W.1	1560	490	£1,650..D £1,050	J. M. Rae, Ph.D. (1970)
Whitgift, Croydon	1596	850	......D £606	D. A. Raeburn (1970)
Winchester College	1382	570	£1,725..D £1,206	J. L. Thorn (1968)

† Pupils

Name of School	F'ded.	No. of Boys	Annual Fees D=Day Boys	Headmaster (With date of Appointment)
Woodhouse Grove Sch., Bradford.....	1812	450	£940.....D£475	D. A. Miller (1972)
Worcester College for the Blind.......	1866	72	£2,265..........	R. C. Fletcher (1959)
Worcester (Royal Gr.).................	1561	740	£645........D*nil*	A. G. K. Brown (1950)
Worksop College, Notts.*...........	1895	410	£1,500..D£1,100	R. J. Roberts (1975)
Worth School, Crawley, Sussex.......	1933	420	£1,500..........	Rev. J. H. D. Gaisford, O.S.B. (1959)
Wrekin Coll., Wellington, Salop.......	1880	395†	£1,560..D£1,040	G. C. L. Hadden (1971)
Wycliffe Coll., Stonehouse, Glos.......	1882	284	£1,296....D£798	R. D. H. Roberts (1967)

Scotland

Name of School	F'ded.	No. of Boys	Annual Fees D=Day Boys	Headmaster (With date of Appointment)
Daniel Stewart's and Melville Coll., Edinburgh (amalgamated, 1973).......	1814	1410	£1,047....D£465	(vacant)
The Edinburgh Academy, Edinburgh...	1824	550	£1,110....D£645	H. H. Mills, M.C., Ph.D. (Rector) (1962)
Fettes College, Edinburgh	1850	458	£1,455....D£873	A. Chenevix-Trench (1971)
George Heriot's, Edinburgh	1628	1580	......D£390	A. S. McDonald (1970)
George Watson's Coll., Edinburgh.....	1723	2400†	£1,047 ......D£345-465	R. W. Young (1958)
Glasgow Academy...................	1846	955	......D£375-525	R. de C. Chapman (1975)
Gordonstoun, Elgin, Morayshire.......	1934	440	£1,620..........	J. W. R. Kempe (1968)
Hutcheson's Gr. Sch. Glasgow.......	1650	820	......D£293	P. Whyte (1966)
Jordanhill College, Glasgow..........	1920	1002†	........D*nil*	W. T. Branston (1956)
Kelvinside Academy, Glasgow.........	1878	696	......D£423	C. J. R. Mair (1958)
Loretto Sch., Musselburgh, Midlothian..	1827	246	£1,305....D£840	R. B. Bruce Lockhart (1960)
Merchiston Castle, Edinburgh	1833	320	£1,245....D£795	D. J. Forbes (1969)
Robert Gordon's Coll., Aberdeen.....	1881	1225	£952....D£352	J. Marshall (1960)
Strathallan, Forgandenny, Perthshire...	1912	350	£1,260..........	C. D. Pighills (1975)
Trinity Coll., Glenalmond, Perthshire...	1841	380	£1,440..........	J. N. W. Musson (Warden) (1972)

Northern Ireland

Name of School	F'ded.	No. of Boys	Annual Fees D=Day Boys	Headmaster (With date of Appointment)
Bangor Gr. Sch., Co. Down..........	1856	790	........D£275	R. J. Rodgers, Ph.D. (1975)
Belfast Methodist College.............	1868	1590†	£807.....D£297	J. Kincade, Ph.D. (1974)
Belfast Royal Academy...............	1785	1510†	........D£315	J. L. Lord (1968)
Campbell Coll., Belfast...............	1894	430	£1,002....D£498	R. M. Morgan (1971)
Coleraine Academical Institution.......	1860	1150	£710....D£255	G. Humphreys, Ph.D. (1955)
Portora Royal Sch., Enniskillen........	1608	497	£810.....D£305	T. J. Garrett (1973)
Royal Belfast Academical Instn........	1810	1030	........D£290	S. V. Peskett (Principal) (1959)

Isle of Man

Name of School	F'ded.	No. of Boys	Annual Fees D=Day Boys	Headmaster (With date of Appointment)
King William's College...............	1668	445	£1,335....D£816	G. R. Rees-Jones (1958)

Channel Islands

Name of School	F'ded.	No. of Boys	Annual Fees D=Day Boys	Headmaster (With date of Appointment)
Elizabeth Coll., Guernsey.............	1563	690	£753.....D£228	R. A. Wheadon (1972)
Victoria Coll., Jersey................	1852	495	£612.....D£210	M. H. Devenport (1967)

Republic of Ireland

Name of School	F'ded.	No. of Boys	Annual Fees D=Day Boys	Headmaster (With date of Appointment)
St. Columba's College, Rathfarnham, Dublin..........................	1843	220	£900.....D£600	D. S. Gibb, O.B.E. (1974)

SOCIETY OF HEADMASTERS OF INDEPENDENT SCHOOLS
Hon. Secretary, S. M. Mischler, M.B.E., 8 Gwarnick Road, Truro, Cornwall

Name of School	F'ded.	No. of Boys	Annual Fees D=Day Boys	Headmaster (With date of Appointment)
Austin Friars, Carlisle (R.C.)...........	1951	297	£975.....D£525	Rev. B. O'Rourke, O.S.A. (1973)
Bearwood Coll., Wokingham, Berks....	1827	345	£1,320....D£870	P. M. Cunningham (1963)
Belmont Abbey, Hereford, (R.C.).....	1926	325	£1,200....D£690	Rev. J. M. Jabale, O.S.B. (1969)
Bembridge, Isle of Wight.............	1919	277	£1,086....D£570	R. L. Whitby, M.V.O. (1974)
Bentham Grammar, Bentham, Lancs...	1726	295	£936.....D£456	J. F. D. Hagan (1972)
Bethany Sch., Goudhurst, Kent........	1866	270	£1,155...D£771	C. A. H. Lanzer (1970)
Carmel College, Wallingford, Berks....	1948	340†	£1,800..........	Rabbi J. Rosen (1971)

† Pupils.   * A Woodard Corporation School.

Name of School	F'ded.	No. of Boys	Annual Fees D=Day Boys	Headmaster (With date of Appointment)
Churcher's College, Petersfield, Hants...	1722	446	£780........Dnil	D. I. Brooks (1973)
Colston's, Bristol.....................	1710	280	£1,194....D£756	G. W. Searle (1975)
Cotton College, Oakamoor, Staffs......	1763	207	£810....D£405	Rev. Mgr. T. J. Gavin (1967)
Fort Augustus School, Invernesshire....	1878	132	£1,335...D£801	Rev. G. F. Davidson, O.S.B. (1972)
Grenville College, Bideford, Devon*...	1954	323	£1,143....D£735	D. C. Powell-Price (1975)
Keil Sch., Dumbarton.................	1915	200	£1,065–1,086 D£664–694	E. S. Jeffs (1962)
Kingham Hill School, Oxford.........	1886	220	£645..........	E. C. Cooper (1954)
King's School, Gloucester.............	1541	436	£1,038–1,098 D£588–648	A. P. David (1969)
Milton Abbey Sch., nr. Blandford, D'set	1954	285	£1,200........	W. M. T. Holland (1969)
Oswestry, Salop.....................	1407	311	£990....D£666	F. E. Gerstenberg (1974)
Pangbourne College, Berks...........	1917	330	£1,395...D£909	P. D. C. Points (1969)
Pierrepont School, Farnham, Surrey....	1947	270	£1,440....D£900	A. G. Hill (1962)
Rannoch School, Perthshire...........	1959	270	£1,140–1,260....	P. T. MacLellan (1967)
Rishworth, nr. Halifax, Yorks.........	1724	760†	£1,086...D£240	Rev. J. Williams (1969)
Royal Russell Sch., Croydon, Surrey...	1853	525†	£1,350...D£790	S. Hopewell (1974)
Royal Wolverhampton Sch., Staffs.....	1850	320	£1,200...D£840	P. G. C. Howard (1961)
Ruthin School, Clwyd...............	1574	255	£1,260....D£630	A. S. Hill (1967)
Ryde School, Isle of Wight...........	1921	460	£1,140...D£510	K. N. Symons (1966)
Scarborough College, Yorks...........	1898	350	£1,230...D£762	R. W. Wilkinson (1975)
Seaford College, Petworth, Sussex.....	1884	430	£1,155..........	Rev. C. E. Johnson (1944)
Shebbear College, Beaworthy, Devon..	1841	340	£1,050...D£501	G. W. Kingsnorth (1964)
Shiplake College, Henley, Oxon.......	1959	256	£......D£....	J. D. Eggar, T.D. (1963)
Sidcot School, Winscombe, Somerset...	1808	300†	£1,320...D£861	R. N. Brayshaw (1957)
Stanbridge Earls School, Romsey.......	1952	152†	£1,545...D£927	R. J. Gould (1959)
Truro Cathedral School, Cornwall......	1549	250	£990....D£600	F. S. G. Pearson (Advocate)
Wells Cathedral Sch., Somerset.......	1180	600†	£1,095...D£618	A. K. Quilter (1964) [(1974)

† Pupils. ★ A Woodard Corporation School. NOTE.—The Headmasters of Abbotsholme School, Bedales School, Lord Wandsworth College, Prior Park College, Rendcomb College, St. Edmund's College, St. George's College, Weybridge and Tettenhall College are also Members of the Society. Details of these schools are included in the list of Headmasters' Conference Schools.

PUBLIC SCHOOLS OVERSEAS

NOTE.—Headmasters of Schools marked (★) are Members of the *Headmasters' Conference*; marked (§) of the *Headmasters' Conference of Australia*.

Name of School	F'ded.	No. of Boys	Annual Fees D=Day Boys	Headmaster (With date of Appointment)
South America				
★Markham Coll., Lima, Peru..........	1946	1000	..........D£250	R. C. Pinchbeck, O.B.E. (1966)
Queen's Coll., Georgetown, Guyana...	1844	720	............Dnil	C. I. Trotz (1974)
★St. George's Coll., Quilmes, Argentine	1898	310	$23,000..D$13,800	C. G. Graham (1968
India				
Mayo College, Ajmer...............	1875	678	Rs.4,000........	S. S. N. Ganju (1974)
★Cathedral and John Connor School, Bombay........................	1860	1600	...DRs.700–1,200	K. K. Jacob (1969)
★St. Joseph's Coll., Darjeeling........	1889	642	Rs.4,000..DRs.990	Rev. H. Nunn, S.J. (1970)
★St. Paul's, Darjeeling................	1823	422	Rs.4,800..........	M. W. Cross (1974)
★Doon Sch., Chand Bagh, Dehra Dun..	1935	516	Rs.3,500..........	E. J. Simeon (1971)
Scindia School, Gwalior.............	1897	634	Rs.3,500...DRs.75	S. P. Sahi (1968)
Canada				
★Ashbury Coll., Ottawa..............	1891	370	$4,100....D$2,200	W. A. Joyce (1966)
★Brentwood Coll. Sch., Vancouver.....	1923	320	$4,500....D$1,700	D. D. Mackenzie (1961)
Hillfield-Strathallan, Hamilton, Ont...	1962	670†	....D$1,700–2,200	M. B. Wansbrough (1969)
Lakefield Coll. Sch., Ontario.........	1879	260	$4,450....D$2,000	J. T. M. Guest (1971)
Lower Canada Coll., Montreal.......	1909	585	D$1,400–2,125	G. H. Merrill (1968)
Ridley Coll., St. Catherine's, Ont.....	1889	480	$4,700...D$2,600	R. A. Bradley (1971)
★St. Andrew's Coll., Aurora, Ont.....	1899	360	$4,750...D$2,650	T. A. Hockin, Ph.D. (1974)
Shawnigan Lake Sch., B.C...........	1916	235	$4,500...D$2,600	Rev. W. H. H. McClelland, [M.B.E. (1975)
★Trinity Coll. Sch., Port Hope, Ont....	1865	335	$4,550...D$2,500	A. C. Scott (1962)
★Upper Canada Coll., Toronto........	1829	857	$3,850...D$1,700	P. T. Johnson (1965)

† Pupils.

School	F'ded.	No. of Boys	Annual Fees D=Day Boys	Headmaster (*With date of appointment*)
Australia				
N.S.W.				
*§The Armidale Sch., Armidale	1894	400	$A2,085..D$A699	A. H. Cash (1962)
*§Barker Coll., Hornsby	1890	1228†	$A2,475–2,595 D$A1,170–1,290	T. J. McCaskill (1963)
*§Sydney C. of E. Gr. Sch., N. Sydney.	1889	1070	$A2,166–2,616 D$A900–1,230	B. H. Travers, O.B.E. (1959)
*§Cranbrook Sch., Sydney	1918	940	$A2,925–3,015 D$A1,365–1,455	M. Bishop (1962)
*§The King's School, Parramatta	1831	891	$A2,600 D$A1,400	Rev. S. W. Kurrle (1965)
§Knox Gr. Sch. Wahroonga	1924	1445	$A2,490 D$A1,245	I. W. Paterson, Ph.D. (1969)
§Newington Coll., Stanmore	1863	1200	$A2,700 D$A1,200	A. J. Rae (1972)
§St. Aloysius Coll. (*R.C.*) Sydney	1879	1036	.....D$A540–660	Rev. G. F. Jordan, S.J. (1974)
§St. Ignatius Coll. (*R.C.*) N.S.W. 2066	1878	883	$A2,007..D$A837	Rev. P. B. Quin, S.J. (1974)
§St. Joseph's Coll. (*R.C.*) Hunter's Hill	1881	850	$A1,650..........	Br. A. Dwyer (1970)
*Scots College, The, Sydney	1893	1130	$A1,935–2,445 D$A615–1,245	G. Wilson, M.C. (1966)
*§Sydney Gr. Sch., Sydney	1854	1085	$A2,580–2,670 D$A1,290–1,380	A. M. Mackerras (1969)
§Trinity Gr. Sch., Sydney	1913	1140	$A2,670–2,910 D$A825–1,320	R. I. West (1975)
Victoria:				
§Ballarat and Clarendon College	1864	720†	$A2,055–2,715 D$A465–1,275	R. M. Horner (1967)
*§Carey Baptist Gr. Sch., Kew	1923	1250	........D$A1,500	G. L. Cramer (1965)
§Caulfield Gr. Sch.	1881	1191	$A2,679 D$A1,416	B. C. Lumsden (1965)
*§Geelong Coll., Geelong	1861	770	$A3,620 D$A1,610	P. N. Thwaites (1960)
*§Geelong C. of E. Gr. Sch., Corio	1855	1202†	$A2,640–3,705 D$A1,020–1,695	Hon. C. D. Fisher (1974)
*§Haileybury Coll., E. Brighton	1892	1250	$A2,670 D$A1,470	A. M. H. Aikman (1974)
§Ivanhoe Gr. Sch.	1915	886	$A2,535 D$A1,185	Rev. C. E. A. Sligo (1975)
*§Melbourne, C. of E. Gr. Sch.	1858	1535	$A3,285 D$A1,635	N. A. H. Creese (1970)
*§Scotch Coll., Hawthorne, Melbourne.	1851	1648	$A3,250 D$A1,500	P. A. V. Roff (1975)
§Trinity Gr. Sch., Kew	1902	990	....D$A864–1,218	J. J. Leppitt (1959)
§Wesley Coll., Melbourne	1865	1250	$A3,555 D$A1,080–1,665	D. H. Prest (1972)
§Xavier Coll. (*R.C.*), Melbourne	1878	793	....	Rev. P. Brennan, S.J. (1974)
Queensland:				
*§All Souls' and St. Gabriel's School, Charters Towers	1920	383	$A1,530..D$A600	Rev. R. W. Gregory (1972)
§Brisbane Boys' Coll., Toowong	1901	680	$A1,470..D$A480	G. E. Thomson (1974)
*Brisbane C. of E. Gr. School	1912	1494	$A2,307..D$A900	W. Hayward (1974)
§Brisbane Grammar Sch.	1868	1124	$A692....D$A292	M. A. Howell (1965)
§Toowoomba Gr. Sch.	1875	543	$A1,500..D$A570	W. M. Dent (1970)
South Australia:				
§Sacred Heart Coll., Somerton Park...	1912	910	$A1,125–1,230 D$A300–405	Br. C. Pratt (1970)
*§St. Peter's College, Adelaide	1847	986	$A2,780 D$A1,445	Rev. J. S. C. Miller (1961)
*§Prince Alfred Coll., Adelaide	1869	692	$A2,520 D$A1,260	G. B. Bean (1970)
§Pulteney Gr. Sch., Adelaide	1847	739	.........D$A1,185	J. A. Mackinnon (1973)
*§Scotch College, Adelaide	1919	880†	....D$A780–1,470	W. M. Miles (1975)
Western Australia:				
*§Christ Church Gr. Sch., Claremont...	1910	845	$A2,160 D$A1,125	P. M. Moyes (1951)
*§Guildford C. of E. Gr. Sch.	1896	679	$A2,130 D$A1,080	D. A. Lawe-Davies (1957)
*§Hale School, Wembley Downs	1858	800	$A2,265 D$A1,185	K. G. Tregonning (1967)
*§Scotch Coll., Swanbourne	1897	839	$A2,277 D$A1,197	W. R. Dickinson (1972)
§Wesley Coll., Perth	1923	757	$A1,520 D$A1,140	C. A. Hamer (1965)
Tasmania:				
§Launceston Church Gr. Sch.	1846	414	$A1,878–2,478 D$A792–1,392	R. P. Hutchings (1971)
*§Hutchins Sch., Hobart	1846	570	$A2,100 D$A1,050	Rev. D. B. Clarke (1971)
§Scotch College, Launceston	1901	307†	$A790....D$A420	J. P. Herbert (1972)
New Zealand				
Auckland Gr. Sch.	1869	1388	$NZ855......Dnil	D. J. Graham (1973)
King's Coll., Otahuhu	1896	684	$NZ1,680 D$NZ867	I. P. Campbell (1973)
*Christchurch Boys' High	1881	1123	$NZ750......Dnil	C. F. S. Caldwell (1959)

† Pupils.

School	F'ded.	No. of Boys	Annual Fees See note (a) D=Day Boys	Headmaster (With date of appointment)
★Christ's Coll., Christchurch.........	1850	587	$NZ579 D $NZ279	A. M. Brough (1970)
★St. Andrew's Coll., Christchurch......	1916	714	$NZ1,425 D $NZ690	I. T. Galloway, C.B.E., E.D. (1962)
★Timaru High Sch...................	1880	684	$NZ775......Dnil	R. J. Welch (1965)
Nelson College, Nelson..............	1856	945	$NZ900......Dnil	E. J. Brewster (1970)
New Plymouth Boys' High School....	1872	934	$NZ945......Dnil	G. R. Cramond (1972)
★Waitaki Boys' High Sch., Oamaru....	1883	904	$NZ800......Dnil	J. H. Donaldson (1961)
★Wanganui Collegiate................	1854	555	$NZ1,770 D $NZ735	T. U. Wells (1960)
Wellington Coll., Wellington........	1867	1000	$NZ795...D $NZ9	S. H. W. Hill (1963)
South Africa				
★St. Andrew's Coll., Grahamstown....	1855	485	R1,776.....DR834	E. B. Norton (1972)
★Diocesan Coll., Rondebosch.........	1849	418	R1,320.....DR780	A. W. H. Mallett (1964)
St. John's Coll., Johannesburg.......	1898	842	R1,683.....DR888	J. J. Breitenbach (1971)
★Hilton College, Natal..............	1872	410	R1,850...........	R. G. Slater (1967)
★Michaelhouse, Balgowan, Natal......	1896	438	R1,700...........	R. F. Pennington (Rector) (1969)
Rhodesia				
★Falcon College, Essexvale...........	1954	370	$1,080...........	D. E. Turner (1962)
★Peterhouse, Marandellas...........	1955	375	$1,305...........	B. R. Fieldsend (1968)
★St. George's College, Salisbury......	1896	700	$900.......D $480	Rev. H. Wardale, S.J. (1974)
Hong Kong				
St. Stephen's College...............	1903	696	$HK4,450 D $HK650	L. J. P. Yip (1974)
Kenya				
Alliance High Sch., Kikuyu.........	1926	600	KSh450/-.........	E. Wangai (1975)
Nairobi School....................	1928	760	KSh.1,965/- DKSh705/-	D. M. Mureithi (1972)
Lenana School, Nairobi..............	1949	692	K£90....DK£30	A. S. Maina (1973)
West Indies				
★Harrison College, Barbados.........	1729	647	D $BDS13.50	A. G. Williams (1965)
Lodge School, St. John, Barbados.....	1721	570	$EC1,288–2,143 D $EC13	C. A. Smith (1972)
★Munro College, Jamaica.............	1856	462	.............Dnil	R. B. Roper (1954)
Malta				
St. Edward's College, Cottonera......	1929	292	£M495 .D £M120	A. Cachia-Carnana (1975)

PRINCIPAL GIRLS' SCHOOLS

NOTES:—(a) "Annual Fees" represents average amount payable annually, *exclusive* of fees for optional subjects. (b) "Headmistress." In certain schools other titles prevail, *e.g.*, St. Paul's, "High Mistress." (c) Headmaster.

Name of School	F'ded.	No. of Girls	Annual Fees See note (a) D=Day Girls	Headmistress See notes (b) and (c)
Abbey School, Malvern Wells........	1880	228	£1,380....D £690	(c) A. P. C. Pollard (1975)
Abbey School, Reading.............	1887	580	.........D £438	S. M. Hardcastle (1960)
Abbots Hill, Hemel Hempstead.......	1912	223	£1,110....D £630	Mrs. J. E. Anderson (1967)
The Alice Ottley School, Worcester....	1883	700	£1,092 D £330–582	E. D. Millest (1964)
All Hallows, Ditchingham, Bungay, Suffolk..........................	1864	160	£1,224....D £720	D. M. Forster (1968)
Ashford, Middlesex, St. David's.....	1716	298	£1,044....D £714	J. M. Gardner (1973)
Ashford Sch. for Girls, Kent.........	1910	755	£1,161....D £645	S. M. Thompson (1972)
Badminton School, Bristol...........	1858	340	£1,260....D £630	M. F. C. Harvey (1969)
Bath, Royal School for Daughters of Officers of the Army...............	1864	409	£1,170....D £630	M. Campbell (1968)
Bedford High School................	1882	700	£942–999 D £471–528	E. K. Wallen (1965)
Bedford, Dame Alice Harpur Sch......	1882	916	£861.....D £381	S. M. Morse (1970)
Bedgebury Park, Goudhurst, Cranbrook	1920	195	£1,125..........	J. M. Nixon (1964)
Benenden, Kent.....................	1923	333	£1,590..........	J. R. Allen (1976)
Berkhamsted Sch. for Girls, Herts......	1888	510	£1,173–1,230 D £483–540	M. R. Bateman (1971)
Bishop's Stortford, Herts. & Essex H.S.	1909	600	.............Dnil	J. Hammersley (1965)
Blackpool, Elmslie Girls' Sch........	1918	530	.........D £390	E. L. Oldham (1952)
Bolton School, Lancs................	1877	658	.........D £357	M. D. Higginson (1954)
Bradford Girls' Gr. Sch.............	1875	611	.........D £361	R. M. Gleave (1976)
Brentwood, Ursuline Convent High (R.C.)............................	1900	660	£607.....D £247	Sr. M. G. O'Driscoll (1969)

School	F'ded.	No. of Girls	Annual Fees (See note (a)) D=Day Girls	Headmistress See notes (b) and (c)
Bridlington High Sch.	1905	555	£450.......D*nil*	D. I. Matthews (1956)
Bruton School for Girls, Som.	1900	572	£1,074....D £621	D. F. Cumberlege (1964)
Burgess Hill, Sussex.	1906	330	£310.....D £190	Mrs. D. E. Harford (1971)
Casterton Sch., Kirkby Lonsdale, Cumbria.	1823	322	£1,257....D £690	(c) T. S. Penny (1973)
Charters Towers, Bexhill on Sea, Sussex	1929	280	£960.....D £525	D. L. Howe (1972)
Chatham, Gr. Sch. for Girls.	1909	536	.............D*nil*	Mrs. L. A. Goulding (1975)
Chelmsford County High Sch.	1906	641	.............D*nil*	P. Pattison (1961)
Cheltenham Ladies College.	1853	859	£1,184....D £704	M. G. Hampshire (1964)
Christ's Hospital, Hertford.	1553	290	Various..........	E. M. Tucker (1972)
Church Schools Company (29 Euston Rd., N.W.1):				
Eothen, Caterham, Surrey.	1892	320	.....D £360–660	D. C. Raine (1973)
Guildford High School.	1887	525	.....D £300–600	M. J. Harley-Mason (1969)
Hull High Sch., Tranby Croft.	1890	475	£540.....D £360	H. W. Thompson (1956)
Southampton, Atherley Sch.	1926	450	.....D £294–555	A. Ward (1973)
Sunderland Church High Sch.	1884	364	.....D £264–510	J. L. Wisbach (1957)
Surbiton High Sch.	1884	470	.....D £300–555	E. M. Kobrak (1964)
York College.	1508	360	.........D £675	M. G. Drury (1967)
Clarendon School, Abergele.	1898	200	£1,230...D £795	S. Haughton (1965)
Clifton High Sch. for Girls.	1877	720	£1,155...D £570	P. M. Stringer (1965)
Cobham Hall, Kent.	1962	290	£1,365...D £855	I. L. Hanson (1972)
Colston's Girls Sch., Bristol.	1891	670	.........D £540	A. M. S. Dunn (1954)
Commonweal Lodge Purley, Surrey.	1916	250	.....D £195–750	J. M. Blunden (1966)
Cranborne Chase Sch., Tisbury, Wilts.	1946	160	£1,575..........	(c) M. D. Neal (1969)
Croft House Sch., Shillingstone, Dorset.	1941	225	£1,500..D £1,000	Mr. & Mrs. E. H. Warley
Croham Hurst, South Croydon, Surrey	1899	500	.....D £240–615	D. J. Seward (1970) [(1971)
Derby High School.	1892	445	.....D £363–465	D. M. Hatch (1957)
Downe House, Cold Ash, Newbury.	1907	270	£1,230...........	Mrs. P. M. Wilson (1967)
Durham High School.	1884	370	.........D £480	C. I. Salter (1958)
Edgbaston C. of E. College.	1886	515	.....D £225–540	M. E. Joice (1967)
Edgehill Coll., Bideford, N. Devon.	1884	543	£1,011...D £582	A. M. Shaw (1955)
Exeter, Maynard's Girl's Sch.	1658	555	.........D £450	J. M. Bradley (1963)
Farnborough Hill, Hants.	1889	520	£915.....D £540	Sr. M. Dawson (1971)
Farringtons School, Chislehurst.	1911	442	£999.....D £600	Mrs. F. V. Hatton (1973)
Felixstowe College, Suffolk.	1929	334	£1,279...D £779	E. M. Manners, T.D. (1967)
Girls' Public Day School Trust (26 Queen Anne's Gate, Westminster, S.W.1.):				
Bath High.	1875	535	£891.....D £435	D. Chapman (1969)
Birkenhead High.	1901	822	.........D £435	F. Kellett (1971)
Blackheath High.	1880	562	.........D £480	F. Abraham (1962)
Brighton and Hove High.	1876	606	£891.....D £435	J. P. Turner (1969)
Bromley High.	1883	670	.........D £480	P. M. F. Reid (1971)
Croydon High.	1874	1119	.........D £480	A. M. McMaster (1975)
Ipswich High.	1878	576	.........D £435	P. M. Hayworth (1971)
Liverpool (Belvedere).	1880	571	.........D £435	S. Downs (1972)
Newcastle (Central) High.	1895	765	.........D £435	C. Russell (1962)
Norwich High.	1875	721	.........D £435	R. H. Standeven (1976)
Nottingham High.	1875	933	.........D £435	L. L. Lewenz (1967)
Notting Hill and Ealing High.	1873	622	.........D £480	M. J. Percy (1974)
Oxford High.	1875	505	£867.....D £435	E. H. Kaye (1972)
Portsmouth High.	1882	572	.........D £435	M. L. Clarke (1968)
Putney High.	1893	702	.........D £480	R. Smith (1963)
Sheffield High.	1878	589	.........D £435	M. C. Lutz (1959)
Shrewsbury High.	1885	581	.........D £435	M. Crane (1963)
South Hampstead High.	1876	613	.........D £480	Mrs. D Burgess (1975)
Streatham Hill and Clapham High.	1887	518	.........D £480	Mrs. N. Silver (1973)
Sutton High.	1884	899	.........D £480	I. A. Wulff (1974)
Sydenham High.	1887	626	.........D £480	M. Hamilton (1966)
Wimbledon High.	1880	654	.........D £480	Mrs. A. Piper (1962)
Godolphin, Salisbury.	1726	300	£1,410...D £759	V. M. Fraser (1968)
Gravesend Sch.	1926	600	.............D*nil*	Mrs. M. H. Dell (1971)
Gt. Crosby, Lancs., Seafield Gr. Sch., Sacred Heart of Mary (*R.C.*).	1908	650	.........D £339	Sr. Bernardine Browne (1975)
Greenacre, Banstead, Surrey.	1933	355	.........D £612	G. W. Steele (1962)
Hampden House Sch., Gt Missenden.	1864	120	£996.....D £558	Mrs. E. A. Scott (1973)
Harrogate College.	1893	430	£421.....D £242	Mrs. J. C. Lawrance (1974)
Haslemere, Royal Naval School.	1840	295	£1,311–1,326 .....D £786–801	D. M. Otter (1970)
Headington Sch., Oxford.	1915	650	£1,227–1,299 .....D £249–666	P. A. Dunn (1959)
Hollington Park, St. Leonard's, Sussex.	1860	158	£1,080....D £720	P. M. E. Garland-Collins (1973)

School	F'ded	No. of Girls	Annual Fees See note (a) D=Day Girls	Headmistress See notes (b) and (c)
Howell's, Denbigh..................	1859	438	£1,167....D£753	J. Sadler (1968)
Howell's, Llandaff.................	1860	674	£897.....D£363	M. Ll. Lewis (1941)
Hunmanby Hall, Yorks...........	1928	385	£1,203...D£753	M. Bray (1967)
King Edward VI High Sch., B'ham....	1883	530	......D£420	J. R. F. Wilkes (1965)
King's High School, Warwick......	1879	600	......D£472	M. Leahy (1970)
Lady Eleanor Holles, Hampton, Middx.	1710	730	......D£570–630	M. C. Smalley (1974)
Leamington, Kingsley Sch...........	1884	375	£945....D£525	N. K. Jones (1961)
Leeds, Girls' High..............	1876	546	......D£520	A. A. Jackson (1970)
Lillesden Sch., Hawkhurst, Kent......	1901	150	£415....D£185	M. Hill (1975)
Liverpool, Huyton College..........	1894	430	£1,287...D£777	Mrs. E. M. Rees (1971)
Liverpool (Everton Valley), Notre Dame Collegiate (R.C.)	1868	590	......D£390	Sr. R. J. Fleming, S.N.D. (1972)
Liverpool (Woolton), Notre Dame High School (R.C.)..............	1850	1100	......Dnil	Sr. M. M. Taylor, S.N.D. [(1970)
London*:				
C. E. Brooke Sch., Langton Rd., S.W. 9	1898	350	......Dnil	C. F. A. Frazer (1970)
Burlington, Wood Lane, W.12.......	1699	570	......Dnil	Mrs. E. Moore (1967)
Camden, Sandall Rd., N.W.5.......	1871	720	......Dnil	Mrs. C. M. Handley (1971)
Channing Sch., Highgate, N.6......	1885	395	......D£615	E. M. Saunders (1964)
City of London, Barbican, E.C.2.....	1894	560	......D£711	L. E. Mackie (1972)
Godolphin and Latymer, W.6.......	1905	690	......D£472	B. F. Dean (1974)
Haberdashers' Aske's, Elstree........	1690	760	......D£526	Mrs. S. Wiltshire (1974)
Haberdashers' Aske's, Hatcham, S.E.14	1690	570	......Dnil	J. A. Kirby (1958)
Francis Holland, Clarence Gate, N.W.1	1878	360	......D£600	A. E. Holt (1974)
Francis Holland, Graham Terr., S.W.1.	1881	285	......D£630	R. Colvile (1965)
James Allen's Girls', Dulwich, S.E.22.	1741	560	......D£510	I. Prissian (1969)
Lady Margaret, Parsons Green, S.W.6.	1917	407	......Dnil	A. E. Cavendish (1971)
Mary Datchelor, Camberwell Green, S.E.5	1877	650	......Dnil	E. B. Godwin (1968)
North London Collegiate, Canons, Edgware	1850	835	......D£390–495	M. M. N. McLauchlan (1965)
Queen's College, Harley St., W.1.....	1848	320	......D£630	Mrs. S. C. P. Fierz (1964)
St. Angela's, Ursuline Convent Sch., Forest Gate, E.7. (R.C.)...........	1872	900	......Dnil	M. M. Walsh, O.S.U. (1971)
St. Paul's Girls' Sch., Brook Grn., W.6.	1904	530	......D£720	Mrs. H. Brigstocke (1974)
St. Saviour's and St. Olave's Gr., New Kent Road, S.E.1.............	1903	500	......Dnil	E. M. Wilson (1959)
Loughborough High Sch., Leics........	1849	600	£723.....D£345	P. J. Hadley (1963)
Loughton City High School..........	1906	600	......Dnil	Mrs. W. J. Delchar (1972)
Lowther College, Nr. Rhyl..........	1890	245	£480....D£295	(c) J. R. Bieneman (1974)
Malvern Girls' College..............	1893	505	£1,350...D£900	V. M. H. Owen (1968)
Manchester High School for Girls......	1874	1000	......D£336	M. Blake (1975)
Manchester, Withington Girls' Sch.....	1890	460	......D£360	M. Hulme (1961)
Merchant Taylors', Gt. Crosby.......	1888	431	......D£360	M. E. Walsh (1963)
Monmouth School for Girls..........	1891	632	£663–693 .D£357	A. Page (1960)
Newcastle upon Tyne Church High Sch.,	1889	605	......D£420	P. E. Davies (1974)
North Foreland Lodge, Sherfield-on-Loddon, Hants..................	1909	160	£1,305....	D. R. K. Irvine (1967)
Northwood Coll, Northwood, Middx..	1878	475	£990–1,110 D£294–600	M. D. Hillyer-Cole (1966)
Oakdene, Beaconsfield..............	1911	490	£810....D£525	A. J. Havard (1959)
Orme Girls' Sch., Newcastle under Lyme	1876	600	......Dnil	Mrs. W. M. G. Buxton (1969)
Overstone Sch., Northampton.......	1929	153	£1,200...D£780	(c) Col. P. B. Clarke, C.B.E.
Pate's Gr. School, Cheltenham......	1905	807	......Dnil	M. M. Moon (1971) [(1974)
Perse Sch. for Girls, Cambridge......	1881	492	......D£450	C. M. Bedson (1967)
Plymouth, Notre Dame High (R.C.)...	1860	410	......D£316	Sr. V. Henderson, S.N.D. (1968)
Polam Hall, Darlington.............	1850	472	£996–1,089 D£345–519	S. M. Owen (1975)
Preston, Winckley Sq. Convent (R.C.).	1908	540	......D£351	Sr. C. Walsh (1968)
Princess Helena Coll., Temple Dinsley, Hitchin, Herts.................	1820	190	£1,152...D£702	(c) D. Clarke, Ph.D. (1971)
Queen Anne's, Caversham...........	1894	325	£1,380....	M. J. Challis (1958)
Queen Ethelburga's, Harrogate‡....	1912	210	£1,450...D£825	(c) J. E. H. Kingdon (1973)
Queen Margaret's, Escrick Park, York‡.	1901	260	£1,320....	B. D. Snape (1960)
Queen Mary, Lytham...............	1930	840	......D£324	J. Charlton (1970)
Queen's School, Chester...........	1878	560	......D£435	M. Farra (1973)
Queenswood, Hatfield, Herts........	1894	420	£1,314....	M. C. Ritchie (1972)
Redland High School, Bristol........	1882	456	......D£399	W. M. Hume (1969)
The Red Maid's, Bristol.............	1634	400	£906—D£423	D. D. Dakin (1961)
Rochester Gr. Sch., Kent...........	1888	700	......Dnil	B. J. Trollope (1973)

---

* See also: Girls' Public Day School Trust, and Church Schools Company.
‡ A Woodard Corporation School.

School	F'ded·	No. of Girls	Annual Fees See note (a) D=Day Girls	Headmistress See notes (b) and (c)
Roedean, Brighton................	1885	430	£1,590.........	(c) J. M. Hunt (1971)
Rosemead, Littlehampton...........	1919	253	£1,170....D £765	Mrs. N. R. Tobenhouse (1967)
Royal Masonic Sch., Rickmansworth Pk.	1788	432	£840......D £300	J. M. Thomson (1972)
Rye St. Anthony, Oxford...........	1930	215	£300.....D £150	I. B. King (1930)
St. Alban's High School, Herts.......	1889	604	.........D £510	M. E. Denham (1966)
St. Anne's School, Windermere.......	1863	335	£975–1,125 D £210–705	(c) C. M. G. R. Jenkins (1972)
St. Clare, Polwithen, Penzance‡.......	1885	205	£1,254....D £750	M. M. Coney (1969)
St. Dominic's High Sch., Stoke-on-Trent (R.C.)................	1857	1020	.........D £318	Sr. M. M. E. House, O.P. (1970)
St. Elphin's, Darley Dale, Matlock.....	1844	458	£1,035....D £558	A. L. Mayhew (1975)
St. Felix, Southwold, Suffolk..........	1897	431	£410.....D £360	M. Oakeley (1958)
St. Helen and St. Katharine, Abingdon .	1904	478	£1,074....D £450	Y. Paterson (1973)
St. Helen's, Northwood..............	1899	710	£921–1,050 D £348–630	J. D. Leader (1946)
St. James's School, West Malvern......	1896	200	£560.........	R. R. Braithwaite (1965)
St. Joseph's Coll., Bradford (R.C.).....	1907	1030	£700.....D £400	Sr. W. M. Daly, C.P. (1965)
St. Margaret's, Bushey, Herts.........	1749	340	£1,245....D £675	B. Scatchard (1965)
St. Mary & St. Anne, Abbots Bromley‡	1874	550	£1,200....D £800	M. E. Roch (1953)
St. Mary Sch., Baldslow, St. Leonard's..	1913	230	£950.....D £435	Sr. B. Allen, C.H.F. (1958)
St. Mary's, Calne, Wilts.............	1873	253	£1,275....D £690	Mrs. J. D. Bailey (1972)
St. Mary's Convent, Cambridge (R.C.)..	1898	600	£785.....D £495	Sr. M. D. Harris (1972)
St. Mary's Hall, Brighton...........	1836	350	£1,305.. D £900	Mrs. E. O. Leslie (1973)
St. Mary's Sch., Gerrard's Cross, Bucks.	1872	240	.....D £130–430	A. Timberlake (1974)
St. Mary's Sch. Wantage, Berks.......	1873	265	£1,380......	Mrs. E. M. Calver (1975)
St. Michael's, Burton Park, Petworth‡..	1844	300	£1,575..D £1,050	F. E. H. Davies (1973)
St. Stephen's College, Broadstairs......	1867	255	£915–1,425 D £255–900	B. Seymour (1974)
St. Swithun's, Winchester...........	1884	365	.........D.....	N. O. Davies (1973)
Salford, Adelphi House (R.C.).........	1852	750	.........D £378	Sr. N. P. Conlan, F.C.J. (1973)
Sheffield, Notre Dame High (R.C.).....	1885	730	.........D £406	Sr. Helen Mary, S.N.D. (1965)
Sherborne Sch. for Girls, Dorset......	1899	444	£1,425....D £810	E. Coulter (1975)
Stamford High Sch., Lincs...........	1876	731	£1,177....D £449	M. L. Medcalf (1968)
Stonar, Atworth, Melksham, Wilts......	1921	385	£1,272....D £693	F. D. Denmark (1962)
Stover Sch., Newton Abbot..........	1932	200	£996.....D £540	C. A. Smith (1970)
Talbot Heath Sch., Bournemouth......	1886	558	£837.....D £379	A. L. Macpherson, Ph.D. (1956)
Teesside High Sch. for Girls, Eaglescliffe.	1970	570	.........D £390	M. E. Hardwick (1971)
Tormead, Cranley Road, Guildford.....	1905	450	£1,080....D £540	M. C. Shackleton (1959)
Truro High School.................	1880	395	£762.....D £348	E. J. Davis (1972)
Tudor Hall, Wykham Park, Banbury....	1850	275	£1,275....D £765	Mrs. M. R. Blyth (1969)
Uplands School, Sandecotes, Poole.....	1903	240	.........D £585	M. P. Poots (1971)
Upper Chine, Shanklin, I.O.W.........	1914	341	£870.....D £540	P. M. Gifford (1955)
Wadhurst College..................	1930	278	£1,194....D £789	D. Swatman (1972)
Walthamstow Hall, Sevenoaks, Kent....	1838	428	£1,005....D £462	E. B. Davies, M.B.E. (1970)
Wentworth Milton Mt., Bournemouth...	1871	300	£990.....D £600	N. A. E. Hibbert (1961)
Westonbirt, Tetbury, Glos...........	1928	326	£1,533....D £927	M. Newton (1965)
Wycombe Abbey, Bucks.............	1896	460	£1,275	P. M. Lancaster (1974)
York, The Mount School............	1785	267	£1,260....D £840	J. Blake (1960)
Scotland				
Craigholme, Glasgow...............	1894	640	.....D £291–393	G. M. MacLean (1962)
Hutcheson's Girls' Gr. Sch., Glasgow...	1876	900	.........D £320	J. G. Knox, M.B.E. (1973)
Laurel Bank, Glasgow..............	1903	590	.......D £88–133	A. J. B. Sloan (1968)
Mary Erskine, Edinburgh............	1694	1,050	.........D £465	J. Thow (1967)
Morrison's Academy, Crieff..........	1860	496	£930.....D £351	A. D. Mackinnon (1972)
Park Sch., 25 Lynedoch St., Glasgow...	1879	530	.........D £430	J. Rutherford (1974)
St. Bride's, Helensburgh.............	1895	380	£1,000....D £420	C. M. Campbell (1972)
St. Columba's, Kilmacolm...........	1897	550	.....D £338–437	E. M. Clark (1966)
St. Denis', Edinburgh..............	1858	477	£1,050–1,200 D £156–570	Mrs. N. E. Law (1971)
St. George's, Garscube Terr., Edinburgh.	1888	712	£966–1,086 D £363–621	Mrs. J. O. Lindsay, Ph.D.(1960)
St. Leonard's, St. Andrews, Fife........	1877	520	£1,470....D £720	M. Hamilton (1970)
Isle of Man, Channel Islands				
Buchan Sch., Castletown, I.O.M.......	1875	236	£876.....D £372	Mrs. J. M. Watkin (1960)
Jersey College for Girls, Jersey........	1880	750	.....D £180–210	Mrs. E. M. Pullin (1974)

‡ A Woodard Corporation School.

NATIONAL REFERENDUM

The figures given in the press for the number of votes cast in the referendum on June 5, 1975, on continued United Kingdom membership of the European Economic Community were as follows:

ENGLAND

Avon
E. 665,484

Yes	310,145
No	147,024
maj	163,121

Bedfordshire
E. 326,566

Yes	154,338
No	67,969
maj	86,369

Berkshire
E. 443,472

Yes	215,184
No	81,221
maj	133,963

Buckinghamshire
E. 346,348

Yes	180,512
No	62,578
maj	117,934

Cambridgeshire
E. 375,753

Yes	177,789
No	62,143
maj	115,646

Cheshire
E. 633,614

Yes	290,714
No	123,839
maj	166,875

Cleveland
E. 392,672

Yes	158,982
No	77,079
maj	81,903

Cornwall
E. 298,706

Yes	137,828
No	63,478
maj	74,350

Cumbria
E. 349,956

Yes	162,545
No	63,564
maj	98,981

Derbyshire
E. 653,005

Yes	286,614
No	131,452
maj	155,162

Devon
E. 676,378

Yes	334,244
No	129,179
maj	205,065

Dorset
E. 429,752

Yes	217,432
No	78,239
maj	139,193

Durham
E. 444,783

Yes	175,284
No	97,724
maj	77,560

Essex
E. 1,010,317

Yes	463,505
No	222,085
maj	241,420

Gloucestershire
E. 347,218

Yes	170,931
No	67,465
maj	103,466

Greater London
E. 5,250,343

Yes	2,201,031
No	1,100,185
maj	1,100,846

Greater Manchester
E. 1,932,717

Yes	797,316
No	439,191
maj	358,125

Hampshire
E. 975,440

Yes	484,302
No	197,761
maj	286,541

Hereford and Worcester
E. 419,866

Yes	203,128
No	75,779
maj	127,349

Hertfordshire
E. 662,177

Yes	326,943
No	137,266
maj	189,677

Humberside
E. 607,890

Yes	257,826
No	122,199
maj	135,627

Isles of Scilly
E. 1,447

Yes	802
No	275
maj	527

Isle of Wight
E. 86,381

Yes	40,837
No	17,375
maj	23,462

Kent
E. 1,035,313

Yes	493,407
No	207,358
maj	286,049

Lancashire
E. 1,000,755

Yes	455,170
No	208,821
maj	246,349

Leicestershire
E. 590,780

Yes	291,500
No	106,004
maj	185,496

Lincolnshire
E. 370,518

Yes	180,603
No	61,011
maj	119,592

Merseyside
E. 1,147,920

Yes	465,625
No	252,712
maj	212,913

Norfolk
E. 485,229

Yes	218,883
No	93,198
maj	125,685

Northamptonshire
E. 351,653

Yes	162,803
No	71,322
maj	91,481

Northumberland
E. 212,846

Yes	95,980
No	42,645
maj	53,335

Nottinghamshire
E. 705,183

Yes	297,191
No	147,461
maj	149,730

Oxfordshire
E. 355,977

Yes	179,938
No	64,643
maj	115,295

Salop
E. 249,463

Yes	113,044
No	43,329
maj	69,715

Somerset
E. 293,191

Yes	138,830
No	60,631
maj	78,199

Staffordshire
E. 706,230

Yes	306,518
No	148,252
maj	158,266

Suffolk
E. 397,626

Yes	187,484
No	72,251
maj	115,233

Surrey
E. 720,440

Yes	386,369
No	120,576
maj	265,793

East Sussex
E. 511,437

Yes	249,780
No	86,198
maj	163,582

West Sussex
E. 464,396
Yes....................242,890
No.................... 75,928
maj............166,962

Tyne and Wear
E. 872,253
Yes....................344,069
No....................202,511
maj............141,558

Warwickshire
E. 327,967
Yes....................156,303
No.................... 67,221
maj............ 89,082

West Midlands
E. 1,972,987
Yes....................801,913
No....................429,207
maj............372,706

Wiltshire
E. 344,833
Yes....................172,791
No.................... 68,113
maj............104,678

North Yorkshire
E. 468,998
Yes....................234,040
No.................... 72,805
maj............161,235

South Yorkshire
E. 954,539
Yes....................377,916
No....................217,792
maj............160,124

West Yorkshire
E. 1,485,749
Yes....................616,730
No....................326,993
maj............289,737

WALES

Clwyd
E. 272,798
Yes....................123,980
No.................... 55,424
maj............ 68,556

Dyfed
E. 241,415
Yes....................109,184
No.................... 52,264
maj............ 56,920

Mid Glamorgan
E. 390,175
Yes....................147,348
No....................111,672
maj............ 35,676

South Glamorgan
E. 275,324
Yes....................127,932
No.................... 56,224
maj............ 71,708

West Glamorgan
E. 272,818
Yes....................112,989
No.................... 70,316
maj............ 42,673

Gwent
E. 314,369
Yes....................132,557
No.................... 80,992
maj............ 51,565

Gwynedd
E. 167,706
Yes.................... 76,421
No.................... 31,807
maj............ 44,614

Powys
E. 76,531
Yes.................... 38,724
No.................... 13,372
maj............ 25,352

SCOTLAND

Borders
E. 74,834
Yes.................... 34,092
No.................... 13,053
maj............ 21,039

Central
E. 188,613
Yes.................... 71,986
No.................... 48,568
maj............ 23,418

Dumfries and Galloway
E. 101,703
Yes.................... 42,608
No.................... 19,856
maj............ 22,752

Fife
E. 235,166
Yes.................... 84,239
No.................... 65,260
maj............ 18,979

Grampian
E. 321,140
Yes....................108,520
No.................... 78,071
maj............ 30,449

Highland
E. 127,925
Yes.................... 40,802
No.................... 33,979
maj............ 6,823

Lothian
E. 548,369
Yes....................208,133
No....................141,456
maj............ 66,677

Orkney
E. 13,157
Yes.................... 3,911
No.................... 2,419
maj............ 1,492

Shetland
E. 13,411
Yes.................... 2,815
No.................... 3,631
maj............ 816

Strathclyde
E. 1,759,889
Yes....................625,959
No....................459,073
maj............166,886

Tayside
E. 282,160
Yes....................105,728
No.................... 74,567
maj............ 31,161

Western Isles
E. 22.432
Yes.................... 3,393
No.................... 8,106
maj............ 4,713

NORTHERN IRELAND
E. 1,030,534
Yes....................259,251
No....................237,911
maj............ 21,340

NOTES.—1. The votes of servicemen and their families were counted in the areas in which they were stationed, and not in the areas in which they were registered to vote. The votes of overseas servicemen and their families with them abroad are included in the Greater London totals.
2. The wording of the question on the ballot paper was "Do yon think that the United Kingdom should stay in the European Community (Common Mrrket)?".

EVENTS OF THE YEAR (OCT. 1, 1974—SEPT. 15, 1975)

THE ROYAL HOUSE

(1974) **Oct. 1.** Princess Margaret was entertained at lunch by the Haberdashers Company at Haberdashers Hall, and later opened Haberdashers' Aske's Girls' School at Elstree. **6.** The Prince of Wales left R.A.F., Brize Norton, in a V.C.10 aircraft of R.A.F. Command to represent the Queen at the centenary celebrations in Fiji of its voluntary cession to Britain, and to participate in the fourth anniversary of its independence. **13.** The Prince flew from Fiji to Canberra for an 18-day visit to Australia. The Duke of Edinburgh left R.A.F., Leuchars to visit Canada and the U.S.A. **15.** The Duke attended a State banquet in Gander, Newfoundland, to celebrate the Island's 25th anniversary of confederation with Canada. The Prince of Wales addressed a joint session of the New South Wales Parliament in Sydney. **16.** The Prince of Wales inaugurated the Anglo-Australian telescope at Siding Springs, New South Wales. Prince Philip arrived in Montreal from New Brunswick, to visit equestrian sites of the 1976 Olympic Games. **17.** The Queen visited the Commonwealth Institute to see the Fiji centennial exhibition and witness a performance by the Dance Theatre of Fiji. **23.** Princess Anne opened the new H.Q. for the Save the Children Fund at Clapham Road, Lambeth. The Queen Mother opened the new Ninewells Hospital and Medical School in Dundee. **24.** The Duchess of Gloucester gave birth to a son at St. Mary's Hospital, Paddington. **25.** The Queen and the Queen Mother were present at the reception at Guildhall given by the Corporation of London to mark the 50th anniversary of the founding of the Royal Auxiliary Air Force. **27.** The Queen Mother was present at a service to mark the 50th anniversary of the founding of the Royal Auxiliary Air Force held in Westminster Abbey. **29.** The Queen, accompanied by the Duke of Edinburgh, Princess Anne, and Capt. Mark Phillips opened the first session of the new Parliament. **31.** The Queen and the Duke of Edinburgh were entertained to dinner by the Lord Mayor of London and the Lady Mayoress at Mansion House. The Prince of Wales arrived at Heathrow Airport at the conclusion of his visit to Australia.

Nov. 8. The Queen Mother conferred upon the Prince of Wales the degree of doctor of laws at a ceremony in the Senate House, University of London. **10.** The Queen and the Duke of Edinburgh, with the Prince of Wales, laid wreaths at the Cenotaph on the occasion of Remembrance Day. The Queen Mother and other members of the Royal Family were also present. The Duke was entertained at lunch by the officers of the Welsh Guards at Chelsea Barracks. Later he attended the regimental service of remembrance of the Welsh Guards at the Guards' Chapel, Wellington Barracks, and took the salute at the Guards' Memorial, Horse Guards. **13.** The Queen visited Bradford and Halifax. The Queen Mother visited York and opened the St. Sampson's Centre for elderly people. **14.** The Queen gave a reception at Buckingham Palace for delegates attending the 20th Annual Session of the North Atlantic Assembly, at which the Prince of Wales was present. **15.** Princess Anne and Capt. Mark Phillips left London in a DC8 aircraft of Air Canada on a four-day visit to Toronto. **19.** The Queen visited Queen Elizabeth's College (the Drapers' Company's Almshouses at Greenwich) to mark the 400th anniversary of its foundation. **25.** The Duke of Edinburgh went to Birmingham to visit victims of the I.R.A. bomb blasts and see the damage caused by the

explosions. **27.** The Queen and the Duke of Edinburgh held an evening reception for the Diplomatic Corps at Buckingham Palace at which the Queen Mother and Princess Alexandra were present. Princess Anne visited Nottingham, Derby, and Leicester.

Dec. 1. The Duke of Edinburgh, President of the Fédération Equestre Internationale, left Gatwick Airport to attend meetings of the bureau of the Fédération and the ordinary general assembly in Brussels. **3.** The Queen Mother visited Lloyd's and honoured the Chairman and members of the committee at luncheon. **6.** The Queen visited Havant and Southampton. **9.** The Duke of Edinburgh, as Colonel-in-Chief, R.E.M.E., visited the Army Apprentices' College, Arborfield, and took the salute at a passing out parade. **10.** The Duke gave a lecture to students of the Royal College of Defence Studies at Seaford House, Belgrave Square. He later attended the bicentenary dinner of the Royal Society of Arts at John Adam Street. **13.** The Prince of Wales arrived at Bangor, Gwynedd, visited the Marine Science Laboratories at Menai Bridge and chaired a meeting of the Prince of Wales' Committee for Wales at University College of North Wales, Bangor. **20.** The Prime Minister of Australia and Mrs. Whitlam were invited to luncheon with the Queen and the Duke of Edinburgh at Buckingham Palace. The Queen arrived at Windsor Castle later and was joined by the Duke of Edinburgh on Dec. 22. **25.** The Queen made her customary Christmas Day broadcast. **28.** The Queen and Duke of Edinburgh and their family moved into Wood Farm, a six-bedroom farmhouse on the Royal Estates at Sandringham, for four weeks because Sandringham House was undergoing rebuilding.

(1975) **Jan. 24.** The Prince of Wales, Princess Margaret, and the Duchess of Kent attended the service in Canterbury Cathedral for the enthronement of Dr. Donald Coggan as Archbishop of Canterbury.

Feb. 3. The Prince of Wales attended the 600th anniversary service at St. Bride's Church, Fleet Street. He was later entertained at dinner at Gray's Inn, was called to the Bar of England and Wales, and elected a Master of the Bench of the Society at Gray's Inn. **6.** The Prince of Wales, Princess Alexandra (who represented the Queen), and Princess Alice, Duchess of Gloucester, attended the funeral of the Duke of Norfolk held at the Cathedral Church of Our Lady and St. Philip Howard, Arundel. **11.** The Queen invested the Prince of Wales with the insignia of a Knight Grand Cross of the Military Division of the Most Honourable Order of the Bath. **12.** The Duke of Edinburgh, as Colonel of the Welsh Guards, visited the 1st Battalion at Caterham and was entertained at luncheon in the Officers' Mess and in the evening, accompanied by the Prince of Wales, was present at a dinner given by the Welsh Guards at the Guards Club to mark his retirement as Colonel. **13.** The Queen made a series of visits in London to meet people who had the responsibility of dealing with bomb outrages, being received at New Scotland Yard, London Fire Brigade H.Q., London Ambulance Service H.Q., and the South Western District Post Office, Victoria. **16.** The Queen and the Duke of Edinburgh left Heathrow Airport in a super VC10 aircraft of British Airways to visit Bermuda, Barbados, the Bahamas, and Mexico. **19.** The Prince of Wales, accompanied by the Duke of Gloucester, and the Earl Mountbatten of Burma, left Heathrow Airport in an R.A.F. Comet to visit New Delhi and Katmandu. **24.** The Queen was represented by the Prince of Wales at the coronation of King Birendra of Nepal in the Old Palace of Hanuman Dhoka, Katmandu.

Mar. 1. The Prince of Wales took part in his first public ceremony as Colonel of the Welsh Guards when he presented the leeks at a St. David's Day drumhead service and parade at Caterham Barracks. **2.** The Queen arrived at Heathrow Airport from Mexico after her two-week visit with the Duke of Edinburgh to the Caribbean and Mexico. **3.** The Prince of Wales was present at a lunch at the House of Commons given by the Parliamentary Press Gallery. He later visited victims of the Moorgate Tube crash in St. Bartholomew's Hospital. **7.** The Queen made a series of visits in Birmingham to meet the people who had had the responsibility of dealing with bomb outrages. **12.** The Prime Minister of Canada (Mr. Pierre Trudeau) lunched with the Queen at Buckingham Palace. **18.** Princess Anne visited Bolton and Rochdale. **19.** The Queen visited the National Federation of Women's Institutes' diamond jubilee exhibition at the Commonwealth Institute. **20.** The Queen Mother opened the new H.Q. of the London City Mission in Tower Bridge Road. **21.** Princess Margaret opened the new community centre at Ashford, Middlesex. **24.** The Duke of Edinburgh arrived at Heathrow Airport from Central America. **28.** Royal Maundy money was distributed by the Queen at Peterborough Cathedral for the first time since the ceremony was performed there by Cardinal Wolsey in 1530.

Apr. 6. The Queen Mother took the salute at a parade of the Territorial Auxiliary and Volunteer Reserve Association for Greater London held in Hyde Park. **10.** The Queen and the Duke of Edinburgh gave a reception at Windsor Castle for the Military Knights of Windsor. **11.** The Queen visited Norwich, when she attended a thanksgiving service for the restoration of the Cathedral. **13.** The Duke of Edinburgh visited The Silverstone Motorracing circuit and declared open the new pits. **14.** The Queen Mother left London Airport for Iran. **16.** Princess Margaret was present at the jubilee celebration of the St. Pancras Housing Association. **20.** The Prince of Wales arrived in Canada to visit Ottawa and the Northwest Territories. **21.** The Queen celebrated her 49th birthday anniversary. Princess Anne and Capt. Mark Phillips left London Airport to visit Australia. **23.** The Queen, the Duke of Edinburgh, the Queen Mother, Prince Andrew, and Princess Margaret were present at the service of thanksgiving in St. George's Chapel, Windsor Castle, to mark the opening of the celebrations of the Chapel's quincentenary. **26.** The Queen and the Duke of Edinburgh began a fourday visit to Jamaica. **27.** The Queen and the Duke of Edinburgh attended morning service at Kingston parish church and laid a wreath on the national war memorial. Later they were guests of the Governor-General at a dinner in his official residence, King's House, which the Queen used to receive Commonwealth heads of Government attending their summit conference in private audience on April 28. **28.** The Queen visited the campus of the University of the West Indies in Kingston to open a new law school. **29.** Thirty-three Commonwealth leaders dined on board the Royal yacht *Britannia* in Kingston harbour as guests of the Queen. **30.** The Queen and the Duke of Edinburgh left Jamaica by air and flew to Honolulu for a brief private stay. Princess Margaret undertook engagements in Portsmouth. In the evening she was present at the annual dinner of the Royal Academy of Arts in Piccadilly.

May 4. The Queen and the Duke of Edinburgh arrived in Hong Kong for a three-day tour, the Queen being the first British sovereign to visit the crown colony. **6.** The Queen Mother visited the London Borough of Enfield, and opened the new civic centre. **7.** The Queen and the Duke of Edinburgh began their State visit to Japan, the first by a British monarch, being met at Tokyo's Haneda Airport by Princess Chichibu, the Emperor's daughter. Princess Anne and Capt. Mark Phillips arrived at London Airport from Australia. **9.** The Queen and the Duke of Edinburgh visited the Hodogaya British Commonwealth War Cemetery in Yokohama and laid a wreath at the foot of the memorial. **11.** The Queen and the Duke of Edinburgh visited the Shinto shrine at Ise, Japan's most sacred place. **13.** The Queen and the Duke of Edinburgh arrived at Heathrow Airport from Japan. Princess Margaret undertook engagements in Glasgow in connection with the City's 800th anniversary celebrations. **15.** The Queen Mother opened the Aboyne Academy and Deeside Community Centre. **16.** The Duke of Edinburgh visited Salford civic centre to present a charter and letters patent to the Metropolitan Borough of Salford. **18.** The Duke of Edinburgh attended the regimental service of remembrance of the Grenadier Guards at the Guard's Chapel, Wellington Barracks. **20.** The Queen and the Duke of Edinburgh visited Greenwich to mark the tercentenary of the Royal Observatory and as part of the celebrations of European Architectural Heritage Year. They embarked in the Port of London Authority's barge *Nore* at Westminster Pier and proceeded to Greenwich Pier. Later they witnessed a demonstration of the 28-inch telescope and toured the special exhibition of 300 years of astronomy in the Great Hall, Queen's House, departing afterwards for the Royal Naval College. After lunch in the Painted Hall, the Queen and the Duke walked through Greenwich town centre to see the improvements scheme and visited St. Alfege's Church and gardens, Ranger's House, Gloucester Circus, Cutty Sark Gardens, and the *Cutty Sark*. The Queen opened the Department of the Environment Exhibition in European Architectural Heritage Year, and later left Greenwich Pier by hydrofoil for Westminster Pier. The Duke of Edinburgh gave the inaugural lecture in the Institute of Building's annual series at Senate House, London University. **21.** The Queen visited the Shropshire and West Midland Agricultural Society's centenary show, and later witnessed a pageant showing life in Shropshire in 1875. The Duke of Edinburgh presided at the annual general meeting of the M.C.C. and was later present at the anniversary dinner. **27.** The Queen Mother embarked in H.M. Yacht *Britannia* at Portsmouth for a visit to the Channel Islands and the Isle of Wight. **28.** The Queen attended the 250th anniversary service of the Order of the Bath in Westminster Abbey, and was present at the ceremony of installation of the Prince of Wales as Great Master of the Order in King Henry VII's Chapel, the Chapel of the Order. The Duke of Edinburgh visited Bristol. The Queen Mother visited Guernsey and lunched with the States, later opening the new extension of the Princess Elizabeth Hospital. **29.** The Duke of Edinburgh toured Shropshire, Hereford, and Worcester in connection with the Duke of Edinburgh's Award. The Queen Mother visited Alderney and Sark. **30.** The Queen visited R.A.F., Cranwell to present the Queen's new colour to the College. The Duke of Edinburgh toured Gwent and Dorset in connection with the Duke of Edinburgh's Award. The Queen

THE STATE VISIT TO JAPAN

The Queen and the Duke of Edinburgh watching women pearl divers during their State visit to Japan in May.

THE QUEEN IN MEXICO

The Queen is seen with the wife of the President of Mexico and other guests, who were in national costume, after a state banquet in Mexico City during the royal visit to Mexico in February.

THE ROYAL OBSERVATORY'S TERCENTENARY

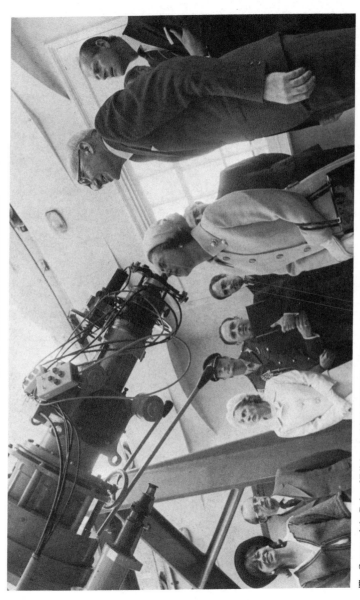

The Queen and the Duke of Edinburgh visited Greenwich on May 20 to mark the tercentenary of the Royal Observatory. Her Majesty is seen looking through a 28-inch telescope.

THE QUEEN MOTHER'S 75th BIRTHDAY

Queen Elizabeth the Queen Mother celebrated her 75th birthday on August 4. She is seen at Royal Lodge, Windsor with two of her grandsons, the Prince of Wales and Prince Andrew.

THE NEW ARCHBISHOP OF CANTERBURY

Dr. Donald Coggan seen at Canterbury Cathedral, where on January 24 he was enthroned as Archbishop of Canterbury.

MRS. MARGARET THATCHER

Mrs. Margaret Thatcher, who was elected leader of the Conservative Party in succession to Mr. Edward Heath on February 11. She became the first woman to lead a British political party.

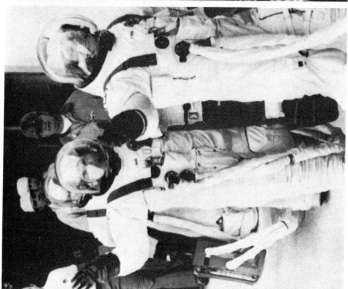

HISTORIC SPACE LINK-UP

The first U.S.-Soviet link-up in space took place on July 17, when an *Apollo* and a *Soyuz* spacecraft docked and the crews met each other. The two Russian cosmonauts and the three American astronauts are seen waving farewell before boarding their spacecraft.

THE MOORGATE TUBE DISASTER

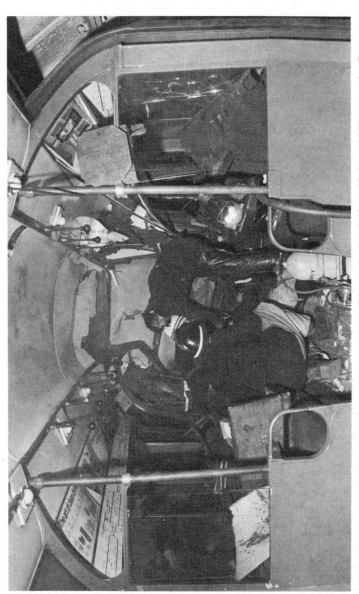

A London Underground train overran the platform at Moorgate station on February 28 and crashed into a blind tunnel, killing 43 people. Firemen are seen at work in one of the carriages.

THE BIRMINGHAM BOMB OUTRAGE

Bombs planted by I.R.A. terrorists exploded in two public houses in the centre of Birmingham on November 21, 1974, killing 21 people and injuring 182. The picture shows the devastated interior of one of the public houses.

THE SUEZ CANAL

Crowds cheer as a destroyer carrying President Sadat of Egypt sails by on the Suez Canal, which was officially reopened to international shipping on June 5. The Canal had been closed since the Arab-Israeli War of 1967.

VANDALS END TEST MATCH

The third Test match between England and Australia at Headingley had to be abandoned on August 19 after vandals had damaged the wicket. The two captains, Ian Chappell and Tony Greig, are seen examining the damage.

TWO WORLD FIGURES

Eamon De Valera, the President of the Republic of Ireland from 1959 to 1973, died on August 29 at the age of 92 and Hailé Selassie, the former Emperor of Ethiopia, died on August 27, aged 83.

THE DEATHS OF FAMOUS MEN

The Duke of Norfolk, the Earl Marshal and Premier Duke and Earl (*top left*), died at the age of 66 on January 31, and Sir Neville Cardus, the music critic and cricket writer (*top right*), died on February 28, aged 85. Two other famous men to die during the year were Sir Arthur Bliss, Master of the Queen's Musick since 1953 (*bottom left*), who died at the age of 83 on March 27, and Sir Pelham (P. G.) Wodehouse, the author, who died on February 14, aged 93.

GRUNDY'S RECORD

Grundy (right), ridden by Pat Eddery, comes home to win the King George VI and Queen Elizabeth Diamond Stakes at Ascot on July 26. This victory increased *Grundy's* prize money to £312,122, a record for an English-trained horse. He had earlier won the Derby.

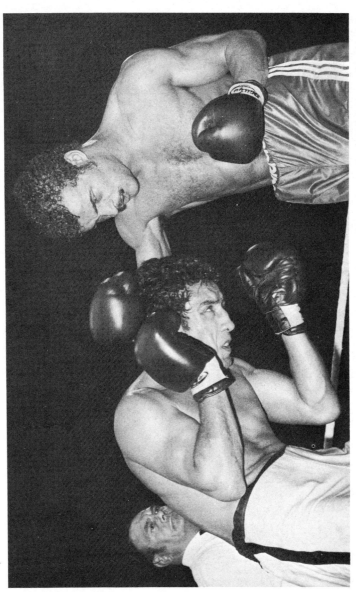

BRITISH WORLD BOXING CHAMPION

John Conteh (*right*), of Liverpool, on his way to a points victory over Jorge Ahumada, of Argentina, in their world light-heavyweight title fight at Wembley Pool on October 1, 1974.

A NEW MILE RECORD

John Walker of New Zealand breasts the tape in Gothenburg, Sweden on August 12 to set a new world record for the mile of 3m. 49·4s.

Mother visited Jersey and named the new Jersey lifeboat, later visiting the States Building.

June 2. The Queen and the Duke of Edinburgh were present at a reception in the Law Society's Hall, Chancery Lane, given by the Law Society to celebrate its 150th anniversary. **4.** The Queen, with the Duke of Edinburgh, accompanied by the Queen Mother, the Duchess of Gloucester, and Princess Alexandra saw the Derby at Epsom. **5.** The Queen drove to the Royal Hospital, Chelsea, and reviewed the In-Pensioners on Founder's Day. Princess Margaret visited Thirsk and Harrogate. **6.** The Queen and the Duke of Edinburgh gave a reception at Buckingham Palace for the teams from Australia, East Africa, England, India, New Zealand, Pakistan, Sri Lanka, and West Indies participating in the international cricket competition. Princess Anne and Capt. Mark Phillips left Heathrow Airport for Germany to visit 14th/20th King's Hussars at Herford. **8.** The Duke of Edinburgh attended the memorial service of the Dunkirk Veterans' Association at Ramsgate, and took the salute at a march past at the East Cliff bandstand. **9.** The Queen opened the northern extension of the National Gallery. **11.** The Duke of Edinburgh. as President of U.K. Council for European Architectural Heritage Year, took part at Thames Television, Euston Road, in the final programme of the series, *A Place in Europe.* **12.** The Prince of Wales visited Windsor to view progress made in restoration work in connection with European Architectural Heritage Year, and also attended the Welsh Guards' Club dinner at the Dorchester Hotel. **13.** The Queen Mother was present at a concert given at the Maltings as part of the Aldeburgh Festival. **16.** The Queen and the Duke of Edinburgh gave a luncheon party at Windsor Castle for the Knights of the Garter, at which the Queen Mother and the Prince of Wales were present. **17.** The Queen, with the Duke of Edinburgh, attended Ascot Races. Princess Anne visited Carlisle, leaving afterwards for Holyroodhouse Palace, Edinburgh. **18.** The Queen, with the Duke of Edinburgh, visited Ascot Races. Princess Anne went to the Royal Highland Agricultural Society of Scotland show at Ingliston, near Edinburgh. **23.** Princess Margaret opened the world conference of the World Association of Girl Guides and Girl Scouts at the University of Sussex, Brighton. **24.** The Queen Mother visited Edinburgh in connection with European Architectural Heritage Year. **25.** The Duke of Edinburgh presided at the International Cricket Conference and was entertained at dinner with the delegates at Lord's Cricket ground. The Prince of Wales spoke in the debate on voluntary service in the community at the House of Lords. **26.** The Queen visited the new Covent Garden Market with the Duke of Edinburgh and declared it open. The Queen and the Duke gave a reception in the evening at Buckingham Palace on the occasion of the golden jubilee of the National Playing Fields' Association. The Duke had been present at a luncheon at Claridge's to celebrate the golden jubilee. **27.** The Queen visited the University of Birmingham to mark its centenary and afterwards left for the Royal Shakespeare Theatre centenary garden at Stratford-upon-Avon, where she unveiled a plaque commemorating its opening. The Queen and the Duke of Edinburgh attended a gala performance at the Royal Shakespeare Theatre in the evening. The Duke earlier carried out engagements in Windsor as president of U.K. Council of European Architectural Heritage Year, and later presented the Civic Trust's Heritage Year awards in Windsor Castle. The Prince of Wales visited the 3rd (Volunteer) Battalion, the Royal Regiment of

Wales, at Jurby Camp, Isle of Man. **30.** The Queen gave a reception at Buckingham Palace for the delegates attending the 22nd conference of the World Association of Girl Guides and Girl Scouts. The Queen Mother and Princess Margaret were also present.

July 1. The Queen left London in the royal train to visit the Duchy of Lancaster estate in Yorkshire. The Duke of Edinburgh visited Architectural Heritage Year schemes in Norwich, King's Lynn, and Sleaford. The Prince of Wales visited the Royal Show at Stoneleigh, Warwickshire. Princess Anne and Capt. Mark Phillips arrived at Heathrow from Boston after having competed in the U.S. international horse trials at Hamilton, Mass. The Queen Mother was present at a garden party given by the National Trust at Montacute, Somerset, to mark the Trust's 80th anniversary. **2.** The Queen and the Duke of Edinburgh visited the Duchy of Lancaster Estate and lunched at Pickering Castle. Later they flew to Turnhouse Airport, Edinburgh, and drove to Holyroodhouse. The Duke afterwards attended the 200th session dinner of the Speculative Society of the Signet Library, Parliament Square. The Prince of Wales was present at the silver jubilee dinner of the Lord's Taverners at Quaglinos. **3.** The Queen opened the new St. Andrew's House, Edinburgh, and visited the St. James shopping arcade. The Queen and the Duke of Edinburgh left in the royal train to visit Dumfriesshire. **4.** The Queen and the Duke of Edinburgh visited Annan, Dumfries and Lockerbie. **6.** The Queen Mother arrived at Holyroodhouse. **7.** The Queen and the Duke gave a luncheon party at Holyroodhouse for the Knights of the Thistle at which the Queen Mother was present. The Prince of Wales and Princess Margaret arrived at Holyroodhouse. **8.** The King of Sweden arrived in Edinburgh on a State visit to the Queen and Duke of Edinburgh at Holyroodhouse. The Queen and the Duke gave a State banquet in honour of the King at which the Queen Mother, the Prince of Wales, and Princess Margaret were among those present, and later held an evening reception in His Majesty's honour. **9.** The King of Sweden was entertained at lunch by the Lord Provost and the members of the City of Edinburgh district council, and later visited oil installations at Grangemouth and Dalmeny. The Queen and the King of Sweden, with the Duke of Edinburgh, the Queen Mother, the Prince of Wales, and Princess Margaret witnessed the ceremony of Beating Retreat in Holyrood Park. The Government gave a dinner and reception in honour of the King of Sweden at Parliament House. The Queen, the Duke of Edinburgh, the Queen Mother, and the Prince of Wales attended the reunion of regiments of the Scottish Division in Holyrood Park. **10.** The King of Sweden toured the Craigvinean Forest of the Forestry Commission, visited Scone Palace, and later flew to Heathrow Airport, London. The Queen flew to R.A.F., Leeming, and drove to Vimy Lines to visit the training brigade of Royal Corps of Signals at Catterick Camp for the 50th anniversary of the Corps' presence in Catterick, later flying to Heathrow. The Queen, the Duke of Edinburgh, the Queen Mother, Princess Anne and Capt. Mark Phillips, Princess Margaret, and other members of the Royal family were entertained at a banquet by the King of Sweden at Claridge's. Earlier the Duke of Edinburgh had visited Beverley and Hull before flying to London. **14.** The Duke of Edinburgh visited Warwickshire cricket ground, Edgbaston, and met members of the Australian and England cricket teams in the first Test. The Prince of Wales visited Monmouth in connection with European

Architectural Heritage Year and the Prince of Wales' Committee for Wales. **15.** The Duke of Edinburgh opened the 1975 conference of the Royal Agricultural Society of the Commonwealth at University College of Wales, Aberystwyth. **18.** The Queen visited 1st Bn. Royal Green Jackets at Dover, and witnessed a tattoo, later touring Connaught Barracks. Princess Anne flew to Herstmonceux Castle, East Sussex, and inaugurated a sundial by unveiling a bust of John Flamsteed, the first Astronomer Royal, and attended a garden party to mark the tercentenary of the foundation of the Royal Observatory at Greenwich. **21.** The Queen and the Duke of Edinburgh visited the Royal Ocean Racing Club to mark its 50th anniversary. **22.** The Queen, with Prince Edward, was present at a performance of the Royal Tournament at Earls Court. The Duke of Edinburgh visited Royal Welsh Agricultural Society Show ground, Builth, Powys, which he opened. The Queen Mother visited Cambridge, lunching with the Master of Trinity College and opened the extension to the Fitzwilliam Museum. **28.** The Prince of Wales played in the Royal Navy polo team at the royal tournament at Earls Court. **29.** The Queen and the Duke of Edinburgh arrived at Doncaster, and later visited Rotherham, Barnsley, and Sheffield. **31.** The Queen was present in afternoon at the Test match between England and Australia at Lord's. The Duke of Edinburgh had been present in the morning.

Aug. 1. The Queen received the President of Guyana and Mrs. Chung at Buckingham Palace. The Duke of Edinburgh flew to Eastney Barracks, Hants, and opened the Royal Marines museum. **4.** Queen Elizabeth the Queen Mother celebrated her 75th birthday. **7.** The Home Secretary (Mr. Roy Jenkins) told the Commons that the Queen's Silver Jubilee of her accession to the throne would be celebrated in the summer of 1977. The Queen, accompanied by Prince Andrew and Prince Edward, arrived at Aberdeen and drove to Balmoral Castle. **11.** The Duke of Edinburgh arrived at Balmoral Castle. **25.** The Duke of Edinburgh left Dyce Airport, Aberdeen, to visit Poland and returned on Sept. 2.

Sept. 4. The Queen and the Duke of Edinburgh arrived at Buckingham Palace from Balmoral Castle; Her Majesty, accompanied by His Royal Highness, opened the Inter-Parliamentary Conference in Westminster Hall; they later returned to Balmoral. **12.** The Prince of Wales left Heathrow Airport to represent the Queen at independence celebrations of Papua New Guinea; the Duke and Duchess of Kent also left for visit to Iran.

BRITISH POLITICS

Oct. 10. The final result of the General Election was: Labour 319, Conservatives 276, Liberals 13, Scottish Nationalists 11, Plaid Cymru 3, United Ulster Unionists 10, Social Democratic and Labour 1, Independent 1, and The Speaker. This gave Labour an overall majority of 3. There was a record number of 2,251 candidates. **17.** Mr. Norman Buchan, 51, Minister of State for Agriculture, and Labour M.P. for Renfrewshire West, resigned from the Government "because of increasingly serious disagreements about certain policy matters and about the control and direction of the department". **18.** The Prime Minister created two new ministerial posts and a special unit to help Mr. Short (Lord President of the Council) to prepare legislation for elected assemblies for Scotland and Wales. These new jobs of Minister of State and Parliamentary Secretary, Privy Council Office, were given respectively to Mr. Gerry Fowler and Mr. William Price and were among 14

ministerial appointments announced by Mr. Wilson in his front bench reshuffle at the beginning of his new administration. The only change to the Cabinet was the addition of Mr. John Silkin, who remained as Minister for Planning and Local Government. **22.** Mr. James Molyneaux, United Ulster Unionist M.P. for Antrim South, was elected as the party's leader at Westminster. When the new House of Commons assembled for the first time since the General Election, the Speaker (Mr. Selwyn Lloyd) was re-elected unopposed for a third term. **23.** Lord Windlesham resigned as Opposition Leader in the House of Lords. **28.** Lord Belhaven and Stenton, a Scottish peer, announced his resignation from the Conservative Party to become the first Scottish Nationalist in the House of Lords. **29.** The first session of the new Parliament was opened by the Queen, and a minimum of 26 bills, an unusually large number, was outlined in the Royal Speech. **30.** The Labour Party's national executive committee agreed to hold a full-scale inquest into the way the B.B.C. reported the October general election on television and radio. The N.E.C. also passed a motion that, whilst welcoming the Foreign Secretary's statement that the British Government was undertaking a thorough review of the Simonstown Agreement, it deplored the Government's action in holding the recent combined naval exercise with South Africa and called upon it to ensure the ministers concerned did not repeat " this gross error ". This N.E.C. motion resulted in the Prime Minister writing the next day (Oct. 31) to three left-wing ministers, unnamed, who voted against the Government on an amendment and asking for an assurance they would adhere to the rule that ministers did not attack the Government. Mr. Wilson received from each of them on Nov. 6 the assurances he sought on acceptance of collective responsibility for Government decisions.

Nov. 4. The Government won its first major division in the Commons when a Conservative amendment regretting " the disastrous proposals " in the Queen's Speech for the nationalisation of the aircraft, shipbuilding and offshore oil industries and the establishment of a National Enterprise Board was defeated by 310 votes to 296, a Government majority of 14, although Liberals, Scottish Nationalists, and Ulster Unionists joined forces with the Opposition. **6.** Mr. Edward du Cann, M.P. for Taunton, was returned unopposed as chairman of the 1922 Committee of Conservative M.P.s. Seven of Uganda's 12 diplomats in London were ordered to leave Britain in retaliation for President Amin's reduction of the British High Commission staff in Kampala from 50 to 5. **7.** Sir Alec Douglas-Home, who disclaimed his hereditary title of Earl of Home on becoming prime minister in 1963, and who retired from the Commons at the general election of October, 1974, was made a life baron. The Opposition leader (Mr. Heath) wrote to the Chairman of the 1922 Committee on the question of a review of the procedure for the election of the leader of the Conservative Party saying " this is one of the important matters I shall be very glad indeed to discuss " with the Committee. **12.** Mr. Healey, Chancellor of the Exchequer, presented his third budget in eight months and told the Commons their new measures must lay the foundation for dealing with Britain's economic problems over the next four years. **14.** The Conservative leader, Mr. Heath, told the 1922 Committee of Conservative M.P.s that he would initiate immediately a discussion of arrangements for a review of the leadership election procedure. Mr. Cledwyn Hughes, M.P. for Anglesey, defeated Mr. Ian Mikardo, M.P. for Bethnal Green and Bow, for the chairmanship of the Parliamentary Labour

Party by 162 votes to 131. **19.** Proposals for taxing revenue from North Sea and other off-shore oil fields were outlined in the Oil Taxation Bill published by the Government. **20.** Three local authorities in the Midlands granted the police special orders banning an I.R.A. funeral procession for James McDade, their action receiving the consent of the Home Secretary. At the request of Mr. Heath, Sir Alec Douglas-Home undertook to chair the special committee to review procedures for the election of the Conservative Party leader. **21.** United States police reported that Mr. John Stonehouse, Labour M.P. for Walsall North and a former minister, was missing, feared drowned, off Miami Beach where his clothes, left in a beach-side changing room, had not been claimed. In the Commons on Dec. 17, the Prime Minister declared that there was no truth whatever in reports that Mr. Stonehouse was being kept under investigation or surveillance by the security services at the time of his disappearance. Mr. Wilson also said that he was advised at the time that there was no evidence to support allegations that Mr. Stonehouse was spying for the Czechoslovakian intelligence service when he held ministerial office and that he had been advised again that no evidence to support the allegations had come to light at any time since then. On Dec. 24 police in Melbourne said that they had detained a man believed to be the missing M.P., under an immigration law. On Dec. 26 a Melbourne magistrate told Mr. Stonehouse that he would be held in custody for seven days while Australia's Immigration Minister considered his case. On Dec. 27 Mr. Stonehouse made a new appeal to be allowed to stay in Australia and not returned as an illegal immigrant. The Australian Government released Mr. Stonehouse from detention on Dec. 28, the Immigration Minister saying that he had not committed any offence in Australia and that members of Commonwealth parliaments did not require permits to enter Australia. On Dec. 30 the Department of Trade announced that it was authorised on Dec. 6 by the Trade Secretary (Mr. Shore) to mke inquiries under the 1967 Companies Act into the London Capital Group and other companies connected with Mr. Stonehouse. London Capital Group announced on Jan, 2, 1975 that Mr. Stonehouse had resigned as director of the bank and all its subsidiaries, this following his dismissal as chairman on the previous Monday. On Jan. 13 the Leader of the House of Commons (Mr. Short) announced that Mr. Stonehouse was resigning as an M.P. by applying for the Manor of Northstead stewardship. Just before this statement some Labour M.P.s tabled a motion saying he had " forfeited his rights to remain a Member of the House of Commons ". But the resignation not having materialised, on Jan. 28 a Government motion to appoint a Select Committee to consider the position of Mr. Stonehouse " as Member for Walsall North " was carried by 237 votes to 30. On March 10 it was revealed in Stockholm that Mr. Stonehouse had written to the Swedish Prime Minister applying for permission to live in Sweden, and stating that he had decided to resign from the House of Commons and renounce his U.K. citizenship and requesting the grant of a Swedish passport. On March 20 the House of Commons select committee which considered his position presented its first report in which it stated that it did not " believe that the House would wish at present to take action against him ". The report added: " Your committee believe if there is no change in Mr. Stonehouse's condition such as would permit him to return within a few months, and he himself takes no steps to resign, the House would then wish to

consider vacating the seat on the grounds of non-representation." On March 21 Mr. Stonehouse was arrested in Melbourne on an extradition warrant issued in London on March 20 and charged with offences of theft, forgery, and deception, being granted bail. On May 6 the House of Commons Select Committee, which had been considering Mr. Stonehouse's position considered that a motion to expel him would now be justified but recommended that it should not be moved earlier than one month after the publication of the report to give him the opportunity to attend the Commons or to resign. On June 9 Mr. Stonehouse was arrested at Tullamarine airport when he attempted to board a London-bound plane. On June 11 the Leader of the House of Commons (Mr. Edward Short) announced that the debate arranged for the following day on a motion seeking the expulsion of Mr. Stonehouse had been withdrawn in order not to prejudice any court proceedings.

Nov. 25. The Home Secretary announced in the Commons what he described as " Draconian measures unprecedented in peacetime " to ban the I.R.A. and combat its activities in Britain, these measures being subject to renewal after six months. More than 60 Conservative M.P.s signed a motion calling for capital punishment of people causing death by planting bombs, and in 24 hours the total reached 155 M.P.s, including one Labour member. **26.** An Opposition attempt to ease the burden of National Insurance contributions to be paid by the self-employed in 1975 was defeated in the Commons by 284–264, a Government majority of 20. **27.** The Home Secretary introduced a bill in the Commons which proscribed the I.R.A., made support for it illegal, and gave powers to make exclusion orders against people involved in terrorism. **28.** The House of Commons gave an unopposed second reading to the Prevention of Terrorism (Temporary Provisions) Bill, giving powers to combat I.R.A. violence and they embarked on detailed examination of its remaining stages which entailed an all-night sitting lasting 17 hours. The House of Lords, who had debated the principle of the bill in a previous debate, passed the measure through all its stages in five minutes on Nov. 29.

Dec. 2. Mrs. Castle announced in the Commons an increase of £29,000,000 in the programme for capital development and renovation of buildings in the National Health Service. **3.** The Defence Secretary (Mr. Roy Mason) announced in the Commons a £4,700,000,000 cut in Britain's defence spending over the next 10 years including a reduction of 35,000 in service manpower and big reductions in forces east of Suez. **4.** The Church of England (Worship and Doctrine) Measure, which gave the Church power to order its own form of worship, was approved in the Commons after a long and controversial debate by 145 votes to 45, a majority of 100. **5.** Nine former M.P.s and two trade union leaders were among those named in a record list of 17 new life peers announced from 10 Downing Street. **9.** The Energy Secretary (Mr. Varley) announced a 50 m.p.h. speed limit on single carriageway roads and 60 m.p.h. on dual carriageways with 70 m.p.h. restrictions on motorways unchanged, compulsory heating restrictions in buildings and curbs to be imposed after Christmas in the use of electricity for external display and advertising during daylight in a series of fuel-saving measures to cut the country's annual oil bill by about £100,000,000. **11.** The Commons rejected a proposal to re-introduce the death penalty for terrorists by 369–217 in a free vote, a majority against of 152. **12.** The Lords debate on the death penalty ended without a vote. **16.**

More than 50 Labour M.P.s voted against the Government's defence policies in the Commons when a motion to take note of the results of the review was carried by 241–58, a Government majority of 183, the Conservatives abstaining, although earlier an Opposition amendment that the proposed cuts would "imperil the nation" was defeated by 316–256, a Government majority of 60. **17.** New rules were announced by a committee headed by Sir Alec Douglas-Home for electing the leader of the Conservative party and provided for the election to be made annually. **18.** The Minister for Overseas Development (Mrs. Judith Hart) announced in the Commons that the Government was to provide £85,000,000 to rescue the Crown Agents, the independent body which conducts large purchasing and investment operations in Britain for overseas governments, from financial difficulties although all money advanced would be recoverable from future earnings. Mr. Wedgwood Benn told the Commons that initial Government aid of up to £50,000,000 for British Leyland would be made to help the company through its immediate crisis, on certain conditions. The Government Chief Whip (Mr. Robert Mellish) tendered his resignation over the level of discipline in the Parliamentary Labour Party but later at the Prime Minister's personal request agreed to withdraw it. **19.** Mr. Short announced in the Commons that the Government would invite Lord Boyle's top salaries review body to undertake a full review of M.P.s' salaries and allowances. **20.** The Prime Minister published in a written Parliamentary answer the Government's decision on top salaries in the public service which meant pay rises of up to £156 a week and averaging 28·8 per cent. for senior civil servants, top Service officers, and judges although in many cases half the increases would be deferred for a year or 19 months while recommended increases of up to £17,200 for heads of nationalised industries were frozen.

(1975) Jan. 8. A Select Committee, in a unanimous report, made recommendations to put into effect the decision of the House of Commons in May 1974, for a compulsory register and disclosure of M.P.s' interests, the main proposal being that the register, open to public inspection, should provide information of any pecuniary interest or other material benefit an M.P. might receive "which might be thought to affect his conduct as a Member", or influence his actions, speeches, or vote in Parliament, but the Committee considered it unnecessary to require the amount of any remuneration or benefits received to be disclosed. **15.** Mr. Wedgwood Benn told the Commons of the Government's proposals to nationalise the aircraft construction industry involving British Aircraft Corporation, Hawker Siddeley Aviation, and Hawker Siddeley Dynamics; Mr. Heath said that Conservatives would fight the forthcoming bill at every opportunity. **23.** Mr. Wilson told the Commons that a referendum on Britain's membership of the E.E.C. would be held not later than the end of June and that Cabinet ministers would be allowed to campaign against the Cabinet's recommendation on whether or not to stay in the Common Market. Mr. Heath announced his approval of the revised procedure to elect the leader of the Conservative Party recommended by the Douglas-Home committee. **29.** The Government sustained its first defeat on the floor of the Commons since the General Election. Nine Labour M.P.s joined with the Opposition in rejecting the Government's amendment to restore a £13-a-week earnings rule for pensioners during the report stage of the Social Security Benefits Bill, voting figures being 280–265,

an Opposition majority of 15. **30.** A Government White Paper, *Public Expenditure to 1978–79*, was published and stated that "absorption of resources last year was about six per cent in excess of national output" and that "the aim must be to close the non-oil deficit as soon as possible".

Feb. 4. The first ballot for the Conservative Party leadership held by the 276 Tory M.P.s resulted as follows: Mrs. Margaret Thatcher 130 votes, Mr. Edward Heath 119, Mr. Hugh Fraser 16. Later Mr. Heath announced his withdrawal from the contest and stood down as leader. Mr. Robert Carr, Shadow Chancellor of the Exchequer, took over the functions of leader until the election procedure was completed. **6.** A formal first reading was given in the Commons to the Air Travel Reserve Fund Bill, providing for the setting-up of a reserve fund to protect holidaymakers travelling abroad by air and for a bonding requirement. **7.** On a free vote, M.P.s voted 203–88 in the Commons to give a second reading to a private member's measure, the Abortion (Amendment) Bill which would amend the 1967 Abortion Act by restricting the law on abortions and ending abuses in the private sector. A motion to refer it to a select committee was carried without a vote. **11.** Mrs. Margaret Thatcher was elected the first woman to become leader of a British political party. In the second ballot for the Conservative Party leadership, the result was: Mrs. Thatcher 146 votes, Mr. William Whitelaw 79, Sir Geoffrey Howe 19, Mr. James Prior 19, Mr. John Peyton 11. **12.** The Prime Minister announced in the Commons that the Queen's income under the Civil List would be increased by £420,000 for the current year and that in view of the current economic situation the Queen had offered to meet £150,000 of the extra expenditure herself. Mr. Wilson told M.P.s that because of inflation the Civil List would be raised from £980,000 to £1,400,000. Mr. Whitelaw was appointed Deputy Leader of the Opposition but Mr. Heath declined Mrs. Thatcher's invitation to join the Shadow Cabinet, indicating that he wished to adhere to his intentions, already announced, of serving in Parliament on the back benches. An Opposition amendment to the Trade Union and Labour Relations (Amendment) Bill to retain provisions in the existing law about union rules, the object being to ensure that a "closed shop" would not necessarily apply to all staff journalists, was defeated by 298 votes to 269, a Government majority of 29. **13.** Mr. Wilson and Mr. Callaghan arrived in Moscow for talks on improving Anglo–Soviet relations, and returned on Feb. 17 with the formal basis of the new relationship set out in a 14-page statement and five other documents. **18.** The Government's Industry Bill, setting up the National Enterprise Board, and providing new controls over industry through planning agreements was given a second reading in the Commons by 313 votes to 299, a majority of 14. **20.** Mrs. Thatcher was confirmed as leader of the Conservative Party at a mass meeting of representatives of all levels of the party in a London hotel. **24.** The Commons decided by 354–182, a majority of 172 in a free vote, in favour of having an experiment in sound broadcasting of its proceedings but rejected by 275–263, a majority of 12, a proposal for a television experiment. **25.** The Government announced that the petroleum revenue tax on North Sea oil developers was to be set at 45 per cent. **26.** Eighty-nine Labour M.P.s and one Liberal M.P. voted against the proposed increase in the Queen's Civil List allowance, the "prayer" by Labour backbenchers to prevent the payment of the additional expenditure being however heavily defeated by 427 votes to 97, a Government majority of 337.

March 11. After an extended debate in the Commons on the White Paper on the Common Market referendum, the Government proposals for the method and conduct of the national poll were carried by 312–262 votes, a Government majority of 50. The Education Secretary (Mr. Prentice) announced in the Commons that direct grant grammar schools were to be given the choice of becoming comprehensive or of going independent, the Government grant to these schools being phased out over a seven-year period starting in September 1976. The Conservative Shadow Education Secretary (Mr. St. John Stevas) pledged that a future Conservative government would restore the grant. The Prime Minister and Mr. Callaghan attended the two-day Common Market summit talks in Dublin when re-negotiations for Britain's continued membership were concluded. **12.** In a statement to the Commons on the conclusion of Common Market re-negotiations, the Prime Minister declared that the Cabinet would decide on its recommendation on whether Britain should remain in the E.E.C. before Easter and claimed that changes of advantage to Britain had been secured in the correcting mechanism for the E.E.C. budget with a substantial improvement on the access for New Zealand butter. Mr. Wedgwood Benn told the Commons that the Government had decided to widen the criteria governing the scope of public ownership of the aeroplane industry and issued a summary of the provisions in the nationalisation bill to safeguard the assets of the aircraft and shipbuilding companies to be taken into public ownership. Mr. Jenkins announced that a visa would be granted for Mr. Alexander Shelepin, former chief of the K.G.B., the Russian secret police, to visit Britain as head of a delegation of Soviet trade unionists invited by the T.U.C. **18.** The Prime Minister announced in the Commons that the Government had decided to recommend the British people to vote for staying in the European Community. The Cabinet majority in favour was 16 votes to 7. **19.** The Government's statement on defence estimates was published showing savings of £4,700,000,000 in defence costs over the next ten years with a reduction in the number of Servicemen by 38,000 and civilian jobs by 30,000. **20.** The Government published the Community Land Bill which would allow agencies to buy land for development to be brought into public ownership. **22.** The Scottish Council of the Labour Party in conference in Aberdeen voted narrowly to campaign against Britain's E.E.C. membership. **24.** The House of Lords carried by 125 votes to 48, a majority against the Government of 77, a group of amendments moved by Lord Goodman, chairman of the Newspaper Publishers' Association, to the Trade Unions and Labour Relations (Amendment) Bill which were regarded as a "Journalists' Charter" to safeguard the rights of editors and other journalists to freedom against extension of closed shop rights. The Housing Finance (Special Provisions) Bill which exempted the 11 Clay Cross councillors and other "rebels" who refused to implement the Conservative Government's Act dealing with fair rents policy from surcharges was given a second reading by 292–267, a Government majority of 25. **28.** The Government White Paper setting out the renegotiated terms of Britain's recommended continued membership of the Common Market was published. **29.** The Co-operative Party voted by a small majority against Britain's membership of the Common Market at its Brighton annual conference.

April 7. The Prime Minister told the Commons that in the "unique circumstances" of the referendum on the Common Market ministers were free to advocate a different view in the country but "this freedom does not extend to Parliamentary proceedings and official business" and that "Government business in Parliament will continue to be handled by all ministers in accordance with Government policy". Plaid Cymru, the Welsh nationalist party, issued a policy document on the Common Market, calling for a free-trade association of self-governing European nations to replace British membership of E.E.C. After a three-day debate in the Commons, the Government motion recommending continued U.K. membership of the Common Market was carried on a free vote by 396–170, a majority in favour of 226, although 145 Labour M.P.s voted against. Because he deliberately spoke against the Government motion and in defiance of the ruling laid down by the Prime Minister for dissenting ministers, Mr. Eric Heffer, Minister of State, Industry, was dismissed by Mr. Wilson. **10.** It was announced that the Common Market referendum would be held on Thursday, June 5, with the result on Sunday, June 8. In the Commons, the Government had a majority of 64 for the second reading of the Referendum Bill, voting being 312 for and 248 against. **15.** Mr. Healey presented his Budget to the Commons, increasing taxation by £1,251,000,000. He announced increases in income tax, value added tax, motor tax and drink and tobacco duties. **22.** An amendment moved by a Labour M.P.—Mr. Roderick MacFarquhar (Belper)—to give British passport holders living abroad the right to vote in the Common Market referendum was defeated in the Commons by 251–211, a Government majority of 40. The Lords approved by a majority of 241 the Government's recommendation that Britain should remain in the E.E.C., voting being 261–20 in favour. **23.** On a free vote, the Commons defeated the Government plan for a national declaration of the E.E.C. referendum result, an amendment by a Labour M.P. that it be declared county by county in England and Wales, Greater London and the Scilly Isles, on a regional basis in Scotland and for Northern Ireland on its own, being carried by 270–153, majority in favour of 117. Mr. Callaghan ordered the closure of the British Embassy in Saigon and the final evacuation of officials from the South Vietnamese capital. **24.** Mr. Wilson announced in the Commons that the Government, accepting the report of the Ryder Committee on British Leyland as a basis of future policy, was to take a majority stake in the Company, and inject up to £1,400,000,000 over the next 7½ years and in return demanding management changes and large reorganisation. **26.** The special Labour Party conference in London polled 3,724,000 votes for the national executive's motion to oppose the U.K.'s continued membership of the Common Market with 1,986,000 votes against it.

May 1. In the 36 Metropolitan district council elections for 856 seats, Conservatives had a net gain of 200 seats while Labour had a net loss of 208 and the Liberals a net loss of 9. **7.** Labour's left-wing M.P.s staged another revolt against the Government in the Commons when backbenchers defied the Whips in protest at the official defence policy, an amendment calling for rejection of the Government's statement in defence estimates being defeated by 489 votes to 57, a Government majority of 432. **13.** Britain recognised the communist provisional revolutionary government of South Vietnam. **14.** Mr. Wedgwood Benn told the Commons that Government was to inject

£15,000,000 new capital into Ferranti, the electrical and electronics group, and in return would take 62½ per cent. of the total equity, including half the ordinary voting capital. 16. It was announced in the Commons that the Government had accepted the review body on armed forces pay recommendations under which the Services would receive a pay increase averaging 29·5 per cent. backdated to April 1 at a cost of £138,816,000 a year. 19. Ten left-wing Labour M.P.s, including two tellers, voted against the Government in the Commons on the order renewing the ban on the I.R.A. in Britain and the making of exclusion orders on suspected terrorists. 20. The Education Secretary (Mr. Prentice) announced in the Commons grant increases for more than 380,000 students of between 20–22 per cent., ranging from £95 to £145 a year, representing from September nearly £25 a week for students at provincial universities and £27 a week for those at London universities with further help for parents with low incomes. 21. Fifty Conservative M.P.'s joined with the Liberals in forcing a Commons vote against the Government's proposed £50,000,000, for guarantees to British Leyland, despite the Shadow Cabinet's decision that there would be no official Opposition vote against the order. 22. Mr. David Steel, Liberal chief whip, announced that he would relinquish his post after the Common Market referendum and would be succeeded by Mr. Cyril Smith, M.P. for Rochdale. Mrs. Castle told the Commons that retirement pensions and other benefits would rise again in November but that the £10 Christmas bonus would stop.

June 5. The U.K. voted in the referendum on continued membership of the Common Market. The votes were counted on June 6 and the final aggregate result was: Yes, 17,378,581 (67·2 per cent.), No, 8,470,073 (32·8 per cent.). Only two of the 68 voting areas said " No ", they being the Shetlands and the Western Isles. 9. Live radio broadcasting of the House of Commons was carried out for the first time jointly by the B.B.C. and Independent Radio News at the start of a four-week experiment. 10. The Prime Minister announced Cabinet changes which involved an exchange of posts between Mr. Eric Varley (Energy Secretary) and Mr. Wedgwood Benn (Industry Secretary). Mr. Prentice became Minister of Overseas Development in place of Mrs. Judith Hart who resigned, and Mr. Fred Mulley took over as Secretary for Education and Science. 12. The Commons approved a motion to establish its own compulsory register of M.P.'s financial interests in a free vote by 181–21. 16. Britain and South Africa formally terminated the 1955 Simonstown naval agreement. 18. The Parliamentary Labour Party decided to end its 2½ year boycott of the European Parliament and to send a delegation of 12 M.P.s and 6 peers to Strasbourg. 23. Conservative and Liberal peers inflicted four defeats on the Government in the Lords on the Housing Finance (Special Provisions) Bill which dealt with the situation of the Clay Cross rent rebels, including one to remove the lifting of civic disqualification on councillors who defied the original Housing Finance Act. 26. The Conservatives gained Woolwich West from Labour in the first by-election of the existing Parliament, with a majority of 2,382 against Labour's general election majority of 3,541, the successful candidate being Mr. P. J. Bottomley.

July 1. Mr. Healey made an unexpected statement in the Commons on proposals to reduce the rate of inflation to 10 per cent. by the end of the next pay round and to single figures by the end of 1976 with a 7-day limit to employers and unions to agree on a voluntary pay policy, dividends also being frozen. 2. The Government sustained two heavy defeats in the Commons on the report stage of the Industry Bill over the disclosure by the Government of economic forecasts—first by 220–149 votes (majority against the Government of 71) and second by 230–147 votes (majority against 83). 9. The Industry Secretary (Mr. Varley) announced that the Government was to take a majority stake in Alfred Herbert, the machine tool group, and provide aid worth £25,000,000. 11. The Prime Minister told the Commons of Government plans to deal with inflation with wage rises limited to £6 weekly maximum to all earning under £8,500 a year and renewal of price controls when they expired in 1976. These plans were also published in a White Paper entitled *The Attack on Inflation.* 16. The Cabinet recommendation to pay increases of £24 a week for M.P.s, raising their salaries from £4,500 to £5,750 a year, with increased allowances, was announced in the Commons by Mr. Short. 17. The Government was defeated by two votes in the Commons in their proposal to impose the new 25 per cent rate of VAT on TV rental contracts entered into before April 16, this meaning a reversion for such contracts to a VAT rate of 8 per cent; the voting was 108–106. 21. Mr. Robert Hughes, Parliamentary Secretary, Scottish Office, resigned from his ministerial post over the Government's pay and anti-inflation policy. 23. M.P.s carried by one vote, 128–127 on a free vote, in the early hours of the morning, a Labour M.P.'s amendment accepting in principle that their pay should be linked after the next General Election to that of Assistant Secretaries in the Civil Service, at present earning between £8,600 and £11,000 a year. M.P.s accepted the proposals for an immediate pay increase of £24 a week and substantial rises in allowances. Mr. Prentice, Overseas Development Minister, was not accepted as Labour candidate for the next general election by 29–19 votes at a meeting of Newham East Labour Party general management committee. The Remuneration Bill, giving legal effect to the Government's anti-inflation policy, was given a second reading in the Commons by 294–16 votes, majority of 278, the Tories abstaining. 24. It was disclosed that the Prime Minister had rejected an application for a salary increase from the heads of nationalised industries who were told to wait until the Diamond report on distribution of income and wealth was produced. 29. The appointment was announced in the Commons of Lord Kearton as first chairman of the British National Oil Corporation which would handle the Government's share of North Sea oil. The Trade Secretary (Mr. Shore) vetoed Skytrain, the walk-on walk-off trans-Atlantic service planned by Mr. Laker, head of Laker Airways and told M.P.s that British Caledonian and British Airways would no longer be allowed to compete on long-haul scheduled services but would have their own spheres of influence. 30. Reports by Sir Alan Marre (Parliamentary Commissioner for Administration) and by two Government appointed inspectors into the collapse of Court Line holidays last year were published but in the Commons the Trade Secretary (Mr. Shore) rejected their criticisms that Mr. Wedgwood Benn had misled holidaymakers over the firm's position.

Aug. 4. The Government was defeated by 268–261 votes, an Opposition majority of 7, in the Commons when M.P.s decided not to disagree with the Lords in their amendment to the Housing Finance (Special Provisions) Bill to ban the holding of local authority office imposed on Clay Cross councillors who did not raise council rents. 5. The

Trade Secretary (Mr. Shore) told the Commons that legislation designed to put worker-directors on the boards of private-sector companies was to be introduced in 1976-77 and that a committee of inquiry would be set up to consider how best to achieve this "radical extension of industrial democracy", while the Government was examining the role of employees relating to decision-making in the nationalised industries. Details of the new temporary employment subsidy scheme involving Government payment of £10 weekly for each full-time worker whose redundancy was deferred were announced in the Commons by the Employment Secretary. **14.** Walsall North constituency Labour Party general management committee passed a resolution not to re-adopt Mr. John Stonehouse, their M.P., and decided "to sever forthwith" all connections with him. **20.** The Prime Minister launched the Government's anti-inflation campaign in a broadcast to the nation. **29.** The Executive committee of Hammersmith North constituency Labour Party voted 14-3 in support of a resolution calling for the retirement at the next general election of their M.P., Mr. Frank Tomney, who had represented the division for 25 years.

Sept. 8. Plans for cuts of up to 40 per cent. in services were revealed by British Rail. **10.** The Prime Minister invited Mrs. Thatcher to hold discussions with him on the situation in Northern Ireland. **12.** Mr. Frank McElhone was appointed Parliamentary Under-Secretary of State, Scottish Office, replacing Mr. Robert Hughes, who had earlier resigned.

IRELAND

(1974) Oct. 10. Two Protestant workmen were machine-gunned in Belfast by masked men and a four-man Army patrol narrowly escaped death in a landmine ambush as election day in Northern Ireland was marked by violence and bomb scares. **15.** Republican internees beat up four prison officers during rioting in the Maze Prison in Northern Ireland and troops were summoned. Prisoners set fire to their huts and CS gas and batons were used by the Army to prevent them damaging the perimeter. **17.** The Governor of Armagh jail and three women prison officers were released unharmed from an attic cell 14 hours after being taken hostage when 100 women inmates joined in an outburst of violence through the prisons of Northern Ireland. The prisoners demanded assurances about the safety of men in the Maze jail. Rubber bullets were used to quell trouble at Crumlin Road prison, Belfast, the previous night when troops also surrounded Magilligan Camp, a jail near Londonderry, where prisoners set fire to the hospital, kitchen and several huts. **21.** Two U.V.F. members in the Carrickfergus area of Co. Antrim were each jailed for 10 years at Belfast City Commission on bombing charges and four Carrickfergus girls involved in the bombing of two bars were each jailed for 2½ years. All six pleaded guilty. **22.** The Ulster Unionist M.P.s elected Mr. James Molyneaux as their leader with Mr. William Craig, leader of the Vanguard Movement, and Mr. Ian Paisley, the Protestant Unionist, as deputy leaders. Four members of a bombing gang received sentences totalling 41 years in Belfast for causing an explosion at a warehouse and possessing a revolver and six rounds of ammunition. **28.** Two soldiers were killed and 30 injured when a 300-lb bomb placed in a parked stolen van destroyed a two-story canteen during morning tea-break at Ballykinler Camp, Co. Down, a man and woman working there also being injured.

Nov. 1. Troops and jail staff unearthed an escape attempt by Protestants in the Maze Prison. **5.** Twenty men, all Republicans, escaped from the Maze Prison by tunnelling their way out, but 18 were quickly recaptured. **6.** Two soldiers were killed in Crossmaglen in a Provisional I.R.A. machine-gun ambush after an escaping prisoner was shot dead in a break-out from the Maze jail **7.** Two staff sergeants were killed, five others wounded, and a R.U.C. policeman seriously injured when a booby-trap bomb exploded at Stewartstown, Co. Tyrone, claimed by the Provisional I.R.A. to be a reprisal for the shooting of the Republican during the jail escape attempt. **11.** The Provisional I.R.A. rejected a demand by leading Republicans for an immediate ceasefire. **17.** Government and Opposition leaders in the Irish Republic met separately to discuss the successor to the country's fourth President, Mr. Erskine Childers, who died earlier of a heart attack after 17 months in office. **21.** The body of James McDade, killed by his own bomb in Coventry, arrived in Dublin on an Aer Lingus plane after the coffin was grounded in Birmingham when Belfast airport workers refused to unload it. Police at Dundalk, on the border, refused to let the coffin stay in the town overnight and a hearse-driver from Dublin declined to take it any further to Belfast for the burial. Ulster security forces detained ten men who travelled in two cars escorting the hearse. **24.** At least seven people were killed by terrorists in Belfast over the week-end, described as the city's worst wave of sectarian killings. **29.** In Ulster more than 50 people were injured when bombs exploded in two Roman Catholic-owned public houses in Newry, Co. Down, and Crossmaglen, Co. Armagh.

Dec. 1. Mr. Cearbhaill O'Dalaigh, a former Chief Justice, was nominated unopposed to succeed Mr. Erskine Childers as President of the Irish Republic. **4.** Anti-I.R.A. proposals which would prevent suspects using Eire as an escape from prosecution were published in Dublin in the Criminal Law Jurisdiction Bill which would empower Irish courts to try people suspected of causing bomb explosions in Britain. Crimes committed in Northern Ireland covered by the Bill included hijackings, murder, manslaughter, arson, kidnapping, and the possession of firearms and ammunition. **13.** Three bombs exploded outside the Belfast homes of two high-ranking civil servants and a senior Post Office official when the Provisional I.R.A. began a new phase in their terror campaign; several people were treated for shock and cuts caused by flying glass. **17.** A 22-year-old mechanic said to have admitted being responsible for between 150 and 200 bombings in Londonderry, Liam Seamus Coyle, of Nicholson Square, Londonderry, was sentenced at Belfast City Commission to 20 years' jail after being found guilty on a series of charges including causing an explosion, sending a letter bomb, and belonging to the I.R.A. **20.** Mrs. Roison McLaughlin, accused of killing a British soldier after he was lured to a "party" in a Belfast flat, was freed in Dublin High Court after Mr. Justice Findlay ruled that she could not be extradited to Northern Ireland since the killing was a "political offence". The Provisionals in Dublin proposed a temporary truce in Britain and Ireland from midnight Dec. 21 until midnight Jan. 2 and said it could become a permanent ceasefire if the British Government accepted certain conditions, but the Ulster Secretary (Mr. Rees) said that no specific undertakings would be given. Later, the Provisional I.R.A. planted bombs in Belfast's shopping centre, two being defused and three exploding without causing casualties. **29.** A riot by Provisional I.R.A. prisoners at Portlaoise jail, Eire's top security prison, ended when Irish Army troops firing rubber bullets stormed the prison with police in riot gear and released 14 warders held hostage.

(1975) Jan. 2. The Provisional I.R.A. extended its Christmas ceasefire by a fortnight with threats to resume its terror campaign if progress towards a lasting solution was not made in that time. Forty-four men convicted of terrorist activity and due to end their sentences by March 31 were released. **6.** The United Ulster Unionist Council unanimously condemned direct or indirect negotiations between the British Government and the I.R.A. and said that the Government should not react to "blackmail and the threat of resumed terrorist action". **13.** James Martin Kearney, of Henry Street, Newry, Co. Down, was jailed for eight years at Belfast for possessing a rifle and ammunition and taking part in the bombing of Newry courthouse in Sept. 1972. **15.** Tax increases on drink, tobacco, and betting were announced by Mr. Richie Ryan, Eire's Finance Minister in his budget, but also average increases of between 21 per cent. and 23 per cent. in social welfare benefits. **16.** The Provisional I.R.A. announced in a statement to Dublin newspapers that the ceasefire which had lasted 25 days would end at midnight. **20.** Patrick Joseph Floyd, of Castlederg, Co. Tyrone, was sentenced at Belfast City Commission to 12 years' jail for possessing a 500-lb bomb and intimidation. **21.** Two people, believed to be terrorists transporting the explosive, were killed when a car bomb exploded in the centre of Belfast, followed by a series of bomb attacks, one being on the British Legion club at Strabane. **22.** Thomas Arthur McCann, of Greenan Trillick, Co. Tyrone, was jailed for 15 years at Belfast City Commission on charges relating to a number of explosions and three other men were each jailed for six years and another for five years on firearms charges. **26.** A 16-year-old Air Training Corps cadet was killed and five others injured when an I.R.A. booby trap bomb exploded in a hut at a Belfast school used as the cadets' H.Q. Londonderry had its first city centre explosion for three months.

Feb. 7. During a search of a cell block in the top security prison at Portlaoise, Eire, where Provisional I.R.A. members were held, a quantity of explosives was found and other items included saws, chisels, knives, gatekeys, and sheet ropes. All visits to the prison were suspended. **9.** A statement issued in Dublin by the Irish Republican Publicity Bureau said that in the light of discussions between the Republican movement and British officials, the Army Council of I.R.A. had renewed the order suspending offensive military action from 6 p.m. on Feb. 10. **13.** Three people, including a mother and her six-year-old daughter, were wounded in Belfast by terrorist letter bombs disguised as St. Valentine's Day cards. The Common Market foreign ministers met in Dublin for the first time for political consultations. **20.** One man died and 23 people were injured in bomb attacks on two Belfast public houses. **21.** Sir Robert Lowry, Ulster's Lord Chief Justice, was appointed chairman of the Northern Ireland Constitutional Convention. **24.** The Northern Ireland Secretary (Mr. Rees) announced the release of 80 more detainees. **25.** The Provisional I.R.A. decided to establish its own police force to operate in Roman Catholic areas of Belfast. **28.** The U.D.A. put patrols in the streets in Protestant areas in protest at the Government's reluctance to allow R.U.C. to enter Roman Catholic areas.

March 5. Ulster Protestants' para-military groups agreed to suspend conditionally their unofficial policing of loyalist areas after receiving Government assurances that the Provisional I.R.A. had not re-established "no-go" areas. **9.** Two trawlers were destroyed and a third badly damaged by fire bombs in a raid by Ulster Protestant extremists on fishing vessels in the harbour at Greencastle, Co. Donegal, near the Northern Ireland border. **10.** Twelve Provisional I.R.A. prisoners escaped from a courthouse in the border town of Newry, Co. Down, by prising apart iron bars and climbing out of a lavatory window; two were recaptured later, with the others believed to have gone to Eire. **13.** The President of Dublin High Court ruled that the murder of an R.U.C. officer by the I.R.A. was a political offence and directed that an extradition order made against Sean Gallagher, an I.R.A. member, be quashed. **16.** The first policewoman reservist to be killed in the Ulster troubles died after a bomb exploded outside a Roman Catholic-owned public house in the seaside resort of Bangor, County Down. **17.** One prisoner was shot dead and two others wounded when an I.R.A. gang tried to organise a mass break-out at Portlaoise jail, Eire, where 140 I.R.A. terrorists were held; police stated that they had arrested two people and that no prisoners had escaped. **18.** The Price sisters, serving life sentences for the London car bombings in 1973, were moved from Durham jail to Armagh prison in Northern Ireland. **26.** The Minister of State, Northern Ireland (Mr. Orme) announced that the Belfast shipyard, Harland and Wolff, was to be nationalised at a cost of about £140,000,000 to save the jobs of 10,300 employees. **28.** Twenty Republican detainees were released by the Northern Ireland Secretary (Mr. Rees) and another twenty were freed on March 29.

April 2. The Provisional I.R.A. admitted responsibility for the bomb attack on the Trans World travel agency in Belfast, this being the first time they had done so since the cease-fire began on Feb. 10. **5.** Eight people were killed and 40 injured in two public house explosions and shootings in Belfast. **12.** Four people were killed and 30 injured when a bomb exploded at the Strand Bar in the Short Strand area of Belfast, rescue workers being hurt when a wall collapsed on them. **14.** Mr. Merlyn Rees, Northern Ireland Secretary of State, revealed in the House of Commons that a few weeks earlier he had ordered the release of a Protestant gunman who tried to assassinate him in May 1974. Irish fishermen were ordered by a judge in Dublin High Court to lift their blockade of Dublin after having laid siege to six of the Republic's bigger ports in protest at cheap foreign imports. **15.** Kevin Mallon, a Provisional I.R.A. leader, was given a 10-year jail sentence in Dublin for encouraging a woman to try to murder a policeman, when being arrested in January 40 days after escaping from Mountjoy Prison by helicopter. **22.** The High Court in London ruled that Kenneth Brian Littlejohn, who was in Winson Green Prison, Birmingham, after escaping from Mountjoy Prison where he was serving 20 years' penal servitude for armed robbery in Eire in 1973, must return to Dublin to finish his sentence. **26.** Troops collected petrol from depots in Dublin docks to ensure vital supplies in Ireland's 10-day strike of oil company lorry drivers. **27.** Three men were shot dead and a fourth seriously wounded in an Ulster darts club at Bleary, near Lurgan. **28.** The Official I.R.A.'s commanding officer in Belfast, Billy McMillan, was shot dead in the Roman Catholic Falls Road area.

May 1. Results in the Ulster Convention election for 78 seats were: United Ulster Unionist Coalition 46 seats, Social Democratic and Labour Party 17 seats, Alliance Party 8 seats, Unionist Party of N .I. 5 seats, N.I. Labour Party 1 seat. Independent Unionists 1 seat. Sir Paget Bourke, a former Chief Justice in the British Colonial Service, who was kidnapped by four armed men the previous night, was released at a police-army checkpoint five miles south of the border at Ballyconnell, Co. Cavan, when his abductors ran away. Lady Bourke was found tied to a chair in their home in Herbert Park, Donnybrook. **6.** Bombs were planted in three Limerick hotels and the city centre was sealed off while they were made safe. **29.** An 18-year-old student from Newtonabbey was jailed for life at Belfast City Commission for the murder of an R.U.C. police inspector during an I.R.A. bank robbery at Rathcoole and a 19-year-old youth, also from Newtonabbey, was sentenced to six years' imprisonment for the armed robbery. **31.** Twenty people were injured by a terrorist bomb thrown at a packed public house in the centre of Newry, Co. Down, the building being completely wrecked.

June 3. Three Protestants on their way home from a Co. Cork dog show were gunned down near the Irish border, two being killed instantly and the other dying from his wounds. **16.** Twelve terrorists made one of their biggest raids on an Army arsenal in Ulster for 20 years when they emptied a U.D.R. armoury including 148 automatic rifles, 33 submachine guns, 35 pistols and some ammunition. **18.** Changes in the procedures for the detention of terrorists in Northern Ireland as recommended by the Gardiner Committee were contained in the Northern Ireland (Emergency Provisions) (Amendment) Bill published by the Government, the main change being detention by executive action by the Northern Ireland Secretary instead of by judicial commissioners. **22.** A farm labourer believed to have been a witness was found stabbed to death near the spot where terrorists tried to blow up a train carrying 300 Official I.R.A. supporters from Dublin to Bodenstown for an annual commemoration at the grave of Wolfe Tone; the explosives blasted the track near Sallins, Co. Kildare, half-an-hour after the train passed.

July 17. Four soldiers were killed and one seriously injured by a terrorist bomb when investigating a suspected bomb, a milk churn surrounded by rocks, placed in a hedge three miles from Forkhill in the south of Co. Armagh, the Provisional I.R.A. unit in Crossmaglen admitting responsibility. **24.** The Ulster Secretary (Mr. Rees) told the Commons that he hoped to release all detainees in the Maze prison by Christmas. **25.** David O'Connell, Provisional I.R.A.'s Chief of Staff, was jailed for a year at the Special Criminal Court in Dublin for belonging to an illegal organisation. **31.** The Dublin-based pop group, the Miami Showband, were ambushed in their minibus near Newry, Co. Down, when returning from an engagement in Ulster. Three of the musicians were killed and two others injured while two of the terrorists posing as soldiers died in a premature explosion.

Aug. 10. A four-year-old girl was shot dead by a terrorist sniper aiming at an army patrol during gun clashes between troops and terrorists in the Lower Falls area of Belfast, the fighting being the culmination of Ulster's most violent week-end since the Provisional I.R.A. ceasefire began eight months earlier. **13.** Four people were killed and 23 injured by terrorists who drove up to Bayardo bar in Shankill Road, Belfast, fired automatic weapons at men on guard outside, threw a bomb which exploded among a crowd of drinkers, and sprayed bullets at a queue waiting at a nearby bus stop while a second bomb blasted at the corner of Percy Street and Shankill Road minutes later. **14.** A resumption of Ulster's Convention due on August 19, was postponed to allow leaders to discuss differences at special committee meetings and in study groups. **15.** A Protestant lorry driver was shot dead and some 59 people injured in two bomb explosions in Belfast during violence between Protestants and Roman Catholic extremists and gangs of youths stoned British troops as rioting increased, a car bomb injuring 35 persons in the Roman Catholic Lower Falls area and a bomb wounding 24 people at a bar used by U.V.F. members. **22.** Three people were killed and over 20 injured in a bomb and gun attack by three terrorists on McGleenan's bar in English Street, Armagh. Four leading I.R.A. Provisionals and a prominent Protestant were barred from entering the United States to attend a conference on Irish affairs near Boston.

Sept. 1. Four men were killed and 16 wounded when two gunmen burst into a meeting of Orangemen in a Protestant hall at Newtownhamilton, Co. Armagh, and opend fire with sub-machine guns; a man was found shot dead in business premises in Upper Donegal Street, Belfast; another man was murdered in a scrapyard at Ballyclare; and another man was shot dead on his doorstep near Dungannon, bringing the day's total killings to seven. **2.** Army and police reinforcements were sent to South Armagh and more roads between Ulster and Eire were being closed after a week of terrorism. The Dublin Government made a special appeal to Roman Catholics living in Ulster to cooperate with the Army and police in stopping the wave of murders in Northern Ireland. The State funeral service in Dublin for Mr. Eamon de Valera, former President of the Irish Republic, was conducted in Irish and Latin at his own request. **4.** It was stated that a further 650 British troops were being sent to Northern Ireland on temporary duty.

ENVIRONMENT AND LOCAL AFFAIRS

(1974) Oct. 7. Mr. William Ross, Secretary of State for Scotland, said that more people were migrating to Scotland than leaving for the first time in 40 years, latest estimates showing a net gain of about 5,000 compared with a loss last year of 10,000. **13.** Greater London Council and the London Boroughs cancelled proposals to celebrate in 1975 the tenth anniversary of the reorganisation of London local government because of the cost. **22.** Greater London Council's planning committee decided in principle to back a modified redevelopment plan for Piccadilly Circus. **30.** Fresh proposals to improve agricultural landscapes were made by the Countryside Commission in a discussion paper, *New Agricultural Landscapes*, which also dealt with the effects of modern farming. There were 7,600,000 visitors to Britain in 1973, a 6 per cent. increase over 1972, according to the British Tourist Authority annual report for year ended March 1974.

Nov. 6. The Environment Secretary (Mr. Crosland) told the Commons that the Government intended to remove the 5-year ban on the 11 Clay Cross, Derbyshire, rebel councillors holding elected office but that they would not have the £7,000 surcharge imposed on them for refusing to raise council rents under the Housing Finance Act cancelled, while the further £120,000 which the local authority lost over the councillors' action was to be recouped from council tenants or the ratepayers. A district auditor's report on the Clay Cross affair published on the same day, said that the 11 rebels had acted " without due regard to the interests of the ratepayers". **8.** Covent Garden Market closed after

300 years and trading began on Nov. 11 on the new 68-acre site at Nine Elms, Vauxhall. **12.** A salmon, 8 lb. 4½ oz, the first caught in the Thames for more than 140 years, was taken in the intake screen at West Thurrock Power Station. **22.** An independent report by a three-man panel of inquiry into the affairs of the Royal Society for the Prevention of Cruelty to Animals was published and listed 38 recommendations aimed at improvements. **26.** The Government announced the scrapping of the planned high-speed rail link between London and the Kent Coast, the Environment Secretary (Mr. Crosland) saying that the estimated cost had soared from £120,000,000 in Feb. 1973 to £373,000,000 in May 1974, and that the French Government and the two Channel Tunnel companies had been asked to put back the time-table for building the tunnel. The Environment Secretary also announced that the Government had agreed to increase the rate support grant paid to councils from 60·5 per cent. in 1974 to " an unprecedented " 66·5 per cent. in 1975 while the expected " formidable " domestic rate rises of between 70 per cent. and 100 per cent. would be cut instead to an average 25 per cent. **28.** A £2,710,000,000 plan for an improved rail system for the London commuter area by the end of the century was published in a report by the London Rail Study Group and commissioned by the last Minister of Transport and the Greater London Council.

Dec. 4. The Great Britain 1971 Census Country of Birth Tables was published and showed that with a population of 53,979,000 in 1971 about 5·5 per cent. (2,983,000) were born outside the U.K., or nearly double the figure in the 1961 census. **10.** In a move to reduce its financial deficit, the B.B.C. decided to cut TV and radio programmes by 10 per cent. in the New Year. **14.** New speed limits came into force at midnight with 70 m.p.h. on motorways, 60 m.p.h. on dual carriageways, and 50 m.p.h. on other roads. **19.** The Transport Minister (Mr. Fred Mulley) announced in the Commons that British Rail would receive about £341,000,000 from the Government next year to meet costs of operating unprofitable rail passenger services and that British Railways Board had been directed " to operate a railway passenger service that will continue to provide a public service comparable generally with that provided at present".

Jan. 13. Government regulations restricting heating in offices, factories, warehouses, and shops to 68° F. (20° C.) and banning the use of electricity during daylight for illuminated signs became effective. **20.** Mr. Crosland announced the abandonment of the Channel Tunnel project and said that the project would be run down as soon as possible although studies, plans, and works would be preserved in case the scheme should be revived. **28.** The British Airport Authority reported that a million fewer passengers used London's three airports in 1974 than in 1973, the first actual reduction since the 1939–45 War. **29.** The G.L.C. decided by 50 votes to 44 against the proposal that it should abolish it film censorship powers for adults of over 18. Mr. Roy Jenkins told the Commons that the B.B.C. licence-fee was to be increased from April 1, 1975, from £7 to £8 for black and white and from £12 to £18 for colour.

Feb. 5. The Government announced their consent for the building of two new nuclear power stations at Sizewell, Suffolk, and at Torness Point, near Dunbar, East Lothian, the first in the new series of British designed steam-generating heavy-water reactors. The Office of Population Censuses reported that an estimated population increase for 1974 in England and Wales was the lowest in

peacetime for half a century, the rise, only 20,000 in 49,000,000, being ten times smaller than in 1973. **6.** Measures to control the use, ferocity, and condition of private guard dogs were announced by the Government in a new voluntary code. **20.** Mr. Crosland rejected in a Commons written reply appeals for a public inquiry into the future of the Criterion site in Piccadilly Circus, this decision meaning that redevelopment could proceed in assurance that the work would not close the theatre for any " financially damaging time".

March 6. The General Medical Council stated that new tests would start on June 1, 1975, for foreign doctors who came from overseas to join the health service and who would have to show that they could read, write, understand and speak English and pass examinations in medical knowledge. **13.** The Independent Hospital Group was inaugurated at the headquarters of British United Provident Association to establish and coordinate a national network of private hospitals to take over when N.H.S. pay beds were phased out. **18.** The Alderman's Court of the City of London confirmed Lady Donaldson as the City's first woman alderman in its 800 years' existence. **25.** Mrs. Castle announced that charges for private beds in N.H.S. hospitals were to be raised by nearly 50 per cent. from April 1.

April 17. Twenty-one former Clay Cross councillors, including the 11 who already faced a £7,000 surcharge for their rent rebellion, were served notices of new surcharges totalling £52,209. The Inner London Education Authority announced that grammar schools under its authority were to be abolished and a fully comprehensive system imposed on all secondary school children by 1977.

May 1. In the 36 Metropolitan District Council elections for 856 seats, Conservative had a net gain of 200 seats, while Labour had a net loss of 208 and Liberals a net loss of 9. **5.** Measures to reduce the number of private pay beds in the National Health Service were announced by Mrs. Castle in the Commons.

July 21. The Home Office announced that fixed penalties for car parking offences would rise from £2 to £6 from Sept. 1, and that if the penalty was not paid the registered owner, whether or not he was the driver at the time, would be held liable.

Aug. 1. The whole Underground system in London was temporarily halted by a power failure in an auxiliary unit at London Transport's Lots Road power station. **5.** A Government spokesman announced that new premises for the British Library were to be built on a former railway site near St. Pancras station in Euston Road. **7.** Plans to abolish the tied farm cottage were published in a counsultative document jointly by the Department of the Environment and the Ministry of Agriculture. **22.** An investigation into the running of the Post Office was ordered by the Government when it approved a further large rise in post, telephone, and telegram charges, although plans to cut services were halted pending further discussions. **29.** The Tobacco Advisory Council announced that cigarette advertising in cinemas was to end except during X film programmes and that tar yield content of cigarettes would be printed on the packets.

Sept. 9. It was announced that the National Trust had acquired the Needles headland at the westernmost point of the Isle of Wight.

ACCIDENTS

(1974) Oct. 8. Two hot-air balloonists plunged 1,500 ft. to their death watched by thousands of spectators at Saltley, Birmingham when their balloon fell on to a canal towpath two minutes after take-off. **30.** Thirty-two of 34 people aboard a Lockheed Electra airliner owned by PanArctic Oils, of Calgary, Alberta, died when it crashed through the ice off Byam Martin Island in the Canadian Arctic.

Nov. 3. When fire occurred in a hotel in eastern Seoul, South Korea, 88 people died, 64 of them being dancers in a night-club on the sixth floor. **8.** Two firemen were killed in a blaze at Chatham Naval Dockyard after a " flashover with explosive force"; four other firemen suffered burns. **10.** Eight young men died when fire damaged a transport hotel in Liverpool Road, Islington, London, used mainly by lorry drivers and building workers. **15.** About 200 people were killed and many others injured when two trains collided head-on near the Dahomey capital of Cotonou. **20.** Fifty-nine people were killed when a Boeing 747 of the West German airline, Lufthansa, crashed and burst into flames when taking off from Nairobi airport, eight Britons being among the dead; another 98 passengers and crew survived, most of them unharmed. Thirty people were buried alive when a sudden eruption occurred on the slopes of the dormant volcano, Mount Argapura, in east Java. **26.** One hundred and forty-two Hindu pilgrims died when a suspension bridge over the River Mahahali in Darchulo district 250 miles north west of Kathmandu collapsed.

Dec. I. A Trans World Boeing 727 crashed into the foothills of the Blue Ridge Mountains, 20 miles from Washington, in the Defence Department's weather communications centre at Mount Weather, Virginia, killing all 93 people aboard who were on a flight from Columbus, Ohio, when the plane was diverted because of high winds. **4.** A Dutch charter DC.8 aircraft carrying 182 Indonesian pilgrims to Mecca and a crew of nine crashed and burst into flames in central Sri Lanka, 60 miles east of Colombo, in a storm and there were no reports of survivors. **5.** Forty-two people were killed when the roof of Mehrabad international airport terminal building at Teheran collapsed on to crowds inside. **8.** Eight people including the pilot were killed when a private plane owned by McAlpine Aviation and carrying ICI personnel en route for Pontypool, South Wales, crashed shortly after taking off from Leeds-Bradford airport, there being no survivors. **15.** Fire in an old people's home, Fairfield, Edwalton, on the outskirts of Nottingham, caused the deaths of 18 people aged between 67 and 91; 31 others were saved. **21.** Nine skiers were killed by an avalanche at Kitzbuehel, Austria. **27.** Thirty-nine men died in a fire-damp explosion 1,500 ft. underground in a coalmine at Liévin, Pas de Calais, Northern France.

(1975) Jan. 5. Twelve people died when a Government-owned bulk carrier, *Lake Illawarra*, collided with the Tasman bridge at Hobart, Tasmania, and sent four cars 150 ft. below into the River Derwent. **23.** Two inter-city express trains collided outside Watford Junction, Herts, killing the driver's mate of the London–Glasgow train and injuring about 14 passengers. **25.** Only two of the 13 crew members of the 1,092-ton British coaster, *Lovat*, survived when she sank in a gale 30 miles south of Penzance. **29.** Four hundred passengers escaped injury when a train from Paddington, to Birmingham was derailed at Oxford as it was moving slowly into the station.

Feb. 27. Three people were killed and 11 injured when two electric passenger trains collided at Lillois between Brussels and Nivelles. **28.** The death toll in London Underground's worst disaster was 42, including the driver, following the crash at Moorgate where the train smashed into a cul-de-sac tunnel. Verdicts of accidental death were returned on all the victims at the end of the four-day inquest on April 18. The 43rd victim died in hospital on June 10.

March 12. A lorry driver found unconscious in his cab at the Pitsea (Essex) waste dump for chemicals where poisonous fumes were discovered was dead on arrival at Basildon hospital. **16.** An Air Force transport plane crashed near Bariloche, Argentina, and all 52 people on board were believed to be killed. **24.** An R.A.F. crewman parachuted to safety as the sole survivor after a Victor refuelling tanker exploded over the North Sea and crashed into the sea 90 miles from Newcastle with four other R.A.F. personnel aboard. **25.** Two Japanese climbers and three Sherpa porters were killed by an avalanche while seeking a new route on Dhaulagiri, a 26,794 ft. peak in the Himalayas, six other climbers escaping unhurt. **31.** Eight people died in one of a series of avalanches which hit Austria and southern Germany when snow buried a group of holiday chalets at Mallnitz in the eastern Tyrol. Lady Hillary, wife of Sir Edmund Hillary, the conqueror of Everest, and their daughter, were killed when a light plane crashed soon after take off from Kathmandu, to fly to the village of Phaphlu, on the lower slopes of Everest; other people including the New Zealand pilot were also killed.

April 2. Twenty-seven people were killed and 16 injured when a bus carrying old people returning from a pilgrimage near Grenoble crashed through a bridge parapet and fell 80 ft. into the River Romanche at Vizille. **4.** About 140 South Vietnamese orphans bound for the United States were among 180 people killed when an American C5A Galaxy crashed soon after leaving Saigon as the first official American airlift of refugees began, 243 orphans and 43 helpers being on board. A blizzard left 47 people dead in the Chicago area and Chicago's O'Hare Airport was closed for 24 hours. **6.** Ten Austrians were killed with three others missing, when a landslide swept over a house near Tamsweg, central Austria; twenty people were feared dead as a result of avalanches in the Swiss Alps; and three persons died when an avalanche hit cars on the road between Solda and Gomagei. **16.** Search for the missing North Sea oil survey ship *Compass Rose III*, with 16 crew aboard which left Dundee on April 5, was abandoned, after a body found two days earlier was identified as a crew member. **27.** Four people were killed and nine injured when a Formula One racing car crashed in the Spanish Grand Prix in Barcelona.

May 12. The findings of the Flixborough court of inquiry into the chemical works disaster on June 1, 1974, when 28 people were killed and 36 injured, were published, the main conclusion being that it was caused by the failure of a large temporary pipe installed as a " rush job " about two months earlier. **27.** Thirty-two people, mostly elderly women, all from Thornaby, Teesside, were killed after their day-trip coach plunged through a bridge parapet into a ravine at Dibble's Bridge, Hebden, in the Yorkshire Dales; 14 people also being injured. **28.** Four Bristish tourists were killed when a concrete balcony above shops collapsed on them as they sheltered from a freak storm in Benidorm, the Spanish seaside resort; a Dutch woman and a Spaniard were also killed and some 14 people injured. **31.** More than 30 passengers were hurt, one seriously, when a six-coach train collided with a cement train two miles from the centre of Glasgow.

June 6. The night Caledonian express from Euston to Glasgow crashed at Nuneaton station, killing five of the 98 passengers and injuring 36 others including the Minister of Agriculture (Mr. Fred Peart). **12.** Five miners were killed and six others were injured after an explosion at Houghton

Main colliery, near Barnsley, Yorkshire. **16.** Ten
people were killed and 36 injured when a coach
taking Brighton pensioners on a Scottish sight-
seeing tour collided with an articulated truck near
Moffat, Dumfriesshire. **24.** A Boeing 727 of
Eastern Airlines flying from New Orleans crashed
in an electric storm near Kennedy International
Airport, New York, with a death toll of 112, the
worst in American aviation history.

July 8. Four men died when fire swept the Edinburgh trawler *Granton Harrier* in the Irish Sea
and nine others were rescued by a survey ship, a
tenth survivor being seriously injured and taken on
board the helicopter cruiser *Tiger*. **11.** Three
children died when a Loch Lomond sandbank
collapsed and buried them; five others were dragged
out alive by rescuers from a camp site, digging
with their hands. **22.** The death toll from a fire in
a guest house at Arbroath, Angus, on July 21, rose
to six when a two-year-old died in hospital, the
victims including three generations of one family.

Aug. 3. All 188 people on board a chartered airliner were killed when it crashed in the Atlas mountains on the approach to Morocco's Agadir airport.
6. Three men were killed by fumes in an effluent tank
at Watney's Brewery, Mortlake. **15.** Six members
of the 46 crew were missing from the British
tanker *Globtik Sun*, which caught fire in the Gulf
of Mexico after ramming an unmanned oil-drilling
platform. **18.** Thirty-four people were killed by a
typhoon which brought up to 24 inches of rain to
south-west Japan in 24 hours; 23 people were missing
and 93 injured and 20,000 houses destroyed, damaged or flooded. **20.** An Ilyushin 62 jet of Czechoslovak Airlines crashed in flames in the Syrian
desert near Damascus, killing 126 people with only
two survivors. A 29-year-old Irish nurse, who went
back into a blazing nursing home at Herne Hill,
London, to rescue two elderly women patients,
died with them in the fire; five other patients were
detained in hospital. **26.** Floods on the river
Ganges and one of its tributaries cut-off Patna,
capital of Bihar State, from the rest of India. **29.** It
was announced that two British boys, aged four and
six, had survived a seven-day ordeal in the African
jungle with the father of one of them and the pilot
after their light plane crashed on a mountainside in
northern Tanzania, the party walking 12 hours a
day and existing on chewing gum and leaves until
found by African farmers.

Sept. 1. Mrs. Caroline Marsh, wife of Mr.
Richard Marsh, British Rail chairman, died in
hospital in Malaga five days after a car crash in
which Mrs. Julia Jacobs, wife of Mr. David Jacobs,
the broadcaster, was killed. **5.** Four young men
fell to their deaths at Peak Cavern, Castleton,
Derbys. **10.** Two divers died in decompression
chamber on oil rig 200 miles north-east of the
Orkneys. **11.** Two trains collided at Bermondsey,
injuring more than sixty people.

CRIMES, TRIALS, ETC.

(1974) Oct. 3. A 31-year-old gunman who
also shot himself dead walked into an employment
exchange at Torquay, produced a shotgun and
killed two men and a woman. **5.** Terrorists who
planted bombs killed five people including four
teenage Army recruits, two of them girls in the
W.R.A.C., and injured 65 in two public houses in
Guildford, Surrey. **11.** Terrorist bombs damaged
the Army & Navy Club in Pall Mall and The
Victory Ex-Service Club in Seymour Street,
Marble Arch. **14.** Barry Robinson, of Longsight,
Manchester, who was first ordered to be detained
for life in Broadmoor in Dec. 1962 and released on
licence in 1969, pleaded guilty at Chester Crown

Court to eight charges connected with the kid-
nappings at Congleton, Cheshire, of a policeman
and two other men in August. He was sentenced
to life imprisonment on three kidnapping charges
and for robbing one victim, and to 10 years for
each of three other charges and five years on a
second burglary charge, all sentences to run concurrently. **18.** Three High Court judges found
Paul Foot, editor of the *Socialist Worker*, son of
Lord Caradon and nephew of Mr. Michael Foot,
Employment Secretary, guilty of contempt of
court and fined him and the publishers £250 each.
Mr. Foot and the publishers were also ordered to
pay costs. Mr. Foot named in his newspaper two
witnesses in the Janice Jones trial at the Old Bailey
after the Judge had directed that their identities
should not be disclosed. **22.** Three people were
injured, one seriously, when a bomb exploded without warning in the dining room of Brooks's Club,
St. James's. The Royal Overseas League building
was also damaged. At Bow Street, London, a
Scottish National Party member, David
Carmichael-Stewart, of Wolverhampton, was
conditionally discharged for a year and ordered to
pay £150 and £75 costs after he admitted
damaging the Coronation Chair while removing
the Stone of Scone from it in Westminster Abbey
on Sept. 4. No evidence was offered against him
on a burglary charge alleging that he stole the
Stone. **23.** A bomb exploded at Harrow School
around midnight and damaged Peterborough
Cottage, a building divided into flats used by
masters, although there were no casualties.
According to statistics published in Home Office
report, crime figures for England and Wales rose
20 per cent. in the first six months of 1974 compared
with the same period in 1973, offences known to
police totalling 798,458 compared with 662,466.
25. A statement from Downing Street said that
personal documents belonging to the Prime
Minister were missing from his home in Lord North
Street, Westminster and that their disappearance
was reported to the police some time earlier.
Scotland Yard confirmed that an investigation was
being carried out and that the loss was being
treated as a theft. **28.** The wife and 10-year-old
son of Mr. Denis Howell, M.P., Minister for Sport,
escaped when a booby trap bomb exploded under
a car as Mrs. Howell started the engine outside their
home in Moseley, Birmingham. Mrs. Howell and
her son were badly shaken but otherwise unhurt.

Nov. 4. Judith Theresa Ward, a former
W.R.A.C. private of Stockport, Cheshire, was jailed
for 30 years at Wakefield Crown Court for her
part in the I.R.A. terror bombing campaign in
England. She was sentenced to 20 years for
murder in the M62 coach blast which killed 12
people and 10 years to run consecutively for
causing an explosion at the National Defence
College at Latimer, Bucks. Ward was further
sentenced to 5 years for causing an explosion at
Euston station and to life on each of 11 other
murder counts relating to the M62 explosions,
these sentences to run concurrently with the 20-
year term. **5.** A high explosive device went off in
the Conservative Party HQ in Edmund Street,
Birmingham, causing extensive damage but no
injuries. **7.** One civilian died and 34 other people
were injured when a bomb was hurled through a
window into the public bar of the King's Arms,
Woolwich, five casualties being off-duty service
personnel including two members of W.R.A.C.
A soldier died from wounds on Nov. 8 and two
men and a girl each had a leg amputated. **8.**
Ronald George Milhench, insurance broker and
property dealer, of Wolverhampton, who admitted

forging a letter purporting to be from the Prime Minister (Mr. Wilson), was imprisoned for three years at Stafford Crown Court for forgery, attempting to obtain money by deception, and firearms offences. Police were trying to trace the Earl of Lucan, 39, 24 hours after his children's nanny had been found battered to death in the Belgravia house where Lady Lucan lived. **14.** Terrorist bombers attacked three times in the Midlands: on a telephone exchange in Coventry where the person planting the bomb was killed, on the Conservative party H.Q. in Solihull, and on an R.A.F. club in Northampton which was badly damaged. **15.** The Chairman and secretary of a Scottish branch of the engineering union were jailed for three years at Glasgow High Court after being found guilty of forging and uttering the signatures of more than 200 members in a ballot. **20.** Twelve people who wore black berets at a Provisional Sinn Fein rally at Speakers' Corner, Hyde Park, were each fined a maximum of £50 at Lambeth, when found guilty of wearing a uniform signifying their association with a political organisation. One of them was also given a suspended three-month jail sentence. **21.** Nineteen people were killed, the death toll later rising to 20, and 184 injured by I.R.A. bombs in Birmingham when explosions occurred in two crowded city centre public houses, the Mulberry Bush and the Tavern in the Town, and damaged a wine bar; unexploded bombs were found in the shopping centre at New Street Station and on a doorstep of a building in Hagley Road. A British Airways super VC.10 was hijacked at Dubai Airport in the Persian Gulf by four armed Arabs as passengers were leaving the aircraft. It was forced to fly to Tunis with 41 hostages aboard and landed there on Nov. 22. Meanwhile Egypt agreed to release certain Palestinian terrorists and the Dutch stated they were prepared to release two Arabs held by the Netherlands. On Nov. 23 the gunmen released 13 passengers after shooting dead a West German banker and freed the rest on Nov. 24 apart from three crew. On Nov. 25 the guerrillas surrendered along with five terrorists released in Cairo and the two Palestinians brought from prison in Holland. **22.** Five Irishmen were arrested at Heysham, Lancashire, as they were about to board a ferry for Belfast and returned to the Midlands by detectives investigating the Birmingham bombs outrages. **25.** Three I.R.A. bombs exploded in pillar boxes in London during the rush hour, injuring 14 people. **27.** Four policemen, two ambulancemen and an explosives expert were among nine people injured in a bombers' ambush in Tite Street, Chelsea, when a second bomb exploded while they were arriving to investigate a pillar-box blast. Sean O'Conaill and Raymond Kane, found guilty of murdering an Army training camp commandant in the name of the I.R.A., were imprisoned for life at Durham Crown Court. O'Conaill also received two sentences of 15 years for the attempted murder of two policemen. Barry Reid was found not guilty of murder but jailed for five years for manslaughter. **28.** A report prepared by Deputy Commissioner James Starritt into the death of Kenneth Lennon, an informant to the I.R.A., who was found shot dead in a ditch near Banstead, Surrey, in April 1974, was published, and stated the Special Branch was not responsible, directly or indirectly. **30.** A bomb was thrown through the window of a public house in Belgravia and four people were hurt.

Dec. 3. Eric Tomlinson and Dennis Warren, who led pickets during the 1972 national building strike, lost their appeal to have their case considered

by the House of Lords, the Appeal Court being unable to certify that a point of law of general public importance was raised by the men's convictions in December 1973 for conspiring to intimidate workers to strike. **4.** At Winchester Crown Court, three members of the para-military Ulster Defence Association were imprisoned for a total of 22 years for their part in an arms smuggling operation which was broken by British detectives working undercover with the Royal Canadian Mounted Police, being convicted of conspiring to import arms and explosives illegally into England. John William Gadd, of Liverpool, the deputy commander of U.D.A. in England, was jailed for 10 years; Roy Ralph Rogers-Forbes, of Leeds, was sentenced to 7 years; and John William Griffiths, of Beeston, Leeds, was imprisoned for 5 years. Miss Pat Arrowsmith appealed in the Criminal Appeal Court against her conviction in May 1974 at the Old Bailey under the 1934 Incitement to Disaffection Act after distributing pamphlets urging soldiers to mutiny and desert if sent to Northern Ireland, when she was jailed for 18 months. The three judges ordered that her conviction should stand but substituted a sentence enabling her to be released immediately. **9.** A bomb shook the centre of Bath after an explosion inside a shop in the Corridor but there were no injuries. **10.** Another victim of the Birmingham bombings died in hospital, bringing the death toll to 21. **11.** A small bomb was thrown through a ground-floor window of the Naval and Military Club, Piccadilly, causing extensive damage but no casualties. Kenneth Littlejohn, who claimed to have been a British agent and who escaped from an Irish jail while serving 20 years for robbing a bank, was recaptured in Birmingham after having been at large for nine months. **14.** Two masked men smashed their way into a milk depot in Swindon and escaped with nearly £4,000 after shooting the supervisor in the face and locking four other employees in an airtight strong room. **17.** One man died and five people were hurt when three terrorist bombs exploded in London. One explosion was near a telephone exchange in Chelsea, the bomb being on a motor-cycle; the second was a car bomb behind a cinema in Soho; and the third was off Tottenham Court Road where a telephone exchange worker was killed and another seriously injured and a policeman was injured. A guard dog was shot dead, a security guard wounded, and staff threatened by a gang of six bank raiders who escaped with more than £100,000 from the Midland Bank in Mitcham Lane, Streatham. **18.** Two bombs exploded in the centre of Bristol slightly injuring 13 people. **19.** Five persons, including a policewoman, were injured when a car bomb exploded near Selfridges in Oxford Street; shop windows were shattered up to 200 yards away. Bernard Silver, a West End club owner, was imprisoned at the Old Bailey for six years and fined £30,000 for his part in running a Soho vice organisation known as the Syndicate; Anthony Mangion and Emmanuel Bartolo were each jailed for five years and fined £10,000 and £15,000 respectively; Frank Melito was jailed for four years and fined £5,000; Victor Micallef was jailed for three years; Joseph Mifsud, two years; and Romeo Saliba, nine months. **20.** A terrorist bomb found at the main railway station at Aldershot as soldiers started Christmas leave was defused by disposal experts. At Leeds Crown Court, Alfred John Merritt, formerly principal regional officer with the Ministry of Health in Leeds, pleaded guilty to 12 charges of corruptly accepting gifts or considerations from John Poulson, the architect, to the total value of more than £4,000 and was fined £2,000 with a suspended 12-month prison sentence. **21.** A carrier-bag bomb exploded on the second floor of Harrods Store, Knightsbridge, badly damaging the motor accessory and the paint and wallpaper departments and starting a fire during a busy shopping period, but there were no injuries. **22.** The Leader of the Opposition (Mr. Heath) arrived at his home in Wilton Street, Victoria, only ten minutes after a 2-lb bomb was lobbed on to the building's first-floor balcony by a man who jumped out of a car which later crashed in Chelsea when chased by a police patrol car, several men running away. There were no personal injuries in the explosion. **23.** P.C. Malcolm Craig was shot in the stomach in Southampton, after going to a house to answer a call for help from a colleague who had been confronted by two armed men who fired at him.

(1975) Jan. 7. A skyjacker seized a BAC 1-11 British Airways airliner while it was flying from Manchester to London, threatened to blow up the plane and the crew after it landed at Heathrow if his demands were not met, held it in the runway seven hours while negotiations were carried on by radio, allowed the 46 passengers to leave but kept the crew of five as hostages, and was finally flown to Stansted, Essex, with £100,000 aboard, instead of to Paris as demanded, and overpowered, the money being recovered. **7.** Graham Frost, of Torquay, pleaded guilty at Exeter to robbing isolated post offices in Wiltshire and Cornwall armed with a toy pistol and to three counts of burgling houses, and asked for 235 other offences to be considered; he was sentenced to seven years' imprisonment. **13.** Balbir Singh Grewal, a Customs Officer, of Hounslow; Jagjit Singh Kalkat, former Customs officer, of Hayes; Ibrahim Issa, and Gulham Patel, both of Notting Hill, were convicted at the Central Criminal Court of conspiracy to evade the ban on importing cannabis resin, and were each jailed for five years, it being stated that they were all members of an international drugs trafficking ring. **14.** Lesley Whittle, aged 17, a student, living with her widowed mother at Highley, near Kidderminster, was kidnapped from her home, a ransom note demanding £50,000 being found on the hearthrug in the lounge with a threat to kill the girl. The prosecution stated at Dudley Crown Court, Worcestershire, that the largest amount of property ever stolen by one postman in the history of the Post Office was taken by John Gillam, of Lye, near Stourbridge, who, it was said, was stealing postal packets at the rate of 100 a week for a year and who admitted four specimen charges of stealing postal packets containing rings, watches, dresses, and other clothing and asked for one other charge involving just under £17,000 worth of goods to be taken into consideration; he was jailed for five years. **19.** Shots were fired from a passing car at the Portman Hotel, central London, and a man and four women were injured although none seriously while some three hours later two women were hurt by flying glass as bullets shattered windows in a dining room of the Carlton Tower Hotel, also in central London. **23.** A bomb blew out windows and doors and destroyed part of the roof of the Metropolitan Waterworks' pumping station in Woodford New Road on the north-east outskirts of London, three persons being slightly injured. **25.** A 14-year-old soccer fan, from Bolton, was cleared at Lancaster Crown Court of murdering another fan, at Blackpool's ground in August 1974. He was also acquitted of manslaughter and discharged. **27.** There were five I.R.A. bomb blasts in London

and another in Manchester where 19 people were injured when resumption of the Provisionals' campaign of violence resumed after a Christmastide cessation of activities.

Feb. 3. Three Irishmen were freed from a charge of murdering an 18-year-old Army girl in the Guildford bombing last October, the charge against them being dropped when they appeared on remand at Guildford Magistrates' Court. A charge against a fourth man of conspiring to cause explosions in the Greater London area was also dismissed. Three other people, including two women, were again remanded in custody accused of the girl's murder. **6.** A 24-year-old unemployed Irish labourer, Patrick Guilfoyle, of Sparkbrook, Birmingham, a member of the I.R.A., was sentenced at Manchester Crown Court to 15 years' imprisonment on each of six counts, the periods to run concurrently; two charges of conspiring to cause explosions, one charge of conspiring to cause arson, and three charges of possessing explosives with intent to endanger life or cause serious injury to property. It was announced that juvenile crime in London increased by 15 per cent. in 1974 when 32,000 children between the ages of 10 and 16 were detained by police and about 1,000 children under the age of 10 came into police hands, offences mainly being thefts and larceny although including muggings, robberies, and burglaries. **7.** A group calling itself the Tartan Army made its second attempt in a week to blow up pylons carrying electrical power from Scotland into England when an attack was made on a pylon near the Cornhill–Berwick road. **12.** The body of 10-year-old Alison Chadwick, of Isleworth, who disappeared on June 22, 1974, was found in a sack beside a water-filled gravel pit at Shepperton, 10 miles from her home. **24.** The murder charge against Mrs. Anne Maguire, of North Kensington, concerning the WRAC who died in the blast of a bomb at the Horse and Groom public-house, Guildford, on Oct. 5, 1974, was dismissed because of insufficient evidence. Two schoolboys aged 15 and 16, both of Cathays, Cardiff, were found guilty at Cardiff Crown Court of unlawfully killing the guard when they dropped a paving stone on to a commuter train while playing on a bridge, and were ordered to be detained at Her Majesty's pleasure. **25.** Sydney Hepworth, a former Mayor of Southport, pleaded guilty at Leeds Crown Court to seven charges involving conspiracy and corruption concerned with the Poulson affair and was jailed for three years. Councillor Tom Roebuck, 49, an N.U.M. branch secretary, was imprisoned for one year. Albert Roy Hadwyn, former Lord Mayor of Newcastle-upon-Tyne, and Peter Ward, journalist, of Rothbury, Northumberland, who had both denied three charges of conspiring to commit corruption were given sentences of nine months, suspended for two years, and fined a total of £600. Peter Godber, former Hong Kong police superintendent, was sentenced in Hong Kong to four years' jail for corruptly receiving £2,000 and conspiring to obtain the promotion of a Chinese police officer. **26.** Police Constable Stephen Tibble, 21, of the Metropolitan Police, died after being shot in the chest while chasing on his motorcycle, although off-duty, a suspected burglar in Hammersmith when he saw two plainclothes officers running after the man. **27.** Two Irish sisters, Eileen Gillespie, aged 22, and Ann Gillespie, aged 25, were each jailed at Manchester for 15 years for their parts in causing explosions in Manchester between April 1 and April 30, 1974, and with conspiracy to cause arson during the same period. Accused with them were Edward Byrne, of Chelmsley

Wood, who was jailed for 18 years, and Martin Coughlan, also of Chelmsley Wood, jailed for 16 years.

March 6. Egon Von Bulow, of Lewisham, was sentenced to life imprisonment at the Central Criminal Court for murdering a Panda car driver, P.C. John Schofield, at Caterham in July 1974, the judge recommending he be detained for a minimum of 20 years. Von Bulow was also found guilty of the attempted murder of the two other members of the Panda car's crew and was jailed for 15 years on each count. For 12 other offences, he was given a total of 74 years to run concurrent with the life sentence. **7.** The body of Leslie Whittle, 17-year-old girl kidnapped from her home in Highley, Shropshire, 52 days earlier, was found in a 60-ft. deep drain shaft in a country park at Kidsgrove, Staffs. **10.** At Winchester Crown Court, Peter James King, of Southampton, was jailed for three years for evading £15,000 tax in the " lump " system. **11.** Raymond McLaughlin, of Sparkbrook, Birmingham, admitted causing an explosion on Nov. 14 and possessing a firearm and was jailed for 12 years at Birmingham Crown Court after evidence was given of the part he played as a look-out for James McDade, who was blown to death when a bomb being planted at Coventry telephone exchange went off prematurely. **12.** French police discovered most of a group of painting masterpieces estimated to be worth £210,000 and stolen from a Paris art gallery in October 1974, at the home of a Corsican. **18.** Eight Irishmen were sentenced to 20 years each at the Central Criminal Court for their parts in I.R.A. bomb plots in London and the Home Counties. **26.** Mrs. Sheila Buckley, secretary to Mr. John Stonehouse, Labour M.P. for Walsall North, was arrested by Victoria State Police in the country town of Sale, Australia, on a Scotland Yard extradition warrant alleging charges of theft. Previously on March 21 Mr. Stonehouse was arrested in Melbourne on an extradition warrant issued in London charged with offences of theft, forgery, and deception. Both were granted bail. On April 29 extradition warrants for Mr. Stonehouse and Mrs. Buckley were granted at Bow Street. On June 29 the Melbourne magistrate decided that there was sufficient evidence on all charges in the extradition warrants against Mr. Stonehouse and Mrs. Buckley to warrant trial by jury and he approved extradition to Britain, Mr. Stonehouse and Mrs. Buckley being brought back by plane on July 18, and charged.

April 2. James White, sentenced to 18 years, and Ronald " Buster " Edwards, sentenced to 15 years, two of the men who participated in the Great Train Robbery in Buckinghamshire in 1963, were released on parole from prison after serving nearly nine years. **24.** Two explosions occurred in the West German Embassy in Stockholm where six German guerrillas at one time held 13 people hostage, after killing the military attaché and demanding the release from German jails of 26 of their fellow members of the Baader-Meinof gang. Five terrorists surrendered, the sixth died from injuries caused by the explosion, and another hostage was found dead. **25.** A bomb in a car exploded outside the British Embassy residence in Buenos Aires, an Argentine police guard being killed and two members of the staff being injured.

May 2. Nine members of the Provisional I.R.A. responsible for the 12-month campaign of bombings in Birmingham which started in 1973 received prison sentences ranging from 10 to 16 years at Birmingham Crown Court, seven being found guilty of conspiracy to cause explosions and the other two admitting the charge. **23.** Major Frederick Boothby, of Biggar, Lanarkshire, was sentenced at Glasgow High Court to three years for his part in seeking to cause violence to property, being one of five leaders of the " Army of the Provisional Government of Scotland " to be imprisoned. William Murray, of Glasgow, received seven years' imprisonment for conspiracy plus eight years concurrently for robbing a Glasgow bank; William Anderson, of Aberdeen, ten years for possessing explosives, eight for conspiracy, and two for carrying explosives in a car, all sentences to run concurrently; William Bell, of Inverness, one year for conspiracy; Tony Tunilla, of Glasgow, twelve years after pleading guilty to bank robbery and illegal possession of firearms. A sixth man was fined £75 for possessing an Army training manual contrary to the Official Secrets Act.

June 5. Four Irish immigrants in Canada who organised arms shipments to the I.R.A. were jailed for up to two years in Toronto, all admitting conspiracy to export arms to Ireland. Nine Post Office counter clerks, four of them trade union officials, were sentenced at the Central Criminal Court to terms ranging from nine months to three years for their part in selling stolen stamps, all except three being also ordered to pay compensation of from £134 to £500. **11.** Kevin Keiran Dunphy, of Cricklewood, a Provisional I.R.A. member, was found guilty at the Central Criminal Court of being involved in causing explosions at Heathrow's No. 1 terminal on May 19, 1974, and at the No. 2 terminal on July 26, 1974, and convicted also of possessing an electric explosive time switch and a canister of chemicals found on him when he was arrested, and stealing two motor-cars used for housing gelignite for the Heathrow blasts. He was jailed for 12½ years. Kenneth Brian Littlejohn, held in Winson Green Prison, Birmingham, after being recaptured in England following his escape in March 1974 from Mountjoy Prison, Dublin, where he was serving 20 years' sentence for armed robbery, was refused leave by the House of Lords to appeal against the High Court's rejection of his application for a writ of *habeas corpus* in April. **16.** Thomas Thompson, of Liverpool, was jailed for 10 years at Winchester Crown Court for conspiring with others to contravene the Firearms and Explosive Substances Act between Jan. 1973 and April 1974; he was also convicted of taking part in the management of the Ulster Defence Association. **19.** The Earl of Lucan, who disappeared some months previously, was named by an inquest jury at Westminster Coroner's Court as the murderer of his children's nannie, Mrs. Sandra Rivett. **20.** An 18-year-old youth who pleaded guilty to raping two women in their homes after threatening them with a knife, and who had spent five months in custody awaiting trial, was freed at the Central Criminal Court by Judge Christmas Humphreys after being given a six-month suspended jail sentence. A Scottish journalist who refused to identify one of the accused in the Tartan Army trial was found guilty of contempt of court and fined £500 in the Scottish High Court.

July 8. Bernard Silver was found guilty at the Central Criminal Court, by a majority verdict of 10-2, of the murder in June 1956 of Tommy " Scarface " Smithson, stated to be an East End protection racketeer, and was jailed for life. Silver was also found guilty by a majority verdict of 10-2 of conspiring to murder Smithson and was sentenced to 10 years concurrently. Saeed Madjd, a Persian, was jailed for seven years at the Central Criminal Court after hijacking a B.A.C. 1-11 flying between Manchester and Heathrow in January with the object of getting to France and by-passing British immigration authorities. 10. A police sergeant was shot and seriously wounded during a gun battle at a suspected I.R.A. " bomb factory " house near Liverpool from which large quantities of explosives, arms, and ammunition were taken. Three Irishmen were later arrested. Another police sergeant was shot in Liverpool 24 hours earlier. 31. Criminal statistics published by the Home Office showed that total indictable offences known to police in England and Wales in 1974 were 1,963,360, an increase of 18 per cent. over 1973.

Aug. 2. Four masked men forced their way at gunpoint into the premises of the Hatton Garden Safe Deposit Co. and held seven persons captive before getting away with jewellery and uncut stones. 4. The Home Secretary announced that more prisoners were to be released early from jail under new guidelines agreed between himself and the Parole Board. 5. The Home Secretary announced his decision to increase the remission which could be earned by boys aged 14–16 sent to junior detention centres with the primary purpose of reducing overcrowding. 15. Six I.R.A. men were sentenced to life imprisonment at Lancaster Crown Court after being found guilty of causing the Birmingham bombings in November 1974, the men being convicted of the murders of 21 people in the blasts at the Mulberry Bush and Tavern in the Town on a unanimous verdict by a jury on all counts, which they denied. Two others were found guilty of conspiring with the six to cause explosions and were each sentenced to nine years, one of these two being also convicted of possessing explosives for which he received a concurrent sentence of five years. A ninth man was acquitted of conspiring to cause explosions but found guilty of possessing explosives and was ordered to be released once a safe place had been found for him to live. 18. A bomb, defused by explosives experts, was found on the steps of the Algerian Embassy in Kensington, being one of three placed at Algerian embassies in Europe by an organisation calling itself, " Soldiers of Algerian Opposition "; the others were in Rome and Bonn. 27. Thirty-three people were injured, including N.C.O.s or guardsmen of 1st Btn., Welsh Guards, when a bomb exploded in a discotheque in the Caterham Arms public-house, Caterham, Surrey. Several of the casualties were seriously injured and two soldiers lost limbs. 28. A bomb went off outside the Prudential Assurance offices in Oxford Street, London, injuring seven people. 29. An Army captain was killed when a terrorist bomb which he was trying to render harmless exploded at a shoe shop in Church Street, Kensington, and also damaged a nearby public-house. 30. The fourth bomb explosion in the London area in four nights occurred in the doorway of the National Westminster Bank in High Holborn, but no one was injured.

Sept. 1. An ambulanceman, a police sergeant, and a woman were killed in a shooting episode in West Knighton, Leicester, and another policeman and a policewoman were injured, a man later being arrested. 3. A Russian Aeroflot IL-62 airliner left Heathrow Airport for Moscow carrying the body of its navigator who died earlier in a mysterious shooting incident when the plane was approaching England; the Russians claimed that the crew-member shot himself with a revolver on the aircraft's flight deck " for an unknown reason ". 5. A man and a woman were killed and over 60 people injured, some seriously, when a bomb exploded in the lobby of London Hilton Hotel in Park Lane. 12. A bomb damaged North Sea oil pipeline near village of Crook of Devon, Tayside. 15. Two book

bombs sent by post from Dublin exploded in London, injuring two women.

LABOUR AND TRADE UNIONS

(1974) Oct. 3. Only four of the 24 executive members of the National Union of Mineworkers present voted against rejection of the National Coal Board's productivity scheme based on bonuses calculated on the potential of each face. The N.U.M. executive demanded a national scheme based on output per manshift and giving the same bonus to everyone in the industry irrespective of job. Thousands of commuters were stranded or delayed when four signalmen on British Rail's Southern Region took an unofficial meal break at Hastings, Wadhurst, St. Leonard's, and Purley in support of a pay increase for 1,200 S.R. signalmen. 7. The 250 clerical workers, members of Association of Professional, Executive, Clerical and Computer Staff, who were employed at the Amalgamated Union of Engineering Workers' head office in Peckham, began limited industrial action over complaints of unreasonable delay in dealing with their claim for increased London weighting allowances. 8. The unofficial strikers from Ford's Dagenham press shop voted to return to work to enable talks to continue on pay negotiations affecting all Ford workers, the Company having offered a £63,000,000 package deal. N.U.M. leaders met N.C.B. negotiators and formally rejected their proposals for a productivity scheme and formed a working party to draw-up an alternative plan. 10. The three-week-old dispute between I.T.V. companies and journalists ended with an agreed all-round pay increase of 19 per cent., management also agreeing to review some journalists' positions and to re-examime the grading system. 11. British Airways cancelled flights from Heathrow by its European Division because of a work-to-rule by 3,500 engineering supervisors and inspectors over restructuring of pay and grades. Normal operations were resumed on Oct. 17. 17. British Caledonian, Britain's biggest independent airline, announced plans to rationalise and cut services with 827 of its 5,673 employees being made redundant, and to prune its operations of all routes except those already satisfactorily developed or capable of profitability in relatively short periods. The aviation section of the Transport Union demanded the immediate nationalisation of British Caledonian. 20. More than 2,500,000 copies of the Sunday People, published by I.P.C., were not printed because of a pay dispute at its London plant. 21. Over 1,400 technicians and draughtsmen at seven Hawker Siddeley plants started a work-in to try to persuade the company to change its decision to scrap the HS 146 Government-supported airbus project. 22. Vauxhall Motors offered its 25,000 workers an interim rise of £5·20 a week from Nov. 4 though the existing agreement did not expire until April 1975; the unions recommended acceptance of the offer, which could cost the firm £11,000,000 a year. 23. Executive of N.U.M. by 15 votes to 11 decided not to press its incentive scheme under which all miners would have received rises up to £22·50 a week for exceeding targets by 20 per cent., and agreed to more meetings with N.C.B. 26. Many flights were delayed and four cancelled through an unofficial 24-hour strike by 80 drivers at Heathrow Airport, who were demonstrating over the London weighting allowance recently announced. 27. Car workers from Ford's Halewood transmission plant voted overwhelmingly to accept the company's £68,000,000 pay offer and men from the Vauxhall plant at Ellesmere Port, Cheshire, also overwhelmingly accepted the company's interim cost-of-living allowance of £5·20 a week. **29.** It was announced that about £5,000,000 State aid was to be given to Alfred Herbert, the machine tool makers. The headquarters of the Amalgamated Union of Engineering Workers in Peckham was picketed by strikers from its own clerical staff in support of better London weighting allowances. **30.** The National Executive Committee of N.U.M. voted by 14–12 votes to recommend miners in a forthcoming ballot to reject the N.C.B.'s revised offer on a productivity deal, thus reversing an earlier decision. The Family Expenditure Survey 1973 was published by the Department of Employment and disclosed that family income kept ahead of spending despite wage restraint with average household spending up by 12·5 per cent. to £39·45 a week and net income by 14·6 per cent. to £41·56. The *Department of Employment Gazette* showed that increases in basic weekly wages during first nine months of 1974 were more than double those in the same period of 1973 and that in the respective periods days lost through strikes were 10,868,000 and 5,512,000. Two thousand fitters at Vickers shipyard at Barrow in Furness voted to accept the £50 a week " no strings " offer made by the company. Eight thousand Scottish lorry drivers overwhelmingly accepted the official Transport Workers Union ruling to return to work immediately after agreement two days earlier to a wages plus mileage bonuses deal, thus ending a four week strike.

Nov. 1. Aircraft refuellers employed by Esso at Heathrow held another 24-hour unofficial strike over their London weighting allowance claim. Mr. Wedgwood Benn granted £3,900,000 to workers at I.P.D. (Industrial) of Liverpool to enable them to take over the plant. Another £8,000,000 was promised to Norton Villiers Triumph motor cycle co-operative launched with £4,950,000 of Government funds earlier in the year. **3.** Production at the steelworks at Llanwern, Monmouth, was at a standstill when over 1,600 craftsmen walked out over proposed changes in the production bonus structure. **4.** Workers at the London refinery at Silvertown of Tate and Lyle began a two-week " blockade " of the plant, continuing to produce and pack sugar but refusing to let it leave the premises because they feared 9,000 jobs would be in jeopardy if the Common Market did not allow Britain to continue importing unrefined sugar from Commonwealth countries. About 30 to 40 signalmen brought chaos to commuters on Southern Railway, mainly from Kent, when they staged a 24-hour strike starting at 2 p.m. over pay and "responsibility payment." A similar number of signalmen also struck in the Liverpool area. About 80 hospital doctors and consultants in the North East began an unofficial work to rule in protest against Government plans to phase out pay beds. Delegates representing 35,000 firemen voted at Blackpool to ban overtime in brigades where not enough men had been recruited for the introduction of a 48-hour week, but accepted a new pay deal giving a qualified fireman a £5·75 increase to £54·55 a week. **5.** By 27–25 votes the Engineering Workers' Union's national committee rejected a resolution calling for £18 increases in the basic weekly rates of pay but instructed the President (Mr. Hugh Scanlon) to seek substantial increases. An estimated 7,000 Scottish teachers went on strike in pursuit of an interim pay demand. The £12,000,000 computerised grain terminal at Seaforth, Liverpool, went into full operation after a delay of over two years because of pay and manning disputes. **6.** Doctors were informed of the Government's proposal to start phasing out pay beds from Jan. 1, 1975, imposing new conditions on fee-paying patients entering State hospitals, and of plans for a new consultants' contract. **7.** The management of the *Evening Standard* announced that it planned to end publication of Saturday editions after the issue of Nov. 30. **8.** Mr. Hugh Scanlon, president of A.U.E.W., called in the police to escort strike-breaking members of his staff through an official picket line of clerical workers belonging to A.P.E.X. outside the Union's London headquarters in Peckham. Farm workers were awarded pay rises of £2·60 a week, 11·2 per cent., bringing the men's rate to £27·80 from January, and the rate for craftsmen increased by £3·80 to £32 a week, higher qualified workers receiving increases of up to £4·61 to £36·15 a week, women's and young workers' rates being raised proportionately. **9.** Normal bus services resumed in Glasgow from midnight following a decision by the City's 3,200 bus and underground staff to end their three-week-old unofficial strike, the men accepting a pay offer adding £1,300,000 to the city's annual transport bill. **10.** Tate and Lyle workers at the Silvertown refinery, East London, called off their week-long ban on sugar distribution. Lorry drivers in the north-east accepted a new wage agreement bringing them up to Scottish rates fixed after the recent strike. **11.** Senior managers in the nationalised steel industry belonging to the Steel Industry Management Association began their first national industrial action by working to rule over a demand for an increase of 14·5 per cent. from Jan. 1, 1975, and a regrading for middle management. **14.** Two one-hour strikes by signalmen produced chaos for thousands of commuters on British Rail's Eastern Region line between Fenchurch Street–Shoeburyness–Southend and Tilbury. The *Birmingham Post* did not appear for the second day after a challenge to the editor's prerogative in a journalists' pay dispute in which National Graphical Association members refused to print an article by the city editor and economics correspondent because he was not a member of N.U.J., which was involved in a pay dispute among 9,000 provincial journalists. **15.** The executive of N.U.J. called a strike of 2,000 London members working on some evening and suburban newspapers in protest at the dismissal of 66 members of the union employed by the *Kentish Times* group. Rolls-Royce settled the unofficial strike of 6,000 workers at its Scottish plants with an £8-a-week all-round pay rise or an increase of 20 per cent. **17.** The miners heavily rejected the National Coal Board's productivity pay scheme when ballot figures were announced as: for the scheme, 77,119 (38·4 per cent.); against, 123,345 (61·5 per cent.), majority against 46,226. **18.** The *Birmingham Post*, produced entirely by its editor, was published for the first time since journalists stopped work six days earlier. London's 23,000 busmen were awarded a £14-a-week increase for " stress and strain ", the first time they had been given a special allowance for working in London; this pay rise also applied to Tube train staff. The National Union of Public Employees rejected the previous month's £160,000,000 pay offer to one million council manual workers, but reached a settlement of £30 a week minimum three days later. **19.** Another 24-hour unofficial strike by signalmen stranded thousands of commuters in the Bournemouth, Weymouth, and Southampton areas. **20.** Figures published by Department of Employment showed that basic wage rates at the end of October had risen by a record 22·8 per cent. over the last 12 months. Another 100,000 commuters were delayed for some three hours during the morning when signalmen again staged a sudden unofficial strike, halting trains in Eastern Region's Liverpool Street and Fenchurch Street lines, and some signalmen staged a one-hour stoppage during the evening rush. **26.** Thousands of Scottish children missed school when 47,000 teachers went on strike in support of a pay claim. **28.** London editions of the *Daily Mirror* were not published because machine managers would not work, claiming no progress had been made over pay demands. Trains in and out of Liverpool Street and Fenchurch Street were halted in a further strike by signalmen who delayed over 100,000 commuters in the Eastern Region for up to three hours. Chrysler announced that it was dismissing 700 white-collar workers and Vauxhall stated that it was stopping overtime at one of its main factories because of falls in car sales. **29.** *Daily Mirror* London editions were halted for second night running. **30.** Some 33,000 staff on bakeries producing more than 80 per cent. of bread supplies in England and Wales started a ban on overtime and Sunday working in support of a 66 per cent. pay claim.

Dec. 2. Delegates representing 70,000 municipal busmen accepted a pay offer giving rises of up to £8·55 a week, basic rates going up to between £30·60 and £39·07 and improvements in shift pay providing about £4 weekly more. **5.** It was announced that Sir Don Ryder was resigning as chairman and chief executive of Reed International to become full-time industrial adviser to the Government. More than 200,000 commuters in Essex and East Anglia were without train services as some Eastern Region signalmen staged an unofficial 24-hour stoppage, halting all trains in and out of Liverpool Street and Fenchurch Street stations in pursuit of a pay dispute. **6.** Mr. Wedgwood Benn announced in the Commons arrangements, including a measure of public ownership, to help British Leyland in its financial difficulties and said that the Government proposed to appoint a high-level team headed by Sir Don Ryder to advise on the company's situation and prospects. Union leaders decided to call on striking bakers to accept the award made after the intervention of the new Conciliation and Arbitration Service giving them £32·90 for a 40-hour week, the offer being worth 19-20 per cent. with increases for some grades much higher. **9.** The Government turned down pleas of trade union leaders not to allow the scrapping of the Hawker Siddeley 146 small jet airliner project for the 1980s. **13.** Most national newspapers published only one edition because of industrial action by the National Graphical Association in a dispute over wages differentials. **17.** Another 24-hour strike by 60 Southern Region signalmen in Hampshire and Dorset halted all trains in the area. A work to contract by hospital consultants began in Blackburn and spread to neighbouring towns in protest at Government delays in negotiating a new contract of employment. **20.** Railway signalmen again practically stopped train commuting in Kent, south-east London and Essex with more unofficial action over pay and conditions. Mr. Wedgwood Benn announced Government assistance of £3,900,000 to Kirkby Manufacturing and Engineering, Liverpool, a worker's cooperative, against expert advice. Teachers were offered their biggest pay rises ever when the recommendations of the Houghton Committee, which examined non-university teachers' salaries, were published and accepted by the Government, a £432,000,000 package providing salaries ranging from £1,677 for teachers on the lowest scale to £12,354 for the principal

of a polytechnic. Teachers' leaders accepted the recommendation on Jan. 6. **22.** Over 800 trawler maintenance men at Hull who had been on strike for eight weeks voted to accept a 20 per cent. pay offer. **30.** It was announced that Aston Martin Lagonda, makers of sports saloons, was to go into liquidation with the loss of nearly 500 jobs.

(1975) Jan. 1. Consultants began a work-to-rule over their contract dispute, junior hospital doctors announced a work-to-contract from the following week unless they received a 40-hour week, and family doctors were refused an interim pay award. Pay increases for doctors and dentists were recommended by the Review Body in a report which supplemented the fourth report published in June, 1974. **3.** Mr. Wedgwood Benn announced the Government would guarantee the overdrafts of Foden's, the commercial vehicle manufacturers, and protect the jobs of 3,000 workers at Sandbach, Cheshire. **8.** Junior hospital doctors called off their threatened work-to-rule when Mrs. Castle promised to give them new contracts from October with a basic working week of 40 hours compared with the existing 80 hours. **9.** The doctors' committee of the B.M.A. decided with reluctance to ask G.P.s to send them their signed but undated resignations form the N.H.S., later action depending on the Government's decision on implementing the next report of the Pay Review Body, while doctors would withhold threatened sanctions although continuing to back consultants in their separate dispute. **15.** Chrysler announced that its next new car for the European market would be produced at its Simca subsidiary in France and that the firm's 21,000 British workers were likely to remain on a three-day week for the rest of the winter. **22.** Three Appeal Court judges dismissed an appeal brought on behalf of 7,000 members of the National Graphical Association against the refusal of a High Court judge to grant an injunction to restrain the *Daily Express*, *Evening Standard*, *Evening News*, and *Times* from regarding N.G.A. members employed by the newspapers as having terminated their employment because of continuing industrial action by the union. **27.** The three-week strike by 250 engine tuners at British Leyland's Cowley plant was referred to an independent inquiry under the Advisory Conciliation and Arbitration Service. **29.** Rolls-Royce announced that work had been resumed on the overhaul of eight Avon engines for Hunter fighters of the Chilean air force at the East Kilbride plant, halted about a year earlier because of a ban by the A.E.W.U. The Department of Industry published figures which showed the number of working days lost through strikes in 1974 was more than double that for 1973 and the second highest total since the 1926 General strike, while basic weekly rates of manual workers increased by a record 28·5 per cent. **30.** Leaders of farmworkers in England and Wales decided not to call a strike in protest against a pay award which became operative on Jan. 20 but the executive of the National Union of Agricultural and Allied Workers agreed to press for the second stage of the award to be advanced. **31.** A meeting of more than 8,000 workers of British Airways voted, against the advice of their shop stewards, to accept the current pay offer of 15 per cent. on the basic wage rates in two stages and against a call for a stoppage.

Feb. 1. British Airways clerical and ticket staff began an unofficial strike at Heathrow Airport over the issue of tickets by stewardesses on the new Glasgow shuttle service. **3.** The four-week-old strike by 250 engine tuners at British Leyland's Cowley plant ended when the men agreed to return to work pending the outcome of an independent inquiry into the dispute. **4.** The Heathrow clerical workers' strike over British Airways' new shuttle service spread to five other airports. Mr. Wedgwood Benn announced that the British Steel Corporation's major plant closure programme was to be slowed down with a job reprieve for 14,300 workers out of 21,200 facing redundancy following an interim report on the B.S.C.'s plans in England and Wales. **5.** Miners' leaders decided unanimously that a 22 per cent. increase in basic rates offered by the National Coal Board was insufficient for their mandate of a substantial pay increase. **6.** Thousands of rail passengers on the Eastern Region and for the first time on the Inter-City and some Midland Region services together with isolated parts of Southern Region were again affected as signalmen staged another 24-hour strike for more pay. **7.** Meetings of clerical staff employed by British Airways at Heathrow, Glasgow, and other airports agreed to end a week-long strike while a joint manpower committee investigated the dispute over who should sell tickets on the new London–Glasgow shuttle service. **11.** Pay increases of between £2·95 and £5·45 for signalmen according to grades were accepted by the National Union of Railwaymen. **12.** Port employers announced new severance arrangements for employees, the present maximum pay-off of £4,000 for dockers leaving the ports being increased by up to £1,250 to a maximum of £5,250. Members of the Association of Broadcasting Staff and the Association of Cinematograph Television and Allied Technicians voted in favour of a trial amalgamation for 18 months. **13.** Pay rises of between 28 per cent. for surface workers and 35·2 per cent. for face-workers were agreed for miners. Rail services were again affected in many parts by signalmen who continued their campaign of one-day strikes for more pay, over one million passengers being involved. **17.** Thousands of railway passengers were stranded or delayed when 450 men at Paddington station started a 24-hour unofficial strike over a pay dispute involving the loading of newspaper trains. **18.** The Ford Motor Company announced indefinite short-time working for 11,000 employees, one-fifth of its labour force, to avoid redundancies. **19.** The December figures published by the Department of Employment showed that the rate of increase of pay over the previous 12 months had set a record for the sixth month running, average earnings for the period being 29·1 per cent. higher than a year earlier. **20.** The weekly unofficial strike by British Rail signalmen caused the worst disruption yet and only the Western Region operated normally. **21.** Three hundred workers began a sit-in at Imperial Typewriters' factory at Hull in protest at the company's decision to close the plant; the shut down of their Leicester factory went off peacefully. **27.** The Ministry of Agriculture, Fisheries and Food announced a Government subsidy of £6,250,000 for the trawling industry. **27.** Railway signalmen staged another Thursday unofficial strike but less than half the number of men involved in the previous week's stoppage failed to report for duty. **28.** The port of London was at a standstill with 9,000 out of 11,500 dockers idle and 28 ships stopped in the internal Transport Union dispute between dockers and lorry-drivers over deliveries to container depots. All 23 areas and groups of the N.U.M. taking part in the pit pay ballot voted overwhelmingly in favour of the recent deal.

March 5. The National Graphical Association announced that members had voted by 2,424 to 2,166 in a 90 per cent. poll among craftsmen on national and London evening newspapers to accept a wages offer by the Newspaper Publishers Association for a 5 per cent. pay rise backdated to Oct. 1, 1974, and a further 2 per cent from April, 1975, with a £2·80 cost-of-living threshold rise being preserved as a fixed house bonus. **6.** A pay rise of 19·1 per cent. plus continuing cost-of-living threshold payments for 200,000 Post-Office workers was agreed between the Post Office and the Union of Post Office Workers. Support for the unofficial signalmen's weekly 24-hour industrial action weakened noticeably and most rail regions ran almost complete services. **7.** Hospital consultants decided to refuse to allow a part-time union official to continue to " vet " the admissions of private patients to Western Europe's largest cancer unit in Manchester, declaring that a committee of consultants would decide who was admitted to the Christie Hospital. **8.** Signalmen in British Rail's eastern region decided to end their series of weekly strikes and to back the " substantial " pay claim of the N.U.R. The National Union of Journalists, in a policy statement from its national executive committee, decided not to insist that newspaper editors should join the Union. **10.** The motor-cycle workers' cooperative at Meriden opened. It was disclosed that consultants at Britain's leading eye hospital, Moorfields, London, had set up a separate unit for private patients because of sanctions by ancillary workers at Wellington Hospital, near Lord's. Work on a multi-million pound oil refinery at Canvey Island, Essex, was to be suspended for two years because of the economic situations, the U.S. firm Occidental stated. **13.** About 800 Port of London tally clerks decided at Tilbury by a majority of only 16 to join the unofficial two-week dock strike over jobs in container depots. **15.** The Glasgow Corporation agreed by 84 votes to 10 to ask for Government help to clear the city's 60,000 tons of rubbish piled up during the 350 corporation dustmen's nine-week strike over pay after being told that there was no alternative because of the growing health hazard. The Government decided to send in troops who began operations on March 19. **21.** More than 400 industrial civil servants whose unofficial strike partially disrupted the work of Parliament and some Whitehall offices for two weeks returned to work after being promised that in the July wage review their pay would be compared with similar jobs outside the Civil Service. Mr. Foot published a consultative document containing Government proposals to extend the national dock labour scheme to " all significant commercial ports " and other cargo-handling activities like container depots. **22.** Fishermen blockaded the ports of Grimsby and Immingham in protest against cut-price fish imports. Tyneside fishermen followed suit on March 23, and other ports on subsequent days. On March 26 the British and Norwegian Governments took action to raise the price of frozen fish imported to the U.K. The blockade was lifted at Immingham and Grimsby after a High Court injunction obtained by the Docks Board. **24.** Basic rates of more than two million engineering workers were increased by 30 per cent. under an agreement reached between employers and the A.E.W.U. **25.** Mirror Group Newspapers, publishers of the *Daily Mirror*, began issuing notices to more than 7,000 employees in London following the dismissal of 1,750 members of S.O.G.A.T. in an industrial dispute. **28.** Holidaymakers heading for the Continent, the Channel Islands and Ireland were hit by a 48-hour strike of officers and men on British Rail Sealink ferries in protest against withdrawal of Heysham–Belfast service. **31.** Mr. Alexander Shepelin, former head of the K.G.B., and now leader of a party of Russian trade unionists visiting London as guests of the T.U.C., arrived at Heathrow on an unpublicised and unscheduled flight from Moscow, amid full-scale security precautions, and mounting demonstrations at the Russian Embassy. Nearly 50 ports were blockaded or affected by inshore fishermen in protest at imports of cheap fish from non-Common Market countries and demanding a 50-mile territorial fishing limit; the blockade involved over 1,000 boats and included the ports of Aberdeen, Newcastle, Preston, Invergordon, Heysham, and Fleetwood. On April 1 action spread to the South coast and trapped the French car ferry, *Valençay* in Newhaven, allowing it to sail later however although the British Rail ferry, *Senlac*, in Dieppe was unable to make the return journey. The blockade was called off on April 3.

April 1. British Rail's 20 per cent. pay offer to 250,000 workers was rejected by the three rail unions and thousands of passengers were delayed or crowded into shortened trains as workshop supervisors banned overtime in protest at differential levels further cut services. **2.** Mr. Shelepin's 48-hour visit to Britain ended after a six-hour visit to Scotland when he flew home from Prestwick Airport in a Russian jet. **3.** Agreement was reached on a pay claim by 105,000 manual workers in the electricity power industry under which increases of 31 per cent. were awarded, an Employment Department official statement saying " The Government regrets that it does not conform to T.U.C. guidelines ". The British Airways shuttle service resumed after a stoppage of five weeks because of an electricians' strike which closed Glasgow airport. **4.** The five-week unofficial stoppage by London dockers ended when they overwhelmingly voted to return to work in the dispute over container depot manning. The annual conference of the Electrical Power Engineers' Association decided at Brighton by 19,716 votes to 11,307 to maintain a ban on Communists holding office. **5.** Publication in London of the *Daily Mirror* and the *Sporting Life* was resumed after a 10-day disruption and settlement of the dispute over reduction of manning levels with S.O.G.A.T. **9.** Leaders of the railway workshop supervisors called off their three-week-old work-to-rule and ban on overtime and rest-day working after accepting a £145-a-year pay offer to improve differentials. Glasgow dustcart drivers decided to end their 12-week-old strike by 505-45 votes and the Scottish Office stated that troops would be withdrawn on April 11. **14.** Pay rises averaging 26 per cent. for 500,000 civil servants were agreed. Mr. James Milne, became the first Communist to be appointed general secretary of Scottish T.U.C., taking up the post at the end of 1975. **17.** Leaders of 100,000 shipbuilding and repair workers accepted a 30 per cent. rise in basic rates. **18.** Increases of up to 38 per cent. were awarded to family doctors, hospital doctors, community physicians, and dentists; family doctors received an extra £2,350 a year, bringing them up to an average £8,485 net of expenses, and dentists £7,643 net, a rise of nearly £2,000 a year. **23.** Merchant Navy officers won a 30 per cent. pay increase from June 1 and the right to take one day's leave for every two days they worked. **25.** London Transport offered 23,000 London busmen a 12-month cost-of-living deal worth about 25 per cent. on basic rates, it being described as a " cost-of-living protection arrangement " by which basic rates would go up 75p for every one per cent. rise in the retail price index. **29.** Rises of over 30 per cent. or up to £17 a week for 6,000 men employed in the London enclosed docks were accepted at a

mass meeting, the basic weekly wage increasing from £44·21 to £55 plus differentials of up to £8·30 a week and a productivity bonus of about £3 a week. Newmarket stable lads began a strike at midnight for an extra £1·47 in addition to a £3 a week rise already agreed to by the trainers.

May 1. Striking stable-lads picketed Newmarket racecourse on the first day of the Guineas meeting. **4.** The first copies of the *Scottish Daily News* were published in Glasgow. **5.** An attempt to abolish the Amalgamated Union of Engineering Workers' postal ballot system of electing officials failed by 27–25 votes at the Union's rules revision conference. **12.** Chrysler shop stewards rejected a plea by union officials to return to work and voted overwhelmingly to continue the strike which had closed the group's engine plant at Stoke, Coventry. Firemen began a three-month ban on all duties except emergency calls in support of a demand for a reduction in the working week from 48 to 40 hours, improved shift allowances, and better week-end work rates. A pay agreement giving 25 per cent. increases, including the consolidation of £4·40 in threshold payments, was reached on behalf of 127,000 Post Office engineers, the deal providing new money of 18 per cent. and a productivity payment of £1 a week. **15.** Normal working was resumed by 82 time-hand members of the N.G.A., whose unofficial industrial action halted printing of London editions of the *Daily Telegraph* for three days, and discussions on a revision of a comprehensive agreement continued. **16.** Clerks at Dunlop's Coventry plant ended their month-long strike by voting overwhelmingly to accept a revised offer which by November would bring increases of £8·50 for men and between £9·12 and £12·72 for women, a new five-grade structure being introduced. The Union of Post Office Workers at a special conference at Blackpool lifted by 6,863 votes to 4,407 their restrictions on mechanisation and cleared the way for immediate talks with the Post Office on the automatic handling programme for which post codes were originally introduced. On the casting vote of its President (Mr. Hugh Scanlon) the Amalgamated Union of Engineering Workers decided to abandon its system of electing its 180 senior officials through postal voting and to revert to branch balloting under which members must attend meetings to vote. **19.** After talks between T.U.C.'s steel committee and the British Steel Corporation, it was announced that B.S.C.'s plans for reducing the number of steelworks were not being pursued and that both sides agreed on a six-point plan for various economies designed to reduce substantially the industry's mounting losses. **21.** It was announced that electricity supply manual workers had voted in favour of a 31 per cent. pay deal, with basic rate increases of between £5·50 and £7·60 weekly backdated to March 17. **23.** Two-thirds of the country was blacked out on Independent T.V. programmes over the holiday week-end by a 72-hour strike called by the Association of Cinematograph, Television, and Allied Technicians over a pay claim. **28.** Thousands of holiday-makers were stranded as seamen and dockers started a 48-hour unofficial strike, halting all ferries between British and French ports, when members of British and French unions protested against a new German-owned ferry service between Southampton and St. Malo. **29.** An arbitration award by the Railway Staff National Tribunal recommended a 27½ per cent. increase on existing basic wage rates.

June 2. The National Union of Railwaymen's executive decided by 21 votes to 3 to call a national rail strike from June 23 unless British Rail improved its pay offer, the independent arbitration award of a 27½ per cent. rise in basic rates and other improvements being rejected. **4.** The six-day strike by 550 British Airways fleet maintenance men and engineers at Heathrow Airport ended when conditions of a flexibility working deal were settled. A.S.L.E.F., the train drivers' union, unanimously accepted the award of the independent arbitration tribunal, the Transport Salaried Staffs Association having already accepted. Strikers at Chrysler's engine factory in Stoke, Coventry, agreed to a recommendation from shop stewards to end the three-week strike which halted all the company's car production, the workers having been offered £8 per week rises from July 1 although the Stoke men demanded more towards a £15 claim. **5.** A pay deal giving 35,000 British Steel Corporation craftsmen and ancillary workers rises of about 35 per cent. was agreed. **11.** Mr. Justice Walton ruled in the High Court in London that Mr. Hugh Scanlon had no power to use his presidential casting vote to abolish the postal ballot system of electing officials in the A.U.E.W. and granted an injunction banning the A.U.E.W. from holding elections other than by postal vote pending a full hearing of the case. **12.** Executive of N.U.R. unanimously decided to proceed with the railway pay strike because of British Railways Board's refusal to improve the arbitration award. **13.** The six-week-long strike which led to a workers' occupation of the Massey-Ferguson tractor factory ended with a vote against shop stewards' advice to reject an improved pay offer, most workers receiving £6·45 increases weekly with highly-skilled men getting £7·89. **17.** A 33 per cent. pay rise over 15 months was agreed for 52,000 white-collar workers in the electricity industry. **20.** The national rail strike was called off after N.U.R. executive accepted an improved pay offer which raised British Rail's annual wages bill by 29·8 per cent., 2·3 per cent. more than the rejected arbitration award. Pay increases averaging 25 per cent. for 491,000 local government staff were agreed by employers and National and Local Government Officers' Association and other unions, and accepted by union delegates on June 27. Members of the N.G.A. voted against executive advice to accept a pay offer by the Newspaper Society and British Printing Industries Federation estimated at 32½ per cent. **21.** Production of the *News of the World* in London was stopped when printers of N.G.A. objected to part of a front-page article by Lord George-Brown. **24.** Leaders of the Engineering union voted to remove the general secretary (Mr. John Boyd) from the T.U.C. general council. **25.** The T.U.C. General Council agreed on a set of six guiding principles for pay increases in the next twelve months, including flat-rate rises all-round, geared to a target for price increases. Workers at Chrysler's plastics factory in Coventry agreed to end their three-week-old strike when their claim that the company failed to honour an agreement by refusing to pay them for the days they were laid off by another dispute was referred to arbitration. Leaders of the 22 unions in the Confederation of Shipbuilding and Engineering Unions voted by a big majority to support a resolution declaring opposition to any Government interference with free collective bargaining. **27.** Pay rises which added 29 per cent. to the wage bill were agreed for 176,000 industrial civil servants working in the royal dockyards, royal ordnance factories and other departments.

July 3. After 25 members were arrested, the N.G.A. agreed to lift all sanctions against the Peterborough-based Sharman weekly newspaper group to enable talks to be resumed. The dispute over introduction of new typesetting equipment which lasted seven weeks was settled on July 4. **4.** N.U.R. accepted an offer of 21 per cent. pay increases for its 15,000 London tube workers. Agreement was reached with N.U.J. members in the *Daily Telegraph* for a salary increase of 11 per cent. additional to the current threshold payment, production of the paper being resumed after a day's stoppage in London. **6.** The *News of the World* was not published because of unofficial industrial action by journalists in support of a pay claim. It was announced that members of S.O.G.A.T. had voted by a large majority in favour of amalgamating with the Scottish Graphical Association. **8.** N.U.M. conference unanimously adopted a compromise over its next wage claim, instructing its national executive to "seek", £100 a week for face workers with consequential increases for others and that if there was an unsatisfactory offer to consult the membership, thus dropping a "demand" for £100 a week as contained originally in the Yorkshire area resolution. **9.** T.U.C. general council voted by 19–13 in favour of voluntary wage restraint but statutory price controls with a flat-rate wage increase of no more than £6 weekly for those earning up to £7,000 a year. N.U.J. voted unanimously for 29-hour, four-day week, to be negotiated immediately. National Union of Seamen's executive voted 11–7 in favour of a 37·3 per cent. pay award agreed by arbitration after pressure from rank-and-file members following the executive's rejection by 10–8 of the same offer a week previously with a decision to hold a strike ballot. **11.** Pay rises of between 18·1 per cent. and 21·2 per cent. backdated to July 1 were agreed for nearly 59,000 white-collar workers in the gas industry. Plans for the introduction of integrated computer techniques resulting in *Financial Times* staff reductions by about one-third were announced by the management to union officials. **13.** Agreement was announced for a closed shop for the three railway unions effective from August 4. **18.** A meeting of British Airways Overseas Division catering staff voted to accept a union recommendation to end their week-old strike over pay parity, on which there would be talks. **24.** It was announced in British Railways Board annual report that it had made a loss of £157,800,000 in 1974 and that industrial action accounted for £18,000,000 or 11 per cent. of the figure. Newmarket stable lads on strike for 13 weeks unanimously voted to return to work after trainers agreed to accept a formula giving them a £37 a week consolidated wage. **30.** British Gas Corporation reported a £44,000,000 loss in 1974 and the Post Office disclosed a record deficit of £307,000,000 for the same period, following the announcement on July 29 of a £257,000,000 electricity loss. **31.** The Government announced that it had decided not to provide any more money to assist Norton-Villiers Triumph, the motor-cycle firm.

Aug. 6. Redundancies caused by closures of out-dated steel plants in Scotland would be cut from 6,500 to 2,115 under a published review of the British Steel Corporation's closure programme although the Government deferred its decision in the future of the Shotton plant in North Wales. **7.** The Government announced that it was making available fresh loans to Govan Shipbuilders of £6,900,000 and was prepared to write-off expected losses of up to £10,300,000 on existing contracts in 1976 and 1977. **8.** The Home Secretary ordered an urgent inquiry into the nationwide work-to-rule by 30,000 firemen and junior officers over a pay claim. **9.** The *Observer* newspaper was not published following a break-down in negotiations over staff reductions. **11.** Police patrol cars were used to answer 999 calls to London Fire Brigade after over 100 fire engines were immobilised by industrial action over pay. **13.** Britain's firemen called-off their work-to-rule after agreement was reached on a national £6-a-week pay rise payable in November. **14.** The *Financial Times* was not published because of action by members of the N.G.A. **19.** British Airways' European Division catering staff, who had been in dispute for three weeks, returned to normal working following talks about a night shift supplement. **21.** The month's unemployment figures showed that the national rate topped the five per cent. mark at 5·4 for the first time since the 1939-45 War with 1,250,334 jobless workers. This represented an increase of 162,464 over July and 558,831 above August, 1974. **26.** The 250 journalists dismissed by the *Birmingham Post* and *Evening Mail* conditionally accepted the offer of a £6-a-week pay increase from Jan. 1st, 1976, but decided to continue the seven-week dispute until agreement was reached on manning levels and redundancies. **28.** The ballot by N.U.M. members resulted in a 3–2 vote in favour of the Government's anti-inflation policy, figures being 116,076 (60·5 per cent.) in support and 75,743 (39·5 per cent.) against in a 77 per cent. total poll. It was announced that British Airways made a net loss in 1974 of £9,400,000 compared with £16,600,000 profit in the previous year to March 31, the Chairman (Sir David Nicolson) stating that unofficial strikes cost the airline £11,000,000.

Sept. 2. Left wing militants caused uproar and rowdily demonstrated at the T.U.C. conference at Blackpool in their campaign for the release of the one Shrewsbury picket remaining in jail; Congress ultimately passed a resolution calling on the General Council to use "the full strength of the British trade union movement to secure the picket's freedom ". **3.** T.U.C. voted on a show of hands to support the Government's £6 a week voluntarily-agreed pay rise limit, a resolution criticising the policy moved by the Technical and Supervisory section of the Engineering Workers being declared " overwhelmingly lost " also on a show of hands and the General Council report detailing the voluntary agreement being approved by 6,945,000 votes to 3,375,000, a majority of 3,570,000. **10.** It was announced that nearly 5,000 workers were to be laid off or not replaced by General Electric Company over next twelve months. **15.** Jensen Motors, the West Bromwich specialist car manufacturer, announced that it was calling in receiver because of labour troubles and general economic problems.

LEGAL

(1974) Oct. 16. The House of Lords ruled that a working men's club which refused admission and service to a coloured member of an affiliated club with reciprocal rights was not committing a breach of the Race Relations Act. Five Law Lords unanimously upheld an appeal by the Dockers' Labour Club of Preston, Lancs., on the grounds that the Act did not apply to the club because it was not offering services to the public or a section of the public.

Nov. 8. Mr. Justice Forbes ruled in the High Court that picketing on a public highway of premises by people not involved in an industrial dispute was illegal, his decision arising out of a complaint by a firm of North London estate agents of

a picketing campaign against them. **20.** Two private detectives and their wives, all from Southmead, Shoreham, Sussex, won appeals in the House of Lords against convictions of conspiring to effect a public mischief by unlawfully obtaining confidential information from councils and government departments by impersonation. Five law lords decided that there was no offence at law of conspiracy to effect a public mischief and quashed the convictions, set aside the sentences, and awarded costs. **21.** The report of the Law Society and comments, and recommendations of the Lord Chancellor's Advisory Committee on Legal Aid and Advice was published, and recommended that legal aid should be available for all tribunals under the supervision of the Council of Tribunals where representation was permitted and the Patents Appeal Tribunal. **22.** Mr. Justice Whitford ruled in the High Court that the N.U.T. was wrong to discipline five members for not attending a mandatory office meeting; he held that the chapel meeting had not been validly called, that the journalists were not bound to attend it, and that issuing cautions as to their future behaviour in the Union was wrong, and he awarded each of the five £2 damages, and ordered the Union to pay costs.

Dec. 11. Appeals by 20 men convicted of wearing I.R.A. uniform were dismissed in the High Court, London, the Lord Chief Justice (Lord Widgery) ruling that black berets constituted a uniform alone. **19.** The Home Secretary (Mr. Jenkins) told the Commons that the law and the facts in the case of the two jailed Shrewsbury pickets had been fully argued before the Court of Appeal and a judicial decision reached on the merits of the sentences and he could not usurp the functions of the court.

Feb. 10. The Court of Appeal decided by a 2–1 majority that a London solicitor paralysed by polio for the past 18 years and who had to live in a specially equipped flat because of paraplegia was entitled to rating relief in the same way that help was given to special institutions for the disabled. **19.** Mr. Justice Templeman ruled in the High Court that a self-employed workman's lunchtime snacks could not be offset as expenses in his tax returns during an Inland Revenue appeal against a tax comissioners' decision in favour of a taxpayer, the dispute being regarded as a test case.

March 12. The House of Lords ruled that an Irishman who claimed he was forced by I.R.A. threats to take part in the killings of an off-duty policeman in Belfast could have his defence of duress put to a jury. By a majority of three to two, the Law Lords held for the first time that duress could be a defence for a person who aided and abetted murder and by the same majority allowed an appeal by Joseph Lynch, who was convicted of murder and sentenced to life imprisonment at Belfast City Commission in June 1972, and quashed his sentence but directed that he should remain in prison pending a new trial to be ordered by the Court of Criminal Appeal in Northern Ireland and at which the defence of alleged duress could be put to the jury. **23.** The Bar Council referred to the Professional Conduct Committee of the Senate of the Inns of Court and the Bar complaint of " mud-slinging " against certain defence counsel by Mr. Justice Melford Stevenson during the I.R.A. court trial at the Central Criminal Court which ended the previous week. **26.** Independent Television News won its appeal against a county court judge's order that it should produce all its film of the 1974 Windsor Pop Festival as evidence in a civil claim against the police. Three Appeal Court judges ruled that although the courts had inherent power to order I.T.N. to produce and show untransmitted film in the interests of justice, its disclosure in this case would be "oppressive".

April 16. A High Court judge ordered a police constable to pay £4 a week for more than 52 years to an ex-policewoman colleague seriously hurt in a car crash, when after awarding £10,929 damages to her he was told that the constable's insurers had gone into liquidation but that the officer offered £4 a week from his £2,200 a year pay.

May 1. By a majority of 3–2 the House of Lords' judicial committee ruled that if a man accused of rape believed the woman consented to intercourse, the jury should not be required to consider the reasonableness of his belief in deciding whether or not there was consent. The issue arose during an appeal by three airmen convicted of raping a mother of two. On May 6 the Home Secretary (Mr. Jenkins) turned down a request by a delegation of Labour and Conservative M.P.s to introduce urgent legislation to reverse the Law Lords' ruling. **5.** Mr. Justice Phillips ruled in the High Court, in a test case brought by a ratepayers' action group, and affecting thousands of people who had been charged on their rates for sewer services even though they were not connected to a local authority main sewer, that charges levied by Devon Council under the Water Charges (Collection of Charges) Order, 1974, as a transitional measure until the 1973 Water Act came into full effect, were not legal.

May 9. Three Appeal Court judges ruled that Sikhs living in Britain could have only one wife, this ruling reversing a previous decision in 1962 which had protected the defendant who came to this country in 1966 and was charged with bigamy after he married again in March 1973. **13.** Record damages for a woman of £122,760 were awarded by Mr. Justice Kilner Brown in Manchester High Court to a 20-year-old Stockport girl stated to have been reduced to "a mental and physical wreck" in a road accident four years previously.

June 17. The Home Secretary announced that he was to appoint a small group to advise if a change was necessary in the law on rape. **27.** Three Appeal Court judges cancelled an injunction granted to the Attorney-General earlier in the day which would have stopped the *Sunday Times* publishing anything in the following four weeks concerning the Crossman Diaries and refused the Attorney-General leave to appeal to the House of Lords after the newspaper gave an undertaking not to publish any new extracts pending a full court hearing of the issue.

July 2. Requests by an all-party deputation of M.P.s for judges to be given rape sentence guidelines were rejected by the Lord Chancellor (Lord Elwyn-Jones). **14.** The Home Secretary asked the Criminal Law Revision Committee to carry out a long-term review of the sexual offence laws, including the penalties for rape. **23.** It was announced in the House of Lords that the duty of a coroner's jury to name the person it found responsible for murder or manslaughter and the coroner's obligation to commit that person for trial were to be abolished.

SPORT

(1974) Oct. 1. John Conteh won the World light-heavyweight championship when he decisively defeated Jorge Ahuenada on points at Wembley Pool. **23.** The International Olympic Committee voted in Vienna to stage the 1980 Olympic Games in the Soviet Union, this being the first time the games will be held behind the Iron Curtain. The winter Olympic Games were awarded to Lake Placid, New York. The Glasgow Rangers club was ordered by Glasgow Sheriff Court to pay damages of £19,621 to a widow and £3,500 to each of her two sons following the

death of her husband who was one of 66 spectators crushed to death at the Rangers *v.* Celtic League match at Ibrox Park in 1971. **29.** South Africa won the Davis Cup international lawn tennis competition by default when India refused to meet them in the 1974 final on racial grounds. **31.** The Sports Council's annual report was presented when it was stated there had been a record public spending of £80,000,000 on sports facilities in 1973–74.

Nov. 29. Gary Player, of South Africa, equalled the world record for a tournament round of golf by completing the second round of the Brazilian Open Championship in 59—10 under par—in Rio de Janeiro.

Dec. 20. Mrs. Theresa Taylor, president of the Zambian Women's Golf Union, who played in the first round of the women's international match tournament at Wentworth while on holiday in England, was told by the Lusaka Government she was forbidden to become involved during 1975 with any organised sport either as a player or an administrator for defying the country's ban on sporting links with Britain.

(1975) Jan. 3. All competitive soccer in Malta was banned following rioting at first division matches in which players and spectators beat up referees and linesmen. **9.** Australia regained the Ashes when they beat England in the fourth test in Sydney by 171 runs to take a winning 3–0 lead in the series. **24.** Eleven spectators and several policemen were injured when rioting broke out during the final Test match between the West Indies and India in Bombay, play on the second day being abandoned at teatime after crowds set fire to benchers and hurled bottles. **26.** Cricketers in the Transvaal decided to introduce racially mixed club cricket later in 1975 although it was stressed that it was intended to stay within South Africa's apartheid law.

Feb. 7. Mr. Boon Wallace, president of South African Cricket Association, was refused a visa to enter Australia where he was due in a few days to discuss Australia's proposed tour of South Africa the following summer because of the Australian Government's opposition to any tour while South Africa remained racially segregated. **18.** The Australian Cricket Board of Control announced that the proposed tour of South Africa later in 1975 by an Australian cricket side would not take place.

March 2. Play on the second day of the second Test between Pakistan and the West Indies was held up for more than two hours when crowds ran on to the field in Karachi's national stadium after Wasim Raja scored his maiden Test century for Pakistan and police used batons and tear gas to quell the crowd. **4.** The South African Government announced agreement to the selection of mixed race rugby and cricket teams to play against touring French and English sides. **16.** The Old Etonians and Royal Engineers played a soccer match at Chatham garrison ground to mark the centenary of their F.A. Cup final at the Oval in which the R.E.s team of 11 officers won 2–0; the Engineers again won 1–0. **26.** William Hill, the bookmakers, announced that subject to police permission, arrangements had been made with the All England Lawn Tennis Club to operate a betting marquee during the Wimbledon championships. **27.** An historic four-day cricket match began when a South African XI for the first time included two non-Whites, when playing Derrick Robins' XI, the crowd on the Table Mountain side of the ground in Cape Town was not segregated, and one umpire was an Indian, K. Kanjee, of Rhodesia.

April 5. Two horses, Beau Bob and Land Lark, were killed in the Grand National won by

L'Escargot, who prevented Red Rum, who came second, the record of a third successive win. 14. The English Rugby Union produced a report rejecting the major alterations proposed by the Mallaby Committee set up to investigate the state of the game in this country. The Welsh Rugby Union announced plans to divide their clubs into three divisions with promotion and relegation within the next seven years.

May 3. The start of the 2,000 Guineas race at Newcastle was stopped for 15 minutes by striking stable-lads. The result of the F.A. Cup Final at Wembley was: Fulham 0, West Ham 2. 15. John Murray, the Middlesex wicket-keeper, took a catch in the match at Lord's against Somerset to break a world record; this was his 1,236th catch, one more than Herbert Strudwick had taken when he retired in 1927. On May 31 Murray, keeping wicket against Surrey at Lord's, passed Strudwick's record for all wicket-keeping dismissals, making his 1,494th dismissal. 17. England visited Windsor Park, Belfast, for the first time in four years to play Northern Ireland in a home international soccer match, the result ending in a 0–0 draw and without incident. 22. Rhodesia was expelled from the International Olympic Committee because " it did not conform to rules governing racial discrimination," according to the Committee.

June 11. Ceylon–Tamil demonstrators stopped play at the Oval to protest that Sri Lanka's team for their Prudential World Cup match with Australia had been selected on an anti-Tamil basis, but police quickly cleared the wicket. 13. Leeds United, whose supporters rioted in the European Cup final against Bayern Munich at the Parc des Princes stadium on May 28 when a Leeds goal was disallowed, were banned from European football competitions for four years by a disciplinary commission of the Union des Associations Européenes de Football. 15. French stable lads disrupted the Chantilly race meeting, forcing the cancellation of all races, including the Prix de Diane, because of a pay and conditions dispute and there were violent scuffles with the Gendarmerie Mobile. 19. About 100 striking Newmarket stable lads marched along the racecourse at Royal Ascot in support of their pay claim. The resumption of racing in France was announced after a settlement in the stable lads' dispute. 23. Bookmakers were allowed at Wimbledon for the tennis championships for the first time.

July 19. The world champion, Emerson Fittipaldi of Brazil, was declared winner of the British Grand Prix after a downpour caused several crashes and stopped the race at Silverstone, Northants. 28. New Zealand Rugby Union rejected a Government request to call off the All Blacks' Rugby Tour of South Africa next year.

Aug. 12. John Walker, the New Zealand middle-distance runner, became the first man in the world to run a mile in less than 3 min. 50 sec. when he recorded 3 min. 49·4 sec. at an international athletics meeting in Gothenburg. 19. Demonstrators caused the England–Australia third Test match to be abandoned by pouring oil on the Headingley wicket and digging holes in it. It was announced that an incident of this nature in the circumstances prevailing did not justify the playing of an additional match. 26. Robin Hobbs, Essex bowler and vice-captain, took 44 minutes to score the fastest first-class century for 55 years and the fifth fastest in history when he hit 100 against the Australians at Chelmsford.

Sept. 3. British Rail announced that it was to withdraw all its " soccer specials " from Sept. 6 in its campaign to combat hooliganism and that the sale of long-distance " Awayday " day return tickets would be banned on Saturdays before 3 p.m.; British Rail stated on Sept. 10, that ban on cheap-day tickets before 3 p.m. would be lifted, except in those areas where football supporters had previously caused trouble. The fourth and final Test at the Oval, Surrey, was the longest game of Test cricket played in England and receipts of £274,000 for the series were a record for England. 7. Niki Lauda of Austria became World Drivers' Champion after finishing third in Italian Grand Prix at Monza. 8. Billy Bremner, captain of Scotland, and four other Scottish internationals, were banned from playing for their country again; Scottish Football Association made decision following incident in Copenhagen night club in previous week after match between Scotland and Denmark. 11. The Cricket Council announced that M.C.C. tour of South Africa, scheduled for 1976–77, would not take place. 14. Britain retained Wightman Cup for tennis in Cleveland, Ohio; it was Britain's first consecutive win since 1924–25. 15. Leicestershire won county cricket championship for first time in their history.

BRITISH COMMONWEALTH
(See also Africa)

(1974) Oct. 2. Australia announced a cut in her immigration quota because of rising unemployment, although she would continue to recruit from Britain and elsewhere special skills needed by industry. 6. Riot police used tear gas in the Central Highlands of Papua New Guinea to quell Yure, Bandi and Dom tribesmen who attacked the Nauru tribe over a land boundary dispute the previous day. Three people were killed and more than 50 injured. 8. An earthquake rocked a wide area of the eastern Caribbean; St. Kitts was reported extensively damaged and Antigua damaged. 22. The Canadian Government announced rule changes in its entry regulations, effective immediately, designed to slow the rate of new immigrants.

Nov. 2. Five major fires raged in the east end of Montreal, the second day of a pay strike by the City's 2,400 firemen; police stopped fighting between strikers and suburban firemen who tried to extinguish the outbreaks while 80 families were driven from their homes and thousands of dollars worth of property was destroyed. The firemen ended their 3-day strike on Nov. 3 when given a £320 cost-of-living bonus they had demanded. 3. Several hundreds of political opponents were reported arrested by the local administrations in New Delhi in an effort to avert a general strike called for the following day by opposition parties in protest against the Government's handling of India's economic problems and alleged corruption. 4. Non-Communist opposition parties in India brought business to a halt in New Delhi and Patna.

Dec. 13. Malta became a republic within the Commonwealth and Sir Anthony Mamo took the oath as President. 17. President Makarios's first effort since his return to Cyprus to make contact with Turkish-Cypriots by trying to visit two refugee camps inside the Episkopi British sovereign base area ended when the Presidential procession was stoned. 20. Rohana Wijeera, 30, leader of Sri Lanka's 1971 youth rebellion, was sentenced in Colombo to rigorous life imprisonment by five Supreme Court judges who also jailed 31 other persons for terms of two to twelve years following the arrests in 1971 of 18,000 youths, the majority of whom were later freed, and who allegedly attempted to overthrow the Government of Mrs. Bandaranaike; Wijeera was stated to have led the revolt. 25. Darwin, capital city of Australia's Northern Territory, was devastated by a cyclone early on Christmas morning, leaving 90 per cent.

of the town in ruins. **28.** The government of Sheikh Mujibar Rahman declared a state of emergency throughout Bangladesh, blaming subversion, lawlessness, and economic havoc.

(1975) Jan. 2. Mr. Lalit Mishra, Indian Minister of Railways, was injured when a bomb exploded after he had opened a new rail line in Bihar and died next day. One other man was killed and 26 persons were seriously hurt. **8.** Greek and Turkish Cypriots agreed after weeks of uncertainty to resume their peace talks, following a meeting between Mr. Denktash, the Turkish-Cypriot leader, and Mr. Clerides, for the Greek-Cypriots, in the presence of U.N. special representative on the island. **13.** It was reported that an unprecedented wave of cold weather had killed more than 500 people in Northern India in the last ten days. **14.** President Makarios of Cyprus formed a new Cabinet including five members of the government overthrown in the coup of July 1974. **17.** A Greek Cypriot high school pupil was killed and 20 people, including British servicemen, were injured during day-long anti-British demonstrations in Cyprus at the British decision to allow 10,000 Turkish Cypriot refugees to be evacuated to Turkey from British bases. **19.** Indian service personnel worked at ports over the week-end to clear urgent food supplies and oil shipments held up by a national dock strike over a pay settlement. **25.** The ruling Awami League used its Parliamentary majority to declare Sheikh Mujibur Rahman, Bangladesh Prime Minister, president and authorised him to establish a one-party state.

Feb. 1. At least eight people were killed and over 80 injured in Delhi when Moslems rioted over the arrest of the Imam of the old city's Jama Masjid mosque. A gun battle between Turkish troops and the Greek Cypriot National Guards occurred close to Nicosia airport and was described by U.N. as a " major violation " of the ceasefire, but the city was quiet again by following day. **13.** The formation of a 50-member constituent assembly to prepare the constitution of a federal Turkish state in Cyprus was announced by Mr. Denktash, Turkish Cypriot leader, and Mr. Irmak, the Turkish Prime Minister. On Feb. 14 President Makarios told thousands of Greek Cypriot demonstrators that his Government would never allow Turkish Cypriots to establish a separate state in the island. **17.** Four of Australia's six State governments rejected the new all-Australia honours award system announced by the federal Labour government to be known as the Order of Australia with three grades, the Governor-General stating that the new awards had been approved by the Queen and reflected her position as Queen of Australia. **24.** Sheikh Mohammad Abdullah, deposed as ruler of Kashmir by India in 1953, returned to power there after his acceptance of the State's accession to India as " final and irrevocable ". Sheikh Mujibur Rahman, President of Bangladesh, launched a national party called the Bangladesh Krishak Sramik Awami League (Bangladesh Peasants' and Workers' League), with himself as chairman, thus introducing one-party rule in his three-year-old republic, other parties being dissolved. **27.** After Mr. Clyde Cameron, the Immigration Minister, replied in the Australian Parliament to Opposition claims about developments in the case of Mr. John Stonehouse, the British M.P. who fled to Australia, there were exchanges between him, the Speaker (Mr. James Cope), and the Prime Minister (Mr. Gough Whitlam), as a result of which the Speaker resigned when the vote to suspend Mr. Cameron was defeated.

March 6. A procession of several hundred thousand people marched on Parliament House,

New Delhi, in an anti-Government rally during which a " charter of demands " was presented calling for the dismissal of the Congress Government in Bihar, the cleansing of alleged corruption, and for sweeping electoral reforms.

April 10. The legislature in the Himalayan kingdom of Sikkim voted to abolish the monarchy and seek full Indian statehood, the Chogyal (ruler) Palden Thondup Namgyal, being in his Gangtok Palace protected by the Indian Army after his personal guards were disarmed on April 9. On April 15 it was announced that the people had voted also to depose the Chogyal and become an Indian State. **25.** It was announced in Wellington, New Zealand, that assisted passages for immigrants were to be ended because of economic and housing problems. **29.** The Commonwealth heads of Government conference opened in Kingston, Jamaica and concluded on May 6.

May 3. Four thousand South Vietnamese refugees, including 1,000 children, who were rescued from a sinking tramp ship in the South China Sea, landed in Hong Kong and were given temporary asylum. **13.** Over 500 European men, women, and children were evacuated from the copper-mining town of Panguna on the Pacific island of Bougainville, which had been held for 24 hours by 1,000 rioting mine workers. **16.** Sikkim formally became an Indian state with Mr. B. B. Lal its first governor. **30.** It was announced that Anguilla, the Caribbean island, was to have a new constitution which the Foreign Office in London stated would fall short of formal separation between it and the neighbouring islands of St. Kitts and Nevis linked as an associated State.

June 5. Papua New Guinea decided to invite the Queen to be head of State when independence from Australia was achieved later in the year. **8.** Turkish Cypriots voted overwhelmingly for the draft constitution of the separate state set up unilaterally in Turkish-occupied Cyprus, 99·4 per cent. voting in favour on a 70 per cent. turn-out. **12.** Mrs. Gandhi, Prime Minister of India, was found guilty in the Allahabad High Court of electoral corruption in 1971 and was debarred from public office for six years although she decided to continue in office pending an appeal. On June 24 she was given only a conditional stay of verdict, with the result that she was not able to vote in Parliament although able to remain in office. **26.** Disturbances followed the arrest of 676 political opponents of Mrs. Gandhi in pre-dawn raids throughout India under the Maintenance of Internal Security Act, the detentions being described as " preventive custody ".

July 2. The Australian Prime Minister (Mr. Gough Whitlam) dismissed his Deputy Prime Minister (Dr. Cairns) after the latter refused to resign over the Government's loan-dealing controversy. **4.** The Indian Government banned 26 political and social organisations both of the Right and the Left under the Defence and Internal Security of India Rules, 1971. **7.** At least 150 people died in the monsoon floods of north and north-east India in the previous two weeks, it was reported. **16.** An Opposition attempt to force a Senate inquiry into alleged Australian Government malpractices in seeking petro-dollar funds failed when witnesses summoned to the Upper House claimed Crown privilege and refused to answer relevant questions. On July 17 the Australian Senate passed a resolution by 26–22 votes demanding a Royal Commission into the Government's loan-seeking activities. **19.** The Indian Government asked foreign correspondents to sign pledges that they would submit their dispatches to censorship, or risk expulsion. **21.** The Labour Party was confirmed as the winner of the South Australian election nine days earlier, the last doubtful seat being retained by Labour to give it 23 seats in the 47-seat Parliament. **22.** Opposition members walked out of the Upper House of the Indian Parliament in a boycott of the remainder of the one-week session after approval by the Congress majority party, supported by the Communist Party of India, of a declaration of an internal emergency. **23.** By 336–59 votes the Lok Sabha (Lower House) decided in New Delhi to continue India's state of emergency, the Congress Party being supported by the Communist Party of India, and Opposition M.P.s announced a boycott of the remainder of the session.

Aug. 1. Britain recognised the new military régime in Nigeria. **5.** The Indian House of Commons gave approval to amendments altering the Representation of the People Act and changing the election law under which Mrs. Gandhi was convicted of corruption two months previously. **9.** The Indian Upper House of Parliament voted in favour of a bill to give immunity to the Prime Minister from criminal and civil court proceedings. **10.** A special crimes tribunal in Rangoon sentenced 52 employees of the state-owned Burma railways to prison terms of between 10–16 years for taking part in labour demonstrations in June. **14.** At least 200 people, including women and children, were swept away by the flooded Mahakali river in Nepal while asleep in their mud huts. **15.** In a dawn coup in Dacca, Army officers in Bangladesh overthrew the government of Sheik Mujibur Rahman, the President, who was assassinated along with most members of his immediate family. The new President was Mr. Khandakar Mostaque Ahmed, formerly Commerce Minister. On Aug. 18 the new régime announced the "complete normalisation" of life in the country. **23.** Bangladesh's former Prime Minister, Mansur Ali, and Vice-President Syed Nazuri Islam, were among 26 leaders of the former régime arrested under new martial law regulations. **26.** The Prime Minister (Mr. Wallace Rowling) announced in Wellington that New Zealand troops stationed in Singapore would be withdrawn during the next two years. A conference of Commonwealth Finance Ministers opened at Georgetown, Guyana. **30.** Bangladesh banned the Awami League, the country's only political party.

Sept. 2. Singapore's Minister for the Environment (Mr. Wee Toon Boon) was imprisoned for 4½ years after being found guilty of corrupt practices and also fined £1,350. Three members of the Trotskyist Lanka Sama Samaja party were formally removed as members of the Sri Lanka Cabinet after refusing to resign voluntarily. **15.** Papua New Guinea became independent nation and member of Commonwealth.

MIDDLE EAST

(1974) Oct. 9. Thousands of orthodox Israelis poured into the West Bank of Jordan to try to force the Government's hand on the issue of settlement in the Judea and Shomron area but most were turned back by police and Army road-blocks while others were forcibly evicted, although a few groups managed to set up provisional settlements south of Schem and Jericho. **10.** Dr. Kissinger, U.S. Secretary of State, held talks in Cairo with President Sadat and the Egyptian Foreign Minister in another attempt to resolve the Middle East impasse. On Oct. 11, he visited Amman for talks with King Hussein before continuing to Tel Aviv. **28.** The Arab countries summit conference in Rabat ended

with the announcement that it recognised that the Palestine Liberation Organisation would "henceforth assume complete responsibility for all Palestinians in the occupied territories both at national and international levels".

Nov. 9. Israel devalued its currency by 42·857 per cent. as one of a series of measures to deal with a worsening economic outlook. Rioting and looting broke out in Tel Aviv on Nov. 10 as a result, and there were renewed demonstrations the following night with the arrest of over 30 teenagers. More youths were arrested as demonstrations continued for a third night on Nov. 11. **16.** Four Egyptian ships entered the Suez Canal on the first trip by commercial vessels since it was closed during the 1967 Middle East War. **19.** A mob of Israelis burned the bodies of a suicide squad of three Arab guerrillas who had burst into a block of flats in the border town of Beit Shean and killed four of the residents, and who died when Israeli troops attacked them. **21.** Mr. Zied Rifai, Jordanian Prime Minister, resigned as King Hussein planned to reorganise his Kingdom following the Rabat meeting of Arab Heads of State. **29.** The U.N. Security Council renewed the mandate of the peace-keeping force of 1,200 on the Golan Heights.

Dec. 1. Two Arab guerrillas surrendered to Israeli troops after a night attack on the border settlement of Rihanyia where they killed a civilian and wounded his wife. **9.** The Greek Catholic Archbishop of Jerusalem, Hilarion Capucci, was sentenced to 12 years' imprisonment by an Israeli court after being found guilty on three counts of gun-running and aiding Arab terrorists. **11.** Two men, believed to be terrorists, were killed and 54 people injured in a bomb attack on a cinema in Tel Aviv. **22.** A 16-year-old girl from Jacksonville, Florida, was the only casualty of the Arab terrorist offensive against tourists visiting the Holy places in Jerusalem for Christmas, being wounded in an attack on a bus with a grenade, and having a leg amputated. **27.** El Al, the Israeli airline, ceased all flights, grounded its entire fleet of planes, and handed dismissal notices to maintenance workers who went on strike for the second time in a few weeks.

(1975) Jan. 26. An Israeli drilling team struck oil in the occupied West Bank near Ramallah, about 20 miles north of Jerusalem. **27.** President Sadat of Egypt arrived in Paris for a three-day official visit, the first by an Egyptian Head of State for 50 years.

Feb. 10. The Israeli negotiating team of three met Dr. Kissinger, American Secretary of State, at a working dinner as another round of Middle East talks on a full settlement began. **12.** Dr. Kissinger held talks with President Sadat of Egypt on the Middle East situation and claimed that Arab and Israeli views could be reconciled.

March 2. Five soldiers were killed, ten others wounded and three civilians died in two-days' fighting in Sidon, Lebanon, in protest at a proposal to award a monopoly fisheries contract to an international firm. **6.** Seven guerrillas, three Israeli soldiers, and eight civilians were killed and eleven wounded when Arab terrorists raided in a commando raid in Tel Aviv bombed an hotel in which they were besieged by Israeli troops after landing at night on the beach, taking some 30 hostages. One guerrilla was captured, as was also the terrorists' mother-ship. **22.** The two-week attempt by Dr. Kissinger to achieve an agreement between Israel and Egypt on a pull-back of forces in Sinai collapsed in Jerusalem, and he suspended his talks to return to Washington.

April 13. Some 30 men were killed in clashes

between Palestinian commandos and members of a Right-wing political party, the Phalangists, in Beirut.

May 7. The first of the 15 ships, including four British, which had been trapped for almost eight years in the Bitter Lakes of the Suez Canal, began their journey out. **22.** Syria decided to extend the mandate of the U.N. peace-keeping force on the Golan Heights for a further six months, Israel having already done so. **26.** Lebanon's military government resigned two days after taking office. On May 28 Mr. Rashid Karami was named Prime Minister-designate after eight days of continued fighting with some 70 dead in Beirut and over 200 injured throughout the country. **31.** Three Moslem extremists were sentenced to death in Egypt for plotting to overthrow President Sadat, being convicted of taking part in a raid on Cairo military academy in April 1974.

June 2. The Israeli Prime Minister (Mr. Rabin) announced in Jerusalem that Israel was to withdraw half her troops and most of her tanks and artillery from the Suez Canal area " to show proof of the desire for peace." **5.** The Suez Canal, closed since the Middle East War, was ceremonially re-opened by President Sadat of Egypt in Port Said. **15.** Four Arab terrorists who seized a farmhouse and held a family as hostages were killed when Israeli soldiers stormed a house at Kfar Yuval near the Lebanese border. One Israeli civilian and one soldier were killed and six Israelis were wounded. **26.** Thousands of Israelis attended a ceremony in Jerusalem for the assassins of Lord Moyne, Britain's resident minister in the Middle East, in 1944. The remains of the two gunmen, returned from Cairo where they were hanged 30 years earlier, were buried with full military honours on Mount Herzl. **29.** Beirut was closed after heavy fighting between Left and Right-wing groups with mortars and machine-guns in action throughout the night and early morning. Two days later 40 people were reported killed and some 200 injured in another day of fighting in the city, bringing the total in six days of street battles to about 95 killed and over 350 wounded. Police stated that the death toll had risen sharply after more fighting on June 29.

July 4. In an Arab terrorist bomb attack inside Israel, 14 people were killed and 65 injured when an abandoned refrigerator filled with gelignite and two mortar shells exploded on a pavement in the centre of Jerusalem. **7.** Thirteen people were reported killed and 37 wounded after three Israeli raids on Palestinian camps in Southern Lebanon. President Sadat of Egypt ordered a general amnesty for all prisoners serving terms in political cases before May 15, 1971, the date of his " corrective revolution." **13.** Israeli planes made a rocket attack on Ain Helweh refugee camp in Southern Lebanon and killed four refugees, wounded 19, and destroyed 40 homes. In the Northern Israel seaside resort of Nahariya, a number of people were wounded by rockets fired from Lebanon. **25.** The Turkish Cabinet decided to take over all United States bases on its territory from July 26 in retaliation for the refusal by the House of Representatives in Washington to lift the ban on military aid and arms sales imposed as a result of Turkey's invasion and partion of Cyprus.

Aug. 1. Agreement was reached in Vienna allowing 9,000 Turkish Cypriots to join their compatriots in the north of Cyprus while 10,000 Greek Cypriots in the Turkish-controlled north would be allowed to remain with another 800 Greeks from the south joining them. **14.** The first British warships to pass through the Suez Canal since its re-opening on June 5 arrived in the Red Sea, comprising three frigates of the Second Flotilla

accompanied by two Royal Fleet auxiliaries. **20.** Dr. Kissinger set off from Washington on his tenth Middle East negotiations to reach an Egyptian-Israeli agreement for an interim settlement in the Sinai. **22.** At the end of a five-day State visit to Syria by King Hussein of Jordan, it was announced that the two countries had formed a supreme command council to direct political and military action against Israel.

Sept. 1. Israel and Egypt reached an interim agreement setting out new demarcation lines in the desert and political commitments and declaring that conflict should be resolved by peaceful means, neither side resorting to the use or threat of force or military blockade, with a permanent mixed commission of Israel and Egyptian officers to supervise the implementation of the settlement.

U.S.A.

(1974) Oct. 1. The Watergate cover-up trial of five former leading figures of the Nixon Administration began in Washington before Judge John Sirica. **8.** President Ford, outlining his new programme to a special televised joint session of Congress, called on it to pass promptly a 5 per cent. surcharge on business firms and all American families with incomes above £6,000, tax concessions to stimulate investment, and a series of measures to cut oil imports by a million barrels a day by Dec. 31, 1975. **16.** In Boston, police guarded newly-integrated classes, with forces standing by in case of reaction in the city. While President Ford refused a request for Federal military help, the Pentagon announced that elements of 82nd Airborne Division had been put on " increased readiness " at Fort Bragg, North Carolina, while Massachusetts had already mobilised two National Guard military police units following 24 days of court-ordered integration of Boston school children of both races. **17.** President Ford became the first American President to submit to formal cross-examination by a Congressional Committee when in a televised appearance before a sub-committee of the Judiciary Committee of the House of Representatives he gave an assurance he had made no deal in granting ex-President Nixon a pardon over Watergate. **18.** Russia agreed with the United States to allow 60,000 Jews to leave the Soviet Union annually, it was announced in Washington. In return for " most favoured nation " trade treatment from America, the Russians also pledged to end the harassment of would-be emigrants. **19.** The U.S. Treasury Secretary (Mr. William Simon announced a 2,200,000-ton grain deal with the Soviet Union to replace the 3,200,000-ton agreement blocked by President Ford earlier in the month. **26.** Four explosions, causing damage but no casualties, shattered offices in New York's Rockefeller Centre and the City's financial district, responsibility being claimed by Puerto Rican militants. **29.** Former President Nixon was said to be in a critical condition following an operation at the Memorial Hospital, Long Beach, California. On Nov. 3 he was taken off the critical list.

Nov. 4. Some 70,000 American Jews attended a mass rally near the United Nations H.Q. in New York to object to the forthcoming appearance at the U.N. of members of the Palestine Liberation Organisation. **5.** Democratic Party candidates scored heavily in America's mid-term congressional elections. They showed a net gain of 4 seats in the Senate, giving them a 62 to 38 control. In the House of Representatives they gained 44 seats to obtain a majority of 292 to 143. **10.** William Calley, former American Army Lieutenant, convicted of murdering 22 civilians in the My Lai massacre in

South Vietnam, was freed on bail after serving one-third of a 10-year sentence. **13.** Yasser Arafat, the Palestinian Liberation Organisation leader, addressed the United Nations in New York. He and his team arrived at U.N. H.Q. in two helicopters amid unprecedented security precautions. **14.** Dr. Kissinger proposed a five-point programme of co-ordinated action by America, Western Europe and Japan to speed-up, *inter alia*, national energy conservation plans, develop new oil supplies and alternative energy sources, and strengthen economic security to protect the world monetary system from the so-called " petrodollar " threat. **17.** President Ford left on an eight-day tour of Japan, South Korea and Russia.

Dec. 4. The original Watergate grand Jury was dismissed after 2½ years of investigation into the burglary at Democratic party headquarters in June 1972. **5.** America's 120,000 striking miners voted to accept a new contract giving them a 64 per cent. rise in wages and fringe benefits over three years. Their stoppage from Nov. 12 had put more than 20,000 steel and rail workers out of a job. **9.** America and East Germany formally opened embassies in each other's capitals, completing the process of recognition 25 years after establishment of the East German state. **10.** It was announced that Johnson Vandyke Grigsby, aged 89, had been released from the Indiana State prison after serving 66 years in jail, believed to be a record, for murdering a man in a saloon fight. **19.** Mr. Nelson Rockefeller was confirmed by Congress as Vice-President of the U.S. by 287 votes to 128. **20.** President Ford signed a bill giving the Government permanent custody over all former President Nixon's White House tapes and documents, including the Watergate affair recordings. The U.S. Senate and House of Representatives approved the Trade Bill which allowed President Ford to lower tariffs levied against Russian goods.

(1975) Jan. 1. Former Attorney General John Mitchell, H. R. Haldeman, ex-President Nixon's chief of staff, and John Ehrlichman, Mr. Nixon's former domestic affairs adviser, were found guilty of taking part in a criminal conspiracy to obstruct justice in the Watergate affair. Kenneth Parkinson, an official of Mr. Nixon's election campaign, was acquitted and a former Assistant Attorney General, Robert Mardian, was convicted of one count of conspiracy. Judge John Sirica released the four convicted men on personal bond and set no date for the sentencing. Mitchell, Haldeman and Ehrlichman were also found guilty of obstruction of justice. They protested their innocence and said that they would appeal. **4.** President Ford announced that he would name a special commission to investigate possible illegal domestic spying activities by the Central Intelligence Agency, and next day appointed Vice-President Rockefeller to head the commission of eight distinguished Americans. **8.** John Dean, chief accuser of ex-President Nixon in the Watergate case, was released from prison after serving only four months of a one-to-four-year sentence and Jeb Magruder, former deputy manager of Mr. Nixon's re-election campaign, and Herbert Kalmbach, once Mr. Nixon's lawyer, were also freed. **14.** Dr. Kissinger announced in Washington that the U.S.S.R. had rejected its trade agreement with the U.S. because of unacceptable demands that the Russians should allow more Jews to emigrate. **15.** In his State of the Union address to Congress, President Ford called for heavy tax cuts and stiff fuel-saving measures, declaring " the State of the Union is not good." **24.** Three people were killed and more than 40 injured in a lunch-time explosion in the Angler's and Tarpon Club, New York, believed

to be the action of the F.A.L.N., an extremist group of Puerto Rican nationalists. **27.** The Senate set up a special select committee to investigate America's intelligence-gathering services. **30.** President Ford and Mr. Wilson met in Washington for the first time since Mr. Ford took office.

Feb. 21. John Mitchell, Mr. Nixon's former Attorney General, and the two chief Nixon White House officials, Robert Haldeman and John Ehrlichman, were sentenced to terms of imprisonment specifying a minimum of 2½ years in jail and a maximum of 8 years for conspiracy to obstruct justice by trying to cover up White House involvement in the Watergate burglary. They were also convicted on perjury charges. Robert Mardian, a former Assistant Attorney-General, received at least 10 months but no more than three years for his part in the conspiracy charge. **24.** The lifting of the U.S. 10-year-old embargo against arms supplies to Pakistan was announced.

April 17. Mr. John Connally, former American Treasury Secretary, was acquitted of accepting two $5,000 pay-offs from the nation's biggest dairy co-operative in return for persuading President Nixon to raise milk subsidies in 1971.

May 12. President Ford ordered the aircraft carrier *Coral Sea* to sail for the Gulf of Thailand after the Cambodian Navy had seized the American merchant ship *Mayaguez* on the high seas and taken it to Koh Tang Island. On May 14 President Ford directed U.S. Marines to board the *Mayaguez* to rescue any crew members on the island. The next day the vessel sailed towards Singapore with the crew of 40 safely aboard, the freighter's crew being handed over to the American destroyer *Wilson* from a small Cambodian boat flying a white flag after 160 Marines landed on Koh Tang. Three Cambodian gunboats were sunk and 17 aircraft and amphibious craft were destroyed in an air raid on a mainland airfield near Kompong Som. On May 18 revised official American casualty figures were: 5 killed in action, 16 men missing, 70 to 80 wounded. **29.** New York's Governor announced the City would receive an emergency transfer in State funds of 200 million dollars (£87 million) to prevent the immediate threat of bankruptcy. A 22-year-old vagrant who severely injured a British girl tourist in a mugging attack at a Miami bus station in August 1973 was jailed in Miami for 150 years " in an attempt to protect society."

June 10. A report by the Rockefeller Commission on the operations of the C.I.A. in the domestic field was issued by the White House. New York City's money crisis eased when the State Legislature approved the creation of the Municipal Assistance Corporation which would re-finance 3,000 million dollars (£1,250 million) of the City's short-term debts and watch future borrowing. **27.** Ex-President Nixon was voluntarily questioned under oath by two Watergate special prosecutors and two grand jurors near his home at San Clemente, California.

July 1. Dustmen began a strike in New York as the city laid off over 19,000 municipal employees under Mayor Abraham Beame's " crisis budget ", but the three-day dispute ended on July 3 following an agreement after " a night of dire danger " from fires. The agreement also ended the six-week deadlock over the City's financial crisis when the governor of New York State concluded a deal with the State's Republican leaders to allow increased taxes to be raised in return for concessions. **8.** President Ford announced officially that he would be a candidate in the 1976 presidential election, promising to conduct " an open and above-board campaign." **9.** The President announced a compromise policy which would permit a resumption of American arms supplies to Turkey, subject to clearance by Congress. **15.** America's *Apollo* spacecraft blasted off from Cape Canaveral at 8.50 p.m. London time, 7½ hours after the launch of Russia's *Soyuz* in the Kazakh desert, as they headed for a rendezvous in space. On July 17 at 140 miles above Amsterdam Brig.-Gen. Thomas Stafford, commander of the American spaceship, exchanged greetings with Col. Alexei Leonov, commander of the Russian craft three hours after the two craft successfully docked at the end of a two-day flight. Stafford and Donald Slayton, " swam " through the airlock hatches of the docking module to greet Leonov and Valeri Kubasov before the four men crammed into the *Soyuz* cabin to hear congratulatory messages from Mr. Brezhnev and President Ford. The third American astronaut, Vance Brand, stayed behind at the controls of *Apollo*, but visited *Soyuz* during the crew transfers next day. On July 18 the Russians and Americans toured one another's craft for the last occasion prior to undocking on July 19. On July 24 the American astronauts splashed down in the Pacific, 300 miles west of Hawaii, thus ending the Russian-American space mission, the Russians having landed on Kazakhstan steppes on July 21. **24.** A move to lift the ban on American arms shipments to Turkey was defeated in the House of Representatives by 233–206 votes. **25.** America's newly-appointed Secretary for the Interior (Mr. Stanley Hathaway) resigned because of ill-health. **27.** President Ford began a 10-day European tour. **28.** The President was forced to withdraw plans to sell Jordan a sophisticated anti-aircraft missile system because of a probable Congressional veto after Senators complained that it would threaten the military balance in the Middle East.

Aug. 1. Earthquakes shook towns and cities in a 250-mile stretch of California from Oroville to Sacramento and Fresno. **18.** America's maritime unions " blacked " grain shipments to Russia until the Ford administration proved that their sales would not drive up the price of food in the U.S. **21.** The ban was lifted which prevented overseas subsidiaries of American firms from trading with Cuba, and the prohibition ended on aid to countries which allowed their ships or planes to carry goods to and from Cuba. **26.** Delivery was blocked of eight C-130 Lockheed cargo planes to Libya because of Libya's refusal to support U.S. Middle East peace efforts.

Sept. 5. Miss Lynette Alice Fromme aimed a gun at President Ford in Sacramento, California; she was quickly disarmed.

COMMON MARKET

(1974) Oct. 2. The E.E.C.'s foreign and agriculture ministers decided in Luxemburg to review the Common Agricultural Policy. **3.** Mr. Peart, British Minister of Agriculture, announced a £34,000,000 boost for Britain's 60,000 hill farmers to help feed bills during the winter as the result of a Common Market meeting in Luxemburg. **15.** British Conservative Group members published an action programme at the European Parliament in Strasburg to guide the Common Market towards political, monetary, and defence union with a directly elected Parliament. Mr. Callaghan attended a meeting of the E.E.C. Council of Foreign Ministers to discuss energy policy, aid, and a trade agreement with Canada, and set out the approximate timetable the Labour Government had in mind for the renegotiations of Britain's membership of the Common Market. **22.** Mr. Peart accepted the E.E.C. offer to supply Britain

with cut-price sugar subsidised from Community funds. Agreement on the sugar import subsidy scheme which was available to all Common Market members with a shortage, but mainly applying to Britain and Italy, was reached after 20 hours of negotiations. **31.** The E.E.C. statistical office in Luxemburg confirmed that a record grain harvest had been gathered by the Common Market countries in 1974.

Nov. 12. The Common Market agreed to admit 1,400,000 tons of sugar from the Commonwealth for a period of at least five years. **18.** M. Carlo Facini, Director General of the Common Market's financial control department, said that unscrupulous businessmen had swindled the E.E.C. Community Farm Fund out of more than £7,500,000 up to mid-1974 and the Common Market Commission urged the nine member States to step up action against frauds. **19.** Mr. Peart agreed to accept the Common Market intervention scheme for beef in return for agreement on sugar supplies and prices. The European Commission earmarked an initial £10,500,000 in a new programme to help to improve housing for steel and coal workers in the Common Market. **21.** The Common Market Commissions called on member Governments to set up a special standing committee to take action at Community level against fiscal frauds and tax evasion.

Dec. 9. The Common Market meeting opened in Paris with a decision to appoint M. Tindemans, Belgian Prime Minister, to investigate the subject of European union and to report with a definition by the end of 1975. **10.** Mr. Wilson achieved agreement at the Common Market summit meeting on the size of Britain's contribution to the Community budget. Agreement was also reached on a three-year regional fund which would give special help to Italy and Ireland and also would mean a share for Britain. **17.** The Common Market social ministers meeting in Brussels formally accepted the principle that women should be paid as much as men for the same work. **19.** The Finance Ministers of the Common Market meeting in Brussels voted in favour of the British plan to re-cycle the revenues of the oil-producing countries by using the machinery of the International Monetary Fund for borrowing money from the Arabs and re-lending it to the needy.

(1975) Feb. 1. The E.E.C. Commission agreed in Brussels a £1,600,000,000 five-year aid and trade package for 46 developing nations including some from the Commonwealth. Mr. Peart also concluded a sugar deal in Brussels with the Commonwealth ministers giving producers £260 a tonne, £10 more than the previous offer. **4.** The Common Market and Comecon, the East European trading organisation, began three days of exploratory talks in Moscow on closer future cooperation. **13.** Common Market foreign ministers met in Dublin to discuss political cooperation, the Middle East and the world's energy crisis. **23.** The Common Market Commission confirmed that Britain would retain her full sovereign rights over her North Sea oil deposits under E.E.C. rules.

March 11. Agreement over the E.E.C. budget and New Zealand's dairy exports to the Community was reached in Dublin after two days of final renegotiations for Britain at the Common Market summit meeting.

April 15. The Agricultural Ministers of the Nine agreed in Luxemburg to buy surplus French and Italian wine for distilling into industrial alcohol at a cost of some £25,000,000.

May 6. The E.E.C. announced a £4,000,000 loan to the British Steel Corporation, bringing to

£98,400,000 the total loans the Corporation had had from the Commission since Britain joined the Common Market. **7.** China became the first Communist country to recognise the Common Market and announced that an ambassador would be sent to Brussels. **20.** The Common Market agreed to make a low interest rate loan of £14,400,000 towards ensuring the jobs of 4,500 steel workers at Ebbw Vale, the money forming part of a £70,000,000 investment in a new tinplate complex. **29.** The European Commission gave another £7,000,000 loan to the British Steel Corporation 24 hours after providing £30,000,000 for the National Coal Board and £12,000,000 for the Distillers Company to increase whisky output.

June 2. More cheap loans to aid development projects in Britain were announced by the Common Market's European Investment Bank.

July 7. Eighteen Labour M.P.s arrived in Strasbourg to take their seats in the European Parliament for the first time as part of the British representation. **22.** E.E.C. agriculture ministers meeting in Brussels agreed on a 5 per cent. devaluation of the " green pound ", the exchange rate for converting Common Market farm prices into sterling, thus increasing food prices by an average 1 per cent., but boosting British farmers' return by over £100,000,000. **28.** Loans and grants totalling over £74,000,000 for the British State-owned steel and coal industries from Common Market institutions were announced.

Aug. 14. E.E.C. authorities reported in Brussels that more than £2,000,000 had been embezzled from the Common Market agricultural fund over the last year and that 136 cases of fraud had been detected, £242,000 having been recovered.

Sept. 4. President Giscard d'Estaing announced a massive programme of new expenditure and credits to reflate the French economy out of recession.

AFRICA

(1974) Oct. 16. Some 100 prominent Africans met Mr. Ian Smith, the Rhodesian Prime Minister, at his invitation at the Chiefs' Hall at Seki near Salisbury for discussions, although African National Council central committee members declined to attend. **22.** Sentence of 14 years' jail was passed in Salisbury, Rhodesia, on Kenneth James Cameron McIntosh, Scottish-born former banking official in Rhodesia who was convicted of contravening the country's Official Secrets Act. He was also sentenced concurrently to three years' imprisonment and fined 30,000 Rhodesian dollars (or two more years in jail) for infringing exchange control regulations. **27.** Mozambique's Provincial Government arrested more than 1,200 people in Lourenço Marques following the previous week's racial violence in which 50 people died. **30.** A triple veto by Britain, U.S.A., and France, saved South Africa from expulsion in the Security Council which voted 10–3 with two abstentions in favour of an African resolution to oust South Africa.

Nov. 3. The Mozambique Government of transition, it was reported, had passed a law providing for up to eight years' imprisonment for people found guilty of spreading rumours affecting public order. **4.** President Bourguiba of Tunisia was re-elected for a fourth five-year term. **5.** President Amin of Uganda ordered the British High Commission in Kampala to reduce its staff from 50 to five immediately. **8.** The South African Prime Minister (Mr. Vorster) announced new plans for the country's £2,000,000 coloured (mixed blood) people giving them more say in government but without full political integration,

and proposing a consultative cabinet with equal numbers of White ministers and Coloured Representative Council members to deal with " all matters of mutual interest." Leaders of the Coloured community and White opposition parties rejected the proposals. **10.** Twenty-five people were reported killed in fighting in Luanda, capital of Angola, where bandits were said to be active. Shooting continued in the suburbs on Nov. 11 and after two days of violence the toll was put at over 50 people killed and more than 100 injured. **12.** Algeria announced the resumption of diplomatic relations with the United States to end a seven-year breach. **13.** South Africa was suspended from the U.N. General Assembly and within an hour ordered the recall of Mr. Botha, its U.N. Ambassador, and the suspension of its £400,000 annual subscription. **24.** Ethiopia's supreme military council in radio broadcasts announced the summary execution of 60 former ministers, officials, and military chiefs, including Lt.-Gen. Aman Andom, who was dismissed as chairman of the provisional government only three days previously, and a grandson of the former Emperor Hailé Selassié. **28.** Brig.-Gen. Tefferi Benti was chosen new Chairman of Ethiopia's ruling provisional military council in succession to Lt.-Gen. Aman Andom who had been shot dead in Addis Ababa some days earlier by his own troops. President Amin of Uganda dismissed Princess Elizabeth Baganya, his Foreign Minister, after making allegations about her behaviour. **30.** Confirmation was given of secret visits in recent months by Mr. Vorster, South African Prime Minister, to three black African countries.

Dec. 3. A Rhodesian Government statement confirmed that two African nationalist leaders, Mr. Joshua Nkomo, of Zapu, and Rev. Ndabanini Sithole of Zanu, both detainees for over 10 years, were flown to Luzaka, Zambia, in November to discuss Rhodesia's future with black Heads of State and were then flown back to resume their detention. **7.** Mr. Ian Smith, Rhodesian Prime Minister, rejected African proposals for a constitutional conference to work out details for immediate majority rule after secret negotiations in the Zambian capital of Lusaka during the week attended by President Kaunda of Zambia, President Nyerere of Tanzania, and President Sir Seretse Khama of Botswana and representatives of Mr. Smith and the Rhodesian African nationalist groups. **8.** Four rival Rhodesian African nationalist organisations— the African National Council, Zanu, Zapu and Frolizi—met in Luzoka and signed a declaration of unity and declared that they recognised " the inevitability of the continued armed struggle and all other forms of struggle until the total liberation of Zimbabwe." Mr. Vorster, South African Prime Minister, promised to continue his efforts to bring black and white political leaders back to the conference table. **11.** Mr. Ian Smith announced that African nationalist leaders had agreed to a ceasefire in their guerrilla war on Rhodesia, and said that his Government would release all political detainees —about 450 Africans—immediately as a gesture of goodwill, and that the nationalists had agreed to a conference without any preconditions. **20.** Radio Ethiopia broadcast a statement by the one-party Government—the Supreme Progressive Council— announcing that the country would be reconstructed as a Socialist State. The Rhodesian Government began to release some of the Black nationalist detainees and those under restriction as part of the Lusaka agreement to hold a conference on Rhodesia's future. **22.** South African Foreign Minister (Dr. Hilgard Muller) said that there would be further relaxation of apartheid in South Africa's efforts to achieve a wide measure of détente with Black Africa. **23.** Six Ethiopian soldiers and five civilians were reported dead after gun battles and a series of explosions in Asmara, capital of Ethiopia's northern province of Eritrea, and disturbances were also reported at Assab, the Red Sea port of Eritrea. **30.** Mr. Callaghan flew from London on a six-nation tour of Africa to survey the prospects of a Rhodesian settlement.

(1975) Jan. 1. The Ethiopian military government announced that it had nationalised all the country's privately-owned banks and insurance companies. **9.** The Rhodesian Minister of Justice, Law and Order (Mr. Desmond Lardner-Burke) said that no more political detainees were being released because African leaders had failed to stop terrorism, and that terrorists had increased their activities in some areas. **31.** Eritrean rebels launched an attack on Asmara, capital of Ethiopia's northernmost province, several men being killed, after a ministerial statement that the ruling military council had no intention of granting independence to Eritrea.

Feb. 2. Ethiopian planes strafed and bombed rebel positions a few miles outside Asmara and in three days of fighting in and around the city damage was reported to be heavy, with a mounting death toll. **3.** The Ethiopian military government announced the nationalisation of major portions of the manufacturing and distributing sector, 72 firms having been totally taken over with a State controlling interest in 29 others. **5.** Col. Richard Ratsimandraya was given full powers as new head of State and head of Government in Madagascar and later swore in a government of seven military officers and nine civilians. **7.** A half-hour battle was reported from Asmara, the Eritrean capital. **10.** Following an Ethiopian Air Force bombing raid on rebel positions north of Asmara, the Eritrean Liberation Front opened a major offensive on the city. South Africa's Foreign Minister confirmed that he had held talks with the foreign ministers of Botswana, Tanzania, and Zambia together with leaders of Rhodesia's African nationalists in Lusaka. **12.** Eritrean rebels launched their first daylight attack on Asmara as thousands of refugees tried to escape from the city. Mr. Ian Smith held discussions with a delegation of executive members of the African National Council on planning the proposed constitutional conference to settle Rhodesia's future. Troops overran a camp defended by police rebels alleged to have assassinated Col. Richard Ratsimandraya, head of the Malagasy Republic (Madagascar), for six days, after a day of shooting and bombing by military aircraft; martial law was declared under a new military council headed by Gen. Gilles Andriamahazo. **15.** Ethiopia declared a state of emergency in Eritrea and extended martial law to all parts of the province. **17.** Mr. Vorster confirmed that he, with his Foreign Minister and his security chief, visited Monrovia, the Liberian capital, the previous week for talks with President Tolbert about détente. **24.** Kenneth McIntosh, who escaped from Salisbury jail three weeks earlier, was handed over to the Rhodesian authorities by Mozambique after he had reached Vila Maniqa, a Mozambique border town.

Mar. 2. In a South African mine tribal clash at Northfield Colliery, Glencoe, Natal Province, 29 Africans were killed. **4.** Ethiopia announced the nationalisation of rural lands which would be the collective property of the people and administered through local and regional peasant associations. **10.** Fifteen supporters of Lesotho's opposition Congress party were imprisoned for three to nine years for treason. **28.** The Zambian Internal Affairs Minister confirmed the arrest and detention of a large number of Zanu members, including many military commanders; the registration of two other Rhodesian nationalist movements, Zapu and Frolizi, was withdrawn and their Lusaka offices closed.

April 7. The Prime Minister (Mr. Vorster) announced that a pilot plant to manufacture enriched uranium had gone into production in South Africa. **13.** Army and gendarmerie units overthrew the Government of the Chad Republic, President Tombalbaye being killed, and the army assumed responsibility for running the country. **17.** The South African Parliament unanimously approved an amendment to the code of military discipline to give Africans, Coloureds and Indians in the defence forces the same status as Whites of equal rank. **25.** The South African Government announced that legislation was to be introduced to enable Blacks to use White hotels, bars, and restaurants and that non-Whites were to be trained for diplomatic posts.

May 2. The South African Government announced legislation under which Blacks would be allowed to buy their own houses in White areas for the first time and be granted other property rights. **23.** The Spanish Government stated that it was ready to give independence to Spanish Sahara. **28.** Fifteen West African nations formed an economic community at the end of a two-day meeting of heads of state and government in Lagos. Nairobi University was closed after a riot in which some 23 students and 37 policemen were injured and over 100 students arrested.

June 1. Eleven Africans were shot dead and 15 wounded in clashes with police during riots in the township of Highfield, Salisbury, and two other African townships in Rhodesia, shops being looted, police and cars stoned, and buildings set on fire. The shootings started after fighting occurred between members of the nationalist parties, Zanu and Zapu. **11.** Denis Hills, a British author and former lecturer, was found guilty by a military tribunal in Uganda of treason in allegedly criticising Gen. Amin in an unpublished manuscript of a book *The White Pumpkin*, and was sentenced to, execution by a firing squad. **12.** Mr. Wilson sent a message to President Amin about the fate of Mr. Hills. On June 19 President Amin's former commanding officers, Lt.-Gen. Sir Chandos Blair and Major Iain Grahame, in his old regiment, 4th King's African Rifles, flew to Uganda with a message from the Queen appealing for a reprieve. On June 23 Mr. Callaghan told the House of Commons that he was not prepared to go to Uganda under duress from President Amin and that it was "utterly wrong" that the life of Mr. Hills "should be bartered against political considerations." On June 25 Mr. Wilson sent a personal message to President Amin and stated that the Foreign Secretary would be ready to review the "whole range of political, economic and cultural problems between the two countries." On July 1 President Amin, on a two-day visit to President Mobutu of Zaire, announced that he had granted clemency to Mr. Hills because of his "confidence" in his host. **13.** All Indians domiciled in South Africa were free to move from one province to another without obtaining prior permission (with the exception of the Orange Free State), it was announced in the South African Parliament. **16.** The Anglican Bishop of Damaraland (Rt. Rev. Richard Wood) was handed a deportation order to leave South West Africa. **25.** President Samora Machel was installed as head of the new People's

Republic of Mozambique in the re-named capital of Can Phumo, formerly Lourenço Marques, after the country achieved independence from Portugal at midnight on June 23.

July 9. After talks in Kinshasa with President Mobutu of Zaire, who had been acting as mediator in the Hills case, Mr. Callaghan flew to Kampala, the Ugandan capital. On July 10 he had talks with President Amin at his command post and 45 minutes later Mr Hills was brought from Bomba Barracks. Two hours later Mr. Hills was flying to London with Mr. Callaghan in an R.A.F. V.C. 10, reaching Heathrow Airport the same night. 9. More than 20 people were killed and many more wounded in the Angolan capital of Luanda when Portuguese troops opened fire as 55 foreigners, including 27 Britons, were being evacuated aboard an R.A.F. V.C. 10, the British Consulate having been closed. **28.** The 12th Organisation of African Unity summit conference opened in Kampala, Uganda, boycotted by Tanzania, Zambia, and Botswana, but with 43 of the 46 member States attending. President Amin of Uganda was elected as O.A.U. Chairman. **29.** General Gowon was ousted as President of Nigeria in a military coup while attending the Organisation of African Unity conference in Uganda, being deposed by officers led by the head of his personal guard, Col. Joseph Nanvan Garba; Brig. Muritala Mohammad was named as new Head of State and Commander in Chief of the Armed Forces. Britain recognised the new military régime on Aug. 1.

Aug. 14. It was announced in Lagos that the visit which the Queen and the Duke of Edinburgh were to have made to Nigeria in October had been postponed. **16.** Chief Fileman Elifas, head of the Ovambo people in South West Africa, was killed by an unknown gunman. **18.** Libya proclaimed a new law imposing the death sentence on anyone who tried to overthrow the Government or belonged to an illegal organisation. **25.** Talks opened between the Rhodesian Government and leaders of the African National Council in a railway coach on the Victoria Falls bridge linking Rhodesia and Zambia to try to achieve a negotiated settlement on Rhodesia. The meeting was attended also by President Kaunda of Zambia and Mr. Vorster. The talks collapsed next day and Mr. Ian Smith said that he would convene a constitutional conference to which the council of the traditional chiefs and other African organisations would be invited, while A.N.C. stated that negotiations had foundered over an amnesty for six key members of its executive.

Sept. 2. Rev. Ndabaningi Sithole, leader of the militant faction of Rhodesia's A.N.C., announced the formation of an " external wing " of A.N.C. known as the Zimbabwe Liberation Council with Mr. James Chikerema, of Frolizi nationalist group, as secretary.

OTHER COUNTRIES
(See also Africa)

(1974) Oct. 1. Herr Genscher, West German Foreign Minister, was elected to lead the Free Democratic Party in succession to Herr Scheel, now Federal President. **3.** A severe earthquake struck central Peru and at least 30 people were reported killed and scores injured, many casualties occurring in Lima, the capital. The Italian coalition government of Signor Mariano Rumor resigned over internal differences after less than seven months in office. **6.** Thailand's new constitution, which cleared the way for a return to parliamentary government after 26 years of military rule, was passed by the National Assembly by 280 votes to six. About 30 people were feared dead and 20 injured after a land-slide struck a coffee workers' camp near Medellin, Colombia. **10.** It was announced that Cuba would open its doors to British tourists in 1975 for the first time in 15 years, under an agreement signed in Havana by a London travel agency. **11.** M. Jacques Soufflet, Defence Minister, announced that France would carry out no further nuclear tests in the atmosphere. Normal radio and television programmes were resumed by the French State broadcasting monopoly, ORTF, when union leaders decided to suspend a strike which began the previous Tuesday. A skeleton crew remained on board the liner *France* at the quayside at Le Havre after more than a month's offshore occupation by seamen on strike. **12.** The Mexican Government announced that rich oil deposits had been found in three fields. **14.** The United Nations General Assembly voted by 105 to 4 with 20 abstentions to invite representatives of the Palestine Liberation Organisation to take part in its forthcoming debate on the future of Palestine. **20.** The French National Assembly voted to allow self-determination to the 300,000 inhabitants of the Comoro Islands in the Indian Ocean. **23.** The four Army officers who seized power in 1967 in Greece, including former President Papadopoulos, were arrested and banished to the Aegean island of Kea. **27.** Conservatives made large gains over Socialists and Liberals in state elections in Bavaria and Hesse although the Socialists and Free Democrats continued their governing coalition formed in 1970. **30.** Moscow received the first Portuguese official delegation to Russia since the days of the Tsars, a five-day visit, led by the Secretary-General of the Portuguese Communist Party, including talks on establishing normal ties and improving cooperation. Herr Schmidt, the West German Chancellor, ended the third and last day of his Moscow visit by signing an agreement supplementing the ten-year pact on economic, industrial, and technical cooperation concluded during the visit of Mr. Brezhnev to Bonn in 1973.

Nov. 4. Thirty people were injured when shooting occurred as police pushed back hundreds of left wingers trying to storm a rally of the Portuguese Centre Democratic Party in Lisbon. **6.** Senora Peron, President of Argentina, declared a state of siege throughout the country after four months of political violence and " as a result of threats against youngsters." **10.** Herr Günter von Drenkmann, President of West Berlin's highest appeal court, was murdered on the doorstep of his Charlottenburg home. **11.** Mr. Tanaka, Japan's Prime Minister, named a new Cabinet in an attempt to retain control of his ruling Liberal Democratic party; 13 out of 21 ministers were replaced although the key senior ministers remained unchanged. **14.** Two groups of Left wing terrorists attacked the American and Russian embassies in Tokyo with home-made petrol bombs. **15.** Two British plane-spotters jailed in Yugoslavia for spying were released on a pardon granted by President Tito and flown to London; their sentences of 4 years hard labour imposed in December 1973 had been reduced to 3 years on appeal in March 1974. **17.** Mr. Constantine Karamanlis, and his New Democratic Party won an overwhelming victory in the Greek parliamentary elections, the first democratically-held for ten years. His party won 220 seats in the 300 member Parliament. **19.** Public transport and services in France were disrupted by the nationwide strike called by leaders of the two most powerful unions. The situation began to improve two days later and M. Chirac, the prime minister, wrote to union chiefs announcing a new and earlier starting date for negotiations on next year's pay. **23.** President Leone of Italy approved the Cabinet list presented by the Prime Minister-designate, Aldo Moro, which showed changes in all but two ministries; this was Italy's 37th government since the fall of fascism and the end of a 51-day political crisis. **25.** Portugal and the liberation movement of Sao Tome and Principe reached agreement on independence for the islands off the West African coast to take effect in July 1975. Mr. Tanaka, the Japanese Prime Minister, resigned after weeks of criticism started by a magazine article which accussed him of corruption. **26.** Mexico broke off diplomatic relations with Chile. **28.** The Cambodian Government of President Lon Nol retained its seat in the United Nations by a vote of 56–54 in the General Assembly. **29.** Ulrike Meinhof, 40 year-old woman leader of the Baader-Meinhof gang of anarchist guerillas, was jailed for eight years by a court in West Berlin after being found guilty of organising and taking part in the freeing from prison of the other leader of the gang in an armed raid in May 1970, and a former lawyer, Horst Mahler, received 14 years on similar charges. The 45-day French postal strike ended. Mr. Sadi Irmak, Turkish Prime Minister, submitted his resignation when his interim Government of independent Parliamentarians failed to win its first vote of confidence from the National Assembly.

Dec. 1. More than 500 Spaniards, mainly Basques, locked themselves inside a church at Bilbao to demand an amnesty for political prisoners and exiles. **2.** The Spanish Prime Minister (Señor Arias Navarro), in a nation-wide television and radio address, announced a draft statute which stipulated that political associations could be formed without discrimination but within the framework of the one party formation, the National Movement. **5.** Three Croat nationalists were sentenced by a Spanish military court to 12-year jail terms for air piracy in 1972 by hijacking a Scandinavian Airline System plane from Malmoe, Sweden, to Madrid with six other Croats released from Swedish prisons as ransom for the 77 passengers. **6.** Portugal was declared free from cholera by the World Health Organisation in Geneva after an epidemic which had caused 2,241 cases, and 38 deaths since mid-May 1974. **7.** The three-month occupation of the liner *France* ended at Le Havre when the 120 members of the crew withdrew their pickets; the occupation was in protest against withdrawal of the ship from service. **8.** With the votes counted in the Greek referendum the figures were: for a Republic 3,236,345 (69·2 per cent.); for a Monarchy 1,443,804 (30·8 per cent.). The Soviet Union's latest rehearsal for the July space link-up with an American Apollo craft ended successfully after six days in earth orbit when the two *Soyuz-16* cosmonauts soft-landed in Northern Kazakhstan. The Swiss, in a week-end referendum, decisively voted down proposed increases in Federal defence and turnover taxes and two different plans to introduce compulsory health insurance but accepted a proposal to restrain the voting of new or increased expenditure by Parliament. **11.** Some 200,000 Basques went on strike in North-West Spain in protest against the Franco régime and more than 20 people were arrested in the various demonstrations. Martial law was declared in Rangoon after thousands of rioters set fire to Government buildings and destroyed police stations, buses, and trains. The Burmese Government radio said that nine people were killed and 74 injured in the rioting. **12.** A bomb exploded in the French Ministry of Education in Paris, causing £100,000 damage but no casualties. **13.** Demonstrators shouting for independence compelled President Giscard d'Estaing to cancel his visit to a city hall reception at Fort de France,

Martinique, hundreds of youths blocking the way to the building. **15.** President Giscard d'Estaing and President Ford met twice in Martinique in an effort to reach agreement on how to deal with the world oil crisis. General Gizikis, who was appointed President of Greece when Papadopoulos was overthrown in November 1973, resigned, and on Dec. 18, Michael Stassinopoulos, of the New Democracy party, was sworn in as temporary President after his election by 206–74 votes. **18.** Eight of the 18 accused in the Bordeaux trial were convicted of doctoring claret and fraud with documents, being fined and given jail sentences of from a month to a year which in all but one case were suspended. **20.** Mun Se-Kwang, Korean resident of Japan, was executed in Seoul for murder of the wife of President Park in August 1974. **23.** The population of the French territory of the Comoro Islands in the Indian Ocean voted in favour of independence from France by 95·6 per cent. against 4·4 per cent. in an electorate of 175,000. **26.** Fifteen terrorists, defeated in their attempt to kidnap two executives of the Argentine subsidary of the British company, Lever Brothers, killed a police bodyguard and wounded another in a gun fight near a bridge south of Buenos Aires. **28.** Some 300 people were feared dead in a severe earthquake which destroyed a remote mountain village, Patan, in northern Pakistan. Another village, Jajal, was also badly damaged. Nine left-wing guerrillas shot their way into a party in Managua, Nicaragua, for the American Ambassador, killed the host and two guards and seized 19 diplomats and Government leaders; the terrorists released all seven women hostages later but held the 12 men. On Dec. 29, the nine terrorists were allowed to fly to Cuba and released their hostages before the plane took off. Sixteen political prisoners were released and allowed to fly out with the guerrillas.

(1975) Jan. 3. Sunday newspapers in East Berlin stopped publication because of soaring newsprint costs and three more East German newspapers announced that they would not publish Sunday editions following similar announcements earlier in the week by two other newspapers. **4.** Communist forces overran the provincial capital of Phuoc Binh, 66 miles north of Saigon, giving them control of the entire province. **5.** In a first formal announcement, a special Cabinet committee stated that the earthquake disaster in the Swat and Hazara districts of Pakistan's North-West Frontier province killed 5,300 people and injured 17,000. **9.** Denmark's general election failed to give any party a clear majority, the Liberal minority government gaining 20 seats with 42 M.P.s in the 197-seat Parliament, the Social Democrats, the largest party, having 53 M.P.s. **10.** A manned Soviet spaceship, *Soyuz 17*, was launched into earth orbit to carry out joint experiments with the research station *Salyut* 4. **13.** One hundred and fifty French Army conscripts marched through the streets of the West German garrison city of Karlsruhe demanding better pay and conditions, this demonstration being the first in the history of French forces serving outside their country. **15.** Portugal and leaders of the three political groups, FLNA, MPLA, and Unita signed an accord to give independence to Angola on Nov. 11 after elections for a constituent assembly, the three movements meanwhile forming a transitional government under rotating leadership. **18.** China announced that its fourth National People's Congress, the first for ten years, had been held and that Chou En-Lai was re-elected premier, Yen Chien-Ying being appointed defence minister. **20.** Three Arab terrorists were flown out of Orly

Airport, Paris, after freeing ten hostages unharmed including a girl aged five, whom they had held the day before when trying to attack an Israeli airliner during which they wounded 20 people in the airport in a 17-hour siege. George Papadopoulos and four of his associates in the military rule of Greece by " the colonels " were taken to jail in Athens after being charged with high treason and insurrection. **25.** Employers and unions agreed that all workers in Italy would get the same cost-of-living bonus in future at 65 p. a month for every point rise. **26.** Three hundred delegates to the first congress of Portugal's Centre Democratic Party were freed by paratroopers after an all-night siege of the conference hall in Oporto by Left wing mobs. A tidal wave caused by a typhoon left 6,000 people homeless in the Southern Philippines with eight deaths. **29.** Denmark's Liberal minority government resigned after Parliament approved a Social Democratic proposal that the Prime Minister should go to make way for the formation of a broad coalition. **31.** Troops supported by armoured cars occupied squares in Lisbon to prevent extreme left-wing organisations holding mass meetings in defiance of a ban imposed by the Armed Forces Movement.

Feb. 2. Troops guarding the first Congress of Portugal's Christian Democratic Party at Figueira da Foz forced it to close because they could not be responsible for the security of the delegates. **3.** Nineteen priests in the archdiocese of Pamplona, Spain, were fined 3,700,000 pesetas (about £25,500) for delivering sermons supporting 12,000 workers on strike in the district the previous month. **4.** The caretaker Turkish Government was officially informed that American military supplies would end at midnight, following demands by U.S. Congress for Turkish concessions in Cyprus as a condition of further supplies. **5.** The Turkish Defence Minister announced that 2,296 non-commissioned officers, had been dismissed, 630 arrested, and 70 retired for showing discontent at a pay award by taking part in demonstrations. Turkey called off Brussels talks with Dr. Kissinger about Cyprus because of the U.S.'s imposition of an arms embargo and a strong protest note was handed to the American Ambassador to Turkey. Tanks entered the centre of Lima, the Peruvian capital, and a state of emergency was declared as thousands of people demonstrated in the streets in protest at an attack by troops in police barracks where 2,000 men on strike for more pay barricaded themselves in but later surrendered; at least 30 people were reported killed and many injured. **6.** Five hundred Spanish Government workers, including high-ranking Ministry officials, made public demands for the country to become " a democratic state in which the political authority comes from the people," this action following stoppages two days earlier by hundreds of Government workers in five ministries. Workers were ordered to stay at home and a dusk-to-dawn curfew was imposed in Lima, Peru, after a night of rioting in the city. **7.** Some 10,000 workers demonstrated through central Lisbon in defiance of a government ban intended to avoid confrontation with 11,000 Nato sailors starting shore leave after naval exercises. **9.** Russia's longest manned space flight ended when Alexei Gubarev and Georgy Grechko returned to earth after a month in orbit, the *Soyuz* 17 mission beating the previous Soviet endurance record by six days. **12.** Russia agreed to resume the protracted negotiations on the frontier dispute and other issues with China, Mr. Leonid Ilyichov, a deputy foreign minister, arriving in Peking to reopen talks after a six-month lapse. **13.** Denmark's two-week old political crisis ended with the new Prime Minister (Mr. Joergensen) and the other 15 members of his

minority Social Democratic government signing the oath of office. **16.** Portugal's biggest newspaper, *O Seculo*, was taken over by left-wing workers who dismissed the editor, locked out the management and set up a workers' committee. **17.** Mr. Bhutto, Pakistan prime minister, dismissed the government of the North West Frontier Province and instituted direct rule from Islamabad. **18.** The Army officers who deposed the Gaetano régime in Portugal in 1974 announced they would stay in power and " institutionalise " their Armed Forces Movement. **19.** A government bill for urgent new measures to protect the country's artistic heritage was rushed through the Italian senate following two big art thefts in 11 days. **20.** Riot police fired warning shots in the air in central Madrid to prevent thousands of students marching on the Education Ministry; police made baton charges with many arrests being made as the protests against closure of certain universities and rising prices mounted. The Portuguese Government published a three-year plan to transform the country's social and economic structure, including the take-over of large estates, majority State control of heavy industry and encouragement of foreign investment. **22.** Fishermen ended their blockade of French ports in protest against the level of French government aid after a promise of a crash programme of assistance. **23.** M. Jacques Chirac, French Prime Minister, was confirmed in the post of secretary-general of the Gaullist party. **25.** Thirty-seven Greek army officers, including six generals, were charged with plotting to overthrow the Greek Government. **26.** Four thousand Christian Democrats were trapped for two hours in Lisbon's sports stadium by a mob of left-wing extremists throwing paving stones until police drove back demonstrators with shots fired in the air. **27.** Herr Peter Lorenz, head of the opposition Christian Democrats in West Berlin, was kidnapped when his car was rammed after he left his home, the abduction coming only three days before the West Berlin elections for city mayor. Riot police entered Madrid Cathedral and evicted some 400 students staging a sit-in in protest against university closures.

March 1. A woman passenger was killed and nine other passengers were wounded in a gun fight between three hijackers and Iraqi security men after an Iraqi Boeing 737 bound for Teheran was seized, the hijackers surrendering to Iranian police. Turkey's caretaker Prime Minister, Sadi Irmak, accepted the task of forming a national coalition after being nominated Prime Minister-elect. **2.** The Shah of Persia declared a one-party system and asked all existing parties to disband and join a new one led by the Prime Minister (Mr. Amir Abbas Hoveyda) called the Persian National Resurrection Party. The leader of three skyjackers who took over an Iraqi Airways Boeing 737 died in hospital in Teheran of wounds received in a shoot out aboard the plane on a flight from Mosul to Baghdad, during which two passengers died and the other two gunmen surrendered. **4.** Herr Peter Lorenz, the West Berlin Opposition leader, was freed by anarchist kidnappers who had held him hostage for six days after five West German urban guerrillas were released from German prisons and given temporary asylum by the South Yemen Government. Four Spanish ministers were dismissed in a Cabinet reshuffle following the resignation of the Vice-Premier and Labour minister (Señor de la Fuente). A bomb explosion caused heavy damage to the Federal Constitutional Court in Karlsruhe, West Germany's highest court. **8.** About 50 policemen were evacuated from their headquarters in Setubal, Portugal, by the army after an 18-hour siege by hundreds of left wing demonstrators demanding "popular justice" after two people died and 26 were hurt in a political party clash. **10.** Presidential rule was imposed in the Indian Ocean republic of the Maldives, Mir Ibrahim Nasis assuming full powers after the arrest of the Prime Minister, Ahmed Zaki, five days earlier and his banishment to a remote atoll. **11.** Portuguese Air Force planes bombed and strafed artillery barracks outside Lisbon in an attempted coup backed by paratroopers and General Spinola, figurehead of the April 25 Revolution a year previously, fled to Spain. Portugal's armed forces set up a supreme revolutionary council with wide powers, headed by President Costa Gomes. **13.** Twenty-three men and women were given prison sentences varying from seven months to five years by a military court in Sao Paulo for their part in trying to reorganise the Communist party of Brazil, 16 being acquitted. **15.** Ex-President Spinola of Portugal landed in Brazil where he, his wife, and 15 fellow officers were given political asylum. **18.** Portugal's Supreme Revolutionary Council banned the Maoist extremists (M.R.P.P.), the rightist Christian Democrats (P.D.C.) and the left-wing Workers and Agricultural Organisation for the whole period of the campaign for the general election on April 12, scheduled to open on March 19; and on that date postponed the poll for 13 days until April 25. **21.** Argentinian security forces arrested more than 150 people after the discovery of an alleged terrorist plot to paralyse heavy industry and take over trade unions. **22.** Communist forces in South Vietnam won two more major victories in their big offensive by capturing Quang Duc province, north-east of Saigon, and Khanh Duong, north-east of Saigon, cutting off thousands of refugees escaping from the Central Highlands. The Kurdish rebellion in the mountains of northern Iraq collapsed after a 13-year struggle for more regional autonomy. **25.** King Faisal of Saudi Arabia, was assassinated at a royal ceremony in Riyadh by his nephew, Prince Museid Crown Prince Khalid bin Abdul Aziz, his brother, was named the new king. On June 18, Prince Museid was publicly beheaded in the main square of Riyadh. A new Portuguese provisional government was announced in Lisbon with an increased left-wing influence. **26.** The ancient imperial capital of Hue fell to the North Vietnamese. Austria signed a consular agreement with East Germany which recognised East German nationality. **28.** Two more South Vietnamese provincial capitals, Bao Loc in the Southern highlands, and Hoi An, in the Northern province of Quang Tin, fell to the Communists. Prince Sihanouk announced in Peking that the Soviet Union had decided to recognise his Cambodian Government in exile as Cambodia's sole government. The French Government banned all imports of Italian wine for one month as a gesture to French growers angry at Italian imports while they could not sell their own produce. **29.** Portugal's extreme left-wing M.R.P.P. party was declared illegal by the Supreme Revolutionary Council. **30.** The Saigon Government asked the United Nations for prompt intervention to evacuate more than a million refugees from combat zones under Communist pressure. Da Nang, a key port on the northern coast of Vietnam, fell to Communist forces. General Mustafa Barzani, leader of the Kurdish rebellion in northern Iraq, fled from his mountain headquarters in Kurdistan to Persia. **31.** Anatoli Marchenko, the dissident Soviet author, was sentenced to four years strict exile within Russia on charges of violating the terms of parole from a previous camp term. Two Soviet Jews, arrested

after taking part in a Moscow demonstration to demand the right to emigrate, were sentenced to five years in exile.

April 1. Qui Nhon and Nha Trang, two coastal cities, were taken by the North Vietnamese. **2.** South Vietnam's Prime Minister, Tran Thien Khiem, submitted his resignation as the North Vietnamese army consolidated its hold. The majority of Saigon's senate called for a new national leadership and formation of a government of national unity. **4.** South Vietnamese troops recaptured the port of Nha Trang, north of Saigon. **6.** Two more ports, Phan Rang and Phan Thiet, were back in the hands of South Vietnamese Government. The manned *Soyuz* spacecraft launched on April 5 was brought back safely to earth south-west of Gorno-Altaisk, western Siberia, when the flight was discontinued automatically after the carrier rocket went off its pre-set course in its third firing stage. The evacuation of dependants and non-essential personnel of British officials and other residents from Saigon began. The first flight of 96 South Vietnamese orphans from Saigon to Britain arrived at Heathrow. **7.** The emergency airlift of orphans from South Vietnam was stopped by the Saigon Government. Persia announced that two Iraqis who hijacked an Iraqi Airways airliner to Teheran from Iraq five weeks earlier and demanded £2,000,000 ransom and the release of 85 Iraqi Kurds, were tried by a military court and executed by firing squad, a third hijacker being killed at the airport. **8.** The Deputy Prime Minister (Dr. Phan Quang Dan) authorised the release for immediate adoption in Australia or elsewhere all South Vietnamese children without parents or whose surviving parent signed a certificate agreeing to adoption. **9.** Eight people convicted by a military court of instigating a student plot to oust the South Korean Government were hanged. **11.** Saigon High Command stated that Xuan Loc, the provincial capital 40 miles from Saigon, had been "completely cleared" of communist forces. The six principal parties contesting the elections in Portugal on April 25 signed an agreement accepting a militarily imposed draft constitution. **12.** Portugal's revolutionary council voted to nationalise basic industries. The acting President of Cambodia (Saukham Khoy) and his family were evacuated from Phnom Penh by the Americans together with the U.S. Ambassador (Mr. John Gunther Dean) who closed the embassy in the capital, and were taken by helicopter to two U.S. carriers before flying on to Thailand; the Prime Minister (Long Boret) who remained behind, announced the setting-up of a seven-man provisional ruling high committee. **14.** South Vietnam's new government was announced, including religious and political interests. **15.** A decree dissolving the National Assembly in Laos was signed by King Savana Vatthana. **16.** Mr. Shelepin, Russian trade union leader and former head of K.G.B., was removed from the ruling Politburo of the Soviet Communist Party. **17.** Cambodia came under the control of the Communist Khmer Rouge forces after the capital, Phnom Penh, surrendered, ending five years of civil war. **18.** Many Italian workers staged a one-day general strike in protest against political violence in Milan during the week when one man was killed and 26 injured. **21.** President Thieu of South Vietnam resigned as Vietnamese Communist forces massed around the capital, Saigon, and handed over power to his Vice-President, Mr. Tran van Huong. **22.** The Honduran armed forces ousted General Oswoldo Lopez Arellano as Head of State after the United Brands Co. admitted paying £540,000 to Honduran officials to gain lower export taxes on bananas. **25.** Portugal held its first free election in 50 years, the first anniversary of the April 25 Revolution. Polling figures were: Socialists 16 seats (37·8 per cent. of votes), Popular Democrats 80 seats (26·3 per cent.) Communists 30 (12.5 per cent.), Centre Democrats 16 (7·6 per cent.). Phnom Penh radio stated that Prince Sihanouk, head of the Royal Government of National Union, would be Chief of State for life and that all foreign diplomats in Cambodia would be replaced, Mr. Penn Nouth remaining Prime Minister. **27.** The South Vietnamese National Assembly voted unanimously for General " Big " Minh as their third President within a week with the task of negotiating surrender terms. **28.** The final evacuation of American civilians from Saigon along with thousands of Vietnamese refugees was successfully accomplished, according to an announcement by President Ford. **29.** The new Communist régime in Cambodia gave permission for the evacuation of the 610 foreigners who had sheltered in the French Embassy in Phnom Penh since the capital was occupied by the Khmer Rouge on April 17. **30.** The South Vietnamese capital of Saigon, renamed Ho Chi Minh City, surrendered to the Viet Cong and North Vietnamese troops.

May 5. The Thai Government announced the withdrawal of American troops from the country and the National Security Council recommended that Bangkok should immediately extend diplomatic recognition to North Vietnam. **9.** A bomb badly damaged the Cannes Festival Palace hours before the film festival was due to start. **10.** A people's court sentenced ex-King Idris of Libya in his absence to seven years' imprisonment for corruption. **14.** Gun fights between police and Basque activists left at least four people dead in the ancient Basque capital of Guernica. The Portuguese Government decreed its third programme of nationalisation, taking into state ownership the cement, tobacco, and paper industries, and fixed an upper earnings limit of 48,900 escudos (£815) a month on salaries, also raising the minimum wage by 21 per cent. to 4,000 escudos (£66) a month. **19.** Portuguese paratroops held back thousands of Socialists in Lisbon trying to " recapture " their daily paper, *Republica*, seized earlier by Communist workers. On May 20 troops closed down the paper, stating that its future had to be decided by the courts. **21.** Two American Air Force officers serving with the Shah's army were shot dead by three gunmen who ambushed their car in Teheran. **22.** An official announcement in Moscow said that Mr. Shelepin, leader of the Soviet trade unions, was relieved of his duties " at his own request." **26.** Queen Margrethe and Prince Henrik of Denmark arrived in Leningrad on a one-week State visit to Russia, the first by a reigning Western monarch to the Soviet Union since the Revolution. **29.** Portugal's armed forces raided the Lisbon headquarters offices in many Portuguese towns of the M.R.P.P., the left-wing movement, and arrested at least 200 of its members. A law giving Spanish workers a limited right to strike came into operation, although strikes for political motives or in support of colleagues in other factories were banned. Gustav Husak, Communist party general secretary since 1969, was appointed President of Czechoslovakia. **31.** The Prime Ministers of Greece and Turkey held their first meeting since the Turkish invasion of Cyprus in July, 1974.

June 2. The new democratically-elected Parliament was formally installed in Lisbon by the Portuguese President Costa Gomes. **12.** Greece applied for full membership of the Common Market. **17.** The Italian Communist Party registered its biggest election success since the 1939-45 war in the elections for 15 regional councils, increasing the size of its vote by 5·1 per cent. to 33·4 per cent., the Christian Democrats losing 3·1 per cent of their support in 35·3 per cent. of the votes. **18.** Professor Constantine Tsatsos, was designated first President of the reconstituted Greek Republic. **23.** French trade union and industry leaders signed a new agreement guaranteeing higher minimum earnings for the 360,000 workers on short time because of a business slump. **24.** The Danish Labour Court ordered the Danish printers' union to pay a £6,000 fine because it had not made any serious effort to prevent wildcat strikes by its members over wages. **27.** Argentine workers demonstrated in front of the presidential palace in Buenos Aires as the Central Trade Union movement called a general strike in defence of new wage agreements providing for rises of up to 130 per cent.; but President Maria Perón later announced an all-round increase of 50 per cent. backed by further rises of 15 per cent. in October and January.

July 2. The Danube burst its banks in Austria, south-east Germany, and Czechoslovakia after four days of torrential rain and hundreds of people were evacuated. **5.** It was announced that farms in Portugal which exceeded 1,729 acres were to be taken over by the Government and all private hunting estates were to be banned. **6.** Argentina began a general strike at midnight over a government-union clash on wages. The French islands of Comoro in the Indian Ocean declared themselves independent. **8.** The Argentine Government agreed to ratify wage increases of up to 150 per cent. and the trade unions called off the general strike. Brazil devalued its currency for the seventh time in 1975. **9.** The Supreme Soviet approved a Government decree imposing a 30 per cent. tax on money reaching Soviet citizens from abroad. **10.** The Portuguese Socialist Party withdrew from the provincial Government in protest against the ruling Revolutionary Council's appointment of a military commission to run the former socialist newspaper, *Republica*, and after earlier rejecting the Armed Forces Movement plans to form a workers' state; the second largest party, the centre-left Popular Democrats who also withdrew. **15.** It was announced that Iceland was to extend its fishing limits from 50 to 200 miles from October 15 and that all foreign vessels would be prohibited from fishing inside the new limit. **17.** Two Molotov cocktail bombs exploded at the feet of Crown Prince Akihito and Princess Nichiko of Japan during a visit to the island of Okinawa, but both escaped unhurt. **20.** A major earthquake occurred in the Pacific Ocean, north of the Solomon Islands, the United States National Earthquake Information Service reported. A blockade of Deauville by French fishing boats in protest against pollution in the Seine estuary continued for the second day, halting an international yachting event which was being conducted from the Normandy port; other ports in Seine Bay had been affected by similar blockades the previous day. **22.** The national council of the Italian Christian Democrat party dismissed Signor Fanfani, the party secretary. **23.** Terrorists threw Molotov cocktails at a four-masted Chilean naval training ship, the *Esmeralda*, and three Japanese vessels which were anchored at the site of the International Ocean Exposition in Okinawa. **24.** A joint communiqué issued in Manila after talks between President Ferdinand Marcos and the visiting Thai Prime Minister, Mr. Kukrit Pramoj, stated that it had been agreed in principle that the South East Asian Treaty Organisation should be phased out to " make it accord with the new realities of the region ". **25.** A triumvirate of three generals—the President (General Costa Gomes), the Prime Minister (General Vasco Gonçalves) and the commander of Copcon (General Otelo de Carvalho)—was formed to take control of Portugal with the 28-member Supreme Revolutionary Council responsible to it. **27.** China announced the successful launch of its third space satellite. **30.** The European Security Conference summit opened in Helsinki with leaders of 35 nations present.

Aug. 1. Former President Thieu of South Vietnam was granted a six-month visa to visit Britain. The European Security Conference in Helsinki ended with the signing by 35 nations of a 30,000 word agreement. **3.** President Ahmed Abdallah of the Comoro Islands was ousted in a bloodless coup, power passing to the National United Front. Leaders of Bougainville's secession movement announced that the Pacific island would break away from the rest of Papua-New Guinea on September 1st. **4.** Japan agreed to the demands of the Japanese Red Army terrorist squad, holding more than 50 hostages in the consulate section of the American Embassy in Kuala Lumpur, and promised to release seven Red Army members from Japanese jails. **9.** President Giscard d'Estaing announced a ban on supplies of "continental" arms by France to South Africa. Athens Court Martial sentenced 14 cashiered Greek Army officers to prison terms ranging from 4 to 12 years for plotting a military coup against the Greek Government in February. Marines with armoured cars broke up a mass Catholic demonstration in Braga, Northern Portugal, after Communists, whom the crowd were besieging, fired on the demonstrators, wounding 20 people. **14.** Portugal took over administrative control of Angola, the Acting High Commissioner stated that in the absence of a functioning government he had assumed full powers of administration. **15.** The doors of the "Queen's Portal" in the Christianborg Palace, the seat of the Danish Parliament in Copenhagen, were blasted by an explosion. **18.** Iceland decided to invite Britain to talks about possible fishing rights within the future 200-mile fisheries limit announced by Iceland. **19.** General Antonio de Spinola, former President of Portugal, announced the formation of the Democratic Movement for the liberation of Portugal in an open letter to the Portuguese President sent from his headquarters in Rio de Janeiro. Two policemen were killed and two wounded when police tried to storm a wine depot in which 50 armed

Corsican separatists were holding four hostages, who were released, the group's leader later giving himself up. **23.** Three leaders of the Greek military junta which seized power in 1967 and ruled for seven years were sentenced to death by an Athens court, the three being the ex-President, Colonel George Papadopoulos, and his two deputies, Nikolaos Makarezos and Stylianos Pattakos. Eight other defendants, including three generals, received life imprisonment, another seven were given prison terms of from 4 to 17 years and two were acquitted. On August 25 the three death sentences were commuted to life imprisonment. **25.** The Argentine peso was devalued 4 per cent., the fourth devaluation in 1975. Some 800 Dutch bargees blockaded the Rhine and entrances to Holland's major ports with their craft to protest against Government plans to reduce the number of cargo craft on inland waterways. **26.** Portugal's military régime surrendered its control over the internal administration of the Azores, local government being transferred from three Lisbon-appointed governors to six Azorian political leaders. **27.** The Governor of Portuguese Timor (Colonel Lemos Pireo) and his staff left the capital town of Dili for Atavro, an island 20 miles to the north, because of rebellion. **29.** Portugal's Prime Minister (General Vasco Gonçalves) was replaced by Admiral Jose Pinheiro de Azevedo, head of the Navy, and appointed Armed Forces Chief of Staff. Two Spanish Basques, members of the separatist movement E.T.A., were convicted at a military court near Burgos of machine-gunning to death a member of the Guardia Civil near San Sebastian and were sentenced to be garotted.

Sept. 1. The island of Bougainville declared itself a separate nation, Dr. Alexis Sarie, chairman of the Republican Government of the North Solomons, announcing unilateral independence. **3.** General Raul Gonzales, leader of the unsuccessful revolt on September 1st against President Guillermo Lara of Ecuador, was granted political asylum in Chile. Communist terrorists threw grenades into a parade of Police Field Force troops in Kuala Lumpur, killing two and wounding 52 others. **6.** Many people lost their lives when earthquake devastated part of eastern Turkey; it was reported on September 10 that death toll was at least 2,300. **9.** Prince Sihanouk, Cambodia's titular head of state, flew home to Phnom Penh after more than five years of exile in Peking.

OBITUARY, OCT. 1, 1974–SEPT. 30, 1975

H.M. Malik Faisal bin Abdul Aziz al Saud, King of Saudi Arabia (*assassinated*), aged 68—*March* 25.

Ashworth, *Hon.* Sir John Percy, Kt., M.B.E., Judge of Queen's Bench Division of High Court since 1954, aged 69—*Sept.* 26.

Barnes, Wally, former footballer, aged 55—*Sept.* 4.

Benny, Jack, comedian, aged 80—*Dec.* 27, 1974.

Birkenhead, Frederick Winston Furneaux Smith, T.D., 2nd Earl of, distinguished biographer, aged 67—*June* 10.

Bliss, Sir Arthur, K.C.V.O., C.H., Master of the Queen's Musick since 1953, aged 83—*March* 27.

Brabin, *Hon.* Sir Daniel James, Kt., M.C., Judge of High Court, Queen's Bench Division, since 1962, aged 62—*Sept.* 22.

Brook, Clive, actor, aged 87—*Nov.* 17, 1974.

Bulganin, *Marshal* Nikolai Alexandrovich, former Russian Prime Minister, aged 79—*Feb.* 24.

Cameron, Basil, C.B.E., conductor, aged 90—*June* 26.

Cardus, Sir Neville, Kt., C.B.E., music critic and cricket writer, aged 85—*Feb.* 28.

Chiang Kai-Shek, *Generalissimo*, former leader of China, aged 87—*April* 5.

Childers, Erskine, President of the Republic of Ireland, aged 68—*Nov.* 17, 1974.

Connolly, Cyril Vernon, C.B.E., author and journalist, aged 71—*Nov.* 26, 1974.

Cottrell, Leonard, author and radio and television producer, aged 61—*Oct.* 6, 1974.

Daubeny, Sir Peter Lauderdale, Kt., C.B.E., distinguished career in the theatre, aged 54—*Aug.* 6.

De Sica, Vittorio, Italian film director and actor, aged 73—*Nov.* 13, 1974.

De Valera, Eamon, President of Republic of Ireland from 1959 to 1973, aged 92—*Aug.* 29.

Elwes, Simon, R.A., notable portrait painter, aged 73—*Aug.* 6.

Finer, *Hon.* Sir Morris, a Judge of High Court of Justice, Family Division and Chairman of Royal Commission on the Press, aged 57—*Dec.* 15, 1974.

Flanders, Michael, O.B.E., actor and writer, aged 53 —*April*.

Fraser of Lonsdale, William Jocelyn Ian Fraser, C.H., C.B.E., Baron, Chairman of the Council of St. Dunstan's since 1921, and former M.P., aged 77 —*Dec.* 19, 1974.

Gluckman, *Prof.* Max, distinguished anthropologist, aged 64—*April* 13.

Gordon, John Rutherford, journalist, aged 84—*Dec.* 9, 1974.

Gregson, John, actor, aged 55—*Jan.* 8.

Griffiths, *Rt. Hon.* James, C.H., former Labour Minister, aged 84—*Aug.* 7.

Hahn, Dr. Kurt Matthias Robert Martin, C.B.E., founder of Gordonstoun School, aged 88—*Dec.* 14, 1974.

Hailé Selassié, former Emperor of Ethiopia, aged 83—*Aug.* 27.

Hailes, Patrick George Thomas Buchan-Hepburn, P.C., G.B.E., C.H., first Baron, distinguished politician, aged 73—*Nov.* 5, 1974.

Hamilton, *Admiral* Sir Frederick Hew George Dalrymple-, K.C.B., naval leader in Second World War, aged 84—*Dec.* 26, 1974.

Hamling, William, Labour M.P. for Woolwich West since 1964, aged 62—*March* 19.

Hepworth, Dame Barbara, D.B.E., sculptor (*accidentally killed*), aged 72—*May* 20.

Hurcomb, Cyril William Hurcomb, G.C.B., K.B.E., 1st Baron, distinguished career in transport, aged 92—*Aug.* 7.

Huxley, Sir Julian Sorell, Kt., F.R.S., D.SC., biologist and writer, aged 87—*Feb.* 14.

Jones, David, C.H., C.B.E., painter, writer and engraver, aged 78—*Oct.* 28, 1974.

Justice, James Norval Harald Robertson-, actor, aged 70—*July* 2.

Krips, Josef, Austrian conductor, aged 72—*Oct.* 13, 1974.

Krishna Menon, Vengalil Krishnan, Indian statesman, aged 78—*Oct.* 5, 1974.

Kuts, Vladimir, famous Russian athlete, aged 48—*Aug.* 16.

Laver, James, C.B.E., author, aged 76—*June* 3.

Linklater, Eric, C.B.E., author, aged 75—*Nov.* 7, 1974.

Lippmann, Walter, writer, aged 85—*Dec.* 14, 1974.

Löhr, Marie, actress, aged 84—*Jan.* 21.

March, Fredric, actor, aged 77—*April* 14.

Maufe, Sir Edward Brantwood, Kt., R.A., architect, aged 92—*Dec.* 12, 1974.

Mindszenty, His Eminence Cardinal Jozsef, former Primate of Hungary, aged 83—*May* 6.

Norfolk, Bernard Marmaduke Fitzalan-Howard, K.G., P.C., G.C.V.O., G.B.E., T.D., Royal Victorian Chain, 16th Duke of, Earl Marshal and Premier Duke and Earl, aged 66—*Jan.* 31.

Oistrakh, David Fyodorovich, famous Russian violinist, aged 66—*Oct.* 24, 1974.

Onassis, Aristotle Socrates, Greek shipowner, aged 69—*March* 15.

Park, *Air Chief Marshal* Sir Keith Rodney, G.C.B., K.B.E., M.C., D.F.C., a leading commander in the Battle of Britain, aged 82—*Feb.* 6.

Potter, Gillie, humorist, aged 87—*March*.

Radhakrishnan, Sarvepalli, O.M. (Hon.)., scholar and statesman, aged 86—*April* 17.

Rahman, Sheikh Mujibur, President of Bangladesh (*assassinated*), aged 55—*Aug.* 15.

Raymond, Harold, O.B.E., M.C., publisher and originator of Book Tokens, aged 87—*July* 17.

Robinson, Sir Robert, Kt., O.M., D.SC., F.R.S., notable scientist, aged 88—*Feb.* 8.

Salter, James Arthur Salter, P.C., G.B.E., K.C.B., 1st Baron, economist and former Minister, aged 94 —*June* 27.

Shostakovich, Dmitry Dmitrievich, great Russian composer, aged 68—*Aug.* 9.

Shuard, Amy, C.B.E., soprano, aged 50—*April* 18.

Slater, John, actor, aged 58—*Jan.* 9.

Steen, Marguerite, novelist and playwright, aged 81—*Aug.* 4.

Tertis, Lionel, C.B.E., virtuoso of the viola, aged 98 —*Feb.* 22.

Taylor, *Prof.* Sir Geoffrey Ingram, Kt., O.M., F.R.S., notable mathematician, aged 89—*June* 27.

Thomson, Sir George Paget, Kt., F.R.S., physicist, aged 83—*Sept.* 10.

Ure, Mary, actress, aged 42—*April* 3.

U Thant, Secretary-General of the United Nations, 1962—71, aged 65—*Nov.* 25, 1974.

Waldron, Sir John Lovegrove, K.C.V.O., Commissioner of Metropolitan Police, 1968—72, aged 65—*Aug.* 24.

Wattis, Richard, actor, aged 62—*Feb.* 1.

Wodehouse, Sir Pelham Grenville, K.B.E., author, aged 93—*Feb.* 14.

THE CENTENARIES OF 1976

In the early part of 1876 the Prince of Wales continued his lengthy and successful visit to India, departing finally from Bombay on March 13. In the course of his journey back to England, he stayed for a week in Cairo as guest of the Khedive of Egypt, and visited Malta and Gibraltar, where he opened a new battery at the head of the Mole. Later he was received at Madrid and Lisbon by the Kings of Spain and Portugal, and finally arrived back in England on May 11. His safe return was marked by a service of thanksgiving in Westminster Abbey, a concert at the Royal Albert Hall and a banquet at the Guildhall.

The Queen opened Parliament in person on February 8, and made another of her comparatively rare public appearances when she visited the East End of London on March 7 to open a new wing of the London Hospital in Whitechapel. On August 17, on her way to Balmoral, she unveiled the memorial to the Prince Consort in Charlotte Square, Edinburgh.

The chief item of legislation during the Parliamentary Session was the Royal Titles Bill, which provided for the Queen to assume the title of Empress of India, and which aroused considerable and unexpected controversy, to some extent misguided because, in spite of repeated explanations by the Government, it did not appear to be understood that, outside India, the traditional title of Queen would be retained. However, in spite of the opposition, which caused much distress to the Queen, the Bill passed through both Houses by April 7. One consequence of the Act was the institution of the Order of the Indian Empire.

The session was otherwise largely devoid of incident, and in spite of opposition by Mr. Gladstone and Mr. Lowe, the vote of £4,000,000 for the purchase of the Khedive's Suez Canal shares was not pressed to a division. The Appellate Jurisdiction Act was passed, as a result of which Lords of Appeal were appointed, and those in question were created the first Law Life Peers in

October. Before the progression it was announced that owing to declining physical strength Mr. Disraeli was retiring from the Commons. He became Earl of Beaconsfield, and continued in office as Prime Minister.

However the subject which dominated the scene during the year, not only in England, but throughout Europe, was the complex Eastern Question. At the end of 1875, Russia, Austria and Germany, in what was known as the Andrassy Note, had urged the Sultan of Turkey to carry out reforms, and in January 1876, the British Government, with some hesitation, gave its support. However, the Note produced little result, and the situation deteriorated, with growing revolt against Turkey in Bosnia and Herzegovina and with the murder of the French and German Consuls at Salonika. The Ministers of Russia, Austria and Germany met again, and produced the Berlin Memorandum, threatening action against Turkey if diplomatic courses failed. Great Britain had not been consulted about this move, and the Government declined to support the Memorandum, but, as a precautionary measure, a detachment of the British fleet was sent to Besika Bay, outside the Dardanelles.

On May 30 the Sultan Abdul Aziz was deposed in favour of his nephew Murad, and it was announced on June 4 that Abdul Aziz had committed suicide. Hopes that his removal might ease the situation were, however, disappointed. On July 1, Servia and Montenegro declared war on Turkey, and at the same time the news became public of Turkish brutality in suppressing an earlier revolt in Bulgaria. The Bulgarian Atrocities, as they were called, aroused great indignation in many circles in Britain, and Mr. Gladstone, who had been in semi-retirement for eighteen months, emerged to lead the attack, demanding that Britain should withdraw support from Turkey, and that Turkish authority should be expelled from the Balkans. Lord Beaconsfield's Government adopted a more cautious attitude, though demanding reparation to the Bulgarians, the punishment of offenders and guarantees against the recurrence of atrocities.

Meanwhile the Turkish forces had been pressing the Servians hard until at the end of October Russia presented an ultimatum to Turkey, demanding an armistice. Sultan Murad, after a reign of four months, had himself been deposed, and was succeeded by his brother Abdul Hamid. The new Sultan accepted the Russian ultimatum, and in the somewhat easier circumstances it was agreed that a Conference of Powers should be held at Constantinople. The conference met on Dec. 23, with Lord Salisbury as the British representative, and at the same time the Sultan announced a new and more liberal constitution.

The troops of King Alfonso enjoyed several successes in February against the Carlist rebels in Spain, and by the end of that month the civil war was over, Don Carlos seeking refuge in France. On March 20 King Alfonso made a triumphal entry into Madrid. The French general elections, which took place under the new Constitution on February 20, resulted in the return of a moderate Republican government. English and French bondholders sent representatives to Egypt during the year, and as a result the Khedive agreed to appoint two Comptrollers-General, one English and one French, to supervise Egyptian finances.

On March 18 occurred the opening of Northumberland Avenue, the new street from Charing Cross to the Embankment, over the site of Northumberland House and its gardens. At Oxford, Keble College Chapel was consecrated on April 24. More than 30 persons were drowned when a

ferry boat capsized on the Dee, at Aberdeen, on April 5, and on July 12 a boiler explosion on H.M.S. *Thunderer*, at Spithead, caused 45 deaths.

The year was celebrated in the United States as the centenary of Independence; General Grant opened the Centennial Exposition at Philadelphia on May 10, and July 4 was kept as a day of general thanksgiving. On June 25, after General George A. Custer had attacked the Sioux Indians on Little Big Horn in Montana, his forces were overwhelmed and he and his body of 264 men were annihilated. After the Presidential election in the autumn between Rutherford B. Hayes (Republican) and Samuel J. Tilden (Democrat), some of the electoral votes were disputed and it was not until later that a commission which had been set up awarded them to Mr. Hayes, who was declared elected.

The famous Balham mystery was a sensation of the year. Charles Bravo, a barrister, was poisoned by tartar emetic, and after two inquests the jury returned a verdict of wilful murder, but no charge was ever brought, and the mystery has caused speculation ever since.

1876 was a prolific year in the world of literature. Sir George Otto Trevelyan's life of his uncle, Lord Macaulay, was one of the most distinguished Victorian biographies. Anthony Trollope added *Phineas Redux* to his series of " political " novels. William Morris published his epic poem *Sigurd the Volsung*. Tennyson continued in the field of drama, adding *Harold* to the series of plays which had begun with *Queen Mary* in 1875. Thomas Hardy wrote *The Hand of Ethelberta*, but this proved to be one of his least successful novels. George Eliot's *Daniel Deronda*, which had begun to appear in parts in 1874, was completed during the year. Lewis Carroll's *The Hunting of the Snark* appeared in 1876, and in the U.S.A. Mark Twain's very popular *Adventures of Tom Sawyer*. It may also be noted that in 1876 C. M. Doughty began his two year sojourn among the Bedouin, from which came his famous *Travels in Arabia Deserta* and that Robert Louis Stevenson made his trip through France by canoe of which he wrote in his first book, *An Inland Voyage*, two years later.

THE CENTENARIES OF 1976

The following is a list of the principal centenaries which will be celebrated in 1976.

Died 1876

Feb. 1.	John Forster. Journalist and author.
April 19.	Samuel Sebastian Wesley. Hymn writer.
May 24.	Henry Kingsley. Novelist.
June 27.	Harriet Martineau. Writer.

Born 1876

Jan. 5.	Konrad Adenauer. German statesman.
Jan 12.	Jack London. Novelist.
Feb. 16.	George Macaulay Trevelyan. Historian.
March 2.	Pius XII. Pope.
March 5.	Visct. Caldecote (Sir Thomas Inskip). Lawyer and politician.
March 23.	Sir Muirhead Bone. Artist.
April 17.	John Hay Beith (" Ian Hay "). Writer.
May 7.	Samuel Courtauld. Art patron.
July 16.	Edward Joseph Dent. Musical scholar.
Aug. 9.	Earl of Lytton. Public servant.
Sept 7.	Bernard Darwin. Golfer and man of letters.
Dec. 30.	Pablo Casals. Cellist.

Died 1776

Aug. 25.	David Hume. Historian.

Born 1776

June 11.	John Constable. Painter.

Nov. 20.	William Blackwood. Publisher.	May 16	Sir Bernard Spilsbury. Pathologist.
Born 1676		May 17	Lord Iliffe. Newspaper proprietor.
Aug. 26.	Sir Robert Walpole. Prime Minister.	May 20	Sir Desmond MacCarthy. Critic.
Died 1576		Aug. 29	Sir Dudley Pound. Admiral of the Fleet.
Aug. 27.	Titian (Tiziano Vecelli). Painter.		
Died 1376		Sept. 9	James Agate. Dramatic critic.
July 8.	Edward the Black Prince.	Sept. 11	Sir James Jeans. Astronomer.
		Oct. 10	Visct. Nuffield. Motor manufacturer and philanthropist.

THE CENTENARIES OF 1977

The following is a list of the principal centenaries which will be celebrated in 1977.

Died 1877

March 13	Charles Cowden Clarke. Man of letters.	Oct. 17	Sir Robert Ensor. Historian.
		Oct. 29	Wilfred Rhodes. Cricketer.
March 24	Walter Bagehot. Author and economist.	Nov. 1	Roger Quilter. Composer.
		Nov. 2	The Aga Khan. Moslem leader and racehorse owner.
May 21	Sir Matthew Digby Wyatt. Architect.		Victor Trumper. Australian cricketer.
May 24	John Lothrop Motley. U.S. historian.	Nov. 25	Harley Granville-Barker. Man of the theatre.
Aug. 29	Brigham Young. Mormon leader.		
Sept. 5	Louis Adolphe Thiers. French statesman.	Dec. 2	Benno Elkan. Sculptor.
Sept. 17	William Henry Fox Talbot. Pioneer of photography.	*Born 1777*	
		July 9	Henry Hallam. Historian.
Born 1877		*Died 1677*	
Feb. 8	Sir Humphrey Milford. Publisher.	Feb. 20	Baruch Spinoza. Philosopher.
April 10	Lord Goddard. Lord Chief Justice.	*Born 1577*	
		June 29	Peter Paul Rubens. Painter.
		Died 1377	
		June 21	King Edward III.

ROMAN EMPERORS

[The *First Triumvirate* (Julius Cæsar, Pompey and Crassus) 60–53 B.C.]

THE TWELVE CÆSARS

I.   Caius JULIUS CÆSAR, *born* A.U.C. 651 (102 B.C.); *Dictator* A.U.C. 705 (48 B.C.); *Assassinated* A.U.C. 709 (44 B.C.).

[The *Second Triumvirate* (Octavian, Antony and Lepidus) 44–31 B.C.]

II.   Caius Julius Cæsar Octavianus AUGUSTUS, *born* 63 B.C.; *Emperor* 27 B.C.; *Died* A.D. 14.
III.   Claudius Nero Cæsar TIBERIUS, *born* 24 B.C.; *Emperor* A.D. 14; *Died* A.D. 37.
IV.   Caius Cæsar CALIGULA, *born* A.D. 12; *Emperor* A.D. 37; *Assassinated* A.D. 41.
V.   Tiberius Drusus CLAUDIUS, *born* 10 B.C.; *Emperor* A.D. 41; *Assassinated* A.D. 54.
VI.   Claudius NERO, *born* A.D. 37; *Emperor* A.D. 54; *Suicide* A.D. 68.
VII.   Servius Sulpicius GALBA, *born* 3 B.C.; *Emperor* A.D. 68; *Assassinated* A.D. 69.
VIII.   Marcus Salvius OTHO, *born* A.D. 32; *Emperor* A.D. 69; *Suicide* A.D. 69.
IX.   Aulus VITELLIUS, *born* A.D. 15; *Emperor* A.D. 69; *Assassinated* A.D. 69.
X.   Titus Flavius VESPASIAN, *born* A.D. 9; *Emperor* A.D. 69; *Died* A.D. 79.
XI.   Flavius Sabinus Vespasianus TITUS, *born* A.D. 48; *Emperor* A.D. 79; *Died* A.D. 81.
XII.   Titus Flavius DOMITIAN, *born* A.D. 52; *Emperor* A.D. 81; *Assassinated* A.D. 96.

NATIONAL INSURANCE AND RELATED CASH BENEFITS

The State insurance and assistance schemes in force from July 5, 1948, comprised schemes of national insurance and industrial injuries insurance, national assistance and non-contributory old age pensions, and family allowances. The Ministry of Social Security Act, 1966, introduced a scheme of non-contributory benefits, termed supplementary allowances and pensions, in place of national assistance and non-contributory old age pensions, and provided for the establishment of a new Ministry of Social Security (now the Department of Health and Social Security), with overall responsibility for the existing insurance schemes and family allowances scheme and the new scheme of supplementary benefits, in place of the Ministry of Pensions and National Insurance and the National Assistance Board, which were abolished.

The Conservative Government's Social Security Act, 1973, which was intended to be brought into force in April, 1975, provided for the replacement of the National Insurance scheme by a basic scheme of social security, offering a range of benefits, including flat-rate basic pensions, similar to those under the existing legislation; a separate reserve pension scheme providing, in addition to the basic pension, earnings-related pensions for those employees not in recognized pensionable employment; and the assimilation of the Industrial Injuries scheme to the basic scheme. It also laid down minimum conditions for recognition of occupational pension schemes so as to exempt the employers and employees concerned from liability to contribute to the reserve pension scheme.

The new Labour Government decided that the basic scheme provisions of the 1973 Act should come into force on April 6, 1975, as planned, but it decided not to bring into effect the provisions of that Act relating to the reserve pension scheme or the recognition tests for occupational pension schemes seeking exemption from the reserve pension scheme (except the provisions relating to the preservation of benefits under occupational schemes). Effect was given to the Government's decisions by an order made in June 1974 under the 1973 Act, and by the Social Security (Amendment) Act, 1974, passed in December, 1974, which provided that the higher rates of national insurance and industrial injuries benefits introduced from July 22, 1974, under the National Insurance Act, 1974, should continue to apply when the new basic scheme came into force. The Social Security (Amendment) Act, 1974, also provided for increases in the rates of contributions laid down in the 1973 Act to enable the income of the new scheme to cover the cost of the July 1974 increases in benefits. The Social Security (Benefits) Act, 1975, enacted in March, 1975, made provision for further increases in national insurance and industrial injuries benefits as well as for the introduction of two new non-contributory benefits (see p. 612) and for increases in family allowances (but not for further changes in contributions) to take effect in the week beginning April 7, 1975.

Three measures—the Social Security Act, 1975; the Social Security (Consequential Provisions) Act, 1975; and the Industrial Injuries and Diseases (Old Cases) Act, 1975—were enacted on March 20, 1975, for the purpose of consolidating the law relating to social security in Great Britain, and corresponding measures were passed for Northern Ireland.

The most recent increases in social security benefits were authorised by the Social Security Benefits Up-rating Order, 1975, made in July, 1975, under the Social Security Act, 1975 (now the principal Act). It is proposed that these new rates should take effect in the week beginning November 17, 1975.

The new Government published in September, 1974, in a White Paper, " Better Pensions fully protected against inflation ", its proposals for a new pensions scheme. The Social Security Pensions Bill based upon these proposals, after consultation with interested bodies, was introduced, with an explanatory memorandum, in February, 1975, and after amendment was passed as the Social Security Pensions Act, 1975, in August, 1975. Preparations are being made for the new scheme to come into force in 1978 (see p. 610).

SOCIAL SECURITY SCHEME, 1975

From April 6, 1975, the National Insurance scheme 1948–1975 was replaced by a new scheme of social security benefits and contributions under the Social Security Act, 1975, and regulations made thereunder. Like the former scheme, the new scheme is financed on a pay-as-you-go basis mainly by contributions but in part out of Exchequer funds (rates of benefit and of contributions being reviewed normally annually in accordance with statutory criteria), but the new scheme contributions, to a greater extent than national insurance contributions, are earnings-related. The graduated pension scheme 1961–1975 has been wound up (existing rights being preserved); otherwise the new scheme provides a pattern of pension and other benefits similar to that of the old scheme. The Industrial Injuries scheme continues with only minor changes, but steps have been taken to assimilate the industrial injuries legislation to the general scheme: thus the separate industrial injuries contribution and the Treasury supplement thereto under the Industrial Injuries Acts have been abolished, and the Industrial Injuries Fund has been merged with the National Insurance Fund.

CONTRIBUTIONS AND CONTRIBUTION CONDITIONS

The funds required for paying benefits payable under the Social Security Act, 1975, out of the National Insurance Fund and not out of other public money; for the making of payments towards the cost of the National Health Service and into the Redundancy Fund; and for paying benefit under the Industrial Injuries and Diseases (Old Cases) Act, 1975, are provided by means of contributions payable by earners, employers and others (such as non-employed persons paying voluntary contributions), together with the Treasury supplement.

Contributions are of four classes:

Class 1, earnings-related:
- (a) primary Class 1 contributions from employed earners; and
- (b) secondary Class 1 contributions from employers and other persons paying earnings;

Class 2, flat-rate, payable weekly by self-employed earners;

Class 3, flat-rate, payable by earners and others voluntarily with a view to providing entitlement to benefit, or making up entitlement; and

Class 4, payable by self-employed persons in respect of the profits or gains of a trade, profession or vocation, or in respect of equivalent earnings.

Particulars of current rates of contributions for each class are given on p. 613.

Regulations state the cases in which earners may be excepted from liability to pay contributions, and the conditions upon which contributions are credited to persons who are excepted.

The Secretary of State for Social Services is empowered by the Social Security Act, 1975, to alter certain rates of contributions by order approved by both Houses of Parliament, and is required by the same enactment to make annual reviews of the general level of earnings in order to determine whether such an order should be made. Increases in contribution rates have so far been made by statutory provisions. When increases were made in social security benefits by the Social Security Benefits Act, 1975, no provision was made for changes in contribution rates. The Government Actuary has pointed out that with a system of mainly earnings-related contributions the income of the National Insurance Fund will rise automatically with increases in the general level of earnings and will broadly be sufficient to meet the cost of corresponding increases in the level of benefits provided the earnings limits for contribution liability and the flat-rate (Classes 2 and 3) contributions are adjusted regularly. Following the decision in the summer of 1975 to make further increases in benefits in November, 1975, it is expected that changes in contributions will become nececessary.

The yearly Treasury supplement to the National Insurance Fund is equal to 18 per cent. of the contributions of the four classes paid during the year after deducting the National Health Service allocation and the allocation to the Redundancy Fund (see p. 613).

BENEFITS

The benefits payable under the Social Security Act, 1975, are as follows:

(1) Contributory Benefits:
  Unemployment benefit.
  Sickness benefit.
  Invalidity pension and allowance.
  Maternity benefit, comprising maternity grant and maternity allowance.
  Widow's benefit, comprising widow's allowance, widowed mother's allowance and widow's pension.
  Child's special allowance.
  Retirement pensions of the following categories:
    Category A.
    Category B.
  Death grant.

(2) Non-contributory Benefits:
  Guardian's allowance (see p. 612).
  Attendance allowance (see p. 612).
  Non-contributory invalidity pension (see p. 612).
  Invalid care allowance (see p. 612).
  Retirement pensions of the following categories.
    Category C (see p. 612).
    Category D (see p. 612).

(3) Benefits for Industrial Injuries and Diseases.

Cash benefits provided under other enactments (supplementary benefits, family allowances and family income supplement) are dealt with on 611–12.

The Social Security Act, 1975, empowers the Secretary of State to increase certain rates of benefit by order approved by both Houses of Parliament, and requires him to increase certain rates by such an order if an annual review shows that they have not retained their value in relation to the general level of earnings and prices obtaining in Great Britain.

Entitlement to the contributory benefits provided by the Act of 1975 (except invalidity benefit) depends on contribution conditions being satisfied either by the claimant or by some other person (depending on the kind of benefit). The class or classes of contribution which for this purpose are relevant to each benefit are as follows:

Short-term benefits

Unemployment benefit	Class 1
Sickness benefit	Class 1 or 2
Maternity grant	Class 1, 2 or 3
Maternity allowance	Class 1 or 2
Widow's allowance	Class 1, 2 or 3

Other benefits

Widowed mother's allowance
Widow's pension
Child's special allowance   Class 1, 2 or 3
Category A retirement pension
Category B retirement pension
Death grant

With the change from a system of flat-rate national insurance and industrial injuries contributions and graduated pension contributions to a system of wholly earnings-related contributions for employed earners the contribution conditions for entitlement to benefit could no longer be based on the number of weekly contributions paid in a contribution year or throughout a working life. The Social Security Act, 1975, introduced a new system of contribution conditions related to yearly levels of earnings on which contributions have been paid. The contribution conditions for different benefits are set out in sections 13 to 33 of and Schedule 3 to the Act, and in summary form in leaflets on the benefits available at local Social Security offices. There are two contribution conditions for most of the benefits. The first condition must be satisfied to qualify for benefit at all; the second condition generally determines whether benefit is paid at the standard rate or at a reduced rate. Under the arrangements made for the transition from the old scheme to the new one, provision has been made for such matters as treating old-style flat-rate contributions as new-style earnings-related contributions and vice versa, and the use of modified contribution tests for short-term benefits for an initial period following the start of the new scheme.

There is one system of adjudication on all claims for benefit under the Act; with certain exceptions, questions as to the right to benefit are decided by independent statutory authorities, consisting of insurance officers, local tribunals and the Chief Commissioner and Commissioners.

The rates of benefit stated below are, unless otherwise indicated, the standard rates having effect from November 17, 1975.

UNEMPLOYMENT BENEFIT

The *standard weekly rates of flat-rate benefit payable to primary Class 1 contributors are as follows*:

	£
Man, single woman or widow	11·10
Married woman: ordinary rate	7·80
Increase of benefit for only child or elder or eldest child (ordinary rate)	3·50
Increase of benefit for each additional child (ordinary rate) in addition to family allowances	2·00
Increase of benefit for wife or other adult dependant (ordinary rate) where payable	6·90

Waiting Period.—Benefit is not payable for the first three days of a period of interruption of employment.

Duration of Benefit.—Benefit is payable in a period of interruption of employment for up to 312 days (a year).

Requalification for Benefit.—A person who has exhausted benefit requalifies therefor when he has again worked as an employed earner for at least 21 hours a week for 13 weeks.

Disqualifications.—There are disqualifications for receiving benefit, e.g. for a period not exceeding six weeks if a person has lost his employment through his misconduct, or has voluntarily left his employment without just cause, or has, without good cause, refused an offer of suitable employment or training.

Earnings-related Supplement.—This supplement is payable to claimants under minimum pension age who are entitled to flat-rate unemployment or sickness benefit. The amount of the supplement depends upon reckonable earnings in the relevant income tax year. Where based on earnings in the 1973–74 income tax year, it is one-third of the amount of reckonable weekly earnings lying between £10 and £30 and 15 per cent. of those lying between £30 and £48. Where it is based on earnings in the 1974–75 income tax year, the upper limit on the band of weekly earnings on which it is paid at 15 per cent. will be increased from £48 to £54. The total benefit, including increases for dependants, is subject to a maximum of 85 per cent. of earnings. The supplement starts from the thirteenth day of a period of interruption of employment and lasts for up to a maximum of six months. Periods of unemployment or sickness not separated by more than 13 weeks are treated as one period of interruption of employment. Where employment is suspended but not terminated by the employer, e.g. short-time working or lay-off, the supplement is not payable for the first six days (except Sundays and holidays) in any continuous period of suspension.

SICKNESS BENEFIT

Standard Rates of flat-rate Benefit payable to primary Class 1 and to Class 2 contributors while incapable of work through illness or disablement.—Same as for unemployment benefit.

Waiting Period.—Same as for unemployment benefit.

Duration of Benefit.—Sickness benefit is payable for 28 weeks of sickness and is then replaced by invalidity benefit (*see below*).

Disqualifications.—Regulations provide for disqualifying a person for receiving sickness or invalidity benefit for a period not exceeding six weeks if he has become incapable of work through his own misconduct or if he fails without good cause to attend for or submit himself to prescribed medical or other examination or treatment, or observe prescribed rules of behaviour.

Earnings-related Supplement.—The supplement and the rules as to duration are the same as for the supplement to unemployment benefit.

INVALIDITY BENEFIT

Normally, after 28 weeks of sickness, sickness benefit is replaced by an *invalidity pension* of £13·30 (£7·90 for a wife) unless the claimant is over pension age and has retired from regular employment. In addition an *invalidity allowance* is payable if incapacity for work begins more than five years before pension age. The allowance varies in amount from 85p to £2·80 a week, according to the age on falling sick, and if still in payment at pension age will continue as an addition to retirement pension. The increases of benefit for children of an invalidity pensioner are at the higher rate, viz., £6·50 for the first child and £5·00 for any other child, in addition to family allowances. Earnings-related supplement is not payable with in-

validity benefit. The dependent wife of an invalidity pensioner residing with him is subject to the same tapered earnings rule as applies to retirement pensioners which begins to operate when earnings exceed £20 (after April 1976 £35). As to the age addition if the pensioner or dependant is 80 or over, and non-contributory invalidity pensions, see p. 612).

MATERNITY BENEFITS

Maternity Grant.—A cash grant of £25 is payable on the mother's own insurance or on her husband's, or late husband's, whether she is confined at home or in hospital. Extra grants are payable, in certain circumstances, if more than one child is born.

Maternity Allowance.—A woman who has been employed or self-employed and paying contributions at the full rate receives in addition a maternity allowance of £11·10 a week normally for 18 weeks beginning eleven weeks before the expected week of confinement, provided that she abstains from work. The rate of allowance is increased where the woman has dependants. Earnings-related supplement is payable with maternity allowance if the claimant's title to the supplement has not been used up in respect of other benefits, see above.

WIDOW'S BENEFITS

Only the late husband's contributions count for widow's benefit in any of its three forms.

Widow's Allowance.—A woman who at her husband's death is under 60 (or over 60, if he had not retired), receives (during the first 26 weeks of widowhood) a cash allowance usually of £18·60 a week with increases of £6·50 for the first or only child and £5·00 for each other child, in addition to family allowances. She may also be entitled to an earnings-related addition to her widow's allowance based on her late husband's earnings (reckoned in the same way as for earnings-related supplements to unemployment and sickness benefit) above.

Widowed Mother's Allowance.—When the 26 weeks of widow's allowance have elapsed, a widow who is left with one or more dependent children receives a cash allowance usually of £19·80 a week as long as she has a child of qualifying age, and in addition £5·00 for each additional child, as well as family allowances. A widowed mother's personal allowance, usually £13·30 a week, is payable to widows who, when their widow's or widowed mother's allowance ends, have living with them a child under 19, who has left school and is not an apprentice.

Widow's Pension.—A widow receives this pension usually of £13·30 a week when widow's allowance ends, if she was over 50 at the time of her husband's death; or (ii) when her widowed mother's allowance or widowed mother's personal allowance ends, if she is then over 50 (40 if widowed before February 4, 1957).

Flat-rate widow's pensions on a graduated scale were introduced in April 1971 for women who are widowed between the ages of 40 and 50, or who cease to be entitled to a widowed mother's allowance between those ages.

Widow's benefit of any form ceases upon re-marriage.

CHILD'S SPECIAL ALLOWANCE

A woman whose marriage has been dissolved or annulled and who has not re-married is paid a special allowance on the ex-husband's death based on his contribution record. The normal condition is that she has a child to whose maintenance he was contributing, or had been liable to contribute, at least 25p a week in cash or its equivalent. The allowance is £6·50 a week for the first or only child and £5·00 for each other child, in addition to family allowances.

RETIREMENT PENSION
(CATEGORIES A AND B)

A *Category A pension* is payable for life to men or women on their own contributions if (a) they are over pension age (65 for a man and 60 for a woman), and (b) they have retired from regular employment. Men aged 70 or over and women aged 65 or over are not required to satisfy condition (b).

The standard flat-rate pension, when the contibution conditions are fully satisfied, is £13·30, *plus* £7·90 for a dependent wife who is not herself qualified for a pension, *plus* £6·50 for the first or only child and £5·00 for each other child, in addition to family allowances. An increase for a dependent wife is reduced, under the earnings rule, below, if she earns more than a certain amount. (As to the age addition payable at 80, see p. 612.)

Where a person does not retire at 65 (60 for a woman) or later cancels retirement, and does not draw a Category A pension, the weekly rate of pension is increased, when he or she finally retires or reaches the age of 70 (65 for a woman), in respect of contributions paid when employed or self-employed during the five years after reaching minimum pension age. For periods of deferred retirement after April 5, 1975, the rate of pension (without any increases except invalidity allowance), when it is finally awarded, will normally be increased by one-eighth of one per cent. for each week of deferment except those weeks in which other benefits (such as sickness or unemployment benefit) were drawn. A married man can also earn extra pension for his wife.

A *Category B pension* is normally payable for life to a woman on her husband's contributions when he has retired, or is over 70, and has qualified for his own Category A pension, and she has reached 60 and retired from regular work or has reached 65. It is also payable on widowhood after 60 whether or not the late husband had retired and qualified for his own pension. The weekly pension is payable at the lower rate of £7·90 while the husband is alive, and at the higher rate of £13·30 on widowhood after 60. Where a woman is widowed before she reaches 60, a Category B pension is paid to her on reaching 60 at the same weekly rate as her widow's pension if she retired. If a woman qualifies for a pension of each category she receives whichever pension is the larger. For periods of deferred retirement after April 5, 1975, a Category B pension will normally be increased by one-sixteenth of one per cent. of the husband's pension rate (apart from any increase other than invalidity allowance) for each week while both husband and wife defer retirement. If the husband dies after April 5, 1975, the extra pension which he earned for his wife by not drawing his pension after she reached 60 will be doubled. She will also receive half of any extra pension he earned for any period before she reached 60. (As to the age addition payable at 80, see p. 612.)

A man aged 65 to 70, or a woman aged 60 to 65, who has qualified for pension will have it reduced if he or she earns more than a certain amount. Until April 1976 the pension will be reduced by 5p for each 10p of net earnings between £20 and £24 and by 5p for each 5p earned over £24. During the twelve months following, the " earnings rule " will start to operate when earnings exceed £35. A man's pension is not affected by his wife's earnings unless he is drawing an increase of his pension for her.

Unemployment, sickness or invalidity benefit is payable to men between 65 and 70 and women between 60 and 65 who have not retired from regular work at the same rate as the retirement pension they would have received had they retired. A retirement pension will be increased by the amount of any invalidity allowance the pensioner was getting within the period of 13 weeks before reaching minimum pension age. As to attendance allowance and invalid care allowance, see p. 612. Persons who do not qualify for a Category A or B pension may qualify for a Category C or D pension at 80 (see p. 612), or for a supplementary pension (see p. 611).

GRADUATED PENSION

The graduated pension scheme under which national insurance contributions and retirement pensions were graduated within specified limits, according to earnings, was discontinued in April, 1975, under the Social Security Act, 1975. Any graduated pension which an employed person over 18 and under 70 (65 for a woman) had earned by paying graduated contributions between April 6, 1961, when the scheme started and April 5, 1975, will be paid when the contributor retires, or at 70 (65 for a woman), in addition to any retirement pension for which he or she qualifies.

Graduated pension is at the rate of 2½p a week for each " unit " of graduated contributions paid by the employee (half a unit or more counts as a whole unit). A unit of contributions is £7·50 for men, and £9·00 for women, of graduated contributions paid.

A wife can get a graduated pension in return for her own graduated contributions, but not for her husband's. A widow gets a graduated addition to her retirement pension equal to half of any graduated additions earned by her late husband, plus any additions earned by her own graduated contributions. If a person defers retirement beyond 65 (60 for a woman), half the graduated pension he or she has forgone by deferring retirement (whether before or after April 5, 1975) will be treated as extra graduated contributions paid, and will count towards further graduated pension on retirement or at 70 (65 for a woman).

DEATH GRANT

A death grant is payable on the death of a qualifying contributor or of his wife, child or widow or, if the contributor is a woman, of her husband, child or widower, and also in respect of the deaths of certain handicapped persons on the insurance of close relatives. The normal grant is for an adult £30, a child aged 6–17 £22·50, a child aged 3–5 £15, a child under 3 £9. For the deaths of people who on July 5, 1948, were between 55 and 65 (men) or between 50 and 60 (women) the grant is £15. No grant is payable for deaths of persons already over pension age on July 5, 1948.

The grant is paid to the deceased person's executors or administrators, if any; otherwise it is paid to the person who meets the funeral expenses or to the next of kin.

FINANCE

Under the National Insurance Acts before April 6, 1975, two funds were set up, viz. the National Insurance Fund, and the National Insurance (Reserve) Fund. The income from contributions, Exchequer grants and interest from both funds were paid into the National Insurance Fund, and payments were made out of the Fund to meet the cost of benefits and administration. Under the National Health Service Contributions Act, provision was made for separate National Health Service contributions to be collected in conjunction with the National Insurance contributions, in place of payments formerly made from the Fund towards the cost of the National Health Service.

Approximate receipts and payments of the National Insurance Fund for the year ended March 31, 1974, were as follows:—

Receipts	£'000
Balance, April, 1973................	334,617
Flat-rate contributions from employers and insured persons...............	1,682,034
Exchequer contribution.............	597,000
Graduated contributions.............	1,933,390
Income from investments............	29,756
Transfer from the Reserve Fund of income from investments, etc.......	38,636
Other receipts......................	75
	4,615,508

Payments		
Benefit:—	£'000	£'000
Unemployment benefit..	174,090	
Sickness benefit........	306,268	
Invalidity benefit.......	241,541	
Maternity benefit.......	42,000	
Widow's benefit........	245,000	
Guardian's allowance...	1,000	
Child's special allowance	140	
Retirement pension.....	2,751,976	
Death grant............	13,388	
Pensioners' lump sum payments............	77,080	
Other payments........	7,800	
		3,860,282(a)
Administration expenses.............		143,401
Other payments....................		37,730
Balance, March 31, 1974.............		574,094
		4,615,508

(a) Including estimated amounts of earnings-related supplement as follows: unemployment benefit £23·0 million; sickness benefit £75·0 million; widow's benefit £7·0 million; graduated retirement benefit £30·0 million.

Receipts exceeded payments during the year by £239 million. Compared with 1972–73 receipts increased by £647 million and payments by £544 million.

The balance in the Reserve Fund at March 31, 1974, was £886·5 million.

INDUSTRIAL INJURIES BENEFITS

The National Insurance (Industrial Injuries) Act, 1946, substituted for the Workmen's Compensation Acts, 1925 to 1945, a system of insurance against personal injury caused by accident arising out of and in the course of a person's employment and against prescribed diseases and injuries due to the nature of a person's employment. The scheme, which insures against personal injuries caused and prescribed diseases and injuries developed on or after July 5, 1948, now operates under the Social Security Act, 1975, and regulations made under the Act. The Social Security Benefits Up-rating Order, 1975, provided for increases in the rates of benefit with effect from November 17, 1975. Rates of benefit are now reviewed annually.

Supplementary allowances payable in certain circumstances in cases arising before the Industrial Injuries scheme started are governed by the Industrial Injuries and Diseases (Old Cases) Act, 1975, and regulations made under the Act. Statutory schemes have also been made providing for the payment of allowances supplementing workmen's compensation in certain circumstances, and for the payment of benefits in certain cases where neither workmen's compensation nor Industrial Injuries benefits are payable.

The scope of " employed earners " and their employments to which the industrial injuries scheme applies is defined in the Social Security Act, 1975, and regulations made under the Act.

Separate industrial injuries contributions were discontinued in April, 1975. The Industrial Injuries Fund was at the same time merged in the National Insurance Fund, and the separate Treasury Supplement to the Industrial Injuries Fund came to an end.

BENEFITS

Injury Benefit is payable for not more than the first 26 weeks of incapacity, but not usually for the first three days. Benefit is payable to persons over 18 and to juveniles with dependant's allowances, at the weekly rate of £13·85 (days being paid for at one-sixth of the weekly rate): with increases of £6·90 for a wife or other adult dependant, and normally £3·50 for the first or only child and £2·00 for each other child, in addition to family allowances. Other juveniles receive lower rates. Where a claimant who is entitled to sickness benefit draws injury benefit instead, any earnings-related supplement to sickness benefit to which he is entitled will be paid with the injury benefit (see p. 607).

Disablement Benefit is payable if at or after the end of the injury benefit period the employed earner suffers from loss of physical or mental faculty such that the resulting disablement is assessed at not less than one per cent. (In cases of pneumoconiosis and byssinosis disablement benefit is paid from the start without a period of injury benefit.) The amount of disablement benefit varies according to the degree of disablement (in the form of a percentage) assessed by a medical board or medical appeal tribunal. In cases of disablement of less than 20 per cent., except in pneumoconiosis or byssinosis cases, benefit normally takes the form of a *gratuity* paid according to a prescribed scale, but not exceeding £1,450. Where the degree of disablement is 20 per cent. or more, or if it is due to pneumoconiosis or byssinosis, the benefit is a weekly *pension* payable either for a limited period or for life, according to the following scale:

Degree of disablement	Weekly Rate
	£
100 per cent.	21·80
90 ,, ,,	19·62
80 ,, ,,	17·44
70 ,, ,,	15·26
60 ,, ,,	13·08
50 ,, ,,	10·90
40 ,, ,,	8·72
30 ,, ,,	6·54
20 ,, ,,	4·36

These are basic rates applicable to adults and to juveniles entitled to an increase for a child or adult dependant; other juveniles receive lower rates.

Basic rates of pension are not related to the pensioner's loss of earning power, and are payable whether he is in work or not. Upon prescribed conditions, however, pension is supplemented for unemployability and in cases of special hardship. There is provision also for increases of pension during approved hospital treatment or if the pensioner requires constant attendance or if his disablement is exceptionally severe. If the beneficiary is entitled to an unemployability supplement there are increases of £6·50 for the first or only child and £5·00 for any other child, and, subject to the earnings rule, £7·90 for an adult dependant. Subject to certain exceptions, a pensioner who is not in receipt of unemployability supplement can draw sickness or invalidity benefit as appropriate, in addition to disablement pension, during spells of incapacity for work.

Death Benefit, in the form of a pension, a gratuity or a weekly allowance for a limited period, available for widows and other dependants in fatal cases, depends in amount upon their relationship to the deceased and their circumstances at the time of death and not upon the deceased's earnings. A widow who was living with her husband at the time of his death receives a pension of £18·60 a week for the first 26 weeks *plus* any earnings-related addition she would have received if she had been entitled to national insurance widow's allowance (*see* p. 607), and thereafter a pension of £13·85 or less a week according to circumstances, *plus* £6·50 for the first or only child and £5·00 for each other child, in addition to family allowances.

Regulations impose certain obligations on claimants and beneficiaries and on employers, including, in the case of claimants for injury or disablement benefit, that of submitting to medical examination and treatment.

Industrial Diseases, etc.—The scheme extends insurance to prescribed industrial diseases and prescribed personal injuries not caused by accident, which are due to the nature of an employed earner's employment and developed on or after July 5, 1948.

Determination of Questions and Claims.—Provision is made for the determination of certain questions by the Secretary of State for Social Services, and of " disablement questions " by a medical board (or a single doctor) or medical appeal tribunal or, on appeal on a point of law, by the Commissioners, subject to leave. Claims for benefit and certain questions arising in connection with a claim for or award of benefit (e.g. whether the accident arose out of and in the course of the employment) are determined by an insurance officer appointed by the Secretary of State, or a local appeal tribunal consisting of a chairman appointed by the Secretary of State and equal numbers of members representing employers and employed earners, or, on appeal, by the Commissioners.

FINANCE

Before April 6, 1975, contributions from employers, insured persons and the Exchequer were paid into, and benefits and administrative expenses were paid out of, a fund established under the Industrial Injuries Act, viz., the Industrial Injuries Fund.

Receipts, 1973–74	£'000
Balance, April 1, 1973	380,599
Contributions from employers and insured persons	125,549
Exchequer contribution	25,872
Income from investments	22,040
Other receipts	5
	554,065

Payments, 1973–74		£'000
Benefit:—		
Injury	33,904	
Disablement	87,339	
Death	13,400	
Other benefits	3,420	
		138,062
Administration expenses		15,410
Other payments		115
Balance, March 31, 1974		400,479
		554,065

PLANS FOR EARNINGS-RELATED PENSIONS

The Social Security Pensions Act, 1975, which became law in August 1975, embodied proposals for the future coordinated development of State and occupational pensions. When the Act comes into force (probably in April 1978), the present flat-rate retirement and other State pensions will be replaced by fully earnings-related pensions for employed earners by fully earnings-related pensions, but it will be twenty years after that before any pensions become payable at the full rate.

The aims of the Act will be, by providing better pensions, to reduce reliance upon means-tested supplementary benefit in old age, in widowhood and in chronic ill-health; to ensure that occupational pension schemes which are contracted out of part of the State scheme fulfil the conditions of a good scheme; that pensions are adequately protected against inflation; and that in both the State and occupational schemes men and women are treated equally.

Under the new State scheme retirement, invalidity and widow's pensions for employees will be related to the earnings on which contributions have been paid. The lower earnings limit for Class 1 contribution liability will be broadly the current level of the basic component of the retirement pension—in April 1975 terms £11·60 a week. Employees with earnings at or above this base level in any week will pay contributions on all their earnings up to a limit of about seven times the base level—in April 1975 terms about £80 a week. The standard rate of contribution set by the Act is 16½ per cent. (which includes 1 per cent. for the National Health Service and 0·2 per cent. for the Redundancy Fund), employees paying 6½ per cent. and employers 10 per cent., instead of the present figures of 5½ per cent. and 8½ per cent. Provision is made for the rate to be reviewed before the new scheme comes into operation. Employees who are contracted out will pay the full rate of contribution on earnings up to the lower limit, but on higher earnings up to the upper limit the rate will be 9½ per cent. (4 per cent. for employees and 5½ per cent. for employers), the rate to be reviewed at intervals of not more than five years. The Treasury supplement will be 18 per cent. of all contributions, calculated so as to include those that would have been received if there had been no contracting out. Self-employed persons will pay contributions towards the basic pension. The non-employed and employees with earnings below the lower limit may contribute voluntarily for basic pension. Women who marry for the first time after the new scheme begins will no longer have a right to elect not to pay the full contribution rate. No primary Class 1 contributions or Class 2 or Class 4 contributions will be payable by persons who work beyond pension age (65 for men, 60 for women), but the employer's liability for secondary Class 1 contributions will continue.

The new system of earnings-related pensions for

retirement, widowhood and invalidity to replace the present flat-rate pensions will provide for employees of either sex with a complete insurance record a category A pension in two parts, a basic and an additional component. The rate of the basic component set by the Act is £11·60 (the flat-rate pension payable under the present system from April 7, 1975): up to this level the pensioner will receive weekly, from the start of the new scheme, £1 for £1 of average weekly earnings on which contributions have been paid. The additional component will be 1¼ per cent. of average earnings above the level of the basic component and up to the upper earnings limit of about £80 for each year of such earnings under the scheme, and will thus build up to 25 per cent. in twenty years. When the number of years exceeds twenty, pensions will be based on contributors' twenty best years of earnings between age 16 and pension age. Actual earnings are to be revalued in terms of the earnings level current in the last complete tax year before pension age (or death or incapacity). In April 1975 terms the total personal retirement pension at maturity under the new scheme would vary from £11·60 for average earnings of £11·60 a week to about £29·00 for average earnings of about £80 or over; a married couple's pension (on the husband's contribution record alone) from £18·50 to £35·90; and a married couple's pension (where both have contributed) from £23·20 to £58·00. The basic component of pensions in payment will be uprated annually in line with the movement of earnings or prices, whichever is increasing the faster, and the additional components in line with the movement of prices. Graduated retirement pensions in payment and rights to such pensions earned by people who are still working will be brought into the annual review of benefits. Among other steps to be taken to give women equal treatment in benefit provision the State scheme will permit years of home responsibilites to count towards satisfying the contribution conditions for retirement pension, widowed mother's allowance and widow's pension, and from April 1979 the " half-test " by which a married woman cannot qualify for a Category A retirement pension unless she has contributed on earnings at the basic level in at least half the years between marriage and pension age is to be abolished. The range of short-term social security benefits and industrial injury benefits under the Social Security Act, 1975, will continue with only minor changes: these will include the repeal of the provision which at present imposes a lower rate of sickness and unemployment benefit on married women.

Members of occupational pension schemes which meet the standards laid down by the Act can be contracted out of a part of the State retirement and widow's benefits. A contracted-out scheme will be required to provide a minimum level of pension calculated on a basis similar to that for the additional component of retirement pension under the State scheme, with a widow's pension at half this rate. The benefits payable from the State scheme will be correspondingly reduced. The State scheme will help in meeting the cost of giving pensions under contracted-out schemes the same protection against inflation as if they had not been contracted out. The Act contains provisions designed to give women the same rights as men to belong to an occupational pension scheme. The Occupational Pensions Board established under the Social Security Act, 1973, will be responsible for deciding whether an occupational scheme should be accepted as a contracted-out scheme, and for ensuring that a contracted-out scheme has adequate financial resources. The Secretary of State for Social Services is empowered to make regulations for requiring

employers to inform employees and their organisations and to have consultations before making an election to contract out.

SUPPLEMENTARY BENEFITS

The Ministry of Social Security Act, 1966, as amended by later measures, enacted a scheme of non-contributory benefits termed supplementary allowances and pensions in place of national assistance and of non-contributory old age pensions, and vested responsibility for these supplementary benefits in a new Ministry of Social Security (now the Department of Health and Social Security). A Supplementary Benefits Commission within the Department is now responsible, subject to Regulations made by the Secretary of State for Social Services, for operating the scheme of supplementary benefits.

The supplementary pension may be claimed by persons over pension age and the supplementary allowance by persons aged 16 or over but under pension age, who are not in full-time work. The benefit payable is the amount, assessed under the provisions of the Act, by which the claimant's income requirements exceed his resources. The basic weekly rates of supplementary benefit (exclusive of rent) since November 17, 1975, are as follows:

	Ordinary	Blind persons
	£	£
Married couple	17·75	19·00 (a)
Single householder	10·90	
Other persons:—		
Aged 18 or over	8·70	12·15
Aged 16–17	6·70	7·60
Aged 13–15	5·60	5·60
Aged 11–12	4·60	4·60
Aged 5–10	3·75	3·75
Aged under 5	3·10	3·10

(a) £19·80 when both are blind.

The long-term weekly rates, which apply, with certain exceptions, to supplementary pensioners, and also to those below pension age, other than the unemployed who are required to register for work, after they have been in receipt of an allowance for two years, are as follows:

	Ordinary	Blind persons
	£	£
Married couple	21·55	22·80 (a)
Single householder	13·70	
Other persons aged 18 or over	11·00	14·95

(a) £23·60 when both are blind.

Where the claimant or a dependant is aged 80 or over a further 25p is added to these long-term rates. Any extra allowances on account of exceptional expenses, other than for heating and certain other items, will be set off against part of the long-term rates, viz., 50p (75p in the case of those over 80). See as to attendance allowances, p. 612.

The amount to be added for rent if the claimant (or his wife or her husband) is the householder is normally the net rent and rates in full; and in the case of the non-householder aged 16 or over, £1·00 a week.

The rules for the computation of resources contain provisions for the treatment of capital and earnings and for certain disregards.

Persons registering for employment as a condition of receiving a supplementary allowance will not generally receive more than is required to bring their total income to what it would be if they were in full-time work in their normal occupation (the " wage stop ").

Individual awards of benefit are determined

by the Commission; a claimant who is dissatisfied with the decision on his claim has a right of appeal to an independant Appeal Tribunal.

The Commission may vary an assessment if there are exceptional circumstances but, in the case of a claim to supplementary pension, may not reduce it. The Commission also has powers, similar to those in the national assistance scheme, to award lumpsum payments to meet non-recurring exceptional requirements, and to meet charges for appliances or services supplied under the National Health Service, *e.g.* for glasses, dentures or dental treatment, and prescriptions.

The number of supplementary benefits in payment at the end of 1973 was: pensions, 1,844,000; allowances 831,000.

In 1973 assistance amounting to £5,914,000 was given to meet charges under the National Health Service for spectacles, dentures and dental treatment.

OLD PERSONS' PENSIONS

The Social Security Act, 1975, provides, subject to a residence test, a non-contributory retirement pension of £7·90 a week (£4·90 for a married woman) for persons who were over pensionable age on July 5, 1948, and for women whose husbands are so entitled if they are over pension age and have retired from regular work, with increases for adult and child dependants (Category C pension); and for others when they reach 80 if they are not already getting a retirement pension of any category or if they are getting that pension at less than these rates (Category D pension). An *age addition* of 25p per week is payable if persons entitled to retirement pension or their dependants are aged 80 or over.

ATTENDANCE ALLOWANCES

The Act of 1975 provides for the payment out of Exchequer funds of a tax-free and non-means-tested attendance allowance to the severely disabled, as determined by the Attendance Allowance Board. The full rate of £10·60 a week is paid to those in need of a great deal of attention or supervision both by day and by night. The allowance is paid at the lower rate of £7·10 a week to those whose need for attention or supervision arises either by day or by night. The allowance is treated as an additional requirement under the supplementary benefits scheme.

NON-CONTRIBUTORY INVALIDITY PENSION

The Social Security Act, 1975, provides for a non-contributory invalidity pension for persons of working age, other than married women supported by their husbands, who have been incapable of work for a period of at least 28 weeks but who do not qualify for a contributory invalidity pension. The benefit has been payable since November 17, 1975, at the rate of £7·90 a week, with additions for dependants. The cost is met from the Consolidated Fund.

INVALID CARE ALLOWANCE

The Social Security Act, 1975, also provides for a non-contributory invalid care allowance for persons of working age, other than married women supported by their husbands, who are not gainfully employed because they are regularly and substanti-ally engaged in caring for a severely disabled relative who is receiving attendance allowance. The benefit has been payable since November 17, 1975, at the rate of £7·90 a week, with additions for dependants. The cost is met from the Consolidated Fund.

GUARDIAN'S ALLOWANCE

Where the parents of a child are dead, the person who has the child in his family receives a guardian's allowance of £6·50 a week while the child is of qualifying age. The allowance is a non-contributory benefit under the Social Security Act, 1975, and, on certain conditions, is payable on the death of only one parent. The allowance cannot be claimed in addition to family allowance or other benefits for children.

FAMILY ALLOWANCES

The scheme provides for a payment out of moneys provided by Parliament of a weekly allowance for each child in a family other than the elder or eldest. The scheme operates under the Family Allowances Act, 1965, as amended. From April 8, 1975, under the Social Security Benefits Act, 1975, the allowance was increased to provide £1·50 a week for each child after the first, and consequential adjustments were made in dependency benefit for second and subsequent children under the Social Security Act, 1975.

The Ministry of Social Security Act, 1966, transferred the administration of the family allowances scheme from the Ministry of Pensions and National Insurance to the new Ministry of Social Security (now the Department of Health and Social Security). The allowance is payable (through the Post Office) while a child is of school age and up to 19 if he or she is undergoing full-time instruction in a school or is an apprentice. Claim forms for allowances can be obtained at any local Social Security Office. Claims are decided by the adjudication authorities under the Social Security Act, 1975.

FAMILY INCOME SUPPLEMENT

A benefit met out of Exchequer funds is payable under the Family Income Supplements Act, 1970, and regulations made thereunder, to families with at least one dependent child under 16 (or over 16 if still at school), whose total family income is below the " prescribed amount " if the head of the family (in the case of a couple, the man) is employed or self-employed, and normally so engaged, in remunerative full-time work (i.e., 30 or more hours a week). The " prescribed amount " is £31·50 if there is one child in the family and rises by £3·50 for each additional child. " Total income " includes gross earnings, family allowances and a wife's earnings. The supplement is one-half of the amount by which the family's total income falls below the " prescribed amount ", subject, since July 22, 1975, to a maximum payment of £7·00 for families with one child, rising by 50p for each additional child: odd amounts are rounded up to the next 10p above, and the minimum amount payable is 20p a week. Usually the supplement is awarded for 52 weeks and is not affected if the claimant's circumstances change during that time. Claim forms can be obtained at a Social Security Office or a Post Office. Claims are decided by the Supplementary Benefits Commission but there is an appeal to an independent Appeal Tribunal.

NATIONAL INSURANCE CONTRIBUTIONS

From April 6, 1975, when the National Insurance and Industrial Injuries schemes were replaced by a new scheme of social security benefits and contributions under the Social Security Act, 1975, combined weekly flat-rate Class 1 contributions ceased to be payable, and the graduated pension scheme was wound up (existing rights being preserved). Under the new scheme employees and their employers both pay wholly earnings-related contributions, based on a percentage of the employee's earnings (Class 1). Self-employed persons continue to pay flat-rate Class 2 contributions, but may also be liable to pay a contribution (Class 4) based on their profits or gains within certain limits. Class 3 contributions are voluntary, and may be paid to help qualify for certain benefits, including retirement pension. The contribution rates and earnings limits stated below apply for the tax year starting on April 6, 1975.

Class 1 contributions.—Primary Class 1 contributions are payable by employed earners and office holders over minimum school-leaving age with gross earnings at or above the lower earnings limit of £11 a week. For those with gross earnings at or above this level, contributions are payable on *all* earnings up to an upper limit of £69 a week. "Gross earnings" include overtime pay, commission, bonus, etc., without deduction of any superannuation contributions. The standard rate of primary contribution is 5·5 per cent. of reckonable earnings (National Insurance Fund 5·1 per cent.; National Health Service 0·4 per cent.). Married women and most widows who have elected not to pay contributions at the full rate pay at a reduced rate of 2 per cent. over the same earnings range: this covers industrial injuries benefits and a contribution of 0·4 per cent. to the National Health Service. An election or change of election relates to complete tax years. No primary contributions are payable by retirement pensioners when in employment, by persons over pension age with no title to pension, or by men over 70 and women over 65 who continue to work. *Secondary* Class 1 contributions are payable by employers of employed earners, and by the appropriate authorities in the case of office-holders, except in the case of persons earning less than the lower earnings limit of £11 a week. The rate is 8·5 per cent. (National Insurance Fund 7·7 per cent; National Health Service 0·6 per cent; Redundancy Fund 0·2 per cent.) over the same earnings range as primary contributions (regardless of the employed earner's contribution rate). Primary contributions are deducted from earnings by the employer, and are paid, together with the employer's contributions, to the Inland Revenue along with income tax collected under the PAYE system, so dispensing with contribution cards for employed earners.

Class 2 contributions.—These contributions are payable by self-employed earners over school-leaving age at a flat-rate normally of £2·41 a week for men and £2·10 for women. The women's rate is to be raised to the men's rate by 1980. Those with earnings below £675 a year can apply for exception from liability to pay Class 2 contributions for the tax year 1975–76. Married women and most widows can choose whether or not to pay Class 2 contributions when self-employed. An election or change of election relates to complete tax years. No Class 2 contributions are payable by retirement pensioners when self-employed, by persons over pension age with no title to pension, or by men over 70 and women over 65 who continue to work. There are special rules for those who are concurrently employed and self-employed. Class 2 contributions may be paid by direct debit of a bank or National Giro account or by stamping a contribution card. People who while self-employed are excepted from liability to pay contributions on the grounds of small earnings may pay either Class 2 or Class 3 contributions voluntarily. Self-employed earners (whether or not they pay Class 2 contributions) may also be liable to pay Class 4 contributions based on profits or gains within certain limits.

Class 3 contributions.—These are voluntary flat-rate contributions payable by persons over school-leaving age who would otherwise be unable to qualify for retirement pension and certain other benefits because they have an insufficient record of Class 1 or Class 2 contributions. The rate is £1·90 a week. Payment may be made by stamping a contribution card or by direct debit through a bank or Giro account. Married women and widows who have elected not to pay Class 1 (full rate) or Class 2 contributions cannot pay Class 3 contributions.

Class 4 contributions.—These contributions are payable by self-employed earners under 70 (65 for women), whether or not they pay class 2 contributions, on annual profits or gains from a trade, profession or vocation chargeable to income tax under Schedule D, starting with the year of assessment beginning on or after April 6, 1975. The rate of contribution is 8 per cent. (including a contribution of 0·6 per cent. to the National Health Service) of such profits or gains falling between £1,600 and £3,600 a year. The maximum Class 4 contribution, payable on profits or gains of £3,600 or more, is £160. The contribution is based on profits or gains subject to certain allowances and relief, which differ in some respects from those for income tax. Class 4 contributions are generally assessed and collected by the Inland Revenue along with Schedule D income tax. Self-employed persons under 16, or who are over pension age and have retired from regular work or are treated as having retired, or do not qualify for a retirement pension on their own contributions, can apply for exception from liability for Class 4 contributions. There are special rules for people who have more than one job, or who pay Class 1 contributions on earnings which are chargeable to income tax under Schedule D.

Leaflets relating to each class of contribution, and an employer's guide to national insurance contributions, are obtainable from local Social Security offices.

MERCHANT SHIPPING

PRINCIPAL MERCHANT FLEETS OF THE WORLD

Source: Lloyd's Register of Shipping

Flag	1959 No.	1959 Tons Gross	1964 No.	1964 Tons Gross	1969 No.	1969 Tons Gross	1974 No.	1974 Tons Gross
Liberia	1,085	11,936,250	1,117	14,549,645	1,731	29,215,151	2,332	55,321,641
Japan	2,775	6,276,689	5,401	10,813,248	7,665	23,987,079	9,974	38,707,659
United Kingdom	5,395	20,756,535	4,538	21,489,948	3,858	23,843,799	3,603	31,566,298
Norway	2,724	10,444,268	2,732	14,477,112	2,848	19,679,094	2,689	24,852,917
Greece	489	2,150,938	1,290	6,887,624	1,700	8,580,753	2,651	21,759,449
U.S.S.R.	1,455	3,155,054	1,674	6,957,512	5,622	13,704,640	7,342	18,175,918
U.S.A.†	4,196	25,287,972	3,537	22,430,249	3,146	19,550,394	4,086	14,429,076
Panama	639	4,582,539	691	4,269,462	823	5,373,722	1,962	11,003,227
Italy	1,325	5,118,764	1,421	5,707,817	1,552	7,037,846	1,710	9,322,015
France	1,409	4,538,370	1,532	5,516,232	1,432	5,961,963	1,341	8,834,519
Germany, Fed. Rep. of	2,501	4,534,441	2,504	5,159,186	2,768	7,027,384	2,088	7,980,453
Sweden	1,210	3,623,423	1,367	4,306,042	1,051	5,029,407	785	6,226,659
Netherlands	1,950	4,743,123	1,889	5,110,022	1,652	5,254,883	1,358	5,500,932
Spain	1,394	1,711,818	1,741	2,047,715	2,119	3,199,035	2,520	4,949,146
Denmark	787	2,204,283	901	2,431,020	1,194	3,490,334	1,349	4,460,219
India	238	749,711	347	1,448,237	397	2,238,344	451	3,484,751
Cyprus	2	905	4	17,435	134	770,463	722	3,304,880
Singapore	124	124,355	Not Recorded		112	233,271	511	2,898,327
Canada	1,079	1,501,025	1,132	1,823,387	1,278	2,433,944	1,231	2,459,998
Brazil	415	952,088	421	1,271,108	414	1,381,458	471	2,428,972
Poland	233	533,895	384	988,382	484	1,535,384	648	2,292,318
Somali Republic**	—	—	4	8,864	58	295,049	276	1,916,273
China, People's Rep. of	262	623,435	216	535,427	237	791,893	360	1,870,567
Yugoslavia	207	495,009	350	966,521	349	1,427,935	398	1,778,423
Finland	337	744,491	411	964,275	388	1,330,488	362	1,597,582
Taiwan	Not Recorded		117	588,355	216	961,807	407	1,416,833
Argentina	358	1,039,307	318	1,284,397	319	1,217,646	366	1,408,129
Portugal	332	579,911	341	701,676	364	825,355	431	1,243,128
Korea (South)	37	103,316	59	122,254	294	767,315	650	1,245,079
German Democratic Rep.	Not Recorded		249	502,240	371	895,932	431	1,223,859
Belgium	212	728,316	213	796,133	228	1,051,882	251	1,214,707
Australia	351	663,885	292	593,700	321	893,613	394	1,166,367
Bermuda	9	59,519	24	167,551	29	354,923	54	1,153,280
WORLD TOTAL	36,221	124,935,479	40,859	152,999,621	50,276	211,660,893	61,194	311,322,626

* Information incomplete.   ** Independence established in 1960.   † Including ships of the United States Reserve Fleet.

TONNAGE CLASSED WITH LLOYD'S REGISTER

At July 1974, 29·7 per cent (92,562,141 tons) of the tonnage owned in the world was classed by Lloyd's Register.

MERCHANT SHIPPING

STEAMSHIPS AND MOTORSHIPS COMPLETED IN THE WORLD* DURING 1974

Source: *Lloyd's Register of Shipping*

Country of Build	Steamships No.	Steamships Tons Gross	Motorships No.	Motorships Tons Gross	Total No.	Total Tons Gross
Japan	67	8,320,040	978	8,573,977	1,045	16,894,017
Sweden	8	1,020,293	32	1,160,926	40	2,181,219
Germany, Federal Rep. of	11	1,319,235	117	822,588	128	2,141,823
Spain	3	452,071	227	1,109,025	230	1,561,096
United Kingdom	3	407,814	113	790,441	116	1,198,255
Denmark	5	752,662	58	323,788	63	1,076,450
France	7	767,289	47	278,848	54	1,046,137
Norway	4	497,765	125	465,966	129	963,731
Italy	7	573,475	47	379,692	54	953,167
Netherlands	6	736,583	121	205,264	127	941,847
U.S.A.	14	570,922	219	162,500	233	733,422
Yugoslavia	..	..	20	719,943	20	719,943
Poland	..	..	90	509,010	90	509,010
†U.S.S.R.	1	75,000	145	318,536	146	393,536
German Democratic Republic	..	..	54	331,982	54	331,982
Korea (South)	2	249,448	47	63,499	49	312,947
Belgium	..	..	17	256,150	17	256,150
Finland	..	..	26	192,332	26	192,332
Canada	..	..	45	184,843	45	184,843
Brazil	..	..	25	164,039	25	164,039
Taiwan	..	..	5	152,883	5	152,883
Greece	..	..	25	143,751	25	143,751
Bulgaria	..	..	8	107,401	8	107,401
Australia	..	..	35	73,073	35	73,073
†Rumania	..	..	17	64,286	17	64,286
Singapore	..	..	51	48,505	51	48,505
Peru	..	..	9	33,337	9	33,337
Portugal	..	..	11	31,117	11	31,117
India	..	..	6	29,973	6	29,973
Argentina	..	..	3	29,538	3	29,538
Other Countries	..	..	76	68,149	76	68,149
Other Commonwealth Countries	..	..	12	3,330	12	3,330
WORLD TOTAL	138	15,742,597	2,811	17,798,692	2,949	33,541,289

For Registration in	Total Steamships and Motorships No.	Total Steamships and Motorships Tons Gross
Liberia	175	8,214,024
United Kingdom	162	3,813,362
Norway	124	3,012,886
Japan	518	2,849,586
France	76	1,647,072
Panama	202	1,441,191
Sweden	48	1,421,864
Germany, Federal Rep. of	68	1,344,264
Greece	72	1,118,963
U.S.S.R.	254	898,946
Italy	45	887,669
U.S.A.	204	724,088
Singapore	52	641,313
Denmark	93	635,278
Spain	185	578,242
Brazil	18	548,381
India	21	493,613
Poland	45	424,906
Bermuda	5	310,974
Netherlands	71	251,684
Korea (South)	61	227,308
Rumania	19	223,400
Belgium	12	186,176
Finland	8	161,561
Libya	6	149,835
China, People's Rep. of	38	144,890
Turkey	30	107,530
Yugoslavia	7	98,809
Canada	42	95,439
Portugal	22	89,305
Other Countries	192	680,410
Other Commonwealth C.	74	119,320
WORLD TOTAL	2,949	33,541,289

Tonnage completed to Lloyd's Register Class.—Of the world tonnage completed during 1974, 27.9 per cent. (9,366,369 tons) was to Lloyd's Register Class. * Excluding People's Republic of China. † Information incomplete.

THE LARGEST SHIPS IN SERVICE
As recorded by Lloyd's Register at December 1974

NAME	Propulsion	Flag	Tons Gross	Length Overall	Breadth Extreme	Draught Summer	Year Built	Owners
*Oil Tankers, etc.**								
Globtik Tokyo	Tb	U.K.	238,252	1243·0	203·6	92·5	1973	Globtik Tankers Ltd.
Globtik London	Tb	U.K.	238,207	1243·0	203·6	92·5	1973	Globtik Tankers Ltd.
Nisseki Maru	Tb	Japan	184,855	1138·6	178·8	88·6	1971	Tokyo Tanker K.K.
Kristine Maersk	Tb	Denmark	167,204	1215·4	185·2	73·6	1974	A. P. Möller
Arteaga	Tb	Spain	163,795	1139·0	175·0	81·5	1972	Petronor S.A.
Butron	Tb	Spain	163,795	1139·0	175·0	81·5	1973	Petronor S.A.
Lagena	Tb	Germany Fed. Rep.	162,026	1153·2	181·9	73·4	1974	Deutsche Shell A.G.
Venpet	Tb	Liberia	152,372	1115·5	175·9	80·7	1973	Venpet Inc.
†Venoll	Tb	Liberia	152,327	1115·5	175·9	80·7	1973	Venoll Inc.
†Svealand	Oe	Sweden	152,068	1108·0	184·0	71·0	1973	Angf. A/B Tirfing
Universe Iran	Tb	Liberia	149,623	1132·8	175·2	81·4	1969	Bantry Transportation Co.
Universe Japan	Tb	Liberia	149,623	1132·8	175·2	81·4	1969	Bantry Transportation Co.
Universe Korea	Tb	Liberia	149,623	1132·8	173·2	81·4	1969	Bantry Transportation Co.
Universe Portugal	Tb	Liberia	149,623	1132·8	175·2	81·4	1969	Bantry Transportation Co.
Universe Ireland	Tb	Liberia	149,609	1132·8	175·2	81·4	1968	Bantry Transportation Co.
Universe Kuwait	Tb	Liberia	149,609	1132·8	175·2	81·4	1968	Bantry Transportation Co.
†Lauderdale	Tb	U.K.	143,959	1101·2	176·0	67·6	1972	P. & O. Steam Nav. Co.
†Nordic Conqueror	Tb	U.K.	143,959	1101·2	176·0	67·6	1972	P. & O. Steam Nav. Co.
Adele	Tb	Liberia	143,686	1140·0	170·0	72·9	1971	Adele Nav. Corp.
Richard Maersk	Tb	Denmark	143,686	1140·0	170·1	72·9	1972	A. P. Möller
Romo Maersk	Tb	Denmark	143,686	1140·0	170·1	72·9	1973	A. P. Möller
Roy Maersk	Tb	Denmark	143,686	1140·0	170·1	72·9	1972	A. P. Möller
Regina Maersk	Tb	Denmark	143,686	1140·0	170·1	72·9	1971	A. P. Möller
Passenger Liners								
France	Tb	France	68,348	1035·2	110·9	34·4	1961	Cie. Générale Transatlantique
Queen Elizabeth 2	Tb	U.K.	65,863	963·0	105·2	32·6	1969	Cunard Line Ltd.
Raffaello	Tb	Italy	45,933	904·6	101·8	30·6	1965	"Italia" Soc. per Azioni di Nav.
Michelangelo	Tb	Italy	45,911	904·9	101·8	30·6	1965	"Italia" Soc. per Azioni di Nav.
Canberra	Te	U.K.	44,807	818·5	102·5	32·7	1961	P. & O. Steam Nav. Co.
Oriana	Tb	U.K.	41,910	804·0	97·2	32·0	1960	P. & O. Steam Nav. Co.
United States	Tb	U.S.A.	38,216	990·0	101·6	31·0	1952	United States Lines Co.
Rotterdam	Tb	Netherlands	37,783	748·6	94·2	29·7	1959	N.V. Nederl.-Amerika Stoomv. Maats.
Windsor Castle	Tb	U.K.	36,277	783·1	92·5	32·1	1960	Union Castle Mail S.S. Co. Ltd.

* All oil tankers unless otherwise stated. † Ore/oil carrier. Oe= Oil engine Tb= Turbine engines. Te= Turbo-electric.

UNITED KINGDOM REVENUE AND EXPENDITURE

Consolidated Fund : revenue
(Years ended March 31)

£ million

	1969–70	1970–71	1971–72	1972–73	1973–74
TAXATION					
INLAND REVENUE: Total	7,476·1	8,174·6	9,133·7	9,245·4	10,633·3
Income Tax	4,899·9	5,728·3	6,449·0	6,475·3	7,135·8
Surtax	255·4	240·3	349·1	340·9	307·3
Profits Tax	2·1	2·3	2·0	0·8	1·0
Corporation Tax.............	1,686·5	1,589·0	1,557·6	1,532·7	2,262·2
Capital Gains Tax...........	126·8	138·8	155·5	208·4	323·6
Death Duties................	365·5	356·3	452·4	458·5	412·2
Stamp Duties................	120·2	116·2	166·3	227·6	190·3
Special Charge..............	19·7	3·4	1·8	1·2	0·9
CUSTOMS AND EXCISE: Total.....	4,952·5	4,709·1	5,325·3	5,743·5	6,219·6
Beer.......................	450·5	466·9	480·0	491·7	365·1
Wines and spirits...........	413·2	464·2	524·0	581·8	588·3
Tobacco....................	1,143·0	1,139·8	1,124·0	1,182·6	1,084·9
Hydrocarbon Oils...........	1,310·7	1,395·2	1,439·0	1,553·2	1,585·1
Protective Duties............	226·2	262·8	269·3	348·5	437·1
Purchase Tax................	1,111·6	1,270·7	1,429·0	1,387·4	379·5
Agricultural Levies..........	—	—	—	4·1	25·4
Betting....................	119·1	130·4	155·0	171·3	185·4
Temporary Charge on Imports.	1·1	—	—	—	—
Import Levies...............	—	—	6·0	16·0	—
V.A.T......................	—	—	—	—	1,447·4
Car Tax....................	—	—	—	—	117·7
Other......................	1·3	2·6	11·0	11·2	9·3
Import Deposits.............	188·2	423·5	112·0	—	—
less Export rebates..........	10·2	—	—	4·3	5·6
MOTOR VEHICLE DUTIES........	416·7	421·2	473·3	485·0	533·5
SELECTIVE EMPLOYMENT TAX.....	1,888·1	1,989·6	1,323·7	993·5	45·0
Total taxation............	14,733·4	15,294·5	16,256·0	16,467·4	17,431·4
MISCELLANEOUS RECEIPTS:					
Interest and Dividends........	92·4	99·6	100·5	99·4	106·5
Broadcast receiving licences....	101·2	100·7	122·0	136·4	152·9
Other.......................	339·6	348·0	453·3	474·9	535·6
Total revenue...........	15,266·6	15,842·8	16,931·8	17,178·1	18,226·4

Consolidated Fund: expenditure
(Years ended March 31)

£ million

	1969–70	1970–71	1971–72	1972–73	1973–74
SUPPLY SERVICES................	12,016·4	13,447·8	14,817·8	16,617·5	18,624·2
CONSOLIDATED FUND STANDING SERVICES:					
National Loans Fund in respect of service of the National Debt	512·8	324·7	333·5	543·6	676·7
Northern Ireland—share of Taxes, etc..................	251·9	277·2	341·6	357·7	349·5
Payments to European Communities, etc...............	—	—	—	37·9	219·3
Contingencies Fund...........	8·0	7·0	26·0	14·0	63·0
OTHER SERVICES:					
War Damage Payments.....	1·0	0·5	0·2	—	—
Repayment of post-war Credits.................	18·0	14·1	18·0	132·6	14·8
Miscellaneous...............	14·0	15·0	11·7	13·8	17·8
Total expenditure........	12,822·1	14,086·3	15,548·8	17,689·1	19,965·3

BRITAIN'S OVERSEAS TRADE

IMPORTS: Section and Division	1973	1974	1975 1st quarter	February	March
	£million	£ million	£ million	£ million	£ million
Food and live animals—	2,710·3	3,372·1	932·2	289·8	272·1
Live animals...........................	80·2	76·9	20·0	7·5	6·0
Meat and meat preparations..............	715·8	681·4	153·9	53·0	41·3
Dairy products and eggs.................	225·1	338·7	109·1	28·4	28·2
Fish and fish preparations...............	132·1	122·1	30·7	9·7	7·6
Cereals and cereal preparations..........	369·8	593·0	136·4	46·5	41·5
Fruit and vegetables....................	561·3	660·7	161·3	49·1	49·8
Sugar, sugar preparations and honey......	174·6	368·9	183·7	47·2	64·9
Coffee, cocoa and preparations, tea and spices	248·6	322·4	89·5	32·7	20·6
Feeding stuffs for animals................	153·6	126·8	23·2	7·7	4·9
Miscellaneous food preparations..........	49·1	81·1	24·4	8·0	7·4
1. *Beverages and tobacco—*.................	383·5	407·0	89·2	30·1	27·7
Beverages.............................	229·8	221·6	41·4	13·0	12·6
Tobacco	153·7	185·4	47·8	17·1	15·1
2. *Crude materials, inedible—*..............	1,833·6	2,364·0	510·6	165·7	142·0
Hides, skins, and furskins, undressed.....	112·5	106·4	29·3	9·3	7·4
Oil seeds, oil nuts and oil kernels........	104·0	142·5	39·5	10·5	14·7
Crude rubber (including synthetic and reclaimed).............................	74·8	100·4	22·2	7·1	6·2
Wood, lumber and cork.................	458·1	589·6	68·8	19·0	17·2
Pulp and waste paper...................	201·0	329·9	100·7	35·7	25·9
Textile fibres, not manufactured and their waste...............................	322·2	310·5	56·1	17·4	18·3
Crude fertilizers and minerals............	80·9	141·3	36·8	11·1	10·7
Metalliferous ores and metal scrap........	389·1	533·5	125·8	46·0	33·0
Crude animal and vegetable materials.....	91·0	110·0	31·5	9·9	8·5
3. *Mineral fuels, lubricants, etc—*...........	1,723·7	4,626·9	1,093·6	354·2	291·9
Petroleum and petroleum products.......	1,678·3	4,533·3	1,058·4	341·7	283·0
4. *Animal and vegetable oils and fats—*.......	129·4	216·2	44·8	10·6	13·0
5. *Chemicals—*...........................	896·6	1,583·7	360·1	112·4	105·8
Chemical elements and compounds.......	360·4	716·8	178·8	57·2	51·7
Essential oils and perfume materials.......	51·5	76·2	16·9	4·7	6·4
Plastic materials and artificial resins.......	204·7	361·1	58·2	18·2	17·3
All other..............................	280·0	429·6	106·2	32·4	30·4
Manufactured goods classified chiefly by materials—	3,379·8	4,789·3	1,173·1	374·1	387·2
Leather, leather manufactures and dressed furs.................................	67·4	60·5	16·1	5·8	5·0
Rubber manufactures...................	57·1	87·7	22·1	7·5	6·7
Wood and cork manufactures............	244·4	232·2	42·4	13·6	13·3
Paper, paperboard and manufactures thereof	401·9	725·9	170·2	53·7	45·3
Textile yarn, fabrics and articles.........	514·6	688·2	166·8	52·3	50·8
Non-metallic mineral manufactures.......	855·2	982·6	238·7	73·2	97·0
Iron and steel.........................	373·3	717·0	242·7	86·1	74·9
Non-ferrous metals.....................	660·6	1,008·6	196·5	57·1	68·4
Other metal manufactures	205·2	286·7	77·7	24·9	25·8
7. *Machinery and transport equipment—*.......	3,292·8	3,901·7	1,083·6	359·9	345·9
Machinery other than electric............	1,526·2	1,959·2	541·3	174·3	174·3
Electrical machinery, apparatus and appliances............................	847·4	1,010·0	246·5	79·9	78·6
Transport equipment...................	919·2	932·5	295·7	105·7	92·9
8. *Miscellaneous manufactured articles—*	1,338·8	1,652·9	429·4	140·7	138·2
Furniture.............................	62·9	70·2	20·4	6·9	7·0
Clothing..............................	333·2	402·4	111·0	36·6	37·1
Footwear.............................	84·3	109·3	39·2	12·9	11·6
Professional, scientific and controlling instruments; photographic and optical goods;	281·7	377·7	103·0	34·1	33·1
Other.................................	576·7	693·4	155·8	50·2	49·4
5–8. *Manufactured goods—*.................	8,908·0	11,927·7	3,046·2	987·2	977·1
9. *Commodities and transactions not classified according to kind*..	151·2	202·8	90·8	33·5	24·8
Total United Kingdom imports..............	15,839·8	23,116·7	5,807·3	1,871·2	1,748·5

BRITAIN'S OVERSEAS TRADE—*continued*

EXPORTS: Section and Division	1973	1974	1975 1st quarter	February	March
Food and live animals—.................	512·1	611·0	205·0	56·8	83·9
Live animals........................	58·8	45·4	11·9	3·8	3·8
Meat and meat preparations.............	79·9	80·1	29·0	8·3	10·7
Dairy products and eggs...............	44·4	41·0	12·1	3·2	4·3
Fish and fish preparations.............	43·1	51·8	13·4	4·9	4·4
Cereals and cereal preparations..........	54·5	76·8	31·0	9·4	12·1
Fruit and vegetables..................	43·3	52·8	18·8	6·4	5·7
Sugar, sugar preparations and honey......	61·5	94·8	43·0	5·1	28·8
Coffee, cocoa preparations, tea and spices..	61·3	91·8	25·8	9·0	6·9
Other food and food preparations........	65·1	76·4	20·1	6·8	7·2
1. *Beverages and tobacco—*................	363·5	452·9	121·9	39·8	42·3
Beverages..........................	305·4	384·1	97·6	31·1	33·8
Tobacco............................	58·1	68·9	24·2	8·6	8·4
2. *Crude materials, inedible—*.............	416·3	545·4	130·3	44·9	42·2
Hides, skins and furskins, undressed......	80·7	91·7	28·8	8·3	9·8
Crude rubber (including synthetic and re-claimed)...........................	37·9	53·7	9·9	3·3	3·0
Textile fibres, not manufactured and their waste.............................	172·1	201·8	43·2	17·2	14·9
Crude fertilizers and minerals...........	60·2	79·5	19·7	6·6	5·5
Metalliferous ores and metal scrap........	36·1	72·7	18·2	5·9	5·8
Other crude materials.................	29·4	46·0	10·6	3·7	3·2
3. *Mineral fuels, lubricants, etc.—*..........	370·1	767·7	201·2	70·8	56·0
Petroleum and petroleum products........	340·6	696·1	168·5	60·2	45·3
Coal, coke, gas and electric energy.......	29·5	71·7	32·7	10·6	10·7
4. *Animal and vegetable oils and fats—*........	17·1	31·5	8·1	2·4	2·4
5. *Chemicals—*........................	1,272·3	2,146·3	540·1	173·9	174·2
Chemical elements and compounds.......	364·4	733·6	156·6	52·9	44·1
Dyeing, tanning and colouring materials...	140·5	213·8	50·8	19·0	14·3
Medicinal and pharmaceutical products ...	221·2	301·6	86·1	26·9	29·7
Essential oils and perfume materials.......	96·8	145·6	39·4	12·6	13·5
Plastic materials and artificial resins.......	225·2	366·8	86·9	28·6	26·7
All other...........................	224·2	384·9	120·3	33·9	45·8
6. *Manufactured goods classified chiefly by materials—*........................	3,258·8	4,005·3	988·5	324·8	331·7
Leather manufactures and dressed furs.....	83·8	94·5	21·7	7·6	6·1
Rubber manufactures, not elsewhere specified...........................	121·2	166·7	48·8	15·8	17·2
Wood and cork manufactures............	15·5	25·3	5·8	1·9	2·0
Paper, paperboard and manufactures thereof	128·8	199·3	50·1	16·3	16·3
Textile yarn, fabrics and articles..........	589·5	745·8	165·1	53·8	53·7
Non-metallic mineral manufactures.......	1,010·1	1,060·4	237·9	80·5	88·0
Iron and steel.......................	433·2	553·5	178·7	58·1	59·7
Non-ferrous metals...................	537·8	689·4	138·0	43·2	43·5
Other metal manufactures	338·9	470·6	142·4	47·6	45·1
7. *Machinery and transport equipment—*.......	4,774·2	6,052·3	1,856·3	601·2	608·2
Machinery other than electric...........	2,413·2	3,081·3	951·7	304·3	314·9
Electric machinery, apparatus and appliances	807·3	1,131·7	357·8	113·4	114·2
Transport equipment..................	1,553·6	1,839·2	546·7	183·5	179·0
8. *Miscellaneous manufactured articles—*.......	1,149·8	1,480·6	395·5	128·2	137·1
Sanitary, plumbing, heating and lighting fittings............................	28·5	43·7	12·6	4·1	4·2
Furniture..........................	44·2	69·5	20·3	6·3	7·6
Clothing...........................	179·6	230·0	52·5	17·5	19·2
Footwear...........................	35·6	47·3	13·0	4·8	4·5
Professional, scientific and controlling instruments, photographic and optical goods, watches and clocks...................	343·8	424·2	121·4	40·1	40·6
Other..............................	518·2	665·9	175·7	55·5	61·1
5–8. *Manufactured goods—*................	10,455·0	13,684·5	3,780·4	1,228·1	1,251·2
9. *Commodities and transactions not classified according to kind*.....................	320·2	401·2	112·5	33·0	39·6
Total United Kingdom exports.............	12,454·3	16,494·3	4,559·1	1,475·7	1,517·5

BRITISH RAILWAY FARES, 1953-1975

The following table shows rail fares for 12 specimen journeys in 1953, in certain other years when a change was made, and the fares current in October, 1975. The fares are 2nd class ordinary returns.

LONDON TO:—	JANUARY				OCTOBER							
	1953	1961	1962	1964	1968	1969	1970	1971	1972	1973	1974	1975
	s. d.	s. d.	s. d.	s. d.	s. d.	s. d.	s. d.	£	£	£	£	£
Birmingham (New St.).....	32 6	47 0	51 0	55 6	64 0	68 0	76 0	4·50	5·10	5·40	6·19	9·25
Bournemouth....	31 6	45 0	50 0	54 0	60 0	60 0	72 0	4·20	4·70	4·90	5·54	8·20
Brighton........	15 0	21 6	23 6	25 6	30 0	30 0	34 0	2·00	2·30	2·40	2·70	4·00
Bristol..........	34 6	50 0	55 0	59 0	65 0	65 0	70 0	4·10	4·55	4·80	5·40	8·08
Edinburgh (Waverley)....	114 8	142 0	142 0	162 0	208 0	208 0	228 0	12·90	14·50	15·20	17·08	25·60
Glasgow (*via* Carlisle)...	117 4	144 0	144 0	168 0	208 0	208 0	228 0	12·90	14·50	15·20	17·08	25·60
Liverpool.......	56 8	81 0	89 0	97 0	116 0	120 0	132 0	7·80	8·80	9·20	10·23	15·45
Manchester.....	53 8	77 0	85 0	92 0	110 0	116 0	128 0	7·55	8·50	8·90	10·23	15·45
Norwich........	33 8	46 0	53 0	57 0	66 0	70 0	76 0	4·40	4·80	5·00	5·63	8·50
Oxford.........	18 8	27 0	29 6	32 0	35 0	36 0	39 0	2·25	2·55	2·70	3·04	4·40
Sheffield........	46 6	67 0	73 0	79 6	88 0	90 0	98 0	5·90	6·70	7·00	7·88	11·70
York...........	55 2	79 0	87 0	94 6	110 0	114 0	122 0	7·10	8·10	8·50	9·41	14·09

LONDON SUBURBAN RAIL AND COACH FARES
London Underground Railway Return Fares

Specimen Journey	JANUARY				OCTOBER							
	1953	1960	1963	1964	1967	1968	1969	1970	1971	1972	1974	1975
	s. d.	s. d.	s. d.	s. d.	s. d.	s. d.	s. d.	s. d.	£	£	£	£
Tottenham Court Rd.-Morden.......	2 0	3 6	4 0	4 8	5 6	5 6	6 0	8 0	0·40	0·50	0·50	0·60
Liverpool Street-Ealing Broadway..........	2 4	3 10	4 4	5 0	5 10	6 0	7 0	8 0	0·40	0·50	0·50	0·70
Tower Hill-Putney Br.....	1 10	2 10	3 4	3 10	4 6	4 6	5 0	6 0	0·30	0·40	0·40	0·60
Piccadilly Circus-Cockfosters....	2 6	4 0	4 8	5 4	6 2	6 6	7 0	8 0	0·40	0·50	0·50	0·70

Southern Region of British Railways 2nd Class Return Fares

Specimen Journey	JANUARY				OCTOBER							
	1953	1961	1962	1964	1968	1969	1970	1971	1972	1973	1974	1975
	s. d.	s. d.	s. d.	s. d.	s. d.	s. d.	s. d.	£	£	£	£	£
Charing Cross-Orpington....	4 2	5 10	6 6	7 0	7 8	7 8	7 2	0·44	0·50	0·52	0·58	0·86
Waterloo-Esher..	4 2	6 4	7 0	7 6	8 2	8 2	8 10	0·52	0·60	0·62	0·70	1·04
Victoria-Sanderstead....	3 10	5 6	6 0	6 6	7 4	7 2	8 0	0·48	0·54	0·56	0·62	0·94
Charing Cross-Bexleyheath...	3 10	5 6	6 0	6 6	7 4	7 2	6 10	0·40	0·46	0·48	0·52	0·80

Green Line Coach Return Fares

Specimen Journey	JANUARY				OCTOBER							
	1953	1960	1963	1964	1968	1969	1970	1971	1972	1973	1974	1975
	s. d.	s. d.	s. d.	s. d.	s. d.	s. d.	s. d.	£	£	£	£	£
Hyde Park Corner-Bromley South Station..	3 6	4 8	5 4	6 0	7 0	8 0	8 0	0·50	0·50	0·50	0·45	0·60
Marble Arch-Purley........	3 10	5 0	5 8	6 4	7 6	8 0	8 0	0·50	0·50	0·50	0·50	0·60
Marble Arch-Enfield Town..	3 0	4 0	4 8	5 4	6 6	7 0	7 2	0·40	0·50	0·50	0·45	0·60
Aldgate-Romford Market Place..	3 4	4 4	5 0	5 8	7 0	7 0	7 0	0·50	0·50	0·50	0·45	0·60

THE UNITED KINGDOM

Area.—The land area of the United Kingdom (England, Wales, Scotland and N. Ireland) is 93,026 sq. miles or 59,537,000 acres. The area of inland water* in the United Kingdom is 1,190 sq. miles. Total 94,216 sq. miles.

	Land Area		Inland water*	Total
	Sq. miles	'ooo acres	Sq. miles	Sq. miles
England........................	50,053	32,034	280	50,334
Wales..........................	7,969	5,100	48	8,016
Scotland.......................	29,798	19,071	616	30,414
Northern Ireland...............	5,206	3,332	246	5,452

*Excluding tidal water

POPULATION: CENSUS RESULTS, 1801–1971

Thousands

	United Kingdom			England and Wales			Scotland			Northern Ireland†		
	Total	Male	Female	Total	Male	Female	Total	Male	Female	Total	Male	Female
1801	11,944	5,692	6,252	8,893	4,255	4,638	1,608	739	869	1,443	698	745
1811	13,368	6,368	7,000	10,165	4,874	5,291	1,806	826	980	1,397	668	729
1821	15,472	7,498	7,974	12,000	5,850	6,150	2,092	983	1,109	1,380	665	715
1831	17,835	8,647	9,188	13,897	6,771	7,126	2,364	1,114	1,250	1,574	762	812
1841	20,183	9,819	10,364	15,914	7,778	8,137	2,620	1,242	1,378	1,649	800	849
1851	22,259	10,855	11,404	17,928	8,781	9,146	2,889	1,376	1,513	1,443	698	745
1861	24,525	11,894	12,631	20,066	9,776	10,290	3,062	1,450	1,612	1,396	668	728
1871	27,431	13,309	14,122	22,712	11,059	11,653	3,360	1,603	1,757	1,359	647	712
1881	31,015	15,060	15,955	25,974	12,640	13,335	3,736	1,799	1,936	1,305	621	684
1891	34,264	16,593	17,671	29,003	14,060	14,942	4,026	1,943	2,083	1,236	590	646
1901	38,237	18,492	19,745	32,528	15,729	16,799	4,472	2,174	2,298	1,237	590	647
1911	42,082	20,357	21,725	36,070	17,446	18,625	4,761	2,309	2,452	1,251	603	648
1921	44,027	21,033	22,994	37,887	18,075	19,811	4,882	2,348	2,535	*1,258*	*610*	*648*
1931	46,038	22,060	23,978	39,952	19,133	20,819	4,843	2,326	2,517	*1,243*	*601*	*642*
1951	50,225	24,118	26,107	43,758	21,016	22,742	5,096	2,434	2,662	1,371	668	703
1961	52,709	25,481	27,228	46,105	22,304	23,801	5,179	2,483	2,697	1,425	694	731
1971	55,515	26,952	28,562	48,750	23,683	25,067	5,229	2,515	2,714	1,536	755	781

NOTES.—1. Before 1801 there existed no official return of the population of either England or Scotland. Estimates of the population of England at various periods, calculated from the number of baptisms, burials and marriages, are: in 1570, 4,160,221; 1600, 4,811,718; 1630, 5,600,517; 1670, 5,773,646; 1700, 6,045,008; 1750, 6,517,035.

2. The last official Census of Population in respect of England and Wales, Scotland, Northern Ireland, the Isle of Man and Guernsey, was taken on the night of April 25, 1971, and in respect of Jersey on April 4, 1971. The figures for 1971 are based on the final results of the 1971 Census.

3.†All figures refer to the area which is now Northern Ireland. Figures for N. Ireland in 1921 and 1931 are estimates based on the Censuses held in 1926 and 1937.

ISLANDS.—*The figures given above do not include islands of the British seas.* Populations of these islands at census years since 1900 were:—

	ISLE OF MAN			JERSEY			GUERNSEY		
	Total	Male	Female	Total	Male	Female	Total	Male	Female
1901............	54,752	25,496	29,256	52,576	23,940	28,636	43,042	21,140	21,902
1911............	52,016	23,937	28,079	51,898	24,014	27,884	45,001	22,215	22,786
1921............	60,284	27,329	32,955	49,701	22,438	27,263	40,529	19,303	21,226
1931............	49,308	22,443	26,865	50,462	23,424	27,038	42,743	20,675	22,068
1951............	55,123	25,749	29,464	57,296	27,282	30,014	45,747	22,094	23,380
1961............	48,151	22,060	26,091	57,200	27,200	30,000	47,198	22,890	24,288
1971............	56,289	26,461	29,828	72,532	35,423	37,109	52,708	25,382	27.326

INCREASE OF THE PEOPLE

Mid-year estimates of the future total population of the United Kingdom are based on estimates by the Registrars General of the total population at mid-1973. The projections have been prepared by the Government Actuary's Department in consultation with the Registrars General. It is assumed in their projections below that, at ages under 60 for males and 70 for females, death rates will decline over the period of the projection until after 40 years, they are three-quarters of present rates. Above these ages the assumed improvement becomes proportionately smaller as age advances until they vanish at ages over 90. Annual live births implied in the projections are 751,000 in mid-1973/74, 735,000 in 1974/75 and 732,000 in 1975/76 followed by a gradual increase in birth and fertility rates until 1983/84 when the number of births reaches 914,000. The projection for 2001/02 is 845,000 and for 2012/ 2013 is 950,000. The ratio of male to female births is taken as 1·06 (N. Ireland 1·07) throughout and allowance has been made for a net outward migration of 19,000 in 1973/74 rising to 50,000 a year from 1978 onwards.

Estimated Future Population of the U.K.
Thousands

1973 (base).56,021	1991 .57,988	2011...60,754	
1981.......56,302	2001 .59,368		

LOCAL GOVERNMENT IN ENGLAND AND WALES

The Local Government Act, 1972 provided for the reorganisation of local government in England (outside Greater London whose local government was reorganised in 1965) and Wales. On April 1, 1974 the former county, county borough, and county district councils were abolished. Two tiers of new local authorities, county and district councils, covering metropolitan and non-metropolitan counties and districts, replaced them.

Structure and Areas in England

Six *metropolitan counties* cover the main conurbations outside Greater London: Tyne and Wear, West Midlands, Merseyside, Greater Manchester, West Yorkshire and South Yorkshire. They range in population from 1,200,000 (Tyne and Wear) to 2,800,000 (West Midlands). Each metropolitan county extends to the edge of the general continuously built-up area of the conurbation. Thus each of the major conurbations outside London has now one local authority to administer strategic functions over the whole conurbation.

The six metropolitan counties are divided into 36 *metropolitan districts*. These range in population from 173,000 (South Tyneside) to 1,100,000 (Birmingham). Most of them have a population of over 200,000 and most include a former county borough. They form compact areas.

There are 39 *non-metropolitan counties* ranging in population from 110,000 (Isle of Wight) and 283,000 (Northumberland) to 1,400,000 (Kent). These counties have generally been formed by combining former administrative counties and associated county boroughs, i.e. they are based on geographical counties. There are, however, three completely new non-metropolitan counties: Avon, Cleveland, and Humberside. Some former counties have been merged to form Cumbria (Cumberland, Westmorland and the Furness area of Lancashire); Hereford and Worcester; Cambridgeshire (Huntingdon and Peterborough and Cambridgeshire and Isle of Ely); and Leicestershire (Leicestershire and Rutland). Smaller boundary adjustments have been made between, e.g. Berkshire and Oxfordshire, Buckinghamshire and Berkshire, and Hampshire and Dorset.

Each of the non-metropolitan counties is divided into *non-metropolitan districts*, of which there are 296. These districts have been formed generally by the amalgamation of former county districts to cover areas with populations broadly between 60,000 and 100,000. About one third of the non-metropolitan districts, however, have populations above this range because of the need to avoid dividing large towns. Some districts, mainly in sparsely populated areas, have populations below 60,000 though only 14 have populations below 40,000 (as compared with three quarters of the 1,210 former authorities).

Permanent Local Government Boundary Commissions for England and Wales have been set up to keep the areas and electoral arrangements of the new local authorities under review.

Constitution and Elections

The new county and district councils consist of directly elected councillors. The broad range of sizes of councils are: county councils 60–100 members; metropolitan district councils 50–80 members; non-metropolitan district councils 30–60 members. The councillors elect annually one of their number as chairman. There are no aldermen under the new system, though councils may give past councillors the title " honorary alderman ". The title carries no right to sit on the council.

All the new authorities were elected *en bloc* in 1973 (as " shadow " authorities until they took on their functions on April 1, 1974). After a transitional period all councillors will be elected for a term of four years. All county councils will be elected *en bloc* in 1977 and every four years thereafter. One third of the councillors for each ward of each metropolitan district will be elected from 1975 in each of the three years between county council elections. Non-metropolitan district councils can choose whether to have elections on the county council or metropolitan district council basis. Most of their electoral areas will need revision and the next elections will therefore be held in 1976 on a whole council basis. If they choose whole council elections these will be held in the mid-year between county council elections. If they choose elections by thirds, for geographical reasons it may not be practicable to arrange for elections by thirds in every ward. Local elections will normally be held on the first Thursday in May.

Greater London (See below) is not affected by reorganisation. Elections to local authorities in Greater London are, however, to be brought into line with the rest of England so that the normal term of office for councillors on the G.L.C. and the London Borough Councils will be four years instead of three. Greater London Council elections will take place in the same year as county council elections in 1977 and every fourth year thereafter. Aldermen will cease to sit as members of the G.L.C. after the 1977 elections. The next London Borough Council elections will be held in May 1978. Aldermen will cease to sit as members of London Borough Councils after the 1978 elections.

Internal Organisation and Local Government Services in England

The council are the final decision making body within any authority. They are free to a great extent to make their own internal organisational arrangements. Normally questions of major policy are settled by the full council, while the administration of the various services is the responsibility of committees of members. Day to day decisions are delegated to the council's officers, who act within the policies laid down by the members.

Many councils have set up corporate management teams of the Chief Executive and chief officers. Such teams consider the operations of their authority as a whole, rather than dealing with each service separately, as was often the case in the past.

Local authorities are empowered or required by various Acts of Parliament to carry out functions in their areas. The legislation concerned comprises public general Acts and " local " Acts which local authorities have promoted as private bills. Functions are divided everywhere between two tiers of authorities, though their allocation within the metropolitan areas is somewhat different from outside, the metropolitan district councils exercising more functions than the non-metropolitan district councils.

Responsibility for the main local government functions is allocated as follows (though responsible authorities may involve other authorities in the provision of certain of their services through agency arrangements):

County councils: Strategic planning (e.g. structure plans; major projects); traffic, transport and highways; police; fire service; consumer protection (other than hygiene); refuse disposal; smallholdings.

Non-metropolitan county and metropolitan district councils: Education; social services; libraries.

District Councils: Local planning: housing; highways (maintenance of certain urban roads and off-street car parks); building regulations; environmental health; refuse collection; cemeteries and crematoria.

Concurrent (county and district councils); Recreation (e.g. parks, playing fields, swimming pools); museums: encouragement of the arts.

The sewerage and sewage disposal functions of local authorities have been transferred to 9 new water authorities and the Welsh National Water Development Authority. Water authorities, however, are expected to make agreements whereby the new district councils discharge sewerage functions on an agency basis. Apart from these functions, the water authorities are responsible for water supply and conservation; river pollution control and river management; fisheries; land drainage; and use of water space for recreation and amenity purposes.

The personal health functions of local authorities have been transferred to area health authorities, whose areas are the same as non-metropolitan and Welsh counties and metropolitan districts. The area health authorities will work within strategies formulated by regional health authorities. They will work in close collaboration with local education, social services and environmental health authorities.

London.—The Greater London Area embraces the old counties of London and Middlesex (except Potter's Bar, Staines and Sunbury-on-Thames) and parts of the neighbouring counties of Essex, Herts., Kent and Surrey and the whole of the county boroughs of Croydon, East Ham and West Ham.

For those functions which need to be considered for the whole of the Area, the Greater London Council is responsible; such functions as traffic, major roads and overall planning. All other matters are the concern of the 32 London borough councils; the City of London, besides retaining its previous functions, has the powers of a London borough.

Parishes

The existing rural parishes in England are generally not affected by local government reorganisation except that the powers of parish councils have been extended and a few of them have been divided by the boundaries of new counties and districts. 300 former small borough and urban district councils have become parish councils with the same powers as other parish councils.

Parishes with 200 or more electors must generally have parish councils, and about three-quarters of the parishes have councils. A parish council comprises at least 5 members, the number being fixed by the district council. All parishes have parish meetings, comprising the electors of the parish.

Parish council functions include; allotments; arts and crafts; community halls, recreational facilities (e.g. open spaces, swimming pools); cemeteries and crematoria; and many minor functions. They must also be given an opportunity to comment on planning applications. They may, like county and district councils, spend up to a 2p rate for the general benefit of the parish. They precept on the district councils for their rate funds. Parish councils will be elected, after a transitional period, every four years, in the year in which the local district councillor is elected.

Civic dignities

District councils may petition for a royal charter granting borough status to the district. In boroughs the chairman of the council is the mayor. The status " city " with or without the right to call the mayor " Lord Mayor " may also be granted

by letters patent. Parish councils may call themselves " town councils ", in which case their chairman is the " town mayor ".

Charter trustees are established for those former boroughs which are too large to have parish councils and are situated in districts without city or borough status. The charter trustees are the district councillors representing the former borough and they elect a mayor, continue civic tradition, and look after the charters, insignia and civic plate of the former borough.

Local Government Elections

Generally speaking, all British subjects or citizens of the Republic of Ireland of 18 years or over, resident on the qualifying date in the area for which the election is being held are entitled to vote at local government elections. A register of electors is prepared and published annually by local electoral registration officers.

A returning officer has the overall responsibility for an election. Voting takes place at polling stations, arranged by the local authority and under the supervision of a presiding officer specially appointed for the purpose. Candidates, who are subject to various statutory qualifications and disqualifications designed to secure that they are suitable persons to hold office, must be nominated by electors for the electoral area concerned.

Local Commissioners for England and Wales

There now exist Local Commissioners for England and Wales whose duty it is to investigate complaints of maladministration in many aspects of local government.

Wales

Wales, including the former Monmouthshire, has been divided into eight counties; Gwynedd; Clwyd; Powys; Dyfed; West, Mid and South Glamorgan; and Gwent. They range in population from 99,000 (Powys) to 536,000 (Mid-Glamorgan). There are 37 new districts in Wales, many of those in the less populated parts reflecting the areas of former Welsh counties. Their populations range from 18,000 (Radnor) to 285,000 (Cardiff).

The arrangements for Welsh counties and districts are generally similar to those for English non-metropolitan counties and districts. There are some differences in functions: Welsh district councils have refuse disposal as well as refuse collection functions and they may provide on-street as well as off-street car parks with the consent of the county council. A few districts have also been designated as library authorities.

In Wales parishes have been replaced by communities. Unlike England, where many areas are not in any parish, communities have been established for the whole of Wales; there is one for each Welsh parish, county borough, borough or urban district (or part where the former area is divided by a new boundary). Community meetings may be convened as and when desired. Community councils already exist where there were formerly parish councils, and also in nearly all the former boroughs and urban districts, and further councils may be established at the request of the community meeting. Community councils have broadly the same range of powers as English parish councils. Community councillors will be elected *en bloc* on the same basis as parish councillors in England, i.e. at the same time as a district council election and for a term of four years.

Local Government Finance

Local government is financed from various sources. (1) *Rates.*—Levied by district councils and in London by the City Corporation and the London boroughs. Sums required by the Greater London Council and by county councils are included in the rates levied by London boroughs and district councils. Rates are levied by a poundage tax on the rateable value of property in the area of the rating authority. Under the General Rate Act, 1967, rating authorities are required to charge a lower rate in the pound on dwellings than on property generally in their area. Differentials of 13p and 18½p for England (33½p and 36p for Wales) respectively were prescribed for 1974–75 and 1975–76. New valuation lists, prepared by valuation officers of the Board of Inland Revenue, came into force on April 1, 1973. These are updated as new property enters the list, and changes to existing property necessitate amendments to the rateable value. The lists remain in force until the next general revaluation due in 1980. Certain types of property are exempt from rates, e.g. agricultural land and buildings, and churches. Some charities and other non-profit making organisations can receive partial exemption. Under the General Rate Act, 1967, as amended by the Local Government Act, 1974, local authorities can resolve to rate specified classes of empty property by an amount up to 100 per cent. of the full rates. Since April 1, 1974 rating authorities must levy a surcharge on empty commercial property at double the normal rates for the first twelve months, treble the rates for the second twelve months and so on progressively during the period of non-use. The Local Government Act, 1974, also makes provision for rate rebates for domestic ratepayers, regardless of the type of property in which they live, eligibility depending on income and family circumstances.

(2) *Government Grants.*—In addition to specific Government grants in aid of revenue expenditure on particular services, from April 1, 1974 grants known as rate support grants are payable to local authorities under the provisions of Part 2 of the Local Government Act, 1974. These grants, which replace the block grants previously paid under the Local Government Act, 1966, consist of three elements: the needs element, the resources element and the domestic element. The needs element, which is payable to non-metropolitan counties, metropolitan districts, London boroughs, the City of London, and the Isles of Scilly, is intended to compensate for variations between authorities in the amount they need to spend per head of population to provide a comparable level of service. The grant is distributed to local authorities on the basis of a distribution formula, which may vary from year to year, using various objective factors for measuring the relative needs of each authority. The resources element is payable to those rating authorities whose rateable resources per head of population fall short of a prescribed national standard for the year, and is so calculated to bring their resources effectively up to that national standard. The domestic element is payable to all rating authorities to reimburse them for the cost of giving the domestic rate relief prescribed for the year.

In order to arrive at the total amount of the rate support grants to local authorities in England and Wales for any year, the aggregate of Exchequer grants to local authorities in respect of their relevant expenditure for the year is determined in advance (housing subsidies and specific grants towards expenditure on rate rebates and mandatory awards to students and trainee teachers are outside this aggregate amount) and from this is deducted the estimated amount of specific grants for the year in aid of revenue expenditure and the supplementary grants for transport purposes and in connection with national parks; the resulting balance is the

amount of rate support grant. This amount can be subsequently increased if there is a substantial increase in the relevant expenditure of local authorities due to an increase in the level of prices, costs or remuneration, or because later legislation has created new areas of expenditure.

Forecasts of local authority relevant expenditure for 1975–76 in England and Wales adopted by the Government for rate support grant purposes were as follows. The amounts given are at November 1974 prices.

Service	£M
Education	£3,947·2
Libraries, Museums and Art Galleries	134·1
Port Health	1·6
Personal Social Services	663·3
Concessionary Fares	35·5
Police	628·0
Fire	176·8
Urban Programme	19·0
Administration of Justice	70·6
Other Home Office Services	16·1
Local Transport Finance	973·4
Refuse	222·3
Recreation, Parks and Baths	234·2
Town and Country Planning	139·3
General Administration	223·8
Housing	392·3
Miscellaneous Services	293·4
Total	8,170·9

The aggregate amount of Exchequer grants for 1975–76 was determined at £5,434,000,000 being 66·5 per cent. of the estimated relevant expenditure. Of this, the specific revenue grants and the transport and National Parks supplementary grants were estimated at £729,000,000 giving a total for rate support grants of £4,705,000,000 of which £2,758,000,000 was in respect of the needs element, £619,000,000 the domestic element and £1,328,000,000 the resources element.

Rates and Rateable Values.—The total rateable value for England and Wales in 1974–75 was £6,660,000,000. The latest estimate of the amount to be raised in rates (net of rate rebates) in 1975–76 is £3,745,000,000.

Average Rates.—The estimated average rates levied in England in 1975–76 were: Inner London Boroughs, *domestic rate* 45·7p, *non-domestic rate* 63·8p; Outer London, 55·8p and 75·4p; Metropolitan Districts, 52·3p and 71·7p; Non-metropolitan districts, 45·9p and 65·6p. In Wales the estimated average rates levied were, *domestic rate* 43·4p, *non-domestic rate*, 80p. The average rates levied in England and Wales were estimated as 48·4p (*domestic*) and 67·9p (*non-domestic*).

SCOTLAND

Under the new structure of local government, in terms of the Local Government (Scotland) Act, 1973, which came into administrative effect on May 16, 1975, Scotland is for local government purposes divided into 9 regions, and 3 island areas covering respectively Orkney, Shetland and the Western Isles. Within the regions there is a second independent tier of 53 districts.

Functions.—Regions and districts have separate responsibility for specific functions. In addition they share responsibility for certain concurrent functions. Islands area councils are all-purpose authorities responsible in these areas for the functions (except police and fire services) which are the separate or concurrent responsibility of regions and districts.

Regional Functions.—The new regional authorities are directly responsible for overall planning strategy and the highly technical or expensive services, e.g. the provision of major infrastructure services including transportation, roads and passenger transport, airports, water, sewerage, river purification, flood prevention, as well as education, social work, police and fire services.

District Functions.—The district authorities deal with more local matters such as local planning; development control; building control; housing; environmental health including cleansing, refuse collection and disposal, food hygiene, inspection of shops, offices and factories, clean air, markets and slaughterhouses, burial and cremation; regulation and licensing, including cinemas and theatres, betting and gaming, taxis, house to house collections; libraries.

Concurrent Functions.—These include country-side and tourism, industrial development, recreation parks, art galleries and museums.

Community Councils.—Provision is also made in the Act for setting up community councils under schemes to be prepared by each district and islands authority. The Act requires that the schemes will be submitted to the Secretary of State for approval, normally by May 16, 1976. Such councils will not be local authorities but will have a statutory base. They will have no statutory functions but will be expected to take such action in the community interest as appears to their members to be desirable and practicable.

Local Government Electors.—In 1975 there were 3,733,232 electors in Scotland. The first ordinary elections of all the new authorities took place on May 7, 1974.

Rates and Rateable Values.—In 1971–72, the latest year for which final figures were available, a total of £239,045,000 was received from the general rates of local government in Scotland and £10,098,000 from domestic water rates. The rateable value on which rates were leviable was £278,395,000 on the general rates and £166,672,000 on the domestic water rates. The average general rate levied was 86p and the domestic water rate levied was 6p.

Provisional figures for 1972–73 show total receipts from general rates of £251,478,000 and £10,424,000 from domestic water rates, and £279,169,000 and £11,913,000 for 1973–74. The rateable value leviable for 1972–73 was £282,779,000 (general) and £165,962,000 (domestic water rate) and £291,492,000 (general) and £166,990,000 (domestic water rate) for 1973–74. The average rate per £ levied for 1972–73 was 89p (general) and 6·5p (domestic water) and 96p (general) and 7p (domestic water) for 1973–74.

NORTHERN IRELAND

On October 1, 1973 a single-tier system of 26 district councils, based on the main centres of population, replaced the former system of two-tier county and district and the single-tier county borough councils.

The new district councils are responsible for a wide range of local services including refuse collection and disposal, the provision and maintenance of recreational and social facilities, street cleansing, environmental health, tourist development, enforcement of building regulations, miscellaneous licensing and registration matters, and gas supply.

They have in addition a consultative function, partly statutory and partly administrative, in relation to roads, housing, water and planning and also nominate representatives as members of public bodies responsible for education, health and housing.

Electors:—The register published on February 15, 1975, contained the names of 1,039,544 local government electors. Of this total, 252,992 related to the City of Belfast and 50,642 to London-derry District.

THE NATIONAL PARKS

The ten National Parks described below in their order of designation have been established in England and Wales. These areas are not public property and visitors are not free to wander over private land within the Park boundaries. They have been marked out for special care aimed at two prime purposes: to preserve and enhance their natural beauty, and to promote their enjoyment by the public.

Peak District National Park (542 sq. miles).— Mainly in Derbyshire but extending into Staffordshire, Cheshire, South Yorkshire, West Yorkshire and Greater Manchester. In the south and east are limestone uplands, and finely wooded dales with swift, clear rivers and unspoilt stone villages. Northwards, moorlands, edged by gritstone crags, attract hill walkers and climbers. There are information centres at Bakewell, Edale, Castleton and at Buxton (just outside the Park) and an information caravan tours the Park

Lake District National Park (866 sq. miles).—In Cumbria. Spectacular mountain scenery with wooded lower slopes enhanced by lakes and tarns. The area includes England's highest mountains (Scafell Pike, Helvellyn and Skiddaw) and largest lakes. Walking and rock-climbing are the principal recreations, but there are fishing, swimming, sailing, boating and winter sports as well. There are information centres at Keswick, Ambleside and Bowness. Information vans are sited at Waterhead, Coniston, Glenridding and Hawkeshead. At Brockhole, Windermere, is a National Park centre.

Snowdonia National Park (800 sq. miles).—In Gwynedd in North Wales. A mountainous region supporting farms, forest, reservoirs and power stations and traversed by high passes, offering some of the finest rock-climbing and mountain walking for both beginner and expert. The main valleys, often finely wooded, hold lakes (or llyns) and are watered by rivers with cascading falls. There are information centres at Aberdyfi, Bala, Blaenau Ffestiniog, Conway, Harlech, Dolgellau, Llanberis and Llanrwst.

Dartmoor National Park (365 sq. miles).—In Devon, the highest area of high moorland in southern England, famous for its granite " tors" often weathered into strange shapes. Fine hanging oak woods adorn the river valleys which lead up into the Moor. The Park is rich in prehistoric relics and offers fine walking and riding. Information vans are sited at Two Bridges, Yelverton, Ashburton and Haytor during summer months.

Pembrokeshire Coast National Park (225 sq. miles).—A spectacular section of Britain's coastline, where rock cliffs alternate with bays and sandy coves. In the north is Mynydd Presely, abounding in prehistoric relics. The Park includes the fine Milford Haven waterway reaches, Tenby, the cathedral of St. David's, and Carew and other Norman castles. There are information centres at Tenby, St. David's, Pembroke, Fishguard, Kilgetty, Milford Haven and Haverfordwest. A countryside unit is open at Broad Haven.

North York Moors National Park (553 sq. miles).— In North Yorkshire and Cleveland, the Park stretches from the Hambleton Hills in the west to the coastline above Scarborough. On the coast sheltered bays and sandy beaches alternate with headlands harbouring villages such as Staithes and Robin Hood's Bay. The heart of the Park offers tracts of open moorland, intersected by beautiful wooded valleys. Mount Grace Priory and the abbeys of Rievaulx and Byland are within the Park.

Yorkshire Dales National Park (680 sq. miles).—An area of upland moors, cut by deep valleys, mostly in North Yorkshire but extending into Cumbria. The Park includes some of the finest limestone scenery in Britain: Kilnsey Crag in Wharfedale, Gordale Scar, and Malham Cove in Malhamdale. In the Park also are Swaledale and Wensleydale, the three peaks of Ingleborough, Whernside and Pen-y-Ghent, and many relics of the past such as the Roman fort at Bainbridge and Bolton Abbey in Wharfedale. There are information centres at Clapham, Aysgarth Falls, Malham and Settle. An information caravan is sited at Hawes.

Exmoor National Park (265 sq. miles).—Mainly in Somerset but extending into Devon, this is a moorland plateau seamed with finely wooded combes. The well-known coastline between Minehead and Combe Martin Bay is exceptionally beautiful. In the east are the Brendon Hills. There are information centres at Minehead, Lynmouth and Dulverton. An information van is sited at Combe Martin.

Northumberland National Park (398 sq. miles).—A region of hills and moorland, stretching from Hadrian's Roman Wall in the south to the Cheviot Hills on the Scottish Border. The area is rich in historic interest. There are information centres at Byrness, Ingram and Once Brewed and an information van tours the Park.

Brecon Beacons National Park (519 sq. miles).—The most recent National Park, established in 1957, is centred on " The Beacons " with its three peaks: Corn Du, Cribyn and Pen y Fan, rising to nearly 3,000 feet. But it includes the Black Mountains to the east and the Black Mountain to the west, thus taking in parts of Gwent and Dyfed as well as southern Powys and a small area of mid-Glamorgan. The Usk Valley, Llangorse Lake, Brecon Cathedral, Carreg Cennen Castle and Llanthony Abbey are all within the Park. There are information centres at Brecon, Abergavenny, Llandovery and a mountain centre near Libanus, Brecon.

AREAS OF OUTSTANDING NATURAL BEAUTY

Anglesey (83 sq. miles).—Except for breaks around the urban areas and in the vicinity of Wylfa, the designated area extends along the entire coastline. The varied scenery is famed for its beauty, as also are the Menai Straits, separating the island from the mainland.

Arnside and Silverdale (29 sq. miles).—Lying along the upper half of Morecambe Bay, the area embraces the Kent estuary where it adjoins the Lake District National Park and includes extensive tidal flats in the Bay. The varied coastal landscape contains several limestone hills, woodland and bog areas locally known as " mosses ". Known for its wildfowl breeding grounds, the whole area is of considerable ecological value.

Cannock Chase (26 sq. miles).—This is an area of high heathland in Staffordshire, relieved by varied scenery in which parklands adjoin farms, woodlands and pleasant villages. Deer continue to roam over the Chase.

Chichester Harbour (29 sq. miles).—Well known for its small boating and sailing facilities, the area extends from Hayling Island in the west to Apuldram in the east and contains the whole of Thorney Island.

Chilterns (309 sq. miles).—The well-known chalk downlands from Goring in South Oxfordshire northeastwards through Buckinghamshire, Hertfordshire and Bedfordshire to Dunstable and Luton, including the outlying group of hills beyond Luton. Contains several National Trust properties and Whipsnade Zoo.

Cornwall (360 sq. miles).—Comprising a number of separate areas including Bodmin Moor and some of the finest and best-known coastal scenery in Britain. Most of the Land's End peninsula; the coast between St. Michael's Mount and St. Austell with Falmouth omitted; and the Fowey Estuary are all included: in north Cornwall most of the coast to Bedruthan Steps, north of Newquay, and between Perranporth and Godrevy Towans.

Cotswold (582 sq. miles).—Contains the great limestone escarpment overlooking the Vales of Gloucester and Evesham. The remainder is high undulating country and narrow wooded valleys traversed by shallow rapid streams. Noted for its beautiful villages.

Dedham Vale (22 sq. miles).—This, the smallest area so far designated, is the flat land of water meadows with hedges and woodland, bordering Essex and Suffolk, where John Constable (1776-1837) painted during most of his life. Flatford Mill, Willy Lott's Cottage and the church of Stoke-by-Nayland still stand.

East Devon (103 sq. miles).—The area comprises the fine stretch of coastline between Orcombe Rocks, near Exmouth, and the Dorset area near Lyme Regis, with Sidmouth, Beer and Seaton omitted. Inland Gittisham Hill, East Hill and Woodbury and Aylebeare Commons are all included.

North Devon (66 sq. miles).—Comprising three sections of fine coastline—the whole of the Hartland peninsula; from Bideford Bar to the western limits of Ilfracombe, and from east of Ilfracombe to the boundary of the Exmoor National Park. Clovelly, Braunton Burrows, Woolacombe and Combe Martin are all included.

South Devon (128 sq. miles).—It includes the magnificent coast between Bolt Head and Bolt Tail. a National Trust property; Salcombe, Slapton Sands and Dartmouth, and the four estuaries and valleys of the Yealm, Erme, Avon and Dart.

Dorset (400 sq. miles).—Takes in the whole of the coastline between Lyme Regis and Poole, with the Isle of Portland and Weymouth omitted, and stretches inland to include the Purbeck Hills and the downs, heaths and wooded valleys of the Hardy country.

Forest of Bowland (310 sq. miles).—A fine tract of high open moorland running westward from near Settle and Bolton by Bowland in the Pennines, to Caton and Scorton in Central Lancashire. A small outlying area east of the River Ribble includes Pendle Hill and Pendleton Moor.

Gower (73 sq. miles).—In the county of West Glamorgan, South Wales, the area is known for its beautiful coastline, its rocky limestone cliffs, sandy bays and coves and for its wooded ravines stretching inland.

East Hampshire (151 sq. miles).—The area stretches from the outskirts of Winchester to the Hampshire/Sussex border at a distance of about 10 miles inland from the south coast.

South Hampshire Coast (30 sq. miles).—14 miles of coastline on the northern shores of the Solent, between Hurst Castle and Calshot Castle, southeast of Fawley, with the central part of the area extending inland up the Beaulieu River for about six miles, including a beautiful part of the New Forest. Along much of the coast woods of oak and

Scots pine stretch down to the water's edge, while at the western end are some attractive salt marshes.

Kent Downs (326 sq. miles).—Running from the Surrey border near Westerham (its boundary adjoining that of the Surrey Hills area), about 60 miles to the coast near Dover and Folkestone, with a coastal outlier at South Foreland and a narrow strip of the old sea cliff escarpment west of Hythe overlooking Romney Marsh. Pleasant pastoral scenery, picturesque villages, ancient churches and castles, with the Downs rising to 600 feet.

Lincolnshire Wolds (216 sq. miles).—The area extends in a south-east direction from Laceby and Caistor in the north to the region of Spilsby, about ten miles west of Skegness. Its charm is derived from the undulating terrain, sparse settlement pattern and the excellent views from the chalk escarpments. The wolds are extensively farmed and contain numerous small, attractive villages.

Lleyn (60 sq. miles).—An isolated peninsula in Gwynedd, North Wales, of unique character, still largely unspoilt by the hand of man.

Malvern Hills (40 sq. miles).—The area embodies the whole range of the Malvern Hills in the county of Hereford and Worcester, just touching Gloucestershire. Such well-known features as the Worcestershire Beacon, North Hill, the Herefordshire Beacon, and Midsummer Hill, a National Trust property, are within the area.

Mendip Hills (78 sq. miles).—Comprising over half of the Mendip Hills, the area stretches, east to west, from Bleadon Hill to the A.39 road north of Wells. Blagdon Lake and Chew Magna Lake are within the boundary which, in the south, takes in Cheddar Gorge. The plateau, rising to over 1,000 ft., commands fine views over the Bristol Channel and surrounding countryside. Noted for its caves, including Wookey Hole, the area is of great scientific and historic interest.

Norfolk Coast (174 sq. miles).—With coastal scenery ranging from salt marsh and mudflats, sand-dunes and shingle ridges to sea cliffs, this area includes six miles of the south-east coast of the Wash, an almost continuous coastal strip three to five miles in depth from Hunstanton to Bacton, with a further small strip between Sea Palling and Winterton-on-Sea. The area, which is rich in wild-life, also includes part of the Sandringham Estate.

Northumberland Coast (50 sq. miles).—Low cliffs and rocky headlands with active fishing villages comprise this area which stretches from just south of Berwick to Amble. It includes Holy Island, with the oldest monastic ruins in the country; the Farne Islands, and the great castles of Bamburgh, Dunstanburgh and Warkworth.

Quantock Hills (38 sq. miles).—The main feature of this area in Somerset is the range of red sandstone hills rising to a height of 1,260 feet at Will's Neck above Crow Combe.

Shropshire Hills (300 sq. miles).—This area includes the fine landscape around Church Stretton, with Caer Caradoc, the Long Mynd, the Stiperstones, and the long ridge of Wenlock Edge from which it extends north-east to the Wrekin and the Ercall.

Soloway Coast (41 sq. miles).—A stretch of beautiful coastline in Cumbria from above Maryport to the estuaries of the Rivers Eden and Esk (with Silloth omitted) backed by the Solway Plain and noted for its historic and scientific interests.

Suffolk Coast and Heaths (151 sq. miles).—Takes in 38 miles of coastline and parts of the Stour and Orwell estuaries, while the Deben, Alde and Blyth flow through it. With heath, woodland, marsh and beaches, the scenery is attractively varied and the area important to ornithologists.

Surrey Hills (160 sq. miles).—The Hog's Back and the ridge of the North Downs from Guildford to Titsey in the east are within this area, as are Leith Hill, Hindhead Common, the Devil's Punch Bowl; the well-known villages of Abinger, Shere, Hambledon and Chiddingfold; Box Hill and Frensham Ponds.

Sussex Downs (379 sq. miles).—The area includes the chalk escarpment of the South Downs from Beachy Head to the West Sussex/Hampshire border, with such well-known features as Firle Beacon and Chanctonbury Ring, and stretches down to the coast between Eastbourne and Seaford. In the west the boundary adjoins the East Hampshire and Surrey Hills areas.

North Wessex Downs (671 sq. miles).—An upland area in Hampshire, Wiltshire, Oxfordshire and Berkshire, bounded by the Marlborough and Lambourn Downs in the west and the Chiltern Hills in the east. To the south of the downs the area is intersected by the Kennet Valley, the Vale of Pewsey and Enbourne Vale, with Savernake Forest in the midst. The southern section comprises the North Downs where they descend to the Test Valley which, together with Salisbury Plain, form the southern limit of what is so far the largest area designated.

Isle of Wight (73 sq. miles).—A number of separate areas comprising unspoiled stretches of coastline, the Yar Valley, the high downland behind Ventnor and the fine chalk downland ridge east of Newport to Culver Cliff and Foreland.

Wye Valley (125 sq. miles).—This area lies within the counties of Gwent, Gloucestershire and Hereford and Worcester. The lower Wye Valley landscape is characterised by its steeply-wooded slopes, cliffs and gorges where the river has cut through limestone outcrops. Further north the valley is broader and the river meanders through pleasant pastureland. Tintern Abbey and the well-known viewpoint from Symonds Yat are within this beautiful area. The flora include many rare species.

BRITISH ISLES

SHETLAND IS.
Lerwick

ORKNEY IS.
Kirkwall
PENTLAND FIRTH

Stornoway

MORAY FIRTH

Inverness

HEBRIDES

SCOTLAND
Aberdeen

Perth Dundee

Oban

Stirling FIRTH OF FORTH

Glasgow Edinburgh

FIRTH OF CLYDE Ayr

ATLANTIC

NORTH

SEA

NORTHERN
IRELAND Belfast

Newcastle
SOLWAY FIRTH Carlisle

ENGLAND

York

ISLE OF MAN Bradford Leeds Hull

IRISH SEA

REPUBLIC OF Liverpool Manchester

IRELAND Sheffield

Dublin Stoke Nottingham THE WASH
ANGLESEY

Leicester Norwich

Birmingham Coventry Cambridge

WALES

Stratford

Cork Oxford

Swansea
Cardiff Bristol
LONDON Canterbury
BRISTOL CHANNEL Calais

Winchester

Southampton Portsmouth

OCEAN Exeter ISLE OF WIGHT

Plymouth

ENGLISH CHANNEL

SCILLY IS

0   50   100 MILES

CHANNEL IS.

FRANCE

THE KINGDOM OF ENGLAND

Position and Extent.—The Kingdom of England occupies the southern position of the island of Great Britain and lies between 55° 46′ and 49° 57′ 30″ N. latitude (from the mouth of the Tweed to the Lizard), and between 1° 46′ E. and 5° 43′ W. (from Lowestoft to Land's End). England is bounded on the north by the summit of the Cheviot Hills, which form a natural boundary with the Kingdom of Scotland; on the south by the English Channel; on the east by the Straits of Dover (Pas de Calais) and the North Sea; and on the West by the Atlantic Ocean, Wales and the Irish Sea. It has a total area of 50,333 sq. miles (land 50,053; inland water 280) and a population (1971 Census) of 46,029,000.

Relief.—There is a natural orographic division into the hilly districts of the north, west and south-west, and the undulating downs and low-lying plains of the east and south-east. In the extreme north the *Cheviot Hills* run from east to west, culminating in the Cheviot, 2,676 feet above mean sea level. Divided from the Cheviots by the Tyne Gap is the *Pennine Chain*, running N. by W. to S. by E., with its highest point in Cross Fell, 2,930 feet above mean sea level. West of the Pennines are the *Cumbrian Mountains*, which contain in Scafell Pike (3,210 feet) the highest land in England, and east of the Pennines are the *Yorkshire Moors*, their highest point being Urra Moor (1,489 feet). South of the Pennines are the Peak of Derbyshire (2,088 feet) and Dartmoor (High Willhays, 2,039 feet). In the western county of Salop are the isolated Wrekin (1,335 feet), Long-mynd (1,666 feet), and Brown Clee (1,792 feet); in Hereford the Black Mountain (2,310 feet), in Worcester the Malvern Hills (1,395 feet); the Cotswold Hills of Gloucestershire contain Cleeve Cloud (about 1,100 feet).

Hydrography.—The *Thames* is the longest and most important river of England, with a total length of 210 miles from its source in the Cotswold Hills to its outflow into the North Sea, and is navigable by ocean-going steamers to London Bridge. The Thames is tidal to Teddington (69 miles from its mouth) and forms county boundaries almost throughout its course; on its banks are situated London, the capital of the British Commonwealth; Windsor Castle, the home of the Sovereign, Eton College, the first of the public schools, and Oxford, the oldest university in the kingdom. The *Severn* is the longest river in Great Britain, rising in the north-eastern slopes of Plinlimmon (Wales) and entering England in Salop with a total length of 220 miles from its source to its outflow into the Bristol Channel, where it receives on the left the Bristol Avon, and on the right the Wye, its other tributaries being the Vrynwy, Tern, Stour, Teme and Upper (or Warwickshire) Avon. The Severn is tidal below Gloucester, and a high bore or tidal wave sometimes reverses the flow as high as Tewkesbury (13½ miles above Gloucester). The scenery of the greater part of the river is very picturesque and beautiful, and the Severn is a noted salmon river, some of its tributaries being famous for trout. Navigation is assisted by the Gloucester and Berkeley Ship Canal (16¾ miles), which admits vessels of 350 tons to Gloucester. The *Severn Tunnel*, begun in 1873 and completed in 1886 (at a cost of £2,000,000) after many difficulties from flooding, is 4 miles 628 yards in length of which 2¼ miles are under the river). A road bridge over the Severn estuary, between Haysgate,

Gwent, and Almondsbury, Glos., with a centre span of 3,240 ft. was opened by Her Majesty the Queen on September 8, 1966. Of the remaining English rivers those flowing into the North Sea are the Tyne, Wear, Tees, Ouse and Trent from the Pennine Range, the Great Ouse (160 miles) from the Central Plain, and the Orwell and Stour from the hills of East Anglia. Flowing into the English Channel are the Sussex Ouse from the Weald, the Itchen from the Hampshire Hills, and the Axe, Teign, Dart, Tamar and Exe from the Devonian Hills; and flowing into the Irish Sea are the Mersey, Ribble and Eden from the western slopes of the Pennines and the Derwent from the Cumbrian Mountains. The *English Lakes* are noteworthy rather for their picturesque scenery and poetic associations than for their size. They lie in Cumbria, the largest being Windermere (10 miles long), Ullswater and Derwentwater.

Islands.—The *Isle of Wight* is separated from Hampshire by the Solent; total area 147 sq. miles, population (estimated 1975) 112,000. The climate is mild and healthy, and many watering places have grown up during the last century. Capital, Newport, at the head of the estuary of the Medina, Cowes (at the mouth) being the chief port; other centres are Ryde, Sandown, Shanklin, Ventnor, Freshwater, Yarmouth, Totland Bay, Seaview and Bembridge. The *Scilly Islands*, 25 miles from Land's End, consist of about 40 islands, with a total area of about 4,000 acres, only St. Mary's, Tresco, St. Martin's, St. Agnes and Bryher being inhabited (population, 1971, 2,428). The capital is Hugh Town, in St. Mary's. The climate is unusually mild, and vegetation luxuriant, semi-tropical plants flourishing in the open. *Lundy* (= Island) 11 miles N.W. of Hartland Point, Devon, is about 2 miles long and about ½ mile broad (average), with a total area of about 1,050 acres (mainly picturesque), and a population of about 20; it became the property of the National Trust in 1969 and has 3 lighthouses (one disused).

Climate.—The *mean annual air temperature* reduced to sea-level varies from 11°C. in the extreme south-west to 9°C. near Berwick-on-Tweed. In January the south and west are warmer than the east, the mean temperature reduced to sea-level being less than 4·5°C. over the eastern half of the country. In July the warmest districts are more definitely in the south and inland, the range being from 17°C. around London to less than 5·9°C. in the extreme north. The decrease of mean temperature with height is about 0.6°C. per 100 metres. The coldest month of the year is January and the warmest July. Sea temperature reaches its maximum rather later than air temperature. The average annual *rainfall* decreases from west to east, owing to the preponderance of south-west winds, and also increases with altitude. The annual average, 1916-1950, varies from 20 in. (500 mm.) in the neighbourhood of the Thames Estuary and locally in Cambridgeshire to more than 100 in. (2,500 mm.) over the mountains of the Lake District. Rather more rain falls in the summer half-year in parts of the east, but in the west much more falls in the winter half-year. The months of least rain are March to June and the wettest months October to January. The mean annual number of hours of bright *sunshine* varies from 1,750 hours along the south-east coast to less than 1,300 hours in the neighbourhood of the Pennine range. June is the sunniest month followed by May, July and August in that order.

EARLY INHABITANTS

Prehistoric Man.—Palæolithic and Neolithic remains are abundantly found throughout England. The Neolithic period is held to have merged into the Bronze Age about 2000 to 1500 B.C., and a date between these years has been given to *Stonehenge* (10 miles N. of Salisbury, Wiltshire) which consists of two circles of menhirs (the largest monolith being 22½ feet in height). The village of *Avebury* and its surroundings were scheduled in 1937, and in 1943 about 1,000 acres of Avebury were purchased by the National Trust, thus preserving the Circle of megalithic monuments, the Avenue, Silbury Hill, etc., relics of Stone Age culture of 1900–1800 B.C., which make this one of the most important archæological sites in Europe. The *Devil's Arrows*, near Boroughbridge, Yorkshire, are regarded as the finest remaining megalithic monoliths in northern Europe; the tallest arrow is 30 ft. 6 in. high and its greatest circumference is 16 ft. In the latter part of the Bronze Age the *Goidels*, a people of Celtic race, and in the Iron Age other Celtic races of *Brythons* and *Belgae*, invaded the country and brought with them Celtic civilization and dialects, place names in England bearing witness to the spread of the invasion over the whole kingdom.

The Roman Conquest.—Julius Cæsar raided Britain in 55 B.C. and 54 B.C. The Emperor Claudius, nearly 100 years later (A.D. 42), dispatched Aulus Plautius, with a well-equipped force of 40,000, and himself followed with reinforcements in the same year.

The British leader from A.D. 48–51 was *Caratacus* (Caractacus), who was finally captured and sent to Rome. By A.D. 70 the conquest of South Britain was completed, a great revolt under *Boadicea*, Queen of the Iceni, being crushed in A.D. 61. In A.D. 122, the Emperor Hadrian visited Britain and built a continuous rampart, since known as *Hadrian's Wall*, from Wallsend to Bowness (Tyne to Solway). The work was entrusted by the Emperor Hadrian to Aulus Platorius Nepos, legate of Britain from 122 to 126, and it is now regarded as "the greatest and most impressive relic of the Roman frontier system in Europe."

The Romans administered Britain as a Province under a Governor, with a well-defined system of local government, each Roman municipality ruling itself and the surrounding territory. Colchester, Lincoln, York, Gloucester and St. Albans stand on the sites of five Roman municipalities, while London was the centre of the road system and the seat of the financial officials of the Province of Britain. Well-preserved Roman towns have been uncovered at (or near) *Silchester* (Calleva Atrebatum), 10 miles south of Reading, *Wroxeter* (Viroconium), near Shrewsbury, and *St. Albans* (Verulamium) in Hertfordshire.

Four main groups of roads radiated from London, and a fifth (the Fosse) ran obliquely from Ermine Street (at Lincoln), through Leicester, Cirencester and Bath to Exeter. Of the four groups radiating from London one ran S.E. to Canterbury and the coast of Kent, a second to Silchester and thence to parts of Western Britain and South Wales, a third (now known as *Watling Street*) ran through Verulamium to Chester, with various branches, and the fourth reached Colchester, Lincoln, York and the eastern counties.

Christianity reached the Roman province of Britain from Gaul in the 3rd century (or possibly earlier), *Alban*, "the protomartyr of Britain," being put to death as a Christian during the persecution of Diocletian (June 22, 303), at his native town Verulamium. The Bishops of Londinium, Eboracum (York), and Lindum (Lincoln) attended the Council of Arles in 314.

The Roman garrison of Britain was much harassed in the 4th century by Saxon pirates, who invaded the eastern areas. A system of coast defence was organized from the Wash to to Southampton Water, with forts at Brancaster, Burgh Castle (Yarmouth), Walton (Felixstowe), Bradwell, Reculver, Richborough, Dover, Stutfall, Pevensey and Porchester (Portsmouth). About A.D. 350 incursions in the north of Irish (Scoti) and Picts became most formidable, and towards the end of the 4th century many troops were removed from Britain for service in other parts of the Roman Empire. Early in the 5th century Gaul was taken from the Romans by Teutonic invaders and Britain was cut off from Rome. The last Roman garrison was withdrawn from Britain in A.D. 442 and the S.E. portion was conquered by the Saxons.

The Latin-speaking Celts of England were replaced by their heathen and Teutonic conquerors, to the submergence of the Christian religion and the loss of Latin speech. According to legend, the British King *Vortigern* called in the Saxons to defend him against the Picts, the Saxon chieftains being *Hengist* and *Horsa*, who landed at Ebbsfleet, Kent, and established themselves in the Isle of Thanet. Bede, a Northumbrian monk, author of the Ecclesiastical History at the opening of the 8th century, described these settlers as Jutes, and there are traces of differences in Kentish customs from those of other Anglo-Saxon kingdoms.

Anglo-Saxons and Normans.—What happened in Britain during the 150 years which elapsed between the final break with Rome and the coming of St. Augustine is shrouded in the deepest mystery. The Jutes, the Saxons and the Angles (whose gods Twi, Woden, Thunor and Frigg are commemorated in " Tuesday, Wednesday, Thursday and Friday ") were converted to Christianity by a mission under Augustine (dispatched by Pope Gregory in 597), which established Archbishoprics at Canterbury and York, and England appears to have been again converted by the end of the 7th century. In the 8th century Offa, King of Mercia, is stated to have built a wall and rampart, afterwards known as *Offa's Dike*, from the mouth of the Dee to that of the Wye, as a protection against the Welsh.

The greatest of the English kingdoms was *Wessex*, with its capital at Winchester, and the greatest of the Wessex kings was *Alfred the Great* (871–899), who resisted the incursions of the Northmen (Danes) and fixed a limit to their advance by the Treaty of Wedmore (878). In the 10th century the Kings of Wessex recovered the whole of England from the Danes, but subsequent rulers were unable to resist the invaders, and England paid tribute (*Danegelt*) for many years, and was ruled by Danish Kings from 1016 to 1042, when Edward the Confessor was recalled from exile. In 1066 Harold (brother-in-law of Edward and son of Earl Godwin of Wessex) was chosen King of England, but after defeating (at Stamford Bridge, Yorkshire, Sept. 25) an invading army under Harald Hadraada, King of Norway (aided by the outlawed Earl Tostig, of Northumbria, younger son of Earl Godwin), he was himself defeated at the *Battle of Hastings* on Oct. 14, 1066, and the Norman Conquest secured the throne of England for Duke William of Normandy.

AREA AND POPULATION OF ENGLISH COUNTIES

County	Administrative Headquarters	Acreage	Population (Reg. Gen's Est.)	Rateable Value 1975
				£
Avon.................	Avon Hse., The Haymarket, Bristol	332,596	915,300	108,546,308
Bedford..............	* Cauldwell St., Bedford	305,094	501,500	70,800,000
Berkshire............	† Reading	310,179	653,400	104,404,393
Buckinghamshire......	* Aylesbury	465,019	497,800	78,254,401
Cambridgeshire........	† Castle Hill, Cambridge	842,433	540,300	67,170,000
Cheshire..............	* Chester	575,375	904,600	114,400,059
Cleveland.............	Municipal Bldgs., Middlesbrough	144,030	565,600	68,642,000
Cornwall.............	* Truro	876,295‡	396,600‡	39,177,232
Cumbria..............	The Courts, Carlisle	1,701,455	475,700	42,052,017
Derbyshire............	County Offices, Matlock	650,146	902,820	91,000,000
Devonshire............	* Exeter	1,658,278	928,800	100,400,000
Dorset................	* Dorchester	664,116	570,500	73,918,300
Durham...............	* Durham	601,939	610,900	51,482,000
Essex.................	* Chelmsford	907,849	1,397,840	203,500,000
Gloucester............	† Gloucester	652,741	485,400	55,615,112
Greater Manchester.....	* Piccadilly Gdns., Manchester	318,580	2,730,000	300,304,732
Hampshire............	The Castle, Winchester	932,468	1,434,700	179,051,113
Hereford and Worcester.	† Worcester	970,203	585,900	72,179,830
Hertford..............	* Hertford	403,797	941,700	151,872,282
Humberside............	Kingston Hse S., Bond St., Kingston-upon-Hull	867,784	848,800	88,374,810
Kent.................	* Maidstone	922,196	1,440,800	161,312,400
Lancashire............	* Preston	751,063	1,370,100	129,610,321
Leicestershire..........	* Glenfield, Leicester	630,842	829,800	96,010,281
Lincoln...............	County Offices, Lincoln	1,454,273	519,500	50,306,577
Greater London........	* S.E.1.	390,302	7,167,600	1,894,543,000
Merseyside............	Metropolitan Hse., Old Hall St., Liverpool	159,750	1,602,700	188,185,505
Norfolk..............	* Martineau Lane, Norwich	1,323,174	650,300	75,143,276
Northampton..........	* Northampton	584,972	496,400	59,191,481
Northumberland.......	* Newcastle-upon-Tyne	1,243,692	285,700	26,480,600
Nottinghamshire.......	* West Bridgford, Nottingham	534,735	981,000	106,697,000
Oxfordshire...........	* New Road, Oxford	645,314	535,300	68,189,009
Salop................	† Abbey Foregate, Shrewsbury	862,479	354,400	36,950,634
Somerset..............	* Taunton	854,488	400,400	42,691,697
Staffordshire..........	County Bldgs., Stafford	671,184	991,100	110,481,000
Suffolk...............	* Ipswich	940,800	567,300	65,759,155
Surrey................	* Kingston upon Thames	414,922	1,005,900	157,606,964
Sussex, East...........	* Pelham Hse., St. Andrew's Lane, Lewes	443,627	661,100	88,696,774
Sussex, West...........	* West St., Chichester	492,068	615,400	83,139,500
Tyne and Wear........	Sandyford Hse., Newcastle	133,390	1,189,500	116,015,956
Warwick.............	† Warwick	489,405	469,500	59,326,588
West Midlands........	* Queensway, Birmingham	222,254	2,779,800	385,726,255
Wight, Isle of.........	* Newport, I.O.W.	94,146	112,000	12,053,718
Wiltshire.............	* Trowbridge	860,109	506,700	51,278,145
Yorkshire, North.......	* Northallerton	2,055,000	648,600	62,281,804
Yorkshire, South........	* Barnsley	385,610	1,317,200	123,733,809
Yorkshire, West........	* Wakefield	503,863	2,082,200	189,033,000

* County Hall † Shire Hall ‡ excluding Isles of Scilly

Lords Lieutenant of Counties.—The actual words used in the Letters Patent relative to these appointments are " Her Majesty's Lieutenant of and in the County of . . ." and this is the official title whether the individual appointed be a Peer or a Commoner. In documents of the highest formality the proper term is therefore " Her Majesty's Lieutenant." In less formal and informal documents and colloquially, the style " Lord Lieutenant " has been applied to H.M. Lieutenants, Peers and Commoners alike, for a great many years. The duties of the Lord Lieutenant are to advise the Lord Chancellor as to the appointment of magistrates to the county bench, to appoint Deputy Lieutenants and to raise the militia, if need be, in time of riot or invasion. The Lord Lieutenant is usually a peer or a baronet and a large landowner and is often appointed *custos rotulorum* (keeper of the records).

ENGLISH COUNTIES AND SHIRES

LORDS LIEUTENANT, HIGH SHERIFFS AND CHAIRMEN OF COUNTY COUNCILS

County or Shire	Lord Lieutenant	*High Sheriff, 1975–76	Chairman of C.C.
(1) Avon............	Sir John V. Wills, Bt., T.D.	J. F. Robinson C.B.E., T.D.	G. Walker
(2) Bedford..........	Maj. Simon Whitbread	R. G. Gale	J. W. Johnson
(3) Berks.............	Maj. the Hon. D. J. Smith, C.B.E.	Lt. Col. R. C. R. Price, D.S.O., O.B.E.	F. D. Pickering, C.B.E.
(4) Bucks............	Maj. J. D. Young	Mrs. J Micklem	J. T. Ireland
(5) Cambridge.......	Lt.-Col. The Hon. P. E. Brassey	K. Beaton	J. R. Horrell, T.D.
(6) Cheshire.........	The Viscount Leverhulme, T.D.	Lt.-Col. J. M. Harrison, T.D.	C. L. S. Cornwall-Leigh, O.B.E.
(7) Cleveland........	Maj. C. Crosthwaite, M.B.E., T.D.	Maj. G. A. B. Jenyns, T.D.	G. W. Groves
(8) Cornwall.........	Col. Sir John C. Pole, Bt., D.S.O., T.D.	Lt.-Col. J. A. M. St. Aubyn, M.B.E.	W. T. H. Rowse
(9) Cumbria.........	J. C. Wade, O.B.E.	M. C. Stanley, M.B.E.	J. Westoll
(10) Derby...........	Col. Sir Ian P. A. M. Walker-Okeover, Bt., D.S.O., T.D.	H. U. Stephenson, T.D.	G. C. Coleman
(11) Devon...........	The Lord Roborough	Field Marshal Sir Richard Hull, G.C.B., D.S.O.	C. A. Ansell
(12) Dorset..........	Col. Sir Joseph Weld, O.B.E., T.D.	Lt.-Col. J. T. A. Wilson	Lt.-Col. G. W. Mansell, T.D.
(13) Durham.........	The Lord Barnard, T.D.	T. R. F. Fenwick	G. Fishburn [C.B.E.
(14) Essex...........	Col. Sir John Ruggles-Brise, Bt., C.B., O.B.E., T.D.	R. E. Tritton	G. C. Waterer
(15) Gloucester.......	Col. The Duke of Beaufort, K.G., P.C.	Lt.-Col. S. R. M. Jenkins, M.C.	Maj. P. D. Birchall
(16) Greater Manchester	W. A. Downward [G.C.V.O.	D. Edwards	T. O. Hammett
(17) Hampshire........	The Earl of Malmesbury, T.D.	Maj. C. H. Liddell, M.C.	Lord Porchester
(18) Hereford & Worcester......	Col. J. F. Maclean	G. H. Heaton	Sir Michael Higgs
(19) Hertford..........	Maj.-Gen. Sir George Burns, K.C.V.O., C.B., D.S.O., O.B.E., M.C.	S. A. Bowes Lyon	P. T. Ireton
(20) Humberside.......	The Earl of Halifax	Col. R. A. Alec-Smith, T.D.	A. F. Clarke
(21) Kent.............	The Lord Astor of Hever	J. G. Phillimore, C.M.G.	J. B. D. Waite
(22) Lancashire........	The Lord Clitheroe, P.C.	Maj. B. Greenwood, T.D.	L. Broughton
(23) Leicestershire......	Col. R. A. St. G. Martin, O.B.E.	J. W. T. Wood	The Duke of Rutland,
(24) Lincoln..........	(vacant)	Col. G. M. Sanders, T.D.	J. H. Lewis [C.B.E.
(25) Greater London....	Marshal of the Royal Air Force, The Lord Elworthy, G.C.B., C.B.E., D.S.O., M.V.O., D.F.C., A.F.C.	M. Baring, C.V.O.	Dame Evelyn Denington, D.B.E.
(26) Merseyside........	Brig. Sir Douglas I. Crawford, C.B. D.S.O., T.D.	Lt.-Col. F. V. Denton, O.B.E., T.D.	W. H. Sefton
(27) Norfolk..........	Col. Sir Edmund Bacon, Bt., K.G., K.B.E., T.D.	D. E. Longe, M.C.	F. H. Stone
(28) Northampton......	Lt.-Col. J. Chandos-Pole, O.B.E.	T. M. Sergison-Brooke	R. E. Warwick
(29) Northumberland...	The Duke of Northumberland, K.G., P.C., T.D.	Lt.-Col. P. R. O. Bridgeman	The Viscount Ridley, T.D.
(30) Nottingham.......	Cmdr. M. B. P. Francklin, D.S.C., R.N.(ret.)	Capt. J. S. Dobson	E. S. Foster
(31) Oxford...........	Col. Sir John Thomson, K.B.E., T.D.	J. E. H. Collins, M.B.E., D.S.C.	R. C. Weir
(32) Salop............	J. R. S. Dugdale	Col. G. M. Thornycroft	Lt.-Col. R. C. G. Morris-Eyton, T.D.
(33) Somerset.........	Col. C. T. Mitford-Slade	M. H. Waley-Cohen, T.D.	W. M. F. Knowles
(34) Stafford..........	A. Bryan	A. S. Monckton	G. W. Newman, C.B.E.
(35) Suffolk..........	Cdr. The Earl of Stradbroke, R.N.(ret.)	R. S. Ryder	The Hon. C. B. A. Bernard,
(36) Surrey...........	The Lord Hamilton of Dalzell, M.C.	Mrs. W. M. M. du Buisson	Brig. S. T. Bastin, C.B.E., T.D.
(37) Sussex, East.......	The Marquess of Abergavenny, O.B.E.	T. E. S. Egerton	T. H. B. Mynors
(38) Sussex, West......	Lavinia, Duchess of Norfolk, C.B.E.	D. D. Scott	E. J. F. Green
(39) Tyne and Wear....	Sir James Steel, C.B.E.	J. M. H. Ross	D. Sleightholme
(40) Warwick..........	C. M. T. Smith-Ryland	B. Gillitt	I. A. B. Cathie
(41) West Midlands.....	The Earl of Aylesford	E. H. Moore	D. A. Birch
(42) Wight, Isle of.....	Admiral of the Fleet, The Earl Mountbatten of Burma, K.G., P.C., G.C.B., O.M., G.C.S.I., G.C.I.E., G.C.V.O., D.S.O.	Rear Adm. J. L. Blackham, C.B.	Rear Adm. J. L. Blackham, C.B.
(43) Wiltshire..........	The Lord Margadale, T.D.	Lt.-Col. R. H. Heywood-Lonsdale, M.B.E., M.C.	Gp. Capt. F. A. Willan, C.B.E., D.F.C.
(44) Yorkshire, North...	The Marquess of Normanby, C.B.E.	Lt.-Col. D. R. Tetley, T.D.	J. T. Fletcher, C.B.E.
(45) Yorkshire, South...	G. F. Young, C.B.E.	E. J. T. Taylor	E. E. Jones
(46) Yorkshire, West...	Brig. K. Hargreaves, C.B.E., T.D.	G. L. Fox	J. S. Bell

* High Sheriffs are nominated by the Queen on November 12 and come into office after Hilary Term.

NOTE.—The office of Chairman of Quarter Sessions was abolished by the Courts Act, 1971, s. 44, effective from Jan. 1. 1972. Jurisdiction of courts of quarter sessions passed to The Crown Court on that date.

ENGLISH COUNTIES AND SHIRES

CHIEF EXECUTIVES OF COUNTY COUNCILS, COUNTY TREASURERS AND CHIEF CONSTABLES

County or Shire	Chief Executive	County Treasurer	Chief Constable
(1) Avon............	W. J. Hutchinson	D. G. Morgan	K. W. L. Steele, O.B.E., K.P.M.
(2) Bedford..........	J. W. Elven	V. F. Phillips	A. Armstrong, Q.P.M.
(3) Berks............	R. W. Gash	M. C. Beasley	} D. Holdsworth, Q.P.M.
(4) Bucks............	J. Stevenson	G. B. Ravens	
(5) Cambridge........	J. K. Barratt	J. E. Barton	F. D. Porter, O.B.E., Q.P.M.
(6) Cheshire.........	J. K. Boynton, M.C.	C. T. Fletcher	W. Kelsall, O.B.E., Q.P.M.
(7) Cleveland........	J. B. Woodham	B. Stevenson	R. Davison, O.B.E., Q.P.M.
(8) Cornwall.........	A. L. Dennis	K. Hyde	J. C. Alderson, Q.P.M.
(9) Cumbria.........	T. J. R. Whitfield	J. R. Ford	W. T. Cavey, O.B.E., Q.P.M.
(10) Derby............	H. Crossley	E. J. Cobb	W. Stansfield, C.B.E., M.C., Q.P.M.
(11) Devon............	C. V. Lucas	O. A. Sanders	J. C. Alderson, Q.P.M.
(12) Dorset...........	K. A. Abel	T. J. J. Emmings	A. Hambleton, O.B.E., M.C., Q.P.M.
(13) Durham..........	J. Procter	J. M. Wright	A. G. Puckering, Q.P.M.
(14) Essex............	J. S. Mills, M.C.	E. A. Twelvetree	Sir John Nightingale, C.B.E., B.E.M.
(15) Gloucester.......	D. G. Rogers	J. V. Miller	B. Weigh
(16) Greater Manchester	Sir George Ogden, C.B.E.	K. J. Bridge	W. J. Richards, C.B.E., Q.P.M.
(17) Hampshire.......	L. K. Robinson	B. Dufton	Sir Douglas Osmond, C.B.E., Q.P.M.
(18) Hereford and Worcester......	J. H. C. Phelips, O.B.E.	A. B. Turner	A. A. Rennie, Q.P.M.
(19) Hertford........	F. P. Boyce	C. C. Jasper	R. N. Buxton, O.B.E., B.E.M., Q.P.M.
(20) Humberside......	J. H. W. Glen, C.B.E.	J. A. Parkes	R. Walton, O.B.E., Q.P.M.
(21) Kent.............	W. U. Jackson	P. E. W. Stoodley	B. N. Pain
(22) Lancashire.......	P. D. Inman, T.D.	W. O. Jolliffe	S. Parr, C.B.E., Q.P.M.
(23) Leicestershire.....	R. R. Thornton, C.B.E.	J. S. Blackburn	A. Goodson, Q.P.M.
(24) Lincoln..........	D. D. Macklin	G. R. Prentice	L. Byford, Q.P.M.
(25) Greater London...	J. C. Swaffield, C.B.E., R.D.	M. F. Stonefrost	(Metropolitan Police Area)
(26) Merseyside.......	Sir Stanley Holmes	P. W. Jenkins	(vacant)
(27) Norfolk..........	B. J. Capon	B. Taylor, M.C.	C. G. Taylor, Q.P.M.
(28) Northampton.....	A. J. Greenwell	H. Lawson	F. A. Cutting, Q.P.M.
(29) Northumberland ..	C. W. Hurley, O.B.E., T.D.	W. H. Foakes	S. Bailey
(30) Nottingham.......	R. F. O'Brien	G. E. Daniel	R. S. Fletcher, Q.P.M.
(31) Oxford...........	A. T. Brown	W. H. P. Davison	D. Holdsworth, Q.P.M.
(32) Salop...........	W. N. P. Jones	R. R. Renville	A. A. Rennie, Q.P.M.
(33) Somerset.........	J. E. Whittaker	(vacant)	K. W. L. Steele, O.B.E., K.P.M.
(34) Stafford	J. B. Brown	G. Woodcock	A. M. Rees, C.B.E., Q.P.M.
(35) Suffolk..........	C. W. Smith	E. T. Knott	A. Burns, D.S.O., Q.P.M.
(36) Surrey...........	F. A. Stone	G. W. Payne-Butler	P. J. Matthews, O.B.E., Q.P.M.
(37) Sussex, East......	R. M. Beechey	J. Unsworth	} G. W. R. Terry, Q.P.M.
(38) Sussex, West......	J. R. Hooley	B. Fieldhouse	
(39) Tyne and Wear	J. J. Gardner	C. J. Davies	S. Bailey
(40) Warwick.........	E. Cust	C. G. McMillan	R. B. Matthews, C.B.E., Q.P.M.
(41) West Midlands....	J. D. Hender	K. E. Rose	P. D. Knights, O.B.E., Q.P.M.
(42) Wight, Isle of....	J. S. Horsnell	D. A. Tuck	Sir Douglas Osmond, C.B.E., Q.P.M.
(43) Wiltshire.........	R. P. Harries	R. L. W. Moon	G. R. Glendinning, O.B.E., Q.P.M.
(44) Yorkshire, North..	H. J. Evans	K. R. Hounsome	R. P. Boyes, Q.P.M.
(45) Yorkshire, South..	F. A. Mallett	D. B. Chynoweth	(vacant)
(46) Yorkshire, West...	P. J. Butcher	G. S. Pollard	R. Gregory, Q.P.M.

GREATER LONDON COUNCIL

The Greater London Council and 32 London Borough Councils were constituted under the London Government Act, 1963. They replaced, on April 1, 1965, the London County Council, the Middlesex County Council, the County Borough Councils of Croydon, East Ham and West Ham, 28 metropolitan borough, 39 non-county borough and 15 urban district councils. The boundaries and constitution of the Corporation of the City of London were not affected.

Under the Act, Greater London became for the first time a clearly defined local government area including, in addition to the former counties of London and the greater part of Middlesex, parts of Metropolitan Essex, Kent, Surrey and Hertfordshire.

The Greater London Council at present consists

of 92 councillors and 15 aldermen. Councillors are elected for single-member electoral divisions which are conterminous with the parliamentary constituencies. Councillors hold office for four years. Aldermen are elected by the councillors from among councillors or persons eligible to be councillors. The Local Government Act 1972 provides for the abolition of the position of alderman at the end of the current term of office. The Chairman, Vice-Chairman and Deputy Chairman are elected annually by the councillors and aldermen. The political head of the administration is the Leader of the Council, elected by the majority party. The Council meets at three-weekly intervals at 2.30 p.m. on Tuesdays except in holiday periods. Most committees and sub-committees meet at three-weekly intervals.

Greater London Council
(Elected April 12, 1973)

Greater London comprises an area of 610 sq. miles and has a population of 7,167,600 (1974 mid-year estimates).

Chairman (1975–76), Dame Evelyn Denington, D.B.E.
Vice-Chairman (1975–76), T. A. Jenkinson.
Deputy-Chairman (1975–76), F. Bennett, C.B.E.
Leader of the Council, Sir Reginald Goodwin, C.B.E.
Leader of the Opposition, H. W. Cutler, O.B.E.
★Abbot, F. (C.) . . . . *Alderman*
★Aplin, G. W. (C.) . . . . *Croydon South*
  Archer, F. W. (*Lab.*) . . . . . *Erith and Crayford*
★Bains, L. A. (C.) . . . . *Hornsey*
  Balfe, R. A. (*Lab.*) . . . . *Dulwich*
★Banks, A. (*Lab.*) . . . . *Fulham*
  Barker, D. E. R. (*Lab.*) . . . *Croydon North West*
  Basset, P. (*Lab.*) . . . . *Carshalton*
★Bell, E. P., O.B.E. (*Lab.*) . . . *Newham South*
★Bell, W. (C.) . . . . *Chelsea*
★Bennett, F., C.B.E. (C.) . . . . *Alderman*
★Black, P. (C.) . . . . *Hendon South*
★Bolton, S. C. (C.) . . . . *Wimbledon*
★Bondy, L. (*Lab.*) . . . . *Islington North*
★Bonham, Mrs. I. (*Lab.*) . . . *Hammersmith North*
★Bramall, Sir Ashley (*Lab.*) . *Bethnal Green and Bow*
★Branagan, J. (*Lab.*) . . . . . . *Stepney and Poplar*
★Brew, R. M. (C.) . . . . *Chingford*
★Brown, B. J. (C.) . . . . *Ruislip-Northwood*
★Carr, E. G., B.E.M. (*Lab.*) . . *Vauxhall*
  Carradice, D. A. (*Lab.*) . . . *Ilford South*
★Chalkley, D. (*Lab.*) . . . . . . *Deptford*
★Chaplin, Mrs. I. (*Lab.*) . . . *Hackney South and*
                                  Shoreditch
★Chorley, A. F. J., M.B.E.
  (*Lab.*) . . . . *Alderman*
★Clack, W. S. (C.) . . . . *Harrow Central*
★Collins, R. (*Lab.*) . . . . *Alderman*
  Cooper, F. A. (*Lab.*) . . . . . *Hendon North*
★Cutler, H., O.B.E. (C.) . . . . *Harrow West*
  Daly, J. (*Lab.*) . . . . *Brentford and Isleworth*
★Denington, Dame Evelyn,
  D.B.E. (*Lab.*) . . . . *Islington Central*
★Dimson, Mrs. G. F. (*Lab.*) *Battersea North*
★Dobson, J. C. (C.) . . . . *Acton*
  Eden, D. (*Lab.*) . . . . *Feltham and Heston*
★Edwards, A. F. G. (*Lab.*) . . *Newham North-West*
★Fielding, D. M. (C.) . . . . . . *Sidcup*
★Freeman, L., O.B.E. (C.) . . . *Alderman*
  Freeman, R. (C.) . . . . *Finchley*
★Garside, Mrs. M. E. (*Lab.*) *Woolwich East*
★Geddes, Hon. Mrs. J. (C.) . *Streatham*
  Gillies, Mrs. L. G. (*Lab.*) . . *Tooting*
★Goodwin, Sir Reginald,
  C.B.E. (*Lab.*) . . . . *Bermondsey*
★Grieves, Mrs. A. Ll. (*Lab.*) . *Lambeth Central*
  Hacker, Mrs. R. (*Lab.*) . . . *St. Pancras North*
★Hardy, A. (C.) . . . . *Brent North*
★Harrington, I. (*Lab.*) . . . . . *Brent South*
★Harris, D. (C.) . . . . *Ravensbourne*
  Harwood, Miss M. (*Lab.*) . *Alderman*
  Haseler, Dr. S. M. (*Lah.*) . . *Wood Green*
  Hatch, S. (*Lab.*) . . . . *Battersea South*
★Henry, J. C. (*Lab.*) . . . . . . *Lewisham East*
★Hichisson, A. J. (C.) . . . . . *Alderman*
★Hillman, E. S. (*Lab.*) . . . . . *Hackney Central*
★Hinds, H. (*Lab.*) . . . . *Peckham*
  Howard, N. (*Lab.*) . . . . . . *Brent East*
★Jenkins, Mrs. M. (*Lab.*) . . *Putney*
  Jenkinson, T. A. (*Lab.*) . . . *Newham North-East*
  Judge, A. (*Lab.*) . . . . *Mitcham and Morden*
  Kay, H. (*Lab.*) . . . . *Dagenham*
★Kazantzis, A. (*Lab.*) . . . . . *Holborn and St. Pancras*
                                  South
★Langton, V. R. M. (C.) . . *Bexleyheath*
  Lemkin, J. (C.) . . . . *Uxbridge*
  Livingstone, K. (*Lab.*) . . . . *Norwood*
  Lourie, S. (*Lab.*) . . . . *Hornchurch*
  McIntosh, A. R. (*Lab.*) . . . *Tottenham*
  Mansfield, Dr. W. K.
  (*Lab.*) . . . . *Alderman*
★Marks, B. (C.) . . . . *Chipping Barnet*
  Mason, B. S. (*Lab.*) . . . . . *Edmonton*
  Mason, Rev. D. (*Lab.*) . . . *Ealing North*
  Mayne, S. (*Lab.*) . . . . *Alderman*
  Merriton, Mrs. J. (*Lab.*) . . *Paddington*
★Mitchell, R. (C.) . . . . *Wanstead and Woodford*
★Mitcheson, T. (C.) . . . . *Southgate*
  Morgan, Miss G. E. (C.) . *Croydon North East*
★Mote, H. T. (C.) . . . . *Harrow East*
★O'Connor, L. P. (*Lab.*) . . . *Alderman*
  Partridge, B. Brook- (C.) . . *Romford*
★Pitt, Lord (*Lab.*) . . . . *Hackney North and*
                                  Stoke Newington
★Plummer, Sir Desmond,
  T.D. (C.) . . . . *St. Marylebone*
★Ponsonby, T. (*Lab.*) . . . . . *Alderman*
  Rees, Mrs. M. (*Lab.*) . . . . *Woolwich West*
  Ridoutt, T. (*Lab.*) . . . . *Ilford North*
★Ripley, S. (C.) . . . . *Kingston upon Thames*
★Roberts, Miss S. (C.) . . . . . *Upminster*
  Rundle, Dr. S. (*L.*) . . . . . . *Richmond*
  Russell, P. F. N. (*Lab.*) . . . *Hayes and Harlington*
★Scorgie, M. C. (C.) . . . . . . *The City of London and*
                                  Westminster South
★Seaton, G. J. D. (C.) . . . . . *Surbiton*
  Shaw, Mrs. R. (*L.*) . . . . . . *Sutton and Cheam*
  Sieve, Mrs. Y. (*Lab.*) . . . . *Southall*
  Simson, W. (*Lab.*) . . . . . . *Lewisham West*

★Smith, F. W. (*C.*)........ *Beckenham*
Stutchbury, O. (*Lab.*).... *Alderman*
Styles, F. W., B.E.M.(*Lab.*) *Greenwich*
Tatham, Mrs. J. (*C.*)..... *Orpington*
★Taylor, Dr. G. W. (*C.*)... *Alderman*
★Townsend, Mrs. L., C.B.E.
  (*C.*)................. *Alderman*
★Tremlett, G. (*C.*)........ *Twickenham*
★Vigars, R. (*C.*).......... *Kensington*
Walsh, J. J. (*Lab.*)........ *Leyton*

★Ward, J. B. (*Lab.*)........ *Barking*
Warren, J. G. (*Lab.*)...... *Alderman*
White, D. (*Lab.*)......... *Croydon Central*
White, Dr. J. (*Lab.*)....... *Enfield North*
★Wicks, A. E. (*Lab.*)....... *Islington South and Finsbury*
Wistrich, Mrs. E. (*Lab.*)... *Hampstead*
Wykes, Mrs. J. (*C.*)...... *Chislehurst*
Young, R. (*Lab.*)........ *Walthamstow*
  ★ Denotes members of the last Council.

Director-General and Clerk to the Council, J. C. Swaffield, C.B.E., R.D.

G.L.C. Services

The services provided by the G.L.C. include planning, roads, traffic management and control, fire services, refuse disposal, housing, parks and licensing. For certain services it shares responsibility with the London Borough Councils and the City Corporation.

Education.—The local education authority for an area corresponding with the area of the twelve inner London boroughs and the City of London is the Inner London Education Authority, a special committee of the G.L.C. consisting of the members of the Council elected for the inner London boroughs together with a representative of each inner London Borough Council and of the Common Council. The Council charges to the rating authorities in the Inner London Education Area the expenditure of the I.L.E.A., the amount being determined by the Authority. This unique arrangement preserves the continuity of the service which has developed since 1870 as a unity without regard to local boundary divisions.

The total number of pupils on the rolls of the Authority's nursery, primary and secondary schools (including special schools for handicapped children) is over 408,000. There are 38 nursery, 725 county (including 2 at Children's homes), 344 voluntary and 118 special schools, staffed by the equivalent of 24,000 full-time teachers. Vocational instruction, cultural studies and recreational activities for persons over compulsory school age are arranged at the various establishments for further education. The Authority maintains 26 colleges and makes grants to 5 polytechnics and 8 other institutions. Non-vocational classes are offered at 31 evening and literary institutes, 1 recreational institute and 67 youth centres, including 2 drama centres. Nine colleges for the training of teachers are also managed by the Authority. The 20 outer London Borough Councils are the education authorities for their Boroughs.

Housing.—The Council shares with the London Borough Councils responsibility for housing in London and it accommodates 15,000 families a year, 4,000 of them in expanding towns many miles from London. The G.L.C. has about 200,000 homes, nearly 50,000 homes having been transferred to the London Borough Councils since 1971.

Planning and Transportation.—The Council as planning authority for Greater London as a whole has prepared a strategic development plan which lays down basic planning policies and principles for the whole area. The Greater London Development Plan has been the subject of a public inquiry whose findings have been published. However, a final decision on the plan is still awaited from the Secretary of State for the Environment, and a number of major amendments have been made by the G.L.C. since its submission. Also, since the submission of the plan, the Transport (London) Act, 1969, has given the G.L.C. responsibility for preparing more detailed transport plans, and, through a London Transport Executive appointed by the Council, for London Transport policies and finance. It is thus now able to consider and co-ordinate priorities for investment in all forms of transport in London.

Within the framework of the Development plan, the London Borough Councils and the City Corporation will prepare their own detailed local development plans. Town planning control of private development proposals is mainly the concern of the London Boroughs but the G.L.C. has some responsibilities in this field. As planner and developer the Council is involved in many major schemes. Notable examples are the Thamesmead project and the Covent Garden area.

The Council is responsible for the construction, improvement and maintenance of principal roads. As the traffic authority for all roads in Greater London it prepares or approves schemes for one-way working, traffic signals, clearways, bus-only lanes, waiting and loading restrictions and speed limits and makes the orders which enforce them. It maintains the Thames tunnels, the Woolwich Free Ferry, and all but four of the Thames bridges (London, Tower, Blackfriars and Southwark, which are maintained by the Corporation of London).

The Transport (London) Act, 1969, gives the Council the primary responsibility for overall transport planning, including the fullest possible integration of all forms of public transport, traffic measures and the development of the most important roads, in close association with land use planning.

Expanding towns.—An important aspect of the Council's policy is the provision of homes for people in housing need from London, willing to move to jobs in towns expanding under agreements with the G.L.C. made under the Town Development Act, 1952. The Council has such agreements with 28 towns.

Parks.—The Council maintains some 5,500 acres of parks and open spaces. The London Borough Councils and the City Corporation between them provide a further 26,500 acres. Up to 1,000 open-air entertainments are arranged in G.L.C. parks each summer and almost all games and sports are provided for. At Crystal Palace, in addition to the Council's 70 acre park is the Crystal Palace National Sports Centre, owned by the Council and managed by the Sports Council.

Other features of the G.L.C.'s administration include its responsibility for the Royal Festival Hall, Queen Elizabeth Hall and Purcell Room and the Hayward Gallery; the maintenance of the Iveagh Bequest, Kenwood, several other buildings of historic interest and two museums. The Greater London Record Office and Library house official records and other manuscripts, books, maps, drawings and photographs relating to London and are open to the public for reference purposes. The Research and Intelligence unit is concerned with information and research on any matters concerning

Greater London. The results of its work will be available to government departments, local authorities and the public.

Refuse disposal.—The Council is responsible for the disposal of refuse throughout Greater London—almost 3,000,000 tons being handled each year. It operates twenty-five transfer stations (where refuse is transferred into bulk road vehicles or barges) and four incinerators. Refuse is used for infilling at some twenty land reclamation sites. The Boroughs continue to be responsible for refuse collection. Well over 20,000 old vehicles and more than 150,000 tons of bulky household refuse (the latter deposited direct by members of the public but included in the total of 3,000,000 tons) are also dealt with as a means of improving the environment under the Civic Amenities Act, 1967.

Land Drainage and Flood Prevention.—The G.L.C. and the Borough Councils exercise land drainage functions on certain watercourses within a 400 sq. mile area in and adjoining Greater London known as the London Excluded Area. The G.L.C. undertakes flood prevention works and maintains unobstructed flows in main metropolitan watercourses including the Ravensbourne, Beverley Brook, Wandle, Crane and Brent rivers. The Council also has flood prevention functions along some 120 miles of riverbank of the Thames and its tidal tributaries. Work has started, and will continue over the next four years, on the construction of a barrier across the Thames at Silvertown which, with associated bank raising schemes, will provide flood protection against surge tides.

Licensing.—The Council is the licensing authority in Greater London for certain places of entertainment, greyhound race tracks and petroleum installations and, as agent for the Department of the

Environment, licenses motor vehicles and drivers.

Fire Services.—The Council runs the fire service for its whole area.

The London Fire Brigade set up on April 1, 1965, under the London Government Act, 1963, consists of the Brigades of the former counties of London and Middlesex (excluding the districts of Staines, Sunbury and Potters Bar), the former county boroughs of East Ham, West Ham and Croydon and of parts of Essex, Herts., Kent and Surrey. *Headquarters,* 8 Albert Embankment, S.E.1.

The Brigade has 114 land and 2 river stations. Wholetime authorized establishment, 6,663. There are 567 fire-fighting appliance vehicles and one fire boat in commission. In 1974, there were 87,270 calls to fires and other emergencies.
Chief Officer, J. Milner, C.B.E., Q.F.S.M.
Deputy Chief Fire Officer, D. R. Burrell, Q.F.S.M.

Finance.—The gross revenue expenditure of the G.L.C. (excluding London Transport) in 1975–76 is estimated in the annual budget at over £595,600,000 and that of the I.L.E.A. £377,700,000, making a total of £973,300,000; of this total about 60 per cent. (£586,300,000) will be met from rates, about 28 per cent. (£274,600,000) from income from rents, services, etc., and the balance of about 12 per cent. (£112,400,000) from central Government grants. The amount levied by the G.L.C. in rate precepts varies for different London Borough Councils according to the services provided.

Gross capital expenditure of the G.L.C. and the I.L.E.A., approved in the annual budget and mainly met by borrowing, amounts to about £429,000,000. Capital expenditure on housing and loans for house purchase accounts for nearly three-quarters of the total.

THE CORPORATION OF LONDON

The City of London is the historic centre at the heart of London known as "the square mile" around which the vast metropolis has grown over the centuries. The City's population is 4,232 (1971 Census, preliminary). The civic government is carried on by the Corporation of London through the Court of Common Council, a body consisting of the Lord Mayor, 25 other Aldermen and 153 Common Councilmen. The legal title of the Corporation is "the Mayor and Commonalty and Citizens of the City of London."

The City is the financial and business centre of London and includes the head offices of the principal banks, insurance companies and mercantile houses, in addition to buildings ranging from the historic interest of the Roman Wall and the 15th century Guildhall, to the massive splendour of St. Paul's Cathedral and the architectural beauty of Wren's spires.

The City of London was described by Tacitus in A.D. 62 as "a busy emporium for trade and traders". Under the Romans it became an important administration centre and hub of the road system. Little is known of London in Saxon times when it formed part of the kingdom of the East Saxons. In 886 Alfred recovered London from the Danes and reconstituted it a burgh under his son-in-law. In 1066 the citizens submitted to William the Conqueror who in 1067 granted them a charter, which is still preserved, establishing them in the rights and privileges they had hitherto enjoyed. The mayoralty was established on the recognition of the corporate unity of the citizens by Prince John in 1191, the first Mayor being Henry Fitz Ailwyn who filled the office for 21 years and was succeeded by Fitz Alan (1212–15). A new charter was granted by King John in 1215, directing the Mayor to be

chosen annually, which has ever since been done, though in early times the same individual often held the office more than once. A familiar instance is that of "Whittington, thrice Lord Mayor of London" (in reality four times, A.D. 1397, 1398, 1406, 1419); and many modern cases have occurred. The earliest instance of the phrase "Lord Mayor" in English is in 1414. It is used more generally in the latter part of the 15th century and becomes invariable from 1535 onwards. At Michaelmas the Liverymen in Common Hall choose two Aldermen who have served the office of Sheriff for presentation to the Court of Aldermen, and one is chosen to be Lord Mayor for the ensuing mayoral year. The Lord Mayor is presented to the Lord Chief Justice at the Royal Courts of Justice on the second Saturday in November to make the final declaration of office, having been sworn in at Guildhall on the preceding day. The procession to the Royal Courts of Justice is popularly known as the *Lord Mayor's Show.*

Aldermen are mentioned in the 11th century and their office is of Saxon origin. They were elected annually between 1377 and 1394, when a charter of Richard II directed them to be chosen for life. The *Common Council,* elected annually on December 17, was, at an early date, substituted for a popular assembly called the *Folkmote.* At first only two representatives were sent from each ward, but the number has since been greatly increased.

Sheriffs were Saxon officers: their predecessors were the *wic-reeves* and *portreeves* of London and Middlesex. At first they were officers of the Crown, and were named by the Barons of the Exchequer; but Henry I (in 1132) gave the citizens permission to choose their own Sheriffs, and the annual election of Sheriffs became fully operative under King John's charter of 1199. The citizens lost this privilege, as far as the election of Sheriff of Middlesex is concerned, by the Local Government Act, 1888; but the Liverymen continue, as heretofore, to choose two Sheriffs of the City of London, who are appointed on Midsummer Day, and take office at Michaelmas.

Officers.—The Recorder was first appointed in 1298. The office of Chamberlain is an ancient one, the first contemporary record of which is 1276. The Town Clerk (or Common Clerk) is mentioned in 1274 and the Common Serjeant in 1291.

Activities.—The work is assigned to a number of committees which present reports to the Court of Common Council. These Committees are:— City Lands and Bridge House Estates, Coal, Corn and Rates Finance, Planning and Communications, Central Markets, Billingsgate and Leadenhall Markets, Spitalfields Market, Police, Port and City of London Health, Library (Library, Records, Art Gallery and Museum), Schools, Music (Guildhall School of Music and Drama), General Purposes, Establishment, Housing, Gresham (City side), Epping Forest and Open Spaces, West Ham Park, Policy and Parliamentary, Privileges, Welfare, Guildhall Reconstruction, Barbican and Central Criminal Court (Extension).

The Honourable the *Irish Society*, which manages the Corporation's Estates in Ulster, consists of a Governor and 5 other Aldermen, the Recorder, and 19 Common Councilmen, of whom one is elected Deputy Governor.

The *City's Estate*, in the possession of which the Corporation of London differs from other municipalities, is managed by the City Lands and Bridge House Estates Committee, the Chairmanship of which carries with it the title of " Chief Commoner."

The Right Honourable the Lord Mayor 1974–1975*

Sir Henry Murray Fox, G.B.E.; *born* 1912; Alderman of *Bread Street*, 1966; *Sheriff of London*, 1971; *Lord Mayor*, 1974.
Secretary, Rear-Admiral C. W. Ellis, C.B.E.

The Aldermen

Aldermen.	Ward	Born.	C.C.	Ald.	Shff.	Lord Mayor
Sir Denis Henry Truscott, G.B.E., T.D.	Bridge Without	1908	1938	1947	1951	1957
Sir Bernard Nathaniel Waley-Cohen, Bt.	Portsoken	1914	....	1949	1955	1960
Sir Robert (Ian) Bellinger, G.B.E.	Cheap	1910	1953	1958	1962	1966
Sir Gilbert (Samuel) Inglefield, G.B.E., T.D.	Aldersgate	1909	....	1959	1963	1967
Sir (Arnold) Charles Trinder, G.B.E.	Aldgate	1906	1951	1959	1964	1968
Sir Peter Malden Studd, G.B.E.	Cripplegate	1916	....	1960	1967	1970
Sir Edward de Coucey Howard, Bt., G.B.E.	Cornhill	1915	1951	1963	1966	1971
The Lord Mais, G.B.E., E.R.D., T.D.	Walbrook	1911	....	1963	1969	1972
Sir Hugh Walter Kingwell Wontner, G.B.E., C.V.O.	Broad Street	1908	....	1963	1970	1973
Sir Henry Murray Fox, G.B.E.	Bread Street	1912	1962	1966	1971	1974

All the above have passed the Civic Chair

Aldermen.	Ward	Born.	C.C.	Ald.	Shff.	Lord Mayor
Lindsay Roberts Ring	Vintry	1914	1964	1968	1967	....
Cdr. Robin Danvers Penrose Gillett, R.D., R.N.R.	Bassishaw	1925	1965	1969	1973	....
Air Cdre. Hon. Peter Beckford Rutgers Vanneck, C.B., O.B.E., A.F.C.	Cordwainer	1922	....	1969	1974	....
Kenneth Russell Cork	Tower	1913	1951	1970	1975	....
Alan Seymour Lamboll	Castle Baynard	1923	1949	1970	....	....
Sir Charles Gundry Alexander, Bt.	Bridge	1923	1969	1970	....	....
Michael Herbert Hinton	Billingsgate	1934	1970	1971	....	....
Peter Drury Haggerston Gadsden	Farringdon Wt.	1929	1969	1971	....	....
Neville Bernard Burston	Farringdon Wn.	....	1961	1971	....	....
Col. Ronald Laurence Gardner-Thorpe, T.D.	Bishopsgate	1917	....	1972	....	....
Christopher Selwyn Priestley Rawson	Lime Street	1928	1963	1972	1971	....
Christopher Leaver	Dowgate	1937	1973	1974	....	....
George Peter Theobald	Queenhithe	1931	1968	1974	....	....
Anthony Stuart Jolliffe	Candlewick	1938	....	1975	....	....
Lady Donaldson	Coleman St.	1921	1966	1975	....	....
Alan T. Traill	Langbourn	....	1970	1975	....	....

* The Lord Mayor for 1975–76 was elected on Michaelmas Day.

The Sheriffs 1975–1976

Alderman Kenneth Russell Cork (*see above*) and Ronald Arthur Ralph Hedderwick, *elected* June 24; *assumed office* September 26, 1975.

THE COMMON COUNCIL OF LONDON

Allday, P. F. (1972) ....*Bishopsgate*
Amies, T. H. C. (1961) ....*Bridge*
Angell, O. D. (1964) ....*Bishopsgate*
Ballard, K. A., M.C. (1969) ....*Castle Baynard*
Balls, H. D. (1970) ....*Cripplegate*
Barratt, *Deputy* T. E. C., C.B.E. (1944) ....*Candlewick*
Batty, J. G. (1968) ....*Portsoken*
Beck, R. T. (1963) ....*Farringdon Wn.*

Bell, A. M. (1971) ....*Bassishaw*
Betty, Capt. F. A. Kemmis-, O.B.E. V.R.D., R.N.R. (1967) ....*Broad St.*
Bowen, I., C.M.G. (1971) ....*Broad St.*
Brewer, H. G. (1970) ....*Langbourn*
Brighton, A. G. (1966) ....*Portsoken*
Brooks, W. I. B. (1967) ....*Cripplegate*
Brown, B. J. (1973) ....*Aldersgate*
Brown, D. T. (1971) ....*Walbrook*

Bull, P. A. (1968)..............Cheap
Burrow, G. W. (1965).........Lime Street
Champness, P. H. (1966)......Walbrook
Charvet, R. C. L., R.D. (1970)....Aldgate
Chubb, *Deputy* S. J. (1966)......Cripplegate
Clackson, *Deputy* D. L., M.B.E.
  (1951)......................Farringdon Wt.
Cleary, F. E., M.B.E. (1959)......Coleman St.
Clements, G. E. (1960).........Farringdon Wt.
Cohen, S. E., C.B.E. (1951)......Farringdon Wt.
Cole, A. C., T.D. (1964).........Castle Baynard
Collett, C. (1973)..............Broad Street
Collett, *Deputy* Sir Kingsley, C.B.E.
  (1945)......................Bridge
Cook, J. E. Evan- (1972)........Lime Street
Cope, Dr. J. (1963)............Farringdon Wt.
Coulson, *Deputy* A. G. (1961)...Broad St.
Coven, *Deputy* Mrs. E. O. (1972).Dowgate
Coward, C. R. (1966)..........Cripplegate
Cresswell, P. H. (1958).........Aldgate
Daltrey, D. H. J. (1973).........Billingsgate
Davis, W. A. (1971)............Queenhithe
Dean, H. R. (1958)............Cordwainer
Deith, *Deputy* R. C. (1944).......Farringdon Wn.
Delderfield, D. W. (1971)........Cripplegate
Denny, A. M. (1971)............Billingsgate
Dewhirst, W. (1971)............Cripplegate
Donelly, T. A., M.B.E. (1973).....Cheap
Duckworth, *Deputy* H. (1960)....Lime St.
Dyer, *Deputy* C. F. W., E.R.D. (1966)Aldgate
Ebbisham, The Lord, T.D., (1947).Candlewick
Ercolani, V. A. (1968).........Broad St.
Eskenzi, A. N. (1971)...........Farringdon Wn.
Evans, D. I., T.D. (1952).........Vintry
Ewin, *Deputy* Sir David Floyd-,
  M.V.O., O.B.E. (1963).........Castle Baynard
Fairweather, C. H. F. (1958)......Queenhithe
Fell, *Deputy* C. A. (1947).........Langbourn
Fellner, L. L. (1973)...........Cripplegate
Fish, H. I. (1950)..............Farringdon Wt.
Fisher, D. G. (1958)...........Cornhill
Fordham, W. E. (1966).........Aldgate
Frankenberg, *Deputy* A. J. (1964)..Portsoken
Frappell, C. E. (1973).........Bread St.
Game, *Deputy* D. S. (1950).......Farringdon Wt.
Gapp, *Deputy* J. G. (1956)........Cheap
Gardener, C. J. (1964)..........Broad St.
Gass, G. J. (1967)..............Coleman St.
Gold, R. (1965)...............Castle Baynard
Goodinge, A. W. (1966).........Aldersgate
Graham, J. (1969)..............Candlewick
Green, A. E. C., M.B.E., T.D. (1971)Bread Street
Gugan, Dr. K. L. (1974).........Dowgate
Hall, N. L., M.B.E. (1952).......Farringdon Wt.
Harding, N. H. (1970)..........Farringdon Wn.
Harris, *Deputy* W. H. Wylie (1957) Farringdon Wt.
Harrowing, *Deputy* T. C. (1940)...Bishopsgate
Hart, C. A. (1973)............Lime Street
Hart, M. G. (1970)............Bridge
Hatfield, A. F. R. (1968).........Bishopsgate
Hayward, *Deputy* R. J., C.B.E.
  (1943)......................Walbrook
Hedderwick, R. A. R. (1968)....Walbrook
Henfrey, Dr. A. W. (1974).......Aldersgate
Hill, *Deputy* E. W. F., T.D. (1962). Tower
Hoare, J. E. (1966)............Bishopsgate
Holland, J. (1972).............Aldgate
Horlock, H. W. S. (1969).......Farringdon Wn.
Howard, D. H. S. (1973)........Cornhill
Hunt, *Deputy* W. G. G. (1962)....Cripplegate
Ide, W. R. (1972)..............Castle Baynard
James, A. J. (1973)............Cordwainer

Jenks, M. A. B. (1972)..........Coleman Street
Keith, J. M., T.D. (1962)........Candlewick
Lascelles, J. C., D.F.C. (1970)......Billingsgate
Last, A. W. (1948)..............Bridge
Lawson, G. C. H. (1972).........Portsoken
Lewis, *Deputy* C. F., C.B.E. (1936). .Coleman Street
Ley, A. H. (1964)..............Bishopsgate
Liss, H. (1965)................Aldersgate
Longman, M. H. (1967).........Langbourn
Luckin, I. F. (1964)...........Candlewick
Luke, A. L. (1968)............Bishopsgate
McAulay, C. (1957)............Bread St.
Mills, A. P. (1969)............Bassishaw
Mitchell, C. R. (1972).........Castle Baynard
Morgan, B. L., C.B.E. (1963)....Bishopsgate
Murkin, C. H. (1969)..........Vintry
Olson, A. H. F. (1972)..........Dowgate
Oram, *Deputy* M. H., T.D. (1963) .Cordwainer
Packard, Brig. J. J. (1973).......Cripplegate
Park, J. W. (1966).............Tower
Parkin, A. M. (1961)...........Cheap
Peacock, *Deputy* R. W., C.B.E.
  (1956)......................Vintry
Peat, G. C. (1973)..............Cheap
Pettit, P. C. F. (1974)..........Queenhithe
Pike, *Deputy* H. T. (1946)........Cornhill
Prince, *Deputy* L. B., C.B.E. (1950). Bishopsgate
Pritchard, F. S. (1961).........Walbrook
Quekett, D. A. F., E.R.D. (1965)..Cornhill
Rayleigh, R. (1973)...........Portsoken
Rayner, N. (1960)............Farringdon Wt.
Reed, J. L., M.B.E. (1967)........Farringdon Wn.
Rigby, P. P. (1972)............Farringdon Wn.
Rodgers, S. C. (1969)..........Farringdon Wt.
Roney, E. P. T. (1974).........Bishopsgate
Rowlandson, Sir Graham, M.B.E.
  (1961)......................Coleman Street
Samuels, Mrs. I. (1972).........Portsoken
Shalit, D. M. (1973)...........Farringdon Wn.
Sharp, Mrs. I. M. (1974).........Queenhithe
Sheppard, *Deputy* S., O.B.E. (1957).Billingsgate
Shillingford, R. G., M.B.E. (1961). Vintry
Shindler, A. B. (1966)..........Billingsgate
Silk, D. (1974)...............Cripplegate
Skilbeck, *Deputy* C. (1948).......Queenhithe
Smith, F. S., T.D. (1958)........Cordwainer
Smith, *Deputy* Sir John Newson-,
  Bt. (1954)..................Bassishaw
Smith, P. A. Revell- (1959).....Vintry
Spurrier, H. J. (1974)..........Dowgate
Steiner, F. N. (1962)..........Bread St.
Stevenson, J. L. (1970).........Coleman Street
Stitcher, G. M. (1966).........Farringdon Wt.
Stunt, F. F. (1967)............Farringdon Wn.
Sudbury, Col. F. A., O.B.E., E.R.D.
  (1963)......................Tower
Sunderland, O., T.D. (1968)......Billingsgate
Titchener, H. B. (1966).........Cripplegate
Tremellen, N. C. (1951).........Langbourn
Trentham, G. D. (1941).........Bread St.
Turner, R. L. (1973)...........Tower
Vine, G. M., C.B.E. (1955).......Farringdon Wt.
Walker, *Deputy* S. R., C.B.E. (1937) Bread St.
Ward, Maj. B. M., M.V.O. (1963)...Bridge
Wilmot, R. T. D. (1973).........Cordwainer
Wilson, *Deputy* A. B. (1960)......Aldersgate
Wilson, E. S. (1971)...........Aldersgate
Wixley, G. R. A., O.B.E. (1964)...Bassishaw
Woodward, C. D. (1972)........Cripplegate
Yates, J. T., M.B.E. (1959).......Cheap

Deputies.—In the preceding list each Common Councilman so described serves as *Deputy* to the Alderman of his Ward.

OFFICERS OF THE CITY OF LONDON

	Elect.
Recorder, James William Miskin, Q.C.......	1975
Chamberlain, John Percival Griggs, M.C.....	1974
Town Clerk, Stanley James Clayton.......	1974
Common Serjeant, John Mervyn Guthrie Griffith-Jones, M.C....................	1964
Commissioner of the City Police, C. J. Page, Q.P.M..................................	1971
Comptroller and City Solicitor, S. F. Heather..	1964
Remembrancer, Geoffrey Arden Peacock....	1968
Secondary and Under Sheriff and High Bailiff of Southwark, R. M. Snagge, M.B.E., T.D....	1969
Medical Officer for the Port and City of London, D. T. Jones............................	1974
Coroner, D. M. Paul.....................	1966
Surveyor, Robert Scott Walker...........	1954
Engineer, G. W. Pickin..................	1973
City Architect, E. G. Chandler.............	1961
Swordbearer, Lt. Col. P. M. Milo...........	1974
Common Cryer and Serjeant-at-Arms, Lt.-Col. St. J. C. Brooke-Johnson, M.B.E.........	1970
Marshal, Col. P. J. C. Ratcliffe, O.B.E......	1974
Head Master of City of London School, J. A. Boyes................................	1965

	Elect.
Head Master of City of London Freemen's School M. J. Kemp..........................	1963
Head Mistress, City of London School for Girls, Miss L. E. M. Mackie................	1972
Principal, Guildhall School of Music and Drama, A. D. Percival, C.B.E..................	1965
Librarian and Curator and Director of the Art Gallery, W. G. Thompson.............	1966
Deputy-Keeper of the Records, Miss B. R. Masters, F.S.A.........................	1970
Deputy Town Clerk, G. W. Rowley.......	1974
Deputy Comptroller and City Solicitor, C. G. Karger.............................	1974
Principal Clerk, Chamberlain's Dept., G. H. Denney.............................	1974
Deputy Remembrancer, A. G. F. Mitchell.....	1972
Market Superintendents:—	
Central, D. J. Noakes, M.B.E.............	1967
Billingsgate and Leadenhall, C. A. Wiard, M.B.E...............................	1956
Spitalfields, C. A. Lodemore............	1967
Supt. Engineer, Tower Bridge, Lt. Cdr. A. P. Rabbitt.............................	1975

ESTIMATED EXPENDITURE ON RATE ACCOUNTS, 1975–1976

The Rateable Value of the City on April 1, 1975, was £243,486,613; rate levied, 1975–76, 65·52p, to provide for estimated expenditure as follows:—POOR RATE ACCOUNT, services administered by G.L.C. and I.L.E.A., net Precept after Grant was £118,693,423. Greater London Rate Equalisation Scheme, £5,750,000. Thames Water Authority Sewerage Levy, £5,930,000. Corporation Services, £19,955. Total Net Expenditure falling upon rates, £130,393,378.

GENERAL RATE ACCOUNT

Services	Net Expenditure excluding Exchequer Grant	Exchequer Grant	Net Expenditure falling upon Rates
	£	£	£
Administration of Justice.....................	1,284,135	186,210	1,097,925
Health & Social Services....................	1,858,980	250	1,858,730
Highways, Lighting etc......................	3,776,315	—	3,776,315
Housing..................................	4,538,675	1,012,670	3,526,005
Library, Museum & Art Gallery..............	1,392,300	—	1,392,300
City Police...............................	6,907,015	2,251,120	4,655,895
Town Planning & Development..............	1,803,705	2,575	1,801,130
Spitalfields Market........................	80,140	—	80,140
Other Services............................	2,993,960	268,005	2,725,690
TOTALS.................................	24,634,960	3,720,830	20,914,130

THE CITY GUILDS (LIVERY COMPANIES)
The Livery Companies of the City of London derive their name from the assumption of a distinctive dress or livery by their members in the 14th century.

The order of precedence (according to 2nd Report of Municipal Corporations' Commissioners, 1837), omitting extinct companies, is given in parentheses after the name of each Company. There are 84 Guilds in existence.

About 10,000 Liverymen of the Guilds are entitled to vote at elections in *Common Hall*.

MERCERS (*1*). *Hall.* Ironmonger Lane, E.C.2. *Livery*, 214.—*Clerk*, G. M. M. Wakeford; *Master*, M. A. O'B. ffrench Blake.

GROCERS (*2*). *Hall*, Princes Street, E.C.2. *Livery* 265.—*Clerk*, A. S. Cox; *Master* J. A. Pott.

DRAPERS (*3*). *Hall*, Throgmorton Street, E.C.2. *Livery*, 220.—*Clerk*, A. O'Neill; *Master* D. A. Harris, M.B.E., M.C.

FISHMONGERS (*4*) *Hall*, London Bridge, E.C.4. *Livery*, 286.—*Clerk*, E. S. Earl; *Prime Warden*, Commodore C. P. C. Noble, C.B.E., D.S.C., V.R.D.

GOLDSMITHS (*5*). *Hall*, Foster Lane, E.C.2. *Livery*, 240.—*Clerk*, C. P. de B. Jenkins, M.B.E., M.C.; *Prime Warden*, Sir Harold Himsworth, K.C.B.

SKINNERS (*6 and 7*). *Hall*, 8 Dowgate Hill, E.C.4. *Livery*, 299.—*Clerk*, M. H. Glover; *Master*, R. M. H. Marriott.

MERCHANT TAYLORS (*6 and 7*). *Hall*, 30 Threadneedle Street, E.C.2. *Livery*, 330.—*Clerk*, J. M. Woolley, M.B.E., T.D.; *Master Deputy* M. H. Oram.

HABERDASHERS (*8*). *Hall*, Staining Lane, E.C.2. *Livery*, 320.—*Clerk*, Cdr. W. R. Miller, R.N., *Master*, D. A. H. Sime, O.B.E., M.C.

SALTERS (*9*). *Livery*, 150.—*Clerk*, J. M. Montgomery, 36 Portland Place, W.1.; *Master* J. S. Wordie, C.B.E., V.R.D.

IRONMONGERS (*10*). *Hall*, Barbican, E.C.2., *Livery*, 37.—*Clerk*, R. B. Brayne, M.B.E., *Master* M. R. Warren.

VINTNERS (*11*). *Hall*, Upper Thames Street, E.C.4. *Livery*, 326.—*Clerk*, Cdr. R. D. Ross, R.N.; *Master*, J. H. Mason, D.S.O., T.D.

CLOTHWORKERS (*12*). *Hall*, Dunster Court, Mincing Lane, E.C.3. *Livery*, 180.—*Clerk*, E. J. Reed; *Master*, Ald. Sir B. Waley-Cohen, Bt.

The above are the Twelve " Great " London Companies in order of Civic precedence..

AIR PILOTS AND AIR NAVIGATORS, GUILD OF (*81*). *Grand Master*, H.R.H. the Prince Philip Duke of Edinburgh, K.G.; *Clerk*, W. T. F. Rossiter, P.O. Box 13, Air Terminal, Buckingham Palace Road, S.W.1; *Master*, Captain C. A. Owens.

APOTHECARIES, SOCIETY OF (*58*), *Hall*, Black Friars Lane, E.C.4. *Livery*, 675.—*Clerk*, E. Busby, M.B.E.; *Master*, E. G. Grey-Turner, M.C., T.D.

ARMOURERS AND BRASIERS (*22*). *Hall*, 81 Coleman Street, E.C.2. *Livery*, 120.—*Clerk*, Col. G. F. H. Archer, M.B.E.; *Master*, R. B. Tippetts.

BAKERS (*19*). *Hall*, Harp Lane, Lower Thames Street, E.C.3. *Livery*, 285.—*Clerk*, H. M. Collinson; *Master*, K. P. W. Stoneley.

BARBERS (*17*). *Hall*, Monkwell Square, E.C.2. *Livery*, 160.—*Clerk*, B. W. Hall, *Master*, R. A. Ottoway.

BASKETMAKERS (*52*). *Livery*, 395.—*Clerk*, B. Stroulger, Battlebridge House, 87–95 Tooley Street, S.E.1; *Prime Warden*, C. E. Hipkins.

BLACKSMITHS (*40*). *Livery*, 201.—*Clerk*, J. Green, 41 Tabernacle Street, E.C.2.; *Prime Warden*, A. J. Beale, M.D.

BOWYERS (*38*). *Livery*, 57.—*Clerk*, M. J. Smyth, Giltspur House, 5–6 Giltspur Street, E.C.1.; *Master*, J. R. Glazier.

BREWERS (*14*). *Hall*, Aldermanbury Square, E.C.2. *Livery*. 32.—*Clerk*, R. C. Stanley-Baker; *Master*, C. J. M. Downes.

BRODERERS (*48*). *Livery*, 106.—*Clerk*, S. G. B. Underwood, 80 Bishopsgate, E.C.2.; *Master*, S. B. Owen.

BUTCHERS (*24*). *Hall*, Bartholomew Close, E.C.1. *Livery*, 387.—*Clerk*, W. M. Collins; *Master*, H. A. Kingwell.

CARMEN (*77*). *Livery*, 428.—*Clerk*, J. M. Donald, 2 Stratford Place, W.1; *Master*, M. W. Harris.

CARPENTERS (*26*). *Hall*, Throgmorton Avenue, E.C.2. *Livery*, 150.—*Clerk*, Capt. G. B. Barstow, R.N.; *Master*, Dr. J. A. Moody, O.B.E.

CITY OF LONDON SOLICITORS (*79*). *Livery*, 450.—*Clerk*, K. S. G. Hinde, 27 Leadenhall Street, E.C.3.; *Master*, R. Chamberlain, T.D.

CLOCKMAKERS (*61*). *Livery*, 248.—*Clerk*, R. C. Pennefather, M.B.E., 38 Bedford Place, Bloomsbury Square, W.C.1.; *Master*, Ald. Sir Hugh Wontner, G.B.E., C.V.O.

COACHMAKERS (*72*). *Livery*, 356.—*Clerk*, A. T. Langdon-Down, 9 Lincoln's Inn Fields, W.C.2; *Master*, C. W. Ward.

COOKS (*35*). *Livery* 75.—*Clerk*, H. J. Lavington, T.D., 49 Queen Victoria Street, E.C.4.; *Master*, P. F. Herbage.

COOPERS (*36*). *Livery*, 230.—*Clerk*, J. W. S. Clark, 13 Devonshire Square, E.C.2; *Master*, I. A. Norman.

CORDWAINERS (*27*). *Livery*, 137.—*Clerk*, E. J. Mander, Eldon Chambers, 30 Fleet Street, E.C.4.; *Master*, J. G. Hooper, O.B.E.

CURRIERS (*29*). *Livery*, 65.—*Clerk*, I. R. McNeil, 43 Church Road, Hove; *Master*, Lord Birkett.

CUTLERS (*18*). *Hall*, 4 Warwick Lane, E.C.4. *Livery*, 100.—*Clerk*, K. S. G. Hinde; *Master*, Rev. Canon D. Webster.

DISTILLERS (*69*). *Livery*, 150.—*Clerk*, H. B. Dehn, Compter House, Wood Street, E.C.2; *Master*, Col. G. V. Churton, M.B.E., M.C., T.D.

DYERS (*13*). *Hall*, 10 Dowgate Hill, E.C.4. *Livery*, 110.—*Clerk*, A. J. Boyall; *Prime Warden*, D. R. B. Park.

FAN MAKERS (*76*). *Livery*, 163.—*Clerk*, E. J. H. Geffen, Africa House, 64–78 Kingsway, W.C.2; *Master*, L. R. Collins.

FARMERS (*80*). *Livery*, 284.—*Clerk*, Dr. B. A. C. Kirk-Duncan; 8 St. Mary at Hill, E.C.3. *Master*, Lt.-Col. C. A. Brooks, O.B.E., T.D. *Senior Warden*, Sir Nigel Strutt, T.D.

FARRIERS (*55*). *Livery*, 310.—*Clerk*, F. E. Birch, 3 Hamilton Road, Cockfosters, Barnet, Herts; *Master*, A. G. Smith.

FELTMAKERS (*63*). *Livery*, 350.—*Clerk*, E. J. P. Elliott, 53 Davies Street, Berkeley Square, W.1; *Master*, C. W. James.

FLETCHERS (*39*). *Livery*, 69.—*Clerk*, F. N. Steiner, Compter House, 4–9 Wood Street, E.C.2.; *Master*, F. G. Peacock.

FOUNDERS (*33*). *Hall*, 13 St. Swithin's Lane, E.C.4. *Livery*, 136.—*Clerk*, H. W. Wiley; *Master*, F. W. Rowe.

FRAMEWORK KNITTERS (*64*). *Livery*, 225.—*Clerk*, H. C. Weale, St. Saviour's School, New Kent Road, S.E.1; *Master*, Dr. G. R. Kershaw, V.R.D.

FRUITERERS (*45*). *Livery*, 220.—*Clerk*, D. L. Hohnen, 49 Berners St., W.1.; *Master*, M. R. Barton.

FURNITURE MAKERS (*83*). *Livery*, 182.—*Clerk*, G. Benbow, T.D., c/o J. Ward & Co., Robertsbridge, Sussex; *Master*, Brig. A. L. W. Newrth, C.B.E.

GARDENERS (66). *Livery,* 250.—*Clerk,* F. N. Steiner, Compter House, 4/9 Wood Street, E.C.2; *Master,* D. M. H. Longman.

GIRDLERS (23). *Hall,* Basinghall Avenue, E.C.2. *Livery,* 80.—*Clerk,* J. A. M. Rutherford; *Master,* Sir Michael Newton, Bt.

GLASS-SELLERS (71). *Livery,* 160.—*Hon. Clerk,* H. K. S. Clark, 6 Eldon Street, E.C.2; *Master,* P. Ide.

GLAZIERS (53). *Livery,* 250.—*Clerk,* Dr. B. A. C. Kirk-Duncan, 8 St. Mary-at-Hill, E.C.3; *Master,* K. S. London.

GLOVERS (62). *Livery,* 180.—*Clerk,* H. M. Collinson, Bakers Hall, Harp Lane, Lower Thames Street, E.C.3; *Master,* E. V. Hawtin.

GOLD AND SILVER WYREDRAWERS (74). *Livery,* 325.—*Clerk,* D. Reid, 40a Ludgate Hill, E.C.4.; *Master,* L. R. S. Cork.

GUNMAKERS (73). *Livery,* 84.—*Clerk,* F. B. Brandt, 12 Devonshire Square, E.C.3; *Master,* E. D. Lawrence.

HORNERS (54). *Livery,* 440.—*Clerk,* G. S. Wood, 28 Bush Lane, E.C.4; *Master,* W. A. Clarke.

INNHOLDERS (32). *Hall,* College Street, Dowgate Hill, E.C.4. *Livery,* 107.—*Clerk,* J. H. Bentley, O.B.E.; *Master,* Dr. I. R. Haire.

JOINERS (41). *Livery,* 85.—*Clerk,* B. J. Turner, 14 Parkway, N.14; *Master,* H. E. Reed.

LEATHERSELLERS (15). *Hall,* 15 St. Helens Place, E.C.3. *Livery,* 150.—*Clerk,* J. Hingtson; *Master,* R. E. C. Powell, M.B.E.

LORINERS (57). *Livery,* 290.—*Clerk,* D. B. Morris, Africa House, 64–78 Kingsway, W.C.2.; *Master,* R. M. Burton.

MASONS (30). *Livery,* 92.—*Clerk,* H. J. Maddocks, 9 New Square, W.C.2; *Master,* R. M. Wood, M.V.O.

MASTER MARINERS, HONOURABLE COMPANY OF (78). H.Q.S. *Wellington,* Temple Stairs, W.C.2. *Livery,* 300.—*Clerk,* D. H. W. Field; *Admiral,* H.R.H. the Prince Philip, Duke of Edinburgh, K.G.; *Master,* Capt. J. L. Watson.

MUSICIANS (50). *Livery,* 220.—*Clerk,* W. R. I. Crewdson, 4 St. Paul's Churchyard, E.C.4.; *Master,* Alderman Sir Gilbert Inglefield, G.B.E., T.D.

NEEDLEMAKERS (65). *Livery,* 240.—*Clerk,* R. H. Lane, 18 Great Marlborough Street, W.1.; *Master,* Lord Ashdown.

PAINTER STAINERS (28). *Hall,* 9 Little Trinity Lane, E.C.4. *Livery,* 350.—*Clerk,* H. N. Wylie; *Master,* A. G. Ingram.

PATTERNMAKERS (70). *Livery,* 152.—*Clerk,* A. J. Hucker, 3 Gray's Inn Square, W.C.1.; *Master,* H. N. E. Alston.

PAVIORS (56). *Livery,* 225.—*Clerk,* F. A. Barragan, 130 Mount Street, W.1.; *Master,* O. A. Aisher.

PEWTERERS (16). *Hall,* Oat Lane, E.C.2. *Livery,* 110.—*Clerk,* C. G. Grant; *Master,* Rev. J. L. Mullens.

PLAISTERERS (46). *Livery,* 164.—*Clerk,* H. Mott, Plaisterers Hall, 1 London Wall, E.C.2; *Master,* A. S. Roberts.

PLAYING CARD MAKERS (75). *Livery,* 150.—*Clerk,* E. K. King, 21A Northampton Square, E.C.1; *Master,* W. E. Tucker, C.V.O., M.B.E.

PLUMBERS (31). *Livery,* 240.—*Clerk,* L. J. D. Jones, 218 Strand, W.C.2; *Master,* Rev. C. Gill.

POULTERS (34). *Livery,* 150.—*Clerk,* I. G. Williamson, 9 Staple Inn, Holborn, W.C.1; *Master,* W. V. Beazley.

SADDLERS (25). *Hall,* Gutter Lane, Cheapside, E.C.2. *Livery,* 90.—*Clerk,* Maj. A. D. Hathway-Jones, R..M (ret.); *Master,* A. G. Sturdy.

SCIENTIFIC INSTRUMENT MAKERS (84). *Livery,* 152. —*Clerk,* H. Mott, Plaisterers Hall, 1 London Wall, E.C.2; *Master,* A. J. Garratt, M.B.E.

SCRIVENERS (44). *Livery,* 136.—*Clerk,* D. V. O'Meara, Lower Court, Stationers Hall, Ludgate Hill, E.C.4.; *Master,* H. M. Temple-Richards.

SHIPWRIGHTS (59). *Livery* 500.—*Hon. Clerk,* D. J. Walker, 14–20 St. Mary Axe, E.C.3; *Permanent Master,* H.R.H. the Prince Philip Duke of Edinburgh, K.G.; *Prime Warden,* Sir Alfred Sims, K.C.B., O.B.E.

SPECTACLEMAKERS (60). *Livery,* 220.—*Clerk,* C. J. Eldridge, Apothecaries' Hall, E.C.4; *Master,* L. E. Evershed Martin, O.B.E.

STATIONERS AND NEWSPAPER MAKERS (47). *Hall,* Stationers' Hall, E.C.4. *Livery,* 425.—*Clerk,* Col. R. A. Rubens; *Master,* L. E. Kenyon, C.B.E.

TALLOWCHANDLERS (21). *Hall,* 4 Dowgate Hill, E.C.4. *Livery,* 145.—*Clerk,* R. H. Monier-Williams; *Master,* W. R. Stevens.

TIN PLATE WORKERS (67). *Livery,* 181.—*Clerk,* H. B. Dehn, Compter House, Wood Street, E.C.2; *Master,* F. Hayes.

TOBACCO PIPE MAKERS AND TOBACCO BLENDERS (82). *Livery,* 200.—*Clerk,* I. J. Kimmins, 9 Red Lion Court, E.C.4; *Master,* F. B. Hooper.

TURNERS (51). *Livery,* 160.—*Clerk,* A. T. Reed, Giltspur House, 5–6 Giltspur Street, E.C.1; *Master,* C. D. L. Smith.

TYLERS AND BRICKLAYERS (37). *Livery,* 90.—*Clerk,* J. C. Peck, 6 Bedford Row, W.C.1; *Master,* Col. F. J. Trumper, O.B.E., T.D.

UPHOLDERS (49). *Livery,* 196.—*Clerk,* U. J. Burke, 26 St. Andrew's Hill, E.C.4; *Master,* D. W. Bishop.

WAX CHANDLERS (20). *Hall,* Gresham Street, E.C.2. *Livery,* 80.—*Clerk,* T. Wood; *Master,* R. J. Fielden.

WEAVERS (42). *Livery,* 125.—*Clerk,* J. G. Ouvry, 53 Romney Street, S.W.1; *Upper Bailiff,* G. Le Marc.

WHEELWRIGHTS (68). *Livery,* 291.—*Clerk,* J. Holland, 31 Copthall Avenue, E.C.2; *Master,* K. H. Williman.

WOOLMEN (43). *Livery,* 119.—*Clerk,* R. J. R. Cousins, 192–198 Vauxhall Bridge Rd., S.W.1; *Master,* L. J. Canham.

PARISH CLERKS (No livery) (Members, 90).—*Clerk,* R. H. Adams, T.D., F.S.A., 108 Dulwich Village, S.E.21; *Master,* Ald. A. S. Lamboll.

WATERMEN AND LIGHTERMEN (No livery).—*Hall,* 18 St. Mary-at-Hill, E.C.3.—*Clerk,* B. G. Wilson; *Master,* G. E. Garrett.

LAUNDERERS (No livery).—*Clerk,* P. H. Jackson, V.R.D., 21 Whitefriars St., E.C.4; *Master,* W. D. C. Robinson.

BUILDERS MERCHANTS OF THE CITY OF LONDON (No livery) (Members, 160).—*Clerk,* V. J. Fanstone, O.B.E., 34–35 Farringdon Street, E.C.4; *Master,* H. J. Hesketh.

NOTE.—In certain companies the election of Master or Prime Warden for the year does not take place till the autumn. In such cases the Master or Prime Warden for 1974–75 is given.

LONDON BOROUGHS

City or Borough *Inner London Borough	Municipal Offices	Population (Reg. Gen.'s Est. June 1972)	Rateable Value April 1, 1975	Rate Levied 1975–76	Town Clerk (*Chief Executive)	Mayor or Lord Mayor
			£	p.		
CITY OF WESTMINSTER*	City Hall, Victoria St., S.W.1.	233,360	311,229,071	63	*Sir Alan Dawtry, C.B.E., T.D.	R. M. Dawe
Barking.........	‡Dagenham, Essex.	158,710	268,600,000	75·5	S. W. Barker.	G. A. Brooker.
Barnet..........	†The Burroughs, Hendon, N.W.4.	305,760	56,595,996	64·5	E. M. Bennett	N. E. Hirshfield.
Bexley..........	†Erith, Kent.	216,980	28,636,820	78	*T. Musgrave.	F. Brearley.
Brent...........	†Forty Lane, Wembley.	275,570	49,265,841	81	K. B. Betts.	R. Dore-Boize
Bromley........	†Bromley, Kent.	306,550	45,668,565	79·8	P. J. Bunting.	A. G. F. Mitchell
Camden*.......	†Euston Road, N.W.1.	197,390	102,955,288	72	B. H. Wilson, C.B.E.	B. J. Taylor.
Croydon........	†Taberner House, Park Lane, Croydon	334,000	66,161,766	57	*A. Blakemore.	J. A. Keeling.
Ealing..........	†Ealing, W.5.	299,440	53,359,218	83·75	*P. J. Coomber.	J. Johnston.
Enfield.........	‡Silver St., Enfield.	265,910	46,296,414	74	*W. D. Day.	J. L. Lindsay.
Greenwich*.....	†Wellington St., Woolwich, S.E.18.	216,180	30,816,770	70	*R. L. Doble.	R. F. Neve
Hackney*.......	†Mare St., E.8.	215,270	36,002,848	60	*L. G. Huddy.	A. Super.
Hammersmith*..	†King St., W.6.	181,880	34,015,361	67	*A. J. R. Ward.	R. Beresford
Haringey........	‡High Road, N.22.	235,490	34,047,297	78·75	*R. C. Limb	Mrs. D. Cunningham.
Harrow.........	‡Station Rd., Harrow.	203,730	33,033,000	80	*R. Hill.	N. G. Hines
Havering........	†Main Road, Romford, Essex.	247,130	36,263,788	74	*R. W. J. Tridgell.	(vacant)
Hillingdon......	†Wood End Green Rd., Hayes.	236,390	53,470,208	81·4	*G. Hooper	L. Sherman
Hounslow.......	†Treaty Rd., Hounslow.	206,460	45,862,353	77·4	D. Mathieson.	W. R. Boyce
Islington*.......	†Upper St., N.1.	194,280	48,337,752	69·4	H. M. Dewing.	D. J. Davies
Kensington and Chelsea (Royal Borough)*.....	‡Kensington, W.8.	183,230	67,416,715	58·3	*R. L. Stillwell, D.F.C., D.F.M.	Mrs. B. Sundius-Smith.
Kingston upon Thames.......	Guildhall, Kingston upon Thames	139,420	27,064,240	69·01	*J. S. Bishop.	F. G. J. Gaisford.
Lambeth*......	†Brixton Hill, S.W.2.	301,690	56,816,247	68	*F. D. Ward.	S. H. Gurney.
Lewisham*.....	†Catford, S.E.6.	262,920	31,915,000	68·9	J. H. French.	L. Lynch.
Merton.........	†Broadway, Wimbledon, S.W.19.	176,820	29,606,757	77·3	*A. G. Robinson, D.F.C.	J. N. Healey.
Newham........	†East Ham, E.6.	232,020	35,481,575	88	*J. J. Warren.	L. A. Wood.
Redbridge.......	†High Rd., Ilford, Essex.	238,300	35,500,000	70·9	*A. McC. Findlay.	T. F. Cobb.
Richmond upon Thames.......	§Twickenham, Mddx.	172,560	29,714,400	74.5	A. W. B. Goode, MC	R. H. Stevens.
Southwark*.....	†Peckham Rd., S.E.5.	253,260	50,161,562	72·5	S. T. Evans.	C. A. G. Halford.
Sutton..........	‡3 Throwley Rd., Sutton, Surrey.	169,050	26,059,038	59	*T. M. H. Scott.	R. J. Slater.
Tower Hamlets*.	†Patriot Square, E.2.	159,200	39,637,483	80	*J. Wolkind.	B. Holmes.
Waltham Forest.	†Walthamstow, E.17.	233,200	30,703,779	79·54	*L. G. Knox.	Mrs. E. Bartram.
Wandsworth*....	†Wandsworth, S.W.18.	287,080	41,264,270	63·4	N. B. White.	A. Jones.

† Town Hall. ‡ Civic Centre. §Municipal Offices.

Public and Private Buildings in London

ADELPHI, Strand, W.C.2.—Adelphi Terrace and district commemorate the four architect brothers, James, John, Robert and William ADAM, who laid out the district (formerly Durham House) at the close of the 18th century. Four of the streets in the Adelphi were formerly called James, John, Robert, and William Streets to commemorate these founders of the Adam style of architecture and internal decoration. They are now Adam Street, John Adam Street, Robert Street and Durham House Street. Extensive rebuilding took place between the two World Wars, and there are now few 18th-century houses left in the district. In the neighbourhood of the Adelphi was York House, built by the Duke of Buckingham in 1625 (the Water Gate of which still stands in Embankment Gardens), the commemorative streets being *Charles* Street, *Villiers* Street, *Duke* Street, *Of* Lane, *Buckingham* Street (Of Lane is now " York Buildings ").

AUSTRALIA HOUSE, Strand, W.C.2.—A handsome and imposing building, erected 1911–14 by the Commonwealth of Australia as the offices of the High Commissioner for the Commonwealth. NEW SOUTH WALES, QUEENSLAND, VICTORIA and WESTERN AUSTRALIA have separate offices in the Strand; TASMANIA at Golden Cross House, Charing Cross, and SOUTH AUSTRALIA at S.A. House, 50 Strand, W.C.2.

BALTIC EXCHANGE, St. Mary Axe, E.C.3.— The world market for the chartering of cargo ships. The present Exchange was built in 1903 and the new wing opened by Her Majesty the Queen on Nov. 21, 1956.

BANK OF ENGLAND, Threadneedle Street, E.C.2. (Not open to sightseers)—The Bank of England, founded in 1694, has always been closely connected with the Government. The present building, completed in 1940 to the designs of Sir Herbert Baker, incorporates features reminiscent of the earlier architects, Sampson (1734), Sir Robert Taylor (1765) and Sir John Soane (1788).

BRIDGES.—The bridges over the Thames (from East to West) are the *Tower Bridge* (built by the Corporation of London and opened in 1894), with it bascules, affording a fine view of the Pool and of the metropolis; *London Bridge* (opened after rebuilding in 1831, and until 1750 the only bridge over the Thames in London), with the London Monument (*q.v.*) and Fishmongers' Hall; the new London Bridge was completed in 1973 and opened by Her Majesty the Queen on March 16, 1973; *Southwark Bridge* (opened in 1819, and rebuilt by the Corporation of London, 1922); *Blackfriars Bridge* (opened in 1869 and widened by the Corporation of London in 1909); *Waterloo Bridge* (Rennie), opened in 1817, commanding a fine view of western London (rebuilt by L.C.C. and re-opened 1944; *Hungerford Bridge* (railway bridge with a footbridge); *Westminster Bridge* (built in 1750 and then presenting a view that inspired Wordsworth's sonnet; rebuilt and re-opened in 1862; width, 84 ft.) with Thornycroft's *Boadicea* at the north-eastern end; this bridge leads from Westminster Abbey and the Houses of Parliament to the County Hall (*q.v.*) and St, Thomas's Hospital; *Lambeth Bridge* (rebuilt by L.C.C. and opened in 1932) leading from Lambeth Palace to Millbank; *Vauxhall Bridge* (rebuilt in 1906). leading to Kennington Oval; *Chelsea Bridge*, leading from Chelsea Hospital to Battersea Park (reconstructed and widened; 1937) and *Albert Bridge* (1873); *Battersea Bridge* (rebuilt in 1890); *Wandsworth Bridge* (opened in 1873; rebuilt and re-opened in 1940); *Putney Bridge* (opened in 1886 and widened in 1933, where the Oxford and Cambridge Boat Race is

started for Mortlake; *Hammersmith Bridge* (rebuilt 1887); *Barnes Bridge* (for pedestrians only, 1933); *Chiswick Bridge* (opened in 1933); *King Edward VII Bridge, Kew* (rebuilt in 1902, opened 1903, leading to the Royal Botanic Gardens, Kew; *Twickenham Lock Bridge; Twickenham Bridge* (opened 1933); *Richmond Bridge* (opened in 1777); *Kingston Bridge* (built 1828 and widened 1914) and *Hampton Court Bridge* (rebuilt, 1933).

BUCKINGHAM PALACE, St. James's Park, S.W.1. (Not open to the public.)—Was purchased by King George III in 1762 from the heir of the Duke of Buckingham, and was altered by Nash for King George IV. The London home of the Sovereign since Queen Victoria's accession in 1837. Refronted in stone (part of the Queen Victoria Memorial) by Sir Aston Webb in 1913.

The Queen's Gallery, containing a changing selection of the finest pictures and works of art from all parts of the royal collection, was opened to the public on July 25, 1962. Open: Tues.–Sat., 11–5 p.m.; Sundays, 2–5 p.m. Admission 30p; *Children, Students, OAPs* 10p, entering from Buckingham Palace Road.

The Royal Mews is open to visitors on Wednesdays and Thursdays throughout the year (except in Ascot Week), 2–4 p.m. The following charges, the net proceeds of which are devoted to charities, are payable on admission: *Adults*, 15p; *Children*, 5p.

CANADA HOUSE, Trafalgar Square, S.W.1.—A conspicuous building on the Western side of the Square, housing the Office of the High Commissioner for Canada in the United Kingdom. Designed by Sir Robert Smirke in 1820, it was renovated and embellished when acquired from the Union Club in 1924. Further major alterations have been completed to incorporate the former Royal College of Physicians building, also designed by Sir Robert Smirke, which was acquired in 1964. The renovated building was re-opened in March, 1967. The exteriors of the two buildings were originally designed to create the appearance of a single building by presenting a common façade facing Trafalgar Square. Certain interior features of the original building are preserved and the spacious, richly furnished room now occupied by the High Commissioner is much admired. Surrounded by Offices of Canadian Banks, Steamship, Railway and other Companies, the Canadian Building is one of London's landmarks. It was opened by King George V. in June, 1925.

CANONBURY TOWER, Canonbury, N.1.—The largest remaining part of a 16th-century house originally built by the Priors of St. Bartholomew, and since 1952 used as the headquarters of a non-professional theatre company. Contains the " Spencer " and " Compton " oak-panelled rooms. Other relics of Canonbury House can be seen nearby.

CARLYLE'S HOUSE, 24 Cheyne Row, Chelsea, S.W.3. The home of Thomas Carlyle for 47 years until his death in 1881, and containing much of his furniture, etc. Now the property of the National Trust. Open daily, except Mondays and Tuesdays, 11–1, 2–6, or dusk, if earlier. Sundays, 2–6. Closed New Year's Day, Good Friday and all December. Admission 25p; Children and Students 12p.

CATHOLIC CENTRAL LIBRARY, St. Francis Friary, 47 Francis Street, S.W.1.—Founded as a private library in 1914, it was taken over in 1959 by the Franciscan Friars of the Atonement. It is an up-to-date lending and research library of over 50,000 volumes, 120 periodicals, for the general reader, student and ecumenist. Books are sent by post when required. Hours of opening: Mon.–Fri. 10.30–6.30; Sat. 10.30–4.30.

CEMETERIES.—In *Kensal Green Cemetery*, North Kensington, W.10 (70 acres), are tombs of W. M. Thackeray, Anthony Trollope, Sydney Smith, Shirley Brooks, Wilkié Collins, Tom Hood, W. Mulready, George Cruikshank, John Leech, Leigh Hunt, Brunel (" Great Eastern "), Ross (Arctic), Charles Kemble and Charles Mathews (Actors). In *Highgate Cemetery*, N.6, are the tombs of George Eliot, Herbert Spencer, Michael Faraday, Karl Marx and G. J. Holyoake. In *Abney Park Cemetery*, Stoke Newington, N.16, are the tomb of General Booth, founder of the Salvation Army, and memorials to many Nonconformist Divines. In the *South Metropolitan Cemetery*, Norwood, S.E.27, are the tombs of C. H. Spurgeon, Lord Alverstone, Douglas Jerrold, John Belcher, R.A., Theodore Watts-Dunton, Dr. Moffat (Missionary), Sir H. Bessemer, Sir H. Maxim, Sir J. Barnby, Sir A. Manns and J. Whitaker, F.S.A. (*Whitaker's Almanack*). In the churchyard of the former *Marylebone Chapel* are buried Allan Ramsay (poet), Hoyle (whist), Ferguson (astronomer), Charles Wesley (hymn writer) and his son Samuel Wesley (musician). The chapel itself was demolished in 1949. CREMATORIA.—*Ilford* (City of London); *Norwood*; *Hendon*; *Streatham Park*; *Finchley* (St. Marylebone) and *Golder's Green* (12 acres), near Hampstead Heath, with " Garden of Rest " and memorials to famous men and women.

CENOTAPH, Whitehall, S.W.1.—(Literally " empty tomb "). Monument erected " To the Glorious Dead ", as a memorial to all ranks of the Sea, Land and Air Forces who gave their lives in the service of the Empire during the First World War. Erected as a temporary memorial in 1919 and replaced by a permanent structure in 1920. Unveiled by King George V on Armistice Day, 1920. An additional inscription was added after the 1939–45 War, to commemorate those who gave their lives in that conflict.

CHARTERHOUSE, The Hospital of King James, Sutton's Hospital, Charterhouse Square, E.C.1 (*Master*, O. Van Oss; *Registrar and Clerk to the Governors*, J. C. Moss), a Carthusian monastery until 1537, purchased from the Earl of Suffolk in 1611 by Thomas Sutton as a hospital for aged " Brothers " and a School (removed to Godalming in 1872). The buildings are partly 14th (but mainly 16th) century. They suffered much damage during the 1939–45 War but are now restored and can accommodate nearly 40 " Brothers ". Visitors can be shown round at 2.45 p.m. on Wednesday during the months of April to July inclusive, except the Wednesdays immediately after Easter and Spring Holiday. (Charge for admission, 30p per person.) Roger Williams, the founder and governor of Rhode Island, U.S.A., was elected a scholar of the Foundation on June 25, 1621. Among many famous Carthusians are John Wesley; the poets Crashaw and Lovelace; Addison and Steele; Sir William Blackstone and Thackeray, who described " Greyfriars School "(Charterhouse) in " The Newcomes "; Baden-Powell and Vaughan Williams.

CHELSEA PHYSIC GARDEN, Royal Hospital Road, S.W.3.—A garden of general botanical research, established in latter part of 17th century by the Society of Apothecaries, occupies site presented in 1722 by Sir Hans Sloane. Transferred in 1899 to the Trustees of the London Parochial Charities. Tickets of admission for *bona fide* students and teachers obtainable from the Clerk to the Trustees, 10 Fleet Street, E.C.4.

CHELSEA ROYAL HOSPITAL (founded by Charles II, in 1682, and built by Wren; opened in 1692), Royal Hospital Road, Chelsea, S.W.3, for old and disabled soldiers. Great Hall, Chapel, Museum open daily 10 to 12 and 2 to 4.30, and on Sunday afternoons. Council Chamber open on Sundays, 11.45 to 12 and 2 to 4 p.m. The extensive grounds include the former Ranelagh Gardens. *Governor*, General Sir Antony Read G.C.B., C.B.E., D.S.O., M.C.,; *Lieut-Governor and Secretary*, Major-Gen. P. R. C. Hobart C.B., D.S.O., O.B.E., M.C.

CITY BUSINESS LIBRARY (formerly Guildhall Commercial Library), 55 Basinghall Street, E.C.2. Open, Mon.–Fri. 9.30–5.30.

COLLEGE OF ARMS OR HERALDS' COLLEGE, Queen Victoria Street, E.C.4.—Her Majesty's Officers of Arms (Kings, Heralds and Pursuivants of Arms) were first incorporated by Richard III, and granted Derby House on the site of the present College building by Philip and Mary. The building now in use was built after the Fire of London. The powers vested by the Crown in the Earl Marshal (The Duke of Norfolk) with regard to State ceremonial are largely exercised through the College, which is the official repository of English coats of arms and pedigrees. Enquiry may be made to the Officer on duty in the Public Office, Mon.–Fri. between 10 a.m. and 4 p.m.

COMMONWEALTH INSTITUTE, Kensington High Street, W.8.— A permanent exhibition opened on Nov. 6, 1962, by Her Majesty the Queen, replacing the former Imperial Institute opened in 1893 in S. Kensington. An interesting feature of the building is its paraboloid copper-sheathed roof. The Institute contains, in 60,000 square feet arranged in 3 galleries, a visual representation of the history and geography of the Commonwealth countries and dependencies: on the ground floor, exhibits of Canada, Australia, New Zealand, India, Sri Lanka and Bangladesh and the smaller island territories in the southern hemisphere; on the middle gallery, the African territories; and on the upper gallery, the other countries of the Commonwealth. Art gallery; Cinema, showing documentary films daily. Open, week-days, 10–5.30; Sundays, 2.30–6. Admission free, Closed Good Friday, Christmas Eve, Christmas Day, Boxing Day and New Year's Day.

COUNTY HALL, Westminster Bridge, S.E.1.— The Headquarters of the Greater London Council (*see* pp. 634–6) built on the Pedlar's Acre, Bishop's Acre, Four Acres and Float Mead, Lambeth, from the designs of Ralph Knott, with a river façade of 750 ft. The foundation stone was laid by King George V on March 9, 1912, and the ceremonial opening took place on July 17, 1922, although the main building was not completed until 1933. The building of the North and South blocks on a site to the East of the main building started in the early 1930s. They were occupied in 1939 but not finally completed until 1963. The main building contains, in addition to office accommodation, the council chamber, a conference hall, committee rooms; education and members' libraries and the county record office. The Council, when in session, meets in public in the council chamber at three-weekly intervals on Tuesday afternoons at 2.30 p.m. The times for public inspection of the building are, on Saturdays and Bank Holidays (except Christmas Day) from 10.30–12; 1.30–3.30 p.m. Admission free.

CUSTOM HOUSE, Lower Thames Street, E.C.3.— Built early in 19th century, with a wide quay on Thames. The *Long Room* is about 190 ft. long.

DICKENS HOUSE, 48 Doughty Street, W.C.1.— In this house Charles Dickens lived from 1837 to 1839, and here he completed *Pickwick Papers*. It is the headquarters of the Dickens Fellowship and contains many relics of the novelist. It is open to the public daily, 10 to 5 (Sundays and Bank Holidays excepted); admission 25p; students, 15p; Children, 10p.

DR. JOHNSON'S HOUSE, Gough Square, Fleet Street, E.C.4.—A tall late 17th-century house in which Samuel Johnson (and his wife) lived. His *Dictionary* was compiled here. The house is furnished with 18th century pieces and there is an excellent collection of Johnsoniana. Open daily (except Sundays and Bank Holidays) from 10.30 to 5 (Winter, 4.30). Admission 20p; Students, 10p.

ELY PLACE, Holborn Circus, E.C.1.—The site of the London house of former Bishops of Ely, Ely Place is a private street whose affairs are administered by Commissioners under a special Act of Parliament. The 14th-century chapel, now St. Etheldreda's (R.C.) Church, is open daily until dusk.

FULHAM PALACE, Bishop's Avenue, Fulham, S.W.6.—The courtyard is 16th century, remainder 18th and 19th century. Residence of the Bishop of London. Grounds of about 9 acres.

GEFFRYE MUSEUM, Kingsland Road, E.2.—Open on Tuesdays to Saturdays 10 to 5, Sundays 2 to 5. Closed on Christmas Day and on Mondays except Bank Holidays. Admission free.

The Museum is housed in a building erected originally as almshouses in 1715. It was eventually purchased by the London County Council and opened as a museum in 1914. The exhibits are shown in a series of period rooms dating from 1600 to 1939, each containing furniture and domestic equipment of a middle-class English home. An 18th century woodworker's shop, an openhearth kitchen and the original chapel are also shown. Temporary exhibitions are held in the Exhibition Hall. There is a reference library of books on furniture, social history and art. Special arrangements for children visiting the Museum in school parties (which must be booked in advance) and in their leisure time. *Curator,* J. Daniels.

GEORGE INN, Southwark.—Near London Bridge Station. Given to National Trust in 1937. Last galleried inn in London, built in 1677. Open during licensed hours.

GUILDHALL, King Street, City, E.C.2.—Scene of civic government for the City for more than a thousand years. Built, 1411-1425, damaged in the Great Fire, 1666, and by incendiary bombs, 1940. The main hall and crypt (the most extensive mediæval crypt in London) have been restored. Events in Guildhall include the annual election of Lord Mayor, election of Sheriffs, receptions in honour of Sovereigns and Heads of State, and the fortnightly meetings of the Court of Common Council (*see* " Corporation of London "). Open free; weekdays, 10-5; Sundays (May to Sept.) 2-5. *Keeper of the Guildhall,* A.J. Marshall.

The New Library and Museum of the Clockmakers' Company adjoining mainly escaped damage, and are open to the public, Mon. to Sat., 10-5. Admission free (entrance in Aldermanbury). The Library contains Plans of London, 1570; Deed of Sale with Shakespeare's signature; first and second, fourth folios of Shakespeare's plays, etc. (*see also* City Business Library).

HONOURABLE ARTILLERY COMPANY'S HEADQUARTERS, City Road, E.C.1.—The H.A.C. (*Sec.* Lt.-Col. P. Massey, M.C.) received its charter of incorporation from Henry VIII in 1537, and has occupied its present ground since 1641. The Armoury House dates from 1735. Four of its members who emigrated in the 17th century, founded in 1638 the Ancient and Honourable Artillery Company of Massachussetts. The H.A.C. is the senior regiment of the Territorial Army Volunteer Reserves, and maintains a Headquarters with an Officer Training Wing, and Artillery and Infantry components.

HORNIMAN MUSEUM AND LIBRARY, London Road, Forest Hill, S.E.23. Open daily except Christmas Eve and Christmas Day, 10.30 to 6, Sundays 2 to 6. Special arrangements on Boxing Day. Admission free. The Museum was presented in 1901 to the London County Council by the founder, Mr. F. J. Horniman, M.P. The Museum has three main departments, anthropology, musical instruments and natural history. In the anthropology department the large collections include exhibits illustrating man's progress in the arts and crafts from prehistoric times. The natural history department includes an aquarium. Reference library (except Mondays). Schools Service. Free concerts and lectures (autumn to spring). *Curator,* D. M. Boston.

HORSE GUARDS, Whitehall, S.W.1.—Archway and offices built about 1753. The mounting of the guard (Life Guards, or the Blues and Royals) at 11 a.m. (10 a.m. on Sundays) and the dismounting at 4 p.m. are picturesque ceremonies. Only those on the Lord Chamberlain's list may drive through the gates and archway into *Horse Guards' Parade* (230,000 sq. ft.), where the Colour is " trooped " on the Queen's Official Birthday. (Trafalgar Square is 168,850 sq. ft. (the island site, 102,050 sq. ft.); Parliament Square, 136,900 sq. ft.; Leicester Square, 100,000 sq. ft.)

HOUSES OF PARLIAMENT, Westminster, S.W.1.—After its destruction by fire in 1834, the Palace of Westminster was re-built in 1840-68 from the designs of Sir Charles Barry and Augustus Welby Pugin, at a cost of over £2,000,000.—Open (free) to visitors on Saturdays, on Easter Monday and Tuesday, Spring and late summer Bank Holiday Mondays and Tuesdays; Mon., Tues. and Thurs. in August and Thurs. in September, if neither House be sitting. Admission at the Sovereign's Entrance, House of Lords, on the above-mentioned days, from 10 a.m. to 4.30 p.m. Closed to visitors on Christmas Day, Boxing Day and Good Friday and the Saturday preceding the State Opening of Parliament. Admission to the Strangers' Gallery of the House of Lords as arranged by a Peer or by queue *via* the St. Stephen's Entrance. Ad·mission to the Strangers' Gallery of the House of Commons, during session by Member's order, or order obtained on personal application at the Admission Order Office in St. Stephen's Hall after the House meets. The present House of Commons was used for the first time on October 26, 1950, the original Chamber having been destroyed by bombs in 1941. The Victoria Tower (House of Lords) is about 330 ft. high, and when Parliament is sitting the Union Jack flies by day from its flagstaff. The Clock Tower of the House of Commons is about 320 ft. high and contains " Big Ben," the Hour Bell, named after Sir Benjamin Hall, First Commissioner of Works when the original bell was cast in 1856. This bell which weighed 16 tons 11 cwt., was found cracked in 1857. The present bell 13½ tons) is a recasting of the original and was first brought into use in July, 1859. A light is displayed from this tower at night when Parliament is sitting.

INNS OF COURT.—The *Inner* and *Middle Temple*, S. of Fleet Street, E.C.4, and N. of Victoria Embankment, to which the gardens extend, have occupied (since early 14th century) the site of the buildings of the Order of Knights Templars. *Inner Temple Hall* is open to the public on Monday-Friday, 10-11.30 a.m. and 2.30-4 p.m., except during Vacations. *Temple Church,* restored in 1958 after severe damage by bombing, is open on weekdays 10-5 p.m. and the public are admitted to Sunday services. *Middle Temple Hall* (sixteenth century) is open to the public when not in use, Monday-Friday, 10-12 and 3-4.30 p.m.;

Saturday, 10–4.30. Closed 1–2 p.m. and Sundays. In Middle Temple Gardens (not open to the public) Shakespeare (Henry VI, Part I) places the incident which led to the " Wars of the Roses " (1455–85). *Lincoln's Inn*, from Chancery Lane to Lincoln's Inn Fields, W.C.2, occupies the site of the palace of a former Bishop of Chichester and of a Black Friars monastery. The records show the Society as being in existence in 1422. The new Hall and Library Buildings are modern, although the Library is first mentioned in 1474, and the old Hall early 16th century, the Chapel (Inigo Jones) early 17th century. *Lincoln's Inn Fields* (7 acres); the Square contains many fine old houses with handsome interiors. *Gray's Inn*, Holborn/Gray's Inn Road, W.C.1. Early 14th century. Hall (16th cent.); Chapel (Services 11.15 a.m. during Law Dining Terms only). Holy Communion 1st Sunday in every month except Aug.–Sept. Public welcome. Library (33,000 vols, mss. and printed books) may be viewed by appointment. Gardens open to the public from 12 noon to 2 p.m. (May–July), 9.30 a.m.–5 p.m. (Aug.–Sept). The Inn, although badly damaged during the last war has been completely restored to its former beauty with gracious red brick buildings overlooking grass covered squares and gardens. Strong Elizabethan associations. No other " Inns " are active, but what remains of *Staple Inn* is worth visiting as a relic of Elizabethan London; though heavy damage was done by a flying-bomb, it retains a picturesque gabled front on Holborn (opposite Gray's Inn Road). *Clement's Inn* (near St. Clement Danes' Church), *Clifford's Inn*, Fleet Street, and *Thavies Inn*, Holborn Circus, are all rebuilt. *Serjeant's Inn*, Fleet Street (damaged by bombing) and another (demolished 1910) of the same name in Chancery Lane, were composed of Serjeants-at-Law, the last of whom died in 1922.

JEWISH MUSEUM, Woburn House, Upper Woburn Place, W.C.1.—Opened in 1932, the Museum contains a comprehensive collection of Jewish antiquities, liturgical items and " Anglo-Judaica ". Open free (Mon.–Thurs.), 2.30–5; (Fri. and Sun.), 10.30–12.45. Closed on Saturdays, Jewish Holy days and Bank Holidays. Conducted tours of parties by arrangement with the Secretary.

KEATS HOUSE, Keats Grove, Hampstead, N.W.3. —In two houses here, now made into one, John Keats lived at various times between 1818 and 1820. Restored 1974–75. Open weekdays, 10 a.m.– 6 p.m.; Sundays and Bank Holidays, 2 p.m.–5 p.m. Closed—Christmas Day, Boxing Day, Good Friday, Easter Eve. The Keats Memorial Library contains 5,000 volumes.

KENSINGTON PALACE, W.8.—The original house was bought by William III in 1689 and rebuilt by Christopher Wren. The birthplace of Queen Victoria in 1819. The state apartments are open to the public and contain pictures and furniture from the royal collections. A suite of rooms devoted to the memory of Queen Victoria is also shown. *Hours of Opening:* (March 1–Sept. 30) 10 a.m.– 6 p.m.; Sundays, 2–6 p.m.; (Feb. and Oct, 10–5; Sundays, 2–5; Jan, Nov. and Dec., 10–4; Sundays, 2–5) *Kensington Gardens* (*q.v.*) adjoin.

LAMBETH PALACE, S.E.1.—The official residence of the Archbishop of Canterbury, on south bank of Thames; the oldest part is 13th century, the house itself is early 19th century. For leave to visit the historical portions, applications should be made by letter to the Archbishop's Chaplain.

LIVERY COMPANIES' HALLS.—The Principal Companies (*see* pp. 640–1) have magnificent halls, but admission to view them has generally to be arranged beforehand. Among the finest or more interesting may be mentioned the following:

Goldsmiths' Hall, Foster Lane. The present hall was completed in 1835, and contains some magnificent rooms. Exhibitions of plate have been shown here periodically in recent years. Fishmongers' Hall, London Bridge (built 1831–3), now admirably restored after severe bomb damage, also contains fine rooms. Apothecaries' Hall, Black Friars Lane, was rebuilt in 1670, after the Great Fire, and has library, hall and kitchen which are good examples of this period, together with a pleasant courtyard. Vintners' Hall, Upper Thames Street, was also rebuilt after the Great Fire, and its hall has very fine late 17th century panelling. The Watermen and Lightermen's Company is not, strictly speaking, a Livery Company, but its hall, in St. Mary at Hill, is a good example of a smaller 18th century building, with pilastered façade. It was completed in 1780. Stationers' Hall, in Stationers' Hall Court, behind Ludgate Hill, another post-Fire Hall, standing in its own court, has a particularly finely carved screen. Barbers' Hall, Monkwell Street, with a Hall attributed to Inigo Jones, was completely destroyed by bombing, but is to be rebuilt. The new hall is to be built some 30 ft. from the old site to enable one of the bastions and part of the wall of the Roman fort to remain exposed to view. Mercers' Hall, Ironmonger Lane, built to replace the hall destroyed by bombing, was opened in 1958.

LLOYD'S, Lime Street, E.C.3.—Housed in the Royal Exchange for 150 years and in Leadenhall Street from 1928–1957. The present building was opened by H.M. Queen Elizabeth the Queen Mother on Nov. 14, 1957. The underwriting space has an area of 44,250 sq. ft.

LORD'S CRICKET GROUND, St. John's Wood Road, N.W.8.—The headquarters (since 1814) of the Marylebone Cricket Club (founded 1787), the premier cricket club in England, the scene of some of the principal matches of the season and Middlesex County headquarters. Tennis court and squash courts in building behind members' pavilion.

The Cricket Memorial Gallery, a museum of cricket, open to the public on match days, until 5 p.m., and on other days by prior arrangement. Adults, 11p, children, 5p. In winter, admission is by prior arrangement.

MANSION HOUSE, City, E.C.4.—(Reconstructed 1930–31.) The official residence of the Lord Mayor; the Egyptian Hall and Ballroom are the chief attractions. Admission by order from the Lord Mayor's Secretary.

MARKETS—The London markets (administered by the Corporation of the City of London) provide foodstuffs for 8,500,000 to 9,000,000 people. The dead meat market at Smithfields is the largest in the world, the supplies marketed amounting to nearly 500,000 tons annually. *Central Meat, Fish, Fruit, Vegetable, and Poultry Markets*, Smithfield; *Leadenhall Market* (Meat and Poultry); *Billingsgate* (Fish), Thames Street; *Spitalfields*, E.1 (Vegetables, Fruit, etc.), enlarged 1928 and opened by the late Queen Mary; *London Fruit Exchange*, Brushfield Street (built by Corporation of London 1928–29) faces Spitalfields Market. Other markets are— *Covent Garden* (now moved to Nine Elms) (established under a charter of Charles II, in 1661) and *Borough Market*, S.E.1, for vegetables, fruit, flowers, etc.

MARLBOROUGH HOUSE, Pall Mall, S.W.1.—The London home of Queen Mary until her death in 1953. Built by Wren for the great Duke of Marlborough and completed in 1711, the house finally reverted to the Crown in 1835. Prince Leopold lived there until 1831, and Queen Adelaide from 1837 until her death in 1849. In 1863 it became the London house of the Prince of Wales. The

Queen's Chapel, Marlborough Gate, begun in 1623 from the designs of Inigo Jones for the Infanta Maria of Spain, and completed for Queen Henrietta Maria, is open to the public for services during part of the year. In 1959 Marlborough House was given by the Queen as a Commonwealth centre for Government conferences and it was opened as such in March, 1962. It is open to the public at certain times when conferences are not taking place.

LONDON MONUMENT (commonly called "The Monument"), Monument Street, E.C.3.—Built from designs of Wren, 1671-77, to commemorate the *Great Fire of London*, which broke out in Pudding Lane, Sept. 2, 1666. The fluted Doric column is 120 ft. high (the moulded cylinder above the balcony supporting a flaming vase of gilt bronze is 42 ft. in addition), and is based on a square plinth 40 ft. high, with fine carvings on W. face (making a total height of 202 ft.). Splendid views of London from gallery at top of column (311 steps). Admission (until 20 minutes before closing time) 5p; children, 2½p, Monday to Saturday, 9 a.m. to 6 p.m. (Oct.–March to 4 p.m.). Sundays—May to Sept. 2–6 p.m. Closed Christmas Day, Boxing Day and Good Friday.

MONUMENTS.—VICTORIA MEMORIAL in front of Buckingham Palace; ALBERT MEMORIAL, South Kensington; AIR, Victoria Embankment; BEACONSFIELD, Parliament Square; BEATTY, JELLICOE and CUNNINGHAM, Trafalgar Square; BELGIAN, Victoria Embankment; BOADICEA (or "Boudicca"), Queen of the Iceni, E. Anglia, Westminster Bridge; BURNS, Embankment Gardens; BURGHERS OF CALAIS (replica of Rodin's statue), Victoria Tower Gardens, Westminster; CAVALRY, Hyde Park; CAVELL, St. Martin's Place; CENOTAPH, Whitehall; CHARLES I. (erected Jan. 29, 1675), Trafalgar Square; CHARLES II. (Grinling Gibbons), inside the Royal Exchange; CHURCHILL, Parliament Square; CLEOPATRA'S NEEDLE (68½ ft. high, erected 1878), Thames Embankment (the Sphinx, W. of pedestal, and the surrounding stone work, bear scars from an air raid); CAPTAIN COOK (Brock), The Mall; CRIMEAN, Broad Sanctuary; OLIVER CROMWELL (Thornycroft), outside Westminster Hall; DUKE OF CAMBRIDGE, Whitehall; DUKE OF YORK (124 ft.), St. James's Park; EDWARD VII (Mackenna), Waterloo Place. ELIZABETH I (1586, oldest outdoor statue in London), Fleet Street; EROS (Shaftesbury Memorial) (Gilbert), Piccadilly Circus; MARECHAL FOCH, Grosvenor Gardens; GEORGE III, Cockspur Street; GEORGE IV (Chantrey), riding without stirrups, Trafalgar Square; GEORGE V, Abingdon Street; GEORGE VI, Carlton Gardens; GLADSTONE, facing Australia House, Strand; GUARDS' (Crimea), Waterloo Place; (Great War), Horse Guard's Parade; HAIG (Hardiman), Whitehall; IRVING (Brock), N. side of National Portrait Gallery; JAMES II. Trafalgar Square; KITCHENER, Horse Guards' Parade; ABRAHAM LINCOLN (St. Gaudens), Parliament Square; LONDON TROOPS, Royal Exchange; MARY, QUEEN OF SCOTS, Fleet Street; MILTON, St. Giles, Cripplegate; MONUMENT, THE (*see above*); NELSON (170 ft. 1½ in.), Trafalgar Square, with Landseer's lions (cast from guns recovered from the wreck of the *Royal George*): FLORENCE NIGHTINGALE, Waterloo Place; "PETER PAN" (Frampton), Kensington Gardens; PORTAL, Embankment Gardens; PRINCE CONSORT, Holborn Circus; RALEIGH, Whitehall; RICHARD COEUR DE LION (Marochetti), Old Palace Yard; ROBERTS, Horse Guards' Parade; FRANKLIN D. ROOSEVELT, Grosvenor Square; ROYAL ARTILLERY (South Africa), The Mall; (Great War), Hyde Park Corner; ROYAL MARINES, The Mall; CAPTAIN SCOTT, Waterloo Place; SHACKLETON, Kensington Gore; SHAKESPEARE (Fontana), Leicester Square; CAPTAIN JOHN SMITH,

Cheapside; SMUTS (Epstein), Parliament Square; TRENCHARD, Victoria Embankment; GEORGE WASHINGTON (Houdon copy) Trafalgar Square; WELLINGTON, Hyde Park Corner; WELLINGTON (Chantrey) riding without stirrups, Royal Exchange; JOHN WESLEY, City Road; WOLSELEY, Horse Guards' Parade.

PERCIVAL DAVID FOUNDATION OF CHINESE ART, 53 Gordon Square, W.C.1.—Set up in 1951 to promote the study and teaching of the art and culture of China and the surrounding regions, and provide facilities necessary to that end. The Foundation contains the collection of Chinese ceramics formed by Sir Percival David and his important library of books on Chinese art. To these was added a gift from the Hon. Mountstuart Elphinstone of part of his collection of Chinese monochrome porcelains. The galleries were opened to the public in 1952. The Foundation is administered on behalf of the University of London by the School of Oriental and African Studies. *Hours of opening:* Galleries, Mon. 2 to 5 p.m.; Tues. to Fri. 10.30 a.m. to 5 p.m.; Sat. 10.30 a.m. to 1 p.m.; Closed Bank Holidays. Library available to ticket holders only; applications in writing to the Curator. *Head of the Foundation,* Prof. W. Watson.

PORT OF LONDON.—The Port of London comprises the tidal portion of the River Thames from Teddington to the seaward limit (Tongue light vessel), a distance of 94 miles and three dock systems and land for redevelopment covering an area of 4,905 acres, of which 512 acres are water. The governing body is the Port of London Authority, whose Head Office is in World Trade Centre, E.1. Particulars of the docks are as follows:— *India & Millwall Docks*, E.14.—Area 449 acres including 127 acres water. Principal commodities handled are hardwood, fruit, plywood, wood pulp and wine in bulk. *Royal Victoria & Albert & King George V Docks*, E.16.—Area 745 acres, including 230 acres water—have special facilities for grain and tobacco. Large quantities of fruit and general cargo are also dealt with. *Tilbury Docks, Essex.*—Area 1,059 acres, including 155 acres water. These docks are 26 miles below London Bridge and are used principally by vessels plying on the Australian, North American, Indian, other Eastern routes, West Africa and the Continent. Tilbury Passenger Landing Stage provides accommodation for liners at all states of the tide and adjoins Tilbury Riverside Station.

A development and extension scheme at Tilbury has added nearly 2 miles of deepwater quays, to provide 13 new berths, of which 6 are for container traffic and 3 for packaged timber. Also included are a freight-liner rail container terminal and a riverside grain terminal which can accommodate vessels up to 65,000 tons deadweight and provide a rated maximum discharge of 2,000 tons per hour. Cost of this development (including Grain Terminal) was estimated at about £35 million.

The St. Katharine Docks were sold to the G.L.C. in 1969 and the London Docks were closed on May 31, 1969. Surrey Commercial Docks were closed in 1970.

PRINCE HENRY'S ROOM, 17 Fleet Street, E.C.4.—Early 17th century timber-framed house containing fine room on first floor with panelling and moulded plaster ceiling. Open Mon. to Fri. 1.45 p.m. to 5 p.m.; Sat. to 4.30 p.m. Admission 10p. Closed Christmas Day and Good Friday. Available occasionally for evening lettings on application to The Town Clerk, Guildhall, E.C.2.

ROMAN LONDON.—Though visible remains are very few, almost every excavation for the foundations of new buildings in the City reveals Roman remains. Sections of the City wall, often however merely a mediæval re-build on the Roman foundations, are the most striking remains still to be seen. Fragments may be seen near the White Tower in the Tower of London, Trinity Square, No. 1 Crutched Friars, All Hallows, London Wall—its semi-circular vestry being built on the remains of a round bastion—St. Alphage, London Wall, recently restored by the Corporation of London and showing a striking succession of building and repairs from Roman till later mediæval times, St. Giles, Cripplegate and, by permission only, the great bastion beneath the pavement of the yard of the G.P.O. in Giltspur Street. Recent excavations in the Cripplegate area have revealed that a fort was built in this area and later incorporated in the town wall in this north-west corner of the City. Evidence from these excavations proves that the fort was not built until about A.D. 100–120 and the date of the town wall must therefore be considerably later. Remains of a bath building are preserved beneath the Coal Exchange in Lower Thames Street and other foundations may be seen in the Crypt of All Hallows Barking by the Tower. The governmental headquarters of the town was a great basilica, more than 400 ft. long from east to west, the massive walls of which have been encountered, extending from Leadenhall Market across Gracechurch Street as far as St. Michael's, Cornhill. Excavations during the past few years have shown that buildings over the river front were erected on huge oaken piles and a framework of timber for a considerable distance both east and west of the present London Bridge. The " Roman Bath", in Strand Lane approached via Surrey Street, which is not now held by most authorities to be of Roman origin, is maintained by the G.L.C. on behalf of the National Trust, and is open to the public on weekdays from 10 a.m. to 12.30 p.m. (*Admission*, 10p). Excavations since 1948 on a bombed site in Walbrook, on the banks of the old Wall Brook, produced interesting discoveries, including a Temple of Mithras, from which the splendid marble statues have been placed in Guildhall Museum, now in the Royal Exchange, where many other relics from the Roman City may be seen.

ROYAL EXCHANGE, E.C.3 (founded by Sir Thomas Gresham, 1566, opened as " The Bourse " and proclaimed " The Royal Exchange " by Queen Elizabeth I, 1571, rebuilt 1667–69 and 1842–44).—Open to the public, free. Statues of Queen Elizabeth I, Charles II, Queen Victoria, Sir Thomas Gresham and others; mural paintings in the ambulatory by Leighton, Abbey, Brangwyn, Wyllie and others. The carillon of the Royal Exchange (reinstated 1950) is temporarily out of use. With the exception of the courtyard and ambulatory (now used for exhibitions, art displays, etc.) and the shops the whole of the building is occupied by departments of the Guardian Royal Exchange Assurance Group and is administered by the Gresham Committee (*Clerk*, Mercers' Hall, Ironmonger Lane, E.C.2).

ROYAL GEOGRAPHICAL SOCIETY, Kensington Gore, S.W. 7.—Map Room open to public, *free.*

ST. JAMES'S PALACE, in Pall Mall, S.W.1.—(Not open to the public.) Built by Henry VIII; the Gatehouse and Presence Chamber remain, and part of the Chapel Royal, which in 1955 was reopened to the public for services during part of the year. A royal residence from 1697 to 1762. Representatives of Foreign Powers are still accredited " to the Court of St. James's " and (by the permission of the Crown) the Conference of the Allies (1921) and later conferences have been held here.

ST. JOHN'S GATE, Clerkenwell, E.C.1.—Now the Chancery of the Order of St. John of Jerusalem, and formerly the entrance of the Priory of that Order, of which the gate house (early 16th century) and crypt of Church (12th century) alone survive, They may be inspected on application to the Curator.

SIR JOHN SOANE'S MUSEUM, 13 Lincoln's Inn Fields, W.C.2. The house and galleries, built 1812–24, are the work of the founder, Sir John Soane (1753–1837) and contain his collections, arranged as he left them, in pursuance of an Act procured by him in 1833. Exhibits include the Sarcophagus of Seti I (*c.* 1290 B.C.), classical vases and marbles, Hogarth's *Rake's Progress* and *Election* series, paintings by Canaletto, Reynolds, Turner, Lawrence, etc., and sculpture by Chantery, Flaxman, etc. Soane's library of 8,000 vols, and a collection of 20,000 architectural drawings are available for study. Open Tues.–Sat. inclusive, 10 a.m. to 5 p.m. Closed Bank Holidays and in August. *Curator*, Sir John Summerson, C.B.E., F.B.A. *Inspectress*, Miss D. Stroud, M.B.E., F.S.A.

SOMERSET HOUSE, Strand, W.C.2, and Victoria Embankment, W.C.2.—The beautiful river façade (600 ft. long) was built at the close of the 18th century from the designs of Sir W. Chambers; the remainder of the building is early 19th century. Somerset House was the property of Lord Protector Somerset, at whose attainder in 1552 the palace passed to the Crown, and it was a royal residence until about the close of the 17th century. The building is now occupied by the *Board of Inland Revenue* and other branches of the Civil Service and by the *Principal Probate Registry.*

STOCK EXCHANGE, E.C.2.—The market floor of the new Stock Exchange building in London opened for trading in June, 1973. A tower, 331 feet high, the new Market, and a separate Public Relations block replace the complex of buildings started in 1801 on the same site. The new building is the headquarters of The Stock Exchange, following the amalgamation of all the Stock Exchanges in Great Britain and Ireland on March 25, 1973.

The Stock Exchange provides a market for the purchase and sale of about 9,000 securities officially listed, and valued at over £210,000,000 and also securities listed on other Stock Exchanges throughout the World. At present the members of The Stock Exchange who consist of brokers (agents for clients) and Jobbers (dealers in specific securities) number about 4,150. The Visitors' Gallery is open between 10.00 a.m. and 3.15 p.m. Monday to Friday. Admission free and without ticket; film show, audio-visual exhibition. Advance bookings can be made; last complete programme begins at 2.50 p.m.

THAMES EMBANKMENTS.—The Victoria Embankment, on the N. side (from Westminster to Blackfriars), was constructed by Sir J. W. Bazalgette for the Metropolitan Board of Works, 1864–70 (the seats, of which the supports of some are a kneeling camel, laden with spicery, and of others a winged sphinx, were presented by the Grocers' Company, and by Rt. Hon. W. H. Smith, M.P., in 1874); the Albert Embankment on the S. side (from Westminster Bridge to Vauxhall), 1866–69; the Chelsea Embankment, 1871–74. The toal cost exceeded £2,000,000. Sir J. W. Bazalgette (1819–91) also inaugurated the London main drainage system, 1858–65. A medallion has been placed on a pier of the Victoria Embankment to commemorate the engineer of the Thames waterside improvements (" Flumini vincula posuit "). The headquarters of the G.L.C. include an embankment on the Surrey side.

THAMES TUNNELS.—The *Rotherhithe Tunnel*, constructed by the L.C.C. and opened in 1908, connects Commercial Road E.14, with Lower

Road, Rotherhithe; the total length is 1 mile 332 yards, of which 474 yards are under the river. The cost of the tunnel and its approaches was £1,506,914. The first *Blackwall Tunnel* (foot passengers and vehicles) was constructed by the L.C.C. and opened in 1897, connecting East India Dock Road, Poplar, with Blackwall Lane, East Greenwich. The cost of the tunnel with its approaches was about £1,323,663. A second tunnel (for southbound vehicles only) was opened in August, 1967, at a cost of about £9,750,000 and the old tunnel was improved at a cost of about £1,350,000 and made one-way northbound. Both tunnels are for vehicles only. The relative lengths of the tunnels measured from East India Dock Road to the Gate House on the south side are 6,215 ft. (old tunnel) and 6,152 feet. *Greenwich Tunnel* (foot passengers only), constructed by the L.C.C. and opened in 1902, connects the Isle of Dogs, Poplar, with Greenwich. The length of the subway is 406 yards, and the cost was about £180,000. The *Woolwich Tunnel* (foot passengers only), constructed by the L.C.C. and opened in 1912, connects North and South Woolwich below the passenger and vehicular ferry from North Woolwich Station, E.16, to High Street, Woolwich, S.E.18. The length of the subway is 552 yards, and its cost was about £86,000. The *Thames Tunnel* (1,300 feet) was opened in 1843 to connect Wapping (N.) with Rotherhithe (S.). In 1866 it was closed to the public, and purchased by the East London Railway Company. The *Tower Subway* for foot passengers was opened in 1870, and has long been closed.

TOWER HILL, E.C.1 and E.C.3, was formerly the place of execution for condemned prisoners from the Tower, the site of the scaffold being marked in the gardens of Trinity Square.

TOWER OF LONDON, E.C.3.—Admission to a general view of the Tower, the White Tower (Armouries), the Beauchamp and Bloody Towers and the Chapels Royal—40p; children, 10p; to the Jewel House, 15p, children 5p. (Nov.–Feb. Adults 10p, children 5p; Jewel House 10p, chidren 5p). On Sundays throughout the year the public is admitted to Holy Communion, 9.15 a.m. and Morning Service, 11 a.m. Open on weekdays, March 1 to October 31, 9.30–5; Nov. 1–Feb. 28, 9.30–4; Sundays, 2 p.m. to 5 p.m., Mar. 1–Oct. 31 only; Tower closed Christmas Eve, Christmas Day, Boxing Day, Good Friday and New Year's Day. CONSTABLE, Field Marshal Sir Geoffrey Baker, G.C.B., C.M.G., C.B.E., M.C., *Lieutenant*, Lieut. Gen. Sir Napier Crookenden, K.C.B., D.S.O., O.B.E.; RESIDENT GOVERNOR AND KEEPER OF THE JEWEL HOUSE, Maj.-Gen. W. D. M. Raeburn, C.B., D.S.O., M.B.E.; MASTER OF THE ARMOURIES, A. R. Dufty, F.S.A.; CHAPLAIN AT THE CHAPEL ROYAL OF ST. PETER AD VINCULA, Rev. J. F. M. Llewellyn.

The White Tower is the oldest and central building in Her Majesty's Royal Palace and Fortress of the Tower of London. It was built at the order of William I and constructed by Gundulph, Bishop of Rochester, in the years 1078–98. The Inner Wall, with thirteen towers, was constructed by Henry III in the 12th century. The Moat was extended and completed by Richard I and the Wharf first mentioned in 1228. The Outer Wall was completed in the reign of Edward I and now incorporates 6 towers and 2 bastions. The last Monarch to reside in the Tower of London was James I. The Crown Jewels came to the Tower in the reign of Henry III. All coinage used in Great Britain was minted in the Outer Ward of the Tower of London until 1810 when the Royal Mint was formed. The Tower of London has had a military garrison since 1078. The Chapel Royal

of St. John the Evangelist, within the White Tower (1080–1088) is the oldest Norman church in London.

WELLINGTON MUSEUM, Apsley House, 149 Piccadilly, at Hyde Park Corner, W.1.—Admission free on weekdays and Bank Holidays, 10 to 6; Sundays, 2.30 to 6. Closed Good Friday, Christmas Eve, Christmas Day, Boxing Day and New Year's Day. Apsley House was designed by Robert Adam for Lord Bathurst and built 1771–8. It was bought in 1817 by the Duke of Wellington, who in 1828–29 employed Benjamin Wyatt to enlarge it, face it with Bath stone and add the Corinthian portico. The museum contains many fine paintings, services of porcelain and silver plate and personal relics of the 1st Duke of Wellington (1769–1853) and was given to the Nation by the 7th Duke. It was first opened to the public in 1952, under the administration of the Victoria and Albert Museum.

WESTMINSTER HALL, S.W.1 (built by William Rufus, A.D. 1097–99 and altered by Richard II, 1394–1401), adjacent to and incorporated in the Houses of Parliament—Westminster Hall is part of the old Palace of Westminster and survived the fire, which destroyed most of the remainder of the Palace (Oct. 16, 1834) and the bombs of 1941 The Hall is about 240 ft. long, 69 ft. wide, and 90 ft. high. The hammer beam roof of carved oak, dating from 1396–98, is one of the principal attractions. King Charles I was tried in the Hall. Extensive repairs to the Hall have recently been carried out. Admission: During sessions—Mon. to Thurs., 10 a.m. until 1.30 p.m., provided neither House is sitting. Sat. 10 a.m.–5 p.m. During Recess—Mon. to Fri., except Good Friday, Christmas Day and Boxing Day, 10 a.m.–4 p.m.; Sat., 10 a.m.–5 p.m.

WHITECHAPEL ART GALLERY, High Street, E.1. Charitable institution founded in 1901 for the organization of temporary exhibitions of art. There is no permanent collection. Open: Tuesdays to Sundays, 11–6; closed Mondays. Admission Free.

PARKS, SPACES AND GARDENS

The principal Parks and Open Spaces in the Metropolitan area are maintained as under:—

By the Crown

BUSHY PARK (1,099 acres).

GREEN PARK (49 acres), W.1.—Between Piccadilly and St. James's Park with *Constitution Hill*, leading to Hyde Park Corner.

GREENWICH PARK (196½ acres), S.E. 10.

HAMPTON COURT GARDENS (54 acres).

HAMPTON COURT GREEN (17 acres)

HAMPTON COURT PARK (622 acres).

HYDE PARK (341 acres).—From Park Lane, W.1, to Kensington Gardens, W.2 containing the Serpentine. Fine gateway at Hyde Park Corner, with Apsley House, the Achilles Statue, Rotten Row and the Ladies' Mile. To the north-east is the *Marble Arch*, originally erected by George IV at the entrance to Buckingham Palace and re-erected in present position in 1851.

KENSINGTON GARDENS (275 acres), W.2.—From western boundary of Hyde Park to Kensington Palace, containing the Albert Memorial.

KEW, ROYAL BOTANIC GARDENS (300 acres).—Accessible by railway and omnibus. Open daily, except Christmas Day and New Year's Day from 10 a.m. The closing hour varies from 4 p.m. in mid-winter to 7 p.m. on week-days, and 8 p.m. at week-ends and Bank Holidays, in mid-summer. Admission, 1p. Museums open 10 a.m.; Glasshouses, 11 a.m. to dusk or 4.50 p.m. (week-days); 1 p.m. to dusk or 5.50 p.m. (Sundays). Dogs not admitted.

REGENT'S PARK and PRIMROSE HILL (464 acres), N.W.1.—From Marylebone Road to Primrose

Hill surrounded by the Outer Circle and divided by the *Broad Walk* leading to the Zoological Gardens.

RICHMOND PARK (2,469 acres).

ST. JAMES'S PARK (93 acres), S.W.1.—From Whitehall to Buckingham Palace. Ornamental lake of 12 acres. The original suspension bridge built in 1857 was replaced in 1957. The *Mall* leads from the Admiralty Arch to the Queen Victoria Memorial and Buckingham Palace. *Birdcage Walk* from Storey's Gate, past Wellington Barracks, to Buckingham Palace.

By the Corporation of London

BURNHAM BEECHES and FLEET WOOD (504 acres), *see* col. 2.
    COULSDON COMMON, Surrey (111 acres).
    EPPING FOREST (6,000 acres).
    FARTHINGDOWN, Surrey (121 acres).
    HIGHGATE WOOD (70 acres).
    KENLEY COMMON, Surrey (80 acres).
    QUEEN'S PARK, Kilburn (30 acres).
    RIDDLESDOWN, Surrey (87 acres).
    SPRING PARK, West Wickham (51 acres).
    WEST HAM PARK (77 acres).
    WEST WICKHAM COMMON, Kent (25 acres).
With smaller open spaces within the City of London, including FINSBURY CIRCUS GARDENS.

By the Greater London Council

ALEXANDRA PARK and PALACE (190 acres), with roller skating and ski slope.

AVERY HILL (87 acres), S.E.9, with Winter Garden.

BATTERSEA PARK (200 acres), S.W.8 to S.W.11, with Festival gardens, concert pavilion, zoo and lake.

BLACKHEATH (271 acres), S.E.3.—*Morden College*, founded in 1695 as a home for " decayed Turkey merchants", is near the S.E. corner. The building was designed by Wren and its Chapel doors have carvings attributed to Grinling Gibbons. Concerts and poetry recitals are held at Rangers House, an early 18th century mansion.

BOSTALL HEATH AND WOODS (159 acres), S.E.2.

CRYSTAL PALACE (199 acres), S.E.19, with concert bowl, ski slope and National Sports Centre. Zoo.

DULWICH PARK (72 acres), with lake, S.E.21.

FINSBURY PARK (115 acres), N.4.

GOLDER'S HILL (36 acres), adjoining West Heath, Hampstead.

HACKNEY MARSH (343 acres), E.5, E.9 and E.10. 112 football pitches.

HAINAULT FOREST (1,108 acres), Hainault, Essex. Country park with two 18-hole public golf courses.

HAMPSTEAD HEATH and Extension (294 acres), N.W.3.

HERNE HILL STADIUM (9 acres), with cycle racing and athletic track.

HOLLAND PARK (55 acres), W.8. Open air theatre and concerts; floodlit gardens; King George VI Memorial Youth Hostel and Restaurant Belvedere.

HORNIMAN GARDENS (21 acres), S.E.23. Adjoining Horniman Museum.

KENWOOD (200 acres), the northern part of Hampstead Heath. Part purchased in 1922 by public subscription. Opened and dedicated by King George V, July 18, 1925. Open air symphony concerts each summer. The Iveagh Bequest, in an 18th-century Mansion (open to the public), includes a fine library and valuable art treasures. Recitals and poetry readings in the Orangery each summer. Ladies' swimming bath.

KING GEORGE'S FIELD (16 acres), E.3, with East London Stadium.

LESNES ABBEY WOODS (215 acres), Erith.—Ruins of an Augustinian abbey.

MARBLE HILL (66 acres).—Twickenham, Middlesex.—A beautiful park, running down to the riverside, on the left bank of the Thames; includes a mansion (open to the public), formerly the residence of Mrs. Fitsherbert, morganatic wife of George IV. Open air theatre.

OXLEAS WOOD (213 acres), S.E.9.

PARLIAMENT HILL (271 acres)—Part of Hampstead Heath. Lido and swimming bath. Important cross-country events are held here.

PARSLOES PARK (118 acres), Becontree, Essex.

TRENT PARK (600 acres), Cockfosters, Enfield. Country park with nature trail, riding school, picnic sites, fishing, etc.

VICTORIA PARK (217 acres), E.9. Lido.

WORMWOOD SCRUBS (193 acres), Hammersmith, W.12 and N.W.10. West London Stadium.

EXHIBITIONS, ETC., IN LONDON

MADAME TUSSAUD'S EXHIBITION, Marylebone Road, N.W.1. Oct.-Mar., Weekdays, 10-5.30; Saturdays and Sundays, 10-6.30; April-Sept., daily 10-6.30.

LONDON PLANETARIUM, Maryebone Road, N.W.1. Presentations hourly from 11 a.m. daily.

ROYAL HORTICULTURAL SOCIETY, Vincent Square, S.W.1, holds regular exhibitions at its Halls in Greycoat Street and in Vincent Square, S.W.1, and the Chelsea Flower Show at the Royal Hospital Grounds, Chelsea (May).

ZOOLOGICAL GARDENS, Regents's Park, N.W.1. —Opened 1828. Admission: (Mar.-Oct.) Mondays to Saturdays, 9-5; Sundays and Bank Holidays, 9-7; (Nov.-Feb.), 10-5. Mondays throughout the year (except Bank Holidays), Adults, 55p; Children under 14, 28p; all other days, Adults, 75p; Children, 40p. Additional charge for admission to the Aquarium and the Children's Zoo. Special rates for parties.

WHIPSNADE ZOOLOGICAL PARK, Whipsnade Park, nr. Dunstable, Beds. (34 miles from London, 8½ miles from Luton and 3 miles from Dunstable). Open from 10 a.m. to 7. p.m., or sunset, whichever is the earlier. Adults, 75p; Children (3-14), 45p. Cars admitted at extra charge. Special rates for parties.

MUSIC

ROYAL OPERA HOUSE, Covent Garden, W.C.2. —Opera and Ballet mid Sept.—early August. The (third) Covent Garden Theatre was opened May 15, 1858 (the first was opened Dec. 7, 1732). *General Administrator*, J. Tooley.

ROYAL ALBERT HALL, Kensington Gore, S.W.7— Regular seasons of Promenade Concerts. Also used for public meetings, concerts and other entertainments. The elliptical hall, one of the largest in the world, was completed in 1871.

ROYAL FESTIVAL HALL, South Bank, S.E.1.— Opened for the Festival of Britain, 1951, and administered by Greater London Council. Concerts and regular ballet seasons. Queen Elizabeth Hall and Purcell Room opened 1967. *Director, South Bank Concert Halls*, J. Denison, C.B.E.

KNELLER HALL, Twickenham.—Royal Military School of Music. A band of up to 250 instrumentalists gives concerts in the grounds on Wednesdays throughout the summer season, commencing at 8 p.m. Members of the public are welcome to attend; admission, 15p. Season tickets available.

ENVIRONS OF LONDON

BARNET AND HADLEY GREEN.—Scene of Battle, A.D. 1471. Hadley Woods.

BURNHAM BEECHES and FLEET WOOD, Bucks.—

Magnificent wooded scenery, purchased by the Corporation of London for the benefit of the public in 1879, includes Fleet Wood (65 acres) presented in 1921. During summer omnibus runs daily. Sundays included, from Slough Station (Western Region), passing within 250 yards of " Gray's Elegy " Church. *See* " Stoke Poges".

BUSHY PARK (1,099 acres).—Adjoining Hampton Court, contains many fine trees and avenue of horse-chestnuts enclosed in a fourfold avenue of limes, planted by King William III. " Chestnut Sunday " (when the trees are in full bloom with their " candles ") is usually about May 1 to 15.

CHEQUERS, a country residence for Prime Ministers, was presented to the Nation (with an endowment to maintain the estate, etc.) by Lord and Lady Lee of Fareham, as the official country residence for the Prime Minister of the day, and the gift was approved by Parliament in the *Chequers Estate Act*, 1917. In 1921 the Chequers Estate of 700 acres was added to the gift by Lord Lee. Chequers is a mansion in Tudor style in the Chilterns about 3 miles from Princes Risborough, Bucks, and contains a collection of Cromwellian portraits and relics.

DARWIN AND DOWN HOUSE, Downe, Farnborough, Kent.—Where Charles Darwin thought and worked for 40 years and died in 1882. Maintained by the Royal College of Surgeons. Open 1 to 6. Closed Mondays (except Bank Holidays), Fridays and Christmas Day. Admission, 50p. Children, 20p.

DORNEYWOOD, country house in 215 acres, near Burnham Beeches, Bucks., was presented to the nation by Lord Courtauld-Thomson (died 1954) as an official residence for any Minister of the Crown chosen by the Prime Minister during office. Administered by the National Trust. Garden and grounds open to the public on Saturdays only. (August and Sept, 2.15–6 p.m.) Admission 10p. Children, 5p.

DULWICH, S.E.21 (5 miles from London), contains *Dulwich College* (founded by Edward Alleyn in 1619), the *Horniman Museum and Dulwich Park* (72 acres). The *Dulwich Picture Gallery*, built by Sir John Soane to house the collection bequeathed by the artist, Sir Francis Bourgeois, was damaged by enemy action in the Second World War. The pictures, however, were saved, and the gallery has been rebuilt with the aid of a grant from the Pilgrim Trust. It was reopened by Queen Elizabeth the Queen Mother on April 27, 1953. In *Dulwich Village* the rural characteristics of the pre-suburban periods are preserved.

ELTHAM, Kent (10 miles from London by Southern Region). Remains of 13th-15th century Eltham Palace, the birthplace of John of Eltham (1316), son of Edward II. The hall, built by Edward IV, contains fine hammer-beam roof of chestnut. In the churchyard of St. John the Baptist is the tomb of Thomas Doggett, the comedian and founder of the Thames Watermen's championship (Doggett's Coat and Badge).

EPPING FOREST (6,000 acres, originally purchased by the Corporation of London for £250,000 and thrown open to the public in 1882; the present forest is 12 miles long by 1 to 2 miles wide, about one-tenth of its original area). LOUGHTON, BUCKHURST HILL, CHINGFORD, HIGH BEECH (London Transport and Eastern Region). Beautiful forest scenery.

ETON COLLEGE.—22 miles from London. The most famous of English schools, founded by Henry VI in 1440, the scholars numbering 1,195 in July, 1970. Buildings date from 1442.

GREENWICH, S.E.10.—*Greenwich Hospital* (since 1873, the Royal Naval College) was built by Charles II, from designs by Inigo Jones, and by Queen Anne and William III, from designs by Wren, on the site of an ancient royal palace, and of the more recent *Placentia*, an enlarged edition of the palace, constructed by Humphrey, Duke of Gloucester (1391–1447), son of Henry IV. Henry VIII, Queen Mary I and Queen Elizabeth I were born in the Royal Palace (which extended to the Crown in 1447) and King Edward VI died there. In the principal quadrangle is a marble statue of George II, by Rysbraeck. (For *National Maritime Museum*, see Index.) *Painted Hall* and *Chapel* open daily except Thursdays from 2.30 p.m. to 5 p.m. (closed on Sundays, Oct.–April inclusive). Visitors are also admitted to Morning Service in the Chapel at 11 a.m., summer and winter, except during College vacations. *Greenwich Park* (196½ acres) was enclosed by Humphrey, Duke of Gloucester, and laid out by Charles II, from the designs of Le Nôtre. On a hill in Greewich Park is the former Royal Observatory (founded 1675). Part of its buildings at Greenwich have been taken over by the Maritime Museum and named *Flamsteed House*, after John Flamsteed (1646–1719), first Astronomer Royal. The Parish church of Greenwich (*St. Alfege*) was rebuilt by Hawksmoor (Wren's pupil) in 1728, and restored after severe damage during the Second World War. General Wolfe (Heights of Abraham) and Tallis (" the father of Church Music ") are buried in the church. Henry VIII was christened in the former church. *Charlton House:* built in the early 17th century (1607–1612) for Adam Newton, tutor to Prince Henry, brother to Charles I. The house is largely in the Jacobean style of architecture. *Cutty Sark*, the last of the famous tea clippers, which has been preserved as a memorial to ships and men of a past era. The ship is fully restored and re-rigged, with a museum of sail on board, Open to visitors: weekdays, 11 to 5 (Summer, 6 p.m.); Sundays and Boxing Day, 2.30 to 5. The yacht *Gipsy Moth IV* in which Sir Francis Chichester sailed single-handed round the world, 1966–67, is preserved alongside *Cutty Sark*.

HAM HOUSE, Richmond.—A notable example of 17th-century domestic architecture, long the home of the Tollemache family (Earls of Dysart). The contents, described as " probably the finest and most varied collection of Charles II's reign to survive", were purchased for the Victoria and Albert Museum which now administers the house. Ham House may be seen on Tues.–Sun. inclusive and on Bank Holidays, 2–6 p.m., April–Sept., 12–4 p.m., Oct.–March. Closed Mon. (except Bank Holidays), Christmas Eve, Christmas Day, Boxing Day and Good Friday and New Year's Day. Admission, 20p; Children and Pensioners, 10p.

HAMPTON COURT.—Sixteenth-century Palace built by Cardinal Wolsey, with additions by Sir Christopher Wren for William and Mary, 15 miles from London. Fine view of river. Beautiful gardens with maze and prolific grape vine (planted in 1769). Old Royal Apartments and collection of pictures. Tennis Court, built by King Henry VIII in 1530. The Palace is *closed* on Christmas Eve, Christmas Day, Boxing Day, New Year's Day and Good Friday. April–September: State Apartments: 30p; Children and OAPs 10p (Oct–March 10p, 5p). Mantegna Paintings 15p; Children and OAPs 5p (Oct.–March 15p, 5p). State Carriages 5p; Children and OAPs 5p. Maze 2p; Children and OAPs 2p. State Carriages, Tennis Court, Banqueting House and Maze *closed* Oct–March. Open May–Sept. 9.30–6 (Sundays 11–6) (Maze 10–6; 11–6). Nov–Feb. 9.30–4 (Sundays 2–4). Oct. and March 9.30–5 (Sundays 2–5).

Grace and Favour Residences.—Hampton Court contains a total of 57 residences occupied by favour of Her Majesty the Queen. The Minister of Public Building and Works reported in Parliament on April 17, 1962, that, of 140 grace and favour residences, the remainder were situated at Windsor Castle (46), Kensington Palace (16), St. James's Palace (8), Marlborough House Mews (9), Bushy Park (2), Kew Palace (1) and Hyde Park (1).

HARROW-ON-THE-HILL.—10 miles by Metropolitan and other railways. Large public school founded by John Lyon in 1571. The " Fourth Form Room " dates from 1608.

HUGHENDEN MANOR, High Wycombe, Bucks.— The home of Disraeli from 1847 till his death and contains much of his furniture, books, etc. Conveyed to the National Trust in 1947. Open daily including Sundays and Bank Holidays, 2–6 or till dusk. Saturdays and Sundays, 12.30 to 6. Closed Tuesdays and all December (1974), January, Good Friday and Christmas Day. Admission (nonmembers), 25p; Children, 12p.

JORDANS AND CHALFONT ST. GILES, near Beaconsfield, Bucks, contain the Old *Quaker Meeting House* (1688) at Jordans, in the burial ground of which lies William Penn (Pennsylvania); a barn built out of the timbers of the *Mayflower* by the 17th-century owner of Jordans (Gardener). At Chalfont St. Giles is the cottage where Milton lived during the Great Plague (1665–1666).

KEW, Surrey, was a favourite home of the early Hanoverian monarchs. Kew House, the residence of Frederick, Prince of Wales, and later of his son, George III, was pulled down in 1803, but the earlier Dutch House, now known as Kew Palace, survives. It was built in 1631 and acquired by George III as an annexe to Kew House in 1781. The famous Kew Gardens (*see* p. 649) were originally laid out as a private garden for Kew House for George III's mother in 1759 and were much enlarged in the nineteenth century, notably by the inclusion of the grounds of the former Richmond Lodge.

MARBLE HILL HOUSE, Twickenham, Middlesex. —Example of the English Palladian style. Reopened 1966, after restoration work on the elevations of the house, entrance hall, main staircase and first floor rooms. The Great Room and mahogany staircase are noteworthy. Open daily except Fri. Admission Free.

NATIONAL ARMY MUSEUM, Royal Hospital Road, S.W.3. Established by Royal Charter (1960). Official Museum for British Army, Honourable East India Company, Indian Services and Colonial Forces. History of British, Indian and Colonial Forces, 1485 to 1914, in new building at Chelsea. Indian Army room remains open at R.M.A. Sandhurst, Camberley, Surrey.

OSTERLEY PARK, Isleworth.—House and park of 140 acres given to the National Trust by the Earl of Jersey in 1949. Part of the Elizabethan house, built in 1577 for Sir Thomas Gresham, remains, but it was largely remodelled by Robert Adam, and the staterooms are among the best examples of Adam decoration. Open daily, except Mondays, (April–Sept.) 2–6 p.m.; (Oct.–Mar.) 12 noon–4 p.m. Closed Monday (except Bank Holidays), Christmas Eve, Christmas Day, Boxing Day, New Year's Day and Good Friday. Admission 20p, children 10p.

RICHMOND, SURREY, contains the red brick gateway of *Richmond Palace* (Henry VIII, 1485–1509) and buildings of the Jacobean, Queen Anne, and early Georgian periods, including *White Lodge* in Richmond Park, the former home of Queen Mary's mother (the Duke of Windsor was born there, June 23, 1894). The *Star and Garter* Home for Disabled Soldiers, Sailors, and Airmen (the

Women's Memorial of the Great War) was opened by Queen Mary in 1924. *Richmond Park* (2,469 acres) contains herds of fallow and red deer.

ROYAL AIR FORCE MUSEUM, Colindale, Hendon.— The museum was established in 1963 and officially opened by the Queen in November 1972. It covers all aspects of the history of the Royal Air Force and its predecessors and most of the history of aviation generally. The museum building is sited on ten acres of the historic former airfield at Hendon. Its aircraft hall, which occupies two hangars dating from the First World War, displays some 40 aircraft from the museum's total collection of over 100 machines. Open weekdays, 10 a.m.–6 p.m., Sundays, 2 p.m.–6 p.m. Admission free.

RUNNIMEDE.—A meadow of about 100 acres, on S. bank of Thames (part of the Crown Lands), between Windsor and Staines. From June 15–23, 1215, the hostile Barons encamped on this meadow during negiotiations with King John, who rode over each day from Windsor. The 48 " Articles of the Barons " were accepted by the King on June 15, and were subsequently embodied in a charter, since known as *Magna Carta*, of which several copies were sealed on June 19. About half a mile N.E. of the meadow is *Magna Carta Island* (claimed as the actual site of the sealing), presented to the National Trust in 1930.

A memorial at *Cooper's Hill*, near Runnimede, to members of the Commonwealth air forces who lost their lives in the Second World War while serving from bases in the United Kingdom and north-western Europe and have no known grave, was unveiled by the Queen on October 17, 1953. Her Majesty on May 14, 1965, unveiled a memorial to the late President of the United States, John F. Kennedy, on ground nearby.

ST. ALBANS.—A city in Hertfordshire, on the River Ver, 22 miles N.W. of London. The abbey church, built partly of materials from the old Roman city of Verulamium by Paul of Caen, was consecrated in 1115. Parts still remain of the Norman structure. The city was the scene of the overthrow of Henry VI in 1455, and of the Earl of Warwick in 1461. The site of the pre-Roman city of King Tasciovanus and the remains of the ancient City of Verulamium, with well preserved theatre and many other features, excavated in recent years.

SYON HOUSE, Brentford.—The summer home of the Duke of Northumberland. The House is built on the remains of the Nunnery of Syon, founded by the order of Henry V in 1415. At the Dissolution of the Monasteries the estate reverted to the Crown. In 1594 it was granted to the 9th Earl of Northumberland, who altered and improved the property. In the eight years, 1762–1770, the interior was transformed and furnished by Robert Adam. Open Easter to Sept.

WALTHAM ABBEY (or WALTHAM HOLY CROSS), 13 miles from London (Eastern Region).—The Abbey ruins, Harold's Bridge (11th century), the Nave of the former cruciform Abbey Church (the oldest Norman building in England (consecrated May 3, 1060) and the traditional burial place of King Harold II (1066), and a Lady Chapel of Edward II, with crypt below. New evidence of the position and style of several buildings, which once stood on the site of the Augustinian monastery, were revealed by the prolonged drought in the summer of 1933. At Waltham Cross, 1 mile from the Abbey, is one of the crosses (partly restored) erected by Edward I to mark a resting place of the corpse of Queen Eleanor on its way to Westminster Abbey. (Ten crosses were erected, but only those at Geddington, Northampton and Waltham remain; "Charing" Cross originally stood near the spot now occupied by the statue of Charles I at Whitehall.)

WINDSOR CASTLE (begun by William the Conqueror, A.D. 1066–87).—22 miles from London, by Western and Southern Regions. The Castle Precincts are open daily, free of charge, from 10 a.m. to one hour before sunset or 4 p.m. (whichever is the later). When the Queen is not in official residence, the *State Apartments* of Windsor Castle are open to the public, during Her Majesty's pleasure, on every weekday and on certain Sunday afternoons during the summer months. When the State Apartments are open, the charges for admission are for Adults, 20p and for Children, 10p. By the Queen's command, the net proceeds go to charities. The hours of admission to the State Apartments are: Jan. to mid-March, mid-Oct. to Dec., 10.30–3; March to mid-Oct., 10.30–5; Sundays, March to mid-Oct. 1.30–5; Closed, Nov.–Feb.

Queen Mary's Doll's House, the *Exhibition of Dolls* and the Exhibition of Drawings by Holbein, Leonardo da Vinci and other artists can be seen on the same days and hours as the State Apartments, admission 5p each person to each. When the State Apartments are closed, Queen Mary's Doll's House and the Exhibition of Drawings remain open to the public. The *Albert Memorial Chapel* is open free throughout the year from 10–1; 2–4; closed on Sundays; Admission free. A fee is charged to visit *St. George's Chapel*. The *Curfew Tower* may be seen under the guidance of the Keeper to whom application must be made at the entrance.

The *Royal Mausoleum*, Frogmore Gardens, Home Park, is open annually on two days in early May, usually the first Wednesday and Thursday in the month, in conjunction with the opening of Frogmore Gardens in aid of the National Garden Scheme, 10 a.m.–dusk. Also open on the Wednesday nearest to May 24 (Queen Victoria's birthday) from 11 a.m. to 4 p.m. Admission free.

HOUSES OPEN TO THE PUBLIC

Times of summer opening and admission fees shown are those which obtained in 1975, and are subject to modification. Space permits only a selection of some of the more noteworthy houses in England which are open to the public. A fuller description of some houses in or near London will be found in the preceding section.

ADLINGTON HALL, Cheshire.—Sun. and Bank Holidays (Sats., July and August), 2.30–6. Admission, 25p.

ALNWICK CASTLE, Northumberland. Seat of the Duke of Northumberland.—May–Sept., Daily (except Fri.) 1–5. Admission, 30p.

ALTHORP Northamptonshire. Seat of Earl Spencer.—Easter–Sept., Sun., Tues., Thurs. and Bank Holidays (May, Suns. only), 2.30–6. Admission, 50p.

*ANGLESEY ABBEY, Cambs.—Easter to second week in Oct., Wed., Thurs., Sat., Sun., and Bank Holidays, 2–6. Admission 40p.

*ANTONY HOUSE, Cornwall.—Tues., Wed., Thurs. and Bank Holidays, 2–6. Admission 40p.

*ARLINGTON COURT, nr. Barnstaple.—April-end Oct., daily, 11–1, 2–6. Admission, 60p.

ARUNDEL CASTLE, Sussex. Seat of the Duke of Norfolk.—Easter to mid-June, Mon.–Thurs., 1–5; mid-June to end of Sept., Mon.–Fri. (and Suns. in August) also Easter Monday and Spring Bank Holiday, 12–5. Admission 50p.

*ASCOTT, Wing, Bucks.—Including Anthony de Rothschild collection of pictures. April–Sept. Wed., Sat. and Bank Holidays (also some Suns. in July and August), 2–6. Admission 50p.

ATHELHAMPTON, Dorset.—Sun., Wed., Thurs. and Bank Holidays, 2–6. Admission 40p.

AUDLEY END, Saffron Walden.—April–early Oct., daily, except Mon. (but including Bank Holidays), 10–5.30. Admission, 25p.

AVEBURY MANOR, Wiltshire. (Adjoining the famous Avebury stone circle, which is also on public view).—May–August, daily except Tues., 2–6; April and Sept., Sat. and Sun. 2–6, Bank Holidays, 10–6. Admission, 30p.

BELVOIR CASTLE, nr. Grantham. Seat of the Duke of Rutland.—April–Sept., Wed., Thurs., Fri. and Tues. following Bank Holidays, 12–6; Bank Holidays, 11–7; Suns., 2–7. Admission, 50p.

BERKELEY CASTLE, Glos.—April–Sept., daily, except Mon., (but including Bank Holidays), 11–5 (April 2–5); also Sun. from May, 2–5; Bank Holidays, 11–5. Admission 40p.

BLENHEIM PALACE. Woodstock. Seat of the

Duke of Marlborough and birthplace of Sir Winston Churchill.—April–Oct. daily, (except Spring Bank Holiday week-end) 11.30–5. Admission, 60p (1974).

*BLICKLING HALL, Norfolk.—Easter–second week in Oct., Tues., Wed., Thurs., Sat., Sun. and Bank Holidays, 2–6 (11–6 mid-May to Sept.). Admission 50p.

*BUCKLAND ABBEY, Tavistock.—Including Drake relics. Easter–Sept. 30, weekdays and Bank Holidays, 11–6. Sun. 2–6. Admission, 17p.

BURGHLEY HOUSE, Stamford. Seat of the Marquess of Exeter. Tues.–Thurs., Sat. and Bank Holidays, 11–5. Sun., 2–5. Admission, 40p, (1974).

CASTLE ASHBY, nr. Northampton. A home of the Marquess of Northampton.—Sundays and Bank Holidays; also Easter week-end. Also Thurs. and Sat., June–Aug., 2–5.30. Admission, 50p.

CASTLE HOWARD, Yorkshire.—Tues., Wed., Thurs., Sat., Sun., 1.30–5; Bank Holidays, 11.30–5.30. Admission, 60p.

*CHARLECOTE PARK, Warwicks. Associations with Shakespeare.—April, Sat., Sun., and daily in Easter Week. May–Sept., daily, except Mon., but incl. Bank Holidays, 11.15–5.45. Admission, 50p.

*CHARTWELL, Kent.—Home of the late Sir Winston Churchill. Sat., Sun. and Bank Holidays, 11–6; Wed. and Thurs., 2–6. Admission, 50p.

CHATSWORTH, Derbyshire. Seat of the Duke of Devonshire.—Wed., Thurs. and Fri., 11.30–4; Sat. and Sun., 1.30–5; Bank Holidays and Tuesdays after Bank Holidays, 11–5. Admission, 50p (1974).

*CLANDON PARK, Surrey.—Sun., Tues. (except day after Bank Holiday), Wed., Thurs., Sat. and Bank Holidays, 2–6. Admission, 50p.

*CLAYDON HOUSE, Bucks.—Daily except Mondays but including Bank Holiday, 2–6. Admission, 35p.

*CLIVEDEN, Bucks.—Wed., Sat. and Sun., 2.30–5.30. Admission, 10p.

*COMPTON CASTLE, nr. Paignton.—Fortified manor house. Mon., Wed. and Thurs., 10.30–12.30, 2–5. Admission, 25p.

COMPTON WYNYATES, Warwickshire. A home of the Marquess of Northampton.—Wed., Sat. and

★ Property of the National Trust.

Bank Holidays. Sundays (June–August only), (also Easter week-end), 2–6. Admission, 50p.

CORSHAM COURT, Wilts.—April to mid-July, and mid-Sept. to Oct., Wed., Thurs., Sun. and Bank Holidays; mid-July to mid-Sept., daily except Mon. and Fri. (but incl. Bank Holiday), 11-12.30, 2–6. Admission, 40p.

★COTEHELE, nr. Calstock, Cornwall.—Daily 11-1, 2–6. Admission, 60p.

★CROFT CASTLE, Herefordshire.—Sun., Wed., Thurs., Sat. and Bank Holiday Mondays, 2.30–5.30 (Oct., Sat. and Sun., 2.15-6). Admission, 30p.

★DYRHAM PARK, Glos. (Avon).—Daily (except Mon. and Tues.), 2–6; Bank Holidays, 12–6 (Oct., Wed., Sat. and Sun., 2–6). Admission, 40p.

EYE MANOR, Herefordshire.—Sun., Wed., Thurs. and Sat. (also Bank Holidays and Tues. following) (July–Sept., daily), 2.30–5.30. Admission, 30p.

★FELBRIGG HALL, Norfolk. Easter–mid-Oct., Sun., Tues.–Thurs. and Bank Holidays, 2–6. Admission, 40p.

GAWSWORTH HALL, Cheshire.—Daily, 2–6. Admission, 30p.

HADDON HALL, Derbyshire.—Tues.–Sat. and Bank Holidays, 11–6; Sun. preceeding Bank Holidays, 2–6. Admission, 50p.

★HARDWICK HALL, Derbyshire.—Wed., Thurs., Sat., Sun. and Bank Holidays, 1–5.30. Admission, 50p.

HAREWOOD HOUSE, Yorks. Seat of the Earl of Harewood.—Easter–mid Oct., daily, 11–6. Admission, 30p (1974).

HATFIELD HOUSE, Hertfordshire. Seat of the Marquess of Salisbury.—Last week in March to first week in Oct., daily except Mon. (but including Bank Holidays), Weekdays, 12–5, Sun. 2–5.30. Admission, 40p.

HEDINGHAM CASTLE, Essex.—May–Sept., Tues., Thurs. and Sat., 2–6. Bank Holidays (incl. Easter Monday), 10–6. Admission, 15p.

HEVENINGHAM HALL, Suffolk.—Sun., Wed., Thurs., Sat. and Bank Holidays (also Tues., June–Aug.), 2–5.30. Admission, 30p.

★HUGHENDEN MANOR, High Wycombe. Former home of Disraeli. Daily, except Tues. Weekdays 2–6; Sat. and Sun., 12.30–6. Admission, 30p.

KNEBWORTH HOUSE, Herts.—Sat. and Sun., Easter–end of May. Daily, June–Sept., except Mon. (but including Bank Holidays) (Oct., Suns. only), 2–5.30. Admission, 30p.

★KNOLE, Sevenoaks.—Wed.–Sat. and Bank Holidays, 10–12, 2–5. Admission 50p.

★LACOCK ABBEY, Wilts.—Daily, except Mon. and Tues., but including Bank Holidays, 2–6. Admission, 40p.

★LITTLE MORETON HALL, Cheshire. Famous example of " black and white " timbering.—Daily except Tuesday and Good Friday, 2–6. Admission, 30p.

LONGLEAT HOUSE, Wilts. Seat of the Marquess of Bath.—Daily, 10–6. Admission, 50p.

LUTON HOO, Beds.—Easter–Sept., Mon., Wed., Thurs. and Sat., 11–6; Sundays 2–6. Admission, 35p.

★MELFORD HALL, Suffolk.—April–Sept., Sun. Wed., Thurs. and Bank Holidays, 2.30–6. Admission, 30p

MILTON MANOR HOUSE, nr. Abingdon.—Easter–Sept., Sat., Sun. and Bank Holidays, 2–6. Admission, 35p.

★MONTACUTE HOUSE, Yeovil.—Daily, except Mon. and Tues. (but including Bank Holidays), 12.30–6 (Oct., Sun., Wed. and Sat., 2–6). Admission, 40p.

NEWBY HALL, Yorks.—Sun., Wed., Thurs., Sat. and Bank Holidays, 2–6. Admission, 50p.

OSBORNE HOUSE, Isle of Wight. State and Private Apartments are shown, including the room in which Queen Victoria died.—Mon.–Fri., 11–5. July and Aug., 10.30–5). Admission, 25p.

★OXBURGH HALL, Norfolk.—Sun., Wed., Thurs., Sat. and Bank Holidays, 2–6. Admission, 35p.

PARHAM, Pulborough, Sussex.—Sun., Wed., Thurs. and Bank Holidays, 2–5.30. Admission, 50p (last Sunday of each month, 70p).

★PAYCOCKE'S, Coggeshall, Essex. Tudor wool-merchant's town house.—April–Sept., Wed., Thurs., Sun. and Bank Holidays, 2–5.30. Admission, 25p.

★PECKOVER HOUSE, Wisbech, Cambs.—Sun., Wed., Thurs., Sat. and Bank Holidays, 2–6. Admission, 30p.

PENSHURST PLACE, Kent. Seat of Visct. De L'Isle, 𝕍𝕮.—Daily, except Mon. and Fri., but including Bank Holidays, 2–6 (July–Sept., 1–6, Bank Holidays, 11.30–6). Admission, 50p.

★PETWORTH HOUSE, Sussex.—Wed., Thurs., Sat. and Bank Holidays, 2–6. Admission, 50p. First and third Tuesday in each month, 60p.

POWDERHAM CASTLE, Devonshire. Seat of the Earl of Devon.—Mid-May to mid-Sept., Sun.–Thurs., 2–5.30. Admission, 40p.

RABY CASTLE, Co. Durham.—Easter week-end and May, Sun. and Spring Holiday week-end; June–Sept., Sun., Wed., Sat. and Bank Holidays (daily in Aug. except Fri.), 2–5. Admission, 35p.

★SALTRAM HOUSE, nr. Plymouth.—April–mid-Oct., daily 11–1, 2–6. Admission, 60p.

★SISSINGHURST CASTLE, Kent.—Daily, 12–6.30 (Sat., Sun. and Bank Holidays, 10–6.30). Admission, 40p.

SKIPTON CASTLE, Yorkshire.—Weekdays, 10–6, Sundays 2–6. Admission, 20p.

STANFORD HALL, Lutterworth.—Thurs., Sat. and Sun., Bank Holidays and Tues. after Bank Holidays, 2.30–6. Admission, 40p.

★STOURHEAD, Wiltshire.—Daily, except Mon. and Tues., but including Bank Holidays (Oct., Wed., Sat. and Sun. only), 2–6. Admission, 40p.

STRATFIELD SAYE, Hants. Seat of the Duke of Wellington. Daily (except Fri.), 11–5.30. Admission, 50p.

SULGRAVE MANOR, Northamptonshire. Former home of members of the Washington family.—Daily, except Weds., 10.30–1, 2–5.30 (closes at 4 p.m., Oct.). Admission, 25p.

★TATTON PARK, Cheshire.—Daily, except Mondays, but including Bank Holidays, 2–5.15 (2–5.45, first week in May to end of Aug.). Admission, 25p.

★UPPARK, nr. Petersfield.—Sun., Wed., Thurs. and Bank Holidays, 2–6. Admission, 35p.

★THE VYNE, Basingstoke.—April–Sept., Wed. and Bank Holidays, 11–1, 2–6; Sun., Thurs. and Sat., 2–6. Admission, 35p.

★WADDESDON MANOR, Bucks.—Wed.–Sun., 2–6. Bank Holidays, 11–6. Admission, 45p (Fri. 65p).

WESTON PARK, Salop. Seat of the Earl of Bradford.—Easter–first week in Sept. Daily, except Mon. and Fri. (but including Bank Holidays), 2–6 (last 3 weeks in Sept., Sat. and Sun. only). Admission, 55p.

WILTON HOUSE, Wilts. Seat of the Earl of Pembroke.—April–Sept., Tues.–Sat. and Bank Holidays, 11–6. Sun., 2–6. Admission, 40p.

WOBURN ABBEY. Seat of the Duke of Bedford.—Daily, 11.30–6.15 (from mid-Sept. 11.30–5.45). Sun., 11.30–6.45. Admission, 50p (1974).

★ Property of the National Trust.

HISTORIC MONUMENTS

A select list of monuments under the control of the Department of the Environment.

Reduced admission prices for retirement pensioners and children under 16. 10 per cent. discount for parties of 11 or more.

Standard hours of opening (marked *) are as follows:

	Weekdays	Sundays
Mar.–April	9.30 a.m.–5.30 p.m.	2–5.30 p.m.
May–Sept.	9.30 a.m.–7.00 p.m.	2–7.00 p.m.
October	9.30 a.m.–5.30 p.m.	2–5.30 p.m.
Nov.–Feb.	9.30 a.m.–4.00 p.m.	2–4.00 p.m.

Those marked † open on Sundays at 9.30 a.m. from April to September.

All monuments are closed on Christmas Eve, Christmas Day, Boxing Day and New Year's Day.

BEESTON CASTLE, Cheshire. 10p†. Thirteenth-century inner ward with gatehouse and towers, and considerable remains of large outer ward.

BERKHAMSTEAD CASTLE, Hertfordshire. 5p.* Extensive remains of a large 11th-century motte-and-bailey castle with later stone wall.

BOLSOVER CASTLE, Derbyshire. 10p.† Established in Norman times, it is now notable for its exceptionally interesting 17th-century buildings.

BOSCOBEL HOUSE, Salop. 5p*. Timber-framed early 17-century hunting lodge with later alterations. Charles II's " Royal Oak " is nearby.

BRINKBURN PRIORY, Northumberland. 5p†. An Augustinian priory; the church (c. 1200, repaired in 1858) and parts of the claustral buildings survive.

BROUGHAM CASTLE, Cumbria. 5p*. Extensive remains of the keep (c. 1170), and of other buildings of periods up to the 17th century.

BUILDWAS ABBEY, Salop. 5p*. Beautiful 12th-century ruin of a Cistercian abbey with early 13th-century vaulted Chapter-house.

BYLAND ABBEY, North Yorkshire. 5p*. Considerable remains of church and conventional buildings date from the abbey's foundation in 1177 by the Cistercians.

CARISBROOKE CASTLE, Isle of Wight. Summer 20p, Winter 10p*. Extensive motte-and-bailey castle with shell keep.

CARLISLE CASTLE, Cumbria. Summer, 20p, Winter 10p†. The castle was begun by William Rufus. The keep houses the Regimental Museum of the Border Regiment.

CASTLE ACRE PRIORY, NORFOLK. 10p†. Extensive remains include the church with its elaborate west front, and the prior's lodgings.

CASTLE RISING, Norfolk. 10p†. A fine 12th-century keep stands in a massive earthwork with its gatehouse and bridge.

CHESTERS ROMAN FORT, Northumberland. Summer 15p, Winter 10p†.

CHYSAUSER ANCIENT VILLAGE Cornwall. 5p†. Iron-Age village of courtyard houses.

CLEEVE ABBEY, Somerset. 10p†. Much of the claustral buildings survive including timber-roofed frater, but only foundations of the church.

CORBRIDGE ROMAN STATION, Northumberland. Summer 15p, Winter 10p†. Excavations have revealed the central area of the Roman town and military base of Corstopitum.

DEAL CASTLE, Kent. 10p†. The largest and most complete of the castles erected by Henry VIII for coastal defence.

DOVER CASTLE, Kent. Keep—Summer 20p, Winter 10p†; Underground Works 10p*; Grounds —free any reasonable time. One of the largest and most important English castles.

DUNSTANBURGH CASTLE, Northumberland. 5p†. The castle, standing on a cliff above the sea, has a 14th-century gatehouse-keep.

FARLEIGH CASTLE, Somerset. 5p†. Late 14th-century castle of two courts. The chapel contains fine tomb of Sir Thomas Hungerford.

FARNHAM CASTLE, Surrey. 5p*. Keep, April–Sept. Built by the Bishops of Winchester, the motte of the castle is enclosed by a large 12th-century shell keep.

FINCHALE PRIORY, Durham. 5p†. Benedictine house on banks of River Wear with considerable remains of the 13th century.

FOUNTAINS ABBEY, North Yorkshire. Summer 20p, Winter 10p. Nov.–Feb. 9.30 a.m.–4 p.m. (Sundays 2–4 p.m.); March, April, Oct., 9.30 a.m.–5.30 p.m.; May, Sept. 9.30 a.m.–7 p.m.; June–Aug. 9.30 a.m.–9 p.m. Finest monastic ruin in W. Europe.

FRAMLINGHAM CASTLE, Suffolk. 10p†. Impressive castle with high curtain-walls of late 12th-century enclosing a poor-house of 1639.

FURNESS ABBEY, Cumbria. 5p*. Founded in 1127 by Stephen, afterwards King of England; extensive remains of church and conventual buildings.

GOODRICH CASTLE, Herefordshire. 10p†. Extensive remains of beautiful 14th-century castle incorporating interesting 12th-century keep.

GRIMES GRAVES, Norfolk. 5p†. Extensive group of flint mines dating from the Stone Age. Several shafts can be inspected.

HAILES ABBEY, Gloucestershire. 5p*. Ruins of a Cistercian monastery founded in 1246. Museum contains some fine architectural fragments.

HELMSLEY CASTLE, North Yorkshire. 5p†. Twelfth-century keep and curtain wall with 16th-century domestic buildings against west wall.

HOUSESTEADS ROMAN FORT, Northumberland. Summer 15p, Winter 10p† Excavation has exposed this infantry fort on Hadrian's Wall with its extra-mural civilian settlement.

KENILWORTH CASTLE, Warwickshire. Summer 15p, Winter 10p†. One of the finest and most extensive castles in England, showing many styles of building from 1155 to 1649.

LANERCOST PRIORY, Cumbria. 5p*. The nave of the priory church is still used and there are remains of other claustal buildings.

LINDISFARNE PRIORY, Northumberland. 10p†. An Anglican monastery destroyed by the Danes, it was re-established by the Benedictine abbey of Durham.

LULLINGSTONE ROMAN VILLA, Kent. Summer 15p, Winter 10p†. A large villa occupied through much of the Roman period; fine mosaics and a unique Christian chapel.

MIDDLEHAM CASTLE, North Yorkshire. 5p*. The fine keep of 1170 stands in the centre of 13th-century inner ward.

MOUNT GRACE PRIORY, North Yorkshire. 10p*, but closed Mon. unless Bank Holiday. Carthusian monastery, with remains of monks' separate houses.

NETLEY ABBEY, Hampshire. 5p*. Extensive remains of 13th-century church, claustral buildings and abbot's house, incorporating much fine detail.

OLD SARUM, Wiltshire. 5p†. Large 11th-century earthworks enclosing the excavated remains of the castle and the cathedral.

ORFORD CASTLE, Suffolk. 10p†. Circular keep of c. 1170 and remains of coastal defence castle built by Henry II.

PENDENNIS CASTLE, Cornwall. 10p†. Well-preserved castle erected by Henry VIII for coast defence and enlarged by Elizabeth I.

PEVENSEY CASTLE, East Sussex. 10p†. Extensive remains of a Roman fort of the Saxon Shore enclosing an 11th-century castle.

PEVERIL CASTLE, Derbyshire. 10p†. In a picturesque and nearly impregnable position, this 12th-century castle is defended on two sides by precipitous rocks.

PORTCHESTER CASTLE, Hampshire. 10p†. A Roman fort of the Saxon Shore enclosing a fine Norman keep and priory church.

RECULVER CHURCH and ROMAN FORT, Kent. 5p. Church†, Fort at any reasonable time. Remains of Saxon church with 12th-century towers standing in a Roman fort.

RICHBOROUGH CASTLE, Kent. 5p†. The landing-site of the Claudian invasion, it became a supply-base and a Saxon Shore fort.

RICHMOND CASTLE, North Yorkshire. 10p†. This very fine 12th-century keep, with 11th-century curtain-wall and gatehouse, commands Swaledale.

RIEVAULX ABBEY, North Yorkshire. 10p†. Extensive remains include an early Cistercian nave (1140) and fine 13th-century choir and claustral buildings.

ROCHESTER CASTLE, Kent. 10.† Eleventh-century wall, partly overlying the Roman city wall, encloses splendid square keep of *c.* 1130.

ST. AUGUSTINE'S ABBEY, Canterbury, Kent. 5p†. Sundays from 9.30 a.m. March to October. Founded by St. Augustine in 598; 7th- and 11th-century churches underly the mediaeval abbey.

ST. MAWES CASTLE, Cornwall. 10p†. Coast defence castle built by Henry VIII consisting of central tower and three bastions.

SCARBOROUGH CASTLE, North Yorkshire. 10p†. Remains of 12th-century keep and curtain-walls dominating the town.

STONEHENGE, Wiltshire. Summer 20p, Winter 10p†. Sundays from 9.30 a.m. all year. World-famous prehistoric monument consisting of central stone circles surrounded by bank and ditch.

TILBURY FORT, Essex. 5p*. Built to guard the Thames against the Dutch, the fort is a fine example of 17th-century fortification.

TINTAGEL CASTLE, Cornwall. Summer 15p, Winter 10p†. Twelfth-century castle on cliff-top site and remains of a Celtic monastery.

TYNEMOUTH PRIORY and CASTLE, Tyne and Wear. 5p†. Anglian monastery destroyed by the Danes and re-established in 1090, with 14th-century defensive system.

WALMER CASTLE, Kent. 10p†. Closed Mon. (unless Bank Holiday) and when Lord Warden is in residence. One of Henry VIII's coast defence

castles, it is the residence of the Lord Warden of the Cinque Ports.

WARKWORTH CASTLE, Northumberland. 10p†. Magnificent early 15th-century keep built by the Percys, with other remains from earlier periods.

WHITBY ABBEY, North Yorkshire. 10p†. A Saxon foundation destroyed by the Danes with considerable remains of fine 13th-century church.

WROXETER ROMAN SITE, Salop. 5p†. The public baths and part of the forum remain of the Roman town of Viroconium.

Wales

BEAUMARIS CASTLE, Anglesey. Summer 15p, Winter 10p†. The finest example of the concentrically planned castle in Britain, it is still almost intact.

CAERLEON ROMAN AMPHITHEATRE, Gwent. 5p†. Late 1st-century oval arena surrounded by bank for spectators with entrance passages.

CAERNARVON CASTLE. Summer 25p., Winter 10p†. The most important of the Edwardian castles, built together with the town wall in 1284.

CAERPHILLY CASTLE, Glamorgan. 10p†. Concentrically planned castle (*c.* 1300) notable for its great scale and use of water defences.

CHEPSTOW CASTLE, Gwent. 10p†. Fine rectangular keep in the middle of the fortifications.

CONWAY CASTLE, Gwynedd. Summer 15p, Winter 10p†. Built by Edward I to guard the Conway ferry, it is a magnificent example of mediaeval military architecture.

CRICCIETH CASTLE, Gwynedd. 10p†. A native Welsh castle of the early 13th century, much altered by Edward I.

DENBIGH CASTLE. 5p†. The remians of the castle, which dates from 1282–1322, include unusual triangular gatehouse.

HARLECH CASTLE, Gwynedd. Summer 15p, Winter 10p†. Well preserved Edwardian castle with a concentric plan sited on rocky outcrop above the former shore-line.

RAGLAN CASTLE, Gwent. 10p†. Extensive and imposing remains of 15th-century castle with moated hexagonal keep.

ST. DAVID'S, BISHOP'S PALACE, Dyfed. 10p†. Extensive remains of principal residence of Bishop of St. David's dating from 1280–1350.

TINTERN ABBEY, Gwent. 10p†. Very extensive remains of the fine 13th-century church and conventual buildings of this Cistercian monastery.

FREEMEN'S GUILDS

London.—Guild of Freemen of the City of London, 4 Dowgate Hill, E.C.4. *Clerk,* D. Reid.

Berwick upon Tweed.—Freemen's Guild of Berwick upon Tweed. *Sec.,* J. R. Reay, 9 Church Street.

Chester.—Freemen and Guilds of the City of Chester. *Hon. Sec.,* K. S. Astbury, The Guildhall, Chester.

Coventry.—City of Coventry Freemen's Guild. *Clerk.*—N. R. Davies, 67 Woodfield Road, Earlsdon.

Grimsby.—Enrolled Freemen of Grimsby. *Clerk,* W. J. Savage, St. Mary's Chambers, Grimsby.

Lincoln.—Lincoln Freemen's Committee. *Clerk,* E. Mason, St. Swithin's Square, Lincoln.

Oxford.—Oxford Freemen's Committee. *Chairman,* S. E. Oswin, 126 High Street, Oxford.

Shrewsbury.—Association of Shrewsbury Freemen. *President,* M. Peele, 20 Dogpole, Shrewsbury.

York.—Guild of Freemen of the City of York. *Hon. Clerk,* L. Buckle, 187 Tadcaster Road, York.

MUSEUMS AND ART GALLERIES OUTSIDE LONDON

BIRMINGHAM.—*City Museum and Art Gallery.* The art collection contains outstanding examples by British and European masters from 14th to 20th centuries, with particularly strong Pre-Raphaelite and Burne-Jones collections, sculpture, prints, drawings and water colours, British and European gold, silver and jewellery, pottery and porcelain, furniture, toys, textiles and costume, archaeology and natural history. Open, free, Weekdays, 10–6; Sundays 2–5.30. Closed Christmas Day, Boxing Day and Good Friday.

Museum of Science and Industry, Newhall Street. Founded 1950, the first provincial museum of its kind devoted to the history of science from the Industrial Revolution to the present. Locomotive Hall (1972) and many working machines under steam, gas, etc. Open, free, Weekdays, 10–5; Saturdays, 10–5.30; Sundays, 2–5.30. Open to 9 on first Wednesday evening of each month. Other Birmingham museums are: *Aston Hall, Blakesley Hall, Cannon Hill Nature Centre, Sarehole Mill, The Smithy* and *Weoley Castle.*

BOWES MUSEUM, Barnard Castle, Co. Durham, Important collections of British and European art, including paintings of Italian, Dutch, French and Spanish schools. Fine porcelain and pottery, tapestries and furniture. English period rooms from Elizabeth I to Victoria; local antiquities from Stone Age to 20th century. Temporary Exhibitions. Open weekdays, May–Sept., 10–5.30; March, April and October, 10–5; Nov.–Feb., 10–4. Sundays, 2–5 (Summer); 2–4 (Winter). Admission 20p; children and OAPs, 5p. Curator, M. H. Kirkby.

BRADFORD.—*Cartwright Hall* contains Italian Old Masters, British paintings, drawings and watercolours from the 18th century onwards. Modern prints. *Bolling Hall* is a furnished Period house and Local History Museum dating from the 15th century. *Industrial Museum,* Moorside Hills, illustrates local industries, particularly wool textiles. *Cliffe Castle,* Keighley. Natural history, local history and folk life. *Manor House,* Ilkley, is an Elizabethan Manor House with a collection of Roman material, and exposed wall of Roman Fort. Admission free. Daily, May to Aug., 10–8; April to Sept., 10–7; Oct. to March, 10–5. *Industrial Museum* 10–5 daily Closed Good Friday and Christmas Day.

BRIGHTON.—The Royal Pavilion, Palace of George IV. Chinoiserie interiors, much of the original furniture returned on loan from H.M. the Queen. Open daily 10–5 (10–8 during annual Regency Exhibition, July to September). Closed Christmas Day, Boxing Day and for three days before Regency Exhibition.

Art Gallery and Museum, Church Street (adjacent Royal Pavilion). Old master paintings; Willett pottery and porcelain collection, 20th-century decorative art and furniture, surrealist paintings; ethnography, archaeology. Open 10–6 winter, 10–7 summer (Sat. open 10–5; Sundays 2–5 winter, 2–6 summer). Closed Christmas, Boxing Day and Good Friday.

Preston Manor, Preston Park. (Thomas-Stanford: Macquoid bequests of English period furniture, furnishings, china and silver.) Closed Christmas Day, Boxing Day and Good Friday. Open weekdays 10–5, Sundays, 2–5. Admission 15p; Children 5p. Gardens open, free.

The Grange, Rottingdean. Art Gallery, Sussex Room, Kipling Room and collections of National Toy Museum. Open, free, 10–7 (winter, 10–6); Saturdays, 10–5; Sundays, 2–6 (winter, 2–5). Closed Christmas Day, Boxing Day and Good Friday.

BRISTOL.—*City Art Gallery.* Collection of Old Masters, 19th cent. and modern paintings, English watercolours, Chinese ceramics, glass, English silver, glass, porcelain and delftware, English and foreign embroideries. Open weekdays, 10–5.30. *Red Lodge,* Park Row. Furnished in style of 17th and very early 18th centuries. Open weekdays, 1–5. *Georgian House,* Great George Street. Furnished in Style of period. Open weekdays, 11–5.

CAMBRIDGE.—Fitzwilliam Museum. The Fine Art collections of the University, and one of the most important museums outside London. The chief collections, largely due to private benefaction, comprise Egyptian, Greek and Roman antiquities, coins and medals, mediæval manuscripts, paintings and drawings, prints, pottery and porcelain, textiles, arms and armour, mediæval and renaissance objects of art, and a library. Open, free, weekdays 10–5; Sundays, 2.15–5. Closed Christmas Day, Boxing Day, New Year's Day and Good Friday. Closed on Mondays, except Easter Monday and the Spring and Summer Bank Holidays

CANTERBURY.—Royal Museum. Collections include archæology, geology and natural history. Much Roman material from post-war excavations of Canterbury. Open free weekdays, 9.30–5.30. Westgate, Armour Museum. Buffs Regimental Museum (both in Stour Street, 2–4 only Oct.–March) Adm. 6p.

CARISBROOKE.—Castle Museum. Former home in Carisbrooke Castle of Governor of Isle of Wight. Collections cover archæology and history of Isle of Wight, and personal relics of Charles I, who was imprisoned in Castle from 1647 to 1648. Open, March–April and Oct. 9.30–5.30 (Sundays, 2–5.30); May–Sept. 9.30–7 (Sundays, 2–7); Nov.–Feb. 9.30–4. (Sundays, 2–4). Admission to Castle and Museum, 20p. (in winter, 10p).

COLCHESTER.—Colchester and Essex Museum, The Castle. The Norman Castle contains local archæological antiquities, expecially the extensive finds from Roman Colchester. The *Holly Trees Mansion* (1718) covers the antiquities of social life of the 18th and 19th centuries. *Natural History Museum,* All Saints Church. Natural history of Essex. *Museum of Social History,* Holy Trinity Church. Domestic life and crafts. Open, weekdays, 10–5 (branches closed 1–2 p.m.); Castle only, Sundays 2.30–5 (April–Sept.) Admission (April–Sept.) 10p Children free. (Oct.–March) free.

DERBY.—Museum and Art Gallery, Strand. Important collection of works by Joseph Wright of Derby, A.R.A., 1734–1797; Derby porcelain. Unique exhibit illustrating the history of the Midland Railway including a working model layout. Open, weekdays, 10–6 (Saturdays, 10–5).

Industrial Museum, Silk Mill, Full Street. Rolls Royce collection of aero engines etc., closed Sundays and Mondays

DORCHESTER.—County Museum. Geology, archæology, local history, natural history and rural crafts of Dorset. Collection of Thomas Hardy's manuscripts, books, notebooks, drawings, etc.

GUILDFORD.—Guildford Museum, Castle Arch. Local museum for archæology and history of Surrey based on collections of the Surrey Archæological Society. Open every day except Sunday, 11–5.

HULL.—*Ferens Art Gallery.* Collection of foreign paintings includes works by Hals, Canaletto and Guardi; British 18th and 19th century works, especially sea-pieces and pictures by the Humberside marine painters, also a representative collection of British paintings to the present day and a constant programme of visiting exhibitions. *Wilberforce House*. Jacobean merchant's house, birthplace of William Wilberforce; collection of slavery relics, period furniture, costume and ceramics. *Old Corn Exchange*. Veteran cars, trams, coaches and velocipedes; archæological finds from Humberside, including Roman mosaics. *Pickering Park Museum*. Maritime collections, relating to the history of trawling, mercantilism and inland waterways. Ferens Art Gallery open weekdays, 10-5.30; Sundays, 2.30-4.30. Museums open weekdays, 10-5; Sundays, 2.30-4.30.

HUNTINGDON.—*Cromwell Museum*. Housed in the only remaining portion of the 12th-century Hospital of St. John. Portraits of Cromwell, his family and Parliamentary notables (by Walker, Lely etc.); as well as reproductions and engravings covering the whole Puritan field. Unique collection of Cromwelliana—objects, documents, armour, coins and medals. Open free, Sundays 2-4; Tuesday to Friday, 11-1, 2-5, Saturday, 11-1, 2-4. Closed Mondays, Christmas Day and Good Friday.

IPSWICH.—*Ipswich Museum*. Refounded 1846. Present buildings 1880/1 with 1901 extension. Art Gallery attached. Collections of Suffolk geology, archaeology and natural history and general collections, including ethnology and industrial. Open weekdays 10-5, Sundays 2.30-4.30. Adm. free. Closed Good Friday, Dec. 24-25. *Christchurch* (Branch Museum) Tudor house, presented 1894. Furniture. Suffolk portraits and works by local artists (Gainsborough, Constable, Munnings, etc). Porcelain, pottery and glass. Modern prints (Picasso). Open weekdays 10-5 (dusk in winter). Sundays 2.30-4.30. Adm. free. Closed Good Friday, Dec. 24-25.

LEEDS.—*City Art Gallery*. Important collection of early English watercolours. British and European painting, modern sculpture, Chinese ceramics etc. Print Room and Art library contains study collection of drawings and prints. Open weekdays, 10.30-6.30, Sundays, 2.30-5. (Print Room and Art Library 9-9, Saturdays, 9-4, closed Sundays.) *Temple Newsam House*. Tudor/Jacobean house altered in mid-18th cent. to make suite of state rooms. Collection of English furniture mostly of 17th and 18th cents., silver, European porcelain and pottery, pictures, etc. Open daily, 10.30-6.15 or dusk; Weds. (May-Sept.), 10.30-8.30. Admission 15p; Children (with adults), 5p. O.A.P.s free. *Lotherton Hall*, Gascoigne art collection, park and gardens, opened 1969. Open daily, 10.30-6.15 (or dusk in winter); Thursdays (May-Sept.), 10.30-8.30. Admission to Hall, 15p; children (with adult) 5p.

LEICESTER.—*Museum and Art Gallery*, New Walk (1849). 18th, 19th and 20th century English paintings, drawings, German expressionists, 19th and 20th century French paintings. Egyptology. English ceramics and silver; reference study collections in biology and geology. *Newarke Houses*, The Newarke. Social history of Leicestershire from 1500 A.D.; musical instruments; local clocks, hosiery machinery. *Jewry Wall Museum*, St. Nicholas Circle. Archæology (prehistoric-1500). Roman Jewry Wall and Baths, mosaics *in situ*. *Belgrave Hall*, Church Road. A Queen Anne house with collection of furniture and garden of note. Coaches and agricultural collection. *Magazine Gateway*, Museum of Royal Leicestershire Regiment in a 14th century gatehouse. *Guildhall*, Guildhall Lane, 14th century timber-framed building. Used as town hall till 1876. *Railway Museum*, Stoneygate. Four locomotives and local railway material. Open Thurs.-Sun.,

2-5.30. *Museum of Technology*, Corporation Road. Horse-drawn vehicles, cycles, motor cycles and motor cars. Beam engines. *Wygston's House*, Museum of Costume, St. Nicholas Circle. Costume from 1789-1924.
All museums open weekdays 10-5.30; Sundays, 2-5.30 unless otherwise stated.

LEWES.—*Barbican House Museum*, near Castle (Sussex Archæological Trust). Prehistoric Roman Saxon and mediæval collections relating to Sussex; local pictures and prints. Open weekdays, 10-5.30, Sundays (April-Oct.), 2-5.30.
Anne of Cleves, House, Southover. Local history and folk museum. Open weekdays (Feb.-Nov.), 10.30-1; 2-5.30. Sundays (April-Oct.), 2-5.30. Admission, 15p; Children, 5p.

LINCOLN.—*Usher Gallery*. Collection of watches, miniatures, porcelain, silver, etc., Peter de Wint collection of oils and watercolours, Tennyson collection of manuscripts, etc. associated with Alfred, Lord Tennyson, collection of pictures relating to the city of Lincoln and small general collection of works of art. Open weekdays, 10-5.30; Sundays, 2.30-5. Admission free. *City and County Museum*. In the Greyfriars, a 13th-cent. Franciscan building. Collections include armour, local archæology with special emphasis on Romano-British collections from the city and county. Open weekdays, 10-5.30; Sundays, 2.30-5. Admission free.

LIVERPOOL.—*Walker Art Gallery*. One of the few Galleries outside London where a representative collection of European painting from the 14th century to the present day can be seen. Particularly strong in early Italian and Northern painting, Pre-Raphaelite and Academic 19th century paintings. Open, weekdays, 10-5; Sundays, 2-5. Closed on Good Friday, Christmas Eve, Christmas Day and Boxing Day. *Sudley Art Gallery* (Emma Holt Bequest), Mossley Hill Road. Collection of 18th and 19th-century paintings, mainly English, including Reynolds, Gainsborough and Romney, Wilkie, Mulready, Turner and Holman Hunt. Open as for Walker Art Gallery. *Merseyside County Museum*, William Brown Street. Founded 1851; buildings destroyed in 1941 and rebuilt 1966-69. The Museum was established on the important Mayer and Derby collections which have been supplemented to form an outstanding collection. These include the Mayer-Fejervary Gothic ivories, the Bryan Faussett group of Anglo-Saxon antiquities and the Lord Derby and Tristram ornithological collections. Gallery displays include material relating to Local History, Shipping, Egyptology, Ethnology, Decorative Art (including clocks and watches, pottery and musical instruments) and Transport. There is also an Aquarium and a Planetarium. Open weekdays, 10-5; Sunday, 2-5. Closed Good Friday, Christmas Day and Boxing Day. *Speke Hall*. A fine half-timbered Tudor house administered by the County Museums for the National Trust. Open weekdays and Bank Holidays 10-5, Sunday 2-7 (2-5 Sept.-April). Adults 25p, Children 10p.

MANCHESTER.—City Art Galleries. Comprising: *City Art Gallery*, Mosley Street, Manchester 2; *Annexe*, Princess Street, and five branches: *Heaton Hall; Platt Hall (Gallery of English Costume); Wythenshawe Hall; Queen's Park Art Gallery; Fletcher Moss Museum*. The City Art Gallery (architect, Sir Charles Barry) was built for the Royal Manchester Institution and opened in 1829; it was presented to the city in 1882. Principal collection of paintings is at the City Art Gallery; ceramics at Annexe; costume at Platt Hall; watercolours at Fletcher Moss Museum; furniture at

Heaton Hall and Wythenshawe Hall; Rutherston Loan Collection, Queen's Park Art Gallery. *Hours of opening*—City Art Gallery: weekdays 10–6, Sundays 2.30–5. Other galleries: weekdays 10–6 (May–Aug.);10–4 (Nov.–Feb.); 10–6 (other months). Sundays opening at 2 p.m. Admission free except to certain temporary exhibitions. Closed Good Friday and Christmas Day.

Whitworth Art Gallery, University of Manchester. —Founded 1889 in memory of Sir Joseph Whitworth (1803–1887). Important collection of English watercolours; Old Master prints and drawings; textiles, including notable examples of Coptic cloths; and contemporary works of art. Hours of opening: daily, 10–5 p.m., except Sundays; Thursdays to 9 p.m.

NEWCASTLE UPON TYNE.—*Laing Art Gallery and Museum*, Higham Place. British oil paintings and watercolours from 17th century to the present day; etchings and engravings; Japanese prints; sculpture; Egyptian, Greek and Roman antiquities; pottery and porcelain; glass; silver; wrought ironwork; Oriental arms and armour; costumes; textiles; and exhibits illustrative of the artistic industries of Tyneside. Open weekdays, 10–6; Tues. and Thurs., 10–8; Sundays 2.30–5.30. *Museum of Science and Engineering*, Exhibition Park, Great North Road. Open, Summer, weekdays, 10–6; Tues. and Thurs., 10–8; Sundays, 2.30–5.30; Winter, weekdays, 10–4.30; Sundays, 1.30–4.30. Admission 5p; Children, 2p. Educational parties free, by arrangement. *Plummer Tower Museum*, furnished in 18th century style. Open weekdays, 10–1, 2.30–6. *John G. Joicey Museum*, City Road. Local historical exhibits; furniture and armour. Open weekdays, 10–1; 2–6. Admission, 5p; Children, 2p.

NORWICH.—*Castle Museum*. Exhibits illustrating art, local archæology, social history and natural history. Open, weekdays 10–5; Sundays 2–5. *Strangers' Hall (Museum of Domestic Life*, Charing Cross). Late mediæval mansion furnished as a museum of urban domestic life, 16th–19th centuries, with displays of costume, transport, shop signs and toys. Open, weekdays, 10–5. *Bridewell Museum*, Bridewell Alley. Exhibits illustrating transport, crafts and industries of Norwich, Norfolk and North Suffolk. Open, weekdays, 10–5. *St. Peter Hungate Church Museum*, Princes Street. Fifteenth century church used for display of church art and antiquities. Open, weekdays, 10–5.

NOTTINGHAM.—*City Art Gallery and Museum*, housed in Nottingham Castle. English and Netherlands paintings and drawings 17th–20th centuries; special collections Bonington and Paul Sandby. English mediæval alabasters; English ceramics and silver; glass; metalwork; furniture; 17th and 18th-century carriages; costume, embroidery and lace, 16th–19th centuries; ethnography; local archæology; the regimental collection of the Sherwood Foresters. Open, Summer, 10–6.45; (Fri. 5.45; Sun., 4.45); Winter, 10 till dusk (Sun. 4.45). Admission free, 4p on Sun. and Bank Holidays.

Industrial Museum, Wollaton Hall. Industries, lace-making machinery, steam engines, transport. Open, Summer, Thurs. and Sat., 10–7; Sunday, 4.45; Winter, Thurs. and Sat., 10–dusk. Admission free.

Natural History Museum (1867) housed in Wollaton Hall. Formal gardens, deer park and lake. Open, Summer 10–7 (Sun. 2–5); Winter, 10 till dusk (Sun. the three hours before dusk). Admission free.

Newstead Abbey, 9 miles N. of Nottingham. Originally a Priory founded *c.* 1170, later property of Byron family, 1540–1817. Collections associated with poet Byron. Abbey open Good Friday to end of September. Monday to Saturday conducted tours at 2, 3, 4 and 5 p.m. On Sundays and Bank Holidays except Good Friday the Abbey is open from 2 to 6.30 p.m. Admission, 11p; children, 5p. Gardens open all year, daily 10 till dusk. Admission, 22p; children, 8p.

OAKHAM, Rutland County Museum, Catmose Street.—Archæology, local history, craft tools and agricultural implements. Open Tues.–Sat., 10–1, 2–5; Sunday 2–5. *Closed* October to March.

OXFORD, Ashmolean Museum.—Department of Western Art, Department of Antiquities, Heberden Coin Room, Department of Eastern Art, Cast Gallery. Open weekdays, 10–4, Sats. 10–5, Sundays 2–4 (Heberden Coin Room, weekdays, 10–12.30 and 2–4; Cast Gallery closed from 1 p.m. Saturdays and all day Sunday).

PLYMOUTH.—*City Museum and Art Gallery*, Drake Circus. Collection of ceramics, including Cookworthy's Plymouth and Bristol hard paste porcelain, collections of paintings, drawings and prints, archæological and natural history collection. Temporary exhibitions arranged. Open weekdays, 10–6 (Fridays, 10–8), Sundays 3–5. Admission free. *Elizabethan House*, 32 New Street. Restored Elizabethan house, furnished according to period. Open 10–1, 2.15–6 (till dusk in winter). Admission free. *See also* Buckland Abbey, p. 651.

PORT SUNLIGHT, Merseyside. *Lady Lever Art Gallery*. Paintings and watercolour drawings, mainly of British School, antique, renaissance and British sculpture, English furniture, mainly 18th cent., Chinese pottery and porcelain, and important collection of old Wedgwood. Open weekdays 10–5, Sundays 2–5.

SHEFFIELD.—*City Museum, Weston Park*. Founded in 1875, the present building was erected in 1937 and extended in 1965. Seven galleries are normally open to the public and the reference library and students' collections may be consulted on request. The exhibits cover a wide range of subjects, and include the Bateman Collection of antiquities from the Bronze Age barrows of the Peak District. The cutlery and Old Sheffield Plate collections are considered to be the finest of their kind in the world. Open, weekdays, Sept.–May, 10–5; June–Aug. 10–8.; Sundays 11–5 (Closed Christmas Eve, Christmas Day and Boxing Day). *Abbeydale Industrial Hamlet*, Abbeydale Road South. A late 18th and early 19th century scythe-works with associated housing. Open, weekdays, 10–5; Sundays, 11–5 (closes at 8 p.m. each day during summer). Closed Dec. 24–26. *Shepherd Wheel*, Whiteley Wood. cutler's water-driven grinding wheel and associated machinery. Open 10–12.30, 1.30–5 (opens at 11 on Sundays) *Closed* Mon. and Tues. *Bishop's House, Meersbrook Park*: museum of local history opened 1975. *Graves Art Gallery* (opened 1934) and *Mappin Art Gallery* (rebuilt 1965).

YORK.—*Castle Museum*. Folk museum of Yorkshire life of the past four centuries. Open weekdays, 9.30–6; Sats. and Bank Holidays 9.30–7.30; Sundays, 10–7.30; Closes 4.30, Oct.–Mar. Admission, 30p; children, 15p (special party rates).

Yorkshire Museum and Gardens, Museum Street. Archæology, decorative arts, geology and natural history. Open weekdays, 10–5; Sundays, 1–5. Admission, 11p; Children, 5p. Gardens, Roman, Anglian and mediæval ruins. Open weekdays, 8 till dusk; Sundays 10 till dusk. Admission free.

Art Gallery, Exhibition Square. European paintings, 14th–20th century; watercolours and prints of Yorkshire; modern English stoneware pottery. Open weekdays, 10–5; Sundays, 2.30–5. Admission free.

THE PRINCIPAL ENGLISH CITIES

BIRMINGHAM

BIRMINGHAM (West Midlands) is the second largest City in Britain and the chief centre of the hardware trade. In local government reorganization effective from April 1, 1974, Birmingham is merged with Sutton Coldfield as a Metropolitan District in the West Midlands Metropolitan County. It is estimated that over 1,500 distinct trades are carried on in the city, the chief industries being the manufacture of buttons, plastic goods, chocolate, chemicals, electroplate, guns, machine tools, glass, motor-cars and motor cycles, motor tyres, nuts and bolts, pens and nibs, tubes, paint and enamels, tools, toys, electrical apparatus, wire, jewellery and brass working, etc.

The first section of Birmingham's Queen Elizabeth Hospital, erected at Edgbaston at a cost of approximately £1,000,000, is claimed to be the finest of its type in Europe. A new maternity hospital adjoining was opened in 1969. The construction of an inner ring road round the centre was completed in 1971, hotel accommodation has been increased and there have been many improvements in the shopping centre including the redevelopment of the old market centre in the Bull Ring at a cost of £8,000,000. A new complex of buildings near the Town Hall includes a School of Music, Central Library, a shopping precinct and Corporation offices. A new television centre is in being and the City's new repertory theatre was opened in October, 1971. The National Exhibition Centre at Bickenhill is due to open early in 1976.

The principal buildings are the Town Hall, built in 1832–1834; the Council House and Corporation Museum and Art Gallery (1878); Victoria Law Courts (1891); the University (1909); the Central Library; the 13th century Church of St. Martin (rebuilt 1873); the Cathedral (formerly St. Philip's Church); the Roman Catholic Cathedral of St. Chad (Pugin) and the Methodist Central Hall. Birmingham was incorporated as a borough in 1838, and was created a city in 1889. The generally accepted derivation of " Birmingham " is the *ham* or dwelling-place of the *ing* or the family of *Beorma* presumed to have been a Saxon. Between the 11th and 16th centuries the de Berminghams were Lords of the Manor.

The Lord Mayor (1975–76), A. L. S. Jackson.
Stipendiary Magistrate, J. F. Milward (1951).
Chief Executive, F. J. C. Amos (1974).

BRADFORD

BRADFORD (West Yorkshire), the principal town in the Metropolitan District of Bradford, is 192 miles N.N.W. of London and 8 miles W. of Leeds. The metropolitan area is 91,444 acres with a population (1974 estimate) 461, 000.

Although the area has always been associated with wool and textiles, industrial activity now covers a much wider range, Together with Keighley and Shipley in the Aire valley it is well known for its engineering and electrical industries, high quality machine tools, mail order firms, iron and printing works and quarries.

The chief public buildings of Bradford in addition to the 15th century Cathedral (formerly the Parish Church) and Bolling Hall (14th century), are the City Hall (1873), the tower of which contains a clock with dials, chimes and a carillon, Cartwright Hall (1904) commemorating the inventor of the power loom, Grammar School (Charter 1662), St. George's Hall (Concert Hall, 1853), Technical College (1882), Wool Exchange (1867), Britannia House (1933) and Bradford University. A new

Central Library, planned on the " subject department " principle was opened in 1967 and the new Magistrates' Courts were opened in 1972. The Civic Precinct was opened in 1974.

The Saxon township of Bradford was created a parliamentary borough in 1832, a borough in 1847, a county borough in 1889, and a city in 1897. The office of Lord Mayor was created in 1907. The Council consists of a Lord Mayor and 92 Councillors.

The Lord Mayor (1975–76), Mrs. D. Birdsall.
Chief Executive, G. C. Moore.

BRISTOL

BRISTOL, situated in the new county of Avon, is the largest non-metropolitan district in population in the country, and is 119 miles W. of London. The present municipal area is 27,068 acres, with a population (1973 estimate) of 421,800.

Among the various industries are aircraft and aero-engine construction, general and nuclear engineering, boot and shoe manufacture, chocolate and cocoa, tobacco, paper bags, cardboard and allied products, printing, chemical industry and shipbuilding and repairing. The principal imports are grain, flour and other cereal products, cocoa, tea, coffee, molasses, feeding stuffs, fruit, provisions, frozen meat, metals, ores, phosphates, paper, petroleum and chemicals, fertilizers, timber, tobacco, wood pulp and other goods, and the chief exports are metals and machinery, chemicals, unmanufactured clay, motor vehicles and parts, carbon black, electrical apparatus, tea, wines and spirits and manufactured goods.

The chief buildings, in addition to the 12th century Cathedral (with later additions), with Norman Chapter House and gateway, the 14th century Church of St. Mary, Redcliffe (described by Queen Elizabeth I as " the fairest, goodliest, and most famous parish church in England "), and Wesley's Chapel, Broadmead, are the Merchant Venturers' Almshouses, the Council House (opened by H.M. the Queen in April, 1956), Guildhall, Exchange (erected from the designs of John Wood in 1743), City Museum and Art Gallery, Central Library, Cabot Tower, the University and Clifton College, Red Lodge (Tudor), Georgian House, and Blaise Castle and Mansion with Folk Museum. The *Clifton Suspension Bridge*, with a span of 702 feet over the Avon, was projected by Brunel in 1836 but was not completed until 1864. The new Roman Catholic Cathedral at Clifton was opened in 1973.

Bristol was a Royal Borough before the Norman Conquest. In 1373 it received from Edward III a charter granting it county statutes and in 1899 its Mayor became a Lord Mayor. The Corporation includes 84 Councillors. The earliest forms of the name are *Brigstowe* and *Bristow*.

The Lord Mayor (1975–76), H. J. Williams.
Chief Executive, P. M. McCarthy.

CAMBRIDGE

CAMBRIDGE, a settlement far older than its ancient University, lies on the Cam or Granta, 51 miles north of London and 65 miles south-west of Norwich. It has an area of 10,060 acres and a population (est., 1974) of 104,000.

The city is a parliamentary borough, county town and regional headquarters. Its industries, which include radio and electronics, flour milling, cement making and the manufacture of scientific instruments are extensive but nowhere obtrusive. Among its open spaces are Jesus

Green, Sheep's Green, Coe Fen, Parker's Piece, Christ's Pieces, the University Botanic Garden, and the Backs, or lawns and gardens through which the Cam winds behind the principal line of college buildings. East of the Cam, King's Parade, upon which stand Great St. Mary's Church, Gibbs' Senate House and King's College Chapel with Wilkins' screen, joins Trumpington Street to form one of the most beautiful thoroughfares in Europe.

University and College buildings provide the outstanding features of Cambridge architecture but several churches (especially St. Benet's, the oldest building in the City, and St. Sepulchre's the Round Church) also make notable contributions. The modern Guildhall (1939) stands on a site of which at least part has held municipal buildings since 1224.

The City Council has 42 members. The District was granted Borough status and reaccorded the style of City from April 1974.

Mayor (1975–76), R. May.
Chief Executive. G. G. Datson.

CANTERBURY

CANTERBURY, the Metropolitan City of the Anglican Communion, has an unbroken history going back to prehistoric times. It was the Roman Durovernum and the Saxon Cant-wara-byrig (stronghold of the men of Kent). Here in 597 St. Augustine began the re-conversion of the English to Christianity, when Ethelbert, King of Kent, was baptized. In 1170 the rivalry of Church and State culminated in the murder in Canterbury Cathedral, by Henry II.'s knights, of Archbishop Thomas Becket, whose shrine became a great centre of pilgrimage as described by Chaucer in his *Canterbury Tales*. After the Reformation pilgrimages ceased, but the prosperity of the City was strengthened by an influx of Huguenot refugees, who introduced weaving. In the first Elizabethan era Christopher Marlowe, the poetic genius and precursor of Shakespeare, was born and reared in Canterbury, and there are literary associations also with Defoe, Dickens and Barham, author of the *Ingoldsby Legends*, and Somerset Maugham.

The Cathedral, with its glorious architecture ranging from the eleventh to the fifteenth centuries, is world-famous. Modern pilgrims are attracted particularly to the Martyrdom, the Black Prince's Tomb and other historic monuments, the Warriors' Chapel and the many examples of mediæval stained glass.

Of the Benedictine St. Augustine's Abbey, burial place of the Jutish Kings of Kent (whose capital Canterbury was) only extensive ruins remain. St. Martin's Church, on the eastern outskirts of the City, is stated by Bede to have been the place of worship of Queen Bertha, the Christian wife of King Ethelbert, before the advent of St. Augustine.

The mediæval City Walls are built on Roman foundations and the fourteenth century West Gate is one of the finest buildings of its kind in the country.

The University of Kent at Canterbury admitted its first students in 1965.

The city has an area of 120 square miles, and a population of 115,000. Before the institution of the Mayoralty in 1448 it was governed by bailiffs and earlier still by prefects or provosts.

Mayor (1975–76), H. J. Alexander.
Sheriff (1975–76), Mrs M. E. Brown.
Chief Executive, C. C. Gay.

COVENTRY

COVENTRY (West Midlands) is a city 92 miles N.W. of London, and an important industrial centre. It has a population (estimated, 1973) of 336,000.

Coventry owes its beginning to Leofric, Earl of Mercia and his wife Godiva in 1043, when they founded a Benedictine Monastery. The beautiful guildhall of St. Mary dates from the 14th century, three of its churches date from the 14th and 15th centuries. Sixteenth century almshouses may still be seen. Coventry's first cathedral was destroyed at the Reformation, its second in the 1940 blitz (its walls remain) and the great new cathedral designed by Sir Basil Spence, consecrated in 1962, now draws innumerable visitors.

Post-war public buildings include the Art Gallery and Museum, Lanchester Polytechnic, the Civic Theatre and new swimming baths. The city centre has been redeveloped.

Coventry returns four M.P.'s. It is governed by a Lord Mayor and a Council of 54. Coventry produces cars, agricultural machinery, machine tools (the world's largest machine tool organization); the telecommunication industry has become the largest employer of industrial labour.

Lord Mayor (1975–76), C. Ward.
Chief Executive, T. Gregory, O.B.E.

KINGSTON UPON HULL

HULL (officially " Kingston upon Hull ") is situated, from April, 1974 in the County of Humberside, at the junction of the River Hull with the Humber, 22 miles from the North Sea and 205 miles N. of London. The municipal area is 17,593 acres, with a population (1971 Census), of 285,970.

Hull is one of the great seaports of the United Kingdom. It has docks covering a water area of over 200 acres, well equipped for the rapid handling of cargoes of every kind, and its many industries include oil-extracting, saw-milling, flour-milling, engineering and chemical industries. New industries, such as electricals, and clothing and textiles are being developed. It also claims to be the premier distant-water fishing port and is an important centre for allied processing activities.

The City, restored after very heavy air raid damage during World War II, is well laid out with fine throughfares. It has good office and administrative buildings, its municipal centre being the Guildhall, its educational centre the University of Hull and its religious centre the Parish Church of the Holy Trinity.

Kingston upon Hull was so named by Edward I. City status was accorded in 1897 and the office of Mayor raised to the dignity of Lord Mayor in 1914. The Lord Mayor presides over a Council of 63 Councillors, representing the 21 wards of the City.

The Lord Mayor (1975–76), Mrs C. E. Ellis.
Stipendiary Magistrate, I. R. Boyd (1973).
Chief Executive, A. B. Wood.

LEEDS

LEEDS (West Yorkshire), a Metropolitan District from April 1, 1974, is a junction for road, rail and canal services and an important commercial centre, situated in the lower Aire Valley, 195 miles by road N.N.W. of London.

Leeds has a wide variety of manufacturing industries, notably cloth and ready-made clothing, heavy and light engineering, leather and chemical products.

The municipal area is 134,916 acres, the population is 748,300.

The principal buildings are the Civic Hall (1933), the Town Hall (1858), the Municipal Buildings and Art Gallery (1884), the Corn Exchange (1863) and the University. The Parish Church (St. Peter's) was rebuilt in 1841; the 17th century St. John's Church has a fine interior with a famous English renaissance screen; the last remaining 18th century church is Holy Trinity, Boar Lane (1727). Kirkstall Abbey (about 3 miles from the centre of the city), founded by Henry de Lacy in 1152, is one of the most complete examples of Cistercian houses now remaining. Temple Newsam, birthplace of Lord Darnley, was acquired by the Corporation in 1922. The present house, a stately building in red brick, was largely re-built by Sir Arthur Ingram in about 1620. Adel Church, about 5 miles from the centre of the city, is a fine Norman structure.

Leeds was first incorporated by Charles I in 1626, made a county borough in 1889, and created a city in 1893. The Lord Mayor presides over 96 Councillors. The earliest forms of the name are *Loidis* or *Ledes*, the origins of which are obscure.

The Lord Mayor (1975–76), A. S. Pedley, D.F.C.
Stipendiary Magistrate, F. D. L. Loy (1972).
Chief Executive, K. H. Potts.

LEICESTER

LEICESTER is situated geographically in the centre of England, 100 miles north of London. The City dates back to pre-Roman times and was one of the five Danish *Burhs*. In 1589 Queen Elizabeth I granted a Charter to the City and the ancient title was confirmed by Letters Patent in 1919. The title of Lord Mayor was conferred upon the Chief Magistrate in 1928. Under local government reorganization Leicester's area remained unchanged at 18,141 acres, and with a population of 287,300 (1975 est.) it is the third largest non-metropolitan district in England and Wales in population. It retains its designation as a City Council.

The principal industries of the city are hosiery, boots and shoes, and light engineering. The growth of Leicester as a hosiery centre increased rapidly from the introduction there of the first stocking frame in 1670; in 1833 there were 14,000 knitting frames in the city, which to-day has some of the largest hosiery factories in the world. Hosiery and knitwear produced includes socks, stockings, dresses, underwear, pullovers, scarves and gloves, much of which is exported. Leicester is also a centre for the ancillary industries.

Engineering, developed partly for the supply of machinery to the hosiery and boot and shoe industries, has become one of the foremost industries in the city. Printing and the manufacture of electronic and plastic goods are also carried on.

The principal buildings in the city are the Town Hall; the University; Leicester Polytechnic; De Montfort Hall, one of the finest concert halls in the provinces, with accommodation for over 3,000 persons, and the Museum and Art Gallery. The ancient Churches of St. Martin (now Leicester Cathedral) St. Nicholas, St. Margaret, All Saints, St. Mary de Castro, and buildings such as the Guildhall, the 14th century Newarke Gate, the Castle and the Jewry Wall Roman site still exist. Leicester has a large number of parks and open spaces. The Sports Centre, which contains an athletics arena and cycle track, was the site of the 1970 World Cycling Championships. The Haymarket Theatre, an integral part of a large new shopping and car-parking complex, was opened in 1973.

The Lord Mayor (1975–76), Mrs. L. R. Marriott.
Chief Executive, J.S. Phipps.

LIVERPOOL

LIVERPOOL (Merseyside) a Metropolitan District, on the right bank of the river Mersey, 3 miles from the Irish Sea and 194 miles N.W. of London, is one of the greatest trading centres of the world and the principal port in the United Kingdom for the Atlantic trade. The municipal area is 27,819 acres (which includes 2,840 acres in the bed of the river Mersey) (about 43 square miles, excluding the bed of the river), with a population of 574,560 (est. June 1973). Quays on both sides of the river are about 38 miles long, and the Gladstone Dock can accommodate the largest vessels afloat. Net tonnage of ships entering and leaving the port annually exceeds 45,000,000 tons. The main imports are petroleum, grain, ores, non-ferrous metals, sugar, wood, oil, fruit and cotton. The new Seaforth Container Terminal was opened in 1972, covering 500 acres and costing £50 m.

The Metropolitan District Council owns large industrial estates at Speke, Kirkby and Aintree, on which many modern factories have been built. These three estates have provided work for some 65,000 people. In 1943 a lease for 99 years was taken of the Elizabethan mansion at *Speke Hall* at a nominal rent.

The principal buildings are the Anglican Cathedral, erected from the designs of Sir Giles Gilbert Scott and consecrated in 1924; when completed this will be the largest ecclesiastical building in England; the Metropolitan Cathedral of Christ the King, designed by Sir Frederick Gibberd and consecrated in 1967; St. George's Hall, erected 1838–1854, and regarded as one of the finest modern examples of classical architecture; the Town Hall, erected 1754 from the designs of Wood; the Walker Art Gallery; Victoria Building of Liverpool University; The Royal Liver, Cunard and Mersey Docks building at Pier Head; the Municipal Offices; and the Philharmonic Hall.

Constructed between 1925 and 1934, the *Mersey Tunnel* connecting Liverpool and Birkenhead was opened to traffic on July 18, 1934, the total cost being estimated at £6,077,800. More than 17,000,000 vehicles pass through the Mersey Tunnel annually. A second tunnel between Liverpool and Wallasey was opened by the Queen on June 24, 1971, and work on a similar tunnel running adjacent to it is nearly complete.

Liverpool was incorporated as a borough early in the 13th century and was created a city in 1880. The Metropolitan District Council consists of a Lord Mayor and 98 Councillors.

The Lord Mayor (1975–76), O. I. Doyle.
Stipendiary Magistrate, Leslie Mervyn Pugh (1965).
Chief Executive, A. J. Stocks.

MANCHESTER

MANCHESTER (Greater Manchester) (the *Mancunium* of the Romans, who occupied it in A.D. 78) is 189 miles N.W. of London. The municipal area is 28,720 acres (about 43 square miles) and the population (estimated 1973), 530,580.

Manchester is a commercial rather than an industrial centre, the industries being largely in the neighbouring towns. Within 25 mile radius, lives a population of 4,500,000 engaged in engineering, chemical, clothing, food processing and textile industries and providing the packing, transport, banking, insurance and other distributive facilities for those industries. The city is connected with the sea by the Manchester Ship Canal, opened in 1894, 35½ miles long, and accommodating ships up to 15,000 tons. Manchester Airport handles approximately 2,318,000 passengers yearly.

The principal buildings are the Town Hall, erected in 1877 from the designs of Alfred Waterhouse, R.A., together with a large extension of 1938; the Royal Exchange, built in 1869 and enlarged in 1921: the Central Library (1934); the Art Gallery; Heaton Hall; the Gallery of English Costume; the

17th century Chetham Library; the Rylands Library (1899), which includes the Althorp collection; the University (Owens College); the University Institute of Science and Technology; the 15th-century Cathedral (formerly the parish church) and the Free Trade Hall. Manchester is one of the principal centres of political, literary and scientific advancement, and the Hallé Concerts have placed the city in the forefront of musical development. as has the Royal Northern College of Music.

The town received its first charter of incorporation in 1838 and was created a city in 1853. The new charter and title of city, under local government reorganization, was presented in May, 1974. The City Council consists of 99 Councillors.

The Lord Mayor (1975–76) Dame Kathleen Ollerenshaw, D.B.E.
Stipendiary Magistrate, J. Bamber (1965).
Chief Executive, R. Calderwood.

NEWCASTLE UPON TYNE

NEWCASTLE UPON TYNE (Tyne and Wear) a Metropolitan District on the north bank of the River Tyne, 8 miles from the North Sea and 272 miles N. of London, has an area of 11,401 acres and a population of 299,800. A Cathedral and University City, it is the administrative commercial and cultural centre for north-east England and the principal port. It is an important manufacturing centre with a wide variety of industries.

The principal buildings include the Castle Keep (12th century), Black Gate (13th century), West Walls (13th century), St. Nicholas's Cathedral (15th century, fine lantern tower), St. Andrew's Church (12th–14th century), St. John's (14th–15th century), All Saints (1786 by Stephenson), St. Mary's Roman Catholic Cathedral (1844). Trinity House (17th century), Sandhill (16th century houses), Guildhall (Georgian), Grey Street (1834–39), Central Station (1846–50). Laing Art Gallery (1904), University of Newcastle Physics Building (1962), Civic Centre (1963) and Central Library (1969). Open spaces include the Town Moor (927 acres) and Jesmond Dene. Seven bridges span the Tyne at Newcastle.

The City derives its name from the " new castle " (1080) erected as a defence against the Scots. In 1400 it was made a County, and in 1882 a City. The City Corporation comprises a Lord Mayor (1906) and 78 Councillors.
Lord Mayor (1975–76), Miss I. Steedman.
Chief Executive, K. Galley.

NORWICH

NORWICH (Norfolk) is an ancient City 110 miles N.E. of London. It grew from an early Anglo-Saxon settlement near the confluence of the Rivers Yare and Wensum, and now serves as provincial capital for the predominantly agricultural region of East Anglia. The name is thought to relate to the most northerly of a group of Anglo-Saxon villages or " wics ". The present City comprises an area of 9,655 acres, with a population (1971 Census, preliminary) of 121,688.

Norwich serves its surrounding area as a market town and commercial centre, banking and insurance being prominent among the City's businesses. Continuously from the fourteenth century, however (when Flemish immigrants helped to establish Norwich as the centre of the woollen industry until the Industrial Revolution) it has combined industry with commerce, and manufactures of a wide variety are now produced in the City. The biggest single industry is the manufacture of shoes and other principal trades are engineering, printing, and the production of chemicals, clothing, confectionery and other foodstuffs. Norwich is accessible to seagoing vessels by means of the River Yare, entered at Great Yarmouth, 20 miles to the east.

Among many historic buildings are the Cathedral (completed in the twelfth century and surmounted by a fifteenth century spire 315 feet in height), the Keep of the Norman Castle (now serving as a museum and also housing the Colman Collection of works by the Norwich School of painters), the fifteenth century flint-walled Guildhall, some thirty mediæval parish churches, St. Andrew's and Blackfriars' Halls, the Tudor houses preserved in Elm Hill and the Georgian Assembly House. The administrative centre of the City is the City Hall, built in 1938. A new central library, opened in 1963, is adjacent to the City Hall. The University of East Anglia has been established in Norwich and received its first students in 1963. The buildings of the University occupy a spacious site at Earlham on the City's western boundary.

The City's first known Charter was granted in 1158 by Henry II and its privileges and form of self government were prescribed successively by later Charters until the enactment of the Municipal Corporations Act, 1835. The City Council consists of 48 Councillors.
The Lord Mayor (1975–76), W. A. J. Spear, T.D.
Chief Executive, G. G. Tilsley.

NOTTINGHAM

NOTTINGHAM (Nottinghamshire) stands on the River Trent, 124 miles N.N.W. of London in one of the most valuable coalfields of the country with excellent railway, water (being connected by canal with the Atlantic and the North Sea), and road facilities. The municipal area is 18,364 acres and population (estimated, 1974) of 287,000.

The principal industries are hosiery, lace, bleaching, dyeing and spinning, tanning, engineering and cycle works, brewing, the manufacture of tobacco, chemicals, furniture, typewriters and mechanical products.

The chief buildings are the 17th century Nottingham Castle (restored in 1878, and now the City Museum and Gallery of Art), Wollaton Hall (1580–88) owned by the City Council and now a Natural History Museum, St. Mary's, St. Peter's, and St. Nicholas's Churches, the Roman Catholic Cathedral (Pugin, 1842–4), the Council House (1929), the Guildhall and Court House (1888), Shire Hall, Albert Hall, the University, Trent Polytechnic and Newstead Abbey, home of Lord Byron.

Snotingaham or *Notingeham*, " the village or home of the sons of Snot " (the Wise), is the Anglo-Saxon name for the Celtic *Tuigogobauc*, " Cave Homes". The City possesses a Charter of Henry II, and was created a City in 1897. Under local government reorganization, the style of city was reaccorded from April, 1974. The City Council consists of 54 Councillors (including the Lord Mayor).
The Lord Mayor (1975–76), Mrs I. F. Matthews.
Chief Executive, M. H. F. Hammond.

OXFORD

OXFORD is a University City, an important industrial centre, and market town. A City from time immemorial, it has an area of 8,785 acres and a population of 115,100. Oxford is a parliamentary constituency returning one member and is governed by a Council of 45 members. Industry played a minor part in Oxford until the motor industry was established in 1912.

It is is for its architecture that Oxford is of most interest to the visitor, its oldest specimens being the reputed Saxon tower of St. Michael's church, the remains of the Norman castle and city walls and the Norman church at Iffley. It is chiefly famous

however, for its Gothic buildings, such as the
Divinity Schools, the Old Library at Merton
College, William of Wykeham's New College,
Magdalen College and Christ Church and many
other college buildings. Later centuries are not
represented by so many examples, but mention
can be made of the exquisite Laudian quadrangle
at St. John's College, the Renaissance Sheldonian
Theatre by Wren, Trinity College Chapel, and
All Saints Church; Hawksmoor's mock-Gothic
at All Souls College, and the superb example of
eighteenth century architecture afforded by Queen's
College. In addition to individual buildings,
High Street and Radcliffe Square, just off it,
both form architectural compositions of great
beauty. Most of the Colleges have gardens, those
of Magdalen, New College, St. John's (designed
by " Capability " Brown) and Worcester being
the largest.

The visitor will always find some of the college
chapels, halls and gardens open for public inspection
between 10 a.m. and 5 p.m.
Lord Mayor (1975–76), W. G. R. Fagg.
Chief Executive, E. J. Patrick.

PLYMOUTH

PLYMOUTH is situated on the borders of Devon
and Cornwall at the confluence of the Rivers
Tamar and Plym, 210 miles from London, with an
area of 19,936 acres and a population (Reg. Gen.
Estimate) of 251,200.

Following extensive war damage, the city centre
comprising a large shopping centre, municipal
offices, law courts and public buildings, has been
re-built. The main employment is provided by
H.M. Dockyard. Many new industrial firms have
become established in the post-war period. In
conjunction with the Cornwall County Council,
the Tamar Bridge was constructed linking the City
by road with Cornwall.

The Lord Mayor presides over a Council of 66
Councillors.
The Lord Mayor (1975–76), W. I. Thompson.
Chief Executive, A. F. Watson.

PORTSMOUTH

PORTSMOUTH, a city, and local government
district, with an area of 14½ sq. miles, occupies
Portsea Island, Hampshire, with boundaries extending to the mainland. Portsmouth is 70 miles by
road from London (90 minutes by electric train).
It has a population (estimated, 1975) of 195,130.

Industries include H.M. Naval Base, the principal
centre of employment with a labour force of 14,000,
which occupies the south-western part of the Island.
The holiday and tourist industry, centred on
the coast at the resort area of Southsea, caters
annually for 200,000 visitors and 1,000,000 day
trippers. Other industries are shipbuilding and
maintenance, electronics, aircraft engineering and
the manufacture of corsets, cardboard boxes, confectionery, baby products, refrigerators and brushes.
The commercial port (the Camber, Flathouse and
Mile End is owned and run by the City Council.

Among many tourist attractions are Lord Nel-
son's flagship, H.M.S. *Victory*; Charles Dickens'
birthplace at 393 Commercial Road, now a
Dickens museum; Southsea Castle, now a museum
of military history, and the Round Tower and
Point Battery, which for hundreds of years have
guarded the entrance to Portsmouth Harbour.
Southsea is particularly noted for its panoramic
views of the busy shipping lanes of the Solent and
Spithead.
Lord Mayor (1975–76), E. H. Taplin.
Chief Executive, J. R. Haslegrave, C.B.E., T.D.

SHEFFIELD

SHEFFIELD (South Yorkshire), the centre of the
special steel and cutlery trades, is situated 159 miles
N.N.W. of London, at the junction of the Sheaf,
Porter, Rivelin and Loxley with the River Don.
The City is set in a beautiful countryside, its resi-
dential suburbs penetrating the Peak District of
Derbyshire.

Sheffield has an area of 91,000 acres (nearly 150
square miles), including 4,065 acres of publicly
owned parks and woodland, and a population (est.
1973) of 561,500. Though its cutlery, silverware
and plate have long been famous, Sheffield has other
and now more important industries—special and
alloy steels, engineering and tools in great variety.
Refractory materials, silver refining, brush making,
the manufacture of confectionery, canning, type-
founding, pharmaceutical products, paper and the
making of snuff are other contrasting industries in
Sheffield. Research in glass, metallurgy, radiotherapy and other fields is carried on.

The parish church of St. Peter and St. Paul,
founded in the twelfth century, became the
Cathedral Church of the Diocese of Sheffield in
1914. Parts of the present building date from
about 1435. The principal buildings are the
Town Hall (1897 and 1923), the Cutlers' Hall
(1832), the University (1905 and recent extensions,
including 19-storey Arts Tower), City Hall (1932),
Central Library and Graves Art Gallery (1934),
City Museum (1937), Castle Market Building
(1959), the new retail market (1973), the rebuilt
Mappin Art Gallery and the Crucible Theatre.

Sheffield was created a borough on Aug. 24,
1843, a county borough in 1888 and a city in 1893,
the Mayor becoming a Lord Mayor in 1897. On
April 1, 1974 Sheffield became a Metropolitan District Council incorporating Stocksbridge and most
of the Wortley Rural area, and retained city status.
The Lord Mayor (1975–76), A. E. Richardson.
Master Cutler (1974–75) 351st *Master of the Company
of Cutlers in Hallamshire*, G. Murray, M.B.E.
Chief Executive, I. L. Podmore.

SOUTHAMPTON

SOUTHAMPTON is Britain's premier passenger port.
As the majority of ocean travellers to this country
arrive at Southampton the City is recognized as
" The Gateway to Britain ". The first Charter was
granted by Henry II and Southampton was created
a county of itself in 1447. In February, 1964, Her
Majesty the Queen granted city status by Royal
Charter. The city has an area of 12,071 acres
excluding tidal waters and a population of 213,000.
The University of Southampton (1952) had 5,010
students in 1974–75.

The Civic Centre, completed in 1939, comprises
four blocks, municipal offices and law courts,
guildhall, library and art galleries. The tower,
which is a notable land-mark for shipping using
Southampton Water and which can be seen for
many miles from vantage points in the surrounding
countryside, incorporates a clock and bells. Public
open spaces total over 1,000 acres in extent and
comprise 9 per cent. of the city's area. The Sports
Centre is 267 acres in extent. The Common
covers an area of 328 acres in the central district of
the city and is mostly natural parkland.

The City Council consists of 51 councillors.
Mayor (1975–76), Mrs. E. I. Pugh.
Chief Executive, D. Scouller.

STOKE-ON-TRENT

STOKE-ON-TRENT (Staffordshire), familiarly
known as The Potteries, stands on the River Trent
157 miles N. of London. The present municipal

area is 22,916 acres (36 square miles), with a population (estimated, 1974) of 258,300. The City is the main centre of employment for the half-million population of North Staffordshire. It is the largest clayware producer in the world (chinaware, earthenware, sanitary goods, refractories, bricks and tiles) and has a large coal mining output drawn from one of the richest coalfields in Western Europe, with proved reserves exceeding one thousand million tons. The City has iron works, steelworks, foundries, chemical works, engineering plants, rubber works, paper mills, and a very wide range of manufactures including textiles, furniture, electrical goods, vehicle components, toys, machinery, plastic materials, metal stampings, glass and glazes.

Extensive reconstruction has been carried on since 1930. A unique feature of the city is that it has six " centres " and more shops and public halls than other areas of comparable size. The City was formed by the federation in 1910 of the separate municipal authorities of Tunstall, Burslem, Hanley, Stoke-upon-Trent, Fenton, and Longton, all of which are now combined in the present City of Stoke-on-Trent. Each of the six areas still has its own public buildings and amenities, but all civic administration is controlled by the City Council.

The City has 72 Councillors and elects 3 Members of Parliament.

The Lord Mayor (1975–76), D. Shotton.
Town Clerk, S. W. Titchener.

STRATFORD UPON AVON

STRATFORD UPON AVON (in Warwickshire, on the banks of the River Avon) had a population of 19,452 at the Census of 1971. As the birthplace of Shakespeare the borough is visited annually by travellers from all parts.

Shakespeare's Birthplace. Half timbered house preserved by Shakespeare Birthplace Trust. Contains period furniture and a collection of rare books, mss. and objects of Shakespearian interest. Garden contains the new Shakespeare centre. *King Edward VI School.* Founded by the mediæval Guild of the Holy Cross of Stratford, and re-endowed by King Edward VI. Here Shakespeare acquired his " small Latin and less Greek." *Anne Hathaway's Cottage.* At Shottery, one mile from the centre of the town, is the thatched farmstead, the early home of Shakespeare's wife, Anne Hathaway. A fine specimen of domestic architecture. *Shakespeare Memorial.* Mainly due to munificence of C. E. Flower (1830–92) and his wife. Group comprises *Library*, with 10,000 volumes of Shakespeare editions and dramatic literature. *Gallery* of pictures. *Gardens. Royal Shakespeare Theatre* burnt down in 1926, rebuilt 1932, with 1,300 seats, chiefly by American generosity. The Shakespeare Festival takes place from spring to autumn each year at this theatre.

Chief Executive, T. J. W. Foy.

WINCHESTER

WINCHESTER, the ancient capital of England, is situated on the River Itchen 65 miles S.W. of London and 12 miles north of Southampton. The City has an area of 3,890 acres and a population (1971 Census, preliminary) of 31,041.

Occupation of the city area can be traced back to 1800 B.C. but organized settlements appeared later. Saxon history is somewhat obscure but Winchester became the capital of Wessex and in the 9th century capital of all England. Alfred the Great made Winchester a centre of education. William the Conqueror marched straight from his victory at Hastings to Winchester where he established a new Palace, his Treasury and his capital.

Here he compiled Domesday Book as the returns came in from the shires. Winchester remained the capital for many years, but its decline as a capital began with the civil war between Stephen and Matilda; and by 1338 it had lost its favourable position.

Winchester is rich in architecture of all types but the Cathedral takes first place. The longest Gothic cathedral in the world, it was built in 1079–1093 and exhibits splendid examples of Norman, Early English and Perpendicular styles. Winchester College, founded in 1382, is one of the most famous public schools, the original building (of 1393) remaining almost unaltered. St. Cross Hospital, the third great mediæval foundation in Winchester, lies 1 mile south of the City. Founded in 1136 by Bishop Henry de Blois, the Almshouses were re-established in 1445 by Cardinal Henry Beaufort. The Chapel and dwellings are of great architectural interest, and visitors may still receive the " Wayfarer's Dole " of bread and ale.

It is not certain when Winchester was first designated a city but it is probable that the term was applied between 650 and 700. Winchester was one of the oldest corporations in the country; the first written record of a Mayor occurs in 1200.

Recent excavations in the Cathedral Close have revealed the sites of two earlier minsters, including the original burial place of St. Swithin, before his remains were translated to a site in the present Cathedral. Excavations in other parts of the city have thrown light on Norman Winchester, notably on the site of the Castle, where new Law Courts are being built.

Mayor (1975–76), A. Cotterill.
Chief Executive, E. M. E. White.

YORK

The City of YORK is a District in the County of North Yorkshire, and is an archiepiscopal seat. The City has an area of 7,295 acres and a population of 103,800. It returns one member to Parliament and is governed by 39 Councillors.

The recorded history of York dates from A.D. 71, when the Roman Ninth Legion established a base under Petilius Cerealis which later became the fortress of Eboracum. By the 14th century the city had become prosperous and was used as the chief base against the Scots. It became a great mercantile centre, chiefly owing to its control of the wool trade, but under the Tudors its fortunes declined, though Henry VIII made it the headquarters of the Council of the North.

With its development as a railway centre in the 19th century the commercial life of York expanded and it is now a flourishing modern city. The principal industries are the manufacture of chocolate, railway coaches, scientific instruments, glass containers and sugar. The City is also an important tourist centre.

It is rich in examples of architecture of all periods. The earliest church (*built*, 627) was succeeded by several others until, in the 12th to the 15th centuries, the present Minster was built in a succession of styles. The finest features are the West front with its two towers, the spacious transepts and the stained glass. Other examples within the city are the mediaeval city walls and gateways, churches and guildhalls. Domestic architecture includes the Georgian mansions of The Mount, Micklegate and Bootham. Its museums are world-famous and include the Castle Museum which is one of the best-known folk museums in Great Britain.

Rt. Hon. Lord Mayor (1975–76), J. P. Birch.
Sheriff (1975–76), G. H. Dean.
Chief Executive, R. Howell.

MUNICIPAL DIRECTORY OF ENGLAND

A list of METROPOLITAN BOROUGH AND CITY COUNCILS. Those accorded CITY status are in SMALL CAPITALS.

Metropolitan Boroughs	Population (Reg. G's Estimate)	Rateable Value 1975 £	Average Rate Levied p.	Chief Executive	Mayor †Lord Mayor 1975–76
GREATER MANCHESTER					
Bolton	261,800	25,754,215	69·6	B. Scholes	J. C. Hanscomb
Bury	181,290	18,009,000	50·5	J. A. McDonald	R. Fletcher
MANCHESTER	530,580	70,424,791	66·6	R. Calderwood	† Dame Kathleen Ollerenshaw, D.B.E.
Oldham	224,700	21,070,297	78	T. M. C. Francis	J. Armitage
Rochdale	210,600	19,168,320	83·1	J. Towey	J. Carroll
SALFORD	273,600	29,921,974	74	R. C. Rees	Mrs. N. Openshaw
Stockport	294,400	35,233,844	60·91	A. L. Wilson	R. G. Crook
Tameside	222,600	19,914,819	—	D. Spiers	
Trafford	227,400	35,576,769	60·9–68	H. W. D. Sculthorpe	G. H. Carnall
Wigan	306,600	28,009,068	50·82–57·42	J. H. Craik	G. MacDonald
MERSEYSIDE					
Knowsley	191,700	21,090,330	81·49	D. Willgoose	S. S. Powell
LIVERPOOL	610,135	71,188,354	69·1	A. J. Stocks	† O. J. Doyle
St. Helens	192,140	20,894,761	51·1–74	T. Taylor, M.C.	Miss. M. McNamera
Sefton	307,200	34,594,109	61·9	J. P. McElroy	E. R. Ball
Wirral	349,200	39,326,000	71·2	I. G. Holt	J. P. Roberts
SOUTH YORKSHIRE					
Barnsley	224,100	16,478,982	74·4–80·9	A. B. Bleasby	H. Brain
Doncaster	280,830	25,584,101	61	W. J. Jackson	G. M. McDade
Rotherham	248,100	20,329,146	53·4–69	L. I. Frost	J. S. Crowther
SHEFFIELD	561,500	61,341,580	70·9–89	I. L. Podmore	† A. E. Richardson
TYNE AND WEAR					
Gateshead	222,300	20,179,848	72·9–91·4	W. Miles	S. J. Nugent
NEWCASTLE UPON TYNE	297,000	37,852,358	76	K. A. Galley	† Miss I. M. Steedman
North Tyneside	206,700	18,900,493	79·83	E. B. Lincoln	H. A. Rutherford
South Tyneside	175,540	15,306,730	72	A. Stansfield	A. M. Campbell
Sunderland	292,600	24,087,269	86	L. A. Bloom	Mrs. M. E. Porter
WEST MIDLANDS					
BIRMINGHAM	1,084,000	155,433,643	72–79	F. J. C. Amos, C.B.E.	† A. L. S. Jackson
COVENTRY	335,000	41,764,916	60·5	T. Gregory, O.B.E.	† C. Ward
Dudley	298,700	39,076,730	62·4	J. F. Mulvehill	J. T. Wilson
Sandwell	320,100	48,385,040	77	K. Pearce	W. H. Walker
Solihull	199,800	25,141,585	67·8	D. W. Chapman, D.F.M.	J. A. Battersby
Walsall	271,000	36,165,342	67·4	J. A. Galloway	H. Ashby
Wolverhampton	268,200	38,696,602	57	K. Williams	E. Mitchell
WEST YORKSHIRE					
BRADFORD	461,000	38,821,775	88·85	G. C. Moore	† Mrs. D. Birdsall
Calderdale	192,400	15,079,056	83·5	A. W. Luke	Mrs. K. M. Cawdry
Kirklees	375,200	29,697,112	75·6–80·6	E. S. Dixon	W. Gregory
LEEDS	748,300	78,719,000	75·5	K. H. Potts	†A. S. Pedley, D.F.C.
WAKEFIELD	305,300	23,650,092	81·8	A. I. Wylie	H. Astbury

DISTRICT COUNCILS

A list of non-Metropolitan District Councils in England. Those accorded CITY status are in SMALL CAPITALS, those with Borough status are distinguished by having § prefixed.

District	Population (Reg. G's Estimate)	Rateable Value 1975 £	Average Rate Levied p.	Chief Executive	Chairman 1975–6 (a) Mayor (b) Lord Mayor
Adur, West Sussex	56,700	7,557,762	60·4	Maj. Gen. R. J. D. E. Buckland	C. Robinson
Allerdale, Cumbria	94,500	7,977,034	61·35	A. C. Crane	W. B. Collins
Alnwick, Northumberland	28,000	2,308,568	65	A. G. A. Groome	H. I. N. Reavell, T.D.
Amber Valley, Derbyshire	107,100	9,891,841	73	J. Ragsdale	T. E. Carrington
Arun, West Sussex	106,000	14,000,000	—	—	—
Ashfield, Nottinghamshire	101,700	8,464,794	60·57	S. Beedham	M. Green
§Ashford, Kent	80,380	8,812,457	72·54	G. H. Redfern	(a) Maj. A. T. Palmer, M.B.E.

§ Civic Centre.

District	Population (Reg. G's Estimate)	Rateable Value 1975 £	Average Rate Levied p.	Chief Executive	Chairman 1975-6 (a) Mayor (b) Lord Mayor
Aylesbury Vale, Bucks.............	117,600	16,125,004	74·7	R. D. W. Maxwell	A. E. Mogford
Babergh, Suffolk..................	67,400	7,547,158	59·9	H. A. Cooper	D. W. Wedgwood
§Barrow-in-Furness, Cumbria.....	75,490	5,841,764	61·9	W. M. Robinson	(a) Mrs. A. L. Shuttleworth
Basildon, Essex....................	137,600	20,250,000	61	R. C. Mitchinson	C. O'Brien
Basingstoke, Hants................	116,800	14,579,969	70·2	D. W. Pilkington, R.D.	J. W. Ludgate
Basserlaw, Notts..................	99,421	12,073,651	65·5	G. A. Yewdall	W. G. Cooper
BATH, Avon.......................	84,700	9,891,887	73	D. C. Beeton	(a) Miss C. M. Edmunds
Beaconsfield, Bucks...............	62,700	12,607,699	52·8	D. P. Harrison	R. M. Scarles
Bedford..........................	129,700	17,214,311	87·2	T. R. B. Tiernay	G. C. W. Beazley
§Berwick upon Tweed, Northumberland................	25,900	2,293,952	64·4	J. Healy	(a) J. A. Marshall
§Beverley, Humberside............	106,700	10,770,829	63	W. J. H. Thomas	(a) C. C. Sonley
§Blaby, Leics.....................	77,200	7,754,927	60	T. Heap	J. Fisher
§Blackburn, Lancs.................	141,700	12,890,764	89	C. H. Singleton	T. Taylor, C.B.E.
§Blackpool, Lancs.................	150,100	17,741,064	61·07	R. O. F. Hickman	(a) H. L. Hoyle, M.B.E.
§Blyth Valley, Northumberland.....	64,270	5,253,103	—		
§Bolsover, Derbys.................	70,990	4,847,609	63·3	E. Edwards	W. Hyatt
Boothferry, Humberside...........	55,800	4,297,213	62·26	Miss M. H. Sindell	A. B. Wise
§Boston, Lincs....................	49,800	5,195,607	—	R. E. Coley	(a) J. J. Parker
§Bournemouth, Dorset.............	146,400	22,514,857	72	K. Lomas	(a) G. H. Masters
Bracknell, Berks..................	70,900	10,898,619	67·6	C. S. McDonald	F. W. Cain
Braintree, Essex..................	101,000	12,180,265	—	P. W. Cotton	D. W. R. Clayton
Breckland, Norfolk................	84,400	8,444,580	60·96	J. B. Heath	E. H. J. Macro
Brentwood, Essex.................	74,290	11,825,627	56	G. Bowden	G. A. Jennings
Bridgnorth, Salop.................	48,700	5,104,393	55	G. C. Nutley	T. Wedge
§Brighton, East Sussex............	160,290	22,970,588	72·2	R. G. Morgan	(a) W. J. C. Clarke
BRISTOL, Avon...................	418,600	55,428,561	83	P. M. McCarthy	(b) H. J. Williams
Broadland, Norfolk...............	91,200	8,322,920	56·6	P. M. Taylor	C. I. Coughtrey
Bromsgrove, Hereford and Worcs....	78,000	9,928,145	68·7	G. F. Badham	R. R. Harvey, O.B.E.
§Broxbourne, Herts................	74,200	10,571,892	—	C. Campbell	G. D. Game
Broxtowe, Notts..................	102,500	10,669,455	50·5-61·5	A. E. Hodder	J. B. Streeter
§Burnley, Lancs...................	93,601	7,643,303	72·53	B. Whittle	(a) Mrs. S. Ennis
CAMBRIDGE......................	100,250	18,066,408	71·6	G. G. Datson	(a) R. May
Cannock Chase, Staffs.............	83,500	8,732,752	48·5	B. E. Rastell	T. E. Cavlishaw
CANTERBURY, Kent...............	116,780	12,799,314	81·2	C. C. Gay	H. J. Alexander
Caradon, Cornwall................	57,050	5,125,707	57·17	H. Enever	J. A. Martin
CARLISLE, Cumbria...............	100,740	9,694,897	67	W. Hirst	A. Graham
Carrick, Cornwall.................	72,000	7,656,123	56·7-60·4	H. P. Dorey	H. W. Hicks
§Castle Morpeth, Northumberland....	47,000	4,631,828	72	M. Cole	(a) G. F. Brown
Castle Point, Essex................	80,500	9,497,179	67·5	A. R. Neighbour	G. A. Pickett
§Charnwood, Leics................	131,000	16,220,826	69	D. L. Harris	(a) L. G. Duncan
Chelmsford, Essex................	128,700	19,104,844	55·7	R. M. C. Hartley	D. H. Clark
§Cheltenham, Glos.................	86,400	13,200,000	52 5	B. N. Wynn	(a) L. F. F. Gaylard
Cherwell, Oxon...................	103,400	12,593,505	59·2	A. M. Brace	H. R. H. Clifton
CHESTER, Cheshire...............	117,000	15,957,448	77·65	D. M. Kermode	(a) F. C. Hignett
§Chesterfield, Derbys..............	95,000	10,141,034	74·4	R. A. Kennedy	(a) J. Wickins
Chester-le-Street, Durham........	48,730	3,809,943	68·5	J. Sanders	J. Willis
CHICHESTER, West Sussex.........	93,610	11,847,564	58	P. G. Lomas	(a) R. S. Hancock
Chiltern, Bucks...................	90,000	13,950,903	61·9	A. T. Rawlinson	W. C. Carvosso
§Chorley, Lancs...................	31,649	7,101,847	59	A. B. Webster	(a) P. Keane
§Christchurch, Dorset.............	34,900	5,445,325	73·95	J. MacFadyen, D.F.C.	(a) J. S. C. Morgan
Cleethorpes, Humberside..........	70,200	8,076,744	61·1-64·6	R. Farmer	A. A. Archer
§Colchester, Essex................	127,500	15,126,889	63·9-67·7	J. Allen	(a) W. G. Ladbrook
§Congleton, Cheshire..............	76,600	8,556,322	71·45	A. Molyneux	(a) E. C. Gill
§Copeland, Cumbria...............	70,960	6,173,179	65·23	P. N. Denson	(a) T. A. Williams
Corby, Northants.................	54,600	8,038,550	72·43	C. E. Chapman	J. Carr
Cotswold, Glos...................	66,500	7,434,792	72·12	D. Waring	D. C. Leadbeater
Craven, North Yorks..............	46,800	4,013,627	56·3	E. G. Sharp	P. N. Willey
§Crawley, West Sussex.............	72,000	12,295,877	57·5	K. J. L. Newell	(a) A. Obbard
§Crewe and Nantwich, Cheshire......	98,900	10,461,221	74·7	A. Brook	J. Nield
Dacorum, Herts...................	122,600	19,706,171	67·78	H. Aughton	J. Johnson
§Darlington, Durham..............	97,500	11,472,175	83·3-85·6	H. Rogers, D.F.C., A.F.C.	(a) J. E. Paterson
Dartford, Kent...................	83,060	9,387,730	56·67	R. J. Duck	L. H. T. Mayne
Daventry, Northants..............	52,000	6,671,350	77·9	R. C. Hutchison	W. A. Wright

§ Civic Centre.

District	Popula- tion (Reg. G's Estimate)	Rateable Value 1975 £	Average Rate Levied p.	Chief Executive	Chairman 1975–6 (a) Mayor (b) Lord Mayor
§Derby............................	217,800	26,803,249	65·4	—	(a) C. Ufton
Derwentside, Durham.............	92,000	7,709,300	80	J. Quinn	J. G. Parkin
Dover, Kent.....................	102,810	9,809,013	63·7	I. J. F. Paterson	P. W. Bean
DURHAM.........................	88,200	7,710,652	84·5	Col. K. G. N. Miller, M.C., T.D.	C. Ellison, B.E.M.
Easington, Durham...............	108,300	6,464,500	60	D. C. Kelly	J. S. Cummings
§Eastbourne, East Sussex..........	73,300	11,093,933	61·5	P. F. Humpherson	(a) C. G. Scott
East Cambridgeshire.............	51,400	4,618,253	60·09	T. T. G. Hardy	Col. J. G. A. Beckett, O.B.E., T.D.
East Devon.....................	100,300	10,626,017	56·37	R. Thompson	J. G. Alford
East Hampshire.................	83,300	9,512,246	66·5	R. H. Moores	Lt.-Col. R. M. Digby, M.B.E.
East Hertfordshire..............	104,400	13,948,001	63·7–70·1	J. J. B. Dutfield	W. H. Stripling
§Eastleigh, Hants...............	80,600	10,767,077	58·4–62·3	D. A. Tranah	(a) N. F. N. Norris
East Lindsey, Lincs.............	99,800	9,827,768	68·7	B. C. V. Spence	R. H. Brackenbury
East Northamptonshire...........	59,800	5,678,078	70·5	D. B. Adnitt	F. C. L. Caress, M.B.E.
East Staffordshire..............	96,500	11,379,395	62	F. N. Brammer	H. Caulton
Eden, Cumbria..................	31,800	3,436,005	61·6	R. S. Bagshaw	T. R. Fetherston- Haugh
§Ellesmere Port, Cheshire.........	83,800	15,783,078	81·09	R. J. Bernie	P. H. Hall
§Elmbridge, Surrey..............	112,800	20,379,244	54·4	E. G. Hubbard	(a) M. R Bygraves
Epping Forest, Essex............	114,800	16,947,328	57·83	D. P. Brokenshire	L. A. Welch
§Epsom and Ewell, Surrey........	72,045	10,655,810	51·1	D. R. Grimes	(a) H. W. Chard
§Erewash, Derbys................	100,000	10,063,289	64	J. M. Parker	(a) W. E. Hart
EXETER, Devon..................	95,729	12,666,636	75·44	(vacant)	(a) W. P. Hutchings
§Fareham, Hants................	85,700	9,371,990	63·33	L. E. Page	(a) F. A. Chamberlain
Fenland, Cambs.................	65,000	6,329,100	—	W. G. E. Lewis	Mrs. D. Fleming
Forest Heath, Suffolk...........	46,700	4,711,228	59·7	J. F. Gale	J. O. Wiggin
Forest of Dean, Glos............	69,100	5,735,627	60·8	L. W. Packer	E. Cooke
§Fylde, Lancs..................	68,910	7,909,923	48–51	R. A. Cork	(a) R. M. Joyce
§Gedling, Notts................	100,200	9,591,890	64·7	W. Brown	(a) H. F. Calladine
§Gillingham, Kent..............	93,000	9,234,850	60·98	G. C. Jones	(a) H. L. King
§Glanford, Humberside...........	61,400	7,510,348	66·4	R. E. Crosby	(a) P. S. Raby
GLOUCESTER.....................	91,000	11,138,367	66·25	H. R. T. Shackleton	(a) P. M. Robins
§Gosport, Hants................	83,430	8,499,982	47·45	G. F. Burndred, T.D.	(a) G. J. Hewitt
§Gravesham, Kent...............	97,300	11,885,335	70·9	J. V. Lovell	(a) E. S. Percy
§Great Yarmouth, Norfolk........	76,200	9,386,982	67·5	K. G. Ward	(a) E. J. Craske
§Grimsby, Humberside............	94,700	10,344,278	64·3	F. W. Ward, O.B.E.	(a) A. Neilson
§Guildford, Surrey..............	124,214	20,575,748	66·68	B. E. Twyford	(a) C. J. K. Boyce
§Halton, Cheshire...............	106,200	13,781,819	53·1–57·5	R. Turton	(a) C. J. Helsby
Hambleton, North Yorks..........	72,000	6,408,886	56·8	D. Parkin	A. W. Herbert
Harborough, Leics..............	56,160	6,176,323	58·3	F. T. Berry	Mrs. M. F. Adcock
Harlow, Essex..................	82,000	12,602,790	69·5	A. W. Medd	T. P. Farr
§Harrogate, North Yorks..........	134,300	13,257,254	54·23	J. N. Knox	(a) J. L. Heaton
Hart, Hants....................	67,900	7,837,662	58·4	E. Robinson	Miss J. Orr
§Hartlepool, Cleveland...........	98,500	10,306,812	76	N. D. Abram	—
§Hastings, East Sussex...........	74,600	8,606,684	54·35	D. J. Taylor	(a) J. Hodgson
§Havant, Hants..................	114,800	13,325,934	75·7	J. L. Stubbs	(a) K. N. Berry
HEREFORD.......................	47,200	5,908,065	67·44	H. G. Culliss	(a) M. K. Prendergast
Hertsmere, Hertfordshire........	90,000	14,801,392	69·22	J. Heath	A. Armstrong
§High Peak, Derbys..............	80,100	8,055,754	70·7–75·4	G. D. Jones	(a) F. S. Kitchen
§Hinckley and Bosworth, Leics......	79,800	8,822,286	70·98	B. D. Ainscough	(a) D. R. Bown
Holderness, Humberside..........	43,200	3,985,434	71·0	D. B. Law	S. Robinson
Horsham, West Sussex...........	90,500	11,093,466	55·3	D. M. Balmford	T. Rowland
§Hove, East Sussex..............	89,200	13,977,600	65·0–76·0	R. Hinton	(a) E. G. P. Rosevear
Huntingdon, Cambs..............	111,300	11,875,686	73·9	N. Godfrey	T. H. Burgess
§Hyndburn, Lancs................	79,900	6,329,833	74·5	D. N. Macgregor	(a) D. J. McNeil
§Ipswich, Suffolk...............	122,500	17,460,828	73·5	R. L. Cross	(a) Mrs. B. C. James
Kennet, Wilts..................	68,900	5,712,041	—	S. L. A. Jaques	R. N. Swanton
Kerrier, Cornwall...............	79,700	6,963,744	57·8	F. J. Pearson	C. L. Hollands
§Kettering, Northants............	70 100	7,029,516	79·66	K. C. Butler	(a) C. T. L. Hakewill
KINGSTON UPON HULL, Humberside..	278,800	25,934,173	66·7	A. B. Wood	(b) Mrs. C. E. Ellis
Kingswood, Avon................	78,000	6,962,715	51·0–58·0	A. Smith	W. G. Lewton
LANCASTER, Lancs...............	125,500	12,200,087	67·2	D. J. Waddell, O.B.E.	(a) Mrs. J. Horner
§Langbaurgh Cleveland...........	150,750	20,409,000	75·5	W. A. Middleham	J. Morgan
LEICESTER......................	287,300	35,577,300	69·5	J. S. Phipps	(b) Mrs. L. R. Marriott
Leominster, Hereford and Worcs.....	34,327	2,934,994	72·82	G. A. Robson	Maj. D. J. C. Davenport
Lewes, East Sussex..............	75,700	10,084,412	71·48	D. N. Thompson	D. A. W. Wheeler

§ Civic Centre.

District	Population (Reg. G's Estimate)	Rateable Value 1975 £	Average Rate Levied p.	Chief Executive	Chairman 1975–6 (a) Mayor (b) Lord Mayor
Lichfield, Staffs...................	86,900	10,086,656	68·8	N. Barton	A. G. Ward
LINCOLN........................	73,100	8,435,102	65·33	P. C. Watts	(a) F. T. Allen
§Luton, Beds....................	165,900	26,658,073	62·5	A. Collins	—
§Macclesfield, Cheshire............	145,620	18,836,928	74·0	J. E. Sandford	(a) J. H. Morris
§Maidstone, Kent................	124,700	14,186,581	44·0–62·5	A. F. Hargraves	(a) H. H. Ashton
Maldon, Essex..................	43,300	5,874,679	55·5	E. Robinson	R. F. Daws
Malvern Hills, Hereford and Worcs...	80,200	8,261,673	73·18	L. J. Martin	J. T. Arnett
Mansfield, Notts................	96,730	8,269,951	63·17	G. R. Cottam	L. Wright
§Medina, Isle of Wight............	65,100	6,730,095	73·12	W. R. Wilks	(a) A. T. Drudge
§Medway, Kent..................	143,080	19,331,938	63·27	R. Hill	(a) R. C. Tomsett
§Melton, Leics..................	40,500	4,570,128	—	J. P. Milburn	(a) G. Y.-C. Green
Mendip, Somerset................	83,450	8,329,910	60·41	C. Riley	R. B. Clark
Mid Bedfordshire.................	93,900	10,727,783	83·0	P. A. Freeman	K. G. Quince
§Middlesbrough, Cleveland..........	153,900	15,172,857	82·5	J. R. Foster	(a) G. A. Burns
Mid Suffolk.....................	62,000	6,236,936	72·7	H. McFarlane	D. J. S. Dyball
Mid Sussex.....................	105,900	13,359,085	56·44	J. A. McGhee	A. L. Whitticks
§Milton Keynes, Bucks............	78,000	10,856,722	75·0	E. C. Ray	(a) C. E. Bowden
Mole Valley, Surrey..............	77,500	11,307,899	73·0	D. C. Hill	S. J. Taylor
Newark, Notts...................	102,100	9,370,094	54·4–73·0	J. R. Spencer	Mrs. M. Beardsley,
Newbury, Berks..................	111,400	15,354,097	—	B. J. Thetford	B. H. Theobald [O.B.E.
§Newcastle under Lyme, Staffs......	121,900	11,581,205	65·25	A. G. Owen	(a) W. E. Welsby
New Forest, Hants................	137,100	19,772,614	68·0	P. A. Bassett	R. H. Alderson
§Northampton...................	137,600	18,965,339	—	A. C. Parkhouse	(a) J. J. Gardner
Northavon, Avon................	112,800	12,542,054	54·5	F. Maude	Col. E. M. K. Mead
North Cornwall..................	59,700	5,743,438	58·78	I. Whiting	J. A. M. Kent
North Devon....................	72,280	6,775,810	61·64	E. Harwood	S. G. Kingdon
North Dorset....................	46,800	4,081,370	62·2	J. L. Guest	C. R. J. Mitchell
North East Derbyshire............	91,900	7,346,906	60·2	R. S. Billington	W. E. Fellows
North Hertfordshire..............	103,700	16,551,856	73·0	M. Kelly	R. A. Lodge
North Kesteven, Lincs............	75,900	6,428,743	60·0	T. L. Hill	K. T. Godson
North Norfolk..................	78,500	8,653,224	59·9	T. V. Nolan	G. S. Allen
North Shropshire................	46,436	4,178,804	76·0	E. G. D. Healey	T. Groom
§North Warwickshire..............	60,090	7,367,499	69·9	R. H. Kealy	(a) P. H. Barlow
North West Leicestershire..........	73,400	8,042,530	63·6–71·8	N. Marson	J. F. Lee
North Wiltshire..................	100,800	8,943,061	55·1	H. F. Hales	The Earl of Shelburne
§North Wolds, Humberside..........	69,500	5,745,557	72·7	E. Hutchinson	(a) Mrs. B. M. D. Wright
NORWICH, Norfolk..............	121,688	19,958,552	63·5	G. G. Tilsey	(b) Mrs. J. L. Morgan
NOTTINGHAM..................	287,000	38,110,207	65·0	M. H. F. Hammond	(b) Mrs. I. F. Matthews
§Nuneaton, Warwickshire..........	110,810	11,684,243	58·7–77·2	B. E. Walters	(a) A. Tallis
§Oadby and Wigston, Leics.........	52,300	5,989,784	59·3	J. B. Burton	(a) J. B. S. Voss
§Oswestry, Salop................	31,720	2,678,133	62·5	D. T. David	(a) Mrs. M. A. Edwards
OXFORD.......................	115,100	18,979,716	62·5	E. J. Patrick	(b) W. G. R. Fagg
Pendle, Lancs...................	86,200	5,760,285	66·11	C. A. Simmonds	Mrs. J. Bebbington
Penwith, Cornwall...............	51,332	5,190,780	63·5	J. R. Eley	D. W. F. Trewern
PETERBOROUGH, Cambs...........	111,300	14,267,756	58·63	C. P. Clarke, O.B.E.	(a) W. R. Cashmore
PLYMOUTH, Devon...............	251,200	26,679,544	59·5	A. F. Watson	(b) W. I. Thompson
§Poole, Dorset..................	112,800	16,385,552	76·5	I. K. D. Andrews	(a) D. Gooding
PORTSMOUTH, Hants..............	195,130	24,871,178	74·0	J. R. Haselgrave, C.B.E., T.D.	(b) E. H. Taplin
§Preston, Lancs..................	132,000	14,223,350	49·77	H. T. Heap	(a) R. Weir
Purbeck, Dorset.................	38,500	4,640,436	70·5	D. R. Sansome	J. Spiller
§Reading, Berks..................	133,280	22,460,691	74·0	W. H. Tee	(a) G. D. Salisbury
Redditch, Hereford and Worcs......	48,000	6,385,000	80·2	P. N. Purvis	Mrs. A. M. Sanders
§Reigate and Banstead, Surrey.....	115,600	17,264,584	66·9–69·2	D. S. Walker	R. V. Stephenson
§Restormel, Cornwall.............	73,800	8,497,440	62·0–80·0	D. W. Cross	Mrs. E. F. A. Clyma
§Ribble Valley, Lancs.............	53,900	4,768,751	64·3–74·4	M. Jackson	(a) T. Robinson
Richmondshire, North Yorks........	46,390	3,812,393	57·8	E. H. Hodge	J. W. Potts
Rochford, Essex.................	69,200	8,699,303	49·3	E. J. Skevington	A. J. Harvey
§Rossendale, Lancs...............	61,583	4,509,685	87·22	W. B. Wolfe	(a) J. Connolly
Rother, East Sussex..............	74,600	9,904,952	74·6	N. C. Walsh	Miss N. C. Frith
§Rugby, Warwicks................	86,500	10,554,419	66·4	J. A. Thwaites	— [M.C.
Runnymede, Surrey..............	75,300	10,669,741	66·6	L. W. Way	I.t.-Col. B. S. Jarvis,
§Rushcliffe, Notts................	88,869	10,178,449	50·3	D. B. Ashford	(a) Mrs. J.M.E. Dixon
§Rushmoor, Hants................	77,270	9,046,655	—	—	—
Rutland, Leics..................	30,400	3,058,103	66·5	R. L. Francis	The Earl of Gainsborough
Ryedale, North Yorks............	75,800	5,843,562	55·85	A. Pearson	M. G. Foster
ST. ALBANS, Herts...............	122,580	18,825,000	—	—	—

§ Civic Centre.

District	Population (Reg. G's Estimate)	Rateable Value 1975 £	Average Rate Levied p.	Chief Executive	Chairman 1975–6 (a) Mayor (b) Lord Mayor
§St. Edmundsbury, Suffolk.........	77,690	8,911,000	64·1	E. G. Thomas	(a) Air Cdre. V. H. B. Roth, C.B., C.B.E.
Salisbury, Wilts..................	101,105	11,405,543	58·1	F. W. Colquhoun	J. J. Paul
§Scarborough, North Yorks........	97,310	9,715,314	87·5	R. Bradley	(a) A. H. Baker
§Scunthorpe, Humberside.........	68,500	11,697,638	74·3	T. M. Lister	(a) H. Hirst
Sedgefield, Durham..............	90,400	7,321,319	76·5	A. J. Roberts	D. Vickers
Sedgemoor, Somerset.............	84,000	9,102,364	48·4	T. J. Shellard	H. P. Choate
Selby, North Yorks..............	68,945	8,816,896	40	J. A. Wakefield	M. G. Patrick
Sevenoaks, Kent.................	101,420	10,891,876	—	—	—
Shepway, Kent..................	86,500	10,322,251	73	K. H. G. Mills	A. E. Burrage
Shrewsbury and Atcham, Salop.....	83,900	10,373,067	61	L. C. W. Beesley	
§Slough, Berks..................	101,805	22,257,000	54·5	M. F. Hulks	(a) D. R. Peters
SOUTHAMPTON Hants............	213,000	28,900,924	84·3	D. Scouller	(a) Mrs. E. I. Pugh
South Bedfordshire..............	94,800	15,077,888	86·9	R. C. Cranmer	F. R. G. Markham
South Cambridgeshire............	97,100	11,746,045	57·25	S. J. Flint	D. J. Allen
South Derbyshire...............	62,800	7,562,067	60·7	R. V. Hawcroft	G. C. Holmes
§Southend-on-Sea Essex..........	160,200	25,209,824	65·5	F. G. Laws	(a) N. Clarke
South Hams, Devon..............	63,000	6,551,858	57·04	S. W. Bradley	L. J. Squire
South Herefordshire.............	45,000	3,671,659	63·09	E, N, Sheldon	W. W. Makin
South Holland, Lincs.............	58,000	5,313,941	61·9	J. T. Brindley	G. R. Hastings
South Kesteven, Lincs............	89,300	9,073,425	44·5	K. R. Cann	G. C. Swanson
South Lakeland, Cumbria..........	93,200	8,929,138	39·5–57·2	N. C. Bizley	W. Dobson
South Norfolk..................	85,800	7,888,349	70·51	R. A. Gorham	B. A. Cook
South Northamptonshire..........	61,400	6,033,902	69·3	C. M. Major	J. M. Heygate
South Oxfordshire...............	138,900	16,825,470	66·2	J. B. Chirnside	E. Howard
§South Ribble, Lancs.............	90,500	7,906,655	61·5	C. E. Lea	(a) H. Kerfoot
South Shropshire...............	33,300	2,802,483	62·5	L. V. Atack	T. H. Pain
South Staffordshire..............	86,400	9,433,527	—		
South Wight, I.O.W.............	45,800	5,064,368	69·7–63·6	C. M. Simpson	(a) R. T. Callis
§Spelthorne, Surrey..............	95,700	19,482,635	48·5	G. F. Hilbert	(a) E. E. J. Wright
§Stafford......................	114,300	13,890,259	66	D. E. Almond	(a) W. Bowen
Staffordshire Moorlands..........	93,200	8,526,640	66·38	H. W. Henson	Mrs. H. M. Gardner
§Stevenage, Herts...............	72,900	12,336,896	70·25	R. E. Hughes	(a) B. P. Hall
§Stockton-on-Tees, Cleveland......	162,500	23,261,749	78	G. F. Lyon	(a) N. Duff
STOKE-ON-TRENT, Staffs..........	258,300	28,621,817	78	S. W. Titchener	(b) D. Shotton
Stratford-on-Avon, Warwicks......	98,440	13,351,674	60·96	T. J. W. Foy	V. A. V. Carr
Stroud, Glos...................	93,400	9,887,728	65·7	H. T. Arnold	D. A. V. Harper
Suffolk Coastal.................	94,500	10,534,295	71	D. C. Blay	N. J. Mumford
§Surrey Heath..................	69,700	10,648,369	50·4	D. J. C. Horn	(a) Mrs. V. Richards
Swale, Kent....................	105,600	10,672,277	58·33	D. Allan	K. H. Burbidge
§Tamworth, Staffs...............	48,900	5,464,659	102	H. B. Leake	(a) D. J. Bonas
Tandridge, Surrey...............	79,750	8,903,040	—		
Taunton Deane, Somerset..........	82,900	9,104,675	79·97	K. A. Horne	(a) Mrs. G. Deacon
Teesdale, Durham...............	24,000	1,896,832	68·26	J. A. Jones	J. L. Armstrong
Teignbridge, Devon..............	94,300	9,541,857	74·14	E. G. Loveys	G. C. C. MacVicker
Tendring, Essex.................	107,700	13,189,140	59	C. H. Ramsden	Lt.-Col. H. Harvey-Williams
Test Valley, Hants..............	86,350	10,360,005	—	G. K. Waddell	H. B. Finmore
§Tewkesbury, Glos...............	77,484	9,364,775	62·45	K. E. S. Smale	Hon. A. A. O. Morrison
§Thamesdown, Wilts.............	141.110	15,817,461	67·7	D. M. Kent	A. J. Masters
Thanet, Kent...................	117,600	13,186,484	69·32	I. G. Gill	H. Anish
Three Rivers, Herts.............	80,610	12,148,506	67·84	J. D. Brown	S. Butchers
§Thurrock, Essex................	126,800	28,611,962	57·6	G. V. Semain	(a) Mrs. E. A. Whalley
Tiverton, Devon................	55,200	4,675,990	70·37	R. C. Greensmith	W. G. Heggadon
Tonbridge and Malling, Kent.......	94,800	11,369,197	60·1	S. W. Stanford, T.D.	M. J. Stone
§Torbay, Devon.................	106,400	15,554,416	64·5	D. P. Hudson	J. Farrell, O.B.E.
Torridge, Devon................	47,300	3,339,644	68·93	J. D. McHardy	C. G. Metherell
§Tunbridge Wells, Kent..........	95,000	10,619,379	74	W. E. Battersby	(a) Lt.-Col. R. J. Smith,
Tynedale, Northumberland........	54,700	4,923,928	82·8	A. Bates	J. C. W. Riddell [M.B.E.
Uttlesford, Essex...............	56,000	7,444,984	—	J. F. Vernon	Mrs. M. R. Davey
Vale of White Horse, Oxon........	96,900	12.631,761	58–59	J. C. N. Wood	E. J. S. Parsons
Vale Royal, Cheshire............	109,500	13,541,821	76·72	W. R. T. Woods	Mrs. J. M. Pollard,
Wansbeck, Northumberland........	62,970	6,710,137	82·6	R. R. Nuttall	R. D. Sanderson [O.B.E.
Wansdyke, Avon................	73,200	7,405,461	71·5	B. L. Clifton	D. G. Miles
§Warrington, Cheshire............	161,000	18,830,974	—		
Warwick.......................	111,100	15,935,779	66·2	M. J. Ward	J. M. W. Savory
§Watford, Herts.................	78,180	15,503,793	70·3	R. B. McMillan	(a) W. T. H. Price
Waveney Suffolk................	94,700	9,705,280	73·8	P. A. Taylor	Air Chief Marshal Sir Alfred Earle, G.C.B., C.B.

§ Civic Centre.

District	Population (Reg. G's Estimate)	Rateable Value 1975 £	Average Rate Levied p.	Chief Executive	Chairman 1975–6 (a) Mayor (b) Lord Mayor
Waverley, Surrey	106,290	15,229,461	72·06	C. J. Wagg	V. R. Goodridge
Wealden, East Sussex	113,000	12,035,488	71	K. Wilson	Air Cdre. H. M. Russell,
Wear Valley, Durham	63,600	5,076,338	80·25	J. R. Passey	D. R. Harburn [O.B.E.
§Wellingborough, Northants	60,900	6,763,223	81·1	J. Huxley	(a) M. R Holmes
Welwyn Hatfield, Herts	93,600	17,183,466	63·82	L. Asquith	J. A. Emmerson
West Derbyshire	66,000	6,127,937	60·75	R. Bubb	G. J. Peach
West Devon	45,000	3,335,614	46·34	G. E. G. Cotton	H. C. Frost
West Dorset	77,410	7,682,763	70·97	E. Andrews	H. W. Haward
West Lancashire	103,400	10,910,102	61·5	J. Cowdall	Miss. E. M. Cropper
West Lindsey, Lincs	73,600	6,032,000	80	W. McIntyre	G. H. Ford
West Norfolk	114,400	12,239,322	70·8	J. E. Bolton	C. L. Burman, M.B.E.
West Oxfordshire	79,060	8,208,961	—		
West Somerset	29,934	3,750,000	59	H. Close	L. K. Axon
West Wiltshire	92,800	9,268,233	58·6	R. Butterworth	M. M. Mortimer
§Weymouth and Portland, Dorset	56,300	5,599,097	67·77	E. J. Jones	(a) J. W. C. Jenner,
Wimborne, Dorset	57,300	7,134,061	73·1	W. G. Press	W. C. Tapper [M.B.E.
WINCHESTER, Hants	87,400	11,101,084	70·45	E. M. E. White	(a) A. Cotterill
§Windsor and Maidenhead, Berks	128,000	19,929,195	61·4	P. A. Welch	(a) C. S. Aston
§Woking, Surrey	77,590	11,958,764	71·1	M. Shawcross	(a) T. A. Molloy
Wokingham, Berks	108,600	13,813,739	61·59	C. G. Cockayne	Air Cdre. Sir Louis Dickens, D.F.C., A.F.C.
Woodspring, Avon	147,800	16,315,630	62·2	R. H. Moon	J. G. Walters
WORCESTER	74,500	11,527,686	64·3	B. Webster, O.B.E.,	(a) R. Blackwell
§Worthing, West Sussex	89,300	12,862,000	63·3	H. Carroll [M.C.	(a) R. D Clapp
Wrekin, Salop	112,500	11,891,686	76·3	A. W. Flockhart	M. Harrison
Wychavon, Hereford and Worcs	85,900	11,002,962	66·7	P. G. Rust	Lt.-Col. R. G. Burlingham, T.D.
Wycombe, Bucks	149,700	23,988,271	72	D. I. Pendrill	J. D. S. Hester
§Wyre, Lancs	98,500	9,774,350	51·5	W. F. Dolman	(a) R. C. Snape
Wyre Forest, Hereford and Worcs	92,200	12,155,671	62·3	N. A. James	H. S. Beresford
Yeovil, North Yorks	121,700	12,146,698	—	K. C. Hermon	Rev. Preb. W. T. Taylor
YORK, North Yorks	103,800	10,237,628	72·5	R. Howell	(b) J. P. Birch [lor

§ Civic Centre.

PARTY REPRESENTATION

Figures given in the press for party representation in England and Wales after the elections of April, 1973: Abbreviations: *C.* = Conservative; *Comm.* = Communist; *D.Lab.* = Democratic Labour; *Ind.* = Independent, including Ratepayers' Association, etc.; *Lab.* = Labour; *Lib.* = Liberal; *P.C.* = Plaid Cymru.

Metropolitan Counties

Greater Manchester. *Lab.* 69, *C.* 23, *Lib.* 13, *Ind.* 1.
Merseyside. *Lab.* 53, *C.* 26, *Lib.* 19, *Ind.* 1.
West Midlands. *Lab.* 74, *C.* 26, *Lib.* 4.
Tyne and Wear. *Lab.* 74, *C.* 26, *Ind.* 3, *Lib.* 1.
South Yorkshire. *Lab.* 82, *C.* 13, *Ind.* 4, *Lib.* 1.
West Yorkshire. *Lab.* 51, *C.* 25, *Lib.* 11, *Ind.* 1.

Non-Metropolitan Counties

Avon. *C.* 36. *Lab.* 32, *Ind.* 3, *Lib.* 2.
Bedfordshire. *Lab.* 39, *C.* 32, *Lib.* 8, *Ind.* 3.
Berkshire. *C.* 42, *Lab.* 26, *Lib.* 13, *Ind.* 5.
Buckinghamshire. *C.* 36, *Lab.* 18, *Ind.* 12, *Lib.* 4.
Cambridgeshire. *C.* 28, *Lab.* 22, *Ind.* 13, *Lib.* 5.
Cheshire. *C.* 31, *Lab.* 29, *Ind.* 6, *Lib.* 1.
Cleveland. *Lab.* 52, *C.* 35, *Ind.* 2.
Cornwall. *Ind.* 75, *C.* 3. *Lab.* 1.
Cumbria. *Lab.* 38, *C.* 31, *Ind.* 11, *Lib.* 1.
Derbyshire. *Lab.* 60, *C.* 26, *Ind.* 7, *Lib.* 5.
Devon. *C.* 54, *Lab.* 20, *Ind.* 12, *Lib.* 11.
Dorset. *C.* 47, *Ind.* 20, *Lab.* 13, *Lib.* 11.
Durham. *Lab.* 56, *Ind.* 7, *Lib.* 6, *C.* 2.
East Sussex. *C.* 48, *Lab.* 19, *Lib.* 9, *Ind.* 8.
Essex. *C.* 50, *Lab.* 40, *Lib.* 5, *Ind.* 2.
Gloucestershire. *C.* 31, *Lab.* 18, *Ind.* 7, *Lib.* 5.
Hampshire. *C.* 44, *Lab.* 27, *Ind.* 20, *Lib.* 6.
Hereford and Worcester. *C.* 37, *Lab.* 30, *Ind.* 17, *Lib.* 8.
Hertfordshire. *C.* 33, *Lab.* 33, *Lib.* 3, *Ind.* 3.
Humberside. *Lab.* 51, *C.* 36, *Ind.* 7, *Lib.* 3.
Isle of Wight. *Ind.* 23, *Lib.* 7, *Lab.* 6, *C.* 6.
Kent. *C.* 63, *Lab.* 31, *Lib.* 7, *Ind.* 2.
Lancashire. *C.* 52, *Lab.* 33, *Lib.* 7, *Ind.* 4.
Leicestershire. *C.* 41, *Lab.* 37, *Ind.* 8, *Lib.* 7.
Lincolnshire. *C.* 34, *Ind.* 22, *Lab.* 10, *D.Lab.* 5, *Lib.* 3.
Norfolk. *C.* 52, *Lab.* 27, *Ind.* 4.
Northamptonshire. *Lab.* 47, *C.* 37, *Ind.* 4.
Northumberland. *Lab.* 28, *Ind.* 21, *C.* 10.
North Yorkshire. *C.* 39, *Ind.* 30, *Lab.* 12, *Lib.* 12.
Nottinghamshire. *Lab.* 54, *C.* 35.
Oxfordshire. *C.* 36, *Lab.* 21, *Ind.* 10.
Salop. *Ind.* 30, *Lab.* 16, *C.* 14, *Lib.* 3.
Somerset. *C.* 35, *Ind.* 12, *Lab.* 7, *Lib.* 2.
Staffordshire. *Lab.* 47, *C.* 28, *Ind.* 9, *Lib.* 1.
Suffolk. *C.* 47, *Lab.* 29, *Lib.* 3, *Ind.* 3.
Surrey. *C.* 46, *Lab.* 12, *Lib.* 9, *Ind.* 5.
Warwickshire. *C.* 27, *Lab.* 21, *Lib.* 5, *Ind.* 2.
West Sussex. *C.* 52, *Ind.* 14, *Lab.* 10, *Lib.* 7.
Wiltshire. *C.* 39, *Lab.* 22, *Ind.* 12, *Lib.* 6.

(Elections of May 1, 1975)

Metropolitan District Councils
(Elections of May 1, 1975)

GREATER MANCHESTER
Bolton............C. 42, Lab. 23, Lib. 3, Ind. 1.
Bury............C. 28, Lab. 16, Lib. 4.
Manchester.......Lab. 54, C. 45.
Oldham..........Lab. 30, C. 15, Lib. 11, Ind. 1.
Rochdale..........Lab. 28, C. 22, Lib. 10.
Salford............Lab. 44, C. 20, Ind. 1. Lib. 1.
Stockport..........C. 34, Lab. 12, Lib. 10, Ind. 4.
Tameside..........Lab. 28, C. 24, Lib. 2.
Trafford............C. 42, Lab. 13, Lib. 8.
Wigan............Lab. 61, C. 10, Ind. 1.

MERSEYSIDE
Knowsley..........Lab. 45, C. 12, Lib. 3, Ind. 2.
Liverpool..........Lib. 43, Lab. 42, C. 14.
St. Helens..........Lab. 30, C. 14, Lib. 1.
Sefton............C. 40, Lab. 22, Lib. 3, Ind. 2.
Wirral............C. 36, Lab. 21, Lib. 9.

SOUTH YORKSHIRE
Barnsley..........Lab. 48, Ind. 9, Lib. 1.
Doncaster..........Lab. 40, C. 15, Ind. 4.
Rotherham........Lab. 44, C. 7, Ind. 3.
Sheffield..........Lab. 66, C. 20, Lib. 4.

TYNE AND WEAR
Gateshead..........Lab. 65, C. 10, Ind. 1, Lib. 1.
Newcastle upon
Tyne..........Lab. 47, C. 27, Ind. 2, Lib. 2.
North Tyneside.....Lab. 46, C. 24, Ind. 4, Lib. 4.
South Tyneside.....Lab. 35, Ind. 23, C. 5, Lib. 3.
Sunderland.....Lab. 52, C. 23, Ind. 2, Lib. 1.

WEST MIDLANDS
Birmingham.......Lab. 63, C. 55, Lib. 8.
Coventry..........Lab. 33, C. 21.
Dudley............Lab. 35, C. 29, Ind. 1, Lib. 1.
Sandwell..........Lab. 58, C. 32.
Solihull............C. 30, Lab. 12, Ind. 7, Lib. 2.
Walsall..........Lab. 37, C. 14, Ind. 9.
Wolverhampton....Lab. 38, C. 21, Ind. 1.

WEST YORKSHIRE
Bradford..........C. 57, Lab. 28, Lib. 8.
Calderdale..........C. 28, Lab. 18, Lib. 5.
Kirklees............Lab. 36, C. 28, Lib. 7, Ind. 1.
Leeds..............C. 43, Lab. 41, Lib. 12.
Wakefield..........Lab. 45, C. 11, Ind. 7.

Non-Metropolitan District Councils

Adur............Lib. 16, C. 13, Lab. 6, Ind. 2.
Allerdale............Ind. 27, Lab. 25, C. 4.
Alnwick..........Ind. 24, Lab. 4.
Amber Valley......Lab. 32, Ind. 21, C. 4, Lib. 3.
Arun..............C. 33, Ind. 10, Lab. 4, Lib. 4.
Ashfield............Lab. 52, Ind. 2, C. 1.
Ashford............C. 22, Lib. 10, Lab. 8, Ind. 4.
Aylesbury Vale.....Ind. 31, Lab. 12, C. 10, Lib. 1.
Babergh............Ind. 20, Lab. 11, C. 7.
Barrow-in-Furness..Lab. 25, C. 6, Ind. 2.
Basildon..........Lab. 31, C. 9, Ind. 6.
Basingstoke........Ind. 20, C. 18 Lab. 14, Lib. 3.
Bassetlaw..........Lab. 29, C. 11. Ind. 11.
Bath............C. 19, Lab. 17, Lib. 9.
Beaconsfield........C. 27, Ind. 11, Lib. 3, Lab. 1.
Bedford............Lab. 22, C. 20, Ind. 12, Lib. 2.
Berwick..........Ind. 26, Lab. 2.
Beverley............Ind. 36, C. 16, Lib. 7, Lab. 1.
Blaby............Ind. 20, C. 8, Lib. 7.
Blackburn..........Lab. 27, C. 19, Lib. 11, Ind. 3.
Blackpool..........C. 40, Lab. 10, Lib. 3, Ind. 3.
Blyth Valley........Lab. 29, Lib. 12, C. 5, Ind. 2.
Bolsover..........Lab. 28, Ind. 7, C. 1.
Boothferry..........Ind. 26, Lab. 5, C. 4.
Boston............Ind. 15, C. 9, Lab. 5, Lib. 5.
Bournemouth......C. 38, Lab. 14, Lib. 3, Ind. 2.
Bracknell..........Lab. 17, C. 9, Ind. 4, Lib. 1.
Braintree..........Ind. 22, Lab. 19, C. 14, Lib. 3.
Breckland..........Ind. 22, C. 19, Lab. 10.
Brentwood........C. 24, Lab. 11, Ind. 2, Lib. 1.
Bridgnorth..........Ind. 31, Lib. 1.
Brighton..........C. 31, Lab. 28.
Bristol............Lab. 56, C. 25, Lib. 3.
Broadland..........Ind. 24, C. 19, Lab. 6.
Bromsgrove........C. 25, Lab. 13, Ind. 4.
Broxbourne........C. 28, Lab. 12.
Broxtowe..........C. 24, Lab. 20, Ind. 2.
Burnley............Lab. 39, C. 12, Ind. 2, Lib. 1.
Cambridge..........Lab. 26, C. 11, Lib. 5.
Cannock Chase.....Lab. 36, C. 1.
Canterbury........C. 34, Ind. 8, Lab. 7, Lib. 2.
Caradon..........Ind. 41.
Carlisle..........Lab. 25, C. 12, Ind. 10, Lib. 1.
Carrick............Ind. 32, Lab. 5, C. 4, Lib. 4.
Castle Morpeth.....Ind. 14, C. 11, Lab. 7, Lib. 2.
Castle Point........Lab. 20, C. 19.
Charnwood........C. 28, Lab. 14, Ind. 11, Lib. 5.
Chelmsford........C. 31, Lab. 16, Lib. 8, Ind. 5.
Cheltenham........C. 21, Lab. 7, Lib. 4, Ind. 3.
Cherwell..........Lab. 16, C. 15, Ind. 14.
Chester............C. 43, Lab. 15, Ind. 4.

Chesterfield..........Lab. 45, C. 7, Lib. 2.
Chester-le-Street......Lab. 23, Lib. 6, Ind. 4.
Chichester..........Ind. 31, C. 13, Lib. 6.
Chiltern............C. 26, Ind. 14, Lab. 11.
Chorley............Lab. 21, C. 17, Ind. 9.
Christchurch........C. 10, Lib. 5, Lab. 4, Ind. 3.
Cleethorpes........Ind. 19, Lab. 14, C. 9, Lib. 6.
Colchester..........C. 28, Lab. 27, Ind. 4, Lib. 1.
Congleton..........C. 18, Ind. 14, Lab. 12, Lib. 1.
Copeland..........Lab. 30, Ind. 12, C. 6.
Corby..............Lab. 29, Ind. 3, C. 1.
Cotswold..........Ind. 42, Lab. 2, C. 1.
Craven..............C. 14, Lib. 9, Lab. 6, Ind. 6.
Crawley............Lab. 25, C. 5, Ind. 2.
Crewe..............Lab. 35, Ind. 21, C. 2, Lib. 2.
Dacorum..........Lab. 33, C. 26, Ind. 3.
Darlington..........Lab. 28, C. 8, Lib. 8, Ind. 5.
Dartford..........Lab. 30, C. 14.
Daventry..........C. 16, Ind. 10, Lab. 9.
Derby..............Lab. 34, C. 14, Lib. 6.
Derwentside......Lab. 45, Ind. 3, Lib. 3, C. 1.
Dover..............C. 29, Lab. 21, Ind. 5.
Durham............Lab. 40, Ind. 14, Lib. 7.
Easington..........Lab. 56, Ind. 4.
Eastbourne..........Lib. 19, C. 10, Lab. 4.
East Cambridgeshire Ind. 33, Lab. 1.
East Devon..........Ind. 42, C. 14, Lib. 3, Lab. 1.
East Hampshire......Ind. 20, C. 16, Lab. 6.
East Hertfordshire...Ind. 22, C. 16, Lab. 10.
Eastleigh..........Lab. 20, C. 13, Lib. 5, Ind. 4.
East Lindsey.......Ind. 49, C. 5, Lib. 3, Lab. 1.
East Northampton-
shire..........Ind. 18, Lab. 14, C. 5.
East Staffordshire....Lab. 24, C. 22, Ind. 14.
Eden..............Ind. 37.
Ellesmere Port........Lab. 27, C. 14, Ind. 1.
Elmbridge..........C. 39, Ind. 14, Lab. 7, Lib. 5.
Epping Forest......C. 44, Lab. 10, Ind. 5.
Epsom and Ewell....Ind. 37, Lab. 3.
Erewash..........Lab. 36, C. 9, Lib. 5, Ind. 4.
Exeter............C. 14, Lab. 13, Lib. 6, Ind. 1.
Fareham............C. 16, Ind. 13, Lib. 5, Lab. 2.
Fenland..........Ind. 18, C. 14, Lab. 8.
Forest Heath.......C. 12, Ind. 12.
Forest of Dean.....Ind. 25, Lab. 21, Lib. 1.
Fylde..............C. 28, Ind. 13, Lab. 2, Lib. 2.
Gedling............C. 32, Lab. 19, Ind. 4.
Gillingham........Lab. 14, C. 13, Lib. 8.
Glanford..........Ind. 33, Lab. 1.
Gloucester..........C. 21, Lab. 12.
Gosport..........Lab. 19, C. 9, Ind. 5.

Gravesham.........Lab. 28, C. 15, Ind. 1.
Great Yarmouth....C. 26, Lab. 17, Ind. 3, Lib. 2.
Grimsby...........Lab. 20, C. 14, Lib. 7, Ind. 1.
Guildford.........C. 29, Lab. 6, Lib. 5, Ind. 2.
Halton............Lab. 30, C. 8, Ind. 4, Lib. 1.
Hambleton.........Ind. 42, C. 4, Lab. 1, Lib. 1.
Harborough........C. 28, Ind. 7, Lab. 2.
Harlow............Lab. 38, Lib. 4.
Harrogate.........C. 35, Lib. 15, Ind. 7, Lab. 2.
Hart..............Ind. 26, C. 7.
Hartlepool........Lab. 30, C. 15, Ind. 1.
Hastings..........C. 12, Lab. 11, Lib. 9, Ind. 1.
Havant............Ind. 16, Lib. 10, C. 8, Lab. 8.
Hereford..........Lab. 10, Lib. 8, Ind. 6.
Hertsmere.........C. 25, Lab. 17, Lib. 13.
High Peak.........C. 23, Lab. 11, Ind. 10, Lib. 2.
Hinckley and Bos-
  worth..........Lab. 14, Ind. 8, Lib. 8, C. 4.
Holderness........Ind. 29.
Horsham...........Ind. 23, C. 18, Lib. 2.
Hove..............C. 24, Lab. 6, Ind. 3.
Huntingdon........Ind. 26, C. 15, Lab. 9.
Hyndburn..........Lab. 24, C. 21, Lib. 3.
Ipswich...........Lab. 36, C. 11.
Kennet............Ind. 28, C. 7, Lib. 2.
Kerrier...........Ind. 34, C. 5, Lab. 3.
Kettering.........Lab. 16, C. 14, Ind. 8, Lib. 7.
Kingston upon Hull.Lab. 55, C. 8.
Kingswood.........Lab. 19, Ind. 16, Lib. 6, C. 4.
Lancaster.........C. 32, Lab. 18, Ind. 9, Lib. 1.
Langbaurgh........Lab. 32, C. 27, Ind. 5.
Leicester.........Lab. 37, C. 11.
Leominster........Ind. 33, Lab. 2, C. 1.
Lewes.............C. 26, Ind. 11, Lab. 10.
Lichfield.........Lab. 25, C. 17, Ind. 14.
Lincoln...........D.Lab. 20, C. 6, Ind. 3, Lab. 1.
Luton.............Lab. 30, C. 12, Lib. 6.
Macclesfield......C. 25, Ind. 17, Lab. 10, Lib. 10.
Maidstone.........Lib. 19, Ind. 16, C. 13, Lab. 12.
Maldon............Ind. 14, C. 9, Lab. 4, Lib. 3.
Malvern Hills.....Ind. 31, Lib. 11, C. 3, Lab. 2.
Mansfield.........Lab. 38, C. 7.
Medina............Ind. 16, Lab. 10, Lib. 4, C. 3.
Medway............Lab. 32, C. 22, Ind. 5.
Melton............C. 12, Ind. 10, Lab. 2.
Mendip............Ind. 23, C. 11, Lab. 7, Lib. 2.
Mid Bedfordshire..Ind. 35, Lab. 8, C. 5, Lib. 1.
Middlesbrough.....Lab. 39, C. 17.
Mid Suffolk.......Ind. 24, Lab. 9, C. 6, Lib. 1.
Mid Sussex........C. 25, Ind. 21, Lib. 5, Lab. 3.
Milton Keynes.....Lab. 27, C. 8, Ind. 5.
Mole Valley.......Ind. 18, C. 16, Lib. 5, Lab. 2.
Newark............Lab. 29, C. 20, Ind. 3.
Newbury...........Lib. 24, Ind. 22, C. 10, Lab. 1.
Newcastle under
  Lyme...........Lab. 31, C. and Ind. 29, Lib. 2.
New Forest........Ind. 40, C. 12, Lib. 7.
Northampton.......Lab. 25, C. 23.
Northavon.........C. 26, Lab. 19, Ind. 6, Lib. 1.
North Cornwall....Ind. 38, Lib. 3.
North Devon.......Ind. 28, Lib. 15, Lab. 1.
North Dorset......Ind. 27, Lib. 4.
North-East Derby-
  shire..........Lab. 32, C. 10, Ind. 9.
Nth. Hertfordshire..C. 23, Lab. 17, Ind. 8.
North Kesteven....Ind. 27, C. 8, Lab. 2.
North Norfolk.....Ind. 37, C. 6, Lab. 4.
North Shropshire..Ind. 36, Lab. 2, Lab. 1.
Nth. Warwickshire.Lab. 19, C. 8, Ind. 6.
North West
  Leicestershire..Lab. 25, Ind. 10, C. 8.
North Wiltshire...C. 24, Ind. 11, Lib. 7, Lab. 4.
North Wolds......Ind. 40, Lab. 2, Lib. 1.
Norwich...........Lab. 37, C. 11.
Nottingham........Lab. 44, C. 10.
Nuneaton..........Lab. 26, C. 7, Lib. 2.
Oadby and Wigston.C. 18, Lib. 7, Lab. 5.

Oswestry..........Ind. 25, Lib. 3, Lab. 3.
Oxford............Lab. 30, C. 12, Lib. 3.
Pendle............Lib. 23, Lab. 19, C. 6, Ind. 3.
Penwith...........Ind. 38, Lab. 1, Lib. 1.
Peterborough......Lab. 28, C. 19, Lib. 1.
Plymouth..........C. 37, Lab. 29.
Poole.............C. 22, Lib. 9, Lab. 3, Ind. 2.
Portsmouth........C. 28, Lab. 17, Ind. 3.
Preston...........Lab. 38, C. 19.
Purbeck...........Ind. 13, C. 5, Lab. 3.
Reading...........Lab. 16, C. 16, Lib. 14.
Redditch..........Lab. 19, C. 6.
Reigate & Banstead.C. 29, Lab. 15, Lib. 4.
Restormel.........Ind. 36, Lib. 2.
Ribble Valley.....C. 30, Ind. 7, Lab. 1.
Richmondshire.....Ind. 35.
Rochford..........C. 19. Lab. 12, Ind. 8, Lib. 1.
Rossendale........C. 17, Lab. 15, Lib. 4.
Rother............Ind. 30, C. 9, Lab. 5, Lib 1.
Rugby.............C. 22, Lab. 18, Ind. 8, Lib. 3.
Runnymede.........C. 23, Lab. 15. Ind. 2.
Rushcliffe........C. 42, Ind. 4, Lab. 3.
Rushmoor..........C. 20, Lab. 9, Ind. 7, Lib. 7.
Rutland...........Ind. 20.
Ryedale...........Ind. 40, Lab. 5.
St. Albans........C. 32, Lab. 14, Lib. 7, Ind. 1.
St. Edmundsbury...C. 26, Lab. 11, Ind. 7.
Salisbury.........Ind. 19, C. 16, Lab. 13, Lib. 8.
Scarborough.......Ind. 16, C. 15, Lib. 11, Lab. 5.
Scunthorpe........Lab. 35, C. 4, Ind. 1.
Sedgefield........Lab. 40, Ind. 8, Lib. 4, C. 1.
Sedgemoor.........C. 19, Lab. 14, Ind. 12, Lib. 3.
Sevenoaks.........C. 28, Ind. 14, Lab. 6, Lib. 6.
Selby.............Ind. 24, C. 16, Lab. 7.
Shepway...........C. 33, Lab. 12, Ind. 8, Lib. 1.
Shrewsbury........Lab. 15, C. 12, Ind. 11, Lib. 7.
Slough............Lab. 34, Lib. 4, C. 2.
Southampton.......Lab. 31, C. 20.
South Bedfordshire.C. 17, Lab. 13, Lib. 8, Ind. 7.
South Cambridge-
  shire..........Ind. 43, Lab. 7, Lib. 3.
South Derbyshire..Ind. 16, Lab. 15, C. 4.
Southend..........C. 24, Lab. 13, Lib. 11.
South Hams........Ind. 40, C. 2.
South Herefordshire.Ind. 35, C. 1.
South Holland.....Ind. 27, C. 6, Lab. 2.
South Kesteven....Ind. 30, C. 13, Lab. 12.
South Lakeland....Ind. 38, C. 7, Lib. 7, Lab. 2.
South Norfolk.....Ind. 33, Lab. 7, C. 6, Lib. 1.
South Northants...Ind. 17, C. 15, Lab. 2, Lib. 1.
South Oxfordshire..C. 25, Ind. 21, Lab. 9, Lib. 7.
South Ribble......C. 30, Lab. 16, Lib. 2, Ind. 1.
South Shropshire..Ind. 35, Lib. 1.
South Staffordshire.C. 22, Ind. 17, Lab. 8, Lib. 1.
South Wight.......Ind. 22, C. 1, Lib. 1.
Spelthorne........C. 39, Lab. 13.
Stafford..........Ind. 24, C. 18, Lab. 15.
Staffordshire
  Moorlands......Ind. 26, Lab. 14, C. 12, Lib. 2.
Stevenage.........Lab. 31, C. 3.
Stockton-on-Tees..Lab. 33, C. 25, Ind. 2.
Stoke-on-Trent....Lab. 60, C. 8, Lib. 3, Ind. 1.
Stratford on Avon.Ind. 32, C. 15, Lib. 5, Lab. 2.
Stroud............Ind. 19, C. 14, Lab. 12, Lib. 8.
Suffolk Coastal...C. 27, Ind. 19, Lab. 9.
Surrey Heath......C. 35, Ind. 1.
Swale.............Lab. 25, C. 17, Ind. 5, Lib. 3.
Tamworth..........Lab. 18, Ind. 6.
Tandridge.........C. 26, Lib. 10, Ind. 3, Lab. 1.
Taunton Deane.....C. 21, Lab. 14, Ind. 13.
Teesdale..........Ind. 29.
Teignbridge.......Ind. 49, Lab. 7, Lib. 1.
Tendring..........C. 31, Ind. 14, Lab. 11, Lib. 4.
Test Valley.......Ind. 21, C. 10, Lib. 7, Lab. 5.
Tewkesbury........Ind. 26, C. 22, Lib. 3.
Thamesdown........Lab. 26, C. 18, Ind. 2.
Thanet............C. 33, Lab. 14, Ind. 11, Lib. 5.

Three Rivers.......*C.* 19, *Lib.* 13, *Lab.* 12.
Thurrock..........*Lab.* 33, *C.* 3, *Ind.* 3.
Tiverton..........*Ind.* 32, *Lib.* 5, *Lab.* 3.
Tonbridge and
  Malling......*C.* 30, *Lab.* 11, *Lib.* 8, *Ind.* 4.
Torbay...........*C.* 30, *Lab.* 6.
Torridge..........*Ind.* 29, *Lib.* 6, *Lab.* 1.
Tunbridge Wells...*C.* 29, *Ind.* 9, *Lab.* 7, *Lib.* 2.
Tynedale.........*Ind.* 28, *Lab.* 10, *C.* 4, *Lib.* 3.
Uttlesford........*C.* 21, *Ind.* 12, *Lab.* 7, *Lib.* 2.
Vale of White Horse *C.* 27, *Ind.* 10, *Lab.* 8, *Lib.* 3.
Vale Royal.......*Ind.* 25, *Lab.* 16, *C.* 10, *Lib.* 6.
Wansbeck.........*Lab.* 44, *Ind.* 1.
Wansdyke.........*Lab.* 22, *C.* 12, *Ind.* 11.
Warrington........*C.* 32, *Lab.* 22, *Ind.* 3, *Lib.* 3.
Warwick..........*C.* 26, *Lab.* 25, *Lib.* 7.
Watford..........*Lab.* 21, *C.* 9, *Lib.* 6.
Waveney..........*Lab.* 27, *C.* 22, *Lib.* 5, *Ind.* 3.
Waverley.........*Lib.* 25, *C.* 24, *Ind.* 10, *Lab.* 2.
Wealdon..........*Ind.* 28, *C.* 25, *Lib.* 2, *Lab.* 1.
Wear Valley......*Lab.* 21, *Ind.* 11, *Lib.* 9.
Wellingborough....*C.* 14, *Lab.* 13, *Ind.* 6.
Welwyn Hatfield...*Lab.* 24, *C.* 19.
West Derbyshire...*C.* 18, *Ind.* 13, *Lab.* 5, *Lib.* 4.
West Devon.......*Ind.* 30.

West Dorset.......*Ind.* 44, *Lib.* 9, *Lab.* 2.
West Lancashire....*Lab.* 23, *Ind.* 14, *C.* 10, *Lib.* 5.
West Lindsey......*Ind.* 25, *Lib.* 6, *Lab.* 5, *C.* 1.
West Norfolk.....*Ind.* 24, *Lab.* 22, *C.* 14.
West Oxfordshire...*Ind.* 36, *Lab.* 7, *C.* 1, *Lib.* 1.
West Somerset.....*Ind.* 27, *C.* 3, *Lab.* 1, *Lib.* 1.
West Wiltshire.....*Ind.* 17, *C.* 13, *Lab.* 10, *Lib.* 2.
Weymouth and
  Portland......*Lab.* 21, *C.* 18.
Wimborne.........*Ind.* 21, *Lib.* 9, *C.* 2.
Winchester........*Ind.* 27, *C.* 14, *Lab.* 5, *Lib.* 5.
Windsor and
  Maidenhead......*C.* 53, *Ind.* 3, *Lab.* 3.
Woking...........*C.* 19, *Lab.* 12, *Lib.* 1.
Wokingham........*C.* 23, *Ind.* 16, *Lib.* 3.
Woodspring........*C.* 40, *Lab.* 10, *Ind.* 8, *Lib.* 3.
Worcester.........*C.* 18, *Lab.* 18.
Worthing.........*C.* 17, *Ind.* 12, *Lab.* 1.
Wrekin............*Lab.* 32, *Ind.* 15, *C.* 8.
Wychavon.........*Ind.* 29, *C.* 10, *Lab.* 4, *Lib.* 2.
Wycombe.........*C.* 30, *Ind.* 14, *Lab.* 12, *Lib.* 3.
Wyre.............*C.* 45, *Ind.* 8, *Lab.* 2.
Wyre Forest......*Lab.* 20, *C.* 13, *Lib.* 9, *Ind.* 3.
Yeovil............*Ind.* 30, *C.* 20, *Lab.* 8, *Lib.* 2.
York.............*C.* 17, *Lab.* 17, *Lib.* 5.

WALES
County Councils

Clwyd...........*Ind.* 30, *Lab.* 20, *C.* 11, *Lib.* 4.
Dyfed..........*Ind.* 41, *Lab.* 29, *Lib.* 8, *P.C.* 1.
Gwent..........*Lab.* 59, *C.* 12, *Ind.* 3, *Lib.* 3, *P.C.* 1.
Gwynedd.........*Ind.* 56, *P.C.* 6, *Lab.* 4.

Mid Glamorgan....*Lab.* 63, *P.C.* 9, *Ind.* 6, *C.* 3, *Comm.* 2, *Lib.* 2.
Powys..........*Ind.* 44, *Lab.* 7, *Lib.* 2.
South Glamorgan...*Lab.* 42, *C.* 35, *Ind.* 3.
West Glamorgan....*Lab.* 52, *C.* 9, *Ind.* 6, *Lib.* 2, *P.C.* 1.

District Councils

Aberconwy........*Ind.* 34, *C.* 4, *Lab.* 3.
Afan............*Lab.* 21, *Ind.* 9.
Alyn and Deeside...*Lab.* 25, *C.* 9, *Ind.* 7, *Lib.* 4.
Arfon..........*Ind.* 27, *Lab.* 8, *P.C.* 5.
Blaenau Gwent.....*Lab.* 31, *Ind.* 13, *Lib.* 3, *P.C.* 3.
Brecknock........*Ind.* 29, *Lab.* 17, *C.* 4, *Lib.* 1.
Cardiff...........*Lab.* 42, *C.* 33.
Carmarthen.......*Ind.* 29, *Lab.* 7.
Ceredigion........*Ind.* 30, *Lib.* 9, *Lab.* 4.
Colwyn..........*Ind.* 22, *Lib.* 10, *C.* 1.
Cynon Valley.....*Lab.* 23, *P.C.* 12, *Ind.* 3.
Delyn...........*Ind.* 26, *Lab.* 11, *P.C.* 2, *C.* 1.
Dinefwr.........*Lab.* 17, *Ind.* 14, *Lib.* 1.
Dwyfor.........*Ind.*, 28, *P.C.* 1.
Glyndwr.........*Ind.* 30, *Lab.* 3.
Islwyn...........*Lab.* 30, *Ind.* 3, *P.C.* 2, *Comm.* 1.
Llanelli..........*Lab.* 29, *Ind.* 4.
Lliw Valley.......*Lab.* 27, *Ind.* 3, *P.C.* 2.
Meirionnydd......*Ind.* 39.
Merthyr Tydfil.....*Lab.* 25, *Ind.* 4, *P.C.* 4.

Monmouth........*C.* 29, *Lab.* 9, *Ind.* 1.
Montgomery.......*Ind.* 44, *Lib.* 3, *Lab.* 2.
Neath............*Lab.* 24, *Ind.* 3, *P.C.* 2.
Newport..........*Lab.* 36, *C.* 8, *Ind.* 5, *Lib.* 2.
Ogwr............*Lab.* 42, *Ind.* 7, *C.* 6, *Lib.* 1, *P.C.* 1.
Preseli............*Ind.* 43.
Radnor............*Ind.* 31.
Rhondda...........*Lab.* 30, *Ind.* 1, *P.C.* 1, *Comm.* 1.
Rhuddlan.........*Ind.* 22, *C.* 9, *Lab.* 4, *Lib.* 1.
Rhymney Valley...*Lab.* 38, *Ind.* 6, *P.C.* 4.
Sth. Pembrokeshire.*Ind.* 30, *P.C.* 1.
Swansea..........*Lab.* 30, *C.* 12, *Ind.* 8, *Lib.* 1.
Taff-Ely..........*Lab.* 30, *Ind.* 12, *Lib.* 4, *P.C.* 2.
Torfaen..........*Lab.* 36, *Ind.* 5, *Comm.* 2.
Vale of Glamorgan..*Lab.* 23, *C.* 15, *Ind.* 11.
Wrexham Maelor...*Lab.* 24, *Ind.* 14, *C.* 14, *Lib.* 2, *P.C.* 1.
Ynys Môn.........*Ind.* 41, *Lab.* 4.

GREATER LONDON BOROUGHS

The figures given in the press for Party Representation in the Greater London Boroughs after the elections of May, 1974, were as follows:

Barking...........*Lab.* 45, *Ind.* 4.
Barnet............*C.* 46, *Lab.* 18, *Ind.* 1.
Bexley...........*C.* 37, *Lab.* 27.
Brent.............*Lab.* 40, *C.* 25.
Bromley..........*C.* 47, *Lab.* 16, *Lib.* 2.
Camden..........*Lab.* 53, *C.* 12.
Croydon..........*C.* 43, *Lab.* 19, *Ind.* 5.
Ealing...........*Lab.* 41, *C.* 24.
Enfield...........*C.* 35, *Lab.* 29, *Lib.* 1.
Greenwich.........*Lab.* 57, *C.* 8.
Hackney.........*Lab.* 65.
Hammersmith.....*Lab.* 53, *C.* 10, *Lib.* 2.
Haringey.........*Lab.* 45, *C.* 19, *Ind.* 1.
Harrow...........*C.* 39, *Lab.* 14, *Ind.* 3.
Havering.........*Lab.* 31, *C.* 20, *Ind.* 9.
Hillingdon........*Lab.* 32, *C.* 28.
Hounslow.........*Lab.* 42, *C.* 23.

Islington...........*Lab.* 65.
Kensington and
  Chelsea.......*C.* 48, *Lab.* 18.
Kingston..........*C.* 44, *Lab.* 15, *Lib.* 6.
Lambeth..........*Lab.* 51, *C.* 14.
Lewisham........*C.* 29, *Lab.* 27, *Ind.* 3.
Merton...........*C.* 29, *Lab.* 27, *Ind.* 3.
Newham.........*Lab.* 56, *Ind.* 9.
Redbridge.........*C.* 49, *Lab.* 16.
Richmond........*C.* 41, *Lib.* 10, *Lab.* 8.
Southwark........*Lab.* 61, *C.* 4.
Sutton...........*C.* 30, *Lab.* 15, *Lib.* 6.
Tower Hamlets....*Lab.* 65.
Waltham Forest....*Lab.* 40, *C.* 12.
Wandsworth......*Lab.* 53, *C.* 12.
Westminster.......*C.* 39, *Lab.* 26.

AERODROMES AND AIRPORTS

There are 170 aerodromes in Great Britain, Northern Ireland, the Isle of Man and the Channel Islands which are either State owned, operated by the Civil Aviation Authority or licensed for use by civil aircraft. A number of unlicensed airfields not included in this list are also available for private use by permission of the owner or controlling authority.

S=Aerodrome owned and operated by the State.
CAA=Aerodrome operated by the Civil Aviation Authority.
BAA=Aerodrome operated by the British Airports Authority.
M=Aerodrome owned or operated by Municipal Authority.
J=Military airfield available for civil use by prior permission.
H=Licensed helicopter station.

Those aerodromes which are designated as Customs airports are printed in bold type. Customs facilities are available at certain other aerodromes by special arrangement.

ENGLAND AND WALES (124)

Abingdon, Oxon. J
Andover, Hants. J
Barrow (Walney Island), Cumbria.
Bembridge, I.O.W.
Benson, Oxon. J
Bicester, Oxon. J
Biggin Hill, Kent.
Binbrook, Lincolnshire. J
Birmingham, W. Midlands. M
Bitteswell, Warwicks.
Blackbushe, Hants.
Blackpool, Lancs. M
Bournemouth (Hurn), Dorset. M
Bristol (Lulsgate). M
Cambridge.
Carlisle, Cumbria.
Chichester (Goodwood), Sussex.
Church Fenton, Yorks. J
Clacton, Essex.
Colerne, Wilts. J
Coltishall, Norfolk. J
Compton Abbas, Dorsetshire.
Coventry, W. Midlands. M
Cranfield, Beds.
Cranwell, Lincs. J
Culdrose, Cornwall. J
Denham, Bucks.
Dishforth, Yorks. J
Doncaster, Yorks.
Dunkeswell, Devon.
Duxford, Cambs.
East Midlands, Leics. M
Elstree, Herts.
Elvington, Yorks. J
Exeter, Devon.
Fair Oaks, Surrey.
Finningley, Yorks. J
Glamorgan (Rhoose). M
Gloucester/Cheltenham (Staverton). M
Great Yarmouth (North Denes), Norfolk.
Grindale Field, Humberside.
Halfpenny Green, Staffs.
Hamble, Hants.
Hatfield, Herts.
Haverfordwest, Dyfed.
Hawarden, Clwyd.
Holbeach (St. John's), Lincs.
Hucknall, Notts.
Humberside, M.
Ipswich, Suffolk.
Kemble, Glos. J
Land's End (St. Just).
Lashenden, Headcorn, Kent.
Leavesden, Herts.
Leconfield, Humberside. J
Leeds and Bradford, Yorks. M
Leeming, Yorks. J
Lee-on-Solent, Hants. J
Leicester East, Leics.

Linton-on-Ouse, Yorks. J
Little Rissington, Gloucs. J
Liverpool, Lancs. M
London (Gatwick). BAA
London (Heathrow). BAA
London (Westland Heliport). H
Luton, Beds. M
Lydd, Kent.
Lyneham, Wilts. J
Manchester. M
Manchester (Barton).
Manston, Kent. J
Nether Thorpe, S. Yorks.
Newcastle, Northumberland. M
Newton, Notts. J
Northampton (Sywell), Northants.
Northolt, Mddx. J
Norwich, Norfolk. M
Nottingham, Notts.
Odiham, Hants. J
Oxford (Kidlington), Oxfordshire.
Paull, Humberside
Penzance Heliport, Cornwall. H
Peterborough (Sibson), Cambs.
Plymouth (Roborough), Devon.
Portland Air Station, Dorset. JH
Redhill, Surrey
Rochester, Kent.
St. Mawgan, Cornwall. J
Scilly Isles (St. Mary's).
Seething, Norfolk.
Shawbury, Salop. J
Sherburn-in-Elmet, Yorks.
Shobdon, Herefordshire.
Shoreham, Sussex. M
Skegness (Ingoldmells), Lincs.
Sleap, Salop.
Southampton, Hants.
Southampton Heliport. H
Southend, Essex. M
Southport (Birkdale Sands), Merseyside. M
Stansted, Essex. BAA
Stapleford Tawney, Essex.
Sunderland, Co. Durham. M
Swansea, Glam. M
Teesside, Co. Durham. M
Tern Hill, Salop. J
Thorney Island, West Sussex. J
Thruxton, Hants.
Topcliffe, Yorks. J
Valley, Anglesey. J
Waddington, Lincs. J
Warton, Lancs.
Wattisham, Suffolk. J
Weston-super-Mare, Avon.
West Raynham, Norfolk. J
White Waltham, Berks.
Wickenby, Lincs.
Wittering, Cambs. J

Woodford, Gtr. Manchester.
Woodvale, Merseyside. J
Wroughton, Wilts. J
Wycombe Air Park (Booker) Bucks.
Yeovil, Somerset.
Yeovilton, Somerset. J

SCOTLAND (37)

Aberdeen (Dyce). BAA
Barra, Hebrides.
Benbecula, Hebrides. CAA
Coll, Inner Hebrides. M
Dornoch. M
Dounreay (Thurso).
Dundee (Riverside Park), Angus. M
Eday. M
Edinburgh. BAA
Fetlar, Shetlands
Glasgow. M
Glenforsa (Mull). M
Glenrothes. M
Hoy, Orkneys. M
Inverness (Dalcross). CAA
Islay (Port Ellen). CAA
Isle of Skye. M
Kinloss. J
Kirkwall. CAA
Lerwick Tingwall, Shetland.
Leuchars. J
Lossiemouth. J
Machrihanish, Kintyre. J Argyll.
North Ronaldsay, Orkneys. M
Papa Westray, Orkneys. M
Perth (Scone).
Prestwick. BAA
Sanday, Orkneys. M
Stornoway, Hebrides. CAA
Stronsay, Orkneys. M
Sumburgh, Shetlands. CAA
Tiree. CAA
Unst. M
Westray, Orkneys. M
Whalsay, Shetlands. M
Wick. CAA

NORTHERN IRELAND (5)

Belfast (Aldergrove). S
Belfast (Harbour).
Enniskillen (St. Angelo). M
Londonderry (Eglington).
Newtownards.

ISLE OF MAN (1)

Ronaldsway.

CHANNEL ISLANDS (3)

Alderney. S
Guernsey. S
Jersey. S

ENGLAND AND WALES

THE PRINCIPALITY OF WALES

Position and extent.—Wales occupies the extreme west of the central southern portion of the island of Great Britain, with a total area of 8,017 sq. miles (5,130,880 acres); it is bounded on the N. by the Irish Sea, on the S. by the Bristol Channel, on the E. by the English counties of Cheshire, Salop, Hereford and Worcester and Gloucester, and on the W. by St. George's Channel. Across the Menai Straits is the Welsh island of *Anglesey* or Ynys Môn (276 sq. miles), communication with which is facilitated by the Menai Suspension Bridge (1,000 ft. long), built by Telford in 1826 (freed from toll as from Jan. 1, 1941) and by the tubular railway bridge (1,100 ft. long) of the former L.M. & S. Railway, built by Stephenson in 1850. Holyheadharbour, on Holy Isle (N.W. of Anglesey), provides accommodation for a fast steam packet service to Dun Laoghaire and Dublin (70 miles).

Population.—The population at the Census of 1971 was 2,723,596 (preliminary figures), compared with 2,644,023 at the 1961 Census.

Relief.—Wales is mostly mountainous, the chief systems being those of North Wales (Snowdon 3,560 ft., Carnedd Llywelyn 3,484 ft., Carnedd Dafydd 3,426 ft.); Berwyn (Aran-mawddwy 2,970 ft.); Powys (Plinlimmon 2,468 ft., Drygan Fawr 2,115 ft., Radnor 2,163 ft.); and the Black Mountain, Brecknock Beacons and Black Forest ranges (Carmarthen Van 2,632 ft., Brecon Beacon 2,906 ft., Pen-y-gader fawr 2,660 ft.).

Hydrography.—The principal river of those rising in Wales is the *Severn* (*see* England), which flows from the slopes of Plinlimmon to the English border. The *Wye* (130 miles) also rises in the slopes of Plinlimmon. The *Usk* (56 miles) flows into the Bristol Channel, through Gwent. The *Dee* (70 miles) rises in Bala Lake and flows through the Vale of Llangollen, where an aqueduct (built by Telford in 1805) carries the Pontcysyllte branch of the Shropshire Union Canal across the valley. The estuary of the Dee is the navigable portion, 14 miles in length and about 5 miles in breadth, and the tide rushes in with dangerous speed over the " Sands of Dee". The *Towy* (68 miles), *Teifi* (50 miles), *Taff* (40 miles), *Dovey* (30 miles), *Taf* (25 miles), and *Conway* (24 miles), the last named broad and navigable, are wholly Welsh rivers.

The largest natural lake in Wales is *Bala* (Llyn Tegid) in Gwynedd, 4 miles long and about 1 mile wide; *Lake Vyrnwy* is an artificial reservoir, about the size of Bala, and forms the water supply of Liverpool, and Birmingham is supplied from a chain of reservoirs in the Elan and Clærwen valleys.

The Welsh Language.—Statistics published on Oct. 1, 1973, show that only 542,400 persons (of three years and over) in Wales were able to speak Welsh at the time of the 1971 Census, compared with 656,000 at the 1961 Census and 715,000 at the 1951 Census. One per cent. of the population could speak Welsh only, compared with 4 per cent. in 1931. The proportion of people speaking Welsh fell from 28·9 per cent. in 1951 to 20·8 per cent. in 1971. As in 1961, the Western Counties (75·9 per cent.), had the highest proportion of Welsh speakers.

Flag.—A red dragon on a green and white field (per fess argent and vert a dragon passant gules). The flag was augmented in 1953 by a royal badge on a shield encircled with a riband bearing the words *Ddraig Goch Ddyry Cychwyn* and imperially crowned. Only the unaugmented flag is flown on Government offices in Wales and, where appropriate, in London. Both flags continue to be used elsewhere.

EARLY HISTORY

Celts and Romans.—The earliest inhabitants of whom there is any record appear to have been subdued or exterminated by the *Goidels* (a people of Celtic race) in the Bronze Age, and a further invasion of Celtic *Brythons* and *Belgae* followed in the ensuing Iron Age. The *Roman* conquest of South Britain and Wales was for some time successfully opposed by *Caratacus* (Caractacus or Caradog), Chieftain of the Catuvellauni and son of *Cunobelinus* (Cymbeline) King of the Trinobantes. In A.D. 78 the conquest of Wales was completed under Julius Frontinus, and communications were opened up by the construction of military roads from Chester to Caerleon-on-Usk and Caerwent, and from Chester to Conway (and thence to Carmarthen and Neath). *Christianity* was introduced (during the Roman occupation) in the 4th century.

The Anglo-Saxon Attacks.—The Anglo-Saxon invaders of South Britain drove the Celtic Goidels and Brythons into the mountain fastnesses of Wales, and into Strathclyde (Cumberland and S.W. Scotland) and Cornwall giving them the name of *Waelisc*, or Welsh (=Foreign). The West Saxons' victory of Deorham (577) isolated Wales from Cornwall and the battle of Chester (613) cut off communication with Strathclyde. In the 8th century the boundaries of the Welsh were further restricted by the annexations of Offa, King of Mercia, and counter-attacks were largely prevented by the construction of an artificial boundary from the Dee to the Wye (Offa's Dike). In the 9th century Rhodri Mawr united the country against further incursions of the Saxons by land and against the raids of Norse and Danish pirates by sea, but at his death his three provinces of *Gwynedd* (N.), *Powys* (Mid.) and *Dehenbarth* (S.) were divided among his three sons—Anarawd, Mervyn and Cadell—the son of the last named being Howel Dda—who codified the laws of the country, while Llewelyn ap Sitsyhlt (husband of the heiress of Gwynedd) again united the provinces and reigned as Prince from 1018 to 1023.

The Norman Conquest.—After the Norman conquest of England, William I created Palatine counties along the Welsh frontier, and Robert FitzHamon, the Norman Earl of Gloucester, raided South Wales and erected fortresses from the Wye to Milford Haven. Henry I introduced Flemish settlers into South Wales, but after his death the Welsh rose under the leadership of Griffith ap Rhys and routed the Norman-Flemish forces at the fords of the Teifi (Cardigan) in 1136. From the early years of the 13th century the house of Gwynedd, in the north, gained an ascendancy over the whole of Wales, and Llewelyn ap Iorwerth was in constant strife with England for recognition as an independent sovereign. Llywelyn ap Gruffydd (grandson of Llywelyn ap Iorwerth), the last native prince, was killed in 1282 during hostilities between the Welsh and English. On Feb. 7, 1301, Edward of Caernarvon, son of Edward I, was created *Prince of Wales*.

The Welsh are a distinct nationality, with a language and literature of their own, and the national bardic festival (Eisteddfod), instituted by Prince Rhys ap Griffith in 1176, is annually maintained. These *Eisteddfodau* (sessions) form part of the *Gorsedd* (assembly), which is believed to date from the time of Prydian, a ruling prince in an age many centuries before the Christian era.

AREA AND POPULATION OF THE WELSH COUNTIES

County	Administrative Headquarters	Acreage	Population Reg. Gen.'s Est.	Rateable Value 1975
				£
Clwyd............	Shire Hall, Mold	599,481	373,300	35,567,642
Dyfed............	*Carmarthen	1,424,668	320,100	27,390,234
Gwent............	*Cwmbran	339,933	440,500	41,517,966
Gwynedd..........	County Offices, Caernarvon	955,244	223,500	19,617,257
Mid Glamorgan....	*Cathays Park, Cardiff	251,732	542,000	33,970,225
Powys............	*Llandrindod Wells	1,254,656	100,200	7,429,057
South Glamorgan...	Newport Rd., Cardiff	102,807	391,100	45,055,132
West Glamorgan....	Guildhall, Swansea	201,476	371,400	35,309,729

*County Hall

MUNICIPAL DIRECTORY OF WALES

District Councils

Those accorded CITY Status are shown in SMALL CAPITALS; those with
Borough Status are distinguished by having § prefixed.

District	Population (Reg. Gen's Estimate)	Rateable Value 1975 £	Average Rate Levied p.	Chief Executive	Chairman 1975–76 (a) Mayor (b) Lord Mayor
§Aberconwy, Gwynedd	50,100	4,843,288	97	J. P. Hughes	(a) K. F. W. Lee
§Afan, West Glamorgan............	58,578	8,777,900	111–116·2	W. E. Griffiths	(a) E. Owen
Alyn and Deeside, Clwyd..........	69,700	8,325,874	73·2	F. N. V. Meredith	E. G. Hett
§Arfon, Gwynedd.................	53,640	3,665,416	—	D. L. Jones	(a) Mrs. M. E. Hughes
Blaenau Gwent, Gwent............	83,900	6,009,093	97·45	R. Leadbeter	E. Hughes
§Brecknock, Powys...............	39,982	2,805,391	77·1	D. H. Hughes, O.B.E.	(a) F. E. Price
CARDIFF, South Glamorgan.........	284,700	34,322,706	77·3	H. Mansfield	(b) Sir Charles Stuart Hallinan, C.B.E.
Carmarthen, Dyfed................	50,100	3,543,410	87·1	J. Thomas	W. D. Evans
Ceredigion, Dyfed................	57,200	4,198,169	74·7	J. K. Harris	Mrs. C. P. Baston
§Colwyn, Clwyd.................	46,300	4,570,997	72·8	G. Edwards, M.B.E.	(a) W. H. Smith
§Cynon Valley, Mid Glamorgan.....	69,660	4,147,828	90·8	C. W. Hosgood	(a) C. Edwards, M.B.E.
§Delyn, Clwyd	61,100	4,999,998	92·5	G. A. McCartney	(a) Mrs. E. M. C. Davies, O.B.E.
§Dinefwr, Dyfed.................	36,700	1,960,618	60·2	E. W. Harries	(a) T. C. Bevan
Dwyfor, Gwynedd................	26,300	2,087,105	92·62	E. Davies	R. Edgar-Jones
Glyndwr, Clwyd.................	38,550	2,942,794	89·52	W. T. Williams	E. R. Davies
§Islwyn, Gwent	66,100	3,774,844	75·5	J. F. Rogers	A. J. F. Rosser
§Llanelli, Dyfed.................	76,800	6,007,049	74·7	A. B. Thomas	(a) C. McLoughlin
§Lliw Valley, West Glamorgan.......	57,800	4,164,544	59·6–95·6	J. C. Howells	(a) H. G. Williams
Meirionydd, Gwynedd.............	30,500	3,093,238	81	E. J. Lloyd-Jones	D. J. Williams
Merthyr Tydfil, Mid Glamorgan......	61,500	3,857,878	91·83	S. Jones	(a) J. Handley
Monmouth, Gwent................	66,090	5,707,193	79–89	G. Cummings	K. C. Lewis
Montgomery, Powys..............	43,900	3,105,031	74·2	I. W. Williams	J. E. Jones
§Neath, West Glamorgan..........	65,200	6,304,407	92·86	I. H. K. Thorne	(a) M. R. Jeffreys
Newport, Gwent.................	134,700	18,610,663	90·7	J. R. Long	(a) R. K. Williams
§Ogwr, Mid Glamorgan...........	128,100	8,876,617	94·4–106	M. Matthews	(a) Mrs. M. Williams
Preseli, Dyfed..................	61,000	6,114,069	—	G. E. Jenkins, M.B.E.	V. J. Lewis
Radnor, Powys..................	19,000	1,757,958	75·9–84·9	W. E. Price	T. E. Ford
§Rhondda, Mid Glamorgan.........	87,100	3,648,406	103·2	G. Evans	W. D. Jones
§Rhuddlan, Clwyd...............	50,000	5,340,012	84·5–92·7	F. J. K. Davies	(a) A. J. Price
Rhymney Valley, Mid Glamorgan....	102,000	6,188,746	—	—	—
South Pembrokeshire, Dyfed........	37,600	5,586,416	81·8	P. F. Klee	T. Griffiths
SWANSEA, West Glamorgan........	189,800	16,629,650	90	A. N. F. Rees	(a) H. T. Morgan
§Taff-Ely, Mid Glamorgan..........	83,038	7,145,360	90	G. Hockin	J. C. Anzani
§Torfaen, Gwent.................	89,100	7,309,035	85·7–91·6	M. B. Mehta	(a) Mrs. M. L. Lee, M.B.E.
§Vale of Glamorgan, South Glamorgan	106,490	10,252,925	87·5	J. C. Colley	(a) J. D. Hinds
§Wrexham Maelor, Clwyd..........	107,200	9,367,867	53·4	T. L. Williams, O.B.E.	(a) Mrs. A. McConville
§Ynys Môn (Isle of Anglesey), Gwynedd......................	63,200	5,928,210	96·3	P. Lloyd	(a) J. G. Jones

LORDS LIEUTENANT, HIGH SHERIFFS AND CHAIRMEN OF COUNTY COUNCILS

County	Lord Lieutenant	High Sheriff (1975–76)	Chairman of C.C.
(1) Clwyd	Brig. H. S. K. Mainwaring, C.B., C.B.E., D.S.O., T.D.	J. W. Bankes	J. O. Davies
(2) Dyfed	Col. The Hon R. H. Philipps, M.B.E.	D. B. Llewellyn-Morgan	H. H. Roberts
(3) Gwent	Col. E. R. Hill, D.S.O.	C. F. Griffin	D. J. Williams
(4) Gwynedd	Sir R. H. D. Williams-Bulkeley, Bt.	R. S. Lloyd, M.B.E.	T. Jones
(5) Mid Glamorgan	Col. Sir Cennydd Traherne, K.G., T.D.	Sir Leslie Joseph	W. J. Kedward, O.B.E.
(6) Powys	Col. J. L. Corbett-Winder, O.B.E., M.C.	Maj. E. A. T. Bonnor-Maurice	The Lord Watkins
(7) South Glamorgan	} as Mid-Glamorgan	A. S. Martyn	Mrs. E. J. Davies
(8) West Glamorgan		C. G. Bellingham	J. Allison

WELSH COUNTY OFFICIALS

County	Chief Executive	County Treasurer	Chief Constable
(1) Clwyd	T. M. Haydn Rees, C.B.E.	W. Hughes	P. A. Myers, Q.P.M. (a)
(2) Dyfed	G. R. Peregrine	R. Silk	R. B. Thomas, Q.P.M. (c)
(3) Gwent	J. A. D. Bray	V. C. Vellacott	W. Farley, O.B.E., M.C., Q.P.M.
(4) Gwynedd	D. E. A. Jones	W. E. Evans	(see Clwyd) (a)
(5) Mid Glamorgan	T. V. Walters	H. S. Parry	T. G. Morris, C.B.E., Q.P.M. (b)
(6) Powys	T. F. G. Young	S. V. Woodhouse	(see Dyfed) (c)
(7) South Glamorgan	W. P. Davey	J. H. Dallard	} (see Mid Glamorgan) (b)
(8) West Glamorgan	M. E. J. Rush	J. L. Couch	

(a) North Wales Police Authority; (b) South Wales Police Authority; (c) Dyfed & Powys Police Authority.

CARDIFF

CARDIFF (South Glamorgan) at the mouth of the rivers Taff, Rhymney and Ely, is the capital City of Wales and one of Britain's major administrative, commercial and office centres. It has many industries including steel works, car component manufacturing, cigars and a flourishing port with a substantial and varied trade, including citrus fruits and timber. There are many fine buildings in the civic centre started early this century which includes the City Hall, the National Museum of Wales, University Buildings, Law Courts, Welsh Office, County Hall, Police Headquarters and the Temple of Peace and Health. Also in the city are Llandaff Cathedral, the Welsh National Folk Museum at St. Fagans and Cardiff Castle.

New buildings include the Sherman Theatre and the Cardiff College of Music and Drama. The City returns four Members to Parliament. Population, 284,700.

Rt. Hon. Lord Mayor (1975–76), Sir Charles Stuart Hallinan, C.B.E.
Stipendiary Magistrate, Hywel ap Robert.
Chief Executive, H. Mansfield.

SWANSEA

SWANSEA (in Welsh, Abertawe), is a City and a seaport of West Glamorgan with its own municipal airport. The beautiful Gower Peninsula was brought within the City boundary under local Government reform on April 1, 1974. The trade of the port includes coal, patent fuel, ores, and the import and export of oil. The municipal area is 60,511 acres, with a population (1974 Census) of 189,800.

The principal buildings are the Norman Castle (rebuilt in 1330), the Royal Institution of South Wales, founded in 1835 (containing Museum and Library), the University College at Singleton and the Guildhall, containing the Brangwyn panels. Swansea was chartered by the Earl of Warwick, *circa* 1158–1184, and further charters were granted by King John, Henry III., Edward II., Edward III. and James II., 2 from Cromwell and 1 Lord Marcher.
Mayor (1975–76), H. T. Morgan.
Chief Executive, A. N. F. Rees.

THE KINGDOM OF SCOTLAND

Position and Extent.—The Kingdom of Scotland occupies the northern portion of the main island of Great Britain and includes the Inner and Outer Hebrides, and the Orkney, Shetland, and many other islands. The Kingdom lies between 60° 51′ 30″ and 54° 38′ N. latitude and between 1° 45′ 32″ and 6° 14′ W. longitude, its southern neighbour being the Kingdom of England, with the Atlantic Ocean on the N. and W., and the North Sea on the E. The greatest length of the mainland (Cape Wrath to the Mull of Galloway) is 274 miles, and the greatest breadth (Buchan Ness to Applecross) is 154 miles. The total area of the Kingdom is 29,798 square miles (or 19,068,724 acres) exclusive of inland water, tidal water and foreshore. The population (1971 Census, prelim.) was 5,227,706, an increase of 48,362 or 0.09 per cent. annually since the census of 1961. The average density of the population in 1971 was 175 persons per square mile, compared with 171 persons per square mile in 1951.

Land's End to John o' Groats.—The customary measurement of the Island of Great Britain is from the site of John o' Groat's house, near Duncansby Head, Caithness (at the N.E. extremity of the island) to Land's End, Cornwall (at the S.W. extremity), a total distance of 603 miles in a straight line and (approximately) 900 by road. But the site of the house of John de Groot (with its 8 doors and octagonal table, to solve the question of precedence between John and his 7 brothers) is about 4 miles S.W. of Duncansby Head, while Dunnet Head (also in Caithness) extends farther N. than Duncansby. John de Groot is believed to have obtained permission to settle in Caithness (from the Netherlands) in the reign of James IV (1488–1513).

Relief.—There are three natural orographic divisions of Scotland. The *Souther Uplands* have their highest points in Merrick (2,764 feet), Rinns of Kells (2,668 feet), and Cairnsmuir of Carsphairn (2,612 feet), in Kirkcudbright; Hartfell (2,651 feet) in Dumfries; and Broad Law (2,754 feet) in Peebles. The *Central Lowlands* include the valleys of the Tay, Forth and Clyde, and the cities of Edinburgh, the capital of the Kingdom, and Glasgow, its principal seaport. The heather-clad *Northern Highlands* extend almost from the extreme north of the mainland to the central lowlands, and are divided into a northern and southern system by the *Great Glen*; they contain, in the central Grampian Hills, *Ben Nevis* (4,406 feet), the highest point in the British Isles, and Ben Muich Dhui (4,296 feet). The *Cheviot Hills* form a natural boundary between Scotland and England, their highest point being The Cheviot (2,676 feet).

Hydrography.—The principal river of Scotland is the *Clyde* (106 miles), one of the most important rivers in the world, with the greatest commercial estuary in Scotland. The Clyde is formed by the junction of Daer and Portrait water, and flows through the city and port of Glasgow to the Firth of Clyde. During its course it passes over the picturesque *Falls of Clyde*, Bonnington Linn (30 feet), Corra Linn (84 feet), Dundaff Linn (10 feet) and Stonebyres Linn (80 feet), above and below Lanark. The *Tweed* (96 miles) has important woollen industries in its valley. The *Tay*, noted for its salmon, and the longest river in Scotland (117 miles, flows into the North Sea, with Dundee (the centre of the jute industry) on the estuary, which is spanned by the *Tay Bridge* (10,289 ft.), opened in 1887, and the *Tay Road Bridge* (7,365 ft.), opened by H.M. Queen Elizabeth the Queen Mother on Aug. 18, 1966. The *Dee* (90 miles), a noted salmon river, flows through scenery of unequalled beauty to the North Sea at Aberdeen. The *Spey* (110 miles),

the swiftest flowing river in the British Isles, and also noted for its salmon and its scenery, flows into the Moray Firth. The *Forth* (66 miles), navigable to Stirling, is spanned by the *Forth (Railway) Bridge* (1890), constructed at a cost of £3,000,000, with a length of 5,330 ft., and the *Forth (Road) Bridge*, with a total length of 6,156 ft. (over water) and a single span of 3,300 ft. The latter was completed in 1964 at a cost of £20,000,000.

The waterfall, *Eas-Coul-Aulin* in Sutherland with a total height of 658 ft. and the *Falls of Glomach* in Ross-shire, with a drop of 370 feet, are the highest in the British Isles; the *Grey Mare's Tail* (Dumfriesshire) is 200 feet.

The *lochs* are the principal hydrographic feature of the Kingdom, both on the mainland and in many of the Islands. The largest in the Kingdom and in Great Britain is *Loch Lomond* (24 miles long), with Lochs Awe, Tay, Rannoch and Ericht in the Grampian valleys; *Loch Ness* (24 miles long and 800 feet deep), with Lochs Oich and Lochy, in the Great Glen; and Lochs Shin (20 miles) and Maree in the northern Highlands.

Climate.—The general climatic values for Scotland are given below, together with the corresponding values for England and Wales within brackets:—mean air temperature reduced to sea level 47.1° F. (49.7); *rainfall*, 50.3 inches (35.2); number of days with rain 217 (188); mean hours per day of bright sunshine, 3.36 (3.96).

Gaelic Language.—The preliminary report on the 1961 Census of Scotland showed that 76,587 persons were Gaelic speakers, compared with 95,447 in 1951. 1,079 persons spoke Gaelic only and not English (compared with 2,178 in 1951). The majority of Gaelic speakers lived in the counties of Ross and Cromarty (38.29 per cent.) and Inverness (24.44 per cent.). 75,508 persons spoke both Gaelic and English, compared with 93,269 in 1951.

Commerce.—The principal exports are machinery, ships and vehicles, iron and steel manufacturers, non-ferrous metals, woollen and worsted yarns and products, food and drink and textile materials. Whisky continues to be the leading export to dollar countries.

THE SCOTTISH ISLANDS

The preliminary report on the 1971 Census of Scotland showed a continued decline in the population of the islands. The populations at April 25, 1971, with 1961 populations in parenthesis, are: Islay, 3,825 (1961, *3,871*); Mull (including Iona, etc.), 1,560 (*1,635*); Coll and Tiree, 1,021 (*1,173*); Harris, 2,879 (*3,418*); Skye 7,372 (*7,772*); Barra, 1,087 (*1,564*); North Uist, 1,732 (*1,982*); South Uist, 3,781 (*4,000*).

Orkney.—About 6 miles N. of the Caithness coast, separated from the mainland by the *Pentland Firth*, is the island county of Orkney, a group of 90 islands and islets (" holms " and " skerries "), of which one-third are inhabited. The total area of the group is 375½ square miles, with a population (1971 Census, preliminary) of 17,075 (1961, *18,888*). 1971 populations of the islands (with 1961 figures in italic) are: Eday, 179 (*202*); Hoy and Walls, 531 (*699*); Mainland, 6,502 (*7,764*); N. Ronaldsay, 134 (*166*); Rousay, 256 (*350*); Sanday, 592 (*682*); Shapinsay, 346 (*432*); S. Ronaldsay, 990 (*1,275*); Stronsay, 440 (*497*); Westray 841 (*1,015*), Kirkwall (4,618), in *Mainland* (Pomona), the largest island of the group, is the capital of the county. Many of the Orkney (and Shetland) Islands contain *brochs* (Pictish towers) and other Pictish and Scandinavian remains. *Scapa Flow*, between *Mainland* and *Hoy*, was the war station of the Grand Fleet from 1914–19 and the scene of the scuttling of the surrendered German High Seas Fleet (June 21, 1919).

Zetland.—About 50 miles N. of Orkney (with the detached Fair Isle at 25 miles N.) is the island county of Zetland or Shetland, a group of about 100 islands and islets, of which one-fifth are inhabited. The total area of the group is 551 square miles, with a population (1971 Census, prelim.) of 17,298 (1961, 17,983). Lerwick (6,107), in *Mainland* (the largest and principal island), is the capital of the county. *Fair Isle*, the southernmost of the group is famous for handknitted hosiery, and *Unst* (with Fair Isle, 1,129) for the finest of the Shetland woollen work for which the county is famous. *Muckle Flugga*, about 1 mile N. of Unst, is the most northerly of the group and of the British Isles (60° 51′ 30″ N. lat.).

Western Islands.—Off the W. coast, at varying distances, and extending from Sutherland to Argyll, are over 500 islands and islets, of which 102 are inhabited. The total area of these Western Islands is 2,812 square miles, but owing to the mountainous surface of the land only about 300 square miles are under cultivation. *The Hebrides.*—Until the closing years of the 13th century " The Hebrides " included other Scottish islands in the Firth of Clyde, the peninsula of Kintyre (Argyllshire), the Isle of Man, and the (Irish) Isle of Rathlin. The origin of the name is stated to be the Greek *Eboudai*, latinized as *Hebudes* by Pliny, and corrupted to its present form. The Norwegian name *Sudreyjar* (Southern Islands) was latinized as *Sodoreness*, a name that survives in the Anglican bishopric of " Sodor and Man." The *Inner Hebrides* include the island of *Skye* (643 square miles—capital, Portree, famous as a refuge of Prince Charlie after his defeat at Culloden, Inverness-shire, in 1746), which contains the *Cuillins* (Sgurr Alasdair 3,309 feet), *Red Hills* (Ben Caillich, 2,403 feet), and many other picturesque mountains; *Mull* (367 square miles), containing *Ben More* (3,169 feet), *Ben Buy* (2,354 feet), and *Ben Creach* (2,289 feet); *Jura* (160 square miles), with a chain of hills culminating in the *Paps of Jura* (Beinn-an-Oir, 2,571 feet and Beinn Chaolais, 2,407 feet); *Islay* (235 square miles), and many smaller islands. The *Outer Hebrides*, separated from the mainland by the *Minch*, include *Lewis with Harris* (770 square miles), celebrated for its homespun " Tweeds," *North Uist*, *South Uist*, *Barra* and other islands. Thirteen miles W. of *Stornoway* (the largest town of Lewis and of the Hebrides) are the " Druidical " remains of *Callanish*, a well-preserved series of monolithic circles, cruciform in general arrangement, but usually regarded as a heathen monument of the remote Stone Age.

EARLY HISTORY

Prehistoric Man.—The Picts, believed to be of non-Aryan origin, and stated to have been named *Picti* by the Romans on account of the tribal habit of painting the body, seem to have inhabited the whole of North Britain and to have spread over the north of Ireland. *Picts' Houses* are most frequent in the northern counties of Caithness and Sutherland and in the Orkney Islands. Celtic *Goidels*, *Brythons* and *Belgae* arrived from Belgic Gaul during the latter part of the Bronze Age and in the early Iron Age, and except in the extreme north of the mainland and in the islands the civilization and speech of the people were definitely Celtic at the time of the Roman Invasion of Britain.

The Roman Invasion.—In A.D. 80 Julius Agricola extended the Roman conquests in Britain by advancing into *Caledonia* as far as the " Grampian " Hills, but after a victory at *Mons Graupius* (since corrupted to " Grampius ") he was recalled, and no further advance was made for about 60 years, when the Roman frontier was carried to the isthmus between the Forth and Clyde and marked by the *Wall of Pius*, towards which ran military roads from the Cheviots. The Roman occupation of Southern Caledonia was not so effective as that of South Britain, and before the close of the second century the northern limit of Roman Britain had receded to *Hadrian's Wall* (Tyne to Solway Firth).

The Scots.—During the later years of the Roman occupation the garrison was continually harassed by Pictish tribes north of the Wall, aided by Scots (the Gaelic tribe then dominant in Ireland), and when the garrison was withdrawn these *Picts* and *Scots* were the principal enemies of the Celtic Brythons, who are believed to have called in the Saxons to protect them from the invasions of their neighbours. A relic of the struggle between Pict and Brython is still to be seen in the *Catrail*, or Picts' Work Dyke, of Roxburgh (from Torwoodlee, near Galashiels, to Peel Fell in the Cheviots). *Christianity* was introduced into Southern Caledonia about 380 by missionaries from Romanized Britain, who penetrated to the northern districts and islands. After the withdrawal (or absorption) of the Roman garrison of Britain there were many years of tribal warfare between the Picts and Scots, the Brythonic Waelisc (Welsh) of Strathclyde (South-west Scotland and Cumberland), and the Anglo-Saxons of the Lothians. The Waelisc were isolated from their kinsmen in Wales by the victory of the West Saxons at Chester (613), and towards the close of the 9th century the Scots under *Kenneth Macalpine* became the dominant power in Caledonia. In the reign of Malcolm I (943–954) the Brythons of Waelisc (Welsh) of Strathclyde were brought into subjection, the lowland kingdom of the English (Lothian) being conquered by Malcolm II (1005–1034). From the close of the 11th century until the middle of the 16th there were constant wars between Scotland and England, the outstanding figures in the struggle being *William Wallace*, who defeated the English at Stirling Bridge (1297) and *Robert Bruce*, who won the victory of Bannockburn (1314). James IV and many of his nobles fell at the disastrous battle of *Flodden* (1513), and in 1603 James VI, the Stuart King of Scotland and the heir to the Tudor line of England (his mother, Mary Queen of Scots, was the great-granddaughter of Henry VII), succeeded Queen Elizabeth I on the throne, his successors reigning as Sovereigns of Great Britain. After the abdication (by flight) of James VII and II, the crown devolved upon William III (grandson of Charles I) and Mary (daughter of James VII and II) and, their issue failing, upon Anne (second daughter of James VII and II). Anne's children died young, and the throne developed upon George I (great-grandson of James VI and I). In 1689 Graham of Claverhouse " roused the Highlands " on behalf of James VII and II, but died after a military success at Killiecrankie. In 1715, armed risings led to the indecisive battle of Sheriffmuir, but the movement died down until 1745, when Prince Charles Edward defeated the Royalist troops under Sir John Cope at Prestonpans and advanced to Derby in England (1746). From Derby, the adherents of " James VIII and III " (the title claimed for his father by Prince Charles Edward) fell back on the defensive, and the *Jacobite* movement was finally crushed by the Royalist troops under the Duke of Cumberland at *Culloden* (April 16, 1746).

The Hebrides did not become part of the Kingdom of Scotland until 1266, when they were ceded to Alexander III by Magnus of Norway. Orkney and Shetland fell to the Scottish Crown as a pledge for the unpaid dowry of Margaret of Denmark, wife of James III, in 1468, the Danish suzerainty being formally relinquished in 1590.

AREA AND POPULATION OF SCOTTISH REGIONAL COUNCILS, ETC.

Region	Administrative Headquarters	Acres	Population	Rateable value	Rate Levied
				£	p
Borders...........	Newtown St. Boswells	1,154,288	99,105	4,700,000	—
Central.............	Stirling	622,080	263,000	19,580,997	90
Dumfries and Galloway........	Dumfries	1,574,400	143,711	6,825,000	88
Fife................	Cupar	322,560	337,690	17,440,441	73
Grampian..........	Aberdeen	2,151,000	447,935	24,100,000	90
Highlands..........	Inverness	6,280,320	176,000	9,000,000	—
Lothian............	Edinburgh	433,920	758,500	48,783,000	108
Orkney............	Kirkwall	240,848	17,462	396,592	92
Shetland...........	Lerwick	352,337	18,445	313,675	—
Strathclyde........	Glasgow	3,422,520	2,527,129	149,206,005	97
Tayside...........	Dundee	1,894,080	401,183	22,578,094	93
Western Isles.......	Stornoway, Lewis	716,800	31,000	661,269	160

CHIEF EXECUTIVES, CHAIRMEN AND CHIEF CONSTABLES

Region	Chief Executive	Chairman (a) Convener	Chief Constable
Borders....................	K. J. Clarke	(a) J. M. Askew, C.B.E.	J. H. Orr, O.B.E.
Central....................	E. Geddes	J. Anderson	E. Frizzell
Dumfries and Galloway......	L. T. Carnegie	(a) J. F. Niven, C.B.E.	A. Campbell, Q.P.M.
Fife......................	J. M. Dunlop	G. Sharp O.B.E.	R. F. Murison, Q.P.M.
Grampian.................	J. L. Russell	A. F. Mutch	A. Morrison
Highlands.................	F. G. Armstrong	Rev. M. J. Nicolson	D. B. Henderson
Lothian...................	R. G. E. Peggie	P. Wilson	J. H. Orr, O.B.E.
Orkney...................	H. A. G. Lapsley.	G. R. Marwick	D. B. Henderson
Shetland.................	I. R. Clark	(a) A. I. Tulloch	D. B. Henderson
Strathclyde...............	L. Boyle, Ph.D.	Rev. G. M. Shaw	D. B. McNee, Q.P.M.
Tayside..................	A. H. Martin	(a) I. A. D. Millar, M.C.	J. R. Little
Western Isles.............	R. MacIver	Rev. D. Macaulay	D. B. Henderson

PRECEDENCE IN SCOTLAND

The Sovereign.

The Prince Philip, Duke of Edinburgh.

The Lord High Commissioner to the General Assembly (while that Assembly *is sitting*).

The Duke of Rothesay (eldest son of the Sovereign). H.R.H. Prince Andrew. H.R.H. Prince Edward.

Nephews of the Sovereign.

Lords Lieutenant of Counties, Lord Provosts of Counties of Cities, and Sheriffs Principal (successively — within their own localities and during holding of office).

Lord Chancellor of Great Britain.

Moderator of the General Assembly of the Church of Scotland.

The Prime Minister.

Keepers of the Great Seal and of the Privy Seal (successively —if Peers).

Hereditary Lord High Constable of Scotland. Hereditary Master of the Household.

Dukes (successively) of England, Scotland, Great Britain and United Kingdom (including Ireland since date of Union).

Eldest sons of Royal Dukes.

Marquesses, in same order as Dukes.

Dukes' eldest sons.

Earls, in order as Dukes.

Younger sons of Dukes of Blood Royal.

Marquesses' eldest sons.

Dukes' younger sons.

Keepers of the Great Seal and of the Privy Seal (successively —if not Peers).

Lord Justice General.

Lord Clerk Register.

Lord Advocate.

Lord Justice Clerk.

Viscounts, in order as Dukes.

Earls' eldest sons.

Marquesses' younger sons.

Lord-Barons, in order as Dukes.

Viscounts' eldest sons.

Earls' younger sons.

Lord-Barons' eldest sons.

Knights of the Garter.

Privy Councillors not included in above ranks.

Senators of Coll. of Justice (Lords of Session).

Viscounts' younger sons.

Lord-Barons' younger sons.

Sons of Life Peers.

Baronets.

Knights of the Thistle.

Knights of other Orders as in England.

Solicitor-General for Scotland.

Lord Lyon King of Arms.

Sheriffs Principal (except as shown in column 1).

Knights Bachelor.

Sheriffs Substitute.

Companions of Orders as in England.

Commanders of Royal Victorian and British Empire Orders.

Eldest sons of younger sons of Peers.

Companions of Distinguished Service Order.

Members (Class 4) Royal Victorian Order.

Officers of British Empire Order.

Baronets' eldest sons.

Knights' eldest sons severally (from Garter to Bachelor).

Members of Class 5 of Royal Victorian Order.

Members of British Empire Order.

Baronets' younger sons.

Knights' younger sons.

Queen's Counsel.

Barons-feudal.

Esquires.

Gentlemen.

LORD LIEUTENANTS IN SCOTLAND

NAME	EXISTING OFFICE	PART OF REGION IN WHICH FUNCTIONS ARE TO BE DISCHARGED
	Lieutenant of:—	Highland Region:—
The Viscount Thurso	The county of Caithness,	The district of Caithness
Col. A. MacD. Gilmour, O.B.E., M.C.	The county of Sutherland	The district of Sutherland
Capt. A. F. Matheson, R.N. (Ret.)	The county of Ross and Cromarty	The districts of Ross and Cromarty and Skye and Lochalsh
Colonel Sir Donald Hamish Cameron of Lochiel, K.T., C.V.O., T.D.	The county of Inverness	The districts of Lochaber, Inverness and Badenoch and Strathspey
The Earl of Leven and Melville	The county of Nairn	The district of Nairn
		Grampian Region:—
Capt. I. M. Tennant	The county of Moray	Such part of the county of Moray as existing before 16th May 1975 as lies within the region.
Colonel T. R. Gordon-Duff of Drummuir, M.C.	The county of Banff	The county of Banff as existing before 16th May 1975
M. Mackie, C.B.E.	The county of Aberdeen	The county of Aberdeen as existing before 16th May 1975 except the electoral divisions of Bucksburn, Newhills Landward, Old Machar and Stoneywood and the Parishes of Dyce and Peterculter
G. A. M. Saunders	The county of Kincardine	The county of Kincardine as existing before 16th May 1975 except the electoral division of Nigg
		Tayside Region:—
The Earl of Dalhousie, K.T., C.B.E., M.C.	The county of Angus	The district of Angus
Maj. D. H. Butter, M.C.	The county of Perth and Kinross	The district of Perth and Kinross
		Fife Region:—
Major The Lord Kilmany, P.C., M.C.	The county of Fife	The whole region
		Lothian Region:—
The Marquess of Linlithgow. M.C.	The county of West Lothian	The district of West Lothian
Sir John Dutton Clerk of Penicuik, Bt. C.B.E., V.R.D.	The county of Midlothian	The district of Midlothian
The Earl of Wemyss and March, K.T.	The county of East Lothian	The district of East Lothian
		Central Region:—
The Earl of Mar and Kellie	The county of Clackmannan	The district of Clackmannan
Colonel The Viscount Younger of Leckie, O.B.E.	The county of Stirling	The districts of Stirling and Falkirk
		Borders Region:—
Sir Robert Heatlie Scott, G.C.M.G., C.B.E.	The county of Peebles	The district of Tweeddale
The Duke of Buccleuch and Queensberry, V.R.D.	The counties of Selkirk and Roxburgh	The district of Ettrick and Lauderdale. The district of Roxburgh
Lt-Col. W. B. Swan, C.B.E., T.D.	The county of Berwick	The district of Berwickshire
		Strathclyde Region:—
The Lord Maclean, K.T., P.C. G.C.V.O., P.C. K.B.E.	The county of Argyll	The district of Argyll and Bute
R. Arbuthnott, M.B.E., T.D.	The county of Dunbarton	The districts of Dumbarton, Clydebank, Bearsden and Milngavie, Strathkelvin and Cumbernauld and Kilsyth
Col. The Lord Clydesmuir, K.T., C.B., M.B.E., T.D.	The county of Lanark	The districts of Monklands, Motherwell, Hamilton, East Kilbride and Lanark
The Viscount Muirshiel K.T., P.C. C.H., C.M.G.	The county of Renfrew	The districts of Eastwood, Renfrew and Inverclyde
Col. B. M. Knox, M.C., T.D.	The county of Ayr	The districts of Cunninghame, Kilmarnock and Loudon, Kyle and Carrick and Cumnock and Doon Valley
		Dumfries and Galloway Region:—
The Earl of Stair, C.V.O., M.B.E.	The county of Wigtown	The district of Wigtown
The Earl of Galloway	The stewartry of Kirkcudbright	The district of Stewartry
Lt.-Gen. Sir William Turner, K.B.E., C.B., D.S.O.	The county of Dumfries	The districts of Nithsdale and of Annandale and Eskdale
Col. R. A. A. S. Macrae, M.B.E.	The county of Orkney	Orkney
R. H. W. Bruce, C.B.E.	The county of Zetland	Shetland

PRINCIPAL SCOTTISH CITIES

EDINBURGH

EDINBURGH, the Capital of Scotland, has a municipal area of 34,781 acres, and a population (estimated, 1973) of 448,682. The city is built on a group of hills and contains in Princes Street one of the most beautiful thoroughfares in the world. The principal buildings are the Castle, which includes St. Margaret's Chapel, the oldest building in Edinburgh, and near it, the Scottish National War Memorial; the Palace of Holyroodhouse; Parliament House, the present seat of the judicature; the University; St. Giles' Cathedral (restored 1879–83); St. Mary's (Scottish Episcopal) Cathedral (Sir Gilbert Scott); the General Register House (Robert Adam): the National and the Signet Libraries; the National Gallery; the Royal Scottish Academy; and the National Portrait Gallery. The city is governed by the City of Edinburgh District Council which includes the area of South Queensferry, Kirkliston, Currie, Ratho and Balerno and tends 7 Members to Parliament.

Rt. Hon. Lord Provost, J. Millar.

Chief Executive, E. G. Glendinning.

GLASGOW

GLASGOW, a Royal Burgh, City and County of a City, and the principal commercial and industrial centre in Scotland, has a municipal area of 49,753 acres and a population of 984,000. The city occupies the north and south banks of the Clyde, one of the chief commercial estuaries in the world. The principal industries include ships, heavy engineering, motor cars, aero and marine engines, chemicals, printing, carpet, cotton thread, food processing, etc. The chief buildings are the Early English former Cathedral, the University (Sir Gilbert Scott), the City Chambers, the Royal Western and Victoria Infirmaries, Kelvingrove Art Gallery and the Mitchell Library. Home of Scottish National Orchestra, Scottish Opera, etc. The city is governed by the City of Glasgow District Council with 72 Members and sends 15 Members to Parliament.

Rt. Hon. Lord Provost, P. T. McCann.
Chief Executive, C. Murdoch.
City Chamberlain, L. Boyle, Ph.D.

ABERDEEN

ABERDEEN, a City and a Royal, Municipal and Parliamentary Burgh, 126 miles N.E. of Edinburgh, received its charter as a Royal Burgh from William the Lion in 1179. The municipal area is 46,557 acres, with a resident population of 212,237. The chief industries are quarrying and granite working, white fish, salmon and herring fisheries, engineering, chemicals, plastics, ship-building, tourism, paper-making, clothing manufacture, wool and linen fabric. The city and surrounding area is now the principal centre of North Sea oil exploration. Aberdeen is famous for its many beautiful buildings, including Marischal College, reputed to be the most imposing white granite building in the world, King's College (1494), St. Machar Church (1378), the Auld Brig o'Balgownie (1320) and the Municipal Buildings. There is a sea beach promenade which stretches for fully two and a half miles along golden sands, and at Hazlehead an open public park of 800 acres, of which 200 are wooded, with one of the finest public golf courses in Scotland and a zoo. The climate is bracing and healthy. The city is governed by a District Council of 48 Members.

The Lord Provost (1975–77), R. S. Lennox.
Chief Executive, J. F. Watt.

DUNDEE

Following the reorganisation of Local Government in Scotland in May 1975, the City of Dundee has an enlarged area of 90 square miles and a population of approximately 207,000. The city, on the River Tay, was inhabited from prehistoric times. Principal buildings are the University, the Institute of Art and Technology, High School, Albert Institute and the Caird Hall Buildings. There is a magnificent public park of 400 acres at Camperdown and other parks of 646 acres and an observatory at Balgay Park. The principal industries are jute manufacture in all its branches, and various forms of linen weaving, the making of tyres, ship-building, engineering, dyeing, fruit, etc., canning, watch and clock making. The City of Dundee District Council consists of 44 members. The City sends 2 Members to Parliament.

The Lord Provost, D. P. Farquhar.
Chief Executive, G. S. Watson.

CHIEFS OF CLANS AND NAMES IN SCOTLAND

THE ROYAL HOUSE: H.M. The Queen.

ARBUTHNOTT: Viscount of Arbuthnott, D.S.C., Arbuthnott House, Laurencekirk, Kincardineshire.

BARCLAY: Peter C. Barclay of that Ilk, Gatemans, Stratford St. Mary, Colchester, Essex.

BORTHWICK: Maj. J. H. S. Borthwick of Borthwick, T.D., Crookston, Midlothian.

BOYD: Lord Kilmarnock, Casa de Mondragon, Ronda (Malaga), Spain.

BRODIE: Ninian Brodie of Brodie, Brodie Castle, Forres.

BRUCE: Earl of Elgin and Kincardine, Broomhall, Dunfermline, Fife.

BUCHAN: David S. Buchan of Auchmacoy, Auchmacoy, Ellon, Aberdeenshire.

BURNETT: J. C. A. Burnett of Leys, Crathes Castle, Kincardineshire.

CAMERON: Col. Sir Donald Hamish Cameron of Lochiel, K.T., C.V.O., T.D., Achnacarry, Spean Bridge, Inverness.

CAMPBELL: Duke of Argyll, Inverary, Argyll.

CARNEGIE: Earl of Southesk, K.C.V.O., Kinnaird Castle, Brechin.

CHISHOLM: Alastair Chisholm of Chisholm (*The Chisholm*), Silver Willows, Bury St. Edmunds.

CLAN CHATTAN: K. A. Mackintosh of Clan Chattan, Maxwell Park, Gwelo, Rhodesia.

COCHRANE: Earl of Dundonald, Lochnell Castle, Ledaig, Argyllshire.

COLQUHOUN: Sir Ivar Colquhoun of Luss, Bt., Rossdhu, Luss, Dunbartonshire.

DARROCH: Captain Duncan Darroch of Gourock. The Red House, Branksome Park Rd., Camberley.

DRUMMOND: Earl of Perth, P.C., Stobhall, Perth.

DUNBAR: Sir Adrian I. Dunbar of Mochrum, Bt., Mochrum Park, Wigtownshire.

DUNDAS: Ian H. Dundas of that Ilk and Inchgarvie, Moreson, Starke Road, Bergvliet, Cape Town, S. Africa.

ELIOTT: Sir Arthur Eliott of Stobs, Bt., Redheugh, Newcastleton, Roxburghshire.

ERSKINE: Earl of Mar and Kellie, Claremont House, Alloa.

FARQUHARSON: Capt. A. A. C. Farquharson of Invercauld, M.C., Invercauld, Braemar.

FERGUSSON: Sir Charles Fergusson of Kilkerran, Bt., Kilkerran, Maybole, Ayrshire.

FORBES: Lord Forbes, K.B.E., Balforbes, Alford, Aberdeenshire.

FRASER: Lord Saltoun, M.C., Cairnbulg Castle, Fraserburgh, Aberdeenshire.

FRASER (OF LOVAT)*: Lord Lovat, D.S.O., M.C., T.D., Beaufort Castle, Beauly, Inverness-shire.

GORDON: Marquess of Huntly, Aboyne Castle, Aberdeenshire.

GRAHAM: Duke of Montrose, Auchmar, Drymen, Stirlingshire.

GRANT: Lord Strathspey, 111 Elms Ride, West Wittering, Sussex.

HAIG: Earl Haig, O.B.E., Bemersyde, Melrose, Roxborough.

HAY: Countess of Erroll, Crimonmogate, Lonmay, Aberdeenshire.

KEITH: The Earl of Kintore, Keith Hall, Inverurie, Aberdeenshire.

KENNEDY: Marquess of Ailsa, O.B.E., Cassillis House, Maybole, Ayrshire.

KERR: Marquess of Lothian, Monteviot, Ancrum, Roxburgh.

KINCAID: A. C. Kincaid of Kincaid, Murarashi, Kenya.

LAMONT: Peter N. Lamont of that Ilk, 63 Patrick Street, Blacktown, Sydney, N.S.W.

LESLIE: Earl of Rothes, Strawberry House, Chiswick Mall, W.4.

LINDSAY: Earl of Crawford and Balcarres, K.T., G.B.E., Balcarres, Colinsburgh, Fife.

McBAIN: H. M. McBain of McBain, Kinchyle House, P.O. Box 2, Hubbard Woods, Illinois, 60093, U.S.A.

MALCOLM (MACCALLUM): Col. George Malcolm of Poltalloch, Duntrune Castle, Argyll.

MACDONALD: Lord Macdonald (*The Macdonald of Macdonald*), Ostaig House, Skye.

MACDONALD OF CLANRANALD★: Ranald A. Macdonald of Clanranald, 55 Compton Road, N.1.

MACDONALD OF SLEAT (CLAN HUSTEAIN)★: Sir Ian Bosville-Macdonald of Sleat, Bt., Thorpe Hall, Rudston, Driffield, Yorks.

MACDONELL OF GLENGARRY★: Air Cdre. Aeneas R. MacDonell of Glengarry, C.B., D.F.C., 5 Sydcote, Rosendale Rd., Dulwich, London S.E.21.

MACDOUGALL: Madame Coline MacDougall of MacDougall, Dunollie, Argyll.

MACGREGOR: Sir Gregor MacGregor of MacGregor, Bt., Edinchip, Lochearnhead, Perthshire.

MACKAY: Lord Reay, 11 Wilton Crescent, S.W.1.

MACKINNON: The Mackinnon of Mackinnon, Field End, Nailsbourne, nr. Taunton, Somerset.

MACKINTOSH: The Mackintosh of Mackintosh, O.B.E., Moy Hall, Inverness.

MACLACHLAN: Madam Marjorie MacLachlan of MacLachlan, Castle Lachlan, Argyll.

MACLAREN: Donald MacLaren of MacLaren and Achleskine, 53 Gordon Mansions, Torrington Place, W.C.1.

MACLEAN: Lord Maclean, P.C., K.T., G.C.V.O., K.B.E., Duart Castle, Mull.

MACLEOD: Dame Flora Macleod of Macleod, D.B.E., Dunvegan Castle, Skye.

MACMILLAN: Gen. Sir Gordon MacMillan of MacMillan, K.C.B., K.C.V.O., C.B.E., D.S.O., M.C., Finlaystone, Langbank, Renfrewshire.

MACNAB: J. C. Macnab of Macnab (*The Macnab*), Kinnell House, Killin, Perthshire.

MACNAGHTEN: Sir Patrick Macnaghten of Macnaghten and Dundarave, Bt., Dundarave, Bushmills, Co. Antrim.

MACNEIL OF BARRA: Ian R. Macneil of Barra (*The Macneil of Barra*), Kismull Castle, Barra.

MACPHERSON: William A. Macpherson of Cluny, Newtown of Blairgowrie, Perthshire.

MACTHOMAS: Andrew P. C. MacThomas of Finegand, The Bell House, Little Wilbraham, nr. Cambridge.

MAITLAND: Earl of Lauderdale, Moberty, Airlie, by Kirriemuir, Angus.

MAR: Earl of Mar, 36 Princes Court, Brompton Rd., London S.W.3.

MARJORIBANKS: William Marjoribanks of that Ilk, Kirklands of Forglen, Banffshire.

MATHESON: Col. B. H. Matheson of that Ilk, M.C., United Service Club, Pall Mall, S.W.1.

MENZIES: David R. Menzies of Menzies, Mundena, Moora, Western Australia.

MONCREIFFE: Sir Iain Moncreiffe of that Ilk, Bt., Easter Moncreiffe, Bridge of Earn, Perthshire.

MONTGOMERIE: Earl of Eglinton and Winton, Skelmorlie Castle, Ayrshire.

MORRISON: Dr. Iain M. Morrison of Ruchdi, Ruchdi, by Lochmaddy, N. Uist.

MUNRO: Patrick G. Munro of Foulis, T.D., Foulis Castle, Ross.

MURRAY: Duke of Atholl, Blair Castle, Blair Atholl, Perthshire.

NICHOLSON OF SCORRYBRECK: Ian Nicholson of Scorrybreck, 18 Hamelin Crescent, Narrabundah. Canberra, A.C.T. 2604, Australia.

OGILVY: Earl of Airlie, Cortachy Castle, Kirriemuir, Angus.

RAMSAY: Earl of Dalhousie, K.T., G.B.E., M.C., Brechin Castle, Angus.

RATTRAY: James S. Rattray of Rattray, Craighall, Rattray, Perthshire.

ROBERTSON: Langton Robertson of Struan (*Struan-Robertson*), 7 Washington Drive, Devon Pen, P.O. Box 337, Halfway Tree P.O., Kingston 10, Jamaica.

ROSE: Miss Elizabeth Rose of Kilravock, Kilravock Castle, Nairn.

ROSS: David C. Ross of that Ilk, Strathdevon House, Dollar, Clackmannanshire.

RUTHVEN: Earl of Gowrie, Castlemartin, Kilcullen, Co. Kildare, Eire.

SINCLAIR: Earl of Caithness, Hampton Court Palace, East Molesey, Surrey.

SWINTON: W. F. H. Swinton of that Ilk, Box 596, Bozeman, Montana, U.S.A.

URQUHART: Kenneth T. Urquhart of that Ilk, 4713 Orleans Blvd., Jefferson, Louisiana, U.S.A.

WALLACE: Lt.-Col. M. R. Wallace of that Ilk, Kirklands of Damside, Auchterarder, Perthshire.

WEMYSS: Michael Wemyss of that Ilk, Wemyss Castle, Fife.

Only chiefs of *whole* Names or Clans are included (except certain special instances (marked ★), who though not chiefs of a " whole name ", were, or are, for some reason, *e.g.* the Macdonald forfeiture, independent). Under decision (*Campbell-Gray*, 1950) that a bearer of a " double or triple-barrelled " surname cannot be held chief of a part of such, several others cannot be included in the list at present.

THE ARMS OF SCOTLAND

ARMS.—*Or*, a lion rampant *gules*, armed and langued *azure*, within a double-tressure flory counter-flory of the second. CREST.—An imperial crown *proper*, surmounted by a lion sejant-guardant *gules* crowned *or*, holding in his dexter paw a naked sword and in the sinister a sceptre both *proper*. SUPPORTERS.—Two unicorns *argent*, armed, tufted and unguled *or*, crowned with imperial and gorged with eastern crowns, chains reflexed over the backs *or*; the dexter supporting a banner charged with the arms of Scotland, the sinister supporting a similar banner *azure*, thereon a saltire *argent*. MOTTOES.—Over the arms, " In Defens "; under the arms " Nemo me impune lacessit."

SCOTTISH DISTRICT COUNCILS

District	Administrative Headquarters	Popula-tion	Rateable Value £	Chief Executive	Chairman a) Convener b) Provost c) Lord Provost
Aberdeen City	Town House, Aberdeen	181,844	10,440,153	J. F. Watt	c) R. S. Lennox
Angus	County Buildings, Forfar	86,849	4,200,000	W. S. McCulloch, M.C.	Col. L. Gray-Cheape
Annandale and Eskdale	Council Chambers, High St., Annan	35,374	1,534,204	G. F. Murray	R. G. Greenhow
Argyll and Bute	Kilmory, Lochgilphead	64,678	2,949,708	M. A. J. Gossip	E. T. F. Spence
Badenoch and Strathspey	36, High St., Kingussie	8,966	602,000	H. G. McCulloch	Maj. A. C. Robertson
Banff and Buchan	Sandyhill Rd., Banff	75,150	3,069,143	N. S. McAlister	W. R. Cruickshank
Bearsden and Milngavie	Boclair, Bearsden	36,500	2,600,000	A. R. Rae	b) W. Hamilton
Berwickshire	8 Newton St., Duns.	20,779	739,926	D. Dunn	J. R. Ford
Caithness	Council Offices, Wick	29,400	826,341	A. Beattie	J. M. Young
Clackmannan	County Bldgs., Alloa	45,546	2,866,316	A. Stewart	A. MacDonald
Clydebank	Municipal Bldgs., Clydebank	60,000	3,350,505	R. A. Nixon	R. A. Calder
Cumbernauld and Kilsyth	Bron Way, Cumbernauld	52,322	3,233,000	R. Kyle, M.B.E.	b) G. S. Murray
Cumnock and Doon Valley	Lugar, Cumnock	49,900	1,677,548	D. T. Hemmings	a) T. P. McIntyre
Cunninghame	Cunninghame Hse., Irvine	129,814	6,461,495	J. M. Miller	D. White
Dumbarton	Crosslet Hse., Dumbarton	79,035	3,785,440	L. MacKinnon	b) J. McKinley
Dundee City	City Chambers, Dundee	207,000	12,700,000	G. S. Watson	c) C. D. P. Farquhar
Dunfermline	City Chambers, Dunfermline	121,000	—	G. Brown	L. G. Wood
East Kilbride	East Kilbride, Glasgow	82,000	5,170,700	W. G. McNay	Mrs. S. Finlayson
East Lothian	Haddington, East Lothian	77,397	4,325,150	D. B. Miller	T. White
Eastwood	Cotton St., Paisley	50,017	3,180,014	M. D. Henry	b) I. S. Hutchison
Edinburgh City	High St., Edinburgh	472,000	34,379,500	E. G. Glendinning	c) J. Millar
Ettrick and Lauderdale	Paton St., Galashiels	32,297	1,509,340	D. H. Cowan	G. R. Johnston
Falkirk	Municipal Bldgs., Falkirk	141,176	—	J. P. H. Paton	W. Ure
Glasgow City	City Chambers, Glasgow	905,000	65,500,000	C. Murdoch	c) P. T. McCann
Gordon	3 High St., Inverurie	50,000	1,012,519	A. C. Kennedy	J. B. Presly
Hamilton	Town Hse., Hamilton	105,000	5,945,308	W. Johnston	R. Sherry
Inverclyde	Municipal Bldgs., Greenock	109,615	—	I. C. Wilson	J. Walsh
Inverness	Town Hse., Inverness	51,897	2,942,999	I. J. Miller	b) I. C. Fraser
Kilmarnock and Loudoun	Civic Centre, Kilmarnock	83,828	4,000,000	J. C. W. Nicol	W. Aitken
Kincardine and Deeside	Viewmount, Stonehaven	34,462	1,400,000	Miss E. M. G. Cockburn	I. M. Frain
Kirkcaldy	Town Hse., Kirkcaldy	148,028	8,085,627	C. D. Chapman, O.B.E.	a) R. King
Kyle and Carrick	Burns Hse., Ayr	110,000	—	J. R. Hill	A. D. Paton
Lanark	57 High St., Lanark	53,534	2,784,000	R. G. Dalkin, E.R.D.	a) R. C. M. Monteith
Lochaber	Fort William, Inverness	19,900	1,116,457	J. T. Ballantyne	Lt.-Col. J. W. Forbes
Midlothian	1 White Hart St., Dalkeith	83,406	4,131,000	D. W. Duguid	a) D. R. Smith
Monklands	Dunbeth Rd., Coatbridge	108,819	5,693,000	J. S. Ness	b) T. Clarke
Moray	High St., Elgin	80,000	3,522,000	J. P. C. Bell	J. M. Anderson
Motherwell	Civic Centre, Motherwell	160,865	10,464,000	F. C. Marks	H. B. Sneddon
Nairn	4 Courthouse Lane, Nairn	8,906	389,677	J. R. McCluskey	b) Lt.-Col. H. McLean, M.B.E.
Nithsdale	Municipal Chambers, Dumfries	55,924	2,925,400	G. D. Grant	F. H. Young
North-East Fife	Cupar, Fife	64,000	3,514,339	H. Farquhar	Capt. D. M. Russell, R.N.
Perth and Kinross	3 High St., Perth	117,911	6,121,201	R. T. Blair	H. Young
Renfrew	Cotton St., Paisley	204,000	—	W. McIntosh	E. G. Conway
Ross and Cromarty	County Bldgs., Dingwall	38,226	1,878,425	T. M. Aitchison	a) The Earl of Cromartie, M.C., T.D
Roxburgh	High St., Hawick	35,789	1,471,000	W. C. Hogg	D. Atkinson, M.B.E.
Skye and Lochalsh	Portree, Isle of Skye	9,519	325,000	D. H. Noble	R. S. Budge
Stewartry	Council Offices, Kirkcudbright	22,411	1,032,500	W. L. Dick-Smith	a) R. F. Maxwell
Stirling	Municipal Bldgs., Stirling	76,091	5,000,000	D. M. Bowie	a) Mrs. L. M. McCaig
Strathkelvin	Kirkintilloch, Glasgow	81,181	—	A. W. Harrower	I. MacBryde
Sutherland	District Offices, Golspie	11,827	349,087	D. W. Mastin	Col. A. A. M. Gilmour
Tweeddale	Rosetta Rd., Peebles	13,584	811,472	G. Gardiner	T. Blyth
West Lothian	District Offices, Bathgate	121,172	6,400,000	D. A. Morrison	a) W. Connolly
Wigtown	Sun St., Stranraer	30,004	1,280,648	D. R. Wilson	D. R. Robinson

NEW TOWNS IN GREAT BRITAIN

(Populations shown are amended 1971 Census preliminary figures; *see also* Municipal Director.

Commission for the New Towns. Glen House, Stag Place, S.W.1.—The Commission was established on October 1, 1961, under the New Towns Act, 1959, to take over new towns in England and Wales from development corporations whose purposes have been achieved or substantially achieved. In each town, the management of residential property is conducted by a local committee appointed by the Commission in accordance with the New Towns Act, 1965 and administration of all property is carried out through the Commission's local staff.

Chairman, Sir Dennis Pilcher, C.B.E.
Deputy Chairman, Mrs. B. F. R. Paterson, C.B.E.
Members, S. R. Collingwood; G. D. Hitchcock; P. G. Grimshaw: W. F. Hodson; C. Macpherson; A. E. Pegler.
Secretary, J. C. O'Neill.

CRAWLEY, Sussex.—*Chairman,* A. E. Pegler. *Manager,* R. M. Clarke, M.C. *Offices,* Broadfield, Crawley, Sussex. Area 6,047 acres. Population, 71,000. Estimated eventual population 85,000.

HATFIELD, Herts.—Hatfield and Welwyn Garden City Local Committee, S. R. Collingwood. *Manager,* M. W. Biggs, C.B.E. *Offices:* Church Road, Welwyn Garden City, Herts. Area, 2,340 acres. Population, 26,000. Estimated eventual population, 29,000.

HEMEL HEMPSTEAD, Herts.—*Chairman,* C. D. Hitchcock. *Manager,* Brig. J. R. Blomfield, O.B.E., M.C. *Offices,* Swan Court, Waterhouse Street, Hemel Hempstead, Herts. Area, 5,910 acres. Population, 74,000. Estimated eventual population, 80,000.

WELWYN GARDEN CITY, Herts. *Chairman,* Hatfield and Welwyn Garden City Local Committee, S. R. Collingwood. *Manager,* M. W. Biggs, C.B.E. *Offices:* Church Road, Welwyn Garden City. Herts. Area, 4,317 acres. Population, 40,700. Estimated eventual population, 50,000.

Development Corporations

AYCLIFFE, Co. Durham.—Formed 1947. *Chairman,* H. D. Stevenson. *General Manager,* G. Philipson, D.F.C. *Offices,* Churchill House, Newton Aycliffe, nr. Darlington, Co. Durham. Area, 3,075 acres. Population, 25,230. Estimated eventual population, 45,000

BASILDON, Essex.—Formed 1949. *Chairman,* A. O. Kelting. *General Manager,* A. H. Mawer, D.F.C. *Offices,* Gifford House, Basildon, Essex. Area, 7,818 acres. Population, 86,300. Estimated eventual population, 134,000.

BRACKNELL, Berks.—Formed 1949. *Chairman.* J. W. Hughes. *General Manager,* G. J. Bryan, C.M.G., C.V.O., O.B.E., M.C. *Offices,* Farley Hall, Bracknell, Berks. Area, 3,303 acres. Population, 42,000. Estimated eventual population, 60,000.

CENTRAL LANCASHIRE NEW TOWN, Lancs.—Formed 1970. *Chairman,* Sir Frank Pearson. *General Manager,* R. W. Phelps. *Offices,* Cuerden Pavillion, Bamber Bridge, Preston, Lancs. Area, 35,225 acres. Population, 242,500. Estimated eventual population, 420,000.

CORBY, Northants.—Formed 1950. *Chairman,* Sir Henry Chisholm, C.B.E. *General Manager,* Brig. H. G. W. Hamilton, C.B.E. *Offices,* 9 Queen's Square, Corby, Northants. Area, 4,423 acres. Population, 53,500. Estimated eventual population, 83,000.

CWMBRAN, Gwent.—Formed 1949. *Chairman,* The Lord Raglan. *General Manager,* R. P. Menday, M.B.E., M.C. *Offices,* Gwent House, Town Centre,

Cwmbran, Gwent. Area, 3,160 acres. Population, 43,500. Estimated eventual population, 55,000.

HARLOW, Essex.—Formed 1947. *Chairman,* B. J. Perkins. *General Manager,* A. T. Bardsley. *Offices,* Gate House, The High, Harlow, Essex. Area, 6,395 acres. Population, 82,000. Estimated eventual population, 90,000.

MILTON KEYNES, Bucks.—Formed 1967. *Chairman,* The Lord Campbell of Eskan. *General Manager,* F. L. Roche. *Offices,* Wavendon Tower, Wavendon, Milton Keynes, Bucks. Area, 22,000 acres. Population, 65,000. Estimated eventual population, 250,000.

NEWTOWN, Powys.—Formed 1967. *Chairman,* E. Roberts. *Chief Executive,* D. P. Garbett-Edwards. *Offices,* Severn Street, Newtown, Powys. Area, 1,497 acres. Population, 7,000. Estimated eventual population 13,000.

NORTHAMPTON.—Formed 1968. *Chairman,* Sir William Hart. *General Manager,* Dr. J. C. Weston. *Offices,* Cliftonville House, Bedford Road, Northampton. Area, 19,966 acres. Population, 147,000. Estimated eventual population 260,000.

PETERBOROUGH.—Formed 1967. *Chairman,* C. T. Higgins. *General Manager,* W. Thomas. *Offices,* Touthill Close, Peterborough. Area, 15,952 acres. Population, 100,000. Estimated eventual population, 182,000.

PETERLEE, Co. Durham.—Formed 1948. *Chairman,* D. H. Stevenson. *General Manager,* G. Philipson, D.F.C. *Offices,* Shotton Hall, Peterlee, Co. Durham. Area, 2,799 acres. Population, 26,500. Estimated eventual population, 30,000.

REDDITCH, Worcs.—Formed 1964. *Chairman,* J. H. C. Chesshire, M.C. *General Manager,* A. M. Grier, C.M.G. *Offices,* Holmwood, Plymouth Road, Redditch, Worcs. Area, 7,180 acres. Population, 49,000. Estimated eventual population, 90,000.

RUNCORN, Cheshire.—Formed 1964. *Chairman,* W. H. Sefton. *General Manager,* D. F. Banwell. *Offices,* Chapel Street, Runcorn, Cheshire. Area, 7,234 acres. Population, 50,311. Estimated eventual population, 100,000.

SKELMERSDALE, Lancs.—Formed 1962. *Chairman,* A. J. E. Taylor, O.B.E. *Managing Director,* I. Gray. *Offices,* Pennylands, Skelmersdale, Lancs. Area, 4,124 acres. Population, 40,000. Estimated eventual population, 80,000.

STEVENAGE, Herts.—Formed 1946. *Chairman,* Dame Evelyn Denington, D.B.E. *General Manager,* J. A. Balchin. *Offices,* Swingate House, Stevenage, Herts. Area, 6,256 acres. Population, 74,800. Estimated eventual population, 100,000.

TELFORD, Shropshire.—Formed 1963. *Chairman,* J. R. S. Dugdale. *General Manager,* E. Thomas. *Offices,* Priorslee Hall, Telford, Salop. Area, 19,300 acres. Population, 94,200. Estimated eventual population, 250,000.

WARRINGTON, Cheshire.—Formed 1968. *Chairman,* The Lord Hamnett. *General Manager,* D. J. Binns. *Offices,* 61 Sankey Street, Warrington, Cheshire. Area, 18,612 acres. Population, 132,750. Estimated eventual population, 188,000.

WASHINGTON, Tyne and Wear.—Formed 1964. *Chairman,* Sir James Steel, C.B.E. *General Manager,* W. S. Holley. *Offices,* Usworth Hall, Washington. Area, 5,610 acres. Population, 38,000. Estimated eventual population, 80,000.

Scotland

CUMBERNAULD, Dunbartonshire.—Formed 1956. *Chairman*, Sir Donald R. Liddle, LL.D. *Chief Executive*, Brig. C. H. Cowan. *Headquarters*, Cumbernauld House, Cumbernauld. Area, 7,788 acres. Population, 42,000. Estimated eventual population, 70,000.

EAST KILBRIDE, Lanarkshire.—Formed 1947. *Chairman*, The Lord Wallace of Campsie. *Managing Director*, G. B. Young. *Offices*, Atholl House, East Kilbride, Lanarkshire. Area, 10,250 acres. Population, 71,800. Estimated eventual population, 82,000.

GLENROTHES, Fife.—Formed 1948. *Chairman*, R. R. Taylor, C.B.E. *General Manager*, Brig. R. S. Doyle, C.B.E. *Offices*, Glenrothes House, Glenrothes, Fife. Area, 5,765 acres. Population, 35,000. Estimated eventual population, 70,000.

IRVINE, Ayrshire.—Designated, 1966. *Chairman*, Sir William S. Gray. *Managing Director*, J. D. Marquis, D.F.C. *Offices*, Perceton House, Irvine, Ayrshire. Area, 12,440 acres. Population, 50,000. Estimated eventual population, 120,000.

LIVINGSTON. West Lothian.—Designated, 1962. *Chairman*, B. D. Misselbrook. *Chief Executive*, S. E. M. Wright. *Offices*, Livingston, West Lothian. Area, 6,692 acres. Population, 24,000. Estimated eventual population, 100,000.

STONEHOUSE, Lanarkshire.—Formed 1973. *Chairman*, The Lord Wallace of Campsie. *Managing Director*, G. B. Young. *Offices*, Atholl House, East Kilbride, Lanarkshire. Area 6,765 acres. Population, 7,250. Estimated eventual population, 70,000.

Northern Ireland

(For geographical and historical notes on Ireland, see Index)

The population of Northern Ireland in 1973 was 1,536,065 (males, 754,676; females, 781,389) compared with a total population of 1,484,775 at the Census of 1966. In 1971 the number of persons in the various religious denominations (expressed as percentages of the total population) were: Roman Catholic, 31·4; Presbyterian, 26·1; Church of Ireland, 22; Methodist, 4·7; others 5·8; not stated, 9·4. Northern Ireland has a total area of 5,452 sq. miles (land, 5,206 sq. miles; inland water and tideways, 246 sq. miles) with a density of population of 293 persons per sq. mile in 1971.

Constitution and Government. A separate parliament and executive Government was established for Northern Ireland in 1921 by the Government of Ireland Act. The Northern Ireland Constitution Act, 1973, abolished the post of Governor and Parliament of Northern Ireland and provided for the transfer of certain legislative functions to a Northern Ireland Assembly and Executive. Elections for a Northern Ireland Assembly took place on June 28, 1973. Devolved Government came into operation with effect from January 1, 1974 but when the Executive collapsed the Northern Ireland Assembly was prorogued on May 29 1974. The Northern Ireland Constitution Act, 1974, which became law in July 1974, made provision for temporary arrangements for the government of Northern Ireland by the Secretary of State for Northern Ireland and also provided for the holding of elections and a Constitutional Convention.

The Privy Council

Senator Sir John Andrews K.B.E. (1957); R. J. Bailie; D. W. Bleakley; R. H. Bradford; Capt. Viscount Brookeborough; W. Craig (1963); Sir Lancelot Curran (1957); J. Dobson (1969); A. B. D. Faulkner (1959); W. K. Fitzsimmons (1965); Sir Maurice Gibson (*Lord Justice*); Senator Col. the Lord Glentoran, H.M.L. (1953); Sir Edward Jones (*Lord Justice*) (1965); B. Kelly, Q.C. (1969); H. V. Kirk (1962); Capt. W. J. Long (1966); Sir Robert Lowry (*Lord Chief Justice*); R. W. B. McConnell (1964); W. B. McIvor (1971); The Lord MacDermott, M.C. (1940); Sir Ambrose McGonigal (*Lord Justice*) (1975); Sir Herbert McVeigh (1965); W. J. Morgan (1961); The Lord Moyola; Ivan Neill (1950); P. R. H. O'Neill; The Lord O'Neill of the Maine (1956); G. B. Newe, D.LITT. (1971); Sir Robert Porter, Q.C.; The Lord Rathcavan (1922); R. Simpson (1969); Capt. Sir Norman Stronge, Bt. M.C., H.M.L. (1946); J. D. Taylor; Judge W. W. B. Topping (1967); H. W. West (1960).

Northern Ireland Constitutional Convention

Elections for the Convention conducted under the single-transferable vote system took place on May 1, 1975. The 78 seats were filled as follows:—Official Unionists 20; Vanguard Unionist Party 14; Democratic Unionist Party 12; Alliance Party 8; Unionist Party Northern Ireland 5; Social and Democratic Labour Party 17; Northern Ireland Labour 1; Independent Unionist 1.

Government Offices

DEPARTMENT OF FINANCE

Permanent Secretary, Sir David Holden, K.B.E., C.B., E.R.D.
Second Secretaries, R. H. Kidd; K. R. Shimeld.
Deputy Secretaries, W. I. Woods; Dr. G. I. Dent.
First Legislative Draftsman, S. F. R. Martin.
Second Legislative Draftsman, T. R. Erskine.
Senior Asst. Secretaries, K. Darwin; S. H. Wightman; S. H. Jamison; Dr. A. T. Park.
Asst. Secretaries, J. Armstrong; F. G. Dougall; J. S. H. Gaw; L. J. Johnston; R. M. McDonald; D. J. Clement; Miss Z. I. Davies; J. Murray; W. H. Hamill; I. Y. Malley, D.S.O., D.F.C.. J. Maguire; L. J. McClelland; W. A. Willis.

DEPARTMENT OF EDUCATION

Permanent Secretary, A. C. Brooke, C.B.
Deputy Secretaries, J. Finney; W. Slinger
Asst. Secretaries, T. R. Meharg; E. J. Kirkpatrick; P. K. McHugh; J. B. McAllister; R. Macdonald; J. Saulters; E. G. Martin.

DEPARTMENT OF HOUSING, LOCAL GOVERNMENT AND PLANNING

Permanent Secretary, K. P. Bloomfield.
Deputy Secretaries, L. V. D. Calvert; J. P. McGrath, *Senior Assistant Secretary*, T. A. D. Higgins.
Planning Director, Town and Country Planning Services, G. Gamblin, O.B.E.
Assistant Secretaries, J. F. Younger; R. B. Spence; W. P. McIlmoyle; J. L. Semple.

ROYAL ULSTER CONSTABULARY
(Knock Road, Belfast 5)
Chief Constable, Sir James Flanagan, C.B.E.

Senior Deputy Chief Constable, K. L. Newman.
Deputy Chief Constable, H. Baillie, O.B.E.

NORTHERN IRELAND AGENT IN LONDON
11 Berkeley Street, W.1.
Agent, Sir Harry Jones, C.B.E.
Assistant Secretary, R. McClelland.

DEPARTMENT OF ENVIRONMENT
Permanent Secretary, W. G. Malcolm.
Deputy Secretaries, J. F. Irvine; J. H. Armstrong.
Senior Assistant Secretaries, G. Hamilton; H. T. Bergin; T. A. N. Prescott.
Assistant Secretaries, B. M. Rutherford; J. M. Beckett; J. G. McKinney; R. E. D. Bain; D. Barry; T. A. Warnock; G. F. Chambers; B. D. Palmer; J. Marsh.

DEPARTMENT OF HEALTH & SOCIAL SERVICES
Permanent Secretary, N. Dugdale.
Deputy Secretaries, D. W. Lowry; J. H. Copeland.
Senior Assistant Secretary, F. A. Elliott.
Assistant Secretaries, R. J. Christie; W. Bell; Dr. A. L. B. Walby; H. Martin; A. Stewart; S. W. McDowell; G. Buchanan; Miss I. M. S. Jordan; J. M. Wilkinson; R. B. Thompson; C. G. Oakes; S. H. O'Fee; N. I. Kells; L. R. Kelly; R. S. Mills; W. S. Long; T. M. Lyness.
Chief Medical Officer, Dr. T. T. Baird.
Deputy Chief Medical Officer, Dr. R. J. Weir.

DEPARTMENT OF COMMERCE
Permanent Secretary, W. E. Bell.
Deputy Secretary, F. T. Mais.
Director of Industrial Development, H. S. Oliver.
Asst. Directors of Industrial Development, E. R. Jolley; W. McC. Taylor; R. J. Henderson; J. T. B. Quan; J. Scott.

Senior Asst. Secretary, Dr. A. J. Howard.
Assistant Secretaries, J. B. M. Thompson; J. A. G. Whitlaw; E. Simpson; D. McVitty.
Economic Adviser, Dr. W. Black.
Financial Controller, J. E. Hawkins.
Senior Industrial Development Officers, N. H. Sherrard; A. I. Devitt; R. J. Browne.
Senior Principal Scientific Officers, Dr. W. McD. Morgan; J. T. McCullins.

DEPARTMENT OF MANPOWER SERVICES
Permanent Secretary, Dr. W. G. H. Quigley.
Deputy Secretary, W. N. Drummond.
Senior Assistant Secretary, D. J. Perham.
Assistant Secretaries, J. H. Scott; J. S. Crozier; T. R. N. Balmer; R. T. O'Connor; T. R. McKnight; J. B. C. Lyttle.

DEPARTMENT OF AGRICULTURE
Permanent Secretary, J. A. Young, C.B.
Deputy Secretary, R. Shaw.
Senior Assistant Secretaries, Dr. W. H. Jack; E. Mayne.
Chief Scientific Officer, Dr. W. O. Brown.
Chief Inspector, T. Moore.
Assistant Secretaries, W. H. Parker; G. H. Hodgins; E. G. Sherrard; T. P. Gibson; J. C. Chalmers; A. J. Kissock.
Chief Forestry Officer, K. F. Parkin.

CENTRAL SECRETARIAT
Senior Assistant Secretary, J. M. C. Parke.
Assistant Secretary, R. Ramsey.
Director of Information, W. E. W. Montgomery, M.B.E.
Head of Press Services, T. E. M. Roberts.

THE JUDICATURE

SUPREME COURT OF JUDICATURE, THE ROYAL COURTS OF JUSTICE (ULSTER), BELFAST.
The Rt. Hon. Sir Robert Lowry, Lord Chief Justice of Northern Ireland............£15,000
Rt. Hon. Lord Justice (Sir Edward Warburton) Jones; The Rt. Hon. Lord Justice (Sir Ambrose Joseph) McGonigal; The Rt. Hon. Lord Justice (Sir Maurice White) Gibson; The Hon. Mr. Justice (Turlough) O'Donnell; The Rt. Hon. Mr. Justice (John William Basil) Kelly; The Hon. Mr. Justice (John Clarke) MacDermott; The Hon. Mr. Justice (D.B.) Murray............each £13,500

Secretariat
Permanent Secretary to Supreme Court and Clerk of the Crown for Northern Ireland, J. A. L. McLean, Q.C.
Asst. Secretary to the Supreme Court and Private Secretary to the Lord Chief Justice, J. W. Wilson.

Registrar's Department
Registrar, D. S. Stephens.
Asst. Registrar, V. A. Care.
Deputy Asst. Registrar, Miss M. Cullen, M.B.E.

Chief Clerk's Department
Chief Clerk (and Registrar in Lunacy), J. K. Davis, O.B.E.
Asst. Chief Clerk and Asst. Registrar in Lunacy, R. L. G. Davison.

Bankruptcy and Chancery Registrar's Department
Registrar, J. M. Hunter.
Asst. Registrar, V. G. Bridges.

Principal Probate Registry
Chief Registrar, T. S. Townley.
Asst. Registrar, Miss M. K. M. Aiken.

Official Assignee's Department
Official Assignee, R. B. Logan.
Deputy Official Assignee, J. B. Kell.

Accountant General's Department
Accountant General, R. A. Guiler.
Chief Clerk, R. J. King.

Taxing Office
Taxing Master, A. E. Anderson.

Recorders
Belfast, Rt. Hon. W. W. B. Topping, Q.C.
Londonderry, D. J. Little, Q.C.

County Court Judges
Judge Babington, D.S.C., Q.C.; Judge Brown, Q.C.; Judge Chambers, Q.C.; Judge Higgins, Q.C.; Judge Johnson, Q.C.; Judge McGrath, Q.C.; Judge Roland, Q.C.; Judge Watt, Q.C.
Crown Solicitor, H. A. Nelson.
Director of Public Prosecutions, C. B. Shaw, C.B., Q.C.

FLAG.—The national flag is that of the United Kingdom.

BELFAST
BELFAST, a City, the seat of Government of Northern Ireland, situated at the mouth of the River Lagan at its entrance to Belfast Lough, has a municipal area of 16,017 acres, exclusive of tidal water (2,034) and a population (1973) of 353,700. The city received its first charter of incorporation in 1613 and has since grown, owing to its easy access by sea to Scottish coal and iron, to be a great industrial centre. The chief industries are ship-building and the manufacture of aircraft, machinery, textiles, ropes and tobacco. Belfast is an important seaport with extensive docks.

The principal buildings are of a relatively recent date and include the Parliament Buildings at Stormont, the City Hall, the Law Courts, the Public Library and the Museum and Art Gallery.

The Queen's University (previously Queen's College) was chartered in 1908.

The city returns 4 members to the House of Commons at Westminster. Belfast was created a city in 1888 and the title of Lord Mayor was conferred in 1892.

Lord Mayor (1975–76), R. E. Myles.
Town Clerk, W. Johnston.

LONDONDERRY

LONDONDERRY, a City situated on the River Foyle, has a population (estimated, 1973) of 51,200 and was reputedly founded in 546 by St. Columba. Londonderry (formerly *Derry*) has important associations with the City of London. The Irish Society, under its royal charter of 1613, fortified the city and was for long closely associated with its administration. On April 2, 1969, the Corporation of Londonderry and Londonderry R.D.C. were dissolved and replaced by the Londonderry Development Commission. The Development Commission was dissolved in Sept. 1973, and its functions were taken over by the newly elected Local District Council and various Government departments and Area Boards.

Famous for the great siege of 1688–89, when for 105 days the town held out against the forces of James II until relieved by sea, Londonderry was an important naval base throughout the Second World War. Interesting buildings are the Protestant Cathedral of St. Columb's (1633) and the Guildhall reconstructed in 1912 and containing a number of beautiful stained glass windows, many of which were presented by the livery companies of London. The famous Walls are still intact and form a circuit of almost a mile around the old city. The manufacture of shirts and collars is the staple industry. Other industries include motor and mechanical engineering and fancy box making. New industries established in Londonderry in the post-war period include the manufacture of synthetic fibre and rubber, tyre cord and light engineering. A large part of Ulster's agricultural export trade passes through the port.

FINANCE

Taxation in Northern Ireland is largely imposed and collected by the United Kingdom Government. After deducting the cost of collections and of Northern Ireland's contributions to the European Economic Community the balance, known as the Attributed Share of Taxation, is paid over to the Northern Ireland Consolidated Fund. Northern Ireland's revenue is insufficient to meet its expenditure and is supplemented by a grant in aid.

	1974–75*	1975–76**
	£	£
Public Income	758,086,640	911,406,900
Public expenditure	758,075,552	911,161,100

* Outturn   ** Estimate

EXTERNAL TRADE*

£'000

	1972	1973	1974
Total imports	937,079	1,303,986	1,722,536
Total exports	916,684	1,174,769	1,365,924

* Including cross-Channel trade with Great Britain.

PRODUCTION

Industries.—The total value of the industrial production of Northern Ireland in 1973 was approximately £1,693,000,000 and employment was given to about 195,000 persons. The products of the engineering, shipbuilding and aircraft industries which employed 47,000 persons, were valued at £208,000,000. The textile industries, employing 37,000 persons, produced yarns, fabrics, household textiles, handkerchiefs, carpets, hosiery, ropes and a wide variety of other products valued at approximately £294,000,000. The food and drink industry, giving employment to 20,000 persons, produced goods valued at £297,000,000 and clothing to the value of £69,000,000 was manufactured in 1973, of which £29,000,000 represented shirts and collars, which are manufactured principally in Londonderry. Other industries of importance to the economy of Northern Ireland are synthetic rubber and products, mineral oil refining, furniture and building materials and cardboard boxes and packing cases.

Minerals.—1,894 persons were employed in mining and quarrying operations in Northern Ireland in 1973 and the minerals raised were valued at £6,934,000.

Fisheries.—The total value of sea and freshwater fish caught in 1973 was £3,687,848.

COMMUNICATIONS

Seaports—The net tonnage of shipping using the principal ports in 1974 was about 12,500,000 tons. Regular services operate to and from ports on the western coast of Great Britain and the continent of Europe. In addition there are frequent, though less regular, calls by many other coastal and foreign going ships. There are roll-on/roll-off services to Liverpool, Ardrossan, and Preston. Specialised container services, with adequate cranage available, operate to Liverpool, Holyhead, Garston, Preston, Glasson Dock (Lancashire), Ardrossan and Southampton and there are weekly sailings catering for palletised and container traffic to ports in France, Germany, Holland, Belgium, Sweden, Norway, Denmark and Italy. Larne—Roll-on/roll-off ferry services carrying passengers, cars and commercial vehicles operate nine times daily to Stranraer, six times daily to Cairnryan and five times weekly to Ardrossan (commercial vehicles only). Container ships operate services five times weekly to Ardrossan and six times weekly to Fleetwood (Liverpool). Warrenpoint—Container services operate to Garston (every other day), Preston (three times weekly), Rotterdam (bi-weekly) and Gothenburg (fortnightly). A roll-on/roll-off berth has almost been completed.

Road and Rail Transport.—The reorganization of public transport in Northern Ireland was completed by the Transport Act (N.I.), 1967, which provided for the abolition of the Ulster Transport Authority and the establishment of the Northern Ireland Transport Holding Company. The Holding Company took over the assets of the Authority and is responsible for the supervision of the subsidiary companies, Northern Ireland Carriers, owned jointly with the National Freight Corporation, which operates road freight services, Ulsterbus Ltd. which operates the public road passenger services, Northern Ireland Railways Co. Ltd., which provides the railway services, and Northern Ireland Airports Ltd. which is responsible for running the main airport at Aldergrove, near Belfast. A few privately operated bus services are provided in rural areas under licence. Citybus Ltd. provides omnibus services in the Belfast area. Road freight services are also provided by a large number of hauliers operating competitively under licence.

Air Transport.—Passenger and freight services operate between Belfast Airport and airports throughout Great Britain. A limited number of services are also operated to North America. In 1974, 1 200,000 passengers, and 20,000 metric tons of freight, including mail, were carried. In 1972 the extension of the main runway to 9,100 ft, was completed.

Counties of Northern Ireland

Counties and County Boroughs	Area* sq. miles	Lord Lieutenant	High Sheriff, 1976
(1) Antrim.....................	1,099	Capt. R. A. F. Dobbs	Col. F. B. S. Maclaran, M.C.
Belfast County Borough............	25	Col. Lord Glentoran, P.C., K.B.E.	J. Stewart.
(2) Armagh....................	489	The Rt. Hon. Sir Charles Norman	H. G. Clendinning, E.R.D.
(3) Down....................	952	Lockhart Stronge, Bt., M.C. The Earl of Clanwilliam	Lt. Col. D. Rowan-Hamilton, M.V.O.
(4) Fermanagh................	657	Maj.-Gen. T. P. D. Scott, C.B., C.B.E., D.S.O.	F. B. Gage
(5) Londonderry†.............	810	Col. M. W. McCorkell, O.B.E., T.D.	Dr. R. W. Temple
Londonderry City...........	3·4	T. F. Cooke	H. M. Bennet, O.B.E.
(6) Tyrone...................	1,218	The Duke of Abercorn	H. F. D. Stevenson

* Excluding tidal waters and large lakes.   † Excluding the City of Londonderry.

Municipal Directory of Northern Ireland

District and § Borough Councils	Estimated Population	Annual Net Value	Council Clerk	Chairman 1975
		£		
Antrim.....................	37,100	515,635	S. J. Magee	J. H. Allen
§ Ards......................	51,000	631,005	W. C. Scott	H. S. Cosbey
Armagh....................	48,000	433,834	N. C. H. Megaw	A. N. Creswell
§ Ballymena.................	52,600	643,576	J. S. McIlroy	G. G. Sloan
Ballymoney................	23,200	207,530	W. J. Regan	F. E. C. Holland
Banbridge.................	29,400	242,575	R. J. Weatherall	W. H. Davison
Belfast City................	374,300	8,219,549	W. J. Johnston	R. E. M. Humphreys
§ Carrickfergus..............	27,800	464,905	R. Boyd	H. McLean
Castlereagh................	65,000	896,682	A. D. Nicol	T. B. S. Hawthorne
§ Coleraine.................	44,900	674,490	W. E. Andrews	Col. A. N. Clarke, O.B.E.
Cookstown.................	27,800	246,075	W. A. Bownes	A. McConnell
§ Craigavon.................	71,200	1,030,970	W. J. Mayes	S. J. McCammick
Down.....................	49,500	499,904	J. Byrne	E. McVeigh
Dungannon................	43,300	333,819	—	Maj. J. H. Hamilton-Stubber
Fermanagh.................	51,000	340,952	J. McGuinness	T. A. Daly
§ Larne.....................	29,400	467,327	R. Lyttle	T. Seymour
Limavady..................	24,700	224,712	M. S. Thompson	Mrs. F. Sloan
Lisburn....................	80,500	927,110	H. A. Duff	G. E. McCartney
Londonderry City...........	86,600	1,124,839	C. M. Geary	H. A. I. Canavan
Magherafelt................	32,500	239,440	W. J. McKinney	P. J. Heron
Moyle.....................	13,900	123,273	J. O'Kane	F. Wheeler
Newry and Mourne...........	75,800	631,246	P. J. O'Hagan	A. Lockhart
Newtownabbey..............	71,200	1,050,575	R. W. Blennerhassett	S. R. Cameron
§ North Down...............	58,800	922,797	R. Wolsey	J. Preston
Omagh....................	41,800	304,650	D. R. D. Mitchell	H. McCauley
Strabane..................	35,500	226,947	J. N. Morran	J. J. McKelvey
Northern Ireland............	1,546,800	21,624,415		

Note.—Since the reorganisation of Local Government, rates in Northern Ireland are now collected by the Department of Finance and consist of two rates. A regional rate of £2·99 was made by the Department of Finance. Each of the 26 District Councils made their own separate rate. The regional rate was subject to subsidy at varying levels to provide a gradual transition from the previous differing rates made by former rating authorities.

THE ISLE OF MAN (MONA)

An island in the Irish Sea, in lat. 54° 3'–54° 25' N. and long., 4° 18'–4° 47' W., nearly equidistant from England, Scotland, and Ireland. The total land area is 141,263 acres (221 sq. miles), of which 76,701 acres are under cultivation. An interim report on the 1971 Census showed a total population of 56,289 (males, 26,461; females 29,828). In 1973 the births numbered 807 and the deaths 921. 165 persons were returned at the Census of 1961 as able to speak the Manx language, compared with 4,657 in 1901 and 355 in 1951. The principal

sector's of the Island's economy in terms of income generated and in order of importance (1971/72 figures) are Manufacturing Industry, Insurance, Banking and Finance, and Tourism.

Government.—The Isle of Man is governed by a Legislature, called the Tynwald, consisting of two branches: the Legislative Council and the House of Keys. The Council consists of the Lieutenant-Governor, the Bishop of Sodor and Man, the First Deemster, the Attorney-General and 7 members appointed by the House of Keys. The House of Keys (possibly from the Scandinavian *keise*= chosen) is one of the most ancient legislative assemblies in the world. It consists of 24 members, elected by the adult male and female population, 13 from the six *sheadings*, 7 from Douglas, 2 from Ramsey, and 1 each from Castletown and Peel. Bills after having passed both Houses are signed by the members, and then sent for the Royal Assent. After receiving the Royal Assent, a Bill does not become law unless promulgated within the ensuing twelve months, and on the first " Tynwald Day " (July 5) following it is announced in the English and Manx languages on the Tynwald Hill. On the promulgation taking place a certificate thereof is signed by the Lieutenant-Governor and the Speaker of the House of Keys. The Isle of Man is associated for certain purposes with the Common Market under Protocol 3 of the Treaty of Accession. Community rules on agricultural trade, customs duties etc., apply to the Island.

Finance.—The Island's Budget for 1975/76 provides for revenue and capital expenditure of £31,765,620. The principal sources of Government revenue are a) Income Tax, charged at the rate of 21·25 per cent of all taxable income and b) Customs and Excise Duties, collected on behalf of the Island under the " Common Purse Agreement " by H. M. Customs and Excise. There are no surtax or death duties, although there is a Company Registration Tax, which is levied at the flat rate of £200 on every company incorporated in the Isle of Man which trades, and there is a Land Speculation Tax payable at the rate of 21·25 per cent.

An annual contribution of 5 per cent of the net " Common Purse " receipts is made towards the cost of defence and other common services provided by the United Kingdom Government.

There are also reciprocal Social Security arrangements with the U.K.

There are 36 primary, 6 secondary schools, a college of further education and a domestic science college, in addition to King William's College and the Buchan School for Girls.

CAPITAL, ΨDouglas. Population (1971), 20,389; ΨCastletown (2,820) is the ancient capital; the other towns are ΨPeel (3,081), and ΨRamsey (5,048).

FLAG.—Three legs in white and gold armed conjoined on a red ground.

Lieutenant-Governor, His Excellency Sir John Paul, G.C.M.G., O.B.E., M.C. (1973).

Government Secretary, T. Kelly.

Speaker, House of Keys, H. C. Kerruish, O.B.E.

THE CHANNEL ISLANDS

Situated off the north-west coast of France (at distances of from ten to thirty miles), are the only portions of the *Dukedom of Normandy* now belonging to the Crown, to which they have been attached ever since the Conquest. They consist of Jersey (28,717 acres) Guernsey (15,654 acres), Alderney (1,962 acres), Brechou (74), Great Sark (1,035), Little Sark (239), Herm (320), Jethou (44) and Lihou (38), a total of 48,083 acres, or 75 square miles. In 1971 the population of Jersey was 72,532, and of Guernsey, etc. 53,734 (Guernsey, 51,458; Alderney, 1,686; Sark, 590).

The climate is mild, and the soil exceptionally productive. The land under cultivation is about 38,765 vergées (2¼ vergées=1 acre) in Jersey, and about 16,500 vergées (2½ vergées=1 acre) in Guernsey, the principal product of the soil of Jersey being potatoes, tomatoes and flowers, and of Guernsey, tomatoes, flowers and fern. The famous Jersey and Guernsey breed of cows have earned a well-deserved celebrity. The Lieutenant-Governors and Commanders-in-Chief of Jersey and Guernsey are the Personal Representatives of the Sovereign and the channel of communication between H.M. Government and the Insular Governments. The Bailiffs of Jersey and Guernsey, appointed by the Crown, are Presidents both of the Assembly of the States (the Insular Legislature) and of the Royal Courts respectively.

The official language is English and a Norman-French *patois* is also in use (except in Alderney). The principal imports are food, beverages, tobacco, manufactured goods, fuels and chemicals, and the chief exports potatoes, tomatoes, grapes, flowers and cattle. The chief town of Jersey is ΨSt. Helier on the south coast; the principal town of Guernsey is ΨSt. Peter Port, on the east coast, and of Alderney is St. Anne's.

JERSEY

Lieutenant-Governor and Commander-in-Chief of Jersey, His Excellency General Sir Desmond Fitzpatrick, G.C.B., D.S.O., M.B.E., M.C. £10,000

Secretary and A.D.C., Lt.-Comdr. O. M. B. de Las Casas, O.B.E., R.N.(ret.).

Baliff of Jersey, H. F. C. Ereaut.

Dean of Jersey, Very Rev. T. A. Goss.

Attorney-General and Receiver-General, V. A. Tomes.

Solicitor-General, P. M. Bailhache.

States Treasurer, J. Clennett.

Year to Dec. 31:	1973	1974
Revenue........	£27,433.357	£33,647,271
Expenditure......	19,508,375	24,889,549
Public Debt......	2,287,211	5,538,940

The standard rate of Income Tax is 20p. in the £. No super tax or death duties are levied.

FLAG.—White, bearing a red diagonal cross.

GUERNSEY AND DEPENDENCIES

Lieutenant-Governor and Commander-in-Chief of Guernsey, His Excellency Vice-Adm. Sir John Martin, K.C.B., D.S.C. (1974). £7,000

Secretary and A.D.C., Capt. M. H. T. Mellish, O.B.E., E.R.D.

Bailiff of Guernsey, Sir John Loveridge, C.B.E.

Dean of Guernsey, Very Rev. F. W. Cogman.

Deputy Bailiff, E. P. Shanks, C.B.E., Q.C.

Attorney-General, C. K. Frossard.

Solicitor-General, G. M. Dorey.

States Supervisor, A. S. Forty.

Receiver-General, R. H. Collenette.

	1973	1974
Revenue........	£12,246,831	£14,793,118
Expenditure......	8,868,419	11,308,363
Net Funded Debt.	2,438,399	2,538,371
Note and Coin issue..........	3,846,800	4,502,360

ALDERNEY

President of the States, G. W. Baron.

Clerk to the States, W. E. Jones.

Clerk to the Court, K. K. Lacey, V.R.D.

SARK

Le Seigneur of Sark, Michael Beaumont.

Deputy Seigneur, B. S. Allen, M.B.E.

Seneschal, B. G. Jones.

FLAG.—White, bearing a red cross of St. George.

The Commonwealth

The Commonwealth is a free association of the 35 sovereign independent states listed below together with their dependencies (mostly small islands which are dependencies of Britain, Australia or New Zealand) and the Associated States of the Eastern Caribbean.

UNITED KINGDOM	LESOTHO
CANADA	MALAWI
AUSTRALIA	MALAYSIA
NEW ZEALAND	MALTA
BAHAMAS	MAURITIUS
BANGLADESH	NAURU (special member)
BARBADOS	NIGERIA
BOTSWANA	SIERRA LEONE
CYPRUS	SINGAPORE
FIJI	SRI LANKA
GAMBIA	SWAZILAND
GHANA	TANZANIA
GRENADA	TRINIDAD AND TOBAGO
GUYANA	UGANDA
INDIA	ZAMBIA
JAMAICA	TONGA
KENYA	WESTERN SAMOA
PAPUA NEW GUINEA	

AREA AND POPULATION.—The total area of the independent British Commonwealth is 9,907,869·6 square miles (excluding the U.K.). Details of the areas and populations of the Member States and dependencies appear in the following pages and are also tabulated on pp. 199-203. The total population of the Commonwealth is estimated to be approaching 900,000,000.

GOVERNMENT.—Most members of the Commonwealth are parliamentary democracies, their laws being made with the consent of a freely elected parliament after discussion in that parliament, the executive government holding office by virtue of majority in parliament. However, Nigeria (1966) has suspended its constitution and is under military rule: the Constitution granted to Lesotho on independence in 1966 was suspended in January, 1970. In January, 1971, Uganda came under military rule.

Queen Elizabeth II is recognized as Queen and Head of State in the following member countries of the Commonwealth: United Kindom, Canada, Australia, New Zealand, Jamaica, Trinidad and Tobago, Fiji, Barbados, Mauritius, Bahamas, Grenada and Papua New Guinea. In each of these countries (except the United Kingdom) Her Majesty is personally represented by a Governor-General, who in many respects holds the same position in relation to the administration of public affairs as is held by the Sovereign in Britain (with the exception of certain constitutional functions which are performed by Her Majesty personally). The Governor-General is appointed by the Queen on the recommendation of the Government of the country concerned and is wholly independent of the British Government; in many cases he is a national of the country in which he holds office.

India, Ghana, Nigeria, Cyprus, Uganda, Tanzania, Kenya, Malawi, Zambia, Singapore, The Gambia, Guyana, Nauru, Sierra Leone, Botswana, Sri Lanka, Bangladesh and Malta are Republics with Presidents as Head of State, Malaysia has one of the State Rulers as elected Monarch (*Yang di-Pertuan Agong*) and Head of State; Lesotho, Tonga and Swaziland are monarchies which have their own Kings. Western Samoa has a Head of State whose functions are analogous to those of a constitutional monarch. All Members of the Commonwealth accept The Queen as the symbol of the free association of the member nations of the Commonwealth and as such, Head of the Commonwealth.

The status of member nations was defined by the Imperial Conference of 1926 and given legal substance by the *Statute of Westminster*, 1931, in which the Commonwealth nations were described as " autonomous communities within the British Empire, equal in status, in no way subordinate one to another, but united by a common allegiance to the Crown and freely associated as members of the British Commonwealth of Nations." Other parts of the Commonwealth, such as the Dependent Territories and Associated States, are regarded as forming part of the Commonwealth by virtue of their relationship with member states of the Commonwealth.

CONSULTATION.—The most important means of consultation between Governments are Heads of Government Meetings. These Meetings, which replaced the more formal pre-war Imperial Conferences, have been held at frequent intervals since 1944. They are a useful means whereby Commonwealth Heads of Government consult together on major issues of international affairs and other matters which affect them all. It is not their practice to pass Resolutions or to seek to formulate common and binding policies on international issues; but they have on occasion made general statements of principle to which they all subscribe—such as the Commonwealth Declaration agreed at Singapore in January 1971 and the statement on Nuclear Weapon Tests issued during the meeting held at Ottawa in August 1973—and the policies of individual Governments are clearly often influenced by the information and ideas exchanged at these Meetings. In addition to meetings of Heads of Government, there are annual meetings of Finance Ministers, as well as less frequent meetings between Ministers or officials responsible for subjects such as trade, education, medicine and law.

RHODESIA.—Southern Rhodesia was united with Northern Rhodesia and Nyasaland in a federation which lasted from 1953 until 1963, since when Nyasaland (as Malawi, 1964) and Northern Rhodesia (as Zambia, 1964) have become independent. Southern Rhodesia made a unilateral declaration of independence on Nov. 11, 1965. Its present constitutional status is as set out in the Southern Rhodesia Act, 1965.

CITIZENSHIP AND NATIONALITY.—Each member of the Commonwealth of Nations defines the citizenship and nationality of its own people and determines the status of other Commonwealth nationals within its own boundaries. In most cases, though not in all, they possess a common status as British subjects (or Commonwealth citizens). Even where there is no such provision for a common status, the Members of the Commonwealth differentiate, in greater or lesser degree, as regards the grant of privileges, between citizens of the Commonwealth and aliens. The Republic of Ireland, which in 1949 ceased to be a member of the Commonwealth, is not regarded by the other Commonwealth nations as a foreign country or her citizens as foreigners.

THE JUDICATURE.—The Supreme Judicial Authority for certain parts of the Commonwealth is the Judicial Committee of the Privy Council. Appeals may be brought to it from the Courts of the dependencies and also from the Courts of certain independent members of the Commonwealth which have not abrogated the right of appeal (i.e. Australian States, New Zealand, Jamaica, Trinidad and Tobago, Malaysia, Singapore, The Gambia, Barbados, Mauritius, Fiji, The Bahamas and Grenada). The Committee consists of such members of the Privy Council as have held or are holding high judicial office in Great Britain or are or have been judges in certain Commonwealth countries. The Supreme Judicial Authority for Great Britain and Northern Ireland is the House of Lords.

DEFENCE.—Each of the independent members of the Commonwealth is completely responsible for its own defence and all are members of the United Nations. The United Kingdom and Canada belong to N.A.T.O.; the United Kingdom, Australia and New Zealand are members of S.E.A.T.O.; Australia and New Zealand are signatories of the Pacific Security Treaty. The United Kingdom has a defence agreement with Malta, and is a signatory to the Treaty of Guarantee of Cyprus. With Australia and New Zealand, the United Kingdom is also a partner in joint defence arrangements with Malaysia and Singapore.

THE ASSOCIATED STATES.—Early in 1967 the former colonies of Antigua, Dominica, Grenada, St. Kitts-Nevis-Anguilla and St. Lucia became " nondependent " States in association with Great Britain. Legal effect was given to this status by the West Indies Act, 1967. In October, 1969, St. Vincent also became an Associated State. The main features of the association are that each State is responsible for its own internal affairs, may amend its own Constitution and may sever the association by unilateral declaration, subject to the observance of procedures contained in the Constitution of each State. Her Majesty's Government retains responsibility for the external affairs and defence of each territory. On February 7, 1974, Grenada left the association on becoming an independent member of the Commonwealth.

OVERSEAS DEPENDENCIES.—The United Kingdom, Australia and New Zealand have dependencies for which they are independently responsible. (*See* following sections.)

Colony (or Settlement): a territory belonging by settlement, conquest or annexation to the British Crown.

Protectorate: a territory not formally annexed, but in respect of which, by treaty, grant, usage, sufferance, and other lawful means, Her Majesty has power and jurisdiction.

Protected State: a territory under a ruler which enjoys Her Majesty's protection, over whose foreign affairs she exercises control but in respect of whose internal affairs she does not exercise jurisdiction.

Condominium: a territory for which responsibility is shared by two administering powers.

Leased Territories: this term applies only to that part of the mainland of China which was in 1898 leased to Great Britain for 99 years and is administered by the Government of Hong Kong.

Other Commonwealth Dependencies.—Australia and New Zealand administer a number of island territories and extensive Antarctic areas.

DEVELOPMENT AND FINANCE.—Complete financial autonomy is enjoyed by all members of the Commonwealth. In some countries, customs tariffs are lower for merchandise of Commonwealth origin than for imports from foreign countries. The British Government provides guarantees for the capital issues made by dependent territories and also provides budgetary assistance in many cases as well as direct loans and grants to assist development.

Under the Colonial Development and Welfare Act, 1940, annual sums of £5,000,000 were made available for developments and £500,000 for research for a ten-year period. Succeeding Acts increased the total sum to be made available and extended the period to be covered. In 1965 the Act was extended for a final 5 years. It authorized Exchequer Loans towards the cost of approved development programmes amounting to £125,000,000 and a ceiling of £390,000,000 for development and welfare assistance in the period 1941–1970. Thereafter the development needs of the remaining dependencies have been dealt with under the provisions of the Overseas Aid Act, 1966.

COMMONWEALTH COUNTRIES NOW MEMBER STATES

1931   Canada; Australia; New Zealand

In 1931 the Statute of Westminster clarified the legal position of Canada, Australia and New Zealand which had long been self-governing and independent states.

1947   India (Republic, 1950)
1948   Sri Lanka (Republic, 1972; but originally a Republic on Ceylon, 1970)
1957   Ghana, *formerly* Gold Coast (Republic, 1960) Malaya (an elective monarchy, now MALAYSIA; *see* Sabah and Sarawak. 1963)
1960   Cyprus (Republic, 1960; Cwlth. Member, 1961)
1960   Nigeria (Republic, 1963)
1961   Sierra Leone (Republic, 1971) Tanganyika (Republic, 1962; united 1964 with Zanzibar as TANZANIA)
1962   Jamaica; Trinidad and Tobago; Uganda, (Republic 1963); Western Samoa
1963   Zanzibar; Kenya (Republic, 1964) Sabah }in Federation of Malaysia (an Sarawak} elective monarchy) Singapore, as State in Federation of Malaysia, seceded as Republic, 1965
1964   Malawi (*formerly* Nyasaland Protectorate; Republic, 1966); Malta Zambia (Republic; *formerly* Northern Rhodesia)
1965   Gambia (The) (Republic, 1970)
1966   Guyana, *formerly* British Guiana (Republic, 1970) Botswana (Republic; *formerly* Bechuanaland Protectorate) Lesotho (*formerly* Basutoland); Barbados
1968   Mauritius; Nauru (Special Membership) Swaziland
1970   Fiji; Tonga
1972   Bangladesh (Republic, 1972; independent, originally as East Pakistan, 1948, although partitioned from India in 1947)
1973   Bahamas
1974   Grenada
1975   Papua New Guinea.

Associated States

From the dates shown, the following are fully self-governing states within the Commonwealth. The United Kingdom continues to be responsible for their defence and external relations:—

Antigua (Feb. 27, 1967); Dominica (March 1, 1967); St. Christopher Nevis and Anguilla (Feb. 27, 1967); St. Lucia (March 1, 1967); St. Vincent (Oct. 27, 1969).

Countries which have left the Commonwealth

1948   Burma; Palestine
1949   *Eire* or Republic of Ireland
1956   Sudan
1960   British Somaliland
1961   South Africa (on becoming a republic). Southern Cameroons
1963   Maldive Islands
1967   Yemen P.D.R. (*formerly* Aden).
1972   Pakistan.

Canada

AREA AND POPULATION

Provinces or Territories and Capitals (with official contractions)	Area (English Sq. Miles). Land and Water	Population Census, 1971	Population Estimated (June 1, 1974)
Alberta, *Alta.* (Edmonton)..................	255,285	1,627,874	1,714,000
British Columbia, *B.C.* (Victoria).............	366,255	2,184,621	2,395,000
Manitoba, *Man.* (Winnipeg).................	251,000	988,247	1,011,000
New Brunswick, *N.B.* (Fredericton)...........	28,354	634,557	662,000
Newfoundland, *Nfld.* (St. John's).............	156,185	522,104	542,000
Nova Scotia, *N.S.* (Halifax)..................	21,425	788,960	813,000
Ontario, *Ont.* (Toronto).....................	412,582	7,703,106	8,094,000
Prince Edward Island, *P.E.I.* (Charlottetown)....	2,184	111,641	117,000
Quebec, *Que.* (Quebec)......................	594,860	6,027,764	6,134,000
Saskatchewan, *Sask.* (Regina)................	251,700	926,242	907,000
Yukon Territory, *Y.T.* (Whitehorse)..........	207,076	18,388	19,000
Northwest Territories, *N.W.T.* (Yellowknife)...	1,304,903	34,807	38,000
Total................	3,851,809	21,568,311	22,446,000

Land Area, 3,560,238 square miles; Water Area, 291,571 square miles. (For areas of individual provinces, excluding freshwater areas, *see* p. 200.)

Of the total immigration of 218,465 in 1974, 26,541 were from the United States, 28,828 from the United Kingdom, 12,704 from Hong Kong, 16,333 from Portugal, and 134,059 from some 180 other countries including Ireland (1,292).

Increase of the People

Census Year	Population Males	Population Females	Population Total	Decennial Increase	Immigrants during Census Year
1901...........	2,751,708	2,619,607	5,371,315	538,076	55,747
1911...........	3,821,995	3,384,648	7,206,643	1,835,328	331,288
1921...........	4,529,643	4,258,306	8,787,949	1,581,306	91,728
1931...........	5,374,541	5,002,245	10,376,786	1,588,837	27,530
1941...........	5,900,536	5,606,119	11,506,655	1,129,869	9,329
1951...........	7,088,873	6,920,556	14,009,429	2,502,774	194,391
1956...........	8,151,879	7,928,912	16,080,791	..	164,857
1961...........	9,218,893	9,019,354	18,238,247	4,228,818	71,689
1966...........	10,054,344	9,960,536	20,014,880	..	194,743
1971...........	10,795,370	10,772,940	21,568,310	3,330,063	121,900

Origins	1961	1971	Religions	1961	1971
British Races.......	7,996,669	9,624,115	Roman Catholic.........	8,342,826	9,974,895
English...........	4,195,175	6,245,970	United Church of Canada	3,664,008	3,768,800
Scottish..........	1,902,302	1,720,390	Anglican Church of Canada	2,409,068	2,543,180
Irish.............	1,753,351	1,581,730	Presbyterian.............	818,558	872,335
Other............	145,841	76,030	Baptist..................	593,553	667,245
European Races.....	9,657,195	11,139,800	Lutheran................	662,744	715,740
French...........	5,540,346	6,180,120	Jewish..................	254,368	276,025
Austrian..........	106,535	42,120	Ukrainian (Greek) Catholic	189,653	227,730
Belgian..........	61,382	51,135	Greek Orthodox.........	239,766	316,605
Czech and Slovak..	73,061	81,870	Mennonite...............	152,452	168,150
Finnish..........	59,436	59,215	Pentecostal.............	143,877	220,390
German...........	1,049,599	1,317,200	Salvation Army..........	92,054	119,665
Hungarian........	126,220	131,890	Mormon................	50,016	66,635
Italian............	450,351	730,820	Church of Christ, Disciples.	19,512	16,405
Jewish............	173,344	296,945	Christian Science.........	19,466	..
Netherlands.......	429,679	425,945	Adventist................	25,999	28,590
Polish............	323,517	316,430	Confucian and Buddhist...	16,700	18,340
Rumanian.........	43,805	27,375	Others..................	543,627	1,567,580
Russian...........	119,168	64,475			
Scandinavian......	386,534	384,795	Totals..............	18,238,247	21,568,310
Ukrainian........	473,337	580,660			
Other............	240,881	448,805			
Asiatic Races.......	121,753	285,540			
Chinese..........	58,197	118,815			
Japanese..........	29,157	37,260			
Other............	34,399	129,460			
Indian and Eskimo...	220,121	312,760	Indian population (1961), 208,286; (1971), 295,215;		
All other.........	242,509	206,095	Eskimo population (1961), 11,835; (1971), 17,550.		
Totals..........	18,238,247	21,568,310			

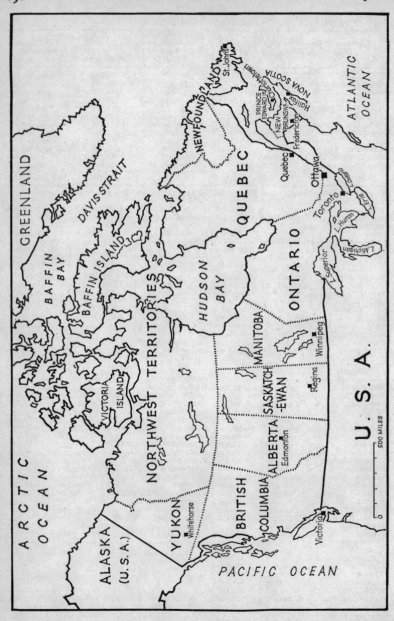

PHYSIOGRAPHY

Canada was originally discovered by Cabot in 1497, but its history dates only from 1534, when the French took possession of the country. The first permanent settlement at Port Royal (now Annapolis), Nova Scotia, was founded in 1605, and Quebec was founded in 1608. In 1759 Quebec was captured by the British forces under General Wolfe, and in 1763 the whole territory of Canada became a possession of Great Britain by the Treaty of Paris of that year. Nova Scotia was ceded in 1713 by the Treaty of Utrecht, the Provinces of New Brunswick and Prince Edward Island being subsequently formed out of it. British Columbia was formed into a Crown colony in 1858, having previously been a part of the Hudson Bay Territory, and was united to Vancouver Island in 1866.

Canada occupies the whole of the northern part of the North American Continent (with the exception of Alaska), from 49° North latitude to the North Pole, and from the Pacific to the Atlantic Ocean. In Eastern Canada, the southernmost point is Middle Island in Lake Erie, at 41° 41′.

Relief.—The relief of Canada is dominated by the mountain ranges running north and south on the west side of the Continent, by the pre-Cambrian shield on the east, with, in between, the northern extension of the North American Plain. From the physiographic point of view Canada has six main divisions. These are: (1) Appalachian-Acadian Region, (2) the Canadian Shield, (3) the St. Lawrence-Great Lakes Lowland, (4) the Interior Plains, (5) the Cordilleran Region and (6) the Arctic Archipelago. The first region occupies all that part of Canada lying southeast of the St. Lawrence. In general, the relief is an alternation of highlands and lowlands, and is hilly rather than mountainous. The lowlands area seldom rises over 600 feet above sea level. The great Canadian Shield comprises more than half the area. The interior as a whole is an undulating, low plateau (general level 1,000 to 1,500 feet), with the more rugged relief lying along the border between Northern Quebec and Labrador. Throughout the whole area water or muskeg-

filled depressions separate irregular hills and ridges, 150 to 200 feet in elevation. Newfoundland, an outlying portion of the shield, consists of glaciated, low rolling terrain broken here and there by mountains. The flat relief of the St. Lawrence-Great Lakes lowland varies from 500 feet in the east to 1,700 feet south of Georgian Bay. The whole area in the western part slopes gently to the Great Lakes. The most striking relief is provided by the eastward facing scarp of the Niagara escarpment (elevation 250 to 300 feet). The interior plains, comprising the Pacific Provinces, slope eastward and northward a few feet per mile. The descent from west to east is made from 5,000 feet to less than 1,000 feet in three distinct levels, with each new level being marked by an eastward facing *coteau* or scarp. Horizontal strata and peneplanation make for slight relief of the level to rolling type. Five fairly well-developed topographic divisions mark out the Cordilleran region of western Canada. These are: (1) coastal ranges, largely above 5,000 feet with deep fiords and glaciated valleys, (2) the interior plateau, around 3,500 feet and comparatively level, (3) the Selkirk ranges, largely above 5,000 feet, (4) the Rocky Mountains with their chain of 10,000 to 12,000-feet peaks, and (5) the Peace River or Tramontane region with its rolling diversified country. The Arctic Archipelago, with its plateau-like character has an elevation between 500 and 1,000 feet, though in Baffin Land and Ellesmere Island the mountain ranges rise to 8,500 and 9,500 feet. Two tremendous waterway systems, the St. Lawrence and the Mackenzie, providing thousands of miles of water highway, occupy a broad area of lowland with their dominant axis following the edge of the shield.

Climate.—The climate of the eastern and central portions presents greater extremes than in corresponding latitudes in Europe, but in the southwestern portion of the Prairie Region and the southern portions of the Pacific slope the climate is milder. Spring, summer, and autumn are of about seven to eight months' duration, and the winter four to five months.

GOVERNMENT

The Constitution of Canada has its source in the British North America Act of 1867 which formed a Dominion, under the name of Canada, of the four provinces: Ontario, Quebec, New Brunswick and Nova Scotia; to this Federation the other Provinces have subsequently been admitted. Under this Act Canada came into being on July 1, 1867 (Dominion Day), and under the Statute of Westminster, which received the royal assent on Dec. 11, 1931, Canada and the Provinces were exempted (in common with other self-governing Dominions of the Commonwealth of Nations) from the operation of the Colonial Laws Validity Act, the Statute of Westminster having removed all limitations with regard to the legislative autonomy of the Dominions. Provinces admitted since 1867 are: Manitoba (1870), British Columbia (1871), Prince Edward Island (1873), Alberta and Saskatchewan (1905) and Newfoundland (1949).

The Executive power is vested in a Governor-General appointed by the Sovereign on the advice of the Canadian Ministry, and aided by a Privy Council.

FLAG.—Red maple leaf with 11 points on white square, flanked by vertical red bars one half the width of the square.

GOVERNOR GENERAL'S HOUSEHOLD

Governor-General and Commander-in-Chief, His Excellency the Right Hon. Jules Léger, C.C., C.M.M., C.D. born April 4,1913, *assumed office* Jan. 14, 1974.
Secretary to the Governor-General, E. U. Butler, C.V.O.
Assistant Secretaries, C. J. Lochnan; R. de C. Nantel, C.D.
Comptroller of the Household, D. C. McKinnon, C.V.O., C.D.
Administrative Secretary, Brig.-Gen. J. C. A. Garneau, C.D.
Press Secretary, P. Cowan.
Attaché, C. Sirois.
Aides-de Camp, Capt. J. A. G. C. Desautels; Capt. N. MacNeil; Capt. P. Collinge.

THE CANADIAN MINISTRY
THE FEDERAL CABINET
Prime Minister, Rt. Hon. Pierre Elliott Trudeau.
President of the Queen's Privy Council for Canada, Hon. Mitchell Sharp.
External Affairs, Hon. Allan Joseph MacEachen.

Science and Technology and Public Works, Hon. Charles Mills Drury.
Transport, Hon. Jean Marchand.
Finance, Hon. John Napier Turner.
President of the Treasury Board, Hon. Jean Chrétien.
Postmaster General, Hon. Bryce Stuart Mackasey.

Energy, Mines and Resources, Hon. Donald Stovel Macdonald.
Labour, Hon. John Carr Munro.
Communications, Hon. Gérard Pelletier.
National Revenue, Hon. Stanley Ronald Basford.
Regional Economic Expansion, Hon. Donald Campbell Jamieson.
Manpower and Immigration, Hon. Robert Knight Andras.
National Defence, Hon. James Armstrong Richardson.
Justice and Attorney General, Hon. Otto Emil Lang.
Supply and Services, Hon. Jean-Pierre Goyer.
Industry, Trade and Commerce, Hon. Alastair William Gillespie.
Agriculture, Hon. Eugene Francis Whelan.
Solicitor General, Hon. Warren Allmand.
Secretary of State, Hon. James Hugh Faulkner.
Consumer and Corporate Affairs, Hon. André Ouellet.
Veterans Affairs, Hon. Daniel Joseph MacDonald.
National Health and Welfare, Hon. Marc Lalonde.
Environment, Hon. Jeanne Sauvé.
Leader of the Government in the Senate, Hon. Raymond Joseph Perrault.
Urban Affairs, Hon. Barnett Jerome Danson.
Indian Affairs and Northern Development, Hon. J. Judd Buchanan.
Fisheries, Hon. Roméo LeBlanc.

The Prime Minister receives remuneration of $33,300; other ministers, each $20,000; without Portfolio, $7,500. In every case—including the Prime Minister's—a sessional allowance of $24,000 per annum is paid to members of the Senate and House of Commons. In addition, for each session of Parliament members of the House of Commons receive an expense allowance of $10,600, while members of the Senate receive an expense allowance of $5,300. A motor vehicle allowance of $2,000 is paid to each Minister of the Crown and to the Leader of the Opposition in the House of Commons and a motor vehicle allowance of $1,000 is paid to the Speakers of the Senate and of the House of Commons. These allowances are not taxable.

CANADIAN HIGH COMMISSION
Macdonald House, 1 Grosvenor Square, W.1.
[01–629–9492]
High Commissioner, His Excellency Rt. Hon. Paul Martin, Q.C.
Deputy High Commissioner, P. A. Bissonnette.
Minister, J. H. Stone (Commercial).
Minister-Counsellors, P. S. Cooper (Administration); P. T. Eastham (Economic).

BRITISH HIGH COMMISSION
80 Elgin Street, Ottawa 4
High Commissioner, His Excellency Sir John Baines Johnston, K.C.M.G., K.C.V.O.
Deputy High Commissioner and Minister (Commercial), A. F. Maddocks, C.M.G.
Counsellors, T. Empson (Head of Chancery); Dr. L. Bovey (Scientific); J. D. Campbell, M.B.E., M.C. (Information); J. F. C. Springford (Cultural Affairs).
Defence Advisers, Brig. D. W. V. P. O'Flaherty, D.S.O.; Air Commodore R. J. Carson, C.B.E., A.F.C.
Military Advisor, Col. T. W. Tilbrook.
Naval Adviser, Capt. J. M. Webster, R.N.
1st Secretaries, J. E. S. Clayden (Admin.); A. R. F. Burgess (Commercial); C. M. Carruthers; I. Woodroffe; D. Cumming (Information); J. J. Taylor; D. Thomson (Defence Sales); H. W. Benstead; J. Moore.
British Council Representative, J. F. C. Springford, O.B.E.

THE LEGISLATURE
Parliament consists of a Senate and a House of Commons. The Senate consists of 104 members,

nominated by the Governor-General (age limit 75). They are distributed between the various provinces thus: 24 each for Ontario and Quebec, 10 each for Nova Scotia and New Brunswick, 6 each for Newfoundland, British Columbia, Manitoba, Alberta, and Saskatchewan and 4 for Prince Edward Island, 1 for North West Territories and 1 for Yukon; each Senator must be at least thirty years old, a resident in the province for which he is appointed, a natural-born or naturalized subject of the Queen, and the owner of a property qualification amounting to $4,000. The Speaker of the Senate is chosen by the Government of the day. The House of Commons is elected every five years at longest.

The House of Commons has 264 members. Representation by provinces is at present as follows: Newfoundland 7, Prince Edward Island 4, Nova Scotia 11, New Brunswick 10, Quebec 74, Ontario 88, Manitoba 13, Saskatchewan 13, Alberta 19, British Columbia 23, Yukon 1, Northwest Territories 1.

The Senate.
Speaker of the Senate, Hon. Renaude Lapointe (with Members' annual indemnity $24,000, residence allowance $3,000, expense allowance $5,300, motor-car allowance $1,000 and Salary $12,000)..... $45,300
Clerk of the Senate & Clerk of the Parliaments, Robert Fortier................. 42,500

The House of Commons.
Speaker of the House of Commons, Hon. James Jerome (with Member's annual indemnity $24,000, expense allowance $10,600, car allowance $1,000, residence allowance $3,000 and salary $20,000)... 58,600
Deputy Speaker, Gérald Laniel (with Member's annual indemnity $24,000, expense allowance $10,600, residence- allowance, $1,500 and salary $8,000)............ 44,100
Clerk of the House of Commons, Alistair Fraser................................ 42,500

THE JUDICATURE
The Judicature is administered by judges following the Civil Law in Quebec Province and Common Law in other Provinces. All Superior and County Court Judges are appointed by the Governor-General, the others by the Lieutenant-Governors of the Provinces, until age 70, except present incumbents who may remain until age 75. Each Province has its Court of Appeal and the highest court is the Supreme Court of Canada, composed of a Chief Justice and eight puisne judges, which holds three sessions each year. There is only one other Dominion Court, the Federal Court of Canada which has both a trial and an appeal division and which replaces the Exchequer Court with expanded jurisdiction.

Supreme Court of Canada.
Chief Justice of Canada, Rt. Hon. Bora Laskin........................... $68,000
Puisne Judges, Hon. R. Martland; Hon. W. Judson; Hon. R. A. Ritchie; Hon. W. F. Spence; Hon. L-P. Pigeon; Hon. B. Dickson; Hon. J. Beetz; Hon. J. de Grandpré...................each $63,000

Federal Court of Canada.
Chief Justice, Hon. W. R. Jackett, P.C.... $60,000
Associate Chief Justice, Hon. C. Noel.
Court of Appeal Judges, Hon. W. F. Ryan; Hon. A. L. Thurlow; Hon. R. Kerr; Hon. L. Pratte.
Trial Division Judges, Hon. A. A. Cattanach; Hon. H. F. Gibson; Hon. A. A. M. Walsh; Hon. J. E. Dubé; Hon. D. J. Heald; Hon. F. U. Collier; Hon. G. A. Addy; Hon. R. G. Decary; Hon. P. M. Mahoney.......................each $55,000

NATIONAL DEFENCE

On Aug. 1, 1964, the Headquarters of the Royal Canadian Navy, the Canadian Army and the Royal Canadian Air Force were integrated to form a single Canadian Forces Headquarters (C.F.H.Q.) under a single Chief of Defence Staff. The role of C.F.H.Q. is to provide military advice to the Minister of National Defence and to control and administer the Canadian Forces, which are organized in seven major commands: *Mobile Command* (units for support of the United Nations or other peacekeeping operations; ground forces, with tactical air support, for the protection of Canadian territory; combat forces in Canada for support of overseas commitments); *Maritime Command* (all sea and air forces on the Atlantic and Pacific coasts for defence of Canada against attack by sea, provision of anti-submarine defence in support of N.A.T.O., conduct of search and rescue operations and sea transport in support of Mobile Command; No. 1 Air Division (the Canadian contribution to strike reconnaissance forces available to the Supreme Allied Commander Europe (SACEUR); *Air Defence Command* (participates with U.S.A. in air defence of North America through NORAD); *Air Transport Command* (air transport for all Canadian forces; search and rescue operations in Ontario and Quebec); *Training Command*; *Canadian Forces Communications System*. In addition there is a *Reserve and Survival Organization* (aid to the civil power, emergency forces for national survival). Armed Forces expenditure for the fiscal year ended March 31, 1975, was $2,302,962,857.

Chief of Defence Staff, Gen. J. A. Dextraze.

On March 31, 1975, the total strength of the Canadian Armed Forces was 78,397.

EDUCATION AND LANGUAGE

Education is under the control of the Provincial Governments, the cost of the publicly controlled schools being met by local taxation, aided by provincial grants. There were (1973–74) 14,814 publicly controlled elementary and secondary schools with 5,477,018 pupils. In addition there were 158,616 pupils in 898 private elementary and secondary schools. There are special schools for Indians with 31,686 pupils (1973–74). In 1973–74 there were 68 degree-granting universities with a full-time university enrolment of 332,412, as well as 210,850 students in other post-secondary, non-university institutions.

Canada has two official languages, English and French. At the 1971 census 67·1 per cent. of the total population gave English as their official language, 18·0 per cent. French, 13·4 per cent. both English and French, and the remaining 1·5 per cent. neither English nor French.

VITAL STATISTICS
BIRTHS, DEATHS AND MARRIAGES, 1973

Province	Births	Deaths	Marriages
Alberta..........	29,288	10,763	16,280
British Columbia.	34,352	18,095	21,303
Manitoba........	16,964	8,196	9,196
New Brunswick..	11,425	5,084	6,357
Newfoundland...	11,906	3,405	5,048
Nova Scotia.....	13,289	6,928	7,273
Ontario.........	123,776	59,876	72,371
P.E.I...........	1,886	1,020	1,014
Quebec.........	84,057	42,666	51,943
Saskatchewan....	14,806	7,646	7,847
Yukon..........	420	111	206
N. W. Territories.	1,204	249	226
	343,373	164,039	199,064

Canada's Birth Rate per 1,000 population (1973) 15·9; Death Rate 7·4; Marriage Rate 9·0; Divorces 36,704.

REVENUE AND EXPENDITURE

Year ended March 31	Total Revenue ($)	Total Expenditure ($)
1971	12,803,051,408	13,182,143,536
1972	14,226,557,770	14,840,865,151
1973	16,601,603,475	16,120,734,605
1974	19,366,756,632	20,039,399,223

DEBT

Year ended March 31	Gross Public Debt ($)	Net Public Debt ($)
1971	42,975,825,289	17,322,374,244
1972	47,723,635,726	17,936,681,625
1973	51,715,635,066	17,455,812,755
1974	55,557,065,787	18,128,455,346

Banking.—There were 10 chartered banks on March 31, 1975, with assets of $98,892,571,000. Deposits were $89,422,229,000 of which $31,366,233,000 were personal savings.

TRADE

Total trade of Canada in 1974 was valued at $31,293,000,000 (exports) and $31,579,000,000 (imports). Value of trade with Canada's largest trading partners in 1974 was as follows:

Country	Imports ($)	Exports ($)
United Stations ..	21,205,838,000	20,629,481,000
Japan...........	1,423,187,000	2,219,206,000
United Kingdom.	1,127,803,000	1,873,274,000
West Germany...	764,388,000	527,246,000
Italy...........	315,968,000	457,068,000
People's Republic of China......	60,895,000	434,148,000
Brazil..........	111,791,000	380,155,000
Netherlands......	162,403,000	379,966,000
Belgium and Luxemburg....	173,383,000	363,380,000
France..........	395,088,000	308,209,000
Australia........	328,500,000	295,681,000
Norway.........	106,304,000	232,329,000
Mexico.........	113,803,000	177,061,000
Venezuela.......	1,289,414,000	175,410,000
Cuba...........	76,764,000	142,474,000
India...........	59,302,000	119,855,000
Spain...........	85,643,000	117,296,000
Switzerland......	136,905,000	95,606,000
Pakistan........	15,674,000	71,455,000
South Korea.....	134,256,000	71,131,000

Canada's Trade with the United Kingdom

	1973	1974
Imports from U.K.	$1,005,397,000	$1,127,803,000
Exports to U.K...	$1,581,845,000	$1,873,274,000

CANADIAN PRODUCTION

Agriculture.—About 7 per cent. of the total land area of Canada is classified as farm land and approximately half of this is under cultivation, the remainder being woodland or suitable only for grazing purposes. More than three-quarters of the land now cultivated is found in the prairie region of Western Canada. Farm cash receipts from the sale of farm products in 1974 were $8,448,140,000. Livestock, poultry and eggs contributed $3,055,370,000; field crops $4,002,519,000 and dairy products $1,085,953,000.

Canadian grain crops (in thousands of bushels):

ALL CANADA	1972	1973	1974
Wheat.......	533,288	604,738	522,513
Oats.........	300,208	326,880	254,745
Barley.......	518,316	469,570	394,286
Corn for grain	99,538	110,365	101,910
Rapeseed.....	57,300	53,200	52,900

Livestock.—In 1974, the livestock included 14,978,500 cattle, 783,500 sheep, 6,564,000 hogs & 36,772,000 poultry. The total milk production in 1974 was 16,670,362,000 lb.; butter, 240,216,000 lb.; factory cheese, 272,046,000 lb.; concentrated milk products 676,675,000 lb.; ice cream mix 30,531,000 gallons.

Fur Production.—Fur farms in Canada in 1973–4 produced 1,066,849 pelts valued at $19,315,582, mink contributing 99 per cent of the total. Wild life pelts totalled 2,773,993 with a value of $32,747,525.

Fisheries.—The total value of fishing products and by-products in 1973 was $772,086,000.

Forestry.—About 1,259,192 square miles, or 35 per cent. of the total land area is in forests, producing in 1973, 673,160,000,000 cubic feet of merchantable timber. The value of forest products in 1972 was: newsprint $1,177,177,000; paper (other than newsprint) $748,017,000; lumber $1,631,668,000; wood pulp $976,146,000.

Minerals.—Canada was, in 1972, the world's leading producer of nickel, silver, zinc and asbestos, and ranked second in gypsum, molybdenum, potash and copper. The total value of mineral production in 1974 was $11,618,098,000. The value of principal minerals produced was: crude petroleum $3,585,090,000; copper $1,400,101,000; nickel $977,687,000; zinc $892,139,000; iron ore $719,036,000; natural gas $686,614,000; natural gas by-products $629,009,000; potash $303,490,000; asbestos $310,680,000; gold $268,981,000; silver $201,965,000; coal $268,000,000; cement $244,711,000; sand and gravel $230,000,000; lead $139,105,000.

COMMUNICATIONS

Railways.—The total first main track mileage of railways in operation on Dec. 31, 1973, was 44,232 miles, the capital of the railways being (1973) $5,853,742,060; operating revenues $2,122,987,515; and operating expenses $2,032,983,640. In 1973 the passengers carried on railways numbered 19,821,933, and revenue freight 130,760,189 ton-miles.

Shipping.—The registered shipping on Dec. 31, 1973 including inland vessels, was 29,539 vessels with gross tonnage 3,900,000. The volume of international shipping handled at Canadian ports in 1973 was 124,558,908 tons loaded and 73,503,191 tons unloaded.

Canals.—The bulk of canal shipping in Canada is handled through the Montreal-Lake Ontario and Welland Canal sections of the St. Lawrence Seaway. Total Seaway transits in 1974 (unduplicated between the two sections) numbered 6,349 carrying 60,136,567 cargo tons. Principal commodities carried were iron ore, wheat, corn, barley, fuel oil, manufactured iron and steel, and coal.

Civil Aviation.—The number of passengers carried in 1973 (all carriers) was 17,160,536. 483,124,363 ton-miles of freight were carried.

Motor Vehicles.—Total motor vehicle registrations numbered 10,158,440 in 1973.

Post.—There were 8,770 postal facilities operating in Canada on March 31, 1974. 5,083,024 points of call were served by letter carriers on 11,159 full and 371 partial letter carrier routes. Mail was delivered to 858,246 customers through 4,984 rural routes and suburban services. Total postal revenue in the fiscal year 1973–74 was $591,133,000; total expenditure $768,305,000.

YUKON TERRITORY

The Yukon Act, 1952, as amended, provides for the administration of the Territory by a Commissioner acting under instructions from time to time given by the Governor in Council or the Minister of Indian Affairs and Northern Development. Legislative powers, analogous to those of a provincial government, are exercised by the Commissioner in Council. The Council comprises seven members elected from electoral districts in the Territory. The area of the Territory is 207,076 square miles with a population (Jan. 1, 1975) of 20,000. Mining is the chief industry, though trapping remains important and there is considerable timber production. Mining production, including asbestos, copper, silver, lead, zinc, gold and nickel, was valued at $185,194,000 in 1974.

SEAT OF GOVERNMENT, Whitehorse. Pop. (1971) 11,217.

Commissioner, J. Smith.

NORTHWEST TERRITORIES

The Northwest Territories Act, 1952, as amended provides for an executive, legislative and judicial structure. Legislative powers are exercised by the Commissioner in Council under the direction of the Minister of Indian Affairs and Northern Development. Council comprises 10 elected and 4 appointed members.

The Northwest Territories are subdivided into the districts of Mackenzie, Keewatin and Franklin.

The area of the Northwest Territories is 1,304,903 square miles with a population of 37,000 (estimated Jan. 1, 1975). The chief industry is mining, with a total value of $228,393,000 in 1974. Zinc and lead contributed 76 per cent. of the total; gold and silver 21 per cent., and natural gas and petroleum 2 per cent.

SEAT OF GOVERNMENT, Yellowknife. Pop. (1971) 6,122.

Commissioner, S. M. Hodgson.

PROVINCES OF CANADA

ALBERTA

Area and Population.—The Province of Alberta has an area of 255,285 square miles, including about 6,485 square miles of water, with a population (estimated January, 1975) of 1,702,485.

Government.—The Government is vested in a Lieutenant-Governor and Legislative Assembly composed of 75 members, elected for five years, representing 75 electoral districts in the Province. At a provincial election held in March, 1975, the Progressive Conservative Party took 69 seats, Social Credit Party (in office for 36 years), 4, the New Democratic Party, one seat and Independent, one seat.

Lieut.-Governor, His Honour Ralph G. Steinhauer
special allowance

Executive

Premier, and President of Council, Hon. Peter Lougheed......................	$40,500
Speaker of the Legislative Assembly, Hon. G. Amerongen......................	21,500
Deputy Speaker, Dr. D. J. McCrimmon..	18,500
Leader of the Opposition, R. C. Clark.....	35,500
Clerk of the Executive Council, H. B. Hobbs.	

Clerk of the Legislative Assembly, W. H. MacDonald.

The Judicature.
The Supreme Court of Alberta.
Appellate Division, Hon. William McGillivray (*C.J.*).......................$55,000*
Judges, Hons. J. M. Cairns; C. W. Clement; N. D. McDermid; G. H. Allen; W. R. Sinclair; D. C. Prowse; A. F. Moir; W. J. Haddad...... each 50,000*
Trial Division, Hon. J. V. H. Milvain (*C.J.*) 55,000*
Judges, Hons. N. Primrose; P. Greschuk; M. E. Manning; W. J. C. Kirby; A. M. Dechene; M. B. O'Byrne; H. J. MacDonald; S. S. Lieberman; A. J. Cullen; J. C. Cavanagh; W. K. Moore; D. H. Bowen; M. E. Shannon; F. H. Quigley; G. A. C. Steer.............. 50,000*
(*=not yet finalised)

London Office, Dept. of Industry and Tourism, 37 Hill Street, W.1.

Production.—The mining, manufacturing and construction industries have increased in economic impact so much more forcibly that agriculture is no longer of prime importance in Alberta.

The net value of production by industries (estimated 1974) is: mining $3,925,000,000; construction $1,299,000,000; manufacturing $1,211,000,000; electric power $199,000,000; agriculture $1,496,000; other $32,000,000. Total: $8,162,000,000.

Mining (1974 preliminary):—Crude oil $3,004,334,000; natural gas $595,809,000; natural gas by-products $611,156,000; coal $80,500,000; sulphur $65,200,000; cement $25,810,000.

Manufacturing.—The value of manufacturing shipments (1974 preliminary) was $2,996,156,647. Number of industrial establishments 2,053, total employees 57,214, salaries and wages $486,869,739. The leading industries are meat packing, oil refining, dairy and poultry products, iron and steel products, industrial chemicals and plastics, flour and feed milling, timber products, pulp and paper mills, printing and publishing, and brewing and distilling.

Finance.—Net Funded Debt. Mar. 31, 1974, $379,947,184; Revenue, March 31, 1974, $1,723,718,676; Expenditure, March 31, 1974, $1,306,035,932.

CAPITAL.—Edmonton. Population (1975 estimates) 445,691. Other centres are Calgary (433,389), Lethbridge (43,612), Medicine Hat (28,152) and Red Deer (28,828).

BRITISH COLUMBIA

Area and Population.—British Columbia has a total area estimated at 366,255 square miles, with a population of 2,184,621 at the census of June 1, 1971.

Government.—The Government consists of a Lieutenant-Governor and an Executive Council together with a Legislative Assembly of 55 members.

Lieut.-Governor, Col. Hon. Walter Stewart Owen, Q.C., Ll.D.

Executive Council
Premier, President of the Council and Minister of Finance, Hon. David Barrett, P.C.................................. $28,000
Provincial Secretary and Minister of Travel Industry, Hon. E. Hall............... 24,000
Attorney-General, Hon. A. B. Macdonald, Q.C.................................. 24,000
Lands, Forests and Water Resources, Hon. R. A. Williams.................... 24,000
Agriculture, Hon. D. D. Stupich........ 24,000
Mines and Petroleum Resources, Hon. L. T. Nimsick............................ 24,000

Transport and Communications, Hon. R. M. Strachan.......................... $24,000
Labour, Hon. W. S. King.............. 24,000
Education, Hon. Eileen E. Dailly...... 24,000
Economic Development, Hon. G. V. Lauk.. 24,000
Municipal Affairs, Hon. J. G. Lorimer.... 24,000
Health, D. G. Cocke.................. 24,000
Public Works, Hon. W. L. Hartley...... 24,000
Human Resources, Hon. N. Levi......... 24,000
Highways, Hon. G. R. Lea.............. 24,000
Recreation and Conservation, Hon. J. Radford.................................. 24,000
Consumer Services, Hon. Phyllis F. Young. 24,000
Housing, Hon. L. Nicolson............. 24,000
Minister without Portfolio, Hon. A. A. Nunweiler.......................... 21,000

Speaker, Legislative Assembly, Hon. G. H. Dowding............................. $11,000

The Judicature.
Court of Appeal—Chief Justice of British Columbia, Hon. J. L. Farris........... $39,000
Justices of Appeal, Hons. E. B. Bull; H. A. Maclean; M. M. McFarlane; A. E. Branca; A. B. Robertson; J. D. Taggart; P. D. Seaton; W. R. McIntyre; A. B. C. Carrothers.......................... 35,000
Supreme Court—Chief Justice, Hon. N. T. Nemetz............................. 39,000
Puisne Judges, Hons. J. G. Ruttan; D. R. Verchere; F. C. Munroe; J. S. Aikins; V. L. Dryer; J. G. Gould; J. A. Macdonald; W. K. Smith; G. G. S. Rae; A. B. Macfarlane; E. E. Hinkson; H. C. McKay; R. P. Anderson; T. R. Berger; D. E. Andrews; K. E. Meredith; A. A. Mackoff; W. A. Craig; E. D. Fulton; J. C. Bouck; S. M. Toy; H. E. Hutcheon; L. G. McKenzie; Hon. R. A. B. Wootton (supernumerary).......each 35,000

Agent-General in London, Rear Adm. M. G. Stirling, British Columbia House, 1 Regent Street, S.W.1.

Finances.—Estimated current Revenue for 1975-76, $3,223,240,000. Estimated current expenditure, $3,222,674,000. There is no direct debt.

Production and Industry.—The production levels of the four leading industries were estimated for 1974 as follows: wood manufactures, $1, 831,200,000; paper and allied industries, $950,400,000; minerals, $1,197,000,000; agriculture, $366,000,000; fisheries, $220,000,000. Manufacturing activity is based largely on the processing of products of the main basic industries. The principal manufacturing centres are Vancouver, New Westminster, Victoria, North Vancouver and Port Moody. Forestry and forest-based industries form the most important economic activity, accounting for approximately 40 per cent. of total production. British Columbia is the leading province of Canada in the quantity and value of its timber and sawmill products. Mining, the second most important economic activity, is based on copper, zinc, lead, iron concentrates, molybdenum, coal, natural gas, crude petroleum, asbestos and nickel. Molybdenum production is approximately 90 per cent. of the Canadian total. The most important agricultural products are livestock, eggs and poultry, fruits and dairy products. Salmon accounts for approximately 75 per cent. of the value of fisheries Other species include halibut, herring, sole, cod, flounder, perch, tuna and shellfish. The climate is healthy, quite moderate on the coast and continental east of the coast mountains. The economy is dependent upon markets outside the province for the disposal of most of the products of her industry.

Canadian and world markets receive forestry, mineral, fishing and agricultural products.

Transport.—The province has deep water harbours which are well serviced by railways and modern paved highways. Vancouver is the base for regular scheduled air routes to other parts of Canada, the United States, Europe, Mexico, South America, Hawaii, Fiji, Australia, Japan, Hong Kong and the Middle East.

Principal Cities.—CAPITAL, ΨVICTORIA, Metropolitan population (1972) 199,000. Ψ Vancouver (founded in 1886), the largest city in the Province, metropolitan population (1972) 1,098,000, is the western terminus of the Canadian Pacific Railway and the Canadian National Railways (the C.N.R. also has a terminus at Prince Rupert) and the southern terminus of the British Columbia Railway, and possesses one of the finest natural harbours in the world, servicing a variety of vessels, including large bulk cargo carriers. Other towns and cities are (1971 Census) Prince George (33,101), Kamloops (54,787) and Kelowna (36,412).

MANITOBA

Area and Population.—Manitoba, originally the Red River settlement, is the central province of Canada. The Province has a considerable area of prairie land but is also a land of wide diversity combining 400 miles of sea-coast, large lakes and rivers covering an area of 39,225 square miles and Precambrian rock which covers about three-fifths of the Province. The total area is 251,000 square miles with a population estimated at 98,000 in 1973.

Government.—The Government is administered by a Lieutenant-Governor, assisted by an Executive Council of 15 Ministers, who are members of the Legislative Assembly of 57 members. Each member of the Legislative Assembly receives an annual sessional indemnity of $9,600.

The New Democratic Party has formed the government of Manitoba since June 25, 1969. The standing in the House at May 1, 1974 was: New Democrats 31, Progressive Conservative 21, Liberal 5. *Lieut.-Governor*, His Honour William John McKeag (1970).

Executive

Premier, President of the Council, Minister of Dominion-Provincial Relations and Urban Affairs, Hon. Edward Schreyer	$16,600
	plus Sessional Indemnity
Minister of Finance, Hon. Saul M. Cherniack, Q.C.	
Labour, Hon. Russell Paulley.	
Attorney-General and Minister of Municipal Affairs, Hon. Howard Pawley.	
Health and Social Development, Hon. Saul Miller.	
Agriculture and Co-operative Development, Hon. Samuel Uskiw.	
Northern Affairs, Hon. Ronald McBryde.	
Tourism, Recreation and Cultural Affairs, Hon. René Toupin.	
Education, Hon. Ben Hanuschak.	
Highways, Hon. Peter Burtniak.	
Industry and Commerce, Hon. Leonard Evans.	
Public Works, Hon. Russell Doern.	
Mines, Resources and Environmental Management, Hon. Sidney Green.	
Consumer, Corporate and Internal Services, Hon. Ian Turnbull.	
Minister responsible for Public Insurance Corporation, Hon. Billie Uruski.	

Ministers each $22,800

Speaker of the Legislative Assembly, Hon. P. Fox.

The Judicature

Court of Appeal:—

Chief Justice of Manitoba, Hon. Samuel Freedman	$39,000
Puisne Judges, Hons. R. D. Guy; A. M. Monninn; G. C. Hall ....each	35,000

Queen's Bench:—

Chief Justice, Q.B.D. Hon. G. E. Tritschler	39,000
Puisne Judges, Hons. I. Nitikman; L. Deniset; J. E. Wilson; R. Matas; J. M. Hunt; J. R. Solomon; A. C. Hamilton ....each	35,000

Finance.—The revenue of the provincial government, 1973–74, is estimated at $694,600,000 and the expenditure $693,500,000.

Agriculture and Livestock.—The total land area in Manitoba is 135,536,000 acres, of which 19,088,000 acres are in occupied farms. The gross value of agriculture production in 1972 was estimated at $669,000,000 and livestock $253,000,000. Farm animals in June 1972, numbered 1,176,000 cattle, 876,000 pigs, 38,000 sheep and 8,530,000 poultry.

Manufactures.—The gross annual value of manufactured products in 1971 was estimated at $1,320,000,000. Manufacturing enterprises employed about 55,000 persons. The chief manufacturing centres are Winnipeg, Brandon and Selkirk. The largest manufacturing industry is the food and beverage industry, followed by the clothing and metal fabricating industries.

CAPITAL.—Winnipeg, population (estimated, 1973), 552,500. Other centres are Brandon (32,463), Thompson (20,623) and Portage la Prairie (13,258). The capital city of Winnipeg was amalgamated with its suburban municipalities on January 1, 1972 to form one city with a central government.

NEW BRUNSWICK

Area and Population.—New Brunswick is situated between 45°–48° N. lat. and 63° 47′–69° W. long. and comprises an area of 28,354 square miles with an estimated population (Jan. 1974) of 658,000. It was first colonized by British subjects in 1761, and in 1783 by inhabitants of New England, who had been dispossessed of their property in consequence of their loyalty to the British Crown.

Government.—The Government is administered by a Lieutenant-Governor, assisted by an Executive Council, and a Legislative Assembly of 58 members elected by the people. At the General Election of November 18, 1974, 33 Conservative and 25 Liberal members were returned.

Lieutenant-Governor, His Honour H. J. Robichaud (1969)	$33,000

Executive

Premier, Hon. Richard B. Hatfield	$38,000
Justice, Hon. P. S. Creaghan.	
Highways, Hon. W. G. Bishop.	
Agriculture and Rural Development, Hon. Malcolm McLeod.	
Economic Growth, Hon. Lawrence Garvie.	
Health, Hon. G. W. N. Cockburn.	
Education and Historical Resources Administration, Hon. G. S. Merrithew.	
Natural Resources, Hon. Roland Boudreau.	
Labour, Hon. R. E. Logan.	
Finance and Chairman, New Brunswick Electric Power Commission, Hon. Edison Stairs.	
Municipal Affairs, Hon. Horace Smith.	
Fisheries and Provincial Secretary, Hon. Omer Leger.	
Tourism and Environment, Hon. Fernand Dube.	
Chairman, Treasury Board, Hon. J. S. Brooks.	
Social Services, Hon. Leslie Hull.	
Youth, Hon. J. P. Ouellett.	

Supply and Services, Hon. George Horton.
Ministers, each $26,500·00.
Speaker of the House, Hon. W. J. Woodroffe
$19,000

The Judicature
Court of Appeal
Chief Justice, C. J. A. Hughes.......... $39,000
Judges of Appeal, Hons. R. V. Limerick;
J. N. Bugold; Hon. H. C. Ryan..each   35,000

Queen's Bench Division
Chief Justice, Q.B.D., Hon. A. J. Cormier. $39,000
Judges, Hons. J. A. Pichette; D. Dickson;
J. P. Barry; C. I. L. Lebere; R. C.
Stevenson; S. G. Stratton........each $35,000
Finance.—The estimated revenue for the year
ending March 31, 1975, is $739,535,015 and
ordinary expenditure, $685,209,458.

Manufactures.—Forest products: pulp, paper and
timber form the major manufacture group, followed by foods, oil refining, shipbuilding and
general manufacturing including electronics, cooking and heating equipment, chemicals and fertilizers
and diversified other products. Saint John is the
principal manufacturing centre. Total value of
manufactured products was $1,096,100,000 in 1973.
Agriculture and Livestock.—The total land area is
17,582,720 acres of which about 85 per cent. is
forested. The Province is the largest potato-pro-
ducing area of Canada, grown chiefly in the upper
Saint John River Valley. Dairy farming is next in
importance with, on Jan. 1, 1975, 104,000 cattle,
7,000 sheep, 45,000 hogs and 2,476,000 (approx.)
poultry. Farm cash receipts $95,571,000 in 1973.
Fishing.—The chief commercial fish are lobsters,
sardines, herring, tuna, crab, plaice, red fish and cod,
with an estimated market value of $90,000,000 in
1974.
Minerals.—Extensive zinc, lead and copper deposits are now being mined in the north-eastern
part of the Province with a lead smelter operating
in conjunction with one mine operation. Total
mineral production was valued at $219,000,000 in
1974. Coal continues to be mined on a decreasing
scale with lesser amounts of non-metallic minerals.
Principal Cities.—CAPITAL ΨFredericton: population (1973), 42,000. Ψ Saint John (pop. 106,745) is
one of the principal winter ports of Canada and is
connected by C.P.R. and Canadian National Railways with Montreal; Moncton (47,890); Bathurst
(16,675); Edmundston (12,365); Campbellton
(10,335).

NEWFOUNDLAND
Area and Population.—The Island of Newfoundland is situated between 46° 37′–51° 37′ N. latitude
and 52° 44′–59° 30′ W. longitude, on the north-
east side of the Gulf of St. Lawrence, and is
separated from the North American Continent by
the Straits of Belle Isle on the N.W. and by Cabot
Strait on the S.W. The island is about 317 miles
long and 316 miles broad and is triangular in shape,
with Cape Bauld (N.), Cape Race (S.E.) and Cape
Ray (S.W.) at the angles. It comprises an area of
156,185 sq. miles (inclusive of Labrador) with a
population (estimated Jan., 1975) of 546,000.
Government.—On March 31, 1949, the island,
with its dependency of Labrador, became the 10th
Province of the Dominion of Canada. The Government is administered by a Lieutenant-Governor,
aided by an Executive Council and a Legislative
Assembly of 42 members.
Lieutenant-Governor, Hon. Gordon A.
Winter (July 2, 1974)................ $18,000

Executive
Premier, F. D. Moores.

President of the Council, Dr. T. C. Farrell.
Minister of Justice, T. A. Hickman.
Education, G. Ottenheimer.
Finance, H. R. V. Earle.
Health, R. Wells.
Mines and Energy, L. Barry.
Social Services, A. H. Murphy.
Municipal Affairs and Housing, B. Pickford.
Transportation and Communication, J. G. Rousseau Jr.
Industrial Development, C. W. Doody.
*Manpower, Industrial Relations, Public Works and
Services,* E. Maynard.
Provincial Affairs and Environment, G. Dawe.
Fisheries, H. Collins.
Rehabilitation and Recreation, T. Doyle.
Tourism, T. Hickey.
Rural Development, J. Reid.
Forestry and Agriculture, H. Collins.
Fisheries and Intergovernmental Affairs, J. C. Crosbie.

Clerk of the Executive Council, J. G. Channing.

The Legislature.
A General Election was held on March 24, 1972,
when 33 Progressive Conservatives and 9 Liberals
were returned. Standings in the Legislature in
June 1975 were 31 Progressive Conservatives, 8
Liberals and 3 empty seats.
Speaker of the House of Assembly, Hon. James Russell.
Finance.—The estimated net general revenue in
the fiscal year ending March 31, 1976, is
$544,292,000 and the net expenditure on current
and capital accounts $705,817,800.
Production and Industry.—With the exception of
Gander, Bishop's Falls, Badger, Millertown,
Buchans, Howley, Deer Lake and that portion of
the West Coast between St. George's and Port aux
Basques the inhabitants are chiefly located on the
coast-line of the shore and bays. In June 1975 there
were ten mines in operation, of which three were
iron, two base metal and five non-metallic mineral
mines. There were also fourteen establishments
mining structural materials such as sand and gravel,
stone, cement and clay. Two pulp and paper mills
were in operation in 1975. Mining is the largest
primary industry in the Province with a total value
of mineral production of $290,610,000 in 1972.
Railways.—The main line of the railway extends
from St. John on the east coast to Port aux Basques
on the west coast—a distance of 547 miles—with
branches connecting with the ports of Argentia,
Carbonear, Bonavista and Lewisporte, a total
mileage of 711. There are also 77 miles of private
line. Communication between various points on
the coast and between Port aux Basques and North
Sydney, Nova Scotia, is maintained by a fleet of 14
freight and passenger vessels and by some 21 freight
vessels, operated by the Railway.
Principal Cities.—The Capital, Ψ ST. JOHN'S
(population, 1971 Census, Greater St. John's
101,161), contains two cathedrals, several banks and
numerous public buildings. The second city of
Newfoundland is Corner Brook (26,309).

LABRADOR
Labrador, the most northerly district in the
Province of Newfoundland, forms the most
easterly part of the North American continent, and
extends from Blanc Sablon, at the north-east
entrance to the Straits of Belle Isle, on the south, to
Cape Chidley, at the eastern entrance to Hudson's
Straits on the north. The territory under the
jurisdiction of Newfoundland has an area estimated
at 112,826 square miles, with a population (1971)
of 28,165. Labrador is noted for its cod fisheries
and also possesses valuable salmon, herring, trout

and seal fisheries. Newfoundland (Labrador) supplies more iron ore than any other province in Canada and the huge hydro-electric plant on the Churchill River will be the largest in the world with a 5,250,000 kW. capacity when completed.

NOVA SCOTIA

Area and Population.—Nova Scotia is a peninsula between 43° 25′–47° N. lat. and 59° 40′–66° 25′ W. long., and is connected with New Brunswick by a low fertile isthmus about thirteen miles wide. It comprises an area of 21,425 square miles including 1,023 square miles of lakes and rivers with a 6,479 miles of shoreline. No place is more than 35 miles from the Atlantic Ocean. Total population (1971 census) 788,960.

Government.—The Government consists of a Lieutenant-Governor and a 46-member elected Legislative Assembly, from which the Executive Council (Cabinet) is selected. The Lieutenant-Governor represents the Queen and is appointed by the Governor-in-Council.

Lieutenant-Governor, Hon. Clarence Gosse,
  M.D. (*plus expense allowance* $12,000)... $35,000

Executive Council
Premier, Hon. Gerald A. Regan, Q.C.
  (*plus members' sessional indemnity* $9,600
  and expense allowance $4,800)......... $25,000
Finance, Hon. P. M. Nicholson, Q.C.
Recreation and Provincial Secretary, Hon. A. Garnet
  Brown.
Attorney-General, Hon. A. E. Sullivan.
Public Works, Hon. B. Comeau.
Social Services, Hon. H. M. Huskilson.
Education, Hon. J. W. Gillis.
Development, Hon. G. M. Mitchell, Q.C.
Labour and Housing, Hon. W. R. Fitzgerald.
Municipal Affairs, Hon. J. Fraser Mooney.
The Environment and Tourism, Hon. G. M. Bagnell.
Lands and Forests, Hon. M. E. De Lory, M.D.
Agriculture and Marketing, Hon. J. Hawkins.
Highways and Mines, Hon. L. L. Pace, Q.C.
Fisheries, Hon. A. H. Cameron.
Public Health, Hon. W. M. MacEachern.
Consumer Services, Hon. Maynard C. MacAskill, M.D.
  Cabinet Ministers receive $21,000 a year, *plus* member's sessional indemnity $9,600 and expense allowance $4,800.

The Judicature
Supreme Court—Appeal Division
Chief Justice, Hon. I. M. MacKeigan..... $55,000
Judges, Hons. T. H. Coffin; A. G. Cooper;
  A. L. Macdonald.................. 50,000

Trial Division
Chief Justice, Hon. G. S. Cowan........ 55,000
Judges, Hons. F. W. Bissett; G. L. S. Hart;
  M. C. Jones; V. A. L. Morrison; A. J.
  MacIntosh........................ 55,000
Finance.—The revenue for the fiscal year ending March 31, 1974, was $576,970,490 and expenditure was $682,587,711. The net direct debt was $298,686,683.

Manufacturing.—Manufacturing constitutes the single most important sector of the economy. Shipments are now worth $1,466,800,000 a year with a total value added of more than $368,800,000. Manufacturing plants provide employment for 43,000 or 16 per cent. of the labour force. Capital expenditure has increased from $612,000,000 in 1972 to $905,000,000 in 1974.

Utilities.—There is one major electrical utility; the Nova Scotia Power Corporation. With less than 2,200 employees, the Corporation delivered over 5 billion kilowatt hours of electrical energy during the year ending March 31, 1974. Power

developed in the province is produced in hydro and fossil-fuelled thermal plants and is supported by an auxiliary 30 mW gas turbine which provides rapid "peak demand" service. The Corporation, an agent of the provincial government, also operates seven retail electrical appliance outlets throughout the province.

Oil and Gas.—By the end of 1974, oil companies spent about $350,000,000 in exploration of the mainland and the Scotian Shelf offshore. 57 wells have been drilled off the coast of Nova Scotia by 3 major licence holders and their partners. 47 were classed as dry and abandoned and 10 suspended as possible oil or gas wells. At the start of that year, 26 companies held petroleum licences.

Tourism.—Between June 1 and October 31, 1974, 1,303,500 visitors spent $75,895,000 in the province. The number of visitors has increased by 70 per cent. in the last five years.

Forest Products.—The estimated gross value of primary and secondary forestry is $185,000,000 annually. Forest lands total 10,762,000 acres or 78·5 per cent. of the land area. About 74 per cent. of forest land is privately owned. Forest based industries employ about 8,000.

Fishing.—The value of fish landed in 1974 was a record $77,903,000. Products have been diversified and enlarged into a variety of processed foods that are increasing in number. Primary fishing and fish processing employ 17,000.

Mining.—The total value of mineral production in 1974 was estimated at $81,367,000, of which $31,200,000 was contributed by coal. Structural materials, gypsum ($14,518,000) and salt ($10,205,000) followed in dollar value.

Agriculture.—Farm cash receipts were estimated at about $101,580,000 in 1974. About 10 per cent. of the total area, or 1,328,875 acres, is classified as agricultural land, dairy products being the major sector.

Principal cities.—Capital Ψ HALIFAX, including the neighbouring city of Dartmouth, has a population of over 225,000. In addition to a 56-acre container-handling terminal, a super autoport has been built at Port Halifax to handle both the export and import of motor vehicles. A second container port will be operational by 1977. A shipyard, with dry-dock, can build and repair the largest ocean-going liners. The harbour, ice-free the year round, it the main Atlantic winter port of Canada. Other cities and towns include Ψ Sydney (33,230), Ψ Glace Bay (22,400), Amherst (9,966) and New Glasgow (10,849).

Strait of Canso.—In the last ten years, $400,000,000 has been invested in industrial development of an area adjacent to the Strait of Canso which once separated the mainland from Cape Breton Island, now linked by road and railway. A 10-mile long, ice-free harbour up to 200 ft. deep can take tankers and other ships of up to 500,000 tons. Existing industry includes an oil refinery, a thermal power generating station, a heavy water plant, bleached sulphate mill and newsprint mill. In 1972 the Nova Scotia Government announced construction of a $39,000,000 common-user dock for the mainland side of the Strait of Canso.

CAPE BRETON ISLAND
This has been part of Nova Scotia since 1819. It is the centre of the steel manufacturing and coal mining industries, and is also noted for its large lakes and beautiful coastal scenery, making it a tourist attraction in Canada.

ONTARIO

Area and Population.—The Province of Ontario contains a total area of 412,582 sq. miles, with a population (estimated April 1974) of 8,031,000.

Government.—The Government is vested in a Lieutenant-Governor and a Legislative Assembly of 117 members elected for five years. The state of the parties in March 1975 was 74 Progressive Conservatives, 23 Liberals, 20 New Democratic Party.

Lieutenant-Governor, Hon. Pauline McGibbon, Q.C. (1974).

Executive Council

Premier and President of the Council, Hon. William G. Davis, Q.C.

Colleges and Universities, Hon. J. A. C. Auld.

Education, Hon. T. L. Wells.

Health, Hon. F. S. Miller.

Community and Social Services, Hon. R. Brunelle.

Agriculture and Food, Hon. W. A. Stewart.

Environment, Hon. W. Newman.

Labour, Hon. J. MacBeth.

Natural Resources, Hon. L. Bernier.

Industry and Tourism, Hon. C. Bennett.

Transport and Communications, Hon. J. R. Rhodes.

Justice and Attorney-General, Hon. J. T. Clement, Q.C.

Correctional and Commercial Relations, Hon. S. B. Handleman.

Solicitor-General, Hon. J. T. Clement, Q.C. (*acting*).

Treasurer, Economics and Intergovernmental Affairs, Hon. W. D. McKeough.

Government Services, Hon. J. W. Snow.

Revenue, Hon. A. K. Meen, Q.C.

Management Board, Hon. E. A. Winkler.

Resources Development, Hon. A. Grossman.

Energy, Hon. D. R. Tumbrell.

Housing, Hon. D. R. Irvine.

Social Development, Hon. Margaret Birch.

Culture and Recreation, Hon. R. Welch, Q.C.

Without Portfolio, Hon. J. White; Hon. R. Beckett.

Secretary to the Cabinet, J. D. Fleck.

Speaker, Legislative Assembly, Hon. R. D. Rowe.

Chief Justice of Ontario, Hon. G. A. Gale.

Chief Justice of the High Court, Hon. W. Z. Estey.

AGENT-GENERAL IN LONDON, W. A. Cornell, 13 Charles II Street, S.W.1.

Livestock.—In June 1974 the numbers of livestock included—cattle, 3,206,000; sheep and lambs, 207,000; pigs, 2,000,000 and poultry, 35,453,000.

Forestry.—Productive forested lands cover 164,000 sq. miles or about 48 per cent. of the land area of the Province. Paper and allied industries are by far the most important sector of Ontario's forest industry.

Manufacture and Minerals.—Ontario is the chief manufacturing province of Canada and leads the other Provinces in mineral production.

CAPITAL.— Ψ Toronto (population, 1971 census Metropolitan area, 2,628,043) has a wide range of manufacturing and service industries and is a centre of education. Other major urban areas are: Ottawa, the national capital (602,510); Ψ Hamilton (498,523), with iron and steel industry, metal fabrication, machinery, electrical and chemical industries; London (286,011), a business, educational and manufacturing centre; Ψ Windsor (258,643); Kitchener (226,846) and Sudbury (155,424).

FEDERAL CAPITAL

OTTAWA, the Federal Capital, 111 miles west of Montreal and 247 miles north-east of Toronto, is a city on the south bank of the Ottawa river. The city was chosen as the Capital of the Province of Canada in 1857 and was later selected as the site of the Dominion capital. Ottawa con-tains the Parliamentary Buildings, the Public Archives, Royal Mint, National Museum, National Art Gallery and the Dominion Observatory.

A National Arts Centre opened on June 2, 1969, near the Parliament buildings. Facilities provided on 6½ acres of terraced land include an opera house with seating for 2,300, a theatre (800 seats), an experimental studio (300 seats) and a hall (100 seats).

Manufacturing is also carried on, food production, printing and publishing being of greatest importance. Ottawa is connected with Lake Ontario by the Rideau Canal. The City population was 302,341 at the Census of 1971; Metropolitan Ottawa (estimated, 1973), 619,000.

PRINCE EDWARD ISLAND

Area and Population.—Prince Edward Island lies in the southern part of the Gulf of St. Lawrence, between 46°–47° N. lat. and 62°–64° 30′ W. long. It is about 130 miles in length, and from 4 to 34 miles in breadth; its area is 2,184 square miles (rather larger than that of the English county of Norfolk), and its population (1971) 111,641.

Government.—The Government is vested in a Lieut.-Governor and an Executive Council, and Legislative Assembly of 32 members elected for a term of 5 years, 16 as Councillors and 16 as Assemblymen. Party representation in 1974 was: Liberal, 26; Conservative, 6.

Lieutenant-Governor, His Honour Gordon L. Bennett (1974) $16,000

Executive

Premier, President of the Executive Council and Minister of Justice, Attorney and Advocate-General, Hon. A. B. Campbell $24,500

Development, Industry and Commerce, Hon. J. H. Maloney, M.D.

Provincial Secretary and Education, Hon. B. Campbell.

Health and Social Services, Hon. Catherine Callbeck.

Highways and Public Works, Hon. B. L. Stewart.

Finance, Hon. T. E. Hickey.

The Environment and Tourism, and Community Services, Hon. G. R. Clements.

Fisheries and Labour, Hon. G. Henderson.

Agriculture, Hon. A. E. Ings.

Without Portfolio, Hon. G. Proude.

Ministers, each $14,500; *without Portfolio,* $3,600 (plus expenses)

Speaker of the Legislative Assembly, Hon. C. A. Miller $1,000

Supreme Court

Chief Justice, Hon. C. St. C. Trainor..... $32,000

Assistant Judges, Hon. G. J. Tweedy; Hon. R. R. Bell; Hon. J. P. Nicholson...each 28,000

Finance.—The ordinary revenue in 1972 was $101,724,546 and the expenditure was $101,540,162.

Education.—A university and a college of applied arts and technology were established in 1969 estimated enrolment for 1973–74 being 1,800; college of applied arts and technology 780 students.

CAPITAL, Ψ Charlottetown (pop. 18,500), on the shore of Hillsborough Bay, which forms a good harbour.

QUEBEC

Area and Population.—The Province of Quebec contains an area estimated at 594,860 square miles with a population (June, 1974), of 6,134,000.

Government.—The Government of the Province invested in a Lieutenant-Governor, a Council of ministers and a National Assembly of 110 members elected for five years. There are at present 100 Liberals, 2 Social Credit Rally, 6 *Parti Quebecois* and one Union National and one Independent.

Lieut-Governor, The Hon. Hughes Lapointe, Q.C. (Feb. 22, 1966).

Executive

Prime Minister and President of the Executive Council, Robert Bourassa.

Vice-Prime Minister and Minister for Inter-Governmental Affairs, Gérard D. Levesque.

Minister for Industry and Commerce, Guy Saint-Pierre.

Education, François Cloutier.

Labour and Manpower, Jean Cournoyer.

Social Affairs, Claude Forget.

Justice, Jérôme Choquette.

Municipal Affairs and the Environment, Victor Goldbloom.

Financial Institutions, Companies and Cooperatives, William Tetley.

Tourism, Fish and Game, Claude Simard.

Transport, Public Works and Supply, Raymond Mailloux.

Communications, Jean-Paul L'Allier.

Lands and Forests, Kevin Drummond.

Revenue, Gérald Harvey.

Cultural Affairs, Denis Hardy.

Immigration, Jean Bienvenue.

Agriculture, Normand Toupin.

Natural Resources, Gilles Massé.

Finance, Raymond Garneau.

Civil Service, Oswald Parent.

(and 6 Ministers of State).

AGENT-GENERAL IN LONDON.—Hon. Jean Fournier, 12 Upper Grosvenor Street, W.1.

The Judicature

Queen's Bench (Montreal):—

Chief Justice, Hon. L. Tremblay.

Puisne Judges (Montreal); Hons. P. C. Casey; G. E. Rinfret; G. R. W. Owen; G. H. Montgomery; R. Brossard; M. Crête; A. Mayrand; F. Kauffman; L. E. Bélanger.

Puisne Judges (Quebec).—Hons. A. Dube; J. Turgeon; F. Lajoie; J. Chouinard; Y. Bernier.

Superior Court:—

Chief Justice, Hon. Jules Deschênes.

Finance.—The revenue for the year 1973–4 was $5,032,850,790; expenditure amounted to $5,290,578,227. The net debt (March 31, 1974) was $2,867,725,689.

Production and Industry.—The principal manufacturing centres are Montreal, Montreal East, Quebec, Trois-Rivières, Sherbrooke, Shawinigan Drummondville and Lachine. Forest lands cover 297,300 sq. miles, of which 206,900 sq. miles are productive. Forest products in 1973 included: wood pulp, 6,147,433 tons; paper and paperboard, 5,941,409 tons.

Total value of shipments in the manufacturing industries in 1974 was $21,682,002,000. Value of 1974 shipments in the chief industries: Food and beverages, $3,878,392,000; Paper and allied industries, $2,358,116,000; Primary metal industries, $1,668,076,000; Textiles, $1,215,978,000; Clothing $1,365,138,000.

Agriculture and Fisheries.—In 1974 total farm receipts were: Crops, $109,140,000; Livestock and livestock products, $861,812,000; Other farm receipts, $136,428,000. 117,386,900 lb. of fish to the value of $13,473,350 were landed in 1974.

Mineral Production.—Minerals to the value of $1,152,083,000 were mined during 1974, compared with $926,083,039 in 1973. Distribution of the 1974 total was: copper, $246,105,000; zinc, $96,091,000; asbestos, $242,175,000.

Principal Cities.—CAPITAL, Ψ Quebec (population, estimated, 1974, 187,400) historic city visited annually by thousands of tourists, and one of the great seaport towns of Canada; and Ψ Montreal (municipal population, 1,216,500) with suburbs, 2,828,795 (Metropolitan Montreal), the commercial metropolis. Other important cities are Laval (238,100); Verdun (75,200) and Sherbrooke (82,700), Montreal-Nord (93,400) and La Salle (76,800).

SASKATCHEWAN

Area and Population.—The Province of Saskatchewan lies between Manitoba on the east and Alberta on the west and has an area of 251,700 square miles (of which the land area is 220,182 sq. miles), with a population (estimated, 1975) of 912,000. Saskatchewan extends along the Canada-U.S.A. boundary for 393 miles and northwards for 761 miles. Its northern width is 276 miles.

Government.—The Government is vested in the Lieutenant-Governor, with a Legislative Assembly of 61 members. There is an Executive Council of 18 members. The Legislative Assembly is elected for 5 years and the state of the parties in July 1975, was: N.P.D., 39; Liberals 15 and Progressive Conservative 7.

Lieut.-Governor, His Honour Stephen Worobetz, M.C., M.D. (1970) $18,000

Executive Council

Premier and President of the Council, Hon. A. E. Blakeney........................ $32,500

Attorney-General and Deputy Premier, Hon. R. Romanow, Q.C.

Industry, Hon. J. R. Messer.

Finance, Hon. E. Cowley.

Health, Hon. W. E. Smishek.

Municipal Affairs, Hon. E. I. Wood.

Labour and Social Services, Hon. G. T. Snyder.

Northern Saskatchewan, Hon. G. R. Bowerman.

Highways and Transport, Hon. E. Kramer.

Education, Hon. G. MacMurchy.

Environment, Hon. N. E. Byers.

Government Services and Telephones, Hon. J. E. Brocklebank.

Agriculture, Hon. E. E. Kaeding.

Culture and Youth, Consumer Affairs and Provincial Secretary, Hon. E. Tchorzewski.

Tourism and Renewable Resources, Hon. J. Kowalchuk.

Minerals, Hon. E. C. Whelan.

Co-operation and Co-operative Development and Consumer Affairs, Hon. W. A. Robbins.

Ministers, each $27,500.

AGENT-GENERAL IN LONDON.—E. A. Boden, 14–16 Cockspur Street, S.W.1.

Chief Justice of Saskatchewan, Hon. E. M. Culliton........................ $31,000

Chief Justice, Queen's Bench, Hon. A. H. Bence........................ $31,000

Finance.—Estimated revenue year ending March 31, 1976, is $1,143,708,620; expenditure, $1,140,643,250.

Agriculture.—In an average crop year, Saskatchewan produces some 60 per cent. of Canada's wheat. Wheat production in 1974 was 326,000,000 bushels. Cash income from the sale of farm products in 1974 was estimated at $1,942,000,000. Livestock population on Jan. 1, 1975, included 2,655,000 cattle and calves, 660,000 hogs and 91,000 sheep.

Industries.—In 1974 net value of commodity production was estimated at $3,055,000,000. Mineral production for 1974 was estimated at $782,425,291.

CAPITAL.—Regina. Population (estimated 1975), 147,000. Other cities: Saskatoon (126,449), Moose Jaw (32,000) and Prince Albert (28,500).

The Commonwealth of Australia

AREA AND POPULATION

States and Capitals	Area English Sq. Miles)	Population		
		Census June 30, 1966	Census June 30, 1971	Estimated Dec. 31, 1974
States				
New South Wales (Sydney)..........	309,433	4,237,901	4,601,180	4,798,000
Queensland (Brisbane)...............	667,000	1,674,324	1,827,065	1,997,700
South Australia (Adelaide)...........	380,070	1,094,984	1,173,707	1,239,300
Tasmania (Hobart)..................	26,383	371,436	390,418	405,000
Victoria (Melbourne)................	87,884	3,220,217	3,502,351	3,672,500
Western Australia (Perth)............	975,920	848,100	1,030,469	1,116,100
Territories				
Australian Capital Territory (Canberra)	939	96,032	144,063	187,600
Northern Territory (Darwin).........	520,280	56,504	86,390	69,700
Total....................	2,967,909	11,599,498	12,755,638	13,485,900

Increase of the People

Year	Increase			Decrease			Net Increase†	Marriages
	Births	‡Overseas Arrivals	Total	Deaths	Overseas Departures	Total		
1968	240,906	771,792	1,012,698	109,547	658,739	768,286	233,300	106,345
1969	250,176	898,858	1,149,034	106,496	769,812	876,308	261,600	112,470
1970	257,516	1,026,675	1,284,191	113,048	903,801	1,016,849	256,300	116,066
1971	276,362	1,078,798	1,355,160	110,650	994,193	1,104,843	244,800	117,637
1972	264,969	1,110,670	1,375,639	109,760	1,082,814	1,192,584	183,100	114,029
1973	247,668	1,290,360	1,538,028	110,823	1,249,942	1,360,765	177,300	112,700

‡ Including the following arrivals under the Australian Government's various schemes for assisted immigration: 1968, 105,102; 1969, 125,958; 1970, 134,428; 1971, 103,811; 1972, 63,710; 1973, 49,822.
† = natural increase (excess of births over deaths), net overseas migration gain; adjusted to make the series of increases agree with total inter-censal increase shown by 1971 census.

Inter-Censal Increases, 1947–1971

Year of Census	Population at Census*			Inter-Censal Increase	Net Immigration during Period
	Males	Females	Total		
1947	3,797,370	3,781,988	7,579,358	949,519	1933–1947 .. 41,106
1954	4,546,118	4,440,412	8,986,530	1,407,172	1947–1954 .. 639,028
1961	5,333,185	5,215,082	10,548,267	1,561,737	1954–1961 .. 584,754
1966	5,841,588	5,757,910	11,599,498	1,051,231	1961–1966 .. 395,485
1971	6,412,711	6,342,927	12,755,638	1,156,140	1966–1971 .. 521,139

*Excludes full-blood Aborigines before 1961. Inter-censal increase figure for 1954–61 excludes full-blood Aborigines.

Races and Religions

Races	1966	1971	Religions	1966	1971
European............	11,453,375	12,541,967	Church of England ...	3,885,018	3,953,204
Aboriginal†.........	80,007	106,288	Roman Catholics*	3,042,507	3,442,634
Torres Strait Islanders.	5,403	9,663	Methodists	1,126,960	1,099,019
Chinese.............	26,723	26,198	Presbyterians	1,045,564	1,028,581
			Other Christians	1,130,308	1,466,941
Other..............	33,790	71,522	Hebrews	63,275	62,208
			Other‡	1,305,811	1,703,051

* Including Catholics, so described, 1,934,190 in 1966 and 1,913,400 in 1971.
† The 1966 figure relates to persons of half or more Aboriginal descent. The 1971 figure is for all persons who reported their race as Aboriginal.
‡ Including 1,159,474 and 781,247 who did not state their religion at the 1966 and 1971 Census respectively.

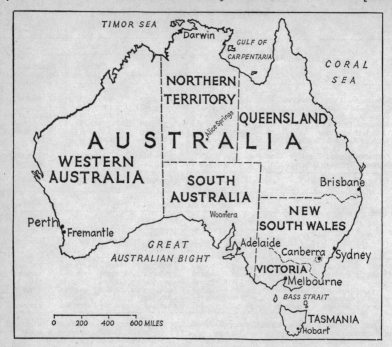

PHYSICAL FEATURES

Australia was separated from the other great land surfaces at a remote period, and exhibits therefore some very archaic types of fauna and flora. It may be regarded as the largest island or the smallest continent, being surrounded by the following waters:—*North*, the Timor and Arafura Seas and Torres Strait; *East*, Pacific Ocean; *South*, Bass Strait (which separates Tasmania from the Continent) and Southern Ocean; and *West*, Indian Ocean. The total area of the mainland is 7,614,500 sq kms, the island of Tasmania having an area of 67,800 sq kms and making a total area for the Commonwealth of 7,682,300 sq kms. The coastline of Australia is approximately 36,800 kms (including Tasmania, 3,200 kms), and its geographical positions is between 10° 41′–39° 8′ (43° 39′, including Tasmania) South latitude and 113° 9′–153° 30′ East longitude; the greatest length East to West is 4,000 kms, and from North to South 3,180 kms (3,680 kms, including Tasmania). Nearest distances from England *via* Cape of Good Hope are East Coast 22,957 and West Coast, 20,048 kms.

From a physical standpoint the continent of Australia is divisible into an eastern and a western area, the former containing a regular coast-line with a good harbourage, roadsteads, rivers, and inland waterways, and a greater development of fauna and flora; the latter a broken coast-line with estuaries rather than rivers, and but little inland water communication. The whole continent is, roughly speaking, a vast, irregular, and undulating plateau, part of which is below the level of the sea, surrounded by a mountainous coast-line, with frequent intervals of low and sandy shore on the north, west and south. The Great Barrier Reef extends parallel with the East coast of Queensland for 1,900 kms ranging in width from 19 kilometres in the north to 240 kilometres in the south. A large part of the interior, particularly in the west, consists of sandy and stony desert, covered with spinifex, and containing numerous salt-marshes, though reaches of grass-land occur here and there. The geological formation of Australia is remarkable for its simplicity and regularity; the *strike* of the rocks is, with a single exception, coincident with the direction of the mountain-chains, from N. to S.; and the tertiary formation to be found in the N., S., and W. develops in the S.E. into a gigantic tertiary plain, watered by the Darling and the Murray Rivers. Nearly all round the coast, however, and in eastern and south-eastern Australia, stretching far inland from the coastal range, is a fertile area devoted to agriculture, beef cattle and dairying, while the inland districts particularly are admirably adapted to the rearing of sheep. The most extensive mountain system takes its rise near the S.E. point, and includes a number of ranges known by different names in different places, none of them being of any great height. The highest peak, Mount Kosciusko, in New South Wales, reaches an elevation of 2,228 metres. The principal rivers are the Murray, which debouches on the south coast, after receiving the waters of its tributaries the Murrumbidgee, Lachlan, and Darling, in the S.E. part of the continent: on the east coast, the Hawkesbury, Hunter, Clarence, Richmond, Brisbane, Mary, Burnett, Fitzroy, and Burdekin; on the west, the

Swan, Murchison, Gascoyne, Ashburton, Fortescue. De Grey, and Fitzroy; on the north, the Drysdale Ord, Victoria and Daly; and the Roper, Flinders, and Mitchell, which debouch into the Gulf of Carpentaria. The scarcity of the natural water supply in the interior has, however, been mitigated by successful borings and by the construction of large dams. The work of conserving the vast quantities of water which run to waste in the wet season is being vigorously prosecuted by a system of locks and weirs on some of the rivers. A major development is the use of the waters of the Snowy River in south-eastern New South Wales for hydro-electricity generation and irrigation.

Significant mineral resources comprise bauxite, coal, copper, crude petroleum, gems, gold, ilmenite, iron ore, lead, limestone, manganese, nickel, rutile, salt, silver, tin, tungsten, uranium, zinc and zircon. Recently, geological exploration has significantly increased the mineral resources of the nation.

Australia now has seven oilfields in production: Moonie, Alton and Bennett, Queensland; Barrow Island, Western Australia; and Barracouta, Kingfish and Halibut in the Gippsland Shelf area offshore from Victoria. In addition, a small amount of oil is being produced from several other wells in the Surat Basin in Queensland. The production of crude oil in 1973 from the Australian oil fields was 22,618,000 cubic metres, approximately 69 per cent. of the country's requirements.

Production from natural gas deposits in Brisbane, Melbourne and Adelaide began during 1969 and in Perth in 1971. Other natural gas reserves have since been discovered in South Australia and Queensland and off the shore of Western Australia and Victoria.

Climate.—The seasons are: summer, December to February; autumn, March to May; winter, June to August, spring, September to November. Australia is less subject to extremes of climate than are regions of similar size in low parts of the world, though the climate varies considerably from the tropical to the alpine.

GOVERNMENT

The Commonwealth of Australia was constituted by an Act of the Imperial Parliament dated July 9, 1900, and was inaugurated Jan. 1, 1901. The Government is that of a Federal Commonwealth within the British Commonwealth of Nations, the executive power being vested in the Sovereign (through the Governor-General), assisted by a Federal Ministry of twenty-seven Ministers of State. Under the Constitution the Federal Government has acquired and may acquire certain defined powers as surrendered by the States, residuary legislative power remaining with the States. Trade and customs passed under Federal control immediately on the establishment of the Commonwealth; posts, telegraphs and telephones, naval and military defence, lighthouses and quarantine on proclaimed dates. The Federal Government also controls such matters as social services, patents and copyrights, naturalization, navigation, &c. The right of a State to legislate on these and other matters is not abrogated except in connection with matters exclusively under Federal control, but where a State law is inconsistent with a law of the Commonwealth the latter prevails to the extent of the inconsistency.

FLAG.—The British Blue Ensign, consisting of a blue flag, with the Union Jack occupying the upper quarter next the staff, differenced by a large white star (representing the six States of Australia and the Territories of the Commonwealth) in the centre of the lower quarter next the staff and pointing direct to the centre of the St. George's Cross in the Union Jack and five white stars, representing the Southern Cross, in the fly.

AUSTRALIA DAY.—January 26.

GOVERNOR-GENERAL AND STAFF

Governor-General, His Excellency the Hon. Sir John Robert Kerr, K.C.M.G., *born* Sept. 24, 1914 *assumed office* July 11, 1974.
Official Secretary, D. I. Smith.
Comptroller, W. H. J. Perring.

MINISTRY

Prime Minister, Hon. E. G. Whitlam, Q.C.
Deputy Prime Minister and Minister for Overseas Trade, Hon. F. Crean.
Minerals and Energy, Hon. R. F. X. Connor.
Treasurer, Hon. W. G. Hayden.
Agriculture and Leader of the Government in the Senate, Senator Hon. K. S. Wriedt.
Foreign Affairs, Senator Hon. D. R. Willesee.
Services and Property and Leader of the House, Hon. F. M. Daly.
Special Minister of State and Manager of Government Business in the Senate, Senator Hon. D. McClelland.
Northern Australia, Hon. R. A. Patterson.
Science and Consumer Affairs, Hon. C. R. Cameron.
Education, Hon. K. E. Beazley.
Manufacturing Industry, Hon. L. F. Bowen.
Social Security and Minister for Repatriation and Compensation, Senator Hon. J. M. Wheeldon.
Urban and Regional Development, Hon. T. Uren.
Postmaster-General, Senator Hon. R. Bishop.
Aboriginal Affairs, Hon. L. R. Johnson.
Transport, Hon. C. K. Jones.
Health, Hon. D. N. Everingham.
Attorney-General, Hon. K. E. Enderby, Q.C.
Labour and Immigration, Senator Hon. J. R. McClelland.
Capital Territory, Hon. G. M. Bryant, E.D.
Media, Hon. M. H. Cass.
Police and Customs, Senator Hon. J. L. Cavanagh.
Defence, Hon. W. L. Morrison.
Tourism and Recreation, and Vice-President of the Executive Council, Hon. F. E. Stewart.
Housing and Construction, Hon. J. M. Riordan.
Environment, Hon. J. M. Berinson.

AUSTRALIAN HIGH COMMISSION

Australia House, Strand, London, W.C.2.
[01-836-2435]

High Commissioner, His Excellency Sir John Bunting, C.B.E.
Deputy High Commissioner, D. W. McNicol.
Minister, A. F. Dingle.
Official Secretary, K. McDonald.
Head, Australian Defence Staff, Maj.-General S. C. Graham.
Special Commercial Adviser, A. L. Paltridge.
Economic Adviser (Treasury), Dr. N. W. Davey.
Migration Officer, G. E. Hitchens, M.B.E.
Defence, Scientific and Technical Representative, Cmdre. W. J. Rourke.
Senior Trade Commissioner, F. G. Atkins.
Trade Commissioners, R. H. Wilson; J. H. Jenkins (*Agriculture*); D. J. Gates (*Minerals*).

BRITISH HIGH COMMISSION

Commonwealth Avenue, Canberra
High Commissioner, His Excellency the Rt. Hon. Sir Morrice James, G.C.M.G., C.V.O., M.B.E. (1971)
Consuls-General, E. W. Cook (Adelaide); G. d' Arnaud-Taylor, O.B.E. (Brisbane); I. F. S. Vincent, C.M.G., M.B.E. (Melbourne); G. E. Dymond, C.B.E. (Perth); J. T. Fearnley (Sydney).
Minister, D. P. Aiers, C.M.G.

Defence Adviser and Head of British Defence Liaison Staff, Maj.-Gen. J. M. W. Badcock, M.B.E.
Counsellors, R. J. Buller (*Technology*); M. H. Callender; H. H. Tucker (*Information*); R. Elphick, O.B.E. (*Agriculture and Food*); B. L. Barder; A.J.V. George, O.B.E. (*Administration*); P. G. P. D. Fullerton (*Commercial*).
First Secretaries, N. E. Buffrey (*Technology*); B. A. Easey; J. M. Hay; G. W. Hewitt; J. F. Holding (*Economic*).
Naval Adviser, Capt. G. M. F. Vallings, R.N.
Military Adviser, Col. A. G. Vicary.
Air Adviser, Group Capt. A. W. Ringer, M.V.O., A.F.C.
Cultural Attaché and British Council Representative, A. MacKenzie Smith, O.B.E., M.C., 203 New South Head Road, Edgecliff, Sydney.

THE LEGISLATURE

Parliament consists of the Queen, a Senate and a House of Representatives. The Constitution provides that the number of members of the House of Representatives shall be, as nearly as practicable, twice the number of Senators. An Act, assented to on May 18, 1948, provided for an increase in the number of members of the Senate from thirty-six to sixty, and as a result the number of members of the House of Representatives was increased from 74 to 123. There are now 127 members in the House of Representatives, including one member for the Northern Territory and two for the Australian Capital Territory. Members of the Senate are elected for six years by universal suffrage, half the members retiring every third year and each of the six States returning an equal number. The House of Representatives, similarly elected for a maximum of three years, contains members proportionate to the population, with a minimum of five members for each State. The state of parties in the House of Representatives after the general election held in May 1974 was Labour 66, Liberal 40, County Party 21. Members of both Houses received $A14,500 per annum, with allowances and free air and rail travel on parliamentary business.
President of the Senate, Senator Hon. J. O'Byrne.
Clerk of the Senate, J. R. Odgers, C.B.E.
Speaker, House of Representatives, Hon. G. G. D Scholes.
Clerk of the House, N. J. Parkes, O.B.E.

THE JUDICATURE

HIGH COURT OF AUSTRALIA

There is a Federal High Court with a Chief Justice and 6 Justices having original and appellate jurisdiction. The principal seat of the Court is at Sydney, New South Wales.
Chief Justice, Rt. Hon. Sir Garfield Edward John Barwick, G.C.M.G.
Justices, Rt. Hon. Sir Edward Aloysius McTiernan, K.B.E.; Rt. Hon. Sir Harry Talbot Gibbs, K.B.E.; Hon. Sir Ninian Martin Stephen, K.B.E.; Hon. Sir Anthony Frank Mason, K.B.E.; Hon. K. S. Jacobs; Hon. Lionel Keith Murphy.
Principal Registrar, L. B. Foley.

INDUSTRIAL COURT

Chief Judge, Hon. Sir John Spicer.
Judges, Hon. E. A. Dunphy; P. E. Joske, C.M.G.; R. A. Smithers; Sir John Nimmo, C.B.E.; A. E. Woodward, O.B.E.; R. J. A. Franki; J. B. Sweeney; P. Evatt; R. J. St. John.

CONCILIATION AND ARBITRATION COMMISSION

President, Hon. J. C. Moore.
Deputy Presidents, Hons. J. T. Ludeke; J. Robinson; P. A. Coldham, D.F.C.; E. A. Evatt; M. G. Gaudron; J. E. Isaac; M. D. Kirby; I. G. Sharp; J. F. Staples.

FEDERAL COURT OF BANKRUPTCY

Judges, Hon. C. A. Sweeny, C.B.E.; Hon. B. J. Riley.

SUPREME COURT OF THE AUSTRALIAN CAPITAL TERRITORY

Judges, Hons. R. W. Fox; E. A. Dunphy; P. E. Joske, C.M.G.; R. A. Smithers; R. A. Blackburn, O.B.E.; F. X. L. Connor; A. E. Woodward, O.B.E.; A. J. A. Franki; J. B. Sweeney; P. G. Evatt; R. J. B. St. John.

SUPREME COURT OF THE NORTHERN TERRITORY

Judges, Hon. W. E. S. Forster; Hon. J. H. Muirhead.
Additional Judges, Hons. E. A. Dunphy; P. E. Joske, C.M.G.; R. A. Smithers; R. E. Woodward, O.B.E.; A. J. A. Franki.

DEFENCE

In December 1972 the Government announced its intention to merge the Defence Group of Departments under a single Minister, and in late 1973 the separate Departments of the Navy, Army and Air were abolished and the staffs of those Departments amalgamated into the Department of Defence. Under the new organization, the Government has given legal status to its Chief Military Adviser and provided him with enlarged authority. The Chief of Defence Force Staff, as the office is now titled, has been given command of the Defence Forces and authority over the Chief of Naval Staff, Chief of General Staff and Chief of Air Staff, who will be the professional heads of each Service.

Within the recognized Defence Department there will be a central organization to advise the Minister on policy and to administer the effective use of resources and the programme. The separate Boards of Management of the three Services will be abolished and substantial authority will pass from them to individual Chiefs of Staff and subordinate commands. The staffs of the separate Departmental organizations will be arranged in functional groupings in the Department of Defence supporting the three Services. As a result, the Secretary of the Department of Defence will be responsible for advice to the Minister on general policy and on the management and utilization of Defence resources. Some responsibilities will be shared between him and the Chief of Defence Force staff.

The separate identities of the Navy, Army and Air Force will be retained.

Royal Australian Navy

The Royal Australian Navy consists of an Anti-Submarine Warfare and strike carrier, 5 destroyers, 6 frigates, 4 submarines, 3 mines counter-measure vessels, 12 patrol boats, 4 survey ships, 2 Fleet support ships, 6 landing craft heavy and one training ship. The Fleet Air Arm is equipped with Skyhawk, Tracker, Macchi and HS748 fixed-wing aircraft, and with Sea King, Wessex and Bell helicopters.

The strength of the Royal Australian Navy on 30 April 1975 was 2,122 officers and 14,089 sailors.

Army

In May 1975 the Australian Army comprised a volunteer Regular Army component of 31,466 and a volunteer Army Reserve component (formerly known as the Citizen Military Force) of 19,888.

The command structure of the Australian Army was reorganized in 1973, replacing the previous geographically based organization with a modernized functional organization.

The major development was the raising of three new functional commands which were invested with Australia-wide responsibilities for the command of units allocated to them and for the conduct of their specialist functions. Field Force Command, with its headquarters in Sydney, commands all field force units and is responsible for the operation of the Army's fighting formations. Logistic Command, with its headquarters in Melbourne, commands all logistic units and is responsible for the broad military functions of transport, supply and repair. Training Command, with its headquarters in Sydney, is responsible for the command of operation of all Army schools and training establishments.

Air

The total strength of the R.A.A.F. on June 1, 1975, was 21,459. There were 18 operational units, 5 maintenance squadrons, 3 control and reporting units, 3 aircraft depots, 3 stores depots, one ammunition depot, 16 training units, 7 Air Training Corps squadrons, 6 university squadrons and 5 auxiliary (Citizen Air Force) squadrons and supporting services. Three flying units, one maintenance squadron and supporting personnel were serving at Butterworth air base in Malaysia.

COMMONWEALTH FINANCE

Revenue and expenditure of the consolidated fund balanced at $A11,975,518,000 in 1973–74, compared with $A9,278,207,000 in 1972–73. Total loan fund expenditure was $A1,828,324,000 in 1973–74 (1972–73, $A1,359,286,000).

The unit of Australian currency is the $A. Rates of exchange in Mar. 1975, were $A1 = £0·565 (buying) and £0·560 (selling).

DEBT

The total of the Commonwealth Debt on June 30, 1974, was $A4,087,517,000. Adding the indebtedness of the States, viz. $A11,218,725,000, the "face" or "book" value of Australian government securities on issue amounted (June 30, 1974) to $A15,306,252,000.

The Debt per head of population at June 30, 1974, was $A1,147·50.

CONSOLIDATED REVENUE FUNDS (a)

State, etc.	1973–74		
	Revenue $A'000	Expend're $A'000	Surplus or Deficit $A'000
N.S.W.	1,878,509	1,895,052	− 16,544
Victoria........	1,361,803	1,364,386	− 2,583
Queensland.....	853,676	855,184	− 1,508
S. Australia.....	611,967	615,368	− 3,401
W. Australia....	567,863	573,414	− 5,731
Tasmania.......	206,947	210,097	− 3,150
Total Six States..	5,480,585	5,513,501	− 32,916
Australian Govt.	11,970,550	11,975,000	

(a) The particulars for the Australian Government and the States' consolidated revenue funds contain duplications of grants made by the Australian Government to the States as well as payments from the National Welfare Fund.

NATIONAL WELFARE FUND EXPENDITURE

Service	1972–73	1973–74
	$A'000	$A'000
Age and Inalid Pensions	1,072,449	1,372,409
Child Endowment.........	253,890	225,392
Commonwealth Rehabilitation Service.............	5,174	7,078
Funeral Benefits...........	1,579	1,578
Maternity Allowances......	7,970	7,782
Unemployment, Sickness Special Benefits.........	77,531	106,637
Widows' Pensions..........	140,505	180,957
Other Welfare	13,773	56,438
Hospital Benefits...........	198,874	226,523
Medical Benefits...........	191,060	198,866
Milk for Children..........	11,717	8,079
Pharmaceutical Benefits.....	177,632	218,296
Tuberculosis Campaign.....	11,635	12,083
Miscellaneous health services.	12,174	19,299
Rental Rebates............	142	123
Home Savings Grants	21,287	24,658
Total.................	2,197,195	2,666,196

BANKING

The average Australian liabilities and assets (excluding shareholders' funds, interbranch accounts and contingencies) of the 7 major trading banks operating in the Commonwealth in April, 1975, were: Liabilities in Australia, $A16,120,300,000 (1974, $A13,500,300,000); Assets in Australia, $A16,756,700,000 (1974, $A13,899,600,000). Total amount on deposit in savings banks in Australia in April 1975, was $A12,258,600,000 or $A914 per head of population (1974, $A10,963,000,000 or $A822 per head).

PRODUCTION AND INDUSTRY

The estimated gross values of production:—

	1972–73 ($A)	1973–74 ($A)
Crops........	1,598,050,000	*p* 2,786,134,000
Livestock slaughterings...	1,547,410,000	*p* 1,782,872,000
Livestock products.	1,829,995,000	*p* 1,862,971,000

p = preliminary. Subject to revision

PRIMARY PRODUCTION

Year	Wool (million kg.)	Wheat ('000 tonnes)	Butter (million kg.)
1970–71	891	7,890	203
1971–72	880	8,510	196
1972–73	736	6,434	185
1973–74	700	11,902	175
1974–75*	777	11,249	..

* Estimated.

Agriculture and Livestock.—The principal crops were:—

Crop	Tonnes
Wheat........................	11,902,416
Oats.........................	1,107,235
Barley.......................	2,397,313
Maize.......................	105,816
Hay.........................	1,034,000
Sugar-cane*..................	19,277,990

* Cut for crushing.

Livestock (in thousands)

	1970	1971	1972	1973	1974
Sheep.	180,080	177,792	162,910	140,029	145,173
Cattle .	22,162	24,373	27,373	29,101	30,839
Pigs...	2,398	2,590	3,199	3,259	2,505

In 1973–74 Australia produced 700,108,000 kg. of wool (as in the grease), estimated value, $A1,231,892,000; 175,498,000 kg. of butter; 95,793,000 kg. of cheese; and 23,035 tonnes of bone-in and 36,397 tons of bone-out bacon and hams. The total meat production (beef, veal, mutton, lamb and pig meat) in terms of fresh meat was 1,977,547 tonnes.

Mines and Minerals.—In 1973–74 the mine production of gold was 16,239 kg. and of black coal 59,343,547 tonnes. Smelter and refinery production of principal metals in 1973 was: pig iron, 7,515,000 tonnes; ingot steel 7,707,000 tonnes; copper (refined), 148,717 tonnes; blister copper, 183,286 tonnes; lead (incl. bullion), 352,975 tonnes; tin, 6,509 tonnes; zinc, 281,586 tonnes; silver, 242,931 kg. Value added by the mining industry in 1972–73 was estimated at $A1,600,900,000.

Manufactures.—In 1972–73 there were in Australia 36,437 industrial establishments, employing 1,297,588 persons; wages paid amounted to $A5,820·0 m; purchases, transfers in and selected expenses $A15,745·9 m; value added by manufacture $A10,746·0 m; and turnover $A26,372·7 m.

Trade Unions.—On December 31, 1974, there were 286 separate trade unions in Australia with a total membership of 2,773,600.

TOTAL EXTERNAL TRADE
(including Bullion and Specie.)

Years	Imports	Exports
1969–70	$A3,881,227,000	$A4,137,222,000
1970–71	4,150,028,000	4,375,757,000
1971–72	4,008,365,000	4,893,368,000
1972–73	4,120,727,000	6,213,727,000
1973–74	6,085,004,000	6,913,746,000

Country	Imports from	Exports to
	1973–74	
United Kingdom	$A848,662,000	$A457,491,000
Canada	191,819,000	173,465,000
India	52,876,000	99,300,000
Pakistan	12,282,000	7,969,000
Malaysia	69,565,000	117,637,000
New Zealand	168,077,000	449,085,000
Hong Kong	159,603,000	114,074,000
Belgium and Luxemburg	57,437,000	59,370,000
China	71,857,000	162,550,000
France	80,156,000	199,060,000
Germany (Fed. Rep.)	450,836,000	181,284,000
Indonesia	16,550,000	106,467,000
Iran	35,914,000	38,944,000
Italy	140,540,000	132,816,000
Japan	1,084,968,000	2,158,141,000
Netherlands	83,842,000	89,430,000
Norway	16,684,000	12,228,000
Papua New Guinea	39,614,000	133,042,000
Poland	8,915,000	50,010,000
Saudi Arabia	53,169,000	24,315,000
South Africa	36,629,000	89,665,000
Sri Lanka	9,448,000	15,390,000
Sweden	109,475,000	20,873,000
Switzerland	90,844,000	15,609,000
U.S.A.	1,348,012,000	749,797,000
U.S.S.R.	5,895,000	154,215,000

IMPORTS FROM ALL COUNTRIES, 1973–74

	$A'000
Live animals	14,212
Meat and meat preparations	3,341
Dairy products and eggs	9,489
Fish	68,633
Cereals	6,386
Fruit and vegetables	50,252
Sugar	3,941
Coffee, tea, cocoa, spices, etc.	63,138
Feeding-stuff for animals	11,164
Miscellaneous preparations chiefly for food	6,223
Beverages	32,073
Tobacco	32,863
Hides and skins	2,461
Oil-seeds, etc.	19,851
Crude rubber	43,061
Wood, timber and cork	115,891
Pulp and waste paper	46,291
Textile fibres	76,622
Crude fertilizers and minerals	67,142
Metalliferous ores and metal scrap	19,897
Crude animal and vegetable materials	23,735
Coal and coke	584
Petroleum and products	376,688
Petroleum gases	105
Oils and fats	28,048
Chemical elements and compounds	212,609
Mineral tar, etc.	2,719
Dyeing, tanning and colouring materials	40,016
Medicinal and pharmaceutical products	75,377
Essential oils and perfume materials	25,213
Fertilizers, manufactured	6,540
Explosives	5,040
Plastic materials, etc.	145,211
Chemical materials and products	67,196
Leather	11,534
Rubber manufactures	83,283
Wood and cork manufactures	35,963
Paper, paperboard and manufactures	167,431
Textile yarn and fabrics	579,065
Non-metallic mineral manufactures	133,666
Iron and steel	214,054
Non-ferrous metals	41,430
Manufactures of metal	137,890
Machinery (except electric)	888,060
Electrical machinery, apparatus and appliances	394,328
Transport equipment	808,962
Sanitary, plumbing, heating and lighting fixtures and fittings	13,057
Furniture	18,942
Travel goods etc.	13,533
Clothing and clothing accessories	122,424
Footwear	43,474
Scientific instruments	192,474
Miscellaneous manufactured articles	317,495
Commodities and transactions of merchandise trade, not elsewhere classified	108,002
Commodities and transactions not included in merchandise trade	57,913

MAJOR EXPORTS 1973–74

Meat and meat preparations	$A795,211,000
Dairy products and eggs	152,125,000
Fish and fish preparations	66,575,000
Cereal grains and cereal preparations	747,473,000
Fruit and vegetables	111,883,000
Sugar, sugar preparations and honey	235,191,000
Hides, skins and fur skins, undressed	150,574,000
Textile fibres and their waste	1,161,648,000
Metalliferous ores and scrap	851,907,000
Coal, coke and briquettes	348,279,000
Petroleum and petroleum products	104,587,000
Animal oils and fats	40,542,000
Chemical elements and compounds	229,494,000
Chemical materials and products, n.e.s.	33,918,000
Non-metallic mineral manufactures, n.e.s.	38,141,000
Iron and steel	214,373,000
Non-ferrous metals	424,320,000
Manufactures of metal, n.e.s.	66,630,000
Machinery (except electric)	148,220,000

Electrical machinery, apparatus and appliances	$A63,735,000
Transport equipment	234,293,000
Miscellaneous manufactured articles, n.e.s.	44,841,000
Commodities and transactions of merchandise trade, not elsewhere classified	89,822,000

FOOD EXPORTS TO U.K. 1973–74

Butter	$A42,000
Cheese	28,000
Eggs	192,000
Meats:—	
Bovine animals	48,088,000
Sheep, lambs and goats	13,128,000
Preserved in airtight containers	14,661,000
Milk and Cream	27,000
Died fruit—grapes	5,363,000
Fruit (preserved in airtight containers)	21,728,000
Flour (wheaten), plain white	21,000
Wheat	..
Sugar-cane	27,989,000

AUSTRALIA'S TRADE WITH U.K.

	Value of Merchandise	
Year	From U.K.	To U.K.
1071–72	$A830,650,000	$A437,789,000
1972–73	764,577,000	575,267,000
1973–74	843,045,000	437,763,000

COMMUNICATIONS

Railways.—Gross earnings during 1973–74:

	Gross Earnings
New South Wales	$A262,691,000 (a)
Victoria	115,613,000 (a)
Queensland	149,844,000
South Australia	39,531,000 (a)
Western Australia	78,480,000
Tasmania	7,674,000
Trans-Australian	26,191,000
Central Australia	7,415,000
Northern Territory	3,302,000
Capital Territory	309,000
Total	$A691,051,000

(a) Excludes certain government subsidies aggregating $A34,699,000.

The gross earnings of all Government lines in 1973–74 were $A691,050,000, working expenses $A903,281,000, and net loss $A212,231,000. In 1973–74 passenger journeys numbered 373,618,000 and 96,966,000 tonnes of goods and livestock were carried.

Shipping.—The entrances and clearances (one entrance and one clearance per voyage, irrespective of the number of ports visited) of vessels engaged in overseas trade at the various Australian ports in 1973–74 were: entered 5,975 (72,041,756 tons); cleared 5,909 (71,462,297 tons).

The total, including local shipping, entering the ports of the capital cities during 1973–74 was: Sydney, 2,971 vessels of 16,576,993 tons; Melbourne, 2,524 (12,708,789); Brisbane, 1,302 (8,068,162); Adelaide, 1,117 (4,038,670); Fremantle, 1,214 (8,531,282); Hobart 534 (1,623,639) tons. At Dec. 31, 1973, the Australian trading fleet vessels 200 tons gross and over comprised 118 vessels with a total 1,293,187 tons gross. Of these, 108 vessels totalling 1,189,015 tons gross were coastal trading vessels.

Posts and Telegraphs.—In the year ended June 30, 1974, there were 6,266 post offices dealing with 2,459,155,000 letters, 321,814,000 packets and newspapers, 11,722,000 registered articles and 25,336,000 parcels. 18,002,000 internal telegrams and 2,661,000 international telegrams were despatched. At June 30, 1974, there were 5,858 telephone exchanges with 3,361,026 services and 4,999,982 instruments.

Broadcasting and Television.—On June 30, 1974, the Australian Broadcasting Commission operated 87 stations, including 6 short-wave stations in Australia. Privately owned commercial broadcasting stations totalled 118. On June 30, 1974, there were in force in Australia 2,851,230 listeners' licences, including 2,546,433 combined broadcast and television receiving licences. On June 30, 1974, 120 television stations were in operation, 25 in the various State capitals (including Canberra), and 95 in country areas. Television licences in force at June 30, 1974, numbered 3,022,006 (including combined licences, as above).

Motor Vehicles.—At June 30, 1974, there were 5,986,100 motor vehicles registered in Australia. These comprised 4,627,200 cars and station wagons, 259,100 motor cycles, and 1,099,900 commercial vehicles; revenue derived from motor registration fees and motor tax, &c. in 1973–74 was $A380,741,000.

Civil Aviation.—At June 30, 1974, there were 473 recognized landing grounds, including 374 licensed public aerodromes, in the various States and Territories, and 8 flying boat bases and alighting areas. Aircraft on the Australian Register at June 30, 1974, numbered 4,023.

CAPITAL

Canberra is the capital of Australia. It is situated in the Australian Capital Territory which has an area of 939 sq. miles and was acquired from New South Wales in 1911. On June 30, 1975, the population was 190,000. Canberra is the seat of the federal government which moved from Melbourne in 1927. Apart from Parliament House, the city also contains other National institutions, such as the Australian War Memorial, National Library, Royal Australian Mint and the Australian National University. Most Government departments now have their headquarters in Canberra. An artificial lake is a central feature of this planned city, based on Walter Burley Griffin's design.

THE NORTHERN TERRITORY

The Northern Territory has a total area of 520,280 square miles, and lies between 129°–138° east longitude and 11°–26° south latitude. The administration was taken over by the Commonwealth on January 1, 1911, from the government of the State of South Australia. The Department of the Northern Territory, created in 1972, with headquarters in Darwin, and the Department of Northern Development, Canberra, were abolished in June 1975 and amalgamated to become the Department of Northern Australia. The new Department covers all that area north of the 26th parallel, and includes in its responsibilities administration of the Northern Territory. In matters related to the specialised development and utilisation of natural resources it works in liaison with the States of Western Australia and Queensland.

The Legislative Council for the Northern Territory, established in 1947 under the provisions of the Northern Territory (Administration) Act, to make Ordinances for the peace, order and good government of the Territory (subject to the assent of the Administrator or Governor General), with 17 members, including 11 elected members, was superseded in October, 1974, by a fully elected Legislative Assembly of 19 members.

The estimated Aboriginal population in the Northern Territory at the 1971 Census was 25,000.

Areas totalling 94,000 square miles, about one-fifth of the Northern Territory, have been set aside as reserves for the use and benefit of the Aboriginal people. Legislation is to be introduced to enable Aboriginal tenure of these lands and as a result of recommendations of a Royal Commission the Government set up land councils which are now operating.

Approximately 16,000 Aboriginals live in communities which are now focal points for education, health and social development.

About 4,000 Aboriginals live permanently on pastoral properties and the government aims to establish communal living areas for these communities. Other Aboriginals live in or around the main towns. In some of the more remote regions, the contact with European Australians has been relatively recent and traditional beliefs and customs are still strong.

The year 1973–74 saw a marked slump in the fortunes of the Territory's major rural industry, beef cattle raising, with total earnings down by 20 per cent. to $A26,300,000 There was a further decline in prices in 1975 with returns to cattlemen the lowest for 12 years. The Territory's two abbatoirs, at Katherine and Darwin, were also affected, and only the Katherine abattoir killed for export in the 1975 season. Low meat prices were a factor in the increase in cattle numbers which at June 30, 1974 stood at 1,198,000—a rise of 38,000 on the previous year. By-products earned $2,400,000 of which $1,600,000 came from the sale of buffalo meat.

Early 1975 saw the start of a new export industry—live feral buffaloes shipped to Nigeria and Venezuela for stud purposes. The attraction of the Territory's buffaloes for overseas buyers is their freedom from serious stock diseases.

Research is going on to evaluate the best agricultural prospects for the Territory. At present agriculture is confined to small farms in the Darwin, Adelaide River, Pine Creek, Daly River, Katherine and Alice Springs districts. One of the most promising crops, with potential for exploitation on a large-scale basis, is grain sorghum, despite the financial failure late in 1974 of the Territory's major sorghum venture at Willeroo 150 km south-west of Katherine.

Mineral industry projects are important to both regional and national economic development. The value of mine and quarry production for 1973–74 was $A126,000,000, derived mainly from iron, manganese, copper, gold, bismuth and aluminium ores. Recently, iron ore production ceased and copper production declined. The rich Alligator Rivers uranium deposits are not yet developed. At the large McArthur River lead–zinc deposit test facilities are being established.

Tourism, an important industry, is estimated to be worth $A28,000,000 a year and expanding by over 12 per cent annually.

The chief rivers of the Territory are the Victoria, Adelaide, Daly, Roper, South Alligator and McArthur. These are navigable from 40–100 miles from their mouths for boats up to 4 ft. draft.

A railway extends from Darwin to Larrimah (311 miles) and Alice Springs is connected by rail with Adelaide. A good bitumen road (the Stuart Highway) links Darwin with Alice Springs (954 miles) and another bitumen road (the Barkly Highway) runs from this road near Tennant Creek to Mount Isa in Queensland (403 miles).

The Government has a continuous programme of improvement and maintenance for these highways which are now included in the National Highway System. A further 3 year programme of $A34,000,000 is proposed to commence in 1975/76. The beef roads completed in 1972 now form part of the development road system throughout the Northern Territory. $A4,200,000 was spent on these roads in 1974/75.

The population of Darwin was estimated at 46,000 in 1974. On Christmas Day a cyclone destroyed 90 per cent. of the city and at the end of the first week of January, 1975, the population had dropped to 11,000. By June, 1975, the population had recovered to 32,500, most people living in makeshift or partially repaired dwellings. Deaths in the cyclone totalled 49, with 16 missing, believed drowned at sea. Darwin, which is 97 ft. above sea level, overlooks Port Darwin. Alice Springs is situated in the MacDonnell Ranges. The climate of the Northern Territory ranges from dry in the south to wet-monsoonal in the north.

Judges of the Supreme Court, Hon. W. E. S. Forster; Hon. J. H. Muirhead; Hon. R. C. Ward.

Additional Judges, Hons. E. A. Dunphy; P. E. Joske, C.M.G.; J. A. Franki.

TERRITORY OF
PAPUA NEW GUINEA

The Papua New Guinea Acts 1949–1974, approved the placing of the Territory of New Guinea under the Trusteeship system of the United Nations with Australia as the sole administering authority, provide for the Administrative Union of that Territory with the Territory of Papua as Papua New Guinea and set up the basic legislative, executive and judicial organs of government for Papua New Guinea.

Papua New Guinea achieved internal self-government on December 1, 1973. In conformity with Papua New Guinean requests responsibility for additional functions of government has since been transferred to Papua New Guinea. Responsibility over the Court system, prosecutions and legal aid was transferred on January 30, 1975, and over defence and foreign relations matters on March 6, 1975. The effect of the transfer of authority over these hitherto reserved matters emphasises Papua New Guinea's position of almost complete independence. The Papua New Guinea House of Assembly has resolved that Papua New Guinea should move to independent nation status as soon as practicable after the enactment of a Constitution and that the House of Assembly should endorse the proposed date of independence. It was expected that Papua New Guinea would enact a Constitution and achieve independence in 1975. The United Nations General Assembly has resolved that on the date on which Papua New Guinea becomes independent, the Trusteeship Agreement will terminate.

The position of the Administrator of Papua New Guinea was abolished and replaced by the office of the High Commissioner of Papua New Guinea on December 1, 1973.

Papua New Guinea has a unicameral legislature, the House of Assembly, elected for a term of four years. The third House of Assembly with 100 members (82 from open Electorates and 18 from Regional Electorates for which candidates must possess educational qualifications) was elected in 1972. There are 19 ministers of the House of Assembly. There is provision for an Executive Council consisting of the High Commissioner and Chief Minister plus not less than nine, nor more than twelve other Ministers. Formal approval of the Executive Council is required for a large range of matters under Papua New Guinea legislation.

The land mass of Papua New Guinea extends from east of the border with Irian Jaya to 160° east longitude. Papua New Guinea lies wholly within the tropics, between the Equator and the 12th parallel of south latitude and is separated from Australia by the Torres Strait. It includes the islands of the Bismarck Archipelago, the two northernmost islands of the Solomon Group, as well as the Trobriand, Woodlark, D'Entrecasteaux and Louisiade Island groups. The land area of Papua New Guinea is 178,260 sq. miles, of which approximately 152,420 are on the main island.

Major towns are Port Moresby, Lae, Rabaul, Madang, Wewak, Goroka and Mount Hagen. At June 30, 1975 the Papua New Guinea population was estimated to be 2,724,740 while the non-indigenous population was estimated to be 37,191.

Most places in Papua New Guinea have an annual average rainfall of over 80 inches and much of its area is drained by a number of large rivers such as the Sepik, Fly, Markham, Ramu, Purari and Kikori. The Sepik is 690 miles long and is navigable for about 300 miles by vessels with a draught of up to 13 ft.

The most important roads are those linking Lae with the populous and developing highlands and with Wau, and in the hinterlands of Port Moresby, Rabaul, Madang and Wewak.

Trans-Australia Airlines and Ansett—A.N.A. operate regular air services from Australia to Port Moresby while internal air services are operated by the newly established Air Niugini, the Papua New Guinea national airline. There are regular services to the British Solomon Islands. Qantas calls at Port Moresby on its Far East Service linking Australia with Manila, and Hong Kong.

Several shipping companies operate regular cargo and passenger services between Papua New Guinea and Australia and the Far East. In the year ended June 30, 1973, overseas shipping entries at the nine main ports totalled 912 ships and approximately two million tons of cargo were handled through these ports.

Papua New Guinea's climate is hot and moist along the coast, becoming cooler and dryer as the higher altitudes are reached. It is suitable for the growth of all tropical products. The main agricultural products are coffee, copra, coconut oil, cocoa, timber, rubber and tea. Oil palm and cattle are expected to increase in importance. Prawns and tuna fishing are also becoming a significant export income earner. The mining of gold has declined considerably, but a copper mine established on Bougainville Island is providing the largest source of export income for Papua New Guinea.

OVERSEAS TRADE
(Papua New Guinea)

	1971–72 $A'000	1972–73* $A'000
Total imports	256,386	228,847
Total exports	127,181	229,614
Imports from U.K.	11,415	9,242
Exports to U.K.	13,045	11,365

*Preliminary.

PUBLIC FINANCE
(Papua New Guinea)

	1973–4 $A,000	1974–5 $A,000
Grants from Australia (a)	135,269	89,172
Local Revenue	136,368	169,466
Loans	41,387	52,612
Total Receipts	313,024	311,250

(a) In addition, Australia provided about $A43,000,000 in 1972–73 and $A50,000,000 in 1973–74 for salaries of overseas officers of the Papua New Guinea Public Service; this amount is not included in the Papua New Guinea budget.

ECONOMIC AID FROM AUSTRALIA

	1973–4 $A,000	1974–5* $A,000
Grants to P.N.G. Govt.	96,173	78,450
Other Economic Aid	80,903	109,482
Total Aid from Australia	177,076	187,932

*Estimated.

SEAT OF ADMINISTRATION.—Administrative Headquarters of the Territory of Papua New Guinea is ΨPort Moresby, the principal port and town of Papua, with a population (estimated, 1971) of 76,507, of whom 59,673 were Papuan New Guineans. ΨRabaul (in New Britain), is the largest port in the Territory, while ΨLae (in Morobe District) is the third largest port and second largest town, being the outlet for the Morobe plywood district and for the Highlands region, and one of the principal air centres in Papua New Guinea.
Chief Minister, M. T. Somare (1972).
High Commissioner, T. K. Critchley (1974).
Port Moresby is 1,800 miles from Sydney.

NORFOLK ISLAND

The island is situated in latitude 29° S. and longitude 168° E., being about 1,042 miles from Sydney and 400 miles north of New Zealand. It is about five miles in length by three in breadth, and was discovered by Capt. Cook in 1774. Its area is 8,528 acres and circumference 20 miles. The climate is mild, with a mean temperature of 68° and an annual rainfall of 53 inches. The descendants of the mutineers of the *Bounty* were brought here from Pitcairn Island in 1856. The island is a popular tourist resort, and a large proportion of the population depends on tourism and its ancillaries for employment. Resident population (1973), 1,546.

Seat of Government and Administration Offices, Kingston. The Norfolk Island Council advises the Administrator on policy and the control of public finance. The island is administered by the Australian Government through the Department of the Capital Territory in Canberra.

Regular air services operate from Australia and New Zealand.
Administrator, Air Cdre. E. T. Pickerd, O.B.E., D.F.C.

COCOS (KEELING) ISLANDS

The Cocos (Keeling) Islands were declared a British possession in 1857. In 1878 they were placed under the control of the Governor of Ceylon and were later annexed to the Straits Settlements and incorporated with the colony of Singapore. On Nov. 23, 1955, their administration was transferred to Australia. They are two separate atolls comprising some 27 small coral islands with a total area of about 5½ square miles, situated in the Indian Ocean in latitude 12° 5′ South and longitude 96° 53′ East. The main islands are West Island (the largest, about 6 miles from north to south) on which are the aerodrome and the administrative centre, and most of the European community; Home Island, the headquarters of the Clunies Ross Estate; Direction Island, on which is situated the Department of Civil Aviation's marine base; and Horsburgh. North Keeling Island, which forms part of the Territory, lies about 15 miles to the north of the group and has no inhabitants. The climate is equable and pleasant, being usually under the influence of the south-east trade winds for about three-quarters of the year. A three weekly air charter service operates between Perth and the Cocos Islands and Christmas Island. Population (estimated June 30, 1974), 643.
Official Representative, C. McManus.

CHRISTMAS ISLAND

Until the end of 1957 a part of the then Colony of Singapore. Christmas Island was administered as a separate colony until October 1, 1958, when it became Australian territory. It is situated in the Indian Ocean about 224 miles S. of Java Head. Area 52 sq. miles. Population (estimated, Dec. 31, 1974) 2,937. The island is densely wooded and contains extensive deposits of phosphate of lime. *Administrator*, C. H. Webb.

THE ANTARTIC CONTINENT

The area of the Antarctic Continent is estimated at approximately 5,750,000 square miles. The greater part of the coastline has been charted, but considerable portions of the interior have not been visited, or at best have been seen only from the air. The question of territorial rights is complicated and there is no general international agreement thereon.

The *Australian Antarctic Territory* was established by an Order in Council, dated February 7, 1933, which placed under the government of the Commonwealth of Australia all the islands and territories, other than Adélie Land, which are situated south of the latitude 60° S. and lying between 160° E. longitude and 45° E. longitude. The Order came into force on August 24, 1936, after the passage of the Australian Antarctic Territory Acceptance Act, 1933. The boundaries of Terre Adélie were definitely fixed by a French Decree of April 1, 1938, as the islands and territories south of 60° S. latitude lying between 136° E. longitude and 142° E. longitude. The Australian Antarctic Territory Act, 1954 declared that the laws in force in the Australian Capital Territory are, so far as they are applicable, in force in the Australian Antarctic Territory.

On February 13, 1954, the Australian National Antarctic Research Expeditions (ANARE) established a station on Mac. Robertson Land at latitude 67° 36′ S. and longitude 62° 53′ E. The station was named Mawson in honour of the late Sir Douglas Mawson and was the first permanent Australian station to be set up on the Antarctic continent. Scientific Research conducted at Mawson includes Upper Atmosphere Physics, Meteorology, Earth Sciences, Biology and Medical Science. Mawson is also the centre for coastal and inland exploration.

A second Australian scientific research station was established on the coast of Princess Elizabeth Land on January 13, 1957, at latitude 68° 34′ S. and longitude 77° 57′ E. The station was named in honour of Captain John King Davis, second in command of two of Mawson's expeditions and master of several famous Antarctic ships. The station was temporarily closed on Jan. 25, 1965 and reopened on Feb. 15, 1969. Scientific programmes carried out at Davis include meteorology, biology, upper atmosphere physics, with field investigations in glaciology and geology. In February, 1959, the Australian Government accepted from the United States Government custody of Wilkes Station on the Budd Coast, Wilkes Land in about 66° 15′ S. and longitude 110° 33′ E. The station was closed in February 1969, and activities were transferred to Casey station. Casey station was named in honour of Lord Casey, former Governor-General of Australia, in recognition of his long association with Australia's Antarctic effort. The station, at 66° 17′ S., 110° 32′ E., is of advanced design and scientific programmes carried out there include upper atmosphere physics, cosmic ray physics, geophysics, meteorology with field programmes in glaciology, geology, etc.

Since 1948 ANARE has also operated a station on Macquarie Island, a dependency of Tasmania, situated at 54° 28′ S. and 158° 57′ E., about 900 miles north of the Antarctic Continent.

On December 1, 1959, Australia signed the Antarctic Treaty with Argentine, Belgium, Chile, France, Japan, New Zealand, Norway, South Africa, the United Kingdom, the United States and U.S.S.R., all countries which have been active in Antarctic operations and research. The Treaty reserves the Antarctic area south of 60° S. latitude for peaceful purposes, provides for international co-operation in scientific investigation and research, and preserves, for the duration of the Treaty, the *status quo* with regard to territorial sovereignty, rights and claims. The Treaty came into force on June 23, 1961, and has been acceded to by another four nations not actively engaged in Antarctic area.

For other Commonwealth dependencies in the Antarctic *see* New Zealand.

STATES OF THE COMMONWEALTH OF AUSTRALIA

NEW SOUTH WALES

The State of New South Wales is situated entirely between the 28th and 38th parallels of S. lat. and 141st and 154th meridians of E. long., and comprises an area of 309,433 square miles (exclusive of 939 sq. miles of Australian Capital Territory which lies within its borders).

POPULATION.—The estimated population at June 30, 1974 was: Males, 2,376,500; Females, 2,367,000. Total, 4,743,400.

Births, Deaths and Marriages

Year	Births	Deaths	Marriages
1971	98,466	41,691	42,928
1972	95,278	41,652	43,038
1973	87,332	41,122	40,722
1974	86,169	43,998	39,327

Vital Statistics.—Annual rate per 1,000 of mean population in 1973:—Births, 18·52; Deaths, 8·72; Marriages, 8·64. Deaths under 1 year per 1,000 live births, 17·07.

Religions

The members of the Church of England in New South Wales, according to the Census of 1971, number 1,639,316. Roman Catholic (including " Catholic ") 1,319,250, Presbyterian 352,107, Methodist 302,856, Congregational 20,902, Baptist 59,541, Orthodox 129,178, Lutheran 33,776, Salvation Army 19,733, and Hebrew 25,971. The religion of 519,125 persons was either not stated in the census schedules or was stated as " none ".

PHYSIOGRAPHY

Natural features divide the State into four strips of territory extending from north to south, viz., the Coastal Divisions; the Tablelands, which form the Great Dividing Range between the coastal districts and the plains; the Western Slopes of the Dividing Range; and the Western Plains. The highest points are Mounts Kosciusko, 7,328 feet, and Townsend, 7,266 feet. The coastal district is well watered by numerous rivers flowing from the ranges into fertile flats which form their lower basins. The western portion of the State is watered by the rivers of the Murray-Darling system and immense reservoirs have been constructed for irrigation purposes, as well as many artesian bores. The Darling, 1,702 miles, and the Murrumbidgee, 981 miles, are both tributaries of the Murray, part of which forms the boundary between the States of New South Wales and Victoria, Other inland rivers are: Lachlan, Macquarie-Bogan, Castlereagh, Namoi and Gwydir.

Climate.—New South Wales is situated entirely in the Temperate Zone. The climate is equable and very healthy. At the capital (Sydney) the average mean shade temperature is 18°C. The mean (shade) temperature ranges for the various divisions of the State are as follows: coastal, 16°C in the south to 20°C in the north; northern and central tableland, 12°C to 16°C; southern tableland, 7°C to 14°C; and for the rest of the State (western slope, central plains, Riverina and western), 15°C in the south to 18°C in the north.

GOVERNMENT

New South Wales was first colonized as a British possession in 1788, and after progressive settlement a partly elective legislature was established in 1843. In 1855 Responsible Government was granted, the present Constitution being founded on the Constitution Act of 1902. New South Wales federated with the other States of Australia in 1901. The executive authority of the State is vested in a Governor (appointed by the Crown), assisted by a Council of Ministers.

GOVERNOR

Governor of New South Wales, His Excellency Sir (Arthur) Roden Cutler, V.C., K.C.M.G., K.C.V.O., C.B.E., *assumed office* Jan. 20, 1966
$A30,000

Lieutenant-Governor, Hon. Laurence Whistler Street.

THE MINISTRY

Premier and Treasurer, Hon. T. L. Lewis, M.L.A.
Deputy Premier, Minister for Local Government and for Tourism, Hon. Sir Charles Cutler, K.B.E., E.D., M.L.A.
Attorney-General and Minister of Justice, Hon. J. C. Maddison, M.L.A.
Planning and Environment, and Vice-President of the Executive Council, Hon. Sir John Fuller, M.L.C.
Public Works and Ports, Hon. L. A. Punch, M.L.A.
Education, Hon. Sir Eric Willis, K.B.E., C.M.G., M.L.A.
Labour, Industry and Consumer Affairs and Minister for Federal Affairs, Hon. F. M. Hewitt, M.L.C.
Agriculture, Hon. G. R. Crawford, D.C.M., M.L.A.
Transport and Highways, Hon. W. C. Fife, M.L.A.
Police and Services, Hon. J. L. Waddy, O.B.E., D.F.C., M.L.A.
Mines and Energy, Hon. G. F. Freudenstein, M.L.A.
Decentralisation and Development, Hon J. C. Bruxner, M.L.A.
Housing and Co-operative Societies, Hon. L. F. McGinty, M.B.E., M.L.A.
Health, Hon. R. O. Healey, M.L.A.
Revenue and Assistant Treasurer, Hon. M. S. Ruddock, M.L.A.
Youth, Ethnic and Community Affairs, Hon. S. G. Mauger, M.L.A.
Culture, Sport and Recreation, Hon. L. J. F. Barraclough, M.L.A.
Lands and Forests, Hon. J. M. Mason, M.L.A.

The annual salaries of Ministers are: Premier, $A38,580; Deputy Premier, $A34,500; other Ministers $A32,400 each. Ministers also receive an expense allowance (Premier, $A8,640. Deputy Premier $A4,320, and other Ministers $A3,888 each) and the Leader and Deputy Leader of the Government in the Legislative Council further special allowances of $A2,520 and $A720 per annum respectively. In addition, Ministers who are members of the Legislative Assembly receive electoral and accommodation allowances (ranging from $A3,960 to $A8,904 according to the location of the electorate).

N.S.W. GOVERNMENT OFFICES IN LONDON,
66 Strand, W.C.2
Agent-General, Hon. Sir Davis Hughes (1972)

THE LEGISLATURE

The Legislature consists of the Sovereign and the two Houses of Parliament (the Legislative Council and the Legislative Assembly). The *Legislative Council* consists of 60 members, elected jointly by both Houses of Parliament. Membership is for 12 years, 15 members retiring in rotation triennially. The *Legislative Assembly* consists of 99 members. Natural-born or naturalized persons 18 years of age, who have resided 6 months in Australia, 3 months in the State and 1 month in the electoral district are entitled to the franchise. Voting is compulsory. At the State General Elections in November, 1973, there were 2,788,733 persons enrolled. In contested elections 2,560,653 persons voted, representing 93 per cent. of the persons enrolled.

President of the Legislative Council, Hon. Sir Harry Budd..... (incl. *allce.*) $A24,480
Chairman of Committees, Legislative Council, Hon. T. S. McKay.. (incl. *allce*). 15,324
Speaker, Legislative Assembly, Hon. J. A. Cameron................(incl. *allce*.) 34,128
Chairman of Committees, Legislative Assembly, J. H. Brown....(incl. *allce*.) 23,880
Leader of Opposition, Legislative Assembly, N. K. Wran, Q.C.........(incl. *allce*.) 34,128
(Office-holders above who are members of the Legislative Assembly also receive electoral and accommodation allowances ranging from $A3,960 to $A8,904 according to the location of the electorate.)

THE JUDICATURE

The judicial system includes a Supreme Court with the Chief Justice, President, eight Judges of Appeal, and 29 Judges), Land and Valuation Court, Industrial Commission, District Courts, Workers' Compensation Commission, Courts of Quarter Sessions, Petty Sessions and Children's Courts.

Supreme Court
Chief Justice, Hon. L. W. Street
(+ *allce* $A2,700)..$A44,400
Judges of Appeal, Hon. A. R. Moffitt (*President, Court of Appeal*) ($A41,820+ *allce*. $A2,100); Hon. K. W. Asprey; Hon. R. M. Hope; Hon. R. G. Reynolds; Hon. F. C. Hutley; Hon. N. H. Bowen (*Chief Judge in Equity*); Hon. H. H. Glass; Hon. G. J. Samuels; Hon. D.L. Mahoney (+ *allce*. $A2,100)   40,620
Judges, Hon. J. H. McClemens (*Chief Judge of Common Law*); Hon. D. M. Selby, E.D. (*Chief Judge of the Family Law Division*); Hon. W. H. Collins; Hon. J. F. Nagle; Hon. R. L. Taylor; Hon. C. E. Begg; Hon. P. H. Allen; Hon. J. O'Brien; Hon. S. Isaacs; Hon. N. A. Jenkyn; Hon. J.A. Lee; Hon. M. M. Helsham; Hon. C. L. D. Meares; Hon. P. B. Toose, C.B.E.; Hon. G. Carmichael; Hon. J. P. Slattery; Hon. A. Larkins; Hon. P. M. Woodward; Hon. K. J. Holland; Hon. I. F. Sheppard; Hon. J. H. Wootten; Hon. A. F. Rath; Hon. A. V. Maxwell; Hon. T. W. Waddell; Hon P. J. Jeffrey; Hon. D. A. Yeldham; Hon. G. D. Needham; Hon. W. P. Ash; Hon. H. L. Cantor (+ *allce*. $A2,100)   40,620
Crown Employees Appeal Board
Chairman, Hon. W. B. Perrignon (+ *allce*. $A2,100)........................   40,620

Industrial Commission

President, Hon. Sir Alexander Beattie
(+ *allce.* $A2,100)..................... $A41,820
Members, J. J. McKeon; J. A. Kelleher;
W. B. Perrignon; C. P. Sheehy;
W. S. Sheldon; J. J. Cahill; F. V.
Watson; J. F. Dey (+ *allce.* $A2,100)
.... *each*   40,620
Land and Valuation Court Judge, Hon.
The Chief Justice.
Workers' Compensation Commission, Chairman, His Honour C. C. Langworth
(+ *allce.* $A2,100)...................   36,600
District Court, Chief Judge, His Honour
J. H. Staunton (+ *allce.* $A2,100).....   36,600

EDUCATION

Education.—Education is compulsory between the ages of 6 and 15 years. It is non-sectarian and free at all state schools. The enrolment in August 1974 in 2,271 state schools was 777,620. In addition to the state schools there were, in 1974, 804 private colleges and schools, with an enrolment of 219,100 scholars. The five universities had an enrolment of 56,109 students in 1974; 17,339 at Sydney (incorporated 1850), 19,594 at New South Wales (1948), 7,001 at New England (1954), 7,998 at Macquarie (1964) and 4,177 at Newcastle (1965). Colleges of Advanced Education (including Teachers' Colleges), which provide courses at tertiary level, but with a more technological emphasis than universities, had 22,470 students enrolled in 1974. Students enrolled in technical colleges in 1974 numbered 207,806. The State expenditure on education was $A603,262,000 in the year 1973–74.

FINANCE

Year ended June 30th	Revenue	Expenditure
	$A	$A
1971...........	1,247,249,000	1,254,634,000
1972...........	1,429,341,000	1,434,825,000
1973...........	1,641,920,000	1,645,117,000
1974...........	1,878,509,000	1,895,052,000

The Public Debt of New South Wales at June 30, 1974, was $A3,654,352,000, of which an amount of $A74,035,000 was repayable in London (interest $A3,678,000), $A20,641,000 was repayable in New York (interest $A1,123,000), $A2,164,000 was repayable in Canada (interest $A124,000), $A3,567,000 was repayable in Switzerland (interest $A160,000), $A1,407,000 was repayable in the Netherlands (interest $A70,000) and $A3,552,538,000 was held in Australia, with an annual interest bill of $A207,480,000.

Banking, etc.—There were (Jan. 1975) 10 trading banks with deposits of $A6,270,700,000. Savings bank deposits amounted to $A3,639,800,000, representing $A762 per head of the population. The amount assured in New South Wales in *Life Insurance* in Jan. 1974 was $A8,127,241,000 ordinary, $A1,408,477,000 superannuation and $A571,687,000 industrial. The membership of *Friendly Societies* was 158,692, and the funds at June 30, 1974 were $A38,749,000. On Dec. 31, 1973, there were 192 separate *Trade Unions* in New South Wales with a total membership of 1,032,000. Balances outstanding on *Instalment Credit* for retail sales on June 30, 1974, were $A714,700,000.

PRODUCTION AND INDUSTRY

Value of Production.—In 1973–4 the net value of production of the primary industries (at place of production), excluding mining and quarrying, was $A1,786,172,000. Of that agriculture contributed $A682,448,000, livestock products (wool, milk etc.) $A535,330,000, livestock slaughterings $A494,311,000 and other industries (forestry, fishing and trapping) $A74,083,000. Value added in mining and quarrying industries and manufacturing industries in 1972–1973 was $A322,386,000 and $A4,293,500,000 respectively.

Agriculture.—The production of wheat in 1973–74 was 3,961,525 tonnes of grain and 52,620 tonnes of hay. Other important crops in 1973–74 were 47,916 tonnes of maize, 327,219 tonnes of oats, 403,446 tonnes of rice, besides other kinds of grain, 124,586 tonnes of potatoes, and 1,252,420 kilograms of dried leaf tobacco. Sugar-cane to the extent of 999,486 tonnes was crushed; while 79,738,329 kilograms of bananas were obtained; almost every kind of fruit and vegetable is grown.

Land Tenure.—The total extent of land virtually alienated and in process of alienation from the Crown on June 30, 1972, was 68,100,000 acres, while the area of land under lease, etc., from the Crown was 110,897,000 acres, and the balance 19,040,000 acres, consisted of reserve and other lands neither alienated nor leased; the total area of the State, exclusive of the Australian Capital Territory, is 198,037,000 acres.

Pastoral, etc.—A large area is suitable for sheep-raising, the principal breed of sheep being the celebrated merino, which was introduced in 1797. On March 31, 1974, there were 8,456,400 cattle, 53,296,223 sheep and lambs, and 834,678 pigs. In 1973–74, 213,224,000 kg. (stated as in the grease) of wool were produced, 13,328,000 kg. of butter, 9,364,000 kg. of cheese, and 22,814,000 kg. of bacon and ham.

Forests.—The estimated forest area is 39,950,000 acres, of which State forests cover 7,510,000 acres and 990,000 have been set aside as timber reserves.

Mining Industry.—The principal minerals are coal, lead, zinc, rutile, zircon, copper and tin. The total value of minerals won in 1973–74 was $A500,750,000; the value of output of the coalmining industry was $A243,406,000 and of the silver-lead-zinc industry, $A108,182,000. The mining industry gave employment to 23,161 miners during 1973–74. In 1973–74, 36,632,000 tonnes of coal were produced.

Manufacturing Industry.—At June 30, 1974, there were 13,857 manufacturing establishments. The average number of persons employed during 1973–74 was 515,572, and the value added to materials was $A5,180,550. Large iron and steel works with subsidiary factories are in operation at Newcastle and Port Kembla in proximity to the coalfields. Products of the regions include iron and steel of various grades, pipes, boilers, steel wire and wire netting, copper wire, copper and brass cables and tin-plate. The production (1973–74) of pig-iron was 6,612,000 tonnes, and of steel ingots 5,688,000 tonnes.

OVERSEAS TRADE

Year ended June 30	Overseas Imports $A(f.o.b.)	Overseas Exports $A(f o.b.)
1961	1,822,118,000	1,113,493,000
1972	1,764,769,000	1,204,938,000
1973	1,810,123,000	1,420,990,000
1974	2,590,179,000	1,513,202,000

The chief exports in 1973–74 were wool, wheat, coal, meat, iron and steel, chemicals, machinery and undressed hides and skins. Chief imports were machinery, textiles, motor vehicles, chemicals, petroleum, paper products, iron and steel, foodstuffs, medical instruments, etc., pharmaceuticals, printed matter and plastic materials.

TRANSPORT AND COMMUNICATIONS.

Shipping.—Excluding coastal trade, 3,716 vessels entered ports of N.S.W. during the year ended June 30, 1974, the net tonnes being 29,311,771. The shipping entries at Sydney, including coastal, were 2,971 vessels of 16,843,054 net tonnes.

Roads and Bridges.—There are 207,971 kilometres of roads and streets in New South Wales, including 42,012 kilometres of natural surface and cleared only. The total expenditure by the Government and the local councils on roads, bridges, &c, in 1972–73 was $A281,853,000. Sydney Harbour Bridge which was completed and opened for traffic in March, 1932, carries eight lanes of roadway with a total width of 25·6m, two footways each 3m wide, and two lines of railway. At mean high water there is a headway of 52·6m.

Motor Vehicles.—At Dec. 31. 1974 there were 2,110,200 registered motor vehicles (cars, 1,377,800).

Railways.—The railways of New South Wales are controlled by the State, which also operates omnibus services. At June 30, 1974, the route kilometres of the State railways open for traffic was 9,754, revenue in the year 1973–74 being $A267,351,000.

Aviation.—Sydney is the principal overseas terminal in Australia. Traffic movements at Sydney airport in 1973–74 were: passengers 6,086,887 (4,679,513 domestic, 1,407,374 international); freight 96,158 tonnes (51,668 domestic, 44,490 international); aircraft, 105,108 (87,181 domestic, 17,837 international).

Posts, Telegraphs and Telephones.—The postal, telegraphic, telephonic and radio services are administered by the Australian Government. At June 30, 1974, there were 2,004 post offices in New South Wales. The postal matter carried during 1973–74 included 819,090,000 letters and registered articles and 122,863,000 newspapers and parcels posted for delivery in Australia. The overseas mails consisted of 48,270,000 registered articles and letters and 4,654,000 newspapers and parcels despatched. 80,824,000 registered articles and letters and 13,982,000 newspapers and parcels received. During the year 6,201,000 telegrams were despatched to places within Australia and 1,289,000 cablegrams to places outside Australia. Transit time between Sydney and London is approximately 2½ days for airborne mail and between 4 and 6 weeks for seaborne mail. The telephone services in operation numbered 1,299,620.

Radio and Television.—In June, 1974, there were 20 National Broadcasting Stations in New South Wales and 39 commercial stations operating under licence. The number of broadcast listeners' licences was 996,248. At June 30, 1974, there were 28 television stations (14 national, 14 commercial) in operation and the number of viewers' annual licences was 1,990,940.

TOWNS.

ΨSYDNEY, the chief city and capital and the largest city in Australia, stands on the shores of Port Jackson, with a water frontage of 245 kilometres; the depth of water at the entrance is not less than 24 m and at the wharves up to 12 m. There are extensive facilities for handling cargo, and for storing and loading grain in bulk or bags. For 21 kilometres Sydney Harbour extends inland, the finest harbour in the world, and is surrounded by scenery of surpassing beauty. The principal wharves are situated in close proximity to the business centre of the city. The total area of water in the harbour is about 55 square kilometres, of which approximately one-half has a depth of not less than 9 m; the average tidal range is 1 m.

The parks in or adjacent to the metropolitan area include the Royal National Park which measures about 36,784 acres, Kuring-gai Chase 36,083 acres, Lane Cove River Park 1,000 acres and Centennial Park 540 acres.

The Sydney Statistical Division embraces an area of approximately 4,077 square kilometres, with a population of 2,898,330 (at June 30, 1974). The Newcastle and Wollongong Statistical Districts contain populations of 360,090 and 208,550 respectively.

The population of principal municipalities located outside the boundaries of these statistical areas are: Albury 31,350, Wagga Wagga 31,160, Broken Hill 28,310, Tamworth 25,090, Orange 24,600, Goulburn 21,910, Lismore 21,550, Blue Mountains 20,090 (part not included in Sydney Statistical Division), Armidale 19,810 and Dubbo 18,750.

DEPENDENCY OF NEW SOUTH WALES.

LORD HOWE ISLAND (702 kilometres north-east of Sydney). Lat. 31° 33′ 4″ S., Long. 159° 4′ 26″ E. Area 17 sq. km. Pop. June 30 1974, 260. The island is of volcanic origin with Mount Gower reaching an altitude of 366 m. The affairs of the Island and the supervision of the Kentia palm seed industry are controlled by an elected Island Committee and a Board at Sydney. *Office*, N.S.W. Department of Lands.

QUEENSLAND

This State, situated in lat. 10° 40′–29° S. and long. 138°–153° 30′ E., comprises the whole northeastern portion of the Australian continent.

Queensland possesses an area of 1,728,000 square kms. (*i.e.*, equal to more than 5½ times the area of the British Isles).

POPULATION.—At Dec. 31, 1974, the population numbered 1,997,700 persons.

Births, Deaths and Marriages

Year	Births	Deaths	Marriages
1972	39,251	16,598	16,066
1973	38,067	16,732	16,490
1974	37,852	18,128	16,086

Vital Statistics:—Annual rate per 1,000 of mean population in 1974; Births, 19·2; Deaths, 9·2; Marriages 8·2. Deaths under 1 year, 16·0 per 1,000 live births.

Religions

At the Census of 1971 there were 544,432 Church of England, 467,203 Roman Catholics (including Catholics undefined), 192,079 Presbyterians, 182,887 Methodists, 45,228 Lutherans, 28,329 Baptists, 15,554 Orthodox, 10,608 Salvation Army, 10,196 Church of Christ, 9,627 Congregationalists, 75,668 other Christians, and 1,491 Hebrews.

PHYSIOGRAPHY

The Great Dividing Range on the eastern coast of the continent produces a similar formation to that of New South Wales, the eastern side having a narrow slope to the coast and the western a long and gradual slope to the central plains, where the Selwyn and Kirby Ranges divide the land into a northern and southern watershed. The Brisbane, Burnett, Fitzroy and Burdekin rise in the eastern ranges and flow into the Pacific, the Flinders

Mitchell, and Leichhardt into the Gulf of Carpentaria, and the Barcoo and Warrego rise in the central ranges and flow southwards.

GOVERNMENT

Queensland was constituted a separate colony with Responsible Government in 1859, having previously formed part of New South Wales. The executive authority is vested in a Governor (appointed by the Crown), aided by an Executive Council of 18 members.

GOVERNOR

Governor of Queensland, His Excellency Air Marshal Sir Colin Thomas Hannah, K.C.M.G., K.B.E., C.B. *appointed* March 21, 1972 ... $35,000

EXECUTIVE COUNCIL.

(H.E. the Governor presides.)

Premier, Hon. J. Bjelke-Petersen $A32,640
Deputy Premier and Treasurer, Hon.
  Sir Gordon Chalk, K.B.E. $A27,990
Mines and Energy, Hon. R. E. Camm.
Minister for Justice and Attorney-General, Hon. W. E. Knox.
Community and Welfare Services and Sport, Hon. J. D. Herbert.
Industrial Development, Labour Relations and Consumer Affairs, Hon. F. A. Campbell.
Primary Industries, Hon. V. B. Sullivan.
Police, Hon. A. M. Hodges.
Water Resources, Hon. N. T. E. Hewitt.
Transport, Hon. K. W. Hooper.
Local Government and Main Roads, Hon. R. J. Hinze.
Tourism and Marine Services, Hon. T. G. Newbery.
Lands, Forestry, National Parks and Wildlife Services, Hon. K. B. Tomkins.
Health, Hon. L. R. Edwards.
Education and Cultural Activities, Hon. V. J. Bird.
Works and Housing, Hon. N. E. Lee.
Aboriginal and Islanders Advancement and Fisheries, Hon. C. A. Wharton.
Survey, Valuation, Urban and Regional Affairs, Hon. W. D. Lickiss.
  Ministers, each $A25,680.

AGENT-GENERAL IN LONDON

Agent-General for Queensland, The Hon. W. A. R. Rae, 392–393 Strand, S.C.2.

THE LEGISLATURE.

Parliament consists of a *Legislative Assembly* of 82 members, elected by all persons aged 18 years and over. Members of the Assembly receive $A15,630 per annum and an electorate allowance ranging from $A2,580 to $A6,310 p.a. The Assembly, as elected on December 7, 1974, was composed of: National Party, 39; Liberal Party, 30; Australian Labour Party, 11; Independent, 1; North Queensland Party, 1. The National and Liberal parties formed a coalition government.
Speaker, Hon. J. E. H. Houghton $A21,460
Chairman of Committees, W. D. Hewitt. $A17,510

THE JUDICATURE

There is a Supreme Court, with a Chief Justice, a Senior Puisne Judge and 12 Puisne Judges; District Courts, with 17 Judges; and Industrial Court, with a Supreme Court Judge as President; a Land Appeal Court and a Medical Assessment Tribunal, each presided over by a Judge of the Supreme Court; a Local Government Court, presided over by a District Court Judge; and the Industrial Conciliation and Arbitration Commission consisting of 5 members; and Inferior Courts at all the principal towns, presided over by Stipendiary Magistrates.
Chief Justice, Supreme Court, Hon.
  Sir Mostyn Hanger, K.B.E. A30,500
Senior Puisne Judge, Hon. Sir Charles
  Wanstall 26,000

Puisne Judges, Hons. N. S. Stable; G. A. G. Lucas; J. A. Douglas; D. M. Campbell; M. B. Hoare, C.M.G.; W. B. Campbell; R. H. Matthews; J. P. G. Kneipp (*Northern Judge*); E. S. Williams; D. G. Andrews; J. L. Kelly (*Central Judge*); J. D. Dunn .... each   26,000

EDUCATION.

Education is compulsory between the ages of 6 and 15, and is free in state primary and secondary schools. On Aug. 1, 1974 there were 1,225 state schools, including 223 providing secondary education, in operation, with 15,192 teachers and an enrolment of 322,318 children, and 329 private and 8 grammar schools, with an enrolment of 91,861. In 1973 tertiary level course enrolments at colleges of advanced education (incl. government teachers' colleges) and technical colleges, were 7,582 full-time and 2,757 part-time. Sub-tertiary level course enrolments at these establishments and rural training schools numbered 1,844 full-time and 30,612 part-time, including correspondence and apprenticeship students. The state-aided Universities had an enrolment of 9,278 full-time students and 9,537 part-time students.

PRODUCTION AND INDUSTRY.

The gross value of primary production (excluding mining) in 1973–74 was $A1,108,919,000 (agriculture $A527,114,000, dairying $A82,186,000, pastoral $A425,098,000, poultry and bee-keeping $A37,595,000, forestry $A20,718,000, fisheries $A15,302,000, hunting and trapping $A906,000.

Agriculture and Livestock.—The most important crop in 1973–74 was sugar-cane, producing 2,405,006 tonnes of raw sugar. Wheat yielded 525,905 tonnes, maize 56,010 tonnes, sorghum 654,225 tonnes and barley 221,051 tonnes. The livestock on March 31, 1974 included 10,296,907 cattle, 529,449 being dairy cattle, 13,118,911 sheep and 441,463 pigs.

Forestry.—At June 30, 1972, 7,718,000 acres were permanently dedicated State forests and 1,726,000 acres were timber reserves. Total Australian grown timber processed in 1974 amounted to 1,135,000 cubic metres.

Minerals.—There are rich deposits of bauxite, coal, copper, lead, phosphate, silver, uranium, and zinc, and deposits of gold, tin, limestone, ironstone, wolfram and mineral sands. Coal is mined extensively in Central Queensland and on a lesser scale in North Queensland and Ipswich districts. Commercial production of oil began at Moonie in South Queensland in 1964 and at Alton nearby in 1966. The output in 1974 included gold, $A2,143,183, coal, $A210,758,501; copper $A226,174,980; tin $A7,083,687; silver $A34,504,342; lead $A49,168,942; zinc $A55,677,425; bauxite $A48,656,507; mineral sands $A33,326,957.

Manufacturing.—At June 30, 1973, 4,212 establishments employed 116,345 persons. During the year value added was $A1,012,595,000. Much production was the processing of primary products, *e.g.* meat, sugar, minerals, timber, fruit and vegetables, flour, and butter. Included in other factory production were the products from engineering, transport equipment, basic and fabricated, chemical fertilizer works, cement, paper and woollen mills and oil refineries.

Year	Revenue	Expenditure	Debt(Gross)[1]
	$A'000	$A'000	$A'000
1972	595,218	592,506	1,347,001
1973	704,109	702,902	1,424,497
1974	853,676	855,184	1,485,255

[1]At par rates of exchange.

Banking.—Advances made by Trading Banks (including the Commonwealth Trading Bank of Australia) at June 30, 1974, totalled $A1,187,857,000. The deposits at the same date amounted to $A1,845,858,000. Depositors' balances in Queensland savings banks at June 30, 1974, $A1,428,411,000, averaged $A734 for each inhabitant. There were 2,480,000 operative accounts.

COMMUNICATIONS

Road and Rail.—The State is served by 9,472 kilometres of railways, practically all of 1,067 millimetres gauge. During 1973–74, 33,723,000 passengers and 25,401,000 tonnes of goods and livestock were carried. At June 30, 1974, there were 131,412 kilometres of formed roads in the State, and 906,000 motor vehicles were on the register.

Aviation.—Regular services operate between Brisbane, the main Queensland coastal and inland towns and the southern capitals. Brisbane is also a port of call on several international services.

Radio and Television.—On June 30, 1974, 21 national and 26 commercial sound broadcasting and 25 national (including 5 microwave repeater stations) and 11 commercial television stations were operating in Queensland.

OVERSEAS TRADE

Year	Imports	Exports
1971–72	$A270,484,273	$A980,954,360
1972–73	311,448,000	305,569,000
1973–74	542,646,000	1,360,701,000

The chief overseas exports are minerals, meat, sugar, wool, alumina, and cereal grains.

TOWNS

CAPITAL, ΨBRISBANE, is situated on the Brisbane River, which is navigable by large vessels to the city, over 23 kilometres from Moreton Bay. The population of the Brisbane Statistical Division at June 30, 1974 was 940,800. This area includes the cities of Brisbane (722,700), Ipswich (66,100) and Redcliffe (38,150).

Other cities and towns with population over 10,000 at June 30, 1974, are: ΨTownsville, 79,500; Gold Coast, 78,600; Toowoomba, 62,250; ΨRockhampton, 51,100; ΨCairns, 34,350; ΨBundaberg, 28,500; Mount Isa,32,500; Ψ Maryborough, 19,100; ΨMackay, 20,400; ΨGladstone, 17,500; Gympie, 11,000.

Transmission of mails from London to Brisbane, by air, 3 days; by sea 5 to 6 weeks.

SOUTH AUSTRALIA

The State of South Australia is situated between 26° and 38° S. lat. and 129° and 141° E. long., the total area being 380,070 sq. miles.

POPULATION.—At 30, June 1974, the population was estimated to be 1,228,100.

Births, Deaths and Marriages

Year	Births	Deaths	Marriages
1971	22,996	9,686	10,833
1972	21,844	9,764	10,829
1973	20,407	9,835	10,806
1974	20,181	10,236	10,767

Religions.

Religion is free and receives no State aid. At the Census, 1971, the persons belonging to the principal religious denominations were as follows: Church of England, 286,754; Methodists, 215,328; Congregationalists, 15,238; Baptists, 22,010; Lutherans, 62,641; Roman Catholics, 242,166; Presbyterians, 39,920; Churches of Christ, 22,802; and Orthodox, 32,636.

PHYSIOGRAPHY

The most important physical features of South Australia are broad plains, divided longitudinally by four great secondary features, which form barriers to east-west movement, and which have thus largely determined the direction of roads and railways, the sites of towns and villages and the manner of distribution of the population. These four barriers are Spencer Gulf, Gulf St. Vincent, the Mt. Lofty-Flinders Ranges and the River Murray. The long, deeply-indented coast-line, which provides a few major, and a multitude of lesser harbours, trends generally south-eastward. Pleasant weather conditions and good rainfall are experienced in most coastal areas.

The north-western portion of the State is mostly desert, while north of latitude 32° S. the country is unpromising by comparison with the fertile land which surrounds the hill country of the east. The Murray, which flows for some 400 miles through the south-eastern corner, is the only river of importance.

The lack of rivers and fresh-water lakes in the settled areas has necessitated the building of a number of reservoirs, which have been supplemented since 1941 by the construction of pipelines from the River Murray.

Climate.—The mean annual temperature at Adelaide is 17·1°C, the winter temperature (June–August) averaging 11·8°C, and the summer (Nov–Mar.) 21·5°C. During the summer months the maximum temperature at times exceeds 40°C, but is associated with a relatively low humidity. The average annual rainfall at Adelaide derived from over 130 years' record is 21 inches. This total is rather higher than the approximate average annual rainfall over the whole of the agricultural areas. In the Mount Lofty Ranges the mean yearly rainfall in places exceeds 40 inches, while in Adelaide precipitation has fallen as low as 10·11 inches.

GOVERNMENT

South Australia was proclaimed a British Province in 1836, and in 1851 a partially elective legislature was established. The present Constitution rests upon a Law of Oct. 24, 1856, the executive authority being vested in a Governor appointed by the Crown, aided by a Council of 11 Ministers.

GOVERNOR

Governor of South Australia, His Excellency Sir Mark Laurence Elwin Oliphant, K.B.E., F.R.S. (1971)

$A20,000

Lieut.-Governor, W. R. Crocker, C.B.E. (1973).

THE MINISTRY

($A244,418 was voted in 1973–74 as salaries and allowances to Ministers.)

Premier and Treasurer, Hon. D. A. Dunstan, Q.C., M.P.

Deputy Premier and Minister of Works and Marine, Hon. J. D. Corcoran, M.P.

Minister of Mines and Energy, Minister of Housing and Special Minister of State for Monarto and Redcliff, Hon. H. R. Hudson, M.P.

Minister of Health and Chief Secretary, Hon. D. H. L. Banfield, M.L.C.

Attorney-General, Minister of Community Welfare and Minister of Prices and Consumer Affairs, Hon. L. J. King, Q.C., M.P.

Minister of Transport and Minister of Local Government, Hon. G. T. Virgo, M.P.

Minister of Lands, Minister of Irrigation, Minister of Repatriation and Minister of Tourism, Recreation and Sport, Hon. T. M. Casey, M.L.C.

Minister for the Environment and Minister for Planning and Development, Hon. G. R. Broomhill, M.P.

Minister of Education, Hon. D. J. Hopgood, M.P.

Minister of Agriculture, Minister of Forests and Minister of Fisheries, Hon. B. A. Chatterton, M.L.C.

Minister of Labour and Industry, Hon. J. D. Wright, M.P.

AGENT-GENERAL IN LONDON

Agent-General and Trade Commissioner for South Australia, J. S. White, C.M.G., South Australia House, 50 Strand, W.C.2.

THE LEGISLATURE

Parliament consists of a *Legislative Council* of 20 members elected for 6 years, one-half retiring every 3 years; and a *House of Assembly* of 47 members, elected for a maximum duration of 3 years. Election is by ballot, with universal adult suffrage for both the Legislative Council and the House of Assembly for all British subjects, male and female. The number of electors in 1974 was 755,095.

The elections to the House of Assembly in March, 1973, returned 26 Labour members, 18 Liberals and Country League, 2 Liberal Movement and 1 Country Party.

President of the Legislative Council, Hon.
Sir Lyell McEwin, K.B.E. $A22,550

Speaker of the House of Assembly, Hon.
J. R. Ryan $A22,550

Leader of the Opposition, Dr. B. C. Eastick.

THE JUDICATURE

Law and Justice.—The Supreme Court is presided over by the Chief Justice and eight Puisne Judges.

EDUCATION

Education at the primary and secondary level is available at State schools controlled by the Education Department and at private schools, most of which are denominational. In 1974 there were 613 State schools with 232,479 students, and 157 private schools with 38,893 students. The Department of Further Education administers the South Australian College of External Studies, apprentice training and contributing education in 8 metropolitan and 4 county technical colleges and 5 metropolitan and 11 county further eduction centres.

There are two universities: the University of Adelaide, founded in 1874, and the Flinders University of South Australia, opened in 1966. In 1974 there was a total enrolment of 8,625 full-time students. There are also eight Colleges of Advanced Education.

FINANCE

Banking.—There are 8 trading banks in Adelaide, including the Commonwealth Trading Bank and the State Bank of South Australia, having total average deposits of $A815,622,000 in June 1974. The eight savings banks had deposits of $A1,174,813,000 at June 30, 1974.

Revenue and Expenditure
(For years ended June 30)

Year	Revenue	Expenditure	Debt
	$A	$A	$A
1971	386,859,000	386,838,000	1,256,337,000
1972	455,245,000	456,312,000	1,333,720,000
1973	520,866,000	524,777,000	1,415,129,000
1974	641,967,000	645,368,000	1,481,337,000

PRODUCTION AND INDUSTRY

The gross value of primary production in 1973–74 was: crops $A374,638,000, livestock slaughterings $A164,074,000, livestock products $A214,443,000, and other primary $A30,209,000.

Land Tenure.—Of the total area of the State (243,000,000 acres), 17,000,000 acres have been sold or are in the process of alienation by the Crown under systems of deferred payment; 127,000,000 acres are held under pastoral leases and 22,800,000 under other miscellaneous leases.

Agriculture.—The total area cultivated in 1971–72 was 14,516,000 acres—under wheat 4,002,640 acres, oats 417,200, barley 1,936,400. Wheat harvest 1973–74, 1,795,000 tonnes; barley, 793,000 tonnes. Oranges, lemons, apples, apricots, peaches, and all stone fruits and olives are successfully grown, and fruit drying is profitable. In 1973–74 164,328,000 litres of wine and 3,196 tonnes of currants and raisins were produced. Considerable quantities of fruits (fresh and dried), wine and brandy, are annually sent to overseas countries, principally Canada, and to other Australian States. Some areas of the State, particularly near Adelaide, are also very suitable for growing all kinds of root crops and vegetables.

Livestock (March 31, 1974).—There were 16,431,000 sheep, 1,692,000 cattle, 385,000 pigs. Wool production (1973–74), 100,155,000 kg.

Minerals.—Iron, pyrite, gypsum, salt, coal, limestone, clay, &c., are found. The total mineral output was valued at $A131,445,000 in 1974, including iron ore valued by the South Australian Director of Mines at $A53,321,000.

Manufactures.—In 1973–74 there were 2,914 factories, employing 121,396 hands, the value of production being $A896,691,000.

Transport and Communications.—There were (June, 1974) 6,121 kilometres of railway in South Australia, 730 kilometres of tram and bus routes and 100,075 kilometres of roads, including roads and tracks outside local government areas. There are a number of excellent harbours, of which Port Adelaide is the most important. The number of vessels (exceeding 200 net tons) entering South Australia from overseas and interstate during 1973–74 was 1,298 with net tonnage of 8,107,488. The total value of shipping at South Australian ports during 1973–74 was 11,061,053 net tons involving 2,462 recorded entries of vessels. The countries of registration of vessels entered were: Australia 1,389; United Kingdom 290; Greece 106; Norway 55; Sweden 49; New Zealand 120; Liberia 70; Japan 72; all other countries 366. There are 786 post offices in the State.

Civil Aviation.—There are 31 Government and licensed airports; the largest of these, Adelaide airport, recorded 1,376,891 passenger movements during 1973–74.

Motor Vehicles.—The registrations on 30 June, 1974, were 577,558, equal to 1 per 2·11 persons.

Wireless and Television (June 30, 1974)—Broadcasting stations 18; listeners' licences 330,868. Television stations 11; viewers' licences 337,731.

OVERSEAS TRADE

Year	Imports	Exports
	$A	$A
1970–71	198,358,301	393,736,947
1971–72	189,748,047	394,063,996
1972–73	199,978,000	521,720,000
1973–74	313,915,000	622,881,000

The principal exports are wool, wheat, barley, meat, lead and lead alloys, and ores and concentrates of iron, lead, zinc and motor vehicles.

Towns

ΨADELAIDE,the chief city and capital, according to population on Census June 30, 1971, 809,482, inclusive of suburbs. Other centres (with 1971 populations) are: Whyalla (32,109); Mt. Gambier (17,934); ΨPort Pirie (15,456); ΨPort Augusta (12,224); and ΨPort Lincoln (9,158).

Transit.—Transmission of mails from London to Adelaide, approximately 29 days by sea and 5 days by air.

TASMANIA

Tasmania is an island state of Australia situated in the Southern ocean off the south-eastern extremity of the mainland. It is separated from the Australian mainland by Bass Strait and incorporates King Island and the Furneaux group of islands which are in the Strait. It lies between 40° 40′–43° 39′ S. lat. and 144° 31′–148° 18′ E. long., and contains an areas of 26,383 square miles.

POPULATION.—The estimated population at June 30, 1974, was 399,500.

Year	Births	Deaths	Marriages
1971	8,321	3,295	3,578
1972	7,824	3,277	3,426
1973	7,326	3,347	3,395
1974	7,398	3,484	3,567

Vital Statistics.—The birth rate in 1973 was 18·5, death rate 8·4, marriage rate 8·6 per 1,000. Infant mortality (1973) 18·7 per 1,000 births.

Religions

In 1971 there were 169,089 members of the Church of England, 77,250 Roman Catholics, 42,173 Methodists, 17,281 Presbyterians, 4,134 Congregationalists and Independents, and 8,039 Baptists.

Physiography

The surface of the country is generally hilly and timbered, with mountains from 1,500 to 5,300 ft. in height, and expanses of level, open plains. There are numerous rivers, the Gordon, Derwent and Tamar being the largest. The climate is fine and salubrious, and well suited to European constitutions; the hot winds of Australia do not often reach the island. At Hobart the mean maximum temperature ranges from about 54°F in winter to 70°F in summer, the minimum from 40°F to 52°F. The western side of the island is very wet, the eastern side being much drier; the average rainfall varies from 20 inches to 140 inches in different parts.

Government

The island was first settled by a British party from New South Wales in 1803, becoming a separate colony in 1825. In 1851 a partly elective legislature was inaugurated, and in 1856 responsible government was established. In 1901 Tasmania became a State of the Australian Commonwealth. The State executive authority is vested in a Governor (appointed by the Crown), but is exercised by Cabinet Ministers responsible to the Legislature, of which they are members.

Governor

Governor of Tasmania, His Excellency Sir Charles Stanley Burbury, K.B.E.; *assumed office* Dec. 5, 1973.

The Ministry

Premier, Treasurer, Hon. W. A. Neilson, M.H.A.

Attorney-General and Minister for Police and Licensing, Hon. B. K. Miller, M.L.C.

Minister for Education, Recreation and the Arts, National Parks and Wildlife, Hon. N. L. C. Batt, M.H.A.

Minister of Transport, Hon. G. D. Chisholm, M.H.A.

Agriculture, Hon. E. W. Barnard, M.H.A.

Lands, Works, Tourism and Immigration, Hon. M. T. C. Barnard, M.H.A.

Health, Hon. H. D. Farquhar, M.H.A.

Industrial Development, Forests, Mines and Hydro-Electric Commission, Hon. S. C. H. Frost, M.H.A.

Chief Secretary and Minister for Planning and Reorganisation, Environment and Local Government Hon. B. A. Lowe, M.H.A.

Housing and Social Welfare, Hon. D. J. Baldock, M.H.A.

Agent-General in London

Agent-General for Tasmania, R. R. Neville, 458–9 Strand, Charing Cross, W.C.2.

The Legislature

Parliament consists of two Houses, a *Legislative Council* of 19 members, elected for six years (3 retiring annually, in rotation, except in every sixth year, when four retire) and a *House of Assembly* of 35 members, elected by proportional representation for five years in five 7–member constituencies, the electors for both Houses being all Tasmanians of 18 years and over who have resided continuously in the State for 6 months. The current term of five years for the House of Assembly will be reduced to four years after the next General Election.

At the election held on April 22, 1972, the Labour Party was returned to power in the House of Assembly after the resignation of the Liberals who had held office for a little under three of the scheduled five year term, which was due to be reduced to three years in 1974. The Labour Party's previous term had lasted for 35 years. The composition of the House of Assembly after the election was: Labour 21; Liberal 14.

President of the Legislative Council, Hon. C. B. M. Fenton.

Clerk of the Council, G. B. Edwards.

Speaker of the House of Assembly, Hon. H. Holgate.

Clerk of the House, B. G. Murphy.

The Judicature

The *Supreme Court of Tasmania,* with civil, criminal ecclesiastical, admiralty and matrimonial jurisdiction, was established by Royal Charter on October 13, 1823.

Chief Justice, Hon. G. S. M. Green.

Puisne Judges, Hon. Sir George Crawford; Hon. F. M. Neasey; Hon. D. M. Chambers; Hon. R. R. Nettlefold.

Local Courts established under the Local Courts Acts, 1896, are held before Commissioners who are legal practitioners with a jurisdiction up to $A1,500 in the case of liquidated claims ($A1,000, unliquidated claims). Courts of General Sessions, constituted by a chairman who is a Justice of the Peace and at least one other Justice, are established in the municipalities for the recovery of debts and demands not exceeding $A100. Courts of Petty Sessions are established under the Justices Act, 1959, constituted by Police Magistrates sitting alone, or any two or more justices. A single justice may hear and determine certain matters.

Education

Government schools are of three main types: primary, secondary and matriculation schools. On Aug. 1, 1974, there were 79,835 scholars enrolled in 279 Government schools. There were also 65 independent schools with an enrolment of 14,407. The University of Tasmania at Hobart, established 1890, had 2,291 full-time students and 1,123 part-time (including external) students in 1974.

FINANCE

Revenue and expenditure of the Consolidated Revenue Fund and debt of Tasmania at current rates of exchange (June 30) was;—

Year	Revenue	Expenditure	Debt
	$A	$A	$A
1970–71	138,228,937	138,206,661	671,323,864
1971–72	157,751,717	160,236,825	709,921,268
1972–73	181,866,413	185,998,130	751,990,198
1973–74	206,946,676	210,096,694	787,618,086

Banking.—The weekly average of depositors' balances in Nov. 1974 was $A227,490,000; the savings bank balances at the end of Nov. 1974, were $A344,454,000.

PRODUCTION AND INDUSTRY

The net values of production in 1973–74 for the following were: agriculture, $A33·5m.; pastoral, $A57·1m.; dairying, $A27·7m.; forestry, $A35·9m.; and other primary industries, $A10·2m. Total value added in manufacturing in 1972–73 was $A283·4m.

Agriculture and Livestock.—The principal crops are potatoes, apples and other fruit, hay, hops, oats, beans, oil poppies, green peas, turnips (for stock feed), barley and wheat. The livestock included (March 31, 1974) 884,000 cattle, 3,964,000 sheep and 68,000 pigs. The wool production (1973–74) was 17,549,000 kg.

Electrical Energy.—Tasmania, the smallest Australian state, ranks fourth as a producer of electrical energy—most of it derived from water power, with an assessed annual capacity of 6,977 million kWh. By reason of its low-cost electrical energy, Tasmania has the large plants producing ferro-manganese and newsprint. A large aluminium plant is situated at Bell Bay and Tasmania is the source of the bulk of Australian requirements of electrolytic zinc and fine papers. The Hydro-electric Commission has completed a network of 22 stations including an oil fired station at Bell Bay. Work is continuing on two hydro-electric developments in the remote western and south-western regions of the state.

Forestry.—The quantity of timber (excluding firewood) of various species cut in 1973–74 was 4,035,390 cubic metres, including 2,961,660 cubic metres for woodchip and wood-pulp.

Minerals.—The chief ores mined are those containing copper, tin, iron, silver, zinc and lead. The gross value of output in all mines and quarries in 1973-74 was $A117·6m.

Manufactures.—The chief manufactures for export are: refined metals, pelletized iron ore, preserved fruit and vegetables, butter, cheese, woollen manufactures, alginates, fish meal, paper, confectionery, wood chips and sawn timber. In 1972–73, 912 manufacturing establishments employed 30,684 persons, including working proprietors. Salaries and wages paid totalled $A130·7m.

COMMUNICATIONS

Road and Rail.—Tasmania is served by a 3 foot 6 inch gauge Government railway system of 984 route kms. An additional 134 route kms of the same gauge is privately operated. During 1973–74 the Government system carried 695,000 passengers and 1,880,000 tonnes of goods and livestock. At Dec. 31, 1974 there were 20,767 kilometres of road

normally open to traffic. Of this total 6,715 kilometres were sealed. Motor vehicles on the register at Dec. 31, 1974 were: cars and station wagons, 147,000; commercial vehicles, 35,100 and motor cycles, 7,400.

Aviation.—Regular services operate between Tasmania and the other Australian States. During 1972–73 687,000 passengers were carried on these services. The main cities and towns in the State are served by regular internal services.

OVERSEAS TRADE

Year	Imports	Exports
	$A'000	$A'000
1971–72	39,749	178,950
1972–73	45,045	218,712
1973–74	69,277	259,745

The principal overseas exports are ores and concentrates, refined metals, fresh fruit, greasy wool, meat and butter.

TOWNS

CAPITAL, ΨHOBART, founded 1804. Population (June 30, 1973), 133,080.

Other towns (with estimated population at June 30, 1974) are ΨLaunceston (63,210), ΨDevonport (19,730), Burnie-Somerset (20,610), Ulverstone (8,360) and New Norfolk (6,860).

VICTORIA

The State of Victoria comprises the south-east corner of Australia, at the part where its mainland territory projects farthest into the southern latitudes; it lies between 34°–39° S. latitude and 141°–150° E. longitude. Its extreme length from east to west is about 493 miles, its greatest breadth is about 290 miles, and its extent of coast-line is about 980 geographical miles, including the length around Port Phillip Bay, Western Port and Corner Inlet, the entire area being 87,884 square miles.

Population.—The population at June 30, 1973, was 3,586,574 (1,792,201 males and 1,794,373 females).

Births, Deaths and Marriages

Year	Births	Deaths	Marriages
1971	75,498	30,598	31,729
1972	71,807	29,856	32,386
1973	67,123	30,696	30,203
1974	66,201	30,875	29,708

Vital Statistics.—Annual rate per 1,000 of population in 1974: Births, 18·25; Deaths,8·51; Marriages, 8·19. Deaths under 1 year per 1,000 births, 14.9.

Religions

Members of the Church of England at the date of the Census in 1971 numbered 892,568, Roman Catholics 1,003,826, Presbyterians 364,338, Methodists 256,058, Orthodox 140,600, Baptists 41,753, Churches of Christ 32,950, Lutheran 39,832 and Hebrew 30,117. The number of persons who did not state their religion was 215,212.

PHYSIOGRAPHY

The *Australian Alps* and the *Great Dividing Range* pass through the centre of the State, and divide it into a northern and southern watershed, the latter sloping down to the ocean and containing, especially in the south-east, well-wooded valleys. The length of the Murray River, which forms part of the northern boundary of Victoria, is about 1,200 miles along the Victorian bank. Melbourne, the capital city, stands upon the Yarra-Yarra, which rises in the southern slopes of the Dividing Range.

Climate.—The climate of Victoria is characterized by warm summers, rather cold winters, and rain in all months with a maximum in winter or spring. Prevailing winds are southerly from November to February inclusive, with a moderate percentage of northerlies often associated with high temperatures. Northerly or westerly winds predominate from March to October inclusive. Rain on an average falls in Melbourne on 143 days per year, the annual average being 25·85 inches.

GOVERNMENT

Victoria was originally known as the Port Phillip District of New South Wales and was created a separate colony in 1851, with a partially elective legislature. In 1855 Responsible Government was conferred. The executive authority is vested in a Governor, appointed by the Crown, aided by an Executive Council of Ministers.

Governor of the State of Victoria, His Excellency Hon. Sir Henry Arthur Winneke, K.C.M.G., O.B.E., *born* Oct. 29, 1908; *assumed office* June 3, 1974) $A20,500
Lieutenant-Governor, Hon. Sir John McIntosh Young, K.C.M.G., Q.C. (1974).

THE MINISTRY

Premier, Treasurer and Minister of the Arts, Hon. R. J. Hamer, E.D.
Deputy Premier and Minister of Education, Hon. L. H. S. Thompson, C.M.G.
State Development and Decentralization, Tourism and Immigration, Hon. Murray Byrne.
Housing, Hon. V. O. Dickie.
Transport, Hon. E. R. Meagher, M.B.E., E.D.
Fuel and Power and Mines, Hon. J. C. M. Balfour.
Chief Secretary, Hon. J. F. Rossiter.
Attorney-General, Hon. V. F. Wilcox, Q.C.
Conservation, Land, Soldier Settlement, Hon. W. A. Borthwick.
Labour and Industry, Consumer Affairs and Federal Affairs, Hon. J. A. Rafferty.
Agriculture, Hon. I. W. Smith.
Public Works, Hon. R. C. Dunstan, D.S.O.
Local Government and Planning, Hon. A. J. Hunt.
Health, Hon. A. H. Scanlan.
Social Welfare, Hon. W. V. Houghton.
Youth, Sport and Recreation, and Assistant Minister of Education, Hon. B. J. Dixon.
Water Supply and Forests, Hon. F. J. Granter.

AGENT-GENERAL IN LONDON

Agent-General for Victoria, Hon. Sir Murray Porter, Victoria House, Melbourne Place, Strand, W.C.2.

THE LEGISLATURE

Parliament consists of a *Legislative Council* of 36 members, elected for the 18 Provinces for 6 years, one-half retiring every 3 years; and a *Legislative Assembly* of 73 members, elected for a maximum duration of 3 years. By virtue of the Electoral Provinces and Districts Act 1974 the number of members of the Legislative Council will be increased to 44 elected for 22 provinces for 6 years, one half retiring every 3 years; the number of members of the Legislative Assembly will be increased to 81 elected for a maximum duration of 3 years. Voting is compulsory. The electors on the rolls at May 30, 1975 numbered 2,162,221.

President of the Legislative Council, Hon.
Sir Raymond Garrett, A.F.C. $A34,125
Speaker of the Legislative Assembly, Hon.
K. H. Wheeler 34,125

THE JUDICATURE

There is a Supreme Court with a Chief Justice and 19 Puisne Judges, a County Court and Magistrates' Courts.

Supreme Court

Chief Justice, Hon. Sir John Young, K.C.M.G. $A42,400
Puisne Judges, Hon. Sir Gregory Gowans; Hon. Sir Oliver Gillard; Hon. J. E. Starke; Hon. E. H. E. Barber; Hon. M. V. McInerney; Hon. G. H. Lush; Hon. C. I. Menhennitt; Hon. H. R. Newton; Hon. F. Nelson; Hon. K. V. Anderson; Hon. W. C. Crockett; Hon W. Kaye; Hon. R. G. De B. Griffith; Hon. B. J. Dunn; Hon. P. Murphy; Hon. W. O. Harris; Hon. B. L. Murray; Hon. R. K. Fullagar; Hon. K. J. Jenkinson .... *each* 38,500

County Court

Chief Judge, Hon. D. Whelan 38,000
Judges, Their Honours T. G. Rapke; H. T. Frederico; N. A. Vickery; A. Adams; D. W. Corson; J. X. O'Driscoll; J. H. Forrest; C. W. Harris; E. E. Hewitt; C. Just; R. J. Leckie; I. F. C. Franich; T. B. Shillito; J. P. Somerville; W. J. Martin; I. Gray; A. J. Southwell; J. R. O'Shea; J. G. Gorman; R. J. D. Wright; H. G. Ogden; G. M. Byrne; N. S. Stabey; B. F. McNab; K. F. Coleman; G. H. Spence; J. Mornane............*each* 31,750
Masters of the Supreme Court, C. P. Jacobs, M.B.E.; S. H. Collie; E. N. Bergere; G. S. Brett....................*each* 26,700

Law Department

Solicitor-General, D. Dawson, Q.C....... 38,500
Secretary to the Law Department, R. Glenister........................... 27,400
Crown Solicitor, J. Downey............ 30,769

EDUCATION

Primary Education is compulsory, secular and free between the ages of 6 and 15. At Aug. 1, 1974, there were 1,724 Government Primary Schools attended by 366,303 pupils, 34 Primary-Secondary Schools with 8,588 pupils, and 262 Secondary Schools (excluding Junior Technical Schools) with an enrolment of 168,987. There were also 101 Government Junior Technical Schools with 61,599 pupils and 40 Special Schools with 3,166 pupils. In addition there are various Senior Colleges and Colleges of Advanced Education.

At Aug. 1, 1974, 196,420 pupils attended 571 non-Government schools, 466 of which were Roman Catholic.

There are three State-aided Universities—Melbourne, Monash and La Trobe. Enrolments for 1974 at Melbourne were 15,539, at Monash 12,837 and at La Trobe 6,481.

PRODUCTION AND INDUSTRY

The gross value of primary production (excluding mining and quarrying) in 1973–74 was $A1,467,007,979, agricultural $A461,231,870, pastoral $A597,851,098, dairying $A276,934,278, poultry and bee-keeping $A69,813,714, trapping $A5,633,632, forestry $A44,478,755 mining and quarries (including oil and natural gas) $A432,949,000, fisheries $A11,064,632. The net value of production of primary industries was $A1,081,611,136. Wool, wheat, flour, butter, live stock, fruits, milk and cream, meats, poultry and eggs are staple products.

Live Stock.—There were on rural holdings in March, 1974, 25,787,000 sheep, 5,840,000 cattle, and

424,000 pigs. The quantity of wool produced in 1973–74 was valued at A248,232,000 (preliminary figures).

Minerals.—Minerals raised include oil and natural gas, brown coal, limestone, clays and stone for construction material. Production of brown coal in 1973–74 amounted to 26,354,577 tonnes.

FINANCE

Year	Consolidated Fund		Debt at end of year
	Receipts	Payments	
	$A'000	$A'000	$A'000
1971–72	1,210,889	1,210,889	2,488,348
1972–73	1,381,153	1,381,153	2,632,910
1973–74	1,610,923	1,610,923	2,746,610

Banking, etc.—State Savings Bank deposits at June 30, 1974, amounted to $A1,861,972,000; in addition, deposits in the Commonwealth Savings Bank (in the State of Victoria) amounted to $A853,858,000, and in other savings banks $A1,214,312,000

Insurance (other than Life).—The total revenue of companies or other bodies transacting business in Victoria during the year 1973–74 amounted to $A522,897,000, made up of premium income $A486,197,000, and other income $A36,699,000. Expenditure totalled $A485,354,000 (excluding taxation), comprising claims $A361,053,000, commission and agents' charges $A39,555,000 and other expenditure $A84,746,000.

Crude Oil and National Gas.—In February, 1965 natural gas was first discovered in commercial quantities in the offshore waters of the Gippsland Basin in eastern Victoria. An even larger gas field was found early in 1966, and during 1967 two valuable oilfields were located in the same general area. These fields are still the largest yet found in Australia. Following the development of the four fields, commercial gas began to flow to consumers in Melbourne during April 1969, and crude oil came on stream in October, 1969. Production from the Gippsland fields during the calendar year 1974 was: stabilized crude oil, 20,136,889 cubic metres; treated natural gas, 2,128,154,045 cubic metres; commercial propane, 918,372 cubic metres and commercial butane, 1,055,219 cubic metres.

Secondary Industry.—In 1972–73 there were 11,734 manufacturing establishments in which 314,269 males and 141,004 females were employed. The principal industrial sub-divisions were: Transport equipment, 60,909 persons; basic and fabricated metal products 51,003 persons; other industrial machinery, 66,603 persons; clothing and footwear, 61,129 persons; and food, beverages and tobacco, 63,847 persons. Manufacturing activity is concentrated in the Melbourne Statistical Division. Important manufacturing centres are Geelong, Ballarat, Bendigo and in the shire of Morwell. Value added in the course of manufacture was $A3,738 million.

TRANSPORT

Victoria State Railways.—At June 30, 1974, there were 6,685 kms of railway open for traffic. The revenue and expenditure for the year ended June 30, 1974, were $A115,612,777 and $A156,119,624 respectively. Total distance travelled was 33,352,420 kms and passenger journeys numbered 114,589,353. The tonnage of goods and livestock carried was 11,231,160.

Shipping.—During the year ended June 30, 1974, 3,530 vessels with net tonnage 22,192,000 entered Victorian ports and 3,530 vessels with total net tonnage of 22,074,695 were cleared.

Motor Vehicle Registration.—The number of vehicles on the register at June 30, 1974, was: cars and stationwagons, 1,301,900; light commercial type vehicles, 150,100; trucks and omnibuses, 111,600, and motor cycles, 45,800.

OVERSEAS TRADE

The export trade (excluding inter-state trade) consists largely of agricultural and mining products. The principal overseas imports of the State are aircraft and parts, apparel and textiles, manufactured fibres, electrical and other machines and machinery, motor vehicles and tractors, metals and metal manufactures, iron and steel, rubber manufactures, crude petroleum, paper, drugs and chemicals, synthetic resins and professional, scientific and controlling instruments.

Year	Imports	Exports
	$A	$A
1969–70	1,347,053,000	912,596,000
1970–71	1,453,583,000	1,034,908,000
1971–72	1,431,076,000	1,139,731,000
1972–73	1,472,602,000	1,495,373,000
1973–74	2,155,908,000	1,594,870,000

CITIES, TOWNS AND BOROUGHS

ΨMELBOURNE, the capital city, which is an archiepiscopal see, was originally laid out in the year 1837 with wisdom and foresight; its wide streets, park lands, public gardens, university, public library, museum, art gallery and large churches are the principal features of the city. At the Census of June 30, 1971, the population of Urban Melbourne was 2,394,117. Other urban centres are ΨGeelong, 115,181; Ballarat, 58,620; Bendigo, 45,936; Moe-Yallourn, 20,863; Shepparton, 19,410; Ψ Warrnambool, 18,684; Morwell 16,858; Wangaratta, 15,586; Traralgon, 14,665.

WESTERN AUSTRALIA

Includes all that portion of the continent west of 129° E. long., the most westerly point being in 113° 9'E. long. and from 13° 44' to 35° 8' S. lat. Its extreme length is 1,480 miles and 1,000 miles from east to west; total area 975,920 sq. miles.

POPULATION.—At June 30, 1974, the population was estimated at 1,094,721 (males, 559,554; females, 535,167). The figures include full-blood Aborigines.

Year	Births	Deaths	Marriages
1970	21,618	7,543	9,227
1971	24,239	7,806	9,382
1972	22,177	7,441	9,120
1973	20,510	7,845	9,102
1974	20,207	7,778	9,295

Religions.—Census of 1971—Church of England 362,759, Roman Catholics 267,990, Methodists 85,283, and Presbyterians 48,367.

Physical Features.—Large areas of the State, for some hundreds of miles inland, are hilly and even mountainous, although the altitude, so far as ascertained, rises nowhere above that of Mount Meharry (4,082 ft) in the north-west division or that of Bluff Knoll (3,640 ft.) in the Stirling Range in the south-west. The coastal regions are undulating, with an interior slope to the unsettled central portion of Australia. The Darling and Hamersley ranges of the west have a seaward slope to the Indian Ocean, into which flow many streams, notably the Preston, Collie, Murray, Swan, Murchison, Gascoyne, Ashburton, Fortescue and De Grey. In the north the Fitzroy flows from the King Leopold ranges into the Indian Ocean, and the Drysdale and Ord into the Timor Sea. The greater portion of the State may be described as an immense tableland, with an average elevation of 1,000 to 1,500 ft. above sea-level, the surface of which varies from stretches of clay soils to the sand dunes of the far interior. The climate is one of the most temperate in the world. The total rainfall at Perth during 1974 was 975 milimetres, the average for the previous 97 years 880. Of the total area two-thirds is suitable for pastoral purposes.

GOVERNMENT

Western Australia was first settled by the British in 1829, and in 1870 it was granted a partially elective legislature. In 1890 Responsible Government was granted, and the Administration vested in a Governor, a Legislative Council, and a Legislative Assembly. The present constitution rests upon the Constitution Act, 1889, the Constitution Acts Amendment Act, 1899, and amending Acts. The Executive is vested in a Governor appointed by the Crown and aided by a Council of responsible Ministers.

The Legislative Assembly (elected March, 1974) is composed of Liberal Party 23, Australian Labour Party 22, Country Party 6.

Governor of Western Australia, Air Chief Marshal Sir Wallace Kyle, G.C.B., C.B.E., D.S.O., D.F,C, (1975).
Lieut.-Governor and Administrator, His Excellency Commodore J. M. Ramsay, C.B.E., D.S.C.

EXECUTIVE COUNCIL

Premier, Treasurer, Minister Co-ordinating Economic and Regional Development, and Minister for Federal Affairs, Hon. Sir Charles Court, O.B.E., M.L.A.
                                                         $A33,700
Deputy Premier, Minister for Works, Water Supplies, and the North West, Hon. D. H. O'Neil, M.L.A.
                                                         $A29,850
Minister for Justice, Chief Secretary and Leader of the Government in the Legislative Council, Hon. Neil McNeil, M.L.C. $A30,370
Minister for Agriculture, Hon. R. C. Old, M.L.A.
Minister for Transport, Police and Traffic, Hon. R. J. O'Connor, M.L.A.
Minister for Education, Cultural Affairs, and Recreation, Hon. G. C. MacKinnon, M.L.C.
Minister for Labour and Industry, Consumer Affairs, and Immigration, Hon. W. L. Grayden, M.L.A.
Minister for Industrial Development, Mines and Fuel and Energy, Hon. A. Mensaros, M.L.A.
Minister for Local Government and Urban Development and Town Planning, Hon. E. C. Rushton, M.L.A.
Minister for Lands, Forests and Tourism, Hon. K. A. Ridge, M.L.A.
Minister for Health, and Community Welfare, Hon. N. E. Baxter, M.L.C.
Minister for Housing, Conservation and the Environment, and Fisheries and Wildlife, Hon. P. V. Jones, M.L.A.
(M.L.A.—Membership of the Legislative Assembly, M.L.C.—Member of the Legislative Council)
Ministers, each $A26,700 to $A31,020, according to location of electorate.

AGENT-GENERAL IN LONDON

Offices, Western Australia House
        115 Strand, London, W.C.2.
Agent-General, J. A. Richards.

THE LEGISLATURE

Parliament consists of a *Legislative Council* and a *Legislative Assembly*, elected by adult suffrage subject to qualifications of residence and registration. The qualifying age for electors for both the Legislative Council and Legislative Assembly was lowered in 1970 from 21 to 18 years. There are 30 members in the Legislative Council, two from each Province, for a period of 6 years, one member from each Province retiring triennially. The Legislative Assembly is composed of 51 members, who are elected for a term of 3 years.
President of the Legislative Council, Hon.
    A. F. Griffith, M.L.C. $A22,280
Speaker of the Legislative Assembly, Hon.
    R. Hutchinson, D.F.C., M.L.A.   21,380

THE JUDICATURE

Chief Justice, Hon. Sir Lawrence Jackson, K.C.M.G. $A32,400
Senior Puisne Judge, Hon. F. T. P. Burt;   29,700
Puisne Judges, Hons. J. M. Lavan; A. R.
    A. Wallace; J. L. C. Wickham; R. E.
    Jones; G. D. Wright   *each* 28,800

EDUCATION

Education.—In 1974 there were 621 government schools and 192 non-government schools (excluding kindergartens) with 188,914 and 42,788 pupils respectively. The total amount expended on education (from State Revenue) during the year ended June 30, 1974, was A135,770,881, including grants of $A4,032,730 to the University of Western Australia (6,033 full-time students in 1974), and $A244,373 to Murdoch University (which commenced in 1974 with 9 full-time students).

PRODUCTION AND INDUSTRY

The gross value of primary production (excluding mining) in 1973–74 was: agricultural $A587,628,000; pastoral $A369,636,000; dairying $A39,290,000; poultry farming $A19,016,000; bee-keeping $A1,343,000; hunting $A1,739,000; forestry $A15,264,000; fishing and whaling $A30,153,000.

Crops and Livestock.—The production of wheat for grain in 1973–74 was 4,210,782 tonnes. On March 31, 1974, the livestock included 2,330,060 cattle, 32,451,073 sheep, and 343,623 pigs. The wool clip in 1973–74 was 142,100,000 kg. in the grease.

Manufacturing Industries.—There were 2,814 manufacturing establishments operating in the State at June 30, 1973. The total number of persons employed (including working proprietors) by these establishments at the end of June, 1973, was 64,074.

Forestry.—The forests contain some of the finest hardwoods in the world. The total quantity of sawn timber produced during 1973–74 was 407,577 cubic metres.

Minerals.—The State has large deposits of a wide range of minerals, many of which are being mined or are under development for production. The ex-mine value of all minerals produced during 1972–73 was $A536,383,000.

Communications.—On June 30, 1974, there were 6,192 kms. of State government railway open for general and passenger traffic; and 731 kms. of the Trans-Australian railway (Kalgoorlie-Port Pirie Junction). In the year ended June 30, 1974, 3,684 vessels (net tonnage 45,959,549) entered Western Australian ports and 3,672 (net tonnage 45,830,588) cleared. The total length of roads at June 30, 1974, was 161,819 kms. The number of registered motor vhicles at June 30, 1974, was 527,091 (389,083 motor cars and station wagons, 116,004 light and heavy commercials, and 22,004 motor cycles and motor scooters).

FINANCE

Total revenue of Western Australia in 1973–74 was $A567,683,368, compared with $A473,840,018 in 1972–73. Expenditure in 1973–74 totalled $A573,414,368 (1972–73 $A477,329,528). The net public debt of the State at June 30, 1974, was $A1,069,211,744 (1973, $A1,029,794,613).

TRADE

Year	Imports	Exports
	$A	$A
1971–72	1,071,050,510	1,084,981,575
1972–73	1,013,446,826	1,313,686,247
1973–74	1,308,271,585	1,612,266,691

Exports in 1973–74 included gold bullion ($A2,483,463), wool ($A268,048,463), wheat ($A211,332,507), salt ($A12,918,049), prawns ($A6,396,673), hides and skins ($A13,535,814), oats ($A5,316,955), timber ($A7,406,954), beef ($A42,536,217), mutton and lamb ($A23,681,560), live animals ($A15,550,541), rock lobster tails ($A18,511,387), apples ($A4,711,459), ilmenite ores and concentrates ($A9,774,384), iron ore ($A488,239,405), barley ($A20,767,207), petroleum and petroleum products ($A45,523,065), iron and steel ($A60,811,011), machines and machinery ($A27,272,684), transport equipment ($A30,004,590), furniture ($A10,075,418).

TOWNS

CAPITAL.—ΨPERTH. Population (estimated, June 30, 1974) of Perth Statistical Division, including the port of Fremantle, 762,600.

Perth, the capital, stands on the right bank of the Swan River estuary, 12 miles from Fremantle. Other towns are ΨFremantle (32,100), Kalgoorlie—Boulder and environs (20,600), ΨBunbury (18,550); ΨGeraldton (15,800); ΨAlbany (12,300).

DISTANCES FROM LONDON BY AIR

A list of the distances in statute miles from London to various places abroad. Distances given are Great Circle distances from London Heathrow Airport to destination airports. They have been supplied by International Aeradio Ltd., a Division of British Airways.

To	Miles	To	Miles	To	Miles
Ajaccio	790	Dublin	279	New York	3,440
Algiers	1,035	Düsseldorf	311	Nice	646
Alicante	911	Entebbe	4,033	Nicosia (Cyprus)	2,008
Amsterdam	231	Faro	1,063	Oporto	806
Ankara	1,765	Frankfurt	406	Oslo	723
Athens	1,500	Geneva	468	Palermo	1,128
Auckland	11,404	Gibraltar	1,084	Palma (Majorca)	836
Baghdad	2,550	Gothenburg	651	Paris	215; (Orly 227)
Bahrain	3,163	Hamburg	463	Perth (Australia)	9,008
Bangkok	5,929	Hanover	437	Pisa	736
Barbados	4,192	Helsinki	1,147	Prague	649
Barcelona	712	Heraklion	1,685	Rangoon	5,581
Basle	447	Hong Kong	5,989	Reykjavik	1,167
Beirut	2,162	Honolulu	7,220	Rhodes	1,743
Bergen	648	Istanbul	1,560	Rome	896
Berlin	593	Johannesburg	5,634	Salzburg	652
Bermuda	3,428	Karachi	3,935	Shannon	369
Bombay	4,478	Khartoum	3,071	Singapore	6,754
Bordeaux	458	Kingston (Jamaica)	4,668	Sofia	1,266
Bremen	406	Kuala Lumpur	6,557	Stockholm	906
Brisbane	10,273	Kuwait	2,903	Stuttgart	469
Brussels	217	Leningrad	1,313	Sydney	10,568
Budapest	923	Lisbon	971	Tangier	1,120
Cagliari	959	Madrid	774	Teheran	2,741
Cairo	2,192	Malaga	1,041	Tel Aviv	2,229
Calcutta	4,958	Malta	1,305	Tokyo	5,955
Chicago	3,942	Marseilles	614	Toronto	3,545
Cologne	331	Mauritius	6,075	Trinidad	4,405
Colombo	5,413	Milan	609	Tripoli	1,468
Copenhagen	608	Montego Bay	4,681	Turin	570
Corfu	1,273	Montreal	3,239	Valencia	826
Dar-es-Salaam	4,661	Moscow	1,557	Venice	715
Darwin	8,613	Munich	588	Vienna	790
Delhi	4,180	Nairobi	4,247	Warsaw	912
Detroit	3,754	Naples	1,011	Zagreb	839
Doha	3,253	Nassau	4,332	Zürich	490

New Zealand
AREA AND POPULATION

Islands	Area (English) Sq. Miles	Population Census Mar. 23, 1971†	Population Estimated Apr. 1. 1974
(a) *Exclusive of Island Territories:*			
North Island	44,281	2,051,363	2,200,500
South Island	58,093	811,268	842,300
Stewart Island	670	414*	410*
Chatham Islands	372	716*	730*
Minor Islands:			
Inhabited—			
Kermadec Islands	13	9*	9*
Campbell Island	44	9*	9*
Uninhabited—			
Three Kings	3	..	..
Snares	1	..	..
Solander	½	..	..
Antipodes	24½	..	..
Bounty		..	..
Auckland	234	..	..
Total exclusive of Island Territories	103,736	2,862,631	3,042,800
(b) *Island Territories:*			
Tokelau Islands	..	1,655	1,574‡
Niue Island	..	4,901	3,992§
Total, inclusive of Island Territories	103,939	2,869,187	3 048,366
(c) Cook Islands¶	..	21,227	19,522§
Ross Dependency	175,000	..	..

Included in North Island and South Island totals.
† Excluding 1,482 members of the Armed Forces overseas.
‡ Sept. 25, 1974.   § March 31, 1974.
¶ The Cook Islands have had complete internal self-government since Aug. 4, 1965, as has Niue since 19 Oct. 1974 but Cook Islanders and Niveans remain New Zealand citizens.
Maori Population included in the totals for New Zealand proper—1971 Census, 227,414 (males 114,948; females 112,466): estimated June 30, 1974, 247,300 (males 124,800; females 122,500).

Increase of the People

Year	Increase Births	Increase Arrivals	Increase Total	Decrease Departures	Decrease Total	Increase	Net Increase	Marriages
1971	64,460	615,774	680,234	24,309	607,051	631,360	48,874	27,199
1972	63,215	698,104	761,519	24,801	674,679	699,480	61,839	26,868
1973	60,727	810,773	871,500	25,315	780,215	805,530	65,970	26,274
1974	59,330	955,986	1,015.316	25,262	923,466	948,728	66,588	25,418

Birth rate (1974) 19·49; death rate 8·30; marriage rate 8·35; infant mortality 16·22 per 1,000.

Inter—censal Increases

Year	Results of Census Males	Results of Census Females	Results of Census Total	Numerical Increase	Net Passenger Arrivals over inter-censal periods
1956	1,093,211	1,080,851	2,174,062	234,590	+27,486
1961	1,213,376	1,201,608	2,414,984	240,922	+68,726
1966	1,343,743	1,333,176	2,676,919	261,935	+48,660
1971	1,430,856	1,431,775	2,862,631	185,712	..

Excluding 2,559 members of the Armed Forces overseas at the time of the 1961 census, 1,936 at the 1966 census and 1,482 at the 1971 census.

Races and Religions

Races	1966	1971	Religions	1966 Per cent.	1971 Per cent.
Europeans	2,426,352	2,561,280	Church of England	33·7	31·3
Maoris	201,159	227,414	Presbyterians	21·8	20·4
Chinese	10,283	12,818	Roman Catholics	15·9	15·7
Polynesians (other than N.Z. Maoris)	26,271	45,413	Methodists	7·0	6·4
Other races	12,854	15,706	Baptists	1·7	1·7

TASMAN SEA

Auckland
Hamilton Tauranga
Rotorua
New Plymouth NORTH ISLAND
Wanganui Napier
Hastings
Palmerston North
Hutt
Wellington

NEW ZEALAND

SOUTH ISLAND
Christchurch

PACIFIC OCEAN

Dunedin
Invercargill
STEWART IS.

0 100 200 MILES

PHYSIOGRAPHY

New Zealand consists of a number of islands of varying size in the South Pacific Ocean, and has also administrative responsibility for a large tract in the Antarctic Ocean. The two larger and most important islands, the North and South Islands of New Zealand, are separated by only a relatively narrow strait. The remaining islands are very much smaller and, in general, are widely dispersed over a considerable expanse of ocean. The boundaries, inclusive of the most outlying islands and dependencies, range from 8° South latitude to south of 60° South latitude, and from 160° East longitude to 150° West longitude.

Geographical Features.—The two principal islands have a total length of 1,040 miles, and a combined area of 102,374 square miles. A large proportion of the surface is mountainous in character. The principal range is that of the Southern Alps, extending over the entire length of the South Island and having its culminating point in Mount Cook (12,349 ft.). The North Island mountains include several volcanoes, two of which are active, others being dormant or extinct. Mt. Ruapehu (9,175 ft.) and Mt. Ngauruhoe (7,515 ft.) are the most important. Of the numerous glaciers in the South Island, the Tasman (18 miles long by 1¼ wide), the Franz Josef and the Fox are the best known. The North Island is noted for its hot springs and geysers. For the most part the rivers are too short and rapid for use in navigation. The more important include the Waikato (270 miles in length); Wanganui (180), and Clutha (210). Lakes (Taupo, 234 sq. miles in area; Wakatipu, 113; and Te Anau 133) are abundant, many of them of great beauty.

Climate.—New Zealand has a moist-temperate marine climate, but with abundant sunshine. A very important feature is the small annual range of temperature which permits of some growth of vegetation, including pasture, all the year round. Very little snow falls on the low levels even in the South Island. The mean temperature ranges from 15° C. in the North to about 9° C. in the South. Rainfall over the more settled areas in the North Island ranges from 35 to 70 inches and in the South Island from 25 to 45 inches. The total range is from approximately 13 to over 250 inches. The number of rainy days is generally in the neighbourhood of 160 to 180 in the North Island and between 110 and 140 in the South, except in the southern portion of the west coast. The amount of sunshine is generally over 2,000 hours per annum and ranges between 1,600 to 2,500 hours.

GOVERNMENT

The west coast of the South Island of New Zealand was discovered by Abel Janszoon Tasman, the navigator (voyaging under the direction of the Netherlands' East India Company), on December 13, 1642.

The islands were visited, and charted, in 1769 by Captain Cook, who returned to them in 1773, 1774 and 1777. From 1800 onwards sealers and whalers settled along the coasts, and trade in timber and flax followed. Christianity was introduced in 1814, and in 1832 a British Resident was appointed. In 1840 British sovereignty was proclaimed, and on May 3, 1841, New Zealand was, by letters patent, created a separate colony distinct from New South Wales. Organized colonization on a large scale commenced in 1840 with the New Zealand Company's settlement at Wellington. On Sept. 26, 1907, the designation was changed to *The Dominion of New Zealand*. The Constitution rests upon the Imperial Act of 1852, and on the New Zealand Constitution (Amendment) Act of Dec. 10, 1947. The Statute of Westminster was formally adopted by New Zealand in 1947. The executive authority is entrusted to a Governor-General appointed by the Crown and aided by an Executive Council, within a Legislature consisting of one chamber, the House of Representatives.

FLAG: Blue ground, with Union Jack in top left quarter, four five-pointed red stars with white borders on the fly. On June 20, 1968, a new naval ensign bearing the Southern Cross was adopted, replacing the British white ensign.

Governor General and Staff

Governor-General and Commander-in-Chief of New Zealand (1972–   ), His Excellency Sir (Edward) Denis Blundell, G.C.M.G., G.C.V.O., K.B.E.
$NZ 26,000

Official Secretary, D. C. Williams, C.V.O.
Comptroller, Lt.-Col. F. B. Bath, M.B.E.
Aide-de-Camp, Capt. R. J. S. Munro, R.N.Z.A.; Lt. P. A. Cozens, R.N.Z.N.
Lady-in-Waiting, Miss M. Ross.

THE EXECUTIVE COUNCIL

His Excellency the GOVERNOR-GENERAL
Prime Minister and Minister of Foreign Affairs, Rt. Hon. W. E. Rowling.
Deputy Prime Minister and Minister of Finance, Hon. R. J. Tizard.
Trade and Industry, Hon. W. W. Freer.
Justice, Dr. Hon. A. M. Finlay.
Works and Development, (vacant).
Maori Affairs and Lands, Hon. M. Rata.
Police, Hon. M. A. Connelly.
Defence, Hon. W. A. Fraser.
Social Welfare, Hon. N. J. King.
Labour and State Services, Hon. A. J. Faulkner.
Agriculture and Fisheries, Forests, and Science, Hon. C. J. Moyle.
Local Government and Internal Affairs, Hon. H. L. J. May.
Transport, Hon. Sir Basil Arthur.
Education, Hon. P. A. Amos.
Tourism and Environment, Hon. Mrs. T. W. M. Tirikatene-Sullivan.
Overseas Trade, Hon. J. A. Walding.
Immigration and Mines, Hon. F. M. Colman.
Railways and Electricity, Hon. T. R. Bailey.

Housing and Customs, Hon. R. O. Douglas.
Health, Hon. T. M. McGuigan.

The Prime Minister receives $27,500 per annum with a tax-free allowance of $5,000 for expenses of his office and the Ministerial residence. The salary of each Minister holding a portfolio is $18,000 with tax-free expense allowance of $2,000 and that of each Minister without portfolio $15,500, with $1,600 tax-free expense allowance.

NEW ZEALAND HIGH COMMISSION

New Zealand House, Haymarket, S.W.1
High Commissioner, Rt. Hon. Hugh Watt.
Deputy High Commissioner, D. B. G. McLean.
Minister (Commercial), W. E. B. Tucker.
Defence and Naval Adviser, Cdre. F. H. Bland, O.B.E.
Counsellors, L. J. Watt (*Politcal*); R. E. Alexander (*Finance*); L. H. Jones (*Administration*); Miss F. M. C. Lee (*Commercial*).
Army Adviser, Col. J. M. Morris, M.B.E.
Air Adviser, Group Capt. B. Stanley-Hunt, A.F.C.
1st Secretaries, Mrs. V. S. Blumhardt; G. D. Malcolm (*Economic*); M. J. Taylor (*Publicity and Information*); J. M. Chetwin (*Economic*).
Agricultural Adviser, M. D. Gould.
Attaché (Scientific), C. M. Palmer.

BRITISH HIGH COMMISSION

Reserve Bank of New Zealand Building,
2 The Terrace (P.O. Box 1812), Wellington, 1
High Commissioner, His Excellency Sir David Aubrey Scott, K.C.M.G. (1973) £15,000
Deputy High Commissioner and Counsellor (Commercial), T. D. O'Leary.
1st Secretary, G. R. Archer (*Head of Chancery*).
Defence Adviser, Capt. C. A. Johnson, R.N.
Asst. do., Squadron Leader P. R. Callaghan, R.A.F.
1st Secretaries, A. F. Baines (*Agriculture and Food*); G. Rutherford (*Commercial*); J. R. E. Carr-Gregg (*Information*).
2nd Secretaries, C. G. Patterson (*Administration*); C. Thompson (*Commercial*); R. D. Lavers.

British Council Representative, P. J. C. Dart.

THE LEGISLATURE

Parliament consists of a House of Representatives consisting of 87 members elected for 3 years. The General Election of November, 1972, returned 55 Labour members and 32 National. Four of the members are Maoris elected by the Maori electors. Women have been entitled to vote since 1893, and to be elected Members of the House of Representatives since the passing of the Women's Parliamentary Rights Act, 1919. There are at present 4 women members, including a woman Cabinet Minister. Members of the House receive $NZ11,000 per annum, with an allowance of $NZ2,395 per annum for expenses, plus an electorate allowance. The Leader of the Opposition receives NZ18,000 per annum and NZ2,000 per annum for expenses, plus travelling allowance or $NZ2,000.

Speaker of the House of Representatives.
Hon. S. A. Whitehead (*plus expense allowance of $NZ1,500 per annum and residential quarters in Parliament House*) $NZ16,500

THE JUDICATURE

The judicial system comprises a Supreme Court and a Court of Appeal; also Magistrates' Courts having both civil and criminal jurisdiction.
Chief Justice, Rt. Hon. Sir Richard Wild, K.C.M.G., E.D.............$NZ23,279

Court of Appeal, Rt. Hon. Sir Thaddeus McCarthy, K.B.E. (*President*) $NZ22,207
Judges, Rt. Hon. Sir Clifford Richmond; Rt. Hon. Sir Arthur Woodhouse...............................   21,130
Supreme Court Puisne Judges, Hons. Sir Alec Haslam; Sir Ian Macarthur; A. C. Perry; J. N. Wilson; L. F. Moller; G. D. Speight; C. M. Roper; J. C. White; D. S. Beattie; J. P. Quilliam; D. W. McMullin; P. T. Mahon; R. B. Cooke; J. B. O'Regan; N. F. Chilwell; N. E. Casey..................   21,130
Supreme Court Administrative Divn., Rt. Hon. Sir Richard Wild (*Chief Justice*); Hons. J. C. White; G. D. Speight.
Judge, Court of Arbitration and Compensation Court, Judge A. P. Blair........   21,130

POLICE

On March 31, 1974 the strength of the Police Force was 3,742 of all ranks, equivalent to 1 for every 800 of the population. The total cost of police protection in 1974–75 was $NZ40,618,000.

DEFENCE

A unified Ministry of Defence was set up on Jan. 1, 1964. The Ministry is responsible, under the Minister of Defence, for the whole field of national defence. Defence expenditure in 1973–74 amounted to $NZ166,854,000.

Navy

The Royal New Zealand Navy was greatly expanded during the Second World War and a number of small vessels were built in New Zealand. The naval forces include the Women's Royal New Zealand Naval Service, and Volunteer Reserve forces in four divisions. The strength is 4 frigates, 1 survey ship. Active naval personnel number 299 officers and 2,845 ratings. A frigate is normally attached to the Far East Station.

Army

The New Zealand Army consists of the Regular Force, the Territorial Force and the Army Reserve. The strength of the Regular Force at March 31, 1974 was 5,553 and of the Territorial Force 4,903.

The Army is now organized on the basis of one integrated Regular/Territorial Brigade Group, with its own logistic support and reserves. In addition, a regular force battalion is stationed as part of the Commonwealth Far East strategic reserve in Malaysia.

Air

Operational elements of the R.N.Z.A.F. include one Strike Squadron, one ground attack squadron, one anti-submarine warfare squadron, one helicopter squadron and three transport squadrons, one of which is based in Singapore. Aircaraft operated by the R.N.Z.A.F. include the Skyhawk, Strikemaster, Orion, Hercules and Bristol Freighter. The strength of the Regular Force at March 31, 1974, was 4,232.

FINANCE

Into the Consolidated Revenue Account (New Zealand's main public account) are paid the proceeds of income tax, sales tax, customs and excise duties and other taxes, also interest, profits from trading undertakings, and departmental receipts (departmental expenditure is included gross). Revenue from taxation is also paid into the National Roads Fund principally from a tax on motor spirits and registration and licence fees for motor vehicles.

Year ended March 31	Revenue	Expenditure
	$NZ	$NZ
1972	1,820,680,922	1,812,328,833
1973	2,135,795,738	2,141,026,641
1974	2,512,164,904	2,509,778,874
1975	3,046,057,941	3,034,889,403*

*Includes:
Education.................	$NZ529,238,000
Social Welfare...........	$NZ710,958,000
Health...................	$NZ491,367,000
Development of Industry....	$NZ183,542,000
Defence..................	$NZ166,854,000
Debt sevices.............	$NZ271,766,000
Law and order...........	$NZ 71,459,000

Revenue from taxation in 1974–75 amounted to $NZ2,865,306,000 of which $NZ2,760, 526,000 represented receipts into the Consolidated Revenue Account, and $NZ104,780,000 receipts into the National Roads Fund.

DEBT

The gross *Public Debt* amounted on March 31, 1975, to $NZ4,199,699,000, of which $NZ682,640,000 was domiciled in London and $NZ128,156,000 in the U.S.A.; $NZ54,955,000 represented World Bank loans.

CURRENCY

A devaluation of the NZ dollar was announced on Sept. 25 1974, following the decision of the Australian Government to devalue by 12 p.c. which, in accordance with the practice whereby the NZ dollar is held stable in value relative to a basket of currencies would have meant an automatic downward adjustment of NZ dollar by c. 3%. The NZ dollar was thus devalued to a point still fractionally below the Australian dollar, the result being an effective devaluation of 9·0 p.c. relative to every country except Australia an appreciation of 3·1 relative to Australia and a weighted average devaluation of about 6·2 p.c.

BANKING

There are five trading banks (with numerous branches) doing business, two of which are predominantly New Zealand banks. Of these the Bank of New Zealand is owned by the State. At Mar. 26, 1975, assets of all trading banks in respect of New Zealand business amounted to $NZ2,225,500,000; liabilities, $NZ2,126,400,000; and the value of notes in circulation amounted to $NZ333,900,000. The Reserve Bank of New Zealand commenced business on August 1, 1934. The note-issuing powers of other banks have since been withdrawn and the Reserve Bank notes are legal tender. New Zealand's official overseas reserves at March 31, 1975, amounted to $NZ567,800,000, of which $NZ317,800,000 represented assets of the New Zealand banking system. Trading banks' advances, including discounts on Mar. 26, 1975, totalled $NZ1,673,300,000 compared with $NZ1,435,100,000 in the previous year. Deposits with trading banks on Mar. 28, 1975, amounted to $NZ2,102,900,000 (1974, $NZ2,000,500,000).

Post-office and trustee savings banks had, at the close of the year 1974–75, over 4 million accounts having $NZ1,952, 370,000 to their credit. Private savings banks have been operated by the trading banks since Oct. 1964, and at March 31, 1975, deposits totalled $NZ468,354,000.

EDUCATION

Schools are free and attendance is compulsory between the ages of 6 and 15. There are opportunities for apt pupils to proceed to university.

In 1973 there were 471,160 pupils attending public primary schools, and 50,711 pupils attending registered private primary schools. The secondary education of boys and girls in the cities and large towns is carried on in 223 state secondary schools, 55 state secondary departments of district high schools and 114 private secondary schools. The total number of pupils receiving full-time secondary education in July 1973 was 202,876 and in addition there were 101,686, students attending technical classes and 17,679 receiving part-time tuition from the Technical Correspondence School. The university system consists of the University of Auckland, the University of Waikato, Massey University of Manawatu, Victoria University of Wellington, the University of Canterbury and the University of Otago. The Lincoln university college of agriculture is associated with the University of Canterbury. The university system is co-ordinated by the University Grants Committee. The Universities had a total of 38,995 students in 1973.

The total expenditure on education out of public funds in 1974–75 was $NZ529,803,189.

PRODUCTION AND INDUSTRY
Gross Farming Income

	1971–72	1972–73
	$NZ(000)	$NZ(000)
Wool..................	161,400	347,790
Mutton and Lamb.......	156,300	325,600
Beef (incl. Dairy Beef)....	209,700	294,800
Dairying..............	313,600	315,300
Pigs..................	26,280	29,800
Grain and Field Crops, Poultry and Bees.......	202,900	220,400
All Farm Produce....	1,070,100	1,553,600

Industrial Production

	1971–72	1972–73
	$NZ	$NZ
Value of Production	3,873,000,000	4,545,000,000

Net Output (Net Value Added), consisting only of the rewards to the factors of production, *i.e.* salaries and wages, interest on borrowed capital, and proprietors' surplus, in 1972–73 amounted to $NZ1,316,000,000, compared with $NZ1,129,000,000 in the previous year.

Agricultural and Pastoral Production

	1972–73	1973–74
Wheat, bushels.........	12,800,000	12,800,000
Wool, metric tons.......	309,000	284,000
Butter, tons...........	235,200	215,900
Cheese, tons...........	99,200	87,856
Stock Slaughtered—	1972–73	1973–74
Lambs, No...........	26,683,000	22,992,000
Sheep, No...........	10,322,000	8,761,000
Cattle, No...........	2,031,000	1,788,000
Calves, No...........	1,052,000	1,244,000
Pigs, No...........	751,000	747,000

Forestry.—The output of sawn timber for 1974 was 904,000,000 board ft., of which 740,000,000 board ft. represented exotic varieties, mainly pine.

Livestock.—Livestock on farms at Jan. 31, 1974, included 3,273,000 dairy cattle (of which 2,140,000 were dairy cows in milk during season), 6,142,000 beef cattle (of which 2,125,000 were beef breeding cows), and 507,000 pigs. At June 30, 1974, sheep numbered 55,883,000, including 40,366,000 breeding ewes.

Manufactures.—Statistics of factory production show (1972–73) 7,668 factories in operation, employing 235,615 persons. Salaries and wages amounted to $NZ875,200,000; cost of materials used, $NZ2.784,500,000. Total value of production, $NZ4,607,800,000.

Minerals.—Coal output in 1974 was 2,564,317 tons. Gold-mining was formerly an important industry, but production has declined greatly in recent years. Gold produced in 1973 was 12,118 oz. Other minerals produced on a relatively small scale are copper, silver, iron ore, manganese ore, zinc, leads, cadmium, tungsten and asbestos. Valuable deposits of natural gas have been discovered in Taranaki, and this has been piped to some main North Island centres. New Zealand has large resources of potential iron ore in the black sands of many of its beaches of which 992,099 tons were exported in 1973 and steelworks have been built near Auckland to utilize such deposits.

TRADE

Provisional figures of New Zealand's trade during the year ended June, 1974, were; Imports (c.i.f.) $NZ2,014,177,000, compared with $NZ1,366,340,000 in 1972–73; Exports, (f.o.b.) $NZ1,787,563,000, compared with $NZ 1,786,989,000 in 1972–73.

Trade with U.K.

	1971	1972
Imports from U.K....	£146,132,000	£146,764,000
Exports to U.K......	226,637,000	251,496,000

New Zealand produce exported to the U.K. in the 12 months ending June, 1974, was valued at $NZ364,218,918 and included butter, valued at $NZ59,202,486, cheese ($NZ14,076,592); meat ($NZ188,839,821); wool ($NZ59,819,309); and fruit ($NZ5,313,569).

Railways.—In March, 1974, there were 2,982 route miles of Government railway in operation. The number of passengers carried on Government lines in 1973–74, including season-ticket holders, was 18,944,000. Goods railed amounted to 13,164,000 tons. Railway total revenue and expenditure were $NZ152,179,000 and $NZ160,832,000 in 1973–74.

Motor Vehicles.—On December 31, 1974, there were 1,804,303 motor vehicles licensed, including 1,222,085 cars and 87,090 motor cycles and power cycles. The number of persons per passenger car was 2·8.

Shipping.—During 1974 the vessels entered from overseas ports numbered 3,831 (net tonnage 20,536,000) and those cleared for overseas 3,817 (net tonnage 20,397,000).

Post Office Statistics.—During 1974–75 internal postal services handled 699,026,000 items, including 351,148,000 letters and 329,605,000 items of printed matter. Overseas mails included 2,583,618 lb. of airmail received and 1,680,056 lb. despatched. Telephone subscribers totalled 980,307 at March 31, 1975.

Civil Aviation.—In 1974 domestic scheduled services flew 15,907,000 miles and carried 2,255,000 passengers. Freight carried amounted to 62,900 tons. In 1974 international services to and from New Zealand carried 1,117,000 passengers, 26,241 tons of freight and 2,055 tons of mail.

CAPITAL, Ψ Wellington, in the North Island (pop. April 1, 1974, Wellington statistical division, 346,900).

Other large centres: ΨAuckland, 775,460; ΨChristchurch, 320,530; ΨDunedin, 119,870; Palmerston North, 85,270; Hamilton, 147,450; ΨWanganui, 38,070; ΨNew Plymouth, 41,840; Ψ Napier-Hastings, 105,460; Rotorua, 45,390; Ψ Tauranga, 46,570.

NATIONAL DAY (Waitangi Day).—Feb. 6.

THE ISLANDS OF NEW ZEALAND

In addition to North, South, Stewart and Chatham Islands:—

The Three Kings (discovered by Tasman on the Feast of the Epiphany), in 34° 9′ S. lat. and 172° 8′ 8″ E. long. (uninhabited). *Auckland Islands*, about 290 miles south of Bluff Harbour, in 50° 32′ S. lat. and 166° 13′ E. long. The islands contain several good harbours, but are uninhabited. *Campbell Island* (used as a weather station). *Antipodes Group* (40° 41′ 15 S. lat. and 178° 43′ E. long.) uninhabited. *Bounty Islands* (47° 4′ 43 S. lat., 170° 01 30 E. long.). *Snares Islands and Solander* (uninhabited).

The Kermadec Group (population 9 in 1971) between 29° 101 to 31° 30′ S. lat., and 177° 45′ to 179° W. long., includes Raoul or Sunday, Macaulay, Curtis Islands, L'Esperance, and some islets. All the inhabitants are government employees at a meteorological station.

Cook and other Islands, included in the boundaries of New Zealand since June, 1901, consist of the islands of Rarotonga, Aitutaki, Mangaia, Atiu, Mauke, Matiaro, Manuae, Takutea, Palmerston, Penrhyn or Tongareva, Manihiki, Rakahanga, Pukapuka or Danger, and Nassau. The total population of the group is 19,522. Niue, which is geographically part of Cook Islands, but which is administered separately, had an estimated population on Sept. 30, 1974 of 3,992. The chief exports of the Cook Islands are fruit juice, clothing, copra, bananas, citrus fruit and pulp, and pearl shell. The trade is chiefly with New Zealand, Australia, Japan, the U.K. and the U.S.A. Financial aid to the Cook Islands and Niue approved by the New Zealand Government totalled $NZ5·5 million for the 1973–74 financial year.

The High Commissioner of the Cook Islands is employed in a dual role, since he represents both the Queen and the New Zealand Government. Since Aug. 4, 1965, the Islands have enjoyed complete internal self-government, execcutive power being in the hands of a Cabinet consisting of the Premier and five other ministers. The new Constitution Act was passed by the New Zealand Parliament in November 1964, but did not come into force until it had been endorsed by the 22-member Legislative Assembly of the Cook Islands, elected in April 1965.

The New Zealand citizenship of the Cook Islanders is embodied in the Constitution, and assurances have been given that the changed status of the Islands will in no way affect the consideration of subsidies or the right of free entry into New Zealand for exports from the group.

A New Zealand Representative is stationed at Niue, which since October 1974 has been self-governing in free association with New Zealand, which is responsible for external affairs and defence. Executive power is in the hands of a Premier and a Cabinet of 3 drawn from the Assembly of 20 members.

Tokelau (or *Union Islands.*—A group of atolls (Fakaofo, Nukunono and Atafu) (population 1,574 in Sept. 1974), proclaimed part of New Zealand as from Jan. 1, 1948.

THE ROSS DEPENDENCY

The *Ross Dependency*, placed under the jurisdiction of New Zealand by Order in Council dated July 30, 1923, and defined as all the islands and territories between 160°E. and 150°W. longitude which are situated south of the 60°S. parallel. The Ross Dependency includes Edward VII Land and portions of Victoria Land. For some years there have been permanent bases in the area, staffed by survey and scientific personnel.

The Bahamas

The Bahama Islands are an archipelago lying in the Atlantic Ocean between 20° 55'–27° 22' N. Lat; 72° 40'–79° 20' W. Long. They extend from the coast of Florida on the north-west almost to Haiti on the south-east. The group consists of 700 islands, of which 30 are inhabited and 2,400 cays comprising an area of more than 5,380 square miles. The population, at the end of 1974, was estimated at 197,000. The principal islands include: Abaco, Acklins, Andros, Berry Islands, Bimini, Cat Cay, Cat Island, Crooked Island, Eleuthera, Exumas, Grand Bahama, Harbour Island, Inagua, Long Cay, Long Island, Mayaguana, New Providence (on which is located the capital, Nassau), Ragged Island, Rum Cay, San Salvador and Spanish Wells. San Salvador was the first landfall in the New World of Christopher Columbus on October 12, 1492.

The Bahamas were settled by British subjects when the islands were deserted. The ownership of the Bahamas was taken over in 1782 by the Spanish, but the Treaty of Versailles in 1783 restored them to the British.

Tourism is the economic mainstay of the Bahamas, whose salubrious climate and fine beaches attract over 1,000,000 visitors annually.

GOVERNMENT

The Bahamas gained independence on July 10, 1973. There are a Senate of 16 members and an elected House of Assembly of 38 members.

Governor-General, His Excellency Sir Milo Boughton Butler, G.C.M.G., G.C.V.O.
Prime Minister and Minister of Economic Affairs, Hon. L. O. Pindling.
Deputy Prime Minister and Minister of Finance, Hon. A. D. Hanna.
Transport, Hon. G. A. Smith.
Education, Hon. L. N. Coakley.
Health, Hon. A. L. Roker.
Agriculture and Fisheries, Hon. R. F. A. Roberts.
Development, Hon. A. Maycock.
Works, Hon. S. L. Bowe.
External Affairs and Attorney General, Hon. P. L. Adderley.
Labour and National Insurance, Hon. C. Darling.
Home Affairs, Hon. D. Rolle.
Tourism, Hon. C. T. Maynard.

Chief Justice, Sir Leonard Knowles.
Puisne Judges, Hon. S. Graham; Hon. K. Potter.

BAHAMAS HIGH COMMISSION
39 Pall Mall, S.W.1.
[01–930 6967]
High Commissioner, His Excellency Sir Alvin Braynen.

BRITISH HIGH COMMISSION
Bitco Building, East St.
P.O. Box N7516, Nassau.
High Commissioner, His Excellency Peter Mennell, C.M.G., M.B.E. (1975).
Deputy High Commissioner, J. G. Doubleday (*Head of Chancery*).

Industries.—A plant for the manufacture of cement and an oil refinery have been established in Freeport, Grand Bahama, where there are also a number of light industries. A rum distillery is in operation in New Providence and a multi-million dollar aragonite operation is in progress off the island of Andros. Other industries are those associated with the treatment of local agriculture and marine produce, salt extraction and handwork, and timber-felling for plywood.

Education.—Education is compulsory between the ages of 5 and 14. More than 57,000 students are enrolled in Ministry of Education and Independent schools in New Providence and the Family Islands.

Civil Aviation.—Facilities for external traffic are provided by Bahamasair, Pan-American World Airways, British Airways, Air Canada, Air Jamaica, Eastern Air Lines, Delta Air Line, National Airlines, International Air Bahama, Flamingo Airways, Lufthansa, Sabena, and Mackey International Airline. Kivin Air provides internal schedule and charter flights to the Family Islands, and Bahamas Air Traders' Island Flying Service provides internal schedule and charter flights to the outlying islands. There are daily return flights between Nassau and Miami, several daily flights between Nassau–Palm Beach–Fort Lauderdale and Tampa, and a regular service between Nassau, Kingston and Montego Bay, Jamaica, besides regular trunk communication with London, New York, Chicago, Toronto, Montreal, Bermuda, Kingston and Haiti.

Communications.—There are a General Post Office in Nassau, 4 branch offices in New Providence and 109 sub-offices in the Family Islands. Wireless and telephone services are in operation to all parts of the world. There are 132 radio-telephone channels among the islands.

FINANCE AND TRADE

	1974	1975*
Public revenue	B$123,500,000	B$133,884,360
Expenditure	115,000,000	131,393,880

	1972	1973*
Total imports	484,894,662	764,260,752
Total exports	343,412,935	529,748,582
		*estimated

	1973	1975
Imports from U.K.	£8,164,000	£8,548,000
Exports to U.K.	19,253,000	10,552,000

The imports are chiefly foodstuffs, manufactured articles, building material, lumber and machinery. The chief exports in 1972 were pulpwood, cement, rum, crawfish, salt and aragonite.

CAPITAL.—Ψ Nassau. Estimated population (1974), 112,000. Nassau is distant from Liverpool 4,000 miles.

Bangladesh

Area, Population, Climate, etc.—The Republic of Bangladesh consists of the territory which was formerly East Pakistan (the old province of East Bengal and the Sylhet district of Assam), covering an area of 55,126 sq. miles in the region of the Gangetic delta, and has a population, according to the 1961 Pakistan census, of 50,840,235, but official estimates place the current figure at 75,000,000.

The country is crossed by a network of navigable rivers, including the eastern arms of the Ganges, the Jumna (Brahmaputra) and the Meghna, flowing into the Bay of Bengal. The climate is tropical and monsoon; hot and extremely humid during the summer, and mild and dry during the short winter. The rainfall is heavy, varying from 50 inches to 135 inches in different districts and the bulk of it falls during monsoon season (from June to September). The mean temperature during the winter (November to February) is about 20°C. (68°F.) and during the hot season 30°C (86°F.).

History.—Prior to becoming East Pakistan, the territory had been part of British India. It acceded to Pakistan in October, 1947, and became a Republic on March 23, 1956. Pakistan had, since March 1969 been under the presidency of General Yahya Khan, who was represented in the East by a Governor. In the first full suffrage elections in West Pakistan in December, 1970, and, in East Pakistan, in January 1971, convincing victories were won respectively by Mr. Zulfikar Ali Bhutto's left-wing Pakistan People's Party and by Sheikh Mujibur Rahman's Awami League, which campaigned for substantial autonomy of the East wing.

The proposed opening of the National Assembly on March 3, 1971, was postponed and a period of civil unrest called forth emergency action by the Army. Sheikh Mujibur Rahman was arrested and imprisoned in West Pakistan. By a proclamation of March 26 Bangladesh purported to secede from the central government, and a government-in-exile was set up in April in Calcutta. The Awami League was outlawed, and guerilla activity in opposition to the Martial Law Authority continued in the province until December 4. The short war that ensued between India and Pakistan, in both the East and the West, and India's overwhelming defeat of the Pakistani Army in the East, brought about a *de facto* secession of the East wing. The Indo-Pakistan war was concluded on December 16, 1971, and Mr. Bhutto succeeded General Yahya Khan as President on December 20. Sheikh Mujib was released early in January and was sworn in as Prime Minister on January 12. Recognition of the new state was accorded swiftly by many countries, but an application for United Nations membership was defeated by a Chinese veto on August 25. Bangladesh was admitted to the Commonwealth on April 18. Pakistan and Bangladesh accorded one another mutual recognition in Feb. 1974 but they have yet to establish diplomatic relations.

Government.—A Constitution was promulgated on December 15, and general elections took place on March 7, 1973, which confirmed the Awami League's ascendancy.

Constitution.—The constitution of Bangladesh promulgated in 1972 provided for a multi-party system of democratic government. In Dec. 1974 the President declared a State of Emergency and suspended certain constitutional privileges. In January 1975 Sheikh Mujib introduced constitutional amendments which empowered him to assume the Presidency and to establish a one-party system of government.

PRESIDENT

CABINET*

Vice-President, Planning and Planning Commission, Syed Nazrul Islam.
Prime Minister and Minister for Home Affairs, Communications, Posts, Telephones, and Telegraphs, M. Mansoor Ali.
Commerce, Khondker Mostaque Ahmed.
Industries, A. H. M. Kamaruzzaman.
Land Administration and Land Reforms, Muhammad-ullah.
Agriculture, Abdus Samad Azad.
Labour and Social Welfare, Cultural Affairs and Sports, Prof. Mohammed Yusuf Ali.
Local Government, Rural Development and Co-operatives, Phani Majumder.
Public Works and Urban Development, Mohammad Sohrab Hossain.
Health and Population Planning, Abdul Mannan.
Foreign Affairs and Petroleum, Dr. Kamal Hossain.
Flood Control, Water Development and Power, Forests, Fisheries and Livestock, Abdur Rab Serneabat.
Law, Parliamentary Affairs and Justice, Monoranjan Dhar.
Food and Civil Supplies, Relief and Rehabilitation, Abdul Momen.
Jute, Asaduzzaman Khan.
Information and Broadcasting, M. Korban Ali.
Finance, Dr. Azizur Rahman Mallik.
Education and Scientific Technological Research and Atomic Energy, Dr. Muzaffer Ahmed Choudhury.

Speaker of the Constituent Assembly, A. Malik Ukil.
Chief Justice of Bangladesh, A. S. M. Sayem.

*On August 14, 1975, Sheikh Mujibur Rahman was overthrown as President by an army-backed coup, in the course of which he was killed. At the time of going to press, the subsequent composition of the Cabinet was not known. The new President is Khondker Mostaque Ahmed.

BANGLADESH HIGH COMMISSION
28 Queen's Gate, S.W.7
[01–584 0081]

High Commissioner, (vacant).
Deputy High Commissioner, Faruq Ahmed Choudhury.
Counsellors, R. I. Choudhury (*Passports*); N. M. Khan (*Consular*); M. R. Akhtar.
1st Secretaries, Q. A. M. A. Rahin; M. A. Choudhury; M. A. L. Matin; Syed Muhammad Hussain.
2nd Secretaries, R. A. Khan; A. K. M. A. Rouf; A. Hai.

BRITISH HIGH COMMISSION
D.I.T. Buildings, Dilkusha (P.O. Box 90),
Dacca 2

High Commissioner, His Excellency Barry Granger Smallman, C.V.O., (1974) . . . . £8,425.
Deputy High Commissioner, R. W. Whitney, O.B.E.
1st Secretaries, F. B. Sedgwick-Jell (*Commercial*); H. A. Moisley (*Aid*); J. H. Owen, O.B.E.; A. Wolstenholme (*Information*); A. S. Payne; A. E. Montgomery; W. A. Tincey (*Immigration*); J. R. Travis (*Aid*); C. K. Woodfield (*Administration*).
2nd Secretaries, N. Veriod (*Administration*); A. Condor (*Consular*); W. D. Townend (*Commercial*).
British Council Representative, E. T. J. Phillips, 5 Fuller Road, Ramna, Dacca 2.

Education.—The present system of education is under thorough review by the National Education Commission. Primary education is free but not universal. There are six Universities: Dacca, Rajshahi, Chittagong, Bangladesh University of Engineering and Technology (at Dacca), Bangladesh Agricultural University (at Mymensingh), and Jahangirnagar (opened in 1970). In 1961 literacy was estimated at 17·6 per cent. of the whole of East Pakistan and 26 per cent of the male population.

Transport and Communications.—Principal seaports with total import and export tonnages for 1969–70 in millions, were: Ψ Chittagong 4·7, and

Ψ Chalma 1·7. The Bangladesh Shipping Corporation has been set up by the Government to operate the Bangladesh merchant fleet. The principal airports with runway lengths in feet are Dacca-Tejgaon (10,500) and Chittagong (7,500); a new international airport outside Dacca is scheduled for completion in 1976. A national airline, Bangladesh Biman, has been established with services to London and Calcutta, and an internal network.

There are about 3,900 miles of roads in Bangladesh; 2,400 miles are metalled. There are 2,600 miles of railway track.

Radio Bangladesh is the main national broadcasting service. A television service was introduced in 1965.

Production.—Bangladesh is the principal producer of raw jute in the world. Other agricultural products are rice, tea, oil seeds, pulses, areca nuts and sugar cane. The chief industries are jute, cotton, paper, fertilizer and sugar.

CAPITAL, Dacca. Population 1,300,000, according to the provisional results of the 1974 census.

Barbados

Barbados, the most easterly of the West India islands, is situated in latitude 13° 14′ N. and longitude 59° 37′ W. The island has a total area of 166 square miles, the land rising in a series of tablelands marked by terraces to the highest point, Mt. Hillaby (1,104 ft.). It is nearly 21 miles long by 14 miles broad. Some 46 acres are covered by forest and 68,875 acres are cultivated. *Climate.*—Barbados has a pleasant climate with annual average temperature 26·5° C. (79·8° F.) and rainfall varying from a yearly average of 75 inches in the high central district to 50 inches in some of the low-lying coastal areas. *Population.*—Since the Census held in April, 1970, the population has risen from 238,141 to an estimated total of 247,506 in 1974.

CAPITAL.— Ψ Bridgetown (population, estimated April, 1971, 18,789). Populations of other administrative areas (parishes) in 1970 were: St. Michael (88,097); Christ Church (36,033); St. Philip (17,230); St George (16,903); St. James (14,658); St. Peter (10,820) and St. Thomas (10,624). Bridgetown, the only port of entry, has a deep-water harbour with berths for 8 ships, opened in 1961. Oil is pumped ashore at one installation on the West Coast. FLAG.—Three vertical stripes, dark blue, gold and dark blue, with trident device on gold stripe. NATIONAL DAY—Nov. 30 (Independence Day).

Government.—Barbados was first settled by the British in 1627 and was a Crown Colony from 1652 until it became an independent state within the Commonwealth on November 30, 1966. The Legislature consists of the Governor-General, a Senate and a House of Assembly. The Senate comprises 21 members appointed by the Governor-General, of whom 12 are appointed on the advice of the Prime Minister, 2 on the advice of the Leader of the Opposition and 7 by the Governor-General at his discretion to represent religious, economic or social interests in the Island or such other interests as the Governor-General considers ought to be represented. The House of Assembly comprises 24 members elected every five years by adult suffrage. In 1963 the voting age was reduced to 18. In September, 1971, seats in the House of Representatives were held as follows: Democratic Labour Party 18, Barbados Labour Party 6.

Governor-General, Sir William Scott, G.C.M.G., G.C.V.O. (1967) (+ duty allowance $16,800) $36,000

CABINET

Premier and Minister of Finance, Rt. Hon. E. W. Barrow.

Deputy Prime Minister and Minister of State for Parliamentary Affairs, Hon. C. E. Talma, C.B.E.

Health and Social Welfare, Dr. the Hon. R. B. Caddle.

Labour, National Insurance, Housing and Lands, Hon. P. M. Greaves.

Trade, Industry and Commerce, Senator the Hon. B. M. Taitt.

Agriculture, Science and Technology, Hon. A. Morrison.

Education, Community Development, Youth Affairs and Sport, Senator L. E. Sandiford.

Communications and Works, Hon. F. G. Smith, Q.C.

Minister without Portfolio, Capt. Hon. G. G. Fergusson.

External Affairs and Attorney-General, Senator the Hon. G. Moe, Q.C.

Tourism, Information and Public Relations, Hon. P. G. Morgan, C.B.E.

President of the Senate, Senator Sir Theodore Brancker, Q.C.

Speaker, House of Assembly, His Hon. N. G. A. Maxwell.

BARBADOS HIGH COMMISSION
[01-235 8686]
6 Upper Belgrave Street, S.W.1
High Commissioner, His Excellency James Cameron Tudor, C.M.G. (1972).

BRITISH HIGH COMMISSION
147-9 Roebuck Street (P.O. Box 676C)
Bridgetown
High Commissioner, His Excellency Charles Stuart Roberts, C.M.G. (1973) £11,000

Deputy High Commissioner, R. P. de Burlet (*Head of Chancery*).

JUDICATURE

There is a Supreme Court of Judicature consisting of a High Court and a Court of Appeal. In certain cases a further appeal lies to the Judicial Committee of H.M. Privy Council. The Chief Justice and Puisne Judges are appointed by the Governor-General on the recommendation of the Prime Minister and after consultation with the Leader of the Opposition. Puisne Judges are appointed by the Governor-General, on the advice of the Judicial and Legal Service Commission.

Chief Justice, Hon. Sir William Douglas . . . $31,200
Puisne Judges, A. J. H. Hanschell, C.M.G.; D. H. L. Ward; D. Williams.

Education.—Primary and secondary education is free in Government-aided schools.

Communications.—Barbados has some 840 miles of roads, of which about 780 miles are asphalted. There is an international airport at Seawell, 12 miles from Bridgetown, and frequent scheduled services connect Barbados with the major world air routes. There are a colour television service, and a radio broadcasting service operated by the Caribbean Broadcasting Corporation, and a wired broadcasting service operated by a local subsidiary of Rediffusion Ltd.

Production, etc.—The principal *exports* are sugar, molasses, rum, clothing, lard and margarine, and the *imports* food, manufactured goods, machinery, transport equipment and chemicals. Barbados' major trading partners are the U.K., U.S.A., CARICOM and Canada. The tourist industry is a major source of revenue.

TRADE

Goods to the value of BDS $172,274,000 were exported in 1974, including sugar ($52,185,000), molasses ($10,822,000), and rum ($4,948,000).

	1974
Total imports	$417,737,000
Total exports	$172,274,000

Trade with U.K.

	1973	1974
Imports from U.K.	£14,123,000	£14,499,000
Exports to U.K.	8,601,000	9,733,000

FINANCE

	1974–5	1975–6 (est.)
Revenue	$165,600,000	$170,900,000
Expenditure	164,000,000	185,700,000

Botswana

Botswana (formerly the British Protectorate of Bechuanaland) lies between latitudes 18° and 26° S. and longitudes 20° and 28° W. and is bounded by the Cape and Transvaal Provinces of South Africa on the south and east, by Rhodesia, the Zambesi amd Chobe (Linyanti) Rivers on the north and north-east and by South West Africa on the west. Botswana extends some 500 miles by 550 miles, with a total area of 220,000 square miles. The climate of the country is generally sub-tropical, but varies considerably with latitude and altitude. A plateau at a height of about 4,000 feet divides Botswana into two main topographical regions. To the east of the plateau streams flow into the Marico, Notwani and Limpopo Rivers; to the west lies a flat region comprising the Kgalagadi Desert, the Okavango Swamps and the Northern State Lands area. The Kgalagadi Desert is a level tract closely covered with thorn bush and grass, extending 300 miles to the west and bounded by the Makgadikgadi salt pans and the Boteti River in the north. Its rainfall varies from 20 inches in the east to 9 inches in the south-west. The Okavango Swamps, 6,500 square miles in area, lie in the remote north-western corner of Botswana, and, apart from the Limpopo and Chobe Rivers, are the only source of permanent surface water in the country. North of the Boteti River and the Makgadikgadi depression the Kgalagadi Desert gives way to forest and dense bush of the Northern State Lands. Large areas of the country support only herds of game. Elephant numbers have been estimated at 10,000.

Population.—At the census in August, 1971, it was recorded that Botswana had a population of 620,000. The eight principal Botswana tribes are Bakgatla, Bakwena, Bangwaketse, Bamalete, Bamangwato, Barolong, Batawana and Batlokwa. CAPITAL.—Gaborone, estimated population 18,000. Other business centres are Francistown (17,000) and Lobatse (12,000). FLAG.—Horizontal bands of blue, white, blue, with a black stripe on the white band.

Government.—On September 30, 1966, Bechuanaland became a Republic within the Commonwealth under the name Botswana. The President of Botswana is Head of State and appoints as Vice-President a member of the National Assembly who is his principal assistant and leader of Government business in the National Assembly. The Assembly consists of the President, 32 members elected on a basis of universal adult suffrage, 4 specially elected members, the Attorney-General (non-voting) and the Speaker. There is also a House of Chiefs.

President, Sir Seretse Khama, K.B.E.
Vice President, Dr. Hon. Q. K. J. Masire.

OFFICE OF THE PRESIDENT
Minister of State for External Affairs, Hon. A. M. Mogwe, M.B.E.
Minister of State for the Public Service and Broadcasting, Hon. D. K. Kwelagobe.
External Affairs Secretary, C. Tibone.

MINISTRY
Minister for Finance and Development Planning, Dr. Hon. Q. K. J. Masire.
Health, Hon. M. P. K. Nwako.
Home Affairs, Hon, B. K. Kgari.
Agriculture, Hon. E. S. Masisi.
Local Government and Lands, Hon. L. Makgekgenene.
Works and Communications, Hon. J. G. Haskins, O.B.E.
Commerce and Industry, Dr. Hon. G. K. T. Chiepe, M.B.E.
Education, Hon. K. P. Morake.
Mineral Resources and Water Affairs, Hon. M. K. Segokgo.

BOTSWANA HIGH COMMISSION
3 Buckingham Gate (6th Floor), S.W.1
High Commissioner, (vacant).

BRITISH HIGH COMMISSION
Private Bag 23, Gaborone
High Commissioner, Her Excellency Miss Eleanor Jean Emery, C.M.G. (1973).
British Council Representative, G. C. Stackhouse.

Chief Justice of Botswana, G. O. L. Dyke.
Attorney-General, M. D. Mokama.

The country is essentially pastoral, although sorghum, maize, beans, pumpkins and melons are sown. Cattle thrive, despite the drought of 1965–66, during which time the numbers of cattle decreased by 350,000. In 1972, after three years of good rain, the national herd numbered about 2,000,000. Plans for the development of agriculture and cattle production, for combating soil erosion, investigating the water resources of the country and improving water supplies are being carried out.

Mineral extraction and processing has recently become a major source of income for the country, following the opening of large mines for diamonds and copper-nickel. Very large deposits of coal have been discovered, and are being mined on a small scale; plans for comprehensive development remain to be formulated. Much of the country has yet to be fully prospected. Manufacturing industry is expected to grow rapidly in the future, as communications improve.

Education.—In 1972, there were 294 primary schools with enrolment of 81,662 and 15 secondary schools with enrolment of 5,564. There were also three teacher training establishments with enrolment of 332. The principal languages in use in the country are English and Setswana.

Communications.—The railway from Kimberley and Mafeking in South Africa to Bulawayo in Rhodesia passes through eastern Botswana. The main roads in the country are the north–south road, which closely follows the railway, and the road running east–west that links Francistown and Maun. A new road from Nata to Kazungula which will provide a direct link to Zambia from

Botswana, is under construction. Air services are provided on a scheduled basis between the main towns, linking with services from South Africa and Zambia. There are telephone and telegraph links to South Africa and Rhodesia.

TRADE

	1971–72	1973–74
Net Imports	R60,700,000	R99,000,000
Exports	33,000,000	64,500,000

FINANCE

	1972–73	1973–74
Actual Revenue	R28,625,642	R42,400,000
Actual Expenditure	28,593,405	40,900,000

Currency: South African rand. R1·50= £1 approx.

Trade with U.K.

	1972	1974
Imports from U.K.	£906,000	£1,322,000
Exports to U.K.	3,820,000	2,532,000

Cyprus

Area, Climate and Population.—Cyprus with an area of 3,572 square miles, is the third largest island in the Mediterranean Sea, exceeded in size by Sicily and Sardinia. Its greatest length is 140 miles and greatest breadth 60 miles. It is situated at the extreme north-east corner of the Mediterranean in latitude 35° N. and longitude 33° 30′ E. It is about 40 miles distant from the nearest point of Asia Minor, 60 miles from Syria and 240 miles from Port Said. The main topographical features of Cyprus are: (a) A narrow limestone range of mountains extending in an unbroken chain for nearly 100 miles along the north coast, at an average height of 2,000 feet; (b) A broad central plain, running for some 60 miles from west to east; (c) An extensive igneous massif rising to over 6,000 feet in the west of the island; and (d) Narrow coastal plains between the mountains and the sea. The rivers are little more than mountain torrents. There is no permanent stream of any volume.

Cyprus has a somewhat intense Mediterranean climate (with a hot dry summer and a variable warm winter). There are two contrasted seasons, winter and summer, while the intermediate ones are short and transitional. The winter is generally sunny with frequent cold spells between the beginning of December and end of February. The mean temperatures of the coldest month range from 36° to 50° F.

The rainy season lasts from October to April with average total rainfall of about 20 inches.

The summers are hot, dry and almost cloudless. July and August are the warmest months, with mean temperatures ranging from 80°–85° F. in the lowlands, to 70° in the mountains. In April 1974 the estimated population was 632,000. There are two major communities, Greek Cypriots (78 per cent.) and Turkish Cypriots (18·2 per cent.); and minorities of Armenians, Maronites and others. The population increases on the average at 0·9 per cent. annually. The birth rate in 1973 was estimated to be 18·2 and the death rate 9·5 per thousand.

CAPITAL.—Nicosia, near the centre of the island, with a population of 235,000 (including suburbs); the other principal towns are Ψ Limassol (population 125,300), Ψ Famagusta (124,300), Ψ Larnaca (60,900), Paphos (57,300) and Kyrenia (32,700). (Since the events of July and August 1974 (see below) there have been significant changes in population distribution). Nicosia is distant from London 2,028 miles by air.

FLAG.—Gold map of Cyprus on a white ground, surmounting crossed olive branches (green).

President, Archbishop Makarios, *elected* Dec. 14, 1959; *assumed office* Aug. 16, 1960; *re-elected* Feb. 25, 1968; *declared re-elected without opposition,* Feb. 8, 1973. [Following an uprising led by Greek Officers of the Cyprus National Guard, on July 15, 1974, Archbishop Makarios left Cyprus. On July 23, Mr. Glafkos Clerides, Speaker of the House of Representatives, was sworn in as Acting President.] Archbishop Makarios returned to Cyprus on Dec. 7, 1974 to resume his presidential functions.

CABINET

A joint Greek-Turkish Cabinet was formed in 1960, but the three Turkish members ceased to attend, following events in Dec. 1963, and their Ministries were taken over by Greek Ministers.

CYPRUS HIGH COMMISSION
[01-499 8272]
93 Park Street, W.1
High Commissioner, His Excellency Costas Ashiotis, M.B.E.

BRITISH HIGH COMMISSION
Alexander Pallis Street (P.O. Box 1978)
Nicosia
High Commissioner, His Excellency Donald Mc-Donald Gordon, C.M.G. (1975) £12,000
British Council Representative, S. C. Alexander, P.O. Box 1995, 3 Museum Street, Nicosia.

GOVERNMENT

Cyprus passed under British administration from 1878. Cyprus was formally annexed to Great Britain on Nov. 5, 1914, on the outbreak of war with Turkey. From 1925 to 1960 it was a Crown Colony administered by a Governor, assisted by an Executive Council and also for a time by a partly-elected Legislative Council. Following the launching in April 1955 of an armed campaign by EOKA in support of ENOSIS (union with Greece), a state of emergency was declared in November, 1955, and Archbishop Makarios was deported. Further proposals for a workable constitution made in 1956 and a seven-year-plan for the government of Cyprus in association with Greece and Greek Cypriots were rejected by the Greek Government and Greek Cypriots. Archbishop Makarios was released in March, 1957, but was not allowed to return immediately to Cyprus. Following a meeting at Zürich between the Prime Ministers of Greece and Turkey, a conference was held in London and an agreement was signed on February 19, 1959, between the United Kingdom, Greece, Turkey and the Greek and Turkish Cypriots which provided that Cyprus would be an independent Republic.

Constitution.—Under the Cyprus Act, 1960, the island became an independent sovereign republic on August 16, 1960. The constitution provides for a Greek Cypriot President and a Turkish Cypriot Vice-President elected for a five-year term by the Greek and Turkish communities respectively. The House of Representatives, elected for five years by universal suffrage of each community separately, consists of 35 Greek and 15 Turkish members. The 1960 Constitution proved unworkable in practice and led to the intercommunal troubles. Talks have been in progress between Greeks and

Turks since 1968 on a new Constitution for the island assisted by the Special Representative in Cyprus of the U.N. Sec.-Gen. and more recently the Secretary General personally. The mandate of the U.N. Peace Keeping Force in Cyprus (UNFICYP) was last renewed for the twenty-seventh time on June 13, 1975, for a further period of six months.

A General Election was held for the 35 Greek Cypriot seats on July 5, 1970, resulting in the following state of parties: *Unified Party*, 15; *Akel* (Communist), 9; *Progressive Front*, 7; *Democratic Centre Union*, 2; and *Independents*, 2. On the same day elections were held in the Turkish sector to elect 15 members for Turkish Cypriot national seats and 15 Turkish communal seats which together form a temporary chamber in the Turkish Cypriot sector first set up in December, 1967, but which is not recognized by the Cyprus Government. On July 15, 1974, mainland Greek officers of the Greek Cypriot National Guard launched a *coup d' état* against President Makarios and installed a former EOKA member Nikos Sampson in his place. Turkey, purportedly acting under the 1960 Treaty of Guarantee by which Britain, Greece and Turkey reserved to themselves the right to maintain constitutional order and the independence and territorial integrity of the island, invaded northern Cyprus on July 20, subsequently moving on August 13, to occupy approximately 40 per cent. of the island. Despite successive U.N. resolutions calling for the withdrawal of all foreign forces from the island and the return of refugees (who number about 210,000) to their homes, much of the northern part of Cyprus remains under Turkish military occupation with a "Turkish Federated State" declared in this area.

British Sovereign Areas.—The United Kingdom retained full sovereignty and jurisdiction over two areas of 99 square miles in all—Akrotiri–Episkopi– Paramali and Dhekelia–Pergamos–Ayios Nicolaos– Xylophagou—and use of roads and other facilities. The British Administrator of these areas is appointed by the Queen and is responsible to the Secretary of State for Defence.

Production and Industries.—About 36 per cent. of those gainfully employed take part in agriculture, the chief agricultural products being:—cereals, vine products, potatoes, carobs, carrots, citrus and other fresh and dried fruit, tobacco and legumes. Various kinds of livestock are raised, principally sheep, goats, pigs and poultry. The value of agricultural and livestock exports in 1974 was about £28,250,000. Mining is an important industry in Cyprus; the value of minerals exported in 1974 was £9,742,000. The principal minerals are cupreous and copper concentrates, copper pyrites, and asbestos. There is no heavy industry, but a wide variety of light manufacturing industries. Tourism prior to July–August 1974, was an important source of revenue. Long-stay visitors to the island in 1973 numbered 257,000.

FINANCE

	1973	1974 (*prov.*)
Ordinary Revenue	C£59,603,000	C£55,208,000
Ord. Expenditure	£55,239,000	£60,840,000
Public Debt	20,235,000	....

TRADE

	1973	1974
Imports	C£157,442,000	C£148,028,000
Exports	63,132,000	55,287,000

	1973	1974
Imports from U.K.	C£35,251,000	C£30,652,000
Exports to U.K.	23,275,000	21,099,000

Fiji

This is a group of 322 islands (of which fewer than half are inhabited) in the South Pacific Ocean, about 1,100 miles north of New Zealand. The gross area of the group, which extends 300 miles from east to west, and 300 north to south, between 15° 45'–21° 10' S. lat. and 176° E.—178° W. long. is 7,083 square miles. The International Date Line has been diverted to the east of the island group. Many of the islands are of volcanic origin, with lofty mountains, and well wooded. The principal are Viti Levu, Vanua Levu, Taveuni and Kandavu. The climate is oceanic. Shade temperatures seldom rise above 93° F. or fall below 60° F. except in the mountains. There is a great contrast in vegetation between the windward and leeward sides of the larger islands with rain forests and luxuriant vegetation giving way in the drier zones to grassland with scattered trees. The chief products are sugar cane, coconuts, gold, rice, bananas, pineapples, yams and dalo or taro (colocasia). Tourism is an increasingly important source of revenue.

The population (1973 estimate) was 540,800 (174,400 Indians, 233,600 Fijians, 9,600 part-Europeans, 4,600 Europeans, 4,700 Chinese and 13,900 other Pacific races).

CAPITAL.— Ψ Suva, in the island of Viti Levu. Population (1966 Census) 54,157.

Government.—Fiji was a British colony from 1874 until October 10, 1970, when it became an independent state and a member of the Commonwealth. Under the Constitution there is a Governor-General appointed by the Queen. An elected House of Representatives (52 members) consists of 12 Fijians, 12 Indians and 3 General members elected on Communal rolls; and 10 Fijians, 10 Indians and 5 General members elected on National rolls, in which members of all races vote on the same register. General members are in the main representatives of the European, part-European and Chinese communities.

There is a Senate of 22 members, 8 appointed by the Great Council of Chiefs, 7 by the Prime Minister, 6 by the Leader of the Opposition and one by the Council of Rotuma, an island dependency 400 miles from Suva, discovered in 1879 and annexed in 1881.

Governor-General, His Excellency Ratu Sir George Cakobau, G.C.M.G., O.B.E. (1973).

CABINET

Prime Minister, Rt. Hon. Ratu Sir Kamisese Mara, K.B.E.

Deputy Prime Minister and Minister for Home Affairs, Hon. Ratu Sir Penaia K. Ganilau, K.B.E., C.M.G., C.V.O., D.S.O.

Attorney-General, Hon. Senator J. N. Falvey, O.B.E., Q.C.

Minister for Communications, Works and Tourism, Hon. E. J. Beddoes.

Finance, Hon. C. A. Stinson, O.B.E.

Agriculture, Fisheries and Forests, Hon. Ratu J. B. Toganivalu.

Labour, Hon. Jonati Mavoa.

Education, Youth and Sport, Hon. J. B. Naisara.

Fijian Affairs and Rural Development, Hon. Ratu W. B. Toganivalu.
Lands and Mineral Resources, Hon. S. N. Waqaniva-valagi.
Commerce, Industries and Co-operatives, Hon. M. T. Khan.
Health, Hon. J. S. Singh, M.B.E.
Urban Development, Housing and Social Welfare, Hon. M. Ramzan, M.B.E.
Information, Hon. Ratu David Toganivalu.

Speaker, House of Representatives, Hon. R. D. Patel.
Deputy Speaker, Hon. Vijay Singh.
President of the Senate, Hon. R. L. Munro, C.B.E.

FIJI HIGH COMMISSION
25 Upper Brook Street, W.1
[01-493 6516]
High Commissioner, His Excellency Josua R. Rabukawaqa, C.B.E., M.V.O.

BRITISH HIGH COMMISSION
Suva
High Commissioner, His Excellency James Stanley Arthur (1974)........................£11,000

JUDICIARY
Chief Justice of Fiji, Hon. C. H. Grant......$8,004
Puisne Judges, Hons. G. Mishra; T. Tuivaga; K. Stuart; J. H. Williams................$7,008

FINANCE

	1972*	1973*
Public Income	$57,686,000	$72,486,000
Public Expenditure	56,776,000	70,401,000
Public Debt (Dec. 31)	48,385,000	51,396,000
* Estimated.		

TRADE

	1972	1973
Total Imports	$131,549,000	$175,360,000
Total Exports	65,582,000	73,605,000

	1973	1974
Imports from U.K.	£9,689,000	£9,744,000
Exports to U.K.	11,301,000	21,474,000

Currency.—Currency is the *Fiji dollar*, against which the £ sterling floats. Exchange rate approx. $1·90 = £1 sterling.

The principal exports are raw sugar, coconut oil, gold, oil seed cake and meal, lumber, copra, ginger, molasses, biscuits, fish, unmanufactured tobacco, veneer sheets, paints and cement. The chief imports are machinery, electrical goods, foodstuffs, all types of fabrics, petroleum products, motor vehicles and miscellaneous manufactured articles. The tourist trade continues to expand.

Communications.—Fiji is approximately 11,000 miles from the United Kingdom; transit time from London *via* Panama Canal about 28–30 days. Air connections are provided between the United Kingdom and Fiji *via* Canada, United States of America, Mexico and the Caribbean, Japan and U.S.S.R., and the Middle East either through New Zealand and Australia or through New Caledonia and Singapore. The following trunk route operators provide services through Nadi Airport; Qantas, Pan American, British Airways, Air New Zealand, U.T.A., and CP Air. Flights connecting with Fiji operate to Auckland, Sydney–Perth and Darwin and points beyond; Honolulu, San Francisco or Los Angeles or Vancouver and points beyond; Tahiti and points beyond; Pago Pago; Noumea and points beyond. Fiji is one of the main aerial crossroads in the Pacific.

Air Pacific Ltd. (previously Fiji Airways Ltd.) is based at Nausori Airport near Suva and with BAC 1-11, HS.748 and DH *Heron* aircraft operates scheduled domestic services within the Fiji islands and from Suva provides connection to Nadi, Labasa, Savusavu and Matei, and there are regional services to Tonga, Western Samoa, Papua, New Guinea (Port Moresby) *via* the New Hebrides (Vila); the Solomon Islands (Honiara) and the Republic of Nauru *via* Funafuti and Tarawa in the Gilbert and Ellice Islands, and Auckland, N.Z., *via* Tonga, Fiji Air Services Ltd. operates Charter flights within the Fiji group of islands and South Pacific and provides scheduled services to the islands of Ovalau, Lakeba and Malolo Lailai and to air-strips on Viti Levu at Korelevu, Natadola, Pacific Harbour and Vatukoula.

The Gambia

The West African river Gambia was discovered by the Portuguese in 1447; and in 1588, the year of the Spanish Armada, Queen Elizabeth I, being then at war with Spain and Portugal, gave a charter to a British Company to trade with the Gambia, and as early as 1618 an effort to do so was made, but it was not success-ful. In 1686 a fort was built upon a rocky island, and, in honour of the new King, was named Fort James; but the English merchants had formidable rivals in the Portuguese and French, and it was not until 1783 that the river was recognized, by the *Treaty of Versailles*, as British. The Colony had no regular political institutions until 1807, when it was put under the Government of Sierra Leone. The Colony of the Gambia was created in 1843, and was constituted a separate government in 1888. It consists of a narrow strip of land, estimated at 4,003 sq. miles, lying on both sides of the River Gambia to a distance of about 300 miles, mainly between 13° 15′–13° 45′ N. and 13° 45′–13° 65′ W. The river is navigable to ocean-going vessels for 150 miles and to river steamers up to 300 miles from its mouth. The capital and chief port, Banjul, formerly Bathurst, is situated at the mouth of the river. The provisional figure for the total population of the country at the 1973 Census was 493,499. The climate of Banjul is extremely pleasant except during the rainy season from June to October, when it sometimes becomes uncomfortably humid. Rainfall, 30–60 inches a year.

CAPITAL.— Ψ Banjul. Population (1973 census), 39,476.
FLAG.—Horizontal stripes of red, blue and green, separated by narrow white stripes.

Government.—On February 18, 1965, the Gambia became an independent monarchy within the Com-monwealth, with the Queen as Head of State. On April 24, 1970, following a referendum, the consti-tution was changed to that of a Republic (within the Commonwealth) with an executive President. The House of Representatives, which elects its own Speaker, consists of 32 elected members, 4 elected Head Chiefs, 3 nominated members and the Attorney General (who is also a nominated member with voting rights). The Vice-President, who is the Government leader in the House, and other

Ministers are appointed by the President. The latter's tenure of office is co-terminous with the life of a Parliament.

PRESIDENT AND CABINET

President, Sir Dawda Jawara.
Vice-President and Minister of External Affairs, Hon. A. D. Camara.
Finance, Commerce and Industry, Alhaji Hon. I. M. Garba Jahumpa.
Education, Youth and Social Welfare, Alhaji Hon. M. C. Cham.
Local Government, Lands and Mines, Alhaji Hon. Yaya Ceesay.
Works and Communications, Alhaji Hon. Sir Alieu Jack.
Agriculture and Natural Resources, Alhaji Hon. A. B. N'Jie.
Health and Labour, Alhaji Hon. K. Singhateh.
Attorney-General, Alhaji Hon. M. L. Saho.
Minister of State (Information, Broadcasting, Tourism), Hon. B. L. K. Sanyang.

Chief Justice, Hon. Sir Phillip Bridges, C.M.G.
Speaker, Dr. S. H. O. Jones.

GAMBIA HIGH COMMISSION
60 Ennismore Gardens, S.W.7.
[01-584 1242]
High Commissioner, His Excellency Bocar Ousman Semega-Janneh, M.B.E. (1971).
BRITISH HIGH COMMISSION
78 Wellington Street, Banjul
High Commissioner, His Excellency, J. R. W. Parker, O.B.E. (1971).

Communications.—Banjul is 2,600 miles from London. There are two direct air services weekly *via* Casablanca and Las Palmas and three weekly, changing at Dakar. There are no regular passenger or mails service by sea. Ocean-going vessels entering the ports in 1972 totalled 282 (net tonnage 668,000). There is an international aerodrome at Yunduz, 17 miles from Banjul. Internal communication is by road and river. There are 794 miles of motor road, including 180 miles of bituminous surface roads, 330 miles of gravel roads and 284 miles of Commissioner's roads. There are eight Government wireless stations and a V.H.F. telephone service linking Banjul with the principal towns in the provinces. There is a broadcasting service.

Education.—There are 96 primary schools and 22 secondary schools, with a total enrolment of 26,338 pupils, including 8,071 girls. There are 73 students, including 15 females, at the Yundum Teacher Training College. A Vocational and Training Centre operates at Banjul.

Production.—Most of the population is engaged in agriculture. the chief product being ground-nuts which is the single important cash crop. Other crops are rice, millet and various kinds of fruit and vegetables. Fishing and livestock production are considerable. No minerals are at present being exploited and there are practically no manufactures other than ground-nut processing and a bottling plant.

FINANCE

	1972–73 (Actual)		1973–74 (Revised estimate)	
	Re-current	Develop-ment	Re-current	Develop-ment
	D'000	D'000	D'000	D'000
Revenue......	23,881	5,992	25,572	9,010
Expenditure...	20,970	4,519	23,692	10,068

The Government financial year begins on July 1.
Currency.—Decimal currency was introduced in the Gambia on July 1, 1971. The new unit is the *dalasi* of 100 *butut*. The present rate of exchange is $D4 = £1$.

TRADE

	1971–72	1972–73
Total imports........	D46,200,000	D54,400,000
Total exports.........	36,000,000	26,500,000

	1973	1974
Imports from U.K...	£3,225,000	£4,437,000
Exports to U.K......	4,204,000	8,438,000

The chief exports are ground-nut products, which account for 95 per cent. of total exports, the main markets being Italy, the United Kingdom, W. Germany, Switzerland and the Netherlands. Other exports are palm kernels, dried fish and hides. Foodstuff imports include rice, sugar, flour and kola nuts. Manufactured goods of all kinds are imported, the chief being textiles and apparel, vehicles, machinery, metal goods and petroleum products.

Ghana

Ghana (formerly the British Colony of the Gold Coast) is situated on the Gulf of Guinea, between 3° 07′ W. long. and 1° 14′ E. long. (about 334 miles), and extends 441 miles north from Cape Three Points (4° 45′ N.) to 11° 11′ N. It is bounded on the north by the Republic of Upper Volta, on the west by the Republic of Ivory Coast, on the east by the Republic of Togo, and on the south by the Atlantic Ocean. Although a tropical country, Ghana is cooler than many countries within similar latitudes.

Area and Population.—Ghana has a total area of 92,100 sq. miles with a total population (Census of 1970) of 8,545,561, some 27 per cent. more than the population at the Census of 1960. Almost all Ghanaians are Sudanese Negroes, although Hamitic strains are common in Northern Ghana.

CAPITAL.—Ψ ACCRA. Population of the Capital District (including Accra Tema City Council area, and Accra Rural area) (provisional, 1970) 851,614. Other towns are Kumasi, Tamale, Sekondi-Takoradi, Cape Coast, Sunyani, Ho, Koforidua, Tarkwa and Winneba. Accra is 3,920 miles by sea from Liverpool, transit 12 to 30 days.

FLAG.—Equal horizontal bands of red over yellow over green; five-point black star on gold stripe.
INDEPENDENCE DAY—March 6.

GOVERNMENT

The Gold Coast region of West Africa was first visited by European traders in the fifteenth century. The Gold Coast Colony, Ashanti, the Northern Territories and Trans-Volta-Togoland, the constituent parts of the new State, came under British administration at various times, the original Gold Coast Colony, the coastal and Southern areas, being first constituted in 1874; Ashanti in 1901; and the Northern Territories Protectorate in 1901. The territory of Trans-Volta-Togoland, part of Togo, a former German colony, was mandated to Britain by the League of Nations after the First World War, and remained under British administration as a United Nations Trusteeship after the Second World War. After a plebiscite in May,

1956, under the auspices of the United Nations, the territory was integrated with the Gold Coast Colony.

The former Gold Coast Colony and associated territories became the independent state of Ghana and a member of the British Commonwealth on March 6, 1957, under the *Ghana Independence Act, 1957,* and adopted a Republican constitution on July 1, 1960.

On Feb. 24, 1966, the Army seized power and Dr. Nkrumah and his ministers were dismissed.

Ghana was administered until October 1, 1969, by a National Liberation Council of four representatives each from the Army and the police, during which time a Constitution for the Second Republic of Ghana was evolved and brought into force by a 150 member Constituent Assembly on Aug. 22, 1969.

General elections were held on August 29, 1969, in which Dr. K. A. Busia's Progress Party won 105 seats and Mr. K. A. Gbedemah's National Alliance of Liberals 29, the remaining 6 seats being won by minority parties. Dr. Busia was appointed Prime Minister on Sept. 3, 1969, and the N.L.C. formally handed over to the civilian government on October 1, 1969. A three-man presidential Commission was appointed under Brigadier Afrifa in September 1969. It was dissolved in July 1970, and a month later Mr. E. Akufo-Addo was elected President.

On January 13, 1972, the Busia administration was ousted in an army *coup d'état* led by Colonel I. K. Acheampong. The Constitution was withdrawn, political acrivity banned and the Presidency abolished. The National Redemption Council is the supreme governing body, assisted by an Executive Council. Rule is by decree.

Head of State and Chairman NRC, Col. I. K. Acheampong.

NATIONAL REDEMPTION COUNCIL

Head of State and Chairman of the NRC.; Commissioner for Defence, Finance and Sport; Commander in Chief of the Armed Forces, Col. I. K. Acheampong.

Labour, Social Welfare and Co-operatives, Lt. Col. K. B. Agbo.

Inspector General of Police and Commissioner for Internal Affairs, E. Ako.

Foreign Affairs, Lt. Col. R. M. Baah.

Economic Planning, Lt. Col. R. J. A. Felli.

Trade and Tourism, Lt. Col. D. A. Iddisah.

Works and Housing, Col. R. E. A. Kotei.

Attorney General and Commissioner for Justice, E. N. Moore.

Chief of Defence Staff and Commissioner for Special Duties, Maj. Gen. L. A. Okai.

Health, Lt. Col. A. H. Selormey.

N.R.C. Affairs, E. K. Buckman.

OTHER CENTRAL GOVERNMENT COMMISSIONERS
(Together with members of the N.R.C. forming the Executive Council.)

Local Government, Maj. Gen. N. A. Aferi.

Transport and Communications, Col. P. K. Agyekum.

Lands and Mineral Resources, Maj. Gen. D. C. K. Amenu.

Cocoa Affairs, Col. F. G. Bernasko.

Industries, Lt. Col. G. Minyila.

Agriculture, Lt. Col. P. K. Nkegbe.

Education and Culture, Col. E. O. Nyante.

Information, Col. C. R. Tachie-Menson.

GHANA HIGH COMMISSION

13 Belgrave Square, S.W.1
[01-235 4142]

High Commissioner, His Excellency Colonel McGal Asante (1975).

BRITISH HIGH COMMISSION

P.O. Box 296, High Street, Accra

High Commissioner, His Excellency Frank Mills, C.M.G. (1975)........................£6,250

Deputy High Commissioner, W. Turner.

British Council Representative, H. R. Crooke, Liberia Road, Accra, and an Office in *Kumasi.*

JUDICIARY

The Judiciary, headed by the Chief Justice, represents the judicial control of Ghana and has authority over all civil and criminal matters, except those heard by military tribunals. Fundamentally the Courts of Ghana consist of two divisions, the *Superior Court of Judicature* and the *Inferior Courts.* The former consist of the Court of Appeal and the High Court. The *Inferior Courts* consist of the Circuit Courts, approximately equivalent to the old British Assize Courts, now Crown Courts, and such courts as deal with judicial matters on a district and juvenile level.

The Court of Appeal, when constituted with five Justices, is the final Court of Appeal in Ghana. The Chief Justice has discretion to create divisions of the Court of Appeal.

The High Court of Justice.—This court has jurisdiction over criminal, industrial and labour matters. Consisting of the Chief Justice and a minimum of twelve Puisne Judges, it may also include any other judge appointed at the discretion of the Chief Justice. Individual courts may consist of up to three judges, with or without a jury.

PRODUCTION, ETC.

Agriculture.—Agriculture forms the basis of Ghana's economy, employing 70 per cent. of the working population. Crops of the *Forest Zone* include cocoa, which is the largest single source of revenue, rice and a variety of other foodstuff crops grown on mixed-crop farms. Fruits such as avocado pears, oranges and pineapples are grown. Cassava is the most important crop of the *Coastal Savannas Zone,* which consists of the Accra Plains (1,400 sq. miles) and Ho-Keta Plains (2,600 sq. miles) of the lower Volta area. Fishing is important in coastal areas and in the Volta itself. Production of pulses such as groundnuts, tiger nuts and cowpeas is widespread. Near the Togo border oil palms, yams, maize, cassava, fruit and vegetables are produced. Livestock is raised in the uncultivated areas. The *Northern Savanna Zone* is Ghana's principal cattle rearing area and other livestock production there is important for home consumption. Corn and millet crops are produced in the far north and maize, yams, rice and groundnut crops in more southerly parts of the Zone.

A State Farms Corporation, established in 1963 to further larger scale farming enterprise, has more than 100 farms in various parts of the country and operates from eight regional centres.

Fisheries.—Some 150,000 of the country's population are engaged in fisheries which now produce about 180,000 tons annually. Ghana's estimated annual requirement is at least 250,000 tons and there are considerable imports of fish products. About 80 per cent of home supply is obtained from sea fisheries, but production from the Volta Lake and other inland fisheries is increasing rapidly thanks to greatly increased fish population.

Mineral Production.—The area within a 60 mile radius of Dunkwa produces 90 per cent. of Ghana's mineral exports. Manganese production from Nsuta ranks among the world's highest and gold, industrial diamonds and bauxite are also produced. Some 30,000 persons are employed by the mining companies.

Manufactures.—Examples of the small-scale traditional industries are tailoring, goldsmithing and carpentry. Priority has been given in recent years to the establishment of a number of "Pioneer Industries" including sawmill furniture, prefabricated doors, plywood, vehicle assembly, cigarettes, boatbuilding, refrigerator assembly, food processing (biscuits, edible oils, confectionery, brewing, etc.), cotton textiles, clothing, footwear, printing and other light industries. A modern industrial complex is growing in the Accra–Tema area.

Volta River Project.—The Volta River is formed at the confluence of the Black and White Voltas, both of which rise in the neighbouring republic of Upper Volta. With its tributaries the Volta drains an area of 150,000 sq. miles of which 61,000 sq. miles lie in Ghana. The Volta Dam at Akosombo was inaugurated in January, 1966, to generate hydro-electric power for the processing of bauxite and feed a power transmission network for the Accra–Kumasi–Takoradi area. Electricity is now also sent to Togo and Dahomey. The lake raised by the Volta Dam has a maximum area of 3,275 sq. miles, a length of 250 miles and a shore line of 4,500 miles. A water transport service from Akosombo to various points on the lake has been instituted.

Power output from Akosombo is planned to reach 768 megawatts, 22 times the country's 1959 generating capacity. Smaller dams with 150 MW. and 93 MW. capacity are to be built at Kpong rapids and at Bui in the Northern Region. Planned aluminium output in Ghana by 1973 was 145,000 tons (1969, 103,000 tons).

COMMUNICATIONS

There are four aerodromes in Ghana, situated at Accra, Takoradi, Kumasi and Tamale. Accra Air-port is an international airport and is the terminus for services from the United Kingdom, the Northern, Ashanti and Western Regions.

Railway communications consist of a main line running from Takoradi to Kumasi thence to Accra, a distance of 357 miles. From Huni Valley on the Kumasi line north of Takoradi a line runs to Kotoku on the railway about 17 miles north of Accra. Branch lines run to Sekondi, Prestea, Kade, Awaso and Tema. Total railway mileage open to traffic is 600. There are 20,245 miles of motorable roads, of which 2,335 are bitumen.

Takoradi Harbour consists of two breakwaters enclosing a water area of 220 acres. Seven quay berths are situated on the lee breakwater—five are used for the handling of general cargo, one is leased specially for manganese exports and one is used for shallow draft colliers. Tema Harbour—Africa's largest artificial harbour and a prospective major port of the South Atlantic—was opened in 1962. There are 10 berths for larger ocean going vessels and the harbour also has the largest dry dock on the West African coast. An oil berth has also been built to serve the Ghaip refinery which has been constructed at Tema.

TRADE

	1971	1974
Total imports...	N¢450,600,000	N¢946,800,000
Total exports....	387,900,000	873,400,000

Trade with U.K.

	1972	1974
Imports from U.K...	£16,474,000	£51,010,000
Exports to U.K......	33,136,000	70,700,000

FINANCE

The currency of Ghana is the *cedi* (¢) (of 100 *pesawas*) equivalent to 35 pence sterling.

Guyana

GUYANA, the former colony of British Guiana, which includes the Counties of Demerara, Essequibo and Berbice, is situated on the north-east coast of South America and has a total area of 83,000 square miles with a seaboard of about 270 miles. The population at December 31, 1970, was estimated at 714,233. There are about 31,460 Amerindians. The territory is bounded on the south by Brazil, on the east by Surinam, on the west by Venezuela, and on the north and N.E. by the Atlantic. The coastline is very like the Netherlands, below the level of the sea, and intersected with canals constructed by its former Dutch owners. At the junction of the Guyana-Venezuela-Brazil boundaries is Mt. Roraima, a flat topped mountain 9,000 feet above sea-level. There are many beautiful waterfalls in Guyana: on the Potaro River (a tributary of the Essequibo) is the *Kaieteur Fall*, with a clear drop of 741 feet and a total fall of 822 feet, and on the Essequibo, the *Horse Shoe Falls* (discovered in 1934); a fall, with a drop of some 500 feet, discovered in 1934 on the Ipobe River, a tributary of the Kuribrong, has been named the *Marina Fall*, and other falls were discovered in 1938 on the Kamarang River, 80 miles north-east of Mt. Roraima.

The seasons are divided into dry and wet, the two dry seasons lasting from the middle of February to the end of April, and from the middle of August to the end of November. The climate on the coast is pleasant and healthy for the greater part of the year. In the Aug.–Oct. period it is hot. The mean temperature is 80·3°, its extremes during 87 years ranging between 68° and 96°, but these are very rare, the usual extremes being 70° and 90°. In the interior the mean temperature is higher—82·6°, its extremes ranging from 66° to 103°. The yearly rainfall is subject to marked variation, its mean on the coast lands averaging about 90 inches with an average of 58 inches on the savannahs. The daily average sunshine is nearly 7 hours and, except when rain is falling, dull and cloudy weather is rarely experienced.

Government.—Guyana became independent on May 26, 1966, with a Governor-General appointed by the Queen. It became a Cooperative Republic on Feb. 23, 1970, and Mr. Arthur Chung was elected first President on March 17, 1970, for a term of six years. The electoral system is a Proportional Representation or "single list" system, each voter casting his vote for a party list of candidates. The Prime Minister and Cabinet are responsible collectively to a National Assembly of 53 members elected by secret ballot; the voting age is 21. Elections to the National Assembly are held every five years; the last election was on July 16, 1973.

An important feature of the Constitution is its provision for the appointment of an *Ombudsman*. The life of the Assembly, presided over by a Speaker, who may or may not be a Member of the Assembly, is five years.

CAPITAL.—Ψ Georgetown. Estimated population, including environs, 168,000. Other towns are: Linden (population 29,000); Ψ New Amsterdam (population 23,000); Corriverton (population 17,000).

FLAG.—Red triangle with black border, pointing from hoist to fly, on a yellow triangle with white border, all on a green field.

President.—His Excellency Arthur Chung, *elected for a six-year term*, March 17, 1970.

CABINET

Prime Minister, L. F. S. Burnham.
Deputy Prime Minister and Minister of National Development and Agriculture, Dr. P. A. Reid.
Finance, F. E. Hope.
Economic Development, H. D. Hoyte.
Education, C. L. Baird.
Health, Dr. O. M. R. Harper.
Works and Housing, S. S. Naraine.
Labour, W. G. Carrington.
Information and Culture, Miss S. M. Field-Ridley.
Co-operatives and National Mobilization, H. Green.
Energy and Natural Resources, H. O. Jack.
Agriculture, G. B. Kennard.
Foreign Affairs and Justice, S. S. Ramphel.
Trade and Consumer Protection, G. A. King.
Parliamentary Affairs and Leader of the House, B. C. Ramsaroop.
Ministers of State, O. E. Clarke; V. Haynes; A. Salim; P. P. Duncan; M. Zaheeruddeen; F. U. A. Carmichael; M. Kasim; C. V. Mingo; C. A. Nascimento.

GUYANA HIGH COMMISSION

3 Palace Court, Bayswater Road, W.2
[01–229 7684]
High Commissioner, His Excellency Sir John Carter.

BRITISH HIGH COMMISSION

44 Main Street (P.O. Box 625),
Georgetown
High Commissioner, His Excellency Peter Gautrey, C.M.G., C.V.O. (1975).

JUDICATURE

The Supreme Court of Judicature consists of a Court of Appeal and a High Court. There are also Courts of Summary Jurisdiction. The Court of Appeal consists of the Chancellor as President, the Chief Justice and such number of Justices of Appeal as may be prescribed by Parliament.

The High Court consists of the Chief Justice, as President, and nine Puisne Judges. It is a court with unlimited jurisdiction in civil matters and exercises exclusive jurisdiction in probate, divorce and admiralty, and certain other matters. It also sits as a Full Court of the High Court of the Supreme Court of Judicature comprising not less than 2 Puisne Judges and then its jurisdiction is almost entirely appellate.

Production, etc.—Much of the country is forest. The cultivated portion (about 600,000 acres, of which 107,182 are under sugar-cane and 316,950 in rice) is largely confined to the narrow coastal alluvial belt. There are extensive deposits of gold, diamonds, bauxite and mica.

Communications.—The Georgetown Automatic Exchange had 7,900 direct extension lines in 1972, involving 12,913 telephones. Twenty-six subsidiary exchanges provided a total of 1,465 direct exchange lines with 2,181 telephone stations. Thirty-nine land-line telegraph stations are maintained at coastal post offices and telegraph stations in the interior, providing communications with the coast. In Georgetown a central radio station, operated by the Guyana Telecommunication Corporation, provides radio-telephone communication with 5 branch offices, 20 stations operated by other Government departments, and 48 by private concerns. Overseas telephone, telex and telegraph services are provided by Cable and Wireless (W.I.) Ltd. in association with the Guyana Telecommunications Corporation. At the end of 1972 there were 50 district post offices (including two mobile post offices) at which all classes of postal business were transacted. There are two broadcasting stations operated on a commercial basis. There are 18 miles of railway and the Guyana Airways Corporation provides internal and coastal air services.

Education.—At the end of the school year 1971–72 there were 390 primary schools with 130,671 pupils receiving first level education, or 81·27 per cent. of the 6–12 age group. Secondary education is offered in three types of school, 31 government-owned, 13 government-aided and approximately 50 privately-owned schools. In August 1972 there were 61,747 pupils receiving secondary education in government schools. This enrolment represented 45·4 per cent of the 12–17 age group. There were also about 10,000 pupils in private institutions.

The University of Guyana is the only institution which provides higher education. In 1971–72 1,232 students were enrolled in the Faculties of Arts, Natural Science, Social Science, Technical Studies and Education as well as in first-year studies in Law and in Diploma and Certificate courses. There are four established technical institutions: Georgetown and New Amsterdam Technical Institutes, the Carnegie School of Home Economics and the Guyana Industrial Training Centre. Besides these, there are 20 Home Economics and Industrial Arts Centres in various parts of the country. There are also Home Economics and Industrial Arts Department in many primary and secondary schools. Government trains teachers for both primary and secondary schools.

It was estimated that in 1973 the Government would spend G$35,200,000 on education, of which G$8,200,000 would be spent on building new schools and improving existing schools.

FINANCE

	1973	1974*
Revenue	G$257,931,000	G$397,196,000
Expenditure	294,736,000	367,727,000
Public debt (Dec. 31, 1973)		381,900,000

*Estimates.

TRADE

	1972	1973
Total imports	G$297,881,000	G$320,245,000
Total exports	289,162,000	247,448,000

The leading exports are bauxite, sugar, alumina, rice, balata, rum, timber, molasses and diamonds.

India

AREA AND POPULATION.—The land area of the Republic of India is 1,261,816 sq. miles, and the population at the census of 1971, was 547,949,809.

FLAG.—The National Flag is a horizontal tricolour with bands of deep saffron, white and dark green in equal proportions. On the centre of the white band appears an Asoka wheel in navy blue.

CAPITAL.—Delhi (population in 1971 was 4,065,698).

NATIONAL DAY.—January 26 (Republic Day).

President of the Republic of India, Fakhruddin Ali Ahmed, *born* 1905, *elected* Aug. 20, 1974.
Vice-President, B. D. Jatti.

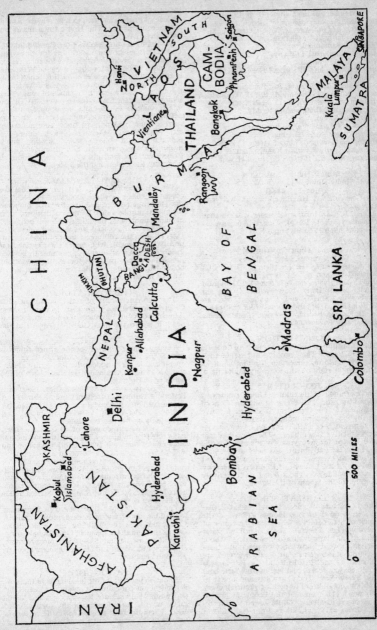

Members of the Cabinet (Feb. 1975)

Prime Minister and Minister of Atomic Energy, Information and Broadcasting, Mrs. Indira Gandhi.
External Affairs, Y. B. Chavan.
Finance, C. Sabramaniam.
Railways, Kamlapati Tripathy.
Defence, Swaran Singh.
Parliamentary Affairs, Works and Housing, K. Raghu Ramaiah.
Tourism and Civil Aviation, Raj Bahadur.
Law and Justice and Company Affairs, H. R. Gokhale.
Petroleum and Chemicals, K. D. Malaviyah.
Home Affairs, K. Brahmanand Reddy.
Industry, T. A. Pai.
Irrigation and Agriculture, Jagjivan Ram.
Communications, S. D. Sharma.
Shipping and Transport, Uma Shankar Dikshit.
Health and Family Planning, Karan Singh.
Education and Social Welfare, S. Nurul Hassan.

INDIAN HIGH COMMISSION

India House, Aldwych, W.C.2.
[01–836 8484]
High Commissioner, His Excellency B. K. Nehru (1973).
Ministers, R. M. Honavar (*Economics*); J. Abraham (*Consular*); Prof. R. N. Dogra (*Education and Scientific Affairs*); Sarup Singh Puri (*Supply*).

BRITISH HIGH COMMISSION

Chanakyapuri, New Delhi, 21.
High Commissioner, His Excellency Sir (Charles) Michael Walker, K.C.M.G. (1974).
British Council Representative in India, S. E. Hodgson, O.B.E., 21 Jor Bagh, New Delhi. Offices also at *Bombay, Madras* and *Calcutta*. There are British Council libraries at these four centres and at *Bangalore, Bhopal, Lucknow, Panta, Poona, Ranchi* and *Trivandrum*.

CONSTITUTION

The Constitution of India came into force on January 26, 1950. The Constitution provides for a single and uniform citizenship for the whole of India, with the right of vote for every adult citizen.

EXECUTIVE

The executive of the Indian Union consists of the President, the Vice-President and the Council of Ministers. The President is elected for five years by an electoral college consisting of all elected members of Parliament and of the various State Legislative Assemblies. The Vice-President is also elected for five years by members of the two Houses of Parliament. As head of the State the President exercises his functions with the aid and advice of the Council of Ministers headed by the Prime Minister. The Council is collectively responsible to the House of the People.

LEGISLATURE

The Legislature of the Union is called Parliament. It consists of two Houses known as the Council of States (*Rajya Sabha*) and the House of the People (*Lok Sabha*). The Council of States consists of not more than 250 members, of whom 12, having special knowledge or practical experience in literature, science, art or social service, are nominated by the President and the rest are indirectly elected representatives of the State and Union Territories. The Council is not subject to dissolution, one-third of its members retiring every two years. The House of the People at present consists of 524 members. Of these, 506 are directly elected from 21 States and 15 from eight Union Territories. One member is nominated by the

President to represent the Union Territory of Arunachal Pradesh and two to represent the Anglo-Indian community. The House has a maximum duration of five years.

Subject to the provisions of the Constitution the Union Parliament can make laws for the whole of India and the State legislatures for their respective units. The distribution of legislative powers is governed by a system of three lists—the Union, the State and the Concurrent—under which all legislative activity has been mapped out. The Union Parliament has exclusive powers to legislate on 97 subjects of all-India importance, such as defence, foreign affairs, communications, railways, currency and banking, insurance, customs duties, etc. The State List contains 66 headings, *e.g.* public order and police, justice, education, public health, local government, agriculture, etc. The Concurrent List contains 47 subjects of common interest to the Union and the States.

OFFICIAL LANGUAGE

The Constitution (Art. 343) provides that the official language of the Union shall be Hindi in the Devanagari script and the form of numerals for official purposes shall be the international form of Indian numerals. English, which was originally to continue as the official language for a period of 55 years from the commencement of the Constitution (January 1950), will, under the Official Language Act, 1963, as amended, continue to be used for all the official purposes for which it was used before Jan. 26, 1965, and also for the transaction of business in Parliament.

THE JUDICATURE

The Supreme Court of India, consisting of a Chief Justice and not more than 13 other judges; is the highest court in respect of constitutional matters. It is also the final Court of Appeal in the country.

DEFENCE

The supreme command of the armed forces is vested in the President. Administrative and operational control resides in the Army, Navy and Air Headquarters under the supervision of the Ministry of Defence.

The Army has five Commands, Southern, Eastern, Northern, Western and Central. A Territorial Force was inaugurated in Oct. 1949. A National Cadet Corps, with senior, junior, and girls' divisions, has also been raised.

The *Indian Navy* consists of an aircraft-carrier, two cruisers, a number of frigate squadrons, including some of the latest type of anti-submarine and anti-aircraft frigates, a squadron of anti-submarine patrol vessels, a minesweeping squdron, conventional type submarines, a submarine depot ship and fast boats carrying surface-to-surface guided missiles. A Naval aviation wing and a hydrographic office have also been set up. India has started building her own naval craft.

The *Indian Air Force* is organized in five major formations, the Western, Eastern and Central Air Commands, and the Training and Maintenance Commands and an independent Operational Group. Aircraft in use include SU-7, Vampire, Mystère, Hunter, Gnat, Mig 21 and HF24; Canberra bomber, helicopter and training planes.

PRODUCTION

About 70 per cent. of the inhabitants of India are dependent on agricultural pursuits. Most of the agricultural holdings are less than 5 acres. Food grains occupy three-fourths of the total cropped area. There are about 176,000,000 cattle, or about a quarter of the world's cattle population.

Production of Principal Crops, 1972–73

Crop	Production ('ooo tonnes)
Rice	38,633
Jowar	6,442
Bajra	3,795
Maize	6,206
Wheat	24,923
Barley	2,327
Ragi	1,913
Small millets	1,474
Pulses	9,488
Total food grains	95,201
Ground-nuts (in shell)	3,924
Castor seed	136
Sesamum	356
Rape and mustard	1,853
Linseed	4,399
Cotton (lint)	5,489
Jute (dry fibre)	4,978
Sugar-cane	123,968
Tobacco	364
Tea	450
Potatoes	4,473

'ooo bales.

Industrial

The output of coal in 1972–73 was 793 lakh tonnes: iron ore 240 lakh tonnes; finished steel 50·8 lakh tonnes; aluminium 174,800 tonnes; cement 155 lakh tonnes; machine tools Rs.62·60 crores; automobiles (commercial vehicles, passenger cars, etc.) 89,700; diesel engines (stationary) 93,500; sewing machines 345,000; sulphuric acid 1,206,000 tonnes; fertilizers 1,384,000 tonnes; petroleum products (refined), 178 lakh tonnes; cotton cloth 792·4 crore metres; cotton yarn, 97·2 crore kg.; rayon yarn 113,000 tonnes.

TRADE
Distribution of Trade, 1972–73

	Imports Rs. lakhs	Exports Rs. lakhs
United Kingdom	22,549	17,253
U.S.A.	22,459	27,574
U.S.S.R.	10,572	30,482
Germany (Federal Republic).	16,072	6,228
Italy	3,560	4,885
Netherlands	3,511	3,540
France	3,690	4,590
Japan	17,022	21,716
Australia	3,239	2,598
Canada	10,507	2,820
Kenya	632	550
Czechoslovakia	1,552	4,610
Egypt	2,887	3,172
Burma	185	436

Trade with U.K.

	1973	1974
Imports from U.K.	£132,911,000	£127,133,000
Exports to U.K.	148,609,000	203,330,000

Imports from All Countries, 1972–73

	Rs. lakhs
Petroleum products	1,521
Machinery other than electric	38,498
Copper	4,865
Metal manufactures	1,713
Electric machinery and appliances	12,399
Medicinal and pharmaceutical products	2,299
Transport equipment	8,711
Chemical elements and compounds	8,890
Textile yarn and thread	327
Raw cotton	9,088
Rice	1,071
Wheat, unmilled	4,816

Exports to All Countries, 1972–73

	Rs. lakhs
Iron and steel	4,176
Cotton manufactures (excluding twist and yarn)	12,671
Iron ore and concentrates	10,979
Textile yarn and thread	3,710
Fresh fruits and nuts (excluding oil nuts)	7,271
Vegetable oils (non-essential)	2,463
Leather	17,045
Jute manufacture (excluding twist and yarn)	24,719
Coffee	3,293
Tea	14,729
Tobacco, unmanufactured	6,107
Floor coverings	2,020
Petroleum products	1,318

FINANCE

The budget estimates for 1974–75, as presented in the Lok Sabha on Feb. 28, 1974, placed expenditure (on revenue account) at Rs.54,07,88 lakhs including States' share of union excise duties as compared to Rs.49,54,75 lakhs (revised) in 1973–74 and revenue at Rs.54,54,76 lakhs as compared to Rs.51,02,95 lakhs (revised) in the previous year, resulting in a surplus of Rs.46,88 lakhs.

Revenue

Tax Revenue	1972–73 (Revised estimate) (in thousands of rupees)	1973–74 (Budget estimate)
Customs	8,10,00,00	9,76,00,00
Union excise duties	24,28,18,00	27,03,42,00
Corporation tax	5,58,00,00	6,08,00,00
Taxes on income	1,09,61,42	1,34,73,06
Estate duty	7,74,40	45,95
Taxes on wealth	43,00,00	43,00,00
Expenditure tax	1,36	..
Gift tax	3,75,00	3,50,00
Other heads	83,59,58	81,96,07
	40,37,89,76	45,51,07,08
Non-Tax Revenue		
Interest receipts	7,19,83,45	7,71,04,81
Administrative services	14,68,80	14,68,76
Social and developmental services	63,79,44	58,22,81
Multipurpose river schemes	10,73,36	16,87,20
Transport and communications	13,87,88	15,08,67
Public Works	7,47,21	7,43,80
Currency and mint	1,46,96,97	1,54,56,71
Miscellaneous	1,19,83,81	50,63,12
Contribution and miscellaneous adjustments	27,54,41	34,35,35
Extraordinary items	9,59,30	3,00,02

Expenditure

	1972–73 (Revised estimate) (in thousands of rupees)	1973–74 (Budget estimate)
Taxes and duties	58,00,72	63,46,30
Debt services	7,68,63,72	8,34,84,60
Administrative services	2,73,87,81	2,79,44,31
Social and developmental services	4,40,81,97	4,58,67,33
Multipurpose river schemes	19,00,24	32,92,86
Public works, etc.	46,91,54	46,95,85
Transport and communications	25,76,62	26,70,85
Currency and mint	21,08,83	20,62,58
Miscellaneous	5,17,10,36	6,75,94,16

Contributions and miscel-		
laneous adjustments	15,70,74,59	15,12,70,44
Extraordinary items.	10,58,95	10,40,35
Defence Services(net).	14,04,13,73	14,04,82,00

Banks and Banking.—The number of scheduled banks was 74 and the number of offices of banks was 15,362 in June 1973. The total credit at the end of 1973 was *Rs.* 6,864 crores.

COMMUNICATIONS

Civil Aviation.—India occupies an important place in civil aviation among the nations of the world. All air lines were nationalized in 1953 and two corporations formed, Indian Airlines and Air India.

Four international aerodromes are managed by the International Airports Authority. The other 84 aerodromes are controlled and operated by the Civil Aviation Department of the Government.

Railways.—The railways are grouped into nine administrative zones, Southern, Central, Western, Northern, North-Eastern, North-East Frontier, Eastern, South-Eastern and South-Central.

Gross Traffic Receipts (1972–73), crores of rupees 1143·10. Working expenses, 935,14. Net railway revenues, 192,23.

Ψ*Ports.*—The chief seaports are Bombay, Calcutta, Madras, Mormugao, Cochin, Visakhapatnam, Kandla, Paradip, Mangalore and Tuticorin. There are 167 intermediate and minor ports with varying capacity.

Shipping.—On April 1, 1974 274 ships totalling 30 90 lakh gross tons were on the Indian Register.

Postal.—On March 31, 1974, there were 116,804 post offices, and 1,629,000 telephones.

Jamaica

Jamaica is situated in the Caribbean Sea south of the eastern extremity of Cuba and lies between latitudes 17° 43′ and 18° 32′ North, and longitude 76° 11′ and 78° 21′ West. The island was discovered by Columbus on May 4, 1494, and occupied by the Spanish from 1509 until 1655 when a British expedition, sent out by Oliver Cromwell, under Admiral Penn and General Venables, attacked the island, which capitulated after a trifling resistance. In 1670 it was formally ceded to England by the Treaty of Madrid. Jamaica became an independent state within the British Commonwealth on August 6, 1962.

Area and Population.—Jamaica is 4,411 square miles in area and is divided into three counties (Surrey, Middlesex and Cornwall) and 14 parishes. The surface of the island is extremely mountainous, the highest peak being 7,402 ft. above sea level. The greatest length from east to west (Morant Point to Negril Point) is 146 miles and the extreme breadth 51 miles. At Dec. 31, 1974 Jamaica's population was estimated to be 2,025,000. Jamaica for climatic and other reasons is a popular tourist resort, attracting visitors mainly from the U.S.A. The total number of visitor arrivals in 1974 was 541,304. Tourist expenditure in 1974 was estimated at J$121.2 millions.

Physical Features.—The topography consists mainly of coastal plains, divided by the Blue Mountain Range in the east, and the hills and limestone plateaux which occupy the central and western areas of the interior. The central chain of high peaks of the Blue Mountains is over 6,000 feet above sea level, and the Blue Mountain Peak, the highest of these, reaches an elevation of 7,402 feet. The rivers flow down from the central mountainous area. Most of the rivers are narrow and fast flowing, and some have rapids. In general those flowing south are longer and are fed by more tributaries than those flowing north. None is navigable except the Black River, and that only for small craft.

CAPITAL.—The seat of government is Kingston, the largest town and seaport (estimated population of the Corporate area of Kingston and St. Andrew in 1971, 572,653). Other towns are Montego Bay (42,800) and Spanish Town (41,600).

FLAG.—Gold diagonal cross forming triangles of green at top and bottom, triangles of black at hoist and in fly. NATIONAL DAY.—First Monday in August (Independence Day).

GOVERNMENT

The Legislative consists of a Senate of 21 nominated members and a House of Representatives consisting of 53 members elected by universal adult suffrage. The number of members cannot be fewer than 45 nor more than 60. The Senate has no power to delay money bills for longer than one month or other bills for longer than seven months against the wishes of the House of Representatives. The Constitution provides for a Leader of the Opposition.

Governor-General, His Excellency Florizel Glasspole.

CABINET

Prime Minister and Minister for External Affairs, Hon. M. N. Manley.
Deputy Prime Minister and Minister of Finance, Hon. D. H. Coore, Q.C.
Industry, Tourism and Foreign Trade, Hon. P. J. Patterson.
Education, Hon. H. F. Cooke.
Pensions and Social Security, Hon. W. V. Jones.
Minister of State, and Leader of Government in the Senate, Senator Hon. D. J. Thompson, Q.C.
Agriculture and Leader of Government Business in the House of Representatives, Hon. K. A. Munn.
Mining and National Resources, Hon. A. St. A. Isaacs.
Health and Environmental Control, Dr. Hon. K. A. McNeill.
Labour and Employment, Hon. E. G. Peart.
Works, Hon. S. R. Pagon.
National Security and Justice, Hon. E. J. Matalon.
Public Utilities, Communications and Transport, Hon. E. C. Bell.

Local Government, Hon. Mrs. R. A. Leon.
Housing, Hon. A. Spaulding.
Ministers of State, Senator D. Manley; Senator C. Rattray.

Speaker, House of Representatives, Hon. R. McPherson.

JAMAICAN HIGH COMMISSION
48 Grosvenor Street, W.1
[01–499 8600]
High Commissioner, His Excellency Dr. Arthur S. Wint, C.D., M.B.E.
BRITISH HIGH COMMISSION
P.O. Box 628, 58 Duke Street, Kingston
High Commissioner, His Excellency John Dunn Hennings, C.M.G. (1973)................£6,875

JUDICATURE
Chief Justice and Keeper of Records, Hon. K. G. Smith.

Judges of the Court of Appeal, Hon. Sir Joseph Luckhoo (*President*); Hons. L. H. Graham-Perkin, C.D.; R. M. Hercules; W. H. Swaby; L. B. Robinson; E. Zacca (*acting*); E. W. Watkins (*acting*).

Puisne Judges, Hons. U. N. Parnell (*Senior Puisne Judge*); V. L. Lopez; V. C. Melville; K. C. Henry; L. Robotham; I. D. Rowe; W. B. Wilkie; H. V. T. Chambers; C. A. B. Ross; R. O. C. White; V. K. G. McCarthy; V. O. Malcolm; W.D. Marsh; B. Carey (*acting*).

COMMUNICATIONS

There are several excellent harbours, Kingston being the principal port. The island is intersected by 2,730 miles of main road, of which 1,890 are asphalted. There are 297 miles of railway open. Telegraph stations and post offices are established in every town and in very many villages.

There are two international airports capable of handling the largest civil jet aircraft, the Norman Manley Airport on the south coast serving Kingston, and the Donald Sangster Airport on the north coast serving the major tourist areas. In addition there are licensed aerodromes at Port Antonio, Ocho Rios and Mandeville, which are used by Jamaica Air Service on scheduled domestic flights. There are nearly 40 private airstrips.

Air Jamaica, the national airline formed by the Government of Jamaica in association with Air Canada, operates scheduled services between the U. K., Canada, U. S.A., Nassau and Jamaica. Eleven other international carriers provide air communication with Europe, North, Central and South America and the Caribbean islands. They are: British Airways, British West Indian Airways, Air Canada, Pan American World Airways, K.L.M., Delta, Lufthansa, Cayman Airways, Mexicana Airlines, Eastern Airlines, TACA International Airlines and Swissair.

Scheduled internal routes are operated by Jamaica. Air Services Ltd. There is also an air taxi service.

PRODUCTION

Most of the staple products of tropical climates are grown. Sugar and rum are manufactured and exported (the latter is still counted the best in the world), and fine quality coffee is grown in certain areas of the Blue Mountains. Sugar production in 1974 amounted to 366,000 tons. There is trade in fruits, chiefly bananas, with U.K. Citrus, cocoa, coffee, pimento and ginger are important export crops. Jamaica has developed a breed of dairy cattle known as Jamaica Hope and a beef breed, the Jamaica Black. Jamaica is the second largest producer of bauxite in the world; output for 1974 was 15,086,000 tons. The bauxite deposits are worked by one of Canadian and five U.S. companies; the Canadian company and a consortium of the U.S. companies process bauxite into alumina. Further expansion of the industry is in progress. Gypsum is also mined, production in 1974 being 204,500 tons. Cement is manufactured locally, the output of the factory being 392,800 tons in 1974. The Esso Oil Refinery is designed to process 26,000 barrels of crude oil daily. The Jamaica Industrial Development Corporation is responsible for implementing the Government's industrial development programme. This Corporation administers incentive legislation which was enacted to stimulate the establishment of industries locally. In addition to undertaking promotional activities both locally and abroad, the Corporation maintains offices in the United States and the United Kingdom. In the last decade, manufacturing has grown from the processing of a few agricultural products into the production of a whole new range of commodities dependent on both local and foreign raw materials.

FINANCE

	1972–73	1973–74
Revenue	£145,000,000	£177,500,000
Expenditure	187,000,000	235,550,000
Public Debt	167,000,000	241,000,000

TRADE

	1972	1973
Total imports	£247,500,000	£302,000,000
Total exports	150,000,000	174,000,000

	1973	1974
Imports from U.K.	£50,469,000	£50,122,000
Exports to U.K.	40,200,000	46,704,000

Chief Exports (1973).—Bauxite and alumina, £113,650,000; sugar, rum and molasses, £19,700,000; bananas, £8,200,000; citrus, coffee, pimento, ginger, £6,050,000; manufactured goods, £14,300,000; clothing, £2,300,000; mineral fuels, etc., £4,100,000.

Kenya

Kenya is bisected by the equator and extends approximately from latitude 4° N. to latitude 4° S. and from longitude 34° E. to 41° E. From the coast of the Indian Ocean in the east, the borders of Kenya are with Somalia in the east and Ethiopia and Sudan in the north and north-west. To the west lie Uganda and Lake Victoria. On the south is Tanzania. The total area is 224,960 square miles (including 5,224 square miles of water). The population is estimated to be 12,934,000 and to be increasing by 3·5 per cent. annually. The country is divided into 7 Provinces (Nyanza, Rift Valley, Central, Coast, Western, Eastern and North-Eastern).

CAPITAL.—Nairobi, situated at latitude 2° S. and longitude 36° 49′ E. at 5,453 feet above sea level, covers an area of 266 sq. miles and has a population of about 509,000. It is 307 miles by road from Mombasa, the country's main port. ΨMombasa (246,000) possesses what is perhaps the finest harbour on the East Coast of Africa and is well served by shipping lines from Europe and Asia besides a frequent coastal service. Other centres are Nakuru (47,800), Kisumu (30,700), Eldoret (16,900), Thika (18,100) and Nanyuki (11,200).

Nairobi: transit from London about 25 days by sea; by air, 10 hrs.

FLAG.—Three equal horizontal bands of black over red over green; red and white spears and shield device in centre. NATIONAL DAY.—December 12.

GOVERNMENT

Kenya became an independent state and a member of the British Commonwealth on December 12, 1963, after six months of internal self-government. The national assembly consists of a single House of Representatives. Kenya became a Republic on Dec. 12, 1964. On July 4, 1974, the executive of the ruling Kenya African National Union decided that Swahili should become Kenya's official language, to be used in the National Assembly and in the country's administration, instead of English.

President, His Excellency Jomo Kenyatta, G.C.B., *elected* 1964; *re-elected* 1969.
Vice-President and Minister of Home Affairs, D. T. arap Moi.

CABINET

Minister of Finance and Economic Planning, M. Kibaki.
Defence, J. S. Gichuru.
Minister of State, Office of the President, M. Koinange.
Agriculture and Animal Husbandry, J. J. M. Nyagah.
Health, J. C. N. Osogo.
Local Government, P. J. Ngei.
Works, N. W. Munoko.
Labour, J. Nyamweya.
Education, Dr. Z. Onyonka.
Tourism and Wildlife, M. J. Ogutu.
Lands and Settlement, J. H. Angaine.
Housing, T. A. Towett.
Power and Communications, I. Omolo Okero.
Attorney-General, C. Njonjo.
Information and Broadcasting, D. M. Mutinda.
Foreign Affairs, Dr. Munyua Waiyaki.
Co-operative Development, R. S. Matano.
Water Development, E. T. Mwamunga.
Commerce and Industry, Dr. J. G. Kiano.
Natural Resources, S. S. Oloitiptip.

KENYA HIGH COMMISSION IN LONDON
45 Portland Place, W.1.
[01-636 2371]
High Commissioner, His Excellency Ng'ethe
Njoroge (1970).
BRITISH HIGH COMMISSION
Bruce House, Standard Street, P.O. Box 30465
Nairobi
High Commissioner, His Excellency Stanley James
Gunn Fingland, C.M.G. (1975).
Deputy High Commissioner, M. P. V. Hannam,
M.V.O. P.O. Box 90360, Mombasa.
First Secretary, T. J. Sigsworth.
British Council Representative, S. R. Smith, P.O.
Box 40751, Kenya Cultural Centre, University
Way, Nairobi. There are offices at *Kisumu* and
Mombasa.

JUDICATURE

Chief Justice, Sir James Wicks.
Puisne Judges, C. B. Madan, Q.C.; E. Trevelyan;
Chana Singh; C. H. E. Miller; A. H. Simpson;
L. G. E. Harris; K. G. Bennett; A. A. Kneller;
J. M. Waiyaki; M. G. Mull; A. R. Hancox;
J. G. Platt.
Registrar, Z. R. Chesoni.

Production.—Agriculture provides about 35 per
cent. of the national income. The great variation
in altitude and ecology provide conditions under
which a wide range of crops can be grown. These
include wheat, barley, pyrethrum, coffee, tea, sisal,
coconuts, cashew nuts, cotton, maize and a wide
variety of tropical and temperate fruits and vegetables. The total area of high potential land on
which concentrated alternate husbandry can be
practised amounts to only 16,761 sq. miles or 11·9
per cent. of the total land area. The remainder is
arid or semi-arid country suitable for stock raising.
In the areas of high potential, most of the old, large
scale farms, formerly farmed by Europeans, have
been bought by the Government for settlement of
landless people and for transfer to African large-
scale farmers.

In 1973 Kenya's forest area totalled 4,621,000
acres, of which 306,000 acres were under plantation.

Prospecting and mining are carried on in many
parts of the country, the principal minerals produced
being soda ash, salt and limestone. Major deposits
of fluorite and galena are now being exploited.
Small amounts of gold are also mined. Value
of all minerals produced in 1973 was £K3,445,000.

Hydro-electric power has been developed, particularly on the Upper Tana River. Owen Falls
Dam scheme in Uganda is connected to the Kenyan
system, and supplies about 30 per cent. of consumption. Work is in progress on the second stage
of the £37,000,000 Seven Forks Project which is
expected to provide 300 MW on completion in the
early 1980s.

There has been considerable industrial development over the last 15 years and Kenya has a wide
variety of industries processing agricultural
produce and manufacturing an increasing range of
products from local and imported raw materials.
New industries have recently come into being such
as steel, textile mills, dehydrated vegetable processing and motor tyre manufacture as well as many
smaller schemes which have added to the country's
already considerable consumer goods. There is an
oil refinery in Mombasa supplying both Kenya and
Uganda, and a fuel pipeline to Nairobi is expected
to open shortly. The market served comprises all
the East African territories and the volume of
exports to adjoining African and Indian Ocean
countries is increasing year by year. Industrial
areas have been developed in all the principal towns
and light industrial estates are being developed for
African *entrepreneurs*. The Kenya Government is
actively encouraging investment in the industrial
sector and has a Foreign Investments Protection
Act to protect such investments.

The main imports are manufactured goods, classified chiefly as materials, machinery and transport
equipment, mineral fuels, lubricants and related
fuels and chemicals.

Communications.—The East African Railways and
Harbours are self-contained and self-financing services of the East African Community; the railway,
which is metre gauge, has a total route mileage of
open line of 3,670 miles (1,270 miles in Kenya). In
addition the East African Railways operate a marine
service on Lakes Victoria and Tanganyika, with a
route mileage of 3,469 miles. There are also 2,367
miles of road services providing regular transport
to the Southern Highlands of Tanzania, and beyond
the railhead at Pakwach in Uganda. East African
Harbours control the four seaports of Mombasa,
Tanga, Dar-es-Salaam amd Mtwara. Mombasa,
Dar-es-Salaam and Mtwara have deep-water berths
and Tanga is a lighterage port.

Scheduled trunk airline services are operated to
and from Kenya, through Nairobi airport, by
East African Airways, British Airways, Air India,
Air France, Scandinavian Airlines System, British
Caledonian Airways, Alitalia, Pan Am, K.L.M.,
Ethiopian Airlines, El Al Israel Airlines, Pakistan
International Airlines, Lufthansa German Airlines,
Sabena, Swissair, Olympic Airways, T.W.A. and
Egyptair, while regional scheduled services are also
run by East African Airways, Ethiopian Airlines,
Air Zaire, Air Malawi, Zambia Airways, Sudan
Airways and Air Madagascar.

The country has approximately 26,000 miles of
road including 3,850 miles of trunk roads and 6,200
miles of secondary roads. There is a total of 2,318
miles of bitumen-surfaced roads, apart from town
streets, etc.

FINANCE

	1973-74	1974-75*
Revenue	K £235,500,000	K £261,130,000
Expenditure	234,960,000	276,690,000

*Estimated

The total public debt at June 30, 1969 was
K £75,111,068.

Trade.—A large part of Kenya's trade is with the
United Kingdom which in 1973 took 16 per cent.
of her exports and supplied 25 per cent. of Kenya's
imports (both figures excluding trade with Uganda

and Tanzania). The principal exports are coffee, tea, petroleum products, maize, meat products, pyrethrum flowers, powder and extract, and hides and skins.

Trade with U.K.	1973	1974
Imports from U.K....	£60,887,000	£78,681,000
Exports to U.K......	38,747,000	44,043,000

Lesotho

Lesotho is a landlocked state entirely surrounded by the Republic of South Africa. Of the total area of 11,716 sq. miles a belt between 20 and 40 miles in width lying across the western and southern boundaries and comprising about one-third of the total is classed as Lowlands, being between 5,000 and 6,000 ft. above sea level. The remaining two-thirds are classed as Foothills and Highlands, rising to 11,425 ft. The land is held in trust for the nation by the King. The population was estimated at 1,181,900 in April, 1975.

CAPITAL.—Maseru, population about 30,000.

FLAG.—Blue with conical white Basotho hat in centre, red and green vertical stripes (next staff).

Government.—Lesotho became a constitutional monarchy within the Commonwealth on October 4, 1966. The independence constitution was suspended in January, 1970, when the country was governed by a Council of Ministers, until the establishment of a National Assembly in April, 1974.

The country is divided into nine administrative districts. In each district there is a District Administrator who co-ordinates all Government activity in the area, working in co-operation with hereditary chiefs.

Judiciary.—The Lesotho Courts of Law consist of: the Court of Appeal, the High Court, Magistrates' Courts, Judicial Commissioners' Court, Central and local Courts. Magistrates' and higher courts administer the laws of Lesotho which are framed on the basis of the Roman–Dutch law. They also adjudicate appeals from the Judicial Commissioner's and Subordinate Courts.

Head of State, His Majesty King Moshoeshoe II.

CABINET

Prime Minister and Minister of Defence and Internal Security, Dr. Hon. Leabua Jonathan.

Deputy Prime Minister and Minister of Works and Communications, Hon. Chief Sekhonyana 'Maseribane.

Minister of Foreign Affairs, Hon. Joseph R. L. Kotsokoane.

Minister to the Prime Minister, Hon. Gabrial C. Manyali.

Finance, Hon. Evaristus R. Sekhonyana.

Health and Social Welfare, Hon. Patrick Mota.

Interior, Hon. Julius Monaleli.

Justice, Hon. Charles D. Molapo.

Agriculture, Hon. Khetla T. J. Rakhetla.

Commerce and Industry, Hon. Joel R. M. Moitse.

Education and Cultural Affairs, Hon. Anthony S. Ralebitso.

———

Chief Justice, Hon. Joseph T. Mapetla.

LESOTHO HIGH COMMISSION
16A St. James's Street (1st Floor), S.W.1
[01–839 1154]
High Commissioner, His Excellency P. M. 'Mabathoana (1973).

BRITISH HIGH COMMISSION
P.O. Box 521, Maseru
High Commissioner, His Excellency Martin John Moynihan, C.M.G., M.C. (1973)
British Council Representative, G. A. Tindale, Hobson's Square, P.O. Box 429, Maseru.

Education.—There are 1,083 primary schools with 218,038 pupils enrolled in 1974, 58 secondary schools with 14,908 students and 7 teacher training colleges, with 383 trainees. There are also two main vocational training schools with 180 students and a training centre for civil servants. There is an Agricultural College with 120 students. The University of Botswana, Lesotho and Swaziland has its headquarters in Lesotho.

Health Services.—There are nine Government General hospitals, the largest being the Queen Elizabeth II Hospital in Maseru, one mental hospital, eight Mission hospitals and a leprosarium as well as 85 health centres and clinics run by Government, Missions and other voluntary organizations.

Communications.—The main north–south road of about 330 km (of which 176 km are bituminised) links Maseru and the lowlands. The mountainous areas are linked by a 1,200 km network of access tracks which are normally only suitable for four-wheel drive vehicles. Gravel roads link border towns in South Africa with the main towns in Lesotho. There is also an extensive network of about 900 km of gravel roads serving the lowlands and foothill areas, with about 1,000 km of bridle paths in the mountains. Maseru is connected by rail with the main Bloemfontein–Durban line of the South African Railways. Scheduled international services are operated three times a week between Maseru and Johannesburg. There are 32 airstrips. Internal scheduled services are operated by the Lesotho Airways Corporation. The telephone network is fully automated in all urban centres. Subscribers can dial direct to telephone exchanges in South Africa. Similar facilities exist for telex subscribers, who can also dial direct to a number of overseas countries. Radio telephone communication is used extensively in the remote rural areas.

Agricultural Production.—The economy of Lesotho is mainly agrarian. At the last enumeration livestock numbers were: cattle 465,500, sheep 1,556,900, goats 961,900, horses 114,000, poultry 578,800, 4,764,158 kg. of wool valued at R3,451,776 and 678,003 kg. of mohair valued at R1,589,162 were exported in 1974. Five large scale integrated agricultural development projects amounting to R25,330,000 are being implemented for increasing agricultural production, with emphasis on cash crops and livestock.

Finance, Trade and Industry.—The main sources of revenue are customs and excise duty. Estimates of expenditure and revenue for 1975–6 are: Recurrent Account, R25,000,000, Capital Account R16,500,000. Lesotho has few known and developed natural resources but it is intended to develop commercially the mineral resources of water and diamonds (the value of diamond exports for 1974–5 is R845,573). Drilling is being carried out for oil. Tourism is being developed and is rapidly playing a major role in the economic progress of the country. A National Park has been established at Sehlabathebe in the Maluti mountains. A number of light industries have recently been established. They include the manufacture of clothing, tapestries, carpets, sheepskin products, jewellery, pharmaceuticals, bricks and building materials; together with milling, diamond cutting and tractor assembly.

Malawi

MALAWI, formerly the Nyasaland Protectorate, comprises Lake Malawi (formerly Lake Nyasa) and its western shore, with the high table-land separating it from the basin of the Luangwa River, the watershed forming the western frontier with Zambia; south of the lake, Malawi reaches almost to the Zambesi and is surrounded by Mozambique) the frontier lying on the west on the watershed of the Zambesi and Shire Rivers, and to the east on the Ruo, a tributary of the Shire, and Lakes Chiuta and Chilwa. This boundary reaches the eastern shore of Lake Malawi and extends up to the mid-point of the lake for about half its length where it returns to the eastern and northern shores to form a frontier with Tanzania.

Malawi has a total area of 45,411 sq. miles (land area, 36,145). The population of Malawi at the Census of August, 1966, was 4,039,583 (52 per cent. female); estimated, 1974, 4,916,000.

CAPITAL.—Lilongwe (population 87,000). The city of Blantyre, incorporating Blantyre and Limbe, is the major commercial and industrial centre and headquarters of the Southern region. Other main centres are: Mzuzu, headquarters of the Northern Region; Thyolo, Mulanje, Mangochi, Mzimba, Nkhota-kota and Zomba, the former capital.

FLAG.—Horizontal stripes of black, red and green, with rising sun in centre of the black stripe.

Government.—Malawi became a republic on July 6, 1966, having assumed internal self-government on February 1, 1963, and is a member of the Commonwealth. There is a Cabinet consisting of the President and other Ministers. The National Assembly consists of 75 members, each elected by universal suffrage. Under the Constitution Act, 1966, the President exercises power to nominate in addition up to fifteen members to represent special interests. Being a one-party State (the Malawi Congress Party), all elected members are required to be members of the Party. The Assembly, which usually meets three times a year, is presided over by a Speaker, who need not himself be a member of it.

President, Minister of External Affairs, Works and Supplies, Defence, Agriculture and National Resources, Hon Dr. H. Kamuzu Banda, *born* 1907, *elected* 1966, *sworn in as* President for Life, July 6, 1971.

CABINET

Minister of State in the President's Office, Hon. A. A. Muwalo Nqumayo.
Minister of Youth and Culture, Hon. G. C. Chakuamba Phiri.
Central Region, Hon. J. T. Kumbweza Banda.
Northern Region, Hon. M. M. Lungu.
Organization of African Unity Affairs, Hon. R. B. Chidzanja Nkhoma.
Finance and Trade, Industry and Tourism, Hon. D. T. Matenje.
Transport and Communications and Labour, Hon. W. B. Deleza.
Education, Hon. R. T. C. Munyenyembe.
Southern Region, Hon. P. L. Makhumula Nkhoma.
Minister of Justice and Attorney-General and Minister of Local Government, Hon. R. A. Banda.
Community Development and Social Welfare, Hon. D. Kainja Nthara.
Health, Hon. E. C. I. Bwanali.
Ministers without Portfolio, Hon. M. Q. Y. Chibambo, Hon. A. E. Gadama.

JUDICIARY

Chief Justice, J. J. Skinner.
Puisne Judges, L. Weston, L. A. Chatsikah.
Solicitor-General, D. R. Barwick.

MALAWI HIGH COMMISSION

47 Great Cumberland Place, W.1
[01–723 6021]
High Commissioner, His Excellency J. Kachingwe (1973).

BRITISH HIGH COMMISSION

Lingadzi Building (P.O. Box 30042), Lilongwe
High Commissioner, His Excellency Kenneth Gordon Ritchie, C.M.G. £12,000
Deputy High Commissioner, O. G. Griffith, O.B.E., M.V.O.
British Council Representative, Dr. G. Howell, P.O. Box 456, Glyn Jones Road, Blantyre. Libraries at *Blantyre, Lilongwe and Zomba.*
Education.—Primary education is the responsibility of local authorities in both urban and rural areas. About 35 per cent. of the population of school age can be taken into schools and only 10 per cent. of those successfully completing primary education can be placed in secondary schools. The Ministry is responsible for policy, school curricula, secondary education teachers' and technical training. Religious bodies, with Government assistance, still play an important part in primary and secondary education and teacher training. Further training is pursued at the University of Malawi, opened in September 1965. For the academic year 1973/74 there were 463 students studying for degrees and 632 for diplomas at the three constituent colleges.

Communications.—A single-track railway runs from the south-western area of Lake Malawi (itself served by two passenger and a number of cargo boats) through Blantyre to the southern frontier into Mozambique, crossing the Zambesi River by a bridge 12,050 feet long, and connecting with the Mozambique port of Beira, which handles the bulk of the country's imports and exports. In 1970 a 70-mile line was opened from Liwonde to Nayuci, linking the Malawi rail system with the Mozambique network to the port of Nacala. Plans are underway and funds are available for a new railway line from Salima through Lilongwe, to Mchinji, which is expected to be completed in 1976. A good class earth road system covers the whole country and is already bituminized from Mulanje through Blantyre and Zomba to Lilongwe, the new capital, and from there to the lakeshore at Salima, the northern terminus of the railway. Plans are under way for a bituminized road from Blantyre to the Mozambique border and onwards to Tete and Salisbury, Rhodesia.

FINANCE

	1972–3	1973–4
Revenue	K56,900,000	K63,100,000
Expenditure	56,100,000	61,700,000

(excluding Development Account)
Decimal currency was introduced on Feb. 15, 1971. The unit is the *kwach* (=50p. sterling), divided into 100 *tambala.*

TRADE

	1973	1974
Imports	K114,900,000	K154,000,000
Exports	79,900,000	101,500,000
	1973	1974
Imports from U.K.	K28,500,000	K34,600,000
Exports to U.K.	26,700,000	30,400,000

Agriculture is the country's mainstay, the principal exports being tea, tobacco, cotton and groundnuts. The value of exports of these crops in 1974 was: tea, K16,908,000; tobacco, K39,125,000; groundnuts, K4,922,000; maize K680,000; cotton K3,023,000. sugar, K7,180,000 Other agricultural exports include tung oil, rice, sisal, casava, coffee and dried vegetables. A total of K78,511,000 of crops was exported in 1974. Imports are mainly clothing materials, vehicles, fuels and machinery.

Malaysia

Malaysia, comprising Malaya, Sabah and Sarawak, forms a crescent well over 1,000 miles long between latitudes 1° and 7° North latitude and longitudes 100° and 119° East. It occupies two distinct regions—the Malay Peninsula which extends from the Isthmus of Kra to the Singapore Strait and the North-West Coastal area of the Island of Borneo. Each is separated from the other by 400 miles of the South China Sea.

Area and Population.—The total area of the 13 states of Malaysia, including the Federal Territory of Kuala Lumpur (94 sq. miles) is estimated to be 130,000 sq. miles, containing a population of 10,434,034 at the Census of Housing and Population of Malaysia held in 1970. Details of individual states appear on p. 201.

Climate.—The whole region is open to maritime influences and is subject to the interplay of wind systems which originate in the Indian Ocean and the South China Sea. The year is commonly divided into the Southwest and Northeast monsoon seasons. Rainfall averages about 100 inches throughout the year, though the annual fall varies from place to place. The average daily temperature throughout Malaysia varies from 70° Fahrenheit to 90° Fahrenheit, though in higher areas temperatures are lower and vary widely.

CAPITAL.—Kuala Lumpur was proclaimed Federal Territory on February 1, 1974. Its population is about 770,000. The chief town of Sarawak is ΨKuching, and of Sabah is ΨKota Kinabalu.

Bahasa Malaysia (Malay) is the national language. In Sarawak English will continue as an official language as well as Bahasa Malaysia until 1979, when the Sarawak State Council will review the position.

RELIGION.—Islam is the official religion of Malaysia, each Ruler being the head of religion in his State, though the Heads of State of Sabah and Sarawak are not heads of the Muslim religion in their States. The Yang di-Pertuan Agung is the head of religion in Malacca and Penang. The Constitution guarantees religious freedom. NATIONAL DAY.—August 31 (*Hari Kebangsaan*).

FLAG.—Equal horizontal stripes of red (7) and white (7); 14 point yellow star and crescent in blue canton.

GOVERNMENT

The Federation of Malaya became an independent country within the Commonwealth on August 31, 1957, as a result of an agreement between H.M. the Queen and the Rulers of the Malay States, whereby Her Majesty relinquished all powers and jurisdiction over the Malay States and over the Settlements of Penang and Malacca which then became States of the Federation. On Sept. 16, 1963, the Federation was enlarged, by the accession of the further states of Singapore, Sabah (*formerly* British North Borneo) and Sarawak, and the name of MALAYSIA was adopted from that date. On Aug. 9, 1965, Singapore seceded from the Federation.

The Constitution was designed to ensure the existence of a strong Federal Government and also a measure of autonomy for the State Governments. It provides for a constitutional Supreme Head of the Federation (His Majesty the *Yang di-Pertuan Agung*) to be elected for a term of five years by the Rulers from among their number, and for a Deputy Supreme Head (His Royal Highness the *Timbalan Yang di-Pertuan Agung*) to be similarly elected. The Malay Rulers are either chosen or succeed to their position in accordance with the custom of the particular state. In other states of Malaysia choice of the Head of State is in the discretion of the *Yang di-Pertuan Agung* after consultation with the Chief Minister of the State. Save in certain instances provided in the Constitution, the Supreme Head acts in accordance with the advice of a Cabinet appointed by him from among the members of Parliament on the advice of the Prime Minister. The Supreme Head appoints as Prime Minister the person who in his judgement is likely to command the confidence of the majority of the members of the House of Representatives. He also has the powers to promulgate emergency ordinances. The National Operations Council was dissolved on February 19, 1971, and the Yang di-Pertuan Agung promulgated the reconvening of Parliamentary democracy the following day.

SUPREME HEAD OF MALAYSIA

His Majesty Tuanku Abdul Halim Mu'azam Shah, *b.* 1927, *assumed office for a term of 5 years*, Sept. 21, 1970. *Deputy Supreme Head of State*, His Royal Highness Tuanku Yahya Putra Ibni-Marhum Sultan Ibrahim (*Sultan of Kelantan*). (*Head of State from* Sept. 21, 1975.)

MINISTRY

Prime Minister, Minister of Foreign Affairs and of Finance, Tun Abdul Haji Razak bin Datak Hussein, G.C.M.G.

Deputy Prime Minister, Minister of Trade and Industry, Datak Hussein bin Onn.

Works and Power, Datuk Haji Abdul Ghani Gilong.

Labour and Manpower, Tan Sri V. Manickavasagam.

Agriculture and Fisheries, Tuan Sri Haji Mohammad Ghazali bin Haji Jawi.

Education, Tuan Haji Mohamed.

Health, Tan Sri Lee Siok Yew.

Culture, Youth and Sports, Encik Ali bin Haji Ahmad.

Technology and Research, Datuk Lee San Choon.

Sarawak Affairs, Ten Sri Temenggong Jugah anak Barieng.

Attorney-General, Tan Sri Abdul Kadir bin Yusoff.

Rural Economic Development, Encik Abdul Ghafar bin Baba.

Minister with Special Functions and Minister of Information, Tengku Ahmad Rithandeen Al-Haj bin Tengku Ismail.

National Unity, Tun V. T. Sambanthan.

Communications, Tan Sri Haji Sardon bin Haji Jubir.

Welfare Services, Puan Hajjah Aishah binti Haji Abdul.

Primary Industries, Datuk Haji Abdul Taib bin Mahmud.

Land Development and Special Functions, Datuk Haji Mohamed Asri bin Haji Muda.

Home Affairs, Tan Sri Muhammad Ghazali bin Shafie.

Local Government and Housing, Datuk Oug Kee Hui.

Defence, Datuk Hamzah bin Datuk Abu Sameh.

Special Functions, Encik Michael Chen Wing Sum.

Without Portfolio, Encik Mohamed Khir Johari.

NOTE.—The words "Tunku/Tengku". "Tun", "Tan Sri", and "Datuk" are titles. The word

"Tunka/Tengku" is equivalent to "Prince". "Tun" denotes membership of a high Order of Malaysian Chivalry and "Tan Sri" and "Datuk" ("Datu Sri" in Perak and "Datu" in Sabah) are each the equivalent of a knighthood. The wife of a "Tun" is styled "Toh Puan", that of a "Tan Sri" is styled "Puan Sri" and of a "Datuk" "Datin". The honorific "Tuan" or "Encik" is equivalent to "Mr." and the honorific "Puan" is equivalent to "Mrs." The words "Al-Haj" or "Haji" indicate that the person so named has made the pilgrimage to Mecca.

MALAYSIAN HIGH COMMISSION
45 Belgrave Square, S.W.1
[01-245 9221]
High Commissioner, His Excellency Datuk Abdallah Ali (1975).

BRITISH HIGH COMMISSION
Wisma Damansara, Jalan Semanton,
(P.O. Box 1030), Kuala Lumpur.
High Commissioner, His Excellency Sir Eric George Norris, K.C.M.G.
Deputy High Commissioner, A. J. M. Craig.

British Council Representative, R. Arbuthnott, Jalan Bukit Aman, Kuala Lumpur, and offices at *Penang, Kota Kinabalu* (Sabah) and *Kuching* (Sarawak).

LEGISLATURE

The Federal Parliament consists of two houses, the Senate and the House of Representatives. The Senate (*Dewan Negara*) consists of 58 members, under a President (*Yang di-Pertua Dewan Negara*), 26 elected by the Legislative Assemblies of the States (2 from each) and 32 appointed by the *Yang di-Pertuan Agung* from persons who have achieved distinction in major fields of activity or are representative of racial minorities, including the Aborigines. The House of Representatives (*Dewan Rakyat*), consists of 154 members (Peninsular Malaysia, 114; Sarawak, 24; and Sabah, 16). Members are elected on the principle of universal adult suffrage with a common electoral roll. The House of Representatives is presided over by a Speaker who is either a member of the House or is qualified to be elected as a member. *Speaker*, C. M. Yusoff.

The Constitution provides that each State shall have its own Constitution not inconsistent with the Federal Constitution, with the Ruler or Governor acting on the advice of an Executive Council appointed on the advice of the *Menteri Besar* or Chief Minister and a single chamber Legislative Assembly. Three *ex officio* members sit in the Executive Council besides these elected members. They are the State Secretary, the State Legal Adviser and the State Financial Officer. The State Constitutions provide for the Ruler or Governor to appoint as *Menteri Besar* or Chief Minister, to preside over the Executive Council, a member of the Legislative Assembly who in his judgement is likely to command the confidence of the majority of the members of the Assembly. The Legislative Assemblies are fully elected on the same basis as the Federal Parliament.

Legislative powers are divided into a Federal List, a State List and a Concurrent List, with residual powers vested in the State Legislatures. The Federal List comprises broadly, external affairs, defence, civil and criminal law and justice, the machinery of government, finance, commerce and industry, communications and transport, power, education, medicine and labour and social security. The State List includes land, agriculture and fores-

try, local government and services and the machinery of state government. In the Concurrent List are, *inter alia*, social welfare, wild-life, animal husbandry, town and country planning, public health and drainage and irrigation.

A State of Emergency was declared after disturbances on May 13, 1969. As Parliament was not then sitting, the *Yang di-Pertuan Agung* did not summon Parliament and instead established the National Operations Council and Y.A.B. Tun Abdul Razak bin Dato Hussein, the then Deputy Prime Minister, was appointed Director of Operations vested with the executive authority of the Federation including the powers to make essential regulations. The *Yang di-Pertuan Agung* remained as the Supreme Head of Federation with powers to promulgate emergency ordinances.

JUDICATURE

The Judicial System consists of a Federal Court and two High Courts, one in Peninsular Malaysia and one for Sabah and Sarawak (sitting alternately in Kota Kinabalu and Kuching). The High Court in Peninsular Malaysia known as the High Court in Malaya has its principal registry in Kuala Lumpur while the High Court in Sabah/Sarawak known as the High Court in Borneo has its principal registry in Kuching.

The Federal Court comprises a President, the two Chief Justices of the High Courts and other judges. This court possesses appellate, original and advisory jurisdiction. In its capacity as an appellate court it has exclusive jurisdiction to determine appeals from the decisions of a High Court or of a judge thereof (except decisions of a High Court given by a registrar or other officer of the court and appealable under federal law to a judge of the Court). This appellate jurisdiction is subject to limitations imposed by or under federal law. It also has jurisdiction to determine disputes between the Federation and any of the States within the Federation, any challenge to the competence of the Federal or any State legislature to enact a particular law and any question as to the effect of any of the provisions of the Constitution which question has arisen in proceedings before another court. It also renders advisory opinions on questions referred to it by the *Yang di-Pertuan Agung* as regards the effect of any provisions of the Constitution which has arisen or is likely to arise.

Each of the High Courts consists of a Chief Justice and not less than 4 other judges. The Federal Constitution allows for a maximum of twelve such judges for Malaya and eight for Borneo. In Peninsular Malaysia the Subordinate Courts consist of the Sessions Courts and the Magistrates' Courts. In Sabah/Sarawak the Magistrates' Courts constitute the Subordinate Courts.

DEFENCE

The Malaysian Armed Forces consist of the Army, Navy and Air Force, together with volunteer forces for each arm. The defence of the country is largely borne by the army in its role of providing defence against external threat and counter-insurgency operations and also to assist the police in the performance of public order duties. The *Royal Malaysian Navy* (*RMN*) has the responsibility of defending the 3,000 miles of the country's coastline and maintaining constant patrol of 500 miles of the high seas that separate Sabah and Sarawak from the mainland. The *Royal Malaysian Air Force* (*RMAF*) is capable of providing close strategic and tactical support to the army and police in the defence and internal security of the country.

FINANCE

	1972	1973
Revenue.......	2,920,000,000	3,304,000,00
Expenditure....	3,068,000,000	3,285,000,00

PRODUCTION AND TRADE

The agricultural sector continues to be the mainstay of the Malaysian economy. However diversification of crops and rapid growth in the manufacturing sector has made Malaysia less vulnerable to fluctuations in the price of its primary crop, natural rubber.

Malaysia is the largest exporter of natural rubber, tin, palm oil and tropical hardwoods. Other major export commodities are manufactured and processed products, petroleum, coconut oil, bauxite, copra and tea.

Exports of the four major primary commodities: rubber, tin, palm oil and tropical hardwoods accounted for 63·3 per cent. of the total exports in 1973. With the rapid expansion in the manufacturing sector, Malaysia is also increasing her export of manufactured products.

Another commodity which is produced throughout Malaysia is rice, the staple food of Malaysians. Total output of *padi* in the 1973 season amounted to 1,281,000 metric tons. The level of self-sufficiency of rice has increased to 90 per cent. in Peninsular Malaysia. To achieve self-sufficiency, various measures aimed at increasing output and productivity are being introduced. They include wider use of improved seeds and fertilizers, expansion of double-cropping through the provisions of large-scale irrigation schemes and research programmes to improve rice yields.

Imports in 1973 consisted mainly of machinery and transport equipment, manufactured goods, food, mineral fuels, chemicals and inedible crude materials for her growing population and to accelerate the pace of her economic growth and development.

	1972 M'000,000	1973 M'000,000
Imports.........	4,538·2	5,899·1
Exports.........	4,854·1	7,372·2
Balance of trade..	+315·9	+1,473·1

Preliminary figures.

Malaysia's Trade by Countries ($M000,000)

Countries	1971			1972			1973		
	Imports	Exports	Total Trade	Imports	Exports	Total Trade	Imports	Exports	Total Trade
Singapore........	335·7	1,124·2	1,459·9	356·5	1,126·8	1,473·3	463·4	1,714·7	2,178·1
Japan............	859·8	912·4	1,772·2	921·9	931·9	1,763·0	1,334·3	1,334·1	2,671·4
U.K.............	642·7	327·7	670·4	581·8	342·4	924·2	604·1	582·9	1,187·0
Other Western Europe........	548·6	627·7	1,176·3	—	—	—	—	—	—
U.S.S.R.........	11·0	152·7	163·3	—	—	—	—	—	—
China (Mainland)	201·4	55·7	257·1	194·6	76·4	271·0	364·7	199·5	564·2
Australia........	255·9	91·8	347·7	338·2	88·7	426·9	420·2	150·8	571·0
Indonesia........	147·2	29·0	176·2	153·1	37·1	191·0	149·3	37·4	186·7

Malta

Malta lies in the Mediterranean Sea, 58 miles from Sicily and about 180 from the African coast, about 17 miles in length and 9 in breadth, and having an area of 94·9 square miles. Malta includes also the adjoining island of *Gozo* (area 25·9 sq. miles); *Comino* and minor islets. The estimated population on Dec. 31, 1973, was 318,481 (including temporary visitors). Malta's climate, although not tropical, is hot in summer.

Malta was in turn held by the Phœnicians, Greeks, Carthaginians, Romans and Arabs. In 1090 it was conquered by Count Roger of Normandy. In 1530 it was handed over to the Knights of St. John, who made of it a stronghold of Christianity. In 1565 it sustained the famous siege, when the last great effort of the Turks was successfully withstood by Grandmaster La Vallette. The Knights expended large sums in fortifying the island and carrying out many magnificent works, until they were expelled by Napoleon in 1798. The Maltese rose against the French garrison soon afterwards, and the island was subsequently blockaded by the British fleet. The Maltese people freely requested the protection of the British Crown in 1802 on condition that their rights and privileges would be preserved and respected. The islands were finally annexed to the British Crown by the Treaty of Paris in 1814.

Malta was again closely besieged in the last war and again withstood the attacks of all its enemies. From June, 1940, to the end of the war, 432 members of the garrison and 1,540 civilians were killed by enemy aircraft, and about 35,000 houses were destroyed or damaged. In recognition of the part played by the Maltese people, King George VI awarded the George Cross to the island, but this honour is no longer used.

Government.—Following the report of a Constitutional Commission under the chairmanship of Sir Hilary Blood, a new Constitution for Malta was introduced by the Malta (Constitution) Order in Council, 1961, under which the Island became known as " the State of Malta ". On Sept. 21, 1964 under the Malta Independence Order, 1964, Malta became an independent state within the Commonwealth; on December 13, 1974, Malta became a republic within the Commonwealth. Elections under the 1964 Order were held in June, 1971, for the 55 seats in the House of Representatives and they resulted as follows: Nationalist Party, 27 seats; Malta Labour Party, 28 seats. The present state of the parties is Malta Labour Party 29 seats, Nationalist Party 26 seats. Maltese and English are the official languages of administration and Maltese is ordinarily the official language in all the courts of law and the language of general use in the islands.

CAPITAL.— Ψ Valletta. Population (estimated, Dec., 1973), 14,152. Valletta Grand Harbour is one of the finest in the world; it is very deep, and large vessels can anchor alongside the shore. It is an important port of call and ship repairing centre for vessels, being half-way between Gibraltar and Port Said.

FLAG.—Equal vertical stripes of white (next staff), and red; a silver George Cross outlined in red in top corner of white stripe.

President, His Excellency Sir Anthony Joseph Mamo, O.B.E., Q.C.

CABINET

Prime Minister and Minister of Commonwealth and Foreign Affairs, D. Mintoff.

Minister of Justice and Parliamentary Affairs, A. Buttigieg.

Labour, Employment and Welfare, Miss A. Barbara.

Finance and Customs, Dr. J. Abela.

Health, A. V. Hyzler, M.D.

Posts and Electricity, D. Piscopo, M.D.

Trade, Industry, and Tourism, P. Xuereb.

Public Building and Works, L. Sant.

Education and Welfare, Dr. J. Cassar.

Development, W. Abela.

Agriculture and Fisheries, F. Micalle.

Housing and Land, Dr. P. Holland.

MALTA HIGH COMMISSION

24 Haymarket, S.W.1
[01-930 9851]

High Commissioner, His Excellency Arthur J. Scerri (1971).

BRITISH HIGH COMMISSION

7 St. Anne Street, Floriana, Malta,

High Commissioner, His Excellency W. R. Haydon, C.M.G. (1974).

British Council Representative, J. A. Roemmele, Piazza Indipendenza, Valletta.

Education.—In 1973/4 there were 107 Government primary schools with 25,520 pupils, 41 secondary and upper secondary schools with 21,461 pupils, 3 Technical Institutions, 8 Trade Schools and 70 Adult Centres. The Malta College of Education (for teacher training) had 138 students in 1974/5. The Malta College of Arts, Science and Technology had 1,205 students in 1973/4 and the Royal University of Malta 1,042. In 1970–71 there were 74 private schools (with 7,861 boys and 7,319 girls), of which 26 were subsidized by the Government. English

and Maltese are taught in all classes in Government primary schools.

In religion the Maltese are Roman Catholics. The Maltese language is of Semitic origin, and is held by some to be derived from the Carthaginian and the Phœnician tongues.

Production.—The islands are intensively cultivated. The chief export crops are potatoes, onions, tomatoes and flowers. Wheat, barley, clover and tomatoes are extensively grown on dry lands, while on irrigated land all the usual temperate climate and sub-tropical vegetables are grown. Tomatoes are grown on irrigated and non-irrigated land. Agriculture and ship repairing are among the principal occupations of the inhabitants.

FINANCE AND TRADE

	1972/3	1973/4
Revenue........	£M49,895,000	£M55,850,000
Expenditure.....	£M41,551,000	£M54,342,000

The Central Bank of Malta has the sole right of issuing legal tender currency notes and coins. The Maltese pound is divided into 100 cents and 1,000 mills. On July 1, 1975 the rate of exchange was £M1 = £sterling 1·216.

Trade.—The principal imports for home consumption are foodstuffs—mainly wheat, meat and bullocks, milk and fruit—fodder, beverages and tobacco, fuels, chemicals, textiles and machinery (industrial, agricultural and transport). The chief domestic exports are scrap-metal, hides and skins, potatoes, tomatoes and onions, smoking requisites, textile fabrics, rubber goods, plastics, gloves, hosiery, beer, mineral waters, edible oil, tallow and fresh flowers. To these may be added exports effected by newly created industries, *viz.* fibres and yarns, rubber seals, flower cuttings, plastic goods, wine, mattresses and knitwear.

Mauritius

Mauritius is an island group lying in the Indian Ocean, 550 miles east of Madagascar, between 57° 17′–57° 46ʹ E. long. and lat. 10° 58ʹ–20° 33′ S., and comprising with its dependencies an area of 805 square miles. The resident population at the census of 1972 was: Mauritius, 826,199; Rodrigues, 24,769; Lesser Dependencies about 500, made up of Europeans (mainly of French extraction), Asiatic races and persons of mixed descent. The total population, including dependencies, was estimated in 1974 at 871,122.

Mauritius was discovered in 1511 by the Portuguese; the Dutch visited it in 1598, and named it Mauritius, in honour of the Stadtholder, Prince Maurice of Nassau. From 1638 to 1710 it was held as a small Dutch colony and in 1715 the French took possession but did not settle it until 1721. Mauritius was taken by a British Force in 1810. A British garrison remained on the island until its withdrawal in June 1960. The French language and French law have been preserved under British rule. English is the official language but French is in common use.

Climate.—Mauritius enjoys a sub-tropical maritime climate, with sufficient difference between summer and winter to avoid monotony; further variation is introduced by the wide range of rainfall and temperature resulting from the mountainous nature of the island. Humidity is rather high throughout the year and rainfall is sufficient to maintain a green cover of vegetation, except for a brief period in the driest districts.

CAPITAL.—Ψ Port Louis, population (1974), 136,800; other centres are Beau Bassin and Rose Hill (80,829); Curepipe (52,709); Vacoas and Phoenix (48,809) and Quatre Bornes (51,638). FLAG.—Red, blue, yellow and green stripes.

Government.—A Crown Colony for 158 years, Mauritius became an independent state within the Commonwealth on March 12, 1968. The Constitution defined by Order in Council in 1964 was slightly altered in 1966 on the recommendation of the Banwell Commission, the effect being to increase the membership of the Legislative Assembly to 70, 62 elected by block voting in multi-member constituencies (including 2 members for Rodrigues) and 8 specially-elected members. Of the latter, 4 seats go to the " best loser " of whichever communities in the island are under-represented in the Assembly after the General Election and the four remaining seats are allocated on the basis of both party and community. The Constitution provides for the appointment of a Governor-General who acts on the advice of the Council of Ministers, collectively responsible to the Legislative Assembly. The present state of the parties in the Assembly is: Government; Labour, 37; *Comité d'Action Museilman* 5; Independent, 2; Opposition; P.M.S.D. (*Parti Mauricien Social Democrate*) 14, Independent Forward Bloc 6, *Union Democratique Mauricienne* 5, *Mouvement Militant* 1. *Socialiste Progressiste* 1.

Governor-General, His Excellency Sir Raman Osman, G.C.M.G., C.B.E. (1973).

COUNCIL OF MINISTERS

Premier and Minister of Defence, Information and Broadcasting, Internal Security, External Affairs, Tourism and Emigration, Dr. the Rt. Hon. Sir Seewoosagur Ramgoolam.

Minister of Finance, Sir Veerasamy Ringadoo.

MAURITIUS HIGH COMMISSION

Grand Bldgs., Northumberland Avenue, W.C.2
[01-930 2895]

High Commissioner, His Excellency Sir Leckraz Teelock, C.B.E. (1968).

Counsellor, Gian Nath.

BRITISH HIGH COMMISSION

Cerne House, Chaussée Street,
Port Louis

High Commissioner, His Excellency (Arthur) Henry Brind, C.M.G. (1974) £5,765

Deputy High Commissioner. R J. C. Pease (*Head of Chancery*).

1st Secretary, P. H. Charters (*Aid*).

British Council Representative, Miss M. E. Platon, O.B.E., Royal Road, Rose Hill.

Education.—At the primary level education is free and is provided for nearly 155,000 children at 185 government primary schools and 55 aided primary schools. Although education is not compulsory it is estimated that about 90 per cent. of children of primary school age attend school. There are 7 government secondary schools—and also 119 private secondary schools, of which 14 are grant-aided. Total enrolment in secondary schools (1974) is 61,000. In addition there are 4 senior primary schools which provide education in practical subjects, 5 rural craft training centres (small scale industries) and 1 Industrial Trade Training Centre. There is a Teacher Training College for the training of primary school teachers. An institute of Education has been set up for the purpose of training secondary school teachers and engaging in curriculum and examination reform. The University of Mauritius consists of a School of Administration, a School of Agriculture and a School of Industrial Technology. There are 1,009 students (1975). Estimated expenditure on education in 1974–5 was: recurrent Rs. 81,757,000; capital Rs. 13,324,000.

Communications.—Port Louis, on the N.W. coast, has an excellent harbour which handles the bulk of the island's external trade. Goods unloaded in 1973 amounted to 731,000 metric tons and goods loaded reached 900,000 metric tons. The international airport is located at Plaisance in the southeast of the island about 2 miles from Mahébourg. Freight unloaded there during 1973 totalled 582 metric tons and freight loaded totalled 1,298 metric tons. Scheduled services are operated by Air France, Air India, Air Malawi, Air Mauritius, British Airways, East African Airways, Lufthansa,

Qantas, South African Airways, Zambia Airways, Air Malagasy and Alitalia. There are 26 telephone exchanges serving 23,500 individual telephone installations on the island. There are 9 daily newspapers published, mostly in French with occasional articles in English, and 3 Chinese daily papers. The Mauritian Broadcasting Corporation has a monopoly of radio broadcasting in the country. Television was introduced in February 1965, and educational television in 1969.

Production.—Of the total cultivated area of about 262,000 acres, in 1972, about 242,000 were under sugar, 14,800 acres under tea, and 5,000 acres under tobacco, vegetables and other crops. The sugar crop in 1974 was 685,800 long tons.

Finance.—The main sources of Government revenue are private and company income tax, customs and excise duties, mainly on imports, but also on sugar exports.

	1973–74	1974–75*
Public revenue...	Rs.515,400,000	Rs.605,900,000
Public expenditure	534,800,000	603,300,000

*Estimated.

The National Debt at Dec. 31, 1974, was Rs.845,787,744.

Currency—*Rs.* = *Rupee* = 7½p.

Trade.—Most foodstuffs and raw materials have to be imported from abroad. Apart from local consumption (about 35,000 long tons per annum), the sugar produced is exported, mainly to Britain and Canada.

	1973	1974
Total imports...	Rs.915,800,000	Rs.1,756,000,000
Total exports....	748,400,000	1,851,600,000

Trade with U.K.

	1972	1973
Imports from U.K..	Rs.131,000,000	Rs.193,000,000
Exports to U.K....	339,500,000	338,600,000

DEPENDENCIES OF MAURITIUS

Rodrigues, 350 miles east-north-east of Mauritius, area, 40 square miles. Population (1972) 25,100. Cattle, salt fish, sheep, goats, pigs and onions are the principal exports. The island is now administered by a Resident Commissioner, who was appointed in June 1974. *Resident Commissioner*, N. Heseltine.

Trade with Mauritius

	1973	1974
Total imports....	Rs.11,322,000	Rs.17,127,000
Total exports.....	3,401,000	6,885,000

In addition to Rodrigues, the islands of Agalea and St. Brandon are dependencies of Mauritius. Other small islands, formerly Mauritian dependencies, including Six Islands, Poros Banhos, Salomon, Diego Garcia and Trois Frères, have since 1965 constituted the British Indian Ocean Territory.

Nigeria

(*For* MAP, *see* Index).

Area and Population.—The Republic of Nigeria is situated on the the west coast of Africa. It is bounded on the south by the Gulf of Guinea, on the west and north by Dahomey and Niger and on the east by Cameroun. It has an area of 356,669 sq. miles with a population (1963 Census) of 55,654,000. (The 1973 census provisional results give 79,760,000.) The population is almost entirely African. There are some 28,000 Europeans, Americans, Lebanese and others engaged in Government posts, commerce and Missionary work.

A belt of mangrove swamp forest 10–60 miles in width lies along the entire coastline. North of this there is a zone 50–100 miles wide of tropical rain forest and oil-palms. North of this the country rises and the vegetation changes to open woodland and savannah. In the extreme north the country is semi-desert. There are few mountains, but in Northern Nigeria the central plateau rises to an average level of 4,000 feet. The Niger, Benue, and Cross are the main rivers.

The climate varies with the types of country described above, but Nigeria lies entirely within the tropics and temperatures are high. Temperatures of over 100° in the north are common while coast temperatures are seldom over 90°. The humidity at the coast, however, is much higher than in the north. The rainy season is from about April to October; rainfall varies from under 25 inches a year in the extreme north to 172 inches on the coast line. During the dry season the *harmattan* wind blows from the desert; it is cool and laden with fine particles of dust.

CAPITAL.—ΨLAGOS, estimated population, 1,000,000. Other important towns are Ibadan, Kano, Ogbomosho, Oyo, Oshogbo, Onitsha, Ife, Abeokuta, Enugu, Aba, Maiduguri, Katsina, ΨPort Harcourt, Sokoto, Zaria, Calabar, Benin, Jos and Ilorin. FLAG.—Three equal vertical bands, green, white and green. NATIONAL DAY.—October 1 (Republic Day).

GOVERNMENT

Following the military take-over of January 16, 1966, the Federal and Regional Constitutions were suspended, in relation to the offices of President, Prime Minister, Regional Governors and Regional Premiers, and Parliament and the Regional Legislatures were dissolved. The country was divided into 12 new States by decree in May, 1967—six in the former Northern Region, three in the former Eastern Region, the former Mid-West Region remaining as before, Western Region (*less* the Colony Province), and a new Lagos State, including the Colony Province formerly part of the Western Region. A Federal Military Government, made up of a Supreme Military Council and a Federal Executive Council (the latter with some civilian members) perform the functions of the former Federal Government and Council of Ministers, while a Military Governor administers each of the 12 States (except East Central State which has a civilian administrator).
Head of State, Brig. Muritala Mohammed.

NIGERIAN HIGH COMMISSION
Nigeria House, 9 Northumberland Avenue, W.C.2
[01-839 1244]
High Commissioner, His Excellency Sule Kolo.

BRITISH HIGH COMMISSION
Kajola House, 62–64 Campbell Street, Lagos.
High Commissioner, His Excellency Sir Charles
Martin LeQuesne, K.C.M.G. (1974)......£18,675

British Council Representative in Nigeria, P. G. Lloyd, O.B.E., 8–10 Yakubu Gowon Street, Lagos. Branch offices at Ibadan, Kano, Kaduna and Enugu; and sub-library at Benin
Education.—There are six Universities, situated in Lagos, Ife, Zaria, Benin, Nsukka (with campuses at Nsukka, Calabar and Enugu) and Ibadan (with campuses at Ibadan and Jos) with a total of 23,228 full-time students in 1973/4. Four more universities are planned. Free and compulsory primary education is to be introduced nationwide on September 1, 1976.
Railways.—The Nigerian railway system, which is controlled by the Nigerian Railway Corporation, is the most extensive in West Africa. There are 2,278 route miles of lines. There are two major bridges, one over the Niger at Jebba and one over the Benue at Makurdi. The latter is 2,624 ft. long, and it is believed to be the second longest in Africa. The North-western main line runs from Lagos to Kano (700 miles) through the important towns of Abeokuta, Ibadan, Ilorin, Jebba, Minna, Kaduna and Zaria. From Kano the line continues in a north-easterly direction to its terminus at Nguru. This line is also linked with Sokoto by a scheduled railway-road service from Gusau. The eastern line runs from Port Harcourt deep-water quay on the Bonny river through the thickly populated oil palm area to Enugu, where its serves the collieries. It then crosses the Benue and joins the north-western line at Kaduna, 569 miles from Port Har-

court. A branch line runs to Bauchi, Gombe and Maiduguri.
Roads.—There are 16,200 miles of motorable road. Most of the roads have gravelled or earth surfaces but about 9,044 miles are tarred. An extensive programme of bituminous surfacing is now being carried out.
Civil Aviation.—Trunk route services operated by Nigerian and the principal international airlines bring Nigeria within less than 12 hours of the Western European capitals and South Africa. There are also services to other parts of Africa and to the United States. A network of internal air services connects the main centres. Comprehensive radio navigational aids are installed at Kano and Lagos airports, and basic radio navigational facilities are provided at the twelve other aerodromes in regular use. Several flying strips are also in use by light aircraft. There is a network of meteorological reporting stations.
Production and Industry.—Nigeria has a traditional but increasingly mixed economy: farming, forestry, and fishing activities contribute just under forty per cent. of the country's gross domestic product but manufacturing industry and, in particular, petroleum are gaining in importance. The export structure is diversified. Mineral oil is the principal source of export revenue, followed by cocoa and palm kernel products. Other crops include benniseed, capsicums, cassava, coffee, copra, cotton, ground nuts, guinea-corn, gum arabic, kola-nuts, maize, millet, piassava, rice, rubber, tobacco, and yams. There are important tin and coal-mining industries at Jós and Eriugu respectively. The coal is mainly used within the country. Nigeria is the principal source of supply of the world's requirements of columbite. Timber and hides and skins are other major exports. Some of the country's more important industrial installations include a steel-rolling mill, a tin smelter, a petroleum refinery, flour mills, a sugar factory, several cement plants and textile factories. Of growing importance is the local assembly of motor vehicles, bicycles, radio sets, fans and sewing machines. Other major manufactures include soap, cigarettes, beer, soft drinks, vegetable oils, canned food, confectionery, metal containers, plywood, footwear, tyres and tubes, paints, pharmaceuticals, plastic goods, glass containers, cement products, and roofing sheets.
Trade.—The principal imports are food, cotton yarn and thread, medicines and drugs, milk, motor vehicles and spares, general machinery and iron and steel bars, electrical goods, pipes and sheets. The principal export is crude oil.

	1973	1974
Total imports....	MN1,224,800,000	1,715,400,000
Total exports....	MN2,227,400,000	5,762,000,000
£1 = Naira 1·45.		

Trade with U.K.

	1973	1974
Imports from U.K..	£172,700,000	£222,400,000
Exports to U.K....	£206,800,000	£368,300,000

Sierra Leone

Area and Population, etc.—The peninsula of Sierra Leone, situated on the West Coast of Africa, was ceded to Great Britain in 1787 by the native chiefs to be used as an asylum for the many destitute negroes then in England. At a somewhat later date the Colony was used as a settlement for Africans from North America and the West Indies, and great numbers of Africans rescued from slave ships have from time to time been liberated and settled there. The total area of Sierra Leone is 27,925 sq. miles, and the total population (1974 Census) is 3,002,426. For administrative purposes, the interior portion of Sierra Leone is divided into 3 Provinces covering 12 Districts, each administered by a Resident Minister. The principal peoples are the Limbas and Korankos in the north, the Temnes in the centre, and the Mendis in the South.

CAPITAL.—Ψ Freetown (population 274,000). FLAG.—Three horizontal stripes of leaf green, white and cobalt blue. NATIONAL DAY.—April 19.

Government.—Sierra Leone became a fully independent state and a member of the British Commonwealth on April 27, 1961. There is a House of Representatives consisting of a Speaker and not fewer than 60 members, elected from constituencies established by an Electoral Commission.

After a period of martial law, and suspension of the Constitution, Parliament re-opened in June 1968.

A Bill instituting republican status for Sierra Leone and providing for the appointment of the interim Governor-General as its first President was approved on April 19, 1971, and the Prime Minister thereupon declared Sierra Leone a republic. A general election was held in May 1973. The Sierra Leone People's Party withdrew from the election and the All Peoples' Congress were unanimously returned. The number of seats actually held in Parliament at present (1975) is 85 elected members, 1 Paramount Chief from each of the 12 Districts, and 2 members elected by the President. There is provision for a third such elected member.

SIERRA LEONE HIGH COMMISSION
33 Portland Place, W.1.
[01–636 6483]
High Commissioner, His Excellency Ralph Emeric Kasope Taylor-Smith (1974)

BRITISH HIGH COMMISSION
Standard Bank Sierra Leone Building,
Wallace Johnson Street, Freetown.
High Commissioner, His Excellency Ian Buchanan Watt, C.M.G.
British Council Representative, J. Mulholland, P.O. Box 124, Tower Hill, Freetown.

Communications.—The public railway has been phased out, but, a mining company, the Sierra Leone Development Company, owns a railway which runs for 52½ miles from the iron ore deposits at Marampa to the shipping port of Pepel. There are about 5,000 miles of road in the country, of which about 2,100 miles are surfaced.

The Freetown international airport is situated at Lungi, across the Sierra Leone River from Freetown. The main port is Freetown, which has one of the largest natural harbours in the world, and where there is a deep water quay

providing about six berths for medium sized ships. There are smaller ports at Pepel and Bonthe. The Sierra Leone Broadcasting Service operates a direct service. Broadcasts are made daily in several of the more important indigenous languages, in addition to English.

Education.—There are 914 primary schools in Sierra Leone and 72 secondary schools. Technical education is provided in the two Government Technical Institutes, situated in Freetown and Kenema, in two Trade Centres and in the technical training establishments of the mining companies. Teacher training is carried out in two universities, one advanced college, five women's primary colleges and four Church training colleges in the Provinces, and in the Milton Margai Training College near Freetown. The University of Sierra Leone (1967), consists of Fourah Bay College (1960) and Njala University College (1964).

Production and Trade.—In the Western area, farming is largely confined to the production of cassava and garden crops, such as maize and vegetables, for local consumption. In the Provincial areas, the principal agricultural product is rice, which is the staple food of the country and export crops such as palm kernels, cocoa beans, coffee and ginger.

The economy depends largely on mineral exports, principally diamonds and iron ore (80 per cent.). Government purchases of diamonds in 1974 totalled Le33,977,073. Exports of iron ore and concentrates in 1973 amounted to 2,366,994 tons (£5,556,111). Bauxite production in 1973 amounted to some 652,459 tons (£1,740,640).

Total exports in 1973 were valued at Le105,977,517; imports Le127,202,528.

	1973	1974
Imports from U.K.	£12,716,000	£18,733,000(F.O.B.)
Exports to U.K.	£40,116,000	£41,897,000(C.I.F.)

Finance.—In August 1964, Sierra Leone adopted decimal currency. The basic unit is the Leone (worth 50p). It is divided into 100 cents.

Total revenue was estimated at Le86,723,492 in 1974/5; expenditure on ordinary budget Le86,723,492. Development expenditure was estimated at Le33,400,000.

Singapore

The Republic of Singapore consists of the island of Singapore and 54 smaller islands, covering a total area of 225·6 square miles. Singapore Island is 26 miles long and 14 miles in breadth and is situated just north of the Equator off the southern extremity of the Malay Peninsula, from which it is separated by the Straits of Johore. A causeway, carrying a road and railway, crosses the three-quarters of a mile to the mainland. The highest point of the island is 581 feet above sea level. *Climate.*—The climate is hot and humid and there are no clearly defined seasons. Rainfall averages 96 inches a year and temperature ranges from 21°–34° C (79°–93°F.). *Population.*—Estimated at 2,219,000 on June 30, 1974, the population is multiracial with a preponderance of Chinese. The racial groups were estimated in 1974 to be divided as follows: Chinese—1,689,500; Malays—334,100; Indians, Pakistanis and Ceylonese—153,500; others (Europeans, Eurasians etc.)—42,000. At least 6 Chinese dialects are used and Malay, Mandarin, Tamil and English are the official languages. FLAG.—Horizontal bands of red over white; crescent with five five-point stars on red band near staff. NATIONAL DAY.—August 9.

Government.—Singapore, where Sir Stamford Raffles had first established a trading post under the East India Company in 1819, was incorporated with Penang and Malacca to form the Straits Settlements in 1826. The Straits Settlements became a Crown Colony in 1867. Singapore fell into Japanese hands in 1942 and civil government was not restored until 1946, when it became a separate colony. Internal self-government and the title " State of Singapore " were introduced in 1959. Singapore became a state of Malaysia when the Federation was enlarged in September, 1963, but left Malaysia and became an independent sovereign state within the Commonwealth on August 9, 1965. Singapore adopted a Republican constitution from that date, the Yang di-Pertuan Negara being re-styled President. There is a Cabinet collectively responsible to a fully-elected Parliament of 65 members.

HEAD OF STATE

President, Benjamin Henry Sheares, G.C.B., *assumed office as President*, Jan. 2, 1971 (*re-elected for second 4-year term from* Jan. 1, 1975).

CABINET

Prime Minister, Lee Kuan Yew, G.C.M.G., C.H.
Deputy Prime Minister and Minister of Defence, Dr. Goh Keng Swee.
Minister for Science and Technology, Dr. Toh Chin Chye.
Finance, Hon Sui Sen.
Foreign Affairs, S. Rajaratnam.
Education, Dr. Lee Chiaw Meng.
Communications, Yong Nyuk Lin.
Culture, Jek Yeun Thong.
Social Affairs, Inche Othman bin Wok.
Law and National Development, E.W. Barker.
Health and Home Affairs, Chua Sian Chin.
Labour, Ong Pang Boon.
Environment, Lim Kim San.

Speaker of Parliament, Dr. Yeoh Ghim Seng.

SINGAPORE HIGH COMMISSION
2 Wilton Crescent, S.W.1
[01-235 8315]
High Commissioner, (vacant)

BRITISH HIGH COMMISSION
Tanglin Circus, Singapore 10
High Commissioner, His Excellency John Peter Tripp, C.M.G. (1974)
British Council Representative. K. I. McCallum, 3rd floor, Cathay Building, Mount Sophia, Singapore 9.

Communications.—Singapore is one of the largest seaports in the world, with deep water wharves and ship repairing facilities. Ships also anchor in the roads, unloading into lighters. 60,400,000 tons of cargo were handled in 1974. Singapore Airport, 7½ miles from the centre of the city, has a runway 11,000 feet long. There are 28 miles of railway connected to the Malaysian rail system by the causeway across the Straits of Johore, and 1,337 miles of roads, 1,026 miles of which are metalled roads maintained by the Government. There are both wireless and wired broadcasting services carrying commercial advertising. Television was introduced in 1963.

Production, etc.—Until 1960 Singapore's trade was primarily based on the distribution and sales of raw materials from surrounding countries and for finished products from developed nations. In the last decade, however, new manufacturing industries have been introduced, including ship building and repairing, iron and steel, textiles, footwear, wood products, micro-electronics, detergents, confectionery, pharmaceuticals, petroleum products, sanitary-ware, building materials, domestic electric appliances, plastic articles, transport equipment, etc. Future developments include the reclaiming of a further 5,000 acres of marshy land at Jurong Industrial Town which when fully developed will cover 12,000 acres; extension to other industrial estates, the building of 130,000 low-cost housing units over the next five years by the Housing and Development Board and the building of reservoirs at Kranji and Ulu Pandan together with associated treatment plant. Growth industries include ship building and repairing, metal working, chemicals, electronics, printing and publishing, aerospace engineering and tourism.

FINANCE

	1974-5	1975-6★
Revenue	S $2,322,950,000	S $2,647,461,000
Estimated	2,299,475,000	2,646,319,000

★Estimated.

Currency.—On June 12, 1967, the Singapore Currency Board began issuing its own currency, the $ *Singapore* (of 100 *cents*) approximately equivalent (May 1975) to 18p sterling. The S $ is freely interchangeable with the $*Brunei* (also issued on June 12, 1967). An interchangeability agreement with Malaysia was cancelled on May 8, 1973.

TRADE

	1973	1974
Total imports.	S $12,513,000,000	S $20,405,000,000
Total exports.	8,907,000,000	14,155,000,000

Trade with U.K.

	1973	1974
Imports from U.K.	£100,601,000	£153,533,000
Exports to U.K.	85,376,000	74,758,000

Sri Lanka

AREA AND POPULATION

Sri Lanka (formerly Ceylon) is an island in the Indian Ocean, off the southern tip of the peninsula of India and separated from it by a narrow strip of shallow water, the Palk Strait. Situated between 5° 55′–9° 50′ N. latitude and 79° 42′–81° 52′ E. longitude, it has an area of 25,332 square miles, including 33 square miles of inland water. Its greatest length is from north to south, 270 miles; and its greatest width 140 miles, no point in Sri Lanka being more than 80 miles from the sea.
At the Census of 1971, the population was 12,747,755.

Races and Religions
The races of Sri Lanka are low-country Sinhalese, Kandyan Sinhalese, Ceylon Tamils, Indian Tamils, Ceylon Moors, Indian Moors, Burghers and Eurasians, Malays and Veddahs. Generally Sinhalese who trace their descent to a low-country district are classified as low-country Sinhalese, others as Kandyan

Sinhalese. The Western and Southern Provinces, the Southern (Chilaw) District and the Western parts of Puttalam District are low-country areas; the Central and North Central Provinces, Uva, Sabaragamuwa and Kurunegala are regarded as Kandyan districts. At the 1953 Census 42·3 per cent. of the population were low-country Sinhalese, 28·8 per cent. Kandyan Sinhalese. The religion of the great majority of inhabitants is Buddhism, introduced from India, according to ancient Sinhalese chronicles, in 247 B.C. Next to Buddhism, Hinduism has a large following.

PHYSIOGRAPHY

Sri Lanka is a compact area, except for the island of Mannar and an almost detached portion in the north, the Jaffna Peninsula and its satellite islands of Delft, Kayts, etc. The relief of the island includes a mountainous area in the south-central region of 3,000 to 7,000 feet above sea level, surrounded by an upland belt of about 1,000 to 3,000 feet and a narrow coastal plain broadening out to a vast tract in the north. The coastal plain continues for a distance out to sea as a continental shelf and a coral reef, for the most part submerged, lies close to the coast. On the Central Ridge of the hill country are some of the highest peaks in Sri Lanka, Pidurutalagala (8,281 ft.), Kirigalpotta (7,857 ft.) and Totapolakanda (7,741 ft.) and the high plains Nuwara Eliya (over 6,000 ft.), Elk Plains (6,000 ft.) and Horton Plains (over 7,000 ft.. The other principal peaks are Adam's Peak (7,360 ft.), Namunukula (6,679 ft.), Knuckles (6,112 ft. and Haycock (2,167 ft.). The Peninsula of Jaffna and the island of Mannar are featureless level stretches.

The Mahaveli-ganga, 208 miles long, is the largest river of Sri Lanka. Rising on the western side of the central hilly ridge, it flows north and east to empty into the Koddiyar Bay on the east coast. Other rivers are the Kelaniganga (90 miles), Aruvi-aru (104), Kala-oya (92), Yam-oya (88) and Deduru-oya (88). Waterfalls girdle the central mountainous massif and offer some of the best scenic features in the island; Dunhinda (Badulla), Diyaluma (Koslanda), Elgin (Hatton Plateau) and Perawella are among the outstanding falls. Forests, jungle and scrub cover the greater part of the island, often being intermingled. The forests, of varying species, extend from fairly near the coast right into the hill country. In areas over 2,000 feet above sea level grasslands (*patanas* or *talawas*) are found. Their total area is some 250 square miles, principally in the Province of Uva.

Climate.—The climate of Sri Lanka is warm throughout the year, with a high relative humidity. Temperatures average 80° F. during the year in the lowlands, falling off in the hills to 60° F. at elevations over 6,000 ft. Day humidity is over 70 per cent. and night humidity over 85 per cent. Temperature ranges vary little between wet and dry seasons. In the hilly areas morning mists something occur. Traces of ground frost appear occasionally at night, at the highest levels, and disappear at sunrise Thunderstorms occasionally give hail, but snow is completely absent. Rainfall is generally heavy, with marked regional variations; the heaviest falls (200–250 inches) are recorded on the south-west slopes of the central hills. Some depressional or cyclonic activity occurs generally during October to December.

GOVERNMENT

Early in the sixteenth century the Portuguese landed in Ceylon and founded settlements, eventually conquering much of the country. Portuguese rule in Ceylon lasted 150 years during which the Roman Catholic religion was established among the Sinhalese inhabitants and to some extent Portuguese modes of living adopted. In 1658, following a twenty-year period of decline, Portuguese rule gave place to that of the Dutch East India Company which was to exploit Ceylon with varying fortunes until 1796.

The Maritime Provinces of Ceylon were ceded by the Dutch to the British on February 16, 1798, becoming a British Crown Colony in 1802 under the terms of the Treaty of Amiens. With the annexation of the Kingdom of Kandy in 1815, all Ceylon came under British rule.

On February 4, 1948, Ceylon became a self-governing state and a member of the British Commonwealth of Nations under the *Ceylon Independence Act* 1947. Under this Act the Parliament of Ceylon consisted of (a) The Queen (represented by the Governor-General) and (b) two houses, namely, the Senate and the House of Representatives. The Executive consisted of the Prime Minister and a Cabinet chosen from the party which had the majority in the House of Representatives. The House of Representatives constituted itself as the constituent Assembly in July, 1970, to draft a republican Constitution for Ceylon. Accordingly, a new republican Constitution was adopted on May 22, 1972, and the country was renamed the Republic of Sri Lanka (meaning 'Resplendent Island'). The new republic continues to be in the Commonwealth.

CAPITAL.—Ψ Colombo, population (1971 Census), 563,705. Other principal towns are Ψ Jaffna (106,856), Kandy (91,942), Ψ Galle (71,060), Ψ Negombo (55,722) and Ψ Trincomalee (38,800).

REPUBLIC DAY.—May 22.

FLAG.—Yellow lion of Kandy on a maroon ground; Sinhalese pinnacle at the corners; yellow border; two vertical stripes of green and saffron at the staff side.

President, WILLIAM GOPALLAWA, *b.* 1897.

CABINET

Prime Minister and Minister of Defence and Foreign Affairs, Planning and Economic Affairs and Plan Implementation, Mrs. Sirimavo R. D. Bandaranaike.
Irrigation, Power and Highways, Maitripala Senanayake.
Foreign and Internal Trade, T. B. Illangaratne.
Education, Badiudin Mahmud.
Shipping and Tourism, P. B. G. Kalugalle.
Labour, M. P. De Z. Siriwardene.
Public Administration, Justice, Local Government and Home Affairs, Felix R. D. Bandaranaike.
Industries and Scientific Research, T. B. Subasinghe.
Finance, Dr. N. M. Perera.

Transport, Leslie S. Goonewardene.
Plantation Industries and Constitutional Affairs, Dr. Colvin R. de Silva.
Agriculture and lands, H. S. R. B. Kobbekaduwa.
Fisheries, George Rajapakse.
Housing and Construction, Pieter G. B. Keuneman.
Posts and Telecommunications, Chelliah Kumarasurier.
Health, W. P. G. Ariyadasa.
Information and Broadcasting, R. S. Perera.
Social Services, T. B. Tennekoon.
Cultural Affairs, S. S. Kulatilake.
Parliamentary Affairs and Chief Government Whip and Minister of Sport, K. B. Ratnayake.
Leader of the House, Maitripala Senanayake.

SRI LANKA HIGH COMMISSION
13 Hyde Park Gardens, W.2
[01–262 1841]
High Commissioner, His Excellency Vernon Mendis
(1975).

BRITISH HIGH COMMISSION
Galle Road, Kollupitiya (P.O. Box 1433),
Colombo 3
High Commissioner, *His Excellency* Harold Smedley,
C.M.G., M.B.E. (1973)................... £6,875
British Council Representative, A. F. Keith. There
are British Council libraries at *Colombo* and *Kandy*.

THE LEGISLATURE
Under the Republican constitution which came
into operation on May 22, 1972, the supreme legislative power is vested in the National State Assembly, a unicameral legislative body.

THE JUDICATURE
The Judicial System includes a Supreme Court
of Appeal, Supreme Court, District Courts,
Magistrates' Courts, Courts of Requests and Rural
Courts. Trial by jury obtains in the Supreme
Court.

PRODUCTION
Agriculture.—The staple products of the island are

agricultural, including paddy, tea, rubber and
coconuts.

Industry.—Factories are established for the manufacture or processing of ceramic ware, vegetable
oils and by-products, paper, tanning and leather
goods, plywood, cement, chemicals, sugar, salt,
textiles, ilmenite, tiles, tyres, fertilizers and hardware and there is a petroleum refinery.

Trade with U.K.

	1973	1974
Imports from U.K....	£10,189,000	£10,042,000
Exports to U.K......	22,957,000	30,436,000

COMMUNICATIONS
There are 11,700 miles of motorable roads in
Sri Lanka. A commercial wireless telegraph station
has a range of 500 miles by day and about 1,000 to
2,000 miles by night and handles ship-to-shore
traffic.

From April 1, 1972, Air Ceylon has been operating a DC-8 aircraft on twice-weekly flights on the
route: London, Paris, Rome, Karachi, Colombo,
Bangkok, Kuala Lumpur, Singapore, Djakarta.
Air Ceylon's regional services are operated direct
to Madras three times weekly and once a week to
Bombay.

Swaziland

Swaziland is the smallest of the former three High Commission Territories in Southern Africa. Geographically and climatically, it is divisible into four physiographic provinces; the broken mountainous
Highveld of the west, adjacent to the Drakensberg, with altitudes averaging over 4,000 ft., the Middleveld
which is mostly mixed farming country, about 2,000 ft. lower and the Lowveld, a hot scrubland region,
bounded on the east by the Lubombo mountains, with an average altitude of 1,500 ft. The Lubombo
mountains form the fourth physiographic province. Four rivers, the Komati, Usutu, Mbuluzi and Ing-
wavuma, flow from west to east, cutting their way through the Lubombo mountains to the Indian Ocean.
The exploitation of these rivers is particularly important to the agricultural development of the middle and
bush veld, where irrigation projects are giving the scenery a different aspect. The total area is 6,704 sq.
miles and the population (estimated, 1971), 465,000.

CAPITAL.—Mbabane (population, estimated, mid-1973, 20,700), the headquarters of the Government, is
situated on the hills at an altitude of 3,800 ft. Other main townships are: Manzini (population 16,000),
Hlatikulu (1,200), Nhlangano (2,400), Pigg's Peak (2,100), Havelock (5,000), Big Bend (3,500) and Mhlume
(2,600). FLAG.—Five horizontal bands, crimson, bearing shield and spears device, bordered by narrow
yellow bands; blue bands at top and foot.

Government.—The Kingdom of Swaziland came into being on April 25, 1967, under a new internal self-
government constitution and became an independent kingdom in membership of the Commonwealth on
September 6, 1968. On April 12, 1973, the King, in response to a motion passed by both Houses of Parliament, repealed the Parliamentary Constitution of 1968 and assumed supreme legislative, executive and
judicial power, to be exercised in collaboration with a Council constituted by his Cabinet Ministers.

King of Swaziland, His Majesty Sobhuza II, K.B.E.

Prime Minister and Minister of Foreign Affairs, Prince
Makhosini Dlamini.

SWAZILAND HIGH COMMISSION
58 Pont Street, S.W.1.
[01–589 5447]
High Commissioner, His Excellency J. M. Fakudze
(1973).

BRITISH HIGH COMMISSION
Mbabane
High Commissioner, His Excellency Eric George Le
Tocq, C.M.G. (1972) £6,475

Education.—In 1973 the primary school enrolment
was 81,259; secondary schools, 12,459.
Communications.—Swaziland's first railway was
completed in 1964. It is about 140 miles long,
starting at Ngwenya, 13 miles north-west of
Mbabane, and connecting at the Mozambique
frontier with an extension to the existing line between Lourenço Marques and Goba. Principal
export traffic on the railway is the iron ore mined
at Bomvu Ridge, near Ngwenya, by the Swaziland
Iron Ore Development Company. A large part of
the country's passenger and goods traffic is carried

by privately-owned motor transport services.
Besides these, the South African Railways Road
Motor Services maintain regular goods and passenger services between Mbabane and Manzini and
the main railheads in South Africa which serve
Swaziland—Breyten, Piet Retief, Komatipoort,
Hectorspruit and Golela. There are post offices,
telegraph and telephone offices at all the chief
centres.

Production.—Exports in 1973 amounted to
R.72,094,900 of which iron ore was worth
R.7,929,600; sugar R.18,490,700; unbleached wood
pulp R.15,323,600; wood and wood products
R.5,710,600; asbestos R.6,766,600; citrus fruit
R.3,388,900; live animals R.767,300; meat and
meat products R.3,552,400; hides and skins
R.2,300,000

Finance.—Government revenue for 1974–75 was
estimated at R.32,807,000 and expenditure at
R.34,877,000. Of a capital budget of R.16,026,000,
R.3,818,000 was estimated as aid funds from the
United Kingdom.

Trade with U.K.

	1973	1974
Imports from U.K...	£150,721	£511,000
Exports to U.K.....	£12,961,645	£16,119,100

Tanzania

Tanganyika, the mainland part of the United Republic of Tanzania (Tanganyika and Zanzibar) occupies the east-central portion of the African continent, between 1°–11° 45′ S. lat. and 29° 20′–40° 38′ E. long. It is bounded on the N. by Kenya and Uganda; on the S.W. by Lake Malawi, Malawi and Zambia; on the S. by Mozambique; on the W. it is bounded by Rwanda, Burundi and Zaire; on the E. the boundary is the Indian Ocean. Tanganyika has a coastline of about 500 miles and an area of 362,820 sq. miles (including 20,650 sq. miles of water). The greater part of the country is occupied by the Central African plateau from which rise, among others, Mt. Kilimanjaro, the highest point on the continent of Africa (19,340 ft.) and Mt. Meru (14,979 ft.). The Serengeti National Park, which covers an area of 6,000 sq. miles in the Arusha, Mwanza and Mara Regions, is famous for its variety and number of species of game.

The African population consists mostly of tribes of mixed Bantu race. The total population of Tanzania at the Census held in August, 1967, was 12,311,991 (estimated, July, 1973, 13,968,000); Africans form a very large majority, while the Europeans, the Asians, and other non-Africans form a small minority. Annual average population growth is 2·7 per cent. The total population of Zanzibar at the 1967 census was 354,815 (estimated, 1973, 403,000). Swahili is the national and official language. English is the second official language, both for educational and government purposes.

Zanzibar.—Formerly ruled by the Sultan of Zanzibar, and a British Protectorate until Dec. 10, 1963. Zanzibar consists of the islands of Zanzibar and Pemba. It has a total area of approximately 1,000 sq. miles The islands produce a large part of the world's supply of cloves and clove oil, and coconuts, coconut oil and copra are also produced.

Zanzibar became internally self-governing on June 24, 1963, and fully independent on Dec. 10, 1963 The revolutionary Afro-Shitazi party seized power on Jan. 12, 1964, and the Sultan was forced to leave the country. Later Zanzibar united with Tanganyika (*see* below).

CAPITAL.—ΨDar es Salaam (population about 300,000). Other towns are ΨTanga (61,061); Mwanza (34,861); Arusha (32,452); Moshi (26,853); Morogoro (25,262); Dodoma (23,559); Iringa (21,746); Tabora (20,994) and Mtwara (20,396). In Zanzibar, the chief town and seaport of that name (population, 68,490) provides facilities for shipping and trade. The principal international airport is Dar es Salaam. Other airports include Zanzibar, Arusha, Mwanza and Tanga. A new international airport has been opened at Kilimanjaro between Arusha and Moshi to take " Jumbo Jets ".

FLAG.—Green (above) and blue; divided by diagonal black stripe bordered by gold, running from bottom (next staff) to top (in fly). NATIONAL DAY.—December 9 (anniversary of independence).

President of the United Republic, Julius Kambarage Nyerere, *b.* 1922; *elected* Nov. 1962; *took office* Dec. 9, 1962; *re-elected* Sept., 1965, and Nov., 1970.

Vice Presidents, Aboud Jumbe; R. M. Kawawa (also Prime Minister).

GOVERNMENT

Following a constitutional conference held in Dar es Salaam in March, 1961, Tanganyika became an independent state and a member of the British Commonwealth on December 9, 1961.

Tanganyika became a Republic, within the Commonwealth, on December 9, 1962, with an executive President, elected by universal suffrage, who is both the Head of State and Head of the Government. A presidential election will be held whenever Parliament is dissolved, and the presidency is closely linked with the official party, the Tanganyika African National Union (TANU), since Tanzania is a one-party state.

On April 25, 1964, following a Parliamentary ratification of an agreement signed by the President of the Republic of Tanganyika and the President of the People's Republic of Zanzibar and Pemba, Tanganyika united with Zanzibar to form a new sovereign state. By this agreement, the President of the United Republic is Julius K. Nyerere; the First Vice-President is Aboud Jumbe (also President of Zanzibar), and the Second Vice-President is Rashidi Mfaume Kawawa (of Tanganyika) who is also Prime Minister and the leader of the Government business in the National Assembly of the United Republic. The Vice-Presidents and Ministers form the Cabinet of the Union Government, which is presided over by the President. There are 4 Zanzibar Ministers and 1 Junior Minister in the Union Government, and 30 others (10 backbenchers nominated from Zanzibar, 15 backbenchers nominated from Members of the Revolutionary Council and 5 Zanzibar Regional Commissioners who are *ex officio* M.P.s) in the National Assembly of the United Republic.

Zanzibar has its own legislature which legislates for matters which are not under the Union Government, *e.g.* education, agriculture, health and community development.

CABINET

The President.
Minister for Foreign Affairs, J. S. Malecela.
Agriculture, J. Mungai.
Commerce and Industries, A. H. Jamal.
Works, J. M. Lusinde.
Economic Affairs and Development Planning, Dr. W. K. Chagula.
Finance, C. Msuya.
Health, A. H. Mwinyi.
Home Affairs, Al-Haj Omari Haji.
Natural Resources and Tourism, H. Makame.
Information and Broadcasting, D. N. Mwakawago.
Water Development and Power, I. Elinewinga.
Lands, Housing and Urban Development, M. Mageni.
National Education, S. Chiwanga.
Defence and National Service, E. N. Sokoine.
Labour and Social Welfare, Gisler Mapunda.
Communications and Transport, Alfred C. Tandau.
National Culture and Youth, Maj.-Gen. M. S. H. Sarakikya.
Ministers of State, P. Siyovelwa; A. S. Mkwawa; H. N. Moyo.

Chief Justice, Hon. A. Saidi.

TANZANIA HIGH COMMISSION
43 Hertford Street, W.1
[01-499 8951]

High Commissioner, His Excellency Amon James Nsekela (1974)

BRITISH HIGH COMMISSION
Dar es Salaam.

High Commissioner, His Excellency Mervyn Brown, C.M.G., O.B.E..........................£9,228

British Council Representative, G. W. Shaw.

EDUCATION

Education, almost entirely under state control, is

characterised by official insistence that education must serve the aims of overall Government policy and planning. All Tanzanian Secondary Schools are expected to include practical subjects in the basic course. All who receive secondary (or equivalent) education are called up for a period of National Service. The school system is administered in Swahili and the intention is for the national language to become the medium at all levels. For higher education most Tanzanian students go to the University of Dar es Salaam, other East African universities, or to Universities and Colleges outside East Africa, mainly in Britain.

PRODUCTION AND TRADE
The economy is based mainly on the production and export of primary produce and the growing of

foodstuffs for local consumption. The chief commercial crops are sisal, cotton, coffee, cashew nuts and oilseeds. The most important minerals are diamonds. Hides and skins are another valuable export. Industry is at present largely concerned with the processing of raw material for either export or local consumption. There is also a healthy growth of secondary manufacturing industries, including factories for the manufacture of leather and rubber footwear, knitwear, razor blades, cigarettes and textiles, and a wheat flour mill.

TRADE WITH U.K.

	1973	1974
Imports from U.K.	£21,754,000	£29,129,000
Exports to U.K.	30,328,000	49,105,000

Trinidad and Tobago

AREA AND POPULATION
Trinidad, the most southerly of the West Indian Islands, lies close to the north coast of the continent of S. America, the nearest point of Venezuela being 7 miles distant. The island is situated between 10° 3′–10° 50′ N. lat. and 60° 55′–61° 56′ W. long., and is about 50 miles in length by 37 in width, with an area of 1,864 sq. miles. *Population.*—Of the population (estimated at 1,027,900 in Dec. 1974), 43 per cent. are African, 36 per cent East Indian, 2 per cent. European, 1 per cent. Chinese, and the rest mixed.

The island was discovered by Colombus in 1498, was colonized in 1532 by the Spaniards, capitulated to the British under Abercromby in 1797, and was ceded to Britain under the Treaty of Amiens (March 25, 1802). Two mountain systems, the Northern and Southern Ranges, stretch across almost its entire width and a third, the Central Range lies somewhat diagonally across its middle portion; otherwise the island is mostly flat. The highest peaks are in the Northern Range (Aripo 3,085 ft., El Tucuche 3,072 ft.). The climate is tropical with temperatures ranging from 82° F. by day to 74° F. by night and a rainfall averaging 82·7 inches a year. There is a well-marked dry season from January to May and a wet season from June to December. The nights are invariably cool. The main tourist season is from December to April.

Tobago lies between 11° 9′ and 11° 21′ N. lat. and between 60° 30′ and 60° 50′ W. long., about 75 miles south-east of Grenada, 19 miles north-east of Trinidad, and 120 miles S.W. of Barbados. It was ceded to the British Crown in 1814 and amalgamated with Trinidad in 1888. The island is 26 miles long, and 7½ wide, and has an area of 116 sq miles. The population was 33,333 in the 1961 census and was estimated at 33,950 in Dec. 1974. It is one of the healthiest of the West Indies and a popular tourist resort. The main town is Ψ Scarborough.

Other Islands.—Corozal Point and Icacos Point, the N.W. and S.W. extremities of Trinidad, enclose the Gulf of Paria, and west of Corozal Point lie several islands, of which Chacachacare, Huevos, Monos and Gaspar Grande are the most important.

CAPITAL.—Ψ Port of Spain (population 100,000), one of the finest towns in the West Indies, with sewerage, electric lighting, omnibus and telephone services. Other towns of importance are Ψ San Fernando (population, 42,000*), about 33 miles south of the capital, and Arima (population, 13,000*).

FLAG.—Black diagonal stripe bordered with white stripes, running from top by staff, all on a red field, NATIONAL DAY.—August 31 (Independence Day).
* Estimated

GOVERNMENT
The Territory of Trinidad and Tobago became an independent state and a member of the British Commonwealth on August 31, 1962, under the Trinidad and Tobago Independence Act, 1962. There is a Parliament consisting of a Senate and a House of Representatives with an elected Speaker and 36 members. The Senate has 24 members of whom 13 are appointed on the advice of the Prime Minister, 4 on the advice of the Leader of the Opposition and 7 on the advice of the Prime Minister after consultation with religious, economic and social organizations.
Governor-General, His Excellency Sir Ellis Emmanuel Innocent Clarke, G.C.M.G. (1973).

CABINET
Prime Minister and Minister of External Affairs and of West Indian Affairs, Rt. Hon. E. E. Williams, C.H., D.Phil.
Public Utilities and Ministry of the Prime Minister, Hon. Shamshuddinq Mohammed.
Agriculture, Lands and Fisheries, Hon. L. M. Robinson.
Works, Hon. V. L. Campbell.
National Security, Hon. O. R. Padmore.

Health and Local Government, Hon. Kamaluddin Mohammed.
Labour, Social Security and Co-operatives, Hon. H. O. N. McClean.
Attorney-General and Legal Affairs, Hon. B. L. B. Pitt.
Finance, Hon. G. M. Chambers.
Education and Culture, Hon. C. Gomes.
Petroleum and Mines, Senator the Hon. F. C. Prevatt.
Tobago Affairs, Hon. W. Winchester.
Industry and Commerce, Hon. E. E. Mahabir.
Planning and Development and Housing, Hon. B. M. Barrow.
Minister in Ministry of External Affairs and of West Indian Affairs, Dr. Hon. C. Joseph.
President of the Senate, Dr. the Hon. W. Ali.
Speaker of the House of Representatives, Hon. C. A. Thomasos.

TRINIDAD AND TOBAGO HIGH COMMISSION
42 Belgrave Square, S.W.1
[01-245 9351]
High Commissioner, His Excellency Dr. Patrick Vincent Joseph Solomon (1971).

Deputy High Commissioner, L. E. Williams.
Counsellors, R. K. Ablack; B. Rambissoon.
BRITISH HIGH COMMISSION
Port of Spain
High Commissioner, His Excellency Christopher
Ewart Diggines, C.M.G. (1973) £8,425

Education.—The system of education has been reformed to co-ordinate more closely the nursery, primary, junior secondary, senior secondary and university stages. The system provides for education of the pupils from 4–5 in nursery schools, 5–11 (or 15) in primary schools. Admission to secondary schools (11–18) is by common entrance examination at 11 years. A Primary School leaving Examination can be taken at 15. Junior secondary schools catering for the 11–14 group are being introduced to ease the shortage of places at secondary level. A General Certificate of Education giving admission to the University of the West Indies is taken in senior secondary schools. The Government Polytechnic Institute was established in 1959. There are two Technical Institutes, a government Vocational Centre and six Teacher Training Colleges. One of three branches of the University of the West Indies is ten miles from Port of Spain, at St. Augustine.

Communications.—There are some 4,000 miles of all-weather roads. The only general cargo port is Port of Spain but there are specialized port facilities elsewhere for landing crude oil, loading refinery products and sugar and for landing, storing and trans-shipping bauxite and cement. Regular shipping services call at Port of Spain, which is also a port for the many small inter-island craft. International scheduled airlines, including the national airline, B.W.I.A., use Piarco International Airport outside Port of Spain. A local airline flies between Piarco and Crown Point Airport in Tobago.

There are two commercial broadcasting stations, one rediffusion station and one commercial television station. There is an internal telephone system and good external telephone and telegraph connections.

Production.—Oil is extracted from land and sea wells for refining locally and large quantities of crude oil are also imported. The most important agricultural crop is sugar, but there is a growing diversification into other crops for local use and export. There is considerable industrialization, which already includes the manufacture of cement, chemicals, tyres, clothing, soap, furniture and foodstuffs.

Total exports in 1974 amounted to *TT* $4,166 million, of which *TT* $3,759 million was on account of exports of crude oil and petroleum products. Other main exports were sugar and sugar preparations, ammonium compounds, tar oils, coffee and cocoa beans and fertilizers. Total imports in 1974 were *TT* $3,777 million, of which *TT* $2,716 million was accounted for by imports of crude oil.

FINANCE

The following statistics are from official Trinidad and Tobago publications: figures in *TT* $ millions (*TT* $4·80= £1).

	1973	1974
Revenue.	923	1,212
Expenditure.	974	1,294
Gross public debt.	619	624

TRADE

	1973	1974
Imports.	1,535	3,777
Exports.	1,365	4,166

	1973	1974
Imports from U.K. . . .	£32,859,000	£37,169,000
Exports to U.K.	16,257,000	15,312,000

Uganda

Situated in Eastern Africa, Uganda is flanked by Zaire, the Sudan, Kenya and on the south by Tanzania and Rwanda. Large parts of Lake Victoria, Idi Amin Daba and Mobutu Sese Seko are within its boundaries, as are Lakes Kyoga and Salisbury and the course of the River Nile from its outlet from Lake Victoria to the Sudan frontier post at Nimule. Despite its tropical location, Uganda's climate is tempered by its situation some 3,000 ft. above sea level, and well over that altitude in the highlands of the Western and Eastern Regions. Temperatures seldom rise above 85° F. (29° C.) or fall below 60°F. (15° C.). The rainfall averages about 50 inches a year which means that the country is covered in a lush green cloak for most of the year. Uganda has three National Parks with a wide variety of wildlife and flora.

Area and Population.—Uganda has an area of 91,000 sq. mile (water and swamp 16,400 sq. miles) and population (estimated, 1972) of 10,400,000. The official language of Uganda is Swahili, although English is commonly spoken and is used in commercial circles. The main local vernaculars are of Bantu, Luo and Hamitic origins. Ki-Swahili is generally understood in trading centres. CAPITAL.—Kampala (population of Greater Kampala, 331,000). FLAG.—Six horizontal stripes of black, yellow and red (repeated) with a crested emblem on a white orb in the centre. NATIONAL DAY.—October 9 (Independence Day).

Government.—Uganda became an independent state and a member of the Commonwealth on October 9, 1962, after some 70 years of British rule. A Republic was instituted on September 8, 1967, under an executive President, assisted by a Cabinet of Ministers.

Early on Jan. 25, 1971, while the President, A. Milton Obote, was in Singapore at the 1971 Commonwealth Prime Ministers' Meeting, the Uganda Army, with the co-operation of the police forces, assumed control of the country. All political activity in Uganda was suspended. On Jan. 26, 1971, Maj.-Gen. Idi Amin, the Army Commander, proclaimed himself Head of State, having previously announced that there would be an early return to civilian rule " after free and fair general elections ". There was some short-lived military

opposition in northern parts of Uganda, by troops loyal to Dr. Obote. On Feb. 2, Gen. Amin announced the suspension of certain parts of the Constitution, dissolution of Parliament and the formation of a Defence Council under his own Chairmanship. An advisory Council of Ministers was sworn in on Feb. 5, 1971.

President and Commander in Chief of the Armed Forces and Minister of Defence, General Al-Hajji Idi Amin Dada, *born* 1926, *assumed office* Jan. 26, 1971.

UGANDA HIGH COMMISSION
Uganda House, Trafalgar Square, W.C.2
[01–839 1963]
Acting High Commissioner. F. K. Isingoma.
Counsellor, J. Luzinda.

BRITISH HIGH COMMISSION
10–12 Parliament Avenue (P.O. Box 7070),
Kampala
Acting High Commissioner, J. P. I. Hennessy, C.M.G.,
O.B.E. (*Commercial Counsellor*).

Education.—Education is a joint undertaking by the Government, Local Authorities and, to some extent, Voluntary Agencies. The education system is divided into three distinct sectors—Primary, Secondary and Post-Secondary. The Primary course covers the first seven years of schooling. There were 641,639 pupils in grant-aided Primary Schools in 1967, which rose to 720,127 pupils in 1970 and to an estimated 735,000 in 1971. Education at secondary level falls into four categories—Secondary schools, which are of the Grammar type of school with a course extending over six years to Higher School Certificate; Technical Schools; Farm Schools; and Primary Teacher Training Colleges. Further education is provided at the Uganda Technical College, the National Teachers' College, the Uganda College of Commerce; and Agricultural Colleges. There are also in addition to these, several departmental training schools training staff for different departments. The Medical Department alone has eight such schools training nurses, midwives, medical assistants, health inspectors, and other medical staff. University level education is available at Makerere University, Kampala: the University College, Nairobi, in Kenya, and the University College, Dar es Salaam, in Tanzania. Uganda students also go to universities and colleges outside East Africa for higher education.

Communications.—There is a first-class international airport at Entebbe, with direct flights to many places in Africa, Asia and Europe. There are 10 other state airports and airfields in Uganda. There are 1,700 kilometres of bituminized and 25,000 kilometres of gravel roads. Nearly 75 per cent. of all trunk roads are metalled, the remainder and all feeder roads are gravel roads of good standard. A railway network joins the capital to the western, eastern and northern centres. Lake, marine, road and rail services are operated by the E. African Railways and Harbours Administration.

Finance.—Currency is the *Uganda shilling* (*Ug. sh.* approx. 17·50 = £1 sterling). Total revenue in 1972–3 was *Ug. sh.*1,525,000,000 and expenditure *Ug. sh.*1,430,000,000.

Trade, etc.—The principal export commodities are coffee, cotton, copper, animal feeding-stuffs, hides and skins and unmanufactured tobacco. Other crops grown include sugar and groundnuts. Hydroelectric power is produced from the Owen Falls power station which has a capacity of 150,000 kWh. Plans are under way for increasing the output of electricity.

	1972	1973
Imports......	*Ug. sh.*1,783,000,000	674,283,000
Exports......	1,857,200,000	2,817,717,000

TRADE WITH U.K.

	1973	1974
Imports from U.K....	£ 4,913,000	£ 7,238,000
Exports to U.K......	20,788,000	24,412,000

Zambia

The Republic of Zambia lies on the plateau of Central Africa between the longitudes 22° E. and 33° 33′ E. and between the latitudes 8° 15′ S. and 18° S. It has an area of 290,587 square miles within boundaries 3,515 miles in length and a population (Census, 1969) of 4,054, 00, including about 50,000 non-Africans.

With the exception of the valleys of the Zambesi, the Luapula, the Kafue and the Luangwa Rivers, and the Luano valley, the greater part of Zambia has a flat to rolling topography, with elevations varying from 3,000 to 5,000 feet above sea level, but in the north-eastern districts the plateau rises to occasional altitudes of over 6,000 feet. In many localities the evenness of the plateau is broken by hills, sometimes occurring as chains which develop into areas of broken country.

Although Zambia lies within the tropics, and fairly centrally in the great land mass of the African continent its elevation relieves it from the extremely high temperatures and humidity usually associated with tropical countries. The lower reaches of the Zambesi, Luangwa and Kafue rivers in deeper valleys do experience high humidity and trying extremes of heat, but these areas are remote and sparsely populated.

Government.—At the dissolution of the Federation of Rhodesia and Nyasaland, on December 31, 1963, Northern Rhodesia (as Zambia was then known) achieved internal self-government under a new constitution. Zambia became an independent republic with the Commonwealth on October 24, 1964—75 years after coming under British rule and nine months after achieving internal self-government. Until December 1972, when the 1964 Constitution was superseded, the country had a multi-party constitution. In July 1973, a new Constitution was introduced, providing that the United National Independence Party shall be the only party.

CAPITAL.—Lusaka, situated in the Central Province. Population (Census, 1969), 238,000. Other centres are Livingstone, Kabwe, Chipata, Mazabuka, Mbala, Kasama, Solwezi, Mongu, Mansa, Ndola, Luanshya, Mufulira, Chingola, Chililabombwe, Kalulushi and Kitwe, the last six towns being the main centres on the Copperbelt. FLAG.—Green with three small vertical stripes, red, black and orange (next fly); eagle device on green above stripes.

President, Dr. Kenneth David Kaunda, *assumed office* October 24, 1964; *re-elected*, December 1973.

CABINET
The President (also *Minister of Defence*).
Prime Minister (also *Minister of National Guidance and Development*), E. H. K. Mudenda.
Minister of Foreign Affairs, R. Banda.
Rural Development, P. Lusaka.
Home Affairs, A. M. Milner.
Local Government and Housing, P. W. Matoka.
Legal Affairs and Attorney-General, M. M. Chona.
Health, Dr. M. M. Bull.
Information and Broadcasting, C. M. Mwanansiku.
Lands, Natural Resources and Tourism, J. Mapoma.
Power, Transport and Works, Dr. N. S. Mulenga.

Education, F. M. Mulikita.
Labour and Social Services, H. D. Banda.
Mines and Industry, A. J. Soko.
Planning and Finance, A. B. Chikwanda.
Commerce, R. Kunda.

ZAMBIA HIGH COMMISSION
7–11 Cavendish Place, W.1
[01–580 0691]
High Commissioner, (vacant)

BRITISH HIGH COMMISSION
Lusaka
High Commissioner, His Excellency Frank Stephen Miles, C.M.G. (1974)................£12,000

British Council Representative, Dr. D. S. Coombs, Heroes Place, Cairo Road, Lusaka.

JUDICATURE

There is a Chief Justice appointed by the President, all other judges being appointed on the recommendation of the Judicial Service Commission consisting of the Chief Justice, the chairman of the Public Service Commission, a senior Justice of Appeal and one Presidential nominee.

Chief Justice of Zambia, Hon. A. M. Silungwe.

Deputy Chief Justice, L. S. Baron.

Justices of the Supreme Court, B. T. Gardener; J. J. Hughes.

Puisne Judges, G. B. Muwo; W. S. Bruce-Lyle; B. Cullinan; G. Care; M. Moodley; B. Bwewpe.

Education.—In 1973 there were 810,740 pupils in primary schools and 65,764 (1974) in secondary schools.

Full-time university enrolment in 1974 was 2,612.

Production and Employment.—The total value of marketed farm produce in 1972 was K63,000,000. Principal products were tobacco, maize, groundnuts, cotton, livestock and vegetables.

Mineral production was valued at K933,599,000 in 1974. The production of copper totalled 702,490 tonnes valued at K874,037,504. In 1973 an oil refinery at Ndola came into operation and the pipeline running through Zambia to Ndola was switched over to the transportation of crude oil.

In Dec. 1973, 383,830 persons were estimated to be in full employment. Included in this figure are: mining and quarrying, 62,590; agriculture, forestry and fishery, 36,500; construction, 75,560; manufacturing, 42,060.

Finance and Currency.—Zambia adopted decimal currency on Jan. 16, 1968, the unit being the *Kwacha.* The exchange rate in June 1974 was about £1 = K1·54, although it varies with the floating of sterling.

	1973	1974
Revenue	K329,300,000	K682,900,000
Expenditure	356,600,000	490,000,000
Capital expenditure	113,900,000	241,800,000

GRENADA

Grenada is situated between the parallels of 12° 13'–11° 58' N. lat. and 61° 20'–61° 35' W. long., and is about 21 miles in length and 12 miles in breadth; it is about 96 miles north of Trinidad, 68 miles S.S.W. of St. Vincent, and 100 miles S.W. of Barbados. Area, about 133 square miles; estimated population (including some of the Grenadines), 106,000 (1973). The country is mountainous and very picturesque, and the climate is healthy. Grenada was discovered by Columbus in 1498, and named Conception. It was originally colonized by the French, and was ceded to Great Britain by the Treaty of Versailles in 1783.

The soil is very fertile, and cocoa, spices, bananas, sugar cane, cotton, coconuts, limes and fruit are grown. The imports are chiefly dry goods, wheat, flour. dried fish, feedstuffs, hardware and rice.

ΨSt. George's (population 8,600) on the southwest coast, is the chief town, and possesses a good harbour.

FLAG.—Tricolour of blue, yellow and green horizontal bands—in centre a nutmeg device on an oval white ground bordered by a brown line.

Trade

Total imports (1972) $42,823,702

Total exports (1972) $10,530,746

Includes Colonial Development and Welfare Grant.

Government

Grenada became an Associated State in association with Great Britain on March 3, 1967. The Legislature became bicameral consisting of Her Majesty, a Senate and a House of Representatives. There is a Premier, with four other Ministers. The Principal Law Officer is *ex officio* a member of the Senate. Grenada became independent on February 7, 1974.

Governor-General, Leo de Gale (1974).

Premier, Eric M. Gairy.

The *Grenadines* are a chain of small islands lying between Grenada and St. Vincent, within which Governments they are included. The largest island is Carriacou, attached to the Government of Grenada, with area of 13 sq. miles and population of 8,179.

GRENADA HIGH COMMISSION
King's House, 10 Haymarket, S.W.1
[01–930 7902]

High Commissioner, His Excellency Oswald M. Gibbs (1974).

British High Commission (*see* Trinidad and Tobago)

REPUBLIC OF NAURU

The Republic of Nauru is an island of 8·2 sq. miles in size, situated in 166° 55' E. longitude and 32' S. of the Equator. It has a population (estimated June, 1972) of 6,768, of whom two-thirds are Nauruans or other Pacific Islanders. There are Chinese and European minorities. About 43 per cent. of Nauruans are adherents of the Nauruan Protestant Church and there is a Roman Catholic Mission on the island.

Nauru was discovered by Capt. Fearn, R.N. in 1798, and was annexed by Germany in 1888. It surrendered to H.M.A.S. *Melbourne* in November, 1914. Until 1968 Nauru was administered by Australia under an international trusteeship agreement which on Nov. 1, 1947, superseded a former League of Nations Mandate.

President, Premier and Minister of Foreign Affairs, Hammer DeRoburt, O.B.E., *born* 1922, *elected* May 19, 1968, *re-elected* Dec. 1973.

Government.—Under Australian administration a Legislative Council of nine elected and five official members was established in 1966 and a four-member Executive Council. After negotiations at Canberra during 1967 between Mr. DeRoburt, then Head Chief of Nauru, and representatives of the Trusteeship powers Australia, New Zealand and the United Kingdom, and with the concurrence of the U.N. Trusteeship Council, Naru became an independent State from February 1, 1968. It was announced in November, 1968, that a limited form of membership of the Commonwealth had been devised for Nauru at the request of its Government. A new Parliament was elected on Jan. 26, 1968.

Judiciary.—The Nauruan judiciary consists of a District Court, a Central Court and a Court of Appeal.

Education and Welfare.—Nauru has a hospital service and other medical and dental services. There is also a maternity and child welfare service. Education is available in 9 primary and 2 secondary schools on the island with a total enrolment of 1,797 pupils.

Production, etc.—There are valuable deposits of phosphates on the island which were purchased from the Pacific Phosphate Company in 1919 by the Governments of Australia, New Zealand and the United Kingdom for £3,500,000 and vested in the British Phosphate Commissioners. Royalties on phosphate exports (about £5,000,000 annually) have been paid partly to the Nauruans and partly into a trust fund which used income from investments abroad to pay for Nauru's administrative and social services. Phosphate mining employs 1,369 persons out of a labour force of 2,208.

The assets on Nauru of the British Phosphate Commissioners have been purchased by the Nauruans, control of mining and marketing passing to the Nauru Phosphate Corporation on July 1, 1970.

Trade.—Phosphate exports in 1969–70 amounted to 2,060,000 tons (Australia, 1,218,300; N.Z., 516,350; Japan, 356,650). Total exports were valued at $A14,500,000 (entirely phosphates). General imports were valued at $A4,502,123, including $A353,385 from the United Kingdom.

Finance.—Total revenue in 1971–72 was $A7,503,900, mainly payments by the British Phosphate Commissioners; expenditure $A7,721,900.

FLAG.—Twelve-point star (representing the 12 original Nauruan tribes) below a gold bar (representing the Equator), all on a blue ground.

TONGA

The Tongan or Friendly Islands, a British-protected state for 70 years, became independent on June 7, 1970.

These islands are situated in the Southern Pacific some 450 miles to the E.S.E. of Fiji, with an area of 270 sq. miles, and population (estimated, 1972) of 92,360. The largest island, Tongatapu, was discovered by Tasman in 1643. Most of the islands are of coral formation, but some are volcanic (Tofua, Kao and Niuafoou or "Tin Can" Island). The limits of the group are between 15° and 23° 30′ S., and 173° and 177° W. Nuku'alofa, on the island of Tongatapu, is the seat of government. The present King Taufa'ahau Tupou IV, G.C.V.O., K.C.M.G., K.B.E., succeeded his mother, the late Queen Salote Tupou III, on December 16, 1965. The constitution provides for a Government consisting of the Sovereign, a privy council and cabinet, a legislative assembly and a judiciary. The legislative assembly has 22 members, with a Speaker, and includes the Ministers of the Crown, the two Governors of Island groups, and the representatives of the Nobles and of the people (seven of each), who are elected triennially.

Premier, Minister of Foreign Affairs and of Agriculture, H.R.H. Prince Fatafehi Tu'ipelehake, C.B.E.

Soil generally is fertile, the principal exports are copra and bananas. Revenue July 1973–June 1974 T$5,081,170; expenditure T$4,248,800. The national debt is T$1,153,200 (June 1974). Total imports (1974) T$11,819,247. Total exports (1974) T$4,561,494. The total shipping cleared in 1972 was 551,347 tons. Tongan currency is at parity with Australia.

CAPITAL.—Nuku'alofa (20,000).

FLAG.—Truncated red cross on rectangular white ground (next staff) on a red field.

TONGAN HIGH COMMISSION
New Zealand House, Haymarket, S.W.1
[01–839 3287]
High Commissioner, His Excellency 'Inoke Fotu Faletau.

BRITISH HIGH COMMISSION
Nuku'alofa
High Commissioner, His Excellency Humphrey Augustine Arthington-Davy, O.B.E.

WESTERN SAMOA

Head of State, H. H. Malietoa Tanumafili II, C.B.E. (April 15, 1963).

Prime Minister, Hon. Tupua Tamasese Lealofi IV.

Formerly administered by New Zealand (latterly with internal self-government), Western Samoa became, on January 1, 1962, the first fully-independent Polynesian State.

The State was treated as a member country of the Commonwealth until its formal admission on August 28, 1970.

Western Samoa consists of the islands of Savai'i (662 sq. miles) and of Upolu, which with nine other islands, has an area of 435 sq. miles. All islands are mountainous. Upolu, the most fertile,

contains the harbours of ΨApia and ΨSaluafata and Savai'i the harbour of ΨAsau. The islanders are Christians of different denominations. In 1973 the population was estimated to be 151,000.

The chief exports are copra, cocoa and bananas.
Total exports 1973 were $4,000,000.
Total imports 1973 were $13,051,000.

TRADE WITH U.K.

	1971	1972
Imports from U.K.	£347,000	£1,116,000
Exports to U.K.	77,000	124,000

CAPITAL.—ΨApia (population 28,800). Robert Louis Stevenson died and was buried at Apia in 1894.

FLAG.—Five white stars (depicting the Southern Cross) on a quarter royal blue at top next staff, and three quarters red.

Associated States, Colonies, Protectorates, etc.

Flags of the Dependencies.—Generally the dependencies use the Union Flag (" Union Jack ") or Blue Ensign bearing a badge of arms of the Dependency (with surrounding garland when used with the Union Flag). In a few cases, e.g. Bermuda, the Red Ensign is used with badge. (See also ANTIGUA (W. Indies); BRUNEI; ST. KITTS (W. Indies); ST. LUCIA (W. Indies).)

ASCENSION
See ST. HELENA

BELIZE

British Honduras, in Central America, was officially renamed Belize on June 1, 1973. It lies within 18° 29′ 50″ to 51° 53′ N. latitude and 89° 13′ 28″

to 87° 21′ 30″ W. longitude. Its extreme length and breadth are approximately 186 m. and 118 m. respectively; it is bounded on the north and northwest by Mexico, on the west and south by Guatemala; and on the east by the Caribbean Sea. The total area (including offshore islands) is about

8,867 sq. miles, with an estimated population (1970) of 122,000. The climate generally is damp and warm, but not unhealthy. The temperature ranges from 47° to 94° F. The average lies between 75° and 80°, but this is considerably tempered by the prevailing sea-breezes.

The greater part of the country is covered by forest, of which 50 per cent. is high rain forest, 15·5 pine forest and dry savannah, 5·5 wet savannah and mangrove forest, the remaining 20 per cent. being existing or recently abandoned cultivation. The wire grass and sedges of the dry savannahs make very poor pasturage for cattle. The north of the territory and the southern coastal plain (8 to 20 miles wide) are nearly flat. Near the sea the plain is low and swampy. The central mountain mass has a general altitude of 2,000 to 3,000 feet and 20 per cent. of the area of the territory is over 1,000 feet in elevation above mean sea-level.

The staple products are obtained from the forests, and include mahogany, cedar, and *chicle* (the basis of chewing-gum), Santa Maria, pine and rosewood. Agricultural crops which grow readily include sugar cane, coconuts, citrus fruit, plantains, pine-apples, mangoes, maize, cucumbers, rice, varieties of beans and peas. Bananas also grow well in certain localities. All varieties of citrus fruits flourish, and in particular grape-fruit, of which a very high grade is exported. Lobster tails and shrimps are also exported.

In 1974 there were 181 Government and grant-aided primary schools and 8 unaided private elementary schools in the country, the total enrolment being 35,000. There are also 21 secondary schools with a total enrolment of 6,000.

There are 50 post offices in the country. A new transmitting and receiving station at Ladyville has been completed. External telegraph and radio telephone and telex services are operated by Cable and Wireless Ltd. Air services are scheduled 5 times weekly to and from the capitals of Panama, Honduras, Mexico, Salvador, Guatemala, Nicaragua, Costa Rica and twice weekly to and from Jamaica. There is a six times weekly service from and to New Orleans, a seven times weekly service from and to Miami and a weekly service to Mexico City. A local scheduled air service links the six districts into which the country is divided.

CAPITAL, Belmopan (estimated population, Dec. 31, 1974, 3,500). The largest city and the former capital is ΨBelize City (population, 1970, 38,000), which was badly damaged by a hurricane in October, 1961. It was announced in 1965 that a new capital would be built, 50 miles inland. Construction is proceeding on the new city, Belmopan, with U.K. aid of $24,000,000. The first phase was completed in 1970. Other towns are ΨCorozal (12,319), Cayo (16,484), ΨStann Creek (13,435) Orange Walk (13,266), Toledo (9,804).

FINANCE

	1974	1975
Revenue	$23,487,200	$31,606,444
Expenditure	23,487,200	27,647,259

Estimated revenue and expenditure on capital projects in 1974 balanced at $16,677,277.

Public Debt (Dec. 31, 1974), $17,469,814.

The Canadian Government has made a loan of $8,000,000 for modern water and sewerage systems in Belize City.

TRADE WITH U.K.

	1973	1974
Imports from U.K.	£3,770,000	£4,218,000
Exports to U.K.	2,730,000	4,975,000

GOVERNMENT

Under the Constitution introduced on Jan. 1, 1964, the Governor retains special responsibility for defence, external affairs, internal security and the safeguarding of the terms and conditions of service of public officers. For so long as the Government continues to receive grant-in-aid from the U.K. Government, the Governor also has special responsibility for maintaining or securing financial and economic stability and for ensuring that any condition attached to any financial grant or loan made by the U.K. Government is fulfilled. The Governor appoints as Premier the person who appears to him to be likely to command the support of a majority in the House of Representatives. Ministers are appointed by the Governor on the advice of the Premier.

The National Assembly comprises a House of Representatives and a Senate. The House of Representatives consists of 18 members elected by universal adult suffrage. The Speaker may be elected by the House from among its own members, or from outside; the Deputy Speaker is elected by the House from among its own members. The Senate consists of 8 members appointed by the Governor (5 on the advice of the Premier, 2 on the advice of the leader of the Opposition and 1 after consulting such persons as he considers appropriate).

Governor and Commander-in-Chief, His Excellency Richard Neil Posnett, O.B.E. (1972)	$25,200
Chief Justice, D. Malone	14,000
Speaker of the House of Representatives, Hon. A. A. Hunter	4,750
Premier and Minister of Finance and Economic Development, Hon. G. C. Price	9,700
Minister of Works and Communications, Hon. F. H. Hunter	9,000
Trade and Industry, Cooperative and Consumer Protection, Hon. S. A. Perdomo	9,000
Local Government and Social Welfare, and Labour, Hon. D. L. McKay	9,000
Education, Housing, Hon. G. Pech	9,000
Deputy Premier and Home Affairs and Health, Hon. C. L. B. Rogers	9,000
Agriculture and Lands, Hon. F. Marin	9,100
Attorney-General and Minister of Economic Planning, Hon. A. Shoman	9,100

Belize is distant from London about 4,700 miles; transit, 17 days by sea, 18 hours by air *via* Miami.

BERMUDA

The Bermudas, or Somers Islands, are a cluster of about 100 small islands (about 20 only of which are inhabited) situated in the west of the Atlantic Ocean, in 32° 18′ N. lat. and 64° 461 W. long., the nearest point of the mainland being Cape Hatteras in North Carolina, about 570 miles distant. The total area is now approximately 20·59 sq. miles which includes 2·3 sq. miles leased to, or reclaimed by, the U.S. authorities between 1941 and 1957 under the terms of the 99 year lease. The civil population was 53,000 at the Census taken in October, 1970. The colony derives its name from Juan Bermudez, a Spaniard, who sighted it before 1515, but no settlement was made until 1609, when Sir George Somers, who was shipwrecked here on his way to Virginia, colonized the islands.

Vegetation is prolific, the principal trees being the Bermuda cedar (juniper), formerly of great importance for shipbuilding, but since 1943 almost entirely destroyed by blight. At one time the islands enjoyed a flourishing export in onions, potatoes, and green vegetables, but the imposition of tariffs in U.S.A. and the growing shortage of arable land made further growing for export unprofitable. The lily bud trade with Canada and U.S.A. and locally manufactured concentrates and pharmaceuticals are now the Colony's leading exports. Little food is produced except vegetables and fish, other foodstuffs being imported.

The Colony's economic structure is based on its importance as a tourist resort and as a naval base and from these sources most of its revenue is derived. Bermuda is now within two hours' air travel from New York, and in 1972 a total of 488,271 visitors arrived in Bermuda. The airport is used by B.O.A.C., Pan-American Airways, Air-Canada, Eastern, North-East and Qantas air lines and most cruise ships dock at Hamilton.

Free elementary education was introduced in May, 1949. Free secondary education was introduced in 1965 for those children in the aided and maintained schools who were below the upper limit of the statutory school age (16 from 1969 onwards).

There are 4 radio and 2 television stations, one daily and 3 weekly newspapers and overseas telephone and telegraph services are maintained.

GOVERNMENT

Internal self-government was introduced on June 8, 1968. There are a Legislative Council of 11 Members and an elected House of Assembly of 40 Members. The Governor retains responsibility for external affairs, defence, internal security and the police.

Voters must be British subjects of twenty-one years of age or older at the time of registration, and if they do not possess Bermudian status, they must have been ordinarily resident in Bermuda for the whole of the period of three years immediately before registration. Registration is held every year during the month of February. Candidates for election must qualify as electors and must possess Bermudian status.

Governor and Commander-in-Chief, His Excellency Sir Edwin Hartley Cameron Leather, K.C.M.G., K.C.V.O. (1973) *(excluding allowances)*..... $28,512

Executive Council
CABINET

Premier, Hon. Sir Edward Richards, C.B.E.
Labour and Immigration, Hon. C. V. Woolridge.
Finance, Hon. J. H. Sharpe, C.B.E.
Education, Hon Mrs. Gloria McPhee.
Tourism and Trade, Hon. de F. Trimingham.
Public Works and Agriculture, Hon. J. M. S. Patton, G.C.
Health and Water, Hon. Q. L. Edness.
Marine and Air Services, Hon. F. J. Barritt.
Planning, Hon. E. W. P. Vesey.
Transport, Hon. R. O. Marshall.
Organization, Hon. J. R. Plowman, C.B.E.
Youth and Sport, Hon. L. I. Swan.

President of the Legislative Council, Hon. Sir George Ratteray, C.B.E.
Speaker of the House of Assembly, Hon. Sir Arthur Spurling, C.B.E.

Chief Justice, Hon. Sir John Summerfield, C.B.E.
Puisne Judge, Hon. E. E. Seaton.
Deputy Governor, I. A. C. Kinnear, C.M.G.

FINANCE

	1973–74
Public revenue	52,245,598
Public expenditure	49,895,419
Public debt (March 31, 1971)	6,093,600

*Estimated.

Currency.—Bermuda Monetary Authority notes ($50, $20, $10, $5 and $1) and metal coinage (50c, 25c, 10c, 5c and 1c) became the currency of Bermuda on Feb. 6, 1970.

TRADE WITH U.K.

	1973	1974
Imports from U.K.	£12,717,000	£14,371,000
Exports to U.K.	5,947,000	4,154,000

Imports: 1970, eight month Figures April–July not reported. †Exports figures refer to years ending on March 31.

CAPITAL, Hamilton, (Population (1970), 3,000).

THE BRITISH VIRGIN ISLANDS

The Virgin Islands are a group of islands at the eastern extremity of the Greater Antilles, divided between Great Britain and the U.S.A. Those of the group which are British number about 42, of which 11 are uninhabited, and have a total area of about 59 square miles. The principal are Tortola, the largest (situate in 18° 27′ N. lat. and 64° 40′ W. long., area, 21 sq. miles), Virgin Gorda (8¼ sq. miles), Anegada (15 sq. miles) and Jost Van Dyke (3½ sq. miles). The 1970 Census of Population showed a total population of 10,030 (Tortola (8,676); Virgin Gorda (904); Anegada (269); Jost Van Dyke (123): and other islands 68). Apart from Anegada, which is a flat coral island, the British Virgin Islands are hilly, being an extension of the Puerto Rico and the U.S. Virgin Islands archipelago. The highest point is Sage Mountain on Tortola which rises to a height of 1,780 feet. The islands are very picturesque and form one of the finest sailing areas in the world on account of their sheltered waters. The sea is rich in gamefish and there are said to be over 400 wrecks off Anegada. Tourism is the main industry, but there is some cattle raising and fishing. Other products are vegetables, fruit, charcoal and a small amount of rum.

The islands lie within the Trade Winds belt and possess a pleasant and healthy sub-tropical climate. The average temperature varies from 71° to 82° F. in winter and 78°–88° F. in summer. The summer heat is tempered by sea breezes and the temperature usually falls by about 10° at night. Average rainfall is 53 inches. Hurricanes are very rare—the last occurrence being in 1928.

The principal airport is on Beef Island, linked by bridge to Tortola, and an extended runway of 3,600 feet, opened in 1969, enables larger aircraft to call. There is a second airfield on Virgin Gorda and a third on Anegada. There are direct shipping services to the United Kingdom and the United States and fast passenger services connect the main islands by ferry.

FINANCE AND TRADE

	1973	1974
Revenue	$U.S.3,776,765	$U.S. 5,016,529
Expenditure	4,776,765	5,999,420
Imports	9,452,896	11,603,836
Exports	440,416	N.A.

GOVERNMENT

The British Virgin Islands are partially internally self-governing, with a ministerial system. The Governor, appointed by the Crown, remains responsible for defence and internal security, external affairs, the civil service, administration of the courts and finance, and acts in accordance with the advice of the Executive Council. The Executive Council consists of the Governor as Chairman, two *ex officio* members (the Attorney-General and the Financial Secretary), the Chief Minister and two other ministers. The Legislative Council consists of a Speaker chosen from outside the Council, two *ex officio* members (the Attorney-General and

Financial Secretary), one nominated member appointed by the Governor after consultation with the Chief Minister and seven elected members returned from seven one-member electoral districts. The islands are proud of their tradition of stable government.

Governor, His Excellency W. W. Wallace (1974).................. U.S.14,030

Chief Minister, Hon. W. Wheatley, M.B.E............................	10,300
Minister of Natural Resources and Public Health, Hon. C. Maduro..........	8,400
Minister of Communications, Works and Industry, Hon. O. Cills............	8,400
Financial Secretary, Hon. J. A. Frost...	12,480
Attorney-General, Hon. Paula Beaubrun	12,828
Chief Education Officer, Enid Scatliffe..	11,784
Chief of Police, R. Jones.............	10,236
Chief Medical Officer, H. P. Watson....	12,384
Chief Engineer, Public Works, P. D. Grace............................	11,784
Chief Electrical Engineer, E. Garner	11,708
Chief Agricultural Officer, N. Vanterpool	7,584

CAPITAL.—Ψ Road Town (on the south-east of Tortola). Population, 2,129.

BRUNEI

Sultan, H. H. Hassanal Bolkiah Mu'izzadin Waddaulah, G.C.M.G., *acceded* 1967, *crowned* Aug. 1, 1968.

Brunei is situated on the north-west coast of the island of Borneo, total area about 2,226 sq. miles, population (estimated 1973), 145,170, of whom 71·7 per cent. are of Malay or other indigenous race and 23·4 per cent. Chinese. The chief town, Bandar Seri Begawan, with its nearby water village (groups of houses on stilts on the Brunei River) has a population of about 38,000. The country has a humid tropical climate.

In 1959, the Sultan of Brunei promulgated the first written Constitution, which provides for a Privy Council, a Council of Ministers and a Legislative Council. Under the 1959 Agreement, as amended in 1971, Britain is responsible for external affairs, and has an obligation to consult the Brunei Government on the defence of the State. The post of British Resident was abolished in 1959 and many of his functions were transferred to the Sultan in Council. A *Mentri Besar* (Chief Minister) is appointed by the Sultan, and is responsible to him for the exercise of executive authority. The Sultan presides over the Privy Council and the Council of Ministers.

FLAG.—Yellow, with diagonal bands of white over narrow black band (from top by staff), with red device on diagonal bands.

BRITISH HIGH COMMISSION
Jalan Residency, Brunei

High Commissioner, His Excellency James Alfred Davidson, O.B.E. (1974)................ £5,765

FINANCE

	1972	1973
Revenue..........	B$256,602,544	B$386,861,494
Expenditure	216,329,741	226,336,451

Including development expenditure.

Currency.—Brunei issues its own currency, the *Brunei dollar* of 100 *cents,* which is fully interchangeable with the currency of Singapore.

Imports from the U.K. in 1974 totalled £5,113,000 (1973, £2,550,000).

FALKLAND ISLANDS

The Falkland Islands, the only considerable group in the South Atlantic, lie about 300 miles east of the Straits of Magellan, between 52° 15'–53° S. lat. and 57° 40'–62° W. long. They consist of East Falkland (area 2,610 sq. miles), West Falkland (2,090

sq. miles) and upwards of 100 small islands in the aggregate, the estimated population at the Census of Dec. 31, 1974 being 1,759. Mount Usborne, the loftiest peak, rises 2,312 feet above the level of the sea. The Falklands were discovered by Davis in 1592, and visited by Hawkins in 1594. A settlement was made by France in 1764; this was subsequently sold to Spain, but the latter country recognized Great Britain's title to a part at least of the group in 1771. The settlement was destroyed by the Americans in 1831. In 1833 occupation was resumed by the British for the protection of the seal-fisheries, and the islands were permanently colonized as the most southerly organized colony of the British Empire. The climate is cool. At Stanley the mean monthly temperature varies between 49° F. in January and 35·5° F. in July. The air temperature has never been known to exceed 77° F. or to fall below 12° F.; it is notably windy. The islands are chiefly moorland. The population is almost totally British, and is principally engaged in sheep-farming to which practically all the land in the colony is devoted, 628,147 sheep being carried in 1973/4. Wool, hides and sheepskins are exported. The only town is Ψ Stanley on the coast of East Falkland.

GOVERNMENT

The Governor is assisted by a Legislative Council of 8 members, with the Governor as President, 2 *ex officio* (Chief Secretary and Financial Secretary), 2 non-official members (nominated by the Governor), and 4 representatives elected by the people.

Governor and Commander-in-Chief, His Excellency Neville Arthur Irwin French, M.V.O. (1975) (+ *duty allce.* £936) £4,500
Chief Secretary, A. J. P. Monk £4,170
Financial Secretary, H. T. Rowlands (+ *allce.* £540) £3,120

FINANCE AND TRADE

	1973/74	1974/75†
Public Revenue.....	£688,977	£862,176
Expenditure........	624,922	790,710

† Estimated.

	1973	1974
Total imports.......	£570,996	£805,237
Total exports........	1 543,735	4,921,746

Falkland Islands and Dependencies
Trade with U.K.

	1973	1974
Imports from U.K....	£478,682	£506,878
Exports to U.K......	1,453,736	4,921,746

CHIEF TOWN, Ψ Stanley, estimated population 1,079. Stanley is distant from England about 8,103 miles. Telegrams by wireless U.K. direct. The journey from U.K. to Falkland Islands can be accomplished in 4 to 5 days travelling to Comodoro Rivadavia, *via* Buenos Aires, thence by air to Stanley.

DEPENDENCIES.—*South Georgia,* an island 800 miles east-south-east of the Falkland group, with an area of 1,450 sq. miles. Some 22 persons reside at the British scientific base which has been established at King Edward Point. The South Sandwich Islands group, which is uninhabited and lies some 470 miles S.E. of South Georgia, is the only other dependency.

GIBRALTAR,

a rocky promontory, 3¾ miles in length, ¾ of a mile in breadth and 1,396 feet high at its greatest elevation, near the southern extremity of Spain, with which it is connected by a low isthmus. It is about 14 miles distant from the opposite coast of Africa. In a total area of $2\frac{1}{4}$ sq. miles, the population at the census of Oct. 1970 was 26,833. The estimated civilian population at the end of 1974 was 29,362.

Gibraltar is a naval base of strategic importance to Great Britain. It was captured in 1704, during the war of the Spanish Succession, by a combined Dutch and English force, under Sir George Rooke, and was ceded to Great Britain by the Treaty of Utrecht, 1713. Several attempts have been made to retake it, the most celebrated being the great siege in 1779–83, when General Eliott, afterwards Lord Heathfield, held it for 3 years and 7 months against a combined French and Spanish force. The town stands at the foot of the promontory on the W. side. Gibraltar enjoys the advantages of an extensive shipping trade. The chief sources of revenue are the port dues, the rent of the Crown estate in the town, and duties on consumer items. Import duties are low and Gibraltar is a popular shopping centre. The gradual change from a fortress city to an attractive holiday centre has led to a flourishing tourist trade.

A total of 2,384 merchant ships (14,178,280 net tons) entered the port during 1974. Of these 1,790 were deep-sea ships (13,973,041 net tons). In addition 1,979 yachts (33,389 net tons) called at the port. There are 26·75 miles of roads.

Education is compulsory and free between the ages of 5 and 15 and scholarships are available for university or further education in Britain. There are 11 Government, 2 private and 2 Services primary schools, with 3,824 pupils in Dec. 1974. The two government secondary schools had 1,549 pupils in 1974. Government expenditure on education in 1974 was £742,441.

FINANCE AND TRADE

	1972/73	1973/74
Revenue	£5,629,642	£6,710,196
Expenditure	5,559,072	6,906,250

	1973	1974
Total imports	£15,511,000	£25,088,714
Total exports	4,663,540	10,484,352

	1973	1974
Imports from U.K.	£9,313,000	£17,875,652
Exports to U.K.	333,000	348,056

GOVERNMENT

The Constitution of Gibraltar, approved in 1969, made formal provision for certain domestic matters to devolve on Ministers appointed from among elected members of the House of Assembly then set up to replace the former Legislative Council. The House of Assembly consists of an independent Speaker, 15 elected members and the Attorney-General and Financial and Development Secretary.
Governor and Commander-in-Chief, His Excellency Marshal of the Royal Air Force Sir John Grandy, G.C.B., K.B.E., D.S.O. (1973)(*including* £1,500 *entertainment allowance*)..................£8,750
Flag Officer, Gibraltar, and Admiral Supr., H.M. Dockyard, Gibraltar, Rear Admiral R. A. Sandford.
Chief Minister, Sir Joshua Hassan, C.B.E., M.V.O., Q.C.
Chief Justice, Sir Edgar Unsworth, C.M.G... £4,890
Speaker, A. J. Vasquez.
Deputy Governor, E. H. Davis, C.M.G., O.B.E.£4,890
Financial and Development Secretary, A. Mackay, C.M.G........................£4,490
Attorney-General, J. K. Havers, O.B.E., Q.C... £4,490
Distance from London 1,209 miles; transit, $3\frac{1}{4}$ days. British Airways operate regular direct air services to the U.K. (Some services are *via* Madrid.) Transit times average 3 hours.

GILBERT AND ELLICE ISLANDS

Until Jan. 1, 1972, the Gilbert and Ellice Islands came under the jurisdiction of the High Commissioner for the Western Pacific.

The Gilbert and Ellice Islands Colony, which includes, in addition, Ocean Island, the Phoenix Islands and the Northern Line Islands, is situated in the south-western Pacific around the point at which the International Date Line cuts the Equator. The Colony consists of 42 coral atolls (of which 29 are permanently inhabited), with a total land area of 324 sq. miles, spread over some 2 million square miles of ocean. Few of the atolls are more than 12 ft. above sea-level or more than half a mile in width. The vegetation consists mainly of coconut palms, breadfruit trees and pandanus. The total population (1973) was 57,960 of whom 47,932 were Micronesians (Gilbertese) and 7,974 Polynesians (Ellice). The Phoenix and Northern Line Islands now have no indigenous populations. Christianity is wide-spread, roughly half the population being Protestants (Congregationalists) and the other half Roman Catholics. Most people still practise a subsistence economy, the main staples of their diet being coconuts and fish.

The Colony is administered by a Governor. The present Constitution was introduced on May 1, 1974, and provides for a House of Assembly consisting of 28 Elected Members and three officials, and a Council of Ministers consisting of a Chief Minister, between four and six appointed members and three officials, as follows: The Chief Minister, elected from among the Elected Members of the House of Assembly; between four and six members from the House of Assembly appointed as Ministers by the Governor acting in accordance with the advice of the Chief Minister; and the three officials who are members of the House of Assembly. Local government services are provided by elected Island Councils. Under an agreement reached in 1939, Canton and Enderbury Islands, in the Phoenix group, are jointly administered by the United Kingdom and the United States.

On the recommendation of a Commissioner appointed by Her Majesty's Government to consider requests by the Ellice leaders to have their island group separated from the Gilberts, a referendum of the Ellice islanders was held in the autumn of 1974. This showed overwhelming support for separation, which was planned to take effect from Oct. 1, 1975. The Ellice islands would then become a separate colony to be known as Tuvalu with the capital at Funafuti. At the time of going to press, however, discussions were still taking place.

The unit of currency is the Australian dollar. Revenue for 1974 was $A15,326,418 and expenditure $A12,701,112. The principal imports are foodstuffs, consumer goods and building materials. The only exports are phosphates from Ocean Island and copra, most of which is produced by small landowners. There are three copra plantations in the Northern Line Islands.

Communication between the islands is mainly by small ships operated by the Development Authority, a non-government organization. There is a weekly air service to Fiji. A few islands are served by an internal air service.

The Government maintains a teacher training college and a secondary school. Four junior secondary schools are maintained by missions. Throughout the Colony there are 111 primary schools. The total enrolment of children of school age (1974) was 14,308. The Marine Training School at Tarawa trains seamen for service with British and foreign shipping lines.

There is a general hospital at Tarawa in the

Gilbert Islands and a smaller one at Funafuti in the Ellice Islands. The British Phosphate Commissioners maintain a general hospital on Ocean Island. The other inhabited islands have dispensaries, the larger ones being in the charge of qualified medical officers.

CAPITAL.— Ψ Tarawa. Estimated population (1973) 14,913.

Governor, His Excellency John Hilary Smith, C.B.E. (1973).

HONG KONG

The Crown Colony of Hong Kong, consisting of a number of islands and of a portion of the mainland, on the south-eastern coast of China, is situated at the eastern side of the mouth of the Pearl River, between 22° 9′ and 22° 37′ N. lat. and 113° 52′–114° 30′ E. long.

The capital city, Victoria, situated on the island of Hong Kong, is about 81 miles S.E. of Canton and 40 miles E. of the Portuguese province of Macau at the other side of the Pearl River. It lies along the northern shore of the island and faces the mainland; the harbour (23 sq. miles water area) lies between the city and the mainland, on which is situated Kowloon with a population equalling that of Victoria. The total area of the territory is 403·8 sq. miles (including recent reclamation) with a population which has varied considerably during recent years owing to unsettled conditions in China: at the end of 1974 it was 4,345,200.

The island of *Hong Kong* is about 11 miles long and from 2 to 5 miles broad, with a total area of 29 square miles; at the eastern entrance to the harbour it is separated from the mainland by a narrow strait (Lei Yue Min), 500–900 yards in width. It was first occupied by Great Britain in January, 1841, and formally ceded by the Treaty of Nanking in 1842; *Kowloon* was subsequently acquired by the Peking Convention of 1860; and the *New Territories*, consisting of a peninsula in the southern part of the Kwangtung province, together with adjacent islands, by a 99-year lease signed June 9, 1898. Hong Kong Island is now linked to the Kowloon peninsula by a mile-long underwater road tunnel opened in 1972.

The island is broken in shape and mountainous, the highest point being Victoria Peak, which is 1,805 feet high. The New Territories contain several peaks higher than this, the highest being Tai Mo Shan, 3,140 ft.

Climate.—Although Hong Kong lies within the tropics it enjoys unusually varied weather for a tropical area. The mean monthly temperature ranges from 15° C. in February to 28° C. in July. Spring is cloudy and humid, often with spells of fog and drizzle. Summer days are hot with temperatures exceeding 33° C. several times in most years. The average annual rainfall is 2,168·8 mm., of which nearly 80 per cent. falls between May and September. Tropical cyclones passing at various distances from Hong Kong sometimes cause high winds and heavy rain, particularly in July, August and September. Autumn and early winter are the most pleasant seasons, with sunny, dry and mild weather. In late winter there is more cloud and strong northerly winds can cause temperatures to drop below 10° C. and frost is not uncommon.

Communications.—Hong Kong, one of the world's finest natural harbours, possesses excellent wharves at which vessels up to 800 ft. in length and 36 ft. draught can be berthed. An ocean terminal pier with an overall length of 1,250 ft. can accommodate large liners and cargo vessels. A recent addition is the Kwai Chung container terminal which opened in 1972. It has three berths, each 1,000 ft.

in length, capable of berthing container ships drawing 40 ft. draught. Excellent dockyard facilities are available and include two floating drydocks, one of which can accommodate vessels up to 100,000 deadweight tons. The net tonnage of ocean-going shipping which entered the port in the year to December 31, 1974, amounted to 32,590,000.

Hong Kong International Airport, Kai Tak, situated on the North shore of Kowloon Bay, is an important link on the main air routes of the Far East. It is regularly used by 31 scheduled airlines and many charter airlines, providing frequent services throughout the Far East, to Europe, North America, Africa, Australia and New Zealand.

British Airways operate 16 passenger services per week to Britain, Australia and Japan. Cathay Pacific Airways, the Hong Kong based airline, operate 97 passenger services to points in the Far East. A total of 1,000 services is operated weekly to and from Hong Kong by scheduled airlines.

During the year ending Dec. 31, 1974, 52,929 aircraft on international flights arrived and departed, carrying 3,662,943 passengers, 100,721 metric tons of freight and 4,524 metric tons of mail.

Education.—In Sept. 1974 there were 2,816 schools with 1,302,838 pupils. About 62·4 per cent. of the pupils are financed wholly or in part by the Government. The University of Hong Kong has a full-time student strength of 3,629 in Faculties of Arts, Science, Medicine, Engineering and Architecture, and Social Sciences and Law. There is also a Centre of Asian Studies and a Department of Extra-Mural Studies. The Chinese University of Hong Kong, inaugurated in Oct. 1963, has a full time enrolment of 3,447 students in Faculties of Arts, Science, Social Science and Business Administration. There is also a Department of Extra-Mural Studies. The Hong Kong Polytechnic has an enrolment of 15,055 full-time and part-time students.

FINANCE

	1973–74	1974–75
Public revenue....	$5,240,805,405	$5,875,309,787
Public expenditure.	5,169,157,030	6,255,150,535

TRADE

Hong Kong is now established as an industrial territory with an economy based on exports rather than the domestic market. Domestic industry, producing mainly light manufactures, has grown rapidly in recent years and now provides the bulk of goods for the export trade; but the secondary role as an *entrepôt*, has also been sustained. In 1974 the value of the re-export trade was 23·7 per cent. of total exports.

Hong Kong produces a wide range of articles, including cotton yarn, cotton piece-goods, garments of all types, woollen and man-made fibre knitwear, electronic products, watches and clocks, footwear, wigs, transistor radios, household enamel and aluminium ware, plastic articles (including household ware, toys and artificial flowers), iron and steel bars, photographic equipment, foodstuffs and beverages, cigarettes, jade, ivory, jewellery and goldsmiths' and silversmiths' ware, and an extensive range of metal products.

Diversification of manufacture continues to be a major feature of recent industrial development, as are industrial partnerships with foreign companies in a wide and varied field of manufactures. New products include quartz watches, shipping containers, air conditioners, automatic telephone dialling equipment, electric household appliances such as rice cookers and toasters, T.V. receiving sets and T.V. tuners and antennae, high grade semiconductors, electronic modules, electronic flash bulbs, electronic desk calculators and other electronic components, steel pipes, rigid P.V.C. tubes and corrugated sheeting, P.V.C. covered fabrics, mixed cotton-synthetic fabrics, extruded aluminium sections, watches and clocks and fibreglass pleasure craft. Modern manufacturing processes have also been introduced to local industry; these include the permanent press for ready-made garments, soil release processing for garments and the manufacture of polyester fabrics. The marked improvement in both quality and output of items for which precision engineering is required, has continued.

The adverse balance on visible trade is offset by a favourable balance on invisible account-remittances from overseas Chinese, investments, exchange, shipping and insurance profits, and the spending of tourists, etc. In 1973 Hong Kong's principal customers for its domestic products, in order of value of trade, were U.S.A., the United Kingdom, the Federal Republic of Germany, Canada, Japan, Australia, Singapore, the Netherlands, Sweden and Taiwan. Japan was its principal supplier, followed by China, U.S.A., the United Kingdom, Taiwan, the Federal Republic of Germany, Singapore, Switzerland, Australia and Pakistan.

	1973 H.K. $	1974 H.K. $
Total Exports	25,999,356,895	30,035,685,777
Total Imports	29,004,698,293	34,120,084,595

	1973	1974
Imports from U.K.	£128,972,793	£160,813,707
Exports to U.K.	211,616,101	228,763,807

$12·1 = £1.

With effect from Nov. 26, 1974, the Hong Kong dollar was allowed to float—that is, market rates would not be maintained within 2¼ per cent. either side of the central rate of HK $5·0850 = US $1. The exchange rate used in the above conversions was the middle market rate on June 10, 1975, based on quotations provided by the Hong Kong Exchange Banks Association.

GOVERNMENT

Hong Kong is administered as a Crown Colony with a Governor, aided by an Executive Council, consisting of 6 official and 8 unofficial members, and a Legislative Council, which consists of 14 official and 15 unofficial members. There is also an Urban Council, financially autonomous, in which is vested, *inter alia*, power of making byelaws in respect of certain matters of public health and sanitation, culture and recreation.

Governor, His Excellency Sir Crawford Murray MacLehose, K.C.M.G., K.C.V.O., M.B.E. (1971) (+ *allce.* £8,393) £26,228
Commander, British Forces, Lt.-Gen. Sir Edwin Bramall, K.C.B., O.B.E., M.C. 20,825
Chief Justice, Hon. Sir Geoffrey Briggs . . . 20,825
Colonial Secretary, Hon. Sir Denys Roberts, K.B.E., Q.C. 20,825
Deputy Colonial Secretary, M. D. A. Clinton, C.M.G., G.M. 18,255
Attorney-General, Hon. J. W. D. Hobley, Q.C. 18,255
Secretary for Home Affairs, Hon. D. C. Bray, C.V.O. 18,255
Financial Secretary, Hon. C. P. Haddon-Cave, C.M.G. 19,514
Secretary for the Civil Service, A. J. Scott. . 16,681
Secretary for Economic Services, D. J. C. Jones 16,681
Secretary for Environment, Hon. J. J. Robson, C.B.E. 16,681
Deputy Financial Secretary, D. G. Jeaffreson 16,681

Secretary for Housing, Hon. I. M. Lightbody, C.M.G. £16,681
Secretary for Security, Hon. L. M. Davis, C.M.G., C.B.E. 16,681
Secretary for Social Services, Hon. Li Fookkow 16,681
Secretary for the New Territories, Hon. D. Akers-Jones 16,681
British Council Representative, K. Westcott, Star House, Kowloon.

LONDON OFFICE
Hong Kong Government Office
6 Grafton Street, W.1.
Commissioner, S. T. Kidd, C.M.G.

THE NEW HEBRIDES

The New Hebrides Group, in the South Pacific Ocean, situated between the 13th and 21st degrees of South latitude and the 166th and 170th degrees of East longitude. It includes 13 large and some 70 small islands, including the Banks and Torres Islands in the North, and has a total land area of about 6,050 square miles. The principal islands are Vanua Lava and Gaua (Banks), Espiritu Santo, Maewo, Pentecost, Aoba, Maleku, Ambrym, Epi, Efate, Erromango, Tanna and Aneityum.

The Territory is administered by an unique British-French Condominium Government. The British Resident Commissioner, exercising powers delegated to him by the High Commissioner for the Western Pacific, and the French Resident Commissioner, representing the High Commissioner for France in the Pacific Ocean, are the joint heads of the Administration. They each have staffs of national officers to assist them in general administrative work and the running of social services (health and education) financed from national funds. In addition they control the " joint " public services (posts and telegraphs, public works, mines, meteorology, etc.) which are financed from funds raised in the Territory. The Resident Commissioners are advised regarding policy and legislation by the Advisory Council, a composite body of New Hebrideans, French and British Nationals, some appointed and some elected, which meets twice a year.

The 1967 Census showed a population of 77,988 of whom 72,243 were New Hebrideans. There were 3,841 French Nationals and 1,629 British Nationals but only 1,773 of these were of European ethnic origin. Estimated population (Dec. 31, 1972), 89,031.

Principal products are frozen fish, copra, timber, frozen and canned meat, coffee, cocoa and manganese. Condominium Budget, 1973 (Recurrent and Development) $A9,000,000; British National Service Budget $A6,150,000; French National Service Budget NHF574,000,000. Two currencies are in use; the New Hebrides Franc and the Australian dollar. They may be converted at the official rate of exchanges as laid down by the Resident Comm'ssioners. On July 15, 1973, 100 NHF = A $1·05.

Seat of New Hebrides Administration— Ŷ Vila, Efate, population of Greater Vila, estimated, 1972, 12,715.

High Commissioner for the New Hebrides, E. N. Larmour, C.M.G.
French High Commissioner, L. Verger.
British Resident Commissioner, (vacant).
French Resident Commissioner, R. Langlois.

PITCAIRN ISLANDS

Pitcairn, a small volcanic island of less than two square miles in area, is the chief of a group of Islands situated about midway between New Zealand and Panama in the South Pacific Ocean at longitude 130° 06′ W. and latitude 25° 04′ S.

The island rises in cliffs to a height of 1,100 feet and access from the sea is possible only at Bounty Bay, a small rocky cove, and then only by whaleboats. Mean monthly temperatures vary between 66° F. in August and 75° F. in Febrary and the average annual rainfall is 80 inches. Moderate easterly and north-easterly winds predominate but short easterly and south-easterly gales occasionally occur from April to September. With an equable climate, the island is very fertile and produces both tropical and sub-tropical trees and crops.

The small community, descendants of the Bounty mutineers and their Tahitian companions who did not wish to remain on Norfolk Island (*see* p. 715) and returned here, numbers about 64 (1975). The Islanders live by subsistence farming and fishing, and their limited monetary needs are satisfied by the manufacture of wood carvings and other handicrafts which are sold to passing ships and to a few overseas customers. Other than small fees charged for gun and driving licences there are no taxes and Government revenue is derived almost solely from the sale of postage stamps. Communication with the outside world is maintained by cargo vessels travelling between New Zealand and Panama which call at irregular intervals in each direction; and by means of a telegraphic link with Fiji.

The other three islands of the group (Henderson lying 105 miles E.N.E. of Pitcairn, Oeno lying 75 miles N.W. and Ducie lying 293 miles E.) are all uninhabited. Henderson Island is occasionally visited by the Pitcairn Islanders to obtain supplies of " miro " wood which is used for their carvings. Oeno is visited for excursions of about a week's duration every two years or so.

Under a scheme of co-operation, New Zealand supplies Pitcairn with a teacher for the one-teacher primary school on the Island. Education is compulsory between the ages of five and fifteen. Secondary education in Fiji and New Zealand is encouraged by the Administration which provides scholarships and bursaries for the purpose. Medical care is provided by a registered nurse and additional help is obtained when required from the surgeons of passing ships. Since 1887 the islanders have all been adherents of the Seventh Day Adventist Church.

Pitcairn became a British Settlement under the British Settlement Act, 1887, and was administered by the Governor of Fiji from 1952 until 1970, when the administration was transferred to the British High Commission in New Zealand and the British High Commissioner was appointed Governor. The local Government Ordinance of 1964 provides for a Council of ten members of whom four are elected.

Governor of Pitcairn, Ducie, Henderson and Oeno Islands, Sir David Scott, K.C.M.G. (*British High Commissioner for New Zealand*).

Commissioner, R. J. Hicks (*British High Commission,* Auckland, New Zealand).
Island Magistrate and Chairman of Island Council, P. Young.
Education Officer and Government Adviser, C. P. B. Shea.

RHODESIA

Rhodesia, comprising Matabeleland, Mashonaland, Manicaland, Midlands and Victoria, is that part of the territory named after Cecil Rhodes lying south of the Zambesi River, its political neighbours being Zambia and Portuguese East Africa on the N.; the Transvaal and Botswana on the S. and W.; Portuguese East Africa on the E. Rhodesia has a total area of 150,820 square miles and a population (estimated, 1974) of 6,100,000 (Europeans, 273,000; Africans, 5,800,000; Asians and Coloured, 29,300).

The majority of Africans of Rhodesia (members of the so-called Bantu race), are known as Mashona. In the Western portion of the territory are the descendants of the Amandebele who conquered and settled down among the Mashona, and from whom the Province of Matabeleland derives its name.

Rhodesia was administered by the British South Africa Company from the date of occupation (1890) to 1923, when responsible government was granted. On this latter date the Company relinquished all rights and interests in the land of Rhodesia except in those estates which it was already developing on July 10, 1923. A Land and Agricultural Bank grants loans for farm development and acquisition of residential property on easy terms of repayment. Under the Land Tenure Act, operative from March 2, 1970, Rhodesia is divided into three areas—European Area (44,950,000 acres), African Area (44,950,000 acres) and National Area (6,600,000 acres).

FINANCE AND TRADE

	1972–73	1973–74
Revenue	$290,100,000	$309,295,000
Expenditure	282,580,000	318,110,000

The expenditure from revenue funds for 1973–74 was estimated at $290,197,000.

TRADE WITH U.K.

	1973	1974
Imports from U.K.	£794,000	£831,000
Exports to U.K.	60,000	105,000

EDUCATION

African education comes under the Minister of Education in the Rhodesian Government. The estimate for African education for 1972–73 was $22,470,000. In 1972 there were 3,516 primary schools, 144 secondary schools, 17 teacher training schools, 8 special schools for the physically handicapped, 16 home-craft schools, 33 evening and part-time schools and 43 study groups. The total enrolment in African schools, exclusive of evening and part-time schools and study groups, was 750,238, of whom 715,588 pupils were in primary schools and 31,088 in secondary schools. At the University of Rhodesia there were 400 Africans out of a total of 978 full-time students. In 1972 there were 18,504 African teachers and 484 European teachers employed in African schools.

GOVERNMENT

Rhodesia (then *Southern Rhodesia*) obtained self-government in 1923 and has a legislative Assembly of 66 members and a Cabinet of 14 members.

Municipal self-government has been established in the cities of Salisbury, Bulawayo, Umtali and Gwelo and the towns of Gatooma, Que Que and Fort Victoria. Smaller areas are administered by Town Management Boards. Over the past ten years local self-government among the Africans has been encouraged.

MINISTRY

The Parliament of Rhodesia, elected on April 10, 1970, consists of 50 Rhodesian Front, 7 Centre Party, 1 National People's Union and 8 Rhodesia Electoral Union Peoples' Party, 2 Democratic Party and 4 Independents.
Prime Minister, Hon. I. D. Smith.
Deputy Prime Minister and Minister of Finance and Posts, Hon. J. J. Wrathall.

Minister of Foreign Affairs, Defence and Public Service, Hon. J. H. Howman.
Justice and Law and Order, Hon. D. W. Lardner-Burke.
Local Government and Housing, Hon. W. M. Irvine.
Agriculture, Hon. D. C. Smith.
Internal Affairs, Hon. L. B. Smith.
Health, Labour and Social Welfare, Hon. I. F. McLean.
Transport, Power, Roads and Road Traffic, Hon. R. T. R. Hawkins.
Information, Immigration, and Tourism, Hon. P. van der Byl.
Education, Hon. A. P. Smith.
Lands, Natural Resources and Water Development, Hon. M. H. H. Partridge.
Mines, Hon. I. B. Dillon.
Commerce and Industry, Hon. B. H. Mussett.

CAPITAL.—SALISBURY, situated on the Mashonaland plateau, altitude 4,850 ft., population (Dec. 1973), 503,000 (European, 122,100; Asian and Coloured, 10,840; African, 370,000). BULAWAYO, the largest town in Matabeleland, altitude 4,450 ft., population (Dec. 1973), 308,000 (European, 58,200; Asian and Coloured, 9,730; African, 240,000). Other centres are Umtali, Gwelo, Gatooma, Que Que, Fort Victoria and Wankie.

Salisbury is 5,600 miles from London (air route) transit 12 hours; by sea, *via* Cape Town, 17 days (approx.).

FLAG.—Vertical stripes of green, white, green; Rhodesian coat of arms in centre of white stripe.

ST. HELENA

Probably the best known of all the solitary islands in the world, St. Helena is situated in the South Atlantic Ocean, 955 miles S. of the Equator, 760 S.E. of Ascension, 1,140 from the nearest point of the African Continent, 1,800 from the coast of S. America and 4,477 from Southampton, in 15° 55′ S. lat. and 5° 42′ W. long. It is 10½ miles long, 6½ broad, and encloses an area of 47 square miles, with a population in 1974 of 4,967.

St. Helena is of volcanic origin, and consists of numerous rugged mountains, the highest rising to 2,700 feet, interspersed with picturesque ravines. Although within the tropics, the south-east " trades " keep the temperature mild and equable. St. Helena was discovered by the Portuguese navigator, João de Nova, in 1502 (probably on St. Helena's Day) and remained unknown to other European nations until 1588. It was used as a port of call for vessels of all nations trading to the East until it was annexed by the Dutch in 1633. It was never occupied by them, however, and the English East India Company seized it in 1659. In 1834 it was ceded to the Crown. During the period 1815 to 1821 the island was lent to the British Government as a place of exile for the Emperor Napoleon Bonaparte who died in St. Helena on May 5, 1821. It was formerly an important station on the route to India, but its prosperity decreased after the construction of the Suez Canal. Since the collapse of the New Zealand flax (*phormuim tenax*) industry in 1965, there have been no significant exports, but a five year development plan, launched in 1974, seeks primarily to increase the island's productivity in its limited land and sea resources. Ψ St. James's Bay, on the north-west of the Island, possesses a good anchorage.

GOVERNMENT

The government of St. Helena is administered by a Governor, with the aid of a Legislative Council, consisting of the Governor, two *ex-officio* mem-

bers (Government Secretary and Treasurer) and twelve elected members. Five committees of the Legislative Council are responsible for general oversight of the activities of Government Departments and have in addition a wide range of statutory and administrative functions. The Governor is also assisted by an Executive Council of the two *ex-officio* members and the Chairmen of the Council committees.

Governor, His Excellency Sir Thomas Oates, C.M.G., O.B.E., (1971) £3,750
Government Secretary, C. B. Kendall, (+*allce.*) 2,700
Colonial Treasurer and Collector of Customs, P. E. Aldous ....(+*allce.*) 2,460
Chief Justice, Sir Peter Watkin Williams. £625 retainer (no fixed salary).
Senior Medical Officer, Dr. J. S. Noaks, O.B.E. ....(+*allce.*) 2,340
Agricultural and Forestry Officer, R. O. Williams ....(+*allce.*) 2,100
Education Officer, C. S. Huxtable ..(+*allce.*) 2,100
Civil Engineer, C. R. Riding .....(+*allce.*) 2,100
Distance from London: 4,472 miles; transit, 9 days.

FINANCE AND TRADE

	1973–4	1974–5
Public revenue	£997,778	£1,356,049
Expenditure	963,795	1,520,101
Total imports	610,834	1,115,341

Imports from U.K. in 1974–75 were valued at £730,535.
CAPITAL, Ψ Jamestown. % Population (1974), 1,475.

ASCENSION

The small island of Ascension lies in the South Atlantic (7° 56′ S., 14° 22′ W.) some 700 miles north-west of the island of St. Helena. It is said to have been discovered by João de Nova, on Ascension Day, 1501, and two years later was visited by Alphonse d'Albuquerque, who gave the island its present name. It was uninhabited until the arrival of Napoleon in St. Helena in 1815 when a small British naval garrison was stationed on the island. The population at December 31, 1974, was 1,137 of whom 708 were St. Helenian. The island remained under the supervision of the Board of Admiralty until 1922, when it was made a dependency of St. Helena by Royal Letters Patent and came under control of the Secretary for the Colonies.

Ascension is a rocky peak of purely volcanic origin, the highest point (Green Mountain) some 2,817 ft. is covered with lush vegetation, which with each rainy season is slowly creeping down to the lower areas. Cable & Wireless Ltd., maintains a farm of some 10 acres on the mountain, permitting the production of vegetables and livestock. The island is famous for Turtles, which land on the beaches from January to May to lay their eggs. It is also a breeding area for the sooty tern, or wideawake, large numbers of which settle on the south-western coastal section every eighth month to hatch their eggs. Other wild life on the island includes feral donkeys and cats, rabbits and francolin partridge. All wild life except rabbits and cats is protected by law. The ocean surrounding the island abounds with shark, barracuda, tuna, bonito and many other fish.

Cable & Wireless Ltd. owns and operates a cable station which connects the Dependency with St. Helena, Sierra Leone, St. Vincent, Rio de Janeiro and Buenos Aires. A B.B.C. relay station was opened on the island in 1966.
Administrator, G. C. Guy, C.M.G., C.V.O., O.B.E.

TRISTAN DA CUNHA

Tristan da Cunha is the chief of a group of islands of volcanic origin lying in lat. 37° 6' S. and long. 12° 2' W., discovered in 1506 by a Portuguese admiral (Tristão da Cunha), after whom they are named. They have a total area of 45 square miles. The main island is about 1,500 miles W. of the Cape of Good Hope, 3,600 miles N.E. of Cape Horn, and about 1,320 miles S.S.W. of St. Helena. It was the resort of British and American sealers from the middle of the 18th century, and in 1760 a British naval officer visited the group and gave his name to Nightingale Island. On August 14, 1816, the group was annexed to the British Crown and a garrison was placed on Tristan da Cunha, but this force was withdrawn in 1817, William Glass, a corporal of artillery (*died* 1853), remaining at his own request, with his wife and two children. This party, with five others, formed a settlement. In 1827 five coloured women from St. Helena, and afterwards others from Cape Colony, joined the party.

The islands form a dependency of St. Helena, being administered by the Foreign and Commonwealth Office through a resident Administrator, with headquarters at the settlement of Edinburgh. Under a new constitution introduced in 1969, he is advised by an elected Island Council of 8 members of whom one must be a woman, with universal suffrage at 18. The population numbered 292 persons in 1974, plus 7 expatriate Government officers and their families.

In October, 1961, a volcano, believed to have been extinct for thousands of years, erupted and mounds of earth were thrown up in some cases to a height of 35 feet. In view of the danger of further volcanic activity, the inhabitants were evacuated and reached the United Kingdom on Nov. 23, 1961, where they remained for nearly two years. An advance party returned to Tristan da Cunha in the spring of 1963, and the main body of the islanders has now returned to the island. Some went back to England in 1966, but most returned in August, 1967.

A boat harbour was completed in 1967. The first freezing factory was re-established in 1966. There are no taxes on Tristan, income being derived from royalties paid by the fishing company and from the sale of stamps. The new Camogli Hospital was opened early in 1971 and a new school was completed in 1974.

Administrator, S. G. Trees, M.V.O., O.B.E.
Chaplain, Rev. E. Buxton.

INACCESSIBLE ISLAND is a lofty mass of rock with sides 2 miles in length; the island is the resort of penguins and sea-fowl. Cultivation was started in 1937, but has been abandoned.

THE NIGHTINGALE ISLANDS are three in number, of which the largest is 1 mile long and ¾ mile wide, and rises in two peaks, 960 and 1,105 ft. above sea-level respectively. The smaller islands, Stoltenhoft and Middle Isle, are little more than huge rocks. Seals, innumerable penguins, and vast numbers of sea-fowl visit these islands.

GOUGH ISLAND (or Diego Alvarez), in 40° 20' S. and 9° 44' W., lies about 250 miles S.S.E. of Tristan da Cunha. The island is about 8 miles long and 4 miles broad, with a total area of 40 square miles, and has been a British possession since 1816. The island is the resort of penguins and sea-elephants and has valuable guano deposits. There is no permanent population, but there is a meteorological station maintained on the island by the South African Government and manned by South Africans.

SEYCHELLES

The Colony of Seychelles, in the Indian Ocean, consists of two distinct collections of islands—the Mahé group, 32 islands in all, granitic with high hills and mountains (highest point about 2,990 ft.) and the outlying islands, the Coralline group, numbering 49 more and, for the most part, only a little above sea-level. Proclaimed as French territory in 1756, the Mahé group began to be settled as a dependency of Mauritius from 1770, was captured by a British ship in 1794 and was finally assigned to Great Britain in 1810. By Letters Patent of September, 1903, these islands, together with the Coralline group, were formed into a separate Colony.

The total area of the Granitic group is 107 square miles, of which Mahé, the largest island and the seat of Government, claims 57. The next largest island is Praslin, home of the unique double coconut, Coco de Mer. Islands of the Coralline group lie at distances from Mahé varying between 60 and 612 miles and have a total area of approximately 18 sq. miles. In 1965 the islands of Farquhar, Desroches and Aldabra were detached from Seychelles and with the Chagos Islands, formerly of Mauritius, formed the new British Indian Ocean Territory. The coralline islands have no permanent population and, where worked, are supplied by contract labour from the Granitic group. The population at the 1971 Census was 52,650. Although only 4° S. of the Equator, the islands are healthy. There are 35 primary schools, 13 secondary schools, four vocational training centres and a teachers' training college.

A new Constitution was introduced in 1970. The Legislative Assembly consists of 15 elected members, three *ex officio* members, and the Speaker.

TRADE

	1971	1972
Imports	Rs.84,003,946	Rs.111,670,529
Exports	7,915,770	9,527,760

The principal imports are rice, mineral oils, cotton piece goods, vehicles, manufactured items and building materials. The chief exports are cinnamon bark and copra; others include cinnamon leaf oil, guano, vanilla, patchouli oil and tortoise shell.

CAPITAL, Ψ Victoria (population, 1971, 13,736), on the N.E. side of Mahé.

Governor and Commander-in-Chief, His Excellency Colin Hamilton Allan, C.M.G., O.B.E. (1973) Rs.69,000
Chief Minister, Hon. J. R. Mancham.
Letters to and from London—5 to 10 days.

SOLOMON ISLANDS

Governor, His Excellency D. C. C. Luddington, C.M.G., C.V.O. (1973)
(+*allce* $A5,000) $A10,875
Chief Justice (vacant) $A6,590*
Deputy Governor, A. J. Clark, M.V.O. $A6,509*
Attorney General, G. P. Nazareth, O.B.E. ... $A5,955*
Financial Adviser, R. J. Wallace, O.B.E.

*Certain allowances are paid in addition under the Overseas Aid Scheme.

The Protectorate (officially called the Solomon Islands since June 1975), established in 1893, includes all the islands in the Solomons Archipelago S. and S.E. of the large island of Bougainville. The main islands in the Protectorate are Choiseul, Santa Isabel, the Shortland Group, Vella Lavella, Kolombangara, Ranongga, Gizo, the New Georgia Group, the Florida Group, Guadalcanal, the Russell Islands, Malaita and San Cristobal, and the outlying islands of Bellona, Rennell, Santa Cruz, Vanikolo, Tikopia, Swallow (or Reef Islands) and Duff

Groups, the Stewart Islands and the Ontong Java Atoll.

The Solomons are situated between 5–13° S. lat. and 155–170° 20′ E. long. They have a total land area of about 11,500 sq. miles. Distribution of population at the Census of 1970 was: Melanesian 149,667; Polynesian 6,399; Micronesian 2,362; European 1,280; Chinese 577; Others 713. Total 160,998.

CAPITAL, Honiara (population 20,000).

FINANCE AND TRADE

Estimated revenue (1975), $A15,498,920 (incl. British Development Aid $A6,604,830 and grant in aid of recurrent expenditure from the United Kingdom $A1,547,460).

The main imports are foodstuffs, consumer goods, machinery and building materials. Principal exports are copra, timber, fish. Other exports include cocoa, marine shells, tobacco and scrap metal.

GOVERNMENT

In 1960 an Advisory Council was replaced by a nominated Legislative Council and Executive Council. In 1964 provision was made for a new Constitution and the first general election was held in 1965. In 1967 a general election was held to elect 14 members of the Legislative Council instead of the previous 8. In 1970 a new Constitution was introduced providing for a single Governing Council comprising the High Commissioner as President, 3 *ex officio* members, up to 6 public service members nominated by the High Commissioner and 17 elected members. No public service members were appointed by the High Commissioner in 1972, and in 1973 the number of elected members was increased to 24.

In 1974 the Governing Council became the Legislative Assembly without change of membership. The 24 elected members then chose their first Chief Minister from among themselves, and he, in turn, selected his ministers. From Sept. 1974 to June 1975 these were limited to six, but the number was then increased to eight, this number to include a Minister of Finance. The Council of Ministers also includes two *ex officio* members.

The report of a special select committee on constitutional development was approved in 1973. The proposed constitution provides for the Governing Council to be retitled the Legislative Assembly and for the 24 elected members to select a Chief Minister who, in turn, would appoint between four and six ministers. These ministers, together with the three *ex officio* members of the Assembly, would then form the Council of Ministers, the equivalent of the Cabinet.

JUDICIARY

The High Court of the Western Pacific constituted by the Western Pacific (Courts) Orders in Council, 1961, consist of a Chief Justice and one Puisne Judge.

The Court is a Superior Court of Record and possesses all the jurisdiction which is vested in Her Majesty's High Court of Justice in England. In addition to the British Solomon Islands Protectorate, the Court has jurisdiction in the Condominium of the New Hebrides and in the Gilbert and Ellice Islands Colony.

EDUCATION

In consequence of his withdrawal of some of the Churches from primary education, a new primary and secondary structure, with a national teaching service, is now being set up. Government participation in technical and teacher training and further education overseas continues.

COMMUNICATIONS

An internal air service, provided by Solair, serves 11 airstrips, but the bulk of the inter-island traffic is by small ships. Air Pacific calls at Henderson Field (Honiara) *en route* from Fiji to Brisbane; Air Niugini has two flights a week from Honiara to Port Moresby, and one to Kieta (Papua New Guinea); Air Nauru flies twice weekly from Melbourne to Naura *via* Honiara and back. There are 221 miles of main roads in the Protectorate of which 14 miles are in Honiara. Guadalcanal has some 70 miles of main road along the north coast, with a further 100 miles of feeder roads; Malaita has 75 miles of main roads around the north of the Island; a coastal road is being built along the north coast of San Cristobal. Except for timber roads, other islands only have short minor roads. All the islands have transceivers (HF) to maintain communications with Honiara and District Headquarters, with VHF between Honiara, Tulagi and District Headquarters, with VHF between Honiara, Tulagi and Auki. There are telex services to Australia and radio telephone services *via* Fiji or Australia. There are overseas airmail services on five days a week.

VIRGIN ISLANDS,
see BRITISH

THE WEST INDIES

The West Indies are a number of islands and islets, some of them mere rocks, situated between 10° to 27° North and 59° 30′ to 85° West. The whole archipelago extends in a curve from the Florida Channel (North America) to within 7 miles of the coast of Venezuela (South America), and is divided into three main groups: I. GREATER ANTILLES, which contain the largest islands, *Cuba* (44,000 sq. miles) and *Hispaniola* (Haiti and the Dominican Republic) (30,000 sq. miles), Jamaica and Puerto Rico; II. BAHAMAS, which is now independent. III. LESSER ANTILLES, which are variously divided; the British islands in the Lesser Antilles are the Leeward and Windward Islands. The total area of the archipelago is nearly 100,000 square miles, of which 72,000 square miles are *Independent*, 12,300 *British*, 3,890 *United States*, 1,350 *French*, 430 *Netherlands*, and 90 *Venezuelan*.

The West India Islands which lie nearest the East have been called the *Windward Islands*; the others the *Leeward Islands*, on account of the winds which in this area generally blow from the east.

COMMISSION FOR THE EASTERN CARIBBEAN
GOVERNMENTS
10 Haymarket, S.W.1
Commissioner, Dr. Claudius C. Thomas.

The British West Indies were governed under a series of federal arrangements, the last of which, a federation of the Leeward and Windward Islands with Barbados, was abandoned in 1966. The islands of Antigua, Dominica, Grenada, St. Kitts-Nevis-Anguilla and St. Lucia became States in association with Britain in February and March 1967. St. Vincent became an Associated State in October, 1969. Grenada became independent on Feb. 7, 1974. Britain's power and responsibilities are limited to defence and external affairs.

West Indies Associated States

The Associated States are described individually in the following sections. The Office of the British

Government Representative is at George Gordon Building (P.O. Box 227), Castries, St. Lucia.
British Government Representative, E. O. Laird, C.M.G., M.B.E. (1972)
Deputy do., C. G. Mortlock.
Development Adviser, Sir Bruce Greatbach, K.C.V.O., C.M.G., M.B.E. (*Resident at* Bridgetown, Barbados).

Supreme Court
Established by Order in Council (1967), which gives the Court additional jurisdiction in Montserrat and the British Virgin Islands. There are two constituents, a Court of Appeal and a High Court. The Chief Justice is appointed by Her Majesty and puisne judges by the Judicial and Legal Services Commission. Expenses of the Supreme Court, after allowing for contributions from Montserrat and the Virgin Islands, are met by the States in equal shares.
Chief Justice, Sir Maurice Davis, O.B.E., Q.C.
Justices of Appeal, E. L. St. Bernard; N. Peterkin (acting).
Puisne Judges, N. Berridge (*St. Vincent*); E. F. Glasgow (*St. Kitts-Nevis* and *British Virgin Islands*); R. A. Nedd (*Antigua and Montserrat*); W. A. Bruno (*St. Lucia*); J. D. B. Renwick (*Dominica*).

ANTIGUA
Antigua lies in 17° 6′ N. lat. and 61° 45′ W. long., and is nearly 108 square miles in area with a coastline of about 70 miles. Antigua was first settled by the English in 1632, and was granted to Lord Willoughby by Charles II. Population in 1963 totalled 61,664; and in 1970, 65,000. Antigua is much less hilly and wooded than the other Leeward Islands. Exports include petroleum products refined in the island. Cotton and rum are also exported. Tourism is the most important industry, with a good choice of resort hotels mostly built to take advantage of the many fine white sand beaches. There are frequent air services to Canada, U.S.A. and the United Kingdom.
FLAG.—Inverted triangle (centred on a red field) divided horizontally into three bands of black over blue over white; rising sun device in gold on black band.

Finance and Trade

	1973
Revenue	EC $27,644,000
Expenditure (recurrent)	23,718,000
Total imports	94,504,000

Governor, Sir Wilfred Ebenezer Jacobs, O.B.E., Q.C. (1967) (*plus* £1,000 *allce. and house*) $22,300

Trade with U.K.

	1972	1973
Imports from U.K.	£3,946,000	£4,215,000
Exports to U.K.	322,000	135,000

Barbuda, formerly a possession of the Codrington family, is situated 30 miles N. of Antigua, of which it is a dependency, in lat. 17° 35′ N., long. 61° 42′ W. Area, 62 square miles. Population, 1,000. The island is flat and mostly stony, producing cotton, corn and ground-nuts. Wild deer are found, and there is good tarpon and other fishing.
Redonda is uninhabited.
CAPITAL Ψ St. John's Population 22,000.

THE CAYMAN ISLANDS
The Cayman Islands, between 79° 44′ and 81° 26′ W. and 19° 15′ and 19° 46′ N., consist of three islands, Grand Cayman, Cayman Brac, and Little Cayman, with a total area of 100 square miles. Population (Census, 1970), 10,652. The constitution provides for a Governor, Legislative Assembly and an Executive Council. The Legislative Assembly consists of the Governor, not fewer than two nor more than three official members and 12 elected members. The Executive Council consists of the Governor and two official members appointed by the Governor, and four elected members, chosen by the elected members of the Assembly from among their own number. The normal life of the Assembly is four years. Supervisory powers over the government of the Islands exercised by the Government of Jamaica came to an end in August, 1962.
The principal town is Ψ George Town, in Grand Cayman, population (1970 census) 3,000.

FINANCE

	1974
Revenue	CI $8,277,837
Expenditure	6,938,380
Public Debt	979,636

TRADE

	1974
Total imports	CI $22,000,059
Total exports	286,699

MONTSERRAT
Situated in 16° 45′ N. lat. and 61° 15′ W. long., 27 miles S.W. of Antigua, the island is about 11 miles long and 7 wide, with an area of 39 square miles; population (1972), 12,905. Discovered by Columbus in 1493, it was settled by Irishmen in 1632, conquered and held by the French for some time, and finally assigned to Great Britain in 1783. It is justly considered one of the most healthy and beautiful of the Antilles; it contains two active soufrières and several hot springs, while the scenery is charmingly diversified. About two-thirds of the island is mountainous, the rest capable of cultivation. The chief exports are sea island cotton, tomatoes and other fruits and vegetables. Real estate development and tourism have done much to aid the island's economy. Revenue (1974) EC $6,307,000; Expenditure EC $7,275,000.
Cabinet government was introduced in Montserrat in 1960. The Executive Council is composed of 4 elected members (the Chief and 3 other Ministers) and two official members (the Attorney-General and the Financial Secretary). The 4 Ministers are appointed from the members of the political party holding the majority in the Legislative Council. The present composition of the Legislative Council consists of the President (the Governor), two official members, one nominated unofficial member and 7 elected members.
Governor, His Excellency Norman Derek Matthews, O.B.E. (1974)

EXECUTIVE COUNCIL
Chairman, The Governor.
Chief Minister and Minister of Finance, Hon. P. A. Bramble.
Minister of Education, Health and Welfare, Hon. Mrs. M. R. Tuitt.
Agriculture, Trade, Lands and Housing, Hon. W. H. Ryan.
Communications and Works, Hon. E. A. Dyer.
Attorney-General, Hon. B. F. Dias, O.B.E.
Financial Secretary, Hon. A. Collings.

Secretary to the Executive Council, K. A. Cassell.
CHIEF TOWN.—Ψ Plymouth (1,300).

ST. KITTS-NEVIS-ANGUILLA
Governor, His Excellency Probyn Ellsworth Innes, M.B.E. (1975).
St. Kitts-Nevis-Anguilla became a State in Association with Britain on February 27, 1967. It

is located at the northern end of the Eastern Caribbean and comprises the islands of St. Kitts (65 sq. miles, population about 35,000), Nevis (36 sq. miles, 13,000), and Anguilla (35 sq. miles, 6,200).

St. Kitts, lat. 17° 18′ N. and long. 62° 48′ W. was the first island in the British West Indies to be colonised (1623). Its economy has been based on sugar for over three centuries. Tourism and light industry is being developed. The central area of the island is forest-clad and mountainous, rising to the 3,792 ft. Mount Misery. The capital, Basseterre, is a port of registry. Golden Rock airport can take large jet aircraft.

Nevis, lat. 17° 10′ N. and long. 62° 35′ W. is separated from the southern tip of St. Kitts by a strait two miles wide. The sea ferry route from Brasseterre, St. Kitts to Charlestown, Nevis is 11 miles. Newcastle airstrip can take small aircraft, e.g. Islanders: no night landing facilities are available. The economy of Nevis centres on small peasant farmers. The island is dominated by the central Nevis Peak, 3,596 ft. The chief town, Ψ Charlestown, is a port of entry.

CAPITAL: Basseterre (St. Kitts), population about 17,000. FLAG: Tricolor of green (next staff), yellow and blue vertical stripes; palm tree device on yellow stripe.

ANGUILLA

Anguilla is a flat coralline island about 70 miles N.W. of St. Kitts. The island is rather less than 16 miles in length, 3½ miles in breadth at its widest point and its area is about 35 sq. miles. The population is 6,500 (1974). Salt and lobster are the principal products.

The island is covered with low scrub and fringed with some of the finest white coral-sand beaches in the Caribbean. The climate is pleasant and healthy with temperatures in the range of 75–85°F. throughout the year.

Three months after the Associated State of Saint Christopher (St. Kitts)-Nevis-Anguilla came into being in 1967 the Anguillans repudiated government from St. Kitts. In 1971 the Anguilla Bill and Anguilla (Administration) Order were enacted, which provide for the administration of Anguilla by a Commissioner who is appointed by Her Majesty The Queen.

H.M. Commissioner for Anguilla, D. F. B. Le Breton (1974).

TURKS AND CAICOS ISLANDS

These West Indian islands geographically form part of the Bahamas group, from which Government they were separated in 1848. From 1873 until 1962 they were annexed to Jamaica, from which they are distant about 450 miles, reverting to U.K. administration on August 6, 1962, upon Jamaica's attainment of independence. On November 5, 1965, the Governor of the Bahamas became also the Governor of the Turks and Caicos. On April 15, 1973, the former Administrator was sworn in as Governor of the Turks and Caicos Islands with the powers previously held by the Governor of the Bahamas. The two Colonies share a Common Bench for their Courts of Appeal. They have an area of 193 sq. miles, and a population (census, 1970) of 6,000. Ψ Grand Turk is an important cable station. A tourist industry is rapidly developing as the climate, beaches and sea sports generally are amongst the finest in the world. Trade in salt, for which the island used to be celebrated, has greatly diminished in recent years. Other exports are crawfish and conchs. A considerable number of men are employed overseas in the Bahamas. There are a U.S. Air Force missile tracking station and a Naval facility at Grand Turk. Airfields at Grand Turk and South Caicos are surfaced. A gravel airstrip at Providenciales is a port of entry in addition to Grand Turk and South Caicos. All three have refuelling facilities.

FINANCE

	1973	1974
Revenue	U.S.$4,849,026	U.S.$5,378,296
Expenditure	4,771,804	5,335,899

TRADE

	1972	1973
Total imports	U.S.$2,732,920	U.S.$3,625,464
Total exports	902,214	504,867

The constitution provides for a Governor and a State Council. The State Council consists of a Speaker, three official members, not less than two nor more than three nominated members and nine elected members. The normal life of the State Council is five years.

Governor, His Excellency A. C. Watson. (+*duty allce.* U.S.$825) $12,400

The Windward Islands

The Windward Islands consist of Grenada, now independent, and the three colonies of St. Vincent, St. Lucia and Dominica with their dependencies. Since March 1967, with the attainment of Associated Statehood, there has been a Governor in St. Lucia and Dominica and in St. Vincent since October, 1969. Each island has its own elected Parliament and Senate and a Premier. The ministerial form of government was introduced in 1956. Grenada became independent in 1974.

ST. LUCIA

St. Lucia, the second largest and the most picturesque of the Windward group, situated in 13° 54′ N. lat. and 60° 50′ W. long., at a distance of about 90 miles W.N.W. of Barbados, 21 miles N. of St. Vincent, and 24 miles S. of Martinique, is 27 miles in length, with an extreme breadth of 14 miles. It comprises an area of 238 square miles with an estimated population (1970) of 100,000. About 56,000 acres are devoted to agriculture. It possesses perhaps the most interesting history of all the smaller islands. Fights raged hotly around it, and it constantly changed hands between the English and the French. It is mountainous, its highest point being 3,145 feet above the sea, and for the most part it is covered with forest and tropical vegetation. The principal exports are bananas, copra, coconuts, cocoa, edible oil. Over 44,130 tons of bananas, valued at $16,500,000, were exported to the U.K. in 1974. The chief imports are flour, machinery, cotton piece goods, building materials and fertilisers.

CAPITAL.— Ψ Castries (estimated population, 43,000) is recognized as being one of the finest ports in the West Indies on account of its reputation as a safe anchorage in the hurricane season. FLAG.— Blue, bearing in centre a device of yellow over black over white triangles having a common base.

Government

There is a Cabinet of Ministers presided over by the premier and consisting of five other Ministers and the Attorney-General. There is a Legislature which consists of Her Majesty and a House of Assembly, of which the normal life is five years. The House of Assembly consists of a Speaker who may be elected from within or without the House, 17 elected and three nominated members and the Attorney General. The Constitution provides for a political Attorney-General if the Legislature or the Premier so decides.

Governor, Sir Allen Montgomery Lewis, Q.C.
Premier, J. G. M. Compton.

ST. VINCENT

St. Vincent achieved Associated Statehood with the United Kingdom on October 27, 1969. The territory of the State of St. Vincent includes certain of the Grenadines, a group of islands set across the Caribbean sea, stretching 40 miles south, some of the larger of which are Bequia, Canouan, Mayreau, Mustique, Union Island, Petit St. Vincent and Isle-a-Quatre. The territory extends 150 square miles (96,000 acres).

The main island, St. Vincent, is situated between 13° 6′ and 14° 35′ N. Latitude and 61° 6′ and 61° 20′ W. Longitude approximately 21 miles South West of St. Lucia and 100 miles West of Barbados. The island is 18 miles long and 100 miles wide at its extremities comprising an area of 133 square miles and an estimated population of 90,000 (1970). St. Vincent was discovered by Christopher Columbus in 1498. It was granted by Charles I to the Earl of Carlisle in 1627 and after subsequent grants and a series of occupations alternately by the French and English, it was finally restored to Britain in 1783. The capital and principal port is Ψ Kingstown, population approximately 23,000.

The economy is based mainly on agriculture but the tourist industry has been rapidly expanding, bringing approximately $5,500,000 to the State in 1972. The main products are bananas, arrowroot, coconuts, cocoa, spices, and various kinds of food crops. The main imports are foodstuffs (meat, rice, sugar, flour, butter and pickled and salted fish), textiles, lumber, cement and other building materials, fertilizers and motor vehicles.

The territory's education system provides a general primary and secondary education. Primary education is free but not compulsory. In 1972 there were 61 primary schools with a total enrolment of 27,609; and 16 secondary schools with a total enrolment of 4,015.

Governor.—As an Associated State St. Vincent has a constitution under which there is a Governor who is Her Majesty's Representative. Except where otherwise provided, the Governor is required to act in accordance with the advice of the Cabinet. Statehood allows St. Vincent the full self-governing control of its internal affairs including the right to amend its own constitution and the power to end the Association and declare itself independent. The United Kingdom Government accepts the responsibility for the State's external affairs and defence.

Governor, His Excellency Sir Rupert Godfrey John.
Chief Minister, Hon. J. F. Mitchell.

The House of Assembly consists of 13 elected members, three nominated members and the Attorney-General. It is presided over by a Speaker elected by the House from within or without it.

DOMINICA

Dominica, the loftiest of the Lesser Antilles, was transferred from the Leeward to the Windward Group on Jan. 1, 1940. It is situated between 15° 20′ and 15° 45′ N. lat. and 61° 13′ and 61° 30′ W. long., 95 miles S. of Antigua, and is about 29 miles long and 15 broad comprising an area of 290 sq. miles, of which about 41,000 acres are under cultivation. The island is of volcanic origin and very mountainous and picturesque, abounding in streams fairly well stocked with fish, and the soil is very fertile. The temperature varies, according to the altitude, from 55° to 85°F. The climate is healthy, and during the winter months is very pleasant. The exports consist almost entirely of agricultural produce, principally bananas, lime oil, lime juice, oranges, bay oil, cocoa, copra and vanilla. Population (estimated, 1972, 71,500). The principal towns are Ψ Roseau, on the south-west coast population, 10,157 and Portsmouth, population, 2,379.

Education.—There are 58 elementary schools, of which 55 are Government and 3 assisted. Of the 5 secondary schools, 3 receive a grant-in-aid and two are maintained by the Government.

Finance and Trade

	1971	1972
Revenue (incl. Grants)	$21,420,427	$19,140,895
Expenditure (do.)....	20,954,862	19,670,419
Public debt.........	4,050,000	4,711,938

Government

On March 1, 1967, Dominica became an Associated State of the United Kingdom. The Queen's Representative was redesignated the Governor.

The new House of Assembly now comprises 21 elected and 3 nominated members, one nominated on the advice of the Leader of the Opposition. The Cabinet (Executive) presided over by the Premier, consists of 5 other Government Ministers and the Attorney-General (Official Member). The Premier is appointed by the Governor from the elected members of the House of Assembly. The other Ministers are appointed by the Governor on the advice of the Premier. The Speaker is elected from among the members of the House or from outside.

Governor, His Excellency Sir Louis Cools-Lartigue, O.B.E. (1967).

Premier, Hon. Patrick John.

PRINCIPAL LAND AREAS OF THE WORLD BELOW SEA LEVEL

(With approx. greatest depth in feet below Mean Sea Level.)

Europe: Netherlands coastal areas (15).
Asia: Jordan Valley, Dead Sea (1290).*
  China: Sinkiang, Turfan Basin (980).
  U.S.S.R.-Iran: Caspian Sea (85).*
  Arabia: Trucial Oman-Qatar (70).
Africa: Libyan Desert Depressions:—
  Qattara (440), Faiyum (150).
  Wadi Ryan (140), Sittra (110).

Africa: Libyan Desert Depressions (*continued*)—
  Areg (80), Wadi Natrun (75).
  Melfa (60), Siwa (55), Bahrein (50).
  Eritrea: Salt Plains depression (385).
  Algeria-Tunisia: Shott Melghir and El
  Gharsa (90).*
America: Death Valley (275), Salton Sea (245).
Australia: Lake Eyre (40).

*Water surface

UNIVERSITIES OF THE COMMONWEALTH

(outside the United Kingdom)
With date of foundation, number of full-time students and name of Executive Head
(*Vice-Chancellor, President or Principal*)

Australia

ADELAIDE (1874). (Full-time students, 6,533).— *Vice-Chancellor*, Prof. G. M. Badger, Ph.D., D.SC.

AUSTRALIAN NATIONAL (1946), Canberra. (3,810).— *Vice-Chancellor*, Prof. D. A. Low, D.Phil.

DEAKIN (1974), Geelong. (First students, 1979).— *Vice-Chancellor designate*, Prof. F. R. Jevons, Ph.D., D.SC.

FLINDERS, SOUTH AUSTRALIA (1966), Bedford Park (2,580).—*Vice-Chancellor*, Prof. R. W. Russell, Ph.D., D.SC.

GRIFFITH (1971), Brisbane.—*Vice-Chancellor*, Emeritus Prof. F. J. Willett, D.SC., LL.D.

JAMES COOK, NORTH QUEENSLAND (1970), Townsville. (1,268).—*Vice-Chancellor*, K. J. C. Back, Ph.D.

LA TROBE (1964), Melbourne. (5,279).—*Vice-Chancellor*, D. M. Myers, D.SC. ENG.

MACQUARIE (1964), Sydney. (4,542).—*Vice-Chancellor*, Emeritus Prof. A. G. Mitchell, Ph.D.

MELBOURNE (1853). (11,079).—*Vice-Chancellor*, Prof. D. P. Derham, C.M.G., M.B.E., LL.D.

MONASH (1958), Melbourne. (9,746).—*Vice-Chancellor*, J. Vaizey, D.Tech.

MURDOCH (1973), Perth. (416).—*Vice-Chancellor*, Prof. S. Griew, Ph.D.

NEWCASTLE (1965). (2,597)—*Vice-Chancellor*, Prof. D. W. George, Ph.D.

NEW ENGLAND (1954), Armidal. (2,935).—*Vice-Chancellor*, Prof. A. Lazenby, Ph.D.

NEW SOUTH WALES (1949), Sydney. (13,769).—*Vice-Chancellor*, Prof. R. H. Myers, Ph.D.

  W. S. & L. B. ROBINSON UNIV. COLL. (1967), Broken Hill.—*Director*, Prof. J. E. Andersen, Ph.D.

QUEENSLAND (1909), Brisbane, (9,508).—*Vice-Chancellor*, Emeritus Prof. Z. Cowen, C.M.G., Q.C., D.C.L., LL.D.

SYDNEY (1850). (13,933).—*Vice-Chancellor*, Prof. B. R. Williams, LL.D.

TASMANIA (1890), Hobart. (2,314).—*Vice-Chancellor*, Sir George Cartland, C.M.G.

WESTERN AUSTRALIA (1911), Perth. (6,283).—*Vice-Chancellor*, Emeritus Prof. R. F. Whelan, M.D., Ph.D., D.SC.

WOLLONGONG (1975 (1,116).—*Vice-Chancellor*, Emeritus Prof, L. M. Birt, Ph.D., D.Phil.

Bangladesh

BANGLADESH AGRICULTURAL (1961), Mymensingh. (Full-time students, 2,730)—*Vice-Chancellor*, Prof. M. U. A. Choudhury.

BANGLADESH U. OF ENGINEERING AND TECHNOLOGY (1961), Dacca. (1,708).—*Vice-Chancellor*, Dr. Wahiduddin Ahmad.

CHITTAGONG (1966). (38,902).—*Vice-Chancellor*, Prof, Abul Fazal.

DACCA (1921). (66,223).—*Vice-Chancellor*, Prof. A. M. Chaudhury, Ph.D.

JAHANGIRNAGAR MUSLIM (1970), Dacca. (904).— *Vice-Chancellor*, Prof. M. E. Huq, Ph.D.

RAJSHAHI (1953). (39,861).—*Vice-Chancellor*, Prof. M. Islam, Ph.D.

Canada

ACADIA (1838), Wolfville. (Full-time students, 2,603).—*President*, J. M. R. Beveridge, M.D., Ph.D., D.SC., LL.D.

ALBERTA (1906), Edmonton. (19,155).—*President*, Prof. H. E. Gunning, Ph.D., D.SC.

BISHOP'S (1843), Lennoxville. (728).—*Vice-Chancellor*, D. M. Healy, D.U., D.C.I.

BRANDON (1967). (959).—*President*, A. L. Dulmage, Ph.D.

BRITISH COLUMBIA (1908), Vancouver. (19,866).— *President*, D. T. Kenny, Ph.D.

BROCK (1964), St. Catherines. (2,295).—*President*, A. J. Earp, LL.D.

CALGARY (1966). (9,578).—*President*, W. A. Cochrane, M.D.

CARLETON (1942), Ottawa. (8,448).—*President*, M. K. Oliver, Ph.D., LL.D.

CONCORDIA (1929), Montreal. (16,099 incl. pt.-time).—*Principal*, J. W. O Brien, Ph.D.

DALHOUSIE (1818), Halifax. (6,784).—*President*, The Hon. H. D. Hicks, C. C., Q.C., Ll.D., D.Ed. D.C.I.

  UNIV. OF KING'S COLL. (1789), Halifax. (253). —*President*, J. G. Morgan, D.Phil.

DOMINICAN COLL. OF PHILOSOPHY AND THEOLOGY (1967), Ottawa. (218).—*President*, Rev. Father G.-D. Mailhoit.

GUELPH (1964). (9,139).—*Vice-Chancellor*, D. F. Forster.

LAKEHEAD (1965), Thunder Bay. (2,356).—*Vice-Chancellor*, A. D. Booth, Ph.D., D.SC.

LAURENTIAN SUDBURY (1960). (2,187).—*President*, E. J. Monahan, Ph.D.

LAVAL (1852), Quebec. (11,071).—*Rector Magnificus*, L. Kerwin, LL.D., D.SC.

LETHBRIDGE (1967). (1,156).—*President*, W. E. Beckel, Ph.D.

McGILL (1821), Montreal. (16,379).—*Principal*, R. E. Bell, C.C., Ph.D., D.SC., LL.D.

McMASTER (1887), Hamilton. (9,421).—*President*, A. N. Bourns, D.SC., Ph.D.

MANITOBA (1877), Winnipeg. (13,776).—*President*, E. Sirluck, M.B.E., Ph.D., LL.D.

  ST. JOHN'S COLL. (1866), Winnipeg.— *Warden*, Rev. Canon J. R. Brown, D.D.

  ST. PAUL'S COLL. (1926), Winnipeg.— *Rector*, Very Rev. V. Jensen.

MEMORIAL, NEWFOUNDLAND (1949), St. John's. (6,415).—*Vice-Chancellor*, M. O. Morgan, C.C., LL.D., D.C.I.

MONCTON (1963). (3,080).—*Rector*, J. Cadieux, D.SC.Econ.

MONTREAL (1876). (15,510).—*Rector*, P. Lacoste, D.U.
MOUNT ALLISON (1858), Sackville. (1,363).—*President*, W. S. H. Crawford, PH.D.
MOUNT ST. VINCENT (1925), Halifax. (1,179).—*President*, Sister Mary Albertus, PH.D.
NEW BRUNSWICK (1785), Fredericton. (5,424).—*President*, J. M. Anderson, PH.D.
NOVA SCOTIA AGRICULTURAL COLL. (1905), Truro. (426).—*Principal*, H. F. MacRae, PH.D.
NOVA SCOTIA COLL. OF ART AND DESIGN (1887), Halifax. (425).—*President*, G. N. Kennedy.
NOVA SCOTIA TECHNICAL COLL. (1909), Halifax. (465).—*Acting President*, A. E. Steeves.
OTTAWA (1848). (10,215).—*Rector*, Rev. R. Guindon, D.Th., LL.D.
   ST. PAUL (1848), Ottawa (330).—*Rector*, Rev. Father M. Patry, D.Ph., PH.D.
PRINCE EDWARD ISLAND (1969), Charlottetown (1,397).—*President*, R. J. Baker, LL.D.
QUEBEC (1968), Chicoutimi, Montreal, Rimouski, and Trois-Rivières. (9,016).—*President*, R. Després.
QUEEN'S KINGSTON (1841). (9,616).—*Principal*, R. L. Watts, D.Phil.
REGINA (1974). (3,505).—*President*, J. H. Archer, PH.D.
ROYAL MILITARY COLL. OF CANADA (1876), Kingston. (679).—*Principal*, J. R. Dacey, M.B.E., PH.D.
RYERSON POLYTECHNICAL INSTITUTE (1963), Toronto. (8,083).—*President*, W. Pitman.
ST. FRANCIS XAVIER (1853), Antigonish. (2,205).—*President*, Rev. M. MacDonell, LL.D.
ST. MARY'S (1841), Halifax. (2,331).—*President*, D. O. Carrigan, PH.D.
SASKATCHEWAN (1907). Saskatoon (9,462).—*President*, R. W. Begg, M.D., D.Phil.
   ST. THOMAS MORE COLL. (1936), Saskatoon.—*Principal*, Rev. P. J. M. Swan, PH.D.
SHERBROOKE (1954). (5,310).—*Rector*, Rt. Rev. Mgr. R. Maltais.
SIMON FRASER (1963), Burnaby. (5,017).—*President*, Pauline Jewett, PH.D.
TORONTO (1827). (29,369).—*President*, J. R. Evans, D.Phil., M.D., LL.D., D.SC.
   UNIV. OF ST. MICHAEL'S COLL. (1852), Toronto. (2,203).—*President*, Rev. J. M. Kelly, PH.D.
   UNIV. OF TRINITY COLL. (1851), Toronto. (934).—*Vice-Chancellor*, G. Ignatieff, C.C., LL.D., D.C.L.
   VICTORIA (1836), Toronto. (2,534).—*President*, G. S. French, PH.D.

ONTARIO INSTITUTE FOR STUDIES IN EDUCATION (1965), Toronto.—*Director*, Dr. C. C. Pitt.
TRENT (1963), Peterborough. (1,820).—*President*, Prof. T. E. W. Nind.
VICTORIA (1963), British Columbia. (4,601).—*President*, H. E. Petch, PH.D.
WATERLOO (1959). (11,731).—*Vice-Chancellor*, B. C. Matthews, PH.D.
   ST. JEROME S COLL., Waterloo.—*President*, C. L. Siegfried, LL.D.
WESTERN ONTARIO (1878), London. (16,210).—*President*, D. C. Williams, PH.D., LL.D.
   BRESCIA COLL. (1919), London.—*Principal*, Sister Frances Ryan, PH.D.
   HURON COLL. (1863), London.—*Principal* Ven. J. G. Morden, D.D., D.Th.
   KING S COLL. (1912), London.—*Principal*, A. F. McKee, D.U.
WILFRED LAURIER (1973), Waterloo. (2,524).—*President*, F. C. Peters, PH.D.
WINDSOR (1857). (5,705).—*Vice-Chancellor*, J. F. Leddy, O.C. D.Phil., D.Litt., D. ès L., LL.D., D.C.L.
WINNIPEG (1967). (2,455).—*President*, H. E. Duckworth, PH.D., D.SC.

YORK (1959), Toronto. (11,220).—*President*, H. I. Macdonald.

Ghana

CAPE COAST (1962). (Full-time students 1,109).—*Vice-Chancellor*, Prof. J. Y. Ewusie, PH.D.
GHANA (1961), Legon. (2,631).—*Vice-Chancellor*, A. A. Kwapong, PH.D.
UNIV. OF SCIENCE AND TECHNOLOGY (1961), Kumasi. (1,885).—*Vice-Chancellor*, E. B. Kwakye, DR.ing.

Guyana

GUYANA (1963), Georgetown. (Full-time students, 388).—*Vice-Chancellor*, D. H. Irvine, PH.D.

Hong Kong

CHINESE UNIV. OF HONG KONG (1963). (Full-time students, 3,094).—*Vice-Chancellor*, C. M. Li, K.B.E.(hon.), PH.D., LL.D., D.SC.
HONG KONG (1911). (3,290).—*Vice-Chancellor*, R. L. Huang, D.Phil., D.SC.

India

AGRA (1927). (Full-time students, 64,248).—*Vice-Chancellor*, C. B. Rao.
AGRICULTURAL SCIENCES (1964), Bangalore. (2,370).—*Vice-Chancellor*, H. R. Arakeri, PH.D.
ALIGARH MUSLIM (1920). (10,298).—*Vice-Chancellor*, A. M. Khusro, PH.D.
ALLAHABAD (1887). (11,198).—*Vice-Chancellor*, R. Sahay.
ANDHRA (1926), Waltair. (9,691).—*Vice-Chancellor*, M. R. Apparow.
ANNAMALAI (1928), Annamalainagar. (5,870).—*Vice-Chancellor*, S. P. Adinarayan, PH.D.
ASSAM AGRICULTURAL (1969), Jorhat. (704).—*Vice-Chancellor*, Dr. L. S. Negi.
AWADHESH PRATAP SINGH VISHWAVIDYALAYA (1968), Rewa. (18,397).—*Vice-Chancellor*, S. N. Shulka.
BANARAS HINDU (1915). (12,620).—*Vice-Chancellor*, K. L. Shrimali, PH.D.
BANGALORE (1964). (32,123).—*Vice-Chancellor*, H. Narasimhaiah, PH.D.
BARODA (1949). (20,005).—*Acting Vice-Chancellor*, Prof. P. J. Madan.
BERHAMPUR (1967). (9,674).—*Vice-Chancellor*, Justice B. K. Patra.
BHAGALPUR (1960). (31,714).—*Vice-Chancellor*, D. P. Singh.
BHOPAL (1970). (13,393).—*Vice-Chancellor*, R. Prakash, PH.D.
BIHAR (1952), Muzaffarpur. (52,554).—*Vice-Chancellor*, K. K. Mandal, PH.D.
BOMBAY (1857). (97,674).—*Vice-Chancellor*, T. K. Tope.
BURDWAN (1960). (59,332).—*Vice-Chancellor*, R. Mukherji, D.Phil., D.Litt.
CALCUTTA (1857). (228,112).—*Vice-Chancellor*, S. N. Sen, PH.D.
CALICUT (1968). (50,440).—*Acting Vice-Chancellor*, Prof. S. Azhicode.
DELHI (1922). (62,932).—*Vice-Chancellor*, R. C. Mehrotra, PH.D., D.Phil.
DIBRUGARH (1965). (32,532).—*Vice-Chancellor*, J. N. Das.
GARHWAL (1973), Srinagar. (12,000).—*Vice-Chancellor*, B. D. Bhatt.
GAUHATI (1948). (43,370).—*Vice-Chancellor*, H. K. Baruah, PH.D.
GORAKHPUR (1956). (63,379).—*Vice-Chancellor*, D. Sharma, PH.D., D.Phil.
GOVIND BALLABH PANT U. of AGRICULTURE AND TECHNOLOGY (1960), Pantnagar. (2,087).—*Vice-Chancellor*, S. P. Pande.
GUJARAT (1949), Ahmedabad. (98,857).—*Vice-Chancellor*, I. J. Patel.
GUJARAT AGRICULTURAL (1969), Ahmedabad. (1,843).—*Vice-Chancellor*, V. R. Mehta.

GUJARAT VIDYAPITH (1920), Ahmedabad. (627).—
Vice-Chancellor, R. Parikh.
GURU NANAK (1969), Amritsar. (45,264).—*Vice-Chancellor*, B. Singh Samundri.
HIMACHAL PRADESH (1970), Simla. (21,965).—*Vice-Chancellor*, R. K. Singh, D.Ed.
INDIAN INSTITUTE OF SCIENCE (1909), Bangalore. (957).—*Director*, S. Dhawan, Ph.D.
INDIAN INST. OF TECHNOLOGY, BOMBAY (1958). (2,088).—*Director*, A. K. De, Ph.D.
INDIAN INST. OF TECHNOLOGY, DELHI (1961). (1,811).—*Director*, Prof. N. M. Swani, Ph.D.
INDIAN INST. OF TECHNOLOGY, KANPUR (1960). (1,983).—*Actg. Director*, J. Lal, Ph.D.
INDIAN INST. OF TECHNOLOGY, KHARAGPUR (1951). (2,047).—*Director*, Prof. C. S. Jha.
INDIAN INST. OF TECHNOLOGY, MADRAS (1959). (2,093).—*Director*, K. A. V. Pandalai.
INDIRA KALA SANGIT VISHWAVIDYALAYA (1956), Khairagarh. (3,150).—*Vice-Chancellor*, G. C. Jain.
INDORE (1964). (17,511).—*Vice-Chancellor*, Dr. P. G. Deo.
JABALPUR (1957). (15,116).—*Vice-Chancellor*, P. D. Agnihotri, Ph.D.
JADAVPUR (1955), Calcutta. (3,225).—*Vice-Chancellor*, A. N. Bose, Ph.D.
JAMMU (1969). (12,245).—*Vice-Chancellor*, J. D. Sharma.
JAWAHARLAL NEHRU KRISHI VISHWA VIDYALAYA (1964), Jabalpur. (2,199).—*Vice-Chancellor*, E. Reinboth.
JAWAHARLAL NEHRU TECHNOLOGICAL (1972), Hyderabad. (3,600).—*Vice-Chancellor*, Prof. T. R. Doss.
JAWAHARLAL NEHRU U. (1969), New Delhi. (1,398). —*Vice-Chancellor*, B. D. Nag Chaudhuri.
JIWAJI (1964), Gwalior. (27,789).—*Vice-Chancellor*, G. N. Tandan.
JODHPUR (1962). (9,550).—*Vice-Chancellor*, Prof. S. C. Goyal.
KALYANI (1960). (1,909).—*Vice-Chancellor*, Prof. P. C. Mukherjee, D.Sc.
KANPUR (1965). (33,842).—*Vice-Chancellor*, B. Darsham.
KARNATAK (1949), Dharwar. (43,054).—*Vice-Chancellor*, R. C. Hiremath, Ph.D.
KASHMIR (1969), Srinagar. (17,848).—*Vice-Chancellor*, R. N. Chishti.
KERALA (1937), Trivandrum. (114,394).—*Vice-Chancellor*, Prof. R. S. Krishnan, Ph.D., D.Sc.
KURUKSHETRA (1956). (94,336).—*Vice-Chancellor*, S. K. Dutta, D.Litt.
LUCKNOW (1921). (30,410).—*Vice-Chancellor*, A. K. Mustafi.
MADRAS (1857). (152,267)—*Vice-Chancellor*, N. D. Sundaravadivelu.
MADURAI (1966). (77,103).—*Vice-Chancellor*, S. V. Chittibabu.
MAGADH (1962), Gaya. (43,378).—*Vice-Chancellor*, Dr. P. Dayae.
MARATHWADA (1958), Aurangabad. (59,427).—*Vice-Chancellor*, S. R. Kharat.
MEERUT (1966). (71,171).—*Vice-Chancellor*, Prof. B. S. Mathur.
MYSORE (1916). (89,199).—*Vice-Chancellor*, Prof. D. J. Gowda.
NAGPUR (1923). (92,009).—*Officiating Vice-Chancellor*, Dr. D. Y. Gohokar.
NORTH BENGAL (1962), Darjeeling. (16,812).—*Vice-Chancellor*, Prof. A. Datta.
NORTH-EASTERN HILL (1973), Shillong. (15,202).—*Vice-Chancellor*, Dr. C. D. S. Devanesan, Ph.D.
OSMANIA (1918), Hyderabad. (69,107).—*Vice-Chancellor*, J. Reddy.

PANJAB (1947), Chandigarh. (130,595).—*Vice-Chancellor*, Prof. R. C. Paul.
PATNA (1917). (12,538).—*Vice-Chancellor*, Prof. D. N. Sharma.
POONA (1948). (94,325).—*Vice-Chancellor*, Dr. D. A. Dabholkar.
PUNJAB AGRICULTURAL (1962), Ludhiana. (2,410)—*Vice-Chancellor*, M. S. Randhawa, D.Sc.
PUNJABI (1961), Patiala. (30,394).—*Vice-Chancellor*, Mrs. I. K. Sandhu.
PUNJABRAO KRISHI VIDYAPEETH (1969) Akola, (3,088).—*Vice-Chancellor*, N. Gopalkrishna.
RABINDRA BHARATI (1962), Calcutta. (4,215).—*Vice-Chancellor*, Mrs. Roma Chaudhuri, D.Phil.
RAJASTHAN (1947), Jaipur. (74,217).—*Vice-Chancellor*, Dr. G. C. Pande.
RANCHI (1960). (42,340).—*Vice-Chancellor*, R. S. Mandal.
RAVISHANKAR (1963), Raipur. (22,222).—*Vice-Chancellor*, J. C. Dikshit.
ROORKEE (1949). (2,037).—*Vice-Chancellor*, Prof. J. Krishna, Ph.D.
SAMBALPUR (1967). (13,430).—*Vice-Chancellor*, Prof. B. Behera.
SAMPURNANAND SANSKRIT VISHWAVIDYALAYA (1958), Varanasi. (30,519).—*Vice-Chancellor*, K. Tripathi.
SARDAR PATEL (1955), Vallabh Vidyanagar. (12,735).—*Actg. Vice-Chancellor*, M. M. Shah.
SAUGAR (1946), Sagar. (22,761).—*Actg. Vice-Chancellor*, Prof. B. Mishra, Ph.D.
SAURASHTRA (1966), Rajkot. (39,431).—*Vice-Chancellor*, Y. P. Shukla.
SHIVAJI (1962), Kolhapur. (63,548).—*Vice-Chancellor*, P. G. Patil.
SHREEMATI N. D. THACKERSEY WOMEN'S (1951), Bombay. (18,722).—*Vice-Chancellor*, Mrs. Maduri R. Shah.
SOUTH GUJARAT (1966), Surat. (23,976).—*Vice-Chancellor*, A. R. Desai.
SRI VENKATESWARA (1954), Tirupati. (22,820).—*Vice-Chancellor*, D. Jaganatha Reddy, M.D.
TAMIL NADU AGRICULTURAL (1971), Coimbatore. (1,352).—*Vice-Chancellor*, G. Rangaswami, Ph.D.
UDAIPUR (1962). (7,544).—*Vice-Chancellor*, P. S. Lamba, Ph.D.
UTKAL (1943), Bhubaneswar. (46,276).—*Administrator*, G. Chand.
VIKRAM (1957), Ujjain. (13,260).—*Vice-Chancellor*, S. M. Singh Suman, Ph.D., D.Litt.
VISVA-BHARATI (1951), Santiniketan. (2,584).—*Vice-Chancellor*, P. C. Gupta, Ph.D.

Kenya

NAIROBI (1970). (Full-time students, 4,205).—*Vice-Chancellor*, J. N. Karanja, Ph.D.
KENYATTA UNIV. COLL. (1972), Nairobi. (1,267).—*Principal*, D. Ireri, Ph.D.

Lesotho

BOTSWANA, LESOTHO AND SWAZILAND (1964), Roma; also campuses in Botswana and Swaziland. (Full-time students, 692).—*Vice-Chancellor*, Prof. C. A. Rogers, Ph.D.

Malawi

MALAWI (1964), Zomba. (1,078).—*Vice-Chancellor*, Prof. G. Hunnings, Ph.D.

Malaysia

UNIV. OF AGRICULTURE, MALAYSIA (1971), Serdang. (Full-time students, 2,109).—*Vice-Chancellor*, Mohd. Rashdan bin Haji Baba, Ph.D.
MALAYA (1962), Kuala Lumpur. (8,646).—*Vice-Chancellor*, Prof. Ungku A. Aziz, D.Econ., D.Litt.H.
NATIONAL UNIV. OF MALAYSIA (1970), Kuala Lumpur. (1,977).—*Vice-Chancellor*, Dr. Anuwar bin Mahmud.
SCIENCE U., MALAYSIA (1969). (1,588).—*Vice-Chancellor*, Prof. Hamzah Sendut, D.Sc., LL.D.

U. OF TECHNOLOGY (1972), Kuala Lumpur. (1,391).
—*Vice-Chancellor*, Ainuddin bin Abdul Wahid.

Malta

ROYAL UNIV. OF MALTA (1769), Valetta. (792).—
Vice-Chancellor, Prof. E. J. Borg Costanzi.

Mauritius

MAURITIUS (1965), Réduit. (717).—*Vice-Chancellor*,
R. Burrenchobay.

New Zealand

AUCKLAND (1882). (Full-time students, 6,487).—
Vice-Chancellor, C. J. Maiden, D.Phil.
CANTERBURY (1873), Christchurch. (4,722).—
Vice-Chancellor, Emeritus Prof. N. C. Phillips,
C.M.G.
    LINCOLN COLL. (1878). (864).—*Principal*,
Emeritus Prof. J. D. Stewart, Ph.D.
MASSEY (1964), Palmerston North. (2,765).—*Vice-Chancellor*, A. Stewart, C.B.E., D.Phil.
OTAGO (1869), Dunedin. (4,852).—*Vice-Chancellor*,
R. O. H. Irvine, M.D.
VICTORIA, WELLINGTON (1897). (3,962).—*Vice-Chancellor*, D. B. C. Taylor, Ph.D.
WAIKATO (1964), Hamilton. (1,842).—*Vice-Chancellor*, D. R. Llewellyn, D.Phil., D.Sc.

Nigeria

AHMADU BELLO (1962), Zaria. (Full-time students,
6,069).—*Vice-Chancellor*, I. S. Audu, L.H.D., D.SC.
BENIN (1970). (417).—*Vice-Chancellor*, Prof. T. M.
Yesufu, Ph.D.
IBADAN (1948). (3,795).—*Vice-Chancellor*, Prof.
H. O. Thomas, C.B.E., D.Sc.
IFE (1961), Ile-Ife. (4,806).—*Vice-Chancellor*, H. A.
Oluwasanmi, Ph.D., D.SC., L.H.D., LL.D.
LAGOS (1962). (3,241).—*Vice-Chancellor*, Prof.
J. F. A. Ajayi, Ph.D.
NIGERIA (1960), Nsukka, with campuses at Enugu
and Calabar. (4,678).—*Vice-Chancellor*, Prof. H.
C. Kodilinye.

Papua New Guinea

PAPUA NEW GUINEA (1965), Port Moresby. (Full-time students, 1,106).—*Vice-Chancellor*, G. B. Gris.
PAPUA NEW GUINEA UNIV. OF TECHNOLOGY (1973),
Lae. (535).—*Vice-Chancellor*, J. A. Sandover,
Ph.D.

Rhodesia

RHODESIA (1955), Salisbury. (Full-time students,
1,116).—*Principal*, Rev. Prof. R. Craig, Ph.D.
D.D.

Sierra Leone

SIERRA LEONE (1966), with colleges at Freetown and
Njala. (1,491).—*Vice-Chancellor*, A. T. Porter,
Ph.D., L.H.D., LL.D.

Singapore

NANYANG (1953). (Full-time students, 2,575).—
Vice-Chancellor, C. M. Lee, Ph.D.
SINGAPORE (1962). (5,560).—*Vice-Chancellor*,
(vacant).

South Pacific

SOUTH PACIFIC (1967), Suva. (Full-time students,
981).—*Vice-Chancellor*, J. A. Maraj, Ph.D.

Sri Lanka

SRI LANKA (1942), with campuses at Colombo
(3,549), Gangodawila (1,889), Jaffna (104),
Katubedde (590), Kelaniya (1,936), and Peradeniya (4,679).—*Vice-Chancellor*, L. H. Sumanadasa.

Tanzania

DAR ES SALAAM (1970). (Full-time students, 2,176).
—*Vice-Chancellor*, P. Msekwa.

Uganda

MAKERERE (1970), Kampala. (Full-time students,
3,660).—*Vice-Chancellor*, Prof. J. S. W. Lutwama.

West Indies

UNIV. OF THE WEST INDIES (1962), Jamaica, with
branches in Trinidad and Barbados. (Full-time
students, 5,609).—*Vice-Chancellor*, A. Z. Preston.

Zambia

ZAMBIA (1965), Lusaka. (Full-time students, 2,605).
—*Vice-Chancellor*, Prof. L. K. H. Goma, Ph.D.

H.M. COASTGUARD

Between Jan. 1, 1974 and Dec. 31, 1974, Coastguards rescued 6,760 persons and took part in 5,572 rescue operations on British coasts.

There are about 600 full-time Coastguards and 7,000 part-time Auxiliary Coastguards on service to save and safeguard the lives of those at sea and around the 2,500 mile coastline of the United Kingdom. H.M. Coastguard is administered by the Department of Trade in 11 Divisions, each with three or four Districts within its boundaries. Each District has a number of stations and lookouts of which there are four types.

Constant Watch Stations are manned at all times, keeping a 24-hour watch, the coastguards working six-hour watches. *Day Watch Stations* are manned by three or four coastguards who each keep a four-hour watch in daylight. Additional watch is kept in bad weather. *Auxiliary Lookout Stations* are manned by Auxiliary Coastguards as and when a need arises. *Auxiliary Rescue Stations* are manned by Auxiliary Coastguards as and when a need arises. *Auxiliary Rescue Stations* are comprehensively equipped for all types of rescue.

Coastguard stations and lookouts are frequently located on bleak and isolated clifftops and headlands from which visual and radio watch is kept. The coastguard records the passage of ships at his post or station and informs the next station so that each ship's progress is noted and followed round the coast from station to station.

The CG66 Boat Safety Report Scheme offers safety coverage to those who regularly use local waters and to those who make longer passages. Its aim is to give the Coastguard a record of the movements of craft and in times of distress provide immediate information vital to the saving of lives.
The scheme consists of two cards, CG66A and CG66B. The "A" card is filled in by the regular user of local waters and the "B" card by the person making a longer journey. In search and rescue action, much time can be lost in the initial stages trying to establish what type of craft is involved and where it is likely to be. With this information to hand the Coastguard can act at once. It is a free service and cards are available, together with more information, at all Coastguard stations, harbour masters' offices and most yacht clubs and marinas.

Coastguards also watch for oil slicks, hazards and almost anything out of the ordinary, taking all necessary action to warn shipping of hazards. They are ready to take action on any distress signal and keep all lights in their area under observation, reporting any fault to the appropriate authority. Coastguard radios are tuned to the "distress frequencies" ready to take action if a ship makes a MAYDAY call. A Bad Weather Watch (BWW) is set whenever the wind exceeds Force 6. A Thick Weather Watch (TWW) is set whenever visibility falls to half a mile or less.

Most Coastguard stations give shipping vital

information about impending bad weather through the Gale Warning Service. The stations hoist cones on their flag masts, usually black, though at Aberdeen, Cromarty, Kildonan, Ardglass and the Mull of Kintyre Lighthouse they are white so that they can be readily distinguished from the background of dark rocks; for the same reason the cones used at St. Ives and Looe are orange and yellow respectively. The direction of the gale forecast is roughly indicated by the position of the cone; where its apex points upwards, the gale is expected from any point North of the East–West line, and where the apex points downwards the gale is expected from any point South of the East-West line.

Members of the public who urgently require the services of the Coastguard should make an emergency " 999 " call and ask for " Coastguard." The call will be routed to the nearest Coastguard Rescue Headquarters which is the co-ordinating authority for Search and Rescue operations and which will alert the appropriate Coastguard stations. As the Coastguard Rescue Headquarters is likely to be some way from the scene of the incident, it is important that the person making the call should give as many details as possible (*e.g.* the nature of the emergency, its position, etc.) and should be prepared, if required, to stay near the telephone, in case additional information is required, or to report any change in the situation. On occasions when larger ships need help the Coastguard will alert the lifeboats of the Royal National Lifeboat Institution or inshore rescue boats, Royal Air Force or Royal Navy helicopters, or R.A.F. aircraft, depending on the circumstances. When ships founder on rocks or beaches the Coastguard commonly organizes a breeches buoy rescue.

THE ZODIAC

The Zodiac is an imaginary belt in the heavens within which lie the apparent paths of the Sun, Moon and major planets. It is bounded by two parallels generally taken as lying 8° on either side of the ecliptic or path of the Sun in its annual course. The Zodiac is divided into twelve equal parts of 30° called Signs, which are not used by astronomers, but have some import in astrology, for which the division of the Zodiac was probably made originally. The Signs of the Zodiac take their names from certain of the constellations with which they once coincided. They are assumed to begin at the vernal equinox or intersection of the plane of the ecliptic with that of the equator. This point is still called the First Point of Aries, although the Sign of Aries now lies in the constellation of Pisces, some 30° to the west. This retrograding of the equinox by about 50″ a year is due to precession; the signs no longer coincide with the constellation; whose names they bear.

A catalogue has been made (Grimaldi, 1905) of all, so far as is known, sculptured or incised representations on ancient monuments or tablets of the traditional constellation figures, either Zodiacal or otherwise, together with many modern pictures of the Zodiac. The first in the list is a roughly shaped upright, black stone about $2\frac{1}{2}$ feet high and $1\frac{1}{2}$ feet broad in the Babylonian room of the British Museum on the front of which are lightly incised ten out of the twelve Signs and other constellation figures. This was found near Baghdad and its date is estimated to be about 1187–1175 B.C.

ARCHBISHOPS OF CANTERBURY SINCE 1414

1414 Henry Chichele	1633 William Laud	1828 William Howley
1443 John Stafford	1660 William Juxon	1848 John Bird Sumner
1452 John Kemp	1663 Gilbert Sheldon	1862 Charles Thomas Longley
1454 Thomas Bourchier	1678 William Sancroft	1868 Archibald Campbell Tait
1486 John Morton	1691 John Tillotson	1883 Edward White Benson
1501 Henry Dean	1695 Thomas Tenison	1896 Frederick Temple
1503 William Warham	1716 William Wake	1903 Randall Thomas Davidson
1533 Thomas Cranmer	1737 John Potter	1928 Cosmo Gordon Lang
1556 Reginald Pole	1747 Thomas Herring	1942 William Temple
1559 Matthew Parker	1757 Matthew Hutton	1945 Geoffrey Francis Fisher
1576 Edmund Grindal	1758 Thomas Secker	1961 Arthur Michael Ramsey
1583 John Whitgift	1768 Hon. Frederick Cornwallis	1974 Frederick Donald Coggan
1604 Richard Bancroft	1783 John Moore	
1611 George Abbot	1805 Charles Manners Sutton	

ARCHBISHOPS OF YORK SINCE 1606

1606 Tobias Matthew	1724 Launcelot Blackburn	1891 William Connor Magee
1628 George Montague	1743 Thomas Herring	1891 William Dalrymple Maclagan
1629 Samuel Harsnett	1747 Matthew Hutton	
1632 Richard Neile	1757 John Gilbert	1909 Cosmo Gordon Lang
1641 John Williams	1761 Robert Hay Drummond	1929 William Temple
1660 Accepted Frewen	1777 William Markham	1942 Cyril Forster Garbett
1664 Richard Sterne	1808 Edward Venables Vernon Harcourt	1956 Arthur Michael Ramsey
1683 John Dolben		1961 Frederick Donald Coggan
1688 Thomas Lamplugh	1848 Thomas Musgrave	1974 Stuart Yarworth Blanch
1691 John Sharp	1860 Charles Thomas Longley	
1714 William Dawes	1862 William Thomson	

Ireland

Position and Extent.—Ireland lies in the Atlantic Ocean, to the West of Great Britain, and is separated from Scotland by the North Channel and from Wales by the Irish Sea and St. George's Channel. The land area of the island is 32,408 sq. miles and its geographical position between 51° 26′ and 55° 21′ N. latitude and from 5° 25′ to 10° 30′ W. longitude. The greatest length of the island, from N.E. to S.W. (Torr Head to Mizen Head), is 302 miles, and the greatest breadth, from E. to W. (Dundrum Bay to Annagh Head), is 174 miles. On the N. coast of *Achill Island* (Co. Mayo) are the highest cliffs in the British Isles, 2,000 feet sheer above the sea. Ireland is occupied for the greater part of its area by the *Central Plain*, with an elevation 50 to 350 ft. above mean sea level, with isolated mountain ranges near the coastline. The principal mountains, with their highest points, are the *Sperrin Mountains* (Sawel 2,240 ft.) of County Tyrone; the *Mountains of Mourne* (Slieve Donard 2,796 ft.) of County Down, and the *Wicklow Mountains* (Lugnaquilla 3,039 ft.); the *Derryveagh Mountains* (Errigal 2,466 ft.) of County Donegal; the *Connemara Mountains* (Twelve Pins 2,695 ft.) of County Galway; *Macgillicuddy's Reeks* (Carrantuohill 3,414 ft., the highest point in Ireland); and the *Galtee Mountains* (3,018 ft.) of County Tipperary, and the *Knockmealdown* (2,609 ft.) and *Comeragh Mountains* (2,470 ft.) of County Waterford. The principal river of Ireland (and the longest in the British Isles) is the *Shannon* (240 miles), rising in County Cavan and draining the central plain. The Shannon flows through a chain of loughs to the city of Limerick, and thence to an estuary on the western Atlantic seaboard. The *Slaney* flows into Wexford Harbour, the *Liffey* to Dublin Bay, the *Boyne* to Drogheda, the *Lee* to Cork Harbour, the *Blackwater* to Youghal Harbour, and the *Suir*, *Barrow* and *Nore*, to Waterford Harbour. As in Scotland, the principal hydrographic feature is the *Loughs*, of which Lough *Neagh* (150 sq. miles) in the north-east is the largest in Ireland and the British Isles, others being the Shannon Chain of *Allen, Boderg, Forbes, Ree* and *Derg*, and the Erne Chain of *Gowna, Oughter, Lower Erne*, and *Erne*; *Melvin, Gill, Gara* and *Conn* in the north-west; and *Corrib* and *Mask* (joined by a hidden channel) in the west. In County Kerry, to the east of Macgillicuddy's Reeks, are the famous *Lakes of Killarney*. The climate of Ireland is more equable than that of Great Britain, the extreme range of temperature readings being from 2° F. to 90° F. (compared with — 17° F. to 100° F. over Great Britain). The average annual rainfall varies from 27 inches at Dublin to more than 100 inches in the mountains of Connemara. The rainfall is also more uniform from year to year than in Great Britain.

Primitive Man.—Although little is known concerning the earliest inhabitants of Ireland, there are many traces of neolithic man throughout the island; a grave containing a polished stone axehead assigned to 2,500 B.C. was found at Linkardstown, Co. Carlow, in 1944, and the use of bronze implements appears to have become known about the middle of the 17th century B.C. In the later Bronze Age a Celtic race of *Goidels* appears to have invaded the island, and in the early Iron Age *Brythons* from South Britain are believed to have effected settlements in the south-east, while *Picts* from North Britain established similar settlements in the north. Towards the close of the Roman occupation of Britain, the dominant tribe in the island was that of the *Scoti*, who afterwards established themselves in Scotland.

History.—According to Irish legends, the island of Ierne was settled by a Milesian race, who came from Scythia by way of Spain, and established the *Kingdom of Tara*, about 500 B.C. The supremacy of the *Ardri* (high king) of Tara was acknowledged by eight lesser kingdoms (Munster, Connaught, Ailech, Oriel, Ulidia, Meath, Leinster and Ossory) ruled by descendants of the eight sons of Miled. The basalt columns on the coast of Antrim, eight miles from Portrush, known as the *Giant's Causeway*, are connected with the legendary history of Ireland as the remnants of a bridge built in the time of Finn M'Coul (Fingal) to connect Antrim with Scotland (Staffa).

Hibernia was visited by Roman merchants but never by Roman legions, and little is known of the history of the country until the invasions of *Northmen* (Norwegians and Danes) towards the close of the 8th century A.D. The Norwegians were distinguished as Findgaill (White Strangers) and the Danes as Dubgaill (Black Strangers), names which survive in " Fingall," " MacDougall " and " Mac-Dowell," while the name of the island itself is held to be derived from the Scandinavian *Ira-land* (land of the Irish), the names of the Provinces being survivals of Norse dialect forms (Ulaids-tir, Laigins-tir, Mumans-tir and Kunnak-tir). The outstanding events in the encounters with the Northmen are the *Battle of Tara* (980), at which the Hy Neill

king Maelsechlainn II defeated the Scandinavians of Dublin and the Hebrides under their king Amlaib Cuarán; and the *Battle of Clontarf* (1014) by which the Scandinavian power was completely broken. After Clontarf the supreme power was disputed by the O'Briens of Munster, the O'Neills of Ulster, and the O'Connors of Connaught, with varying fortunes. In 1152 Dermod MacMurrough (Diarmit MacMurchada), the deposed king of Leinster, sought assistance in his struggle with Ruaidhri O'Connor (the high king of Ireland), and visited Henry II, the Norman king of England. Henry authorized him to obtain armed support in England for the recovery of his kingdom, and Dermod enlisted the services of Richard de Clare, the Norman Earl of Pembroke, afterwards known as *Strongbow*, who landed at Waterford (Aug. 23, 1170) with 200 knights and 1,000 other troops for the reconquest of Leinster, where he eventually settled, after marriage with Dermod's daughter. In 1172 (Oct. 18) Henry II himself landed in Ireland. He received homage from the Irish kings and established his capital at Dublin. The invaders subsequently conquered most of the island and a feudal government was created. In the 14th and 15th centuries, the Irish recovered most of their lands, while many Anglo-Irish lords became virtually independent, royal authority being confined to the " Pale," a small district round Dublin. Though under Henry VII, Sir Edward Poynings, as Lord Deputy had passed at the *Parliament of Drogheda* (1494) the act later known as *Poynings' Law*, subordinating the Irish Legislature to the Crown, the Earls of Kildare retained effective power until, in 1534, Henry VIII began the reconquest of Ireland. Parliament in 1541 recognized him as King of Ireland and by 1603 English authority was supreme.

Christianity.—Christianity did not become general until the advent of St. Patrick. St. *Patrick* was born in Britain about 389, and was taken to Ireland as a slave about sixteen years later escaping to Gaul at the age of 22. In 432 he was consecrated Bishop at Auxerre and landed in Wicklow to establish and organize the Christian religion throughout the island.

Republic of Ireland

Area and Population.—The Republic has a land area of 26,600 sq. miles, divided into the four Provinces of LEINSTER (Carlow, Dublin, Kildare, Kilkenny, Laoighis, Longford, Louth, Meath, Offaly, Westmeath, Wexford and Wicklow); MUNSTER (Clare, Cork, Kerry, Limerick, Tipperary and Waterford); CONNACHT (Galway, Leitrim, Mayo, Roscommon and Sligo); and part of ULSTER (Cavan, Donegal and Monaghan). Total population of the Republic at the Census held on April 18, 1971, was 2,978,248 (males, 1,495,760; females 1,482,488), a density of 112 persons per sq. mile (Census, 1966, 2,884,002). Provisional figures showed 68,784 births, 22,643 marriages and 34,468 deaths in the year 1974.
Uachtarn-na-hEireann (President), Erskine H. Childers, *born* 1906, *assumed*, June 25, 1973.

THE PRESIDENT

Uachtarn-na-hEireann (President),Cearbhall O' Dálaigh (Carroll Daly), *born* 1911, *assumed office*, Dec. 19, 1974.

A new Irish Government took office on March 14, 1973. Following the victory of the National Coalition of the Fine Gael and Labour in the general election held on February 28, the leader of Fine Gael, Mr. Liam Cosgrave, was elected *Taoiseach* (Prime Minister) when the new *Dáil* (Lower House of Parliament) met for the first time on March 14. Later that evening, following his formal appointment by the President, Mr. de Valera, the new *Taoiseach*, Mr. Cosgrave, announced his Cabinet to the *Dáil*.

MEMBERS OF THE GOVERNMENT

Taoiseach, Liam MacCosgair (Liam Cosgrave).
Tanaiste and Minister for Health and Minister for Social Welfare, Brendán Mac Fheórais (Brendan Corish).
Minister for Defence, Padraig S. Ó Donnagáin (Patrick S. Donegan).
Minister for Local Government, Seamus Ó Táithligh (James Tully).
Finance and the Public Service, Risteárd O Riain (Richie Ryan).
Agriculture and Fisheries, Marcus Mac Giollafhionntáin (Mark Clinton).
Labour, Micheál Ó Laoire (Michael Ó'Leary).
Minister for the Gaeltacht, Tomás Ó Domhnaill (Tom O'Donnell).
Lands, Tomás Mac Giolla Phádraigh (Tom Fitzpatrick).
Foreign Affairs, Gearóid Mac Gearailt (Garret Fitz-Gerald).
Posts and Telegraphs, Conchubhar Crús O Brian (Conor Cruise-O'Brien).
Transport and Power, Peadur de Barra (Peter Barry).
Industry and Commerce, Saorbhreathach Céitinn (Justin Keating).
Education, Risteard de Búrca (Dick Burke).
Justice, Padraigh Ó Cuana (Patrick M. Cooney).

Parliamentary Secretaries

Parliamentary Secretary to the Taoiseach and to the Minister for Foreign Affairs, Seán Ó Ceallaigh (John Kelly).
Do. to the Minister for Agriculture and Fisheries, Micheál Pádraigh Ó Murchadha (Michael Pat Murphy).
Do. to the Minister for Health, Risteárd de Barra (Richard Barry).
Do. to the Minister for Finance, hAnnraoi Ó Cionaith (Henry Kenny).
Do. to the Minister for Social Welfare, Proinsias Mac Bhloscaidh (Frank Cluskey).
Do. to the Minister for Local Government, and to the Minister for Defence, Micheál Ó Beaglaoi (Michael Begley).
Do. to the Minister for Education and to the Minister for Industry and Commerce, John Bruton.
Attorney-General, Declan Costello.
Secretary to the Government, Dónal Ó Súilleabháin (Daniel O'Sullivan).

Irish Embassy

17 Grosvenor Place, S.W.1
Ambassador Extraordinary and Plenipotentiary, His Excellency Dr. Donal O'Sullivan.

British Embassy

33 Merrion Road, Dublin 4
Ambassador Extraordinary and Plenipotentiary, His Excellency Sir Arthur Norman Galsworthy, K.C.M.G. (1973)......................£15,000
Counsellor, J. K. Hickman.
First Secretaries, M. F. Daly (*Information*); R. K. McKenzie (*Commercial*); J. White (*Agriculture*); W. N. Wenban-Smith (*EEC*).

GOVERNMENT

The Constitution.—The constitution approved by a plebiscite on July 1, 1937, came into operation on December 29, 1937.

The Constitution declares that Ireland is a sovereign independent democratic State and affirms the right of the Irish Nation to choose its own form of Government, to determine its relations with other nations, and to develop its life, political, economic and cultural, in accordance with its own genius and traditions. The national territory is declared to be the whole island of Ireland, its islands and the territorial seas. Pending the re-integration of the national territory, and without prejudice to the right of the Parliament and the Government established by the Constitution to exercise jurisdiction over the whole of the national territory, the laws enacted by that Parliament shall have the like area and extent of application as those of the Irish Free State, which did not include the six counties of Northern Ireland. The national flag is the tricolour of green, white and orange. The Irish language, being the national language, is the first official language. The English language is recognized as a second official language.

The President.—The President—*Uachtarán na hEireann*—is elected by direct vote of the people for a period of seven years. A former or retiring President is eligible for a second term. The President summons and dissolves Dáil Éireann on the advice of the *Taoiseach* (Head of the Government). He signs and promulgates laws. The supreme command of the Defence Forces is vested in him, its exercise being regulated by law. He has the power of pardon. The President, in the exercise and performance of certain of his constitutional powers and functions, is aided and advised by a Council of State.

The Legislature.—The National Parliament—*Oireachtas*—consists of the President and two Houses: a House of Representatives—*Dáil Eireann*—and a Senate—*Seanad Eireann*.

Dáil Eireann is composed of 144 members elected by adult suffrage on a basis of proportional representation.

Seanad Éireann is composed of 60 members, of whom 11 are nominated by the Taoiseach and 49 are elected; three by the National University of Ireland three by the University of Dublin, and 43 from panels of candidates, established on a vocational basis.

Members of Dáil Éireann are paid an allowance of £4,661 per annum (and members of Seanad Éireann £2,650); are allowed free travelling facilities between Dublin and their constituencies and are, subject to certain restrictions granted free telephone and postal facilities from Leinster House and allowances for overnight stays in Dublin.

The Executive.—The executive authority is exercised by the Government subject to the Constitution. The Government is responsible to Dáil Éireann, meets and acts as a collective authority, and is collectively responsible for the Departments of State administered by the Ministers.

The Taoiseach is appointed by the President on the nomination of Dáil Éireann. The other members of the Government are appointed by the President on the nomination of the Taoiseach with the previous approval of Dáil Éireann. The Taoiseach appoints a member of the Government to be the *Tánaiste* who acts for all purposes in the place of the Taoiseach in the event of the death, permanent incapacitation, or temporary absence of the Taoiseach. The Taoiseach, the Tánaiste and the Minister for Finance must be members of Dáil Éireann. The other members of the Government must be members of Dáil Éireann or Seanad Éireann, but not more than two may be members of Seanad Éireann.

THE LEGISLATURE

The Legislature (*Oireachtas*) consists of the President and two Houses—a House of Representatives (*Dáil Eireann*) and a Senate (*Seanad Eireann*). Dáil Éireann has 144 Members, elected on the system of Proportional Representation by means of the single transferable vote. All citizens who have reached the age of 18 years and are not disqualified by law have the right to vote. Each Dáil may continue for a period not exceeding five years from the date of election.

The result of the general election on Feb. 28, 1973 was as follows: *Fine Gael and Labour Coalition*, 73; *Fianna Fáil*, 69; *Independent*, 2. Total membership including the *Ceann Comhairle* (Chairman),144.

THE JUDICIARY

The Judiciary consists of Courts of First Instance and a Court of Final Appeal called the Supreme Court—*Cúirt Uachtarach*. The Courts of First Instance include a High Court—*Ard-Chúirt*—invested with full original jurisdiction in and power to determine all matters and questions, whether of law or fact, civil or criminal, and also Courts of local and limited jurisdiction, with a right of appeal as determined by law. The High Court alone has original jurisdiction to entertain the question of the validity of any law having regard to the provisions of the Constitution. The Supreme Court has appellate jurisdiction from all decisions of the High Court, subject to exceptions and regulations prescribed by law. No law may, however, be enacted excepting the question of the vaildity of any law from the appellate jurisdiction of the Supreme Court.

Chief Justice. Hon. Thomas F. O'Higgins	£14,210
President of the High Court, Hon. Thomas A. Finlay	12,315
Judges, Supreme Court, Hon. Brian Walsh; Hon. F. G. Budd; Hon. Seamus Henchy; Hon. Francis Griffin	11,999
Judges, High Court, Hon. George Murnaghan; Hon. Seán Kenny; Hon. Seán Butler; Hon. John M. Gannon; Weldon R. C. Parke; Hon. Thomas A. Doyle; Hon. Liam Hamilton; Hon. John C. Conroy .... *each*	10,419

DEFENCE

Under the direction of the President, and subject to the provisions of the Defence Act, 1954, the military command of the Defence Forces is exercisable by the Government through the Minister for Defence. To aid and counsel the Minister for Defence there is a Council of Defence consisting of the Parliamentary Secretary to the Minster, the Secretary of the Department of Defence, the Chief of Staff, the Adjutant-General and the Quartermaster-General. Establishments provide at present for a Permanent Defence Force of approximately 14,000 all ranks, including the Air Corps and the Naval Service. The Defence Estimates for the period April 1, 1974 to Dec. 31, 1975, provide for approximately 22,800 all ranks of the Reserve Defence Force. Recruitment is on a voluntary basis. The maximum term of enlistment for the Army is three years in the Permanent Defence Force *or* three years in the Permanent Defence Force and nine years in the Reserve Defence Force. For the Naval Service, enlistment is for four years in the Permanent Defence Force *or* six years in the Permanent Defence Force and six years in the Reserve Defence Force. There are at present six Brigades in the Army. Each comprises three infantry battalions and a squadron or company from each Corps (except Ordnance and Air). The Naval Service has three coastal minesweepers and a patrol vessel. The Air Corps has a small number of Chipmunk, Provost, Vampire, Dove and Cessna aircraft and Alouette helicopters. The Defence Estimates for the year ending Dec. 31 1975 provide for an expenditure of £48,946,000.

FINANCE

	1974 (April-Dec.) (Actual)	1975 (April-Dec.) (Estimated)
Revenue	£651,400,000	£1,126,300,000
Expenditure	743,700,000	1,251,700,000

In addition to the Expenditure figures shown above there were certain services of a capital nature regarded as proper to be met from borrowing. Issues for these services in 1974 (9 months) amounted to £201,130,000, and for 1975 are estimated at £317,800,000.

The estimated *Revenue* for 1975 includes Customs Duties, £179,700,000; Excise Duties, £157,600,000; Estate etc. Duties, £13,000,000; Income Tax, including Surtax, £351,206,000; Corporation Profits Tax, £23,000,000; Motor Vehicle Duties, £28,700,000; Stamp Duties, £13,100,000; Post Office Services, £71,600,000; Value-added Tax, £198,800,000; Agricultural Levies, £3,500,000; Capital Taxes, £3,000,000.

The principal items of estimated current *Expenditure* for 1975 are Debt Service, £224,100,000; Agriculture, £84,800,000; Defence, £48,900,000; Police and Justice, £44,500,000; Education, £159,400,000; Social Welfare, £211,900,000; Health Services, £171,300,000; Transport, £45,100,000; Post Office, £59,800,000; Superannuation, £36,800,000; Industry, £31,100,000.

The Gross Debt on December 31, 1975 will be £1,958,000,000 with capital assets of £973,000,000 at that date.

RELIGION
(Census of 1971)

Catholic	2,795,596
Church of Ireland	97,741
Presbyterians	16,054
Methodists	5,646
Others	63,211
Total	2,978,248

EDUCATION

Primary education is directed by the State. There were 3,688 State-aided primary schools with an average enrolment of 521,805 and average daily attendance 90·2 per cent. in 1973-74.

In 1973–74 there were 554 recognized secondary schools with 167,309, pupils under private management (mainly religious orders). Also, 62,549 full-time pupils (and approximately as many part-time pupils) received secondary education in 278 permanent secondary vocational schools (and a large number of temporary centres), and 7 Regional Technical Colleges—all these schools and colleges are controlled by some 38 statutory local Vocational Education Committees. In addition there were 8 residential schools for home economics under these committees. State comprehensive schools were in operation in 1973–74 with a total enrolment of 5,791 students, and twelve Community Schools with an enrolment of 4,202 students.

Third-level education is catered for by five University Colleges, a National Institute for Higher Education, and also by third-level courses offered by the Technical Colleges and Regional Technical Colleges. There were 20,360 full-time university students in 1973–74.

The estimated State expenditure on education in the period April 1, 1975 to Dec. 31, 1975, excluding administration and inspection, is Primary £77,323,000; Secondary £76,228,000. The vote for Universities and third-level Colleges amounted to £21,127,000, while, in addition, grants of £2,686,984 were provided in respect of the Facilities of General Agriculture, Veterinary Medicine and Dairy Science.

PRODUCTION AND INDUSTRY

Agriculture and Livestock.—In 1973 there were 874,800 acres under corn crops, 311,600 under root and green crops, 9,500 under fruit and 2,510,600 under hay, a total of 3,706,500 acres. The principal produce in 1973 was: oats, 159,700 tons; wheat, 225,300 tons; barley, 890,300 tons; turnips, 1,413,800 tons; potatoes, 1,311,200 tons; sugar beet, 1,300,200 tons; and hay, 4,278,400 tons. The live-stock included, 6,969,800 cattle, 4,261,000 sheep, 1,107,600 pigs and 103,300 horses and ponies.

Minerals.—300 persons were employed in the coal mines in 1974 and 67,000 tons of coal won.

Sea Fisheries.—6,696 persons were employed in the fisheries in 1974, the total value of all fish (excluding salmon) landed being £5,735;590.

COMMUNICATIONS

Railways.—In the year ended March 31, 1974, there were 1,361 miles of railway all of standard (5 ft. 3 in.) gauge; 12,695,155 passengers and 3,672,202 tons of merchandise were conveyed; the receipts were £17,125,272 and expenditure £25,211,858. These figures are in respect of railway working by *Coras Iompair Eireann*, the national transport undertaking which is now the only concern operating a rail service in the State.

Road Motor Services.—In 1974 road motor (omnibus) vehicles carried 233,303,306 passengers, the gross receipts being £20,006,620.

Shipping.—In 1974 the number of ships with cargo and in ballast in the foreign trade which arrived at Irish ports was 13,287 (38,127,022 net registered tons); of these 1,780 (2,612,131 net registered tons) were of Irish nationality.

CIVIL AVIATION

Shannon Airport, 15 miles W. of Limerick, is on the main transatlantic air route. In 1974 the airport handled 984,186 passengers, 58,835 tonnes of cargo and 2,014 tonnes of mail.

Dublin Airport, 6 miles N. of Dublin, serves the cross-channel and European services operated by the Irish national airline *Aer Lingus* and other air-lines. During 1974 the airport handled 2,075,136 passengers, 51,867 tonnes of cargo and 2,438 tonnes of mail.

Cork Airport, 5 miles S. of Cork, serves the cross-Channel and European services operated by *Aer Lingus* and other airlines. During 1974 the airport handled 245,504 passengers and 1,828 tonnes of cargo and 15 tonnes of mail.

There are 23 private aerodromes.

Trade with U.K.

	1973	1974
Imports from U.K.	£576,668,096	£758,248,133
Exports to U.K...	475,331,792	634,225,137

OVERSEAS TRADE

Year	Imports	Exports	Trade Balance
	£	£	£
1967..	414,663,869	314,504,050	100,159,819
1968..	516,124,308	363,689,163	152,435,145
1969..	613,639,642	404,246,194	209,393,448
1970..	676,652,175	466,671,557	209,980,618
1971..	754,913,123	538,661,654	216,251,469
1972..	838,053,271	647,548,503	190,504,768
1973..	1,137,236,398	869,186,046	268,050,352

PRINCIPAL ARTICLES

Imports (1972)

The principal groups were: live animals, £21,545,085; food, drink and tobacco, £122,415,939; petroleum and petroleum products, £66,961,941; chemicals, £123,289,317; machinery (non-electric), £142,865,726; electrical machinery, £64,127,801; transport equipment, £100,311,679; metal and manufactures, £99,229,204; textiles and clothing, £129,814,177; paper, paperboard and manufactures, £30,959,449; professional, scientific, etc. goods, £18,501,480.

Domestic Exports (1973)

Principally live animals, £84,637,941; meat and meat preparations, £132,432,493; other food, drink, and tobacco, £158,797,196; machinery and transport equipment, £85,662,140; clothing, headgear and footwear, £40,463,406; textiles, £74,013,006; metal ores and scrap, £23,073,519; metals and manufactures, £21,759,409; non-metallic mineral manufactures, £15,645,421; chemicals, £58,691,766; professional, scientific, etc. goods, £21,364,457.

CAPITAL.—Dublin (*Baile Atha Cliath*) is a City and County Borough on the River Liffey at the head of Dublin Bay. In April, 1971, its population was 567,866. There are many notable public buildings in the City, among them the two Cathedrals of Christ Church and St. Patrick, the Bank of Ireland (formerly the House of Parliament) and Trinity College (the only constituent College of the University of Dublin). University College is a constituent college of the National University of Ireland. A large export trade of agricultural products passes through the city and there is a considerable brewing industry, while there is an increasing amount of light manufacturing.

Other cities and towns, with populations at the Census of 1971 are Ψ Cork (128,645); Ψ Limerick (57,161); Ψ Dun Laoghaire (53,171); Ψ Waterford (31,968); Ψ Galway (27,726); Ψ Dundalk (21,672); ΨDrogheda (19,762); Ψ Sligo (14,080); Bray (14,467); Wexford (11,849); ΨTralee (12,287); Clonmel (11,622); Kilkenny (9,838); Athlone (9,825).

FLAG.—Equal vertical stripes of green, white and orange.

NATIONAL DAY.—March 17 (St. Patrick's Day).

The United States of America

Area and Population

Population.—The total resident population of the United States on March 1, 1975 was estimated at 212,515,000, excluding Armed Forces stationed abroad. Civilian resident population at the same date was estimated at 210,811,000. Including Armed Forces stationed abroad (March 1, 1975), 213,015,000.

	Land Area, 1970 (sq. miles)	Population	
		Census 1960	Census 1970
The United States*	3,536,855	179,323,175	203,211,926
Commonwealth of Puerto Rico.....	3,435	2,349,544	2,712,033
Possessions......................	463	123,151	..
Guam..........................	212	67,044	84,996
Virgin Islands of U.S.............	133	32,099	62,468
American Samoa.................	76	20,051	27,159
Midway Islands.................	2	2,356	2,220
Wake Island....................	3	1,097	1,647
Canton Island and Enderbury Island	27	320‡	..
Johnston Island and Sand Island....	—	156‡	1,007
Swan Islands....................	1	28‡	22
Other Outlying areas:			
Panama Canal Zone.............	553	42,122	44,198
Corn Islands....................	4	1,872	..
Pacific Islands Trust Territory.....	717	70,724‡	90,940
Population Abroad..............		1,374,421	1,737,836
Total........................	3,542,481	183,285,009	207,682,378

* The 50 States and the Federal *District of Columbia* (see p. 795).

‡ The islands of Enderbury, Sand, Little Swan and Little Corn were uninhabited at the time of enumeration.

REGISTERED BIRTHS AND DEATHS

Cal-endar Year	Live Births		Deaths	
	Number	Rate per 1,000	Number	Rate per 1,000
1965	3,760,358	19·4	1,828,136	9·4
1966	3,606,274	18·4	1,863,149	9·5
1967	3,520,959	17·8	1,851,323	9·4
1968	3,501,564	17·5	1,930,082	9·7
1969	3,571,000	17·7	1,921,990	9·5
1970	3,731,386	18·4	1,921,031	9·5
1971	3,555,970	17·2	1,927,542	9·3
1972	3,258,411	15·6	1,963,944	9·4
1973	3,136,965	14·9	1,973,003	9·4
1974*	3,166,000	15·0	1,933,000	9·1

Births based on 50 per cent. sample. *Provisional.

Note.—Figures tabulated are for the United States. Deaths exclude fœtal deaths. Rates are based on the population as estimated on July 1 (1970, April 1).

IMMIGRATION AND NATURALIZATION

From 1820 to 1974, 46,712,725 immigrants were admitted to the United States. Of the 394,861 admitted during fiscal year 1974, 71 per cent. were born in the following countries: Mexico (71,586), the Philippines (32,857), Italy (15,884), Greece (10,824), Cuba (18,929), Jamaica (12,408), the United Kingdom (10,710), China and Taiwan (18,056), Canada (7,654), Portugal (11,302), the Dominican Republic (15,680), India (12,779), Korea (28,028), Trinidad and Tobago (6,516) and Colombia (5,837). During 1974, 131,655 aliens residing permanently in the United States were naturalized, an increase of nine per cent. over 1973, and 33,856 persons acquired citizenship status at birth abroad, after birth by the naturalization of parents, through marriage, or by other reasons.

MARRIAGE AND DIVORCE

Laws of marriage and of divorce are within the exclusive jurisdiction of each State. Each State legislature enacts its own laws prescribing rules and qualifications pertaining to marriage and its dissolution.

Year	Marriages	Per 1,000 Pop.§	Estimated Divorces	Per 1,000 Pop.§
1965	1,800,000	9·3	479,000	2·5
1966	1,857,000	9·5	499,000	2·5
1967	1,927,000	9·7	523,000	2·6
1968	2,069,000	10·4	584,000	2·9
1969	2,145,000	10·6	639,000	3·2
1970	2,159,000	10·6	708,000	3·5
1971	2,190,481	10·6	773,000	3·7
1972	2,282,154	11·0	845,000	4·1
1973	2,284,108	10·9	915,000	4·4
1974*	2,223,000	10·5	970,000	4·6

* Provisional.

§ Population as estimated on July 1.

Increase of the People

Year of Census	Total Population				Increase over preceding census	Inter-Censal Immigrants*
	White	Negro	Other Races	Total		
1930	110,395,753	11,891,842	915,065	123,202,660	17,181,092	4,107,209
1940	118,357,831	12,865,914	941,384	132,165,129	8,962,409	528,431
1950	135,149,629	15,044,937	1,131,232	151,325,798	19,161,229	1,035,039
1960	158,831,732	18,871,831	1,619,612	179,323,175	27,997,377	2,515,479
1970	177,748,975	22,580,289	2,882,662	203,211,926	23,888,751	3,321,677

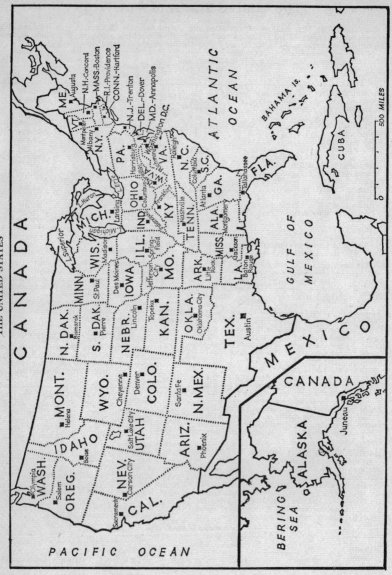

THE UNITED STATES

THE UNITED STATES

State (with date and *order* of admission)	Area Sq. M.*	Population, Census 1970	Capital	Governor (term of office in years, and starting year)	
Alabama (Ala.) (1819) (*22*)........	51,609	3,444,165	Montgomery...	George C. Wallace (D) (4—1975)......	$25000
Alaska (1959) (*49*)...............	586,400	302,173	Juneau......	Jay S. Hammond (R) (4—1974)......	50,000
Arizona (Ariz.) (1912) (*48*)......	113,909	1,772,482	Phoenix......	Raul H. Castro (D) (4—1975)......	40,000
Arkansas (Ark.) (1836) (*25*)......	53,104	1,923,295	Little Rock...	David H. Pryor (D) 2—1975........	10,000
California (Cal.) (1850) (*31*)......	158,693	19,953,134	Sacramento....	Edmund G. Brown, Jr. (D) (4—1975) .	49,100
Colorado (Colo.) (1876) (*38*).....	104,247	2,207,259	Denver......	Richard D. Lamm (D) (4—1975)......	40,000
Connecticut (Conn.) § (1788) (*5*)....	5,009	3,032,217	Hartford......	Ella T. Grasso (D) (4—1975)......	42,000
Delaware (Del.) § (1787) (*1*)......	2,057	548,104	Dover......	Sherman W. Tribbett (D) (4—1973)...	35,000
Dist. of Columbia (D.C.) (1791)....	69	756,510	..	†	
Florida (Fla.) (1845) (*27*)........	58,560	6,789,443	Tallahassee...	Reubin O'D. Askew (D) (4—1975)...	50,000
Georgia (Ga.) § (1788) (*4*)........	58,876	4,589,575	Atlanta........	George Busbee (D) (4—1975	50,000
Hawaii (1959) (*50*)...............	6,423	769,913	Honolulu....	George R. Ariyoshi (D) (4—1974)...	42,000
Idaho (1890) (*43*)..............	83,557	713,008	Boise.......	Cecil D. Andrus (D) (4—1975)......	33,000
Illinois (Ill.) (1818) (*21*)........	56,400	11,113,976	Springfield....	Dan Walker (D) (4—1973).........	50,000
Indiana (Ind.) (1816) (*19*)......	36,291	5,193,669	Indianapolis...	Otis R. Bowen (R) (4—1973)......	36,000
Iowa (1846) (*29*)...............	56,290	2,825,041	Des Moines ..	Robert D. Ray (R) (4—1975)......	40,000
Kansas (Kan.) (1861) (*34*)......	82,276	2,249,071	Topeka......	Robert F. Bennett (R) (4—1975)...	35,000
Kentucky (Ky.) (1792) (*15*)......	40,395	3,219,311	Frankfort....	Julian M. Carroll (D) (4—1974)...	35,000
Louisiana (La.) (1812) (*18*)......	48,523	3,643,180	Baton Rouge...	Edwin W. Edwards (D) (4—1972)...	50,000
Maine (Me.) (1820) (*23*)........	33,215	993,663	Augusta......	James B. Longley (I) (4—1975)...	35,000
Maryland (Md.) § (1788) (*7*)......	10,577	3,922,399	Annapolis....	Marvin Mandel (D) (4—1975)......	45,000
Massachusetts (Mass.) § (1788) (*6*) .	8,257	5,689,170	Boston......	Michael S. Dukakis (D) (4—1975)...	40,000
Michigan (Mich.) (1837) (*26*).....	58,216	8,875,083	Lansing......	William G. Milliken (R) (4—1975)...	47,250
Minnesota (Minn.) (1858) (*32*)....	84,068	3,805,069	St. Paul......	Wendell R. Anderson (D) (4—1975)..	41,000
Mississippi (Miss.) (1817) (*20*)....	47,716	2,216,912	Jackson......	William L. Waller (D) (4—1975)...	43,000
Missouri (Mo.) (1821) (*24*)......	69,674	4,677,399	Jefferson City..	Christopher S. Bond (R) (4—1973)...	37.500
Montana (Mont.) (1889) (*41*).....	141,138	694,409	Helena......	Thomas L. Judge (D) (4—1973).....	30,000
Nebraska (Nebr.) (1867) (*37*).....	77,227	1,483,791	Lincoln......	J. James Exon (D) (4—1975).......	25,000
Nevada (Nev.) (1864) (*36*)........	110,540	488,738	Carson City...	Mike O'Callaghan (D) (4—1975 .) ..	30,000
New Hampshire (N.H.) § (1788) (*9*) .	9,304	737,681	Concord......	Meldrim Thomson, Jr. (R) (2—1975) .	33,741
New Jersey (N.J.) § (1787) (*3*)......	7,836	7,168,164	Trenton......	Brendan T. Byrne (D) (4—1974)......	57,500
New Mexico (N. Mex.) (1912) (*47*)..	121,666	1,016,000	Santa Fé.....	Jerry Apodaca (D) (4—1975)......	26,000
New York (N.Y.) § (1788) (*11*)......	49,576	18,190,740	Albany......	Hugh L. Carey (D) (4—1975)......	85,000
North Carolina (N.C.) § (1789) (*12*) .	52,712	5,082,059	Raleigh......	James E. Holshouser, Jr. (R) (4—1973)	38,500
North Dakota (N. Dak.) (1889) (*39*)	70,665	617,761	Bismarck....	Arthur A. Link (D) (4—1973)......	18,000
Ohio (1803) (*17*)................	41,222	10,652,017	Columbus....	James A. Rhodes (R) (4—1975)......	50,000
Oklahoma (Okla.) (1907) (*46*).....	69,919	2,559,253	Oklahoma City.	David L. Boren (D) (4—1975)......	42,500
Oregon (Oreg.) (1859) (*33*).......	96,981	2,091,385	Salem......	Robert W. Straub (D) (4—1975)......	35,000
Pennsylvania (Pa.) § (1787) (*2*).....	45,333	11,793,909	Harrisburg....	Milton J. Shapp (D) (4—1975)......	60,000
Rhode Island (R.I.) § (1790) (*13*) ..	1,214	949,723	Providence....	Philip W. Noel (D) (2—1975).......	42,500
South Carolina (S.C.) § (1788) (*8*)...	31,055	2,590,516	Columbia....	James B. Edwards (R) (4—1975)......	37,000
South Dakota (S. Dak.) (1889) (*40*).	77,047	666,257	Pierre........	Richard F. Kneip (D) (4—1975)......	27,500
Tennessee (Tenn.) (1796) (*16*).....	42,244	3,924,164	Nashville....	Ray Blanton (D) (4—1975).........	50,000
Texas (Tex.) (1845) (*28*)..........	267,339	11,196,730	Austin......	Dolph Briscoe (D) (4—1975)........	63,000
Utah (1896) (*45*)...............	84,916	1,059,273	Salt Lake City .	Calvin L. Rampton (D) (4—1973).....	33,000
Vermont (Vt.) (1791) (*14*)........	9,609	444,732	Montpelier....	Thomas P. Salmon (D) (2—1975).....	36,100
Virginia (Va.) § (1788) (*10*).......	40,815	4,648,494	·Richmond....	Mills E. Godwin, Jr. (R) (4—1974)...	50,000
Washington (Wash.) (1889) (*42*)...	68,192	3,409,169	Olympia......	Daniel J. Evans (R) (4—1973)......	34,300
West Virginia (W. Va.) (1863) (*35*).	24,181	1,744,237	Charleston....	Arch A. Moore, Jr. (R) (4—1973).....	35,000
Wisconsin (Wis.) (1848) (*30*)......	56,154	4,417,933	Madison......	Patrick J. Lucey (D) (4—1971)......	25,000
Wyoming (Wyo.) (1890) (*44*)......	97,914	332,416	Cheyenne....	Ed Herschler (D) (4—1975).........	37,505

OUTLYING TERRITORIES AND POSSESSIONS

Puerto Rico (1899)	3,435	2,712,033	San Juan......	Rafael Hernández-Colón (4—1973)....	35,000
Guam (1899)...................	206	86,926	Agaña	Ricardo J. Bordallo (D) (4—1975)....	35,000
Samoa (1900)..................	76	27,769	Fagatogo....	Earl B. Ruth (R) (2—1975)	24,500
Virgin Islands (1917)............	133	63,200	Charlotte Amalie	Cyril E. King (I) (4—1975)........	35,505

D.—Democratic Party.   *R.—Republican Party.*   §   The 13 Original States.

* Gross area, including water.

† The capital territory is governed by Congress through a Commissioner and City Council (*see* p. 796).

Largest Cities (Metropolitan Areas: Census 1970 (April)).

Ψ New York............	9,973,716	Ψ Cleveland, Ohio.........	2,063,729	Denver–Boulder, Colo....	1,239,477
Ψ Los Angeles–Long Beach, Calif.................	7,041,980	Ψ Newark, N.J............	2,057,468	Riverside–San Bernardino– Ontario, Calif..........	1,141,307
		Ψ Houston, Texas.........	1,999,316		
ΨChicago, Ill............	6,977,611	Minneapolis–St. Paul,		Indianapolis, Ind........	1,111,352
Ψ Philadelphia...........	4,824,110	Minn.–Wis	1,965,391	Ψ Tampa–St. Petersburg, Fla.	1,088,549
Ψ Detroit, Mich...........	4,435,051	Atlanta, Georgia.........	1,595,517	ΨSan José, Calif.........	1,065,313
ΨBoston, Mass...........	3,376,328	Anaheim–Santa Ana–		Ψ New Orleans, La........	1,046,470
Ψ San Francisco	3,108,782	Garden Grove, Calif....	1,421,233	Columbus, Ohio.........	1,017,847
ΨSan Francisco–Oakland, Calif.................	3,108,782	Ψ Seattle–Evett,Wash.....	1,424,605	Ψ Portland, Oreg.–Wash ...	1,007,130
		Ψ Milwaukee, Wis........	1,403,884	Phoenix, Ariz...........	969,425
Washington, D.C........	2,909,355	Cincinatti, Ohio–Ky–Ind.	1,385,103	Ψ Rochester, N.Y.........	961,516
Nassau–Suffolk, N.Y......	2,555,868	Ψ San Diego, Calif.........	1,357,854	San Antonio, Texas......	888,179
St. Louis, Mo.–Ill........	2,410,492	Ψ Buffalo, N.Y...........	1,349,211	Louisville, Ky.–Ind......	867,330
Pittsburgh, Pa..........	2,401,362	Kansas City, M.–Kans ...	1,273,296	Dayton, Ohio...........	852,531
Dallas–Fort Worth, Texas	2,378,353	ΨMiami, Florida..........	1,267,792		
ΨBaltimore, Md...........	2,071,016				

Ψ Seaport

PHYSIOGRAPHY

The conterminous States of the Republic occupy nearly all that portion of the North American Continent between the Atlantic and Pacific Oceans, in latitude 25° 07'–49° 23' North and longitude 66° 57'–124° 44' West, its northern boundary being Canada and the southern boundary Mexico. The separate State of Alaska reaches a latitude of 71° 23' N., at Point Barrow (2,502 miles from the U.S. geographic centre).

The general coastline of the 50 States has a length of about 2,069 miles on the Atlantic, 7,623 miles on the Pacific, 1,060 miles on the Arctic, and 1,631 miles on the Gulf of Mexico.

The principal river is the mighty Mississippi-Missouri-Red Rock, traversing the whole country from north to south, and having a course of 3,710 miles to its mouth in the Gulf of Mexico, with many large affluents, the chief of which are the Yellowstone, Platte, Arkansas, Ohio, and Red Rivers. The rivers flowing into the Atlantic and Pacific Oceans are comparatively small; among the former may be noticed the Hudson, Delaware, Susquehanna, Potomac, James, Roanoke and Savannah; of the latter, the Columbia-Snake, Sacramento, and Colorado. The Nueces, Brazos, Trinity, Pearl, Mobile-Tombigbee-Alabama, Apalachicola-Chattahoochee, Suwannee and Colorado of Texas fall into the Gulf of Mexico, also the Rio Grande, a long river partly forming the boundary with Mexico. The areas of the water-basins have been estimated as follows:—Rivers flowing to the Pacific, 647,300 square miles; to the Atlantic, 488,877; and to the Gulf of Mexico, 1,683,325 square miles, of which 1,234,600 are drained by the Mississippi-Missouri-Red Rock. The chain of the Rocky Mountains separates the western portion of the country from the remainder, all communication being carried on over certain elevated passes, several of which are now traversed by railroads; west of these, bordering the Pacific coast, the Cascade Mountains and Sierra Nevada form the outer edge of a high tableland, consisting in part of stony and sandy desert and partly of grazing land and forested mountains, and including the Great Salt Lake, which extends to the Rocky Mountains. Eastward the country is a vast, gently undulating plain, with a general slope southwards towards the partly marshy flats of the Gulf of Mexico, extending to the Atlantic, interrupted only by the Appalachian Highlands, of inferior elevation, in the Eastern States. Nearly the whole of this plain, from the Rocky Mountains to some distance beyond the Mississippi, consists of immense prairies. In the Eastern States (which form the more settled and most thickly inhabited portion of the country) large forests of valuable timber, as beech, birch, maple, oak, pine, spruce, elm, ash, walnut; and in the south, live oak, water-oak, magnolia, palmetto, tupil-tree, cypress, etc., still exist, the remnants of the forests which formerly extended over all the Atlantic slope, but into which great inroads have been made by the advance of civilization. The mineral kingdom produces much ore of iron, copper, lead, zinc, and aluminium, the non-metallic minerals include immense quantities of coal, anthracite, petroleum, stone, cement, phosphate rock, and salt. The highest point is Mount McKinley (Alaska), 20,320 ft. above sea level and the lowest point of dry land is in Death Valley (Inyo, California), 282 ft. below sea-level.

THE PRESIDENTS OF THE UNITED STATES OF AMERICA

Name (*with Native State*)	Party	Born	Inaug.	Died	Age
1. George Washington, *Va.*	Fed.	1732, Feb. 22	1789	1799, Dec. 14	67
2. John Adams, *Mass.*	,,	1735, Oct. 30	1797	1826, July 4	90
3. Thomas Jefferson, *Va.*	Rep.	1743, April 13	1801	1826, July 4	83
4. James Madison, *Va.*	,,	1751, Mar. 16	1809	1836, June 28	85
5. James Monroe, *Va.*	,,	1758, April 28	1817	1831, July 4	73
6. John Quincy Adams, *Mass.*	,,	1767, July 11	1825	1848, Feb. 23	80
7. Andrew Jackson, *S.C.*	Dem.	1767, Mar. 15	1829	1845, June 8	78
8. Martin Van Buren, *N.Y.*	,,	1782, Dec. 5	1837	1862, July 24	79
9. William Henry Harrison†, *Va.*	Whig.	1773, Feb. 9	1841	1841, April 4	68
10. John Tyler (*a*), *Va.*	,,	1790, Mar. 29	1841	1862, Jan. 17	71
11. James Knox Polk, *N.C.*	Dem.	1795, Nov. 2	1845	1849, June 15	53
12. Zachary Taylor† *Va.*	Whig.	1784, Nov. 24	1849	1850, July 9	65
13. Millard Fillmore (*a*), *N.Y.*	,,	1800, Jan. 7	1850	1874, Mar. 8	74
14. Franklin Pierce *N.H.*	Dem.	1804, Nov. 23	1853	1869, Oct. 8	64
15. James Buchanan, *Pa.*	,,	1791, April 23	1857	1868, June 1	77
16. Abraham Lincoln†§, *Ky.*	Rep.	1809, Feb. 12	1861	1865, April 15	56
17. Andrew Johnson (*a*), *N.C.*	,,	1808, Dec. 29	1865	1875, July 31	66
18. Ulysses Simpson Grant, *Ohio*	,,	1822, April 27	1869	1885, July 23	63
19. Rutherford Birchard Hayes, *Ohio*	,,	1822, Oct. 4	1877	1893, Jan. 17	70
20. James Abraham Garfield†§, *Ohio*	,,	1831, Nov. 19	1881	1881, Sept. 19	49
21. Chester Alan Arthur (*a*), *Vt.*	,,	1830, Oct. 5	1881	1886, Nov. 18	56
22. Grover Cleveland, *N.J.*	Dem.	1837, Mar. 18	1893	1908, June 24	71
23. Benjamin Harrison, *Ohio*	Rep.	1833, Aug. 20	1889	1901, Mar. 13	67
24. William McKinley†§, *Ohio*	Rep.	1843, Jan. 29	1897	1901, Sept. 14	58
25. Theodore Roosevelt (*a*), *N.Y.*	,,	1858, Oct. 27	1901	1919, Jan. 6	60
26. William Howard Taft, *Ohio*	,,	1857, Sept. 15	1909	1930, Mar. 8	72
27. Woodrow Wilson, *N.J.*	Dem.	1856, Dec. 28	1913	1924, Feb. 3	67
28. Warren Gamaliel Harding†, *Ohio*	Rep.	1865, Nov. 2	1921	1923, Aug. 2	57
29. Calvin Coolidge (*a*), *Vt.*	,,	1872, July 4	1923	1933, Jan. 5	60
30. Herbert Clark Hoover, *Iowa*	,,	1874, Aug. 10	1929	1964, Oct. 20	90
31. Franklin Delano Roosevelt††, *N.Y.*	Dem.	1882, Jan. 30	1933	1945, April 12	63
32. Harry S. Truman (*a*), *Missouri*	,,	1884, May 8	1945	1972, Dec. 26	88
33. Dwight D. Eisenhower, *Texas*	Rep.	1890, Oct. 14	1953	1969, Mar. 28	78
34. John F. Kennedy, *Mass.*†§	Dem.	1917, May 29	1961	1963, Nov. 22	46
35. Lyndon B. Johnson (*a*), *Texas*	,,	1908, Aug. 27	1963	1973, Jan. 22	64
36. Richard M. Nixon, *California*	Rep.	1913, Jan. 9	1969	..	..
37. Gerald R. Ford *Michigan*	,,	1913, July 14	1974	..	..

† Died in office. § Assassinated. (*a*) Elected as Vice-President.

‡ Re-elected Nov. 5, 1940, the first case of a third term; re-elected for a fourth term Nov. 7. 1944.

GOVERNMENT

The United States of America is a Federal Republic consisting of 50 States and 1 Federal District (of which 13 are Original States, 7 were admitted without previous organization as Territories, and 30 were admitted after such organization), and of organized Territories. Hawaii formally entered the Union as the 50th State on Aug. 21, 1959, from which date the flag of the United States has 13 stripes and 50 stars in 9 horizontal rows of six and five alternatively. July 4 (Independence Day) is observed as the National Day.

THE CONSTITUTION.—By the Constitution of Sept. 17, 1787 (to which ten amendments were added on Dec. 15, 1791, and eleventh to twenty-sixth, Jan. 8, 1798, Sept. 25, 1804, Dec. 18, 1865, July 28, 1868, March 30, 1870, Feb. 25, 1913, May 31, 1913, Jan. 16, 1920, Aug. 26, 1920, Feb. 6, 1933, Dec. 5, 1933, Feb. 26, 1951, March 29, 1961, Jan. 23, 1964, Feb. 10, 1967 and June 30, 1971), the government of the United States is entrusted to three separate authorities—the Executive, the Legislative, and the Judicial.

THE EXECUTIVE

THE *Executive* power is vested in a President, who is elected every four years, and is eligible for re-election for one additional term. The mode of electing the President is as follows:—Each State appoints, in such manner as the Legislature thereof directs (they are now elected by popular vote on the *first Tuesday after the first Monday in November* of the year preceding the year in which the Presidential term expires), a number of electors, equal to the whole number of Senators and Representatives to which the State may be entitled in the Congress; but no Senator or Representative, or anyone holding office under Government, shall be appointed an elector. The electors for each State meet in their respective States on the *first Monday after the second Wednesday in December* following, and there vote for a President by ballot. The ballots are then sent to Washington, and opened on the *sixth day of January* by the President of Senate in presence of Congress, and the candidate who has received a majority of the whole number of electoral votes cast is declared President for the ensuing term. If no one has a majority, then from the highest on the list (not exceeding three) the House of Representatives elects a President, the votes being taken by States, the representation from each State having one vote. There is also a Vice-President, who, on the death of the President, becomes President for the remainder of the term. Under the XXth Amendment to the Constitution the terms of the President and Vice-President end at noon on the 20th day of January of the years in which such terms would have ended if the Amendment had not been ratified, and the terms of their successors then begin. In case of the removal or death of both President and Vice-President, a statute provides for the succession.

The President must be at least 35 years of age and a native citizen of the United States. He receives a taxable salary of $200,000 with a taxable expense allowance of $50,000 and a non-taxable travelling allowance not exceeding $40,000. Under the XXIInd Amendment to the Constitution, the tenure of the Presidency is limited to two terms. Executive duties:—(1) He is Commander-in-Chief of the Army and of the Navy (and of the Militias when they are in Federal service), and he commissions all officers therein. (2) With the consent of the Senate, he appoints the Cabinet officers and all the chief (and many minor) officials. (3) He exercises a general supervision over the whole Federal Administration and sees that the Federal Laws are duly carried out. Should disorder arise in any State which the authorities thereof are unable to suppress, the aid of the President is invoked. (4) He conducts the Foreign Policy of the Republic, and has power, " by and with the Advice and Consent of the Senate to make Treaties, provided two thirds of the Senators present concur." The Declaration of War rests with Congress. (5) He makes recommendations of a general nature to Congress, and when laws are passed by Congress he may return them to Congress with a veto. But if a measure so vetoed is again passed by both Houses of Congress by a two-thirds majority in each House, it becomes law, notwithstanding the objection of the President.

President of the United States, GERALD RUDOLPH FORD, *born* July 14, 1913, *Sworn in* August 9, 1974. Republican.

Vice-President, Nelson A. Rockefeller, *born* July 8, 1908, *sworn in* Dec. 19.1974.

THE CABINET (each $60,000)

Secretary of State, Henry A. Kissinger, *(born* May 27, 1923), *appointed* Sept. 1973.
Secretary of the Treasury, William E. Simon *(born* 1927), *appointed* May 8, 1974.
Secretary of Defence, James R. Schlesinger *(born* 1929), *appointed* May 10, 1973.
Attorney-General, Edward H. Levi *(born* 1911), *appointment confirmed* Feb. 5, 1975.
Secretary of the Interior, Stanley Hathaway *(born* 1924), *appointment confirmed* June 11, 1975.
Secretary of Agriculture, Earl L. Butz *(born* 1909), *appointed* Nov. 11, 1971.
Secretary of Commerce, Rogers C. B. Morton *(born* 1914), *appointment confirmed* April 25, 1975.
Secretary of Labor, John T. Dunlop *(born* 1914), *appointment confirmed* March 6, 1975.
Secretary of Health, Education and Welfare, F. David Mathews *(born* 1935), *nominated* June 27, 1975.
Secretary of Housing and Urban Development, Carla A. Hills *(born* 1934), *appointment confirmed* March 5, 1975.
Secretary of Transportation, William T. Coleman *(born* 1920), *appointment confirmed* March 3, 1975.

UNITED STATES EMBASSY
Grosvenor Square, W.1
[01-499 9000]

Ambassador Extraordinary and Plenipotentiary, His Excellency Elliot L. Richardson (1975).
Minister, Hon. Ronald L. Spiers.
Counsellors, William K. Miller *(Economic and Commercial Affairs);* William M. Woessner *(Political Affairs);* Michael M. Conlin *(Administration);* Michael T. F. Pistor *(Public Affairs);* John R. Diggins, Jr. *(Consular Affairs);* Borrie L. Hyman *(Commercial).*
Defence Attaché, Naval Attaché and Naval Attaché for Air, Rear Admiral James C. Longino, U.S.N.

Army Attaché, Col. James M. McGarity, U.S.A.
Air Attaché, Col. Thomas G. McInerney, U.S.A.F.
1st Secretaries, Harry Pollack; William P. Clappin; *(Economic);* George H. Thigpen; William G. Hamilton, Jr. *(Public Affairs);* Lucien L. Kinsolving *(Politico-Military Affairs);* Larry C. Williamson *(Commercial);* Elwood J. McGuire *(Administration);* Raymond G. H. Seitz; Samuel Karp *(Consular);* Bruce R. Koch *(Cultural Affairs);* C. Edward Dillery.
Second Secretary, Denis A. Sandberg.
Attachés, William L. Rodman *(Agriculture);* Alden C. McCray *(Legal);* James E. Ammerman *(Finance);* Cord Meyer, Jr.; Charles R. Ritcheson

(*Cultural Affairs*); Thomas C. Colwell (*Civil Air*); Michael G. MacDonald (*Politico-Military Affairs*); William M. McGhee; Tobias J. Boyd (*Administration*); Charles A. Bakey, Jr. (*Administration*); Ellen V. Watson (*Administration*); Charles M. Shaw (*Commercial*).

CAPITAL OF THE UNITED STATES

In 1790 Congress ratified the cession of 100 sq. miles by the States of Maryland and Virginia as a site for a Federal City to be the national capital of the United States. In 1791 it was decided to name the capital *Washington* and in 1793 the foundation-stone of the Capitol building was laid. In 1800 the seat of government was removed to Washington, which was chartered as a city in 1802. In 1846 the Virginia portion was retroceded and the present area of the *District of Columbia* (with which the City of Washington is considered co-extensive) is 61 square miles, with a population at the Census of 1970 of 756,510.

The District of Columbia has hitherto been governed by a Commissioner and assistant and a 9-member City Council, all appointed by the President. From Nov. 5, 1974, this body has been replaced by an elected mayor and City Council.

The *City of Washington* is situated on the west central edge of Maryland, opposite the State of Virginia, on the left bank of the Potomac at its confluence with the Anacostia, 107 miles from Chesapeake Bay and 186 from the Atlantic Ocean.

THE CONGRESS

The Legislative power is vested in two Houses, the Senate and the House of Representatives, the President having a *veto* power, which may be overcome by a two-thirds vote of each House. The Senate is composed of two Senators from each State, elected by the people thereof for the term of six years, and each Senator has one vote; and Representatives are chosen in each State, by popular vote, for two years. The average number of persons represented by each Congressman is 1 for 469,088. The *Senate* consists of 100 members. The salary of a Senator is \$42,500 per annum, with mileage at 20 cents per mile each session. The *House of Representatives* consists of 435 Representatives, a resident commissioner from Puerto Rico and a delegate from the District of Columbia, Guam and the Virgin Isalnds. The salary of a Representative is \$42,500 per annum, with mileage as for Senators. By the XIXth Amendment, sex is no disqualification for the franchise. On Nov. 1, 1972, there were 139,642,000 persons of voting age, excluding members of the armed forces overseas.

THE NINETY-FOURTH CONGRESS

Noon of Jan. 3, 1975 to Noon of Jan. 3, 1976.
President of the Senate, Nelson A. Rockfeller (*Vice-President of the United States*).
Speaker of the House of Representatives, Carl Albert, Oklahoma.
Secretary of the Senate, Francis R. Valeo, *District of Columbia*.
Clerk of the House of Representatives, W. Pat Jennings, *Va.*
Members of the 94th Congress were elected on Nov. 5, 1974.
The 94th Congress is constituted as follows:
Senate.—Democrats 62; Republicans, 38; Total, 100. *House of Representatives.*—Democrats, 291; Republicans, 144. Total, 435.

THE JUDICATURE

The *Federal Judiciary* consists of three sets of Federal Courts: (1) The *Supreme Court* at Washington, D.C., consisting of a Chief Justice and eight Associate Justices, with original jusrisdiction in cases affecting Ambassadors, etc., or where a State is a party to the suit, and with appellate jurisdiction from inferior Federal Courts and from the decisions of the highest Courts of the States. (2) The *United States Courts of Appeals*, dealing with appeals from District Courts, and consisting of the Justice of the Supreme Court for the Circuit and all the Circuit Judges within the circuit. (3) The 94 *District Courts* served by 400 District Court Judges.

THE SUPREME COURT

(U.S. Supreme Court Building, Washington, D.C.)
Chief Justice, Warren E. Burger, *Minn.*, *born* Sept. 17, 1907, *appointed* June 23, 1969.

Associate Justices

Name	Born	Apptd
Wm. O. Douglas, *Conn.*	1898	1939
William J. Brennan, Jr., *N.J.*	1906	1956
Potter Stewart, *Ohio.*	1915	1958
Byron R. White, *Colo.*	1917	1962
Thurgood Marshall, *N.Y.*	1908	1967
Harry Blackmun, *Minn.*	1908	1970
Lewis F. Powell, Jr., *Va.*	1907	1971
William R. Rehnquist, *Ariz.*	1924	1971

Clerk of the Supreme Court, Michael Rodak, Jr.

CRIMINAL STATISTICS, U.S.

	No. of offences	
Crime	1972	1973
Murder	18,550	19,510
Rape	46,480	51,000
Robbery	374,790	382,680
Aggravated Assault	389,000	416,270
Burglary	2,352,800	2,540,900
Larceny—Theft	4,109,600	4,304,000
Thefts of Automobiles	882,200	923,600
Total	8,173,400	8,638,400

DEFENCE

Department of Defence

Secretary of Defence (in the Cabinet), James R. Schlesinger.
Secretary of the Army, Howard H. Callaway.
Secretary of the Navy, J. W. Middendorf II.
Secretary of the Air Force, John L. McLucas.
Chairman, Joint Chiefs of Staff, Gen. George S. Brown, U.S.A.F.

The Department of Defence includes the Secretary of Defence as its head, the Deputy Secretary of Defence, the Defence staff offices, the Joint Chiefs of Staff and the Joint Staff, the three military departments and the military services within those departments, the unified and specified commands, and other Department of Defence agencies as the Secretary of Defence establishes to meet specific requirements. The Defence staff offices and the joint Chiefs of Staff, although separately organized function in full coordination and cooperation. They include the offices of the Director of Defence Research and Engineering, the nine Assistant Secretaries of Defence, the General Counsel of the

Department of Defence and such other staff offices as the Secretary of Defence may establish. The Joint Chiefs of Staff, as a group, are directly responsible to the Secretary of Defence for the functions assigned to them. Each member of the Joint Chiefs of Staff, other than the Chairman, is responsible for keeping the Secretary of his military department fully informed on matters considered or acted upon by the Joint Chiefs of Staff.

Each military department is separately organized under its own Secretary and functions under the direction, authority and control of the Secretary of Defence.

The Department of Defence maintains and employs armed forces: (1) to support and defend the Constitution of the United States against all enemies, foreign and domestic; (2) to insure, by timely and effective military action, the security of the United States, its possessions, and areas vital to its interests; (3) to uphold and advance the national policies and interest of the United States; and (4) to safeguard the internal security of the United States. All functions in the Department of Defence and its component agencies are performed under the direction, authority and control of the Secretary of Defence.

Commanders of unified and specified commands are responsible to the President and the Secretary of Defence for the accomplishment of military missions assigned to them.

Unified Defence Commands

Commanders-in-Chief

U.S. European Command, Brussels.—Gen. Alexander M. Haig, Jr. (*U.S.A.*) (concurrently *N.A.T.O. Supreme Allied Commander*).

U.S. Southern Command, Quarry Heights, Panama Canal Zone.—Gen. William B. Rosson (*U.S.A.*).

Atlantic, Norfolk, Virginia.—Adm. Ralph Cousins (*U.S. Navy*) (concurrently *N.A.T.O. Supreme Allied Commander, Atlantic*).

Pacific, Hawaii.—Adm. Noel A. M. Gayler (*U.S. Navy*).

†*U.S. Naval Forces, Europe*, London.—Adm. David Baglay (*U.S. Navy*).

North American Air Defence Command, Colorado Springs.—Gen. Lucius D. Clay, Jr. (*U.S.A.F.*).

★*Strategic Air Command*, Omaha.—Gen. Russell E. Dougherty (*U.S.A.F.*).

Alaskan Command, Anchorage, Alaska.—Lt.-Gen. James C. Sherrill (*U.S.A.F.*).

U.S. Readiness Command, MacDill, Florida.—Gen. John J. Hennessey (*U.S. Army*).

★ A Specified Command.

† A subordinate component of *U.S. European Command*.

Army.—The Army of U.S. had a strength of 8,293,766 (including 2,310,436 Air Force) on V.E. Day, reduced by June 30, 1959, to 861,964 (excluding Air Force). The strength on March 31, 1975,

was 775,310. Stationed in Germany were four divisions. There was one division in Korea. Combat units were on duty in the Caribbean and in Alaska and other combat units were in Italy as part of the NATO force.

Chief of Staff of the Army, Gen. Fred C. Weyand.

Navy.—The peak strength of the Navy (including Marine Corps in 1945, was 3,855,497. The strength of the U.S. Navy in 1974, was 545,900. Strength of the Marine Corps, 188,800.

The U.S. Navy had in service in 1975, 500 active fleet ships, including 14 attack carriers, 27 cruisers, 69 destroyers, 64 frigates, 117 submarines (64 nuclear, 41 SSBN and 12 diesel), 65 amphibious, 3 mine warfare, 127 auxiliaries and 14 patrol craft, *Chief of Naval Operations*, Adm. James Holloway.

Air.—The United States Air Force was established as a separate organization on September 18, 1947. At June 30, 1974, there were 643,795 officers and airmen on active duty, with 273,602 civilian employees. Air Force Reserve and Air National Guard numbered 145,560 on June 30, 1974.

To deter aggression the Air Force has about 140 strategic bombers maintaining constant alert as well as 1,054 inter-continental ballistic missiles in hardened silos. In addition, the Air Force maintains the capability to carry out limited war and special warfare operations. In March, 1961, the Air Force was assigned primary responsibility for the Department of Defence space development programmes and projects. By June 8, 1975, the United States had placed a total of 2,241 space-craft into earth orbit or deep space. These included Air Force, Army and N.A.S.A. shots.

Chief of Staff of the U.S. Air Force, Gen. David C. Jones.

NATIONAL ORIGINS OF THE POPULATION

About 102,200,000 of the approximately 205 million persons in the United States reported on a sample survey conducted in March, 1972, that they were of one of eight specific origin categories. Approximately 25.5 million persons reported German origin; 29.5 million, English, Scottish or Welsh; 16.4 million Irish; 9.2 million, Spanish; 8.8 million, Italian; 5.1 million, Polish; and 2.2 million, Russian. About 11 million persons living in the United States at the time of an earlier survey of 1969 were foreign born, Germany, Italy, Mexico and the United Kingdom were the major contributing countries. Two-thirds of them reported English as the language usually spoken in their homes. Ther were 23 years older on the average, than the native population.

Countries of birth of the foreign-born population (1969) were: Austria (236,000), Cuba (504,000), Germany (1,004,000), Ireland (277,000), Italy (1,353,000), Mexico (938,000), Poland (550,000), Russia (412,000), Sweden (166,000), United Kingdom (1,006,000); other countries, 4,434,000.

SOCIAL WELFARE EXPENDITURE

The total value of government expenditure on social welfare (federal, state and local government) in 1973 was $214,178,900,000 compared with $192,350,200,000 in 1972 and $52,293,000,000 in 1960. 57.2 per cent. of the 1973 total was Federal expenditure. In 1973 expenditure per person (of the total population of U.S.A.) was $1,002—social insurance, $402; education, $306; public aid, $135; health and medical services, $59; veterans' welfare, $60; other services, $30 per person. Total expenditure by programmes was:

		$ million	
	1960	1972	1973
Social insurance.......	19,307	75,063	86,118
Education............	17,626	61,093	65,258
Public aid...........	4,101	25,606	28,697
Health and medical...	4,464	12,361	12,640
Veterans............	5,479	11,503	12,951
Other welfare services.	1,139	5,666	6,335
Housing.............	177	1,448	2,180
TOTAL.......	52,293	192,740	214,179

FINANCE

THE UNITED STATES BUDGET

[Fiscal years]

Description	Actual	
	1974	1975 Preliminary
Receipts by Source	$	$
Individual income taxes	118,951,031,000	122,321,565,000
Corporation income taxes	38,619,654,000	40,626,750,000
Social insurance taxes and contributions:		
Employment taxes and contributions	65,892,164,000	75,203,856,000
Unemployment insurance	6,836,545,000	6,764,177,000
Contributions for other insurance and retirement	4,051,342,000	4,460,650,000
Excise taxes	16,843,668,000	16,541,971,000
Estate and gift taxes	5,034,640,000	4,589,361,000
Customs	3,334,138,000	3,665,929,000
Miscellaneous	5,368,613,000	6,746,724,000
Total	264,932,400,000	280,920,983,000
Outlays by Function		
National defence	78,568,540,000	88,288,891,000
International affairs and finance	3,593,005,000	4,214,921,000
General science, space, and technology	4,154,043,000	4,156,821,000
Natural resources, environment, and energy	6,390,241,000	8,020,450,000
Agriculture	2,230,029,000	2,008,766,000
Commerce and transportation	13,100,014,000	15,545,907,000
Community and regional development	4,910,094,000	4,482,364,000
Education, manpower, and social services	11,600,144,000	15,060,808,000
Health	22,073,035,000	27,447,554,000
Income security	84,431,067,000	109,315,276,000
Veterans benefits and services	13,386,006,000	16,598,623,000
Law enforcement and justice	2,462,102,000	2,759,392,000
General government	3,327,174,000	3,582,264,000
Revenue sharing and general purpose fiscal assistance	6,746,029,000	6,695,095,000
Interest	28,072,121,000	31,035,387,000
Undistributed offsetting receipts	−16,651,661,000	−14,079,865,000
Total	$268,391,983,000	$325,132,657,000

PUBLIC DEBT

On June 30, 1975, the total gross *Federal Debt* of the United States stood at $544,131,472,000; the equivalent debt for 1974 was $486,247,088,000.

COST OF LIVING IN U.S.A.

The Consumer Price Index (for city wage-earner and clerical workers—single persons and families—in 50 cities representative of all cities in the United States) showed a monthly average during the calendar year 1974 of 147·7 (the basic figure of 100 being the 1967 average). The Consumer Price Index rose 4·3 per cent. in 1971, 3·3 per cent in 1972, 6·2 per cent. in 1973 and 11·0 per cent. in 1974. From June 1974 to June 1975 the index rose 9·3 per cent. for all items, 8·8 per cent. for food, 9·3 per cent. for other commodities, 5·1 per cent. for rent and 10·5 per cent for other services.

The Wholesale Price Index of all commodities averaged 160·1 in 1974 (compared to the base of 100·0 in 1967) and was 173·7 in June, 1975. From June, 1974 to June, 1975 the index rose 11·6 per cent. for all items, 10·4 per cent. for farm products, 14·2 per cent. for processed foods and feeds and 11·1 per cent. for industrial commodities.

PERSONAL INCOMES IN U.S.A.

Personal incomes in the United States rose from $944·9 billion in 1972 to $1,055·0 billion in 1973, $1,150·5 billion in 1974 and $1,220·8 billion in the second quarter of 1975. In the latter period, labour income was $885·5 billion, 4·4 per cent. above the level of the previous year. Business proprietors, professional and farm income totalled $86·0 billion in the second quarter of 1975 (4·2 per cent. decrease on previous year) and dividends, interest, and rent totalled $176·7 billion (up 10·6 per cent.). Transfer payments were $177·9 billion and personal contributions to social insurance, which are offsets to income, were $49·7 billion.

Disposition of personal incomes.—Personal taxes were $142 billion in the second quarter of 1975, leaving households with $1,078·8 billion of disposable income. Consumption expenditures were $938·1 billion; $130·0 billion for durable goods, $408·5 billion for non-durable goods and $399·6 billion for services. Personal saving was $114·6 billion. Disposable income per capita was $5,056 in the second quarter of 1975.

Private domestic investment.—The total gross private domestic investment rose from $179·3 billion in 1972 to $209·4 billion in 1973, and to $213·0 billion in the second quarter of 1974. It declined to $147·3 billion in the second quarter of 1975. Fixed investment in new residential construction declined to $46·0 billion in 1974 (1973 $57·2 billion) and other construction rose to $52·0 billion (1973 $47·0 billion). Investment in producers' durable equipment rose from $89·18 billion in 1973 to $97·1 billion in 1974.

EXTERNAL TRADE OF THE UNITED STATES

Year	General Imports	Total Exports and Re-exports excluding military aid	Balance of Exports and Imports
	$	$	$
1970	39,952,000,000	42,659,000,000	+ 2,707,000,000
1971	45,563,000,000	43,549,000,000	− 2,014,000,000
1972	55,583,000,000	49,199,000,000	− 6,364,000,000
1973	69,121,000,000	70,823,000,000	+ 1,702,000,000
1974	100,972,000,000	97,907,000,000	− 3,065,000,000

EXPORTS BY PRINCIPAL COMMODITIES OF DOMESTIC ORIGIN, 1973

Commodity	Value
	$
Food and Live Animals	13,983,000,000
Meat and Meat Preparations	381,000,000
Dairy Products and Eggs	67,000,000
Wheat and Wheat Flour	4,589,000,000
Rice	852,000,000
Corn and other grains	4,890,000,000
Fruit and Nuts	757,000,000
Vegetables	391,000,000
Soybean oil-cake and meal	944,000,000
Beverages and Tobacco	1,247,000,000
Cigarettes	301,000,000
Crude Materials (inedible), except fuels	10,934,000,000
Synthetic rubber	290,000,000
Raw cotton	1,335,000,000
Mineral fuels, etc.	3,442,000,000
Coal	2,436,000,000
Petroleum and products	792,000,000
Animal and Vegetable Oils and Fats	1,423,000,000
Chemicals	8,822,000,000
Machinery and Transport Equipment	38,189,000,000
Other Manufactured Goods	16,516,000,000

UNITED STATES IMPORTS BY PRINCIPAL COMMODITIES, 1974

Commodity	Value
	$
Food and Live Animals	9,379,000,000
Meat and Meat Preparations	1,344,000,000
Fish	1,499,000,000

	$
Fruit, Nuts, Vegetables	1,014,000,000
Sugar	2,256,000,000
Coffee (green)	1,504,000,000
Beverages and Tobacco	1,321,000,000
Whisky	556,000,000
Crude materials (inedible), except fuels	5,915,000,000
Rubber (including latex)	507,000,000
Textile fibres and wastes	225,000,000
Ores and metal scrap	1,838,000,000
Mineral Fuels, etc.	25,350,000,000
Petroleum and Products	24,210,000,000
Animal and Vegetable Oils, Fats	544,000,000
Chemicals	3,991,000,000
Machinery and Transport Equipment	24,713,000,000
Electrical apparatus	5,417,000,000
Motor vehicles and parts	10,640,000,000
Other manufactured goods	27,507,000,000
Paper and manufactures	1,831,000,000
Metals and manufactures	11,383,000,000
Textiles other than clothing	1,629,000,000

UNITED STATES FOREIGN TRADE BY ECONOMIC CLASS 1974

Class	Imports	Exports*
	$	$
Crude Materials	19,995,000,000	11,150,000,000
Crude Foodstuffs	3,720,000,000	10,246,000,000
Manufactured Foods	6,810,000,000	4,196,000,000
Semi-manufactures	22,067,000,000	14,913,000,000
Finished Manuf.	48,380,000,000	56,638,000,000
Total	100,972,000,000	97,143,000,000

* Excluding total military grant-aid of $96,544,000,000.

UNITED STATES FOREIGN TRADE BY PRINCIPAL COUNTRIES, 1974

Country	Exports and Re-exports to	General Imports from	Country	Exports and Re-exports to	General Imports from
	$	$		$	$
Australia	2,157,000,000	1,042,000,000	Japan	10,679,000,000	12,455,000,000
Belgium and Luxemburg	2,285,000,000	1,681,000,000	Korea	1,546,000,000	1,460,000,000
Brazil	3,089,000,000	1,705,000,000	Mexico	4,855,000,000	3,386,000,000
Canada	19,932,000,000	22,282,000,000	Netherlands	3,979,000,000	1,453,000,000
France	2,942,000,000	2,305,000,000	Spain	1,160,000,000	609,000,000
Germany, W.	4,986,000,000	6,428,000,000	Sweden	908,000,000	876,000,000
India	760,000,000	561,000,000	Switzerland	1,150,000,000	900,000,000
Israel	1,206,000,000	282,000,000	United Kingdom	4,574,000,000	4,021,000,000
Italy	2,752,000,000	2,593,000,000	Venezuela	1,768,000,000	4,679,000,000

UNITED STATES STOCK OF MONEY

$ million

June 30	Gold*	Dollars†	Subsidiary Coin	Minor Coin	Silver Certificates§	United States Notes	Federal Reserve Notes	Total‡
1970	11,156·5	484·7	4,703·3	1,174·3	219·9	322·5	50,430·5	68,572·6
1971	10,184·2	484·7	5,056·0	1,260·6	217·4	322·5	54,494·4	72,098·9
1972	10,401·1	711·9	5,394·8	1,344·0	215·2	322·5	58,285·5	76,761·5
1973	10,410·2	767·4	5,714·3	1,437·4	213·4	322·5	63,653·4	82,594·8
1974	11,566·8	792·5	5,969·3	1,553·0	211·9	322·5	69,489·3	89,980·4

* Held by U.S. Treasury only.
† Standard silver dollars only up to 1971. 1972, 1973 and 1974 figures consist of $481·8 m in standard silver and the balance in cupronickel clad dollars.
‡ Totals include value of early issue notes in process of withdrawal, not separately shown. Value, June 1974, $75·1 m.
§ In process of withdrawal. Not redeemable in silver.

AGRICULTURE AND LIVESTOCK

Agriculture.—The total land surface, including Hawaii and Alaska, is 2,263,591,000 acres of which about 50 per cent. is in farms. The total number of farms in 1975 was 2,818,580. The cash income from crops in 1974 was $52,677,000,000, and in 1973, $42,346,000,000. Cash income from livestock and livestock products in 1973 was $46,244,000,000 and in 1974 $42,327,000,000.

Combined production of all crops in 1974 was about 8 per cent. less than in 1973. There were record outputs of wheat, rice, dry beans, peanuts, potatoes, and citrus fruits. Yields per acre were at new high levels for peanuts and potatoes. Farm output of livestock and livestock products was up 4 per cent. due largely to record high meat animal production.

Livestock on Farms, Jan. 1

	1973 '000 head	1974 '000 head	1975 '000 head
Cattle	121,534	127,670	131,826
Cows	52,541	54,293	56,637
Hogs*	59,180	61,106	55,062
Stock sheep	14,852	13,744	12,480
Chickens*	406,241	412,503	382,793
Turkeys, hens	3,303	3,553	2,970

* Dec. 1, preceding year.

MINERALS

The value of mineral production in the United States in 1974 totalled an estimated $54·9 billion compared with $36·8 billion in 1973 and $32·2 billion in 1972.

Lead output declined 3 per cent. from that of 1973 and primary aluminium production at 4·9 million tons increased 8 per cent over 1973. Production of zinc decreased and iron dropped 5 per cent.; uranium concentrate production decreased by 13 per cent.

About 75 per cent. of the mineral production of the United States (in value) consists of fuels. In 1973 U.S. production of crude petroleum amounted to 3·2 billion barrels. Total demand (domestic plus exports) averaged 12·2 million barrels daily, a slight decrease from 1973.

In the three principal oil-producing States in 1973 daily average production declined in Louisiana by 165,214 barrels (total average daily production, 2,278,000 barrels), declined by 19,216 barrels in Texas (average daily production, 3,547,000 barrels), and decreased by 29,992 barrels in California (average daily production 920,050 barrels).

Production of anthracite again decreased in 1974, reflecting continued declines in major markets at home and abroad. Pennsylvania anthracite production fell 8·0 per cent. below the 1973 figure. The continued loss in the domestic market was due to competition from other fuels, principally oil and gas.

Bituminous coal and lignite produced in 1974 totalled 588 million tons, a decrease of almost 2 million tons from 1973. Exports rose from the 1973 level of 53,000,000 tons to 61,000,000 tons.

LABOUR

Organized Labour.—On December 5, 1955, the American Federation of Labour (AFL), founded in 1881, and the Congress of Industrial Organizations (CIO), formally established in 1928, merged into an organization called the American Federation of Labour and Congress of Industrial Organizations. The combined membership in 1972 was 16,507,000. There are also 4,387,000 members of unions not affiliated to the AFL-CIO. Of the 20,894,000 members of national and international unions with headquarters in U.S.A., 1,458,000 were employed in Canada.

Approximately 26·7 per cent. of the non-agricultural labour force of the United States is estimated to be organized.

Work Stoppages.—There were 6,074 stoppages recorded in 1974. There were 48,044,600 man-days of idleness, representing 0·2 per cent. of estimated working time of all non-agricultural workers.

Employment and Unemployment.—The civilian labour force (working population) was 92,340,000 in June, 1975. This includes self-employed, wage and salary-earners, and unpaid family workers, employed and unemployed. Unemployment was estimated at 7,896,000 in June 1975 (8·6 per cent.)

Wages.—In April, 1975, gross average weekly earnings in industry ranged from $299·70 per week

Wages (Preliminary Figures) April 1975	Average Weekly Earnings	Hours per Week	Average Hourly Earnings
	$		$
Manufacturing	182·75	38·8	4·71
Durable	198·29	39·5	5·02
Non-durable	161·41	37·8	4·27
Coal Mining	255·60	36·0	7·10
Bituminous Coal and Lignite Mining	255·96	36·0	7·11
Gen. Bldg. Contractors	250·14	36·2	6·91
Gas, Electricity and Sanitary Services	240·02	41·1	5·84
Wholesale trade	183·46	38·3	4·79
Retail trade (incl. eating and drinking places	104·63	31·9	3·28
Laundries, Cleaners	103·75	34·7	2·99

in electrical work to $70·15 in eating and drinking places (28·4 hours and $2·47 average hourly earnings). The average for all manufacturing was $182·75 compared with $174·50 in May, 1973.

On Jan. 1, 1975, the minimum wage set by federal law became $2·00 an hour for most non-agricultural employees subject to the Fair Labour Standards Act. This law covers employees engaged in or producing goods for interstate commerce and employees of certain large enterprises. The law requires at least time and a half of an employee's regular rate of pay for all hours over 40 a week for most covered workers.

Other non-agricultural employees employed in enterprises or occupations made subject to the minimum wage provisions on or after February 1, 1967, became subject to a $2·00 minimum wage rate also on Jan 1, 1975. The minimum wage for hired farmworkers was increased to $1·80 an hour on the same date. The minimum wages for the three employment categories will be increased to $2·30 an hour over a 2 to 4 year period.

There are certain exemptions from these requirements in specific occupations and industries.

In addition to cash wages, most workers receive some type of " fringe " benefits—the most common forms being paid vacations, and public holidays, various types of insurance and health benefits financed by the employer or by employer and employees jointly.

COMMUNICATIONS
RAILWAYS

Data pertaining to Class I and II Carriers and their non-operating subsidiaries:—

	1972 $	1973 $
Capital Stock outstanding	5,904,814,000	5,894,304,000
Funded Debt outstanding	7,063,411,000	7,197,571,000
Total Rly. capital actually outsdg.	12,968,225,000	13,091,875,000
Dividends declared	531,908,000	482,362,000
Interest accrued...	600,903,000	624,120,000
Total dividends and interest....	1,132,811,000	1,106,482,000
Railway operating revenues	13,821,880,000	15,243,795,000
Railway operating expenses	11,016,037,000	12,067,957,000
	Number	*Number*
Number of passengers carried earning revenue.	262,010,000	255,444,000
Number of passenger-train cars in service	7,762	7,362
Number of freight-train cars in service	1,415,004	1,391,448
Number of railway employees	537,038	533,766
Miles operated....	218,024	216,405

ROADS

In 1972 there were 3,786,713 miles of roads and streets in the United States, of which 3,173,287 miles were in rural areas and 613,426 miles were in municipal areas. Surfaced roads and streets account for 3,021,552 miles of the total; 765,361 miles were unimproved and graded and drained. State primary roads, including extensions in municipal areas, total 470,849 miles (467,718 surfaced). Other roads and streets under State control total 321,210 miles (291,073 surfaced), 2,785,483 miles are under local control (2,199,342 surfaced); and 209,171 miles (63,255 surfaced) are under Federal control (in national forests and parks).

An estimated total of $22,187,000,000 was spent in 1973 for roads and streets in the United States. Of this total $14,503,000,000 was spent for State highways, $3,295,000,000 was spent for county and local rural roads, $3,812,000,000 was spent for city streets and $577,000,000 was spent on roads in Federal areas. Capital outlay accounts for 53·4 per cent. of the total expenditure; 26·4 per cent. was spent for maintenance, and 7·1 per cent. for administration; 8·5 per cent. for highway police and safety; and 4·6 per cent. for interest on highway bonds.

Motor Vehicles and Taxation.—The number of motor vehicles registered in 1973 in the United States was 125,156,876, an increase of 5·5 per cent. over the 1972 total of 118,626,190. The State governments received $11,974,221,000 in 1972 from motor fuel, motor vehicle and motor-carrier taxes. In 1973 the Federal Government received $6,082,881,000 from excise taxes on motor vehicles and parts, tyres and tubes, petrol, diesel and special fuels and lubricating oils.

Accidents.—In 1973 there were 55,600 deaths caused by motor vehicle accidents. The death rate per 100,000,000 vehicle-miles of travel was 4·3 in 1973, compared with 4·5 in 1972.

SHIPPING

The ocean-going Merchant Marine of the U.S. on April 1, 1975, consisted of 910 vessels of 1,000 gross tons and over, of which 553 were privately owned and 357 were government-owned ships. Of the 553 privately owned active vessels, 168 were freighters, 6 were combination passenger and cargo, 223 were tankers, 16 were bulk carriers and 140 were intermodal types. There were 310 ships in the National Defense Reserve Fleet of inactive government-owned vessels, of which 78 were to be sold for scrap.

AIR TRANSPORT

United States domestic and international scheduled airlines in 1974 were estimated to have carried 207,449,000 passengers over 162,917,241,000 revenue passenger miles. The freight flown by the scheduled airlines during 1974 totalled 4,890,074 ton miles and express 80,845,000 ton miles. In addition, the airlines flew 1,150,832,000 ton miles of mail, a decrease of 3·9 per cent. over 1973.

Total operating revenues of all U.S. scheduled airlines reached the record figure of $14,699,125,000 in 1974, an increase of 18·4 per cent. over 1973. Similarly, total operating expenses rose to a record high total of $13,973,385,000 last year, or a 11·9 per cent. increase over 1973. The net operating income (*i.e.* before deduction of taxes, interest, etc.). was $725,740,000, an increase of 24·0 per cent. from the previous year, resulting in a profit of $321,641,000 compared with a profit of $226,693,000 in 1973.

Ten principal classes of commercial air carriers can be distinguished in the United States. (a) The Domestic Trunk Lines (11); (b) Local Service Carriers, operating routes of lesser traffic density between the smaller traffic centres and between small and large centres (8); (c) The International and Territorial Carriers, including all U.S. flag air carriers authorized to operate between the U.S.A. and foreign countries, other than Canada, and over international waters; also between foreign countries and into Mexico, the Caribbean (10); (d) Intra-Hawaiian Air Carriers, operating in

Hawaii (2); (e) Intra-Alaskan Carriers, providing service within Alaska (4); (f) All Cargo Carriers (3); (g) Helicopter Carrriers (3); (h) Supplement Air Carriers (14); (i) Air Freight Forwarding Companies (181) and Air Taxi operators; and (j)

Intra-State Carriers, with operations limited to State boundaries.

In 1974, 3,307,318 persons were employed by the domestic and international airlines, 1·3 per cent. more than in 1973.

U.S. SCHEDULED AIRLINE INDUSTRY STATISTICS, 1974 (Thousands)

	Domestic Trunk Airlines	Local Service Airlines	Intra-Hawaiian Carriers	Heli-copter Carriers	International and Territorial Airlines	Intra-Alaskan Carriers	All Cargo Carriers
Revenue passengers carried	147,993	35,200	4,675	592	17,725	1,107	..
Revenue passenger miles..	117,616,261	10,808,141	644,685	10,298	33,186,199	635,222	..
Air mail ton miles........	620,348	33,432	1,182	4	337,060	11,647	147,159
Express ton miles.........	70,961	6,929	..	2	857	206	1,885
Freight ton miles.........	2,245,262	68,599	5,687	2	1,338,199	24,213	1,208,004
Revenue ton miles........	15,076,887	1,211,754	112,446	1,058	5,788,488	102,518	1,645,694
Revenue plane miles......	1,589,077	262,216	9,192	1,085	330,248	18,660	44,675

EDUCATION

State School Systems

Almost every State in the Union has a compulsory school attendance law. In general, children are obliged to attend school from 7 to 16 years of age, and those from 14 to 16 must attend school or be lawfully employed. In the States there are, connected with the local administrative units, officers charged with enforcing the compulsory attendance law, known in the majority of States as the truant or attendance officers.

In Oct. 1973 the total number of children in the United States of 5 to 17 years of age was 50,760,000, of whom 48,567,000 were enrolled in public elementary and secondary schools. The average daily attendance in the public schools which 90 per cent. of students attend was 45,056,000 for the 1974-75 school year.

The 1972-73 total revenue receipts for school purposes, were about $52,117,930,000. Of this amount, $4,525,000,000 were received from Federal sources, $20,843,520,000 from State sources and $26,749,412,000 from county and local sources. Current expenditures were $54,342,000,000; $5,492,000,000 expended for sites, buildings, furniture and equipment, and $1,795,000,000 for interest on school debt.

Estimates for the 1973-74 school year were: 51,009,000 children aged 5-17 in the United States in autumn 1973; a public elementary and secondary enrolment of 45,499,000; 2,060,000 teachers; an average teacher salary of $10,690; $49,258,000,000 for current expenditure; $5,201,000,000 for sites, buildings, furniture and equipment expenditures; and $1,700,000,000 expenditure for interest.

Institutions of Higher Education

In the autumn of 1974 enrolment in institutions of higher education numbered 9,023,446.

Institutions of higher education include universities, colleges, professional schools, and two-year colleges. The 1974 survey of enrolments covered 2,747 institutions classified as follows: 1,744 universities, colleges and professional schools enrolling 6,825,152 students; and 1,003 two-year colleges enrolling 2,198,294 students. Publicly controlled institutions of higher education enrolled 75·8 per cent. (6,838,324) of the students and privately controlled 24·2 per cent. (2,185,122).

During the school year 1972-73, an estimated 941,000 bachelor's degrees were conferred, 526,000 to men and 415,000 to women; 50,200 first-professional degrees, 46,000 to men and 4,200 to women; 251,400 master's degrees, and 34,400

doctorates, 28,700 to men and 5,700 to women. There were 164,020 bachelor's degrees in Education. 190,570 in Social Sciences and 129,600 in Accounting and other Business and Management. The three leading fields of study for the master's degree were Education (93,810), Accounting and other Business and Management (30,980) and Social Sciences (18,040). The most popular fields of study on the doctorate level were Education (7,390), Physical Sciences (4,270) and Social Sciences (3,850).

Particulars of some of the Universities (with opening autumn enrolment figures, 1974) are: *Harvard* (20,830 students, including 7,648 women), founded at Cambridge, Mass. on Oct. 28, 1636, and named after John Harvard of Emmanuel College, Cambridge, England, who bequeathed to it his library and a sum of money in 1638; *Yale* (9,736 students, including 2,934 women), founded at New Haven, Connecticut, in 1701; *Bowdoin*, Brunswick, Me. (founded 1794; 1,297, including 393 women); *Brown*, Providence, R.I. (founded 1764; 6,740 students, including 2,668 women); *Columbia*, New York, N.Y. (founded 1754; 23,611 students, including 5,802 women); *Cornell* (founded at Ithaca, N.Y., 1865); 16,857 students, including 5,802 women); *Dartmouth*, Hanover, N.H. (founded 1769, 4,214 students, including 871 women); *Georgetown*, Washington, D.C. (founded 1789; 10,517 students, including 3,627 women); *North Carolina*, Chapel Hill, N.C. (founded in 1789; 19,952 students, including 8,497 women); *Pennsylvania*, Philadelphia, Pa. (founded 1740; 20,220 students, including 7,509 women); *Pittsburgh*, Pa. (founded 1787; 28,157 students, incl. 11,620 women); *Princeton*, N.J. (founded 1746; 4,232 men and 1,644 women); *Tennessee*, Knoxville, Tenn. (founded 1794; 28,011 students, including 11,797 women); *William and Mary*, Williamsburg, Va. (founded 1693; 5,840 students, including 2,703 women); *New York University*, founded in 1831 at New York, had 28,683 students, including 12,065 women.

WEIGHTS AND MEASURES

The weights and measures in common use in the United States are of British origin. They date back to the American Revolution when practically all the standards were intended to be equivalent to those used in England at that period. The principal units were the yard, the avoirdupois pound, the gallon, and the bushel. More or less authentic copies of the English standards of the denominations mentioned had been brought over and adopted by the different colonies. Divergencies in these weights and measures were, however, quite common, due no doubt to the fact that the system of weights and measures in England was not itself well established, and hence the copies brought to this country were often adjusted to different standards.

Because of these discrepancies, the system of weights and measures in the United States (U.S. Customary System) is not identical with the British system. The U.S. bushel and the U.S. gallon, and their subdivisions differ from the corresponding British units. Also the British ton is 2,240 pounds, whereas the ton generally used in the United States is the short ton of 2,000 pounds. The American colonists adopted the English wine gallon of 231 cubic inches. The English of that period used this wine gallon and they also had another gallon, the ale gallon of 282 cubic inches. In 1824 these two gallons were abandoned by the British when they adopted the British Imperial gallon, equivalent to 277.42 cubic inches. At the same time, the bushel was redefined as 8 gallons. In the British system the units of dry measure are the same as those of liquid measure. In the United States these two are not the same, the gallon and its subdivisions being used in the measurement of liquids, while the bushel, with its subdivisions, is used in the measurement of certain dry commodities. The U.S. gallon is divided into 4 liquid quarts

and the U.S. bushel into 32 dry quarts. All the units of capacity mentioned thus far are larger in the British system than in the U.S. system. But the British fluid ounce is smaller than the U.S. fluid ounce, because the British quart is divided into 40 fluid ounces, whereas the U.S. quart is divided into 32 fluid ounces.

The rapidly diminishing world-wide use of the U.S. Customary and British Systems of measurement and the corresponding rise in metric usage, promoted the passage of Public Law 90–472. Pursuant to this law, the National Bureau of Standards conducted a programme of investigation, research and survey to determine the impact on U.S.A. of such increasing world-wide and domestic use of the metric system (SI), reporting back to Congress in July, 1971. The study recommended a concerted, co-ordinated, but voluntary national effort to make the SI the predominant form of measurement in the United States. Legislation to effect this recommendation has been introduced in Congress.

The International System of Units—officially abbreviated SI—is a modernized version of the metric system. It was established by international agreement to provide a logical and interconnected framework for all measurements in science, industry and commerce.

TERRITORIES, ETC. OF THE UNITED STATES

The territories and the principal islands and island groups under the sovereignty of the United States of America comprise: Palmyra Island; Kingman Reef (about 1 sq. mile); Johnston (or Cornwallis) Island and Sand Island (about 1 sq. mile in all); Canton and Enderbury Islands (jointly administered with Great Britain); Midway Islands; Wake Island; Guam, Howland, Baker and Jarvis Islands (about 3 sq. miles in all); American Samoa (including the island of Tutuila, the Manua Islands, and all other islands of the Samoan group east of longitude 171° west of Greenwich together with Swains Island); the Commonwealth of Puerto Rico; the Virgin Islands of the United States, and Navassa Island (2 sq. miles).

The Canal Zone is under the jurisdiction of the United States.

The Trust Territory of the Pacific Islands is under the jurisdiction of the United States pursuant to a trusteeship agreement between the U.S. Government and the Security Council of the United Nations. It consists of the Mariana (except Guam), Caroline and Marshall Islands, with a land area of 687 square miles and a population of 101,592 in 1970. Nine individual languages are spoken in the Territory. Copra is the principal export of importance.

There are certain small guano islands, rocks, or keys which, in pursuance of action taken under the Act of Congress, August 18, 1856, subsequently embodied in Sections 5570–5578 of the Revised Statutes are considered as appertaining to the United States. Responsibility for territorial affairs generally is centred in the Director, Office of Territorial Affairs, Dept. of the Interior, Washington, D.C.

CANTON AND ENDERBURY

Under the Anglo-American Pact of Aug. 10, 1938, Canton and Enderbury (of the Phoenix Island Group in the Central Pacific) were declared to be for the common use of Great Britain and U.S.A. for aviation and communication. The

islands, which are about midway between Hawaii and Australia, extend to a total of 27 sq. miles.

On April 6, 1939, the U.S. and Great Britain agreed to set up a joint regime for Canton and Enderbury Islands. Provision for the joint control of these islands was made by exchange of notes between the two Governments on April 6, 1939.

Canton Island was successively used for aviation support activities and as a missile tracking station by the U.S. National Aeronautics and Space Administration. These activities have been terminated. Enderbury has been uninhabited since World War II.

GUAM

Guam, the largest of the Ladrone or Mariana Islands in the North Pacific Ocean, lies in 13° 26′ N. lat. and 144° 39′ E. long., at a distance of about 1,506 miles east of Manila. The area of the island is estimated at 209 square miles, with an estimated civilian population (1974) of 105,000.

The Guamanians are of Chamorro stock mingled with Filipino and Spanish blood. The Chamorro language belongs to the Malayo-Polynesian family, but has had considerable admixture of Spanish. English is the language used throughout the island, although Chamorro is also used in Guamanian homes.

Guam was occupied by Japanese in Dec., 1941 but was recaptured and occupied throughout by U.S. forces before the end of August, 1944. Under the Organic Act of Guam of August 1, 1950 (Public Law 630 of the 81st Congress), Guam has statutory powers of self-government, and Guamanians are United States citizens. The Governor is popularly elected. In 1972 a non-voting delegate was elected to serve in the U.S. House of Representatives. A 21-member unicameral legislature is elected biennially. There is also a District Court of Guam, with original jurisdiction in cases under federal law.
Governor, Ricardo J. Bordallo; *elected* Nov. 1974.
Lt. Governor, Rudolph G. Sablan; *elected* Nov. 1974.
CAPITAL, Agaña. Port of entry, ΨApra.

WAKE AND MIDWAY ISLANDS

Wake Island, annexed in 1898, has an area of about 3 sq. miles and lies in the N. Pacific about 2,300 miles from Hawaii on the direct route to Hong Kong. Wake Island was occupied by Japanese, Dec. 27, 1941; it was re-occupied by U.S. on Sept. 15, 1945. Population (1970), 1,647.

Midway Islands, with a total area of 28 sq. miles and a population (1970) of 2,220, lie in the N. Pacific about 1,300 miles from Hawaii. There is no indigenous population.

PUERTO RICO

Puerto Rico (Rich Port) is an island of the Greater Antilles group in the West Indies, and lies between 17° 50'–18° 30' N. lat. and 65° 30'–67° 15' W. long., with a total area of 3,435 square miles and a population (1973 Census preliminary) of 2,913,000. The majority of the inhabitants are of Spanish descent and Spanish and English are the official languages. The island is about 100 miles from west to east, and 35 miles from north to south at the western end, narrowing towards the eastern extremity. The capital is 1,600 miles distant from New York, and 1,000 miles from Miami. Puerto Rico was discovered in 1493 by Christopher Columbus. It was explored by Ponce de León in 1508. It continued a Spanish possession until Oct. 18, 1898, when the United States took formal possession as a result of the Spanish-American War. It was ceded by Spain to the United States by the Treaty ratified on April 11, 1899. Sugar is grown along the coastal plain and tobacco and coffee on the slopes of the hills; fruits, cotton, maize, sweet potatoes and yams are also grown. The trade is principally with the U.S. In 1973 there were 3,972 miles of highway under maintenance. There are good harbours at San Juan, Mayaguez and Ponce.

The Constitution approved by the Congress and the President of the United States, which came into force on July 25, 1952, establishes the Commonwealth of Puerto Rico with full powers of local government. Legislative functions are vested in the Legislative Assembly, which consists of 2 elected houses; the Senate of 29 members (2 from each of 8 senatorial districts and 13 at large) and the House of Representatives of 54 members (1 from each of 40 representative districts and 12 at large). Membership of each house may be increased slightly to accommodate minority representatives. The term of the Legislative Assembly is 4 years. The Governor is popularly elected for a term of 4 years. A Supreme Court of 9 members is appointed by the Governor, with the advice and consent of the Senate. There are 10 similarly appointed Secretaries at the head of permanent departments, but the selection of the Secretary of State must be approved also by the House of Representatives. The Governor appoints all judges. Puerto Rico is represented in Congress by a Resident Commissioner, elected for a term of 4 years, who has a seat in the House of Representatives, but not a vote, although he has a right to vote on certain committees within the House of Representatives. Great improvement has been made in the progress, industrialization and welfare of the island during the last two decades. A programme of tax exemption has raised income from industry to a level higher than that from agriculture. Public schools in established throughout—enrolment in 1973 was 711,030.

CAPITAL.—Ψ San Juan, population 851,247; Other major towns are: Ψ Ponce (158,981); Bayamón (156,192); Ψ Mayagüez (85,857); and Ψ Arecibo (73,283).

TRADE

	1972–73
Total Imports	$3,496,000,000
Total Exports	2,465,000,000

Trade with U.K.

	1971	1972
Imports from U.K.	£11,855,000	£9,537,000
Exports to U.K.	3,048,000	9,759,000

Governor, Rafael Hernández Colón, *elected* 1972.
Resident Commissioner, Jaime Benítez (1972).

AMERICAN SAMOA

American Samoa consists of the island of Tutuila, Aunu'u, Ofu, Olosega, Ta'u, Rose and Swains Islands, with a total area of 76·5 square miles and a population of 27,769 in 1970.

Tutuila, the largest of the group, has an area of 52 square miles and contains a magnificent harbour at Ψ Pago Pago (pop. 1960, 1,251). The constitution of American Samoa designates the village of Fagatogo as the seat of government. The remaining islands have an area of about 24 square miles. Tuna and copra are the chief exports.

Under an Executive Order of the President, which became effective on July 1, 1951, civilian administration under the Department of the Interior replaced the Naval administration which had existed since 1900. At present the Government consists of an executive, a bicameral legislature and a judiciary. Most of the Samoans are U.S. nationals, but some have acquired citizenship through service in the United States armed forces or other naturalization procedure.

Governor, Earl B. Ruth.

TRUST TERRITORY OF THE PACIFIC ISLANDS

The Trust Territory of the Pacific Islands consists of the Mariana (excluding Guam), Caroline and Marshall Islands which extend from latitude 1° to 20° north and from longitude 130° to 172° east. They cover an ocean area of 3,000,000 square miles but have a total land area of only 687 square miles. There are 96 separate islands and island groups in the Trust Territory. The population in 1970 was 101,592. The inhabitants of the Trust Territory are broadly classed as Micronesians. The native cultures vary considerably among island groups and even more among islands and atolls in the same geographic area. Nine different languages are spoken in the territory.

The Trust Territory is administered by the United States pursuant to a Trusteeship Agreement with the Security Council of the United Nations of July 18, 1947, administration being under the general jurisdiction of the Secretary of the Interior.

For administrative purposes, the territory is divided into six districts: The Marianas, Palau, Yap, Truk, Ponape and the Marshalls. Local governments exist within each district.

High Commissioner, Edward E. Johnston.
Deputy High Commissioner, Peter T. Coleman.
CAPITAL (Provisional).—Saipan, Mariana Islands.

VIRGIN ISLANDS

Purchased by the United States from Denmark for the sum of $25,000,000, and proclaimed, January 25, 1917. The total area of the islands is 133 sq. miles, with a population (estimated 1972), of 90,000. *St. Thomas* (28 sq. miles) had a population of 29,565; *St. Croix* (84 sq. miles) had a population of 31,892; *St. John* (20 sq. miles) had a population of 1,743.

Ψ Seaport.

CAPITAL, Ψ Charlotte Amalie contains one of the finest harbours in the West Indies. The government of the Virgin Islands is organized under the provisions of the Revised Organic Act of the Virgin Islands, enacted by the Congress of the United States on July 22, 1954. Legislative power is vested in the Legislature of the Virgin Islands, a unicameral body composed of 15 senators popularly elected for two-year terms. Virgin Islanders are citizens of the United States. From the elections of November, 1970, the Governor has been popularly elected. In 1972, a non-voting delegate was elected to serve in the U.S. House of Representatives. The Virgin Islands are now a favourite tourist area in the Caribbean. The climate of the islands is delightful at all times, and particularly so during the winter months.

Governor, Cyril E. King, *elected* Nov. 1974.
Lieut.-Governor, Juan F. Luis, *elected* Nov. 1974.

THE PANAMA CANAL

The Panama Canal, including the related commercial enterprises in the Canal Zone, are operated by the Panama Canal Company, which was

Fiscal Year	No. of Transits	Canal, Net Tons	Cargo Tons
1964	11,803	69,707,102	70,550,090
1965	11,835	74,853,264	76,573,071
1966	11,926	78,918,013	81,712,940
1967	12,413	88,266,343	86,193,430
1968	13,199	96,487,843	96,550,165
1969	13,150	100,603,265	101,391,132
1970	13,658	108,141,640	114,257,260
1971	14,020	111,006,363	118,626,906
1972	13,766	112,971,058	109,233,725
1973	13,841	126,203,549	126,104,029
1974	14,033	135,715,628	147,906,914

formed on July 1, 1951, under the provisions of the Panama Canal Company Act. The Canal Zone is governed by the Canal Zone Government, which was established simultaneously with the new Canal Company. Both organizations are headed by Major-General H. R. Parfitt, U.S.A., who holds the joint title of Governor of the Canal Zone and President of the Panama Canal Company.

The Canal Zone has an area of 647 sq. miles (about 1 per cent. of the total area of Panama) (land area, 372 sq. miles) and a population in 1970 of 51,000.

Chief Towns.—Balboa Heights, Balboa, Ancon and Margarita.

Including only ocean-going commercial vessels, 300 Panama Canal net tons measurement or over, against which tolls were collected, the volume of commercial traffic passing through the Canal during each of the last 10 fiscal years (*see* table in col. 1). In 1974 the 14,033 vessels using the canal carried the highest tonnage so far recorded.

The canal is fifty statute miles long (44.08 nautical miles), and the channel is from 500 to 1,000 feet wide at the bottom. It contains 12 locks in twin flights; 3 steps at Gatun on the Atlantic side, 1 step at Pedro Miguel and 2 at Miraflores on the Pacific side. Each lock chamber is 1,000 feet long and 110 feet wide. Transit from sea to sea takes on average 13 to 15 hours. The least width is in Gaillard Cut, and the greatest in Gatun Lake, where the channel can be made much broader at any time by the cutting down of trees and a small amount of dredging.

The Panama Canal Company is engaged in a Canal improvement programme. The widening of Gaillard Cut from 300 to 500 feet was completed in August, 1970. The maximum draft allowable for ships using the Panama Canal is determined by the level of Lake Gatun, which is an average of 85 feet above sea level. During dry season, from December to April, the lake level drops, imposing draft restrictions. The all-time high maximum tropical fresh water draft was 40 feet for certain types of vessels in 1967.

BRITISH EMBASSY

3100 Massachusetts Avenue, N.W.
Washington, D.C. 200008

Ambassador Extraordinary and Plenipotentiary, His Excellency the Hon. Sir Peter Edward Ramsbottom, K.C.M.G. (1974) £14,000

Ministers, J. O. Moreton, C.M.G., M.C.; A. K. Rawlinson (*Economic*); G. N. Gadsby, C.B. (*Defence, Research and Development*); H. A. H. Cortazzi, C.M.G. (*Commercial*).

Head of British Defence Staff and Defence Attaché, Vice-Admiral Sir Ian Easton, K.C.B., D.S.C.

Naval Attaché, Rear Admiral R. W. Halliday, D.S.C.

Military Attaché, Brigadier A. L. Watson.

Air Attaché, Air Cdre. N. S. Howlett.

Counsellors, W. J. A. Wilberforce; A. H. B. Herman (*Hong Kong Commercial Affairs*); J. L. B. Garcia (*Labour*); B. D. Airey (*Defence Supply*); A. R. Gordon-Cumming, C.V.O. (*Civil Aviation and Shipping*); J. Gaunt; J. C. McKane; I. B. Bott (*Defence Research and Development*); C. T. Brant (*Energy*); R. A. Fyjis-Walker (*Information*); J. C. Harrison; T. Sharp (*Commercial*); J. Parker; H. M. Griffiths (*Economic*); R. M. Russell; G. L. Scullard, O.B.E. (*Admin.* and *H.M. Consul-General*); R. A. Browning (*Overseas Develop-*

ment); R. C. Samuel; P. Robinson (*Asst. Defence Research and Development*); A. Smith (*Science and Technology*); Brig. J. P. Ferry (*Asst. Defence Research and Development*); D. A. Payne (*Civil Aviation Operations*); E. P. D. P. Hall (*Civil Aviation Telecommunications*); D. J. Walters (*Asst. Defence Research and Development*); G. R. Sanderson (*Education*); M. E. Pike.

1st Secretaries, A. Reeve; J. M. Knight; J. G. MacDonald (*Commercial*); S. H. Broadbent (*Economic*); M. A. Cowdy (*Financial*); J. Thomas (*Commercial*, A. J. Pryor (*Civil Aviation and Shipping*); M. S. Baker-Bates (*Information*); C. M. Clarkson (*Defence Supply*); J. E. Cornish; J. P. Millington; J. Davidson; D. C. Walker; Dr. T. M. Moynehan (*Asst. Attaché* (*Science*); J. Q. Greenstock (*Private Secretary to the Ambassador*); P. W. Murphy (*Agriculture and Commercial*); J. McAuley (*Technology*); Miss O. Goodinson (*Consul*); W. H. Fletcher, M.B.E.; T. E. Colquhoun; A. I. Glasby (*Energy*); A. Lovell; J. Smallwood (*Information*); Miss C. J. Tasch (*Administration*); R. Murphy; G. A. Gillespie (*Accountant*); A. B. N. Morey (*Commercial*).

The United Nations

CHARTER OF THE UNITED NATIONS

The foundations of the Charter of the United Nations were laid at the Conference of Foreign Ministers in Moscow in 1943, and upon those foundations a structure was built at the meetings at Dumbarton Oaks, Washington, D.C., Aug. 21–Oct. 7, 1944. The design was discussed and criticized at San Francisco from April 25 to June 26, 1945, on which date representatives of 50 Allied Nations appended their signatures to the Charter.

The United Nations formally came into existence on October 24, 1945. It was later decided that its seat should be in the United States. Permanent headquarters have been erected at Manhattan, New York. October 24 has been designated "United Nations Day".

The following 138 states are members of the United Nations:—

Afghanistan, Albania, Algeria, Argentina,★ Australia,★ Austria, Bahamas, Bahrain, Bangladesh, Barbados, Belgium,★ Bhutan, Bolivia,★ Botswana, Brazil,★ Bulgaria, Burma, Burundi, Byelorussian Soviet Socialist Republic,★ Cambodia, Cameroon, Canada,★ Central African Republic, Chad, Chile,★ China,★ Colombia,★ Congo (Pop. Repub.), Costa Rica,★ Cuba,★ Cyprus, Czechoslovakia,★ Dahomey, Denmark,★ Dominican Republic,★ Ecuador,★ Egypt,★ El Salvador,★ Equatorial Guinea, Ethiopia,★ Fiji, Finland, France,★ Gabon, Gambia, Germany (East), Germany (West), Ghana, Greece,★ Guatemala,★ Guinea, Guyana, Haiti,★ Honduras,★ Hungary, Iceland, India,★ Indonesia, Iran,★ Iraq,★ Republic of Ireland, Israel, Italy, Ivory Coast, Jamaica, Japan, Jordan, Kenya, Kuwait, Laos, Lebanon,★ Lesotho, Liberia,★ Libya, Luxemburg,★ Madagascar, Malawi, Malaysia, Maldive Islands, Mali, Malta, Mauritania, Mauritius, Mexico,★ Mongolia, Morocco, Nepal, Netherlands,★ New Zealand,★ Nicaragua,★ Niger, Nigeria, Norway,★ Oman, Pakistan, Panama,★ Paraguay,★ Peru,★ Philippines,★ Poland,★ Portugal, Qatar, Rumania, Rwanda, Saudi Arabia,★ Senegal, Sierra Leone, Singapore, Somalia, South Africa,★ Spain, Sri Lanka, Sudan, Swaziland, Sweden, Syria,★ Tanzania, Thailand, Togo, Trinidad and Tobago, Tunisia, Turkey,★ Uganda, Ukrainian Soviet Socialist Republic,★ Union of Soviet Socialist Republics,★ United Arab Emirates, United Kingdom,★ United States of America,★ Upper Volta, Uruguay,★ Venezuela,★ Yemen (Arab Repub.), Yemen (P.D.R.), Yugoslavia,★ Zaïre, Zambia.

★ Original member (*i.e.* from 1945). (From October 25, 1971, "China" was taken to mean the People's Republic of China.)

The principal organs of the United Nations are:— (1) The General Assembly; (2) The Security Council; (3) The Economic and Social Council; (4) The Trusteeship Council; (5) The International Court of Justice; (6) The Secretariat.

1. The General Assembly

The General Assembly consists of all the Members of the United Nations. Each Member is entitled to be represented at its meetings by five representatives, but has only one vote. The General Assembly meets once a year in regular session normally beginning on the third Tuesday in September. Special Sessions may also be held.

The work of the General Assembly is divided among seven Main Committees, on each of which every Member has the right to be represented:— (1) Political and Security (including the regulation of armaments); (2) Economic and Financial; (3) Social, Humanitarian and Cultural; (4) Trusteeship (including Non-Self Governing Territories); (5) Administrative and Budgetary; (6) Legal. There is also a Special Political Committee, to relieve the burden on the first Committee.

The Main Committees consider items referred to them by the General Assembly and recommend draft resolutions for submission to the Assembly's plenary meetings.

The Assembly has two procedural committees— a General Committee and a Credentials Committee; and three standing committees—an Advisory Committee on Administrative and Budgetary Questions, a Committee on Contributions and a Disarmament Commission.

The General Assembly appoints such *ad hoc* committees as may be required from time to time for special purposes. The Assembly is also assisted in its work by subsidiary bodies such as a Board of Auditors, an Investments Committee, a United Nations Staff Benefit Committee, and an International Law Commission. In 1964 the General Assembly set up the United Nations Conference on Trade and Development (UNCTAD) as a permanent body.

The United Nations Industrial Development Organization (UNIDO) was set up on Jan. 1, 1967, to promote industrialization and co-ordinate United Nations activities in this field.

President of the United Nations General Assembly, Abdelaziz Bouteflika (*Algeria*) (1974).

2. The Security Council

The Security Council consists of fifteen Members, each of which has one representative and one vote. There are five *permanent* Members (China, France, U.K., U.S.A., U.S.S.R.) and ten non-permanent Members elected for a two-year term.

The Security Council bears the primary responsibility for the maintenance of peace and security. Decisions on procedural questions are made by an affirmative vote of seven Members. On all other matters the affirmative vote of nine Members must include the concurring votes of the *permanent Members*, and it is this clause which makes the *Veto* possible. The only exception to this rule is that with regard to measures for peaceful settlement a party to a dispute may refrain from voting.

The General Assembly, any member of the United Nations, or the Secretary-General, can bring to the Council's attention any matter considered to threaten international peace and security. A non-member State can bring a dispute before the Council provided it accepts in advance the U.N. Charter obligations for peaceful settlement.

A *Committee on the Admission of New Members* was set up by the Security Council on May 17, 1946, for the purpose of examining applications for admission to membership in the United Nations which may be referred to it by the Security Council. It is composed of a representative of each of the members of the Security Council.

The Security Council also establishes *ad hoc* committees and commissions which may be required from time to time for special purposes.

3. The Economic and Social Council

This body is responsible under the General Assembly for carrying out the functions of the United Nations with regard to international economic, social, cultural, educational, health and related matters.

It has established the following Commissions: Statistical, Human Rights, Social, Status of Women, Narcotic Drugs, Population, Regional Economic Commissions for Europe, Asia and the Pacific, Western Asia, Latin America and Africa. The Council also supervises and co-ordinates the work of fourteen related agencies.

United Nations Children's Fund (UNICEF).— UNICEF embraces all aspects of child welfare and assists the governments of the developing countries in developing maternal and child health services, the prevention and treatment of disease, nutrition and the preparation of children for adult life. It is financed by voluntary contributions from Governments and from the public and its work is carried out in co-operation with the relevant technical members of the United Nations.

4. Trusteeship Council

The Trusteeship Council is composed of countries administering Trust Territories, permanent members of the Security Council, and one other country elected by the General Assembly for a three-year term.

The Trusteeship Council considers reports from administering authorities; examines petitions in consultation with the administering authority; makes periodic inspection visits; and checks conditions with an annual questionnaire on the political, economic, social, and educational advancement of the inhabitants of trust territories.

5. International Court of Justice

The International Court of Justice is the principal judicial organ of the United Nations. The Statute of the court is an integral part of the Charter and all Members of the United Nations are *ipso facto* parties to it. The Court is composed of 15 judges, no two of whom may be nationals of the same State, and meets at The Hague.

If any party to a case fails to adhere to the judgment of the Court, the other party may have recourse to the Security Council.

THE SECRETARIAT

Secretary-General (1972–77), Kurt Waldheim (*Austria*).

Under-Secretaries-General

Inter-Agency Affairs and Co-ordination, C. V. Narasimhan (*India*).
Special Political Affairs, B. E. Urquhart (*U.K.*); Roberta Guyer (*Argentina*).
Conference Services, B. Lewandowski (*Poland*).
Economic and Social Affairs, Gabriel Van Laetham (*France*).
Political Affairs and Decolonization, Ming-Chao Tang (*China*).
Political and Security Council Affairs, A. Shevchenko (*U.S.S.R.*).
Director-General, U.N. Office, Geneva, V. Winspeare Guicciardi (*Italy*).
Office or Administration and Management, G. Davidson (*Canada*).
Legal Counsel, E. Suy (*Belgium*).

U.N. Information Centre, 14–15, Stratford Place, W.1.

BUDGET OF THE UNITED NATIONS

The budget is now approved for periods of two years, and the appropriation for the biennium 1974–75 is U.S.$540,473,000. The scale of assessments for 1974–76 includes: Australia, 1·44 per cent.; Canada, 3·18 per cent.; India, 1·20 per cent.; New Zealand, 0·28 per cent.; United Kingdom, 5·31 per cent. The United States contribution is 25·00 per cent.; U.S.S.R. is 12·97 per cent.; France is 5·86 per cent.; Italy is 3.60 per cent and Japan is 7·15 per cent.

UNITED KINGDOM REPRESENTATIVES

845 Third Avenue, New York

Permanent Representative to the United Nations and Representative on the Security Council, Ivor Seward Richard, Q.C. (1974).
Minister and Deputy Permanent Representative, James Murray, C.M.G.
Minister (Economic and Social Affairs), P. R. H. Marshall, C.M.G.
Counsellors, J. C. Thomas (*Head of Chancery*); H. Steel, O.B.E. (*Legal Adviser*); C. A. Lovitt, M.B.E. (*Administration*); M. F. H. Stuart (*Treasury Adviser*).
1st Secretaries, A. D. Baighty; B. D. Donnelly; A. J. C. E. Rellie; S. P. Day; Miss S. E. Harden, M.B.E.; C. C. A. Battiscombe; R. J. Dalton; D. B. C. Logan; T. L. Richardson; D. Broad; Miss E. C. Wallis, M.B.E.; F. C. G. Hohler.

INTERNATIONAL ATOMIC ENERGY AGENCY

Kärntnerring 11–13, P.O. Box 590, Vienna

Set up on July 29, 1957, to accelerate and enlarge the contribution of atomic energy to peace, health and prosperity throughout the world and to ensure that assistance provided by it or under its supervision is not used to further any military purpose. Agreements have been reached concerning the Agency's working relationship with the United Nations and some of the specialized agencies. In June, 1975, 106 states were members.

A General Conference of all members meets in regular annual session and in such special session as may be necessary. A Board of Governors (34 members) carries out the functions of the Agency and meets usually four times a year. The Budget in 1975 amounted to $29,675,000.

Director-General, Sigvard Eklund (*Sweden*).

INTERNATIONAL AGENCIES

Fourteen other international organizations, having wide responsibilities in economic, social, cultural, educational and other related fields, carry out their functions in co-operation with the United Nations under agreements made with a standing committee of the Economic and Social Council.

International Labour Organization (ILO) Geneva (London Branch Office, 87–91 New Bond Street, W.1.). Established with the League of Nations in 1919 under the Treaty of Versailles, the ILO became in 1946 the first specialized agency associated with the United Nations. In June, 1975, the Organization had 126 member States. The aim of the ILO is to promote lasting peace through social justice, and to this end it works for better economic and social conditions everywhere. It was awarded the Nobel Peace Prize in 1969.

The ILO establishes international labour standards, which set guidelines for improving working conditions and protecting basic human rights; runs a world-wide programme of technical assistance to developing countries (with funds from all sources amounting in 1974–75 to about $80 million); conducts research and disseminates information on the human aspects of economic activity, with a view to improving social and economic well-being. Through its World Employment Programme, the ILO is attacking unemployment and its associated ills by aiding national and international efforts to provide productive work for the world's fast-growing population.

The International Labour Conference, composed of national delegations of two government delegates, one worker delegate and one employer delegate, meets at least once a year. It formulates international labour standards and broad policies of the Organization, provides a forum for discussion of world labour and social problems, and approves the ILO's work programme and budget, which is financed by member States.

A 56-member Governing Body, composed of 28 government members, 14 worker members and 14 employer members, acts as the Organization's executive council. Ten governments hold seats on the Governing Body because of their industrial importance. These are Canada, China, France, the Federal Republic of Germany, India, Italy, Japan, U.S.S.R., the United Kingdom and the United States of America.

The International Labour Office, the secretariat of the Organization, collects and distributes information, assists governments on request in drafting legislation on the basis of international labour standards, directs technical co-operation activities, and issues publications.

Director-General, Francis Blanchard (*France*).

Food and Agriculture Organization of the United Nations (FAO), Viale delle Terme di Caracalla, Rome.—Established on October 16, 1945, to raise levels of nutrition and standards of living, to secure improvements in the efficiency of the production and distribution of all food and agricultural products and to better the condition of rural populations, thus contributing to the expansion of world economy and ensuring man's freedom from hunger. Among its many activities the Organization promotes the global exchange of information in the fields of agriculture, forestry and fisheries, facilitates international agreement in these fields and provides technical assistance in such subjects as nutrition and food management, soil erosion control, re-afforestation, the establishment of paper industries, irrigation engineering, control of infestation of stored foods, production of fertilizers, control of crop pests and diseases, and improvement of fishing vessels, fish distribution and marketing. As well as its work as an intergovernmental agency the Organization also mobilizes the efforts of private individuals and associations through the world-wide *Freedom from Hunger Campaign*. Jointly with the United Nations it administers a $1,000,000,000 World Food Programme using food as capital backing for development programmes in developing countries. The 1973 session of the governing Conference approved a budget of $107,000,000 for the two years 1974–75. In addition FAO is carrying out field programmes involving expenditure of about $100,000,000 under the U.N. Development Programme and other aid programmes. Through its co-operative programme with the World Bank it is helping to increase international investment in agriculture and allied fields.

The policy of the Organization is directed by a two-yearly Conference of the 131 member countries. A council (42 members) acts for the Conference between its sessions.

Director-General, Dr. A. H. Boerma (*Netherlands*).

United Nations Educational, Scientific and Cultural Organization (UNESCO), 9 Place de Fontenoy, Paris 75700.—Under its constitution, the Organization makes its contribution to peace and security by promoting collaboration among its Member States in the fields of education, science, culture and communications. It aims at furthering a universal respect for justice, for the rule of law and for human rights, without distinction of race, sex, language or religion, in accordance with the Charter of the United Nations.

Unesco continues to work for the advancement of mutual knowledge and understanding of peoples ... to give fresh impulse to popular education and to the spread of culture ... to maintain, increase and diffuse knowledge.

The Organization is composed of three organs: (i) the *General Conference*, consisting of representatives of Member States, which meets biennially to decide the programme and budget; (ii) the *Executive Board*, composed of 40 members elected by the General Conference to supervise the execution of the approved programme and (iii) the *Secretariat*, which is responsible for Unesco's day-to-day functioning and the execution of the programme. In most Member States National Commissions serve as a link with Unesco and help carry out the programme. The broad objectives of Unesco: in education, its democratization and regeneration; in science, the development of science policy, the application of science and technology to development and the intensification of international programmes of scientific co-operation; in culture, the evolution of cultural policy; in communication, the improvement and development of the mass media in Member States as a means of increasing the flow of information. Member States in July, 1975, 136.

Director-General, Amadou-Mahtar M'Boa (*Senegal*).

U.K. National Commission for UNESCO, Ministry of Overseas Development, Stag Place, S.W.1.

Secretary, D. Bell.

World Health Organization (WHO),   1211 Geneva 27. Established on April 7, 1948, the aim of the World Health Organization is the attainment by all peoples of the highest possible level of health. Through its advisory services, it helps its member governments to develop health manpower, streamline health services, control communicable diseases, promote family health—including mother and child care, family planning, nutrition and health education—and strengthen environmental health. Its other services include the International Pharmacopoea, drug evaluation and monitoring, biological standardization, epidemiological surveillance, medical research and scientific publications. Approved budget for 1976, $137,100,000. Membership (May 1975), 145.

Organs are a *World Health Assembly* meeting annually to frame policy, an *Executive Board* (30 members), meeting at least twice a year, and a *Secretariat*.

Director-General, H. T. Mahler (*Denmark*).

International Bank for Reconstruction and Development (*The World Bank*), 1818 H Street, Washington, D.C.; European office, 66 Ave. d'Iéna, 75116, Paris, France.—Established on Dec. 27, 1945, to assist in the reconstruction and development of territories of member countries by facilitating the investment of capital for productive purposes; to promote private foreign investment and, when private capital is not readily available on reasonable terms, to supplement private investment by providing loans for productive purposes out of its own capital, funds raised by it, and its other resources. The 1,161 loans made by the Bank since its inception to June 30, 1975, totalled $27,595,000,000. Subscribed capital, June 30, 1975, $30,820,879,000.

The *Board of Governors* consists of one Governor and one alternative appointed by each of the 125 member countries.

Twenty *Executive Directors* exercise all powers of

the Bank except those reserved to the Board of Governors: The *President*, selected by the Executive Directors, conducts the business of the Bank, with the assistance of an international staff.
President, Robert S. McNamara (*U.S.A.*).

International Development Association (IDA), 1818 H Street, Washington, D.C.; European office, 66 Ave. d'Iéna, 75116 Paris, France—an affiliate of the World Bank established in September 1960. Its purposes are to promote economic development, increase productivity and thus raise standards of living in the less developed areas of the world included within the Association's membership, in particular by providing finance to meet their important developmental requirements on terms which are more flexible and bear less heavily on the balance of payments than those of conventional loans, thereby furthering the objectives of the World Bank and supplementing its activities. IDA's Board of Governors and Executive Directors are the same as those holding equivalent positions in the World Bank, serving *ex officio* in IDA. By June 30, 1975, IDA had extended 595 development credits totalling $8,346,000,000 in 69 countries for improved transportation, agriculture, electric power facilities, industry, education and municipal water supplies. The credits were for terms of 50 years, free of interest.

International Finance Corporation (IFC), 1818 H Street, Washington, D.C.; European office, 66 Ave. d'Iéna, 75116 Paris, France—The IFC was established in 1956 as an affiliate of the World Bank to assist less developed member countries by promoting the growth of the private sector of their economies. IFC's share capital of $107,331,000 at June 30, 1975, had been subscribed by 100 countries. In addition, *IFC* is empowered to borrow up to approximately $685,000,000 from the World Bank for use in its lending programme. At the end of June, 1975, IFC had made commitments totalling more than $1,262,000,000 in 57 countries.
President, Robert S. McNamara (*U.S.A.*).

International Monetary Fund, 19th and H Streets, N.W. Washington, D.C.—Established on Dec. 27, 1945, the Fund exists to promote international monetary co-operation and the expansion of international trade; to promote exchange stability, maintain orderly exchange arrangements and avoid competitive exchange depreciations; and to assist in the establishment of a multilateral system of payments in respect of current transactions between members and in the elimination of foreign exchange restrictions which hamper world trade. 126 countries were in membership of the Fund in June, 1975.

The Fund's financial assistance takes the form of a foreign exchange transaction. The member pays to the Fund an amount of its own money equivalent to the amount of foreign currency it wishes to purchase. The member is expected to " repurchase " its own currency from the Fund within three, or at the outside five years, with a payment of gold or dollars or convertible currency acceptable to the Fund. These arrangements are subject to certain charges which rise in proportion to the amount of foreign exchange involved, and the length of time it is held.

Currencies drawn from the Fund may be used in a flexible way to relieve the member's payments difficulty, but its assets are not intended to be used for military purposes, or for programmes of economic development.

Each member of the Fund is assigned a quota which approximately determines its voting power and the amount of foreign exchange that it may draw from the Fund. The subscription of each member is equal to its quota, and is payable partly in gold and partly in the member's own currency.
Managing Director, H. Johannes Witteveen (*Netherlands*).

International Civil Aviation Organization (ICAO), International Aviation Square, 1,000 Sherbrooke Street, W., Montreal, Quebec, Canada.—In existence since April 4, 1947, to study problems of international civil aviation and the establishment of international standards and regulations for civil aviation, ICAO encourages the use of safety measures, uniform regulations or operation, and simpler procedures at international airports. It promotes the use of new technical methods and equipment. With the co-operation of members, it has evolved a pattern for meteorological services, traffic control, communications, radio beacons and ranges, search and rescue organization, and other facilities required for safe international flight. It has secured much simplification of government customs, immigration, and public health regulations as they apply to international air transport. 129 states are now members of ICAO.

An *Assembly* of delegates from member states meets at least once every three years. A *Council* of 30 members is elected by the Assembly, taking into account the countries of chief importance in air transport and the need for representation of the main geographical areas of the world. The Council is the executive body, working through subsidiary committees.
President of Council, Walter Binaghi (*Argentina*).
Secretary-General, Dr. A. Kotaite (*Lebanon*).

Universal Postal Union (UPU), Weltpoststrasse 4, 3000 Berne 15.—Established on October 9, 1874, by the postal Convention of Berne and in operation from July 1, 1875, UPU exists to form a single postal territory of all the countries, members of the Union, for the reciprocal exchange of correspondence in order to secure the organization and improvement of the various postal services and to promote in this sphere the development of international collaboration. Every member agrees to transmit the mail of all other members by the best means used for its own mail. The Union includes almost all the countries of the world. Budget, 1975, $U.S.5,286,000. A *Universal Postal Congress* meets at five-yearly intervals, the last Congress was held at Lausanne in 1974. The next is due to be held in Brazil in 1979.
Director-General, Mohammed J. Sobhi (*Egypt*).

International Telecommunication Union (ITU), Place des Nations, Geneva.—Founded at Paris in 1865 as the International Telegraph Union. ITU became a U.N. Specialized Agency in 1947 and as from Jan. 1, 1975, is governed by the Convention adopted by the Torremolinos Conference held in 1973. ITU exists to set up international regulations for telegraph, telephone and radio services to further their development and extend their utilization by the public, at the lowest possible rates; to promote international co-operation for the improvement and rational use of telecommunications of all kinds; the development of technical facilities and their most efficient operation. ITU allocates the radio frequency spectrum and registers radio frequency assignments. It studies, recommends, collects and publishes information on telecommunication matters, including space radio communications. The Budget for 1976 is 63,266,500 *Swiss francs*.
Secretary-General, M. Mili (*Tunisia*).

World Meteorological Organization (WMO), Geneva.—Came into existence in 1951. The present membership is 130 States and 11 Territories. WMO exists to facilitate world-wide co-operation in establishing networks of stations making observations related to meteorology, and to promote the establishment and maintenance of centres providing meteorological services; to promote the establishment of systems for the rapid exchange of weather information; to promote standardization of meteorological observations and to ensure their uniform publication; to further the application of meteorology to aviation, shipping, water problems, agriculture, and other human activities; to encourage research and training in meteorology and to coordinate their international aspects. Budget (1976–79), $U.S.40,542,000. A *World Meteorological Congress* meets at least once every four years. An *Executive Committee* (24 members), meeting at least annually carries out the resolutions of the Congress, initiates studies and makes recommendations on matters requiring international action. Other organs are six *Regional Meteorological Associations* (Africa, Asia, S. America, N. and Central America, Europe and South-West Pacific), eight technical commissions and a Secretariat. *Secretary-General*, D. A. Davies (*U.K.*).

Inter-Governmental Maritime Consultative Organization (IMCO), 101–104 Piccadilly, W.1. A United Nations Specialized Agency established on March 17, 1958, to provide means for co-operation and exchange of information among governments on technical matters related to international shipping, especially with regard to safety at sea and preventing marine pollution caused by ships. IMCO is responsible for calling maritime conferences and drafting maritime agreements, *e.g.* Load Line Convention, 1966 and Convention on Tonnage Measurement of Ships. It has produced International Maritime Dangerous Goods Code; Code of Safe Practice for Bulk Cargoes; revised International Code of Signals, and fire safety measures for ships. In June, 1975, 89 nations were in membership. Budget, 1974–75, $5,995,000 *Secretary-General*, C. P. Srivastava (*India*).

International Trade. *General Agreement on Tariffs and Trade* (GATT), Villa le Bocage, Palais des Nations 1211, Geneva 10. A multilateral treaty, in operation since 1948, to which 83 countries are parties; a further 20 countries apply GATT *de facto*. Its rules thus govern over four-fifths of the world trade. Objectives of GATT are to expand international trade and promote economic development. GATT provides a permanent forum for discussion and solution of particular international trade problems, and for multilateral negotiations to reduce tariffs and other obstacles to the expansion of international trade. In September 1973, 102 countries agreed in Tokyo to launch comprehensive new negotiations in GATT, aimed at further reductions in both tariff and non-tariff barriers to industrial and agricultural trade. Special attention is given to trade problems of developing countries. An International Trade Centre, set up by GATT in 1964 to aid developing countries in export promotion, is now operated jointly by GATT and UNCTAD. *Director-General*, O. Long (*Switzerland*).

VEHICLE LICENCES

From October 1, 1974, registration and first licensing of vehicles has been done through local offices (known as Local Vehicle Licensing Offices) of the Department of the Environment's Driver and Vehicle Licensing Centre in Swansea. The records of existing vehicles are now being transferred to Swansea in stages. Local facilities for relicensing will remain available as follows:—

   (i) Before transfer of the record to the centralised system through local authority Local Taxation Offices (on behalf of the Secretary of State for the Environment), and

   (ii) after transfer through DOE Local Vehicle Licensing Offices and the Driver and Vehicle Licensing Centre at Swansea.

In certain circumstances licences are also issued by post offices. Details of the present duties chargeable on motor vehicles are set out in the Finance Act, 1975. The Vehicles (Excise) Act, 1971 provides inter alia that any vehicle kept on a public road but not used on roads is chargeable to excise duty as if it were in use.

Rates of duty for motor car and motor cycle licences are shown below. For Hackney Carriages the rates of duty are: Hackney Carriage with seating capacity not exceeding 20 persons, £20.00; additional for each person above 20 (excluding the driver) for which the vehicle has seating capacity, 50p.

Type of Vehicle	Exceeding	Not Exceeding	12 Months	4 Months
MOTOR CARS				
Electric and those first registered before January 1, 1947......	—	7 hp	28·80	10·55
Other than the above	—	—	40·00	14·65
MOTOR CYCLES				
With or without sidecar......................................	—	150 c.c.	4·00	—
With or without sidecar......................................	150 c.c.	250 c.c.	8·00	—
With or without sidecar......................................	250 c.c.	—	16·00	5·85
THREE WHEELERS				
Other than pedestrian-controlled............................	—	—	16·00	5·85
PEDESTRIAN-CONTROLLED VEHICLES..................	—	—	8·00	—

Rates

*Three-year Driving Licence..........	£1·00
*Replacement of lost or defaced licence	0·25
*Amendment of licence (*e.g.* for additional Group of vehicles), for the unexpired period..................	0·25
Provisional Driving Licence: 12 months..	1·00
Public Service Vehicle Driving Licence:	
3 years†.............................	0·15

  * But see opposite.

  † Additional to ordinary driving licence.

Driving Licences

The Road Traffic Act 1974 contains provision for driving licences to run until the age of 70 with renewals on application at 3-yearly intervals thereafter. These licences will be issued after January 1, 1976, to new drivers passing the driving test and to full licence holders upon renewal of their licences. There will be a new once-and-for-all fee of £5 (£1 for people aged 65 and over) for a " till 70 " licence. This fee will also cover subsequent issues. Drivers of any age with certain disabilities may be granted licences for one, two or three years.

Foreign Countries

THE following Articles have been revised under the direction of the various Governments or of the British Representatives at Foreign Capitals, to whom the Editor desires to express his warmest thanks. The Editor is also greatly indebted to the Embassies and Consulates-General in London for various corrections and additions.

Salaries and Allowances

The Salaries of Officers of H.M. Diplomatic Service are shown below. In addition foreign allowances are assigned to officers serving abroad:—

Grade 1—£18,675.
Grade 2—£14,000.
Grade 3—£12,410.
Grade 4—£9,060 to £11,410.
Grade 5—£6,090 to £7,860.
Grade 6—£5,310 to £6,310.
Grade 7A—£4,814 to £5,843.
Grade 7E—£4,310 to £5,110.
Grade 8—£2,805 to £4,080.
Grade 9—£2,275 to £4,080.
Grade 10—£1,610 to £2,950.

NOTE.—Salaries of Ambassadors and of Ministers Plenipotentiary at British Embassies and Legations abroad shown in the following articles are in each case the maximum salary for the post and exclude *Frais de Représentation.*

ABYSSINIA. *See* Ethiopia

AFGHANISTAN
(Afghänistän)

Head of State (President), Mohammad Daoud, *born* 1909, *assumed office*, July 17, 1973. (Also *Prime Minister, Minister of National Defence and Foreign Affairs.*)

COUNCIL OF MINISTERS

Prime Minister, Mohammad Daoud.
Deputy Prime Minister, Dr. Mohammad Hussañ Sharq.
Justice, Abdul Majid.
Finance, Sayed Abdul Ellah.
Interior, Faiz Mohammad.
Education, Prof. Dr. Abdul Qayum.
Frontier Affairs, (vacant).
Commerce, Mohammad Khan Jalalar.
Mines and Industries (vacant).
Public Works, Ghausuddin Faeq.
Communications (vacant).
Health, Prof. Dr. Nazar Mohammad Sekandar.
Information and Culture, Prof. Dr. Abdul Rahim Navin.
Agriculture and Irrigation, Ghulam Jaili Bakhtari.
Planning, Ali Ahmad Khoram.

EMBASSY IN LONDON
31 Princes Gate, S.W.7.
[01-589-8891]

Ambassador in London, His Excellency Hamidollah Enayat-Seraj (1974).

1st Secretary, Mohammed Yussuf Samad.

Afghanistan lies to the N. and W. of Pakistan. Its ancient name was Aryana, by which title it is referred to by Strabo, the Greek geographer who lived in the 1st century B.C. The estimated area is 250,000 sq. miles, and the population (U.N. estimate, 1969) 16,516,000. The population is very mixed. The most numerous race is the Pathan which predominates in the South and West, the main divisions being the Durranis, from whom the Royal Family came, and the Ghilzais. Then come the Tadjiks, an Iranian people mainly cultivators and small traders. There are also Uzbeks and Turkomen in the North, Hazaras in the centre, Baluchis in the South-West and the Nuristanis who live near the Chitral border. All are Sunni Moslems, except the Hazaras and Kizilbashes, who belong to the Shia sect.

Afghanistan is bounded on the W. by Iran (boundary fixed 1857 and 1904), on the S. by Baluchistan (now Pakistan) (boundary fixed 1896–7), on the N. by Asiatic Russia (boundary fixed 1886–7 and 1893–5), and on the E. by the N.W. Frontier Province (now Pakistan) (boundary fixed 1895). The northern boundary runs from Zulfikar on the Iran frontier to Kushk, the Russian railway terminus, to the Oxus (or Amu Darya, " Mother of Rivers ") which forms the boundary from Khamiab to Lake Victoria, whence the line to the Chinese frontier on the branch line from Mary and thence N.E. was fixed by the Pamir agreement of 1895. The Russo-Afghan frontier was demarcated by the Tashkent Boundary Commission in 1948. An Afghan-Chinese border treaty was signed in 1963 and the border demarcation in 1964. The Pakistan-Afghan frontier was settled by the Durand agreement of 1893.

Mountains, chief among which are the Hindu Kush, cover three-fourths of the country, the elevation being generally over 4,000 feet. There are three great river basins, the Oxus, Helmand, and Kabul. The climate is dry, with extreme temperatures.

Afghanistan is divided into 26 provinces each under a Governor.

Government.—The constitutional monarchy, introduced by the 1964 Constitution, was overthrown by a *coup d'état* on July 17, 1973. Pending a new constitution, the country is under rule by Presidential Decree.

By treaty of Nov. 22, 1921 (renewed in 1930), Great Britain and Afghanistan agreed to respect one another's internal and external independence; to recognize boundaries then existent, subject to a slight re-adjustment near the Khyber; and to establish Legations and consular offices. As successor state to the British Government, Pakistan has agreed that her relations with Afghanistan shall be based on the 1921 treaty.

Judiciary.—Hitherto Afghanistan has been ruled on the basis of Shariat or Islamic law. However, the Constitution introduced in 1965 provided for the creation of a legal code, and for a new structure of courts, consisting of a lower court in each *wuluswal* (sub province), and a court of appeal in each province, with a Supreme Court in Kabul. The complete separation of executive and judiciary in this constitution was abolished by Presidential Decree in July, 1973.

Defence.—The Army has been reorganized and is recruited by yearly calls. Service is for one year for officers and 2 years for other ranks. The peace strength is about 80,000. A military academy and military colleges are located in Kabul; and provision is made for training of regular officers abroad. A small Air Force is maintained. All military and air force equipment is now of Russian pattern.

Production.—Agriculture and sheep raising are the principal industries. There are generally two crops a year, one of wheat (the staple food), barley, or lentils, the other of rice, millet, maize, and *dal*. Sugar beet and cotton are grown. Afghanistan is rich in fruits. Sheep, including the Karakuli, and transport animals are bred. Silk, woollen and hair cloths and carpets are manufactured. Salt, silver, copper, coal, iron, lead, rubies, lapis lazuli, gold, chrome and talc are found.

The following main roads are open to motor traffic. (*a*) Internal: Kabul–Kandahar (310 miles); Kandahar–Herat (350 miles); Herat–Maimana to Mazar-i-Sharif (500 miles); Mazar-i-Sharif–Kabul (380 miles). Also Kabul–Khanabad–Faizabad (450 miles); Kabul–Gardez (80 miles); Kabul–Bamian (140 miles). The road from Kabul to the North has now been shortened by the completion in 1964 of the Salang pass. (*b*) Roads to the frontiers: Kabul–Khyber (175 miles); Kandahar–Chaman (70 miles) and roads from Herat to the Russian and Iranian borders. Five of the major roads in Afghanistan have been surfaced by U.S. and Soviet Aid. The Kabul–Khyber, Kandahar–Spin Baldak and Kabul–Kunduz–Qizil Qala roads are also surfaced. A network of minor roads fit for motor traffic in fine weather links up all important towns and districts.

Motor transport has taken the place of pack transport as the chief means of conveyance. The chief trade routes to Pakistan and India are the Khyber Pass route, from Kabul to Peshawar (190 miles), and the road from Kandahar to Chaman (70 miles). Internal air services between the main towns are being developed.

Language and Literature.—The languages of the country are Persian and Pushtu, and Turki (spoken by Uzbeks and Turkoman tribes in the North). The Turki language is unwritten in Afghanistan. All schoolchildren learn both Persian and Pushtu. The Government is encouraging the spread of Pushtu, the language of the Pathans. Education is free and nominally compulsory, elementary schools having been established in most centres; there are secondary schools in large urban areas and a university (established in 1932) at the capital.

The annual revenue consists largely of payments in kind, There are taxes on land, sales of animals, a grazing tax, customs duties, stamps, fines, receipts from State lands, monopolies, and factories and mining royalties; in addition certain businesses and individuals have become eligible for income-tax.

Trade with U.K.

	1973	1974
Imports from U.K.	£2,905,000	£3,345,000
Exports to U.K.	11,592,000	12,887,000

Exports are mainly Persian lambskins (Karakul), fruits, cotton, raw wool, carpets, spice and natural gas, while the imports are chiefly oil, cotton yarn and piece goods, tea, sugar, machinery and transport equipment.

CAPITAL, Kabul (about 500,000). The chief commercial centres are Kabul and Kandahar (125,000). Other provincial capitals are Herat (86,000), Mazar-i-Sharif (42,000), Jalalabad (22,000).

FLAG.—Vertical stripes of black, red and green, with gold emblem.

NATIONAL DAY.—July 17.

BRITISH EMBASSY
(Kabul)

Ambassador Extraordinary and Plenipotentiary, His Excellency John Kenneth Drinkall, C.M.G. (1974).
1st Secretary, J. A. Birch (*Consul*).
Oriental Secretary, Miss K. J. Himsworth.
2nd Secretary, B. W. V. Tomsett (*Commercial*).

British Council Representative.—P. A. Connell, P.O. Box 453, 855 Shehabuddin Wat, Kabul (British library).
Kabul is distant 5,000 miles from London, transit 21 days; by air 12 hours.

ALBANIA

Head of State, Haxhi Lleshi, *assumed office*, July 24, 1953.

Chairman, Council of Ministers, Mehmet Shehu.
Labour (= *Communist*) Party
Politbureau of the Central Committee, R. Alia; B. Balluku; A. Carcani; K. Hazbiu; Enver Hoxha; H. Kapo; A. Kellezi; S. Koleka; R. Marko; M. Myftiu; M. Shehu; K. Theodhosi; H. Toska (*full members*); P. Dume; P. Dodbiba; P. Peristeri; X. Spahiu (*candidate members*).
Secretariat of the Central Committee, Enver Hoxha (*First Secretary*); R. Alia; H. Kapo; H. Toska; P. Dode.

Situated on the Adriatic Sea, Albania is bounded on the north and east by Yugoslavia and on the south by Greece. The area of the Republic is estimated at 10,700 sq. miles, with a population (1974) of 2,377,600.

On Nov. 10, 1945, the British, U.S.A. and U.S.S.R. governments decided to recognize the Albanian administration under Colonel-General Enver Hoxha as the provisional government of Albania on the understanding that free elections would be held at an early date, in order that a truly representative government could be formed. Elections were held in December, 1945; on Jan. 11, 1946, the Constituent Assembly declared Albania an independent Republic. It was admitted to the United Nations in 1955. United Kingdom diplomatic relations with Albania ceased in 1946.

Although Albania was almost entirely an agricultural country (staple crops are wheat and maize), industrial expansion of her natural resources is now in process.

CAPITAL, Tirana (pop. 200,000).

FLAG.—Black-two-headed eagle surmounted by yellow outline star, all on a red field.

ALGERIA
(Republic of Algeria)

President of the Council of Revolution and Minister of National Defence, Houari Boumedienne, *assumed office* June 19, 1965.

CABINET
Minister of State, Cherif Belkacem.
Minister of State responsible for Transport, Rabah Bitat.
Minister of the Interior, Mohamed Ben Ahmed Abdelghani.
Foreign Affairs, Abdelaziz Bouteflika.
Information and Culture, Ahmed Taleb.
Health, Dr. Omar Boudjellab.
Justice, Boualem Benhamouda.
Industry and Energy, Belaid Abdesselam.
Public Works, Abdelkader Zaibek.
Agriculture and Agrarian Reform, Mohamed Larbi Tayebi.
Commerce, Layachi Yaker.
Labour and Social Affairs, Mohamed Said Mazouzi.
Higher Education and Scientific Research, Mohamed Benyahia.
Tourism, Abdelaziz Maoui.
Primary and Secondary Education, Abdelkrim Ben-mahmoud.
Religious Affairs, Mouloud Kassim.
Ex-Servicemen, Mahmoud Guennez.
Posts and Telecommunications, Said Ait Messaoudene.
Youth and Sports, Abdallah Fadel.
Finance, Smail Mahroug.

ALGERIAN EMBASSY IN LONDON
6 Hyde Park Gate, S.W.7
[01–584–9502–5]
Ambassador Extraordinary and Plenipotentiary, His Excellency Lakhdar Brahimi (1971).
Minister Plenipotentiary, Abdelkrim Chitour.
1st Secretary, Mohamed Larbi Tebbal.
Attachés, Lamri Khelif; Hamid Haraigue; Abdelkader Mesbahi; Abdelhamid Ghomari.

Algeria lies between 8° 45′W. to 12° E. longitude, 37° 6′ N. to a southern limit about 19° N. Area, 855,900 sq. miles (estimated). The population (U.N. estimate, 1970) is 13,547,000, of which 30 per cent. are urban dwellers.

Government,—Algiers surrendered to a French force on July 5, 1830, and Algeria was annexed to France in Feb. 1842. From 1881 the three northern departments of Algiers, Oran and Constantine formed an integral part of France. Between 1955 and 1960 these were reorganized to form 13 departments: Algiers, Tizi-Ouzou, Orleansville, (now El-Aznam) Médéa, Constantine, Bône (*now* Annaba), Setif, Batna, Oran, Tlemcen, Mostaganem, Saida and Tiaret. The Southern Territories of the Sahara, formerly a separate colony,

became an integral part of Algeria on the attainment of independence, forming the two additional departments of the Saoura and the Oasis. An armed rebellion led by the Moslem *Front de Libération Nationale (F.L.N.)* against French rule broke out on Nov. 1, 1954. French control of Algeria came to an end when President de Gaulle declared Algeria independent on July 3, 1962; by October, 1963, all agricultural land held by foreigners had been expropriated and by 1965 more than 80 per cent. of the French population had left Algeria. More have left since.

Ben Bella was elected President of the Republic in Sept., 1963, but was deposed and a Council of the Revolution presided over by Col. Boumedienne assumed power on June 19, 1965.

Development in Algeria is regulated by a series of national development plans. The 1970–73 plan provided for expenditure of approximately £3,200 million, with particular emphasis being placed on industrial development. The 1974–77 Plan provides for expenditure of the order of £13,000 million, and places greater emphasis on infrastructure development, and the social services.

Trade with U.K.

	1973	1974
Imports from U.K.	£37,900,000	£54,700,000
Exports to U.K.	45,700,000	36,100,000

Algeria's main exports are crude oil and liquefied natural gas. Principal imports from the United Kingdom are capital plant and equipment for industrial use.

Algeria's main industry is the hydrocarbons industry. Oil and natural gas are pumped from the Sahara to terminals on the coast before being exported; the gas is first liquefied at liquefaction plants at Skikda and Arzew.

Other major industries being developed include a steel industry, motor vehicles, building materials, paper making, chemical products and metal manufactures. All major industrial enterprises are now under State control.

Algeria has a rapidly expanding network of roads and railways. Considerable sums are also being spent on the development of the State airline, the national shipping company and telecommunications.

CAPITAL.— Ψ Algiers, population (census of 1966), 943,000. The large numbers of French inhabitants who left the country have largely been replaced by an influx of Algerians to the city. Other towns include Ψ Oran (328,000); Constantine (254,000); Ψ Annaba (*formerly* Bône) (168,000); Blida (99,000); Setif (98,000); Sidi-Bel-Abbès (91,000); Tlemcen 87,000); Mostaganem (75,000); Ψ Skikda (*formerly* Philippeville) (72,000); El Aznam (*formerly* Orleansville) (70,000) and Tizi Ouzou (53,000).

FLAG.—Red crescent and star on a vertically divided green and white background.

NATIONAL DAY.—November 1.

BRITISH EMBASSY
Résidence Cassiopée, 7 Chemin de Glycines,
Algiers.
Ambassador Extraordinary and Plenipotentiary, His Excellency John Armstrong Robinson, C.M.G. (1974).............................£6,925
Counsellor, D. J. Brown, M.B.E. (*Commercial*).
1st Secretary and Consul, D. C. Lees.
Cultural Attaché, British Council Representative, K. R. Hunter, 6 Avenue Souidani Boudjemaa, R. A. Hack, 6 Avenue Souidani Boudjemaa, Algiers. There is a British Council library in Algiers.

ANDORRA

A small, neutral principality situated on the southern slopes of the Pyrenees, between Spain and France, with an approximate area of 180 square miles and population of about 25,000, one-third of whom are native Andorrans. It is surrounded by mountains of 6,500 to 10,000 feet. Historians place the origin between the eight and ninth centuries. Andorra is divided into six Parishes, each of which has four Councillors elected by vote to the Valleys of Andorra Council of Twenty-four. Constitutionally, the sovereignty of Andorra is vested in two " Co-Princes ", the President of the French Republic and the Spanish Bishop of Urgel. These two " co-princes " can veto certain decisions of the Council of the Valleys but cannot impose their own decisions without the consent of the Council. They are represented by Permanent Delegates of whom one is the French Prefect of the Pyrenees Oriental Department at Perpignan and the other is the Spanish Vicar-General of the Diocese of Urgel. They are in turn represented in Andorra la Vella by two resident " Viguiers " known as the Viguier Français and the Viguier Episcopal, who have a joint responsibility for law and order and overall administration policy, together with judicial powers as members of the Supreme Court.

The official language of the country is Catalan, but French and Spanish are also spoken. Spanish *pesetas* and French *francs* are the accepted currency and the Budget is expressed in *pesetas*. A good road crossing the Valleys from Spain to France is open all year. Andorra has deposits of iron and quantities of alum and lead, stone quarries, granite, jasper and marble. Slate is abundant. Timber includes pine, fir, oak, birch and box-tree. Potatoes are produced in the highlands and tobacco in the plains. The climate is naturally cold for six months, but mild in spring and summer. The mountain slopes are suitable for skiing, and it is estimated that 2,250,000 tourists visit the Valleys during the year.

There are two radio stations in Andorra, one privately-owned and one operated by a French Government corporation. Both pay dues to the Council of the Valleys.

CAPITAL: Andorra la Vella (population 10,200).

FLAG.—Three vertical bands, blue, yellow, red; Andorran coat of arms frequently imposed on central (yellow) band but not essential.
H.M. Consul-General, L. J. Evans (Resident at Barcelona).

ANGOLA

Angola, which has an area of 488,000 square miles lies on the western coast of Africa; its population in 1970 was 5,673,046 although in the wake of fighting between the rival liberation movements, the white population, formally of several hundred thousand has been greatly reduced, by a mass exodus.

After a Portuguese presence of at least four centuries, and an anti-colonial war since 1961, Angola is due to receive full independence on November 11, 1975. However the transitional government under the Portuguese High Commissioner Brigadier-General Antonio Silva Cardoso set up on January 31 is in disarray. The three liberation movements, the Marxist M.P.L.A., the F.N.L.A. and UNITA previously " united " against Portugal are now engaged in bitter internecine fighting. Other factions support separate independence for Kabinda, the Angolan enclave on the Congo-Zaire coast (that in fact lacks any common border with Angola).

Angola exports diamonds, iron ore, oil and coffee.

CAPITAL.—Ψ(St. Paul de) Luanda (346,763 in 1970).

Nova Lisbôa is the capital-designate. There is a British Consulate-General at Luanda.
Consul-General, S. E. Croft, T.D.

ARABIA

Arabia is a peninsula in the south-west of the Asiatic continent, forming the connecting link between Asia and Africa, and lies between 30° 30′ —60° E, long. and 12° 45′—34° 50′ N. lat. The north-western limit is generally taken from 'Aqaba at the head of the Gulf of 'Aqaba, to a point in the Syrian Desert about 150 miles north-east, and thence northwards to a point about 50 miles due east of Damascus. The remaining land boundaries are in the form of a horse-shoe, encompassing the Syrian Desert, and descending in a south-easterly direction to the head of the Persian Gulf, and thus excluding the whole of Mesopotamia and the Euphrates Valley. The other boundaries of Arabia are the Red Sea and Gulf of Aden, the Arabian Sea, and the Persian Gulf and Gulf of Oman. Generally speaking, the peninsula consists of a plateau sloping from south-west to north-east towards the Euphrates Valley, except that the broad south-eastern promontory, which encloses the Persian Gulf, contains a coastal range in Oman.

The total area is estimated at 1,200,000 sq. miles (of which nearly one-half is occupied by the Syrian, Nafud, Dahana, and Rub Al Khali deserts), and the total population is believed to be about 10,000,000.

Language and Literature.—Arabic is spoken not only in Arabia, but in many other countries, either as the principal or auxiliary tongue, notably in Egypt and the Sudan, Libya, Morocco, Algeria, Iraq, Jordan, Syria, Lebanon; and to some extent also in Nigeria, Madagascar and Zanzibar. Owing to Moorish incursions it was formerly spoken in Spain, the Balearic Islands and Sicily. There are anthologies of pre- and post-Islamic poetry and a considerable prose literature, including popular romances and story cycles (such as " The Thousand Nights and One Night "), historical and biographical studies, and, resulting from the westernizing movement, there is a general revival of learning among Arabic speaking peoples. Many daily newspapers are published in Arabic and there is a native Arabic drama.

See also—BAHRAIN; KUWAIT; OMAN; QATAR; SAUDI ARABIA; THE YEMEN REPUBLICS: UNITED ARAB EMIRATES.

ARGENTINE REPUBLIC

(República Argentina)
President (acting) Sr. Halo Argentino Luder, acceded, September 14, 1975.
Interior, Sr. Angel Robledo.
Defence, Sr. Tomas Vottero.
Foreign (vacant).

EMBASSY IN LONDON.
9 Wilton Crescent, S.W.1.
[01–235–3717
Ambassador Extraordinary and Plenipotentiary, His Excellency Dr. Manuel Norberto Jose de Anchorena (1974).
Minister Plenipotentiary, Rafael M. Gowland (Chargé d'Affaires).
Naval Attaché, Rear Adm. Jorge Isaac Ariaya.
Military and Air Attaché, Cdre. Jorge A. van Thienen.
Economic Minister (vacant).
Economic and Commercial Counsellor, Antonio E. Seward.
Asst. Naval Attachés, Capt. Rafael M. Chechi; Cdr. Raúl A. Marino; Cdr. Arico H. Taladriz.
1st Secretary, Horacio R. Basso.
2nd Secretaries, Domingo Cullen; Federico Mirré.
3rd Secretaries, Luis D. Mendiola; Raymond Villagra.
Consulate-General, 53 Hans Place, S.W.1 (01–584–1701).
Counsellor, Alejandro H. Pineiro.
2nd Secretary, Señor Rosellini.
There is also a Consulate in Liverpool.

Argentina is a wedge-shaped country, occupying the greater portion of the southern part of the South American Continent, and extending from Bolivia to Cape Horn, a total distance of nearly 2,300 miles; its greatest breadth is about 930 miles. It is bounded on the north by Bolivia, on the north-east by Paraguay, Brazil, and Uruguay, on the south-east and south by the Atlantic, and on the west by Chile, from which Republic it is separated by the Cordillera de los Andes. On the west the mountainous Cordilleras, with their plateaux, extend from the northern to the southern boundaries: on the east are the great plains. Those in the north are thickly wooded and are known as El Gran Chaco, and further south lie the treeless pampas extending from the Bolivian boundary in the north to the Río Negro; and south of the

Río Negro are the vast plains of Patagonia. Argentina thus contains a succession of level plains, broken only in Córdoba by the San Luis and Córdoba ranges, in the north-western states by the eastern spurs of the Andes, and in the southern portion of the Province of Buenos Aires by the Tandil Hills (about 1,000 ft.) and the Sierra Ventana, near Bahia Blanca (about 3,000 ft.). The Paraná River, formed by the junction of the Upper Paraná with the Paraguay River, flows through the north-eastern states into the Atlantic, and is navigable throughout its course in Argentina; the Pilcomayo, Bermejo, and Salado del Norte are also navigable for some distance from their confluence with the Paraná. In the Province of Buenos Aires the Salado del Sud flows south-east for some 300 miles into Samborombon Bay (Atlantic). In the south Colorado and Río Negro rise in the extreme west and flow across the pampas into the Atlantic, many similar streams in Patagonia (notably the Chubut and Santa Cruz) traversing the country from the Andes to the Atlantic. The climate ranges from sub-tropical to cold temperate.

The Republic consists of 22 provinces, one territory (Tierra del Fuego) and one federal district (Buenos Aires), comprising in all an area of 1,079,965 square miles, with a population (Census of 1970) of 23,360,000 (male 11,600,000; female 11,760,000).

Government.—The estuary of La Plata was discovered in 1515 by Juan Díaz de Solís, but it was not until 1534 that Pedro de Mendoza founded Buenos Aires. This city was abandoned and later founded once more by Don Juan de Garay in 1580. In 1810 (May 25) Spanish rule was defied, and in 1816 (July 9), after a long campaign of liberation conducted by General Jos de San Martín, the independence of Argentina was declared by the Congress of Tucumán.

A revolt in September, 1955, overthrew the Government under the presidency of General Juan D. Perón and an interim Provisional Government was formed by the late General Eduardo Lonardi. This Provisional presidency passed to General Pedro Aramburu in November, 1955.

A Constituent Assembly, elected on July 28, 1957, decided that the country should revert to the 1853 Constitution. General Elections were held in February, 1958, and Dr. Arturo Frondizi was elected President. Following Perónist victories in the partial elections of March, 1962, the armed forces took over the Government and appointed the Chairman of the Senate, Dr. Guido, President. He held office until 1963. After general elections of July 7, Dr. Arturo Illia was elected President in July, 1963, and took office in October, 1963, for a period of six years. But after the bloodless revolution by the Armed Services of June 27–28, 1966, the Presidency was offered to and accepted by General Ongania. Congress was dissolved and the president then ruled by decree. A bloodless *coup* was carried out by the Commanders-in-Chief in June, 1970, and Brigadier General Levingston was appointed President. In March, 1971, another bloodless *coup* took place and the Commander-in-Chief of the Army, General Lanusse, became President and undertook to restore constitutional government. Elections were held in March, 1973, and Dr. Campora, candidate of the Perónist-led front, *Frejuli*, became President on May 25. On June 20, former-dictator General Juan Perón returned to Argentina after 18 years exile, and on July 13, Dr Campora resigned as President, so that elections could be held in which General Perón could stand as a candidate. Pending elections in September, Sr. Raul A. Lastiri was appointed Provisional President.

Elections were held on September 23, 1973, and Gen. Perón was elected with the highest number of votes ever gained by an Argentine President (62 per cent.), and an absolute majority in both Houses of Congress.

Gen. Perón was sworn in as President on October 12, 1973, with his wife, Señora Maria Estela Perón as Vice-President. Gen. Perón suffered from ill-health throughout most of his third Presidency, and on June 29, 1974, following a heart attack, he relinquished the Presidency in favour of his wife. Following Perón's death on July 1, 1974, Señora Perón was confirmed as President.

Following months of crisis, marked by political and economic uncertainty, and continuous violence from guerilla forces, President Perón temporarily relinquished her powers on September 14, 1975, and handed over power to her constitutional successor, Sr. Italo Argentino Luder, speaker of the Senate.

Agriculture.—Of a total land area of approximately 700,000,000 acres, farms occupy about 425,000,000. About 60 per cent. of the farmland is in pasture, 10 per cent. in annual crops, 5 per cent. in permanent crops and the remaining 25 per cent. in forest and wasteland. A large proportion of the land is still held in large estates devoted to cattle raising but the number of small farms is increasing. The principal crops are wheat, maize, oats, barley, rye, linseed, sunflower seed, alfalfa, sugar, fruit and cotton. Argentina is pre-eminent in the production of beef, mutton and wool, being self-sufficient in basic foodstuffs and conducting a large export trade in many others. Pastoral and agricultural products provide about 85 per cent. of Argentina's exports and they originate mainly from the pampas or rich central plain which embraces the provinces of Buenos Aires, Santa Fé, Entre Rios, Córdoba and La Pampa.

The following table shows the yield of some of the more important crops:

	1972-73 metric tons
Maize	10,300,000
Wheat	6,560,000
Linseed	297,000
Oats	561,000
Barley	732,000
Rye	613,000
Rice	316,000
Sunflower seed	1,070,000
Cotton (gross bulk production)	424,000
Sugar cane	17,600,000
Millet	233,000
Tobacco	84,000

Livestock.—Livestock population in 1974 was: cattle, 60,000,000; sheep, 44,000,000; and pigs, 4,000,000. Meat exports to UK fell from 57,676 tons in 1973 to 38,373 tons in 1974. 10,000,000 cattle were slaughtered in 1974 (1973, 9,800,000).

Mineral Production.—Oil is found in various parts of the Republic and is obtained to a considerable extent at Comodoro Rivadavia (Chubut), Mendoza, Plaza Huincul (Neuquen), Tartagal (Salta) and in other districts. A natural gas pipeline between Comodoro Rivadavia and Buenos Aires has been in operation since 1949. An oil pipeline from Campo Duran (Salta) to a refinery in San Lorenzo (Santa Fé) was put in service in March, 1960, as was also a natural gas pipeline from the same source to the outskirts of Buenos Aires. Another project of importance was the construction of the natural gas pipeline between Neuquén and Bahía Blanca, completed in 1970. The production of oil is of first importance to Argentina's rapidly expanding industries and, to some extent, to her economic and financial development. Total petroleum output for 1974 was 24,247,000 cubic metres compared with 24,441,000 cubic metres in 1973.

Coal, lead, zinc, tungsten, iron ore, sulphur, mica and salt are the other chief minerals being exploited. There are small worked deposits of beryllium, manganese, bismuth, uranium, antimony, copper, kaolin, arsenate, gold, silver and tin. Coal production in 1974 was 695,000 tons, compared with 561,000 tons in 1973; this is produced at the Rio Turbio mine in the province of Santa Cruz. The output of other materials is not large but greater attention is now being paid to the development of these natural resources, especially copper for which the Government and private companies are carrying out exploration.

Industries.—Meat-packing is one of the principal industries; flour-milling, sugar-refining, and the wine industry are also important. In recent years great strides have been made by the textile, plastic and machine tool industries and engineering, especially in the production of motor vehicles and steel manufactures.

Communications.—There are 25,386 miles of railways of which 14,000 miles are broad gauge (5′ 6″), 2,000 miles standard (4′ 8½″), 8,720 miles of narrow 1 metre, 537 miles of 0·75 metre and 129 miles of 0·60 metre. They are all State property. Plans are in hand for complete re-organization of the railways in order to improve their operating efficiency and reduce a very large financial deficit. The combined national and provincial road network totals approximately 137,000 miles of which 23,180 miles are surfaced. There are air services between Argentina and all the neighbouring republics, Europe, Asia, Canada and the U.S.A. Total tonnage entering Argentine ports in 1973 was 11,471,745.

There are 16 short-wave broadcasting stations, 150 medium wave (of which 65 are official). In addition there are 65 television stations, of which 4 are in Buenos Aires. About 3·8 million television receivers are in use.

Defence.—The Army consists of four corps organized into ten brigades, including mountain, jungle, airborne and armoured troops. It numbers about 5,000 officers, 15,000 N.C.O.s and 65–70,000 conscripts who serve 1 year.

The Navy consists of 2 cruisers, 1 aircraft carrier, 9 destroyers, 4 frigates/corvettes, 4 submarines, 4 minesweepers, 1 minehunter and ancillary craft.

The Air Force consists of 5 brigades and a training force, with a strength of 1,600 officers, 15,000 other ranks and 20,000 civilians. Aircraft total 321, including Meteor IV's, Skyhawk A.4 BS1, Lockheed C130, Fokker F27, HS.748 and Mirage III.

Education—Primary and Secondary. The educational reform programme has been frozen since early 1971. The government is formulating a new education policy. At the moment, education is compulsory for the 7 grades of primary school (6 to 13). Secondary schools (14 to 17+) are available in and around Buenos Aires and in most of the important towns in the interior of the country. Most secondary schools are administered by the Central Ministry of Education in Buenos Aires, while primary schools are administered by the Central Ministry or by Provincial Ministries of Education. Private schools, of which there are many, are also loosely controlled by the Central Ministry. *Teacher-Training* now takes place at post school level, courses lasting from 2 to 4 years. *Universities*—Many new universities have been created over the last two years. The total is now over 50 with 24 national (including the Federal Technological University), 25 private and a small number of provincial universities.

Language and Literature.—Spanish is the language of the Republic and the literature of Spain is accepted as an inheritance by the people. There is little indigenous literature before the break from Spain, but all branches have flourished since the latter half of the nineteenth century, particularly journalism. Under the first Perón régime many newspapers and reviews were closed down and others turned into Government mouthpieces. About 450 daily newspapers are published in Argentina, including 7 major ones in the city of Buenos Aires. The English language newspaper is the *Buenos Aires Herald* (daily). There are several other foreign language newspapers.

TRADE

	1972	1973
	Dollars U.S.	
Total Imports....	1,904,682,000	2,235,331,000
Total Exports....	1,941,098,000	3,266,204,000

Trade with U.K.

	1973	1974
Imports from U.K..	£41,732,000	£49,204,000
Exports to U.K.....	106,132,000	98,467,000

For Exchange Rate *see* p. 83.

CAPITAL.—Ψ Buenos Aires, Pop. (Dec. 1970), Metropolitan area 2,972,453; with suburbs, 8,774,529. Other large towns are: Ψ Rosario de Santa Fé (798,292), Córdoba (798,663), Ψ La Plata (408,300), Ψ Mar del Plata (317,444), San Miguel de Tucuman (326,000), Santa Fé (312,427) and Mendoza (118,568).

FLAG.—Horizontal bands of blue, white blue; gold sun in centre of white band.

NATIONAL DAY.—July 9.

Dr. Luis Agote 2412, Buenos Aires.
Ambassador Extraordinary and Plenipotentiary, His Excellency, Derick Rosslyn Ashe, C.M.G. (1975).
Minister, E. F. G. Maynard (*Commercial*).
Counsellors, J. W. R. Shakespeare, M.V.O. (*Consul-General*; D. N. Higginbottom.
1st *Secretaries*, J. Illman (*Head of Chancery*); J. R. Cowling (*Information*); I. I. Morgan, M.B.E. (*Administration*); R. A. M. Hendrie (*Commercial*).
2nd *Secretaries*, D. G. Alexander; H. E. Bicheno; H. J. S. Pearce.
Defence and Air Attaché, Col. R. W. Millo.
Naval Attaché, Capt. J. Thomas, R.N.
Veterinary Attaché, R. W. Steele.

BRITISH CONSULAR OFFICES
There are British Consular Offices at *Buenos Aires*, *Cipolletti*, *Comodoro Rivadavia*, *La Plata*, *Rio Gallegos* and *Rio Grande* (*Tierra del Fuego*).

BRITISH COUNCIL
Representative in Argentine, P. B. Naylor, Marcelo T de Alvear, 590 Buenos Aires.

BRITISH CHAMBER OF COMMERCE
Calle 25 de Mayo 444, (5° Piso), Buenos Aires.
Buenos Aires is 7,160 miles from Southampton; transit, 19 days by steamship; 18 hours by air.

AUSTRIA

President of the Austrian Republic, Dr. Rudolf Kirchschläger, *born* 1915; *elected* June 23, 1974.
CABINET
Chancellor, Dr. Bruno Kreisky.
Vice-Chancellor and Minister of Social Affairs, Ing. Rudolf Häuse.
Minister for the Interior, Otto Rösch.
Justice, Dr. Christian Broda.
Transport, Erwin Lanc.
Foreign Affairs, Dr. Erich Bielka-Karltreu.
Finance, Dkfm. Hannes Androsch.
Agriculture, Dip. Ing. Dr. Oskar Weihs.
Defence, Brig. Karl Lütgendorf.
Education, Dr. Fred Sinowatz.
Trade and Industry, Dr. Josef Staribacher.

Building, Josef Moser.
Science and Research, Frau Dr. Hertha Firnberg.
Health and Environment, Frau Dr. Ingrid Leodolter.
AUSTRIAN EMBASSY IN LONDON
18 Belgrave Square, S.W.1
[01-235 3731]
Ambassador Extraordinary and Plenipotentiary, His Excellency Dr. Kurt Enderl (1975).
Minister-Counsellor, Dr. Ingo Mussi, M.V.O.
Counsellor, Dr. Helga Winkler-Campagna.
3rd *Secretary*, Dr. P. Lang.
Defence Attaché, Brig.-Gen. H. Wingelbauer.
Attachés, Dr. Ernst Menhofer (*Press*); Mrs. M. Ballod (*Consular Affairs*); Mrs. A. Schmidt; Mrs. B. Neider (*Administration*).

Austria is a country of Central Europe bounded on the north by Czechoslovakia, on the south by Italy and Yugoslavia, on the east by Hungary, on the north-west by Germany and on the west by Switzerland. Its area is 32,376 square miles and its population (estimated June, 1975), 7,456,403.

Government.—The Austrian Federal Republic comprises nine provinces (Vienna, Lower Austria, Upper Austria, Salzburg, Tyrol, Vorarlberg, Carinthia, Styria and Burgenland) and was established in 1918 on the break-up of the Austro-Hungarian Empire. In March 13, 1938, as a result of the *Anschluss*, Austria (*Oesterreich*) was incorporated into the German *Reich* under the name *Ostmark*. After the liberation of Vienna in 1945, the Austrian Republic was reconstituted within the frontiers of 1937 and, after a period of provisional government, a freely-elected Government took office on December 20, 1945. The country was divided at this time into four zones occupied respectively by the U.K., U.S.A., U.S.S.R. and France, while Vienna was jointly occupied by the four Powers. On May 15, 1955, the Austrian State Treaty was signed in Vienna by the Foreign Ministers of the four Powers and of Austria. This Treaty recognized the re-establishment of Austria as a sovereign, independent and democratic state, having the same frontiers as on January 1, 1938. It entered into force on July 27, 1955.

There is a National Assembly of 183 Deputies. In the elections of October, 1971, the Socialists won an overall majority of the votes.

The state of the parties in June 1975, was:

Socialist Party...................	93
People's Party...................	80
Freedom Party (right wing)........	10

Religion and Education.—The predominant religion is Roman Catholic. Elementary education is free and compulsory between the ages of 6 and 15 and there are good facilities for secondary, technical and professional education. There are Universities at Vienna, Graz, Innsbruck, Salzburg, Linz and Klagenfurt.

Language and Literature.—The language of Austria is German, but the rights of the Slovene- and Croat-speaking minorities in Carinthia, Styria and Burgenland are protected. The press is free. There are 6 daily papers in Vienna and 24 in the provinces, as well as numerous weeklies and monthlies.

Communications.—Internal communications in Austria are partly restricted because of the mountainous nature of the country, and road and rail routes must, of necessity, follow the river valleys. The railways in Austria are state-owned and have 5,901 km. of track of which 2,660 km. had been electrified by June, 1975. While road surfaces in many cases are not up to British standards, the main roads linking the major towns are generally good and relatively fast. The *Westautobahn*, completed in 1967, links Munich, Salzburg, Linz and Vienna. A second major autobahn (*Inntal Autobahn*) is now complete between Kufstein, Innsbruck and the Brenner Pass, thus linking the West German and Italian autobahn networks through Austria. A third major autobahn (*Südautobahn*) linking Vienna with Graz, Klagenfurt and Villach is under construction and about half of it is already open for use.

Production and industry.—Agriculture is an important industry, the arable land producing wheat, rye, barley, oats, maize, potatoes, sugar beet, turnips, and miscellaneous crops. Many varieties of fruit trees flourish and the vineyards produce excellent wine. The pastures support horses, cattle and pigs. Timber forms a valuable source of Austria's indigenous wealth, about 39 per cent. of the total land area consisting of forest areas. Coniferous species predominate and account for more than 80 per cent. of the timber under cultivation. Hardwood trees are mainly confined to Lower Austria. Spruce is the most common among the conifers (about 60 per cent. of the total) and beech is the most prevalent of the broad leaf trees.

Austria has important heavy industries. Production figures for 1974 include (in thousands of metric tons): pig iron 3,443, steel 4,699, rolled products 3,372. Raw magnesite, nitrogenous fertilizers, paper, chemical pulp and synthetic fibres are produced in quantity. In addition, motor cycles, scooters, buses, tractors and motor lorries are produced.

Energy.—Of Austria's energy requirement in 1974, 47 per cent. was supplied from internal sources. Production of crude oil in Northern and Eastern Austria amounted to 2·6 million metric tons in 1974, 25 per cent. of annual consumption. Oil imports came from Iraq (58·5 per cent.), Libya (15·1 per cent.), the U.S.S.R. (13·2 per cent.) and Iran (9·2 per cent.). Austria imported 2·0 thousand million cubic metres of gas in 1974 (52 per cent. of annual consumption) nearly all of which came from the U.S.S.R. Many hydro-electric power sites have already been developed in Austria and a long run plan has been evolved for further development. Production in 1974 was 22,662 million kWH (73 per cent. of total electricity consumption).

Since these resources are limited, a 700 mW nuclear power station is under construction, due to commence operation in September 1976 and tenders have been issued for a second.

Minerals.—There are iron ore and oil deposits. In addition there are useful deposits of brown coal, magnesite, salt and lead. There are also limited deposits of copper.

FINANCE.	1973	1974
	Schillings	*'000,000*
Ordinary Budget:		
Expenditure.............	135,285	160,303
Revenue.................	128,267	148,531
Extraordinary Budget:		
Expenditure.............	5,857	6,836
Revenue.................	43	104

Trade with U.K.

	1973	1974
Imports from U.K..	£136,709,000	£153,139,000
Exports to U.K.....	178,228,000	203,659,000

Currency.—The unit of currency is the *Schilling* of 100 *Groschen*, reintroduced in December, 1945. The rate of exchange (June 1975) was 37·80 Austrian *schillings* = £1, at par.

CAPITAL, Vienna, on the Danube, population 1,614,841. Other towns are Graz (248,500), Linz (202,874), Innsbruck (115,197), Salzburg (128,845), and Klagenfurt (82,512).

FLAG.—Horizontal stripes of red, white, red, with eagle crest on white stripe. NATIONAL DAY.—October 26.

BRITISH EMBASSY
Vienna.

Ambassador Extraordinary and Plenipotentiary, His Excellency Sir Denis Seward Laskey, K.C.M.G., C.V.O. (1972)

Counsellor (*Commercial*), R. Brash.

Counsellor (IAEA/UNIDO), D. Slater.

1st Secretaries, M. F. Chapman (*Head of Chancery*); J. D. M. Blyth; R. Harrison; J. W. Cox; D. K. Urquhart (*Commercial*); P. J. Kirchner, M.B.E. (*H.M. Consul*); H. J. Bowe (*Information*).

Defence Attaché, Lt.-Col. B. A. Stewart-Wilson.

There are British Consular Offices at *Vienna* and *Innsbruck*.

British Council Representative, T. F. Hibbett, Schenkenstrasse 4, 1010 Vienna.

BAHRAIN

Amir, H. H. Shaikh Isa bin Sulman Al Khalifah, K.C.M.G., *born* 1932; *acceded* Dec. 16, 1961.

CABINET

Prime Minister, H.E. Shaikh Khalifa Isa bin Sulman Al-Khalifa.

Minister of Defence, H.E. Sheikh Hamed bin Isa Al-Khalifa (*Heir Apparent*).

Finance, Sayed Mahmud Al-Alawi.

Foreign Affairs and (acting) *Information*, Sheikh Mohammed bin Mubarak Al-Khalifa.

Education, Shaikh Abdul Aziz bin Mohamed Al-Khalifa.

Justice, Sheikh Khalid bin Mohammed Al-Khalifa.

Development and Engineering Services, Yusuf Ahmed Shirawi.

Labour and Social Affairs, Ibrahim Humaidan.

Health, Dr. Ali Fakhroo.

Legal Affairs, Dr. Husain Mohamed Al-Baharna.

Municipalities and Agriculture, Sheikh Abdulla bin Khalid Al-Khalifa.

Minister of State for the Cabinet, Jawad Salim Al-Arrayedh.

Secretary to the Cabinet, Saeed Zeera.

EMBASSY IN LONDON
98 Gloucester Road, S.W.7
[01-370 5132/3]

Ambassador Extraordinary and Plenipotentiary (vacant).
Counsellor, Dr. Wasfi Nimer.
2nd Secretary, Ali Mohamed Al-Arrayed.
3rd Secretary, Ebrahim Salahudin Ebrahim.

Bahrain consists of a group of low-lying islands situated halfway down the Persian Gulf some 20 miles off the east coast of Arabia. The largest of these, Bahrain Island itself, is about 30 miles long and 10 miles wide at its broadest. The two most important towns are Manama (89,608) and Muharraq (49,387). The latter is situated on a separate island of the same name which is connected with Bahrain Island by a causeway 1½ miles long. The population of the islands at the Census held in 1971 was 216,000, of whom about half belong to the Shia Sect, the remainder, including the ruling family being Sunnis. There are 6,000 Europeans and Americans and 30,000 non-Bahrainis of whom about half are Iranians, Indians and Pakistanis. The standard of living is high among the large and influential merchant class and steadily rising among the lower social groups.

Bahrain enjoys a typical Persian Gulf climate with long, mild winters and an annual rainfall of about 3″. Summer extends from May to October, with temperatures between 100° F. and 115° F. and humidity often approaching 100 per cent. The surrounding sea abounds in a variety of fish, and some of the best prawns in the world inhabit the warm sheltered waters.

Local government is the responsibility of six municipalities. There is free primary and secondary education and free medical treatment. The new town of Madinat Isa, planned to rehouse nearly 18 per cent. of the population, was formally opened by the Ruler in 1968.

In earlier days the only industry was the pearl trade, of which Bahrain was an important centre, but this has declined since the advent of the cultured pearl and petroleum dominates the scene. Oil was discovered in 1932 and The Bahrain Petroleum Company, Limited (BAPCO), has its headquarters in Awali, some eleven miles from Manama. The company also operates a refinery and about 70 per cent. of the oil refined is piped from Saudi Arabia.

The second source of revenue is that of Bahrain's traditional *entrepôt* trade. The island is conveniently situated to handle goods in transit to the mainland and it is estimated that not less than 70 per cent. of the imports unloaded at Bahrain were, up to a few years ago, destined for onward movement. In 1966 Bahrain re-exported 30 per cent. of its imports compared to the 28·3 per cent. in 1965 and by 1968 re-exports had risen to 35·5 per cent. To encourage the *entrepôt* trade, free transit facilities were introduced in the port of Bahrain on January 1, 1958. A new harbour, named the Mina Sulman after the late Ruler, was opened in May, 1962.

Bahrain is being developed as a major manufacturing state, the first important enterprise being the Aluminium Bahrain smelter, operated by a company whose shareholders include the Bahrain Government and British, Swedish, German and United States interests. The aluminium operation is one of the largest non-oil industries in the Middle East. Ancillary industries being developed around aluminium smelting include the production of aluminium powder and paste. Other projects at present under consideration include the further development of marine industries and the expansion of Bahrain's tourist potential.

Bahrain International Airport is the Gulf's main air communication centre. The runway has been extended to 12,000 feet—and a new terminal building constructed to meet the demands of the Jumbojets which use Bahrain as a main stopping point on the routes between the Far East and Australia on the one side and Europe and the Middle East on the other. The new terminal building is designed to handle 500 passengers an hour.

The principal imports and re-exports are household goods, foodstuffs, piece-goods, timber and building materials (especially cement), wearing apparel, vehicles and machinery.

Trade with U.K.

	1970	1971
Imports from U.K.	£24,340,000	£25,181,000
Exports to U.K.	1,554.000	4,046,000

Manama, the capital and commercial centre, extends for two miles along the northern shore of Bahrain Island. Banking services are provided by the Chartered Bank, the British Bank of the Middle East, the National Bank of Bahrain, and the Bank of Bahrain and Kuwait, among others. There is an excellent world-wide telephone service, via satellite, and telex service. Electricity and water supply is available in all towns and villages.

FLAG: Red, with vertical serrated white bar next to staff.

CAPITAL, Ψ Manama; population 89,608.

BRITISH EMBASSY
P.O. Box 114, Manama.
Ambassador Extraordinary and Plenipotentiary, His Excellency Robert Mathieson Tesh, C.M.G. (1972).

British Council Representative, W. E. Brook, P.O. Box 452, Manama.

BELGIUM
(Royaume de Belgique.)

King of the Belgians, H.M. King Baudouin, K.G., *born* Sept. 7, 1930; *succeeded* July 17, 1951, on the abdication of his father, King Leopold III, after having acted as Head of the State since August 11, 1950; *married* Dec. 15, 1960, Doña Fabiola de Mora y Aragòn.

Heir Presumptive, H.R.H. Prince Albert, *born* June 6, 1934, *brother* of the King; *married* July 2, 1959, Donna Paola Ruffo di Calabria, and has *issue* Prince Philippe Léopold Louis Marie, *b.* April 15, 1960; Princess Astrid Josephine-Charlotte Fabrizia Elisabeth Paola Marie, *b.* June 5, 1962; Prince Laurent, *b.* Oct. 20, 1963.

CABINET
(October 4, 1974)

Prime Minister, M. Léo Tindemans (*CVP*).
Defence and Brussels Affairs, M. Paul Vanden Boeynants (*PSC*).
Finance, M. Willy de Clerq (*PVV*).
Foreign Affairs and Development Co-operation, M. Renaat van Elslande (*CVP*).
Health and Family Affairs, M. Joseph de Saeger (*CVP*).
Social Security, M. Placide de Paepe (*CVP*).
Justice, M. Herman Vanderpoorten (*PVV*).
Foreign Trade, M. Michel Toussaint (*PLP*).
Interior, M. Joseph Michel (*PSC*).
Agriculture, M. Albert Lavens (*CVP*).
Communications, M. Jozef Chabert (*CVP*).
Middle Classes, M. Louis Olivier (*PLP*).
Public Works, M. Jean Defraigne (*PLP*).
Economic Affairs (vacant).
Labour and Employment, Walloon Affairs, Housing and Land Use, M. Alfred Califice (*PSC*).
Dutch Culture and Flemish Affairs, Rita de Backer-Van Ocken (*CVP*).
French Culture, M. Henri-François Van Aal (*PSC*).
Education (Dutch), M. Herman de Croo (*P.V.C.*).
Education (French), M. Antoine Humblet (*PSC*).
Institutional Reform (French), M. François Perin (*RW*).

Institutional Reform (Flemish), M. Robert Vandekerckhove (*CVP*).

STATE SECRETARIES

Wallon Regional Economy, M. Jean Gol (*RW*).
Flemish Regional Economy, Land Use and Housing, M. Luc Dhoore (*CVP*).
Regional Economy, assistant to the Minister for Brussels Affairs, M. August De Winter (*PVV*).
Civil Service, assistant to the Prime Minister, M. Louis d'Haeseleer (*PVV*).
Environment, assistant to the Prime Minister, M. Karel Poma (*PVV*).
Budget and Scientific Policy, assistant to the Prime Minister, M. Gaston Geens (*CVP*).
Economic Affairs assistant, M. Etienne Knoops (*RW*).
Social Affairs, assistant to the Minister for Walloon Affairs, M. Robert Moreau (*RW*).

[*CVP*= Christelijke Volkspartij
PSC= Parti social-chrétien
PVV= Partij voor Vrijheid en Vooruitgang
PLP= Parti pour la liberté et le progrès
RW= Rassemblement Wallon]

BELGIAN EMBASSY IN LONDON.

Chancery and Passport Office, 103 Eaton Square, S.W.1.
[01-235 5422]
Ambassador Extraordinary and Plenipotentiary, His Excellency Robert Rothschild, K.C.M.G. (1973).
Minister Counsellors, M. R. Six; M. J. Kadijk (*Economic Affairs*).
Counsellors, M. Georges Van der Espt (*Culture and Information*); M. Roger P. Martin; M. A. Adam; M. Maurice Cammaerts (*Agriculture*).
Naval, Military and Air Attaché, Colonel Jules E. H. H. G. Kaisin.
Economic Attaché, M. Eric Duchéne.

A Kingdom of Western Europe, with a total area of 11,775 square miles and a population, (Dec., 1970) of 9,650,944. The Kingdom of Belgium is bounded on the N. by the Kingdom of the Netherlands, on the S. by France, on the E. by Germany and Luxemburg, and on the W. by the North Sea.

Belgium has a frontier of 898 miles, and a seaboard of 41 miles. The Meuse and its tributary, the Sambre, divide it into two distinct regions, that in the west being generally level and fertile, while the table-land of the Ardennes, in the east, has for the most part a poor soil. The " polders " near the coast, which are protected by dykes against floods, cover an area of 193 sq. miles. The highest hill, Signal de Botranges, rises to a height of 2,276 feet, but the mean elevation of the whole country does not exceed 526 feet. The principal rivers are the Scheldt and the Meuse. Brussels has a mean temperature of 49° F. (summer 65°, winter 37°).

Belgium is divided linguistically between those who speak Dutch (the Flemings, who occupy the North) and those who speak French (the Walloons, who occupy the South) with a small Germanspeaking region east of Liège. Nearly all Belgians are Roman Catholics.

Government.—The kingdom formed part of the " Low Countries " (Netherlands) from 1815 until Oct. 14, 1830, when a National Congress proclaimed its independence, and on June 4, 1831, Prince Leopold of Coburg was chosen hereditary king. The separation from the Netherlands and the neutrality and inviolability of Belgium were guaranteed by a Conference of the European Powers, and by the *Treaty of London* (April 19, 1839), the famous " Scrap of Paper," signed by Austria, France, Great Britain, Prussia, The Netherlands, and Russia. On Aug. 4, 1914, the Germans invaded Belgium, in violation of the terms of the treaty.

The Kingdom was again invaded by Germany on May 10, 1940. The whole Kingdom eventually fell into enemy hands and was occupied by Nazi troops until the victorious advance of the Allies in September 1944. A monument at Hertain in the province of Hainault (where British forces crossed the frontier on Sept. 3, 1944), set up by the Anglo-Belgian Union, was unveiled on St. George's Day, 1949.

According to the Constitution of 1831 the form of government is a constitutional representative and hereditary monarchy with a bicameral legislature, consisting of the King, the Senate and the Chamber of Representatives. The Senate is partly directly and partly indirectly elected (or co-opted) for 4 years. 106 members out of 181 are directly elected. The Chamber of Representatives consists of not more than 1 per 40,000 inhabitants and is elected directly by all adult nationals.

The last election for the Chamber of Deputies was held on March 10, 1974, and M. Tindemans's Social Christians' Party won 32 per cent. of the votes. The results were as follows:

	Seats	
	1974	(1971)
Social Christians.........	72	(67)
Socialist.................	59	(61)
Liberals.................	30	(31)
French-speaking bloc......	25	(27)
Flemish Nationalist " People's Union "...............	21	(21)
Communists.............	4	(5)

Elections were also held for the Senate, 106 of whom were directly elected, 50 were appointed by the newly-elected provincial councils, and 25 co-opted by secret ballot. The overall distribution of seats in the Senate was as follows (1971 results in parentheses): Social Christians, 66 (61); Socialists, 50 (49); Liberals, 27 (29); French-speaking bloc, 21 (19); Flemish Nationalists, 16 (19); Communists, 1 (1). H.R.H. Prince Albert is also a member of the Senate.

On April 24, 1974, M. Tindemans formed a minority coalition Government of Social Christians and Liberals, who were sworn in on April 25. M. Tindemans has since re-shuffled his Government on two occasions, and he has enlarged it to include the French-speaking Rassemblement Wallon.

Production.—Belgium is essentially a manufacturing country. With no natural resources except coal, annual production of which formerly averaged some 30,000,000 tons but which dropped to 8,841,000 metric tons in 1973 following the closing of uneconomic pits, industry is based largely on the processing for re-export of imported raw materials. In 1973 about 4·1 per cent. of the active population was engaged in agriculture and forestry, the former supplying four-fifths of the population's needs. Principal industries are coal, steel and metal products (Mons, Charleroi, Liège, Namur, Hainault, Brabant and Limburg), textiles (Ghent, Bruges, Courtrai, Verviers, etc.), glass nitrogen, heavy chemicals, sugar, breweries, etc. Crude steel output in 1973 was 15,527,000 metric tons.

Education.—The budget for education (over 100,000,000,000 Belgian francs) represents approximately a quarter of the national budget and does not include the amount spent by the Communes, provinces and the church in subsidized schools. 5453 nursery schools provide free education for the 2½ to 6 age group. Of the 8368 primary schools (6 to 12 years) approximately 5000 are administered by the State, province or commune and the remainder are free institutions (predominantly Roman Catholic). Of the 1134 secondary schools offering a general academic education slightly over half are free institutions (predominantly Roman Catholic but subsidized by the State) and the remainder official institutions. The official school leaving age is 14. There are 3437 technical and vocational institutions of which 2700 cater for students in the secondary sector.

Language and Literature.—Dutch is spoken in the provinces of West Flanders, East Flanders, Antwerp, Limburg, and the northern half of Brabant, and French in the provinces of Hainault, Namur Luxemburg, Liège and the southern half of Brabant. Dutch is recognized as the official language in the northern areas and French in the southern (Walloon) area and there are guarantees for the respective linguistic minorities. Brussels is officially bi-lingual.

In July, 1971, the Belgian Parliament passed three Bills together implementing the constitutional amendments introduced in December 1970, to ease friction between the French-speaking and Dutch-speaking communities. The first Bill established a cultural council for each linguistic group, in operation from Dec. 1, 1971, all members of the Chamber of Representatives and the Senate being members of one council or the other. A Cultural Council for the German-speaking community also has since been established. The second Bill defined the powers of the cultural councils, providing that the councils would be responsible for certain aspects of cultural life; commissions for co-operation with the other council would be set up, with a statutory obligation to hold at least two meetings with the other council in each Parliamentary session. The third Bill provided for the establishment of five " agglomerations " of municipalities centred on Antwerp, Brussels, Charleroi, Ghent and Liège and the federation of small municipalities, with special provision in respect of the border boroughs of Brussels (which have a predominantly Flemish population) designed gradually to reduce the influence of the French speakers in that area. Regional councils for Flanders, Wallonia and Brussels were established in 1974.

The literature of France and the Netherlands is supplemented by an indigenous Belgian literary activity, in both French and Dutch. Maurice Maeterlinck (1862–1949) was awarded the Nobel Prize for Literature in 1911. Emile Verhaeren (1855–1916) was a poet of international

standing. Of contemporary Belgian writers, perhaps the most celebrated is Georges Simenon (*born* at Liège in 1903). There are 45 daily newspapers (French, Dutch and some German) in Belgium.

FINANCE

Ordinary Budget	1973	1974
	B. Fr. (millions)	
Revenue..................	406,642	472,623
Expenditure..............	406,642	473,363
Extraordinary Budget		
Revenue..................	802	604
Expenditure..............	86,900	82,610

The unit of currency is the Belgian *franc*. Since June 1972 there has been no fixed rate. (*See also* p. 83)

TRADE

	1972	1973
	(*'000 Francs*)	(*'000 Francs*)
Total Imports......	681,772,789	852,639,796
Total Exports......	710,979,595	870,244,933

Trade with U.K.

	1972	1973
Imports from U.K...	£385,700,000	£612,200,000
Exports to U.K......	309,500,000	434,300,000

COMMUNICATIONS.—On Dec. 31, 1972, there were 4,080 kilometres of normal gauge railways operated by the Belgian National Railways, of which 1,232 kilometres were electrified; the length of regional railways operated in 1973 was 215·8 kilometres. Belgian National Railways also operate 4,425 kilometres of regular bus routes. Other operators run 14,179 km. of bus routes. On Dec. 31,1973, there were 1,625, 726 telephone subscribers in Belgium.

Ship canals include *Ghent-Terneuzen* (18 miles, of which half is in Belgian and half in the Netherlands; constructed 1825–27) which permits the passage to Ghent of ships up to 60,000 tons; the Canal of Willebroek Rupel-Brussels (20 miles, by which ships drawing 18 ft reach Brussels from the sea; opened in 1922); and *Bruges* (from Zeebrugge on the North Sea to Bruges, 6½ miles; opened in 1922). The *Albert Canal* (79 miles), which figured prominently in the fighting (Sept. 1944) for the relief of Belgium and the Netherlands and for the invasion of Germany, links Liège with Antwerp; it was completed in 1939 and accommodates barges up to 1,350 tons. The modernization of the port of Antwerp begun in 1956 is well advanced. Inland waterway approaches to Antwerp are also to be improved. The river Meuse from the Dutch to the French frontiers, the river Sambre between Namur and Monceau, the river Scheldt from Antwerp-Ghent and the Brussels-Charleroi Canal are being widened or deepened to take barges up to 1,350 tons.

In 1973 there were 12,830 km. of trunk roads of which about 1,030 km. are motorways. Most of the maritime trade of Belgium is carried in foreign shipping, the mercantile marine consisting (1973) of 89 vessels (1,091,984 metric tons), in addition to which there were 268 fishing boats.

The Belgian National Airline *Sabena* operates regular services between Brussels and London, and many continental centres, as well as overseas services to the United States, Zaire, Canada, Mexico, Guatemala, Middle East, Far East, India, etc. Many foreign airlines call at Brussels.

CITIES AND TOWNS

The Capital, BRUSSELS, had an estimated population (Dec. 31, 1971) of 1,075,000 (with suburbs). Other towns are ΨAntwerp, the chief port (67,259); Ψ Ghent (229,687), which has large cotton and flax spinning mills, and is the second port of importance after Antwerp, while its flower shows are famous; Liège (446,990), the centre of the iron industry, and Charleroi (218,089), the important coal-mining and metallurgical centre; ΨBruges (118,000); ΨOstend (47,230); Malines (67,730). Brussels is 224 miles from London; transit, by rail and sea, 8 hrs.; by air, 1 hr.

NATIONAL FLAG.—Three vertical bands, black, yellow, red.

NATIONAL DAY.—July 21 (Accession of King Leopold I, 1831).

BRITISH EMBASSY.

28 Rue Joseph II, 1040 Brussels.

Ambassador Extraordinary and Plenipotentiary, His Excellency David Francis Muirhead, C.M.G., C.V.O. (1974)

Counsellors, I. S. Winchester (*Commercial*); The Viscount Dunrossil; C. P. H. T. Isolani, C.B.E., M.V.O. (*Information*).

Defence (Military and Naval) Attaché, Col. W. H. Atkins, O.B.E.

Air Attaché, Wing Cdr. J. D. Evans.

1st Secretaries, A. C. D. S. MacRae (*Head of Chancery*); G. S. McWilliam, O.B.E. (*Consul*); J. N. Elam (*Commercial*); C. Marshall, O.B.E. (*Labour*); J. Doorbar, O.B.E. (*Commercial*); Miss E. M. Hodges, O.B.E.; A. D. F. Findley (*Agriculture*); N. M. McCarthy (*Information*).

2nd Secretaries, R. W. James; A. R. Nuttall (*Commercial*); M. D. Cuthbertson.

3rd Secretaries, J. M. Cresswell; K. Mackenzie.

BRITISH CONSULAR OFFICES

There are British Consular Offices at *Brussels, Antwerp, Ostend, Ghent* and *Liège*.

British Council Representative to Belgium and Luxembourg, P. L. Roussel, O.B.E., Galilée Building, Avenue Galilée 5, 1030, Brussels (Council Library at *Brussels*).

BRITISH CHAMBER OF COMMERCE, 30 Rue Joseph II, 1040 Brussels.

BHUTAN

King of Bhutan, Jigme Singye Wangchuck, *born* 1955; *succeeded his father*, July, 1972; *crowned*, June 2, 1974.

Bhutan, with an area of about 18,000 sq. miles and an estimated population (1972) of 1,010,000, mainly Buddhists, is an independent State bounded on the North and East by Tibet, on the South by India, and on the West by Sikkim, which is now a State of the Indian Union. In 1949, a treaty was concluded with the Government of India under which the Kingdom of Bhutan agreed to be guided by the Government of India in regard to its external relations, but it still retains complete independence, issues its own passports and has diplomatic representatives at the United Nations as well as in India. It also receives from the Government of India an annual payment of *Rs*.500,000 as compensation for portions of its territory annexed by the British Government in India in 1864. The principal cottage industries are weaving, metal works and crafts, and the main exports are timber, rice and wheat. A motor road runs 107 miles from Paro, the winter capital, to Phuntsholing in W. Bengal. Three other roads linking Bhutan with India are under construction or projected. The Government of India has a diplomatic representative in Bhutan.

CAPITAL. Thimphu. FLAG.—Orange and crimson divided diagonally, with dragon device in centre.

BOLIVIA
(República de Bolivia)

President, Col. Hugo Banzer, *assumed office* Aug. 22, 1971.

BOLIVIAN EMBASSY IN LONDON
106 Eaton Square, S.W.1.
[01–235 4248]

Ambassador Extraordinary and Plenipotentiary, His Excellency General Rogelio Miranda Baldivia (1974).

Consulate, 106 Eccleston Mews, S.W.1.

Counsellor, Sr. Jorge Soruco Villaneuva.

1st Secretary, Srta. Marta Bosacoma Bonel.

Mining Attaché, Sr. H. Zannier.

There are Bolivian Consular Offices in *Liverpool, Birmingham* and *Hull*.

The Republic of Bolivia extends between lat. 10° and 23° S. and long. 57° 30' and 69° 45' W. It has an area estimated at 415,000 square miles with an estimated population (1970) of 4,658,000. (*For* MAP, *see* Index.) The Republic derives its name from its liberator, Simón Bolivar born 1783, died 1830).

The chief topographical feature is the great central plateau (65,000 square miles) over 500 miles in length, at an average altitude of 12,500 feet above sea level, between the two great chains of the Andes, which traverse the country from south to north, and contain, in Illampu, Illimani, and Sajama, three of the highest peaks of the western hemisphere. The total length of the navigable streams is about 12,000 miles, the principal rivers being the Itenez, Beni, Mamore and Madre de Dios.

President Barrientos, who had held office since his election on July 3, 1966, was killed in a helicopter accident on April 27, 1969, and in accordance with the Constitution was succeeded by Vice-President Dr. Luis Adolfo Siles Salinas. On Sept. 26, 1969, the armed forces overthrew the constitutional Government and set up a civilian-military government under the Presidency of General Ovando. On October 7, 1970, Gen. Torres assumed the Presidency after defeating the right-wing military group which had overthrown the Government of Gen. Ovando the day before, and held office until August 22, 1971.

A *coup d'état* occurred in August 1971, when, after reported heavy fighting, the President was ousted by Army leaders headed by Col. Hugo Banzer, Gen. Florentino Mendieta and Col. Andres Selich. Col. Banzer was proclaimed President in La Paz on Aug. 22, and subsequently formed a national front embracing the Armed Forces and the two leading political parties (M.N.R. and F.S.B.).

Mining, petroleum and agriculture are the principal industries. The ancient silver mines of Potosí are now worked chiefly for tin, but gold, partly dug and partly washed, is obtained on the Eastern Cordillera of the Andes; the tin output is, after that of Malaysia, the largest in the world. Copper, antimony, lead, zinc, asbestos, wolfram, bismuth salt and sulphur are found, and petroleum is also produced.

The Republic is now a net oil exporter. Production of crude oil in 1974 totalled 16,000,000 barrels (of 42 U.S. gallons). The Bolivian Gulf Oil Company was nationalised on October 17, 1969, and shortly afterwards exports diminished (4,662,004 barrels in 1970 compared with 8,807,834 barrels in 1969). Exports rose in 1974 to 30,000 barrels per day. Bolivia's agricultural produce consists chiefly of rice, barley, oats, wheat, sugarcane, maize, cotton, indigo, rubber, cacao, potatoes, cinchona bark, medicinal herbs, brazil nuts, etc. The development of manufacturing industry progresses slowly. However, Bolivia has joined the Latin American Free Trade Area, and on May 26, 1969, signed the Andean Pact which is designed to secure economic integration and co-operation within the Andean Group of countries. Total

Exports (F.O.B.) doubled in 1974 to U.S.$560 million as a result of the surge in oil and mineral prices.

Transport and Communications.—There are 2,200 miles of railways in operation including the lines from Corumbá to Santa Cruz (405 miles) and from Yacuiba to Santa Cruz (312 miles). There are about 10,950 miles of telegraphs, and wireless services between Riberalta, La Paz, Cobija, Capitandi (Chaco). There is direct railway communication to the sea at Antofagasta (32 hours), Arica (10 hours), and Mollendo (2 days), and also to Buenos Aires (3½ days); branch lines run from Oruro to Cochabamba, and from Río Mulato to Potosí, and from Potosí to Sucre, the legal capital. The Antofagasta (Chile) and Bolivia Railroad was formerly an all-British concern, but the Bolivian sector has now been nationalised. Communication with Peru is effected by rail to Guaqui and thence by steamer across Lake Titicaca to the railhead at Puno.

Commercial aviation in Bolivia is conducted by Braniff International Airways (American), Lufthansa, Iberia, Aerolineas Argentinas, and Lloyd Aereo Boliviano (Bolivian), the five former providing international connections with U.S.A., West coast South American countries, Canal Zone, Europe and Argentina; Lloyd Aereo Boliviano, maintaining a service to Lima, São Paulo, Buenos Aires and Arica, and attending to local flights, links La Paz with Oruro, Cochabamba, Santa Cruz and Trinidad, etc. and connects with LAN of Chile, Argentine Airlines and Cruzeiro do Sul of Brazil.

Bolivia is without a sea-coast, having been deprived of the ports of Tocopilla, Cobija, Mejillones and Antofagasta by the "Pacific War" of 1879–1884.

Language and Literature.—The official language of the country is Spanish, but many of the Indian inhabitants (about two-thirds of the population) speak Quechua or Aymará, the two linguistic groups being more or less equal in numbers.

The Roman Catholic religion was disestablished in 1961 but relations between it and the State are good. Elementary education is compulsory and free and there are secondary schools in urban centres. Provision is also made for higher education; in addition to St. Francisco Xavier's University at Sucre, founded in 1624, there are six other universities, the largest being the University of Sant Andres at La Paz. Bolivian literature has not yet produced authors of world-wide renown. There are twelve principal daily newspapers in Bolivia, with an estimated daily circulation of 150,000.

FINANCE

The Budget for 1974, which included State industrial organisations (except the State Mining Corporation) and local authorities, envisaged an expenditure of $b26,742,172,500 showing a small deficit of just over $b349,000,000.

The Bolivian currency, after remaining stable for 15 years at 12 pesos to the U.S. dollar, was devalued in October 1972; the new rate is 20 pesos. A stand-by credit of U.S.$30,000,000 was granted by the I.M.F. and a stabilisation programme set up to effect a faster rate of growth and a balancing of the National Budget. Exchange cross-rate $bs48·2 = £1 (1974) (*see also* p. 83).

Bolivia has benefited considerably from the high prices of basic materials, notably oil, gas and tin, and her foreign exchange earnings for 1974 were U.S.$560,000,000.

Trade with U.K.

	1973	1974
Imports from U.K....	£2,200,000	£4,300,000
Exports to U.K.......	20,000,000	9,700,000

The principal exports are tin ore (most of which is exported to the U.K.), oil and gas, lead and antimony ores, silver, copper, wolfram, zinc, gold, nuts, hides and skins, cotton and coffee. The chief imports are wheat and flour, iron and steel products, machinery, vehicles and textiles.

Seat of Government.—La Paz. Population (estimated 1970) 553,000. Other large centres are Cochabamba (149,000), Oruro (119,700), Santa Cruz (124,900), Potosí (96,800), Sucre, the legal capital and seat of the judiciary (84,900) and Tarija (35,700).

FLAG: Three horizontal bands; Red, yellow, green.

NATIONAL DAY.—August 6 (Independence Day).

BRITISH EMBASSY.

Casilla 694, La Paz.

Ambassador Extraordinary and Plenipotentiary, His Excellency Ronald Christopher Hope-Jones, C.M.G. (1973).

1st Secretary, M. S. Green (*Commercial and Head of Chancery*).

Defence Attaché, Captain D. L. G. James, R.N. (*resident in Lima, Peru*).

2nd Secretaries, Miss J. D. Robertson (*Aid and Information*); B. A. Barrett (*Administration and Consul*).

Attaché, H. Kershaw (*Commercial*).

BRITISH CONSULAR OFFICES

There are British Consular Offices at *La Paz* and *Cochabamba*.

BRAZIL

(The Federative Republic of Brazil)

President, General Ernesto Geisel, *born*, August 3, 1908; *appointed*, Jan. 15, 1974; *acceded*, March 15, 1974.

Vice-President, General Adalberto Pereira dos Santos.

MINISTRY

(Feb. 21, 1974)

External Relations, Sr. Antônio F. A. da Silveira.
Interior, Sr. Maurício Rangel Reis.
Finance, Sr. Mário E. Simonsen.
Justice, Sr. Armando Falcão.
Planning, Sr. João P. dos R. Velloso.
Mines and Energy, Sr. Shigeaki Ueki.
Education, Sen. Ney Braga.
Agriculture, Sr. Alysson Paulinelli.
Labour, Sr. Arnaldo da C. Prieto.
Communications, Cdr. Euclides Q. de Oliveira.
Health, Dr. Paulo de A. Machado.
Industry and Trade, Sr. Severo F. Gomes.
Transport, Gen. Dirceu de A. Nogueira.
Air Force, Gen. Joelmir de A. Macedo.
Army, Gen. Silvio Coetho de Frota.
Navy, Adm. Geraldo de A. Henning.
Social Security, Lunz Nascimento e Silva.

BRAZILIAN EMBASSY IN LONDON

32 Green Street, W.1.
[01–629 0155–58]

Ambassador Extraordinary and Plenipotentiary, His Excellency Roberto de Oliveira Campos (1975).
Minister-Counsellor, Ronaldo Costa.
Naval Advisers, Rear-Admiral T. B. Reifschneider; Captain M. Brasil; Captain F. M. B. da Costa.
Minister, Marcelo Rafaelli (*Economic Affairs*).
Air Attaché, Colonel F. W. Derschum.
Naval and Military Attaché, Capt. M. H. B. de Carvalho.
Assistant Air Attaché, Col. S. Rodrigues.

1st Secretaries, J. Ferreira-Lopes (*Administrative*);
J. G. Merquior; R. V. Sobrino; B. M. F. Neele
(*Commercial*); D. Flusser.

2nd Secretaries, F. C. de Garcia; F. Cezar de Araujo,
M.V.O.; M. E. Côrtes Costa; L. F. O. C. Benedini
(*Consular Affairs*); F. C. de Araujo; L. A. de C.
Neves; V. A. Cleaver.

Consular Section, 6 Deanery Street, W.1 (01-499-
7441).

Commercial Section, 15 Berkeley Street, W.1
(01-499-6706).

There are also a Brazilian Consulate-General at
Liverpool and honorary consular offices at *Cardiff*,
Newcastle-upon-Tyne, and *Glasgow*.

POSITION AND EXTENT

Brazil, the most extensive State of South America,
discovered in 1500 by Pedro Alvares Cabral,
Portuguese navigator, is bounded on the north by
the Atlantic Ocean, the Guianas, Colombia and
Venezuela; on the west by Peru, Bolivia Paraguay, and Argentina; on the south by Uruguay;
and on the east by the Atlantic Ocean. Brazil
extends between lat. 5° 16′ N. and 33° 45′ S.
and long. 34° 45′ and 73° 59′ 22″ W., being 2,685
miles from north to south, and 2,690 from west to
east, with a coast-line on the Atlantic of 4,604 miles.
The Republic comprises an area of 3,289,440 square
miles, with a population (1975 est.) of 108,000,000.

The northern States of Amazonas and Pará are
mainly wide, low-lying, forest-clad plains. The
central state of Mato Grosso is principally plateau
land and the eastern and southern States are
traversed by successive mountain ranges interspersed with fertile valleys. The principal ranges are
Serra do Mar in São Paulo; the *Serra Geral* (Caparao
9,393 feet) between Minas Gerais and Espirito Santo,
the *Serra da Mantiqueira* (Itatiaia, 9,163 feet) and the
Serra do Espinhaco (Itacolumi, 5,748 feet), in the
south-east of Minas Gerais; the *Serra do Paraná*,
between Goiás and Minas Gerais, the *Serra dos
Aimorés*, which divide Espírito Santo from Minas
Gerais; and the *Serra do Gurgueia, Branca* and
Araripe, which envelop Piaui.

Brazil is unequalled for its rivers. The River
Amazon has tributaries which are themselves great
rivers, and flows from the Peruvian Andes to the
Atlantic, with a total length of some 4,000 miles.
Its principal northern tributaries are the *Rio Branco,
Río Negro*, and *Japurá*; its southern tributaries are the
Jurúa, Purus, Madeira and *Tapajós*, while the *Xingú*
meets it within 200 miles of its outflow into the
Atlantic. The *Tocantins* and *Araguaia* flow north-
wards from the Plateau of Mato Grosso and the
mountains of Goiás to the Gulf of Pará. The
Parnaiba flows from the encircling mountains of
Piaui into the Atlantic. The *São Francisco* rises in

the South of Minas Gerais and traverses Bahia on is way to the eastern coast, between Alagoas and Sergipe. The *Paraguai*, rising in the south-west of Mato Grosso, flows through Paraguay to its confluence with the *Paraná*, which rises in the mountains of that name and divides Brazil from Paraguay. On the *Iguaçu or Iguassú*, which unites with the Upper Paraná at the Brazil-Argentine-Paraguay boundary, are the majestic *Falls of the Iguaçu* (200 ft.), and on the *São Francisco* are the no less famous falls of *Paulo Afonso* (260 ft.).

Government.—Brazil was colonized by Portugal in the early part of the sixteenth century, and in 1822 became an independent empire under Dom Pedro, son of the refugee King Joao VI. of Portugal. On Nov. 15, 1889, Dom Pedro II., second of the line, was dethroned and a republic was proclaimed.

In 1964 President Goulart was deposed in a bloodless coup and Marshal Castello Branco became President. He was in turn succeeded in 1967 by Marshal Costa e Silva. When the latter became incapacitated by illness in 1969, the three Ministers for the Armed Forces took over the leadership of the Government. In October 1969, Congress confirmed the appointment of General Emilio Media as President for five years. A series of amendments to the Constitution came into effect on October 30, which codified the powers assumed by the régime, and which laid down that subsequent Presidents should be elected by an electoral college; previously the President had been chosen by the military, and approved by Congress. In January 1974, 66 Senators, 310 Deputies, and 127 delegates from the State Legislatures elected General Ernesto Geisel, the candidate of the Government party, to succeed President Medici, whose term of office was due to expire in March 1974.

Production.—There are large and valuable mineral deposits including among others, iron ore (hematite), manganese, bauxite, beryllium, chrome, nickel, tungsten, cassiterite, lead, gold, monazite (containing rare earths and thorium) and zirconium. Diamonds and precious and semi-precious stones are also found. The mineral wealth is being exploited to an increasing extent. The iron ore deposits of Minas Gerais and the untapped ones of the Amazon region are particularly rich and plans for mining them are advanced. Production is increasing all the time.

In 1974 10,114,294 cubic metres of oil was produced; 7,504,000 tons of steel ingots and almost 23,000,000 cubic metres of refined petroleum (including refining of imported oil); 59,000,000 tons of iron ore were exported at a value of U.S. $571,000,000.

Total foreign private investment in Dec. 1974 was estimated at almost U.S. $6,027,000,000.

In 1974 the Brazilian automobile industry produced 858,500 vehicles.

The main exports of agricultural produce in 1974 were:

	Metric tons	Value U.S.$
Coffee	731,000	1,002,000,000
Sugar	2,249,000	1,259,000,000
Soya	4,754,000	888,000,000

Coffee is grown mainly in the States of São Paulo and Paraná and to a lesser extent in Minas Gerais and Espírito Santo.

Defence.—The peace-time strength of the Army is 180,000 of which some 70 per cent are doing military service, with an immediate reserve of 250,000. The Navy consists of 1 Aircraft Carrier, 14 Destroyers and Escorts, 8 Submarines, 6 Minesweepers, 6 Survey Vessels, 10 Corvettes (tugs), 45 other vessels and 3 helicopter squadrons. The strength of the

Navy is 57,000 including 13,000 marines. The Air Force, with a strength of 44,000, including approximately 1,600 pilots and aircrew, has 650 aircraft and is the largest in South America.

Education.—*Primary* education is compulsory and is the responsibility of State governments and municipalities. At this level approximately 10 per cent attend private schools. In 1973, 19,939,144 children were enrolled in 188,056 primary schools.

Secondary education is largely the responsibility of the State and Municipal Governments, although a small number of very old foundations (the Pedro II Schools) remain under direct Federal control. Over 50 per cent. of all pupils at this level attend Private Schools.

In 1973 a total of 1,476,288 pupils were enrolled in the various types of secondary school, including normal and technical schools.

Higher education is available in Federal State, Municipal and private universities and faculties. In 1973 a total of 772,800 students were enrolled in some 797 institutions (57 of which were universities).

Language and Literature.—Portuguese is the language of the country, but Italian, Spanish, German, Japanese and Arabic are spoken by immigrant minorities, and newspapers of considerable circulation are produced in those languages. English and French are currently spoken by educated Brazilians.

Until the second quarter of the nineteenth century Brazilian literature was dominated by Portugal. French influence is traceable for the next half century, since when a national school has come into existence and there are many modern authors of high standing. Public libraries have been established in urban centres and there is a flourishing national press with widely circulated daily and weekly newspapers.

Communications.—In 1973 there were about 30,394 kilometres of railways in service, largely of 1 metre gauge, but including 3,880 kilometres of other gauges. Traffic carried in 1972 was—Passengers 313,760,000; Freight 47,918,000 metric tons. During 1974, the ports of Brazil were used by 31,331 vessels, shipping a total of 110,348,000 tons. There are 7,800 kilometres of navigable inland waterways.

Varig of Brazil and 11 foreign airlines operate services between Brazil and Europe, 3 between Brazil and U.S.A., and there are connections with all Latin American countries. Four major domestic airlines, as well as the Brazilian Air Force, maintain services throughout the country. During 1970, more than 4 million passengers passed through Brazilian airports; 34 m. kg of cargo were transported and 3m. kg. of mail. The airports of Rio de Janeiro and São Paulo alone handled 4,400,000 passenger arrivals and departures in 1972.

Postal facilities in Brazil include approximately 4,042 post offices. In 1971, 2,123,760 telephones were in use, of which a large proportion are dial operated.

FINANCE

	1972 Cruzeiros '000	1973 Cruzeiros '000
Revenue	39,419,929	52,726,000
Expenditure	38,198,339	50,767,000

In Dec. 1974, Brazil's foreign debt stood at U.S. $16,100,000,000. Reserves in Feb. 1975 were $4,750,000,000. The rate of exchange in May 1975 was Cr $7·9 = U.S.$1.

TRADE (1974)

Total imports	U.S.$12,531,000,000
Total exports	U.S.$ 7,968,000,000

Trade with U.K. (1974)

Imports from U.K.	£143,100,000
Exports to U.K.	195,500,000

The principal imports in 1971 and 1972 were machinery and aircraft, foodstuffs, raw materials, oil and chemicals, and manufactured goods. Principal exports were coffee, manufactured goods, iron ore and other minerals, foodstuffs and fruits.

CAPITAL.—Brasilia (inaugurated on April 21, 1960). Population (estimated 1970), 544,862. Other important centres are São Paulo (5,901,553); the former capital ΨRio de Janeiro (4,296,782); ΨBelo Horizonte (1,232,708); ΨRecife (1,078,819); ΨSalvador (1,000,647); ΨPorto Alegre (885,567); and ΨFortaleza (842,231).

FLAG.—Green, with yellow lozenge in centre; blue sphere with white band and stars in centre of lozenge.

NATIONAL DAY.—September 7 (Independence Day).

BRITISH EMBASSY

Avenida das Nacóes, Lote 8, Brasilia, D.F.

Ambassador Extraordinary and Plenipotentiary, His Excellency Sir Derek Sherborne Lindsell Dodson, K.C.M.G., M.C. (1973)

Counsellor, D. P. M. S. Cape.

1st Secretaries, T. J. Bellers(*Aid and Head of Chancery*); J. W. G. Ridd; A. L. S. Coltman (*Commercial*); R. J. Chase (*Information*).

2nd Secretaries, T. T. Macan; A. Ferguson (*Admin.*); D. N. Simmons (*Commercial*).

Defence and Military Attaché, Col. P. J. L. Wickes.

Naval Attaché, Capt. A. K. Hall, R.N.

Air Attaché, Wing Cdr. J. Cheesbrough.

BRITISH CONSULAR OFFICES

There are British Consulates-General at Rio de Janeiro (*Consul-General*, A. G. Munro) and São Paulo (*Consul-General*, G. E. Hall) and Consular Offices at *Belém* (Para), *Belo Horizonte*, *Vitória*, *Salvador* (Bahia), *Manàus*, *Fortaleza*, *Pôrto Alegre*, *Rio Grande*, *Santos* and *Recife*.

BRITISH COUNCIL.—*Representative in Brazil*, J. W. L. Gale, C.B.E., Avenida Portugal 360, Rio de Janeiro. Regional Directors in *Brasilia*, *Curitiba*, *Recife* and *São Paulo*. Book supply to libraries of *Sociedade Brasiliera de Cultura Inglesa* at *Rio de Janeiro* and *São Paulo*.

BRITISH AND COMMONWEALTH CHAMBER OF COMMERCE IN SÃO PAULO, Rua Barão de Itapetininga 275, Caixa Postal 1621, São Paulo. (Correspondents at *Santos* and *Porto Alegre*).

Rio de Janeiro, 5,750 miles distant from London: transit, 15 days.

BULGARIA
(Bulgariya)

COUNCIL OF STATE

Chairman of the Council of State, Todor Zhivkov, elected July 7, 1971 (*Head of State*).

First Deputy Chairman, Krustyn Trichkov; Petus Tanchev.

Deputy Chairmen, Peko Takov; Georgi Dzhagarov; Ivan Popov; Mitko Grigorov.

Secretary, Mincho Minchev.

Chairman of the Committee for State and Popular Control, Krustyn Trichkov.

COUNCIL OF MINISTERS

Chairmen, Stanko Todorov.

First Deputy Chairman, Tano Tsolov.

Deputy Chairmen, Pencho Kubadinski; Zhivko Zhivkov; Ognyan Doynov; Prof. Mako Dakov.

Minister of National Education, Nencho Stanev.

National Defence, Dobri Dzhurov (*Army General*).

Internal Trade and Services, Georgi Karamanev.

Foreign Trade, Ivan Nedev.

Light Industry, Stoyan Zhulev.

Transport, Vassil Tsanov.

Foreign Affairs, Petur Mladenov.

Internal Affairs, Maj.-Gen. Dimitur Stoyanov.

Information and Communication, George Andreev.

Agriculture and Food Industry, Gancho Krustev.

Mineral Resources, Stamen Stamenov.

Forest and Environmental Protection, Yanko Markov.

Machine Building and Metallurgy, Toncho Chakurov.

Supply and State Reserves, Nicolay Zhishev.

Public Health, Dr. Angel Todorov.

Construction and Architecture, Grigor Stoichkov.

Finance, Dimitur Popov.

Justice, Svetla Daskalova.

Labour and Social Welfare, Kiril Zarev.

Electronics and Electrical Engineering, Yordan Mladenov.

Power, Petur Danailov.

Chemical Industry, Georgi Pankov.

Chairmen of the Committees, Kiril Zarev (*State Planning*); Pavel Matev (*Art and Culture*); Nacho Papazov (*Science, Technical Progress and Higher Education*); Ivan Vrachev (*Recreation and Tourism*).

THE COMMUNIST PARTY

The Politbureau of the Central Committee, T. Tsolov; Ts. Dragoycheva; P. Kubadinski; I. Mihailov; T. Pavlov; I. Popov; S. Todorov; B. Velchev; T. Zhivkov; Zh. Zhivkov; G. Filipov; A. Lilov (*full members*); P. Takov; K. Trichkov; D. Dzhurov; D. Vulcheva; P. Mladenov; T. Stiochev (*candidate members*).

The Secretariat of the Central Committee, Todor Zhivkov (1st); G. Filipov; P. Kiratsov; A. Lilov; I. Prumov; K. Tellalov; B. Velchev (*Secretaries*); G. Bokov; V. Bonev; G. Yordanov; S. Dulbokov; Misho Mishev (*Members*).

BULGARIAN EMBASSY AND CONSULATE IN LONDON

12 Queen's Gate Gardens, S.W.7.

[01–584–9400]

Ambassador Extraordinary and Plenipotentiary, His Excellency Alexander Yankov (1972).

Counsellors, Ivan Moutafchiev; Asparouh K. Mladenov (*Commercial*); Ilia I. Iliev (*Economic*).

Military, Naval and Air Attaché, Lt.-Col. Dimitar Petkov Toskov.

Deputy Commercial Counsellor, Plamen A. Despatov.

1st Secretary, Mladen Galabov.

2nd Secretaries, Stanislav V. Baev (*Cultural Affairs*); Kolio Trankov (*Consular*); Ivan Nedev.

Attaché, Svetlomir V. Baev.

The Republic of Bulgaria is bounded on the

north by Rumania, on the west by Yugoslavia, on the east by the Black Sea, and on the south by Greece and Turkey. The total area is approximately 43,000 square miles, with a population in December, 1972 of 8,594,493. The largest religion of the Bulgarians is the Bulgarian Orthodox Church. The Gregorian (Western) Calendar is in use.

A Principality of Bulgaria was created by the *Treaty of Berlin* (July 13, 1878) and in 1885 Eastern Roumelia was added to the newly-created principailty. In 1908 the country was declared to be an independent kingdom, the area at that date being 37,202 square miles, with a population of 4,337,500. In 1912–13 a successful war of the *Balkan League* against Turkey increased the size of the kingdom, but in August, 1913, a short campaign against the remaining members of the League reduced the acquired area, and led to the surrender of Southern Dobrudja to Rumania. On Oct. 12, 1915, Bulgaria entered the War on the side of the Central Powers by declaring war on Serbia. She thus became involved in the defeats of 1918, and on Sept. 29, 1918, made an unconditional surrender to the Allied Powers. On Nov. 29, 1919, she signed the *Treaty of Neuilly*, which ceded to the Allies her Thracian territories (later handed over to Greece) and some territory on the western frontier to Yugoslavia.

Nazi troops entered the country on March 3, 1941, and occupied Black Sea ports, but Bulgaria was not officially at war with the Soviet Union. On August 26, 1944, the government declared Bulgaria to be " neutral in the Russo-German war " and delegates to Cairo sought terms of peace from Great Britain and the United States. The Soviet Union refused to recognize the so-called " neutrality " and called upon Bulgaria to declare war against Germany, and no satisfactory reply being received on Sept. 5, 1944, the U.S.S.R. declared war on Bulgaria. Bulgaria then asked for an armistice and on Sept. 7 declared war on Germany, hostilities with U.S.S.R. ending on Sept. 10. The armistice with the Allies was signed in Moscow, Oct. 28. On Sept. 9 a *coup d'état* gave power to the Fatherland Front, a coalition of Communists, Agrarians, Social Democrats and Republican officers and intellectuals. In August, 1945, the main body of Agrarians and Social Democrats left the Government. The Peace Treaty with Bulgaria was signed on Feb. 22, 1947, and came into force on Sept. 15, 1947. It recognized the return of Southern Dobrudja to Bulgaria.

On Sept. 8, 1946, a referendum was held, at which, according to the published results, an overwhelming majority declared for the abolition of the Monarchy and the setting up of a Republic. On Oct. 27, a general election to a Grand National Assembly (with power to make a constitution) was held; the Opposition won 101 seats out of 465.

On May 16, 1971 a referendum was held, at which a new Constitution was adopted. According to the Constitution the legislature is a single chamber National Assembly of *Subranie* elected by adult suffrage for a maximum term of 5 years and consisting of 400 deputies representing constituencies of equal size. The 1971 Constitution also established the Council of State, being the supreme permanent body of the National Assembly with both legislative and executive functions. The opposition Agrarian Party was suppressed in 1947, but its remnant was later revived as the Agrarian Union which now constitutionally shares power with the Communist Party.

Production.—Until 1939 Bulgaria was a predominantly agricultural country, but has since pursued an elaborate programme of industrialization. About 90 per cent. of the country's agriculture has been turned over to co-operatives, and a smaller proportion mechanized. The principal crops are wheat, maize, beet, tomatoes, tobacco, oleaginous seeds, fruit, vegetables and cotton. The livestock includes cattle, sheep, goats, pigs, horses, asses, mules and water buffaloes.

There is now a substantial engineering industry producing *inter alia* machine tools, electric trucks of all kinds, agricultural machinery, cranes, electric motors and electronic components, which accounts for about a third of Bulgaria's exports; and considerable production of lead, zinc and copper (1971, 93,000 tons; 63,000 tons and 24,000 tons respectively). In 1973 production of electricity was 21,952 million kilowatt-hours, of steel 2,246,000 tons and of coal 26,810,000 tons (of which a large proportion is soft coal).

There are mineral deposits of varying importance. Bulgaria's heavy industry includes the Kremikovtsi Metallurgical Plant near Sofia, whose first blast furnace, with an annual output of 560,000 tons, was put into operation in 1963, the petrochemical plant at Burgas with an annual capacity of 6 million tons of processed oil, a nitrogenous fertilizer plant, and other chemical and metallurgical works.

Defence.—Under the Peace Treaty signed between Bulgaria and the Allies, the Bulgarian Army is limited to 55,000 men, but it is believed at present to be at least 152,000 strong.

Education.—Free basic education is compulsory for children from 7 to 15 years inclusive. The Bulgarian educational system was reorganized on Soviet lines in September, 1950, and in 1971–72 there were 7,641 kindergartens, 1,167 elementary schools (Grades (I–IV), 81 preparatory schools (Grades V–VIII), 2,532 primary schools (Grades I–VIII), 138 secondary schools (gymnasia) 147 vocational training schools, 241 technical colleges, 21 post-secondary institutions, 27 institutes of higher education and three universities (at Sofia, Plovdiv and Veliko Turnovo). There were 1,850,557 pupils, including 93,713 students in higher education, and 98,527 teachers.

Language and Literature.—Bulgarian is a Southern Slavonic tongue, closely allied to Serbo-Croat and Russian (*see* U.S.S.R.) with local admixtures of modern Greek, Albanian and Turkish words. There is a modern literature chiefly educational and popular. The alphabet is Cyrillic. In 1967 there were 8 daily newspaper in Sofia.

Finance.—Estimated budget revenue for 1974 is 8,510,000,000 *leva*, expenditure 8,360,000,000 *leva* Currency in Bulgaria is the *lev*. Rate of exchange (in May 1974) was 3·9*Lv*= £1 (Tourist), 2·30*Lv*= £1 (Official).

TRADE

The principal imports are industrial and agricultural machinery, industrial raw materials, machine tools, chemicals, dyestuffs, drugs, rubber, paper. The principal exports are cereals, tobacco, fruit, vegetables, oil seeds, oils, fats, textiles, eggs, chemicals, essential oils including attar of roses, non-ferrous metals, electric trucks and motors, pumps, ships, accumulators and machine tools. In 1974 73 per cent. of Bulgaria's foreign trade was with the Soviet bloc, including about 50 per cent. with the Soviet Union.

Trade with U.K.

	1973	1974
Imports from U.K.	£13,150,000	£18,042,000
Exports to U.K.	9,340,000	13,549,000

CAPITAL.—Sofia, Pop. (1972), 927,833, at the foot of the Vitosha Range, the capital and commercial centre is on the main railway line to

Istanbul, 338 miles from the Black Sea port of Ψ Varna (251,588) and 125 miles from Lom (28,500), on the Danube; Ψ Burgas (142,137) is also a Black Sea Port, those on the Danube being Ψ Rusé (163,012), Ψ Svishtov (18,537), Ψ Vidin (43,000). Other important trading and industrial centres are Plovdiv (261,732), Pleven (108,180), and Stara Zagora (117,543).

FLAG.—3 horizontal bands, white, green, red; national emblem on white stripe near hoist.

NATIONAL DAY.—Sept. 9 (Day of Freedom).

BRITISH EMBASSY
Residence, 65 Boulevard Tolbuhin, Sofia.
Ambassador Extraordinary and Plenipotentiary, His Excellency Edwin Bolland, C.M.G. (1973).
1st Secretaries, J. W. D. Gray (*Consul and Head of Chancery*); W. B. Powell (*Commercial*).
2nd Secretary, K. Q. F. Manning (*Cultural Attaché*).
Defence, Naval, Military and Air Attaché, Lt.-Col. R. H. Chappell, O.B.E.
3rd Secretaries, I. Vella; B. V. Sims; Miss A. Adams.

BURMÁ
(The Socialist Republic of the Union of Burma)

Government of the Union
President, U Ne Win.

BURMESE EMBASSY AND CONSULATE
19A Charles St., Berkeley Square, W.1.
[01-499 8841]
Ambassador Extraordinary and Plenipotentiary, (vacant).
Military, Naval and Air Attaché, Lt.-Col. Soe Myint.
Cultural Attaché, U Maung Maung Soe Tint.
2nd Secretaries, U Kyaw Shein; U Soe Thinn.

Area and Population.—Burma forms the western portion of the Indo-Chinese district of the continent of Asia, lying between 9° 58′ and 28° N. latitude and 92° 11′ and 101° 9′ E. longitude, with an extreme length of approximately 1,200 miles and an extreme width of 575 miles. It has a sea coast on the Bay of Bengal to the south and west and a frontier with Bangladesh along the Naaf River, defined in 1964 by a Memorandum of Agreements, and India to the north-west defined in 1967, in the north and east the frontier with China was determined by a treaty with the People's Republic in October, 1960, and has since been demarcated; there is a short frontier with Laos in the east, while the long finger of Tenasserim stretches southward along the west coast of the Malay Peninsula, forming a frontier with Thailand to the east. (*For* MAP, *see* Index). The total area of the Union is about 262,000 square miles, with an officially estimated population of 29,512,000 in 1974—about 113 persons to the square mile.

Political Divisions.—The Socialist Republic of the Union of Burma is comprised of fourteen States and Divisions. Amongst the former are the Kachin State (34,000 sq. miles), Kayah State (4,500 sq. miles); Karen (formerly Kawthoolei) State (12,000 sq. miles), Chin State (14,000 sq. miles), Mon State, Arakan State and the Shan State (60,000 sq. miles).

Physical Features.—Burma falls into four natural divisions, Arakan (with the Chin Hills region) the Irrawaddy basin, the old Province of Tenasserim, including the Salween basin and extending southwards to the Burma-Siam peninsula, and the elevated plateau on the east made up of the Shan States. Mountains enclose Burma on three sides, the highest point being Hka-kabo Razi (19,296 ft.) in the northern Kachin hills. Mt. Popa, 4,981 ft., in the Myingyan district is an extinct volcano and a well-known landmark in Central Burma. The principal river systems are the Kaladan-Lemro in Arakan, the Irrawaddy-

Chindwin and the Sittang in Central Burma, and the Salween which flows through the Shan Plateau.

Races, Language and Religions.—The indigenous inhabitants who entered Burma from the north and east are of similar racial types and speak languages of the Tibeto-Burman, Mon-Khmer and Thai groups. The three important non-indigenous elements are Indians, Chinese and those from the former East Pakistan. Numbers of resident foreigners have shown a sharp decline in recent years. Burmese is the official language, but minority languages include Shan, Karen, Chin, and the various Kachin dialects. English is still spoken in educated circles in Rangoon and elsewhere. Buddhism is the religion of 85 per cent. of the people, with 5 per cent. Animists, 4 per cent. Moslems, 4 per cent. Hindus and rather less than 2 per cent. Christians.

Government.—Burma became an independent republic outside the British Commonwealth on January 4, 1948, and remained a parliamentary democracy for 14 years.

On March 2, 1962 the army took power, and suspended the parliamentary Constitution. A Revolutionary Council of senior officers under General Ne Win took measures to create a Socialist State in accordance with their policy statement " The Burmese Way to Socialism ". The Burmese Socialist Programme or Lanzin Party was founded to provide political leadership for the country.

In January 1974 a new Constitution was adopted after a national referendum. In February elections to the People's Assembly and local councils were held. On March 2 the Revolutionary Council transferred power to the bodies elected under the new Constitution. The highest authority is the People's Assembly (450 representatives) which is expected to meet twice a year. When the Assembly is not in session the Council of State (29 members) is vested with wide powers. The senior executive body is the Council of Ministers. The Chairman of the Council of State (U Ne Win) is also President of the Socialist Republic of the Union of Burma.

Education.—The literacy rate is high compared with other Asiatic countries, there is no caste system and women engage freely in social intercourse and play an important part in agriculture and retail trade.

Under the University Education Law of 1964, the Government reorganized the higher education system to encourage the expansion of medical and technical studies. The four existing Universities (Rangoon, Mandalay, Moulmein and Bassein) have been decentralized and the faculties of Medicine (at present there are 2 Medical Institutes in Rangoon and one in Mandalay), Economics, Engineering, Agriculture, Veterinary Science and Education have been reconstituted as independent Institutes. The remaining faculties are grouped together as the Arts & Science University of the city concerned.

There are teachers' training colleges in Rangoon, Moulmein and Mandalay which train junior assistant teachers and 13 State Teachers Training Institutes for primary assistant teachers. The Institute of Education in Rangoon trains senior assistant teachers and awards degrees. There are three Government technical institutes at Insein (near Rangoon), Mandalay and Kalaw. There are 6 technical high schools, 2 in Rangoon, 1 in Mandalay, 1 in Maymo, 1 in Taunggyi and 1 in Moulmein. Under the Colombo Plan, New Zealand financed the construction of a school at Taunggyi at a cost of £100,000 sterling and Britain provided the school with equipment valued at £45,000. British aid to Burma under the Colombo Plan amounts to some

£300,000 annually, over half of this being devoted of technical assistance awards.

Finance.—The chief sources of revenue are profits on state trading, income-tax, customs duties, commercial taxes and excise duties; the chief heads of expenditure are general administration, defence, education, police and development. The budget estimates for 1975–6 were: Revenue, K14,472,000,000; Expenditure, K15,521,000,000. The monetary unit is the *Kyat* of 100 *Pyas.* (For rate of exchange, *see* p. 83).

Production, Industry and Commerce.—Three-quarters of the population depend on agriculture; the chief products are rice, oilseeds (sesamum and groundnut), maize, millet, cotton, beans, wheat, grain, tea, sugarcane, Virginia and Burmese tobacco, jute and rubber. Rice has traditionally been the mainstay of Burma's economy but the poor harvest of 1972–73 and increased home consumption have greatly reduced the quantity of exported rice. Exports in 1974 amounted to 374,600 tons, including by-products.

The net area sown to all crops in 1974–75 was 23,519,000 acres and reserved forests covered 37,414 square miles. The principal export after rice is teak, of which some 200,000 tons were exported annually before the war. The 1974 figure was 112,800 cubic tons.

Burma is rich in minerals, including petroleum, lead, silver, tungsten, zinc, tin, wolfram and gemstones. Of these, petroleum products are the most important. Oil is now being produced from oilfields in Myanaung, Prome and Shwepyitha and at Chauk, Yenangyaung, Mann, and Letpando. Production of crude oil in 1973–74 totalled 217,390,000 gallons. There is a refinery at the main oilfield, Chauk, and another at Syriam near Rangoon. Their combined output of petroleum products is sufficient for most of Burma's needs. The production and distribution of petroleum and the importation of oil products is a monopoly of Myanna Oil Corporation (formerly Burmah Oil Company (1954), Ltd.) which is owned by the Government of Burma.

Under the Government's development plan, a cement plant, a brick and tile factory, a steel rolling mill, a jute bag and twine mill, four cotton spinning and weaving mills, a pharmaceutical plant, a large hydro-electric scheme, five sugar factories, a paper factory and a plywood factory are in operation. West German soft loans have been made available to finance construction of a glass factory, a fertilizer plant, a textile mill, a natural gas liquefying plant, a soda ash factory and a formaldahyde plant, as well as a seismic survey for crude oil sources and technical assistance in the general field of mineral exploitation.

The Japanese Government has approved a third commodity loan of US $22,000,000. Loans amounting to US $95,000,000 have been extended by the World Bank for rail and water transport services, whilst the Asian Development Bank has loaned US $16,300,000 for the fishing and rice products industries. The UNDP Governing Council has approved US $35,000,000 towards the Second Country Programme for Burma covering 1974 to 1978, and consisting of 52 large scale and 25 small scale projects.

Burma joined the Colombo Plan in 1952 and is now receiving important assistance from member countries and through the specialized agencies of the United Nations.

Communications.—The Irrawaddy and its chief tributary, the Chindwin, form important waterways, the main stream being navigable beyond Bhamo (900 miles from its mouth) and carrying much traffic.

Ψ The chiefs eaports are Rangoon, Moulmein, Akyab and Bassein. Transit from London to Rangoon: by sea, 35 days; by air, 16 hours.

The Burma Railways network covers 2,688 route miles, extending to Myitkyina, on the Upper Irrawaddy. The first diesel locomotives were introduced in 1958 and there are now 164 diesel locomotives in service, as well as 217 steam. There were 2,452 miles of Union highways and 11,051 miles of other main roads in 1973–74. Since the war a considerable network of internal air services has come into being. The airport at Mingaladon, about 11 miles north of Rangoon, has been reconstructed and handles international traffic.

CAPITAL.—The chief city of Lower Burma, and the seat of the government of the Union is Rangoon, on the left bank of the Rangoon river, about 21 miles from the sea. The city contains the Shwe Dagon pagoda, much venerated by Burmese Buddhists. Population (1973), 3,186,886.

Mandalay, the chief city of Upper Burma, had a population of 781,819 in 1973, Moulmein of 679,484 and Bassein of 335,588. Pagan, on the Irrawaddy, S.W. of Mandalay, contains many sacred buildings of interest to antiquaries.

FLAG.—The Union flag is red, with a canton of dark blue, inside which are a cogwheel and two rice ears surrounded by 14 white stars.

NATIONAL DAY.—January 4.

BRITISH EMBASSY
(80 Strand Road, Rangoon.)

Ambassador Extraordinary and Plenipotentiary, His Excellency Terence John O'Brien, C.M.G., M.C. (1974)................................ £6,925
1st Secretaries, J. S. Chick (*Head of Chancery and Consul*); T. K. Blackman (*Commercial*).
Defence and Military Attaché, Lt.-Col. M. E. A. Berryman.
2nd Secretary, J. A. Stevens.

BURUNDI
(Republic of Burundi)

President, Michel Micombero, *assumed office,* Nov. 28, 1966.
Foreign Affairs, Gilles Bimazubute.

Formerly a Belgian trusteeship under the United Nations, Burundi was proclaimed an independent State on July 1, 1962. Situated on the east side of Lake Tanganyika, the State has an area of 10,747 sq. miles and a population (estimated, 1969) of 3,475,000. There are some 2,500 Europeans and 1,500 Asians. The majority of the population are of the Bahutu tribe, but power rests in the hands of the minority Batutsi tribe.

Burundi became independent as a Constitutional monarchy but this was overthrown on November 28, 1966. The Constitution and Parliament were also abolished. The President rules through a Cabinet of Ministers and the UPRONA party apparatus. Burundi is a one-Party State.

The chief crop is coffee, representing about 80 per cent. of Burundi's export earnings, some 87 per cent. of which is exported to the United States. Cotton is the second most important crop. Minerals and hides and skins exports are also important. Joint economic arrangements of Burundi with Rwanda ended in 1964 and each country now has its own national bank, coffee organization, etc.

Trade with U.K.

	1973	1974
Imports from U.K...	£1,116,000	£590,000
Exports to U.K.....	464,000	964,000

Trade with U.K.

	1973	1974
Imports from U.K...	£3,767,000	£4,366,000
Exports to U.K.....	6,979,000	4,099,000

The currency is the Burundi *Franc*. The rate of exchange was *Bu. Fr.* 203= £1 (June 1973). Government expenditure for 1972 was *Bu. Fr.* 2,400,000,000 and revenue the same.

CAPITAL.—Bujumbura (*formerly* Usumbura), with about 70,000 inhabitants. Gitega (7,000 inhabitants) is the only other sizeable town. Official languages are Kirundi, a Bantu language, and French. Kiswahili is also used.

FLAG.—White diagonal cross on green and red quarters, with a circular white panel in the centre.

NATIONAL DAY.—July 1.

British Ambassador, His Excellency Richard James Stratton, C.M.G. (1974) (*resident at* Kinshasa, Zaire).

CAMBODIA
(*formerly* Khmer Republic)

Prime Minister, Penn Nouth.

Head of State of the Royal Government of the National Union of Cambodia, Prince Norodom Sihanouk.

CAMBODIAN EMBASSY
26 Townshend Road, N.W.8.
[01–722 8802]

Ambassador Extraordinary and Plenipotentiary, His Excellency Douc Rasy.

Minister Counsellor, Unn Saoeum.

Counsellor, So Yandara.

Area and Population.—Situated between Thailand and South Vietnam and extending from the border with Laos on the north to the Gulf of Thailand, Cambodia covers an area of some 70,000 square miles. It has a population (estimated, 1973) of 7,300,000. (*For* MAP, *see* Index.)

History.—Once a powerful kingdom, which, as the Khmer Empire, flourished between the tenth and fourteenth centuries, Cambodia became a French protectorate in 1863 and was granted independence within the French Union as an Associate State in 1949. Two years earlier Prince (then King) Norodom Sihanouk had promulgated a constitution providing for parliamentary government. Full independence was proclaimed on November 9, 1953. The Geneva Conference of 1954 took Cambodia further along the road to independence by ensuring the withdrawal of French and Vietminh forces from the country, and the process was completed when, in January, 1955, the Kingdom of Cambodia became financially and economically independent not only of France but also of Laos and Vietnam. For the next fifteen years the political life of the country was dominated by Prince Norodom Sihanouk, first as King, then as Head of Government after he had abdicated in favour of his father and finally (following his father's death in 1960) as Head of State. Although the *Sangkum Reastr Nyum* or Popular Socialist Community, which he set up to embody his political views still won all the seats in the National Assembly elections of September, 1966, his initial popularity was, towards the end of the sixties, increasingly dimmed by criticism both of his management of the economy and of the pro-communist slant of the neutralist policy he proclaimed, which condoned extensive use of Cambodian territory by the North Vietnamese in their military operations against South Vietnam.

On March 18, 1970, during his absence from the country, Prince Sihanouk was deposed as Head of State by a vote of the National Assembly. A Republic was declared on October 9, 1970, and the name of the country changed to the Khmer Republic. A constitution was adopted by referendum on April 30, 1972 and Marshal Lon Nol elected President. A bicameral parliament was elected in September 1972. Prince Sihanouk has however maintained a rival government-in-exile in Peking (Royal Government of National Union of Cambodia—GRUNC).

In April 1970 widespread fighting developed between communist Viet-Namese and Khmer forces which gradually developed into a general civil war with republican forces controlling the major centres of population and large areas of the country falling under the control of insurgents supported by North Viet-Namese. With large-scale assistance from the United States the armed forces of the Republic were increased from 35,000 in 1970 to 250,000 in 1973.

In March 1973 a State of National Emergency was declared, various clauses of the constitution were suspended and a coalition " government of exception " formed under the premiership of In Tam. Following In Tam's resignation in December 1973, Long Boret, formerly Foreign Minister, was appointed Prime Minister.

In April 1975 Phnom Penh fell to the insurgents. Khien Samphan, ran the government and Prince Sihanouk returned to Cambodia on September 9, to resume his role as Head of State.

Geography, Economy and Communications.—Cambodia has an economy based on agriculture, fishing and forestry, the bulk of its people being rice-growing farmers living in the basins of the Mekong and Tonlé Sap rivers. In addition to rice, which is the staple crop, the major products are rubber, livestock, maize, timber, pepper, palm sugar, fresh and dried fish, kapok, beans, soya and tobacco. Rice and rubber are normally the main exports though rubber production was brought to a standstill by the hostilities, and rice exports ceased in 1972, the country becoming for the first time a substantial importer. Fifty per cent. of the total land area is forest or jungle, abounding in wild life of all kinds, including big game. The climate is tropical monsoon with a rainy season from May to October.

The country has over 5,000 kilometres of roads, of which nearly half are hard-surfaced and passable in the rainy season. There are two railways. One runs from Phnom-Penh to the Thai border; the other from Phnom-Penh to Kampot and on to Sihanoukville (*formerly* Kompong Som). Both railways and much of the road system have been damaged and badly neglected since 1970. Phnom-Penh is a river capable of receiving ships of up to 2,500 tons all the year round. The deep water port at Sihanoukville on the Gulf of Thailand can receive ships up to 10,000 tons. The port is linked to Phnom-Penh by a modern highway.

There is no heavy industry but factories processing local produce or designed to reduce dependence on imports were established prior to 1970, several of them with aid from communist countries. They include jute, sugar, plywood, tyre, textile, bottle, cement and paper factories as well as a brewery, oil refinery and vehicle assembly plant. Production of all such industry has been greatly reduced or suspended altogether as a result of military activity. In addition the new régime appears to be pursuing a deliberately anti-industrial line, expelling the city-dwellers into the country-side.

Khmer's foreign aid previously came mainly from France and the Communist bloc. Much of this aid has been suspended since the deposition of Prince Sihanouk but French cultural influence and education are still prominent. U.S. economic aid was instituted late in 1970, and was running at the rate of about $280,000,000 a year. U.S. military aid amounted to about $350,000,000 a year.

Religion and Education.—The state religion is Buddhism of the " Little Vehicle ". There are also small Muslim and Christian communities. The national language is Khmer, although French is widely spoken. In the years preceding the civil war considerable efforts had been devoted to the development of education and new schools, colleges and technical institutes had been established. Until April 1975 there was a Buddhist University in Phnom-Penh, where there were also Faculties of Arts, Medicine and Law and a Technological Institute. Several residential teachers' training colleges were in operation.

Trade with U.K.

	1973	1974
Imports from U.K....	£1,100,000	£872,000
Exports to U.K......	—	269,000

CAPITAL, Phnom-Penh.

FLAG.—Red, with a broad strip of dark green at top and bottom; in centre a white emblem of the Temple of Angkor Wat.

NATIONAL DAY.—October 9.

BRITISH EMBASSY
96 Moha Vithei 9 Tola,
Phnom-Penh.
(temporarily closed)

CAMEROUN REPUBLIC
(United Republic of Cameroun)

President, Ahmadou Ahidjo, *elected for* 5 *years*, May 5, 1960; *re-elected for* 5 *years*, May 7, 1965 and Mar. 20, 1970.

CAMEROUN EMBASSY
84 Holland Park, W.11.
[01-727 0771]

Ambassador Extraordinary and Plenipotentiary, His Excellency Michel Koss Epanqué (1975).
2nd Counsellor, Nkuo Thaddeus.
1st Secretary, Francis Isidore Wainchom Nkwain.

The United Republic of Cameroun lies on the Gulf of Guinea between Nigeria to the west, Chad and the Central African Republic to the east and Congo and Gabon and Equatorial Guinea to the south. It has an area of 183,381 sq. miles (432,000 sq. km.) and a population estimated (1970) at 5,836,000. Principal products are cocoa, coffee, bananas, cotton, timber, ground-nuts, aluminium, rubber and palm products. There is an aluminium smelting plant at Edéa with an annual capacity of 50,000 tons. Annual trade of the United Republic is approximately, Exports, £87,000,000; Imports, £105,000,000.

Trade with U.K.

	1973	1974
Imports from U.K......	£464,000	£964,000
Exports to U.K........	1,116,000	590,000

The whole territory was administered by Germany from 1884 to 1916. From 1916 to 1959, the former East Cameroun was administered by France as a League of Nations (later U.N.) trusteeship. On Jan. 1, 1960 it became independent as the Republic of Cameroun. The Republic was joined on October 1, 1961, by the former British administered trust territory of the Southern Cameroons, after a plebiscite held under United Nations auspices. Cameroun became a Federal Republic governed by a President, Vice-President and 19 Federal Ministers, with separate East and West Cameroun state governments. Subsequently in a plebiscite held in May, 1972, there was an overwhelming vote in favour of the proposal that Cameroun should become a United Republic and on July 3, 1972, the President appointed the first government of the United Republic, comprising 24 ministers.

CAPITAL.—Yaoundé (180,000). Ψ Douala (250,000), is an important commercial centre.

FLAG.—Vertical stripes of green, red and yellow with two five-pointed stars in upper half of green band.

NATIONAL DAY.—January 1 (Independence Day).

BRITISH EMBASSY
Yaoundé

Ambassador Extraordinary and Plenipotentiary, His Excellency Edward Ferguson Given, C.M.G. (1972).................................£6,925
1st Secretaries, P. J. C. Radley (*Head of Chancery and Consul*); S. A. Priddle (*Labour*).
2nd Secretaries, Miss L. P. Walker; R. Canning.
British Council Representative, H. F. Grant.

CAPE VERDE ISLANDS

President, Aristides Pereira *born* 1924, *assumed office*, July 5, 1975.

The Cape Verde Islands, off the west coast of Africa, consist of two groups of islands, *Windward* (Santa Antão, São Vicente, Santa Luzia, São Nicolau Boa Vista and Sal) and *Leeward* (Maio, São Tiago, Fogo and Brava) with a total area of 1,516 sq. miles and a population (1970) of 272,071. *Capital*, Ψ Praia (1970, 6,000).

The Islands colonised in c. 1460 achieved independence from Portugal on July 5, 1975, after the decision of the Armed Forces Movement to give up the Portuguese colonies. Elections for a constituent assembly were held on June 30. President Pereira favours an eventual political union of the islands with neighbouring Guinea-Bissau and Article 1 of the latter's constitution expresses a similar wish. (Till 1879 Guinea-Bissau and the Islands were a single administrative unit).

CENTRAL AFRICAN REPUBLIC

President, Marshal Jean Bedel Bokassa, *assumed office* Jan. 1, 1966.

Formerly the French colony of Ubanghi Shari, the Republic lies just north of the Equator between the Cameroun Republic and the southern part of Sudan. It has a common boundary with the Republic of Chad in the north and with Zaire in the south. The Republic has an area of about 234,000 sq. miles and a population of 2,255,536 (Census of 1968). On December 1 1958, Ubanghi Shari elected to remain within the French Community and adopted the title of the Central African Republic. It became fully independent on August 17 1960. The first President of the Central African Republic, M. David Dacko, held office from 1960 until Jan. 1, 1966, when he was replaced by the then Col. Bokassa after a *coup d'état*. Imports from U.K. 1974, £409,000; Exports to U.K., £515,000.

CAPITAL.—Bangui, near the border with the Congolese Republic (301,793).

FLAG.—Four horizontal stripes blue, white, yellow, green, crossed by central vertical red stripe; a yellow star in centre of blue half-stripe next staff.

CHAD REPUBLIC

Head of State, Gen. Felix Malloum, *assumed office*, May, 1975.

Situated in north-central Africa, the Chad Republic extends from 23° N. latitude to 7° N. latitude and is flanked by the Republics of Niger and Cameroun on the west, by Libya in the north, by the Sudan on the east and by the Central African Republic on the south. (*For* MAP, *see* Index.) It has an area of 487,920 sq. miles and a population now estimated at 4,000,000. Chad became a member state of the French Community on Nov. 28, 1958, and was proclaimed fully independent on August 11, 1960. On April 14, 1962, a new Constitution was adopted involving a presidential-type régime. Mr. Tombalbaye accepted the formal title of President on April 23, 1962. He was killed in the military coup on April 13, 1975.

Trade with U.K.

	1973	1974
Imports from U.K.	£170,000	£209,000
Exports to U.K.	476,000	1,378,000

CAPITAL.—Ndjaména (formerly known as Fort Lamy) south of Lake Chad (126,000).

FLAG.—Vertical stripes, blue, yellow and red.

CHILE
(República de Chile)

Head of State, General Augusto Pinochet (Ugarte), *born*, November 25, 1915, Army Commander-in-Chief and President of the Military Junta that took power on September 11, 1973.

Other Junta Members, Admiral José Toribio Merino (Castro), C.-in-C. Navy; General Gustavo Leigh (Guzmán), C.-in-C. Air Force; General César Mendoza (Durán), Director-General of Carabineros.

CABINET
(April 14, 1975)

Foreign Affairs, Vice Adm. Patricio Carvajal.
Interior, Gen. César Benavides.
Defence, Gen. Herman Brady Roche.
Education, Rear Adm. Arturo Troncoso Daroch.
Mines, Sr. Luis E. Valenzeuela Blanquier.
Economic Co-ordination, Sr. Raúl Sáez.
Finance, Sr. Jorge Cauás.
Economy, Sr. Sergio de-Castro Spikula.
Justice, Sr. Miguel Schweitzer Speisky.
Public Works, Sr. Hugo Leon Puelma.
Transport, Gen. Enrique Garín.
Agriculture, Gen. Tucapel Vallejos.
Land and Settlement, Gen. Mario Mackay.
Labour, Gen. Nicanor Diaz.
Health, Gen. Francisco Herrera.
Housing, Sr. Carlos Granifo Harms.
Minister without Portfolio, Gen. Hernan Bejares Gonzalez (*Secretary General to the Government*).

CHILEAN EMBASSY AND CONSULATE IN LONDON
12 Devonshire Street, W.1
[01-580 6392]

Ambassador Extraordinary and Plenipotentiary, His Excellency Admiral Kaare Olsen.
Minister-Counsellor, Sr. Alberto Besa.
Counsellor, Sr. Carlos Costa-Nora (*Consular*).
Naval Attaché, Rear Adm. Raúl Lopez.
Air Attaché, Col. Juan Cerda.
1st Secretary, Sr. Fernando Cousiño.
2nd Secretary, Sr. Jaime Pardo.

3rd Secretary, Sr. Jorge Montero.
Asst. Naval Attaché, Capt. Jorge Le May.
Cultural and Press Attaché, Sr. Jorge Navarrate.

A State of South America, of Spanish origin, lying between the Andes and the shores of the South Pacific, extending coastwise from just north of Arica to Cape Horn south, between lat. 17° 15' and 55° 59' S. and long 66° 30' and 75° 48' W. Extreme length of the country is about 2,800 miles, with an average breadth, north of 41°, of 100 miles. The great chain of the Andes runs along its eastern limit, with a general elevation of 5,000 to 15,000 feet above the level of the sea; but numerous summits attain a greater height. The chain, however, lowers considerably towards its southern extremity. The Andes form a boundary with Argentina, and at the head of the pass where the international road from Chile to Argentina crosses the frontier, has been erected a statue of *Christ the Redeemer,* 26 feet high, made of bronze from old cannon, to commemorate the peaceful settlement of a boundary dispute in 1902. There are no rivers of great size, and none of them is of much service as a navigable highway. In the north the country is arid. (*For* MAP, *see* p. 815.)

Among the island possessions of Chile are the *Juan Fernandez group* (3 islands) about 360 miles distant from Valparaiso, where a wireless station has been erected. One of these islands is the reputed scene of Alexander Selkirk's (Robinson Crusoe) shipwreck. *Easter Island* (27° 8' S. and 109° 28' W.), about 2,000 miles distant in the South Pacific Ocean, contains stone platforms and hundreds of stone figures, the origin of which has not yet been determined. The area of the island is about 45 sq. miles.

Chile is divided into 25 provinces and 13 administrative and economic regions and the total area of the Republic is estimated at 290,000 square miles, with a population (estimated, 1971) of 10,000,000. Two of these provinces, Arica and Antofagasta, were annexed from Peru and Bolivia respectively after the War of the Pacific (1879–84). The province of Tacna was also annexed but under a treaty signed in 1929 was returned to Peru which at the same time received payment of £1,200,000 for Arica. The Chilean population has four main sources: (*a*) Spanish settlers and their descendants; (*b*) indigenous Araucanian Indians, Fuegians, and Changos; (*c*) mixed Spanish Indians; and (*d*) European immigrants. Only the few remaining indigenous Indians and some originally Bolivian Indians in the north are racially separate. Following extensive inter-marriage there is no effective distinction among the remainder.

Government.—Chile was discovered by Spanish adventurers in the 16th century, and remained under Spanish rule until 1810, when a revolutionary war, culminating in the *Battle of Maipu* (April 5, 1818), achieved the independence of the nation. Chilean women obtained equal voting rights with men on Dec. 21, 1948, before which they only participated in municipal elections

At a general election held on Sept. 4, 1970, the Marxist candidate Dr. Allende was elected President by a narrow margin. A new Cabinet took office on Oct. 30, 1970.

Severe industrial unrest, notably a crippling strike by the National Confederation of Lorry Owners, which began in July 1973, led to sympathy strikes in other occupations; there were widespread violent incidents and a congressional vote of censure against the Government, with resultant resignations from the Cabinet. The Government of Dr. Salvador Allende was overthrown on September 11, 1973, by a *coup* planned, and carried out within a few hours, by leaders of the Armed Forces and National Police. President Allende was said to have committed suicide.

Although the Constitution of 1925 is still notionally in force, the National Congress has been dissolved, Marxist parties have been banned, as have all political activities. As a temporary expedient the Government has assumed wide-ranging civil powers. Inflation is still the main problem; in April 1975 the *Escudo* was devalued for the 34th time since the military assumed power.

Production.—Wheat, maize, barley, oats, beans, peas, rice, lentils, wines, tobacco, hemp, chili-pepper, potatoes, sugar beet, onions and melons are grown extensively and livestock accounts for nearly 40 per cent. of agricultural production. The vine and all European fruit trees flourish in the central zone and fruit is a fairly important export item. Good wines are produced and exported and are becoming more widely known in world markets. Sheep farming predominates in the extreme south (Province of Magallanes). There are large timber tracts in the central and southern zones of Chile, some types of which are exported, along with wood derivatives such as cellulose, to Europe and the Argentine and other markets. The mineral wealth is considerable, the country being particularly rich in copper-ore, iron-ore and nitrate. Uranium is also said to have been discovered in small quantities. Copper production in 1973 totalled 768,860 metric tons. Copper provides over 70 per cent. of Chile's exports earnings, the remainder of which are derived mainly from other minerals, wool, fruit, fish and forestry derivatives. The rainless north is the scene of the only commercial production of nitrate of soda (Chile saltpetre) from natural resources in the world. Production in 1973 (including potassium nitrate) was 676,000 metric tons. Chile also produces iodine, manganese ore, coal, mercury, molybdenum, zinc, lead and a small quantity of gold. 1,309,800 metric tons of coal and 9,314,200 long tons of iron ores were produced in 1973. The country has also large deposits of high grade sulphur, but mostly around high extinct volcanoes in the Andes Cordillera, difficult of access. Production of refined sulphur has hitherto been in relatively small quantities, but reached 96,323 metric tons in 1972. Oil was struck in Magallanes (Tierra del Fuego) in December, 1945. Production in 1973 was 1,817,000 cu. metres of crude oil and 7,376,000,000 cu. metres of natural gas—all in the Magallanes area. This total production, and imported crude oil, amounting in 1973 to about 70 per cent. of the input, is refined at Concon and San Vicente in the central part of the country. A large steel plant was completed and started operation during 1950 at Huachipato, near Concepción. Current production capacity is about 600,000 metric tons of steel ingots per year, to be increased to one million metric tons per year.

Most consumer goods are manufactured locally— copper, steel and oil derivatives, pulp and paper, cement and other building materials, tobacco, cutlery, food products and beverages, sugar refining, textiles, clothing and footwear, plastic products, household equipment, tyres and other rubber products, radio and television sets, chemicals, pharmaceutical products, soaps, detergents and cosmetics. New classes of manufacture being developed are in the fields of motor-vehicle assembly, chemicals and petrochemicals, cellulose, metallurgy and some electrical, electronic and mechanical equipment.

Communications.—Chilean ships have a virtual monopoly in the coastwise trade, though, with the improvement of the roads, an increasing share of internal transportation is moving by road and rail. Foreign trade continues to be carried on mostly by foreign steamship lines operating either directly to the West Coasts of North and South America, or *viâ* the Straits of Magellan. Chilean vessels have also been participating for many years in foreign trade with North America and Europe. The Chilean mercantile marine numbers about 63 vessels (of over 100 tons gross) with a total deadweight tonnage of about 570,313. Under a law promulgated in June, 1956, 50 per cent. of Chile's foreign trade must be carried by Chilean vessels with the intention of this figure eventually reaching 100 per cent. of bulk and refrigerated cargoes.

The first railway was opened in 1851 and there are now 6,575 miles of track. A metre-gauge line (the *Longitudinâl*) runs from La Calera, just north of Santiago, to Iquique. The wide gauge railway (1·676 metres) runs from Valparaiso through La Calera, 60 miles inland, and after passing through Santiago ends at Puerto Montt.

With the completion of a section of 435 miles from Corumba, Brazil, to Santa Cruz, Boliva, the Trans-Continental Line will link the Chilean Pacific port of Arica with Rio de Janeiro on the Atlantic. Another line from Antofagasta to Salta (Argentine) was opened in 1948. Further south, the Trans-Andine Railway connects Valparaiso on the Pacific with Buenos Aires, crossing the Andes at 11,500 ft.

Chile is served by 15 international airlines. The domestic traffic is carried almost exclusively by the State-owned Linea Aerea Nacional, which also operates internationally. Chile has an extensive system of airports which are being modernized with international financial assistance.

Chile's road system is about 65,000 kilometres in length, but only an estimated 7,000 kilometres are first-class paved highways. At the end of 1970 there were registered 216,000 cars and taxis, 15,773 buses and coaches and 143,000 goods vehicles, excluding about 11,000 tractors.

Defence.—Military service is compulsory, but not all those who are liable are required. Recruitment for the Navy is voluntary. The Army has 5 infantry divisions and 1 cavalry division with a total strength of 1,760 officers, 11,000 regular other ranks plus 20,000 conscripts. In addition there is a police force of " Carabineros " of 30,000 officers and men. The Air Force has 800 officers and 8,700 other ranks with a strength of 200 aircraft. The Navy consists of 3 cruisers, 4 destroyers, 2 destroyer escorts, 4 submarines and 4 motor torpedo boats, all operational. There is a support force of transports, tankers, 1 submarine depôt ship and ancillary small craft. The strength of the Navy is 915 officers and 12,500 men, plus a Marine Force of 60 officers and 2,000 men.

Education.—Elementary education is free, and has been compulsory since 1920. There are 8 Universities (3 in Santiago, 2 in Valparaiso, 1 in Antofagasta, 1 in Concepción and 1 in Valdivia). The religion is Roman Catholic.

Language and Literature.—Spanish is the language of the country, with admixtures of local words of Indian origin. Recent efforts have reduced illiteracy and have thus afforded access to the literature of Spain, to supplement the vigorous national output. The Nobel Prize for Literature was awarded in 1945 to Señorita Gabriela Mistral, for Chilean verse and prose, and in 1971 to the poet Pablo Neruda. There are over 100 newspapers and a large number of periodicals, including some devoted to professional, scientific and social subjects.

Finance.—Total revenue for 1973 was estimated at $E°165,168,400,000$ and expenditure at $E°286,132,300,000$. Foreign debt in May 1975 was estimated at some U.S. $3,750,000,000.

The official rate of exchange, 1975, was about $E°9,911 = £1$ (banker's rate) and $E°11,065 = £1$ (broker's rate).

EXTERNAL TRADE
(Final figures)

	1973	1974
Total imports .	$U.S.1,691,000,000	2,178,400,000
Total exports .	1,356,000,000	2,043,400,000

Trade with U.K.

	1973	1974
Imports from U.K...	£16,805,000	£36,878,000
Exports to U.K.....	57,293,000	86,516,000

The principal exports are metallic and non-metallic minerals (refined copper, ingots and bars, iron ore, etc.), wood derivatives, some metal products, vegetables, fruit and wool. The principal imports are wheat and other food products, industrial raw materials, machinery, equipment and spares, oil fuels, transportation equipment and raw cotton.

CAPITAL, Santiago, 4,000,000 (Greater Santiago). Other large towns are:—Ψ Valparaiso (500,000), Concepción (170,000), Temuco (110,000), Ψ Antofagasta (110,000), Chillán (79,461), Ψ Talcahuano (75,643), Talca (75,354); Ψ Valdivia (70,000), Ψ Iquique (50,000), Ψ Punta Arenas (50,000). Punta Arenas, on the Straits of Magellan, is the southernmost city in the world.

FLAG.—2 horizontal bands, white, red; in top sixth a white star on blue square, next staff.

NATIONAL DAY.—September 18 (National Anniversary).

BRITISH EMBASSY.
Avenida La Concepción 177, Piso 4° Santiago (Casilla 72D)

Ambassador Extraordinary and Plenipotentiary, His Excellency Reginald Louis Secondé, C.M.G., C.V.O. (1973).

1st Secretaries, P. W. Summerscale (*Head of Chancery*); R. Bedford (*Commercial*).

Defence Attaché, Capt. P. B. Archer, R.N.

2nd Secretaries, A. W. Shave (*Commercial*); P. Langmead (*Information*); M. I. P. Webb (*Chancery*); D. Fernyhough (*Consul/AO*).

BRITISH CONSULAR OFFICES
There are British Consular Offices at *Santiago, Antofagasta, Arica, Valparaiso, Concepción, Coquimbo* and *Punta Arenas.*

BRITISH COUNCIL
Representative in Chile, V. A. Atkinson, Calle Eliodoro Yañez 832, Santiago (Casilla 154-D).

The Council supplies books to the libraries of the *Instituto Chileno-Britanico* in *Santiago* and in *Viña del Mar/Valparaiso.*

Valparaiso is distant from London 9,000 miles *viâ* Panama, and 11,000 *viâ* the Strait; transit 28 to 45 days; by air, 22 hrs.

CHINA

(Zhonghua Renmin Gongheguo—
The People's Republic of China.)

Chairman of the Standing Committee of the Fourth National People's Congress, Chu Teh.

Secretary-General of the Fourth NPC Standing Committee, Chi Peng-fei.

Premier, Chou En-lai.

Vice-Premiers, Teng Hsiao-ping; Chang Chun-chiao; Li Hsien-nien; Chen Hsi-lien; Chi Teng-kuei; Hua Kuo-feng; Chen Yung-kuei; Wu Kuei-hsien; Wang Chen; Yu Chiu-li; Ku Mu; Sun Chien.

MINISTERS

Foreign Affairs, Chiao Kuan-hua.
National Defence, Yeh Chien-ying.
State Planning Commission, Yu Chiu-li.
State Capital Construction Commission, Ku Mu.
Public Security, Hua Kuo-feng.
Foreign Trade, Li Chiang.
Economic Relations With Foreign Countries, Fang Yi.
Agriculture and Forestry, Sha Feng.
Metallurgical Industry, Chen Shao-kun.
Machine Building, Li Shui-ching, (*1st Ministry*); Liu Hsi-yao (*2nd*); Li Chi-tai (*3rd*); Wang Cheng (*4th*); Li Cheng-fang (*5th*); Pien Chiang (*6th*); Wang Yang (*7th*).
Coal Industry, Hsu Chin-chiang.
Petroleum and Chemical Industries, Kang Shih-en.
Water Conservancy and Power, Chien Cheng-ying.
Light Industry, Chien Chih-kuang.
Railways, Wan Li.
Communications, Yeh Fei.
Posts and Telecommunications, Chung Fu-hsiang.
Finance, Chang Ching-fu.
Commerce, Fan Tzu-yu.
Culture, Yu Hui-yung.
Education, Chou Jung-hsin.
Public Health, Liu Hsiang-ping.
Physical Culture and Sport, Chuang Tse-tung.

THE CHINESE COMMUNIST PARTY

Chairman of the Central Committee, Mao Tse-tung.
Vice-Chairmen of the Central Committee, Chou En-lai; Wang Hung-wen; Kang Sheng; Yeh Chien-ying; Teng Hsiao-ping.
The Standing Committee of the Politbureau of the Central Committee, Mao Tse-tung; Wang Hung-wen; Yeh Chien-ying; Chu Teh; Chang Chun-chiao; Chou En-lai; Kang Sheng; Teng Hsiao-ping.
The Politbureau, Mao Tse-tung; Wang Hung-wen; Wei Kuo-ching; Yeh Chien-ying; Liu Po-cheng; Chiang Ching; Chu Teh; Hsu Shih-yu; Hua Kuo-feng; Chi Teng-kuei; Wu Teh; Wang Tung-hsing; Chen Yung-kuei; Chen Hsi-lien; Li Hsien-nien; Li Te-sheng; Chang Chun-chiao; Chou En-lai; Yao Wen-yuan; Kang Sheng; Teng Hsiao-ping (*full members*); Wu Kuei-hsien; Su Chen-hua; Ni Chih-fu; Saifudin (*alternate members*).

EMBASSY IN LONDON
31 Portland Place, W.1
[01-636 5726]

Ambassador Extraordinary and Plenipotentiary, His Excellency Sung Chih-kuang.
Counsellors, Chu Chi-yuan; Peng Jun-min (*Commercial*); Hu Ting-yi; Ting Wen-pin.
Military, Naval and Air Attaché, Shih Hsin-Jen.
1st Secretaries, Hung Lung (*Consular*); Hou Ping-Lin; Liu Ching-hua; Lin Hsiang-ming.
2nd Secretaries, Madame Hsieh Heng; Hu Nan-sheng; Sung Kuei-pao; Lei Wei-tsung; Wu Sheng-yuan.

AREA AND POPULATION.—The area of China is about 4,300,000 square miles. Estimates of the present population vary considerably, but the U.N. estimate for 1972 gave a figure of 800,721,000. The Chinese also now make public reference to a population of 800,000,000. According to figures published in 1957 by the National Bureau of Statistics, the total population of China was 656,630,000, not including Chinese living in Hong Kong, Macau or abroad. A birth-rate of 32 per 1,000 and death rate of 17 per 1,000 were estimated for 1970. In 1953 the percentage distribution of the population was as follows:

Han, 94·13; Mongolian, 0·26; Tibetan, 0·48; Manchu, 0·41; Tribal, 3·57; Others, 1·15. There is no reason to suppose that the proportions have significantly changed.

THE PROVINCES OF CHINA.

Population figures made public in 1967–71 were as follows:

Anhwei	35,000,000
Chekiang	31,000,000
Chinghai	2,000,000
Fukien	18,000,000
Heilungkiang	25,000,000
Honan	50,000,000
Hopei	43,000,000
Hunan	38,000,000
Hupeh	38,000,000
Kansu	13,000,000
Kiangsi	25,000,000
Kiangsu	47,000,000
Kirin	20,000,000
Kwangsi Chuang Autonomous Region	24,000,000
Kwangtung	43,000,000
Kweichow	20,000,000
Liaoning	28,000,000
Inner Mongolian Autonomous Region	13,000,000
Ningsia Autonomous Region	2,000,000
Shansi	20,000,000
Shantung	57,000,000
Shensi	21,000,000
Sinkiang Uighur Autonomous Region	8,000,000
Szechuan	70,000,000
Tibet	1,000,000
(Taiwan	15,000,000)
Yunnan	23,000,000

Sinkiang is the largest region or province in area (about 1/6th of the whole area of the country) and Szechuan the most populous.

Government.—On October 10, 1911, the party of reform forced the Imperial dynasty to a "voluntary" abdication, and a Republic was proclaimed at Wuchang. Events leading up to the end of the war with Japan are briefly described in earlier issues of WHITAKER'S ALMANACK.

On September 30, 1949, the Chinese People's Political Consultative Conference (C.P.P.C.C.) met in Peking and appointed the National People's Government Council under the Chairmanship of Mao Tse-tung. On October 1, Mao proclaimed the inauguration of the Chinese People's Republic. The Soviet Union broke off relations with the Nationalists and established relations with the new *régime* on October 2. The *régime* was recognized by all the Communist *bloc* countries in quick succession, and soon after by the Asian countries of the Commonwealth, the United Kingdom and by a number of other countries. France recognized the Chinese People's Republic on January 27, 1964. Canada agreed to recognize the People's Republic in October 1970. From 1970 to 1975 the Chinese People's Republic has established or renewed diplomatic relations with over 50 countries. The United States and certain other countries continue to recognize the Nationalist *régime* in Formosa.

The C.P.P.C.C. continued to be the supreme legislative body of the new state until September 20, 1954, when a new constitution was adopted. It was then replaced as the highest organ of state power by the National People's Congress which exercised legislative power.

With the adoption of the 1954 Constitution, the National People's Government Council was replaced by the State Council, composed of the Premier, 16 Vice-Premiers and the heads of ministries and commissions. This body was the supreme administrative body, responsible for the day-to-day running of the country.

In January 1975 a new Constitution was adopted by the Fourth National People's Congress, which established the leading role of the Chinese Communist Party in all spheres of national life. Institutions such as the National People's Congress and the State Council and the system of People's Congresses remain, but their powers are less clearly defined under the new Constitution, or are curtailed. The post of State Chairman has been abolished, and the Standing Committee of the National People's Congress now appears to act as a kind of collective Head of State. Among its powers is that of acting for the country in its dealings with foreign states, i.e. in the despatch and recall of Chinese representatives abroad and the reception of foreign diplomatic envoys. The National People's Congress, which is supposed to hold one session a year, is empowered to amend the Constitution, make laws, appoint and remove the Premier and members of the State Council on the recommendation of the Party Central Committee, and to approve the national economic plan, the state budget and the final state accounts. Command over the armed forces is now vested in the Chairman of the Chinese Communist Party.

The system of elections to local People's Congresses and to the National People's Congress is maintained under the new Constitution; but there is no reference to deputies to congresses at the primary level being " directly elected by the voters ". Deputies to congresses at all levels are now to be elected " through democratic consultation ". Deputies to the National People's Congress are, as before, elected by provinces, autonomous regions, municipalities directly under the Central Government and by the armed forces, but no longer by Chinese resident abroad.

Local government is now entrusted to local Revolutionary Committees. These bodies, which emerged during the Cultural Revolution to replace the former People's Councils, were firmly established under the new Constitution as the permanent organs of the local people's congresses by which they are elected and to which they are accountable, in each instance at the corresponding level. They are also accountable to the " organ of state at the next higher level " (this would appear to mean the people's congress at the next higher level).

Autonomous regions, prefectures and counties continue to exist for national minorities and are described as self-governing. The system prevailing is that found elsewhere, i.e. people's congresses and revolutionary committees. Peking, Shanghai and Tientsin continue to come directly under the central government.

It is only in the 1975 Constitution that the leading role of the Chinese Communist Party is spelt out; but its complete dominance over the Government, which includes " united-front " figures from lesser parties, has always been achieved by ensuring that all the really important positions at whatever level have been filled by Party members.

During the Cultural Revolution both Party and State organs were disrupted. The system of " Revolutionary Committees " was devised to replace the People's Councils at provincial level and below. Party Committees have been reconstituted at all levels. The leadership in both Party and Revolutionary Committees is for the most part identical, thus providing for an interlocking relationship between the two bodies. Until April, 1959, Mao Tse-tung was Chairman both of the Republic and the Communist Party. When he stood down from his position as Head of State his place was taken by Liu Shao-ch'i who was then First Vice-Chairman of the Party. In October 1968, the Party's Central Committee resolved to strip Liu of all his posts both in the Party and in the State. The 10th Congress of the Chinese Communist Party was held in Peking from August 24 to 28, 1973. The Congress was unusual in several respects; the Party Constitution provides that congresses should normally be held every five years, and only four years had passed since the previous one; the Congress was unusually short, lasting only five days compared to 24 days for the ninth congress, and its also took place in unusual secrecy, no official announcement being made until after it had finished. It was stated that 1,249 delegates, representing 28,000,000 party members, attended. The agenda consisted of three items, adoption of the Central Committee's political report, which was presented by Chou En-lai, a report on the revision of the new party constitution adopted in 1969, presented by Wang Hung-wen and election of a new Central Committee of 195 full and 124 alternate members.

Armed Forces.—All three military arms in China are parts of the People's Liberation Army (P.L.A.) The size of this body has not been formally given, but it is estimated that China has between 2½ and 3 million men under arms, with a further 12 million (or perhaps many more) reserves who take part in militia activities. Until 1955 the P.L.A. did not have a rank structure, but one was introduced in that year similar to that of the Russian Army. In the same year compulsory military service was introduced for all men between the ages of 18 and 40. This service was on a selective basis. In January, 1965, the length of service for those conscripted was increased by one year, to four years for the Army, five years for the Air Force and six years for the Navy; and with effect from June 1, 1965, the rank structure was abolished, together with all marks of distinction of branch of service (although members of the services may still be distinguished from one another by the colour of their uniforms). This means a reversion to the previous system by which members of the armed forces are known only by their appointment.

China exploded her first experimental nuclear device on October 16, 1964 and made further tests in 1965 and in May, October and December, 1966. Her first hydrogen bomb was tested in June, 1967, and further tests of nuclear devices were detected up to October, 1970. China launched her first earth-satellite in April, 1970, and a second one in March, 1971.

Religion.—The indigenous religions of China are Confucianism (which includes ancestor worship), Taoism (originally a philosophy rather than a religion) and, since its introduction in the first century of the Christian era, Buddhism. There are also Chinese Moslems and Christians. Since 1949, the practice of all religions has been severely curtailed, although not actually prohibited.

Education.—Although primary education was compulsory under the Nationalists, mass education did not become a fact until after the Communists had taken over. All major educational establishments closed down at the start of the Great Proletarian Cultural Revolution in 1966. Primary and middle school education was interrupted and it was announced that the entire education system was to be reformed. School classes are being resumed, and, among the reforms observable are a reduction in the number of years in primary and middle schools, and the application of the principle of part-work part-study. In the summer of 1970 some of the major institutes of higher education started to enrol new students, and courses started in the autumn. Students are being selected from among workers, peasants, soldiers and also middle-school

graduates who have had two-three years experience of manual labour in factories or in the rural areas. The new courses are from 2–3 years duration.

Language and Literature.—The Chinese language has many dialects, Cantonese, Hakka, Swatow. Foochow, Wenchos, Ning-po and Wu (Shanghai). The Common Speech or *Putonghua* (often referred to as "Mandarin") which is being taught throughout the country is based on the Peking dialect. The Communists, when they came into power, continued the Kuomintang policy of promoting it as the national language and made much more intensive efforts to propagate it throughout the country. Since the most important aspect of this policy is the use of the spoken language in writing, the old literary style of writing has fallen into disuse.

Chinese writing is ideographic and not phonetic. The number of sounds in *Putonghua* is strictly limited; each sound may have a large number of different characters and meanings. Whereas originally the language was monosyllabic and confusion was avoided by the use of different characters, thus producing texts which were visually clear but ambiguous to the ear, with the increasing use of the spoken language for writing people are increasingly making use of polysyllabic compounds both in speech and writing in order to avoid confusion. In 1956, after some 4 years of study, the Government decided to introduce 230 simplified characters with a view to making reading and writing easier, The list was enlarged; there are now about 1,000 simplified characters in use. In January, 1956, all Chinese newspapers and most books began to appear with the characters printed horizontally from left to right, instead of vertically reading from right to left, as previously.

In November 1957, after some experimentation, the Government introduced a system of Romanization, using 25 of the letters of the Latin alphabet (not v). This has been used within the country largely for assisting school children and others to learn the pronunciation of characters in *Putonghua*. It has been announced that there is no intention of using the alphabet to replace characters.

Although the pinyin system of romanisation of names was due to be brought into use from Sept. 1, 1975, it was announced in Peking on Aug. 27 that it would not then be introduced.

Chinese literature is one of the richest in the world. Paper has been employed for writing and printing for nearly 2,000 years. The Confucian classics which formed the basis of the traditional Chinese culture date from the Warring States period (4th–3rd centuries B.C.) as do the earliest texts of the rival tradition, Taoism. Histories, philosophical and scientific works, poetry, literary and art criticism, novels and romances survive from most periods. Many have been translated into English. In the past all this considerable literature was available only to a very small class of *literati*, but with the spread of literacy in the 20th century, a process which has received enormous impetus since the Communists took over in 1950, the old traditional literature has been largely superseded by modern works of a popular kind and by the classics of Marxism and modern developments from them.

Three daily (and one monthly) newspapers are published in Peking of which the most important is the People's Daily, the organ of the Chinese Communist Party.

Currency.—The *yuan* was revalued with effect

from March 1, 1955, on the basis 10,000 old *yuan* for one new *yuan*. (*See also* p. 83.)

Production and Industry.—China is essentially an agricultural and pastoral country: peasants constitute about 80 per cent. of the population. After the establishment of the Chinese People's Government at which time land for the most part was privately owned, there occurred several stages of land reform culminating in the formation of the people's communes in 1958. With the exception of a few State farms, the communes embrace the whole rural population. In all there are 74,000 communes and each is sub-divided into production brigades and teams. Work is assigned on a collective basis and the production team (of about 45 families) is the normal unit of accounting and labour. Wheat, barley, maize, millet and other cereals, with peas and beans, are grown in the northern provinces, and rice and sugar in the south. Rice is the staple food of the inhabitants. Cotton (mostly in valleys of the Yangtze and Yellow Rivers), tea (in the west and south), with hemp, jute and flax, are the most important crops.

Livestock is raised in large numbers. Silkworm culture is one of the oldest industries. Cottons, woollens and silks are manufactured in large quantities. The mineral wealth of the country is very great. Coal of excellent quality is produced. Iron ore, tin, antimony, wolfram, bismuth and molybdenum are also abundant. Oil is produced in Kansu, Sinkiang, Sining and three new major oilfields located in the northeast and east of the country. No reliable figures for industrial production have been published since 1959. The figures given below are those published for 1958.

Steel, 8,000,000 tons; Pig Iron, 9,530,000 tons; Coal, 270,000,000 tons; Electric Power, 27,530,000,000 kWh.; Crude Petroleum, 2,264,000 tons; Cement, 9,300,000 tons; Timber, 35,000,000 cubic metres; Sulphuric Acid, 740,000 tons; Chemical Fertilizers, 811,000 tons; Machine Tools, 50,000; Motor Vehicles, 16,000; Paper, 1,630,000 tons; and Cotton Cloth 5,700,000,000 metres.

Following the Great Leap Forward in 1958 and during three subsequent years of difficult conditions for agriculture, there was a cut back in both agricultural and industrial production which then recovered to its pre-1958 level. During the Cultural Revolution there was some economic dislocation. Industrial policy is governed by the need to build up agriculture, and some branches of industry, especially those such as machine tools and chemical fertilizers which have a direct relevance to agriculture have gone ahead more quickly. China is now virtually self-sufficient in petrol and oil.

A new (third) Five Year Plan began in 1966. No details of the Plan were published, but it was announced in 1970 that it had been completed. The Fourth Five Year Plan began in 1971, but no details of the Plan have as yet been published.

The principal articles of export are animals and animal products; oils; textiles; ores, metals and tea. The principal imports are raw cotton, cotton yarn and thread; motor vehicles; machinery; chemical fertilizer plants; wheat; aircraft; books, paper and paper-making materials; chemicals; metals and ores; and dyes.

Trade with U.K.

	1970	1971
Imports from U.K.	£44,586,000	£28,352,000
Exports to U.K.	33,538,000	31,671,000

Communications.—Of the total area of China about half consists of tableland and mountainous areas where communications and travel are generally difficult. By 1949 the communications system, as a result of years of neglect and civil war,

was more or less completely paralysed. In any case such roads and railways as did exist were largely confined to the eastern plains. After the Communists achieved complete control they devoted much attention to restoring and improving the communication system. By the end of 1958 the total length of railways was 19,000 miles (42 p.c. more than 1949), the total length of roads was 250,000 miles (about 5 times as much as in 1949) and of inland waterways about 100,000 miles (twice as much as 1949). In addition, internal civil aviation has been developed; routes total more than 20,000 miles. As a result the communications network now covers most of the country. In the past where roads did not exist the principal means of communications east to west was provided by the rivers, the most important of which are the Yangtze (3,400 miles long), the Yellow River (2,600 miles long) and the West River (1,650 miles). These, together with the network of canals connecting them are still much used, but their overall importance is less than it was. In the past 10 years great progress has been made in developing postal services and telecommunications. It is now claimed that 95 p.c. of all rural communes are on the telephone and that postal routes reach practically every production brigade headquarters.

SPECIAL TERRITORY

Tibet, a plateau seldom lower than 10,000 feet, forms the northern frontier of India (boundary imperfectly demarcated), from Kashmir to Burma, but is separated therefrom by the Himalayas. The area is estimated at 463,000 square miles with a population (estimated, 1957) of 1,270,000.

From 1911 to 1950, Tibet was virtually an independent country but its status was never officially so defined. In October, 1950, Chinese Communist forces invaded Eastern Tibet. The Dalai Lama later left Lhasa and set up his Government at Yatung, near the Sikkim frontier. On May 23, 1951, an agreement was reached whereby the Chinese army was allowed entry into Tibet. A Communist military and administrative headquarters was set up. In 1954 the Government of India recognized that Tibet was an integral part of China, in return for the right to maintain trade and consular representation there.

A series of revolts against Chinese rule over several years culminated on March 17, 1959, in a rising in Lhasa. Heavy fighting continued for several days before the rebellion was suppressed by Chinese troops and military rule imposed. The Dalai Lama fled to India where he and his followers were granted political asylum. On May 4, the Indian Government announced that an estimated 9,000 Tibetans had entered India or the Himalayan hill states. On March 28, 1959, the Chinese Prime Minister issued an order dissolving the Tibetan Government. In its place the 16-member Preparatory Committee for the Tibetan Autonomous Region, originally set up in 1955 with the Dalai Lama as Chairman, was to administer Tibet under the State Council. The Preparatory Committee was to have the Panchen Lama as Acting Chairman and also to include 4 Chinese Officials. Elections were held to choose local People's Congresses in Tibet, thus indicating that the government organization there no longer differed significantly from that of any ordinary province in China. The Dalai Lama, now exiled in India, announced a "new constitution" in March, 1963.

In December, 1964, the Dalai Lama, although absent, was declared to be a traitor, and both he and the Panchen Lama were dismissed. The position of Acting Chairman of the Preparatory Committee was assumed by Jigme, who had long been the most prominent secular figure in Tibet. This move marked the end of the period of co-operation by the Chinese Government with the traditional religious authorities, and the eclipse of the latter. The Preparatory Committee completed its work with the setting up of Tibet as an Autonomous Region of China on Sept. 9, 1965.

CAPITAL.—Peking, population (U.N. estimate, 1972), 7,570,000. The population of ΨShanghai was estimated at 10,820,000 (U.N. 1972); Nanking, 2,000,000 (Chinese est.); figures for the other principal towns are those for 1957; Tientsin, 3,220,000; Shenyang (Mukden), 2,411,000; Wuhan (*formerly* Hankow, Hanyang and Wuchang), 2,146,000; Chungking, 2,121,000; ΨCanton, 1,840,000; Harbin, 1,552,000; ΨPort Arthur (Lushun)/Dairen, 1,508,000; Sian, 1,310,000; ΨTsingtao, 1,121,000; Chengtu, 1,107,000; Taiyuan, 1,020,000.

FLAG.—Red, with large gold five-point star and four small gold stars in crescent, all in upper quarter next staff.

NATIONAL DAY.—October 1 (Founding of People's Republic).

BRITISH EMBASSY
11 Kuang Hua Lu,
Chien Kuo Men Wai, Peking.

Ambassador, His Excellency Edward Youde, C.M.G., M.B.E. (1974).

Counsellors, N. M. Fenn (*Head of Chancery*); R. D. Clift (*Commercial*).

Defence Attaché, Col. P. J. L. Tustin.

1st Secretaries, J. D. I. Boyd; R. E. Allen (*Commercial*); J. H. C. Gerson.

2nd Secretaries, W. H. H. Sanders; Miss S. Pares; D. G. Martin; R. C. Fursland.

Attachés, Miss M. J. Frude; R. J. Shaw; A. J. Slater; F. A. Doherty; D. A. McKellar; A. Nash; D. H. Hugill; J. B. Cave; M. Evans.

FORMOSA
(Taiwan)

President, Dr. C. K. Yen (Yen Chia-kan), *sworn in*, April 6, 1975.

Premier, Gen. Chiang Ching-kuo (June 1, 1972).

An island of some 13,800 sq. miles in the China Sea, Formosa lies 90 miles east of the Chinese mainland in latitude 21° 45′ N.—25° 38′ N. The population (15,353,291 in March, 1973), is almost entirely Chinese in origin and includes about 2,000,000 mainlanders who came to the island with Chiang Kai-Shek in 1947–49. The territory of Formosa includes the Pescadores Islands (50 sq. miles), some 35 miles west of Formosa, as well as Quemoy (68 sq. miles) and Matsu (11 sq. miles) which are only a few miles from the mainland. Settled for centuries by the Chinese, the island has been known as Ryukyu and Taiwan. It was administered by Japan as a province from 1895 to 1945. General Chiang Kai-shek withdrew to Formosa in 1949, towards the end of the war against the Communist *régime* accompanied by 500,000 Nationalist troops, since when the territory continued under his presidency. Gen. Chiang Kai-Shek died on April 5, 1975 and was succeeded by the Vice-President, Dr. C. K. Yen. A mutual defence treaty between the United States and Formosan Governments was signed in 1954.

The eastern part of the main island is mountainous and forest covered. Mt. Morrison (Yu Shan) (13,035 ft.) and Mt. Sylvia (Tzu'ukaoshan) (12,972 ft.) are the highest peaks. The western plains are watered by many rivers and the soil is very fertile, producing sugar, rice, tea, bananas, pineapples and tobacco. Coal, sulphur, iron, petroleum, copper and gold are mined. There are important fisheries. The principal seaports ΨKee-

lung (305,545) and ΨKaohsiung (724,222) are situated in the northern and southern sections of the island.

Trade with U.K.

	1970	1971
Imports from U.K.	£6,630,000	£10,115,000
Exports to U.K.	5,869,000	12,646,000

CAPITAL.—Taipei (population March, 1973, 1,921,736). Other towns are ΨKaohsiung (915,035); Tainan (495,454); Taichung (490,992); and ΨKeelung (333,998).

FLAG.—Red, with blue quarter at top next staff, bearing a twelve-point white sun.

BRITISH CONSULATES
The British Consulate was withdrawn from Taiwan on March 31, 1972.

COLOMBIA
(República de Colombia)

President (1974–78), Alfonso López Michelsen, *elected* April 21, 1974; *assumed office*, August 7, 1974.

EMBASSY
3 Hans Crescent, S.W.1
[01-589 9177]

Ambassador Extraordinary and Plenipotentiary, His Excellency Alfredo Vázquez-Carrizosa.

Counsellors, Srta. N. Millán; Dr. J. C. Restrepo (*Coffee Affairs*).

1st Secretary, A. Arango.

2nd Secretaries, S. B. de Perdorno; Dr. J. M. Santos (*Coffee Affairs*).

There are *Consulates-General* (1975) in London and Liverpool.

The Republic of Colombia lies in the extreme north-west of South America, having a coastline on both the Atlantic and Pacific Oceans. It is situated between 4° 13′ S. to 12° 30′ N. lat. and 68° to 79° W. long., with an approximate area of 440,000 square miles, and a population (estimated 1970) of 22,000,000.

The Colombian coast was visited in 1502 by *Christopher Colombus*, and in 1536 a Spanish expedition under Jiménez de Quesada penetrated to the interior and established on the site of the present capital a government which continued under Spanish rule until the revolt of the Spanish-American colonies of 1811–1824. In 1819 *Simón Bolívar* (born 1783, died 1830) established the Republic of Colombia, consisting of the territories now known as Colombia, Panama, Venezuela and Ecuador. In 1829–1830 Venezuela and Ecuador withdrew from the association of provinces, and in 1831 the remaining territories were formed into the Republic of New Granada. In 1858 the name was changed to the Granadine Confederation and in 1861 to the United States of Colombia. In 1886 the present title was adopted. In 1903 Panama seceded from Colombia, and became a separate Republic.

There are three great ranges of the Andes, known as the Western, Central, and Eastern Cordilleras; the second contains the highest peaks, but the latter is the most important, as it consists of a series of vast tablelands, cool and healthy. This temperate region is the most densely peopled portion of the Republic. The highest mountain in Colombia is Cristobal Colon (18,946 feet) in the Sierra Nevada de Santa Marta on the Caribbean coast.

The principal rivers are the Magdalena, Guaviare, Cauca, Atrato, Caquetá, Putumayo and Patia. The Patia flows through the famous *Mínima Gorge* of the Western Cordilleras, and one of its tributaries (the Carchi, or Upper Guiatara) is spanned by the Rumichaca Arch, or *Inca's Bridge*, of natural stone.

On the Rio Bogotá is the great *Fall of Tequendama*, 482 ft. in height.

Government.—During the early nineteenth-fifties Colombia suffered a period of virtual civil war between the supporters of the traditional political parties, the Conservatives and the Liberals. The dictatorship of Gen. Rojas Pinilla (1953–57) put an end to the worst of the violence and on May 10, 1957, a military junta took over, preparing the way for a return to democratic government. Congressional elections were held on March 16, 1958, which yielded a Liberal majority. This led, the same year, to the institution of the National Front system, to run for a period of 16 years. The Presidency alternated every four years between the Liberals and Conservatives while parity of appointment was maintained between the two parties in Congress, the Government and all Government Departments.

During the presidency of Dr. Carlos Lleras (May, 1966 to April, 1970) the country made considerable economic advances, but the National Front system was nearly overthrown at the 1970 presidential election, when Gen. Rojas, with his political movement, the National Popular Alliance, almost defeated the Government candidate, Dr. Misael Pastrana.

In 1974 the first election not subject to the National Front system for the Presidency and Congress was won by the Liberal candidate, Alfonso Lopez Michelsen; parity in administrative appointments between the traditional parties will continue, however, until 1978.

Production.—The Colombian forests are extensive; among the trees are mahogany, cedar, fustic, and other dye-woods and medicinal plants. The mineral productions are emeralds, gold, silver, platinum, copper, iron, lead and coal. In 1972 the country was producing 192,000 barrels of oil per day after a peak production figure of 218,000 in 1970. Prospecting for new reserves continues apace but since early 1975 Colombia has exchanged its rôle of net-exporter for that of net-importer of crude oil. The principal agricultural products are coffee (which accounts for nearly 50 per cent. of total exports by value) cotton, bananas, rice, cocoa, sugar, tobacco, maize, cut flowers, wheat and other cereals. Manufactures (mainly for home consumption, but with an increasing export trade) consist of woollen, cotton and artificial silk textiles, leather goods, chemicals, asbestos-cement goods, many pharmaceutical products, rubber goods, including motor tyres, furniture, boots and shoes, confectionery, cigarettes, beer, cement, glass containers and steel. Over the last four years the Government, backed by massive international finance and technical aid, has been encouraging the development of new industries, including the local assembly and partial manufacture of motor vehicles, radio sets and office machinery. The importation of many consumer goods is restricted.

Defence.—The Army peace effective strength is 41,000; war effective 300,000. The Navy consists of 4 destroyers, 4 frigates, some gunboats and other small craft, with personnel about 5,000, including one battalion of marines; a battalion of the Colombian army and elements of the Navy served with the United Nations forces in Korea. The Air Force, with 4,000 personnel, has jet trainers and a front-line squadron equipped with Mirage fighters.

Communications.—The first railway was opened in 1855, about 1,914 miles being open in 1949. The "Atlantic Railway" running through the Magdalena Valley, which links the departmental lines running down to the river, and completes the connection between Bogotá and Santa Marta, was opened in July,

1961. There are about 2,200 miles of rail in use at present. The total road network (1973) consists of 39,900 km. of roads of all types, of which 7,000 km. are classified as main trunk and transversal roads. A programme of road improvement and construction is under way, financed by a tax on petrol. The national telephone and telegraph system consists primarily of wireless links between the more important centres. Large appropriations have been made for modernization of the country's telecommunication system. There are daily passenger and cargo air services between Bogotá and all the principal towns. There are daily services to the U.S.A., frequent services to other countries in South America, and services to London daily *via* Miami, *via* Paris and once a week by British Airways to London. Air mail is delivered to the United Kingdom 3 to 5 days after leaving Bogotá. There are wireless stations in the main cities, and a television station in Bogotá with relays to most parts of the country.

Roman Catholicism is the established religion.

Language and Literature.—Spanish is the language of the country and education has been free since 1870. Great efforts have been made in reducing illiteracy and it is estimated that about 60 per cent. of those over 10 years of age can read and write. In addition to the National University with headquarters at Bogotá there are 26 other universities. There is a flourishing press in urban areas and a national literature supplements the rich inheritance from the time of Spanish rule.

Finance.—For rate of exchange, *see* p. 83.

	1973 $U.S.
Total imports (c.i.f.)	876,000,000
Total exports (f.o.b.)	1,084,000,000

Trade with U.K.

	1973	1974
Imports from U.K...	£15,494,000	£24,213,000
Exports to U.K.....	9,687,000	12,458,000

CAPITAL, Bogotá, population (estimated, 1974 2,900,000. Bogotá is an inland city in the Eastern Cordilleras, at an elevation of 8,600 to 9,000 ft. above sea level. Other centres are Medellin (1,100,000); Cali (950,000); Barranquilla (700,000); Bucaramanga (320,000); Manizales (300,000); Cúcuta (230,000); ΨCartagena (340,000).

FLAG.—Broad yellow band in upper half, surmounting equal bands of blue and red.

NATIONAL DAY.—July 20 (National Independence Day).

BRITISH EMBASSY

Calle 38, No. 13–35, Bogotá.

Ambassador Extraordinary and Plenipotentiary, His Excellency Geoffrey Allan Crossley, C.M.G.

1st Secretaries R. B. Hervey (*Head of Chancery and Consul*); R. G. Osborn, M.B.E. (*Commercial*).

Defence Attaché, Cdr. C. M. Jenne.

2nd Secretaries, A. R. Powell (*Commercial*); Mrs. M. F. Dar (*Technical Assistance*).

3rd Secretary, D. A. Lloyd.

There are British Consular Offices at *Bogotá, Barranquilla, Medellin* and *Cali.*

British Council Representative, R. S. Newberry, Calle 11, No. 5–16, Bogotá.

CONGO
(People's Republic of the Congo)

President of the Republic, Marien N'gouabi.

Prime Minister, Henri Lopes.

Vice-Prime Minister and Minister of Agriculture, Charles Ngouoto-Moukolo.

Minister of Foreign Affairs. M. Charles David Ganao.

The Republic lies on the Equator between

Gabon on the west and Zaire on the east, the River Congo and its tributary the Ubanghi forming most of the eastern boundary of the state. The Congo has a short Atlantic coast-line. Area of the Republic of Congo is 129,960 sq. miles, with a population of approximately 2,100,000. Formerly the French colony of Middle Congo, it became a member state of the French Community on November 28, 1958, and was pro-claimed fully independent on August 17, 1960.

M. Fulbert Youlou held office as President of the Republic from Aug. 7, 1960. Growing discontent with the *régime* culminated in riots in Brazzaville and led to the President's resignation on Aug. 15, 1963, and the dissolution by the Army of the National Assembly. A provisional Government led by M. Alphonse Massemba-Débat took office on Aug. 16, and a new constitution, giving the provisional Government full powers, came into operation in December, 1963.

On Jan. 12, 1968, the President dismissed the Prime Minister, M. Noumazalay, with three other members of his Cabinet and himself assumed office as Prime Minister with a reformed Ministry. He was himself arrested after heavy fighting during the last few days of August and resigned on Sept. 4 1968. Conduct of affairs was assumed by a National Council of Army officers.

Commandant Marien N'Gouabi became Presi-dent of the Republic on December 31, 1968. The Parti Congolais du Travail (*PCT*) was created by the Congress of December 29-31, 1969. The People's Republic of the Congo was established, and a new Constitution was promulgated. Follow-ing the Second Extraordinary Congress of the Party in December 1972, a new Constitution and a re-organization of the structures of the Party and the State were submitted to a people's referendum, in July 1973.

Trade with U.K.

	1973	1974
Imports from U.K...	£1,448,0000	£5,266,000
Exports to U.K.....	3,231,000	1,324,000

CAPITAL.—Brazzaville (156,000); Ψ Pointe Noire (76,000). FLAG.—Red, with hammer and sickle in centre.

BRITISH EMBASSY
Ambassador Extraordinary and Plenipotentiary, His Excellency Richard James Stratton, C.M.G. (1974). (Resident at *Kinshasa, Zaire*).

COSTA RICA
(República de Costa Rica)
President (1974–78), Lic. Daniel Oduber Quirós, *born* 1923, *elected* February 8, 1974; *assumed office*, May 8, 1974.

COSTA RICAN EMBASSY
55 Eaton Place, S.W.1.
[01–286 7898]
Ambassador Extraordinary and Plenipotentiary, His Ex-cellency Sr. Don Eduardo Echeverría-Villafranca (1975).
Minister-Counsellor, Sr. F. von Hacke-Prestinary (*Economic and Consular*).
Counsellor, Sra. F. de M. M. de Brenes (*Cultural Affairs*).
2nd Secretary, Sra. P. C. Gutiérrez.

The Republic of Costa Rica, in Central America extends across the isthmus between 8° 17′ and 11° 10′ N. lat. and from 82° 30′ to 85° 45′ W. long., contains an area of 19,653 English sq. miles, and a population (estimated January, 1974) of 1,875,000. The population is basically of European stock, in which Costa Rica differs from most Latin American countries. The Republic lies between Nicaragua and Panama and between the Caribbean Sea and the Pacific Ocean.

For nearly three centuries (1530–1821) Costa Rica formed part of the Spanish-American dominions, the seat of government being at Cartago. In 1821 the country joined in the War of Independence, and from 1824 to 1839 it was one of the United States of Central America.

On Dec. 1, 1948, the Army was abolished, the President declaring it unnecessary, as the country loved peace.

The coastal lowlands by the Caribbean Sea and Pacific have a tropical climate but the interior plateau, with a mean elevation of 4,000 feet, enjoys a temperature climate. The capital is 103 miles from the Atlantic and 72 miles from the Pacific by rail.

The principal agricultural products are coffee (of a high quality), bananas. rice, maize, sugar-cane, potatoes, cocoa beans and hemp, the soil being extremely fertile. Increasing attention is being paid to cattle raising.

The chief ports are Ψ Limón, on the Atlantic coast, through which passes most of the coffee exported, and Ψ Puntarenas on the Pacific coast.

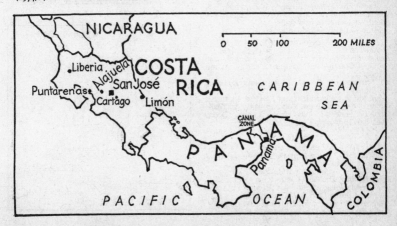

Bananas are exported from Golfito, on the Pacific Coast, by the United Fruit Co., and from Limón by the Standard Fruit Co. In 1973, 1,605 ships entered at Costa Rican ports bringing in approximately 1,539,000 tons of goods. About 500 miles of railroad are open. The country is well provided with airways, and Pan-American Airways, TACA, SAHSA and COPA call at San José, while feeder services link the main centres of population with the capital. LACSA is the national airline with BAC-111 flights to Miami, Mexico, Central American capitals and Caracas, Barranquilla and Maracaibo in South America, besides internal flights to local airports.

Spanish is the language of the country. Education is compulsory and free. The literacy rate is the highest in Latin America. In post-war years there has been a big advance in the provision of social services.

FINANCE

	1972	1973
	Colones, millions	
Revenue	1,390·8	2,029·0
Expenditure	1,414·3	1,865·4
Public Debt	2,628·2	3,351·2

Currency is the *colon* of 100 *centimes*. Exchange rate in 1973 was C8·54=U.S. $1.

TRADE

	1972	1973
	$U.S., millions	
Total imports	390·5	454·7
Total exports	287·3	342·2

Trade with U.K.

	1973	1974
Imports from U.K.	£7,257,000	£7,025,000
Exports to U.K.	771,000	1,085,000

The chief exports (1973) were coffee, bananas, meat, chemical products, sugar and cacao. The imports, 32 per cent. from U.S.A., 20 per cent. from other Central American Common Market countries, 7 per cent. from Germany and 10 per cent. from Japan, consisted of machinery, motor vehicles, bicycles, chemicals, textiles, fuel and lubricants, rubber manufactures, non-ferrous metals, etc.

CAPITAL, San José pop. (May 1973), 215,441; Alajuela (96,325); ΨPuntarenas (65,562); Cartago (65,310); ΨLimón (40,830); Heredia (36,487); Liberia (21,781). (Populations shown are of the Central Cantons of provincial capitals at May, 1973.)

FLAG.—Five horizontal bands, blue, white, red, white, blue (the red band twice the width of the others with emblem near staff).

NATIONAL DAY.—September 15.

BRITISH EMBASSY

3202 Paseo Colon, Apartado 10056, San José
Ambassador Extraordinary and Plenipotentiary and Consul-General, His Excellency Keith Hamylton Jones (1974).
1st Secretary and Consul, J. R. Duffy (*Head of Chancery*).

San José is 5,687 miles from London; sea transit direct 18 days; *via* New York, 20 days; Air Mails (*via* New York) 3 to 5 days from London. Ocean Mail, 8 to 16 weeks.

CUBA
(Republica de Cuba)
President, Dr. Osvaldo Dorticós Torrado, *appointed* July 17, 1959.
COUNCIL OF MINISTERS
Prime Minister, Dr. Fidel Castro Ruz.
First Deputy Prime Minister and Minister for Armed Forces, Cdte de Div. Raúl Castro Ruz.
Minister of Foreign Affairs, Dr. Raúl Roa Garcia.
Justice, Dr. Armando Torres Santrayill.

Interior, Sergio del Valle.
Communications, Sr. Pedro Guelmes González.
Foreign Trade, Marcelo Fernandez Font.
Internal Trade, Serafín Fernández Rodriguez.
Chemical Industry, Antonio Esquivel Yedra.
Mining and Geology, Manuel Cespedes
Sidero-Mechanic Industry, Herrandez.
Light Industry, Sra. Nora Frometa Silva.
Public Health, Dr. José A. Gutiérrez Muñiz.
Education, Sr. José Fernandez Alvarez.
Labour, Sr. Oscar Fernandez Padilla.
Merchant Marine, Sr. Angel Joel Chaveco Morales.
Ports, Sr. Lester Rodriguez Pérez.
Transport, Enrique Lussón Battle.
Sugar Industry, Ing. Marcos Lage Cuello.
Food Industry, Sr. José A. Naranjo Morales.
President, National Bank, Sr. Raúl León Torras.

CUBAN EMBASSY IN LONDON
57 Kensington Court, W.8
[01–937 8226]
Ambassador Extraordinary and Plenipotentiary, His Excellency Dr. Lionel Soto Prieto (1973).

Cuba (the largest of the "West India" Islands) lies between 74° and 85° W. long., and 19° and 23° N. lat., with a total area of 44,178 sq. miles and a population at the Census of 1970 of 8,553,395.

The island of Cuba was visited by Christopher Columbus during his first voyage, on October 27, 1492, and was then believed to be part of the Western mainland of India. Early in the 16th century the island was conquered by the Spaniards, to be used later as a base of operations for the conquest of Mexico and Central America, and for almost four centuries Cuba remained under a Spanish Captain-General. [The island was under British rule for one year, 1762–1763, when it was returned to Spain in exchange for Florida.] Separatist agitation culminated in the closing years of the 19th century in a fierce and blood-thirsty war. In 1898 the government of the United States intervened and despatched the battleship *Maine* to Havana harbour, where in February of that year the vessel was sunk by an explosion, the cause of which remains an unsolved mystery. On April 20, 1898, the U.S. Government demanded the evacuation of Cuba by the Spanish forces, and a short Spanish–American war led to the abandonment of the island, which was occupied by U.S. troops. From Jan. 1, 1899, to May 20, 1902, Cuba was under U.S. military rule, and reforms of the widest and

most far-reaching character were instituted. On May 20, 1902, an autonomous government was inaugurated with an elected President, and a legislature of two houses. The island was, however, again the prey of revolution from Aug. to Sept., 1906, when the U.S. Government resumed control. On Jan. 28, 1909, a republican government was again inaugurated. In 1933 a revolution was followed by provisional government until May, 1936, when a constitutional government was elected. A new Constitution was promulgated in 1940, but its operation was suspended for various periods until February 24, 1955, when the Government elected on November 1, 1954, took office.

A revolution led by Dr. Fidel Castro overthrew the Government of General Batista on January 1, 1959. A provisional government was set up and elections were promised within four years. Dr. Castro has since proclaimed the revolution to be Socialist and himself to be a Marxist-Leninist.

In October, 1965, the Communist Party of Cuba was formed to succeed the United Party of the Socialist Revolution. It is the only authorized political party. Elections are no longer to be held. A new Socialist constitution has also been promised, but no date has been set for its introduction.

The Revolutionary Government has carried out programmes of land and urban reform and of nationalization of the means of production and distribution. By June, 1963, 90 per cent. of industrial production, all foreign trade and about 50 per cent. of small commercial companies were in state hands. In March, 1968, virtually all remaining private commercial enterprises were nationalized. About 70 per cent. of the cultivated land is in state farms or co-operatives. Private smallholders, who own the remainder, also come under a measure of Government control.

Although efforts are being made to diversify the economy, sugar is still its mainstay and Cuba's principal source of foreign exchange. It still accounts for some 80 per cent. in value of total Cuban exports. The largest sugar harvest ever, was produced in 1969/70, when total production reached about 8,500,000 tons. This was achieved at considerable expense to the rest of the economy, however, and the declared target of 10 million tons, which was to have been reached in 1970, has been delayed. Cuba's other main exports are nickel, tobacco and rum, while increases are expected shortly in the availability of fish, meat and citrus fruit.

Despite increased trade with Western Europe and Japan, the Communist countries, particularly the Soviet Union, form Cuba's main trading partners, covering about 80 per cent. of imports and exports. In addition, the U.S.S.R. offers substantial aid from an imbalance in the annual trade profits in Cuba's favour which has recently been in the region of 250 to 350 million roubles.

11,915 miles of railway are open (public service 4,880; sugar plantations and mining areas 7,035) and about 12,000 miles of telegraph line. There are about 8,291 miles of road. At present scheduled international air services run to Mexico City, Moscow, Prague, Madrid, Rabat and Algiers.

Language and Literature.—Spanish is the language of the island, but English is widely understood. Education is compulsory and free. The University of Havana was founded in 1728, but until its enlargement under American auspices in the first quarter of the twentieth century no great progress was made in secondary or higher education. There are universities at Santiago de Cuba and Santa Clara. Public libraries have been established. The daily press and broadcasting and television are under the control of the Government.

Finance.—The public revenue rose from an estimated $365,247,946 in 1958 to $2,399,006,000 for 1964, including profits from State trading concerns, etc. No up-to-date figures are available for the public debt—at the end of 1958 this stood at $760,300,000.

Currency—Average, Pesos 1·95= £1, U.S. currency ceased to be legal tender in Cuba on June 30, 1951 (*see also* p. 83).

Trade.—Exports in 1968 were valued at $649,900,000, compared with $710,800,000, in 1967; imports, 1968, $1,094,000,000 (1967, $997,800,000). No statistics are available for subsequent years.

Trade with U.K.

	1973	1974
Imports from U.K...	£17,538,000	£23,926,000
Exports to U.K	13,250,000	19,952,000

The exports are principally sugar and tobacco; the imports are mainly machinery.

CAPITAL, ΨHavana (pop., Census 1970), 1,755,360; other towns are ΨSantiago (292,251), Santa Clara (213,296), Camagüey (196,854), Holguín (183,115), and ΨCienfuegos (164,061).

FLAG.—Five horizontal bands, blue and white (blue at top and bottom) with red triangle, close to staff, charged with 5-point white star.

NATIONAL DAY.—January 1 (Day of Liberation).

BRITISH EMBASSY

Edificio Bolívar, Capdevila No. 101, e Morro y Prado, Apartado 1069, Havana.

Ambassador Extraordinary and Plenipotentiary, (vacant).

Counsellor, A. S. Papadopoulos, M.V.O., M.B.E. (*Head of Chancery*).

1st Secretary, M. W. Marshal (*Commercial and H.M. Consul*).

2nd Secretaries, A. J. Terry (*Commercial*); D. S. Stingemore (*Administration*).

Defence Attaché, Lt.-Col. B. D. O. Smith (*Resident at Mexico City*).

Attaché, A. V. Stonham.

Vice Consul, Miss M. L. Reid, M.B.E.

There is a British Consular Office at *Havana.*

CZECHOSLOVAKIA
(Československá Socialistická Republika)

President, Gustav Husak, *born* Jan. 10, 1913; *elected,* May 29, 1975.

Federal Government

Prime Minister, Lubomír Štrougal.

Deputy Prime Ministers, Petr Colotka; Jan Gregor; František Hamouz; Václav Hůla; Josef Korčák; Karol Laco; Matej Lučan; Rudolf Rohlíček; Josef Šimon; Jindřich Zahradnik.

Ministers

Agriculture and Food, Boshuslav Večeřa.

Finance, Leopold Ler.

Foreign Affairs, Bohuslav Chňoupek.

Foreign Trade, Andrej Barčák.

Fuel and Power, Vlastimil Ehrenberger.

Interior, Jaromír Obzina.

Labour and Social Affairs, Michal Štancel.

Metallurgy and Heavy Engineering, Zdeněk Půček.

National Defence, Martin Dzúr.

Telecommunications, Vlastimil Chalupa.

Technical and Investment Development. Ladislav Šupka.

Transport, Štefan Šutka.

People's Control, Josef Machačka.

Prices, Michal Sabolčík.

General Engineering, Pavol Bahyl.

Deputy Chairman of State Planning Commission, Vladimír Janza.

Prime Minister of the Czech Socialist Republic, Josef Korčák.
Prime Minister of the Slovak Socialist Republic, Dr. Petr Colotka.

CZECHOSLOVAK COMMUNIST PARTY
Presidium of the Central Committee, V. Bilak; P. Colotka; K. Hoffman; G. Husák; A. Indra; A. Kapek; J. Kempny; J. Korčák; J. Lenárt; L. Štrougal; L. Svoboda (*full members*); M. Hruskovic; V. Hůla (*alternate members*).
Secretariat of the Central Committee, Gustáv Husák (*General Secretary*); V. Bilak; J. Fojtik; J. Kempny; F. Ondřich; O. Švestka; J. Baryl (*secretaries*); J. Lenart; M. Moc (*members*).

CZECHOSLOVAK EMBASSY
25 Kensington Palace Gardens, W.8.
[01–229 1255]
Ambassador Extraordinary and Plenipotentiary, Mečislav Jablonský (1974).
Minister-Counsellor, Dr. František Telička.
Commercial Counsellor, Martin Sakal.
Military and Air Attaché, Col. Jiří Boušek.
1st Secretary, Pavel Stulrajter.
2nd Secretaries František Pavlis; Jiri Novotný.
Commercial Attachés, Vaclav Levora; Josef Maruniak.
3rd Secretaries, Jan Prikopa; Dr. Miloslav Jezel.
Area and Population.—Czechoslovakia, formerly part of the Austro-Hungarian Monarchy, declared its independence on Oct. 28, 1918 (Czechoslovak Independence Day), the territory affected having an area of 53,700 square miles, reduced, by the cession of Ruthenia to U.S.S.R. in 1945, to 49,400 square miles. The population of Czechoslovakia was 14,526,268 in December, 1972.
Government.—The Communist Party, with the aid of Action Committees, seized power in Czechoslovakia in February, 1948, and Communist control of the country is now unqualified. On July 11, 1960, a new constitution was proclaimed, replacing that of 1948. Its purpose was to express the fact that Czechoslovakia is now deemed to have completed the construction of Socialism and to be on the road to true Communism. The official title of the State was accordingly changed to " The Czechoslovak Socialist Republic ".
In January, 1968, pressures for reform of the system were realized with the removal of the First Secretary of the Communist Party, Novotný, and his replacement by Alexander Dubček. They

were translated into a Party Action Programme adopted in April. Shortly afterwards the country's supreme legislative body, the National Assembly, began work on new legislation, which envisaged the democratisation of the country's political life, greater guarantees of fundamental liberties and the establishment of a federal system.
The speed of events and their implications for the internal development of the other communist regimes in Eastern Europe and the Soviet Union, as well as for the system of alliances among these countries, alarmed the Soviet Union. On the night of August 20, Czechoslovakia was invaded by Soviet, Polish, East German, Hungarian and Bulgarian troops, the capital and all major towns being occupied.
The Russians were unable to depose the Czechoslovak leadership, but forced them to sign on August 26 an Agreement modifying their policies and, on October 18, a treaty legalising the presence of Soviet troops on Czechoslovak territory.
On April 17, 1969, Gustáv Husák took over the leadership of the Communist Party, and the reforms of 1968 were abandoned with exception of the Federal system of government, which had been set up in October 1968. Czechoslovakia now consists of the Czech Socialist Republic and the Slovak Socialist Republic, each of which has its own government responsible to its legislative body—the National Council. Areas such as the Constitution, Defence, Foreign Affairs, State Material Reserves and Currency are the responsibility of the Federal Administration. The Federal Government is responsible to the Federal Assembly, which is composed of two Chambers, the Chamber of the People, whose duties are elected throughout the Federation, and the Chamber of the Nations, consisting of an equal number of Czech and Slovak Deputies. The federal system was not extended to the organization of the Communist Party.
The Economic System.—Czechoslovakia has long been one of the most highly-industrialised countries of Central Europe. Under the present political system industry is state-owned, while nearly all agricultural land is cultivated by state or co-operative farms. Economic planning is centralised, and state economic plans have the force of law. In 1965 the system was reformed to allow for a greater devolution of responsibility to enterprises and factories, and greater emphasis was placed on profitability and competition within a centrally

planned economy. After the events of 1968–69 there was a sharp swing back to the present highly centralised system.

Language and Literature.—Czech and Slovak are the official languages, each having its own literature. The Reformation gave a wide-spread impulse to Czech literature, the writings of Jan Hus (who was martyred in 1415 as a religious and social reformer) familiarizing the people with Wyclif's teaching. This impulse endured to the close of the 17th century when Jan Amos Komensky or Comenius (1592–1670) was expelled from the country. He is still recognized as an outstanding educationist and a thinker of first magnitude. Under Austrian repression and with the persistent pursuit of Germanization, there was a period of stagnation until the national revival in the first half of the 19th century. Modern prose, drama and fiction, penned between the Wars, are represented by several authors, of international reputation, notably K. M. Capek-Chod (1860–1927), Viktor Dyk (1877–1931), Jaroslav Hašek (1883–1923) Karel Capek (1890–1938), Vladimír Vančura (1891–1942), and Ivan Olbracht (1882–1952). Liberty of the press ceased with the loss of independence and the Nazi occupation in 1939. It was temporarily restored on the liberation of the country. After the Communist take-over of February, 1948, however, freedom of the press was curtailed. All papers and periodicals were forced to follow the Party line and a number of publications were banned. Following the thaw of 1956 and after the relapse into dogmatism after the Hungarian Revolution, the new wave of freedom started in 1962–1963 and led to increased recognition of Czech and Slovak literature in the world. Greater international recognition is hampered by translation difficulties. In 1966 nearly 250 Czech and Slovak books were published abroad, including roughly one-third in non-Socialist countries. The prominent writers include Frantisek Hrubín (b. 1910), Bohumil Hrabal (b. 1914), Václav Havel (b. 1936), Ladislav Mňačko (b. 1919), Ladislav Novomesky (b. 1904), Arnošt Lustig (b. 1926), Jiří Mucha (b. 1915), and others. Poetic writing ranges from traditional lyric (Jaroslav Seifert) to " concrete " and typographic modernism (Jiří Kolář, Josef Hiršal). In the present political conditions few of these writers are published in Czechoslovakia.

Education.—Education is compulsory and free for all children from the ages of 6 to 15. The number of pupils in basic nine-year schools is 1,890,081 (1973–74). There are 127,451 students in the secondary grammar schools and the number given for technical schools of all kinds is 277,945. There are five universities in Czechoslovakia of which the most famous is Charles University in Prague (founded 1348), the others being situated at Bratislava, Brno, Olomouc and Košice. In addition there are a considerable number of other institutions of university standing, technical colleges, agricultural colleges, etc. In 1973–74, there were 135,874 students in centres of higher education of which 23,811 were part-time.

Finance.—The Czechoslovak currency is the Czechoslovak *Koruna* (*Kčs*= Czechoslovak crown) of 100 *heller*. The present Czechoslovak rate of exchange is Kčs. 12·50=£1 (July 1975) with a bonus of 75 per cent. for non-commercial travellers (*see also* p. 83).

Trade with U.K.

	1973	1974
Imports from U.K.	£39,090,000	£55,300,000
Exports to U.K.	27,190,000	44,770,000

CAPITAL, Prague (Praha), on the Vltava (Moldau), the former capital of Bohemia with a population (1973) of 1,091,449. Other towns are Brno (Brünn), capital of Moravia (353,866), Bratislava (Pressburg), capital of Slovakia (325,035), Ostrava (290,828), Košiče (163,359) and Plzen (Pilsen) (153,119).

FLAG.—Two equal horizontal stripes, white (above) and red; a blue triangle next to staff.

NATIONAL DAY.—May 9.

BRITISH EMBASSY

Thunovská Ulice 14, Prague 1.

Ambassador Extraordinary and Plenipotentiary, His Excellency Edward Gervase Willan, C.M.G. (1974)

Counsellor, K. G. Macinnes (*Head of Chancery*).

Defence and Military Attaché, Col. B. D. Underwood, M.B.E.

Air Attaché, Wing-Cdr. B. M. Burley.

1st Secretaries, P. J. George, O.B.E. (*Commercial*); D. S. Broucher; R. B. Dearlove; R. E. Escritt (*Commercial*).

2nd Secretary (*Consul/AO*), P. H. Johnson.

3rd Secretaries, D. T. Cox; M. W. Powles (*Commercial*); Miss P. A. Marshall; B. M. Bennett (*Press*).

Cultural Attaché, K. L. Pearson.

DAHOMEY
(Republic of Dahomey)

President of the Military Revolutionary Government and Head of State, Lt.-Col. Mathieu Kerekou; assumed office, October 26, 1972.

A republic situated in West Africa, between 2° and 3° W. and 6° and 12° N., Dahomey has a short coast line of 78 miles on the Gulf of Guinea but extends northwards inland for 437 miles. It is flanked on the west by Togo, on the north by Upper Volta and Niger and on the east by Nigeria. It has an area of about 47,000 square miles and a population (estimate, 1973) of 2,948,000. Although poor in resources, Dahomey is one of the most thickly populated areas in West Africa, with a high level of education. It is divided into four main regions running horizontally: a narrow sandy coastal strip, a clay belt and a sandy plateau in the north.

The first treaty with France was signed by one of the kings of Abomey in 1851 but the country was not placed under French administration until 1892. Dahomey became an independent republic within the French Community on Dec. 4, 1958; full independence outside the Community was proclaimed on August 1, 1960. In October, 1963, a popular revolution led to the fall of the government of the first President of Dahomey, Hubert Maga. The Army held power until Sourou-Migan Apithy was elected President and Justin Ahomadegbé Chief of Government in January, 1964, after a new constitution had been agreed. This government was overthrown in November, 1965, following a long-standing disagreement between Maga and Apithy. It was replaced by President Tahirou Congacou, who was in turn dismissed in December of the same year by the Army. Christophe Soglo then assumed control and dismissed the Assembly. Soglo was in his turn overthrown by an Army *coup d'état* on December 17, 1967. Seven months later Dr. Zinsou was installed, with the support of the Army, as President, an appointment which was confirmed by a national referendum on July 28, 1968.

Dr. Zinsou was overthrown by a military coup on December 10, 1969 and for five months the country was ruled by a military " Directoire ". Following abortive elections in March, 1970, a Presidential Council was set up in May, 1970 consisting of MM. Maga, Ahomadégbé and Apithy, with M. Maga as President of the Council and Head of State. He was succeeded in May, 1972 by M. Ahomadégbé, who in turn would have been succeeded in May 1974 by M. Apithy, but for the *coup d'état* of October 26, 1972 which brought the Military Revolutionary Government, headed by Lt.-Col. Kerekou, to power.

Dahomey is a member of the *Conseil de l'Entente*, the *Organisation Commune Africaine et Malgace* (OCAM) and the Organization of African Unity (O.A.U.). The official language is French.

Finance.—The currency of Dahomey is the *Franc CFA* (*Francs CFA* 50=1 French *Franc*) (*Francs CFA* 450= £1 June, 1975).

Trade.—The principal exports are palm products (80 per cent.) followed by ground nuts, shea-nuts and coffee. Small deposits of gold, iron and chrome have been found.

Trade with U.K.

	1973	1974
Imports from U.K.	£2,032,006	£3,605,289
Exports to U.K.	53,595	457,891

CAPITAL.—Porto Novo (85,000). Principal commercial town and port, Ψ Cotonou (120,000).

FLAG.—Three stripes, one vertical, green, two horizontal yellow and red.

NATIONAL DAY.—August 1.

British Embassy (see Togo).

DENMARK
(Kongeriget Danmark)

Queen, Margrethe II, eldest daughter of King Frederik IX, *born* April 16, 1940, *succeeded* Jan. 14, 1972, *married* June 10, 1967, Count Henri de Monpezat (Prince Henrik of Denmark) and has issue Crown Prince Frederik *born* May 26, 1968; and Prince Joachim, *born* June 7, 1969.

CABINET

Prime Minister, Anker Jørgensen.
Foreign Affairs, K. B. Andersen.
Finance, Knud Heinesen.
Economic Affairs, Per Hækkerup.
Labour, Erling Dinesen.
Foreign Economic Affairs, Ivar Nørgaard.
Housing and Environment, Helge Nielsen.
Interior, Egon Jensen.
Public Works and Cultural Affairs, Niels Matthiasen.
Social Affairs, Eva Gredal.
Commerce, Erling Jensen.
Justice and Defence, Orla Møller.
Education, Ritt Bjerregaard.
Inland Revenue, Svend Jakobsen.
Ecclesiastical Affairs and Greenland, Jørgen Peder Hansen.
Agriculture and Fisheries, Poul Dalsager.

ROYAL DANISH EMBASSY IN LONDON
29 Pont Street, S.W.1
[01–584 0102]

Ambassador Extraordinary and Plenipotentiary, His Excellency Erling Kristiansen, G.C.V.O. (1964).
Minister Plenipotentiary, K. E. Willumsen, K.C.V.O.
1st Secretaries, E. H. Schmiegelow, M.V.O.; E. Hedegard.
Minister Plenipotentiary, Press and Culture, H. Agerbak, C.V.O.
Minister-Counsellor, P. B. Søndergaard, C.V.O. (*Economic and Consular Affairs*).
Agricultural Counsellor, M. Munch, M.V.O.
Defence Attaché, Col. H. H. Prince Georg of Denmark K.C.V.O.
Commercial Counsellor, N. Buch-Hansen, M.V.O.

Area and Population.—A Kingdom of Northern Europe, consisting of the islands of Zeeland, Funen, Lolland, etc., the peninsula of Jutland, and the outlying island of Bornholm in the Baltic, the Faroes and Greenland. Denmark is situated between 54° 34′–57° 45′ N. lat., and 8° 5′–15° E. 12′ long.,

with an area of 17,000 square miles, and a population estimated (April 1975) of 5,054,909. In 1972 there were 75,505 live births, 50,445 deaths and 31,073 marriages.

Government.—Under the Constitution of the Kingdom of Denmark Act of June 5, 1953, the legislature consists of one chamber, the *Folketing,* of not more than 179 members, including 2 for the Faröes and 2 for Greenland. Voting age has been 18 since 1971.

Mr. Jorgensen, the Prime Minister, dissolved Parliament on Nov. 8, 1973, after his Social Democrat minority Government was defeated in a vote on taxation, and called an election for Dec. 4. Following the election, it was announced on Dec.

17 that Mr. Poul Hartling, leader of the Liberal Party, would form a Liberal minority Government. Mr. Hartling called an election at the end of 1974. Although his party substantially increased its representation in the *Folketing,* it was unable to continue in office after the election and a Social Democrat minority Government was formed in February 1975. The representation in the *Folketing* was as follows; Social Democrats 53; Venstre 42; Progress Party 24; Radicals 13; Conservatives 10; Christian People's Party 9; Socialist People's Party 9; Communists 7; Centre Democrats 4; Left Socialists 4; Greenland 2; Faroes 2.

In 1973 Denmark joined the European Economic Community. Denmark is also a member of NATO, and the Nordic Council.

Education is free and compulsory, the schools being maintained by taxation. Special schools are numerous, technical and agricultural predominating. There are Universities at Copenhagen (founded in 1478), Aarhus (1933), Odense (1966), Roskilde (1972) and Aalborg (1974). A further University at Esjerg is planned.

Language and Literature.—The Danish language is akin to Swedish and Norwegian. Danish literature, ancient and modern, embraces all forms of expression, familiar names being Hans Christian Andersen (1805–1875), Sören Kierkegaard (1813–1855) and Georg Brandes (1842–1927), with Henrik Pontoppidan (1857–1943) and Karl Gjellerup (1857–1919), who shared the Nobel

Prize for Literature in 1917, and Johannes V. Jensen (1873–1950), who received the same award in 1944. Among recent authors of note are Klaus Rifbjerg (b. 1931) and Leif Panduro (b. 1923). Some 52 newspapers are published in Denmark. 10 daily papers are published in Copenhagen.

Production and Industry.—Nine per cent. of the labour force is engaged in agriculture, fishing, forestry, etc.; 35 per cent. in manufacturing, building and construction; 17 per cent. in commerce and 28 per cent. in administration, the liberal professions, etc. The chief agricultural products are pigs, cattle, dairy products, poultry and eggs, seeds, cereals and sugar beet; manufactures are mostly based on imported raw material but there are also considerable imports of finished goods.

COMMUNICATIONS.—Mercantile marine (ships above 100 gross tonnage) at end of 1972, 1,567 ships, with a gross tonnage of 4,069,017. On March 31, 1973, there were 2,522 km. of railway. In 1973 the capacity of the telecommunications network in circuit km. was 12,366,000.

FINANCE   1975–76
Revenue (*Budget estimate*)..... Kr. 62,055,098,400
Expenditure (*Budget estimate*).. 67,933,028,400
Denmark's balance of payments showed a deficit for 1974 of Kr. 6,145,000 (1973,— Kr 2,945,000,000).
Rate of Exchange—Kr. 12·30= £1 (July 1975) (*see also* p. 83).

TRADE

	1973	1974
	Kr. million	
Total Imports..............	46,969	60,138
Total Exports..............	37,549	46,915

Trade with U.K.

	1973	1974
Imports from U.K..	£329,174,000	£427,074,000
Exports to U.K....	477,946,000	577,115,000

The principal imports are petroleum and its products, machinery, vehicles and textile products. The chief exports are agricultural produce, fish products, butter, bacon, eggs, meat and livestock and machinery.

CAPITAL, Ψ Copenhagen, pop. (1970), 802,226; Greater Copenhagen, 1,380,118. Other centres are: Ψ Aarhus, 198,980; Ψ Odense 137,288; Ψ Aalborg, 100,255; Ψ Esbjerg, 68,085; Ψ Randers, 58,411; Roskilde, 44,245; Ψ Kolding, 41,612; Ψ Horsens, 44,121; Ψ Fredericia, 36,154; Ψ Vejle, 43,876.

FLAG.—Red, with white cross
NATIONAL DAY.—June 5 (Constitution Day).
Copenhagen, distant from London 728 miles; transit 36 hours by sea.

BRITISH EMBASSY
Offices, Kastelsvej 36–40, Copenhagen.
Residence, Bredgade 26, Copenhagen.
Ambassador Extraordinary and Plenipotentiary, His Excellency Sir Andrew Alexander Steel Stark, K.C.M.G., C.V.O. (1971).
Counsellor, Hon. R. J. T. McLaren.
Counsellor (Commercial), G. W. Marshall, C.M.G., M.B.E., B.E.M.
Defence, Naval, Military and Air Attaché, Cdr. D. Monsell, R.N.
1st Secretaries, J. P. Davies; E. G. B. Allen (*Administration and Consular*); F. S. Napier (*Information*); M. W. R. Mustoe, M.B.E. (*Commercial*); C. P. Carter, M.B.E.; G. L. Jones (*Agric. and Fisheries*); R. O. Barritt (*Labour*) (resident in Stockholm).
Asst. Military Attaché, Major C. F. Cooper.
Asst. Air Attaché, Sqn. Ldr. C. P. Russell-Smith (resident in Stockholm).
2nd Secretary, D. G. Parker (*Commercial*).
3rd Secretary, D. A. Rogers.

Attachés, Miss M. M. Tinman, M.B.E. (*Consular*); Miss B. Brett-Rooks (*Commercial*).
Chaplain, Rev. D. H. T. Picton.
There are Consulates at *Aabenraa, Aalborg, Esbjerg, Aarhus* and *Odense*; and at *Thorshavn* and *Klaksvig* (Faröes). There is a British Trade Office at *Aarhus.*

British Council Representative and Cultural Attaché, J. D. W. Hughes, O.B.E., Møntergade 1, Copenhagen.

Outlying Parts of the Kingdom
The outlying parts of Denmark have about 81,000 inhabitants. The FARÖES, or Sheep Islands (540 sq. m.; pop. (1969) 38,000), capital, Thorshavn, are governed by a *Lagting* of 26 members, a *Landstyr* of 4 members which deals with special Faröes affairs, and send 2 representatives to the *Folketing* at Copenhagen. On Sept. 14, 1946, the *Lagting,* with the consent of the Danish Government, for its own guidance held a plebiscite on the Faröes. About one-third of the electors did not, however, take part in the voting: of the rest a little more than half the votes cast were in favour of separation from Denmark and the establishment of a republic. At a subsequent general election for the *Lagting* a great majority voted in favour of remaining part of the Kingdom of Denmark with a certain measure of home rule and in 1948 the Faröes received this. Trade with U.K. in 1970 totalled: Imports, £941,000; Exports, £1,221,000. GREENLAND (ice-free portion about 132,000 sq. m., total area about 840,000 sq. m., population, 1965, 48,792) is divided into 3 provinces (West, North and East). Greenland (capital, Godthaab) has a *Landsraad* of 17 members and sends 2 representatives to the *Folketing* at Copenhagen. The trade of Greenland is mainly under the management of the Royal Greenland Trade Department. Mineral and oil prospecting revealed deposits of lead, zinc, iron ore, oil and gas. Commercial exploitation of these resources has not yet begun. The United States of America has acquired certain rights to maintain air bases in Greenland.

DOMINICAN REPUBLIC
(República Dominicana)
President, Joaquin Balaguer, *born* Sept. 1, 1907; *elected* June 1, 1966; *re-elected* May 16, 1970; *re-elected,* May 16, 1974.

EMBASSY AND CONSULATE
4 Braemar Mansions, Cornwall Gardens, S.W.7
[01–937 1921]
Ambassador Extraordinary and Plenipotentiary (vacant).
There are also Consular Offices at *Liverpool, Birmingham, Manchester, Nottingham, Grimsby, Southampton, Plymouth, Cardiff, Edinburgh, Glasgow* and *Belfast.*

The Dominican Republic, formerly the Spanish portion of the island of Hispaniola, is the oldest settlement of European origin in America. The western part of the island forms the Republic of Haiti. (*For Map, see* p. 871.)

The island lies between Cuba on the west and Puerto Rico on the east and the Republic covers an area of about 19,322 square miles, with a population (U.N. estimate, 1970) of 4,012,000. The climate is tropical in the low lands and semi-tropical to temperate in the higher altitudes.

Government.—Santo Domingo was discovered by Christopher Columbus in December, 1492, and remained a Spanish Colony until 1821. In 1822 it was subjugated by the neighbouring Haitians who remained in control until 1844 when the Dominican Republic was proclaimed. The country was occupied by American marines from

1916 until the adoption of a new Constitution in 1924. In July, 1924, a properly elected Constitutional Government was installed. From 1930 until May 30, 1961 (when he was assassinated) Generalissimo Rafael Trujillo ruled the country.

A Council of State headed by Rafael F. Bonnelly was set up in 1962, and Professor Juan Bosch, elected President in December 1962, held office until September, 1963, when he was deposed by a military junta. A revolt in favour of ex-President Bosch in April, 1965, developed into civil war lasting until September the same year when a provisional President was elected. At a further election on June 1, 1966, Dr. Joaquin Balaguer was elected President; re-elected May 16, 1970 and again on May 16, 1974.

Communications.—According to local classification there are 2,932 miles of first class and 1,392 miles of second class and inter-communal roads in the Republic. There is a direct road from Santo Domingo to Port-au-Prince, the capital of Haiti, but that part of it in the border area has fallen into disuse and although road travel is possible, it is preferable to travel direct between the two capitals by air. The frontier has been closed since Sept., 1967, except for that section crossed by the main road linking the two capitals. A telephone system connects practically all the principal towns of the republic and there is a telegraph service with all parts of the world. There are more than 90 commercial broadcasting stations and there is a television station operated by Radiotelevision Dominicana, which with the help of relay stations provides receptions of its programmes in the major cities. Three other television stations in Santo Domingo—Rahintel, Tele-Inde and Color-Vision —transmit to the local area.

Spanish is the language of the Republic.

The Republic is served by two national and six foreign airlines, and an international airport 18 miles to the east of the capital is in operation. Another is being constructed near Puerto Plata on the north coast.

Sugar, coffee, cocoa, and tobacco are the most important crops. Other products are peanuts, maize, rice, bananas, molasses, salt, cement, ferro-nickel, bauxite, gold, silver, cattle, sisal products, honey and chocolate. There is a growing number of light industries producing beer, tinned foodstuffs, glass products, nylon and cotton textiles, soap, cigarettes, construction materials, plastic articles, shoes, papers, paint, rum, matches, peanut oil and other products.

FINANCE

	1974 (est.)	1975 (est.)
Budget		
Revenue.....	RD$470,636,070	RD$486,308,238

One *Dominican Peso* = $1·00 U.S.

TRADE

	1973	1974
Imports......	RD$407,100,000	RD$673,000,000
Exports......	447,714,290	650,000,000

Trade with U.K.

	1973	1974
Imports from U.K....	£4,666,000	£6,396,000
Exports to U.K.......	4,716,000	10,553,000

The chief imports are machinery, food stuffs, iron and steel, cotton textiles and yarns, mineral oils (including petrol), cars and other motor vehicles, chemical and pharmaceutical products, electrical equipment and accessories, construction material, paper and paper products, and rubber and rubber products; the chief exports are sugar, coffee, cocoa, tobacco, chocolate, molasses, bauxite, ferro-nickel and gold.

The principal export to U.K. over a number of years has been sugar by-products; ferro-nickel and

bauxite are also exported in considerable quantities to the U.S.A. and Europe.

CAPITAL, ♱ Santo Domingo, population of the Capital District (1970 census), 817,000. Other centres, with populations (1970 census); Santiago de los Caballeros (245,000); La Vega (156,000); San Francisco de Macoris (126,000); San Juan (114,000); San Cristóbal (106,000).

FLAG.—Red and blue, with white cross bearing an emblem at centre.

NATIONAL DAY.—February 27 (Independence Day, 1844).

BRITISH EMBASSY

Avenida Independencia 84, Santo Domingo
Ambassador Extraordinary and Plenipotentiary, His Excellency, Paul Victor St. John Killick, O.B.E. (1972).
First Secretary and Consul, J. E. T. Thorne, M.V.O.

BRITISH CONSULAR OFFICES

There are British Consular Offices at *Santo Domingo, Puerto Plata* and *San Pedro de Macoris.*

ECUADOR
(Republica del Ecuador)

President, Brig. Gen. Guillermo Rodriguez Lara, *assumed office* Feb. 16, 1972.

EMBASSY AND CONSULATE

Flat 3B, 3 Hans Crescent, S.W.1
[01–584 1367]
Ambassador Extraordinary and Plenipotentiary, His Excellency Gustavo Ycaza.
1st Secretary, Dr. J. Ortiz.
Counsellor (Commercial), Sr. J. Marchan.
3rd Secretary, Srta. G. Moreno.

There are consulates at *Liverpool, Birmingham* and *Glasgow.*

Area and Population.—Ecuador is an equatorial State of South America, the mainland extending from lat. 1° 38′ N. to 4° 50′ S., and between 75° 20′ and 81° W. long., comprising an area reduced by boundary settlements with Peru (Jan. 29, 1942) to about 226,000 sq. miles. (*For* MAP, *see* Index.)

The Republic of Ecuador is divided into 20 provinces. It has a population estimated (1973) at 7,000,000, mostly descendants of the Spaniards, aboriginal Indians, and Mestizoes. The territory of the Republic extends across the Western Andes, the highest peak of which is Aconcagua, in the Chilean sector (22,976 ft.), the highest peaks in Ecuador being Chimborazo (20,408 ft.), Ilinza (17,405 ft.), Carihuairazo (16,515 ft.), Cotocachi (16,301 ft.), and Pichincha (16,000 ft.) in the Western Cordillera; and Cotopaxi (19,612 ft.), Antisana (18,864 ft.), Cayambe (19,160 ft.), Altar (17,730 ft.), Sangay (17,464 ft.), Tungurahua (16,690 ft.), and Sincholagua (16,365 ft.) in the Eastern Cordillera. Ecuador is watered by the Upper Amazon, and by the rivers Guayas, Mira, Santiago, Chone, and Esmeraldas on the Pacific coast. There are extensive forests, and the cinchona bark tree is common.

The *Galápagos* (Giant Tortoise) *Islands* forming the province of the Archipelago de Colón, were annexed by Ecuador in 1832. The archipelago lies in the Pacific, about 500 miles from Saint Elena peninsula, the most westerly point of the mainland. There are 12 large and several hundred smaller islands with a total area of about 3,000 sq. miles and an estimated population (1973) of 4,000. The capital is San Cristobal, on Chatham Island. Although the archipelago lies on the equator, the temperature of the surrounding water is well below equatorial average owing to the *Antarctic Humboldt Current.* The province consists for the most part of National Park Territory, where unique marine birds, iguanas, and the giant tortoises are conserved. There is some local subsistence farming; the main industry, apart from tourism, is tuna and lobster fishing.

Government.—The former *Kingdom of Quito* was conquered by the Incas of Peru in the latter part of the 15th century. Early in the 16th century Pizarro's conquests led to the inclusion of the present territory of Ecuador in the Spanish Vice-royalty of Peru. The independence of the country was achieved in a revolutionary war which culminated in the battle of Mount Pichincha (May 24, 1822). At elections held on June 2, 1968, Dr. José María Velasco (Ibarra) was elected President and assumed office on Sept. 1, 1968. He dismissed Congress on June 22, 1970, and assumed supreme power. President Velasco was deposed on Feb. 15, 1972. A National Revolutionary Government of the Armed Forces was formed under Brig.-Gen. Guillermo Rodriguez Lara and the 1945 constitution was reintroduced.

Production and Industry.—The chief products are petroleum, bananas, cocoa, coffee, sugar, rice, straw hats, pyrethrum, xanthophyll, scopolamine, vegetable ivory and balsa wood. The oil deposits in the Oriente are estimated at between 10–15,000,000,000 barrels. The oil is evacuated by a trans-Andean pipeline to the port of Balao (near Esmeraldas). In the highlands the principal crops are maize, wheat, potatoes and other temperate products. Small amounts of gold, silver and lead are mined, and emeralds and rubies are occasionally found. A Five-Year industrialisation programme was introduced in 1973, and industry is being rapidly diversified; textiles have traditionally been predominant.

Communications.—There are 23,256 km. of permanent roads and 5,044 km. of roads which are only open during the dry season. There are about 750 miles of railway, including the railway from Quito to Guayaquil. Nine commercial airlines operate international flights, linking Ecuador with New York, Miami, Panama, Lima, Santiago, Rio de Janeiro, Paris, Frankfurt, Madrid, etc. There are internal services between all important towns.

Defence.—The standing Army has a strength of about 15,000. There is an Air Force of some 90 aircraft of various kinds and a small Navy.

Language and Literature.—Spanish is the language of the country. The electorate is confined to adult male and female citizens who can read and write, and in recent years considerable headway has been made in reducing the high figure of illiteracy. 3 daily newspapers are published at Quito and 4 at Guayaquil. Elementary education is free and compulsory. In 1973 there were 8,062 primary schools with 1,091,102 pupils and 894 high schools with 278,400 pupils. The 9 Universities, at Quito (2), Guayaquil (3), Cuenca, Machala, Loja and Portoviejo, the Polytechnic Schools at Quito and Guayaquil and the 8 technical colleges in other provincial capitals had 70,138 students in the same year.

FINANCE 1973
Revenue(*Budget Estimates*).. *Sucres* 8,700,000,000
Expenditure(*Budget Estimates*)..... 8,700,000,000
 1974
Revenue (*Budget Estimates*).... *Sucres* 9,427,000,000
Expenditure (*Budget Estimates*)..... 9,427,000,000
Internal Debt (Sept. 30, 1967)..... 4,516,570,000
External Debt (Dec. 31, 1972).. U.S.$343,295,000

The official rate of Exchange: *Sucres* 57= £1, is used for most legal imports and exports. There is also a free rate of exchange. *See also* p. 83.

TRADE

Import licences are required for all merchandise and these are issued by the Central Bank of Ecuador.

	1971	1972
Imports....	$U.S.289,793,000	$U.S.279,128,000
Exports....	221,544,000	279,783,000

Trade with U.K.

	1973	1974
Imports from U.K.....	£11,822,000	£13,600,000
Exports to U.K........	2,250,000	2,170,000

The chief exports are petroleum, bananas, cocoa, coffee and sugar. Other exports are rice, balsa wood, castor-oil seeds, hats, pharmaceuticals, fish, ivory, nuts and pyrethrum. Manufactured goods and machinery are the main imports.

CAPITAL.—Quito. Population (estimated 1972), 700,000; Ψ Guayaquil (1,000,000) is the chief port; other centres are Cuenca (100,000); (est. 1968) Ambato (69,766); Riobamba (50,710); ΨEsmeraldas (51,573); and ΨManta (42,750). The foregoing figures of urban populations have been revised by the Census and Statistics Office to exclude from 1968 figures for rural areas of the cities (*i.e.* areas not supplied by city fuel or water services).

FLAG.—Three horizontal bands, yellow, blue and red (the yellow band twice the width of the others); emblem in centre.

NATIONAL DAY.—August 10 (*Dia de la Independencia*).

BRITISH EMBASSY
Calle G. Suarez, 111 (P.O. Box No. 314), Quito.

Ambassador Extraordinary and Plenipotentiary, His Excellency Norman Ernest Cox, C.M.G. (1974)

1st Secretary, D. V. Thornley (*Commercial, Head of Chancery*).

There is a British Consular Office at *Guayaquil*.

EGYPT
(Arab Republic of Egypt)

It was announced in Cairo on Sept. 2, 1971, that the country had resumed its ancient name of Egypt.
President and Prime Minister, Anwar El Sadat, *elected President*, Oct. 15, 1970.
Vice-President, Air Marshal Hosni Mubarak.

CABINET
Prime Minister, Mamduh Salem.
Deputy Prime Ministers
Higher Education, Dr. Muhammad Hafiz Ghanim.
Foreign Affairs, Ismail Fahmi.
War, General Muhammad el Gamassy.

Manpower and Training, Abdul Latif Bultia.
Power, Ahmad Sultan.
Tourism, Ibrahim Naguib.
Social Affairs, Dr. Aisha Ratib.
Agriculture and Sudan Affairs, Dr. Uthman Badran.
Information, Ahmad Kamal Abul Magd.
War Production, Ahmad Kamal el Badri.
Culture, Yussuf al Sibai.
Health, Dr. Fuad Muhieddin.
Petroleum, Ahmed Izzedin Hilal.
Justice, Adel Yunis.
Maritime Transport, Mahmud Abdul Rahman Fahmi.
Planning and Administrative Development, Dr. Ibrahim Hilmi Abdul Rahman.
Interior, Major General Sayyid Hussein Fahmi.
Trade, Zakaria Tawfik Abdul Fattah.
Irrigation, Abdul Azim Abdullah Abul Atta.
Industry, Issa Abdul Hamid Shaheen.
Scientific Research and Nuclear Power, Dr. Muhammad Abdul Maabud el Gibaily.
Finance, Dr. Ahmad Abu Ismail.
Economy and Economic Cooperation, Dr. Muhammad Zaky Shafei,.

Communications, Muhammad Kamaluddin Hassanain.

WAQFS and Azhar Affairs, Dr. Muhammad Hussain el Zahaby.

Transport, Muhammad Gamaluddin Sidqi.

Civil Aviation, Hamdi Abu Zaid.

Ministers of State, Abdul Fattah Abdullah (_Cabinet Affairs and Control_); Albert Barsum Salama (_People's Assembly Affairs_); Uthman Ahmad Uthman (_Housing and Reconstruction_); Muhammad Abdul Fattah Ibrahim (_Insurance_); Dr. Mustafa Kamal Hilmi (_Education_); Muhammad Hamid Mahmud (_Local Government and People's Organisations_); Abdul Rahman al Shazli (_Supply_).

EMBASSY IN LONDON
26 South Street, W.1
[01-499 2401]

Ambassador Extraordinary and Plenipotentiary, His Excellency Mohammed Samih Anwar (1974).

Ministers, Amin Sami (_Consul General_); Abdel Halim Abdel Hamid Badawi (_Minister Counsellor_); Anwar Mohamed Koreitem (_Cultural_); Abdel Moneim Ahmed Abd-Rabbo (_Commercial_); Ahmed Ibrahim Khalil Anis (_Press_).

Counsellors, Gamel Mohamed Said; Mahmoud Abdel Rahim Pasha; Hassan Shaker Abdel-Aal; Emad Edin Aly El-Kadi; Mohamed Salah El-Din; Mohamed Abboud; Ahmed Amin Waly.

1st Secretaries, Mohammed Abdel Rahim Mohamed (_Consular_); Nabil Rihan (_Consular_); Farouk El Kadi (_Consular_).

2nd Secretaries, Ali Muturali Heqazi; Farouk Helmi Ali Helmi; Hamdi Mohamed Nada; Farouk El-Sadek.

AREA AND POPULATION.—The total area of Egypt is estimated at 1,000,000 square kilometres (385,110 square miles), the inhabited area being only 35,168 square kilometres (13,578 square miles), with a population (estimated May, 1971) of 34,000,000.

There are three distinct elements in the native population. The largest, or " Egyptian " element, is a Hamito-Semite race, known in the rural districts as _Fellahin_ (_fellâh_—ploughman, or tiller of the soil). The _Fellahin_ have been mainly of the Moslem faith since the conquest of the country in the 7th century. A second element is the _Bedouin_, or nomadic Arabs of the Libyan and Arabian deserts,

of whom about one-seventh are real nomads, and the remainder semi-sedentary tent-dwellers on the outskirts of the cultivated end of the Nile Valley and the Fayüm. The third element is the _Nubian_ of the Nile Valley between Aswân and Wadi-Halfa of mixed Arab and Negro blood. The Bedouin and Nubians are Moslems.

The territory of Egypt comprises (1) _Egypt Proper_, forming the N.E. corner of the African continent, divisible into (_a_) the valley and delta of the Nile, (_b_) the Libyan or Western Desert, and (_c_) the Arabian or Eastern Desert; (2) _The Peninsula of Sinai_, forming part of the continent of Asia; and (3) a number of _Islands_ in the Gulf of Suez and Red Sea, of which the principal are Jubal, Shadwan, Gafatin and Zeberged (or St. John's Island). This territory lies between 22° and 32° N. lat. and 24° and 37° E. long. The northern boundary is the Mediterranean, and in the south Egypt is conterminous with the Sudan. The western boundary runs from a point on the coast 10 kilometres N.W. of Sollüm to the latitude of Siwa and thence due S. along the 25th meridian to the parallel of 22° N. (the N. boundary of the Sudan) at 'Uweinat Mountain. The E. boundary follows a line drawn from Rafa on the Mediterranean (34° 15' E. long.) to the head of the Gulf of 'Aqaba, from which point the remainder of the E. boundary is washed by the waters of the Gulf of 'Aqaba and the Red Sea. The " settled land area " is stated officially at 7,667,000 _feddâns_ (12,431 square miles) and the area of lakes at 641,000 _feddâns_ (1,039 square miles), a total of 8,308,000 _feddâns_ (13,470 square miles).

Physical Features.—The Nile valley varies in width from less than half a mile in the southern granitic region to over 10 miles in the northern limestone region, and the cliffs in some places rise to heights of over a thousand feet above the river. The fertile lands, on which the prosperity of the country depends, occupy the floor of the valley between the river and the bounding cliffs, while to the north of Cairo they spread out into the irregular fan-shaped formation of the Delta which comprises the six provinces of Lower Egypt, with the richest soil in the country.

The _Nile_ has a total length of 4,160 miles. In the 960 miles of its course through Egypt it receives not a single tributary stream. The river formerly had a regular yearly rise and fall of about 13 feet at Cairo, but since the commencement of storage in the reservoir of the Aswan High Dam in 1965, there has been no flood downstream of the Dam and the water level remains almost constant throughout the year. Westward from the Nile Valley into Tripolitania stretches the _Libyan Desert_, an arid region, containing some depressions, whose springs irrigate small areas known as _Oases_, of which the principal, from S.E. to N.W., are known as Kharga, Dakhla, Farafra, Baharia and Siwa.

On the eastern edge of the Libyan Desert, a few miles south-west of Cairo stand the Pyramids of Gizeh, of which the highest, the _Great Pyramid_, is 451 feet high. Close to the pyramids is the _Great Sphinx_, 189 feet long. In the Eastern Desert a great backbone of high and rugged mountains extends north-westwards from Ethiopia to near Suez, and reappears as a detached mass in the Peninsula of Sinai. Flanking this mountain chain on the west, between the axis of the range and the Nile, are plateaux of sandstones and limestones, dissected by _wadis_ (dry water-courses), often of great length and depth, with some wild vegetation and occasional wells and springs. The roads follow the course of the main _wadis_ from well to well, and here and there are to be found small encampments of wandering Arabs.

Religions.—The predominant religion is Islam but there are about 2,000,000 Christians (mainly Copts). By 1968 nearly all the Jews had left the country. The chief Moslem religious authorities in Egypt are the *Sheik el Gami el Azhar* and the *Mufti Gumhuriya Misr al Arabiya.*

Government.—From 30 B.C. to A.D. 639 Egypt was a province of the Roman Empire, but in A.D. 640 the Christian inhabitants were subjugated by Moslem invaders and Egypt became a province of the Eastern Caliphate. In 1517 the country was incorporated in the Ottoman Empire under which it remained until early in the 19th century.

A British Protectorate over Egypt declared on Dec. 18, 1914, lasted until Feb. 28, 1922, when Sultan Ahmed Fuad was proclaimed King of Egypt. Following closely on the accession of King Farouk, the *Anglo-Egyptian Treaty* was signed in London (Aug. 26, 1936) and the military occupation by British troops was terminated.

The security of Egypt was threatened after the outbreak of war in 1939 and reinforcements were sent from Britain and the Dominions. Axis troops invaded Egypt in 1940 and fierce fighting ensued, with Allied victories and reverses, until the decisive victory in " The Battle of Egypt " (Oct.–Nov. 1942) drove the enemy out of the country. In July, 1952, following a military *coup d'état,* King Farouk abdicated in favour of his infant son, who became King Ahmed Fuad II. In June, 1953, however, Gen. Neguib's military council deposed the young king and declared Egypt a Republic, Gen. Neguib himself assuming the Presidency. In November, 1954, General Neguib was deposed by Lt.-Col. Gamal Abdel Nasser and the military council. On June 23, 1956, Col. Nasser assumed office as President, after an election at which voting was compulsory, and he was the only candidate.

A union with Syria was affected in 1958 and lasted until September, 1961, when Syria seceded after a *coup d'état.* The title and flag of the United Arab Republic were, however, retained for Egypt.

President Nasser died suddenly on Sept. 28, 1970, and the duties of Head of State were assumed by Mr. Anwar Sadat who was elected President in a referendum on Oct. 15. After initially making few Ministerial changes, President Sadat took the opportunity of an alleged plot against him in April, 1971, to remove many of the Ministers and officials he had inherited from Nasser. On March 26, 1973, he announced the formation of a government of which he was Prime Minister as well as President. He retained the Premiership in the new Cabinet formed in April 1974.

Agriculture.—Despite increased industrialization and the discovery of new oil fields, agriculture continues to provide the most substantial contribution to the national economy. Cotton (10 million *kanbars* in 1974) is the most important export, but sugar cane, onions, potatoes and citrus fruits are also sold extensively to overseas markets. Nearly all cultivation is carried out by peasant farmers whose operations are funded and generally controlled by co-operative organizations. Productivity is usually good. Irrigation and land reclamation schemes have contributed to a small increase in the cultivable area, and a $147 million drainage project, financed partly by the International Bank for Reconstruction and Development, is intended ultimately to irrigate nearly one million acres.

Railways.—The principal lines radiate from Cairo to Alexandria (and on to Rosetta), Damietta and Ismailia (continuing northwards to Port Said and southward to Suez). From Cairo the line runs southwards for a distance of 554 miles to a new port being constructed upstream of the High Dam. At this point a steamer connection runs to New Halfa, connecting Egypt with the Sudan Government Railways. Westwards from Alexandria (and close to the coast) runs a line to the frontier at Sollûm, thus joining Libya to Egypt. The gauge is standard (4 ft. 8½ in.).

Roads and Caravan Routes.—A sea coast motor road exists from Alexandria to Mersa Matruh, with an extension along the coast to Sollûm and thence to connect with the coast road in Libya. A bitumen road leads to Kharga and Dakhla, from the former of which there is a route, known as the Darb el 'Arbain, leading to Dar Fûr and the south of the Sudan. There are many well-known routes across the Arabian Desert to the Red Sea, that from Qena to Qoseir, a metalled road, being probably the most frequently used.

Shipping.— Ψ Apart from the three great seaports of Alexandria, Port Said and Suez, the last two of which are now undergoing reconstruction following several years of disuse after the 1967 war, Egypt has but few harbours and anchorages adapted for large craft; the principal are those of Sollûm and Matruh on the Mediterranean, Tor, Abu Zenima, Zeitia, Jemsa and Hurghada in the Gulf of Suez, and Safaga and Qoseir on the Red Sea.

Currency.—£E (Egyptian *pound* of 100 *piastres*) =97p sterling. Floating Official Rate of Exchange, plus a Preferential Rate of Exchange for visitors, about 50 per cent. above the Official Rate.

Trade with U.K.

	1973	1974
Imports from U.K.	£27,100,000	£52,000,000
Exports to U.K.	23,700,000	27,000,000

The principal imports are metals, and manufactures thereof, chemicals and pharmaceuticals, machinery and transport equipment, foodstuffs, beverages and textile fibres. The exports are principally raw cotton, textile yarns, rice, fruit and vegetables, petroleum products and a growing list of secondary exports, many of them manufactured goods.

CAPITAL.—Cairo (population, estimated in 1975 at 8,143,000), stands on the E. bank of the Nile, about 14 miles from the head of the Delta. Its oldest part is the fortress of Babylon in old Cairo, with its Roman bastions and Coptic churches. The earliest Arab building is the Mosque of 'Amr, dating from A.D. 643, and the most conspicuous is the Citadel, built by Saladin towards the end of the 12th century and containing in its walls the Mosque of Mohamed Ali built in the 19th century.

Ψ ALEXANDRIA (estimated population, 1,900,000), founded 332 B.C. by Alexander the Great, was for over 1,000 years the capital of Egypt and a centre of Hellenic culture which vied with Athens herself. Its great *pharos* (lighthouse), 480 feet high, with a lantern burning resinous wood, was one of the " Seven Wonders of the World ". Other towns are: Ismailia; Ψ Port Said; Mansura (102,709); Asyût (284,000); Faiyûm (162,000); Tanta (139,965); Mahalla el Kubra (115,509); Ψ Suez; Ψ Damietta (97,000).

CAIRO is 2,520 miles from London: transit *via* Trieste, 5 days; *via* Marseilles, 6 days.

FLAG.—Horizontal bands of red, white and black, with two 5-point green stars in white band. NATIONAL DAY.—July 23 (Anniversary of Revolution in 1952).

BRITISH EMBASSY

Kasr el Doubara, Garden City, Cairo

Ambassador Extraordinary and Plenipotentiary, His Excellency Willie Morris, C.M.G. (1975).

Counsellor, R. S. Faber.

Defence and Military Attaché, Col. W. C. Deller, O.B.E.

1st Secretaries, D. A. S. Gladstone (*Head of Chancery*); D. J. F. Barwell (*Information*); H. R. Leach, M.B.E.; D. Parker (*Aid*); A. J. Ramsay (*Economic*); D. H. G. Rose (*Consul*); B. S. T. Eastwood.
2nd Secretaries, T. Airey (*Administration*); D. Cartwright (*Commercial*); P. W. Ford.
Cultural Attaché, N. A. Daniel, C.B.E.
  British Consulate-General, Alexandria
Consul-General, F. W. Hall.
Vice-Consul, G. B. B. Chavasse.

EQUATORIAL GUINEA
President, Francisco Macias (Nguema), *elected* October 12, 1968.
Formerly the territory of "Spanish Guinea", Equatorial Guinea consists of the Island of Macias Nguema (formerly known as Fernando Póo), an island in the Bight of Biafra about 20 miles from the west coast of Africa, Pagalu Island (formerly Annobon) in the Gulf of Guinea, the Corisco Islands (Corisco, Elobey Grande and Elobey Chico) and Rio Muni, a mainland area between Cameroun and Gabon. It has a total area of about 11,000 sq. miles and a population (U.N. estimate, 1969) of 286,000.
Macias Nguema is a mountainous island with forests of oil palm, ebony, mahogany and oak, and sugar-cane, cotton and indigo. Cocoa, coffee, sugar, tobacco, vanilla nut and kola nut are cultivated and large quantities of cocoa and other products are exported.
Government.—Former colonies of Spain, the territories now forming the Republic of Equatorial Guinea were from April 1, 1960, constituted as two provinces of Metropolitan Spain, the inhabitants having the same rights as Spanish citizens. As a result of a plebiscite held on Dec. 15, 1963, an autonomous *régime* was instituted on June 2, 1964, with the approval of the Spanish Government. Equatorial Guinea became fully independent on October 12, 1968, after a referendum on the new constitution held in August, 1968, and presidential elections on Sept. 22, 1968. The latter were supervised by a U.N. Mission. The first President, Señor Francisco Macias, assumed office on Independence Day, having two days earlier formed a coalition ministry. The President took the Defence portfolio and appointed Ministers of Commerce and Foreign Affairs.
Severe disorders occurred during February and March, 1969, following incidents at the town of Bata (in Rio Muni). Spanish residents left Equatorial Guinea in large numbers, having had to seek the protection of residual Spanish forces while awaiting evacuation to Spain. In a statement to the United Nations Security Council on April 4, the Secretary-General reported that all Spanish troops had left Equatorial Guinea by March 28, together with all civilians who wished to leave. Some 600 Spanish civilians elected to remain in Macias Nguema and about 80 in Rio Muni.
CAPITAL, ΨMalabo (formerly known as Santa Isabel) on the island of Macias Nguema (population 9,000). ΨBata is the principal town and port of Rio Muni. FLAG.—Three horizontal bands, green over white over red; blue triangle next staff; coat of arms in centre of white band.
British Ambassador, His Excellency, Edward Ferguson Given, C.M.G. (1972) (Resident at *Yaoandé, Cameroun*).

ETHIOPIA
Provisional Military Administrative Council
Chairman, Brig.-Gen. Teferi Barite.
First Vice-Chairman, Major Mengistu Haile Mariam.
2nd Vice-Chairman, Lt.-Col. Atnafu Abate.

EMBASSY IN LONDON
17 Prince's Gate, S.W.7
[01–589 7212]
Ambassador Extraordinary and Plenipotentiary (vacant).
Counsellor, Ato Zaudie Makuria.
1st Secretary, Ato Yohannes Meshesha.
2nd Secretary, Ato Zelleke Bellete.
3rd Secretary, Ato Getatiun Dessalegn.

Position and Extent.—Ethiopia, with which Eritrea was federated from 1952 to 1962 when it was incorporated as a province, is in North-Eastern Africa, bounded on the north west by the Sudan; on the south by Kenya; on the east by Afars and Issas Territory and the Republic of Somalia; and on the north-east by the Red Sea. The area is estimated at 400,000 square miles, with a population of 26,000,000 of whom about one-third are of the ruling race of Semitic origin (Amharas and Tigres) and the remainder mainly Gallas, Guraghi, Sidama, Agao, negro tribes on the west and south frontiers, and Danakil and Somalis on the east.
Ethiopia is mainly a mountainous country, volcanic in origin, with several peaks of about 14,000 ft., notably in the centre and in the Simien range in the north; many other mountains exceed 10,000 ft. Eritrea consists of a mountainous hogsback range up to 10,000 ft., interposed between the Red Sea and the Sudan, flanked on east and west by flatter territory. The lower country and valley gorges are very hot; the higher plateaux are well watered, with a genial climate. On the high plateaux there are two main seasons in the year, a dry winter, October to May, and a rainy summer from June to September, with a season of "small rains" occurring generally in March. The chief river is the Blue Nile, issuing from Lake Tana; the Atbara and many other tributaries of the Nile also rise in the Ethiopian highlands.
Those of Semitic origin (Amharas and Tigres), who inhabit the southern highlands of Eritrea, provinces of Tigre, Begemdir, Gojjam, parts of Shoa, and many of the Gallas, are Christians of the Ethiopian Orthodox Church, which was formerly led by the head of the Coptic Church, the Patriarch at Alexandria. Since 1959, however, the Ethiopian Church has been autocephalous and the new Patriarch, Abuna Theophilos, was enthroned by the Ethiopian archbishops in May, 1971. Moslems predominate in some areas, notably northern Eritrea, Harar and Jimma and Arussi, the Moslem

centre being at Harar. The province of Gamu Gofa and parts of Sidamo and Arussi have considerable pagan elements.

Following considerable military and civil unrest in early 1974 the Emperor Hailé Selassié I announced on March 5 the convening of a commission to revise the Constitution, and the setting up within six months of a conference to consider the commission's proposals. It appeared likely that more power would devolve on to Parliament. Internal unrest continued through the summer, however, and at the end of June, the armed forces assumed effective control of the country by establishing an "Armed Forces Committee" now entitled the Provisional Military Administrative Council. Their demands for far-reaching reforms were acceded to by the Government, with the agreement of the Emperor, who was finally deposed on Sept. 12, 1974.

Eritrea.—Eritrea was administered by Great Britain from the end of the Second World War until September 15, 1972, when in accordance with a resolution of the United Nations Assembly of December 2, 1950, it was federated with Ethiopia under the Ethiopian Crown, becoming a province of Ethiopia in 1962. An armed campaign for independence has accompanied the collapse of the imperial régime.

Production and Industry.—The principal pursuits are agriculture and cattle breeding. In the hotter regions, sugar-cane, cotton, &c., flourish; in the middle zone maize, wheat, barley, coffee, oranges and other fruit trees, tobacco, potatoes and oil seeds are cultivated; and above 6,000 feet are excellent pastures with some corn cultivation. Coffee provided approximately 64 per cent. of the country's total exports by value in 1974. The forests are a potential source of wealth. Horses, mules, donkeys, cattle, oxen, goats, and sheep, and camels in the lowlands, form a large portion of the wealth of the people. Industry is small, the main products being textiles, foodstuffs, tyres, beer and cement. Hydro-electric power production and telecommunications are expanding rapidly, however, mainly with loans from the World Bank, which in 1971 had approved a number of loans for agricultural development.

Communications.—A railway links Addis Ababa, the capital, via Dire Dawa, with Djibouti, 486 miles away. It carried 361,000 passengers and 393,000 tons of freight in 1971–72. In Eritrea a narrow gauge line runs from Massawa to Asmara and on to Agordet. Several roads were constructed before and during the Italian occupation; the principal road runs from Addis Ababa to Dessie and on to Asmara, with a branch from Dessie to Assab on the Red Sea Coast. Addis Ababa and Asmara are linked by a road running through Gondar and along Lake Tana. Others run from Addis Ababa west to Lekempti, south-west to Jimma, Gore and Gambela, south to the Kenya frontier, and in the East to Dire Dawa, Harar and the northern region of the Somali Republic. Partly financed by large loans from the International Bank for Reconstruction and Development, much further improvement and extension of roads is being undertaken. The Ethiopian Air Lines maintain regular services from Addis Ababa to many provincial towns. External services are operated to Athens, Frankfurt, Rome, Paris, Aden, Djibouti, Sana'a, Taiz, Jedda, Cairo, Khartoum, Nairobi, Dar-es-Salaam, Entebbe, Lagos, Accra, Douala, Kigali, Kinshasa, Bombay, New Delhi, Peking and London.

Defence.—Under the Ministry of Defence the armed forces comprise the Army, including the Bodyguard, the Air Force and the Navy. The Army consists of four infantry divisions, including one mechanized brigade with armour, with normal artillery, engineer units and supporting arms including a parachute battalion. An American Military Advisory and Assistance Group (MAAG) assists the forces, mainly the Army, with training and advice, under an agreement signed with the Ethiopian Government. There is a military academy at Harar and a military training centre at Holleta with a specialist training wing. The Air Force comprises a transport squadron, a bomber squadron, three fighter squadrons, a training squadron, a jet conversion squadron, and an elementary training unit. The Air Force Headquarters is situated at Debre Zeit. The aircraft are mostly of American manufacture but also include Canberras. The Navy has a headquarters in Addis Ababa with a main base at Massawa and a smaller one at Assab. The principal units are an ex-U.S. seaplane tender (*Ethiopia*), a patrol craft squadron of 5, an MTB squadron of 4, and an ex-Dutch minesweeper.

Education.—Elementary education is provided without religious discrimination by Government schools in the main centres of population; there are also Mission schools, and cadet-schools for the Army, Air Force, and Police. Government secondary schools are found mainly in Addis Ababa, but also in most of the provincial capitals. In 1961 the Hailé Selassié I University was founded to co-ordinate the existing institutions of higher education (University College, Engineering, Building and Theological Colleges in Addis Ababa, Agricultural College at Alemaya, near Harar, and Public Health Centre in Gondar, etc.) and to provide a framework for future development. There is also a Catholic-run university in Asmara. Amharic is the official language of instruction, with English as the first foreign language. Arabic is taught in Koran Schools; and Ge'ez (the ancient Ethiopic) in Christian Church Schools, which abound. Adult education is met to some extent by institutes which provide evening classes in Addis Ababa. In 1971 the International Development Agency granted a loan of U.S. $95 million for the development of secondary education.

Finance.—Total revenue for 1974–75 was estimated at £180 m., while expenditure was expected to reach £188 m. The Ethiopian dollar has a value of 5.52 grains of fine gold and is divided into 100 cents. At Jan. 31, 1975, the combined note and coin issue amounted to £128,000,000. Foreign exchange and gold reserves of the National Bank amounted to £115,000,000 at the same date. Eth. $4·90= £1 (May 1975). (*See also* p. 83.)

Trade.—The chief imports by value are machinery and transport equipment, manufactured goods, chemicals, beverages and tobacco (from U.K.); the principal exports by value being coffee, oilseeds, hides and skins, and pulses.

TRADE

	1973	1974
Total Imports......	£85,000,000	£116,000,000
Total Exports......	122,000,000	143,000,000
	1973	1974
Imports from U.K.....	£7,000,000	£9,800,000
Exports to U.K.......	3,600,000	4,800,000

CAPITAL, Addis Ababa (population, estimated 912,000), also capital of the province of Shoa; Asmara (population 250,000) is the capital of the Province of Eritrea. Dire Dawa is the most important commercial centre after Addis Ababa and Asmara, Ψ Massawa and Ψ Assab (recently enlarged) are the two main ports. There are ancient architectural remains at Aksum, Gondar, Lalibela and elsewhere.

ETHIOPIAN FLAG.—Three horizontal bands; green, yellow, red; bearing crowned lion at centre.

NATIONAL DAY.—July 23.

BRITISH EMBASSY
(Addis Ababa)

Ambassador Extraordinary and Plenipotentiary, His Excellency Derek Malcolm Day, C.M.G. (1975).

Counsellor, R. A. R. Barltrop.

Defence Attaché, Lt.-Col. R. Smith.

1st Secretaries, E. M. Smith, B.E.M.; Miss C. B. Dowds, M.B.E.

2nd Secretaries, A. Vittery (*Information*); P. A. Penfold.

BRITISH CONSULAR OFFICES

There are British Consular Offices at *Addis Ababa* and *Asmara*.

Hon. Consul, Asmara, B. H. Burwood-Taylor.

British Council Representative, E. C. Pugh, Artistic Building, Hailé Selassié Avenue, Addis Ababa.

FINLAND
(Suomi)

President, Dr. Urho Kaleva Kekkonen, G.C.B., *born* 1900, *elected* Feb. 15, 1956; re-elected 1962 and 1968; term extended until 1978 by Act of Parliament (1973).

CABINET

Prime Minister, Kalevi Sorsa (*S.D.P.*).
Minister of Labour, Valde Nevalainen (*S.D.P.*).
Foreign Affairs, Ahti Karjalainen (*C.P.*).
Justice, Matti Louekoski (*S.D.P.*).
Interior, Heikki Tuominen.
Defence, Kristian Gestrin (*S.P.P.*).
Finance, Johannes Virolainen (*C.P.*), *Deputy Minister of Finance*, Esko Niskanen (*S.D.P.*).
Education, Ulf Sundqvist (*S.D.P.*), *Deputy Minister*, Marjatta Väänänen (*C.P.*).
Agriculture, Heimo Linna (*C.P.*).
Communications, Pekka Tarjanne (*L.P.*).
Trade, Jermu Laine (*S.P.D.*).
Industry, Jan-Magnus Jansson (*S.P.P.*).
Social Affairs, Seija Karkinen (*S.D.P.*), *Deputy Minister of Social Affairs*, Pentti Pekkarinen (*C.P.*).
[*C.P.*= Centre Party; *S.D.P.*= Social Democratic Party; *S.P.P.*= Swedish People's Party; *L.P.*= Liberal Party.]

FINNISH EMBASSY AND CONSULATE
38 Chesham Place, S.W.1
[01–235 9531]

Ambassador Extraordinary and Plenipotentiary, His Excellency, Richard Bjornson Tö Herman, K.C.V.O., O.B.E. (1975).

Counsellor, Erkki Mäentakanen.

Counsellor, Raimo Salmi.

1st Secretary, Unto Turunen.

Attaché, Esko Hamilo.

Press Counsellor, Kristofer Gräsbeck.

Military, Naval and Air Attaché, Capt. Erik Wihtol.

Area and Population.—A country situated on the Gulfs of Finland and Bothnia, with a total area of 130,165 square miles, of which 70 per cent. is forest, 10 per cent. cultivated, 9 per cent. lakes and 11 per cent. waste and other land, population (1974), 4,698,000. In 1974 the birth rate was 13·3, death rate 9·6 per 1,000. The infant mortality rate was 10·2 per 1,000 live births. 92·6 per cent of the people are Lutherans, 1·2 per cent. Greek Orthodox and 6·2 per cent. others.

The Aland Archipelago (Ahvenanmaa), a group of small islands at the entrance to the Gulf of Bothnia, covers about 572 square miles, with a population (1973) of 21,800 (96·3 per cent. Swedish-speaking). The islands have a semi-autonomous status.

Government.—Under the Constitution there is a single Chamber (*Eduskunta*) for which women are

eligible, composed of 200 members, elected by universal suffrage of both sexes. The legislative power is vested in the Chamber and the President. The highest executive power is held by the President who is elected for a period of 6 years.

A coalition government was formed on Sept. 4, 1972, but a temporary, non-political, caretaker government was appointed by the President on June 13, 1975, to hold office until the elections on Sept. 21–22, 1975. It was led by Mr. Keijo Liinamaa.

Defence.—By the terms of the Peace Treaty (Feb. 10, 1947) with U.K. and U.S.S.R., the Army is limited to a force not exceeding 34,400. The Navy is limited to a total of 10,000 tons displacement with personnel not exceeding 4,500. The Air Force, including naval air arm, is limited to 60 machines with a personnel not exceeding 3,000. Bombers or aircraft with bomb-carrying facilities are expressly forbidden. The Defence Forces contain a cadre of regular officers and N.C.O.'s, but their bulk is provided by conscripts who serve for 8–11 months. None of the Defence Forces has the full complement permitted.

Education.—Primary education is compulsory for children from 7 to 16 years, and free in certain State and municipal schools. In the autumn of 1974, there were 189,100 in primary schools, 312,872 in comprehensive schools, 49,964 in experimental comprehensive schools and 246,000 in secondary schools. There are 11 Higher Schools and 6 Universities (1974); Helsinki University (1974), 21,104 students. Combined enrolment at Higher Schools and Universities was 68,135.

Language and Literature.—Most Finns are bilingual. 93·2 per cent. speak Finnish as their first language, 6·6 Swedish and the remaining 0·2 per cent. other languages (mainly Lapps living a nomadic life in the North). Since 1883 Finnish has been on an equal footing with Swedish as the official language of Finland, but since independence in 1917 Finnish has slowly been displacing Swedish. In literature also, until the close of the eighteenth century, Swedish was dominant, but awakening Finnish nationalism in the early years of the nineteenth century and the establishment of an association for the promotion of Finnish literature in 1831 gave Finnish the status of a literary language. There is a vigorous modern literature. Eemil Sillanpää was awarded the Nobel Prize for Literature in 1939. There are 62 daily newspapers in Finland which appear on 4 or more days per week (55 Finnish language, and 7 Swedish).

Production and Industry.—Finland is a highly industrialised country producing a wide range of capital and consumer goods. Timber and the products of the forest-based industries remain the backbone of the economy, accounting for over a half of her export earnings, but the importance of the metal-working, shipbuilding and engineering industries is growing. This sector in 1974 accounted for over a quarter of Finland's exports. The textile industry is well developed and Finland's glass, ceramics and furniture industries enjoy international reputations. Other important industries are rubber, plastics, chemicals and pharmaceuticals, footwear, foodstuffs and electronic equipment.

Communications.—There are 5,900 kilometres of railroad and a well-developed telegraph and telephone system. There is railway connection with Sweden and U.S.S.R., passenger boat connection with Sweden, Denmark and West Germany. Vessels on the London to Leningrad route call at Helsinki. There are also passenger/cargo services between Britain and Helsinki, Korka and other Finnish ports. External civil air services are maintained by British Airways, Finnair, Kar Air, Scandinavian Airlines, Maley, Lufthansa, Interflug, Pan American, LOT (Polish Airlines), Aeroflot, Czechoslovak Airlines and Swiss Air. The merchant fleet at the end of 1974 totalled 449 vessels, (1,623,000 tons gross); 27 steamers (13,800 tons gross); 361 motor vessels (756,700) and 61 tankers (853,400).

FINANCE

	1974	1975*
	Finnmarks	*Finnmarks*
Revenue (*Budget*)	19,940,000,000	24,055,000,000
Expenditure (*Budget*)	20,060,000,000	25,420,000,000

* Proposed budget figures for 1975.

TRADE

	1973	1974
	Finnmarks	*Finnmarks*
Total Imports	16,597,391,000	25,676,000
Total Exports	14,608,525,000	20,687,000

	1973	1974
Imports from U.K.	£167,800,000	£228,000,000
Exports to U.K.	331,600,000	493,000,000

The principal imports are raw materials, foodstuffs, machinery and manufactured goods. The exports are principally the output of the timber and forest based industries and metal industry (*e.g.* paper-working machinery and ships).

CAPITAL.—Ψ Helsinki (Helsingfors). Population 526,896; other towns are Tampere (Tammerfors), 156,380; Ψ Turku (Abo), 153,300; Lahti, 88,715; Ψ Oulu (Uleaborg) 82,366; Ψ Pori (Björneborg) 73,665; Jyväskylä, 57,148; Kuopio, 64,398; Lappeenranta, 50,950; and Ψ Vaasa (Vasa) 44,316.

NATIONAL DAY.—December 6 (Day of Independence).

FLAG.—White with blue cross.

BRITISH EMBASSY
Helsinki

British Ambassador's Residence, It. Puistotie 15. *Chancery Offices,* Uudenmaankatu 16–20.

Ambassador Extraordinary and Plenipotentiary, His Excellency James Eric Cable, C.M.G. (1975).

Counsellor (Commercial), M. S. Berthoud (*and Consul-General*).

1st Secretaries, R. C. Beetham; C. H. Godden (*Commercial*); H. O. Spankie; P. J. Monk (*Consul*).

Defence, Military Attaché and Air, Lt.-Col. J. O. Lawes, M.C.

Naval Attaché, Capt. R. J. F. Turner, R.N.

2nd Secretaries, J. B. Midgley (*Commercial*); G. Berg; R. O. L. Fraser-Darling.

3rd Secretaries, M. Edwards (*Vice-Consul*); Miss E. A. Sketchley.

There are British Consular offices at *Helsinki, Tampere, Turku, Pori, Kotka, Oulu,* and *Vaasa.*

British Council Representative, R. B. Lodge, E. Esplanaadikatu 22A, Helsinki 13.

FRANCE
(La République Française)

President of the French Republic, Valéry Giscard d'Estaing, *born* Feb. 2, 1926, *elected* May 19, 1974, assumed office, May 27, 1974.

CABINET

Prime Minister, M. Jacques Chirac.
Minister of State for Interior, M. Michel Poniatowski.
Defence, M. Yvon Bourges.
Commerce and Small Trades, M. Vincent Ansquer.
Justice, M. Jean Lecanuet.
Foreign Affairs, M. Jean Sauvagnargues.
Education, M. René Haby.
Economy and Finance, M. Jean-Pierre Fourcade.
Foreign Trade, M. Norbert Ségard.
Quality of Life, M. André Jarrot.
Health, Mme. Simone Veil.
Industry, M. Michel d'Ornano.
Co-operation, M. Pierre Abelin.
Equipment, M. Robert Galley.
Agriculture, M. Christian Bonnet.
Labour, M. Michel Durafour.
Secretaries of State, M. André Bord (*Ex-Servicemen*); M. Aymar Achille-Fould (*Posts and Telecommunications*); M. Marcel Cavaille (*Transport*); M. Michel Guy (*Culture*); Gen. Marcel Bigeard (*Defence*); M. Jean-Pierre Soisson (*Universities*); M. Olivier Stirn (*Overseas Departments and Territories*), M. Réne Tomasini (*Relations with Parliament*); M. Gabriel Peronnet (*Civil Service*); M. Paul Granet (*Professions*); M. André Rossi (*Government Spokesman*); Mme. Hélène Dorlhac (*Prisons*); Mme. Annie Lesur (*Pre-Elementary Education*); M. Bernard Destremau (*Foreign Affairs*); M. Christian Poncelet (*Budget*); M. Jacques Barrot (*Housing*); Mme. Françoise Guroud (*Condition of Women*); M. Pierre Mazeaud (*Youth and Sport*); M. Gérard Ducray (*Tourism*); M. Paul (Didoud (*Immigrant Workers*); M. Réne Lenoir (*Social Action*); M. Jean François Denian (*Agriculture*).

FRENCH EMBASSY IN LONDON

Residence: 11 Kensington Palace Gardens, W.8 [01–229 9411]

Chancery: 58 Knightsbridge, S.W.1. [01–235 8080].

Ambassador Extraordinary and Plenipotentiary, His Excellency Monsieur Jacques de Beaumarchais (1972).

Minister-Counsellor, M. Philippe Cuvillier.

2nd Counsellors, Comte Tristan d'Albis; M. François Bujon; M. Samuel Le Caruyer de Beauvais; M. Robert Delos Santos.

Press Counsellor, M. Daniel Contenay.

1st Secretaries, M. Jean Fargue; M. Denis Nardin.

2nd Secretary, M. Philippe Selz.

Area and Population.—The largest state in Central Europe, extending from 42° 20′ to 51° 5′ N. lat., and from 7° 85′ E. to 4° 45′ W. long., bounded on the north by the English Channel and the Straits of Dover (*Pas de Calais*), which separate it from England. Its circumference is estimated at about 3,000 miles and its area at 213,000 sq. miles divided into 95 departments, including the island of Corsica, in the Mediterranean, off the west coast of Italy. The population of France (estimated) in 1975 was 52,590,000.

DEPARTMENTS AND REGIONS
(Estimated March 1, 1968)

Paris	2,590,000	Nièvre	247,702	Pyrénées-	
Seine-et-		Saône-et-		Orientales.	281,976
Marne	604,340	Loire	550,364		
Yvelines	854,382	Yonne	283,376	*Languedoc-*	
Essonne	674,157			*Roussillon*	
Hauts-de-		*Bourgogne*	1,502,632		1,707,500
Seine	1,461,619	Nord	2,417,899	Alpes-de-	
Seine-Saint-		Pas-de-		Haute-	
Denis	1,249,606	Calais	1,397,159	Provence	104,813
Val-de-				Alpes (Hautes)	91,790
Marne	1,121,340	Nord	3,815,058	Alpes-Mari-	
Val-d'Oise	693,269	Meurthe-et-		times	722,070
		Moselle	705,413	Bouches-du-	
Paris		Meuse	209,513	Rhône	1,470,271
Region	9,248,713	Moselle	971,314	Var	555,926
Ardennes	309,380	Vosges	388,201	Vaucluse	353,966
Aube	270,325				
Marne	485,388	*Lorraine*	2,274,441	*Provence-Côte:*	
Marne		Rhin (Bas)	827,367	*d'Azur*	3,298,836
(Haute)	214,336	Rhin (Haut)	596,633	*Corsica*	273,173
Champagne	1,273,429	*Alsace*	1,412,385		
Aisne	526,346	Doubs	426,363		
Oise	540,988	Jura	233,547		
Somme	512,113	Saône (Haute)	214,176		
		Belfort (Terr.			
Picardie	1,519,447	de)	118,450		
Eure	383,385	*Franche-*			
Seine-		*Comté*	992,536		
Maritime	1,113,977	Corrèze	237,858		
		Creuse	156,876		
Haute-Nor-		Vienne			
mandie	1,497,962	(Haute)	341,589		
Cher	304,601				
Eure-et-Loir	302,207	*Limousin*	736,323		
Indre	247,118	Ain	339,262		
Indre-et-		Ardèche	256,927		
Loire	447,132	Drôme	342,891		
Loir-et-Cher	267,896	Isère	768,450		
Loiret	430,629	Loire	722,443		
		Rhône	1,325,611		
Centre	1,990,381	Savoie	288,921		
Loire-Atlan-		Savoie			
tique	861,452	(Haute)	378,550		
Maine-et-					
Loire	556,272	*Rhône-*			
Mayenne	252,762	*Alpes*	4,422,995		
Sarthe	461,839	Charente	331,016		
Vendée	421,250	Charente-			
		Maritime	483,622		
Pays de la		Sèvres (Deux)	326,462		
Loire	2,533,575	Vienne	340,256		
Côtes-du-					
Nord	506,102	*Poitou-Char-*			
Finistère	768,929	*entes*	1,481,356		
Ille-et-		Dordogne	374,073		
Vilaine	652,722	Gironde	1,009,390		
		Landes	277,381		
Morbihan	540,474	Lot-et-			
		Garonne	290,592		
Bretagne	2,468,200	Pyrénées			
Calvados	532,897	(*Atlantiques*)	508,734		
Manche	451,939				
Orne	288,524	*Aquitaine*	2,460,170		
		Ariège	141,768		
Basse-Nor-		Aveyron	281,568		
mandie	1,294,145	Garonne			
Côte-d'Or	421,192	(Haute)	690,712		

Additional middle column entries:

Gers	181,577
Lot	151,198
Pyrénées	
(Hautes)	225,730
Tarn	332,011
Tarn-et-Gar-	
onne	183,572
Midi-Py-	
renees	2,184,846
Allier	386,533
Cantal	169,330
Loire (Haute)	208,337
Puy-de-Dôme	547,743
Auvergne	1,311,943
Aude	278,323
Gard	478,544
Hérault	591,397
Lozère	77,258

Government.—The monarchical system of government was overthrown by the *French Revolution* (1789–1793), and the *First Republic* lasted until the Great Napoleon (born Aug. 15, 1769, died May 5, 1821) founded the First Empire in 1804. The monarchy was restored in 1814, and also after the "Hundred Days" of Napoleon (March 20–June 29, 1815), until the *Second Republic* of 1848, which became the Second Empire on Nov. 22, 1852. On Sept. 4, 1870, the Emperor Napoleon III (nephew of the Great Napoleon) was deposed, and the *Third Republic* was set up. The constitution of the Third Republic vested the legislative power in a Chamber of Deputies and a Senate. The executive was vested in the President, who was elected for 7 years by the Senate and Chamber assembled in Congress.

On Sept. 1, 1939, Germany invaded Poland thus precipitating war with France and Great Britain, which had (March 31, 1939) given an open pledge to support Poland against aggression.

On June 17, 1940, the late Maréchal Pétain sought terms of surrender from the Germans. A number of French troops had reached British ports after the evacuation of the British Expeditionary Force from Dunkirk and St. Valéry, and on June 23, 1940, after stating that the French Government had capitulated before all means of resistance had been exhausted, General Charles de Gaulle announced the formation of a Provisional National Committee "to defend that part of the French Empire which has not yet been conquered by Germany and to free that part of France still under the yoke of the invader."

On June 3, 1943, after prolonged negotiation, there was set up a *French Committee of National Liberation*, which was recognized by the allied nations on August 26, 1943.

Paris was liberated on August 25, 1944, and on October 13, 1944, the de Gaulle administration was recognized by the allied nations as the government of France.

Under the de Gaulle administration there was a single chamber legislature (The National Consultative Assembly) which met at Algiers until France was liberated. The enlarged Consultative Assembly met in the Luxemburg Palace (Paris), formerly the Senate House, on Nov. 7, 1944.

Following a national referendum on Oct. 21, 1945, a Constituent Assembly was elected with the task of drafting a new constitution. This was duly drawn up and adopted at a further referendum on Oct. 13, 1946. A National Assembly and Council of the Republic, elected on a territorial basis, were set up. With amendments made in 1954, the Constitution of the Fourth Republic was in force from 1946 until Oct. 5, 1958. From the liberation

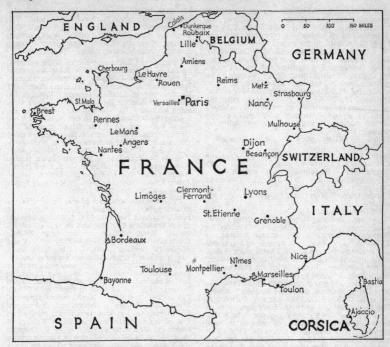

of Paris in 1944 until the Fourth Republic came to an end in 1958, 26 Cabinets were formed with an average life of 5½ months. The Government of M. Mollet for 16 months in 1956–57 was the longest in office, that of M. Queuille in 1950 the shortest, being in office for only three days.

Insurrections took place in Algeria and in the Metropolitan Department of Corsica in May, 1958, and, faced by a threat of imminent insurrection among the armed forces at home, President Coty warned the nation that it was on the brink of civil war and invited General de Gaulle to form a Government. M. Pflimlin formally resigned the office of Prime Minister on May 31. On June 1, by 329 votes to 224, Gen. de Gaulle was invested in the National Assembly as Prime Minister, with power to govern by decree for a period of six months during which time proposals for constitutional reform would be submitted to a national referendum.

The Fifth Republic.—The Constitution of the Fifth Republic, embodying important changes, was adopted by an overwhelming majority at a referendum held on Sept. 28 in Metropolitan France and all overseas departments and territories.

The *President* was elected for a term of 7 years by an electoral college consisting of both Houses of Parliament, the departmental general councils, overseas assemblies and elected representatives of the municipal councils. As the result of a referendum in October, 1962, future Presidents are to be elected by direct universal suffrage. Presidents are eligible for re-election. The President appoints the Prime Minister. He may dissolve the National

Assembly after consultation with the Prime Minister and Presidents of both Houses, but may not do so more than once in twelve months. He may submit disputed legislation to a national referendum at the request of the Government or of both Houses of Parliament. The President may assume special powers in an emergency. At the presidential elections held on Dec. 21, 1958, General de Gaulle was elected President by an overwhelming majority and took office on Jan. 8, 1959, as first President of the Fifth French Republic. He was re-elected in December, 1965, for a second presidential term. In May, 1968, a major internal crisis was precipitated by a student rebellion, which led to a generalized strike and the virtual collapse of the Government. General de Gaulle then held parliamentary elections at which the Gaullists won the largest majority in living history.

The General remained President until April 27 1969, when a referendum on regional and Senate reform on which he had staked his personal future as President, was lost. Alain Poher (*Centrists and President of the Senate*) became interim President and stood for election against MM. Pompidou (*Gaullist*), Duclos (*Communist*), Defferre (*Socialist*) and three other candidates. On the second round M. Pompidou was elected with 58 per cent. of the vote and assumed office as President on June 20, 1969.

President Pompidou died on April 2, 1974. Following his death, M. Poher (*President of the Senate*) for the second time became acting Head of State. The first ballot for the election of a new President was held on May 5, 1974. Of the twelve candidates, M. François Mitterand won 43·24 per cent. of the vote, and M. Giscard d'Estaing won 32·60 per cent., and since no overall majority had been achieved, these two went forward to the second round of voting, the other ten candidates being eliminated. In the second vote, on May 19, M. Giscard d'Estaing defeated M. Mitterand by 424,599 votes, out of a total poll of 26,724,595, which represented a turn-out of 87 per cent. M. Giscard d'Estaing's share of the vote was 50·81 per cent., and M. Mitterand's was 49·19 per cent. M. Giscard d'Estaing assumed office on May 27, and appointed M. Chirac as Prime Minister. After the most recent parliamentary elections held on March 4 and 11, 1973, the strengths of the party groups in the National Assembly were established as follows:—

Union of Democrats for the Republic (Gaullist) 183
Socialists and left-wing Radicals 102
Communists 73
Independent Republicans (Government Supporters) 55
Reformers 34
Central Union (Government Supporters) 30
Others 13

Parliament consists of the National Assembly and the Senate. Bills may be presented in either House, except money bills, which must originate in the National Assembly. The normal session of Parliament is confined to 5½ months each year and it may also meet in extraordinary session for 12 days at the request of the Prime Minister or a majority of the Assembly. Voting rights are personal and can only be delegated in special circumstances.

The *Prime Minister* is appointed by the President, as is the Cabinet on the Prime Minister's recommendation. They are responsible to Parliament. But the executive is constitutionally separate from the legislature and Ministers may not sit in Parliament. The Prime Minister is assumed to have the Assembly's confidence unless the Opposition moves a censure motion signed by not less than one-tenth of the deputies; such motion must be approved by an absolute majority; if defeated, its sponsors must not introduce another no-confidence motion in the same session.

A *Constitutional Council* is responsible for supervising all elections and referenda and must be consulted on all constitutional matters and before the President of the Republic assumes emergency powers. At the request of the Government, the *Economic and Social Council* gives advice on bills, ordinances or decrees referred to it. Any economic or social plan or bill must be submitted to it.

Production.—The chief agriculture products are wheat, barley, rye, maize, oats, potatoes, beet-root (for the manufacture of sugar), hops, &c. Rice is being grown in parts of the Camargue (Rhône delta). Fruit trees abound, and are very productive, the principal being the olive, chestnut, walnut, almond, apple, pear, citron, fig, plum, &c.
The harvest in 1972 was:—

	(Quintals)
Wheat	176,735,000
Oats	24,259,000
Barley	104,635,000
Rye	3,308,000
Maize	85,963,000

Forestry is an important industry, the principal forests being those of the Ardennes, Compiègne, Fontainebleau, and Orléans, consisting chiefly of oak, birch, pine, beech, elm, chestnut and the cork-tree in the south. The vine is cultivated to a very great extent, as the names Bordeaux, Burgundy, Champagne, &c., universally testify. Production of wine in 1973 was 60,100,000 hectolitres. Cider-making is also an important industry. The mineral

resources include coal, natural gas, pig iron, bauxite, lead, silver, antimony and salt. The most important manufactures are of metals, cars, aircraft, watches, jewellery, cabinet-work, carving, pottery, glass, chemicals, dyeing, paper making, cottons, woollens, carpets, linen, silk and lace.

Language and Literature.—French is the universal language of France and of a large proportion of the people of Belgium, Luxemburg, Switzerland, Tunisia, Algeria, Mauritius, Haiti and the Province of Quebec, Canada, to whom the almost inexhaustible literature of France is a treasured heritage. The work of the *French Academy*, founded by Richelieu in 1635, has established *le bon usage*, equivalent to " The King's English " in Great Britain. French authors have been awarded the Nobel Prize for Literature on 11 occasions—R.F.A. Sully-Prudhomme (1901), F. Mistral (1904), Romain Rolland (1915), Anatole France (1921), Henri Bergson (1927), Roger M. du Gard (1937), André Gide (1947), François Mauriac (1952), Albert Camus (1957), St. John Perse (Alexis Léger) (1960) and Jean Paul Sartre (1964).

Defence.—The personnel of the Defence Forces in September 1973 totalled: ARMY 326,982; AIR FORCE 101,175; NAVY 67,833; Common Services 77,817 (including GENDARMERIE 66,533). National nuclear forces include medium-range ballistic missiles, submarine-launched ballistic missiles and *Mirage* IV medium bombers. The Army has a variety of new French-made equipment in service, including medium tanks, field and anti-aircraft SP guns, trucks and radio equipment. A road-mobile tactical nuclear weapon is expected to enter service in 1974. The Air Force is equipped with *Mirage* IV nuclear bombers, C135F tanker/transports, *Mirage* IIIC, IIIE and 5 fighters and *Transall* and DC8 transports. In June 1973 it also received its first squadron of *Jaguar* strike attack fighters of which 160 are due for delivery by 1975. Later, in 1974, *Mirage* F1 fighters will enter service to replace the *Vautours* and *Super Mystères*. The Air Force also now has in service the STRIDA 2 air defence control and reporting system, which is a part of the NATO air defence system. The Navy includes 2 aircraft carriers, 2 helicopter carriers, 3 GW destroyers, 17 Fleet escorts, 18 fast escorts, 9 escort frigates, 3 nuclear missile launching submarines, 20 conventional submarines, 2 LSD, 5LST, 13 ocean minesweepers, 5 modern minehunters, and 57 coastal and inshore minesweepers.

Education.—The educational system is highly developed and centralized. It is administered by the Ministry of National Education, comprising (a) the *Direction des Enseignements Supérieurs; Direction de la Pédagogie, des Enseignements Scholaires et de l'Orientation; Direction des Personnels d'Enseignement Général Technique et Professionnel; Direction des Services Administratifs et Sociaux; Direction de l'Equipement Scolaire, Universitaire et Sportif; Direction des Bibliothèques et de la Lecture Publique; Direction de la Coopération*; (b) the Superior Council of National Education (consultative); and (c) the Inspectorate. *Local Administration* comprises 25 Territorial Academies, with inspecting staff for all grades, and Departmental Councils presided over by the *Préfet*, and charged especially with *primary* education.

Primary and secondary education are compulsory, free and secular, the school age being from 6 to 16. Schools are for boys, for girls, or mixed. (i) *Primary* education is given in *écoles maternelles* (nursery schools), *écoles primaires élémentaires* (primary schools) and *collèges d'enseignement général* (4-year secondary modern course); (ii) *Secondary* education in *collèges d'enseignement technique, collèges d'enseignement secondaire* and *lycées* (7-year course leading to one of the five *baccalauréats*). *Baccalauréat A* consists largely of philosophy and languages with a little mathematics, and provides entry into the faculties of Letters and Law. *Baccalauréat B* groups languages, mathematics and economics with philosophy classes oriented towards psychology and sociology. It provides entry to the faculties of Letters for the social sciences and to the faculty of Law for economics. *Baccalauréat C*, consisting of mathematics and physics with some languages, provides entry to the faculty of Sciences for those studying for a degree in mathematics and physics. *Baccalauréat D* has the same language component as *Baccalauréat C*, but its main feature is the natural sciences. It provides entry to the faculty of Sciences for natural science degrees, and also to the Medicine and Pharmacy Faculties. *Baccalauréat E* is largely scientific and technical with a language element, and provides entry to engineering schools and the Faculty of Science. (iii) *Special schools* are numerous. (iv) There are numerous *Grandes Ecoles* in France which award diplomas in many subjects not taught at university, especially applied science and engineering. Most of them are State institutions but have a competitive system of entry, unlike the universities. (v) The reform of the French university structure continues, and there are now universities in twenty-four towns in France. In the major provincial towns the existing university has been reorganized to form two, or three universities, and in Paris and the immediate surrounding district there are, since autumn 1970, thirteen universities.

Archæology, etc.—There are dolmens and menhirs in Brittany, prehistoric remains and cave drawings in Dordogne and Ariège, and throughout France various megalithic monuments erected by primitive tribes, predecessors of Iberian invaders from Spain (now represented by the Basques), Ligurians from northern Italy and Celts or Gauls from the valley of the Danube. Julius Cæsar found Gaul " divided into three parts " and described three political groups—Aquitanians south of the Garonne, Celts between the Garonne and the Seine and Marne, and Belgae from the Seine to the Rhine. Roman remains are plentiful throughout France in the form of aqueducts, arenas, triumphal arches, &c., and the celebrated Norman and Gothic Cathedrals, including Notre Dame in Paris, and those of Chartres, Reims, Amiens (where Peter the Hermit preached the First Crusade for the recovery of the Holy Sepulchre), Bourges, Beauvais, Rouen, etc., have survived invasions and bombardments, with only partial damage, and many of the renaissance and the XVIIth and XVIIIth century châteaux survived the French Revolution.

Roads.—The length of the *Routes Nationales* at the end of 1972 was 82,730 km. and of motorways 1,880 km. The principal rivers of France are the Seine, Loire, Garonne, and Rhône, the navigable waterways in general use in 1972 were 8,625 km.

Railways.—The system of railroads in France is very extensive. The length of lines of general interest, exclusive of local lines, open for traffic at the end of 1972 was 37,350 km., of which 9,356 km. were electrified. Traffic at the end of 1973 totalled 44,510,000,000 passenger-km. and 73,823,000,000 ton-km.

Shipping.—The French mercantile marine consisted on Jan. 1, 1973, of 531 ships of 7,440,004 tons gross, of which 26 were passenger vessels (229,696 tons gross), 129 tankers (4,658,995 tons gross) and 376 cargo vessels (2,551,313 tons gross).

FINANCE

	1971	1972
	F. millions	
Total revenue (*Budget*)	170,693	187,464
Total expenditure (*do.*)	168,358	186,376

The *Public Debt* on Dec. 31, 1972, was F.87,810,000,000 of which the external debt amounted to F.8,400,000,000.

Currency.—The unit of currency is the *franc* of 100 *centimes*, which was devalued on Aug. 10, 1969. Bank notes in 10, 50, 100 and 500 *franc* denominations and coins in 1, 5, 10 and 20 *francs* are issued.

EXCHANGE RATE (at July 3, 1973).—F.10·62 = £1 (*see also* p. 83).

COMMERCE

The principal imports are machinery, mineral fuels, chemical products, automobiles, iron, electrical equipment, minerals and non-ferrous metals, textile and leather goods, meat, fish, poultry and other agricultural products and precision instruments. The principal exports are automobiles, chemical products, iron and steel, textile and leather goods, machinery, electrical equipment, cereals and flour, wine and other agricultural products.

FRENCH FOREIGN TRADE

	1972	1973
	Francs	*Francs*
Imports	127,446,000,000	155,833,000,000
Exports	133,387,000,000	162,461,000,000

Trade with U.K.

	1973	1974
Imports from U.K.	£678,330,000	£914,639,000
Exports to U.K.	979,552,000	1,349,153,000

OVERSEAS DEPARTMENTS

With effect form Jan 1, 1947, the colonies of Guyane (French Guiana), Martinique, Guadeloupe and La Réunion with its dependencies have been theoretically administered in exactly the same way as the Metropolitan Departments, but in practice somewhat greater discretion is allowed to the Prefects and the locally elected bodies.

La Réunion.—Formerly Ile de Bourbon, about 420 miles E. of Madagascar, Réunion has been a French possession since 1643. Area, about 1,000 sq. miles. Population (1970), 445,500. Capital, St. Denis (85,992). Assigned to the administration of Réunion are the distant islands of St. Paul (3 sq. miles), New Amsterdam (27 sq. miles) and Kerguelen containing whaling and fishing stations 1,100 sq. miles). The Crozet Islands (200 sq. miles) and Adélie Land in the Antarctic Continent are also dependencies of Réunion. Imports from U.K., 1971, £611,000.

Martinique.—An island situated in the Windward Islands group of the West Indies, between Dominica in the north and St. Lucia in the south. Population (U.N. estimate, 1969), 332,000. Capital ΨFort de France (60,600). Other towns are ΨTrinité (39,173) and ΨMarin (31,369).

Guadeloupe.—In the Leeward Islands of the West Indies, the island of Guadeloupe, together with Marie Galante, the Ile des Saintes, Petite Terre, St. Barthélemy and St. Martin, form the other West Indian Department of France. Population (U.N. estimate, 1969), 323,000. Capital ΨPointe à Pitre 39,000). Other towns are ΨBasse Terre (16,000) in Guadeloupe and ΨGrand Bourg (12,827) in Marie Galante.

French Guiana.—Area, 35,000 sq. miles. Population (U.N. estimate, 1969), 48,000. Capital, ΨCayenne (20,000). Situated on the north-eastern coast of South America, French Guiana is flanked by

Netherlands Guiana on the west and by Brazil on the south and east. Under the administration of French Guiana is a group of islands (St. Joseph, Ile Royal and Ile du Diable), known as Iles du Salut. On Devil's Isle, Captain Dreyfus was imprisoned from 1894 to 1899. Imports from U.K. in 1971 were valued at £5,516,000.

CAPITAL OF FRANCE. Paris, on the Seine.
Population (estimated, 1975), 3,978,000 (incl. inner suburbs).
District of Paris.—Created by legislation promulgated on August 10, 1966, the District consists of 8 Departments one of which is the City of Paris (*see* list of Departments, p. 856).
Paris is administered by the Council of Paris which is composed of 90 members elected for six years by popular vote within the city/Department. The President and four Vice-Presidents of the Council are elected for one year by the members. The President presides over the meetings of the Council and is the representative of Paris on all official occasions. The administrative functions exercised in all other towns by the Mayor are exercised in Paris by two Government nominees: the Prefect of Paris, and the Prefect of Police. But Mayors are elected in each of the 20 arrondissements of Paris to carry out local civil duties.
At the Census of 1968 nineteen towns had a population of over 150,000 inhabitants:—Paris (2,590,000); Ψ Marseilles (893,771); Lyons (535,000); Toulouse (380,340); Ψ Nice (325,400); Ψ Bordeaux (270,996); Ψ Nantes (265,009); Strasbourg (254,038); Saint-Etienne (216,020); Ψ Le Havre (200,940); Lille (194,948); Rennes (188,515); Ψ Toulon (178,489); Montpellier (167,211); Grenoble (165,902); Ψ Brest (159,857); Reims (158,634); Clermont-Ferrand (154,110); Dijon (150,791). 37 towns in France have a population of over 100,000.
The chief towns of Corsica are Ψ Ajaccio (44,659) and Ψ Bastia (51,022).
Paris is distant from London 267 miles; transit by air, 1 hr.
FLAG.—The "tricolour", three vertical bands, blue, white, red (blue next to flagstaff).
NATIONAL DAY.—July 14.

BRITISH EMBASSY
(35 rue du Faubourg St. Honoré, Paris 8e)
Ambassador Extraordinary and Plenipotentiary, His Excellency Sir Nicholas Henderson, K.C.M.G., (1975).
Minister, C. T. E. Ewart-Biggs, C.M.G., O.B.E.
Minister (Economic), R. Arculus, C.M.G.
Counsellor and Consul-General, J. McAdam Clark, C.V.O., M.C.

BRITISH CONSULAR OFFICES
There are British Consular Offices in Metropolitan France at Paris, Bordeaux, Biarritz-Bayonne, Lille, Calais, Boulogne, Dunkirk, Lyons, Marseilles, Perpignan, Nice, Ajaccio, Cherbourg, Epernay, Le Havre, Nantes, Strasbourg, Metz.

BRITISH CHAMBER OF COMMERCE
6 Rue Halévy, Paris 9e
President, O. G. Longley, M.C.
Vice-Presidents, D. H. Goodchild; K. G. W. Bartell.

BRITISH COUNCIL
Representative in Paris, G. L. H. Hitchcock, C.B.E. rue des Ecoles 36, Paris 5e.
There is a British Council office at *Toulouse;* British Council libraries at *Paris, Bordeaux, Lille, Lyons* and *Strasbourg.*

THE FRENCH COMMUNITY
The Constitution of the Fifth French Republic promulgated on Oct. 6, 1958, envisaged the establishment of a French Community of States closely linked with common institutions. A number of the former French States in Africa have seceded from the Community but for all practical purposes continue to enjoy the same close links with France as those that remain formally members of the French Community. The Community Institutions in fact never operated as envisaged. Nevertheless, with the exception of Guinea, which opted out of the Community in the 1958 referendum, all the former French African colonies are closely linked to France by a series of financial, technical and economic agreements.

Francophone Countries.
In the following countries French is either the official or national language or the language of instruction; where there is another national language the name of it is shown after the name of the country:—Algeria (*Arabic*); Belgium (*Flemish*); Burundi (*Kirundi*); Cambodia (*Khmer*); Cameroun (*English*); parts of Canada (in Quebec, parts of Ontario and New Brunswick) (*English*); Central African Republic (*Sangho*); Chad; Congo (P.D.R.); Dahomey; France; Gabon; Guinea; Haiti (*Creole*); Ivory Coast; Laos (*Laotian*); Lebanon (*Arabic*); Luxemburg (*German and Letzeburgesch*); Madagascar (*Malagasy*); Mali; Morocco (*Arabic*); Mauritania (*Arabic*); Niger; Rwanda (*Kinyarwanda*); Senegal; Switzerland (1,000,000 French speaking); Togo; Tunisia (*Arabic*); Upper Volta; Vietnam (*Vietnamese*); Zaire. French is also spoken in the Overseas Departments (*see* above).

OTHER TERRITORIES
French Territory of the Afars and Issas.—Situated on the north-east coast of Africa, the Territory has an area of 9,000 sq. miles with a population (U.N. estimate, 1969) of about 81,000.
Formerly French Somaliland, the Territory was renamed on July 6, 1967, to emphasize the existence of the two main ethnic groups in the population. A renamed Chamber of Deputies succeeded the former territorial assembly to which a governing council is responsible for the administration of the territory. The French High Commissioner retains responsibility for foreign policy, defence, currency, credit, citizenship and law, other than traditional civil law. Capital, Ψ Djibouti (62,000).
New Caledonia.—Area, 7,200 sq. miles. Population (U.N. estimate, 1969), 98,000. Capital, Ψ Noumea (12,000). A large island in the Western Pacific, 700 miles E. of Queensland. Dependencies are the Isle of Pines, the Loyalty Islands (Mahé, Lifou, Urea, etc., the Huon islands and Alofis). New Caledonia was discovered in 1774 and annexed by France in 1854; from 1871 to 1896 it was a convict settlement. It is the world's third largest producer of nickel, after Canada and U.S.S.R.
Wallis and Futuna Islands.—Following a request from local kings and chiefs, it was decided by referendum (Dec. 27, 1959) that the islands would become the sixth Overseas Territory of France. Population of the islands, formerly dependencies of New Caledonia, is about 9,500, mostly Polynesians.
French Polynesia.—Area, 2,500 sq. miles. Population (U.N. estimate, 1970), 109,000. Capital, Ψ Papeete (15,220), in Tahiti. Includes the Society Islands (Tahiti, Moorea, Makatea, etc.), the Marquesas (Nukahiva, Hiva-oa, etc., 500 sq. miles, population, 3,000); the Leeward Isles (Huahine, Raiatea, Tahaa, Bora Bora, Maupiti, etc.); the Gambier Islands (Mangareva, etc.); the Tubuai Islands (Tubuai, Rurutu, Raivavae, Rimatara and Rapa Island; and Maiao Island).
Comoro Archipelago.—Area, 800 sq. miles. Population (estimated 1970), 275,227. Capital, Moroni. Includes the islands of Great Comoro, Anjouan, Mayotte and Mohilla and certain islets in

the Indian Ocean. Except for Mayotte, the islands voted in favour of independence in a referendum in December, 1974.

St. Pierre and Miquelon—Area, 93 sq. miles. Population (1967), 5,000. Two small groups of Islands off the coast of Newfoundland.

GABON
(Gabonese Republic)
(*For* MAP, *see* Index).

President, Omar Bongo, *assumed office,* December, 1967.

EMBASSY IN LONDON
66 Drayton Gardens, S.W.10.
[01-370 6441]

Ambassador Extraordinary and Plenipotentiary, His Excellency Joseph N'Goua.

Gabon lies on the Atlantic coast of Africa at the Equator and is flanked on the north by Equatorial Guinea and Cameroun and on the east and south by the People's Republic of Congo. It has an area of 101,400 sq. miles and a population (estimated 1972) of 500,000. Gabon elected on Nov. 28, 1958, to remain an autonomous republic within the French Community and was proclaimed fully independent on August 17, 1960.

Trade with U.K.

	1973	1974
Imports from U.K.	£2,833,000	£3,565,000
Exports to U.K.	10,258,000	28,397,000

CAPITAL.—Libreville (31,000).

FLAG.—Horizontal bands, green, yellow and blue.

NATIONAL DAY.—August 17.

British Ambassador (vacant).

Chargé d'Affaires, 1st Secretary and Consul, J. K. Gordon (resident at Yaourdé).

GERMANY
⋆ Deutsches Reich (German Realm)

THE HISTORY OF GERMANY from 1863-1945 is marked by wars of aggression. In 1864, Prussia, in company with Austria, attacked Denmark, and after a short campaign annexed the peninsula of Schleswig-Holstein. In 1866, as a result of war with Austria (the Seven Weeks' War), Prussia acquired the hegemony of the North Germanic Confederation from Austria. After the Franco-Prussian War of 1870, when Prussia wrested Alsace-Lorraine from France, the North Germanic Confederation and three South German States became the Germanic Confederation, the King of Prussia being proclaimed German Emperor at Versailles on Jan. 18, 1871.

At the outbreak of the War of 1914-1918, Germany was a Confederate League bearing the name German Empire under the hereditary presidency of the King of Prussia holding the title of German Emperor. At the close of the war, Germany lost most of the gains she had acquired since 1863, including all her colonies.

GERMANY BETWEEN THE TWO WARS.—On Nov. 9, 1918, two days before Germany sued for an Armistice from the victorious Allies, the German Emperor abdicated, and the Government of the country was taken over by the Council of the People's Commissioners in Berlin. In January, 1919, elections were held to a National Assembly on the basis of universal adult suffrage (male and female). The Assembly met at Weimar (Feb. 5, 1919), and elected Friedrich Ebert President of the Republic, a position he occupied until his death (Feb. 28, 1925) when Field Marshal Paul von Hindenburg was elected in his stead. Von Hindenburg was re-elected April 10, 1932, the rival candidate being Adolf Hitler, who was born at Braunau, Austria (April 20, 1889) and had migrated as a young man to Bavaria. A General Election of 1933 provided Hitler's party, the *Nationalsozialistische Deutsche Arbeiter Partei* (National Socialist German Workers' Party, or *Nazis*) with an absolute majority in the legislature (*Reichstag*) and Hitler became Prime Minister (Chancellor), a position which became fused with that of President at the death of von Hindenburg (Aug. 2, 1934), and Adolf Hitler exercised supreme and uncontrolled authority in the Reich.

THE WAR OF 1939-1945.—After concluding a Treaty of Non-Aggression with Soviet Russia (Aug. 24, 1939), Germany invaded Poland (Sept. 1, 1939), thus precipitating war with France and Great Britain, which had (March 31) given a pledge to support Poland against aggression.

Germany invaded and occupied Denmark and Norway (April, 1940), Belgium, the Netherlands, Luxemburg and France (May, 1940). Norway capitulated on June 9, France sued for peace in mid-June. The lightning war against Britain began on August 11, 1940, but the *Luftwaffe* attack, which was to prepare the way for invasion, was defeated. In April, 1941, Yugoslavia was invaded and Germany joined Italy in attacking Greece and Crete. On June 22, 1941, the U.S.S.R. was invaded. In 1942 the Nazi empire reached its height. The boundaries of Greater Germany included Alsace-Lorraine, Luxemburg, Eupen-Malmédy, large areas of Poland, Memelland and Slovenia; Germany and her satellites controlled all European countries except the British Isles, Spain, Portugal, Switzerland, Sweden and parts of European Russia, as well as large tracts of North Africa. The turning point came in November, 1942, with the Soviet victory at Stalingrad and the British at El Alamein. In 1943 a Soviet offensive threw the invader back almost to the Polish frontier, and the Western Allies, after defeating the Axis in North Africa, landed in Italy. In June, 1944, the Second Front opened on the Normandy beaches and by September, 1944, Germany itself was the battlefield. On May 8, 1945, the unconditional surrender of all German forces was accepted by representatives of the Western Allied and Soviet Supreme Commanders.

Hitler committed suicide on April 30, 1945.

In 1962 the Federal Statistical Office reported that during the course of the war from 1939 to 1945, 593,000 persons were killed during allied air attacks on Germany and 403,000 dwellings were destroyed. 537,000 civilians were killed, some 15 per cent. children under 14, and 56,000 foreign civilians, members of the police and armed forces. In the area now covered by the Federal Republic persons injured numbered 486,000, including 16,000 foreigners and prisoners of war.

THE POST WAR PERIOD.—After the surrender the Allied Powers assumed supreme authority in Germany. Power was to be exercised by the Commanders-in-Chief, each in his own zone of occupation and jointly in matters affecting Germany as a whole through a Control Council. Berlin was to be governed jointly by the four occupying powers. The guiding lines of policy were laid down in the agreement reached between the U.K., U.S. and U.S.S.R. Governments at Potsdam in August, 1945, which was to remain in force until a Peace Treaty should confirm or revise its directives. It

---

⋆ Nazi historians referred to the National Socialist régime as *Drittes Reich*. The *First* was the Holy Roman Empire, established in A.D. 962 by Otto I of Saxony, enduring until 1806. The *Second* was established by Prince Otto von Bismarck, after the Franco-Prussian war in 1871, and endured until 1918. The *Third* was established by Adolf Hitler in 1933.

was decided that "for the time being no Central German Government shall be established," but that central German administrative departments acting under the direction of the Control Council should be established in the fields of finance, transport, communications, foreign trade and industry. The Eastern frontier of Germany was provisionally redrawn (pending final settlement in the Peace Treaty) to transfer the northern area of East Prussia, including Königsberg (now Kaliningrad), to the U.S.S.R. and the rest of East Prussia and all the area lying east of the Oder and Western Neisse rivers to Polish control. On Oct. 15, 1947, the Saar, enlarged at the expense of German territory, voted for economic union with France, but following a plebiscite was incorporated in the Federal Republic of Germany on Jan. 1, 1957. The Potsdam agreement also laid down that Germany should be disarmed and prohibited from producing armaments, that production of certain other goods should be limited to the amount needed to support a peacetime economy and that existing capital equipment surplus to these requirements should be removed as reparations and distributed by the Inter Allied Reparations Agency among the nations who had suffered war damage, in proportion to their losses. (The proportions were fixed by the Paris Conference of November, 1945.) The agreement further dealt with denazifi-

cation, democratization, refugees, restitution, decartelization, etc.

Though certain details of the Potsdam agreement (not yet superseded by a Peace Treaty) have been carried out, differences in interpretation among the Allies have made it impossible to apply the provisions in full. Quadripartite control became a dead letter when the Russians withdrew from the Control Council in March, 1948.

Federal Republic of Germany

President, Walter Scheel, *born July 8, 1919, elected July 1, 1974, for five years.*

CABINET

Federal Chancellor, Helmut Schmidt (*SPD*).
Foreign Minister and Vice-Chancellor, Hans Dietrich Genscher (*FDP*).
Interior, Dr. Werner Maihofer (*FDP*).
Justice, Jochen Vogel (*SPD*).
Finance, Hans Apel (*SPD*).
Economics, Dr. Hans Friderichs (*FDP*).
Food, Agriculture and Forestry, Josef Ertl (*FDP*).
Labour and Social Affairs, Walter Arendt (*SPD*).
Defence, Georg Leber (*SPD*).
Transport, Posts and Telecommunications, Kurt Gscheidle (*SPD*).
Regional Planning, Building and Urban Development, Karl Ravens (*SPD*).

Intra-German Relations, Egon Franke (*SPD*).
Health, Family and Youth Questions, Dr. Katharina Focke (*SPD*).
Education and Science, Hans Rohde (*SPD*).
Research and Technology, Hans Matthöfer (*SPD*).
Economic Co-operation, Egon Bahr (*SPD*).
FDP = Free Democrats; *SPD* = Social Democrats.

EMBASSY IN LONDON
23 Belgrave Sq., S.W.1
[01–2315 5033]
(*Consular, Passports, etc.*:
6 Rutland Gate, S.W.7.)
Ambassador Extraordinary and Plenipotentiary, His Excellency Karl-Günther von Hase, K.C.M.G. (1970).
Minister Plenipotentiary, H. H. Noebel.
Minister-Counsellor, Dr. K. Stöckl.
Minister, Herr Hans Freiherr von Stein (*Head of Economic Dept.*).
1st Counsellors, Dr. Rolf Breitenstein (*Press*); Frau Dr. Brigitte Lohmeyer (*Cultural*); Dr. Hans-Peter Lorenzen (*Scientific Affairs*).
Counsellors, Herr Hans Wolfgang Neugebauer; Dr. Manfred Giesder; Dr. Christian Hofman (*Agriculture*); Dr. Gunter Behrendt (*Commodities*); Dr. Rudolf Schrader (*Defence Research*); Herr Niemöller (*Legal and Consular*).
1st Secretaries, Fräulein Margarete Stark; Dr. Rudolf Vollmer (*Labour*); Dr. Wilhelm Dünwald; Herr B. Oetter; Herr Günter Habelt; Frau Dr. Jutta Grützner.

NOTE.—Except where otherwise indicated statistical data on the Federal Republic of German include Berlin (West).

Area and Population.—The area of the Federal Republic is approximately 95,985 sq. miles. Total population of the Federal Republic on December 31, 1974, was 61,991,500. Distribution of the population among the *Länder* in 1974 was:

Schleswig-Holstein	2,584,300
Hamburg	1,733,800
Lower Saxony	7,264,800
Bremen	724,000
North Rhine Westphalia	17,217,800
Hessen	5,576,100
Rhineland Palatinate	3,688,100
Baden-Wurttemberg	9,226,200
Bavaria	10,849,100
Saarland	1,103,300
Berlin (West)	2,024,000

The population of the principal cities and towns in the Federal Republic on Dec. 31, 1973, was:

Berlin (West)	2,047,948	Augsburg	256,908
ΨHamburg	1,751,621	Wiesbaden	252,457
Munich	1,336,576	Aachen	241,362
Cologne	832,396	Oberhausen	240,702
Essen	674,000	ΨLübeck	236,047
Frankfurt/Main	663,422	Krefeld	221,240
Dortmund	632,317	Brunswick	218,939
Düsseldorf	628,498	Kassel	212,575
Stuttgart	624,835	Münster	199,748
ΨBremen	584,265	Hagen	196,764
Nuremberg	514,657	Mülheim/Ruhr	190,783
Hanover	505,106	Mainz	183,363
Duisburg	435,281	Solingen	175,923
Wuppertal	409,715	Freiburg	174,997
Gelsenkirchen	338,022	Ludwigshaven	173,141
Bochum	333,202	Osnabrück	164,060
Mannheim	325,386	Mönchen-	
Bielefeld	321,200	Gladbach	150,274
Bonn	283,260	ΨBremerhaven	144,578
ΨKiel	265,587	Darmstadt	140,509
Karlsruhe	261,250	Remscheid	135,587

Oldenburg	134,168	Würzburg	113,450
Wolfsburg	133,971	Leverkusen	109,520
Regensburg	133,806	Heilbronn	105,767
Recklinghausen	124,383	ΨWilhelms-	
Saarbrücken	123,006	haven	104,305
Heidelberg	120,925	Fürth	103,559
Göttingen	120,435	Bottrop	103,458
Offenbach/		Kaiserslautern	102,450
Main	120,092	Herne	102,229
Koblenz	119,476	Trier	102,221
Salzgitter	119,181	Rheydt	100,939
Neuss	118,607		

Vital Statistics.—There were 10·1 live births per 1,000 inhabitants in the Federal Republic in 1974, compared with 19·5 per 1,000 for the same area in 1938.

Government.—The Federal Republic grew out of the fusion of the three western zones. The economic union of the U.K. and U.S. zones followed the Fusion Agreement of December, 1946. The Bizone was later joined by the French zone and in 1948-49 Parliamentary Council, elected by the Diets of the three zones, drafted a provisional democratic federal constitution for Germany. This Basic Law came into force in the three western zones on May 23, 1949. It provides for a President, elected for a five-year term, a Lower House, with a four-year term of office, elected by direct universal suffrage, and an Upper House composed of delegates of the *Länder*, without a fixed term of office.

The results of the elections held for the lower House (*Bundestag*) on November 19, 1972, were as follows:

Party	Numbers
Social Democrats	230
Christian Democratic Union	177
Christian-Social Union	48
Free Democrats	41
Total	496

with an additional 22 representatives of Berlin elected by the Berlin Chamber of Deputies (Social Democrats, 12; Christian Democrats, 9; Free Democrats, 1). The Social Democrats form a coalition with the Free Democrats. The Christian Democratic and the Christian Social Unions are the Parliamentary Opposition.

When the Federal Government took office the Allied Military Governors were replaced by High Commissioners. In 1952 a contractual agreement was signed between the Federal Republic and the western Allies, whereby the Republic, in return for certain promises regarding a defence contribution, a foreign debt settlement, and the continuation of allied policies concerning decartelization, democratization, restitution, etc., regained virtual sovereignty in May, 1955, after ratification by all the parties concerned. The High Commissioners then became Ambassadors.

The Prime Ministers of the *Länder* governments in June, 1974, were:—

Ministers-President
Baden-Württemberg.—Dr. Hans Filbinger.
Bavaria.—Dr. Alfons Goppel.
Berlin.—Klaus Schütz (*Governing Mayor*).
Bremen.—Hans Koschnick (*Mayor*).
Hamburg.—Peter Schulz (*Mayor*).
Hessen.—Albert Osswald.
Lower Saxony.—Alfred Kubel.
North Rhine-Westphalia.—Heinz Kühn.
Rhineland-Palatinate.—Dr. Helmut Kohl.
Saarland.—Dr. Franz-Josef Röder.
Schleswig-Holstein.—Dr. Gerhard Stoltenberg.
Economic position.—Despite the difficulties arising

from the division of Germany, which cut off from the Federal Republic the main food producing areas of Eastern Germany and some of the principal centres of light industry, German economic recovery has made rapid strides since the currency reform of 1948. As a result of United States and British economic aid and of successful economic policies pursued by the Federal Government, Germany has regained her position as the main industrial power on the Continent, and is the most economically powerful member of the European Common Market. The Gross National Product at current prices in 1974 was estimated at *DM*.995·5 milliard, an increase of *DM*.65·2 milliard or 7·0 per cent. over 1973.

Agriculture.—In 1974 total area of farmland was 13,344,100 hectares, of which 7,553,100 hectares were arable land. Forest areas cover 7,144,600 hectares. The 1974 harvest yielded 10,426,100 metric tons of bread grains, 11,706,200 metric tons of potatoes. The livestock population at the end of 1974 included 14,419,739 cattle, 325,151 horses, 1,040,133 sheep, 20,213,231 pigs and 91,537,927 fowl.

Industrial Production.—The index of industrial net production adjusted for irregularities of the calendar (1970 = 100) has developed in the Federal Republic, including Berlin, as follows:

	1972	1973	1974
Mining	93·3	92·3	91·4
Manufacturing industry	105·2	112·6	110·6
(i) Basic materials	106·0	116·3	116·0
(ii) Capital goods	102·3	110·3	107·2
(iii) Consumer goods	109·6	112·2	107·7
(iv) Foodstuffs	107·2	111·9	113·7
Power (electricity and gas)	123·7	139·8	159·8
Building Industry	109·0	110·3	104·8
Total industry	105·9	113·1	111·5

Productivity of labour in industry (excluding electricity, gas and building industries) per man-hour: 1968, 90·5; 1969, 96·5; 1970, 100; 1971, 106·1; 1972, 114·6; 1973, 122·7; 1974, 128·3 per cent.

Some production figures are shown below (monthly averages):

	1973	1974
	Number	
Passenger cars	279,896	214,607
Commercial vehicles	22,830	18,786

	1973	1974
	Tons	
Sulphuric acid (SO3)	344,819	348,983
Chlorine	209,785	227,094

	1973	1974
	Tons	
Artificial plastic material	536,321	522,601
Man-made fibres	981,630	78,302
Cotton yarn	17,954	17,831
Woollen yarn	5,422	4,565

604,100 new dwellings were completed in 1974 in the Federal Republic (1973, 714,226).

Labour.—Of 26,231,000 employed in 1974, (annual average), 16,612,000 were men. The average number of unemployed was 582,481 of whom 324,685 were men (1973 = 273,000 and 150,000). On September 30, 1974, 2,350,000 foreign workers were employed in the Federal Republic. An average of 8,143,537 (1973 = 8,368,439 were employed in industry (establishments employing 10 or more persons).

	1973	1975
Coal mining	232,229	224,422
Iron and steel production	315,689	316,046
Mechanical engineering	1,712,132	1,700,155
Chemicals	587,344	600,498
Textiles and clothing	793,764	703,997

Finance.—As from January 1, 1970, the distribution of taxes in the Fed. Rep. of Germany between Federation, Länder, communities and local authorities has been regulated by an amendment of the Basic Law (Constitution) as follows:—
(1) Of the yields of wage tax and assessed income tax, Federation and Länder receive 43 per cent. each, and the communities 14 per cent. The yields of capital yield tax and corporation tax are distributed to Federation and Länder with 50 per cent. each.
(2) The turnover taxes have been made joint taxes of which the Federation obtains 63 per cent. and the Länder 37 per cent.
(3) Of the trade tax which so far had been fully allocated to the communities, the Federation and the Länder receive equal shares (about 20 per cent. of the trade tax receipts).
(4) The yields of capital transactions taxes, insurance and bill taxes, which so far went to the Länder, now accrue to the Federation.

Customs and excise duties, other than the beer tax, accrue to the Federal Government, all other taxes (with the exception of local taxes, *i.e.* particularly taxes on land and buildings) to the *Länder*.

Preliminary figures of budgetary expenditure in 1974 are: total expenditure *DM*.136,392,000,000 (1973, *121,757,000,000*); Defence *DM*.28,661,000,000 (1973, *27,334,000,000*); Social expenditure, *DM*.39,084,000,000 (1973, *32,077,000,000*) (about 30 per cent.); Agriculture and food, *DM*. 2,465,000,000 (1973, *2,855,000,000*) (about 4 per cent.); Transport, *DM*.10,918,000,000 (1973, *10,067,000,000*).

Currency.—The currency of the Federal Republic is the *Deutsche Mark* of 100 *Pfennig*, the rate of exchange with sterling being at Dec. 31, 1974, *DM*.5·660=£1. The rate of exchange of the pound sterling has been floating since 23 June 1972. (*See also* p. 83.)

Foreign Trade.—In 1974, imports were valued at *DM*.179,732,599,000 (1973, *145,417,467,000*); and exports at *DM*.230,578,246,000; 16·3 per cent. of imports consisted of foodstuffs and 19·3 per cent. of industrial raw materials; 47·9 per cent. came from the Common Market* countries; 8·4 per cent. from the E.F.T.A.† and 8·9 per cent. from the United States and Canada. The Common Market countries took 44·9 per cent. of all exports, the E.F.T.A. 14·9 per cent. and the United States and Canada 8·3 per cent.

Trade with U.K.

	1973	1974
Imports from U.K.	£785,167,000	£1,011,271,000
Exports to U.K.	1,351,236,000	1,892,651,000

Communications.—In December, 1974, the state-owned railways of the Federal Republic measured 17,948 miles of which 6,029 miles were electrified, and the privately owned railways 2,063 miles, a total of 20,011 miles. In 1974 the railways handled 404,264,037 tons of goods and the inland waterways 252,108,243 tons. Railway rolling stock (*Deutsche Bundesbahn*) included, in 1974, 616 steam locomotives, 2,572 electric locomotives, 3,013 diesel locomotives, 17,762 passenger coaches, 737 rail buses and 285,236 goods waggons. Classified roads measure 104,487 miles. On Jan. 1, 1975, there were registered 17,356,276 cars, 1,304,941 commercial vehicles (incl. buses) and 1,424,949 tractors.

*Common Market: Belgium and Luxemburg, Denmark, France, Italy, Netherlands, Rep. of Ireland, U.K., W. Germany.

† E.F.T.A. (European Free Trade Association): Austria, Iceland, Norway, Portugal, Sweden, Switzerland.

Ocean-going shipping under the German flag in Dec., 1974, amounted to 8,308,090 tons gross (1,805 ships). Civil aircraft in service at the same date totalled 160 aircraft.

Social Welfare.—There is compulsory insurance against sickness, accident, old age and unemployment. Children's allowances are payable in respect of the second and subsequent children. Pension schemes for widows and orphans of public servants are in operation. Public assistance is given to persons unable to earn their living, or with insufficient income to maintain a decent standard of living.

Law and Justice.—Judicial authority is exercised by the Federal Constitutional Court, the Supreme Federal Court, and the courts of the *Länder.* Judges are independent and subject only to the law. The death sentence has been abolished.

Language and Literature.—Modern (or New High) German has developed from the time of the Reformation to the present day, with differences of dialect in Austria and Alsace and in the German-speaking cantons of Switzerland. The literary language is usually regarded as having become fixed by Luther and Zwingli at the Reformation, since which time many great names occur in all branches, notably philosophy, from Leibnitz (1646–1716) to Kant (1724–1804), Fichte (1762–1814), Schelling (1775–1854) and Hegel (1770–1831); the drama from Goethe (1749–1832) and Schiller (1759–1805) to Gerhart Hauptmann (1862–1946); and in poetry, Heine (1797–1856). German authors have received the Nobel Prize for Literature on seven occasions—Theodore Mommsen (1902), R. Eucken (1908), P. Heyse (1909), Gerhart Hauptmann (1912), Thomas Mann (1929), N. Sachs (1966) and Heinrich Böll (1972). In 1973 there were 404 daily papers.

Education.—School attendance is compulsory for all children and juveniles between the ages of 6 and 18. Compulsory education comprises 9 years of schooling at primary schools (*Volksschulen*)—full-time compulsory education—and 3 years of compulsory vocational education on a part-time basis. Preliminary figures showed that in autumn, 1973, there were in the Federal Republic 18,561 primary schools (*Volksschulen*) with 217,859 teachers and 6,499,824 pupils. Intermediate schools (*Realschulen*) numbered 2,252 with 42,942 teachers and 1,043,570 pupils. There were 2,465 secondary schools (*Gymnasien* including *Gesamtschulen*) with 90,760 teachers and 1,793,208 pupils.

There were also 2,593 special schools (*Sonderschulen*) for retarded, physically and mentally handicapped and socially maladjusted children in the Federal Republic with 28,093 teachers and 377,767 pupils.

The secondary school leaving examination (*Abitur*) entitles the holder to a place of study at a university or another institution of higher education. The number of examinations passed in 1973 was 96,390.

Juveniles below the age of 18 who are not attending an intermediate school, a secondary or a full-time vocational school (*Berufsfachschule*) are obliged to take a three-year course (part-time) at a vocational school. In November, 1973, there were 1,772 part-time vocational schools (*Berufsschulen*) and 488 vocational extension schools (*Berufsaufbauschulen*) with 26,033 teachers and 1,678,915 pupils, 2,780 full-time vocational schools with 9,103 teachers and 254,839 pupils, 1,384 advanced vocational schools (*Fachschulen*) with 5,596 teachers and 124,486 pupils; 781 schools for secondary technical studies (*Fachoberschulen/Fachgymnasien*) with 3,787 teachers and 115,024 students and 1,764 Public Health Schools with 23,274 full-time and part-time teachers and 73,051 pupils. [State expenditure for primary schools per annum amounted

to $DM.1,700$ per pupil, for intermediate schools $DM.2,200$ and for grammar achools $DM.3,100.$ State expenditure per pupil for part-time vocational, full-time vocational and advanced vocational schools per annum amounted to $DM.1,200.$] According to preliminary results, in the winter term 1973/74 there were 52 universities—including a college for physical education (*Sporthochschule*) —(415,967 students), 9 technical universities (*Technische Universitäten*) (96,642 students), 11 colleges of theological philosophy (*Theologische Hochschulen*) (1,194 students), 39 teachers' training colleges (*Pädagogische Hochschulen*) (78,479 students), 30 colleges of arts (*Kunsthochschulen* (14,943 students) and 147 vocational colleges (*Fachhochschulen*) (121,982 students); a total of 288 institutions of higher education with 729,207 students. The largest universities were in Munich, Hamburg, Münster (Westf.), West Berlin, Cologne, Bonn and Frankfurt-am-Main.

Religion.—In 1970 there were 29,696,571 Protestants in the Republic, 27,060,826 Roman Catholics, 31,684 Jews and 3,861,518 others.

CAPITAL, Bonn, in North Rhine Westphalia, 15 miles distant from Cologne. Population 283,891 (Dec. 31, 1974).

FLAG.—Horizontal bars of black, red and gold.

BRITISH EMBASSY

Friedrich-Ebert Allee 77, 53 Bonn

Ambassador Extraordinary and Plenipotentiary, His Excellency Sir (John) Oliver Wright, K.C.M.G., D.S.C (1975).

Ministers, J. L. Bullard, C.M.G.; H. T. A. Overton, C.M.G.

Counsellors, P. C. Petrie (*Head of Chancery*); F. R. MacGinnis (*Political and Public Affairs*); J. R. Rich (*Commercial*); J. S. P. MacKenzie, O.B.E. (*Labour*); C. A. Alldis, C.B.E., D.F.C., A.F.C. (*Defence Supply*); R. I. T. Cromartie; P. W. Unwin (*Economic*); W. C. Lyall, M.B.E. (*Administration*); P. H. Towers-Picton, O.B.E.

1st Secretaries, R. J. Dowle; P. Yarnold; B. L. Crowe; D. M. Edwards; J. D. N. d. R. Clibborn; C. A. K. Cullimore; C. D. Powell; E. J. Mitchell; H. L. Davies; D. J. Hall; H. Davies; G. Brook; W. E. J. Groves; Dr. J. K. Duxbury; D. J. Alexander; A. K. Mineeff, O.B.E.; D. J. Couvell; A. F. Blake-Pauley; G. Hay, M.B.E.

2nd Secretaries, Miss P. Lambe; A. E. Gay; P. A. McDermott, M.V.O.; E. Dixon; C. Smith; T. G. Longdon-Griffiths; R. Tempest; R. C. Cutler.

Defence and Military Attaché, Brig. G. H. Hoerder, M.B.E.

Asst. Military Attaché, Lt.-Col. M. C. Sweeney.

Naval Attaché, Captain B. J. Williams, R.N.

Asst. Naval Attaché, Lt.-Cdr. S. J. Barry, R.N.

Air Attaché, Air Cdre. L. G. P. Martin.

Head of Visa Section (Düsseldorf), Miss D. M. Symes.

Chaplain, Rev. F. H. Mountney.

There are British Consulates-General at *Berlin, Hamburg, Hanover, Düsseldorf, Frankfurt, Munich* and *Stuttgart* and a British Consulate at *Bremen.*

BRITISH COUNCIL

Representative, Dr. J. M. Mitchell, Hahnenstrasse 6, Cologne. Offices at *Berlin, Hamburg* and *Munich* and British Council libraries at *Berlin, Cologne* and *Munich.*

BERLIN

G.O.C. British Sector, Maj.-General D. W. Scott-Barrett, M.B.E., M.C.

Minister and Deputy Commandant, J. H. Lambert, C.M.G.

Counsellor, J. F. Walker, M.B.E. (*Political Adviser and Head of Chancery*).

GERMAN DEMOCRATIC REPUBLIC
(East Germany)
(For Map, *see* p. 862)

Area and Population.—The German Democratic Republic comprises the five former German *Länder* of Brandenburg, Mecklenburg, Saxony, Saxony-Anhalt and Thuringia (an area of 41,768 sq. miles). The seat of Government is East Berlin (156 sq. miles). The population of East Germany (mid 1973) is 16,979,600. In 1952 the former *Länder* were replaced by fourteen *Bezirke* (regions): Potsdam, Cottbus and Frankfurt (*formerly* Brandenburg); Rostock, Schwerin and Neubrandenburg (*formerly* Mecklenburg); Karl-Marx-Stadt, Dresden and Leipzig (*formerly* Saxony); Halle and Magdeburg (*formerly* Saxony-Anhalt); Erfurt, Gera and Suhl (*formerly* Thuringia.)

The present Constitution, which defines the GDR as a Socialist state, came into force on April 9, 1968 after endorsement by a referendum. It replaced the first Constitution of October 7, 1949. Among items of the 1949 Constitution omitted from that of 1968 were the rights of trade unions to strike, of citizens to emigrate and of newspapers to publish without censorship. Further amendments came into force on October 7, 1974 after adoption by the *Volkskammer* on September 27, 1974. They mainly involved (*a*) the deletion of all references to the German nation and to the possibility of reunification, and (*b*) the recording of the transfer of certain governmental functions from the State Council to the Council of Ministers which had their origin in the Law on the Council of Ministers of October 16, 1972. The supreme organ of State power is the *Volkskammer*, which has power to elect and dismiss the State Council, the Council of Ministers, the Chairman of the National Defence Council, the Supreme Court and the Procurator-General. The State Council retains the presidential powers which it has exercised since the abolition of the office of President on September 12, 1960, together with responsibility for the organization of defence with the help of the National Defence Council. The Council of Ministers is responsible to the *Volkskammer* for the conduct of State policy. The present *Volkskammer* is that elected on November 14, 1971.

Council of State
Chairman, Herr Willi Stoph.
Deputy Chairmen, Herr Friedrich Ebert; Herr Gerald Götting; Dr. Heinrich Homann; Dr. Manfred Gerlach; Herr Hans Rietz.
Members, Herr K. Anclam; Herr F. Clermont; Prof. E. Correns; Herr W. Grandetzka; Herr E. Grützner; Frau B. Hanke; Prof. Lieselott Herfurth; Herr E. Honecker; Herr F. Kind; Frau M. Müller; Herr B. Quandt; Prof. H. Rodenberg; Herr K. Sorgenicht; Herr P. Strauss; Frau I. Thiele; Herr P. Verner; Frau R. Walther; Herr H. Tisch.

Council of Ministers
Prime Minister, Herr Horst Sindermann.
1st Deputy Prime Ministers, Dr. Günter Mittag; Herr Alfred Neumann.

Total membership of the Council is 41, including 9 other Deputy Prime Ministers, 13 holding principal portfolios and 15 holding portfolios of a mainly technical nature.
GERMAN SOCIALIST UNITY (= *Communist*) PARTY
Politbureau of the Central Committee, H. Axen; F. Ebert; G. Grüneberg; K. Hager; Gen. H. Hoffmann; E. Honecker; W. Krolikowski; W. Lamberz; G. Mittag; E. Mückenberger; A. Neumann; A. Norden; H. Sindermann; W. Stoph; P. Verner; H. Tisch (*full members*); G. Ewald; W. Felfe; J. Herrman; W. Jaro-

winsky; G. Kleiber; Frau I. Lange; E. Mielke; Frau M. Mueller; K. Naumann; G. Schürer (*candidate members*).
Secretariat of the Central Committee, E. Honecker (*First*); H. Axen; G. Grüneberg; K. Hager; W. Jarowinsky; W. Lamberz; G. Mittag; A. Norden; P. Verner; W. Krolikowski; I. Lange; H. Dohlus (*secretaries*).

EMBASSY IN LONDON
34 Belgrave Square, S.W.1
[01–235 9941]
Ambassador Extraordinary and Plenipotentiary, His Excellency Karl-Heinz Kern.
Economic Position.—Before the 1939–45 war, the economy of the area at present occupied by the GDR was largely devoted to agriculture and light industry, most heavy industry being concentrated in other parts of the Reich. In spite of this imbalance, compounded by severe war damage, a declining population, a shortage of labour and a lack of basic raw materials, East Germany has made considerable economic progress and is now in the world's top ten industrial nations in terms of G.N.P., and is second to the U.S.S.R. in Eastern Europe as a major producer of industrial goods. East Germany has a number of highly developed industries including basic chemicals and petro-chemicals, machine tools and industrial plant, ship-building and transport equipment, electronic and engineering equipment, precision tools and optical instruments.
The East German economy, including the control of industry and foreign trade, is centrally planned and administered. The State Planning Commission, which is subordinate to the Council of Ministers, is responsible for drawing up the 5- and 1-Year Plans. The 5-Year Plans determine the future development and structure of the economy; the 1-Year Plans have to achieve these aims. The implementation of these plans is the responsibility of the State Production Enterprises under the supervision of the economic and industrial Ministries.
The economy is very closely integrated with those of other member countries of C.M.E.A. and particularly with the U.S.S.R.

Trade with U.K.

	1973	1974
Imports from U.K...	£13,690,000	£39,230,000
Exports to U.K.....	£26,380,000	£44,880,000

Principal cities and towns (population, 1973): East Berlin (1,088,827); Leipzig (575,913); Dresden (505,408); Karl-Marx-Stadt (Chemnitz) (301,826); Magdeburg (273,567); Halle/Saale (248,561); Rostock (205,803); Erfurt (201,249); Zwickau (124,371).
FLAG.—Horizontal bands of black, red, gold; hammer, compasses and corn device at centre.

BRITISH EMBASSY
(108 Berlin, Unter den Linden 32/34)
Ambassador Extraordinary and Plenipotentiary, His Excellency H. B. C. Keeble, C.M.G.

GREECE
(Hellas)
President of the Hellenic Republic, Constantine Tsatsos, *born* 1899 (*assumed office* June 20, 1975).
CABINET
Prime Minister, Constantine Karamanlis.
Coordination and Planning, Panayotis Papaligouras.
Alternate Minister of Coordination and Planning, John Boutos.
Minister to the Prime Minister, George Rallis.
Foreign Affairs, Dimitiros Bitsios.
National Defence, Evangelos Averoff-Tositsas.
Interior, Constantine Stephanopoulos.
Justice, Constantine Stephanakis.

Public Order, Solon Ghikas.
Culture and Science, Constantine Trypanis.
Education and Religion, Panayotis Zepos.
Finance, Evangelos Devletoglou.
Agriculture, Hippocrates Iordanoglou.
Industry, Constantine Konofagos.
Commerce, John Varvitsiotis.
Employment, Constantine Laskaris.
Social Services, Constantine Chrysanthopoulos.
Public Works, Christophoros Stratos.
Transport and Communications, George Voyatzis.
Merchant Marine, Alexandros Papadongonas.
Northern Greece, Nikolaos Martis.

GREEK EMBASSY IN LONDON
1a Holland Park, W.11
[01–727 8040]
Ambassador Extraordinary and Plenipotentiary, His
Excellency Stavros Georgiou Roussos (1974).
Minister, N. E. Athanassiou.
Counsellors, L. Mavromichalis (*Consular Affairs*);
G. Christoyannis; A. Philon; A. Zaphiropoulos
(*Commercial*); C. Kondoyiannis (*Agricultural*).
Armed Forces Attaché, Capt. C. Paizis-Paradelis.
Tourist Adviser, Mlle. C. Angelopoulou.

There are Honorary Consulates at *Birmingham,*
Bradford, Bristol, Falmouth, Hull, Immingham,
Leeds, Liverpool, Manchester, Newcastle, Plymouth,
Portsmouth, Southampton, Cardiff, Edinburgh and
Glasgow, and at *Belfast.*

A maritime State in the south-east of Europe,
bounded on the N. by Albania, Yugoslavia and
Bulgaria, on the S. and W. by the Ionian and
Mediterranean seas, and on the E. by Turkey, with
an estimated area of 51,182 sq. miles. A census
held throughout the country on March 14, 1971,
recorded a population of 8,768,641.

The area of the mainland is 41,328 sq. miles,
and of the islands 9,854 sq. miles. The main
divisions are: *Macedonia* (which includes Mt. Athos
and the island of *Thasos*), *Thrace* (including the
island of *Samothrace*), *Epirus, Thessaly, Continental*
Greece (which includes the island of *Euboea* and the
Sporades, or "scattered islands," of which the largest
is *Skyros*), the *Peloponnese* (or *Morea*), the *Dodecanese*
or *Southern Sporades* (12 islands occupied by Italy in
1911 during the Italo-Turkish War and ceded to
Greece by Italy in 1947) consisting of Rhodes,
Astypalaia, Karpathos, Kassos, Nisyros, Kalymnos,
Leros, Patmos, Kos, Symi, Khalki and Tilos,
the *Cyclades* (a circular group numbering about
200, with a total area of 923 sq. miles; the chief
islands are Syros, Andros, Tinos, Naxos, Paros,
Santorini, Milos and Serifos), the *Ionian Islands*
(Corfu, Paxos, Levkas, Ithaca, Cephalonia, Zante
and Cerigo), the *Aegean Islands* (Chios, Lesbos, Lim-
nos and Samos). In *Crete* there was for over 1,500
years (300 to 1400 B.C.) a flourishing civilization
which spread its influence far and wide throughout
the Aegean, and the ruins of the palace of Minos at
Cnossos afforded evidence of astonishing comfort
and luxury. Greek civilization emerges about 1300
B C. and the poems of Homer, the blind poet of
Chios, which were probably current about 800 B.C.,
record the 10-year struggle between the Achaeans of
Greece and the Phrygians of Troy (1194–1184 B.C.).

Government.—A military *coup* on April 21, 1967,
suspended parliamentary government and, following an unsuccessful royal counter *coup* on December
13, 1967, King Constantine went into voluntary
exile in Rome. A new constitution was approved
in 1968 in a national referendum. On June 1, 1973,
following allegations of a plot within the Navy to
overthrow the government, the monarchy was
abolished and a republic established under the
Presidency of Mr. George Papadopoulos.

A referendum held on July 29, 1973, confirmed
the new presidential Constitution with Mr.
Papadopoulos as President until 1981. In early
October a civilian government, headed by Mr.
Markezinis, was appointed. Following student
demonstrations in early November the Army, on
November 17, was called in to restore order and
martial law was declared. On November 25,
following an Army coup, the Markezinis Government was overthrown and General Gizikis was
sworn in as President of the Republic.

The overthrow of Archbishop Makarios, President of Cyprus, on July 15, by a military coup led
by Greek Officers of the Cypriot National Guard
caused an international crisis, in the wake of which
the heads of the Greek armed forces decided, on
July 23, to relinquish power. President Gizikis
called upon Mr. Konstantinos Karamanlis, Prime
Minister between 1955 and 1963, to return from
his self-imposed exile in Paris and form a provisional Government. On Austust 1, Mr. Karamanlis
announced that the Constitution of 1952 would be
reintroduced, pending a new Constitution.

The first elections for ten years were held
on November 17, 1974. Mr. Karamanlis' New
Democracy Party polled 54·3 per cent. of the
vote and gained 220 out of the 300 seats in Parliament (this was later reduced in by-elections to
216 seats). Mr Karamanlis formed a new Government on November 21.

The constitutional position of the King, however,
remained unsettled until December 8, when by a
referendum, the Greek people rejected " crowned
democracy " by 69·2 per cent. to 30·8 per cent. and
Greece became a republic.

On December 18, 1974 Mr. Michael Stassinopoulos was elected by Parliament President of the
Hellenic Republic until a new constitution should be
passed. The draft of the new constitution was presented by the Government to Parliament in January
1975 and was formally passed on June 7, coming into force on June 11, 1975.

On June 19 the Greek Parliament elected Mr.
Constantine Tsatsos President of the Hellenic Republic under the new constitution. He assumed
office on June 20, 1975.

Defence.—The Navy has 55 major war vessels, of
U.S., French and German origin, and is a balanced
fleet of destroyers, submarines, fast patrol boats and
amphibious warfare vessels. The strength of the

Army is 122,000. The Air Force consists of 23,000 men, ten offensive squadrons, two transport squadrons and one helicopter, together with the necessary support, training and maintenance organizations.

Communications.—The 2,650 kilometres of Greek railways are State-owned with the exception of the Athens-Piraeus Electric Railway. The railway from Athens to the Peloponnese, serving Patras and southern Greece, is metre gauge, but the other lines, except one or two minor ones, are standard gauge. Greek roads total somewhat over 35,500 kilometres, of which about 25 per cent. are classified as national highways and just under 30,000 km. are classified as provincial roads.

On February 28, 1975, the Greek Mercantile fleet numbered 3,154 ships with a total tonnage of 24,422,681 tons gross. On the same day Greek-owned ships registered under foreign flags numbered 1,298 with a total tonnage of 20,426,039 tons gross. Athens has direct airline links with Australasia, North America, most countries in Europe, Africa and the Middle East.

Religion.—Over 97 per cent. of the people are adherents of the Greek Orthodox Church, which is the State religion, all others being tolerated and free from interference. The Church of Greece recognizes the spiritual primacy of the Œcumenical Patriarch of Constantinople, but is otherwise a self-governing body administered by the Holy Synod under the Presidency of the Archbishop of Athens and All Greece. It has no jurisdiction over the Church of Crete, which has a degree of autonomy under the Œcumenical Patriarch, nor over the Monastic Community of Mount Athos and the Church in the Dodecanese, both of which come directly under the Œcumenical Patriarch.

Education is free and compulsory from the age of 6 to 12 and is maintained by State grants. There are four Universities, Athens, Salonika, Patras and Joannina. There are several other institutes of higher learning, mostly in Athens.

Language and Literature.—The *spoken* language of modern Greece is descended by a process of natural development from the " Common Greek " of Alexander's empire. Official and technical matter is mostly composed in *Katharevousa*, a conservative literary dialect evolved by Adamantios Corais (Diamant Coray), who lived and died in Paris (1748–1833) but novels and poetry are mostly composed in *dimotiki*, a progressive literary dialect which owes much to John Psycharis (1854–1929). The poets Solomos, Palamas, Cavafis, Sikelianos and Seferis have won a European reputation.

Production.—Though there has in recent years been a substantial measure of industrialization, Greece is still largely an agricultural country. Agriculture employs about 40 per cent. of the working population, the most important product and export being tobacco, which accounts for about one-tenth of the value of total visible exports from Greece. Since the war the production of wheat, cotton, sugar and rice has been greatly increased, partly in an attempt to make the country's economy less dependent upon tobacco. The most important of the fruit trees are the olive, vine, orange, lemon, fig, peach, almond, pomegranate and currant-vine, and considerable efforts have lately been made to develop exports of Greek fresh fruit and vegetables as well as currants and other dried fruits. Currants, grown mainly around Patras, remain one of Greece's main exports, the United Kingdom being the principal purchaser.

The principal minerals mined in Greece are nickel, bauxite, iron ore, iron pyrites, manganese, magnesite, chrome, lead, zinc and emery, and prospecting for petroleum is being carried on. Oil refineries are in operation near Athens and at Salonika, where there is also a petro-chemical plant. The chief industries are textiles (cotton, woollen, silk and rayon), chemicals, cement, glass, metallurgy, shipbuilding, domestic electrical equipment and footwear. In recent years new factories have been opened for the production of aluminium, nickel, iron and steel products, tyres, chemicals fertilizers and sugar (from locally-grown beet). Food processing and ancillary industries have also grown up throughout the country. The development of the country's electric power resources, irrigation and land reclamation schemes and the exploitation of Greece's lignite resources for fuel and industrial purposes are also being carried out, and the television network is being expanded. Tourism is developing rapidly. Greece has announced her intention of becoming a full member of the E.E.C., but has yet to negotiate transitional arrangements.

Currency.—The Greek *drachma* has a floating exchange rate of about 71= £1 (July 1974) and 30= $1 U.S.

(*See also* p. 83)

TRADE

	1973	1974
Total imports.....	$3,095,693,000	$4,635,200,000
Total exports.....	1,427,053,000	1,774,100,000

Trade with U.K.

	1973	1974
Imports from U.K...	£99,241,000	£105,079,000
Exports to U.K.....	46,757,000	68,180,000

CAPITAL, Athens. Population (including × Piraeus and suburbs), 2,540,241 (1971 Census). Other large towns are Ψ Salonika (557,360); Ψ Patras (111,607), Ψ Volos (71,245); Larissa (72,336); and Ψ Kavalla (46,234); in Crete—Ψ Heraklion or Candia (77,506), Ψ Canea (40,564), and Ψ Rethymnon (14,969); in the Ionian Islands—Ψ Corfu (28,630); in the Dodecanese—Ψ Rhodes (32,092); in the Cyclades—Ψ Syros Hermoupolis (13,502); in Lesbos—Ψ Mytilene (23,426); in Chios—Ψ Chios (24,084).

FLAG.—9 horizontal bands, alternately blue and white, with white cross, on blue ground, at top next hoist.

NATIONAL DAY.—March 25 (Independence Day).

BRITISH EMBASSY
(Ploutarchou 1, Athens)

Ambassador Extraordinary and Plenipotentiary, His Excellency Francis Brooks Richards, C.M.G., D.S.C. (1974).

Counsellors, J. B. Denson, C.M.G., O.B.E. (*Political and Consul-General*); T. J. Everard (*Commercial*).

1st Secretaries, P. W. M. Vereker; C. C. Smellie, C.B.E., M.V.O.; C. W. Wainwright (*Information*); S. T. Corcoran (*Labour*); D. T. Wallis (*Commercial*); D. Pragnell (*Administration*).

2nd Secretaries, E. W. Wise (*Consul*); M. J. H. Wood.

3rd Secretary, M. D. Hanman (*Commercial*).

Defence and Military Attaché, Brig. P. R. Body.

Naval and Air Attaché, Capt. D. G. Mather, R.N.

Attachés, E. C. Duckworth, M.B.E. (*Commercial*); E. Tragoutsi, O.B.E.; H. Byatt, M.B.E. (*Press*).

Embassy Chaplain, Ven. S. R. Skemp.

Hon. Attaché, H. W. Catling, D.PHIL. (*Director, British School of Archæology*).

BRITISH CONSULAR OFFICES
There are British Consular Offices at *Athens, Piraeus, Corfu, Samos, Rhodes, Salonika, Heraklion, Kavalla* and *Patras*.

BRITISH COUNCIL
17 Filikis Etairias Street, Kolonaki Square, Athens 138

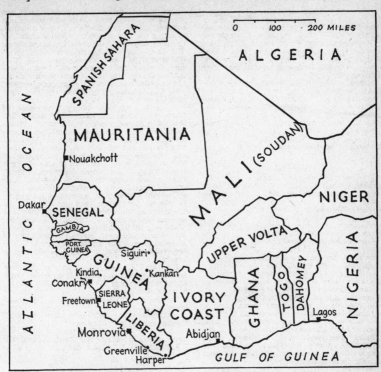

Representative and Cultural Attaché, I. G. I. Fraser, O.B.E.

There is also an office at *Salonika* and British Council libraries at both centres.

GUATEMALA
(República de Guatemala)

President, Gen. Kjell Eugenio Laugerud García, *elected*, March, 1974; *assumed office*, July 1, 1974.

Guatemala, the most northerly of the Republican States of Central America, is situated in N. lat. from 13° 45′ to 17° 49′, and in W. long. from 88° 12′ 49″ to 92° 13′ 43″, and has an area of 42,042 square miles, and a population (1970) of 5,400,000 (*for* Map, *see* p. 872). The constitutionally elected president, Gen. Miguel Ydígoras Fuentes, who had taken office on March 3, 1958, was overthrown on March 31, 1963, by the Army, which handed executive and legislative powers to the Minister of Defence, Col. Enrique Peralta Azurdia. Important changes were included in a new constitution promulgated on Sept. 15, 1965, including the reduction of the presidential term from 6 to 4 years and the establishment of a Council of State under the chairmanship of a Vice-President. Elections for a new Congress and for President and Vice-President took place on March 6, 1966. Dr. Mendez was chosen as President at the first meeting of the new Congress and was succeeded by Col. Arana in 1970.

The Republic is divided into 22 departments, and is traversed from W. to E. by an elevated mountain chain, containing several volcanic summits rising to 13,000 feet above the sea; earthquakes are frequent, and the capital (which is at an altitude of 4,800 ft.) was destroyed by an upheaval in Dec. 1917. The country is well watered by numerous rivers; the climate is hot and malarial near the coast, temperate in the higher regions. The rainfall in the capital is 57 in. per annum. The chief seaports are San José de Guatemala and Champerico on the Pacific and Livingston, Santo Tomás de Castilla and Puerto Barrios on the Atlantic side.

Language and Literature.—Spanish is the language of the country, and since the establishment of the University in the capital education has received a marked impulse and the high figure of illiteracy is being reduced. The National library contains about 80,000 volumes in the Spanish tongue.

Finance.—Actual revenue and expenditure in 1973 were *Quetzales* 214,706,800 and *Quetzales* 253,484,000 respectively, compared with *Quetzales* 186,618,400 and *Quetzales* 238,857,600 in 1972.

At par 1 *Quetzal*= $1 U.S. (*See also* p. 84).

TRADE

	1972 Quetzales	1973 Quetzales
Imports (c.i.f.)	323,984,500	431,002,200
Exports (f.o.b.)	327,484,700	436,151,300

Trade with U.K.

	1973	1974
Imports from U.K......	£5,100,000	£6,900,000
Exports to U.K.........	4,700,000	7,400,000

The principal export is coffee, other articles being manufactured goods, bananas, cotton, *chicle* (chewing gum), essential oils, zinc and lead. The chief imports are textiles, petroleum, vehicles, machinery and foodstuffs.

CAPITAL, Guatemala. Population: 790,311. Quezaltenango (second city of the Republic), has a pop. of 54,487. Other towns are Ψ Puerto Barrios (29,435), Mazatenango (23,932), and Antigua (17,270).

FLAG.—Three vertical bands, blue, white, blue; coat of arms on white stripe.

BRITISH EMBASSY
(Diplomatic relations suspended, July 31, 1963).

GUINEA
(Republic of Guinea)

President, Ahmed Sékou Touré, *elected* for seven year terms, January 1961, 1968 and on Dec. 27, 1974.
President of National Assembly, Léon Maka.
SUPER MINISTERS
Prime Minister, Dr. Lansara Beavogui.
Interior and Security, Moussa Diakite.
Culture and Education, Mamady Keita.
Social Domain, Alpha Bocar Barry.
Exchanges Domain, N. Famara Keita.
Economy and Finance, Ismael Touré

As from the Government changes of May 22, 1975, there were 31 Ministers in the domains of the Super Ministers, including the President.

Formerly part of French West Africa, Guinea has a coastline on the Atlantic Ocean between Portuguese Guinea and Sierra Leone and in the interior is adjacent to Senegal, Mali, Ivory Coast, Liberia and Sierra Leone (*see* below). Area, 96,865 sq. miles. The population (U.N. estimate, 1969) is 3,890,000, mostly the Fullah, Malinké and Soussou tribes. It is estimated that there are about 2,000 Europeans in the country.

Government.—Guinea was separated from Senegal in 1891 and administered by France as a separate colony until 1958. In the referendum held in Metropolitan France and the overseas territories on Sept. 2, 1958, Guinea rejected the new French Constitution. Accordingly, on Sept. 28, it was declared that Guinea had separated itself from the other territories of French West Africa which had adopted the Constitution. French administrative and financial assistance was terminated; and Guinea left the French Community. On October 2, 1958, Guinea became an independent republic governed by a Constituent Assembly. M. Sékou Touré, Prime Minister in the Territorial Assembly, assumed office as head of the new Government.

A provisional constitution, adopted on Nov. 12, 1958, declared Guinea "a democratic, secular and social republic", powers of government being exercised by a president assisted by the Cabinet. The President, eligible for a term of 7 years and for re-election, is head of state and of the armed forces. M. Sékou Touré was elected President of the Republic by an overwhelming vote in an election (in which he was the sole candidate) in January, 1961 and re-elected in 1968. General recognition of Guinea as an independent state was followed by her admission to membership of the United Nations in December, 1958.

Guinea withdrew from the Franc Zone on March 1, 1960, and established her own currency, the *Guinea franc* (at par with the *franc C.F.A.*). This led to the rupture of commercial relations with France, hitherto her most important supplier and purchaser. Guinea is in receipt of economic aid and technical assistance from a number of countries, including the United States, Federal Republic of Germany, Yugoslavia, the Soviet Union and China. The Government's foreign policy is one of "positive neutralism" and non-alignment. In May, 1963, Guinea signed agreements with France covering *inter alia* the settlement of Governmental claims and technical co-operation. Diplomatic relations with U.K., suspended in December, 1965, were resumed on Feb. 20, 1968.

Production, etc.—The principal products of Guinea are alumina, iron-ore, palm kernels, millet, rice, coffee, bananas, pineapples and rubber. Principal imports are cotton goods, manufactured goods, tobacco, petroleum products, sugar, rice, flour and salt; exports, alumina, iron-ore, diamonds, coffee, hides, bananas, palm kernels and pineapples. In the mountains in the hinterland of Guinea (Fouta Djalon, 4,970 feet), where the rivers Senegal, Gambia and Niger have their sources, large deposits of bauxite (the raw material of aluminium) are worked and alumina is produced for export. Bauxite has been worked and exported from the Conakry area where there are also rich deposits of iron-ore and large-scale mining is carried on. There are a British-built cotton mill and a Chinese-built cigarette and match factory. Guinea imported goods to the value of £1,692,000 from U.K. and exported to U.K. goods to the be value of £409,000 in 1974.

CAPITAL.—Ψ Conakry (120,000). Other towns are Kankan (29,000), which is connected with Conakry by a railway, Kindia (25,000), N'Zérékoré, Mamou, Siguiri and Labé.

FLAG.—Three vertical stripes of red, yellow and green.

NATIONAL DAY.—October 2 (Anniversary of Proclamation of Independence.

BRITISH EMBASSY
Ambassador Extraordinary and Plenipotentiary, His Excellency D. I. Dunnett, C.M.G., O.B.E. (*resident at Dakar*).

GUINEA–BISSAU

President of the Council of State, Sr. Luis Cabral.

Guinea-Bissau, formerly Portuguese Guinea, lies in western Africa, between Senegal and Guinea; it has an area of 14,000 sq. miles and had a population in 1972 of 544,000 (est. 1975—600,000).

Guinea-Bissau achieved independence on Sept. 10, 1974.

Currency, it is planned to replace the *escudo* in 1978 by Guinea-Bissau's own unit of currency, the *peso*.

Economy, The country produces rice, coconuts and ground-nuts. Cattle are raised, and there are bauxite deposits in the south.

Provisional Capital, Medina de Boe. The former capital and chief port is Ψ Bissau.

HAITI
(République d'Haiti)

President, Jean Claude Duvalier, *born* 1951, *installed as President for life*, April 21, 1971.
EMBASSY AND CONSULATE
17 Queen's Gate, S.W.7
[01–581 0577]
Ambassador Extraordinary and Plenipotentiary, Dr Hervé Boyer.

The Republic of Haiti occupies the western third of the island of Hispaniola, which, next to Cuba, is the largest island in the West Indies.

The area of the Republic, including off-shore islands, is about 10,700 sq. miles with a population (estimated, 1969) of 4,768,000. The people are

oils, sisal, cocoa and cotton. Coffee accounts for about one third of total exports and is still a mainstay of the country's economy though exports now rarely exceed 300,000 bags (of 60 kg.). Exports of bauxite began in 1957. Production of copper in the Terre Neuve area started in 1960, but was suspended as uneconomic at the end of 1971. Industry is still on a small scale but the last few years have seen a steady and considerable expansion of light industry (the so-called transformation industries) taking advantage of cheap local labour (minimum wage $U.S.1.30 per day) to assemble or manufacture labour-intensive goods for the U.S. market (baseballs, brassieres, electronic equipment, etc.). Exports of manufactures now rank second after coffee at about 40 per cent. of total exports. The tourist industry is again expanding and many French Canadians are now attracted to Haiti for winter holidays. The country is one of the most beautiful in the Caribbean.

mainly negroes but there are numbers of mulattoes and others with some admixture of European blood. About 250 British subjects, many of West Indian origin, reside in Haiti.

A French colony under the name of Saint-Domingue from 1697, the slave population, estimated at 500,000, revolted in 1791 under the leadership of Toussaint L'Ouverture, who was born a slave and made himself Governor-General of the colony. He capitulated to the French in 1802 and died in captivity in 1803. Resistance was continued by Jean Jacques Dessalines, also a former negro slave, who, on January 1, 1804, declared the former French colony to be an independent state. It was at this time that the name Haiti, an aboriginal word meaning mountainous, was adopted. Dessalines became Emperor of Haiti, but was assassinated in 1806. In 1915, following a period of political upheaval, the country was occupied by a force of U.S. marines. The occupation came to an end in 1934, and U.S. control of the revenue of Haiti officially ended on October 1, 1947.

The six-year term of General Magloire having ended in December 1956, he attempted to stay in power for a further period but was forced to resign and go into exile. A period of political upheaval followed and for many months there was no effective government. A military junta took over in June, 1957, and elections were held in September, following which Dr. François Duvalier was installed as the new president of the Republic. He began a second term in 1961 and in May, 1964, a new constitution granting absolute power to the President was adopted by the National Assembly. Dr. Duvalier was re-elected as President for life on June 15, 1964. He died on April 21, 1971. He was succeeded as President for life on the same day by his son, Jean Claude Duvalier, whom he had nominated as his successor under Article 102 of the Constitution of 1964 as amended on January 14, 1971.

Production, Industry, etc.—In French colonial times, Haiti was one of the most productive countries in the world and the richest French possession. Improvident methods of peasant agriculture succeeded the plantation system and resulted in the gradual impoverishment of natural resources through exhaustion of the soil, deforestation and erosion. In recent years measures for agricultural rehabilitation have been taken with the aim of a gradual restoration of productivity. The main project is a scheme for the irrigation of more than 70,000 acres of the Artibonite valley.

The principal products are coffee, sugar, essential

Communications.—There are very few asphalted roads and internal communications are bad although the situation is improving. Air services are maintained between the capital and the principal provincial towns. The principal towns and villages are connected by telephone and/or telegraph. The telephone company is now state owned (51 per cent.) and the service both in Port-au-Prince and Inter-urban has been greatly improved. External telegraph, telephone and postal services are normal. There are several commercial radio stations and a television station at Port-au-Prince.

Haiti is very well served by air from New York, Miami and Kingston to the North and from Martinique, Puerto Rico and other points to the South, with daily services by one line or another in both directions. The airlines touching Port-au-Prince International Airport include Pan American, Air France, American Air Lines, Eastern Airlines, and A.L.M. Regular passenger liner services to New York have ceased, but cruise ships call regularly, one Norwegian line operating a weekly cruise service to Kingston and Miami. Freight sailings are frequent for the U.S.A., Canada, Europe, Latin America (except Cuba) and the main Caribbean ports. (Airmail: U.K./Port-au-Prince, 4–14 days—extremely variable.)

Climate.—The climate is tropical with comparatively little difference in the temperatures between the summer (March-Oct.) and the winter (Nov.-Feb.). The temperature at Port-au-Prince rarely exceeds 95° F., but the humidity is high, especially in the autumn.

Language and Literature.—French is the language of the government and the press, but it is only spoken by the educated minority. The usual language of the people is Creole. Education is free but estimates of illiteracy are as high as 75 per cent. There are 3 French daily newspapers and one monthly in English. The total circulation is very small.

Finance.—The International Monetary Fund has granted Haiti a stand-by credit of $U.S.4,000,000

	1973–74 $U.S.	1974–75* $U.S.
Revenue	33,200,000	38,916,000
Expenditure	33,200,000	38,916,000

* Haitian budget figures: there is also non-fiscal revenue—e.g. from the Tobacco Monopoly.

Exchange Rate: 5 Gourdes = $1 (U.S.). (*See also* p. 84.)

Trade.—Value of imports 1973 $U.S. 68,500,000 (est.); exports 1973 $U.S. 46,900,000 (est.)

Trade with U.K.

	1973	1974
Imports from U.K.	£1,470,000	£2,000,000
Exports to U.K.	154,000	199,000

The principal exports are listed above; the prinicpal imports are foodstuffs, machinery, vehicles, chemicals and miscellaneous manufactured goods.

CAPITAL, Ψ Port-au-Prince. Population (estimated, 1974), 400,000. Other centres are: Ψ Cap Haitien (24,957); Ψ Gonaives (13,534); Ψ Les Cayes (11,835); Jérémie (11,138); Ψ St. Marc (10,485); Ψ Jacmel (8,545); Ψ Port de Paix (6,309) (1960 Census figures).

FLAG.—Two vertical bands, black (next staff) and red; arms in centre on a white background.

NATIONAL DAY.—January 1.

BRITISH EMBASSY
(Port-au-Prince)

Ambassador Extraordinary and Plenipotentiary, His Excellency John Dunn Hennings, C.M.G. (1973) (*resident at* Kingston, Jamaica).

1st Secretary and Consul, J. D. Murray, C.M.G. (*Port-au-Prince*).

HEJAZ, *see* Saudi Arabia

HONDURAS
(Republica de Honduras)

Head of State, Colonel Juan Alberto Melgar Castro, *assumed office* April 22, 1975.

CABINET
[April 23, 1975]

Interior and Justice, Col. Alonso Flores Guerra.
Defence, Col. Mario Carcamo Chinchilla.
Economy and Commerce, Capt. Armando San Martin.
Finance, Sr. Porfirio Zabala.
Foreign Affairs, Sr. Virgilio Gálvez.
Education, Sra. Lídia Arias de Williams.
Health and Social Security, Dr. Enrique Aguilar Paz.
Natural Resources, Sr. Fernando Montes Matamoros.
Labour and Social Affairs, Sr. Enrique Flores Valeriano.
Economic Planning, Sr. Arturo Corletto.

HONDURAS EMBASSY IN LONDON
48 George Street, W.1.
[01–486 3380]

Ambassador Extraordinary and Plenipotentiary, His Excellency Carlos Lopez-Contreras (1973).

Honduras, one of the five Republican States of Central America, lies between lat. 13° and 16° 30′ N. and long. 83° and 89° 41′ W. with a seaboard of about 400 miles on the Caribbean Sea and an outlet, consisting of a small strip of coast 77 miles in length on the Pacific. Its frontiers are contiguous with those of Guatemala, Nicaragua and El Salvador.

The Republic contains a total area of approximately 43,278 sq. miles and a population (preliminary, March 1974, census) of 2,646,828, of mixed Spanish and Indian blood. There is a strong foreign negro (British West Indian) element in Northern Honduras. The country is very mountainous, being traversed by the Cordilleras. Most of the soil is poor and acid, except for a few acres along the North coast and in the interior. Rainfall is seasonal, May to October being wet and November to

April dry. The climate varies with the altitude, being tropical throughout the year in the coastal belts and temperate and mainly healthy in the uplands.

Originally discovered and settled by the Spaniards at the beginning of the sixteenth century Honduras formed part of the Spanish American Dominions for nearly three centuries until 1821 when independence was proclaimed.

On December 4, 1972, General López Arellano took over the Government from the previous National/Liberal Coalition headed by Dr. Ramón Ernesto Cruz, in a bloodless *coup*, and set up a military régime. President López Arellano was removed on April 22, 1975, and replaced by Colonel Juan Alberto Melgar Castro. The coup followed allegations of corruption, involving bribes alleged to have been paid by the American banana concern, United Brands, to obtain a reduction in a banana export tax.

The Republic is divided into 18 departments, the newest of which, Gracias a Dios, formed in Feb. 1957, covers all the territory previously known as La Mosquitia, together with portions of the Departments of Olancho and Colón. It is inhabited by Indian tribes and largely unexplored.

The chief industry is the production of bananas. Other products are coffee, tobacco, beans, maize, rice, cotton, sugar cane, cement and tropical fruits. Cattle raising is becoming an increasingly important industry, a number of cattle being exported to the neighbouring countries every year. Honduras is also a timber producing country, the most important woods being pine, mahogany and cedar. There are large tracts of uncultivated land.

There are about 730 miles of railway in operation, chiefly to serve the banana plantations and the Caribbean ports. There are 5,943 km. of roads, of which 1,228 are paved. Improvements are being made and new roads built. There are 33 unpretentious airports and three international airports in use in Honduras. A new international airport suitable for jet aircraft has been built near San Pedro Sula. There are numerous small landing and emergency fields. There are four international air services (AVIATECA, SAHSA, PAA and TAN) and 3 domestic air services (SAHSA, Aero Servicios and LANSA).

The language of the country is Spanish. Primary and secondary education is free, primary education being compulsory, and, although there is still a great deal of illiteracy, it is gradually diminishing.

Ψ The chief ports are Puerto Cortes, Tela and La Ceiba on the North Coast, through which passes the bulk of the trade with the United States and Europe, and Amapala, situated on Tiger Island in the Gulf of Fonseca, on the Pacific side.

FINANCE	1974
Revenue (*Budget estimate*)	*Lempiras* 329,142,174
Expenditure................ ,,	329,142,174
Public Debt—	Dec. 31, 1973
External...........	*Lempiras* 240,215,508
Internal........................	267,350,000

The unit of currency is the *Lempira* (named after a native chief), value of 50 cents, U.S. and *Lps* 5·20 to the £. (*See also* p. 84.)

TRADE	1973
Imports....................	*Lempiras* 534,485,920
Exports.................... ,,	473,595,714

Trade with U.K.

	1973	1974
Imports from U.K....	£1,522,000	£3,321,000
Exports to U.K.......	400,000	447,000

CAPITAL.—Tegucigalpa. Pop. 267,754 (March 1974 census); other towns are San Pedro Sula

(146,842), ΨLa Ceiba (38,582), ΨPuerto Cortes (25,661), Choluteca (25,120) and ΨTela (19,268).

FLAG.—Three horizontal bands, blue, white, blue (with five blue stars on white band).

NATIONAL DAY.—September 15.

BRITISH EMBASSY
Tegucigalpa

Ambassador Extraordinary and Plenipotentiary and Consul-General, His Excellency David Morris Pearson, O.B.E.

1st Secretary and Consul, J. D. Perris.

3rd Secretary, H. Parkinson (*Vice-Consul*).

Tegucigalpa is 5,930 miles from London; transit, *via* New York, 14 days; *via* Panama 20 days. By air *via* New York or Miami 2 days.

HUNGARY
(Magyarország)

President of the Presidential Council of the Republic, Pál Losonczi, elected April, 1967.

COUNCIL OF MINISTERS

Prime Minister, György Lázár.

Deputy Prime Ministers, György Aczél; János Borbándi; Ferenc Havasi; István Huszár; Gyula Szekér.

Foreign Affairs, Frigyes Puja.

Interior, András Benkei.

Defence, Lajos Czinege.

Finance, Lajos Faluvégi.

Justice, Mihály Korom.

Metallurgy and Machine Industry, Tivadar Nemeslaki.

Heavy Industry, Pál Simon.

Light Industry, Mrs. János Keserü.

Foreign Trade, József Biró.

Internal Trade, István Szurdi.

Agriculture and Food, Pál Romány.

Health, Dr. Emil Schultheisz.

Education, Dr. Károly Polinszky.

Culture, László Orbán.

Building and Town Planning, Jozsef Bondor.

Labour, László Karakas.

Transport and Communications, Károly Rödönyi.

President National Planning Office, István Huszár.

President, Technical Development Committee, Miklos Ajtai.

THE COMMUNIST PARTY

Politbureau of the Central Committee, G. Aczél; A. Apró; V. Benke; B. Biszku; J. Fock; S. Gáspar; J. Kádár; I Huszár; G. Lázár; P. Losonczi; L. Marothy; D. Nemes; K. Németh; M. Ovári; I. Sárlos.

Secretariat of the Central Committee, Janos Kádár (*1st Secretary*); B. Biszku; I. Györi; A. Geyenes; K. Nemeth; M. Ovári; A. Pullai.

HUNGARIAN EMBASSY AND CONSULATE
35 Eaton Place, S.W.1

[01–235 4048, 7191; Consulate: 01–235 4462]

Ambassador Extraordinary and Plenipotentiary, His Excellency Dr. Vencel Házi (1970).

Counsellors, M. Tibor Antalpéter (*Commercial*); M. Dezsö Kiss; Mrs. E. Abri (*Cultural Affairs*).

Military and Air Attaché, Col. Károly Mészáros.

1st Secretaries, M. Bela Szombati; M. Dezsö Takács; Miss Piroska Szögyéni (*Administration*); M. Attila Kövesdy (*Commercial*).

3rd Secretary, M. Laszlo Merklin (*Consul*).

Attaché, Dr. Istvan Földesi.

Area and Population.—The area of Hungary may be stated as approximately 36,000 sq. miles with a population (1972) of 10,415,000.

Government.—Hungary was reconstituted a kingdom in 1920 after having been declared a republic on Nov. 17, 1918. She joined the Anti-Comintern Pact on Feb. 24, 1939, and entered the 1939–45

War on the side of Germany in 1941. On Jan. 20, 1945, a Hungarian provisional government of liberation, which had been set up during the preceding December, signed an armistice under the terms of which the frontiers of Hungary were withdrawn to the limits existing in 1937.

For the first four years after the liberation, Hungary was governed by a coalition of the Small-holder, National Peasant, Social Democrat and Communist parties. During this time land reform was carried out, the great landowners being dispossessed and their estates partitioned among peasants; mines, heavy industry, banks and schools were nationalized. By 1949 the Communists, under the leadership of Mr. Rákosi, having compelled the Social Democrat Party to merge with them, and having disrupted the peasant parties, had succeeded in gaining a monopoly of power. Elections in that year, in which candidates for the National Assembly were drawn from a single list, resulted in 95·6 per cent. of the votes cast being obtained by the Communist-dominated People's Front. A campaign was opened to collectivize agriculture and by 1952 practically the entire economy had been "socialized".

In mid-1953 Mr. Imre Nagy replaced Mr. Rákosi as Prime Minister, though the latter continued to hold his post as First Secretary of the Party. Mr. Nagy introduced a more moderate policy based largely on the development of agriculture rather than heavy industry; but in April, 1955, Mr. Rákosi succeeded in turning the tables on his rival who was removed from his position as Prime Minister and subsequently expelled from the Party. But after the 20th Congress of the Soviet Communist Party, opposition to Mr. Rákosi within the Hungarian Communist Party mounted and on July 18, 1956, he was removed from his post as First Secretary and succeeded by Mr. Gerö, who had been one of his closest associates.

The period from July to the outbreak of the national revolution on Oct. 23, 1956, was marked by growing ferment in intellectual circles and increased discord within the Party. The immediate signal for the revolt was a series of students' demonstrations, first in Szeged on Oct. 22 and in Budapest a day later. The chief demands put forward by students and other demonstrators were for the return of Mr. Nagy as Prime Minister, for the withdrawal of Soviet troops from the country and for free elections. Fighting broke out on the night of Oct. 23 between demonstrators, who had been joined by large numbers of factory workers, and the State Security Police (A.V.H.). Soviet forces intervened in strength early the next morning. By Oct. 30 Soviet troops had withdrawn from Budapest and on Nov. 3 Mr. Nagy formed an all-party coalition government. This government was overthrown and the revolution suppressed as the result of a renewed attack by Soviet forces on Budapest in the early hours of Nov. 4. Simultaneously the formation of a new Hungarian Revolutionary Worker Peasant Government under the leadership of Mr. Kádár, Mr. Gerö's successor as First Secretary of the Party, was announced. The trial and execution of Imre Nagy and three of his associates was announced on June 17, 1958.

Dr. Ferenc Münnich succeeded as President of the Council of Ministers on Jan. 27, 1958, and held office until Sept. 13, 1961, being replaced by Mr. Kádár. Several other Ministers were replaced at the same time. Mr. Kádár relinquished the post of President of the Council of Ministers in June, 1965, but continued as First Secretary of the Hungarian Socialist Workers' Party.

Industrialization has made considerable progress in the last decade and now produces together with the building industry 55 per cent. of national income. Industry is mainly based on imported raw materials, but Hungary has her own coal (mostly brown), bauxite, considerable deposits of natural gas (some not yet under full exploitation), some iron ore and oil. Output figures in 1974 (1,000 tons), coal, 25,800; bauxite, 2,751; steel 3,466; crude oil, 1,997; cement, 3,437. Natural gas production totalled 5,094 million cubic metres.

Agriculture still occupies an important place in the Hungarian economy and 54 per cent. of the total area of the country is arable land. 10·7 per cent. of the entire land area is owned by State farms and 60·2 per cent. by co-operative farms. Production of the most important crops in 1974 was as follows (1,000 tons): wheat, 4,968; rye 175; barley 894; maize 5,911; rice 56; oats 78; sugar beet 3,662; green maize and silage maize 4,337; lucerne 2,193. In 1974 most plan targets were just fulfilled. National income grew by 6 per cent., as did industrial production, while agricultural production was 3–4 per cent. higher than in 1973. The index of retail prices rose 2·4 per cent.

Since 1968 the Hungarian economy has been run according to a system which allows more decentralized decision-making than in some other Eastern European countries. More difficult economic circumstances have led to some slight moves to more central control in vital areas such as the allocation of fuels and raw materials.

Religion and Education.—About two-thirds of the population are Roman Catholics, and the remainder mostly Calvinist. There are five types of schools under the Ministry of Education—infant schools 3–6, general schools 6–14 (compulsory), vocational schools (15–18), secondary schools (15–18), universities and adult training schools (over 18). In the academic year 1973–74 there were 98,122 students at higher education institutions, 348,473 (incl. 212,734 attending day courses) at secondary schools, and 1,032,800 at general schools.

Language and Literature.—Magyar, or Hungarian, is one of the Finno-Ugrian languages. Hungarian literature began to flourish in the second half of the sixteenth century. Among the greatest writers of the nineteenth and twentieth centuries are Mihály Vörösmarty (1800–1855), Sándor Petöfi (1823–1849), János Arany (1817–1882), Endre Ady (1877–1918), Attila József (1905–1937), Mihály Babits (1883–1941) and Dezsö Kosztolányi (1885–1936).

Finance.—The budget estimates for the year

1975 were: Revenue, *Forints* 318,500,000,000; Expenditure, *Forints* 323,400,000,000. The tourist rate of exchange for the *Forint* (of 100 *Filler*) was 49·07 *Forints*= £1 (June, 1975).

TRADE

	1973 Forints	1974 Forints
Imports	37,229,000,000	51,010,000,000
Exports	42,038,000,000	46,927,000,000

Trade with U.K.

	1973	1974
Imports from U.K.	£26,467,000	£44,050,000
Exports to U.K.	16,830,000	25,007,000

CAPITAL: Budapest, on the Danube; population (1974), 2,049,132. Other large towns are: Miskolc (193,717); Debrecen (176,665); Szeged (164,647) and Pecs (158,802).

FLAG.—Red, white green (horizontally).

NATIONAL DAY.—April 4 (Anniversary of Liberation, 1945).

BRITISH EMBASSY

6 Harmincad Utca, Budapest V

Ambassador Extraordinary and Plenipotentiary, His Excellency The Hon. (Richard) John (McMoran) Wilson, C.M.G. (1973).

1st Secretaries, C. W. Long (*Head of Chancery*); S. N. P. Hemans (*Commercial*), M. J. Reynolds.

2nd Secretaries, C. C. Hayward (*Commercial*); D. M. Merry (*Information*); J. W. O. Smith, M.V.O., M.B.E. (*Administration*).

Consul and Visa Officer, Miss E. A. Urquhart, M.B.E.

Defence Attaché, Lt.-Col. K. H. J. Reynolds.

Air Attaché, Wing Cdr. R. J. Linford, O.B.E.

Cultural Attaché, J. M. E. Took, M.B.E.

Budapest is distant 1,126 miles from London, transit by rail 30 hours; by air 2 hrs. 20 mins.

ICELAND
(Island)

President, Dr. Kristjan Eldjarn, *born* 1917, *elected* July 1, 1968, *for a term of 4 years; assumed office* Aug.1, 1968, *re-elected* 1972, *for a term of 4 years*.

Prime Minister, Geir Hallgrimsson (*Ind*).

Foreign Affairs, Einar Augustsson (*Pr.*).

Industries and Social Affairs, Gunnar Thoroddsen (*Ind.*).

Finance, Matthias A. Mathiesen (*Ind.*).

Fisheries, Health and Social Security, Matthias Bjarnason (*Ind.*).

Justice and Commerce, Ólafur Jóhanneson (*Pr.*).

Agriculture and Communications, Halldór Sigurdsson (*Pr.*).

Education, Vilhjalmur Hjalmarsson (*Pr.*).

(*Ind*,—Independence Party; *Pr.*—Progressive Party).

EMBASSY IN LONDON

1 Eaton Terrace, S.W.1

[01–730 5131–2]

Ambassador Extraordinary and Plenipotentiary, His Excellency Niels P. Sigurdsson (1971).

Minister-Counsellor, M. Eirikur Benedikz.

1st Secretary, M. Helgi Ágústsson.

Iceland is a large volcanic island in the North Atlantic Ocean, extending from 63° 23′ to 66° 33′ N. lat., and from 13° 22′ to 24° 35′ W. long., with an estimated area of 40,500 square miles, or about one-sixth greater than that of Ireland. The population was 216,172 on Dec. 1, 1974.

Iceland was uninhabited before the ninth century, when settlers came from Norway. For several centuries a form of republican government prevailed, with an annual assembly of leading men called the *Althing*, but in 1241 Iceland became subject to Norway, and later to Denmark. During the colonial period, Iceland maintained its cultural integrity but a deterioration in the climate, together with frequent volcanic eruptions and outbreaks of disease led to a serious fall in the standard of living and to a decline in the population to little more than 40,000. In the nineteenth century a struggle for independence began which led first to home-rule for Iceland under the Danish Crown (1918), and later to complete independence under a republican form of rule in 1944.

The Icelandic Cabinet normally consists of seven Ministers, responsible to the *Althing*, a Parliamentary assembly of 60 members. A coalition of Progressives, Left Wing Liberals and members of the People's Alliance (Communists) held office from 1971 until the general election of June 30, 1974, in which government and opposition parties obtained an equal number of seats. After prolonged discussions between the party leaders, a new coalition of members of the Independence Party (25 seats) and Progressives (17 seats) took office on Aug. 28, 1974.

The principal exports are frozen fish fillets, fresh fish on ice, frozen scampi, fishmeal and oil, skins and aluminium; the imports consist of almost all the necessities of life, the chief items being petroleum products, transport equipment, textiles, foodstuffs, animal feeds, timber, and alumina.

At January 1, 1974, the mercantile marine consisted of 651 vessels of under 100 gross tons and 332 ships of 100 gross tons and over; a total of 983 vessels (154,168 gross tons), of which 902 were fishing boats and trawlers and 37 were coasters. There is a regular shipping service between Reykjavik and Felixstowe and between Reykjavik and Weston Point on the Mersey and the Continent.

In the period since Iceland attained independence in 1944, relations between Britain and that country have come under strain on three occasions as a result of unilateral action by Iceland to extend the area of her exclusive fishery jurisdiction. In 1952, Iceland extended her fishing limits from 3 miles to 4 miles from new base lines across bays and estuaries, and the consequent dispute with Britain lasted until 1956. In 1958, Iceland extended her fishing limits from 4 to 12 miles. The ensuing dispute with Britain (and West Germany) was settled in March 1961 by an Exchange of Notes in which it was agreed, *inter alia*, that Iceland would give Britain 6 months' notice of any further extension of her fisheries jurisdiction and that in the event of a dispute about such extension the matter could be referred to the International Court of Justice at the request of either party.

The Icelandic Government which came to power in July 1971, declared their intention of extending the fishing limits to 50 miles from September 1, 1972, and on February 15, 1972, passed legislation purporting to have this effect. Britain then referred the matter to the International Court. As an interim measure, the Court granted Britain an injunction restraining Iceland from enforcing the 50 mile limit against British vessels and at the same time ordered Britain to limit her catch in the area to 170,000 tons a year (the average for 1967–1971). The Court subsequently decided that it had jurisdiction, but the Icelandic Government refused to recognize the Court's competence in the matter and sought to apply the new fishing limit by force. After September 1, 1972, British trawlers were subjected to warp cutting and harassment by Icelandic Coastguard vessels. On May 19, 1973, the British Government ordered naval vessels into the disputed zone to provide protection for British trawlers. An interim settlement, without prejudice to the legal position of either government, was, however, reached on November 13, 1973, by an Exchange of Notes establishing maximum numbers for British trawlers fishing off Iceland and a system of rotating areas around the coast in which it was agreed that they should fish, with certain other areas reserved for conservation purposes. This agreement is valid for 2 years.

A regular air service is maintained between Glasgow and London and Reykjavik. There are also air services from the island to Scandinavia, U.S.A., Germany and Luxemburg.

Road communications are adequate in summer but greatly restricted by snow in winter. Only roads in town centres and a few key highways are metalled the rest being of gravel, sand and lava dust. The climate and terrain make first-class surfaces for highways out of the question. Total number of vehicles licensed is about 58,000 (private cars, 50,000).

Language and Literature.—The ancient Norraena (or Northern tongue) presents close affinities to Anglo-Saxon and as spoken and written in Iceland to-day differs little from that introduced into the island in the ninth century. There is a rich literature with two distinct periods of development, from the middle of the eleventh to the end of the thirteenth century and from the beginning of the nineteenth century to the present time.

FINANCE

	1973 *Krónur ('000)*	1974 *Krónur ('000)*
Revenue	20,448,000	29,178,000
Expenditure	19,868,000	29,402,000
External Debt	7,878,000	—
Internal Debt	3,368,000	—

TRADE

	1973 *Krónur ('000)*	1974 *Krónur ('000)*
Exports	26,039,000	32,877,000
Imports	31,856,000	52,568,000

TRADE WITH U.K.

	1973	1974
Imports from U.K.	£15,690,000	£24,575,000
Exports to U.K.	12,520,000	12,059,000

The Icelandic *Krónur* was devalued by 10·7 per cent. on Dec. 19, 1972, by 10 per cent. on Feb. 15, 1973, by 3·6 per cent. on Sept. 14, 1973, by 4 per cent. on May 17, 1974, and by 20 per cent. on Feb. 14, 1975, the present par value being expressed as *Krónur* 154= $U.S. 1. (*see also* p. 83).

CAPITAL: ⚓Reykjavik. Population (Dec. 1, 1974), 85,000.

Other centres in approximate order of importance are Akureyri, Kopavogur, Hafnarfjördur, Keflavik, Westmann Islands, Akranes, Isafjördhur and Siglufjördur.

FLAG.—Blue, with white-bordered red cross.

NATIONAL DAY.—June 17.

BRITISH EMBASSY
Laufasvegur 49, Reykjavik
Ambassador Extraordinary and Plenipotentiary and Consul-General, His Excellency Kenneth Arthur East, C.M.G. (1975).
1st Secretary and Consul, E. Young.

BRITISH CONSULAR OFFICES
There are Consular Offices at *Reykjavik, Akureyri* and *Isafjördhur.*

INDONESIA
(Republic of Indonesia)

President, General Soeharto, *born* June 9, 1921. Acting President, March 12, 1967; confirmed as President, Mar. 28, 1968, re-elected for a term of 5 years, March, 1973.
Vice-President, Sultan Hamengku Buwono IX.

SECOND DEVELOPMENT CABINET
Ministers of State
Economic, Financial and Industrial Affairs, Prof. Dr. Widjojo Nitisastro.
Administrative Reform, Dr. Johanes Baptista Sumarlin.
Research, Prof. Dr. Sumitro Djojohadikusumo.
Public Welfare, Prof. Dr. Sunawar Sukowati, S.H.
State Secretary, Maj.-Gen. Sudharmono, S.H.
Ministers
Home Affairs, Lt.-Gen. Amir Machmud.
Foreign Affairs, Hadji Adam Malik.
Defence/Security, Gen. Maraden Panggabean.
Justice, Prof. Dr. Muchtar Kusumaatmadja.
Information, Mashuri S.H.
Finance, Prof. Dr. Ali Wardhana.
Trade, Drs. Radius Prawiro.
Agriculture, Prof. Dr. Ir. Thojib Adiwadjaja.
Industry, Lieut.-Gen. M. Jusuf.
Mining, Prof. Dr. Ir. M. Sadli.
Public Works and Electricity, Ir. Sutami.
Communications, Prof. Dr. Emil Salim.
Education and Culture, Dr. Syarif Thayeb.
Health, Prof. Dr. G. A. Siwabessy.
Religion, Prof. Dr. H. A. Mukti Ali.
Manpower, Transmigration, Co-operatives, Prof. Dr. Subroto.
Social Affairs, H. M. S. Mintaredja S.H.

INDONESIAN EMBASSY AND CONSULATE
38 Grosvenor Square, W.1.
[01-499 7661]
Ambassador Extraordinary and Plenipotentiary, His Excellency Admiral Ricardus Subono (1974).
Minister, K. Noermattias (*Political*).
Minister-Counsellor, U. Notodirdjo (*Economic*).
Defence, Air and Military Attaché, Col. J. H. Sumarjono.
Naval Attaché, Lt.-Col. Aboe.
Attachés, K. Sunoto (*Information*); S. Boedjang (*Commercial*);
Counsellor, M. Sja'roni (*Economic*).
1st Secretary, J. Sutantio (*Political*).
3rd Secretaries, S. Narjadi, J. Soenarjo (*Protocol*); A. Rahman Siata (*Economic*); E. S. Suryodiningrat (*Consular*).

Situated between latitudes 6° North and 11° South and between longitudes 95° and 141° East, Indonesia comprises the islands of *Java* and *Madura*, the island of *Sumutra*, the *Riouw-Lingga Archipelago* which with Karimon, Anambas, Natuna Islands,

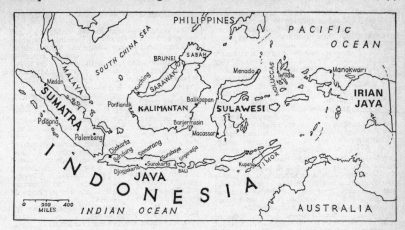

Tambelan, and part of Sumatra, forms the province of Riau), the islands of *Bangka* and *Billiton*, part of the island of *Borneo* (Kalimantan), *Sulawesi* (*formerly* Celebes) *Island*, the *Molucca Islands* (Ternate, Halmahera, Buru, Seram, Banda, Timor-Laut, Larat, Bachiam, Obi, Kei, Aru, Babar, Leti and Wetar), part of *Timor Island*, the islands of *Bali* and *Lombok* and the western half of the island of New Guinea (*Irian Jaya*), with a total area of 735,000 sq. miles, and a population of about 129,000,000.

From the early part of the 17th century much of the Indonesian Archipelago was under Netherlands rule. Following the World War 1939-45, during which the Archipelago was occupied by the Japanese, a strong nationalistic movement manifested itself and after sporadic fighting the formal transfer of sovereignty by the Netherlands of all the former Dutch East Indies except W. New Guinea took place on December 27, 1949.

Dr. Sukarno was elected President of Indonesia and held office until his deposition in 1967. He died on June 21, 1970.

Following the establishment of Malaysia (including Sabah and Sarawak) in 1963, President Sukarno pursued a policy of " confrontation " against it, involving border incursions in both West and East Malaysia. Commonwealth forces assisted Malaysian resistance. Western New Guinea became part of Indonesia in 1963 under the name West Irian (now Irian Jaya), this interpretation being confirmed in an " Act of Free Choice " in July, 1969, of which the United Nations took note in November 1969.

On Sept. 30, 1965, an attempted *coup d'état* assisted by the Palace Guard resulted in the murder of six generals. The Indonesian Communist Party was charged with plotting to destroy the power of the Army and to set up a Peking-oriented régime, nominally under President Sukarno. The coup was swiftly crushed and a widespread massacre of Communists and their supporters followed. Sukarno remained in office but his Foreign Minister, Dr. Subandrio, among others, was arrested and later sentenced to death. The sentence had not been carried out by the summer of 1974.

Following a three-week period of unrest and violent student demonstrations the Minister of the Army, General Soeharto, took over effective political power in March, 1966, and announced the banning in Indonesia of the Communist Party. The new régime concluded an agreement ending the " confrontation " with Malaysia on Aug. 11, 1966, and Indonesia resumed membership of the United Nations Organization which it had left in 1965. General Soeharto was made Acting President with full powers, on March 11, 1967.

Using his powers as Acting President, General Soeharto revised the membership of the two Houses of Parliament, and on March 28, 1968, the MPRS (Provisional People's Consultative Congress), the highest constitutional body, appointed him full President for a period of five years. The 1971 elections resulted in the Government faction Golkar (functional groups) achieving a large majority.

In accordance with another instruction General Soeharto on June 6 replaced the Ampera Cabinet with the Development Cabinet, *i.e.* one which was intended to reflect the emphasis to be placed henceforward on the development of the country, economic affairs, efficiency and expertise in general, and to reduce the direct influence of the military in the Government.

From March 12-24, 1973, the M.P.R. (Peoples' Consultative Assembly) met at Jakarta, the first time that it had assembled in its proper form during Indonesian independence. The primary outcome was the re-election of President Soeharto for a further term of 5 years, the election of Hamengku Buwono IX, Sultan of Yogyakarta, as Vice-President, and the determination of the broad lines of State policy. In March a new Cabinet, called the Second Development Cabinet, was sworn in. The next elections are due in 1977 and the next meeting of the M.P.R. in 1978.

Finance.—Following new measures introduced by the Government in October, 1966, inflation declined from the rate of 600 per cent. in 1966 to about 2 per cent. in 1971. At the end of 1972, a rice shortage, followed by a rise in other prices, increased inflationary pressure on the economy and inflation rose to 27 per cent. in 1973 and 40 per cent. in early 1974 but special measures reduced this to about 2 per cent. for the year. Following the agreement on the re-scheduling of Indonesia's debts in 1966, Western creditor nations agreed to make available aid amounting to $200,000,000 as balance of payments support. Commitments undertaken by these countries in May 1974 amounted to over $900,000,000.

The new measures adopted by the Government in October, 1966, included the abolition of State controls and the introduction of a free market policy with more realistic exchange rates geared to a floating rate for the purchase of foreign exchange in the form of bonus export certificates for essential imports. The rate had risen to a peak of *Rps.*480= $1 by mid-1968, but fell to *Rps.*378 = $1 by mid-1969. It has remained stable since then even though on April 17, 1970, the Government abolished the bonus exports certificate system and introduced a free market for foreign exchange. *Rps.*415= U.S. $1 (July 1974).

Production.—Nearly 70 per cent. of the population of Indonesia is engaged in agriculture and related production. Copra, kapok, nutmeg, pepper and cloves are produced, mainly by smallholders; palm oil, sugar, fibres and cinchona are produced by large estates. Rubber, tea, coffee and tobacco are also produced by both in large quantities. Timber is now the second largest foreign exchange earner after oil. Rice is a traditional staple food for the people of Indonesia and the islands of Java and Madura are important producers, but production is only gradually rising and up to 1975 has been insufficient to meet home demands.

Oil is the most important asset with production in 1974 earning some U.S. $7,000,000,000 in foreign exchange.

Indonesia is rich in minerals; petroleum, tin, coal and bauxite are the principal products; gold, silver, manganese phosphates, nickel and sulphur were produced in quantity before the Second World War and there are considerable deposits. Aid to Indonesia is channelled through the Inter-Governmental Group on Indonesia (IGGI), which pledged U.S. $940,000,000 in May 1975.

The first five-year development programme announced on Dec. 30, 1968, concentrating particularly on agriculture and communications, was inaugurated on April 1, 1969. The second five-year plan began in April 1974 and envisages a fivefold increase in the Government's development expenditure and a 7½ per cent. annual rate of growth in Gross National Product.

Trade with U.K.

There was a progressive decline in British exports to Indonesia after 1960. This became more marked during Indonesia's policy of "confrontation" against Malaysia which resulted in a disruption of normal commercial relations and stringent import controls due to lack of foreign currency, but exports have improved markedly since the restoration of normal commercial relations in 1967.

	1973	1974
Direct Imports from U.K. £	32,834,000	46,693,000
Exports to U.K.	14,947,000	14,419,000

Principal exports to the United Kingdom are rubber, tea, coffee, spices and sugar. Imports from the United Kingdom are mainly of machinery, chemicals, electrical equipment, motor vehicles, cycles, lubricating and heavy oils, and metal goods

Language.—The National Language is Bahasa Indonesia; common spelling for Malay and Bahasa Indonesia was introduced in August 1972.

Transport.—In Java a main line connects Jakarta with Surabaya in the East of Java and there are several branches, including a line from Semarang on the North coast to Yogyakarta in the South. In Sumatra the important towns of Medan, Padang and Palembang are the centres of short railway systems.

Sea communications in the archipelago are maintained by the State-run shipping companies Djakarta-Lloyd (ocean-going) and Pelni (coastal and inter-island) and other smaller concerns. Transport by small craft on the rivers of the larger islands plays an important part in trade. Air services in Indonesia are operated by Garuda Indonesian Airway and other local airlines, and Jakarta is served by various international services. There are approximately 50,000 miles of roads.

CAPITAL.—Ψ Jakarta, formerly Batavia (population 5,000,000). Other important centres are: (Java), Ψ Surabaya, Ψ Semarang, Bandung, Ψ Cirebon, Ψ Surakarta and Yogyakarta; (1971 *populations*) (Madura) Pamekesan (180,000); (Sumatra) Palembang (582,961); Medan (800,000); and Ψ Padang; (Sulawesi) Ψ Ujung Pandang (*formerly* Makassas) (600,000); and Ψ Menado; (Kalimantan, Borneo) Banjarmasin, Ψ Balikpapan and Ψ Pontianak; (Moluccas) Ternate (70,000); (Bali) Denpasar and Singaraya (120,000); (W. Timor) Kupang (10,000); (W. Irian) Jayapura.

NATIONAL DAY.—August 17 (Anniversary of Proclamation of Independence).

FLAG.—Equal bands of red over white.

BRITISH EMBASSY
Jakarta

Ambassador Extraordinary and Plenipotentiary, His Excellency John Archibald Ford, C.M.G., M.C. (1975).

Counsellors, A. C. Stuart; R. B. Crowson (*Commercial*).

Defence and Military Attaché, Col. D. T. Grantham, O.B.E.

Naval Attaché, Cdr. C. F. Le Mesurier, R.N.

1st Secretaries, G. A. Duggan (*Head of Chancery*); S. Muir; J. G. S. Curtis; Miss S. M. Bull, M.V.O. (*Information*); R. K. Buist (*Commercial*); Miss M. Clay (*Aid*); T. E. F. Williams (*Consul*).

2nd Secretaries, R. J. C. Allen; P. J. Torry (*Commercial*).

3rd Secretaries, R. H. Gozney; A. Godson (*Commercial*); Miss V. B. M. Steele (*Vice-Consul*); R. C. Huxley (*Aid*); R. D. Leighton.

BRITISH CONSULAR OFFICES
There are British Consular Offices at *Jakarta* and *Medan*.

BRITISH COUNCIL
Representative, Dr. J. H. F. Villiers, Jalan Imam Bonjol 57–59 Jakarta. There is also an office at *Bandung*.

IRAN
(Persia)

Shanshah of Iran, H.I.M. Mohammed Reza Pahlavi, *born* Oct. 26, 1919; *acceded* Sept. 16, 1941 (on abdication of his father Reza Shah Pahlevi); *married* (March 15, 1939), Princess Fawzieh, sister of ex-King Farouk of Egypt (marriage dissolved Nov. 17, 1948). and has issue a daughter *born* 1940. The Shah *married* (Feb. 12, 1951) Suraya Esfandiari Bakhtiari (marriage dissolved, April 6, 1958); *married* Dec. 21, 1959, Farah Dibah (Empress Farah Pahlevi) and has issue Crown Prince Reza, *born* Oct. 31, 1960; Princess Farahnaz, *b.* March 12, 1963; Prince Ali Reza, *b.* April 28, 1966; Princess Leila, *b.* Mar. 27, 1970.

Prime Minister, Amir Abbas Hoveida

IRANIAN EMBASSY IN LONDON
16 Princes Gate, S.W.7
[01–584 8101]
Ambassador Extraordinary and Plenipotentiary, His

Excellency Dr. Mohammad Reza Amirteymour (1974).

Minister-Counsellor, C. Behname.

Armed Forces Attaché, Col. H. Ghaffari.

Counsellors, S. Gondarzuia; J. Bahar; J. Moinzadeh; R. Basiji; M. R. Noor-Salehi.

Naval Attaché, Cdr. F. Fiuzi.

1st Secretaries, Mrs. V. B. Tehrani; M. Kakhi.

Area and Population.—Iran has an area of 628,000 sq. miles, with a population of 25,781,090 (Census of 1966); U.N. estimate, March, 1970, 28,448,000. It is mostly an arid table-land, encircled, except in the east, by mountains, the highest in the north rising to 18,934 ft. The central and eastern portion is a vast salt desert.

The Iranians are mostly Shi'ah Moslems but among them are a few hundred thousand Zoroastrians, Bahais, Sunni Moslems and Armenian and Assyrian Christians. There is also a substantial Jewish community. Civil and Penal codes based on those of France and Switzerland are in force.

Government.—Iran was ruled from the end of the 18th century by Shahs of the Qajar Dynasty, with despotic power, subject only to the influence of interpreters of the sacred law. A nationalist movement became active in Dec., 1905, and in Aug., 1906, the Shah, Muzaffer-ud-Din, admitting the need for reforms, granted a Constitution. After the war of 1914-18, the subsequent troubles and the signature of the Soviet-Iranian Treaty of 1921, a vigorous Prime Minister, Reza Khan, formerly an officer of the Persian Cossack Regiment, re-established general order. On Oct. 31, 1925, the last representative of the Qajar Dynasty, Sultan Ahmed Shah, who had been absent from the country for some time, was deposed by the National Assembly, which handed over the government to the Prime Minister, Reza Khan, who was elected Shah on Dec. 13, 1925, by the Constituent Assembly, and took the title Reza Shah Pahlavi.

Owing to Nazi German penetration before and during the early part of the war of 1939-45, the Shah and his Government tended so far to favour the Axis powers that, after the German invasion of the U.S.S.R. in 1941, counter-measures became necessary; British and Soviet Forces entered the country from south and north on August 25, 1941, and expelled the agents of the Axis. On September 16, 1941, Reza Shah abdicated and left the country,

nominating the Crown Prince as his successor. The Prince ascended the throne under the title of Mohammed Reza Shah Pahlavi.

In March 1949, the Shah issued an Imperial Farman convoking a Constituent Assembly to make certain revisions to the Constitution and the Assembly was duly elected and convened on April 21. After this Assembly the Senate was formed for the first time.

On February 26, 1963, the Shah announced his six point " White Revolution ". The six points are: 1. A land reform designed to redistribute land and place it in the hands of the peasants. 2. Nationalization of all forest land. 3. The sale of government shares in factories and industrial enterprises to raise money for the implementation of the land reform. 4. The distribution of factory profits among the factory employees. 5. The granting of the vote to women. 6. The creation of a Literacy Corps to bring basic education to the rural areas. Six additional points have since been added.

On March 2, 1975, the Shah dissolved the two-party system, and announced the formation of the *Rastakhiz* (National Resurrection) Party, which would be the only political party. On June 20, general elections were held for the *Majhs* (Chamber of Deputies) and the Senate.

For the purposes of local government the country is divided into 14 Provinces (Ustans) and 8 Countries (*Farmandariye Kol*), comprising 147 Sub-Provinces (*Shahristans*), under Governors-General and Governors, respectively.

Defence.—The Army has a strength of about 175,000 men, in 3 armoured divisions, 2 infantry divisions and 4 independent brigades. Two years' military service is compulsory. The Air Force has a strength of about 50,000, with over 200 aircraft. The Navy, with personnel of about 13,000, consists of 3 destroyers, 4 frigates, 4 corvettes, 6 mine-sweepers, and patrol boats, landing craft and hover-craft. The Gendarmerie is an all regular, para-military force of about 70,000 men which provides frontier guards and mans small posts throughout the country.

Education.—Since 1943 primary education has been compulsory and free, but there is large scale absenteeism, particularly outside the towns. The establishment in 1963 of the Literacy Corps (a body of National Servicemen who are seconded to the Ministry of Education to work as Primary School teachers in rural districts) has brought schooling to hitherto deprived villages and is making a valuable contribution in increasing educational opportunities for country people. During the academic year 1970-71 there were 4,200,000 pupils attending 21,800 schools. About 2,500,000 of these were at Primary School. There are in Iran eight universities (Tehran 3, Tabriz, Meshed, Isfahan, Shiraz, Rezayeh and Ahwaz) and there were over 50,000 students in higher education in 1970.

Language and Literature.—Persian, or Farsi, the language of Iran, and of some other areas formerly under Persian rule, is an Indo-European tongue with many Arabic elements added; the alphabet is mainly Arabic, with writing from right to left. Among the great names in Persian literature are those of Abu'l Kásim Mansúr, or Firdausi (A.D. 939-1020), Omar Khayyám, the astronomer-poet (died A.D. 1122), Muslihu'd-Din, known as Sa'di (born A.D. 1184) and Shems-ed-Din Muhammad, or Hafiz (died A.D. 1389).

Finance.—The budget for the Iranian year beginning March 21, 1971, including development expenditure, balanced at Rls. 481,000,000,000 an increase of 18 per cent. over 1970-71. The unit of currency is the *Rial* of 100 *Dinars* (for rate of exchange, *see* p. 84).

Production and Industry.—While petroleum is the principal product and by far the greatest export Iran, except for its desert areas, is primarily an agricultural country and more than half of the inhabitants depend of their living on the land. Wheat is the principal crop, using about half the area under cultivation. Other important crops are barley, rice, cotton, sugar beet, fruits and vegetables. Wool is also produced—sheep, as well as goats, being numerous. There are extensive forests in the north and west, the conservation of which is an urgent problem. Rapid progress has been made in the development of industry. Apart from oil, the principal industrial products are carpets, textiles (mainly cotton), sugar, cement and other construction materials, ginned cotton, vegetable oil and other food products, leather and shoes, metal manufactures, pharmaceuticals, automobiles, fertilizers, plastics, matches and cigarettes. A steel mill at Isfahan began the production of pig iron at the end of 1971. There are now three petrochemical plants in operation, producing fertilizers plastics, detergents, sulphur and liquid petroleum gas. Large-scale copper deposits have been found in the south-eastern part of the country.

The oilfields had produced over 200,000,000 metric tons of oil from their first output to Dec. 31, 1946. Production had risen to a total of 35,000,000 metric tons in 1950, the last full year before nationalization. Oil shipments ceased in 1951 and were not resumed until Oct. 30, 1954.

The former functions of A.I.O.C. (now renamed " British Petroleum Company ") in Iran were taken over for an initial period of 25 years by a consortium of 8 oil companies (including A.I.O.C., one French, one Dutch and five U.S.), A.I.O.C. receiving from Iran £25,000,000 cash in the 10 years from Jan. 1. 1957, in compensation for its oil assets in Northern Iran and in settlement of losses since 1951; and from the other members of the consortium for their shares, about £214,000,000 payable over 20–25 years. The consortium is responsible for the production, refining and sale of Iranian oil through two operating companies, while " non-basic " operations are undertaken by the National Iranian Oil Company.

Oilfields outside the Consortium area are being developed by several oil companies formed jointly by N.I.O.C. with western oil companies, notably S.I.R.P., I.P.A.C., L.A.P.C.O. and I.M.I.N.C.O. Production from offshore oil wells in the Persian Gulf developed by these companies is increasing rapidly.

Recent oil production figures are (in long tons): 1966, 105,100,000; 1967, 129,300,000; 1968, 142,200,000; 1969, 168,100,000; 1970, 194,000,000.

Communications.—The principal roads are from the frontier of Iraq at Khosravi to Tehran; from Tehran *via* Saveh and Hamadan to Ahwaz and Khorramshahr; from Tehran *via* Qum, Isfahan and Shiraz to Bushire; from Tehran into Azerbaijan, through Tabriz to Julfa (on the Soviet frontier) with a branch road into Turkey; from Tehran to Meshed; three roads through the Elbruz mountains to the Caspian coast and the Soviet borders east and west of the Caspian Sea; and from Isfahan, *via* Yezd and Kerman to Zahidan and thence to Meshed. Zahidan is connected by road with Quetta (Pakistan). Meshed is connected by road with Herat (Afghanistan). Some of these roads traverse extremely difficult mountainous country; others are desert tracks. The *Trans-Iranian Railway*, from Bandar Shah, on the Caspian Sea, to Bandar Shahpur, on the Persian Gulf, was inaugurated in 1938; this line has a total length of 872 miles, the total cost, after eleven years' work, being approximately £30,000,000. The branch lines from

Tehran to Meshed and to Tabriz have now been completed. There are also railroads from Tabriz to Julfa and from Zahidan to Mirjawa and thence to Quetta and branch lines from Ahwaz to Khorramshahr and Khorramshahr to Tanuma in Iraq (on the Shatt al Arab, opposite Basrah) were opened during the war. An extension from Qum to Yezd *via* Kashan is now in operation as is one from Bandar Shah to Gorgan. Extensions from Yezd to Kerman and from Tabriz to Van (Turkey) are being built. It is hoped to connect the Iranian rail system with the Turkish and with the Pakistan systems, thereby offering a through route from Europe to Pakistan.

Civil Aviation.—In May, 1946, a Department of Civil Aviation was created, subordinate to the Ministry of Roads. Progress has been made towards establishing first-class International Airports at Tehran and Abadan, with secondary airfields in accordance with ICAO standards. The *Iranian National Airlines Corporation* was formed from the former *Iranian Airways* and *Persian Air Services* in February, 1962. The Company is 51 per cent. Government-owned and operates internal and international routes. Air France, K.L.M., S.A.S., Iraqi, M.E.A., P.A.A., Lufthansa, British Airways, Quantas, P.I.A., Aeroflot, Alitalia, Aryana Airways and El Al operate services to Tehran.

TRADE

	1968–9	1969–70
Imports.	Rials106,723,875,715	Rials115,567,000,000
Exports.	16,268,001,537	18,533,000,000

These figures are calculated at the commercial rate of exchange and exclude oil exports. Total exports, including oil exports for 1969–70, Rials 612,357,000,000.

Trade with U.K.

	1973	1974
Imports from U.K.	£169,412,000	£278,580,000
Exports to U.K.	237,331,000	513,270,000

Imports into Iran consist mainly of industrial and agricultural machinery, iron and steel (including manufactures), electrical machinery and goods, sugar, chemicals and pharmaceuticals, motor vehicles and certain textile fabrics and yarns. The principal exports, apart from oil, are cotton, carpets, dried fruits and nuts, hides and skins, mineral ores, wool, gums, caviare, cummin seed and animal casings. West Germany, the U.S.A. and the U.K. are Iran's three leading suppliers. West Germany, the U.S.S.R., the U.K. and the U.S.A. are the main customers for non-oil exports.

CAPITAL: Tehran, population (1970), 3,150,000. Other large towns are Tabriz (388,000), Isfahan (340,000), Meshed (312,000), Shiraz (206,000), Resht (119,000), Kerman (73,000), Hamadan (115,000), Yezd (74,000), Kermanshah (152,000), Ψ Abadan (273,000), Ahwaz (145,000).

FLAG.—Equal horizontal bands of green, white and red; with arms (lion and sun) in centre.

NATIONAL DAY.—October 26 (Anniversary of Birthday of the Shahanshah).

BRITISH EMBASSY

Avenue Ferdowsi, Tehran

Ambassador Extraordinary and Plenipotentiary, His Excellency Sir Anthony Derrick Parsons, K.C.M.G., M.V.O., M.C. (1974).

Counsellors, G. B. Chalmers; M. K. O. Simpson-Orlebar (*Commercial*); A. B. Milne, O.B.E.

Defence and Military Attaché, Col. J. A. Cowgill.

Naval Attaché, Capt. M. E. Lane, R.N.

Air Attaché, Group Capt. B. A. Primavesi, C.V.O.

BRITISH COUNCIL

Representative, J. G. Hanson, 58 Avenue Ferdowsi, Tehran. Centres and libraries at *Isfahan, Meshed, Shiraz, Tabriz* and *Tehran*.

IRAQ

REVOLUTIONARY COMMAND COUNCIL

Chairman, President of the Republic, and *Supreme Commander of the Armed Forces,* Field Marshal Ahmad Hasan al Bakr, *assumed* office July 17, 1968.

Members, Saddam Hussain (*Vice-Chairman*); General Sa'dun Ghaidan (*Minister of Communications*); Dr. Izzat Mustafa (*Minister of Health*); Sd Izzat Ibrahim al Duri (*Minister of the Interior*); Sd Taha al Jazrawi (*Minister of Industry and Minerals*).

In addition to those members of the R.C.C. holding departmental portfolios listed above, there are 23 other ministers, including 8 ministers of State.

IRAQ EMBASSY IN LONDON
21–22 Queen's Gate, S.W.7
[01–584 7141]

Ambassador Extraordinary and Plenipotentiary, H. E. Abdul Malik Ahmed Ali-Yasin.

Area, etc.—Traversed by the Rivers Euphrates and Tigris, Iraq extends from Turkey on N. and N.E. to the Persian Gulf on the S. and S.E. and from Iran on E. to Syria and Arabian Desert on W. the approximate position being between $37\frac{1}{2}°$ to $48\frac{1}{2}°$ E. long., and from $37\frac{1}{2}°$ to 30° N. lat. (*see* MAP, p. 879). The area of Iraq is officially estimated at 172,000 sq. miles of which 37 per cent. is desert land. About 35 to 40 per cent. of the remainder is potentially cultivable either by rainfall or by irrigation.

Population.—At the Census of 1965 Iraq had a total population of 8,097,230; estimated 1970, 9,498,362.

The *Euphrates* (which has a total length of 1,700 miles from its source to its outflow in the Persian Gulf) is formed by two arms, of which the Murad Su (415 miles) rises in the slopes of the Ala Dagh, a mountain of Eastern Erzurum, and flows westwards to a junction with the Kara Su, or Frat Su (275 miles); the other arm rises in the north-west of Erzurum in the Dumlu Dagh. The *Tigris* has a total length of 1,150 miles from its source to its junction with the Euphrates at Qurna, 70 miles from the Persian Gulf, and rises in two arms south of the Taurus mountains, in Kurdistan, uniting at Til, where the boundaries of the districts of Diarbekir, Van and Bitlis conjoin.

Antiquities.—In 1944 excavations at Tell Hassuna, near Shura (on the Tigris in North Iraq) unearthed abundant traces of culture dating back to 5000 B.C. Excavations in 1948 at Tel Abu Shahrain, 14 miles south of " Ur of the Chaldees," confirm Eridu's claim to be the most ancient city of the Sumerian world. Hillah, the ancient city on the left bank of the Shatt el Hillah. a branch of the Euphrates, about 70 miles south of Baghdad, is near the site of Babylon and of the " house of the lofty-head " or " gate of the god " (Tower of Babel). Mosul *Liwa* covers a great part of the ancient kingdom of *Assyria,* the ruins of Ninevah, the Assyrian capital, being visible on the banks of the Tigris, opposite Mosul. Qurnar, at the junction of the Tigris and Euphrates, is the traditional site of the *Garden of Eden.* The " *Tree of Knowledge,*" which had stood there " from time immemorial," withered and died in December, 1946. It has been replaced by a shoot said to be from the original tree.

Government.—Under the Treaty of Lausanne 1923), Turkey renounced the sovereignty over Mesopotamia. A provisional Arab Government was set up in Nov., 1920, and in Aug., 1921, the Emir Fisal was elected King of Iraq. The country was a monarchy until July, 1958, when King Faisal II was assassinated. From 1958 Iraq has been under Presidential rule.

Diplomatic relations with the United Kingdom were broken in June 1967 and resumed in May 1968 They were again broken in Dec. 1971 and resumed once more in April 1974.

Language.—The language is mainly Arabic (*see* Arabia) and English is widely used in commerce, science and the arts.

Education.—In 1969–70 Iraq had 130 infant schools, with 619 teachers and 15,697 pupils; 5,172 primary schools, with 48,290 teachers and 1,040,968 pupils; and 836 intermediate and preparatory secondary schools, with 10,116 teachers and 302,611 full-time students. There were 5 universities and 4 other public institutes of higher education, with 49 teachers and lecturers and 1,146 students. In 1969–70 there were 48 vocational schools (agriculture, commerce and industry, home economics).

Communications and Trade.—New roads are being rapidly built, and communications between Baghdad and the provincial capitals are being improved and secured. The port of Basrah is not at present able to handle expeditiously all seaborne traffic. Continuous dredging of the Shatt-al-Arab has provided a navigable channel of $22\frac{1}{2}$ feet at low water (as compared with 9 feet before dredging was begun). The port of Um Qasr near the Kuwaiti border has been developed for freight and sulphur handling. Road routes from Turkey and the Mediterranean are well used, and carry through traffic to Kuwait and the south.

There are international airports at Baghdad and Basrah. Iraqi Airways provide a London/Baghdad service six days a week. British Airways and other European airlines operate weekly. Iraqi Airways and Middle East Airlines operate within the area, including (Iraqi) services to Basrah and Mosul. Iraqi Republican Railways provide regular passenger and goods services on a standard gauge line between Basra, Baghdad and Mosul, which links up through Syria and Turkey with the Mediterranean and the Bosphorus. There is also a metre gauge line connecting Baghdad with Khannaqin, Kirkuk and Arbil.

Agriculture and Industry.—Iraq is capable of supporting a considerably greater population if irrigation is developed and extended. The Government's concern with agricultural development is shown in the large financial allocations made to the sector. Apart from the valuable revenues to be derived from oil the wealth of the country depends upon agricultural development and two harvests can usually be gathered in the year. Production fluctuates from year to year according to rainfall. During the five years 1964–69 crops of barley, millet, rice, wheat, dates, cotton and tobacco were produced in sufficient quantities to allow a margin for export. However, due to a poor harvest in 1969–70 dates were the only important agricultural export. All crops improved in 1971–72 but fell to 1970 levels in 1973.

Few industries with the exception of the oil industry are yet established on any scale, but increasing industrialization is taking place, mainly in the public sector. Priority is being given to petrochemicals, food industries, construction industries and engineering. Existing industries include cement, building materials, flour milling, cigarettes, soap, beer, steel fabrications, furniture, tanning, textiles, footwear and vegetable oils. In 1972 there were 1,319 industrial eatablishments employing an average number of 121,409 persons annually. Turnover of these establishments was *ID.*235,986,000. Iraq's major industry is oil production, and this accounts for approximately 98 per cent. of the country's foreign exchange receipts, 90 per cent. of total government revenue and 45 per cent. of the

Gross National Product. Production figures in long tons are:

1970.....75,241,000   1972.....71,207,000
1971.....82,450,046   1973.....97,802,000

Total revenues from exports of crude oil have not been published since 1972, but they are believed to have been worth some ID.2,120,000,000 in 1974. The Iraq Petroleum Company was nationalized on June 1, 1972, but its associate, Basrah Petroleum Company, is still 24 per cent. foreign-owned. Following nationalization, Iraq's oil production fell to an estimated 65,000,000 long tons in 1972. However, as a result of an agreement reached between the Iraq Petroleum Company and the Government in March 1973 Iraq's oil production has since risen to meet market requirements and reached some 97,800,000 long tons in 1973.

FINANCE

	1973–74	1974–75*
Total revenue	ID1,270,300,000	ID2,747,851,776
Total expenditure	1,375,200,000	2,993,458,195

* Budget estimates.

The Iraqi *Dinar* (of 1,000 *Fils*= £1·40 sterling. Exchange rate (May, 1974), 705 *Fils*= £1 (*see also* p. 84).

TRADE
(Excluding oil)

Trade with U.K.

	1972	1973
Total imports	ID234,680,003	ID270,316,788
Total exports	28,614,060	32,522,820
	1973	1974
Imports from U.K.	£27,057,000	£59,838,000
Exports to U.K.	30,678,000	106,577,000

In 1974, petroleum accounted for some £103,000,000 of exports to the U.K.

The principal imports are iron and steel, mechanical and electrical machinery, motor cars, cotton and rayon piecegoods, sugar and tea; and the chief exports are crude petroleum, dates, cement, raw wool, raw hides and raw cotton.

CAPITAL.—Baghdad. Population of the governorate (estimated 1970), 2,696,000. Other towns of importance are Ψ Basrah and Mosul.

FLAG.—Horizontal stripes of red, white and black, with three green stars on the white stripe.

BRITISH EMBASSY
Sharia Salah Ud-Din,
Karkh, Baghdad

Ambassador Extraordinary and Plenipotentiary, His Excellency John Alexander Noble Graham, C.M.G. (1974).
Counsellor, R. G. Giddens.
Commercial Secretary, N. W. Lomas.
Defence Attaché Lt.-Col. J. Y. Sanders.
Consul, W. J. Dixon.
Second Secretaries, K. D. Temple; F. G. Carter.
Attachés, D. White (*Commercial*); S. H. Palmer (*Consular*).
There are no British Consular Offices outside Baghdad.

British Council Representative, R. A. K. Baker, 7/2/9 Waziriya, Baghdad.

ISRAEL
(Yisrael)

President of Israel, Professor Ephraim Katzir, *born* 1916, *elected President* May 24, 1973.

CABINET

Prime Minister, Yitzhak Rabin.
Deputy Prime Minister and Minister for Foreign Affairs, Yigal Allon.
Interior and Social Welfare, Dr. Joseph Burg.
Education and Culture, Aharon Yadlin.
Agriculture and Communications, Aharon Uzan.
Labour, Moshe Bara'm.
Defence, Shimon Peres.
Police, Shlomo Hillel.
Health, Victor Shemtov (*Mavam*).
Finance, Yehoshua Rabinowitz.
Commerce and Industry, Haim Bar-Lev.
Transport, Gad Yaacobi.
Justice, Haim Yosef Zadok.
Housing, Avraham Offer.
Immigration Absorption, Shlomo Rosen (*Mapam*).
Religious Affairs, Itzhak Raphael.
Tourism, Moshe Kol (*I.L.P.*).
Information, (*vacant*).
Without Portfolio, Israel Galili; Gideon Hausner (*I.L.P.*).

Apart from Ministers marked otherwise, members of the Cabinet belong to the Israel Labour Party, a merger (Jan. 21, 1968) of the former *Mapai*, *Ahdut Avodah* and *Rafi* parties. *Mapam*= United Workers' Party; *I.L.P.*= Independent Liberal Party.

EMBASSY IN LONDON
2 Palace Green, Kensington, W.8
[01–937 8050]

Ambassador Extraordinary and Plenipotentiary, His Excellency Gideon Rafael.
Consular Section, 2A Palace Green, W.8.
Consul-General, Ze'ev Suffot.

Area and Population.—Israel lies on the western edge of the continent of Asia at the eastern extremity of the Mediterranean Sea, between lat. 29° 30′–33° 15′ N. and longitude 34° 15′–35° 40′ E. Its political neighbours are Lebanon on the North, Syria on the North and East, Jordan on the East and the Egyptian province of Sinai on the South-West.

The area is estimated at 7,992 square miles out of the 10,429 square miles comprised in the whole of Palestine (the remainder being occupied by Israel since the Six Day War in June, 1967, together with the Sinai Peninsula and the Golan Heights in Syria). The population was estimated in 1973 at 3,230,000. Jewish immigration has made rapid progress since the establishment of the State in 1948. In 1912 there were only 83,790 Jews in Palestine out of a total population of 752,048. During the upheavals of 1948–49 some 6,000 Arabs left the country as refugees and settled in neighbouring countries. Since 1948 the population of Israel has more than trebled.

Hebrew and Arabic are the official languages of Israel. Arabs are entitled to transact all official business with Government Departments in Arabic, and provision is made in the *Knesset* for the simultaneous translation of all speeches into Arabic.

Physical Features.—Israel comprises four main regions: (*a*) the hill country of Galilee and Judæa and Samaria, rising in places to heights of nearly 4,000 feet; (*b*) the coastal plain from the Gaza strip to North of Acre, including the plain of Esdraelon running from Haifa Bay to the south-east, and cutting in two the hill region; (*c*) the Negev, a semi-desert triangular-shaped region, extending from a base south of Beersheeba, to an apex at the head of the Gulf of 'Aqaba: and (*d*) parts of the Jordan valley, including the Hula Region, Tiberias and the south-western extremity of the Dead Sea. The principal river is the Jordan, which rises from three main sources in Israel, the Lebanon and Syria, and flows through the Hula valley and the canals which have replaced Lake Hula, drained in 1958. Between Hulata and Tiberias (Sea of Galilee) the river falls 926 ft. in 11 miles and becomes a turbulent stream. Lake Tiberias is 696 ft. below sea-level and liable to sudden storms. Between it and the Dead Sea the Jordan falls 591 ft. The other principal rivers are the Yarkon and Qishon. The

largest lake is the *Dead Sea* (shared between Israel and Jordan); area 393 sq. miles, 1,286 feet below sea-level, 51·5 miles long, with a maximum width of 11 miles and a maximum depth of 1,309 ft.; it receives the waters of the Jordan and of six other streams, and has no outlet, the surplus being carried off by evaporation. The water contains an extraordinarily high concentration of mineral substances. The highest mountain peak is Mount Meron, 3,962 feet above sea-level, near Safad, Upper Galilee.

Climate.—The climate is variable, similar to that of Lower Egypt, but modified by altitude and distance from the sea. The summer is hot but tempered in most parts by daily winds from the Mediterranean. The winter is the rainy season lasting from November to April, the period of maximum rainfall being January and February.

Antiquities.—The following are among the principal historic sites in Israel: Jerusalem: the Church of the Holy Sepulchre; the Al Aqsa Mosque and Dome of the Rock, standing on the remains of the Temple Mount of Herod the Great, of which the Western (wailing) Wall is a fragment; the Church of the Dormition and the Cœnaculum on Mount Zion; Ein Karem: Church of the Visitation, Church of St. John the Baptist. Galilee: The Sea; Church and Mount of the Beatitudes, ruins of Capernaum and other sites connected with the life of Christ. Mount Tabor: Church of the Transfiguration. Nazareth: Church of the Annunciation and other Christian shrines associated with the childhood of Christ. There are also numerous sites dating from biblical and mediæval days, such as Ascalon, Cæsarea, Atlit, Massada, Megiddo and Hazor. Other antiquities in the West Bank of Jordan, Sinai or the Golan Heights at present occupied by Israel can now be visited from Israel.

Government.—There are a Cabinet and a single-chamber Parliament (*Knesset*) of 120 members. A general election is held at least once every four years. The last took place on Dec. 31, 1973.

A " Government of National Unity " was formed on December 11, 1969, headed by Mrs. Golda Meir. It was a broad coalition and, with one exception, embraced the same parties as were in the two previous governments formed in June, 1967, and March, 1969, by the late Mr. Levi Eshkol and Mrs. Meir respectively. In August, 1970, the *Gahal* bloc left the Government because they were opposed to a resumption of the Jarring negotiations. Following the General Election held on December 31, 1973 (postponed from October 30 owing to the outbreak of war), there was a prolonged ministerial crisis, finally resolved when Mrs. Meir succeeded in forming a new Coalition Government, and the Cabinet was chosen on March 6. The Government received a vote of confidence in the Knesset on March 10. However, on April 10, Mrs. Meir announced her resignation; on April 22 the Labour Party chose General Itzhak Rabin as Prime Minister-designate, and on April 26 President Katzir asked him to form a new Government, which was chosen on May 28, and received a vote of confidence in the Knesset on June 3. The present coalition government commands 57 seats in the Knesset, as follows: *Alignment*, 50; *Arab & Druse Lists* (affiliated to Labour Party), 3; *Independent Liberals* 4. The Opposition commands 59 seats in the Knesset as follows: *Likud*, 39; *National Religious*, 10; *Agudat Blo*, 5; *Ya'ad* (the former C.R.M. with *Lyiova Fliar* from the Labour Party) 4; *New Communists*, 4; *Israel Communists*, 1.

Immigration.—The Declaration of Independence of May 14, 1948, laid down that " the State of Israel will be open to the immigration of Jews from all countries of their dispersion." The Law of Return, passed by the *Knesset* on July 5, 1950, provides that an immigrant visa shall be granted to every Jew who expresses his desire to settle in Israel. From the establishment of the State until April 1973, 1,480,000 immigrants had entered Israel from over 100 different countries.

Education.—Elementary education for all children from 5 to 15 years is compulsory. The Law also provides for working youth, age 15–18 who, for some reason, have not completed their primary education, to be exempted from work in order to do so.

In 1974–75 enrolment in all educational establishments was 1,012,300: kindergartens 192,600 (including 37,000 in private schools; elementary education, 503,500; teacher's training colleges, 11,100; secondary education, 175,300; academic institutions, 51,000.

Finance.—Government expenditure for the fiscal year 1974–75 totalled I£40,650,000,000.

The unit of account is the Israel pound of 100 *agorot*. Exchange rate, *see* p. 84.

COMMUNICATIONS

Railways and Roads.—Israel State Railways started operating in August, 1949. Towns now served are Haifa, Tel Aviv, Jerusalem, Lod, Nahariya, Beersheba, Domona, Oron, Ashdod and intermediate stations. In March 1973 the total railway network amounted to 795 km. There were over 10,000 km. of paved road and 375,340 licensed vehicles in 1974.

Shipping.—Israel's merchant marine had reached a total of 3,435,076 tons deadweight by December, 1973.

The chief ports are Haifa, a modern harbour, with a depth of 30 ft. alongside the main quay; the new harbour on the Red Sea at Eilat, inaugurated in September, 1965, has a capacity of 10,000 tons a day; Acre has an anchorage for small vessels; the deep-water port at Ashdod, 20 miles south of Tel Aviv, which started operations at the end of 1965, handled 3,363,000 million tons of cargo in 1973. In 1974 Israel's three main ports handled 9,989,000 tons of cargo (excluding petroleum).

Civil Aviation.—In 1974, El Al carried 862,000 passengers. El Al operates Boeing jets exclusively and has bought three Boeing 747's. Arkia, the internal airline, has had a steep increase in traffic since the Six-Day War and in 1974 carried 363,000 passengers. Arkia uses five Heralds and five Viscounts.

PRODUCTION AND INDUSTRY

Agriculture.—The country is generally fertile and climatic conditions vary so widely that a large variety of crops can be grown, ranging from temperate crops, such as wheat and cherries, to subtropical crops such as sorghum, millet and mangoes. The famous " Jaffa " orange is produced in large quantities mostly in the coastal plain for export; other kinds of citrus fruits are also grown and exported. The citrus yield during the 1972–73 season was 1,495,038 tons. Of this total, 846,770 tons

were exported, of which 182,000 tons went to the U.K. Olives are cultivated, mainly for the production of oil used for edible purposes and for the manufacture of soap. The main winter crops are wheat and barley and various kinds of pulses, while in summer sorghum, millet, maize, sesame and summer pulses are grown. Large areas of seasonal vegetables are planted; potatoes can be grown in autumn and in the winter. Since the establishment of the State of Israel, beef, cattle and poultry farming have been developed and the production of mixed vegetables and dairy produce has greatly increased. Tobacco and medium staple cotton are now grown. Fishing has also been extended, and production (mostly from fish ponds) reached 23,737 tons in 1973. All kinds of summer fruits such as figs, grapes, plums and apples are produced in increasing quantities for local consumption. Water supply for irrigation is the principal limiting factor to greater production. The area under cultivation during 1972–73 was 4,225,000 dunams, of which 1,815,000 were under irrigation. The largest of these is the Kinneret-Negev Project. Much of the dairy industry is dependent on the production of fodder crops under irrigation; areas under fodder crops have doubled. The Israel land measure is the *dunam*, equivalent to 1,000 square metres (approximately a quarter of an acre).

Industry.—In value polished diamonds now account for more than one-third of Israel's total exports. Amongst the most important of her exporting industries are textiles, foodstuffs, chemicals (mainly fertilisers and pharmaceuticals). Her metal-working and science-based industries have been developed to a highly sophisticated and technologically advanced level. These include the aircraft and military industries. Other important manufacturing industries include plastics, rubber, cement, glass, paper and oil refining.

TRADE

	1971	1972
Imports..	§U.S.1,785,000,000	§U.S.1,947,814,000
Exports..	957,000,000	1,148,027,000

Trade with U.K.

	1973	1974
Imports from U.K..	£187,248,000	£219,206,000
Exports to U.K.....	69,942,000	78,701,000

The principal imports are foodstuffs, crude oil, machinery and vehicles, iron, steel and manufactures thereof, and chemicals. The principal exports are citrus fruits and by-products, polished diamonds, plywood, cement, tyres, minerals, finished and semi-finished textiles.

CAPITAL.—Most of the Government departments are in Jerusalem (population, 1971, 301,000). A resolution proclaiming Jerusalem as the capital of Israel was adopted by the Israel parliament on Jan. 23, 1950. It is not, however, recognized as the capital by the United Nations. Other principal towns are Ψ Tel Aviv-Jaffa (383,000); Ψ Haifa and district (219,000); Ramat Gan (119,000) and Beersheba (81,000).

FLAG.—White, with two horizontal blue stripes, the Shield of David in the centre. NATIONAL DAY (1976)—May 5.

JERUSALEM

Until 1967 Jerusalem was divided between Israel and Jordan, two of the 36 recognized Christian Holy Places (in the New City) being under Jewish administration, the remainder under Arab administration in the Old City. At the conclusion of hostilities between Israel and the surrounding Arab countries in 1967 the entire city was under Israeli control.

BRITISH EMBASSY
192 Hayarkon Street, Tel Aviv.
Ambassador Extraordinary and Plenipotentiary, His
Excellency, Thomas Anthony Keith Elliott,
C.M.G. (1975).
Counsellor, M. J. Newington (*Head of Chancery and
Consul-General*).
Defence and Air Attaché, Group Capt. R. J. F.
Dickenson, A.F.C.
Counsellor, E. V. Vines, O.B.E. (*Commercial*).

British Council Representative, E. H. Semmens, 140
Hayarkon Street, Tel Aviv. There is an office
and library in *Tel Aviv*; libraries at *Ha'fa* and
Jerusalem.

ITALY
(Repubblica Italiana)
President of the Italian Republic, Giovanni
Leorne, *born* at Naples in 1908. *Elected* December
24, 1971.

COUNCIL OF MINISTERS
(November 23, 1974)
Prime Minister, Aldo Moro (*CD*).
Foreign Affairs, Mariano Rumor (*CD*).
Interior, Luigi Gui (*CD*).
Grace and Justice, Oronzo Reale (*PRI*).
Budget and Economic Planning, Giulio Andreotti
(*CD*).
Finance, Bruno Visentini (*PRI*).
Treasury, Emilio Colombo (*CD*).
Defence, Arnaldo Forlani (*CD*).
Education, Franco Maria Malfatti (*CD*).
Public Works, Pietro Bucalossi (*PRI*).
Agriculture, Giovanni Marcora (*CD*).
Transport and Civil Aviation, Mario Martinelli
(*CD*).
Posts and Telecommunications, Giulio Orlando (*CD*).
Industry, Commerce and Arts and Crafts, Carlo Donat
Cattin (*CD*).
Labour and Social Security, Mario Toros (*CD*).
Foreign Trade, Ciriaco De Mita (*CD*).
Merchant Marine, Giovanni Gioia (*CD*).
State Participation, Antonio Bisaglia (*CD*).
Health, Nino Gullotti (*CD*).
Tourism and Entertainment, Adolfo Sarti (*CD*).
Ministers without Portfolio:
Regions, Tommaso Morlino (*CD*).
Scientific Research, Mario Pedini (*CD*).
Administrative Reform, Francesco Cossiga (*CD*).
Culture and Environment, Giovanni Spadolini
(*PRI*).
CD= Christian Democrat.
PRI= Republican.

ITALIAN EMBASSY IN LONDON
14 Three Kings Yard, Davies Street, W.1
[01-629 8200]
Ambassador Extraordinary and Plenipotentiary, His
Excellency Signor Roberto Ducci (1975).
Minister, Signor R. Paolini.
Minister-Counsellor, Sig. M. Egidi (*Commercial*).
First Counsellor, Sig. G. Borga.
Counsellors, Sig. L. M. Falconi (*Labour*); Sig. C.
Civiletti (*Press*).
1st Secretary, Sig. B. Uguccioni (*Commercial*).
2nd Secretaries, Sig. P. B. Francese; Sig. F. Mistretta;
Sig. F. Trupiano.
Defence and Naval Attaché, Rear-Admiral F.
Mottolese.
Asst. Defence and Naval Attaché, Lt.-Cdr. C. Bruno.
Military Attaché, Lt.-Col. L. Caligaris.
Asst. Military Attaché, Lt.-Col. N. Russo.
Air Attaché, Col. C. d'Antonio.
Asst. Air Attaché, Lt.-Col. T. Lusi.
Financial Attaché, Sig. E. Battiati.
Cultural Attaché, Prof. M. Montuori.

Italian Consulate General, 38 Eaton Place, S.W.1.
(01-235 4831).
Consul General, Sig. S. M. Siggia.
Italy is a Republic in the South of Europe, consisting of a peninsula, the large islands of Sicily and
Sardinia, the island of Elba and about 70 islands
(with certain dependencies noted below). Italy is
bounded on the N. by Switzerland and Austria, on
the S. by the Mediterranean, on the E. by the
Adriatic and Yugoslavia, etc., and on the W. by
France and the Ligurian and Tyrrhenian Seas.
The total area is about 324,000 sq. kilometres
(131,000 sq. miles).
The peninsula is for the most part mountainous,
but between the Apennines, which form its spine,
and the East coastline are two large fertile plains; of
Emilia/Romagna in the north and of Apulia in the
south. The Alps form the northern limit of Italy,
dividing it from France, Switzerland, Austria and
Yugoslavia. *Mont Blanc* (15,782 feet), the highest
peak, is in the French Pennine Alps, but partly within the Italian borders are Monte Rosa (15,217 feet),
Matterhorn (14,780 feet) and several peaks from
12,000 to 14,000 feet.
The chief rivers are the Po (405 miles), which
flows through Piedmont, Lombardy and the
Veneto and the Adige (Trentino and Veneto) in the
north, the Arno (Florentine Plain) and the Tiber
(flowing through Rome to Ostia). The *Rubicon*, a
small stream flowing into the Adriatic near Rimini
(and now usually identified with the Fiumicino)
formed the boundary between Italy and Cisalpine
Gaul: "crossing the Rubicon" (as Cæsar did in
49 B.C., thus "invading" Italy in arms) is used to
indicate definite committal to some course of action.
Population.—Italy has a resident population
estimated at 54,683,136 in October, 1970, about
417 persons per sq. mile. Live births in 1970
totalled 917,496, deaths, 528,622 and marriages
395,321 (estimated).
Government.—Italian unity was accomplished
under the House of Savoy, after an heroic struggle
from 1848 to 1870, in which the great patriots
Mazzini (1805-72), Garibaldi (1807-82) and
Cavour (1810-61) were the principal figures. It
was completed when Lombardy was ceded by
Austria in 1859 and Venice in 1866, and through
the evacuation of Rome by the French in 1870.
In 1871 the King of Italy entered Rome, and
that city was declared to be the capital.
Benito Mussolini, known as *Il Duce* (The
Leader) was born July 29, 1883, and was continuously in office as Prime Minister from June 30,
1925, until July 25, 1943, when the Fascist *régime*
was abolished. He was captured by Italian
partisans while attempting to escape across the
Swiss frontier and was put to death on April 28,
1945.
In fulfilment of a promise given in April, 1944,
that he would retire when the Allies entered Rome
a decree was signed on June 5, 1944, by the late King
Victor Emmanuel III under which Prince Umberto,
the King's son, became "Lieutenant-General of the
Realm." The King remained head of the House
of Savoy and retained the title of King of Italy until
his abdication on May 9, 1946, when he was succeeded by the Crown Prince.
A general election was held on June 2, 1946,
together with a referendum on the question of
Republic or Monarchy. The Referendum resulted in 12,717,923 votes for a Republic and
10,719,284 for a Monarchy. The Royal Family
left the country on June 13, and on June 28, 1946,
a Provisional President was elected.
Constitution.—The constitution of the Republic
of Italy, approved by the Constituent Assembly
on December 22, 1947, provides for the election of

the President by an electoral college which consists of the two Houses of Parliament (the Chamber of Deputies and the Senate) sitting in joint session together with three delegates from each region (one in the case of the Valle d'Aosta). The President, who must be over 50 years of age, holds office for 7 years. He has numerous carefully defined powers, the main one of which is the right to dissolve one or both Houses of Parliament, after consultation with their Speakers.

The elections for the sixth President began on December 9, 1971. The Christian Democrats nominated Senator Amintore Fanfani as their candidate, and the Socialists Francesco de Martino, Deputy Prime Minister. There were other candidates, including the retiring President. Neither of the two main candidates could secure the majority required for election—two-thirds on the first three ballots and a simple majority subsequently—and both eventually withdrew. Instead, the Christian Democrats nominated Senator Giovanni Leone, who had been the party's unsuccessful candidate in 1964, and the Socialists, Senator Pietro Nenni. Senator Leone was elected President at the twenty-third ballot on December 24 with 518 votes (the required majority was 505). Senator Nenni received 408 votes. The new President was sworn in before Parliament in joint session on December 29, 1971.

Since the General Election of 1948, governments have been formed by Signor de Gasperi (1948–53, coalition); Signor Pella (1953–54, *Christian Democrat*); Signor Scelba (1954–55, coalition); Signor Segni (July, 1955–May, 1957, coalition); Signor Zoli (June, 1957–May, 1958, *Christian Democrat*); Signor Fanfani (May, 1958–Feb., 1959, coalition); S. Segni (Feb., 1959–Feb., 1960, *Christian Democrat*, with *Liberal* support). Signor Tambroni (March 25–July 1960, *Christian Democrat*, with Neo-Fascist support); Signor Fanfani (July 27, 1960–Feb., 1962, *Christian Democrat*); Signor Fanfani (Feb. 1962–June, 1963, coalition); Signor Leone (June–Nov., 1963, *Christian Democrat*); Signor Moro (coalitions formed, Nov., 1963; July, 1964; Feb., 1966); Sen. Leone (May, 1968–December, 1968, *Christian Democrat*); Sig. Rumor (December, 1968–June, 1969, Centre Left coalition); Sig. Rumor (second Government) (August, 1969–April, 1970, *Christian Democrat*); Sig. Rumor (third Government, April–Aug., 1970, Centre Left coalition); Sig. Colombo (Aug., 1970–Feb., 1972, Centre Left coalition); Sig. Andreotti (Feb., 1972, *Christian Democrat*); Sig. Andreotti (June, 1972–June, 1973, *Christian Democrat, Social Democrat* and *Liberals*); Sig. Rumor (July, 1973–March, 1974) (*Centre Left Coalition*); Sig. Rumor (March 1974–Oct. 1974) (*Centre Left Coalition*); Sig. Moro (Nov., 1974, *Christian Democrat and Republican*).

Following the general election in May, 1972, the President called on Sig. Andreotti (*CD*) to try to form a government. It proved impossible to reconstitute a centre-left coalition on the lines of the Government headed earlier by Sig. Colombo, mainly owing to differences between the Christian Democrats and the Socialists, or a government which included the Socialists and the Liberals. After lengthy negotiations Sig. Andreotti did succeed in forming a centre coalition which consisted of the Christian Democrats (not all sections of the party agreed to serve in the government), Social Democrats and Liberals. This government, which the Republicans agreed to support in Parliament, won votes of confidence in the two Houses on July 7 (Chamber of Deputies) and July 14 (Senate).

From the outset Sig. Andreotti's government suffered from the disadvantage of a small majority in Parliament. From early 1973 onwards it ran into serious difficulties when it was repeatedly defeated in Chamber and Senate Votes on various issues, because some of the left-wing members of the Christian Democrat party were voting with the opposition, and on May 29 the Republicans withdrew their Parliamentary support from the government. The Christian Democrat Congress in early June agreed that the party should seek to reconstitute a Centre Left government with the Socialists, and Sig. Andreotti resigned on June 12. Negotiations for the formation of a new Centre Left achieved success after the Socialists had decided, on July 4, to join the new coalition. On July 7 Sig. Rumor formed a new government consisting of Christian Democrats, Socialists, Social Democrats and Republicans. It received votes of confidence in the Senate on July 18 and in the Chamber of Deputies on July 20. On March 1, 1974, the Republicans withdrew from the coalition, following the resignation of their secretary as Treasury Minister. On March 6, Sig. Rumor accepted an invitation by President Leone to form a new coalition government. After fundamental disagreements on economic and political issues, the coalition broke down, and the Government was forced to resign on June 10. However, President Leone refused to accept the resignation, and called on the coalition parties to reconcile their differences.

A Government crisis was averted when the coalition parties reached a temporary agreement on economic policy, and on July 6, Sig. Rumor's government introduced a new package of fiscal measures which was subsequently approved (in a modified form) by Parliament. However, the differences among the coalition parties broke out again shortly afterwards, and Sig. Rumor was forced to resign on Oct. 3. After an unsuccessful attempt by Sig. Fanfani to form a Government, Sig. Moro (CD) formed a two-party coalition of Christian Democrats and Republicans, supported in Parliament by the Socialists and Social Democrats, which received its final vote of confidence in the National Assembly in December, 1974.

Defence.—The period of conscription is 18 months for the Army and Air Force and 12 months for the Navy. The *Army* consists of 300,000 men including 22,000 officers. It has two armoured divisions, five infantry divisions, four independent infantry brigades, five Alpine brigades, one independent armoured brigade, one missile brigade, one parachute brigade and one amphibious regiment. There is also a para-military force, the *Carabinieri*, about 84,000 strong. The *Navy* consists of 3 cruisers, 37 escorts including four G.W. destroyers, 10 submarines, 60 minesweepers and also coastal craft and fleet auxiliaries. Approximate strength: 43,000 uniformed personnel. The *Air Force* consists of 500 aircraft; approximate strength: 75,000 men.

REGIONS OF ITALY

Rome and Central Italy.—Rome was founded, according to legend, by Romulus in the year now known as 753 B.C. It was the focal point of Latin civilization and dominion under the Republic and afterwards under the Roman Empire and became the capital of Italy when the Kingdom was established in 1871. With a metropolitan population of 2,842,616, Rome has been recreating herself as a major capital in the 100 years since Italy's reunification. The capital is concerned mainly with tourism and government, but due partly to the fact that the power of the Central Government is increasingly felt by industry, and that the headquarters of the giant State and parastatal companies are located there, Rome's importance as a business centre, although far from rivalling that of Milan, is steadily increasing.

Lombardy and Milan.—In the small area around Milan, which has a metropolitan population of 1,724,819, are to be found some 22 per cent. of Italy's commercial and banking services and some 30 per cent. of her industry. Here too, a market for consumer goods greatly exceeds that of any other comparable area in Italy. Lombardy's population of some 8·3 million is growing fast, both naturally and by immigration, and enjoys a *per capita* income some 40 per cent. above the national average. The whole range of Italian industry is there. Most important are the steel, machine tool and motor car factories.

Turin and Piedmont.—Turin between 1861 and 1865 was Italy's first capital as the home of the Piedmontese Royal Family. Now with a metropolitan population of 1,187,832 it is famous as the headquarters of Europe's largest manufacturer of motor cars, produces 75 per cent. of Italy's motor vehicles and over 80 per cent. of its roller bearings. Turin is also Italy's second largest steel producing city. Piedmont is the centre of the Italian textile industry based mainly on Biella.

Genoa and the Ligurian Riviera.—Genoa, with a metropolitan population of 842,114, is Europe's fourth largest port and handles one-third of Italy's foreign trade. About 80 per cent. of the goods handled are imports. Anglo-Genoese trade goes back to the 13th century and 20 per cent. of Genoa's imports still come from Britain. Genoa is Italy's third most important industrial city.

Venice and the North-East.—Venice, with a metropolitan population of 367,528 is primarily a tourist attraction of unique beauty. It was founded in the middle of the 5th century by refugees from the mainland fleeing from Barbarian attacks. At the beginning of the 16th century it was one of the strongest and richest states of Europe, dominating Eastern Mediterranean trade. It lost its independence in 1797 when Napoleon handed it over to Austria. Industry is now developing in the Venice area, particularly on the autostrada linking Venice with her historical and now developing rivals, Verona, Vicenza, Padua and in the areas around Pordenone. Padua is known for mechanical equipment. Verona for paper and stationery, Treviso for consumer goods, and Valdagno for its woollen industry. An important electrical appliance industry is based near Treviso and at Pordenone. Near Trieste, which has a population of 277,135, is the modern Monfalcone shipyard. Present-day Trieste itself consists of Zone A, the area which was administered by the Allied Military Government from June 12, 1945, to October 26, 1954, when it was handed over to the Italian authorities. The remainder of the area of Trieste was administered by Yugoslavia after the War and handed over to that country in 1954 after the free territory of Trieste, an arrangement agreed in the

Italian Peace Treaty of 1947, had proved to be un-workable.

Tuscany, Emilia and Romagna.—In 1940–45 this area was the agricultural centre of Italy and there was little industry. Now there are large industrial centres at Bologna (metropolitan population, 493,700), Florence (metropolitan population, 460,944), Modena, Pistola and Ravenna. Most of the new firms are small or medium-sized. In Prato there are about 1,000 textile firms. The footwear industry is based on Florence, reproduction furniture at Cascina and Poggibonsi, ceramics at Sassuolo, and glass and pottery at Empoli and Montelupo. Bologna is an important centre for the food industry. Florence, the capital of Tuscany was one of the greatest and most creative cities in Europe from the 11th to the 16th centuries. Under the Medici family in the 15th century flourished many of the greatest names in Italian art, including Filippo Lippi, Botticelli, Donatello and Brunelleschi. In the 16th century the tide turned to Rome where great Florentine artists like Michelangelo and Leonardo da Vinci flourished.

Naples and the Toe of Italy.—Naples (metropolitan population 1,258,721), formerly the capital and administrative centre of the Kingdom of Naples and Sicily, remains the dominant city in the area, but it is beset with great problems of unemployment and the need for modernization. Around it, however, helped by Government incentives, industry is slowly developing, northwards to Caserta, southwards to Salerno and eastwards to Benevento.

Puglia.—Bari (metropolitan population, 356,250) has always been a commercial centre. Fairly rapid industrial development is now taking place in the areas of Taranto, Bari, Brindisi and Foggia. At Taranto there are a highly-mechanized steel-works and a modern oil refinery. The Bari industrial zone has factories producing electronic and pneumatic valves, specialized vehicle bodies and tyres, etc. The main industry of Brindisi is a petro-chemical plant. At Foggia there is a textile factory.

Sicily.—The main source of income is agriculture, particularly citrus fruits, almonds and tomatoes, but this faces severe competition. Oil and oil products have recently supplanted citrus fruits as Sicily's main exports. The island is the scene of intense activity in the fields of oil, natural gas and petro-chemicals. Small and medium sized industries, benefiting from the Government's incentives, are developing. Of the island's 279 factories, some 90 are in the Catania area and 60 around Palermo (metropolitan population, 657,326), the capital of the island. Tourism is bringing an increasing amount of revenue to Sicily.

Sardinia.—Sardinia is another autonomous region, with its capital at Caliari (metropolitan population, 225,812). Six main industrial development areas have been officially designated; they are at Cagliari, Porto Vesme, Oristano, Sassari, Olbia and Arbatax. Lead and zinc mining are important. At Porto Vesme, a large smelting plant has been constructed. In the same area, a company is investing some £60 million in an aluminium plant. There is a flourishing tourist industry.

THE ECONOMY

Italian gross national income in 1974 was *lire* 97,182 milliards, as compared with *lire* 80,963 milliards in 1973. The economy developed fast in the fifties and early sixties with an average real annual increase in the gross national output of about 7 per cent. But its recovery after a setback caused by labour unrest in the last quarter of 1969, has been slower than was expected. After a partial recovery came the energy crisis of 1973/74. In 1975 the balance of payments deficit was reversed and

inflation halved but this was accompanied by stagnation and increasing unemployment.

Currency.—The market rate of exchange on July 10, 1975 stood at *lire* 1,394= £1.

Industry.—The general index of industrial production (1970= 100) stood at 119·4 in 1974, and 107·9 by March 1975. The State-owned sector of Italian industry is important, dominated by the holding companies IRI (mechanical, steel airlines), ENI (petro-chemicals) and ENEL (electricity).

Mineral Production.—Italy is generally poor in mineral resources but since the war deposits of natural methane gas and smaller deposits of oil have been discovered and rapidly exploited. Production of lignite has also increased. Other minerals produced in significant quantities include iron ores and pyrites, mercury (over one-quarter of the world production), lead, zinc and aluminium. Marble is a traditional product of the Massa Carrara district. Tobacco is still a Government monopoly.

Agriculture.—Agriculture accounted for 9·2 per cent. of gross domestic product in 1972, and at the end of 1974 employed about 16·5 per cent. of the working population. Some three-quarters of the 3,785,000 farms and small holdings are privately owned and operated. In the period 1964–71 Italy was a net exporter of rice, vegetables, fresh and dried fruit and wine, but the rising standard of living has increased imports of foodstuffs, particularly meat and animal food.

Tourist Traffic.—About 32,910,000 visitors entered Italy in 1974, a decline of 9 per cent. from 1973.

Communications.—The main railway system is State-run by the *Ferrovia dello Stato*. A network of motorways (*autostrade*) covers the country, built and operated mainly by the IRI State-holding company and ANAS the State highway authority. The autostrada network covered 5,176 kms. in 1974. *Alitalia*, the principal international and domestic airline, is also State-controlled by the IRI group. Other smaller companies, including ATI (an *Alitalia* subsidiary) and *Iravia* operate on domestic routes. The Italian mercantile marine total of 8,378,000 tons in December, 1972, compared with 3,500,000 tons before the War.

FOREIGN TRADE

Total Italian imports in 1974 were 26,603 milliard *lire* (an increase of 64 per cent. over 1973). Exports amounted to 19,683 milliard *lire* (up 51·8 per cent. over 1973).

The main markets for Italian exports were West Germany (22·9 per cent.), France (14·2 per cent.) and U.S.A. (9·8 per cent.). The U.K. accounted for 4·3 per cent. of Italian exports. The main commodities exported were: machinery, motor vehicles, iron and steel, footwear, textiles and clothing, plastic and artificial resins and materials. The main commodities imported were petroleum products, iron and steel, meat, copper and motor vehicles. The E.E.C. provides the largest share in Italy's imports (55·7 per cent. in 1974). The U.K.'s share has decreased from 6·3 per cent. in 1963 to 3 per cent. in 1974.

Trade with U.K.

	1973	1974
Imports from U.K.	£386,100,000	£510,000,000
Exports to U.K.	504,400,000	723,800,000

Language and Literature.—Italian is a Romance language derived from Latin. It is spoken in its purest form at Siena (Tuscany), but there are numerous dialects, showing variously French, German, Spanish and Arabic influences. Sard, the dialect of Sardinia, is accorded by some authorities the status of a distinct Romance language. Italian literature (in addition to Latin literature, which is the common inheritance of the civilized world) is one of the richest in Europe, particularly in its golden age (Dante, 1265–1321; Petrarch, 1304–1374; and Boccaccio, 1313–1375) and in the renaissance during the fifteenth and sixteenth centuries (Ariosto, 1474–1533; Machiavelli, 1469–1527; Tasso, 1544–1595). Modern Italian literature has many noted names in prose and verse, notably Manzoni (1785–1873), Carducci (1835–1907) and Gabriele d'Annunzio (1864–1938). The Nobel Prize for Literature has been awarded to Italian authors on four occasions—G. Carducci (1906), Signora G. Deledda (1926), Luigi Pirandello (1934) and Salvatore Quasimodo (1959). In 1971, there were 85 daily newspapers published in Italy, of which 22 were published in Rome and 10 in Milan.

Education.—Education is free and compulsory between the ages of 6 and 14; this comprises five years at primary school and three in the "middle school", of which there are about 8,000. Pupils who obtain the middle school certificate may seek admission to any "senior secondary school", which is roughly equivalent to a U.K. grammar school but may be a lyceum with a classical or scientific or artistic bias, or may be an institute or school for teacher training, or may be an institute directed at technology (of which there are eight different types) or trade or industry (including vocational schools). Courses at the lyceums and technical institutes usually last for five years and success in the final examination qualifies for admission to university. There are 35 State and 14 private universities, some of ancient foundation; those at Bologna, Modena, Parma and Padua were started in the 12th century. University education is not free, but entrants with higher qualifications are charged reduced fees according to a sliding scale. In general, schools, lyceums and universities are financed by local taxation and central government grants.

CAPITAL, Rome. Metropolitan population (estimated Oct. 1971), 2,842,616.

Oct. 1971 estimates of the metropolitan population of the principal cities and towns are Milan, 1,724,819; Ψ Naples 1,258,721; Turin, 1,187,832; Ψ Genoa, 842,114; Bologna, 493,007; Florence, 460,944; Ψ Venice, 367,528; Ψ Bari, 356,250; Ψ Trieste, 277,135; Verona, 262,014; Padua, 228,854; Ψ Taranto, 223,392; Brescia, 209,659; Modena, 170,450; Ψ Reggio Calabria, 167,087; Ψ Salerno, 152,780; and Bergamo, 126,504; in *Sicily*; Ψ Palermo, 657,326; Ψ Catania, 414,619; Ψ Messina, 274,740; in *Sardinia*; Ψ Cagliari, 225,812.

ISLANDS.—*Pantelleria Island* (part of Trapani Province) in the Sicilian Narrows, has an area of 31 sq. miles and a population of 9,601. The *Pelagian Islands* (Lampedusa, Linosa and Lampione) are part of the Province of Agrigento and have an area of 8 sq. miles, pop. 4,811. The Tuscan Archipelago (including Elba), area 293 sq. km., pop. 31,861; Pontine Archipelago (including Ponza, area 10 sq. km., pop. 2,515); Flegrean Islands (including Ischia, area 60 sq. km., pop. 51,883); Capri; Eolian Islands (including Lipari, area 116 sq. km., pop. 18,636); Tremiti Islands (area 3 sq. km., pop. 426).

FLAG.—Vertical stripes of green, white and red.
NATIONAL DAY.—June 2.

BRITISH EMBASSY
Via XX Settembre 80a, Rome.
Ambassador Extraordinary and Plenipotentiary, His Excellency Sir Guy Elwin Millard, K.C.M.G., C.V.O. (1974).

Ministers, A. J. Williams, C.M.G., A. A. W. Landymore, C.B.E. (FAO).
Defence and Military Attaché, Col. P. E. B. Madsen.
Naval Attaché, Capt. C. E. T. Baker, M.B.E., R.N.
Air Attaché, Group-Capt. R. G. Churcher, D.S.O., M.V.O., D.F.C.
Counsellors, A. Brooke Turner (*Head of Chancery*); A. F. R. Harvey, O.B.E. (*Commercial*); M. R. Morland (*Economic*); K. Kenney, O.B.E. (*Labour*); C. de L. Herdon, O.B.E.
1st Secretaries, A. M. Layden; Sir Joseph Cheyne, Bt. (*Information*); N. H. Young (*Administration*); E. F. Macleod; J. H. Bailey (*Consul*); A. A. C. Nash, M.B.E. (*Commercial*); P. M. Scola (*Agriculture*); R. A. Fulton.
2nd Secretaries, J. Smith; C. P. P. Baldwin.
Asst. Defence Attaché, Maj. B. A. S. Leishman.
3rd Secretary, H. R. Mortimer.
Chaplain, Rev. D. Murfet.

BRITISH CONSULAR OFFICES
There are British Consular Offices at *Milan, Rome, Naples, Genoa, Florence, Palermo, Turin, Venice, Trieste, Messina* and *Cagliari* and a trade representative at *Bari*.

British Council Representative, R. E. Cavaliero, Palazzo del Drago, Via delle Quattro Fontane 20, 00184, Rome.
There are *British Council Institutes* at Milan and Naples, each with a library.

IVORY COAST
(République de Côte d'Ivoire)

President, Félix Houphouët-Boigny, *elected* for five years in 1960; *re-elected* 1965 and 1970.
President of National Assembly, Philippe Yacé.
President of Economic and Social Council, Mamadou Coulibaly.
President of Supreme Court, Alphonse Boni.
Ministers of State, Auguste Denise; Mathieu Ekra; Blaise N'Dia Koffi; Koffi Gadeau; Loua Diomandé.
Minister for Foreign Affairs, Arsène Assouan Usher.

IVORY COAST EMBASSY IN LONDON
2 Upper Belgrave Street, S.W.1
[01–235 6991]
Ambassador Extraordinary and Plenipotentiary, His Excellency Louis-Antoine Aduko (1973).
1st Counsellor, M. Patrice K. Anoh.
Counsellors, M. Georges N'Dia (*Head of Commercial Section*). M. Benjamin Amuah.
2nd Secretary, M. Raymond T. Diecket.
3rd Secretary, M. Kouakou G. Loukou.
Financial Attaché, M. Gérard Biatchon.

The Ivory Coast is situated on the Gulf of Guinea between 5° and 10° N. and 3° and 8° W. and is flanked on the West by Guinea and Liberia, on the North by Mali and Upper Volta and on the East by Ghana. It has an area of about 127,000 square miles—tropical rain forest in the southern half and savannah in the northern—and a population of 5,400,000 (1972 estimate) divided into a large number of ethnic and tribal groups.

Although official French contact was made in the first half of the 19th century, the Ivory Coast became a Colony only in 1893 and was finally pacified in 1912. It decided on December 5, 1958 to remain an autonomous republic within the French Community; full independence outside the Community was proclaimed on August 7, 1960. Special agreements with France, covering financial and cultural matters, technical assistance, defence, etc., were signed in Paris on April 24, 1961. The Ivory Coast was a founder member of the *Conseil de l'Entente*, established on May 29, 1959, as a loose union embracing also, without abrogation of sovereignty, Dahomey, Niger and Upper Volta. Togo also adhered in June, 1966. The Ivory Coast is also an Associated State of E.E.C. and a member of the *Organisation Commune Africaine et Malgache* (O.C.A.M.), the Organization of African Unity (O.A.U.) and the Communauté Economique de l'Afrique de l'Ouest (C.E.A.O.). The official language is French.

The Ivory Coast has a presidential system of government modelled on that of the United States and the French Fifth Republic. The single Chamber National Assembly of 100 members was elected in 1970 for five years. The defence of the Constitution which was promulgated on Nov. 3, 1960, is vested in a Supreme Court.

Finance.—The unit of currency of the Ivory Coast is the *Franc CFA (Francs CFA* 50= 1 French franc). In 1975, the Ivory Coast Budget totalled *Francs CFA* 180,841,000,000.

Trade.—The principal exports are coffee, cocoa, timber and bananas. The United Kingdom imports Ivory Coast timber, coffee, cocoa and bananas. Diamonds are exported. There are a few deposits of minerals including manganese and iron. Trade in 1974 was valued at: Imports, *Francs CFA* 232,286,000,000; Exports, *Francs CFA* 291,770,000,000.

Trade with U.K.

	1973	1974
Imports from U.K....	£3,937,000	£6,528,000
Exports to U.K.......	15,249,000	19,928,000

CAPITAL, Ψ Abidjan (population, 600,000) which is also the main port.

FLAG.—3 vertical stripes, orange, white and green.
NATIONAL DAY.—December 7.

BRITISH EMBASSY

Immeuble Shell, Abidjan, B.P. 2581.
Ambassador Extraordinary and Plenipotentiary, His Excellency Paul Cecil Henry Holmer, C.M.G. (1972).
(also Ambassador to *Niger* and *Upper Volta*).
1st Secretary, F. M. A. Cargill (*Commercial*).
2nd Secretary, P. J. Wilson (*Vice Consul*).
3rd Secretary, J. Bentley (*Admin.*).

JAPAN
(Nippon Koku—Land of the Rising Sun)

Emperor of Japan, His Majesty Hirohito, *born* April 29, 1901; *succeeded* Dec. 25, 1926; *married* (1924) Princess Nagako (*born* March 6, 1903), daughter of the late Prince Kuniyoshi Kuni, and has issue two sons and four daughters.

Heir-Apparent, His Imperial Highness Prince Akihito, *Crown Prince, born* Dec. 23, 1933; *married* April 10, 1959, Miss Michiko Shoda and has issue Prince Naruhito Hironomiya, *born* Feb. 23, 1960, Prince Fumihito, *born* Nov. 30, 1965 and Princess Sayako, *born* April 18, 1969.

CABINET

Prime Minister, Takeo Miki.
Deputy Prime Minister (and Director-General, Economic Planning Agency), Takeo Fukuda.
Justice, Osamu Inaba.
Foreign Affairs, Kiichi Miyazawa.
Finance, Masayoshi Ohira.
Education, Michio Nagai.
Health and Welfare, Masami Tanaka.
Agriculture, Shintaro Abe.
International Trade and Industry, Toshio Komoto.
Transport, Mutsuo Kimura.
Posts and Telecommunications, Isamu Murakami.
Labour, Takashi Hasegawa.
Construction, Tadao Kariya.
Home Affairs, Hakime Fukuda.
Ministers of State, Ichitaro Ide (*Chief Cabinet Secre-*

tary); Mitsunori Ueki (*Prime Minister's Office, and Director-General, Okinawa Development Agency*); Yuzo Matsuzawa (*Director General, Administrative Management Agency*); Michita Sakata (*Director-General, Defence Agency*); Yoshitake Sasaki (*Director-General, Science and Technology Agency*; *Chairman, Atomic Energy Commission*); Tatsuo Ozawa (*Director-General, Environment Agency*); Shin Kanemaru (*Director-General, Land Development Agency*).

JAPANESE EMBASSY AND CONSULATE

43–46 Grosvenor Street, W.1
Information Centre: 9 Grosvenor Square, W.1
[01–493 6030]

Ambassador Extraordinary and Plenipotentiary, His Excellency, Tadao Kato (1975).
Minister, Toshijiro Nakajima.
Minister, Yasuhiko Sano (*Commercial*).
Minister, Yoshihito Amano (*Financial*).
Counsellor, Hiroshi Hashimoto (*Consul General*).
Counsellors, Noboru Nakahira; Eiichi Fujita (*Agriculture*); Michihiko Kunihiro; Masanori Ito (*Consular*); Tatsuro Suzuki (*Financial*); Rokuro Nagaoka (*Home Affairs*); Masahiko Kashiwagi (*Commercial*).
1st Secretaries, Capt. Hideo Sato (*Defence Attaché*); Mitsumasa Iwata (*Transport*); Yutaka Kubota (*Agriculture*); Hiroshi Ota (*Press and Information*); Minoru Matsui; Yasuo Yashima (*Labour*); Takaya Suto (*Economic*); Issei Nomura; Kenji Ogawa (*Transport*); Yasuo Ebisawa; Koichi Kikuchi; Moto Uwano (*Press and Information*); Kazuo Ichinose; Ryusuke Sakai; Yasuhide Hayashi (*Commercial*); Masaharu Wakasa (*Scientific*).

Area and Population.—Japan consists of 4 large and many small islands situated in the North Pacific Ocean between longitude 128° 6' East and 145° 49' East and between latitude 26° 59' and 45° 31' N., with a total area of 142,812 square miles and a population (1974) of 110,050,000.

Japan Proper consists of *Honshū* (or Mainland), 230,448 sq. k. (88,839 sq. m.), *Shikoku*, 18,757 sq. k. (7,231 sq. m.), *Kyūshū*, 42,079 sq. k. (16,170 sq. m.), *Hokkaido*, 78,508 sq. k. (30,265 sq. m.). Formosa and the Kwangtung Province, which had been throughout the years of Japanese expansion and aggression leased or annexed, reverted to Chinese sovereignty after the War of 1939–45.

After the unconditional surrender to the Allied Nations (Aug. 14, 1945), Japan was occupied by Allied forces under General MacArthur (Sept. 15, 1945). A Japanese peace treaty conference opened at San Francisco on Sept. 4, 1951, and on Sept. 8, 48 nations signed the treaty, which became effective on April 28, 1952. Japan then resumed her status as an independent power.

British participation in the occupation of Japan was virtually over by May, 1950. However, the outbreak of hostilities in Korea in June, 1950, resulted in the despatch to Korea of British Forces, from the United Kingdom, Australia, New Zealand and Canada to participate in the United Nations action. The main base of this force was established in Japan at Kure. On July 1, 1956, the base was moved to Inchon, Korea, and all Commonwealth troops had left Japan by the middle of 1957.

Under the terms of the Japan–U.S.A. Security Treaty of Sept. 8, 1951, United States forces remained to assist in the defence of Japan. However, as Japan's own Self Defence Forces have been built up, U.S. ground troops have been withdrawn. A revised version of the security treaty, which went into effect on June 23, 1960, was the subject of considerable controversy in the summer of that year.

Vital Statistics.—The birth rate in 1973 was 19·4 per 1,000 (1947, 34 per 1,000; 1967, 19·7 per 1,000). It has been stated that a considerable part in reducing the birth rate to its present level was played by drastic methods, induced abortion and sterilization, the legal sanction for which had been extended by the Eugenics Law, 1948, to include economic and social hardships. The improving standard of living has also played an important part in keeping the birthrate down.

The death rate in 1973 was 6·6 per 1,000, compared with 17 per 1,000 in per-war years, natural increase of the population being 1,382,500 in 1973.

Physiography.—The coastline exceeds 17,000 miles and is deeply indented, so that few places are far from the sea. The interior is very mountainous, and crossing the mainland from the Sea of Japan to the Pacific is a group of volcanoes, mainly extinct or dormant. Mount Fuji, the loftiest and most sacred mountain of Japan, about 60 miles from Tokyo, is 12,370 ft. high and has been dormant since 1707, but there are other volcanoes which are active, including Mount Aso in Kyūshū. There are frequent earthquakes, mainly along the Pacific coast near the Bay of Tokyo. Japan proper extends from sub-tropical in the south to cool temperate in the north. Heavy snowfalls are frequent on the western slopes of Hokkaidō and Honshū, but the Pacific coasts are warmed by the Japan current. There is a plentiful rainfall and the rivers are short and swift-flowing, offering abundant opportunities for the supply of hydro-electric power.

Government.—According to Japanese tradition, Jimmu, the First Emperor of Japan, ascended the throne on Feb. 11, 660 B.C. Under the constitution of Feb. 11, 1889, the monarchy was hereditary in the male heirs of the Imperial house. A new constitution approved by the Supreme Allied Commander was published on March 6, 1946, superseding the " *Meiji Constitution* " of 1889, and containing many radical changes based on the constitutional practices of the United Kingdom, U.S.A. and France.

The new constitution came into force on May 3, 1947. Legislative authority rests with *The Diet*, which is bicameral, consisting of a *House of Representatives* and a *House of Councillors*, both Houses

being composed of elected members. Executive authority is vested in the Cabinet which is responsible to the Legislature.

A General Election was held in December 1972, in which the Liberal Democratic Party was once more returned to power. The strength of the parties in the House of Representatives on July 15, 1975, was: Liberal Democratic Party, 276; Japan Socialist Party, 114; Japan Communist Party, 39; Komeito, 30; Democratic Socialist Party, 20; Independent, 1; vacant, 11.

A regular election for the House of Councillors was held in 1974. The Liberal Democratic Party maintained their overall majority in the Upper House. The state of the parties there is now: Liberal Democratic Party, 130; Japan Socialist Party, 61; Komeito, 24; Japan Communist Party, 20; Democratic Socialist Party, 10; Niin Club, 4; Independent, 3.

Ryuku Islands (Okinawa).—Since World War II the appointment of a Chief Executive, chosen by the local legislature, had been subject to the approval of the United States High Commissioner. After reversion, the former Chief Executive, Mr. Chobyu Yara, was re-elected as Governor of Okinawa Prefecture.

Agriculture and Livestock.—Owing to the mountainous nature of the country not more than one-sixth of its area is available for cultivation. The forest land included Cryptomeria japonica, Pinus massoniana, Zeikowa keaki, and Pawlonia imperialis, in addition to camphor, trees, mulberry, vegetable wax tree and a lacquer tree which furnishes the celebrated lacquer of Japan. The soil is only moderately fertile, but intensive cultivation secures good crops. The tobacco plant, tea shrub, potato, rice, wheat and other cereals are all cultivated: rice is the staple food of the people, about 12,292,000 metric tons being produced in 1974. The floral kingdom is rich, beautiful and varied. Fruit is abundant, including the mandarin, persimmon, loquat and peach; European fruits such as apples, strawberries, pears, grapes and figs are also produced.

Minerals.—The country has mineral resources, including gold and silver, and copper, lead, zinc, iron chromite, white arsenic, coal, sulphur, petroleum, salt and uranium, but iron ore, coal and crude oil are among the principal post-war imports to supply deficiencies at home.

Industry.—Japan is the most highly industrialized nation in the Far East, with the whole range of modern light and heavy industries, including mining, metals, machinery, chemicals, textiles (cotton, silk, wool and synthetics), cement, pottery, glass, rubber, lumber, paper, oil refining and shipbuilding. The labour force of Japan in 1970 was 51,530,000, of which only 590,000 were unemployed. Of the total labour force, some 42,510,000 were engaged in non-agricultural industries, 8,860,000 in agriculture, forestry and fisheries.

Communications.—There were 26,796 kilometres of Government and private railroad (steam and electric) in March, 1973. The merchant fleet (ocean-going ships over 3,000 tons gross) consisted of 1,152 vessels totalling 31,230,000 tons gross in April, 1974.

Armed Forces.—After the unconditional surrender of August, 1945, the Imperial Army and Navy were disarmed and disbanded and all aircraft confiscated by the occupying forces.

Although the Constitution of Japan prohibits the maintenance of armed forces, an internal security force, known as the National Police Reserve, came into being in August, 1950, and a Maritime Safety Force was established in April,

1952. In August, 1952, these Forces were renamed the National Safety Force and the Coastal Safety Force and were placed under a National Safety Agency. In July, 1954, the Agency was renamed the Defence Agency, the Forces under it the Ground Self Defence Force and the Maritime Self Defence Force respectively, and a new arm, the Air Self Defence Force, was created. At the same time the mission of the forces was extended to include the defence of Japan against direct and indirect aggression.

A Treaty of Mutual Co-operation and Security between Japan and the U.S.A. was signed in January, 1960, replacing an earlier Security Treaty signed in 1951 at the same time as the Peace Treaty. By this Treaty each country recognised that an armed attack against either in the territories under the administration of Japan would be dangerous to its own safety and declared that it would act to counter the danger.

The defence budget allocated for the fiscal year 1975/76 amounted to Yen 1,327 billion, equivalent to 0·84 per cent. of Japan's Gross National Product, or 6·23 per cent. of the total budget. The authorised uniformed strength was: Ground Self-Defence Force (GSDF) 180,000 (Reserve 36,000); Maritime Self-Defence Force (MSDF) 41,388 (Reserve 300); Air Self-Defence Force (ASDF) 44,575 (Reserve 490).

In 1975 the GSDF was organised into five Armies of thirteen Divisions. In addition, in the Northern Army there were one Artillery Brigade, one Anti-Aircraft Artillary Brigade and one Tank Brigade; the Eastern Army had one Airborne Brigade and all five Armies had one Engineer Brigade, Under the Ground Staff Office there were one Helicopter Brigade and one Signal Brigade, Seven divisions had an authorised strength of almost 9,000 (four combat groups) and the remainder of about 7,000 (three combat groups). Major equipment included 610 tanks, 465 APCs, 4,620 artillery pieces, 50 missiles, 130 Hawks, and 390 aircraft. Equipment is now largely manufactured in Japan.

The MSDF has 161 warships totalling 159,775 tons and including two DDH, two TARTAR-equipped GMDs, 45 escort ships, 16 submarines and 96 others. The MSDF has a total of 286 aircraft (75 helicopters, 30 S2F-1, 30 P2V-7, 46 P2J-1, 14 PS1 A/S flying boats and 91 others).

The ASDF has about 950 aircraft (160 F104J, 280 F86F, 40 F4EJ, 14 RF4E; 260 trainers T34, Fuji T-1, T-33, F104DH; 50 transports and about 100 search and rescue and communications). The principal fighter is the F104J augmented by the F4EJ. Domestically designed and built supersonic T2 trainers and C1 cargo planes have entered service. There are about 5 Nike surface to air missile units.

Religion.—All religions are tolerated. The principal religions of Japan are Mahayana Buddhism and Shinto. The Roman Catholic Church has 1 Cardinal, 1 archbishop and 14 bishops. The Nippon Seikokai (Holy Catholic Church of Japan) has 11 Japanese bishops (1968) and is an autonomous branch of the Anglican communion. There is also a United Protestant Church.

Education.—Under the Education Law of 1948 education at elementary (6 year course) and lower secondary (3 year course) is free, compulsory and co-educational. They have courses in general, agricultural, commercial, technical, mercantile marine, radio-communication and home-economics education, etc. 32·2 per cent. of upper secondary school leavers went on to higher education in 1973. There are 2 or 3 year junior colleges and

4 year universities. Some of the 4 year universities have graduate schools. In May 1973 there were 905 universities and junior colleges, 101 state maintained, 78 local authority maintained and 726 privately maintained. The most prominent universities are the seven State Universities of Tokyo, Kyoto, Tohoku (Sendai), Hokkaido (Sapporo), Kyushu (Fukuoka), Osaka and Nagoya, and the two private universities, Keio and Waseda.

Language and Literature.—Japanese is said to be one of the Uro-Altaic group of languages and remained a spoken tongue until the fifth–seventh centuries A.D., when Chinese characters came into use. Japanese who have received school education (99·8 per cent. of the population) can read and write the Chinese characters in current use (about 1,800 characters) and also the syllabary characters called Kana. English is the best known foreign language. It is taught in all middle and high schools. By 1973, the number of public libraries was 915, with 33,587,084 volumes. In addition there are 1,059 university libraries with 66,485,099 volumes. There are 123 daily newspapers in Japan. Japan's total newspaper circulation was estimated at 39,847,332 copies and 1·25 per household at the end of 1973. The National Diet Library contained in 1973 2,866,956 books; 135,602 atlases; 140,098 public records; 47,382 items of microfilm; and 26,695 periodicals.

FINANCE

The Budget for the financial year 1974–75, ending on March 31, was initially estimated to balance at Yen 21,288,800,000,000 for revenue and expenditure on the general account, an increase of 24·5 per cent. over the preceding financial year, before the Supplementary Budget and 10·9 per cent. after the Supplementary Budget.

The market rate of exchange with Sterling in July 1975, was Yen 653= £1. (*see also* p. 83).

PRODUCTION AND TRADE

Being deficient in natural resources, Japan has had to develop a complex foreign trade. Principal imports consist of mineral oils (30·4 per cent.), raw materials (23·4 per cent.) e.g. metal ores, 8·6 per cent., timber, 5·9 per cent.; raw cotton, 1·7 per cent.; and soya beans, 1·4 per cent.), foodstuffs (13·1 per cent.) (e.g. wheat and sugar) machinery (7·6 per cent.), chemicals (4·3 per cent.) and textiles (2·9 per cent.). Principal exports consist of steel (24·7 per cent.), ships (10·1 per cent.), automobiles (9·4 per cent.), electric machinery and appliances (12·1 per cent.), non-electric machinery (10·7 per cent.), chemicals (7·3 per cent.) and textile goods (7·3 per cent.).

FOREIGN TRADE

	1973 ($1,000)	1974 ($1,000)
Total imports........	38,313,604	62,110,456
Total Exports........	36,929,971	55,535,755

TRADE WITH U.K.

	1973	1974
Imports from U.K...	£272,598,000	£319,047,000
Exports to U.K......	443,394,000	570,009,000

CAPITAL.—TOKYO. Population (estimated March 1, 1971), 11,403,744. The other chief cities had the following populations at the beginning of 1971: Ψ Osaka (2,980,409); Ψ Nagoya (2,037,952); Ψ Yokohama (2,273,209); Kyoto, the ancient capital (1,415,880); Ψ Kobé (1,294,373); Kita-Kyushu (1,042,319); Ψ Sapporo (1,010,123); Ψ Kawasaki (973,486); Ψ Fukuoka (853,270).

FLAG.—White, charged with sun (red).

NATIONAL DAY.—April 29 (Birthday of the Emperor).

Yokohama, by sea *via* Cape Town, 14,653 miles (50 days); *via* Panama, 12,544 miles (35 days); Tokyo, by air (B.O.A.C., polar route), 8,382 miles distant from London: transit, 17 hrs.; (B.O.A.C. trans-Siberia route (13 hrs.).

BRITISH EMBASSY
(Ichiban-cho, Chiyoda-ku, Tokyo)

Ambassador Extraordinary and Plenipotentiary, His Excellency Kenneth Michael Wilford, C.M.G. (1975).

Minister, P. A. G. Westlake, C.M.G., M.C.

Minister (Commercial and Economic), C. S. R. Giffard.

Counsellors, R. A. H. Duke, C.V.O., C.B.E. (*Cultural*); H. A. J. Prentice (*Scientific*); R. E. G. Burges Watson (*Economic*); B. Thorne, M.B.E. (*Commercial*); N. J. Barrington, C.V.O. (*Head of Chancery*); W. K. Slatcher, C.V.O. (*Information*).

1st Secretaries, L. Pickles, O.B.E. (and *Consul-General*); R. A. Kidd; F. M. Beatty, M.B.E. (*Cultural*); G. R. H. Geoghegan, O.B.E. (*Atomic Energy*); R. G. Farrar, M.V.O.; E. J. Field (*Commercial*); C. A. Axworthy (*Administration*); J. G. Dearlove; Dr. P. E. Roe (*Scientific*); Miss H. B. Reid; A. N. R. Millington (*Economic*); P. W. Denison-Edson, M.V.O.; A. E. Lewis; P. M. Newton (*Economic*); J. W. MacDonald (*Commercial*).

2nd Secretaries, R. S. Howe, M.B.E. (*Commercial*); T. Havey (*Administration*); A. F. Pinnell (*Commercial*); C. T. W. Humfrey (*Economic*); J. A. Towner; P. B. Preece; R. F. Cooper, M.V.O. (*Commercial*); S. J. Gomersall (*Information*); D. F. Parsons; Mrs. C. E. Coates (*Commercial*).

3rd Secretaries, S. D. M. Jack; G. H. Fry.

Defence and Military Attaché, Col. D. L. Heffill.

Naval Attaché, Captain C. McK. Little, A.F.C., R.N.

Air Attaché, Group Captain R. H. B. Dixon.

Financial Attaché, J. E. W. Kirby.

Assistant Defence Attaché, Lt.-Col. D. O. Caton.

There is a British Consulate-General at *Osaka* and Honorary Consulates at *Nagoya* and *Kita Kyushu*.

JORDAN
(The Hashemite Kingdom of The Jordan)

King of the Jordan, Hussein, G.C.V.O., *born* November 14, 1935, *succeeded* on the deposition of his father, King Talal, Aug. 11, 1952, *assumed constitutional powers*, May 2, 1953, *on coming of age.*

Crown Prince, Prince Hassan, third son of King Talal of Jordan, *born* 1948, *appointed Crown Prince*, April 1, 1965.

CABINET
(Nov. 24, 1974)

Prime Minister, Foreign Affairs and Defence, Sayid Zeid al Rifai.

Reconstruction and Development, Dr. Subhi Amin Amr.

Culture and Information, Sayid Salah Abu Zeid.

Transport, Sayid Khaled al Haj Hassan.

Education, Sayid Dhouqan al Hindawi.

Social Affairs and Labour, Sayid Sami Ayoub.

Finance, Sayid Salem al Masa'deh.

Tourism and Antiquities, Sayid Ghaleb Barakat.

Communcations, Sayid Ahmad al Shobaki.

Supply, Sayid Ali Hassan Odeh.

Agriculture, Sayid Marwan al Hmoud.

Wakfs, Islamic Affairs and Shrines, Dr. (Sheikh) Abdul Aziz al Khayyat.

Public Works, Sayid Mahmoud al Hawamdeh.

Interior, Sayid Tharwat al Talhouni.

Justice, Sayid Naji Hussein al Tarawneh.

Health, Dr. Trad Se'oud al Qadi.

Interior for Municipal and Rural Affairs, Dr. Muhammad 'Addoub al Zaben.

National Economy, Dr. Rajai al Mu'asher.

Ministers of State, Sayid Sadeq al Share (*Foreign Affairs*); Sayid Rakan 'Inad al Jazi (*Prime Minister's Office*).

JORDANIAN EMBASSY AND CONSULATE
6 Upper Phillimore Gardens, W.8
[01-937 3685]

Ambassador Extraordinary and Plenipotentiary, His Excellency, Ma'an Abu Nowar.

Minister Plenipotentiary, Hani B. Tabbara.

Counsellor, Hassan Abu Nimah.

First Secretary, Miss Zein Samir Rifai (*Press.*).

Military, Naval and Air Attaché, Colonel Hassan Shawki Dia.

Service Office: 16 Upper Phillimore Gardens, W.8. (01-937-9611).

Area and Population.—The Kingdom, which covers 37,700 sq. miles, is bounded on the north by Syria, on the west by Israel, on the south by Saudi Arabia and on the east by Iraq. Since the hostilities of June, 1967, that part of the country lying to the west of the Jordan River has been under Israeli occupation. The majority of the population are Sunni Moslems and Islam is the religion of the State. Total population (1974) is 2,660,000, of whom 1,890,000 live in East Jordan and the remainder on the West Bank and in East Jerusalem. (*For* MAP, *see* p. 883).

History and Government.—After the defeat of Turkey in the First World War the Amirate of Transjordan was established in the area east of the River Jordan as a state under British mandate. The mandate was terminated after the Second World War and the Amirate, still ruled by its founder, the Amir Abdullah, became the Hashemite Kingdom of Jordan. Following the 1948 war between Israel and the Arab States, that part of Palestine remaining in Arab hands (but excluding Gaza) was incorporated into the Hashemite Kingdom. King Abdullah was assassinated in 1951; his son Talal ruled briefly but abdicated in favour of the present King, Hussein, in 1952. All of Jordan west of the River has been under Israeli occupation since 1967. As a result of the wars of 1948 and 1967 there are about 750,000 refugees and displaced persons living in East Jordan, about 200,000 of whom live in refugee and displaced persons camps established by the U.N. Relief and Works Agency (UNRWA). In addition there are some 300,000 entirely self-supporting Palestinian members of the East Jordanian community. It was largely among the refugee population that the Palestinian *fedayeen* (commando) movement which had come into existence some years earlier grew considerably in strength during 1969 and 1970. The *fedayeen* organizations conducted a number of operations against Israel but during 1970 came more and more into conflict with the Jordanian Government. After the civil war between the Jordan Army and the *fedayeen* the Jordan Government re-established its authority. The *fedayeen* were finally expelled from Jordan in the summer of 1971. In March 1972 King Hussein put forward a plan for the " United Arab Kingdom " which was to be implemented after liberation of the West Bank. The plan provides for the creation of a federal State, composed of two autonomous regions, Palestine and East Jordan. During the war of October 1973 between the Arab countries and Israel, Jordan sent two armoured brigades into Syria to support the Syrian campaign on the Golan Heights.

The present constitution of the Kingdom came into force in 1952. It provides for a senate of 30 members (all appointed by the King) and an elected House of Representatives of 60 persons. The

King himself appoints the members of the Council of Ministers. Crown Prince Hassan normally acts as Regent when King Hussein is away from Jordan.

Production and Industry.—West Jordan is fertile, though many areas have suffered from soil erosion. In East Jordan the main agricultural areas are the east part of the Jordan Valley, the hills overlooking the Valley and the flatter country to the south of Amman and around Madaba and Irbid. The rest of the country is desert and semi-desert. The principal crops are wheat, barley, vegetables, olives and fruit (mainly grapes and citrus fruits). Agricultural production in the Jordan Valley has suffered from the continued hostilities in the area, though the East Ghor Canal, vital to the irrigation of the area, has now been restored and is being extended. The only important industrial product is raw phosphates (production 1974: 1,674,800 tons), most of which is exported. There are schemes under consideration for the production of copper, potash and phosphate fertilizers. Tourism was a major industry and foreign currency earner before the 1967 war but dwindled considerably as most of the tourist sites are now in Israeli occupied territory. In recent years it has begun to increase once more, with numbers of tourists visiting the archæological sites of East Jordan and the resort of Aqaba. The Trans-Arabian oil pipeline (Tapline) runs through North Jordan on its way from the eastern province of Saudi Arabia to the Lebanese coast of Sidon. A branch pipeline feeds a refinery at Zerqa (production 1974: 748,400 tons) which meets most of Jordan's requirements for refined petroleum products.

Communications.—The trunk road system is good. Amman is linked to Damascus, Baghdad and Jedda by tarred roads which are of considerable importance in the overland trade of the Middle East. The former Hejaz Railway enters Jordan east of Ramtha and runs through Zerqa and Amman to Ma'an with a spur to the top of the Raz al-Naqb escarpment. The formerly abandoned section from Ma'an to Medina in Saudi Arabia has been partially reconstructed. A total of 299 vessels called at Aqaba in 1974 and 1,483,300 tons of cargo were handled. Much of Jordan's trade moves overland to and from the ports in Syria and Lebanon. The Royal Jordanian Airline (ALIA) operates from Amman Airport to other cities in the Middle East and to Rome, London, Paris, Frankfurt, Athens, Istanbul and Madrid. There is a service to the newly constructed airport at 'Aqaba.

FINANCE

	1974 JD (Million)	1975 JD (Million)
Expenditure	165·7	218·2
Domestic Revenue	56·7	95·8
Budgetary Supports	51·4	60·4
Compensatory Finance	3·2	Nil
Development Loans	45·0	50·2
Deficit	12·6	11·9

Trade with U.K.

Britain has been a leading source of supply of imported goods to Jordan for some time. Jordan's exports to U.K. are negligible.

	1973	1974
Imports from U.K.	£13,400,000	£20,600,000
Exports to U.K.	—	£1,600,000

CAPITAL.—Amman. Population, 615,000 (1974).

FLAG.—Black, white and green horizontal stripes, surcharged with white seven-point star on red triangle.

NATIONAL DAY.—May 25 (Independence Day).

BRITISH EMBASSY, AMMAN
Ambassador Extraordinary and Plenipotentiary, His Excellency John Campbell Moberly (1975).

Counsellor, M. R. Melhuish (*Development*).
Defence, Naval and Military Attaché, Col. J. D. Wellings, O.B.E.
Asst. Military Attaché, Maj. B. C. O'Hara.
Air Attaché, Wing-Cdr. J. E. Vickery.
1st Secretaries, M. St. E. Burton (*Head of Chancery and Consul*), J. A. N. Brehony; W. B. Lello (*Civil Air*) (*resident in Beirut*).
2nd Secretaries, B. J. McDowell (*Commercial*); A. J. R. Pitt (*Administration*).
3rd Secretaries, P. Willis (*Development*); B. E. Stewart (*Information*).

BRITISH COUNCIL
Representative, J. G. Mills, Box 634. Jebel Amman, Amman.

KOREA

Korea is situated between 124° 11″ and 130° 57′ E. long., and between 33° 7′ and 43° 1″ N. lat. It has an area of 85,256 sq. miles with an estimated population of about 48,000,000, of whom about 33,500,000 live south of the present dividing line. The southern and western coasts are fringed with innumerable islands, of which the largest, forming a province of its own, is Chejudo (Quelpart).

Agriculture.—The soil is fertile, but the arable land is limited by the mountainous nature of the country. The staple agricultural products are rice, barley, and other cereals, beans, cotton, tobacco and hemp. Fruit-growing and seri-culture are also practised. Gingseng, a medicinal root much affected by the Chinese, forms a rich source of revenue.

Minerals.—Gold, copper, coal, iron, graphite, tungsten and other minerals are distributed throughout the country, but are more abundant in the north. In pre-war days the south was mainly agricultural and most of the limited industries were in the north. Since 1966, however, rapid industrialization has taken place in the south.

History.—The last native dynasty (Yi) ruled from 1392 until 1910, in which year Japan formally annexed Korea. The country remained an integral part of the Japanese Empire until the defeat of Japan in 1945, when it was occupied by troops of the U.S.A. and the U.S.S.R.; the 38th parallel being fixed as the boundary between the two zones of occupation. The U.S. Government endeavoured to reach agreement with the Soviet Government for the creation of a Korean Government for the whole country and the withdrawal of all Russian and American troops. These efforts met with no success, and in September, 1947, the U.S. Government laid the whole question of the future of Korea before the General Assembly of the United Nations. The Assembly in November, 1947, resolved that elections should be held in Korea for a National Assembly under the supervision of a temporary Commission formed for that purpose by the United Nations and that the National Assembly when elected should set up a Government. The Soviet Government refused to allow the Commission to visit the Russian Occupied Zone and in consequence it was only able to discharge its function in that part of Korea which lies to the south of the 38th parallel.

The Korean War.—The country remained effectively divided into two along the line of the 38th parallel until the aggression of June 25, 1950, when the North Korean forces invaded South Korea. On the same day, at an emergency meeting of the United Nations Security Council, a resolution was adopted calling for immediate cessation of hostilities, and the withdrawal of the North Korean armed forces to the 38th parallel. The Communist

CHINA

SEA OF JAPAN

KOREA

YELLOW SEA

Inchon • Seoul

Taegu

Pusan

0   100   200 MILES

forces ignored this demand and continued their advance. In response to a Security Council recommendation that United Nations members should furnish assistance to repel the attack, 16 nations, including the United States of America and the United Kingdom, came to the aid of the Republic of Korea. A unified command under the leadership of the United States was established on July 8. Shortly afterwards U.S. troops were landed in Korea but were at first unable to stem the Communists' onslaught. Finally the United Nations and South Korean forces were able to stabilize a front around the Pusan perimeter. On September 15, U.S. Marines made a successful surprise landing at Inchon which was quickly followed by a breakout from the Pusan perimeter and a general advance to the north. The Communist forces had been pushed back almost to the Manchurian frontier when, at the beginning of November, hordes of Chinese " Volunteers " began to pour over the Yalu River and by sheer weight of numbers forced the U.N. troops to withdraw once again south of Seoul. However, the latter quickly regrouped and threw the Communist forces back to approximately the old dividing line.

The fighting was ended by an armistice agreement signed by the U.N. Commander-in-Chief and the commanders of the North Korean army and the Chinese People's " Volunteers " on July 27, 1953. By this agreement (which was not signed by the government of the Republic of Korea) the line of division between North and South Korea remained in the neighbourhood of the 38th parallel. The Geneva Conference discussed Korea from April 26 to June 15, 1954, but failed to agree on measures for reunifying the country.

Republic of Korea

President, Park, Chung Hee, *assumed office*, March 22 1962; *re-elected for four years* 1963, 1967 and 1971
Prime Minister, Kim Jong Pil (1971).

KOREAN EMBASSY
4 Palace Gate, W.8.
[01-581 0247]
Ambassador Extraordinary and Plenipotentiary, His Excellency Yong Shik Kim (1974).
Ministers, Jong Ick Choi; Dong Kun Kim.

Counsellors, Jai Sung Kim; Chu Won Yoon.
Defence Attaché, Col. Dong Yull Seo.

The Republic of Korea has been officially recognized by the Governments of the United States, France, Great Britain, and most other countries except the U.S.S.R. and its satellites. It has an area of 38,452 sq. miles and a population of 33,459,000.

A general election was held on May 10, 1948, and the first National Assembly met in Seoul on May 31. The Assembly passed a Constitution on July 12, and on July 20 elected the late Dr. Syngman Rhee as the first President of the Republic of Korea, an office which he held until 1960. On August 15, 1948, the Republic was formally inaugurated and American Military Government came to an end.

President Syngman Rhee was overthrown by a widespread popular rising in 1960. After a year of unstable and ineffectual governments a new régime was set up by an army officers' coup on May 16, 1961 led by Major-Gen. Park Chung Hee. On March 22, 1962, he took over as acting President, retaining his post as Chairman of the Supreme Council. Elections were originally promised for May and August, 1963, respectively, but when political activities were allowed to start again at the beginning of that year there was considerable confusion, so that the military government decided to retain power until December, 1963. Elections were then held in which General Park was elected and the Democratic Republican Party secured a majority. At further elections held in 1967, Pres. Park was returned by a comfortable majority for a new four-year term. In 1969 a constitutional amendment was passed to enable Pres. Park to stand for a third term and he was re-elected on April 27, 1971.

In 1972 a new constitution was inaugurated under which there was no limit to the number of terms which the President could serve. President Park was then elected in December 1972 to a six-year term.

The Republic of Korea has an army of about 550,000 men, a small navy mainly for coast protection duties, a small air force and a Marine Corps which includes one division trained in amphibious operations.

Finance.—The Budget for 1975 totalled *Won* 1,291·9 billion, of which 25 per cent. was for defence.

The unit of Korean currency is the *Won*. In 1975 the rate of exchange was about 1,122 *Won* to £1.

Trade.—The Republic of Korea's main exports are textiles, plywood and wood products, fish and fish preparations, electrical and electronic equipment, chemicals, footwear, rubber, petroleum products, cement, ships, musical instruments, toys, sports goods, iron and steel products and metalliferous ores and scrap. Her main customers are Japan and the U.S.A. Imports greatly exceed exports. In 1974 exports totalled $U.S. 4,460,370,000; imports amounted to $U.S. 6,851,848,000.

Trade with U.K.

	1973	1974
Imports from U.K.	£28,722,000	£36,045,000
Exports to U.K.	31,211,000	50,985,000

CAPITAL.—Seoul, population (1973), 6,289,556. Other main centres are Ψ Pusan (pop. 2,015,162), Taegu (pop. 1,082,750) and Ψ Inchon (pop. 646,013), Pusan on the south-east coast, and Inchon on the west coast, only 28 miles from Seoul, are the main ports but the development of Inchon is hampered by a tide variation of 28–30 feet.

FLAG.—White, with red over blue device in centre, three black parallel bars, some broken, in each quarter.

NATIONAL DAY.—August 15 (Independence Day).

BRITISH EMBASSY
Seoul

Ambassador Extraordinary and Plenipotentiary, His Excellency William Stanley Bates, C.M.G. (1975).

1st Secretaries, H. W. Sturdy, O.B.E. (*Commercial*); I. C. Sloane (*Head of Chancery and Consul*).

Defence Attaché, Brig. K. Neely, M.B.E.

2nd Secretaries, P. J. D. Whitehead (*Political*); R. J. Griffiths (*Commercial*).

Vice-Consul, R. D. Stainton.

Attachés, P. Fluck (*Commercial*); F. A. Wilson (*Administration*).

Cultural Attaché, C. W. Perchard (British Council Representative). There is an Honorary British Consul at Pusan.

Democratic People's Republic of Korea.—Meanwhile in the Russian-occupied zone north of the 38th parallel the Democratic People's Republic had been set up with its capital at Pyongyang; a Supreme People's Soviet was elected in September 1948, and a Soviet-style Constitution adopted. Recognition had been given by the U.S.S.R. and its satellites. The population is around 14,500,000.

FLAG.—Broad red horizontal band bordered by white lines bearing a five-point red star on a white disc in centre; blue horizontal bands at top and bottom.

Korean Workers (= *Communist*) Party

Political Committee of the Central Committee, Kim Il Song; Choe Yong Kun; Kim Il; Pak Song Chol; Kim Yong Chu; O Chin U; Kim Tong Kyu; So Chol; Kim Chung Im; Han Ik Su, Yi Kun Mo; Yang Hyang Soh; Yi Yong Mu (*full members*); Hyon Mu Kwang; Kim Man Kim; Kang Song San; Ch'oe Chae U; Kim Yong Nam; Yu Chang Sik; Chan Mun Sop (*alternate members*).

Secretariat of the Central Committee, Kim Il Song (*Secretary-General*); Choe Yong Ko; Kim Il; Kim Yong Chu; O Chin U; Kim Tong Kyu; Kim Chung Im; Han Ik Su; Hyon Mu Kwang; Yang Hyong Sop; Yon Hyong Muk; Kim Yong Nam; Yu Chang Sik.

KUWAIT
(The State of Kuwait)

Amir, H.H. Shaikh Sabah as-Salem as-Sabah, *born* 1915; acceded Nov. 24, 1965.

Crown Prince and Prime Minister (Dec. 1965), H.H. Shaikh Jabir al-Ahmed-as-Sabah; *appointed Crown Prince*, May 31, 1966.

KUWAIT EMBASSY IN LONDON
40 Devonshire Street, W.1
[01-580 8471]

Ambassador Extraordinary and Plenipotentiary, His Excellency Sheikh Saud Nasir Al-Sabah (1975).

Area and Population.—Kuwait extends along the shore of the Persian Gulf from Iraq to Saudi Arabia, with an area of about 7,500 square miles and a population (Census, 1975) of 990,000. It is officially estimated that about 47 per cent. of this total are Kuwaitis, the remainder being large numbers of other Arab peoples, Persians, Indians and Pakistanis. The total European and American population is about 7,000. Kuwait has a hot, dry climate with a summer season extending from April to September. During the coldest month (January) the temperatures can fall below freezing, but normally range between 50° to 60°F. Shade temperatures are about 85°F; and can reach 130°F.; 180°F. has been recorded in the sun. Humidity rarely exceeds 60 per cent. except in July and August.

Government.—Although Kuwait had been independent for some years, the " exclusive agreement " of 1899 between the Shaikh of Kuwait and the British Government was formally abrogated by an exchange of letters dated June 19, 1961. This exchange was immediately followed by Iraqi claims to sovereignty over Kuwait and, in accordance with the terms of the exchange, the Amir requested British military assistance to help him maintain his sovereignty and independence, which was immediately supplied. British troops were withdrawn in October, 1961, and replaced by the Arab League Security Force composed of contingents from various Arab States. The withdrawal of this Force was completed in January, 1963. On May 7, 1963, Kuwait was admitted to the United Nations and on Oct. 4, 1963, Iraq recognized Kuwait's independence. On May 13, 1968, an exchange of Notes was signed giving notice that the 1961 defence agreement with the United Kingdom would end on May 13, 1971.

Elections were held in December, 1961, for a Constituent Assembly, which held its first meeting in January, 1962. A council of Ministers including non-members of the ruling family was formed in January, 1962, to replace the former Supreme and Joint Councils. Under the Constitution drafted by the Constituent Assembly, the first 50-member National Assembly was elected in January, 1963. The present National Assembly was elected for four years in January, 1975. The Constitution provides that the Assembly must pass all laws and approve the Heir Apparent nominated by the Amir. The Prime Minister is appointed by the Amir and can appoint his Ministers from the members of the Assembly or from outside. The Assembly has the right to pass a vote of no confidence in any Minister except the Prime Minister.

Education, etc.—As a result of the very considerable oil revenues, the Kuwait Government embarked on a large scale development scheme and plans for social services. Education and medical treatment are free. New hospitals and schools continue to be built. Kuwait University was opened in 1966. In 1972, 385 students graduated out of a total 2,600. In 1972 there were over 137,309 pupils at 161 government schools.

Public Utilities.—Kuwait has a domestic water supply from water distillation plants which operate on waste natural gas from the oil fields. These plants can produce over 40,000,000 gallons of fresh water daily. For storage there are two 15,000,000 gallon reservoirs and one of 3,000,000 gallons. There are also two 7,500,000 gallon reservoirs at Shuaiba and two of similar capacity at Abraq Kheitan.

In 1961 a natural source of fresh water was discovered at Raudhatain in the north of the State. This has been developed to produce 5,000,000 gallons per day for at least 20 years and a pipeline has been built to carry the water to Kuwait town. Kuwait signed an agreement with Iraq on Feb. 11, 1964, allowing her to draw up to 120,000,000 gallons of sweet water a day from the Shatt-al-Arab, but this has yet to be implemented. Electricity is produced by three power stations in Kuwait (160 MWh) and two at Shuaiba (400 MWh). Twal town is served by a network of dual carriageway roads and more are under construction.

Communications.—Ships of British, Dutch, Kuwaiti and other lines make regular calls at Kuwait. British Airways, Kuwait Airways, K.L.M., Lufthansa and several international and Middle Eastern airlines operate regular air services, and other companies make non-scheduled flights to Kuwait under charter. Wireless communications, telephone and postal services are conducted by the Kuwait Government, which has built an earth satellite station.

Finance.—Banking is carried out by the National Bank of Kuwait, the Commercial Bank, the Gulf Bank, the Ahli Bank, and by the Bank of Kuwait and the Middle East. The banking system is controlled by the Central Bank of Kuwait.

Revenue for the financial year 1974–75 was budgeted at KD2,552,000,000. Total expenditure for 1974–75 was KD886,700,000. It included KD31,400,000 on health, KD168,400,000 on defence, KD62,500,000 on education, and KD 50,600,000 on public works.

Production and Trade.—The centre of the Kuwait Oil Company's production is at Burgan, south of Kuwait town. An oil port has been constructed by the company at Mina-al-Ahmadi, about five miles from Ahmadi, the company's administrative and residential centre. Production of crude oil in 1972 totalled 143,724,505 long tons. The Company is jointly owned by the British Petroleum Company and the American Gulf Oil Corporation. It has about 3,300 employees, including British, Americans, Indians, Pakistanis, Kuwaitis and Arabs from neighbouring territories. In May, 1962, the Company relinquished about half of its original concession area, and further areas were relinquished in 1971. At the end of 1972 an agreement was signed providing for an eventual 51 per cent. participation by the State of Kuwait in the concession. In May 1974 an agreement was signed for a 60 per cent. participation and early in 1975 negotiations were started on a 100 per cent. take over by the Kuwait government. Oil was also struck in the Kuwait-Saudi Arabian Neutral Zone to the south of the State early in 1953. Concessions for this area are held by the American Independent Oil Co. (Aminoil) from Kuwait and the Getty Oil Company from Saudi Arabia. Aminoil's production for 1972 (*i.e.*, Kuwait's share from the Neutral Zone) was approximately 3,658,083 long tons.

The Arabian Oil Company, of Japan, having been awarded in 1958 the oil concession for the Partitioned Zone offshore sea-bed by Kuwait and Saudi Arabia for their respective half shares, commenced exploratory drilling in the summer of 1959 and struck oil in commercial quantity early in 1960. The first shipment of crude oil was made in March 1961; production in 1972 was nearly 10,214,814 long tons. A concession covering the off-shore area of Kuwait proper was awarded to the Shell Company in Nov. 1960, and the concession agreement in the name of The Kuwait Shell Petroleum Development Co. was signed in Kuwait on Jan. 15, 1961. Exploratory drilling began in 1962 but was suspended in the autumn of 1963. The establishment of a Kuwait company, The Kuwait National Petroleum Co., was authorized by an Amiri Decree on October 5, 1960. This company took over the distribution of petroleum products in Kuwait from the Kuwait Oil Co., on June 1, 1961, and was, in partnership with the Spanish Company Hispanoil, awarded the concession to exploit the area relinquished by the K.O.C. Ltd. in 1962.

In addition to petroleum products, skins and wool are also exported. Trade in 1974 amounted to: Imports, KD331,300,000; Exports (including re-exports), KD79,100,000, excluding oil.

Trade with U.K.

	1973	1974
Imports from U.K.	£36,101,000	£59,800,000
Exports to U.K.	235,305,000	600,000,000

CAPITAL.—ΨKuwait (population, excluding suburbs, 300,000).

FLAG.—Three horizontal stripes of green, white and red, with black trapezoid next to staff.

NATIONAL DAY.—February 25.

BRITISH EMBASSY

Arabian Gulf Street, Kuwait

Ambassador Extraordinary and Plenipotentiary, His Excellency Albert Thomas Lamb, C.M.G., M.B.E., D.F.C.

Counsellor, G. E. Fitzherbert.

1st Secretaries, P. R. M. Hinchcliffe (*Head of Chancery*); J. Stark, M.B.E. (*Consul*); J. Gallacher; J. S. Khoury (*Commercial*); A. S. M. Marshall.

2nd Secretaries, A. H. Ellis (*Admin.*); H. G. Hogger.

British Council Office, P.O. Box 345 Kuwait. *Representative*, R. L. S. Tong.

There is a library in *Kuwait*.

LAOS

(*For* MAP, *see* Index).

King, H.M. Sri Savang Vatthana, *born* 1907, proclaimed King, Nov. 1, 1959.

Prime Minister, Prince Souvanna Phouma (June 23, 1962).

EMBASSY IN LONDON

5 Palace Green, W.8

Ambassador Extraordinary and Plenipotentiary (vacant).

Position and Extent.—Laos is a kingdom in the northerly part of Indo-China, lying between Vietnam, on the north and east, and Burma and Thailand on the west. Laos has a common boundary with Cambodia to the south. The area of the kingdom is approximately 90,000 sq. miles, with a population (estimated, 1970) of about 2,700,000.

History.—The Kingdom of Lane Xang, the Land of a Million Elephants, was founded in the 14th century, but broke up at the beginning of the 15th century into the separate kingdoms of Luang Prabang and Vientiane and the Principality of Champassac, which together came under French protection in 1893. In 1945 the Japanese executed a *coup de force* and suppressed the French administration. Under a new Constitution of 1947 Laos became a constitutional monarchy under King Sisavang Vong of the House of Luang Prabang, father of the present King, and an independent sovereign state in 1949.

The past twenty years in Laos have been marked by power struggles and civil war. International conferences were held in Geneva in 1954 and 1961–2 to produce a settlement based on neutrality and independence. But the resulting Coalition Governments were short-lived. Personalities involved include the present Prime Minister, Prince Souvanna Phouma, who in 1957 formed a Government of National Union, including Pathet Lao (Communist) ministers, and has held office as Prime Minister with intervals since 1962; Prince Boun Oum of Champassac who formed a rightist Government in December 1960; and Prince Souphannouvong, a *Pathet Lao* leader, who took part in a later coalition with Souvanna Phouma and Boun Oum in 1962–63. Attempts to seize power by Capt. Kong Le (1960), Gen. Phoumi Nosavan (1965) and Gen. Thao Ma (1966 and 1973) were unsuccessful.

Recent Events.—After 1967 North Vietnamese forces steadily increased their military activities in Laos. Although there were regular seasonal fluctuations in the fighting, which resulted in many areas of the country changing hands several times, Government forces gradually lost ground. By February 21, 1973, when a ceasefire agreement was signed in Vientiane between the *Pathet Lao* and the Government in Vietiane, Communist forces had occupied or dominated most of the strategic areas of Laos, including the Plain of Jars in the north, and the Bolovens Plateau in the south. The 1973 Vietiane Agreement and its Protocol of September 1973, provided for a cease-fire; a timetable for the withdrawal of foreign forces; a halt to U.S. bombing and the " neutralization " of Vientiane and of the Royal capital, Luang Prabang. The agreement also made provisions for a Provisional Government of National Union and for a Political Consultative Council (eventually formed on April 5, 1974) with equal representation from the *Pathet Lao* (now known as the Lao Patriotic forces) and the Vientiane Government, which would hold office until new elections could be held. After the fall of Saigon in April 1975, internal resistance to the Pathet Lao crumbled; Communist troops occupied the whole country and, though still paying lip-service to the 1973 Agreement and maintaining a façade of coalition, the *Pathet Lao* took over the government and began to implement an authoritarian régime with policies of austerity and economic self-sufficiency.

Finance.—Budget estimates for the fiscal year 1974–75 are: Revenue, *K*19,600,000,000; Expenditure, *K*37,046,000,000 of which the military budget will absorb *K*14,445,000,000. The unit of currency is the *Kip* (*K*). In July 1975 there were two official rates of exchange, 750 and 1,200 *Kip* to US$1 and a blackmarket rate of *Kip* 2,400 to US $1.

CAPITAL.—Vientiane (the administrative capital), population (estimated 1973) 174,000. The Royal Capital is at Luang Prabang.

FLAG.—Three-headed white elephant on 5 steps, surmounted by parasol, all on a red ground.

NATIONAL DAY.—May 11 (Independence Day).

BRITISH EMBASSY
Vientiane

Ambassador Extraordinary and Plenipotentiary, His Excellency Alan Eaton Davidson, C.M.G. (1973)
£6,925

1st Secretaries, P. S. Fairweather (*Head of Chancery and Consul*); M. F. H. Scrase-Dickins.

Defence, Military and Air Attaché, Col. J. P. Cross, M.B.E.

2nd Secretaries, A. T. J. Lovelock (*Commercial and Aid*); D. G. Taylor (*Admin. and Vice-Consul*).

3rd Secretary, P. K. C. Thomas (*Chancery, Information*).

LEBANON
President of the Republic of Lebanon, Suleiman Franjieh, *elected* Aug. 17, 1970.

CABINET
[July 1, 1975]

Prime Minister, Finance, Defence and Information, Rachid Karamé.

Interior, Post, Telephones and Telegraphs and Hydro-electric Resources, Camille Chamoun.

Justice, Public Works and Transport, and Economy and Commerce, Adel Osseiran.

Health, Agriculture, Housing and Co-operatives, Emir Magid Arslan.

Foreign Affairs, Education and Fine Arts, and Planning, Philippe Takla.

Labour and Social Affairs, Tourism, Industry and Oil, Ghassan Toueini.

LEBANESE EMBASSY IN LONDON
21 Kensington Palace Gardens, W.8
[01–229–7265]

Ambassador Extraordinary and Plenipotentiary, His Excellency Nadim Dimechkie (1966).

Counsellors, Mahmoud Hammoud; Chawki Nicholas Choueri.

1st Secretary, Nizar Farhat.

2nd Secretary, Gilbert Aoun.

Attaché (*Tourism*), Mounir El-Sheikh.

Military Attaché, Col. Fouad El-Houssami.

Consular Section, 15 Palace Gardens Mews, W.8 (01–229 8485).

Area and Population.—Lebanon forms a strip about 120 miles in length and varying in width from 30 to 35 miles, along the Mediterranean littoral, and extending from the Israel frontier on the south to the Nahr al Kebir (15 miles north of Tripoli) on the north; its eastern boundary runs down the Anti-Lebanon range and then down the Great Central depression, the *Beqaa*, in which flow the rivers Orontes and Litani. It is divided into 5 districts, North Lebanon, Mount Lebanon, Beirut, South Lebanon and Beqaa. The seaward slopes of the mountains have a Mediterranean climate and vegetation. The inland range of Anti-Lebanon has the characteristics of steppe country. There is a mixed Arabic-speaking population of Christians, Moslems and Druses. The total area of Lebanon is about 4,300 sq. miles, population (U.N. estimate, 1969), 2,645,000. (*For MAP, see* p. 885.)

Government.—Lebanon became an independent State on Sept. 1, 1920, administered under French Mandate until Nov. 26, 1941. Powers were transferred to the Lebanese Government from Jan. 1, 1944, and French troops were withdrawn in 1946.

Suleiman Franjieh was elected President in 1970, for a term of six years. In April 1975, serious fighting broke out in Beirut between members of the predominantly Christian Phalangist Party and Palestinian guerrillas based in Lebanon. On May 15, the Government of M. Rashid Solh resigned, and the President appointed a military government led by Brig. Noureddin Rifai on May 23, which lasted only three days. After a renewed outbreak of violence on June 24, the country was on the verge of civil war. On June 30, a new cabinet was formed with the sole intention of restoring peace. It was led by Rachid Karamé, and contained a representative of each of the main religious communities.

It was estimated that over 2,000 people were killed and 16,000 injured between April and July, 1975.

Production.—Fruits are the most important products and include citrus fruit, apples, grapes, bananas and olives. There is a small but growing industry, geared mainly to the production of consumer goods. The most important industries are foods and drinks (confectionery, jams, sugar, wines and beer, etc.), textiles, chemicals, furniture, plastics, leather, clothing and footwear, refrigerators, cast and forged metal products, and building materials. There is little remaining of the famous cedars of Lebanon.

Railways.—A narrow-gauge railway runs from Beirut to Damascus, connecting at Rayak with a branch of the standard-gauge line which runs from Tripoli through Homs, Hama and Aleppo to the Turkish frontier, from Nusaybin to the Iraq frontier at Tel Kotchek. A standard gauge railway also runs up the coast from Beirut to Tripoli.

Civil Aviation.—Beirut International Airport is one of the most important traffic centres in the Middle East. Numerous international air services to all parts of the world pass through it, and local services connect with all Middle Eastern capitals except Tel Aviv. Lebanon has two international airlines of its own, Middle East Airlines/Air Liban, primarily a passenger carrier, and Trans Mediterranean Airways, specializing in freight.

Archæology, etc.—Lebanon has some important historical remains, notably Baalbek (Heliopolis) which contains the ruins of first to third century Roman temples and Jubail (Biblos), one of the oldest continuously inhabited towns in the world, and ancient Tyre which is in course of excavation.

Language and Literature.—Arabic is the principal language (*see* Arabia), and French is also widely used. The use of English is increasing. About 40 daily papers are published, including 2 in French, 1 in English and 4 in Armenian; and a further 30 periodicals.

Education.—There are four universities in Beirut, the American and the French (R.C.) Universities established in the last century, and the Lebanese National University and the Arab University which are recent foundations in the early stages of development. There are several institutions for vocational training and there is a good provision throughout the country of primary and secondary schools, among which are a great number of private schools.

Finance.—Revenue and Expenditure, 1974 (Estimated) £L1,385,300,000. The monetary unit is the Lebanese £(L). (*See also* p. 84.)

Principal Imports.—Gold and precious metals, machinery and electrical equipment, textiles and yarns, vegetable products, iron and steel goods, motor vehicles, mineral products, chemicals and chemical products, pharmaceuticals, prepared foods, beverages, tobacco products, live animals and animal products.

Principal Exports.—Gold and precious metals, fruits and vegetables, textiles, building materials, furniture, plastic goods, foodstuffs, tobacco and wine.

Trade with U.K.

	1973	1974
Imports from U.K.	£41,958,000	£60,800,000
Exports to U.K.	8,010,000	28,600,000

There is also a considerable transit trade through Beirut, including gold, crude oil and a wide range of machinery and consumer goods. Lebanon is the terminal for two oil pipe lines, one belonging to the Iraq Petroleum Company, debouching at Tripoli, the other belonging to the Trans-Arabian Pipeline Company, at Sidon. There are refineries at the end of each pipeline which can supply Lebanon's needs.

CAPITAL.— Ψ Beirut (population, excluding suburbs, about 600,000). Other towns are Ψ Tripoli (210,000), Zahlé (45,000), Ψ Sidon (42,000), Aley (14,500), Ψ Tyre (12,000).

FLAG.—Horizontal bands of red, white and red with a green cedar of Lebanon in the centre of the white band.

NATIONAL DAY.—November 22.

BRITISH EMBASSY
Beirut

Ambassador Extraordinary and Plenipotentiary, His Excellency Peter George Arthur Wakefield, C.M.G. (1975)

Counsellors, A. J. D. Stirling; G. F. Hancock.

1st Secretaries, A. Shepherd (*Commercial*); P. T. Gardner, M.B.E. (*Consul*); A. C. Thorpe; B. R. Berry; D. A. Marston (*Information*); D. A. McAlindon; W. B. Lello.

Defence, Naval and Military Attaché, Lt.-Col. A. M. MacFarlane.

The British Embassy houses the Office of the Middle East Development Division of the Overseas Development Administration.

British Council Representative, R. F. Hitchcock.

LIBERIA
(Republic of Liberia)

President, Dr, William R. Tolbert.
Speaker of the House, R. Henries.
Vice President, J. E. Greene.
Presidential Affairs, E. R. Townsend.

Finance, Edwin Williams.
Foreign Affairs, C. Cecil Dennis.
National Defence, A. H. Williams.
Health and Welfare, O. Bright.
Commerce, Industry and Transportation, W. E. Dennis.
Planning and Economic Affairs, D. F. Neal.
Public Works, G. J. Tucker.
Agriculture, J. T. Philips.
Education, Jackson F. Doe.
Local Government, Rural Development and Urban Reconstruction, E. J. Goodridge.
Mines and Lands, Dr. Nyema Jones.
Information, Cultural Affairs and Tourism, Dr. E. B. Kesselly.
Labour and Youth, J. J. Peal.
Postmaster-General, M. A. DeShield.
Attorney General, L. A. Morgan.
Chairman of Public Utilities Authority, Benjamin Darpoh.

LIBERIAN EMBASSY IN LONDON
21 Prince's Gate, S.W.7
[01-589 9405]

Ambassador Extraordinary and Plenipotentiary, His Excellency Herbert Richard Wright Brewer (1975).

Counsellor, C. W. Birch.
1st Secretary and Consul, W. E. Greaves.
2nd Secretary and Vice-Consul, J. D. Moulton.

An independent republic of Western Africa, occupying that part of the coast between Sierra Leone and the Ivory Coast, which is between the rivers Mano in the N.W. and Cavalla in the S.E., a distance of about 350 miles, with an area of about 43,000 square miles, and extending to the interior to latitude 8° 50′, a distance of 150 miles from the seaboard. It was founded by the American Colonization Society in 1882, and has been recognized since 1847 as an independent State. The population at the Census of 1974 was 1,481,524.

The executive power is vested in a President elected for 4 years (8 years in the first instance) assisted by a Cabinet; there are two houses of Legislature, the Senate and the House of Representatives. The Senate is composed of eighteen members elected from each of the nine Counties. They hold office for a period of six years. The House of Representatives is composed of fifty-two members, each member holding office for four years. William V. S. Tubman, President of Liberia since 1944, died on July 23, 1971, and was succeeded by Mr. Tolbert (*see* above). The Army of Liberia consists of one division of 2 brigades of militia, three regular infantry battalions, one engineer battalion and a small coastguard. The artificial harbour and free port of Monrovia was opened on July 26, 1948. There are 9 ports of entry, including 3 river ports.

Liberia is receiving assistance from the U.S. A.I.D. (successor to I.C.A.), and technicians have been sent from U.S.A. to advise on various projects. Technical assistance is also being provided by several other countries, including the United Kingdom. UNESCO, WHO and FAO have missions in the country providing technical assistance. The U.S.A. and more recently I.B.R.D., has also made loans for the improvement of power and water supplies, roads and hospitals.

FINANCE

	1974	1975
Revenue	$96,000,000	$117,000,090
Expenditure	96,000,000	117,200,000

$=U.S. Dollar.

TRADE

	1972	1973
Imports	$178,683,359	$193,468,586
Exports	244,393,820	324,039,251

Trade with U.K.

	1973	1974
Imports from U.K....	£17,625,000	£13,990,000
Exports to U.K......	7,381,000	6,494,000

The principal exports are iron ore, crude rubber, uncut diamonds, palm kernels, cocoa and coffee. The chief imports are manufactured goods of all kinds, transport and iron-ore mining equipment and foodstuffs.

The language of the Republic is English. American weights and measures are used.

CAPITAL, Ψ Monrovia. Est. Pop. 201,600. Other ports are Ψ Buchanan, Ψ Greenville (Sinoe) and Ψ Harper (Cape Palmas).

FLAG.—Alternate horizontal stripes (5 white, 6 red), with 5-pointed white star on blue field in upper corner next to flagstaff.

NATIONAL DAY.—July 26.

BRITISH EMBASSY
Monrovia

Ambassador Extraordinary and Plenipotentiary and Consul-General, His Excellency John Henry Reiss, O.B.E. (1973).

1st Secretary and Consul, J. D. Maher, M.B.E.

3rd Secretary and Vice-Consul, G. Tippett.

Monrovia, 3,650 miles distant; transit by English steamers from Liverpool, 11 to 20 days; also by French, Netherlands, German and U.S. vessels from Continent and U.S.A., British Caledonian, U.T.A., Pan American Airways, Nigerian Airways, K.L.M., Sabena, S.A.S., Swissair, Middle East Airlines and Air Afrique aircraft call at Robertsfield, 35 miles from Monrovia. Ghana and Nigerian Airways call at Spriggs Payne airfield, on the outskirts of Monrovia.

LIBYA

King Idris I, who had ruled Libya since its independence in 1951, was deposed on September 1, 1969, by a group of Army officers, who formed a Revolutionary Command Council and declared the country a Republic. The Revolutionary Command Council (RCC) is the highest authority in Libya. The Cabinet, containing five members of the Revolutionary Command Council was reformed on November 14, 1974, to include:

Chairman of the RCC, Commander in Chief of the

Armed Forces and Minister of Defence, Col. Mu'ammar al-Qadhafi (or "Gaddafi".)

Prime Minister, Maj. Abdul Salam Jalud.

Minister of the Interior, Maj. Khweldi al Humaidi.

Foreign Minister, Maj. Abdul Munim al Huni.

Minister of Planning and Scientific Research, Maj. Omar al Muhaishi.

LIBYAN EMBASSY IN LONDON
58 Prince's Gate, S.W.7
[01–589 5235]

Ambassador, His Excellency Mahmood Suleiman Maghribi (1973).

Minister Plenipotentiary, Suleiman Grada.

Counsellors, Ahmed Abdalla Bughula; Khalifa A. Bazelya; Syed M. Ghadaf-Addam.

2nd Secretary, Salah Eddin M. Msallem.

Libya, on the Mediterranean coast of Africa, is bounded on the East by Egypt and the Sudan, on the South by the Republics of Chad and Niger, and on the West by Algeria and Tunisia. It consists of the three former provinces of Tripolitania, Cyrenaica and the Fezzan, with a combined area of approximately 810,000 square miles and a population (1973 Census preliminary results) of 2,257,037. The people of Libya are principally Arab with some Berbers in the West and aboriginal tribes in the Fezzan. Islam is the official religion of Libya, but all religions are tolerated. The official language is Arabic.

Vast sand and rock deserts, almost completely barren, occupy the greater part of Libya. The Southern part of the country lies within the Sahara Desert. There are no rivers, and, as rainfall is precarious, a good harvest is infrequent. Agriculture is confined mainly to the coastal areas of Tripolitania and Cyrenaica, where barley, wheat, olives, almonds, citrus fruits and dates are produced, and to the areas of the oases, many of which are well supplied with springs supporting small fertile areas. Among the important oases are Jagabub, Gadames, Jofra, Sebha, Murzuch, Brach, Gat, Jalo and the Kufra group in the South-East. Exports from Libya are dominated by crude oil, but some wool, cattle, sheep and horses, esparto grass, olive oil, sponges and hides and skins are also exported. Principal imports are foodstuffs, including sugar, tea and coffee and most constructional materials and consumer goods. The major producing companies are Esso, Oasis, Mobil, Um Al Jawah (*formerly* Amoseas), A.G.I.P., Occidental, Aquitane and Libyan National Oil Co. In September 1973, the Libyan Government announced that it would be taking a 51 per cent. share in all foreign-owned companies. A few companies have been completely nationalized. In addition to the Esso main pipeline from Zelten to the terminal at Mersa Bregha and the Oasis Company's pipeline from Dahra to Ras-es-Sider, Mobil operates a 176-mile pipeline from Amal to Ras Lunuf and the Occidental line from Intisar field to Zuetina. A new gas liquefaction plant run by Esso was opened at Mersa Bregha in June 1970. Production of crude oil in 1973 was approximately 105 million tons (2·1 million barrels per day) which was a decrease of 4·6 per cent. over 1972.

The ancient ruins in Cyrenaica, at Cyrene, Ptolemais (Tolmeta) and Apollonia, are outstanding, as are those at Leptis Magna near Homs, 70 miles from Tripoli and at Sabratha, 40 miles west of Tripoli. An Italian expedition has found in the S.W. of the Fezzan a series of rock-paintings more than 5,000 years old. The Museum in the Castello at Tripoli has been completely re-organized and is of great interest to visitors.

Communications in Libya are good in the coastal area where a motor road (of international standards) runs from the Tunisian frontier through Tripoli to Benghazi, Tobruk and the Egyptian border, serving the needs of the main population centres. A road from the coast to Sebha, in the Fezzan, was completed in Oct. 1962. A Czech-built road between Nalut and Ghadames was completed in 1972. Elsewhere roads are poor and the transport inland is confined to caravan and occasional motor bus routes. There are airports at Tripoli and Benghazi (Benina), Tobruk (El Adem), Mersa Bregha, Sebha, Ghadames and Kufra regularly used by commercial airlines and military airfields at El Adem and Okba ben Nafi' (formerly Wheelus Field near Tripoli).

Government.—Libya was occupied by Italy in 1911–12 in the course of the Italo-Turkish War, and under the Treaty of Ouchy (Oct. 1912) the sovereignty of the province was transferred by Turkey to Italy. In 1939 the four Provinces of Libya (Tripoli, Misurata, Benghazi and Derna) were incorporated in the national territory of Italy as *Libia Italiana.* After the Second World War Tripolitania and Cyrenaica were placed provisionally under British and the Fezzan under French administration, and in conformity with a resolution of the General Assembly on Nov. 21, 1949, Libya became on Dec. 24, 1951, the first independent state to be created by the United Nations. The monarchy was overthrown by a revolution on Sept. 1, 1969, and the country was declared a republic. In 1971 a Libyan Arab Socialist Union was created as the country's sole political organisation.

Local Government.—Until the amendment of the Constitution in 1963, Libya was a Federal State, each of the three Provinces, Tripolitania, Cyrenaica and Fezzan, being administered by a Governor assisted by Executive and Legislative Councils. In April 1963, however, comprehensive unity was proclaimed and the Federal system (together with the Governors and the Executive and Legislative Councils) abolished. The country is now divided into ten divisions, each administered by an Inspectorate (*Muraaqiba*).

Currency.—The Libyan *pound* was abolished in August, 1971, and a new currency the Libyan *dinar* of 1,000 *dirham* was introduced. *Dinar=* £1·42 sterling (*see also* p. 83).

Technical assistance is being provided by the United Nations to foster Libya's economic and educational development.

A treaty of alliance and friendship between the United Kingdom and Libya, together with military and financial agreements, was signed at Benghazi on July 29, 1953, but terminated in January, 1972.

Trade with U.K.

	1973	1974
Imports from U.K...	£61,100,000	£62,500,000
Exports to U.K....	164,500,000	390,132,000

CAPITAL.—Tripoli.

The principal towns with the latest available estimates of population are: ΨTripoli (551,477); ΨMisurata (103,302); ΨBenghazi (282,192); Homs-Cussabat (88,695); Zawia (72,207); Gharian (65,439); ΨTobruk (58,869).

FLAG.—Libya uses the flag of the Confederation of Arab Republics (Libya, Egypt, Syria) which is a red, white and black tricolor with an eagle in gold in the centre. NATIONAL DAY.—Sept. 1.

BRITISH EMBASSY
30 Trigal Fatah, Tripoli.

Ambassador Extraordinary and Plenipotentiary, His Excellency Donald Frederick Murray, C.M.G. (1974).

Counsellor and Head of Chancery, J. M. Brown.

1st Secretaries, D. J. Easton; G. H. Boyce; I. S. Lockhart, M.B.E. (*Commercial*); C. O. Wood (*Consul*).

2nd Secretary, K. Farnworth (*Administration*).

3rd Secretary, T. Millson (*Commercial*).

There is a British Consular Office at *Tripoli.*

LIECHTENSTEIN
(Fürstentum Liechtenstein)

Prince, Franz Josef II., *b.* Aug. 16, 1906; *suc.* Aug. 25, 1938; *married* March 7, 1943, Countess Gina von Wilczek. *Heir*, Crown Prince Hans Adam, *b.* Feb. 14, 1945; *married* July 30, 1967, Countess Marie Kinsky.

_____

Prime Minister, Dr. Walter Kieber.

Liechtenstein is represented in diplomatic and consular matters in the United Kingdom by the Swiss Embassy, *q.v.*

At the General Election on Feb. 1 and 3, 1974, the Progressive Citizens' Party won 8 seats and Patriotic Union Party 7. Dr. Walker Kieber was asked to form a new Government.

A Principality on the Upper Rhine, between Vorarlberg (Austria) and Switzerland, with an area of 65 square miles and a population in 1973 of 23,156. The main industries are metal goods, cotton spinning and weaving, measuring instruments, coating of lenses, manufacture of vacuum apparatus, electronic microscopes, ceramics, artificial teeth and sausage casings, textiles, various apparatus, foodstuffs, leatherware and woodwork. The chief products are cotton yarn, cotton material, screws, bolts and bolt-shooting apparatus, needles, knitting machinery, ceramics, artificial teeth, precision measuring instruments, vacuum pumps, coated lenses, shoes, leather gloves, bed down, conveyor belts, boilers, preserves, damask cloth, socks and stockings, and furniture. Revenue 1973, *Swiss francs* 90,128,626. Expenditure 1973, *Swiss francs* 90,104,348.

The language of the Principality is German.

CAPITAL, Vaduz. Pop. (1973), 4,326.

FLAG.—Equal horizontal bands of blue over red; gold crown on blue band near staff.

British Consul General, James Ernest Reeve (*office at Dufourstrasse 56, 8008 Zürich*) *Consul*, O. E. Goddard (*office at Bellerivestrasse 5, 8008 Zürich*).

LUXEMBURG
(Grand-Duché de Luxembourg)

Grand Duke, H.R.H. Jean, *born* Jan 5, 1921, *married*, April 9, 1953, Princess Joséphine-Charlotte of Belgium, and has issue, 3 sons and 2 daughters; *succeeded* (on the abdication of his mother) Nov., 1964. *Heir Apparent*, Prince Henri, *born* April 16, 1955.

Prime Minister and Minister for Foreign Affairs and Sport, M. Gaston Thorn.

Deputy Prime Minister and Minister of Finance, of the Budget and of Planning, M. Raymond Vouel.

Minister of Economic Affairs, of the Middle Classes, of Transport, of Energy and of Tourism, M. Marcel Mart.

Minister of Employment and Social Affairs, M. Benny Berg.

Minister of Public Health, of the Environment, of the Civil Service and of the Armed Force, M. Emile Krieps.

Minister of Agriculture, of Viticulture and of Public Works, M. Jean Hamilius.

Minister of the Interior, M. Jos. Wohlfart.

Minister of Justice and of National Education, M. Robert Krieps.

State Secretaries, M. Maurice Thoss; M. Guy Linster; M. Albert Berchem.

EMBASSY AND CONSULATE
27 Wilton Crescent, S.W.1
[01–235 6961]

Ambassador Extraordinary and Plenipotentiary, His Excellency André Philippe, G.C.V.O. (1972).

A Grand Duchy in Western Europe, bounded by Germany, Belgium, and France. Established as an independent State under the sovereignty of the King of the Netherlands as Grand Duke by the Congress of Vienna in 1815, it formed part of the Germanic Confederation, 1815–66, and was included in the German " Zollverein ". In 1867 the Treaty of London declared it a neutral territory. On the death of the King of the Netherlands in 1890 it passed to the Duke of Nassau. The territory was invaded and overrun by the Germans at the beginning of the war in 1914, but was liberated in 1918. By the *Treaty of Versailles*, 1919, Germany renounced her former agreements with Luxemburg in respect of the customs union, etc., and in 1921 an economic union was made with Belgium (B.L.E.U.). The Grand Duchy was again invaded and occupied by Germany on May 10, 1940. The constitution of the Grand Duchy was modified on April 28, 1948, and the stipulation of permanent neutrality was then abandoned. Luxemburg is now a fully effective member of the Western association of powers and a signatory of the Brussels and North Atlantic Treaties. She is also a member of the European Communities.

Besides B.L.E.U., Luxemburg is also a member of the Belgium–Netherlands–Luxemburg Customs Union (Benelux, 1960). The Court of the European Communities has its seat in Luxembourg, as does the Secretariat of the European Parliament, the European Investment Bank and the European Monetary Co-operation fund.

The area is 1,000 square miles; the population (Jan. 1975) 357,300, nearly all Roman Catholics, There is a Chamber of 59 Deputies, elected by universal adult suffrage for 5 years. Legislation is submitted to the Council of State. The Grand Duchy is rich in iron-ore and possesses an important iron and steel industry with an annual productive capacity over 6,000,000 tons. The revenue for 1975 was estimated at L.F. 25,663,000,000, expenditure L.F. 25,301,000,000. The Luxembourg *franc* has at present the same value as the Belgian *franc* and the latter is legal tender in the Grand Duchy. Approximate Exchange Rate, 82·75 *Francs*= £1 (June 1, 1975). There are 170 miles of railway.

Trade with U.K.

	1972	1973
Imports from U.K....	£8,030,000	£8,580,000
Exports to U.K......	6,363,000	7,847,000

The capital, Luxemburg, pop. (1972), 78,300, is a dismantled fortress. The country is well wooded, with many deer and wild boar. The language is Letzeburgesch but French is the official language; all speak German and many English.

FLAG.—Three horizontal bands, red, white and blue. NATIONAL DAY.—June 23.

BRITISH EMBASSY
Luxemburg

Ambassador Extraordinary and Plenipotentiary, His Excellency Antony Arthur Acland (1975).
1st Secretary and Consul, J. M. Crosby.
2nd Secretary, Miss S. M. Griffith-Jones.
3rd Secretary and Vice Consul, W. F. Harris.

MADAGASCAR
(Ny Repoblika Malagasy)

Head of State, Capt. de Frégate Didier Ratsiraka.
Minister of Foreign Affairs, M. Rémi Tiandraza.

MALAGASY EMBASSY IN LONDON
33 Thurloe Square, S.W.7
[01–584 3714]

Ambassador Extraordinary and Plenipotentiary, His Excellency Benjamin Razafintseheno.

Madagascar lies 240 miles off the east coast of Africa and is the fifth largest island in the world. It has an area of 228,000 sq. miles and a population of about 8,000,000. It became a French protectorate in 1895, and a French colony in 1896 when the former queen was exiled. Republican status was adopted on October 14, 1958. Independence was proclaimed on June 26, 1960, when agreements confirming Madagascar's membership of the French community and co-operation with France on defence, monetary, judicial, educational and other matters were signed.

Following demonstrations in Tananarive on May 13, 1972, the Parti Social Democrate (*PSD*) Government which had been in power since independence under Monsieur Tsiranana (*President* 1959–1972) was replaced by a military government under General Ramanantsoa who resigned in January 1975. His successor, Col. Ratsimandrava, was assassinated on February 11 after only 6 days in office. A mutiny in a gendarmerie camp in the capital was put down with about 20 casualties. A *Directoire Militaire* under General Andriamahazo then took over and martial law was declared. The *Directoire* was replaced by a Supreme Council of the Revolution of 8 members of the armed forces under Capitaine de Frégate Didier Ratsiraka on June 15, 1975. Twelve civilian ministers whose activities are coordinated and directed by the Supreme Council were also appointed. The first act of the new Government was to nationalise insurance and banking.

Both houses of the Malagasy Parliament, and the activities of political parties were suspended.

Revised agreements with France were signed on June 4, 1973, providing for the withdrawal of the French forces stationed in the country since independence. The French naval base at Diégo Suarez has been turned into a civilian ship repair yard and French influence has been greatly reduced. Madagascar has also withdrawn from the Franc Zone and has announced a claim to the Islands of Juan de Nova, Glorieuses, Isle de l'Europe, Bassa da India and Tromelin which had remained integral parts of the French Republic after independence.

The people are of mixed Polynesian, Arab and Negro origin. The languages spoken are Malagasy and French. There are sizeable French, Chinese and Indian communities.

The island's economy is still almost wholly based on agriculture, which accounts for three-quarters of its exports. Development plans have placed emphasis on increasing agricultural and livestock production, the improvement of communications and the creation of small industries.

Total exports in 1973 amounted to *FMG* 44·7 million. The principal exports in order of value were coffee (25 per cent. of total), cloves (10 per cent.), vanilla, rice, meat and meat products, sugar and butter beans. Minerals exported include chrome ore, graphite and mica.

Total imports in 1973 amounted to *FMG* 45·1 million compared with *FMG* 51 million in 1972. The main imports are manufactures, petroleum, fertilizers, cement and rice.

TRADE WITH U.K.

	1972	1973
Imports from U.K......	£817,000	£763,000
Exports to U.K........	1,213,000	1,902,000

The rate of exchange is about Malagasy francs (FMG) 460= £1 (June 1975).

CAPITAL.—Tananarive (population about 400,000). Other main towns are the chief port Tamatave (55,000); Majunga (50,000); Fianarantsoa (47,000); Diégo Suarez (41,000).

FLAG.—Equal horizontal bands of red (above) and green, with vertical white band by staff.

NATIONAL DAY.—June 26 (Independence Day).

BRITISH EMBASSY

41 Lalana Razanakombana, Tananarive
(P.O. Box 167)

Ambassador Extraordinary and Plenipotentiary and Consul-General, (vacant).
1st Secretary and Consul, R. B. Hammond.
Commercial Officer and Vice-Consul, A. J. Marcelin.

THE MALDIVES

President, His Excellency Amir Ibrahim Nasir.

Area, etc.—The Maldives are a chain of coral atolls, some 400 miles to the south-west of Sri Lanka, stretching from just south of the equator for about 600 miles to the north. There are 12 clearly defined atolls, separated from each other by deep channels through which the currents run strongly. No point in the entire chain of islands is more than 8 feet above sea-level. The total number of islands is over 2,000, some being very small; about 220 of them are inhabited. The population of the islands (estimated, 1975) is 123,000. The people are Moslems and the Maldivian language is akin to Elu or old Sinhalese. They are highly civilized and are great navigators and traders.

Government.—The Maldives form a Republic which is elective. There is a Parliament (the *Citizens' Majlis*) with representatives elected from all the atolls. The life of the Majlis is 5 years. The Government consists of a Cabinet, which is responsible to the Majlis. By the agreement signed with the British Government in 1965, the Maldives form a composite sovereign and fully independent state, free to conduct their own external relations with other countries.

On March 6, 1975, the Prime Minister, Ahmed Zaki, was arrested and exiled, and presidential rule was imposed.

With the agreement of the Maldivian Government, the R.A.F. maintain a staging post on Gan Island, in Addu Atoll, the most southerly atoll, lying just south of the equator.

Production, etc.—The islands are thickly covered with coconut palms, and coir and ropes are exported. The principal industry is fishing and considerable quantities of fish are exported to Japan. Dried fish is exported to Sri Lanka, where it is a delicacy. The tourist industry is expanding very rapidly.

CAPITAL.—Malé (population, estimated 1970, 13,610). There is an air strip on Hulule Island about 1 mile from Malé.

FLAG.—Green field bearing a white crescent, with wide red border.

BRITISH REPRESENTATION

Ambassador Extraordinary and Plenipotentiary, His Excellency Harold Smedley, C.M.G., M.B.E. (1973) (*concurrently British High Commissioner to Sri Lanka*).

MALI
(Republic of Mali)

Chairman, National Liberation Committee, Lt. Moussa Traore, *born* 1937, *assumed office* Nov. 20, 1968.

The Republic of Mali, an inland state in north-west Africa has an area of 465,000 square miles and a population (U.N. estimate, 1969) of 4,929,000.

Formerly the French colony of Soudan, the

territory elected on Nov. 24, 1958, to remain as an autonomous republic within the French Community. It associated with Senegal in the Federation of Mali which was granted full independence on June 20, 1960. The Federation was effectively dissolved on August 22 by the secession of Senegal. The title of the Republic of Mali was adopted on Sept. 22, 1960. The Republic is no longer a member of the French Community. On July 1, 1962, a Mali *franc* equal in value to the *Franc CFA* was introduced and a new State bank set up.

The *régime* of Modibo Keita was overthrown on Nov. 19, 1968, and the President arrested by a group of Army officers, who then formed a National Liberation Committee and appointed a Prime Minister. Lieut. Traore assumed the functions of Head of State. A new civil constitution to come into being in 1979 was approved in a national referendum on June 21, 1974.

Mali's principal exports are groundnuts (raw and processed), cotton fibres, meat and dried fish. The principal rivers are the Niger and the Senegal. Goods to the value of £1,436,000 were imported from the United Kingdom in 1974 (1973 £431,000). Exports to U.K. 1974 £2,505,000 (1973 £782,000).

CAPITAL.—Bamako (170,000). Other towns are Gao, Kayes, Mopti, Sikasso and Segou (all regional capitals), and Timbuktu.

FLAG.—Vertical stripes of green (by staff), yellow and red. NATIONAL DAY.—September 22.

BRITISH EMBASSY

Ambassador Extraordinary and Plenipotentiary, His Excellency Denzil Inglis Dunnett, C.M.G., O.B.E. (resident at *Dakar*).

MAURITANIA
(Islamic Republic of Mauritania)

President and Prime Minister, Moktar Ould Daddah, *assumed office* Nov. 28, 1958; *re-elected for 5 years,* 1966 and 1971.

Mauritania lies on the north-west coast of Africa between Spanish Sahara and the Republic of Senegal. It is bounded on the east and south by the Republic of Mali. Area 419,000 sq. miles. The population of Mauritania was estimated at 1,140,000 in 1969. (*For MAP, see* p. 869.) The Republic of Mauritania elected on November 28, 1958, to remain within the French Community as an autonomous republic. It became fully independent on Nov. 28, 1960. Mauritania's main source of potential wealth lies in rich deposits of iron ore around Fort Gouraud, in the north of the country. Exports began in 1963, *via* a railway laid for the purpose from the mine to the port of Nouadhibou. The deposits are being exploited under the aegis of the *Société Nationale Industrielle Minière* following the nationalisation on November 28, 1974 of the internationally based company MIFERMA. There are copper deposits at Akjoujt which are being exploited by SOMIMA, a company which had an international base but was nationalised on Feb. 25, 1975.

Trade with U.K.

	1973	1974
Imports from U.K....	£857,000	£4,554,000
Exports to U.K.......	14,463,000	13,303,000

FLAG.—Yellow star and crescent on green ground.
NATIONAL DAY.—November 28.
CAPITAL.—Nouakchott (30,000).
British Ambassador, His Excellency Denzil Inglis Dunnett, C.M.G., O.B.E. (*Resident at Dakar*.)

MEXICO
(Estados Unidos Mexicanos)

President (1970–76), Lic. Luís Echeverría Alvarez, *born* 1922, *assumed office*, Dec. 1, 1970.

CABINET

Minister of the Interior, Lic. Mario Moya Palencia.
Foreign Affairs, Lic. Emilio O. Rabasa.
National Defence, Dr. Hermenegildo Cuenca Díaz.
Navy and Marine, Almirante C. G. Luís M. Bravo Carrera.
Finance, Lic. José López Portillo.
National Patrimony, Lic. Francisco Javier Alejo.
Industry and Commerce, Lic. José Campillo Sainz.
Agriculture and Livestock, Dr. Oscar Brauer Herrera.
Communcations and Transport, Ing. Eugenio Méndez Docurro.
Public Works, Ing. Luís Enriquez Bracamontes.
Hydraulic Resources, Ing. Leandro Rovirosa Wade.
Education, Ing. Victor Bravo Ahuja.
Labour and Social Affairs, Lic. Porfirio Muñoz Ledo.
Secretariat of the Presidency, Lic. Hugo Cervantes del Río.
Agrarian Affairs, Lic. Augusto Gómez Villanueva.
Federal District, Lic. Octavio Senties Gomez.
Health and Public Welfare, Dr. Ginés Navarro Díaz de León.
Attorney-General, Lic. Pedro Ojedo Paullada.
Tourism, Lic. Julio Hirschfield Aimada.

MEXICAN EMBASSY IN LONDON
48 Belgrave Square, S.W.1
[01–235 2522]

Ambassador Extraordinary and Plenipotentiary, His Excellency Hugo B. Margain, G.C.V.O.
Minister-Counsellor, Donaciano Gonzalez.
Consul-General, Sr. Mario Tapia Ponce.
Naval Attaché, Capt. Carlos López Sotelo.
Counsellors, Sra. Francisca Celis-Campos, M.V.O. (*Information*); Sr. Jorge E. Martin, M.V.O. (*Commercial*); Sr. Horacio Flores-Sánchez (*Cultural*).
1st Secretary, Sr. Andrés Rozental.

Area and Population.—Mexico occupies the southern part of the continent of North America, with an extensive seaboard to both the Atlantic and Pacific Oceans, extending from 14° 33' to 32° 43' N. lat. and 86° 46' to 117° 08' W. long., and comprising one of the most varied zones in the world. It contains 31 states and the federal district of Mexico, making in all 32 political divisions, covering an area of 761,530 square miles. At the Mexican General Census taken on Jan. 28, 1970, the total population was 48,313,000, but a present day estimate is 57,000,000.

The two great ranges of North America, the Sierra Nevada and Rocky Mountains, are pro-

longed from the north to a convergence towards the narrowing Isthmus of Tehuantepec, their course being parallel with the west and east coasts. The surface of the interior consists of an elevated plateau between the two ranges, with steep slopes both to the Pacific and Atlantic (Gulf of Mexico). In the west is the Peninsula of Lower California, with a mountainous surface, separated from the mainland by the Gulf of California. The Sierra Nevada, known in Mexico as the *Sierra Madre*, terminates in a transverse series of volcanic peaks, from Colima on the west to Citlaltepetl ("El Pico de Orizaba") on the east. The low-lying lands of the coasts form the *Tierra Caliente*, or tropical regions (below 3,000 ft.), the higher levels form the *Tierra Templada*, or temperate region (from 3,000 to 6,000 ft.), and the summit of the plateau with its peaks is known as *Tierra Fria*, or cold region (above 6,000 ft.). The only considerable rivers are the *Rio Grande del Norte* which forms part of the northern boundary, and is navigable for about 70 miles from its mouth in the Gulf of Mexico, and the *Rio Grande de Santiago*, the *Rio Balsas* and *Rio Papaloapan*. The remaining streams are governed by the formation of the land, and run in mountain torrents between deep-cut cañons or "barrancas". The largest fresh-water lakes are *Chapala* (70 miles long and 20 miles wide), and *Pátzcuaro*. In the north-west are saline lakes amid bare and dry regions. The climate varies according to the altitude, the rainy season lasting from June to October.

History and Archæology.—The present Mexico and Guatemala were once the centre of a remarkable indigenous civilization, which had unknown beginnings in the centuries before Christ, flowered in the periods from A.D. 500 to 1100 and A.D. 1300 to 1500 and collapsed before the little army of Spanish adventurers under Hernán Cortés in the years following 1519. Pre-Columbian Mexico was divided between different but connected Indian cultures, each of which has left distinctive archæological remains: the best-known of these are Chichén Itzá, Uxmal, Bonampak and Palenque, in Yucatan and Chiapas (Maya); Teotihuacán, renowned for the Pyramid of the Sun (216 feet high) in the Valley of Mexico (Teotihuacáno); Monte Albán and Mitla, near Oaxaca (Zapotec); El Tajín in the State of Vera Cruz (Totonac); and Tula in the State of Hidalgo (Toltec). The last and most famous Indian culture of all, the Aztec, based on Tenochtitlán, suffered more than the others from the Spaniards and only very few Aztec monuments remain.

A few years after the Conquest, the Spaniards

built Mexico City on the ruins of Tenochtitlán, and appointed a Viceroy to rule their new dominions, which they called New Spain. The country was largely converted to Christianity, and a distinctive colonial civilization, representing a marriage of Indian and Spanish traditions, developed and flourished, notably in architecture and sculpture. In 1810 a revolt began against Spanish rule. This was finally successful in 1821, when a precarious independence was proclaimed. Friction with the United States in Texas led to the war of 1845–48, at the end of which Mexico was forced to cede the northern provinces of Texas, California and New Mexico. In 1862 Mexican insolvency led to invasion by French forces which installed Archduke Maximilian of Austria as Emperor. The empire collapsed with the execution of the Emperor in 1867 and the austere reformer, Juárez, restored the republic. Juárez's death was followed by the dictatorship of Porfirio Diaz, which saw an enormous increase of foreign, particularly British and United States, investment in the country. In 1910 began the Mexican Revolution which reformed the social structure and the land system, curbed the power of foreign companies and ushered in the independent industrial Mexico of today.

Government.—Under the Constitution of Feb. 5, 1917 (as subsequently amended), Congress consists of a Senate of 60 members, elected for six years, and of a Chamber of Deputies, at present numbering 213, elected for three years. Presidents, who wield full executive powers, are elected for six years; they cannot be re-elected.

There are four political parties registered in Mexico, of which by far the largest and most influential is the *Part do Revolucionario Institucional* (P.R.I.) which has for many years constituted the government party.

Communications.—Veracruz, Tampico and Coatzacoalcos are the chief ports on the Atlantic, and Guaymas, Mazatlán, Manzanillo, Puerto Lázaro, Cárdenas, Acapulco, Salina Cruz and Puerto Madéro on the Pacific. The total tonnage of registered merchant marine at the end of 1972 was 732,000 tons. There were 24,119 kilometres of railway track open in Mexico in 1968. Work is proceeding on the reorganization, rehabilitation and re-equipment of the whole system; help in this has been forthcoming from the World Bank, the Export-Import Bank and private sources in the United States. The railways were completely nationalized in 1970.

The total length of road at the end of 1972 was 93,289 kilometres, of which 55,260 kilometres were paved, 21,775 dressed and 16,254 gravelled. Mexico City may be reached by at least three excellent roads from the United States, and work is complete on roads southward from Mexico City to Yucatán and the Guatemalan border.

At the end of 1971 the national telegraph system's lines were 200,000 kilometres in length. International telegraph services to the United States frontier are provided by the Government-owned Mexican Telegraph Company and then through the United States to Canada and Europe. Telephone communications are similar, with over 3,000,000 km. of long distance lines.

There is a good national and international network of air services. There are 1,202 airports and landing fields in Mexico. 24 airfields are equipped to receive turbojets and 26 to receive medium sized aircraft. There are 77 Mexican airlines including two trunk lines *Aeronaves de Mexico S.A.* and *Mexicana de Aviacion S.A.* which both have turbojets.

Production.—The total area of arable land is estimated at 24,000,000 hectares, of which an increasing amount is under cultivation. The principal agricultural crops are maize, beans, wheat, sugar cane, coffee, cotton, tomatoes, chili, tobacco, rice, chick-peas, groundnuts, sesame, alfalfa, vanilla, cocoa and many kinds of fruit, both tropical and temperate. The maguey, or Mexican cactus yields several fermented drinks, mezcal and tequila (distilled) and pulque (undistilled). Another species of the same plant supplies sisal-hemp (henequen). The forests abound in mahogany, rosewood, ebony and chicle trees.

The principal industries (apart from agriculture) are mining and petroleum, but during recent years there has been very considerable expansion of both light and heavy industries, over 80 per cent. of all consumer goods now being made in Mexico. Most of the remaining 20 per cent. is in fact made up of bulk imports of industrial equipment and motor vehicles for assembly, so that the true figure for local manufacture of consumer goods is nearer to 95 per cent. The steel industry has expanded rapidly and produced 4,637,000 tons of steel in 1973. The mineral wealth is great, but in recent years the low world market prices have caused a slump in the mining industry. The principal minerals are gold, silver, copper, lead, zinc, quicksilver, iron and sulphur. Substantial reserves of uranium have been found. Production in 1973 amounted to: gold, 4,122 kilograms; silver, 1,206 tons; lead, 79,296 tons.

The total petroleum reserves were said to be 397,000 m. metric tons in 1971. Total production of petroleum and natural gasoline reached 30,116 and 9,379 thousands of cubic metres respectively in 1973. Oil reserves were increased substantially due to very important new discoveries in Tabasco and Chiapas states.

Woollen and cotton spinning and weaving, the making of footwear and clothing and of domestic appliances of all kinds have made such progress in recent years that all these industries are protected by high import duties and import licence restrictions.

An indication of the rapid industrial expansion of Mexico is that output of electricity increased from 4,423 million kWh in 1950 to 37,084 million kWh in 1973.

Defence.—The regular army has a strength of 58 infantry battalions, one infantry brigade and a Presidential Guard of three battalions, 20 cavalry regiments, 3 parachute battalions and a small number of artillery and engineer units. There is also a conscript army of about 250,000 men organized into National Service divisions, each 6,000–7,000 strong. The Navy has some 60 ships of all kinds and the Air Force some 200 aircraft.

Language and Literature.—Spanish is the official language of Mexico and is spoken by about 95 per cent. of the population. About 1,005,000 inhabitants speak Indian languages only and of those about 30 per cent. speak Nahuatl, 9 per cent. Maya, 8 per cent. Zapotec, 7 per cent. Otomi and 10 per cent. Mixtec, the remainder speaking other varieties of the minor linguistic families. The National Library in the capital contains about 600,000 volumes. The Press of Mexico is in a flourishing condition with many daily newspapers in the capital and in other urban centres. The first printing press and the first regularly issued newspaper in the New World were established by the Spaniards in Mexico City.

Education.—Education is divided into primary, secondary and university. Primary education is free, secular and nominally compulsory. In 1974 there were 53,649 primary schools with 15,216,627 pupils, 7,642 secondary schools with 2,024,042 pupils. Other schools (preparatory, vocational, normal (for teachers), technical and commercial) numbered 1,325, with 590,089 students. The National University of Mexico (1533) had 100,000 students in 1970. There were 323 professional schools including universities, with 194,090 students. The prevailing religion is Roman Catholic. In 1965, 21 per cent. of the population above 6 years old were illiterate; while progress in reducing illiteracy has been steady over the last few years, it has barely kept pace with the rapidly increasing population. Between 1964 and 1970 the number of schools increased by 22 per cent. and the number of pupils by 43 per cent.

FINANCE (*Pesos*)

The proposed budget expenditure for 1975 amounts to 346,658,425,000 *pesos*, 187,107,539,000 from the Federal Government and 160,550,886,000 from the decentralised agencies. 51·7 per cent. is to be spent on economic growth, 32·7 per cent. on investment and social welfare, 10 per cent. on public debt and the remainder on administration and military expenses. This budget is a new record and represents a substantial increase over the 1974 budget.

As from April 19, 1954, by agreement with the International Monetary Fund, the Rate of Exchange has been fixed at 12·50 *pesos*=1 \$U.S. (*See also* p. 84.)

TRADE

	1973
Total Imports	*Pesos* 47,101,250,000
Total Exports	,, 26,050,000,000

Trade with U.K.

	1973	1974
Imports from U.K.	£39,650,000	£60,012,000
Exports to U.K.	10,268,000	17,868,000

The imports (mainly from U.S.A.) consist largely of machinery and implements for industry, mining and agriculture, and raw materials for industry. Principal exports are cotton, coffee, sisal (henequen), sugar, tomatoes and shrimps, lead, silver, zinc and other metals, tobacco, sulphur and heavy fuel oil.

CAPITAL.—Mexico City, est. pop. 1974 10,000,000. Other towns (est. pop. 1974) are: Guadalajara (2,000,200); Monterrey (1,350,000); Ciudad Juarez (436,000); Mexicali (390,400); Puebla (321,900); Léon (454,000); Chihuahua (363,800); Ψ Merida (253,800); and San Luis Potosi (230,300).

FLAG.—Three vertical bands, green, white, red, with shield of Mexico in centre. NATIONAL DAY.—September 16 (Proclamation of Independence).

BRITISH EMBASSY

(Calle Río Lerma 71, Colonia Cuauhtémoc, Mexico 5, D.F.)
Ambassador Extraordinary and Plenipotentiary, His Excellency Sir John Edgar Galsworthy, K.C.V.O., C.M.G. (1972).   £12,000
Counsellor, A. J. Payne.
Defence, Naval, Military and Air Attaché, Lt.-Col. B. D. O. Smith, M.V.O.
1st Secretaries, P. J. Streams (*Head of Chancery*); E. V. Nelson, M.V.O. (*Information*); Dr. I. Baker (*Scientific*); G. H. B. Kaye (*Cultural*); R. F. Stimson (*Commercial*).
2nd Secretaries, A. C. W. Culbert (*Consul*); W. G. Doherty; A. S. Green, M.V.O. (*Administration*); G. Thomas (*Cultural*); D. Hardinge (*Cultural*).
Assistant Information Officer, A. Estavillo.
Vice-Consul, A. D. Morales.
There are British Consular Offices at *Mexico City, Guadalajara, Acapulco, Mérida, Monterrey, Tampico,* and *Veracruz.*
British Council Representative.—I. P. Allnutt, *Guadalajara, Acapulco, Mazatlán, Mfrida, Monterrey,* Calle M. Antonio Caso 127, Mexico 4, D. F. The Council supplies books to the *Instituto Anglo-Mexicano de Cultura* in Mexico City.

BRITISH CHAMBER OF COMMERCE, Calle Tiber 103, 6th Floor, Mexico, D.F.—*Manager*, D. Hennessy.

Transit from London to Mexico City:—By air, 13 hours; By sea, U.K.–New York, 5 to 10 days; New York–Mexico City, by rail, 3 days; by air, 6 hours. There is a direct freight service from Liverpool to ports on both the Mexican Gulf and the Pacific Coast.

MONACO
(Principauté de Monaco)

Sovereign Prince, H.S.H. Rainier III-Louis-Henri-Maxence Bertrand, *born* May 31, 1923, *succeeded his grandfather* (H.S.H. Prince Louis II), May 9, 1949; *married* April 19, 1956, Miss Grace Patricia Kelly and has issue Prince Albert Alexandre Louis Pierre, *born* March 14, 1958, Princess Caroline Louise Marguerite, *born* January 23, 1957; and Princess Stephanie Marie Elisabeth, *born* Feb. 1, 1965.
President of the Crown Council, M. Pierre Blanchy.
President of the National Council, M. Auguste Medecin.

Minister of State, André Saint-Mleux, *appointed* 1972.

CONSULATE-GENERAL IN LONDON
4 Audley Square, W.1
[01–629 0734]
Consul-General, I. S. Ivanović.
Consul, A. J. Hucker, 3 Gray's Inn Square, W.C.1
[01–242 5323].

A small Principality on the Mediterranean, with land frontiers joining France at every point, and consisting of the old town of Monaco, La Condamine, and Monte Carlo, where is the famous casino. The Principality comprises a narrow strip of country about 2 miles long (area approx. 467 acres), with 24,500 inhabitants (est. 1975) and a yearly average of over 600,000 visitors. The whole available ground is built over, so that there is no cultivation, though there are some notable public and private gardens. Monaco has a small harbour (30 ft. alongside quay) and the import duties are the same as in France. The National Council consists of 18 members and the Council of Government of the Minister of State, as President, and three State Counsellors. There is a local police force of 160 men.

A new constitution was promulgated by Prince Rainier on Dec. 17, 1962, which is subject to modification only with the approval of the elected National Council. It maintains the traditional hereditary monarchy and gives guarantees for the right of association, trade union freedom and the right to strike.

CAPITAL.—Monaco-viller (2,422).
FLAG.—Two equal horizontal stripes, red over white.

British Consul-General, I. C. L. Alexander, O.B.E (*Resident at Nice*).

(OUTER) MONGOLIA
(Mongolian People's Republic—
Bugd Nairamdakh Mongol Ard Uls)

President: Yu Tsedenbal.
Prime Minister: J. Batmonkh.

Mongolian People's Revolutionary
(= *Communist*) **Party**

Politbureau of the Central Committee, Yu Tsedenbal; J. Batmonkh; S. Luvsan; D. Molomjamts; N. Jagvaral; D. Maidar; N. Luvsanravdan; S. Jalanajar (*full members*); T. Ragchaa; B. Altangerel (*deputy members*).

Secretariat of the Central Committee, Yu Tsedenbal (1st); D. Molomjamts; N. Jagvaral; S. Jalanajav; D. Chimidorj.

MONGOLIAN EMBASSY
7 Kensington Court, W.8
[01–937 0150]

Ambassador Extraordinary and Plenipotentiary, His Excellency Denzengiin Tserendondov (1973).
2nd Secretary, Mrs. L. Ider.
Attaché, Luvsandorjin Dawagiv.

Area and Population.—The Mongolian People's Republic (Outer Mongolia) is a large and sparsely populated country to the north of China. Its area is over 600,000 square miles. Its population, 1975 is about 1,300,000. However, this total constitutes only part of the Mongolians of Asia, a number of whom are to be found in China and in the neighbouring regions of the Soviet Union (especially the Mongolian Buryat Autonomous Region). This country, which is almost nowhere below 1,000 feet above sea level, forms part of the Central Asiatic Plateau and rises towards the west in the high mountains of the Mongolian Altai and Khanggai Ranges. The Khentai Mountain Range, situated to the north-east of the capital Ulan Bator, is less high. The Gobi region covers the southern half of the country. It contains some sand deserts, but between these less hospitable areas there is steppe land which provides pasture for great numbers of cattle, sheep, goats, camels and horses (the latter is still the characteristic means of transport for the population). There are several long rivers and many lakes, but good water is scarce since much of the water is salty. The climate is hard, with a short mild summer giving way to a long winter when temperatures can drop as low as minus 50° Centigrade.

History.—Mongolia, under Genghis Khan the conqueror of China and much of Asia, was for many years a buffer state between Tsarist Russia and China, although it was under general Chinese suzerainty. The outbreak of the Chinese Revolution in 1911 was the signal for a declaration of independence which was confirmed by the Sino-Russian Treaty of Kiakhta (1915), but cancelled by a unilateral Chinese declaration in 1919. Later the country became a battleground of the Russian Civil War, and Soviet and Mongolian troops occupied Ulan Bator in 1921: this was followed by another declaration of independence. However, in 1924 the Soviet Union in a Treaty with China again recognized the latter's sovereignty over Mongolia; but this was never properly exercised because of China's pre-occupation with internal affairs, and later by the anti-Japanese war. The Mongolian People's Republic was formally established in 1924. Under the Yalta Agreement, Chiang Kai-shek agreed to a plebiscite, held in 1945, in which the Mongolians declared their desire for independence; this was granted. The country entered the United Nations in 1961. The heroes of Mongolian history during the earlier part of the century were Sukhebator, who died in 1923, and the Communist Choibalsang (died 1952), who did much to turn the country into the Communist state it is today, and carried out a systematic destruction of the power of the Lamas and the old princely houses which had previously been the dominant force in both the economy and the government.

Production, etc.—The total of Mongolia's livestock was planned to reach 52 million in 1975. Traditionally the Mongolian is a herdsman, tending his flock of sheep, goats and horses, cows and camels and leading a totally nomadic life. With the coming of the Communist régime (under the Mongolian People's Revolutionary Party) and especially since 1952, great efforts have been made to settle the population, but a large proportion still live nomadically or semi-nomadically in the traditional *ger* (circular tent). The pastoral population was collectivized at the end of the 1950s into huge *negdels* (co-operatives) and State farms which have hastened the process of settlement, but within these the herdsmen and their families still move with their *gers* from pasture to pasture as the seasons change. The country, except for the capital, is today divided into 18 *aimaks* (provinces) and beneath these into more than 300 *somons* (counties), and these form the basis of the State organization of the country, parallel with which runs the apparatus of the Revolutionary Party.

Membership of the Communist bloc has brought Mongolia considerable quantities of aid from other Socialist countries, especially the Soviet Union and China, both of which supplied many thousands of workers to help with various construction projects. Mongolia's support of the Soviet Union in the Sino-Soviet dispute resulted in the cessation of Chinese aid and a halt in the supply of Chinese workers. Mongolia is now relying on eastern European, especially Czech, Polish and East German aid to supplement the massive assistance from the Soviet Union. Soviet and Bloc aid is hastening the process of industrialization; for although the economy remains based on the herds of animals, and the principal exports of the country are still animal by-products (especially wool, hides and furs) and cattle, factories serving the needs of the country have been started up and the coal and electricity industries are being developed to provide an industrial base. A joint Mongolian/Soviet enterprise for copper and molybdenum mining has been started in northern Mongolia.

Ulan Bator, which contains a sixth of the country's population, is the main seat of industry. Under the third 5-year plan, a new industrial centre was founded at Darkhan, north of the capital near the Soviet frontier. This was being continued in the fourth 5-year plan (1966–70), and a start has been made with the development of Choibalsan in the east as a third industrial town (mostly for the processing of animal and agricultural products). Agriculture, formerly little practised, is now being extended. Communication is still difficult in the country as there are virtually no roads. The trans-Mongolian railway, following the line of the old north-south trade route, was opened in 1955 and links Mongolia with both China and Russia. Mongolia's fundamental difficulty is its very small population and labour force.

Foreign trade is dominated by the Soviet Union, with the eastern European countries taking most of what is left. Trade with western countries is developing slowly.

CAPITAL.—Ulan Bator. (Pop. 195,300.)

FLAG.—Vertical tri-colour red, blue, red and in the hoist the traditional Soyombo symbol in gold.

NATIONAL DAY.—July 11 (Anniversary of the Mongolian People's Republic).

BRITISH EMBASSY
Ulan Bator

Ambassador Extraordinary and Plenipotentiary, His Excellency Myles Walker Ponsonby, C.B.E. (1974)
3rd Secretary, R. G. Lewington.
Attachés, K. McWilliam; J. N. C. Church.

MOROCCO
(Kingdom of Morocco)

King, H.M. King Hassan II, *born* July 9, 1929; *acceded* February 26, 1961, *on the death of his father,* King Mohammad V. *Heir,* Crown Prince Sidi Muhammad, *b.* August 21, 1963.

CABINET
(April 1974)

Prime Minister, Ahmed Osman.
Cultural Affairs, Hadj M'Hamed Bahnini.
Co-operation and Training of Cadres, Dr. Mohamed Benhima.
Foreign Affairs, Dr. Ahmed Laraki.
Information, Ahmed Taibi Benhima.
Justice, Abbas El Kissi.
Interior, Mohamed Haddou Echiguer.
Religious Endowments and Islamic Affairs, Dey Ould Sidi Baba.
Posts, Telegraphs and Telephones, Gen. Driss Ben Omar el Alami.
Finance, Abdelkader Benslimane.
Agriculture and Agrarian Reform, Salah M'Zily.
Urbanism, Housing, Tourism and the Environment, Hassan Zemmouri.
Administrative Affairs and Secretary General of the Government, M'Hamed Benyakhlef.
Public Health, Dr. Abolerrahman Touhami.
Commerce, Industry, Mines and Merchant Marine, Abdellatif Ghissassi.
Public Works and Communications, Ahmed Tazi.
Higher Education, Abdellatif Ben Abdeljalil.
Primary and Secondary Education, Mohamed Bouamoud.
Labour and Social Affairs, Mohamed Larbi el Khattabi.
Secretaries of State, Abdallah Gharnit (*National Co-operation and Traditional Industry*); Kamal Raghaye (*Finance*); Abdeslam Znined (*General Affairs*); Mohamed Belkhayat (*Economic Affairs*); Tayeb Bencheikh (*Planning and Regional Development*); Dr. Mohamed Tahiri Jotti (*Youth and Sports*); Driss Basri (*Interior*); Jalal Said (*Urbanism, Housing, Tourism and Environment*); Mohamed Mahjoubi (*Information*); Hassan Loukach (*Religious Endowments and Islamic Affairs*); Moussa Saadi (*Commerce, Industry, Mines and Merchant Marine*); Moulay Ahmed Cherkaoui (*Foreign Affairs*).

ROYAL MOROCCAN EMBASSY AND CONSULATE
49 Queen's Gate Gardens, S.W.7
[01–584 8827]

Ambassador Extraordinary and Plenipotentiary, His Excellency M. Abdellah Chorfi.
Minister Counsellor, Khalil Haddaoui.
Military, Naval and Air Attaché, Col. Ahmed Benomar Sbay.

Area and Population.—Morocco is situated in the north-western corner of the African continent between latitude 27° 40′–36° N. and longitude 1°–13° W. with an area estimated at approximately 180,000 sq. miles, and a population (1971) of 15,379,259. It is traversed in the north by the Riff Mountains and in a general S.W. to N.E. direction, by the Middle Atlas, the High Atlas, the Anti-Atlas and the Sarrho ranges. The northern flanks of the Middle and High Atlas Mountains are well wooded but their southern slopes, exposed to the dry desert winds, are generally arid and desolate, as are the whole of the Anti-Atlas and Sarrho ranges. The north-westerly point of Morocco is the peninsula of Tangier which is separated from the continent of Europe by the narrow strait of Gibraltar. The Jebel Mousa dominates the promontory and, with the rocky eminence of Gibraltar, was known to the ancients as the *Pillars of Hercules*, the western gateway of the Mediterranean.

Climate.—The climate of Morocco is generally good and healthy, especially on the Atlantic coast, (where a high degree of humidity is, however, prevalent) the country being partially sheltered by the Atlas mountains from the hot winds of the Sahara. The rainy season may last from November to April. The plains of the interior are intensely hot in summer. Average summer and winter temperatures for Rabat are 81° F. and 45° F.; for Marrakesh 101° F. and 40° F. respectively.

Government.—Morocco became an independent sovereign state in 1956, following joint declarations made with France on March 2, 1956, and with Spain on April 7, 1956. The Sultan of Morocco, Sidi Mohammad ben Youssef, adopted the title of King Mohammad V.

A constitution, adopted by referendum on December 7, 1962, was in force from December 14, 1962, until June 7, 1965.

Following serious disturbances in Casablanca in March, 1965, attempts were made by King Hassan, in consultation with all political parties, to form a government of national union. These efforts were unsuccessful and on June 7, 1965, the King proclaimed a "state of exception" and suspended Parliament. Assuming himself the office of Prime Minister, he announced the formation of a new government and indicated that constitutional changes were to follow. A revised Constitution was approved by a national referendum on July 24, 1970 and brought into effect soon after. It was superseded by another constitution, also approved by a national referendum, on March 1, 1972. This provides that not only political parties, but trade unions, chambers of commerce and professional bodies will participate in the organization of the State and representation of the people; specifies that the King is the supreme representative of the people; makes changes in the composition of the Regency Council and the Sovereign's rights; establishes a unicameral legislature in which members' tenure of office is six years. The new Chamber is to have 240 members, 180 elected by direct universal suffrage and 60 members elected by electoral colleges representing local government, industry, agriculture and working class groups. However the election expected in April 1973 did not take place.

Defence.—The Moroccan army, formed in 1956, is about 50,000 strong. A Moroccan air force was formed in 1959 and a navy in 1960. The armed forces possess quantities of French, Soviet and American equipment, including aircraft.

Production and Trade.—Morocco's main sources of wealth are agricultural and mineral. The current Five Year Plan (1973–77) for economic development places particular emphasis on social improvement. Other priority sectors are industrial development, agriculture and tourism.

Agriculture employs more than 70 per cent. of the working population and accounts for about 40 per cent. of Morocco's exports. The main agricultural products are cereals, citrus fruits, olives, grapes, tomatoes and vegetables. Dates and figs are also grown and exported. Cork and wood-pulp are the most important commercial forest products. Esparto grass is also produced. There is a fishing industry and substantial quantities of canned fish, mainly sardines, are exported. Livestock in 1972 included about 11,900,000 sheep, 4,600,000 goats, 2,785,000 horned cattle and smaller numbers of donkeys, camels, horses and pigs.

Morocco's mineral exports are phosphates, anthracite, manganese, iron ore, lead and zinc, while the following are also produced: petroleum, cobalt, graphite, copper, molybdenum, tin, antimony, ochre and gypsum. Production of phosphates totalled 19,721,237 tons in 1974. There are oil refineries at Mohammedia and Sidi Kacem, and oil sold in Morocco in 1974 amounted to 2,270,117 cu. metres. Production of crude oil in 1974 amounted to 25,159 tons.

Morocco's main import requirements are petroleum products, motor vehicles and tyres, building materials, fabrics, agricultural and other machinery, chemical products, clothing, householdware, sugar, green tea and other foodstuffs.

The trade of Morocco, which is chiefly with France, the U.S.A., W. Germany, Italy, the United Kingdom and Spain, was valued in 1974 at Imports, DH 4,683,587,000; Exports, DH 3,745,948,000 (both involving very small variations on 1973).

Trade with U.K.

	1973	1974
Imports from U.K....	£14,192,000	£28,127,000
Exports to U.K.......	23,123,000	52,506,000

There is a British Chamber of Commerce at Casablanca (c/o B.B.M.E., 80 Avenue Lalla Yacout).

Finance and Currency.—The unit of currency is the *dirham.* Exchange rate (*see* p. 84).

The 1975 Ordinary Budget amounted to DH 8,849,000,000 (1974: DH 4,951,000,000).

Communications.—The railway runs south from Tangier to Sidi Kacem. From this junction, one line runs eastwards through Fez and Oujda to Algeria, and another continues southwards, through Rabat and Casablanca, to Marrakesh. A line running due south from Oujda skirts the Morocco-Algeria frontier and reaches Colomb-Bechar in Algeria, the beginning of the Mediterranean–Niger project. Moroccan railroads cover 1,250 miles and traction is electric or diesel. An extensive network of well-surfaced roads covers all the main towns in the kingdom.

Tangier is distant from London about 1,200 miles or a matter of hours by air, 4 days by sea. Royal-Air-Maroc and British Caledonian Airways operate services between Casablanca and London. There are air services between Tangier, Agadir, Marrakesh (seasonal) and London, and also between Tangier and Gibraltar connecting with London. Royal Air Inter operates internal services. There are also regular services by many airlines with many parts of the world.

Language.—Arabic is the official language. Berber is the vernacular mainly in the mountain regions. French and Spanish are also spoken, mainly in the towns. The foreign population is estimated at 112,000 (1971). The national daily press consists of 3 Arabic and 4 French newspapers.

Education.—There are government primary, secondary and technical schools. At Fez there is a theological university of great repute in the Moslem world. There is a secular university at Rabat. Schools for special denominations, Jewish and Catholic, are permitted and may receive government grants.

CAPITAL.— Ψ Rabat (population 565,000). The other chief towns are: Ψ Casablanca (1,638,000); Marrakesh (407,000); Fez (399,000); Meknes (376,000); Oujda (323,000); Tetuan (285,000). Ψ Tangier (187,894), Ψ Kenitra (139,105). The towns of Fez, Marrakesh and Meknes were capitals at various times in Morocco's history.

FLAG.—Red, with green pentagram (the Seal of Solomon). NATIONAL DAY.—March 3 (Anniversary of the Throne).

BRITISH EMBASSY
Rabat

Ambassador Extraordinary and Plenipotentiary, His Excellency John Spenser Ritchie Duncan, C.M.G., M.B.E. (1975).
1st Secretaries, M. A. Marshall (*Head of Chancery*), J. J. Beale (*Economic and Consul*).
Defence Attaché, Lt.-Col. B. Henderson.
2nd Secretary, Mrs. A. Massouh.
3rd Secretary, C. P. M. Griffith.
Vice-Consul, J. S. Taylor.

BRITISH CONSULAR OFFICES
There are British Consular Offices at *Tangier* and *Casablanca.*

British Council Representative, W. E. N. Kensdale, P.O. Box 427, 6 Avenue Moulay Youssef, Rabat.

MOZAMBIQUE
(Moçambique)

President, Samora Moïses Machel.

Area and Population.—The People's Republic of Mozambique lies on the east coast of Africa, and is bounded by South Africa in the south and west, Rhodesia in the west, Zambia and Malawi in the north-west and Tanzania in the north. It has an area of 297,657 square miles, with a population (census 1970) of 8,233,834.

Government.—Mozambique, discovered by Vasco da Gama in 1498, and colonized by Portugal in 1505, achieved complete independence from Portugal on June 25, 1975. The date had been agreed in September 1974 by Portugal and *Frelimo,* (*Frente da Libertação de Moçambique*) the Marxist liberation movement. A transitional government, containing Portuguese and *Frelimo* elements, had been sworn in on Sept. 20, 1974.

A constitution was published on June 25, 1975, which stated, *inter alia,* that the President of *Frelimo* would be President of the People's Republic of Mozambique, and head of state. The legislative body would be the People's Assembly, consisting of 210 members.

It was announced that the basis of the economy would be collectivised agriculture. Main exports are sugar, cashew nuts, copra, cotton, tea and sisal.

CAPITAL.— Ψ Lourenço Marques (pop. 441,363). Other main ports are Beira, Moçambique, and Nacala.

FLAG.—Red, green, black, white and yellow; central motif of a rifle crossed with a hoe, on a book inside a cog-wheel.

There is a *British Consulate-General* at Lourenço Marques.
Consul-General, S. F. St. C. Duncan.
There is also a *British Consulate* at Beira.

(NEJD. *See* Saudi Arabia)

NEPAL

Sovereign, King Birendra Bir Bikram Shah Deva, born 1945, *succeeded* January 31, 1972.

COUNCIL OF MINISTERS

Prime Minister and Minister for Palace Affairs and General Administration, Nagendra Prasad Ryal.
Commerce and Industry, Chaturbhuj Prasad Singh.
Foreign Affairs, Krishna Raj Aryal.
Home, Panchayat, Law and Justice, Bhoj Raj Ghimire.
Land Reform, Jog Meher Shrestha.
There are also seven State Ministers and nine Assistant Ministers.

ROYAL NEPALESE EMBASSY IN LONDON
12A, Kensington Palace Gardens, W.8.
[01–229 6231]

Ambassador Extraordinary and Plenipotentiary, His Excellency The Rt. Hon. General Kiran Shumshere J. B. Rana, K.C.V.O., K.B.E. (1974).
1st Secretary, Bhanu Prasad Thapliya.
Military Attaché, Lt.-Col. Madan Krishna Kharel.
Attaché, Khadqa Bahadur Khadka.

Nepal lies between India and Tibet on the slopes of the Himalayas, and includes Mt. Everest (29,028 ft.). It has a total area of 54,362 sq. miles and a population (1971 census) of 11,289,000. Amid the mountains lie many fertile valleys. The lower hills and Terai Plains are covered with jungle, in which wild animals abound. Rice, wheat, maize, etc., are grown. (*For* MAP, *see* p. 745.) Kathmandu, the capital, is connected with India by a road, the mountain section of which was built by India under the Colombo Plan, and to Tibet by a road from Kathmandu to Kodari on the border, which was built by the Chinese and opened on May 26, 1967. The Indian-aided Sunauli Pokhara road (128 miles) was inaugurated in April, 1972, and construction by the Chinese of a road between Kathmandu and Pokhara was opened in 1973. The East–West Highway (*Mahendra Raj Marg*) to run the length of the country, is now under construction in the following sections: Jhapa to Janakpur (173 miles and Butwal to Nepalgunj (148 miles) by Indian aid team; Narayanghat-Butwai (75 miles) by British aid team. The Russian-aided Janakpur-Simra (73 miles) section was opened in April, 1972.

Nepal exports rice and other grains, hides, oilseeds, *ghi*, cattle, jute, large quantities of timber, etc., and imports cotton goods and yarn, sugar, salt, spices, petrol, metals, etc. Nepalese imports from U.K. were valued at £670,000 in 1971 (1970 £1,767,000); exports to U.K., £371,000 (1970, £857,000).

Finance.—Revenue for the fiscal year 1974–75, mainly from land rent and taxes, is estimated at N.Rs.959,748,000, compared with a revised figure of N.Rs.729,420,000 in 1973–74. A State Bank was inaugurated on April 26, 1956, to issue bank notes, regulate the Nepalese currency, fix foreign exchange rates and help in the preparation of a national budget. Since the sterling pound was floated, the exchange rate has fluctuated. On June 2, 1975, it was NRs.24·27 Buying Rate and NRs.24·77 Selling Rate= £1. There are three commercial banks with branches throughout Nepal.

The inhabitants are of mixed stock with Mongolian characteristics prevailing in the north and Indian in the south, and their religions are Hinduism and Buddhism. They were originally divided into numerous hill clans and petty principalities, one of which, Gorkha, whose ruler founded the present Nepalese dynasty, became predominant in 1768. During the 1914–18 and the 1939–45 wars, the Nepalese Government rendered unstinted and unconditional assistance to the British Government.

From the middle of the nineteenth century, Nepal was ruled by the Rana family which provided the hereditary prime ministers of the country.

After the Second World War, a revolutionary movement in 1950 and 1951 achieved the aim of breaking the hereditary power of the Ranas and of restoring to the monarchy the powers which it had lost 104 years before. After ten years, during which various parties and individuals tried their hand at government, the late King Mahendra resumed direct powers on December 16, 1960, with the object of leading a united country to basic democracy.

The state of emergency ended on April 13, 1963, the King appointing a Cabinet consisting of a Prime Minister and seven other ministers, all of whom have seats in the indirectly elected *Rastriya Panchayat* (Parliament). A State Council (*Raj Sabha*) of 69 members, to advise the King on state affairs, constitutional matters and on the choice of the heir to the throne was also appointed on April 2, 1963. An Act was passed at the same time maintaining the existing ban on political parties.

CAPITAL.—Kathmandu, population (1971) 353,756. Other towns of importance are Morang (301,557), Lalitpur (154,998) and Bhaktapur (110,157). These population figures include some adjacent rural areas.

FLAG.—Double pennant of crimson with blue border on peaks; white moon with rays in centre of top peak; white quarter sun, recumbent in centre of bottom peak. NATIONAL DAY.—February 18.

BRITISH EMBASSY

Ambassador Extraordinary and Plenipotentiary, His Excellency Michael Scott, M.V.O. (1974).
1st Secretaries, R. E. Holloway (*Head of Chancery and Consul*); D. A. Spain, O.B.E. (*Information*).
Defence Attaché, Lt.-Col. J. A. Lys, M.C.
2nd Secretary, M. H. Connor.
Vice-Consul, P. H. Chase.

British Council Representative, D. M. Waterhouse, P.O.Box 640, Kanti Path, Kathmandu.

NETHERLANDS (or HOLLAND)
(Koninkrijk der Nederlanden)

Queen of the Netherlands, Her Majesty JULIANA, K.G., born April 30, 1909; *married* January 7, 1937, Prince Bernhard of Lippe Biesterfeld, G.C.B., G.C.V.O., G.B.E. (THE PRINCE OF THE NETHERLANDS), born June 29, 1911; *succeeded*, September 4, 1948, upon the abdication of her mother Queen Wilhelmina who died Nov. 28, 1962. Issue:

(1) H.R.H. Princess Beatrix Wilhelmina Armgard, G.C.V.O., *born* Jan. 31, 1938; *married* March 10, 1966, H.R.H. Prince Claus George Willem Otto Frederik Geert of the Netherlands, Jonkheer van Amsberg; and has issue, Prince Willem Alexander, *b.* April 27, 1967; Prince Johan Friso, *b.* Sept. 25, 1968; Prince Constantijn Christof, *b.* Oct. 11, 1969.

(2) H.R.H. Princess Irene Emma Elizabeth, *born* Aug. 5, 1939; *married* April 29, 1964, Prince Hugo Carlos of Bourbon-Parma and has issue, Prince Carlos, *b.* Jan. 27, 1970; Princess Margarita and Prince Jaime, b. Oct. 14, 1972; and Princess Maria Carolina Christina, *b.* June 23, 1974.

(3) H.R.H. Princess Margriet Francisca, *born* (at Ottawa, Canada), Jan. 19, 1943; *married* Jan. 10, 1967, Mr. Pieter van Vollenhoven; and has issue, Prince Maurits, *b.* April 17, 1968; and Prince Bernhard, *b.* Dec. 25, 1969; and Prince Pieter, *b.* March 22, 1972; and Prince Floris, *b.* April 10, 1975.

(4) H.R.H. Princess Maria Christina, *born* Feb. 18, 1947. *married* June, 28, 1975, Jorge Guillermo.

CABINET

Prime Minister and Minister of General Affairs, J. M. den Uyl (*Labour*).
Deputy Prime Minister and Minister of Justice, A. A. M. van Agt (*Catholic*).
Foreign Affairs, M. van der Stoel (*Labour*).
Home Affairs, W. F. de Gaay Fortman (*Anti-Revolutionary*).
Education and Sciences, J. A. Kemenade (*Labour*).
Finance, W. F. Duisenberg (*Labour*).
Defence, H. Vredeling (*Labour*).
Housing and Planning, H. Gruijters (*Democrats '66*).
Transport and Waterways, Th. E. Westerterp (*Catholic*).
Economic Affairs, R. F. M. Lubbers (*Catholic*).
Agriculture and Fisheries, A. P. J. J. M. van der Stee (*Catholic*).
Social Affairs, J. Boersma (*Anti-Revolutionary*).
Culture, Recreation and Social Welfare, H. W. van Doorn (*Radical*).
Public Health and Environment, Mrs I. Vorrink (*Labour*).
Development Co-operation, J. P. Pronk (*Labour*).
Without Portfolio in charge of Science Policy, F. H. P. Trip (*Radical*).

NETHERLANDS EMBASSY IN LONDON
38 Hyde Park Gate, S.W.7
[01–584 5040]

Ambassador Extraordinary and Plenipotentiary, His Excellency Baron W. J. G. Gevers, G.C.V.O. (1971).
Minister Plenipotentiary, H. Th. Schaapveld.
1st Secretary, D. V. Schaafsma.
2nd Secretary, J. Huisman (*Administration*).
3rd Secretary, R. M. F. van der Kroon.
Naval Attaché and Air Attaché, Capt. J. R. Roele.
Assistant Naval Attaché and Assistant Air Attaché, Cdr. H. Prinselaar.
Military Attaché, Col. W. Epke.

NETHERLANDS

NORTH SEA

Groningen

Haarlem · Amsterdam · Enschede
The Hague · Leiden · Hilversum · Apeldoorn
· Rotterdam · Utrecht · Arnhem
Nijmegen
· Breda · Tilburg
Eindhoven

BELGIUM

GERMANY

0   20   40   60   80 MILES

Counsellor (Press and Cultural Affairs), D. J. van Wijnen, C.V.O.
1st Secretary for Cultural Affairs, J. A. F. S. van Alphen.
Attaché for Cultural Affairs, Miss A. Stenfert Kroese.
Minister Plenipotentiary, (Economic), C. H. A. Plug.
1st Secretaries, J. Schoen; J. A. Krijgsman.
Civil Air Attaché, Dr. D. Goedhuis.

Area and Population.—The Kingdom of the Netherlands is a maritime country of Western Europe, situated on the North Sea, in lat. 50° 46′–53° 34′ N. and long. 3° 22′–7° 14′ E., consisting of 11 provinces plus Eastern and Southern Flevoland (reclaimed parts of the Ysselmer) and containing a total area of 13,500 sq. miles (34,830 sq. km). The population in Jan. 1975 was estimated at 13,599,092. The live birth rate in Jan., 1974 was 13·8 per 1,000 of the population, and the death-rate was 8·0.

The land is generally flat and low, intersected by numerous canals and connecting rivers—in fact, a network of water courses. The principal rivers are the Rhine, Maas, Yssel and Scheldt.

The chief agricultural products are potatoes, wheat, rye, barley, corn, sugar beet, cattle, pigs, milk and milk products, cheese, butter, poultry, eggs, beans, peas, flax seed, vegetables, fruit, flower bulbs, and cut flowers and there is an important fishing industry. Among the principal industries are engineering, both mechanical and electrical, electronics, nuclear energy, petro-chemicals and plastics, shipbuilding, steel, textiles of all types, leather goods, electrical appliances, metal ware, furniture, paper, cigars, sugar, liqueurs, beer, clothing, rubber products, etc.

Production of coal (1974) was 758,000,000 kg., crude oil 14,610,000,000 K.cal and refined oil 637,190,000,000 K.cal; steel 5,840,000,000 kg. and gas 83,725,000,000 cubic metres. Diamond cutting, though still an important industry, has declined considerably in importance, employing about 154 persons at the end of 1971.

Government.—In 1815 the Netherlands became a constitutional Kingdom under King William I, a Prince of Orange-Nassau, a descendant of the house which has taken a leading part in the destiny of the nation since the 16th century. The States-General comprise the *Eerste Kamer* (First Chamber) of 75 members, elected for 6 years by the Provincial Council; and the *Tweede Kamer* (Second Chamber) of 150 members, elected for 4 years by men and women voters of 18 years and upwards. Members of the *Tweede Kamer* are paid.

General elections were held on Nov. 29, 1972 for the Second Chamber of the States-General. Party Representation is: Labour Party, 43; Catholic People's Party, 27; Liberal, 22; Anti-Revolutionary, 14; Democrats '66, 6; Christian Historical Union, 7; Democratic Socialists '70, 6; Communists, 7; Radicals, 7; Political Reformed, 3; Reformed Political Union, 2; Pacifist Socialists, 2; Farmers' Party, 3; Roman Catholic National Party, 1.

The First (Upper) Chamber of the States-General was elected by the Provincial Councils in June, 1974 Party Representation is: Labour, 21; Catholic People's Party, 16; Liberal, 12; Christian Historical Union, 7; Anti-Revolutionary, 6; Radicals, 4; Communists, 4; Democrats '66, 3; Political Reformed, 1; Farmers' Party, 1.

Defence.—The armed forces are almost entirely committed to NATO. As a result of a far-reaching defence review recently completed the three services are expected to be reduced in size but to be re-equipped over the next decade with new ships, aircraft and Army vehicles. Under this plan, the Royal Netherlands Navy is to be modernised to provide three escort groups, each consisting of a Command ship and six frigates, for use under NATO Command in the Atlantic and North Sea. The Royal Netherlands Army is to be reorganised into two active and one reserve Divisions each containing three Brigades. These units are fully integrated into the NATO Central Army Command. The Royal Netherlands Air Force comprises nine squadrons of jet aircraft, the principal roles of which are offensive support, air defence, and reconnaissance. All these squadrons are assigned to the NATO Central Region. In addition there are various missile units stationed in Germany, also assigned to NATO.

Language and Literature.—Dutch is a West-Germanic language of Saxon origin, closely akin to Old English and Low German. It is spoken in the Netherlands and the northern part of Belgium. It is also used in the Netherlands Antilles. Afrikaans, one of the two South African languages, has Dutch as its origin, but differs from it in grammar and pronunciation. There are eight national papers, four of which are morning papers, and there are many regional daily papers.

Education.—Illiteracy is practically non-existent. Primary and secondary education is given in both denominational and State schools, the denominational schools being eligible for State assistance on equal terms with the State schools. Attendance at primary school is compulsory. Secondary schools are numerous, well equipped and well attended. The principal Universities are at Leiden, Utrecht, Groningen, Amsterdam (2), Nijmegen (R.C.) and Rotterdam, and there are technical Universities at Delft (polytechnic); Eindhoven (polytechnic), Enschede (polytechnic) Wageningen (agriculture).

Communications.—The total extent of navigable rivers including canals, is 4,354 km. and of metalled roads 82,877 km. In 1974 the total length of the railway system amounted to 3,832 km., of which 1,646 km. were electrified. The mercantile marine in 1974 consisted of 702 ships of total 3,355,000 gross registered tons. The total length of air routes covered by K.L.M. (Royal Dutch Airlines) in the course of April, 1973, to April, 1974, was 364,232 km.

FINANCE
Estimates, 1975
Aggregate Budget Revenue....Fls.58,222,000,000
Aggregate Budget Expenditure. 62,815,000,000
See also p. 83.

TRADE
The Dutch are traditionally a trading nation. *Entrepôt* trade, banking and shipping are of particular importance in their economy. The geographical position of the Netherlands, at the mouths of the Rhine, Meuse and Scheldt, brings a large volume of transit trade to and from the interior of Europe to Dutch ports.

Principal trading partners are the Federal Republic of Germany and Belgium/Luxemburg. Britain supplied 6·29 per cent. of Netherlands imports in 1974 (Fls. 4,790,403,000) and took 10·6 per cent. of Netherlands exports (Fls.8,018,465,000).

In common with other members of the European Economic Community, the Netherlands on July 1, 1968, removed remaining duties on imports from EEC countries and brought down duties on imports from other countries into line with the Common External Tariff of the EEC.

Excluding the building industry, the index of industrial production in the Netherlands (1970= 100) rose from 111 in 1972 to 121 in 1974 and the index of industrial production per worker (1970= 100) rose from 116 in 1972 to 132 in 1974. In 1974 Dutch imports amounted to Fls.76,155,411,000 and exports to Fls.75,630,455,000 (excluding Belgium and Luxemburg).

Trade with U.K.
	1973	1974
Imports from U.K..	£603,568,000	£982,300,000
Exports to U.K.....	911,732,000	1,637,000,000

SEAT OF GOVERNMENT, The Hague (Den Haag or, in full, 's-Gravenhage). Pop. (Sept., 1974) 487,120.

PRINCIPAL TOWNS.—Ψ Amsterdam, 770,805; Ψ Rotterdam, 625,361; Utrecht, 269,574; Eindhoven, 191,842; Haarlem, 168,243; Groningen, 167,571; Tilburg, 152,500; Nijmegen, 148,219; Enschede, 142,851; Arnhem, 126,585; Leiden, 97,154; Breda, 119,186; Maastricht, 111,314; Dordrecht, 101,279; Apeldoorn 131,979; Hilversum, 96,841.

FLAG.—Three horizontal bands of red, white and blue. NATIONAL DAY.—April 30 (The Queen's Birthday).

BRITISH EMBASSY
(Lange Voorhout, 10, The Hague)
Ambassador Extraordinary and Plenipotentiary, His Excellency Sir John Barnes, K.C.M.G., M.B.E. (1972).
Counsellors, J. A. Sankey; D. F. Ballentyne (*Commercial*).
Defence and Naval Attaché, Capt. J. R. Hill, R.N.
Air Attaché, Wing-Comdr. D. W. Smith.
Military Attaché, Lt.Col. P. G. Duffield.
1st Secretaries, D. J. Moss (*Head of Chancery*); J. G. Dixon (*Chancery*); A. D. F. Findlay (*Agriculture*); W. K. Prendergast (*Economic*); K. H. Jones (*Commercial*); Miss P. M. Kelly (*Information*).

BRITISH CONSULAR OFFICES
Amsterdam, Johannes Vermeerstraat 7.—*Consul-General,* T. J. Trout, M.B.E.
Rotterdam, Parklaan 18.—*Consul-General,* W. F. B. Price.
There are Honorary British Consuls at *Curaçao and Aruba,* Netherlands Antilles.
British Council Representative, C. N. P. Powell, D.S.O., O.B.E., Keizergracht 343, Amsterdam (Library).

OVERSEAS TERRITORIES
The Netherlands West Indies formerly comprised *Surinam* in South America and certain islands in the West Indies known as the *Netherlands Antilles* (Curaçao, Bonaire, Aruba, part of St. Martin, St. Eustatius, and Saba). The area of the Netherlands Antilles is 394·1 sq. miles with a population of 234,400 at December, 1974. Under the Realm Statute which took effect on December 29, 1954, Surinam and the Netherlands Antilles received autonomy in domestic affairs as parts of the Netherlands Realm under the Crown. The statute was amended in 1975 to provide for the full independence of *Surinam* on November 25, 1975. Henceforth the Realm will comprise the Netherlands and the Netherland Antilles only.

Governor
Netherlands Antilles, Dr. B. M. Leito (1970).

Trade with U.K.
Netherlands Antilles	1973	1974
Imports from U.K.....	£10,236,000	£8,684,000
Exports to U.K........	14,220,000	38,760,000

The capital of Curaçao is Ψ Willemstad (pop. 154,000), of Aruba, Ψ Oranjestad; of Bonaire, Ψ Kralendijk; of St. Martin, Philipsburg; of Statius (St. Eustatius), Oranjestad; and of Saba, Bottom.

NICARAGUA
(República de Nicaragua)
President of the National Emergency Committee and Supreme Chief of the Armed Forces, Gen. Anastasio Somoza Debayle, *assumed office,* Dec. 1, 1974.
Foreign Affairs, Dr. Alejandro Montiel Arguello.

NICARAGUAN EMBASSY AND CONSULATE GENERAL
8 Gloucester Road, S.W.7
[01–584 3231]
Ambassador Extraordinary and Plenipotentiary (vacant).
Counsellors, Dr. José Rizo Castellon; Lic. Benjamín Marín Abaúnza.

Area and Population.—Nicaragua is the largest State of Central America, with a long seaboard on both the Atlantic and Pacific Oceans, situated between 10° 45′–15° N. lat. and 83° 40′–87° 38′ W. long., containing an area of 57,145 English square miles (see MAP, p. 872). It has a population of 2,400,000 of whom about threequarters are of mixed blood. Another 15 per cent. are white, mostly of pure Spanish descent and the remaining 10 per cent. are Indians or negroes. The latter group includes the Mosquitos, who live on the Atlantic coast and were formerly under British protection.

Government.—The eastern coast of Nicaragua was touched by Columbus in 1502, and in 1519 was overrun by Spanish forces under Davila, and formed part of the Spanish Captaincy-General of Guatemala until 1821, when its independence was secured. From 1972 the country was headed by a three-man National Governing Council   A new Constitution, adopted in April 1974, provided for presidential elections to be held on Sept. 1, 1974. General de Division Anastasio Somoza, Debayle was re-elected President (formerly in office, 1967–72) of the Republic, and took office on December 1, 1974 for a term expiring on April 31, 1981. Nicaragua is now a democratic representative republic divided into sixteen Departments and the National District, which includes Maragua and its surroundings. The Government is divided into four branches: Legislative, Executive, Judicial and Electoral.   Legislative power is vested in a Senate of 30 members and the ex-President, and a chamber of Deputies with not less than 70 members.

Agriculture and Industry.—The country is mainly agricultural. The major crops are cotton, coffee, sugar, sesame and bananas.   Beans, rice, maize and ipecacuanha are also important.   Livestock and timber production, already considerable, are expanding. Nicaragua possesses deposits of gold and silver, both of which are mined and exported by United States and Canadian concessionaires.

Communications.—There are 252 miles of railway, all on the Pacific side and approximately 5,500 miles of telegraph. There are 27 radio stations and two television stations in Managua.   An automatic telephone system has been installed in the capital and extended to the provincial towns of León, Granada, Matagalpa, Chinandega, Diriamba and Jinotepe.   The system in the capital, however, suffered heavy damage as a result of the earthquake in December 1972.   A ground station for satellite communication was inaugurated in 1973. Transport except on the Pacific slope, is still attended with difficulty but many new roads have either been opened or are under construction. The Inter-American Highway runs from the Honduras frontier in the north to the Costa Rican border in the south; the interoceanic highway runs from the Corinto on the Pacific coast viâ Managua to Rama, where there is a natural waterway to Bluefields on the Atlantic. The country's main airport is at Managua. It is used by several airlines, including Panam and Lanica, the Nicaraguan national airline.

Language and Literature.—The official language of the country is Spanish. There are 2 daily newspapers published at Managua, apart from the official Gazette (*La Gaceta*) and 4 in the provinces. About 40 per cent. of the population are illiterate. There are universities at León and Managua.

Trade with U.K.

	1973	1974
Imports from U.K.	£3,050,000	£7,706,000
Exports to U.K.	302,000	1,385,000

Considerable quantities of foodstuffs are imported as well as cotton goods, jute, iron and steel, machinery and petroleum products. The chief exports are cotton, coffee, beef, gold, sugar, cottonseed, bananas, copper and soluble coffee.

CAPITAL, Managua, population post-earthquake, 400,000. The centre was almost totally destroyed in the earthquake of December 1972, and reconstruction will take several years. León, 119,347; Granada, 100,334; Masaya, 96,830; Chinandega, 95,437; Ψ Bluefields, 17,706; Matagalpa, 65,928; Jinotepe, 15,957. Ψ Corinto (9,650), on the Pacific is the chief port, handling about 70 per cent. of the total trade; Bluefields and Puerto Somoza on the E. coast are mainly concerned in the fish, banana and timber trade to the United States.

FLAG.—Three horizontal bands, blue, white, blue (the arms of the Republic on the white band, displaying five volcanoes surmounted by a cap of liberty under a rainbow).

BRITISH EMBASSY
Managua

Ambassador Extraordinary and Plenipotentiary and Consul-General, His Excellency David Francis Duncan.

1st Secretary, S. E. Warder (*Head of Chancery and Consul*).

NIGER
(République du Niger)

President, Lt.-Col. Seyni Kountché, *assumed power* April 15, 1974.
Minister of State, Major Sani Souna Sido.
Minister of Foreign Affairs, Capt. Moumouni Djermakoye Adamou.

Situated in West Central Africa, between 12° and 24° N. and 0° and 16° E., Niger has common boundaries with Algeria and Libya in the north, Chad, Nigeria, Dahomey, Mali and Upper Volta.

It has an area of about 459,000 square miles with a population (U.N. estimate, 1972) at 4,030,000. Apart from a small region along the Niger Valley in the south-west near the capital the country is entirely savannah or desert. The main races in Niger are the Haussas in the east, the Djermas in the south-west and the nomadic Touaregs in the north.

The first French expedition arrived in 1891 and the country was fully occupied by 1914. It decided on December 18, 1958, to remain an autonomous republic within the French Community; full independence outside the Community was proclaimed on August 3, 1960. Special agreements with France, covering financial and cultural matters, technical assistance, defence, etc., were signed in Paris on April 24, 1961.

The constitution of Niger, adopted on November 8, 1960, provided for a presidential system of government, modelled on that of the United States and the French Fifth Republic, and a single Chamber National Assembly. In April 1974 Lt.-Col. Seyni Kountché seized power, suspended the Constitution, dissolved the National Assembly, and suppressed all political organizations. He then set up a Supreme Military Council with himself as President and eleven other officers together with a temporary Government in which all the major portfolios are held by military officers. Niger is a member of the United Nations, the *Conseil de l'Entente*, O.C.A.M., O.A.U. and C.E.A.O. (*see* Ivory Coast).   The official language is French.

Finance.—The currency of Niger is the *franc CFA* (Francs CFA 50 = 1 French Franc). In 1975 the total budget amounted to *Francs CFA* 16,670,000,000.

Trade.—The cultivation of ground-nuts and the production of livestock are the main industries and provide the two main exports.   A company formed by the Government, the French Atomic

Energy Authority and private interests is exploiting uranium deposits at Arlit. Total value of trade in 1973 was: Imports, *Francs CFA* 15,281,000,000; Exports, *Francs CFA* 12,697,000,000. Imports from U.K. (1974) — £3,380,000; exports to U.K. (1975) — £1,381,000.

CAPITAL.—Niamey (100,000).

FLAG.—Three horizontal stripes, orange, white and green with an orange disc in the middle of the white stripe. NATIONAL DAY.—December 18.

British Ambassador, His Excellency Paul Cecil Henry Holmer C.M.G. (*resident at Abidjan*).

NORWAY
(Norge)

King, Olav V, K.G., K.T., G.C.B., G.C.V.O., b. July 2, 1903; *succeeded*, Sept. 21, 1957, on death of his father King Haakon VII; *married* March 21, 1929, Princess Marthe of Sweden (*born* March 29, 1901; *died* April 5, 1954); having issue, Harald (*see below*) and two daughters.

Heir-Apparent, H.R.H. Prince Harald, G.C.V.O., b. Feb. 21, 1937; *m.* Aug. 29, 1968, Sonja Haraldsen, and has issue Princess Märtha Louise, b. Sept. 22, 1971; and Prince Haakon Magnus, b. July 20, 1973.

CABINET
Prime Minister, Trygve Bratteli.
Foreign Affairs, Knut Frydenlund.
Agriculture, Thorstein Treholt.
Justice, Fru Inger Louise Valle.
Education and Ecclesiastical Affairs, Bjartmar Gjerde.
Defence, Alv Jakob Fostervoll.
Commerce and Shipping, Einar Magnussen.
Industry and Handicrafts, Ingvald J. Ulveseth.
Consumer Affairs and Administration, Odd G. Sagør.
Transport and Communications, Fru Annemarie Lorentzen.
Fisheries, Eivind Bolle.
Labour and Municipal Affairs, Leif J. Aune.
Social Affairs, Tor Halvorsen.
Environment, Fru. Gro Harlem Brundtland.
Finance and Customs, Per Kleppe.
Without Portfolio, Jens Evensen.

ROYAL NORWEGIAN EMBASSY IN LONDON
Offices: 25 Belgrave Square, S.W.1
[01–235 7151]
Ambassador Extraordinary and Plenipotentiary, His Excellency Frithjo Halfdan Jacobsen (1975).
Minister-Counsellor, Kjell Rasmussen.

Counsellors, Herman Pedersen (*Press and Information*), Olav Sole; Semund Remøy (*Fisheries*); Øivind Johnsen (*Consular*); Hans Høegh Henrichsen (*Commercial*).
Cultural Attaché, Tor Neumann.
1st Secretaries, Jan Wessel Hegg; C. F. Prebensen (*Press and Information*); D. R. Nielson (*Commercial*).
Defence Attaché, Lt.-Col. Jorgen Mørtvedt.
Asst. Defence Attaché, Cdr. Chr. Bøgh-Tobiassen.
2nd Secretary, Ole F. Knudsen (*Commercial*),
Consular Attachés, Thor Torvik; Oscar Torgersen.

Area and Population.—Norway (" The Northern Way "), a kingdom in the northern and western portion of the Scandinavian peninsula, was founded in 872. It is 1,752 km. in length, its greatest width about 430 km. The length of the coastline is 2,650 km., and the frontier between Norway and the neighbouring countries is 2,531 km. (Sweden 1,619 km., Finland 716 km. and U.S.S.R. 196 km.). It is divided into 19 counties (*fylker*) and comprises an area of 323,877 sq. km. (125,016 sq. miles) with a population (estimated, Dec., 1973) of 3,972,990. In 1972 there were for every 1,000 inhabitants: 16·1 live births; 10·0 deaths; 11·8 deaths during first year of age (per 1,000 live births); 7·2 marriages.

The Norwegian coastline is extensive, deeply indented with numerous fiords, and fringed with an immense number of rocky islands. The surface is mountainous, consisting of elevated and barren tablelands, separated by deep and narrow valleys. At the North Cape the sun does not appear to set from the second week in May to the last week in July, causing the phenomenon known as the *Midnight Sun*; conversely, there is no apparent sunrise from about Nov. 18 to Jan. 23. During the long winter nights are seen the multiple coloured *Northern Lights* or *Aurora Borealis*, which have a maximum intensity in a line crossing North America from Alaska to Labrador and Northern Europe to the Arctic coast and Siberia.

Production.—The cultivated area is about 10,000 sq. km. (3·4 per cent. of total surface area); forests cover nearly 25 per cent.; the rest consists of highland pastures or uninhabitable mountains.

The *Gulf Stream* pours from 140 to 170 million cubic feet of warm water per second into the sea around Norway and causes the temperature to be higher than the average for the latitude. It brings shoals of herring and cod into the fishing grounds and causes a warm current of air over the west coast, making it possible to cultivate potatoes and barley in latitudes which in other countries are perpetually frozen.

The chief industries are manufactures, agriculture and forestry, fisheries, mining and shipping. In the fourth quarter of 1973, 1,660,000 persons were employed in Norwegian industry. Manufactures are aided by great resources of water power, estimated at 14,120 MW. Actual production in 1972 amounted to 67·8 GW★. Oil was discovered on the Norwegian continental shelf in 1968. In normal years the quantity of fish caught by Norwegian fishing vessels is greater than that of any other European country except U.S.S.R. In 1973 the total catch amounted to 2,692,392 metric tons. In 1972 herring oil production amounted to 189,549 metric tons.

Government.—From 1397 to 1814 Norway was united with Denmark, and from Nov. 4, 1814, with Sweden, under a personal union which was dissolved on June 7, 1905, when Norway regained complete independence. Under the constitution of May 17, 1814, the *Storting* (Parliament) itself elects one-quarter of its members to constitute the *Lagting* (Upper Chamber), the other three-quarters forming the *Odelsting* (Lower Chamber). Legislative questions alone are dealt with by both parts in separate sittings.

On April 8–9, 1940, Germany invaded Norway, and it was not until June 7, 1945, that the late King Haakon was able to return from Great Britain to Oslo.

On October 14, 1973, Mr. Trygve Bratteli, leader of the Labour Party, formed his second minority Government since March 1971, in succession to the three-party coalition of Mr. Lars Korvald, which resigned on October 12.

Defence.—Norway is a member of the North Atlantic Treaty Organization, and the Headquarters of Allied Forces, Northern Europe, is situated near Oslo. The period of compulsory national service is 15 months (without refresher training) in the Navy and Air Force, and 12 months (with refresher training) in the Army.

Education from 7 to 16 is free and compulsory in the "basic schools" maintained by the municipalities with State grants-in-aid. From 1976 all schools catering for the 16–19 age groups will be organised along comprehensive lines, the aim being to offer facilities for some 85–90 per cent. of the age groups. In 1971 47·4 per cent. of all 18 year olds received full time schooling. In addition to the many specialized schools and industrial and technical institutes, there are 29 colleges of education and 7 new regional colleges. There are 4 universities and 7 state colleges of university level, with a total in autumn 1973 of 36,694 students, 32·4 per cent. of them women. Oslo University (founded 1811) had 19,367; Bergen University (1948) 7,351, and Trondheim University (created in 1968 by merging the State Institute of Technology, the State College for Teachers, and the Royal Norwegian Society of Science Museum) 6,230; the newest, Tromsø University, started teaching in 1972 with 871 students in science, the humanities and medicine.

Language and Literature.—Norwegian is one of the Scandinavian languages and is the language of the mainland and of Svalbard. Old Norse literature is among the most ancient (and the richest) in Europe. Modern Norwegian became formed in the time of the Reformation and Ludvig Holberg (1684–1754) is regarded as the founder of Norwegian literature, although modern Norwegian literature dates from the establishment of a national university at Christiania (Oslo) in 1811 and with the writings of Henrik A. Wergeland (1805–1845). Some of the famous names are Henrik Ibsen (1828–1906) the dramatist, Björnstjerne Björnson (1832–1910) journalist, dramatist and novelist and Nobel Prizewinner in 1903, Jonas Lie (1833–1908) novelist, Knut Hamsun (1859–1952) novelist and Nobel Prizewinner in 1920, and Sigrid Undset (1882–1949), champion of Norwegian womanhood and herself a Nobel Prizewinner in 1928. In 1973 there were 67 daily newspapers in the country with a total circulation of 1,555,000, and 77 newspapers published 1 to 5 times a week with a total circulation of 331,000.

Communications.—The total length of railways open at the end of 1971 was 4,242 km., excluding private lines. The extension of the main line from Fauske to Bodö, 60 miles north of the Arctic Circle, was completed in 1962 and opened on June 7 by King Olav. The number of telephones at the end of 1972 was 1,262,254 which is 32 telephones per 100 inhabitants. There are 74,796 km. of public roads in Norway (including urban streets). At the end of 1973, 1,468,517 road motor vehicles were registered.

Civil Aviation.—Scheduled airlines are operated by Scandinavian Airlines System (SAS) on behalf of Det Norske Luftfartselskap (DNL), by Braathens South American and Far East Airtransport (SAFE), and by Wideröes Flyveselskap A.S.

Mercantile Marine.—The Mercantile Marine, December 31, 1972, consisted of 2,117 vessels of 23,328,000 gross tons (vessels above 100 gross tons, excluding fishing boats, floating whaling factories, tugs, salvage vessels, icebreakers and similar types of vessel). The fleet ranks fourth among the merchant navies of the world.

FINANCE

	1974	1975
	million *Kroner*	
Revenue	29,720	34,724
Expenditure	29,720	34,724
National Debt	25,671★	29,521★

★ Voted budget

Rate of Exchange (June 1, 1973) *Kr.*14·43 = £1. See also p. 83.

TRADE

	1972	1973
	million *Kroner*	
Total imports	28,808	36,041
Total exports	21,625	27,085

Trade with U.K.

	1973	1974
Imports from U.K.	*Kr.*240,897,000	£333,611,000
Exports to U.K.	325,217,000	408,394,000

The chief imports are raw materials, motor vehicles, chemicals, motor spirit, fuel and other oils; coal, ships and machinery; together with manufactures of silk, cotton and wool. The exports consist chiefly of fish and products of fish (as canned fish, whale oils), pulp, paper, iron ore and pyrites, nitrate of lime, stone, calcium carbide, aluminium, ferro-alloys, zinc, nickel, cyanamide, etc.

CAPITAL.—Ψ Oslo (incl. Aker). Pop. (Jan. 1, 1974), 468,514. Other towns are Ψ Trondheim,

---

★ Gigawatt = 1,000 million watts.

133,213; Ψ Bergen, 214,580; Ψ Stavanger, 84,359;
Ψ Kristiansand, 58,975; Ψ Drammen, 50,573;
Ψ Tromsö, 42,253; Ψ Aalesund, 40,662; Ψ Hauge-
sund, 27,283; Moss, 25,523.

FLAG.—Red, with white-bordered blue cross.

NATIONAL DAY.—May 17 (Constitution Day).

AIR TRANSIT FROM U.K.—London–Bergen or
Oslo, 1 hr. 50 mins.

BRITISH EMBASSY

Thomas Heftyesgate, 8 Oslo 2.

Ambassador Extraordinary and Plenipotentiary, His
Excellency Charles Peter Scott, C.M.G., O.B.E.
(1975).

BRITISH CONSULAR OFFICES

There are British Consular Offices at *Bergen*
and *Oslo* and Honorary Consulates at *Tromso,
Aalesund, Kristiansand N., Narvik, Stavanger, Trondheim, Tønsberg, Kristiansand S.* and *Haugesund*.

BRITISH COUNCIL

Representative, J. D. Edmondston, O.B.E., Fridtjof
Nansen Plass 5, Oslo 1.

SVALBARD

(*Spitsbergen and Bear Island*)

By Treaty (Feb. 9, 1920) the sovereignty of
Norway over the Spitsbergen (" Pointed Mountain ") Archipelago was recognized by the Great
Powers and other interested nations, and on Aug.
14, 1925, Norway assumed sovereignty. In
September, 1941, Allied forces (British, Canadian
and Norwegian) landed on the main island. After
destruction of the accumulated stocks of coal and
dismantling of mining machinery and the wireless
installation, the Norwegian inhabitants (about 600)
were evacuated to a British port and the Russians
(about 1,500) to the U.S.S.R. After the war the
Norwegian mining plants were rebuilt. 873,406
metric tons of coal were shipped from Norwegian
and Russian mines in Svalbard in 1973 (Norwegian
mines, 411,503 metric tons).

The Svalbard Archipelago lies between 74°–81°
N. lat. and between 10°–35° E. long., with an
estimated area of 24,295 square miles. The archipelago consists of a main island, known as Spitsbergen (15,200 sq. miles); North East Land,
closely adjoining and separated by Hinlopen Strait;
the Wiche Islands, separated from the mainland
by Olga Strait; Barents and Edge Islands, separated from the mainland by Stor Fjord (or Wybe
Jansz Water); Prince Charles Foreland, to the W.;
Hope Island, to the S.E.; Bear Island (68 square
miles) 127 miles to the S.; with many similar
islands in the neighbourhood of the main group.
In addition to those engaged in coal-mining, the
archipelago is also visited by hunters for seal, foxes
and polar bears.

South Cape is 355 miles from the Norwegian
Coast. Ice Fjord is 520 miles from Tromsö, 650
miles from Murmansk, and 1,300 miles from
Aberdeen. Transit from Tromsö to Green Harbour 2 to 3 days; from Aberdeen 5 to 6 days.

JAN MAYEN, an island in the Arctic Ocean
(70° 49′–71° 9′ N. lat. and 7° 53′–9° 5′ W. long.)
was joined to Norway by law of Feb. 27, 1930.

Norwegian Antarctic

BOUVET ISLAND (54° 26′ S. lat. and 3° 24′ E.
long.) was declared a dependency of Norway
by law of Feb. 27, 1930.

PETER THE FIRST ISLAND (68° 48′ S. lat. and
90° 35′ W. long.), was declared a dependency of
Norway by resolution of Government, May 1,
1931.

PRINCESS RAGNHILD LAND (from 70° 30′ to
68° 40′ S. lat. and 24° 15′ to 33° 30′ E. long.' has
been claimed as Norwegian since Feb. 17, 1931.

QUEEN MAUD LAND.—On Jan. 14, 1939, the
Norwegian Government declared the area between
20° W. and 45° E., adjacent to Australian Antarctica,
to be Norwegian territory.

OMAN
(The Sultanate of Oman)

Sultan, Qaboos bin Said, *succeeded* on deposition of
Sultan Said bin Taimur, July 23, 1970.

COUNCIL OF MINISTERS
(November, 1974)

Personal Adviser and Governor of the Capital, Sayyid
Thuwaini bin Shihab.

Communications, Abdul Hafidh Salim Rajab.

Public Works, Karim Ahmad al Haremi.

Diwan Affairs, Sayyid Hamad bin Hamud.

Education, Sayyid Faisal bin Ali al-Said.

Health, Dr. Mubarak al-Khadduri.

Information and Tourism, Sayyid Fahd bin Mahmoud
al-Said.

Justice, Sayyid Hilal bin Hamad al-Sammar.

Interior, Sayyid Fahr bin Taimur al-Said.

Land Affairs, Sayyid Muhammad bin Ahmad.

Social Affairs and Labour, Khalfan bin Nasr al-
Wahaibi.

Awkaf and Islamic Affairs, Shaikh Walid bin Zahir
al Hinai.

Commerce and Industry, Mohamed Zubair.

Agriculture, Fisheries, Petroleum, and Minerals, Said
Ahmed al-Shanfari.

Minister of State (Foreign Affairs), Qais Abdul Muris
al-Sammar.

Ministers without Portfolio, Dr. Asim al-Jamali;
Shaikh Braik bin Hamud al-Ghafari.

(The Sultan acts as his own Minister of Foreign
Affairs and Defence.)

OMAN EMBASSY IN LONDON
64 Ennismore Gardens, S.W.7.
[01–584 6782]

Ambassador, His Excellency Nassir Seif El Bualy.

The independent Sultanate of Oman lies at the
eastern corner of the Arabian Peninsula. Its seaboard is nearly 1,000 miles long and extends from
near Tibat on the west coast of the Musandam
Peninsula round to Ras Darbat Ali, with the exception of the stretch between Dibba and Kalba on the
east coast which belongs to Sharjah and Fujairah
of the United Arab Emirates. Ras Darbat Ali
marks the boundary between the Sultanate and the
People's Democratic Republic of Yemen. The
Sultanate extends inland to the borders of the Rub
al Khali, or "Empty Quarter" as the South
Eastern Arabian Desert is called.

Physically and historically modern Oman can
be split into two main parts, the North and the
South, divided by a large tract of desert. *Northern
Oman* has three main sections. The *Batinah*, the
coastal plain, varies in width from 30 miles in the
neighbourhood of Suwaiq to almost nothing at
Muscat where the mountains descend abruptly to
the sea. The plain is fertile, with date gardens
extending over its full length of 150 miles. The
dates, which ripen in early July, well before the
Basra product, are famous for their flavour. The
Hajjar, a mountain spine running from North East
to South West, reaching nearly 10,000 feet in
height on Jabal Akhdar. For the most part the
mountains are barren, but numerous valleys penetrate the central massif of Jabal Akhdar and in these
there is considerable cultivation irrigated by wells
or a system of underground canals called *falages*
which top the water table. The two plateaus
leading from the western slopes of the mountains,
the *Dhahirah* or back, in the north and the *Sharqia*

in the south east also have centres of settlements and cultivation. They fall from an average height of 1,000 feet into sands of the Empty Quarter. Camels raised in this area are prized throughout Arabia. The *Wahiba Sands* separate the North from the South with nearly 400 miles of inhospitable country crossed by one motorable track, the only land link. *Dhofar*, the Southern Province, is the only part of the Arabian Peninsula to be touched by the South West Monsoon. Temperatures are more moderate than in the North and sugar cane and coconuts are grown on the coastal plain, while cattle are bred on the mountains.

Muscat is the original capital of Oman, but Matrah, 3 miles away, where a new port has been built and where there is more room for expansion, is the commercial centre, and government offices and private houses are moving out to Ruwi and Qurum along the road to Seeb Airport. The other main towns on the northern coast are Sur, Khaburah and Sohar, all of which are ports but without sheltered anchorage. In the interior Nizwa and Rostaq, both former capitals, are the centres of population. The main town of Dhofar is Salalah, and Raysut and Murbat are the ports.

The area of Oman has been estimated at 120,000 sq. miles and the population at 650,000 (official estimates put the latter figure as high as 1,500,000). The inhabitants of the North are for the most part Arab but along the coast there is a strong infusion of negro blood, while in the Capital Area which stretches from Muscat to Seeb there are large communities of Hindus, Khojas and Baluch, in addition to Zanzibaris of Omani origin. In Dhofar there is also an infusion of negro blood around Salalah, but in the mountains the inhabitants are either of pure Arab descent or belong to tribes of pre-Arab origin, the Qarra and Mahra, who speak their own dialects of semitic origin.

Since 1972 ships have been using Port Qaboos at Matrah, where 8 deep water berths have been constructed as part of the new harbour facilities (£20m.). In 1974, 361 vessels entered the port. 169 tankers called at the oil company port at Mina al Fahal and carried away over 106 million barrels of crude oil.

The telegraph office, an automatic telephone service in Muscat and Matrah and an international telephone service have been operated since January 1975 by OMANTEL. The Sultanate of Oman and Cable & Wireless share in the company in the ratio of 60/40. There are cleared or graded motorable tracks linking most main population centres of the country with the coast and with the towns of the United Arab Emirates. Over 300 miles of tarmac road are now open linking the capital area with the new international airport at Seeb and the town of Sohar and others are being built, for example to link Muscat and Nizwa.

Finance.—On May 7, 1970, a new currency was brought into circulation. The main unit is the *Rial Oman* RO 0·770 = £1 (July 1975). Each *Rial* is divided into 1,000 new *Baiza*. There are notes of *Rials* 10, 5, 1, ½, ¼ and 100 *Baiza* and coins of *Baiza* 100, 50, 25, 10, 5 and 2. The Indian External Rupee ceased to be legal tender from May 21, 1970. The metric system was introduced in 1975 but there is also a local system in which one *kiyas*=the weight of six dollars or 5·9375 oz.; 24 *liyas*=one Muscat *maund*; 10 *maunds*=one *Farasala*; 200 *maunds*=1 *Bahar*. Rice is sold by the bag, other cereals by the following measurement: 40 *Palis*=one *Farrah*; 20 *Farrahs*=one *Khandi*.

Trade with U.K.

	1973	1974
Imports from U.K.	£22,200,000	£42,900,000
Exports to U.K.	15,900,000	32,800,000

Commerce and Trade.—Trade is mainly with the United Kingdom, Japan, the Netherlands, U.S., West Germany and India. Imports for the year 1974 exceeded *RO* 135m. Chief imports were machinery, cars, building materials, refined petroleum and food and telecommunications equipment.

Petroleum Development (Oman) Ltd. (owned 60 per cent. by Oman Government and 34 per cent. by Shell) began exporting oil on Aug. 1, 1967. Exports are currently at a rate of 335,000 barrels a day. Wintershall A.-G., Sun Oil and ELF-ERAP have off-shore concessions and Eif-Aquitane Sumitomo has a new inland oil concession.

Development.—For many years the Sultanate was a poor country with a total annual income of less than £1,000,000. The advent of oil revenues since 1967 and the change of régime in 1970 have improved prospects and have enabled the initiation of a wide-ranging development programme, especially concerned with health, education and communications. New hospitals have been completed in the main provincial centres. 180 primary schools were in operation in Sept. 1974. At Salalah, the main coastal town of the southern province of Dhofar, a new civil airport is planned. A metalled road joins Salalah to Taqa and the port of Rayzut and several housing schemes have been completed. A thermal power station and desalination plant is under construction near Muscat and work has recently begun on a flour mill. There are also plans to build a cement factory near Muscat.

CAPITAL.—Ψ Muscat, population (estimated), 7,000.

FLAG.—Red, green and white with crossed daggers in red sector.

BRITISH EMBASSY
Muscat

Ambassador Extraordinary and Plenipotentiary, His Excellency Charles James Treadwell, C.M.G. (1975).
First Secretary, D. E. Tatham (*Head of Chancery*).
Defence Attaché, Col. P. F. G. Allardyce.
Air Attaché, Wing Cdr. J. A. Horrell.
1st Secretaries, D. R. Gallwey; B. V. White.
3rd Secretary, E. G. M. Chaplin.
British Council Representative M. R. W. Dexter.

PAKISTAN

President, Fazal Elahi Chaudhry, *born* 1905, *elected* Aug. 10, 1973.
Prime Minister, Defence and Foreign Affairs, Zulfikar Ali Bhutto.
Interior and States and Frontier Regions, Abdul Qaiyum Khan.
Labour, Health, Social Welfare and Population Planning, Hafeezullah Cheema.
Education, Science and Technology, Abdul Hafiz Pirzada.
Law and Parliamentary Affairs, Malik Meraj Khalid.
Communications, Mumtaz Ali Bhutto.
Production, Industries and Town Planning, Rafi Raza.
Religious Affairs, Maulana Kausar Niazi.
Finance Planning and Economic Affairs, Rana Mohammad Hanij.
Fuel, Power and Natural Resources, Mohammad Yusuf Khattak.
Commerce, Meer Ajzal.
Ministers of State.—Aziz Ahmed (*Defence, Foreign Affairs*); Qaim Ali Shah (*Industries*); Maj.-Gen. Jamaldar Khan (*Establishment and Kashmir Affairs*); Malik Mohammad Akhtar (*Parliamentary Affairs*); Abdul Sattar Gabol (*Labour*); Chaudhry Jehangir Ali (*Works*); Malik Mohammad Jaffer (*Minority Affairs and Tourism*); Taj Mohammad Khan Jamali (*Natural Resources*); Shahzada Saeedur Rashid Abbasi (*Science and*

Technology); Sardur Abdul Aleem (*States and Frontier Regions*); Mian Mohammad Ataullah (*Railways*).

PAKISTAN EMBASSY

35 Lowndes Square, S.W.1
[01-235 2044]

Ambassador Extraordinary and Plenipotentiary, His Excellency Mian Mumtaz Mohammad Khan Daultana.

Counsellors, Zafar Hussain Qureshi; Abdul Qayyum (*Press*); Abdul Karim Lodhi (*Economic*); Sher Mohammad Zaman (*Education*); Nasim Ahmed; Javaid Quyum Khan.

Area and Population.—The Islamic Republic of Pakistan consists of country situated to the northwest of the Indian sub-continent, bordered by Iran, Afghanistan, the disputed territory of Kashmir and India. It covers a total area of 310,403 sq. miles. The Government of Pakistan census in 1972 showed a population figure of 64,892,000. Of these, about 88 per cent. are Moslems, about 6 per cent. Scheduled Caste Hindus, 5 per cent. Caste Hindus, under 1 per cent. Christians, and ½ per cent. Buddhists.

Running through Pakistan are five great rivers, the Indus and its tributaries, Thelum, Chenab, Ravi and Sutlej. The upper reaches of these rivers are in Kashmir, and their sources in the Himalayas.

Government.—Until April 17, 1972, when the Republic of Bangladesh seceded and was formally created to replace East Pakistan, Pakistan consisted of two geographical units, West and East Pakistan, which were separated by about 1,100 miles of Indian territory. Pakistan was constituted as a Dominion under the Indian Independence Act, 1947, which received Royal Assent on July 18, 1947.

In terms of the Act the Dominion of Pakistan consisted of former territories of British India. The Punjab States of Bahawalpur and Khairpur, with a Muslim population of almost 80 per cent. and with Muslim rulers, acceded to Pakistan in October, 1947. Boundaries of the Provinces of East Bengal and of Punjab (West Punjab) were defined by a Boundary Commission presided over by Sir Cyril Radcliffe, K.B.E., Q.C. (now Viscount Radcliffe). The following States also acceded to Pakistan: the Baluchistan States of Kalat, Mekran, Las Bela and Kharan, and the North-West Frontier States of Amb, Chitral, Dir and Swat. The States of Junagadh and Manavadar which had acceded to Pakistan were occupied by India on November 8, 1947.

Pakistan became a Republic on March 23, 1956, when the provisions of the Constitution came into force. On October 7, 1958, however, this Constitution was abrogated and Pakistan came under martial law. General (later Field Marshal) Mohammed Ayub Khan, Commander-in-Chief of the Pakistan Army, was appointed the Chief Martial Law Administrator. On October 28, 1958, General Ayub Khan also became President of Pakistan. Following a period of unrest in both East and West Pakistan, marked by rioting and massed strikes, President Ayub Khan on March 24, 1969, announced his resignation and handed over control of the country to the armed forces. The Commander-in-Chief, General Yahya Khan, proclaimed martial law on March 25 and appointed military governors for East and West Pakistan. The Constitution was abrogated, National and Provincial Assemblies dissolved and Provincial Governors dismissed. Law and order were rapidly restored. On March 31, 1969, Gen. Yahya Khan assumed the Presidency and formed a Council of Administration.

A *Legal Framework Order*, published by the President in March, 1970, laid down the principles on which a new Constitution for Pakistan would be based, including the division of West Pakistan into four provinces—The Punjab, Sind, Baluchistan and the North-West Frontier Province.

The first general elections ever held in Pakistan on a basis of " one man, one vote ", were held on Dec. 7, 1970, with a postponement until January 17, 1971, in 9 East Pakistan constituencies which had been severely affected by the cyclone disaster in the Ganges delta. The Awami League in East Pakistan, led by Sheikh Mujibur Rahman, and the Pakistan People's Party in West Pakistan, led by Zulfikar Ali Bhutto, won large majorities, the latter party in Punjab and Sind. Following the elections there was total disagreement between the two main parties on the question of a new Constitution for Pakistan, Sheikh Mujib insisting on complete autonomy for East Pakistan. The proposed opening of the National Assembly at Dacca on March 25, 1971, was postponed by the President. Civil war broke out.

The unofficially styled " Bangladesh " seceded from the Government of Pakistan by unilateral declaration on March 26. 1971, and Sheikh Mujibur Rahman was flown to West Pakistan where he was in due course tried for treason. Meanwhile, in East Pakistan, fierce and brutal fighting continued between West Pakistan forces and Bengali guerrillas. Several million Bengali refugees fled to India. Fighting in East Pakistan intensified towards the end of the year and on December 3 it spread to West Pakistan where Pakistan and Indian forces were engaged. On December 16 the Pakistan forces on the eastern front surrendered, and the following day Pakistan accepted a cease-fire in the West. Following the resignation of Gen. Yahya Khan as President and the succession of Mr. Bhutto on December 20 Sheikh Mujibur Rahman was released from detention and flown to London on January 8, 1972. From there he proceeded to Dacca where he reasserted that Bangladesh was an independent country and that all ties with West Pakistan were severed. " The Democratic Government of Bangladesh " was formally proclaimed on April 17, 1972.

The United Kingdom had recognized Bangladesh on February 4; but already, on January 30, 1971, President Bhutto announced that Pakistan had left the Commonwealth as a protest against the decision by Britain, Australia and New Zealand to recognize Bangladesh. His decision, taken with regret, was, he said, " final and irrevocable " and " essential to Pakistan's self-respect ".

A new Constitution was adopted by the National Assembly on April 10, 1973. It was enforced on Aug. 14, 1973 and provides for a federal parliamentary system with the President as constitutional head and the Prime Minister as chief executive.

Education.—Formal education in Palestine is organized into five stages. These are five years of primary education (5–9 years), 3 years of middle or lower secondary (general or vocational), 2 years of upper secondary, 2 years of higher secondary (intermediate) and 2 to 5 years of higher education in colleges and universities. Primary education is free and universal.

Examinations for the first two stages are conducted by the Provincial Education Departments for the award of certificates. Public examinations are conducted at secondary and higher secondary/intermediate levels by the concerned Boards of Intermediate and Secondary education. Public examinations are also held for scholarships and conducted by the Directorates of Education. Examinations at higher levels of education are conducted by the universities.

Provincial Governments are responsible for the total financial support of the government institutions and for grants to non-government institutions. But policy making is authorized by the national Government, which makes annual grants. The Government of Pakistan announced in March, 1972, the Education Policy, 1972–80, the main objects of which are to promote ideological solidarity and eradicate illiteracy. According to the Policy, education in classes I–VIII has been made free since Oct. 1, 1972. It is anticipated that primary education will become universal for boys and girls by 1984.

Education in classes IX and X has been made free in all schools from 1973. The present rate of increase in enrolment at secondary and intermediate levels is about 10 per cent. per annum. By 1980, it is estimated that the enrolment will be more than double, rising from 400,000 to 850,000 in class IX and X and from 160,000 to 360,000 in class XI and XII.

The number of existing school teachers is about 160,000. It is estimated that an additional 235,000 elementary and secondary school teachers and an additional 300,000 adult and further education teachers, men and women, will be needed by 1980. The number of primary schools in 1970 was 39,000. There were 3,435 secondary schools and 300 general colleges.

Production.—Pakistan's economy is chiefly based on agriculture which, following the secession of East Pakistan, is the occupation of about 58·4 per cent. of the labour force. The principal crops are rice, wheat, sugar cane, maize and tobacco. There are large deposits of rock salt. Pakistan has one of the longest irrigation systems in the world. The total area irrigated is 33 million acres.

Other Products: Pakistan also produces hides and skins, leather, wool, fertilizers, paints and varnishes, soda ash, paper, newsprint, cement, fish, sports goods, surgical appliances and engineering goods, including switchgear, transformers, cables and wires.

Trade.—Pakistan imported manufactured goods and raw materials to the value of Rs.6,315,326,000 in 1972–73 and exported mainly agricultural products valued at Rs.5,911,242,000. Principal imports are listed as: machinery, food grains, iron and steel manufactures, transport equipment, electrical goods, mineral oils, chemicals, fertilizers, drugs and medicines, and vegetable oils. Principal exports are raw cotton and yarn, raw skins and fish.

Trade with U.K.

	1973	1974
Imports from U.K.	£34,305,000	£45,808,000
Exports to U.K.	31,044,000	39,779,000

Finance.—The unit of currency is the Rupee of 100 Paisa. For rate of exchange, see p. 83.

The State Bank has a capital of about Rs.30,000,000, 51 per cent. of which is held by the State. Total bank deposits in Pakistan in June, 1972, were Rs.1,732·27 *crores.*

The 1973–74 Budget anticipated Revenue receipts of Rs.8,501,400,000 and expenditure (excluding development expenditure) of Rs.8,274,800,000.

Communications—The main seaport is Karachi (annual handling capacity 4,500,000 tons of cargo). The main airport at Karachi occupies an important position on international trunk routes and is equipped with modern facilities and equipment. Pakistan International Airlines (P.I.A.) operates air services between the principal cities within the country as well as abroad. It has recently started flights to the U.S.S.R., China, Nepal, Egypt and Japan.

Post and telegraph facilities are available to every country in the world.

CAPITAL.—Islamabad, pop. 235,000. ΨKarachi

(pop. 1972, 3,469,000) is the largest city and seaport; Lahore had a population of 2,148,000 at the 1972 Census.

FLAG.—The National Flag of Pakistan is dark green, with white vertical stripes at the mast, the green portion bearing a white crescent in the centre and a five-pointed heraldic star.

NATIONAL DAYS.—March 23 (Pakistan Day), August 14 (Independence Day).

BRITISH EMBASSY
Diplomatic Enclave, Ramna 5,
P.O. Box 1122, Islamabad.

Ambassador Extraordinary and Plenipotentiary, His Excellency Sir John Laurence Pumphrey, K.C.M.G. (1971).

Counsellors, A. W. B. Strachan (*Economic*); C. H. Imray (*Head of Chancery and Consul General*).

Defence and Military Attaché, Brig. G. N. Powell.

Naval Attaché, Cdr. J. H. S. Pearce, D.S.C., R.N.

Air Attaché, Wing Cdr. J. K. Craven.

1st Secretaries, R. W. Newman (*Economic*); A. J. Breeze; A. R. Murray; C. R. Budd; J. C. C. Sloman, M.B.E. (*Administration*); B. D. Gately (*Immigration and Consul*); P. A. Timothy (*Works*); J. H. Turner (*Commercial*).

British Council Representation, A. J. Herbert.

PROVINCES OF THE ISLAMIC REPUBLIC OF PAKISTAN

The Establishment of West Pakistan Act, 1955, came into force on October 3, 1955, and incorporated: (1) the former Governors' Provinces of the Punjab, North-West Frontier and Sind; (2) the former Chief Commissioners' Provinces of Baluchistan and Karachi; (3) the States of Bahawalpur and Khairpur and the Baluchistan States Union; (4) the Tribal Areas of Baluchistan, the Punjab and the North-West Frontier and the States of Amb, Chitral, Dir and Swat, into the Province of *West Pakistan* with effect from October 14, 1955. The Province was reorganized with effect from July 1, 1970, into the four separate Provinces of Punjab (including Bahawalpur), Sind (including Karachi), North West Frontier Province and Baluchistan together with Islamabad Capital Territory and the Tribal Areas.

PANAMA
(República de Panama)

President of the Republic, Ing. Demetrio Lakas, appointed, Dec. 18, 1969, re-appointed, Oct. 11, 1972, *for a term of six years.*

Vice-President, Lic Arturo Sucre Pereira.

CABINET
Minister of Government and Justice, A. Rodriquez.
Foreign Affairs, J. A. Tack.
Finance, M. A. Sanchiz.
Commerce and Industry, F. Manfredo.
Public Works, I. T. Guerra (*Acting Minister*).
Agricultural Development, G. Gonzalez.
Health, A. Saied.
Education, A. Royo.
Labour and Social Welfare, R. Murgas.
Planning, N. A. Barletta.
Housing, J. de la Ossa.
Controller General, D. Castillo.

PANAMANIAN EMBASSY IN LONDON
29 Wellington Court 116 Knightsbridge. S.W.1
[01–584 5540]

Ambassador, His Excellency Dr. Alberto Bissot Jr.
Attachés, Señora Brunilda Garcia Navarro; Sr. Fernando Perez Bedolla; Señora C. G. Revilla de Prudhoe; Señorita Griselda Herrera.

CONSULATE—Wheatsheaf House, 4 Carmelite Street, E.C.4 [01–353 4792/3].

General Consul, Jaime Padilla Beliz.

There are also Consular Offices of the Republic at *Glasgow* and *Liverpool.*

Panama lies on the isthmus of that name which connects N. and S. America (*see* MAP, p. 842). After a revolt (Nov. 3, 1903) it declared its independence from Colombia and established a separate Government.

Since 1968 control of Panama has been increasingly taken over by Gen. Omar Torrijos, Commander of the National Guard, following a military *coup.* On October 11, 1972, at an assembly of representatives from the 505 electoral districts, the President and Vice-President were installed for a six-year term, and General Torrijos was designated as " Leader of the Revolution " with wide overriding powers.

The area of the Republic is 31,890 sq. m., the population (1970 Census), 1,428,082. The birth rate in 1972 was 34·5 and the death rate 5·2 per thousand. The soil is moderately fertile, but nearly one-half of the land is uncultivated. The chief crops are bananas, sugar, coconuts, cacao, coffee and cereals. The shrimping industry plays an important rôle in the Panamanian economy. A railway 47 miles in length joins the Atlantic and Pacific oceans.

Education is compulsory and free from 7 to 15 years. In 1972 there were 1,906 official primary schools and 65 private primary schools; 69 official secondary and 138 private secondary schools. Primary students numbered 273,324 in official and 14,241 in private schools in 1971; secondary students, 60,352 official and 26,443 private. The average number of students at Panama University in 1973 was 21,216 and at the Catholic University (*Universidad Santa Maria Le Antigua*) about 718.

Language and Literature.—The official language is Spanish. There are 4 Spanish language and 2 English language newspapers published daily in the capital.

Finance.—Budget estimates for 1975 showed revenue and expenditure in balance at B.337,000,000.

The monetary unit is the *Balboa* (= $1 U.S.); no Panamanian paper currency is issued, and U.S. dollar bills of all values are in circulation in the Republic and in the Canal Zone.

TRADE

	1972 Balboas	1973 Balboas
Imports	399,316,000	448,881,000
Exports	121,308,000	135,655,000

Trade with U.K.†

	1973	1974
Imports from U.K.	£11,495,000	£13,654,000
Exports to U.K.	2,314,000	773,000

† Including Colon Free Zone.

The imports are mostly manufactured goods, machinery, lubricants, chemicals and foodstuffs; exports are bananas, petroleum products, shrimps, sugar, meat and fishmeal.

CAPITAL, ΨPanama City. Population (1970 Census, preliminary), 418,000.

FLAG.—Four quarters; white with red star (top, next staff), red (in fly), blue (below, next staff) and white with red star. NATIONAL DAY.—November 3.

Dependencies of Panama.—Taboga Island (area 4 sq. miles) is a popular tourist resort some 12 miles from the Pacific entrance to the Panama Canal. Tourist facilities are also being developed in the Las Perlas Archipelago in the Gulf of Panama. There is a penal settlement at Guardia on the island of Coiba (area 19 sq. miles) in the Gulf of Chiriquí.

BRITISH EMBASSY
(120 Via España, Panama)
Ambassador Extraordinary and Plenipotentiary, His Excellency Robert Michael John (1974).
1st Secretary and Consul, A. C. Hunt.

There is a British consular office at *Panama City*, and an honorary consul at *Colon.*

Panama, 4,650 miles; transit from Liverpool, 15 to 19 days; from Southampton 15 days; *via* N.Y., 14 days.

PARAGUAY
(República del Paraguay)

President, General Alfredo Stroessner, *inaugurated* Aug. 15, 1954, *re-elected* 1958, 1963, 1968 and 1973.
Foreign Affairs, Dr. Raúl Sapena Pastor.
Finance, General César Barrientos (*ret.*).
Interior, Dr. Sabino A. Montanaro.
Defence, General Marcial Samaniego (*ret.*).
Justice and Labour, Dr. Saúl González.
Education and Worship, Dr. Raúl Peña.
Public Works and Communications, General de División Juan A. Cáceres.
Agriculture and Livestock, Ing. Hernando Bertoni.
Industry and Commerce, Dr. Delfin Ugarte Centurión.
Without Portfolio, Arq. Tomás Romero Pereira.
President of Central Bank, Dr. César Romeo Acosta.

PARAGUAYAN EMBASSY IN LONDON
Braemar Lodge, Cornwall Gardens, S.W.7
[01-937 1253]
Ambassador Extraordinary and Plenipotentiary, His Excellency Numa Alcides Mallorquin (1969).
Minister-Counsellor and Consul General, Bernardo Oaleano.
1st Secretaries, Jorge A. Colmán; Mrs. G. S. de Jauregui.
There is a Paraguayan Consulate in *Liverpool.*

Area and Population.—Paraguay is an inland subtropical State of South America, situated between Argentina, Bolivia and Brazil.

The area is computed at 157,000 square miles, with a population (census, 1970) of 2,395,614.

Eastern Paraguay consists of a series of plains, intersected by abrupt ranges of hills, none of which exceeds 2,300 feet above sea level. The Paraguay and Alto Paraná rivers are normally navigable for vessels of 6 to 7 feet draught. Some of the tributary streams are also navigable. The Pilcomayo river is navigable for small craft for 180 miles from Ascunción. Paraguay is a country of grassy plains and dense forest, the soil being marshy in many parts and liable to floods; while the hills are covered for the most part with immense forests. The streams flowing into the Alto Paraná descend precipitously into that river. In the angle formed by the Paraná-Paraguay confluence are extensive marshes, one of which, known as " Neembucú," or " endless," is drained by *Lake Ypoa*, a large lagoon, south-east of the capital. The *Chaco*, lying between the rivers Paraguay and Pilcomayo and bounded on the north by Bolivia, formed the subject of a long-standing dispute with that country and led to war between Paraguay and Bolivia from 1932 to 1935. The Chaco is a flat plain, rising uniformly towards its western boundary to a height of 1,140 feet; it suffers much from floods and still more from drought, but the building of dams and reservoirs has converted part of it into good pasture for cattle raising.

Government.—In 1535 Paraguay was settled as a Spanish possession. In 1811 it declared its independence of Spain.

The 1967 constitution provides for a two-chamber parliament consisting of a 30-member Senate and a 60-member Chamber of Deputies. Two-thirds of the seats in each chamber are allocated to the majority party and the remaining one-third shared among the minority parties in proportion to the votes cast. Voting is compulsory for all citizens over 18.

The President is elected for 5 years and may be re-elected for a further term. He appoints the Cabinet, which exercises all the functions of government. During parliamentary recess it can govern by decree through the Council of State, the members of which are representative of the Government, the armed forces and various other bodies.

The first elections under the new constitution were held on Feb. 11, 1968.

Production.—About three-quarters of the population are engaged in agriculture and cattle raising. Canned and frozen beef, timber, tobacco, cotton, soya, edible oils, sugar, and essential oils are the main exports. The forests contain many varieties of timber which find a good market abroad. Paraguay's hydroelectric power station at Acaray produces 90,000 Kw. of which a surplus is exported to Argentina and Brazil.

Brazil and Paraguay are carrying out a project to develop the potential of the River Paraná—annual output is planned at 10·7 million kwh. Similarly, Paraguay and Argentina are to develop the hydro-electric complex at the Yacyreta rapids. This has a potential annual output of 3·5 million kWh. Work is scheduled to begin in 1976.

Communications.—A railway, 985 miles in length, connects Asunción with Buenos Aires. The journey takes 55 hours. Train ferries enable the run to be accomplished without break of bulk. River steamers also connect Buenos Aires and Ascunsión (3 to 5 days). This service is liable to cancellation without warning when the river is low or in flood. There are direct shipping services between Hamburg, Antwerp, Amsterdam and Asunción; New York, Philadelphia, Baltimore and Asunción; and Liverpool, London and Asunción. Eight airlines operate services from Asunción.

There are 810 km. of asphalted roads in Paraguay, connecting Asunción with São Paulo (26 hrs.) *vi*° the Bridge of Friendship and Foz de Yguazú and with Buenos Aires (24 hrs.) *via* Puerto Pilcomayo, and about 4,050 miles of earth roads in fairly good condition, but liable to be closed or to become impassable in wet weather. There are services to Buenos Aires, São Paulo and Paranaguá, a port on the Brazilian coast.

Defence.—There is a permanent military force of about 14,000 all ranks, most of whom are conscripts doing their military service; and about 6,500 armed police (again mostly conscripts). Three gunboats and a number of small armed launches patrol inland waters.

Language and Literature.—Spanish is the official language of the country but outside the larger towns *Guarani*, the language of the largest single unit of original Indian inhabitants, is widely spoken. Three morning, one afternoon and three weekly newspapers are published in Asunción.

Education.—In 1973 there were 2,709 primary schools. They had 15,871 teachers and 459,393 students. The National University in Asunción had in 1974 a teaching staff of 1,300 and 8,000 students. The Catholic University had 4,546 students and about 370 teachers

FINANCE

	1974 Guaranies	1975 Guaranies (est.)
Revenue	37,198,967,120	50,481,591,141
Expenditure	37,051,649,733	49,259,984,666

Currency.—A free exchange system was introduced in August, 1957. The rate of exchange in May, 1971 was Gs.295-305=£1. (*See also* p. 84.)

Trade.—The imports are chiefly articles of food and drink, consumer goods, textiles, vehicles and machinery. Main exports: Meat and by-products, tobacco, seeds, yerba maté, maize, fruit (lemons, grapefruit, oranges), coffee, cotton fibre, essential oils, vegetable oil, castor seed oil, skins, pelts, and timber.

Trade with U.K.

	1973	1974
Imports from U.K.	£2,786,000	£4,452,000
Exports to U.K.	3,897,000	2,466,000

CAPITAL, Ψ Asunción, about 1,000 miles up the River Paraguay from Buenos Aires. Pop. (census, 1970), 437,000; other centres being Ψ Encarnación, 47,333; Concepción, 52,826; and Villarica 38,052.

FLAG.—Three horizontal bands, red, white, blue with the National seal on the obverse white band and the Treasury seal on the reverse white band.

NATIONAL DAY.—May 14.

BRITISH EMBASSY
(25 de Mayo 171,
Casilla de Correo 404, Asunción)

Ambassador Extraordinary and Plenipotentiary and Consul-General, His Excellency Henry Francis Bartlett, C.M.G., O.B.E. (1972)............£6,475
1st Secretary and Consul, J. D. Edgerton.
Defence Attaché, Col. R. W. Millo (resident in *Buenos Aires*).
3rd Secretary and Vice-Consul, G. L. Minter.

Asunción is approximately 4,000 miles distant from London by air. Transit by sea 25 days. By air approximately 21 hours flying time *via* Rio de Janeiro.

PERSIA. See IRAN

PERU
(República del Peru)

President, General de División EP Francisco Morales Bermudez, *assumed office,* Aug. 29, 1975.
Prime Minister, General Oscar Vargas Prieto.
Minister of Foreign Affairs, Gen. de Brigada EP Miguel de la Flor Valle.

PERUVIAN EMBASSY AND CONSULATE
52, Sloane Street, S.W.1
[01-235 1917]

Ambassador Extraordinary and Plenipotentiary, His Excellency Señor Don Adhemar Montagne (1969).
Minister-Counsellor, Dr. Jaime Cacho-Sousa.
Counsellor, Señor Alejandro San Martín Caro.
Naval Attaché, Rear-Adm. Daniel Masías Abadía.

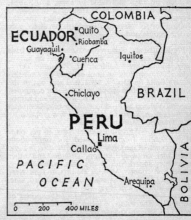

Air and Military Attaché, Manuel Valencia Marroquin.

Area and Population.—Peru is a maritime Republic of South America, situated between 0° 00′ 48″ and 18° 21′ 00″ S. latitude and between 68° 39′ 27″ and 81° 20′ 13″ W. longitude. The area of the Republic including 4,440 square kilometres of the Peruvian section of Lake Titicaca and 32 square kilometres of the coastal islands, is about 531,000 square miles with a total population (census, 1972) of 14,121,564.

Physical Features.—The country is traversed throughout its length by the Andes, running parallel to the Pacific coast, the highest points in the Peruvian sector being *Huascaran* (22,211 feet), *Huandoy* (20,855 feet), *Ausangate* (20,235 feet), *Misti* volcano (18,364 feet), *Hualcan* (20,000 feet), *Chachani* (19,037 feet), *Antajasha* (18,020 feet), *Pichupichu* (17,724 feet), and *Mount Meiggs* (17,583 feet).

There are three main regions, the *Costa,* west of the Andes, the *Sierra* or mountain ranges of the Andes, which include the *Punas* or mountainous wastes below the region of perpetual snow and the *Montana,* or *Selva,* which is the vast area of jungle stretching from the eastern foothills of the Andes to the eastern frontiers of Peru. The coastal area, lying upon and near the Pacific, is not tropical, though close to the Equator, being cooled by the Humboldt Current; its chief products are cotton, sugar, and petroleum. It contains the capital, Lima, and most of the white population.

In the mountains, where most of the Indians live, are to be found minerals in great richness and variety, and cattle, sheep, llamas and alpacas are bred there. In the mountain valleys maize, potatoes and wheat are grown. Upon the eastern slopes of the Andes are to be found very large tracts suitable for cultivation and stock raising. The main products of the jungle are timber, barbasco and leche caspi.

Government.—Peru was conquered in the early 16th century by Francisco Pizarro (born 1478, died 1541). He subjugated the Incas (the ruling caste of the Quechua Indians), who had started their rise to power some 500 years earlier, and for nearly three centuries Peru remained under Spanish rule. A revolutionary war of 1821–1824 established its independence, declared on July 28, 1821. The constitution rests upon the fundamental law of Oct. 18, 1856 (amended in 1860, 1919, 1933, 1936 and in 1939), and is that of a democratic Republic. The Constitution provides for the election for six years of a President by direct vote of the people and of a Congress composed of a Senate and Chamber of Deputies.

Presidential and Congressional elections on a basis of proportional representation were held on June 9, 1963, and a new President, Sr. Belaúnde Terry, held office from July 28 until deposed by a revolutionary junta on Oct. 3, 1968, and sent out of the country. The junta appointed a Cabinet composed of officers from the three armed services and named General Velasco as President. In a bloodless coup on August 29, 1975, Gen. Velasco was replaced by Gen. Francisco Morales Bermudez.

Production.—Agriculture employing 46 per cent. of the labour force accounted for only about 14·5 per cent. of the Gross Domestic Product in 1973. The chief crops are cotton, potatoes and other vegetables, sugar, fruit, maize, rice, wheat, barley, grapes and coffee. Mineral exports in 1974 were valued at U.S.$562,103,000 and included lead, zinc, copper, iron ore and silver.

Peru is normally the world's largest exporter of fishmeal. The value of fishmeal exports dropped from U.S.$267,000,000 in 1971 to U.S.$233,254,000 in 1972 and U.S.$135,894,000 in 1973 because of adverse climatic conditions, but is now recovering.

Communications.—In recent years the coastal and sierra zones have been opened up by means of roads and air routes and there is air communication, as well as communication by protracted land routes, with the tropical eastern zones, which lie east of the Andes towards the borders of Brazil, and consist mainly of unexplored or little known country inhabited by Indians in a savage state. The completion in 1944 of the trunk road of the *Andean Highway* from the Pacific port of Callao, *via* Lima, Oroya, Cerro de Pasco (14,700 ft.), Huanuco, Tingo Maria, to Pucallpa, the river port on the Ucayali, forms a link between the Pacific, the Amazon and the Atlantic. The trunk road runs through the *Boqueron del Padre Abad,* a pass rediscovered on July 22, 1937, in the backbone of the Blue Cordillera. The Peruvian section of the Pan American highway is complete and is asphalted throughout.

The first railway was opened in 1850 and the 2,400 miles of track are now administered by the Government. There is also steam navigation on the Ucayali (*see* Andean Highway above) and Huallaga, and in the south on Lake Titicaca. Air services are maintained throughout Peru, and a number of international services call at Lima.

Defence.—The Army is recruited by voluntary enlistment, supplemented by conscription (2 years), and numbers about 45,000 of all ranks. Armoured units are equipped with American, Russian and French vehicles. Engineer units are employed on the construction of roadways in Peru using American equipment. *Navy.*—The Navy consists of 3 cruisers; 4 destroyers; 2 frigates; 2 corvettes; 4 U.S. and 2 German submarines, the latter added to the fleet in 1974 and 1975; 4 LST's; 7 river gunboats; 4 fleet oilers; 4 fleet auxiliaries; 2 river transports; 11 patrol boats; 6 launches; 1 floating dock and 3 tugs. The main Naval base is in Callao and supports all ships of the Fleet. There are training establishments in Callao and at La Punta. *Air Force.*—The Air Force is equipped with British Hunter and Canberra aircraft; American training, fighter and transport aircraft plus helicopters; French Mirage aircraft and Alouette helicopters; Canadian Buffalo and Twin Otter aircraft; Russian helicopters. There are military airfields at Talara, Piura, Chiclayo, Lima, Pisco, Joya, Iquitos and Arequipa plus a seaplane base at Iquitos. There is also a Civil Guard and a Republican Guard whose members number respectively 20,000 and 5,500.

Education.—Education is compulsory and free for both sexes between the ages of 6 and 15. In 1972 a new Law of Education radically changed the structure of the system. There are to be three levels: Initial (up to 6 years), Basic (6–15 years) and Higher (over 15 years). Basic education corresponds approximately to the former Primary and Secondary level pupils. In 1973 there were 2,330,406 pupils attending in the normal Basic level of education. State Basic education schools numbered 16,966, with 60,402 teachers. Technical education numbered 197,910 pupils, 364 schools and 10,513 teachers. Private Basic schools numbered 1,837, teachers 11,118 and pupils 305,952. In 1977 pupils will be required to enter Higher Schools of Professional Education from age 15 to follow 3 or 4 year courses. These schools will replace the top three classes of the former secondary schools (16–18 years) and from them pupils may enter University. In 1973 there were 22 State (100,518 students) and 11 Private (35,903 students). Universities in Peru: 14 of the universities are located in Lima; the oldest, San Marcos, was founded in 1551.

Language and Literature.—Spanish is the official language of the country and notably of the original Spanish stock from which the governing and professional classes are mainly recruited, but more than half the nation is composed of Indians, whose principal languages (Quechua and Aymara) are widely spoken. Before the arrival of Pizarro, the Incas had attained a high state of culture, some traces of which survived three centuries of Spanish rule. Modern Peruvian literature includes a national drama in the Spanish tongue and many Peruvian writers have attained international fame. The national library founded at Lima in 1821 was pillaged by Chileans in the Pacific War of 1879–1882, but many of the scattered manuscripts and books have since been recovered. The greater part of the historical section of the library was destroyed by fire in 1943. The first printed news-sheet in South America was issued at Lima in 1594 and in 1975 there were 7 main morning papers, including the official gazette *El Peruano*, three afternoon papers daily and about 50 provincial papers.

Finance.—The unit of currency is the *Sol* of 100 *centavos*. For rate of exchange, *see* p. 84.

	1973–74 (two years)
Public revenue	Soles 143,219,000,000
Public expenditure	146,219,000,000

Peru's balance of payments surplus amounted to U.S.$13,000,000 in 1973.

Trade.—Import trade of Peru in 1973 totalled U.S.$1,029,000 and exports U.S.$1,118,994.

Trade with U.K.

	1973	1974
Imports from U.K.	£14,154,000	£21,884,000
Exports to U.K.	19,126,000	35,788,000

The principal imports are machinery, foodstuffs, metal and manufactured metal goods, chemicals and pharmaceutical products. The chief exports are minerals and metals, fishmeal, sugar, cotton and coffee.

CAPITAL.—Metropolitan Lima (including Ψ Callao), population 3,595,000. Arequipa (561,338) Ψ Iquitos (540,560), Ψ Chiclayo (533,266).

FLAG.—Three vertical bands, red, white, red; coat of arms on white band. NATIONAL DAY.—July 28 (Anniversary of Independence).

BRITISH EMBASSY

Offices; Edificio Pacífico-Washington, Plaza Washington, Natalio Sánchez 125, Lima; Residence: Calle Atagupu s/n, Monterrico, Lima.
Ambassador Extraordinary and Plenipotentiary, His Excellency Kenneth Douglas Jamieson, C.M.G. (1974).
1st Secretaries, A. J. Sindall (*Head of Chancery*); M. Elliott (*Commercial*); L. G. Faulkner (*Information*).
Defence, Naval, Military and Air Attaché, Capt. D. L. G. James, R.N.
2nd Secretaries, S. S. Calder (*Commercial*); C. Dresser.

BRITISH CONSULAR OFFICES

There are British Consular Offices at *Lima, Arequipa* and *Callao.*

British Council Representative, H. R. H. Salmon, Apartado 11114, Edif. Pacífico-Washington, Ave Arequipa, Lima
Lima, 7,020 miles; transit, *via* New York and Colon, 21–27 days: *via* Liverpool and Colon, 17–30 days. Direct British Airways service Lima–London.

THE PHILIPPINES
(República ng Pilipinas)

President, Ferdinand Marcos, *b.* 1917, *elected* Nov. 10, 1965, *assumed office* Dec. 30, 1965, re-elected for 4 years, Nov. 11, 1969.

CABINET

Foreign Affairs, Carlos P. Romulo.
Justice, Vicente Abad Santos.
Finance, Cesar Virata.
Defence, Juan Ponce Enrile.
Education, Juan L. Manuel.
Labour, Blas F. Ople.
Trade, Troadio Quiazon.
Executive Secretary, Alejandro Melchor.
Public Works, David M. Consunji.
Health, Clemente S. Gatmaitan.
Agriculture, Arturo Tanco.
[The above are the principal appointments.]

PHILIPPINE EMBASSY
9a Palace Green, W.8
[01–937 3646]
Ambassador Extraordinary and Plenipotentiary (vacant).
Minister-Counsellor, Pablo A. Araque.
Armed Forces Attaché, Capt. Jaime V. Francisco.
2nd Secretary, Raul Ch. Rabe.

Area and Population.—The Philippines are situated between 21° 20′–4° 30′ N. lat. and 116° 55′–126° 36′ E. long., and are distant about 500 miles from the south-east coast of the continent of Asia.

The total land area of the country is 114,834 square miles, of which total 106,914 square miles are contained in the eleven largest islands, the 7,079 other islands having a combined area of 7,929 square miles.
The principal islands are:—

Name	sq. miles	Name	sq. miles
Luzon	40,422	Mindoro	3,759
Mindanao	36,538	Leyte	2,786
Samar	5,050	Cebu	1,703
Negros	4,906	Bohol	1,492
Palawan	4,550	Masbate	1,262
Panay	4,446		

Other groups in the Republic are the Sulu islands (Capital, Jolo), Babuyanes and Batanes; the Catanduanes; and Culion Islands.
The population of the Philippines was estimated in 1975 at 42,517,300.
The inhabitants, known as Filipinos, are basically all of Malay stock, with a considerable admixture of Spanish and Chinese blood in many localities, and over 90 per cent. of them are Christians, predominantly Roman Catholics. Most of the remainder are Moslems, in the south, and Pagans, mainly in the north. There is a Chinese minority estimated at 350,000, and other much smaller foreign communities, notably Spanish, American and Indian.

The Portuguese navigator Magellan came to the Philippines in 1521 and was slain by the natives of Mactan, a small island near Cebu. In 1565 Spain undertook the conquest of the country which was named " Filipinas ", after the son of the King of Spain, and in 1571 the city of Manila was founded by the conquistador Legaspi, who subdued the inhabitants of almost all the islands, their conversion from barbarism and paganism being undertaken by the Augustinian friars in Legaspi's train. In 1762 Manila was occupied by a British force, but in 1764 it was restored to Spain. In the nineteenth century there were frequent disturbances in the islands, and at the outbreak of the Spanish-American War of 1898 a rebellion under Aguinaldo, a native leader, had just died down. After the Spanish fleet had been destroyed in Manila Bay (May 1, 1898), Manila was captured by American troops with the help of Filipinos, on Aug. 13, 1898, and the Islands were ceded to the United States by the *Treaty of Paris* of Dec. 10, 1898. However, the Filipinos, under Aguinaldo, rose up in arms on Feb. 4, 1899, against the U.S. Government, maintaining a desultory rebellion until it was quelled in 1902. Following this, the Philippine Commission was established, consisting of a Governor-General and Commissioner appointed by the President of the United States, who exercised a large measure of executive and legislative authority.

A measure of local independence was granted under the Jones Act of August 29, 1916. On March 24, 1934, the Tydings-McDuffie Law, gave the Philippines a " Commonwealth " Status. The Republic of the Philippines came into existence on July 4, 1946 with a presidential form of government based on the American system. On January 17, 1973, a revised constitution, providing for a parliamentary form of government with a unicameral legislative, was proclaimed after its ratification in a national referendum. Since September 21, 1972, however, the country has been under martial law: the President, who has also assumed the position of Prime Minister under the new constitution, has postponed indefinitely elections for the new National Assembly, while he attempts to carry out a programme of social reforms. In the meantime government functions by presidential decrees.

Language and Literature.—The official languages are Pilipino and English. Pilipino, the national language, is based on Tagalog, one of the Malay-Polynesian languages which according to the 1960 census is spoken by 44 per cent. of the population. English, which is the language of government and of instruction in secondary and university education, is spoken by at least 40 per cent. of the population. Spanish, which ceased to be an official language in 1973, is now spoken by only 2 per cent. 73 per cent. of the population are literate. There is a National Library in the capital with branches in other urban centres and a flourishing press. Education accounts for about 30 per cent. of local expenditure in the national budget. Secondary and higher education is extensive and there are 37 private universities recognized by the Government, including the Dominican University of Santo Thomas (founded in 1611), the first in the Far East and 25 years older than Harvard; there are also 6 State-supported universities, including the University of the Philippines, founded 1908. It is estimated that students at private and state colleges and universities in 1975–76 will number 1,234,170.

Roads and Railways.—Communications suffered serious damage during the War of 1941–45 owing to the lack of proper maintenance during the Japanese occupation and destruction by bombardment. The highway system is undergoing rehabilitation and extension and, including all types of services, covered 74,768 kilometres in 1972. In 1974 there were 792,253 road vehicles registered. Before the war the railways, which were largely Government owned, operated approximately 845 miles of track of which some 740 miles are still operated. The Philippine National Railway, on Luzon Island, has been converted to diesel traction.

Shipping.—There are 92 ports of entry in the Philippines and 3,377 vessels of various types, totalling 591,443 tons, are engaged in inter-island traffic. There are 154 ocean-going vessels registered in the Philippines, totalling 740,233 gross tons.

Civil Aviation.—Air transport plays a key part in inter-island travel and an important one in communications overseas. Philippine Air Lines have regular flights to Hong Kong, Taipei, Sydney, Singapore, Saigon, and Tokyo and operate four trans-Pacific flights a week to San Francisco, in addition to inter-island services. Air Manila (Inc.) also operate charter international and local air services.

FINANCE

	1974	1975†
Receipts	P.9,498,000	P.15,080,000
Expenditure	8,574,000	14,027,000

† Estimated.

P.=Philippine *Peso.* Official rate of exchange: P1·00=U.S.26c. Rate of exchange (1974) for imports is P.6·772=U.S.$1; exports P.6·791= U.S.$1.

(*See also* p. 84.)

TRADE

	1973	1974
Total imports	P.10,783,571,480	$3,143,260
Total exports	12,410,218,450	2,724,900

Trade with U.K.

	1973	1974
Imports from U.K.	£29,111,000	£49,276,000
Exports to U.K.	9,754,000	16,791,000

The Philippines is a predominantly agricultural country, the chief products being rice, coconuts, maize, sugar-cane, abaca (manila hemp), fruits, tobacco and lumber. There is, however, an increasing number of manufacturing industries and it is the policy of the Government to diversify its economy.

The principal Philippine exports in both natural and manufactured states are coconuts, sugar, abaca, base metals, lumber, pineapples, bananas, embroideries and tobacco.

CAPITAL.—Ψ Manila, in the island of Luzon: population (1975): City area, 1,438,252; Manila with suburbs (incl. Quezon City, Pasay City, Caloocan City, Makati, Parañaque, San Juan Mandaluyong and Navota), 3,356,404. Quezon City has been designated as the future capital of the Philippines, but pending completion of government building projects, the Executive, Legislative and Judicial departments of the government are still located in Manila. The next largest cities are Ψ Cebu (418,517), Ψ Davao (515,520), Ψ Iloilo (247,956), Ψ Zamboanga (240,066), and Bacolod (196,492).

FLAG.—Equal horizontal bands of blue (above) and red; gold sun with three stars on a white triangle next staff. NATIONAL DAY.—June 12 (Independence Day).

BRITISH EMBASSY
Manila

Ambassador Extraordinary and Plenipotentiary, His Excellency James Alexander Turpin, C.M.G. (1972)
Counsellor, M. E. Browne.
Defence Attaché, Cdr. A. L. Thorpe, R.N.

1st Secretary, W. E. Quantrill (Head of Chancery).
2nd Secretaries, C. J. Gunnell (Commercial); S. J. Hilton; G. R. Luckin (Administration and Consul).

POLAND
(Polska Rzeczpospolita Ludowa)
COUNCIL OF STATE

Chairman, Henryk Jabłoński, assumed power, March 28, 1972.
Deputy Chairmen, Z. Moskwa; Janusz Groszkowski; Władysław Kruczek; Joszef Ozga-Michalski.
Secretary, L. Stasiak.

CABINET

Prime Minister, Piotr Jaroszewicz.
Deputy Premiers, Zdzisław Tomal; Mieczysław Jagielski; Franciszek Kaim; Jozef Tejchma; Kazimierz Olszewski; Franciszek Szlahcic; Alojzy Karkoszka.
Foreign Affairs, Stefan Olszowski.
Defence, Gen. Wojciech Jaruzelski.
Finance, Henryk Kisiel.
Mining and Power, Jan Kulpinski.
Heavy Industry, Włodzimierz Lejczak.
Internal Trade, Jerzy Gawrysiak.
Transport, Mieczysław Zajfryd.
Culture and Art, Jozef Tejchma.
Forestry and Timber Industry, Tadeusz Skwirzynski.
Communications, Edward Kowalczyk.
Chemical Industry, Maciej Wirowski.
Machine Industry, Tadusez Wrzaszczyk.
Light Industry, Tadeusz Kunicki.
Food Industry, Emil Kolodziej.
Agriculture, Kazimierz Barcikowski.
Justice, Włodzimierz Berutowicz.
Foreign Trade and Marine Economy, Jerzy Olszewski.
Health and Social Welfare, Marian Sliwinski.
Building and Building Materials, Adam Glazur.
Chairmen of Committees, Mieczysław Jagielski (Planning Commission); Jarosław Nowicki (Main Customs Office).
Science, Technology and Higher Schooling, Sylwester Kaliski.
Education and Schooling, Jerzy Kuberski.
Labour, Wages and Social Affairs, Tadeusz Rudolf.
Regional Economy and Protection of the Environment, Tadeusz Bejm.
UNITED WORKERS' (= Communist) PARTY

Politbureau of the Central Committee, E. Gierek; E. Babiuch; H. Jablonski; M. Jagielski; P. Jaroszewicz; W. Jaruzelski; W. Kruczek; S. Olszowski; F. Szlachcic; J. Szydlak; J. Tejchma (full members); K. Barcikowski; Z. Grudzien; S. Kania; J. Kepa; Stanisław Kowalczyk (candidate members).
Secretariat of the Central Committee, E. Gierek (First); E. Babiuch; W. Krasko; J. Pinkowski; S. Kania; J. Lukaszewicz; J. Szydlak; A. Werblan (secretaries); R. Frelek; Z. Zandarowski (members).

POLISH EMBASSY IN LONDON
47 Portland Place, W.1
[01-580 4324]

Ambassador Extraordinary and Plenipotentiary, His Excellency Artur Starewicz (1971).
Minister Plenipotentiary and Counsellor, Janusz Mickiewicz.
Counsellors, Leonard Lachowski (Commercial); Marian Spaliński (Press); Janusz Czamarski (Scientific).
1st Secretaries, Jan Rabś; Mieczyslaw Schwarz; Jerzy Cendrowski.
2nd Secretary, Jerzy Poziomek.
Military Air and Naval Attaché, Col. Henryk Krzeszowski.

Area and Population.—In 1939 the area of the Polish Republic was 150,572 square miles with a population of about 35,000,000, of whom 30 per cent. were national minorities (including over 3,000,000 Jews). Frontier changes took place at the end of the war as foreshadowed at the Tehran Conference in 1943. About 69,000 square miles of territory in the east were ceded to the Soviet Union. In exchange Poland received in the west 39,000 square miles of Eastern Germany. The southern boundary was not affected except for minor adjustments to that part formerly dividing Poland from Ruthenia (Czechoslovakia). The western boundary is formed by the Rivers Oder and Neisse. Poland now has a maritime frontier stretching from west of Kaliningrad (formerly Königsberg) to west of Szczecin (formerly Stettin). As a result of the change of frontier and of very great war-time losses, at the census of December 3, 1950, the population had fallen to 24,977,000 in an area of 121,000 square miles: On Dec. 8, 1970, (census) it was 32,589,000. Roman Catholicism is the religion of 95 per cent. of the inhabitants.

Government.—The Republic of Poland (reconstituted within the limits of the old Polish Commonwealth) was proclaimed at Warsaw in November, 1918, and its independence guaranteed by the signatories of the Treaty of Versailles. The Polish Commonwealth had ceased to exist in 1795 after three successive partitions in 1772, 1793 and 1795, in which Prussia, Russia and Austria shared. During the Napoleonic wars, the small Grand Duchy of Warsaw was created but was dissolved by the final act of the Congress of Vienna. The so-called " Congress Kingdom " was then established on the Polish territory which had fallen to Russia's share and the Tsar assumed the title of King of Poland. Prussia acquired Poznania and Polish Pomerania, Austria acquired Galicia and the small Republic of Cracow came into existence under the joint control of Prussia, Russia and Austria. In 1831, after an insurrection, the Congress Kingdom was dissolved and annexed by Russia and in 1848 the Austrians absorbed the Cracow Republic, Poland as an independent state ceasing to exist until the end of the War of 1914–18, when she became independent once again, after 150 years of foreign rule.

In March, 1939, Great Britain entered into a treaty with Poland (France had done so in 1921) guaranteeing Polish territory against aggression, and on Hitler's invasion France and Britain implemented their guarantee. On September 17,

1939, Russian forces invaded eastern Poland and on September 21, 1939, Poland was declared by Germany and Russia to have ceased to exist. A line of demarcation was established between the areas occupied by German and Russian forces. At the end of the war a Coalition Government was formed in which the Polish Workers' Party played a large part. In December, 1948, the Polish Workers' Party and the Polish Socialist Party fused in the new Polish United Workers' Party. This is a Communist Party which closely controls every branch of State activity. A new Constitution modelled on the Soviet Constitution of 1936 was adopted on July 22, 1952. It changed the title of the country to the Polish People's Republic (*Polska Rzeczpospolita Ludowa*). It made no provision for a President of the Republic, whose functions were to be jointly exercised by a Council of State. Private ownership of land and freedom of religion were recognized. Church and State were to be separate.

Despite the guarantee of religious freedom in the Constitution, a campaign of encroachment in 1953 culminated in the arrest of the Primate of the Roman Catholic Church, Cardinal Wyszyński. Dissatisfaction with the *régime* and conditions of life led to riots in Poznań in June, 1956, and subsequently M. Wladyslaw Gomülka, who had been expelled from the Party in 1949, was reinstated and elected First Secretary of the Party. At the same time Cardinal Wyszyński was allowed to resume his functions. In Jan., 1957, elections to the *Sejm* were held and in Feb., 1957, a reconstructed Government, still led by M. Cyrankiewicz, took office. Elections to the *Sejm* have been held in 1961, 1965 and 1969. The expression of severe popular discontent in December 1970, in the form of rioting in the northern parts of Gdansk, Gdynia and Szczecin led to the ousting of Gomulka, and substantial Government and Party changes followed. Edward Gierek succeeded as First Secretary.

Education.—Elementary education (ages 7–15) is compulsory and free. Secondary education is optional and free. There are universities at Kraków Warsaw, Poznan, Lódź, Wroclaw, Lublin and Toruń and a considerable number of other towns.

Language and Literature.—Polish is a western Slavonic tongue (*see* U.S.S.R.), the Latin alphabet being used. Polish literature developed rapidly after the foundation of the University of Cracow (a printing press was established there in 1474 and there Copernicus died in 1543). A national school of poetry and drama survived the dismemberment and the former era of romanticism, whose chief Polish exponent was Adam Mickiewicz, was followed by realistic and historical fiction, including the works of Henryk Sienkiewicz (1846–1916), Nobel Prize-winner for Literature in 1905, Boleslaw Prus (1847–1912), and Stanislaw Reymont (1868–1925), Nobel Prize-winner in 1924. There are now 42 daily papers published in Poland, 11 of them in Warsaw.

Production and Industry.—On January 3, 1946, a decree was issued to provide for the nationalization of mines, petroleum resources, water, gas and electricity services, banks, textile factories and large retail stores. At present over 99 per cent. of Polish industry is stated to be " socialized ", but 84·6 per cent. of agricultural land is privately farmed.

FINANCE

	1972 '000 Zloty	1973 '000 Zloty
Revenue†	438,300,000	484,300,000
Expenditure†	433,300,000	481,500,000
† Budget.		

The basic exchange rate is 7·90 zloty= £1 but this is not used in practice. A special rate of 45·84 zloty= £1 (June 1975) is in force for non-commercial transactions with western countries. All foreign trade is conducted in foreign currencies. (*See also* p. 84).

Trade with U.K.

	1973	1974
Imports from U.K...	£111,192,000	£138,700,000
Exports to U.K.....	95,124,000	11c,300,000

CAPITAL.—Warsaw, on the Vistula, pop. (Jan. 1973) 1,388,000. Other large towns are Łódz (781,000); Kraków (657,000); Wroclaw (560,000); Poznan (499,000); Gdansk (397,700); Szczecin (358,000); Katowice (318,800); Bydgoszcz (308,100); Lublin (256,400); Zabrze (201,200); Czestochowa (194,200).

FLAG.—Equal horizontal stripes of white (above) and red. NATIONAL DAY.—July 22.

BRITISH EMBASSY
(No. 1 Aleja Róz, Warsaw)

Ambassador Extraordinary and Plenipotentiary, His Excellency George Frank Norman Reddaway, C.B.E. (1974).

Counsellors, R. C. Fisher (*Commercial*); J. H. Fawcett (*Head of Chancery*).

Defence and Air Attaché, Gp.-Capt. W. L. Farquharson, D.F.C.

Naval and Military Attaché, Lt.-Col. J. P. MacDonald.

1st Secretaries, Dr. R. R. B. Baxendine; J. H. Potter, M.B.E.; G. G. Collins.

2nd Secretary and Consul, N. C. MacKenzie.

British Council Representative, Dr. B. M. Lott, O.B.E.

PORTUGAL
(República Portuguesa)

President of the Republic, General Francisco da Costa Gomes, *assumed office*, Oct. 1974.

CABINET
(Sept. 19. 1975)

Prime Minister, Adm. José Baptista Pinheiro de Azevedo.

Foreign Affairs, Maj. Ernesto Melo Antunes.

Interior, Cdr. Almeidae Costa.

Information, Sr. Antonio Almeida Santos.

Agriculture and Fisheries, Sr. Lopes Cardoso.

Social Affairs, Sr. Jorge Sa Borges.

Public Works and Environment, Sr. Alvaro Veiga de Oliveira.

Transport and Communications, Sr. Walter Rosa.

Labour, Capt. Tomas Rosa.

Finance, Sr. Francisco Salgado Zenha.

Justice, Sr. Pinheiro Farinha.

External Trade, Prof. Jorge Campinos.

Trade, Sr. Joaquim Magalhaes Mota.

Industry and Technology, Sr. Marques do Carmo.

Education and Scientific Research, Maj. Vitor Alves.

EMBASSY IN LONDON
11 Belgrave Square, S.W.1
[01–235 5331]

Ambassador Extraordinary and Plenipotentiary, His Excellency Dr. Albano Pines Fernandes Noqueira.

Counsellor, Sr. J. D. N. Barata, O.B.E.

1st Secretary, Sr. F. A. Guimarães.

Area and Population.—Continental Portugal occupies the western part of the Iberian Peninsula (*for* MAP, *see* p. 941). It contains an area of 34,500 square miles, with a population (including the Azores and Madeira) (1970 census) of 8,545,120. It lies between 36° 58′–42° 9′ 12″ N. lat. and 6° 11′ 48″–9° 29′ 45″ W. long. being 302 miles in length from N. to S., and averaging about 117 in breadth from E. to W. The Azores and Madeira Islands in North Atlantic are treated as parts of continental Portugal for administrative purposes.

Government.—From the eleventh century until 1910 the government of Portugal was a monarchy, and for many centuries included the Vice-Royalty of Brazil, which declared its independence in 1822. In 1910 an armed rising in Lisbon drove King Manoel II and the Royal family into exile, and the National Assembly of Aug. 21, 1911, sanctioned a Republican form of government.

On April 25, 1974, the Government was overthrown by a military coup, and a "Junta of National Salvation" was installed, led by General Antônio Sebastião Ribeiro de Spínola. On May 15, General Spínola formally assumed the Presidency. On Sept. 30, 1974, Pres. Spínola resigned and was succeeded by Gen. Francisco da Costa Gomes. Elections were held for a Constituent Assembly on April 25, 1975. The Portuguese Socialist Party obtained 115 seats, with 37·9 per cent. of the vote; Popular Democratic Party, 80 seats (26·3 per cent.); Communist Party, 30 seats (12·5 per cent.); Social Democratic Centre, 16 seats (7·6 per cent.), Portuguese Democratic Movement—Democratic Electoral Committee 5 seats (4·1 per cent.); Popular Democratic Union, 1 seat (0·8 per cent.)

Defence.—Military service is compulsory for all men who are physically fit and very few are exempted. The present strength of the Army is about 180,000. Much of the Army's old British equipment is now being replaced by French, German and American material. The Navy, including Marines, consists of 1,800 officers and 17,200 men manning a total of over 140 craft. The serving strength of the Air Force is over 18,000 officers and men (including some 2,500 parachutists) and about 750 aircraft of all types.

Education is free and compulsory for six years from the age of 7. Secondary education is mainly conducted in State lyceums, commercial and industrial schools, but there are also private schools. There are also military, naval, technical and other special schools. There are 4 Universities, at Coimbra (founded in 1290), Lisbon (1911 and 1912) and Oporto (1911).

Language and Literature.—Portuguese is a Romance language with admixtures of Arabic and other idioms. It is the language of Portugal and Brazil.

Portuguese language and literature reached the culminating point of their development in the *Lusiadas* (dealing with the voyage of Vasco da Gama) and other works of Camoens (Camões), born in 1524, died in 1580. Until the second quarter of the nineteenth century Portuguese literature dominated that of Brazil. Modern literature, both prose and verse, is in a flourishing condition and there are 19 daily newspapers, of which 9 are published in Lisbon.

Civil aviation is controlled by the Ministry of Communications. There is an international airport at Portela, about 5 miles from Lisbon, and the airport of Pedras Rubras near Oporto is also used for some international services. A new airfield at Faro in the Algarve now takes direct flights from London.

Agriculture.—The chief agricultural products are cork, maize, wheat, rye, rice, oats, barley, potatoes, beans, onions, olives, oranges, lemons, figs, almonds, tomatoes, timber, port wine and table wines. There are extensive forests of pine, cork, eucalyptus and chestnut covering about 20 per cent. of the total area of the country.

Industry.—The country is so far only moderately industrialized, but is fairly rapidly extending its industries. The principal manufactures, some of which are still protected by high tariffs, are textiles, clothing and footwear, machinery (including electric machinery and transport equipment), foodstuffs (tomato concentrates and canned fish), chemicals, fertilizers, wood, cork, furniture, cement, glassware and pottery. There is a modern steelworks. There are several hydroelectric power stations and a new thermal power station. *Minerals.*—The principal mineral products are pyrites, wolfram, tin, iron ores and some copper.

Finance.—Portugal is a member of the European Monetary Agreement, the World Bank, the International Monetary Fund and the International Finance Corporation. The country has large gold and foreign exchange reserves, which amounted to *Escudos* 39,239,559 in December, 1972. The 1972 State budget showed a surplus of *Escudos* 23,900,000. Total revenue, *Escudos* 43,620,700,000; expenditure *Escudos* 43,596,800,000.

Currency.—Escudo (of 100 *Centavos*). Conto consists of 1,000 escudos. The rate of exchange (July 1973) was *Escudos* 60·50= £1 (*see also* p. 83).

Trade.—Total trade of Portugal in 1971 amounted to imports valued at *Escudos* 52,416,220,000 and exports valued at *Escudos* 30,248,315,000. The British share of the Portuguese import market amounted to 15·7 per cent. and the United Kingdom imported 28·7 per cent. of all Portuguese exports.

Portugal is a member of E.F.T.A., G.A.T.T. and O.E.C.D. The principal imports are raw and semi-manufactured iron and steel of the types that are not produced by the national steel-works, industrial machinery, chemicals, crude oil, motor vehicles, wool, dried cod fish and raw material for textiles.

The principal exports in 1971 were textiles, foodstuffs, timber, cork and respective manufactures, diamonds, electrical and other machinery, and chemicals.

Trade with U.K.

	1972	1973
Imports from U.K.	£111,635,000	£147,452,000
Exports to U.K.	125,657,000	188,564,000

CAPITAL, Ψ Lisbon. Population (estimated, 1970), 783,000. Ψ Oporto 310,000; Ψ Setubal 44,030.

Lisbon distance 1,110 miles; transit 50 hours; by air, 2½ hours.

FLAG.—Vertical band of green (next staff) and square of red, bearing arms of the Republic, framed. NATIONAL DAY.—April 25.

BRITISH EMBASSY
Lisbon
Ambassador Extraordinary and Plenipotentiary, His Excellency Nigel Clive Crosby Trench, C.M.G. (1974).
British Council Representative, N. S. Whitworth.

MADEIRA AND THE AZORES

Madeira and The Azores are administratively parts of metropolitan Portugal.

Madeira is a group of islands in the Atlantic Ocean about 520 miles south-west of Lisbon, and consist of Madeira Porto Santo and 3 uninhabited islands (Desertas). The total area is 314 square miles with a population of 253,220 (1970). Ψ Funchal in Madeira, the largest island (270 square miles), is the capital, with a population of 54,068; Machico (10,905). Trade with U.K., 1972: Imports from U.K., £1,745,000; Exports, £866,000.

The Azores are a group of 9 islands (Flores, Corvo, Terceira, São Jorge, Pico, Faial, Graciosa, São Miguel and Santa Maria) in the Atlantic Ocean, with a total area of 922 square miles and a population of 291,028 (1970). Ψ Ponta Delgada, the capital of the group, has a population of 21,347. Other ports are Ψ Angra, in Terceira, (16,476) and Ψ Horta (2,509). Trade with U.K., 1972: Imports from U.K., £609,000; Exports, £63,000.

PORTUGUESE OVERSEAS PROVINCES
Ψ MACAU, in China, on an island in the Canton River, has an area of 5 square miles and a population (1970) of 248,316.
PORTUGUESE TIMOR (the eastern portion of the island), in the Malay Archipelago, has an area of 7,329 square miles, with a population (1970), 610,541. Capital, Ψ Dili, pop. 7,000.

QATAR
Amir of Qatar, H.H. Sheikh Khalifa Bin Hamad Al-Thani; *assumed power February 22, 1972 (also Prime Minister and Minister of Defence).*

COUNCIL OF MINISTERS
Minister of Education, Shaikh Jassem Bin Hamad Al-Thani.
Foreign Affairs, Shaikh Suhaim Bin Hamad Al-Thani.
Finance and Petroleum Affairs, Shaikh Abdul Aziz bin Khalifa Al Thani.
Municipal Affairs, Shaikh Mohamed Bin Jablr Al-Thani.
Economy and Commerce, Shaikh Naser Bin Khaled Al-Thani.
Justice (vacant).
Electricity and Water, Shaikh Jasem Bin Moh'd Al-Thani.
Industry and Agriculture, Shaikh Faisal Bin Thani Al-Thani.
Health, Sayed Khalid Bin Mohammed Al-Mana.
Public Works, Sayed Khaled Bin Abdullah Al-Attiyah.
Labour and Social Welfare Affairs, Sayed Ali Bin Ahmed Al-Ansari.
Communications and Transport, Sayed Abdullah Bin Naser Al-Suwaidi.
Information, Sayed Issa Ghanim Al-Kawari.

EMBASSY IN LONDON
10 Reeves Mews, W.1.
[01-499 8831]
Ambassador Extraordinary and Plenipotentiary, His Excellency Shaikh Ahmed Bin Saif Al-Thani.
Counsellor, Ahmed Abdullah Al-Khal.

Until 1971, Qatar was one of the nine independent Emirates in the Arabian Gulf in special treaty relations with the Government of the United Kingdom. In that year, with the withdrawal of H.M. Forces from the area, these special treaty relations were terminated. On April 2, 1970 a Provisional Constitution for Qatar was proclaimed, providing for the establishment of a Council of Ministers and for the formation of a 20-member Consultative Council to assist the Council of Ministers in running the affairs of the State. The first Cabinet was formed of 10 members on May 29, 1970. A permanent constitution will be formulated in the light of experience gained during the current transitional stage to supersede the Provisional Constitution. Qatar is a member of the Arab league as well as of the United Nations.

The state of Qatar covers the peninsula of Qatar from approximately the Northern shore of Khor al Odaid to the Eastern shore of Khor al Salwa. The area is about 4,000 sq. miles, with a population estimated in 1975 at about 180,000.

The great majority of the population is concentrated in the urban district of the capital Doha. Only a small minority still pursue the traditional life of the semi-nomadic tribesmen and fisherfolk.

There are townships on the coast at Khor, Dukhan, Wakra and Umm-Said. There are many gardens and farms near Doha and to the North and encouragement is being given to the development of agriculture. Qatar is self-sufficient in most vegetables, exporting a surplus to the other Gulf States.
Doha is an expanding town with good shopping facilities and services and an airport built to international standards. Regular air services connect Qatar with Bahrain and the United Arab Emirates, Kuwait, Muscat, Iran, Saudi Arabia, Jordan, Lebanon, Egypt, the Indian sub-continent and Europe.
In April, 1973, the new Qatar *Riyal* was introduced.
Current industrial development projects include a fertilizer plant, a cement factory, and a natural gas liquids plant. In addition the government is developing an iron and steel and ore reduction plant, and a petrochemical complex. The township of Umm-Said is being developed as an industrial area. Qatar is also rapidly expanding its infrastructure including electrical generation and water distillation, roads, ports, hotels, houses, and Government buildings.
The Qatar Broadcasting Authority transmits on medium, shortwave, and V.H.F. Regular television transmissions in colour began in 1974 and a second channel is planned.
Oil deposits on land are being exploited by the Qatar Petroleum Company who first shipped oil on December 31, 1949. An offshore concession is held by the Shell Company of Qatar which is exporting oil from its terminal on Halul Island at a rate of about 7,000,000 long tons per annum. Further offshore concessions are held by a consortium headed by Wintershall, who also hold an onshore concession. On January 1, 1975, the Amir signed an act establishing the Qatar General Petroleum Corporation, empowering it to establish subsidiaries, offices or agencies inside or outside Qatar. It will be responsible for all oil production in the country once current negotiations for a 100 per cent. takeover of Q.P.C. and Shell Company of Qatar are completed.

Trade with U.K.
	1973	1974
Imports from U.K.	£19,400,000	£22,100,000
Exports to U.K.	47,300,000	166,000,000

CAPITAL.—Doha. Population (estimated) 120,000.
FLAG.—White and maroon, white portion nearer the mast; vertical indented line comprising 17 angles divides the colours.

BRITISH EMBASSY
(Doha)
Ambassador Extraordinary and Plenipotentiary, His Excellency David Gordon Crawford (1974).
1st Secretary and Consul, R. D. Gordon.
2nd Secretary, D. A. Wright (*Commercial*).
Attaché, D. Meadowcroft (*Commercial*).
3rd Secretary, R. Woodward.
British Council Representative, W. H. Jefferson.

RUMANIA
(Republica Socialistâ România)
President of the Republic, Nicolae Ceauşescu, *elected*, March 28, 1974.
State Council, N. Ceauşescu (*President*); Emil Bodnăras; Emil Bobu; Stefan Voitec (*Vice-Presidents*); Constantin Stătescu (*Presidential Secretary of the State Council*).

COUNCIL OF MINISTERS
Prime Minister, Manea Manescu.
Deputy Prime Ministers, Emil Drăgănescu; Janos Fazekas; Mikhai Marinescu; Angelo Miculescu; Paul Niculescu; Ion Pătan; George Rădulescu.

Minister of National Defence, General of the Army
Ion Ioniță.
Interior, Teodor Coman.
Foreign Affairs, George Macovescu.
President of the State Planning Committee, Mihai
Marinescu.
Finance, Florea Dumitrescu.
Metallurgical Industry, Neculai Agachi.
Machine Building, Ioan Avram.
Chemical Industry, Mihai Florescu.
Petroleum Industry, Bujor Almășan.
Transport and Telecommunications, Traian Dudas.
Light Industry, Gheorghe Cazan.
Industrial Construction, Matei Ghigiu.
Timber Industry, Vasile Patilineț.
Food Industry, Angelo Miculescu.
Health, Radu Păun.
Labour, Petre Lupe.
Internal Trade, Janos Fazekas.
Foreign Trade, Ion Pățan.
Education, Paul Niculescu.
Justice, Emil Nicolcioiu.
Presidents:
  Council for Economic and Social Organisation,
  Gheorghe Pană.
  State Committee for Prices, Gheorghe Gaston
  Marin.
  Agriculture, Food Industry and Waters, Angelo
  Miculescu.
  Local Economy and Administration, (vacant).
  *Central Council of the General Union of Trade
  Unions*, Gheorghe Pană.
  Council of Socialist Culture and Education, Dumitru
  Popescu.
  National Union of Agricultural Co-operatives, Aldea
  Militaru.
  National Council for Science and Technology, Ioan
  Ursu.
  National Council of Waters, Florin Iorgulescu.
  State Department for Food Industry, Constantin Iftodi.
  Department for Agriculture, Marin Capisizu.

The Communist Party

Executive Political Committee, N. Ceaușescu; E.
Bodnaras; M. Mănescu; E. Ceaușescu; G. Cioara;
L. Ciobanu; E. Bobu; C. Burtică; G. Oprea;
I. Pățan; I. Uglar; E. Drăgănescu; J. Fazekas;
P. Lupu; P. Niculescu; G. Pană; D. Popescu;
G. Rădulescu; L. Răutu; V. Trofin; I. Verdet;
V. Vîlcu; S. Voitec (*full members*); I. Banc; M.
Dalea; M. Dobrescu; I. Iliescu; S. Andrei; N.
Giosan; I. Ioniță; V. Patilineț; R. Winter; I.
Ursu; M. Telescu (*alternate members*).
Secretariat of the Central Committee, N. Ceaușescu
(*Secretary General*); G. Pană; D. Popescu; I.
Verdet; C. Burtică; I. Uglar; E. Bobu; I. Banc;
S. Andrei.

Rumanian Embassy in London
4 Palace Green, W.8
[01-937 9666]
Ambassador Extraordinary and Plenipotentiary, His
Excellency Pretor Popa (1973).
Counsellors, Constantin Rădulescu (*Commercial*);
Vasile Tilincă; Nicu Bujor (*Political*).

Area and Population.—Rumania is a republic of
South-Eastern Europe, formerly the classical *Dacia*
and *Scythia Pontica*, having its origin in the union
of the Danubian principalities of *Wallachia* and
Moldavia under the *Treaty of Paris* (April, 1856).
The area of Rumania is 237,500 sp. kms. and the
population in July, 1973 was 20,827,525.

Government.—The principalities remained separate entities under Turkish suzerainty until 1859,
when Prince Alexandru Ion Cuza was elected
Prince of both, still under the suzerainty of Turkey.
Prince Cuza abdicated in 1866 and was succeeded

by Prince Charles of Hohenzollern-Sigmaringen, in
whose successors the crown was vested. By the
Treaty of Berlin (July 13, 1878) the Principality
was recognized as an independent State, and part
of the *Dobrudja* (which had been occupied by the
Rumanians) was incorporated. On March 27,
1881, it was recognized as a Kingdom.
The outcome of the War of 1914–18 added
Bessarabia, the Bukovina, Transylvania, The Banat
and Crisana–Maramures, these additions of territory
being confirmed in the Treaty of St. Germain, 1919,
and the Treaty of Petit Trianon, 1920.
On June 27, 1940, in compliance with an ultimatum from U.S.S.R., Bessarabia and Northern
Bukovina were ceded to the Soviet Government,
the area affected being about 20,000 sq. miles, with
a population of about 4,000,000.
In August, 1940, Rumania ceded to Bulgaria
the portion of Southern Dobrudja (about 3,000
sq. miles) taken from Bulgaria in 1913. Rumania
became "The Rumanian People's Republic" in
December, 1947, on the abdication of King
Michael.
A new Constitution, modelled on the Soviet
Constitution of 1936, was adopted unanimously on
September 24, 1952, by the Grand National
Assembly. The Assembly was later dissolved and
elections were held for a new Grand National
Assembly on November 30, 1952; in each con-
stituency there was only one candidate for election,
representing the People's Democratic Front.
Further elections on similar lines were held in
February, 1957; in March, 1961, and in March, 1965.
A new Constitution was approved by the Grand
National Assembly in 1965 when the name of the
state was changed to The Socialist Republic of
Rumania. The Constitution states (Art. 3) that the
leading political force of the whole society is the
Rumanian Communist Party. The Constitution
was modified in March, 1974.

Agriculture.—The soil of Wallachia and Moldavia
is among the richest in Europe producing wheat,
maize, millet, oats, barley, rye, beans, peas and
other vegetables. Grape vines and fruits are abundant. The fertile plain of Transylvania yields large
crops of maize, wheat, rye, oats, flax and hemp.
Agriculture and sheep and cattle raising are the
principal industries of Rumania, but the climate
of this part of South-Eastern Europe is of the
Continental character, and the intense winter cold
and summer heat, and fierce summer drought sometimes defeat these principal industries. The forests

of the mountainous regions are extensive, and the timber industry is important.

Socialization of agriculture was completed when plans for collectivization were fulfilled in the spring of 1962, some three years ahead of the planned date.

Natural Resources and Industry.—Before the war petroleum and agriculture were the backbone of the Rumanian economy. Though the production of both industries has increased, they no longer hold the same dominant position. Rumania's oil resources enabled her to produce 14,287,000 tons of crude oil in 1973 and there are plentiful supplies of natural gas, together with various mineral deposits including coal, iron ore, bauxite, lead, zinc, copper and uranium in quantities which allow a substantial part of the requirements of industry to be met from local resources. Since 1948 industrialization has proceeded rapidly and the State is well on the way to establishing a mixed industrial economy. Heavy investments have been made in electrical power, the chemical industry, the metallurgical industry and the engineering industry and growing attention is being paid to light industry. The economy is certainly organized on the basis of Five-Year Plans which cover all branches of national activity including investment and production.

1973 production figures were: crude oil, 14,287,000 tons; coal, 26,664,000 tons; electric power, 46,779 million kWh; methane gas, 23,639 million cu. metres; steel, 8,161,000 tons; pig iron, 5,713,000 tons; wheat, 5,528,500 tons; maize, 7,397,200 tons; sugar-beet, 4,380,200 tons.

Language and Literature.—Rumanian is a Romance language with many archaic forms and with admixtures of Slavonic, Turkish, Magyar and French words. The folk-songs and folk-lore, composed by the people themselves, and transmitted orally through many centuries (and collected in the 19th century), form one of the most interesting of such collections. The publication of all books and reviews is controlled and authorized by the Council for Socialist Culture and Education, which has the status of a Ministry. In 1972, 75 daily newspapers were published. The leading religion is that of the Rumanian Orthodox Church; the Roman Catholics and some Protestant denominations are of importance numerically. The Jewish community has declined through emigration.

Education is free and nominally compulsory, with 3,308,381 in attendance in 1973–74, including 143,656 in higher education. There are Universities at Bucharest, Iasi, Cluj, Timisoara, Craiova and Brasov. A "Marxist-Leninist" University was opened in Bucharest in 1951. There are polytechnics at Bucharest, Timisoara, Cluj, Brasov, Galati and Iasi, two commercial academies at Bucharest and Brasov, and agricultural colleges at Bucharest, Iasi, Cluj, Craiova and Timisoara.

Communications.—In 1972 there were 11,023 km. of railway open for traffic. The mercantile marine, as a result of war losses, seizure and reparations, was reduced to a few moderate-sized sea-going steamers and a number of coastal and river craft. The number of sea-going ships had been increased by 1970. The principal ports are Constanta (on the Black Sea), Sulina (on the Danube Estuary), Galati, the most important, Braila, Giurgiu and Turnu Severin. Rumania is a member of the Danube Commission whose seat is at Budapest.

FINANCE

	1971	1973
	Lei	Lei
Revenue	153,382,200,000	175,972,100,000
Expenditure	145,432,300,000	168,090,700,000

Up-to-date figures of the Public Debt are not available. No foreign loans (other than short-term commercial loans) are known to have been contracted since March, 1947. The internal debt was virtually wiped out by stabilization in August, 1947; there has been no internal loan issue since that date.

The Rumanian *Lei* (of 100 *Bani*) had been revalued three times since the war by Feb. 1, 1954. With a 189·33 per cent. premium on all "capitalist" currencies for non-commercial transactions, the effective exchange rate on May 1975 was *Lei* 28·08= £1. (*See also* p. 84.)

TRADE

	1972	1973
	Lei	Lei
Imports	14,465,200,000	17,417,700,000
Exports	14,373,000,000	18,575,000,000

No complete figures for foreign trade have been published since the start of the Communist *régime*. Imports are chiefly semi-manufactured goods, raw materials, machinery and metals; exports consist principally of maize, wheat, barley, oats, petroleum, timber, cattle, machines and industrial equipment. Trade with U.K., although relatively small, has increased notably since the signature of an Anglo-Rumanian trade arrangement in 1960. External trade with Communist countries dropped from 80 per cent. in 1960 to 50 per cent. in 1970.

Trade with U.K.

	1973	1974
Imports from U.K.	£34,160,000	£33,485,000
Exports to U.K.	31,710,000	34,252,000

CAPITAL, Bucharest, on the Dimbovita, population (1975), 1,528,562. Other large towns are: Cluj (212,690); Timisoara (204,687); Iasi (202,052); Brasov (193,089); ψ Galati (191,111); Craiova 188,333); Ploiesti (171,668); ψ Braila (161,057). Oradea (148,587); Arad (142,960); Sibiu (127,146); Tirgu-Mures (109,873); Baia Mare (86,602).

FLAG.—Three vertical bands, blue, yellow, red, with the emblem of the Republic in the centre band. NATIONAL DAY.—August 23 (Liberation Day, 1944).

BRITISH EMBASSY
24 Strada Jules Michelet, Bucharest 22
Ambassador Extraordinary and Plenipotentiary, His Excellency Jeffrey Charles Petersen, C.M.G. (1975).
Counsellor, R. Dorman (*Commercial*).
Defence, Naval and Military Attaché, Lt.-Col. B. A. Allum.
1st Secretaries, M. Shea (*Head of Chancery*); R. G. H. Fletcher (*Information*); R. T. L. Watkins (*Cultural*).
2nd Secretaries, A. Brown, M.B.E. (*Consul*); T. J. Duggin (*Commercial*).

RWANDA
(Republic of Rwanda)

President, Grégoire Kayibanda, *born* 1925; *elected* Oct. 26, 1961; *assumed office*, July 1, 1962; *re-elected*, 1965 and 1969.

Rwanda became an independent republic on July 1, 1962. Formerly part of the Belgian-administered trusteeship of Ruanda-Urundi, it has an area of 10,169 sq. miles and a population (estimated, 1969) of 3,500,000, mainly of the Bahutu tribe, with Batutsi and Batwa minorities. Coffee, cotton and tea are grown and there is some mineral production. Hides, extract of quinine and pyrethrum flowers are also exported.

The currency is the *Rwanda franc*. In 1970 total imports were valued at *Rw.Fr.*2,537,700,000; total exports, *Rw.Fr.*2,458,200,000; imports from U.K. 1972, £348,000; exports to U.K., £514,000. Revenue in 1970 totalled: *Rw.Fr.* 1,944,200,000; Expenditure *Rw.Fr.* 1,756,700,000.

At a referendum held in September, 1961, under supervision of the United Nations, a large majority voted against the retention of the monarchy which was accordingly abolished on Oct. 2, 1961. Elections for a new Legislative Assembly were also held in September, 1961, and the Assembly elected M. Kayibanda as President of the National Council, to hold office as Head of State and Head of the Government. Admission of Rwanda to membership of the United Nations was approved on July 26, 1962.

CAPITAL.—Kigali (7,000).

FLAG.—Three vertical bands, red, yellow and green with letter R on yellow band.

NATIONAL DAY.—July 1.

British Ambassador, vacant.

EL SALVADOR
(República de El Salvador)

President, Col. Arturo Armando Molina; *elected* February 20, 1972; *assumed office* July 1, 1972, *for* a five-year term.

Vice-President, Dr. Enrique Mayorga Rivas.

Minister of Foreign Affairs, Ing. Mauricio Borgonovo.

SALVADOREAN EMBASSY AND CONSULATE
9B Portland Place, W.1.
[01-636 9563]

Ambassador Extraordinary and Plenipotentiary, His Excellency Alvaro Ernesto Martínez (1974).

Secretary and Consul, Señor Lic. Oscar Manuel Gutiérréz-Rosales.

Attachés, Dr. David Castro-Escobar; Dr. Rafael Lemus-Corleto.

Area and Population.—The Republic of El Salvador extends along the Pacific coast of Central America for 160 miles with a general breadth of about 50 miles, and contains an area of 7,722 square miles with a population (July 1973) of 3,863,793. El Salvador is therefore a densely populated country with some 460 persons per square mile. It is divided into 14 Departments. (*For* MAP, *see* p. 84.)

The surface of the country is very mountainous, many of the peaks being extinct volcanoes. The highest peaks are the Santa Ana volcano (7,700 ft.) and the San Vicente volcano (7,200 ft.). Much of the interior has an average altitude of 2,000 feet. The lowlands along the coast are generally hot, but towards the interior the altitude tempers the severity of the heat. Much has been done in recent years to improve sanitary conditions and services. There is a wet season from May to October, and a dry season from November to April. Earthquakes have been frequent in the history of El Salvador, the most recent being that of May 3, 1965, when considerable damage was done to San Salvador.

The principal river is the Río Lempa. There is a large volcanic lake (Ilopango) a few miles to the east of the capital, while farther away and to the west lies the smaller but very picturesque lake of Coatepeque, which appears to have been formed in a vast crater flanked by the Santa Ana volcano.

Government.—El Salvador was conquered in 1526 by Pedro de Alvarado, and formed part of the Spanish vice-royalty of Guatemala until 1821. Under a new Constitution adopted in 1950, the President is elected for six years and the Legislature for two. In the legislative elections held in March, 1974, the result was, 36 deputies of the Official party, and 16 opposition deputies. In the presidential elections held on February 20, 1972, the candidate of the Official Party, Col. Arturo Armando Molina, secured a narrow margin over his closest opponent, Ingeniero José Napoléon Duarte, therefore his election had to be confirmed by the National Assembly.

Agriculture.—The principal cash crops are coffee which is grown under shade-trees principally on the slopes of the volcanoes, cotton, which is cultivated on the coastal plains, and cane sugar. Also cultivated are maize, sesame, indigo, rice, balsam, etc. In the lower altitudes towards the east, sisal is produced and used in the manufacture of coffee and sugar bags. Diversification and modernization of agriculture are in progress, including the exportation of meat, principally to the U.S.A.

Industry.—There is growing industrialization and existing factories make textiles, constructional steel, furniture, cement and household items. El Salvador is a leading exporter to the Central American Common Market, of which she is a member. The first trade zone was inaugurated in November 1974 and the National Assembly approved a new Export Development Law. The free-trade scheme is expected to attract some 52 new industries.

Education.—The illiteracy rate is about 50 per cent. Primary education is nominally compulsory, but the number of schools and teachers available is too small to enable education to be given to all children of school age. In recent Budgets, however, a high percentage of the national revenue has been devoted to education and great efforts are being made to eliminate the existing shortage of schools and teachers.

Language and Literature.—The language of the country is Spanish. Indigenous literature has not yet produced work of international repute. There are 4 daily newspapers published at the capital, and 4 in the provinces.

Communications.—The former El Salvador Railways and the Salvadorean Section of International Railways of Central America have been merged under the Executive Autonomous Port Commission (CEPA) which will also administer the previously foreign-owned port of Cutoco. The new railroad organisation is styled FENADESAL. There is continuous railway communication between San Salvador and Guatemala City and Puerto Barrios on the Caribbean coast. The roads are paved and in good condition. There are good motor roads between Acajutla, the principal port, and the capital (23 miles), and between the capital and Guatemala City. The Pan-American Highway from the Guatemalan frontier follows this route and continues to the Honduran frontier. Pan American Airways, TACA, LANICA, COPA, AVIATECA, SAM, Iberia and LACSA connect El Salvador with the rest of the world. British Airways, SABENA and other important airway companies are represented in San Salvador. The Ilopango international airport can receive jet aircraft.

There are post and telegraph offices throughout the country. There are many broadcasting stations and six television stations.

FINANCE

	1973 Colones	1974 Colones
Revenue (*Budget*)	488,881,000	596,723,000
Expenditure (*do.*)	449,961,000	594,504,000
Surplus	38,920,000	2,209,000
Public Debt (Dec.,31.):	460,100,000	565,500,000
External Debt	321,600,000	404,062,000
Internal Debt		
Direct Governmental	79,500,000	91,500,000
Guaranteed by		
Government	59,000,000	69,900,000

TRADE

	1972 Colones	1973 Colones
Imports	694,234,043	934,679,609
Exports	693,232,968	896,038,414

Trade with U.K

	1973	1974
Imports from U.K...	£3,393,000	£3,857,000
Exports to U.K.....	297,000	897,000

Par of Exchange 2·50 *Colones*= $1 (U.S.) (*see also* p. 84).

Coffee to the value of ₡480,300,000 was exported in 1974. Exports of cotton were valued at ₡120,500,000. Other exports are shrimps (₡20,600,000), sugar (₡95,200,000), sisal (in the form of the bags used for exporting coffee, sugar, etc.), gold, indigo, sesame, balsam, hides and skins. The chief imports are iron and steel goods, motor cars, fertilizers, manufactured goods, chemical products and petrol.

CAPITAL.—San Salvador. Population, 620,000. Other towns are Santa Ana (204,000), San Miguel (120,700), Ψ La Union (Cutoco), Ψ La Libertad and Ψ Acajutia.

FLAG.—Three horizontal bands light blue, white, light blue; coat of arms on white band. NATIONAL DAY.—September 15.

BRITISH EMBASSY

11A Avenida Norte (Continuación), Colonia Dueñas, (Apartado 2350), San Salvador

Ambassador Extraordinary and Plenipotentiary and Consul-General, His Excellency Albert Henry Hughes, O.B.E. (1975).

1st Secretary, J. F. Taylor (*Head of Chancery and Consul*).

San Salvador is 5,700 miles from London.

SAN MARINO
(Repubblica di San Marino)
Regents, Two " Capitani Reggenti ".

CONSULATE GENERAL IN LONDON
166 High Holborn, W.C.1.
Consul General, Sir Charles Forte.
Vice-Consul, R. E. Rudge.

A small Republic in the hills near Rimini, on the Adriatic, founded, it is stated, by a pious stonecutter of Dalmatia in the 4th century. The Republic always resisted the Papal claims, and those of neighbouring dukedoms, during the 15th–18th centuries, and its integrity and sovereignty is recognized and respected by Italy. The Republic is governed by a State Congress of 10 members, under the Presidency of two Heads of State. The Great and General Council, a legislative body of 60 members, is elected by a universal suffrage for a term of 5 years. A Council of Twelve forms in certain cases a Supreme Court of Justice. The area is approximately 23 square miles, the population (June, 1973) is 19,000. There is a ceremonial guard of about 180. The city of San Marino, on the slope of Monte Titano, has three towers, a fine church and Government palace, a theatre and museums. The principal products are wine cereals, and cattle, and the main industries are ceramics, lime, concrete, cotton yarns, colour and paints. A Treaty of Extradition between the Governments of Great Britain and the Republic of San Marino has been in force since 1899.

FLAG.—Two horizontal bands, white, blue (with coat of arms of the Republic in centre).

SÃO TOMÉ AND PRÍNCIPE
President, Dr. Manuel Pinto da Costa.
Prime Minister, Sr. Miguel Trouvoada.

The islands of São Tomé and Príncipe are situated in the Gulf of Guinea, off the west coast of Africa. They have an area of 372 square miles, and a population (1970) of 74,500.

Following Portugal's decision to grant independence, a transitional government was installed on Dec. 21, 1974, and the islands became an independent democratic republic on July 12, 1975.

Cacao is the main product.

CAPITAL.— Ψ São Tomé (3,187).

SAUDI ARABIA
(Al Mamlaka al Arabiya as-Sa'udiyya.)
King of Saudi Arabia, H.M. King Khalid bin Abdul Aziz Al Saud, *born* 1912, *ascended the throne* March 25, 1975.
Crown Prince, H.R.H. Amir Fahd bin Abdul Aziz, *born* 1921.

COUNCIL OF MINISTERS
Prime Minister and Foreign Minister, H.M. King Khalid bin Abdul Aziz.
First Deputy Prime Minister and Minister of Interior, H.R.H. Amir Fahd bin Abdul Aziz.
Second Deputy Prime Minister and Commander of the National Guard, H.R.H. Amir Abdullah bin Abdul Aziz.
Defence and Aviation, H.R.H. Amir Sultan bin Abdul Aziz.

Finance and National Economy, H.R.H. Amir Musa'id bin Abdul Rahman.
Agriculture, Shaikh Hasan al-Mishari.
Education, Shaikh Hasan Al al-Shaikh.
Commerce and Industry, Shaikh Muhammad al-Awadi.
Communications, Shaikh Muhammad Umar Tawfiq.
Petroleum and Mineral Resources, Shaikh Ahmad Zaki Yamani.
Justice, Shaikh Muhammad Ali al-Harakan.
Labour and Social Affairs, Shaikh Abdul Rahman Aba al-Khail.
Information, Shaikh Ibrahim al-Anqary.
Health, Sahikh Abdul Aziz Khuwaitir.
Pilgrimage and Trusts, Shaikh Hasan Kutbi.
Deputy Minister of Interior, H.R.H. Amir Naif bin Abdul Aziz.
Deputy Minister of Defence and Aviation, H.R.H. Amir Turki bin Abdul Aziz.
Ministers of State, H.R.H. Amir Saud al-Faisal; Shaikh Hisham Nazir; Shaikh Muhammad Aba al-Khail; Sayyid Salih Hussayin; Shaikh Abdul Aziz Quraishi; Shaikh Abdul Wahhab Abdul Wasi.

SAUDI ARABIAN EMBASSY
27 Eaton Place, S.W.1
[01–235 8431]
Ambassador Extraordinary and Plenipotentiary, His Excellency Sheikh Abdul Rahman Al Helaissi, G.C.V.O. (1966).

Counsellor, Salem Azzam, C.V.O.
1st Secretaries, Saleh al-Fouzan; Yasien Khalil Allaf; Hassan M. Attar: Amin Malki.
Defence Attaché, Brig.-Gen. Abdulla I. al-Saheal.
Cultural Counsellor, Abdul Aziz Mansour Al-Turki.

The Kingdom of Saudi Arabia, so named since Sept. 20, 1932, is a personal union of two countries, the Sultan of Nejd being also King of the Hijaz.

By the *Treaty of Jedda* (May 20, 1927) Great Britain recognized Ibn Saud as an independent ruler, King of the Hijaz and of Nejd and its Dependencies.

The total area of the Kingdom is about 927,000 sq. miles, with a population (U.N. estimate, 1969) of 7,200,000.

In the 18th century Nejd was an independent State and the stronghold of the Wahhabi sect. It subsequently fell under the Turkish yoke, but in 1913 Ibn Saud threw off Turkish rule and captured from the Turks the Province of Hasa. In 1921 he added to his dominions the territories of the Rashid family of Jebel Shammar, which he captured by force of arms; in 1925 he completed the conquest of the Hijaz, and in 1926 accepted the surrender of the greater part of Asir, the whole of which is now part of the Kingdom.

Nejd (" Plateau ") has no definite frontiers, but may be said to extend over about 800,000 square miles of Central Arabia, including the Nafud and Dahana Deserts, and reaches eastward to the Persian Gulf (Hasa). The population is largely nomadic and is estimated at about 3,500,000, the majority being Muslims of the Wahhabi persuasion. There is little agriculture, but wheat and barley are grown, and there is an experimental farm, irrigated from natural deep pools and covering 3,000 acres, at al-Kharj, about 50 miles south of Riyadh. The principal occupation of the bulk of the population is camel and sheep raising, but oil makes by far the largest contribution to the economy of the country. Oil was found in commercial quantities at Dammam, near Dhahran in the Hasa, in 1938, and in 1973 total production of crude oil for the whole country, including offshore concessions, averaged some 8,000,000 barrels per day. Exports other than oil are negligible. The capital is Riyadh (450,000), and the principal trading centres are Hofuf (the chief town of the Hasa province) (100,000). Ψ Al Khobar and Ψ Dammam on the Persian Gulf littoral, Anaiza, Buraida, Hail (20,000), and Jauf. The old ports (Persian Gulf) were Ψ Qatif, Ψ Uqair and Ψ Al Khobar, which were suitable only for sailing craft, but the Arabian-American Oil Company, which is exploiting the Hasa oil under a 60 years' lease, has built a deep-water port for its own purposes at Ψ Ras Tannura, and a civil deep-water port, with a pier seven miles long, was brought into use at Ψ Dammam in 1950. A railway is in operation from Dammam through Hofuf to Riyadh.

The *Hijaz* (" The Boundary "—between Nejd and Tihama) extends from Asir in S. to Jordan in N., and from the Red Sea and the Gulf of 'Aqaba in the W. to the ill-defined boundaries of Central Arabia. The coastline on the Red Sea is about 800 miles, and the total area is about 112,500 sq. miles, with a population of from 1,000,000 to 1,500,000, including many nomad tribes. On the coast are the small ports of Al-Wajh, Yanba'u, Raabigh and Jizzan. Jedda contains the ruins of the reputed " tomb of Eve, the mother of mankind "; and inland are many settlements through which runs the course of the disused Saudi-Arabian section of the Hijaz Railway. The *Oasis of Khaibar*, east of the railway, contains a considerable population, descendants of former negro slaves, with a centre at Kast al Yahudi. The importance of the Hijaz depends upon the pilgrimages to the holy cities of Medina and Mecca. *Medina* (*al Madinah al Munawwarah*, " The City of Light "), once the terminus of the Hijaz Railway, 820 miles from Damascus, has a permanent population of about 137,000 and is celebrated as the burial place of Muhammad, who died in the city on June 7, 632 (12 Rabia, A.H. 11). The Mosque of the Prophet (500 feet in length and over 300 in breadth) contains the sacred tomb of Muhammad. *Mecca*, the birthplace of the Prophet, is 45 miles east of the seaport of Jedda, and about 200 miles south of Medina, and has a population estimated at 301,000. The city contains the great mosque surrounding the *Kaaba*, or sacred shrine of the Muslim religion, in which is the black stone " given by Gabriel to Abraham ", placed in the south-east wall of the Kaaba at such a height that it may be kissed by the devout pilgrim. Ψ Jedda (381,000) is the principal port and commercial centre of Saudi Arabia. A new deep-water port was completed in 1971.

Asir (" The Inaccessible ") extends, geographically, from a line drawn inland from Birk on the southern limit of Hijaz to the northern boundary of the Yemen, some 12 miles N. of the port of Meidi. Its breadth extends about 180 miles eastwards to Bisha in the north and to the boundary of the Beni Yam in the south. The territory includes the Farsan Islands, where prospectors have searched for oil, but without success. The maritime lowland is interspersed with fertile areas near the wadis, which afford pasturage and bear grain. Capital, Abha.

Finance and Trade.—Oil is the main source of the country's wealth, though customs revenues and other taxes, as well as the foreign exchange accruing from the annual Pilgrimage to Mecca, also bring in a significant income. In the fiscal year 1973–74 the budget was balanced at *SR* 28,810,000,000 of which 92·5 per cent. was derived from oil. 62·5 per cent. of total Government expenditure was allocated to development projects in the fiscal year 1972–73. The rate of exchange was *SR* 8.50=£1 (June 1974). (*See also* p. 84.) The currency is strong, and backed by gold and foreign exchange reserves of over £1,000,000,000. With few exceptions, such as the ban on alcohol, there are no restrictions on trade or payments including foreign exchange transactions. There is no public debt. Imports in 1972 were valued at *SR* 4,708,000,000, the United States of America being the leading supplier followed by Japan, Lebanon, the United Kingdom and W. Germany.

Trade with U.K.

	1973	1974
Imports from U.K.	£58,466,000	£119,698,000
Exports to U.K.	322,183,000	1,178,149,000

Communications.—The railway from the port of Dammam to the oilfields at Abqaiq and through Hofuf to Riyadh was opened late in 1951. Metalled roads connect all the main cities in the northern half of the country, and a road linking Abha, in the south, to this network is under construction. The Government-owned Saudi Arabian Airlines, in association with Transworld Airlines operate Douglas DC3, Convair 340, and Boeing 707, 720 and 737 aircraft. Scheduled services are flown to all the main towns of the country. There are first class airports at Dhahran, where a new airport was opened in 1962, and at Jedda. A new airport is under construction at Jedda and a new airport is planned for Riyadh; other airports for internal flights, are also in the planning stage. Saudi Arabian Airlines have an extensive overseas operation including five flights to London per week.

A large nember of international airlines operate into Jedda and Dhahran.

Education.—In 1972 there were 2,106 Government schools (including elementary, intermediate and secondary institutions for boys and girls). There is an Islamic University of Medina, a college of Islamic law at Mecca, a college of Petroleum and Minerals at Dhahran and universities at Riyadh and Jedda.. With three exceptions all schools are maintained by the Government. Education at all levels is free.

CAPITAL.—Riyadh, population about 450,000.

SAUDI ARABIAN FLAG.—Green oblong, white Arabic device in centre: " There is no God but God, Muhammad is the Prophet of God," and a white scimitar beneath the lettering.

BRITISH EMBASSY
Kilo 5, Medina Road, Jedda

Ambassador Extraordinary and Plenipotentiary, His Excellency Alan Keir Rothnie, C.M.G. (1972)
Counsellors, J. C. Kay; R. O. Miles.
1st Secretaries, J. M. A. Herdman (*Head of Chancery*); T. Quinlan (*Commercial*); M. J. Moore, M.B.E.
2nd Secretaries, M. J. Copson (*Commercial*); D. Plumbly; W. I. Rae (*Consul*); P. W. James, M.B.E.
3rd Secretaries, A. R. Michael (*Commercial*); T. Rooney(*Archivist*).
Defence and Military Attaché, Col. D. C. Lees.

British Council Representative, B. Vale, P.O. Box 2701, Riyadh.

SENEGAL
(République du Sénegal)

President and Head of Government, Léopold Senghor, elected President, Sept. 5, 1960; re-elected for five years, 1973.
Prime Minister, Abdou Diouf.
MINISTERS OF STATE
Relations with the Assemblies, Magatte Lô.
Interior, Jean Collin.
Finance and Economic Affairs, Babacar Bâ.
National Education, Doudo Ngom.
There are also 13 Ministers and 2 Secretaries of State, following Cabinet reorganization on March 26, 1975.

SENEGAL EMBASSY IN LONDON
11 Phillimore Gardens, W.8.
[01-937 0925]
Ambassador Extraordinary and Plenipotentiary, His Excellency Abdourahmane Dia (1974).

Senegal lies on the west coast of Africa between Mauritania in the north and the Republic of Guinea in the south. (*For* MAP, *see* p. 871.) It has an area of 77,814 sq. miles and a population (estimated, 1970) of 3,800,000.

Formerly a French colony, Senegal elected on Nov. 25, 1958, to remain within the French Community as an autonomous republic. Foundation of a Federation of Mali, to consist of the State of Senegal, (French) Soudan, Dahomey and Upper Volta, was announced in January, 1959, and the Federation came into existence on April 4, consisting of Senegal and the Sudanese Republic only, the others having meanwhile withdrawn. Mali was proclaimed fully independent by the President of the Federal Assembly, M. Léopold Senghor, on June 20, 1960. However, these arrangements proved short-lived as on August 22, 1960, the Senegal Legislative Assembly formally approved measures to secede from the Federation and continue as an independent state. In March, 1963 (after an attempted *coup d'état* by the then Prime Minister in the previous December) a new constitution was approved giving executive powers to the President, on the lines of the present French constitution.

Senegal's principal exports are ground-nuts (raw and processed) and phosphates.

Trade with U.K
	1973	1974
Imports from U.K.	£2,717,000	£3,260,000
Exports to U.K.	3,003,000	9,637,000

CAPITAL.— Ψ Dakar (581,000).

FLAG.—Three vertical bands, green, yellow and red; a green star on the yellow band. NATIONAL DAY.—April 4.

BRITISH EMBASSY
B.P. 6025, Dakar.

Ambassador Extraordinary and Plenipotentiary, His Excellency Denzil Inglis Dunnett, C.M.G., O.B.E. (1973).
1st Secretaries, A. E. Furness (*Head of Chancery*); D. M. St. G. Saunders.
2nd Secretaries, R. M. J. Lyne; C. Dyer.
3rd Secretary, R. Daly.
Cultural Attaché (*British Council Representative*), D. N. Nuttall.

SIAM. *see* Thailand

SOMALIA
(Somali Democratic Republic)

President of the Supreme Revolutionary Council, Maj.-Gen. Mohamed Siad Barre, *assumed office* Oct. 21, 1969.

EMBASSY
60 Portland Place, W.1
[01-580 7148]
Ambassador Extraordinary and Plenipotentiary, His Excellency Ahmed Haji Dualeh (1970).
1st Secretary, Abdi Haji Ahmed Liban.

The Somali Democratic Republic occupies part of the north-east horn of Africa, with a coast-line on the Indian Ocean extending from the boundary with Kenya (2° South latitude) to Cape Guardafui (12° N.); and on the Gulf of Aden to the boundary with the Territory of the Afars and Issas. Somalia is bounded on the west by the Territory of the Afars and Issas, Ethiopia and Kenya and covers an area of approximately 246,000 sq. miles. The population, of which a large proportion is no-madic, is estimated (June, 1969) at 2,730,000. Livestock raising is the main occupation in Somalia and there is a modest export trade in livestock on the hoof, skins and hides. Italy imports the bulk of the banana crop, the second biggest export under agreement with the Somali Government. Imports from U.K. in 1973 totalled £2,050,000.

Government.—The Somali Republic, consisting of the former British Somaliland Protectorate and the former Italian trust territory of Somalia, was set up on July 1, 1960. British rule in Somaliland lasted from 1887 until June 26, 1960, with the exception of a short period in 1940–41 when the Protectorate was occupied by Italian forces. Somalia, formerly an Italian colony, was occupied by the United Kingdom from 1941 until the end of 1950, when it was placed under Italian administration by resolution of the United Nations. This trusteeship came to an end on July 1, 1960, when Somalia became independent and united with the former British Somaliland Protectorate under the title of the Somali Republic. Aden Abdulle Osman was returned to office as the first substantive President of the Republic in 1961, after a year as provisional President. Following national elections on June 10, 1967, Dr. Shermarke suceeded to the Presidency and on July 6 appointed Mr. Egal as Prime Minister. On October 15, 1969, the President was assassinated and Army commanders assisted by the police took over the Government without resistance. A Revolutionary Council under Major. Gen. Siad assumed full control of the state. The 19 member Supreme Revolutionary Council is assisted by a Council of Secretaries comprising 20 holders of Ministerial office, mostly civilians.

CAPITAL.— Ψ Mogadishu (Mogadiscio), population (estimated 1971), 220,000. Other towns are Hargeisa (50,000), Kisimayu (18,000), Ψ Berbera (19,000) and Burao (10,000).

FLAG.—Five-pointed white star on blue ground.
NATIONAL DAY.—October 21.

BRITISH EMBASSY
Ambassador Extraordinary and Plenipotentiary, His Excellency John Dennis Bolton Shaw, M.V.O. (1973).
1st Secretary and Consul, A. B. Gundersen (*Head of Chancery and Commercial*).
3rd Secretary, P. H. Palmer (*Administration, Information and Vice-Consul*).

SOUTH AFRICA
(Republiek van Suid-Afrika)

State President, Dr. Nicolaas Diederichs, *elected President*, Feb. 21, 1975; *inaugurated* April 10, 1975.

CABINET
Prime Minister, B. J. Vorster.
Minister of Foreign Affairs, Dr. H. Muller.
Information, Interior, Social Welfare and Pensions, Dr. C. P. Mulder.
Justice, Prisons and Police, J. T. Kruger.
Transport, S. L. Muller.
Economic Affairs, J. C. Heunis.
Finance, Senator O. P. F. Horwood.
National Education, Sen. J. P. van der Spuy.
Agriculture, H. Schoeman.
Defence, P. W. Botha.
Community Development and Public Works, A. H. du Plessis.
Water Affairs, Forestry and Power, S. P. Botha.
Labour, Posts and Telegraphs, M. Viljoen.
Indian Affairs and Tourism, S. J. Marais Steyn.
Bantu Affairs, M. C. Botha.
Planning, Environment and Statistics, J. J. Loots.
Health, Coloured Relations and Rehoboth Affairs, Dr. S. W. van der Merwe.
Mines, Immigration, Sport and Recreation, Dr. P. G. J. Koornhof.

EMBASSY AND CONSULATE
South Africa House, Trafalgar Square, W.C.2
[01-930 4488]
Ambassador Extraordinary and Plenipotentiary, His Excellency Dr. The Hon. Carel de Wet (1972).
Ministers, J. F. Wentzel; J. S. J. Kruger (*Commercial*).
Counsellors, A. A. Pienaar (*Commercial*); T. F. Wheeler.
1st Secretaries, A. H. Bouwer; J. M. Sterban.
2nd Secretaries, Miss A. de K. Joubert; J. L. Russouw; C. van N. Scholtz; W. van W. de Vries; J. N. Sounes (*Commercial*).
3rd Secretaries, J. P. Verster; Miss B. Harrison; P. J. H. Cilliers; Miss N. D. Theron.
Armed Forces Attaché, Maj.-Gen. H. R. Meintjes.
Naval Attaché, Capt. D. F. Silberbaur.
Army Attaché, Cdt. D. Hamman.
Air Attaché, Cdt. P. H. Groenewald.

Area and Population.—The Republic occupies the southernmost part of the African continent from the courses of the Limpopo, Molopo and Orange Rivers (34° 50′ 22″ South latitude) to the Cape of Good Hope, with the exception of Lesotho, Botswana and Swaziland, and part of Mozambique. It has a total area of 472,359 square miles,

and a total population (census of May, 1970, preliminary) of 21,282,000 (White 3,779,000; African, 14,893,000; Coloured, 1,996,000; and Asian, 614,000). Populations of the Provinces at the 1960 census were: Cape Province (278,380 sq. miles), 5,360,234; Natal (33,578 sq. miles), 2,977,084; Transvaal (109,621 sq. miles), 6,270,711; Orange Free State (49,866 sq. miles), 1,386,202.

Zululand, annexed in 1897, comprises about two-thirds of the country formerly under Zulu kings, and is bounded on the south and south-west by the Tugela River; on the south-east by the Indian Ocean; on the north by the Portuguese possessions; and on the west by the districts of Babanango, Vryheid and Ngotshe and by Swaziland. In 1951, the appointment was confirmed of Cyprian Bekuzulu, grandson of Dinizulu and great-grandson of Cetewayo, as Paramount Chief of the Zulus in Natal.

The southernmost province contains many parallel ranges, which rise in steps towards the interior. The south-western peninsula contains the famous *Table Mountain* (3,582 feet), while the *Great Swartberg* and *Langeberg* run in parallel lines from west to east of the Cape Province. Between these two ranges and the *Roggeveld* and *Nieuwveld* ranges to the north is the Great Karroo Plateau, which is bounded on the east by the *Sneeuberg*, containing the highest summit in the province (Kompasberg, 7,800 feet). In the east are ranges which join the *Drakensberg* (11,000 feet) between Natal and the Orange Free State.

The Orange Free State presents a succession of undulating grassy plains with good pasture-land, at a general elevation of some 3,800 feet, with occasional hills or kopjes. The Transvaal is also mainly an elevated plateau with parallel ridges in the *Magaliesberg* and *Waterberg* ranges of no great height. The veld or plains of this northernmost province is divisible into the High Veld of the south, the Bankenveld of the centre, and the Low Veld of the north and east, the first and second forming the grazing and agricultural region of the Transvaal and the last a fertile sub-tropical area. The eastern province of Natal has pastoral lowlands and rich agricultural land between the slopes of the Drakensberg and the coast, the interior rising in terraces as in the southern provinces. The *Orange*, with its tributary the *Vaal*, is the principal river of the south, rising in the Drakensberg and flowing into the Atlantic between the Territory of South West Africa and the Cape Province. The *Limpopo*, or Crocodile River, in the north, rises in the Transvaal and flows into the Indian Ocean through

Portuguese East Africa. Most of the remaining rivers are furious torrents after rain, with partially dry beds at other seasons.

Government.—The self-governing colonies of the Cape of Good Hope, Natal, the Transvaal and the Orange River Colony became united on May 31, 1910, under the South Africa Act, 1909, in a legislative union under the name of the Union of South Africa, the four colonies becoming Provinces of the Union. The Union of South Africa continued as a member of the British Commonwealth until 1961. A referendum held among white voters on October 5, 1960, decided by a narrow majority in favour of Republican status. 1,633,772 votes were cast—a poll of 90·73 per cent.—with 52·05 per cent. in favour. The Union of South Africa became a republic on May 31, 1961, and withdrew from the Commonwealth.

The *Senate* as reconstituted by the Senate Act, 1960, consists of 54 members, appointed or elected for a term of five years. Eleven are appointed by the Government (8 for the Republic, 2 for South West Africa and a Coloured representative). Forty-three are elected (Transvaal, 14; Cape Province, 11; Natal and Orange Free State, each 8; and South West Africa, 2). The Act of 1960 reintroduced proportional representation at elections to the Senate and excluded Native representation.

The *House of Assembly* consists of 171 elected members, 55 of whom represent the Cape of Good Hope, 20 Natal, 76 Transvaal, 14 the Orange Free State, and 6 South West Africa. Members of both Houses must be South African citizens of white descent. White female franchise was introduced under the provision of Act No. 18 of 1930. Cape Bantu voters ceased to be entitled to elect 3 members in Nov. 1959.

After the General Election on April 24, 1974 and two subsequent by-elections, the party representation in the House of Assembly was as follows: Nationalist Party, 123; United Party, 41; National Union, 1; Progressive Party, 7.

Defence.—The South Africa Defence Act, 1957, became law on Nov. 1, 1958. This Act, as amended in 1961, provides that every citizen between the ages of 17 and 65 is liable to render personal service in time of war, and those between 17 and 25 are liable to undergo a prescribed course of peace training with the Citizen Force or Commandos spread over a period of four consecutive years. Thereafter citizens are required to serve with the Reserve for a prescribed period of time.

Education.—The Provinces have been relieved of all vocational education (technical and industrial), and the Departments of Cultural Affairs and Higher Education under the Minister are concerned with universities, technical colleges, schools of industries, reformatories and State technical, housecraft and commercial high schools. State-aided vocational schools and State and State-aided special schools for the physically handicapped.

Communications.—The total open mileage of Government-owned railway lines at the end of March 1973 was 22,196 km. of which 4,501 km. were electrified. Working expenditure (excluding depreciation) amounted to *R*.1,140,219,242 (railways, harbours airways and pipelines). Internal air services are operated between all the major centres in South and South West Africa.

Production and Trade.—Final figures for the principal crops produced in 1972–73 were: Wheat, 1,746,000 metric tons; Maize, 416,000 mt.; Barley and oats, 105,000 mt.; ground nuts, 138,000 mt.

Mineral production is of the greatest importance in the South African economy. Value of mineral production in 1973: gold, *R*.1,789,290,145; dia-

monds, *R*.7,565,374; silver, *R*.7,331,163. Production in 1973: coal, 62,351,942 metric tons; copper, 175,797 metric tons; tin, concentrates and metallic, 5,930 metric tons.; asbestos, 332,650 metric tons.

Value of trade in 1973, Imports, *R*.3,301,100,000; Exports, *R*.2,410,600,000.

Trade with U.K.

	1973	1974
Imports from U.K.	£374,400,000	£526,291,000
Exports to U.K.	399,514,000	465,194,000

Currency.—The South African £ reached parity with the £ sterling in 1946. A new decimal currency the *Rand* (*R.*) was introduced in South Africa on Feb. 14, 1961, with a par value of 10*s*. Sterling.

Finance.—Estimated revenue for the year ended March 31, 1974, was *R*M3,235 (1972 *R*M2,864); total estimated expenditure *R*M3,461 (1972 *R*M2,825). The total government debit as at December 31, 1973 was *R*M7,506.

CAPITAL.—The administrative seat of the Government is PRETORIA, Transvaal; population (census 1970), 561,703; the seat of the Legislature is Ψ CAPE TOWN, population (1970), 1,096,597. Cape Town is 5,979 miles from Southampton; transit by mail steamship 11 days, and by air mail two days. There is a modern and well-equipped aerodrome seventeen miles by road from the centre of the city. Cape Town's harbour and docking facilities, existing and projected, are in keeping with its status as a world port of commercial and strategic importance. Other large towns are Johannesburg, Transvaal (1,432,643); Ψ Durban, Natal, the largest seaport (843,327); Ψ Port Elizabeth, Cape (468,577); Germiston, Transvaal (272,965); BLOEMFONTEIN, capital of Orange Free State (146,200); Springs, Transvaal (143,177); Benoni Transvaal (135,818); ΨEast London, Cape (136,757); Welkom, O.F.S. (73,362); and PIETERMARITZBURG, capital of Natal (112,693).

FLAG.—Three horizontal stripes of equal width; from top to bottom, orange, white, blue; in the centre of the white stripe, the old Orange Free State flag hanging vertical, towards the pole the Union Jack horizontal, away from the pole the old Transvaal Vierkleur, all spread full. The national flag was adopted by the Union in 1927 and was flown side by side with the Union Jack. This practice was expected to be continued in Natal.

NATIONAL DAY.—May 31.

BRITISH EMBASSY

6 Hill Street, Pretoria
91 Parliament Street, Cape Town (Jan.–June)
Ambassador Extraordinary and Plenipotentiary, His Excellency Sir James Reginald Alfred Bottomley, K.C.M.G., (1972).
Minister, D. M. Summerhayes. C.M.G.
Counsellors, J. M. O. Snodgrass (*Head of Chancery*); R. Carter.
Defence and Air Attaché, Air Cdre. G. A. Mason, D.F.C.
Naval Attaché, Cdre. A. F. C. Wemyss, O.B.E. R.N.
Military Attaché, Col. P. G. Howard-Harwood.
Cultural Attaché and British Council Representative, D. J. Sharp, 170 Pine Street, Pretoria.
There are British Consular Offices at *Cape Town, Johannesburg, Durban, East London* and *Port Elizabeth.*

South West Africa

Administrator, B. J. van der Walt.
South West Africa stretches from the southern border of Angola (lat. 17° 23′ S.) to part of the northern (Orange River) and north-western borders of the Cape Province of the Republic of South

Africa; and from the Atlantic Ocean in the west to Botswana in the east.

The territory has an area of 318,261 sq. miles, including the area of Walvis Bay (434 sq. miles) which, although part of the Republic of South Africa, is for convenience administered as part of South West Africa. The population was 746,328 in 1970 (Census) and the main population groups are: Ovambo (342,455), Whites (90,658), Damara (64,973), Kavango (49,577), Herero (49,203), Nama (32,853), Coloured (28,275), East Caprivians (25,009), Bushmen (21,909), Rehoboth Baster (16,474), Kaokovelders (6,457), Tswana (3,719) and others (14,766).

Government.—A German protectorate from 1880 to 1915, South West Africa was administered until the end of 1920 by the Union of South Africa. In terms of the Treaty of Versailles the Territory was declared a "C" Mandate and entrusted to South Africa with full powers of administration and legislation over the Territory. After the dissolution of the League of Nations and in the absence of a trusteeship agreement, South Africa informed the United Nations that she would continue to administer South West Africa in the spirit of the Mandate. Since the establishment of the United Nations, South West Africa has been the subject of dispute.

The South African Government announced on Oct. 2, 1968, the formation of a Legislative Council of 42 members for Ovamboland, six members nominated by each of the seven tribal authorities in the territory and a nominated Executive Council of seven members, with a Chief Councillor elected by the Legislative Council. Certain administrative powers held in South West Africa were in February, 1969, transfered to the South African Government. On June 21, 1971, the International Court of Justice at The Hague delivered an advisory opinion as requested by the U.N. Security Council on the legal consequences for States of the continued presence of South Africa in " Namibia " (South West Africa). The Court decided by 13 votes to 2, that (*inter alia*) " the continued presence of South Africa being illegal, South Africa is under obligation to withdraw its administration from Namibia immediately and thus put an end to its occupation of the Territory ". Dissenting opinions were submitted by the British and French judges; several other judges issued separate opinions in respect of parts of the Court's advisory opinion. A member of the South African legal team had contended at the hearings that South Africa had no obligation to submit to general international supervision of its administration of South West Africa, as the Mandate by the League of Nations had come to an end at the dissolution of that organization. The South African Prime Minister rejected the Court's majority opinion in a statement also made on June 21, 1971.

Production and Education.—Mining, agriculture and fisheries are important. Animal husbandry accounts for 99 per cent. of the total gross output of commercial agriculture. The average rainfall over 70 per cent. of the Territory is below 400 mm. per annum. In 1970 there were 480 native schools, with 2,649 teachers and 107,572 Native pupils. For the Whites there were 83 schools with 1,155 teachers and 22,253 pupils.

Trade with U.K.

	1973	1974
Imports from U.K.	£535,000	£1,735,000
Exports to U.K.	32,637,000	21,857,000

CAPITAL.—Windhoek (estimated population, 60,000). The ports are Ψ Walvis Bay and Ψ Lüderitz.

SPAIN
(España)

Head of the Spanish State, Generalisimo Don Francisco Franco Bahamonde, *born* Dec. 4, 1892, *assumed office*, Oct. 1, 1936.
President of the Government, Sr. Carlos Arias Navarro, *appointed* Dec. 29, 1973.

CABINET
(March 4, 1975)

1st Deputy Prime Minister, Interior, Sr. José García Hernández.
2nd Deputy Prime Minister, Finance, Sr. Rafael Cabello de Alba y Gracia.
3rd Deputy Prime Minister, Labour, Sr. Fernando Suárez González.
Foreign Affairs, Sr. Pedro Cortina Mauri.
Justice, Sr. José María Sánchez Ventura y Pascal.
Army, Lt.-Gen. Francisco Coloma Gallegos.
Air, Lt.-Gen. Mariano Cuadra Medina.
Navy, Adm. Gabriel Pita de Veiga y Sanz.
Economy and Development, Sr. Joaquín Gutiérrez Cano.
Education and Science, Sr. Cruz Martínez Esteruelas.
Relations with Trade Unions, Sr. Alejandro Fernández Sordo.
Information and Tourism, Sr. Léon Herrera Esteban.
Secretary-General of the Movement, Sr. José Solis Ruiz.
Public Works, Sr. Antonio Valdés González Roldán.
Agriculture, Sr. Thomás Allende y García-Baxter.
Housing, Sr. Luis Rodríguez de Miguel.
Industry, Sr. Alfonso Alvarez de Miranda.
Commerce, Sr. José Luis Cerón Ayuso.
Under-Secretary of the Presidency, Sr. Antonio Carro Martínez.

SPANISH EMBASSY IN LONDON
24 Belgrave Square, S.W.1
[01-235 5555]

Ambassador Extraordinary and Plenipotentiary, His Excellency Don Manuel Fraga Iribarne (1973).
Minister-Counsellor Sr. Don Manuel Gómez Acebo.

Area and Population.—A National State in the south-west of Europe, between 36°–43° 45′ N. lat. and 4° 25′ E. – 9° 20′ W. long., bounded on the south and east by the Mediterranean, on the west by the Atlantic and Portugal, and on the north by the Bay of Biscay and France, from which it is separated by the Pyrenees. Continental Spain occupies about eleven-thirteenths of the Iberian peninsula, the remaining portion forming the Republic of Portugal. Its coast-line extends 1,317 miles—712 formed by the Mediterranean and

605 by the Atlantic—and it comprises a total area of 196,700 square miles, with a population (1970) of 34,032,801. Returns for 1970 gave 656,102 births, 281,777 deaths and 247,492 marriages.

Physical Features.—The interior of the Iberian Peninsula consists of an elevated tableland surrounded and traversed by mountain ranges—the Pyrenees, the Cantabrian Mountains, the Sierra Guadarrama, Sierra Morena, Sierra Nevada, Montes de Toledo, &c. The principal rivers are the Douro, the Tagus, the Guadiana, the Guadalquivir, the Ebro and the Minho.

Government.—In April, 1931, the last monarch of Spain, Alfonso XIII, left the country; a Republic was immediately proclaimed and a Provisional Government, drawn from the various Republican and Socialist parties, was formed. The Republican Assembly (*Cortes*) was a single Chamber Congress of Deputies. On July 18, 1936, a counter-revolution broke out in many military garrisons in Spanish Morocco and spread rapidly throughout Spain. The principal leader was General Francisco Franco Bahamonde, formerly Governor of the Canary Islands. The struggle, in its later phases, threatened to embroil some of the European Powers, those of Nazi-Facist tendency lending aid to General Franco (leader of the Military-Fascist fusion, or *Falange*) while those of Communist views supported the Azaña (*Popular Front*) government. In October, 1938, many of the supporting troops were withdrawn, and on March 29, 1939, the Civil War was declared to have ended, the popular Front Governments in Madrid and Barcelona surrendering to the *Nationalists* (as General Franco's followers were then named). On June 5, 1939, the Grand Council of the *Falange Española Tradicionalista y de las Juntas Ofensivas Nacional-Sindicalistas*, which replaced the former *Cortes*, met at Burgos to legislate for the reorganization of the country under the Presidency of General Franco, who had assumed the title of *Caudillo* (*Leader*) *of the Empire and Chief of the State*. In the Civil War of 1936–39 over 1,000,000 lives were lost.

On July 1, 1942, General Franco announced the reinstitution of the *Cortes de España*. This was re-organized by an Organic Law of 1966 and is composed of approximately 564 members—ministers, 19; members of the National Council of the Movement, 109; Presidents of various State bodies, 5; representatives of the national syndicates, 150; 100 members elected by heads of families and married women; university rectors, 12; representatives of professional, academic and scientific bodies, 28; representatives of local administration, 116; and 25 members directly appointed by the Head of State.

A referendum held in 1967 approved an Organic Law of the State introducing a number of changes in state institutions. The offices of Head of State and Head of Government were separated, but General Franco still holds both offices.

On July 22, 1969, General Franco nominated Prince Juan Carlos (Alfonso) of Bourbon (*born* Jan. 5, 1938; grandson of the late King Alfonso XIII) to succeed him as head of state at his death or retirement. The nomination was approved in the *Cortes* by a large majority.

Defence.—Army: There are in Spain one armoured, one mechanized, one motorized, and two mountain divisions; one cavalry brigade, two artillery brigades, one air-transportable brigade, 1 parachute brigade, 11 infantry brigades, 2 artillery brigades, 1 mountain brigade (Independent) and 1 battalion surface to air missiles. The *Guardia Civil* also forms part of the Army though it operates as a gendarmerie in the rural areas under the control of the Ministry of the Interior.

The active Spanish *Navy* consists of 1 cruiser, 1 helicopter carrier, 20 destroyers, 11 frigates and corvettes, 3 anti-submarine launches, 23 minesweepers, 6 submarines, 14 landing craft, 4 squadrons of helicopters, and a large number of auxiliary and small craft.

The *Air Force* is divided geographically into 3 Regions covering Spain plus an Air Zone for the Canaries. There are also separate functional Air Defence, Tactical and Transport Commands. The Air Force consists of 11 fighter-bomber squadrons, one anti-submarine squadron, and one search and rescue squadron. There are also a variety of training and miscellaneous aircraft and some helicopters.

Education.—A new law of education (1970) providing free education for all children aged 6 to 13 is now in the process of implementation. 30 per cent. of primary schools and 80 per cent. of secondary schools are still run privately, although state spending on education multiplied fourfold between 1960 and 1970. There are eighteen state universities, the oldest of which, Salamanca, was founded in 1230. Other ancient foundations are Valencia (1245), Oviedo (1317), Valladolid (1346), Barcelona (1450), Zaragoza (1474), Santiago (1501), Seville (1502), Granada (1526), and Madrid (1590). Private universities are Deusto in Bilbao, and Navarra in Pamplona. Student numbers in the universities have risen to over 200,000.

Language and Literature.—Castilian is the language of more than three-quarters of the population of Spain and is the form of Spanish spoken in Mexico, Central and (except in Brazil) Southern America. Basque, reported to have been the original language of Iberia, is spoken in the rural districts of Vizcaya, Guipuzcoa and Alava. Catalan is spoken in Provençal Spain, and Galician, spoken in the north-western provinces, is allied to Portuguese. The literature of Spain is one of the oldest and richest in the world, the *Poem of the Cid*, the earliest and best of the heroic songs of Spain, having been written about A.D. 1140. The outstanding writings of its golden age are those of Miguel de Cervantes Saavedra (1547–1616), Lope Felix de Vega Carpio (1562–1635) and Pedro Calderón de la Barca (1600–1681). The Nobel Prize for Literature has three times been awarded to Spanish authors—J. Echegaray (1904), J. Benavente (1922) and Juan Ramón Jimenez (1956).

FINANCE

	1970 million Pesetas	1971 million Pesetas
Estimated Revenue	309,758	370,169
Estimated Expenditure	309,758	370,169

Public Debt (Dec. 31, 1964) excluding parastatal organizations and State-guaranteed issues: *Pesetas* 186,928,600,000.

The rate of exchange for the *peseta* in September, 1974, was 134 *pesetas*= £1 sterling (*see also* p. 83).

Production and Industry.—The country is generally fertile, and well adapted to agriculture and the cultivation of heat-loving fruits—olives, oranges, lemons, almonds, pomegranates, bananas, apricots and grapes. The agricultural products include wheat, barley, oats, rice, hemp and flax. The orange crop is exported mainly to Germany, France and the United Kingdom. The vine is cultivated widely; in the south-west, Jerez, the well-known sherry and tent wines are produced.

Spain's mineral resources of coal, iron, wolfram, copper, zinc, lead and iron ores are variously exploited. Many of the richer and more easily worked deposits have been exhausted, but the authorities are actively engaged in stimulating the exploitation of hitherto unworked or lower grade deposits. In 1970 the coal output amounted to

13,150,000 metric tons. 4,150,000 metric tons of iron ore and 7,366,000 metric tons of steel were produced in 1970. Other production figures included (ʼ000 metric tons): cement, 16,500; sulphuric acid, 2,015; cotton yarn, 117 and wool yarn, 37. Production of electric power was 56,484 million kWh. The fishing industry is important.

The principal goods produced are manufactured goods, textiles, chemical products, footwear and other leather goods, ceramics, sewing machines and bicycles. 24,105,000 tourists visited Spain in 1970 and spent £700,000,000. The Gross National Product was approximately £13,400 million.

Communications.—In 1970 there were over 13,402 km. of railways in service and 138,670 km. of paved roads. The sea-going mercantile marine in 1970 (excluding fishing boats) registered a total on 3,338,190 gross tons. Civil aviation is under the control of the Air Ministry; there are several inland and international services in operation.

TRADE

	1969 $ million	1970 $ million
Imports (c.i.f.)	4,233	4,747
Exports (f.o.b.)	1,900	2,387

The balance of payments surplus in 1970 was $600 (provisional) and reserves stood at $1,730 m. at the end of the year.

Trade with U.K.

	1973	1974
Imports from U.K.	£199,286.000	£260,292,000
Exports to U.K.	203,864,000	261,826,000

Inclusion of the Canary Islands trade with U.K. raises the 1974 figures to: Imports from U.K., £294,519,000; Exports, £301,143,000.

The principal imports are cotton, tobacco, cellulose, timber, coffee and cocoa, fertilizers, dyes, machinery, motor vehicles and agricultural tractors, wool and petroleum products. The principal exports include iron ore, cork, salt, vegetables, citrus fruits, wines, olive oil, potash, mercury, pyrites, tinned fruit and fish, bananas and tomatoes.

CAPITAL, Madrid. Population 3,146,071. Other large cities are Ψ Barcelona (1,750,000), Valencia (648,000), Ψ Seville (546,000), Zaragoza (470,000), Ψ Málaga (361,000), Bilbao (410,000); Murcia (244,000).

FLAG.—Three horizontal bands, red, yellow and red, with coat of arms on yellow band. NATIONAL DAY.—July 18 (*Fiesta Nacional Espanola*).

AIR TRANSIT FROM U.K.—London–Barcelona (713 miles), 2 hrs. 25 mins.; Madrid (775 miles), 2 hrs. 5 mins.; Valencia, 2 hrs. 10 mins.

BRITISH EMBASSY

(Calle Fernando el Santo, 16, Madrid)
Ambassador Extraordinary and Plenipotentiary, His Excellency Charles Douglas Wiggin, C.M.G., D.F.C., A.F.C. (1974).
Minister, R. L. Wade-Gery.
British Council Representative, J. G. G. Muir, O.B.E., D.S.C.

The BALEARIC ISLES form an archipelago off the east coast of Spain. There are four large islands (Majorca, Minorca, Ibiza and Formentera), and seven smaller (Aire, Aucanada, Botafoch, Cabrera, Dragonera, Pinto and El Rey). The islands were occupied by the Romans after the destruction of Carthage and provided contingents of the celebrated Balearic slingers. The total area is 1,935 square miles, with a population of 558,287. The archipelago forms a province of Spain, the capital being Ψ Palma in Majorca, pop. 234,098; Ψ Mahon (Minorca), pop. 16,547.

The CANARY ISLANDS are an archipelago in the Atlantic, off the African coast, consisting of 7 islands and 6 uninhabited islets. The total area is 2,807 square miles, with a population of 1,170,224. The Canary Islands form two Provinces of Spain.—*Las Palmas* (Gran Canaria, Lanzarote (38,500), Fuerteventura (19,500) and the islets of Alegranza, Roque del Este, Roque del Oests, Graciosa, Montaña Clara and Lobos), with seat of administration at Ψ Las Palmas (pop. 287,038) in Gran Canaria, where major oil companies have installations for re-fuelling shipping; and *Santa Cruz de Tenerife* (Tenerife, La Palma (76,000), Gomera (31,829), and Hierro (10,000)), with seat of administration at Ψ Santa Cruz in Tenerife, pop. 151,361.

Trade with U.K.

	1973	1974
Imports from U.K.	£27,812,000	£34,227,000
Exports to U.K.	29,667,000	39,317,000

ISLA DE FAISANES is an uninhabited Franco-Spanish condominium, at the mouth of the Bidassoa in La Higuera bay.

Ψ CEUTA is a fortified post on the Moroccan coast, opposite Gibraltar. The total area is 5 square miles, with a population (1970) of 67,187.

Ψ MELILLA is a town on a rocky promontory of the Rif coast, connected with the mainland by a narrow isthmus. Melilla has been in Spanish possession since 1492. Population (1970) 64,942. Ceuta and Melilla are parts of Metropolitan Spain.

OVERSEAS TERRITORIES

The former provinces of Spanish Guinea, Fernando Póo and Rio Muni achieved independence on October 12, 1968, under the title of Equatorial Guinea.

Ifni, the former enclave in Morocco was incorporated in the latter state by treaty, on June 30, 1969.

SPANISH SAHARA.—The province of Spanish Sahara extends from 27° 40′ N. lat. in the north to La Agüera (Cape Blanco) in the south, though the main southern boundary runs along latitude 21° 20′. The land area is approximately 125,000 square miles. Spanish Sahara is divided into two regions separated by latitude 26° which passes south of Cape Bojador. The northern region is the Seguia el Hamra (Rio Rojo) of which the capital is Aaiun. It extends eastward to approximately 8° 40′ W. long. The southern region is the Rio de Oro, of which the capital is Villa Cisneros. Its eastern boundary is approximately 12° W. long. Total population was estimated in 1969 at 63,000. There are rich deposits of potash.

Spain has accepted, but not implemented, a series of United Nations resolutions enjoining her to determine the wishes of the inhabitants as to their future. Both Morocco and Mauritania have claims on the territory.

SPANISH MOROCCO.—In addition to Ceuta and Melilla, Spain exercised until 1956 a protectorate over a part of Northern Morocco. Moroccan independence was proclaimed after negotiations with France and Spain in 1956 (*see* "Morocco"). Remaining Spanish settlements on the Moroccan seaboard are:—

Alhucemas, the bay of that name includes six islands: population 366.

Peñon de la Gomera (or *Peñon de Velez*) is a fortified rocky islet about 40 miles west of Alhucemas Bay; population 450.

The Chaffarinas (or *Zaffarines*) are a group of three islands near the Algerian frontier about 2 miles north of Cape del Agua; population 610.

SUDAN

(Democratic Republic of the Sudan)

President, Major-General Gaafar Mohamed El
Nimeri, *assumed office* May 25, 1969.
Minister of Foreign Affairs, Sayed Gamal Mohammed
Ahmed.

SUDANESE EMBASSY IN LONDON

3 Cleveland Row, S.W.1.

[01–839 8080]

Ambassador Extraordinary and Plenipotentiary, His
Excellency Mohamed Kheir Osman (1975).

Area and Population.—The Sudan extends from
the southern boundary of Egypt, 22° N. lat., to the
northern boundary of Uganda, 3° 36′ N. lat., and
reaches from the Republic of Chad about 21°
49′ E. (at 12° 45′ N.) to the north-west boundary of
Ethiopia in 38° 35′ E. (at 18° N.). The greatest
length from north to south is approximately 1,300
miles, and east to west 950 miles.

The northern boundary is the 22nd parallel of
North latitude; on the east lie the Red Sea and
Ethiopia; on the South lie Kenya, Uganda and
Zaire; and on the west the Central African Re-
public, Chad, and Libya.

The *White Nile* enters from Uganda at the Sudan
frontier post of Nimule in Equatoria Province, as
the *Bahr el Jebel,* and leaves the Sudan at Wadi
Halfa. The *Blue Nile* flows from Lake Tana on the
Ethiopian Plateau. Its course in the Sudan is
nearly 500 miles long, before it joins the White Nile
at Khartoum. The next confluence of importance
is at Atbara where the main Nile is joined by the
River Atbara. The total length of the Nile, now
accepted as the longest river in the world, is estimated to be 4,160 miles from its source to the Mediterranean Sea. Between Khartoum and Wadi
Halfa lie five of the six *Cataracts.*

The estimated area is about 967,500 sq. miles with
a population (estimated, 1974) of 16,900,000, partly
Arabs, partly Negroes, and partly of mixed Arab-
Negro blood, with a small foreign element, in-
cluding some 8,000 Europeans. The Arabs are
Moslems. The Nilotics of the Bahr el Ghazal and
Upper Nile Valleys are generally animists, but some
have been converted to Christianity and others are
Moslems.

Government.—The Anglo-Egyptian Condominium over the Sudan which had been established in

1899 ended when the Sudan House of Representatives on Dec. 19, 1955, voted unanimously a
declaration that the Sudan was a fully independent
sovereign state. A Republic was proclaimed on
Jan. 1, 1956, and was recognized by Great Britain
and Egypt, a Supreme Commission being sworn
in to take over sovereignty. The Sudan was under
military rule from Nov., 1958, until 1964 when a
new civilian Cabinet was appointed. Following a
crisis in the coalition Cabinet of Mr. Mahgoub, the
Prime Minister resigned on April 23, 1969, and was
unable to form a new coalition. Government of
the country was taken over on May 25, 1969, by a
ten-man revolutionary council headed by Col.
Jaafar Mohammed al Nimeri. A *coup d'état* by a
Communist group on July 19, 1971, was short-lived.
The leader of the group, Lt.-Col. Babikr al Noor,
had been in London for medical treatment when
power was seized by Maj. Hashem Atta. The
B.O.A.C. plane in which the former was returning
to Khartoum on July 22 was forced down at
Benghazi by Libyan fighter aircraft and Lt.-Col.
Noor and an aide were arrested. They were later
returned to the Sudan and executed. Maj.-Gen.
Nimeri was overwhelmingly elected President in an
uncontested election in October 1971. In February
1972 an agreement was signed at Addis Ababa
which brought to an end nearly 17 years of insurrection and civil war in the three southern provinces, and which recognized southern regional
autonomy within a unified Sudanese State.

Education.—School education is free for most
children, but not compulsory, beginning with
Primary School (of which there are 4,000) which
continues for 6 years. The final examination at
Primary School is highly competitive and selects
children for General Secondary Schools (of which
there are 700) which continues for 3 years. The
Higher Secondary Stage comprises 80 academic
Higher Secondary schools (3 years); 15 vocational
schools—Technical (4 years); Agricultural and
Commercial (3 years) and 15 Primary Teacher
Training Colleges (4 years). The medium of
instruction is Arabic. English is taught as the
principal foreign language in all schools.

Teacher Training is carried out in 15 Primary
Teacher Training Colleges, 2 General Secondary
Teacher Training Institutes and 1 Higher Teacher
Training Institute.

Khartoum University is the largest educational
institution and had 9 faculties and 5,478 students in 1971–72. There is an Islamic University
at Omdurman.

Selection for higher education is normally based
on the Sudan School Certificate.

In addition to the three universities there are
various technical post-secondary institutes as well
as professional and vocational training establishments.

Production.—The principal grain crops are wheat
and *dura* (great millet), the staple food of the people
in the Sudan. Sesame and ground-nuts are other
important food crops, which also yield an exportable surplus and a promising start has been made
with castor seed. The principal export crop is cotton. Main production is of long-staple (mainly
Egyptian type) cotton of which the Sudan is a major
producer, but increasing quantities of short and
medium staple (American) type cotton are being
grown. Production in 1974–75 totalled 1,200,000
bales. Much of the high quality, long-staple cotton
is provided by the Sudan Geziza Scheme (a Government-controlled project irrigated from the
Sennar Dam on the Blue Nile) and its extension,
the Managil Scheme. The Sudan also produces
the bulk of the world's supply of gum arabic.

Sugar is an increasingly important crop. The Sudan aims to be self-sufficient in sugar by 1976 and then to produce an exportable surplus; Livestock is the mainstay of the nomadic Arab tribes of the desert and the negro tribes of the swamp and wooded grassland country in the South. A new dam at Khashm el Girba began to store water in May, 1964, and will eventually provide irrigation to about 500,000 acres, most of which is being used to resettle the population of the Wadi Halfa area which has been flooded by the reservoir of the Egyptian High Dam. Another dam at Roseires on the Blue Nile will enable new or increased irrigation on a further 3,000,000 acres as well as providing hydro-electric power.

Communications.—The railway system (3 ft. 6 in. gauge) has a route length of about 3,200 miles, linking Khartoum with Wadi Halfa, Port Sudan, Wad Medani, Sennar, Kosti, El Obeid and Nyala. A line branches out southwards to Wau from the Sennar/Nyala western line. Regular rail and Nile steamer services connect Khartoum with Juba in Equatoria Province which in turn is connected by a bus service with Nimule on the Uganda border. Ψ Port Sudan is a well-equipped modern seaport. Sudan Airways fly regular services from Khartoum to many parts of the Sudan and to Egypt, Greece, Italy, the Lebanon, the United Kingdom, Ethiopia, Uganda and W. Germany, Iraq and Bahrain and are equipped with 2 Boeing 707's and 4 Fokker F27 aircraft as well as some smaller machines; they have contracted to buy 2 Boeing 737.

FINANCE

	1972–73	1974
Revenue	£S 191,286,658	£S 268,291,000
Expenditure	190,136,658	264,791,000

£S = Sudanese *Pound* of 100 Piastres.
Exchange Rate £S. 0·847 = £1 sterling, £S. 0·349 = U.S.$1. (May 1974) (*see also* p. 84).

TRADE

	1972	1974
Total Imports	£S 123,100,000	£S 223,580,000
Exports	125,500,000	122,010,000

Trade with U.K.

	1973	1974
Imports from U.K.	£26,900,000	£36,000,000
Exports to U.K.	8,400,000	8,000,000

The principal exports are cotton and cotton seed, ground-nuts and gum arabic. The chief imports are cotton piece goods, base metals, vehicles and transport equipment, machinery, petroleum products, sugar, tea, coffee, chemicals and pharmaceuticals.

CAPITAL, Khartoum (est. pop. 194,000). The town contains many mosques, a Catholic cathedral and an Anglican cathedral, which is no longer open for worship, and the University with extensive government buildings. Khartoum North and Omdurman have estimated populations of 58,000 and 167,000 respectively.

FLAG.—Three horizontal stripes of red, white and black with a green triangle next to the hoist.
NATIONAL DAY.—January 1 (Independence Day).

BRITISH EMBASSY
Khartoum

Ambassador Extraordinary and Plenipotentiary, His Excellency John Fleetwood Stewart Phillips, C.M.G. (1973).
Counsellor, J. L. Y. Sanders (*Head of Chancery*).
Defence and Military Attaché, Col. P. L. F. Baillon.
1st *Secretaries*, W. H. Stevens; J. G. Douglas (*Commercial*).
2nd *Secretaries*, H. J. Taylor (*Administration and Consul*); D. Lamb; D. G. Lambert (*Development*); S. R. Bonde (*Commercial*).

British Council Representative, J. Lawrence, O.B.E., Gama'a Avenue, P.O. Box 1253, Khartoum. There are British Council libraries at *Khartoum*, *El Fasher*, *El Obeid*, *Omdurman* and *Wad Medani*.

SURINAM

Governor, Dr. J. H. E. Ferrier (1968).

Surinam is situated on the north coast of South America and is bounded by French Guiana in the east, Brazil in the south and Guyana in the west. It has an area of 54,000 square miles, with a population of 480,000 (December, 1971).

Formerly known as Dutch Guiana, Surinam remains part of the Netherlands West Indies until November 25, 1975, when it achieves complete independence. Surinam had received autonomy in domestic affairs under the Realm Statute which took effect on December 29, 1954.

Surinam has large timber resources. Rice and sugar cane are the main crops. Bauxite is mined, and is the principal export.

TRADE

	1971	1972
		Surinam Guilders
Imports	237,800,000	258,200,000
Exports	294,500,000	305,700,000

Trade with U.K.

	1973	1974
Imports from U.K.	£2,904,000	£4,409,000
Exports to U.K.	£4,071,000	4,873,000

CAPITAL.—Ψ Paramaribo (population, 1971, 110,000).

There is a *British Consulate* at Paramaribo.
Honorary Consul, J. J. Healy.

SWEDEN
(Sverige)

King of Sweden, Carl XVI Gustaf, *grandson* of the late King Gustaf VI Adolf, *born* April 30, 1946.

CABINET

Prime Minister, Olof Palme.
Justice, Lennart Geijer.
Foreign Affairs, Sven Andersson.
Defence, Eric Holmquist.
Social Affairs, Sven Aspling.
Local Government and Planning, Hans Gustafsson.
Communications, Bengt Norling.
Finance, Gunnar Sträng.
Housing, Ingvar Carlsson.
Labour, Ingemund Bengtsson.
Agriculture, Svante Lundkvist.
Education, Bertil Zachrisson.
Industry, Rune Johansson.
Trade Kjell-Olof Feldt.
Ministers of State, Carl Lidbom (*Cabinet Office*); Anna-Greta Leijon (*Labour*); Gertrud Sigurdsen (*Aid*); Lena Hjelm-Wallén (*Education*).

SWEDISH EMBASSY IN LONDON

Residence, 27 Portland Place, W.1; *Chancery*, 23 North Row, W.1.
[01-499 9500]
Ambassador Extraordinary and Plenipotentiary, His Excellency Ole Jödahl (1972).
Minister Plenipotentiary, B. Åkerrén.
Counsellors, Baron C. G. von Platen (*Economic and Financial*); L. Arnö (*Press*); G. Westin (*Consular*).
1st *Secretaries*, N. G. Revelius; L. G. Carlsson (*Consular*); Miss K. Rosenström (*Administration*).
Naval Attaché, Capt. N. Rydström.
Military Attaché, Col C. Hasselgren.
Air Attaché, Col. J. Winqvist.
Trade Commissioner, S. Widenfelt (14 Trinity Square, E.C.4).
Area and Population.—Sweden occupies the eastern

area of the Scandinavian peninsula in N.W. Europe and comprises 24 local government districts, *"Län"*, with an area of 173,436 sq. miles, and population Jan. 1, 1975 of 8,177,000. In 1973 there were 109,663 births (13·8 per 1,000 inhabitants); death rate was 10·52 per 1,000 inhabitants and infant mortality rate (under one year of age) 0·9 per cent. of all live births.

Government. Under the Act of Succession of June 6, 1809 (with amendments) the throne is hereditary in the House of Bernadotte. Jean-Baptiste Jules Bernadotte, Prince of Ponte Corvo, a Marshal of France, was invited to accept the title of Crown Prince, with succession to the throne. He landed at Hälsingborg on Oct. 20, 1810, and succeeded Charles XIII in 1818. There is a uni-cameral Diet (*Riksdag*) of 350 members elected for 3 years. The Council of Ministers (*Statsrad*) is responsible to the *Riksdag.*

Production and Industry.—Since the end of the First World War Sweden has become one of the leading industrial nations of Europe. Agriculture is still one of the main activities, but its relative importance is declining and in 1974 less than 6 per cent. of the working population was engaged in farming and forestry. The country's rising indus-trial prosperity is based on an abundance of natural resources in the form of forests, mineral deposits and water power. The forests are very extensive, cover-ing about half the total land surface, and sustain flourishing timber, pulp and paper milling indus-tries. The mineral resources include iron ore of excellent quality, lead, zinc, sulphur, granite and marble. There are also extensive deposits of low grade uranium ore. Important industries based on mining include iron and steel, aluminium, and copper. The engineering industry has expanded largely on the basis of products invented or de-veloped by Swedish engineers. Sweden has now one of the most important shipbuilding industries in the world. Motor car manufacturing is a major industry. The establishment of a petro-chemicals industry has led to a rapid expansion in the output of chemicals and plastics.

Communications.—The total length of Swedish railroads is about 7,500 miles. At the end of 1973 there were 580 telephones for every 1,000 of the population, and in January, 1975, the number of broadcast receiving licences issued had reached 2,841,000. The number of private cars in use on January 1, 1974, was 2,637,800.

The Mercantile Marine (March 1974) consisted of 649 vessels of 100 tons gross and over with a total tonnage of 5,954,000. The Board of Civil Aviation under the control of the Ministry of Communications handles civil aviation matters. Regular domestic air traffic is maintained by the Scandinavian Airlines System and by A. B. Linje-flyg. Regular European and inter-continental air traffic is maintained by the Scandinavian Airlines System.

Defence.—A period of service in the Defence Forces is compulsory and about 40,000 National Servicemen are called up each year. In addition some 45,000 reservists receive training each year. However, the regular strength of the *Army* is only about 9,700 all ranks. There are some 500,000 trained reserves. Weapons and equipment are modern and the Army is highly mechanized. The *Navy* has 8 destroyers, 5 frigates, 22 submarines, 42 F.P.S.'s and a large number of minor craft and auxiliaries. Only about one-third of this force is commissioned in normal times. The *Air Force* is equipped with modern supersonic jet fighters, attack and reconnaissance aircraft of Swedish manu-facture. There are 7 fighter, 3 attack and 2 recon-

naissance wings, supported by a modern control and reporting organization and a network of dispersed air bases.

Religion.—The State religion is Lutheran Pro-testant, to which over 95 per cent. of the people officially adhere.

Language and Literature.—Swedish belongs, with Danish and Norwegian, to the North Germanic language group. Swedish literature dates back to King Magnus Eriksson, who codified the old Swedish provincial laws in 1350. With his transla-tion of the Bible, Olaus Petri (1493–1552) formed the basis for the modern Swedish language. Litera-ture flourished during the reign of Gustavus III, who founded the Swedish Academy in 1786. Swedish literature is studded with names such as Kellgren (1751–1795), Atterbom (1790–1855), Almquist (1795–1866), Rydberg (1828–1895), Levertin (1862–1906), Strindberg (1849–1912) and Lagerlöf (1858–1940), Nobel Prize Winner in 1909. Contemporary authors include Lagerquist (1891–1973), Nobel Laureate in 1951, Martinson (b 1904) and Johnson (b. 1900), Nobel Laureates jointly in 1974. The Swedish scientist Alfred Nobel (1833–1896) founded the Nobel Prizes for Literature, Science and Peace. In 1974 there were 146 daily newspapers with a total circulation of 4,602,800 copies, 4 major papers being published at Stock-holm, 2 at Göteborg and 4 at Malmö.

Education.—Well developed and recently re-organized to provide (i) 9 years' compulsory school-ing from the age of 7 to 16 in the *Grundskolan;* (ii) further education from 16 to 18/19 in the *Gym-nasia,* which offer a number of courses preparing for entry to the universities, other centres of higher education, the professions, etc.; (iii) the universities. There are five State universities—Uppsala (founded 1477); Lund (founded 1668); Stockholm (founded 1878); Göteborg (founded 1887); Umea (founded 1963). In 1967 University branches, empowered to grant first degrees in the humanities, social sciences and natural sciences were

established in Örebro (University of Uppsala), Växjö (University of Lund), Karlstad (University of Gothenburg) and Linköping (University of Stockholm). Since 1970 the Linköping branch has ranked as an autonomus institution of university standing. Tuition within the State system, which is maintained by the State and by local taxation, is free.

FINANCE

	1974–75 '000 Kronor	1975–76 '000 Kronor
Revenue (Estimated)	73,033,000	81,318,000
Expenditure (Estimated)	84,886,000	93,224,000

The Swedish *Krona* (of 100 *Ore*) exchanges at about 8.72 *Kronor*= £1 sterling (June, 1975). (*See also* p. 83.)

TRADE

	1973 '000 Kronor	1974 '000 Kronor
Imports	46,302,000	69,993,000
Exports	53,019,300	70,390,600

Trade with U.K.

	1973	1974
Imports from U.K.	£514,300,000	£723,340,000
Exports to U.K.	739,996,000	929,112,000

The chief imports from Britain are machinery and engineering goods, transport equipment, petroleum products, chemicals, plastics, raw materials, iron and steel and other metals, textile fabrics, clothing, instruments and some foodstuffs. Sweden's chief exports to Britain are timber, pulp and paper, machinery, motor vehicles, iron ore, and iron and steel.

CAPITAL.— Ψ Stockholm. Population (1973): City 681,318; Greater Stockholm, 1,349,892; Ψ Gothenburg (Göteborg) (449,470); Ψ Malmö (251,431); Västerås (117,936); Uppsala (136,067); Ψ Norrköping (120,341); Örebro (117,835); Ψ Helsingborg (101,033); Linköping (107,033); Ψ Gävle (84,576); Borås (106,287); Eskilstuna (92,095).

FLAG.—Yellow cross on a blue ground. NATIONAL DAY.—June 6 (Day of the Swedish Flag).

BRITISH EMBASSY

(*Residence*, Laboratoriegatan 8; *Chancery*, Skarpögatan 8, Stockholm.)

Ambassador Extraordinary and Plenipotentiary, His Excellency Sir Samuel Falle, K.C.V.O., C.M.G., D.S.C. (1974).

Counsellors, B. A. Flack (*Commercial*) P. L. V. Mallett (*Head of Chancery*).

1st Secretaries, J. G. B. Weait (*Commercial*); R. O. Barritt, O.B.E. (*Labour*); D. G. H. Brookfield, M.B.E.; R. R. Best (*Economic*); A. Lindsay (*Consul*); P. R. Holmes (*Information*).

2nd Secretaries, M. Cederlund (*Information*); C. R. L. de Chassiron.

Defence and Air Attaché, Gp. Capt. K. J. Barratt.
Naval Attaché, Cdr. J. A. Palmer, R.N.
Military Attaché, Lt.-Col. R. F. Dorey.
Assist. Air Attaché, Sqn.-Ldr. C. P. Russell-Smith.
Archivist, A. Treadell.
British Council Representative, D. H. Spencer.

BRITISH CONSULAR OFFICES

There are British Consular Offices at *Gävle*, *Göteborg*, *Hälsingborg*, *Luleå*, *Malmö*, *Norrköping*, *Stockholm* and *Sundsvall*.

British-Swedish Chamber of Commerce in Sweden: Birger Jarlsgatan 6B, Stockholm.

SWITZERLAND

(Schweizerische Eidgenossenschaft—Confédération Suisse—Confederazione Svizzera.)

CABINET

President of the Swiss Confederation (1975) *and Head of the Swiss Federal Political Department* (*Foreign Affairs*), M. Pierre Graber, *born* 1908.

Vice-President (1975) *and Defence*, M. Rudolf Gnaegi.
Justice and Police, M. Kurt Furgler.
Economics, M. Ernst Brugger.
Transport and Power, M. Willi Ritschard.
Interior, M. Hans Huerlimann.
Finance and Customs, M. Georges-André Chevallaz.
Federal Chancellor, M. Karl Huber.

SWISS EMBASSY IN LONDON
16–18 Montagu Place, W.1.
[01–723 0701]

Ambassador Extraordinary and Plenipotentiary, His Excellency, Dr. Albert Weitnauer.
Minister Plenipotentiary, Dr. K. Fritschi.
Counsellors, Dr. von Tscharner (*Economic and Labour*); J.-J. Indermuehle (*Cultural Affairs*); M. R. Serex.
Defence Attaché, Col. Hans W. Fischer.
1st Secretary, Paul A. Ramseyer.
Counsellor, J. F. Lüthi (*Commodities and Agriculture*).
Asst. Defence Attaché, Capt. Peter Bürgisser.
Consul and Head of Administration, C. Glauser.
There is a Swiss Consulate-General in *Manchester*.

Area and Population.—The Helvetia of the Romans, a Federal Republic of Central Europe, situated between 45° 50'–47° 48' N. lat. and 5° 58'–10° 3' E. long. It is composed of 22 Cantons, 3 subdivided, making 25 in all, and comprises a total area of 15,950 square miles with a population (estimated Jan. 1, 1973) of 6,385,000. In 1972 there were 91,342 (1973, 84,187) live births, 56,489 deaths and 43,081 marriages. The infant mortality rate was 13 per 1,000 live births. In 1970, out of a

total of 6,169,800, 47·8 per cent. of the population was Protestant, 49·4 per cent. Roman Catholic and 0·3 per cent. Jewish.

Physical Features.—Switzerland is the most mountainous country in all Europe. The Alps, covered with perennial snow and from 5,000 to 15,217 feet in height, occupy its southern and eastern frontiers, and the chief part of its interior; and the Jura mountains rise in the north-west. The Alps occupy 61 per cent., and the Jura mountains 12 per cent., of the country. The *Alps* are a crescent-shaped mountain system situated in France, Italy, Switzerland, Bavaria and Austria, covering an area of 80,000 square miles from the Mediterranean to the Danube (600 miles). The highest peak, Mont Blanc, Pennine Alps (15,732 feet) is partly in France and Italy; Monte Rosa (15,217 feet) and

Matterhorn (14,780 feet) are partly in Switzerland and partly in Italy. The highest wholly Swiss peaks are Dufourspitze (15,203 ft.), Finsteraahorn (14,026), Aletschhorn (13,711), Jungfrau (13,671), Mönch (13,456), Eiger (13,040), Schreckhorn (13,385), and Wetterhorn (12,150) in the Bernese Alps, and Dom (14,918), Weisshorn (14,803) and Breithorn (13,685).

The Swiss lakes are famous for their beauty and include Lakes Maggiore, Zürich, Lucerne, Neuchâtel, Geneva, Constance, Thun Zug, Lugano, Brienz and the Walensee. There are also many artificial lakes.

Production and Industry.—Agriculture is followed chiefly in the valleys, where wheat, oats, maize, barley, flax, hemp, and tobacco are produced, and nearly all English fruits and vegetables as well as grapes are grown. Dairying and stock-raising are the principal industries, about 3,000,000 acres being under grass for hay and 2,000,000 acres pasturage. The forests cover about one-quarter of the whole surface. The chief manufacturing industries comprise engineering and electrical engineering, metal-working, chemicals and pharmaceuticals, textiles, watchmaking, woodworking, foodstuffs and footwear. Banking, insurance and tourism are major industries.

Government.—The legislative power is vested in a Parliament, consisting of two Chambers, a National Council (*Nationalrat*) of 200 members, and a Council of States (*Ständerat*) of 44 members; both Chambers united are called the Federal Assembly, and the members of the National Council are elected for four years, an election taking place in October. The executive power is in the hands of a Federal Council (*Bundesrat*) of 7 members, elected for four years by the Federal Assembly and presided over by the President of the Confederation. Each year the Federal Assembly elects from the Federal Council the President and the Vice-President. Not more than one of the same canton may be elected member of the Federal Council; on the other hand, there is a tradition that Italian and French-speaking areas should between them be represented on the Federal Council by at least two members.

Defence.—All Swiss males must undertake military service in the Army. *Elite* (ages 20 to 32) initial training, 118 days. Subsequently 8 training periods of 21 days; then *Landwehr* (33–42) and *Landsturm* (43 to 50). Flying personnel of the Air Force, which is part of the Army (ages 20–36): Initial training 1 year, totalling 200 hours of flying. 6 weeks with squadron each year and completion of 80 to 100 hours of flying. After 36 revert to ground duties with Air Force or Army. Swiss Army equipment includes many British items, notably Centurion tanks, Bloodhound missiles, and Venom, Vampire and Hunter aircraft.

Communications.—By the end of 1973 there were 4,979 km of railway tracks (Swiss Federal Railways, 2,927 km; Swiss privately owned railways, 2,052 km); the whole system is electrified. At the end of 1973, there were 89,940 km of telegraph and telephone lines. By December 1973, the number of telephone subscribers amounted to 2,284,368 and the network was fully automatic throughout the country. In 1973 there were 2,003,204 licensed radio receivers and 1,627,410 television receivers.

At the end of 1972 the total length of motorways was 770·2 km. The number of motor vehicles licensed at the end of 1973 was 1,934,029.

A merchant marine established in 1940, consisted in 1973 of 27 vessels with a total displacement of 237,003 tons (gross). In addition 507 vessels with a total tonnage of 584,644 were engaged in Rhine shipping. In 1973, goods handled at the Basle Rhine port amounted to 8,203,931 tons. 123 lake vessels transported 9,060,000 passengers and 332,846 tons of freight in 1972. The national airline, Swissair, has a network covering 226,949 km and in 1973 carried a total of 5,152,106 passengers. Its fleet of 43 aircraft includes 2 Jumbojets, with 14 aircraft on order (10 DC 9's and 4 DC 10's). It flies to and from the Swiss airports at Zürich, Geneva and Basle.

Education.—Control by cantonal and communal authorities. No central organization. Illiteracy practically unknown. (i) *Primary:* Free and compulsory. School age varies, generally 7 to 14. (ii) *Secondary:* Age 12–15 for boys and girls. Schools numerous and well-attended, and there are many private institutions. (iii) *Special schools* make a feature of commercial and technical instruction. (iv) *Universities:* Basle (founded 1460), Berne (1834), Fribourg (1889), Geneva (1873), Lausanne (1890), Zürich (1832), and Neuchâtel (1909), and the technical University of Zürich and commercial University of St. Gall.

Language and Literature.—There are three official languages: French, German and Italian. In addition Romansch is recognized as a national, but not an official language. German is the dominating language in 19 of the 25 cantons; French in Fribourg, Geneva, Neuchâtel, Valais and Vaud; Italian in Ticino, and Romansch in parts of the Grisons.

Many modern authors, alike in the German school and in the Suisse Romande, have achieved international fame. Karl Spitteler (1845–1924) and Hermann Hesse (1877–1962) were awarded the Nobel Prize for Literature, the former in 1919, the latter in 1946.

FINANCE

	Budget 1974	Budget 1975
	Swiss Francs	*Swiss Francs*
Revenue	12,656,000,000	12,908,000,000
Expenditure	12,851,000,000	13,366,000,000
Federal Public Debt (Dec., 1974):		
Internal consolidated		1,284,000,000

The approx. rate of exchange is Sw. Frs. 6 = £1 (*see also* p. 83).

TRADE

	1973	1974
	Sw. Frs.	*Sw. Frs.*
Total Imports	36,588,562,179	42,909,358,510
Total Exports	29,948,317,321	35,353,101,852

Trade with U.K.
(including Liechtenstein)

	1973	1974
Imports from U.K.	£520,873,000	£600,450,000
Exports to U.K.	591,582,000	717,143,000

The principal imports are machinery, electrical and electronic equipment, textiles, motor vehicles, non-ferrous metals, chemical elements, clothing, food, medicinal and pharmaceutical products. The principal exports are machinery, chemical elements, non-ferrous metals, watches, electrical and electronic equipment, textiles, dyeing, tanning and colouring equipment. Switzerland is a member of E.F.T.A.

CAPITAL, Berne. Population (1973) 157,700. Other large towns are Zürich (410,100), Basle (204,900), Geneva (168,600), Lausanne (137,700), Winterthur (92,900), St. Gallen (81,700), Lucerne (69,500), Bienne (62,700) and La Chaux-de-Fonds (42,400).

FLAG—Red, with white cross. NATIONAL DAY.—August 1.

AIR TRANSIT FROM U.K.—London-Basle (446 miles), 1 *hr.* 20 *mins.*; Geneva (468 miles), 1 *hr.* 20 *mins.*; Zürich (491 miles), 1 *hr.* 20 *mins.*

RAIL TRANSIT FROM U.K.—London-Berne, 16 *hrs.*

BRITISH EMBASSY
(Thunstrasse 50, 3005 Berne)

Ambassador Extraordinary and Plenipotentiary, His Excellency John Richard Wraight, C.M.G.

Counsellor, P. A. Grier, O.B.E.

1st Secretary, H. L. O'Bryan-Tear, O.B.E.

2nd Secretaries, A. V. Hill; G. D. Darby (*Consul*).

Defence, Naval, Military and Air Attaché, Lt.-Col. A. A. Taylor.

Attaché, D. L. Wetton, M.B.E. (*Commercial*).

Press Attaché, P. A. Arengo-Jones.

BRITISH CONSULAR OFFICES

There is a Consular Section at H.M. Embassy, Berne; British Consular Offices at *Basle, Geneva, Lugano* and *Montreux*; and a Directorate of British Export Promotion in Switzerland and Consulate-General in *Zürich.*

BRITISH COUNCIL.—Rämistrasse 34, 8001, *Zürich* (*Representative,* N. H. Ashmere, M.C.).

BRITISH-SWISS CHAMBER OF COMMERCE FOR SWITZERLAND, Durfourstrasse 51, 8008 *Zürich* (Branch at 1 Galeries Benjamin Constant, 1,000 *Lausanne*).

SWISS-BRITISH SOCIETY, Berne.—*President,* Dr. Th. von Mandach.

SWISS-BRITISH SOCIETY, Zürich.—*President,* Dr. R. Schneebeli.

SWISS-BRITISH SOCIETY, Basle.—*President,* Mr. Simons.

SYRIA
(Syrian Arab Republic)

President, Lt.-Gen. Hafez el Assad, *b.* 1930, *assumed office March 14, 1971, for a term of 7 years.*

MINISTERS
(Aug. 31, 1974)

Prime Minister, Mahmoud Ayoubi.

Deputy Prime Minister, Foreign Affairs, Abdel Halim Khaddam.

Deputy Prime Minister, Economic Affairs, Mohammed Haidar.

Defence, Maj.-Gen. Mustapha Tlass.

Interior, Col. Ali Zaza.

Local Administration, Adib Milhem.

Information, Ahmed Iskandar.

Public Works and Water Resources, Abdel Ghani Karrout.

Euphrates Dam, Sobhi Kahalé.

Education, Dr. Shaker Fahham.

Planning, Dr. Nourallah Awad Nourallah.

Economy and Foreign Trade, Mohammed Inadi.

Culture and National Guidance, Fawzi Kayali.

Justice, Adib Nahawi.

Communications, Omar Sebai.

Food and Internal Trade, Ahmed Kablane.

Religious Affairs, Sheikh Abdel Sattar al Sayyed.

Labour and Social Affairs, Hussein Koueider.

Health. Madani al Khyami.

Tourism, Abdullah al Khani.

Higher Education, Mohammed Ali Hashem.

Housing, Abdel Razzak Abdel Baki.

Industry, Chteoui Seifo.

Transport, Naaman Zein.

Electricity, Hani Sawaz.

Finance, Mohammed Cherij.

Agriculture, Mousel Abdou Omar.

Oil and Mineral Resources, Adnane Moustapha.

Ministers of State, Fayez Nasser (*Prime Minister's Office*); Zahir Abdel Samad; Anwar Hamdane.

SYRIAN EMBASSY IN LONDON
5 Eaton Terrace, S.W.1.
[01-730 0384]

Ambassador Extraordinary and Plenipotentiary, His Excellency Adnan Omran (1974).

Area and Population.—Syria is in the Levant, covering a portion of the former Ottoman Empire, with an estimated area of 70,800 sq. miles and a population (Census of 1970) of 6,294,000, Arabic speaking and mainly Moslems. (*For Map, see* p. 883.) The Orontes flows northwards from the Lebanon range across the northern boundary to Antakya (Antioch, Turkey). The Euphrates crosses the northern boundary near Jerablus and flows through north-eastern Syria to the boundary of Iraq.

Archæology, etc.—The region is rich in historical remains. Damascus (*Dimishq ash-Sham*) is the oldest continuously inhabited city in the world, having an existence as a city for over 4,000 years. It is situated on the river Abana (now known as Barada), in an oasis at the eastern foot of the Anti-Lebanon, and at the edge of the wide sandy desert which stretches to the Euphrates. The city contains the Omayyed Mosque, the Tomb of Saladin, and the " Street Called Straight " (Acts ix. 11), while to the North-East is the Roman outpost of Dmeir and further east is Palmyra.

On the Mediterranean coast at Amrit are ruins of the Phœnician town of Marath, where the *well* has been found and is being excavated and also ruins of Crusaders' fortresses at Markab, Sahyoun, and Krak des Chevaliers. At Tartous (also on the coast) the cathedral of Our Lady of Syria, built by the Knights Templars in the 12th and 13th centuries has been restored as a museum.

Hittite cities dating from 2,000 to 1,500 B.C., have recently been explored on the west bank of the Euphrates at Jerablus and Kadesh.

Government.—Syria, which had been under French mandate since the 1914–18 war, became an independent Republic during the 1939–45 war. The first independently elected Parliament met on August 17, 1943, but foreign troops were in part occupation until April, 1946. Syria remained an independent Republic until February, 1958, when it became part of the United Arab Republic. It seceded from the United Arab Republic on Sept. 28, 1961.

A new Constitution was promulgated in March 1973; this declared that Syria is a " democratic, popular socialist State ", and that the Ba'ath Party, which has been the ruling party since 1963, is " the leading party in the State and society ". Elections to the 186-seat Peoples' Council in May 1973 resulted in a large majority for the Ba'ath Party.

Production and Industry.—Agriculture is the principal source of production; wheat and barley are the main cereal crops, but the cotton crop is the highest in value. Tobacco is grown in the maritime plain in Sahel, the Sahyoun and the Djebleh district of Lattakia; skins and hides, leather goods, wool and silk, textiles, cement, vegetable oil, glass, soap, sugar, plastics and copper and brass utensils are locally produced. There are also some light assembly plants. Mineral wealth is small but oil has been found at Karachuk in the north-eastern corner of the country and drilling is continuing. A pipeline is to be built to the Mediterranean port of Tartous, *viâ* Homs. An oil refinery is in production at Homs and revenue is derived from the Kirluk-Banias oil pipeline and the pipeline from the oilfields of Saudi-Arabia to Sidon in Lebanon (Tapline). Syria also has deposits of phosphate and rock salt.

Language and Literature.—Arabic is the principal language (*see* Arabia), but a few villages still speak

Aramaic, the language spoken by Christ and the Apostles. There are 2 daily newspapers and several periodicals in Arabic published in Damascus and one daily newspaper in Aleppo.

Education.—Education in Syria is under State control and, although a few of the schools are privately owned, they all follow a common system and syllabus. Elementary education is free at State Schools, and is compulsory from the age of seven. Secondary education is not compulsory and is free only at the State Schools. Because of the shortage of places, entry to these State Schools is competitive. Damascus University, founded in 1924, has faculties of law, medicine, engineering, science, arts, commerce, agriculture, divinity, fine arts, and a Higher Teachers' Training College. The number of students has risen from a few hundred in 1943 to about 20,000. There are also over 4,500 students at Aleppo University (founded 1961). Approximately 10 per cent. of all students receive scholarships, and at the present time Palestinian refugees are admitted free. The rest pay fees.

Communications.—A narrow-gauge railway runs from Beirut in the Lebanon to Damascus, connecting at Rayak (Lebanon) with the standard-gauge line which runs from Beirut and Tripoli (in the Lebanon) through Homs, Hama and Aleppo to the Turkish frontier, from Nusaybin to the Iraq frontier at Tel Kotchek. From Damascus the Hejaz railway runs southwards to Jordan. Railway lines are under construction to link the ports of Lattakia and Tartous with Aleppo and Qamishli. All the principal towns in the country are connected by roads of varying quality. An internal air service operates between Damascus and Aleppo, and between Aleppo and Qamishli. There are also flights from Damascus to Palmyra and Deir-ez-Zor. Damascus is also on international air routes.

Currency.—The monetary unit is the Syrian paper pound (£Syr.). Exchange rate, see p. 84.

Trade.—The principal imports are foodstuffs (fruit, vegetables, cereals, meat and dairy products, tea, coffee and sugar), mineral and petroleum products, yarn and textiles, iron and steel manufactures, machinery, chemicals, pharmaceuticals, fertilizers and timber.

Principal Exports.—Raw cotton, cereals, fruit, livestock and dairy products, other foodstuffs, textiles and raw wool.

Trade with U.K.

	1973	1974
Imports from U.K.	£11,630,000	£20,854,000
Exports to U.K.	1,154,000	20,572,000

CHIEF TOWNS.—Damascus (population (estimate, 1971), 557,252) is the capital of Syria. Other important towns being Aleppo (population 425,467), Homs (137,217) and Hama (97,390), and the principal port is Ψ Lattakia (67,604).

FLAG.—Red over white over black horizontal bands, with three green stars on central white band.

NATIONAL DAY.—April 17.

BRITISH EMBASSY
(Quartier Malki, 11 rue Mohammad Kurd Ali, Imm. Kotob, Damascus.)

Ambassador Extraordinary and Plenipotentiary, His Excellency David Arthur Roberts (1973).

THAILAND (Siam)

King, His Majesty Bhumibol Adulyadej, *born* 1927; *succeeded his brother*, June 9, 1946; *married* Princess Sirikit Kityakara, April 28, 1950; *crowned* May 5, 1950; daughter *born*, April 6, 1951; son and heir *born*, July 28, 1952; second daughter *born* April 2, 1955; third daughter *born* July 4, 1957.

CABINET
(March 1975)

Prime Minister, Kukrit Pramoj.
Defence and Deputy Prime Minister, Maj. Gen. Pramarn Adireksarn.
Minister to Prime Minister's Office, Preeda Patanathabutr.
Finance, Boonchu Rojanasathien.
Foreign Affairs, Maj. Gen. Chatichai Choonhavan.
Agriculture and Co-operatives, Tavich Klinpratoom.
Communications, Maj. Gen. Siri Siriyodhin.
Commerce, Thongyod Chittavera.
Interior, Boonthenj Thongswasdi.
Justice, Yai Switachata.
Education, Nibondh Sasidhorn.
Health, Prachoom Ruttanapian.
Industry, Surin Thepkanjana.
State Universities, Lt. Gen. Chan Ansuchote.

There are also 13 Deputy Ministers.

ROYAL THAI EMBASSY IN LONDON
30 Queen's Gate, S.W.7
[01–589 0173]

Ambassador Extraordinary and Plenipotentiary, His Excellency Konthi Suphamongkhon, G.C.V.O. (1970).

Area and Population.—The Kingdom of Thailand, or Muang Thai, formerly known as Siam, has an area of 198,247 sq. miles with a population (estimated 1973) of 41,000,000. For position, *see* MAP, p. 745. It has a common boundary with Malaysia in the south, and is bounded on the west and north-east and east by the Kingdom of Laos and Cambodia, which was formerly part of the French Colony of Indo-China. Although there is no common boundary between Thailand and China, the Chinese province of Yunnan is separated from the Thai northern border only by a narrow stretch of Burmese and Laotian territory.

The country slopes southwards from the north-west and from the great mountains of Tibet. The principal rivers are the Salween (which forms a boundary with Burma for 200 miles), the Menam Chao Phraya with its tributary the Meping (which are Thai throughout) and the Mekong and its tributaries, which water the eastern plateau.

Government.—The military Government of Field-Marshal Thanom Kitlikachorn resigned on Oct. 14, 1973, after mass demonstrations, in protest at the Government's refusal to hasten the drafting of a new constitution (the previous constitution having been suspended in 1971), led to violence and riots.

A National Assembly was convened and a new constitution providing for an elected House of Representatives of 269 members, and an appointed Senate of 100 members, was promulgated in October 1974. Following the subsequent General Election held on January 26, 1975, the interim Government of Dr. Sanya Dharmasakt resigned and was succeeded on March 17 by the present coalition Government under Kukrit Pramoj.

Language, Religion and Education.—Thai is basically a monosyllabic, tonal language, a branch of the Indo-Chinese linguistic family, but its vocabulary especially has been strongly influenced by Sanskrit and Pali. It is written in an alphabetic script derived from ancient Indian scripts. The principal religion is Buddhism. In 1973 93.6 per cent. of the population were Buddhists, 3.9 per cent. Moslems, 0.6 per cent. Christians and 1.9 per cent. other religions. Primary education is compulsory and free and secondary education in Government Schools is free. In 1974 there were 33,448 schools of all kinds with 7,321,797 pupils and 250,300 teachers. There are 10 Universities attended by 136,349 students, 34 training colleges and 196 vocational schools (all types). New universities were opened at Chiengmai and Khon Kaen in 1966 and a further university has subsequently been opened at Songkhla in the south. In 1972 an open university (Ramkhamhaeng) was established in Bangkok with some 45,000 students.

Production and Industry.—The agricultural sector provides just under half the national income and employs about 70 per cent. of the working population. Rice remains the most important crop, accounting for 64 per cent. of the area planted. After rice (13,000,000 tons in 1974) the main crops are cassava (6,600,000 tons of roots), maize (2,500,000 tons), and rubber (9,000,000 tons). Other crops of some importance are sugar cane, kenaf, groundnuts, tobacco, and coconuts. There is also a substantial forest extraction industry the most valuable product of which is teak.

Mineral resources are mainly tin, antimony, gypsum and fluorite. The most important of these, tin, is seeing something of a decline, mainly because of the exhaustion of reserves. The importance of lignite as a source of energy is now increasing with higher oil prices.

Before the war, industry was mainly confined to the basic processing industries—sawmilling, ricemilling, etc. After the war, the Government set up a number of factories run by the Civil Service or the Armed Forces. The Government still has a sizeable stake in industry—notably the tobacco monopoly and factories for the manufacture of cement, glass, paper, jute, textiles, sugar and beer and spirits.

The then Government in 1962 instituted a policy of encouraging the private sector to invest in industry, by means of tax reliefs and other incentives. The private sector industries are almost entirely of a secondary nature; soap products, gunny bags, textiles, car assembly pharmaceutical preparations and packaging, dry batteries, etc. Over the last few years the size of the manufacturing sector has grown rapidly and now provides 18 per cent. of national income.

Communications.—Rivers and canals provide the traditional mode of transport for much of the country. Navigable waterways have a length of about 1,100 km. in the dry season and 1,600 km. in the wet season. About 3,830 km. of State-owned railways were open to traffic in 1974. The track is metre gauge. Main lines run from Bangkok to Aranya Pradet, linking up with the Cambodian state railway at this border town (160 miles E.); *via* Korat to Ubol (about 352 miles E.) and to Nongkhai (415 miles N.E.) the ferry terminal on the River Mekong opposite Vientiane, capital of Laos; to Chiengmai (411 miles N.); and to Haadyai (600 miles S.), whence lines go down the eastern and western sides of the Malay Peninsula, *via* Sungei Golok and Penang respectively, to Singapore.

Thailand has about 17,686 km. of highways and provincial roads, of which about 63 per cent. are paved.

Bangkok has an international airport of importance, and services connect it with Europe, America, India, Pakistan, Japan and Australasia, as well as other parts of S.E. Asia. Thai Airways International (THAI), was formed in 1960 in association with SAS to operate international routes. Domestic routes are operated by Thai Airways Corporation. A private airline, Air Siam, operates a limited number of services to Hong Kong, Japan, Singapore and the West Coast of the United States. There are some 22,000 km. of telegraph lines and parts of a countrywide micro-wave communications system are coming into operation. The harbour at Bangkok, which can take vessels up to 10,000

tons dead weight is congested, but six new berths are presently being constructed. A new deep-water port is proposed for the east side of the Gulf of Thailand.

FINANCE

	1973	1974
	millions of *Baht*	
Total revenue	26,900	38,900
Total expenditure	32,300	35,600

The exchange rate for the *Baht* was officially fixed at *Baht* 20·8= $1 U.S. (*See also* p. 84.)

TRADE

	1973	1974
	millions of *Baht*	
Total imports	42,184	64,051
Total exports	32,226	50,330

Trade with U.K.

	1973	1974
Imports from U.K.	£36,000,000	£57,000,000
Exports to U.K.	11,600,000	18,300,000

Thailand's main exports in 1974 (in millions of *Baht*) were: rice, 9,792, maize 6,047, rubber 5,036, tapioca 3,386, sugar 3,757, and tin 3,071. Other exports include jute, shrimps, cement, teak, tobacco and beans. Main imports for the same period were machinery 20,463 and lubricants 12,573, manufactured goods 12,061, chemicals 9,316 and raw materials 4,277.

CAPITAL, ΨBangkok (population 4,130,000); in the delta of the Chao Phraya. Other centres are Chiengmai, Nakorn Sawan, Korat and Haadyai, but no other town approaches Bangkok in size or importance.

FLAG.—Five horizontal bands, red, white, dark blue, white, red (the blue band twice the width of the others). NATIONAL DAY.—December 5 (King's Birthday).

BRITISH EMBASSY
(Bangkok)

Ambassador Extraordinary and Plenipotentiary, His Excellency Sir David Lee Cole, K.C.M.G., M.C. (1973).

Counsellors, H. A. J. Staples; J. P. Law.

Defence and Military Attaché, Col. I. T. C. Wilson, M.B.E., M.C.

Naval and Air Attaché, Cdr. P. J. F. Moore, R.N.

1st Secretaries, F. J. Sharland (*Head of Chancery*); A. V. Hastley, O.B.E.; P. B. Cormack; J. N. Howard (*Consul*); J. Greaves (*Commercial*); W. McAllister, M.B.E.; Miss C. Swan.

British Council Representative, I. Ll. Watts.

TOGO
(Republic of Togo)

President and Minister of Defence, Gen. Gnassingbé Eyadéma, *born* 1937, *assumed office as Head of State*, April 14, 1967.

Minister for Foreign Affairs, M. Houenou Hunlédé.

The Republic is situated in West Africa between 0°–2° W. and 6°–11° N., with a coastline only 35 miles long on the Gulf of Guinea, and extends northward inland for 350 miles. It is flanked on the west by Ghana, on the north by Upper Volta and in the east by Dahomey (*see* MAP, p. 953). It has an area of 21,000 sq. miles and a population (estimate, Dec. 1972) of 2,089,900, including people of several African races.

The first President of Togo, Sylvanus Olympio, assassinated on January 13, 1963, was succeeded by Nicolas Grunitzky, who was himself overthrown by an army *coup d'état* on January 13, 1967. On April 14, 1967, the Commander-in-Chief of the Togolese army, Lt. Colonel (later promoted General) Eyadéma named himself President.

Togo is a member of the *Conseil de l'Entente*, the *Organisation Commune Africaine et Malgache* (O.C.A.M.), and the Organization of African Unity (O.A.U.). The official language is French.

Finance.—The currency of Togo is the *Franc C.F.A.* (*Francs C.F.A.* 50= 1 *French Franc*) (*Francs C.F.A.* 450= £1, at June, 1975).

Production and Trade.—Although the economy of Togo remains largely agricultural exports of phosphates have superseded agricultural products as the main source of export earnings, being 75 per cent. of the total in the first 10 months of 1974 compared with 11 per cent. for cocoa and 6 per cent. for coffee. Other exports include palm kernels, copra and manioc. The production of phosphates entirely for export was begun by a Franco-American consortium in 1958 but the Togolese Government has increased its participation in recent years and took over completely in February 1974.

Trade with U.K.

	1973	1974
Imports from U.K.	£3,008,958	£3,333,933
Exports to U.K.	173,896	542,210

CAPITAL.—Ψ Lomé, population (1974), 214,200.

FLAG.—Five alternating green and yellow horizontal stripes; a quarter in red at top next staff bearing a white star. NATIONAL DAY.—April 27 (Independence Day).

BRITISH EMBASSY

Boulevard Circulaire, P.O. Box 892, Lomé
Ambassador Extraordinary and Plenipotentiary and Consul-General, His Excellency Alan James Brown (1973).
2nd Secretary, D. J. Peate (*Vice-Consul*).

TUNISIA
(Tunisian Republic)

President, Habib Bourguiba, *elected* July 25, 1957; *re-elected* 1959, 1964, 1969 and 1974.

CABINET

Prime Minister, Hédi Nouira.
Minister delegué in the Prime Minister's Office, Mohamed Sayah.
Justice, Slaheddine Baly.
Foreign Affairs, Habib Chatti.
Interior, Tahar Belkhodja.
National Defence, Hedi Khefacha.
Finance, Mohamed Fitouri.
National Economy, Abdelaziz Lasram.
Agriculture, Hassan Belkhodja.
National Education, Driss Guiga.
Public Health, Mohamed M'Zali.
Cultural Affairs, Mahmoud Messadi.
Transport and Communications, Abdallah Farhat.
Social Affairs, Mohamed Ennaceur.
Youth and Sport, Fouad M'Bazaa.
Equipment, Lassaad Ben Osman.
In addition there are 9 Secretaries of State.

TUNISIAN EMBASSY IN LONDON
29 Princes Gate, S.W.7
[01-584 8117]
Ambassador, His Excellency Brahim Turki (1974).
Counsellor, Mohamed Mahrezi.
1st Secretaries, Hamid Zaouche; Mohamed Trabelsi (*Consular*).
Attaché, Hassen Sediri; Belgacem Gabchoug.

Area and Population.—Tunisia lies between Algeria and Libya and extends southwards to the Sahara Desert, with a total area of 63,380 sq. miles and the estimated population at the end of 1972 was 5,409,000.

Government.—A French Protectorate from 1881 to 1956, Tunisia became an independent sovereign State with the signing on March 20, 1956, of an agreement whereby France recognized Tunisia's independence and right to conduct her own foreign policy and to form a Tunisian Army. The United Kingdom formally recognized Tunisia as an independent and sovereign state on May 10, 1956.

Following a first general election held on March 25, 1956, a Constituent Assembly met for the first time on April 8. On July 25, 1957, the Constituent Assembly deposed the Bey, abolished the monarchy and elected M. Bourguiba first President of the Republic. On June 1, 1959, the Constitution was promulgated and on December 7, 1959, the National Assembly held its first session. In March 1975 the National Assembly proclaimed M. Bourguiba as President for life.

Important changes in the system of local government were decreed on June 16, 1956. The country was divided into 13 regions (*gouvernorats*) each administered by a Governor. In 1972, the number of regions was increased to 14 by the division of the Tunis region into two regions. By 1974, the number increased to eighteen.

Production, Trade, etc.—The valleys of the northern region support large flocks and herds, and contain rich agricultural areas, in which wheat, barley, and oats are grown. The vine and olive are extensively cultivated.

The chief exports are crude oil, olive oil, phosphates and wine. The chief imports are machinery, food-stuffs, iron and steel, textiles and crude petroleum, etc. Some oil has been discovered in Tunisia and production is running at about 4,000,000 tons a year. In 1974 Tunisia's total imports were equal in value to *Dinars* 488,658,000 and total exports *Dinars* 397,695,000. France remains Tunisia's main trading partner, supplying 31 per cent. of the country's imports and purchasing 22 per cent. of Tunisia's exports.

Trade with U.K.

	1973	1974
Imports from U.K.	£7,554,000	£11,465,000
Exports to U.K.	3,563,000	6,192,000

Currency.—The Tunisian *dinar* was adopted on Nov. 3, 1958. At the same time a new Central Bank of Tunisia became responsible for the issue of notes. Although Tunisia remains in the Franc Zone the *dinar* is not tied to the French *franc*. The current rate of exchange is *dinars* 0·880= £1 (July, 1975).

So far as trade is concerned Tunisia was effectively part of metropolitan France until September, 1959, when she abrogated the Customs Union with the latter and a new trade and payments agreement was negotiated. This reduced or eliminated the tariff advantages enjoyed by certain French goods. Under commercial agreements concluded in November, 1962, and February, 1964, import quotas were established for certain French goods. In June, 1964, however, following Tunisian measures regarding the take-over of foreign-owned lands in Tunisia, France gave notice that she would not renew the 1959 Trade Agreement, due to expire on Sept. 30, 1964. In May 1966, France opened import quotas for a wide range of Tunisian goods (but excluding wine). Within these quota limits these goods can be admitted into France customs-free. In 1966 a policy of severe import restriction was adopted in order to reduce the country's chronic imbalance of trade. An ambitious programme of co-operative schemes for most areas of the economy was reserved in

September, 1969, and gave way to a more orthodox economic policy. Tunisia became an associate member of EEC early in 1969.

CAPITAL, Ψ Tunis, connected by canal with La Goulette on the coast, has a population of 1,127,000. The ruins of ancient Carthage lie a few miles from the city. Other towns of importance are: Ψ Sfax (482,000); Ψ Bizerta (316,000); Ψ Sousse (586,000); Kairouan (302,000).

FLAG.—Red crescent and star in a white orb, all on a red ground. NATIONAL DAY.—June 1.

BRITISH EMBASSY
Place de la Victoire, Tunis

Ambassador Extraordinary and Plenipotentiary and Consul-General, His Excellency John Ewart Marnham, C.M.G., M.C., T.D. (1973) £12,000
1st Secretary, R. Goring-Morris, O.B.E. (*Head of Chancery*).
2nd Secretary (Consular), G. F. Noble.
Commercial Attaché, J. Cummins.

British Council Representative, J. E. Lankester. There is a British Council Library in *Tunis*.

TURKEY

President of the Republic, Fahri Korutürk, *born* 1903; *elected President* April 6, 1973.

Prime Minister, Süleyman Demirel (*JP*).
Deputy Prime Ministers, Prof. Necmettin Erbakan (*NSP*); Prof. Turhan Feyzioglu (*RRP*); Col. Alpaslan Türkes (*NAP*).
Justice, Ismail Müftüoglü (*NSP*).
Defence, Sen. Ferit Melen (*RRP*).
Interior, Oguzhan Asiltürk (*NSP*).
Foreign Affairs, Sen. Ihsan Sabri Caglayangil (*JP*).
Finance, Yilmaz Ergenekon (*JP*).
Education, Ali Naili Erdem (*JP*).
Public Works, Fehim Adak (*NSP*).
Trade, Halil Başol (*JP*).
Health, Dr. Kemal Demir (*RRP*).
Customs and Monopolies, Orhan Öztrak (*RRP*).
Food, Agriculture and Animal Breeding, Prof. Korkut Özal (*NSP*).
Communications, Nahit Menteşe (*JP*).
Labour, Ahmet Tevfik Paksu (*NSP*).
Energy, Selähattin Kiliç (*JP*).
Tourism, Sen. Lütfü Tokoglu (*JP*).
Housing, Nurettin Ok (*JP*).

Villages, Sen. Vefa Poyraz (*JP*).
Forestry, Sen. Turan Kapanli (*JP*).
Youth and Sports, Ali Sevki Erek (*JP*).
Culture, Rifki Danişman (*JP*).
Social Security, Ahmet Mahir Ablum (*JP*).
Industry, Abdülkerim Doğru (*NSP*).
Ministers of State, Soyfi Özturk (*JP*); Hasan Aksay (*NSP*); Mustafa Kemal Erkovan (*NAP*); Giyasettin Karaca (*JP*).

(*JP*=Justice Party; *NSP*=National Salvation Party; *RRP*=Republican Reliance Party; *NAP*= Nationalist Action Party).

TURKISH EMBASSY IN LONDON
Chancery: 43 Belgrave Square, S.W.1
[01–235 5252]

Ambassador Extraordinary and Plenipotentiary, His Excellency Turgut Menemencioğlu (1972).

Area and Population.—Turks are to be found scattered throughout a wide belt extending from China through the Soviet Union, Afghanistan and Iran to the present day Turkish State.

Turkey itself extends from Edirne (Adrianople) to Transcaucasia and Iran, and from the Black Sea to the Mediterranean, Syria and Iraq. Total population at the Census of October, 1970 was estimated at 35,666,549.

Turkey in Europe consists of Eastern Thrace, including the cities of Istanbul and Edirne, and is separated from Asia by the Bosphorus at Istanbul and by the *Dardanelles*—about 40 miles in length with a width varying from 1 to 4 miles—the political neighbours being Greece and Bulgaria on the west. Population (Census, 1970), 3,165,629.

Turkey in Asia comprises the whole of Asia Minor or *Anatolia* (" Land of the Rising Sun " or Orient), and extends from the Aegean Sea to the western boundaries of Georgia, Soviet Armenia and Iran, and from the Black Sea to the Mediterranean and the northern boundaries of Syria and Iraq. Population (Census, 1970), 32,500,920.

Government.—On October 29, 1923, the National Assembly declared Turkey a Republic and elected Gazi Mustafa Kemal (later known as Kemal Ataurk) President. Following the introduction of a multi-party régime in 1945, the Democrat Party was returned to power in 1950 and re-elected in 1954 and 1957. On May 27, 1960, the D.P. Government was overthrown by the Turkish Armed

Forces which ruled through the Committee of National Union, a body of military officers. The committee ruled from January to November, 1961, in conjunction with a civilian House of Representatives, the two bodies together forming the Constituent Assembly.

At elections held in October, 1969, the Justice Party obtained 256 seats, the People's Republican Party 143 and the Reliance Party 15. Mr. Demirel's Justice Party Government (in office since Oct., 1965) resigned on March 12, 1971, following a memorandum to the President by the Chiefs of Staff of the Armed Forces. Three all-party governments, two under Prof. Erim and the third under Senator Ferit Melen were in office between March 26, 1971 and April 1973. After the resignation of the latter Senator Naim Talu formed a further government drawn mostly from the Justice and Republican Reliance Parties. Elections were held in October 1973 and PRP obtained 185 seats, JP 149 seats, DP 45 seats and NSP 48 seats. After several unsuccessful attempts to form a government, a coalition under PRP party leader Mr. Bülent Ecevit with NSP as minority partner was formed on January 25, 1974.

However, this coalition collapsed in September, but continued to rule Turkey on a caretaker basis until a new administration was formed by Senator Prof. Sadi Irmak in November. This largely technocratic government was denied a vote of confidence by Parliament, but continued in office until March 31, 1975, when a right-wing coalition of the Justice, National Salvation, Republican Reliance and Nationalist Action Parties was formed, under the Premiership of Süleyman Demirel, Chairman of the Justice Party.

Turkey is divided for administrative purposes into 67 *vilayet* with subdivisions into *kaza* and *nahiye*. Each *vilayet* has a governor (*vali*) and elective council.

Religion and Education.—98·99 per cent. of the population are Moslems. The main religious minorities, which are concentrated in Istanbul and on the Syrian frontier, are: Orthodox, 107,000; Armenian Apostolic, 71,000; Catholic, 25,000; Protestant, 17,000; others, 10,000 (Total Christians, 230,000); Jewish, 44,000. On April 10, 1928, the Grand National Assembly passed a law in virtue of which Islam ceased to be the State religion of the Republic. Education is compulsory, free, and secular. There are elementary, secondary and vocational schools.

In 1971–72 there were 38,952 primary schools, with 5,032,949 pupils. There are two universities at Istanbul (one being a Technical University), three in Ankara, one each at Izmir, Erzurum and Trabzon. There is also a Faculty of Agriculture at Adana. The expenditure allocated to education in the 3rd Five Year Plan (1973–77) is TL14,000,000,000, compared with TL7,002,000,000 actually spent from 1968–72, but past experience has shown that targets in this field are not always met.

Language and Literature.—Until 1926, Turkish was written in Arabic script, but in that year the Roman alphabet was substituted for use in official correspondence and in 1928 for universal use, with Arabic numerals as used throughout Europe. Mainly as a consequence of this change the number of Turks who can read and write is rising steadily, from about 10 per cent. in 1927 to nearly 80 per cent. by 1970. Ancient Turkish literature aped the Arabic manner, but the revolution of 1908 was followed by a popular reaction against the writings of the past (which appealed only to a small class) and led to the introduction of a native literature free from foreign influences and adapted to the understanding of the people. The vehicle first

employed was the newspaper, printed in the neo-Latin alphabet, with supplements for prose and dramatic fiction, poetry and literary criticism. The leading Turkish newspapers are centred in Ankara and Istanbul, although most provincial towns have their own daily papers. There are foreign language papers in French, Greek, Armenian and English and numerous magazines and weeklies on various subjects, but few trade commercial publications.

Agricultural Production.—In 1973 agricultural production declined by 9 per cent., the first substantial reduction for ten years and for the first time was exceeded in value by industrial output. Agricultural production still accounted for 24·4 per cent. of the gross national product while exports of agricultural commodities represented 62 per cent. of the total exports. Over 9,000,000, about 70 per cent. of the working population, are in the rural sector, but agriculture is still primitive in many areas and agricultural productivity is low. Preliminary production figures for the principal crops in 1973 were ('000 tons): Cereals, 13,970; sugar beet, 5,095; cotton, 498; tobacco, 140; olives 487; filberts (unshelled), 240; tea (fresh leaves), 220; sultanas, 800. With the important exception of wheat, which is mostly grown on the arid Central Anatolian Plateau, most of the crops are grown on the fertile littoral. Tobacco, sultana and fig cultivation is centred around Izmir, where substantial quantities of cotton are also grown. The main cotton area is in the Çukurova Plain around Adana. In 1970 it was estimated that there were 73,000,000 head of livestock, including sheep, 36,471,000; goats, 19,483,000; and cattle, 13,873,000. The forests which lie between the littoral plain and the Anatolian Plateau, contain beech, pine, oak, elm, chestnut, lime, plane, alder, box, poplar and maple. During recent years the Government has attempted, so far not altogether successfully, to combat the depredations of peasant and goat which threaten to destroy the existing forests within the next 25 years.

Industry.—After agriculture, Turkey's second most important industry is based on her considerable mineral wealth which is, however, as yet comparatively unexploited. The most important developments are in coal, of which over 15,000,000 metric tons are produced annually (of which 7,000,000 metric tons are lignite) for domestic needs. The main export mineral is chromite. Production of iron ore in 1972 was 2,073,708 tons; chrome ore, 649,273 tons; manganese, 20,000 tons; sulphur, 55,000 tons; blister copper, 17.038 tons and boracite, 429,432 tons. The research and exploitation of the principal mineral deposits are mainly in the hands of the Mineral Research and Exploration Institute of Turkey and the State-owned Etibank respectively. The latter controls directly, on behalf of the Government, all the copper, sulphur and pyrite output of Turkey, as well as much of the colemenite and chrome production. Since State-sponsored industrialization began in 1935, industry has played an increasing part in the Turkish economy. Here, also, as in the case of minerals, much of the industry of the country is controlled by the Government.

The progress made in the manufacture of sugar, cotton, woollen and silk textiles, and cement, has been such that the bulk of the country's requirements can now be produced locally, while other industries contributing substantially to local needs include vehicle assembly, paper, glass and glassware, iron and steel, leather and leather goods, sulphur refining, canning and rubber goods, soaps and cosmetics, pharmaceutical products, prepared foodstuffs and a host of minor industries. Legislation was passed in 1954 to encourage the investment of foreign capital in Turkey and to promote the exploitation of Turkey's petroleum resources by foreign countries. Local production of crude petroleum in 1972 totalled 3,388 177 tons.

General Economic Factors.—The improvement in the balance of payments observed in 1971 and 1972 continued in 1973. Both exports and remittances from Turkish workers abroad rose to unforeseen levels. The latter increased remarkably to U.S. $1·2 billion, almost equal to the whole of visible exports. Reserves rose to $2 billion. These favourable trends began to be offset at the end of 1973 by the oil crisis. There is also the difficulty of increasing exports which are mainly agricultural products, and minor raw materials for which world markets are rather weak. At the same time, Turkey's population is growing at an estimated rate of about 2·6 per cent. per annum. Since the Second World War the United States Government has given Turkey financial aid totalling over 5 billion dollars, half of which has been for military and half for economic purposes. The other main official sources of foreign aid have been the O.E.C.D., and more recently the I.B.R.D., while the I.M.F. has made medium term loans for balance of payment support. The United Kingdom has pledged nearly £66,000,000 of aid to Turkey since 1963.

The third of Turkey's three Five Year Development Plans, for the years 1973-77, began in January 1973. The basic economic objective of the third plan is to achieve an average growth rate of 7·9 per cent. per annum in the gross national product.

COMMUNICATIONS

Railways.—The complete network became the property of the State Railways Administration in 1948. The total length of lines in operation at the end of 1972 was 8,132 kilometres. In 1971, the railways carried 110,712.000 passengers and 15,264,000 metric tons of freight.

Roads.—At the end of 1970 there were 35.016 km. of national roads (17,214 of which were hard-surfaced). Total all-weather roads, both national and provincial, amounted to 48,125 km. The number of motor vehicles in use at the end of 1970 was 147,014 passenger cars, 126,827 trucks, 37,481 buses and 105,865 tractors.

Posts.—In mid-1972 the number of telephone subscribers in Turkey was over 450,000. There is a considerable shortage of telephone lines in some of Turkey's major cities.

Shipping.—At the end of 1970, the Turkish Merchant Navy consisted of 2,275 dry cargo ships of 18 tons gross and over totalling 530,498 tons, 163 passenger ships of a gross tonnage of 111,790 tons and 82 tankers with a gross tonnage of 145,353 tons.

Civil Aviation.—The State airlines (T.H.Y.) operate all internal services and have services to London, Paris, Athens, Beirut, Brussels, Amsterdam, Zürich, Frankfurt, Munich, Rome, Milan, Geneva, Copenhagen, Nicosia, Tel Aviv and Vienna. Most of the leading foreign airlines, including British Airways, operate services to Istanbul and some also to Ankara. The T.H.Y. fleet is composed of D.C.10's, D.C.9's, Fokker Friendships, Fokker Fellowships and Boeing 707's.

FINANCE

(Financial year, March 1 to February 28)

	1974-5	1975-76
	TL'000,000	
Estimated Expenditure	83,092	108,442
Estimated Revenue	77,092	99,442

Currency.—The Turkish *Lira* (*TL*) is divided into 100 *Kurus*. The official rate of exchange is TL33 = £1 (Nov. 1974) and TL14 = U.S.$1. (*See also* p. 84.)

TRADE

	1973	1974 (prov.)
Total imports....	$2,099,000,000	$3,777,000,000
Total exports.....	1,318,000,000	1,532,000,000

All imports are subject to licence and the issue of licences is limited to goods considered necessary for the country's economy. Lists of permitted imports are published annually at the beginning of January. The main imports are machinery, crude oil and petroleum products, iron and steel, vehicles, medicines and dyes, fabrics and yarns. The principal exports are cotton, tobacco, fruits, nuts, minerals, livestock and textiles.

Trade with U.K.

	1973	1974
Imports from U.K..	£81,770,000	£104,600,000
Exports to U.K.....	33,872,000	35,200,000

CAPITAL OF TURKEY, ANKARA (Angora), an inland town of Asia Minor, about 275 miles E.S.E. of Istanbul, with a population (Census, Oct. 1970) of 1,440,779. Ankara (or Ancyra) was the capital of the Roman Province of *Galatia Prima*, and a marble temple (now in ruins), dedicated to Augustus, contains the *Monumentum* (*Marmor*) *Ancyranum*, inscribed with a record of the reign of Augustus Cæsar. A new city was laid out on modern lines, with parks, statues and avenues. ΨISTANBUL (2,312,751), the former capital, was the Roman city of Byzantium. It was selected by Constantine the Great as the capital of the Roman Empire about A.D. 328 and renamed Constantinople. Istanbul contains the celebrated church of St. Sophia, which, after becoming a mosque, was made a museum in 1934; it also contains Topkapi, former Palace of the Ottoman Sultans, which is also a museum. Other cities are ΨIzmir (753,443); Adana (529,926); Bursa (415,348); Gaziantep (329,087); and Eskişehir (246 071).

FLAG.—Red, with white crescent and star. NATIONAL DAY.—October 29 (Republic Day).

BRITISH EMBASSY
(Ankara)

Ambassador Extraordinary and Plenipotentiary, His Excellency Sir Horace Phillips, K.C.M.G. (1973) £11,000

Counsellors, A. B. Ball, O.B.E. (*Commercial*); D. N. Lane.

1st Secretaries, W. H. Fullerton; L. C. R. Seeley; R. M. James; M. A. Goodfellow; J. R. Leeland; J. Waller; A. H. G. Amy.

2nd Secretaries, H. E. P. Lewis; H. Warren-Gash.

Consul, J. Hanratty.

Defence and Military Attaché, Brig. J. P. Sellers, D.F.C.

Naval Attaché, Cdr. M. T. H. Styles, R.N.

Air Attaché, Wing-Cdr. K. J. Ryall, D.F.C.

BRITISH CONSULAR OFFICES
There are British Consular Offices at *Istanbul Izmir* and *Iskenderun.*

BRITISH COUNCIL.—27 Adakale Sokak, Yenisehir, Ankara, *Representative*, J. Goatly, O.B.E.—There are also a centre and library at *Istanbul* and a library at *Ankara*.

BRITISH CHAMBER OF COMMERCE OF TURKEY INC., Mesrutiyet Caddessi No. 34, Tepebasi Beyoğlu, Istanbul (Postal Address, P.O. Box 190 Karaköy, Istanbul). *Chairman*, A. M. Mansur.

UNITED ARAB REPUBLIC. *See* EGYPT.

UNITED ARAB EMIRATES

President, Shaikh Zaid bin Sultan Al Nahayyan (Abu Dhabi).

Vice-President, Shaikh Rashid bin Sa'id Al Maktum (Dubai).
Prime Minister, Shaikh Maktum bin Rashid Al Maktum (Dubai).
Minister of Finance, Economy and Industry, Shaikh Hamdan bin Rashid Al Maktum (Dubai).
Minister of Interior, Shaikh Mubarak bin Mohammad Al Nahayyan (Abu Dhabi).
Minister of Defence, Shaikh Muhammed bin Rashid Al Maktum (Dubai).
Minister of Foreign Affairs, Sayed Ahmed Khalifa Al Suwaidi (Abu Dhabi).

EMBASSY IN LONDON
30 Prince's Gate, S.W.7
[01–581 1281]
Ambassador Extraordinary and Plenipotentiary, His Excellency Sayed Mohamed Mahdi Al-Tajir.

The United Arab Emirates (formerly the Trucial States) is composed of seven Emirates (Abu Dhabi, Ajman, Dubai, Fujairah, Ras al Khaimah, Sharjah and Umm al Qaiwain) which came together as an independent state on December 2, 1971, when they ended their special treaty relationships with the British Government (Ras al Khaimah joined late on February 10, 1972).

The British Government, by virtue of a treaty made in 1892, had been responsible for the external affairs of the states through the British Political Resident in the Persian Gulf and the British Political Agents in the Trucial States, but on independence the Union Government assumed responsibility for all the Union's internal and external affairs. Six of the states lie on the coast of the Gulf between the Musandam peninsula in the East and the Qatar peninsula in the West and one, Fujairah, lies on the Gulf of Oman.

Area and Population
The approximate area of the U.A.E. is 32,000 square miles and the population (estimated 1972) is about 300,000. Security in the area is maintained by the Union Defence Force (formerly the Trucial Oman Scouts), the Force having its headquarters at Sharjah, and in Abu Dhabi by the Abu Dhabi Defence Force. Dubai, Sharjah and Ras al Khaimah also have their own local defence forces. There are police forces in all seven Emirates.

Revenue is chiefly derived from oil and from customs dues on imports. Other formerly important sources of revenue, such as export of dried fish and pearling, are now almost negligible.

TRADE WITH U.K.

	1973	1974
Imports from U.K....	£49,400,000	£103,800,000
Exports to U.K......	69,200,000	220,300,000

Abu Dhabi is the largest Emirate of the U.A.E. in area, stretching from Khor El Odaid in the west to the borders with Dubai in the region of Jebel Ali. It includes six villages of the Buraimi oasis and a number of settlements in the series of oases known as the Liwa.

Several oil companies are operating in Abu Dhabi territory; the two most important are Abu Dhabi Petroleum Co. Ltd. on land and Abu Dhabi Marine Areas Ltd. in the Abu Dhabi offshore concession area. Oil has been discovered off Das Island, where Abu Dhabi Marine Areas had its headquarters and where production started in 1962. Production from the on-shore Murban oilfield commenced in December 1963. Abu Dhabi oil revenues are estimated at about £1,600 million for 1974. With all this new wealth Abu Dhabi is a rapidly expanding and developing town. There are airfields at Abu Dhabi and at Das Island and an airstrip at Buraimi. The population of the Emirate is approximately 100,000.

Dubai is the next largest Emirate in the U.A.E. with a population estimated at about 70,000. It is the main port for the import of goods into the U.A.E. and the interior of Oman and there is also a lively entrepôt trade. The value of imports in the year 1974 was £560,000,000 and in 1973 £240,000,000. Oil was discovered offshore in 1966 and production began in September 1969. Dubai Marine Areas Ltd. have relinquished their concession to the Government but remain responsible as contractors for production and marketing. The production facilities are entirely offshore and include three giant underwater storage tanks. Development has proceeded fast. A fifteen-berth new deep water harbour was completed by October, 1972, and an international airport terminal opened in May, 1971. A £94,000,000 supertanker dry dock is now under construction. Telegraphic and telex communications are good and managed by Cable and Wireless Ltd. Ten international airlines fly regular scheduled services into Dubai and two have regular freight services. Eighteen banks are now operating in Dubai.

Sharjah, with a present population of about 35,000, has declined from its position of 50 years ago as principal town in the area. However, Sharjah became the third oil producing Emirate in the Union in the Summer of 1974 following the discovery of oil in commercial quantities in its offshore areas. On Sharjah's west coast the offshore oil concession is held by Buttes Gas and Oil Company and the on-shore oil concession by Shell Hydrocarbons, while on Sharjah's east coast both the onshore and offshore concessions are held by Shell Minerals. The town is linked to Dubai, Ras al Khaimah and the oasis of Daid by metalled roads and the number of new businesses is increasing rapidly. The harbour has a new deep water jetty and a £1 million improvement scheme to deepen the creek and the harbour is almost complete. A small international air terminal is served by Gulf Aviation and Syrian Arab Airlines.

Ras al Khaimah has a population of about 30,000 of whom about half live in the town. It is an ancient sea port near which some remains of archæological interest have been found. Dates, vegetables, fruit and tobacco are grown. The seat of the government has now moved from its exposed position on the shore to the inland side of the creek. The offshore oil concession is held by Union Oil and the onshore concession by Shell Hydrocarbons, but so far no oil in marketable quantities has been found.

Fujairah has a population of about 10,000 and its inhabitants are spread between the inland hills and the town of Fujairah which lies on the comparatively fertile plain of the Gulf of Oman coast. The onshore and offshore oil concessions are held by Shell Minerals.

Ajman and Umm al Qaiwain are the smallest Emirates, having a population of only about 5,000 each. Ajman has inland enclaves at Manama and Masfut. Occidental of Ajman Incorporated hold both the onshore and offshore oil concessions. In Umm al Qaiwain the offshore concession is held by Occidental of Umm al Qaiwain Incorporated and the onshore by Shell Hydrocarbons.

BRITISH EMBASSY
(Abu Dhabi)
Ambassador Extraordinary and Plenipotentiary, His Excellency Daniel John McCarthy, C.M.G. (1973).
British Council Representative, M. A. Evans, P.O. Box 1636, Dublai.

UPPER VOLTA
(République de Haute Volta)
President, Gen. Sangoulé Lamizana, *assumed power* in 1966.
Minister of Foreign Affairs, Maj. Saye Zerbo.

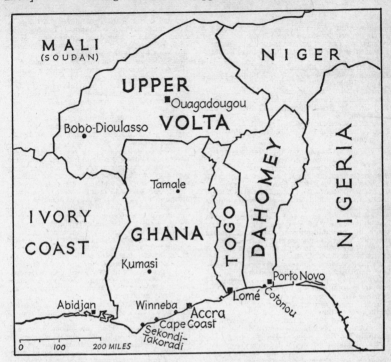

Upper Volta is an inland savannah state in West Africa, situated between 9° and 15°N and 2°E and 5°W with an area of about 100,000 square miles and a population estimated in 1972 at 5,514,000. It has common boundaries with Mali on the west, Niger and Dahomey on the east and Togo, Ghana and the Ivory Coast on the south. The largest tribe is the Mossi whose king, the Moro Naba, still wields a certain moral influence.

Upper Volta was annexed by France in 1896 and between 1932 and 1947 was administered as part of the Colony of the Ivory Coast. It decided on December 11, 1958, to remain an autonomous republic within the French Community; full independence outside the Community was proclaimed on August 5, 1960. Special agreements with France, covering financial and cultural matters, technical assistance, etc., were signed in Paris on April 24, 1961. Upper Volta is a member of the *Conseil de l'Entente, OCAM, OAU* and *C.E.A.O.* (*see* Ivory Coast). The official language is French. The 1960 constitution provided for a presidential form of government with a single chamber National Assembly, but in January, 1966, the Army assumed power after popular demonstrations in Ouagadougou against the *régime* of the former President Yaméogo. A new constitution allowing for a partial return to civilian rule but with the Army still in effective control was adopted by a referendum held on June 14, 1970. Following internal political manoeuvering the President suspended the constitution on Feb. 8, 1974 and dissolved the National Assembly. A Government of National Renewal was formed, with a majority of military members.

Finance and Trade.—The currency of the Republic is the *Franc CFA* (*Francs CFA* 50 = 1 *French Franc*). The 1974 Budget totalled *Francs CFA* 12,490,000,000.

The principal industry is the rearing of cattle and sheep and the chief exports are livestock, groundnuts, shea-nuts and cotton. Small deposits of gold, manganese, copper, bauxite and graphite have been found. Value of trade in 1972 amounted to: Imports, *francs CFA* 15,311,000,000; Exports, *francs CFA* 5,141,000,000. Imports from U.K.— £417,000 (1974); Exports to U.K. — £356,000 (1974).

CAPITAL.—Ouagadougou (125,000). Other principal town: Bobo-Dioulasso (80,000).

FLAG.—Three horizontal stripes, black over white over red.

NATIONAL DAY.—December 11.

BRITISH REPRESENTATION
Ambassador Extraordinary and Plenipotentiary, His Excellency Paul Cecil Henry Holmer, C.M.G. (*resident in Abidjan*).

URUGUAY
(República Oriental del Uruguay)
President, Juan María Bordaberry, *born* 1928 (1972).

CABINET
(July 13, 1974)

Minister of Interior, General Hugo Linares Brun.
Foreign Affairs, Dr. Juan Carlos Blanco.
Economy and Finance, Sr. Alejandro Vegh Villegas.
Transport and Public Works, Ing. Eduardo Crispo Ayala.
Public Health, Justo Alonso.
Labour and Social Security, Dr. José Enrique Etcheverry Stirling.
Agriculture and Fishing, Hector Albuquerque.
Education and Culture, Dr. Daniel Darracq.
Housing and Social Development, Sr. Federico Soneira.
National Defence, Dr. Walter Ravenna.
Director of Planning and Budget, Sr. Juan José Anichini.

URUGUAYAN EMBASSY AND CONSULATE
48 Lennox Gardens, S.W.1
[01–589 8835]

Ambassador Extraordinary and Plenipotentiary (vacant).
1st Secretary, Senor Alfredo Cazes.

Area and Population.—The smallest Republic in South America, on the east coast of the Rio de la Plata situated in lat. 30°-35°S. and long. 53° 25′-57° 42′ W., with an area of 72,172 square miles, and a population of 2,763,964, almost entirely white and predominantly of Spanish and Italian descent. Many Uruguayans are Roman Catholics. There is complete freedom of religion and no church is established by the State.

Physical Features.—The country consists mainly (and particularly in the south and west) of undulating grassy plains. The principal chains of hills are the Cuchilla del Haedo, which cross the Brazilian boundary and extend southwards to the Cuchilla Grande of the south and east. In no case do the peaks exceed 2,000 feet.

The principal river is the *Rio Negro* (with its tributary the Yi), flowing from north-east to south-west into the *Rio Uruguay*. The boundary river *Uruguay* is navigable from its estuary to Salto, about 200 miles north, and the Negro is also navigable for a considerable distance. Smaller rivers are the Cuareim, Yaguaron, Santa Lucia, Queguay and the Cebollati. On the south-east coast are several lagoons, and the north-east boundary crosses the (Brazilian) Lake Merin.

The climate is reasonably healthy. The summer is warm, but the heat is often tempered by the breezes of the Atlantic. The winter is, on the whole, mild, but cold spells characterized by winds from the South Polar regions are experienced in June, July and August. Rainfall is regular throughout the year, but there are occasional droughts.

Government.—Uruguay—or the *Banda Oriental*, as this territory lying on the eastern bank of the Uruguay River was then called—resisted all attempted invasions of the Portuguese and Spaniards until the beginning of the 17th century, and 100 years later the Portuguese settlements were captured by the Spaniards. From 1726 to 1814 the country formed part of Spanish South America and underwent many vicissitudes during the Wars of Independence. In 1814 the armies of the Argentine Confederation captured the capital and annexed the province, and it was afterwards annexed by Portugal and became a province of Brazil. In 1825, the country threw off the Brazilian yoke. This action led to war between Argentina and Brazil which was settled by the mediation of the United Kingdom, Uruguay being declared an independent state in 1828. In 1830 a Republic was inaugurated.

Elections were held on Nov. 28, 1971, which gave the Colorado Party a narrow majority.

According to the Constitution the President appoints a council of 11 ministers and the Vice-President presides over Congress. The legislature consists of a Chamber of 99 deputies and a Senate of 30 members (plus the Vice-President), elected for five years by a system of proportional representation. Voting is obligatory and extends to all citizens of good repute and certain long standing residents who are not citizens, from the age of 18. However, since February, 1973 the country has been governed by presidential rule with military support.

The Republic is divided into 19 Departments each with a chief of police and a Departmental Council. The most important cities of the interior are Salto and Paysandu, both situated on the River Uruguay, which forms the main line of division from Argentina.

Production and Industry.—Wheat, barley, maize, linseed, sunflower seed and rice are cultivated. The wealth of the country is obtained from its pasturage, which supports large herds of cattle and sheep, the wool of which is of excellent quality. The 1970 livestock census showed figures of 8,563,747 cattle, 19,892,758 sheep, 420,972 horses, 418,709 hogs. It was estimated that in 1973 the number of cattle rose to 11,000,000. In addition to the meat packing industry, other foodstuffs, wine, beer and textiles are of importance.

The development of local industry continues and during and since the Second World War, in addition to the greatly augmented textile industry, marked expansion in local production is notable in respect of tyres, sheet-glass, three-ply wood, cement, leather-curing, beet-sugar, plastics, household consumer goods, edible oils and the refining of petroleum and petroleum products.

Mineral Deposits.—Iron is now being quarried; estimated yearly production is 1,000,000 tons of first quality pellets.

Communications.—There are about 7,820 km. of national highways, and about 12,083 km. of telegraph, with 48,375 miles of telephones.

There are about 2,398 km. of standard gauge railway in use in Uruguay. A State Autonomous Entity was formed to administer the railway systems purchased by the Government from four British companies in 1948.

An airline, PLUNA, which is owned by the State, runs a limited daily service to southern Brazil, Paraguay and Argentina. The principal capitals of the interior and a limited freight service are connected to Montevideo by TAMO, another State owned airline, using principally military aircraft and personnel. International passenger and freight services are maintained by American, South American and European airlines. The air-port of Carrasco lies 12 miles outside Montevideo.

Education and Social Services.—Uruguay is one of the most advanced of the South American states, with old-age pensions, maternity and child welfare centres, accident insurance, etc. Primary education is compulsory and free, and technical and trade schools and evening courses for adult education are state controlled. There are about 322,053 pupils in the 2,362 state schools. In 1969 there were 140,700 pupils in secondary schools. The University at Montevideo (founded in 1849) had, in 1969, 18,000 students enrolled in its ten faculties.

Language and Literature.—Spanish is the language of the Republic. Modern literature has provided some authors with international reputations and the literature of Spain is accessible in all public libraries. Four daily newspapers are published in Montevideo with an estimated total circulation of 200,000. Most of them are distributed throughout the country.

Finance.—No recent figures of revenue and expenditure are available. The national debt at Dec. 31, 1972 amounted to $Ur. 61,597,140,427.

Currency.—The monetary unit is the *peso*. In May, 1963, the gold content of the *peso* was fixed at 0·059245 grammes of pure gold. After several devaluations the commercial exchange rate stood at June 2, 1975 at Ur.$2·525 = $U.S.1. Sterling exchange stood at June 2, 1975 at $Ur.5·870 = £1. The quotations of the U.S. dollar and pound sterling in the financial (fluctuating) market as at the same date were 1·360 and 3·280 Uruguayan *pesos* respectively. Sterling exchange, *see p.* 84.

TRADE

	1973	1974
Total exports	$U.S.319,190,000	$U.S.381,182,000
Total imports	294,976,000	481,259,000

Trade with U.K.

	1973	1974
Imports from U.K....	£4,562,000	£6,694,000
Exports to U.K.....	10,150,000	9,211,000

† Unadjusted figures.

The major exports are meat and by-products, wool and by-products, hides and bristle and agricultural products. The principal imports are raw materials, construction materials, oils and lubricants, automotive vehicles, kits and machinery.

The principal export item to the U.K. is wool and the main imports are automotive vehicles, kits, machinery, raw materials and metals.

CAPITAL, Ψ Montevideo. Population (1975 census 1,229,748). Other centres (with 1967 estimates) are Ψ Salto (60,000) Ψ Paysandu (60,000), Ψ Mercedes (34,000), Minas (34,000), Melo (30,000), and Rivera (40,000).

FLAG.—Four blue and five white horizontal stripes surcharged with sun on a white ground in the top corner, next flagstaff. NATIONAL DAY.—August 25 (Declaration of Independence, 1825).

Time of transit from London to Montevideo, by air, 20–22 hours.

BRITISH EMBASSY
Montevideo

Ambassador Extraordinary and Plenipotentiary, His Excellency Peter Richard Oliver, C.M.G. (1972).
2nd Secretary, R. Backhouse.
Naval Attaché, Capt. J. Thomas, R.N. (*resident at Buenos Aires*).
Defence and Air Attaché, Gp. Capt. R. W. Millo (*resident at Buenos Aires*).

BRITISH CONSULAR OFFICES
There is a British Consular Office at *Montevideo*.

ANGLO-URUGUAYAN CULTURAL INSTITUTE, San José 1426, Montevideo.
There are branch Institutes at Salto, Paysandú, Fray Bentos, Rivera, Las Piedras, Melo, Mercedes, Trinidad and Treinta y Tres.
BRITISH–URUGUAYAN CHAMBER OF COMMERCE, Avenida Agraciada 1641, Piso 2°, *Montevideo*.

U.S.S.R.
**Soyuz Sovetskikh Sotsialisticheskikh Respublik=
Union of Soviet Socialist Republics**
THE COMMUNIST PARTY OF THE SOVIET
UNION
(K.P.S.S.=Kommunisticheskaya Partiya
Sovetskogo Soyuza)
Constitutionally, the highest executive organ of the C.P.S.U. is its *Central Committee*, as elected by the *Party Congress*. The present Central Committee (elected at the XXIVth Party Congress in April, 1971) consists of 241 members; there are also 155 " candidates for membership " with a consultative

voice and 81 members of the *Central Auditing Commission*. The real power in the Party is vested, however, in the *Politbureau*, the *Secretariat* and the permanent Departments of the Central Committee:

Politbureau, Yu. V. Andropov; L. I. Brezhnev; A. A. Grechko; V. V. Grishin; A. A. Gromyko; A. P. Kirilenko; A. N. Kosygin; F. D. Kulakov; D. A. Kunayev; K. T. Mazurov; A. Ya Pel'she; N. V. Podgorny; D. S. Polyansky; V. V. Shcherbitsky; M. A. Suslov: (*full members*); P. N. Demichev; P. M. Masherov; B. N. Ponomarev; Sh. R. Rashidov; G. V. Romanov; M. S. Solomentsev; D. F. Ustinov (*candidates for membership*).

Secretariat, Leonid Ilyich Brezhnev (*General Secretary*) (*since* October 14, 1964); P. N. Demichev; V. I. Dolgikh; I. V. Kapitonov; K. F. Katushev; A. P. Kirilenko; F. D. Kulakov; B. N. Ponomarev; M. A. Suslov; D. F. Ustinov.
Committee of Party Control, A. Ya Pel'she (*Chairman*).
Komsomol (*Young Communist League*). Ye. M. Tyazhelnikov (*1st Secretary*).

GOVERNMENT OF THE U.S.S.R
The Presidium of the Supreme Soviet of the

U.S.S.R.
Chairman (=President of the U.S.S.R.), Nikolay Viktorovich Podgorny (*since* December 9, 1965).
Secretary, M. P. Georgadze.
The Supreme Soviet (=Parliament) consists of two chambers.
Chairman (= *Speaker*) *of the Council of the Union*, A. P. Shitikov.
Chairman (= *Speaker*) *of the Council of Nationalities*, V. P. Ruben.

The Council of Ministers of the U.S.S.R.
Chairman (= *Prime Minister*), Alexei Nikolayevich Kosygin (*since* October 14, 1964).
1st Vice-Chairman, K. T. Mazurov.
Vice-Chairmen, I. V. Arkhipov; N. K. Baybakov; V. E. Dymshits; V. A. Kirillin; M. A. Lesechko; I. T. Novikov; V. N. Novikov; Z. N. Nuriyev; N. A. Tikhonov; L. V. Smirnov.
Ministries.—There are three groups of departmental ministries, with a total of 76 ministers—31 All Union Ministries, *i.e.* federal ministries, 31 Union Republican Ministries (co-ordinating ministries of individual republics) and 14 Chairmen of State committees, etc., ranking as Ministers. The more important posts are occupied by:
Foreign Affairs, A. A. Gromyko.
Defence, Marshal A. A. Grechko.
Foreign Trade, N. S. Patolichev.
Internal Affairs, N. A. Shchelokov.
Planning, N. K. Baybakov.
Science and Technology, V. A. Kirillin.
Buildings, I. T. Novikov.
State Security, Yu V. Andropov.
The Prime Ministers of the 15 constituent republics belong to the Council *ex officio*.

EMBASSY OF THE U.S.S.R. IN LONDON
13 Kensington Palace Gardens, W. 8.
[01–229 2666]
Ambassador Extraordinary and Plenipotentiary, His Excellency Nikolai M. Lunkov (1973).

AREA AND POPULATION
The U.S.S.R. is composed of 15 Union Republics (*see* below). Before the outbreak of the Second World War (1941–45 in U.S.S.R.), the U.S.S.R. consisted of 11 Republics—the Russian Socialist Federal Soviet Republic (R.S.F.S.R.) and the Ukrainian, Belorussian, Armenian, Azerbaidjan, Georgian, Turkmen, Uzbek, Tadjik, Kazakh and Kirghiz Soviet Socialist Republics. After the

collapse of Poland in September, 1939, the Soviet Government by agreement with Germany seized five-eighths of Poland's territory, the so-called _Western Ukraine_ and _Western Belorussia_, subsequently incorporated into the Ukrainian and Belorussian Republics respectively.

In March, 1940, some territories ceded by Finland under the 1940 Treaty were joined to the Karelian Autonomous Soviety Socialist Republic to form a Karelo-Finnish S.S.R. which became the 12th constituent Republic of the U.S.S.R., while others, including the town of Viipuri (Vyborg), were added to the R.S.F.S.R. Similarly, in August of the same year, the major part of _Bessarabia_ ceded by Rumania in June was joined to the Moldavian A.S.S.R. to form a Moldavian S.S.R. as the 13th Soviet Republic, while a smaller part of Bessarabia, including the Danube estuary port of Izmail, and _Northern Bukovina_, also ceded by Rumania, became part of the Ukraine. The new Soviet-Rumanian frontier was confirmed by the 1947 Peace Treaty with Rumania.

In August, 1940, the three independent Baltic States, _Estonia, Latvia_ and _Lithuania_, were forcibly incorporated into the Soviet-Union to form the 14th, 15th and 16th Republics respectively. In June, 1945, _Ruthenia_ was ceded by Czechoslovakia and became part of the Ukranian S.S.R. under the name of _Transcarpathia_. After the defeat of Germany, a part of _East Prussia_ with its capital Königsberg (renamed Kaliningrad in July, 1946) became part of the R.S.F.S.R., while the port and district of _Memel_ (Klaipeda) was incorporated into the Lithuanian S.S.S. By the 1947 Peace Treaty with Finland, the district of _Petsamo_ (Pechenga) was added to the territory of the R.S.F.S.R. In the Far East, the southern half of _Sakhalin_ and the whole of the _Kurile Islands_ were incorporated into the last-named Republic in 1945, after the defeat of Japan. In October, 1944, _Tannu-Tuva_, until the Second World War a nominally independent state lying to the N.W. of Outer Mongolia, became the autonomous province of _Tuva_ and, in 1961, the Autonomous Republic of Tuva, within the R.S.F.S.R.

In July, 1956, the Karelo-Finnish Republic reverted to the status of an Autonomous (_Karelian_) Republic within the R.S.F.S.R.

Area and population (January 1, 1974 estimate) of the constituent Republics of the U.S.S.R. with their capitals:—

Republic (Capital)	Sq. miles	Population
I. R.S.F.S.R.		
(Moscow)	6,593,391	132,913,000
II. Ukraine (Kiev)	252,046	48,521,000
III. Belorussia (Minsk)	80,300	9,268,000
IV. Uzbekistan		
(Tashkent)	157,181*	13,289,000*
V. Kazakhstan		
(Alma-Ata)	1,064,980*	13,928,000*
VI. Georgia (Tbilisi)	26,911	4,878,000
VII. Azerbaidjan (Baku)	33,436	5,514,000
VIII. Lithuania (Vilnius)	26,173	3,262,000
IX. Moldavia (Kishinev)	13,912	3,764,000
X. Latvia (Riga)	24,695	2,454,000
XI. Kirghizia (Frunze)	76,642	3,219,000
XII. Tadjikistan		
(Dushanbe)	54,019	3,283,000
XIII. Armenia (Erevan)	11,306	2,728,000
XIV. Turkmenistan		
(Ashkhabad)	188,417	2,430,000
XV. Estonia (Tallinn)	17,413	1,418,000

* (Adjusted to include transfer of 3 border regions —888 sq. miles and 162,000 inhabitants—by Uzbek S.S.R., Kazakh S.S.R. and U.S.S.R. decrees of May–June 1971.)

The total area of the U.S.S.R. is 8,620,822 sq. miles; the total population: 250,869,000.

A striking demographic feature is the rapid urbanization. While in 1939 the proportion of urban population was 32 per cent. of the total, in 1974 it reached 60 per cent., owing to migration to the towns, growth of new towns, incorporation of villages into conurbations and a higher birth-rate in urban areas. There are now 36 towns with over 500,000 (11 in 1939).

The proportion of women to men is 53·7 to 46·3. (In 1973 the birth-rate was 17·6; the mortality rate, 8·6; the natural increase, 9·0 per 1,000.

More than four-fifths of the people were born after the 1917 Revolution.

Main Nationalities
(1970 Census)

The most numerous national groups of U.S.S.R. are: Russian, 129 m and Ukrainian, 41 m. There are between 5 and 9 million Belorussians, Uzbeks, Kazakhs, and Tatars respectively. Azerbaidjani, Armenians and Georgians number between 3 and 5 million each group. There are some 2·5 million Lithuanians, Jews, Moldavians and Tadjiks respectively. In each of the following nationality groups the population numbers between 1·05 and 1·8 millions: Germans, Chuvashes, Latvians, Poles, Mordovians, Turkmens, Kirghizians, Bashkirs and Estonians.

The 1970 census revealed a remarkable difference between the growth rates of individual nationalities: while the Slav nations showed an annual increase of roughly one per cent., certain Central-Asian and Caucasian (mostly Moslem) nations recorded an annual net growth of three to four per cent.

Constitution

Under the 1936 ("Stalin") Constitution, the _Union of Soviet Socialist Republics_ is "a socialist state of workers and peasants" (§ 1) in which "all power belongs to the working people as represented by the Soviets [Councils] of Working People's Deputies" (§ 3), while its economy is based on "the socialist ownership of the instruments and means of production" (§ 4). "The land, its mineral wealth, waters, forests, mills, factories, mines, rail, water and air transport, banks, communications, large state-organized agricultural enterprises, as well as municipal enterprises and the bulk of dwelling-houses in the cities and industrial localities, are state property" (§ 6), while "the joint enterprises of collective farms and co-operative organizations . . . constitute the common, socialist property of the collective farms and co-operative organizations" (§ 7). "The law [also] permits the small private economy of individual peasants and handicraftsmen based on their own labour and precluding the exploitation of the labour of others" (§ 9). "The personal property right of citizens in their incomes and savings from work, in their dwelling-houses and subsidiary home enterprises, in household articles . . . as well as the right of citizens to inherit personal property, is protected by law" (§ 10). The whole economic life, however, is subordinated to the state economic plan (§ 11).

The U.S.S.R. is a federal state, "formed on the basis of a voluntary union of equal Soviet Socialist Republics" (§ 13); every Republic has "the right to secede from the U.S.S.R." (§ 17).

"The highest organ of state power in the U.S.S.R. is the Supreme Soviet of the U.S.S.R." (§ 30) which exercises exclusively the legislative power (§ 32). It consists of two Chambers, the _Soviet of the Union_ (elected on the basis of one deputy for every 300,000 of the population) and

ALASKA

WRANGEL I.

ARCTIC CIRCLE

NORTH PACIFIC OCEAN

0 200 400 600 800 1000 MILES

NEW SIBERIAN IS.

KAMCHATKA

OCEAN

SAKHALIN

Okhotsk

Nikolayevsk

Vladivostok

JAPAN

UNION OF SOVIET
SOCIALIST REPUBLICS

Krasnoyarsk

Irkutsk

MONGOLIA

ARCTIC

Novosibirsk

Omsk

CHINA

NOVAYA ZEMLYA

Perm
Sverdlovsk
Chelyabinsk

PAKISTAN
INDIA

BARENTS SEA

Kazan
Ufa

Kuibyshev
Saratov
Volgograd

IRAN

AFGHANISTAN

Gorky

CASPIAN SEA

Leningrad

Moscow

Voronezh
Rostov

BLACK SEA

TURKEY

FINLAND

POLAND
CZECH.
RUMANIA
YUGO. BULG.

the *Soviet of Nationalities* (elected at the ratio of 25 deputies from each Union Republic, 11 from each Autonomous Republic, 5 from each Autonomous Province and 1 from each National Territory) (§§ 33–35). At elections held on June 16, 1974, for the two Chambers, approximately 161 million persons voted *for* candidates (99·82 per cent. of voters) and under 400,000 against. The *Supreme Soviet* which, as a rule, meets four to five times a year for about a week, delegates most of its power to its *Presidium* which acts as a kind of collective President of the U.S.S.R. between the sessions.

" The highest executive and administrative organ of state power is the Council of Ministers of the U.S.S.R." (§ 64). It is appointed by the Supreme Soviet (§ 70) and is accountable to it, or, in the intervals between the sessions, to its Presidium (§ 65).

The Supreme Court of the U.S.S.R. and the Special Courts of the U.S.S.R. are elected by the Supreme Soviet for a term of five years (§ 104). Similarly, the Procurator-General, who exercises " supreme supervisory power to ensure the strict observance of law " (§ 113), is appointed by the Supreme Soviet for a term of seven years.

Citizens of the U.S.S.R. have the right to work, to rest and leisure, to maintenance in old age and sickness and disability relief and to education (§§ 118–121). " Women are accorded equal rights with men " (§ 122). Citizens are accorded equal rights irrespective of their nationality or race (§ 123). The citizens are also guaranteed freedom of speech, of the press, of assembly and of street processions and demonstrations, " in conformity with the interests of the working people and in order to strengthen the socialist system " (§ 125).

Section 126 of the Constitution is remarkable for containing the only reference to the real master of the country, the Communist Party. It says that " the most active and politically conscious citizens in the ranks of the working class and other sections of the working people unite in the Communist Party of the Soviet-Union, which is the vanguard of the working people in their struggle to strengthen and develop the socialist system and is the leading core of all organizations of the working people, both public and state." The new Party programme, adopted in November, 1961, envisages a great increase of the economic capacity of the country and promises the transition to " full Communism " some time after 1980.

A special committee was set up in November, 1961, to draft a new constitution,

Local Government.—The State power in regions, provinces, autonomous provinces, territories, districts, towns and rural localities is vested in the *Soviets of Working People's Deputies* (§ 94), elected by the working people of the respective administrative units for a term of two years (§ 95). The executive and administrative organ of a Soviet is its Executive Committee elected by it (§ 99). The Union Republics and the Autonomous Republics have Supreme Soviets and Councils of Ministers of their own (§§ 57–63 and 79–88), although their jurisdiction is severely circumscribed in favour of the central Government. Since February, 1944, the Union Republics have had the right to enter into direct relations with foreign states and to conclude agreements and exchange diplomatic and consular representatives with them (§ 18A). So far, however, the only important activity of this kind has been the individual membership of the Ukraine and of Belorussia in the United Nations Organization. Similarly, the 1944 law allowing each Union Republic to possess its own Republican

military formations (§ 18B) seems to have remained a paper provision.

The Union Republics possess Ministries of their own for internal affairs, certain branches of heavy and light industry, agriculture, public health, trade, finance and the like. The work of these Ministries is co-ordinated by respective federal Ministries and/or the *Gosplan*. Nominally, the Union Republics possess exclusive jurisdiction over such matters as motor transport, housing, social security, municipal affairs, local industry, education and, since 1956, inland water transport and justice.

Religion.—Section 124 of the Constitution lays down that " in order to ensure to citizens freedom of conscience, the church in the U.S.S.R. is separated from the state, and the school from the church," and that " freedom of religious worship and freedom of anti-religious propaganda is recognized for all citizens." Churches have remained open in virtue of contracts concluded between the congregations and the local authorities. The clergy live on voluntary donations from their parishioners. A new *modus vivendi* between the Government and the religious communities was created during the War of 1939–1945. In September, 1943, Stalin agreed to the election of the Patriarch of Moscow and All Russia, a post which had been vacant since the death of Patriarch Tikhon in 1925. Patriarch Sergius, elected by the Council of the Russian Church in 1943, died in May, 1944, and was succeeded in February, 1945, by Patriarch Alexius (*d.* 1970). A new Patriarch, Pimen, was elected in 1971.

The proselytizing successes of the religious communities have become of great concern to the authorities; there has been a great increase of anti-religious articles in the press since 1959, and a number of religious institutions were once again closed or banned. Harassment of individuals active in all religions and denominations continues.

Education.—Under the Constitution, citizens of the U.S.S.R. have the right to education. Since 1956 the entire educational course, including higher education at universities, technical colleges, etc., has been free.

The state controls all educational institutions, theatres, cinemas, museums, libraries and picture galleries, as well as the press and the radio. The main centre of research and learning is the Academy of Sciences of the U.S.S.R., which is in effect a vast government-controlled pool of scientists. *President,* (vacant).

Chronological System.—On February 14, 1918, the Soviet Government adopted the Gregorian (Western) Calendar, and by a decree of June 16, 1930, the Soviet Government advanced all the clocks in the Union by one hour, thus adopting permanent Summer Time. The country is divided into several time zones (Moscow time is 3 hours ahead of G.M.T.).

LANGUAGE, LITERATURE AND ARTS

Language and Literature.—Russian is a branch of the Slavonic family of languages which is divided into the following groups: *Eastern*, including Russian, Ukrainian and White Russian; *Western*, including Polish, Czech, Slovak and Sorbish (or Lusatian Wendish); and *Southern*, including Serbo-Croat, Slovene, Macedonian and Bulgarian. The Western group and part of the Southern group are written in the Latin alphabet, the others in the Cyrillic, said to have been instituted by SS. Cyril and Methodius in the ninth century, and largely based on the Greek alphabet. Before the Westernization of Russia under Peter the Great (1682–1725), Russian literature consisted mainly of folk ballads (*byliny*), epic songs, chronicles and works of moral theology. The eighteenth and particularly the nineteenth centuries saw a brilliant development of Russian poetry and fiction. Romantic poetry reached its zenith with Alexander Pushkin (1799–1837) and Mikhail Lermontov (1814–1841). The 20th century produced great poets like Alexander Blok (1880–1921), the Nobel Prize laureate of 1958 Boris Pasternak (1890–1960), Vladimir Mayakovsky (1893–1930) and Anna Akhmatova (1888–1966). Realistic fiction is associated with the names of Nikolai Gogol (1809–1852), Ivan Turgenev (1818–1883), Fedor Dostoyevsky (1821–1881) and Leo Tolstoy (1828–1910), and later with Anton Tchekhov (1860–1904), Maxim Gorky (1868–1936), Ivan Bunin (1870–1953) and Alexander Solzhenitsyn (b. 1918).

Great names in music include Glinka (1804–1857), Borodin (1833–87), Mussorgsky (1839–1881), Rimsky-Korsakov (1844–1908), Rubinstein (1829–1894), Tchaikovsky (1840–1893), Rakhmaninov (1873–1943), Skriabin (1872–1915), Prokofiev (1891–1953), Stravinsky (1882–1971) and Shostakovich (1906–1975). Performers include Igor and David Oistrakh, M. Rostropovich, and S. Richter and the famous conductor Rozhdestvensky.

FINANCE

A new "heavy" Rouble was introduced on January 1, 1961. Prices and wages have been changed accordingly at the rate of 10 old Roubles = 1 new Rouble. The official exchange rate is now approx. £1=R.1·6. It bears little relation to the actual purchasing power of the two currencies. Banknotes in circulation are those valuing R. 1, 3, 5, 10, 25, 50 and 100. There are also coins valuing Kopecks 1, 2, 3, 5, 10, 15, 20 and R. 1.

DEFENCE

No official defence estimates are published in the U.S.S.R., although estimated defence expenditure in 1974/75 is put at $96 billion. The general trend is a continuing emphasis on nuclear weapons, but without any reduction in the level of conventional arms.

The basic military service is two years in the Army and Air Force and two to three years in the Navy and Border Guards.

The total size of the Soviet regular forces is now estimated to be about 3,525,000.

Operational ICBMs, i.e. Inter-Continental Ballistic Missiles, now total about 1,575. SLBMs number 720. The number of MRBMs and IRBMs appears to be fixed at about 600. The operational personnel of the Strategic Rocket Forces totals about 350,000.

The Air Forces comprise about 11,790 operational aircraft (including about 8,250 combat aircraft). The total strength of the Air Forces, excluding the Naval Air Force, is about 550,000 men. The total personnel of the separate Air Defence Command is estimated at 500,000 men.

The total size of the Soviet Army is estimated at 1,800,000 men. It is thought to be organized in 167 divisions, distributed as follows: 63 divisions in European U.S.S.R., 28 in Central and Southern U.S.S.R., 45 in the Sino-Soviet border area, 31 in Eastern Europe.

The total strength of the Soviet Navy and Naval Air Force is 475,000 men. In total tonnage, it is the second largest navy in the world, and its main strength lies in the submarine fleet. There are now 70 nuclear-powered and 175 diesel-powered submarines.

The Soviet Navy is reported to be building its first two aircraft-carriers, one of which was expected to come into service at the end of 1975. The land-based Naval Air Force comprises about 650 bombers and 420 other aircraft. The surface ships comprise 33 cruisers and 78 destroyers.

The para-military forces number some 130,000 security and 180,000 border troops. There are also about 2½ million DOSAAF members who participate in such activities as athletics, shooting and parachuting.

Minister of Defence, Marshal A. A. Grechko.
Chief of General Staff, Army General V. G. Kulikov.
Chief, Political Administration, Soviet Armed Forces, Army Gen. A. A. Yepishev.

On May 14, 1955, a Treaty of Friendship, Mutual Assistance and Co-operation was signed in Warsaw between the Soviet Union and its European associates (Bulgaria, East Germany, Hungary, Poland, Rumania, and Czechoslovakia) (and Albania which left the Pact in Sept. 1968) to serve as a counterpoise to NATO. A united military command was set up in Moscow (*Secretary-General*, N. P. Firyubin; *C.-in-C.*, Marshal I. I. Yakubovsky; *Chief of Staff*, Army Gen. S. M. Shtemenko).

INDUSTRY AND AGRICULTURE

One of the most remarkable aspects of the Soviet economy has been the transformation of an essentially agricultural country into the second-strongest industrial power in the world. The 1974 output amounted to 99,900,000* tons of pig-iron, 136,000,000* tons of steel, 109,000,000* tons of rolled metal, 684,000,000* tons of coal, 459,000,000* tons of crude oil, 115,000,000* tons of cement, 975,000 million kW/h of electricity and 1,846,000 motor vehicles.

Agricultural development has been far slower, mainly owing to lack of incentives among peasants organized in *kolkhozy* (collective farms). Repeated droughts, such as in 1965, were a contributing factor to a permanent shortage of grain. Stock breeding has also suffered from the general mismanagement of farming. The livestock at Jan. 1, 1975 included 109,100,000 cattle, including 41,900,000 cows, and 151,100,000 sheep and goats. The level of productivity remains very low. It remains to be seen whether new incentives for peasants introduced in 1966 and 1970 and a variety of administrative reforms recently introduced in Moldavia and elsewhere will bring about a radical change in the situation. *Forests* cover nearly 40 per cent. of the whole area of the Union and form a considerable source of wealth.

Trade with U.K.

	1973	1974
Imports from U.K.	£97,387,000	£110,016,000
Exports to U.K.	331,362,000	395,457,000

COMMUNICATIONS

European Russia is relatively well served by railways, Leningrad and Moscow being the two main focal points of rail routes. The centre and south have a good system of north-south and east-west lines, but the eastern part (the Volga lands), traversed as it is by trunk lines between Europe and Asia which enter Siberia *via* Sverdlovsk, Chelyabinsk, Magnitogorsk and Ufa, lacks north-south routes. In Asia, there are still large areas of the U.S.S.R., notably in the Far North and Siberia, with few or no railways. Railways built since 1928 include the Turkestan-Siberian line (*Turksib*) which has made possible a large-scale industrial exploitation of Kazakhstan, a number of lines within the system of the *Trans-Siberian Railway* (Magnitogorsk-Kartaly-Troitsk, Sverdlovsk-Kurgan, Novosibirsk-Proyektnaya, etc.), which are of great importance for the industrial development in the east, the Petropavlovsk-Karaganda-Balkhash line

---

* Metric.

which has made possible the development of the Karaganda coal basin and of the Balkhash copper mines, and the Moscow–Donbass trunk line. In the northern part of European Russia, the North Pechora Railway has been completed, while in the Far East a second Trans-Siberian line (the Baikal-Amur Railway) is under construction; it will follow a more northerly alignment than the existing Trans-Siberian and will terminate in the Pacific port of Sovetskaya Gavan.

Sea Ports and Inland Waterways.—The most important ports (Odessa, Nikolayev, Batumi, Taganrog, Rostov, Kerch, Sevastopol and Novorossiisk) lie around the Black Sea and the Sea of Azov. The northern ports (Leningrad, Murmansk and Archangel) are, with the exception of Murmansk, ice-bound during winter. Several new ports have been built along the Arctic Sea route (between Murmansk and Vladivostok) and are now in regular use every summer. The great Far Eastern port of Vladivostok, the Pacific naval base of the U.S.S.R., is kept open by icebreakers all the year round. Inland waterways, both natural and artificial, are of great importance in the country, although all of them are icebound in winter (from 2½ months in the south to 6 months in the north). The great rivers of European Russia flow outwards from the centre, linking all parts of the plain with the chief ports, an immense system of navigable waterways which carried about 419,000,000 tons of freight in 1973. They are supplemented by a system of canals which provide a through traffic between the White, Baltic, Black and Caspian Seas. The most notable of them, built largely by forced labour, are the *White Sea-Baltic Canal*, and the *Moscow-Volga Canal.* The 63-miles long *Volga-Don Canal* linking the Baltic and the White Seas in the North to the Caspian, the Black Sea and the Sea of Azov in the South, was completed in May 1952.

FLAG OF THE U.S.S.R.—Red, with five-pointed star above hammer and sickle.

NATIONAL DAY OF THE U.S.S.R.—November 7 (Commemorating the October Bolshevist Revolution of 1917).

BRITISH EMBASSY

(Naberezhnaya Morisa Toreza 14, Moscow)

Ambassador Extraordinary and Plenipotentiary, His Excellency Howard Frank Trayton Smith, C.M.G. (1975).

Minister, I. J. M. Sutherland, C.M.G.

Counsellors, K. J. Uffen (*Commercial*); Dr. J. Thynne (*Scientific*); C. L. G. Mallaby (*Head of Chancery*); B. Spencer (*Admin.*).

1st Secretaries, D. J. Johnson; R. D. McM. Williams; Dr. M. J. Llewellyn-Smith; L. V. Appleyard (*Commercial*); A. J. Longrigg; Miss J. Dimond; Dr. D. H. Woodhead (*Medical Officer*).

Defence and Air Attaché, Air Cdre. D. D. Thorne, O.B.E., D.F.C.

Asst. Air Attachés, Sqn. Ldr. G. P. Taylor; Flt.-Lieut. R. A. Bealer.

Military Attaché, Brig. D. H. Bush.

Asst. Military Attaché, Maj. A. R. Cattaway.

Naval Attaché, Capt. R. J. F. Turner, R.N.

Asst. Naval Attachés, Lt.-Cdr. W. M. Caswell, R.N.; Lt.-Cdr. A. E. Johnson-Newell, R.N.

British Council Representative, A. A. Edmondson (*Asst. Cultural Attaché*).

There are no British Consulates in the U.S.S.R. apart from the Consular Section attached to the Embassy.

I.—R.S.F.S.R.

(The Russian Soviet Federal Socialist Republic)

Chairman of the Presidium of the Supreme Soviet, M.A. Yasnov.

Chairman of the Council of Ministers, M. S. Solomentsev.

The R.S.F.S.R. has no Communist Party Central Committee of its own.

The R.S.F.S.R., the largest and the most important of the Republics, occupies the major half of the European part of the U.S.S.R. and the major northern half of its Asiatic part and makes up 77 per cent. of the total territory of the U.S.S.R. with 53 per cent. of the total population. It consists of 16 Autonomous Republics (the Bashkir, Buryat, Checheno-Ingush, Chuvash, Daghestan, Kabardin-Balkar, Kalmyk, Karelian, Komi, Mari, Mordovian, North-Osetian, Tatar, Tuva, Udmurt and Yakut A.S.S.R.s); 6 regions (Altai, Khabarovsk, Krasnodar, Krasnoyarsk, Maritime and Stavropol) containing in their turn 5 autonomous provinces; 49 provinces (Amur, Archangel, Astrakhan, Belgorod, Bryansk, Chelyabinsk, Chita, Gorky, Irkutsk, Ivanovo, Kalinin, Kaliningrad, Kaluga, Kamchatka, Kemerovo, Kirov, Kostroma, Kuibyshev, Kurgan, Kursk, Leningrad, Lipetsk, Magadan, Moscow, Murmansk, Novgorod, Novosibirsk, Omsk, Orel, Orenburg, Penza, Perm, Pskov, Rostov, Ryazan, Sakhalin, Saratov, Smolensk, Sverdlovsk, Tambov, Tomsk, Tula, Tyumen, Ulyanovsk, Vladimir, Volgograd, Vologda, Vorenezh and Yaroslavl).

Physical Features.—The R.S.F.S.R. may be conveniently divided into three areas, a low-lying flat Western part stretching eastwards up to the Yenisei and divided in two by the Ural ridge; an eastern part, between the Yenisei and the Pacific, consisting of a number of tablelands and ridges, and a southern mountainous part. Climatically, the R.S.F.S.R. extends over all zones, except the tropics, and may be divided into the following belts (from north to south): Arctic, Tundra, Forest, Mixed Forest-Steppe, Steppe, Sub-Tropics.

The Republic has a very long coast-line, including the longest Arctic coast-line in the world (about 17,000 miles). The most important rivers in the European Part of the R.S.F.S.R. are the Volga with its tributaries Kama and Oka, the Northern Dvina and the Pechora, the short but wide Neva, the Don and the Kuban, and in the Asiatic part, the Obi with the Irtysh, the Yenisei, the Lena and the Amur, and, further north, Khatanga, Olenek, Yana, Indigirka, Kolyma and Anadyr. Lakes are abundant, particularly in the north-west. The huge Baikal Lake in Eastern Siberia is the deepest lake in the world. There are also two large artificial water reservoirs within the Greater Volga canal system, the Moscow and Rybinsk " Seas."

Minerals.—The Republic occupies one of the first places in the world for mineral wealth. Coal is mined in the Kuznetsk area, in the Urals, south of Moscow, in the Donets basin (its Eastern part lies in the R.S.F.S.R.) and in the Pechora area in the North. Oil is produced in the Northern Caucasus, in the area between the Volga and the Ural (the so-called " Second Baku ") and in Western Siberia. The Ural mountains contain a unique assortment of minerals—high-quality iron ore, manganese, copper, aluminium, gold, platinum, precious stones, salt, asbestos, pyrites, coal, oil, etc. Iron ore is mined, in addition to the Urals, near Kursk, Tula, Lipetsk, Khopper, in several areas in Siberia and in the Kola Peninsula. Non-ferrous metals are found in the Altai, in Eastern Siberia, in the Northern Caucasus, in the Kuznetsk-Basin, in the Far East and in the Far North. Nine-tenths of all U.S.S.R. forests are located in the R.S.F.S.R.

Production and Industry.—The vastness of the territory of the Republic and the great variety in climatic conditions cause great differences in the structure of agriculture from north to south and from west to east. In the Far North stag breeding, hunting and fishing are predominant. Further south, timber industry is combined with grain growing. In the southern half of the forest zone and in the adjacent forest-steppe zone, the acreage under grain crops is far larger and the structure of agriculture more complex. An extensive programme of land improvement mainly involving this zone, announced early in 1974, aims to double its total agricultural output by 1990. In the eastern part of this zone, between the Volga and the Urals, cericulture is predominant (particularly summer wheat), with cattle breeding next. Beyond the Urals, we find another important grain-growing and stock-breeding area in the southern part of the Western-Siberian plain. The southern steppe zone is the main wheat granary of the U.S.S.R., containing also large acreages under barley, maize and sunflower. In the extreme South (Krasnodar region, Stavropol region) cotton is now cultivated. Vine, tobacco and other Southern crops are grown on the Black Sea shore of the Caucasus.

Industrially, the R.S.F.S.R. occupies the first place among the Soviet Republics. Major changes in the location of industry have occurred since the revolution and again since the war with two new industrial areas being developed in the Urals and in the Kuznetsk basin, although Moscow and Leningrad are still the two largest industrial centres in the country. Most of the oil produced in the U.S.S.R. now comes from two areas in the R.S.F.S.R.—the Bashkir and Tatar Autonomous Republics. All industries are represented in the R.S.F.S.R., including iron and steel and engineering. Industrial centres include Magnitogorsk, Chelyabinsk, Novokuznetsk, Tula, Komsomolsk, Perm, Ufa, Irkutsk, Kuibyshev, Krasnoyarsk, Nizhny-Tagil, Novosibirsk, Omsk, Volgograd, Gorky, Saratov, Grozny, Rostov and Taganrog.

CAPITAL, MOSCOW. Population 7,368,000 (Jan. 1, 1974). Moscow, founded about A.D. 1147 by Yuri Dolgoruki, became first the centre of the rising Moscow principality and, later, in the 15th century, the capital of the whole of Russia (Muscovy). In 1325, it became the seat of the Metropolitan of Russia. In 1703 Peter the Great transferred the capital to the newly built St. Petersburg, but on March 14, 1918, Moscow was again designated as the capital. Ψ Leningrad (before the First World War " St. Petersburg " and from 1914–1924 " Petrograd ") has a population of 3,786,000 (Jan. 1, 1974).

Other towns with populations exceeding 500,000 are:—

Gorky (Nizhny-Novogorod)	1,260,000
Novosibirsk (Novonikolayevsk)	1,243,000
Kuibyshev (Samara)	1,140,000
Sverdlovsk (Yekaterinburg)	1,122,000
Chelyabinsk	947,000
Omsk	935,000
Kazan	931,000
Perm (Molotov)	920,000
Volgograd (Stalingrad; Tsaritsyn)	885,000
Ufa	871,000
Ψ Rostov-on-Don	867,000
Saratov	820,000
Voronezh	729,000
Krasnoyarsk	728,000
Yaroslavl	558,000
Novokuznetsk	519,000
Krasnodar	519,000

Ψ Seaport.

About 83 per cent. of the population are Russians.

II.—UKRAINE

First Secretary of the Party Central Committee, V. V. Shcherbitsky.
Chairman of the Presidium of the Supreme Soviet, I. S. Grushetsky.
Chairman of the Council of Ministers, A. P. Lyashko.

This Republic, second largest in population, lying in the south-western part of the European half of the U.S.S.R., was formed in December, 1917. It consists of 25 provinces—Cherkassy, Chernigov, Chernovtsy, Crimea, Dnepropetrovsk, Donetsk, Ivano-Frankovsk, Kharkov, Kherson, Khmelnitsky, Kiev, Kirovograd, Lvov, Nikolayev, Odessa, Poltava, Rovno, Sumy, Ternopol, Transcarpathia, Vinnitsa, Volhynia, Voroshilovgrad, Zaporozhye and Zhitomir.

Physical Features.—The larger part of the Ukraine forms a plain with small elevations. The Carpathian mountains lie in the south-western part of the Republic. The climate is moderate, with relatively mild winters (particularly in the south-west) and hot summers. The main rivers are the Dnieper with its tributaries, the Southern Bug and the Northern Donets (a tributary of the Don).

Production and Industry.—The main centre of Soviet coal mining and iron and steel industry is situated in the southern part of the Ukraine. Engineering and chemical industry have been greatly developed under the Soviet régime. In 1970, the Ukraine provided 40 per cent of the total Soviet steel, 40 per cent. of metal goods and 33 per cent. of coal. The central forest-steppe region (mainly on the right bank of the Dnieper) is the greatest sugar-producing area in the U.S.S.R. The Ukraine also leads in grain-growing and stock-raising.

There are large deposits of coal and salt in the Donets Basin, of iron ore in Krivoy Rog and near Kerch in the Crimea, of manganese in Nikopol, and of quicksilver in Nikitovka.

CAPITAL (since 1934), Kiev, the oldest city in the U.S.S.R. founded in the 9th century A.D., was the capital of the Russian State from 865 to 1240. Population (Jan. 1, 1974), 1,887,000. Other towns with population over 500,000 are:—

Kharkov	1,330,000
Ψ Odessa	981,000
Dnepropetrovsk (Yekaterinoslav)	941,000
Donetsk (Stalino; Yuzovka, *i.e.* Hughesovka)	934,000
Zaporozhye (Aleksandrovskaya)	729,000
Krivoy-Rog	620,000
Lvov (Lviv; Lwow; Lemberg)	605,000

III.—BELORUSSIA
(White Russia)

First Secretary of the Party Central Committee, P. M. Masherov.
Chairman of the Presidium of the Supreme Soviet, F. A. Surganov.
Chairman of the Council of Ministers, T. Ya. Kiselev.

The Belorussian S.S.R., lying in the western part of the European area of the U.S.S.R., was formed early in 1919. It now consists of six provinces (Brest, Gomel, Grodno, Minsk, Mogilev and Vitebsk. It is largely a plain with many lakes, swamps and marshy land. Before the revolution of 1917 the area was one of the most backward parts of European Russia. Since then, agriculture has been greatly developed, thanks to draining of swamps. Most of the Republic's industry is also of recent growth. Woodworking is of great importance, but engineering has also been greatly extended with several major plants built in Gomel and Minsk.

The main rivers are the upper reaches of the Dnieper, of the Niemen and of the Western Dvina.

CAPITAL, Minsk. Population 1,082,000 (Jan. 1, 1974).

Belorussians make up four-fifths of the population, with Russians and Poles coming next.

IV.—UZBEKISTAN

First Secretary of the Party Central Committee, Sh. R. Rashidov.

Chairman of the Presidium of the Supreme Soviet, N. M. Matchanov.

Chairman of the Council of Ministers, N. D. Khudayberdyev.

The Uzbek S.S.R. was formed in 1924 and consists of the Kara-Kalpak A.S.S.R. and of 11 provinces (Andizhan, Bokhara, Dzhizak, Ferghana, Kashka-Darya, Khorezm, Namangan, Samarkand, Surkhan-Darya, Syr-Darya and Tashkent). It lies between the high Tienshan Mountains and the Pamir highlands in the east and south-east and sandy lowlands in the west and north-west. The major part of the territory is a plain with huge waterless deserts and several large oases, which form the main centres of population and economic life. The largest is the Ferghana valley, watered by the Syr-Darya. Other oases include Tashkent, Samarkand, Bokhara and Khorezm. The climate is continental and dry. Minerals include gold, natural gas, oil, copper, lead, zinc and coal.

The Uzbeks, a Turkic people, make up 65·5 per cent. of the population the Russians (12·5 per cent.), Tatars (5 per cent.) and Kazakhs (4 per cent.) come next.

There are major agricultural and textile machinery plants and several chemical combines. Uzbekistan is the main cotton-growing area of the U.S.S.R. producing more than 60 per cent. of all Soviet cotton. Irrigation has always been of decisive importance in this area, and the Soviet Government has done much in this field, including the contruction of the Great Ferghana Canal (230 miles).

CAPITAL, Tashkent. Population 1,595,000 (Jan. 1, 1975). Samarkand contains the Gur-Emir (Tamerlane's Mausoleum), completed A.D. 1400 by Ulugbek, Tamerlane's astronomer-grandson, and a 15th-century observatory. Heavy damage was done to Tashkent by the series of earthquakes in April and May, 1966.

V.—KAZAKHSTAN.

First Secretary of the Party Central Committee, D. A. Kunayev.

Chairman of the Presidium of Supreme Soviet, S. B. Niyazbekov.

Chairman of the Council of Ministers, B. A. Ashimov.

The Kazakh S.S.R., the second-largest Union-Republic, stretching from the lower reaches of the Volga and the Caspian in the west to the Altai and Tienshan in the east, and bordering on China, was formed in 1920 as an autonomous republic (under the name of the Kirghiz A.S.S.R.) within the R.S.F.S.R., and was constituted a Union Republic in 1936. It consists of the 19 Provinces: Aktyubinsk, Alma-Ata, Chimkent, Djambul, Dzhezkazgan, East-Kazakhstan, Guryev, Karaganda, Kokchetav, Kustanay, Kzyl-Orda, Mangyshlak, Semipalatinsk, Taldy-Kurgan, Tselinograd, North-Kazakhstan, Pavlodar, Turgay and Uralsk.

Kazakhstan is a country of arid steppes and misedeserts, flat in the west, hilly in the east and mountainous in the south-east (Southern Altai and Tienshan). The climate is continental and very dry. The main rivers are the (Upper) Irtysh, the Ural, the Syr-Darya and the Ili. Kazakhstan is very rich in minerals: copper in Kounrad and Dzhezkazgan, lead and zinc in the Altai and Karatau mountains, iron ore in Radryg and Lisakovsk, coal in Ekibastuz and Karaganda and oil and natural gas in the Mangyshlak peninsula. Major centres of

metal industry exist now in the Altai Mountains, in Chimkent, north of the Balkhash Lake and in Central Kazakhstan. Stock-raising is highly developed, particularly in the central and south-western parts of the Republic. Grain is grown in the north and north-east and cotton in the south and south-east. In 1954 an ambitious programme of development of " virgin " lands in the steppes was launched by the Government to increase grain production.

The Kazakhs (a Turkic people) are now in a minority in the Republic named after them; they constitute only 33 per cent. of its population. Russian settlers make up 42 per cent. and Ukrainians 7 per cent.

CAPITAL, Alma-Ata (formerly Verny). Population, 837,000 (Jan. 1, 1975). Karaganda, a major mining centre, has a population of 565,000 (Jan. 1, 1975).

VI.—GEORGIA

First Secretary of the Party Central Committee, E. A. Shevardnadze.

Chairman of the Presidium of the Supreme Soviet, G. S. Dzotsenidze.

Chairman of the Council of Ministers, G. D. Djavakhishvili.

The Georgian S.S.R., occupying the north-western part of Transcaucasia, lies on the shore of the Black Sea and borders in the south-east on Turkey. It was formed in 1921; in 1922 it joined the Transcaucasian Federation which, in its turn, adhered to the U.S.S.R. in the same year. After the liquidation of the Transcaucasian S.F.S.R. in 1936 Georgia became a Union Republic. It contains two Autonomous Republics (Abkhazia and Adjaria) and the South-Ossetian Autonomous Province. Georgia is a country of mountains, with the Greater Caucasus in the north and the Smaller Caucasus in the south. A relatively low-lying land between these two ridges is divided into two parts by the Surz Ridge: Western Georgia with a mild and damp climate and Eastern Georgia with a more continental and dry climate. The Black Sea shore and the Rion lowlands are subtropical in their climatic character. The most important mineral deposits are manganese (Chiatura), coal (Tkibuli and Tkvarcheli) and oil (Kakhetia). Georgia is leading as regards production of manganese in the U.S.S.R. There are also many oil refineries. Viniculture and tobacco-growing are the two main agricultural industries. The Black Sea coast harbours many famous holiday resorts. Georgians make up 67 per cent. of the population, the remainder being composed of Armenians, Russians, Azerbaidjani and Osetians.

CAPITAL, Tbilisi (Tiflis), population 1,006,000 (Jan. 1, 1975).

VII.—AZERBAIDJAN

First Secretary of the Party Central Committee, G. A. Aliyev.

Chairman of the Presidium of the Supreme Soviet, K. A. Khalilov.

Chairman of the Council of Ministers, A. I. Ibragimov.

The Azerbaidjan S.S.R. occupies the eastern part of Transcaucasia, on the shore of the Caspian Sea, and borders on Iran. It was formed in 1920. Between 1922 and 1936 it formed part of the Transcaucasian Federation. In 1936 it became a Union Republic. It contains the Nakhichevan Autonomous Republic and the Nagorno-Karabakh Autonomous Province.

The north-eastern part of the Republic is taken up by the south-eastern end of the main Caucasus ridge, its south-western part by the smaller Caucasus hills, and its south-eastern corner by the spurs of the Talysh Ridge. Its central part is a depression irrigated by the Kura and by the lower reaches of its tributary Araks. Sheltered by the mountains from the humid west winds blowing from the Black Sea, Azerbaidjan has a continental climate. The land requires artificial irrigation. Industry is dominated by oil and natural gas extraction and related chemical and engineering industries centred on Baku and Sumgait. A large power station on the Kura (Mingechaur) was completed in 1954. Azerbaidjan is also important as a cotton growing area. The Azerbaidjani (Turks) make up three-quarters of the population of the Republic, Armenians, about 9 per cent., and Russians, 10 per cent.

CAPITAL, Ψ Baku. Population 1,383,000 (Jan. 1, 1975).

VIII.—LITHUANIA

First Secretary of the Party Central Committee, P. P. Grishkyavichus.
Chairman of the Presidium of the Supreme Soviet, M. Yu Shumauskas.
Chairman of the Council of Ministers, I. A. Manyushis.

Lithuania, formerly a Province of the Russian Empire, was declared an independent Republic at Vilna in 1918 and was incorporated into the U.S.S.R. in August, 1940. It was occupied by German forces from June, 1941, until the autumn of 1944. The Republic forms a plain with a large number of lakes and swamps. The forests occupy 19 per cent. of the whole area. The main river is the Niemen with its tributaries.

The chief industries are agriculture and forestry, the chief products being rye, oats, wheat, barley, flax, sugar-beet and potatoes. Before its incorporation into the Soviet Union, Lithuania exported a large quantity of meat and dairy produce.

The Lithuanians make up four-fifths of the population, Russians and Poles, 8–9 per cent. each.

CAPITAL, Vilnius (Vilna, restored to Lithuania by U.S.S.R. after the collapse and partition of Poland in 1939, and recaptured by Soviet forces in 1944). Population 420,000 (Jan. 1, 1974).

IX.—MOLDAVIA

First Secretary of the Party Central Committee, I. I. Bodyul.
Chairman of the Presidium of the Supreme Soviet, K. F. Ilyashenko.
Chairman of the Council of Ministers, P. A. Paskar.

Moldavia occupying the south-western corner of the U.S.S.R., borders in the west on Rumania with the Pruth forming the frontier. In 1918, Rumania seized the Russian Province of Bessarabia. In 1924 a Moldavian Autonomous Republic was formed within the Ukraine, and in 1940 the U.S.S.R. forced Rumania to give back Bessarabia, the major part of which was merged with the Moldavian A.S.S.R. to form a Moldavian Union Republic. Moldavia was occupied by the Germans and Rumanians from 1941 to 1944.

The northern part of the Republic consists of flat steppe lands, now all under plough. Some forests skirt the Dniester. Further south, around Kishinev, there are woody hills and further south again, low-lying steppe lands. The climate is moderate. The main river is the Dniester, navigable along the whole course.

The main industry is agriculture (viniculture, fruit-growing and market-gardening). Industry is insignificant in both parts of Moldavia, but the Republic has the densest population in the U.S.S.R. Moldavians make up 64 per cent. of the population, with Ukranians, and Russians next.

CAPITAL, Kishinev (Chisinau). Population, 432,000 (Jan. 1, 1974).

X.—LATVIA

First Secretary of the Party Central Committee, A. E. Voss.
Chairman of the Presidium of the Supreme Soviet, P. Ya. Strautmanis.
Chairman of the Council of Ministers, Yu. Ya. Ruben.

The Latvian S.S.R., lying on the shores of the Baltic and of the Gulf of Riga, was formerly a Baltic Province of the Russian Empire. It was proclaimed an independent state in 1918 and was forcibly incorporated into the U.S.S.R. in August 1940. Between 1941 and 1944 the Republic was occupied by the German forces.

The surface of the country is generally flat, interspersed by occasional chains of hills. The climate is moderately-continental. The main rivers are the lower reaches of the Western Dvina and its tributaries. Forests occupy 20 per cent. of the total territory.

The Latvians make up 57 per cent. of the Republic's population, Russians 30 per cent.

Latvian industry was always highly developed, with shipbuilding, engineering, chemical industry, textile industry, wood-working and dairying being the chief occupations. Both Riga and Liepaja (Libava, Liebau) are important sea-ports.

As in other newly-acquired Republics an agrarian reform was carried out in Latvia in 1940–41 and again after 1944.

CAPITAL, Ψ Riga. Population, 776,000 (Jan. 1, 1974).

XI.—KIRGHIZIA

First Secretary of the Party Central Committee, T. U. Usubaliyev.
Chairman of the Presidium of the Supreme Soviet, T. Kulatov.
Chairman of the Council of Ministers, A. S. Suyumbayev.

The Kirghiz S.S.R. occupies the north-eastern part of Soviet Central Asia and borders in the south-east on China. In 1924, a Kara-Kirghiz Autonomous Province was formed within the R.S.F.S.R. In 1926 it became a Kirghiz Autonomous Republic, and in 1936 a Union Republic. It contains three provinces, Issyk-Kul, Naryn and Osh. The Kirghiz Republic is a mountainous country, the major part being covered by the ridge of the Central Tienshan, while mountains of the Pamir-Altai system occupy its southern part. There are a number of spacious mountain valleys, the Alai, Susamyr, the Issyk-kul lake and others. The majority of the population is concentrated in plains, lying at the foot of mountains—Chu, Talass, part of the Ferghana Valley where agriculture prospers. Crops include sugar beet and cotton, and sheep are important in the mountains. Industry is being developed and some mining is done. The Kirghiz constitute 44 per cent. of the population, the Russians 29 per cent. The Uzbeks (in Eastern Ferghana) amount to 11 per cent.

CAPITAL, Frunze (formerly Pishpek). Population, 486,000 (Jan. 1, 1975).

XII.—TADJIKISTAN

First Secretary of the Party Central Committee, D. Rasulov.
Chairman of the Presidium of the Supreme Soviet, M. Kholov.
Chairman of the Council of Ministers, R. N. Nabiev.

The Tadjik S.S.R. lies in the extreme south-east of Soviet Central Asia and borders in the south on Afghanistan and in the east on China. It was originally formed in 1924 as an Autonomous Republic within the Uzbek S.S.R. and became a Union Republic in 1929. It includes the Gorno-Badakhshan Autonomous Province and the Kulyab and Leninabad Provinces.

The country is mountainous: in the east lie the Pamir highlands with the highest point in the U.S.S.R., Pik Communizmu (24,500 feet), in the centre the high ridges of the Pamir-Altai system. Plains are formed by wide stretches of the Syr-Darya valley in the north and of the Amu-Darya in the south.

Like the other Central-Asiatic Republics, Tadjikistan is a cotton-growing country. Its climatic conditions favour the cultivation of Egyptian cotton. Irrigation is of great importance. Fifty-six per cent. of the population are Tadjiks (linguistically and culturally akin to the Persians), 23 per cent. Uzbeks, the rest Russians and others.

CAPITAL, Dushanbe (formerly Stalinabad; Dyushambe). Population, 436,000 (Jan 1, 1975).

XIII.—ARMENIA
First Secretary of the Party Central Committee, A. Ye. Kochinyan.
Chairman of the Presidium of the Supreme Soviet, N. Kh. Arutyunyan.
Chairman of the Council of Ministers, G. A. Arzumanyan.

The Armenian S.S.R. occupies the south-western part of Transcaucasia: it was formed in 1920. In 1922 it joined the Transcaucasian Federation, and on its liquidation in 1936 became a Union Republic. In the south it borders on Turkey. It is a mountainous country consisting of several vast table lands surrounded by ridges. The population and the economic life are concentrated in the low-lying part of Armenia, the Aras valley and the Erevan hollow; the climate is continental, dry and cold, but the Aras valley has a long, hot and dry summer. Irrigation is essential for agriculture. At the junction of the former Turkish, Persian and Russian boundaries is *Mount Ararat* (17,160 ft.), the traditional resting place of "Noah's Ark." Industrial and fruit crops are grown in the low-lying districts, grain in the hills. Armenia is traditionally noted for her wine. There are large copper ore and molybdenum deposits and other minerals. The Armenian Church centred in Etchmiadzin is the oldest established Christian Church, Christianity having been recognized as the State religion in A.D. 300.

Nearly 90 per cent. of the population is Armenian.

CAPITAL, Erevan. Population, 870,000.

XIV.—TURKMENISTAN
First Secretary of the Party Committee, M. Gapurov.
Chairman of the Presidium of the Supreme Soviet, A.-M. Klychev.
Chairman of the Council of Ministers, O. N. Orazmukhamedov.

Turkmenia occupies the extreme south of Soviet Central Asia, between the Caspian and the Amu-Darya and borders in the south on Iran and Afghanistan. It was formed in 1924 and contains five Provinces, Ashkhabad, Chardjou, Knasnovodsk, Mary and Tashauz). The country is a low-lying plain, fringed by hills in the south. Ninety per cent. of the plain is taken up by the arid Kara-Kum desert. Of all Central-Asiatic Republics, Turkmenia is the lowest and driest. The principal industries are agriculture and stock-raising, cotton, wool, astrakhan furs, carpets and horses being the principal products. Minerals include natural gas, oil and sulphur. Most of the land under plough is artificially irrigated. Silk industry is of an old standing. There are also some fisheries in the Caspian.

Turkmens nomadic in the past, make up two-thirds of the population, Russians 15 per cent., and Uzbeks eight per cent.

CAPITAL, Ashkhabad (formerly Askhabad, Poltoratski). Population, 289,000 (Jan. 1, 1975).

XV.—ESTONIA
First Secretary of the Party Central Committee, I. G. Kebin.
Chairman of the Presidium of the Supreme Soviet, A. P. Vader.
Chairman of the Council of Ministers, V. I. Klauson.

Estonia, formerly a Baltic province of the Russian Empire, was proclaimed an independent Republic in 1918. In 1940, it was forcibly incorporated into the U.S.S.R. It lies on the shores of the Baltic and of the Finnish Gulf in the north and of the Gulf of Riga in the south-west. Some 800 islands, among them Dagö and Ösel, form part of Estonian territory. Between 1941 and 1944, Estonia was occupied by the German forces.

The country forms a low-lying plain with many lakes, among them the Chud (or Pskov) Lake, on the border with the R.S.F.S.R. Forests take up about one-fifth of the territory. Agriculture and dairy-farming are the chief industries, rye, oats, barley, flax and potatoes being the chief crops, and butter, bacon and eggs the chief products of dairy farming. There are important manufactures, including textiles, engineering, shipbuilding, wood-working, etc.

The population consists of Estonians (68 per cent.) and Russians (25 per cent.).

CAPITAL, Ψ Tallinn (formerly Reval). Population, 392,000 (Jan. 1, 1974).

THE VATICAN CITY STATE
(Stato della Città del Vaticano)
Sovereign Pontiff, His Holiness Pope Paul VI (Giovanni Battista Montini), *born* at Concesio (Brescia), Sept. 26, 1897, *elected* Pope (in succession to John XXIII), June 21, 1963.
Secretary of State, Cardinal Jean Marie Villot, *appointed* April 30, 1969.

The office of the ecclesiastical head of the Roman Catholic Church (Holy See) is vested in the Pope, the Sovereign Pontiff. For many centuries the Sovereign Pontiff exercised temporal power, and in 1859 the Papal States had an area of 17,218 square miles, with a population of 3,124,688. During the reign of Pius IX (1846–1878), the Papal States of Romagna, Umbria and the Marches were incorporated in the Kingdom of Sardinia and with the remaining States (Rome, Comacchio, Viterbo, Civita Vecchia, Velletri and Frosinone) became part of unified Italy in 1870. The territory of the Papacy was confined to the palaces of the Vatican and the Lateran and the Villa of Castel Gandolfo and the temporal power of the Pope was in suspense until the treaty of Feb. 11, 1929, which recognized the full and independent sovereignty of the Holy See in the City of the Vatican. Accompanying the treaty were conventions regulating the condition of religion and the Catholic Church in Italy and agreeing to pay 750,000,000 *lire* in cash and the income at 5 per cent. on 1,000,000,000 *lire* State bonds as a final settlement of the claims of the Holy See against Italy for the loss of temporal power. The population of the Vatican City in 1974 was 1,000.

FLAG.—Square flag; equal vertical bands of yellow (next staff), and white; crossed keys and triple crown device on white band.

BRITISH LEGATION
(91 Via Condotti, Rome)
Envoy Extraordinary and Minister Plenipotentiary to the Holy See, His Excellency Dugald Malcolm, C.M.G., C.V.O., T.D. (1975).
1st Secretary, R. M. Purcell.

VENEZUELA
(La Republica de Venezuela)

President, Sr. Carlos Andrés Pérez, *elected* Dec. 9, 1973, *assumed office* March 12, 1974.

CABINET
(June 1975)

Home Affairs, Dr. Octavio Lepage.
Foreign Affairs Dr. Ramón Escovar Salom.
Finance, Dr. Héctor Hurtado Navarro.
Defence, General de División Homero Ignacio Leal Torres.
Public Works, Dr. Arnoldo José Gabaldón Berti.
Development, Dr. José Ignacio Casal.
Education, Dr. Luis Manuel Peñalver.
Health and Social Assistance, Dr. Antonio Parra León.
Agriculture, Dr. Carmelo Contreras.
Labour, Dr. Antonio Leídenz.
Communications, Ing. Leopoldo Sucre Figarella.
Justice, Dr. Armando Sánchez Bueno.
Mines and Hydrocarbons, Dr. Valentín Hernández Acosta.
Minister of State for Planning, Dr. Gumersindo Rodríguez.
Minister of State for Information, Dr. Guido Grooscors.
Governor of Federal District, Dr. Diego Arria.
Governor of Miranda State, Dr Manuel Mantilla.

VENEZUELAN EMBASSY IN LONDON
3 Hans Crescent, S.W.1
[01-584 4206]

Ambassador Extraordinary and Plenipotentiary, His Excellency Dr. Carlos Pérez de la Cova (1970).
Counsellor, Lic. José Miguel Quintana.
2nd Secretary, Srta. Hedy Hernández-Ortega.
3rd Secretary, Lic. Rafael Hernández-Sanchez.

Consulate-General: 71A Park Mansions, S.W.1.
Consul, Señor Elias Casado.
There is also a Consulate-General at *Liverpool*.

Area and Population.—A South American Republic, situated approximately between 0° 45′ S. lat. and 12° 12′ N. lat. and 59° 45′–73° 09′ W. long. It consists of one Federal District, 20 states and 2 territories. Venezuela has a total area of 353,894 sq. miles and a population (estimate, 1975) of 11,992,700 increasing annually at a rate of 3·4 per cent.

Venezuela lies on the north of the South American continent, and is bounded on the north by the Caribbean Sea, west by the Republic of Colombia, east by Guyana, and south by Brazil. Included in the area of the Republic are 72 islands off the coast, with a total area of about 14,650 square miles, the largest being *Margarita*, which is politically associated with Tortuga, Cubagua and Coche to form the State of *Nueva Esparta*. Margarita has an area of about 400 square miles. In 1942 Great Britain ceded to Venezuela the small island of *Patos* (170 acres) about 3 miles from the mainland.

Physical Features.—The Eastern Andes from the south-west cross the border and reach to the Caribbean Coast, where they are prolonged by the Maritime Andes of Venezuela to the Gulf of Paria on the north-east. The main range is known as the Sierra Nevada de Merida, and contains the highest peaks in the country in Pico Bolivar (16,411 feet) and Picacho de la Sierra (15,420 feet), the maritime ranges containing the Silla de Caracas (8,531 feet). Near the Brazilian border the Sierras Parima and Pacaraima, and on the eastern border the Sierras de Rincote and de Usupamo, enclose the republic with parallel northward spurs, between which are valleys of the Orinoco tributaries. The Sierra Parima contains Yaparana

(7,175 feet) and Duida (8,120 feet), and Pacaraima contains Maraguaca (8,228 feet) and Roraima (9,000 feet), the latter being on the Venezuela-Guyana boundary. The slopes of the mountains and foothills are covered with dense forests, but the basin of the Orinoco is mainly *llanos*, or level stretches of open prairie, with occasional woods.

The principal river of Venezuela is the *Orinoco*, with innumerable affluents, the main river exceeding 1,600 miles in length from its rise in the southern highlands of the republic to its outflow in the deltaic region of the north-east.

A Franco-Venezuelan Expedition, led by Major Frank Risquez, claimed to have discovered the source of the Orinoco, on Nov. 27, 1951, at 63° 15′ W. long., 2° 18′ N. lat., and about 1,100 metres above sea-level.

The Orinoco is navigable for large steamers from its mouth for 700 miles, and by smaller vessels as far as the Maipures Cataract, some 200 miles farther up-stream. Dredging operations completed at the beginning of 1954 opened the Orinoco to ocean-going ships, of up to 40 ft. draft, as far as Puerto Ordaz (about 150 miles up-stream), which with the adjacent town of San Felix is now officially known as Ciudad Guayana. Among the many tributaries of the main stream are the Ventuari, Caura and Caroni from the south, and the Apure (with its tributary the Portuguesa), Arauca, Meta, and Guaviare from the west, the Meta and Guaviare being principally Colombian rivers. The upper waters of the Orinoco are united with those of the Rio Negro (a Brazilian tributary of the Amazon) by a natural river or canal, known as the *Casiquiare*. A British scientific expedition travelled in April-May, 1968, by Hovercraft from Manaos in Brazil *viâ* the Rio Negro, Casiquiare canal and Orinoco River to Trinidad. The coastal regions of Venezuela are much indented and contain many lagoons and lakes, of which *Maracaibo*, with an area of 8,296 square miles, is the largest lake in South America. Other lakes are Zulia (290 square miles), south-west of Maracaibo, and Valencia (216 square miles) about 1,400 ft. above sea-level in the Maritime Andes. The *llanos* also contain lakes and swamps caused by the river floods, but they are dry in the summer seasons.

The climate is tropical and, except where

modified by altitude or tempered by sea breezes, is unhealthy, particularly in the coastal regions and in the neighbourhood of lowland streams and lagoons. The hot, wet season lasts from April to October, the dry, cooler season from November to March.

Government.—On January 23, 1958, the military dictatorship of Maj-Gen. Marcos Pérez Jiménez, which had lasted since 1953 and covered a period of remarkable economic expansion due to the Venezuelan oil boom, was overthrown by a popular and military uprising. Since 1958 Venezuela has had a freely-elected democratic government. In elections in December, 1958, *Accion Democratica* (A.D.) gained a clear majority and Sr. Rómulo Betancourt of A.D. was elected President. For most of his five-year term of office Sr. Betancourt governed in coalition with the Christian Socialist Party, *Copei*. Further national elections were held on December 1, 1963, in which A.D. retained a reduced majority. Dr. Raúl Leoni of A.D. was elected President. The inauguration of the new Government took place on March 11, 1964. Formation of a broad-based coalition government composed of A.D., U.R.D. (*Union Republicana Democratica*) and F.N.D. (*Frente Nacional Democratico*) was announced on Nov. 5, 1964. The F.N.D. left the Government in 1965 and U.R.D. in April, 1968. A general election held in Dec., 1968, was narrowly won by *Copei* and Dr. Rafael Caldera assumed the Presidency in March, 1969. *Copei*, however did not have a majority in Congress, and to some extent governed with the consensus of A.D., who were returned to power with a Congressional majority in the General Election of Dec. 1973. President Carlos Andrés Pérez's term of office lasts until March 1979.

Language and Literature.—Spanish is the language of the country. Some Venezuelan literature is of international repute. There are 44 daily newspapers in Venezuela, of which ten are published in Caracas, and about 60 to 70 weekly news magazines. There are also a large number of fortnightly, monthly and quarterly publications.

Education is free and primary education compulsory from the age of 7 years. There are ten universities in Venezuela, five in Caracas and the others in Maracaibo, Mérida, Valencia, Cumaná and Barquisimeto.

Production and Industry.—The produce of Venezuelan forest and fields includes the following: (*a*) Tropical forest region: orchids, wild rubber, timber, mangrove bark, balata gum and tonka beans. (*b*) Agricultural areas: cocoa beans, coffee, cotton, rice, maize, sugar, sesame, groundnuts, potatoes, tomatoes, other vegetables, sisal and tobacco. There is an extensive beef and dairy farming industry. The country does not produce all the grain it requires but is practically self-sufficient for its other food requirements.

The principal industry is that of *Petroleum*, which last year contributed 97 per cent. of Venezuela's foreign exchange income. Daily production of the oilfields was reduced by direct government policy in 1974, and this policy of reduction in offtake is to continue until 1976 as a conservation measure. Before the war of 1939–45 over 80 per cent. of the crude oil was exported to Netherlands Antilles refineries. In 1942 small refineries were established in Venezuela, capable of handling about 200,000 barrels daily. The large Shell plant at Punta Cardon went into production in February, 1949, and the Creole refinery at Amuay a year later. Both companies have invested heavily in desulphurization plant to satisfy anti-pollution measures in Eastern U.S.A., whither most of their product goes in the form of fuel oil. Other refineries are being operated at Caripitó, San Lorenzo, Puerto La Cruz,

Tucupido, El Chaure and El Palito. New contracts have been signed for exploitation of petroleum resources in parts of the Maracaibo region. The Venezuelan Government has unified income tax on firms involved in mining and petroleum at 60 per cent, and reformed the basis on which tax is calculated. In 1973, as a result of united action by the OPEC countries, the posted price of Venezuelan oil rose from U.S. $3·14 per barrel in January to U.S. $14·08 per barrel by December. The two iron mining companies were nationalised in 1974 and the oil industry is expected to come under state ownership in 1975.

Rich iron ore deposits in Eastern Venezuela have been developed and production was 17,000,000 metric tons in 1972. Secondary processes for pelletizing and briquetting ore for export have been installed. The government-owned steel mill at Matanzas in the Guayana uses local iron ore and obtains its electric power from hydro-electric installations on the Caroni River. It produces seamless steel tubes, billets, wire and profiles. The production of more steel products is planned over the next few years. A new mill at Ciudad Guayana for the production of centrifugally-cast iron pipe came into operation at the end of 1970, with an annual capacity of 30,000 tons. It is planned to increase steel production to 15,000,000 tons a year by 1985.

Other industries include petrochemicals, gold, diamonds and asbestos; textiles and clothing; plastics; manufacture of paper, cement, glass and plate glass; beer and other alcoholic beverages; tyres, cigarettes, soap, animal feeding concentrates, non-alcoholic drinks, simple steel products, shoes, tins, jewellery, rope, metal and wooden furniture, sacks, paint and motor-vehicle assembly; preparation of pharmaceutical goods, lard, powdered milk, vegetable oil, flour, biscuits and other foods; fishing and fish-canning; pearl fishing, sanitary ware, electric home appliances, pumps, aluminium and aluminium products, toys, agricultural machinery, bicycles, electronic components, cosmetics and many others.

Communications.—There are about 39,563 km. of all-weather roads. The State has now acquired all but a very few of the railway lines, whose total length is only some 372 kilometres. Road and river communications have made railways of negligible importance in Venezuela except for carrying iron-ore in the south-east. However, the government now plans a new railway from Guayana to the industrial zones round Valencia for carrying steel. British, U.S. and European airlines provide Venezuela with a wide range of services. There are three Venezuelan airlines (two of them state-owned) which between them have a comprehensive network of internal lines and also connect Caracas with the United States, Central America, South America, the Caribbean and Europe. In 1972 the Venezuelan state-owned merchant fleet had 16 ships with a total deadweight tonnage of 115,950. Foreign vessels are not permitted to engage in the coast trade. The telegraph, radio-telegraph and radio-telephone services are state-owned. There are one government-controlled, 96 commercial and one cultural, FM, broadcasting stations. There are three television stations in Venezuela, all in Caracas. One is government controlled.

FINANCE

	1972	1973
	(in millions of *Bs.*)	
Revenue	12,450	16,440
Expenditure	12,618	14,036

National income per head in Venezuela in 1973 was $U.S.1260, the highest in Latin America.

Currency.—The unit of currency is the gold *Bolivar* of 100 *centimos*. The selling rate for foreign exchange for all purposes is *Bs.* 4·30= U.S. $1. The rates for other currencies fluctuate according to their quotations against the U.S. dollar. The Government still subsidises the imports of certain basic commodities.

TRADE

	1972	1973†
Imports	Bs.9,301,000,000	Bs.10,895,000,000
Exports	13,060,000,000	23,418,000,000

† Estimate.

The principal imports are machinery, foodstuffs, durable and non-durable consumer goods, iron, steel and chemicals. The principal exports are petroleum and petroleum products, iron ore, coffee and cocoa, and diamonds.

Trade with U.K.

	1973	1974
Exports from U.K.	£39,235,000	£50,311,000
Imports to U.K.	58,690,000	135,226,000

CAPITAL.—Caracas (3,000 ft.). Population, 1971, 2,183,935. Other principal towns are ΨMaracaibo (650,000), Barquisimeto (330,000), Valencia (360,000), Maracay (250,000), San Cristobal (150,000), Cumaná (120,000) and Ciudad Guayana (150,000).

FLAG.—Three horizontal bands, yellow, blue, red (with seven white stars on blue band and coat of arms next staff on yellow band). NATIONAL DAY.—July 5.

BRITISH EMBASSY

Edificio La Estancia, Apartado 1246, Ciudad Comercial Tamanaco, Caracas.
Ambassador Extraordinary and Plenipotentiary, His Excellency John Lang Taylor, C.M.G. (1975).
Counsellors, J. A. Snellgrove; D. A. Hamley (*Commercial*).
Defence Attaché, Cdr R. D. G. Williams, R.N.
1st Secretaries, D. Joy (*Information*); C. M. Wilkes; M. Hickson; D. Mellor (*Commercial*).
Consul, R. D. Baird Fraser.
British Council Representative, D. Aspinall.

BRITISH CONSULAR OFFICES

There are British Consular Offices at *Caracas, Maracaibo, Puerto La Cruz* and *Valencia.*

VIETNAM
REPUBLIC OF SOUTH VIETNAM

Since the beginning of May 1975, following the military overthrow of the former government, South Vietnam has been jointly controlled by the Provisional Revolutionary Government (PRG) and a number of local Military Management Committees. At the time of going to press, details of the composition of the PRG, first set up in opposition to the former government in 1969, have still not yet been formally announced.

South Vietnam has an area of 66,281 sq. miles and a population of approximately 20,000,000. Rice, rubber, timber and fishery products are the chief products. Trade in 1973 (excluding trade financed or assisted under American aid programmes) was: Imports $U.S.382,700,000; Exports $U.S.60,600,000.

Trade with U.K.

	1972	1973
Imports from U.K.	£1,295,000	£2,182,000
Exports to U.K.	115,000	229,000

On October 23, 1955, a referendum showed a large majority in favour of the deposition of the former Chief of State, Bao Dai, and the election of Ngo dinh Diem to his place. The latter was accordingly proclaimed Chief of State on October 26, and his first act was to declare South Vietnam a Republic of which he became the President.

On November 1, 1963, the Government of President Diem was overthrown by a military *coup d'état* during which the President was killed. General Duong Van Minh assumed power as Chairman of the Military Revolutionary Council and Head of State, but the former position was wrested from him on January 30 by General Ngu yen Khanh who assumed the function of Prime Minister and on Aug. 17 the Presidency.

A period of governmental instability followed, with rule by military junta being interrupted by shortlived attempts to form civilian administrations. Eventually, under the supervision of the army controlled national leadership committee led by General Nguyen van Thieu, elections to a constituent assembly were held on Sept. 11, 1966, and a new democratic constitution was promulgated on April 1, 1967. Presidential elections were held on Sept. 3, 1967.

At his presidential inauguration on October 30, 1967, President Nguyen Van Thieu proclaimed the Second Republic of Vietnam. On January 27, 1973, an agreement on ending the war and restoring the peace in Vietnam was signed in Paris. This provided, *inter alia*, for a ceasefire throughout Vietnam, the withdrawal of all U.S. forces within 60 days, the return of all U.S. prisoners-of-war held by North Vietnam, and the exchange of Vietnamese prisoners-of-war and civilian detainees. The agreement also provided for the establishment of an international commission with the participation of Canada, Hungary, Indonesia and Poland, to supervise the implementation of the agreement, and for the holding of an international conference, which the United Kingdom attended, to endorse the terms of the agreement. Finally, it provided for the holding of talks between the Government of Vietnam and the "Provisional Revolutionary Government of South Vietnam" (PRG) on the political future of Vietnam.

Canada later withdrew from the international commission, and was replaced by Iran.

Although the provisions of the Paris Agreement regarding the withdrawal of U.S. troops and the return of U.S. prisoners-of-war were respected, other provisions of the Agreement were not fulfilled to the satisfaction of all the parties. Hostilities continued, albeit at a reduced level, the exchange of Vietnamese personnel was acrimonious and long drawn-out, and the political talks, having made no perceptible progress, were suspended in April 1974.

A carefully prepared offensive by Communist forces in March 1975 led to the collapse of the Thieu Government in the following month. Thieu himself resigned on April 21 and his automatic successor, Vice-President Tran Van Huong, also resigned after only a few days in order to enable General Duong Van Minh, a former president and a neutral figure, to assume power and attempt to seek a peaceful solution to the war. Saigon fell to the Communist forces on April 30, shortly after President Minh had announced the unconditional surrender of his forces. The Provisional Revolutionary Government thereupon took over control of South Vietnam. The British Government recognized the Provisional Revolutionary Government as the Government of South Vietnam on May 12.

CAPITAL.— Ψ Saigon, population 3,000,000 (Saigon/Cholon, 1973). Other principal towns are Ψ Danang (500,000) and Hué (150,000). Saigon and Danang are the main ports.

FLAG.—Top half red, bottom half light blue, with yellow five-point star in centre.

BRITISH EMBASSY
25 Dai Lo Thong Nhut, Saigon
NOTE.—The Staff of the Embassy were withdrawn on April 24, 1975 because Saigon was about to fall into the war zone. The British Government and the PRG agreed on June 23, 1975 to establish diplomatic relations at Embassy level, but at the time of going to press no Staff had yet returned to the Embassy.

DEMOCRATIC REPUBLIC OF VIETNAM
(NORTH VIETNAM)
President, Ton Duc Thang, *elected* Sept. 24, 1969.
Prime Minister, Pham Van Dong (1955).
Minister of Foreign Affairs, Nguyen Duy Trinh.

VIETNAMESE WORKERS' (= Communist) PARTY
1st Secretary, Le Duan.
Politbureau of the Central Committee, Hoang Van Hoan; Le Duc Tho; Le Duan; Le Thanh Nghi; Vo Nguyen Giap; Nguyen Duy Trinh; Pham Hung; Pham Van Dong; Truong Chinh; Tran Quoe Hoan; Van Tien Dung.
Secretariat of the Central Committee, Le Duan (1st); Hoang Anh; Le Duc Tho; Nguyen Van Tran; To Huu; Le Van Luong; Nguyen Con; Xuan Thuy.

EMBASSY IN LONDON
89 Belsize Park Gardens, N.W.3
[01-586 2577]
Chargé d'Affaires, Lai Văn Ngoc.
North Vietnam (north of the 17th parallel) has an area of approximately 63,000 sq. miles and a population (April 1974 census) of 23,780,375 The capital is Hanoi (1,378,335) and the chief port is Ψ Haiphong. The chief crop is rice, of which the production in 1965 was claimed to be 4,660,000 tons. No figures have been given since but it is believed that, with a drop in the intervening wartime years, production again reached this level in 1974. The chief industrial products are coal, cement and apatite (phosphate). A number of new factories have been built with foreign aid, mainly from the U.S.S.R., China and East Europe.

Power is wielded by the *Lao Dong* (Workers' Party) which is Communist in character, and which can exert its influence through another mass organization known as the Fatherland Front (which some years ago superseded the " Vietminh "). The policy of the northern government has been to work for unification of Vietnam on Communist lines. Although the South fell to Communist forces in April 1975, formal unification may take some time to achieve. The reconstruction of North Vietnam is still in progress after the heavy damage inflicted by wartime bombing. Assistance is coming mainly from Communist countries but also others, notably Japan and Sweden. The government has diplomatic relations with the U.S.S.R., China and other States of the Sino-Soviet bloc, and since early 1973, with an increasing number of non-Communist countries.

FLAG.—Red, with yellow five-point star in centre.
NATIONAL DAY.—September 2.

BRITISH EMBASSY
Hanoi
British Chargé d'Affaires, John Anthony Benedict Stewart, O.B.E.

YEMEN
(Yemen Arab Republic)
Chairman of Command Council, Lieutenant-Colonel Ibrahim Mohammed al Hamdi, *assumed office*, June 13, 1974.
Prime Minister, Abdul Aziz Abdul Ghani.

YEMENI EMBASSY
41 South Street, W.1
[01-499 5246]
Ambassador, His Excellency Mohammed Abdullah al-Eryani (1974).
Minister-Plenipotentiary, Hashem al-Hauthi.

Yemen, the *Arabia Felix* of the ancients, occupies the S.W. corner of Arabia between the kingdom of Saudi Arabia and the People's Democratic Republic of Yemen, with an estimated area of 75,000 square miles and a population of about 6,000,000 including more than 1,000,000 emigrant workers in the Arabian peninsula. The highlands and central plateau of Yemen, and the highest portions of the maritime range, form the most fertile part of Arabia, with an abundant but irregular rainfall.

Trade.—The main exports are cotton, hides and skins, and cotton seeds. Imports from U.K. in 1974 were valued at £6,100,000.

The ruins of Marib, the ancient Sabæan capital and its dam are in the Yemen.

Government.—Following a bloodless military coup in Sana'a on June 13, 1974, a Military Command Council seized power. The Presidential Council resigned. The Constitution and the Consultative Council were suspended, but provisionally restored on October 23, 1974, except that the Command Council, no longer exclusively formed of military members, replaced the Republican Council as the Supreme Constitutional body.

A new government was formed in February, 1975.

CAPITAL, Sana'a (pop. 135,000). Other main cities are Taiz (80,000) and Hodeida (80,000).

FLAG.—Horizontal bands of red, white and black, with 5-point green star in centre of white band. (Adopted Dec., 1962).

BRITISH EMBASSY
Sana'a
Ambassador Extraordinary and Plenipotentiary, His Excellency Derrick Charles Carden (1973).
1st Secretary, C. J. H. Keith, M.B.E. (*Commercial Head of Chancery and Consul*).
Military Attaché, Lt.-Col. B. M. Lees.
Attaché, C. S. M. Shelton (*Technical Assistance*).
Vice-Consul, S. N. Lee.
British Council Representative, C. K. Smith.

YEMEN
(People's Democratic Republic of Yemen)
Presidential Council, Salim Rubi'a Ali (*Chairman*); Ali Nasser Muhammed; Abdul Fattah Isma'il.

Prime Minister and Minister of Defence, Ali Nasser Muhammed.
Foreign Affairs, Mohammed Saleh Yafai Muti. There are 14 other departmental Ministers.

EMBASSY
57 Cromwell Road, S.W.7
[01-584 6607]
Ambassador Extraordinary and Plenipotentiary, His Excellency Muhammed Hadi Awad.
Area and Population.—The Democratic Republic of Yemen lies at the southern end of the Arabian peninsula, having a frontier with the Yemen Arab Republic, and a coastline extending 700 miles from the Red Sea eastwards along the Gulf of Aden. The area is largely composed of mountains and desert. Rainfall is generally scarce and unpre-

INDO-CHINA

dictable. The population outside Aden is concentrated in the fertile districts. In the more extensive desert and near-desert areas nomadic communities depend on their livestock for a livelihood.

Included in the State are the offshore islands of Perim (in the Bab al-Mandeb Straits) and Socotra, formerly part of the sultanate of Qishn and Socotra, now merged in the People's Republic. Sovereignty over the island of Kamaran (area 70 sq. miles) in the Red Sea is under dispute following its occupation by forces of the Yemen Arab Republic during border conflicts in October, 1972. The area of the People's Democratic Republic is 180,000 sq. miles, with a population of 1,598,275 (Census, May 1973). The population of Aden alone (75 sq. miles) is about 250,000. The principal districts of Aden township are: Crater, Khormaksar,

Tawahi, and Ma'alla. Neighbouring communities are at Sheikh Othman, Medinat al-Shaab, and Little Aden, which is linked to the main town by a sandy strip of coastline, and is the site of a British Petroleum oil refinery. The other major coastal town is Mukalla.

Government.—The People's Republic of South Yemen was set up on Nov. 30, 1967 when the British government ceded power to the National Liberation front, thus bringing to an end 129 years of British rule in Aden and some years of protectorate status in the hinterland. Its name was changed to People's Democratic Republic of Yemen on Nov. 30, 1970. Territory of the Republic is that of the former Federation of South Arabia and the Aden Protectorates, consisting of the State of Aden and some 17 sultanates and emirates. It is now divided into six Governorates. Negotiations held between the British Government and representatives of the N.L.F. at Geneva from Nov. 21-29, 1967, ended in agreement on financial aid to South Yemen for civil and military purposes for a period of six months from the date of independence. Evacuation of British military forces which had begun in April, 1967, was completed on Nov. 29.

The Secretary-General of the National Liberation Front, Mr. Qahtan as-Shaabi, who had been appointed President from Nov. 30, 1967, held office until June 22, 1969, when he was deposed in a bloodless *coup d'état* and replaced by a Presidential Council led by Salim Rubi' a Ali. Under a constitution promulgated on Nov. 30, 1970, a Supreme People's Council of 101 members was appointed in May, 1971.

The Government receives substantial development and other aid from China, U.S.S.R. and other Socialist Bloc countries.

Kuria Muria Islands.—The Kuria Muria Islands, which had been administered by Gt. Britain from Aden although 200 miles distant from Yemen territory, were retroceded to the Sultanate of Oman on Nov. 30, 1967.

Production.—Agriculture is the main occupation of the inhabitants of the 60,000 square miles of the Republic, outside Aden town. This is largely of a subsistence nature, sorghum, sesame and millets being the chief crops, with wheat and barley widely grown at the higher elevations. Of increasing importance, however, are the cash crops which have been developed since the Second World War, by far the most important of which is long-staple cotton, which is now a major export, and revenue from which averages about £1,500,000 annually.

Under the Five Year Development Plan 1974-79 much importance is attached to the development of agricultural and fisheries projects. It is expected, that together, there will be a production increase of 54·1 per cent. by 1978-80 over the base year 1972-73. Light industries are being established which will replace imports and use locally produced raw materials.

Trade with U.K.

	1973	1974
Imports from U.K.	£4,500,000	£6,000,000
Exports to U.K.	3,400,000	8,100,000

Following the closure of the Suez Canal in 1967 the once prosperous trading economy of Aden fell into a steady decline. It is now hoped that the re-opening of the Canal in June will arrest and reverse this decline. The British Petroleum refinery exports almost 2,500,000 tons of petroleum products annually. In the main harbour, cargo handling for larger vessels is by lighter, but wharves at Maalla can accommodate alongside vessels up to 300 feet in length and 18 feet in draught.

Finance and Currency.—In the financial year 1974-75 revenue was estimated at about £18,000,000 and expenditure £38,000,000. Currency is the South Yemen *dinar* (SYD), the total circulation of which is about £48,000,000.

Communications.—There are no railways in the Republic. Aden has 400 miles of good roads and construction of a further 300 miles will proceed under the Five Year Plan. A system of undeveloped but motorable roads links the towns and villages outside Aden. There is an international airport at Aden (Khormaksar) into which a limited number of international airlines operate.

CAPITAL.—Aden (population, 250,000).

FLAG.—A tricolour, red, white and black horizontal bands, with a triangle of light blue at the hoist pointing towards the fly and charged with a five pointed red star.

NATIONAL DAYS.—Independence Day, Nov. 30; Revolution Day, Oct. 14.

BRITISH EMBASSY
Khormaksar, Aden.
Chargé d'Affaires, John Single Martyn Roberts.
1st Secretary, W. J. A. Buckley (*Consul*).
3rd Secretary, S. J. McEvoy (*Vice Consul*).

YUGOSLAVIA
(Socijalistička Federativna Republika Jugoslavije)

President of the Republic, President of the Presidency, President of the League of Communists of Yugoslavia, Chairman of the National Defence Council and Supreme Commander of the Armed Forces, Josip Broz Tito, *assumed office,* Jan. 14, 1953, *re-elected for* 4 *years,* 1954, 1958, 1963, 1967 *and July* 29, 1971 (5 yrs.). In May, 1974 he was elected President of the Federal Republic for an unlimited term.

Vice President of the Republic, Vladimir Bakarić (*elected May, 1974 for one year*)
President of the SFRJ Assembly, Kiro Gligorov.
President of the Federal Executive Council, Džemal Bijedić.
President of the Socialist Alliance of the Working People of Yugoslavia, Dušan Petrović.
Vice-Presidents of the SFRJ Assembly, Marijan Cvetković; Peko Dapčević; Sinan Hasani; Branko Pešić; Rudi Kolak.
Vice-Presidents of the Federal Executive Council, Anton Vratusa; Dobrosav Ćulafić; Borislav Šefer; Miloš Minić.
Secretary of the Federal Executive Council, Ivica Čačić.
Foreign Affairs, Miloš Minić.
Defence, Nikola Ljubičić.
Internal Affairs, Franjo Herljević.
Finance, Momčilo Cemović.
Foreign Trade, Dr. Emil Ludviger.
Justice and General Administrative Matters, Ivan Franko.
Market and Prices, Imer Pulja.
President of the Constitutional Court, Nikola Sekulić.
Federal Committee Presidents:—
Social Planning, Milorod Birovljev.
Power and Energy, Dušan Ilijević.
Agriculture, Ivo Kuštrak.
Tourism, Milan Vukasović.
Transport and Communications, Boško Dimitrijević.
Economic Cooperation with Developing Countries, Stojan Andov.
Labour and Employment, Svetozar Pepovski.
War Veterans, Mara Radić.
Health and Social Policy, Zora Tomić.
Science and Culture, Trpe Jakovlevski.
Information, Muharem Berberović.

LEAGUE OF YUGOSLAV COMMUNISTS
President, Josip Broz Tito.
Praesidium, R. Albreht; D. Alimpić; M. Bakali; V. Bakarić; I. Balint; M. Baltić; D. Bijedić; J. Billić; A. Cemerski; D. Ćulafić; R. Dugonjič; S. Dolanc; S. Doronjski; V. Djuranović; K. Gligorov; A. Grličkov; F. Hodža; E. Kardelj; L. Koliševski; I. Kukoč; T. Kurtović; N. Ljubičić; K. Markovski; M. Mesihović B. Mikulić; C. Mijatović; M. Minić; D. Petrović; M. Popović; D. Popović; F. Popit; M. Planinć; M. Ravnik; D. Ristić; D. Šarac; V. Sizentić; P. Stambolić; M. Spiljak; D. Stavrev; J. Smole; A. Šukrija; D. Vidić; J. Vrhovec; T. Vlaškalić; J. Vujadinović; V. Zarković.

Executive Committee, J. Bilić; S. Dolanc; T. Kurto-
vić; M. Popović; V. Srzentić; A. Grličkov;
I. Kukoč; M. Mesihović; D. Popović; D.
Stavrev; A. Šukrija; D. Vidić.

YUGOSLAV EMBASSY IN LONDON
5–7 Lexham Gardens W.8.
[01–370 6105]
Ambassador Extraordinary and Plenipotentiary, His Ex-
cellency Gen. Bogdan Orescanin (1973).
Minister-Counsellor, Dušan Gaspari.
Minister Plenipotentiary, Branko Komatina (*Eco-
nomic*).
Counsellors, Dušan Bogdanović (*Press and Culture*);
Momcilo Bajcetić (*Consular*).
Defence Attaché, Col. Milos Surlan.
Asst. Defence Attaché, Lt.-Col. Miroslav Ribner.
First Secretary, Jovan Cvejić (*Consular*).
2nd Secretaries, Radoslav Maksimović (*Press and
Culture*); Mrs. Rahela Altaras (*Consular*).
3rd Secretary, Gojko Skopelja (*Economic*).
Attaché, J. Prodanović (*Political*).
Consulate, 7 Lexham Gardens, W.8.

Area and Population.—Yugoslavia is a Federation
comprising the Socialist Republics of Serbia,
Croatia, Slovenia, Montenegro, Bosnia and Herzegovina, and Macedonia, Serbia includes the Socialist
Autonomous Provinces of the Vojvodina and
Kosovo. In July, 1946, Pelagosa and adjacent
islands with all territory east of the line known as
the *French Line* in Istria (including Pola and Fiume)
were ceded by Italy to Yugoslavia. By an agreement concluded in London on Oct. 5, 1954,
between Yugoslavia, Italy, the United Kingdom
and the United States, Zone B of the Trieste
Territory was transferred to the civil administration
of Yugoslavia, under whose military administration it had been since 1945. Zone B, an area of
200 square miles with a population of 73,500, in
cluded the towns of Kopar (Capodistria), Piran
(Pirano) and Novi Grad (Cittanuova). The area
has now been divided between the Republics of
Slovenia and Croatia. The area of Yugoslavia is
estimated at 255,804 square kilometres (98,725
square miles) and the population in April, 1971,
at 21,500,000. As a result of the war there was a
decrease of nearly 2,000,000 in the population of
Yugoslavia, and this loss has only recently been
made up.

Government.—On Nov. 29, 1945, the Constituent
Assembly of Yugoslavia at a joint session of the
Skupšatina and the House of Nationalities, proclaimed Yugoslavia a Republic. In January, 1953,
a new Constitution became effective, under which
two houses (the Federal Council and Council of
Producers) were established. Elections to these
houses were held in November, 1953 and March,
1958.

On April 7, 1963, a new Constitution was proclaimed under which the official name of the country
was changed to " The Socialist Federal Republic of
Yugoslavia". The existing two Councils of the
Federal Assembly were replaced by five Chambers
of 120 members each (Federal Chamber, Economic
Chamber, Educational-Cultural Chamber, Social
Welfare and Health Chamber, and Organizational/
Political Chamber), plus a Chamber of Nationalities
of 70 members. A Constitutional Court was
created. Elections to the new Federal Assembly
were held in 1963 and in April, 1967.

In 1969 the Federal Assembly was reconstructed
by the abolition of the Federal and Organizational/
Political Chambers and the addition of one new
chamber, the Social/Political. All Chambers continued to have 120 members each except the Chamber of Nationalities which doubled its size to 140.
Elections to this Assembly were held in April, 1969.

Several amendments to the Constitution were
made in 1971. The most important formed a new
ruling body called the Presidency. The intention
is that its members will take it in turns to become
President of the Republic for a period of 12 months
each. President Tito will however have the title
of Life President. A new Constitution was proclaimed in 1974 followed by the reconstitution of
the Federal Assembly, after elections based on the
new delegatory system, into two chambers consisting of the Federal Chamber (220 delegates) and
the Republican Provincial Chamber (88 delegates).
A new Federal Executive Council (i.e. government)
was also formed.

Defence.—The Army, Navy and Air Force on a
peace footing consist of 222,000 officers and men.

Religion and Education.—The Orthodox, Roman
Catholic, Protestant, Islamic and Judaic faiths are
recognized by the State. The 1953 Census revealed
that 2,127,875 of the population were without
religion, 6,984,686 were Orthodox, 5,370,760

Catholic, 157,702 Protestant, 61,274 other Christians, 2,090,380 Moslem, 2,565 Jews, 495 other non-
Christians, 10,096 undecided and 130,740 unknown.
The Church is separated from the State. All religious instruction in schools has been forbidden
since January 1952. Priests are allowed to teach in
churches. Eight years' elementary education is
compulsory and all education is free. In 1969–70
there were 14,043 elementary schools with 116,895
teachers and 2,854,579 pupils and 2,974 secondary
schools (including adult and special schools) with
33,702 teachers and 801,169 pupils. In addition, in
the 1970–71 academic year there were 13 art
academies with 483 teachers and 2,225 pupils, 10
high schools with 557 teachers and 7,456 pupils, and
119 higher schools with 3,986 teachers and 79,325
pupils. There are eight universities: Belgrade,
Zagreb, Ljubljana, Sarajevo, Skopje, Novi Sad,
Niš and Priština.

Language and Literature.—The languages of the
country are Serbo-Croat, Slovenian and Macedonian, all South-Slav tongues. Serbo-Croat predominates and is the language of the Federal
Government. In Serbia, Macedonia and Montenegro the Cyrillic script is used and in the rest of
the country the Latin; Hungarian, Rumanian,
Albanian, Italian, Slovak and Ruthenian are also
used in certain districts. The desire for the political

union of the South Slavs led to a cultural unity and a revival of Slav literature. There are 4 Serbian daily newspapers in Belgrade, 2 Slovene dailies in Ljubljana (Laibach), 2 Croat dailies in Zagreb, 2 dailies in Novi Sad, one in Hungarian, 2 dailies in Rijeka, one in Italian and daily papers at Skopje, Sarajevo, Priština, Split, Maribor and Osijek.

Production and Industry.—About 50 per cent. of the population is engaged in agriculture, although in recent years industry has expanded rapidly and industrial production has grown sevenfold since 1939. Recent emphasis has been on the integration of small industrial enterprises into more efficient complexes. In agriculture the main emphasis is on increased investment in mechanization and fertilizers in the large socially-owned agricultural combines but now the private sector is being encouraged to mechanize and become more efficient and small size tractors, farm machinery and implements are being supplied.

The main crops are wheat and maize, of which the yields in 1974 were 6,282,000 and 7,989,000 tons respectively. The forest areas produced 17,430,000 cubic metres of cut timber in 1973. According to Yugoslav official estimates, the livestock population in 1974 was approximately as follows: cattle, 5,681,000; sheep, 7,852,000; pigs 7,401,000; poultry, 54,685,000. Minerals are an important source of wealth particularly in the central and south-eastern regions. Estimated production in 1974 included the following ('000 tons): coal 33,583; coke 1,315; electrolytic copper 150; pig iron 2,126; steel (total) 2,833; aluminium 147; zinc 56; mercury 546 and crude petroleum 3,458.

Communications.—In 1973 there were approximately 10,400 kms of standard and narrow gauge railway and approximately 97,800 kms of classified roads. In 1973 there were 1,004,000 telephones in use in the country. The principal Ψ ports on the long Adriatic seaboard of Yugoslavia are Rijeka, Šibenik, Split, Zadar, Ploće, Dubrovnik, Bar, Kotor (Carraro) and Koper. A new port is still under construction at Bakar. The Danube forms a great commercial highway and the tributary rivers Sava and Tisa provide other shipping routes.

FINANCE

	1972	1973
	million *Dinars*	
Revenue	50,173	59,314
Expenditure	49,951	58,742

The rate of exchange is variable, but has been steady since Jan. 1974 at approx. 36 *dinars*= £1 (*see also* p. 84).

Trade with U.K.

	1973	1974
Imports from U.K.	£56,200,000	£83,100,000
Exports to U.K.	24,500,000	30,600,000

The chief exports to the United Kingdom are meat and meat products, furniture and timber. The main imports from the United Kingdom are machinery of all kinds, iron and steel, chemicals, wool tops and metal manufactures.

CAPITAL.—Belgrade, population (Greater Belgrade, 1971), 1,204,000. Other towns are Zagreb (602,000); Skopje (388,000); Ljubljana (258,000); Sarajevo (292,000); Novi Sad (214,000); Priština (153,000); Ψ Split (152,000); Ψ Rijeka (133,000); Titograd (99,000).

FLAG.—Five-point red star outlined by narrow yellow stripe, on a ground of three horizontal bars, blue, white and red. NATIONAL DAY.—November 29.

BRITISH EMBASSY

Generala Zdanova 46, Belgrade.
Ambassador Extraordinary and Plenipotentiary, His Excellency Sir Dugald Leslie Lord Stewart, C.M.G. (1971).
Counsellors, C. L. Booth; J. Middleton (*Economic and Commercial*).
Defence Attaché, Col. B. A. M. Pielow.
Naval and Air Attaché, Wing-Cdr. I. Scott.
1st Secretaries, G. D. G. Murrell (*Information*); D. A. Burns; J. M. Candlish (*Commercial*); S. T. Corcoran (*Labour*) (*resident at* Athens); D. J. Young (*Admin. and Consular*).
2nd Secretary, P. Thomas.
3rd Secretaries, M. H. F. Legg; H. S. M. Clark; Miss J. Oldershaw; N. A. S. Jones.

BRITISH CONSULAR OFFICES

There are British Consular Offices at *Belgrade*, *Zagreb* and *Split*.

British Council Representative, E. Evans, M.B.E., Generala Ždanova 34, Belgrade. British Council Reading Room Knez Mihajlova 45, Belgrade. There are also a centre and library at *Zagreb*.

ZAIRE
(The Republic of Zaire)

President of the Republic and Minister of Defence, Gen. Mobutu Sésé Seko, *born* Oct. 30, 1930; *assumed office* November 25, 1965; *elected for* 7-year term, Nov. 5, 1970.

CABINET
(As at June 1975)

Political Affairs, Engulu Baangampongo Bakokele Lokanga.
Foreign Affairs and International Cooperation, Mandungu Bula Nyati.
National Orientation, Bokonga Ekanga Botombele.
Justice, Kabuita Nyamabu.
Youth and Sports, Elonga Mali Mazungu.
Finance, Bofosa W'Amb'Ea Nkoso.
National Economy and Industry, Tshimpumpu Kanyinda.
Mines, D'Zbo Kalogi.
Agriculture, Kayinga Onsi Ndal.
Commerce, Citoyenne Mata'a Nkumu Wa Bowango Nanganda Diowo.
National Education, Mabolia Inengo Tra Bwato.
Public Works and Land Management, Takizala Luyanu Musimbingi.
Transport and Communications, Inonga Lokongo L'ome.
Public Service, Mulenda Shamwange Mutebi.
Energy, Muntu Kakubi Tshiondo Kabanza Wa Mintenge.
Public Health, Ngwete Kikhela.
Social Affairs, Mama Mobutu Sésé Seko.
Labour and Social Security, Bintu'a Tshiabola.
Posts and Telecommunications, Tchomba Somwa Kimbayo.
Culture and Arts, Citoyenne Mkemba Yowa Mabinda Kapinga.
Environment, Conservation of Nature and Tourism, Citoyenne Lessedjina Kiaba Lema.
Without Portfolio, Mambu Ma Khenzu Makwala.

ZAIRE EMBASSY

26 Chesham Place, S.W.1.
[01–235 6137]
Ambassador Extraordinary and Plenipotentiary, His Excellency Kaninda Mpumbua Tshingomba, G.C.V.O.

The State of the Congo, founded in 1885, became a Belgian Colony on Nov. 15, 1908, and was administered by Belgium until June 30, 1960, when it

became the Democratic Republic of the Congo. In October 1971 the name changed to the Republic of Zaire. Situated between long. 12°–31° E. and lat. 5° N.–13° S., the Zairian Republic comprises an area of 905,582 sq. miles, with a population (Census, 1970) of 21,637,000, including 932,000 foreigners. The State is divided into 8 provinces (*see* below).

Government.—On June 30, 1960, the Belgian Congo became an independent unitary state under the Presidency of M. Kasavubu with a provisional constitution, the *Loi Fondamentale*, drawn up by the metropolitan Belgian Parliament. On July 11, M. Moise Tshombe announced the independence of the State of Katanga although he failed to obtain international recognition. Katanga did not come under the Government at Leopoldville until January 14, 1963.

The constitutional and political situation remained unsettled, the United Nations having mixed forces in the country until 1964. By the middle of 1965, the Congolese Government formed by M. Tshombe in July, 1964, had succeeded in gaining control of all the towns from the rebels and depriving them of military aid from outside the Congo. At elections held in the spring of 1965 the Government party won an overall majority of 86, but the elections in three provinces were annulled on the grounds that they had been irregularly conducted. Following fresh elections held in these provinces in August, 1965, M. Tshombe's Government was dismissed by the President. A new Cabinet was formed by M. Evariste Kimba on October 19 and held office until the deposition on Nov. 25 of the President.

General Joseph-Desiré Mobutu, Commander-in-Chief of the Congolese National Army, announced on November 25, 1965, that he had assumed the Presidency. After re-organizations in Dec. 1966, and Oct. 5, 1967, a new Cabinet, with the President again as Prime Minister, took office on Mar. 5, 1969.

The office of Prime Minister was later dropped and a Presidential régime instituted. The *Mouvement Populaire de la Révolution*, formed in 1967, was made the sole political party. With its deliberative assembly, the Party Congress, it is the supreme political institution of the country. Its executive body, the 15-man Political Bureau, is headed by the President and takes precedence over the single-chamber 420-person National Assembly as well as over the Government. The President changed his name to Mobutu Sésé Séko Kuku Ngbendu Wa Zabanga in 1972, but is usually known by the first three of these names only.

Climate.—Apart from the coastal district in the West which is fairly dry, the rainfall averages between 60 and 80 inches. The average temperature is about 80° F., but in the South the winter temperature can fall nearly to freezing point. There has been some increase in sleeping-sickness since independence. Malaria, formerly under control in Leopoldville (*now* Kinshasa) and Matadi, has also begun to increase.

Extensive forest covers the central districts.

Provinces.—On December 24, 1966, the number of provinces was reduced from 21 to 8, each under a Governor and provincial administration. They have recently been redesignated as " regions " and are now as follows with names of capitals in brackets: Bas-Zaire (*Matadi*); Bandundu (*Bandundu*); Equateur (*Mbandaka*); Haut-Zaire (*Kisangani*); Kivu (*Bukavu*); Shaba, *formerly* Katanga (*Lubumbashi*); East Kasai (*Mbuji-Mayi*); West Kasai (*Kananga*).

Production.—The cultivation of oil palms is widespread, palm oil being the most important agricultural cash product. Rubber, coffee, cocoa and timber are the next most important agricultural exports. The production of cotton, pyrethrum and copal fell sharply on independence but is now increasing. The country is rich in minerals, particularly Shaba (*ex*-Katanga) province. Copper is widely exploited and is the country's major source of foreign exchange earnings. Extensive radium deposits exist near Lubumbashi and reef-gold exists in the north-east of the country.

There is a wide variety of small but flourishing secondary industries, the main products being: cotton fabrics, blankets, sacks, footwear, beer, cigarettes, cement, paint, sugar, furniture, metal goods and tyres, and local assembly of motor vehicles is now beginning. There are very large reserves of hydro-electric power and the huge Inga dam on the river Zaire is now supplying electricity to Matadi and Kinshasa.

The chief exports are copper, palm oil and palm-kernels, coffee, diamonds, rubber, cobalt, cassiterite, zinc and other metals.

Currency.—The present unit of currency, the Zaire, was introduced in 1967, replacing 1,000 Old Congolese francs. Since then it has retained its rate of U.S. \$2= 1 Zaire. Rate against the Pound, Z1·28= £1 (July 1973).

Trade with U.K.

	1973	1974
Imports from U.K....	£11,568,000	£20,428,000
Exports to U.K......	22,214,000	36,496,000

Language, Religion and Education.—The people are mainly of Bantu-Negro stock, divided into semi-autonomous tribes, each speaking a Bantu tongue. Swahili, a Bantu dialect with an admixture of Arabic, is the nearest approach to a common language in the East and South, while Lingala is the language of Kinshasa, and of a large area along the river and in the north. It is estimated there are 5,000,000 African Christians in the Republic (Roman Catholic 4,200,000, Protestant 800,000). The local Kimbanguist religion has over a million adherents. The National University of Zaire has campuses in Kinshasa, Kisangani and Lubumbashi, with approximately 12,000 students.

CAPITAL, Kinshasa (*formerly* Leopoldville), population (estimated, 1971) 1,300,000. Principal towns, Lubumbashi (*formerly* Elisabethville) (182,638); Kisangani (*formerly* Stanleyville) (79,941); Likasi (74,478); Kananga (59,935); Ψ Matadi (59,184); Kolwezi (47,712); Mbandaka (37,587); and Ψ Boma (31,598).

FLAG.—Dark brown hand and torch with red flame in yellow roundel on green background. NATIONAL DAY.—June 30.

BRITISH EMBASSY
Kinshasa.
Ambassador Extraordinary and Plenipotentiary, His Excellency Richard James Stratton, C.M.G. (1974).
Counsellor, D. J. Reid (*Consul General*).

Defence, Naval, Military and Air Attaché, Col. R. C Wigglesworth.
1st Secretaries, B. Sparrow (*Head of Chancery*); T. E. Martin (Commercial); E. K. Green (*Vice Consul*).

EUROPEAN FREE TRADE ASSOCIATION (EFTA)

Member States: Austria, Iceland, Norway, Portugal, Sweden, Switzerland. Associate Member: Finland.

Following the unsuccessful attempt to create a European Free Trade Area linking the E.E.C. with other members of the O.E.E.C., seven European States above came together in 1959 to form the European Free Trade Association. The seven were Austria, Denmark, Norway, Portugal, Sweden, Switzerland and the United Kingdom. The EFTA Convention became effective on May 3, 1960, and just over a year later, on June 26, 1961, Finland became an associate member. Iceland applied for full membership in November, 1968, and acceded to the Association and to the Finland–EFTA Agreement on March 1, 1970.

In 1973 all the EFTA Member States entered into a new relationship with the EEC. Two—Denmark and the United Kingdom—withdrew from EFTA at the end of December 1972 to become members of the EEC on January 1, 1973. Agreements establishing industrial free trade between five of the other EFTA Member States (Austria, Iceland, Portugal, Sweden and Switzerland) and the EEC came into force on that same date. Similar agreements with Norway and Finland came into force on July 1, 1973, and January 1, 1974, respectively.

The Convention defines the objects of the Association as (1) to promote economic expansion in the area of the Association and in each member state; (2) to ensure that trade between member states takes place in conditions of fair competition; (3) to avoid significant disparity between member states in the condition of supply of raw materials produced within the area; and (4) to contribute to the harmonious development and expansion of world trade and to the progressive removal of barriers to it.

Members agreed to reduce progressively their tariffs on imports of industrial goods originating in the Area with a view to their complete elimination by January 1, 1970. They also undertook to abolish quantitative restrictions on imports of goods from the free trade area. Provision was made for alterations in these timetables and in May, 1963, when tariffs had been reduced to 50 per cent. of the original rates, members agreed to bring forward the date when tariffs and quotas would be finally eliminated to December 31, 1966. Since that date therefore the member countries of the Association have constituted a virtually complete industrial free trade area. There is no common external tariff for the Association, each member country being free to fix the level of its tariffs against countries outside the area. The Convention includes rules governing the origin of goods manufactured in the area. It also contains provisions relating to the " rules of competition "—government subsidies, restrictive business practices, etc. There are special provisions relating to trade in agricultural and fish products.

The Council of EFTA consists of one ministerial or official representative from each member country. Each state has a single vote and recommendations must normally be unanimous. Decisions of the Council are binding on member countries.

Secretary-General, Bengt Rabaeus (*Sweden*), 9–11 rue de Varembé, 1211 Geneva 20.

EUROPEAN COMMUNITY

The nine member states: Belgium, Denmark, France, Germany, Ireland, Italy, Luxemburg, The Netherlands, the United Kingdom.

The beginnings of the European Community date from May 9, 1950, when Robert Schuman, France's Foreign Minister, proposed that France and Germany should pool their coal and steel industries under an independent (" supranational ") High Authority, in a Community open to the membership of any other European country wishing to join. Not only Germany, but also Italy, Belgium, the Netherlands, and Luxemburg accepted this invitation.

The Coal and Steel Community (ECSC), Common Market and Euratom share a single institutional framework: a Commission, Council of Ministers, Parliament and Court of Justice. The core of the Community policymaking process is the " dialogue " between the Commission, which initiates and implements policy, and the Council of Ministers, which takes major policy decisions. The beginnings of democratic control are excercised by the European Parliament, while the Court of Justice ensures the rule of law and is the final arbiter in all matters arising from the Community Treaties.

Since the start of the Common Market and Euratom in 1958, the Parliament and Court of Justice have been common to all three Communities. Up to July, 1967, each Community had its own executive body (the EEC and Euratom Commissions, and the ECSC High Authority) and its own Council of Ministers.

In April, 1965, the Six signed a treaty providing for the merger of the three executive bodies in a single Commission and the three Councils in a single Council, with a view to the eventual merger of the three Communities themselves. The merger treaty came into force on July 1, 1967; the single Commission and single Council then took office. They enjoy the same powers under the three Community Treaties as did their predecessors.

On December 1 and 2, 1969, the Heads of State or Government of the Six met at the Hague and decided on the completion, strengthening, and, provided that other European countries wished to accept the Treaties of Rome, enlargement of the Community. They instructed the Commission to draw up a plan for economic and monetary union, and the Foreign Ministers to report by the end of July on possible moves towards political unification. They also resolved to intensify the co-ordination of research and development programmes.

In accordance with the Hague decisions the Council of Ministers agreed in April, 1970, that as from 1975 the Community would have its own revenue, independent of national contributions. The Foreign Ministers agreed (May, 1970) to hold formal political consultations twice a year.

In June, 1970, the Six invited Britain, the Irish Republic, Denmark and Norway to open negotiations on June 30 at Luxemburg on their applications to join the Community. Negotiations continued in 1971 and were concluded with the United Kingdom Government for all major questions by the end of June; on July 8, H.M. Government issued a White Paper on the results. On Jan. 22, 1972, the four applicant countries signed the Treaty of Accession in Brussels. Norway conducted a referendum on its Common Market entry and as a result withdrew its application. The enlarged Community of the Nine came into existence on Jan. 1, 1973.

The Commission

On July 1, 1970, the Commission was reduced from 14 members to nine, two each from Germany, France, and Italy, and one each from Belgium, the Netherlands and Luxemburg. After the three new countries joined, the number rose to 13, with two sets each from Britain, France, Germany, and Italy and one each for the other members.

The members of the Commission are appointed by agreement among the six member governments for a four-year renewable term; the president and vice-presidents are appointed from among the members for a two-year term, also renewable.

The members of the Commission are pledged to independence of the governments and of national or other particular interests. They accept joint responsibility for their decisions, which are taken by majority vote.

In addition to being the initiator of Community action and having specific powers, the Commission acts as a mediator between the member governments in Community affairs and is the guardian of the Community Treaties.

Commission of the European Communities
200 Rue de la Loi, Brussels 1049

President, François-Xavier Ortoli (French).
Vice-Presidents, Wilhelm Haferkamp (German); Carlo Scarascia Mugnozza (Italian); Sir Christopher Soames (British); Patrick Hillery (Irish); Henri Simonet (Belgian).

The Commission maintains information offices in London (20 Kensington Palace, Gardens, W.8), Washington (Suite 707, 2100 M Street, N.W., Washington, D.C. 20037), New York (277 Park Avenue, New York, N.Y. 10017) and other cities.

The new 13-member Commission was appointed by the Government of the Nine and was sworn in on Jan. 9, 1973.

The Council of Ministers
170 Rue de la Loi, 1040 Brussels

This consists of ministers from each member government, the ministers concerned depending on the subject under discussion. It is the Community's main decision-taking body but its authority is not as great in ECSC matters as in those relating to the Common Market and Euratom. The powers of the Commission are proportionately greater under the ECSC Treaty. For coal and steel, decisions are usually by majority vote; on Common Market and Euratom matters decisions usually had to be unanimous in the early stages, but most decisions can now be taken by a qualified majority vote. For certain vital questions, however, unanimity is still required. (Admission of new members is not decided by the Council, but by a unanimous decision of the member governments.) Although the Council is the Community's ultimate decision-taking body, in almost all cases it can act only on the basis of proposals submitted by the Commission. The Council acts by issuing (a) " regulations " which are generally and directly binding throughout the Community; (b) " directives " which set out the aims of policy but leave

national governments to implement; (c) " decisions " which bind only those addressed (normally member states); and (d) " recommendations ", which have no binding force. The meetings of the Council are prepared by a Committee of Permanent Representatives of the member states.

The Presidency of the Coucil is held in rotation for periods of six months.

European Parliament
Secretariat: Centre Européen, Kirchberg, Luxemburg.

The European Parliament consists of 198 members nominated by the national parliaments of the nine member countries—36 members each from France, Germany, Italy, and the United Kingdom, 14 each from Belgium and the Netherlands, 10 each from Ireland and Denmark, and 6 from Luxemburg. Set up under the terms of the ECSC Treaty of 1952, its authority was extended by the Treaty of Rome 1957 to cover also the European Economic Community and Euratom. The Parliament must be consulted on all major issues and has the right to dismiss the Commission by a vote of no confidence. In April, 1970, it was agreed that as part of the financial arrangements giving the Community its own direct revenue, the Parliament would have after 1975 a degree of control over the Community's budget. The Parliament now has the right to reject the Community Budget as a whole, and to amend certain items classed as "non-obligatory" expenditure—about 20 per cent. of the whole. The Treaty of Rome provides for direct election of the members of the European Parliament. At the summit conference of December 1974 the date for the first such elections was set for "any time in or after 1978". In January 1975 the Parliament itself drew up a new draft convention for direct elections which would enlarge the Parliament to 355 members, of which the United Kingdom would have 67. The members of the Parliament have formed six political groups—*Socialist* (67 in July 1975), *Christian Democrat* (51), *Liberal* (25), *Conservative* (17) *Progressive Democrat* (17) and *Communist* (15). There are also six independents.
President, Georges Spénale (*Socialist, France*).

European Court of Justice
Boite postale 1406, Luxemburg

The European Court superseded the Court of Justice of ECSC and is common to the three European Communities. It exists to safeguard the law in the interpretation and application of the Community treaties, to decide on the legality of decisions of the Council of Ministers or the Commission and to determine violations of the Treaties. Cases may be brought to it by the member States, the Community institutions, firms or individuals. Its decisions are directly binding in the member countries. The nine judges of the court are appointed by the member Governments in concert and are partially replaced every three years, being eligible for re-appointment.
Judges, R. Lecourt (*President*); A. M. Donner; R. Monaco; J. Mertens de Wilmars; H. Kutscher; Lord Mackenzie Stuart; M. Sørensen; A. O'Keeffe.
Advocates-General, G. Reischl; H. Mayras; A. Trabucchi, J.-P. Warner.
Registrar, A. Van Houtte.

The European Investment Bank
2 Place de Melz, Luxemburg

The European Investment Bank (EIB) was set up in 1958 under the terms of the Treaty of Rome with the essential function that of contributing to the balanced development of the Common Market.

It grants long-term loans to enterprises, public authorities and financial institutions to finance projects which assist the development of less advanced regions and areas where the conversion or modernisation of older, exhausted industries is required. Another important role of the EIB is that of helping to finance projects which serve the interests of the Community as a whole or more than one member country (such as motorways, railways and telecommunications, development and diversification of the EEC's energy sources).

The members of the European Investment Bank are the nine member countries of the Community, who have all subscribed to the Bank's capital, which currently stands at 2,025 million units of account.* The funds required to carry out its tasks are borrowed on the capital markets of the Community and non-member countries, and on the international markets.

As it operates on a profit-making basis, the interest rates charged by the E.I.B. are therefore close to the average rates charged on the markets where it obtains its funds.

The Board of Governors of the European Investment Bank consists of Ministers nominated by the member countries, usually the Finance Minister, who lay down general directives on the policy of the Bank and appoint members to the Board of Directors, which takes decisions on the granting and raising of loans and the fixing of interest rates.

A Management Committee, also appointed by the Board of Governors, is responsible for the day-to-day operations of the Bank.

President, Yves Le Portz.

Vice-Presidents, Sjoerd Boomstra; Luca Rosania; Horst-Otto Steffe; Sir Raymond Bell.

Secretary General, Henri Lenaert.

* The financial statements of the European Investment Bank are drawn up in units of account, which in January 1975, were £0·52.

EUROPEAN COAL AND STEEL COMMUNITY

This, the first of the European Communities, was established in 1952. Since then, for coal, iron ore and scrap, it has abolished customs duties, quantitative restrictions, the dual pricing system whereby prices charged on exported coal or steel differed from those charged to home consumers, currency restrictions and discrimination in transport rates based on the nationality of customers and the special frontier charges which made international transport of these goods within the Community dearer than transport within national frontiers. It has applied rules for fair competition and a harmonized external tariff for the whole Community.

In the period 1952 to 1968 Community steel production rose rapidly from 41·9 to 99 million tons. The coal industry, however, after expanding initially in conditions of acute energy shortage, found that a growing share of the energy market was being won by oil. The task of the ECSC thus came to be to ensure the orderly retreat of coal at a price which would avoid social or economic dislocation. So far, since the start of the crisis, in 1957, the Community's coal industry has lost a third of its labour force. The ECSC has been especially active in meeting the social problems raised by such changes.

Between 1954 and 1973 joint expenditure in retraining and resettling or assisting the retirement of workers came to over £228 millions. ECSC loans in the same period helped to provide over 120,000 new jobs. New priorities, for avoiding

further rundown in the coal industry and enhancing its status, have been put forward since 1973. The ECSC also conducts its own housing programme for coal and steel workers.

Decisions of the European Commission in ECSC matters are directly binding on the industries concerned. The Commission now supervises the smooth working of the common market in ECSC products, ensures that the Treaty rules of fair competition are observed, stimulates investment and research, and aids workers threatened with unemployment. The Paris Summit of 1972 recognized the need for the EEC to prepare an energy policy covering all sources. Attempts to formulate such a policy have become a dominant issue in EEC affairs since the energy crisis. Of the various forms of energy, coal falls within the competence of the ECSC, nuclear energy within that of Euratom and all others within the EEC.

The United Kingdom, Ireland and Denmark joined the ECSC on Jan. 1, 1973.

EUROPEAN ECONOMIC COMMUNITY (THE COMMON MARKET)

Discussions were held at Messina, Sicily, in 1955 between the foreign ministers of the six member states of ECSC (Belgium, France, Germany, Italy, Luxemburg and The Netherlands) on proposals for further advances towards economic integration in Europe, and after intensive study of these proposals, a treaty was signed at Rome on March 25, 1957, setting up the European Economic Community.

The Treaty aimed to lay the foundations of an enduring and closer union between the European peoples by gradually removing the economic effects of their political frontiers. The Common Market was established during a transition period of twelve years which ended on Dec. 31, 1969. The Treaty provides for the elimination of customs duties and quotas in trade between member states; the establishment of a common customs tariff and a common trade policy towards third countries; the abolition of the obstacles to free movement of persons, services and capital between member states; the inauguration of common policies for agriculture and transport; the establishment of a system ensuring that competition shall not be distorted in the Common Market; the co-ordination of economic policies; the harmonization of social and economic legislation to the extent necessary in order to enable the Common Market to work; the creation of a European Social Fund in order to improve the possibilities of employment for workers and to contribute to the raising of their standard of living; the establishment of an Economic and Social Committee which must be consulted on major proposals, consisting of representatives of employers, workers, consumers and other groups; the establishment of a European Investment Bank intended to aid investment in underdeveloped areas and help to finance modernization; and the association of overseas countries and territories with the Community with a view to increasing trade and to pursuing jointly their effort towards economic and social development.

To date, this programme has been put into effect as follows:

Reduction of trade barriers.—A first 10 per cent. reduction in customs duties between member countries took place on January 1, 1959. Decisions taken by the Council of Ministers in May, 1960, and July, 1963, resulted in a speeding up of the rate of tariff cutting. On May 11, 1966, the Council of Ministers agreed that the abolition of internal duties should be completed on July 1, 1968, and this advanced target date was met. Quota restrictions on trade within the Common Market were completely removed on January 1, 1962. Customs tariffs between the three new member states and the original Six will be phased out by three stages ending in July 1977. A determined effort is being made to speed up the removal of non-tariff barriers to trade, *e.g.* different safety regulations and technical specifications.

Common external tariff.—The Common Market has a common external tariff (CET) which came into effect in July 1968 along with the abolition of customs duties among the Six, thus forming a customs union. The CET is based on the arithmetical average of those national tariffs it replaced, and after two international tariff-cutting rounds now stands at an average of 6 per cent. The three new members are gradually aligning their industrial tariffs up or down towards the CET and should join in full customs union by 1977.

In international tariff and trade negotiations in the GATT framework, the Community is represented by the Commission, which negotiates under a mandate from the Council of Ministers. New GATT talks began in September 1973 in Tokyo.

Trade between the member countries of the Common Market increased from $6,864 million in 1958 to $49,100 million in 1971. Internal trade in 1972 was up to 112,251 million u/a (equivalent to pre-1971 US dollars). Community exports to the rest of the world increased from $15,911 million in 1958 to $50,600 million in 1971 and $56,681 million u/a in 1972. Imports from the rest of the world in 1971 were $49,100 million, leaving the Community as a whole with a surplus of $1,500 million against a deficit of $423 million in 1970 and a deficit of $25 million in 1969. In 1972, imports were up to 52,526 million u/a, giving a surplus of 4,155 million u/a. The 1973–74 oil crisis severely upset the balance of payments situation of several member States; the EEC external deficit in 1974 amounted to some $18,000 million compared with a surplus of 1,000 million units of account in 1973. The situation was redressed during 1974–75.

Free movement of labour.—Freedom of movement for workers was achieved within the Common Market in July 1968, and those who work in member countries other than their own are ensured of rights equal to those of local workers, and of full tranferability of social security benefits. They enjoy equal treatment in applying for jobs and receive equal priority over workers from non-member countries.

Services.—The right of Community firms to establish business in member countries other than their own is being progressively freed, as is the right of Community citizens to engage in professional activities in member countries other than their own. In parallel with this programme, the mutual recognition of professional qualifications is being achieved. Freedom of establishment for a number of liberal professions was delayed for years, but with provision made in 1975 for doctors to practise throughout the Community, progress elsewhere should be rapid.

Capital.—So far unconditional and complete freedom of movement has been achieved for direct investments, transfers of personal funds and emigrants' remittances, short and medium term commercial loans and the buying and selling of stocks and shares. For other transactions, such as capital issues, there is conditional liberalization. Progress is being made towards equalizing access to domestic capital markets within the Nine.

Rules for Fair Competition.—The Common Market Treaty bans agreements which prevent, restrain or distort competition and, in particular, price-fixing, market-sharing, restriction of production or of technical development and discriminatory supply conditions if they are likely to affect trade between member states. The abuse of a dominant position in the market by a firm or firms is also banned. Implementing regulations adopted by the Council have caused some 36,000 restrictive agreements to be registered with the Commission. Decisions banning or authorizing particular agreements have begun to be taken, and a body of case-law is being established.

Agriculture.—The basic machinery for a common organization of agricultural markets throughout the Community was established by decision of the Council of Ministers in January 1962. It involved the setting of target prices, support buying, levies on imports, and export rebates. Community funds can be allotted for the modernization of farming and the improvement of agricultural productivity in the Community. The common agricultural policy came into effect in July, 1962, for grains, eggs and poultry, pigmeat, fruit and vegetables, and wine. It was extended in September, 1964, to rice, and in November 1964 to beef, veal, and dairy produce, thus covering 90 per cent. of total Community agricultural output.

Under a decision reached in December, 1964, common price levels throughout the Community came into effect in July, 1967, for grains, pigmeat, and eggs and poultry. Further decisions taken on July 24, 1966, established common marketing regulations and common price levels for fruit and vegetables, sugar, dairy produce and fats and oils; to come into force between July 1, 1967, and July 1, 1968. On July 24, also, common price levels were fixed for beef and veal, milk and other dairy produce.

On July 1, 1967, grains, pigmeat, eggs and poultry reached the full single-market stage, thus bringing half the Community's farm production under the common agricultural policy's marketing and financial provisions. On May 29, 1968, the Six agreed on the pricing system for dairy produce and beef and veal in the single-market stage from July 1, 1968, having failed to agree by the original planned date of May 1.

Firm proposals accepted in principle in March, 1971 and formally adopted in March, 1972 provided for Community part-financing of pensions for farmers retiring between the ages of 55 and 65 and other measures to reduce the number of small, scattered farms and to improve agricultural efficiency by offering modernization aid. The Community has now adopted a hill farming policy which applies to difficult farming areas throughout the Nine.

Economic Policy.—Member States are required by the Treaty to consider their economic policies as a matter of common concern and to consult their partners and the Commission in the concertation of these policies. From 1959 regular discussions took place in the Monetary Committee (senior officials from the national treasuries and Central Banks), the Central Bank Committee and others devoted to economic policy (later, in 1974, replaced by a single committee, the Economic Policy Committee). Regular finance ministers' meetings were held.

Following the currency crisis of 1969 and the Hague Summit, a short-term reserve fund of $2,000 millions was set up. Then, in 1971, the Six embarked on the first steps towards Economic and Monetary Union. The Werner Plan (named after the Luxemburg Prime Minister who chaired the

Committee) laid down the path to be followed in the first phase up to 1973; establishment of a $2,000 million medium-term reserve pool; intensification of short-term monetary policy co-ordination; concertation in international affairs; the progressive harmonisation of taxes and budgetary affairs; and the centrepiece, the narrowing of the permitted margin of fluctuation of members' currencies from the central rate from 4·5 per cent. (world margin) to 2·25 per cent.

The goal of economic and monetary union was affirmed by the 1972 Summit of the Nine, and the target date of 1980 affixed. But by this time (long before the Nine were due to move towards the second phase in December 1973) the international monetary crisis, devaluation of the dollar and floating of the EEC currencies in 1971 had curtailed further progress towards EMU. The floating, first of the Pound Sterling and then of the Lira in 1972, outside the joint float of EEC currencies, left only six countries effectively coordinating their monetary policies. Between January 1974 when France allowed the franc to float separately and July when the franc rejoined the " snake " or fluctuation margin, there were only five.

During 1973 the Nine set up the embryonic Monetary Cooperation Fund but at the end of the year failed to consolidate this action by a significant pooling of reserves. By this time they were faced with the impact of quadrupling oil prices on their economies and prospects of world-wide recession. During 1974 and 1975 inflation, balance of payments deficits and their financing through " recycling ", the coordination of policies internationally and structural economic problems occupied the centre of discussions. On October 21, 1974, the Finance Ministers agreed to launch an initial $3,000 million EEC loan to assist member states in balance of payments difficulties and help recycle " petrodollars " accumulating to the oil-exporting countries. The Nine heads of Government reaffirmed the goal of Economic and Monetary Union at the September 1974 Summit.

Industrial Policy.—On March 21, 1970, the Commission published proposals (the " Colonna Plan ") for a joint industrial policy calling for the removal of technical barriers to trade; the throwing open of public contracts to any firm in the Community; the creation of a European company statute; the encouragement, where efficiency would be improved, of industrial mergers across Europe's frontiers; the strengthening of Community regional policy; the extension of the European Social Fund; and the improvement of business education.

Transport.—The Treaty aims to establish a common policy on transport, with common rules for international transport within the Common Market, covering road, rail and inland water transport. Rates for freight which discriminate as to the national origin or destination of goods transported are to be eliminated within the transitional period. In June, 1965, the Council adopted a Commission proposal setting out the principles of a common policy to be put into force by the end of the transition period. The member governments did not agree on the implementation of these principles, but late in 1967 and early in 1968 a number of steps were agreed, on controlling social and economic conditions in intra-Community transport, especially road-haulage. Other measures covering railways were agreed by the Commission later in 1968 and early in 1969. In December, 1974, the Council agreed to lay down a uniform basis for calculating costs and financing railways. In the middle of 1974 substantial new road haulage quotas were agreed for the three new Member States.

Social Policy.—Under the Treaty, member states agree upon the necessity to promote improvement of the living and working conditions of labour so as to permit the equalization of such conditions in an upward direction. They also cooperate closely on matters relating to employment, labour legislation and working conditions, occupational training, social security, industrial accidents and diseases, industrial hygiene and trade union law. The main instrument for social policy is the Social Fund, established under the Treaty and reformed in 1972. Since then, the Nine's agreement in 1974 on the principles of a social action programme has enlarged the scope for the Fund's operation, which now includes special provisions for migrants, the handicapped, young and redundant workers. Between September 1960 and December 1973 £364 million went from the Social Fund to finance half the cost of retraining and resettling workers in the EEC. In 1974–75 £350 millions were allocated to the Social Fund.

Regional development policy.—On December 10, 1974, the Summit of the Nine meeting in Paris approved a Regional Development Fund of 1,300 million units of account (£540 million) to be spent over the three years (1975–77). The money will be used to help to provide or maintain jobs in the poorer areas of the Community; during the three years the Community will seek to coordinate the regional development policies of the Nine.

The Community's external relations.—Under its common external trade policy the EEC has trade agreements of varying kinds with the following countries: Argentine, Brazil, Uruguay, Mexico, India, Pakistan, Bangladesh, Thailand, Sri Lanka, Philippines, Spain, Yugoslavia, Egypt, Lebanon, Israel, Malta, Cyprus, Morocco and Tunisia. Some of these arrangements are being remade and new trade agreements being considered or negotiated with other countries including Syria, Jordan and Algeria in the context of the EEC's Mediterranean policy which would lead to links with 14 countries bordering on the Mediterranean.

In January 1975 the EEC completed negotiations for a trade, aid and cooperation agreement (Lomé Convention) with 46 developing countries of Africa, the Caribbean and the Pacific, among them 22 ex-Commonwealth countries. (Protocol 22 of Britain's accession Treaty had held out the offer of a relationship with the enlarged Community for these countries equivalent to that associating the 18 African French-speaking countries with the EEC under the Yaoundé Convention.) A different kind of association—holding out the possibility of eventual membership—with Greece and Turkey dates back to 1961 and 1963.

Separate agreements, leading to an industrial free trade area by 1977, were concluded in 1972 with those members of the European Free Trade Association which did not seek candidature for EEC membership when Britain, Denmark and Norway filed their applications: Sweden, Finland, Iceland, Austria, Switzerland, Portugal. These were joined by Norway when the referendum went against entry in the autumn of 1972.

Member states' bilateral agreements with the East European state-trading countries (which was officially due to expire at the end of 1974) are still due to be reshaped into a common commercial policy. The first steps have been made towards this with agreement among the Nine on the draft outlines, or models, for agreements with each of these countries.

Political cooperation.—Cooperation on general foreign policy questions began through the machinery set up in 1970 (Davignon Committee), and takes the form of frequent meetings of the foreign affairs ministers of the Nine. They worked closely together at ministerial level and committee level during the years of preparation and the final summit at Helsinki of the Conference on Security and Cooperation in Europe. Actual military matters are not within the scope of political cooperation: all the members of the EEC except for Ireland are members of the Atlantic Alliance, although France is no longer a member of NATO's integrated military organization. Consultation on foreign affairs is exemplified by the EEC's joint positions on the Middle East, Cyprus and United Nations matters.

Scientific and technical collaboration.—In March, 1970, Britain and eight other European countries accepted an invitation by the Six to start discussing concrete projects for Europe-wide scientific and technical collaboration. Seven working parties have so far been set up covering data-processing, telecommunications, new forms of transport, metallurgy, pollution, meteorology and oceanography. The Paris Summit of October 1972 affirmed the aim of increasing collaboration in the fields of scientific research and advanced technology.

Enlargement.—The question of possible enlargement of the Community has played an important part in its development since the Autumn of 1961 when Britain, the Irish Republic, Denmark and Norway first sought membership, and Austria, Sweden, Switzerland, Spain and Cyprus sought association with the Community. The negotiations were vetoed by France in January, 1963. In May, 1967, Britain, the Irish Republic and Denmark formally submitted applications for Community membership. In July Norway followed suit and Sweden announced that it would seek to participate in the enlargement of the Community on terms compatible with its neutrality. These applications made very slow progress and appeared to come to a standstill when in December, 1967, France declared that Britain's economy would have to be strengthened before negotiations could begin. But shortly after taking office as President of France, Georges Pompidou stated in July, 1969, that there was no objection in principle to the admission of Britain to the Community. At the Hague " summit " meeting in December, 1969 (*see above*) the Six decided that provided that the completion of the Community was not prejudiced, and provided that the Community was strengthened to provide for enlargement, then the entry of other European countries would be desirable. After deciding on a common negotiating position, the Six invited Britain and the other applicants to begin negotiations for membership, and these were opened in Luxemburg on June 30, 1970, and settled in outline, as far as Britain is concerned, on June 23, 1971.

The Entry Terms.—A single overall transitional period of five years, during which the Three were to adopt Community rules and regulations, started on January 1, 1973, giving time for the gradual integration of the economics of the Three with the Six. The five-year period covers both agriculture and industry. The industrial tariff reductions take the form of five moves of 20 per cent., the first on April 1, 1973, a further three on January 1 of 1974, 1975 and 1976, and the final reduction on July 1, 1977.

The first 40 per cent. alignment on the Community's Common External Tariff (CET)—i.e. 40 per cent. of the difference between the new members' tariffs and the CET—was made at the beginning of 1974, and three further alignments of 20 per cent. each will follow the same rhythm as internal tariff-cutting, so that from July 1, 1977, the Three will apply the same tariffs as the Six on goods from non-member states.

EUROPEAN ATOMIC ENERGY COMMUNITY (EURATOM)

A second treaty, arising from the Messina discussions between the ECSC powers on additional means of co-operation, was signed in Rome on March 25, 1957, setting up the European Atomic Energy Community. The task of *Euratom*, defined in detail in the Treaty, is to create within a short period the technical and industrial conditions necessary to utilize nuclear discoveries and especially to produce nuclear energy on a large scale. Other sections of the Treaty cover the establishment and growth of nuclear industries, the procurement, ownership and control of nuclear materials, matters affecting health and safety, including training, and external relations, the stimulation of scientific research and the training of specialists, to assure through a Supply Agency adequate supplies of nuclear fuels, the supervision of the nuclear common market, inspection and control of the use of fissile material, and the safeguarding of both workers and the population at large by laying down basic standards for the protection of health. The United Kingdom, Denmark and Ireland joined Euratom on Jan. 1, 1973.

CURRENCIES OF THE WORLD

Country	Monetary Unit	Denominations in Circulation	
		Notes	Coins
Afghanistan.......	*Afghani of* 100 *Puls*	*Afghanis* 1,000, 500, 100, 50, 20, 10	*Afghanis* 5, 2, 1; *Puls* 50, 25
Albania.........	*Lek of* 100 *Qindarka*	*Leks* 100, 50, 25, 10, 5, 3, 1	*Lek* 1; *Qintars* 50, 20, 10, 5
Algeria..........	*Dinar of* 100 *Centimes*	*Dinars* 500, 100, 50, 10, 5	*Dinars* 5, 1; *Centimes* 50, 20, 10, 5, 2, 1
Angola..........	*Escudo of* 100 *Centavos*	*Escudos* 1,000, 500, 100, 50, 20	*Escudos* 20, 10, 2½, 1; *Centavos* 50, 20, 10
Argentina.......	*Peso of* 100 *Centavos or* 100 *Old Pesos*	*Pesos* 1,000, 500, 100, 50, 10, 5, 1; *Old Pesos* 10,000, 5,000, 1,000, 500, 100, 50, 10	*Old Pesos* 25, 10, 5, 1; *Centavos* 50, 20, 10, 5, 1
Australia.........	*Dollar of* 100 *Cents*	$*A* 50, 20, 10, 5, 2, 1	*Cents* 50, 20, 10, 5, 2, 1
Austria..........	*Schilling of* 100 *Groschen*	*Schillings* 1,000, 500, 100, 50, 20	*Schillings* 100, 50, 25, 10, 5, 1; *Groschen* 50, 10, 5, 2, 1
Bahamas.........	*Bahamian Dollar of* 100 *Cents*	*B.*$ 100, 50, 20, 10, 5, 3, 1; *Cents* 50	*B.*$ 5, 2, 1; *Cents* 50, 25, 15, 10, 5, 1
Bahrain..........	*Dinar of* 1,000 *Fils*	*Dinars* 10, 5, 1, ½, ¼; *Fils* 100	*Fils* 500, 250, 100, 50, 25, 10, 5, 1
Bangladesh.......	*Bangladesh: Taka =* 100 *Paise*	*Taka* 100, 10, 5, 1	*Paise* 50, 25, 10, 5, 2, 1
Barbados.........	*Dollar of* 100 *Cents*	$100, 20, 10, 5, 1	$1; *Cents* 25, 10, 5, 1
Belgium..........	*Belgian Franc of* 100 *Centimes*	*Frs.* 5,000, 1,000, 500, 100, 50, 20	*Frs.* 100, 50, 10, 5, 1; *Centimes* 50, 25
Bermuda.........	*Dollar of* 100 *Cents*	$50, 20, 10, 5, 1	*Cents* 50, 25, 10, 5, 1
Bolivia...........	*Peso of* 100 *Centavos*	*Pesos* 100, 50, 20, 10, 5, 1	*Peso* 1; *Centavos* 50, 25, 20, 10, 5
Brazil...........	*Cruzeiro of* 100 *Centavos*	*Cruzeiros* 500, 100, 50, 10, 5, 1	*Cruzeiros* 300, 20, 1; *Centavos* 50, 20, 10, 5, 2, 1
Belize...........	*Dollar of* 100 *Cents*	$20, 10, 5, 2, 1	*Cents* 50, 25, 10, 5, 1
Brunei...........	*Brunei Dollar of* 100 *Sen*	$100, 50, 10, 5, 1	*Sen* 50, 20, 10, 5, 1
Bulgaria.........	*Lev of* 100 *Stotinki*	*Léva* 20, 10, 5, 2, 1	*Léva* 2, 1; *Stotinki* 50, 20, 10, 5, 2, 1
Burma..........	*Kyat of* 100 *Pyas*	*Kyats* 20, 10, 5, 1	*Pyas* 50, 25, 10, 5, 1; *Kyat* 1.
Burundi..........	*Burundi Franc*	*Frs.* 5,000, 1,000, 500, 100, 50, 20, 10	*Frs.* 10, 5, 1
Cameroon (Federal Republic of)	*Franc C.F.A.*	*Frs.* 10,000, 5,000, 1,000, 500, 100	*Frs.* 100, 50, 25, 10, 5, 2, 1
Canada..........	*Dollar of* 100 *Cents*	*Dollars* 1,000, 100, 50, 20, 10, 5, 2, 1	*Dollars* 1; *Cents* 50, 25, 10, 5, 1
Cape Verde Islands	*Escudo of* 100 *Centavos*	*Esc* 500 $00, 100 $00, 50 $00, 20 $00	*Esc* 10 $00, 5 $00, 2 $50, 1 $00, *Centavos* $50, $20, $10, $05,
Cayman Islands...	*Dollar of* 100 *Cents*	$25, 10, 5, 1	*Cents* 25, 10, 5, 1
Chile............	*Escudo of* 100 *Centésimos* (= 1,000 *Pesos*)	*Escudos* 5,000, 1,000, 500, 100, 50, 10, 5, 1, 0'50	*Centesimos* 10, 5, 1, ½
China...........	*Renminbi or Yuan of* 10 *Jiao or* 100 *Fen*	*Yuan* 10, 5, 2, 1; *Jiao* 5, 2, 1	*Fen* 5, 2, 1
Colombia........	*Peso of* 100 *Centavos*	*Pesos* 500, 100, 50, 20, 10, 5, 2, 1	*Pesos* 5, 1; *Centavos* 50, 20, 10, 5, 1
Congo	*Franc C.F.A.*	*Frs.* 5,000, 1,000, 500, 100	*Frs.* 100, 50, 25, 10, 5, 2, 1
Costa Rica.......	*Colon of* 100 *Céntimos*	*Colones* 1,000, 500, 100, 50, 20, 10, 5	*Colones* 2, 1; *Céntimos* 50, 25, 10, 5
Cuba...........	*Peso of* 100 *Centavos*	*Pesos* 100, 50, 20, 10, 5, 1	*Centavos* 40, 20, 5, 2, 1
Cyprus...........	*Cyprus Pound of* 1,000 *Mils*	£5, £1; *Mils* 500, 250	*Mils* 500, 100, 50, 25, 5, 3, 1
Czechoslovakia....	*Koruna (Crown) of* 100 *Haléru (Heller)*	*Korunas* 500, 100, 50, 20, 10	*Korunas* 5, 2, 1; *Heller* 50, 20, 10, 5, 3, 1
Dahomey (Republic of)	*Franc C.F.A.*	*Frs.* 5,000, 1,000, 500, 100	*Frs.* 100, 50, 25, 10, 5, 2, 1
Denmark.........	*Krone of* 100 *Ore*	*Krone* 1,000, 500, 100, 50, 10	*Kroner* 5, 1; *Ore* 25, 10, 5
Dominican Republic	*Peso of* 100 *Centavos*	*Pesos* 1,000, 500, 100, 50, 20, 10, 5, 1	*Peso* 1; *Centavos* 50, 25, 10, 5, 1
East Caribbean Territory	*East Caribbean Dollar of* 100 *Cents*	$100, 20, 5, 1	*Cents* 50, 25, 10, 2, 1
Ecuador..........	*Sucre of* 100 *Centavos*	*Sucres* 1,000, 500, 100, 50, 20, 10, 5	*Sucre* 1; *Centavos* 50, 20, 10, 5
Egypt............	*Egyptian Pound of* 100 *Piastres or* 1,000 *Millièmes*	£*E* 10, 5, 1, ½, ¼; *Piastres* 10, 5	*Piastres* 10, 5; *Millièmes* 20, 10, 5, 2, 1
El Salvador.......	*Colón of* 100 *Centavos*	*Colones* 100, 25, 10, 5, 2, 1	*Centavos* 50, 25, 10, 5, 3, 2, 1
Ethiopia..........	*Ethiopian Dollar of* 100 *Cents*	*Dollars* 500, 100, 50, 20, 10, 5, 1	*Cents* 50, 25, 10, 5, 1

Country	Monetary Unit	Denominations in Circulation	
		Notes	Coins
Falkland Islands...	Pound of 100 Pence	£5, £1; 50p	As in U.K., except no 50p
Faröe Islands......	Krone	Kr. 100, 50, 10*	As in Denmark
Fiji..............	Fiji Dollar of 100 Cents	$20, 10, 5, 2, 1; Cents 50	Cents 50, 20, 10, 5, 2, 1
Finland...........	Markka of 100 Penniä	Markkas 100, 50, 10, 5, 1	Markkas 5, 1; Penniä 50, 20, 10, 5, 1
Formosa..........	New Taiwan Dollar of 100 Cents	NT$ 100, 50, 10, 5, 1	$5, $1; Cents 50, 20, 10
France...........	Franc of 100 Centimes (1 Franc = 100 old Francs)	Francs 500, 100, 50, 10	Francs 10, 5, 1, ½; Old Francs 2, 1; Centimes 20, 10, 5, 1
French Community (Republics of Gabon, Congo Central Africa and Chad)	Franc C.F.A.	Frs. 10,000, 5,000, 1,000, 500, 100	Frs. 100, 50, 25, 10, 5, 2, 1
Gambia (The).....	Dalasi of 100 Bututs	Dalasis 25, 10, 5, 1	Dalasi 1; Bututs 50, 25, 10, 5, 1
Germany (East)....	Mark der Deutschen Demokratischen Republik (M.) of 100 Pfennig	M. 100, 50, 20, 10, 5	M. 20, 10, 5, 2, 1; Pfennig 50, 20, 10, 5, 1
Germany (Federal Republic of)	Deutsche Mark of 100 Pfennig	D.M. 1,000, 500, 100, 50, 20, 10, 5	D.M. 10, 5, 2, 1; Pfennig 50, 10, 5, 2, 1
Ghana...........	Cedi of 100 Pesewa	Cedis 10, 5, 2, 1	Pesewas 20, 10, 5, 2½, 1, ½
Gibraltar.........	Pound of 100 pence	£5, £1	As in U.K.
Greece...........	Drachma of 100 Lepta	Drachmae 1,000, 500, 100, 50	Drachmae 20, 10, 5, 2, 1; Lepta 50, 20, 10, 5
Guatemala........	Quetzal of 100 Centavos	Quetzales 100, 50, 20, 10, 5, 1; Centavos 50	Centavos 25, 10, 5, 1
Guinea (Republic of)	Syli	Sy 100, 50, 25, 10	Sy 5, 2, 1, ½
Guinea-Bissau (Republic of)	Escudo of 100 Centavos	Escs. 1,000, 500, 100, 50	Escs. 20, 10, 5, 2·50, 1; Centavos 50, 20, 10, 5
Guyana..........	Guyana Dollar of 100 Cents	Dollars 20, 10, 5, 1	Cents 100, 50, 25, 10, 5, 1
Haiti.............	Gourde of 100 Centimes*	Gourdes 500, 250, 100, 50, 10, 5, 2, 1	Centimes 50, 20, 10 5
Honduras.........	Lempira of 100 Centavos	Lempiras 100, 50, 20, 10, 5, 1	Lempira 1; Centavos 50, 20, 10, 5, 2, 1
Hong Kong......	Hong Kong Dollar of 100 Cents	Dollars 100, 50, 10, 5, 1; Cents 1	Dollar 1; Cents 50, 10, 5
Hungary.........	Forint of 100 Fillér	Forints 500, 100, 50, 20, 10	Forints 10, 5, 2, 1; Fillér 50 20, 10, 5, 2
Iceland...........	Króna of 100 Aurar	Króna 5,000, 1,000, 500, 100	Króna 50, 10, 5, 1
India.............	Rupee of 100 Paise	Rupees 10,000, 5,000, 1,000, 100, 10, 5, 2, 1	Rupees 10, 1, ½, ¼; Paise 50, 25, 20, 10, 5, 3, 2, 1
Indonesia........	Rupiah of 100 Sen	Rupiahs 10,000, 5,000, 1,000, 500, 100, 50, 25, 10, 5, 2½, 1; Sen 50, 25, 10, 5, 1	Rupiahs 100, 50, 25, 10, 5, 2, 1
Iran.............	Rial of 100 Dinars	Rials 10,000, 5,000, 1,000, 500, 200, 100, 50, 20, 10	Rials 20, 10, 5, 2, 1; Dinars 50
Iraq.............	Iraqi Dinar of 1000 Fils	Dinars 10, 5, 1, ½, ¼	Dinars 5, 1; Fils 500, 250, 100, 50, 25, 10, 5, 1
Ireland (Republic of)	Pound of 100 Pence	£100, 50, 20, 10, 5, 1; 10s.	New Pence 50, 10, 5, 2, 1, ½
Israel.............	Israel Pound of 100 Agorot (formerly 1,000 Prutot)	Pounds 100, 50, 10, 5, 1, ½; Prutot 500, 250, 100, 50	Pounds 1, ½; Agorot 25, 10, 5, 1; Prutot 250, 100, 50, 25, 10, 5, 1
Italy.............	Lira	Lire 100,000, 52,000, 10,000, 5,000, 1,000, 500	Lire 1,000, 100, 100, 50, 20 10, 5, 2, 1
Ivory Coast (Republic of)	Franc C.F.A.	Frs. C.F.A. 5,000, 1,000, 500, 100	Frs. C.F.A. 100, 50, 25, 10, 5, 2, 1
Jamaica..........	Jamaican Dollar of 100 Cents	$10, 5, 2, 1; Cents 50	$1, Cents 50, 25, 20, 10, 5, 1
Japan............	Yen	Yen 10,000, 5,000, 1,000, 500	Yen 1,000, 100, 50, 10, 5, 1
Jordan (Hashemite Kingdom of)	Jordanian Dinar of 1,000 Fils	J. Dinars 10, 5, 1, ½	Fils 250, 100, 50, 25, 20, 10, 5, 1
Kenya...........	Kenya Shilling of 100 Cents	Shillings 100, 20, 10, 5	Shillings 1; Cents 50, 10, 5

* U.S.A. Currency also used.

Country	Monetary Unit	Denominations in Circulation	
		Notes	Coins
Khmer Republic (*formerly* Cambodia)	*Riel* of 100 *Sen*	*Riels* 500, 100, 50, 20, 10, 5, 1	*Sen* 50, 20, 10
Korea, Republic of (South Korea)	*Won* of 100 *Jeon*	*Won* 5,000, 500, 100, 50, 10, 5, 1; *Jeon* 50, 10	*Won* 100, 10, 5, 1
Korea (North).....	*Won* of 100 *Jeon*	*Won* 100, 50, 10, 5, 1; *Jeon* 50	*Jeon* 10, 5, 1
Kuwait...........	*Kuwait Dinar* of 1,000 *Fils*	*Dinars* 10, 5, 1, ½, ¼	*Fils* 100, 50, 20, 10, 5, 1
Laos.............	*Kip* of 100 *Ats*	*Kips* 1,000, 500, 200, 50, 20, 10, 5, 1	——
Lebanon..........	*Lebanese Pound* of 100 *Piastres*	*Pounds* 100, 50, 25, 10, 5, 1	*Piastres* 50, 25, 10, 5, 2½, 1
Liberia...........	*Liberian* $ of 100 *Cents*	*Dollars* 20, 10, 5, 1 (U.S. notes)	*Dollar* 1; *Cents* 50, 25, 10, 5 1*
Libya............	*Libyan Dinar* of 1,000 *Dirhams*	*Libyan Dinars* 10, 5, 1, ½, ¼	*Dirham* 100, 50, 20, 10, 5, 1
Luxembourg......	*Franc* of 100 *Centimes*†	*Francs* 100, 50, 20, 10	*Francs* 250, 100, 10, 5, 1; *Centimes* 25
Macau...........	*Pataca* of 100 *Avos*	*Patacas* 500, 100, 50, 10	*Patacas* 5, 1; *Avos* 50, 10, 5
Malagasy Republic	*Franc Malgache* (*F.M.G.*)	*Frs.* 5,000, 1,000, 500, 100, 50	*Frs.* 20, 10, 5, 2, 1
Malawi..........	*Malawi Kwacha* of 100 *Tambala*	*KM.* 10, 5, 2, 1; *Tambala* 50	*Tambala* 20, 10, 5, 2, 1
Malaysia.........	*Malaysian Dollar* (*Ringgit*) of 100 *Cents*	*Dollars* 1,000, 100, 50, 10, 5, 1	*Dollar* 1; *Cents* 50, 20, 10, 5, 1
Mali (Republic of)	*Franc Malien*	*Frs.* 10,000, 5,000, 1,000, 500, 100	*Frs.* 25, 10, 5
Malta............	*Maltese Pound* of 100 *cents* or 1,000 *Mils*	*£M*10, *£M*5, *£M*1	*Cents* 50, 10, 5, 2, 1; *Mils* 5, 3, 2
Mauritania........	*Ouguiya* of 5 *Skhoums*	*UM* 1,000, 200, 100	*UM* 20, 10, 5, 1, ⅕
Mauritius.........	*Rupee* of 100 *Cents*	*Rs.* 50, 25, 10, 5	*R.* 1; *Cents* 50, 25, 10, 5, 2, 1
Mexico..........	*Peso* of 100 *Centavos*	*Pesos* 10,000, 1,000, 500, 100, 50, 20, 10, 5, 1	*Peso* 25, 10, 5, 1; *Centavos* 50, 20, 10, 5, 1
Mongolian People's Republic	*Tugrik* of 100 *Mongo*	*Tugriks* 100, 50, 25, 10, 5, 3, 1	*Tugrik* 1; *Mongo* 50, 20, 15, 10, 5, 2, 1
Morocco.........	*Dirham* of 100 *Centimes*	*Dirham* 100, 50, 10, 5	*Dirham* 5; *Centimes* 50, 20, 10, 5, 2, 1
Mozambique......	*Escudo* of 100 *Centavos*	*Escudos* 1,000, 500, 100, 50	*Escudos* 20, 10, 5, 2½, 1; *Centavos* 50, 20, 10
Nepal............	*Rupee* of 100 *Paisa*	*Rupees* 1,000, 500, 100, 10, 5, 1	*Rupee* 1; *Paisa* 50, 25, 10, 5, 2, 1
Netherlands (The).	*Florin* (*Guilder*) of 100 *Cents*	*Florins* 1,000, 100, 25, 10, 5, 2½, 1	*Florins* 10, 2½, 1; *Cents* 25, 10, 5, 1
Netherlands Antilles (The)	*N.A. Guilder* of 100 *Cents*	*Guilders* 500, 250, 100, 50, 25, 10, 5, 2½, 1	*Guilders* 2½, 1, ½, ¼, 1/10; *Cents* 5, 2½, 1
New Zealand.....	*New Zealand Dollar* of 100 *Cents*	N.Z.$ 100, 20, 10, 5, 2, 1	*Cents* 50, 20, 10, 5, 2, 1
Nicaragua........	*Córdoba* of 100 *Centavos*	*Córdobas* 1,000, 500, 100, 50, 20, 10, 5, 2, 1	*Centavos* 50, 25, 10, 5; *Córdobas* 1
Niger (Republic of)	*Franc C.F.A.*	*Frs. C.F.A.* 5,000, 1,000, 500, 100	*Frs. C.F.A.* 100, 50, 25, 10, 5, 2, 1
Nigeria (Federal Republic of)	*Naira* = 100 *Kobo*	N.10, 5, 1 and *Kobo* 50	k.25, 10, 5, 1, ½
Norway..........	*Krone* of 100 *Ore*	*Kroner* 1,000, 500, 100, 50, 10, 5	*Kroner* 5, 1; *Ore* 50, 25, 10, 5, 2, 1
Oman...........	*Rial Omani* of 1,000 *Baiza*	*Rial Omani* 10, 5, 1, ½, ¼; *Baiza* 100	*Baiza* 100, 50, 25, 10, 5, 2
Pakistan.........	*Rupee* of 100 *Paisa*	*Rupees* 100, 50, 10, 5, 2, 1	*Rupee* 1, ½, ¼; *Paisa* 50, 25, 10, 5, 2, 1
Panama..........	*Balboa* of 100 *Cents* (= *U.S.*$)	As in U.S.A.	*Balboa* 1, ½, ¼, 1/10, 1/20, 1/40; *Cent* 1.*
Papua New Guinea	*Kina* = 100 *Toea*	*Kina* 10, 5, 2	*Kina* 1; *Toea* 20, 10, 5, 2, 1
Paraguay.........	*Guaraní* of 100 *Céntimos*	*Guaranies* 10,000, 5,000, 1,000, 500, 100, 50, 10, 5, 1	——
Peru.............	*Gold Sol* of 100 *Centavos*	*Soles* 1,000, 500, 200, 100, 50, 10, 5	*Soles* 10, 5, 1; *Centavos* 50, 25, 10, 5
Philippines........	*Philippine Peso* of 100 *Centavos*	*Pesos* 100, 50, 20, 10, 5	*Peso* 1; *Centavos* 50, 25, 10, 5, 1

* U.S. coins also circulate. † Belgian currency is also legal tender.

Country	Monetary Unit	Denominations in Circulation: Notes	Denominations in Circulation: Coins
Poland	*Zloty* of 100 *Groszy*	*Zlotys* 1,000, 500, 100, 50, 20	*Zlotys* 100, 50, 10, 5, 2, 1; *Groszy* 50, 20, 10, 5, 2, 1
Portugal	*Escudo* of 100 *Centavos*	*Escudos* 1,000, 500, 100, 50, 20	*Escudos* 50, 20, 10, 5, 2½, 1; *Centavos* 50, 20, 10
Portuguese Timor	*Escudo* of 100 *Centavos*	*Escs.* 1,000, 500, 100, 50, 20	*Escs.* 10, 5, 2½, 1; *Centavos* 50, 20, 10
Qatar	*Qatar Riyal* of 100 *Dirhams*	*Q.R.* 500, 100, 10, 5, 1	*Dirhams* 50, 25, 10, 5, 1
Reunion Island	*Franc* (*C.F.A.*)	*Frs.* 5,000, 1,000, 500	*Frs.* 100, 50, 20, 10, 5, 2, 1
Rhodesia	*Dollar* of 100 cents	*RH$* 10, 5, 2, 1	*Cents* 2½, 1, ½
Rumania	*Leu* of 100 *Bani*	*Lei* 100, 50, 25, 10, 5, 3, 1	*Lei* 3, 1; *Bani* 25, 15, 10, 5, 3, 1
Rwanda	*Rwanda Franc*	*Frs.* 1,000, 500, 100, 50, 20	*Frs.* 10, 5, 2, 1, ½
Samoa (Western)	*Tala* of 100 *Sene*	*Tala* 10, 2, 1	*Sene* 50, 20, 10, 5, 2, 1
St. Tomé and Principé	*Escudo* of 100 *Centavos*	*Escs.* 1,000, 500, 100, 50, 20	*Escs.* 10, 5, 2½, 1; *Centavos* 50, 20, 10
Saudi Arabia	*Riyal* of 20 *Qursh* or 100 *Halalas*	*Riyals* 100, 50, 10, 5, 1	*Qursh* 4, 2, 1; *Halala* 50, 25, 10, 5, 1
Seychelles	*Rupee* of 100 *Cents*	*Rs.* 100, 50, 20, 10, 5	*Rupees* 5, 1; *Cents* 50, 25, 5, 1
Sierra Leone	*Leone* of 100 *Cents*	*Leone* 5, 2, 1; *Cents* 50	*Cents* 50, 20, 10, 5, 1, ½
Singapore	*S. Dollar* of 100 *Cents*	$10,000, 1,000, 500, 100, 50, 25, 10, 5, 1	$10, 1; *Cents* 50, 20, 10, 5, 1
Somali Democratic Republic	*Somali Shilling* of 100 *Cents*	*S. Shillings* 100, 20, 10, 5	*Shillings* 1, ½; *Cents* 10, 5, 1
South Africa (Republic of)	*Rand* of 100 *Cents*	*Rands* 20, 10, 5, 2, 1; *£SA* 100, 20, 10, 5, 1; 10*s.*	*Rand* 1; *Cents* 50, 20, 10, 5, 2, 1, ½
Spain	*Peseta* of 100 *Céntimos*	*Pesetas* 1,000, 500, 100	*Pesetas* 100, 50, 25, 5, 2½, 1; *Céntimos* 50, 10
Sri Lanka (Ceylon)	*Rupee* of 100 *Cents*	*Rupees* 100, 50, 10, 5, 2	*Rupees* 5, 2, 1; *Cents* 50, 25, 10, 5, 2, 1
Sudan	*Sudanese Pound* of 100 *Piastres* or 1,000 *Milliemes*	*£S* 10, 5, 1; *Piastres* 50, 25	*Piastres* 10, 5, 2; *Milliemes* 10, 5, 2, 1
Surinam	*Guilder* of 100 *Cents*	*Guilders* 1,000, 100, 25, 10, 5, 2½, 1	*Guilder* 1; *Cents* 25, 10, 5, 1
Sweden	*Krona* of 100 *Ore*	*Kronor* 10,000, 1,000, 100, 50, 10, 5	*Kronor* 10, 5, 2, 1; *Ore* 50, 25, 10, 5, 2, 1
Switzerland	*Franc* of 100 *Centimes*	*Francs* 1,000, 500, 100, 50, 20, 10, 5	*Francs* 5, 2, 1; *Centimes* 50, 20, 10, 5, 2, 1
Syria	*Syrian Pound* of 100 *Piastres*	*Pounds* 500, 100, 50, 25, 10, 5, 1	*Pound* 1, ½; *Piastres* 50, 25, 10, 5, 2½
Tanzania	*T. Shilling* of 100 *Cents*	*Shillings* 100, 20, 10, 5	*Shilling* 5, 1; *Cents* 50, 20, 5
Thailand	*Baht* of 100 *Stangs*	*Bahts* 100, 20, 10, 5, 1; *Stangs* 50	*Baht* 1; *Stangs* 50, 25, 20, 10, 5, 1, ½
Togo (Republic of)	*Franc C.F.A.*	*Frs. C.F.A.* 5,000, 1,000, 500, 100	*Frs. C.F.A.* 100, 50, 25, 10, 5, 2, 1
Tonga	*Pa'anga* (*T$*) of 100 *Seniti*	*Pa'anga* 10, 5, 2, 1, ½	*Pa'anga* 2, 1; *Seniti* 50, 20, 10, 5, 2, 1
Trinidad and Tobago	*Trinidad and Tobago Dollar* of 100 *Cents*	*Dollars* 20, 10, 5, 1	*Dollar* 1; *Cents* 50, 25, 10, 5, 1
Tunisia	*Tunisian Dinar* of 1,000 *Millimes*	*Dinars* 10, 5, 1, ½	*Dinar* ½; *Millimes* 100, 50, 20, 10, 5, 2, 1
Turkey	*Turkish Lira* of 100 *Kuru*	*TL* 1,000, 500, 100, 50, 20, 10, 5	*TL* 10, 5, 2, 1; *Kuru* 50, 25, 10, 5, 1
Uganda	*U. Shilling* of 100 *Cents*	*Shillings* 100, 50, 20, 10	*Shillings* 5, 2, 1; *Cents* 50, 20, 10, 5
United Arab Emirates	*Dirham* of 100 *Fils*	*Dirhams* 100, 50, 10, 5, 1	*Dirham* 1; *Fils* 50, 25, 10, 5, 1
United Kingdom (*See* pp. 1209–10)	*Pound* of 100 *new pence*	*£*20, *£*10, *£*5, *£*1	*Pence* 50, 10, 5, 2, 1, ½; 5*s.* (25*p*); 6*d.* (2½).
United States of America	*Dollar* of 100 *Cents*	$100, 50, 20, 10, 5, 1	$1; *Cents* 50, 25, 10, 5, 1
Upper Volta (Republic of)	*Franc C.F.A.*	*Frs. C.F.A.* 5,000, 1,000, 500, 100	*Frs. C.F.A.* 100, 50, 25, 10, 5, 2, 1
Uruguay	*Peso* of 100 *Centésimos*	*Pesos* 10,000, 5,000, 1,000, 500, 100, 50	*Pesos* 1,000, 50, 20, 10, 5, 1
U.S.S.R.	*Rouble* of 100 *Copecks*	*Roubles* 100, 50, 25, 10, 5, 3, 1	*Rouble* 1; *Copecks* 50, 20, 15, 10, 5, 3, 2, 1
Venezuela	*Bolivar*	*Bolivares* 500, 100, 50, 20, 10, 5	*Bolivares* 100, 20, 10, 5, 2, 1, ½, ¼, ⅛, $\frac{1}{20}$

Country	Monetary Unit	Denominations in Circulation	
		Notes	Coins
Vietnam (North)...	Dong of 10 Hào or 100 Xu	Dong 10, 5, 2, 1; Hào 5, 2, 1; Xu 2	Xu 5, 2, 1
Vietnam (South)...	Dong of 100 Cents	Dong 1,000, 500, 200, 100, 50, 20, 10, 5, 1	Dong 20, 10, 5, 1
Yemen (Arab Republic).........	Riyal of 100 Fils	Riyals 50, 20, 10, 5, 1;	Fils 50, 25, 10, 5, 1
Yemen (People's Democratic Republic)	Southern Yemen Dinar (YD) of 1,000 Fils	YD 10, 5, 1; Fils 500, 250	Fils 50, 25, 5, 2½, 1
Yugoslavia.......	Dinar of 100 Paras.....	Dinars 500, 100, 50, 10, 5	Dinar 5, 2, 1; Paras 50, 20, 10,
Zaire (Congolese Republic)	Zaire of 100 Makuta or 10,000 Sengi	Zaires 10, 5, 1; Makuta 50, 20, 10	Makuta 5, 1; Sengi 10
Zambia..........	Kwacha of 100 Ngwee	Kwacha 20, 10, 5, 2, 1; Ngwee 50	Ngwee 50, 20, 10, 5, 2, 1

THE COUNCIL OF EUROPE

Headquarters: 67006 Strasbourg, France.   *Secretary-General,* G. Kahn-Ackermann.

A European organization founded in 1949 whose aim is to achieve greater unity between its Members to safeguard their European heritage and to facilitate their economic and social progress. The aim of the Council is pursued through discussion and common action in economic, social, cultural, educational, scientific, legal and administrative matters and in the maintenance and furtherance of human rights and fundamental freedoms.

The following 18 countries belong to the Council: Austria, Belgium, Cyprus, Denmark, France, the Federal Republic of Germany, Greece, Iceland, the Republic of Ireland, Italy, Luxemburg, Malta, Netherlands, Norway, Sweden, Switzerland, Turkey and the United Kingdom.

The organs are the Committee of Ministers, consisting of the Foreign Ministers of member countries: and the Parliamentary Assembly of 147 members, elected or chosen by the national parliaments of member countries in proportion to the relative strength of political parties. There is also a Joint Committee of Ministers and Representatives of the Consultative Assembly.

The Committee of Ministers is the executive organ of the Council. Certain of its conclusions take the form of international agreements or recommendations to governments. On certain major matters the Committee votes by unanimity but abstentions are permitted. Decisions of the Ministers may also be embodied in partial agreements to which a limited number of member governments are party. The Committee of Ministers meets twice yearly. All Ministers have appointed Deputies to act on their behalf. The Committee of Deputies meets monthly to transact business and to take decisions on behalf of Ministers. Member governments accredit Permanent Representatives to the Council in Strasbourg, who are also the Ministers' Deputies.

The Committee is a forum for discussion between member governments on political and other matters, supervises the work of the technical expert committees and considers recommendation received from the Parliamentary Assembly. The Assembly's conclusions may take the form of recommendations to the Committee of Ministers or resolutions. Ministers, including Ministers other than those for Foreign Affairs, may address the Assembly and take part in its debates.

The Assembly holds three week-long sessions a year. It debates reports on, *inter alia,* political, economic, agricultural, social, educational, legal and regional planning affairs. The Chairman in office of the Committee of Ministers presents a report at each session. The Assembly also debates reports received annually from the O.E.C.D., other European organizations and certain specialized agencies of the United Nations. It holds an annual joint meeting with the members of the European Parliament of the " Nine ". Matters of mutual interest to the Committee of Ministers and the Assembly are discussed in the joint Committee. The Council's budget is voted annually in December and is met by agreed contributions of member countries.

One of the principal achievements of the Council of Europe is the European Convention on Human Rights (1950) under which was established the European Commission and the European Court of Human Rights. These organs have built up a valuable system of European jurisprudence in the field of Human Rights. Other major achievements of the Council of Europe are the European Cultural Convention (1953) and the European Social Charter (1960). Over 80 conventions and agreements have been concluded by the Council covering matters in all the fields of its competence, such as social insurance, equivalence of European diplomas for university entrances, equivalence of university degrees, public health patents, extradition, etc.

The Council's cultural and educational programme is administered by the Council for Cultural Co-operation to which in addition to members of the Council of Europe belong Finland, Greece, Spain and the Holy See. A European Committee for Legal Co-operation administers the Council's legal programme. A few non-member states take part as observers in several of the Council's intergovernmental activities.

The Committee of Ministers approves annually the Council of Europe Programme of Activities handled by the intergovernmental committees of experts. The Programme lists the various projects on which the Council is working and thus provides a guide to the intergovernmental work of the Council.

Permanent U.K. Representative, His Excellency Peter John Foster, C.M.G. (1974) £6,475
Deputy Representative, G. R. Lee.

RETROSPECT OF SPORT 1974–75
OLYMPIC GAMES

The XXIst Olympic Games are scheduled to take place in Canada from July 17 to August 1, 1976. The Main Events will be held in Montreal, and the Yachting in Kingston, Ontario. The following 22 Sports will be included: Archery, Athletics, Basketball, Boxing, Canoeing, Cycling, Equestrian, Football, Gymnastics, Handball, Hockey, Judo, Modern Pentathlon, Rowing, Shooting, Swimming, Volley Ball, Water Polo, Weight-lifting, Wrestling, and Yachting.

Previous Games have been held as follows: I, 1896, Athens; II, 1900, Paris; III, St. Louis, 1904; IV, London, 1908; V, Stockholm, 1812; VII, Antwerp, 1920; VIII, Paris, 1924; IX, Amsterdam, 1928; X, Los Angeles, 1932; XI, Berlin, 1936; XIV, London, 1948; XV, Helsinki, 1952; XVI, Melbourne, 1956; XVII, Rome, 1960; XVIII, Tokyo, 1964; XIX, Mexico, 1968; XX, Munich, 1972.

The VIth Games scheduled for Berlin in 1916, the XIIth for Tokyo and then Helsinki in 1940, and the XIIIth did not take place owing to World Wars.

OLYMPIC RECORDS TRACK AND FIELD
Athletics—Men's Events

Metres		min.	sec.
100—J. Hines (U.S.A.)			9·9
200—T. Smith (U.S.A.)			19·8
400—L. Evans (U.S.A.)			43·8
800—R. Doubell (Australia)		1	44·3
1,500—K. Keino (Kenya)		3	34·9
5,000—L. Viren (Finland)		13	26·4
10,000—L. Viren (Finland)		27	38·4
110 Hurdles—R. Milburn (U.S.A.)			13·2
400 Hurdles—J. Akii-Bua (Uganda)			47·8
Steeplechase—K. Keino (Kenya)		8	23·6
4 × 100 Relay—U.S.A.			38·2
4 × 400 Relay—U.S.A.		2	56·1
20,000 Walk*—P. Frenkel (G.D.R.)	1 hr 26		42·4
Marathon*—A. Bikila (Ethiopia)	2 hr 12		11·2

	metres	ft.	in.
High Jump—R. Fosbury (U.S.A.)	2·24	7	4
Pole Vault—W. Nordwig (G.D.R.)	5·50	18	0½
Long Jump—R. Beamon (U.S.A.)	8·90	29	2½
Triple Jump—V. Saneyev (U.S.S.R.)	17·39	57	0½
Shot—W. Komar (Poland)	21·18	69	6
Discus—A. Oerter (U.S.A.)	64·78	212	6
Hammer—A. Bondarchuk(U.S.S.R.)	75·50	247	8
Javelin—K. Wolfermann (Germany)	90·48	296	10
Decathlon—N. Avilov (U.S.S.R.)	8,454 points		
* Best Performances.			

Athletics—Women's Events

Metres		min.	sec.
100—W. Tyus (U.S.A.)			11·0
200—R. Stecher (G.D.R.)			22·4
400—M. Zehrt (G.D.R.)			51·1
800—H. Falck (Germany)		1	58·6
1,500—L. Bragina (U.S.S.R.)		4	01·4
4 × 100 Relay—U.S.A. and Germany			42·8
4 × 400 Relay—G.D.R.		3	22·9

	metres	ft.	in.
High Jump—U. Meyfarth (Germany)	1·92	6	3½
Long Jump—H.Rosendahl(Germany)	6·78	22	3
Shot—N. Chizhova (U.S.S.R.)	21·03	69	0
Discus—F. Melnik (U.S.S.R.)	66·62	218	7
Javelin—R. Fuchs (G.D.R.)	63·88	209	7
Pentathlon—M. Peters (G.B.)	4,801 points		

WORLD'S ATHLETIC RECORDS

* (All the world records given below have been accepted by the International Amateur Athletic Federation with the exception of those marked thus (*) which await ratification and are likely to be accepted.)

Running

Distance	Time hr. min. sec.	Name	Nation	Year
100 yards	9·0	I. Crockett	U.S.A.	1974
100 yards	9·0*	H. McTear	U.S.A.	1975
100 metres	9·9	C. Greene	U.S.A.	1968

Equalled in 1968 by J. Hines (*U.S.A.*) and R. R. Smith (*U.S.A.*); in 1972 by E. Hart (*U.S.A.*) and R. Robinson (*U.S.A.*); in 1974 by S. Williams (*U.S.A.*) and in 1975 by S. Leonard (*Cuba*) and S. Williams (*U.S.A.*) twice.

Distance	Time hr. min. sec.	Name	Nation	Year
200 metres (straight)	19·5	T. Smith	U.S.A.	1966
200 metres (turn)	19·8	T. Smith	U.S.A.	1968
200 metres (turn)	19·8	D. Quarrie	Jamaica	1971 and 1975
200 metres (turn)	19·8	S. Williams	U.S.A.	1975
220 yards (straight)	19·5	T. Smith	U.S.A.	1966
220 yards (turn)	19·9	D. Quarrie	Jamaica	1975
220 yards (turn)	19·9	S. Williams	U.S.A.	1975
400 metres	43·8	L. Evans	U.S.A.	1968
440 yards	44·5	J. Smith	U.S.A.	1971
800 metres	1 43·7	M. Fiasconaro	Italy	1973
880 yards	1 44·1	R. Wohlhuter	U.S.A.	1974
1,000 metres	2 13·9	R. Wohlhuter	U.S.A.	1974
1,500 metres	3 32·2	F. Bayi	Tanzania	1974
1 mile	3 51·0	F. Bayi	Tanzania	1975
1 mile	3 49·4*	J. Walker	New Zealand	1975
2,000 metres	4 56·2	M. Jazy	France	1966
3,000 metres	7 35·2	B. Foster	G.B.	1974
2 miles	8 13·8	B. Foster	G.B.	1973
3 miles	12 47·8	E. Puttemans	Belgium	1972
5,000 metres	13 13·0	E. Puttemans	Belgium	1972
6 miles	26 47·0	B. Clarke	Australia	1965
10,000 metres	27 30·8	D. Bedford	G.B.	1973
10 miles	46 04·2	W. Polleunis	Belgium	1972

World's Athletic Records—*continued*

20,000 metres		57	44·4	G. Roelants	Belgium	1972
20,784 metres						
(12 miles 1,610 yards)	1	00	00·0	G. Roelants	Belgium	1972
15 miles	1	11	52·6	P. Paivarinta	Finland	1975
25,000 metres	1	14	16·8	P. Paivarinta	Finland	1975
30,000 metres	1	31	30·4	J. Alder	G.B.	1970
3,000 metres steeplechase		8	09·8	A. Garderud	Sweden	1975

Hurdling

Hurdles	sec.			
120 yards (3 ft. 6 in.)	13·0	R. Milburn	U.S.A.	1971
120 yards	13·1	R. Milburn	U.S.A.	1973
120 yards	13·0*	G. Drut	France	1975
110 metres	13·0*	G. Drut	France	1975
200 metres (2 ft. 6 in.)				
(straight)	21·9	D. Styron	U.S.A.	1960
200 metres (turn)	22·5	M. Lauer	Germany	1959
200 metres (turn)	22·5	G. Davis	U.S.A.	1960
220 yards (straight)	21·9	D. Styron	U.S.A.	1960
400 metres	47·8	J. Akii-Bua	Uganda	1972
440 yards	48·7	J. Bolding	U.S.A.	1974

Relay Racing

Distance	*Time* min. sec.	*Nation*	*Year*
4 × 100 metres	38·2	U.S.A.	1968
4 × 110 yards	38·6	U.S.A.	1967
4 × 200 metres	1 21·5	Italy	1972
4 × 220 yards	1 21·7	U.S.A.	1970
4 × 400 metres	2 56·1	U.S.A.	1968
4 × 440 yards	3 02·4	U.S.A.	1975
4 × 800 metres	7 08·6	Germany	1966
4 × 880 yards	7 10·4	U.S.A.	1973
4 × 1,500 metres	14 49·0	France	1965
4 × 1 mile	16 02·8	New Zealand	1972

Jumping and Throwing

	ft.	in.	metres	*Name*	*Nation*	*Year*
High Jump	7	6½	2·30	D. Stones	U.S.A.	1973
Pole Vault	18	6½	5·65	D. Roberts	U.S.A.	1975
Long Jump	29	2½	8·90	R. Beamon	U.S.A.	1968
Triple Jump	57	2¾	17·44	V. Sanyeyev	U.S.S.R.	1972
Shot	71	7	21·82	A. Feuerbach	U.S.A.	1973
Discus	226	8	69·10	J. Powell	U.S.A.	1975
Hammer	260	2	79·30	W. Schmidt	Germany	1975
Javelin	308	8	94·08	K. Wolfermann	Germany	1973
Decathlon		8,524 points		B. Jenner	U.S.A.	1975

Walking

Distance	*Time* hr. min. sec.	*Name*	*Nation*	*Year*
20,000 metres	1 24 45·0	B. Kannenberg	Germany	1974
27,153 metres				
(16 miles 1,535 yards)	2 00 00·0	B. Kannenberg	Germany	1974
30,000 metres	2 12 58·0	B. Kannenberg	Germany	1974
20 miles	2 30 38·6	G. Weidner	Germany	1974
30 miles	3 51 48·6	G. Weidner	Germany	1973
50,000 metres	4 00 27·0	G. Weidner	Germany	1973

WOMEN'S EVENTS

Running

Distance	*Time* min. sec.	*Name*	*Nation*	*Year*
60 metres	7·2	B. Cuthbert	Australia	1960
60 metres	7·2	I. Bochkareva	U.S.S.R.	1960
60 metres	7·2	A. Lynch	G.B.	1974
100 yards	10·0	Chi Cheng	Taiwan	1970
100 metres	10·8	R. Stecher	G.D.R.*	1973
200 metres	22·1	R. Stecher	G.D.R.*	1973
220 yards	22·6	Chi Cheng	Taiwan	1970
400 metres	49·9	I. Szewinska	Poland	1974
440 yards	52·2	K. Hammond	U.S.A.	1972
440 yards	52·2	D. Sapenter	U.S.A.	1974
800 metres	1 57·5	S. Zlateva	Bulgaria	1973
880 yards	2 02·0	D. Willis	Australia	1962

Women's Events—*continued*

880 yards	2	02·0	J. Pollock	Australia	1967
1,500 metres	4	01·4	L. Bragina	U.S.S.R.	1972
1 mile	4	29·5	P. Cacchi	Italy	1973
3,000 metres	8	46·6	G. Andersen	Norway	1975
100 metres hurdles (2 ft. 0 in.)		12·3	A. Ehrhardt	G.D.R.★	1973
400 metres hurdles		56·5	K. Kasperczik	Poland	1974

★ German Democratic Republic (East Germany).

Relays

Distance	Time min. sec.		Nation	Year
4 × 100 metres		42·5	G.D.R.	1974
4 × 110 yards		44·1	Germany	1975
4 × 200 mertres	1	33·8	G.B.	1968
4 × 220 yards	1	35·8	Australia	1969
4 × 400 metres	3	23·0	G.D.R.	1972
4 × 440 yards	3	30·3	Germany	1975
4 × 800 metres	8	05·2	Bulgaria	1975

Women's Jumping and Throwing

	ft.	in.	metres	Name	Nation	Year
High Jump	6	4¾	1·95	R. Witschas	G.D.R.	1974
Long Jump	22	5¼	6·84	H. Rosendahl	Germany	1970
Shot Putt	70	10½	21·60	M. Adam	G.D.R.	1975
Discus	230	4	70·20	F. Melnik	U.S.S.R.	1975
Javelin	220	6	67·22	R. Fuchs	G.D.R.	1974
Pentathlon		4,932 pts.		B. Pollak	G.D.R.	1973

Electric Timing for World Records

At the Rome Congress in 1974, the I.A.A.F. decided that in events in metric distances up to 400 metres, where the best fully-automatic electric times were slower than the human timed records, the electric times should also be accepted as world records. Naturally where the electrically timed records are faster than the human timed, the latter are ignored.

The following electrically timed records have been accepted. Times to 1/100th second are included in brackets, though the times for official purposes are converted to 1/10ths.

Distance	Time	Name	Nation	Year
		Men		
	sec.			
100 metres	10·0 (9·95)	J. Hines	U.S.A.	1968
400 metres	43·9 (43·86)	L. Evans	U.S.A.	1968
		Women		
100 metres	11·1 (11·07)	W. Tyus	U.S.A.	1968
100 metres	11·1 (11·07)	R. Stecher	G.D.R.	1972
200 metres	22·2 (22·21)	I. Szewinska	Poland	1974

UNITED KINGDOM (ALL COMERS') RECORDS
(Records made in the United Kingdom of Great Britain and Northern Ireland by any athlete.)

Distance	Time hr. min. sec.			Name	Nation	Year
				MEN		
100 yards			9·4	K. A. Gardner	Jamaica	1958
100 yards			9·4	P. F. Radford	G.B.	1960
100 metres			10·3	W. H. Dillard	U.S.A.	1948
100 metres			10·3	P. F. Radford	G.B.	1960
100 metres			10·3	B. Green	G.B.	1972
100 metres			10·3	S. Schenke	G.D.R.	1973
100 metres			10·3	A. Kornelyuk	U.S.S.R.	1973
100 metres			10·3	D. Quarrie	Jamaica	1975
200 metres			20·3	D. Jenkins	G.B.	1972
200 metres			20·3	S. Williams	U.S.A.	1975
220 yards			20·5	P. F. Radford	G.B.	1960
400 metres			45·0	C. Asati	Kenya	1970
440 yards			45·9	W. Mottley	Trinidad	1966
800 metres		1	45·1	A. Carter	G.B.	1973
880 yards		1	47·2	C. Carter	G.B.	1968
1,500 metres		3	36·6	K. Keino	Kenya	1969
1 mile		3	53·4	K. Keino	Kenya	1966
3,000 metres		7	35·2	B. Foster	G.B.	1974
2 miles		8	13·8	B. Foster	G.B.	1973
3 miles		12	52·0	D. Bedford	G.B.	1972
5,000 metres		13	17·2	D. Bedford	G.B.	1972
6 miles		26	51·6	D. Bedford	G.B.	1971

U.K. (All Comers') Records—*continued*

10,000 metres	27 30·8	D. Bedford	G.B.	1973
10 miles	46 44·0	R. Hill	G.B.	1968
12 miles 1268 yards	1 00 00·0	R. Hill	G.B.	1968
15 miles	1 12 48·2	R. Hill	G.B.	1965
3,000 metres steeplechase	8 18·2	B. Malinowski	Poland	1975
120 yards hurdles	13·6	B. Price	G.B.	1975
110 metres hurdles	13·6	B. Price	G.B.	1975
200 metres hurdles (curve)	23·0	A. Pascoe	G.B.	1975
220 yards hurdles (straight)	23·3	P. B. Hildreth	G.B.	1955
220 yards hurdles (curve)	23·3	E. Gilbert	U.S.A.	1957
400 metres hurdles	48·9	A. Pascoe	G.B.	1975
440 yards hurdles	49·7	G. A. Potgieter	S. Africa	1958
4 × 100 metres	39·4	——	Jamaica	1970
4 × 100 metres	39·4	——	U.S.S.R.	1975
4 × 110 yards	40·0	——	G.B.	1963
4 × 220 yards	1 26·0	——	London Team	1959
4 × 400 metres	3 03·6	——	Kenya	1970
4 × 440 yards	3 06·4	——	U.S.A.	1960
4 × 880 yards	7 16·0	——	U.S.S.R.	1966
4 × 1500 metres	15 12·6	——	England Team	1975
4 × 1 mile	16 28·2	——	England Team	1961

	ft. in.			
High Jump	7 3¼	J. Beers	Canada	1973
Pole Vault	17 9½	W. Kozakiewicz	Poland	1975
Long Jump	26 10	R. Boston	U.S.A.	1965
Triple Jump	55 7¼	V. Saneyev	U.S.S.R.	1975
Shot	70 1½	A. Feuerbach	U.S.A.	1974
Shot	70 1½	G. Capes	G.B.	1974
Discus	212 5	R. Bruch	Sweden	1973
Hammer	252 3	V. Dmitrenko	U.S.S.R.	1975
Javelin	297 6	K. Wolfermann	Germany	1973
Decathlon	7,985 pts.	W. Toomey	U.S.A.	1968

Walking

	hr. min. sec.			
20,000 metres	1 28 45·8	K. Matthews	G.B.	1964
16 miles 315 yards	2 00 00·0	R. Wallwork	G.B.	1971
30,000 metres	2 28 44·0	P. Nihill	G.B.	1972
20 miles	2 40 42·16	P. Nihill	G.B.	1972
30 miles	4 8 11·6	D. Thompson	G.B.	1960
50,000 metres	4 17 29·8	D. Thompson	G.B.	1960

WOMEN

Distance	Time min. sec.	Name	Nation	Year
60 metres	7·2	A. Lynch	G.B.	1974
100 yards	10·6	M. Willard	Australia	1958

Equalled in 1958 by H. J. Young (*G.B.*); by W. Rudolph (*U.S.A.*) in 1960; in 1962 and 1964 by D. Hyman (*G.B.*); in 1964 by D. Arden (*G.B.*) and M. Rand (*G.B.*); and in 1968 by V. Peat (*G.B.*).

100 metres	11·2	R. Boyle	Australia	1974
200 metres	22·8	R. Stecher	G.D.R.	1973
220 yards	23·6	M. Willard	Australia	1958
220 yards	23·6	D. Arden	G.B.	1964
400 metres	50·3	I. Szewinska	Poland	1975
440 yards	54·2	G. Kraan	Netherlands	1962
800 metres	1 58·9	G. Hoffmeister	G.D.R.	1973
880 yards	2 04·2	A. Smith	G.B.	1966
1,500 metres	4 08·5	T. Kazankina	U.S.S.R.	1975
1 mile	4 35·1	G. Reiser	Canada	1973
3,000 metres	8 54·0	I. Knutsson	Sweden	1975
4 × 100 metres	43·	——	G.D.R.	1973
4 × 110 yards	45·0	——	G.B.	1968
4 × 200 metres	1 33·8	——	G.B.	1968
4 × 220 yards	1 39·9	——	G.B.	1953
4 × 400 metres	3 28·5	——	U.S.S.R.	1975
4 × 800 metres	8 27·0	——	G.B.	1970
100 metres hurdles	13·0	A. Ehrhardt	G.D.R.	1973
400 metres hurdles	58·0	D. Piecyk	Poland	1974

	ft. in.			
High Jump	6 2¼	R. Witschas	G.D.R.	1974
Long Jump	22 0¾	S. Sherwood	G.B.	1972
Shot	68 1¾	N. Chizhova	U.S.S.R.	1973
Discus	227 11	F. Melnik	U.S.S.R.	1973
Javelin	216 10	R. Fuchs	G.D.R.	1973
Pentathlon	4,630 pts.	M. Peters	G.B.	1972

UNITED KINGDOM (NATIONAL) RECORDS

(Records made anywhere by athletes eligible to represent Great Britain and Northern Ireland)

Men

100 *yards*—9·4 sec. (P. F. Radford, 1960).
100 *metres*—10·1 sec. (B. Green, 1971).
200 *metres*—20·3 sec. (D. Jenkins, 1972).
220 *yards*—20·5 sec. (P. F. Radford, 1960).
400 *metres*—44·9 (D. Jenkins, 1975).
440 *yards*—45·9 sec. (R. I. Brightwell, 1962).
800 *metres*—1 min. 45·1 sec. (A. Carter, 1973).
880 *yards*—1 min. 47·2 sec. (C. Carter, 1968).
1,000 *metres*—2 min. 18·2 sec. (J. P. Boulter, 1969).
1,500 *metres*—3 min. 37·4 sec. (F. Clement, 1974).
1 *mile*—3 min. 55·0 sec. (F. Clement, 1975).
2,000 *metres*—5 min. 03·0 sec. (B. Foster, I. Stewart, 1975).
3,000 *metres*—7 min. 35·2 sec. (B. Foster, 1974).
2 *miles*—8 min. 13·8 sec. (B. Foster, 1973).
3 *miles*—12 min. 52·0 sec. (D. Bedford, 1972).
5,000 *metres*—13 min. 14·6 sec. (B. Foster, 1974).
6 *miles*—26 min. 51·6 sec. (D. Bedford, 1971).
10,000 *metres*—27 min. 30·8 sec. (D. Bedford, 1973).
10 *miles*—46 min. 44·0 sec. (R. Hill, 1968).
20,000 *metres*—58 min. 39·0 sec. (R. Hill, 1968).
12 *miles* 1,268 *yards*—1 hr. (R. Hill, 1968).
15 *miles*—1 hr. 12 min. 48·2 sec (R. Hill, 1965).
25,000 *metres*—1 hr. 15 min. 22·6 sec. (R. Hill, 1965).
30,000 *metres*—1 hr. 31 min. 40·4 sec. (J. Alder, 1970).
3,000 *metres Steeplechase*—8 min. 22·6 sec. (J. Davies, 1974).
120 *yards Hurdles*—13·5 sec. (B. Price, 1973).
110 *metres Hurdles*—13·5 sec. (B. Price, 1973).
200 *metres Hurdles* (*curve*)—23·0 sec. (A. Pascoe, 1975).
220 *yards Hurdles* (*straight*)—23·3 sec. (P. B. Hildreth, 1955).
220 *yards Hurdles* (*curve*)—23·7 sec. (P. A. L. Vine, 1955).
400 *metres Hurdles*—48·1 sec. (D. P. Hemery, 1968).
440 *yards Hurdles*—50·2 sec. (D. P. Hemery, 1968).
4× 100 *metres Relay*—39·3 sec. (British Team, 1968).
4× 110 *yards*—40·0 sec. (British Team, 1963).
4× 200 *metres*—1 min. 24·1 sec. (British Team, 1961).
4× 220 *yards*—1 min. 26·0 sec. (London Team, 1959).
4× 400 *metres*—3 min. 00·5 sec. (British Team, 1972).
4× 440 *yards*—3 min. 06·5 sec. (English Team, 1966).
4× 800 *metres*—7 min. 17·4 sec. (British Team, 1970).
4× 880 *yards*—7 min. 17·4 sec. (British Team, 1970).
4× 1,500 *metres*—15 min. 06·6 sec. (G.B. Team, 1971).
4× 1 *mile*—16 min. 24·8 sec. (English Team, 1961).
High Jump—7 ft. 0¼ in. (M. Butterfield, A. Mackenzie, 1975).
Pole Vault—17 ft. 2¾ in. (M. Bull, 1973).
Long Jump—27 ft. 0 in. (L. Davies, 1968).
Triple Jump—54 ft. (F. J. Alsop, 1964).
Shot—70 ft. 1½ in. (G. Capes, 1974).
Discus—209 ft. 11 in. (W. Tancred, 1973).
Hammer—233 ft. 9 in. (B. Williams, 1973).
Javelin—278 ft. 7 in. (C. Clover, 1974).
Decathlon—7,903 pts. (P. Gabbett, 1971).

Walking

20,000 *metres*—1 hr. 28 min. 45·8 sec. (K. Matthews, 1964).
2 *Hours*—16 miles 315 yds. (R. Wallwork, 1971).
30,000 *metres*—2 hr. 24 min. 18·2 sec. (R. Thorpe, 1974).
20 *miles*—2 hr. 34 min. 25·4 sec. (R. Thorpe, 1974).
30 *miles*—4 hr. 2 min. 49·2 sec. (R. Dobson, 1974).
50,000 *metres*—4 hr. 11 min. 22·0 sec. (R. Dobson, 1974).
8 *miles*, 1,187 *yards*—1 hr. (P. Embleton, 1972).

Women

60 *metres*—7·2 sec. (A. Lynch, 1974).
100 *yards*—10·6 sec. (H. Young, 1958; D. Hyman, 1962, 1964; D. Arden, M. Rand, 1964; V. Peat, 1968).
100 *metres*—11·1 sec. (A. Lynch, 1974).
200 *metres*—23·0 sec. (H. Golden, 1974).
220 *yards*—23·6 sec. (D. Arden, 1964).
400 *metres*—51·3 sec. (D. Murray, 1975).
440 *yards*—54·1 sec. (D. Watkinson, 1966).
800 *metres*—2 min. 00·2 sec. (R. Stirling, 1972).
880 *yards*—2 min. 04·2 sec. (A. Smith, 1966).
1,500 *metres*—4 min. 04·8 sec. (S. Carey, 1972).
1 *mile*—4 min. 36·2 sec. (J. Allison, 1973).
3,000 *metres*—8 min. 55·6 sec. (J. Smith, 1974).
100 *metres Hurdles*—13·0 sec. (J. Vernon, B. Thompson, 1974).
400 *metres Hurdles*—58·0 sec. (C. Warden, 1974).
4× 100 *metres Relay*—43·7 sec. (G.B. Team, 1968, 1972, and 1975).
4× 110 *yards Relay*—45·0 sec. (G.B. Team, 1968).
4× 200 *metres Relay*—1 min. 33·8 sec. (G.B. Team, 1968).
4× 220 *yards Relay*—1 min. 39·9 sec. (G.B. Team 1953).
4× 400 *metres*—3 min. 26·6 sec. (G.B. Team, 1975).
4× 800 *metres Relay*—8 min. 23·8 sec. (G.B. Team, 1971).
High Jump—6 ft. 1½ in. (B. Lawton, 1973).
Long Jump—22 ft. 2¼ in. (M. Rand, 1964).
Shot—53 ft. 6¼ in. (M. Peters, 1966).
Discus—190 ft. 4 in. (R. Payne, 1972).
Javelin—182 ft. 5 in. (S. Platt, 1968).
Pentathlon—4,801 pts. (M. Peters, 1972).

GREAT BRITAIN *v.* BELGIUM

Indoor—Held in Cosford, February 15,1975

Men's Events

Metres	min.	sec.
60—D. Roberts (G.B.)		7·0
400—B. Brijdenbach (B.)		48·3
800—I. Van Damme (B.)	1	49·0
1,500—P. Banning (G.B.)	3	41·9
5,000—A. Simmons (G.B.)	8	01·8
4× 200 *Relay*—Great Britain	1	28·9
60 *Hurdles*—B. Price (G.B.)		8·1
	ft.	in.
High Jump—P. De Preter (B.)	7	0¼
Pole Vault—B. Hooper (G.B.)	16	4¾
Long Jump—A. Lerwill (G.B.)	24	7¾
Triple Jump—D. Johnson (G.B.)	50	7¼
Shot—G. Capes (G.B.)	67	1½

Great Britain beat Belgium by 76 points to 52.

Women's Events

Metres	min.	sec.
60—L. Alaerts (B.)		7·7
400—V. Elder (B.)		53·2
800—A. Van Nuffel (B.)	2	08·7
1,500—F. Peeters (B.)	4	20·1
4× 200 *Relay*—Great Britain	1	38·0
60 *Hurdles*—L. Booth (G.B.)		8·7
	ft.	in.
High Jump—D. Brown (G.B.)	5	10¾
Long Jump—M. De Voeght (B.)	19	0
Shot—B. Bedford (G.B.)	48	8¼

Great Britain beat Belgium by 53 points to 42.

GREAT BRITAIN *v.* FRANCE

Indoor—Held in Orleans, February 23, 1975

Men's Events

Metres	min.	sec.
60—A. Sarteur (F.)		6·9
400—J. Chivers (G.B.)		48·5
800—P. Browne (G.B.)	1	51·7
1,500—W. Wilkinson (G.B.)	3	44·2
3,000—I. Stewart (G.B.)	7	56·8
60 *Hurdles*—G. Drut (F.)		7·7
Relay—France	1	30·5
	ft.	in.
High Jump—P. Poaniewa (F.)	7	1¼
Pole Vault—J-M. Bellot (F.)	16	0¼
Long Jump—J. Rousseau (F.)	26	0¼
Triple Jump—C. Valetudie (F.)	53	3¼
Shot—G. Capes (G.B.)	65	2¼

France beat Great Britain by 68 points to 58.

Women's Events

Metres	min.	sec.
60—A. Lynch (G.B.)		7·3
400—V. Elder (G.B.)		53·8
800—M. Thomas (F.)	2	06·6
1,500—M. Stewart (G.B.)	4	21·8
60 *Hurdles*—C. Rega (F.)		8·5
Relay—Great Britain	1	46·0
	ft.	in.
High Jump—M-C. Debourse (F.)	5	10¾
Long Jump—J. Curtet (F.)	19	5
Shot—L. Bertimon (F.)	51	5

France beat Great Britain by 53 points to 42.

GREAT BRITAIN *v.* SPAIN

Indoor—Held in Madrid, February 25, 1975

Metres	min.	sec.
60—J. Carbonell (S.)		6·8
400—C. O'Neill (G.B.)		48·5
800—P. Browne (G.B.)	1	51·2
1,500—I. Stewart (G.B.)	3	48·6
3,000—A. Burgos (S.)	8	16·2
60 *Hurdles*—G. Gower (G.B.)		8·0
	ft.	in.
High Jump—G. Marqueta (S.)	6	9
Pole Vault—B. Hooper (G.B.)	16	9½
Long Jump—A. Lerwill (G.B.)	25	1¼
Triple Jump—D. Johnson (G.B.)	52	6¼
Shot—G. Capes (G.B.)	65	4¾

Great Britain beat Spain by 70 points to 51.

EUROPEAN INDOOR CHAMPIONSHIPS

Held in Katowice, Poland, March 8/9, 1975

Men's Events

Metres	min.	sec.
60—V. Borzov (U.S.S.R.)		6·6
400—H. Kohler (Germany)		48·8
800—G. Stolle (G.D.R.)	1	49·8
1,500—T. Wessinghage (Germany)	3	44·6
3,000—I. Stewart (G.B.)	7	58·6
60 *Hurdles*—L. Wodzynski (Poland)		7·7
	ft.	in.
High Jump—V. Maly (Czechoslovakia)	7	3
Pole Vault—A. Kalliomaki (Finland)	17	6½
Long Jump—J. Rousseau (France)	26	0¾
Triple Jump—V. Saneyev (U.S.S.R.)	55	9¾
Shot—V. Stoev (Bulgaria)	66	7

Women's Events

Metres	min.	sec.
60—A. Lynch (G.B.)		7·2
400—V. Elder (G.B.)		52·7
800—A. Barkusky (G.D.R.)	2	05·6
1,500—N. Andrei (Rumania)	4	14·7
60 *Hurdles*—G. Rabsztyn (Poland)		8·0
	ft.	in.
High Jump—R. Ackermann (G.D.R.)	6	3½
Long Jump—D. Catineanu (Rumania)	20	8½
Shot—M. Adam (G.D.R.)	65	9½

BRITISH INTERNATIONAL GAMES

Held at Crystal Palace, May 31, 1975

Men's Events

	min.	sec.
100 *Metres*		
1 A. Cornaby		10·7
2 I. Matthews		10·7
3 G. Edwards		10·7
200 *Metres*		
1 R. Kennedy		21·5
2 D. Hill		21·7
3 B. Jones		21·8
400 *Metres*		
1 P. Hoffmann		47·8
2 R. Benn		48·2
3 D. Laing		48·5
800 *Metres*		
1 A. Settle	1	49·3
2 P. Browne	1	49·5
3 W. Matosz (Poland)	1	50·6
"*Emsley Carr*" *Mile*		
1 F. Bayi (Tanzania)	3	55·5
2 I. Stewart	3	57·4
3 B. Malinowski (Poland)	3	57·5
2 *Miles*		
1 D. Black	8	27·2
2 B. Ford	8	29·4
3 J. Goater	8	34·4
Steeplechase		
1 C. Thomas	8	44·4
2 J. Bicourt	8	45·6
3 D. Coates	8	47·6
110 *Hurdles*		
1 B. Price		14·0
2 L. Wodzynski (Poland)		14·0
3 G. Gower		14·5
400 *Hurdles*		
1 J. Hewelt (Poland)		51·2
2 W. Hartley		51·6
3 C. O'Neill		51·6
	ft.	in.
High Jump		
1 M. Butterfield	7	0¼
2 A. Mackenzie	7	0¼
3 B. Burgess	6	8
Pole Vault		
1 J. Gutteridge	16	0¾
2 A. Williams	16	0¾
3 J. Fenge	14	9
Long Jump		
1 G. Hignett	24	9¼
2 R. Mitchell	24	7¼
3 D. Cole	24	5¾
Triple Jump		
1 A. Moore	53	2¼
2 D. Johnson	52	7¼
3 J. Phillips	50	11
Discus		
1 T. Tuomola (Finland)	201	3
2 W. Tancred	194	2
3 P. Tancred	186	3
Hammer		
1 H. Huhtala (Finland)	222	1
2 C. Black	219	8
3 J. Whitehead	210	10
Javelin		
1 B. Roberts	244	6
2 L. Pusa (Finland)	240	2
3 D. Travis	235	4

Women's Events

		min.	sec.
100 *Metres*			
1	A. Lynch		11·3
2	A. Annum (Ghana)		11·6
3	S. Colyear		11·7
200 *Metres* (A)			
1	I. Szewinska (Poland)		23·0
2	A. Lynch		23·2
3	A. Annum (Ghana)		23·6
200 *Metres* (B)			
1	J. Pusey (Jamaica)		24·0
2	E. Barnes		24·0
3	H. Afriyie (Ghana)		24·1
400 *Metres* (A)			
1	D. Murray		52·6
2	V. Elder		53·1
3	J. Roscoe		53·5
400 *Metres* (B)			
1	E. Barnes		53·8
2	A. Robertson		55·9
3	J. Pusey (Jamaica)		56·4
800 *Metres*			
1	L. Kiernan	2	05·0
2	M. Coomber	2	06·0
3	A. Creamer	2	06·7
1,500 *Metres*			
1	H. Hollick	4	15·7
2	J. Allison	4	16·1
3	M. Stewart	4	16·4
100 *Hurdles*			
1	A. Colyear		13·7
2	L. Boothe		13·8
3	M. Nimmo		13·8
400 *Hurdles*			
1	J. Roscoe		59·5
2	J. Stokoe		59·7
3	S. Howell		61·1
		ft.	in.
High Jump			
1	V. Harrison	5	10½
2	B. Lawton	5	10½
3	F. Stacey	5	8
Long Jump			
1	M. Nimmo	20	10¾
2	S. Reeve	20	7
3	S. Mapstone	20	1
Javelin			
1	T. Sanderson	169	10
2	P. Carter	156	10
3	V. Fountain	155	8

GREAT BRITAIN *v.* GERMAN DEMOCRATIC REPUBLIC

Held in Dresden, June 21/22, 1975

Men's Events

Metres	min.	sec.
100—E. Ray (G.D.R.)		10·6
200—E. Ray (G.D.R.)		21·0
400—G. Arnold (G.D.R.)		46·2
800—H. Ohlert (G.D.R.)	1	47·0
1,500—H. Ohlert (G.D.R.)	3	42·1
5,000—N. Rose (G.B.)	13	41·4
10,000—W. Cierpinski (G.D.R.)	28	52·2
400 *Relay*—G.D.R.		39·1
1,600 *Relay*—G.D.R.	3	04·6
110 *Hurdles*—T. Munkelt (G.D.R.)		13·7
400 *Hurdles*—A. Pascoe (G.B.)		49·9
Steeplechase—F. Baumgarti (G.D.R.)	8	26·2
20-*km Walk*—H-G. Reimann (G.D.R.)	89	36·2
	ft.	in.
High Jump—R. Beilschmidt (G.D.R.)	7	4¼
Pole Vault—W. Reinhardt (G.D.R.)	17	0¾
Long Jump—P. Rieger (G.D.R.)	26	1
Triple Jump—J. Drehmel (G.D.R.)	55	8½
Shot—U. Beyer (G.D.R.)	68	9¾
Discus—W. Schmidt (G.D.R.)	219	2
Hammer—J. Sachse (G.D.R.)	242	11
Javelin—A. Katterle (G.D.R.)	271	9

German Democratic Republic beat Great Britain by 147 points to 75.

Women's Events

Metres	min.	sec.
100—R. Stecher (G.D.R.)		11·4
200—R. Stecher (G.D.R.)		22·8
400—E. Streidt (G.D.R.)		51·2
800—U. Klapezynski (G.D.R.)	2	00·5
1,500—W. Strotzer (G.D.R.)	4	09·4
400 *Relay*—G.D.R.		42·9
1,600 *Relay*—Great Britain	3	27·8
100 *Hurdles*—A. Ehrhardt (G.D.R.)		13·2
	ft.	in.
High Jump—R. Ackermann (G.D.R.)	6	3½
Long Jump—A. Voigt (G.D.R.)	21	4¾
Shot—M. Adam (G.D.R.)	65	11¾
Discus—G. Hinzmann (G.D.R.)	210	5
Javelin—R. Fuchs (G.D.R.)	210	8

German Democratic Republic beat Great Britain by 91 points to 44.

MATCH *v.* ROUMANIA

Same date and venue as above.

Women's Events

Metres	min.	sec.
100—A. Lynch (G.B.)		11·6
200—H. Golden (G.B.)		23·5
400—M. Suman (R.)		51·8
800—M. Suman (R.)	2	01·4
1,500—N. Andrei (R.)	4	09·5
Hurdles—S. Colyear (G.B.)		13·5
100 *Relay*—Great Britain		44·3
1,600 *Relay*—Great Britain	3	27·8
	ft.	in.
High Jump—V. Ioan (R.)	5	11¼
Long Jump—M. Nimmo (G.B.)	21	2
Shot—V. Cioltan (R.)	59	5½
Discus—A. Menis (R.)	204	5
Javelin—I. Pecec (R.)	178	10

Roumania beat Great Britain by 70 points to 65.

GREAT BRITAIN *v.* FRANCE

("A" MATCH)

Held in Dieppe on July 12/13, 1975

Men's Events

Metres	min.	sec.
100—J. Amoureux (F.)		10·7
200—C. Ducasse (F.)		21·2
400—R. Velasquex (F.)		47·3
800—P. Meyer (F.)	1	48·6
1,500—J. McGuinness (G.B.)	3	40·3
5,000—D. Lowes (G.B.)	13	52·4
10,000—N. Tijou (F.)	28	32·2
Steeplechase—J. Villain (F.)	8	35·0
100 *Relay*—France		40·1
400 *Relay*—Great Britain	3	09·1
110 *Hurdles*—E. Raybois (F.)		14·0
400 *Hurdles*—J. N'Lomo (F.)		51·1
20-*km Walk*—O. Flynn (G.B.)	90	31·0
	ft.	in.
High Jump—F. Bonnet (F.)	6	10¾
Pole Vault—J. Bellot (F.)	17	4½
Long Jump—D. Porter (G.B.)	25	6¾
Triple Jump—R. Le Goupil (F.)	52	10¼
Shot—M. Winch (G.B.)	62	11¼
Discus—M. Winch (G.B.)	188	2
Hammer—C. Black (G.B.)	226	8
Javelin—D. Ottley (G.B.)	243	8

France beat Great Britain by 239 points to 191.

Women's Events

Metres	min.	sec.
100—D. Ramsden (G.B.)		11·9
200—D. Camus (F.)		23·8
400—A. Smyth (G.B.)		54·4

800—A. Creamer (G.B.)	2	05·2
1,500—H. Hollick (G.B.)	4	22·7
3,000—P. Yeoman (G.B.)	9	21·4
100 *Relay*—France		45·7
400 *Relay*—France	3	39·1
100 *Hurdles*—C. Prevost (F.)		13·6
	ft.	in.
High Jump—G. Hitchen (G.B.)	5	9¼
Long Jump—J. Curtet (F.)	20	8
Shot—S. Creantor (F.)	48	0¾
Discus—M. Ritchie (G.B.)	176	4
Javelin—S. Corbett (G.B.)	166	9

Great Britain beat France by 150 points to 128.

EUROPEAN CUP
Held in Nice, August 20/21, 1975

Men's Events

Metres	min.	sec.
100—V. Borzov (U.S.S.R.)		10·4
200—P. Mennea (Italy)		20·4
400—D. Jenkins (G.B.)		45·5
800—S. Ovett (G.B.)	1	46·6
1,500—T. Wessinghage (Germany)	3	39·1
5,000—B. Foster (G.B.)	13	36·2
10,000—K. Leiteritz (G.D.R.)	28	37·2
4×100 *Relay*—G.D.R.		39·0
4×400 *Relay*—Great Britain	3	02·9
110 *Hurdles*—G. Drut (France)		13·6
400 *Hurdles*—A Pascoe (G.B.)		49·0
Steeplechase—M. Karst (Germany)	8	16·4
	ft.	in.
High Jump—A. Griguriev (U.S.S.R.)	7	4¼
Pole Vault—W. Kozakiewicz (Poland)	17	10¾
Long Jump—G. Cybulski (Poland)	26	9
Triple Jump—V. Saneyev (U.S.S.R.)	55	8¼
Shot—G. Capes (G.B.)	68	1
Discus—W. Schmidt (G.D.R.)	207	3
Hammer—K. Riehm (Germany)	254	3
Javelin—N. Grebnev (U.S.S.R.)	276	7

Result: 1. German Democratic Republic, 112 points; 2. U.S.S.R., 109; 3. Poland, 101; 4.* Great Britain, 85; 5. Germany, 85; 6. Finland, 85; 7. France, 80; 8. Italy, 68.

* 4th, 5th, and 6th places decided by wins: G.B. (6); Germany (3).

Women's Events

Metres	min.	sec.
100—R. Stecher (G.D.R.)		11·3
200—R. Stecher (G.D.R.)		22·1
400—I. Szewinska (Poland)		50·5
800—R. Suman (Roumania)	2	00·6
1,500—W. Strotzer (G.D.R.)	4	08·0
4×100 *Relay*—G.D.R.		42·8
4×400 *Relay*—G.D.R.	3	24·0
Hurdles—A. Ehrhardt (G.D.R.)		12·8
	ft.	in.
High Jump—R. Ackermann (G.D.R.)	6	4¼
Long Jump—L. Alfeyeva (U.S.S.R.)	22	2¼
Shot—M. Adam (G.D.R.)	69	11½
Discus—F. Melnik (U.S.S.R.)	218	4
Javelin—R. Fuchs (G.D.R.)	212	7

Result: 1. German Democratic Republic, 97 points; 2. U.S.S.R., 77; 3. Germany, 64; 4. Poland, 57; 5. Roumania, 52; 6. Bulgaria, 47; 7. Great Britain, 38; 8. France, 35.

GREAT BRITAIN *v.* NETHERLANDS *v.* HUNGARY
Held in Drachten, August 3, 1975

Women's Events

Metres	min.	sec.
100—G. Taylor (G.B.)		11·8
200—D. Murray (G.B.)		24·3
400—V. Elder (G.B.)		53·3
800—M. Lazar (H.)	2	03·3
1,500—J. van Gerven (N.)	4	17·6
Hurdles—M. Sterk (N.)		13·9
4×100 *Relay*—Hungary		45·4
4×400 *Relay*—Great Britain	3	35·5
	ft.	in.
High Jump—M. van Doorn (N.)	5	11½
Long Jump—I. Szabo (H.)	21	7¼
Shot—M. Iranyi (H.)	52	11½
Discus—R. Stahlman (N.)	178	11
Javelin—I. Vago (H.)	161	2

Team Result: Hungary, 108 points; Great Britain, 91; Netherlands, 69.

GREAT BRITAIN *v.* FRANCE (JUNIOR)
Held in Warley, August 9/10, 1975

Men's Events

Metres	min.	sec.
100—E. Guy (F.)		10·7
200—M. Machaby (F.)		21·6
400—B. Jones (G.B.)		47·5
800—G. Gabrielli (F.)	1	50·0
1,500—S. Coe (G.B.)	3	50·8
3,000—M. East (G.B.)	8	17·0
5,000—M. Deegan (G.B.)	14	37·8
Steeplechase—M. Morris (G.B.)	5	44·6
110 *Hurdles*—M. Hatton (G.B.)		14·9
400 *Hurdles*—W. Greaves (G.B.)		52·7
4×100 *Relay*—France		40·6
4×400 *Relay*—Great Britain	3	12·6
10,000 Walk—D. Cotton (G.B.)	45	35·4
	ft.	in.
High Jump—B. Burgess (G.B.)	6	10¼
Pole Vault—Y. Nanot (F.)	15	9
Long Jump—F. Charles (F.)	24	9¾
Triple Jump—A. Moore (G.B.)	53	6¼
Shot—L. Viudes (F.)	56	6
Discus—P. Buxton (G.B.)	174	11
Hammer—P. Surriray (F.)	198	6
Javelin—P. Kuentz (F.)	233	2

Great Britain beat France by 233 points to 195 (3 competitors from each side in each event).

Women's Events

Metres	min.	sec.
100—W. Clarke (G.B.)		11·8
200—W. Clarke (G.B.)		24·1
400—R. Kennedy (G.B.)		55·0
800—K. Colebrook (G.B.)	2	07·4
1,500—A Robinson (G.B.)	4	25·0
4×100 *Relay*—France		46·0
4×400 *Relay*—Great Britain	3	43·3
Hurdles—L. Lebeau (F.)		14·1
	ft.	in.
High Jump—G. Hitchen (G.B.)	5	9¾
Long Jump—A. Manley (G.B.)	19	10½
Shot—J. Oakes (G.B.)	44	7½
Discus—V. Watson (G.B.)	143	4
Javelin—A. Bocle (F.)	163	5

Great Britain beat France by 161 points to 93.

GREAT BRITAIN *v.* SPAIN (JUNIOR)
Held in Warley, August 9/10, 1975

Men's Events

Metres	min.	sec.
100—J. Carbonell (S.)		10·8
200—M. Arnau (S.)		21·7
400—B. Jones (G.B.)		47·5
800—M. Edwards (G.B.)	1	50·4
1,500—S. Coe (G.B.)	3	50·8
3,000—D. Dominquez (S.)	8	15·2
5,000—J. Gonzalez (S.)	14	31·2
Steeplechase—M. Morris (G.B.)	5	44·6
110 *Hurdles*—J. Moracho (S.)		14·7
400 *Hurdles*—J. Alonso (S.)		52·3
4×100 *Relay*—Spain		40·9
4×400 *Relay*—Great Britain	3	12·6

	ft.	in.
High Jump—B. Burgess (G.B.)	6	10¼
Pole Vault—J. Gutteridge (G.B.)	15	9
Long Jump—I. De Coq (S.)	24	5¾
Triple Jump—A. Moore (G.B.)	53	6¼
Shot—P. Buxton (G.B.)	50	8¾
Discus—P. Buxton (G.B.)	174	11
Hammer—P. Buxton (G.B.)	187	6
Javelin—L. Evans (G.B.)	196	1

Great Britain beat Spain by 114 points to 96 (2 competitors).

GREAT BRITAIN *v.* U.S.S.R.

Held at Crystal Palace, August 24/25, 1975

Men's Events

Metres	min.	sec.
100—J. Siloys (U.S.S.R.)		10·4
200—A. Bennett (G.B.)		20·9
400—D. Jenkins (G.B.)		45·8
800—V. Ponomaryov (U.S.S.R.)	1	47·4
1,500—B. Foster (G.B.)	3	42·2
5,000—E. Sellik (U.S.S.R.)	13	27·2
10,000—M. Tagg (G.B.)	28	31·0
4×100 *Relay*—U.S.S.R.		39·4
4×400 *Relay*—Great Britain	3	08·1
110 *Hurdles*—B. Price (G.B.)		13·7
400 *Hurdles*—A. Pascoe (G.B.)		50·1
Steeplechase—A. Velichko (U.S.S.R.)	8	33·0
	ft.	in.
High Jump—V. Kiva (U.S.S.R.)	7	1¾
Pole Vault—Y. Isakov (U.S.S.R.)	17	0¾
Long Jump—A Pereverzev (U.S.S.R.)	26	2¼
Triple Jump—V. Saneyev (U.S.S.R.)	55	7¼
Shot—V. Voykin (U.S.S.R.)	65	11½
Discus—V. Penzikov (U.S.S.R.)	207	3
Hammer—V. Dmitrenko (U.S.S.R.)	247	1
Javelin—N. Grebnyev (U.S.S.R.)	177	10

U.S.S.R. beat Great Britain by 225 points to 181 (3 competitors from each side per event).

Women's Events

Metres	min.	sec.
100—A. Lynch (G.B.)		11·4
200—A. Lynch (G.B.)		23·2
400—D. Murray (G.B.)		51·8
800—N. Morgunova (U.S.S.R.)	2	01·3
1,500—T. Kazankina (U.S.S.R.)	4	08·5
4×110 *Relay*—U.S.S.R.		43·8
4×400 *Relay*—U.S.S.R.	3	28·5
Hurdles—N. Lebedyeva (U.S.S.R.)		13·2
	ft.	in.
High Jump—D. Brown (G.B.)	5	10½
Long Jump—L. Alfeyeva (U.S.S.R.)	21	3½
Shot—E. Krachevskaya (U.S.S.R.)	65	1½
Discus—F. Melnik (U.S.S.R.)	217	7
Javelin—S. Babich (U.S.S.R.)	198	0

U.S.S.R. beat Great Britain by 141 points to 114.

EUROPEAN JUNIOR CHAMPIONSHIPS

Held in Athens, August 22, 23, and 24, 1975

Men's Events

Metres	min.	sec.
100—W. Bastians (Germany)		10·5
200—W. Bastians (Germany)		21·3
400—H. Galant (Poland)		46·9
800—G. Gabrielli (France)	1	49·8
1,500—A. Paunonen (Finland)	3	44·8
3,000—Y. Naessens (Belgium)	8	10·6
5,000—P. Chernuk (U.S.S.R.)	14	18·0
Steeplechase—M. Morris (G.B.)	5	34·8
110 *Hurdles*—A. Pouchkov (U.S.S.R.)		14·1
400 *Hurdles*—A. Muench (G.D.R.)		51·3
10,000 *Walk*—T. Wieser (G.D.R.)	43	11·4
4×100 *Relay*—France		40·1
4×400 *Relay*—G.D.R.	3	08·7
	ft.	in.
High Jump—J. Wszola (Poland)	7	3¼
Pole Vault—A. Dolgov (U.S.S.R.)	16	4¾
Long Jump—L. Dunecki (Poland)	26	2¼
Triple Jump—A. Moore (G.B.)	53	0¼
Shot—V. Kissilev (U.S.S.R.)	59	11½
Discus—H. Klink (G.D.R.)	182	0
Hammer—D. Gerstenberg (G.D.R.)	229	11
Javelin—I. Gromov (U.S.S.R.)	255	8

Decathlon—E. Muller (Germany), 7,706 points

Women's Events

Metres	min.	sec.
100—P. Koppetsch (G.D.R.)		11·3
200—P. Koppetsch (G.D.R.)		23·2
400—C. Brehmer (G.D.R.)		51·3
800—O. Commandeur (Netherlands)	2	05·8
1,500—A. Kuhse (G.D.R.)	4	18·6
100 *Hurdles*—L. Lebeau (France)		13·8
4×100 *Relay*—G.D.R.		44·1
4×400 *Relay*—G.D.R.	3	33·7
	ft.	in.
High Jump—A. Fedorchuk (U.S.S.R.)	6	2
Long Jump—I. Shidova (U.S.S.R.)	20	10½
Shot—V. Vasselinova (Bulgaria)	56	9¼
Discus—K. Wenzel (G.D.R.)	180	8
Javelin—L. Blodnietse (U.S.S.R.)	198	11

Pentathlon—B. Holzapfel (Germany), 4450 points.

GREAT BRITAIN *v.* SWEDEN

Held at Meadowbank, Edinburgh, September 13 and 14, 1975

Men's Events

Metres	min.	sec.
100—C. Garpenborg (S.)		10·5
200—D. Jenkins (G.B.)		21·2
400—R. Jenkins (G.B.)		46·7
800—P. Browne (G.B.)	1	48·8
1,500—D. Moorcroft (G.B.)	3	54·9
5,000—A. Simmons (G.B.)	13	59·4
10,000—J. Brown (G.B.)	28	54·4
110 *Hurdles*—A. Pascoe (G.B.)		14·2
400 *Hurdles*—B. Hartley (G.B.)		51·0
Steeplechase—D. Glans (S.)	8	31·4
4×100 *Relay*—Sweden		40·7
4×400 *Relay*—Great Britain	3	07·6
	ft.	in.
High Jump—R. Almen (S.)	6	11½
Pole Vault—R. Thorstensson (S.)	15	1½
Long Jump—U. Jarfelt (S.)	25	2¾
Triple Jump—B. Nyberg (S.)	51	4¼
Shot—G. Capes (G.B.)	65	7¾
Discus—K. Akesson (S.)	191	5
Hammer—P. Dickenson (G.B.)	226	11
Javelin—P.-E. Smiding (S.)	254	7

Great Britain beat Sweden by 113 points to 99.

Women's Events

Metres	min.	sec.
100—S. Lannaman (G.B.)		11·6
200—S. Lannaman (G.B.)		23·6
400—V. Elder (G.B.)		53·5
800—R. Wright (G.B.)	2	08·0
1,500—R. Wright (G.B.)	4	19·8
3,000—I. Knutsson (S.)	8	54·0
100 *Hurdles*—E. Sutherland (G.B.)		13·9
400 *Hurdles*—J. Roscoe (G.B.)		59·3
4×100 *Relay*—Great Britain		44·5
4×400 *Relay*—Great Britain	3	38·4
	ft.	in.
High Jump—R. Few (G.B.)	5	8¾
Long Jump—M. Nimmo (G.B.)	20	7¼
Shot—B. Bedford (G.B.)	49	5
Discus—M. Ritchie (G.B.)	179	5
Javelin—T. Sanderson (G.B.)	169	6½

Metres	min.	sec.
10,000—P. Nihill (G.B.)	44	23·2
10,000 *Junior*—B. Simonsen (S.)	44	35·6
3,000 *Women*—B. Holqvist (S.)	14	09·2

Great Britain beat Sweden by 103 points to 54.

Walking Match won by Sweden by 19 points to 13.

A.A.A. INDOOR CHAMPIONSHIPS

Held in Cosford, January 31 and February 1, 1975

Metres	min.	sec.
60—D. Roberts (Cardiff)		6·8
200—C. Monk (Leicester)		22·5
400—J. Chivers (Wolverhampton)		48·4
800—P. Browne (TVH)	1	52·4
1,500—P. Banning (Andover)	3	42·2
3,000—I. Stewart (Birchfield)	8	01·0
Steeplechase—D. Coates (Gateshead)	5	30·8
60 *Hurdles*—B. Price (Cardiff)		8·0
	ft.	in.
High Jump—C. Boreham (Birmingham)	6	6¾
Pole Vault—B. Hooper (Borough Rd.)	17	0¾
Long Jump—P. Scott (Bristol)	23	10¾
Triple Jump—D. Johnson (Sheffield)	51	0
Shot—G. Capes (Enfield)	65	4¼

W.A.A.A. INDOOR CHAMPIONSHIPS

Held in Cosford, January 31 and February 1, 1975

Metres	min.	sec.
60—A. Lynch (Mitcham)		7·3
400—V. Elder (Wolverhampton)		53·5
800—M. Barrett (Verlea)	2	11·5
1,500—M. Stewart (Birchfield)	4	21·4
3,000—C. Haskett (Stretford)	9	40·2
60 *Hurdles*—L. Boothe (Mitcham)		8·5
	ft.	in.
High Jump—R. Few (Mitcham)	5	10¾
Long Jump—J. Jay (Bristol)	18	11¾
Shot—B. Bedford (Mitcham)	49	5¾

WOMEN S A.A.A. CHAMPIONSHIPS

Held at Crystal Palace, July 18/19, 1975

Metres	min.	sec.
100—A. Lynch (Mitcham)		11·7
200—H. Golden (Edinburgh)		24·2
400—D. Murray (Southampton)		51·9
800—A. Creamer (Rotherham)	2	05·1
1,500—M. Stewart (Birchfield)	4	14·7
3,000—M. Purcell (Eire)	9	08·0
100 *Hurdles*—E. Damman (Canada)		13·9
400 *Hurdles*—J. Roscoe (Stretford)		58·3
5,000 *Walk*—V. Lovell (Birchfield)	25	02·8
	ft.	in.
High Jump—D. Brown (Kent)	5	8¾
Long Jump—M. Nimmo (Maryhill)	20	8
Shot—B. Bedford (Mitcham)	48	10¼
Discus—M. Ritchie (Edinburgh)	174	3
Javelin—T. Sanderson (Wolverhampton)	178	6

Pentathlon†—S. Wright (Essex), 4,196 points

* 5 ft. 10½ in. in jump off.

† Held at Crystal Palace on May 25.

A.A.A. CHAMPIONSHIPS

Held at Crystal Palace, August 1/2, 1975

Men's Events

Metres	min.	sec.
100—S. Riddick (U.S.A.)		10·4
200—S. Riddick (U.S.A.)		20·8
400—D. Jenkins (Gateshead)		45·9
800—S. Ovett (Brighton)	1	46·1
1,500—D. Malan (S. Africa)	3	38·1
5,000—M. Liquori (U.S.A.)	13	32·6
10,000—D. Black (Small Heath)	27	54·2
*Marathon**—J. Norman (Notts) ....2 hr.	15	50·0
3,000 *Walk*†—P. Nihill (Surrey)	12	43·2
10,000 *Walk*—B. Adams (Leicester)	42	40·0
110 *Hurdles*—B. Price (Cardiff)		13·9
400 *Hurdles*—W. Hartley (Liverpool)		49·7
Steeplechase—A. Staynings (Bristol)	8	30·0
	ft.	in.
High Jump—R. Schiel (S. Africa)	6	10¾
Pole Vault—R. Boyd (Australia)	16	4¾
Long Jump—A. Lerwill (Enfield)	25	6
Triple Jump—M. McGrath (Australia)	52	10¾
Shot—G. Capes (Enfield)	66	3¼
Discus—J. Van Reenen (S. Africa)	204	3
Hammer—A. Barnard (S. Africa)	241	5
Javelin—H. Potgieter (S. Africa)	256	4

Decathlon§—P. Zeniou (North London), 6,931 points.

* Held at Stoke-upon-Trent on June 1.

† Held at West London on March 29.

§ Held at Cwmbran on August 29/30.

A.A.A. JUNIOR (UNDER 20) CHAMPIONSHIPS

Held in Kirby, July 26/27, 1975

Metres	min.	sec.
100—D. Thompson (Essex)		10·9
200—A. Harley (Pitreavy)		21·9
400—B. Jones (Liverpool)		47·3
800—P. Forbes (Edinburgh)	1	50·7
1,500—S. Coe (Hallamshire)	3	47·1
3,000*—J. Treacey (Eire)	8	15·0
5,000—J. Treacey (Eire)	14	04·6
Steeplechase—M. Morris (Cwmbran)	5	37·8
110 *Hurdles*—M. Hatton (Reading)		14·9
400 *Hurdles*—W. Greaves (Ilford)		54·3
	ft.	in.
High Jump—M. Palmer (Wolverh'pton)	6	6¾
Pole Vault—K. Stock (Croydon)	15	7
Long Jump—B. Cronin (Lee)	22	8
Triple Jump—B. Cronin (Lee)	49	0¼
Shot—P. Buxton (Edinburgh)	52	10¾
Discus—P. Buxton (Edinburgh)	172	10
Hammer—P. Buxton (Edinburgh)	196	10
Javelin—L. Evans (Stretford)	184	7

Decathlon†—D. Thompson, 7,008 points.

* Held at Crystal Palace on August 2.

† Held at Cwmbran, August 29/30.

ENGLISH SCHOOLS CHAMPIONSHIPS

Held in Durham, July 11/12, 1975

Boys' Events

Metres	min.	sec.
100—J. Jankenfields (Middx)		11·1
200—F. Thompson (London)		22·6
400—M. Francis (Manchester)		49·3
800—S. Morley (Sussex)	1	53·3
1,500—M. Wilson (Somerset)	3	53·8
5,000—R. Callan (Leicester)	14	40·0
Steeplechase—D. Warren (Surrey)	5	47·6
110 *Hurdles*—M. Hatton (Berks)		14·7
400 *Hurdles*—J. Longman (Hants)		55·3
100 *Relay*—London		43·4
	ft.	in.
High Jump—C. Dean (Lancs)	6	3½
Pole Vault—R. Goodall (Cheshire)	13	5¼
Long Jump—S. Peglar (Manchester)	22	8½
Triple Jump—N. Stoppard (Derby)	46	7½
Shot—I. Lindley (W. Yorks)	53	11
Discus—R. Wheway (Devon)	153	4
Hammer—M. Fenton (Suffolk)	177	11
Javelin—T. Smith (Middx)	203	4

Girls' Events

Metres		min.	sec.
100—K. Harrison (Manchester)			12·3
200—D. Heath (Cheshire)			25·1
400—E. Eddy (West Midlands)			56·3
800—P. Byrne (West Midlands)		2	11·4
1,500—B. Schofield (Manchester)		4	40·3
Hurdles—J. Bowerman (Surrey)			14·5

		ft.	in.
High Jump—C. Mathers (Middx)		5	5¼
Long Jump—A. Manley (Surrey)		19	5½
Shot—J. Oakes (Kent)		45	7
Discus—L. Smith (Dorset)		141	2
Javelin—B. Richardson (Durham)		139	8

INTERNATIONAL CROSS COUNTRY
Held in Rabat, Morocco, March 16, 1975

Senior Men

1	I. Stewart (Scotland)	35	20
2	M. Haro (Spain)	35	21
3	B. Rodgers (U.S.A.)	35	27
4	J. Walker (New Zealand)	35	45
5	E. Robertson (New Zealand)	35	46
6	F. Fava (Italy)	35	47

Team Result

		points
1	New Zealand (4, 5, 25, 26, 33, 34)	127
2	England (7, 14, 37, 39, 50, 51)	198
3	Belgium (10, 16, 21, 45, 57, 62)	211

4. U.S.A. (249 points); 5. G.D.R. (273); 6. Scotland (292); 7. Algeria (301); 8. France (303); 9. Germany (308); 10. Italy (325); 11. Australia (325); 12. Spain (379); 13. Tunisia (453); 14. Morocco (480); 15. Wales (510); 16. Eire (571); 17. Northern Ireland (678); 18. Sudan (728); 19. Iran (824); 20. Libya (889); 21. Syria (892); 22. Gibraltar (984); 23. Saudi-Arabia (1,005). Egypt and Finland Teams did not finish.

Junior Men

		min.	sec.
1	B. Thomas (U.S.A.)	21	00
2	J. Gonzales (Spain)	21	18
3	J. Treacy (Eire)	21	23

Team Result—1. U.S.A. (29 points); 2. Eire (35); 3. Spain (61); 5. Scotland (95); 6. England (99).

Women

		min.	sec.
1	J. Brown (U.S.A.)	13	42
2	B. Ludwichowska (Poland)	13	47
3	C. Valero (Spain)	13	48

Team Result—1. U.S.A. (44 points); 2. New Zealand (50); 3. Poland (61); 4. England (64); 10. Scotland (129); 12. Wales (251).

NATIONAL CROSS COUNTRY CHAMPIONSHIPS
Held at Luton, March 1, 1975

Senior Race, 9 miles

		min.	sec.
1	A. Simmons (Luton)	46	24
2	B. Ford (Aldershot)	46	32
3	G. Tuck (Cambridge)	47	08
4	R. Smedley (Birchfield)	47	17
5	T. Wright (Wolverhampton)	47	20
6	M. Beevor (Luton)	47	27

Team Result

		points
1	Gateshead H. and A.C. (12, 15, 48, 50, 62, 77)	264
2	Liverpool H. and A.C. (20, 46, 49, 80, 89, 134)	418
3	Airedale and Spen Valley A.C. (27, 39, 87, 108, 110, 137)	508

Junior Race, 6 Miles
Won by S. Ovett (Brighton and Hove), 32 min. 06 sec. Team: Birmingham University A.C., 91 points.

Youth's Race, 4 Miles
Won by J. Mills (Gateshead), 22 min. 58 sec. Team: Gateshead H. and A.C., 108 points.

NATIONAL 10–MILES WALK
Held in Southwick, March 15, 1975

		min.	sec.
1	O. Flynn (Basildon)	71	15
2	B. Adams (Leicester)	71	38
3	R. Mills (Ilford)	71	59

Team Result—Ilford, 40 points.

NATIONAL 20–Km WALK
Held at Coventry, May 10, 1975

		min.	sec.
1	O. Flynn (Basildon)	88	58
2	R. Mills (Ilford)	89	28
3	B. Adams (Leicester)	133	54

Team Result: Southend, 36 points

NATIONAL 20–MILES WALK
Held at Castletown, Isle of Man, June 14, 1975

		hr.	min.	sec.
1	R. Dobson (Southend)	2	36	26
2	R. Thorpe (Sheffield)	2	37	09
3	J. Warhurst (Sheffield)	2	38	21

Team Result—1. Sheffield United (28 points); 2. Southend (47); 3. Brighton and Hove (66).

RWA 50–Km WALK
Held in Leicester, July 19, 1975

		hr.	min.	sec.
1	J. Warhurst (Sheffield)	4	20	32
2	J. Lees (Brighton and Hove)	4	26	13
3	C. Fogg (Enfield)	4	27	44

Team Result—1. Sheffield (43 points); 2. Southend (50); 3. Belgrave (71).

OXFORD v. CAMBRIDGE

Cambridge beat Oxford in the Annual Oxford v. Cambridge Sports, held at the West London Stadium on May 14, 1975, by 111 points to 99. Of the 101 contests held since 1864, Oxford have won on 50 occasions, Cambridge on 44. There have been 7 draws. The first women's contest was held on the same date, Cambridge winning by 67 points to 61.

Oxford won the Cross Country (1974) by 30 points to 49, and in Field Events (also 1974), by 4 events to 3.

BRITISH ATHLETICS LEAGUE

Div. I—Wolverhampton and Bilston, 24 points; Thames Valley, 18.
Div. II—Edinburgh A.C., 22; Sale, 21.
Div. III—Stretford, 18; Swansea, 18.
Div. IV—Essex Beagles, 18; Metropolitan Police, 15½.
" Pye " Gold Cup—Edinburgh Southern Harriers.
British Women's Cup—Edinburgh Southern Harriers.

THE TURF

The Turf in Great Britain is under the control of the Jockey Club.

The *Jockey Club* (incorporating the National Hunt Committee, 42 Portman Square, London, W.I.). Stewards are: The Viscount Leverhulme, T.D. (*Senior Steward*); Capt. H. M. Gosling; T. F. Blackwell, M.B.E. (*Deputy Senior Stewards*); Lt. Col. P. H. G. Bengough, O.B.E.; J. Hambro; Major E. M. Cameron; Sir John Thompson, K.B.E., T.D.; The Earl of Ranfurly, K.C.M.G.; Major M. G. Wyatt, M.B.E.

Leading Owners and Trainers, 1975
(Flat Season up to Oct. 3)

Winning Owners		Winning Trainers	
Dr. C. Vitta-dini	£208,664	P. Walwyn	£366,671
C. d'Alessio	77,366	H. Cecil	155,177
R. Tikkoo	67,215	R. Price	105,468
D. Robinson	64,743	B. Hills	93,626
C. St. George	64,586	W. Hern	89,145
G. Williams	51,476	J. Tree	69,493
J. Morrison	48,608	M. V. O'Brien	68,723
N. B. Hunt	44,700	B. Hobbs	67,784
W. Zeitelhack	39,296	M. Jarvis	64,743
Lady Beaver-brook	34,642	M.W.Easterby	58,531
Lord Howard de Walden	28,080	J. Hindley	57,668
G. Reed	28,897	G. Pritchards-Gordon	57,057

Leading Breeders, 1975
(Up to Oct. 3)

	Horses	Races won	Value
Overbury Stud	6	10	£194,135
Woodpark Ltd	7	10	70,976
Barretstown Estates	2	4	54,743
G. P. Williams	3	9	52,074
Fonthill Stud	2	3	49,223
Cleaboy Farms Co.	9	11	41,136
N. B. Hunt	3	3	40,895
Gestut Rottgen	1	1	39,296
Cragwood Estates Inc.	8	13	33,154
J. Dillon	2	4	31,619
Dalham Stud Farm Ltd.	8	13	30,170
F. Feeney	3	9	29,531

Winning Jockeys, 1975
(Up to Oct. 3)

	1st	2nd	3rd	Unpl.	Total Mts.
P. Eddery	143	107	78	376	704
W. Carson	105	118	92	419	734
L. Piggott	101	79	55	225	460
J. Mercer	85	74	59	281	499
G. Lewis	80	46	54	290	470
A. Murray	75	56	53	327	511
F. Durr	72	58	74	292	496
B. Raymond	69	62	64	292	487
A. Bond	57	54	38	265	414
E. Hide	55	43	39	196	333
R. Hutchinson	53	28	31	166	278
E. Johnson	52	49	37	238	376

Winning Sires, 1975
(Up to Oct. 3)

	Horses	Races won	Value
Great Nephew (1963), by Honeyway	15	28	£290,142
Habitat (1966), by Sir Gaylord	24	32	99,257
Blakeney (1966), by Hethersett	8	14	80,455
Balidar (1966), by Will Somers	8	13	75,420
Busted (1963), by Crepello	20	38	66,351
Sea Hawk II (1963), by Herbager	12	16	64,347
Track Spare (1963), by Sound Track	16	29	45,979
Appiani II (1963), by Herbager	8	9	45,116
Jukebox (1966), by Sing Sing	17	30	42,388
Tower Walk (1966), by High Treason	16	40	42,120
Supreme Sovereign (1964), by Sovereign Path	11	14	42,022
Vaguely Noble (1965), by Vienna	4	5	41,839

THE DERBY, 1965-1975
For particulars of the Derby from 1780–1964 see 1921–65 editions.

The *Distance* of the Derby course at Epsom is 1½ miles. Lord Egremont won Derby in 1782, 1804, 5, 7, 26 (also, 5 Oaks); Duke of Grafton, 1802, 9, 10, 15 (also, 9 Oaks); Mr. Bowes, 1835, 43, 52, 3; Sir J. Hawley, Teddington (1851), Beadsman (1858), Musjid (1859), and Blue Gown (1868), the 1st Duke of Westminster, Bend Or (1880), Shotover (1882), Ormonde (1886), and Flying Fox (1899). Lady James Douglas was the first lady to win the Derby—War Substitute at Newmarket (1918); at Epsom, Mrs. G. B. Miller (1937). First winner was Sir Charles Bunbury's Diomed in 1780. From 1940 to 1945 a substitute Derby was run at Newmarket. By winning his 5th Derby, the late Aga Khan equalled Lord Egremont's record. He also won 2 Oaks.

Year	Owner and Name of Winner	Betting	Jockey	Trainer	No. of Run'rs
1965	M. J. Ternynck's Sea Bird II (Fr.)	7 to 4 F.	T. P. Glennon	E. Pollet	22
1966	Lady Zia Wernher's Charlottown	5 to 1	A. Breasley	G. Smyth	25
1967	Mr. H. J. Joel's Royal Palace*	7–4 F.	G. Moore	N. Murless	22
1968	Mr. R. R. Guest's Sir Ivor* (Ir.)	4–5 F.	L. Piggott	M. V. O'Brien	13
1969	Mr. A. M. Budgett's Blakeney	15–2	E. Johnson	A. M. Budgett	26
1970	Mr. C. W. Engelhard's Nijinsky*° (Ir.)	11–8 F.	L. Piggott	M. V. O'Brien	11
1971	Mr. P. Mellon's Mill Reef	100–30 F.	G. Lewis	I. Balding	21
1972	Mr. J. Galbreath's Roberto (Ir.)	3–1 F.	L. Piggott	M. V. O'Brien	18
1973	Mr. A. M. Budgett's Morston	25–1	E. Hide	A. M. Budgett	25
1974	Mrs. N. Phillips' Snow Knight	50–1	B. Taylor	P. M. Nelson	18
1975	Dr. C. Vittadini's Grundy	5–1	P. Eddery	P. Walwyn	18

Marked* also won the Two Thousand Guineas; °the St. Leger.

Record times, 2 min. 34 secs. by Hyperion in 1933; Windsor Lad in 1934; 2 min. 33·8 sec. Mahmoud in 1936.

TWO THOUSAND GUINEAS. First Run, 1809. Rowley Mile. Newmarket. 9 st.

Year	OWNER AND NAME OF WINNER	Betting	Jockey	Trainer	No. of Run'rs
1971	Mrs. J. Hislop's Brigadier Gerard....	11 to 2	J. Mercer.......	W. R. Hern.....	6
1972	Sir Jules Thorn's High Top...........	85 to 40F.	W. Carson.....	B. van Cutsem...	12
1973	Mrs. B. Davis's Mon Fils...........	50 to 1	F. Durr.......	R. Hannon.....	18
1974	Mme. M. Berner's Nonoalco (Fr.)....	19 to 2	Y. Saint-Martin.	F. Boutin.....	12
1975	Mr. C. d'Alessio's Bolkonski.........	33 to 1	F. Dettori....	H. Cecil.....	24

ONE THOUSAND GUINEAS. 1814. Rowley Mile. Newmarket. Fillies. 9 st.

Year	OWNER AND NAME OF WINNER	Betting	Jockey	Trainer	No. of Run'rs
1971	Mr. F. Hue-Williams's Altesse Royale	25 to 1	Y. Saint-Martin.	N. Murless......	10
1972	Mrs. R. Stanley's Waterloo...........	8 to 1	E. Hide.......	B. Watts.......	18
1973	Mr. G. H. Pope's Mysterious.........	11 to 1	G. Lewis......	N. Murless.....	14
1974	H.M. the Queen's Highclere.........	12 to 1	J. Mercer......	W. R. Hern.....	15
1975	Mrs. D. O'Kelly's Nocturnal Spree...	14 to 1	J. Roe........	N. Murless.......	16

OAKS. 1779. Epsom. 1½ Mile. Fillies. 9 st.

Year	OWNER AND NAME OF WINNER	Betting	Jockey	Trainer	No. of Run'rs
1971	Mr. F. Hue-Williams's Altesse Royale	6 to 4 F.	G. Lewis.......	N. Murless......	11
1972	Mr. C. St. George's Ginevra.........	8 to 1	A. Murray......	H. R. Price.....	17
1973	Mr. G. H. Pope's Mysterious.........	13 to 8 F.	G. Lewis......	N. Murless.....	10
1974	Mr. L. Freedman's Polygamy........	3 to 1 F.	P. Eddery......	P. Walwyn.....	15
1975	Mr. J. Morrison's Juliette Marny.....	12 to 1	L. Piggott.......	J. Tree........	12

ST. LEGER. 1776(8). Doncaster. 1¾ mile, 127 yards.

Year	OWNER AND NAME OF WINNER	Betting	Jockey	Trainer	No. of Run'rs
1971	Mrs. J. Rogerson's Athens Wood.....	5 to 2	L. Piggott.......	T. Jones........	8
1972	Mr. O. Phipps's Boucher (Ir.)........	3 to 1	L. Piggott.......	M. V. O'Brien...	7
1973	Col. W. Behrens's Peleid.............	28 to 1	F. Durr..........	W. Elsey.......	13
1974	Lady Beaverbrook's Bustino........	11 to 10 F.	J. Mercer.......	W. R. Hern.....	10
1975	Mr. C. St. George's Bruni..........	9 to 1	A. Murray......	R. Price.....	12

	Lincolnshire Handicap Doncaster—1 mile.	Free Handicap Newmarket—3yrs.—7f.	Jockey Club Stakes Newmarket—1½ miles.	Coronation Cup Epsom—1½ miles.
1972	Sovereign Bill 6y 8st 12 lb.	Panama Canal 7st 11lb ...	Knockroe 4y 8st 13 lb...	Mill Reef 4y 9st.........
1973	Bronze Hill 4y 7st 9lb.....	Pitskelly 8st 5lb...........	Our Mirage 4y 9st 3lb....	Roberto (Ir.) 4y 9st 3lb...
1974	Quizair 5y 7st 13lb.....	Charlie Bubbles 8st 3lb....	Relay Race 4y 8st 9lb.....	Buoy 4st 9lb.........
1975	Southwark Star 4y 7st 3lb.	Green Belt 8st 9lb	Shebeen 4y 8st 10lb......	Bustino 4y 9st.......

	Ascot Stakes 2½ miles.	Gold Cup Ascot—2½ miles.	Coventry Stakes Ascot—2 yrs—6 furlongs.	Grand Prix de Paris 1 mile 7½ furlongs.
1972	Balios 4y 8st 10lb.........	Erimo Hawk 4y 9st......	Perdu 8st 11lb..........	Pleben ....
1973	Full of Beans 5y 7st 11lb...	Lassalle (Fr.) 4y 9st.......	Doleswood 8st 11lb.......	Tennyson...............
1974	Kambalda 4y 8st 9lb......	Ragstone 4y 9st..........	Whip it Quick 8st 11lb.....	Sagaro.................
1975	Crash Course 4y 9st 4lb...	Sagaro 4y 9st..........	Galway Bay 8st 11lb......	Matahawk..............

	Chester Cup Chester—2¼m. 97yd.	Jubilee Handicap Kempton Park—1¼m.	Eclipse Stakes Sandown Park—1¼m.	King George VI and Queen Elizabeth Stakes Ascot—1½ miles.
1972	Eric 5y 7st.............	Grandrew 6y 8st 8lb.....	Brigadier Gerard 4y 9st 5lb	Brigadier Gerard 4y 9st 7lb
1973	Crisalgo 5y 7st 7lb.......	Brigade Major 4y 8st 5 lb .	Scottish Rifle 4y 9st 5lb...	Dahlia 3y 8st 4lb.........
1974	Attivo 4y 7st 5lb.........	Jumpabout 4y 7st 12lb....	Coup de Feu 5y 9st 5lb....	Dahlia 4y 9st 4lb.........
1975	Super Nova 5y 7st 7lb....	Jumpabout 5y 8st 5lb.....	Star Appeal 5y 9st 7lb	Grundy 3y 8st 7lb.......

	Prix de L'Arc de Triomphe Longchamp—1½ m.	Cheltenham Gold Cup abt. 3¼ m.	Cambridgeshire Newmarket—9f.	Middle Park Stakes Newmarket—2yrs.—6f.
1972	San San 3y 8st 7lb......	Glencaraig Lady 8y 12st...	Negus 5y 9st...........	Tudenham 9st........
1973	Rheingold 4y 9st 6lb	The Dikler 10y 12st.......	Siliciana 4y 8st 5lb.......	Habat 9st...........
1974	Allez France 4y 9st 3lb....	Captain Christy 7y 12st...	Flying Nelly 4y 7st 7lb....	Steel Heart 9st.........
1975	Star Appeal 5y 9st 6lb....	Ten Up 8y 12st..........	Lottogift 4y 8st 7lb......	Hittite Glory 9st........

	Cesarewitch Newmarket—2¼m.	Washington Int'national Laurel Park—1½ m.	Champion Stakes Newmarket—1¼ m.	Grand National Liverpool—4m. 856 yds.
1972	Cider with Rosie 4y 7st 11lb	Droll Role (U.S.A.)........	Brigadier Gerard 4y 9st 3lb	Well To Do 9y 10st 11lb....
1973	Flash Imp 4y 7st 13lb.....	Dahlia (France)..........	Hurry Harriet (Ir.)3y8st7lb	Red Rum 8y 10st 5lb.....
1974	Ocean King 8y 7st 7lb....	Admetus (France)........	Giacometti 3y 8st 10lb.....	Red Rum 9y 12st........
1975	Shantallah 3y 8st 10lb.....	....	Rose Bowl 3y 8st 7lb......	L'Escargot 12y 11st 3lb....

CRICKET

Marylebone Cricket Club (1787), Lord's, N.W.8. *Pres.*, C. G. A. Paris; *Sec.*, J. A. Bailey; *Asst. Sec. Admin.*, Gp. Capt. W. R. Ford, C.B.E., R.A.F.(ret.); *Asst. Sec. Cricket*, J. G. Lofting; *Curator*, S. E. A. Green.

TEST MATCHES
Australia v. England, 1974–75

First Test.—(Brisbane, Nov. 29–Dec. 4). Australia won by 166 runs. Australia 309 and 288 for 5 (dec.); England 265 and 166.

Second Test.—(Perth, Dec. 13–17). Australia won by nine wickets. England 208 and 293; Australia 481 and 23 for 1.

Third Test.—(Melbourne, Dec. 26–31). Drawn. England 242 and 244; Australia 241 and 238 for 8.

Fourth Test.—(Sydney, Jan. 4–9). Australia won by 171 runs. Australia 405 and 289 for 4 (dec.); England 295 and 228.

Fifth Test.—(Adelaide, Jan. 25–30). Australia won by 163 runs. Australia 304 and 272 for 5 (dec.); England 172 and 241.

Sixth Test.—(Melbourne, Feb. 8–13). England won by an innings and 4 runs. Australia 152 and 373; England 529.

AUSTRALIA BATTING

Batsmen	Innings	Times not out	Runs	Highest Score	Average
G. S. Chappell	11	0	608	144	55·27
T. J. Jenner	3	1	100	74	50·00
M. H. N. Walker	8	3	221	41*	44·20
I. R. Redpath	12	1	472	105	42·90
K. D. Walters	11	2	383	103	42·55
R. B. McCosker	5	0	202	80	40·40
I. M. Chappell	12	1	387	90	35·18
R. W. Marsh	11	2	313	55	34·77
R. Edwards	9	1	261	115	32·62
J. R. Thomson	5	2	65	24*	21·66
D. K. Lillee	8	2	88	26	14·66
A. A. Mallett	7	2	61	31	12·20
W. J. Edwards	6	0	68	30	11·33

Also batted: G. Dymock 0 and 0.

BOWLING

Bowlers	Overs	Maidens	Runs	Wickets	Average
J. R. Thomson	175·1	34	592	33	17·93
A. A. Mallett	140·6	47	339	17	19·94
D. K. Lillee	182·6	36	596	25	23·84
M. H. N. Walker	218·7	46	684	23	29·73
K. D. Walters	56·3	14	175	5	35·00

Also bowled: I. M. Chappell 22—3—83—1; G. Dymock 39—6—130—1; T. J. Jenner 42—10—136—3.

ENGLAND BATTING

Batsmen	Innings	Times not out	Runs	Highest Score	Average
J. H. Edrich	7	1	260	70	43·33
A. W. Greig	11	0	446	110	40·54
A. P. E. Knott	11	0	364	106*	36·40
K. W. R. Fletcher	9	0	324	146	36·00
M. H. Denness	9	0	318	188	35·33
D. Lloyd	8	0	196	49	24·50
D. L. Amiss	9	0	175	90	19·44
M. C. Cowdrey	9	0	165	41	18·33
F. J. Titmus	8	0	138	61	17·25
C. M. Old	3	0	50	43	16·66
R. G. D. Willis	10	5	76	15	15·20
B. W. Luckhurst	4	0	54	27	13·50
D. L. Underwood	9	0	111	30	12 33
P. Lever	3	1	24	14	12·00
M. Hendrick	4	2	12	8*	6·00
G. G. Arnold	7	1	22	14	3·66

* Not out.

BOWLING

Bowlers	Overs	Maidens	Runs	Wickets	Average
P. Lever	61	8	214	9	23·77
R. G. D. Willis	140·4	15	522	17	30·70
D. L. Underwood	185	42	595	17	35·00
C. M. Old	51·6	4	210	6	35·00
G. G. Arnold	141·1	22	528	14	37·71
A. W. Greig	168·6	19	681	17	40·05
F. J. Titmus	122·3	30	360	7	51·42

Also bowled: M. Hendrick 35—6—119—2.

New Zealand v. England, 1975

First Test.—(Auckland, Feb. 20–25). England won by an innings and 83 runs. England 593 for 6 (dec.); New Zealand 326 and 184.

Second Test.—(Christchurch, Feb. 28–March 5). Drawn. New Zealand 342; England 272 for 2.

India v. West Indies, 1974–75

First Test.—(Bangalore, Nov. 22–27). West Indies won by 267 runs. West Indies 289 and 356 for 6 (dec.); India 260 and 118.

Second Test.—(New Delhi, Dec. 11–15). West Indies won by an innings and 17 runs. India 220 and 256; West Indies 493.

Third Test.—(Calcutta, Dec. 27–Jan. 1). India won by 85 runs. India 233 and 316; West Indies 240 and 224.

Fourth Test.—(Madras, Jan. 11–15). India won by 100 runs. India 190 and 256; West Indies 192 and 154.

Fifth Test.—(Bombay, Jan. 23–29). West Indies won by 201 runs. West Indies 604 for 6 (dec.) and 205 for 3 (dec.); India 406 and 202.

Pakistan v. West Indies, 1975

First Test.—(Lahore, Feb. 15–20). Drawn. Pakistan 199 and 373 for 7 (dec.); West Indies 214 and 258 for 4.

Second Test.—(Karachi, March 1–6). Drawn. Pakistan 406 for 8 (dec.) and 256; West Indies 493 and 1 for no wkt.

England v. Australia, 1975

First Test.—(Edgbaston, July 10–14). Australia won by an innings and 85 runs. Australia 359; England 101 and 173.

Second Test.—(Lord's, July 31–Aug. 5). Drawn. England 315 and 436 for 7 (dec.); Australia 268 and 329 for 3.

Third Test.—(Headingley, Aug. 14–19). Abandoned. England 288 and 291; Australia 135 and 220 for 3.

Fourth Test.—(The Oval, Aug. 28–Sept. 3). Drawn. Australia 532 for 9 (dec.) and 40 for 2; England 191 and 538.

ENGLAND BATTING

Batsmen	Innings	Times not out	Runs	Highest Score	Average
D. S. Steele.........	6	0	365	92	60·83
R. A. Woolmer......	4	0	218	149	54·50
J. H. Edrich.........	8	0	428	175	53·50
A. P. E. Knott.......	8	1	261	69	37·28
A. W. Greig.........	8	0	284	96	35·50
B. Wood.............	6	0	146	52	24·33
K. W. R. Fletcher.....	4	0	79	51	19·75
C. M. Old...........	6	1	60	25*	12·00
J. A. Snow..........	7	0	84	34	12·00
P. H. Edmonds......	4	1	32	13*	10·66
G. A. Gooch.........	4	0	37	31	9·25
D. L. Amiss.........	4	0	19	10	4·75
D. L. Underwood.....	7	3	16	10	4·00

Also batted: G. R. J. Roope 0 and 77; J. H. Hampshire 14 and 0; M. H. Denness 3 and 8; G. G. Arnold 0* and 6*; P. Lever 4.

BOWLING

Bowlers	Overs	Maidens	Runs	Wickets	Average
D. S. Steele..........	11·4	5	21	2	10·50
J. A. Snow...........	135·5	29	355	11	32·27
R. A. Woolmer.......	34	9	72	2	36·00
P. H. Edmonds......	81·1	20	224	6	37·33
A. W. Greig.........	97	23	322	8	40·25
C. M. Old...........	91	22	283	7	40·42
D. L. Underwood.....	131	51	266	6	44·33

Also bowled: G. G. Arnold 33—3—91—3; P. Lever 35—5—138—2; B. Wood 6—2—16—0.

AUSTRALIA BATTING

Batsmen	Innings	Times not out	Runs	Highest Score	Average
R. B. McCosker.......	7	2	414	127	82·80
I. M. Chappell........	6	0	429	192	71·50
R. Edwards..........	6	1	253	99	50·60
D. K. Lillee.........	4	2	115	73*	57·50
K. D. Walters........	5	1	125	65	31·25
R. W. Marsh.........	5	0	133	61	26·60
A. A. Mallett........	4	3	23	14	23·00
G. S. Chappell.......	7	2	106	73*	21·20
J. R. Thomson.......	4	0	82	49	20·50
A. Turner...........	5	0	77	37	15·40
M. H. N. Walker.....	0	0	25	7	6·25

Also batted: G. J. Gilmour 6.

BOWLING

Bowlers	Overs	Maidens	Runs	Wickets	Average
K. D. Walters........	12·5	3	40	5	8·00
G. J. Gilmour........	51·2	15	157	9	17·44
D. K. Lillee.........	207	72	460	21	21·90
J. R. Thomson........	175·1	56	457	16	28·56
M. H. N. Walker......	204·1	59	486	14	34·71
A. A. Mallett........	161	57	386	9	42·88
I. M. Chappell........	29	8	82	1	82·00

Also bowled: G. S. Chappell 12—2—53—0; R. Edwards 2—0—20—0.

* Not out.

County Championship Table, 1975

County Order for 1975 1974 in brackets	Played	Won	Lost	Drawn	Bonus Btg.	Bonus Blng.	Points
Leicestershire (4)........	20	12	1	7	61	59	240
Yorkshire (11)........	20	10	1	9	56	68	224
Hampshire (2)........	20	10	6	4	51	72	223
Lancashire (8)........	20	9	3	8	57	72	219
Kent (10).............	20	8	4	8	59	70	209
Surrey (7)............	20	8	3	9	55	67	202
Essex (12)............	20	7	6	7	61	67	198
Northamptonshire (3).....	20	7	9	4	40	72	182
Glamorgan (16)......	20	7	8	5	45	66	181
Worcestershire (1).....	20	5	6	9	55	63	168
Middlesex (6)........	20	6	7	7	45	59	164
Somerset (5).........	20	4	8	8	51	65	156
Nottinghamshire (15).....	20	3	9	8	59	67	156
Warwickshire (9)......	20	4	10	6	48	65	153
Derbyshire (17)......	20	5	7	8	33	69	152
Gloucestershire (14).....	20	4	10	6	43	62	145
Sussex (13)............	20	2	13	5	37	62	119

Prudential World Cup Final.—West Indies beat Australia by 17 runs at Lord's on June 21, 1975. West Indies 291 for 8; Australia 274.

Gillette Cup Final.—Lancashire beat Middlesex by seven wickets. Lancashire 182 for 3; Middlesex 180 for 8.

Benson and Hedges Cup Final.—Leicestershire beat Middlesex by five wickets. Middlesex 146; Leicestershire 150 for 5.

John Player Sunday League Competition.—Hampshire won with 52 points from 16 games.

Universities.—Cambridge University drew with Oxford University. Cambridge 302 for 7 (dec.) and 131 for 5; Oxford 256 for 9 (dec.) and 251 for 8 (dec.).

Eton v. Harrow.—Harrow won by an innings and 151 runs. Harrow 303 for 2 (dec.); Eton 96 and 56.

MISCELLANEOUS CRICKET RECORDS

Highest Individual Scores.—In first-class cricket in England: A. C. MacLaren, 424, for Lancashire *v.* Somerset at Taunton, July, 1895. In Australia: D. G. Bradman (Australia), 452 (not out) for N.S.W. *v.* Queensland, Sydney, 1929–30. In India: B. B. Nimbalkar (Maharashtra *v.* W. Indian States), Poona, 1948–49, 443 (not out). In Pakistan: Hanif Mohammad, 499, Karachi *v.* Bahawalpur, 1959. In a minor inter-county match: F. E. Lacey (Hampshire *v.* Norfolk), Southampton, 1887, 323 (not out). In other minor matches: A. E. J. Collins, aged 13, scored 628 (not out) in a Junior House match playing for Clarke's House *v.* North Town at Clifton College in 1899.

Highest Team Innings.—Australia: Victoria 1,107 *v.* N.S.W., Melbourne, 1926; England: England 903 (for 7 dec.) *v.* Australia, 1938.

Smallest Totals.—Oxford University (one man absent), 12 *v.* M.C.C. at Oxford, May 1877; Northamptonshire *v.* Gloucestershire, June 11, 1907.

Highest Aggregate.—Bombay, 651 and 714 for 8 dec. *v.* Maharashtra, 407, 604, Poona, 1948–49. Total: 2,376 (38 wkts.).

Highest Partnership.—Gul Mahomed (319) and V. S. Hazare (288) made 577 for 4th wkt. for Baroda *v.* Holkar, March 7, 1947.

BATTING AND BOWLING AVERAGES

English Batting Averages, 1975
(Qualifications, 8 Innings)

Batsmen	Number of Innings	Times not out	Total Runs	Highest Innings	Average
R. B. Kanhai	22	9	1,073	178*	82.53
G. Boycott	34	8	1,915	201*	73.65
C. H. Lloyd	27	4	1,423	167*	61.86
B. A. Richards	37	5	1,621	135*	60.03
G. M. Turner	29	5	1,362	214*	56.75
B. F. Davison	34	6	1,498	189	53.50
J. M. Brearley	39	8	1,656	150	53.41
D. S. Steele	39	3	1,756	126*	48.77
Asif Iqbal	30	4	1,262	140	48.53
P. A. Todd	9	1	385	178	48.12
J. H. Edrich	38	5	1,569	175	47.54
Zaheer Abbas	31	1	1,426	123	47.53
A. W. Greig	37	1	1,699	226	47.19
R. W. Tolchard	31	10	973	106	46.33
R. Illingworth	33	11	997	88	45.31
D. L. Amiss	37	2	1,564	158*	44.68
B. L. d'Oliveira	34	6	1,225	97*	43.75
B. R. Hardie	42	7	1,522	162	43.48
R. M. C. Gilliat	34	4	1,299	113	43.30
J. A. Ormrod	37	4	1,406	134	42.60
R. A. Woolmer	29	1	1,193	149	42.60
A. Kennedy	29	5	1,022	114*	42.58
G. R. J. Roope	35	5	1,277	102	42.56
F. C. Hayes	29	3	1,103	104	42.42
Majid J. Khan	37	3	1,413	170*	41.55
C. G. Greenidge	27	0	1,120	259	41.48
R. G. Lumb	44	7	1,532	118	41.40
Mushtaq Mohammad	40	3	1,531	138	41.37
D. W. Randall	34	5	1,197	153*	41.27
B. Dudleston	37	3	1,365	172	40.14
D. B. Close	38	6	1,284	138*	40.12
A. P. E. Knott	27	7	799	105*	39.95
C. T. Radley	39	5	1,351	152*	39.73
B. Wood	22	2	792	135	39.60
M. H. Denness	29	1	1,099	171	39.25
A. I. Kallicharran	33	1	1,247	137	38.96
R. D. V. Knight	33	5	1,091	128*	38.96
P. M. Roebuck	28	6	857	158	38.95
J. F. Steele	38	4	1,302	158	38.29
J. H. Hampshire	35	5	1,138	127	37.93
Younis Ahmed	38	3	1,314	183*	37.54
D. Nicholls	18	6	450	68	37.50
Sadiq Mohammad	35	1	1,268	117	37.29
J. D. Morley	8	1	261	94	37.28
J. C. Balderstone	38	5	1,222	168*	37.03
C. M. Old	30	7	850	115*	36.95
D. Lloyd	29	1	1,014	100*	36.21
G. W. Johnson	42	2	1,438	142	35.95
J. B. Bolus	38	4	1,220	151	35.88
A. Jones	44	3	1,464	167*	35.70
I. V. A. Richards	34	1	1,174	217*	35.57
P. A. Slocombe	37	5	1,125	132	35.15
N. G. Featherstone	37	4	1,156	147	35.03
M. J. Harris	37	2	1,223	163	34.94
D. R. Turner	32	2	1,047	150*	34.90
K. S. McEwan	38	4	1,174	145	34.52
N. M. McVicker	24	10	482	83*	34.42
J. M. Parker	33	2	1,061	133	34.22
B. E. A. Edmeades	37	2	1,190	93	34.00
J. Abrahams	10	2	271	60	33.87
M. J. Smith	40	2	1,278	144	33.63
J. Whitehouse	30	1	970	170	33.44
G. R. Cass	27	5	731	172*	33.22
S. B. Hassan	35	2	1,095	133*	33.18
C. E. B. Rice	37	2	1,155	112	33.00
P. W. Denning	39	2	1,199	81	32.40
M. J. Smedley	36	1	1,128	114	32.22
P. D. Johnson	35	2	1,063	103	32.21
J. N. Shepherd	30	7	735	116	31.95
B. W. Luckhurst	39	2	1,180	141	31.89
M. H. Page	34	1	1,037	103	31.42
C. J. Aworth	35	1	1,057	135	31.08
M. C. Cowdrey	31	6	777	151*	31.08
R. C. Davis	42	2	1,243	131	31.07
W. Snowden	16	2	435	107*	31.07
P. J. Sainsbury	31	4	834	105	30.88
B. W. Reidy	23	3	614	80	30.70
M. J. K. Smith	24	1	703	122	30.56
K. R. Pont	21	1	672	110	30.54
M. J. J. Faber	36	1	1,060	176	30.28

English Bowling Averages, 1975
(Qualifications, 10 Wickets in 10 Innings)

Bowlers	Overs	Maidens	Runs	Wickets	Average
A. M. E. Roberts	418.3	141	901	57	15.80
M. Hendrick	493.1	148	1,077	68	15.83
B. D. Julien	270	76	707	40	17.67
P. Lever	419.1	115	1,098	61	18.00
D. L. Underwood	576.1	233	1,210	67	18.05
K. D. Boyce	461	100	1,309	72	18.18
P. Lee	799.5	193	2,067	112	18.45
B. Wood	127	45	244	13	18.76
T. E. Jesty	383.5	108	960	50	19.20
K. Shuttleworth	307.5	86	717	37	19.37
A. G. Nicholson	106.5	31	253	13	19.46
J. W. Solanky	436.3	107	1,154	59	19.55
P. Willey	292	76	791	39	20.28
Sarfraz Nawaz	728.4	173	2,051	101	20.30
R. Illingworth	459.1	158	1,068	51	20.94
P. Carrick	642	224	1,673	79	21.17
J. K. Lever	704.1	155	1,807	85	21.25
S. Venkataraghavan	505.5	128	1,457	68	21.42
G. G. Arnold	588.1	149	1,547	72	21.48
P. J. Sainsbury	566.1	241	1,133	52	21.78
G. A. Cope	624.3	201	1,509	69	21.86
H. P. Cooper	380	106	912	41	22.24
R. W. Hills	237	49	698	31	22.51
R. M. Ratcliffe	350.4	84	895	39	22.94
B. S. Bedi	773.2	227	1,973	85	23.21
J. Simmons	406.2	110	1,027	44	23.34
F. W. Swarbrook	612.1	166	1,667	71	23.47
M. N. S. Taylor	309.1	85	847	36	23.52
M. A. Nash	735.2	192	2,002	85	23.55
C. M. Old	459.1	113	1,279	54	23.68
J. C. J. Dye	519.4	110	1,480	62	23.87
J. F. Steele	354.5	112	816	34	24.00
G. I. Burgess	407.1	110	987	41	24.07
E. J. O. Hemsley	117.1	29	292	12	24.33
J. A. Snow	567	126	1,505	61	24.67
J. N. Graham	243.5	56	653	26	25.11
R. D. Jackman	556.2	115	1,821	72	25.29
H. R. Moseley	549	132	1,341	52	25.78
N. M. McVicker	455.4	109	1,188	46	25.82
J. C. Balderstone	454	136	1,111	43	25.83
P. H. Edmonds	814.5	238	1,946	75	25.94
C. E. B. Rice	433.1	95	1,377	53	25.98
P. I. Pocock	713.4	204	1,752	67	26.14
D. P. Hughes	403.5	119	1,101	42	26.21
J. Davey	570.4	116	1,681	64	26.26
J. M. Rice	529.5	156	1,306	49	26.65
D. J. Brown	657.4	135	1,957	73	26.80
Imran Khan	400	60	1,235	46	26.84
J. W. Southern	491.5	186	1,193	44	27.11
B. M. Brain	405	51	1,417	52	27.25
P. J. Lewington	639.3	168	1,801	66	27.28
A. A. Jones	537.5	104	1,621	59	27.47
I. T. Botham	605.3	132	1,704	62	27.48
J. N. Shepherd	579.2	146	1,465	52	28.17
A. L. Robinson	394.1	100	1,031	36	28.63
M. W. W. Selvey	666.4	141	1,842	64	28.78
Mushtaq Mohammad	272.4	56	957	33	29.00
J. Birkenshaw	523	163	1,279	44	29.06
K. Higgs	559.4	140	1,458	50	29.16
P. E. Russell	434.5	105	1,176	40	29.40
A. S. Brown	438.1	104	1,238	42	29.47
K. Jarvis	383.2	74	1,186	40	29.65
F. J. Titmus	724.5	221	1,811	61	29.68
A. Sidebottom	151	41	417	14	29.78
N. Gifford	758.5	192	1,941	65	29.86
T. M. Lamb	368.1	69	1,107	37	29.91
S. Perryman	531	128	1,480	49	30.20
G. Miller	325.5	80	886	29	30.55
H. C. Latchman	250	46	887	29	30.58
J. Spencer	650.2	159	1,715	56	30.62
G. W. Johnson	506.5	151	1,257	41	30.65
T. J. Mottram	215	66	522	17	30.70
R. A. Woolmer	332.4	84	921	30	30.70
A. Hodgson	168.4	30	493	16	30.81
B. Stead	544.3	98	1,734	56	30.86
G. D. Armstrong	397.3	79	1,395	45	31.00
E. E. Hemmings	897.4	238	2,456	79	31.08
D. A. Graveney	581.2	152	1,630	52	31.34
A. E. Cordle	533.5	131	1,541	49	31.44
C. P. Phillipson	354.3	83	976	31	31.48

★ Denotes not out.

LIST OF COUNTY CRICKET CHAMPIONS.

1934	Lancashire			1960	Yorkshire	1971	Surrey
1935	Yorkshire	1950	{Lancashire	1961	Hampshire	1972	Warwickshire
1936	Derbyshire		{Surrey	1962	Yorkshire	1973	Hampshire
1937	Yorkshire	1951	Warwickshire	1963	Yorkshire	1974	Worcestershire
1938	Yorkshire	1952	Surrey	1964	Worcestershire	1975	Leicestershire
1939	Yorkshire	1953	Surrey	1965	Worcestershire		
1946	Yorkshire	1954	Surrey	1966	Yorkshire		
1947	Middlesex	1955	Surrey	1967	Yorkshire		
1948	Glamorgan	1956	Surrey	1968	Yorkshire		
1949	{Middlesex	1957	Surrey	1969	Glamorgan		
	{Yorkshire	1958	Surrey	1970	Kent		
		1959	Yorkshire				

RUGBY FOOTBALL

International Union Table, 1974–75

Country	Played	Won	Lost	Drawn	Points Scored		Points
					For	Against	
Wales..................	4	3	1	0	87	30	6
Scotland..............	4	2	2	0	47	40	4
Ireland................	4	2	2	0	54	67	4
France................	4	2	2	0	53	79	4
England..............	4	1	3	0	40	65	2

CALCUTTA CUP
England v. Scotland

1967	England 27–14
1968	England 8–6
1969	England 8–3
1970	Scotland 14–5
1971	Scotland 16–15
1972	Scotland 23–9
1973	England 20–13
1974	Scotland 16–14
1975	England 7–6

COUNTY CHAMPIONSHIP

Surrey and Durham.
Middlesex.
Lancashire.
Staffordshire.
Surrey.
Gloucestershire.
Lancashire.
Gloucestershire.
Gloucestershire.

INTERNATIONAL MATCHES, 1974–75

1974
Sept. 28 Edinburgh: Scotland 44 Tonga 8
Oct. 19 Cardiff: Wales 26 Tonga 7
Nov. 23 Dublin: Ireland 6 N.Z. 15
Nov. 23 Toulouse: France 4 S. Africa 13
Nov. 30 Paris: France 8 S. Africa 10

1975
Jan. 18 Dublin: Ireland 12 England 9
Paris: France 10 Wales 25
Feb. 1 Twickenham: England 20 France 27
Edinburgh: Scotland 20 Ireland 13
Feb. 15 Paris: France 10 Scotland 9
Cardiff: Wales 20 England 4
Mar. 1 Edinburgh: Scotland 12 Wales 10
Dublin: Ireland 25 France 6
Mar. 15 Cardiff: Wales 32 Ireland 4
Twickenham: England 7 Scotland 6
May 24 Sydney: Australia 16 England 9
May 31 Brisbane: Australia 30 England 21
June 14 Auckland: N.Z. 24 Scotland 0

COUNTY CHAMPIONSHIP FINAL
Gloucestershire beat Eastern Counties 13–9

OTHER CHIEF MATCHES, 1974–75
Universities. 1974. Cambridge University beat Oxford University 16–15 at Twickenham on Dec. 10.
Hospitals Cup Final.—Westminster beat St. Mary's 12–3.
Services.—R.A.F. beat Royal Navy 20–7; Royal Navy beat Army 19–0; Army beat R.A.F. 41–13.
Club Knock-out Competition.—Bedford beat Rosslyn Park 28–12 at Twickenham on April 26, 1975.
Middlesex Seven-a-Side Final.—Richmond beat Loughborough Colleges 24–8.

RUGBY FOOTBALL LEAGUE (Est. 1895)
INTERNATIONAL MATCHES

Triangular Competition
1975
Jan. 19 Perpignan: France 9 England 11
Feb. 16 Swansea: Wales 21 France 8
Feb. 25 Salford: England 12 Wales 8

World Championship
1975
Mar. 2 Toulouse: France 14 Wales 7
16 Leeds: England 20 France 2
June 1 Brisbane: Australia 36 N. Zealand 8
10 Brisbane: England 7 Wales 12
14 Sydney: Australia 30 Wales 13
16 Auckland: N.Z. 27 France 0
21 Auckland: N.Z. 17 England 17
22 Brisbane: Australia 26 France 6
28 Sydney: Australia 10 England 10
28 Auckland: N. Zealand 13 Wales 8

Rugby League Challenge Cup.—Final. Widnes beat Warrington 14–7 pts. at Wembley Stadium on May 10, 1975.
County Champions.—Lancashire.
Premiership.—Leeds beat St. Helens 26–11 at Wigan.
First Division Champions.—St. Helens.
Second Division Champions.—Huddersfield.

HOCKEY, 1974–75
MEN'S HOCKEY
INTERNATIONAL CHAMPIONSHIP

	P.	W.	D.	L.	Goals F.	A.	Pts.
England...........	3	3	0	0	10	3	6
Ireland............	3	1	1	1	5	5	3
Scotland..........	3	1	1	1	4	5	3
Wales.............	3	0	0	3	3	10	0

Universities.—Oxford University beat Cambridge University 3–1.
County Championship Final.—Kent beat Hertfordshire 3–0.
Services Championship.—R.A.F.
National Club Championship.—Final. Southgate beat Nottingham 4–0.

WOMEN'S HOCKEY
LEADING MATCHES, 1974–75
England drew with Ireland 1–1; England beat Wales 2–0; England beat Scotland 1–0; England drew with Netherlands 1–1.

ASSOCIATION FOOTBALL
International Table, 1974–75

Country	Played	Won	Drawn	Lost	Goals		Points
					For	Against	
England............	3	1	2	0	7	3	4
Scotland............	3	1	1	1	6	7	3
Ireland.............	3	1	1	1	1	3	3
Wales..............	3	0	2	1	4	5	2

ENGLAND v. SCOTLAND
g. g.
1966 England....4—3
1967 Scotland...3—2
1968 Draw.......1—1
1969 England....4—1
1970 Draw.......0—0
1971 England....3—1
1972 England....1—0
1973 England....1—0
1974 Scotland....2—0
1975 England....5—1

FOOTBALL ASSOCIATION CUP
g. g.
Everton b. Sheffield W......3—2
Tottenham H. b. Chelsea...2—1
W.B.A. b. Everton.........1—0
Manchester C. b. Leicester.1—0
Chelsea b. Leeds U.........2—1
Arsenal b. Liverpool.......2—1
Leeds U. b. Arsenal.......1—0
Sunderland b. Leeds U......1—0
Liverpool b. Newcastle.....3—0
West Ham U. b. Fulham....2—0

LEAGUE COMPETITION, 1974–75
Div. I.—Derby Co., 53 pts. Runners-up: Liverpool, 51 pts. Relegated: Luton T., 33 pts.; Chelsea, 33 pts.; and Carlisle U., 29 pts.
Div. II.—Promoted: Manchester U., 61 pts.; A. Villa, 58 pts.; and Norwich C., 53 pts. Relegated: Millwall, 32 pts.; Cardiff C., 32 pts.; and Sheffield W., 21 pts.
Div. III.—Promoted: Blackburn R., 60 pts.; Plymouth A., 59 pts.; and Charlton A., 55 pts. Relegated: Tranmere R., 37 pts.; Watford, 37 pts.; Huddersfield T., 32 pts.; and Bournemouth, 38 pts.
Div. IV.—Promoted: Mansfield T., 68 pts.; Shrewsbury T., 62 pts.; Rotherham U., 59 pts.; and Chester, 57 pts.

SCOTTISH LEAGUE.—Div. 1 Champions: Rangers, 56 pts. Div. II Champions: Falkirk, 54 pts.

REPRESENTATIVE MATCHES, 1974–75
HOME INTERNATIONALS
1975
May 17 Cardiff: Wales 2 Scotland 2
       Belfast: Ireland 0 England 0
May 20 Hampden Scotland 3 Ireland 0
       Park
May 21 Wembley: England 2 Wales 2
May 23 Belfast: Ireland 1 Wales 0
May 24 Wembley: England 5 Scotland 1

OTHER INTERNATIONAL
1975
Mar. 12 Wembley: England 2 W. Germany 0

EUROPEAN CHAMPIONSHIP
1974
Oct. 30 Wembley: England 3 Czechoslovakia 0
Nov. 20 Wembley: England 0 Portugal 0
1975
April 16 Wembley: England 5 Cyprus 0
May 11 Limassol: Cyprus 0 England 1

EUROPEAN UNDER-23 CHAMPIONSHIP
1974
Oct. 29 Selhurst England 3 Czechoslovakia 1
      Park
Nov. 19 Lisbon: Portugal 2 England 3

OTHER UNDER-23 INTERNATIONALS
1974
Dec. 18 Aberdeen: Scotland 0 England 3
1975
Jan. 21 Wrexham: Wales 0 England 2

CUP FINALS, 1974–75
F.A. CUP.—*S.F.:* April 9 (Maine Road), Fulham beat Birmingham 1–0 (after 1–1 draw); (Stamford Bridge), West Ham beat Ipswich 2–1 (after 0–0 draw).
Final: May 3 (Wembley Stadium), West Ham beat Fulham 2–0. Attendance 100,000. Receipts £303,000.

FOOTBALL LEAGUE CUP. *Final:* March 1 (Wembley Stadium), Aston Villa beat Norwich City 1–0. Attendance 100,000.

F.A.VASE. *Final:* Hoddesdon beat Epsom 2–1 at Wembley Stadium.

F.A. CHALLENGE TROPHY.—*F.:* Matlock beat Scarborough 4–0 at Wembley Stadium.

F.A. YOUTH.—*F.:* Ipswich T. beat West Ham (on aggregate) 5–1.

SCOTTISH F.A. CUP.—*S.F.:* Celtic beat Dundee 1–0; Airdrie beat Motherwell 1–0 (after 1–1 draw).
Final: May 3 (Hampden Park), Celtic beat Airdrie 3–1. Attendance 75,457.

SCOTTISH LEAGUE CUP.—*F.:* Celtic beat Hibernian 6–3.

EUROPEAN CUP.—*S.F.:* Leeds beat Barcelona (on aggregate) 3–2; Bayern Munich beat St. Etienne (on aggregate) 2–0.
F.: Bayern Munich beat Leeds 2–0 in Paris.

EUROPEAN CUP-WINNERS' CUP.—*S.F.:* Ferencvaros beat Red Star Belgrade (on aggregate) 4–3; Dynamo Kiev beat PSV Eindhoven (on aggregate) 4–2.
F.: Dynamo Kiev beat Ferencvaros 3–0 in Basle.

U.E.F.A. CUP.—*F.:* Borussia Munchengladbach beat Twente Enschede (on aggregate) 5–1.

Universities.—Oxford University beat Cambridge University 3–1.
Arthur Dunn Cup.—O. Malvernians beat O. Foresters 2–1.
Services Championship.—Royal Navy.

WORLD CUP WINNERS, 1930–1974
1930 (*Played in Uruguay*)...............Uruguay
1934 (*Italy*)................................Italy
1938 (*France*)..............................Italy
1950 (*Brazil*)............................Uruguay
1954 (*Switzerland*)...............West Germany
1958 (*Sweden*)...........................Brazil
1962 (*Chile*).............................Brazil
1966 (*England*)........................England
1970 (*Mexico*)...........................Brazil
1974 (*West Germany*)............West Germany

GOLF, 1974–75

CHAMPIONSHIPS.

OPEN
(Instituted 1860)

1966 J. Nicklaus (U.S.A.), 282.
1967 R. de Vicenzo (Argentina), 278.
1968 G. Player (S. Africa), 289.
1969 A. Jacklin (G.B.), 280.
1970 J. Nicklaus (U.S.A.) beat D. Sanders (U.S.A.) after tie, 283.
1971 L. Trevino (U.S.A.), 278.
1972 L. Trevino (U.S.A.), 278.
1973 T. Weiskopf (U.S.A.), 276.
1974 G. Player (S. Africa), 282.
1975 T. Watson (U.S.A.) beat J. Newton (Australia) after tie, 279.

PROFESSIONAL MATCH PLAY TOURNAMENT
1966 P. W. Thomson (Aust.).
1967 P. W. Thomson (Aust.).
1968 B. Huggett.
1969 M. Bembridge.
1970 T. Horton.

1972 J. Garner.
1973 N. C. Coles.
1974 J. Newton (Aust.).
1975 E. Polland.

AMATEUR
(1885)

1966 R. Cole (S. Africa).
1967 B. Dickson (U.S.A.).
1968 M. F. Bonallack.
1969 M. F. Bonallack.
1970 M. F. Bonallack.
1971 S. N. Melnyk (U.S.A.).
1972 T. Homer.
1973 R. Siderowf (U.S.A.).
1974 T. Homer.
1975 M. Giles (U.S.A.).

LADIES
(1893)

1966 Miss D. E. Chadwick.
1967 Miss D. E. Chadwick.
1968 Mlle. B. Varangot (France).
1969 Mlle. C. Lacoste (France).
1970 Miss D. L. Oxley.
1971 Miss M. Walker.
1972 Miss M. Walker.
1973 Miss A. Irvin.
1974 Miss C. Semple (U.S.A.).
1975 Mrs. N. Syms (U.S.A.).

WALKER CUP
(St. Andrews, May, 1975)

U.S.A. won by 14 matches to 7, with 3 halved.

Winners—

Singles—U.S.A.—G. Koch (2); J. Grace (2); M. Giles; J Haas; C. Strange; C. Stadler; W. C. Campbell.
Great Britain and Ireland—M. James; P. Mulcare; I. C. Hutcheon; J. C. Davies.

Foursomes—U.S.A.—G. Burns and C. Stadler (2); M. Giles and G. Koch; J. Haas and C. Strange (2).
Great Britain and Ireland—M. James and G. R. D. Eyles (2); P. Mulcare and I. C. Hutcheon.

RYDER CUP
(Laurel Valley, September, 1975)

U.S.A. won by 18 matches to 8, with 6 halved.

Winners—

Singles—U.S.A.—R. Murphy (2); G. Littler; T. Weiskopf; W. Casper; R. Floyd; H. Irwin.
British Isles—P. Oosterhuis (2); B. Barnes (2); T. Horton; N. Wood.

Foursomes—U.S.A.—J. Nicklaus and T. Weiskopf; G. Littler and H. Irwin; J. Miller and A. Geiberger; L. Trevino and J. C. Snead; T. Weiskopf and J. Miller; H. Irwin and W. Casper; A. Geiberger and L. Graham.
British Isles—A. Jacklin and B. Huggett.

Fourballs—U.S.A.—T. Weiskopf and L. Graham; J. Nicklaus and J. C. Snead; G. Littler and L. Graham; L. Trevino and H. Irwin.
British Isles—A. Jacklin and P. Oosterhuis.

OTHER GOLF EVENTS, 1974–75

Australian Open.—G. Player (S. Africa).
President's Putter.—C. Weight.
Halford Hewitt Cup (Final).—Harrow beat Merchant Taylors, 3½–1½.
English Amateur.—N. Faldo.
Piccadilly Medal Knock-out Tournament.—R. Shearer (Australia).
Brabazon Trophy.—A. W. Lyle.
Penfold P.G.A. Championship.—A. Palmer (U.S.A.).
Madrid Open.—R. Shearer (Australia).
MacGregor Club Professionals' Championship.—D. N. Sewell.
Berkshire Trophy.—N. Faldo.
World Cup Championship (Caracas, Nov. 1974).—1, S. Africa, 554; 2, Japan, 559; 3, U.S.A., 563.
Women's World Amateur Team Championship.—U.S.A.
Eisenhower Trophy.—U.S.A.
Golf Illustrated Gold Vase.—M. F. Bonallack.
Martini International Tournament.—C. O'Connor Jnr. tied with I. Stanley (Australia).
Scottish Amateur.—D. Greig.
Welsh Amateur.—J. Toye.
P.G.A. Seniors' Championship.—K. Nagle (Australia).
U.S.A. Masters.—J. Nicklaus.
U.S.A. Open.—L. Graham.
U.S.A., P.G.A. Championship.—J. Nicklaus.
Universities.—Cambridge beat Oxford 9½–5½.
English County Championship.—Staffordshire.
Women's County Championship.—Glamorgan.
British Youth Championship.—N. Faldo.
British Boys' Championship.—B. Marchbank.
British Girls' Championship.—Miss S. Cadden.
Girls' Home International Series.—England.
Home International Championship.—Scotland.
English Women's Championship.—Miss B. Huke.
Women's Home International Championship.—England.
South African Open.—G. Player.
French Open.—B. Barnes.
Spanish Open.—A. Palmer (U.S.A.).
Lytham Trophy.—G. Macgregor.
Benson and Hedges Festival.—V. Fernandez (Argentina).
British Women's Open Amateur Stroke Play.—Miss J. Greenhalgh.
Women's European Team Championship.—France.
English Girls' Championship.—Miss M. Burton.
German Open.—M. Bembridge.
Swiss Open.—D. Hayes (S. Africa).
Dutch Open.—H. Baiocchi (S. Africa).
Women's European Open.—Mrs. D. Young (U.S.A.).
Sumrie Better-Ball Tournament.—J. Newton and J. O'Leary.
Carrolls Irish Open.—C. O'Connor Jnr.
Scandinavian Open.—G. Burns (U.S.A.).
Portuguese Open.—H. Underwood (U.S.A.).
P.G.A. Under-25.—D. Hayes (S. Africa).
Canadian Open.—T. Weiskopf (U.S.A.).
Dunlop Masters.—B. Gallacher.
World Open.—J. Nicklaus.
Piccadilly Match-Play.—F.: H. Irwin (U.S.A.) beat A. Geiberger (U.S.A.) 4 and 2.

LAWN TENNIS
THE DAVIS CUP CHALLENGE ROUNDS
(Founder—Dwight Filley Davis (1879–1945), First Played, 1900.)

1931 France beat Great Britain....3–2	1949 U.S.A. beat Australia........4–1	1962 Australia beat Mexico........5–0
1932 France beat U.S.A..........3–2	1950 Australia beat U.S.A.........4–1	1963 U.S.A. beat Australia........3–2
1933 Great Britain beat France...3–2	1951 Australia beat U.S.A.........3–1	1964 Australia beat U.S.A.........3–2
1934 Great Britain beat U.S.A....4–1	1952 Australia beat U.S.A.........4–1	1965 Australia beat Spain.........4–1
1935 Great Britain beat U.S.A....5–0	1953 Australia beat U.S.A.........3–2	1966 Australia beat India.........4–1
1936 Great Britain beat Australia..3–2	1954 U.S.A. beat Australia........3–0	1967 Australia beat Spain.........4–1
1937 U.S.A. beat Great Britain....4–1	1955 Australia beat U.S.A.........5–0	1968 U.S.A beat Australia.........4–1
1938 U.S.A. beat Australia.......3–2	1956 Australia beat U.S.A.........5–0	1969 U.S.A. beat Rumania.........5–0
1939 Australia beat U.S.A........3–2	1957 Australia beat U.S.A.........3–2	1970 U.S.A. beat W. Germany.....5–0
1946 U.S.A. beat Australia.......5–0	1958 U.S.A. beat Australia........3–2	1971 U.S.A. beat Rumania.........3–2
1947 U.S.A. beat Australia.......4–1	1959 Australia beat U.S.A.........3–2	1972 U.S.A. beat Rumania.........3–2
1948 U.S.A. beat Australia.......5–0	1960 Australia beat Italy.........4–1	1973 Australia beat U.S.A.........5–0
	1961 Australia beat Italy.........5–0	1974 S. Africa won by default.

THE CHAMPIONSHIPS (WIMBLEDON)
1975

Men's Singles.—A. R. Ashe (U.S.A.) beat J. S. Connors (U.S.A.), 6–1, 6–1, 5–7, 6–4.

Women's Singles.—Mrs. L. W. King (U.S.A.) beat Mrs. R. Cawley (Australia), 6–0, 6–1.

Men's Doubles.—V. Gerulaitis and A. Mayer (U.S.A.) beat C. Dowdeswell (Rhodesia) and A. J. Stone (Australia), 7–5, 8–6, 6–4.

Women's Doubles.—Miss A. K. Kiyomura (U.S.A.) and Miss K. Sawamatsu (Japan) beat Miss F. Durr (France) and Miss B. F. Stove (Netherlands), 7–5, 1–6, 7–5.

Mixed Doubles.—M. C. Riessen (U.S.A.) and Mrs. B. M. Court (Australia) beat A. J. Stone and Miss Stove, 6–4, 7–5.

All England Plate:
Men's Singles.—T. Koch (Brazil) beat V. Gerulaitis, 6–3, 6–2.
Women's Singles.—Miss D. L. Fromholtz (Australia) beat Miss V. A. Burton (G.B.), 6–4, 6–2.

Junior International Invitation Tournament:
Boys' Singles.—C. J. Lewis (N.Z.) beat R. Ycaza (Ecuador), 6–1, 6–4.
Girls' Singles.—Miss N. Y. Chmyriova (U.S.S.R.) beat Miss R. Marikova (Czechoslovakia), 6–4, 6–3.
Veterans' Doubles.—L. Bergelin (Sweden) and B. Patty (U.S.A.) beat J. D. Budge and G. Mulloy (U.S.A.), 6–3, 6–3.

WIGHTMAN CUP, 1974
(Deeside, October)
Great Britain won by 6 matches to 1.

WIGHTMAN CUP, 1975
(Cleveland, Ohio, September)
Great Britain won by 5 matches to 2.

Singles.—Miss S. V. Wade (G.B.) beat Miss M. Schallau (U.S.A.), 6–2, 6–1; Miss C. Evert (U.S.A.) beat Miss G. Coles (G.B.), 6–4, 6–1; Miss S. Barker (G.B.) beat Miss J. Newberry (U.S.A.), 6–4, 7–5; Miss Evert beat Miss Wade, 6–3, 7–6; Miss Coles beat Miss Schallau, 6–3, 7–6.
Doubles.—Miss Wade and Mrs. A. Jones (G.B.) beat Miss Newberry and Miss J. Anthony (U.S.A.), 6–2, 6–3; Miss Coles and Miss Barker beat Miss Evert and Miss Schallau, 7–5, 6–4.

BRITISH HARD COURT CHAMPIONSHIPS
(Bournemouth)

Men's Singles.—M. Orantes (Spain).
Women's Singles.—Miss J. Newberry (U.S.A.).
Doubles—Men's: M. Orantes and J. Gisbert (Spain).

Women's: Miss L. J. Charles and Miss S. Mappin (G.B.). *Mixed:* D. Lloyd (G.B.) and Miss S. Walsh (U.S.A.).

U.S.A. Championships:
Men's Singles.—M. Orantes (Spain).
Women's Singles.—Miss C. Evert (U.S.A.).

French Championships:
Men's Singles.—B. Borg (Sweden).
Women's Singles.—Miss C. Evert (U.S.A.).
Men's Doubles.—R. Ramirez (Mexico) and B. Gottfried (U.S.A.).
Women's Doubles.—Miss C. Evert (U.S.A.) and Miss M. Navratilova (Czechoslovakia).
Mixed Doubles.—T. Koch (Brazil) and Miss F. Bonicelli (Uruguay).

Federation Cup.—Czechoslovakia.
Public Schools—Youll Cup: Magdalen College School, Oxford beat Sevenoaks, 3–2, *Clark Cup.*—Millfield beat Manchester G.S., 2–0.
Inter-Services Tournament.—Royal Air Force.

GREEN SHIELD JUNIOR CHAMPIONSHIPS
(Eastbourne)

Boys' Singles.—P. Bourdon beat P. Littlewood, 6–1, 6–7, 6–2.
Girls' Singles.—Miss L. Mottram beat Miss M. Tyler, 5–7, 7–6, 6–0.
Boys' Doubles.—W. J. Gowans and N. C. Sears beat C. D. Best and R. C. Bevan, 3–6, 6–1, 6–4.
Girls' Doubles.—Miss A. Cooper and Miss C. Harrison beat Miss J. Cox and Miss L. Robinson, 6–4, 6–1.

TENNIS, 1975

Amateur Singles Championship.—H. R. Angus beat A. Lovell, 3–0.
Open Singles Championship.—H. R. Angus beat F. Willis, 7–6.
Henry Leaf Cup.—Winchester beat Rugby, 3–0.
Universities.—Oxford University beat Cambridge University, 3–0.

BADMINTON, 1975
ALL-ENGLAND CHAMPIONSHIPS, 1975

Men's Singles.—S. Pri (Denmark) beat R. Hartono (Indonesia), 2–0.
Ladies' Singles.—Miss H. Yuki (Japan) beat Mrs. M. A. Gilks (England), 2–0.
Men's Doubles.—Tjun Tjun and J. Wahjudi (Indonesia) beat C. and A. Chandra (Indonesia), 2–0.
Ladies' Doubles.—Miss M. Anzowa and Miss E. Takanaka (Japan) beat Miss T. Widiastuti and Miss I. Wigoeno (Indonesia), 2–1.
Mixed Doubles.—E. C. Stuart and Miss N. C. Gardner (England) beat R. Maywald and Mrs. B. Steden (Germany), 2–0.

SQUASH RACKETS, 1974–75

British Open Championship.—Qamar Zaman (Pakistan) beat G. Alauddin (Pakistan), 3–0.
British Amateur Championship.—Mohibullah Khan (Pakistan) beat Qamar Zaman (Pakistan), 3–1.
Women's Championship.—Mrs. H. McKay (Australia) beat Mrs. M. Jackman (Australia), 3–0.
University Match.—Oxford University beat Cambridge University, 3–1.
Londonderry Cup.—Barnard Castle beat Lancing, 4–1.
British Isles Professional Championship.—A. Safwat (Egypt) beat B. Patterson (G.B.), 3–1.
Inter-County Championship.—Sussex beat Yorkshire, 3–2.
Drysdale Cup.—P. Kenyon (Lancashire).

FENCING, 1974–75

British Championships:
Foil.—B. Paul (Salle Paul).
Sabre.—J. Deanfield (Polytechnic).
Epée.—Lt. T. Belson (Thames).
Ladies Foil.—Miss S. Wrigglesworth (Salle Paul).
Sporting Record Cup.—Salle Paul.
Granville Cup.—Salle Paul.
Magrini Cup.—Polytechnic.
Public Schools Championship:
Foil.—E. M. R. Raynolds (St. Paul's).
Epée.—S. J. S. Webb (St. Paul's).
Sabre.— C. F. Webb (Brentwood).
Inter-Schools (Graham Bartlett Cup).—St. Paul's.
Savage Shield.—Salle Boston.
Martin Edmunds Cup.—Thames.
Universities.—Oxford beat Cambridge, 15–12.

RACKETS, 1974–75

British Open Championship.—H. R. Angus beat W. Surtees, 4–1.
Amateur Singles Championship.—H. R. Angus beat D. Norman, 3–1.
Amateur Doubles Championship.— C. T. M. Pugh and W. R. Boone beat H. R. Angus and C. J. Hue Williams, 4–3.
Public Schools Championship.—*Singles (H. K. Foster Cup).*—M. Nicholls (Malvern) beat M. Szarf (Harrow), 3–2. *Doubles:* Malvern (M. Tang and P. Nicholls) beat Harrow (A. Piggott and P. Greig), 4–0.
Noel Bruce Cup.—P. Gracey and M. Smith (Tonbridge) beat A. Milne and W. Boone (Eton), 4–2.
Universities.—Oxford University beat Cambridge University, 3–0.
Swallow Cup.—J. A. N. Prenn beat B. R. Wetherill, 3–1.

ETON FIVES, 1975

Amateur Championship.—*Kinnaird Cup.* A. Hughes and A. J. G. Campbell (O. Edwardians) w.o. G. S. May and D. C. Frith (O. Berkhamstedians).
Public Schools Championship.—King Edward's, Birmingham (D. Barnes and P. M. Smith) beat Highgate (D. B. Wainwright and P. G. Dunbar), 3–1.
Alan Barber Cup.—O. Cholmeleians beat O. Salopians, 3–0.
Universities.—Oxford University beat Cambridge University, 2–1.

RUGBY FIVES, 1975

Universities.—Oxford University beat Cambridge University by 255 to 224 pts.

Schools Competition.—*Singles.*—I. G. Peck (Bedford) beat A. M. Lloyd-Williams (Bedford), 2–0.
Doubles: St. Paul's (R. L. Vainer and T. Mackaskie) beat Oundle (T. King-Smith and I. Wilson), 2–1.
Open Doubles Championship.—J. H. M. East and G. W. Enstone beat D. Gardner and S. Reid, 2–0.
Open Singles Championship.—G. W. Enstone beat J. East, 2–0.

POLO, 1975

Queen's Cup.—Foxcote beat Sladmore 9–6½.
Cowdray Park Gold Cup.—Greenhill Farm beat Jersey Lilies 9–5.
Cowdray Park Challenge Cup.—Jersey Lilies beat Cowdray Park 10½–5.
Royal Windsor Cup.—Jersey Lilies beat Los Locos 5–2.
Harrison Cup.—Bucket Hill beat Lea Grange 5½–5.
Brecknock Cup.—Cowdray Park beat Polo Cottage 4–3½.
Benson Cup.—Polo Cottage beat Rangatiki 4–2.
Royal Horse Guards Cup.—Jersey Lilies beat Bucket Hill 7–5½.
Barrett Cup.—Rangatiki beat Maidensgrove 10–7.
Bass Charrington Cup.—Greenhill Farm beat Jersey Lilies 6–5.
Jersey Lilies Challenge Cup.—Jersey Lilies beat Polo Cottage 4½–3.
Aotea Cup.—Cowdray Park beat Peover Park 7–1½.
Tyro Cup.—Jersey Lilies beat Cowdray Park 5½–4.
Maidensgrove Cup.—Rangatiki beat Foxcote 5–2½.
Midhurst Town Cup Final.—San Flamingo beat Sladmore 7–6.
Holden White Cup.—Brookers beat Los Locos 4–3½.
Cicero Cup.—Jersey Lilies beat Rangatiki 10–4.
Ruins Cup.—Golden Eagles beat Maidensgrove 6–5.

TABLE TENNIS, 1975

INTERNATIONAL CHAMPIONSHIPS
(Brighton)

Singles.—*Men:* A. Strokatov (U.S.S.R.) beat J. Secretin (France).
Women: E. Antonian (U.S.S.R.) beat Liu Hsin-Yen (China).
Doubles.—*Men:* S. Gomozkov and S. Sarkhoyan (U.S.S.R.) beat Li Ching-Kuang and Kuo Yao-Hua (China).
Women: Yen Kui-Li and Yu Ching-Chia (China) beat Liu Hsin-Yen and Li Ming (China).
Mixed: Li Ching-Kuang and Yen Kui-Li (China) beat J. Secretin and C. Bergeret (France).
Swaythling Cup.—China.
Corbillon Cup.—China.

WRESTLING, 1975

British Amateur Championships

Flyweight.—A. Dobrozsky (London); *Bantamweight.*—A. Singh Gill (Bradford); *Featherweight.*—J. Henson (U.S.A.); *Lightweight.*—J. Gilligan (Manchester); *Welterweight.*—K. Haward (London); *Middleweight.*—C. Kelly (Scotland); *Light Heavyweight.*—M. Allan (Scotland); *Mid-Heavyweight.*—K. Peache (London); *Heavyweight.*— R. Bradley (Margate).

CANOEING, 1975

Devizes–Westminster Race (124 miles) *Senior Class.*—1, B. Perrett and B. Greenham (Leighton Park School and Royal C.C.), 17 hr. 50 m. 23 s.; 2, A. Haskey and E. Waterton (Royal Engineers C.C.), 18 hr. 2 m. 24 s.; 3, W. Wallace and J. Rycroft (Royal Marine C.F.), 18 hr. 42 m. 50 s.

ANGLING
National Championship

Year	Venue	No. of teams	Individual Winner	Weight	Team winners	Points	Division
				lb. oz.			
1972	Bristol Avon, Wilts.	80	P. Coles (Leicester)	33 8	Birmingham A.A.	248 pts.	(1st Div.)
	R. Welland, Spalding	80	J. Hart (Whittlesey)	54 14½	Coleshill A.C.	216 pts.	(2nd Div.)
1973	R. Witham, Lincs.	—	A. Wright (Derby)	41 10½	Grimsby	717 pts.	(1st Div.)
	Gt. Ouse Relief Channel, Norfolk	92	J. Wilkinson (Elthorn)	43 1½	Leigh	826 pts.	(2nd Div.)
1974	R. Welland and Coronation Channel, Lincs.	80	P. Anderson (Cambridge F.P. & A.S.)	40 2½	Leicester A.S.	—	(1st Div.)
	R. Avon, between Bidford and Tewkesbury	115	C. Hibbs (Leigh Miners)	47 3½	Stockport Federation	—	(2nd Div.)
1975	R. Nene, Peterborough	78	M. Hoad-Reddick (Rotherham)	63 7	—	—	(1st Div.)
	R. Trent, Nottingham	71	A. Webber (Wigan)	16 2½	—	—	(2nd Div.)

SWIMMING

World's Amateur Swimming Records, 1974

Men—Free Style
100 metres.—M. Spitz (U.S.A.), 51·22 s.
200 metres.—M. Spitz (U.S.A.), 1 m. 52·78 s.
400 metres.—R. Demont (U.S.A.), 3 m. 58·18 s.
1,500 metres.—S. Holland (Australia), 15 m. 31·85 s.
Free Style Relay:
  4 × 100 metres.—U.S.A., 3 m. 26·42 s.
  4 × 200 metres.—U.S.A., 7 m. 35·78 s.

Men—Breast Stroke
100 metres.—J. Hencken (U.S.A.), 1 m. 04·02 s.
200 metres.—D. Wilkie (G.B.), 2 m. 19·28 s.

Men—Butterfly Stroke
100 metres.—M. Spitz (U.S.A.), 54·27 s.
200 metres.—M. Spitz (U.S.A.), 2 m. 00·70 s.

Men—Back Stroke
100 metres.—R. Matthes (E. Germany), 56·3 s.
200 metres.—R. Matthes (E. Germany), 2 m. 01·87 s.
Individual Medley:
  200 metres.—D. Wilkie (G.B.), 2 m. 06·32 s.
  400 metres.—A. Hargitay (Hungary), 4 m. 28·29 s.
Medley Relay:—U.S.A., 3 m. 48·16 s.

Women—Free Style
100 metres.—K. Ender (E. Germany), 56·96 m.
200 metres.—K. Ender (E. Germany), 2 m. 03·22 s.
400 metres.—K. Rothhammer (U.S.A.), 4 m. 18·07 s.
800 metres.—J. Turrall (Australia), 8 m. 50·1 s.
Free Style Relay:
  4 × 100 metres.—E. Germany, 3 m. 52·45 s.
Medley Relay:—4 × 100 metres.—E. Germany, 4 m. 13·78 s.

Individual Medley:
  200 metres.—U. Tauber (E. Germany), 2 m. 18·97 s.
  400 metres.—U. Tauber (E. Germany), 4 m. 52·42 s.

Women—Breast Stroke
100 metres.—C. Justen (W. Germany), 1 m. 12·55 s.
200 metres.—C. Linke (E. Germany), 2 m. 34·99 s.

Women—Butterfly Stroke
100 metres.—R. Kother (E. Germany), 1 m. 01·99 s.
200 metres.—R. Kother (E. Germany), 2 m. 13·76 s.

Women—Back Stroke
100 metres.—U. Richter (E. Germany), 1 m. 03·08 s.
200 metres.—U. Richter (E. Germany), 2 m. 17·35 s.

Amateur Swimming Association Championships, 1975
Men:
200 metres Back Stroke.—J. Carter, 2 m. 10·81 s.

400 metres Free Style.—B. Brinkley, 4 m. 4·03 s)
100 metres Butterfly.—B. Brinkley, 57·03 s.
100 metres Breast Stroke.—D. Leigh, 1 m. 8·05 s.
200 metres Individual Medley.—B. Brinkley, 2 m. 10·89 s.
200 metres Free Style.—B. Brinkley, 1 m. 55·39 s.
100 metres Back Stroke.—J. Carter, 1 m. 0·37 s.
1,500 metres Free Style.—P. Nash, 16 m. 28·19 s.
200 metres Butterfly.—B. Brinkley, 2 m. 5·68 s.
200 metres Breast Stroke.—B.O'Brien, 2 m. 31·02 s.
100 metres Back Stroke.—J. Carter, 1 m. 0·37 s.
400 metres Individual Medley.—J. Carter, 4 m. 38·06 s.
100 metres Free Style.—B. Brinkley, 52·30 s.
Free Style Team Relay.—1, Modernians, 3m. 46·05 s.; 2, Southampton, 3 m. 48·10 s.; 3, City of Cardiff, 3 m. 49·48 s.
Medley Team Relay.—1, Southampton, 4 m. 7·57 s.; 2, Paisley, 4 m. 14·11 s.; 3, Modernians, 4 m. 16·16s.
Women:
800 metres Free Style.—K. Skilling, 9 m. 10·86 s.
100 metres Back Stroke.—J. Carter, 7·44s.
200 metres Breast Stroke.—M. Kelly, 2 m. 42·13 s.
200 metres Free Style.—W. Lee, 2 m. 9·58 s.
200 metres Butterfly.—J. Bonner, 2 m. 22·96 s.
400 metres Individual Medley.—S. Richardson, 5 m. 8·82 s.
100 metres Free Style.—D. Hill, 1 m. 1·21 s.
200 metres Individual Medley.—H. Boivin, 2 m. 25·72 s.
100 metres Breast Stroke.—M. Kelly, 1 m. 16·18 s.
400 metres Free Style.—K. Skilling, 4 m. 29·51 s.
100 metres Butterfly.—H. Boivin, 1 m. 5·22 s.
200 metres Back Stroke.—G. Labouceur, 2 m. 26·09 s.
Free Style Team Relay.—1, Beckenham Ladies, 4 m. 13·48 s.; 2, St. James's Ladies, 4 m. 16·14 s.; 3, Newcastle, 4 m. 16·28 s.
Medley Team Relay.—1, City of Cardiff, 4 m. 35·98 s; 2, Beckenham Ladies, 4 m. 40·59 s.; 3, Ruislip and Northwood, 4 m. 46·36 s.

HENLEY REGATTA, 1975
Grand Challenge Cup.—Leander and Thames Tradesmen beat Harvard Univ. (U.S.A.) by 2 lengths, 6 m. 16 s.
Ladies Challenge Plate.—Univ. of London beat Isis by 1½ lengths, 6 m. 31 s.
Princess Elizabeth Cup.—Ridley College (Canada) beat St. Paul's School, Concord (U.S.A.) by 1 length, 6 m. 32 s.
Thames Cup.—Garda Siochana (Eire) beat Quintin by 1 length, 6 m. 37 s.

Stewards' Cup.—Potomac (U.S.A.) beat Lady Margaret, Cambridge by 2½ lengths, 6 m. 50 s.

Prince Philip Cup.—Univ. of London beat Vesper (U.S.A.) by 1⅜ lengths, 7 m. 2 s.

Visitors' Cup.—Ealing High School beat Hampton G.S. by 3½ lengths, 7 m. 12 s.

Wyfold Cup.—Thames Tradesmen beat Leander by 1¼ lengths, 6 m. 57 s.

Britannia Challenge Cup.—Leander beat Tideway Scullers School by 2 lengths, 7 m. 18 s.

Silver Goblets.—H. A. Droog and R. J. Luynenburg (Holland) beat G. A. Locke and F. J. Smallbone (Leander and Thames Tradesmen) by ⅓ length, 7 m. 36 s.

Double Sculls.—M. J. Hart and C. L. Baillieu (Leander) beat P. Levy and K. B. Gee (Weybridge and Molesey), easily, 7 m. 23 s.

Diamond Sculls.—S. Drea (Neptune R. C., Eire) beat J. W. Dietz (New York), by 2½ lengths, 7 m. 56 s.

THE UNIVERSITY BOAT RACE
(Putney-Mortlake, 4m. 1f. 180 yds)

Year	Winner	m. s.	Won by
1962	Cambridge....	19 46	5 lengths
1963	Oxford.......	20 47	5 lengths
1964	Cambridge....	19 18	6½ lengths
1965	Oxford.......	18 45	4 lengths
1966	Oxford.......	19 12	3¾ lengths
1967	Oxford.......	18 52	3½ lengths
1968	Cambridge....	18 22	3½ lengths
1969	Cambridge....	18 4	4 lengths
1970	Cambridge....	20 22	3½ lengths
1971	Cambridge....	17 58	10 lengths
1972	Cambridge....	18 36	9½ lengths
1973	Cambridge....	19 21	13 lengths
1974	Oxford.......	17 35	5½ lengths
1975	Cambridge....	19 27	3¾ lengths

Cambridge have won 68 times, Oxford 52 and there has been 1 dead-heat.

OTHER AQUATIC EVENTS

Head of the River (*Thames, Mortlake-Putney*).—1, National Squad; 2, Tideway Scullers I; 3, Tideway Scullers II.

Oxford Torpids.—Oriel.

Oxford Summer Eights.—Christ Church.

Cambridge Lents.—Lady Margaret.

Cambridge Mays.—Lady Margaret.

Wingfield Sculls (*Putney-Mortlake*).—1, K. V. Dwan, 24 m. 16 s.; 2, M. S. Spencer, 24 m. 34 s.; 3, J. McCarthy, 24 m. 45 s.

Doggett's Coat and Badge (Estab. 1715, 261st Race, *London Bridge-Chelsea*, 4½ miles).—1, C. M. Drury (Battersea); 2, J. C. Dwan (Northfleet); 3, A. L. Macpherson (Blackwall).

SKATING, 1974–75
WORLD CHAMPIONSHIPS
(Colorado Springs)

Men's Figure.—S. Volkov (U.S.S.R.).

Ladies' Figure.—Miss D. De Leeuw (Holland).

Pairs.—A. Zaitsev and Miss I. Rodnina (U.S.S.R.).

Ice Dancing.—A. Minenkov and Miss I. Moiseeva (U.S.S.R.).

EUROPEAN CHAMPIONSHIPS
(Copenhagen)

Men's Figure.—V. Kovalev (U.S.S.R.).

Ladies' Figure.—Miss C. Errath (E. Germany).

Pairs.—A. Zaitsev and Miss I. Rodnina (U.S.S.R.).

Ice Dancing.—A. Gorschkov and Miss L. Pakhomova (U.S.S.R.).

World Speed Skating Championship.—H. Kuipers (Netherlands).

European Championship.—S. Stensen (Norway).

BRITISH CHAMPIONSHIPS (Ice)

Men's Figure.—J. Curry.

Ladies' Figure.—Miss G. Keddie.

Pairs.—C. Taylforth and Miss L. McCafferty-Myles.

Dancing.—G. Watts and Miss H. Green.

(Roller)

Men's Figure.—C. Stirling.

Ladies' Figure.—Miss V. Woolsey.

Pairs.—G. Cubitt and Miss J. Gray.

Dancing.—I. Watkins and Miss P. Bruce.

SHOOTING–BISLEY, 106th N.R.A., 1975

Queen's Prize.—1, C. M. Y. Trotter, 284 pts; 2, J. S. Spaight, 284; 3, F. R. Miles, 284.

St. George's Challenge Vase.—A. St G. Tucker, 142.

Grand Aggregate.—1, J. S. Spaight, 579; 2, M. T. Heathcote, 584; 3, K. O. Pugh, 574.

Elcho Challenge Shield.—1, England, 1,520; 2, Scotland, 1,486; 3, Ireland, 1,453.

The Kolapore.—1, Mother Country, 1,151; 2, Canada, 1,146; 3, Guernsey, 1,116; 4, Jersey, 1,113; 5, Zambia, 1,064.

Universities—Chancellor's Challenge Plate.—1, Cambridge University, 1,120; 2, Oxford University, 1,078.

Inter-Services Long Range.—1, R.N., 546; 2, R.A.F., 545; 3, T.A.V.R., 541.

United Services.—1, Regular Army, 1,211; 2, R.N., 1,191; 3, R.M., 1,176.

Ashburton Shield.—1, Oakham, 499; 2, Christ's Hospital, 491; 3, Lancing, 490.

National Match.—1, England, 2,006; 2, Scotland, 1,954; 3, Ireland, 1,943; 4, Wales, 1,936.

CLAY PIGEON SHOOTING, 1975

International Cup.—1, England, 7,151/7,500; 2, Scotland, 7,081; 3, Ireland, 7,043; 4, Wales, 6,843.

Mackintosh Trophy.—1, Australia, 7,393/7,500; 2, South Africa, 7,255; 3, Canada, 7,239.

British Open Down-the-Line Championship.—P. G. Woodward (Cambs), 295/300.

British Open Skeet Championship.—B. J. Wells (Worcs), 99/100.

British Open Sporting Championship.—P. R. Howe (Norfolk), 91/100.

Coronation Cup.—T. Poskitt (Yorks), 377/400.

Grand Prix of Great Britain (Olympic Trap).—P. Boden (Warwicks), 192/200.

Grand Prix of Great Britain (International Skeet).—W. J. Sykes (Suffolk), 196/200.

European Sporting Championship.—A. B. Hebditch (Wilts), 180/200.

BOXING, 1975
A.B.A. CHAMPIONSHIPS
(Winners)

Light-Flyweight.—M. Lawless (Grangemouth); *Flyweight.*—C. Magri (Arbour Youth); *Bantam.*—S. Ogilvie (Camperdown); *Feather.*—R. Beaumont (Hull Fish Trades); *Light.*—P. Cowdell (Warley); *Light-Welter.*—J. Zeraschi (Fitzroy Lodge); *Welter.*—W. Bennett (New Tredegar); *Light-Middle.*—C. Harrison (Denbeath); *Middle.*—D. Odwell (Repton); *Light-Heavy.*—M. Heath (Hull Fish Trades); *Heavy.*—G. McEwan (Rum Runners).

THE UNIVERSITIES
Oxford University beat Cambridge University by 5 bouts to 4.

PROFESSIONAL BOXING
WORLD CHAMPIONS
Title Holders in Sept. 1975

Semi-Flyweight.—F. Udella (Italy); *Flyweight.*—M. Canto (Mexico); *Bantamweight.*—R. Martinez (Mexico); *Featherweight.*—D. Kotey (Ghana); *Semi-Lightweight.*—A. Escalera (Puerto Rico); *Light-Welterweight.*—S. Muansurin (Thailand); *Lightweight.*—G. Ishimatsu (Japan); *Welterweight.*—J. Napoles (Mexico); *Light-Middleweight.*—M. De Oliveira (Brazil); *Middleweight.*—R. Valdez (Colombia); *Light-Heavyweight.*—J. Conteh (England); *Heavyweight.*—Muhammad Ali (U.S.A.).

BRITISH CHAMPIONS
Title Holders in Oct. 1975

Flyweight.—J. McCluskey (Scotland); *Bantamweight.*—D. Needham (England); *Featherweight.*—V. Sollas (Scotland); *Lightweight.*—J. Watt (Scotland); *Light Welterweight.*—J. Singleton (England); *Welterweight.*—vacant; *Light Middleweight.*—M. Hope (England); *Middleweight.*—vacant; *Light-Heavyweight.*—C. Finnegan (England); *Heavyweight.*—R. Dunn (England).

COMMONWEALTH CHAMPIONS
Title Holders in Sept. 1975

Flyweight.—vacant; *Bantamweight.*—P. Ferrari (Australia); *Featherweight.*—D. Kotey (Ghana); *Junior Lightweight.*—B. Moeller (Australia); *Lightweight.*—J. Dele (Nigeria); *Light Welterweight.*—H. Thompson (Australia); *Welterweight.*—vacant; *Light Middleweight.*—vacant; *Middleweight.*—M. Bethan (N.Z.); *Light-Heavyweight.*—S. Aczel (Australia); *Heavyweight.*—R. Dunn (England).

EUROPEAN CHAMPIONS
Title Holders in Sept. 1975

Flyweight.—F. Udella (Italy); *Bantamweight.*—D. Trioulaire (France); *Featherweight.*—E. Cotena (Italy); *Junior Lightweight.*—Sven-Erik Paulsen (Norway); *Lightweight.*—vacant; *Light Welterweight.*—J. R. Gomez-Fouz (Spain); *Welterweight.*—J. Stracey (England); *Light Middleweight.*—E. Dagge (Germany); *Middleweight.*—G. Tonna (France); *Light Heavyweight.*—D. Adinolfi (Italy); *Heavyweight.*—J. Bugner (England).

BILLIARDS AND SNOOKER
World Professional Billiards Championship.—A. L. Driffield (England) beat A. Johnson (Australia) by 9,204 to 4,696.

World Open Billiards Championship.—A. L. Driffield (England) beat P. Morgan (Ireland) by 3,055 to 2,404.

World Professional Snooker Championship.—R. Reardon beat E. Charlton (Australia) by 31–30 frames.

World Amateur Snooker Championship.—R. Edmonds (England) beat G. Thomas (Wales) by 11–9 frames.

World Amateur Billiards Championship.—N. Dagley (England) beat M. Ferreira (India) by 3,386 to 2,268.

English Amateur Billiards Championship.—N. Dagley beat R. Close by 2,917 to 2,693.

English Amateur Snooker Championship.—S. Hood beat W. Thorne by 11–6 frames.

Women (Amateur).—*Billiards:* Mrs. V. Selby; *Snooker:* Mrs. V. Selby.

BOWLS, 1975
English Bowling Association Championships (Worthing).

Fours.—*S.F.*: Cromer (Norfolk) beat Basingstoke Town (Hants) 24–14; L.T.A.S.S.A. (Middx) beat Borough Park (Yorkshire) 26–11; *F.*: Cromer beat L.T.A.S.S.A. 23–19.

Triples.—*S.F.*: British Legion, Farnborough (Hants) beat Newquay Trenance (Cornwall) 18–11; City of Ely (Cambs) beat Margaret Catchpole (Suffolk) 20–13; *F.*: British Legion, Farnborough beat City of Ely 23–15.

Pairs.—*S.F.*: W. A. Campbell and P. Inch (Middlesbrough Co-op, Yorks) beat D. Dennis and D. Hockley (St. Neots, Cambs) 21–13; G. Davis and J. Nelson (North Shields West End, Northumberland) beat T. A. Thomas and J. A. Rodwell (Liberty of Havering, Essex) 20–19; *F.*: Davis and Nelson beat Campbell and Inch 22–14.

Singles.—*S.F.*: D. J. Bryant, M.B.E. (Clevedon, Somerset) beat A. Ridington (Parsons Green, Middlesex) 21–12; R. A. Gibbins (L.T.A.S. S. A. Middlesex) beat S. Bunting (Courtfield, Cumberland) 21–16; *F.*: Bryant beat Gibbins 21–15.

Inter-County Championship (Middleton Cup).—*S.F.*: Surrey beat Essex 125–87; Hampshire beat Yorkshire 125–114; *F.*: Surrey beat Hampshire 109–105.

International Championship.—*Winners:* Scotland.—*Results:* Scotland beat England 91–82; Ireland beat Wales 107–83; Scotland beat Ireland 94–78; England beat Wales 90–88; England beat Ireland 120–80 and Scotland beat Wales 101–82.

BRITISH SHOW JUMPING, 1975
ROYAL INTERNATIONAL HORSE SHOW. WEMBLEY

King George V Gold Cup.—1, A. Schockemohle on Rex the Robber; 2, D. Broome on Philco; 3, P. McMahon on Penwood Forge Mill.

Horse and Hound Cup.—1, G. Fletcher on Tauna Dora; 2, D. Broome on Philco; 3, H. Snoek on Rasputin.

Queen Elizabeth II Cup.—1, Mrs. J. Davenport on Hang On; 2, Mrs. P. Dunning on Sugar Plum; 3, Miss D. Johnsey on Speculator.

Moss Bros. Puissance.—A. Schockemohle on Warwick and T. Newbery on Snaffles, equal first.

John Player Trophy.—1, A. Schockemohle on Rex the Robber; 2, Mrs. B. Crago on Brevitt Bouncer; 3, D. Broome on Philco.

Daily Mail Cup.—1, E. Macken on Boomerang; 2, G. Fletcher on Tauna Dora; 3, T. Newbery on Warwick III.

OXFORD AND CAMBRIDGE
Principal Events and Winners, 1974–75

Event (with date of first meeting)	Summary of Results			Results 1974–75
	Ox.	Camb.	Drawn	
Cricket (1827)..........	44	51	36	Draw
Boat Race (1829)........	52	68	1	Camb.
Athletics (1864).........	49	45	7	Camb.
Football—				
Association (1873–4)...	32	41	19	Oxford
Rugby (1871–2)........	42	38	13	Camb.
Golf (1878).............	34	45	5	Camb.
Hockey (1890)..........	26	32	14	Oxford

OTHER UNIVERSITY EVENTS AND WINNERS
1974–75
Rugby Fives..........................Oxford
Squash Rackets.......................Oxford
Eton Fives...........................Oxford
Boxing...............................Oxford
Shooting.............................Cambridge
Real Tennis..........................Oxford
Rackets..............................Oxford

CYCLING, 1975

Tour de France.—B. Thevenet (France).
Tour of Britain.—B. Johansson (Sweden).
World Championships:—
  Professional Sprint.—J. Nicholson (Australia).
  Professional Pursuit.—R. Schuiten (Holland).
  Professional Road Race.—H. Kuiper (Holland).
  Ladies' Sprint.—S. Novara (U.S.A.).
  Ladies' Pursuit.—K. Van Oosten-Hage (Holland).
  Ladies'Road Race.—T. Fopma (Holland).
National Championships:—
  Amateur Sprint.—P. Medhurst.
  Ladies' Sprint.—F. Murray.
  Amateur Pursuit.—S. Hefferman.
  Ladies' Pursuit.—D. Burton.
  Amateur Road Race.—K. Apter.
  Ladies' Road Race.—J. Westbury.

MOTOR CYCLING, 1975

Senior T.T., Isle of Man.—1, M. Grant (Kawasaki), 2 hr. 15 m. 27·6 s. (100·27 m.p.h.); 2, J. Williams (Yamaha), 2 hr. 15 m. 58·8 s.; 3, C. Mortimer (Yamaha), 2 hr. 18 m. 22·8 s.
Junior 350 c.c. TT., Isle of Man.—1, C. Williams (Yamaha), 1 hr. 48 m. 26·4 s. (104·38 m.p.h.); 2, C. Mortimer (Yamaha), 1 hr. 49 m. 51 s.; 3, T. Herron (Yamaha), 1 hr. 50 m. 35·4 s.
250 c.c. Lightweight T.T., Isle of Man.—1, C. Mortimer (Yamaha), 1 hr. 28 m. 57·8 s. (101·78 m.p.h.); 2, D. Chatterton (Yamaha), 1 hr. 29 m. 20 s.; 3, J. Williams (Yamaha), 1 hr. 29 m. 42·2 s.
Manx Grand Prix (Isle of Man).—*Senior:* 1, S. McClements (Yamaha), 2 hr. 14 m. 25·6 s. (101·04 m.p.h.); 2, K. Trubshaw (Yamaha), 2 hr. 15 m. 24·2 s.; 3, J. Higham (Yamaha), 2hr. 16 m. 37·6 s.

MOTOR RACING, 1974–75

24-hours (Le Mans).—1, D. Bell and J. Ickx (Gulf-Ford), 118·9 m.p.h.; 2, J. L. Lafosse and G. Chasseuil (Ligier-Ford); 3, V. Schuppan and J. P. Jaussand (Gulf-Ford).
Monaco Grand Prix.—1, N. Lauda (Ferrari), 2 hr. 1 m. 21·31 s. (75·52 m.p.h.); 2, E. Fittipaldi (McLaren), 2 hr. 1 m. 24·09 s.; 3, C. Pace (Brabham), 2 hr. 1 m. 39·12 s.
French Grand Prix.—1, N. Lauda (Ferrari), 1 hr. 40 m. 18·84 s. (116·6 m.p.h.); 2, J. Hunt (Hesketh), 1 hr. 40 m. 20·43 s.; 3, J. Mass (McLaren), 1 hr.40 m. 21·15 s.
British Grand Prix (Silverstone).—1, E. Fittipaldi (McLaren); 2, C. Pace (Brabham); 3, J. Scheckter (Elf Tyrrell).
German Grand Prix.—1, C. Reutemann (Brabham), 1 hr. 41 m. 14·1 s. (117·73 m.p.h.); 2, J. Laffite (Williams-Ford), 1 hr. 42 m. 51·8 s.; 3, N. Lauda (Ferrari), 1 hr. 43 m. 37·4 s.
South African Grand Prix.—1, J. Scheckter (Elf Tyrrell), 1 hr. 43 m. 16·90 s. (115·5 m.p.h.); 2, C. Reutemann (Brabham), 1 hr. 43 m. 20·64 s.; 3, P. Depailer (Elf Tyrrell), 1 hr. 43 m. 33·82 s.
Argentine Grand Prix.—1, E. Fittipaldi (McLaren), 1 hr. 39 m. 26·29 s.; 2, J. Hunt (Hesketh), 1 hr. 39 m. 32·20 s.; 3, C. Reutemann (Brabham), 1 hr. 39 m. 43·35 s.
Brazilian Grand Prix.—1, C. Pace (Brabham), 1 hr. 44 m. 41·17 s. (113·39 m.p.h.); 2, E. Fittipaldi (McLaren), 1 hr. 44 m. 46·96 s.; 3, J. Mass (McLaren), 1 hr. 45 m. 17·83 s.
Swedish Grand Prix.—1, N. Lauda (Ferrari), 1 hr. 59 m. 18·31 s. (100·41 m.p.h.); 2, C. Reutemann (Brabham), 1 hr. 59 m. 24·60 s. ; 3, C. Regazzoni (Ferrari), 1 hr. 59 m. 47·41 s.
Italian Grand Prix.—1, C. Regazzoni (Ferrari), 1 hr. 22 m. 42·6 s. (135·67 m.p.h.); 2, E. Fittipaldi (McLaren), 1 hr. 22 m. 52·9 s.; 3, N. Lauda (Ferrari), 1 hr. 23 m. 5·8 s.
Austrian Grand Prix.—1, V. Brambilla (Beta March); 2, J. Hunt (Hesketh); 3, T. Pryce (UOP Shadow).
Belgian Grand Prix.—1, N. Lauda (Ferrari), 1 hr. 43 m. 53·98 s. (107·04 m.p.h.); 2, J. Scheckter (Elf Tyrrell), 1 hr. 44 m. 13·20 s.; 3, C. Reutemann (Brabham), 1 hr. 44 m. 35·80 s.
U.S. Grand Prix.—1, N. Lauda (Ferrari), 116·10 m.p.h.; 2, E. Fittipaldi (McLaren); 3, J. Mass (McLaren).
Dutch Grand Prix.—1, J. Hunt (Hesketh), 1 hr. 46 m. 57·40 s. (109·86 m.p.h.); 2, N. Lauda (Ferrari); 3, C. Regazzoni (Ferrari).

SPORTS REPRESENTATIVE BODIES

ANGLING.—National Federation of Anglers. *Sec.-Gen.,* J. W. Warner, Haig House, 87 Green Lane, Derby.
ASSOCIATION FOOTBALL.—The Football Association. *Sec.,* E. A. Croker, 16 Lancaster Gate, W.2.
ATHLETICS.—Amateur Athletic Association. *Hon. Sec.,* B. E. Willis, 70 Brompton Road, S.W.3.
— British Amateur Athletic Board. *Hon. Sec.,* A. Gold, C.B.E., 70 Brompton Road, S.W.3.
— Women's Amateur Athletic Association. *Hon. Sec.,* Miss M. Hartman, M.B.E., 70 Brompton Road, S.W.3.
BADMINTON.—Badminton Association of England. *Sec.,* J. B. H. Bisseker, 44/45 Palace Road, Bromley, Kent.
BASKET BALL.—English Basket Ball Association. *Sec.,* K. K. Mitchell, Dept. of Physical Education, The University, Leeds.
BILLIARDS.—Billiards and Snooker Control Council. *Chairman,* W. H. Cottier, Alexandra Chambers, 32 John William Street, Huddersfield.
BOBSLEIGH.—British Bobsleigh Association. *Hon. Sec.,* G. Renwick, 515 Watford Way, N.W.6.
BOWLS.—English Bowling Association. *Secs.,* J. F. Elms, 4 Lansdowne Crescent, Bournemouth, Hants.
BOXING.—Amateur Boxing Association, 70 Brompton Road, S.W.3.—*Hon. Sec.,* F. J. Warren.

— British Boxing Board of Control, Ramillies Buildings, Hills Place, W.1.—*Gen. Sec.,* R. L. Clarke.
CANOEING.—British Canoe Union, 70 Brompton Road, S.W.3.
CLAY PIGEON SHOOTING.—Clay Pigeon Shooting Association. *Dir.,* A. P. Page, 107 Epping New Road, Buckhurst Hill, Essex.
CRICKET.—Marylebone Cricket Club, Lord's Ground, N.W.8. *Sec.,* J. A. Bailey.
CYCLING.—British Cycling Federation, 70 Brompton Road, S.W.3.—*Sec.* L. Unwin.
FENCING.—Amateur Fencing Association. *Sec.,* Cmdr. F. A. Booth, R.N., 83 Perham Road, W. Kensington, W.14.
GOLF.—Royal and Ancient Golf Club, St. Andrews. *Sec.,* K. R. T. Mackenzie, M.C.
— English Golf Union. *Sec.,* I. R. H. M. A. Erskine, 12A Denmark Street, Wokingham, Berks.
— Ladies' Golf Union. *Sec.,* 2 Fairways, Sandwich Bay, Kent.
GYMNASTICS.—British Amateur Gymnastics Association. *Gen. Sec.,* Lt. Cdr. B. W. C. Middleton, R.N. *(ret.),* 23A High Street, Slough, Bucks.
HOCKEY.—Hockey Association. *Sec.* R. I. W. Struthers, M.B.E., 70 Brompton Road, S.W.3.
— All England Women's Hockey Association, 160 Great Portland Street, W.1.

JUDO.—British Judo Association, 70 Brompton Road, S.W.3. *Gen. Sec.*, A. J. Reay.

LACROSSE.—English Lacrosse Union. *Hon. Sec.* R. Balls, 64 Broad Walk, Hockley, Essex.

LAWN TENNIS.—Lawn Tennis Association. *Sec.*, P. M. Johns, Barons Court, West Kensington, W.14.

— International Lawn Tennis Federation, *Gen. Sec.* S. B. Reay, O.B.E., International Lawn Tennis Federation, Barons Court, West Kensington, W.14.

MOTOR CYCLING.—Auto-Cycle Union, 31 Belgrave Square, S.W.1. *Sec. Gen.*, K. E. Shierson.

MOUNTAINEERING.—British Mountaineering Council, Crawford House, Precinct Centre, Booth Street East, Manchester.

NETBALL.—All England Netball Association. *Sec.*, Mrs. J. Holman, 70 Brompton Road, S.W.3.

RACING.—The Jockey Club (incorporating National Hunt Committee), 42 Portman Square, W.1. *Sec.*, S. M. Weatherby.

RIFLE SHOOTING.—National Rifle Association, *Sec.*, Air Commodore A. B. Riall, C.B.E., R.A.F. (*ret.*), Bisley Camp, Brookwood, Woking, Surrey.

— National Small-bore Rifle Association. *Sec.*, R. C. Russell, Codrington House, 113 Southwark Street, S.E.1.

ROWING.—Amateur Rowing Association. *Dir.- Sec.*, M. C. Stamford, 6 Lower Mall, W.6.

RUGBY FIVES.—Rugby Fives Association. *Sec.*, T. Wood, Fairbourne Lodge, Epping Green, Essex.

RUGBY FOOTBALL.—The Rugby Football Union, Whitton Road, Twickenham, Middx. *Sec.*, Air Commodore R. H. G. Weighill, C.B.E., D.F.C.

— The Rugby Football League, *Sec.*, D. S. Oxley, 180 Chapeltown Road, Leeds.

SKATING.—National Skating Association of Great Britain. *Gen. Sec.*, A. R. Drake, Charterhouse, E.C.1.

SKI-ING.—National Ski Federation of Great Britain. *Sec.*, Maj. Gen. I. R. Graeme, C.B., O.B.E., 118 Eaton Square, S.W.1.

SQUASH RACKETS.—Squash Rackets Association. *Sec.*, E. P. Woods, 26 Park Crescent, W.1.

— Women's Squash Rackets Association. *Sec.*, Miss C. Myers, 345 Upper Richmond Road West East Sheen, Surrey.

SWIMMING.—Amateur Swimming Association, Harold Fern House, Derby Square, Loughborough Leics.

TABLE TENNIS.—English Table Tennis Association, *Gen. Sec.*, E. R. Taylor, 21 Claremont, Hastings, East Sussex.

TOBOGANNING.—British Racing Tobogganing Association.—*Pres.*, Dr. R. Liversedge, 82 Firtree Road, Banstead, Surrey.

UNDERWATER SWIMMING.—British Sub-Aqua Club. *Dir.-Gen.*, R. L. Vallintine, 70 Brompton Road, S.W.3.

WATER SKI-ING.—British Water Ski Federation, 70 Brompton Road, S.W.3.—*Sec. Gen.*, S. J. Primo.

WEIGHT-LIFTING.—British Amateur Weight Lifters Association. *Hon. Sec.*, W. W. R. Holland, 3 Iffley Turn, Iffley, Oxford.

WRESTLING.—British Amateur Wrestling Association. *Sec.*, A Wishart, 60 Calabria Road, N.5.

YACHTING.—Royal Yachting Association, Victoria Way, Woking, Surrey. *Sec.- Gen.*, J. Durie.

DUKE OF EDINBURGH'S AWARD SCHEME

The Duke of Edinburgh's Award Scheme is meant to provide an incentive and a challenge to young people to reach certain standards in leisure-time activities with the voluntary help of adults. Entrants in the United Kingdom and in other Commonwealth countries, must be between their 14th and 23rd birthdays and can enter through their school, the firm where they work a youth organization, or on their own. Bronze, Silver and Gold Awards can be gained by those who qualify in four of the five sections of the Scheme: Service, Expeditions, Interests, Design for Living, and Physical Activity. The qualifying standards are expressed in terms of proficiency, perseverance or sustained effort, participants being assessed on the use they make of their personal abilities and aptitudes and not in competition with others.

In 1974, there were 70,529 new entrants from the United Kingdom (40,441 boys, 30,088 girls) and 19,849 from overseas; a total of 28,295 Awards were gained in the U.K. and 9,693 overseas. There have now been more than a million entrants since the Scheme began.

Head Office: 2 Old Queen Street, Westminster, London SW1. Director: A. Blake, C.V.O., M.C., Ll.B.

TOPICS OF THE DAY

THE TERCENTENARY OF THE ROYAL GREENWICH OBSERVATORY

The upsurge of the spirit of scientific inquiry in the seventeenth century in Europe was marked in England in 1660 by the founding of the Royal Society and in 1675 by the founding of the Royal Observatory at Greenwich.

John Flamsteed was appointed by King Charles II to be " our astronomical observator, forthwith to apply himself with the most exact care and diligence to the rectifying the tables of the motions of the heavens, and the places of the fixed stars, so as to find out the so-much-desired longitude of places for the perfecting of the art of navigation ". Flamsteed's appointment, carrying with it a salary of one hundred pounds a year, dated from St. Michael's Day, 1674. The building of the Observatory, designed by Sir Christopher Wren, a former professional astronomer, was commenced in 1675. In May of the following year Flamsteed was able to move into the building which is now known as Flamsteed House and his first observations were obtained on September 19, 1675.

At this time the most likely method of determining longitude at sea appeared to be that of " lunar distances ". The idea was that the Moon's apparent motion in front of the stars could be used as the hands of a clock. Flamsteed's observations, made before his appointment as " astronomical observator " had shown that errors of over 5 minutes of arc existed in even the best available star catalogues whilst the Moon's predicted position could be in error by as much as 20 minutes of arc. Since an error of 5 minutes of arc in a celestial position leads to a corresponding error of about $2\frac{1}{2}°$ in the terrestrial longitude, it was obvious that the method of lunar distances was impractical until both the positions of the stars and the orbit of the Moon were known to a greatly improved accuracy. This is the justification for Flamsteed's labours over the next four decades, culminating in the publication (by his widow) of the star catalogue *Historia coelestis britannica* in 1725.

Halley succeeded Flamsteed in 1720 and continued with the idea of improving the orbit of the Moon, and observed about 1500 transits of the Moon between 1722 and 1740.

Flamsteed had observed a variation in position of gamma Draconis close to the zenith and thought he had found a parallax for this star. Later on, in 1729, Bradley rediscovered this effect for several stars but correctly deduced that it was caused by a phenomenon known as the aberration of light. Bradley succeeded Halley in 1742 and six years later published his great work on the discovery of nutation—a wobbling of the Earth's axis caused by the gravitation of the Moon. Bradley died in 1762. He was followed by Bliss who died two years later.

The fifth Astronomer Royal, Maskelyne, was appointed in 1765. Two years earlier he had published the *British Mariner's Guide* concerning the use of lunar distances, so it was not surprising to learn that in 1766, shortly after his appointment, he published for the year 1767 the first Nautical Almanac.

Pond succeeded Maskelyne in 1811 and was renowned for increasing the accuracy of the observations made at Greenwich. Oddly enough the Nautical Almanac, for which he was also responsible, at the same time became renowned for the errors in its published figures!

Airy, Astronomer Royal from 1835 to 1881, replaced the existing instruments of the Observatory by new ones of his own design. The most famous of these was the transit circle which was later adopted as marking the zero meridian.

Christie succeeded Airy in 1881 and retired in 1910, having arranged that Greenwich would be one of the 18 observatories to participate in a programme to photograph the whole sky down to a magnitude 14.

Dyson followed Christie and held office until 1933. He introduced the method of determining stellar parallaxes photographically. His successor, Spencer Jones, will be remembered for his work establishing the non-uniform rotation of the Earth and for his successful removal of the observatory from Greenwich to Herstmonceux. Woolley succeeded Spencer Jones in 1956 and by the time of his retirement in 1971 had the satisfaction of knowing that the construction of the new observatory was complete, including the erection of the Isaac Newton Telescope, the largest in western Europe. Woolley was the last director of the Observatory to hold the title of Astronomer Royal. Since then his successors (Burbidge and Hunter) have been referred to as Directors.

Professor Graham Smith has been appointed the new director from January 1, 1976, and will be faced with a major task—the construction of a new large observatory in the northern hemisphere, expected to be either in Palma, Canary Islands, or Madeira, or Hawaii. There are to be three main telescopes of apertures 1·0, 2·5 and 4·5 metres.

The tercentenary celebrations consisted of a number of separate events during 1975.

From January onwards there was an exhibition on " The Measurement of Time " in Flamsteed House, Old Royal Observatory, while another exhibition on "300 years of Astronomy" opened in March in the Queen's House at Greenwich. In April there was an issue of commemorative medals in gold, silver, and bronze, by the Royal Mint. On April 23 the Post Office issued a set of stamps to mark the European Architectural Heritage Year. The stamp shows Flamsteed House and bears the words " The Royal Observatory Greenwich " but unfortunately makes no reference to the tercentenary.

On May 20 the Queen visited Greenwich to inaugurate the new " onion " dome housing the 71 cm refractor. The old dome was irreparably damaged during the war and the telescope was taken to Herstmonceux but returned to Greenwich in 1971. The anniversary of King Charles II's warrant establishing the Royal Observatory at Greenwich occurred on June 22. Two different commemorative covers were issued at Greenwich and at Herstmonceux.

A week of visits to the Observatory at Herstmonceux by various scientific societies started on June 23. At Burstow Church, Surrey (where John Flamsteed was rector) a commemoration service was held on July 13.

Between July 14–17 the National Maritime Museum held a symposium on " The Origins, Achievements and Influence of the Royal Observatory, Greenwich, 1675–1975 ".

On July 18 a garden party was held in the grounds of Herstmonceux Castle. Princess Anne, the guest of honour, unveiled a bust of Flamsteed and inaugurated a large, stainless steel sundial which had been erected to commemorate the tercentenary. The dial is called a reclining equiangular sundial and it is believed that it was the first of its type to be erected. It is set daily and always shows the Greenwich Mean Time (correct to the nearest minute) and thus serves as a reminder of the link between the observatory and Greenwich.

On July 20 there was a special service to mark the

tercentenary, linked with statutory evensong, in Westminster Abbey. During the following week there was a symposium on " The Galaxy and the Local Group " at Herstmonceux. Also in July the planetarium at Greenwich started showing its special programme " 300 years of the Observatory".

During the period August 2–17 the Observatory at Herstmonceux, including some telescope domes and the interior of the Castle, was thrown open to the public—the first time since the Observatory took over the historic site after the war.

A three volume *History of the Observatory* was issued written by Forbes, Meadows and Howse, and also a smaller publication *The Royal Greenwich Observatory* by McCrea. Wedgwood issued a commemorative plate in the autumn.

EUROPEAN ARCHITECTURAL HERITAGE YEAR

In May, 1972, the Council of Europe formally agreed to designate 1975 as European Architectural Heritage Year (EAHY), in the hope of reaffirming the merits of "conservation" for the final quarter of this century. Its sponsors set themselves certain objectives: initially simply to invoke interest and then build on that, to "protect and enhance" historic buildings, preserve their more nebulous "character", and "assure for ancient buildings a living rôle in contemporary society". The U.K. Council, under the presidency of HRH, The Duke of Edinburgh, in addition, aimed to improve the flow of capital for restoration schemes and to encourage ideas that would enhance Britain's 3,500 odd conservation areas declared under the Civic Amenities Act of 1967.

Following the declaration of intent in 1972, EAHY was anticipated in many ways. Sir Nikolaus Pevsner, after 25 years of unstinting application, completed the final 46th volume of his *Buildings of England* series in 1974, an achievement unique in Europe. An old-established classic, Sir Bannister Fletcher's book on architectural history, passed into a record 18th edition. In 1973 Adam Fergusson drew attention to the 2,000 demolitions in twenty years at Bath whilst Christopher Booker wrote about the similar pressure on London. EAHY also received legislative as well as literary groundwork; The Town and Country Amenities Act of 1974, a private member's measure involving The Civic Trust, brought the demolition of all buildings and the felling of trees in conservation areas under stricter control and allowed central as well as local government to declare such areas in the first place. The Housing Act of 1974 intensified the disfavour into which wholesale bulldozing had fallen as a means of slum clearance; and finally the practice of listing buildings of architectural or historic interest was extended to Northern Ireland (in 1975, the work of The Ulster Architectural Heritage Society, formed eight years ago, was recognised by a Special Heritage Year Award from the Civic Trust). Also, in Europe itself in April 1973 the Italian Parliament voted £200m. to be spent on securing the survival of Venice.

Back in Britain, the museum world was active; a sad toll was tabulated in the major exhibition, late in 1974, at the Victoria and Albert Museum entitled "The Destruction of the English Country House 1875–1975". Its clear message was the need to call a halt to a frightening number of demolitions; 76 in 1955 alone. The names of the lost houses are now largely forgotten; it is the philistinism entailed in putting a pickaxe to carved staircases and gently-modelled plasterwork that remains the hardest fact to forget; yet disturbing too is the realisation that the threat remains; Fonthill House,

Wilts, only came down in 1972 and in EAHY itself the fate of Barlaston Hall, Staffs, became a *cause célèbre*. The exhibition also pointed out a secondary menace; that entirely undiscriminating element, fire; 110 country houses have been consumed by it in about as many years, and its capacity to commit dreadful damage was evidenced late in 1974 by the complete gutting of one of Ireland's noblest houses, Powerscourt, built about 1720. In urban areas too the spirit of EAHY was heralded by decisions to cancel, shelve or trim four major redevelopment schemes in London—at Piccadilly Circus, Covent Garden, Whitehall and the once-intended British Library site in Bloomsbury (now moved to railway land at Somers Town). Elsewhere, however, the proximity of EAHY seemed to mean little; the Georgian Woburn Square in Bloomsbury was all but completely swept away and in 1974 some 400 listed buildings were destroyed and an equal number condemned.

Once EAHY had been launched in 1975 all sorts of bodies made contributions. The Civic Trust provided the U.K. Secretariat and having sifted the 1,377 submissions, made 285 Heritage Year Awards (52 in Scotland, 11 in Wales, one in Northern Ireland), including 16 for schemes "of exceptional merit" such as the restoration of York Minster, and scholarly reconstructions at Chevening House, Kent (the intended home of the Prince of Wales), the long gallery at Burton Agnes Hall, Humberside and at Makerstoun House, Kelso. Furthermore 20 awards were made for "continuing contributions to conservation"; to the National Trust, for example, which marked EAHY by restoring gardens at Ham, near Richmond, Surrey, and at Osterley, and coincidentally acquired new properties like Lutyens' Castle Drogo of 1911–30 (built for Julius Drewe, the last of the medievally-minded millionaires), negotiating also to take over Arundel and Dunster Castles. The National Trust for Scotland, also an award-winner, opened Adam's 7 Charlotte Square, in Edinburgh. Another recipient, the Landmark Trust, continued its good work in preserving as holiday accommodation certain architectural oddities such as a martello tower and an Egyptianising house at Penzance. A wide range of institutions staged exhibitions—The Royal Society of Arts, the Arts Council, the Council for the Care of Places of Worship, and individuals like the Duke of Bedford. The Greater London Council, overseer for 26,000 of the nation's 240,000 listed buildings, commemorated EAHY by restoring the simple Georgian chapel at the Geffrye Museum, converting the Ranger's House at Blackheath into an arts gallery and renovating an early Georgian terrace in Albury St., Deptford. Elsewhere in London, Greenwich, the location for Wren's Royal College and Royal Observatory, Hawksmoor's St. Alfege's Church and Vanbrugh's Castle acted as a showpiece for the Year.

Attention was also diverted on to four pilot projects; Poole, Edinburgh's Georgian " New Town ", Fife's " Little Houses Improvement Scheme " (begun 1960) and Chester. The last two, especially, deserved close European scrutiny. The Fife scheme operates on the basis of a " revolving fund "; that is consecutive restoration schemes financed by means of the ploughed-back profits gained from post-renovation sales. In Chester finance derives from a specific conservation rate first levied in 1969, bringing in now at its maximum £200,000 p.a.; and superintended by a conservation officer. EAHY has been celebrated there by work at Gamul House (c1620) and " The Dutch Houses " and the opening of an architectural heritage centre in the converted St. Michael's Church (1850); an idea followed up at York (St.

Mary, Castlegate), at Faversham, Kent (in the former Fleur de Lis Inn) and at Oxford. Also of importance in the way many hands and monies were coordinated is the £2m. Heritage over The Wensum project at Norwich. In Wales a sum total of £450,000 is going towards conservation on the Margam Abbey estate. Haslemere Estates, one of the few property development firms that can be called an ally of conservationists, published a fine book for EAHY to illustrate its adaptation for contemporary use of urbane Georgian and exuberant Victorian property; buildings that might otherwise have succumbed to progress of the root-and-branch variety. The RIBA marked the Year by instituting a children's educational scheme (with the *Sunday Times* and WATCH) and a £1m. appeal for its world-renowned architectural library.

Quite clearly the will to conserve is widespread but money is often lacking. It was fortunate, therefore, that the Government, as the nation's greatest source of capital, announced a more open-handed financial policy on conservation, in 1975. Having already in 1974 handed down £1½m. in grants for repairs to historic properties, as well as another £1m. for other improvements, it agreed, for EAHY, both to contribute 50 per cent. (£500,000) of a National Heritage Fund, and to donate £180,000 to finance small schemes of improvement in " non-outstanding " conservation areas. In addition the usual " Conservation Grants " totalled £1m. in 1974/75. An agreement in principle was also announced for governmental (i.e. secular) money of up to £1m. p.a. to be set aside for the upkeep of historic churches still in ecclesiastical use; a complete and welcome break with tradition.

Two sectors of the British architectural heritage, freshly retrieved from unwarranted scorn and/or neglect received duly unprejudiced treatment in EAHY, viz: Victorian architecture (secular and ecclesiastical) and those adjuncts of the Industrial Revolution, mills, warehouses and their kind.

The Victorian Society, founded in 1958 amid general apathy, was in a position in EAHY to move into its own premises in Norman Shaw's suburb at Bedford Park and was able to witness the National Trust negotiate for the same architect's Cragside in Northumberland and acquire Burges' Knightshayes Court, Devonshire and Philip Webb's Standen, Sussex, of the mid and late nineteenth century respectively. The Heritage Year Awards included the sensitive handling of Victoriana at St. John's, Liverpool, the Cambridge Halls, Stockport, the country house at Wykehurst and even a former prison at Dornoch in Sutherland. The Redundant Churches Fund, having taken over its first Victorian buildings—Studley Royal Church, Yorkshire, for example spent EAHY handling the receipt of more. To pick further cases at random: 1975 also saw the completion of a new piazza to set off Westminster Cathedral (1899), loud protests at threats to Brighton and Southend Piers, the use of Morris glass in the rebuilding to an award-winning design of Haddington church in East Lothian and further action over the establishment of a stained glass museum at Ely (this art form being quantitatively a mainly Victorian preserve). Finally mention must be made of the expenditure of £2,000 on the tent-shaped stone tomb of the Victorian explorer, Sir Richard Burton, at Mortlake.

Historic utilitarian architecture also did not pass ignored in EAHY. The restoration of relics of Britain's nascent industrialism before the " Revolution " like the Elizabethan Kingsbury watermill at St. Albans and the 1632 windmill at Chesterton, Warwickshire, were commended as was the open-air museum at Singleton near Chichester where examples of medieval vernacular housing, stores and a market hall have been reinstated. Industrial buildings that came with the " Revolution ", have become fascinating to an age interested in primitive technology and early " honest " functionalism in design. Maltings, a bleachworks, the Clock Mill of 1817 at Newham, the lighthouse of 1818 at Harwich and the water tower at Kenilworth all have or are to be lovingly saved from decay for EAHY, the last metamorphosed into something akin to Eric Mendelssohn's Einstein Tower. Victorian railway stations have been restored at Huddersfield, Darlington (North Road), Richmond, Yorks, Lisburn Co. Antrim and Monkwearmouth. Industrial museums, following that at Coalbrookdale, have emerged at Bradford, Sheffield and Stoke-on-Trent; and this pattern is being repeated abroad. In Europe industrial archaeology has also come of age: one of the Swedish pilot projects involved ironworks at Engelsberg and a mining village at Falun. EAHY saw interest too focused, in Britain, upon four fairly humble houses of the last century, because of their literary associations: the residences of Keats at Hampstead, Dickens at Portsmouth and Chatham, and D. H. Lawrence at Eastwood, which were all improved or restored. Finally, those unaware of the swing into fashion of English suburbia from the 1920s and 1930s, may be surprised to see included among the holders of Heritage Year Awards a " semi- " 40 Beeches Avenue Carshalton, Surrey: the home of Frank Dickinson (d.1961) a disciple of Voysey and Morris.

Ancient churches have always been close to the English heart and the implications of EAHY were probably discussed in many a parish; for the Church has architectural problems as well as blessings; dwindling congregations for one, leading to the need to dispose of " redundant " churches. Ideas for reuse are legion and EAHY spurred the search for satisfactory solutions. The late medieval St. Mary's Lambeth, and St. Mark's Widcombe (Bath) are to become community centres; two York churches and St. George's, Gt. Yarmouth (early Georgian) are earmarked as arts centres. Holy Trinity, Southwark (of the 1820s) is being transformed into an orchestral rehearsal hall and St. John's, Smith Square, Westminster (of the 1720s) has already become a BBC chamber concert hall. (During the 1975 " Proms " season the very far from redundant and highly impressive St. Augustine's, Kilburn, from the High Victorian period, found an additional use as the perfect venue for a concert of medieval music). Holy Trinity, Colchester serves as a museum of social history, St. Nicholas, Bristol as one on ecclesiology and All Saints, Oxford (c1710) now houses a college library. Not all the several hundred churches declared redundant since 1969 have found a new use, by any means; some like the late medieval St. Nicholas, Gloucester and others still officially consecrated like Christ Church, Spitalfields in East London (c1714) remain in a state of semi-dereliction despite protests connected with EAHY. Major churches at Tunbridge Wells and Maidstone, for example, faced demolition in 1975. The other main problem for The Church also much discussed in EAHY was restoration; even as funds were being sought to finish off cathedrals at Liverpool, Belfast, Portsmouth and Bury St. Edmunds, the custodians of their older counterparts also sought money in order to stave off structural collapse; Canterbury Cathedral has launched an appeal for £3,500,000 and £40,000 is required to reinforce the Perpendicular spire that survived the bombing at the old Coventry Cathedral. Moreover the dilemma is not reserved to the Anglicans; at Bristol, the Roman Catholics have decided to demolish their Victorian cathedral in Clifton while the Methodists are divided on the decision, confirmed in EAHY, to spend £750,000 on restoring Wesley's Chapel, City Road, London. Statistically, also churches run a greater risk from fire than does for example the average home and in the Metropolis alone EAHY was marked by the gutting of historic parish churches at Putney and Streatham.

If the ecclesiastical aspects of conservation presented many problems for EAHY a less troubled field was that of the ruin. A greater concentration in this century on the historic as opposed to the poetic qualities of ruins, on the wall that is well-labelled and remortared rather than crumbling and ivy-covered, has led to the resolve to spend more money than was previously felt necessary, but the fire danger for example is virtually non-existent. For EAHY several aspects of the preservation of ruins were discussed in detail—where only the foundations remained, as with Runcorn Priory and Baynard's Castle near the Thames at Blackfriars—where later ages had abused the remains as at Greyfriars, Gloucester—and finally where the shell has survived intact, as at Southsea Castle.

In the year of confirmation for British entry into The Common Market it was appropriate that the perspective decided on for a year devoted to conservation, should have been European. All seventeen members of the Council of Europe participated; from behind the Iron Curtain, the USSR, Hungary and Poland expressed their solidarity and the nation straddling that great divide, Yugoslavia, presented the ancient town of Dubrovnik, freed of cars and insensitive development, as an exemplar. Even in Western Europe, in Communist-controlled Bologna bold progress was publicised during EAHY, in methods of reconciling our century to the demands of an historic town.

Certainly the greatest architectural disaster at the Year's début was impending not in Britain but in Venice, its façades eroded by chemicals, its foundations undermined by rising waters. There was some comforting news in the Summer from the scientists about the rate of sinkage but the menace of attritive decay from polluted air remains. Through organisations like Britain's " Venice in Peril " in fact European attention has been directed to the plight of this noble Italian city throughout 1975. In addition, via UNESCO, Europeans also expressed concerted anxiety over the fate of one of the architectural wonders of Asia, the complex of temples at Angkor Wat in Cambodia, which fortunately did survive the civil war, relatively unscathed.

The pilot projects run all over Europe were a further means of focusing interest on to given examples; among the centres chosen for such " control " experiments in conservation were Salzburg, Bruges, Nicosia, Elsinore, Rouen, Holycross and Limerick in Ireland, Verona, Luxemburg, Medina (the old Maltese capital), Amsterdam, Stavanger (Norway), Istanbul, Ephesus and three areas in Spain.

Britain certainly can learn from European demonstrations. It was Sweden that first institutionalised the protection of historic buildings in 1643, followed by France in 1840, and it is undeniably instructive to contrast France's Malraux Act of 1962 with British statutes or to compare the conservation campaign at Chester with that at Middelburg in the Netherlands—where there are plans to restore the town centre at the rate of 35 noteworthy buildings a year through a special office. In Czechoslovakia, interestingly, there exists a category of building eligible for protection where the property in question " shows the develop-

ment of society and science ". Moreover Warsaw provides the *locus classicus* of painstaking rebuilding after mass destruction (in its case, the War).

There was a certain unkind irony in the fact that The Year coincided with such economic troubles in Britain; concentration on the buildings of the past becomes easier when the pace of modern examples slackens. Yet paucity of funds hits all buildings, intended or erected, and some authorities could only afford to give nominal recognition to EAHY. It is indeed the case that where renovation was required, economic problems did impede conservation, but there was compensation in the restraints they simultaneously imposed on the far-ranging schemes of " comprehensive development " so much a feature of the 'sixties. The petroleum crisis did have some effect in reducing the difficulties created in historic towns by the motor car. There was the additional unfortunate coincidence of EAHY with the rampages of the virulent Dutch Elm Disease, which bedevilled several landscaping schemes, and of course a good measure of the Ulster effort was merely the repair of bomb damage, occasionally undone again by subsequent outrages. The Year however was certainly of some value. Its messages reached many through television programmes, articles in the local press, conferences, competitions, books and handouts, " Heritage Walks " and even commemorative postage stamps, while its physical impact, admittedly often merely minimal, was at least far flung. All over the country there have been modest schemes: for example, to re-install granite setts, Victorian gas lamps, verandahs and railings and reintroduce the original glazing bars into windows; or repaint and clean façades (and complement the new-found cleanliness by floodlighting); put underground unsightly overhead wires, ban cars from sensitive areas, tidy up church-yards and erect plaques to inform the inquisitive.

There is no denying the attraction of " living history "—well over 2m. visited the Tower of London in 1975; about ½m. were members of the National Trust; EAHY did not create that interest but it has certainly stimulated it and were that public interest to require a further boost 1977 should also prove something of a conservationists' jamboree as the Society for the Protection of Ancient Buildings, the Georgian Group and the Civic Trust celebrate respectively a century, forty and twenty years of campaigning.

THE APOLLO–SOYUZ SPACE LINK-UP

American tourists on the streets of Moscow on the evening of July 17 found themselves swept up and hugged by passing Moscovites. Detente had come to space with the link-up of a U.S. Apollo spacecraft and a Soviet Soyuz spaceship and the symbolic exchange of flags. ASTP—Apollo–Soyuz Test Project—had its origins three years earlier in the Space Agreement signed by President Nixon and Mr. Kosygin. Article 3 had laid down that compatible docking mechanisms should be developed and that 1975 should see astronauts and cosmonauts visiting each others' craft in space. Docking two such dissimilar craft was no simple operation. They differed in size, Apollo being much the larger, in shape, in docking equipment, and even had different atmospheres. Apollo used oxygen at reduced pressure and Soyuz had oxygen and nitrogen at near normal pressure. For the joint flight the Soyuz pressure could be reduced by almost half but there would still have to be an airlock between the craft. The two problems of different docking equipment and the airlock were solved with a docking tunnel, ten feet long and five feet across, designed to join with Apollo at one end and Soyuz at the other and to equalise the two pressures as the spacemen crawled through. The spacemen themselves had to be fluent in each other's language, familiar with the other's procedures and equipment and able to cope with any problem that might occur. After joint training in the U.S.A. and Russia the two commanders were locked up in a simulated spaceship and given, bilingually, twenty difficult problems to solve, which they did within seconds.

The launch of Soyuz 19 from the Baikonur cosmodrome in Central Asia, which set off the operation, was the first Soviet launching to be shown live on television. It could not have been a more successful debut for it was only seven thousandths of a second off schedule at blast-off. The Americans achieved an equally successful launch seven and a half hours later. However, there were difficulties. The television coverage of the Soyuz take-off was interrupted when faults developed with an inboard television camera, but Colonel Alexei Leonov and Flight Engineer Valery Kubasov, the two man crew, dealt with it. For their part the three Americans, Brigadier Thomas Stafford, Vance Brand and Donald Slayton found themselves coping with a more vital problem, a fault in the docking tunnel. This would not have prevented docking but it would have rendered it pointless by preventing any transfer between the two craft. However, with advice from the ground this was also rectified. For two days Apollo overtook and homed on Soyuz, using radar, radio and getting optical guidance from flashing beacons on the Russian craft. First, though, Soyuz had to fire its engines to go into a circular orbit 225 kilometres above the Earth. The orbit it achieved was accurate to within a tenth of one per cent. Early on July 17 the two ships were still 1500 kilometres apart. The distance was reduced rapidly as Apollo moved first into an orbit which kept it at a constant distance below the height of Soyuz and then into one which would intercept it. The final 50 metres was covered under manual control with a U.S. communications satellite relaying progress reports to the control headquarters. There came a slight jolt and a one word comment from Leonov —"Captured"—which signalled success.

The docking took place at 4.09 p.m. GMT. Three hours later Stafford and Leonov were shaking hands across the threshold of Soyuz and giving an elementary display of their linguistic powers. Stafford and Slayton then entered Soyuz, President Ford and Mr Brezhnev sent their congratulatory messages and certificates were signed to claim the first international space flight record. The astronauts and cosmonauts then celebrated with a Soviet-American dinner of bortsch and turkey with cranberry sauce. The two craft remained locked together for almost two days during which time the crews visited each other's craft and carried out joint experiments. After undocking Apollo withdrew and then returned for a second docking in which Soyuz played the active role. The Apollo engines were then fired again to take the craft out of the common orbit in which the spaceships had flown for more than fifty hours. Leonov and Kubasov made their descent, again watched by television viewers around the world, on July 21. A great cloud of fire and dust rising from the Central Russian desert signalled that the braking rockets had fired eight feet above the ground to cushion the landing.

The U.S. astronauts remained in orbit for three more days, making the fullest use of what could be the last manned spaceflight by the U.S.A. this decade. As they came in to splash down, it was announced

that they had made one scientific discovery to excite astronomers. In the last minutes of their experimental work they picked up an unexpectedly intense beam of ultra-violet radiation from a distant star, the first extreme ultra-violet source found outside our solar system. The only bad moment in an almost faultless flight came for the three Americans as they descended. Poisonous nitrogen tetroxide fumes from an outside motor seeped into their craft. Brand lost consciousness and all three, it was reported later, had been in danger of death. They subsequently developed breathing troubles, but these cleared up.

Both crews had been busy with scientific experiments, individually and jointly. One of the more important joint experiments was an artificial eclipse of the Sun, carried out between the first undocking and the second docking. Apollo withdrew on a line between Soyuz and the Sun, covering the Sun's disc and exposing the corona. The eclipse it achieved was better for scientific observations than those rare events which earth-bound astronomers pursue around the globe. The Soyuz observations were made without the interference of the Earth's atmosphere and for longer than the one to two minutes of total eclipse seen on Earth. At the same time Apollo studied Soyuz's own "atmosphere". In space, gases, water and other absorbed substances leave the spacecraft surface. The surface itself is eroded by micrometeors and solar radiation. All this produces a sort of comet's tail around a spaceship which has never been thoroughly examined before but which could affect observations carried out from orbiting observatories. Soyuz's own observations of the Sun were to be corrected, if necessary, in the light of the studies of its own atmosphere. Joint experiments also included the welding of special alloys in weightless conditions in a furnace carried by Apollo, using metallic mixtures brought by Soyuz. Biological experiments included a check on the transfer of microbes in space and one ingenious experiment designed to increase knowledge of biorhythms, the "internal clocks" which, when upset, cause such troubles as "jet lag". Weightlessness also produces biorhythm problems for astronauts. For this experiment a fungus was used which grows rhythmically, in rings like a tree but one a day instead of one a year. Two lots of the same fungus, from America and Russia, with a built-in time difference of nine hours were photographed regularly to see how differently they were affected by space hazards such as radiation, occurring at different times in their cycles.

ASTP was an event of undoubted political significance. Sceptics might doubt whether it was of equal scientific significance or whether it provided material value for the £250,000,000 it was said to have cost. However it did demonstrate the possibility of space rescue, in the event of some future calamity, some of the experiments could only have been carried out on such a joint flight, and it also encouraged hopes of future cooperation of more obvious scientific and economic worth.

LAST TRIAL OF DIETS
Having newly celebrated its double centenary, the institution of the annual Trial of Diets (begun in 1774) was held in 1975 for the final time. On this occasion samples or " scrapings " of gold and silver submitted for hallmarking and sent in by all assay offices outside London were tested chemically at The Royal Mint. In future the operation will be continued but under a measure of decentralisation; in accordance with the Hallmarking Act of 1973 Mr. E. G. V. Newman, The Queen's Assay Master and Chemist and Assayer at the Mint, will inspect each of the assay departments himself.

DRAMATIC SUMMARY, 1974-75

Among London productions between Oct. 1, 1974 and Sept. 30, 1975, were the following:

ADELPHI: (1975) *Apr. 15. A Little Night Music*, with Jean Simmons, Hermione Gingold and Joss Ackland.

ALBERY: (1974) *Nov. 28. What Every Woman Knows*, by J. M. Barrie (Dorothy Tutin, Dorothy Reynolds, Clive Morton and Peter Egan). (1975) *June 16. The Gay Lord Quex*, by Pinero (Judi Dench, Daniel Massey, Sian Phillips and directed by Sir John Gielgud). *Aug. 13. Travesties*, by Tom Stoppard (3 week transfer from the R.S.C. season at the Aldwych).

ALDWYCH: (1974) *Nov. 19. The Marquis of Keith* by Wedekind, directed by Ronald Eyre (Ian McKellen, Ian Richardson and Sara Kestelman). *Dec. 19.* Ian Richardson in Shakespeare's *Cymbeline*. (1975) *Jan. 9.* Shakespeare's *King John* (Emrys James and Ian McKellen. Director: John Barton). *Feb. 5. Twelfth Night* (Nicol Williamson, Frank Thornton, David Waller, Jane Lapotaire and Patricia Hayes). *March 5.* Macbeth (Nicol Williamson and Helen Mirren). World Theatre Season: *March 31.* Cracow Stary Theatre in *November Night* by Wyspianski, directed by Andrzej Wajda. *Apr. 7.* Gothenburg Stadsteater in *Gustav III*, by Strindberg. *Apr. 14.* Trino Buazzelli Company in *Regeneration*, by Svevo and (*Apr. 16*) Ibsen's *Enemy of the People*. *Apr. 21.* Uganda's Batumi Company in *Renga Moi*, by Serumaga. *May 1. Love's Labours Lost*, directed by David Jones (Ian Richardson, Estelle Kohler, Susan Fleetwood, Tony Church and Norman Rodway). *May 29. Travesties*, by Tom Stoppard, director Peter Wood (John Wood, Robert Powell, Meg Wynn Owen and Beth Morris). *July 17. Hedda Gabler*, by Ibsen (Glenda Jackson). *Aug. 19. Jingo*, by Charles Wood, directed by Ronald Eyre. *Sept. 18. The Marrying of Ann Leete*, by Harley Granville-Barker, directed by David Jones.

AMBASSADORS: (1975) *March 7. Grandson of Oblomov*, with Bernard Bresslaw. *Apr. 14. There Goes the Bride.* Transferred from the Criterion. *Sept. 10. Happy as a Sandbag.* A musical by Ken Lee.

APOLLO: (1975) *Apr. 10. A Family and A Fortune*, with Margaret Leighton and Alec Guinness.

CAMBRIDGE: (1975) *Feb. 5. Sankofa Sunshine.* *Feb. 18. Jack the Ripper.* Transferred from Ambassadors. *Apr. 24. The Black Mikado.*

COMEDY: (1974) *Nov. 7. The Pay-Off* (Nigel Patrick, Dulcie Gray, Peter Sallis and Peter Vaughn). (1975) *Apr. 2. The Exorcism*, by Don Taylor (Honor Blackman, Mary Ure, Anna Cropper, Brian Blessed and Ronald Hines). *May 13. A Touch of Spring*, by Samuel Taylor (Hayley Mills, Francis Matthews and Leigh Lawson).

CRITERION: (1974) *Oct. 7. There Goes The Bride*, by Ray Cooney and John Chapman (Bernard Cribbens, Geoffrey Sumner, Terence Alexander, Jane Downs, Bill Pertwee and Peggy Mount). (1975) *Apr. 14.* Marty Brill in *Lenny. June 5. Oh! Coward!* with Geraldine McEwan, Roderick Cook and Jamie Ross. *Aug. 11. Rosencrantz and Guildenstern Are Dead*, by Tom Stoppard, transferred from the Young Vic.

DUKE OF YORK'S: (1974) *Oct. 16. The Little Hut*, by André Roussin (Geraldine McEwan, Gerald Harper and James Villiers). (1975) *Feb. 17.* Anna Neagle, Tony Britton and Alan Gifford in *The Dame of Sark*, by William Douglas-Home. *June 2. Entertaining Mr. Sloane*, transferred from Royal Court.

GARRICK: (1975) *Feb. 3. Aspects of Max Wall.* *March 12. Murderer*, by Anthony Shaffer with

Robert Stephens. *July 23. Absent Friends*, by Alan Ayckbourne, with Richard Briers.

HAYMARKET: (1975) *Feb. 4.* Emlyn Williams as Charles Dickens. *March 10. The Case in Question*, by Ronald Miller and C. P. Snow (John Clements and Zena Walker).

HER MAJESTY'S: (1975) *Apr. 22. Jeeves*, by Alan Ayckbourne and Andrew Lloyd Webber (David Hemmings and Michael Aldridge).

MAYFAIR: (1974) *Dec. 10. An Evening with Hinge and Brackett*, transferred from Theatre Upstairs. (1975) *Apr. 8. Alphabetical Order*, by Michael Frayn with Billie Whitelaw.

MERMAID: (1975) *Apr. 21. The Doctor's Dilemma*, by Shaw. *June 19. The Merry Wives of Windsor.*

OLD VIC: (1974) *Oct. 30.* Jonathan Miller's production of *The Marriage of Figaro. Dec. 3. Grand Manoeuvres*, by A. E. Ellis, directed by Michael Blakemore, with Alan McNaughton. (1975) *Jan. 28.* Ibsen's *John Gabriel Borkman*, directed by Peter Hall (Ralph Richardson, Peggy Ashcroft and Wendy Hiller). *Feb. 25.* Shaw's *Heartbreak House*, directed by John Schlesinger (Eileen Atkins, Colin Blakely, Anna Massey, Paul Rogers and Graham Crowden). *March 13. Happy Days*, by Samuel Beckett (Peggy Ashcroft and Alan Webb). *Apr. 23. No Man's Land*, by Harold Pinter, with John Gielgud and Ralph Richardson. *July 9. The Misanthrope*, by Molière, directed by John Dexter (Diana Rigg and Alec McCowen). *Aug. 7. Engaged*, by W. S. Gilbert. *Sept. 9. Phaedra Britannica*, by Tony Harrison, after Racine's *Phèdre.*

PHOENIX: (1974) *Oct. 23. The Gingerbread Lady*, by Neil Simon, with Elaine Stritch. (1975) *Apr. 10. Norman, is That You?* (Harry Worth, Avril Angers). *May 27. Diary of a Madame*, with Miriam Karlin.

PICCADILLY: (1974) *Oct. 22. The Male of the Species*, by Alan Owen (Edward Woodward and Michele Dotrice). *Dec. 21. The Gentle Hook*, by Francis Durbridge (Dinah Sheridan, Jack Watling and Raymond Francis). (1975) *May 7. The Sunshine Boys*, by Neil Simon, with Jimmy Jewel and Alfred Marks. *July 16. Clarence Darrow*, by David W. Rintels (Henry Fonda).

PRINCE OF WALES: (1975). *Apr. 9.* James Stewart in *Harvey.*

QUEENS: (1974) *Oct. 8. Saturday, Sunday, Monday*, by Eduardo di Filippo (Joan Plowright and Frank Finlay). Directed by Franco Zeffirelli. (1975) *June 18. Ardele*, by Jean Anouilh (Vincent Price, Coral Browne and Charles Gray). *July 30. Otherwise Engaged*, by Simon Gray (Alan Bates).

ROYAL COURT: (1974) *Oct. 9. The Great Caper*, by Ken Campbell (Warren Mitchell). *Nov. 12. The City:* The Tokyo Kid Brothers. (1975) *Jan. 2. Objections to Sex and Violence*, by Caryl Churchill, with Rosemary McHale and Anna Calder-Marshall. *Jan. 29. Not I*, by Samuel Beckett (Billie Whitelaw) and *Statements*, by Athol Fugard (Yvonne Bryceland and Ben Kingsley). *March 4. Don's Party*, by David Williamson directed by Michael Blakemore. *Apr. 17.* Start of the Joe Orton Festival, with *Entertaining Mr. Sloane* (Malcolm McDowell, Beryl Reid and Ronald Fraser). *June 3. Loot* (Jill Bennett and Philip Stone, directed by Albert Finney). *July 16. What The Butler Saw*, directed by Lindsay Anderson. *Sept. 2. Teeth 'N' Smiles*, by David Hare, with Helen Mirren and Dave King.

SAVOY: (1975) *Apr. 29. The Clandestine Marriage* (Alastair Sim, Ron Moody, Dandy Nichols and Ian McKellen). *July 28. Murder at the Vicarage*, by Agatha Christie (Barbara Mullen and Derek Bond).

SHAFTESBURY: (1974) *Dec. 19. West Side Story.*

SHAW: (1974) *Oct. 7. The Taming of the Shrew*

(Susan Hampshire and Nicky Henson). *Dec.* 4. *Old King Cole*, by Ken Campbell. (1975) *Jan.* 8. *The Birthday Party*, by Harold Pinter (John Alderton and Sidney Tafler). *March* 18. *Night Must Fall* by Emlyn Williams (Hywel Bennett). *May* 12. *A Certain Vincent*, with Jules Croiset. *June* 4. Shakespeare's *As You Like It* (Susan Hampshire).

THEATRE UPSTAIRS: (1974) *Oct.* 17. *Lord Nelson Lives in Liverpool 8*, by Philip Martin. *Nov.* 6. *Fourth Day Like Four Long Months of Absence*, by Colin Bennett. *Nov.* 26. *An Evening with Hinge and Brackett. Dec.* 18. *Remember The Truth Dentist*, by Heathcote Williams. (1975) *Feb.* 11. *Mrs. Grabowski's Academy*, by John Antrobus. *March* 7. *Loud Reports*, by John Burrows and John Harding. *March* 26. *The Doomduckers' Ball. Apr.* 28. *Paradise*, by David Lan. *May* 28. *Echoes from a Concrete Canyon*, by Wilson John Haire. *June* 4. *Homage to Bean Soup*, by David Lan. *July* 1. *Heroes*, by Stephen Poliakoff. *July* 3. *Black Slaves, White Chains*, by Mustapha Matura. *July* 28. *Sex and Kinship in a Savage Society*, by Seabrook and O'Neill. *July* 29. *Mean Time*, by Richard Crane.

WYNDHAMS: (1974) *Oct.* 17. *The Dame of Sark*, by William Douglas-Home (Celia Johnson, Tony Britton and Alan Gifford). (1975) *Feb.* 20. Paul Schofield in Shakespeare's *The Tempest. July* 15. *No Man's Land*, transferred from the Old Vic.

Royal Shakespeare Company at Stratford upon Avon: (1975) *Apr.* 8. *Henry V*, directed by Terry Hands (Alan Howard as Henry). *Apr.* 24. *Henry IV, Part I*, with Brewster Mason as Falstaff, Alan Howard as Prince Hal and Emrys James as the King. *June* 24. *Henry IV, Part II* (Brewster Mason, Alan Howard and Emrys James).

CHICHESTER: (1975) *May* 14. *Cyrano de Bergerac*, by Rostand (Keith Michell and Barbara Jefford). *May* 26. *An Enemy of the People* (Donald Sinden, Bill Fraser, Donald Houston and Barbara Jefford). *July* 15. *Made in Heaven* (Patrick McNee and Michael Bates). *July* 29. *Othello* (Topol and Hannah Gordon).

This last year has been a particularly barren one for Theatre. The economic situation in Britain has brought many hardships to it. Increased taxation has hit not only ticket prices, which have rocketed, but also production costs, items like paint, scenery and lights included. The worst blow was found to be Value Added Tax. Finding themselves paying out vast amounts every week in VAT, fairly ordinary shows in the West End were forced to stay open for far longer than would normally be the case in order to clear a profit. When the musical *Jeeves* was taken off prematurely, incurring a large loss, the hint was taken by a lot of people and very soon old favourites were revived like *Godspell*, *Hair* and *Murder at the Vicarage*. Another trend has been to put on plays with small casts and little setting; in the cases of *Aspects* of Max Wall, Emlyn Williams as Charles Dickens and Henry Fonda as the lawyer Clarence Darrow, entirely one-man shows.

Experiment has become almost totally impossible. A wonderful season at the Theatre Upstairs passed seemingly unnoticed as the Royal Court intend to close it for financial reasons. In June the Royal Shakespeare Company warned the owners of the Aldwych that activities there would have to terminate in December if an extra £200,000 was not added to the current grant. The artistic director, Trevor Nunn, outlined the measures he had had to use to try and save his theatre: 30 productions in 1974 were cut to 20 in 1975; he found it necessary to discontinue the existing permanent company-

repertoire system and opt for a cheaper repertory system. Stars like Nicol Williamson and Ian McKellen were engaged to attract audiences and the attempts to create an ensemble were shelved. Williamson was given Macbeth and Malvolio while McKellen (who had a tremendous range of experience in 1975, from the Royal Shakespeare Company to directing Alastair Sim in *The Clandestine Marriage* and appearing in David Rudkin's *Ashes at the Young Vic*) played the Marquis of Keith. All three virtuoso performances were highly imaginative.

The National Theatre saw Peter Hall take over as director and inherit a host of financial and administrative difficulties. His main worry must have been the incompletion of the new complex on the South Bank, the opening date still undecided. Plans for Albert Finney to open there with his first Hamlet were shelved. Mr. Hall still found time to direct a couple of plays himself: *John Gabriel Borkman* and *Happy Days*. Both seemed to mirror the atmosphere of the year at the Old Vic, a reliance on huge, solid, mainly classical pieces (Shaw, Beckett, Ibsen). However, he housed as a great highlight in the year the new Pinter masterpiece, *No Man's Land*. One of our best contemporary playwrights brought us to the stage two wonderful new characters: the rich Hirst played by Ralph Richardson and Spooner (John Gielgud) a minor poet, seedy and dilapidated. Their lives cross and cross and neither can escape from their exitless No Man's Land. The imagery is disturbing, the atmosphere menacing and the acting tremendous.

The Young Vic's production of *Rosencrantz and Guildenstern Are Dead* went to the Criterion, while at their home in The Cut, Frank Dunlop's black magic orientated *Macbeth* was a great success and *Ashes* by David Rudkin brought out some superb acting from Gemma Jones and Ian McKellen as a childless couple. At the Greenwich Theatre, two outspoken playwrights featured highly in the past year's repertoire. Max Wall played Archie Rice, John Osborne's *Entertainer*; a new Osborne play, *The End Of Me Old Cigar* starred Rachel Roberts and Jill Bennett; and Osborne's adaptation of Oscar Wilde's story *The Portrait of Dorian Gray* was followed by Wilde's own *Importance of Being Earnest*, directed by Jonathan Miller and featuring Irene Handl as a frumpish Prussian Lady Bracknell.

The Royal Shakespeare Company's production of Tom Stoppard's latest play *Travesties* was one of the hits of the year; it was brought back by public demand for a nine-week-only run before it visited Broadway. It is an intellectual and witty farce, funny on a variety of levels. John Wood played the lead, Henry Carr, a retired diplomat, while famous historical figures, James Joyce, Lenin, Tristan Tzara, litter the cast list. They are together in Zürich during the First World War, and are used by Stoppard to put over some valuable ideas on the role of the artist in society. Another notable London production was a most magical interpretation of *Twelfth Night*, with Jane Lapotaire enchanting as Viola. At Stratford, the Centenary play was *Henry the Fifth*, a good choice, to which Terry Hands brought its splendour and also a lot of his own originality. Alan Howard playing Henry saw him as a king very much in need of personal comfort, knowing that he must face a terrible situation without it.

Some outstanding performances have been Paul Schofield's Prospero in *The Tempest*, Alec Guinness as Uncle Dudley in *A Family and A Fortune* and Marty Brill as Lenny (Bruce).

LITERATURE OF THE YEAR

Jane Austen was born 200 years ago on December 16, 1775, and when she died in 1817, she left eleven chapters of an unfinished novel, which was known to her family as *Sanditon*, although it has been said that she had intended to call it *The Brothers*. The fragment was published in 1925, but it has now been completed, and published as *Sanditon* by Jane Austen and Another Lady, the anonymity of the new author reflecting that which Jane Austen sought for her own work in her lifetime. Whilst aspiring to her style, the finished work lacks her inspiration, but is a competent attempt at completion from the characters and clues given, in the pattern of the previous novels. Although considered a sacrilege by some Austen devotees, it has been generally well received.

Charles Kingsley, eminent theologian, historian, social reformer, poet and novelist died on January 23, 1875, but is now best remembered for *The Water Babies*, and the Devon village named after one of his novels. His centenary has been marked by the publication of several works. In *The Beast and The Monk* Susan Chitty has been fortunate in having access to some unpublished sketches of Kingsley's, 300 letters and a diary of Mrs. Kingsley's, which are remarkable for their intimacy. The letters to Fanny Grenfell, later his wife, reveal Kingsley's suppressed sexuality struggling against Victorian restraints, and moreover revelling in it, and finding expression in his mildly erotic drawings, with rigorous self-imposed scourgings to cleanse his impure thoughts. Without doubt, Kingsley's life and works will be seen in a different light as a result of these revelations, and it appears that he meant it to be so. It is thus unfortunate that Brenda Colloms, who has written a competent centenary biography in *Charles Kingsley*, has not had access to the new material, for her work has thus been more than overshadowed by that of Lady Chitty.

John Buchan, first Baron Tweedsmuir, was born on September 26, 1875. He reached distinction in several fields, notably as Director of Information under the Prime Minister in the First World War, and in 1935 as Governor-General of Canada, but his books are his lasting memorial. Buchan was as prolific as his interests were varied. He wrote short stories, poetry, historical romances, thrillers such as *The Thirty-Nine Steps*, biographies including his excellent life of Sir Walter Scott, and even had time in 1905 to write on *The Taxation of Foreign Income*. In *The Interpreter's House: A Critical Assessment of John Buchan*, David Daniell has examined in detail all Buchan's works, and convincingly demonstrates his skills and achievements. His centenary was also marked by an exhibition of books and manuscripts in the National Library of Scotland.

JOHNSON AND BOSWELL.—*Samuel Johnson* by John Wain, Professor of Poetry at Oxford, is a successful attempt to discover the real Johnson as opposed to " The Great Cham of Literature ", or the figure presented by Boswell. Addressed to " the intelligent general reader ", it is a fine analysis of Johnson's genius, and the creation of his great works, notably his *magnum opus*, the *Dictionary of the English Language* and his excellent ten volumes of *Lives of the Poets*, and fills a large gap in Johnson scholarship. The man is presented in all his aspects, and is revealed as an interesting, benevolent and compassionate figure. Boswell in comparison is a minor writer and figure, whose fame was gained at Johnson's expense. More interesting than the man is the saga of his literary archives, and in *The Treasures of Auchinleck, The Story of the Boswell Papers*, David Buchanan relates the intriguing, and

as yet incomplete, story of the hunt for the large collection of manuscripts, documents, letters and journals which Boswell had accumulated at his Scottish home, Auchinleck, during his lifetime. After his death, it was long assumed that the collection had been burned, but in fact it had been widely dispersed, from Malahide Castle to Kincardine. When eventually the existence of some of the papers became known, an American, Colonel Ralph Isham, dedicated himself to an obsessive, twenty-five year search to find and buy all the papers, in order to recreate the collection for the Library at Yale. In this he largely succeeded, but the correspondence between Boswell and Johnson is still undiscovered.

LITERARY LIVES.—Thomas Hardy ensured that most of his letters and documents were destroyed, so that the biographical details known about him should be those of which he approved. His official biography, *The Early Life of Thomas Hardy, 1840–1891* and *The Later Years of Thomas Hardy, 1892–1928*, supposedly by his second wife Florence, was in fact written by Hardy himself. In *Young Thomas Hardy*, Robert Gittings has scrupulously tracked down Hardy's background and early life from official records, newspapers, letters, diaries and discussions with surviving relatives, from which it would appear that his secretiveness was more than a passion for privacy, but symptomatic of his shame for his humble origins, which he considered a handicap when he became successful.

In *The Tennysons: Background to Genius*, Sir Charles Tennyson and Hope Dyson write of the forbears of Alfred, Lord Tennyson, and his eleven brothers and sisters. The family were conspicuous for their talents, for apart from Alfred, his two elder brothers Frederick and Charles were noted poets; for their eccentricities, which in the case of Edward at least veered into insanity, and caused him to spend 60 years in an asylum; and their longevity, the Tennysons being credited with " weak health and strong constitutions ". Sir Charles himself was in his 96th year when this book was published.

In *Laurence Sterne: the Early and Middle Years*, Arthur H. Cash has written an excellent account of the early life of the author of the comic masterpiece, *The Life and Opinions of Tristram Shandy*. Extensively researched, it portrays the Reverend Mr. Sterne as a somewhat irreverent figure, who late in life discovered a talent for satire in his *Political Romance*, which soon became transformed to comic genius in his great novel. It is pleasing to note that Sir Joshua Reynolds' marvellous portrait of Sterne has now been sold to the National Portrait Gallery.

Wilfred Owen was killed a week before the Armistice in 1918 in a bold but futile military action. Jon Stallworthy has written an excellent biography entitled simply *Wilfred Owen*; the poems are treated perceptively, with the manuscripts reproduced in the text where appropriate. It becomes evident that Owen was not merely a soldier inspired to poetry by the horror of war, but a poet who became great when he found in war a subject to match his unique talent.

Other literary figures to be the subject of major biographies during the year were William Faulkner and Evelyn Waugh. In *Faulkner: A Biography*, Joseph Blotner has written a massive work in two volumes, of some 2,000 pages, examining in minute detail the life and works of one of America's most distinguished novelists. Christopher Sykes knew Evelyn Waugh from 1930 until his death, and in *Evelyn Waugh: A Biography*, he writes affectionately but not uncritically about one of the great English writers.

THREE EDWARDS.—Edward IV was unique as the only English King to lose and then regain his crown, and for his failure to establish his elder son's succession. Much maligned, the benefits of his reign have often been overlooked, and the shortage of contemporary accounts has hindered a fair assessment. However Dr. Charles Ross has written what seems certain to become the standard life. His *Edward IV* is a reappraisal of the reign and achievements of a complex figure, and shows that Edward was a popular, if avaricious monarch, sound in politics and finance, whose main achievement was to restore the prestige of the monarchy after Henry VI.

Much more is known of Edward VII, but in a fascinating study entitled *Uncle of Europe: the Social and Diplomatic Life of Edward VII*, Gordon Brook-Shepherd has drawn on unpublished diaries, papers and letters of families the King knew, notably of the Marquis de Soveral, better known as " The Blue Monkey ", and Sir Ernest Cassel, and he has unearthed much new information. Edward is shown as both playboy and politician, a sympathetic character and an influential statesman, who on his own initiative, whether it was on his triumphant State Visits to Lisbon, Rome and Paris in 1903, or during his regular sojourns at Marienbad and Biarritz, led European diplomacy as surely as he dominated European society. In *The King, the Press and the People: A Study of Edward VII*, Kinley Robey has analysed contemporary accounts to examine the attitude of the Press to Edward throughout his life, his impact on the age and the influence of the press in shaping his relationship with the nation.

Edward VIII is best remembered for his abdication. Over the years his reputation has been inflated, and he has achieved a stature undeserved by his actions or on merit. In *Edward VIII*, Frances Donaldson shows clearly that Edward was totally unsuited to the role of constitutional monarch. Although he undoubtedly possessed charm, he was of nervous disposition and always immature in outlook. During the Abdication crisis, the magnitude of his actions was beyond his comprehension, and he demonstrated a lack of judgment that was often reflected elsewhere, notably in his attitude to Nazi Germany. It is significant that Baldwin, who has been considered by some the villain of the Abdication, is here shown as tactful and sympathetic throughout in his dealings with Edward, who by contrast was often remarkably callous in his treatment of his friends.

WRITTEN OUT OF REPUTATION.—One man whose reputation has not been posthumously enhanced is Lord Reith. *The Reith Diaries*, edited by Charles Stuart, have come as a surprise to those who knew him. Reith asked for suggestions as to what use he should make of his diaries, when he advertised their existence in *The Times* in 1961. He was ill-advised to publish them. Reith was first general-manager and director-general of the B.B.C., which he left in 1938, apparently to his everlasting regret. His later posts included Minister of Works and Buildings in the war-time cabinet of Churchill, whom he hated, and Chairman of Imperial Airways, but Reith was an egotistical megalomaniac, never satisfied with the job he had and always waiting for the summons that never came to a post that would match his own estimate of his talents. His diaries show him to be petty and narrow-minded in the extreme, always full of bitter resentment for what he felt to be his failures, and hatred for those whom he judged to have blocked his ambitions. As he said of himself in a rare moment of self-

analysis, he was a man " stifled and strangled and submerged by the pettiness of (his) own preoccupations ".

From *Thurber: A Biography* by Burton Bernstein, it becomes apparent that the man is best remembered by his writings and drawings, notable for their comic fantasy, for his life was grim in contrast, from his loss of an eye at the age of 6, to his blindness in later years, and his frequent drinking bouts.

CHURCHILL.—The fourth volume of the official biography of Churchill was published during the year. *Winston S. Churchill, Vol. IV: 1917–1922* by Martin Gilbert begins with Churchill's return to office in 1917 as Minister of Munitions, followed by the posts of Secretary of State for War and for the Colonies; it ends with his removal from Parliament in 1922, with the loss of the seat he had held at Dundee since 1908, his campaign being conducted by his wife as he was ill with appendicitis. As in previous volumes, Churchill's actions are fully recorded throughout, in a detailed and fair analysis, one of the dominant themes to emerge being Churchill's hatred of the Bolsheviks.

Also published was *Poor, Dear Brendan: the Quest for Brendan Bracken* by Andrew Boyle. Bracken was one of public life's great enigmas. At the age of 20, the Irish-born Bracken presented himself at Sedbergh, with a bag of sovereigns, purporting to be a 15-year-old Australian orphan. He left after two terms, and following a spell as a master at a preparatory school, he progressed from Member of Parliament to Minister of Information, director of a publishing house and Viscount. A life-long friend and confidant of Churchill, and companion of Beaverbrook, Bracken the man begins to emerge from his self-imposed shroud of obscurity in this well-researched biography. There are unlikely to be further significant revelations, as Bracken's private papers were destroyed after his death at his command. Also published was *Roosevelt and Churchill: their Secret Wartime Correspondence*, edited by Francis L. Loewenheim, Harold D. Langley and Manfred Jonas.

IN GENERAL.—Field Marshal Leberecht von Blücher was an eccentric whose shortcomings off the field of battle became positive virtues on it. Tough, fearless, impetuous and often drunk, he was an inspired and inspiring cavalry commander who hated the French and fought them for twenty years, fighting nine battles against Napoleon. Roger Parkinson has written the first full-length biography of this bizarre Prussian General in *The Hussar General: The Life of Blücher, Man of Waterloo*, so entitled because his timely intervention in that battle, following a forced march after a severe defeat at Ligny, gave Wellington the extra power needed to make his victory decisive.

In contrast, General Sir Hubert Gough was a model of restraint, notably when he was made the scapegoat and dismissed from his command following the Fifth Army's strategic retreat in 1918; faced by the final offensive of Ludendorff's numerically superior forces, retreat was inevitable. Gough's conduct was not questioned, but an official enquiry was never held, and he was not exonerated until he was awarded the G.C.B. by George VI in 1937. *Goughie: the Life of General Sir Hubert Gough* is a perceptive account of the life of a popular and respected soldier by Anthony Farrar-Hockley, himself a major-general. The author has drawn on unpublished private letters and War Office and Cabinet Papers.

The Marquess of Anglesey has written his second volume of *A History of the British Cavalry*. Dealing with the years 1851 to 1871, the main events covered in this definitive and well-researched work are the Crimean War and the Indian Mutiny, in which the role of the cavalry is explored. Also published during the year were *A Concise History of the British Army* by Major C. J. D. Haswell and *A Military History of Germany: From the Eighteenth Century to the Present Day* by Martin Kitchen. In *Where Soldiers Fear to Tread* Captain Ranulph Fiennes describes his two year secondment to the forces of the Sultan of Oman. *Destroyer Captain* by Roger Hill relates the author's experiences in command of destroyers during the Second World War, and his participation in some of the most important naval actions of the War. In *The German Occupation of the Channel Islands* Charles Cruickshank examines that controversial period in the Islands' history. He justifies the policy of passive resistance to the occupying forces as saving unnecessary bloodshed, as did England's demilitarization of the Islands, and the decision not to attempt to recapture them. It is apparent that Hitler had seriously over-estimated their strategic importance, and wasted valuable manpower and resources on them.

A Kind of Survivor is the autobiography of Guy Chapman, so called because, having served throughout the First World War, he thereafter saw himself as " Essentially, on the deepest level of my being . . . a survivor of the 13th battalion of the Royal Fusiliers ". His varied life included reading for the bar, publishing, writing, taking a degree at the London School of Economics at the age of 41 and becoming Professor of History at Leeds University.

Judge Leon is perhaps better known as the author Henry Cecil. However, in *Just Within the Law: Memories and Reminiscences* the two roles are combined, and Henry Cecil Leon offers his views on the law and the legal system. As always he writes well, and comes across as an interesting person and compassionate judge.

OXFORD.—*The Oxford Book of Literary Anecdotes*, edited by James Sutherland, is a splendidly amusing and interesting compendium of some 500 anecdotes by and about the famous figures of English literature. *The Oxford Companion to Sports and Games*, edited by John Arlott, contains more than 5,000 entries, including main entries for more than 200 sports and games from aquabobbing to yachting, with biographies of leading players, individual entries for important events, clubs and venues, and copious illustrations. The Companion is too wide ranging for the average spectator, but too perfunctory for the specialist. Although it provides enough information to make a game comprehensible, it is not detailed enough to enable a game to be played.

WODEHOUSE.—P. G. Wodehouse was knighted and died at the age of 93. Before his death, yet another of his inimitable Jeeves novels was published. *Aunts Aren't Gentlemen* is the usual excellently crafted concoction, involving Bertie Wooster, his Aunt Dahlia, Jeeves, a cat and a couple of racehorses. In the hermetic world Wodehouse created, the present rarely intruded, and although Bertie mentions muggings in New York, and gets involved with a left-wing Vanessa, to whom he had once proposed marriage, it is evident that time had stood still for Wodehouse and his characters since the turn of the century. *P. G. Wodehouse: A Portrait of a Master* by David A. Jasen shows that apart from the infamous Berlin broadcasts, which although tactless were hardly traitorous, Wodehouse led a dull life. However as a humorous writer and craftsman he was unmatched in a writing career that spanned over 70 years.

CRIME.—Dick Francis has followed a distinguished career as a National Hunt jockey, where his failure to win the 1956 Grand National

on Devon Loch would have taxed the powers of many of his characters, with an even more successful career as a writer of thrillers. His latest novel *Knock Down* confirms his reputation; well-written, with the finely-observed racing background that is his hallmark, it concerns a bloodstock agent whose honesty makes him unpopular with other dealers.

Sherlock Holmes has been the inspiration behind several recent novels. In the ingenious *A Three Pipe Problem* by Julian Symons, a television actor who portrays Holmes becomes obsessed with the character, and takes on his mantle to solve three murders. *The Seven Per Cent Solution* by Nicholas Meyer purports to be a manuscript written by Doctor Watson in 1939, which relates Holmes's involvement with Sigmund Freud, and is a clever and entertaining novel. In *The Return of Moriarty*, John Gardner has Holmes's arch adversary alive and continuing his life of crime, having survived the struggle that had originally been supposed to have led to the death of both of them.

Dame Agatha Christie has released for publication a novel written thirty years ago, concerning Poirot's last case. Entitled *Curtain*, it places the little Belgian detective, now sick and dying, with his faithful old companion Captain Hastings, back in the Essex country house where they made their debut in 1920 in *The Mysterious Affair at Styles*. A classic in the genre, it was written when Dame Agatha was at the peak of her powers. It is reported that at the same time she also wrote Miss Marple's last case, both novels originally having been intended for publication after her death.

REMARKABLE FEET.—In her *Autobiography*, Dame Margot Fonteyn relates modestly how the girl born Margaret Hookham in 1919 became one of the greatest ever ballerinas. She declares that her " happiest moments on stage have been in ballets by Frederick Ashton ", and she writes frankly of her marriage, the shooting of her husband in 1964 and his subsequent paralysis, and her relations with Nureyev. Also published was *Ballerina: Portraits and Impressions of Nadia Nerina*, edited by Clement Crisp, which contains excellent photographs, with short pieces by Nerina and others.

AT SEA.—*The Walkabouts* by Mike Saunders is a humorous and affectionate tale of the 18-month voyage of himself and his wife and their four young children from Rhodesia to England in a 33 foot ketch. Dougal Robertson, author of *Survive the Savage Sea*, in which he described how he and his family survived 38 days in the Pacific in a nine-foot dinghy after their yacht was sunk by whales, has crystallized what he learned from the experience in *Sea Survival*, a manual designed to enable others to survive a similar disaster.

FICTION.—With the publication of the twelfth volume, *Hearing Secret Harmonies*, Anthony Powell has now completed his mammoth enterprise *A Dance to the Music of Time*, which he initiated in 1951 with *A Question of Upbringing*. The whole sequence is skilfully and plausibly brought up to date, and its consistently high quality, in style and content, and its humour and richness of invention will ensure its place as one of the great works of English literature.

Richard Adams, author of the widely-acclaimed bestseller *Watership Down*, has published his second novel. Entitled *Shardik*, it is a lengthy mythical fantasy of less immediate appeal than his first book, but obviously a product of the same fertile imagination. Concerning a giant bear, taken on his appearance among the Ortelgan people to be a long-awaited god reincarnate, the novel describes the effect of the bear Shardik on these people, and in particular on the hunter Kelderek who captured him.

SCIENCE, DISCOVERY AND INVENTION IN 1975

International cooperation in science is one of the more heartening features of the 'seventies. In 1975 it provided the biggest scientific news of the year with the link-up of American astronauts and Soviet cosmonauts in the Apollo-Soyuz mission which brought spaceflight back to newspapers and television screens in the biggest possible way (*See* Topics of the Day). That was undoubtedly the most glamorous and expensive example of scientific and technological cooperation so far, but it was still just one expression of a general trend. Hopefully, at least as important for mankind, ultimately, as U.S.-Soviet space cooperation, is U.S.-Soviet cooperation in cancer research. An agreement to extend this was reached during the year and the *communiqué* emphasized that the results would be available to cancer research workers in all countries. To doctors, too, for the research was concerned not only with the "science" of pure research into the origins of the cancerous cell, genetic, virological, environmental or whatever it might be, but the "technology" of treatment of the disease. Breast cancer was singled out for one joint project to be started. Cancer experts also hoped for useful results from an epidemiological study of the disease in the two countries. With two such large populations, both enjoying close medical scrutiny, such a study should disclose or throw fresh light on many factors of environment and life-style important in the disease. Fishery research, climatological research, geological research, rheumatology and pollution were among the other areas where U.S.-Soviet cooperation received extra impetus during the year. One other, of especial interest to some British scientists,

was in transport. Russian and American engineers began working out a joint programme for research into very high speed railways using linear motors—a subject in which Britain led the world until the main work was abruptly stopped in 1974 for lack of money.

Britain has had an important share in the development of East-West scientific cooperation. In a sense it can be said to have started here, springing from a meeting between Russian and British nuclear physicists which took the subject of fusion research off the top secret list and made it into perhaps the prime example of international cooperation for the benefit of mankind. Anglo-Soviet cooperation now extends from such fields as nuclear power to the study of Man's past—an Anglo-Soviet symposium on archaeology took place at Cambridge. One outcome of a meeting between Mr. Wilson and Mr. Brezhnev was the publication of a most detailed programme for extending scientific and technological research.

The benefits of two way exchange in medicine were experienced during the year by a Russian "blue" baby and a 7-year-old Northumberland girl, threatened with blindness. The Russian baby suffered from a heart defect which British surgeons are especially skilled in treating and was successfully operated on in London. The Northumberland girl suffered from pigmentary dystrophy of the retina, a condition caused by disruption in the structure of the genes. It is the largest single cause of blindness and is generally regarded as incurable. The girl was taken to Moscow where a technique had been devised of introducing into an affected person nucleic acids which are missing because of the genetic defect. She returned with an encouraging improvement in her sight.

East-West technological cooperation, hardly to be thought about when the North Atlantic Treaty Organization was founded, is now a fitting subject for a Nato conference, to be held in 1976, and for a survey in its journal *Nato Review*. In that survey Prof. Edwin Mansfield, of the University of Pennsylvania, pointed to the cost of "going it alone" in rivalry, a spending of 21 billion (U.S.) dollars by the Soviet Union and of 25 billion by the U.S.A. on research and development in 1970, much of it military spending resulting from the days when cooperation was nil and competition everything.

Spaceflight

Expense has singled out spaceflight as the most suitable field for cooperation for some years. Smaller or less wealthy countries have been providing specialist scientific experiments for the satellites of the two super-powers or even whole satellites to be launched on American or Russian

rockets. That sort of cooperation chalked up at least a minor triumph and possibly one of considerable importance, when the British Aerial 5 satellite, launched on an American rocket, picked up X-ray signals from 30,000 light years away on the X-ray telescope it carried. When telescopes on the ground were pointed in that direction they picked up a second star pulsating at a strange frequency, too slow for a pulsar, too fast for a normal binary star system. One suggestion was that what had been located was a double system of stars denser than any found before, possibly a white dwarf revolving around a black hole, the X-rays resulting from the black hole tearing matter out of the white dwarf.

Perhaps significantly in a year when there were launch windows for sending probes to both Venus and Mars the Americans occupied themselves solely with Mars and the Russians with Venus. At a cost of 850 million dollars to mount and run, an American project to land an automatic laboratory on Mars to seek out any traces of life was undoubtedly the most expensive unmanned space venture the country had undertaken. Originally the plan was to send two Viking craft, each of which would divide into an "Orbiter" and a "Lander" after reaching the vicinity of the planet. The Orbiter would map the surface of Mars and carry out studies of its atmosphere, seeking information on water concentration, surface temperatures, clouds, dust storms and the shape and colour of surface features. The Lander would study the physical, chemical, magnetic and seismological features of the planet from its surface, also its biological features if it has any. The search for life would not be directed at finding intelligent Martians, builders of the famous "canals", now known to be just natural surface features, but primitive organisms or even the basic molecules of life which might exist below the surface. To do this the Lander has devices to dig up soil samples for analysis in the craft's own Laboratory, the resultant information to be radioed back to Earth. This laboratory, one cubic foot in size, crammed with 40,000 parts though weighing only 25 pounds, cost £25,000,000 to develop. Originally it had been hoped to launch the first Viking on August 11 for it to land on July 4, 1976, the 200th anniversary of the Declaration of Independence, and the official bicentenary of the United States. It would have been followed by a second Viking to land in August. Mechanical and electrical trouble meant the launch was delayed and the first spacecraft had to be removed from its rocket and replaced by the second. It was launched ten days late but it was hoped still to make the celebratory landing on the anniversary day. The Russian craft was the ninth in the series of Venus probes. The little information given at its launch—

ing, in June, indicated that it was intended to land and had a toughened version of the instrument package which Venus 8 put on the surface three years before, one able to survive the intense heat and pressure on the Venusian surface for longer than the fifty minutes that Venus 8 endured.

One planetary probe which had proved a resounding success was the American Mariner 10. This made its third close approach to the planet Mercury since it was launched in November 1973. It had then passed close to Venus and been swung by the gravitational pull of the planet into an orbit which took it near to Mercury every six months. Ground controllers had again been able to manoeuvre it close enough to the planet in 1975 for photographs to be taken, though this would be the last time because fuel for the probe's engines had been exhausted. While things worked perfectly in the probe after a journey of hundreds of millions of miles a fault in the ground receiver meant that 75 per cent. of the image in the 500 photographs transmitted did not appear. Another example of spacecraft longevity was shown by the Russian Luna 22 which had been orbiting the Moon for over a year. Its engines were fired again to bring it swooping to within 18 miles of the surface for pictures to be taken. It was then transferred back into a more suitable orbit for its other experiments.

ANTIPODEAN WEATHER UPSET.—The one thing on which Northern Hemisphere meteorologists seem to be agreed is that the weather is getting cooler. Some, looking further ahead, predict a new ice age. Others, with their thoughts closer to the present, say that current problems, such as the southward spread of Saharan conditions, bringing widespread drought to countries such as Ethiopia, Mediterranean weather stretching into North Africa and a general cooling of northern Europe, indicate that weather bands are being squeezed towards the Equator. Something similar should be happening in the Southern Hemisphere.

Climatic data from the South is in much shorter supply than that from the North, simply because there is less land with fewer people on it to carry out weather checks. Two New Zealanders, Dr. M. J. Salinger and Dr. J. M. Gunn, of Otago University, reported in *Nature* conclusions from an analysis of weather reports during this century which could cause rethinking of theories about climatic change. New Zealand is a good base for studying the circulation of the atmosphere. Its long, narrow islands stretch over a broad belt of latitude, from 34 degrees to 47 degrees South, and, for good measure, Drs. Salinger and Gunn included reports from Campbell Island, a further five degrees to the South. Also the basic atmospheric circulation and, therefore, the weather pattern of the South, is unaffected by any nearby continental land mass. The records showed that during the first part of this century New Zealand experienced a climatic decline, the weather was then the worst recorded in the country and the temperatures the lowest. From 1935, the weather has improved until today the country is enjoying its warmest spell since temperature measurements began. This is almost exactly the opposite of the experience in the Northern Hemisphere. Far from the Southern Hemisphere undergoing the same " squeezing-up " of climate bands as the North, it seems that the weather bands move in the same direction, north or south, in both hemispheres.

BETTER X-RAYS.—A new British machine for taking pictures of the soft interior of the body was described as the greatest advance in diagnostic aids since the discovery, itself, of X-rays. The only problem, apparently, was whether the British National Health Service would be able to afford it or would just have to watch enviously as the machine was exported to wealthier countries. Conventional medical X-rays give good pictures of hard objects, such as bones and metallic interlopers in the body. To have his internal organs shown up, though, the patient has to swallow, or have injected, some chemical which is opaque to X-rays. Probably the best known of the many methods devised for doing this is the barium meal. All, however, have their unpleasant if not outright dangerous disadvantages and none is entirely satisfactory. To have his kidneys, liver, intestines, and so on, revealed with the new technique, the patient simply stands in front of the machine. Instead of the usual single beam of X-rays passing through his body several hundred small beams converge from all sides. Changes in the beams are detected by sensitive crystals, instead of photographic film, and their information is fed into a computer to produce an accurate picture of the interior of the body. Despite the number of beams the total X-ray dose is said to be low.

The machine, developed by EMI laboratories at Hayes, Middlesex, had been expected since EMI introduced, three years ago, a similar scanner for examination of the brain. This has already revolutionized diagnosis of brain disease in specialist units and won EMI orders worth more than £27,000,000 from all parts of the world. So far, though, the NHS has lagged behind in acquiring brain scanners, largely because of the cost. There are fewer than ten in Britain but almost 200 in North America.

BEYOND PLUTO.—The astronomical debate on whether or not there are other planets beyond the orbit of Pluto could be resolved by evidence from a comet within the next decade, a leading Soviet specialist on celestial mechanics reported. Professor Gleb Chebotaryov of the Institute of Theoretical Astronomy in Leningrad reported that he had become convinced of the existence of a Transplutonian planet after carrying out a series of computer calculations dealing with the comet listed in astronomical references as 1862–3. The parameters of the orbit showed clearly that it was drawn to a planetary body. Its reappearance, in 1982, should show if his conclusions are right. According to those calculations there is one planet beyond Pluto about the same size as the Earth but 54 times more distant from the Sun. There is also indirect existence of another twice as big as Earth and a hundred times as far from the Sun.

BIGGEST TELESCOPE.—The world's biggest telescope, a 240 inch Russian reflector, began functioning on Mount Pastukhov, nearly 7,000 feet above sea level in the North Caucasus. From the first design work to completion had taken fifteen years. The BTA, as it is called, for "big telescope, azimuthal", is a full 40 inches larger in diameter than the Mount Palomar instrument in California, the biggest for a quarter of a century, with 50 per cent. more light gathering capacity, and 90 inches bigger, with 2½ times the light capacity, than the joint Anglo-Australian instrument in New South Wales. While design work was still in progress, expeditions had been sent out from the Pulkovo Observatory in Leningrad to find the best place to mount it. Possible sites had been assessed in the Crimea, Pamirs, Eastern Siberia, Kazakhstan and the Far East as well as in the Caucasus. The Mt. Pastukhov site was chosen primarily for its climatic suitability. The mountain top enjoys over a hundred cloudless days a year with very little atmospheric turbulence. Wind velocities are low and there are no airfields nor industrial establishments in the area to interfere with seeing conditions. The designer, Bagrat Ioannisiani, chose an azimuthal mounting, rather than the normal equatorial mounting, because of the great weight of the telescope, over 850 tons and several times that of other giant telescopes. An azimuthal mount requires a much more complicated system of rotating the instrument but to offset this computer control enables objects to be located and tracked automatically. The BTA has a focal length of just over 79 feet and so a prime focus of F_4, carrying an observer's cell at the prime focus, the first Soviet telescope to do so. Twenty eight tons of glass had to be pulverized and removed from the great pyrex disc used for the mirror in the process of grinding and polishing. For comparison, just under a ton was removed in the making of Britain's 90 inch Isaac Newton telescope, itself no mean feat. From all reports, moving the 42 ton completed mirror demanded as much care and effort as making it. It had to be taken 2,000 miles from where it was made near Moscow, protected all the time against temperature fluctuations and the slightest vibration, the last stage being along a narrow winding, mountain road. The observatory, named the Special Astrophysical Observatory of the Soviet Academy of Sciences, also houses a giant radio telescope.

A few months earlier the 150 inch Anglo-Australian telescope went into regular operation at Siding Spring Mountain in New South Wales, a site also chosen for its natural advantages and for the absence of human industrial interference. This was the first of the modern giants to be established south of the Equator and so able to study the important objects in the southern sky, including the centre of our own galaxy, out of sight of northern instruments. The first moves to build a giant Southern Hemisphere telescope were taken in 1960 but a firm decision by the Australian and United Kingdom Governments was not made until 1967—the actual building was completed in seven and a half years. The telescope was based on the design for the 150 inch instrument at Kitts Peak, Arizona, completed in 1974, itself based on the Mount Palomar 200 inch. Both retain the horseshoe mounting and the prime focus observer's cage which are features of the Palomar instrument. Stiffening of the horseshoe and computer controlled tracking are said to have made it possible to point the telescope with extreme accuracy. Construction work was shared between Grubb Parsons of Newcastle, and the Japanese firm of Mitsubishi. The mirror, part of the Grubb Parsons share, was made from Cervit, a synthetic, low-expansion, quartz-like material and the total error in the final figuring was so small it was said it would have been a creditable achievement for a ten inch flat mirror, let alone a 150 inch in the hyperboloid form chosen. It is one of the two or three best large mirrors ever made. Apart from that it has the benefit of modern instrumentation which would enable a 50 inch telescope today to outperform a 150 inch telescope of the 1960's.

BRITISH ASSOCIATION.—The belief that material progress comes automatically with scientific discovery is one of the tragic myths of our age, Sir Bernard Lovell told members of the British Association in his presidential address to the 138th annual meeting in Guildford. Continuing the recent tendency of eminent scientists to discuss the rationale and ethos of science—with heartsearchings rather than unquestioning optimism about its worth to mankind—Sir Bernard stated that he had changed his position in the debate about the responsibility of the scientist. Though he would neither say that science was a magic wand nor a poisoned arrow he

did not believe, as he had in the past, that it was neutral in its impact. Through technology it was an immensely powerful force, for evil as well as for good. He gave as an instance the researches into the structure of the atom. Half a century ago it was just an advance, a tremendous one, in Man's search for pure knowledge. Within a few years the technological application of this new knowledge produced the weapons that destroyed Nagasaki and Hiroshima. At the same time, though, the development of rockets to carry bombs led to Man's triumphal progress in the exploration of space.

"Today the delicacy of the balance for good or evil these devices establish paralyses the imagination," he said. "As in war, so in peace. But today the distress of the human spirit is enhanced not merely by the inequalities amongst the peoples of the world but especially by our failure to achieve the integration of science to meet this challenge. The mind of man is adrift and the peoples of the civilized world derive their satisfactions from activities that are so often alien to, and destructive of, both the physical and intellectual environment. We have deluded ourselves that through science we find the only avenue to true understanding about nature and the universe. We have persuaded the society in which we work to support our activities in the belief that our discoveries will inevitably, in some way, be of practical benefit."

Science was a powerful and vital human activity but people were now bewildered and confused about the motives of scientists. The present antagonisms of society to scientific activity could deepen further, he warned.

He illustrated the conflict of interests with the latest attempts to explore Earth's neighbouring planets, then under way, the Russian probes on their way to land on Venus and the American attempt to reach Mars, which had as their primary objectives the search for life. It was sad and ironical that this search for life elsewhere in the universe stemmed from the development of weapons to destroy life here. Just as it was not peaceful endeavour in either the U.S. or the U.S.S.R. which had given men the power to launch scientific instruments into space, so it should not be imagined that the space activities of the two countries were innocent of military interest. Two-thirds of U.S. payloads placed in orbit were under the control of the Department of Defence and of the 834 space missions launched by the U.S.S.R., 516 were for military activities, he said.

The 138th annual meeting of the British Association, in 1976, will be held at the University of Lancaster.

The presidents of sections and the titles of their addresses at the Guildford meeting were—Physics and Mathematics: Prof. L. Fox, " Computers, mathematics and problem-solving "; Chemistry: Prof. J. Chatt, " Nitrogen and food supply "; Geology: Prof. F. Hodson, " Clays as sediments "; Zoology: Prof. E. J. W. Barrington, " Hormones and evolution; New paths in a molecular landscape "; Geography: Prof. Eila M. J. Campbell, " Maps and leisure "; Economics: Rt. Hon Aubrey Jones, " The economics of equality "; Engineering: Dr. O. A. Kerensky, " Civil Engineering and research "; Anthropology: Prof. J. Littlejohn, " European thought and anthropological specimens "; Biomedical Sciences: Prof. V. Marks, " Biochemistry, the key to modern medicine "; Psychology: Prof. R. L. Gregory, " Physiological psychology—a war of nerves "; Botany: Dr. L. Fowden, " A chemist among plants "; Forestry: D. R. Johnson " Forestry in a changing world "; Education: Sir Hugh Springer, " Education, development and the quality of life "; Agriculture: Prof. E. H. Roberts, " Protein production in the future "; Sociology: Prof. R. E. Pahl, " The myth of independence in a dependent society "; General: Sir Alan Cottrell, " Contribution of science to the national economy ".

BUMBLEBEE ENERGETICS.—Discoveries about the remarkable powers of the bumblebee, one of the most beneficial of all insects, could provide fresh and safer weapons to fight harmful insect pests, according to a report from the Agricultural Research Council. Not only has the bumblebee puzzled students of aerodynamics by being able to fly at all with its unaerodynamic shape. it has also puzzled beekeepers by being able to fly and gather nectar when it is too cold for the honeybee which stays in the hive. It is all a matter of energetics, it seems. Bumblebees fly because they are extremely efficient producers of energy. Their flight muscles produce more power, weight for weight, than aero engines. Studies of the processes involved, at the ARC's Unit of Muscle Mechanism and Insect Physiology, in Oxford University's Zoology Department, have revealed that the bumblebee's efficiency is even greater than previously believed and have provided the answer to the beekeeper's puzzle. The metabolism of energy release depends on two processes, glycolysis and oxidative phosphorylation. These processes, previously studied in detail only for vertebrates, have been found to differ between insects. In particular the bumblebee has displayed a fascinating ability to change the direction of the process and instead of using it to produce the considerable amounts of energy needed for flight to turn it to producing heat. With this internal source of warmth it is able to be out and about, engaged on its useful work among the earliest blossoms of the spring, long before the honeybee. While the scientists hold out little hope of being able to transfer this ability to the honeybee they do believe that understanding it might enable them to devise ecologically safer ways of dealing with harmful insects by interfering with their energy metabolism.

CHANGEABLE WEATHER.—Greenland is an ice land and Iceland is a green land. The question is, then, why did the Vikings, who first visited the lands and named them, get it wrong? The answer, it seems, is that they did not. When they were discovered, Iceland was icy, and Greenland was green. That does not mean that the climates of the two places have reversed in the thousand or so years since they were discovered. The north Atlantic was going through a particularly cold spell when Iceland was discovered but it was warmer when Greenland was discovered. Professor W. Dansgaard of Copenhagen University reported this in *Nature*. He and his colleagues at the University base their explanation on a core of ice 404 metres long taken from the crest of an ice sheet 3,172 metres above sea level in central Greenland. That took 1,420 years to be laid down, the Danes reported, and so gives a climatic history from A.D. 554 to the present day.

The Danes are expert at reading climatic history from the ice. Basically their technique depends on determining the ratio of two isotopes of oxygen, oxygen-18 and oxygen-16, present. This ratio depends on the temperature when the ice was deposited. Others have used this as a broad guide to temperature variations over long periods of time but the Danes have refined the technique to pick out seasonal variations in temperature between summer and winter. That means it is possible to count the years down through the ice, rather like counting the annual growth rings in the trunk of a tree. Although the task is too laborious to carry out on

every ice core, Professor Dansgaard's group have been able to deduce a formula which can give the age of an ice sample to an accuracy of ten years just by measuring its depth below the present day surface.

According to Professor Dansgaard, in A.D. 865, when Iceland was discovered and named, the country was experiencing a cold spell which lasted for several decades. The warming which took place after that explains why settlers in Iceland did so well, despite the name of their new home. Greenland, though, was in the middle of the warming up phase when it was discovered. The Vikings also explored America during that favourable period. When, a couple of centuries or so later, the little Ice Age set in the Vikings' voyagings were over. If the two islands had been discovered at the same time, then surely the names would have been reversed, argued the Professor. His work also has some hint for our future. According to his climatic studies the pleasant warm conditions of the northern hemisphere during the first half of this century were exceptional. The norm is closer to those of the past few years and that is what we should expect and prepare for. Studies of a mere 1420 years are little to go on, the professor admits. He hopes, in 1977, to drill a still better core going back 100,000 years.

CHEAPER STAINLESS STEEL.—Cheaper stainless steel is the promised outcome of research going on at Sheffield University, with the backing of the Science Research Council. Dr. L. G. M. Sparling and a team of three, from the University's Department of Engineering, were given financial backing by the Council for a three year programme of research into the production of a steel sandwich. This would have a core of a strong but cheap alloy steel and would be faced by thinner layers of stainless steel made by hot rolling from powder compacts. Success should extend the use of stainless steel to articles for which it is too expensive at the moment. If all went well, said Dr. Sparling, the new process could be in use by the mid-1980s. The British Steel Corporation was already showing interest.

Dr. Sparling had already perfected a new method of producing stainless steel strip from stainless steel powder which should cut the cost by about a third while maintaining or even improving quality. The powders are produced by directing high pressure jets of air or water at a stream of molten metal as it pours from a ladle. The powders have been compacted, at the University and elsewhere, into a form of strip known as " greenstrip ". Though easily broken it can be handled. When heated in an Argon atmosphere to orange heat and then hot rolled, a good quality stainless steel strip is produced which can be further improved when it is conventionally annealed and cold rolled. Work was going on to demonstrate that this was an industrially viable process by producing wider strip than had already been made at the University. In the course of this work hydraulic mills of a new design were being installed.

Not the least attractive outcome of the work, if all goes well, it was claimed, was a reduction in the size of the enormous slab and strip rolling mills now in use, perhaps to one third.

CLEVER CRICKET.—The cricket is not only a remarkably indefatigable sound producer, and a powerful one, too, it is also a remarkable acoustic engineer. At least this is the case with one species of South African tree cricket which has found a way of amplifying its song so that it is at least twice as loud and doing so while eating.

Entomologists from Pretoria reported in *Nature* seeing a solitary *Oecanthus burmeisteri*, as the cricket is scientifically called, in a small sunflower leaf.

They used a microphone to compare the volume of sound it produced when singing from within the hole in the leaf and when it was calling from the leaf surface. Singing within the hole, they found, increased the volume of sound between two and a half and three and a half times. The cricket, like most engineers, appears to be a good mathematician. It takes care that the size of the hole, left when it has eaten into the leaf, and the size of the leaf itself are the best for its purpose. The hole measures 8 millimetres by 14 millimetres and this means that when the cricket sits in it the front wings are pressed against the inner edge. As the cricket's call is produced by rubbing a stridulatory file or row of teeth on one wing against the edge of the other this means the sound is conveyed directly to the leaf so that it can act as a baffle. The frequency of the cricket's call is about 2,000 cycles a second, giving a wavelength of 170 millimetres. Acoustic theory shows that a baffle is most efficient when its diameter is about half a wavelength—which is just what the sunflower leaf chosen usually measures.

CLEVER PEN.—A ballpoint pen has been developed that gives the alarm when a would-be forger uses it. The pen will detect any false attempt at any signature—provided, of course, the signature has been fed into a computer. The device was developed in the U.S.A. by the Stanford Research Institute, as a means of making the popular method of personal identification, signature verification, a more foolproof one. The pen is linked to the computer which is primed, by that pen or a similar one, with a genuine signature, taking note not just of the appearance of the signature but also the motions and pressures used by the writer on the pen as he signs his name. Each succeeding time the signature is written the computer compares motions and pressures with its own memory of that genuine signature. Of course, no-one signs his or her own name exactly the same way each time, but it has been found that on a scale on which zero represents a perfect match people duplicate their own signatures with an error or two. The best forger cannot get closer than three or four. This, admittedly, is based on the premise that the forger will not have been able to observe, in microscopic or computer detail, all the actions taken in producing the signature he is trying to forge.

COLD TIMES FOR CHIMPS.—The forests of northwest Russia hardly seem to be the place to meet chimpanzees swinging through the trees, yet a thriving colony has been established on a desolate island in a lake there. It is a summer only home as yet, pointed out Leningrad physiologist, Leonid Firsov. The chimps have not been exposed to the full rigours of the Russian winter, but even in summer the forests make a cool home compared to the African jungle, the apes' natural home, with temperatures falling at night to 6 degrees Centigrade. Despite this and the cold rains none of the apes caught cold. All the apes, though brought up in captivity, had been born in Africa. It seemed that they had their own central heating system. For the cold weather they use branches to make homes resembling armchairs and hammocks and it turned out that their beds were warmed to 37 degrees by the animals' bodies. How this was done is yet to be fathomed. The chimps, experimenters themselves as well as the subject of experiments, found that almost half the 180 plants growing on the island were edible and they also ate ants and dragonflies. An analysis of their diet showed they were seeking out the vitamins their bodies needed. The experiments, conducted by the Anthropoid Centre of the Academy of Science's Institute of Physiology, showed that the chimpanzees were skilful in the use of sticks, branches and stones as working implements. They remembered what to do in situations which presented problems they had already coped with. Only in one thing were they altogether helpless. They were quite incapable of working together to solve a task. The experiment, said Firsov, director of the Anthropoid Centre, showed that the area of Pskov, where it was conducted, was quite suitable for establishing a primatology centre.

CORAL BEAUTY SECRET.—Coral reefs, as everyone knows, are remarkably beautiful. Why this is so is a puzzle for marine biologists, though, for this beauty depends on an abundance of life where life should not be abundant. Coral reefs are islands of plenty in the midst of tropical seas which generally provide little more than a starvation diet. The seas which wash over the reefs are the source of nutrients for the multitudinous life which flourishes on them, yet tropical oceans are especially poor in the nitrogen which is essential for the plant life which forms the foundation of any living system. The answer lies in another form of reef, drab and colourless, an ugly sister to the coral reef yet the source of all its beauty, as an American expedition to Enewetok Atoll, in the Marshall Islands, found. Three biologists, Dr. W. J. Wiebe and Dr. R. E. Johannes, of the University of Georgia, and Dr. K. L. Webb, of the Virginia Institute of Marine Science at West Point, noticed that water flowing over a shallow reef between two islands had become enriched with nitrogen. They traced the nitrogen to thin yellowbrown films of algae that covered large areas of the windward intertidal reef flats at Enewetok Atoll. One species, *Calothrix crustacea*, was a blue-green alga, one of the small group of algae and bacteria which can fix nitrogen directly from the air into compounds, such as ammonia, nitrites and nitrates, which can be used by plants. This alga existed above the low-tide mark where, although it was alternately wetted by the sea and dried by the scorching sun, also, occasionally, wetted by rainwater instead of salt, it survived in dense, black, felt-like mats. The average rate of nitrogen fixation over the reef's surface was 1.8 kilograms a hectare a day, among the highest ever recorded in a marine environment. Even higher rates were recorded low down the reef, where the alga was almost continuously wet and where the continual grazing by fish kept it growing.

Some of the nitrogen is released directly by *Calothrix* into the water where it is taken up by the microscopic plankton animals and plants. Some is utilised by animals that feed on the fragments of algae broken off the mat. Some becomes available to inhabitants of the coral reef in the faeces of the fish that graze on the algae and need only a small part of the nitrogen they consume.

CUTTING IT FINE.—The knife that never needs sharpening could cut costs, save waste in valuable raw materials and make factory life more pleasant for workers. This is the argument put forward by the Shoe and Allied Trades Research Association laboratories, at Kettering, Northants, where the knife—a high-power water jet—was installed to help carry out an eighteen month £320,000 Government research contract. The virtues of cutting by fluid jet will be investigated not just for shoe leather and its substitutes but for other materials as well. In the matter of cutting costs it was pointed out that materials represent 40 to 50 per cent. of the cost of footwear and computer controlled fluid jet cutting should mean a saving of 5 to 6 per cent. in materials.

Cutting by fluid jet is simple, it was claimed. The water is mixed with a liquid consisting of long-chain molecules, to ensure a " solid " jet free of spray, and brought to a high pressure by a pump. It goes to an accumulator to smooth out the pump impulses and ensure that the water is at a constant pressure. In use the high pressure liquid passes through a very fine hole in sapphire by way of a pneumatic valve which can switch the jet on or off instantaneously. The width of the cut is determined by the size of the sapphire orifice, the smallest practical so far achieved being three thousandths of an inch. At these sizes the cut is so small that it can be difficult to separate the cut out pieces from the original sheet unless the correct size of orifice is chosen. After doing its work the water enters a drain. Unless the material being cut is itself a polluent there is no problem with the effluent, the liquid originally added to the water is easily destroyed by natural processes.

In a typical large scale installation there would be nine pumping units, each using 40 hp, to provide 40 gallons of fluid an hour at 40,000 pounds a square inch pressure. Each unit could supply six 0.005 inch nozzles, each taking 6½ gallons an hour, three 0.007 inch (13 gal/hour), one 0.010 inch (28 gal/hour) or one 0.012 inch (38 gal/hour). Maximum pressures have reached 70,000 psi, at which point the fluid is travelling at twice the speed of sound. Since the pumps would normally be distant from the work the only noise audible to the worker would be caused by air being trapped in the jet, though this could well be unnoticeable as the working distance between orifice and material being cut is normally only one quarter of an inch. No dust is produced, no pilot holes are needed to start a cut, cuts can be started and stopped at any point and the whole process is easily automated. The only thing to wear out is the sapphire orifice and these average a 100 hour life and cost £10 to replace.

The machine installed, to be followed by two more, the second at the laboratory and the third at a shoe factory, was American, the product of the McCartney Manufacturing Company of Baxter Springs, Kansas. Fluid cutting started in the USA about four years ago, with cardboard. The materials they now cut include plywood, rubbers, foams, textiles, laminated paper, gypsum boards and asbestos sheets. The cost varies with the task, from £10,000 to about £100,000 a machine, those used at Kettering costing £17,000. One jigsaw puzzle maker has found the investment in the machines worth while as they cut out ten puzzles at a time. Mr. O. M. Walstead, vice-president of McCartney Manufacturing, reported they were experimenting with a view to incorporating abrasive materials in the jet to cut very hard materials but, so far, were finding the abrasives were wearing out the nozzles too quickly.

From Russia also came news of a water cutting, machine but one designed for massive rather than fine work. From the description it appeared to be designed to make use of the pump impulses, not to smooth them out. It was said to discharge a quart of water in six thousandths of a second, with a force that would send it crashing through quarter inch steel plate, doing this once every three to four seconds. In a demonstration it had cut a hole big enough for a car to go through in a two metre wall of granite blocks embedded in concrete in 2½ hours. It was designed by the Donets Institute of Mining for coal mining, though its designers, without specifying what, said there were other industrial activities which could use that cutting power. One side effect, in mining, though, was that hydraulic coal cutting eliminated dust.

Water power, it seems, is equally at home doing fine cutting or carving out chunks of solid granite. But when it comes to boring holes, light is even more effective than fluids and Ferranti announced their Mark 2 laser micro-driller. This can bore holes as small as 0.0004 of an inch or ten microns in most common metals and plastics as well as in brittle and hard-to-machine materials such as ceramics and tungsten carbide. The largest hole the laser is capable of drilling is one twentieth of an inch in diameter. It is not limited to round holes, though, the beam can be adjusted to produce non-circular shapes. Nor is it limited to boring in a straight line. Just as the laser light can be reflected, so can the laser drill, to reach awkward spots at difficult angles.

ELECTRONIC POSTMAN.—An answer to postal inflation is the electronic postman unveiled by the Data Communications Division of Muirhead, a Kent firm, at the World Telecommunications Exhibition in Geneva. Known as Mufaxgram it consists of a compact desk-top receiver and transmitter. Plugged into the firm's own PBX or into the public telephone network it will, it is claimed, transmit correspondence and inter-office memoranda at considerably less cost, to say nothing of much higher speed, than the postal services. Letters do not have to be typed, handwriting appears at the receiving end just as legible as it was when transmitted. The standard piece of paper takes a communication about 200 words long and this can be transmitted rather faster than it could be dictated to a shorthand typist and she, of course, would still have to transcribe it. Where ordinary telephone links are not possible radio-telephone can be used. Cost for a 200 word message can be as little as a third of a penny, where the connection is by private wire, reaching, at most, 12½p for long-distance deliveries over the public network. As well as saving money the electronic letter dispenser also saves in space, standing less than six inches high it takes up just a square foot.

ELECTRIC VEHICLES.—Phase Two of an extensive development programme for the development of electric vehicles, announced by Lucas during the year, was the operation of one ton vans by the Post Office and other important users. Phase One was the entry into service in Manchester, earlier in the year, of a 34 passenger electric bus. The vans, capable of more than 50 m.p.h. and with 0 to 30 m.p.h. acceleration times of about ten seconds, were powered by 50 h.p. motors designed to operate from 216 volts. The motor drives the rear wheels through a conventional propeller shaft and back axle but no gearbox is required. Supply from battery to motor is through solid state switches which switch on and off so rapidly, several hundred times a second, that the motor just " sees " an average of the chopped up voltages. By adjusting the open to closed times of the switch this average voltage is varied and power is automatically adjusted to suit the demand and the vehicle's speed. The batteries are of the lead-acid type, Lucas feeling that this is the only battery currently available which enables viable vehicles to be produced and also one which can be still further improved. A special traction battery gives 10 watt-hours per pound of battery weight at a two-hour discharge rate and can be charged about 1500 times. The ordinary SLI (starting, lighting and ignition) car battery with a hard rubber case gives about 12 watt-hours per pound weight and will stand up to about 100 charges. Polypropylene SLI batteries give 13.6 watt-hours. Polypropylene batteries have been chosen for the vans, Lucas aiming to improve further the power–weight ratio and also to extend the life of several hundred cycles. Regenerative braking is provided through the motor, the kinetic energy of the vehicle being used to drive the traction motor and operate it as a generator, providing some degree of charge and so returning some of the energy of motion to the battery. Greater braking than is available from the motor is provided by normal hydraulic brakes, brought into operation by pressing the brake pedal down further. During trials it was found that when driven in traffic the high performance electric vehicle's accelerator pedal is released, so drawing no power from the batteries, for a surprisingly large proportion of the time. One main aim of the development programme is to ensure that losses in these conditions are as low as possible.

FILTERING OUT THE LEAD.—A dual benefit was claimed for a " second generation " exhaust filter for cars, announced during the year. Not only was it said to be better at reducing lead pollution, but it would also help to conserve fuel resources, compared with less advanced equipment. The filter, produced by the Associated Octel Company engine laboratory at Bletchley, reduces overall lead emissions by about 50 per cent. rising to a staggering figure of 96 per cent. under town driving conditions. This, it was suggested, would mean a reasonable answer to the problem of lead emissions without the need for reducing the efficiency of engines and so increasing fuel consumption. Lead from car exhausts is an emotive matter. Without any strong factual evidence to show it does great harm—and, indeed, with the near certainty that other sources provide a vastly greater part of Man's lead intake—countries round the world have been placing limits on the amount of lead that can be used in refining the high octane petrol needed for high performance and high efficiency engines. Each drop of one in the octane number, it has been stated, leads to an increase in fuel consumption of 1.4 per cent. Lead can give an extra eight to ten octane numbers, so banning it altogether would increase petrol consumption by 12.6 per cent. in the U.K., about 2 million tons of oil a year. Cutting lead in petrol by about 30 per cent. as called for under Common Market proposals would mean £50 million on the country's oil bill.

The new filter is based on a lead trap patented by Texaco in 1966. The expansion and silencer boxes on a conventional exhaust system are replaced with boxes filled with stainless steel wool coated with alumina. The original design was subject to " purging ". Under open throttle conditions filtration was less efficient and the first few miles spent " burning up " the motorway could mean the release of lead trapped during gentler driving. Lead emission could reach higher levels, during those miles, than that from unfiltered exhausts. Purging is prevented in the new model by treating the aluminised stainless steel core with phosphate. It has also been redesigned to reduce the back pressure which motor manufacturers objected to in the original design. Work on a third generation filter is directed to reducing the cost by using only one filter box in an exhaust system instead of the two needed at present. Even so, it is claimed that the second generation filter, though it costs twice as much, has twice the life of a standard exhaust system.

FIRST PLANT-ANIMAL HYBRID.—Scientists have shown that the basic building blocks of plant and animal life are not incompatible. They have managed to fuse them together. Hybrids between cells from different animals have become a well-established technique over the past decade for research into the working of the cells, using the nucleus from one cell and the protoplasm from another can reveal the relative role of the two in controlling the functions and activity of the cell. Hybrids of this type have also been used to throw light on the role of the membrane which marks the boundary of all living cells and is yet the point of contact between the cells making up a single organic entity. Plant cells with their rigid walls have proved a little more difficult to hybridize but they also have been fused.

The latest success, the first plant-animal hybrid, was announced in *Nature* by two teams, one from the Royal Free Hospital School of Medicine, led by Prof. J. A. Lucy, and the other from the Nottingham University Department of Botany, led by Prof. E. C. Cocking. Their achievement was to fuse red blood cells taken from a hen with protoplasts derived from yeast cells. Yeast is a fungus and like higher plant cells has a cell wall which had to be dissolved by enzymes to leave the protoplast, that is the cell denuded of its wall but still bounded by its membrane. The blood cells and the yeast protoplasts were then treated with a chemical agent, polyethylene glycol, which has been found to promote fusion in both animal cells and plant protoplasts. When the animal and plant matter were mixed in the right proportions, with an excess of protoplasts over blood cells of about ten to one, they fused relatively readily. Inspection under the microscope showed nuclei from both parents with a smooth continuous membrane surrounding the hybrid cell.

Eventually, said the scientists, they hoped to culture the hybrid cells and carry out experiments to elucidate problems which have resisted research with simple animal-animal and plant-plant hybrids. In particular it is hoped to discover more about the structure and role of the cell membrane. Fusion of animal cells has shown that this structure is in many ways more like a fluid than a solid. When membranes from fusing cells have been labelled with different dyes the colours have intermingled in the membrane of the hybrid, showing that membrane components diffuse freely among each other. Fusion of membranes from two such different cells as those of animal and plant origin could throw fresh light on the structure. One of the most important fields of research in biology, too, is into the function of the membrane and the part it plays in receiving information from the world outside the cell and how that information is processed. This is at the root of the mysteries of how organisms, from primitive plants to higher animals grow and, within limits, repair themselves and how different parts are developed to take over different functions.

FIXING NITROGEN.—Hopes of stimulating protein production for the hungry mouths of future generations were raised by several lines of research during the year. Protein depends on a ready supply of nitrogen to plants and though our atmosphere is mostly nitrogen this is useless to plants until it is "fixed" to other chemicals in a form that plants can use. Only a few forms of bacteria and blue algae are believed to do this naturally and the explosion of agricultural production in recent years has depended on a ready supply of plant food in artificial nitrogen fertilisers. The increasing cost of these, due to the rising price of fuel, has led to intensified research into the natural methods and into means of extending them. The best known form of nitrogen fixing bacteria, *Rhizobia*, lives in a symbiotic relationship with the pea family, carrying out their vital role in nodules on the roots of peas, beans, clovers, lupins and their relatives. It if could prove possible to get these bacteria to enter into a similar relationship with wheat, for example, then high-protein grains could be produced without the heavy dressings of nitrogen fertilisers now necessary. Standing in the way of that, though, has been the long accepted belief that the *rhizobia* only fix nitrogen when in those nodules. Away from their natural hosts, cultured in a laboratory, they grew but never fixed nitrogen. It seemed that some missing component might be provided by the plant. The good news, for plant breeders, that this is not so, came from three groups of scientific workers, two Australian and one Canadian, who reported in *Nature* that they had independently succeeded in getting *rhizobia* to fix nitrogen. It turned out that what the bacteria needed were supplies of special plant sugars and also a little ready fixed nitrogen. With this success scientists will be able to study the bacteria engaged on their life-giving work in the test-tube and this should speed research considerably.

The legume-rhizobia relation is not the only one, though it is the best known. Other nitrogen-fixing bacteria, *Azotobacter* and *Spirillum*, seem to find a preferential environment among the roots of some tropical grasses and even enter into a primitive symbiotic relationship with them in some cases. Maize is one such grass and Dr. J. F. W. von Bulow and Dr. Johanna Dobereiner, of Rio de Janeiro University, reported in *Nature* that the strength of the association is genetically controlled and selected lines of maize are as self-reliant in the matter of nitrogen as the soya bean.

In plants they bred they found the nitrogen fixing ability to be up to twenty times as great as in the parent plant. More work still remains to be done, they reported, in determining the conditions in which maize is best able to produce its own nitrogen and in breeding still better varieties.

From Washington it was reported that an international panel of scientists, including British agricultural specialists, were recommending a major effort to turn the winged bean, *Psophocarpus Tetragonolobus*, into a main crop for the tropics where protein deficiency is high. At the moment the winged bean is just a backyard crop in Papua, New Guinea and parts of Southeast Asia but is suitable, they claimed, for widespread cultivation in Central and South America, Africa and Asia. The secret of the plant's value lay in the great number of extra-large nodules on its roots. These accounted for the high protein content. Also, while the beans, said to be highly palatable in the green phase, are as protein rich as soya beans, the whole of the plant, pods, leaves and roots as well, is edible. The tuberous roots contain 20 per cent. protein, compared with a mere one per cent. in that common tropical crop, cassava, and two per cent. in potatoes, sweet potatoes and yams.

Back in England Professor J. Chatt, director of the Agricultural Research Council's Nitrogen Fixation Unit, described in *Nature* how he had produced ammonia from nitrogen. In nature nitrogen-fixing bacteria do this with an enzyme, nitrogenase, containing molybdenum as well as iron atoms. Prof. Chatt achieved the same result by bonding nitrogen with molybdenum, or tungsten which behaves similarly, in a metalloorganic compound and then steeping the compounds in a solution of methanol and sulphuric acid. The nitrogen then acquired excess electrons from the molybdenum which enabled it to pick up hydrogen ions from the methanol to produce ammonia. With molybdenum he obtained a 30 to 40 per cent. yield and with tungsten 90 per cent. On the face of it this could replace the present industrial methods of producing ammonia which depend on fossil fuel for the supply of hydrogen. At the moment, unfortunately, the process results

in the destruction of the molybdenum. If, or when, it proves possible to recycle the molybdenum and if it becomes possible to use water as the hydrogen supplier instead of methanol then ammonia production by simple electrolysis could become a commercial proposition.

FLYING MONSTER.—The finding of a flying reptile, from the days of the dinosaurs, with a wingspan larger than that of a modern jet fighter, was reported from the U.S.A. Measuring 51 feet from wingtip to wingtip it more than doubled the previous record for a pterosaur, or pterodactyl, and would have had almost six times the span of the largest flying bird of today, the condor. The measurements were computed from fragments and complete bones found in the Big Bend National Park, Brewster County, Texas. Mr. Douglas Lawson, a graduate student at the University of California, reported in *Science* how he made the first finds while hunting for fossils as a student at the University of Texas. Over a period of three years, as his searches continued under the auspices of the University's palaeontology department, he found parts of the skeletons of three of the monsters, including remains of four wings, a neck, hindlegs and jaws, which were toothless. One novelty about the find, apart from the size of the creature, was that it was made in non-marine sediments, suggesting that the pterosaur lived well away from the sea. This does not fit the familiar pictures, in books on dinosaurs, of pterosaurs and pterodactyls feeding on fish scooped out of the sea. Mr. Lawson in his report, stated that the long neck suggested that the creature was a carrion eater, feeding on dead dinosaurs, the counterpart in those days of giants of the vultures and condors of today.

Announcement of the discovery reopened the old controversy on whether pterodactyls could fly, in the sense of lifting themselves into the air and propelling themselves through it by flapping their wings, or whether they just spread those wings to soar on air currents, perhaps launching themselves from high perches. One expert on dinosaurs and pterosaurs, Mr. Adrian Desmond of the Harvard University Museum of Comparative Zoology, gave his view that the creature would not have flown by flapping its wings, which would have been too heavy for it to cope with. It was a soarer and glider, not a powered flyer. He also corrected another of the popular views of pterosaurs. The wings would not have been the leathery membranes they are so often pictured as being. A find in Kazakhstan in 1970 had shown conclusively that pterodactyls had furry wings and were warm-blooded. In that they resembled mammals though they were called reptiles.

Efforts in Britain to solve that old controversy on whether pterodactyls soared or flew came to naught when the first attempt at a powered wing-flapping model crashed on being launched from the cliffs at Rhossili in South Wales. Palaeontologists and engineers who said they had made the first mathematical studies of the aerodynamics of the pterodactyl and shown that it would have been able to flap and fly, reported that they would continue with their attempts to duplicate what it had achieved 60 million years ago.

FROTHING WITH IDEAS.—A glass of beer was the inspiration behind the idea of a Swedish inventor which should have the double benefit of cutting pollution as well as industrial costs. It was English beer which provided food for his thought as he was travelling by train through the Midlands. Bruno Javorsky called for the beer after watching the chimneys of the factories beside the line. The froth on the beer did him more good than he expected. For, as he watched the steady release of gas bubbles he noticed particles of matter travelling, as steadily if not as quickly, the other way, being precipitated to the bottom of the glass. That glass of beer did initiate what could become a widely used technological advance, the foam cleaning of gases. When he checked his idea in the laboratory he found that unwanted particles—sometimes wanted, too, if they are of materials worth reclaiming—can be removed. As the gas to be cleaned is passed through a bed of foam the particles in it are trapped by individual bubbles. First a particle adheres to a bubble and then it punctures the wall of the bubble. As the bubble collapses the particle falls with it through the foam.

The principle is simple but the application is rather more difficult. The foam has to be prepared with a different gas from that being cleaned and special foaming agents are needed to suit different applications. The liquid used to make the foam can be salvaged, as well as the dust, when the system is used on a large scale. The first major test of the equipment showed that it could eradicate problems experienced by a large foundry with coarse particles of iron oxide produced in the grinding and powder cutting of castings. Many advantages were found, compared with conventional wet scrubbing plant. Electrical consumption was reduced to less than one third, installation costs and space requirements were less and the equipment, called a Foamator, was also able to remove an extensive range of dust particles. The efficiency of the method results from the enormous surface area presented by the bubbles, though produced from only a small amount of liquid. The Foamator, it was said, could also carry out cleaning tasks not possible with conventional wet cleaning equipment, where, previously only dry clean was thought possible. The inventor, after having his idea in England, took it back to Sweden where the equipment was produced by Temporator AB, a firm near Stockholm. Its first application in Britain was at a large chemical plant in East Anglia where a Foamator completed six months successful operation.

GLASS ROADS?.—What to do with the waste glass that is one of the products of the affluent society is a worry not only for conservationists, but for the glass-makers too. About $1\frac{1}{2}$ million tons of glass containers are produced in Britain each year, most of them non-returnable. If environmental pressure results in non-returnable bottles being banned the glass makers could lose some of their customers to the can business—heavier bottles would put up the price of drinks noticeably. Thinking hard about what use waste glass could be, Cardiff University scientists, sponsored by the Glass Manufacturers' Federation, came up with the idea of spreading it on roads. Hardly likely to appeal to the motorist, one might think, but the scientists say glass could make better roads. Ground to a fine, sand-like texture it would provide an ideal filling for asphalt. As well as having good wearing qualities it could be produced in the optimum sizes for giving a good-grip surface in all weathers.

GOOD SMOG.—Every cloud has its silver lining, even a cloud of smog, it seems. Smog, long condemned as a man-made pestilence, lethal as well as unsightly exists in nature, Soviet scientists reported. In nature, though, it can be beneficial to man. The smog of Los Angeles and similar afflicted places which sets people gasping is the result of photochemical reactions between sunlight and pollutants such as exhaust fumes. Scientists of the USSR Institute of Meterological Physics reported that the mysterious haze to be seen over fields in summer consists of minute particles formed also as the result of photo-chemical reactions, this time involving salts and organic substances given off by living plants. Investigations carried out on an island in the Baltic showed that this phenomenon is not a definite, unchanging state of the atmosphere but a continuing process. The particles making up the smog go through the stages of birth, development and decay. Each one is a tiny chemical retort in which photochemical reactions take place under the action of sunlight but regulated by the meteorological situation. A study of this natural process, the Russians suggested, should help to produce effective ways of dealing with city smogs. Unlike industrial smog, certain natural smogs have a beneficial effect on the organism. The well-established benefits of living in pine woods for sufferers from tuberculosis are, it seems, due to smog. Particles produced by solar rays in the thick of a pine forest kill tuberculosis bacilli.

GRAVITY WAVES, QUARKS AND MONOPOLES.—Research during the year provided a damper for those who thought gravity waves had been found, a boost for those who believe in quarks and perhaps the first real tidings of a basic magnetic particle sought for almost a century. Gravitational waves have been a matter of deep controversy since the American astronomer, Professor Joseph Weber, first reported detecting them some years ago. Nobody who believes in the General Theory of Relativity doubts that gravitational waves exist but they should be so weak in our part of the universe as to be virtually undetectable. Professor Weber claimed, however, that he had detected them after ten years of searching and others who copied his methods agreed with his findings. A careful study by a group at Glasgow University, however, has shown in meticulous experiments that there is no trace of the very large pulses of gravitational energy which would be needed to account for Prof. Weber's results. There still remained the possibility that what was being picked up was the sum of thousands of very small pulses but a report from Glasgow during the year ruled that out too.

All the efforts of following Prof. Weber's reported results, however, seemed to have brought the equipment halfway to the point of picking up those waves previously thought undetectable. They would show themselves by minute changes in the dimensions of massive metal rods, changes so small that they would be swallowed up by those produced by traffic vibrations or normal thermal changes. The answer would seem to be to cool the bars to near absolute zero or set them up in space.

Quarks are hypothetical "building blocks" from which atomic particles are made, more fundamental than any so far detected. They have been in the position of providing an elegant explanation for the behaviour of atomic particles in the giant accelerators without having any observed physical existence. Now it seems that other experiments can only be explained by postulating other particles named "partons". The two types of objects, partons and quarks, postulated to explain two entirely different observations, show remarkable similarities and, some physicists believe, must be identical. It could be that they are on the point of having observed existence. To the original three quarks which were needed to explain things originally there has been added, theoretically, a fourth a "charmed" quark. Two particles, with a lifetime of less than a millionth of a millionth of a millionth of a second, which appeared in two American accelerators could be this delightfully named object.

For years scientists have postulated a unit particle of magnetism, a monopole or single magnetic pole, which would bear the same relation to magnetism as the electron does to electricity. It eluded detection for almost a century but it was tracked down this year, if an announcement by the American Institute of Physics and the University of California is confirmed. Its track was left, according to the announcement, in layers of photographic emulsion hung beneath a balloon over Iowa almost two years before in a hunt for superheavy elements in cosmic rays. If the particle could be captured and controlled, it was claimed, it could produce revolutionary advances in providing new sources of energy, new types of motors and even new medical treatments.

HEAT-RESISTANT PLASTIC.—A new type of polyamide resin, able to withstand the sort of temperatures which make steel glow cherry-red, was developed by the Hughes Aircraft Company in California during a four-year research programme supported by the U.S. Air Force Materials Laboratory. Claimed to withstand temperatures of 800 degrees Fahrenheit and to be stable for long periods at 700 degrees, the plastic was expected to find many applications in motor vehicle parts, aircraft structures, jet engines, and also in the home. According to Hughes it is also a good adhesive for the titanium alloys used in aircraft. Its excellent mechanical and electrical properties are also said to be little affected by exceptionally high temperatures. The special properties of the material, described as an " addition-curable thermosetting polyamide ", are said to come from its ability to cross-link its molecules with little or no off-gassing, so yielding structures which are homogeneous and free from cavities.

The Russians claimed to have devised an additive to prolong the life of polymers several times. These plastics tend to disintegrate when heated because of a reaction with oxygen. Scientists at the Institute of Chemical Physics suggested including in the basic material of the polymer substances which would interact to stabilize the polymer before oxidation took place. Tests showed their idea worked in practice and as a result, it was stated, it has proved possible to prolong the service life of practically all heat-resistant polymers. ·The additives consist of finely dispersed compounds of copper and other metals. Polymers responding to the treatment include synthetic rubbers and graphitic materials. Tests in industrial conditions have shown they can be used for a long time without disintegrating at temperatures of 600 to 900°F.

INFRA-RED FIRE SPOTTER.—The flickering effect caused by air rising over a fire or a heated surface is put to work in an infra-red fire detector shown by the security firm of Chubb at a London fire-prevention exhibition. A beam of infra-red rays, in pulses lasting only a minute fraction of a second, are sent by a transmitter to a photo-sensitive detector on a path just below the ceiling of the premises to be protected. Hot air or gases rising from a fire break up the beam to produce a low-frequency flicker. When the receiver notes this it continues checking for long enough to rule out any false effect and then sounds a heat alarm. The device also acts as a smoke detector. In this case the overall brightness of the beam, as received, is continually compared, by computer, with that of ten minutes earlier. Any reduction of more than half in that time sets off the alarm. Changes caused by dirt collecting on the lenses or by the beam going out of alignment occur much more slowly, so the system, claim the makers, cannot be confused by this. The more stable alignment of the beam is said to give the device an advantage over laser systems, where the beam is so narrow that it can move off target because of minute shifts in the structure of the building. The infra-red beam, however, spreads out to a diameter of one metre over a pathway of 100 metres. One Beam Master, as the device is called, is claimed to give the same cover as twelve conventional smoke detectors or 24 heat detectors.

MAGNETIC CORPUSCLES.—Iron is an essential ingredient of the red blood pigment haemoglobin and this fact was utilised by a research team at the University of Southampton in devising a new magnetic technique for separating red corpuscles from the rest of the blood. It was claimed to offer advantages over current methods of separation such as spinning or centrifuging and, so, could be of value in blood transfusion, organ transplantation and cell research. In a laboratory demonstration of the technique, blood was passed through a filter consisting of smooth stainless steel wool. The filter was set in a magnetic field and so became magnetic itself, attracting the iron in the haemoglobin. Red blood corpuscles caught on the filter may be washed off when the field is removed with no permanent damage, according to preliminary checks. This was believed to be the first time magnetic separation had been used in this way.

MAGNETIC MIGRATION.—Support for the belief that birds navigate when they are migrating by " reading " the Earth's magnetic field came from tests in the U.S.A. A new very low-frequency radio communication system is being developed by the U.S. Navy to communicate with submarines. Project Sanguine, as it is known, will eventually consist of two long radio antennae, each 55 miles long, with an interconnecting grid. Conservationists, however, have expressed concern about possible effects on bird life and Dr. William Southern, a biologist from Northern Illinois University, tested the effects while the project was in an early experimental phase. It then consisted of two antennae, each a mere 15 miles long, arranged in a cross with a transmitting unit at the centre. One antenna ran north to south 3 feet below the surface of the ground, the other, aligned east to west, was supported on 35-feet high pylons.

Dr. Southern carried out his tests with young chicks of the ring-billed gull, taking them from a colony in Michigan to the military site in Wisconsin, situated west and north of the colony. Groups of birds were released at times when the radio system was not functioning and others when it was, with the buried antenna being energized at frequencies of 45 and 76 cycles a second with currents of 200 and 300 amps. The birds were released on the ground immediately over the buried antenna. The trials were carried out on clear days when natural interference with the geomagnetic field was minimal and tests with and without the system functioning were carried out on the same day. Birds were released in groups of sixty at a time. At the end of four days of tests it was found that 250 control groups, released when the military system was not functioning, all tended to fly to the south-east and behaved in a manner similar to that shown by birds in the colony at Michigan.

The 642 groups released when the antenna was energized, did not favour any particular direction and tended to disperse at random. Whether the effect produced on the birds released immediately over the aerials would be repeated fully on birds flying at height is unlikely, the magnetic fields generated fall off with height.

MAN IN SPACE.—It was a busy year for spaceflight but mainly because of Russian activity.

Apart from the American share in the joint Apollo-Soyuz mission all the manned flights were Russian, as they are likely to be for the next four years or so until the Americans start a new era with their space shuttle. This reusable vehicle, which will take off like a rocket and return to Earth like a plane, will be able to ferry crews and supplies to space stations at about one third of the cost of the rockets on which spaceflight has depended so far. A space station featured in the Russian flights, Salyut 4, the fourth in the series of purpose built laboratories which can either be operated automatically or with a human crew. Salyut 4 was launched in December, to take over from Salyut 13 which had just come to the end of its six month operational life, this being twice as long as envisaged under the initial flight programme.

A fortnight after it was launched Lt. Col. Alexei Gubarev and Flight Engineer Georgy Grechko boarded Salyut 4 from the Soyuz 17 ferry vehicle to begin 28 days of experiments. They returned after a 30 day spaceflight, setting a new Soviet endurance record by six days, though this was still well inside the overall record, the 84 day flight of one U.S. crew of the Skylab space station in 1974. On board Salyut, Gubarev and Grechko went through an arduous working day, sometimes lasting 15 to 20 hours, with tasks that ranged from advanced astronomy to gardening. Experiments in germinating peas and onion seeds and breeding wine flies were reported to have been successful. The principal astronomical instrument on the space station was a solar telescope, Ost-1, whose "sight" was claimed to have proved dozens of times sharper than that of ground-based instruments. It also reported on the Sun in a field of the spectrum inaccessible from the Earth yet one of great importance because it is one in which the behaviour of hydrogen, the main fuel of the Sun, reveals itself most vividly. X-ray telescopes were used to study stars, with particular attention to X-1 in the constellation of Scorpio, one of the most powerful of all sources of X-rays. New instruments for the spectral sounding of the upper atmosphere in the infra-red and ultra-violet were designed to provide further knowledge of the distribution of water vapour, ozone and nitrogen oxides. From their base 200 miles out in space the cosmonauts were reported to be "exploring" the Earth, by photography and spectrometry. Geology, geography, agriculture, forestry, land improvement, glaciology and even fishing, through increased knowledge of the biological resources of the sea could all benefit from this, Russian scientists claimed. To help keep them fit the cosmonauts had a bicycle ergonometer, said to provide pleasure as well as helping stave off the ill effects of weightlessness, still the prime problem in human adaptation to spaceflight. For their return the cosmonauts wore special gravity-suits, similar to those used by American astronauts.

The second attempt to board Salyut 4 almost ended in disaster when the third rocket stage sent the ferry vehicle off course 80 miles above the Earth. An automatic device coped with the situation, however, discontinuing the flight and ejecting the re-entry capsule with its two man crew, Colonel Vasili Lazarev and Oleg Makarev. They landed safely in Western Siberia.

The Russians were quick to declare that this failure would not affect plans for Apollo-Soyuz and that the incident, in fact, demonstrated the efficiency of the automatic equipment. In May another attempt to put a second crew on board the space station was successful and Lt. Col. Pyotr Klimuk and Vitali Sevastianov, a technical scientist, proceeded to break the Russian endurance record again. Their flight lasted 63 days. It was the

Russians' fifth manned spaceflight in twelve months. The two cosmonauts were aloft during the Apollo-Soyuz operation and some Americans had expressed doubts about whether the Russian control headquarters could cope with two complicated flights at the same time. To answer these doubts the Russians revealed that there was a separate control centre for Salyut, in other words that they had two control centres capable of handling simultaneous flights, an indication that they probably plan more ambitious flights shortly. Following the example set with the Russian half of the Apollo-Soyuz flight the landing of Klimuk and Sevastianov was shown live on television from the arid plains of Central Asia. Checks on the two cosmonauts after their two months in space showed their blood pressure was normal but they had lost some weight. According to Academician V. Glushko, a leading Soviet space scientist, weightlessness remains the main stumbling block in the way of creating long-duration space stations. Artificial gravity could be produced by rotating the stations but this would limit their use and make it difficult to carry out the many observations which require a stable platform. Salyut 4 had what was called the "Cascade" system for maintaining its orientation automatically with the use of only a fraction of the fuel previously required. The station also carried out automatically, by means of its own computer, many navigational tasks which had previously to be tackled by big computers on the ground. This sort of capacity, merely useful in a station going round the other side of the Earth, would be indispensable on flights to Mars. Salyut also moved a step nearer a closed life support system. In Salyut 3 water for domestic purposes had included a purified condensate enriched with mineral salts. In Salyut 4 cosmonauts drank purified used water for the first time. The hot houses on board were prototypes for future biological systems which would not only enable air and water to be used time and time again but would also supply cosmonauts with fresh vegetables, fruit and wheat.

In the U.S.A., scientists at a conference at Princeton University discussed seriously proposals to build space cities, self-contained communities of 10,000 people or more. Professor Gerald O'Neill, professor of physics at the University, produced detailed studies of such a station, positioned a quarter of a million miles from the Earth, at one of a number of points where the gravitational pulls of Earth and Moon act jointly to make assembly easier. The colonies would be housed in gigantic cylinders, 1,000 yards long and 200 yards across, probably made into as Earth-like a habitat as possible, with meadows, trees and animals. The inhabitants, who, in time, might outnumber those staying behind on Earth, would be engaged in manufacture, using materials obtained cheaply from the Moon. They would supply Earth not only with such things as electronic goods which can be made more easily or better in weightless conditions but also electricity obtained from "free" solar energy. All that talk of energy supplies drying up soon is put into perspective when one realises that the sunlight intercepted by the Earth's atmosphere each year, most of it going to waste, amounts to over 5,000 Q units while the total reserves of oil, gas and coal amount to only 200 Q, just enough to replace Earth's minute share of sunlight for a fortnight. The only problem, of course, is how to trap that solar energy in a form Man can use.

PAINLESS PICNICKING.—That bane of the picnicker, the unwelcome insect visitor, could become a thing of the past with one of the latest marvels of electronics. Though named Nimrod—the mighty hunter—it stays still and just draws the insects to itself, using the well known principle that insects are attracted to light. A central ultra-violet light attracts the insects by day or by night. Surrounding the light are two concentric metal grids, separated by a half inch gap. The outer grid acts as a protective cage. The inner grid is charged to a voltage that is not dangerous for humans or animals but is instantly fatal to insects flying against it. Nimrod is the brainchild of Electronic Pest Controls, of Staines, who produce it in five sizes, designed to give protection over areas from 500 square yards to 2,000 square yards. Though primarily intended for industrial, farming and catering concerns, there is one model which could appeal to the picnicker. This has its own built-in rechargeable battery pack and is portable.

PATCHING SKULLS.—One piece of good blown by the ill wind of Ulster violence is a technique for repairing gunshot shattered skulls. This, claimed the surgeons at the Royal Victoria Hospital, Belfast, who introduced it, should have far reaching consequences in offering new chances of life to victims of road and industrial accidents and to people suffering from brain tumours. The surgeons had been faced with the problem of coping with gaping holes in skulls left by bullets from high-velocity weapons, such as the Armalite rifle, introduced during the conflict. As one surgeon put it, " The difference between low and high velocity weapons is as marked as the difference between a blow from a feather and a blow from a sledgehammer." What was needed was a very strong, very light plate that would match precisely the missing part of the skull. After some research titanium was chosen because, apart from being tough and light, it does not cause any reaction in the body. First a mould is taken of the patient's skull and then, after various intermediate processes, the plate is shaped under hydraulic pressure of 6,000 lbs per square inch. When it emerges from the press it matches exactly the missing bone. The operation has been successfully carried out on patients who have lost the greater part of the skull. One plate measured thirty square inches. At the time of the report more than 60 people had been treated in this way and the plates were being used in operations other than those for gunshot wounds.

PICK-A-BACK SUBMARINE.—The exploitation of seabed oil and other new marine technologies have given an enormous boost to diving. However, expensive divers can only be used for about 100 days in the year in the North Sea. The conditions down below, where the diver works, are not the trouble but it is the rough seas of the surface, where the diver's support ship operates, that are the problem. The idea of a Swedish firm, though, could end that. Why not have the support ship down below, too, where it is calm, is how that idea expressed itself—and how the pick-a-back submarine came to be born. The system was announced by the Swedish firm of Kockums at a conference in Houston, Texas. It consists of a 1,600 ton " mother " submarine carrying a 50-ton " baby " that can be launched and taken back while underwater. With it, it was claimed, divers would be able to work for 300 days a year and would also be far better protected, with access to a complete diving centre under the sea. The 50 ton submersible was developed with the aid of the French diving company Comex. Larger than the conventional civilian working submarine, it can carry a cargo of three tons and is fitted with a lock-out system for passing out and taking on two divers.

Its price was estimated at about £1,300,000. It would be carried in a compartment of the submarine support vessel which was priced at something over £10,000,000.

The larger vessel would operate down to 400 feet, where the water is always calm and where launching and taking aboard the small submarine could be carried out without lifting gear. The smaller craft would be able to descend to depths of 1,500 feet for its crew to carry out visual inspections and work with manipulators. Its divers would be released at depths of down to 1,000 feet. For launching it would be lifted by a hydraulic platform from its " garage " inside the larger submarine to a launching position on the hull When it is taken on board the platform would lower it to its carrying compartment, immediately below which would be locks and decompression chambers, a medical treatment chamber and workshops and stores. The mother submarine would have a captain, cook and three shifts of three men for round the clock operation. It would also provide accommodation for the thirteen men required to man the working unit and carry out underwater operations. While the small submarine was operating the larger craft could hover beneath the surface for up to 50 hours at a time. More usually, though, it would operate on the surface or at snorkel depth, keeping out a watch for surface craft with sonar and radar but still keeping in touch with the submersible by underwater communications. A normal tour of duty would be three weeks, of which 19 days could be spent on operations. Apart from reducing costs by trebling working days the submarine pick-a-back system is also expected to be at least as able as other systems to meet the new safety regulations proposed to counter underwater dangers and reduce the toll of divers' lives.

PLANT POLLUTION.—It is known that plants such as peas and beans take up microscopic amounts of such metals as zinc, copper and lead and release them through their leaves. Now, three scientists, Dr. Beauford and Dr. Barber, of Imperial College, London, and Dr. A. R. Barringer, of Barringer Research Ltd., Ontario, have shown the size of the plants' contribution by measuring it.

The amounts given off are so small—an estimate for zinc is one-millionth of a gram from a square metre of vegetation an hour—that ordinary collecting systems are ruled out. In the experiments they reported in *Nature* the scientists used a radioactive labelling technique which enabled them to follow the course of the metals from the soil into the plant's roots and out through its leaves into the atmosphere. They built separate compartments around the roots and foliage of pea and broad bean plants and pine seedlings. Into the root compartments they put a liquid culture containing radioactive zinc-65. The compartment containing the foliage was designed so that air could be flushed through it and into a counter which would detect the radioactive decay of the zinc. First they showed that the decay the counter measured really did come from the leaves and had not leaked from the root compartment by a control experiment in which the roots were severed from the foliage of plants just above the point where the two compartments joined. After that was done no zinc was found in the air flushed through the foliage. They also showed that the zinc had to be picked up from the environment by the roots by shutting off the supply of zinc-65. The release then ceased abruptly, even though there should still have been quite a high concentration of the radioactive zinc still in the plant. This also indicated that the plant maintains a reserve of zinc for some purpose not yet understood. One other matter not perfectly understood is the form in which the zinc is given off. Electron microscope studies suggest that it is contained in tiny wax-like rods about one-fifth of a millionth of a metre by a third of a millionth.

Experiments with copper and lead showed that these metals are also emitted by plants, though in much smaller quantities. For the same concentration of a culture of lead only between one-tenth and one-fiftieth as much was given off as with zinc.

PLASTIC POLLUTION.—Large brittle sheets of plastic brought up in the nets of Swedish fishermen while they were trawling in the Skagerak proved, on analysis, to have had their origin in the vast quantities of polythene wrappings thrown overboard from ships. Dr. Arne Holmstrom, of Gothenburg University, provided an explanation how this low-density material finds its way to the bottom of the sea. According to his researches, reported in *Nature*, the polythene does float for a while, but in the presence of sunlight and water it becomes degraded and brittle. As this happens a calcareous marine organism, *bryozoan*, which lives between the surface and a depth of 15 metres, starts to colonize the sheets. Under the extra weight they begin slowly to sink. Eventually, however, they reach the pycnocline, the level, about 15 metres down, where the density of seawater increases rapidly. For a while they hover at that level. But that is the level where another organism, a brown algae, *Lithoderma*, starts to appear. It also begins to add its weight as it grows on the sheet, upsetting the balance and starting the sinking process off again. *Lithoderma* ceases to be abundant at about 30 metres, but by that point the plastic sheet is well set on its downward drift to the sea floor, between 180 and 400 metres deep. The colonizing process appears to take about eight months as both organisms show about four months' growth. The process is obviously extensive; fishermen from one fleet alone are said to be finding up to 750 pieces of plastic a week, some several metres across. Restrictions on the dumping of plastic from ships seem bound to come after this discovery, though there is one hopeful sign that plastic pollution may not be as long-lived in the sea as it has proved to be on land. Some of the sheets had large holes in them and Dr. Holmstrom believes that these were caused by molluscs which feed on the algae and, probably involuntarily, find themselves eating the plastic base as well.

REFINED BY MICROBES.—Microbes that could refine gold, producing it economically from low-grade ores, are just one possible product from the latest ICI laboratory. At Runcorn in Cheshire, it was claimed to be the first purpose-built laboratory for work in genetic engineering, the transfer of genes and the qualities and attributes they carry from one organism to another. In this case it was intended to produce new useful micro-organisms by transferring genetic material between bacteria or from animal cells to bacteria. Apart from using the ability possessed by some bacteria of concentrating valuable minerals—the Russians have been reported to mine copper in this way—ICI scientists hope to produce bacteria that can produce valuable drugs, such as insulin, process such pollutants as waste oil into harmless and, possibly, useful products and convert household garbage into fuel.

ICI was able to move to experiments on an industrial scale before anybody else, so far as is known, because of its collaborative research schemes with universities. The technique of transferring genes has been devised by geneticists at the Department of Molecular Biology, Edinburgh University. Work there has been done with simple and harmless strains of bacteria. It is a subject, however, which has caused grave concern because of the possibility of transferring some harmful quality to a previously harmless organism, turning, for example, bacteria that live quietly and even beneficially in humans into dangerous pathogens. Because of this, warnings have been issued by scientific bodies in the USA and Britain and some scientists have even called for a moratorium on all such work. Elaborate security arrangements have been made at Runcorn. Access to the laboratory, which is within an existing research centre, can be obtained only by entering a code on a keyboard controlling the lock on an armour plated door. Every item of equipment has been designed to ensure that any spillage is unable to escape and the strains of organisms selected for the preliminary investigations would destroy themselves if they did succeed in leaking out. Using microorganisms to do such work is just another recognition of the continually rediscovered fact that whenever Nature and man find themselves in competition in carrying out some such procedure as the synthesis of complex substances, Nature proves to do it far more economically and efficiently.

SAVING VENICE.—The sea which threatens to submerge the city of Venice, can be held at bay—and held at bay by its own water. So claimed the Italian firms of Pirelli and Furianis after six months operational trials on the Adriatic coast of an inflatable dam which could be rapidly brought into operation whenever the sea, which has been eroding the city for centuries, threatens it again. The dam consists of rubber-coated nylon tubes, up to 1000 yards long, to span the three channels, Lido, Chioggia and Malamocco, that link the Venetian lagoon with the open sea. When not in use the barriers would lie uninflated and out of sight on the sea bed. A computer, fed with meteorological and hydrographic information, would be programmed so that, on deducing that the sea was about to rise to danger level, it would set turbopumping stations on both sides of each channel mouth to the task of inflating each barrier with water. This would raise the dams to a sufficient height above sea level to block off wind-whipped waves as well as the rising sea, ensuring that the level of the Venetian lagoon remains consistent and the city free of flooding.

The system was tested with a 220 foot long dam across a Po delta channel mouth at Punta Pila. Despite a constant tidal current speed of over 3 feet a second the dam successfully resisted heavy waves, wind and the abrasiveness of the sea bed. The dam is designed to conform to sudden changes in the sea bed caused by strong currents but, to make the tests even more severe Pirelli engineers dug additional craters into the bed. The dam, however, adhered strongly to the sea bottom, adapting itself to the most uneven surface without leaking. The tests, it was claimed, showed the system's effectiveness not only as a solution to the problem of the erosion of Venice but as a cheap, quickly installed and durable dam which could supersede traditional steel and concrete structures for many industrial, agricultural and civil projects.

SOPHISTICATED SCRAP MERCHANTS.—The scrap merchant's business becomes ever more sophisticated and one of the latest pieces of technology to find a place in it is the deep-freeze.

A new Belgian technique for converting low grade scrap into high purity ferrous fragments depends on the fact that, cooled to the temperature of liquid nitrogen, ordinary steel becomes as brittle as glass. It was claimed to be the ideal way of re-

claiming such things as old cars, washing machines
and other domestic appliances, consisting mainly of
steel but heavily contaminated by such metals as zinc,
copper and aluminium and also by plastics and other
non-metallic materials. They are first crushed and
then the bales so produced are cooled in the liquid
nitrogen. The resistance to impact of the steel is
dramatically reduced, so that, when hit, it shatters
into pieces the size of potato crisps. All the trapped
impurities are released and the steel becomes available in a form suitable for high quality steel manufacture. The system was developed by Belgium's
major scrap company, George et Cie, and offered
in the UK by British Oxygen.

SUNHOUSES.—Two thirds of the energy used in
running the average home can be saved, claimed
Phillips scientists and engineers in West Germany,
and, with the realization that 40 per cent. of the
country's fuel bill ultimately goes in domestic space
and water heating, the Government there was prepared to contribute towards proving it. The proof,
it was hoped, would come with the Phillips Energy
Conservation House which began operating at
Aachen. "Operating" was the right word. No
one was living in it, computers were used to simulate
the presence of mere human beings and to record
exactly what would happen if there were people
in it. Strips of punched tape set in train such energy
consuming activities as cooking, bathing, washing
and washing up and the computers monitored their
effect on the house and its equipment and weighed
it all up against differing weather conditions. Apart
from using the sun's heat to warm water the house
also possessed a heat pump to extract heat from the
ground beneath it and a heat exchanger to reuse the
residual warmth of waste water. Heat was also
taken out of stale air and, in the summer, from
warm air drawn into the house—in winter the same
equipment warmed the incoming cold air. Studies
of all this equipment were intended to show which
was the most effective and so enable engineers to
devise packages for fitting into new buildings and,
possibly, existing ones.

The key item in the experiment, though, was
Phillip's latest solar panel. This uses the vacuum
tube principle, like a thermos flask, but to capture
heat not just conserve it. Water is heated by the
sun as it passes through a black indium oxide coated
water tube which runs inside a larger, evacuated
tube of ordinary glass. Eighteen solar panels were
built into the roof at 45 degrees to the horizontal,
connected in series to a giant hot water tank. These
solar panels, it was claimed, are far more efficient
than the normal metal panel used for solar heat
collection by water, particularly in overcast conditions. The array was expected to produce, on
average, three kilowatts. Performance during the
day is one thing. The house also has to be heated
and serviced at night. The only way to store the
necessary amount of heat, it seemed, was to have
that giant water tank, holding 40 cubic metres or
over 8,000 gallons. Despite its size the tank's contents should be kept at about 90 degrees Centigrade
by the solar panel, claimed the company.

Insulation, naturally, is of prime importance.
The interior surface of the house is a layer of plasterboard attached to beams and backed by a thick layer
of chipboard. Glass fibre fills the spaces between
plasterboard and chipboard. Next comes a six inch
layer of glass fibre and then the external wall, three
inches of asbestos cement. Windows and doors are
double glazed, the glass being oxide-coated on the
inside to prevent infra-red loss. The window frames
were made of a polyurethane moulding with a steel
spine and also conduct little heat. The capital cost
of the house was £150,000 which included the two

computer occupants. Running it for three years is
likely to cost £2 million, the Government and a
power company, between them, providing more
than half. The West German State is spending a
further £20 million in the next five years on similar
projects, including a multi-family dwelling and a
swimming pool.

In its way the idea of a Southampton builder, for
which he was awarded a prize at an international
exhibition in Geneva, is even more ambitious. His
house would not only cut the cost of fuel but the
cost of food—and rates, too. Mr. Bill Sandey has
designed an "autonomous" house to provide its
occupants with free heat, gas, electricity, water,
food—even wine. At ground level there would be
quarters for chickens, rabbits and a goat. Living-
quarters for the human occupants would be on the
first floor and the second floor, a greenhouse, would
be given up to vegetable and fruit production.
Rainwater would be collected and stored, a windmill on the roof would provide electricity and all
the waste would go through a digester to produce
methane gas for cooking and heating as well as
compost for the plants. Most of the heat would
also come from sunlight, with the house being
glazed all over. The north wall would be double
glazed and the other walls would have special
venetian-style blinds, either to let the slanting rays
of the sun through or to act as insulators to keep in
the warmth. Near-tropical conditions could be
produced in the greenhouse in this way, claims Mr
Sandey, basing that claim on the results he has already achieved with ordinary glasshouses.

A house of this type with a third of an acre of
garden could produce enough food for the average
family, he states. His design, for which he won
the international award, was for a "living village", a circular structure to house 650 families. He
planned a one-bedroom version, just big enough for
his wife and himself. Even on that scale, he states,
the greenhouse would produce 2000 lbs of vegetables and fruit a year and a thousand bunches of
grapes for wine. Unfortunately, though, he was
deprived of his chance of proving his idea for cutting the cost of living and also the rates. The
Southampton Corporation, which dignified the
previous house he built for himself in Bitterne Park
by sending along the mayor to open it, refused permission for him to build this new, rate-cutting one
on the grounds that it might upset the neighbours.
He had planned to build it in the garden of his
existing house.

SWEETLY CLEAN.—Sugar should sweeten life for
water and sewage engineers, with an invention
announced by Tate and Lyle during the year. Their
research scientists on the campus at Reading University succeeded in formulating an entirely new
detergent, based on sugar. One important advantage claimed for it over the petroleum-based
detergents which still dominate the market, was in
what is called biodegradability. It is easily broken
down by natural organisms. The resistance of oil-
based detergents to natural processes of destruction
has been blamed for rivers that froth like the wash-
ing-up water, lakes that choke themselves with
weeds and the increasing cost of treating water for
use by water undertakings. The detergent was
also said to be cheaper to produce than conventional
ones. It came successfully through tests for any
adverse effects on the articles it would have to clean
and for poisonous effects on people using it. A
pilot plant with a capacity of 5,000 tons a year was
built near Reading. Initially all supplies would go
to the industrial market.

TALL GRASS STORY.—It was reported at the 12th
International Botany Congress in Leningrad that

specialists have been testing over fifty wild plants from various parts of the Soviet Union for their productivity and food value as fodder crops. Those which have stood the test and been recommended for mass planting include cowparsnip, oil radish and the Helianthus. The leaves of a cowparsnip, it was pointed out, weigh two to three kilograms, the plants can grow without re-seeding for seven or eight years and yield two crops a year.

Another talking point at the Congress was a handful of violet-coloured wheat grains which amazed not so much by their colour but by their origin. Delegates were told they were taken from a field sown four years previously to a perennial wheat bred by Academician Nikolai Tsitsin, a noted selectionist. The future of agriculture, he declared, was linked with the breeding of new crops produced by distant hybridization, in this case wheat crossed with couch grass. Unlike conventional wheat varieties it does not complete its life cycle after maturing but sprouts new shoots from the lower tilloring node. This process continues for two to five years. The plant has the peculiarity of ripening, not from bottom to top, but from top to bottom. More important, it not only yields weighty grains, with one thousand tipping the scales at fifty grams, but also green straw fodder containing up to seven per cent. protein. Perennial wheats are resistant to fungus and virus diseases, he stated, and have a strong stalk, making them suitable for mechanized cultivation. Another fodder wheat has been obtained in Tsitsin's laboratory by crossing with wild rye. This rapidly growing crop makes it possible to obtain three hay harvests a summer in Central Russia, yielding up to twenty tons an acre of green mass. It also resists frosts of minus 30°C.

The total weight of the Earth's vegetation was given at the conference as 141,000,000,000 tons. South America ranks first among the continents, followed by Africa, Asia, Europe and North America. The Australian flora have the lowest productivity potential according to the survey. The highest productivity is found in the tropical jungles of South America, in the basins of the Amazon and Orinoco, and the foothills of the Cordillera. The annual growth of trees, grasses and lianas, from top to roots, is over twenty tons an acre, four times as much as the productivity of vegetation on the same geographical latitude in Equatorial Africa. For comparison meadows sown to Fyodorov's giant grass should, according to his results, yield eighty tons of vegetable mass an acre each year.

Even that could be bettered, according to work done by the Henry Doubleday Research Association. The favoured crop in this case is comfrey. Though sometimes called Russian comfrey, it is not another of those new Soviet fodder crops; it was grown in Britain around the turn of the century, according to Mr. Lawrence Hills of the Association. It reputedly grew crops of seventy tons or more an acre, but fell out of favour, possibly,

he suggests, because those giant yields were the result of an accidental hybridization which seed raisers then were unable to repeat. It lingered on in hedgerows, though, for it has two virtues. A feed of comfrey makes a horse look fit and it grows readily from odd bits of root.

Surviving plants are probably the relics of feeds given by gypsy horse-dealers to their horses before a sale. New trials with the plant have led to claims that in England it could match the performance of Fyodorov's grass, providing a leaf with a host of uses from a first-class mulch and natural compost for blackcurrants to a high protein feed for pigs. Heavier crops have been produced in the better growing areas of the U.S.A. and in the whole-year-round growing season of Kenya yields have topped a hundred tons an acre. One particular advantage claimed for comfrey is rare if not unique in the vegetable world. It provides the essential protein vitamin B_{12}. This fact has led to experiments in producing a high yielding protein food by growing yeasts and fungi on the leaf, with American, British, Japanese and Australian scientists experimenting with different micro-organisms

THRIFT PAYS WITH RICE.—Two Egyptian scientists reported finding how discarded rice husks could help a country move on to the path of industrialization. Dr. Ahmed El Bouseily, of the University of Alexandria, and Dr. Tayseir El Shamy, from the University of Tanta, described in *Nature* how the useful chemical water-glass, sodium silicate, can be made from the ash left after burning the husks.

Water-glass is used in many industrial processes, including the manufacture of detergents, adhesives, ceramics, papers and textiles. The usual process for making it requires high temperatures and high pressures, fusing sodium carbonate and sand at 1,400 degrees to form a soda-silica glass and then converting that to the syrupy liquid of water-glass by subjecting it to water vapour under high pressure. It can also be made, however, by treating non-crystalline forms of silica with sodium hydroxide at much lower temperatures, between 100 and 200 degrees. Rice hull ash, it seems, is an ideal source of silica for this process. The dry paper hulls of rice, discarded when the crop is milled, make up about twenty per cent. of the grain. Because their silica content is so high they are of little value as animal feed and their main use has been to provide the heat, by burning, to power the rice-mills where they are removed from the grain. This act of burning drives off the organic material as carbon dioxide and water, leaving behind a loose skeleton of non-crystalline silica. This does not suffer from the disadvantage of crystalline silica, from the water-glass maker's point of view, of being very reluctant to react with water or alkalis. It is ideally suited to the low temperature and low pressure reaction.

ARCHÆOLOGY IN 1974–75

The Council for British Archaeology's 24th Annual Report for the year ended June 30, 1974, was published during the winter of that year, and in it is explained the important organisational changes that have taken place within the Council; the Executive Committee is restyled the Executive Board and there are three subsidiary boards for Finance and General Purposes, Research, and Education; each of these boards will be responsible for co-ordinating the activities of five or six full committees. Of particular interest is the fact that the period committees are being disbanded and, as the Report notes, " the titles of the Committees reporting to the Research Board—Urban, Countryside, Churches, Industrial, Scientific—are an indication of the re-orientation in archaeological thought in the past decade."

The Churches Committee has been especially active, having made written submissions to the Committee of the General Synod of the Church of England, which is considering revising the Pastoral Measure No. 1 of 1968; the Churches Committee hopes that in due course it will be possible to apply normal historic building procedures to ecclesiastical buildings. The Department of the Environment has clarified the status of excavations carried out for archaeological purposes in churches that are still in use; in the right circumstances they could be regarded as normal rescue excavations and therefore qualify for Department of the

Environment funding; the financing of the York Minster excavations in this way is a precedent. To assess the scale of the threat to the archaeology of churches, both those in use and those made redundant, the Churches Committee supported a survey of the problem in the Diocese of Chelmsford financed by a grant from the Department of the Environment. The need for local knowledge and expertise is acknowledged and the Council for the Care of Places of Worship now backs the Churches Committee of the C.B.A. in its campaign to establish archaeological links with Diocesan Advisory Committees throughout the land; the C.B.A. now has an official consultant in every diocese.

Details are given of various projects in the C.B.A. Report and one of the most interesting is the Butser Ancient Farm Research Project, the aim of which is to study the development of early agriculture on an experimental basis. It is noted that one round-house has been built and successfully stood up to the force of two full hurricanes and several days of gale-force winds; Soay sheep are now living on the site and will be joined by some Dexter cattle which will be trained as draught animals. It is reported that " the first complete growing season gave initial crop yield figures for spring emmer which are far in advance of those popularly assumed. Furthermore, the yield was obtained under intense weed and rabbit infestation." Rare cereals are propagated at Butser and it is hoped that it will be possible to plant " celtic-sized " fields with the seed; a " slash and burn " experiment is being undertaken developing land obtained by clearance of secondary woodland. In an effort to obtain information about possible Iron Age practices grain continues to be stored in underground pits as part of a controlled experiment.

The activities of the Moated Sites Research Group are also noted in the C.B.A. Report; the Group keeps a central index of moated sites and as a result of field work this central archive continues to expand. It is considered that the number of moated sites is much higher than at first thought by members of the Research Group; for example, in Essex alone over 600 have been recorded, while 500 are estimated for Norfolk and 700 moated sites have been indexed in Ireland.

Still concerned with the medieval period, the C.B.A. Report notes the extensive activities of the Medieval Village Research Group; research is being carried out at the Public Record Office to list references to deserted villages in documents not previously examined. A start has been made in Rutland and Huntingdonshire and it is hoped to continue with Bedfordshire, Cambridgeshire and Nottinghamshire. Fieldwork has recently been undertaken in counties where no work had previously been done, for example Cumberland and Westmorland, and over 60 sites were visited in Lancashire; from all these researches a provisional list of deserted medieval villages in northwest

England has been produced. During the 24th season of the Group's research excavation at Wharram Percy in north Yorkshire, work was continued on the church, glebe terrace, and mill-dam; the investigation of the general settlement pattern continued with the excavation of the medieval headland, and earlier lynchet, and a second-century Roman ditch. In addition to all this work, the Group advised the Department of the Environment on priorities on over 40 threatened sites and recommended major excavations at five Saxon settlement sites and eight deserted medieval villages.

Ancient Monuments Board

The 21st Annual Report of the Ancient Monuments Board for England, covering the year 1974, was ordered to be printed in June 1975. Made to the Secretary of State for the Environment, the Report includes a description of a tour by the Ancient Monuments Board based on Matlock Bath in Derbyshire, which included the inspection of two pre-historic henges, Peveril Castle, the ruins of Sutton Scarsdale Hall, Bolsover Castle (" this remarkable example of early Stuart antiquarianism "), Wingfield Manor, a 15th century courtyard house, and Hardwick Old and New Halls, the former being a ruin of buildings erected in 1587–90 in the care of the Department of the Environment, while the latter, started in 1590, is maintained by the National Trust; the Board's members " warmly congratulate the Department's architects and the Trust on their work to preserve it with the help of grants made on the recommendation of the Historic Buildings Council."

By way of contrast the Board also examined two industrial monuments; first, the Abbeydale Industrial Hamlet near Sheffield, maintained by the Museums Department of that City, which " is probably unique in that it is possible to trace in one place the manufacture of a steel-edged tool from the raw materials to the finished products ". Secondly, the Board visited the National Coal Board's Newcomen engine at Elsecar which " is unique among surviving Newcomen-type engines in that it is still on its original site and in what is believed to be its original housing."

In the section on individual cases, it is reported that two monuments have been removed from the list, namely Orsett Roman Camp at Thurrock in Essex and a cave at Cannington Park in Somerset; the former was threatened by a new link road and the latter by quarrying.

Six cases of the use of compulsory powers by the Secretary of State are recorded; the sites range in date from Bronze Age to Medieval times and include the Albert Road Round Barrow at Farnborough in Hampshire described as " this fine example of a Bronze Age bowl barrow "; as it is threatened by building work an Interim Preservation Notice was issued. Then there are the group of round barrows at Little Cressingham in Norfolk, of which it is stated by the Board that " the importance of these monuments lies in their relationship with the Wessex Culture, indicated by the results of an excavation carried out in 1849, and in the rarity of such a group in East Anglia "; although three of the seven barrows are now flat, two are still some four to five feet in height, and the other two are " in generally good condition ". For the Roman period, sites included the Romano-British settlements at Bullocks Haste Common in Cambridgeshire, for which an Interim Preservation Notice has been served to save that part of the site not already subject to arable cultivation, for, as the Board notes, " very few of the once numerous Roman farms in the Fens now survive as visible antiquities." An Interim Preservation Notice was also issued to protect from levelling the rectangular manorial earthwork and shrunken medieval village at Church Farm, Hockliffe, Bedfordshire.

The Ancient Monuments Board advised on some seven cases during the year including the preservation of a complex of sites at Shaugh Prior, near Shaugh Cross in Devon, threatened by china clay extraction and tipping. The Board also recommended that now that three " relatively unspoilt stretches " have been scheduled, " action be taken to preserve as much as possible of the remainder of this remarkable industrial monument of Roman times ", namely the Car Dyke which connects the River Witham near Lincoln with the River Nene at Peterborough and is a Roman canal with a central channel and upcast banks on either side, in all some hundred feet wide; connections project it further south and a direct link from the Fens to York is made by another canal north of Lincoln, which joins the River Witham to the River Trent. So far as later sites are concerned, the Board's members " deeply regret the Department's action in grant aiding the construction by the County Council of a car and coach park for visitors to the hitherto unspoilt area " in the vicinity of Goodrich Castle in the County of Hereford and Worcester. At Tilbury Fort, Essex, " the only surviving example of a late 17th century fort with the outworks virtually unaltered since their construction, and characteristic of Low Countries fortifications of the period," the Board were asked to advise upon the archaeological implications of two schemes for flood defences along the north bank of the River Thames; members favoured the proposals, which would involve the construction of defences in the former of an earth bank and concrete wall round the landward side of the Fort. Coming into the 20th century, the Board considered the future of the decaying Fairbairn Crane at Hartlepool Docks in Cleveland, for " this swan-necked steam-driven crane is believed to have the greatest lifting capacity of any of this type ever built. It was supplied to Hartlepool Docks in 1904 and can be regarded as an outstanding industrial monument." Members of the Board agreed that if possible it should be preserved and moved to another waterfront site.

It is noted in the Report that the year in question saw an innovation in that *ad hoc* committees of the Board were appointed " to inspect excavations where criticisms of excavations techniques and standards had been made." One case was at Wiggery Wood, Gestingthorpe, Essex where the owner objected to the scheduling of a Roman site on his land discovered by him twenty five years ago because it would prevent his carrying out further excavations; after a meeting between three members of the Board and the owner it was agreed that the scheduling of the site should proceed and that the publication of a report on the excavations to date should be encouraged. The second case of an *ad hoc* committee being formed by the Board was to report on the current situation at Vindolanda at the invitation of the Vindolanda Trust following a discussion of the latter body's excavations and standards at the Vindolanda Roman Fort and civil settlement at Chesterholm in Northumberland; a detailed eight page report of the committee is published as an appendix to the Board's Report and the main recommendations are that an improved site supervision and recording system should be introduced, the responsibility and knowledge of the site supervisory staff should be broadened, and the planning, recording and excavations of the deep deposits should be reorganised more systematically; in addition the Board felt that at least one trained conservation officer on site was desirable, as was the employment of a full-time environmentalist when the excavations were in progress; in addition, the carrying out of a hydrographic survey was recommended. The Committee's final verdict on the criticisms of the way in which the Vindolanda project was conducted is as follows: " while appreciating the need for vigilance and the obligation of ensuring that archaeological excavations of important sites is up to a proper standard, and while commending the Department of the Environment on its initiative and stand in this matter, we deplore the hostile and negative attitude of some of the criticism we have heard, and the spreading of damaging rumours on insufficient investigation, which in our view, can cause great harm to archaeology."

In noting that the Secretary of State for the Environment had further increased by £250,000 the sum allocated for rescue archaeology, so bringing the total provision in 1974-75 up to £1,063,000, the Board " whole heartedly welcomed " the Secretary of State's plan to constitute a committee of the Ancient Monuments Board for rescue archaeology and to establish area archaeological advisory committees on a regional basis throughout England. It is noted that the Secretary of State's scheme is an extension of proposals made by the Ancient Monuments Board in 1972. The functions of the Board's Committee and the Area Committees " are to advise the Department on policies and priorities for surveys and excavations, on applications for grants and on back-up facilities to ensure early completion and publication of reports." At its constitution in July 1974 the Board's Committee had fourteen members, of whom six were members of the Board, who will serve for a term of two years initially.

This year the Ancient Monuments Board returned to a consideration of the problem of Industrial Monuments noting that since 1966 125 have been scheduled, including aqueducts, viaducts, cast-iron bridges, canal structures, engine houses, furnaces, ironworks, blowing houses, a railway arch, a gas-works, cranes, kilns, a stretch of iron railway and a glass-works cone. Particular attention is paid in Appendix 3 to the need to preserve those industrial monuments which relate to the iron and steel industry, in which it is noted that " in selecting industrial monuments there are two principal and related criteria. Firstly there are those sites associated with an ' historic first ', by virtue either of their own construction as buildings, or of the process that went on within them, or both. Often these remains date from that period during the 18th and 19th centuries when the technicological, economic and social conditions in England were unique in the world. Sites selected against the second criterion are those which are more generally illustrative of the technology of the period of industrialisation and particularly in those industries where Britain was in the van of invention and development. There is no terminal date precluding sites from consideration."

The blast furnace was not invented in Britain but was imported from France in the early 16th century and most of the early blast furnace sites, especially those in the Weald, have been researched and some excavated, while it is probable that the one at Pippingford will be preserved. The major British contribution sprang from Abraham Darby first smelting iron with coke in about 1709, thereby developing a major iron working area on the River Severn between Bridgnorth and Shrewsbury. As the area did not survive as a major industrial centre into the 20th century, it has been possible to incorporate into the Ironbridge Gorge Museum the sites at Coalbrookdale where Darby first smelted iron with coke, Bedlam furnaces built in 1756 beside the River Severn and their successors at Blists Hill, which were built after 1832 and remained in blast until the Great War. With the establishment of the Museum, other items have been moved into the area including the earliest surviving blowing engine, dated 1841, which was removed from the Lilleshall Ironworks. The Department of the Environment has grant aided schemes at Ironbridge and is taking into its care the famous Bridge itself at Coalbrookdale which dates from 1779. The Report notes that in all nine blast furnaces are scheduled in England, but none are in guardianship, although one is in guardianship in Scotland and negotiations are proceeding for one in Wales. In contrast to blast furnaces, the number of forges is not high, because the latter were often situated away from the furnaces and needed considerable water power for bellows and hammers. The Appendix includes in a very useful summary details of other monuments in the history of iron and steel technology, mentioning particularly the "outstandingly important" contribution of the Sheffield area where in Handsworth Benjamin Huntsman worked on the production of high quality crucible or cast steel from blister steel in the 1740's. Mention is also made of the co-operation with the Department of the Environment of the British Steel Corporation " in an attempt to establish which sites and items of equipment are worthy of preservation to illustrate the progress of the iron and steel industry during the later 19th and early 20th centuries. It is hoped that sufficient material will be preserved to show developments at least until the First World War."

It is recorded in the Report that six monuments have been taken into the care of the Department of the Environment during the year under review, and these include two deserted medieval villages at Gainsthorpe, Hibaldstow, Humberside, and Wharram Percy in north Yorkshire, as well as Bushmead Priory near Eaton Socon in Bedfordshire; the Department also took over the Powder Magazine, Garrison, St. Mary's, Isle of Scilly, Stott Park Bobbin Mill at Finsthwaite in Cumbria and a timber seasoning shed at Chatham Dockyard in Kent.

Some 319 monuments were recommended for scheduling by the Ancient Monuments Board during 1974, of which 47 are in Cornwall, 37 in Devon and 27 in Cumbria. These 319 monuments are divided up into the following categories: Prehistoric burial mounds or groups of mounds, 59; camps, settlements and other pre-historic sites, 62; Roman remains, 33; linear earthworks, 4; ecclesiastical sites and crosses, 35; castles and other secular buildings, 47; industrial monuments, 21; deserted villages, settlements, moated sites and mounds, 49; bridges, 9.

Archæological Excavations 1974

The Department of the Environment published a summary of pre-historic, Roman and medieval sites excavated in advance of destruction under the title of *Archæological Excavations 1974*. In the introduction it is stated that in 1974 out of the total provision for rescue archæology in England, Scotland and Wales, £802,450 was made available towards the costs of surveys and excavations in England, £142,676 for post-excavation work and £23,993 towards publication costs; for Scotland £34,566 was provided in grants and £42,035 in Wales; further, fees for supervisors and assistants working on direct and sponsored excavations totalled £64,726, £18,966 going to those engaged on post-excavation work. Although the economic state of the nation caused the delay or postponement of some development schemes, requests for financial aid for the investigation for threatened sites totalled double the amount of money available; this led to the rigorous selection of projects to be supported and large scale work was carried on especially in Lincoln, the City of London, Southampton and York; in addition, "special attention has been given to projects for surveys to assess the overall threats, especially in areas where little work has been organised hitherto." The Report further notes that "increasing support and participation have been provided by local authorities, both from the organisational standpoint and in the provision of services and financial support. With their co-operation, and that of other interests, full-time rescue excavation units have been established in a number of counties and districts, but financial restraints have limited further developments. University Departments, Museums and local Committees and Societies and other bodies continue to provide the greater part of the rescue archæology efforts beyond the Department's contributions."

During the year five major schemes were undertaken which were concerned more with the evolution of a landscape than with concentrating on the excavation of individual sites or on a limited period of the past; at Garton Slack in Humberside the investigation of the first 100 acres threatened by mineral extraction was finished, revealing more Bronze Age barrows and Iron Age houses with related pits and granaries. A further expanse of an Iron Age landscape was uncovered at Mucking in Essex, while at Beckford in the County of Hereford and Worcester a "straggling village" of ditched enclosures surrounding huts and storage-pits was examined, and inside one enclosure a hoard of ten currency-bars was discovered. In Hampshire, Bronze Age Romano-British cemeteries and Iron Age and later settlements and agrarian systems were examined along the line of the M.3 extension, while in Somerset the Somerset Levels Project continues its examination of pre-historic trackways in advance of peat cutting.

Among the more important pre-historic sites noted in the Report were two Mesolithic settlements at Darenth in Kent and West Heath in Sussex, as well as a scattered Neolithic occupation at Dover in Kent. At Butterbump in Lincolnshire excavation of a barrow revealed three more secondary burials including one in a barrel urn, and at Callis Wold in Humberside the re-excavation of Mortimer's barrow 275 revealed a Neolithic mortuary enclosure below a small barrow as well as traces of Beaker occupation; at Burton Fleming, also in Humberside, more square barrows were examined and additional sword-burials were discovered. Bronze Age cemeteries were excavated at Grendon in Northamptonshire, Martlesham in Suffolk, and Roxton in Bedfordshire. So far as pre-historic settlements are concerned, Iron Age farmsteads were excavated in a number of counties and particularly noteworthy is the important investigation of a 15,000 sq. m. Iron Age farmstead at the Portway at Andover in Hampshire. Hill forts also received attention and the investigation of the one at Thwing in Humberside disclosed occupation within the fort and the post-sockets of a box-rampart, while in Norfolk the hill fort at Wighton would seem to have remained in use long after the Iceni had been subdued. The only hill fort investigation in southern England was at Danebury in Hampshire, now in its sixth season.

An excavation in advance of road works near Corbridge in Northumberland produced what the Report describes as the year's " most important Roman military discovery ", namely the probable supply base or depot for Agricola's Scottish campaign. A river improvement scheme at Watercrook in Cumbria provided the opportunity for an investigation which has revealed a civil settlement developing at the same time as the early phase of the fort at the end of the first century. So far as the large Roman towns are concerned, at Lincoln an unexpected Postern gate and a stretch of late wall incorporating inscriptions was found in Saltergate, while at Leicester more details of the south wing of the forum were recovered. A large timber-box quay of late 2nd century date was found during a series of excavations along the Roman waterfront in the City of London, and at Colchester in Essex excavations in the Balkern Lane area produced evidence for an elaborate water supply system. Excavations on Roman rural sites included the villa at Barton Court Farm in Oxfordshire where an Iron Age/Roman/Anglo-Saxon sequence of land use can be detected. At North Cave in Humberside an aisled building and field ditches were found overlying a number of circular Iron Age houses, while at Sapperton in Lincolnshire extensive buildings lining a Roman road were investigated and there were found traces of iron working and also suggestions that Sapperton may be a small town; at Earith in Cambridgeshire there was what the Report describes as " one of the rare attempts to examine a Roman fenland farm ". Substantial work was also done on industrial sites of the Roman period, including five Roman pottery kilns at Bessecar, Doncaster, and on an iron working site at Crawley in Sussex, while at Ickham in Kent a watermill was discovered of late 4th century A.D. date.

From the earlier medieval period may be noticed the excavations of Anglo-Saxon settlement sites,

for example, at Thirlings in Northumberland where a second building was revealed, and in Durham City where there was the " unexpected " discovery of an Anglo-Saxon settlement apparently earlier than the traditional date of foundation, 995 A.D. At Osbournby in Lincolnshire the excavation of a Middle-Saxon settlement produced postholes of a bow-sided building and a fine series of stratified pottery. Pagan Saxon cemeteries were examined at Sowerby in Humberside where nine burials were recovered from areas near the 1959 excavation and at Empingham in Leicestershire where 129 graves were found aligned on a Roman trackway. Among ecclesiastical sites a number of churches were investigated including Hadstock, Essex, which involved the complete excavation of the interior of a church still in use revealing a complex sequence, including a Middle Saxon church which may have been part of St. Botolph's monastery. From work in major urban centres may be noted the excavation in Ripon in North Yorkshire where within the grounds of the Deanery was found substantial stone building of 14th century date overlying 12th century timber structures, while in Nottingham further work at Fisher Gate disclosed extensive traces of medieval buildings including a fine aisled hall. In the City of London the Roman timber waterfronts which had been rebuilt during the later Saxon period were reconstructed again in the 13th century and the 14th century saw a major rebuilding of the waterfront with the Roman system of box-framing being replaced by diagonally-braced uprights linked by plates. The main excavation of a castle during the year was at Stamford in Lincolnshire where the hall was examined and a complex sequence of rebuilding was revealed; at Goltho in Lincolnshire continued excavation below the 11th century ringwork disclosed four superimposed halls with camerae dating to the 9th and 10th centuries, and below the lowest hall was a Romano-British farmstead with circular huts and a series of enclosure sites.

Work on post-medieval sites included the continued investigation of the site of John Dwight's factory at Fulham in London, while at Woolwich was discovered a stone-ware kiln which predates Dwight by at least a generation and which " may represent the earliest successful attempt to produce stoneware in this country ". Another noteworthy post-medieval excavation was at Pippingford in Sussex where an early 18th century blast furnace for gun casting was excavated next to a unique wood lined gun casting pit.

EDUCATION IN THE UNITED KINGDOM

ENGLAND AND WALES
The present pattern of education in England and Wales derives from the Education Act of 1944 (Butler Act) modified later by minor Acts.

Department of Education and Science
The responsibilities of the Secretary of State for Education and Science which relate to civil science and (exercised through the University Grants Committee) the universities cover the whole of Great Britain, but his functions in connection with schools, further education and teachers relate to England and Wales only, except that responsibility for primary and secondary education in Wales is in the hands of the Secretary of State for Wales. Most of the work of the 520 H.M. Inspectors (who inspect schools and other educational establishments apart from universities, and provide the Secretary of State with information and advice) is in the local education authority areas. The Department of Education and Science does not run any schools or colleges, or engage any teachers, or prescribe textbooks or curricula, but it does set minimum standards of educational provision; control the rate, distribution, nature and cost of educational building; and control the training, supply and distribution of teachers. The Secretary of State's requirements under the Act are issued, and guidance is given, mainly in the form of regulations, orders and circulars addressed to local education authorities and other bodies, and in booklets. A report and six volumes of statistics are published annually.

Local Education Authorities
The educational service is a national service locally administered. Among its main features are:—

(a) Its administration is decentralized, the responsibility for providing state primary, secondary and further education (but not university education) to meet the needs of their areas being that of the 162 local education authorities (L.E.A.'s).

These elected councils appoint education committees consisting of some of their own members (a majority of the committee) and other people with experience in education and knowledge of the local education situation. The L.E.A.'s maintain schools and colleges and build new ones, employ teachers and provide equipment. Most of the public money spent on education is disbursed by the local authorities. Education is the largest item of their expenditure. L.E.A.'s are financed by rate support grants from the Department of the Environment and from the rates; and employ more than one million people, half of them teachers, whose salaries account for almost half of the national expenditure on education.

Voluntary Agencies
(b) Voluntary agencies play an important part in educational provision often in co-operation with the State. Some indication of its nature and extent is given below.

SCHOOLS AND PUPILS
Schooling is compulsory for all children between 5 and 16 years. No fees are charged in any publicly maintained school.

There are four main categories of school: (a) those maintained by local education authorities, the authorities meeting their expenditure partly from local rates and partly from grants made by the Department of the Environment; (b) direct grant schools which are assisted by grants from the Department of Education and Science; (c) recognized independent schools, i.e. independent schools which have sought and obtained recognition as efficient after inspection by H.M. Inspectors of Schools; (d) other independent schools.

County and Voluntary Schools
Maintained schools are of two types: (i) county schools (19,000) which are built, maintained and staffed by local education authorities. Their managers (primary schools) and governors (secondary schools) are appointed by the L.E.A.'s. (ii) Voluntary schools (9,100) which although built by voluntary bodies (mainly religious denominations) are maintained by an L.E.A. About two-thirds of the voluntary schools are Church of England schools and about 2,600 are Roman Catholic. Voluntary schools are of three kinds: controlled, aided, and special agreement. In controlled schools the L.E.A. nominates two-thirds of the managers or governors (the rest are nominated by the voluntary body), bears all costs and appoints the teachers.

In aided schools the managers or governors (two-thirds appointed by the voluntary interest and one-third by the L.E.A.) are responsible for repairs to the outside of the school building and for improvements and alterations to it though the Department of Education and Science may reimburse up to four-fifths of approved capital expenditure. The L.E.A. meets all running costs. The managers or governors control the appointment of teachers. Special agreement schools are those where the L.E.A. may, by special agreement, pay between one-half and three-quarters of the cost of building a new, or extending an existing, voluntary school, almost always a secondary school. Two-thirds of the governors are appointed by the voluntary body and the remainder by the L.E.A. Expenditure is normally apportioned between the authority and the voluntary body as for an aided school.

Direct Grant Schools
A direct grant grammar school has an independent governing body with L.E.A. representatives and receives maintenance grants direct from the Department of Education and Science in return for which a quarter of its places ("free places") are offered to pupils who have attended a grant-aided primary school for not less than two years. The remainder of the places may be available for fee-payers, except that up to a further 25 per cent. ("reserved places") may be claimed by the authority. The authority's proportion of the admissions may not, unless the governors agree, exceed one half. Fees are paid by the L.E.A.'s for the places they take up and they pay for about 60 per cent. of direct grant pupils. The fees paid by the parents of all other pupils are assessed according to the parents' means, any balance being paid to the school by the Department of Education and Science. The maintenance grant from the D.E.S. to the school comprises a capitation grant for every boy and girl in the school together with an additional sum for each sixth-former.

Direct grant grammar schools are to be phased out starting from September 1976. The 174 schools involved will have to become independent, close, or join the maintained sector.

Public Schools
By the term public schools is usually meant the independent schools in the membership of the Headmasters' Conference, the Governing Bodies

Association or the Governing Bodies of Girls' Schools Association.

Independent schools charge fees and do not receive grants from the State. *Preparatory schools* are mainly for boys from about 8 to 13 years who wish to enter public schools. All independent schools are open to inspection and must register with the Department of Education and Science which lays down certain minimum standards and can make schools remedy any unacceptable features of their building or instruction and exclude any unsuitable teacher or proprietor. To be designated " recognized as efficient ", an independent school must satisfy the D.E.S. that its standards are broadly comparable with those of grant-aided schools.

The State System

Nursery Education is for children under 5 years who may attend a nursery school or a nursery class attached to a primary school. In the public sector there are some 550 nursery schools accommodating about 42,000 children over half of whom attend part-time. In addition there are more than 290,000 boys and girls under compulsory school age who attend maintained primary schools full-time.

Primary Stage.—This begins at 5 years and the transfer to secondary school is generally made at 11 years. Over half the primary schools take 5 to 11-year olds; about a quarter are schools for infants (up to 7 years only); and most of the rest take juniors only (7 to 11 year olds). Most primary schools take both boys and girls. More than half have between 100 and 300 children each; most of the rest are smaller.

Middle Schools.—In some areas, middle schools are being developed which cover the age-ranges 8 to 12, 9 to 12, 9 to 13, 10 to 13 or 10 to 14.

Secondary Stage.—Secondary Schools are for children aged 11 to 16 and over. The largest have over 2,000 pupils but more than half the schools take between 300 and 600 pupils. In January, 1973, when there were 3,362,554 pupils in maintained secondary schools the main types were: (*a*) *comprehensive* schools (1,580,406 pupils), whose admission arrangements are without reference to ability or aptitude and cater for the secondary education of all pupils in an area; (*b*) *secondary modern* schools (965,753 pupils) providing mainly a general education with a practical bias, with an increasing number of pupils staying on after the school-leaving age; (*c*) *grammar* schools (496,766 pupils) providing an academic course from 11 to 16-18 years; and (*d*) *technical* schools (25,321 pupils) providing an integrated academic and technical course.

In a circular on *The Organization of Secondary Education* the Government in April 1974 told local education authorities and school governors of its intention to develop a fully comprehensive system of secondary education and of ending selection at eleven plus or at any other stage.

The *Further Stage* is treated separately below.

Primary and Secondary Schools

In January, 1973, there were 33,129 schools, of which 30,303 were maintained by local education authorities, 303 were direct grant schools, 1,390 were independent schools recognized as efficient, and 1,133 were other independent schools. There were at school in 1973, 9,190,030 children (4,720,366 boys and 4,469,664 girls) of whom 8,648,276 were in maintained schools, 130,090 in direct grant schools, 315,391 in recognized independent schools and 96,273 in other independent schools. Of those in maintained schools, 5,148,965 were in primary, 3,362,554 in secondary schools and the rest in nursery (15,450) or special (119,098) schools includ-

ing hospital. Almost all maintained primary schools and nearly two-thirds of the maintained secondary schools, are for both boys and girls. At secondary level most recognized independent schools are for boys only or girls only.

The total number aged 15 years or over (excluding those under the school-leaving age was 726,912; of these 618,149 were in maintained schools, 40,176 were in direct grant schools, 63,853 in recognized independent schools and 4,734 in other independent schools. 379,530 of the 726,912 were boys.

Middle Schools.—Numbers in this new type of school rose from 4,750 pupils (15 schools) in 1969 to 205,606 pupils (544 schools) in 1973. Pupils come to middle schools from " first schools " and usually go on to comprehensive upper schools.

Handicapped Pupils.—In January 1973 there were 119,098 handicapped pupils in 1,423 maintained special schools (including 9,112 in hospital); 14,866 of them were boarding. Of the 119,098, 85,241 were classified as " educationally sub-normal ".

A government Committee was set up in 1974, under the chairmanship of Mrs. Mary Warnock, to review the education of handicapped children and young people.

Class sizes.—In January, 1973, the average number of pupils to each qualified teacher in primary schools was 25.5 and in secondary schools 17.0. The average size of classes as registered in primary schools was, however, 30.8; and in secondary schools the average size as taught was 22.3.

School Meals.—L.E.A.'s must provide school dinners to all maintained school pupils who require them. In October 1974, 5,773,000 or 70.1 per cent. of pupils at maintained schools took the school dinner; 13 per cent. of the dinners were free of charge. Free school milk is available to pupils in special schools, children in other maintained schools up to the end of the summer term after they become seven, and other junior children for whom it is recommended on health grounds by a school medical officer.

Work Experience.—Many schools provide opportunities for pupils in their later secondary years to see something of the work and other activities of their neighbouring communities, as part of their curriculum. In recent years there has been a marked growth in the provision of " work experience " schemes which involve the participation of pupils in the work of industrial, commercial and other firms.

Examinations.—Secondary school pupils (and others) can take the General Certificate of Education (G.C.E.) or the Certificate of Secondary Education (C.S.E.). The examinations for the G.C.E., which are conducted by eight examining bodies (most connected with universities) are set at two levels: Ordinary level (" O ") and Advanced level (" A "). " A " level is usually taken after two years in the sixth form following " O " level, which is normally taken at 16 years (earlier only if the head teacher agrees). The G.C.E. is not a " grouped subject " examination and candidates at either level may take one or more subjects as they wish. At " A " level passes are awarded in five grades. " A " level candidates may take Special papers which are usually set on the same syllabus as the basic " A " level papers but contain more searching questions.

A new grading system for " O " level has been introduced. Under it, attainment in an " O " level subject is indicated by a grade A, B, C, D or E of which grade A is the highest and grade E the lowest. Candidates awarded grade A, B or C have reached the standard of the former subject pass at " O " level. Grades D and E indicate lower levels of attainment.

Like the G.C.E. the Certificate of Secondary Education (C.S.E.) can be taken in one or more subjects. It is open to boys and girls in any school completing five years of secondary education, and is meant for pupils of about 16 years who are around the average in terms of ability for their age groups. Five grades are awarded. The C.S.E. can be examined in a number of ways, internal and external, and is controlled largely by serving teachers sitting on the 14 regional examining boards. More than a quarter of a million candidates take the C.S.E. examinations each summer.

Co-ordinating the work of the G.C.E. and C.S.E. examining boards, and advising them, is the *Schools Council for the Curriculum and Examinations* which was established in 1964 by the Secretary of State for Education and Science as an independent advisory body financially supported by the D.E.S. and the L.E.A.'s and representing all educational interests with teachers forming a majority of its members. The Council is particularly concerned with promoting and encouraging curriculum study and development. Among its major programmes of work are those relating to English teaching at all school stages, and sixth-form curricula and examinations. It is also concerned *inter alia* with maintaining comparability of standards between boards and also between the two examinations (grade 1 in the C.S.E. is intended to indicate a standard such that a candidate achieving it might reasonably have been expected to obtain a pass at " O " level in the G.C.E. had he followed a course leading to that examination).

In January 1973, 268,995 pupils at 3,292 schools were following G.C.E. " A " level courses; 145,443 were boys and 123,552 girls. 97,235 of the 268,995 were in maintained grammar schools, 34,619 in recognized independent schools, 24,346 in direct grant grammar schools, 96,446 in comprehensive schools, 3,591 in technical schools, 5,601 in secondary modern schools and 7,157 in other maintained schools.

Of the 416,400 boys and girls who left school in 1972–73, 385,000 had obtained a C.S.E. or G.C.E. qualification and 131,000 planned to enter full-time further education (including university education).

TEACHERS

Although it is the duty of each Local Education Authority to ensure that there is efficient education to meet the needs of the local population, what is taught in the schools is normally decided on their behalf by the head teachers of schools.

Teachers are appointed by local education authorities, school governing bodies or managers. Those in maintained schools must (except student teachers and instructors) be approved as "qualified " by the Department of Education and Science. Most teachers become qualified by successfully completing a course at a college of education or university department of education. Those who, after 1973, obtain a university degree or one of certain specialized qualifications must take a one-year course of professional training before they can teach in a maintained school.

The estimated number of teachers (including the full-time equivalent of part-time teachers) in maintained primary and secondary schools in March 1975 is 442,000. This is 16,000 more than a year earlier and about 150,000 more than in 1965. The Government is planning a further increase to 480,000–490,000 teachers by 1981.

In October, 1972, teachers were being trained in a total of 206 institutions of various types: 121 maintained by local education authorities, 52 by voluntary bodies and 33 by universities. These included 30 university departments of education providing mainly one-year courses for graduates; 152 colleges of education providing mainly three- and four-year courses, 7 departments of education in polytechnics, which also offered mainly three- and four-year courses, 13 art teacher training centres offering one-year specialist courses, and 4 colleges of education (technical) providing one-year and 4-term specialist courses and initial training courses for serving teachers. At the voluntary colleges (provided mainly by religious denominations) up to 80 per cent. of approved capital expenditure and 100 per cent. of running costs are paid by the Government.

There were 123,195 students in training in October 1972 (39,055 men and 84,140 women) of whom 7,221 were in university departments of education, 110,534 in colleges of education, 2,598 in departments of education in polytechnics, and 1,863 in colleges of education (technical). Many colleges now provide for suitably qualified students a four-year course leading to a B.Ed. degree awarded by the university of whose institute of education the college is a member or by the Council for National Academic Awards.

In March 1972 there were some 365,305 full-time teachers in maintained primary and secondary schools, including 29,186 heads; in further education there were an additional 55,813 full-time teachers and in colleges of education 10,742.

Because in the next ten years or so the number of newly trained teachers required to meet the needs of the schools will decline substantially, the teacher training capacity outside the universities will be contracted to about 60,000 places. As a result, some 30 colleges may have to give up initial teacher training, though as many as possible will be used for other educational purposes.

Salaries.—The payment of full-time teachers in maintained schools is negotiated through the Burnham Primary and Secondary Committee set up under the Remuneration of Teachers Act 1965. The committee has two sides, one (teachers' panel) representing teachers and the other (management panel) the Secretary of State for Education and Science and the local authorities, with an independent Chairman. Its agreed recommendations are transmitted to the Secretary of State who must give effect to them. If the committee is unable to agree on a new salary award the matter is referred to independent arbitration and the Secretary of State must give effect to the arbitrators' recommendations unless they are set aside by Parliament. There is a superannuation scheme administered by the Department of Education and Science.

FURTHER EDUCATION

The term " Further Education " usually means all post-school education except that provided by universities and colleges of education.

Local Education Authorities are responsible, under the 1944 Education Act, for providing full-time and part-time courses of post-secondary education (other than university education) in their areas. There are ten Regional Advisory Councils which co-ordinate further education in their regions and nominate a majority of the members of the National Advisory Council on Education for Industry and Commerce which advises the Secretary of State for Education and Science on national educational policy relating to industry and commerce.

The 7,086 further education establishments (November 1972 enrolment: 3,388,528 students, more than half of them women) other than the colleges of education, may be grouped in the following main categories of which all, except the last, are grant-aided:—

1. *Polytechnics.*—Thirty major centres (some single colleges and others combinations of colleges) in which a wide range of full-time, sandwich and part-time courses are being developed and which aim to become " comprehensive academic communities " catering for students at all levels of higher education, and entirely or almost entirely for those of 18 years or more. They have governing bodies with a large measure of autonomy and are mainly teaching institutions though provision is made for certain research where it is essential to the proper fulfilment of teaching functions and the maintenance of close links with industry. As part of the sector of higher education within the Further Education system they complement the universities and colleges of education. By November 1972 there were 159,292 students enrolled in polytechnics, 114,147 of them taking advanced courses.

2. *Other Maintained and Assisted Major Establishments* (579).—Including all major establishments, other than polytechnics, maintained or assisted by local education authorities and providing courses in art, agricultural, commercial, technical and other subjects. 1,616,888 students.

3. *Direct-Grant Establishments* (16) which receive financial aid direct from the D.E.S. 4,761 students.

4. *Evening Institutes* (6,361) offering a wide range of courses, many of them recreational, for evening students, and often housed in premises used by day for other educational purposes.—1,590,056 students.

5. *Independent Establishments* which may apply to the Department of Education and Science for recognition as efficient; in 1972 there were 100 such recognized establishments with 17,531 students.

For Colleges of Education, *see* under " Teachers " above.

The number of students taking advanced courses (full-time, part-time, sandwich, or evening only) leading to recognized qualifications at grant-aided establishments was 203,481 (165,291 men and 38,190 women) in 1972. Of these 62,565 were on full-time courses, 33,715 were sandwich course students, 70,591 were taking part-time day courses and 36,610 were attending evening only classes. 11,746 of the total were working for a university first degree, 31,304 for a C.N.A.A. first degree (*see below*), 1,582 for a university higher degree and 739 for a C.N.A.A. higher degree.

In 1973 there was set up a *Technician Education Council* to develop a unified national system of courses for technicians in industry; and in 1974 the *Business Education Council* which will be concerned with the development of policies for a uniform national system of courses, in further and higher education, for people in business and commerce.

An important body with few, if any, parallels in other countries is the *Council for National Academic Awards* (C.N.A.A.) which awards degrees to students taking courses approved by it in non-university institutions. Following a recommendation of the Robbins Committee it was established by Royal Charter in 1964 as an autonomous body. More than 100 colleges in Great Britain conduct a total of some 700 courses leading to its degrees: B.A., B.Sc., and the higher degrees of M.A. and M.Sc. (for post-graduate course work) and M.Phil, and Ph.D. (for research which may be undertaken jointly in industry and college). Although these degrees are mainly in science and applied science subjects they can be awarded in any field and include at present degrees in economics, law, languages, librarianship, psychology, social science and business studies. In 1973–74, 40,781 students were working

for C.N.A.A. first degrees in the U.K. and 2,082 for a master's degree or Ph.D.

In 1974 the National Council for Diplomas in Art and Design merged with the C.N.A.A. and the diploma in art and design which was awarded by the N.C.D.A.D. has been superseded by the award of a C.N.A.A. B.A. hons. degree.

A *Further Education Information Service* is provided each summer by the local education authorities in cooperation with the polytechnics and other colleges offering full-time degree and higher national diploma courses, and the Department of Education and Science. Its purpose is to provide up-to-date information and advice about full-time degree, H.N.D. and Dip.H.E. courses in the colleges for those who find themselves, late in the summer, without a place on a course. It operates during August and September each year. A list of 400 local advisory officers is available from the D.E.S.

Adult Education.—A wide variety of courses for the education and recreation of adults is provided by local education authorities, the Workers' Educational Association and other voluntary bodies, the extra-mural departments of universities and certain residential colleges. In November 1974 the total number of students enrolled by local education authorities at adult education centres and evening institutes was about 1,747,000. There were also many students engaged in non-vocational classes at major further educational establishments. In 1973–74 there were some 272,000 students attending courses provided by the university extra-mural departments and W.E.A. districts. 470 students were admitted to long-term residential colleges from 1973–74.

The Youth Service.—Provides for the spare-time activities of young people. The Local Education Authorities co-operate with voluntary bodies in their areas and may maintain their own youth clubs. There are various national voluntary youth organizations which receive grants from the Department of Education and Science. By the end of 1974 there were about 2,500 full-time youth leaders on the Department's register. In addition there are many thousands of part-time paid and unpaid workers.

The new *Diploma of Higher Education* (Dip.H.E.) is a two-year diploma intended to serve as either a a terminal qualification or as a stepping stone to a degree or other further study; it has a normal entry requirement of two " A " levels. The first Dip.H.E. courses began in 1974–75.

SCOTLAND

The educational system of Scotland has developed independently of that of England and has a number of distinctive features. The general supervision of the national system of education, except for the universities, is the responsibility of the Secretary of State for Scotland acting through the Scottish Education Department. The Duty of providing education locally rests with the nine regional councils and three islands councils. Educational facilities of various kinds are also provided by the governing bodies of grant-aided schools, independent schools, " central institutions ", and national voluntary organizations in the field of informal further education.

Schools in Scotland fall into three main categories, viz. *education authority schools* which are managed by education authorities and financed partly from local rates and partly from rate support grant; *grant-aided schools*, conducted by voluntary managers who receive grants direct from the department; and *independent schools* which receive no direct grant, but which are subject to inspection and registration. As at January 1973 there were 3,138 education authority and grant-aided schools of which 127 were nursery schools, 2,348 primary, 492 secondary and 171 special schools. There were also 107 registered independent schools. The total number of pupils in education authority and grant-aided schools (including special schools) was 1,025,311 (524,027 boys, 501,284 girls), 16,751 children received nursery education.

Schooling normally starts at the age of 5, and the primary school course lasts for 7 years. Primary schools usually take both boys and girls. Pupils transfer from the primary course to secondary courses about the age of 12.

A large and increasing proportion of pupils at the secondary stage attend schools which offer a full range of non-certificate courses and of certificate courses leading to the Scottish Certificate of Education at Ordinary and Higher grade. There are also a number of other types of schools—those providing 3-year non-certificate courses, those providing 4-year courses leading to the Ordinary grade of the Scottish Certificate of Education; and senior secondary schools providing 6-year courses leading to the Higher grade of the Scottish Certificate of Education and post-certificate work.

The Scottish Certificate of Education examination is conducted by the S.C.E. Examination Board. Pupils may attempt as many of a wide range of subjects as they are capable of, on either the Ordinary grade which corresponds to the Ordinary level of the General Certificate of Education, or on the Higher grade which is normally taken a year earlier than the G.C.E. Advanced level and is therefore not of so high a standard. The Board grants a Certificate of Sixth Year Studies designed to give direction and purpose to sixth-year work by encouraging pupils who have completed their main subjects at Higher grade to study a particular subject in depth.

Further Education.—Facilities for further education are provided by 13 Central Institutions (grant-aided colleges administered by independent Boards of Governors) and by 82 further education centres managed by education authorities. The Central Institutions provide mainly advanced courses in science and technology, commerce, art, music, domestic science, and other subjects, leading to their own diplomas, to professional qualifications or, in certain cases, to C.N.A.A. degrees.

The further education centres normally provide less advanced courses which are mainly part-time covering vocational and non-vocational subjects, but a few offer courses of degree level. Courses are offered in a wide variety of subjects but to make the most economic use of resources, provision of certain courses is made on a regional or even a national basis.

Teachers.—All teachers in permanent posts in public or grant-aided schools in Scotland are required to be registered with the General Teaching Council for Scotland (which is independent of the Scottish Education Department) and normally to hold a teaching qualification awarded by a Scottish college of education. There are ten of these colleges and six, including two Roman Catholic residential colleges for women, provide both one- and three-year courses leading to a teaching qualification (primary education) or a teaching qualification (secondary education). Four of these colleges, in conjunction with local universities, also provide four-year combined courses leading to the degree of B.Ed. and to a teaching qualification (primary and/or secondary education). One of the Roman Catholic colleges also admits men to the three-year non-graduate course for primary teachers. Of the remaining four colleges, one is a residential college of physical education for women and the other three train only non-graduate primary teachers.

The basic scales of teachers' salaries are non-graduate, graduate and honours graduate, with additional payment for posts of special responsibility.

NORTHERN IRELAND

The statutory system of education in Northern Ireland is broadly comparable to that in Great Britain. Under the 1947 Act (and later amendments) primary education is provided for children up to about 11½ years of age when they are transferred to secondary school. The main types of secondary school are: grammar and secondary (intermediate). Selection for secondary education is based on verbal reasoning tests at eleven-plus combined with teachers' assessments of performance in school subjects. Fees are charged at grammar schools but qualified pupils there receive scholarships from their local education authority.

In January 1973 there were 1,182 primary (including nursery) schools with 214,924 pupils and 7,719 full-time teachers; 177 secondary (intermediate) schools with 89,163 pupils and 4,887 full-time teachers; 1 technical intermediate school with 12 pupils; 81 grammar schools with 46,577 pupils and 2,703 full-time teachers; 27 special schools with 2,291 pupils and 227 full-time teachers.

In 1973–74, 31,655 students were enrolled in institutions of further education; of these 10,146 were full-time, 9,076 were on day-release, and 12,433 were other part-time. The training of teachers is carried out in 5 colleges, and in the department of education of the Queen's University of Belfast and the education centre of the New University of Ulster.

Expenditure from public funds on education in Northern Ireland during 1972–73 was £101,651,000.

UNIVERSITIES

There are 44 universities in the United Kingdom (*see* pp. 501–10). Of these, 33 are in England, eight in Scotland, two in Northern Ireland and one (a federal institution) in Wales. In addition, there is the " Open University " which provides courses leading to degrees by a combination of television, radio, correspondence, tutorials, short residential courses and local audio-visual centres. The Open University offers undergraduate (no qualifications needed for entry), post-experience and post-graduate courses. It is grant-aided directly by the Department of Education and Science and does not come within the University Grants Committee system. More than 5,000 students graduate each year from the Open University.

A University College at Buckingham, the nucleus of an Independent University, will admit its first students in February 1976; it will provide a two-year course leading to a Licence and its tuition fees will be £1,500 for the first year (which will consist of 4 terms of 10 weeks each).

In 1972–73 there were 246,813 full-time students enrolled at universities in the United Kingdom; of these, 76,298 were women, 46,902 were postgraduates (including 11,140 women). The number of new undergraduate entrants (full-time) in 1972–73 was 68,057; the corresponding figures for 1958–59 and 1965–66 were 29,054 and 52,446. The full-time total of 246,813 in 1972–73 compares with just over 50,000 in 1938–39. In 1971–72, 51,782 first degrees (including honours degrees) and 11,282 higher degrees were awarded by universities. In 1972–73 there were 36,522 full-time teaching and research staff in U.K. universities; 3,851 of them were professors, 6,909 readers or senior lecturers, 23,769 lecturers or assistant lecturers.

By October 1974 the full-time student population had risen to about 251,400.

Students applying for admission to a first degree course at a university do so through the Universities Central Council on Admissions (U.C.C.A.) which was set up by the universities in 1961 on the initiative of the Committee of Vice-Chancellors and Principals. All universities participate fully in the U.C.C.A. Scheme except certain Scottish universities. The U.C.C.A. office is in Cheltenham.

The requirements for entry to first degree courses may vary somewhat from one university to another but the universities publish co-operatively an annual Compendium which describes these requirements in detail.

Students who are normally resident in Britain, have certain minimum qualifications and have been admitted to a university in the United Kingdom are entitled to an award from public funds; the amount varies according to the financial circumstances of the students and their parents.

In 1971–72 the total income of universities in the U.K. was £361,984,430 of which 1 per cent. came from endowments and donations, 74 per cent. from exchequer grants, 6 per cent. from students' fees, and 12 per cent. from research grants and contracts. Non-recurrent grants for capital expenditure paid by the Exchequer to universities in Great Britain totalled £71,716,532 in 1971–72; of that sum, £24,664,036 was for building works, £22,959,700 for scientific equipment and £10,484,946 for teaching hospitals.

The University Grants Committee advises the Secretary of State for Education and Science on university matters. Most of its members are academics or businessmen.

Although the universities have freedom in academic matters, the Government, through the U.G.C., determines the total size of the university student population, strongly influences its distribution between arts, science, medicine, etc., and determines the part which the university sector plays in the whole higher education system.

The Comptroller and Auditor General has access to the books and records of the U.G.C. and of the universities.

SCHOOLS COUNCIL FOR CURRICULUM AND EXAMINATIONS
160 Great Portland Street, W.1

Established in 1964, the Schools Council is an independent body representing all sections of the education service in England and Wales—with a majority of teacher members on its main committees. It undertakes research and development in the curriculum and keeps under review teaching methods and examinations in schools, including aspects of school organization in so far as they affect the curriculum.

The Schools Council is jointly financed by the Department of Education and Science and local education authorities.

Chairman, Sir Alex Smith.

Joint Secretaries, V. H. Stevens; J. G. Raitt; Dr. L. J. Stroud.

THE STOCK EXCHANGE IN THE UNITED KINGDOM AND IRELAND
THE STOCK EXCHANGE

Broker Members of the Stock Exchange buy and sell shares for members of the public. This is done for individual investors, for their advisers such as bank managers, solicitors and accountants, and for investing institutions like insurance companies, pension funds, unit trusts and merchant banks. For this the stockbroker is paid a fixed scale of commission based on the value of the securities. In addition to this service, brokers advise their clients, according to their particular circumstances and needs, on how to invest their money to greatest advantage. In addition, they will undertake to review periodically the portfolios of their clients. Often this service is backed up by a regular news-letter, keeping the investors up-to-date with economic developments and current recommendations.

The Stock Exchange provides facilities for raising capital for industry. Any Broker will give advice on how a company can finance its growth by getting a listing. For companies already listed, other methods are possible—such as rights issues and debenture or loan stocks—for obtaining additional funds. Brokers' advice is also available to industrialists on matters such as mergers and acquisitions.

All listed British companies are incorporated under the Companies' Acts, which contain stringent regulations for their management and control. They are limited liability companies, which means that if you are a shareholder in such a company you cannot be called upon to pay any part of its debt or liabilities if it gets into difficulties, unless, in quite exceptional cases, you are a holder of partly-paid shares, in which event your liability is limited to the amount required to make the shares fully paid. The Stock Exchange serves investors, whether inexperienced or expert, big or small, and the authorities of the Stock Exchange insist on compliance with stringent regulations to ensure that the public are fully informed of the constitution and record of every company whose securities are admitted to the market.

Furthermore, Firms of the Stock Exchange contribute to the Compensation Fund, a discretionary fund established to protect members of the public in the event of the default of a Member Firm.

In London the foundation stone of the present building was laid in 1801, but the building was almost entirely reconstructed in 1854 from the designs of Thomas Allason. The Stock Exchange has now been rebuilt as a large tower block, 331 feet high with a new Trading Floor to the west of the block.

There are other Trading Floors in Liverpool, Manchester, Birmingham, Glasgow, Belfast and Dublin.

The Stock Exchange provides a market for the purchase and sale of about 9,000 securities valued at over £210,000,000,000, and also securities listed on overseas Exchanges. At present, the Members of the Stock Exchange, consisting of Brokers (agents for clients) and Jobbers (dealers in specific securities), number about 4,150. Visitors' Gallery in London is open between 10 a.m. and 3.15 p.m. from Monday to Friday. Admission free and without ticket. Film show.

There are also Visitors' Galleries in Liverpool, Manchester, Birmingham, Glasgow and Dublin.

The Stock Exchange

Chairman, R. M. H. Marriott; *Deputy Chairmen,* D. H. LeRoy-Lewis; J. Dundas Hamilton; G. R. Simpson, D.S.O., T.D.; *Chief Exec.,* R. Fell, C.B.E.

Administrative Units

The Stock Exchange, London, E.C.2; the Stock Exchange, Margaret Street, Birmingham; the Stock Exchange, Norfolk Street, Manchester; the Stock Exchange, 69 St. George's Place, Glasgow; the Stock Exchange, 28 Anglesea Street, Dublin 2; the Stock Exchange, Northern Bank House, 10 High Street, Belfast; the Stock Exchange, Melrose House, 3 St. Sampson's Square, York.

THE NOBEL PRIZES

The Nobel Prizes are awarded each year from the income of a trust fund established by the Swedish scientist Alfred Nobel, the inventor of dynamite, who died on December 10, 1896, leaving a fortune of £1,750,000. They are awarded to those who have contributed most to the common good in the domain of (a) Physics; (b) Chemistry; (c) Physiology or Medicine; (d) Literature; (e) Peace. The first awards were made in 1901 on the fifth anniversary of Nobel's death. The awarding authorities are the Swedish Academy of Sciences: (a) Physics—(b) Chemistry; the Royal Caroline Institute, Stockholm—(c) Physiology or Medicine; the Swedish Academy—(d) Literature; a committee of five persons elected by the Norwegian Storting—(e) Peace. The Trust is administered by the Board of Directors of the Nobel Foundation, Stockholm. The Board consists of five members and three deputy members. The Swedish Government appoints a chairman and a deputy chairman, the remaining members being appointed by the awarding authorities.

The nationality of prizewinners is indicated as follows: (a) Great Britain; (b) U.S.A.; (c) France; (d) Sweden; (e) Belgium; (f) U.S.S.R.; (g) Germany; (h) Netherlands; (i) Switzerland; (k) Denmark; (l) Norway; (m) Spain; (n) Poland; (o) Austria; (p) Italy; (q) India; (r) Hungary; (s) Finland; (t) Canada; (u) Chile; (v) Argentina; (w) Japan; (x) Portugal; (y) Irish Free State; (z) Republic of Ireland; (aa) South Africa; (bb) Iceland; (cc) China; (dd) Czechoslovakia; (ee) Australia; (ff) Yugoslavia; (gg) Greece; (hh) Israel; (ii) Guatemala. The distribution by nationalities is shown at foot of table.

For prize winners for the years 1901–1963, *see* earlier editions of WHITAKER'S ALMANACK.

Year	(a) PHYSICS	(b) CHEMISTRY	(c) PHYSIOLOGY OR MEDICINE	(d) LITERATURE	(e) PEACE
1964	C. H. Townes (b) N. G. Basov (f) A. M. Prochorov (f)	Dorothy Crow-foot Hodgkin (a)	K. Bloch (b) F. Lynen (g)	J. P. Sartre (c)	Rev. M. L. King, Jr. (b)
1965	S. I. Tomonaga (w) J. Schwinger (b) R. P. Feynman (b)	R. B. Woodward (b)	A. Lwoff (c) F. Jacob (c) J. Monod (c)	M. Sjolochov (f)	U.N. Children's Fund
1966	A. Kastler (c)	R. S. Mulliken (b)	P. Rous (b) C. B. Huggins (b)	S. Y. Agnon (hh) N. Sachs (g)	No award
1967	Prof. H. A. Bethe (b)	Prof. M. Eigen (g) Prof. G. Porter (a) Prof. R. Norrish (a)	Prof. R. Granit (d) Prof. H. K. Hart-line (b) Prof. G. Wald (b)	M. A. Asturias (ii)	No award
1968	Prof. L. W. Al-varez (b)	Prof. L. Onsager (b)	R. W. Holley (b) H. G. Khorana (b) M. W. Nirenberg (b)	Y. Kawabata (w)	R. Cassin (c)
1969	M. Gell-Mann (b)	D. H. Barton (a) O. Hassel (l)	M. Delbrück (b) A. D. Hershey (b) S. E. Luria (b)	S. Beckett (z)	International Labour Organization
1970	H. Alfven (d) L. Néel (c)	L. F. Leloir (v)	Sir Bernard Katz (a) U. von Euler (d) J. Axelrod (b)	A. Solzhenitsyn (f)	N. E. Boriaug (b)
1971	Prof. D. Gabor (a)	G. Herzberg (t)	E. W. Sutherland (b)	P. Neruda (u)	W. Brandt (g)
1972	J. Bardeen (b) L. N. Cooper (b) J. R. Schrieffer (b)	C. H. Anfinsen (b) S. Moore (b) W. H. Stein (b)	G. R. Porter (a) G. M. Edelman (b)	H. Böll (g)	No award
1973	B. D. Josephson (a) L. Esaki (w) I. Giaever (b)	G. Wilkinson (a) E. O. Fischer (g)	K. Lorenz (o) N. Tinbergen (h) K. von Frisch (o)	P. V. M. White (ee)	H. A. Kissinger (b)
1974	Sir Martin Ryle (a) A. Hewish (a)	P. J. Flory (b)	A. Claude (b) C. de Duve (e) G. E. Palade (e)	E. Johnson (d) H. Martinson (d)	S. McBride (z) E. Sato (w)

The awards have been distributed as follows: PHYSICS (101).—U.S.A. 32; Gt. Britain, 19; Germany, 14; France, 9; U.S.S.R. 6; Netherlands, 5; Austria, 3; Japan, 3; Sweden, 3; China, 2; Italy, 2; Denmark, 1; India, 1; Ireland, 1.

CHEMISTRY (86).—Germany, 23; U.S.A., 20; Gt. Britain 19; France, 6; Sweden, 4; Switzerland, 3; Netherlands, 2; Austria, 1; Czechoslovakia, 1; Finland, 1; Hungary, 1; Italy, 1; Norway, 1; U.S.S.R., 1; Argentina, 1; Canada, 1.

PHYSIOLOGY OR MEDICINE (113).—U.S.A., 42; Gt. Britain, 17; Germany, 10; France, 6; Austria, 5; Belgium, 4; Denmark, 4; Sweden, 4; Switzerland, 4; Netherlands, 3; Australia, 2; Canada, 2; Hungary, 2; Italy, 2; U.S.S.R., 2; Argentina, 1; Portugal, 1; South Africa, 1; Spain, 1.

LITERATURE (71).—France, 11; Germany, 7; Gt. Britain, 6; Sweden, 6; U.S.A., 6; Italy, 4; U.S.S.R., 4; Denmark, 3; Norway, 3; Spain, 3; Chile, 2; Ireland, 2; Poland, 2; Switzerland, 2; Australia, 1; Belgium, 1; Finland, 1; Greece, 1; Guatemala, 1; Iceland, 1; India,1; Israel, 1; Japan, 1; Yugoslavia, 1.

PEACE (68).—U.S.A., 16; Institutions, 10; France, 9; Gt. Britain, 7; Germany, 4; Sweden, 4; Belgium, 3; Switzerland, 3; Austria, 2; Norway, 2; Argentina, 1; Canada, 1; Denmark, 1; Ireland, 1; Italy, 1; Japan, 1; Netherlands, 1; South Africa, 1.

In 1969 a Nobel Prize for Economic Sciences was instituted. Prize-winners have been: 1969, J. Tintergen (h) and R. Frisch (1); 1970, P. A. Samuelson (b); 1971, S. Kuznets (b); 1972, Sir John Hicks (a) and K. J. Arrow (b); 1973, W. Leontief (b); 1974, F. von Hayek (a) and G. Myrdal (d).

BRITISH ARCHITECTURE OF 1974–75

WOLFSON COLLEGE, OXFORD

The firm of Powell & Moya were entrusted with the task of designing a post-graduate college bearing the name of the benefactors, the Wolfson family. This was a difficult and challenging task, made all the more so by a site on which any large building complex would intrude upon the Cherwell Valley at its best and upon Edwardian North Oxford alike. Add the expectations which the building, a complete new Oxford college, aroused and the sheer magnitude of the task becomes apparent.

A built-in baby alarm system, a pram store and a children's play area are not usually found in the plans of a new Oxford College, but Wolfson College is not an ordinary college. It is a graduate college catering for older students and responds to this by providing houses and flats on the site for married couples and their families. The new college provides teaching and residential accommodation for graduate students and fellows (mainly scientists) with study bedrooms, small flats and houses for families, 2 offices, a dining hall to seat 250,with a large seminar room opening off it to increase the total dining capacity to 380.

In true Oxford style, its focal point is a main quadrangle, but there the similarity ends. The sides of the quadrangle are made up of offices, the library and hall. From here, two wings of bed-sitters and flats run down towards the river, one in a straight line, the other curving gently. Beyond one wing is a block of flats and close by three rows of terraced maisonettes.

Wolfson College overflows with interesting features from the pyramid hall roof with its glass top to the unusual layout of the library and its 40 individual studies, named carrels after the monks' cells they resemble. There is even a punt harbour which is on a bend in the river forming a lagoon with an opening into the stream at either end and an island in the middle. As far as possible the trees on the site have been kept and at one point a quadrangle has been built around them. The result is extremely attractive. There are more than 100 single rooms in the college, grouped in self-contained sets of two or four, each room a study-bedroom, some of them opening out on to shared sitting rooms.

The greatest attention has been paid to the married quarters, particularly the 20 terraced houses. They are, in actual fact, two and three bedroomed maisonettes built in terraces facing each other across tiled courtyards. They are designed on the fringes of the college—so that small children will not have the run of the main areas—but not be isolated from it.

Wolfson has the makings of an unusual academic community; no other mixed graduate college at Oxford is geared to the needs of the family in the same way. It is fortunate to have had the opportunity to start from scratch with a generous amount of money. It began in 1965 as a college for dons without fellowships at the established colleges but whose services were needed in the university. A site was set aside at Iffley and the college was to take the name " Iffley College ". But the endowments changed all that. The Wolfson Trust offered £1,500,000 for buildings and the Ford Foundation gave a similar amount for the long running of the college. The University accepted the gifts and gave as its contribution Cherwell, formerly the home of Professor J. S. Haldane, as land for the building. The idea, and the name, Wolfson College, was born.

The permanent Fellowship is of 60 (plus 30 other visiting and research fellows) and the number of graduate students will reach 250. It has a bias towards the sciences, particularly the biological sciences. Its internal structure is almost self-consciously democratic. The allocation of rooms is to be on the grounds of need rather than prestige.

The main college buildings are mostly three or four storeys high of reinforced concrete construction, faced externally with crushed grey granite reinforced concrete panels. A consistent use of concrete was one of the reasons why the building won not only an RIBA award but also the Concrete Society Award.

Structurally the building is an amalgam of various well tried techniques. In the administration wing circular precast columns support *in situ* plate roof and floor slabs but on one elevation, where windows are not required, load bearing storey height precast concrete panels are used. The library displays a similar pragmatic approach in the choice of structure. The first floor is supported on columns; above this an *in situ* roof slab is supported on a combination of two-storey height precast panels and *in situ* walls and roof beams. The residential blocks use yet another technique with flat slabs bearing on brick cross-walls, while on the corridor side of the block the slabs are supported on pre-cast columns.

The roof to the square dining room is structurally more unusual, consisting of inclined struts rising from each corner to form a truncated pyramid supporting at the top a rectangular frame around a central roof light.

A crushed grey Cornish granite exposed aggregate was chosen, its use being limited to the extreme outer face of the building. Soffits and reveals have been painted white and the circular columns which are set back from the face of the building have a smooth white, calcined flint finish.

The proportions of the concrete structural frame are very elegant and the use of glass as a reflective surface and curtaining to give controlled but lively colour is most imaginative. " The buildings ", said the RIBA jury, " show a rare sensitivity in the use of concrete as a facing material and the crushed granite facing to precast panels gives every sign of weathering pleasantly in the English climate."

WARWICK UNIVERSITY ARTS CENTRE

The architects' brief was to provide a building to be the social, cultural and theatrical hub of the University and contain a performance theatre to seat 550, a music centre, studio theatre, conference hall, coffee shop, university bookshop, workshops, dressing rooms and ancillary accommodation.

The building, sited centrally on the students' main pedestrian route across the campus, provides spaces for the wide spectrum of artistic activities available to the University. The foyer acts as a covered multi-level meeting place, most students walking through four or five times a day, to and from lectures. The route passes all the various activity areas which display information about forthcoming events.

The stage and auditorium (which seats up to 577) are designed to high standards to meet the requirements of professional touring companies, but the theatre is in the first instance designed for the University. It will need to be used for a variety of events, from ceremonial academic functions, conference and lecture use to full theatrical productions.

The site is between the library and science buildings to the North and Rootes Hall and the residential accommodation to the South. It is a very open site, sloping gently to the East towards Coventry, and is bounded visually to the West by the triangular wood across Gibbet Hill Road.

The plan meets all the requirements set out in the brief and achieves the aim of allowing for future expansion for other cultural buildings and of providing a social focus astride the main pedestrian route. It consists of two faceted buildings connected by a foyer and circulation space which will eventually link further elements of the complex. The administration and other proposed buildings enclose courtyards accessible from the Arts Centre foyer.

Entrance to all elements of the Arts Centre is made from a large connecting concourse. The North part of the foyer is designed to be used as an exhibition area. A coffee shop seating 200 forms part of this foyer at the South and is easily accessible for pedestrians passing along the main concourse or through the sculpture court. From the head of the staircase, balcony foyers lead to the four auditorium entrances; in this way, theatre audiences are kept separate from the general users of the concourse while still being in the same place. Similarly, since there are entrances from the concourse to all the other elements of the design, this will ensure a considerable cross-movement of users, allowing meetings and refreshment. The concrete blockwork finishes in the large foyer areas are enlivened by gloss-painted ceilings, planting and coarse graphics. The variety of levels is the key to the success of this vast space.

Four gangways serve the auditorium for the four separate entrance points. The seats are arranged in one bank of fourteen rows with a variable rate of eighteen to twenty-six degrees. The theatre is designed for optimum use with a forestage and 529 seats. To effect the provision of proscenium productions by visiting companies, the forestage can be lowered and thirty-eight extra seats fitted. For musical productions an orchestra of up to forty-five musicians can be accommodated in the forestage space and understage area; for concerts the side screen periaktoid construction can be rearranged to produce suitable acoustic conditions. A 60 ft. fly tower provides adequate flying and lighting facilities for all productions and a point suspension grid at the front of the fly tower can be used for lifting props and scenery off the forestage.

A 24 ft. high antespace with soundproof doors connects both the main auditorium stage and the studio theatre scenery entrance with the workshop proper. This workshop has a central area for the construction of scenery 24 ft. high and an area for the storage of flats.

The music department is a self-contained unit with an external entrance from the main forecourt for large instruments. A lobby which can be used as a common room opens on to the ensemble room which can accommodate soloists and chamber orchestras. This room is separated by a corridor from four practice rooms, on the first floor are a further five practice rooms.

Opening off the concourse, the conference hall is laid out with stepped rake and tables and fixed swivel seats. It allows for 200 places.

The bookshop is planned to provide up to 1,900 ft. of shelving and a 25 ft. long sales counter. Service desks and offices are arranged to give maximum surveillance by the bookshop staff. The long wall of the bookshop runs along the pedestrian route and provides an extensive area for display. 100 per cent expansion of the bookshop is envisaged, partly by an increase in area and partly by introducing a mezzanine level.

The exterior of the building is of white Forticrete blockwork, glass reinforced plastic cladding panels and aluminium windows and louvres. Inside are white fairfaced walls, melamine faced panels, and painted render. The floors are precast pavings, carpet, stained chipboard and vinyl tiles. The total cost of the building was £900,260.

The Architects, Renton, Howard, Wood Levin Partnership, received one of the RIBA's coveted awards for this scheme. The jury considered it to be a very stimulating yet human meeting place. The interior is considered to be more interesting than the exterior but " it is recognised that landscaping would have a significant effect on both the form and appearance of the building ".

HALLIFAX BUILDING SOCIETY
HEAD OFFICE

The Society's considerable growth rate and the inadequacy of its existing premises gave an opportunity to reappraise its methods and social climate. The principal decisions were: That the mortgage, application and administration process should be in one single level Burolandschaft space; That storage of title deeds should be in a secure vault with an automated retrieval system; That amenity and social areas should be provided at ground level for after-hours use; That full air-conditioning, the most modern service installations and high quality low maintenance materials should be used.

There was no statutory control over density, height or light angles. The local authority did require the provision of parking within the site for essential users and the use of York stone on external walls as it is the established material of the town.

The site, 54,000 sq. ft. of irregular quadrilateral shape, is on the edge of the central area of Halifax, closing the vista of a major commercial street. Most of the centre lies below or on the same level as the site with residential areas rising steeply to the West in the bowl-like valley in which Halifax stands. It was formerly the site of a brewery. The Society owns the adjacent land to the West and had built a seven-storey building for computer operations in 1967. A link-up between sites to create a single unit was sought. Apart from the office tower, buildings around the site do not rise above third floor and are a mixture of commercial and domestic buildings and a Masonic lodge.

The slope of the site enabled vehicular and plant areas to be concealed below a landscaped podium above the deed storage vault. Ground level had to contain social facilities and reception, while the first floor needed to link with the adjacent office building to provide common services. The two floors cover only half the site and leave extensive open spaces to North and South. The general office area required coincided with the site area. A complete floor following the irregular quadrilateral slope of the site was needed. The general office is on the third floor, from where there are fine views over the town and surrounding country. On the top floor are executive offices, the board suite and overnight and residential accommodation.

The structure of the building is a massive reinforced concrete box sunk 50 ft. into the rock which forms the base of the building and contains the automatic filing system. Rising at the corners of the site are four pairs of triangular concrete service and stair towers.

Erected from the basement slab to span between the towers, a 14 ft. steel girder structure carries the concrete office floors. The central part of the building, continuous through all floors, is a flat slab concrete frame.

A building of these proportions fits more readily into a Yorkshire mill town than to any Southern town. The looseness of grain provides convincing sites and because the townscape is already dotted with great mills, heroic size does not shock or dwarf. Despite its size, the building adopts a servant role towards the other buildings in the town centre. The overhang which points towards the town is so high that the space beneath is generally referred to as " the piazza ". As it stands, it is majestic and yet human, almost intimate.

The external finish of the building is limited to York stone for pavings, podium works and towers and bronze glass in bronze-anodised aluminium framing for walls to occupied spaces. Internally there is tile, bronze on the core, buff on the columns. Ash panelling or vinyl cloth is used on the walls and a warm yellow carpet, tile and broadloom on all floors except utility areas.

The jury of the RIBA were strong in their praise of the Architects, Building Design Partnership. Their opinion, when giving it an award was that "the Client is rewarded with one of the finest office environments in Britain today and one which is likely to remain so for a long time to come. Finally it is a building which could not have happened without the guiding hands of a team of gifted designers ... It is a building of which the Society can be proud, the town can be proud and our profession must surely be proud."

UNIVERSITY OF LEICESTER LIBRARY

The building has been designed to house centralised library services with open access to the stacks for all readers. It was planned for construction in two stages with the possibility of further extension at an unspecified date. The first stage accommodates half a million books and 800 readers: when the second stage is added the building will provide accommodation for one million books and over 1,500 readers. Initially, the library has been arranged on a traditional " functional " basis with the possibility that other systems of library organisation can be accommodated in the future. A linear plan was chosen primarily to facilitate the parallel growth of the various elements of the building: the stacks, technical services, staff areas and core can all be extended *pari passu*, so maintaining the same relationship with each other.

The site for the new library presented the Architects, Castle, Park, Hook & Partners, with a difficult task—to insert a building (capable of 100 per cent. future expansion) between two buildings of strong individual character, on the one side the classical early Victorian Fielding Johnson building housing the main administration offices of the University and on the other Stirling and Gowan's engineering building.

The front portion, constructed in 1837, is a protected building, but two sides of the courtyard—sections of no architectural or historical interest—were demolished for the first stage of the library and the third side will have to be demolished for the next stage. The entrance to the building is on the north-east face and is approached over a new forecourt bounded on one side by the Attenborough Building and the Engineering Buildings.

The structure consists of hollow *in situ* concrete columns and beams with precast floor units. The accommodation is fully air-conditioned by roof mounted package units connected to these hollow structural members. The building has been designed to give a high level of thermal insulation: the external walls are insulated and faced with solar heat reflecting glass, whilst the asphalte roof is kept covered with water.

The restrained external appearance in dark coloured glass designed to reflect and act as a foil to the surrounding buildings has not only made the library visually sympathetic with its neighbours, but has in some interesting way united all three build-

ings around the well proportioned forecourt, forming the entrance to the library. The use of the reflective surfaces reduces the bulk of the building, creating surprise, arousing interest and fascination. It is a very strong and convincing design solution.

The roof, usually a forgotten dimension in the building and important because a number of tall buildings overlook the library, has been very carefully handled with neat assembly of plant and protective glazed canopies.

The approach to the main entrance is quite theatrical, a double set of well detailed revolving doors set below a simple suspended canopy with exposed structure and solid deck.

The simplicity evident in the elevations is in fact repeated throughout the whole building; the basic floor plan is flexible usable space around the central core; the structural system naturally accommodates the mechanical services, so much so that suspended ceilings are almost non-existent and sensible window sizing allows the most economical use of energy to heat and cool the building. It is quite obvious that very close communication existed between client and architect.

The interior is well controlled, if rather severe, and lack of finance has necessitated re-using existing library furniture. Despite this, the RIBA award for the East Midlands Region was deservedly won by the architects of this very fine building.

PILLWOOD HOUSE, FEOCK

The architects brief was to design a house with holiday use in mind and a plan arrangement that could be modified to suit the varying numbers of people who might use it (4 to 8 people). It had to be as compact as possible, at the same time ensuring that the living areas took advantage of the view of the Fal river to the south-east.

The wooded western slope of the site limits the amount of sunshine it receives to winter mornings and up to mid afternoon in the summer. The local climate is exceptionally mild in Feock and there is rarely any frost. It is also well sheltered from prevailing winds. The site slopes steeply to the water's edge, but the area available for building is level and terraced into the slope.

Many of the nineteenth century houses in the locality have glazed porches and large conservatories and this, together with the topographical and climatic conditions, gave rise to the form and choice of the elements in the design.

In order to take advantage of the view, the living area and kitchen have been located at first floor level with an adjoining terrace. Half of this living area is enclosed, the other half forms the upper part of the conservatory space. Sliding partitions can close off the rear part of the living area to complete the enclosure and thus provide a contrast to the openness of the glazed area.

The bedrooms on the ground floor are arranged with direct access to the outside. The sub-divisible children's bedrooms open on to the play area, which has large sliding doors to the lower terrace. The play space forms the lower level of the conservatory and connects with the living area by means of an open spiral staircase. The adults' bedroom has a second spiral staircase which gives access to the enclosed living area above. The bedroom spaces can be changed by re-arranging the position of the sliding partitions.

Three-fifths of the floor area is enclosed and due to the good insulation of the walls and floor slab, there is little heat loss. These spaces are heated by means of underfloor heating. The remaining two-fifths, the conservatory space, gives unrestricted views of the wood and the river and at the same time its height and the arrangement of the louvred windows at the apex and in the opposite and lower surface in the play space, through ventilation by stack effect. This minimises heat gain in the summer months.

Internal blinds have been fitted which give additional local control to restrict glare. The pitch of the glazed roof, as well as aiding ventilation, also re-establishes the angle of the slope of the land and the resulting tree line. In the summer the trees form an external "room" and act as a screen to the house.

This holiday home combines in a very pleasing and original way, the selected materials of steel, aluminium, glass and white glass reinforced plastic panels, and uses colour in a restrained but exciting manner.

The theme is consistent throughout and great care and attention have been given to the detailing to ensure a first-class standard of design and finish in all the component parts. The building sits well on the site and affords the occupants excellent views of the creek, while the surrounding trees afford adequate privacy.

This building also won a Royal Institute of British Architects award, the jury considering, " this small building is excellent of its type and well deserving of an award ".

VICARAGE, PARISH HALL AND OFFICES, TRING

Tring Vicarage in Hertfordshire is a Grade II listed building in Jacobean revival style, erected in the 1820's. It was no longer suitable for use as a vicarage as it cost too much to maintain and was in an advanced state of dilapidation.

This was the problem faced by the firm of architects, Melvin, Lansley and Mark, who were instructed to design a new parsonage house in the grounds of the existing vicarage, for the Vicar of Tring. The original intention was to demolish the existing vicarage, but the planning authority counselled strongly against demolition.

While the building of the new vicarage was taking place, the architects were instructed by the Diocese of St. Albans to examine the possibilities of retaining the existing house as part of a comprehensive development plan for the remainder of the site.

In 1971, planning and listed building consent was granted for a scheme involving the conversion and restoration of the old vicarage, a new wing of offices, a new parish hall (for use both by the Anglican and Methodist congregations) and the restoration of the vicarage gatehouse.

Work started five years ago and the parish hall was the last part of the development. The result is that the vicarage is the focal point of the complex with the new buildings linked to it to form a collegiate type of development.

Traditional materials and construction have been used throughout the project, namely load-bearing brick walls, pitched roofs with dark concrete tiles on the new vicarage and blue/black asbestos slates elsewhere. Great care has been taken to match brickwork and adopt rendering and plasterwork to blend with the original.

The jury of the Royal Institute of British Architects were very impressed by the blending of new work with existing buildings of a different period. " The use of traditional materials and careful detailing successfully achieve affinity between old and new without stylistic concessions. Fortunately the architects' sensitive detailing is matched by a high standard of workmanship." This opinion won for the firm one of the seven highly coveted awards of the Royal Institute of British Architects for 1975.

CHRIST'S HOSPITAL ARTS CENTRE, HORSHAM

The "Religious, Royal and Ancient foundation" of Christ's Hospital was established by King Edward VI in 1553. For centuries, beneficent almoners financed and supervised the education of the " Bluecoat boys " in the City of London. In the late 19th century the school moved out to the present rural site near Horhsam in Sussex, into new buildings designed by Aston Webb which were started in 1896 and finished by 1902. These buildings are built in a hybrid, red-brick, stone-trimmed Elizabethan/Gothic style.

The new buildings surround the old music school which lies to the south-east of the main quadrangle of the school. The buildings are on the far side of a fine avenue of limes from the rest of the school and form the last small blob on the axis of a grand axial design. The theatre is set between the classrooms and the music school, the whole complex forming a three-sided courtyard.

The school wanted nine classrooms for history, geography and economics and a small subject library and a seminar room; a theatre for 450–500 with ancillary accommodation: an enlarged music school to provide ten teaching rooms, forty-one practice rooms, a band room, library and a small recital room.

The grouping of the buildings is based on a decision that the theatre should be between the classrooms and music school. The music practice rooms back on to the stage end of the theatre thus providing forty-five individual dressing rooms, as well as a range of chorus and orchestra assembly spaces. The arrangement obviates the need for masses of accommodation that is unused a great deal of the time. A large changing room with showers, etc. is alongside the theatre for everyday use.

The *raison d'être* of the Christ's Hospital buildings is the new theatre. Professor Bill Howell (who was tragically killed before the theatre was fully in operation) had quietly made a bit of theatrical history with his cheap " temporary " Young Vic theatre in London. Here at Christ's Hospital he was able to develop his ideas further with a more generous budget. The result is a unique theatre that successfully solves the almost intractable problem of flexibility, and is a building where arena, thrust or proscenium productions are all possible. This has been achieved by deciding to move the audience about, not mechanically and expensively, but by using the ever-present manual strength of Christ's Hospital boys. Sturdy timber rostra form the stages and a mobile " fourth wall " of towers that carry the lines of the three balconies is the elementary and practical solution. When the towers are in place, the theatre is a large room with three, one-row deep galleries on all sides and a central playing area.

Entering the theatre is a great surprise; one is prepared for it to be octagonal, but one is not prepared for the vivid red timber galleries, benches stained red, walls dark and a ceiling enlivened by red-stained timber " egg-crates ". It is a genuinely cheerful building which, filled with Bluecoat boys, takes on the character of some latter-day Globe and it will surely be ideal for some of Shakespeare's most robust plays.

The adjoining new buildings are well finished and in the case of the octagonal recital room and the octagonal library, make elegant small consorts for the theatre. Red brick walls are used externally and the interior is painted white throughout the classroom block. Wood is natural inside the classrooms, stained brown in the corridors and green in the library. All important doors are painted red.

Door frames are pressed metal, windows galvanised steel painted dark brown. The new rooms of the music school cluster round the Webb practice rooms and provide sound-sealed space for the multifarious musical talents of the school.

The building sits handsomely among the existing landscape of fine trees and grass and it is planned to plant creepers on the large area of brick wall. Evergreen honeysuckle has been chosen for the north walls and clematis, vines and virginia creeper elsewhere.

The new buildings are remarkable for the way they fit into the grandeur of a late Victorian public school, by using forms that link with the past by the powers of association, while being new in themselves. The Royal Institute of British Architects selected Christ's Hospital Arts Centre for one of their 1975 awards, naming the firm of Howell, Killick, Partridge and Amis, adding that it was a fitting memorial to a fine architect.

THE COST OF LIVING

The first cost-of-living index to be calculated in Great Britain was the one which took July, 1914, as 100 and was based on the pattern of expenditure of working class families in 1904. Since 1947 the Index of Retail Prices has superseded the cost-of-living index, although the older term is still often popularly applied to it. This index is designed to reflect the month-by-month changes in the average level of retail prices of goods and services purchased by the " majority " of households in the United Kingdom, including practically all wage-earners and most small and medium salary-earners. For spending coming within the scope of the index, a representative list of items is selected and the prices actually charged for these items are collected at regular intervals. In working out the index figure, the price changes are " weighted "—that is, given different degrees of importance—in accordance with the pattern of consumption of the average family.

A more widely used guide when considering changes in the average level of prices of all consumer goods and services, particularly over a number of years, is the consumer price index, now renamed the consumers' expenditure deflator. This index, which has been calculated back to 1938, covers the expenditure of all consumers as defined for national income purposes, and compares the price of goods and services actually purchased in a given year with the prices of the same goods and services in a base year.

During 1973 the Central Statistical Office constructed an annual index of prices of consumer goods and services over the period 1914 to 1972. This index has been constructed by linking together the pre-war cost of living index for the period 1914–1938, the consumers' expenditure deflator for the period 1938 and 1946–62* and the General Index of Retail Prices for the period 1962–1972.

In 1974 the index was rebased taking January 1974 = 100. Using this index the following table has been constructed:

	Price Index Jan. 1974 = 100	Comparable Purchasing power of £1 in 1974
1914........	11·1	9·77
1915........	13·7	7·92
1920........	27·7	8·91
1930........	17·6	6·19
1938........	17·4	6·24
1946........	29·4	3·69
1950........	35·6	3·05
1955........	44·1	2·46
1960........	49·6	2·19
1961........	51·0	2·09
1962........	53·0	2·05
1963........	54·0	2·01
1964........	55·8	1·94
1965........	58·4	1·86
1966........	60·7	1·79
1967........	62·3	1·74
1968........	65·2	1·66
1969........	68·7	1·58
1970........	73·1	1·48
1971........	80·0	1·36
1972........	85·7	1·27
1973........	93·5	1·16
1974........	108·5	1·00

By employing this table an annual purchasing power of the pound index may be derived by taking the inverse of the price index. So, for example, if the purchasing power of the pound is taken to be 100p in 1938, then its comparable purchasing power in 1974 would be:

$$100 \times \frac{17·4}{108·5} = 16p$$

It should be noted that these figures can only be approximate.

*There are no official figures for 1939–45.

TEMPERATURE AND RAINFALL RECORDS

WORLD: The maximum air temperature recorded is 57·8° C. (136° F.) at San Louis, Mexico on Aug. 11, 1933; the minimum air temperature recorded is −88·3° C. (−127° F.) at Vostok Antarctica on Aug. 24, 1960. The greatest rainfall recorded in one day is 1870 mm. (73·62 ins.) at Cilaos, Ile de Réunion on Mar. 16, 1952; the greatest rainfall in one calendar month is 9,300 mm. (366·14 ins.) at Cherrapunji, Assam in July 1861; the greatest annual total being 22,990 mm. (905·12 ins.) also at Cherrapunji in 1861.

UNITED KINGDOM: The maximum air temperature recorded is 38·1° C. (100·5° F.) at Tonbridge, Kent on July 22, 1868; the minimum air temperature recorded is −27·2° C. (−17° F.) at Braemar, Aberdeen on Feb. 11, 1895. The greatest rainfall recorded in one day is 280 mm. (11 ins.) at Martinstown, near Dorchester on Jul. 18, 1955; the greatest annual total is 6,528 mm. (257 ins.) at Sprinkling Tarn in 1954.

THE QUEEN'S AWARD TO INDUSTRY

The Queen's Award to Industry was instituted by Royal Warrant in 1965 in accordance with the recommendations of a committee chaired by the Duke of Edinburgh. The Award Scheme was reviewed in 1970 in the light of five years' experience by a committee chaired by Lord McFadzean, which considered all aspects of the Award and made a number of recommendations that were accepted by the Government. The most important was the extension of the scheme to include "invisible" exporters and merchants. The reports of both committees are available from Her Majesty's Stationery Office.

The Award is designed to recognize and encourage outstanding achievements in exports or in technological innovation or both. It differs from a personal Royal honour in that it is given to a unit as a whole—management and employees working as a team.

It may be applied for by an organization within the United Kingdom, the Channel Islands or the Isle of Man producing goods or services which meet the Awards criteria. Eligibility is not influenced in any way by the particular activities of the unit applying, its location, or size. Units or agencies of central and local government with industrial functions, as well as research associations, educational institutions and bodies of a similar character, are also eligible, provided that they can show they have contributed to industrial efficiency.

The criteria on which recommendations for the Award are based are:

(i) A substantial and sustained increase in export earnings to a level which is outstanding for the products or services concerned and for the size of the applicant unit's operations, taking into account any special market factors described in the application. Export earnings include receipts by the applicant unit in this country, services to non-residents and profits remitted to this country from overseas branches, subsidiaries or associates in the same general line of business.

(ii) A significant advance, leading to increased efficiency, in the application of technology to a production or development process in British industry or the production for sale of goods which incorporate new and advanced technological qualities.

The Award is formally conferred by a Grant of Appointment, and is symbolized by a representation of the emblem cast in stainless steel and encapsulated in a transparent acrylic block. It is held for a period of five years but units can continue to display the emblem of previous Awards during the life of any Awards. Presentations are usually made on behalf of the Queen by Her Majesty's Lieutenants of Counties at the unit's principal place of business or production unit. Holders are entitled to fly the Award flag and to display the emblem on the packaging of goods produced in this country, on the goods themselves, on office stationery, in advertising and in articles used by employees

Awards are announced on April 21 each year—the actual birthday of Her Majesty the Queen—and published formally in a special supplement to the London Gazette.

All enquiries about the scheme and requests for application forms should be made to:

The Secretary,
Office of the Queen's Award to Industry,
1 Victoria Street,
London S.W.1.
[01-222 2277]

Increased Exports Awards

In 1975, the Queen's Award was conferred on the following 78 concerns for achievement in increasing exports: The Marchon Division (UK) of Albright & Wilson Ltd., Whitehaven; Allied Colloids Ltd., Bradford; Anderson Mavor Ltd., Motherwell; Asprey and Co., W.1.; W. S. Atkins Group Ltd., Epsom; Beckman Instruments, Ltd., Glenrothes; Bowater Treatment Co. Ltd., Dorking; George Blair & Co. Ltd., Newcastle upon Tyne; Blue Anchor Caravan Mfg. Division Ltd., Skegness; Booth Bros. Ltd., Bradford; Guided Weapons Division of British Aircraft Corporation, Stevenage; British Celanese Ltd., W.1.; British Hovercraft Corporation Ltd., East Cowes; Power Cables Division, Wrexham and Supertension Cables Division, Belvedere, British Insulated Callender's Cables; Burberrys Ltd., E.9; Colchester Lathe Co. Ltd., Colchester; Brian Colquhoun & Partners, W.1.; Concargo Ltd., Weston-Super-Mare; Crabtree Denims Ltd., Todmorden; R. Croan & Sons Ltd., Edinburgh; John Dewar & Sons Ltd., Perth; Dominick Hunter Engineers, Birtley; Donaghadee Carpets Ltd., Donaghadee; X-Ray Systems Division of EMI Ltd., Hayes; Telecommunications Division of EMI Sound and Vision Equipment Ltd., Hayes; Clay Division of English China Clays Ltd., St. Austell; Ethicon Ltd., Edinburgh; Eurotherm Ltd., Worthing; Evans Electroselenium Ltd., Halstead; Federal Electric Ltd., Wolverhampton; Reinforcements Division of Fibreglass Ltd., St. Helens; Financial Times Ltd., E.C.4; James Garnar & Sons Ltd., S.E.1; Turbocharger Division of Garrett Airesearch Ltd., Skelmersdale; Bankfield Division, Bilston, and Wheel Division, Telford, of GKN Sankey Ltd.; Glaxo Holdings Ltd., W.1.; Ilford Ltd., Ilford; Organics Division Manchester, Pharmaceutical Division, Macclesfield and Methanol Group of Imperial Chemical Industries; Instron Ltd., High Wycombe; International Harvester Co. of Great Britain Ltd., E.C.1; Consumer Division of James A. Jobling & Co. Ltd., Sunderland; K.E.F. Electronics Ltd., Maidstone; Kina Engineering Ltd., Ipswich; Kirkpatrick of Ballyclare, Ltd., Ballyclare; Knoll Spinning Co. Ltd., Oldham; P. Leiner & Sons Ltd., Treforest; Letraset International Ltd., S.E.1; Lewmar Marine Ltd., Havant; Loewy Robertson Engineering Co. Ltd., Poole; London & Overseas Freighters Ltd., W.1; Luxfer Ltd., Nottingham; Massey-Ferguson Holdings Ltd. W.1; Matra-Malic Co., Ltd., Nottingham; Mechema Ltd., W.1; Mirrlees Blackstone Ltd., Stockport; Mitchell Beazley Ltd., W.1; Tobacco Machinery Division of Molins Ltd., S.E.8; Morgan Grenfill & Co. Ltd., E.C.2; Morganite Crucible Ltd., Norton; Mullard Ltd., W.C.1; Ogdens (Otley) Ltd., Otley; Parsons Peebles Ltd., Edinburgh; Peel Jones Copper Products Ltd., Cardiff; Pig Improvement Co. Ltd., Abingdon; Proprietary Perfumes Ltd., Ashford; Rank Cintel Division of Rank Precision Industries Ltd., Ware; Rank Xerox Ltd., N.W.1; Rapid Metal Developments Ltd., Aldridge; R.I.C. Capacitors Ltd., Romsey; Ernest Scragg & Sons Ltd., Macclesfield; Setpoint Ltd., S.W.8; Sevcon Ltd., Gateshead; Aircraft Division of Short Brothers & Harland Ltd., Belfast; Sinclair Radionics Ltd., St. Ives; Stanhay (Ashford) Ltd., Ashford; Magnesia Divison of Steetley (Mfg.) Ltd., Hartlepool, W. S. Unkles (Seafoods) Ltd., Hartlepool; Howson-Algraphy Groups of Vickers Ltd., Leeds.

Awards for Technological Innovation

In 1975, the following 19 concerns received the Queen's Award for achievement in technological innovation: Allen & Hanburys Research Ltd., Ware (*development of Geclomethasone diproprionate for treatment of bronchial asthma*); Autoflow Engineering Ltd., Rugby (*Ophthalumic lens grinding machines*); Foundry Machine Division of Baker Perkins Ltd., Peterborough (*foundry mixing machines*); Guided Weapons Division, British Aircraft Corporation Ltd., Stevenage (*high performance flight radomes*); Research Division of British Aluminium Co. Ltd., Gerrards Cross (*removal of gas and inclusions from molten aluminium*); Britten-Norman (Bembridge) Ltd., Bembridge (*development of Trislander aircraft*); Dowty Hydraulic Units Ltd., Cheltenham (*high performance hydraulic pumps*); Glacier Metal Co., Wembley (*ship stern gear*); Marconi-Elliott Avionic Systems Ltd., Rochester (*navigaton and weapon aiming system for aircraft*); Micro Consultants Ltd., Caterham (*high speed analogue and digital converters*); Micron Sprayers Ltd., Bromyard (*agricultural spraying equipment*); Mini Tunnels International Ltd., Old Woking (*small diameter shield driven tunnelling system*); Netlon Ltd., Blackburn (*plastic net and net-like fabrics*); Plant Breeding Institute, Trumpington (*breeding of new varieties of brassica crops*); Scott Bader Co. Ltd., Willingborough (*high gloss emulsion paints*); Sinclair Radionics Ltd., St. Ives (*scientific electronic calculators*); Kelvin Hughes Division of Smiths Industries Ltd. Hainault (*marine radar*); Spembly Ltd., Andover (*cryogenic instruments for use in radar*); Vickers Oceanics Ltd., S.W.1 (*submersibles in offshore operations*).

THE POST OFFICE

Crown services for the conveyance of Government letters and despatches by posts or stages were set up under a Master of the Posts about 1516. Public correspondence was officially accepted for the first time for conveyance by these services at fixed postage rates in 1635, but they were still under direct Crown control. In 1657 a Post Office was created under a Postmaster-General by Oliver Cromwell, and responsibility foi the carrying of all letters was thus transferred to Parliament, Charles II ratified this arrangement by statute in 1660.

A Money Order Office was inaugurated in 1792, uniform Penny Post in 1840, the Book Post in 1848, the Post Office Savings Bank in 1861, Post Office Telegraphs in 1870, Postal Orders and

the Post Office Telephone Service in 1881 and the Parcel Post in 1883.

The Post Office also acts as agent for many Government Departments in the collection and payment of money.

The financial arrangements brought into effect by the Post Office Act, 1961, separated Post Office finances from the Exchequer and established the Post Office Fund on April 1, 1961.

By the Post Office Act 1969, the Post Office was formally set up as a public corporation, and ceased to be a Government Department run by civil servants. It is now headed by a chairman and board of control, appointed by and responsible to the Secretary of State for Industry.

POST OFFICE FINANCIAL RESULTS
(£ million)

	1973–74				1974–75				
	Telecom-munications	Posts	GRS*	DPS†	Telecom-munications	Posts	GRS*	DPS†	Total (1974/75)
INCOME									
Main Services........	1,118·1	498·4	23·3	21·4	1,348·2	609·1	26·6	27·2	2,011·1
Agency Services.....	31·9	81·0	—	—	27·0	99·7	—	—	126·7
Other..............	10·5	52·0	10·9	0·4	13·4	64·4	14·5	0·4	92·7
TOTAL....	1,160·5	631·4	34·2	21·8	1,388·6	773·2	41·1	27·6	2,230·5
EXPENDITURE									
Plant Maintenance...	134·1	8·9	—	—	167·6	11·5	—	—	179·1
Operating and Ad-ministration.......	233·8	545·7	9·2	14·8	318·2	710·4	12·0	19·3	1,059·9
Accommodation.....	74·0	24·0	0·6	2·2	95·7	30·5	0·6	2·6	129·4
Motor Transport....	23·0	15·5	—	—	29·1	21·0	—	—	50·1
Interest Payable.....	214·6	16·8	4·0	1·8	286·8	24·0	4·9	1·9	317·6
Depreciation	286·9	13·3	0·4	2·4	367·9	16·4	0·5	3·1	387·9
Other‡..............	255·5	64·8	29·8	—	317·9	68·6	26·4	0·3	413·2
TOTAL....	1,221·9	689·0	44·0	21·2	1,583·2	882·4	44·4	27·2	2,537·2

Note: These figures include inter-business charges of £107·9m. for 1974–75 and £85·4m for 1973–74.
* Giro and Remittance Services.
† Data Processing Service.
‡ Includes expenditure on purchasing and supply services, research and development and payment in respect of external traffic.

WEATHER IN THE UNITED KINGDOM, 1974–1975

(1974) *July*.—Monthly rainfall totals were near or above average in the southern half of Northern Ireland, most of northern Scotland and parts of southern Scotland. Most districts of Wales, northern England and East Anglia were also wet. Some parts of north Wales and northwestern England received about twice their normal rainfall. Other districts were drier and small areas of eastern Scotland, East Anglia and southwestern England received only 50 per cent. of the average amount or even less. Showers and outbreaks of rain were sometimes heavy and prolonged particularly in Wales and some western and northern districts of England and Scotland. Winds were often fresh or strong with a few local gales and fog was frequent on high ground and on the coasts of Wales and southwestern England. On the 1st a gust of 82 knots (94 m.p.h.) with a mean wind speed of 66 knots (76 m.p.h.) was recorded at Snaefell (Isle of Man) and during widespread rain on the 2nd daily falls of 62 mm. (2·4 ins.) at Llantrisant (Mid Glamorgan) and 58 mm. (2·3 ins.) at Neudd Reservoir (Powys) were recorded. Two days later there were heavy falls of rain in northern districts of England and Wales and 57·2 mm. (2·2 ins.) fell at Revesby Reservoir (Lincolnshire). On the afternoon of the 12th four waterspouts were observed to the west of Hartland Point (Devon) and on the 30th rain was again heavy in places in central areas of the country. 63 mm. (2·5 ins.) were recorded on that day at Minafon (Gwynedd). Monthly mean temperatures were below average over most of the country. There were only two short warm spells. The first of these occurred during the second week in the Midlands and most of eastern and southern England. Jersey (Channel Islands) had a maximum temperature of 26·3° C. (79·3° F.) on the 8th. From the 19th to 22nd warm weather was more general but the highest temperatures occurred in eastern Scotland and the eastern, central and southern districts of England and Wales. At Littlehampton (West Sussex) the temperature rose to 26·4° C. (79·5° F.) on the 20th and at Aldenham (Hertfordshire) it reached 25·9° C. (78·6° F.) on the 21st. Sunshine totals for the month were mostly near or below average but one or two places in northern and eastern Scotland had between 120 and 130 per cent. of average. On the 1st, Falmouth (Cornwall) had 15·6 hours and on the 15th Ringway (Greater Manchester) and Squires Gate (Lancashire) each recorded 15 hours of sunshine.

August.—Rainfall was near or above average in the extreme west of Northern Ireland, western Scotland, the southernmost districts of Wales, most of the Midlands and eastern and southern England. In small parts of East Anglia and southwest England rainfall was about twice the average. Other districts were drier, particularly eastern Scotland where some places had less than half the average. On the 4th thunderstorms were widespread in the Midlands, southern and eastern districts of England. A man was killed by lightning in Felixstowe (Suffolk) and in Cambridgeshire, houses were damaged and electricity supplies disrupted. Flooding occurred in several places and 63·9 mm. (2·5 ins.) of rain fell near Sittingbourne (Kent). From the 7th to 18th showers or periods of rain occurred frequently and thunder and hail were reported at times mainly in the Midlands, southern and eastern England and south Wales. On the 7th, 70 mm. (2·8 ins.) of rain fell at Stansted Nurseries (Essex) and on the 9th and 10th there was lightning damage and local flooding. On the 14th and 15th gusts of

60 knots (69 m.p.h.) or over were recorded in northern England and the Isle of Man. On the 17th and 18th there was more lightning damage and local flooding. On the 18th, five small waterspouts were seen south of Peacehaven (East Sussex) and a ship reported a large waterspout just south of the Isle of Wight. Another waterspout was seen on the 19th in St. Margarets Bay (Kent). On the 25th outbreaks of thundery rain in Scotland spread to the Midlands and southwest England and gales occurred on the coasts of Northern Ireland, Scotland and northern England. A gust of 58 knots (67 m.p.h.) was recorded at Stornoway (Highland Region). On the 26th thunderstorms became widespread. Some hail fell and torrential rain caused flooding in one or two districts. In Woking (Surrey) a small tornado uprooted a tree and caused considerable damage to a market garden. Waterspouts were seen in the Ribble Estuary (Lancashire). On the 30th, 78·7 mm. (3·1 ins.) of rain fell at Creech Grange (Dorset). Monthly mean temperatures were near or below average except in Orkney and Shetland and the northern and eastern coasts of Scotland. On the 6th, a temperature of 27° C. (80·6° F.) was recorded at Stratford-upon-Avon (Warwickshire) and on the 15th a similar temperature was recorded at East Dereham (Norfolk). Sunshine totals were above average in most districts and at Baltasound (Shetland), the monthly total of 166 hours was the highest August total since 1947. Parts of western Scotland however were rather dull and Onich (Highland Region) with 73 hours had its lowest August total since 1943.

September.—Rainfall was generally above average and in most of southern England well over twice the normal amount fell. Parts of northern, central and eastern Scotland and a few small areas of eastern England however received less than normal. At Hartley Reservoir (Devon), 216·8 mm. (8·5 ins.) was the highest September total since 1909. Showers or outbreaks of rain occurred frequently and at times rainfall was very heavy. Some showers were of hail and later in the month a little snow or sleet fell in Scotland and north Wales. Thunderstorms were most frequent over England and Wales. On the 2nd, gales were severe in southern districts and a gust of 62 knots (71 m.p.h.) occurred at Plymouth (Devon). On the same day 80 mm. (3·1 ins.) of rain fell at Foffany Reservoir (Co. Down) and on the 4th, 73 mm. (2·9 ins.) fell at Woking (Surrey). Gales were widespread on the 7th and gusts of 60 knots (69 m.p.h.) or more occurred in many places. In the Midlands, two men were killed by falling trees and in Margate (Kent) a man was killed by an advertising sign when it was blown down. A train was derailed at Liphook (Hampshire) by an uprooted tree and electricity supplies were disrupted in East Anglia and southeast England as power lines were broken. Crops and fruit trees were extensively damaged. 86·6 mm. (3·4 ins.) of rain fell at Dinas Mawddwy (Gwynedd) and in southern England many acres of farmland and several roads were flooded. On the 12th thunderstorms occurred widely. Lightning damage occurred and there were heavy downpours in many localities. At Oxford, 20 mm. (0·8 ins.) of rain fell in 15 minutes and at Cally Market Gardens (Dumfries and Galloway Region), 76·1 mm. (3·0 ins.) were measured for the day. On the 23rd, 67·5 mm. (2·7 ins.) fell at Blaraidh (Highland Region) and gusts of around 70 knots (80 m.p.h.) were reported from several coastal places in southwest England. A whirlwind occurred at Folkestone (Kent). On the 26th, 64·7 mm. (2·5 ins.) of rain fell in 17 hours at Winstitchen (Somerset). Further floods occurred in southern England and on the 28th, 19 cows were saved from drowning by helicopter when caught in floods at Sturminster Marshall (Dorset). Monthly mean temperatures were below average generally and in one or two places in Wales and southwest England they were as much as 2·5° C. (4·5° F.) below normal. On the 16th, the temperature reached 25° C. (77° F.) at East Dereham (Norfolk), but during the night 27th/28th it fell to −6° C. (21·2° F.) at Braemar (Grampian Region), the lowest September temperature there since 1942. In spite of the rain, monthly sunshine totals were mostly near or above average. In Shetland and Outer Hebrides, sunshine was around 140 per cent. of average.

October.—Rainfall was near or below average in Northern Ireland and most of Scotland where some central and southwestern districts had less than half the average amount. Parts of northeast and southeast Scotland however had well above the average amount and parts of the Midlands and eastern England had nearly three times the average. Northern and western Wales and Cornwall were also wetter than normal. Showers occurred frequently sometimes accompanied by hail. Thunder was often reported in England and Wales. Throughout the month snow or sleet showers occurred, mainly in northern districts over high ground. On the 3rd lightning damaged a church tower in Derby. The 7th was a wet day particularly in England and Wales and 55·7 mm. (2·2 ins.) fell at Barnetby-le-Wold (Humberside). Snow fell in a few places in East Anglia and southeast England. From the 12th to the 18th fog occurred frequently at night in the Midlands, East Anglia and southern England and less often in parts of central and southern Scotland. Hill fog was widespread and fog also affected the coasts of northern Scotland and southern Wales at times. On the 18th, 59·4 mm. (2·3 ins.) of rain fell at Honister Pass (Cumbria). Gales were occasionally widespread and on the 27th gusts of 60 knots (69 m.p.h.) or more were reported at a number of places in Scotland and northern England. At Snaefell (Isle of Man) a gust of 96 knots (110 m.p.h.) with a mean wind speed of 81 knots (93 m.p.h.) was recorded. After these gales, snow drifts nearly 1 metre (39 ins.) deep were reported on some mountain roads in Scotland. Monthly mean temperatures were well below average everywhere. It was probably the coldest October in Northern Ireland this century, in England and Wales since 1917 and in Scotland since 1926. Monthly sunshine totals were above average in most of Northern Ireland, the Isle of Man, Shetland and western Scotland. Some places round the Firth of Clyde had their sunniest October for 35 years. By contrast, sunshine was below average in northern and eastern Scotland and at Nairn the total of 34 hours was the lowest recorded in October since 1906. Over England and Wales sunshine was mostly near or below average, the dullest districts being in the extreme north of England and in northern and southwestern Wales.

November.—Rainfall was about or below average in the extreme east of Scotland, parts of northeastern and eastern England and in a small area of western Wales. It was above average elsewhere and in East Anglia and southeastern England some places had more than twice the average amount. Showers or outbreaks of rain occurred repeatedly in all districts and the rain was often heavy with hail and thunder after the first week. Fog was widespread at times, usually in heavy rain. On the 10th, 111·5 mm. (4·4 ins.) of rain fell at Achnagart (Highland Region) and on the 11th many roads were flooded in the West Country. Gales were severe in Scotland on the 11th and a gust of 80 knots

(92 m.p.h.) was recorded at Tiree (Strathclyde Region). Even in Dorset two vehicles were overturned by strong gusts. Gales later swept western and southern coasts of England and Wales and The Lizard (Cornwall) had a gust of 77 knots (88 m.p.h.) on the 13th. On the 14th, a whirlwind was reported at Thorpe (Norfolk). On the 19th snowfall was prolonged in places and undrifted depths of 5–8 cm. (2–3 ins.) were measured in parts of southwestern Scotland and the northern Midlands. On the 21st, 12–18 cm. (5–7 ins.) of snow accumulated on the mountains in north Wales. Between the 19th and 23rd, widespread flooding was reported in East Anglia, the Midlands and southern England. 93·2 mm. (3·7 ins.) of rain fell at Forest Lodge (Tayside Region) on the 22nd. On the 24th and 25th gales were severe in exposed places in Northern Ireland, Scotland and northern England and a gust of 65 knots (75 m.p.h.) was recorded at Ballypatrick Forest (Co. Antrim) on the 24th. Gales were renewed on the 27th and 28th and a gust of 71 knots was recorded at Coningsby (Lincolnshire) on the 27th. Monthly mean temperatures were above average in northeastern Scotland, most of the Midlands, East Anglia and southern England, but below average in all other districts. On the 9th, the temperature rose to 14·4° C. (57·9° F.) at Elgin (Grampian Region) and to 15·8° C. (60·4° F.) at Cannington (Somerset). The third week was particularly cold in central and southern Scotland and northern England. Frosts occurred frequently and were severe at times. On the 20th, the temperature at Abbotsinch (Strathclyde Region) did not rise above 0° C. (32° F.) all day. Sunshine totals were below average in the southeastern half of England, northwestern England and in a few places in southwestern England, western Wales and northern and western Scotland. Elsewhere sunshine totals were mostly above average and in parts of Northern Ireland it was the sunniest November this century.

December.—Rainfall was above average in parts of northwestern and southwestern England and most of Northern Ireland, Wales and Scotland. Some places in the northwest Highlands had more than twice the average amount. Elsewhere it was drier and in small areas of eastern Scotland, eastern and southern England and the Midlands, rainfall was less than half the average. There were scattered thunderstorms on a few days. Gales were frequent and occurred widely at times but Northern Ireland, western and northern Scotland and western and northern districts of England and Wales were the most affected. On the 6th, 74·7 mm. (2·9 ins.) of rain fell at Camusrory (Highland Region). On the 11th thundery squalls crossed England and Wales and gusts of 60 knots (69 m.p.h.) or more were recorded at a number of places. At Kew (Greater London), a gust of 78 knots (90 m.p.h.) was probably the highest recorded since records began in 1871. On the same day an aircraft at London Airport was lifted and blown into another one by a gust of wind. Also on the 11th, an undrifted snow depth of 27 cm. (10·6 ins.) was measured at Leadhills (Strathclyde Region) and three people were injured when the roof of a house collapsed in Ramsgate (Kent) after being struck by lightning. On the 17th gales were severe on coasts and over high ground and cross-winds made driving hazardous on motorways. Several mountain roads in Scotland were blocked by snowdrifts and some roads in East Anglia were blocked by fallen trees. On the 21st, 83·8 mm. (3·3 ins.) of rain fell at Lluest Wen Filters (Mid Glamorgan) and on the 25th, 77·1 mm. (3·0 ins.) fell at Thirlmere (Cumbria). On the 27th a gust of 74 knots (85 m.p.h.) was recorded at The Lizard (Cornwall) and on the 28th, 83 knots (95 m.p.h.)

was recorded near Middlesbrough (Cleveland). 92·1 mm. (3·6 ins.) of rain fell at Honister Pass (Cumbria) on the 28th and at Eskdalemuir (Dumfries and Galloway Region) a gust of 83 knots (95 m.p.h.) occurred on the 29th. Monthly mean temperatures were well above average in most districts. In England, Wales and Northern Ireland together it was probably the mildest December since 1934. In many places roses were still blooming at Christmas. On the 23rd, the temperature reached 15·8° C. (60·4° F.) at Inverpolly (Highland Region) and on the 28th it rose to 16·2° C. (61·2° F.) at Elmstone (Kent). 15·2° C. (59·4° F.) at Edgbaston (West Midlands) on the 28th was the highest December temperature there since records began in 1885. Sunshine was mostly below average but eastern and central districts of England and Scotland were sunnier than normal. At Stonehaven (Grampian Region) 78 hours of sunshine was the highest total recorded in December since 1931.

Year (1974).—Annual rainfall was above average in Wales, much of Scotland and most of England. It was about average in Northern Ireland and slightly less than normal in northern and eastern coastal districts of Scotland, northeast England and parts of the Midlands. The most notable features of the rainfall were the dry spring and wet autumn. This was particularly marked in England and Wales where the April and May period was the driest since 1896 and the period September to November was the wettest since 1960 and the fifth wettest this century. The first six weeks of the year were mild, wet and very windy with frequent gales. Heavy rain caused flooding in widely separated places and several people were killed in gales. Road and rail services were disrupted and the sea-front railway station at Dawlish (Devon) was partly demolished by heavy seas. The latter half of February was drier, much less windy and more foggy. March was also a quiet month but snow or sleet occurred further south than in the first two months of the year. April was a very dry month and many places had long sunny periods by day with frost at night. In May, rainy periods alternated with drier spells. Monthly mean temperatures from March to May were about average, but June was a little cooler. Thunderstorms were widespread in the Midlands, eastern and southern England in the latter half of June and intense rain led to flooding in some areas. Floodwater near Bristol was over a metre (39 ins.) deep on one occasion. Showers or periods of rain occurred frequently in July and in August, torrential rain caused flooding in some districts. Both July and August were cool. September was wet, windy and rather cold, but in spite of the frequent rain most places had sunny periods. During gales two men were killed by falling trees, another man was killed by an advertising sign and an uprooted tree derailed a train. The unsettled weather continued into October which was unusually cold in all districts. Snow or sleet showers fell throughout the month, mostly in Scotland and northern England. November was less cold but wet. Showers or outbreaks of rain occurred in all districts, often heavy and with hail and thunder at times. There was widespread flooding in southern England, the Midlands and East Anglia. Both November and December were often very windy. December was remarkable for its exceptionally mild weather which contrasted so strikingly with the cold of October. Annual mean temperatures were near average almost everywhere, most districts being slightly above average but Northern Ireland, parts of Wales, southwest England and East Anglia and a few places in Scotland being a little below average. Annual sunshine totals were also near normal. Central southern England, the Midlands, the Isle of Man, Northern Ireland and

Scotland were generally a little sunnier than average and eastern districts of East Anglia and southeast England and some places in southwest England and Wales were a little less sunny than normal.

(1975) *January*.—Rainfall was below average in eastern Scotland, northeast England and the west and north Midlands but most other areas had more than average. It was the wettest January in Scotland since 1928 and at Dumfries (Dumfries and Galloway Region) since 1909. Gales, severe at times on coasts, were frequent and on the 2nd and 6th some ships ran aground with loss of life. On the 4th, 100 mm. (3·9 ins.) of rain fell at Camusrory (Highland Region). On the 12th whirlwinds caused structural damage at Flintham (Nottinghamshire) and at Chipping Warden (Northamptonshire) where the whirlwind cut a 23 metre (75·5 ft.) path through the village. A tornado struck the village of Clay Coton (Northamptonshire) and an Elizabethan barn was completely demolished killing a pig and a calf. On the 18th fog formed from the Midlands northwards and was particularly dense and freezing in the Glasgow area where it lasted well into the 19th. On the 19th a girl was drowned after a large wave swept her into gale whipped seas near Newquay (Cornwall) and a man was drowned at Shoreham (West Sussex) when a dinghy overturned. On the 21st, 96·2 mm. (3·8 ins.) of rain fell at Honister Pass (Cumbria) and 92 mm. (3·6 ins.) fell at Nant Peris (Gwynedd). On the 22nd a gust of 96 knots (110 m.p.h.) was recorded at Snaefell (Isle of Man) and a coaster was wrecked after going aground in Orkney and another sank off Lundy in the Bristol Channel. On the night of the 22nd/23rd, East Kilbride (Strathclyde Region) was cut off by a snowstorm for 5 hours. On the 25th widespread gales swept across England, Wales and southern Scotland and on the 27th, gusts of 77 knots (88 m.p.h.) were recorded at The Lizard (Cornwall). On the 28th snow affected many areas and Buxton (Derbyshire) was cut off for about 3 hours. Monthly mean temperatures were well above average almost everywhere. It was probably the mildest January in Scotland since 1916 and in England and Wales since 1932. Shrubs and ornamental trees blossomed and daffodils in Kew Gardens had not bloomed so early for 20 years. The temperature reached 14·6° C. (58·3° F.) at Dinnet (Grampian Region) on the 4th and at Aberdeen/Dyce Airport on the 5th, the highest January temperature there since 1950. On the 15th the temperature rose to 15·2° C. (59·4° F.) at Stanstead Abbots (Hertfordshire). Sunshine was generally below average, particularly in western Scotland and the Borders, where it was the dullest January for 50 years. Eskdalemuir (Dumfries and Galloway Region) had its dullest January since 1913. Shetland, Orkney, north and east Scotland, northeast England and the coast of north Wales were sunnier than normal.

February.—Rainfall was below average almost everywhere. North and northeast Scotland and parts of the Borders were particularly dry with only about a quarter of the average amount. Some places in these districts had less than 10 mm. (0·4 ins.) of rain and one or two places in northeast Scotland had their driest February for 50 years. Most of the rain fell in the middle of the month. Overnight fog occurred frequently, especially in south and northeast Scotland, east Wales and districts of England away from the west coasts. The fog was dense and freezing at times and slow to clear. Fog persisted all day in parts of northeast England on the 3rd and in the Moray Firth area of Scotland on the 4th, 8th, 9th and also on the 10th, when fog affected 30 counties in England and Scotland. There were collisions involving many vehicles and resulting in fatalities on several days mostly in the north of

England and the Midlands. Gusts exceeding 60 knots (69 m.p.h.) were reported from Scottish coasts and Islands in the northwest and north on the 16th and from places in the Isle of Man and northern England on the 16th and 17th. 51·8 mm. (2 ins.) of rain fell at Coniston (Cumbria) on the 16th, but apart from this there were no falls exceeding 50 mm. (2 ins.) anywhere during the month. On the 24th fog again persisted all day in parts of northeast England. Although some snow fell around mid-month, mainly in central and northern Scotland and the Welsh mountains, a notable feature of February, 1975 was the absence of snowfall in most districts. Monthly mean temperatures were mainly above average but not so markedly as in January. The absence of prolonged cold spells, combined with the mildness of the previous two months, brought an early spring to some parts of the country. In the south of England fruit trees blossomed in Kent and vegetables in market gardens were a month to six weeks early. The temperature reached 16·0° C. (60·8° F.) at Dinnet (Grampian Region) on the 16th and rose to 14·8° C. (58·6° F.) at East Dereham (Norfolk) on the 24th and at Pen-y-Ffridd (Gwynedd) on the 28th. By contrast the temperature fell to −6·3° C. (20·7° F.) at Santon Downham (Norfolk) on the night of 27th/28th. Sunshine totals were less than half the average in central and northeast districts of England and parts of Scotland bordering the Firth of Tay but were above average in most other areas. The north of Scotland was particularly sunny and Baltasound (Shetland) with almost twice the normal amount had its sunniest February since records began there in 1907.

March.—Rainfall was generally below average in Scotland, western districts of Wales, northwest England and Northern Ireland. Much of England was considerably wetter and the east Midlands and parts of central southern, southeast and eastern England had more than twice the average amount. A few places in southeast Kent had over three times the average. Rain or drizzle affected many areas at the beginning of the month and became more general between the 4th and 8th. On the 1st, 4th and 5th dense and freezing fog became widespread in central, eastern and northern England and southern Scotland. On the 8th and 9th rain became persistent and heavy at times in south and east England with occasional thunderstorms. A funnel cloud was reported near Honington (Norfolk) on the 9th. On the 10th there were widespread floods in eastern England and the Midlands. Floods in the west Midlands were the worst for 10 years. On the 19th and 20th a few local gales occurred on exposed coasts and a man was killed at Rochford (Essex) on the 20th when his moped was blown in front of a car. On the same day a ferry-boat sank at her moorings during the gales, putting the Portsmouth–Hayling Island ferry service out of action. Rough weather halted cross-channel services in and out of Folkestone (Kent) and at Lowestoft (Suffolk) a 15 metre (49 ft.) stretch of sea wall collapsed after being pounded by heavy seas. Showers of snow, sleet or hail occurred in the second half of the month and southeast England had heavy rain on the 20th. Wintry showers became more general towards the end of the month and there were a few thunderstorms. From the 27th to the 29th undrifted snow depths of 19–25 cms. (7·5–9·8 ins.) were measured in the central highlands of Scotland. Monthly mean temperatures were mostly below average. An unusual feature for March was that the end of the month was generally colder than the beginning. On the 4th the temperature reached 14·7° C. (58·5° F.) at Hadlow College (Kent). During the night of the 13th/14th the temperature fell to

−11° C. (12·2° F.) at Lagganlia (Highland Region) and the 14th was the coldest day in London since March 9, 1974. Sunshine was above average in Northern Ireland where it was the sunniest March since 1955. One or two places in the Province had their sunniest March this century. Sunshine was also above average in most of Scotland, Cornwall and much of northern England. Most other districts had below average sunshine.

April.—Rainfall was mainly above average but some widely separated areas had less than normal. Coastal districts were the wettest and some places in East Anglia and the Grampian Region (where it was the wettest April at a number of places since 1934) had more than twice the average amount. This was the wettest April generally since 1970 and at Gisla Power Station (Western Islands Region) it was the wettest since 1959. The first 10 days of the month were cold with wintry showers and snowfall was sometimes prolonged and heavy in Scotland. Orchards which had blossomed early, because of the mild winter, were damaged by frost, pear blossom in southern England being particularly affected. Gales occurred in exposed places in northern districts from the 7th to the 9th and the Orkney mail boat was unable to make its usual crossing on the 8th because of rough seas. Gusts of 79 knots (91 m.p.h.) were recorded at Snaefell (Isle of Man) on the 7th and 8th. High winds were also reported during blizzards which swept the Cairngorms on the 8th. A skier lost his life at Aviemore. The severe weather disrupted air and rail services in northeast Scotland and the central highlands. Main roads were blocked with snow and there were power failures. A level depth of 47 cms. (18·5 ins.) of snow was measured at Glenmore Lodge (Highland Region) on the 8th. Kent was also affected by snow and a depth of 15 cms. (5·9 ins.) was measured at Doddington on the 9th. Air services were cancelled in Jersey on the night of 13th/14th because of fog and on the 18th a British Rail hovercraft was damaged when she struck a ramp in Dover Harbour in thick fog. All districts had wet weather at times from the 11th to the 22nd. Heavy rain delayed crop sowing and some farmers were working throughout the 24 hours during the drier weather of the 4th week. Monthly mean temperatures were near or a little below average in most districts but slightly above average in southern Scotland, Northern Ireland, parts of northern England and much of the Midlands. On the 6th the temperature fell to −9·1° C. (15·6° F.) at Dall (Tayside Region) and to −6·0° C. (21·2° F.) at Winfrith (Dorset). The temperature rose to 23·1° C. (73·6° F.) at Southampton (Hampshire) on the 22nd, at Brynamman (Dyfed) on the 24th and at Milltown (Belfast) on the 25th. On the 25th a temperature of 22·7° C. (72·9° F.) at Armagh (Co. Armagh) was the highest April temperature recorded there since 1840. Sunshine was below average almost everywhere. Wick (Highland Region) and Kirkwall (Orkney) had their dullest April since 1945 and 1947 respectively.

May.—Rainfall was well below in western areas but eastern districts had more than the normal amount. This was particularly marked in England where the east of the country had 100 to 150 per cent. of average, whilst western districts had less than 50 per cent. of average. A few places in Cumbria had less than 20 per cent. of normal. In Northern Ireland it was the driest May this century and some places in Scotland had their driest May for over 50 years. Showers or periods of rain occurred in many districts on the 1st and 2nd. Gales occasionally occurred on exposed coasts and affected southern and eastern England and the Midlands in the first week. On the 7th a tree was blown on to a bus near Corsham (Wiltshire) killing the driver. Showers or periods of rain occurred again in most districts from the 7th to the 14th. On the 14th, 55·7 mm. (2·2 ins.) of rain fell in 4 hours 18 minutes at Sheffield (South Yorkshire). It was wet in southern England, East Anglia and the Midlands until the 17th when floods affected roads and railways. During severe thunderstorms on the 23rd, accumulations of hailstones to depths of 10 cms. (3·9 ins.) were measured in the villages of Chulmleigh and Chawleigh in Devon. A few hailstones as large as marbles were reported. On the 30th a funnel cloud was observed over the sea north of Alderney (Channel Islands). Monthly mean temperatures were below average almost everywhere. There were some cold nights and air frosts were reported from time to time. Ground frosts occurred with above average frequency in Northern Ireland and were widespread in Scotland, northern England and northern Wales. The temperature fell to −5·1° C. (22·8° F.) at Leadhills (Strathclyde Region) on the 15th and at Carnwath (Strathclyde Region) on the 31st. By contrast, the temperature rose to 23·2° C. (73·8° F.) at Gloucester and East Dereham (Norfolk) on the 20th and to 23·0° C. (73·4° F.) at Corpach (Highland Region) on the 28th. Sunshine totals were above average in Northern Ireland, Wales and much of northern England and most of Scotland. Several places in Scotland had their sunniest May for 50 years and in Northern Ireland generally it was the sunniest May since 1946. Sunshine was below normal in East Anglia, the east and south Midlands, central southern and southeast England.

June.—Rainfall was less than normal over Scotland and in some northern and eastern parts of England. At Gloucester, where it was the driest June since 1962, and Torquay (Devon), only 6 per cent. of average was recorded. At Watnall (Nottinghamshire) it was the driest June since records began there in 1941. In other areas rainfall was generally less than half the normal amount with less than 20 per cent. of average in much of Wales and southern England. The month started with night frosts in many areas with gales in northern districts. On the 2nd a gust of 95 knots (109 m.p.h.) was recorded at Middlesbrough (Cleveland) and 85 knots (98 m.p.h.) was recorded at Snaefell (Isle of Man). There were moderate falls of snow over high ground and sleet or snow showers reached as far as the London area. This is the first time since July 1888 that sleet or snow showers have been reported so widely and so far south in summer. By the 7th, temperatures of between 22° C. (71·6° F.) and 26° C. (78·8° F.) were being reported from many parts of the country and such a spectacular change of weather type has probably only occurred three times in the last 100 years. Northern areas had some rain or showers from the 12th which later spread to southern areas with thunderstorms in places. Some northern and western areas had rain on the 18th and 19th but other districts were dry. On the 23rd thunderstorms occurred in southeast England. Coastal fog patches affected some western areas during the last 10 days of the month. Monthly mean temperatures were near normal over most of the country. Daytime maxima were above normal in many areas while night temperatures were below normal in parts of the Midlands and near normal elsewhere. Sunshine totals were generally well above average and it was the sunniest June in central London since records began there in 1929.

Average and General Values, 1973–1975 (June)

Month	Rainfall (mm.)				Temperature (°C.)				Bright Sunshine (hrs. per day)			
	Aver. 1916–1950	1973	1974	1975	Aver. 1941–1970	1973	1974	1975	Aver. 1941–1970	1973	1974	1975
					England and Wales							
January	92	44	117	117	4·0	5·2	6·5	7·2	1·6	1·1	1·7	1·3
February	66	40	99	32	4·2	5·0	6·1	5·2	2·4	2·8	2·3	2·3
March	57	24	47	82	6·2	6·9	6·4	5·3	3·7	4·5	3·4	3·0
April	60	67	14	71	8·8	7·5	8·3	8·6	5·3	5·1	5·1	4·5
May	63	84	40	47	11·6	11·8	11·3	10·1	6·3	5·6	6·7	6·3
June	55	63	65	21	14·7	15·3	14·0	14·8	6·8	7·6	6·7	9·2
July	79	92	77	—	16·3	15·9	15·5	—	5·9	5·2	5·4	—
August	81	63	95	—	16·1	16·9	15·7	—	5·5	5·7	6·1	—
September	76	86	144	—	14·3	14·8	12·6	—	4·4	4·8	4·7	—
October	92	57	99	—	11·2	9·8	8·2	—	3·3	2·9	2·9	—
November	95	52	125	—	7·2	6·7	7·2	—	1·9	2·8	1·8	—
December	88	67	72	—	5·1	5·7	8·3	—	1·5	1·8	1·5	—
YEAR	904	793	994	—	10·0	10·2	10·0	—	4·0	4·1	4·0	—
					Scotland							
January	154	103	228	243	3·5	5·2	5·9	5·3	1·4	0·9	1·1	1·2
February	106	98	118	48	3·7	4·0	5·4	4·8	2·5	2·6	1·8	3·0
March	89	65	73	58	5·4	6·4	5·4	4·5	3·4	3·6	3·3	3·8
April	88	83	18	99	7·5	6·2	7·6	7·3	5·0	4·7	6·0	3·9
May	87	107	78	48	9·9	9·7	10·3	8·6	5·7	4·7	5·5	7·2
June	87	83	71	66	12·7	13·3	12·3	12·6	5·8	4·8	6·4	7·5
July	114	89	102	—	14·1	14·4	13·4	—	4·8	4·4	4·7	—
August	122	107	97	—	14·0	14·2	13·9	—	4·5	4·9	4·5	—
September	128	95	141	—	12·5	12·3	11·0	—	3·7	3·4	4·0	—
October	158	82	106	—	9·9	8·4	7·7	—	2·7	2·7	2·5	—
November	143	155	190	—	6·3	5·0	6·1	—	1·7	1·7	1·7	—
December	143	169	226	—	4·6	4·0	6·5	—	1·1	0·9	1·1	—
YEAR	1,419	1,236	1,448	—	8·7	8·5	8·8	—	3·5	3·3	3·5	—

TEMPERATURE, RAINFALL AND SUNSHINE
IN THE UNITED KINGDOM

The following table gives mean air temperature (°C.) total monthly rainfall (mm.) and mean daily bright sunshine (hrs.) at a representative selection of climatological reporting stations in the United Kingdom during the year July 1974 to June 1975. The heights (metres) of the reporting stations above mean sea level are also given. Fuller details of the weather are given in the Monthly Weather Report published by the Meteorological Office.

Station	Ht. in mtrs.	July Temp. °C	July Rain mm.	July Sun hrs.	August Temp. °C	August Rain mm.	August Sun hrs.	September Temp. °C	September Rain mm.	September Sun hrs.	October Temp. °C	October Rain mm.	October Sun hrs.
Aberporth	133	14·1	54	5·6	14·1	48	5·7	11·6	124	4·0	8·8	114	2·1
Aberystwyth	4	—	91	—	—	61	—	—	149	—	—	90	—
Aldergrove	68	13·8	83	4·1	14·3	56	5·1	10·7	117	3·5	7·5	55	3·5
Bath	118	15·3	43	—	15·3	79	—	12·0	193	—	8·1	37	—
Birmingham	163	15·2	60	5·1	15·3	90	5·9	11·9	93	4·3	7·7	66	2·7
Bournemouth	40	15·5	44	6·7	15·5	87	7·3	12·9	177	5·6	8·2	54	4·1
Braemar	339	11·7	45	4·4	11·8	49	4·4	8·7	50	3·4	5·5	99	1·0
Buxton	314	13·1	137	5·0	13·2	104	5·7	10·2	179	—	5·7	151	—
Cambridge	26	15·6	40	6·9	15·9	117	6·7	12·8	67	5·7	7·7	85	3·1
Cardiff	62	—	—	—	—	—	—	12·3	219	4·1	8·5	55	3·2
Cheltenham	65	15·9	39	5·3	15·9	78	6·4	12·5	106	4·5	7·9	52	2·7
Clacton-on-Sea	16	16·3	31	5·8	16·8	64	6·7	13·5	87	5·3	8·0	67	2·9
Douglas	87	13·5	103	5·9	14·1	78	6·1	11·5	189	4·5	8·5	110	3·6
Dumfries	49	13·6	91	5·0	13·9	89	4·9	10·7	155	3·7	7·3	31	3·2
Dundee	45	14·1	63	5·5	14·3	76	5·1	11·1	71	4·1	7·7	33	2·7
Durham	102	14·0	65	4·4	14·1	48	5·2	11·1	65	3·8	7·2	76	2·1
Eastbourne	7	16·1	56	7·2	16·6	85	8·2	14·1	193	6·1	8·5	141	3·6
East Malling	37	15·8	53	6·6	15·9	90	6·6	12·8	137	5·5	7·7	77	2·5
Edinburgh	134	13·7	62	5·3	13·9	52	4·4	10·7	76	3·8	7·1	46	1·5
Falmouth	51	15·1	58	5·9	—	—	—	—	—	—	—	—	—
Glasgow	107	13·3	87	4·8	13·9	78	4·3	10·3	138	3·6	7·1	32	3·2
Hartland Point	91	14·1	51	4·5	15·1	100	6·8	12·3	185	4·1	9·6	77	2·7
Hastings	45	15·7	51	5·9	16·7	65	7·5	13·7	179	5·2	8·3	106	3·5
Huddersfield	99	15·1	71	5·2	15·2	64	5·3	12·0	134	4·4	7·7	80	2·4
Hull	2	15·9	67	5·2	16·3	95	6·1	12·9	87	4·7	8·3	129	3·1
Inverness	4	13·7	62	3·7	14·1	58	4·8	11·3	53	3·5	7·9	54	1·3
Lincoln	7	14·8	86	4·5	15·5	83	6·5	11·9	56	4·7	7·1	103	3·1
Llandrindod Wells	235	—	—	—	—	—	—	—	—	—	—	—	—
London (Kew)	6	16·7	34	6·7	15·8	62	6·7	12·9	124	5·7	8·1	69	2·9
Lowestoft	25	15·7	45	5·3	16·2	99	6·9	12·9	116	5·0	7·8	109	2·9
Manchester Airport	75	14·7	129	4·5	15·1	82	5·6	11·9	95	4·3	7·7	91	2·6
Margate	16	16·1	63	7·0	16·3	71	7·7	—	100	5·7	—	86	2·7
Morecambe	7	15·1	144	4·2	—	—	—	12·5	185	3·8	8·3	72	2·7
Newton Rigg	171	13·6	82	4·3	13·7	74	4·9	10·5	107	3·5	6·4	46	1·6
Nottingham	59	—	—	—	—	—	—	13·1	62	4·4	8·6	48	2·8
Oxford	63	16·1	42	6·1	15·9	97	6·4	12·8	156	4·9	7·9	66	3·4
Penzance	19	15·5	59	5·5	15·5	141	5·9	13·1	167	5·1	10·2	131	3·8
Plymouth	36	—	—	—	—	—	—	12·7	153	4·3	—	—	—
Prestwick	16	13·6	58	5·0	14·3	62	5·2	11·1	109	4·2	7·1	45	3·5
Ross-on-Wye	68	15·4	45	4·9	15·1	64	6·1	12·2	103	4·2	8·1	36	3·1
St. Mawgan	103	14·6	55	4·7	15·1	149	6·2	12·2	179	4·0	9·4	114	3·2
Sandown	4	16·5	41	7·2	16·8	103	7·5	14·1	211	6·1	9·0	72	4·1
Scarborough	53	14·7	76	5·6	15·0	64	6·6	12·0	74	4·7	8·0	130	3·1
Scilly	48	—	—	—	15·9	138	6·2	13·3	136	4·6	10·5	61	3·5
Sheffield	131	15·2	68	5·3	15·5	81	5·8	12·3	91	4·6	7·7	56	2·9
Shoeburyness	2	16·9	51	6·6	16·9	55	6·8	13·8	84	5·6	8·2	73	2·7
Shrewsbury	56	15·5	51	5·8	—	—	—	—	—	—	7·9	53	2·5
Skegness	5	15·3	41	5·1	16·2	86	6·3	12·7	59	4·9	8·1	115	2·8
Southampton	3	16·3	48	6·1	16·3	80	6·5	13·5	161	5·3	8·9	50	3·8
Stornoway	3	12·0	93	4·3	12·9	70	5·0	10·1	87	4·9	7·7	110	2·8
Tiree	9	12·7	72	4·9	13·5	103	5·0	11·3	137	4·1	8·9	63	3·0
Torbay	8	16·2	37	6·0	15·9	128	6·9	13·0	159	5·2	9·3	35	3·7
West Kirby	8	15·7	103	5·0	15·3	45	4·6	12·9	125	3·9	8·9	73	2·6
Weymouth	23	15·9	27	6·7	15·7	132	6·8	13·3	154	5·5	9·1	60	3·8
Worthing	2	15·7	46	6·4	15·9	64	7·4	13·3	181	5·6	8·2	86	5·6
York	20	14·9	59	5·6	14·9	58	5·6	11·7	66	4·4	7·5	56	2·7

TEMPERATURE, RAINFALL AND SUNSHINE IN THE UNITED KINGDOM

Mean Temperature of the air (°C.), Rainfall (mm.) and Bright Sunshine (as mean hours per day) at a representative selection of reporting stations during the year July, 1974 to June, 1975. Fuller details of the weather are given in the *Monthly Weather Report* published by the Meteorological Office.

Station	1974						1975					
	November			December			January			February		
	Temp. °C.	Rain mm.	Sun hrs.	Temp. °C.	Rain mm.	Sun hrs.	Temp. °C.	Rain mm.	Sun hrs.	Temp. °C.	Rain mm.	Sun hrs.
Aberporth	7·2	89	2·0	8·3	79	0·9	7·1	132	1·0	5·9	32	4·3
Aberystwyth	—	121	—	—	114	—	—	132	—	—	56	—
Aldergrove	5·5	87	2·5	6·8	82	1·0	5·7	110	1·5	5·3	24	3·1
Bath	7·3	89	—	—	8·0	69	—	7·1	102	—	4·9	26	—
Birmingham	6·5	79	1·7	7·7	42	1·8	6·6	78	1·1	4·5	20	1·7
Bournemouth	8·3	151	2·3	8·5	46	1·8	7·8	112	1·6	5·7	26	3·5
Braemar	3·5	126	1·1	4·7	120	0·9	2·7	173	0·9	1·9	36	—
Buxton	5·0	158	—	6·1	138	—	5·1	180	—	2·7	38	—
Cambridge	—	126	1·9	8·1	28	1·7	7·0	52	1·2	4·7	25	1·9
Cardiff	—	—	—	8·3	113	1·4	7·1	154	1·1	5·3	43	2·3
Cheltenham	7·2	72	1·7	—	—	—	7·5	87	1·5	5·3	26	2·5
Clacton-on-Sea	7·4	96	1·6	7·5	27	1·7	6·7	74	1·0	5·5	19	3·3
Douglas	7·0	127	2·2	7·6	91	1·4	6·6	187	1·7	5·4	90	2·3
Dumfries	5·9	146	2·0	7·1	119	1·4	5·8	231	1·3	4·3	42	3·2
Dundee	5·6	79	2·5	6·2	59	1·9	5·2	90	1·6	4·4	48	1·3
Durham	5·7	55	2·2	6·6	36	2·0	5·6	44	2·0	3·5	22	1·4
Eastbourne	8·9	169	2·1	8·7	69	1·9	8·2	131	1·3	6·1	33	3·8
East Malling	7·5	115	1·4	8·3	41	1·5	7·1	100	1·2	4·9	21	3·4
Edinburgh	5·4	68	2·4	6·1	85	1·4	5·0	88	1·4	3·9	28	2·5
Falmouth	—	—	—	—	—	—	8·1	140	1·4	7·7	26	2·0
Glasgow	4·7	106	1·5	5·9	157	1·1	4·8	173	0·8	3·8	38	2·3
Hartland Point	8·7	117	1·6	8·8	69	0·9	8·1	102	1·3	6·7	28	3·7
Hastings	8·2	131	2·0	8·1	55	1·8	7·5	191	1·1	6·1	27	4·0
Huddersfield	6·1	110	1·6	7·5	97	1·2	6·6	89	—	3·8	28	1·1
Hull	6·3	52	1·9	7·6	40	—	6·5	54	—	4·5	15	1·1
Inverness	5·9	71	1·6	6·5	103	1·0	4·9	99	1·3	3·6	13	3·3
Lincoln	5·9	61	1·6	7·5	33	1·7	6·2	49	1·1	4·1	21	1·4
Llandrindod Wells	—	—	—	—	—	—	—	—	—	—	—	—
London (Kew)	7·7	138	1·5	8·7	35	1·9	7·6	84	1·4	5·3	26	3·1
Lowestoft	6·6	97	1·5	7·3	25	1·1	6·4	88	1·5	4·8	17	3·3
Manchester Airport	6·5	80	1·3	8·1	61	1·8	6·7	103	0·9	4·6	32	3·5
Margate	—	86	—	8·6	—	—	7·5	83	1·0	5·7	17	2·8
Morecambe	6·5	119	1·4	7·5	81	1·0	6·7	152	1·2	5·1	32	4·1
Newton Rigg	5·2	155	1·4	6·5	179	0·9	5·4	179	0·9	3·7	23	3·4
Nottingham	6·5	74	1·5	8·1	32	1·7	6·8	58	1·0	4·5	19	1·0
Oxford	7·5	95	1·8	8·3	33	1·9	7·2	69	1·4	4·9	30	2·1
Penzance	9·3	186	2·6	9·5	110	1·4	8·5	177	1·7	8·2	59	2·5
Plymouth	8·9	107	2·3	9·2	68	1·0	8·1	109	1·2	7·3	34	2·8
Prestwick	6·0	121	1·7	7·3	140	0·9	6·0	162	0·9	4·7	27	4·0
Ross-on-Wye	7·1	83	2·1	8·7	32	1·7	7·3	92	—	4·5	35	—
St. Mawgan	8·7	124	2·3	9·1	81	1·1	8·0	145	1·5	7·1	26	3·1
Sandown	9·1	174	2·5	8·9	57	2·1	8·1	144	1·5	6·5	24	2·8
Scarborough	5·9	59	2·0	7·2	37	2·0	6·0	41	1·4	4·1	20	1·3
Scilly	9·9	130	2·8	9·7	73	1·5	8·8	111	1·9	8·9	23	2·7
Sheffield	6·2	121	1·6	7·5	71	1·4	6·3	73	1·0	4·1	16	0·9
Shoeburyness	8·1	84	1·6	8·5	23	1·7	7·7	73	1·2	5·5	22	3·2
Shrewsbury	6·5	75	2·0	8·5	36	1·4	7·1	61	1·3	4·3	20	1·2
Skegness	6·7	75	1·8	7·4	31	1·9	6·4	57	1·2	4·5	19	1·5
Southampton	8·7	166	2·0	8·8	45	1·8	7·9	129	1·6	6·1	25	3·5
Stornoway	5·9	153	1·6	5·7	211	0·5	4·5	194	1·1	5·3	25	3·8
Tiree	6·8	137	1·8	7·1	179	0·5	5·9	229	0·8	6·3	38	3·3
Torbay	8·9	137	2·8	9·4	75	1·8	8·1	128	1·7	7·5	30	2·1
West Kirby	7·3	81	1·7	8·7	38	1·5	7·5	79	1·2	4·7	28	2·4
Weymouth	8·9	191	2·2	8·9	50	1·2	8·3	114	1·6	6·3	23	3·0
Worthing	8·5	144	1·8	8·2	59	1·8	7·5	130	1·3	5·9	33	4·0
York	5·3	55	2·0	7·4	41	2·0	6·3	45	1·5	3·5	12	0·9

TEMPERATURE, RAINFALL AND SUNSHINE IN THE UNITED KINGDOM

Mean Temperature of the air (°C.), Rainfall (mm.) and Bright Sunshine (as mean hours per day) at a representative selection of reporting stations during the year July 1974 to June, 1975. Fuller details of the weather are given in the *Monthly Weather Report* published by the Meteorological Office.

	1975											
	March			April			May			June		
Station	Temp. °C.	Rain mm.	Sun hrs.	Temp. °C.	Rain mm.	Sun hrs.	Temp. °C.	Rain mm.	Sun hrs.	Temp. °C.	Rain mm.	Sun hrs.
Aberporth.........	5·2	42	3·7	7·7	71	4·9	9·6	24	8·6	13·7	4	9·2
Aberystwyth.......	—	42	2·4	—	86	4·0	—	14	—	—	4	—
Aldergrove........	5·0	49	4·7	8·1	65	5·4	9·3	10	8·5	13·9	25	8·4
Bath..............	5·1	83	—	8·7	58	—	10·6	28	—	—	—	—
Birmingham.......	4·4	87	2·3	8·3	62	3·5	9·8	22	5·4	15·0	18	8·7
Bournemouth......	5·6	89	3·2	8·1	43	5·7	10·5	37	7·1	15·4	2	11·3
Braemar..........	1·9	32	3·4	5·3	71	4·0	7·9	39	6·5	11·9	43	7·2
Buxton...........	3·0	83	—	6·5	102	—	7·9	63	—	12·7	19	—
Cambridge........	5·0	92	2·3	8·6	80	4·3	10·1	49	5·8	14·9	18	9·4
Cardiff...........	5·7	61	3·5	9·0	54	4·8	11·3	14	6·4	16·3	10	8·9
Cheltenham.......	5·5	82	2·6	9·2	37	4·2	10·9	19	6·0	16·1	11	8·9
Clacton-on-Sea....	4·9	74	1·9	7·5	43	4·3	9·8	44	5·1	14·3	23	9·0
Douglas...........	5·1	43	5·1	7·8	77	6·3	9·5	37	9·2	13·5	35	10·1
Dumfries..........	4·5	27	4·2	7·7	44	4·9	8·8	35	8·5	13·7	42	8·6
Dundee...........	4·7	14	3·6	7·7	41	3·5	9·5	15	7·1	13·7	25	6·3
Durham...........	4·1	45	3·1	7·7	71	3·9	7·9	50	5·0	13·1	25	7·3
Eastbourne........	5·9	106	2·3	8·1	47	5·7	10·7	56	6·1	15·3	19	11·0
East Malling.......	5·1	95	1·9	8·6	41	4·8	10·1	68	5·1	14·5	12	9·3
Edinburgh.........	3·9	27	3·0	7·6	50	4·0	8·3	47	7·3	13·6	29	6·9
Falmouth.........	6·3	66	4·7	8·7	64	5·6	10·7	33	7·9	14·9	11	10·4
Glasgow..........	4·2	23	3·5	7·8	65	4·4	9·4	29	8·2	13·8	56	7·8
Hartland Point.....	5·9	62	4·1	7·8	86	5·5	10·3	17	8·5	14·3	17	10·4
Hastings..........	5·5	113	2·3	7·9	38	5·0	10·5	63	5·7	15·2	13	10·6
Huddersfield.......	4·6	58	3·2	8·6	50	3·9	9·4	33	6·2	14·6	23	8·1
Hull..............	5·3	81	3·4	8·9	56	4·4	9·7	57	6·4	14·7	13	8·5
Inverness.........	4·1	12	3·3	7·3	47	3·5	8·7	50	5·4	13·1	45	6·3
Lincoln...........	4·5	70	—	8·3	68	—	9·1	41	6·1	13·6	10	8·8
Llandrindod Wells ..	—	—	—	—	—	—	—	—	—	—	—	—
London (Kew)....	5·5	72	2·1	8·7	37	5·1	10·3	67	5·5	14·7	17	10·1
Lowestoft.........	4·7	67	2·4	7·4	39	4·0	9·2	43	6·0	13·3	17	9·2
Manchester Airport..	4·9	45	3·2	8·1	68	3·8	10·1	34	7·1	14·7	22	9·1
Margate..........	5·5	85	1·9	7·9	45	4·3	9·8	55	4·8	13·9	16	9·3
Morecambe........	5·5	46	4·2	8·3	68	4·3	10·7	27	8·6	15·2	33	9·7
Newton Rigg......	3·4	33	3·6	7·3	44	4·1	8·0	26	8·1	13·4	33	8·4
Nottingham.......	—	71	2·4	8·7	55	3·8	9·9	43	—	15·1	11	8·4
Oxford...........	5·1	95	2·3	9·1	47	4·4	10·3	49	5·1	15·5	18	10·0
Penzance.........	6·9	89	4·9	9·1	81	6·5	11·5	39	8·2	15·1	6	10·1
Plymouth.........	6·3	75	4·3	8·9	63	5·9	11·9	50	7·0	15·9	5	10·9
Prestwick.........	4·4	20	4·9	7·7	55	4·9	8·5	21	9·4	12·9	36	9·6
Ross-on-Wye.....	5·2	71	—	9·0	37	—	10·5	32	—	15·1	15	—
St. Mawgan......	5·9	91	4·6	8·5	89	6·1	10·9	29	8·8	14·8	12	10·4
Sandown..........	5·7	102	3·3	8·0	56	6·2	11·0	40	6·4	15·7	1	11·1
Scarborough......	4·8	86	3·2	7·7	77	4·1	8·5	65	5·9	13·2	18	8·8
Scilly............	7·9	65	5·1	9·3	68	5·8	11·3	34	8·6	15·0	10	10·3
Sheffield..........	4·3	59	2·9	8·7	47	4·4	9·7	86	6·1	14·9	12	8·4
Shoeburyness......	5·5	84	2·0	8·2	36	4·5	9·9	56	5·1	14·1	33	9·4
Shrewsbury.......	4·6	44	2·8	8·3	53	3·7	9·6	34	5·8	14·4	16	7·7
Skegness.........	4·9	60	3·0	7·9	62	3·5	9·9	52	6·5	13·1	35	8·8
Southampton......	6·1	98	2·9	9·3	32	5·4	11·7	41	5·8	16·9	17	10·7
Stornoway........	4·3	57	3·6	6·6	104	3·7	7·4	20	8·3	11·1	57	7·2
Tiree............	5·1	54	5·1	7·4	90	4·5	9·0	15	10·7	12·0	43	6·7
Torbay...........	6·5	55	4·3	9·3	40	6·0	11·5	26	7·8	15·9	3	11·3
West Kirby.......	5·4	63	3·6	8·5	68	4·2	10·3	29	7·5	15·1	16	9·5
Weymouth........	6·3	74	3·6	8·6	50	5·8	11·1	18	7·2	15·5	1	10·4
Worthing.........	5·7	85	2·5	7·7	59	5·6	10·5	40	6·3	15·4	14	10·8
York.............	4·1	39	3·3	7·8	51	3·9	8·9	32	5·8	13·7	12	8·2

Weather Record, July, 1974

Day	Temperature Max. °C.	Min. °C.	Wind Speed knots	Rainfall mm.	Sunshine hrs.
1	20·2	13·5	12·0	0·0	14·3
2	19·2	6·3	7·3	6·1	4·3
3	18·5	13·0	11·6	0·3	6·0
4	15·5	10·9	11·5	1·3	0·0
5	20·5	14·1	12·2	0·0	5·7
6	20·2	13·6	9·7	0·0	13·9
7	22·7	7·4	5·0	0·0	8·0
8	23·1	15·7	8·3	0·0	10·4
9	22·2	14·2	9·5	0·0	10·1
10	18·4	12·8	9·2	0·6	0·8
11	18·2	13·7	9·7	0·0	2·3
12	19·0	9·4	5·0	4·6	5·0
13	15·4	11·7	3·0	5·7	0·2
14	19·0	9·8	6·1	0·5	8·8
15	16·5	12·1	14·0	0·9	0·1
16	17·3	12·6	11·6	3·7	3·7
17	18·8	12·2	7·8	0·1	5·4
18	19·4	6·9	5·1	0·0	10·1
19	20·2	5·8	5·2	0·0	6·6
20	23·1	16·5	7·8	0·0	9·1
21	24·3	8·3	5·5	0·0	13·8
22	21·9	14·1	12·0	0·2	11·0
23	21·2	15·3	8·2	0·0	9·7
24	18·1	12·6	6·0	9·4	3·3
25	20·3	8·6	7·3	0·1	9·5
26	22·2	14·2	8·6	0·0	6·2
27	20·0	12·7	9·3	0·0	1·7
28	22·4	13·6	11·0	0·4	7·5
29	22·1	10·3	8·0	0·0	13·9
30	22·7	14·5	9·5	0·0	4·6
31	21·5	15·8	13·7	0·0	2·8
Total	—	—	—	33·9	208·8
Mean	20·1	12·0	8·7	—	—
Temp. °F.	68·2	53·6	—	—	—
Average	21·6	13·4	6·8	62	197

Weather Record, August, 1974

Temperature Max. °C.	Min. °C.	Wind Speed knots	Rainfall mm.	Sunshine hrs.	Day
21·4	15·5	8·3	0·0	6·0	1
21·6	8·1	3·6	0·0	12·4	2
21·2	8·0	8·0	3·7	2·4	3
14·3	13·0	12·3	4·0	0·0	4
20·5	11·1	4·0	0·0	9·8	5
21·9	6·9	3·8	0·0	10·5	6
24·0	7·8	5·7	3·6	4·4	7
21·8	14·4	8·9	1·2	7·6	8
21·3	14·6	8·6	2·7	6·6	9
19·3	13·1	11·5	3·8	7·1	10
20·4	11·2	8·7	10·2	11·8	11
20·4	14·0	9·3	2·1	3·8	12
19·4	12·7	4·3	0·2	1·4	13
20·9	14·4	8·7	0·1	1·1	14
23·9	17·0	10·5	0·1	11·1	15
20·8	14·2	5·8	0·0	2·5	16
20·4	11·5	5·7	5·1	11·0	17
17·2	8·3	3·1	3·6	0·3	18
20·7	8·9	6·6	0·0	5·5	19
21·8	5·8	3·8	0·0	11·7	20
22·4	5·7	1·5	0·0	9·8	21
22·9	9·5	1·8	0·0	10·3	22
20·5	8·8	6·9	0·0	5·3	23
22·9	15·4	7·9	0·0	8·9	24
23·3	11·5	9·4	11·3	5·1	25
19·6	13·8	7·8	1·0	6·4	26
19·1	8·9	5·2	0·0	10·7	27
20·3	3·2	5·1	0·0	11·2	28
21·3	9·8	6·9	0·0	6·0	29
20·2	9·4	6·2	6·5	1·1	30
18·6	8·0	5·9	2·5	5·0	31
—	—	—	61·7	206·6	.. Total
20·8	10·8	6·6	—	—	.. Mean
69·4	51·4	—	—	—	Temp. °F.
21·0	13·1	6·2	57	183	.. Average

Weather Record, September, 1974

Day	Temperature Max. °C.	Min. °C.	Wind Speed knots	Rainfall mm.	Sunshine hrs.
1	18·0	12·3	8·5	9·7	2·3
2	19·4	7·0	13·5	6·1	4·3
3	17·8	13·5	16·3	0·9	6·7
4	18·7	12·2	13·0	31·2	0·6
5	15·3	10·5	6·8	4·9	0·0
6	18·2	10·7	11·4	6·9	9·6
7	16·8	11·7	19·5	0·9	6·8
8	19·0	11·7	13·4	0·4	7·6
9	18·1	11·1	7·1	0·0	7·5
10	18·5	4·7	5·9	0·0	7·9
11	19·8	4·3	4·0	1·5	4·6
12	20·8	13·7	5·9	1·6	3·1
13	20·4	14·6	9·5	0·0	2·3
14	20·1	5·6	3·4	0·0	9·5
15	17·8	10·4	3·7	5·8	1·9
16	20·9	12·3	3·7	0·0	4·2
17	18·3	8·3	5·4	0·0	5·6
18	16·7	7·4	6·3	0·0	10·5
19	17·3	3·1	4·1	0·0	8·9
20	16·7	7·3	5·5	0·0	9·2
21	14·8	10·3	8·8	3·8	1·0
22	15·4	6·0	9·3	8·5	9·8
23	16·0	8·7	10·3	7·0	3·5
24	14·3	9·5	10·0	3·8	8·5
25	13·8	7·8	9·8	2·2	4·5
26	13·5	7·0	7·4	19·7	6·1
27	15·2	8·2	7·6	8·6	0·0
28	13·3	6·1	7·5	0·3	7·6
29	12·9	3·0	4·0	0·1	7·8
30	14·3	0·5	3·1	0·0	7·8
31					
Total	—	—	—	123·9	169·7
Mean	17·1	8·6	8·2	—	—
Temp. °F.					
Average	18·5	11·4	6·6	50	143

Weather Record, October, 1974

Temperature Max. °C.	Min. °C.	Wind speed knots	Rainfall mm.	Sunshine hrs.	Day
12·9	0·3	4·1	2·1	7·3	1
9·1	5·7	5·7	8·4	0·4	2
12·8	5·9	10·3	3·9	6·5	3
9·8	6·9	8·6	4·4	0·0	4
11·8	7·7	5·8	0·0	1·1	5
11·6	5·8	8·3	7·2	0·0	6
10·4	3·1	8·8	7·2	0·8	7
13·0	8·2	9·1	0·0	5·9	8
13·2	8·6	6·2	0·0	4·3	9
9·4	1·4	3·0	2·9	1·0	10
10·7	5·8	6·7	0·0	0·8	11
10·9	4·1	5·9	0·0	7·7	12
11·3	0·1	3·1	0·0	2·1	13
12·5	-1·7	0·6	0·0	6·9	14
11·6	-0·5	1·0	11·3	0·1	15
10·4	8·0	1·5	1·5	0·0	16
9·0	8·1	1·3	0·2	0·0	17
11·7	5·5	10·0	12·8	0·0	18
11·8	5·8	6·7	3·4	7·3	19
10·3	6·4	8·1	1·5	1·3	20
10·7	3·7	7·8	0·4	8·7	21
10·7	7·2	12·0	0·1	3·2	22
10·2	7·5	14·1	0·0	0·0	23
10·0	7·7	7·2	0·0	1·4	24
11·9	8·1	0·0	0·0	3·5	25
12·8	9·1	6·7	0·0	0·3	26
11·8	9·8	11·5	1·1	1·9	27
10·0	5·5	14·2	0·0	6·8	28
7·4	4·4	15·0	0·1	2·8	29
6·2	3·5	10·1	0·5	1·6	30
8·1	1·3	2·9	0·0	4·5	31
—	—	—	69·4	89·2	.. Total
10·8	5·3	7·2	—	—	.. Mean
					Temp. °F.
14·7	8·5	6·6	57	102	.. Average

Entries of Maximum Temperature cover the day period 9–21 h.; Minimum Temperature the night period 21–9 h. entered to the day of reading: Rainfall is for the 24 hours commencing at 9 h. on the day of entry: Sunshine is for the 24 hours 0–24 h.: Mean Wind Speed 10 metres above the ground.

100 knots = 115·1 m.p.h.; 100 mm = 3·94 ins.; °F = 9/5°C + 32

Weather Record, November, 1974

Day	Temperature Max. °C.	Min. °C.	Wind Speed knots	Rainfall mm.	Sunshine hrs.
1	10.2	2.9	1.7	0.2	0.7
2	11.2	2.4	3.9	1.5	0.0
3	10.4	6.4	7.7	5.8	2.9
4	9.6	4.0	7.9	0.0	2.3
5	9.5	5.9	4.3	0.0	1.4
6	10.5	2.4	6.0	0.3	2.5
7	10.2	7.0	6.5	0.4	0.0
8	12.8	9.3	9.4	0.2	0.0
9	14.0	8.1	11.8	1.4	0.0
10	10.0	6.1	11.8	0.0	4.5
11	11.8	9.4	15.2	12.4	0.0
12	8.4	4.2	10.3	0.2	4.0
13	11.2	4.5	14.7	26.6	0.0
14	12.1	7.6	17.0	7.3	2.1
15	11.5	7.4	5.9	8.7	3.4
16	9.6	7.2	5.0	3.1	3.5
17	10.2	2.6	3.3	19.3	0.7
18	7.4	6.8	5.7	3.5	0.0
19	8.3	2.2	4.5	7.0	4.5
20	9.5	-1.7	4.4	6.4	0.1
21	10.5	2.8	7.3	30.0	0.0
22	11.0	8.8	7.1	0.2	0.0
23	12.6	6.6	9.3	0.0	0.3
24	10.8	3.1	11.9	0.0	0.0
25	8.7	6.0	13.4	0.0	5.9
26	8.0	4.2	6.8	0.2	1.2
27	11.2	-1.8	10.7	0.6	0.4
28	9.2	5.1	15.4	0.2	0.9
29	7.9	6.1	9.2	2.7	1.2
30	12.3	4.8	8.2	0.0	2.0
31					
Total ..				138.2	44.5
Mean ..	10.4	5.0	8.5	—	—
Temp. °F.	50.7	41.0			
Average	9.8	5.3	6.8	63	58

Weather Record, December, 1974

Temperature Max. °C.	Min. °C.	Wind Speed knots	Rainfall mm.	Sunshine hrs.	Day
13.0	6.2	9.0	0.0	0.1	1
13.2	11.4	11.0	0.0	0.0	2
12.2	11.8	9.2	0.0	0.0	3
12.1	10.0	11.1	0.0	3.1	4
9.5	6.0	9.6	0.0	2.6	5
11.0	7.4	8.1	0.0	0.2	6
13.0	9.9	9.0	0.0	0.7	7
11.4	10.3	9.6	0.0	0.0	8
10.0	7.9	9.5	0.0	0.0	9
8.8	0.8	13.0	3.7	0.7	10
5.3	2.4	13.5	2.9	6.3	11
10.5	1.5	10.5	1.9	0.0	12
5.8	1.4	9.4	0.0	5.2	13
10.6	5.7	9.6	0.0	2.8	14
8.2	0.8	7.5	0.0	5.1	15
12.0	4.0	12.9	1.7	0.0	16
7.4	5.1	16.4	0.0	5.7	17
7.5	4.8	10.5	0.1	0.6	18
10.5	6.6	11.4	0.0	0.1	19
12.0	9.2	16.5	0.0	0.5	20
12.0	10.5	17.4	1.3	0.0	21
12.3	9.2	14.3	1.7	0.9	22
12.0	10.5	13.0	3.6	5.0	23
9.1	7.5	10.0	1.0	3.4	24
13.1	1.4	12.0	8.7	0.0	25
12.0	11.1	17.3	7.3	2.1	26
11.5	7.8	14.2	0.4	2.0	27
15.2	8.9	17.3	0.5	2.8	28
12.0	11.9	14.4	0.0	2.7	29
6.7	1.1	7.0	0.0	4.6	30
9.2	4.5	9.9	0.0	1.7	31
—	—	—	34.8	58.9	.. Total
10.6	6.7	11.7	—	—	.. Mean
51.1	44.1				Temp. °F.
7.2	3.4	7.6	52	43	.. Average

Weather Record, January, 1975

Day	Temperature Max. °C.	Min. °C.	Wind Speed knots	Rainfall mm.	Sunshine hrs.
1	9.1	6.6	7.6	2.6	0.0
2	9.3	7.4	2.3	0.0	0.0
3	9.2	6.9	4.4	0.0	0.0
4	7.5	1.5	6.3	0.0	3.4
5	11.1	5.2	10.0	0.0	0.0
6	10.4	9.1	15.0	0.4	0.0
7	8.9	6.7	7.9	0.2	0.0
8	9.4	7.6	4.3	0.0	0.1
9	9.9	8.2	8.5	0.0	0.0
10	9.5	8.5	9.6	0.0	0.0
11	12.7	7.6	13.2	0.0	1.3
12	10.7	7.5	12.9	3.5	0.6
13	10.4	3.9	10.5	0.0	0.0
14	12.6	8.6	12.6	2.2	0.3
15	13.9	3.0	14.7	1.0	4.1
16	7.1	5.2	7.4	7.4	0.5
17	8.1	3.6	7.7	0.0	3.0
18	7.0	2.3	5.7	14.3	0.0
19	7.6	-0.7	8.1	4.3	6.6
20	8.7	7.5	11.8	13.6	0.0
21	8.6	2.4	11.9	2.3	6.7
22	11.3	5.1	17.2	2.3	0.0
23	9.9	3.5	16.0	0.5	4.0
24	8.2	3.1	9.5	4.0	4.0
25	12.5	6.4	14.7	0.4	3.2
26	8.8	-2.3	8.3	7.9	3.0
27	10.1	6.8	12.9	3.0	0.1
28	8.6	2.9	9.2	9.1	0.0
29	9.7	3.5	5.7	1.4	0.0
30	12.7	9.5	12.4	0.5	0.3
31	10.6	10.5	12.7	3.5	1.1
Total ..	—	—	—	84.4	42.3
Mean ..	9.8	5.4	10.0	—	—
Temp. °F.	49.6	41.7			
Average	6.1	2.3	8.1	55	48

Weather Record, February, 1975

Temperature Max. °C.	Min. °C.	Wind Speed knots	Rainfall mm.	Sunshine hrs.	Day
11.5	3.2	5.2	0.0	0.0	1
10.5	1.8	2.5	0.0	0.0	2
7.6	5.5	10.1	0.0	0.7	3
5.3	4.4	13.3	0.0	0.0	4
6.5	4.1	11.4	0.0	1.8	5
8.4	-0.4	8.7	0.0	4.4	6
10.2	2.4	10.2	0.0	4.8	7
7.0	4.1	10.5	0.0	3.4	8
8.6	2.3	7.3	0.0	6.2	9
8.4	-3.0	2.0	0.4	0.0	10
10.0	6.8	4.3	5.4	0.0	11
10.1	6.8	3.0	5.0	0.0	12
8.9	5.5	9.3	0.1	3.9	13
7.5	-0.4	4.7	9.9	0.6	14
4.6	2.5	8.9	0.1	0.0	15
6.7	-1.1	8.4	0.1	0.0	16
12.4	6.5	11.2	0.4	0.0	17
8.9	4.5	5.6	4.9	0.0	18
8.1	2.4	5.6	0.0	6.7	19
8.6	-2.3	5.3	0.0	5.5	20
8.0	-0.6	4.9	0.0	5.1	21
11.5	-4.0	3.4	0.0	6.0	22
13.0	-1.5	0.8	0.0	5.4	23
12.5	-2.9	3.5	0.0	8.3	24
7.8	-1.8	11.5	0.0	1.7	25
9.5	3.8	9.2	0.0	6.5	26
12.3	-4.1	5.4	0.0	9.0	27
12.3	-2.3	6.9	0.0	6.6	28
					29
					30
					31
—	—	—	26.3	86.6	.. Total
9.2	1.5	6.9	—	—	.. Mean
48.6	34.7				Temp. °F.
6.8	2.3	8.3	39	65	.. Average

Weather Record, March, 1975

Day	Temperature Max. °C.	Min. °C.	Wind Speed knots	Rain-fall mm.	Sun-shine hrs.
1	13·7	4·1	6·7	1·2	3·1
2	12·1	6·9	10·0	2·8	1·4
3	12·0	8·1	9·5	0·0	0·8
4	12·5	2·3	7·2	1·2	1·8
5	8·5	6·4	6·7	0·0	0·0
6	11·3	0·6	9·1	7·6	0·6
7	10·7	5·4	7·6	6·4	1·9
8	9·2	-0·8	7·9	12·8	0·0
9	8·3	5·6	6·1	0·3	0·1
10	6·1	3·8	5·5	0·1	0·0
11	8·5	2·8	5·7	1·9	0·0
12	7·4	5·1	9·7	1·9	0·0
13	5·6	4·3	10·1	4·8	0·0
14	5·4	3·2	10·1	0·0	0·0
15	5·7	2·6	7·8	1·3	2·0
16	6·5	1·6	7·7	0·1	3·2
17	7·2	-2·4	9·0	0·1	7·0
18	5·6	0·2	11·4	0·6	7·9
19	4·5	0·1	17·0	1·6	0·8
20	5·7	4·0	16·1	0·0	0·0
21	7·8	5·0	5·0	6·9	0·0
22	9·2	3·4	8·4	2·1	1·2
23	9·5	4·4	7·8	0·0	4·0
24	9·7	5·5	11·4	0·0	3·4
25	8·9	2·5	8·5	0·0	4·4
26	9·0	4·5	6·6	9·9	0·1
27	4·1	0·4	6·9	5·6	0·1
28	6·5	-0·2	8·7	0·0	7·7
29	7·4	-1·2	7·0	1·8	3·1
30	5·7	0·6	8·0	0·8	6·2
31	8·9	-0·2	6·7	0·0	5·7
Total	—	—	—	71·8	66·5
Mean	8·2	2·9	8·6	—	—
Temp. °F.	46·8	37·2	—	—	—
Average	9·8	3·4	8·0	37	112

Weather Record, April, 1975

Temperature Max. °C.	Min. °C.	Wind Speed knots	Rain-fall mm.	Sun-shine hrs.	Day
7·6	2·8	7·8	1·9	3·7	1
7·4	6·0	10·0	3·0	0·1	2
6·3	0·6	10·1	2·1	4·6	3
6·1	0·8	9·0	1·0	1·5	4
6·0	-1·1	5·2	0·4	3·0	5
8·2	-2·9	3·3	0·0	8·0	6
9·5	-0·7	11·0	0·7	2·2	7
7·3	1·6	11·0	2·1	8·1	8
6·3	0·2	8·7	0·6	10·6	9
8·0	-1·7	6·8	1·7	6·6	10
11·3	4·7	7·0	0·1	1·2	11
15·1	6·8	7·0	0·0	4·0	12
16·6	2·4	6·0	0·1	3·0	13
12·4	8·8	11·4	5·8	1·9	14
13·0	7·3	7·6	0·9	1·3	15
14·7	5·4	5·5	1·0	6·4	16
14·1	8·4	7·9	0·5	0·0	17
15·9	9·7	5·3	10·8	7·3	18
14·2	9·9	10·4	0·0	4·6	19
15·5	3·1	8·1	0·0	9·4	20
15·5	7·1	8·5	0·0	2·2	21
20·8	1·4	3·7	0·0	12·7	22
15·2	9·6	9·1	0·0	3·9	23
19·8	5·1	6·4	0·0	11·0	24
18·3	5·9	4·3	0·4	4·7	25
18·1	7·6	3·0	0·0	6·2	26
15·2	7·8	5·3	0·0	2·9	27
19·2	9·5	7·5	0·0	7·9	28
12·4	7·4	9·1	0·2	2·9	29
13·6	3·2	8·9	3·2	10·3	30
					31
—			36·5	152·2	Total
12·8	4·6	7·5	—	—	Mean
55·0	40·3	—	—	—	Temp. °F.
13·3	5·7	8·1	46	162	Averag

Weather, Record, May, 1975

Day	Temperature Max. °C.	Min. °C.	Wind Speed knots	Rain-fall mm.	Sun-shine hrs.
1	14·0	7·4	13·1	0·0	2·5
2	16·1	10·4	8·9	4·1	3·1
3	12·7	4·4	10·0	0·0	13·0
4	12·9	4·4	10·5	0·0	11·1
5	14·1	4·3	15·4	0·0	10·7
6	15·7	6·4	16·5	0·0	4·0
7	16·9	7·2	14·3	7·7	2·1
8	16·9	9·1	10·2	0·0	8·3
9	14·2	7·3	4·9	0·0	1·5
10	15·1	7·9	6·5	0·0	1·3
11	12·4	8·0	5·8	0·0	2·8
12	13·6	1·2	8·2	5·8	3·0
13	15·2	10·0	9·2	0·6	5·6
14	14·4	7·5	6·7	0·0	5·4
15	13·2	7·3	5·4	11·0	1·4
16	9·2	7·4	9·2	33·2	0·0
17	8·7	7·5	7·6	4·2	0·0
18	11·2	7·6	5·3	0·0	0·0
19	18·4	2·6	4·6	0·0	13·0
20	21·0	1·1	3·7	0·0	13·0
21	17·5	6·4	7·4	0·0	12·5
22	11·8	1·8	2·3	0·0	0·1
23	13·5	0·8	3·8	0·0	9·8
24	10·9	1·0	7·2	0·1	2·3
25	14·0	7·2	7·2	0·0	2·1
26	17·5	8·0	13·2	0·0	10·5
27	18·3	8·7	13·9	0·0	10·2
28	19·8	11·5	11·0	0·0	8·7
29	13·5	6·9	9·7	0·1	0·4
30	11·4	6·7	8·1	0·0	0·5
31	13·6	-0·1	5·5	0·0	11·8
Total	—	—	—	66·8	170·7
Mean	14·4	6·1	8·5	—	—
Temp. °F.	57·9	43·0	—	—	—
Average	16·8	8·4	7·4	46	203

Weather, Record, June, 1975

Temperature Max. °C.	Min. °C.	Wind Speed knots	Rain-fall mm.	Sun-shine hrs.	Day
13·5	2·3	5·6	0·1	9·4	1
13·4	4·8	10·1	8·6	5·6	2
14·5	6·0	10·4	0·0	13·6	3
15·2	0·6	4·7	0·1	8·4	4
17·7	4·3	6·4	0·0	2·4	5
24·2	12·1	6·6	0·0	13·9	6
25·8	10·3	5·8	0·0	14·9	7
23·5	6·2	6·1	0·0	15·1	8
23·2	9·5	8·3	0·0	14·8	9
23·2	8·7	7·9	0·0	13·6	10
25·2	10·3	8·5	0·0	14·3	11
26·2	11·1	5·9	0·0	14·0	12
25·4	10·3	4·1	0·0	13·5	13
22·4	11·4	4·5	0·2	1·2	14
18·2	14·2	5·6	0·5	3·5	15
16·4	5·9	6·0	0·6	9·2	16
19·0	7·3	4·1	0·6	6·7	17
21·0	5·0	5·4	0·0	12·5	18
19·9	11·8	9·3	0·0	6·6	19
23·8	11·2	3·7	0·0	10·4	20
24·8	9·4	8·3	0·0	14·5	21
22·8	13·2	11·9	0·0	12·6	22
19·1	11·0	6·1	6·7	1·8	23
24·8	9·3	8·6	0·0	12·7	24
21·7	10·3	6·1	0·0	14·3	25
26·2	5·2	4·8	0·0	14·0	26
18·4	13·0	11·0	0·0	7·9	27
15·2	11·2	9·6	0·0	2·2	28
19·5	6·6	8·4	0·0	7·9	29
21·9	6·0	3·9	0·0	10·5	30
					31
—	—	—	17·4	302·0	Total
20·9	8·8	6·9	—	—	Mean
69·6	47·5	—	—	—	Temp. °F.
20·2	11·5	7·2	44	214	Average

Principal Book Publishers and Their Addresses

More than 8,000 firms, individuals and societies have published one or more books in recent years. The list which follows is a selective one comprising, in the main, those firms whose names are most familiar to the general public. An interleaved list containing some 2,000 names and addresses is available, price 70p post free, from the publishers of "Whitaker."

Abelard-Schumann, Intertext House, 450 Edgware Rd., W.2.
Allan (Ian), Terminal House, Shepperton, Mddx.
Allen (J. A.), 1 Lower Grosvenor Pl., S.W.1.
Allen, (W. H.), 44 Hill St., W.1.
Allen & Unwin, 40 Museum St., W.C.1.
Angus & Robertson, 2 Fisher St., W.C.1.
Architectural Press, 9 Queen Anne's Gate, S.W.1.
Arlington Books, 38 Bury Street, S.W.1.
Armada Books, 14 St. James's Place, S.W.1.
Arms & Armour Press, 2 Hampstead High St., N.W.3.
Arnold (E.), & Co., 25 Hill St., W.1.
Arnold (E. J.) & Son, Butterley St., Leeds.
Arrow Books, 3 Fitzroy Square, W.1.
Athlone Press, 4 Gower St., W.C.1.
Autobooks, Golden Lane, Brighton.
Baillière, Tindall, 8 Henrietta St., W.C.2.
Baker (John), 4 Soho Square, W.1.
Barker (Arthur), 11 St. John's Hill, S.W.11.
Barrie & Jenkins, 24 Highbury Cresc., N.5.
Bartholomew & Son, Duncan St., Edinburgh.
Batsford, 4 Fitzhardinge St., Portman Square, W.1.
Bell (Geo.) & Sons, 6 Portugal St., W.C.2.
Benn (Ernest), Sovereign Way, Tonbridge, Kent.
Bingley (Clive), 16 Pembridge Rd., W.11.
Black (A. & C.), 4 Soho Sq., W.1.
Blackie, Glasgow, and 5 Fitzhardinge St., W.1.
Blackwell (Basil), 108 Cowley Rd., Oxford.
Blackwood (W.), 32 Thistle St., Edinburgh.
Blandford Press, West St., Poole, Dorset.
Blond & Briggs, 56 Doughty St., W.C.1.
Bodley Head, 9 Bow St., W.C.2.
Bowes & Bowes, 9 Bow St., W.C.2.
Brown, Son & Ferguson, 52 Darnley St., Glasgow.
Burke Pub. Co., 14 John St., W.1.
Butterworth & Co., 88 Kingsway, W.C.2.
Calder & Boyars, 18 Brewer St., W.1.
Cambridge Univ. Press, 200 Euston Rd., N.W.1, and Cambridge.
Cape (Jonathan), 30 Bedford Square, W.C.1.
Cassell & Co., 35 Red Lion Sq., W.C.1.
Centaur Press, Fontwell, Arundel, Sx.
Chambers (W. & R.), 11 Thistle St., Edinburgh.
Chapman & Hall, 11 New Fetter Lane, E.C.4.
Chapman (Geoffrey), 35 Red Lion Sq., W.C.1.
Chatto & Windus, 40-42 William IV St., W.C.2.
Churchill Livingstone, 23 Ravelston Terr., Edinburgh.
Collier-Macmillan, 35 Red Lion Sq., W.C.1.
Collins, Sons & Co., 14 St. James's Place, S.W.1.
Constable & Co., 10 Orange St., W.C.2.
Cooper (Leo), 196 Shaftesbury Ave., W.C.2.
Corgi Books, 57 Uxbridge Road, W.5.
Darton, Longman & Todd, 85 Gloucester Rd., S.W.7.
David & Charles, Brunel House, Newton Abbot, Devon.
Davies (Christopher), 4 Thomas Row, Swansea.
Davies (Peter), 15 Queen St., W.1.
Davis (R. Hart-), MacGibbon, Frogmore, St. Albans, Herts.
Dean & Son, 43 Ludgate Hill, E.C.4.
Dent (J. M.) & Sons, 26 Albemarle St., W.1.
Deutsch (A.), 105 Gt. Russell St., W.C.1.
Dobson Books, 80 Kensington Church St., W.8.
Dolphin Pub. Co., Milton Rd., Aylesbury, Bucks.
Duckworth & Co., 43 Gloucester Crescent, N.W.1
E.P. Group, 10 Snow Hill, E.C.1.

Elek, 54 Caledonian Rd., N.1.
Elliot Right Way Books, Kingswood Bldg., Kingswood, Surrey.
Encyclopædia Britannica, 156 Oxford St., W.1.
English Universities Press, Warwick Lane, E.C.4.
Evans Bros., Montague House, Russell Sq., W.C.1.
Eyre & Spottiswoode, 11 New Fetter Lane, E.C.4.
Faber & Faber, 3 Queen Square, W.C.1.
Focal Press, 31 Fitzroy Square, W.1.
Fontana, 14 St. James's Place, S.W.1.
Foulis (G. T.), Sparkford, Yeovil, Som.
Foulsham & Co., Yeovil Rd., Slough, Berks.
Fountain Press, Hemel Hempstead, Herts.
French (Samuel), 26 Southampton St., W.C.2.
Frewin (Leslie), 5 Goodwin's Court, W.C.2.
Gall & Inglis, 12 Newington Road, Edinburgh, 9.
Garnstone, 59 Brompton Rd., S.W.3.
Gee & Co., 151 Strand, W.C.2.
Geographia, St. Albans, Herts.
Gibbons (Stanley), 391 Strand, W.C.2.
Gibson (Robert), 17 Fitzroy Place, Glasgow.
Ginn & Co., Elsinore Ho., Buckingham St., Aylesbury, Bucks.
Gold Lion Books, 138 Park Lane, W.1.
Gollancz (Victor), 14 Henrietta St., W.C.2.
Gower Press, Epping, Essex.
Graham (Frank), 6 Queen's Terrace, Newcastle.
Green (W.), St. Giles St., Edinburgh.
Griffin (Charles), 5A Crendon St., High Wycombe, Bucks.
Guinness Superlatives, 2 Cecil Court, London Road, Enfield.
H.M. Stationery Office, Atlantic House, Holborn Viaduct, E.C.1.
Hale (Robert), Clerkenwell Green, E.C.1.
Hamilton (Hamish), 90 Gt. Russell St., W.C.1.
Hamlyn, Astronaut Ho., Hounslow Road, Feltham, Mddx.
Harrap (G. G.) & Co., 182 High Holborn, W.C.1.
Harvill Press, 30A Pavilion Rd., S.W.1.
Haynes (J. H.), Sparkford, Yeovil, Som.
Heffer & Sons, 20 Trinity Street, Cambridge.
Heinemann (Wm.), 15 Queen St., W.1.
Hodder & Stoughton, Warwick Lane, E.C.4.
Hodge & Co., 34 N. Frederick St., Glasgow.
Hogarth Press, 40-42 William IV St., W.C.2.
Hollis & Carter, 9 Bow St., W.C.2.
Holmes-Macdougall, 137 Leith Walk, Edinburgh.
Holt-Saunders, 120 Golden Lane, E.C.1.
Hughes & Son, 29 Rivulet Rd., Wrexham.
Hurst & Blackett, 3 Fitzroy Square, W.1.
Hutchinson & Co., 3 Fitzroy Square, W.1.
Independent Press, 86 Tavistock Pl., W.C.1.
Jackdaw Publications, 30 Bedford Sq., W.C.1.
Jarrold & Sons. Barrack Street, Norwich.
Jarrolds, 3 Fitzroy Square, W.1.
Johnson Pubns., 55 Langley Pk. Rd., Sutton, Sy.
Johnston & Bacon, 35 Red Lion Sq., W.C.1.
Jordan & Sons, 15 Pembroke Rd., Bristol.
Joseph (Michael), 52 Bedford Sq., W.C.1.
Kaye & Ward, 21 New St., E.C.2.
Kelly's Directories, Neville House, Eden St., Kingston, Surrey.
Kimber (Wm.), 22A Queen Anne's Gate, S.W.1.
Kimpton (Henry), 106 Hampstead Rd., N.W.1.
Ladybird, Beeches Rd., Loughborough.
Lane (Allen), 17 Grosvenor Gdns., S.W.1.
Lawrence & Wishart, 46 Bedford Row, W.C.1.

Lewis (H. K.), 136 Gower St., W.C.1.
Lockwood (Crosby), Park St., St. Albans, Herts.
Long (John), 3 Fitzroy Square, W.1.
Longman Group, Burnt Mill, Harlow, Essex.
Low (S.), Marston & Co., Queen St., Maidenhead, Berks.
Lund Humphries, 12 Bedford Sq., W.C.1.
Lutterworth Press, Farnham Rd., Guildford, Sy.
Macdonald & Evans, 8 John St., W.C.1.
Macdonald & Jane's, 8 Shepherdess Walk, N.1.
McGraw-Hill, Shoppenhangers Rd., Maidenhead, Berks.
Machinery Pub. Co., New England St., Brighton.
Macmillan Publishers, Little Essex St., W.C.2.
Marshall Cavendish, 58 Old Compton St., W.1.
Marshall, Morgan & Scott, 116 Baker St., W.1.
Mayflower, Frogmore., St. Albans, Herts.
Methodist Publishing, Wellington Rd., S.W.19.
Methuen & Co., 11 New Fetter Lane, E.C.4.
Mills & Boon, 17 Foley St., W.1.
Mitchell Beazley, 14 Manette St., W.1.
Mowbray, The Alden Press, Osney Mead, Oxford.
Muller (F.), Victoria Works, Edgware Rd., N.W.2.
Murray (John), 50 Albemarle St., W.1.
Museum Press, 39 Parker St., W.C.2.
National C.E.C., Robt. Denholm House, Nutfield, Surrey.
Nelson (T.), 36 Park St., W.1.
New Authors, 3 Fitzroy Square, W.1.
New English Library, Barnard's Inn, E.C.1.
Nisbet & Co., Digswell Pl., Welwyn, Herts.
Nonesuch Library, 9 Bow St., W.C.2.
Novello & Co., Borough Green, Sevenoaks, Kent.
Oak Tree Press, 116 Baker St., W.1.
Octopus Books, 59 Grosvernor St., W.1.
Odhams Books, Astronaut Ho., Hounslow Rd., Feltham, Mddx.
Oliphants, 116 Baker St., W.1.
Oliver & Boyd, 23 Ravelston Terr., Edinburgh.
Owen (Peter), 20 Holland Park Ave., W.11.
Oxford Univ. Press, 37 Dover St., W.1.
Pall Mall Press, 5 Cromwell Pl., S.W.7.
Pan Books, 18 Cavaye Place, S.W.10.
Panther, Frogmore, St. Albans, Herts.
Paul (Kegan), 39 Store St., W.C.1.
Paul (Stanley), 3 Fitzroy Square, W.1.
Pelham Books, 52 Bedford Sq., W.C.1.
Penguin Books, Harmondsworth, Mddx.
Pergamon Press, Headington Hill Hall, Oxford.
Phaidon Press, 5 Cromwell Place. S.W.7.
Pharmaceutical Press, 17 Bloonsbury Sq., W.C.1.
Philip (George), 12 Long Acre, W.C.2.
Photo Precision, Caxton Rd., St. Ives, Hunts.
Pickering & Inglis, 26 Bothwell St., Glasgow, C.2.
Pitkins, 11 Wyfold Rd., S.W.6.
Pitman Publishing, Parker St., W.C.2.
Purnell Books, Queen St., Maidenhead, Berks.

Putnam & Co., 9 Bow St., W.C.2.
Quartet Books, 27 Goodge St., W.1.
Queen Anne Press, 12 Vandy St., E.C.2.
Rapp & Whiting, 105 Great Russell Street, W.C.1.
Reinhardt (Max), 9 Bow St. W.C.2.
Religious Education Press, Hennock Rd., Exeter.
Rider & Co., 3 Fitzroy Square, W.1.
Rivingtons, Montague House, Russell Sq., W.C.1.
Routledge & Kegan Paul, 68–74 Carter Lane, E.C.4.
Scripture Union & C.S.S.M., 47 Marylebone Lane, W.1.
Secker & Warburg, 14 Carlisle St., W.1.
Seeley Service, 196 Shaftesbury Av., W.C.2.
Sheed & Ward, 6 Blenheim St., W.1.
Sheldon Press, Holy Trinity Church, Marylebone Rd., N.W.1.
Sidgwick & Jackson, 1 Tavistock Chambers, W.C.1.
Smith (M. Temple), 37 Gt. Russell St., W.C.1.
Smythe (Colin), Gerrards Cross, Bucks.
S.P.C.K., Holy Trinity Church, Marylebone Rd., N.W.1.
Souvenir Press, 43 Gt. Russell St., W.C.1.
Spearman (N.), 112 Whitfield St., W.1.
Sphere Books, 30 Gray's Inn Rd., W.C.1.
Spon (E. & F. N.), 11 New Fetter Lane, E.C.4.
Sporting Handbooks, 13 Bedford Square, W.C.1.
Stanford Maritime, 12–14 Long Acre, W.C.2.
Stephens (Patrick), Bar Hill, Cambridge.
Stevens & Sons, 11 New Fetter Lane, E.C.4.
Student C. M. P., 58 Bloomsbury St., W.C.1.
Studio Vista, 35 Red Lion Sq., W.C.1.
Sweet & Maxwell, 11 New Fetter Lane, E.C.4.
Tabard Press, 10 Snow Hill, E.C.1.
Talbot Press, Ballymount Rd., Dublin.
Tavistock Publications, 11 New Fetter Lane, E.C.4.
Technical Press, Freeland, Oxford.
Thames & Hudson, 30 Bloomsbury St., W.C.1.
Turnstone Press, 37 Upper Addison Gdns., W.14.
University of London Press, Warwick Lane, E.C.4.
University of Wales Press, James St., Cardiff.
University Tutorial Press, 9 Gt. Sutton St., E.C.1.
Vallentine, Mitchell, 67 Gt. Russell St., W.C.1.
Ward, Lock, 116 Baker St., W.1.
Warne, 40 Bedford Square, W.C.1.
Watts & Co., 39 Parker St., W.C.2.
Weidenfeld & Nicolson, 11 St. John's Hill, S.W.11.
Wheaton (A.), Hennock Rd., Exeter.
"Whitaker," 13 Bedford Square, W.C.1.
Wildwood House, 29 King St., W.C.2.
Witherby (H. F. & G.), 5 Plantain Place, S.E.1.
Wolfe Publishing, 10 Earlham St., W.C.2.
World Distributors, 12 Lever St., Manchester.
World's Work, Kingswood, Tadworth, Surrey.
Wright (John), 42 Triangle West, Bristol.

Most of the principal book publishers are members of The Publishers Association, whose address is 19 Bedford Square, London, W.C.1.—*President*, Peter Allsop (Associated Book Publishers, Ltd.); *Secretary*, R. E. Barker.

BOOK PRODUCTION AND BOOK EXPORTS

These figures for book production and exports are issued by the Department of Industry. The totals for the years 1963 to 1974 are shown below:

Year	Total value of Books produced in U.K.	Total value of Books exported from U.K.	Year	Total value of Books produced in U.K.	Total value of Books exported from U.K.
1963	£90,142,709	£39,043,851	1969	£145,893,000	£68,523,000
1964	98,489,220	43,225,649	1970	153,676,000	67,842,000
1965	104,876,998	46,123,190	1971	179,099,000	77,856,000
1966	119,578,145	51,417,786	1972	205,266,000	81,207,000
1967	125,782,262	53,838,418	1973	230,106,000	95,855,000
1968	137,748,324	61,741,160	1974 (Provisional)	283,373,000	120,334,000

BOOKS PUBLISHED IN GREAT BRITAIN IN 1974

This table, from *The Bookseller* of January 4, 1975, shows the books published in 1974 with the number of new editions, translations and limited editions.

Books and pamphlets priced at less than 12½p have been omitted, as are also all Government publications except the more important issued by H.M. Stationery Office.

	Total	Reprints and New Editions	Translations	Editions de Luxe
Aeronautics	98	24	2	—
Agriculture and Forestry	242	48	5	—
Architecture	356	65	7	—
Art	1,130	147	47	5
Astronomy	62	21	6	1
Bibliography and Library Economy	563	61	3	4
Biography	1,024	243	54	4
Chemistry and Physics	679	74	43	—
Children's Books	2,618	662	110	2
Commerce	721	185	3	1
Customs, Costume, Folklore	118	31	13	—
Domestic Science	451	122	17	—
Education	908	167	7	—
Engineering	928	239	13	—
Entertainment	465	86	14	—
Fiction	4,154	1,904	133	6
General	200	32	12	1
Geography and Archæology	270	85	6	1
Geology and Meteorology	225	20	18	—
History	1,193	385	46	2
Humour	83	8	—	1
Industry	410	118	8	—
Language	282	62	6	—
Law and Public Administration	893	203	11	—
Literature	757	140	58	3
Mathematics	450	77	21	—
Medical Science	1,466	306	21	1
Military Science	137	18	1	—
Music	272	75	11	—
Natural Sciences	1,091	181	56	4
Occultism	250	50	12	—
Philosophy	296	85	37	—
Photography	180	80	5	—
Plays	225	65	27	1
Poetry	812	85	60	118
Political Science and Economy	2,412	359	69	1
Psychology	408	71	13	—
Religion and Theology	1,011	310	98	3
School Textbooks	1,712	262	6	—
Science, General	65	8	4	—
Sociology	757	116	26	1
Sports and Outdoor Games	519	147	14	1
Stockbreeding	182	57	2	1
Trade	359	101	—	1
Travel and Guidebooks	580	243	8	—
Wireless and Television	180	24	—	—
Totals	32,194	7,852	1,133	163

COPYRIGHT

The Government Department dealing with Copyright is the *Industrial Property and Copyright Dept., Department of Trade*, 25 Southampton Bldgs., W.C.2.

Subject to the provisions of the Copyright Act, 1956, copyright subsists automatically in every original literary, dramatic, musical and artistic work and continues to subsist until the end of the period of fifty years from the end of the calendar year in which the author died and shall then expire. *No registration nor other formalities are required in order to obtain the protection of the Act.* Protection is conferred not only against reproduction but also against the public performance of a work without permission. Copyright may also subsist in sound recordings, cinematograph films and television and sound broadcasts. Libraries entitled, under a provision still in force of the Copyright Act, 1911, to receive free copies of books published in the United Kingdom are the British Library, the Bodleian Library, Oxford, University Library, Cambridge, the National Library of Wales, the National Library of Scotland and Trinity College, Dublin.

Voluntary Registration at Stationers' Hall.—Compulsory registration at Stationers' Hall was terminated by the Copyright Act of 1911, but in 1924 the Stationers' Company established a *new* Register in which Books and Fine Arts can be registered. A copy has to be filed at Stationers' Hall and certified copies of the entries are issued, the fees being £2 for a Book, or a Fine Art; certified copies £2 in either case. The fee for a search is 50p.

ANNUAL REFERENCE BOOKS

Advertiser's Annual.—Mercury House, 103–119 Waterloo Road, S.E.1. (May.) £8.00.

Aircraft.—Terminal House, Shepperton, Middx. £2·75.

Annual Art Sales Index.—Pond Ho., Weybridge, Sy. (Nov.) £18·50.

Annual Register of World Events.—Longman Ho., Burnt Mill, Harlow, Essex. £12·00.

Antiques in Britain.—2 High St., Wendover, Bucks. (Jan.) £2·74.

Architects & Planners, Directory of Official.—2 Catherine Street, W.C.2. £6·50

Astronomical Ephemeris.—H.M. Stationery Office, Atlantic House, Holborn Viaduct, E.C.1. (Jan.) £3·80

Automobile Year.—Bar Hill, Cambridge. (Feb.) £9·95.

B.B.C. Handbook.—35 Marylebone High St., W.1. £0·75.

Baily's Hunting Directory.—1 Lower Grosvenor Place, S.W.1 (Oct.) £5·25.

Banker's Almanac & Year Book.—R.A.C. House, Lansdowne Rd., Croydon. (Feb.) £15·50.

Bloodstock Breeders Annual Review.—26 Charing Cross Rd., W.C.2. £15·50.

Boat World—39 East St., Epsom, Surrey. (Jan.) £1·95.

Boxing News Annual.—St. Crispin's Way, Thurmaston, Leicester. (Feb.) £1·00

Brassey's Defence Year Book.—81A Endell St., W.C.2. £8·50.

British Books in Print.—13 Bedford Square, W.C.1. £23·00.

British Film & Television Year Book.—142 Wardour St., W.1. (Jan./Feb.) £6·00.

British Industry & Services in the Common Market.—Neville Ho., Eden St., Kingston-upon-Thames, Sy. £10·00.

British Plastics Yearbook.—Paris Gdn., Stamford St., S.E.1. £5·00.

British Rubber Industry, Directory of.—90 Tottenham Court Road, W.1. (Aug.). £3·00.

British Textile Register.—R.A.C. House, Lansdowne, Rd., Croydon. (Mar.) £10·50.

Brown's Nautical Almanack.—52 Darnley St., Glasgow S.1. (Sept.) £3·40.

Building Societies Yearbook.—2–3 Burgon St., E.C.4. (July.) £7·60.

Buses Annual.—Terminal Ho., Shepperton, Mddx. £2·00.

Caravan Sites and Mobile Home Parks.—Link House, Dingwall Ave., Croydon. (Feb.) 40p.

Carpet Annual.—54 Regent St., W.1. (Jan.). £7·95.

Catholic Directory.—21 Fleet St., E.C.4. £5·00.

Charities Digest.—88 Kingsway, W.C.2. (Jan.) £2·80.

Chemical Industry Directory & Who's Who.—Sovereign Way, Tonbridge, Kent. (Nov.) £12·50.

Christies' Review of the Season.—3 Fitzroy Sq., W.1. (Dec.) £9·50.

Church of England Year Book.—Church House, Dean's Yard, Westminster, S.W.1. (Jan.) £3·00.

Church of Scotland Year Book.—121 George St., Edinburgh 2. (Apr.) £1·00.

City Connections, Directory of.—15–16 New Burlington St., W.1. £17·50.

Clean Air Year Book.—134 North St., Brighton. (May.) £1·25.

Clothing Export Council Directory.—1–5 Bath St., E.C.1. £7·50.

Commercial Television Yearbook & Directory.—103–119 Waterloo Road, S.E.1. £5·00.

Commonwealth Universities Year Book.—36 Gordon Square. W.C.1. (Sept.) £17·00.

Computer Users' Year Book.—18 Queen's Rd., Brighton, Sx. £13·50.

Concrete Year Book.—Wexham Springs, Slough, Bucks. £3·00.

Consulting Engineers Who's Who.—10–16 Elm St., W.C.1. £3·75.

Contractors and Public Works Annual, Directory of.—68 High St., Northwood, Middx. (Apr.) £5·00.

Coventry Evening Telegraph Year Book and Who's Who.—Coventry Newspapers Ltd., Corporation St., Coventry. (Nov.) £2·00.

Current Law Year Book.—11 New Fetter La., E.C.4. £12·50.

"Daily Mail" Year Book.—Carmelite House, Fleet St., E.C.4. (Dec.) 80p; 50p.

Debrett's Peerage.—Neville House, Eden St., Kingston-on-Thames. (May.) £26·50.

Decorating Contractor Annual Directory.—2 Queensway, Redhill, Surrey. £3·20.

Decorative Art in Modern Interiors.—35 Red Lion Sq., W.C.1. £9·95.

Diplomatic Service List.—H.M.S.O., Atlantic House, Holborn Viaduct, E.C.1. (April.) £3·25.

Directory of Directors.—R.A.C. House, Lansdowne Rd., Croydon. (Apr.) £9·00.

Directory of Opportunities for Graduates.—54 Regent St., W.1. £6·00.

Do-it-Yourself Annual.—Link House, Dingwall Ave., Croydon. (Jan.) 25p.

Dod's Parliamentary Companion.—39 East St., Epsom, Surrey. (Sept.) £7·00.

Education Authorities' Directory and Annual.—Derby House, Bletchingley Rd., Merstham, Surrey. (Jan.) £8·00.

Electrical & Electronic Trader Year Book.—Paris Gdn., Stamford St., S.E.1. £5·00.

Electrical & Electronics Trades Directory.—P.O. Box 8, Southgate House, Stevenage. (Feb.) £16·50.

Electrical Contractor's Yearbook.—55 Catherine Place, S.W.1. £2·00.

Electricity Supply Handbook.—P.O. Box 147, 40 Bowling Green Lane, E.C.1. (Apr.). £1·50.

"Engineer" Buyers' Guide, 30 Calderwood St., S.E.18. £2·30.

Europa Year Book.—18 Bedford Square, W.C.1. 2 vols. (Apr.) £24·00.

Export Data: Exporter's Year Book.—Sovereign Way, Tonbridge, Kent. (Dec./Jan.) £10·00.

Extel Issuing House Year Book.—37–45 Paul St., E.C.2. £16·50.

Farm and Garden Equipment Guide.—161 Fleet St., E.C.4. £2·60.

Finishing Handbook and Directory.—4 Ludgate Circus, E.C.4. £5·65.

Fire Protection Directory.—Sovereign Way, Tonbridge, Kent. (Nov.) £6·00.

Fishing Industry Index International.—54 Regent St., W.1. £5·50.

"Fishing News" Directory and Equipment Guide.—110 Fleet St., E.C.4. (Feb.) £4·00.

"Flight" Directory of British Aviation.—Neville House, Eden St., Kingston-upon-Thames. Surrey. (Mar.) £3·00.

Food Processing and Packaging Directory.—1–6 Paris Gdn., Stamford St., S.E.1. £7·00.

Frozen Foods Yearbook.—2 Queensway, Redhill, Surrey. £3·00.

Fruit Trades World Directory.—54 Regent St., W.1. (Jan.) £5·57.

Furnishing Trade, Directory to the.—Sovereign Way, Tonbridge, Kent. (Jan.) £12·50.

Games & Toys Yearbook.—30–31 Knightrider St., E.C.4. (Dec.) £2·00.

Gas Directory.—Sovereign Way, Tonbridge, Kent. (Jan.) £7·50.

Gibbon's Stamps of the World Catalogue.—391 Strand, W.C.2. (Oct.) £5·50.

Girls' School Year Book.—4–6 Soho Square, W.1. (May.) £2·25.

Glass Directory & Buyer's Guide, European.—2 Queensway, Redhill, Surrey. £5·25.

Good Food Guide.—14 Buckingham St., W.C.2. £2·95.

Government & Municipal Contractors Register.—39 East St., Epsom, Surrey. (Jan.) £5·00.

Guild of Agricultural Journalists Year Book.—152 Fleet St., E.C.4. £1·50.

Guinness Book of Records.—2 Cecil Court, London Rd., Enfield. (Oct.) £2·50.

Hard's Yearbook for Clothing Industry.—42–43 Gerrard St., W.1. £2·50.

Hardware Directory.—Sovereign Way, Tonbridge, Kent. £8·50.

Harper's Directory & Manual of Wine & Spirit Trades.—Southbank House, Black Prince Rd., S.E.1. (June.) £4·00.

Harper's Guide to the Sports Trade.—Southbank House, Black Prince Rd., S.E.1. (Jan.) £2·50.

Hi-fi Year Book.—1–6 Paris Gdn., Stamford St., S.E.1. £1·75.

Hollis Press and P.R. Annual.—Contact House, Lower Hampton Rd., Sunbury-on-Thames. (Oct.) £4·50.

Horse & Hound Yearbook.—P.O. Box 21, Tower House, Southampton St., W.C.2. (Winter.) £2·50.

Horseman's Year.—52 Bedford Sq., W.C.1. (Apr.) £5·00.

Hospitals & Health Services Yearbook.—75 Portland Place, W.1. (Nov.) £9·85.

Hotel Catering and Institutional Managers' Yearbook.—116A Pentonville Rd., N.1. £4·25.

Hotel, Restaurant & Canteen Supplies.—39 East St., Epsom, Sy. £2·50.

Hutchins' Priced Schedules.—33 Station Rd., Bexhill-on-Sea. £7·25.

Hydraulic Handbook.—Crown House, Morden, Surrey. £14·00.

I.T.V. Guide to Independent Television.—70 Brompton Rd., S.W.3. £1·30; £1·60.

Insurance Directory & Yearbook.—12–13 Henrietta St., W.C.2. (April.) £5·25.

International Antiques Yearbook.—29 Maddox St., W.1. (Jan.). £4·00.

International Finishing Industries Manual.—157 Hagden La., Watford. (Jan.) £5·50.

International Shipping & Shipbuilding Directory.—Sovereign Way, Tonbridge, Kent. £16·00.

International Yearbook & Statesman's Who's Who.—Neville Ho., Eden St., Kingston-upon-Thames, Surrey (Apr.). £15·00.

Iron & Steel Year Book.—Atlantic House, Holborn Viaduct, E.C.1. £2·10.

Jane's All The World's Aircraft.—49 Poland St., W.1. (Sept.) £16·50.

Jane's Fighting Ships.—49 Poland St., W.1. (Aug.) £19·50.

Jane's Freight Containers.—49 Poland St., W.1. £15·95.

Jane's Major Companies of Europe.—49 Poland St., W.1. £25·00.

Jane's Surface Skimmer Systems.—49 Poland St., W.1. (Sept.) £10·95.

Jane's Weapon Systems.—49 Poland St., W.1. £16·50.

Jane's World Railways.—49 Poland St., W.1. (Nov.) £15·95.

Jewish Year Book.—33–37 Moreland St., E.C.1. (Jan.) £2·15.

Journal of Commerce Annual Review.—213 Tower Bldg., 22 Water St., Liverpool. 75p.

Kelly's Handbook to the Titled, Landed and Official Classes.—Neville House, Eden St., Kingston-upon-Thames, Surrey. £8·50.

Kelly's Post Office London Directory.—Neville House, Eden St., Kingston-upon-Thames, Surrey. (Jan.) £8·65.

Kempe's Engineers Year Book.—30 Calderwood St., S.E.18. £11·00.

Kemp's Directory.—1–5 Bath St., E.C.1. (Sept.) £12·00.

Kemp's International Film & T.V. Directory.—1–5 Bath St., E.C.1. (May.) £6·50.

Kime's International Law Directory.—170 Sloane St., S.W.1. (June.) £3·50.

Law List.—11 New Fetter Lane, E.C.4. (May.) £6·00.

Law List: Commonwealth and International.—88 Kingsway, W.C.2. (Jan.) £5·25.

Laxton's Building Price Book.—Neville House, Eden St., Kingston-upon-Thames, Surrey. £3·30.

Library Association Yearbook.—7 Ridgmount St., Store St., W.C.1. (May.) £6·00.

Lloyd's Calendar.—Lime St., E.C.3. (Oct.). £2·00.

Local Government Manual & Directory.—Shaway House, Lower Sydenham, S.E.26. (Nov.) £8·25.

London Chamber of Commerce and Industry Directory.—2 Queensway, Redhill, Surrey. (Nov.) £5·00.

Manufacturers & Merchants Directory.—Neville House, Eden St., Kingston-upon-Thames, Surrey. £9·85.

Markets (Retail) Yearbook.—Union St., Oldham. 90p.

Master Printers Annual.—11 Bedford Row, W.C.1. (Jan.) £5·35.

"Mechanical World" Electrical Year Book.—13–35 Bridge St., Hemel Hempstead, Herts. £2·50.

"Mechanical World" Year Book.—13–35 Bridge St., Hemel Hempstead, Herts. £2·75.

Medical Annual.—42–44 Triangle West, Bristol. (Sept.) £7·00.

Medical Directory.—23 Ravelston Terr., Edinburgh. (Apr.) £15·00.

Medical Register.—44 Hallam St., W.1. (Mar.) £10·00.

Metal Bulletin Handbook.—46 Wigmore St., W.1. £7·00.

Middle East & North Africa.—18 Bedford Sq., W.C.1. (Oct.) £12·00.

Mining Annual Review.—15 Wilson St., Moorgate, E.C.2. (May.) £5·00.

Mining International Yearbook.—10 Cannon St., E.C.4. (June.) £8·00.

Modern Publicity.—35 Red Lion Sq., W.C.1. (Sept.) £10·00.

Motor Industry of Great Britain.—Forbes House, Halkin St., S.W.1. (Oct.) £11·50.

Municipal Yearbook & Public Services Directory, 178 Gt. Portland St., W.1. (Dec.) £12·50.

Music Trades Directory.—157 Hagden Lane, Watford. £4·50.

Music Yearbook.—Little Essex St., W.C.2. (June.) £6·50.

Nautical Almanac.—H.M.S.O., Atlantic House, Holborn Viaduct, E.C.1. (Oct.) £1·60.

Newspaper Press Directory.—Sovereign Way, Tonbridge, Kent. (Feb.) £15·00.

Oil & Gas International Yearbook.—10 Cannon St., E.C.4. (Dec.) £9·00.

Old Moore's Almanac.—Yeovil Rd., Slough, Bucks. (July.) 7p.

Owen's Commerce and Travel and International Register.—886 High Rd., N.12. (Mar.) £7·00.

Packaging Directory.—9 Chiswick High Rd., W.4. 2v. ea. £4·00.

Paper Trade Directory of the World, Phillips'.— Sovereign Way, Tonbridge, Kent. (Jan.) £16·00.

Paperbacks in Print.—13 Bedford Sq., W.C.1. £6·50.

Pears Cyclopedia.—52 Bedford Square, W.C.1. £3·50.

Penrose Annual.—10–16 Elm St., W.C.1. (Apr.) £7·95.

Personnel & Training Management Year Book.— 116A Pentonville Rd., N.1. £6·95.

Photography Year Book.—Station Rd., King's Langley, Herts. £5·50.

Plastics Materials Guide.—33–39 Bowling Green Lane, E.C.1. (Jan.) £3·00.

Polymers, Paint, Colour Year Book.—2 Queensway, Redhill, Surrey. £3·25.

Ports of the World.—Sovereign Way, Tonbridge, Kent. £16·00.

Printing Trades Directory.—Sovereign Way, Tonbridge, Kent. £10·00.

Public and Preparatory Schools Year Book.—4–6 Soho Square, W.1. (Apr.) £3·10.

Publishers in the United Kingdom and their Addresses.—13 Bedford Square, W.C.1. (Feb.) 70p.

Publishing, Directory of.—35 Red Lion Square, W.C.1. (Oct.) £3·50.

R.A.C. Guide & Handbook.—85 Pall Mall, S.W.1. (Apr.) £2·00.

Raceform Up-to-date Form Book: Flat Racing. —Thomson Ho., Withy Grove, Manchester. (Dec.) £2·00.

Raceform Up-to-date Form Book: National Hunt. —Thomson Ho., Withy Grove, Manchester. (Aug.) £2·00.

Radio & Television Year Book.—Paris Gdn., Stamford St., S.E.1. £1·00.

Railway Directory & Year Book.—Dorset Ho., Stamford St., S.E.1. (Dec.) £5·00.

Reed's Nautical Almanac.—36–37 Cock Lane, E.C.1. (Oct.) £3·60.

Register of Defunct & Other Companies.—R.A.C. House, Lansdowne Rd., Croydon. £5·00.

RIBA Directory of Practices.—Royal Institute of British Architects, 66 Portland Place, W.1. (Oct.) £5·00.

Royal Society Year Book.—6 Carlton Ho. Terr., S.W.1. (Feb.) £3·20.

Ruff's Guide to the Turf.—9 New Fetter Lane, E.C.4. (Dec.) £6·00.

Salvation Army Year Book.—117–121 Judd St., W.C.1. (Nov.) £1·50.

Scottish Current Law Year Book.—St. Giles St., Edinburgh. £15·00.

Scottish Law Directory.—34–36 North Frederick St., Glasgow. £5·00.

Screen World.—Victoria Works, Edgware Rd., N.W.2. £5·50.

Sell's British Aviation.—39 East St., Epsom, Surrey. £4·50.

Sell's British Exporters Register & National Directory.—39 East St., Epsom, Surrey. £6·00.

Sell's Building Index.—39 East St., Epsom, Surrey· £6·50.

Sell's Directory of Products and Services.—39 East St., Epsom, Surrey. (July.) £8·80.

Sheet Metal Industries Year Book.—2 Queensway, Redhill, Surrey. £4·00.

Shipowners, Shipbuilders & Marine Engineers. Directory of.—Paris Gdn., Stamford St., S.E.1. (Apr.) £8·50.

Soap, Perfumery & Cosmetics Yearbook & Buyers Guide.—42–43 Gerrard St., W.1. £4·00.

Sociological Yearbook of Religion in Britain.— 56–58 Bloomsbury St., W.C.1. (May.) £2·80.

Specification.—9–13 Queen Anne's Gate, S.W.1. (May.) £8·50.

Spon's Architects' & Builders' Price Book.— 11 New Fetter La., E.C.4. (Oct.) £4·50.

Spon's Mechanical & Electrical Services Prices Book.—11 New Fetter La., E.C.4. £6·00.

Statesman's Yearbook.—Little Essex St., W.C.2. (Aug.) £5·95.

Stock Exchange Official Year Book.—R.A.C. Ho., Lansdowne Rd., Croydon. £20·50.

Stone's Justices' Manual.—88 Kingsway, W.C.2. 2v. (May.) £25·00.

Stores, Shops, Supermarkets Retail Directory.—48 Poland St., W.1. £15·00.

Tanker Register.—52 Bishopsgate, E.C.2. (May.) £15·00.

Theatre.—3 Fitzroy Sq., W.1. (Oct.) £4·50.

Trader Handbook.—Paris Gdn., Stamford St., S.E.1. £3·50.

Trades Register of London.—1–5 Bath St. E.C.1. (Jan.) £4·50.

Travel Trade Directory.—30 Calderwood St., S.E.18. (July.) £4·50.

U.K. Kompass Register of British Industry & Commerce.—R.A.C. House, Lansdowne Rd., Croydon. £20·75.

Unit Trust Year Book.—3 St., Andrew Hill, E.C.4. (Mar.) £2·75.

United Reformed Church Year Book.—86 Tavistock Pl., W.C.1. (Sept.) £2·70.

Veterinary Annual.—42–44 Triangle West, Bristol. (Dec.) £8·00.

Water Engineer's Handbook.—2 Queensway, Redhill, Surrey. (Oct.) £3·75.

Which Company?—116A Pentonville Rd., N.1. (Mar.) £1·00; £3·00

Which University?—54 Regent St., W.1. £12·00.

Whitaker's Almanack.—13 Bedford Sq., W.C.1. (Dec.) £1·60, £3·50, £4·75.

Who Owns Whom?—24 Tufton St., S.W.1. £21·00.

Who's Who.—4 Soho Sq., W.1. (May.) £15·00.

Who's Who, International.—18 Bedford Sq., W.C.1. (Sept.) £16·00.

Willing's Press Guide.—R.A.C. House, Lansdowne Rd., Croydon. (Apr.) £6·00.

Wine & Spirit Trade Directory.—19 Eastcheap, E.C.3. (May.) £3·00.

Wisden Cricketers' Almanack.—13 Bedford Square, W.C.1. (Apr.) £2·75, £3·00.

World of Learning.—18 Bedford Square, W.C.1. (Jan.) £18·50.

Writers' & Artists' Year Book.—4 Soho Square, W.1. (Mar.) £1·50.

Year Book of World Affairs.—11 New Fetter Lane, E.C.4. £6·60.

Principal Daily Newspapers

LONDON

The Times (*Ind.*) Gray's Inn Road, W.C.1.
Daily Express (*Ind.*) Fleet St., E.C.4.
Daily Mail (*Ind.*) Northcliffe House, E.C.4.
Daily Mirror (*Ind.*) Holborn Circus, E.C.1.
Daily Telegraph and Morning Post (*Cons.*) 135 Fleet St., E.C.4.
Financial Times (*Ind.*) 10 Cannon St., E.C.4.
The Guardian (*Ind.*) 192 Gray's Inn Rd., W.C.1.
Lloyd's List, Lloyd's, E.C.3.
Morning Advertiser (*Ind.*) 57 Effra Rd., S.W.2.
Morning Star (*Communist*) 75 Farringdon Rd., E.C.1.
Sporting Life, 9 New Fetter Lane, E.C.4.
The Sun, 30 Bouverie St., E.C.4.
Evening News (*Ind.*) Carmelite House, E.C.4.
Evening Standard (*Ind*) 47 Shoe Lane, E.C.4.

ABERDEEN........Press and Journal (*Ind.*)
　　　　　　　　Evening Express (*Ind.*)
BARROW.........North-Western Evening Mail (*Ind.*)
BATH...........Bath and West Evening Chronicle (*Cons.*)
BELFAST.........News Letter (*Un.*)
　　　　　　　　Belfast Telegraph (*Ind.*)
　　　　　　　　Irish News (*Nat.*)
BIRMINGHAM.....Birmingham Post (*Ind.*)
　　　　　　　　Evening Mail (*Ind.*)
BLACKBURN.....Lancs. Evening Telegraph (*Ind.*)
BLACKPOOL......W. Lancs. Ev. Gazette (*Ind.*)
BOLTON........Evening News (*Ind.*)
BOURNEMOUTH..Evening Echo, Bournemouth (*Ind.*)
BRADFORD.......Telegraph and Argus (*Ind.*)
BRIGHTON......Evening Argus (*Ind.*)
BRISTOL.........Evening Post
　　　　　　　　Western Daily Press (*Ind.*)
BURNLEY........Evening Star (*Ind.*)
BURTON........Burton Daily Mail (*Un.*)
CAMBRIDGE......Cambridge Evening News (*Ind.*)
CARDIFF.........South Wales Echo (*Ind.*)
　　　　　　　　Western Mail (*Ind.*)
CARLISLE.........Cumberland Evening News (*Ind.*)
CHELTENHAM.....Gloucestershire Echo (*Ind.*)
CLEVELAND.....Evening Gazette (*Ind.*)
COLCHESTER.....Evening Gazette (*Ind.*)
COVENTRY.......Coventry Evening Telegraph (*Ind.*)
DARLINGTON.....Northern Echo (*Ind.*)
　　　　　　　　Evening Despatch (*Ind.*)
DERBY...........Derby Evening Telegraph (*Ind.*)
DONCASTER......Doncaster Evening Post (*Ind.*)
DUNDEE.........Courier and Advertiser (*Ind.*)
　　　　　　　　Evening Telegraph and Post (*Ind.*)
EDINBURGH.......Scotsman (*Ind.*)
　　　　　　　　Evening News (*Ind.*)
EXETER..........Express and Echo (*Ind.*)
GLASGOW........Glasgow Herald (*Ind.*)
　　　　　　　　Daily Record (*Ind.*)
　　　　　　　　Evening Times (*Ind.*)
GLOUCESTER......Citizen (*Ind.*)
GREENOCK.......Greenock Telegraph (*Lib.*)
GRIMSBY........Evening Telegraph (*Ind.*)
GUERNSEY........Guernsey Evening Press and Star (*Ind.*)
HALIFAX.........Halifax Evening Courier (*Ind.*)
HUDDERSFIELD....Huddersfield Daily Examiner (*Lib.*)

HULL............Daily Mail (*Ind.*)
IPSWICH.........East Anglian Daily Times (*Ind.*)
　　　　　　　　Evening Star (*Ind.*)
JERSEY............Evening Post (*Ind.*)
KETTERING.......Northants Evening Telegraph (*Ind.*)
LEAMINGTON SPA..Leamington Spa Morning News (*Ind.*)
LEEDS...........Yorkshire Post (*Cons.*)
　　　　　　　　Evening Post (*Cons.*)
LEICESTER........Leicester Mercury (*Ind.*)
LINCOLN.........Lincolnshire Echo (*Ind.*)
LIVERPOOL.......Liverpool Daily Post (*Ind.*)
　　　　　　　　Liverpool Echo (*Ind.*)
　　　　　　　　Journal of Commerce (*Ind.*)
LUTON..........Evening Post (*Ind.*)
MANCHESTER.....Manchester Evening News (*Ind.*)
　　　　　　　　Sporting Chronicle
NEWCASTLE......Evening Chronicle (*Ind.*)
　　　　　　　　Journal
NEWPORT........South Wales Argus (*Ind.*)
NORTHAMPTON...Chronicle and Echo (Northampton) (*Ind.*)
NORWICH.......Eastern Daily Press (*Ind.*)
　　　　　　　　Eastern Evening News (*Ind.*)
NOTTINGHAM.....Evening Post (*Ind.*)
NUNEATON......Nuneaton Evening Tribune (*Ind.*)
OLDHAM........Oldham Evening Chronicle (*Lib.*)
OXFORD.........Oxford Mail (*Ind.*)
PAISLEY.........Paisley Daily Express (*Ind.*)
PETERBOROUGH...Peterborough Evening Telegraph (*Ind.*)
PLYMOUTH.......Western Morning News (*Ind.*)
　　　　　　　　Western Evening Herald (*Ind.*)
PORTSMOUTH.....The News (*Ind.*)
PRESTON.........Lancashire Evening Post (*Ind.*)
READING........Evening Post (*Ind.*)
SCARBOROUGH....Scarborough Evening News (*Ind.*)
SHEFFIELD........Morning Telegraph (*Ind.*)
　　　　　　　　Star (*Ind.*)
SOUTH SHIELDS...Shields Gazette and Shipping Telegraph (*Ind.*)
SOUTHAMPTON....Southern Evening Echo (*Ind.*)
STOKE...........Evening Sentinel (*Ind.*)
SUNDERLAND.....Echo (*Ind.*)
SWANSEA........South Wales Evening Post (*Ind.*)
SWINDON........Evening Advertiser (*Ind.*)
TORQUAY........Herald Express (*Ind.*)
WATFORD........Evening Echo (*Ind.*)
WEYMOUTH......Dorset Evening Echo (*Ind.*)
WOLVERHAMPTON.Express and Star (*Ind.*)
WORCESTER......Evening News (*Ind.*)
YORK ....Yorkshire Evening Press (*Ind.*)

SUNDAY NEWSPAPERS

News of the World (*Ind.*)—30 Bouverie St., E.C.4.
Observer (*Ind.*)—160 Queen Victoria St., E.C.4.
Sunday Express (*Ind.*)—Fleet St., E.C.4.
Sunday Mail (*Ind.*)—Anderston Quay, Glasgow.
Sunday Mercury (*Ind.*)—Colmore Circus, Birmingham.
Sunday Mirror (*Ind.*)—Holborn Circus, E.C.1.
Sunday News (*Ind.*)—51–59 Donegall St., Belfast.
Sunday People (*Ind.*)—9 New Fetter Lane, E.C.4.
Sunday Post (*Ind.*)—144 Port Dundas Road, Glasgow.

Sunday Sun (*Ind.*)—Groat Market, Newcastle-on-Tyne.
Sunday Telegraph (*Cons.*)—135 Fleet St., E.C.4.
Sunday Times (*Ind.*)—200 Gray's Inn Rd., W.C.1.

RELIGIOUS PAPERS

[*W.* = Weekly; *M.* = Monthly; *Q.* = Quarterly]

Baptist Times—4 Southampton Row, W.C.1. *W.*
British Weekly and Christian World—69 Fleet St., E.C.4. *W.*
Catholic Herald—63 Charterhouse Street, E.C.1. *W.*
Challenge—Revenue Buildings, Chapel Rd., Worthing, Sussex. *M.*
Christian Herald—4 Western Esplanade, Portslade, Brighton, Sussex. *W.*
Church of England Newspaper—69 Fleet St., E.C.4. *W.*
Church of Ireland Gazette—Windsor Avenue, Lurgan, Co. Armagh. *W.*
Church Times—7 Portugal St., W.C.2. *W.*
Crusade—19 Draycott Pce, S.W.3. *M.*
English Churchman—St. Marks's Church Chmbrs, Kennington Park Rd., S.E.11. *Alt. W.*
Friend—Drayton House, Gordon St., W.C.1. *W.*
Inquirer—1-6 Essex St., W.C.2. *Alt. W.*
Jewish Chronicle—25 Furnival St., E.C.4. *W.*
Jewish Gazette—18 Cheetham Parade, Manchester, 8. *W.*
Jewish Telegraph—Levi House, Bury Old Road, Manchester, 8. *W.*
Life and Work—121 George St., Edinburgh 2. *M.*
Methodist Recorder—176 Fleet St., E.C.4. *W.*
Sunday—Udimore Vicarage, Rye, Sussex. *M.*
Tablet—48 Great Peter St., S.W.1. *W.*
Universe—Universe House, 21 Fleet St., E.C.4. *W.*
War Cry—101 Queen Victoria St., E.C.4. *W.*

PERIODICALS, MAGAZINES AND REVIEWS

[*W.* = Weekly; *M.* = Monthly; *Q.* = Quarterly]

Amateur Gardening—189 High Holborn, W.C.1. *W.*
Amateur Photographer—161 Fleet St., E.C.4. *W.*
Angler's Mail—Fleetway House, Farringdon St., E.C.4. *W.*
Angling—135 Wardour St., W.1. *M.*
Angling Times—Oundle Rd., Woodston, Peterborough. *W.*
Antiquaries' Journal—Oxford U. Press, Press Rd., N.W.10. *Twice a year.*
Antique Collector—49 Great Marlborough St., W1. *M.*
Apollo—10 Cannon St., London, E.C.4. *M.*
Art and Antiques Weekly—40 Craven St., W.C.2.
Art and Artists—75 Victoria St., S.W.1. *M.*
Asia and Africa Review—38 Kennington Lane, S.E.11. *M.*
Autocar—Dorset House, Stamford St., S.E.1. *W.*
Birds and Country Magazine—79 Surbiton Hill Park, Surbiton, Surrey. *Q.*
Blackwood's Mag.—32 Thistle St., Edinburgh. *M.*
Books & Bookmen—75 Victoria St., S.W.1. *M.*
Boxing News—135 Wardour St., W.1. *W.*
Brain—Macmillan (Journals) Ltd., 4 Little Essex St., W.C.2. *Q.*
Brides and Setting-up Home—Vogue House, Hanover Sq., W.1. *Alt. M.*
British Birds—10 Merton Rd., Bedford. *M.*
British Book News—The British Council, 59 New Oxford St., W.C.1. *M.*
Bunty—186 Fleet St., E.C.4. *W.*

Burlington Mag.—10-16 Elm St., W.C.1.
Buses—Terminal House, Shepperton. *M.*
Cage and Aviary Birds—161 Fleet St., E.C.4. *W.*
Caravan—Link House, Dingwall Ave., Croydon, Surrey. *M.*
City Press—4 Moorfields, E.C.2. *W.*
Classical Quarterly—The Clarendon Press, Oxford. *Twice a Year.*
Classical Review—The Clarendon Press, Oxford. *Twice a Year.*
Coal News—Hobart House, Grosvenor Place, S.W.1. *M.*
Coin Monthly—Sovereign House, High St., Brentwood, Essex.
Coins—Link House, Dingwall Ave., Croydon, Surrey. *M.*
Connoisseur—Chestergate House, Vauxhall Bridge Road, S.W.1. *M.*
Contemporary Review—37 Union St., S.E.1. *M.*
Cornhill Mag.—50 Albermarle St., W.1. *Q.*
Country Life—2-10 Tavistock St., W.C.2. *W.*
Countryman—23/27 Tudor St., E.C.4. *Q.*
Cricketer—Beech Hanger, Ashurst, Kent. *M.*
Criminologist—9 Old Bailey, E.C.4. *Q.*
Cycling—161 Fleet Street, E.C.4. *W.*
Dalton's Weekly—Windsor Ave., Merton, S.W.19. *W.*
Dance and Dancers—75 Victoria St., S.W.1. *M.*
Dancing Times—18 Hand Court, W.C.1. *M.*
Disc—161-166 Fleet St., E.C.4. *W.*
Dog World—32 New St., Ashford, Kent. *W.*
Do It Yourself—Link House, Dingwall Ave, Croydon. *M.*
Drama—9 Fitzroy Sq., W.1. *Q.*
Drive—Berkeley Sq. House, Berkeley Sq., W.1. *Q.*
Economic Journal—4 Little Essex St., W.C.2. *Q.*
Economica—Lond. Sch. of Economics, Houghton St., Aldwych, W.C.2. *Q.*
Economist, The (*Ind.*)—25 St. James's St., S.W.1. *W.*
Edinburgh Gazette (*Official*)—Exchequer Offices, 102 George St., Edinburgh 2. *Twice a week.*
Encounter—59 St. Martin's Lane, W.C.2. *M.*
English Historical Review—5 Bentinck St., W.1. *Q.*
Exchange and Mart—Pembroke House, Wellesley Rd., Croydon, Surrey. *W.*
Family Circle—Elm House, Elm St., W.C.1. *M.*
Field, The—8 Stratton St., W.1. *W.*
Films and Filming—75 Victoria St., S.W.1. *M.*
Freethinker, The—698 Holloway Rd., N.19. *M.*
Fur and Feather—Idle, Bradford. *Alt. W.*
Gardeners' Chronicle—5 Winsley St., W.1. *W.*
Garden News—Park House, 117 Park Rd., Peterborough. *W.*
Geographical Journal—Kensington Gore, S.W.7. *Three times a year.*
Geographical Magazine—128 Long Acre, W.C.2. *M.*
Golf Illustrated—8 Stratton St., W.1. *W.*
Golf Monthly—113 St. Vincent St., Glasgow. *M.*
Good Health—Stanborough Press, Ltd., Alma Park, Grantham. *Alt. M.*
Good Housekeeping—Chestergate House, Vauxhall Bridge Road, S.W.1. *M.*
Good Motoring—2 Elis St., S.W.1. *M.*
Gramophone—179 Kenton Road, Kenton, Mx. *M.*
Greece and Rome—The Clarendon Press, Oxford. *Twice a year.*
Guider—17-19 Buckingham Palace Rd., S.W.1. *M.*
Harper's Queen—Chestergate House, Vauxhall Bridge Rd., S.W.1. *M.*
Health & Strength—20-30 Holborn, E.C.1. *M.*

Health Education Journal—78 New Oxford St., W.C.1

Hers—30-32 Southampton St., W.C.2. *M.*

History—59A Kennington Park Road, S.E.11. *Three times a year.*

History Today—388-389 Strand, W.C.2. *M.*

Homefinder—10 East Road, N.1. *M.*

Homemaker—189 High Holborn, W.C.1. *M.*

Homes and Gardens—Tower House, Southampton St., W.C.2. *M.*

Homoeopathy—27A Devonshire St., W.1. *M.*

Honey—Tower House, Southampton St., W.C.2. *M.*

Horse and Hound—189 High Holborn, W.C.1. *W.*

House and Garden—Vogue House, Hanover Sq., W.1. *Ten times a year.*

Ideal Home—189 High Holborn, W.C.1. *M.*

Illustrated London News (*Ind.*)—Elm House, Elm Street, W.C.1. *M.*

In Britain—B.T.A., 4 Bromells Rd., S.W.4. *M.*

International Affairs—Chatham House, St. James's Square, S.W.1. *Q.*

Jazz Journal—27 Willow Vale, W.12. *M.*

Kennel Gazette—1-4 Clarges St., Piccadilly, W.1. *M.*

Labour Monthly—134 Ballards Lane, N.3.

Lady—39-40 Bedford St., W.C.2. *W.*

Land and Liberty—177 Vauxhall Bridge Rd., S.W.1. *Alt. M.*

Lawn Tennis—Lowlands, Wenhaston, Suffolk. *M.*

Liberal News—7 Exchange Ct., Strand, W.C.1. *W.*

Light (*Psychic*)—16 Queensbury Place, S.W.7. *Q.*

Light Horse—19 Charing Cross Rd., W.C.2. *M.*

Listener, The—35 Marylebone High St., W.1. *W.*

Living—Elm House, Elm St., W.C.1. *M.*

Local Government Chronicle (*Ind.*)—11-12 Bury St., St. Mary Ave., E.C.3. *W.*

London Gazette (*Official*)—First Avenue House, Warwick Court, High Holborn, W.C.1. *Four times a week.*

London Magazine—30 Thurloe Place, S.W.7. *Six times a year.*

London Weekly Advertiser—5 Winsley St., W.1.

London Weekly Diary of Social Events—39 Hertford St., W.1.

Look and Learn—Fleetway House, Farringdon St., E.C.4. *W.*

Look and Listen—75 Victoria St., S.W.1. *M.*

Man—36 Craven St., W.C.2. *Q.*

Mayfair—95A Chancery Lane, W.C.2. *M.*

Meccano Magazine—Binns Rd., Liverpool 13. *Q.*

Melody Maker—166 Fleet Street, E.C.4. *W.*

Meteorological Magazine—Atlantic House, Holborn Viaduct, E.C.1. *M.*

Mind—108 Cowley Rd., Oxford. *Q.*

Mirabelle—30-32 Southampton St., W.C.2. *W.*

Model Boats—13-15 Bridge St., Hemel Hempstead, Herts. *M.*

Model Railway Constructor—Terminal House, Shepperton. *M.*

Model Railways—13-15 Bridge St., Hemel Hempstead, Herts. *M.*

Modern Caravan—Link House, Dingwall Avenue, Croydon. *M.*

Modern Languages—35 Lewisham Way, S.E.14.

Month—114 Mount St., W.1. *M.*

Monthly Digest of Statistics (*Official*)—Atlantic House, Holborn Viaduct, E.C.1.

Mother—189 High Holborn, W.C.1. *M.*

Motor Cycle News—Dryland St., Kettering. *W.*

Movie Maker—13-15 Bridge Street, Hemel Hempstead, Herts. *M.*

Municipal & Public Services Journal—178-202 Gt. Portland St., W.1. *W.*

Municipal Engineering and Environmental Technology—178-202 Gt. Portland St., W.1. *W.*

Municipal Review—36-38 Old Queen St., Westminster, S.W.1. *M.*

Museums Journal—87 Charlotte St., W.1. *Q.*

Music and Letters—32 Holywell, Oxford. *Q.*

Music and Musicians—75 Victoria St., S.W.1. *M.*

My Weekly—186 Fleet St., E.C.4.

Nature—4 Little Essex St., W.C.2. *W.*

Nautical Magazines—52 Darnley Street, Glasgow, *M.*

Navy International—River Hall Farm, Biddenden, Kent. *M.*

Needlewoman—Bromley Cross, Bolton, Lancs. *Q.*

New Middle East—68 Fleet St., E.C.4. *M.*

New Musical Express—128 Long Acre, W.C.2. *W.*

New Scientist—128 Long Acre, W.C.2. *W.*

New Society—128 Long Acre, W.C.2. *W.*

New Statesman (*Ind.*)—10 Great Turnstile, High Holborn, W.C.1. *W.*

19—Tower House, Southampton St., W.C.2. *M.*

Notes and Queries—Oxford U. Press, Press Rd., N.W.10. *M.*

Nova—Tower House, Southampton St., W.C.2. *M.*

Nursery World—Clifford's Inn, Fetter Lane, E.C.4. *W.*

Opera—6 Woodland Rise, N.10. *M.*

Our Dogs—Oxford Road, Station Approach, Manchester. *W.*

Oxford—8 Wellington Square, Oxford. *Twice a year.*

Parade—135 Wardour Street, W.1. *M.*

Parliamentary Debates (Lords) (Hansard)—Atlantic House, Holborn Viaduct, E.C.1. *Daily during Session.*

Parliamentary Debates (Commons) (Hansard)—Atlantic House, Holborn Viaduct, E.C.1. *Daily during Session.*

Penthouse—2 Bramber Rd., W.14. *M.*

People's Friend—7 Bank Street, Dundee. *W.*

Philosophy—4 Little Essex St., W.C.2. *Q.*

Photography—13-15 Bridge St., Hemel Hempstead, Herts. *M.*

Photoplay Film Monthly—12-18 Paul St., E.C.2. *M.*

Pins and Needles—Elm House, Elm Street, W.C.1. *M.*

Playhour—Fleetway House, Farringdon St., E.C.4. *W.*

Plays and Players—75 Victoria St., S.W.1. *M.*

Poetry Review—21 Earls Court Square, S.W.5. *Three times a year.*

Political Quarterly, The—Elm House, Elm Street, W.C.1.

Pony—19 Charing Cross Rd., W.C.2. *M.*

Popular Gardening—189 High Holborn, W.C.1. *W.*

Poultry World—16 Fleet St., E.C.4. *W.*

Practical Boat Owner—54 Stamford Street, S.E.1.

Practical Camper—5 Winsley St., W.1. *M.*

Practical Caravan—5 Winsley St., W.1. *M.*

Practical Gardening—Mercury House, Waterloo Rd., S.E.1. *M.*

Practical Householder—Fleetway House, Farringdon St., E.C.4. *M.*

Progress (Braille Type)—224-8 Great Portland St., W.1. *M.*

Punch (*Ind.*)—23-27 Tudor St., E.C.4. *W.*

Racing Calendar—42 Portman Sq., W.1. *W.*

Radio Control Models and Electronics—13-15 Bridge St., Hemel Hempstead, Herts. *M.*

Radio Times—35 Marleybone High St., W.1. *W.*

Railway Magazine—Dorset House, Stamford St., S.E.1. *M.*

Railway World—Terminal House, Shepperton. *M.*

Readers Digest—25 Berkeley Sq., W.1. *M.*

Record and Recording—75 Victoria St., S.W.1. *M.*

Red Star Weekly—185 Fleet St., E.C.4.

Riding—Tower House, Southampton St., W.C.2. *M.*

Round Table—18 Northumberland Ave., W.C.2. *Q.*

Scotland's Magazine—114-116 George St., Edinburgh. *M.*

Scots Independent—9 Upper Bridge St., Stirling. *M.*

Scottish Field—57-59 Buchanan St., Glasgow. *M.*

Scouting—Baden Powell House, Queen's Gate, S.W.7. *M.*

Seafarer—207 Balham High Rd., S.W.17. *Q.*

She—Chestergate House, Vauxhall Bridge Road, S.W.1. *M.*

Shoot!—Fleetway House, Farringdon St., E.C.4. *W.*

Shooting Times and Country Magazine—Clivemont Rd., Maidenhead. *W.*

Socialist Leader—197 King's Cross Rd., W.C.1. *Alt. W.*

Sociological Review—University of Keele, Staffs. *Q.*

Spectator (*Ind.*)—99 Gower Street, W.C.1. *W.*

Sporting Chronicle Handicap Book—Thomson House, Manchester 6. *M.*

Stitchcraft—Belmont Rd., W.4. *M.*

Strad—1 Upper James St., W.1. *M.*

Studio International—14 West Central St., W.C.1. *M.*

Tatler and Bystander—15 Berkeley St., W.1. *M.*

Tennis World—Lancaster Rd., Hinckley, Leics. *Ten times a year.*

Theatre Quarterly—39 Goodge St., W.C.1.

Time (British Isles)—Time and Life Bldg., New Bond St., W.1. *W.*

Time & Tide (*Ind.*)—13 New Bridge St., E.C.4. *M.*

Times Educational Suppl't.—Gray's Inn Rd., W.C.1. *W.*

Times Higher Education Suppl't.—Gray's Inn Rd., W.C.1. *W.*

Times Literary Suppl't.—Gray's Inn Rd., W.C.1. *W.*

Tribune—24 St. John St., E.C.1. *W.*

Trout and Salmon—21 Church Walk, Peterborough. *M.*

True Magazine—Tower House, Southampton St., W.C.2. *M.*

True Romances and True Story Magazine—12-18 Paul St., E.C.2. *M.*

TV Times—247 Tottenham Court Rd., W.1. *W.*

Universities Quarterly—10 Gt. Turnstile, W.C.1.

Vacher's Parliamentary Companion—15 Cochrane Mews, N.W.8. *Q.*

Vogue—Vogue House, Hanover Square, W.1. *Sixteen times a year.*

Weather—Cromwell House, Bracknell, Berks. *M.*

Weekend—Carmelite House, E.C.4. *W.*

Welsh Nation—8 Heol Frenhines, Caerdydd, Cardiff. *W.*

West Africa (*Ind.*).—Cromwell House, Fulwood Pl., W.C.1. *W.*

Woman—189 High Holborn, W.C.1. *W.*

Woman and Home—40 Long Acre, W.C.2. *M.*

Woman's Journal—Tower House, Southampton St., W.C.2. *M.*

Woman's Own—Tower House, Southampton St., W.C.2. *W.*

Woman's Realm—189 High Holborn, W.C.1. *W.*

Woman's Weekly—40 Long Acre, W.C.2.

World Today—Chatham House, St. James's Sq., S.W.1. *M.*

Yachting Monthly—Hatfield House, Stamford St., S.E.1.

Yachting World—Dorset House, Stamford St., S.E.1. *M.*

Yachts and Yachting—196 Eastern Esplanade, Southend-on-Sea. *Alt. W.*

TRADE, PROFESSIONAL AND BUSINESS JOURNALS

[*W.*=Weekly; *M.*=Monthly; *Q.*=Quarterly]

Accountancy—56 Goswell Rd., E.C.1. *M.*

Accountant—151 Strand, W.C.2. *W.*

Accountants' Magazine—27 Queen St., Edinburgh. *M.*

Achievement—13 New Bridge St., E.C.4. *M.*

Advertising Quarterly—Abford House, Wilton Rd., S.W.1.

Adweek (Advertiser's Weekly)—110 Fleet St., E.C.4.

Agricultural Machinery Journal—161 Fleet St., E.C.4. *M.*

Anti-Corrosion—127 Stanstead Rd., S.E.23. *M.*

Antique Dealer and Collector's Guide—1 Wine Office Court, Fleet St., E.C.4. *M.*

Architects' Journal—9-13 Queen Anne's Gate, S.W.1. *W.*

Architectural Review—9-13 Queen Anne's Gate, S.W.1. *M.*

Artist—33 Warwick Sq., S.W.1. *M.*

Bakers' Review—886 High Rd., Finchley, N.12. *M.*

Banker—10 Cannon St., E.C.4. *M.*

Bankers' Magazine—49 Great Marlborough St., W.1. *M.*

Bookseller—13 Bedford Square, W.C.1. *W.*

Brewer's Guardian—93-99 Goswell Rd., E.C.1. *M.*

Brewing Review—42 Portman Square, W.1. *M.*

British Baker—69-77 High St., Croydon. *W.*

British Clothing Manufacturer—20 Soho Sq., W.1. *M.*

British Dental Journal—64 Wimpole St., W.1. *Twice a month.*

British Food Journal—Peterson House, Livery St., Birmingham, 3. *Alt. M.*

British Jeweller and Watch Buyer—27 Frederick St., Birmingham. *M.*

British Journal for Philosophy of Science—Farmers Hall, Aberdeen. *Q.*

British Journal of Photography—24 Wellington Street, W.C.2. *W.*

British Knitting Industry—1 Ford Lane, Salford, Manchester. *M.*

British Medical Journal—Tavistock Square, W.C.1. *W.*

British Printer—30 Old Burlington St., W.1. *M.*

British Steelmaker—886 High Rd., Finchley, N.12. *M.*

British Sugar Beet Review—134 Piccadilly, W.1. *Q.*

British Tax Review—11 New Fetter Lane, E.C.4. *Alt. M.*

British Veterinary Journal—7-8 Henrietta St., W.C.2. *Bi-monthly.*

Brushes—157 Hagden Lane, Watford. *M.*

Builders' Merchants Journal—Sovereign Way, Tonbridge, Kent. *M.*

Building—4 Catherine St., W.C.2. *W.*

Cabinet Maker and Retail Furnisher—25 New Street Square, E.C.4. *W.*

Cage and Aviary Birds—161 Fleet St., E.C.4. *W.*

Campaign—5 Winsley St., W.1. *W.*

Canoe-Camper—Bulls Green, Knebworth, Herts. *Q.*

Carpet and Floor Covering World—25 New Street Square, E.C.4. *W.*

Carpet Review—5 Winsley St., W.1. *M.*

Caterer and Hotel Keeper—40 Bowling Green Lane, E.C.1. *W.*

Catering and Hotel Management—167 High Holborn, W.C.1. *M.*

Catering Times—Northwood House, 93–99 Goswell Rd., E.C.1. *W.*

Chemical Age—Morgan Grampian House, Calderwood St., S.E. 18. *W.*

Chemist and Druggist—25 New Street Square, E.C.4. *W.*

Chemistry and Industry—14 Belgrave Sq., S.W.1. *Twice a month.*

Chemistry in Britain—Burlington House, W.1. *M.*

Child Education—Montague House, Russell Sq., W.C.1. *M.*

Chiropodist—8 Wimpole St., W.1. *M.*

Civil Engineering and Public Works Review—Morgan Grampian House, Calderwood St., S.E.18. *M.*

Club Mirror—18 Queen's Rd., Brighton. *M.*

Colliery Guardian—Queensway House, Redhill, Surrey. *M.*

Commerce International—69 Cannon St., E.C.4. *M.*

Commercial Grower—Sovereign Way, Trowbridge, Kent. *W.*

Commercial Motor—Dorset House, Stamford St., S.E.1. *W.*

Computer Survey—42–43 Gerrard St., W.1. *W.*

Concrete—52 Grosvenor Gdns., S.W.1. *M.*

Contact Journal—32 Southwark Bridge Rd., S.E.1. *W.*

Control and Instrumentation—Morgan Grampian House, Calderwood St., S.E.18. *M.*

Cordage, Canvas and Jute World—157 Hagden Lane, Watford. *M.*

C.S.E. News (Camping and Sports Equipment)—4 Spring St., W.2. *M.*

Dairy Farmer—Fenton House, Ipswich. *M.*

Dairy Industries—42–43 Gerrard St., W.1. *M.*

Design—28 Haymarket, S.W.1. *M.*

Display International—167 High Holborn, W.C.1. *M.*

Dock and Harbour Authority—19 Harcourt St., W.1. *M.*

Drapers' Record—20 Soho Sq., W.1. *W.*

Education—10 Queen Anne St., W.1. *W.*

Education Equipment—125 High St., Colliers Wood, S.W.19. *M.*

Electrical & Electronic Trader—Dorset House Stamford St., S.E.1. *W.*

Electrical and Radio Trading—Dorset House, Stamford St., S.E.1. *W.*

Electrical Review—Dorset House, Stamford St., S.E.1. *W.*

Electrical Times—Dorset House, Stamford St., S.E.1. *W.*

Electronic Engineering—Morgan Grampian House, Calderwood St., S.E.18. *M.*

Electronics Weekly—Dorset House, Stamford St., S.E.1. *W.*

Embroidery—73 Wimpole St., W.1. *Q.*

Engineer—Morgan Grampian House, Calderwood St., S.E.18. *W.*

Engineering—28 Haymarket, S.W.1. *M.*

Engineers' Digest—120 Wigmore St., W.1. *M.*

Estates Gazette—151 Wardour St., W.1. *W.*

Export News, Benn's—Lyon Tower, Colliers Wood, S.W.19. *W.*

Fairplay International Shipping Weekly—1 Pudding Lane, E.C.3. *W.*

Far East Trade & Development—3 Belsize Crescent., N.W.3. *M.*

Farmers' Weekly—161–166 Fleet St., E.C.4. *W.*

Financial World—100 Fleet St., E.C.4. *Alt. W.*

Fire (British Fire Service)—34 Dudley Rd., Tunbridge Wells, Kent. *M.*

Fire Protection Review—125 High St., Colliers Wood, S.W.19. *M.*

Fish Friers' Review—289 Dewsbury Road, Leeds. *M.*

Fish Trade Gazette—17–19 John Adam St., Adelphi, W.C.2. *W.*

Flight International—Dorset House, Stamford St., S.E.1. *W.*

Food Trade Review—7 Garrick St., W.C.2. *M.*

Forestry and Home Grown Timber—25 New Street Square, E.C.4. *Alt. M.*

Foundry Trade Journal—Queensway House, Redhill, Surrey. *W.*

Frozen Foods—17–19 John Adam St., W.C.2. *M.*

Fruit Trades Journal—6–7 Gough Square, E.C.4. *W.*

Fuel—32 High St., Guildford. *Q.*

Funeral Service Journal—King & Hutchings, Cricketfield Rd., Uxbridge, Middx. *M.*

Fur & Leather Review—27 Garlick Hill, E.C.4. *M.*

Furniture and Bedding Production—157 Station Rd. East, Oxted, Surrey. *M.*

Fur Weekly News—87 Lamb's Conduit St., W.C.1.

Games and Toys—30–31 Knightrider St., E.C.4. *M.*

Gas Marketing and Domestic Gas—25 New Street Square, E.C.4. *M.*

Gas World and Gas Journal—25 New Street Square, E.C.4. *W.*

Gifts—Lyon Tower, Colliers Wood, S.W.19. *M.*

Glass—Queensway House, Redhill, Surrey. *M.*

Greek Review—34 Bush Hill Rd., N.21. *Q.*

Grower—49 Doughty St., W.C.1. *W.*

Grocer—19 Eastcheap, E.C.3. *W.*

Hair and Beauty—62 Oxford St., W.1. *M.*

Hairdressers' Journal—40 Bowling Green Lane, E.C.1. *W.*

Handy Shipping Guide—12–16 Laystall St., E.C.1. *W.*

Hardware Trade Journal—Sovereign Way, Tonbridge, Kent. *W.*

Harper's Sports and Camping—Southbank House, Black Prince Rd., S.E.1. *Alt. W.*

Harper's Wine and Spirit Gazette—Southbank House, Black Prince Rd., S.E.1. *W.*

Heating and Ventilating Engineer—11–13 Southampton Row, W.C.1. *M.*

Hospital and Health Services Review—75 Portland Place, W.1. *M.*

Ice Cream & Frozen Confectionery—90 Grays Inn Rd., W.C.1. *M.*

Industrial Daily News—28 Upper St., N.1. *Four times a week.*

Industrial Society—48 Bryanston Square, W.1. *Bi-monthly.*

Insurance Mail—44 Fleet St., E.C.4. *M.*

Insurance Record—75 Carter Lane, E.C.4. *M.*

Investor's Chronicle and Stock Exchange Gazette—30 Finsbury Sq., E.C.2. *W.*

Investors' Review—100 Fleet St., E.C.4. *Alt. W.*

Jeweller—39 High St., Wheathampstead, Herts. *M.*

Journalist—314 Gray's Inn Rd., W.C.1. *M.*

Journal of the Chemical Society—Burlington House, W.1. *In six parts.*

Journal of the Institute of Bankers—10 Lombard St., E.C.3. *Alt. M.*

Junior Age—167 High Holborn, W.C.1. *M.*

Justice of the Peace—Little London, Chichester. *W.*

Knitting and Haberdashery Review—6 Ludgate Square, E.C.4. *Alt. M.*

Lancet—7 Adam Street, W.C.2. *W.*

Law Quarterly Review—11 New Fetter Lane, E.C.4.

Law Reports—3 Stone Buildings, Lincoln's Inn, W.C.2. *M.*

Law Society's Gazette—113 Chancery Lane, W.C.2. *W.*

Leather—125 High St., Colliers Wood, S.W.19. *M.*

Leathergoods—125 High St. Colliers Wood, S.W.19. *M.*

Library Review—98–100 Holm St., Glasgow. *Q.*

Light and Lighting—York House, Westminster Bridge Road, S.E.1. *Alt. M.*

Lithoprinter—5 Winsley St., W.1. *M.*

Lloyd's Loading List—Lloyd's, E.C.3. *W.*

Locomotive Journal—9 Arkwright Rd., N.W.3. *M.*

London Corn Circular—63 Crutched Friars, E.C.3. *W.*

Machinery Market—146A Queen Victoria St., E.C.4. *W.*

Maker-Up and Women's Wear Manufacturer—42 Gerrard St., W.1. *M.*

Management Accounting—63 Portland Place, W.1. *M.*

Management Decision—200 Keighley Rd., Bradford. *Six times a year.*

Management Today—5 Winsley St., W.1. *M.*

Manufacturing Chemist and Aerosol News—Morgan Grampian House, Calderwood St., S.E.18. *M.*

Manufacturing Clothier—42 Gerrard St., W.1. *M.*

Marine and Air Catering—125 High St., Colliers Wood, S.W.19. *M.*

Marketing—5 Winsley St., W.1. *M.*

Master Builder—3 Chalk Hill, Oxhey, Watford, Herts. *M.*

Materials Reclamation Weekly—69–77 High St. Croydon. *W.*

Meat Trades Journal—49 Hatton Garden, E.C.1. *W.*

Mechanical Handling—33–40 Bowling Green Lane, E.C.1. *M.*

Medico-Legal Journal—Coroner's Court, 65 Horseferry Rd., S.W.1. *Q.*

Men's Wear—20 Soho Sq., W1. *W.*

Metal Bulletin—46 Wigmore St., W.1. *Twice a week.*

Metallurgia and Metal Forming—Queensway House, Redhill, Surrey. *M.*

Milk Industry—20 Eastbourne Terrace, W.2. *M.*

Mining Journal—15 Wilson St., Moorgate, E.C.2. *W.*

Mining Magazine—15 Wilson St., Moorgate, E.C.2. *M.*

Model Engineer—13–15 Bridge St., Hemel Hempstead, Herts. *Twice a month.*

Modern Law Review—11 New Fetter Lane, E.C.4. *Alt. M.*

Modern Railways—Terminal House, Shepperton. *M.*

Motor—Dorset House, Stamford St., S.E.1. *W.*

Motor Boat and Yachting—Dorset House, Stamford St., S.E.1. *Twice a month.*

Motor Cycle—161 Fleet St., E.C.4. *W.*

Motor Cycle and Cycle Trader—74 Mildred Ave., Watford. *Alt. W.*

Motor Trader—Dorset House, Stamford Street, S.E.1. *W.*

Motor Transport—Dorset House, Stamford St., S.E.1. *W.*

Musical Times—1–3 Upper James St. W.1. *M.*

National Builder—82 New Cavendish St., W.1. *M.*

National Guardian—113 St. Vincent St., Glasgow, C.2. *W.*

Natural Gas—25 New Street Square, E.C.4. *M.*

New Law Journal—88 Kingsway, W.C.2. *W.*

Nuclear Engineering International—Dorset House, Stamford St., S.E.1. *M.*

Nurseryman & Garden Centre—Sovereign Way, Tonbridge, Kent. *W.*

Nursing Mirror—166 Fleet St., E.C.4. *W.*

Nursing Times— Little Essex St., W.C.2. *W.*

Off Licence Journal—66 Queens Road, Watford, Herts. *M.*

Off Licence News—19 Eastcheap, E.C.3. *W.*

Official Journal (Patents)—Patent Office, St. Mary Cray, Orpington. *W.*

Ophthalmic Optician—65 Brook St., W.1. *Alt. W.*

Optician—40 Bowling Green Lane, E.C.1. *W.*

Packaging—75 Carter Lane, E.C.4. *M.*

Packaging Review—33–40 Bowling Green Lane, E.C.1. *M.*

Paint Manufacture—Morgan Grampian House, Calderwood St., S.E.18. *M.*

Painting and Decorating Journal—30 Princes St., Southport, Lancs. *M.*

Paper—Lyon Tower, Colliers Wood, S.W.19. *Alt. W.*

Personnel Management—Mercury House, Waterloo Rd., S.E.1. *M.*

Petroleum Times—33–40 Bowling Green Lane, E.C.1. *Alt. W.*

Pharmaceutical Journal—17 Bloomsbury Square, W.C.1. *W.*

Philatelic Magazine—42 Malden Lane, W.C.2. *M.*

Philatelic Trader—42 Malden Lane, W.C.2. *Alt. W.*

Photographer, The—Amwell End, Ware, Herts. *Six to Ten issues a Year.*

Physics Bulletin—Netherton House, Marsh St., Bristol. *M.*

Physics Education—Netherton House, Marsh St. Bristol. *Seven issues a Year.*

Physics in Technology—Netherton House, Marsh St., Bristol. *Alt. M.*

Plumbing Equipment News and Heating Engineer—Peterson House, Livery St., Birmingham. *M.*

Police Review—14 St. Cross St., E.C.1. *W.*

Policy Holder—Waterloo Rd., Stockport. *W.*

Post Magazine and Insurance Monitor—12–13 Henrietta St., W.C.2. *W.*

Power Farming—161 Fleet St., E.C.4. *M.*

Power Laundry—40 Bowling Green Lane, E.C.1. *Alt. W.*

Practical Wireless—Fleetway House, Farringdon St., E.C.4. *M.*

Practical Woodworking—Fleetway House, Farringdon St., E.C.4. *M.*

Practitioner—5 Bentinck St., W.1. *M.*

Printing Trades Journal—Sovereign Way, Tonbridge, Kent. *M.*

Printing World—Lyon Tower, Colliers Wood, S.W.19. *W.*

Product Finishing—127 Stanstead Rd., S.E.23. *M.*

Professional Administration—388/389 Strand, W.C.2. *M.*

Public Law—11 New Fetter Lane, E.C.4. *Q.*

Public Ledger—11 Tokenhouse Yard, E.C.2. *Daily.*

Public Service—Nalgo House, 8 Harewood Row, N.W.1. *M.*

Quarry Management and Products—7 Regent St., Nottingham. *M.*

Quarterly Journal of Experimental Psychology—24-28 Oval Rd., N.W.1.

Quarterly Journal of Medicine—The Clarendon Press, Oxford.

Railway Gazette International—Dorset House, Stamford Street, S.E.1. *M.*

Railway Review—205 Euston Rd., N.W.1. *W.*

Rating and Valuation Reporter—2 Paper Bldgs., Temple, E.C.4. *W.*

Resale Weekly—Unit 4, Sewell St., Plaistow, E.13.

Retail Jeweller—93/99 Goswell Rd., E.C.1. *Alt. W.*

Retail Newsagent—21-25 Earl Street, E.C.2. *W.*

Review (Insurance)—42-43 Gerrard St., W.1. *Alt. W.*

Review of Economic Studies—Faculty of Economics, Sidgwick Ave., Cambridge. *Q.*

Review of English Studies—The Clarendon Press. Oxford. *Q.*

Safety at Sea International—Queensway House, Redhill, Surrey. *M.*

Scottish Farmer—39 York St., Glasgow. *W.*

Scottish Grocer—34-6 North Frederick St. Glasgow, *W.*

Scottish Schoolmaster—41 York Place, Edinburgh 1. *Alt. M.*

Service Station—178-202 Gt. Portland St., W.1. *M.*

Sheet Metal Industries—Queensway House, Redhill, Surrey. *M.*

Shipping World and Shipbuilder—125 High St., Colliers Wood, S.W.19. *M.*

Shoe and Leather News—84-88 Great Eastern St., E.C.2. *W.*

Soap, Perfumery and Cosmetics—42-43 Gerrard St., W.1. *M.*

Solicitors' Journal—237 Long Lane, S.E.1. *W.*

Sports Trader—125 High St., Colliers Wood, S.W.19. *M.*

Stage and Television Today—19 Tavistock St., W.C.2. *W.*

Structural Engineer—11 Upper Belgrave Sq., S.W.1. *M.*

Surveyor and Local Government Technology—Dorset House, Stamford St., S.E.1. *W.*

Tableware International—17 John Adam St., W.C.2. *M.*

Taxation—98 Park St., W.1. *W.*

Teacher—Derbyshire House, St. Chad's St., W.C.1. *W.*

Teacher's World—Montague House, Russell Sq., W.C.1. *W.*

Teaching History—59A Kennington Park Rd., S.E.11. *Twice a year.*

Television—Fleetway House, Farringdon St., E.C.4. *M.*

Textile Institute and Industry—10 Blackfriars St., Manchester, 3. *M.*

Textile Manufacturer—33 King St. Manchester. *M.*

Textile Month—Statham House, Talbot Rd., Stretford, Manchester. *M.*

Timber and Plywood—21 New St., E.C.2. *W.*

Timber Trades Journal—25 New Street Square, E.C.4. *W.*

Tobacco—17-19 John Adam St., Adelphi, W.C.2. *M.*

Tooling—127 Stanstead Rd., S.E.23. *M.*

Town and Country Planning—17 Carlton House Terrace, S.W.1. *M.*

Town Planning Review—Dept. of Civic Design, Liverpool University. *Q.*

Toy Trader—157 Hagden Lane, Watford. *M.*

Trade and Industry (*Official*)—1 Victoria St., S.W.1. *W.*

Trade Marks Journal—25 Southampton Bldgs., W.C.2. *W.*

Traffic Engineering and Control—29 Newman St., W.1. *M.*

U.K. Press Gazette—2-3 Salisbury Ct., Fleet St., E.C.4. *W.*

Ultrasonics—32 High St., Guildford. *Alt. M.*

Universities Quarterly—10 Great Turnstile, W.C.1.

Watchmaker, Jeweller and Silversmith—40 Bowling Green Lane, E.C.1. *M.*

Weekly Law Reports—3 Stone Buildings, Lincoln's Inn, W.C.2.

Welding and Metal Fabrication—IPC House, 32 High St., Guildford. *M.*

Which ?—14 Buckingham St., W.C.2. *M.*

Whitaker's Books of the Month and Books to Come—13 Bedford Sq., W.C.1. *M.*

Whitaker's Cumulative Book List—13 Bedford Sq., W.C.1. *Q.*

Wire Industry—157 Station Road East, Oxted, Surrey. *M.*

Wireless World—Dorset House, Stamford St., S.E.1. *M.*

Woodworker—13-35 Bridge St., Hemel Hempstead. *M.*

Woodworking Industry—25 New Street Square, E.C.4. *M.*

Wool Record and Textile World—Dorset House, Stamford St., S.E.1. *Alt. W.*

World Crops—9 Botolph Alley, E.C.3. *Bi-monthly.*

World's Fair—Union St., Oldham. *W.*

NORTHERN IRISH NEWSPAPERS

LONDON OFFICES:

Ballymena Observer—30 Fleet St., E.C.4.

Banbridge Chronicle—30 Fleet St., E.C.4.

Belfast Telegraph (and Weekly Telegraph)—Greater London Hse, Hampstead Rd., N.W.1.

Coleraine Chronicle—30 Fleet St., E.C.4.

Derry Journal—30 Fleet St., E.C.4.

Down Recorder—30 Fleet St., E.C.4.

Impartial Reporter (Enniskillen)—30 Fleet St., E.C.4.

Irish News—70 Hatton Garden, E.C.1.

Irish Weekly—70 Hatton Garden, E.C.1.

Londonderry Sentinel—30 Fleet St., E.C.4.

Lurgan Mail—30 Fleet St., E.C.4.

Mid Ulster—30 Fleet St., E.C.4.

Northern Constitution (Coleraine)—30 Fleet St., E.C.4.

Portadown News—30 Fleet St., E.C.4.

Portadown Times—54-55 Wilton Rd., S.W.1.

Strabane Weekly News—30 Fleet St., E.C.4.

Tyron Constitution—30 Fleet St., E.C.4.

Ulster Gazette (Armagh)—30 Fleet St., E.C.4.

Ulster Herald (Omagh)—Drayton House, Gordon St., W.C.1.

REPORTING AND NEWS AGENCIES IN LONDON

ASSOCIATED PRESS LTD.,
  83–86 Farringdon Street, E.C.4. 01–353 1515.

BRENARD PRESS LTD.,
  Heathrow Airport, Hounslow, Middx. 01–759 1235.

CAPEL COURT PRESS AGENCY LTD.,
  20 Copthall Avenue, E.C.2. 01–628 3580.

CENTRAL PRESS FEATURES,
  80 Fleet Street, E.C.4. 01–353 7792.

EXCHANGE TELEGRAPH CO., LTD.,
  Extel House, East Harding Street, E.C.4.

HAYTERS SPORTS, 01–353 1080.
  41–42 Slave Lane, E.C.4. 01–353–0971.

NATIONAL PRESS AGENCY LTD.,
  Newspaper House, 8–16 Great New Street, E.C.4. 01–353 1030.

PARLIAMENTARY NEWS SERVICES.
  92 Fleet Street, E.C.4. 01–583 7848.

PRESS ASSOCIATION LTD.,
  85 Fleet Street, E.C.4. 01–353 7440.

REUTERS LTD.,
  85 Fleet Street, E.C.4. 01–353 6060.

UNITED PRESS INTERNATIONAL, LTD.,
  8 Bouverie St., E.C.4. 01–353 2282.

UNIVERSAL NEWS SERVICES, LTD.,
  Gough Square, Fleet St., E.C.4. 01–353 5200.

LETTER POST SINCE 1972

The following list shows the cost of sending within the United Kingdom an ordinary letter not exceeding the weight shown:

Feb., 1972			First-Class		Second-Class
2 oz.	for	..	3p	..	2½p
4 oz.	for	..	4p	..	3½p
6 oz.	for	..	6p	..	5½p
8 oz.	for	..	8p	..	6½p
10 oz.	for	..	10p	..	7½p
12 oz.	for	..	13p	..	8½p
14 oz.	for	..	15p	..	9½p
1 lb.	for	..	17p	..	11½p
1 lb. 8 oz. for		..	24p	..	13½p
2 lb.	for	..	34p	..	Limit of weight
Each extra lb.		..	17p	..	1 lb. 8 oz.

Sept., 1973			First-Class		Second-Class
2 oz.	for	..	3½p	..	3p
4 oz.	for	..	5p	..	4p
6 oz.	for	..	8p	..	5½p
8 oz.	for	..	10p	..	7p
10 oz.	for	..	12p	..	8½p
12 oz.	for	..	14p	..	10p
14 oz.	for	..	16p	..	11½p
1 lb.	for	..	18p	..	13p
1 lb. 8 oz. for		..	27p	..	18½p max.
2 lb.	for	..	36p	..	—
each additional					
½ lb.	for	..	9p	..	

June, 1974			First-Class		Second-Class
2 oz.	for	..	4½p	..	3½p
4 oz.	for	..	6½p	..	5p
6 oz.	for	..	10p	..	7p
8 oz.	for	..	12½p	..	9p
10 oz.	for	..	15p	..	11p
12 oz.	for	..	17½p	..	13p
14 oz.	for	..	20p	..	15p
1 lb.	for	..	22½p	..	17p

			First-Class		Second-Class
1 lb. 8 oz. for		..	32½p	..	22½p max.
2 lb.	for	..	42½p	..	—
each additional					
½ lb.			10p		

March, 1975			First-Class		Second-Class
2 oz.	for	..	7p	..	5½p
4 oz.	for	..	10p	..	8p
6 oz.	for	..	12½p	..	9½p
8 oz.	for	..	15p	..	11p
10 oz.	for	..	17½p	..	13p
12 oz.	for	..	19½p	..	14½p
14 oz.	for	..	22p	..	16½p
1 lb.	for	..	24p	..	18p
1 lb. 8 oz. for		..	34p	..	24p max.
2 lb.	for	..	44p	..	
each additional					
½ lb or part ½ lb: 10p				..	—

Sept., 1975			First-Class		Second-Class
60 g (2.1 oz.)	for	..	8½p	..	6½p
100 g (3.5 oz.)	for	..	11½p	..	9p
150 g (5.3 oz.)	for	..	15p	..	11p
200 g (7.1 oz.)	for	..	18p	..	13½p
250 g (8.8 oz.)	for	..	21p	..	16p
300 g (10.6 oz.)	for	..	24p	..	18½p
350 g (12.3 oz.)	for	..	27p	..	21p
400 g (14.1 oz.)	for	..	30p	..	23½p
450 g (15.9 oz.)	for	..	33p	..	26p
500 g (1.1lb.)	for	..	36p	..	28½p
750 g (1.7 lb.)	for	..	51p	..	42p max.
1000 g (2.2 lb.)	for	..	66p	..	
each additional					
250 g (8.8 oz.)			15p		

THE PRESS COUNCIL

In April, 1947, a Royal Commission was appointed to enquire into the control, management and ownership, etc., of the Press and news agencies and to make recommendations thereon. The Commission, in its report of June, 1949, recommended *inter alia* that a voluntary Press Council be formed.

A constitution ultimately set up provided for the establishment of such a council on July 1, 1953. This constitution was materially amended in 1963 by the introduction of an independent chairman and up to 20 per cent. lay membership. In 1973, the Council was increased to 30, of whom one-third were lay members, excluding the Chairman. The objects of the Council are (1) to preserve the established freedom of the British press; (2) to maintain the character of the British Press in accordance with the highest professional and commercial standards; (3) to consider complaints about the conduct of the Press or the conduct of persons and organizations towards the Press; to deal with these complaints in whatever manner might seem practical and appropriate and record resultant action; (4) to keep under review developments likely to restrict the supply of information of public interest and importance; (5) to report publicly on developments that may tend towards greater concentration or monopoly in the Press (including changes in ownership, control and growth of Press undertakings) and to publish statistical information relating thereto; (6) to make representations on appropriate occasions to the Government, organs of the United Nations and Press organizations abroad; and (7) to publish periodical reports recording the Council's work and to review, from time to time, developments in the Press and the factors affecting them.

The membership of the Council consists of editorial and managerial nominees of The Newspaper Publishers Association Ltd. (5), The Newspaper Society (3), The Periodical Publishers Association Ltd. (2), The Scottish Daily Newspaper Society (1), Scottish Newspaper Proprietors' Association (1), The Guild of British Newspaper Editors (2), The National Union of Journalists (4) and The Institute of Journalists (2).

Chairman, The Lord Shawcross, P.C., G.B.E., Q.C.

Vice-Chairman, D. R. W. Greenslade.

Professional Members, W. J. Bailey; W. R. A. Breare; H. R. Douglas; H. French; C. D. Hamilton, D.S.O.; A. V. Hare; W. Heald; A. A. Jenner; F. P. M. Johnston; I. McColl; A. Miles; K. J. Peters; E. Pickering; A. E. Simpson; R. Swingler; R. M. Taylor; J. S. Wallwork; G. Withy; one vacancy.

Lay Members, Capt. G. C. Baldwin, C.B.E.; P. Bartlett; Dr. A. C. Copisarow; D. Ellis, O.B.E., T.D.; T. Jackson; Mrs. J. Martin; Sir Ian Morrow; Dame Jean Rivett-Drake, D.B.E.; Mrs. B. Thompson; Rt. Rev. W. J. Westwood.

Secretary, N. S. Paul, New Mercury House, 81 Farringdon Street, E.C.4.

THE ARTS COUNCIL
105 Piccadilly, W.1

The Arts Council of Great Britain is incorporated under Royal Charter with the following objects, (*a*) to develop and improve the knowledge, understanding and practice of the arts; (*b*) to increase the accessibility of the arts to the public throughout Great Britain; and (*c*) to advise and cooperate with Departments of Government, local authorities and other bodies on any matters concerned directly or indirectly with the foregoing objects.

The members of the Council, who may not exceed twenty in number, are appointed by the Minister responsible for the Arts after consultation with the Secretary of State for Scotland and the Secretary of State for Wales. With the approval of the two latter the Council appoints separate committees for Scotland and Wales known as the Scottish Arts Council and the Welsh Arts Council respectively.

The Council receives a grant-in-aid from the Government, and for the year 1975–76 the amount was £26,150,000.

Chairman, The Lord Gibson.
Secretary-General, R. Shaw

WEATHER INFORMATION AND FORECASTS

Recorded weather forecasts for the areas listed below are available by telephoning the numbers shown:

Bedford area	Bedford 8091	Lancs. Coast	Southport 8091	South Devon and	
	Bishops Stortford 8091	Leeds/Bradford and		East Cornwall	Exeter 8091
	01–246 8099	Huddersfield area	Bradford 8091		Plymouth 8091
	Peterborough 8091		Huddersfield 8091		Torquay 8091
	Luton 8091		Leeds 8091	Southern Hants. and I.O.W.	
Belfast area	Belfast 8091	London area	01–246 8091	(including coastal area	
Birmingham area	021–246 8091		Tunbridge Wells 8091	between Poole Harbour and	
	Coventry 8091		Guildford 8091	Chichester) Bournemouth 8091	
Bristol area	Bristol 8091	Norfolk and Suffolk			Portsmouth 8091
	Swindon 8091		Norwich 8091		Southampton 8091
Cardiff area	Cardiff 8091		Ipswich 8091	South Lancs. and	
Central Lancs.	Blackburn 8091	North Lincs. and		North Cheshire	051–246 8091
Edinburgh area	031–246 8091	Retford area	Grimsby 8091		061–246 8091
Essex Coast	Chelmsford 8091		Lincoln 8091	South-West Midlands	
	01–246 8096	North Wales Coast			Cheltenham 8091
	Colchester 8091	from Conway	051–246 8093		Gloucester 8091
	Southend 8091	to Chester	061–246 8093		Hereford 8091
Glasgow area	041–246 8091		Chester 8091	Sussex Coast	01–246 8097
Kent Coast	01–246 8098		Colwyn Bay 8091		Brighton 8091
	Canterbury 8095	Notts., Leics. and		Thames Valley	01–246 8090
	Medway 8091	Derby	Nottingham 8091		High Wycombe 8091
Lancs. Coast	051–246 8092		Leicester 8091		Oxford 8091
	061–246 8092		Derby 8091		Reading 8091
	Blackburn 8092	Sheffield area	Sheffield 8091	Tyne-Tees	Newcastle 8091
	Blackpool 8091		Doncaster 8091		Middlesbrough 8091

Principal London Clubs

Club and Address	Secretary	Subscription Entr.	Subscription Ann.	Remarks
		£	£	
Alpine (1857), 74 S. Audley St., W.1.	M. F. Baker (Hon.)...	4·00	4·00 to 6·50	Mountaineering.
American (1919), 95 Piccadilly, W.1.	J. Levak.............	100·00	75·00	Americans in London.
American Women's (1899), 1 Cadogan Gardens, S.W.3.	Mrs. K. E. Hayward..	10·00	5·00 to 25·00	American Women in London.
Anglo-Belgian (1955), 6 Belgrave Square, S.W.1.	Baron de Gerlache de Gomery, M.V.O.	13·20	22·00	Social and Residential.
Army and Navy (1837), 36 Pall Mall, S.W.1.	J. Gordon...........	Nil	32·00	Commissioned officers of H.M. Forces.
Arts (1863), 40 Dover Street, W.1.	A. E. Eldon-Edington.	10·00	70·00	Art, Literature, Science.
The Athenæum (1824), 107 Pall Mall, S.W.1.	G. L. E. Lindlow.....	52·50	87·40 to 36·80	Literature and Science, Public Services, The Arts.
Authors' (1891), 1 Whitehall Place, S.W.1.	E. Walsh............	..	Various	Social.
The Bath (1896), 41–43 Brook St., W.1.	H. A. Style..........	110·00	110·00	Social: non-political.
Beefsteak (1876), 9 Irving Street, W.C.2.	W. E. Usher........	30·00	30·00	Dining and Social.
Boodle's (1762), 28 St. James's St., S.W.1.	R. J. Edmonds.......	100·00	100·00	Social: non-political.
Brooks's (1764), St. James's Street, S.W.1.	J. O. Robson........	55·00	88·40	Social: non-political.
Buck's (1919), 18 Clifford Street, W.1.	R. C. Gilbert........	100·00	90·00	Social: non-political.
Caledonian (1897), 9 Halkin St., S.W.1.	Capt. G. G. Wilson, C.B.E., R.N.	Nil	50·00 to 5·00	Strictly Scottish.
Canning (1910), 42 Half Moon Street, W.1.	R. B. Baker.........	50·00	45·00	Social: S. American.
Carlton (1832), 69 St. James's St., S.W.1.	R. P. McDouall......	50·00	100·00	Conservative and Unionist.
Cavalry (1891), 127 Piccadilly, W.1.	Sqn.-Ldr. A. F. O'Connor (Hon.)	34·65	41·00	Offices of Mounted Services.
Challoner (1949), 61 Pont Street, S.W.1.	Brig. P. B. Cuddon, C.B.E., M.C. (Hon.)	15·00	Various	Roman Catholic residential.
Chelsea Arts (1891), 143 Old Church Street, S.W.3.	A. G. Hartmann......	..	30·00	Arts and Literature.
Chemical (1918), 1 Whitehall Place, S.W.1.	P. F. Corbett........	Nil	25·00 & 20·00	Chemical and Social.
City Livery (1914), Sion College, E.C.4.	B. L. Morgan, C.B.E.	25·00	25·00	Liverymen of City only.
City of London (1832), 19 Old Broad Street, E.C.2.	P. Merritt...........	200·00	90·00	Merchants, Bankers, &c.
City University (1885), 50 Cornhill, E.C.3.	G. O. Puckle........	55·00	55·00	Oxford and Cambridge Graduates.
Civil Service (1953), 13–15 Great Scotland Yard, S.W.1.	E. G. Roberts (Manager)	Nil	1·50	Serving or pensioned Civil Servants.
Constitutional (1883), 86 St. James's Street, S.W.1.	S. F. Head...........	Nil	75·00	Social and Political.
Devonshire (1874), 50 St. James's Street, S.W.1.	Miss D. Wallace......	Nil	100·00	Social.
East India, Sports and Public Schools (1848), 16 St. James's Square, S.W.1.	P. H. Wallace........	50·00	50·00	Social.
Eccentric (1890), 9 Ryder Street, S.W.1.	L. E. Newman.......	50·00	50·00	Social.
Farmers' (1842), 3 Whitehall Ct., S.W.1.	Vacant..............	30·00 to 15·00	30·00 to 5·00	Agricultural Interests.
Flyfishers' (1884), 86 St. James's Street, S.W.1.	H. A. Rickett........	50·00	25·00 to 8·00	Flyfishing and Social.
Garrick (1831), Garrick Street, W.C.2.	M. Harvey..........	125·00	100·00	Dramatic and Literary.
Golfers' (1893), 10 Old Burlington Street, W.1.	Mrs. M. A. Pearse....	..	11·55 to 6·93	Members of Golf Clubs.
Green Room (1877), 9 Adam Street, W.C.2.	Vacant..............	10·00	25·00	Dramatic Profession.
Gresham (1843), 15 Abchurch Lane, E.C.4.	P. N. Owen.........	100·00	70·00	Bankers, Merchants, Social.

Club and Address	Secretary	Entr. £	Ann. £	Remarks
Guards (1810), 16 Charles Street, W.1.	J. E. Savage..........	Nil	40·00	Guards Officers and their families only.
Helena (1922), 52 Lower Sloane Street, S.W.1.	Mrs. G. D. Lawson...	4·00	10·00	Social and Residential.
Hurlingham (1869), Ranelagh Gardens, S.W.6.	D. F. A. Trewby.....	100·00	65·00	Tennis, Swimming, Croquet, Squash, Bowls, Social, Golf, Cricket.
Irish (1948), 82 Eaton Sq., S.W.1.	J. Sheehy (Hon.)......	1·05	10·50 & 6·30	Social: Non-political.
Junior Carlton (1864), 30 Pall Mall, S.W.1.	W. A. Jolly..........	Nil	75·00	Conservative.
Kempton Park (1878), Sunbury-on-Thames.	Mrs. V. J. Blackford..	..	40·00	Racing.
Kennel (1873), 1 Clarges St., W.1.	Lt.-Cdr. J. S. Williams.	25·00	15·00	For improving breed of dogs.
Lansdowne (1935), 9 Fitzmaurice Place, Berkeley Square, W.1.	Brig. R. F. B. Hensman, C.B.E.	Nil	Various	Social, Sports and Residential.
London Fencing (1848), 83 Perham Road, W.14.	E. J. Morten (Hon.)...	Nil	20·00	Fencing.
London Rowing (1856), Embankment, Putney, S.W.15.	K. C. W. King.......	2·00	Various	Amateur Rowing.
M.C.C. (Marylebone Cricket Club) (1787), Lord's Cricket Ground, N.W.8.	J. A. Bailey..........	10·00	20·00	Headquarters of Cricket.
Mining (1910), 3 London Wall Bldgs., E.C.2.	G. Sumner..........	10·00	25·00 to 5·00	Mining and metallurgical interests.
National (1845), c/o Constitutional Club (q.v.).	E. Scott (Hon.).......	Nil	22·00 & 14·00	Clerical and social.
National Liberal (1882), 1 Whitehall Place, S.W.1.	C. Billson...........	10·00	45·00 to 30·00	Social and political.
Naval (1943), 38 Hill Street, W.1.	Lt.-Cdr. L. A. d'E. Lloyd, M.B.E., R.N.	Nil	Various	Serving and retired Naval Officers, R.M. and yacht club members.
Naval and Military (1862), 94 Piccadilly, W.1.	Maj. W. E. Anderson, M.B.E., M.C.	54·00	48·60	Officers of R.N., Army, Marines, R.A.F.
Oriental (1824), Stratford House, Stratford Place, W.1.	R. N. Rapson, M.V.O..	55·00	50·00 to 10·00	Social.
Portland (1816), 42 Half Moon Street, W.1.	Cdr. D. A. Becker, R.N. (ret.)	100·00	70·00	Social: Non-political.
Pratt's (1841), 14 Park Place, S.W.1.	Maj. G. C. Hackett, M.B.E.	Nil	20·00	Social.
Press (1882), International Press Centre, 76 Shoe Lane, E.C.4.	J. H. Horrocks.......	10·00	25·00	Strictly Journalistic.
Queen's (1886), Palliser Road, W. Kensington, W.14.	N. K. Haugh........	64·00 to 80·00	81·00 to 15·00	Lawn Tennis, Tennis, Rackets and Squash Rackets.
Railway (1899), 112 High Holborn, W.C.1.	C. F. Wells (Hon).....	1·00	4·00	Railway interests.
Reform (1832), 104–5 Pall Mall, S.W.1.	R. G. Tennant.......	55·00	90·00	Social.
Roehampton (1901), Roehampton Lane, S.W.15.	J. Maples............	70·00 to 20·00	75·00 to 25·00	Golf, Lawn Tennis, Squash, Croquet, Swimming.
Royal Air Force (1918), 128 Piccadilly, W.1.	E. A. Jeffreys.........	27·00*	9·90*	Officers of R.A.F., R.A.F.V.R., W.R.A.F., etc.
Royal Automobile (1897), 89–91 Pall Mall, S.W.1.	G. E. Samson........	34·00 to 10·00	60·00 to 12·00	And at Woodcote Park, Epsom.
Royal Cruising (1880), 42 Half Moon Street, W.1.	A. P. Gray (Hon.).....	10·00	7·00	Cruising and Social.
R.A.F. Reserves (1948), c/o Naval Club, 38 Hill Street, W.1.	Sqn. Ldr. H. C. Room, M.B.E. (Hon.)	Nil	5·25 to 1·00	Officers of R.A.F., R.A.F.V.R., R.A.F. Reserve and ex-officers.
Royal Ocean Racing (1925), 20 St. James's Place, S.W.1.	Mrs. M. Pera........	6·00	24·00	Off-shore Yacht Racing.
Royal Thames Yacht (1775), 60 Knightsbridge, S.W.1.	Capt. K. Stobbs......	35·00 & 75·00	105·00 to 50·00	Yachting and Social.

* Non-Serving Officers.

Club and Address	Secretary	Subscription		Remarks
		Entr.	Ann.	
		£	£	
St. James' (1859), 106 Piccadilly, W.1.	P. K. Hiller..........	26·25	52·50	Diplomatic and Social.
St. Stephen's (1870), 34 Queen Anne's Gate, S.W.1.	Maj. P. J. Browning..	20·00 & 10·00	40·00 to 5·00	Conservative and Social.
Sandown Park (1875), Esher, Surrey.	F. J. Bates...........	Nil	27·50	Racing.
Savage (1857), 9 Fitzmaurice Place, Berkeley Square, W.1.	A. Wykes (Hon.).....	25·00	30·00 & 15·00	Drama, Literature, Art, Music, Science, Law.
Savile (1868), 69 Brook Street, W.1.	R. W. Guy..........	65·00	78·00	Social: Non-political.
Sesame Pioneer and Lyceum (1895), 49 Grosvenor Street, W.1.	Miss C. Sutton.......	15·00	22·00 to 9·00	Social and Residential: Men and Women.
Ski Club of G.B. (1903), 118 Eaton Square, S.W.1.	Brig. L. E. Madrell...	2·00	8·00 or 6·00	Ski-ing and Social.
Spanish (Centro Español de Londres) (1913), 5 Cavendish Sq., W.1.	J. R. Roca..........	Nil	0·75 to 1·50	Social and Residential.
Thames Rowing (1860), Embankment, Putney, S.W.15.	S. Falvey...........	2·00	14·50	Men and Women.
Travellers' (1819), 108 Pall Mall, S.W.1.	R. A. Williams......	55·00	100·00	Social: Non-political.
Turf (1868), 5 Carlton House Terrace, S.W.1.	J. D. Thomson.......	80·00 to 35·00	80·00 to 35·00	Social: Non-political.
United Nursing Services (1921), 40 South Street, W.1.	W. Oakes...........	3·50	9·25	Social.
United Oxford & Cambridge University (1972), 71–7 Pall Mall, S.W.1.	D. J. McDougall.....	Nil	55·00	Oxford & Cambridge.
United Wards (1877), 20 Chivelston Parkside, Wimbledon, S.W.19.	D. Munro...........	1·15	5·00	Freemen, Liverymen, Ward Club members, Civic.
University Women's (1867), 2 Audley Square, W.1.	Miss M. F. Lindsay...	10·80	15·12 to 10·80	University Graduates.
V.A.D. Ladies (1920), 44 Great Cumberland Place, W.1.	Miss M. A. Sample...	2·20	13·20 & 8·80	Social and residential.
Victoria (1863), 150–162 Edgware Road, W.2.	L. A. Holland........	Nil	36·75	Sporting and Social.
Victory Services (1907), 63–79 Seymour Street, W.2.	D. G. Stovey........	Nil	3·00	Social and residential; Serving and Ex-Service Men and Women.
White's (1693), 37–8 St. James's St., S.W.1.	W. H. West.........	100·00	80·00	Social: Non-political.
Wig and Pen (1908), 229–230 Strand, W.C.2.	R. A. Brennan.......	7·00	7·50	Law and Journalism.

CLUB AND LIBRARY EDITION OF WHITAKER, 1976

The Club and Library Edition of Whitaker's Almanack, 1976, contains 1,220 pages, illustrations and additional coloured maps (The World, The British Isles, Baltic States, Russia and her neighbours, Germany and her neighbours, France and Spain, The Far East, India, Pakistan and Burma, Africa, Canada, and Newfoundland, The United States, South America, Australia, New Zealand) in strong leather binding, with gilt top and silk headband. Price £4·75 net.

Club and Address (with date of foundation)	Secretary or *Hon Sec.	Subscription	
		Entr.	Ann.
		£	£
Aldershot (Officers) (1846), Farnborough Road.	B. A. Harvey........	15·00	20·00
Bath (Bath and County) (1858), 21–22 Queen Square.	R. A. L. Belben......	Nil	25·00
Birmingham—			
(Birmingham Club) (1888), Winston Churchill House, 8 Ethel Street.	N. J. Masterton......	Nil	46·00
(Chamber of Commerce) (1922), 75 Harborne Road.	J. R. Dixon..........	Nil	16·50
(St. Paul's) (1859), 34 St. Paul's Square.	A. E. Shipton........	Nil	45·00
(Union) (1850), 87 Colman Row	*J. McFea	Nil	Various
Bishop Auckland (The Club) (1868), Victoria Street.	T. W. Walton........	5·00	9·00
Bradford (The Club) (1870), 41 Bank Street.	*W. E. B. Holroyd; D. R. Hobbs	5·00	42·00
Union (1857), Piecehall Yard.	C. D. M. Roberts....	10·50	39·60
Bridport and West Dorset (1921), 12 South Street.	R. M. Mayles........	Nil	10·00
Bristol (Clifton) (1882), 22 The Mall.	Lt.-Col. A. W. Thompson, O.B.E., M.C., T.D.	Nil	40·00 or 12·00
(Constitutional) (1885), Marsh Street,	Brig. H. A. Hardy, M.B.E., M.C.	11·05	35·00
(The Bristol Club) (1889), 38a Corn Street.	*C. W. Lawson......	Nil	25·00 to 12·00
Buxton (Union) (1886), 3 St. John's Road.	*J. Brady............	Nil	15·75 to 12·00
Cambridge (Amateur Dramatic) (1855), Park Street.	G. B. Skelsey........	Nil	3·00
(Hawks) (1874), Jesus Lane.	*D. B. Williams, Ph.D.	3·00 to 6·50	†25·00
(Union) (1815), Bridge Street.	R. F. Thompson (Chief Clerk)	Nil	9·50
(University Pitt) (1835), Jesus Lane.	*A. C. L. Campbell...	3·00	21·00
Canterbury (Kent and Canterbury) (1868), 17 Old Dover Road.	D. F. Andrews, M.B.E..	10·00	20·00
Cardiff (Cardiff and County) (1866), 2 Westgate Street.	*G. V. Wynne-Jones, O.B.E.	40·00	50·00
Cheltenham (The New Club) (1890), Mountpellier Parade.	*J. V. Venn..........	Nil	30·00
Chester (Grosvenor) (1866), 3 Vicars Lane.	M. J. D. Roberts.....	Nil	18·90
(City) (1807), St. Peter's Church Yard.	R. Edwards..........	20·00	20·00
Chichester (W. Sussex County) (1873), 38 East St.	C. W. Hayden.......	..	11·00 & 5·50
Colchester (The Club) (1874), 3–5 Culver Street, E.	P. A. Witard........	Nil	15·00
Devizes (Devizes & District) (1932), 17 St. John Street.	*C. S. D. Hall.......	5·50	4·62 & 2·31
Douglas, Isle of Man (Ellan Vannin Club) (1893), 20 Finch Road.	*T. E. Osborne......	1·05	20·00
Durham (County) (1894), 52 Old Elvet.	*J. T. Culley........	Nil	12·00
Eastbourne (Devonshire) (1872), Westdown House, Hartington Place.	J. B. Neal...........	9·00	9·00
Exeter (Exeter and County) (1871), 5 Cathedral Close.	M. P. Saunders.......	5·00	22·00
Folkestone (Radnor Club) (1874), 136 Sandgate Rd.	Vacant.............	5·50	13·20
Harrogate (The Club) (1857), 36 Victory Avenue.	*C. L. Leslie.........	..	25·00 & 5·25
Haverfordwest (Pembrokeshire County) (1877), 48 High Street.	*B. J. Radley.......	4·00	6·00
Henley-on-Thames (Leander) (1818), Henley.	*H. R. P. Steward....	10·00 & 5·00	11·00 & 6·00
(Phyllis Court) (1906), Marlow Road.	D. C. Ferguson......	Nil	28·00
Hove (The Hove Club) (1882), 28 Fourth Avenue.	Sqn. Ldr. G. A. Inveranty, D.F.C.	5·00	15·75
Jersey (United) (1846), Royal Sq.; St. Helier.	*R. J. Michel........	20·00	20·00
(Victoria) (1853), Beresford St., St. Helier.	C. G. Mitchell.......	10·00	15·00
Leamington (Tennis Court) (1847), 50 Bedford Street.	*Maj. J. Dolan, M.B.E..	Nil	16·50
Leeds (The Leeds Club) (1850), 3 Albion Place.	*J. W. Bosomworth..	Nil	40·00
(Leeds & County Conservative) (1882), 13 South Parade.	*P. Jones............	Nil	31·00
Leicester (Leicestershire Club) (1873), 9 Welford Place.	A. B. Proctor........	10·00	33·00
Liverpool (Artists) (1886), 5 Eberle Street.	*M. S. Dawson	11·00	45·00
(Athenæum) (1797), Church Alley.	*F. J. Smith.........	Nil	35·00
(Lyceum) (1800), 1 Bold Street.	G. F. Harnden.......	Nil–5·25	36·00
(Racquet) (1877), 102 Upper Parliament Street.	*R. L. Packer........	Nil	50·00

† Life Membership.

Club and Address (with date of foundation)	Secretary or *Hon. Sec.	Subscription	
		Entr.	Ann.
		£	£
Manchester (The Manchester Club) (1871), 50 Spring Gardens.	F. C. T. Baker.......	27·50	50·00 to 7·00
(St. James's) (1825), 7 Charlotte Street.	H. F. Kennedy.......	24·00	49·50
Newcastle upon Tyne (Northern Constitutional) (1908), 37 Pilgrim Street.	Mrs. G. Whitham....	Nil	44·00
Northampton (Northampton and County) (1873), George Row.	Sqdn. Ldr. J. V. Hadland, D.F.C.	5·00 to 20·00	12·00 to 25·00
Norwich (Norfolk) (1864), 17 Upper King Street.	Mrs. S. M. Gostling...	15·00	45·00 to 15·00
Nottingham (Nottinghamshire) (prior to 1850), Bottle Lane.	B. C. Weldon.......	21·00	25·00
Oxford (Clarendon) (1863), 121 High Street.	*R. Ellis............	22·00	22·00
(Frewen) (1869), 98 St. Aldate's.	*W. H. Miller, B.E.M..	11·00	11·00
(Vincent's) (1863), King Edward Street.	G. J. Brazier (Steward).	..	..
Peterborough (City and Counties) (1867), 21 Priestgate.	D. A. S. Parker......	2·00	20·00
Portsmouth (Royal Naval and Royal Albert Yacht) (1867), 17 Pembroke Road.	Capt.D.J.Bateman,R.N.	10·00	25·00 to 8·00
Preston (Conservative) (1878), Guildhall Street.	*L. M. C. Waller.....	Nil	6·00 & 3·00
Reading (Berkshire Athenæum) (1842), 28 Friar St.	*B. H. Powell.......	Nil	16·50
Rochester (Castle) (1865), 3 Esplanade.	*L. F. Fagg..........	15·00	24·00
Rugby (The Rugby) (1865), 35 North Street.	*V. M. Roberts, O.B.E.	15·00	5·00
Rye (Dormy House) (1896), East Cliff, Rye.	*H. A. Fowler.......	2·10	6·30 & 4·20
St. Leonards on Sea (East Sussex) (1884), 1 Warrior Square.	*S. G. Bradbury......	1·05	10·50
Sheffield (The Club) (1843), George Street.	Lt.-Col. J. R. Pattison.	30·00	50·00 to 12·00
Shrewsbury (Salop) (1972), 6 The Square.	S. Davies............	Nil	21·00 to 7·00
Teddington (Royal Canoe) (1866), Trowlock Island, Middx.	Mrs. G. Barnard......	..	..
Torbay (The Paignton Club) (1882), The Esplanade. (Torbay) (1906), Hyde Road.	P. Grafton...........	15·00	8·00
	F. Greenwood.......	3·15	4·20
Tunbridge Wells (Tunbridge Wells) (1872), 40 London Road	Sqn.-Ldr. D. S. Leete..	3·00	7·00
Winchester (Hampshire Club) 32 Southgate Street.	*R. D. Utting.......	5·00	20·00
Worcester (Union and County) (1861), 49 Foregate Street.	*P. J. Seward........	Nil	12·00
Yeovil (Ivel Club) (1884), Frederick Place.	B. A. Collins........	3·15	9·45 to 3·15
York (Yorkshire) (1839), River House, Museum St.	S. A. Free...........	22·00	40·00
(City) (1876), 4 Museum Street.	*I. R. Washington....	3·00	30·00

Scotland

Ayr (County) (1872), Savoy Park Hotel.	*W. W. McHarg.....	Nil	8·00
Dundee (Eastern) (1865), 2 Euclid Street.	G. S. McInroy.......	Nil	40·00
Edinburgh (Caledonian) (1877), 32 Abercromby Place.	Mrs. M. W. Hutton...	Nil	30·00 to 15·00
(Ladies' Caledonian) (1908), 13–14 Charlotte Square.	Miss P. D. Bremmer..	10·50	25·00 to 5·50
(New) (1787), 86 Princes Street.	R. Pettie, T.D........	35·00	24·50 to 45·00
(Queen's) (1897), 13 Frederick Street.	(vacant)..............	5·00	15·00
Glasgow (Art) (1867), 185 Bath Street.	G. Cowan...........	5·00	20·00 & 26·00
(Royal Scottish Automobile) (1899), 11 Blythswood Square.	Maj. R. T. Reid, M.C..	34·00 or 17·00	40·00 or 15·00
(The Western Club) (1825), 32 Royal Exchange Square.	Lt.-Col. A. Gordon, M.C.	25·00	50·00
Inverness (Highland) (1870), 39 High Street.	C. J. Sedgwick.......	25·00	25·00
Stirling (Stirling and County), (1877), 5 Melville Terrace.	*R. Heathwood......	10·50	10·50

Northern Ireland

Belfast (Ulster) (1837), River House, High Street.	*S. M. P. Cross.......	10·50	61·56
(Ulster Reform) (1885), 4 Royal Avenue.	S. F. Hodge, M.B.E....	Nil	40·00

YACHT CLUBS

Club and Address (with date of foundation)	Secretary or *Hon. Sec.	Subscription Entr.	Ann.
		£	£
Beaumaris (Royal Anglesey) (1802), 6–7 Green Edge.	*R. R. M. Jones.....	12·00 to 8·00	10·00 to 1·05
Bembridge, I. of W. (Sailing) (1886), Isle of Wight.	K. J. Hawker........	15·00	19·80
Birkenhead (Royal Mersey) (1844), 8–10 Bedford Road, Rock Ferry.	*C. J. Kay...........	20·00	15·00
Bridlington (Royal Yorks) (1847), 1 Windsor Crescent.	*Lt.-Col. G. R. Saltoustall, O.B.E.	10·00 to 6·50	25·30 to 12·10
Burnham-on-Crouch (Royal Burnham) (1897), The Royal Burnham Yacht Club.	J. T. Derry	..	..
(Royal Corinthian) (1872), Burnham-on-Crouch.	Cdr. I. McL. Methven, R.N. (ret.)	..	..
Caernarvon (Royal Welsh) (1847), Porth-yr-Aur.	*T. W. Williams.....	5·00	8·00
Cowes (Royal Yacht Squadron) (1815), The Castle, Cowes	Maj. J. D. Dillon, D.S.C., R.M.	200·00	65·00
(Royal London) (1838), The Parade.	Sqn.-Ldr. C. A. A. Davis (ret.).	50·00	35·00 to 1·50
Dover (Royal Cinque Ports) (1872), 4–5 Waterloo Crescent.	Mrs. E. A. Parker.....	5·00	15·00 to 4·50
Essex (1890), Leigh-on-Sea.	Lt.-Cdr. C. Stokes, M.B.E.	..	..
Fishbourne, I. of W. (Royal Victoria) (1848), Fishbourne.	Mrs. A. Gilbert.......	3·15	8·00 to 2·00
Fowey (Royal Fowey) (1894), Fowey.	*T. K. Jones.........	Various	Various
Harwich (Royal Harwich) (1843), Woolverstone, nr. Ipswich.	Cdr. R. D. Sterndale-Bennett, R.N.	15·00	15·00
Jersey (R.C.I.) (1862), Le Boulevard, St. Aubin, Jersey.	F. J. Houillebecq.....	10·00	10·00 to 4·00
Kingswear (Royal Dart.) (1866), Kingswear, S. Devon.	*Miss A. M. Hine-Haycock, M.B.E.	10·00	10·00 to 2·00
London (Cruising Association) (1908), Ivory House, St. Katharine Dock, E.1.	Miss E. Rider........	5·00	12·00 to 2·00
(Royal Cruising) (1880), 42 Half Moon Street, W.1.	*A. P. Gray.........	10·00	7·00
Lowestoft (Royal Norfolk and Suffolk) (1859), Royal Plain.	Capt. I. A. B. Quarrie.	10·00	35·00
Penarth (Penarth) (1880), The Esplanade.	D. E. Morse........	5·00	15·00
Plymouth (Royal Western) (1827), 9 Grand Parade, West Hoe.	Sqn.-Ldr. J. E. R. Vosper (ret.).	Various	28·00
(Royal Plymouth Corinthian) (1877), Madeira Road.	*P. J. Crowther......	..	..
Poole (East Dorset Sailing) (1875), Sandbanks Rd.	Mrs. B. V. Okey.....	10·50	9·00
(Parkstone) (1895), Pearce Avenue, Parkstone.	Col. T. A. Hunt......	22·50	20·00
(Poole Harbour) (1949), Salterns Way, Lilliput.	Mrs. E. M. Perry.....	Various	Various
(Royal Motor Yacht) (1905), Sandbanks.	Mrs. M. C. Hardie....	26·25	21·00
(Yacht) (1865), New Quay Road, Hamworthy.	G. E. Thornton.......	20·00	15·00
Ramsgate (Royal Temple) (1857), West Cliff Mansions.	C. R. De Silva.......	Various	Various
Southampton:			
(Royal Air Force) (1932), Riverside Ho., Hamble.	Mrs. V. P. Hill.......	25·00	18·00
(Royal Southern) (1837), Hamble, Hants.	Mrs. W. J. F. Clampett	33·00	Various
(Royal Southampton) (1875), 10 Northlands Rd.	Maj. J. J. Batchelor, (ret.).	Various	Various
(Royal Thames) (1775), Shore House, Warsash, Hants.	Capt. K. R. Stobbs...	52·50 & 26·25	105·00 to 35·00
Southend (Alexandra) (1873), The Cliffs, Clifton Terrace.	*E. Green...........	Nil	14.00
Southsea (Royal Naval and Royal Albert) (1864), 17 Pembroke Road, Portsmouth.	Capt. D. J. Bateman, R.N. (ret.).	10·00	Various
Swansea (Bristol Channel) (1875), 744 Mumbles Road, Mumbles.	*P. G. Cawker.......	30·00	30·00 to 20·50
Torbay (Royal Torbay) (1875), Beacon Hill, Torquay.	Lt.-Col. D. R. Large..	8·50	8·50
Westcliffe-on-Sea (Thames Estuary) (1947), 3 The Leas.	*C. E. Hutchings.....	Various	Various
Weymouth (Royal Dorset) (1875), 51 The Esplanade.	*J. C. T. Plummer....	10·00	15·00
Windermere (Royal Windermere) (1860), Fallbarrow Road.	*A. Murdoch.........	25·00	17·00 & 14·00
Yarmouth (Royal Solent) (1878), Yarmouth, I.O.W.	Col. R. W. Stephenson, O.B.E.	14·00 to 20·00	24·00 to 1·00

Scotland

Club and Address (with date of foundation)	Secretary or *Hon. Sec.	Subscription	
		Entr.	Ann.
		£	£
Dundee (Royal Tay) (1891), 34 Dundee Road, Broughty Ferry.	J. D. A. Sey.........	10·00	8·00
Edinburgh (Royal Forth) (1868), 1 Boswall Road, Edinburgh, 5.	G. Laing............	20·00	25·00
Glasgow (Royal Clyde) (1856), Rhu, Dunbarton-shire.	J. Colvill, 175 West George Street, Glasgow	5·00	9·00
(Royal Western) (1875), (None).	*R. Cockburn, West-croft, Kilmacolm.	1·00	1·00
Oban (Royal Highland) (1881).	W. Melville.........	Nil	2·10
Rhu (Royal Northern) (1824), Rhu, Dunbarton-shire.	S. L. Revett, D.S.C., V.R.D.	30·00	Various

Northern Ireland

Bangor (Royal Ulster) (1866), Clifton Road, Bangor, Co. Down.	G. D. Ralston........	12·00	40·00

PRESIDENTS OF THE ROYAL SOCIETY

The Royal Society received a charter from Charles II on April 22, 1662, when it was incorporated as a body politic and corporate under the appellation of The President, Council and Fellowship of the Royal Society of London, for improving Natural Knowledge.

Sir Robert Moray......................	1660	Lord Wrottesley........................	1854
Viscount Brouncker....................	1662	Sir Benjamin Brodie, Bt.................	1858
Sir Joseph Williamson.................	1677	Maj.-Gen. Sir Edward Sabine...........	1861
Sir Christopher Wren..................	1680	Sir George Biddell Airy.................	1871
Sir John Hoskins, Bt...................	1682	Sir Joseph Dalton Hooker...............	1873
Sir Cyril Wyche.......................	1683	William Spottiswoode...................	1878
Samuel Pepys..........................	1684	Thomas Henry Huxley..................	1883
Earl of Carbery........................	1686	Sir George Stokes, Bt..................	1885
Earl of Pembroke......................	1689	Lord Kelvin...........................	1890
Sir Robert Southwell..................	1690	Lord Lister...........................	1895
Earl of Halifax........................	1695	Sir William Huggins	1900
Lord Somers...........................	1698	Lord Rayleigh.........................	1905
Sir Isaac Newton......................	1703	Sir Archibald Geikie...................	1908
Sir Hans Sloane, Bt....................	1727	Sir William Crookes...................	1913
Martin Folkes.........................	1741	Sir Joseph John Thomson...............	1915
Earl of Macclesfield...................	1752	Sir Charles Scott Sherrington...........	1920
Earl of Morton........................	1764	Lord Rutherford.......................	1925
Sir James Burrow......................	1768	Sir Frederick Gowland Hopkins.........	1930
James West............................	1768	Sir William Henry Bragg................	1935
Sir John Pringle, Bt...................	1772	Sir Henry Hallett Dale.................	1940
Sir Joseph Banks, Bt...................	1778	Sir Robert Robinson...................	1945
William Hyde Wollaston...............	1820	Lord Adrian...........................	1950
Sir Humphry Davy, Bt.................	1820	Sir Cyril Hinshelwood.................	1955
Davies Gilbert........................	1827	Lord Florey...........................	1960
The Duke of Sussex....................	1830	Lord Blackett..........................	1965
Marquess of Northampton..............	1838	Sir Alan Hodgkin......................	1970
Earl of Rosse..........................	1848		

Principal British and Irish Societies and Institutions

THE ROYAL ACADEMY OF ARTS (1768), Burlington House, W.1.—*President*, Sir Thomas Monnington (1966); *Keeper*, Peter Greenham, R.A.; *Treas.*, The Lord Holford, R.A.; *Sec.*, Sidney C. Hutchison, M.V.O., F.S.A.; *Reg.*, K. J. Tanner.

Royal Academicians

1972 Adams, Norman, C.B.E.
1963 Aldridge, John
1970 Ardizzone, Edward, C.B.E.
1955 Bawden, Edward, C.B.E.
1975 Blamey, Norman
1975 Bowey, Miss Olwyn
1971 Bratby, John R.
1937‡Brockhurst, G. L.
1972 Brown, Ralph
1955 Buhler, Robert
1962*Burn, Rodney J.
1972 Butler, James
1970 Casson, Sir Hugh
1975 Brown, H. T. Cadbury-, O.B.E.
1973 Clatworthy, Robert
1972 Coker, Peter
1972 Cooke, Miss Jean
1938 Cowern, Raymond T.
1974 Cuming, Frederick
1969 de Grey, Roger
1955 Dring, William
1968 Dunstan, Bernard
1953 Eurich, Richard
1974 Fell, Miss Sheila
1954 Fitton, James
1942‡Frampton, Meredith
1965 Freeth, H. Andrew
1972*Fry, E. Maxwell, C.B.E.
1969 Gibberd, Sir Frederick, C.B.E.
1972 Gore, Frederick
1960 Greenham, Peter G.
1970 Hayes, Colin
1961 Hepple, Norman

1971 Hermes, Miss Gertrude
1967 Hillier, Tristram
1968 Holford, Lord
1965*Jones, Allan Gwynne, D.S.O.
1973 Jones Ivor Roberts
1974 Kneale, Bryan
1962*Lowry, L. S.
1963 McFall, David
1955 Machin, Arnold, O.B.E.
1933*McMillan, W., C.V.O.
1973 MacTaggart, Sir William
1973 Middleditch, Edward
1938 Monnington, Sir Thomas
1951*Nash, John, C.B.E.
1967*Nimptsch, Uli
1953*Pitchforth, R. V.
1966*Roberts, William
1969 Rosoman, Leonard
1961 Sanders, Christopher C.
1972 Sheppard, Richard, C.B.E.
1963*Sisson, Marshall A., C.V.O., C.B.E.
1959 Skeaping, John R
1969 Soukop, Willi
1954 Spear, Ruskin
1960 Spence, Sir Basil, O.M., O.B.E., T.D.
1945*Thomson, A. R.
1954 Tunnicliffe, C. F.
1965 Ward, John
1965 Weight, Carel, C.B.E.
1974 Williams, Kyffin
1945*Woodford, James, O.B.E.
1972*Wolfe, Edward

Associates

1971 Blackadder, Miss Elizabeth V.
1974 Blake, Peter
1971 Blow, Miss Sandra
1974 Bowyer, William
1974 Camp, Jeffrey
1975 Chamberlin, Peter
1970 Clarke, Geoffrey
1970 Dickson, Miss Jennifer
1975 Fraser, Donald Hamilton

1971 Frink, Miss Elizabeth, C.B.E.
1974 Goldfinger, Ernö
1971 Green, Anthony
1974 Harpley, Sydney
1974 Hogarth, Paul
1975 Levene, Ben
1972 Paolozzi, Eduardo
1973 Phillipson, Robin
1972 Powell, Sir Philip, O.B.E.
1975 Stephenson, Ian
1972 Swanwick, Miss Betty
1973 Tindle, David

Former Presidents of the Royal Academy

Sir J. Reynolds, 1768	Sir A. Webb, 1919
Benjamin West, 1792	Sir F. Dicksee, 1924
James Wyatt, 1805	Sir W. Llewellyn, 1928
Benjamin West, 1806	Sir E. Lutyens, 1938
Sir T. Lawrence, 1820	Sir A. J. Munnings, 1944
Sir M. A. Shee, 1830	
Sir C. Eastlake, 1850	Sir G. F. Kelly, 1949
Sir F. Grant, 1866	Sir A. E. Richardson, 1954
Lord Leighton, 1878	
Sir J. Millais, 1896	Sir C. Wheeler, 1956
Sir E. Poynter, 1896	

ROYAL CAMBRIAN ACADEMY OF ART (1881), Plas Mawr, Conway.—*Pres.*, K. Williams, R.A.; *Hon. Sec.*, J. R. Webster; *Curator and Sec.*, L. H. S. Mercer.

THE ROYAL SCOTTISH ACADEMY (1826), Princes Street, Edinburgh—*Pres.*, R. Philipson, R.S.A.; *Sec.*, E. Gordon, R.S.A.; *Treas.*, J. Cumming, R.S.A.; *Librarian*, J. Houston, R.S.A.; *Asst. Sec.*, J. Marshall.

Hon. Retired Academicians:
1937 Cursiter, Stanley, C.B.E.
1939 McGlashan, Arch. A.
1946 Thomson, Adam B., O.B.E.
1964 Miller, James

Royal Scottish Academicians

1958 Armour, Mrs. Mary
1966 Armour, William
1972 Blackadder, Elizabeth
1971 Cameron, Gordon S.
1962 Coia, J. A., C.B.E.
1974 Collins, Peter
1956 Crawford, H. Adam
1974 Crosbie, William
1970 Cumming, James
1962 Donaldson, David A.
1956 Fleming, Ian
1967 Gordon, Esmé
1973 Henderson, Ann
1972 Houston, John
1966 Johnston, Ninian

1956 Kininmonth, Sir William
1973 Littlejohn, William
1957 Lorimer, Hew
1971 McClure, David
1946 MacDougall, Leslie Graham
1948 MacTaggart, Sir William
1972 Michie, David
1963 Morrocco, Alberto
1957 Patrick, J. McIntosh
1966 Peploe, Denis
1962 Philipson, Robin
1937 Schotz, Benno
1970 Sutherland, Scott
1975 Wheeler, H. Anthony, O.B.E.

Associates

Baillie, W. J. L.	Malcolm, Ellen
Balmer, Barbara	Morris, James
Bone, W. Drummond	Morrison, James
Brown, Neil Dallas	Morrocco, Leon
Buchan, Dennis	Reeves, Philip
Butler, Vincent	Reiach, Alan, O.B.E.
Campbell, A. Buchanan	Richards John
Campbell, Alex.	Robertson, James
Dick, Miss Alix	Robertson, R. Ross
Dods, Andrew	Scott, William
Donald, George	Shanks, Duncan F.
Evans, David	Smith, Ian McKenzie
Fraser, Alexander	Snowdon, Michael
Glover, John Hardie, O.B.E.	Steedman, Robert R.
Johnstone, Miss Dorothy	Stewart, S. Birnie
Johnstone, John	Thomson, Sinclair
Knox, John	Walker, Frances
	Whiston, Peter
	Womersley, Peter

Hon. Retired Associates, Miss Elizabeth Dempster; J. H. Clark. *Non-Resident Associates*, Charles Pulsford; Sir Basil Spence, O.M., O.B.E., T.D., R.A.

---

*Senior Academician.
‡ Honorary Retired Academician.

ROYAL IRISH ACADEMY (1786), 19 Dawson Street, Dublin.—*Pres.*, D. W. Greene; *Treas.*, P. Lynch; *Sec.*, T. Walsh, Ph.D., D.SC.

ABBEYFIELD SOCIETY, 35A High Street, Potters Bar, Herts.—Provides small households for lonely elderly people.—*Gen. Sec.*, D. A. L. Charles

ACCOUNTANTS, INSTITUTE OF CHARTERED, in England and Wales (1880), Chartered Accountants' Hall, Moorgate Place, E.C.2.—*Pres.* (1975–76), J. P. Grenside; *Secretary*, J. P. Hough.

ACCOUNTANTS AND AUDITORS, BRITISH ASSOCIATION OF (1923), Stamford House, W.4.—*Sec.*, G. F. Garrad.

ACCOUNTANTS, ASSOCIATION OF CERTIFIED (1904), 22 Bedford Square, W.C.1.—*Pres.*, H. Hill; *Sec.*, R. A. Dudman.

ACCOUNTANTS OF SCOTLAND, THE INSTITUTE OF CHARTERED (1854), 27 Queen Street, Edinburgh 2.—*Pres.*, Prof. D. Flint; *Sec.*, E. H. V. McDougall.

ACCOUNTANTS IN IRELAND, INSTITUTE OF CHARTERED (1888), 7 Fitzwilliam Place, Dublin 2, and 11 Donegall Square, South, Belfast.—*Dir.*, R. F. Hussey.

ACCOUNTANTS, SOCIETY OF COMPANY AND COMMERCIAL (1974), 11 Portland Road, Edgbaston, Birmingham.—*Exec. Dir.*, J. H. Tresman.

ACTORS' BENEVOLENT FUND (1882), 6 Adam Street, W.C.2.—*Sec.*, Miss A. G. Marks.

ACTORS' CHARITABLE TRUST (incorporating DENVILLE HALL), Gloucester House, 19 Charing Cross Road, W.C.2.—Assists children of theatrical parentage who are in need; home for elderly and infirm actors and actresses.—*Pres.*, The Lord Olivier; *Admin. Sec.*, Miss M. M. Brisley.

ACTORS' CHURCH UNION (1899), St. Paul's Church, Bedford Street, Covent Garden, W.C.2.—*Senior Chaplain*, Rev. J. Hester.

ACTUARIES IN SCOTLAND, THE FACULTY OF (1856), Hall and Library, 23 St. Andrew Square, Edinburgh.—*Sec.*, W. W. Mair.

ACTUARIES, INSTITUTE OF (1848), Staple Inn Hall, W.C.1.—*Pres.*, G. V. Bayley; *Hon. Secs.* M. H. Field: F. B. Corby.

ADDICTION (TO ALCOHOL AND OTHER DRUGS), SOCIETY FOR THE STUDY OF (1884).—*Sec.*, N. H. Rathod, c/o 1 Wimpole St., W.1.

ADDITIONAL CURATES SOCIETY; HOME MISSIONS OF CHURCH OF ENGLAND AND THE CHURCH IN WALES (1837), St Mark's Church House, 264a Washwood Heath Road, Birmingham.—*Sec.*, Rev. A. J. Prescott.

ADMINISTRATIVE MANAGEMENT, INSTITUTE OF (1915), 205 High Street, Beckenham, Kent.—*Sec.*, J. L. Cousins.

ADMINISTRATIVE ACCOUNTING, INSTITUTE OF (1916), Walter House, 418–422 Strand, W.C.2.—*Sec.-Gen.*, D. W. Bradley.

ADVERTISING ASSOCIATION, Abford House, 15 Wilton Road, S.W.1.—*Director-General*, J. S. Williams, O.B.E.; *Sec.*, R. C. G. Hunt-Taylor.

ADVERTISING BENEVOLENT SOCIETY, NATIONAL (1913), 3 Crawford Place, W.1.—*Gen. Sec.*, Miss R. Bell.

ADVERTISING, INSTITUTE OF PRACTITIONERS IN, 44 Belgrave Square, S.W.1.—*Dir.*, J. P. O'Connor.

ADVERTISEMENT MANAGEMENT ASSOCIATION, Incorporated (founded 1932, inc. 1958), 5 Claremont Park Road, Esher, Surrey.—*Exec. Offr.*, D. St. C. McBride.

AERONAUTICAL SOCIETY, ROYAL (1866) (incorporating the Institution of Aeronautical Engineers and the Helicopter Association of Great Britain), 4 Hamilton Place, W.1.—*Pres.*, (1965–76) Air

Marshal Sir Charles Pringle, K.B.E.; *Sec.*, E. M. J. Schaffter.

AFRICAN INSTITUTE, INTERNATIONAL (1926), 210 High Holborn, W.C.1—*Sec.* B. Wheeler.

AFRICAN MEDICAL AND RESEARCH FOUNDATION, 9 Upper Grosvenor Street, W.1.—*Administrator*, Mrs E. Young.

AGED PILGRIMS' FRIEND SOCIETY (1807), 175 Tower Bridge Road, S.E.1.—*Sec.*, G. Reid.

AGED POOR SOCIETY (1708) AND ST. JOSEPH'S HOUSE, 39 Eccleston Square, S.W.1.—*Sec.*, Major A. R. W. Shipley.

AGRICULTURAL BENEVOLENT INSTITUTION, ROYAL, Vincent House, Vincent Square, S.W.1.—*Hon. Treas.*, J. D. S. Ainscow; *Sec.*, Cdr. O. C. Wright.

AGRICULTURAL BENEVOLENT INSTITUTION, ROYAL SCOTTISH (1897), 8 Dublin Street, Edinburgh.—*Sec.*, K. M. Campbell, W.S.

AGRICULTURAL BOTANY, NATIONAL INSTITUTE OF (1919), Huntingdon Road, Cambridge.—*Director*, P. S. Wellington, D.S.C., Ph.D.; *Sec.*, K. Batchelor.

AGRICULTURAL ENGINEERS ASSOCIATION, LIMITED (1877), 6 Buckingham Gate, S.W.1.—*Dir.-Gen.*, F. D. Swift, O.B.E.

AGRICULTURAL SOCIETY, EAST OF ENGLAND, East of England Showground, Peterborough.—*Sec.*, R. W. Bird.

AGRICULTURAL SOCIETY, GLASGOW (1826).—*Sec.*, S. Gilmour, 24 Beresford Terrace, Ayr.

AGRICULTURAL SOCIETY, ROYAL ULSTER (1826), The King's Hall, Balmoral, Belfast.—*Sec.*, J. T. Kernohan, O.B.E.

AGRICULTURAL SOCIETY OF THE COMMONWEALTH, ROYAL (1957).—*Hon. Sec.*, F. R. Francis, M.B.E., Robarts House, Rossmore Road, N.W.1.

AGRICULTURE, ASSOCIATION OF (1947), 78 Buckingham Gate, S.W.1.—*Gen. Sec.*, Miss J. Bostock.

AIRBROKERS ASSOCIATION (1949), 25 Bury Street, E.C.3.—*Sec.*, G. E. K. Ireland.

AIRCRAFT NOISE, BRITISH ASSOCIATION FOR THE CONTROL OF, 30 Fleet Street, E.C.4.

AIR LEAGUE, THE (1909), 142 Sloane Street, S.W.1. —*Dir.*, J. Motum.

ALEXANDRA ROSE DAY FUND, 1 Castelnau, Barnes, S.W.13.—*Organizer*, Mrs. E. Day.

ALMSHOUSES, NATIONAL ASSOCIATION OF, Billingbear Lodge, Wokingham, Berks.—*Gen. Sec.*, L. A. Hackett, O.B.E.

AMATEUR CINEMATOGRAPHERS, INSTITUTE OF (1932), 63 Woodfield Lane, Ashtead, Surrey.—*Admin. Sec.*, Mrs. B. Wood.

ANAESTHETISTS OF GREAT BRITAIN AND IRELAND, ASSOCIATION OF (1932). Room 475, Tavistock House South, Tavistock Square, W.C.1.

ANCIENT BUILDINGS, SOCIETY FOR THE PROTECTION OF (1877), 55 Great Ormond Street, W.C.1.—*Sec.*, Mrs. M. Dance, M.B.E.

ANCIENT MONUMENTS SOCIETY (1924).—*Sec.*, Mrs. J. Jenkins, 33 Ladbroke Square, W.11.

ANGLO-ARAB ASSOCIATION (1961), 33 Cavendish Square, W.1.

ANGLO-BELGIAN UNION (1918), 6 Belgrave Square, S.W.1.—*Hon. Sec.*, Mrs. M. Taylor.

ANGLO-BRAZILIAN SOCIETY (1943), 2 Belgrave Square, S.W.1.—*Sec.*, Mrs. E. C. Skinner.

ANGLO-DANISH SOCIETY (1924), 7 St. Helen's Place, Bishopsgate, E.C.3.—*Chairman*, Sir Robert Bellinger, G.B.E.

ANGLO-NORSE SOCIETY, 25 Belgrave Square, S.W.1.

ANGLO-SWEDISH SOCIETY, 4 Staple Inn, High Holborn, W.C.1.

ANGLO-THAI SOCIETY (1962).—*Hon. Sec.*, Miss B. J. Crewe, 95 Kennington Park Road, S.E.11.

ANIMAL HEALTH TRUST, 24 Portland Place, W.1.—*Chief Exec. Offr.*, Brig. J. Clabby, C.B.E., M.R.C.V.S.

ANTHROPOLOGICAL INSTITUTE, ROYAL (1843); 36 Craven Street, W.C.2.—*Hon. Sec.*, Prof. Lucy Mair.

ANTHROPOSOPHICAL SOCIETY IN GREAT BRITAIN, Rudolf Steiner House, 35 Park Road, N.W.1.

ANTIQUARIES, SOCIETY OF (1717), Burlington House, W.1.—*Pres.*, A. J. Taylor; *Treas.*, R. M. Robbins; *Director*, Prof. J. D. Evans; *Sec.*, I. H. Longworth.

ANTIQUARIES OF SCOTLAND, SOCIETY OF (1780), National Museum of Antiquities of Scotland, Queen Street, Edinburgh.—*Sec.*, B. C. Skinner; *Treas.*, J. A. Donaldson.

ANTI-SLAVERY SOCIETY FOR THE PROTECTION OF HUMAN RIGHTS (1839), 60 Weymouth Street, W.1.—*Sec.*, Col. J. R. P. Montgomery, M.C.

ANTI-VIVISECTION: BRITISH UNION FOR THE ABOLITION OF VIVISECTION (INC.) (1898), 47 Whitehall, S.W.1.—*Gen. Sec.*, S. Hicks.

ANTI-VIVISECTION SOCIETY, THE NATIONAL (1875), 51 Harley Street, W.1.

ANTI-VIVISECTION SOCIETY, SCOTTISH, 121 West Regent Street, Glasgow.

APOSTLESHIP OF THE SEA (1920). For active seafarers. *National Headquarters.*—Anchor House, 81 Barking Road, E.16.—*Dir.*, Rt. Rev. D. McGuinness.

APOTEHCARIES, SOCIETY OF (1617).—Black Friars Lane, Queen Victoria Street, E.C.4.—*Clerk and Registrar*, E. Busby, M.B.E.

ARBITRATORS, THE INSTITUTE OF (1915), 16 Park Crescent, W.1.—*Sec.*, B. W. Vigrass, O.B.E.

ARCHÆOLOGICAL ASSOCIATION, BRITISH (1843), 61 Old Park Ridings, Winchmore Hill, N.21.—*Hon. Asst. Treas.*, Miss I. B. McClure.

ARCHÆOLOGICAL ASSOCIATION, CAMBRIAN (1846).—*President* (1975–76) Dr H. N. Savory, F.S.A.; *Gen. Sec.*, H. D. Rees, Llyswen, Bow Street, Dyfed.

ARCHÆOLOGICAL INSTITUTE, ROYAL (1843).—*Hon. Sec.*, S. D. T. Spittle, M.A., F.S.A., A.R.I.B.A.; *Asst. Sec.*, Miss W. E. Phillips, 304 Addison House, Grove End Road, N.W.8.

ARCHÆOLOGY, COUNCIL FOR BRITISH (1944), 7 Marylebone Road, N.W.1.—*President*, N. Thomas; *Hon. Sec.*, P. J. Fowler, F.S.A.; *Dir.*, H. F. Cleere, F.S.A.

ARCHITECTS, THE ROYAL INSTITUTE OF BRITISH (1834), 66 Portland Place, W.1.—*President*, E. Lyons; *Sec.*, P. K. Harrison.

ARCHITECTS REGISTRATION COUNCIL OF THE UNITED KINGDOM, 73 Hallam Street, W.1.—*Chairman*, D. Waterhouse; *Registrar*, Mrs. N. Dawson, M.B.E.

ARCHITECTS AND SURVEYORS, INCORPORATED ASSOCIATION OF (1925), 29 Belgrave Square, S.W.1.—*Pres.*, F. Didsbury; *Sec.*, J. H. Callingham.

ARCHITECTS AND SURVEYORS, THE FACULTY OF, LTD: (incorporating The Institute of Registered Architects Ltd), 68 Gloucester Place, W.1.—*Sec.*, W. O. Jones.

ARCHITECTS BENEVOLENT SOCIETY (1850), 66 Portland Place, W.1.—*Hon. Sec.*, Howard Lobb, C.B.E.

ARCHITECTS IN SCOTLAND, ROYAL INCORPORATION OF (1922), 15 Rutland Square, Edinburgh.—*Sec. and Treas.*, P. G. D. Clark.

ARCHITECTURAL ASSOCIATION (INC.) (1847), 34–36 Bedford Square, W.C.1.—*Pres.*, R. Andrews, M.B.E.; *Sec.* E. Le Maistre.

ARCHIVISTS, SOCIETY OF (1946), *Hon. Sec.*, P. Walne, County Hall, Hertford.

AREA MEDICAL OFFICERS, ASSOCIATION OF (1974).—*Hon. Sec.*, Dr P. C. Moore, The Limes, Belle Vue Road, Shrewsbury, Salop.

ARLIS (Art Libraries Society) (1969).—*Sec.*, Miss F. Martin, Bath Academy of Art Library, Corsham, Wilts.

ARMY BENEVOLENT FUND (1944), "G" Block, Duke of York's H.Q., Chelsea, S.W.3.—*Controller*, Maj.-Gen. D. N. H. Tyacke, C.B., O.B.E.

ARMY CADET FORCE ASSOCIATION (1930), 58 Buckingham Gate, S.W.1.—*Sec.*, W. F. L. Newcombe, O.B.E., T.D.

ARMY HISTORICAL RESEARCH, SOCIETY FOR (1921). *Hon. Sec.*, Maj. B. Mollo, T.D., c/o The Library, Old War Office Building, Whitehall, S.W.1.

ART-COLLECTIONS FUND, NATIONAL (1903), Hertford House, Manchester Square, W.1.—*Sec.*, J. Christian, F.S.A.

ART EDUCATION, NATIONAL SOCIETY FOR (1888), 3rd Floor, Champness Hall, Drake Street, Rochdale, Lancs.—*Gen. Sec.*, G. F. Williams.

ART WORKERS GUILD (1884), 6 Queen Square, Bloomsbury, W.C.1.—*Master*, R. Enthoven; *Sec.* R. Murry.

ARTHRITIS AND RHEUMATISM COUNCIL FOR RESEARCH, Faraday House, 8–10 Charing Cross Road, W.C.2.—*Gen. Sec.*, M. C. G. Andrews.

ARTISTS' GENERAL BENEVOLENT INSTITUTION (1814) AND ARTISTS' ORPHAN FUND (1871), Burlington House, Piccadilly, W.1.—*Sec.*, Miss D. P. Laidman.

ARTS COUNCIL OF GREAT BRITAIN, 105 Piccadilly, W.1.—*Chairman*, The Lord Gibson; *Secretary-General*, R. Shaw.

ASLIB (1924). (Formerly Association of Special Libraries and Information Bureaux), 3 Belgrave Square, S.W.1.—*Director*, L. Wilson, M.A.

ASSISTANT MASTERS ASSOCIATION, 29 Gordon Square, W.C.1.—*Sec.*, A. W. S. Hutchings, C.B.E., M.A.

ASSISTANT MISTRESSES, ASSOCIATION OF, 29 Gordon Square, W.C.1.—*Sec.*, Miss S. D. Wood, O.B.E.

ASTHMA RESEARCH COUNCIL, 12 Pembridge Square, W.2.—*Chairman*, D. M. Walters, M.B.E., M.P.

ASTRONOMICAL ASSOCIATION, BRITISH.—*Office*, Burlington House, Piccadilly, W.1. Meetings at 23 Savile Row, W.1.—*President*, H. G. Miles; *Sec.*, Mrs. G. E. Stone; *Asst. Sec.*, J. L. White.

ASTRONOMICAL SOCIETY, ROYAL (Incorporated (1820), Burlington House, W.1.—*Pres.*, Prof. F. G. Smith, F.R.S.; *Secs.*, Dr J. A. Hudson; Prof. R. J. Tayler; Dr. J. R. Shakeshaft.

A.T.S. and W.R.A.C. BENEVOLENT FUNDS (1964), Queen Elizabeth Park, Guildford, Surrey.—*Sec.*, Mrs E. Laurence-Smith.

AUDIT BUREAU OF CIRCULATIONS LTD., 19 Dunraven Street, W.1.—*Dir.*, K. Derbyshire.

AUTHORS, PLAYWRIGHTS AHD COMPOSERS, INCORPORATED SOCIETY OF, 84 Drayton Gardens, S.W.10.—*Secs.*, G. D. Astley; V. Bonham-Carter; Phillippa MacLiesh.

AUTOMOBILE ASSOCIATION (1905), Fanum House, Basingstoke, Hants.—*Chairman*, The Lord Erroll of Hale, P.C.; *Dir.-Gen.*, A. C. Durie, C.B.E.; *Sec.*, W. Lynch.

AVICULTURAL SOCIETY (1894).—*Hon. Sec.*, H. J. Horswell, 20 Bourdon Street, W.1.

AYRSHIRE CATTLE SOCIETY OF GREAT BRITAIN AND IRELAND (1877), 1 Racecourse Road, Ayr.—*Gen. Sec.*, J. Lawson.

BALTIC EXCHANGE (1903), St. Mary Axe, E.C.3.—*Chairman*, B. H. F. Fehr; *Sec.*, D. J. Walker.

BANKERS, THE INSTITUTE OF (1879), 10 Lombard Street, E.C.3.—*Pres.*, Sir John Prideaux, O.B.E.; *Sec.-Gen.*, G. H. Dix.

BANKERS IN SCOTLAND, THE INSTITUTE OF (1875), 20 Rutland Square, Edinburgh.—*Sec.* W. W. Jamieson.

BAPTIST MISSIONARY SOCIETY (1792), 93–97 Gloucester Place, W.1.—*Secs.*, Rev. A. S. Clement, B.A., B.D. (*Home*); Rev. E. G. T. Madge, B.A., B.D. (*Overseas*).

(DR.) BARNARDO'S (1866), *Head Offices:* Tanner's Lane, Barkingside, Essex. More than 217,000 children have been helped. 7,000 boys and girls are helped in residential and non-residential settings.

BARONETAGE, STANDING COUNCIL OF THE (1898), Kent House, Telegraph Street, E.C.2.—*Sec. and Regr.*, P. L. Forwood.

BARRISTERS' BENEVOLENT ASSOCIATION (1873), 3 Raymond Buildings, Grays Inn, W.C.1.—*Hon. Treasurers*, M. Nolan, Q.C.; P. Medd, Q.C.; *Sec.*, Miss K. M. Hopper.

BEIT MEMORIAL FELLOWSHIPS (for Medical Research) (1909).—*Sec.*, Prof. W. G. Spector, Pathology Dept., St. Bartholomew's Hospital, E.C.1.

BIBLE AND MEDICAL MISSIONARY FELLOWSHIP (formerly Zenana Bible and Medical Mission) (1852), 352 Kennington Road, S.E.11.—*Gen. Sec.*, A. M. S. Pont.

BIBLE CHURCHMEN'S MISSIONARY SOCIETY (1922), 157 Waterloo Road, S.E.1.—*Gen. Sec.*, Rev. Canon A. S. Neech.

BIBLE SOCIETY, BRITISH AND FOREIGN (1804), 146 Queen Victoria Street, E.C.4. The Bible has been published in whole or in part in over 1,520 languages and dialects. Bible Societies distribute 250,000,000 copies a year.

BIBLIOGRAPHICAL SOCIETY (1892), c/o British Academy, Burlington House, W.1.—*Hon. Sec.*, R. J. Roberts.

BIBLIOGRAPHICAL SOCIETY, EDINBURGH (1890), c/o National Library of Scotland, Edinburgh, 1.—*Hon. Sec.*, J. R. Seaton.

BIOCHEMICAL SOCIETY, THE (1911), 7 Warwick Court, W.C.1.—*Sec.*, A. I. P. Henton.

BIOLOGICAL ENGINEERING SOCIETY.—*Hon. Sec.*, K. Copeland, Biophysics Dept., Faculty of Medical Sciences, University College London, Gower Street, W.C.1.

BIOLOGISTS, ASSOCIATION OF APPLIED.—*Hon. Gen. Sec.*, A. J. Cooper, Glasshouse Crops Research Institute, Rustington, Littlehampton, Sussex.

BIOLOGY, INSTITUTE OF, 41 Queen's Gate, S.W.7.—*Pres.*, Prof. J. Heslop-Harrison, F.R.S.; *Gen. Sec.*, D. J. B. Copp.

BIRD PRESERVATION, INTERNATIONAL COUNCIL FOR (BRITISH SECTION), c/o Natural History Museum, Cromwell Road, S.W.7.—*Hon. Sec.*, Miss Phyllis Barclay-Smith, C.B.E.

BLIND, GREATER LONDON FUND FOR THE, 2 Wyndham Place, W.1.—*Pres.*, The Lord Mayor of London; *Gen. Sec.*, A. C. Jay, D.S.C.

BLIND, GUIDE DOGS FOR THE, ASSOCIATION, Alexandra House, 113 Uxbridge Road, Ealing, W.5. *Director-Gen.*, A. R. Clark.

BLIND, INCORPORATED ASSOCIATION FOR PROMOTING THE GENERAL WELFARE OF THE (1854), 8–22 Curtain Road, E.C.2.

BLIND, LONDON ASSOCIATION FOR THE (1857), 14–16 Verney Road, S.E.16. A national voluntary organization helping the blind and partially-sighted both in London and country. Training and employment; homes, holiday hotels and hostels; self-contained flats; benevolent and pensions fund.—*Gen. Sec.*, G. W. Guy.

BLIND, ROYAL COMMONWEALTH SOCIETY FOR THE (1950), Commonwealth House, Haywards Heath, Sussex.—*Dir.*, Sir John Wilson, C.B.E.

BLIND, ROYAL NATIONAL INSTITUTE FOR THE (1868), 224 Great Portland Street, W.1.—*Director-General*, E. T. Boulter. Branches of the Institute: *Queen Elizabeth Homes of Recovery, Homes for Blind and Deaf Blind, School of Physiotherapy, Schools for Blind Girls and Boys, School for Shorthand-Typing and Telephony, Sunshine Home Nursery Schools, Braille and Moon Periodicals and Books, Braille Music, Talking Books, Students' Library, Professional, Commercial and Industrial Placement, Vocational Assessment Centre for Blind Adolescents, Apparatus and Appliances, Personal Services, Prevention of Blindness, etc.*

BLIND, NATIONAL LIBRARY FOR THE (1882), 35 Great Smith Street, S.W.1.—Books in embossed and large type are sent free on loan and post free to blind and partially-sighted readers. Stock of volumes, 400,000.—*Director-General*, W. A. Munford, M.B.E., PhD.

BLIND, ROYAL LONDON SOCIETY FOR THE (1838), *Head Office and Workshops*, 105–9 Salusbury Road, Brondesbury, N.W.6; *School*, Dorton House, Seal, nr. Sevenoaks, Kent; *Home Workers' Scheme* and *Residential Clubs.*—*Hon. Sec.*, W. W. Woods.

BLIND, ROYAL NORMAL COLLEGE (1872). Further education for visually-handicapped. Rowton Castle and Albrighton Hall, nr. Shrewsbury.—*Principal*, A. W. Laurie.

BLIND, ROYAL SCHOOL FOR THE INDIGENT (1799), Leatherhead.—*Resident Principal and Chaplain*, Rev. B. G. Bartlett.

BLIND, SOCIETY FOR GRANTING ANNUITIES TO THE POOR ADULT, c/o The Clothworkers' Company, Clothworkers' Hall, Dunster Court, Mincing Lane, E.C.3.

BLIND (LONDON) SPORTS CLUB FOR THE (1932), *Chairman*, R. D. Birrell, Grants, Grants Lane, Limpsfield, Oxted, Surrey.

BLOOD TRANSFUSION. *See* GREATER LONDON RED CROSS BLOOD TRANSFUSION SERVICE.

BLUE CROSS, THE (Incorporating Our Dumb Friends' League) (1897), Animals' Hospital, Hugh Street, Victoria, S.W.1.—*Sec.*, Peter Carpmael.

BODLEIAN, FRIENDS OF THE, Bodleian Library, Oxford.—*Sec.*, D. H. Merry.

BOOK-KEEPERS, INSTITUTE OF (1916), (see under Administrative Accounting, Institute of).

BOOKSELLERS ASSOCIATION OF GREAT BRITAIN AND IRELAND (1895), 154 Buckingham Palace Road, S.W.1.—*Dir.*, G. R. Davies.

BOOK TRADE BENEVOLENT SOCIETY (1967), 19 Bedford Square, W.C.1, formerly the National Book Trade Provident Institution (1962).—*Pres.*, T. Joy, F.R.S.A.; *Hon. Sec.*, R. E. Barker, O.B.E.

BOTANICAL SOCIETY OF THE BRITISH ISLES (1836), c/o Dept. of Botany, British Museum (Natural History), S.W.7.

BOTANICAL SOCIETY OF EDINBURGH, Royal Botanic Garden, Edinburgh.—*Hon. Gen. Sec.*, R. Watling, PhD.

BOY SCOUTS ASSOCIATION, *see* SCOUT ASSOCIATION, THE.

BOYS' BRIGADE, THE (INCORPORATED) (1883), Brigade House, Parsons Green, S.W.6. Membership: British Isles, 162,488; Overseas, 105,671 in 58 countries; World strength, 268,159.—*Sec.*, A. A. J. Hudson.

BOYS' CLUBS, NATIONAL ASSOCIATION OF, INCORPORATED (1925), 17 Bedford Square, W.C.1. Responsible for the development and co-ordination of boys' club work throughout the country, and has affiliated to it, either directly or through local organizations, 1,970 clubs—*Gen. Sec.*, Brig. E. G. B. Davies-Scourfield, C.B.E., M.C.

BOYS' CLUBS, NORTHERN IRELAND ASSOCIATION OF (1940), 28 Bedford Street, Belfast.—*Gen. Sec.*, C. E. Larmour.

BREWING, INSTITUTE OF (1886), 33 Clarges Street, W.1.—*Sec.*, Capt. S. Le H. Lombard-Hobson, C.V.O., O.B.E., R.N.

BRIDEWELL ROYAL HOSPITAL, King Edward's School, Witley, Surrey (1553).—*Treas.*, The Earl of Selborne; *Clerk to the Governors*, Lt.-Col. S. A. Faith.

BRITISH ACADEMY, THE (1901), Burlington House, Piccadilly, W.1.—*President*, Sir Isaiah Berlin, O.M., C.B.E.; *Treas.* Sir Roy Allen, C.B.E.; *Sec.*, D. F. Allen, C.B.; *Foreign Sec.*, Prof. A. G. Dickens, C.M.G.

BRITISH AND FOREIGN SCHOOL SOCIETY (1808). 7 Stone Buildings, Lincoln's Inn, W.C.2.—*Sec.*, G. G. G. Robb.

BRITISH ASSOCIATION FOR THE ADVANCEMENT OF SCIENCE (1831), Fortress House, 23 Savile Row, W.1.—*President*, Sir John Baker, O.B.E., F.R.S.; *Gen. Secs.*, Sir Lincoln Ralphs; Dr. T. Emmerson; Sir Gordon Cox, K.B.E., F.R.S., T.D.; *Gen. Treas.*, Sir Eric Mensforth, C.B.E.; *Sec.* Dr. Magnus Pyke, F.R.S.E.

BRITISH ASSOCIATION FOR EARLY CHILDHOOD EDUCATION (formerly Nursery School Association of Gt. Britain and N. Ireland), Montgomery Hall, Kennington Oval, S.E.11.—*Sec.*, Miss D. E. Warren, O.B.E.

BRITISH ASSOCIATION OF THE HARD OF HEARING.—*Hon. Sec.*, C. H. Mardell, M.B.E., Briarfield, Syke Ings, Iver, Bucks.

BRITISH BEE-KEEPERS' ASSOCIATION (1874), 55 Chipstead Lane, Riverhead, Sevenoaks, Kent.—*Gen. Sec.*, O. Meyer.

BRITISH BOARD OF FILM CENSORS, 3 Soho Square, W.1.—*Sec.*, J. Ferman.

BRITISH COMMONWEALTH EX-SERVICES LEAGUE, 49 Pall Mall, S.W.1.—*Sec.-Gen.*, Air Commodore B. J. R. Roberts.

BRITISH COTTON GROWING ASSOCIATION LTD. (1904), Stanley Hall, Edmund Street, Liverpool.—*Managing Director*, R. Derbyshire.

BRITISH CYCLING FEDERATION (1878), 70 Brompton Road, S.W.3.—*Sec.*, L. Unwin.

BRITISH DENTAL ASSOCIATION (1880), 64 Wimpole Street, W.1.—*Pres.*, R. G. Hunt; *Sec.*, R. B. Allen.

BRITISH DIABETIC ASSOCIATION (1934), 3–6 Alfred Place, W.C.1.—*Sec.-Gen.*, R. Allard.

BRITISH DRIVING SOCIETY, 10 Marley Avenue, New Milton, Hants.—*Sec.*, Mrs. P. Candler.

BRITISH EQUESTRIAN FEDERATION, National Equestrian Centre, Kenilworth, Warwicks.—*Dir.-Gen.*, Maj.-Gen. J. R. Reynolds, C.B., O.B.E.

BRITISH FIELD SPORTS SOCIETY (1930), 26 Caxton Street, S.W.1.—*Sec.*, Lt.-Gen. Sir Richard Goodwin, K.C.B., C.B.E., D.S.O.

BRITISH FILM INSTITUTE (1933), 81 Dean Street, W.1.—*Director*, K. Lucas; *Deputy Dir.*, A. Hill; *Controller, National Film Theatre*, L. Hardcastle.

BRITISH GLIDING ASSOCIATION (1930), affiliated to United Service and Royal Aero Club. Kimberley House, Vaughan Way, Leicester. *Gen. Secs.*, B. Rolfe.

BRITISH GOAT SOCIETY (1879). *Sec.*, Mrs. T. T. F. May, Lion House, Rougham, Bury St. Edmunds, Suffolk.

BRITISH HEART FOUNDATION (1963), 57 Gloucester Place, W.1.—*Sec.*, D. A. Blake, M.B.E.

BRITISH HORSE SOCIETY, National Equestrian Centre, Kenilworth, Warwicks.—*Dir.*, Col. N. F. Grove-White.

BRITISH INDUSTRY, CONFEDERATION OF, 21 Tothill Street, S.W.1.—*Director-General*, W. O. C. Adamson.

BRITISH INSTITUTE OF ARCHÆOLOGY AT ANKARA, c/o British Academy, Burlington House, W.1.—*Hon. Sec.*, A. S. Hall, F.S.A.

BRITISH INSTITUTE OF INTERNATIONAL AND COMPARATIVE LAW, 32 Furnival Street, E.C.4.—*Sec.*, H. H. Marshall, C.M.G.

BRITISH INSTITUTE OF PERSIAN STUDIES (1961), *Asst. Sec.*, Mrs. M. E. Gueritz, 85 Queen's Road, Richmond, Surrey.

BRITISH INSTITUTE OF RADIOLOGY, 32 Welbeck Street, W.1.—*Gen. Sec.*, Miss B. J. Bashford.

BRITISH INSTITUTE OF RECORDED SOUND (1948), 29 Exhibition Road, S.W.7.—*Dir.*, P. Saul.

BRITISH INTERPLANETARY SOCIETY (1933), 12 Bessborough Gardens, S.W.1.—*Exec. Sec.*, L. J. Carter.

BRITISH ISRAEL WORLD FEDERATION (1919), 6 Buckingham Gate, S.W.1.—*Sec.*, H. E. Stough.

BRITISH LEGION, ROYAL. *Headquarters*, Pall Mall, S.W.1. *Pres.*, Gen. Sir Charles Jones, G.C.B., C.B.E., M.C.; *Gen. Sec.*, D. E. Coffer, C.B.E.—*British Legion Poppy Fund*, £1,950,000 raised on Poppy Day, 1973, exclusive of Scotland. Grand total for years 1921 to 1973. £45,325,000.

BRITISH LEGION SCOTLAND, ROYAL, Haig House, 23 Drumsheugh Gardens, Edinburgh.—*Gen. Sec.*, Brig. F. H. Coutts, C.B.E.

BRITISH MEDICAL ASSOCIATION (1832), B.M.A. House, Tavistock Square, W.C.1.—*President*, Sir John Stallworthy, F.R.C.S.; *Sec.* D. P. Stevenson, C.B.E.

BRITISH MUSIC INFORMATION CENTRE, 10 Stratford Place, W.1.—*Sec.*, Miss E. Yeoman.

BRITISH NATURALISTS' ASSOCIATION (1905).—*Hon. Sec.*, Mrs. L. K. Butcher, Willowfield, Boyneswood Road, Four Marks, Alton, Hants.

BRITISH NUTRITION FOUNDATION (1967), 93 Albert Embankment, S.E.1.—*Dir. Gen.* Miss D. Hollingsworth, O.B.E.

BRITISH OPTICAL ASSOCIATION, THE, 65 Brook Street, W.1.—*Sec.*, P. A. Smith.

BRITISH POULTRY BREEDERS AND HATCHERIES ASSOCIATION LTD., 52–54 High Holborn, W.C.1.—*Gen. Sec.*, T. J. Aley.

BRITISH PROPERTY FEDERATION (formerly National Association of Property Owners), 35 Catherine Place, S.W.1; *Sec.*, C. E. F. Gough.

BRITISH RECORDS ASSOCIATION (1932), The Charterhouse, Charterhouse Square, E.C.1.—*Pres.*, The Master of the Rolls; *Hon. Sec.*, A. J. Farrington.

BRITISH RECORD SOCIETY (1887).—*Hon. Sec.*, P. Spufford, Dept. of History, The University, Keele, Staffs.

BRITISH RED CROSS SOCIETY (1870).—*National Headquarters*, 9 Grosvenor Crescent, S.W.1.—*Dir.-Gen.*, D. E. Barson (*acting*).

BRITISH RHEUMATISM AND ARTHRITIS ASSOCIATION (1947), 1 Devonshire Place, W.1.

BRITISH SCHOOL AT ATHENS—*Chairman of the Managing Committee*, R. A. Higgins, F.B.A., F.S.A.; *Director*, H. W. Catling, D. Phil.; *Sec.*, Mrs. S. Bicknell, 31–34 Gordon Square, W.C.1.

BRITISH SCHOOL AT ROME (1901).—*Chairman of Executive Committee*, A. G. Shepherd Fidler, C.B.E.; *Director*, D. B. Whitehouse, F.B.A.; *Hon. Sec.*, C. A. H. James, 1 Lowther Gardens, Exhibition Road, S.W.7.

BRITISH SCHOOL OF ARCHÆOLOGY IN JERUSALEM (1919), 2 Hinde Mews, Marylebone Lane, W.1.—*Pres.*, Sir Mortimer Wheeler, C.H., C.I.E., M.C.; *Dir.*, Mrs. C-M. Bennett.

BRITISH SEAMEN'S BOYS' HOME, Rock House, Brixham.—*Supt.*, Capt. W. G. Parry, R.N.

BRITISH SHIP ADOPTION SOCIETY (1936), 207 Balham High Road, S.W.1.—*Sec.* R. R. Ryder, M.B.E.

BRITISH SHIPPING, GENERAL COUNCIL OF (1975), 30–32 St. Mary Axe, E.C.3.—*Pres.* (1975–76) F. B. Bolton, M.C.; *Dir.-Gen.*, J.-N. Wood, O.B.E.; A. Watson, O.B.E.

BRITISH SOCIAL BIOLOGY COUNCIL, 69 Eccleston Square, S.W.1.—*Sec.*, H. M. Thomas.

BRITISH STANDARDS INSTITUTION, 2 Park Street, W.1.—*Dir.-Gen.*, G. B. R. Feilden, C.B.E., F.R.S.

BRITISH THEATRE ASSOCIATION (*formerly* British Drama League) (1919), 9-10 Fitzroy Square, W.1.—*Dir.*, W. Lucas.

BRITISH THORACIC AND TUBERCULOSIS ASSOCIATION 30 Britten Street, S.W.3. *Admin. Sec.*, A. N. Hutchins.

BRITISH UNITED PROVIDENT ASSOCIATION LIMITED Provident House, 24 Essex Street, W.C.2.— *Chief Exec.*, D. V. Damerell.

BRITISH VETERINARY ASSOCIATION (1881), 7 Mansfield Street, W.1.—*Sec.*, P. B. Turner, M.A.

BUILDING, INSTITUTE OF (1834), Englemere, King's Ride, Ascot, Berks.—*Exec. Dir.*, D. A. Neale, O.B.E., M.C.

BUILDING SOCIETIES ASSOCIATION, 14 Park Street, W.1.—*Sec.-Gen.*, N. E. Griggs.

BUILDINGS SOCIETIES INSTITUTE, Fanhams Hall, Ware, Hertfordshire.—*Sec.*, D. J. Keenan.

BULWER LYTTON CIRCLE, 125 Markyate Road, Dagenham, Essex.—*Sec.* E. F. J. Ford.

BUSINESS AND PROFESSIONAL WOMEN'S CLUBS OF GREAT BRITAIN AND NORTHERN IRELAND, NATIONAL FEDERATION OF (1938), 54 Bloomsbury Street, W.C.1.—*Gen. Sec.*, Miss E. M. Young.

BUSINESS ARCHIVES COUNCIL, 37-45 Tooley Street, S.E.1.—*Hon. Sec.*, Dr. D. Avery.

BUTCHERS' CHARITABLE INSTITUTION (1828).—*Sec.*, J. A. Fordyce, 61 West Smithfield, E.C.1.

BUYERS, THE INSTITUTION OF (1974) (see Sales Engineers).

CALOUSTE GULBENKIAN FOUNDATION, LISBON, United Kingdom and British Commonwealth Branch (1956), 98 Portland Place, W.1.—*Dir.*, P. Brinson.

CAMBRIDGE FUND AND WILLIAM WOODMAN CHARITY. (Applicants must be ex-soldiers who served as Regulars before the 1914-18 War.) *Address*, The Deputy Under-Secretary of State (C.2(AD)), Ministry of Defence, Old War Office Building, Whitehall, S.W.1.

CAMBRIDGE PRESERVATION SOCIETY (1929).—*Chairman*, S. C. Bowles; *Sec.*, N. Clark, Gatehouse Lodge, Gog Magog Hills, Babraham, Cambridge.

CAMERA CLUB (1885). 8 Great Newport Street, W.C.2.—*Sec.*, F. J. Reid.

CANADA UNITED KINGDOM CHAMBER OF COMMERCE (1921), British Columbia House, 1-3 Lower Regent Street, S.W.1.—*Pres.*, J. E. Marks, C.B.E.; *Sec. Gen.*, K. R. S. Leadlay.

CANCER RESEARCH CAMPAIGN (Brit. Empire Cancer Campaign for Research), 2 Carlton House Terrace, S.W.1.—For research into the disease of cancer in all its forms.—*Sec. Gen.*, Brig. K. D. Gribbin, M.B.E.

CANCER COUNCIL, BRITISH (1968).—*Sec.*, Dr. Graham Bennette, 19 St. Michael's Road, S.W.9.

CANCER RELIEF, NATIONAL SOCIETY FOR (1911), Michael Sobell House, 30 Dorset Square, N.W.1. —*Sec.* Miss S. Porter.

CANCER RESEARCH FUND, IMPERIAL (1902), Lincoln's Inn Fields, W.C.2. Research into causes, prevention, treatment and cure of all forms of cancer; in own laboratories and extra-mural units.—*Sec.*, A. B. L. Clarke, O.B.E.

CANCER RESEARCH, INSTITUTE OF: ROYAL CANCER HOSPITAL (1911), Fulham Road, S.W.3.—*Sec.*, N. P. Hadow, O.B.E.

CARAVAN MISSION TO VILLAGE CHILDREN (1893), 47 Marylebone Lane, W.1.—*Sec.*, H. P. M. Warde.

CARNEGIE DUNFERMLINE TRUST (1903) (social and cultural purposes in Dunfermline).—*Sec.*, F. Mann, Abbey Park House, Dunfermline, Fife.

CARNEGIE HERO FUND TRUST (1908). Income £40,000. Makes grants and allowances to people injured or the dependants of people killed in saving human life within the British Isles and territorial waters.—*Sec.*, F. Mann, Abbey Park House, Dunfermline, Fife.

CARNEGIE UNITED KINGDOM TRUST (1913). Comely Park House, Dunfermline, Fife.—*Object*, The improvement of the well-being of the masses of the people of Great Britain and Ireland by means which are " charitable " in law and are to be selected by the Trustees themselves. The Trust is particularly concerned with social welfare schemes of a pioneer or experimental kind; grants are not made to individuals or in response to general appeals for subscriptions. Management—By trustees. *Sec.*, M. Holton.

CAREER TEACHERS, ASSOCIATION OF, Hillsboro. Castledine Street, Loughborough, Leics.—*Gen. Sec.*, Miss R. Yaffé.

CATHEDRALS ADVISORY COMMITTEE, 83 London Wall, E.C.2.—*Sec.*, D. C. Mandeville, O.B.E.

CATHOLIC MARRIAGE ADVISORY COUNCIL (National Office), 15 Lansdowne Road, W.11; (London Centre), 33 Willow Place, Francis Street, S.W.1. *Chairman*, G. Steer (*acting*).

CATHOLIC RECORD SOCIETY (1904).—*Hon. Sec.*, Miss R. Rendel, c/o 114 Mount Street, W.1

CATHOLIC TRUTH SOCIETY (1868), P.O. Box 422, 38-40 Eccleston Square, S.W.1.—*Gen. Sec.*, D. Murphy, M.A.

CATHOLIC UNION OF GREAT BRITAIN.—*Pres.*, The Duke of Norfolk, C.B., C.B.E. M.C.; *Sec.*, Mrs. J. Stuyt, 18 The Boltons, S.W.10.

CATTLE BREEDER'S CLUB, BRITISH (1949), Lavenders, Isfield, nr. Uckfield, Sussex.—*Sec.*, C. R. Stains.

CATTLE VETERINARY ASSOCIATION, BRITISH.—*Sec.*, M. H. Hinton, Langford House, Langford, Bristol.

CECIL HOUSES (Inc.), 190-192 Kensal Road, W.10. —*Sec.*, Mrs. J. M. Bolton.

CEREALS AND BALTIC FRIENDLY SOCIETY (1908), 14/20 St. Mary Axe, E.C.3.—*Sec.*, R. T. Wheelans.

CERAMIC SOCIETY, BRITISH (1900), Shelton House, Stoke Road, Shelton, Stoke-on-Trent, Staffs.— *Pres.*, Dr. W. C. Gilpin.

CERAMICS, INSTITUTE OF (1955), Shelton House, Stoke Road, Shelton, Stoke-on-Trent, Staffs.— *Sec.*, W. A. Evans.

CEYLON ASSOCIATION IN LONDON, 2/3 Crosby Square, Bishopsgate, E.C.3.—*Sec.*, R. J. Barber.

CHADWICK TRUST (1895) (for the promotion of health and prevention of disease), 13 Grosvenor Place, S.W.1.—*Clerk*, D. S. Wilson.

CHAMBERS OF COMMERCE.—See COMMERCE.

CHANTREY BEQUEST (1875).—*Sec. to the Trustees*, The Secretary, Royal Academy of Arts, Burlington House, Piccadilly, W.1.

CHARTERED SECRETARIES AND ADMINISTRATORS, INSTITUTE OF (1891), 16 Park Crescent, W.1.— *Sec.*, J. F. Phillips, O.B.E.

CHEMICAL ENGINEERS, INSTITUTION OF (1922), 15 Belgrave Square, S.W.1.—*Pres.*, Prof. J. F. Richardson; *Gen. Sec.*, Maj. Gen. A. M. McKay.

CHEMICAL INDUSTRY, SOCIETY OF, 14 Belgrave Square, S.W.1.—*Pres.*, E. L. Streatfield; *Sec.* D. H. Sharp.

CHEMICAL SOCIETY, Burlington House, Piccadilly, W.1.—*Pres.*, Prof. F. A. Robinson; *Gen. Sec.*, J. R. Ruck Keene, M.B.E., T.D.

CHEMISTRY, THE ROYAL INSTITUTE OF, 30 Russell Square, W.C.1.—*Pres.*, Prof. C. Kemball, F.R.S.; *Sec. and Registrar*, R. E. Parker, PH.D.

CHESS FEDERATION, BRITISH, P.O. Box 54, Norwich. *Gen. Sec.* P. Buswell.

CHEST AND HEART ASSOCIATION (1899), Tavistock House North, Tavistock Square, W.C.1.—*Dir. Gen.*, Air Marshal Sir Ernest Sidey. K.B.E., C.B., M.D.

CHILDREN'S COUNTRY HOLIDAYS FUND, 1 York Street, W.1.—*Gen. Sec.*, Mrs. J. M. Meekins, M.B.E.

CHILDREN'S RELIEF INTERNATIONAL (1959), Overstream House, Cambridge.—*Dir.*, T. Hardy.

CHINA ASSOCIATION (1889), 18 Diamond House, Hatton Garden, E.C.1.—*Sec.*, E. S. Bush.

CHIROPODISTS, THE SOCIETY OF 8 Wimpole Street, W.1.—*Sec.*, G. C. Jenkins.

CHOIR SCHOOLS ASSOCIATION (1921).—*Hon. Sec.*, Rev. D. Thomson, Cathedral Choir School, Ripon, Yorks.

CHRISTIAN ACTION (1949), 2 Amen Court, E.C.4. —*Sec.*, Mrs. F. Champion.

CHRISTIAN EDUCATION MOVEMENT (1965), 2 Chester House, Pages Lane N.10. *Gen. Sec.*, Rev. J. M. Sutcliffe.

CHRISTIAN EVIDENCE SOCIETY (1870), St. Margaret-Pattens, Eastcheap, E.C.3.—*Hon. Sec.*, Rev., S. E. Alford.

CHRISTIAN KNOWLEDGE, SOCIETY FOR PROMOTING (1698), Holy Trinity Church, Marylebone Road, N.W.1.—*Gen. Sec.*, P. N. G. Gilbert.

CHRISTIANS AND JEWS, COUNCIL OF (1942), 41 Cadogan Gardens, S.W.3.—*Gen. Sec.*, Rev. P. Jennings.

CHURCH ARMY, C. S. C. House, North Circular Rd., N.W.10. *Chief Sec.*, Rev. A. M. A. Turnbull.

CHURCH BUILDING SOCIETY, INCORPORATED (1818), St. Matthew's Chapel, 24 Great Peter Street, S.W.1.—*Sec.*, W. A. Carter.

CHURCH EDUCATION CORPORATION, The Oyster Building, Horsebridge, Whitstable, Kent.—*Sec.*, W. F. Holmes.

CHURCH HOUSE (1888), Dean's Yard, S.W.1.—*Sec.*, Maj. G. C. Hackett, M.B.E.

CHURCH LADS' BRIGADE (1891), *National Headquarters*, 15 Etchingham Park Road, N.3.—*Gen. Sec.*, Rev. J. H. S. Burton, M.A.

CHURCH MISSIONARY SOCIETY (1799), 157 Waterloo Road, S.E.1. Income, 1974 £1,423,424.—*Secs.*, Rev. S. Barrington-Ward (*General*); A. P. E. Paton (*Depy. Gen. Sec.*); J. J. Hillman (*Africa*); Rev. J. B. Carden (*Asia*); W. R. Billington (*Medical*); Rev. H. W. M. Moore (*Home*); Miss M. H. Beaver (*Candidates*); G. A. Hill (*Financial*).

CHURCH OF ENGLAND CHILDREN'S SOCIETY (1881) (formerly Waifs and Strays), Old Town Hall, Kennington Road, S.E.11.—*Dir.*, D. F. T. Bowie.

CHURCH OF ENGLAND MEN'S SOCIETY (1899). 24 Tufton Street, S.W.1.—*Gen. Sec.*, Rev. C. D. S. Woodhouse.

CHURCH OF ENGLAND PENSIONS BOARD (1926), 53 Tufton Street, S.W.1.—*Sec.*, D. Thackray.

CHURCH OF ENGLAND SOLDIERS', SAILORS' AND AIRMEN'S CLUBS (1891), and CHURCH OF ENGLAND SOLDIERS', SAILORS' AND AIRMEN'S HOUSING ASSOCIATION LTD. (1974), 1 Shakespeare Terrace, 126 High Street, Portsmouth. *Chairman*, Rear-Adm. J. L. Blackham, C.B.; *Gen. Sec.*, Group Capt. J. A. S. Brown.

CHURCH OF SCOTLAND DEPT. OF SOCIAL SERVICE, 121 George Street, Edinburgh 2.—*Dir.*, Rev. L. Beattie Garden, M.A.,

CHURCH PASTORAL AID SOCIETY (1836), Falcon Court, 32 Fleet Street, E.C.4.

CHURCH UNION (1859), 7 Tufton Street, S.W.1. —*Sec.*, G. Evans.

CHURCHES, BRITISH COUNCIL OF (1942), 10 Eaton Gates, S.W.1.—*Gen. Sec.*, Rev. H. O. Morton, M.A.

CHURCHES, COUNCIL FOR CARE OF, (see Places of Worship, Council for).

CHURCHES, FRIENDLESS, FRIENDS OF (1957), 12 Edwards Square, W.8.—*Hon. Dir.*, I. Bulmer-Thomas; *Hon. Sec.*, L. E. Jones.

CHURCHES MAIN COMMITTEE (1941), Fielden House, Little College Street, S.W.1.—*Sec.*, A, E. L. Parnis, C.B.E., M.A.

CIRCUS PROPRIETORS OF GREAT BRITAIN, ASSOCIATION OF, The Pheasantry, Longleat, Warminster, Wilts.—*See* R. Cawley.

CITY PAROCHIAL FOUNDATION (Trustees of the London Parochial Charities), 10 Fleet Street, E.C.4.

CIVIC TRUST FOR THE NORTH WEST, 56 Oxford Street, Manchester 1.—*Chairman*, Prof. G. Ashworth.

CIVIL DEFENCE, INSTITUTE OF (1942). P.O. Box 229, 3 Little Montague Court, E.C.1.—*Asst. Sec.* (*Admin.*), V. G. B. Atwater.

CIVIL DEFENCE AND EMERGENCY PLANNING OFFICERS, ASSOCIATION OF, 8 Meadow Road, Harborne, Birmingham 17.—*Hon. Gen. Sec.*, E. E. Alley.

CIVIL ENGINEERS, INSTITUTION OF (1818), Great George Street, S.W.1.—*Pres.*, Sir Norman Rowntree; *Sec.* J. G. Watson, C.B.

CIVIL LIBERTIES, NATIONAL COUNCIL FOR (1934), 186 King's Cross Road, W.C.1.—*Sec.*, Miss P. Hewitt.

CIVIL SERVICE COUNCIL FOR FURTHER EDUCATION.—*Sec.*, R. W. Farrington, 140 Gower Street, W.C.1.

CLASSICAL ASSOCIATION (1903).—*Hon. Treas.*, G. R. Watson, Dept. of Classical and Archæological Studies, The University, Nottingham.

CLASSICAL TEACHERS, JOINT ASSOCIATION OF (1962) 31–34 Gordon Square, W.C.1.—*Exec. Sec.*, M. R. F. Gunningham.

CLAY TECHNOLOGY INSTITUTE OF (1927), c/o Butterley Building Materials Ltd., Wellington Street, Ripley, Derbyshire.—*Acting Sec.*, B. A. Robinson.

CLERGY FRIENDLY SOCIETY (1882), Aldwych House, Aldwych, W.C.2.

CLERGY ORPHAN CORPORATION (1749), 5 Verulam Buildings, Gray's Inn, W.C.1.—*Sec.*, Miss V. B. Warters.

CLERKS OF THE PEACE OF SCOTLAND, ASSOCIATION OF (1908).—*Hon. Sec.*, J. B. McGowan, 135 Irish Street, Dumfries.

CLERKS OF WORKS OF GREAT BRITAIN INCORPORATED, INSTITUTE OF (1882), 6 Highbury Corner, N.5.—*Sec.*, A. P. Macnamara.

CLYDESDALE HORSE SOCIETY OF GREAT BRITAIN AND IRELAND (1877), 24 Beresford Terrace, Ayr.

COACHING CLUB (1871), 65 Medfield Street, S.W.15.—*Sec.*, R. A. Brown, O.B.E.

COAL TRADE BENEVOLENT ASSOCIATION (1889), 63 Narrow Street, Limehouse, E.14.—*Sec.*, R. W. Porcas, M.B.E., T.D.

COKE OVEN MANAGERS' ASSOCIATION, Waveney House, Adwick Road, Mexborough, South Yorks.

COLLEGE OF THE SEA (Seafarers Education Service) (1938), Mansbridge House, 207 Balham High Road, S.W.17.

COMBINED CADET FORCE ASSOCIATION (1952), 58 Buckingham Gate, S.W.1.—*Sec.*, W. F. L. Newcombe, O.B.E., T.D.

COMMERCE, ASSOCIATION OF BRITISH CHAMBERS OF (1860).—*Pres.*, The Earl of Limerick; *Dir-Gen.*, W. A. Newsome, 75 Cannon Street, E.C.4.

COMMERCE AND INDUSTRY, LONDON CHAMBER OF (1881), 69 Cannon Street, E.C.4.—*Pres.*, The Lord Mais, G.B.E. E.R.D., T.D.; *Dir.*, W. F. Nicholas, O.B.E.

COMMERCE, ASSOCIATION OF SCOTTISH CHAMBERS OF, 30 George Square, Glasgow.—*Sec.*, M. Neil.

COMMERCE AND MANUFACTURES, EDINBURGH CHAMBER OF (1786), 20 Hanover Street, Edinburgh 2.—*Chief Executive*, D. M. Mowat.

COMMERCE AND MANUFACTURES, GLASGOW CHAMBER OF (1783), 30 George Square, Glasgow.—*Sec.*, M. Neil.

COMMERCIAL AND INDUSTRIAL EDUCATION, BRITISH ASSOCIATION FOR (BACIE), 16 Park Crescent, W.1.—*Dir.*, P. J. C. Perry, O.B.E.

COMMERCIAL TRAVELLERS' BENEVOLENT INSTITUTION (1849), No. 1 London Bridge, S.E.1.—*Sec.*, E. B. Auger.

COMMISSIONAIRES, THE CORPS OF (1859), founded by the late Captain Sir Edward Walter; for the employment of ex-Soldiers, Sailors and Airmen and ex-police, fire service and merchant navy servicemen. *Headquarters*, Exchange Court, 419A Strand, W.C.2. *Outquarters*, War Memorial Building, Waring St., Belfast 1.; Room 53, Guildhall Buildings, Navigation Street, Birmingham; 87 Park Street, 1st Floor, Bristol; 99 Shandwick Place, Edinburgh; 180 W. Regent Street, Glasgow; Room 23, 10–12 East Parade, Leeds; 21 Dale Street, Liverpool; 2 St. John Street, Deansgate, Manchester; 10 Bigg Market, Newcastle-upon-Tyne 1. Total strength, 3,900—*Commandant*, Col. G. L. V. Pring; *Adjutant*, Col. A. M. Thorburn.

COMMONS, OPEN SPACES AND FOOTPATHS PRESERVATION SOCIETY (1865), Suite 4, 166 Shaftesbury Avenue, W.C.2.—*Sec.* (*vacant*).

COMMONWEALTH AND CONTINENTAL CHURCH SOCIETY (1823), 175 Tower Bridge Road, S.E.1.—*Secs.*, Rev. S. R. Beesley; D. R. Steele.

COMMONWEALTH GAMES FEDERATION.—*Hon. Sec.*, K. S. Duncan, O.B.E., 12 Buckingham Street, W.C.2.

COMMONWEALTH INDUSTRIES ASSOCIATION, LTD., 6/14 Dean Farrar Street, S.W.1.—*Dir.*, E. Holloway.

COMMONWEALTH PARLIAMENTARY ASSOCIATION.—*Sec., U.K. Branch*, P. G. Molloy, M.C., Westminster Hall, S.W.1.

COMMONWEALTH PRESS UNION (1909), Studio House, 184 Fleet Street, E.C.4.—*Sec.*, Lt.-Col. T. Pierce-Goulding, M.B.E., C.D.

COMMONWEALTH PRODUCERS' ORGANIZATION (1916), 25 Victoria Street, S.W.1.—*Dir.*, S. Stanley-Smith.

COMMONWEALTH SETTLEMENT, CHURCH OF ENGLAND COUNCIL FOR (1925), (see OVERSEAS SETTLEMENT, C. of E. COMMITTEE FOR).

COMMONWEALTH SOCIETY FOR THE DEAF (1959), 83 Kinnerton Street, S.W.1.—*Exec. Chairman*, Lady Templer.

COMMONWEALTH UNIVERSITIES, ASSOCIATION OF, 36 Gordon Square, W.C.1.—*Sec.-Gen.*, Sir Hugh Springer, K.C.M.G., C.B.E.

COMMUNIST PARTY OF GREAT BRITAIN EXECUTIVE COMMITTEE (1920), 16 King Street, W.C.2.—*Gen. Sec.*, G. McLennan.

COMMUNITY MEDICINE, SOCIETY OF (1856), (*formerly* Society of Medical Officers of Health), Tavistock House South, W.C.1.—*Pres.*, Dr. A. M. Nelson; *Sec.*, N. G. T. Taylor.

COMPOSERS' GUILD OF GREAT BRITAIN, THE (1945), 10 Stratford Place, W.1.—*Sec.*, Miss E. Yeoman.

COMPUTER SOCIETY, BRITISH (1957), 29 Portland Place, W.1.—*Sec.-Gen.*, M. C. Ashill.

CONFEDERATION OF BRITISH ROAD PASSENGER TRANSPORT (1974), Sardinia House, 52 Lincoln's Inn Fields, W.C.2.—*Dir.-Gen.*, D. R. Quin.

CONGREGATIONAL AND REFORMED, COUNCIL FOR WORLD MISSION (1973), Livingstone House, Carteret Street, S.W.1.—Formerly the Congregational Council for World Mission, the London Missionary Society, the Commonwealth Missionary Society and the Presbyterian Church of England Overseas Mission.—*Gen. Sec.*, The Rev. B. G. Thorogood.

CONSERVATION OF HISTORIC AND ARTISTIC WORKS, INTERNATIONAL INSTITUTE FOR, 608 Grand Buildings, Trafalgar Square, W.C.2.—*Pres.*, S. Keck; *Sec. Gen.*, N. Brommelle.

CONSERVATION SOCIETY (1966), 12 London Street, Chertsey, Surrey.—*Dir.*, Dr. J. Davoll.

CONSERVATIVE AND UNIONIST ASSOCIATIONS, NATIONAL UNION OF (1867), 32 Smith Square, S.W.1.—*Sec.*, J. A. Smith: *Women's National Advisory Committee.*—*Sec.*, Mrs. S. Hewitt; *Young Conservative and Unionist National Advisory Committee.*—*Sec.*, P. Houlden.

CONSERVATIVE AND UNIONIST CENTRAL OFFICE, 32 Smith Square, S.W.1.—*Chairman*, The Lord Thorneycroft, P.C.; *Deputy Chairman*, The Lord Fraser of Kilmorack, C.B.E.; *Vice-Chairmen*, A. Grant, M.P.; W. G. Clark, M.P.; A. E. U. Maude, M.P., R. E. Eyre, M.P.; G. Finsberg, M.P.; J. E. M. Moore, M.P.; The Baroness Young; *Treasurers*, The Lord Chelmer, M.C., T.D.; Lord Ashdown; A. McAlpine; *Dir. of Organization*, Sir Richard Webster, D.S.O.

CONSERVATIVE CLUBS, LTD., ASSOCIATION OF (1894), 32 Smith Square, S.W.1.—*Sec.*, L. G. Waterman.

CONSTRUCTION SURVEYORS' INSTITUTE (1952), 203 Lordship Lane, S.E.22.—*Exec. Dir.*, S. L. J. Cook.

CONSULTING ENGINEERS, ASSOCIATION OF (1913), Hancock House, 87 Vincent Square, S.W.1.—*Sec.*, Maj.-Gen. M. W. Prynne, C.B., C.B.E.

CONSULTING SCIENTISTS, ASSOCIATION OF, 47 Belgrave Square, S.W.1.—*Asst. Sec.*, F. B. Lucas.

CO-OPERATIVE SOCIETIES AND ASSOCIATIONS:—

Central Council for Agricultural and Horticultural Co-operation, 301–344 Market Towers, New Covent Garden Market, 1 Nine Elms Lane, S.W.8.—*Chief Exec.*, P. R. Dodds.

Co-operative Party, 158 Buckingham Palace Road, S.W.1.—*Sec.*, D. Wise.

Co-operative Productive Federation (1882), 42 Western Road, Leicester.—*Sec.*, J. Leonard.

Co-operative Union (1869), Holyoake House, Hanover Street, Manchester.—*Gen. Sec.*, D. L. Wilkinson.

Co-operative Wholesale Society (C.W.S.) (1963), New Century House, Manchester 4.—*Chief Exec. Officer*, A. Sugden; *Sec.*, T. H. Taylor.

Co-operative Women's Guild, 342 Hoe Street, Walthamstow, E.17.—*Gen. Sec.*, Mrs. K. Kempton.

Fisheries Organization Society, Ltd. (1914), 558 London Road, Sutton, Surrey.—*Gen. Sec.*, E. B. Hamley.

International Co-operative Alliance (1895), 11 Upper Grosvenor Street, W.1.—*Dir.*, S. K. Saxena.

Plunkett Foundation for Co-operative Studies (1919), 31 St. Giles, Oxford.—*Sec.*, F. H. Webster.

COPYRIGHT COUNCIL, BRITISH (1953), 29–33 Berners Street, W.1.—*Sec.*, R. Wreford.

CORONERS' SOCIETY OF ENGLAND AND WALES (1846).—*Hon. Sec.*, J. Burton, Coroner's Court, 77 Fulham Palace Road, W.6.

CORPORATE TRUSTEES, ASSOCIATION OF, Juxon House, St. Paul's Churchyard E.C.4.—*Sec.*, J. S. Rawlings.

CORRESPONDENCE COLLEGES, ASSOCIATION OF BRITISH (1955), 4 Chiswell Street, E.C.1.—*Sec.*, F. L. Cowham.

COTTON RESEARCH CORPORATION (1921), 14 Grosvenor Place, S.W.1.—*Dir.*, M. A. Choyce, O.B.E.

COUNTRY LANDOWNERS' ASSOCIATION (1907), 16 Belgrave Square, S.W.1.—*Gen. Sec.*, J. M. Douglas.

COUNTY CHIEF EXECUTIVES, ASSOCIATION OF.—
Hon. Sec., W. U. Jackson, County Hall, Maidstone, Kent.

COUNTY COUNCILS, ASSOCIATION OF (1973), Eaton House, 66A Eaton Square, S.W.1.—*Sec.*, A. C. Hetherington, C.B.E.

COUNTY SECRETARIES, SOCIETY OF.—*Hon. Sec.*, R. W. Adcock, County Hall, Chelmsford, Essex.

COUNTY SURVEYORS' SOCIETY (1884).—*President*, L. F. Crossley, Eastgate, Beverley. *Hon. Sec.*, J. H. Scarlett, County Hall, Aylesbury.

COUNTY TREASURERS, SOCIETY OF (1903), Shire Hall, Reading, Berks.—*Hon. Sec.*, M. C. Beasley.

CRAFT EDUCATION, INSTITUTE OF.—*Gen. Sec.*, H. N. Deslow, 59 Dovedale Avenue, Clayhall, Ilford, Essex.

CRAFTS CENTRE, BRITISH (1948), 43 Earlham Street, W.C.2.—*Dir.*, M. Sellers.

CRUELTY TO ANIMALS, ROYAL SOCIETY FOR THE PREVENTION OF. *See* "ROYAL."

CRUELTY TO ANIMALS, CENTRAL COUNCIL OF SOCIETIES IN SCOTLAND FOR PREVENTION OF (1950), 19 Melville Street, Edinburgh 3.—*Hon. Sec.*, G. F. S. Brian.

CRUELTY TO CHILDREN. *See* "NATIONAL" and "ROYAL SCOTTISH."

CULTURAL EXCHANGE, ASSOCIATION FOR (1958), 9 Emmanuel Road, Cambridge.—*Sec.* P. B. Barnes.

CURATES' AUGMENTATION FUND (1866), East Wing, Fulham Palace, S.W.6.—*Sec.*, Rev. M. L. Nicholas.

CYCLISTS TOURING CLUB (1878), Cotterell House, 69 Meadrow, Godalming, Surrey.—*Sec.*, Leslie C. Warner.

CWMNI URDD GOBAITH CYMRU (Welsh League of Youth) (1922), Swyddfa'r Urdd, Aberystwyth.—*Dir.*, J. C. Hughes.

CYMMRODORION, THE HONOURABLE SOCIETY OF (1751).—*Hon. Sec.*, J. Haulfryn Williams, 118 Newgate Street, E.C.1.

DAIRY ASSOCIATION, UNITED KINGDOM (1950), Giggs Hill Green, Thames Ditton, Surrey.—*Sec.*, R. D. Lemmer.

DAIRY TECHNOLOGY, SOCIETY OF (1943), 172A Ealing Road, Wembley, Middx.—*Sec.*, S. W. Stilton.

D DAY AND NORMANDY FELLOWSHIP.—*Hon. Membership Sec.*, St. John's Cottage, Shedfield, Southampton.

DATA PROCESSING, INSTITUTE OF (1966), Walter House, 418–422 Strand, W.C.2.—*Sec.-Gen.*, D. W. Bradley.

DEAF ASSOCIATION, BRITISH (1890), 38 Victoria Place, Carlisle.—*Gen. Sec.*, A. B. Hayhurst, M.B.E.

DEAF, ROYAL NATIONAL INSTITUTE FOR THE (1911) 105 Gower Street, W.C.1.—*Sec. Gen.*, R. Sydenham.

DEAF AND DUMB, ROYAL ASSOCIATION IN AID OF, To promote the general, social and spiritual welfare of deaf and blind/deaf people in Greater London, Essex, Surrey and West Kent, 7–11 Armstrong Road, W.3.—*Director*, Rev. I. Scott-Oldfield.

DEAF AND DUMB WOMEN, BRITISH HOME FOR, 36 Clapton Common, E.5.—*Matron and Sec.*, Miss E. Cheverall.

DEAF CHILDREN, ROYAL SCHOOL FOR (1792), Margate. *Office*, Victoria Road, Margate, Kent.—*Sec.* D. E. Downs.

DEAF WELFARE EXAMINATION BOARD.—*Hon. Registrar*, Rev. Canon A. F. Mackenzie, Corscombe Rectory, Dorchester, Dorset.

DECORATORS AND INTERIOR DESIGNERS, INCORPORATED INSTITUTE OF BRITISH (1899), 162 Derby Road, Stapleford, Nottingham.—*Sec.*, N. Parker.

DEER SOCIETY, BRITISH.—*Sec.*, F. J. T. Page, Forge Cottage, Askham, Penrith, Cumbria.

DELINQUENCY, INST. FOR THE STUDY AND TREATMENT OF (1931), 8 Bourdon Street, W.1.—*Gen. Sec.*, Miss E. Saville, M.B.E.

DENTAL COUNCIL, GENERAL, 37 Wimpole Street, W.1.—*Registrar*, D. Hindley-Smith, C.B.E.

DENTAL HOSPITALS OF GREAT BRITAIN AND NORTHERN IRELAND, ASSOCIATION OF (1942).—*Hon. Sec.*, Dr. R. G. Mitchell, Dental Hospital, St. Chad's Queensway, Birmingham 4.

DESIGN AND INDUSTRIES ASSOCIATION (1915), 12 Carlton House Terrace, S.W.1.—*Hon. Dir.*, R. Plummer.

DEVON AND CORNWALL RECORD SOCIETY (1904).—c/o Devon and Exeter Institution, 7 The Close, Exeter.

DICKENS FELLOWSHIP, Dickens House, 48 Doughty Street, W.C.1.

DIRECTORS, INSTITUTE OF (1903), 10 Belgrave Square, S.W.1.—*Dir. Gen.*, Sir Richard Powell, Bt., M.C.

DISABLED, BRITISH COUNCIL FOR REHABILITATION OF THE (1944), Tavistock House (South), Tavistock Square, W.C.1.—*Sec. Gen.*, I. R. Henderson.

DISABLED, CENTRAL COUNCIL FOR THE (1919), 34 Eccleston Square, S.W.1.—*Dir.*, G. Wilson.

DISPENSING OPTICIANS, ASSOCIATION OF (1925), 22 Nottingham Place, W.1.—*Sec.*, M. G. Aird.

DISTRESS, SOCIETY FOR THE RELIEF OF (1860).—*Hon. Sec.*, Mrs. W. F. Poper, 51 The Chine, N.21.

DISTRESSED GENTLEFOLKS' AID ASSOCIATION (1897), (Headquarters and London Nursing Home), Vicarage Gate House, Vicarage Gate, Kensington, W.8.

DISTRICT COUNCILS ASSOCIATION OF (1974), Eggington House, 25 Buckingham Gate, S.W.1.—*Sec.*, S. Rhodes, O.B.E.

DITCHLEY FOUNDATION, Ditchley Park, Enstone, Oxford.—*Dir.*, Sir Michael Stewart, K.C.M.G., O.B.E.

DOGS HOME BATTERSEA, THE (1860), Battersea Park Road, S.W.8. *Hours:* Monday to Friday, 9.30–5. Claims only, Saturday and Sunday and Public Holidays, 2–4 p.m.—*Sec. and Gen. Manager*, Col. H. J. Sweeney, M.C.

DOMESTIC SERVANTS' BENEVOLENT INSTITUTION (1846), Royal Bank of Scotland, Burlington Gardens, W.1.—*Sec.*, J. H. Thyme.

DOMINION STUDENTS' HALL TRUST (see Overseas Graduates, London House for).

DOWSERS, BRITISH SOCIETY OF (1933).—*Hon. Sec.*, P. B. Smithett, 19 High Street, Eydon, Daventry, Northants.

DRAINAGE AUTHORITIES, ASSOCIATION OF (1937).—*Sec.* H. E. G. Wells, O.B.E., 12 The Plain, Thornbury, Bristol.

DRINKING FOUNTAIN ASSOCIATION (formerly Metropolitan Drinking Fountain and Cattle Trough Association) (1859), 426 Lewisham High Street, S.E.13.—*Sec.*, Brig. J. M. Rymer-Jones, C.B.E., M.C., Q.P.M.

DRUG DEPENDENCE, INSTITUTE FOR THE STUDY OF, Kingsbury House, 3 Blackburn Road, N.W.6.—*Hon. Dir.*, F. Logan.

DUKE OF EDINBURGH'S AWARD, 5 Prince of Wales Terrace, W.8.—*Director*, A. L. Blake, C.V.O., M.C.

DYERS AND COLOURISTS, SOCIETY OF (1884), Perkin HOUSE, P.O. Box 244, 82 Grattan Rd., Bradford, Yorks.—*Gen. Sec.*, M. Tordoff, PH.D., F.R.I.C.

EARL HAIG'S (BRITISH LEGION) APPEAL FUND. *See* "BRITISH LEGION."

EARL HAIG FUND (SCOTLAND). Established for the relief of distress among ex-service personnel and their dependants in Scotland. Applicants may apply to either of the following: *North, South and East Area*, 23 Drumsheugh Gardens, Edinburgh.

—*Gen. Sec.*, Brig. F. H. Coutts, C.B.E.; or *Glasgow and South-West Area*, 1 Fitzroy Place, Glasgow, C.3.—*Sec.*, Maj. J. B. A. Smyth.

EARLY ENGLISH TEXT SOCIETY (1864).—*Hon. Director*, Prof. N. Davis, F.B.A.; *Exec. Sec.*, Dr. A. Hudson, Lady Margaret Hall, Oxford.

ECCLESIASTICAL HISTORY SOCIETY.—*Sec.*, Dr. Janet Nelson, King's College, W.C.2.

ECCLESIOLOGICAL SOCIETY (Founded in 1839 as the Cambridge Camden Society).—*Hon. Sec.*, S. Chapman, C.B.E., c/o St. Ann's Vestry Hall, Carter Lane, E.C.4.

EDUCATION COMMITTEES, ASSOCIATION OF, 10 Queen Anne Street, W.1.—*Sec.*, The Lord Alexander of Potterhill, Ph.D.

EDUCATION COUNCIL OF THE SOCIETY OF FRIENDS, Friends House, Euston Road, N.W.1.—*Sec.*, J. P. Wragge.

EDUCATION, NATIONAL COMMITTEE FOR AUDIO-VISUAL AIDS IN, 33 Queen Anne Street, W.1.—*Dir.*, G. C. Marchant.

EDUCATION OFFICERS, SOCIETY OF.—*Sec.*, C. W. W. Read, 10 Queen Anne Street, W.1.

EDUCATION OFFICERS' SOCIETY, COUNTY.—*Hon. Sec.*, J. A. Springett, Threadneedle House, Market Road, Chelmsford, Essex.

EDUCATION, SCOTTISH COUNCIL FOR RESEARCH IN, 16 Moray Place, Edinburgh, 3.

EDUCATION THROUGH ART, SOCIETY FOR, Bath Academy of Art, Corsham, Wilts.—*Chairman*, D. Pope.

EDUCATIONAL CENTRES ASSOCIATION, Walthamstow Adult Education Centre, Greenleaf Road, E.17.—*Sec.*, Ray Lamb, M.B.E.

EDUCATIONAL FOUNDATION FOR VISUAL AIDS, 33 Queen Anne Street, W.1.—*Dir.*, G. C. Marchant.

EDUCATIONAL INSTITUTE OF SCOTLAND (1847), 46 Moray Place, Edinburgh.—*Gen. Sec.*, J. D. Pollock.

EDUCATIONAL RESEARCH IN ENGLAND AND WALES, NATIONAL FOUNDATION FOR, The Mere, Upton Park, Slough, Berks.—*Dir.*, A. Yates.

EDUCATIONAL VISITS AND EXCHANGES, CENTRAL BUREAU FOR, 43 Dorset Street, W.1.—*Dir.*, J. Platt.

EGYPT EXPLORATION SOCIETY (1882), 3 Doughty Mews, W.C.1.—*Chairman*, Prof., E. G. Turner; *Sec.*, Miss M. Crawford.

ELDERLY INVALIDS FUND AND OLD PEOPLES ADVISORY SERVICE, 10 Fleet Street, E.C.4.

ELECTORAL REFORM SOCIETY OF GREAT BRITAIN AND IRELAND (founded 1884 as Proportional Representation Soc.), 6 Chancel Street, S.E.1.—*Dir.*, Miss E. Lakeman.

ELECTRICAL AND ELECTRONICS TECHNICIAN ENGINEERS, INSTITUTION OF (1965), 2 Savoy Hill, W.C.2.—*Sec.*, A. C. Gingell.

ELECTRICAL ENGINEERS, INSTITUTION OF (1871), Savoy Place, W.C.2.—*Sec.*, Dr. G. F. Gainsborough.

ELECTRONIC AND RADIO ENGINEERS, INSTITUTION OF (1925), 8–9 Bedford Square, W.C.1.—*Sec.*, G. D. Clifford, C.M.G.

EMPLOYMENT FELLOWSHIP (formerly WINTER DISTRESS LEAGUE) (1922), Drayton House, Gordon Street, W.C.1. Assists in the setting-up of sheltered workrooms for the elderly.—*Dir.*, T. H. Oakman.

ENGINEERING DESIGNERS, INSTITUTION OF (1945), Courtleigh, Westbury Leigh, Westbury, Wilts.—*Gen. Sec.*, W. E. Walters.

ENGINEERING INDUSTRIES ASSOCIATION, Equitable House, Lyon Road, Harrow, Middx.—*Dir.*, T. R. Wade.

ENGINEERING INSTITUTIONS, COUNCIL OF (1965), 2 Little Smith Street, S.W.1.—*Sec.*, M. W. Leonard.

ENGINEERS AND SHIPBUILDERS IN SCOTLAND, INSTITUTION OF (1857), 183 Bath Street, Glasgow, C.2.—*Pres.*, Prof. A. W. Scott; *Sec.*, W. McLaughlin.

ENGINEERS AND SHIPBUILDERS, N.E. COAST INSTITUTION OF (1884), Bolbec Hall, Newcastle upon Tyne 1.—*Sec.*, Capt. H. G. S. Brownbill, D.S.C., R.N.

ENGINEERS' GUILD, LTD. (for Chartered Engineers), 400–403 Abbey House, 2 Victoria Street, S.W.1.

ENGINEERS, INSTITUTION OF BRITISH (1928), Regency House, 3 Marlborough Place, Brighton.—*Sec.*, Mrs. D. Henry.

ENGINEERS, SOCIETY OF (Incorporated) (1854), Artillery Mansions, 75 Victoria Street, S.W.1.—*Sec.*, L. T. Griffith.

ENGLISH ASSOCIATION (1906), 29 Exhibition Road, S.W.7.—*Sec.* Lt. Col. R. T. Brain, M.C.

ENGLISH FOLK DANCE AND SONG SOCIETY (1932), Cecil Sharp House, 2 Regent's Park Road, N.W.1.—*Sec.*, Mrs. C. B. Pennington.

ENGLISH PLACE-NAME SOCIETY (1923).—*Hon. Director*, Prof. K. Cameron, Ph.D., The University, Nottingham.

ENGLISH-SPEAKING UNION OF THE COMMONWEALTH (1918), 37 Charles Street, Berkeley Square, W.1.—*Chairman*, Sir Patrick Dean, G.C.M.G.; *Dir.-Gen.*, W. N. Hugh Jones, M.V.O.

ENGLISH WOODLANDS LTD., 109 Upper Woodcote Road, Caversham Heights, Reading.

ENHAM VILLAGE CENTRE (1918), The White House, Enham Alamein, Andover, Hants. For rehabilitation, employment and housing of the physically handicapped.—*Sec.-Gen.*, D. Benwell.

ENTOMOLOGICAL SOCIETY OF LONDON, ROYAL (1833), 41 Queen's Gate, S.W.7.—*Hon. Sec.*, P. E. S. Whalley.

ENTOMOLOGY, COMMONWEALTH INSTITUTE OF (1913), 56 Queen's Gate, S.W.7.—*Director*, A. H. Parker, Ph.D.

ENVIRONMENTAL (*formerly Public*) HEALTH OFFICERS ASSOCIATION, 19 Grosvenor Place, S.W.1.—*Sec.*, R. Johnson.

EPILEPSY ASSOCIATION, BRITISH, 3–6 Alfred Place, W.C.1.—*Dir.*, L. Fitzgibbon.

EPILEPTICS, THE NATIONAL SOCIETY FOR (1892), Chalfont Centre for Epilepsy, Chalfont St. Peter, Bucks.—*Sec.*, Col. H. V. Trewhella.

ESPERANTO ASSOCIATION (LTD.), BRITISH (1907), 140 Holland Park Avenue, W.11.—*Sec.*, H. E. Platt.

EUGENICS SOCIETY (1907), 69 Eccleston Square, S.W.1.—*Gen. Sec.*, Miss S. E. Walters.

EVANGELICAL ALLIANCE (1846), 19 Draycott Place, S.W.3.—*Gen. Sec.*, G. J. T. Landreth.

EVANGELICAL LIBRARY, THE, 78A Chiltern Street, W.1.—*Librarian*, G. R. Sayer.

EXAMINERS UNDER SOLICITORS (SCOTLAND) ACTS (1933–1965), Law Society's Hall, 26–27 Drumsheugh Gardens, Edinburgh.—*Clerk*, R. B. Laurie, O.B.E., W.S.

EXECUTIVES ASSOCIATION OF GREAT BRITAIN (1929), 16 West Central Street, W.C.1.—*Sec.*, M. C. Waddilove.

EXPORT, INSTITUTE OF, World Trade Centre, E.1. *Dir.-Gen.*, A. J. Day.

EX-SERVICES MENTAL WELFARE SOCIETY (for ex-Service men and women suffering from psychoses and neuroses arising from active or long regular service), 37 Thurloe Street, S.W.7.

FABIAN SOCIETY (1884), 11 Dartmouth Street, S.W.1.—*Gen. Sec.*, T. Ponsonby.

FAIRBRIDGE SOCIETY (1909) (formerly Fairbridge Farm Schools), 119–125 Bush House (N.E.), Aldwych, W.C.2.—*Dir.*, Maj.-Gen. W. T. Campbell, C.B.E.

FAIR ISLE BIRD OBSERVATORY TRUST, 21 Regent Terrace, Edinburgh.—*Hon. Sec.*, George Waterson, O.B.E.

FAMILY PLANNING ASSOCIATION, 27–35 Mortimer Street, W.1.—*Chief Exec. Officer*, T. E. Parker.

FAMILY SERVICE UNITS, 207 Old Marylebone Road, N.W.1.—*Dir.*, J. R. Halliwell.

FAMILY WELFARE ASSOCIATION Ltd. (Founded 1869 as CHARITY ORGANIZATION SOCIETY), 501–5 Kingsland Road, E.8.—*Dir.*, Mrs. P. A. Thomas.

FAUNA PRESERVATION SOCIETY (1903).—*Office*, c/o Zoological Society of London, Regent's Park, N.W.1.—*Hon. Sec.*, R. S. R. Fitter.

FAWCETT SOCIETY (1866), 27 Wilfred Street, S.W.1.—*Sec.*, O. Braman.

FELLOWSHIP HOUSES TRUST (Flatlets for the elderly) (1937), Clock House, Byfleet, Surrey.—*Sec.*, L. P. Leech.

FIELD LANE FOUNDATION (1841), Vine Hill, Clerkenwell Road, E.C.1; HOMES FOR OLD PEOPLE; COMMUNITY CENTRE, 32 Cubitt Street, W.C.1.—*Gen. Sec.*, A. C. Ash.

FIELD STUDIES COUNCIL (1943), 9 Devereux Court, W.C.2.—*Sec.*, R. S. Chapman.

FIRE ENGINEERS, INSTITUTION OF, 148 New Walk, Leicester.—*Gen. Sec.*, D. S. Ramsey.

FIRE PROTECTION ASSOCIATION, Aldermary House, Queen Street, E.C.4.—*Dir.*, N. C. Strother Smith, O.B.E., T.D.

FIRE SERVICES ASSOCIATION, BRITISH, 86 London Road, Leicester.—*Gen. Sec.*, D. G. Varnfield.

FIRE SERVICES NATIONAL BENEVOLENT FUND (1943), Marine Court, Fitzalan Road, Littlehampton, Sussex.—*Hon. Organizing Sec.*, R. W. Greene, M.B.E.

FOLKLORE SOCIETY, c/o University College London, Gower Street, W.C.1.—*Hon. Sec.*, Mrs. V. J. Newall.

FORCES HELP SOCIETY AND LORD ROBERTS WORKSHOPS (1899), 118–122 Brompton Road, S.W.3. *Comptroller*, Maj. L. F. E. James, M.B.E.

FOREIGN BONDHOLDERS, COUNCIL OF (1873), 68 Queen Street, E.C.4.—*Director-General*, C. E. N. Wyatt, M.C.

FOREIGN PRESS ASSOCIATION IN LONDON, 11 Carlton House Terrace, S.W.1.—*Pres.*, W. Kornacki.

FORENSIC SCIENCES, BRITISH ACADEMY OF (1959).—*Sec.-Gen.*, Prof. J. M. Cameron, Dept. of Forensic Medicine, The London Hospital, Turner Street, E.1.

FORESTERS OF GREAT BRITAIN, INSTITUTE OF (1973), 6 Rutland Square, Edinburgh.—*Sec. and Treas.*, T. R. Moffat.

FORESTRY ASSOCIATION, COMMONWEALTH (1921). Royal Commonwealth Society, Northumberland Avenue, W.C.2.—*Editor-Sec.*, C. W. J. Pitt.

FORESTRY SOCIETY OF ENGLAND, WALES AND NORTHERN IRELAND, ROYAL (1882), 102 High Street, Tring, Herts.—*Sec.*, E. H. M. Harris.

FORESTRY SOCIETY, ROYAL SCOTTISH (1854), 26 Rutland Square, Edinburgh.—*Sec. and Treas.*, W. B. C. Walker.

FRANCO-BRITISH SOCIETY, 1 Old Burlington Street, W.1.—*Sec.*, Miss M. Coate, M.B.E.

FREE CHURCH FEDERAL COUNCIL, 27 Tavistock Square, W.C.1.—*Moderator*, Rev. D. R. Lee, M.B.E.; *Gen. Sec.*, Rev. G. A. D. Mann.

FREEMASONS, GRAND LODGE OF SCOTLAND (1736), (Freemasons' Hall, Edinburgh.—*Grand Master Mason of Scotland*, Capt. R. Wolrige Gordon of Esslemont; *Grand Sec.*, E. S. Falconer.

FREEMASONS, UNITED GRAND LODGE OF ENGLAND, Freemasons' Hall, Great Queen Street, W.C.2.—*Grand Master*, H.R.H. the Duke of Kent, G.C.M.G., G.C.V.O.; *Pro Grand Master*, The Earl Cadogan, M.C.; *Deputy Grand Master*, Maj.-Gen. Sir Allan Adair, Bt., K.C.V.O., C.B., D.S.O., M.C.;

Asst. Grand Master, Hon Fiennes Cornwallis, O.B.E.; *Grand Wardens*, The Earl of Elgin and Kincardine; Lord Fisher of Camden; *Grand Chaplain*, The Dean of Gloucester, *Grand Sec.*, J. W. Stubbs.

FREEMEN OF CITY OF LONDON, GUILD OF (1908), 4 Dowgate Hill, E.C.4.—*Master*, C. R. Coward; *Clerk*, D. Reid.

FREEMEN OF ENGLAND (1966), 4 Lindsay Close, Epsom, Surrey.—*Pres.*, H. Ward.

FREIGHT FORWARDERS LTD., THE INSTITUTE OF, Suffield House, 9 Paradise Road, Richmond, Surrey.

FRESHWATER BIOLOGICAL ASSOCIATION (1932), The Ferry House, Far Sawrey, Ambleside, Cumbria.—*Sec. and Director of Laboratories*, E. D. Le Cren, M.A.

FRIENDS OF THE CLERGY CORP. (incorporating the Friend of the Clergy Corp. and the Poor Clergy Relief Corp.), 27 Medway Street, S.W.1.—*Sec.*, C. L. Talbot.

FRIENDLY SOCIETIES, NATIONAL CONFERENCE OF—*Sec.*, P. M. Madders, Room 341, Hamilton House, Mabledon Place, W.C.1.

FRIENDS OF CATHEDRAL MUSIC (1956), Holy Trinity Church, Marylebone Road, N.W.1.—*Hon. Gen. Sec.*, N. T. Barnes.

FRIENDS OF THE NATIONAL LIBRARIES, c/o The British Library, W.C.1.—*Chairman*, The Lord Kenyon, C.B.E.; *Hon. Sec.*, T. S. Blakeney.

FRIENDS OF THE ELDERLY & GENTLEFOLK'S HELP (1905), 42 Ebury Street, S.W.1.—*Gen. Sec.*, Miss P. M. Lethbridge.

FUEL, INSTITUTE OF (1927), 18 Devonshire Street, Portland Place, W.1.—*Sec.*, H. M. Lodge.

FURNITURE HISTORY SOCIETY (1964).—*Hon. Sec.*, Dr. L. Boynton, c/o Dept. of Furniture, Victoria and Albert Museum, S.W.7.

GAME CONSERVANCY, Fordingbridge, Hants.—*Dir.*, C. L. Coles.

GARDEN HISTORY SOCIETY (1965).—*Hon. Sec.*, Mrs. M. Batey, 12 Charlbury Road, Oxford.

GARDENERS' ROYAL BENEVOLENT SOCIETY (1839), Palace Gate, Hampton Court, East Molesey, Surrey.—*Dir.*, W. J. Hayward.

GAS ENGINEERS, INSTITUTION OF (1863), 17 Grosvenor Crescent, S.W.1.—*Sec.*, A. G. Higgins.

GEMMOLOGICAL ASSOCIATION OF GREAT BRITAIN (1931), St. Dunstan's House, Carey Lane, E.C.2.—*Sec.*, H. J. Wheeler.

GENEALOGICAL RESEARCH SOCIETY, IRISH.—*Sec.*, Mrs. P. J. Sainthill, 82 Eaton Square, S.W.1.

GENEALOGISTS AND RECORD AGENTS, ASSOCIATION OF (1968).—*Hon. Sec.*, Miss I. Mordy, 123 West End Road, Ruislip, Middx.

GENEALOGISTS, SOCIETY OF (1911), 37 Harrington Gardens, S.W.7.—*Sec.*, Mrs. C. M. Mackay.

GENERAL PRACTITIONERS, ROYAL COLLEGE OF (1952), 14 Princes Gate, S.W.7.—*Sec.*, J. Wood, D.S.C.

GENTLEPEOPLE, GUILD OF AID FOR (1904), 10 St. Christopher's Place, W.1.—*Sec.*, Miss P. Roden.

GEOGRAPHICAL ASSOCIATION, 343 Fulwood Road, Sheffield.—*Joint Hon. Secs.*, W. R. A. Ellis; G. M. Lewis.

GEOGRAPHICAL SOCIETY, ROYAL (1830), Kensington Gore, S.W.7.—*Pres.*, Sir Duncan Cumming, K.B.E., C.B.; *Hon. Secs.*, Prof. W. R. Mead; Dr. G. C. L. Bertram; *Hon. Foreign Sec.*, Lt.-Col. D. N. Hall; *Hon. Treas.*, H. Gould; *Director and Sec.*, J. Hemming; *Keeper of the Map Room*, Brig. R. A. Gardiner, M.B.E.; *Librarian*, G. S. Dugdale.

GEOGRAPHICAL SOCIETY, MANCHESTER (1884), 274, The Corn Exchange Buildings, Manchester.—*Sec.*, Mrs. A. Wood.

GEOGRAPHICAL SOCIETY, ROYAL SCOTTISH (1884), 10 Randolph Crescent, Edinburgh 3.—*Sec.*, D. G. Moir.

GEOLOGICAL SOCIETY (1807), Burlington House, Piccadilly, W.1.—*Pres.*, Sir Peter Kent, D.SC., PH.D., F.R.S., F.R.S.E.; *Secs.* A. H. B. Stride, PH.D.; P. McL. D. Duff, PH.D., F.R.S.E.; *Foreign Sec.*, J. V. Hepworth, PH.D.; *Exec. Sec.*, D. G. Clayton.

GEOLOGISTS' ASSOCIATION.—*Hon. Gen. Sec.*, F. H. Moore, B.SC., PH.D., F.G.S., 278 Fir Tree Road, Epsom, Surrey.

GEORGIAN GROUP (1937), 2 Chester Street, S.W.1.

GIFTED CHILDREN, NATIONAL ASSOCIATION FOR (1966), 27 John Adam Street, W.C.2.—*Dir.*, H. Collis, T.D.

GILBERT AND SULLIVAN SOCIETY.—*Hon. Sec.*, C. Lambert, 273 Northfield Avenue, W.5.

GIRL GUIDES ASSOCIATION.—An organization founded by the first Lord Baden-Powell as a sister movement to the Scouts and incorporated by Royal Charter in 1922. In 1974 the total membership in Great Britain and Northern Ireland was 791,931. *Commonwealth Headquarters*, 17-19 Buckingham Palace Road, S.W.1.

GIRLS' BRIGADE, THE, Brigade House, 8 Parsons Green, S.W.6.—*Brigade Sec. for Eng. & Wales*, Miss M. I. Taylor.

GIRLS' FRIENDLY SOCIETY AND TOWNSEND FELLOWSHIP (1875), 126 Queens Gate, S.W.7.

GIRLS OF THE REALM GUILD (1900).—Educational grants towards schooling or initial training of single girls. Applications before February for ensuing academic year to: Mrs. L. Jennens, Wistaria, Church Street, Chiswick, W.4.

GIRLS' VENTURE CORPS, 33 St. George Drive, S.W.1. A uniformed youth movement for girls between 13 and 20.

GLADSTONE MEMORIAL LIBRARY (1895), St. Deiniol's Library, Hawarden, Flintshire.—*Warden*, Rev. Dr. R. S. Foster.

GLASS TECHNOLOGY, SOCIETY OF (1916), 20 Hallam Gate Road, Sheffield.—*Hon. Sec.*, T. S. Busby.

GORDON BOYS' SCHOOL (1885), West End, Woking. —*Headmaster*, G. Leadbeater.

GRAPHIC ARTISTS, SOCIETY OF (1919), 17 Carlton House Terrace, S.W.1.—*Sec.*, D. A. L. Playfair.

GREATER LONDON PLAYING FIELDS ASSOCIATION (1926), Playfield House, 57B Catherine Place, S.W.1.—*Sec.*, Capt. D. N. Forbes, D.S.C., R.N. (ret.).

GREATER LONDON RED CROSS BLOOD TRANSFUSION SERVICE (1921), 4 Collingham Gardens, S.W.5 [01-373 1056/7]. Hours, 9 a.m. to 10 p.m. every day.

GREEK INSTITUTE (1969), 34 Bush Hill Road, N.21. —*Dir.*, Dr. Kypros Tofallis.

GRENFELL ASSOCIATION OF GREAT BRITAIN AND IRELAND, Hope House, 45 Great Peter Street, S.W.1. For medical and social work among the fishermen, Eskimos and Indians of Labrador and N. Newfoundland.—*Sec.*, Miss S. A. Yates.

GULBENKIAN FOUNDATION, *see* CALOUSTE.

HAKLUYT SOCIETY (1846), c/o Map Library, The British Library, Ref. Div., Great Russell Street, W.C.1—*Joint Hon. Secs.*, Dr. T. E. Armstrong; Prof. E. M. J. Campbell.

HANSARD SOCIETY FOR PARLIAMENTARY GOVERNMENT (1944), 12 Gower Street, W.C.1.—*Sec.*, Mrs. M. Vlieland.

HARLEIAN SOCIETY (1869), Ardon House, Mill Lane, Godalming, Surrey.—*Hon. Sec.*, J. P. Heming.

HARVEIAN SOCIETY OF LONDON.—*Hon. Sec.*, Dr. Marion Smith, 11 Chandos Street, Cavendish Square, W.1.

HEAD MASTERS, INCORPORATED ASSOCIATION OF, 29 Gordon Square, W.C.1.—*Pres.* (1976), P. W. Martin; *Joint Hon. Secs.*, B. H. Holbeche; D. P. M. Michael; *Hon. Treas.*, A. R. Barnes; *Sec.*, E. J. Dorrell; *Deputy Sec.*, B. C. Harvey.

HEAD MISTRESSES, ASSOCIATION OF, 29 Gordon Square, W.C.1.—*President*, Miss E. J. Bradbury, C.B.E.; *Sec.*, Miss S. M. Chapman.

HEADMISTRESSES OF PREPARATORY SCHOOLS, ASSOCIATION OF.—*Hon. Sec.*, Miss M. McVicar, Rookesbury Park, Wickham, Hants.

HEAD TEACHERS, NATIONAL ASSOCIATION OF.—*Gen. Sec.*, R. J. Cook, Maxwelton House, 41-43 Boltro Road, Haywards Heath, Sussex.

HEALTH EDUCATION COUNCIL, THE (1968), 78 New Oxford Street, W.C.1—*Dir.-Gen.*, A. C. L. Mackie, C.B.E.

HEALTH EDUCATION, INSTITUTE OF.—*Sec.*, F. St. D. Rowntree, 35 Victoria Road, Sheffield.

HEALTH, GUILD OF (1904), Edward Wilson House, 26 Queen Anne Street, W.1.—*Chairman*, Rev. B. Coote.

HEALTH SERVICE ADMINISTRATORS, INSTITUTE OF (1902), 75 Portland Place, W.1.—*Sec.*, J. F. Milne.

HEATING AND VENTILATING ENGINEERS, INSTITUTION OF (1897), 49 Cadogan Square, S.W.1.—*Sec.*, B. A. Hodges, O.B.E.

HELLENIC STUDIES, SOCIETY FOR THE PROMOTION OF (1879), 31-34 Gordon Square, W.C.1.—*Pres.*, Prof. R. Browning; *Hon. Sec.*, Prof. R. P. Winnington-Ingram, F.B.A.

HENRY GEORGE FOUNDATION, 177 Vauxhall Bridge Road, S.W.1.—*Sec.*, V. H. Blundell.

HERALDIC AND GENEALOGICAL STUDIES, INSTITUTE OF (1961), 80-82 Northgate, Canterbury, Kent.—*Dir.*, C. R. Humphery-Smith.

HERALDRY SOCIETY, THE (1947), 28 Museum Street, W.C.1.—*Sec.*, Mrs. L. M. Biermann.

HIGHWAY ENGINEERS, INSTITUTION OF (1930), 14 Queen Anne's Gate., S.W.1.—*Sec.*, Miss P. A. Steel.

HISPANIC AND LUSO BRAZILIAN COUNCIL (1943), Canning House, 2 Belgrave Square, S.W.1.—*Dir. Gen.*, S. M. Mackenzie, C.B.E., D.S.C.

HISTORICAL ASSOCIATION (1906), 59A Kennington Park Road, S.E.11.—*Sec.*, Miss C. M. Povall.

HISTORICAL SOCIETY, ROYAL (1868), University College, London, Gower Street, W.C.1.—*Pres.*, Prof. G. R. Elton, M.A., PH.D., D.Litt, F.B.A.; *Sec.*, Mrs. P. Burn.

HOMELESS CHILDREN'S AID AND ADOPTION SOCIETY, and F. B. Meyer Children's Home (1920), 54 Grove Avenue, Muswell Hill, N.10.—*Gen. Sec.*, Rev. R. H. Johnson.

HONG KONG ASSOCIATION (1961), 18 Diamond House, Hatton Garden, E.C.1.—*Sec.*, E. S. Bush.

HORATIAN SOCIETY (1933).—*Hon. Sec.*, Lady Templeman, Manor Heath, Knowl Hill, The Hockering, Woking, Surrey.

HOROLOGICAL INSTITUTE, BRITISH (1858), Upton Hall, Upton, Newark, Notts.—*Sec.*, F. West, M.B.E.

HOROLOGICAL SOCIETY, ANTIQUARIAN (1953), New House, High Street, Ticehurst, Wadhurst, Sussex.—*Hon. Sec.*, Cdr. G. Clarke.

HORTICULTURAL ADVISORY BUREAU, INTERNATIONAL, Arkley Manor, Arkley, nr. Barnet, Herts.—*Dir.*, W. E. Shewell-Cooper, M.B.E., D.Litt.

HOSPITAL FEDERATION, INTERNATIONAL (1947), 24 Nutford Place, W.1.—*Dir. Gen.*, M. C. Hardie.

HOSPITALS CONTRIBUTORY SCHEMES ASSOCIATION, BRITISH (1948), 30 Lancaster Gate, W.2.—*Hon. Sec.*, Air Vice-Marshal A. A. Case, C.B., C.B.E.

HOSPITAL SATURDAY FUND, THE (1873).—*Head Office*, 192-198 Vauxhall Bridge Road, S.W.1.—*Sec.*, Miss I. Gleeson.

HOSPITAL SAVING ASSOCIATION, THE, 30 Lancaster Gate, W.2.—*Gen. Sec.*, Air Vice-Marshal A. A. Case, C.B., C.B.E.

HOTEL CATERING AND INSTITUTIONAL MANAGEMENT ASSOCIATION, 191 Trinity Road, S.W.17.—*Sec.*, M. A. Nightingale.

HOTELS, RESTAURANTS AND CATERERS ASSOCIATION, BRITISH (1907), 20 Upper Brook Street, W.1. *Chief Exec.*, C. Derby.

HOUSE OF HOSPITALITY LTD., Holy Cross Priory, Cross-in-Hand, Heathfield, Sussex. Twenty homes for old people.—*Sec.*, Sister Mary Garson.

HOUSE OF ST. BARNABAS IN SOHO (House of Charity for Distressed Women in London) (1846), 1 Greek Street, Soho Square, W.1.

HOUSING AID SOCIETY, CATHOLIC (1956), 189a Old Brompton Road, S.W.5.—*Dir.*, D. Pollard.

HOUSING AND TOWN PLANNING COUNCIL, NATIONAL (1900), 34 Junction Road, N.19.— *Sec. Gen.*, A. H. Small.

HOUSING ASSOCIATION FOR OFFICERS' FAMILIES (1916), Alban Dobson House, Green Lane, Morden, Surrey.—*Gen. Sec.*, R. Davis.

HOWARD LEAGUE FOR PENAL REFORM (1866), 125 Kennington Park Road, S.E.11. For the advancement of knowledge of constructive penal and social policies.—*Dir.*, M. Wright.

HUGUENOT SOCIETY OF LONDON (1885), c/o Barclays Bank, Ltd., 1 Pall Mall East, S.W.1.— *Hon. Sec.*, Miss I Scouloudi, M.SC., F.S.A., F.R.Hist.S.

HUNTERIAN SOCIETY, The Hunterian Room, The Wellcome Building, Euston Road, N.W.1. *Secs.*, Dr. N. Thorne; Dr. Anne Jepson.

HUNTERS' IMPROVEMENT AND NATIONAL LIGHT HORSE BREEDING SOCIETY (1885), 8 Market Square, Westerham, Kent.—*Sec.*, G. W. Evans.

HYDROFOIL SOCIETY, INTERNATIONAL, 17 Melcombe Court, Dorset Square, N.W.1.—*Chairman*, M. Thornton.

ILLUMINATING ENGINEERING SOCIETY (1909), York House, Westminster Bridge Road, S.E.1.—*Sec.*, G. F. Cole.

INCOME TAX PAYERS' SOCIETY, 5 Plough Place, Fetter Lane, E.C.4.—*Dir.*, E. C. L. Hulbert-Powell.

INDEPENDENT SCHOOLS CAREERS ORGANIZATION (*formerly* Public Schools Appointments Bureau), 12A–18A Princess Way, Camberley, Surrey.— *Dir.*, R. F. B. Campbell, M.A.

INDEPENDENT SCHOOLS INFORMATION SERVICE (I.S.I.S.) (1972), 47 Victoria Street, S.W.1.—*Dir.*, D. D. Lindsay, C.B.E.

INDEXERS, SOCIETY OF, 25 Leyborne Park, Kew Gardens, Surrey.—*Hon. Sec.*, J. A. Gordon.

INDIA, PAKISTAN AND CEYLON, ROYAL SOCIETY FOR (1966), c/o Inchcape & Co. Ltd., 40 St. Mary Axe., E.C.3.—*Hon. Sec.*, J. W. N. Baldock.

INDUSTRIAL ARTISTS AND DESIGNERS, SOCIETY OF (1930), 12 Carlton House Terrace, S.W.1.—*Sec.*, G. V. Adams.

INDUSTRIAL CHRISTIAN FELLOWSHIP (1877), St. Katharine Cree Church, Leadenhall Street, E.C.3. —*Gen. Sec.*, Rev. N. F. P. Brown.

INDUSTRIAL MARKETING RESEARCH ASSOCIATION.— *Admin. Sec.*, 11 Bird Street, Lichfield, Staffs.

INDUSTRIAL PARTICIPATION ASSOCIATION (1884), 25–28 Buckingham Gate, S.W.1.—*Sec.*, D. Wallace Bell.

INDUSTRIAL SAFETY OFFICES, INSTITUTION OF, 222 Uppingham Road, Leicester.—*Sec.*, Maj. A. Poole (*ret.*).

INDUSTRIAL SOCIETY, THE (1918), Robert Hyde House, 48 Bryanston Square, W.1.—*Dir.*, W. J. P. M. Garnett, C.B.E.; *Sec.*, D. Fazakerley.

INLAND WATERWAYS ASSOCIATION, 114 Regent's Park Road, N.W.1.—*Gen. Sec.*, R. J. Taunton.

INNER WHEEL CLUBS IN GREAT BRITAIN AND IRELAND, ASSOCIATION OF (1934), 51 Warwick Square, S.W.1.—*Sec.*, Miss J. Dobson.

INSURANCE AGENTS, CORPORATION OF (1906), 63 Gt. Cumberland Place, W.1.—*Sec.*, G. Leigh.

INSURANCE ASSOCIATION, BRITISH (1917), Aldermary House, Queen Street, E.C.4.—*Sec. Gen.*, R. C. W. Bardell.

INSURANCE BROKERS, CORPORATION OF (1906), 15 St. Helen's Place, E.C.3.—*Sec.*, J. E. Fryer.

INSURANCE INSTITUTE, CHARTERED (1897), 20 Aldermanbury, E.C.2.—*Sec.*, D. C. McMurdie.

INTERNATIONAL LAW ASSOCIATION (1873), 3 Paper Buildings, Temple, E.C.4.—*Chairman*, The Lord Wilberforce, P.C., C.M.G., O.B.E.; *Sec.-Gen.*, J. B. S. Edwards.

INTERNATIONAL POLICE ASSOCIATION (British Section).—*National Headquarters*, 1 Fox Road. West Bridgford, Nottingham.—*Chief Exec, Officer*, K. H. Robinson.

INTERNATIONAL SHIPPING FEDERATION (1909), 146–150 Minories, E.C.3.—*President*, F. B. Bolton, M.C.; *Gen. Manager*, J. K. Rice-Oxley; *Sec.*, J. Lusted.

INTERNATIONAL SOCIETY FOR THE PROTECTION OF ANIMALS (1959), *Headquarters*, 106 Jermyn Street, S.W.1.—*Exec. Dir.*, T. H. Scott.

INTERNATIONAL STUDENTS TRUST (1962), 229 Gt. Portland Street, W.1.—*President*, The Duke of Grafton; *Dir.*, H. A. Shaw, O.B.E

INTERNATIONAL UNION FOR LAND VALUE TAXATION AND FREE TRADE, 177 Vauxhall Bridge Road, S.W.1.—*Sec.*, V. H. Blundell.

INTERNATIONAL VOLUNTARY SERVICE (1920), 91 High Street, Harlesden, N.W.10.

INVALID CHILDREN'S AID ASSOCIATION (LONDON), INCORPORATED (1888), 126 Buckingham Palace Road, S.W.1.—Advisory service on care of handicapped children; family social work in London and Home Counties; special schools. *Gen. Sec.*, Miss M. Coubrough.

INVALIDS-AT-HOME (1966).—*Hon. Sec.*, Mrs. J. Pierce, 23 Farm Avenue, N.W.2. Helps seriously disabled people living at home.

IRAN SOCIETY (1936), 42 Devonshire Street, W.1.— *Pres.*, The Lord Carrington, P.C., K.C.M.G., M.C.

IRISH LINEN MERCHANTS' ASSOCIATION (1872), Lambeg, Lisburn, N. Ireland.—*Sec.*, E. O. L. Seccombe.

IRISH SOCIETY, THE HONOURABLE THE (1613), Irish Chamber, Guildhall Yard, E.C.2.—*Sec.*, E. H. Shackcloth; *Representative (N. Ireland)*, Cmdr. P. C. D. Campbell-Grove, M.V.O., R.N.

JAPAN ASSOCIATION (1950), 18 Diamond House, Hatton Garden, E.C.1.—*Sec.*, E. S. Bush.

JAPAN SOCIETY OF LONDON (1891), 630 Grand Buildings, Trafalgar Square, W.C.2.—*Hon. Sec.*, Mrs. E. F. Dobson.

JERUSALEM AND THE MIDDLE EAST CHURCH ASSOCIATION (1887), 24 The Borough, Farnham, Surrey.—*Gen. Sec.*, J. B. Wilson.

JEWISH ASSOCIATION FOR THE PROTECTION OF GIRLS, WOMEN AND CHILDREN (administered by the Jewish Welfare Board) (1885).

JEWISH WELFARE BOARD (1859), Lionel Cohen House, 315 Ballards Lane, N.12.

JEWISH HISTORICAL SOCIETY OF ENGLAND, Mocatta Library, University College, W.C.1.—*Hon. Sec.*, Dr. J. Israel, 33 Seymour Place, W.1.

JEWISH RELIGIOUS EDUCATION, CENTRAL COUNCIL FOR, Woburn House, Upper Woburn Place, W.C.1.

JEWISH YOUTH, ASSOCIATION FOR (1899), 192/6 Hanbury Street, E.1.—*Gen. Sec.*, Michael Goldstein, M.B.E.

JEWS, CHURCH'S MINISTRY AMONG THE, Vincent House, Vincent Square, S.W.1.—*Secs.*, Rev. W. F. Barker; Rev. B. F. Adeney.

JEWS AND CHRISTIANS, LONDON SOCIETY OF (1927), 28 St. John's Wood Road, N.W.8.—*President*, The Very Rev. E. S. Abbott, K.C.V.O., M.A., D.D.;

Joint Chairman, Rabbi Leslie I. Edgar, M.A., D.D.; The Dean of Westminister; *Sec.*, Mrs. E. Hathan.

JOHN INNES INSTITUTE (1910), Colney Lane, Norwich.—*Director*, Prof. R. Markham, Ph.D., F.R.S.

JOURNALISTS, THE INSTITUTE OF, 1 Whitehall Place, S.W.1.—*Gen. Sec.*, R. F. Farmer.

JUSTICES' CLERKS' SOCIETY (1839).—*Hon. Sec.*, P. J. Halnan, County Hall, Hobson Street, Cambridge.

KEEP BRITAIN TIDY GROUP (1954), Bostel House, 37 West Street, Brighton, Sussex.—*Dir. Gen.*, D. J. Lewis.

KING EDWARD'S HOSPITAL FUND FOR LONDON (1897), 14 Palace Court, W.2.—A charity which uses its annual income to help hospitals improve the effectiveness and efficiency of their service to patients. The Fund divides its income between several major activities: making grants to hospitals both within and outside the National Heath Service but confined to those in or serving the Greater London Area; providing education for hospital staffs through the King's Fund College; sponsoring experiment and enquiry and providing information through its various experts and through the King's Fund Centre; providing the special service of the Emergency Bed Service.—*Chairman of Management Committee*, The Lord Hayter; *Treasurer*, R. J. Dent; *Secretary*, G. A. Phalp.

KING GEORGE'S FUND FOR SAILORS (1917), 1 Chesham Street, S.W.1. The central fund for all charities which support seafarers in need and their families. Distributes over £350,000 in grants annually.—*Gen. Sec.*, Capt. E. G. Brown, R.N.

KING GEORGE'S JUBILEE TRUST, 39 Victoria Street, S.W.1.—Inaugurated in 1935 in commemoration of the Silver Jubilee of King George V. Its objects are the advancement of the physical, mental and spiritual welfare of the younger generation.—*Sec.*, Maj. Sir Michael Hawkins, K.C.V.O., M.B.E.

KING'S FUND, THE (1940), 10 John Adam Street, W.C.2.—To give temporary assistance in directions which are beyond the province of State liability to war-disabled members of the Navy, Army, Air Force, Auxiliary Services, Home Guard, Merchant Navy and Civil Defence organizations and to widows, children and other dependants of those who lost their lives through war service. *Sec.*—K. R. Blundell.

LABOUR PARTY, Transport House, Smith Square, S.W.1.—*Gen. Sec.*, R. G. Hayward, C.B.E.

LADIES IN REDUCED CIRCUMSTANCES, SOCIETY FOR THE ASSISTANCE OF (1886), Lancaster House, Malvern, Worcs.—*Sec.*, Mrs. A. R. White.

LANCASTRIANS IN LONDON, ASSOCIATION OF (1892), Burnley House, 129 Kingsway, W.C.2.—*Hon. Sec.*, W. H. Butler.

LANDSCAPE ARCHITECTS, INSTITUTE OF, 12 Carlton House Terrace, S.W.1.—*Registrar*, K. J. Halifax.

LAND-VALUE TAXATION LEAGUE, 177 Vauxhall Bridge Road, S.W.1.—*Pres.*, V. G. Saldji.

LAW REPORTING FOR ENGLAND AND WALES, INCORPORATED COUNCIL OF (1865), 3 Stone Buildings, Lincoln's Inn, W.C.2.

LEAGUE OF THE HELPING HAND, Edgeleys, Manor Farm, East Worldham, Alton, Hants.—*Sec.*, Mrs. L. E. M. Stacey.

LEAGUE OF REMEMBRANCE, 48 Great Ormond Street, W.C.1.—*Hon. Administrator*, Mrs. D. A. Jeffreys.

LEAGUE OF WELLDOERS (incorporated) (1893), 119 & 133 Limekiln Lane, Liverpool, 5.—*Warden and Sec.*, W. J. Horn.

LEATHER AND HIDE TRADES' BENEVOLENT INSTITUTION (1860), 82 Borough High Street, S.E.1.—*Sec.*, H. G. Forward.

LEGAL EXECUTIVES, INSTITUTE OF, Ilex House, Barrhill Road, S.W.2.—*Sec.*, L. W. Chapman, M.B.E.

LEISURE GARDENERS, NATIONAL SOCIETY OF (*formerly* National Allotments and Gardens Society), 22 High Street, Flitwick, Beds.

LEPROSY GUILD (St. Francis) (1895), 20 The Boltons, S.W.10.

LEPROSY MISSION, THE (*formerly* The Mission to Lepers) (1874), 50 Portland Place, W.1.—*Chairman*, Sir E. Richardson, C.B.E., Ph.D.; *Int. Gen. Sec.*, A. D. Askew.

LEUKAEMIA RESEARCH FUND (1962), 43 Great Ormond Street, W.C.1.—*Dir.*, G. J. Piller.

LIBERAL PARTY ORGANIZATION, 7 Exchange Court, Strand, W.C.2.—*Head of Organization*, E. Wheeler, O.B.E.

LIBERAL PUBLICATION DEPARTMENT (1887), 7 Exchange Court, Strand, W.C.2.—*Sec.*, Mrs. E. Hill.

LIBRARY ASSOCIATION (1877), Ridgmount Street, W.C.1.—*Sec.*, R. P. Hilliard.

LIFEBOATS. *See* " ROYAL NATIONAL."

LIFE OFFICES' ASSOCIATION, THE (1889), Aldermary House, Queen Street, E.C.4.—*Sec. Gen.*, T. H. M. Oppé.

LINGUISTS, INSTITUTE OF (1910), 91 Newington Causeway, S.E.1.—*Sec.*, G. H. Smith, O.B.E.

LINNEAN SOCIETY OF LONDON (1788), Burlington House, W.1.—*Pres.*, Prof. Irene Manton, Sc.D., F.R.S.; *Treas.*, J. C. Gardiner; *Secs.*, Dr. F. H. Perring (*Botany*); Dr. B. Gardiner (*Zoology*); D. C. McClintock, T.D. (*Editorial*); *Exec. Sec.*, T. O'Grady.

LIVERPOOL COTTON ASSOCIATION, 620 Cotton Exchange Buildings, Edmund Street, Liverpool. —*Sec.*, I. R. A. Daglish.

LLOYD'S Lime Street, E.C.3.—*Chairman* (1975), H. H. T. Hudson; *Deputy Chairmen*, L. R. Dew; A. W. Higgins; *Sec. Gen.*, C. G. Wastell, C.B.E.; International Insurance Market, Office of *Lloyd's List, Shipping Index, Loading List, etc.*

LLOYD'S PATRIOTIC FUND (1803), Lloyd's, Lime Street, E.C.3.—*Sec.*, A. J. Carter.

LLOYD'S REGISTER OF SHIPPING (1760), 71 Fenchurch Street, E.C.3.—*Chairman*, R. A. Huskisson; *Deputy Chairman and Chairman of the Sub-Committees of Classification*, R. M. Turnbull; *Deputy Chairman and Treas.*, J. N. S. Ridgers; *Exec. Director*, C. M. Glover; *Technical Director*, B. Hildrew; *Chief Ship Surveyor*, J. McCallum; *Chief Engineer Surveyor*, N. Chambers; *Secretary*, W. T. Leadbetter; Office of *Lloyd's Register Book, Lloyd's Register of Yachts, etc.*

LOCAL AUTHORITIES, INTERNATIONAL UNION OF (1913), British Section, 36 Old Queen Street, S.W.1.—*Joint Secs.*, A. C. Hetherington, C.B.E.; R. H. McCall, O.B.E.; S. Rhodes, O.B.E.

LOCAL GOVERNMENT ADMINISTRATORS INSTITUTE OF.—*Hon. Sec.*, B. J. N. Gleave, 127 Lexden Road, Colchester, Essex.

LOCAL GOVERNMENT BARRISTERS, SOCIETY OF.—*Hon. Sec.*, N. A. L. Rudd, Council Offices, Pontypool, Gwent.

LONDON APPRECIATION SOCIETY (1932), 17 Manson Mews, S.W.7. Visits to places of historic and modern interest in and around London.—*Hon. Sec.*, H. L. Bryant Peers.

LONDON BOROUGHS ASSOCIATION (1964), Westminster City Hall, Victoria Street, S. W.1.—*Hon. Sec.*, Sir Alan Dawtry, C.B.E., T.D. (*Chief Exec. of Westminster*).

LONDON CITY MISSION (1835), 175 Tower Bridge Road, S.E.1.—*Gen. Sec.*, Rev. D. M. Whyte.

LONDON CORNISH ASSOCIATION (1898), *Hon. Gen. Sec.*, N. S. Bunney, 119 Warwick Road, N.11.

LONDON COURT OF ARBITRATION (1892), 69 Cannon Street, E.C.4.—*Chairman*, L. B. Prince, C.B.E.; *Registrar*, E. H. Spalding (*acting*).

LONDON DIOCESAN FUND AND LONDON DIOCESAN HOME MISSION, 33 Bedford Square, W.C.1.—*Sec.*, Ven. J. D. R. Hayward.

LONDON LIBERAL PARTY, St. Margaret's Mansions, 53 Victoria Street, S.W.1.—*Hon. Sec.*, George B. Patterson.

LONDON LIBRARY, THE (1841), 14 St. James's Square, S.W.1.—*Librarian*, S. G. Gillam.

LONDON MAGISTRATES' CLERKS' ASSOCIATION (1889), *Hon. Sec.*, J. A. Laing, Deputy Chief Clerk, Camberwell Green Magistrates' Court, D'Eynsford Road, S.E.5.

LONDON MISSIONARY SOCIETY, *see* CONGREGATIONAL COUNCIL.

"LONDON OVER THE BORDER" CHURCH FUND (1878), Guy Harlings, New Street, Chelmsford. —*Sec.*, H. R. Lovell.

LONDON PLAYING FIELDS SOCIETY (1890), Headquarters, Boston Manor Playing Field, Boston Gardens, Brentford, Middlesex. *Sec.*, Lt.-Col. C. E. B. Sutton, T.D.

LONDON SOCIETY, THE (1912), Wheatsheaf House, 4 Carmelite Street, E.C.4.

LONDON TOPOGRAPHICAL SOCIETY, 50 Grove Lane, S.E.5.—*Hon. Sec.*, S. N. P. Marks.

(LORD MAYOR) TRELOAR TRUST (incorporating Lord Mayor Treloar College and Florence Treloar School for physically handcapped boys and girls), Froyle, nr. Alton, Hants.—*Sec.*, *and Bursar*, B. E. T. Roberts.

LORD'S DAY OBSERVANCE SOCIETY (1831), 55 Fleet Street, E.C.4.—*Gen. Sec.*, H. J. W. Legerton.

LORD'S TAVERNERS, THE, 1 St. James's Street, S.W.1.—*Gen. Sec.*, Capt. J. A. R. Swainson, O.B.E., R.N.

MAGISTRATES' ASSOCIATION (1920), 28 Fitzroy Square, W.1.—*Pres.*, The Lord Chancellor; *Sec.*, A. J. Brayshaw, C.B.E.

MALAYSIA-SINGAPORE COMMERCIAL ASSOCIATION INC. (1955), Cereal House, 58 Mark Lane, E.C.3. —*Sec.*, I. Stemson.

MALAYSIAN RUBBER PRODUCERS' RESEARCH ASSOCIATION (1938), 19 Buckingham Street, W.C.2. —*Sec.*, P. O. Wickens

MALCOLM SARGENT CANCER FUND FOR CHILDREN.— *Gen. Administrator*, Miss S. Darley, 56 Redcliffe Square, S.W.10.

MALONE SOCIETY (for the study of Early English Drama).—*Hon. Sec.*, Miss K. M. Lea, 2 Church Street, Beckley, Oxford.

MANAGEMENT, BRITISH INSTITUTE OF, Parker Street, W.C.2.—*Gen. Manager*, P. J. S. Churchill.

MARINE BIOLOGICAL ASSOCIATION OF THE U.K. (1884), The Laboratory, Citadel Hill, Plymouth. —*Sec. to Council and Director of Plymouth Laboratory*, E. J. Denton, C.B.E., Sc.D., F.R.S.

MARINE ENGINEERS, INSTITUTE OF (1889), 76 Mark Lane, E.C.3.—*Dir. and Sec.*, J. Stuart Robinson.

MARKET AUTHORITIES, NATIONAL ASSOCIATION OF BRITISH, Cattle Market, Gloucester.

MARKETING, INSTITUTE OF (1911), Moor Hall, Cookham, Maidenhead, Berks.—*Sec.*, W. E. Hinder.

MARK MASTER MASONS, GRAND LODGE OF (1856), Mark Masons' Hall, 40 Upper Brook Street, W.1.—*Grand Master*, The Earl of Stradbroke; *Deputy Grand Master*, Col. E. Perry Morgan, M.B.E., T.D.; *Grand Sec.*, Lt.-Col. Hon. M. G. Edwards, M.B.E.

MASONIC BENEVOLENT INSTITUTION, ROYAL (1842), 20 Great Queen Street, W.C.2.—*Sec.*, Sqn.-Ldr. D. A. Lloyd, D.F.C., D.F.M.

MASONIC BENEVOLENT INSTITUTIONS IN IRELAND; *Masonic Girls' School* (1792); *Masonic Boys' School* (1867); *Victoria Jubilee Masonic Annuity Fund* (1887).—*Sec.*, R. J. Clinton, 19 Molesworth Street, Dublin 2.

MASONIC DEGREES—ORDER OF THE TEMPLE, Mark Masons' Hall, 40 Upper Brook Street, W.1.— *Grand Master*, Lt.-Col. J. L. B. Leicester-Warren, T.D.; *Great Vice-Chancellor*, Lt.-Col. Hon. M. G. Edwardes, M.B.E.

MASONIC INSTITUTION FOR BOYS, ROYAL (Incorporated) (1798), 26 Great Queen Street, W.C.2.— *Sec.*, A. R. Jole.

MASONIC INSTITUTION FOR GIRLS, ROYAL (1788). *School*, Rickmansworth; *Offices*, 31 Great Queen Street, W.C.2.—*Sec.*, A. A. Huckle.

MASTER BUILDERS, FEDERATION OF, 33 John Street, W.C.1.—*Nat. Dir.*, W. S. Hilton.

MASTERS OF FOXHOUNDS ASSOCIATION (1856), The Elm, Chipping Norton, Oxon.—*Hon. Sec.*, Lt.-Col. J. E. S. Chamberlayne.

MATERNAL AND CHILD WELFARE, NATIONAL ASSOCIATION FOR (1911), Tavistock House (North), Tavistock Square, W.C.1.—*Gen. Sec.*, W. Rice.

MATHEMATICAL ASSOCIATION (1871), 259 London Road, Leicester.—*Pres.* Prof. R. L. Goodstein; *Hon. Secs.*, Miss N. L. Squire; Dr. A. G. Howson.

MATHEMATICAL SOCIETY, LONDON (1865), Burlington House, W.1.—*Hon. Sec.*, D. A. Brannan; J. L. Briton.

MATHEMATICS AND ITS APPLICATIONS, INSTITUTE OF (1964), Maitland House, Warrior Square, Southend, Essex.—*Sec.*, N. Clarke.

MEASUREMENT AND CONTROL, INSTITUTE OF (1944), 20 Peel Street, W.8.—*Sec.*, E. Eden.

MECHANICAL ENGINEERS, INSTITUTION OF, 1 Birdcage Walk, S.W.1.—*Pres.*, P. T. Fletcher, C.B.E.; *Sec.*, K. H. Platt, C.B.E.

MEDIC-ALERT FOUNDATION, 9 Hanover Street, W.1.—*Chairman*, A. J. Hart. For the protection, in emergencies, of those with a medical disability; to prevent mistakes.

MEDICAL AUXILIARIES, THE BOARD OF REGISTRATION OF (1936), B.M.A. House, Tavistock Square, W.C.1.

MEDICAL COUNCIL, GENERAL, 44 Hallam Street, W.1.—*Registrars*, M. R. Draper (*General Council of England and Wales*); W. Russell (*Branch Council for Scotland*), 8 Queen Street, Edinburgh; Miss M. Hoolan (*Branch Council for Ireland*), 6 Kildare Street, Dublin 2.

MEDICAL SOCIETY OF LONDON (1773), 11 Chandos Street, Cavendish Square, W.1.—*Pres.*, J. S. Richardson, F.R.C.S.; *Hon. Sec.*, J. Glyn; *Registrar*, Maj. H. R. Mitchell, T.D.

MEDICAL WOMEN'S FEDERATION (1917), Tavistock House (North), Tavistock Square, W.C.1.—*Pres.*, Mrs. J. Williamson; *Hon. Sec.*, Dr. Jean Lawrie.

MEN OF THE TREES (1922), Crawley Down, Crawley, Sussex.

MENTAL AFTER CARE ASSOCIATION (1879), for the care and rehabilitation of those recovering from mental illness.—*Sec.*, Mrs. J. Moore, 110 Jermyn Street, S.W.1.

MENTAL HEALTH TRUST AND RESEARCH FUND (1940), 8 Wimpole Street, W.1.—*Dirs.*, Maj.-Gen. C. M. F. Deakin, C.B., C.B.E.; Air Vice-Marshal A. A. Adams, C.B., D.F.C.

MERCANTILE MARINE SERVICE ASSOCIATION (1857) (Shipmasters in command). Affiliated to the Officers (Merchant Navy) Federation. Nautilus House, Mariners' Park, Wallasey, Merseyside.— *Gen. Sec.*, Capt. W. W. P. Lucas; *London Office*, 750/760 High Road, Leytonstone, E.11.

MERCHANT NAVY WELFARE BOARD, 19–21 Lancaster Gate, W.2.—*Sec.*, R. E. Haerle.

MERSEY MISSIONS TO SEAMEN (1857). *Headquarters, Hotel and Registered Office*, Kingston House, James Street, Liverpool 2.

METALLURGISTS, THE INSTITUTION OF, Northway House, High Road, Whetstone, N.20.—*Registrar-Sec.*, D. W. Harding.

METALS SOCIETY, THE (1974) (*Amalgamation of Institute of Metals and Iron and Steel Institute*), 1 Carlton House Terrace, S.W.1.—*Sec.-Gen.*, M. J. Hall.

METEOROLOGICAL SOCIETY, ROYAL (1850), James Glaisher House, Grenville Place, Bracknell, Berks.—*Pres.*, R. Hide, SC.D., F.R.S.; *Hon. Secs.*, D. E. Pedgley; A. J. Gadd, PH.D.

METHODIST MISSIONARY SOCIETY (1786), 25 Marylebone Road, N.W.1. Income, 1974 £1,717,596.

METROPOLITAN AND CITY POLICE ORPHANS FUND (1870), 30 Hazlewell Road, Putney, S.W.15.—*Sec.*, E. R. Hall.

METROPOLITAN AUTHORITIES, ASSOCIATION OF (1974), 36 Old Queen Street, S.W.1.—*Sec.*, R. H. McCall, O.B.E.

METROPOLITAN HOSPITAL-SUNDAY FUND (1872), P.O. Box 15, 206b Station Road, Edgware, Middx. In 1974, £38,200 was distributed as maintenance grants and grants for specific purposes to Hospitals and Homes not controlled by the State; £26,700 to State Hospitals for the use of their medical and psychiatric social workers; £3,050 to other medical charities.—*Sec.*, Miss B. F. Ambler.

METROPOLITAN PUBLIC GARDENS ASSOCIATION (1882), 4 Carlos Place, W.1.

MIDDLE EAST ASSOCIATION (1961), Bury House, 33 Bury Street, S.W.1.—*Dir.-Gen.*, Sir Richard Beaumont, K.C.M.G., O.B.E.

MIDWIVES, ROYAL COLLEGE OF (1881), 15 Mansfield Street, W.1.—*Gen. Sec.*, Miss B. D. Mee.

MIGRAINE SOCIETY, BRITISH, Evergreen, Ottermead Lane, Ottershaw, Chertsey, Surrey.

MIGRAINE TRUST (1965), 23 Queen Square, W.C.1.—*Dir.*, D. R. Mullis.

MILITARY HISTORICAL SOCIETY.—*Hon. Sec.*, J. Gaylor, Duke of York's Headquarters, Chelsea, S.W.3.

MIND (National Association for Mental Health), 22 Harley Street, W.1.—*Dir.*, A. Smythe.

MINERALOGICAL SOCIETY (1876).—*Pres.* (1976), Sir Kingsley Dunham, F.R.S.; *Hon. Gen. Sec.*, J. E. T. Horne, 41 Queen's Gate, S.W.7.

MINIATURE PAINTERS, SCULPTORS AND GRAVERS, ROYAL SOCIETY OF (1895), 17 Carlton House Terrace, S.W.1.—*Pres.*, R. Lister; *Sec.*, C. de Winter.

MINIATURISTS, SOCIETY OF (1895), R. W. S. Galleries, 26 Conduit Street, W.1.—*Sec.*, M. Fry.

MINING AND METALLURGY, INSTITUTION OF (1892), 44 Portland Place, W.1.—*Pres.*, F. D. Richardson; *Sec.*, M. J. Jones.

MINING ENGINEERS, THE INSTITUTION OF (1889), Hobart House, Grosvenor Place, S.W.1.—*Pres.* (1975-76) L. J. Mills; *Sec.*, G. R. Strong.

MINING INSTITUTE OF SCOTLAND, c/o National Coal Board, Green Park, Greenend, Edinburgh.—*Sec.*, E. R. Rodger.

MISSIONS TO SEAMEN, THE, AND ST. ANDREW'S WATERSIDE CHURCH MISSION FOR SAILORS, St. Michael Paternoster Royal, College Hill, E.C.4.—*Gen. Sec.*, Rev. W. J. D. Down.

MODERN CHURCHMEN'S UNION (1898), for the Advancement of Liberal Religious Thought—*Pres.*, The Dean of Westminster; *Hon. Sec.*, Rev. F. E. Compton, Caynham Vicarage, Ludlow, Salop.

MODERN LANGUAGE ASSOCIATION, 33-35 Lewisham Way, S.E.14.—*Hon. Sec.*, S. R. Ingram.

MONUMENTAL BRASS SOCIETY (1887), *Hon. Sec.*, W. Mendelsson, 57 Leeside Crescent, N.W.11.

MORAVIAN MISSIONS, LONDON ASSOCIATION IN AID OF (1817), Moravian Church House, 5/7 Muswell Hill, N.10.—*Sec.*, Rev. R. S. Burd.

MORDEN COLLEGE (1695), Blackheath, S.E.3. *Clerk to the Trustees*, M. S. Graham, M.B.E.

(WILLIAM) MORRIS SOCIETY AND KELMSCOTT FELLOWSHIP (1918).—*Hon. Sec.*, R. C. H. Briggs, Kelmscott House, 26 Upper Mall, W.6.

MOTOR INDUSTRY, THE INSTITUTE OF THE (1920), Fanshaws, Brickendon, Hertford.—*Dir.*, E. V. Tipper.

MOUNTBATTEN (EDWINA) TRUST, 1 Grosvenor Crescent, S.W.1.—*Sec.*, Miss V. W. Henderson, M.B.E.

MULTIPLE SCLEROSIS SOCIETY, 4 Tachbrook Street, S.W.1.—*Gen. Sec.*, A. C. Waine, M.B.E., T.D.

MUNICIPAL ENGINEERS, INSTITUTION OF (1873), 25 Eccleston Square, S.W.1.—*Sec.*, A. Banister, O.B.E., B.SC.

MUSEUMS ASSOCIATION (1889), 87 Charlotte Street, W.1.—*Sec.*, Miss B. Capstick.

MUSICIANS' BENEVOLENT FUND, St. Cecilia's House, 16 Ogle Street, W.1. *Convalescent Home*, Westgate-on-Sea. *Permanent Homes*, Westgate, Hereford and Bromley.

MUSICIANS, INCORPORATED SOCIETY OF (1882), 48 Gloucester Place, W.1.—*Gen. Sec.*, S. M. Alcock.

MUSICIANS OF GREAT BRITAIN, ROYAL SOCIETY OF (1738), 10 Stratford Place, W.1.—*Sec.*, Mrs. M. E. Gleed.

MUSIC SOCIETIES, NATIONAL FEDERATION OF (1935), 29 Exhibition Road, S.W.7.—*Sec.*, J. Crisp.

MYCOLOGICAL SOCIETY, BRITISH.—*Sec.*, B. E. J. Wheeler, PH.D., Imperial College Field Station, Silwood Park, Sunninghall, Berks.

NATIONAL ADULT SCHOOL UNION (1899), Drayton House, Gordon Street, W.C.1.—*Gen. Sec.*, L. A. Sanders.

NATIONAL ALLIANCE OF PRIVATE TRADERS (1943), 388 Corn Exchange, Hanging Ditch, Manchester 4.

NATIONAL AND UNIVERSITY LIBRARIES, STANDING CONFERENCE OF (1950).—*Sec.*, A. J. Loveday, c/o The Library, School of Oriental and African Studies, Malet Street, W.C.1.

NATIONAL ASSOCIATION OF ESTATE AGENTS (1962), Walton House, 11-15 The Parade, Royal Leamington Spa.—*Sec.*, A. R. Taylor.

NATIONAL ASSOCIATION OF FIRE OFFICERS, 6 Westow Hill, S.E.19.—*Gen. Sec.*, W. R. J. Hitchin.

NATIONAL ASSOCIATION OF LOCAL COUNCILS (1947), 100 Great Russell Street, W.C.1.—*Sec.*, C. Arnold-Baker, O.B.E.

NATIONAL BENEVOLENT INSTITUTION (1812), 61 Bayswater Road, W.2.—*Sec.*, Lt.-Col. G. G. Robson.

NATIONAL BIRTHDAY TRUST FUND (1928), 57 Lower Belgrave Street, S.W.1. For Extension of Maternity Services.—*Consultant Adviser*, Miss D. V. Riddick, M.B.E.

NATIONAL BOOK LEAGUE (1925), 7 Albemarle Street, W.1.—*Dir.*, M. Goff.

NATIONAL CATTLE BREEDERS' ASSOCIATION, Brierley House, Summer Lane, Combe Down, Bath.—*Sec.*, A. S. R. Austin.

NATIONAL CHILDREN'S HOME (1869). *Chief Office*, 85 Highbury Park, N.5. Cares for 5,000 socially mentally, or physically handicapped children annually in residental homes, special schools, family centres and community projects in the U.K. and Jamaica.—*Principal*, Rev. G. E. Barritt.

NATIONAL CHRISTIAN EDUCATION COUNCIL (*incorporating* International Bible Reading Association and Denholm House Press), Robert Denholm House, Nutfield, Redhill, Surrey.

NATIONAL CORPORATION FOR THE CARE OF OLD PEOPLE, Nuffield Lodge, Regent's Park, N.W.1. —*Sec.*, H. W. Mellor.

NATIONAL COUNCIL OF LABOUR COLLEGES, 5 Mount Boone, Dartmouth, Devon.—*Gen. Sec.*, J. P. M. Millar.

NATIONAL COUNCIL OF SOCIAL SERVICE, 26 Bedford Square, W.C.1.—*Dir.*, J. K. Owens.

NATIONAL COUNCIL OF WOMEN OF GREAT BRITAIN, 36 Lower Sloane Street, S.W.1.—*Gen. Sec.*, Mrs. J. Simpson.

NATIONAL FEDERATION OF OLD AGE PENSIONS ASSOCIATIONS, 91 Preston New Road, Blackburn, Lancs.—*Sec.*, Mrs. M. Green.

NATIONAL FEDERATION OF OWNER-OCCUPIERS' AND OWNER-RESIDENTS' ASSOCIATIONS.—*Hon. Sec.*, J. W. Clark, 29 Norview Drive, East Didsbury, Manchester.

NATIONAL FEDERATION OF YOUNG FARMERS' CLUBS, Y.F.C. Centre, National Agricultural Centre, Kenilworth, Warwicks.

NATIONAL FUND FOR RESEARCH INTO CRIPPLING DISEASES (1952), Vincent House, 1 Springfield Road, Horsham, Sussex.—*Dir.*, D. Guthrie.

NATIONAL MARKET TRADERS' FEDERATION (1899).— *Pres.*, H. Cross; *Gen. Sec.*, J. Coates, 87 Spital Hill, Sheffield 4.

NATIONAL MARRIAGE GUIDANCE COUNCIL, Herbert Gray College, Little Church Street, Rugby, Warwicks.—*Chief Officer*, N. J. Tyndall.

NATIONAL MONUMENTS RECORD (*incorporating* the National Buildings Record) (1941), Fortress House, 23 Savile Row, W.1.—*Curator*, C. Farthing. O.B.E., F.S.A.

NATIONAL OPERATIC AND DRAMATIC ASSOCIATION (1899), 1 Crestfield Street, W.C.1.—*Dir.*, B. J. Soul.

NATIONAL PEACE COUNCIL (1908), 29 Great James Street, W.C.1.—*Gen. Sec.*, Miss S. Oakes.

NATIONAL PURE WATER ASSOCIATION (1960).— *Sec.*, Mrs. A. R. Cooper, 225 Newtown Road, Worcester.

NATIONAL SECULAR SOCIETY (1866), 698 Holloway Road, N.19.—*Gen. Sec.*, W. McIlroy.

NATIONAL SOCIETY FOR CLEAN AIR (1899), 136 North Street, Brighton, Sussex.—*Sec.-Gen.*, Rear-Adm. P. G. Sharp, C.B., D.S.C.

NATIONAL SOCIETY (CHURCH OF ENGLAND) FOR PROMOTING RELIGIOUS EDUCATION (1811), Church House, Dean's Yard, S.W.1.—*Gen. Sec.*, Rev. Canon R. T. Holtby.

NATIONAL SOCIETY FOR THE PREVENTION OF CRUELTY TO CHILDREN (1884), *Headquarters*, 1 Riding House Street, W.1.—*Chairman*, Lady Holland-Martin, O.B.E., *Treas.*, G. Edmiston; *Director*, Rev. Arthur Morton, O.B.E.

NATIONAL TRUST for places of Historic Interest or Natural Beauty (1895), 42 Queen Anne's Gate, S.W.1.—*Dir. Gen.*, J. D. Boles.

NATIONAL TRUST FOR SCOTLAND for places of historic interest or natural beauty (1931), 5 Charlotte Square, Edinburgh 2.—*Dir.*, J. C. Stormonth Darling, C.B.E., M.C., T.D., W.S.

NATIONAL UNION OF STUDENTS, 3 Endsleigh Street, W.C.1.—*Admin. Sec.*, D. G. Metheringham.

NATIONAL VIEWERS' AND LISTENERS' ASSOCIATION. —*Hon. Gen. Sec.*, Mrs. M. Whitehouse, Blacharnae, Ardleigh, Colchester, Essex.

NATION'S FUND FOR NURSES, 1a Henrietta Place, W.1.—*Sec.*, Mrs. M. Wynne Williams.

NATURE RESERVES, SOCIETY FOR PROMOTION OF (1912).—*Hon. Sec.*, A. E. Smith, O.B.E., The Green, Nettleham, Lincs.

NAUTICAL RESEARCH, SOCIETY FOR (1911), c/o National Maritime Museum, Greenwich, S.E.10. —*Hon. Sec.*, G. P. B. Naish.

NAVAL, MILITARY AND AIR FORCE BIBLE SOCIETY (1780), Radstock House, Eccleston Street, S.W.1. Copies and portions of the Scriptures circulated to the Forces (1974), 123,254.—*Sec.*, N. Brown.

NAVAL ARCHITECTS, ROYAL INSTITUTION OF (1860), 10 Upper Belgrave Street, S.W.1.—*Sec.*, P. W. Ayling.

NAVIGATION, ROYAL INSTITUTE OF, c/o Royal Geographical Society, 1 Kensington Gore, S.W.7. *Dir.*, M. W. Richey, M.B.E.

NAVY LEAGUE (INC.) (1895), Broadway House, Broadway, S.W.19.—*Pres.*, The Earl Cairns, G.C.V.O., C.B.; *Dir.-Gen.*, Rear Adm. I. G. W. Robertson, C.B., D.S.C.

NAVY RECORDS SOCIETY, Royal Naval College, Greenwich, S.E.10.—*Hon. Secs.*, E. F. Bunt; A. N. Ryan.

NEWCOMEN SOCIETY (1920), for the Study of the History of Engineering and Technology, Science Museum, S.W.7.—*Exec. Sec.*, J. W. Butler.

NEW ENGLISH ART CLUB (1886), 17 Carlton House Terrace, S.W.1.—*Sec.*, C. de Winter.

NEWMAN ASSOCIATION (1942), Newman House, 15 Carlisle Street, W.1.

NEWSPAPER EDITORS, GUILD OF BRITISH (1946), Whitefriars House, Carmelite Street, E.C.4.— *Pres.*, T. H. Cooke (*St Regis Newspapers, Bolton*); *Sec.-Treas.*, C. Gordon Page.

NEWSPAPER PRESS FUND (1864), Dickens House, 35 Wathen Road, Dorking, Surrey.—*Sec.*, S. C. Reynolds, O.B.E.

NEWSPAPER PUBLISHERS ASSOCIATION (1906), 6 Bouverie Street, E.C.4.—*Dir.*, J. Dixey.

NEWSPAPER SOCIETY (1836), Whitefriars House, Carmelite Street, E.C.4.—*Pres.*, D. R. W. Greenslade (*Chronicle Advertiser, Mansfield*); *Dir.*, D. Lowndes.

NEWSVENDORS' BENEVOLENT INSTITUTION (1839), Dutch House, 307 High Holborn, W.C.1.—*Sec.*, J. E. Llewellyn-Jones.

NEW TOWNS ASSOCIATION (1970), Glen House, Stag Place, S.W.1.—*Sec.*, P. B. Holden.

NOISE ABATEMENT SOCIETY, 6 Old Bond Street, W.1.—*Chairman*, John Connell.

NONSMOKERS, NATIONAL SOCIETY OF (1926)—*Sec.*, Rev. H. V. Little, 125 West Dumpton Lane, Ramsgate, Kent.

NORE R. N. and R. M. CHILDREN'S TRUST, H.M.S. *Pembroke*, Chatham.—*Sec.*, Lt.-Cdr. H. Blease, R.N. (ret.).

NORTHERN IRELAND TOURIST BOARD, River House, 48 High Street, Belfast 1.—*Chief Executive*, R. C. C. Hall.

NORTHUMBERLAND AND DURHAM ASSOCIATION IN LONDON (1920).—*Hon. Sec.*, H. J. Luxton, 7 Havannah Street, E.14.

NORWOOD HOMES FOR JEWISH CHILDREN (Jewish Orphanage) (1795), 315/317 Ballards Lane, N.12. —*Exec. Dir.*, H. Altman.

NUCLEAR ENERGY SOCIETY, BRITISH (1962), 1-7, Great George Street, S.W.1.—*Sec.*, J. G. Watson, C.B.

NUFFIELD FOUNDATION (1943), Nuffield Lodge, Regent's Park, N.W.1.—*Dir.*, J. Maddox.

NUFFIELD PROVINCIAL HOSPITALS TRUST (1939), 3 Prince Albert Road, N.W.1.—*Gen. Sec.*, G. McLachlan, C.B.E.

NUMISMATIC SOCIETY, BRITISH.—*Hon. Sec.*, W. Slayter, 63 West Way, Edgware, Middx.

NUMISMATIC SOCIETY, ROYAL, c/o Dept. of Coins and Medals, The British Museum, W.C.1.—*Pres.*, R. A. G. Carson; *Hon. Sec.*, Miss M. M. Archibald.

NURSES', RETIRED, NATIONAL HOME, Riverside Avenue, Bournemouth.

NURSES, ROYAL NATIONAL PENSION FUND FOR, 15 Buckingham Street, W.C.2.—*Manager and Actuary*, C. M. O'Brien.

NURSING COUNCIL FOR ENGLAND AND WALES, GENERAL, 23 Portland Place, W.1.—*Registrar*, Miss E. Bendall.

NURSING COUNCIL, GENERAL, for Scotland, 5 Darnaway Street, Edinburgh 3.—*Registrar*, Miss J. G. M. Main, R.G.N.

NURSING, ROYAL COLLEGE OF, Henrietta Place, W.1.—*Gen. Sec.*, Miss C. M. Hall, C.B.E.

NUTRITION SOCIETY (1941).—*Hon. Sec.*, G. L. S. Pawan, D.Sc., Middlesex Hospital Medical School, W.1.

OBSTETRICIANS AND GYNAECOLOGISTS, ROYAL COLLEGE OF (1929), 27 Sussex Place, Regent's Park, N.W.1.—*Pres.*, Prof. Sir Stanley Clayton; *Sec.*, N. Catterall, M.B.E.

OFFICERS' ASSOCIATION, THE (1920), 28 Belgrave Square, S.W.1. Affords relief to ex-officers of The Royal Navy, Army and R.A.F. or their widows and dependants in distress; assists such persons with disability pension and other claims, and to find accommodation in homes for the elderly; helps unemployed ex-officers to find employment.—*Gen. Sec.*, Maj.-Gen. M. Janes, C.B., M.B.E.

OFFICERS' FAMILIES FUND (1899), 28 Belgrave Square, S.W.1.—*Sec.*, Mrs. E. R. Sword.

OFFICERS' PENSIONS SOCIETY, LTD., 15 Buckingham Gate, S.W.1.—*Gen. Sec.*, Rear Adm. F. B. P. Brayne-Nicholls, C.B., D.S.C.

OIL PAINTERS, ROYAL INSTITUTE OF (1883), 17 Carlton House Terrace, S.W.1.—*Pres.*, M. Noakes; *Sec.*, D. de Winter.

OILSEED, OIL AND FEEDINGSTUFFS TRADES BENEVOLENT ASSOCIATION, THE, 14–20 St. Mary Axe, E.C.3.

OLYMPIC ASSOCIATION, BRITISH (1905), 12 Buckingham Street, W.C.2.—*Gen. Sec.*, G. M. Sparkes.

ONE PARENT FAMILIES, NATIONAL COUNCIL FOR (*formerly* National Council for the Unmarried Mother and Her Child), 255 Kentish Town Road, N.W.5.—*Dir.*, Mrs. E. Bramall, O.B.E.

OPEN-AIR MISSION (1853), 19 John Street, W.C.1.—*Sec.*, A. J. Greenbank.

OPTICAL COUNCIL, GENERAL, 41 Harley Street, W.1.—*Registrar*, J. D. Devlin.

ORDERS AND MEDALS RESEARCH SOCIETY.—*Gen. Sec.*, N. G. Gooding, 11 Maresfield, Chepstow Road, Croydon.

ORIENTAL CERAMIC SOCIETY (1921), 31B Torrington Square, W.C.1.—*Sec.*, Vice-Admiral Sir John Gray, K.B.E., C.B.

ORNITHOLOGISTS' CLUB, THE SCOTTISH, 21 Regent Terrace, Edinburgh.—*Sec.*, Maj. A. D. Peirse-Duncombe.

ORNITHOLOGISTS' UNION, BRITISH, c/o Zoological Society of London, Regent's Park, N.W.1.—*Hon. Sec.*, P. J. S. Olney.

ORNITHOLOGY, BRITISH TRUST FOR (1932), Beech Grove, Tring, Herts.—*Administrator*, C. W. N. Plant.

ORNITHOLOGY, FIELD, THE EDWARD GREY INSTITUTE OF (1938), Dept. of Zoology, South Parks Road, Oxford.

ORTHOPÆDIC ASSOCIATION, BRITISH (1918), c/o Royal College of Surgeons, Lincoln's Inn Fields, W.C.2.—*Hon. Sec.*, R. Q. Crellin, F.R.C.S.

OUTWARD BOUND TRUST, Iddesleigh House, Caxton Street, S.W.1.—*Exec. Dir.*, Lt. Col. C. Wylie.

OVERSEAS DEVELOPMENT INSTITUTE LTD. (1960), 10–11 Percy Street, W.1.—*Dir.*, R. N. Wood.

OVERSEAS GRADUATES, LONDON HOUSE FOR, Mecklenburgh Square, W.C.1.

OVERSEAS SERVICE PENSIONERS' ASSOCIATION (1960), 408–412 Coastal Chambers, 172 Buckingham Palace Road, S.W.1.—*Sec.*, K. M. Cowley, C.M.G., O.B.E.

OVERSEAS SETTLEMENT, CHURCH OF ENGLAND COMMITTEE OF (1925), Church House, Dean's Yard, S.W.1.—*Admin.-Sec.*, Miss P. J. Hallett.

OWNERS OF CITY PROPERTIES, ASSOCIATED.—*Sec.*, C. E. F. Gough, 35 Catherine Place, S.W.1.

OXFORD AND CAMBRIDGE SCHOOLS EXAMINATION BOARD (1873). *Offices*, 10 Trumpington Street, Cambridge and Elsfield Way, Oxford.—*Secs.*, A. R. Davis, Oxford; H. F. King, Cambridge.

OXFORD PRESERVATION TRUST (1927), 10 Turn Again Lane, St. Ebbes, Oxford.—*Sec.*, R. S. W. Malcolm.

OXFORD SOCIETY (1932), 8 Wellington Square, Oxford.—*Sec.*, Mrs. D. M. Lennie.

PAINTER-ETCHERS AND ENGRAVERS, ROYAL SOCIETY OF (1880), 26 Conduit Street, W.1.—*Pres.*, H. N. Eccleston; *Sec.*, M. Fry.

PAINTERS IN WATER COLOURS, ROYAL INSTITUTE OF (1831), 17 Carlton House Terrace, S.W.1. —*Pres.*, A. Sykes; *Treas.*, E. Wesson; *Sec.-Gen.*, M. B. Bradshaw.

PAINTERS IN WATER COLOURS, ROYAL SOCIETY OF (1804), 26 Conduit Street, W.1.—*Pres.*, A. Freeth, R.A.; *Sec. and Curator*, M. Fry.

PAINTERS, SCULPTORS AND PRINTMAKERS, NATIONAL SOCIETY OF (1930), 17 Carlton House Terrace, S.W.1.—*Pres.*, K. Barratt; *Sec.*, C. de Winter.

PALÆONTOGRAPHICAL SOCIETY (1847). *Sec.*, F. G. Dimes, c/o Institute of Geological Sciences, Exhibition Road, S.W.7.

PALÆONTOLOGICAL ASSOCIATION (1957).—*Sec.*, Dr. C. T. Scrutton, Dept. of Geology, The University, Newcastle upon Tyne.

PALESTINE EXPLORATION FUND (1865), 2 Hinde Mews, Marylebone Lane, W.1.—*Chairman*, Brig. A. Walmesley White, C.B.E., M.A., F.R.G.S.

PARENTS' NATIONAL EDUCATIONAL UNION, P.N.E.U. (1888), Murray House, Vandon Street, S.W.1.—*Dir.*, C. S. Smyth.

PARKINSON'S DISEASE SOCIETY (1969), 81 Queens Road, S.W.19.—*Exec. Dir.*, C. A. A. Kilmister.

PARLIAMENTARY AND SCIENTIFIC COMMITTEE.— *Sec.*, Lt.-Cdr. C. Powell, 30 Farringdon Street, E.C.4.

PARLIAMENTARY LABOUR PARTY.—*Leader*, Rt. Hon. J. H. Wilson, O.B.E., M.P.; *Deputy Leader*, Rt. Hon. E. W. Short, M.P.; *Chief Whip*, Rt. Hon. R. J. Mellish, M.P.; *Chairman*, Rt. Hon. Cledwyn Hughes, M.P.; *Leader of Labour Peers*, The Lord Shepherd, P.C.; *Sec.*, F. H. Barlow, C.B.E.

PASTEL SOCIETY (1899), 17 Carlton House Terrace, S.W.1.—*Pres.*, A. Sykes; *Sec.*, M. B. Bradshaw.

PASTORAL PSYCHOLOGY, GUILD OF (1936).—*Hon. Sec.*, Mrs. R. Cole, 9 Phoenix House, 5 Waverley Road, N.8.

PATENT AGENTS, CHARTERED INSTITUTE OF (1882), Staple Inn Buildings, W.C.1.—*Sec.*, P. E. Lincroft, M.B.E.

PATENTEES AND INVENTORS, INSTITUTE OF (1919), Whiteley Building, 165 Queensway, W.2.— *Sec.*, A. L. T. Cotterell, M.B.E.

PATHOLOGISTS, ROYAL COLLEGE OF, 2 Carlton House Terrace, S.W.1.

PATIENTS ASSOCIATION (1963), 335 Gray's Inn Road, W.C.1.—*Pres.*, Dame Elizabeth Ackroyd, D.B.E.

PEACE SOCIETY, INTERNATIONAL (1816), Fellowship House, Browning Street, S.E.17. (*Continental Offices*, 5 rue Charles Bonnet, Geneva).—*Director and Sec.*, Rev. H. Rathbone Dunnico.

PEARSON'S FRESH AIR FUND, 112 Regency Street, S.W.1.—*Gen. Sec.*, G. Franklin, O.B.E.

PEDESTRIANS' ASSOCIATION FOR ROAD SAFETY, 166 Shaftesbury Avenue, W.C.2.—*Sec.* (vacant).

P.E.N., INTERNATIONAL (1921), 62–3 Glebe Place, S.W.3. World association of writers.—*Gen. Sec.*, P. Elstob.

PENSION FUNDS, NATIONAL ASSOCIATION OF (1923), —*Sec.*, J. D. Cran, Prudential House, Wellesley Road, Croydon, Surrey.

PEOPLE'S DISPENSARY FOR SICK ANIMALS (1917), P.D.S.A. House, South Street, Dorking, Surrey. —*Gen. Sec.*, E. Rowling.

PERFORMING RIGHT SOCIETY LTD. (1914), 29–33 Berners Street, W.1.—*Gen. Manager*, M. J. Freegard; *Sec.*, G. M. Neighbour.

PERIODICAL PUBLISHERS ASSOCIATION LTD., Imperial House, Kingsway, W.C.2.—*Dir.-Gen.*, D. Burnett.

PERSONNEL MANAGEMENT, INSTITUTE OF (1913), Central House, Upper Woburn Place, W.C.1.—*Dir.*, E. Tonkinson.

PESTALOZZI CHILDREN'S VILLAGE TRUST, Sedlescombe, Battle, Sussex.—*Sec.*, S. G. Dibley.

PETROLEUM, INSTITUTE OF (1913), 61 New Cavendish Street, W.1.—*Gen. Sec.*, D. C. Payne.

PHARMACEUTICAL SOCIETY OF GREAT BRITAIN, 17 Bloomsbury Square, W.C.1.—*Pres.*, J. P. Bannerman; *Sec.*, D. F. Lewis.

PHARMACOLOGICAL SOCIETY, BRITISH.—*Gen. Sec.*, Prof. J. F. Mitchell, Dept. of Pharmacology, The Medical School, University Walk, Bristol.

PHILOLOGICAL SOCIETY (1842), University College, Gower Street, W.C.1.—*Hon. Secs.*, Prof. H. L. Shorto; Prof. R. H. Robins.

PHILOSOPHY, ROYAL INSTITUTE OF, 14 Gordon Square, W.C.1.—*Director*, Prof. G. N. A. Vesey.

PHOTOGRAPHERS, INSTITUTE OF INCORPORATED (1901), Amwell End, Ware, Herts.—*Gen. Sec.*, E. I. N. Waughray.

PHYSICAL EDUCATION ASSOCIATION OF GREAT BRITAIN AND N. IRELAND, THE, Ling House, 10 Nottingham Place, W.1.—*Hon. Sec.*, P. Sebastian.

PHYSICAL RECREATION, CENTRAL COUNCIL OF (1935), 70 Brompton Road, S.W.3.

PHYSICIANS, ROYAL COLLEGE OF (1518), 11 St. Andrew's Place, N.W.1.—*Pres.*, Sir Cyril Clarke, K.B.E., M.D., P.R.C.P., F.R.S.; *Treas.*, N. D. Compston, M.D.; *Registrar*, D. A. Pyke, M.D.; *Sec.*, G. M. G. Tibbs.

PHYSICIANS AND SURGEONS, ROYAL COLLEGE OF (Glasgow) (1599), 242 St. Vincent Street, Glasgow.—*Pres.*, Sir Ferguson Anderson; *Hon. Sec.*, Dr. N. Mackay.

PHYSICIANS OF EDINBURGH, ROYAL COLLEGE OF (1681), *Hall and Library*, 9 Queen Street, Edinburgh 2.—*Sec.*, J. Syme.

PHYSICS, INSTITUTE OF (1874), 47 Belgrave Square, S.W.1.—*Pres.*, Prof. A. B. Pippard, F.R.S.; *Sec.*, L. Cohen, Ph.D.

PHYSIOLOGICAL SOCIETY (1876), Physiological Laboratory, Downing Street, Cambridge.—*Hon. Sec.*, S. M. Hilton, Ph.D., M.B.

PIG BREEDERS ASSOCIATION, NATIONAL (1884), 51a Clarendon Road, Watford, Herts.—*Sec.*, A. J. Manchester.

PILGRIM TRUST, THE (1930), Fielden House, Little College Street, S.W.1.—*Sec.*, Sir Edward Ford, K.C.B., K.C.V.O.

PILGRIMS OF GREAT BRITAIN, THE (1902), Savoy Hotel, W.C.2.—*Chairman*, The Lord Astor of Hever; *Hon. Sec.*, Lt.-Col. S. W. Chant-Sempill, O.B.E., M.C.

PILGRIMS OF THE U.S., THE (1903).—*Pres.*, Hugh Bullock, K.B.E., 74 Trinity Place, New York, N.Y. 10006, U.S.A.

PLACES OF WORSHIP, COUNCIL FOR, 83 London Wall, E.C.2. (*formerly* Council for the Care of Churches) —*Sec.*, D. C. Mandeville, O.B.E.

PLANT ENGINEERS, INSTITUTION OF, 138 Buckingham Palace Road, S.W.1.—*Sec.*, J. K. Bennett.

PLASTICS AND RUBBER INSTITUTE, THE (1931), 11 Hobart Place, S.W.1.—*Sec.*, J. N. Ratcliffe.

PLAYING FIELDS ASSOCIATION, NATIONAL (1925), 25 Ovington Square, S.W.3.—*Chairman*, The Lord Luke, T.D.; *Gen. Sec.*, Lt. Col. R. G. Satterthwaite, O.B.E.

POETRY SOCIETY (1909), 21 Earl's Court Square, S.W.5.—*Gen. Sec.*, M. S. Mackenzie.

POLIO FELLOWSHIP, BRITISH (1939), Bell Close, West End Road, Ruislip, Middlesex.—*Gen. Sec.*, D. S. Powell.

POLITICAL AND ECONOMIC PLANNING (PEP) (1931), 12 Upper Belgrave Street, S.W.1.—*Jt. Dirs.* J. Pinder, O.B.E.; R. Davies.

POLYTECHNICS, COMMITTEE OF DIRECTORS OF, St. Katherine's House, 204 Albany Street, N.W.1.— *Chairman*, Sir Alex Smith; *Sec.* P. L. Flowerday.

POLYTECHNIC TEACHERS, ASSOCIATION OF (1973), 11 Queen's Keep, Clarence Parade, Southsea, Hants.—*Chief Executive*, Miss V. S. Gay.

POULTRY CLUB, THE (1877) (incorporating the British Bantam Association).—*Gen. Sec.*, Mrs. S. Jones, 72 Springfields, Gt. Dunmow, Essex.

PRECEPTORS, COLLEGE OF, Bloomsbury House, 130 High Holborn, W.C.1. All persons engaged in education who have obtained a Diploma of the College or have passed an examination satisfactory to the Council are admissible as members.— *Secretary*, J. V. Chapman.

PREHISTORIC SOCIETY (1908).—*Hon. Sec.*, I. M. Stead, M.A., Ph.D., F.S.A., Dept. of Prehistoric and Romano-British Antiquities, British Museum, W.C.1.

PRESBYTERIAN HISTORICAL SOCIETY OF ENGLAND (1913), c/o United Reformed Church, 86 Tavistock Place, W.C.1.

PRESBYTERIAN HOUSING LIMITED (1929), 86 Tavistock Place, W.C.1.—*Sec.*, C. M. Manning.

PRESS ASSOCIATION (1868), 85 Fleet Street, E.C.4.— *Chairman* (1975–76), H. R. Dickinson (*Bristol United Press*); *General Manager*, I. H. N. Yates; *Sec.*, J. Purdham.

PRINCESS LOUISE SCOTTISH HOSPITAL FOR LIMBLESS SAILORS AND SOLDIERS (1916), Erskine, Bishopton, Renfrewshire.—*Sec. and Tres.*, Maj. G. A. Rankin, 201 W. George Street, Glasgow.

PRINTERS' CHARITABLE CORPORATION (1827), 31 Doughty Street, W.C.1. Homes for elderly printers and widows at Basildon and Bletchley, holiday hotel and convalescence at Eastbourne.— *Gen. Sec.*, A. Reynolds.

PRINTING HISTORICAL SOCIETY (1964), St. Bride Institute, Bride Lane, E.C.4.—*Hon. Sec.*, D. Chambers.

PRINTING, INSTITUTE OF (1961), 10–11 Bedford Row, W.C.1.—*Sec.*, M. A. Smith.

PRISON VISITORS, NATIONAL ASSOCIATION OF (1922), 47 Hartington Street, Bedford.—*Gen. Sec.*, Mrs. A. G. McKenna.

PRIVATE LIBRARIES ASSOCIATION (1957), Ravelston, South View Road, Pinner, Middlesex.—*Hon. Sec.*, F. Broomhead.

PRIVATE PATIENTS PLAN (The Provident Association for Medical Care Ltd.), Eynsham House, Tunbridge Wells, Kent.—*Man. Dir.*, G. D. Lock.

PROCURATORS IN GLASGOW, ROYAL FACULTY OF (1600).—*Treas.*, *Clerk and Fiscal*, A. F. Ferguson, T.D., 55 West Regent Street, Glasgow.

PRODUCTION CONTROL, INSTITUTE OF, Beaufort House, Rother Street, Stratford-upon-Avon, Warwickshire.—*Gen. Sec.*, K. Roberts.

PRODUCTION ENGINEERS, INSTITUTION OF, Rochester House, 66 Little Ealing Lane, W.5.—*Sec.*, S. Caselton, V.R.D.

PROFESSIONAL CIVIL SERVANTS, INSTITUTION OF (1919), 3–7 Northumberland Street, W.C.2.— *Gen. Sec.*, W. McCall.

PROFESSIONAL CLASSES AID COUNCIL, 10 St. Christopher's Place, W.1.—*Sec.*, Miss P. Roden.

PROFESSIONAL SALESMEN— *See* Sales Engineers.

PROFESSIONAL WORKERS, NATIONAL FEDERATION OF (1920), 30a Station Road, Harpenden, Herts.

PROFESSIONS SUPPLEMENTARY TO MEDICINE, COUNCIL FOR, York House, Westminster Bridge Road, S.E.1.—*Registrar*, J. S. Tapsfield.

PROPAGATION OF THE GOSPEL, UNITED SOCIETY FOR THE (U.S.P.G.), 15 Tufton Street, S.W.1.—*Sec.*, Canon James Robertson, M.A.

PROTECTION OF LIFE FROM FIRE, SOCIETY FOR THE (1836), Chichester House, 278–82 High Holborn, W.C.1.—*Sec.*, W. E. Chantler.

PROTESTANT ALLIANCE, THE (1845), 112 Colin Gardens, N.W.9.—*Sec.*, Rev. A. G. Ashdown.

PROVINCIAL NOTARIES SOCIETY (1907), 132 High Street, Portsmouth, Hants.—*Sec.*, G. E. Delafield.

PSYCHIATRISTS, ROYAL COLLEGE OF (1971, *formerly* Royal Medico-Psychological Association founded in 1841), 17 Belgrave Square, S.W.1.—*Registrar*, M. Markowe, M.D.

PSYCHICAL RESEARCH, SOCIETY FOR (1882), 1 Adam and Eve Mews, W.8.—*Pres.*, Dr. J. Beloff.

PSYCHOLOGICAL SOCIETY, THE BRITISH (1901), 18–19 Albemarle Street, W.1.—*Pres.*, Prof. J. Tizard; *Sec. Gen.*, R. R. Hetherington.

PUBLIC ADMINISTRATION, ROYAL INSTITUTE OF (1922), Hamilton House, Mabledon Place, W.C.1 —*Dir.-Gen.*, R. Nottage, C.M.G.

PUBLIC FINANCE AND ACCOUNTANCY, CHARTERED INSTITUTE OF (1885) (*formerly* Institute of Municipal Treasurers and Accountants).—*Sec.*, R. A. Emmott, 1 Buckingham Place, S.W.1.

PUBLIC HEALTH AND HYGIENE, THE ROYAL INSTITUTE OF (1937), Postgraduate Medical School, 28 Portland Place, W.1.; Harben Laboratories, 23 Queen Square, W.C.1.—*Sec.*, A. R. Horsham.

PUBLIC HEALTH ENGINEERS, INSTITUTION OF (1895), 32 Eccleston Square, S.W.1.—*Sec.*, I. B. Muirhead.

PUBLIC RELATIONS, INSTITUTE OF (1948), 1 Great James Street, W.C.1.—*Dir.*, B. V. Tolputt.

PUBLIC SCHOOLS, ASSOCIATION OF GOVERNING BODIES OF (BOYS) (1941).—*Sec.*, F. J. Walesby, 2 Church Road, Steep, Petersfield, Hants.

PUBLIC SCHOOLS, ASSOCIATION OF GOVERNING BODIES OF GIRLS' (1942).—*Sec.*, F. J. Walesby (*see above*).

PUBLIC SCHOOLS BURSARS' ASSOCIATION (1932).— *Sec.*, Capt. I. G. Mason, R.N., 69 Crescent Road, Alverstoke, Gosport, Hants.

PUBLIC TEACHERS OF LAW, SOCIETY OF (1908).— *Pres.*, Prof. F. R. Crane; *Hon. Sec.*, Prof. P. B. Fairest, Faculty of Law, The University, Hull.

PUBLISHERS ASSOCIATION (1896), 19 Bedford Square, W.C.1.—*Pres.*, P. Allsop; *Sec.*, R. E. Barker, O.B.E.

PURCHASING AND SUPPLY, INSTITUTE OF (1967), York House, Westminster Bridge Road, S.E.1.— *Dir.-Gen.*, A. M. Taylor.

QUALITY ASSURANCE, INSTITUTE OF (*formerly* the Institution of Engineering Inspection), 54 Princes Gate, Exhibition Road, S.W.7.—*Sec.*, R. Knowles, C.B.E.

QUANTITY SURVEYORS, INSTITUTE OF, 98 Gloucester Place, W.1.—*Dir.*, Brig. F. H. Lowman.

QUARRIER'S HOMES (1871), Bridge of Weir, Renfrewshire, Scotland.

QUARRYING, INSTITUTE OF (1917), 7 Regent Street, Nottingham.—*Sec.*, R. Oates.

QUEEN ELIZABETH'S FOUNDATION FOR THE DISABLED (1967), Leatherhead, Surrey.—*Dir.*, R. N. Smith, O.B.E., M.C., T.D. Incorporating Queen Elizabeth's Training College (1934), Banstead Place

Assessment and Further Education Centre for Handicapped School Leavers (1973), Dorincourt Residential Sheltered Workshop (1958) and Lulworth Court Holiday and Convalescent Home (1959).

QUEEN VICTORIA CLERGY FUND (1897), *Central Fund*, Church House, Dean's Yard, S.W.1.— *Sec.*, Maj. G. C. Hackett, M.B.E.

QUEEN VICTORIA SCHOOL, Dunblane, Perthshire.— *Headmaster*, J. R. F. Melluish, M.A.

QUEEN'S NURSING INSTITUTE (1887), 57 Lower Belgrave Street, S.W.1.—*Gen. Sec.*, Miss M. Faulkner.

RADIO SOCIETY OF GREAT BRITAIN (Incorporated), 35 Doughty Street, W.C.1.—*Gen. Manager*, G. R. Jessop.

RADIOLOGISTS, FACULTY OF (1934), Royal College of Surgeons, Lincoln's Inn Fields, W.C.2.—*Hon. Sec.*, J. W. Laws.

RAILWAY AND CANAL HISTORICAL SOCIETY.—*Hon. Sec.*, A. P. Voce, Littlemoor, Puddington, nr. Tiverton, Devon.

RAILWAY BENEVOLENT INSTITUTION (1858), 29 John Street, W.C.1.; Railway Children's Home at Derby and Old People's Home near Dorking. —*Gen. Sec.*, E. A. Palmer.

RAILWAY INVIGORATION SOCIETY (1954), BM-RIS, W.C.1.—*Gen. Sec.*, J. M. Stanley.

RAINER FOUNDATION, 89a Blackheath Hill, S.E.10. A voluntary society providing residential and remedial help for children and young people.— *Gen. Sec.*, R. Howell.

RAMBLERS' ASSOCIATION (1935), 1–4 Crawford Mews, York Street, W.1.—*Sec.*, A. Mattingly.

RATEPAYERS' ASSOCIATIONS, NATIONAL UNION OF, 47 Victoria Street, S.W.1.

RATING AND VALUATION ASSOCIATION (1882), 115 Ebury Street, S.W.1.—*Sec.*, B. L. Hill.

RED CROSS SOCIETY, BRITISH. See BRITISH.

RED POLL CATTLE SOCIETY AND BRITISH DANE CATTLE SOCIETY, 28 Riseholme Lane, Riseholme, Lincoln.—*Sec.*, W. Dunnaway.

REEDHAM SCHOOL (Incorporated) (1844), Purley, Surrey.—*Sec.*, Mrs. M. J. Pupius.

REED'S SCHOOL (1813), *Offices*, 8 Little Trinity Lane, E.C.4.—*Sec.*, D. Cooper.

REFRIGERATION, INSTITUTE OF (1899), 272 London Road, Wallington, Surrey.—*Sec.*, D. T. Lee.

REGULAR FORCES EMPLOYMENT ASSOCIATION (1885), 25 Bloomsbury Square, W.C.1. Finds employment for non-commissioned ex-Regulars.— *General Manager*, Maj.-Gen. P. F. Claxton, C.B., O.B.E.

REINDEER COUNCIL OF THE UNITED KINGDOM (1949), Newton Hill, Harston, Cambridge.— *Hon. Sec.*, Dr. E. J. Lindgren, M.A.

RELIGION AND MEDICINE, INSTITUTE OF (1964).— *Organizing Sec.*, Mrs. E. A. Wye, St. Mary Abchurch, Abchurch Lane, E.C.4.

RENT OFFICERS, INSTITUTE OF.—*Hon. Sec.*, D. A. G. Sargent, D.F.C., Moulsham House, 48 Moulsham Street, Chelmsford, Essex.

RESEARCH DEFENCE SOCIETY, 11 Chandos Street, Cavendish Square, W.1.—*Hon. Sec.*, Prof. H. Barcroft, M.D., F.R.C.P., F.R.S.; *Sec.*, Mrs. C. Ewen.

RETAIL ALLIANCE, 3 Berners Street, W.1.—*Sec.*, J. Hussey.

RICHARD III SOCIETY.—*Gen. Sec.*, Mrs. P. Hester, 65 Howard Road, Upminster, Essex.

RIVER AUTHORITIES, ASSOCIATION OF, National Water Council, 1 Queen Anne's Gate, S.W.1.

RIVERS PROTECTION, CENTRAL COUNCIL FOR, Fishmongers' Hall, E.C.4.—*Joint Hon. Secs.*, E. S. Earl; Leonard Millis, C.B.E.

ROAD SAFETY OFFICERS, INSTITUTE OF (1971), Road Safety Centre, 8 Meadow Road, Harborne, Birmingham.—*Sec.*, D. E. Clarke.

ROADS IMPROVEMENT ASSOCIATION, Comet Way, Southend-on-Sea, Essex.

ROAD TRANSPORT ENGINEERS, INSTITUTE OF (1945), 1 Cromwell Place, S.W.7.—*Sec.*, J. A. Fletcher, M.B.E.

ROMAN AND MEDIAEVAL LONDON EXCAVATION COUNCIL.—*Hon. Sec.*, R. A. Woods, F.S.A., 31 Goodyers Avenue, Radlett, Herts.

ROMAN STUDIES, SOCIETY FOR PROMOTION OF, 31–34 Gordon Square, W.C.1.—*Pres.*, A. N. Sherwin-White, F.B.A.; *Sec.*, Mrs. P. Gilbert.

ROTARY INTERNATIONAL IN GREAT BRITAIN AND IRELAND (1911), Sheen Lane House, Sheen Lane, S.W.14.—*Sec.*, J. H. Jackson.

ROYAL AFRICAN SOCIETY (1901), 18 Northumberland Avenue, W.C.2.—*Sec.*, M. Edgedale.

ROYAL AGRICULTURAL SOCIETY OF ENGLAND (1838), National Agricultural Centre, Stoneleigh, Kenilworth, Warwicks.—*Chief Exec.*, J. D. M. Hearth.

ROYAL AIR FORCE BENEVOLENT FUND (1919), 67 Portland Place, W.1.—*Controller*, Air Marshal Sir Denis Crowley-Milling, K.C.B., C.B.E., D.S.O., D.F.C.

ROYAL AIR FORCES ASSOCIATION, 43 Grove Park Road, W.4.—*Sec. Gen.*, G. R. Boak, O.B.E.

ROYAL ALEXANDRA AND ALBERT SCHOOL (1758), Offices, Gatton Park, Reigate, Surrey.—*Comptroller*, E. A. Corner.

ROYAL ALFRED MERCHANT SEAMEN'S SOCIETY (1865), Weston Acres, Woodmansterne Lane, Banstead, Surrey. Home for aged seamen, Belvedere, Kent; Flatlets for retired seafarers and widows at Banstead, Surrey. Out-pensions for retired seamen of limited means. Samaritan and War Fund for general relief. Allowances for widows in distress and Home for widows and retired stewardesses, Eastbourne.—*Gen. Sec.*, D. J. Lafferty, M.B.E.

ROYAL ARMOURED CORPS BENEVOLENT FUND, *Headquarters*, R.A.C. Centre, Bovington Camp, Wareham, Dorset; *Sec.*, Lt.-Col. C. H. Rayment, M.B.E.

ROYAL ARTILLERY ASSOCIATION, Artillery House, Connaught Barracks, Grand Depot Road, S.E.18.—*Gen. Sec.*, Maj. F. C. Emery, M.B.E.

ROYAL ASIATIC SOCIETY, 56 Queen Anne Street, W.1.—*Sec.*, Miss D. Crawford.

ROYAL ASSOCIATION OF BRITISH DAIRY FARMERS (1876), Robarts House, Rossmore Road, N.W.1.—*Sec.*, F. R. Francis, M.B.E.

ROYAL BRITISH NURSES ASSOCIATION, 94 Upper Tollington Park, N.4.—*Hon. Sec.*, Mrs. H. M. Vorstermans, M.B.E.

ROYAL CALEDONIAN SCHOOLS (1815), Bushey, Herts.—*Chief Exec.*, George Deans.

ROYAL CAMBRIDGE HOME FOR SOLDIERS' WIDOWS, 82–84 Hurst Road, East Molesey, Surrey.—*Sec.*, Miss E. M. Bennett, M.B.E.

ROYAL CELTIC SOCIETY (1820), 49 Queen Street, Edinburgh.—*Sec.*, J. G. S. Cameron, W.S.

ROYAL CENTRAL ASIAN SOCIETY (1901), 42 Devonshire Street, W.1.—*Pres.*, The Earl of Selkirk, P.C. G.C.M.C., G.B.E., A.F.C.; *Sec.*, Miss M. FitzSimons.

ROYAL CHORAL SOCIETY (1871), Royal Albert Hall, S.W.7.—*Gen. Man.*, M. de Grey.

ROYAL COLLEGE OF VETERINARY SURGEONS, 32 Belgrave Square, S.W.1.—*Pres.*, A. G. Beynon; *Registrar*, A. R. W. Porter.

ROYAL COMMONWEALTH SOCIETY (1868), Northumberland Avenue, W.C.2.—*Chairman*, The Lord Astor of Hever (30,000 members).—*Sec.-Gen.*, A. S. H. Kemp, O.B.E.

ROYAL DESIGNERS FOR INDUSTRY, FACULTY OF (1936) (Royal Society of Arts), John Adam Street, W.C.2.—*Master*, J. Howe, R.D.I., F.R.I.B.A.; *Sec.*, K. Grant.

ROYAL DRAWING SOCIETY (1902), 17 Carlton House Terrace, S.W.1.—*Pres.*, J. Mills, F.R.S.A.; *Sec.*, D. Flanders.

ROYAL ECONOMIC SOCIETY (1890), P.O. Box 86, Cambridge.—*Sec.-Gen.*, R. C. Tress.

ROYAL ENGINEERS ASSOCIATION, *Headquarters*, R.S.M.E., Chatham, Kent.—*Controller*, Col. R. R. L. Harradine, T.D.

ROYAL ENGINEERS, THE INSTITUTION OF (1875), Chatham.—*Sec.*, Col. E. E. Peel.

ROYAL HIGHLAND AND AGRICULTURAL SOCIETY OF SCOTLAND (1784), Ingliston, Edinburgh.—*Sec.*, T. W. M. Alder.

ROYAL HORTICULTURAL SOCIETY (1804).—*Offices*, Vincent Square, S.W.1. *Garden*, Wisley, Ripley, Woking, Surrey.—*Sec.*, J. R. Cowell.

ROYAL HOSPITAL AND HOME FOR INCURABLES, PUTNEY (1854), West Hill, S.W.15.—*Sec.*, Col. N. F. Gordon-Wilson, M.B.E.

ROYAL HOSPITAL SCHOOL, Holbrook, nr. Ipswich, Suffolk.—*Headmaster*, N. B. Worswick.

ROYAL HUMANE SOCIETY (1774).—In 1974, 748 persons were rewarded by the R.H.S. for saving 469 lives, and attempting to save the lives of 77 others.—*Offices*, Watergate House, York Buildings, Adelphi, W.C.2.—*Sec.*, J. M. Leadbitter, O.B.E.

ROYAL INSTITUTE OF INTERNATIONAL AFFAIRS (1920), Chatham House, St. James's Square, S.W.1.—*Director*, A. Shonfield.

ROYAL INSTITUTION OF GREAT BRITAIN (1799), 21 Albemarle Street, W.1.—*Pres.*, The Lord Kings Norton, PH.D., D.SS., D.Tech.; *Dir.*, Prof. Sir George Porter, F.R.S.; *Sec.*, J. S. Porterfield, M.D.

ROYAL INSTITUTION OF SOUTH WALES, Swansea (1835).—*Hon. Sec.*, F. M. Gibbs.

ROYAL LIFE SAVING SOCIETY, THE (1891), Desborough House, 14 Devonshire Street, W.1.—*Dir. and Sec.*, Brig. P. de C. Jones, O.B.E.

ROYAL LITERARY FUND (1790), 11 Ludgate Hill, E.C.4. Grants to necessitous authors of some published work of approved literary merit or to their immediate dependants.—*Pres.*, J. Lehmann, C.B.E.; *Sec.*, V. Bonham-Carter.

ROYAL MEDICAL BENEVOLENT FUND (1836), 24 King's Road, Wimbledon, S.W.19.—*Dir.*, Col. A. J. S. Crockett, O.B.E.

ROYAL MEDICAL SOCIETY (1737), Students Centre, Bristo Street, Edinburgh.—*Secs.*, Miss J. Duvall; D. Smith.

ROYAL METAL TRADES BENEVOLENT SOCIETY (1843), 223 Cranbrook Road, Ilford, Essex.—*Sec.*, L. H. Lindsay, M.B.E.

ROYAL MICROSCOPICAL SOCIETY, 37–38 St. Clements, Oxford.—*Administrator*, Lt.-Col. P. G. Fleming.

ROYAL MILITARY POLICE ASSOCIATION (1946), Regimental Headquarters, Corps. of Royal Military Police, Roussillon Barracks, Chichester, Sussex.—*Sec.*, Major R. J. R. Whistler.

ROYAL MUSICAL ASSOCIATION (1874) c/o British Museum, W.C.1.—*Sec.*, M. Turner.

ROYAL NATIONAL LIFE-BOAT INSTITUTION, THE (1824).—*Income* (1974) £4,944,781, expenditure £4,669,118; total number of lives rescued, over 100,000; rescued in 1974, 1,353. 135 life-boats and 122 fast inshore lifeboats are maintained on the coasts of Great Britain and Ireland. *Offices*, West Quay, Poole, Dorset.—*Dir.*, Capt. N. Dixon, R.N.

ROYAL NATIONAL MISSION TO DEEP SEA FISHERMEN (1881), 43 Nottingham Place, W.1.—*Sec.*, J. C. Lewis, O.B.E.

ROYAL NATIONAL ROSE SOCIETY, Chiswell Green Lane, St. Albans, Herts.—*Sec.*, L. G. Turner.

ROYAL NAVAL AND ROYAL MARINE CHILDREN'S HOME (1834), Waterlooville.—*Sec.*, Mrs. P. A. Hopper, H.M.S. *Nelson*, Portsmouth.

ROYAL NAVAL BENEVOLENT SOCIETY (1739), 1 Fleet Street, E.C.4.—*Sec.*, Capt. R. C. Steele, R.N. (*ret.*).

ROYAL NAVAL BENEVOLENT TRUST (1922) (Grand Fleet and Kindred Funds), High Street, Brompton, Gillingham, Kent (Local Committees at Chatham, Devonport and Portsmouth).—*Gen. Sec.*, Lt.-Cdr. D. C. Lawrence, R.N. (*ret.*).

ROYAL NAVAL FUND (1891). Administered by the Royal Naval Benevolent Trust. *See above.*

ROYAL NAVY OFFICERS, ASSOCIATION OF (Trafalgar Day, 1925), 70 Porchester Terrace, W.2.—*Sec.-Comptroller*, Cdr. D. J. Calnan, R.N.

ROYAL PATRIOTIC FUND CORPORATION (1854), 1 Cambridge Gate, N.W.1. Administers funds for the benefit of widows, children and other dependants of deceased officers and servicemen of the Armed Forces.—*Sec.*, Brig. H. E. Boulter, C.B.E., D.S.O.

ROYAL PHILANTHROPIC SOCIETY'S SCHOOL, Redhill, Surrey.—*Princ.*, L. H. Crew.

ROYAL PHILATELIC SOCIETY, LONDON (1869), 41 Devonshire Place, W.1.—*Hon. Sec.*, J. O. Griffiths.

ROYAL PHILHARMONIC SOCIETY (1813), 29 Exhibition Road, S.W.7.—*Hon. Sec.*, W. Cole, M.V.O., D.Mus., F.R.A.M., F.R.C.O.

ROYAL PHOTOGRAPHIC SOCIETY (1853), 14 South Audley Street, W.1.—*Sec.*, K. R. Warr.

ROYAL PINNER SCHOOL FOUNDATION, 110 Old Brompton Road, S. Kensington, S.W.7. Assists by grants and bursaries in the education of commercial travellers' children where families are struck by misfortune.—*Sec.*, W. H. Drayton.

" ROYAL SAILORS' RESTS " (Miss Agnes Weston's) (1876). *Head Office*, South Street, Gosport, Hants. Rests for naval personnel at Devonport and Singapore; Christian Community centres for Naval families at Gosport and Plymouth.

ROYAL SCHOOL OF NEEDLEWORK (1872), 25 Princes Gate, S.W.7.—*Dir.*, D. Lloyd.

ROYAL SCOTTISH COUNTRY DANCE SOCIETY (1923), 12 Coates Crescent, Edinburgh.—*Sec.*, Mrs. A. Burt.

ROYAL SCOTTISH SOCIETY FOR PREVENTION OF CRUELTY TO CHILDREN (1884), 16 Melville Street, Edinburgh.—*Gen. Sec.*, A. M. M. Wood.

ROYAL SCOTTISH SOCIETY OF ARTS (1821) (Science and Technology).—*Sec.*, G. Brash, 70 Cumberland Street, Edinburgh.

ROYAL SEAMEN'S PENSION FUND (Incorporated) (1919), 58 High Street, Sutton, Surrey.—*Sec.*, R. F. Van Houten

ROYAL SIGNALS INSTITUTION (1950), Cheltenham Terrace, S.W.3.—*Sec.*, Lt.-Col. E. G. Day, O.B.E., T.D.

ROYAL SOCIETY, THE (1660), 6 Carlton House Terrace, S.W.1.—*Pres.*, Sir Alan Hodgkin, O.M., K.B.E.; *Treas. and Vice-Pres.*, Sir James Menter; *Secretaries and Vice-Presidents*, Sir Bernard Katz; Sir Harrie Massey; *Foreign Secretary and Vice-Pres.*, Sir Kingsley Dunham; *Executive Sec.*, Sir David Martin, C.B.E.

ROYAL SOCIETY FOR THE PREVENTION OF ACCIDENTS, Cannon House, Priory Queensway, Birmingham. —*Dir.-Gen.*, J. P. Weston; *Sec.*, R. F. B. Fenn.

ROYAL SOCIETY FOR THE PREVENTION OF CRUELTY TO ANIMALS (1824), Causeway, Horsham, Sussex. *Exec. Dir.*, Maj. R. F. Seager.

ROYAL SOCIETY FOR THE PROTECTION OF BIRDS (1889), The Lodge, Sandy, Beds.—*Dir.*, I. Prestt.

ROYAL SOCIETY OF ARTS (1754), 6-8 John Adam Street, Adelphi, W.C.2.—*Chairman*, Sir Brian Batsford; *Sec.*, K. Grant.

ROYAL SOCIETY OF BRITISH ARTISTS (1823), 17 Carlton House Terrace, S.W.1.—*Pres.*, P. Greenham, R.A.; *Vice-President*, D. J. Winfield; *Keeper*, C. de Winter.

ROYAL SOCIETY OF BRITISH SCULPTORS (1904), 8 Chesham Place, S.W.1.—*Pres.*, M. Clark; *Sec.*, Mrs. F. McGregor-Eadie.

ROYAL SOCIETY OF EDINBURGH (1783), 22 George Street, Edinburgh 2.—*Pres.*, The Hon. Lord Cameron, D.S.C.; *Gen. Sec.*, Prof. A. E. Ritchie, M.D.; *Treas.*, The Lord Balerno, C.B.E., T.D., D.SC.; *Curator*, H. E. Butler, Ph.D.

ROYAL SOCIETY OF HEALTH (1876), to promote the health of the people, 13 Grosvenor Place, S.W.1. —*Sec.*, D. S. Wilson.

ROYAL SOCIETY OF LITERATURE (1823), 1 Hyde Park Gardens, W.2.—*Sec.*, Mrs. J. M. Patterson.

ROYAL SOCIETY OF MEDICINE (1805), 1 Wimpole Street, W.1.—*Pres.*, Dr. G. E. W. Wolstenholme, O.B.E., F.R.C.P.; *Exec. Dir.*, R. T. Hewitt, O.B.E.

ROYAL SOCIETY OF PORTRAIT PAINTERS (1891), 17 Carlton House Terrace, S.W.1.—*Pres.*, E. Halliday, C.B.E.; *Sec.*, M. B. Bradshaw.

ROYAL SOCIETY OF ST. GEORGE (1894), 4 Upper Belgrave Street, S.W.1.—*Gen. Sec.*, Mrs. W. M. Bourne.

ROYAL STATISTICAL SOCIETY (1834), 21 Bentinck Street, W.1.—*Pres.*, Miss S. V. Cunliffe; *Sec.*, I. H. Blenkinsop.

ROYAL TANK REGIMENT ASSOCIATION and BENEVOLENT FUND, H.Q. R.A.C. Centre, Bovington Camp, Wareham, Dorset.—*Sec.*, Lt.-Col. C. H. Rayment, M.B.E.

ROYAL UNITED KINGDOM BENEFICENT ASSOCIATION (1863), 6 Avonmore Road, W.14.—*Gen. Sec.*, Maj.-Gen. R. D. Houghton, C.B., O.B.E., M.C.

ROYAL UNITED SERVICES INSTITUTE FOR DEFENCE STUDIES, Whitehall, S.W.1.—*Dir.-Gen.*, Air Vice-Marshal S. W. B. Menaul, C.B., C.B.E., D.F.C., A.F.C.

RURAL ENGLAND, COUNCIL FOR THE PROTECTION OF (1926), 4 Hobart Place, S.W.1.—*Dir.*, C. Hall.

RURAL SCOTLAND, ASSOCIATION FOR PROTECTION OF (1927), 20 Falkland Avenue, Newton Mearns, Renfrewshire.—*Sec.*, R. Livingstone.

SAILORS' CHILDREN'S SOCIETY, THE (1821), Newland, Hull. Cares for British seamen's children who have lost a parent and for short periods during a mother's illness if father is at sea. Provides welfare facilities for seamen in Humber area, including Homes for aged seafarers at Hull, Goole, Grimsby, and S. Shields.

ST. DUNSTAN'S, for men and women blinded on War Service, P.O. Box 58, 191 Old Marylebone Road, N.W.1. In March 1975, the number of blinded men and women in the care of the organization was 1,807.—*Pres.*, Sir Neville Pearson, Bt.; *Chairman*, I. Garnett-Orme; *Hon. Treas.*, M. D. Morgan; *Sec.*, C. D. Wills.

ST. GILES CHRISTIAN MISSION (1860), 60 Bride Street, N.7.—*Superintendent*, Pastor J. B. Jones.

ST. JOHN AMBULANCE ASSOCIATION AND BRIGADE, 1 Grosvenor Crescent, S.W.1.—*Chief Commander*, Sir Maurice Dorman, G.C.M.G., G.C.V.O.; *Commissioner-in-Chief*, Maj.-Gen. D. S. Gordon, C.B., C.B.E. *Brigade Strengths* (U.K. 1974), Men, 22,397; Women, 16,708; Boy Cadets, 20,056; Girl Cadets, 35,466.—*Registrar*, G. W. Woodhill, M.B.E.

SALES ENGINEERS, INSTITUTION OF (1966), Concorde House, 24 Warwick New Road, Royal Leamington Spa. *Dir.-Gen.*, J. E. Fenton.

SALMON AND TROUT ASSOCIATION (1903), Fishmongers' Hall, E.C.4.—*Sec.*, B. H. Catchpole.

SALTIRE SOCIETY (1936), Gladstone's Land, 483 Lawnmarket, Edinburgh 1. *Org. Sec.*, A. C. Davis.

SALVAGE CORPS (FIRE)—
London (1866), 140 Aldersgate Street, E.C.1.
Chief Officer, K. G. Smith.
Liverpool (1842), 46 Derby Road, Liverpool.
Chief Officer, A. H. Jones.
Glasgow (1873), 90 Maitland Street, Glasgow.
Chief Officer, W. C. Borland.

SAMARITANS, THE (to help the suicidal and despairing).—*Gen. Sec.*, Miss J. Burt, 17 Uxbridge Road, Slough, Bucks.

SANITARY ENGINEERS, INSTITUTION OF. *See* PUBLIC HEALTH ENGINEERS.

SAVE THE CHILDREN FUND (1919), 157 Clapham Road, S.W.9.—*Dir. Gen.*, Sir John Lapsley, K.B.E., C.B., D.F.C., A.F.C.

SAVINGS BANKS INSTITUTE, Knighton House, 52–66 Mortimer Street, W.1.—*Sec.*, A. J. F. Miller.

SCHOOL LIBRARY ASSOCIATION, Victoria House, 29–31 George Street, Oxford.—*Hon. Sec.*, C. A. Waite.

SCHOOL NATURAL SCIENCE SOCIETY, 2 Bramley Mansions, Berrylands Road, Surbiton, Surrey.—*Hon. Gen. Sec.*, M. Jenny Sellers.

SCHOOLMASTERS' ASSOCIATION, SCOTTISH, 41 York Place, Edinburgh.—*Gen. Sec.*, R. McClement.

SCHOOLMASTERS, NATIONAL ASSOCIATION OF, P.O. Box 65, Swan Court, Waterhouse Street, Hemel Hempstead, Herts.

SCHOOLMASTERS, SOCIETY OF (1798) (for the relief of Necessitous Schoolmasters and of their Widows and Orphans), 308 Galpins Road, Thornton Heath, Surrey.—*Sec.*, Mrs. H. E. Closs.

SCHOOLMISTRESSES AND GOVERNESSES BENEVOLENT INSTITUTION, 39 Buckingham Gate, S.W.1. Helps schoolmistresses, matrons and secretaries in independent schools, and self-employed women teachers; annuities, grants, a home.—*Sec.*, C. J. Page.

SCHOOLS MUSIC ASSOCIATION, THE (1938), 4 Newman Road, Bromley, Kent.—*Sec.*, S. S. Moore.

SCIENCE AND LEARNING, SOCIETY FOR THE PROTECTION OF, 3 Buckland Crescent, N.W.3.—*President*, Prof. A. V. Hill, C.H., O.B.E., F.R.S.; *Sec.*, Miss E. Simpson, O.B.E.

SCIENCE EDUCATION, ASSOCIATION FOR (1963), College Lane, Hatfield, Herts.

SCOTTISH ASSESSORS' ASSOCIATION. *Sec.*, J. S. Gardner, 30/31 Queen Street, Edinburgh.

SCOTTISH CONSERVATIVE AND UNIONIST ASSOCIATION, 11 Atholl Crescent, Edinburgh 3.—*Sec.*, A. Strang, M.B.E.

SCOTTISH CONSERVATIVE AND UNIONIST CENTRAL OFFICE, 11 Atholl Crescent, Edinburgh 3.—*Dir.*, A. M. G. Macmillan.

SCOTTISH GENEALOGY SOCIETY (1953).—*Hon. Sec.*, Miss J. P. S. Ferguson, 21 Howard Place, Edinburgh.

SCOTTISH HISTORY SOCIETY (1886).—*Hon. Sec.*, T. I. Rae, PH.D., c/o National Library of Scotland, George IV Bridge, Edinburgh.

SCOTTISH LANDOWNERS' FEDERATION (1906).—*Dir.*, A. F. Roney Dougal, 26 Rutland Square, Edinburgh.

SCOTTISH LAW AGENTS SOCIETY, 61 High Street, Dunblane, Perthshire.

SCOTTISH LIBERAL PARTY (1946), 2 Atholl Place, Edinburgh.—*Admin. Sec.*, Mrs. M. Aitken.

SCOTTISH MARINE BIOLOGICAL ASSOCIATION (1914), Dunstaffnage Marine Research Laboratory, P.O. Box 3, Oban, Argyll.—*Dir.*, *and Sec.*, R. I. Currie, F.R.S.E.

SCOTTISH NATIONAL BLOOD TRANSFUSION ASSOCIATION (1940), 5 St. Colme Street, Edinburgh.—*Sec.*, Neil A. Milne, W.S.

SCOTTISH NATIONAL PARTY, 6 North Charlotte Street, Edinburgh.—*Sec.*, Miss M. M. Gibson.

SCOTTISH RECORD SOCIETY, Scottish History Dept., Univ. of Glasgow.—*Hon. Sec.*, Dr. J. Kirk.

SCOTTISH SECONDARY TEACHERS' ASSOCIATION, 15 Dundas Street, Edinburgh.—*Gen. Sec.*, J. Docherty.

SCOTTISH SOCIETY FOR PREVENTION OF CRUELTY TO ANIMALS (1839), 19 Melville Street, Edinburgh, 3.—*Sec.*, G. F. S. Brian.

SCOTTISH SOCIETY FOR THE PROTECTION OF WILD BIRDS (1927), 125 Douglas Street, Glasgow.—*Sec.*, James M. MacKellar.

SCOTTISH TOURIST BOARD (1969), 23 Ravelston Terrace, Edinburgh.—*Chief Exec.*, P. Taylor.

SCOTTISH WOMEN'S RURAL INSTITUTES (1917), 42 Heriot Row, Edinburgh.—*Gen. Sec.*, Mrs. J. A. Noble.

SCOUT ASSOCIATION, THE, *Headquarters*, Baden-Powell House, Queen's Gate, S.W.7.—*Chief Scout*, Sir William Gladstone, Bt.; *Sec.*, E. W. Hayden. Membership in U.K. (1974), 596,852; World Membership over 13,000,000 in over 100 countries.

SCRIBES AND ILLUMINATORS, THE SOCIETY OF.—*Hon. Sec.*, J. M. Cackett, Art Workers Guild Hall, 6 Queen Square, W.C.1.

SCRIPTURE GIFT MISSION (1888), Radstock House, Eccleston Street, S.W.1. Copies and selections of the Scriptures circulated (1974), 16,079,226.—*Sec.*, N. Brown.

SCRIPTURE UNION (1867), 47 Marylebone Lane, W.1.—*Gen. Dir.*, N. W. H. Sylvester.

SEAFARERS EDUCATION SERVICE (1919), Mansbridge House, 207 Balham High Road, S.W.17 (incorp. Marine Society).—*Director*, R. Hope, O.B.E., D.Phil.

SEAMEN'S CHRISTIAN FRIEND SOCIETY (1846), 87 Brigstock Road, Thornton Heath, Surrey.

SELDEN SOCIETY (1887), Faculty of Laws, Queen Mary College, Mile End Road, E.1. To encourage the study and advance the knowledge of the History of English Law.—*Pres.*, Sir Richard Southern, F.B.A.; *Sec.*, V. Tunkel.

SENATE OF THE INNS OF COURT AND THE BAR, 11 South Square, Gray's Inn, W.C.1.—*Pres.*, Hon. Mr. Justice Templeman, M.B.E.; *Chairman*, Rt. Hon. Sir Peter Rawlinson, Q.C., M.P.; *Sec.*, Sir Arthur Power, K.C.B., M.B.E.

SHAFTESBURY HOMES AND *Arethusa* (founded 1843); *Headquarters*, 3 Rectory Grove, S.W.4.; *Gen. Sec.*, Maj. R. P. A. de Berniere-Smart.

SHAFTESBURY SOCIETY (1844), Shaftesbury House, 112 Regency Street, S.W.1.—Engaged in social service among the physically handicapped and the poor. Maintains Residential Schools for physically handicapped children, Hostels for Muscular Dystrophy sufferers over 16 years, Holiday centres for the disabled and Missions in Greater London.—*Sec.*, G. A. Franklin, O.B.E.

SHAW SOCIETY (1941), 125 Markyate Road, Dagenham, Essex.—*Sec.*, E. F. J. Ford.

SHEEP ASSOCIATION, NATIONAL, Jenkins Lane, St. Leonards, nr. Tring, Herts.—*Sec.*, J. Thorley.

SHELLFISH ASSOCIATION OF GREAT BRITAIN, Fishmongers' Hall, E.C.4.—*Hon. Sec.*, E. S. Earl.

SHELTER (National Campaign for the Homeless), 86 Strand, W.C.2.

SHERLOCK HOLMES SOCIETY (1951), 5 Manor Close, Warlingham, Surrey.—*Hon. Sec.*, Capt. W. R. Michell, R.N. (*ret.*).

SHIPBROKERS, INSTITUTE OF CHARTERED (1911), 25 Bury Street, E.C.3.—*Sec.*, J. H. Parker.

SHIPWRECKED FISHERMEN AND MARINERS' ROYAL BENEVOLENT SOCIETY (1839), 1 North Pallant, Chichester, Sussex.—*Sec.*, Lt.-Cdr. H. E. Pinchin, R.N.

SHIRE HORSE SOCIETY (1878), East of England Showground, Peterborough.—*Sec.*, R. W. Bird.

SIMPLIFIED SPELLING SOCIETY (1908).—*Hon. Sec.*, G. O'Halloran, 83 Hampden Road, Hornsey, N.8.

SIR OSWALD STOLL FOUNDATION, 446 Fulham Road, S.W.6.—*Sec.*, Maj. L. F. H. Kershaw, D.S.O.

SMALL INDUSTRIES IN RURAL AREAS, COUNCIL FOR, 11 Cowley Street, S.W.1.—*Sec.*, S. A. Jackson.

SOCIAL CREDIT CENTRE.—*Hon. Sec.*, V. R. Hadkins, Montagu Chambers, Mexborough, Yorkshire.

SOCIAL WORKERS, BRITISH ASSOCIATION OF (1970), 16 Kent Street, Birmingham 5.—*Gen. Sec.*, C. A. Andrews.

SOCIALIST PARTY OF GREAT BRITAIN (1904), 52 Clapham High Street, S.W.4.—*Gen. Sec.*, K. Knight.

SOIL ASSOCIATION, Walnut Tree Manor, Haughley, Stowmarket, Suffolk.—*Pres.*, Dr. E. F. Schumacher; *Gen. Sec.*, Brig, A. W. Vickers, D.S.O., O.B.E.

SOLDIERS' AND AIRMEN'S SCRIPTURE READERS ASSOCIATION, THE (1838), 75–79 High Street, Aldershot, Hants.—*Gen. Sec.*, G. H. Stokes.

SOLDIERS' DAUGHTERS' SCHOOL, ROYAL (1855) 65 Rosslyn Hill, Hampstead, N.W.3.—*Sec.*, Col. J. G. Palmer.

SOLDIERS', SAILORS' AND AIRMEN'S FAMILIES ASSOCIATION (1885), 27 Queen Anne's Gate, S.W.1.—*Chairman*, Lt.-Gen. Sir Napier Crookenden, K.C.B., D.S.O., O.B.E.; *Controller*, D. Smithers; *Sec.*, Lt.-Cdr. R. G. Brown, V.R.D., R.N.R.

SOLDIERS, SAILORS AND AIRMEN'S HELP SOCIETY (Incorporated) (1899), *see* FORCES HELP SOCIETY.

SOLICITORS' BENEVOLENT ASSOCIATION (1858), 58 Clifford's Inn, Fetter Lane, E.C.4.—*Sec.*, Lt.-Col. P. B. Wakelin, M.C.

SOLICITORS IN THE SUPREME COURTS OF SCOTLAND, SOCIETY OF.—*Sec.*, A. R. Brownlie, 2 Abercromby Place, Edinburgh 3; *Treas.*, A. Stewart.

S.O.S. SOCIETY, THE (1929), 13 Culford Gardens, S.W.3. Old people's homes (5), Mental Rehabilitation homes, Ex-offenders and Homeless Men's hostel (1), Young's Men's Hostel (1).—*Gen. Sec.*, Lt.-Col. P. Rew.

SOUTH AMERICAN MISSIONARY SOCIETY, Allen Gardner House, Pembury Road, Tunbridge Wells, Kent.—*Gen. Sec.*, Rev. P. D. King.

SOUTH WALES INSTITUTE OF ENGINEERS (1857), Institute Buildings, Park Place, Cardiff.—*Hon. Sec.*, T. G. Dash.

SPASTICS SOCIETY, THE (1952), 12 Park Crescent, W.1.—*Sec.*, A. V. M. Diamond

SPORTS MEDICINE, INSTITUTE OF (1963), Ling House, 10 Nottingham Place, W.1.—*Hon. Sec.*, P. Sebastian.

SPURGEON'S HOMES (1867), Park Road, Birchington, Kent.—*Sec.*, P. E. Johnson.

STAIR SOCIETY (to encourage the study and advance the knowledge of the history of Scots Law).—*Sec.*, G. R. Thomson, T.D., Ph.D., 2 St. Giles' Street, Edinburgh.

STAR AND GARTER HOME FOR DISABLED SAILORS, SOLDIERS, AND AIRMEN (1916), Richmond-upon-Thames.—*Sec.*, Maj.-Gen. J. Sheffield, C.B., C.B.E.

STATISTICIANS, INSTITUTE OF (1948), St. Edmunds House, Lower Baxter Street, Bury St. Edmunds, Suffolk.—*Hon. Sec.*, E. Hunter.

STEWART SOCIETY (1899), 48 Castle Street, Edinburgh.—*Hon. Sec.*, D. F. Stewart, W.S.

STRUCTURAL ENGINEERS, INSTITUTION OF (1908), 11 Upper Belgrave Street, S.W.1.—*Sec.*, C. D. Morgan, O.B.E.

STUDENT CHRISTIAN MOVEMENT OF GREAT BRITAIN AND IRELAND (1889), Wick Court, Wick, Bristol.

SURGEONS OF ENGLAND, ROYAL COLLEGE OF (1800), Lincoln's Inn Fields, W.C.2.—*Pres.*, Sir Rodney Smith; *Sec.*, R. S. Johnson-Gilbert.

SURGEONS OF EDINBURGH, ROYAL COLLEGE OF (1505), 18 Nicolson Street, Edinburgh.—*Sec.*, I. F. MacLaren, F.R.C.S.Ed.

SURGICAL AID SOCIETY, ROYAL (1862), 1 Dorset Buildings, Salisbury Square, E.C.4.—*Sec.*, Maj. R. F. Crichton, M.C.

SURGICAL TECHNICIANS, BRITISH INSTITUTE OF, 21 Tothill Street, S.W.1.—*Sec.*, R. Nunn.

SURVEYORS, ROYAL INSTITUTION OF CHARTERED (1868), 12 Great George Street, S.W.1.—*Pres.*, (1975–76), D. Doig.

SUSSEX CATTLE SOCIETY (1887), Station Road, Robertsbridge, E. Sussex.—*Sec.*, H. J. Hancorn.

SUTTON HOUSING TRUST (1901), Sutton Court, Tring, Herts.—*Gen. Manager*, R. G. Poulter.

SWEDENBORG SOCIETY (1810), 20–21 Bloomsbury Way, W.C.1.—*Sec.*, Madeline G. Waters.

TAIL WAGGERS' CLUB TRUST, 4–6 Cannon Street, E.C.4.—*Sec.*, J. Minister.

TAVISTOCK INSTITUTE OF HUMAN RELATIONS, Tavistock Centre, Belsize Lane, N.W.3.—*Sec.*, S. G. Gray.

TAXATION, INSTITUTE OF (1930), 3 Grosvenor Crescent, S.W.1. *Sec.*, A. A. Arnold.

TEACHERS IN COLLEGES AND DEPARTMENTS OF EDUCATION, ASSOCIATION OF, 3 Crawford Place, W.1.—*Gen. Sec.*, K. Baird.

TEACHERS IN COMMERCE LTD., FACULTY OF, 141 Bedford Road, Sutton Coldfield, West Midlands. —*Sec.*, J. Snowdon.

TEACHERS IN TECHNICAL INSTITUTIONS, ASSOCIATION OF (1904), Hamilton House, Mabledon Place, W.C.1.—*Sec.*, T. Driver.

TEACHERS OF DOMESTIC SCIENCE, ASSOCIATION OF, Hamilton House, Mabledon Place, W.C.1.— *Gen. Sec.*, G. S. Large.

TEACHERS OF MATHEMATICS, ASSOCIATION OF.— c/o *Sec.*, Market Street Chambers, Nelson, Lancs.

TEACHERS OF SPEECH AND DRAMA, SOCIETY OF, St. Bride Institute, Fleet Street, E.C.4.—*Hon. Sec.*, Marguerite Turnbull, Abbot's Lodging, Marshside, Canterbury.

TEACHERS OF THE DEAF, NATIONAL COLLEGE OF.— *Hon. Sec.*, E. Brown, Needwood School, Rangemore Hall, Burton-on-Trent.

TEACHERS' UNION, ULSTER (1919), 94 Malone Road, Belfast.—*Sec.*, B. K. Toms.

TELEPHONE USERS' ASSOCIATION (1965), 35 Connaught Square, W.2.—*Sec.*, M. Elwes.

TELEVISION SOCIETY, ROYAL, Tavistock House North, Tavistock Square, W.C.1.—*Hon. Sec.*, A. J. Pilgrim.

TEMPERANCE SOCIETIES:—

British National Temperance League (1834), Livesey-Clegg House, 44 Union Street, Sheffield, 1.—*Sec.*, Miss M. Daniel.

British Women's Temperance Association, S.C.U. (1876), 8 North Bank Street, Edinburgh 1.— *Hon. Sec.*, Mrs. G. M. McKinlay.

Church of England Council for Social Aid, Church House, Dean's Yard, S.W.1.—*Gen. Sec.*, Rev. J. B. Harrison, O.B.E.

Division of Social Responsibility of the Methodist Church No. 1 Central Buildings, Matthew Parker St., S.W.1.—*Gen. Sec.*, Rev. J. H. Atkinson.

Independent Order of Rechabites, Salford Unity Friendly Society, London District (1870), No. 30, 18 Doughty Street, W.C.1.

National Association of Temperance Officials (1897), 207 London Road, Reading. *Hon. Sec.*, F. E. H. Jackson.

National Unitarian and Free Christian Temperance Association (1893), 35 Oakington Manor Drive, Wembley.—*Hon. Sec.*, Rev. W. M. Long.

Order of the Sons of Temperance, 21 Victoria Avenue, Harrogate.—*Sec.*, K. Unsworth.

Royal Naval Temperance Society (auxiliary of Royal Sailors' Rests), The Bus Station, South Street, Gosport, Hants.

Social Service Board of the Episcopal Church in Scotland (1919).—*Sec.*, I. D. Stuart, 21 Grosvenor Crescent, Edinburgh.

Temperance Council of the Christian Churches (1915) (incorporating the Overseas Temperance Council), Drayton House, Gordon Street, W.C.1.—*Gen. Sec.*, Rev. A. C. Davies.

Temperance Education Board (Ireland) (1918), c/o 27 Russell Park, Belfast.—*Sec.*, H. C. Jones.

United Kingdom Band of Hope Union, Hope House, 45 Great Peter Street, S.W.1.—*Gen. Sec.*, A. Candler Page.

TERRITORIAL, AUXILIARY AND VOLUNTEER RESERVE ASSOCIATIONS, COUNCIL OF (1908), Centre Block, Duke of York's Headquarters, Chelsea, S.W.3.—*Sec.*, Brig. B. T. V. Cowey, D.S.O.

TEXTILE INSTITUTE (1910), 10 Blackfriars Street, Manchester.—*Gen. Sec.*, J. T. Wenham.

THEATRE RESEARCH, SOCIETY FOR (1948).—*Hon. Secs.*, Miss K. M. Barker, J. Reading, 14 Woronzow Road, N.W.8.

THEATRICAL FUND ASSOCIATION, ROYAL GENERAL (1839), 11 Garrick Street, W.C.2.—*Sec.*, G. S. Hall.

THEATRICAL LADIES' GUILD OF CHARITY (1892) Gloucester House, 19 Charing Cross Road W.C.2.—*Sec.*, Mrs. G. Hammill.

THEATRICAL MANAGEMENT ASSOCIATION, Gloucester House, 19 Charing Cross Road, W.C.2.—*Sec.*, C. R. L. Thompson.

THEOSOPHICAL SOCIETY IN ENGLAND (1875), 50 Gloucester Place, W.1.—*Gen. Sec.*, Miss I. H. Hoskins, M.A.

THISTLE FOUNDATION, THE (1945), 22 Charlotte Square, Edinburgh 2.—*Secs.*, Graham, Smart and Annan, Chartered Accountants.

THORACIC SOCIETY, THE.—*Hon. Sec.*, J. E. Cotes, M.D., Llandough Hospital, Penarth, Glamorgan.

TIBET SOCIETY OF THE UNITED KINGDOM AND TIBET RELIEF FUND (1959), c/o B.C.A.R., 35 Great Peter Street, S.W.1.

TIN RESEARCH INSTITUTE (1932), Fraser Road, Perivale, Greenford, Middlesex.—*Dir.*, D. A. Robins, Ph.D.

TOC H (TALBOT HOUSE) (1915), Headquarters, 1 Forest Close, Wendover, Bucks.—*Gen, Sec.*, G. A. Francis.

TOWN AND COUNTRY PLANNING ASSOCIATION, 17 Carlton House Terrace, S.W.1.—*Dir.*, D. Hall.

TOWN PLANNING INSTITUTE, ROYAL (1914), 26 Portland Place, W.1.

TOWNSWOMEN'S GUILDS, NATIONAL UNION OF (1929), 2 Cromwell Place, S.W.7.—*Nat. Sec.*, Mrs. M. Erskine-Wyse.

TRADE MARK AGENTS, INSTITUTE OF (1934), 69 Cannon Street, E.C.4.—*Sec.*, R. A. Marshall.

TRADE, NATIONAL CHAMBER OF (1897), Enterprise House, Henley-on-Thames, Oxon.—*Dir. Gen.*, L. E. S. Seeney.

TRADES UNION CONGRESS (T.U.C.).—*See* p. 1117.

TRADING STANDARDS ADMINISTRATION, INSTITUTE OF—*Admin. Officer*, J. T. Fisher, Estate House, 319D London Road, Hadleigh, Essex.

TRAFFIC ADMINISTRATION, INSTITUTE OF (1944), 8 Cumberland Place, Southampton.—*National Sec.*, G. C. McCarthy.

TRANSPORT, CHARTERED INSTITUTE OF (1919), 80 Portland Place, W.1.—*Dir.-Gen.* Brig. D. N. Locke, O.B.E.

TRAVEL AGENTS, ASSOCIATION OF BRITISH (1950), 53–54 Newman Street, W.1.—*Chief Exec.*, M. A. Elton.

TROPICAL MEDICINE AND HYGIENE, ROYAL SOCIETY OF (1907), Manson House, 26 Portland Place,

W.1.—*Pres.*, C. E. Gordon Smith, C.B., M.D., F.R.C.P., *Sec.*, Mrs. B. Harrison.

TRUSTEE SAVINGS BANKS ASSOCIATION LTD. (1887), Knighton House, 52–66 Mortimer Street, W.1.—*Chief Gen. Man.*, J. Bryans, M.B.E.

UFAW (Universities Federation for Animal Welfare) (1926), 6 Hamilton Close, Potters Bar, Herts.—*Sec.*, Mrs. C. Brockhurst.

ULSTER SOCIETY IN LONDON, THE, 11 Berkeley Street, W.1.—*Pres.*, The Lord Rathcavan, P.C.; *Hon. Sec.*, Miss P. Bell.

UNIT TRUST MANAGERS, ASSOCIATION OF (1959), Park House, 16 Finsbury Circus, E.C.2.—*Sec.*, W. J. Burnett.

UNITED COMMERICAL TRAVELLERS' ASSOCIATION OF GREAT BRITAIN AND IRELAND (U.K.C.T.A.), (1883), Bexton Lane, Knutsford, Cheshire.—*Gen. Sec.*, R. Tomlinson.

UNITED NATIONS ASSOCIATION OF GREAT BRITAIN AND NORTHERN IRELAND (1945), 93 Albert Embankment, S.E.1.—*Dir.*, F. Field.

UNITED SOCIETY FOR CHRISTIAN LITERATURE, THE, Luke House, Farnham Road, Guildford, Surrey. —*Gen. Sec.*, Rev. D. R. Chesterton; *Gen. Manager*, M. E. Foxell.

UNITED SYNAGOGUE (1870).—*Pres.*, A. Woolf.—*Sec.*, N. Rubin, Woburn House, Upper Woburn Place, W.C.1.

UNIVERSITIES CENTRAL COUNCIL ON ADMISSIONS (1961), P.O. Box 28, Cheltenham, Glos.—*Sec.*, L. R. Kay.

UNIVERSITY TEACHERS, ASSOCIATION OF (1917), United House, 1 Pembridge Road, W.11.—*Sec.* L. J. Sapper.

UNIVERSITY WOMEN, BRITISH FEDERATION OF (LTD.) (1907), Crosby Hall, Cheyne Walk, S.W.3.—*Sec.*, Mrs. E. Bianco, LL.B.

VALUERS AND AUCTIONEERS, INCORPORATED SOCIETY OF, 3 Cadogan Gate, S.W.1.—*Sec.*, J. A. Crockett.

VEGETARIAN SOCIETY (U.K.) LTD., Parkdale, Dunham Road, Altrincham, Cheshire.

VENEREAL DISEASES, MEDICAL SOCIETY FOR THE STUDY OF, 11 Chandos Street, W.1.—*Hon. Sec.*, C. B. S. Schofield, M.D., F.R.C.P., The Clinic, 67 Black Street, Glasgow.

VICE-CHANCELLORS AND PRINCIPALS OF THE UNIVERSITIES OF THE UNITED KINGDOM, COMMITTEE OF, 29 Tavistock Square, W.C.1.—*Chairman*, Prof. Sir Arthur Armitage.

VICTORIA LEAGUE FOR COMMONWEALTH FRIENDSHIP (1901), 18 Northumberland Avenue, W.C.2. —*Sec.*, Mrs. C. Barnett, O.B.E.

VICTORIAN SOCIETY (1958), 1 Priory Gardens, Bedford Park, W.4.—*Sec.*, Mrs. E. Fawcett, M.B.E.

VICTORY (SERVICES) ASSOCIATION LTD. AND CLUB, THE, 63–79 Seymour Street, W.2.—*Sec.*, D. G. Stovey.

VIKING SOCIETY FOR NORTHERN RESEARCH, University College, Gower Street, W.C.1.—*Hon. Secs.*, Prof. G. Turville-Petre, M.A., B.Litt.; Prof. P. G. Foote, M.A.

VITREOUS ENAMELLERS, INSTITUTE OF, Ripley, Derby.—*Sec.*, J. D. Gardom.

VOLUNTARY SERVICE OVERSEAS (1958), 14 Bishop's Bridge Road, W.2.—*Dir.*, D. W. A. Collett.

WAR BLINDED, SCOTTISH NATIONAL INSTITUTION FOR THE. Workshops at Edinburgh, Glasgow and Linburn. *Appeals Director*, Maj. D. F. Callander, M.C., P.O. Box 304, 38 Albany Street, Edinburgh.

WATER ENGINEERS AND SCIENTISTS, INSTITUTION OF, 6–8 Sackville Street, W.1.—*Pres.* (1975–76), C. A. Serpell; *Sec.*, J. P. Banbury, M.B.E.

WELDING INSTITUTE, THE, Abington Hall, Cambridge and 54 Princes Gate, S.W.7.—*Dir.-Gen.*, Dr. R. Weck, C.B.E., F.R.S.

WELFARE OFFICERS, INSTITUTE OF (1945), Red Cross House, 73 Penrhyn Road, Kingston upon Thames, Surrey.—*Gen. Sec.*, Mrs. B. Amos.

WELLCOME TRUST (1936), 1 Park Square West, N.W.1.—*Dir.*, P. O. Williams, M.B., F.R.C.P.

WELLS (H. G.) SOCIETY INTERNATIONAL, 125 Markgate Road, Dagenham, Essex.—*Sec.*, E. F. J. Ford.

WELSH JOINT EDUCATION COMMITTEE (1948), 245 Western Avenue, Cardiff.—*Sec.*, D. A. Davies.

WELSH NATIONAL PARTY (Plaid Cymru), 8 Heol y Frenhines, Cardiff.—*Gen. Sec.*, D. Williams.

WESLEY HISTORICAL SOCIETY (1893).—*Gen. Sec.*, Rev. T. Shaw, 39 Fair Street, St. Columb Major, Cornwall.

WEST AFRICA COMMITTEE (1956), Chronicle House, 72–78 Fleet Street, E.C.4.—*Sec.*, W. G. Syer, C.V.O., C.B.E.

WEST END THEATRE MANAGERS, SOCIETY OF, 19 Charing Cross Road, W.C.2.—*Sec.*, C. R. L. Thompson.

WEST INDIA COMMITTEE (1750), 18 Grosvenor Street, W.1.—*Sec.*, Lt.-Col. M. R. Robinson, D.S.O., O.B.E.

WEST LONDON MISSION (1887), Kingsway Hall, W.C.2.—*Supt.*, Rev. The Lord Soper, M.A., Ph.D.

WIDOWS, SOCIETY FOR THE RELIEF OF DISTRESSED (1823) (residing within five miles of Charing Cross and applying within two months of widowhood), 175 Tower Bridge Road, S.E.1.—*Sec.*, W. N. Barr.

WINE AND SPIRIT ASSOCIATION OF GREAT BRITAIN (INC), Five King's House, Kennet Wharf Lane, Upper Thames Street, E.C.4.—*Dir.*, R. H. Insoll, E.R.D.

WOMEN ARTISTS, SOCIETY OF (1855), 17 Carlton House Terrace, S.W.1.—*Sec.*, M. Bradshaw.

WOMEN, NATIONAL ADVISORY CENTRE ON CAREERS FOR (formerly Women's Employment Federation) (1933), 251 Brompton Road, S.W.3.—*Dir.*, Miss K. M. Menon.

WOMEN PILOTS' ASSOCIATION, BRITISH (1955), c/o P.O. Box 13, British Airways Victoria Terminal, S.W.1.

WOMEN, SOCIETY FOR PROMOTING THE TRAINING OF (1859) (Women's Loan Training Fund), Court Farm, Hedgerley, Bucks.—*Sec.*, Mrs. W. M. Golding.

WOMEN'S ENGINEERING SOCIETY (1920), 25 Foubert's Place, W.1.—*Sec.*, Miss T. Davison.

WOMEN'S HOLIDAY FUND (1895), 125 Wilton Road, S.W.1.—*Sec.*, Mrs. U. Muirhead.

WOMEN'S INSTITUTES, NATIONAL FEDERATION OF (1915), 39 Eccleston Street, S.W.1.—*Gen. Sec.*, Mrs. A. Ballard, M.A.

WOMEN'S INTERNATIONAL LEAGUE FOR PEACE AND FREEDOM (1915), British Section, 29 Great James Street, W.C.1.—*Sec.*, Miss R. Adams.

WOMEN'S LIBERAL FEDERATION, 7 Exchange Court, Strand, W.C.2.—*Pres.*, The Baroness Seear; *Sec.*, Mrs. H. Bainbridge.

WOMEN'S NATIONAL CANCER CONTROL CAMPAIGN, 9 King Street, W.C.2.—*Senior Administrator*, Mrs. M. K. Cooper.

WOMEN'S PROTESTANT UNION (INC.), WORLD PROTESTANT UNION, and THE SENTINELS' UNION, Sentinels Court, 130 South Coast Road, Peacehaven, Newhaven, Sussex.

WOMEN'S ROYAL NAVAL SERVICE BENEVOLENT TRUST, 2 Lower Sloane Street, S.W.1.

WOMEN'S ROYAL VOLUNTARY SERVICE (WRVS) (1938), 17 Old Park Lane, W.1.

WOMEN'S TRANSPORT SERVICE (FANY) (1907), Duke of York's H.Q., King's Road, S.W.3.—*Corps Commander*, Mrs. S. Y. Parkinson.

WOOD PRESERVING ASSOCIATION, 62 Oxford Street, W.1.—*Dir.*, J. Bick.

WORCESTERSHIRE ASSOCIATION (1926).—*Hon. Sec.*, S. Driver White, 5 Deansway, Worcester.

WORK STUDY, ORGANIZATION AND METHODS, INSTITUTE OF PRACTIONERS IN (1975), 9–10 River Front, Enfield, Middx.—*Dir., and Gen. Sec.*, E. A. King.

WORKERS' EDUCATIONAL ASSOCIATION, 9 Upper Berkeley Street, W.1.—*Gen. Sec.*, R. J. Jeffries.

WORKS AND HIGHWAYS TECHNICIAN ENGINEERS, INSTITUTION OF, 26 Bloomsbury Way, W.C.1.—*Gen. Sec. and Registrar*, Lt.-Col. W. H. Bush.

WORKS MANAGERS, INSTITUTION OF, 45 Cardiff Road, Luton, Beds.

WORLD CONGRESS OF FAITHS (1936), Younghusband House, 23 Norfolk Square, W.2.—*Chairman*, Rt. Rev. G. Appleton.

WORLD EDUCATION FELLOWSHIP (1921), *International Headquarters*, 33 Kinnaird Avenue, W.4.

WORLD ENERGY CONFERENCE (1924). *Central Office*, 5 Bury Street, S.W.1.—*Sec.-Gen.*, *International Executive Council*, E. Ruttley.

WORLD SHIP SOCIETY (1946).—*Sec.*, S. J. F. Miller, 35 Wickham Way, Haywards Heath, Sussex.

WRITERS TO H.M. SIGNET, SOCIETY OF, PARLIAMENT Square, Edinburgh.—*Deputy Keeper of the Signet*, P. J. Oliphant, T.D.; *Sub-Keeper and Clerk*, P.C. Millar.

YEOMANRY BENEFIT FUND, 206 Brompton Road, S.W.3.—*Sec.*, Mrs. M. L. Bernard, O.B.E.

YORKSHIRE AGRICULTURAL SOCIETY (1837), Great Yorks Showground, Hookstone Oval, Harrogate.—*Sec.-Gen.*, R. G. G. English.

YORKSHIRE FIELD STUDIES LTD.—*Gen. Sec.*, D. H. Smith, Westland, Westfields, Kirbymoorside, York.

YORKSHIREMEN IN LONDON, SOCIETY OF (1899), AND THE YORKSHIRE SOCIETY (1812), 200 High Street, Brentford, Middx.—*Sec.*, G. G. Prince.

YOUNG MEN'S CHRISTIAN ASSOCIATION, *National Council*, 640 Forest Road, E.17.—*Gen. Sec.*, S. Charlesworth.

YOUNG WOMEN'S CHRISTIAN ASSOCIATION (1855), *National Headquarters*, 2 Weymouth Street, W.1. —*Nat. Gen. Sec.*, Miss B. Cowderoy.

YOUTH CLUBS, NATIONAL ASSOCIATION OF, P.O. Box 1 Blackburn House, Bond Gate, Nuneaton, Warwicks. (London Centre—30 Devonshire St., W.1.)—*Chief Exec. Officer*, J. M. Butterfield.

YOUTH CLUBS, NORTHERN IRELAND ASSOCIATION OF, Hampton, Glenmachan Road, Belfast.—*Dir.*, M. A. Brown.

YOUTH HOSTELS ASSOCIATION (ENGLAND AND WALES) (1930), *National Office*, Trevelyan House, St. Albans, Herts.—*Sec.*, H. B. Livingstone.

YOUTH HOSTELS ASSOCIATION (SCOTTISH) (1931), *National Office*, 7 Glebe Crescent, Stirling.

YOUTH HOSTELS ASSOCIATION OF NORTHERN IRELAND LTD. (1931), 93 Dublin Road, Belfast.—*Hon. Sec.*, E. R. Henderson.

ZOOLOGICAL SOCIETY OF LONDON, Regent's Park, N.W.1.—*Sec.*, Prof. Lord Zuckerman, O.M., K.C.B., D.SC., F.R.S. Attendances (1974), Regent's Park, 1,958,000, and Whipsnade Park, 547,000.

ZOOLOGICAL SOCIETY OF SCOTLAND, ROYAL, Scottish National Zoological Park, Murrayfield, Edinburgh 12.—*Dir.*, R. J. Wheater.

THE CIVIC TRUST

17 Carlton House Terrace, S.W.1
[01-930 0914]

Founded in 1957 with the object of improving the appearance of town and country. The Trust is a recognized charity, supported by voluntary contributions. Four Associate Trusts are linked with it in Scotland, Wales, the North West and the North East.

The Trust gives support and advice to some 1,200 local civic and amenity societies throughout Britain. It has initiated hundreds of schemes to brighten and tidy up drab streets. It has promoted new techniques for moving semi-mature trees as part of a wider campaign to plant more trees. It stimulates voluntary action to remove eyesores

which mar town and countryside. It makes awards annually for good development of all kinds. Its proposals led to the creation of the Lee Valley Regional Park Authority. It was closely associated with the drafting of the Civic Amenities Act 1967 and of the Town and Country Amenities Act 1974. It makes available on hire films, photographs, slides and exhibitions. By conferences, projects and reports, it focuses attention on major issues in town planning and architecture. The Trust also provided the central Secretariat for the United Kingdom campaign for European Architectural Heritage Year, 1975.

LOCAL ARCHAEOLOGICAL SOCIETIES

England and Wales

Anglesey.—ANGLESEY ANTIQUARIAN SOCIETY. Hon. Sec., D. O. Jones, 22 Lôn Ganol, Menai Bridge, Anglesey.

Bedfordshire.—SOUTH BEDFORDSHIRE ARCHÆOLOGICAL SOCIETY. Hon. Sec., D. H. Kennett, 55 Mount Grace Road, Stopsley, Luton.

Berkshire.—BERKSHIRE ARCHÆOLOGICAL SOCIETY. Hon. Sec., F. M. Underhill, F.S.A., Turstins, High Street, Upton, Didcot, Oxfordshire.

Berkshire.—NEWBURY DISTRICT FIELD CLUB, Donnington Dene, Newbury. Hon. Sec., Mrs. M. E. Kaines-Thomas, D.Litt., F.S.A.

Buckinghamshire.—BUCKS ARCHÆOLOGICAL SOCIETY. Hon. Sec., E. Viney, County Museum, Church Street, Aylesbury, Bucks.

Cambridgeshire. — CAMBRIDGE ANTIQUARIAN SOCIETY. Sec., Miss J. Liversidge, 20 Manor Court, Grange Road, Cambridge.

Cardiganshire. — CEREDIGION ANTIQUARIAN SOCIETY. Hon. Sec., D. M. Jones, 26 Alban Square, Aberaeron.

Cheshire.—CHESTER ARCHÆOLOGICAL SOCIETY, Grosvenor Museum, Chester.—Hon. Sec., J. T. Driver, 25 Abbot's Grange, Chester. *See also under Lancashire.*

Cornwall.—ROYAL INSTITUTION OF CORNWALL, County Museum and Art Gallery, Truro. Hon. Sec., A. J. Lyne.

Cumberland and Westmorland.—CUMBERLAND AND WESTMORLAND ANTIQUARIAN AND ARCHÆOLOGICAL SOCIETY. Hon. Sec., Mrs. J. Cherry, 68 Scanton Way, Seascale, Cumbria.

Derbyshire.—DERBYSHIRE ARCHÆOLOGICAL SOCIETY, 36 St. Mary's Gate, Derby. Hon. Sec., M. A. B. Mallender.

Devonshire.—DEVON ARCHÆOLOGICAL SOCIETY. Hon. Sec., Miss S. M. Pearce, City Museum, Queen Street, Exeter.

Dorset.—DORSET NATURAL HISTORY AND ARCHÆOLOGICAL SOCIETY, Dorset County Museum, Dorchester. *Curator and Sec.*, R. N. R. Peers.

Durham. — DURHAM AND NORTHUMBERLAND ARCHITECTURAL AND ARCHÆOLOGICAL SOCIETY, Hon. Sec., C. D. Morris, F.S.A.(Scot.), Dept of Archæology, Old Fulling Mill, The Banks, Durham.

SUNDERLAND ANTIQUARIAN SOCIETY.—Hon. Sec., J. R. Salkeld, 72 The Broadway, Grindon Sunderland.

Essex.—ESSEX ARCHÆOLOGICAL SOCIETY, Hollytrees Museum, High Street, Colchester. Hon. Sec., J. E. Sellers.

Gloucestershire.—BRISTOL AND GLOUCESTERSHIRE ARCHÆOLOGICAL SOCIETY, 9 Pembroke Road, Bristol 8. Hon. Sec., Miss E. Ralph.

Hampshire.—HAMPSHIRE FIELD CLUB AND ARCHÆOLOGICAL SOCIETY, Hon. Sec., Miss E. R. Lewis, City Museum, The Square, Winchester, Hants.

Herefordshire.—WOOLHOPE NATURALISTS' FIELD CLUB. Hon. Sec., c/o The Hereford Library, Broad Street, Hereford.

Hertfordshire. — EAST HERTFORDSHIRE ARCHÆOLOGICAL SOCIETY. Hon. Sec., C. L. Lee, 107 Queen's Road, Hertford.

ST. ALBANS AND HERTFORDSHIRE ARCHITECTURAL AND ARCHÆOLOGICAL SOCIETY.—Hon. Sec., G. L. Wilde, 5 Townsend Drive, St. Albans.

Kent.—KENT ARCHÆOLOGICAL SOCIETY. Gen. Sec., c/o The Museum, Maidstone.

Lancashire.—HISTORIC SOCIETY OF LANCASHIRE AND CHESHIRE. Hon. Sec., P. J. Andrews, c/o Liverpool City Libraries, William Brown Street, Liverpool.

Leicestershire.—LEICESTERSHIRE ARCHÆOLOGICAL AND HISTORICAL SOCIETY, The Guildhall, Guildhall Lane, Leicester. Hon. Sec., D. Tomkins.

Middlesex.—LONDON AND MIDDLESEX ARCHÆOLOGICAL SOCIETY, Bishopsgate Institute, 230 Bishopsgate, E.C.2. Hon. Sec., E. E. F. Smith.

Northumberland.—SOCIETY OF ANTIQUARIES OF NEWCASTLE UPON TYNE. Admin. Sec., Dr. C. M. Fraser, c/o Department of Adult Education, University of Newcastle upon Tyne.

Norfolk.—NORFOLK AND NORWICH ARCHÆOLOGICAL SOCIETY. Hon. Gen. Sec., I. Cresswell, F.S.A., The Old Rectory, Shelton, Norwich.

Nottinghamshire.—THOROTON SOCIETY OF NOTTINGHAMSHIRE, Bromley House, Angel Row, Nottingham. Hon. Sec., M. G. Dobbin.

Oxfordshire.—OXFORDSHIRE ARCHITECTURAL AND HISTORICAL SOCIETY. Hon. Sec., Mrs. N. Stebbing, c/o Ashmolean Museum, Oxford.

Powys: Montgomery District; POWYSLAND CLUB. Hon. Sec., W. G. J. Hughes, County Branch Library, Red Bank, Welshpool, Powys.

Radnor District; RADNORSHIRE SOCIETY. Hon. Secs., E. V. Howells, The White House, Cefnllys Lane, Llandrindod Wells; C. W. Newman, Wynberg, Dyffryn Road, Llandrindod Wells.

Somerset.—SOMERSET ARCHÆOLOGICAL AND NATURAL HISTORY SOCIETY, Taunton Castle, Taunton. Secretary, H. L. M. Patten.

Staffordshire.—NORTH STAFFORDSHIRE FIELD CLUB, Hon. Sec., R. A. Tribbeck, Dept. of Chemistry, North Staffordshire Polytechnic, Stoke-on-Trent.

CITY OF STOKE-ON-TRENT MUSEUM ARCHÆOLOGICAL SOCIETY, City Museum, Stoke-on-Trent. Chairman, A. R. Mountford.

SOUTH STAFFORDSHIRE ARCHÆOLOGICAL AND HISTORICAL SOCIETY. Hon. Sec., Dr. J. G. L.

Cole, 11 Bracebridge Road, Sutton Coldfield, West Midlands.

Suffolk.—SUFFOLK INSTITUTE OF ARCHÆOLOGY.—Hon. Sec., D. G. Penrose, Suffolk Record Office, County Hall, Ipswich.

Surrey.—SURREY ARCHÆOLOGICAL SOCIETY, Castle Arch, Guildford.—Hon. Sec., D. J. Turner, F.S.A.

Sussex.—SUSSEX ARCHÆOLOGICAL SOCIETY, Barbican House, High Street, Lewes.

Warwickshire.—BIRMINGHAM AND WARWICKSHIRE ARCHÆOLOGICAL SOCIETY, Birmingham and Midland Institute, Margaret Street, Birmingham 3.—Hon. Sec., Mrs. R. Taylor.

Wight.—ISLE OF WIGHT NATURAL HISTORY AND ARCHÆOLOGICAL SOCIETY.—Sec., Miss H. Blount, 50 Queen's Road, Ryde, I.o.W.

Wiltshire. — WILTSHIRE ARCHÆOLOGICAL AND NATURAL HISTORY SOCIETY, The Museum, 41 Long Street, Devizes. Sec., C. P. Barber.

Worcestershire.—WORCESTERSHIRE ARCHÆOLOGICAL SOCIETY.—Hon. Sec., R. F. Panton, Birchdale, 4 Orchard Road, Gt. Malvern.

Yorkshire.—HUNTER ARCHÆOLOGICAL SOCIETY. Hon. Sec., F. L. Preston, Grove Cottage, Moorgate Grove, Rotherham.

  YORKSHIRE ARCHÆOLOGICAL SOCIETY.—Hon. Sec., F. A. Aberg, Claremont, 23 Clarendon Road, Leeds.

  HALIFAX ANTIQUARIAN SOCIETY. Hon. Sec., R. L. Sunderland, 37 Lombard Street, King Cross, Halifax.

THORESBY SOCIETY, Claremont, 23 Clarendon Road, Leeds 2.—Hon. Sec., D. Keighley.

Isle of Man and Channel Islands

ISLE OF MAN NATURAL HISTORY AND ANTIQUARIAN SOCIETY, c/o The Manx Museum, Douglas.

SOCIÉTÉ JERSIAISE, The Museum, Pier Road, St. Helier, Jersey. Hon. Sec., Mrs. W. E. Macready.

Scotland

AYRSHIRE ARCHÆOLOGICAL AND NATURAL HISTORY SOCIETY. Carnegie Library, Ayr.—Hon. Sec., R. Waite, Ph.D., 74 Doonfoot Road, Ayr.

DUMFRIESSHIRE AND GALLOWAY NATURAL HISTORY AND ANTIQUARIAN SOCIETY. Hon. Sec., Mrs. E. Adamson, 39 Westerlea, Roberts Crescent, Dumfries.

GLASGOW ARCHÆOLOGICAL SOCIETY. Hon. Secs., Miss H. C. Adamson, Art Gallery and Museum, Glasgow; E. J. Talbot, Dept. of Archæology, University of Glasgow.

HAWICK ARCHÆOLOGICAL SOCIETY. Hon. Sec., T. I. Storie, 6 Park Terrace, Hawick.

SHETLAND ARCHÆOLOGICAL AND HISTORICAL SOCIETY, County Museum, Lerwick.—Pres., T. Henderson.

EMPLOYERS' AND TRADE ASSOCIATIONS

AEROSPACE COMPANIES, SOCIETY OF BRITISH (1916), 29 King Street, S.W.1.—Dir., Vice-Adm. Sir Richard Smeeton, K.C.B., M.B.E.

ALUMINIUM FEDERATION LTD., Broadway House, Calthorpe Road, Five Ways, Birmingham 15.

BAKERS, CONFECTIONERS AND CATERERS, NATIONAL ASSOCIATION OF MASTER, Queen's House, Holly Road, Twickenham, Middx.—Dir., M. F. Zimmerman.

BAKERS, THE FEDERATION OF, 20 Bedford Square, W.C.1.

BOOT TRADES ASSOCIATION, LTD., ST. CRISPINS, St. Crispin's House, Desborough, nr. Kettering, Northants.—Gen. Sec., Mrs. P. J. Copley.

BRUSH MANUFACTURERS' ASSOCIATION, BRITISH, 4 Southampton Row, W.C.1.—Sec., R. F. Knox, M.B.E.

BUILDING AND ALLIED HARDWARE MANUFACTURERS FEDERATION, NATIONAL, 5 Greenfield Crescent, Edgbaston, Birmingham 15.—Dir. and Sec., E. C. Skelding.

BUILDING TRADES EMPLOYERS, NATIONAL FEDERATION OF (1878), 82 New Cavendish Street, W.1.—Sec., H. L. Foster.

CEMENT MAKERS' FEDERATION, Terminal House, 52 Grosvenor Gardens, S.W.1.—Dir., Rear Adm. C. K. T. Wheen, C.B.

CERAMIC MANUFACTURERS' FEDERATION, BRITISH, Federation House, Station Road, Stoke-on-Trent.—Sec., D. Turner, M.B.E.

CHEMICAL INDUSTRIES ASSOCIATION LTD. (1966), Alembic House, 93 Albert Embankment, S.E.1.—Dir.-Gen., M. E. Trowbridge.

CHINA AND GLASS RETAILERS' ASSOCIATION, 21 John Adam Street, W.C.2.—Sec., W. E. V. Burch, T.D.

CINEMATOGRAPH EXHIBITORS' ASSOCIATION OF GREAT BRITAIN AND IRELAND, 22-25 Dean Street, W.1.—Gen. Sec., R. S. Camplin.

CIVIL ENGINEERING CONTRACTORS, FEDERATION OF, Romney House, Tufton Street, S.W.1.—Dir., D. V. Gaulter.

CLOTHING MANUFACTURERS' FEDERATION OF GREAT BRITAIN LTD., 14-16 Cockspur Street, S.W.1.—Dir., M. K. Reid, O.B.E.

COAL MERCHANTS' FEDERATION OF GREAT BRITAIN, Victoria House, Southampton Row, W.C.1.—Dir., L. R. Chambers, O.B.E.

COCOA, CHOCOLATE AND CONFECTIONERY MANUFACTURERS' INDUSTRIAL GROUP, 11 Green Street, W.1.—Sec., E. T. Beauchamp.

COLD STORAGE FEDERATION, NATIONAL, 272 London Road, Wallington, Surrey.—Sec., D. T. Lee.

CONFECTIONERS ASSOCIATION, RETAIL, LTD., 53 Christchurch Avenue, North Finchley, N.12.—Sec., C. J. Southam.

COOPERAGE FEDERATION, NATIONAL, 27 Queen Charlotte Street, Leith, Edinburgh 6.—Sec., J. Steven.

CUTLERY AND SILVERWARE MANUFACTURERS ASSOCIATION, UNITED KINGDOM, Light Trades House, Melbourne Avenue, Sheffield, 10.—Sec., Miss M. Arnold, M.B.E.

CYCLE AND MOTOR CYCLE TRADERS, NATIONAL ASSOCIATION OF, 31A High Street, Tunbridge Wells, Kent.—Gen. Sec., J. E. F. Davies.

DAIRY TRADE FEDERATION, 20 Eastbourne Terrace, W.2.—Sec., Miss E. Gadsby.

DECORATORS ASSOCIATION, BRITISH, 6 Haywra Street, Harrogate, N. Yorks.—Dir., K. A. C. Blease.

DRAPERS' CHAMBER OF TRADE, North Bar, Banbury, Oxfordshire.—Sec., S. D. Russell.

ELECTRICAL AND ALLIED MANUFACTURERS ASSOCIATION, BRITISH (1905), 8 Leicester Street, W.C.2.—Chief Executive, G. C. Stebbing.

ELECTRICAL APPLIANCE ASSOCIATION (R.T.R.A.) LTD., 100 St. Martin's Lane, W.C.2.

ELECTRICAL CONTRACTORS' ASSOCIATION, 55 Catherine Place, S.W.1.—Dir., B. E. Gray.

ENGINEERING EMPLOYERS' FEDERATION, Broadway House, Tothill Street, S.W.1.—Sec., H. K. Mitchell.

FARMERS' UNION, NATIONAL (1908), Agriculture House, Knightsbridge, S.W.1.—*Dir. Gen.*, G. H. B. Cattell.

FILM PRODUCTION ASSOCIATION OF GREAT BRITAIN, 27 Soho Square, W.1.—*Sec.*, I. Mitchell.

FISH FRIERS, NATIONAL FEDERATION OF, 289 Dewsbury Road, Leeds 11.—*Gen. Sec.*, P. Worthington.

FISHMONGERS, NATIONAL FEDERATION OF, 21 John Adam Street, W.C.2.—*Sec.*, R. W. Stote.

FLAT GLASS ASSOCIATION, THE, 6 Mount Row, W.1.—*Sec.*, M. G. Stretton-Hill.

FOOD MANUFACTURERS FEDERATION, 1–2 Castle Lane, Buckingham Gate, S.W.1.—*Gen. Sec.*, J. P. Burney.

FOOD AND DRINK, NATIONAL FEDERATION OF (incorp. National Grocers' Federation and the National Off-Licence Federation), 17 Farnborough Street, Farnborough, Hants.—*Chief. Exec.*, L. E. Reeves-Smith.

FOOTWEAR MANUFACTURERS FEDERATION, BRITISH, Royalty House, 72 Dean Street, W.1.—*Dir. Gen.*, J. R. Parr.

FRESH MEAT WHOLESALERS, FEDERATION OF, Columbia House, 69 Aldwych, W.C.2.

FURNISHERS, NATIONAL ASSOCIATION OF RETAIL, 3 Berners Street, W.1.—*Dir.*, H. L. Calder-Jones, O.B.E.

GLASS MANUFACTURERS FEDERATION, 19 Portland Place, W.1.—*Dir.*, O. C. T. R. Normandale.

GRAIN, SEED, FEED AND AGRICULTURAL MERCHANTS, BRITISH ASSOCIATION OF, 3 Whitehall Court, S.W.1.—*Sec.*, H. S. Leech.

GROCERS AND PROVISION MERCHANTS, NATIONAL FEDERATION OF WHOLESALE, 18 Fleet Street, E.C.4.—*Sec.*, D. Ellam.

HYDRAULIC EQUIPMENT MANUFACTURERS LTD., ASSOCIATION OF (1959), 54 Warwick Square, S.W.1.—*Dir.*, L. F. Nosworthy.

JEWELLERY AND GIFTWARE FEDERATION LIMITED, BRITISH, St. Dunstan's House, Carey Lane, E.C.2. —*Dir.-Gen.*, S. R. Simmons.

JUTE SPINNERS AND MANUFACTURERS ASSOCIATION, Kandahar House, 71 Meadowside, Dundee.— *Dir.*, D. A. Borrie.

LAUNDERERS AND CLEANERS, ASSOCIATION OF BRITISH, LTD., Lancaster Gate House, 319 Pinner Road, Harrow, Middlesex.—*Dir.*, E. W. Swetman, O.B.E.

LEATHER PRODUCERS' ASSOCIATION, Leather Trade House, 82 Borough High Street, S.E.1.

LONDON CLEARING BANK EMPLOYERS, FEDERATION OF, 10 Lombard Street, E.C.3.—*Dir. and Sec.*, E. S. Richards.

MALTSTERS' ASSOCIATION OF GREAT BRITAIN, Prince Rupert House, 64 Queen Street, E.C.4.—*Sec.*, Group Capt. V. Fairfield, O.B.E.

MEAT TRADERS, NATIONAL FEDERATION OF, 29 Linkfield Lane, Redhill, Surrey.

MENSWEAR ASSOCIATION OF BRITAIN LTD., Palladium House, 1–4 Argyll Street, W.1.—*Dir.*, K. E. Smith.

MILLERS, NATIONAL ASSOCIATION OF BRITISH AND IRISH, LTD. (1878), 21 Arlington Street, S.W.1.— *Sec.*, E. T. J. Hurle.

MINES OF GREAT BRITAIN, FEDERATION OF SMALL, 9 Winchester Road, Billinge, Wigan, Lancs.— *Chairman and Sec.*, J. Wainwright.

MOTOR AGENTS' ASSOCIATION, LTD., 201 Great Portland Street, W.1.—*Dir.-Gen.*, F. E. Higham, O.B.E.

MOTOR MANUFACTURERS AND TRADERS, SOCIETY OF (1902), Forbes House, Halkin Street, S.W.1.— *Sec.*, M. G. Feather.

PAINTMAKERS ASSOCIATION OF GREAT BRITAIN LIMITED, Prudential House, Wellesley Road, Croydon, Surrey.—*Dir.*, W. P. G. Wilson.

PAPER AND BOARD INDUSTRY FEDERATION, BRITISH, (Industrial Relations Division), 1 Clements Inn, W.C.2.—*Dir.*, W. J. Bartlett.

PAPER MERCHANTS, NATIONAL ASSOCIATION OF, 35 New Bridge Street, E.C.4.—*Dir.*, S. R. W. Bailey.

PLUMBING, HEATING AND MECHANICAL SERVICES CONTRACTORS NATIONAL ASSOCIATION OF, 6 Gate Street, W.C.2.—*Sec.*, H. Leighton.

PORT EMPLOYERS, NATIONAL ASSOCIATION OF, 3/5 Queen Square, W.C.1.—*Gen. Manager*, E. Bainbridge.

PRECAST CONCRETE FEDERATION, BRITISH, 60 Charles Street, Leicester.—*Dir.*, J. P. Metcalfe.

PRINTING INDUSTRIES FEDERATION, BRITISH, 11 Bedford Row, W.C.1.—*Dir.*, H. W. Kendall.

PROPRIETARY ASSOCIATION OF GREAT BRITAIN, Victoria House, Southampton Row, W.C.1.— *Dir.*, J. P. Wells.

RADIO AND TELEVISION RETAILERS' ASSOCIATION, 100 St. Martin's Lane, W.C.2.

READY MIXED CONCRETE ASSOCIATION, BRITISH, Shepperton House, Green Lane, Shepperton, Middlesex.—*Dir.-Gen.*, K. Newman.

ROAD HAULAGE ASSOCIATION LTD., 22 Upper Woburn Place, W.C.1.—*Dir.-Gen.*, G. K. Newman.

ROOFING CONTRACTORS, NATIONAL FEDERATION OF, High Holborn House, 52/54 High Holborn, W.C.1.—*Gen. Sec.*, H. S. Kitching.

SAND AND GRAVEL ASSOCIATION LIMITED, 48 Park Street, W.1.—*Sec. Gen.*, A. C. F. Hey.

SAWMILLING ASSOCIATION, NATIONAL, Clareville House, Whitcomb Street, W.C.2.—*Sec.*, P. A. T. Smith.

SCIENTIFIC INSTRUMENT MANUFACTURERS' ASSOCIATION OF GREAT BRITAIN, 20 Peel Street, W.8.

SCOTCH WHISKY ASSOCIATION, 20 Atholl Crescent, Edinburgh.—*Dir. Gen. and Sec.*, Col. H. F. O. Bewsher. *Information Office*, 17 Half Moon Street, W.1.

SHIPBUILDERS AND REPAIRERS NATIONAL ASSOCIATION, 21 Grosvenor Place, S.W.1.—*Dir.*, C. H. Baylis.

TAILORS, FEDERATION OF MERCHANT, Alderman House, 37 Soho Square, W.1.—*Exec. Sec.*, C. W. Allen.

TEXTILE EMPLOYERS' ASSOCIATION, BRITISH, 5th Flr., Royal Exchange, Manchester.—*Sec.*, J. Platt, M.B.E.

TIMBER TRADE FEDERATION, Clareville House, Whitcomb Street, W.C.2.—*Sec.*, H. J. Bocking.

TOBACCONISTS, FEDERATION OF RETAIL, 546–548 Commercial Road, E.1.—*Sec.*, G. J. Alden.

TRAWLERS FEDERATION LTD., BRITISH, Trinity House Chambers, 12 Trinity House Lane, Hull. *Sec.*, I. C. Thorburn.

VEHICLE BUILDERS AND REPAIRERS ASSOCIATION, Belmont House, 102 Finkle Lane, Gildersome, Leeds.—*Sec.*, J. G. Mellar.

WATER COMPANIES ASSOCIATION, THE 14 Great College Street, S.W.1.—*Sec.*, R. P. Owen.

CLUB AND LIBRARY EDITION OF WHITAKER, 1976

The Club and Library Edition of Whitaker's Almanack, 1976, contains 1,220 pages, including illustrations and coloured maps (The World, The British Isles, Baltic States, Russia and her neighbours, Germany and her neighbours, France and Spain, The Far East, India, Pakistan and Burma, Africa, Canada and Newfoundland, The United States, South America, Australia, New Zealand) in strong leather binding, with gilt top and silk headband. Price £4.75 net.

CONFEDERATION OF BRITISH INDUSTRY
21 Tothill Street, London, S.W.1.

The Confederation of British Industry was founded in August 1965 to promote the prosperity of British Industry and those elements of British business closely associated with it. It combines in a single, democratic and voluntary association the rôles previously played by the British Employers' Confederation, the Federation of British Industries and the National Association of British Manufacturers.

The C.B.I. is recognized nationally and internationally as the representative organization of the management side of industry for the United Kingdom. It acts as a national point of reference for all those who seek the views of industry and management and it advises the Government on all aspects of Government policy which affect the interests of industry and business, both at home and abroad.

Membership of the C.B.I. consists of some 12,000 companies and over 200 trade associations and employers' organizations. In addition to these most of the nationalized industries are in membership as public sector members and thereby able to work with the C.B.I. on problems that are the concern of all management.

The governing body of the C.B.I. is the Council, which meets monthly in London. It is assisted by some 30 expert standing committees which advise on the main aspects of policy. There is a C.B.I. Regional Council and eight C.B.I. offices in the administrative regions of England and offices and Councils covering Scotland, Wales and Northern Ireland. These Regional Councils send their representatives to the governing body. The C.B.I. is represented in more than 100 centres overseas.

The C.B.I. provides its members with a wide range of services and practical advice on economic, industrial relations, commercial, technical, social and export questions. The organization is financed by the subscriptions of its members.

President, Sir Ralph Bateman, K.B.E.

Vice-Presidents, Sir Michael Clapham, K.B.E., Sir John Partridge, K.B.E.

Director-General, Campbell Adamson.

Secretary, E. M. Felgate.

NATIONAL BUILDING AGENCY
N.B.A. House, Arundel Street, W.C.2
(North St. Andrew Street, Edinburgh; Bedford House, Bedford Street, Belfast; 115 Portland Place, Manchester; Caerwys House, Windsor Place, Cardiff; Newton House, Sauchiehall Street, Charing Cross, Glasgow 2; 187A West Street, Sheffield.)

The NBA is a Government-sponsored, non-profit distributing Agency, whose aims are to encourage improved methods of design, construction and management in the building industry. Founded in 1964 it was initially concerned with the appraisal of building systems (which it now does jointly with the Agrément Board) with metrication and with demonstration housing projects. Currently it provides a wide range of technical and building management services to public authorities, housing associations, government departments and private clients. It receives a grant from the Department of the Environment for certain services to the local authorities and the Housing Corporation, but charges normal fees for its consultancy work.

Chairman (part-time), The Lord Goodman, C.H.

Managing Director, A. W. Cleeve, Barr, C.B.E., F.R.I.B.A.

HOME-GROWN CEREALS AUTHORITY
Hamlyn House, Highgate Hill, N.19.

Constituted under the Cereals Marketing Act, 1965, the Authority consists of 9 members representing cereal growers, 9 representing dealers in, or processors of, grain and 5 independent members. The purpose of the Authority is to improve the marketing of home-grown cereals. Production now exceeds 15 million tons per annum; at full E.E.C. prices this is valued at over £825,000,000. The Authority is empowered by the Act to provide a market intelligence service; to operate schemes for the encouragement of forward sales, and the orderly phasing of supplies according to market needs; and to undertake research aimed at the expansion of the market for home-grown cereals. It has been appointed executive agent for the Intervention Board for Agricultural Produce in respect of the denaturing of wheat and intervention buying,

storage and disposal of cereals under the Common Agricultural Policy of the E.E.C. It submits advice to Ministers on matters affecting cereals marketing.

Chairman, Sir Henry Hardman, K.C.B.

Deputy Chairman, Dr. Clare Burgess.

Members (Independent), The Lord Collison, C.B.E.; Prof. D. K. Britton; O. G. Williams.

(*Cereal Growers*), R. Ankers; G. E. Daniels; K. Deighton; J. Macaulay; S. W. Passmore; E. Richards; P. Savory; S. Shaw; J. Stobo.

(*Merchants, Dealers & Processors*), K. J. Arnott; N. B. Baird; F. S. D. Brown; J. Gray, O.B.E., T.D.; P. A. Metaxa; W. J. Oldacre; H. Paul; B. C. Read; L. J. Wright.

General Manager and Secretary, H. Pitchforth.

PERIODS OF GESTATION AND INCUBATION
The table shows approximate periods of gestation or incubation for some common animals and birds. In some cases the periods may vary and where doubt arises professional advice should be sought.

Species	Shortest Period. Days	Usual Period. Days	Longest Period. Days	Species	Shortest Period. Days	Usual Period. Days	Longest Period. Days
Human	240	273	313	Turkey	25	28	28
Mare	305	336	340	Duck	28	28	32
Ass	365	—	374	Goose	28	30	32
Cow	273	280	294	Pigeon	17	18	19
Ewe	140	147–50	160	Canary	12	14	14
Goat	147	151	155	Guinea Pig	63	—	70
Sow	109	112	125	Mouse	18	—	19
Bitch	55	63	70	Rat	21	—	24
Cat	53	56	63	Elephant		2 years	
Rabbit	30	32	35	Camel		45 weeks	
Hen	20	21	22	Zebra		56 weeks	

TRADES UNION CONGRESS (T.U.C.)

Congress House, 23–28 Great Russell Street, W.C.1.

[01-636-4030]

The Trades Union Congress, founded in 1868, is a voluntary association of Trade Unions, the representatives of which meet annually to consider matters of common concern to their members. The Congress has met annually since 1871 (with the exception of 1914) and in recent years has met normally on the first Monday in September, its sessions extending through the succeeding four days. Congress is constituted by delegates of the affiliated unions on the basis of one delegate for every 5,000 members, or fraction thereof, on whose behalf affiliated fees are paid. Affiliated unions (in 1974/5) totalled 110 with an aggregate membership of 10,363,724.

The main business of the annual Congress is to consider the report of its General Council dealing with the activities of the Congress year, along with motions from affiliated societies on questions of policy and organization. Some of these unions, especially in cotton, are themselves federal bodies including over 100 more unions.

One of the important responsibilities of the annual Congress is to elect a General Council to keep watch on all industrial movements, legislation affecting labour and all matters touching the interest of the trade union movement, with authority to promote common action on general questions, and to assist trade unions in the work of organization. The General Council is elected by Congress and is composed of 38 members (36 representing 18 trade groups and two representing women workers). Following is a list of these trade groups with the aggregate membership of unions in each group and with the number of representatives each group is entitled to have on the General Council. *Women Members.*—In 1975, a total of 2,772,819 women were members of unions in the T.U.C. The largest groups were members of the National Union of General and Municipal Workers (285,357), National Union of Public Employees (321,302), Transport and General Workers' Union (286,829), National Union of Teachers (197,453), National and Local Government Officers' Association (218,100), and Union of Shop, Distributive and Allied Workers (203,952).

Among the powers vested in it by consent of the Unions in Congress is the responsibility of adjusting disputes and differences between affiliated organizations; such cases being dealt with by a Disputes Committee of the General Council which investigates matters referred to it and issues its findings thereon, which are invariably accepted by the parties to the dispute. The General Council has power also, if there appears to be justification, to institute an investigation into the conduct of any affiliated organization on the ground that its activities are detrimental to the interests of the trade union movement or contrary to the declared principles and policy of the Congress; but membership of the Congress is voluntary and Unions retain full control of their own affairs, and a penalty of suspension from membership of the Congress or exclusion from membership is the only measure that can be taken to enforce Congress decisions. Through the General Council, the trade union movement maintains systematic relations with the Government and Government Departments, with the Confederation of British Industry and with a large number of other bodies. The General Council is represented on the National Economic Development Council, established to examine problems associated with faster economic growth. The Council includes Ministers dealing with economic and industrial affairs, representatives of public and private industry and independent members. The General Council nominates members to serve on numerous other bodies, e.g., Manpower Services Commission, Health and Safety Commission and the Council of the Advisory, Conciliation and Arbitration Service.

Chairman (1975–76), C. T. H. Plant, C.B.E.
General Secretary, L. Murray, O.B.E.

Trade Group (with numbers of unions)	Membership
Mining and Quarrying (2)	276,636
Railways (3)	272,762
Transport (other) (6)	1,966,303
Shipbuilding (1)	129,598
Engineering, Founding and Vehicle Building (10)	449,511
Technical Engineering and Scientific (5)	523,242
Electricity (1)	414,189
Iron and Steel and Minor Metal Trades (10)	144,473
Building, Woodworking and Furnishing (5)	346,830
Printing and Paper (6)	306,582
Textiles (17)	130,092
Clothing, Leather and Boot and Shoe (6)	262,553
Glass, Ceramics, Chemicals, Food, Drink, Tobacco, Brushmaking, and Distribution (9)	495,506
Agriculture (1)	90,000
Public Employees (9)	1,615,452
Civil Servants and Post Office (10)	785,696
Professional, Clerical and Entertainment (9)	270,489
General Workers (1)	883,810
TOTAL (111)	10,363,724

SCOTTISH TRADES UNION CONGRESS

12 Woodlands Terrace, Glasgow, C.3.

The Congress was formed in 1897 and acts as a national centre for the trade union movement in Scotland. In 1975 it consisted of 68 unions with a membership of 896,892 and 46 directly affiliated Trades Councils. The majority of the unions organize throughout Britain and affiliate on their membership in Scotland.

The Annual Congress in April elects a 20-member General Council on the basis of 11 industrial sections. Congress has been prominent in pressing for economic expansion and full employment in Scotland and the development of the social services, most of which are separately organized in Scotland.

Chairman (1975–76) A. Forman.
General Secretary, J. Jack, C.B.E.

TRADE UNIONS AFFILIATED TO T.U.C.

A list of the Trade Unions affiliated to the Trades Union Congress in September, 1975. The number of members of each Union is shown in parenthesis.

ACTORS' EQUITY ASSOCIATION, BRITISH (22,014).— *Gen. Sec.*, P. Plouviez, 8 Harley St, W.1.

AGRICULTURAL AND ALLIED WORKERS, NATIONAL UNION OF (90,000).—*Sec.*, R. N. Bottini, C.B.E., 308 Gray's Inn Road, W.C.1.

ASPHALT WORKERS, THE AMALGAMATED UNION OF (2,890).—*Sec.*, H. M. Wareham, Jenkin House, 173A Queen's Road, Peckham, S.E.15.

BAKERS UNION (55,886), Station House, Darkes Lane, Potters Bar, Herts.—*Gen. Sec.*, C. T. Child.

BAKERS AND ALLIED WORKERS, SCOTTISH UNION OF (9,249).—*Sec.*, A. H. Mackie, Baxterlee, 127 Fergus Drive, Glasgow 20.

BEAMERS, TWISTERS AND DRAWERS (HAND AND MACHINE), AMALGAMATED ASSOCIATION OF (949).—*Gen. Sec.*, F. Sumner, 27 Every Street, Nelson, Lancs.

BLASTFURNACEMEN, ORE MINERS, COKE WORKERS AND KINDRED TRADES, THE NATIONAL UNION OF (16,261).—*Sec.*, H. C. Smith, 93 Borough Road West, Middlesbrough. Cleveland.

BLIND AND DISABLED, NATIONAL LEAGUE OF THE (4,250).—*Sec.*, T. J. Parker, O.B.E., Tottenham Trades Hall, 7 Bruce Grove, N.17.

BOILERMAKERS, SHIPWRIGHTS, BLACKSMITHS AND STRUCTURAL WORKERS, AMALGAMATED SOCIETY OF (125,598).—Lifton House, Eslington Road, Newcastle-upon-Tyne 2.—*Pres.*, D. McGarvey, C.B.E.

BOOT, SHOE AND SLIPPER OPERATIVES, ROSSENDALE UNION OF (6,054).—*Sec.*, T. Whitaker, 7 Tenterfield Street, Waterfoot, Rossendale, Lancs.

BRITISH AIR LINE PILOTS ASSOCIATION (4,454).— *Gen. Sec.*, M. Young, 81 New Road, Harlington, Hayes, Middlesex.

BROADCASTING STAFF, ASSOCIATION OF (12,852), King's Court, 2 Goodge Street, W.1.—*Gen. Sec.*, D. A. Hearn.

BRUSHMAKERS AND GENERAL WORKERS, NATIONAL SOCIETY OF (2,034).—*Sec.*, A. W. Godfrey, 20 The Parade, Watford.

BUILDING TECHNICIANS, ASSOCIATION OF (3,696).— *Sec.*, F. E. Shrosbree, Ucatt House, 177 Abbeville Road, S.W.4.

CARD SETTING MACHINE TENTERS' SOCIETY (150). —*Sec.*, G. Priestley, 36 Greenton Avenue, Scholes, Cleckheaton, Yorks.

CARPET TRADE UNION, NORTHERN (2,209).—*Gen. Sec.*, L. R. Smith, 22 Clare Road, Halifax, Yorks.

CERAMIC AND ALLIED TRADES UNION (44,404).— *Sec.*, L. R. Sillitoe, 5 Hillcrest Street, Hanley, Stoke-on-Trent.

CIGARETTE MACHINE OPERATORS' SOCIETY (352).— W. D. Brunt, 9 Wootton Crescent, St. Anne's Park, Bristol 4.

CINEMATOGRAPH, TELEVISION AND ALLIED TECHNICIANS, ASSOCIATION OF (18,690).—*Sec.*, A. Sapper, 2 Soho Square, W.1.

CIVIL AND PUBLIC SERVICES ASSOCIATION (215,144). —*Sec.*, W. L. Kendall, 215 Balham High Road, S.W.17.

CIVIL SERVANTS, SOCIETY OF (86,460) *including Customs and Excise Group*).—*Gen. Sec.*, B. A. Gillman, 124–6 Southwark Street, S.E.1.

CIVIL SERVICE UNION (43,624).—*Sec.*, J. O. N. Vickers, 17–21 Hatton Wall, E.C.1.

CLOTH PRESSERS' SOCIETY (120).—*Sec.*, G. Kaye, 34 Southgate, Honley, Huddersfield, Yorks.

COLLIERY OVERMEN, DEPUTIES AND SHOTFIRERS, NATIONAL ASSOCIATION OF (21,340).—*Sec.*, A. E. Simpson, Argyle House, 29–31 Euston Road, N.W.1.

CONSTRUCTION, ALLIED TRADES AND TECHNICIANS, UNION OF (257,796).—*Sec.*, G. F. Smith, C.B.E., Ucatt House, 177 Abbeville Road, S.W.4.

CO-OPERATIVE OFFICIALS, NATIONAL UNION OF (5,462).—*Sec.*, A. W. Potts, Saxone House, 56 Market Street, Manchester 1.

COOPERS' FEDERATION OF GREAT BRITAIN (1,380).— *Gen. Sec.*, D. Hutchison, 13 Gayfield Square, Edinburgh 1.

CUSTOMS AND EXCISE GROUP.—*Gen. Sec.* J. E. Morrish, 193 Fleet Street, E.C.4. (incorporated in Society of Civil Servants).

DOMESTIC APPLIANCE & GENERAL METAL WORKERS, NATIONAL UNION OF (5,238).—*Sec.*, J. Higham, M.B.E., Imperial Bldgs., Corporation Street, Rotherham.

DYERS, BLEACHERS AND TEXTILE WORKERS, NATIONAL UNION OF (55,324), National House, Sunbridge Road, Bradford 1.—*Sec.*, F. Dyson.

ELECTRICAL, ELECTRONIC, TELECOMMUNICATION, AND PLUMBING UNION (414,189).—*Sec.*, F. J. Chapple, Hayes Court, West Common Road, Hayes, Bromley, Kent.

ELECTRICAL POWER ENGINEERS' ASSOCIATION (33,157).—*Gen. Sec.*, J. Lyons, Station House, Fox Lane North, Chertsey, Surrey.

ENGINEER SURVEYORS' ASSOCIATION (2,525).—*Sec.*, E. J. Metcalfe, Parsonage Chambers, 3 Parsonage, Manchester 3.

ENGINEERING WORKERS, AMALGAMATED UNION OF (1,211,000), 110 Peckham Road, S.E.15.—*Gen. Sec.*, J. M. Boyd, C.B.E.

> CONSTRUCTIONAL SECTION (27,291).—*Sec.*, (vacant). Construction House, 190 Cedars Road, Clapham, S.W.4.

> FOUNDRY SECTION (62,186).—*Sec.*, R. Garland, 164 Chorlton Road, Manchester 16.

> TECHNICAL, ADMINISTRATIVE AND SUPERVISORY SECTION (127,362).—*Sec.*, K. Gill, Onslow Hall, Little Green, Richmond, Surrey.

FELT HATTERS AND ALLIED WORKERS, AMALGAMATED SOCIETY OF JOURNEYMEN (843).—*Sec.*, H. Walker, 14 Walker Street, Denton, nr. Manchester.

FELT HAT TRIMMERS, WOOL FORMERS AND ALLIED WORKERS, AMALGAMATED (743).—*Sec.*, H. Walker, 14 Walker Street, Denton, nr. Manchester.

FILM ARTISTES' ASSOCIATION, THE (1,497).—*Sec.*, S. Brannigan, 61 Marloes Road, W.8.

FIRE BRIGADES UNION, THE (30,000).—*Sec.*, T. Parry, O.B.E., 59 Fulham High Street, S.W.6.

FOOTWEAR, LEATHER AND ALLIED TRADES, NATIONAL UNION OF (66,069). The Grange, Earls Barton, Northampton.—*Sec.*, W. G. T. Jones.

FUNERAL SERVICE OPERATIVES, NATIONAL UNION OF (1,179).—*Sec.*, D. R. Coates, 16 Woolwich New Road, S.E.18.

FURNITURE, TIMBER AND ALLIED TRADES UNION (83,585).—Fairfields, Roe Green, Kingsbury, N.W.9.

GENERAL AND MUNICIPAL WORKERS UNION (883,810), Thorne House, Ruxley Ridge, Claygate, Esher, Surrey.—*Gen. Sec.*, D. Basnett.

GOLD, SILVER AND ALLIED TRADES, NATIONAL UNION OF (3,196).—*Gen. Sec.*, B. H. Bridge, Kean Chambers, 11 Mappin Street, Sheffield 1.

GOVERNMENT SUPERVISORS AND RADIO OFFICERS, ASSOCIATION OF (11,487).—*Sec.*, P. L. Avery, 90 Borough High Street, S.E.1.

GRAPHICAL AND ALLIED TRADES, SOCIETY OF (193,804).—*Sec.*, W. H. Keys, 74 Nightingale Lane, S.W.12.

GRAPHICAL ASSOCIATION, SCOTTISH (6,418).—*Gen. Sec.*, F. Smith, 136 West Regent Street, Glasgow G.2.

GREATER LONDON COUNCIL STAFF ASSOCIATION (18,279).—*Sec.*, F. T. Hollocks, 164–8 Westminster Bridge Road, S.E.1.

HEALDERS AND TWISTERS TRADE AND FRIENDLY SOCIETY, HUDDERSFIELD (231).—*Sec.*, G. Booth, 20 Uppergate, Hepworth, Huddersfield.

HEALTH SERVICE EMPLOYEES, CONFEDERATION OF (143,479).—*Gen. Sec.*, E. A. G. Spanswick, Glen House, High Street, Banstead, Surrey.

HEALTH VISITORS' ASSOCIATION (7,172).—*Sec.*, Mrs. J. Wyndham-Kaye, 36 Eccleston Square, S.W.1.

HOSIERY AND KNITWEAR WORKERS, NATIONAL UNION OF (72,723).—*Sec.*, D. A. C. Lambert, 55 New Walk, Leicester.

INLAND REVENUE STAFF FEDERATION (54,920).—*Sec.*, C. T. H. Plant, C.B.E., 7 St. George's Square, S.W.1.

INSURANCE WORKERS, NATIONAL UNION OF (25,740).—*Sec.*, F. H. Jarvis, 185 Woodhouse Road, N.12.

IRON AND STEEL TRADES CONFEDERATION (106,048). —*Sec.*, W. Sirs, Swinton House, 324 Gray's Inn Road, W.C.1.

JOURNALISTS, NATIONAL UNION OF (29,433).—*Sec.*, K. Morgan, Acorn House, 314–320 Gray's Inn Road, W.C.1.

JUTE, FLAX AND KINDRED TEXTILE OPERATIVES, UNION OF (2,500).—*Sec.*, Mrs. M. Fenwick, M.B.E., 93 Nethergate, Dundee.

LAMINATED AND COIL SPRING WORKERS' UNION (230).—*Sec.*, F. M. Hynes, 144 Rural Lane, Wadsley, Sheffield.

LITHOGRAPHIC ARTISTS, DESIGNERS, ENGRAVERS AND PROCESS WORKERS, SOCIETY OF (16,925).—*Sec.*, J. A. Jackson, 55 Clapham Common (South Side), S.W.4.

LOCK AND METAL WORKERS, NATIONAL UNION OF (6,537).—*Sec.*, J. Martin, Bellamy House, Wilkes Street, Willenhall, Staffs.

LOCOMOTIVE ENGINEERS AND FIREMEN, ASSOCIATED SOCIETY OF (28,899).—*Sec.*, R. W. Buckton, 9 Arkwright Road, N.W.3.

LOOM OVERLOOKERS, THE GENERAL UNION OF ASSOCIATIONS OF (3,231).—*Gen. Sec.*, A. Howcroft, 6 St. Mary's Place, Bury.

MACHINE CALICO PRINTERS, TRADE SOCIETY OF (420).—*Sec.*, J. Eckersley, Middle Room, 2nd Floor, 1B Cooper Street, Manchester 2.

MANAGERS AND OVERLOOKERS' SOCIETY (1,477).—*Sec.*, L. Smith, Textile Hall, Westgate Bradford.

MERCHANT NAVY AND AIRLINE OFFICERS' ASSOCIATION (26,100).—*Sec.*, E. Nevin, 750–760 High Road, Leytonstone, E.11.

METALWORKERS' UNION, ASSOCIATED (5,024).—*Sec.*, E. Tullock, 92 Deansgate, Manchester 3.

METAL MECHANICS, NATIONAL SOCIETY OF (43,650). —*Sec.*, J. H. Wood, 70 Lionel Street, Birmingham 3.

MILITARY AND ORCHESTRAL MUSICAL INSTRUMENT MAKERS TRADE SOCIETY (120).—*Gen. Sec.*, G. W. Lock, 56 Avondale Crescent, Enfield, Middx.

MINEWORKERS, NATIONAL UNION OF (255,296).—*Sec.*, L. Daly, 222 Euston Road, N.W.1.

MUSICIANS' UNION (34,721).—*Gen. Sec.*, J. Morton, 29 Catherine Place, Buckingham Gate, S.W.1.

NATIONAL AND LOCAL GOVERNMENT OFFICERS ASSOCIATION (541,918).—*Sec.*, G. A. Drain, Nalgo House, 1 Mabledon Place, W.C.1.

PATTERNMAKERS AND ALLIED CRAFTSMEN, ASSOCIATION OF (10,667).—*Sec.*, G. Eastwood, 15 Cleve Road, W. Hampstead, N.W.6.

PATTERN WEAVERS' SOCIETY (170).—*Gen. Sec.*, D. G. Hawley, 21 Kaye Lane, Almondbury, Huddersfield.

POST OFFICE ENGINEERING UNION (125,738).—*Sec.*, B. C. Stanley, Greystoke House, Hanger Lane, Ealing, W.5.

POST OFFICE EXECUTIVES, SOCIETY OF (21,000).—*Gen. Sec.*, J. K. Glynn, 116 Richmond Road, Kingston-on-Thames, Surrey.

POST OFFICE MANAGEMENT STAFFS ASSOCIATION (19,668).—*Gen. Sec.*, L. F. Pratt, 52 Broadway, Bracknell, Berks.

POST OFFICE WORKERS, UNION OF (190,000).—*Sec.*, T. Jackson, U.P.W. House, Crescent Lane, Clapham Common, S.W.4.

POWER LOOM CARPET WEAVERS AND TEXTILE WORKERS' ASSOCIATION (5,650).—*Sec.*, A. Hatton, Callows Lane, Kidderminster.

POWER LOOM OVERLOOKERS, YORKSHIRE ASSOCIATION OF (1,402).—*Sec.*, E. D. Sleeman, Textile Hall, Westgate, Bradford.

POWER LOOM OVER-LOOKERS, SCOTTISH UNION OF (350).—*Sec.*, A. Stobie, 1 Osnaburg Street, Forfar.

PRINTERS, GRAPHICAL AND MEDIA PERSONNEL, NATIONAL SOCIETY OF OPERATIVE (55,992).—*Sec.*, O. O'Brien, Caxton House, 13–16 Borough Road, S.E.1.

PRISON OFFICERS' ASSOCIATION (17,625).—*Sec.*, K. A. Daniel, Cronin House, 245 Church Street, N.9.

PROFESSIONAL, EXECUTIVE, CLERICAL AND COMPUTER STAFF, ASSOCIATION OF (137,716).—*Gen. Sec.*, R. Grantham, 22 Worple Road, S.W.19.

PUBLIC EMPLOYEES, NATIONAL UNION OF (507,826). —*Sec.*, A. W. Fisher, Civic House, Aberdeen Terrace, Blackheath, S.E.3.

RADIO AND ELECTRONIC OFFICERS UNION (3,441), 4–6 Branfill Road, Upminster, Essex.—*Sec.*, K. A. Murphy.

RAILWAYMEN, NATIONAL UNION OF (172,558).—*Sec.*, S. Weighell, Unity House, Euston Road, N.W.1.

ROLL TURNERS' TRADE SOCIETY, BRITISH (863).—*Sec.*, B. W. Johnson, 44 Collingwood Avenue, Corby, Northants.

SAWMAKERS' PROTECTION SOCIETY, SHEFFIELD (270). —*Sec.*, A. Marples, 27 Main Avenue, Totley, Sheffield.

SCALEMAKERS, NATIONAL UNION OF (1,958).—*Gen. Sec.*, S. W. Parfitt, Herbert Morrison House, 195 Walworth Road, S.E.17.

SCHOOLMASTERS, NATIONAL ASSOCIATION OF (59,429).—*Sec.*, T. A. Casey, P.O. Box 65, Swan Court, Waterhouse Street, Hemel Hempstead, Herts.

SCIENTIFIC, TECHNICAL AND MANAGERIAL STAFFS, ASSOCIATION OF (351,000).—*Gen. Sec.*, C. Jenkins, 10–26A Jamestown Road, N.W.1.

MEDICAL PRACTITIONERS' SECTION (5,502).—*Sec.*, Dr. H. Faulkner, 10–26A Jamestown Road, N.W.1.

SCREW, NUT, BOLT AND RIVET TRADE UNION (2,524).—*Sec.*, H. Cater, 368 Dudley Road, Birmingham 18.

SEAMEN, NATIONAL UNION OF (50,000).—*Gen. Sec.*, J. Slater, Maritime House, Old Town, Clapham, S.W.4.

SHEET METAL WORKERS, COPPERSMITHS AND HEATING AND DOMESTIC ENGINEERS, NATIONAL UNION OF (79,718).—*Gen. Sec.*, L. W. Buck, 75–77 West Heath Road, N.W.3.

SHOP, DISTRIBUTIVE AND ALLIED WORKERS, UNION OF (352,610).—*Sec.*, The Lord Allen of Fallowfield, C.B.E., "Oakley," 188 Wilmslow Road, Fallowfield, Manchester 14.

SHUTTLEMAKERS, SOCIETY OF (135).—*Gen. Sec.*, E. V. Littlewood, 21 Buchan Towers, Manchester Road, Bradford.

SPINNERS AND TWINERS, THE AMALGAMATED ASSOCIATION OF OPERATIVE COTTON (880).—*Sec.*, J. Richardson, 115 Newton Street, Manchester 1.

SPRING TRAPMAKERS' SOCIETY (90).—*Sec.*, J. Martin, Bellamy House, Wilkes Street, Willenhall, Staffs.

TAILORS AND GARMENT WORKERS, NATIONAL UNION OF (116,121), Radlett House, West Hill, Aspley Guise, Milton Keynes.—*Gen. Sec.*, J. Macgougan.

TEACHERS, NATIONAL UNION OF (264,349).—*Sec.*, F. Jarvis, Hamilton House, Mabledon Place, W.C.1.

TEACHERS IN TECHNICAL INSTITUTIONS, ASSOCIATION OF (43,000).—*Gen. Sec.*, T. Driver, Hamilton House, Mabledon Place, W.C.1.

TEXTILE WORKERS' UNION, AMALGAMATED (45,243).—*Gen. Secs.*, F. G. Hague; J. King, O.B.E., Textile Union Centre, 5 Caton Street, Rochdale, Lancs.

TEXTILE WAREHOUSEMEN, AMALGAMATED (3,201).—*Gen. Sec.*, A. Birtwistle, 4 Hall Street, Colne, Lancs.

TEXTILE WORKERS AND KINDRED TRADES, AMALGAMATED SOCIETY OF (6,178).—*Gen. Sec.*, H. Lisle, O.B.E., Foxloe, Market Place, Leek, Staffs.

THEATRICAL, TELEVISION AND KINE EMPLOYEES, THE NATIONAL ASSOCIATION OF (16,100).—*Gen. Sec.*, vacant, 155 Kennington Park Road, S.E.11.

TOBACCO WORKERS' UNION, THE (21,295).—*Sec.*, C. D. Grieve, 9 Station Parade, High Street, E.11.

TRANSPORT AND GENERAL WORKERS' UNION (1,857,308).—*Sec.*, J. L. Jones, M.B.E., Transport House, Smith Square, S.W.1.

TRANSPORT SALARIED STAFFS' ASSOCIATION (71,305).—*Gen. Sec.*, D. A. Mackenzie, Walkden House, 10 Melton Street, N.W.1.

TRANSPORT UNION, UNITED ROAD (25,000).—*Sec.*, J. Moore, 76 High Lane, Manchester 21.

WALLCOVERINGS, DECORATIVE AND ALLIED TRADES, NATIONAL UNION OF (5,200).—*Gen. Sec.*, R. W. Tomlins, 223 Bury New Road, Whitefield, Manchester.

WIRE DRAWERS AND KINDRED WORKERS, THE AMALGAMATED SOCIETY OF (10,954).—*Sec.*, L. Carr, Prospect House, Alma Street, Sheffield 3.

WOOL SHEAR WORKERS' TRADE UNION, SHEFFIELD (24).—*Sec.*, J. Billard, 19 Rivelin Park Drive, Sheffield 6.

WOOL SORTERS' SOCIETY, NATIONAL (827).—*Sec.*, N. Newton, M.B.E., 40 Little Horton Lane, Bradford 5.

WRITERS GUILD OF GREAT BRITAIN (1,159).—*Sec.*, P. Ralph, 430 Edgware Road, W.2.

OTHER TRADE UNIONS

The following Trade Unions were not affiliated to the Trades Union Congress at the time of going to press.

BANK EMPLOYEES, NATIONAL UNION OF (103,314).—*Gen. Sec.*, L. A. Mills, 2 Holly Road, Twickenham, Middlesex.

CHAIN MAKERS AND STRIKERS' ASSOCIATION (228).—*Sec.*, A. E. Head, M.B.E., Unity Villa, Sidney Road, Cradley Heath, Warley, West Midlands.

ENGINEERS' AND FIREMEN'S UNION, GRIMSBY STEAM AND DIESEL FISHING VESSELS (200).—10 Orwell Street, Grimsby.

PROFESSIONAL FOOTBALLERS' ASSOCIATION (2,160).—*Sec.*, C. Lloyd, O.B.E., 124 Corn Exchange Buildings, Manchester 4.

RETAIL BOOK, STATIONERY AND ALLIED TRADES EMPLOYEES' ASSOCIATION, THE (3,580).—*Gen. Sec.*, A. J. Johnson, 152–3 Temple Chambers, Temple Avenue, E.C.4.

TEXTILE CRAFTSMEN, YORKSHIRE SOCIETY OF (925).—*Sec.*, C. Hall, Textile Hall, Westgate, Bradford 1.

INDUSTRIAL RESEARCH ASSOCIATIONS

A notable development in modern industry is the growth in numbers and importance of Industrial Research Associations and their increasing influence on the scientific and economic life of the country. The total income of these Associations exceeds £18,000,000 per annum.

The Government Scheme for Co-operative Industrial Research was launched by the Department of Scientific and Industrial Research in 1917. Its aim was to stimulate the industries of the United Kingdom to undertake co-operative research as a means of increasing their efficiency.

Research Associations formed under this scheme are registered companies, limited by guarantee of a nominal sum and working without the division of profits in the form of dividends. To assist the formation of such Associations the Department of Trade and Industry kept a model Memorandum and Articles of Association, to which Research Associations under the scheme conform in all essential points.

The Research Associations are autonomous bodies free to determine their own policy for the development of their research programmes and the use to be made of the results of their research. Membership is open to any British firm in the particular industry, subject to the approval of the Councils of the Research Associations.

Brushes.
BRITISH BRUSH MANUFACTURERS' RESEARCH ASSOCIATION, 90 Cowcross Street, E.C.1.—*Dir.*, D. I. Fothergill.

Cast Iron.
BRITISH CAST IRON RESEARCH ASSOCIATION, Bordesley Hall, Alvechurch, Birmingham.— *Dir.*, H. Morrogh, C.B.E., F.R.S.

Ceramics.
BRITISH CERAMIC RESEARCH ASSOCIATION, Queen's Road, Penkhull, Stoke-on-Trent.—*Dir.*, A. Dinsdale.

Civil Engineering.
CONSTRUCTION INDUSTRY RESEARCH AND INFORMATION ASSOCIATION, Old Queen Street House, 6 Storey's Gate, S.W.1.—*Dir.*, A. R. Collins, M.B.E., D.SC., Ph.D.

Coke and Tar.
BRITISH CARBONIZATION RESEARCH ASSOCIATION, Research Centre, Wingerworth, Chesterfield, Derbyshire.—*Dir.*, J. P. Graham.

Cotton, Silk, etc.
COTTON, SILK AND MAN-MADE FIBRES RESEARCH ASSOCIATION, Shirley Institute, Didsbury, Manchester, 20.—*Dir.*, L. A. Wiseman, O.B.E.

Cutlery.
CUTLERY AND ALLIED TRADES RESEARCH ASSOCIATION, Henry Street, Sheffield, 3.—*Dir.*, E. A. Oldfield.

Drop Forging.
DROP FORGING RESEARCH ASSOCIATION, Shepherd Street, Sheffield, 3.—*Director*, S. E. Rogers, Ph.D.

Electrical.
ELECTRICAL RESEARCH ASSOCIATION, Cleeve Road, Leatherhead, Surrey.—*Man. Dir.*, B. C. Lindley, Ph.D.

Flour Milling and Baking.
FLOUR MILLING AND BAKING RESEARCH ASSOCIATION, Research Station, Chorleywood, Rickmansworth, Herts.—*Dir.*, C. T. Greenwood, D.SC., Ph.D.

Food Manufacture.
BRITISH FOOD MANUFACTURING INDUSTRIES RESEARCH ASSOCIATION, Randalls Road, Leatherhead, Surrey.—*Dir.*, A. W. Holmes, Ph.D.

Fruit and Vegetable Canning.
CAMPDEN FOOD PRESERVATION RESEARCH ASSOCIATION, Chipping Campden, Glos.—*Dir.*, H. R. Hinton.

Furniture.
FURNITURE INDUSTRY RESEARCH ASSOCIATION, Maxwell Road, Stevenage, Herts.—*Dir.*, D. M. Heughan.

Glass.
BRITISH GLASS INDUSTRY RESEARCH ASSOCIATION, Northumberland Road, Sheffield 10.—*Dir.*, C. Thorpe.

Heating and Ventilating.
BUILDING SERVICES RESEARCH & INFORMATION ASSOCIATION, Old Bracknell Lane, Bracknell, N. S. Billington, O.B.E.

Hosiery.
HOSIERY AND ALLIED TRADES RESEARCH ASSOCIATION (HATRA), Thorneywood, 7 Gregory Boulevard, Nottingham.—*Dir.*, W. A. Dutton.

Hydromechanics.
BRITISH HYDROMECHANICS RESEARCH ASSOCIATION, Cranfield, Bedford.—*Dir.*, G. F. W. Adler.

Industrial Powders, Chalk & Lime.
WELWYN HALL RESEARCH ASSOCIATION, Edgewoth House, Arlesey, Beds.—*Dir.*, R. R. Davidson.

Instrumentation.
SIRA INSTITUTE LTD., South Hill, Chislehurst, Kent.—*Man. Dir.*, S. S. Carlisle.

Laundering.
BRITISH LAUNDERERS' RESEARCH ASSOCIATION, The Laboratories, Hill View Gardens, Hendon, N.W.4.—*Dir.*, J. Leicester, O.B.E.

Leather.
BRITISH LEATHER MANUFACTURERS' RESEARCH ASSOCIATION, Milton Park, Egham, Surrey.— *Dir.*, R. L. Sykes, Ph.D.

Linen.
LAMBEG INDUSTRIAL RESEARCH ASSOCIATION, Research Institute, Lambeg, Lisburn, Co. Antrim, N. Ireland.—*Dir.*, H. A. C. Todd, O.B.E.

Machine Tools.
MACHINE TOOL INDUSTRY RESEARCH ASSOCIATION, Hulley Road, Hurdsfield, Macclesfield, Cheshire. —*Dir.*, A. E. De Barr, O.B.E.

Motor Vehicles.
MOTOR INDUSTRY RESEARCH ASSOCIATION, Watling Street, Nuneaton, Warwickshire.—*Dir.*, R. H. Macmillan.

Mycology.
COMMONWEALTH MYCOLOGICAL INSTITUTE, Ferry Lane, Kew, Surrey.—*Dir.*, A. Johnson.

Non-Ferrous Metals.
BRITISH NON-FERROUS METALS TECHNOLOGY CENTRE, The Grove Laboratories, Denchworth Road, Wantage, Berks.—*Dir.*, A. J. Kennedy, D.SC., Ph.D.

Paint.
PAINT RESEARCH ASSOCIATION, Paint Research Station, Waldegrave Road, Teddington, Middlesex.—*Dir.*, G. de W. Anderson, Ph.D.

Paper, Board, Printing and Packing.

RESEARCH ASSOCIATION FOR THE PAPER AND BOARD, PRINTING AND PACKAGING INDUSTRIES, Randalls Road, Leatherhead, Surrey.—*Dir.*, N. K. Bridge, Ph.D.

Production Engineering.

PRODUCTION ENGINEERING RESEARCH ASSOCIATION OF GREAT BRITAIN, Melton Mowbray, Leics.— *Dir.*, D. F. Galloway, C.B.E., Ph.D.

Rubber and Plastics.

RUBBER AND PLASTICS RESEARCH ASSOCIATION OF GREAT BRITAIN, Shawbury, Shrewsbury, Shropshire.—*Dir.*, W. F. Watson, D.SC., Ph.D.

Ships.

BRITISH SHIP RESEARCH ASSOCIATION, Research Station, Wallsend, Northumberland.—*Dir.*, R. Hurst, G.M., C.B.E., Ph.D.

Shoes.

SHOE AND ALLIED TRADES RESEARCH ASSOCIATION, Satra House, Rockingham Road, Kettering, Northants.—*Dir.*, A. R. Payne, D.SC.

Springs.

SPRING RESEARCH ASSOCIATION, Henry Street, Sheffield 3.—*Dir.*, J. A. Bennett.

Steel Castings.

STEEL CASTINGS RESEARCH AND TRADE ASSOCIATION. East Bank Road, Sheffield 2.—*Director* J. C. Wright, Ph.D.

Timber.

TIMBER RESEARCH AND DEVELOPMENT ASSOCIATION, Hughenden Valley, High Wycombe, Bucks.— *Dir.*, J. S. McBride.

Toxicology.

BRITISH INDUSTRIAL BIOLOGICAL RESEARCH ASSOCIATION, Woodmansterne Road, Carshalton, Surrey.—*Dir.*, R. F. Crampton, Ph.D.

Water.

WATER RESEARCH CENTRE, Ferry Lane, Medmenham, Marlow, Bucks.—*Dir.*, R. G. Allen, O.B.E., Ph.D.

Welding.

WELDING INSTITUTE, Abington Hall, nr. Cambridge.—*Dir.-Gen.*, R. Weck, C.B.E., Ph.D.

Wool.

WOOL INDUSTRIES RESEARCH ASSOCIATION (WIRA), Headingley Lane, Leeds 6.—*Dir.*, B. E. King, Ph.D.

AGRICULTURAL RESEARCH INSTITUTES AND UNITS

The following research institutes are under the direct control of the Agricultural Research Council (*see* p. 372):—

Unit Of Animal Genetics, Institute of Animal Genetics, West Mains Road, Edinburgh 9.— *Director*, Prof. D. S. Falconer, SC.D., F.R.S.

Unit of Developmental Botany, 181A Huntingdon Road, Cambridge.—*Director.*, Prof. P. W. Brian, SC.D., F.R.S.

Unit of Invertebrate Chemistry and Physiology, University of Sussex, Falmer, Brighton.—*Hon. Director*, Prof. A. W. Johnson, F.R.S.

Unit of Invertebrate Chemistry and Physiology (Subgroup), University of Cambridge, Zoology Dept., Downing Street, Cambridge.—*Associate Director*, J. E. Treherne, Ph.D., SC.D.

Unit of Muscle Mechanism and Insect Physiology, Dept. of Zoology, University of Oxford, South Parks Road, Oxford.—*Hon. Dir.*, Prof. J. W. S. Pringle, M.B.E., SC.D., F.R.S.

Unit of Nitrogen Fixation, University of Sussex, Brighton.—*Director*, Prof. J. Chatt, Ph.D., SC.D., F.R.S.

Unit of Reproductive Physiology and Biochemistry, 307 Huntingdon Road, Cambridge.—*Director*, Prof. T. R. R. Mann, C.B.E., M.D., SC.D., Ph.D., F.R.S.

Unit of Soil Physics, 219C Huntingdon Road, Cambridge.—*Dir.*, E. G. Youngs, Ph.D. (*acting*).

Unit of Statistics, University of Edinburgh, 21 Buccleuch Place, Edinburgh 8.—*Hon. Director*, Prof. D. J. Finney, SC.D., F.R.S., F.R.S.E.

Statistics Group, Dept. of Applied Biology, Downing Street, Cambridge.

Systemic Fungicide Unit, Wye College, Ashford, Kent.—*Hon. Director*, Prof. R. L. Wain, C.B.E., D.SC., Ph.D., F.R.S.

Institute for Research on Animal Diseases, Compton, Newbury, Berks.—*Director*, J. M. Payne, Ph.D.

Institute of Animal Physiology, Babraham, Cambs.—*Director*, B. A. Cross, Ph.D., SC.D., F.R.S.

Animal Breeding Research Organisation, West Mains Road, Edinburgh 9.—*Director*, J. W. B. King, Ph.D.

Poultry Research Centre, King's Buildings, West Mains Road, Edinburgh, 9.—*Director*, T. C. Carter, O.B.E., Ph.D., D.SC., F.R.S.E.

Letcombe Laboratory, Letcombe Regis, Wantage, Oxon.—*Director*, R. Scott Russell, D.SC., Ph.D.

Weed Research Organisation, Begbroke Hill, Sandy Lane, Yarnton, Oxford.—*Director*, J. D. Fryer.

Food Research Institute, Colney Lane, Norwich.— *Director*, Prof. S. R. Elsden, Ph.D.

Meat Research Institute, Langford, nr. Bristol.— *Director*, J. R. Norris, Ph.D. (also Weston Laboratory, Bridge Road, Weston-super-Mare).

GRANT-AIDED RESEARCH INSTITUTES

In addition to the above there are other institutes which, while retaining their own individuality, are financed wholly or in the main by grants made from Government funds. Most of these Institutes have governing bodies of their own to which they are directly responsible. The maintenance grants for Institutes in England and Wales are met from funds voted by Parliament and administered by the Agricultural Research Council; the Scottish Institutes are borne on the vote of the Department of Agriculture and Fisheries for Scotland.

Long Ashton Research Station, Bristol.—*Director*, Prof. J. P. Hudson, M.B.E., G.M., Ph.D.

Animal Diseases Research Association (Scotland), Moredun Institute, 408 Gilmerton Road, Edinburgh.—*Dir.*, J. T. Stamp, D.SC., F.R.S.E.

Animal Virus Research Institute, Pirbright, Surrey. —*Director*, J. B. Brooksby, C.B.E., D.SC., Ph.D., F.R.S.E.

East Malling Research Station, Maidstone, Kent.— *Director*, A. F. Posnette, Ph.D., SC.D., F.R.S.

Glasshouse Crops Research Institute, Worthing Road, Rustington, Littlehampton, Sussex.—*Director*, D. Rudd-Jones, ph.d.

Grassland Research Institute, Hurley, nr. Maidenhead, Berks.—*Director*, Prof. E. K. Woodford, o.b.e., ph.d.

Hannah Research Institute, Ayr.—*Director*, Prof. J. A. F. Rook, ph.d., d.sc.

Hill Farming Research Organisation, Bush Estate, Penicuik, Midlothian.—*Director*, J. M. M. Cunningham, ph d.

Hop Research Centre, Wye College, Ashford, Kent. *Head of Dept.*, R. A. Neve, ph.d.

Houghton Poultry Research Station,* Houghton, Huntingdon.—*Director*, P. M. Biggs, ph.d.

John Innes Institute, Colney Lane, Norwich.—*Director*, Prof. R. Markham, ph.d., f.r.s.

Macaulay Institute for Soil Research, Craigiebuckler, Aberdeen.—*Director*, R. L. Mitchell, ph.d., f.r.s.e.

National Institute of Agricultural Engineering, Wrest Park, Silsoe, Bedford.—*Director*, Prof. C. J. Moss.

Scottish Institute of Agricultural Engineering, Scottish Station, Bush Estate, Penicuik, Midlothian.—*Director*, W. J. West, f.r.s.e.

National Institute for Research in Dairying, Shinfield, nr. Reading.—*Director*, Prof. B. G. F. Weitz, o.b.e., d.sc.

National Vegetable Research Stn. Wellesbourne, Warwick.—*Director*, Prof. D. W. Wright.

Plant Breeding Institute, Maris Lane, Trumpington, Cambridge.—*Director*, Prof. R. Riley, d.sc., f.r.s.

Welsh Plant Breeding Station, Plas Gogerddan, nr. Aberystwyth.—*Director*, Prof. J. P. Cooper, ph.d., d.sc.

Scottish Plant Breeding Station, Pentlandfield, Roslin, Midlothian.—*Director*, N. W. Simmonds, sc.d., f.r.s.e.

Rowett Research Institute, Bucksburn, Aberdeen. —*Director*, K. L. Blaxter, d.sc., f.r.s.

Rothamsted Experimental Station, Harpenden, Herts.—*Director*, L. Fowden, ph.d., f.r.s.

Scottish Horticultural Research Institute, Invergowrie, Dundee.—*Director*, C. E. Taylor, ph.d.

*Financed jointly by the Agricultural Research Council and the Animal Health Trust.

PROGRESS OF THE NEW TOWNS (To Dec. 31, 1974)

Town	New Industries		New Shops and Offices	New Houses and Flats	Net + Expenditure for all purposes £
	Number of firms	Number Employed			
Aycliffe....................	—	—	103	6,860	28,600,000
Basildon...................	185	20,966	428	24,742	135,100,000
Bracknell..................	74	9,589	277	13,429	63,295,000
Central Lancs..............	—	—	—	4,549	22,500,000
Corby.....................	55	5,720	294	11,687	32,108,000
Crawley...................	93	18,319	357	20,421	51,120,000
Harlow....................	302	20,450	441	24,104	92,000,000
Hatfield...................	20	1,568	135	6,706	14,585,000
Hemel Hempstead...........	77	14,000	371	19,161	49,226,000
Milton Keynes..............	102	—	44	27,498	92,817,000
Northampton...............	153	6,220	148	9,524	45,250,000
Peterborough..............	—	4,800	—	6,472	56,174,000
Peterlee...................	49	4,100	156	7,683	30,280,000
Redditch..................	235	5,812	122	10,990	41,226,000
Runcorn..................	81	3,775	140	7,593	53,375,000
Skelmersdale..............	100	10,600	217	8,202	63,212,000
Stevenage.................	49	16,200	435	21,474	63,460,000
Telford...................	232	20,800	114	9,666	68,000,000
Warrington...............	13	475	—	6,601	16,000,000
Washington...............	186	7,795	130	7,655	48,343,000
Welwyn Garden	24	4,002	182	8,379	26,003,000
Cwmbran..................	110	5,053	216	11,517	37,341,000
Newtown..................	27	815	5	592	7,810,000
Cumbernauld...............	149	7,400	160	11,488	62,851,000
East Kilbride..............	306	19,410	309	20,927	86,300,000
Glenrothes................	141	8,979	139	9,151	42,000,000
Irvine....................	81	7,000	80	4,249	22,703,000
Livingston................	774	5,570	70	6,249	47,674,000
Stonehouse................	—	—	—	139	2,020,000
TOTAL.................	2,918	229,516	5,073	327,708	1,401,373,000

PRINCIPAL CHARITABLE BEQUESTS OF THE YEAR

Capital Transfer Tax has replaced Estate Duty since our last issue. New legislation enables gifts made to charity more than a year before the death of the donor to be free of tax, although gifts totalling over £100,000 made within a year of death and at death will carry the tax.

The following alphabetical list shows the principal charitable bequests since our last issue. Legacies and other charges have to be deducted from gross estates before the amount to charities can be arrived at.

The Duke of Norfolk left Arundel Castle and Castle Park to the National Trust, or some other similar body, together with such sum as his Trustees decide as an endowment, and Olive, Lady Baillie, left her home, Leeds Castle, near Maidstone, one of, the oldest inhabited historic fortresses in Britain, for the benefit of the nation. She also left about £1,400,000 to provide for its upkeep.

The National Gallery received nearly £100,000 from its former director, Sir Martin Davies, the income from which is to be used to buy books, manuscripts, photographs and photographic copies for the library, furniture and sculpture, as well as providing grants to staff to enable them to travel to widen their knowledge of the history of art.

St. Hughes College, Oxford, was left the residue from the estate of Miss Mary E. Seaton, a Fellow and Tutor of the college, to be used for a schoolmistress studentship. Mr. Gavin M. MacFarlane-Grieve, an Hon. Fellow of Magdalene College, Cambridge, left his entire estate of £316,979 to the college and £10,000 was left to Cheltenham Ladies College under the will of Prof. Norman B. Capon, Emeritus Professor of Child Health at Liverpool University.

The 1st Baron Heyworth of Oxton, who joined Lever Brothers Ltd. at 18 as a clerk and became the company chairman, left £50,000 for charitable purposes as his executors decide, and hotel owner Mr. Peter Peters left the bulk of his £779,894 estate to the State of Israel.

Two communities benefited by large bequests— the Fylde village of Freckleton received £136,000 under the will of retired insurance broker Mr. Robert Rawstorne, to be used as the Parish Council think fit, and Mr. Horace Taylor, a Driffield timber merchant, left £50,000 for charities in Driffield and district as his executors decide.

A retired Oldham electrical engineer, Mr. Harry Hind, left his estate of £9,000 to the RAF Benevolent Fund, and the Magpie Children's Home at Teddington Lock, Middlesex, received all of Mr. Alfred T. Hine's property.

The RSPCA, Sheffield, will have to wait for one of their bequests as Mrs. Ivy Blackhurst left the £22,000 residue of her estate for the benefit of her cat " Blackie " for life, only on its death will the charity receive the balance.

The principal figure in the list below is that of the *gross* estate.

Mr. Hugh Carson Andrews, of Bournemouth
£117,815
(Several small charitable legacies and £25,000 each and the residue equally between the RNLI and Imperial Cancer Research Fund.)

Hon. Olive Cecilia, Lady Baillie, of Leeds Castle, near Maidstone....................£4,360,976
(Leeds Castle and endowment to Leeds Castle Trust.)

Mrs. Ivy Mabel Blackhurst, of Sheffield... £28,168
(Residue to RSPCA after the death of her cat "Blackie.")

Elsie Matilda Bowler, of Bedford.........£25,545
(All property equally between Arthritis and Rheumatism Council, Missions to Seamen and Imperial Cancer Research Fund.)

Mrs. Edith Mary Burgess, of Ventnor.....£20,527
(All property to Dr. Barnardo's.)

Mrs. Florence Winifred Burrows, of Woodthorpe, Notts.......................£96,196
(Residue to Nottingham General Hospital.)

Prof. Norman Brandon Capon, of Ruthin. £39,079
(£10,000 to Cheltenham Ladies College and several smaller charitable legacies.)

Mr. Kenneth Cleave, of Poole.........£176,951
(Residue equally between RSPCA, NSPCC, and National Trust.)

Sir Martin Davies, of London..........£109,308
(Residue to National Gallery)

Marian Vaughan Dunlop, of Newbury....£76,878
(£20,000 to Fellowship of Meditation, Guildford.)

Mr. Samuel Fishel Epstein, of London... £120,345
(Residue equally between Cancer Research Campaign and Jewish National Fund.)

Miss Elizabeth Evans, of Allestree........£30,820
(Residue to Cancer Research Campaign.)

Miss Margaret Evans, of Newton Abbot.. £24,890
(Residue to Help the Aged.)

Miss Freda Fletcher, of London.........£87,277
(Residue to Pestalozzi Children's Village Trust.)

Mr. Gavin Malcolm MacFarlane-Grieve, of Toft, Cambs............................£316,979
(All property to Magdalene College, Cambridge.)

Major Harold Wesley Hall, of Downton, Lymington, and London............£514,431
(£50,000 to D'Arcy Hall Charitable Trust.)

Mrs. Harry Gordon Roy Hancher, of Beckenham................................£26,955
(All property to Cheshire Homes.)

Miss Alice Barbara Holroyd Haywood, of Oxford..............................£32,784
(Residue to RSPCA.)

Mrs. Helen Christian Drawhill Heffer, of Bideford..........................£41,152
(All property equally between PDSA and Dr. Barnardo's.)

Mr. William Arthur Herbert, of Laleham on Thames............................£88,877
(£10,000 each to NSPCC, Pharmaceutical Society of Great Britain, British Epilepsy Association and Imperial Cancer Research Fund, £5,000 to RNLI.)

1st Baron Heyworth of Oxton, of London
£195,574
(£50,000 for charitable purposes as executors decide.)

Mr. Harry Hind, of Oldham.............£9,232
(All property to RAF Benevolent Fund.)

Mr. Alfred Thomas Hine, of Prestbury, Ches.
£17,932
(All property to Magpie Children's Home, Teddington Lock.)

Mr. Frederick Hodges, of Frinton on Sea
£1,099,873
(£25,000 to the British Diabetic Association, £12,500 each to RNIB and Help the Aged.)

Margaret Emily Silcock Howes, of Stithians, Truro................................£47,332
(Residue equally between Children's Society, Dr. Barnardo's and Shaftesbury Homes.)

Major Frank Julius Jebens, of London....£60,822
(£10,000 to RSPCA.)

Mr. Percy Andrew Hall Kerr, of Frinton on Sea...................................£16,929
(Residue to RNIB.)

Mrs. Margaret Ellen Marshall, of Farnborough, Hants................................£27,554
(Residue to St. John Parish Church, Cove.)

Jessie Janet Maycock, of Bournemouth..£151,109
(Residue to Cheshire Homes.)

Mrs. Ada Maude Nicoll, of Rottingdean. £154,072
(£25,000 to Institute of Cancer Research.)

16th Duke of Norfolk, of Arundel....£3,536,537
(Arundel Castle, Castle Park and sum for endowment to National Trust, or some similar body.)

Mrs. Irene Nutt, of Harrogate..........£27,070
(All property equally between St. Dunstan's and Star and Garter Home, Richmond.)

Mr. Peter Peters, of London...........£779,894
(Residue to the State of Israel.)

Miss Vera Jane Pitt, of Seaford........£251,472
(Residue variously to ten charities.)

Mr. Robert Rawstorne, of Fulwood, Lancs.
£147,044
(Several small charitable legacies and residue to Freckleton Parish Council.)

Olive Agnes Richard, of Stanford le Hope. £52,725
(Residue equally between RSPCA, PDSA, and Carter Foundation.)

Mr. Carl Robert Rudolf, of London....£598,034
(Large bequest to Hunterian Society.)

Mr. John Eric William Graves Sandars, of Gainsborough....................£1,557,991
(£50,000 to charitable trust.)

Miss Mary Ethel Seaton, of Oxford......£46,446
(Residue to St. Hugh's College, Oxford.)

Mr. Geoffrey Newton Sharp, of Barnston, Dunmow.........................£104,397
(Large bequest to St. Loye's College, Exeter.)

Mr. Alfred Belton Smith, of Bristol.....£36,804
(All property to RNIB.)

Eileen Fenimore Somers, of Chislehurst...£84,207
(Residue as to three parts to Guide Dogs for the Blind Association and one part to Imperial Cancer Research Fund.)

Mr. Horace Taylor, of Driffield........£558,852
(£50,000 to charities in Driffield and District.)

Miss Doris Irene Turner, of London.....£454,338
(Residue equally between Royal Agricultural Benevolent Institution and National Mission to Deep Sea Fishermen.)

Mr. Richard Sydney Hansford Ward, of Horsham...........................£29,968
(All property to Christ's Hospital.)

Mrs. Mary Watts, of Glossop...........£25,944
(All property to the Imperial Cancer Research Fund.)

Mrs. Gwendoline Dorothy Wheeler, of Tankerton.........................£96,173
(Residue to Royal College of Surgeons of England.)

Mrs. Olive Wookey, of Liverpool.......£50,710
(Several small charitable legacies and residue to North West Cancer Research Fund.)

Mr. Sydney Price Woolley, of Southampton
£64,892
(All property equally between the Salvation Army Men's Hostel and Church Army Men's Social Department, both of Southampton, and Dr. Barnardo's.)

CAR PRODUCTION IN MAIN PRODUCING COUNTRIES (thousands)

	1964	1965	1966	1967	1968	1969	1970	1971	1972	1973
United Kingdom...	1,868	1,722	1,604	1,552	1,816	1,717	1,641	1,742	1,921	1,747
France............	1,390	1,423	1,786	1,777	1,833	2,168	2,458	2,694	2,993	3,202
W. Germany......	2,650	2,734	2,830	2,296	2,862	3,313	3,528	3,697	3,521	3,650
Italy.............	1,029	1,134	1,282	1,439	1,545	1,477	1,720	1,701	1,732	1,823
Sweden..........	162	182	173	194	223	243	279	287	318	342
Japan............	580	696	878	1,376	2,056	2,611	3,179	3,718	4,022	4,471
USA (Factory sales).	7,752	9,306	8,598	7,437	8,849	8,224	6,550	8,584	8,828	9,668
Canada..........	561	711	702	721	901	1,035	937	1,095	1,147	1,235
Total............	15,992	17,908	17,853	16,792	20,085	20,788	20,292	23,308	24,482	26,138
UK % of total....	12	10	9	9	9	8	8	9	9	8

BRITISH MOTOR VEHICLE PRODUCTION AND EXPORTS

Year	Weeks	Passenger Cars (including taxis)			Commercial Road Vehicles		
		For Export	Total	Weekly average	For Export	Total	Weekly average
1969	...53...	824,315	1,717,073	32,398	192,778	465,776	8,788
1970	...52...	722,857	1,640,966	31,557	190,125	457,532	8,799
1971	...52...	714,479	1,741,940	33,499	187,927	450,206	8,773
1972	...52...	613,430	1,921,311	36,948	135,470	408,019	7,848
1973	...52...	605,105	1,797,316	33,602	159,049	416,626	8,012

BRITISH INSURANCE COMPANIES IN 1974

In 1974, companies experienced an underwriting loss on their worldwide general insurance business of £115 million (3·4% of premiums) against a profit of £19 million in 1973. The deterioration was most marked in fire and accident (non-motor) business transacted in overseas territories, where there was a loss of £85 million, while the loss on motor business overseas rose to £53 million.

Worldwide investment income from general insurance funds, stockholders funds and free reserves was £377 million, producing an overall profit before tax for general insurance of £262 million.

RESULTS IN MAJOR TERRITORIES
United Kingdom

UK motor insurance produced only a marginal underwriting profit of £1·8 million on premium income which increased by 10% to £507 million.

Garage charge out rates and spare parts prices continued to rise rapidly, by 29% and 36% respectively, increases which were inevitably reflected in the rising cost of claims.

Fire and accident (non-motor) business contributed a profit of £21·4 million (2·7% of premiums) compared with £44·7 million (6·6% of premiums) in 1973. Premiums increased from £676 million to £789 million. The estimated cost of fire damage, covering both insured and uninsured damage, rose from £179 million in 1973 to £237 million. This included the Flixborough disaster in June, which accounted for an estimated £36 million damage to the plant and surrounding property. The estimated cost of fire damage for the first four months of 1975 (£54·4 million) has been approximately the same as the same period in 1974.
United States

Underwriting operations in the United States produced a loss of £44·3 million (5·9% of premiums), compared with a profit of 5·7 million (0·8%) in 1973. Of this total, £33 million arose from fire and accident (non-motor) business, caused largely by severe windstorm damage and by adverse experience in the liability classes. Motor results further deteriorated, particularly in the last quarter, to produce a loss of £11·3 million.

Premium income from general business increased by only 7% to £748 million in 1974 against £702 million in 1973, reflecting the increasingly selective underwriting approach of British companies in the United States market during a period of intense competition and inadequate rates.
Rest of the World

Results in other overseas territories were also

disappointing, with a loss of £41·6 million on motor business and £52·3 million on fire and other accident classes. Significant factors in overseas results were natural disasters such as Cyclone Tracy and the Queensland floods in Australia and unsatisfactory underwriting conditions there on Motor Act and Workers Compensation business.

In Canada, where there was particularly severe competition, results deteriorated in both motor and property business.

In Europe, general business in the other 8 EEC countries grew by 38% to £422 million with the results varying by class of business and by territory.
Overseas Earnings

Despite the disappointing underwriting results in all major territories, insurance companies continued to make a major contribution to the invisible earnings of the insurance industry—comprising the company market, Lloyd's and brokers. In 1973 (the latest year for which figures are available), these earnings amounted to £372 million—representing investment income, underwriting profit and commission from all insurance activities.

MARINE, AVIATION AND TRANSPORT

Worldwide premium income for maritime and aviation business rose by 18·6% to £347 million and transfers to profit and loss accounts totalled £9·8 million. Competition in world markets continued partly as a result of increased capacity. Several major disasters occurred such as the constructive total loss through fire of the liner " Cunard Ambassador " and the crash at Nairobi of a Boeing 747, the first fatal operational loss of this class of aircraft. Losses of this magnitude (where the hull values alone were over £8 million and £13 million respectively) make clear the need for adequate premiums.

INVESTMENTS

The invested funds of the insurance companies arising from long term insurance totalled £18,293 million at book values at 31 December 1974. Income from these funds was £1,459 million.

Invested sums of worldwide general insurance funds, stockholders funds and free reserves totalled £5,272 million at book values at 31 December 1974. Income from these funds was £377 million.

Although the market values of these investments at the end of 1974 were below the corresponding book values, the rise in stock market prices since the end of 1974 has more than made good the year-end shortfall between book and market values.

WORLDWIDE GENERAL PREMIUMS 1973 AND 1974

	1973	1974	Increase
	£m	£m	%
Fire and Accident (non-motor)	1,907	2,246	17·8
Motor	1,159	1,265	9·2
Marine, Aviation and Transport	293	347	18·6
TOTAL	3,359	3,858	14·9

NOTE: 1. These figures include business transacted by specialist reinsurers, and business written on a 3 year account basis which is not included in later tables.
    2. The 1973 figures in all appropriate tables incorporate slight upwards adjustments to include business of new members of BIA, thus enabling direct comparisons between 1973 and 1974.

WORLDWIDE UNDERWRITING RESULTS 1973 AND 1974

	1973			1974		
	Premiums	Profit/ Loss	% of Premiums	Premiums	Profit/ Loss	% of Premiums
	£m	£m	%	£m	£m	%
Fire and Accident (non-motor)	1,819	+ 38·1	+ 2·1	2,154	− 63·9	− 3·0
Motor	1,146	− 19·1	− 1·7	1,252	− 51·1	− 4·1
TOTAL	2,965	+ 19·0	+ 0·6	3,406	− 115·0	− 3·4

WORLDWIDE LONG TERM PREMIUMS 1973 AND 1974

	1973	1974	Increase
	£m	£m	%
Ordinary long term U.K............................	1,719	1,887	9·8
Ordinary long term (Overseas)......................	387	489	26·4
Industrial long term (U.K.)....................,.....	356	382	7·3
TOTAL..................................	2,462	2,758	12·1

U.K. UNDERWRITING 1973 AND 1974

	1973			1974		
	Premiums	Profit/ Loss	% of Premiums	Premiums	Profit/ Loss	% of Premiums
	£m	£m	%	£m	£m	%
Fire and Accident (non-motor)...	676	+44·7	+6·6	789	+21·4	+2·7
Motor........................	461	+12·7	+2·8	507	+1·8	+0·4
TOTAL..................	1,137	+57·4	+5·0	1,296	+23·2	+1·8

U.S.A. UNDERWRITING 1973 AND 1974

	1973			1974		
	Premiums	Profit/ Loss	% of Premiums	Premiums	Profit/ Loss	% of Premiums
	£m	£m	%	£m	£m	%
Fire and Accident (non-motor)...	448	+7·7	+1·7	486	−33·0	−6·8
Motor........................	254	−2·0	−0·8	262	−11·3	−4·3
TOTAL	702	+5·7	+0·8	748	−44·3	−5·9

REST OF THE WORLD UNDERWRITING 1973 AND 1974

	1973			1974		
	Premiums	Profit/ Loss	% of Premiums	Premiums	Profit/ Loss	% of Premiums
	£m	£m	%	£m	£m	%
Fire and Accident (non-motor)...	695	−14·3	−2·1	879	−52·3	−5·9
Motor........................	431	−29·8	−6·9	483	−41·6	−8·6
TOTAL..................	1,126	−44·1	−3·9	1,362	−93·9	−6·9

LLOYD'S OF LONDON

Lloyd's of London is an international market for almost any type of insurance. Ships, aircraft, oil rigs, cargo of all descriptions, motor cars, civil enginering projects, fire, personal accident and third party liability are a few random examples of the everyday risks placed at Lloyd's which bring some £750 million of premiums to underwriters each year. Two thirds of this business comes from outside Great Britain and makes a valuable contribution to the country's balance of payments.

Today, as it was three centuries ago, a policy is subscribed at Lloyd's by private individuals with unlimited liability. Now that Lloyd's members are numbered in their thousands, however, the method of underwriting is the same only in principle. The merchant of the past, signing policies in a coffee house as a sideline to his main business, has long since given way to the specialist underwriter who accepts risks at Lloyd's on behalf of members grouped in a syndicate. There are currently about 270 syndicates of varying sizes, some with up to several hundred names and each managed by a full-time underwriting agent.

Lloyd's membership today is drawn from many sources. Industry, commerce and the professions are strongly represented while many members are, of course, actively engaged at Lloyd's either on the broking or the underwriting side.

Underwriting membership of Lloyd's is open to men and women of any nationality provided that they meet the stringent financial requirements of the Committee of Lloyd's. Assets of at least £75,000 have to be shown and a minimum deposit of £10,000 must be lodged with the Corporation of Lloyd's as security for underwriting liabilities.

Lloyd's also provides the most comprehensive shipping intelligence service available in the world. The enormous volume of shipping information received from Lloyd's agents, radio stations, shipowners and other sources is collated and distributed to newspapers, radio and television services, and throughout the marine and commercial communities in general.

This information is edited, printed and published at Lloyd's and sent all over the world. " Lloyd's List " is London's oldest daily newspaper and contains news of general commercial interest as well as shipping information. " Lloyd's Shipping Index " also published daily, lists some 18,000 ocean-going vessels in alphabetical order and gives the latest known report of each.

LLOYD'S UNDERWRITERS

SUMMARY OF ACCOUNTS AS AT DECEMBER 31, 1973

In the summaries: (1) Premiums include the reinsurance premium (if any) received from a previous closed account; and (2) Claims include the reinsurance premium paid or amount placed to reserve at close of third year.

	Net Premium Income	Interest and other credits	Claims	Expenses and other debits	Balance
	£	%	%	%	%
1971 A/C (end year 3)					
Life	966,483	5·98	78·02	9·90	18·06
Motor	52,078,934	3·40	89·57	9·96	3·87
Marine, Aviation and Transit		3·85	87·72	3·43	12·70
Other than Aviation	336,410,895		89·15		
Aviation	83,646,809		81·98		
All other	398,162,435	3·58	95·24	2·83	5·51
	871,265,556	3·70	91·26	3·55	8·89
1972 A/C (end Year 2)					
Life	929,313	2·87	60·81	12·43	29·63
Motor	66,333,656	1·73	40·46	9·38	51·89
Marine, Aviation and Transit		1·32	23·47	2·77	75·08
Other than Aviation	362,637,499		23·53		
Aviation	85,561,588		23·22		
All other	442,019,411	1·09	21·72	2·36	77·01
	957,481,467	1·24	23·88	3·05	74·31
1973 A/C (end Year 1)					
Life	874,604	0·91	14·90	9·07	76·94
Motor	55,885,358	0·84	15·84	11·67	73·33
Marine, Aviation and Transit		0·84	23·05	5·46	72·33
Other than Aviation	180,968,302		22·71		
Aviation	34,480,695		24·83		
All other	169,200,510	0·84	13·65	5·89	81·30
	441,409,469	0·84	18·52	6·42	75·90

LIFE ASSURANCE IN 1974

In 1974 yearly premiums paid by policyholders for life assurance and annuities totalled £2,420 million, an increase of 16% over £2,090 million in 1973. Single premium payments improved by £20 million from £870 million to £890 million.

Investment income earned on the life assurance and annuity funds totalled £1,570 million in 1974 against £1,340 million the previous year.

Total benefits paid out to policyholders amounted to £2,190 million, equivalent to approximately £42 million per week. Benefit payments have virtually quadrupled over the last ten years.

During 1974, premiums received from policyholders together with investment income exceeded outgo by way of payments to policyholders, management expenses and taxation by £1,520 million. This figure represents the amount of money made available for new investment through life assurance savings in 1974. In a normal year, this would roughly coincide with the growth of the funds held by life offices against future claims, but in 1974, reflecting the increased percentage yields arising from the depreciation in the market value of assets at the year end, some offices valued their liabilities at an appropriately higher rate of interest and used the resulting reduction in the value of liabilities to offset depreciation in asset values.

The net result of this was that the value of the life assurance funds decreased by £600 million from £20,200 million in 1973 to £19,600 at the end of 1974. Because of the long term nature of life assurance, the market value of assets on any particular date is of much less importance than the income which these assets produce.

These figures take into account all forms of ordinary and industrial life assurance, including business written under occupational pension and life assurance arrangements and business written overseas by UK offices and their subsidiary companies.

INDUSTRIAL LIFE ASSURANCE 1974

The following figures are based on returns from 18 " home service " insurance offices, which together transact over 99% of all industrial assurance business. While they, unlike all other insurers, transact industrial life assurance, they also carry on a very considerable volume of ordinary life and general insurance business, much of it in policyholders' homes.

	Figures for 1974	Comparable figures for 1973		Figures for 1974	Comparable figures for 1973
Industrial Life Business	£m	£m	*Industrial Life Business*	£m	£m
1. Premium Income.....	382·0	356·2	5. Payments to policy-holders:		
2. Investment Income (Gross)..............	214·0	198·5	(a) on Death.........	88·5	84·1
3. Industrial Assurance Fund at the end of the year (after transfers to and from investment reserves, etc.)........	2,643·4	2,737·9	(b) on Maturity......	135·4	127·6
			(c) on Surrender.....	74·1	65·3
			Total:.......	298·0	277·0
4. New Business:			6. Expenses including pension fund contri-butions, staff bonuses and Selective Employ-ment Tax...........	149·8	131·3
(a) New Sums Assured	1,201·2	1,039·1			
(b) New Premiums per annum...............	72·9	62·9			

NEW BUSINESS IN LINKED LIFE ASSURANCE POLICIES

	Year ended Dec. 31, 1973 £m	Year ended Dec. 31, 1974 £m
1. *New Annual Premiums*		
(a) Ordinary business.........................	42·832★	35·668
(b) Pension (including retirement annuity)...................	7·577★	17·583
Total New Annual Premiums....................	£50·409★	£53·251
2. *New Single Premiums*		
(a) Ordinary business.........................	356·101★	100·690
(b) Pension (including retirement annuity)...................	10·677★	11·510
Total New Single Premiums......................	£366·778★	£112·200
3. Number of policies in force at end of period.................	1,889,581★	2,233,800
(a) Number of policies involving investment directly or indirectly, and wholly or partly, in authorised unit trusts.............	996·404★	1,142,187
Investment in authorised unit trusts in respect of policies falling under 3 (a)		
4. Net amount invested during period.......................	96·769★	50·822
5. Aggregate market value at end of period..................	351·672★	239·968

★ Corrected figure

INSURANCE COMPANY INVESTMENTS
Long Term Funds

	1973		1974	
	£m	%	£m	%
British Government authority securities...............	2,843	15·5	2,496	13·6
Foreign and Commonwealth Government, provincial and municipal stocks............................	673	3·7	693	3·8
Debentures, loan stocks, preference and guaranteed stocks and shares......................................	2,871	15·7	2,771	15·2
Ordinary stocks and shares............................	5,109	27·9	4,203	23·0
Mortgages..	2,909	15·9	3,079	16·8
Real property and ground rents.......................	2,932	16·1	3,649	19·9
Other investments...................................	949	5·2	1,402	7·7
TOTAL....................................	18,286	100·0	18,293	100·0
INCOME....................................	1,254		1,459	

INSURANCE COMPANY INVESTMENTS

Other Funds

	1973		1974	
	£m	%	£m	%
British Government authority securities	333	7·0	345	6·5
Foreign and Commonwealth Government, provincial and municipal stocks.............................	724	15·3	818	15·5
Debentures, loan stocks, preference and guaranteed stocks and shares.....................................	826	17·4	884	16·8
Ordinary stocks and shares...........................	1,583	33·4	1,407	26·7
Mortgages..	301	6·4	366	6·9
Real property and ground rents......................	448	9·5	547	10·4
Other investments..................................	520	11·0	905	17·2
TOTAL....................................	4,735	100·0	5,272	100·0
INCOME..............................	292		377	

THE LIFE ASSURANCE COMPANIES

The list on the following pages contains the names of all the more important British life offices, and of Commonwealth offices (marked C) which transact life business in this country.

Class of business. The second column shows whether the company is conducted on the mutual system whereby the whole of the divisible profit is allotted to participating policyholders (M), or whether the company has proprietors by whom part (usually a very small proportion) of such profits received (P). Life offices transacting other business are marked (O) in this column. In such cases the life funds are kept separately, and are not liable for the claims of other departments. The share capital is usually liable for the claims of all branches. Those having an industrial branch are indicated by letter (I).

Figures. These are taken from the latest annual accounts available at date of going to press and in the majority of cases refer to annual reports for the financial year ended December 31, 1972.

Life funds. The amounts of these funds, though of interest, are not in themselves a sufficient indication of the financial stability of a company, which cannot be judged unless liabilities are actually compared with assets.

Premium income. The annual premium income is in all cases stated after deduction of the amount paid to other companies for reassuring parts of the risk.

Consideration for annuities.—These are the amounts received to provide various types of annuities.

Interest.—The rate of interest earned is important for comparison with the rate assumed in valuing liabilities, since the greater the margin between these rates the greater is the surplus available from this source bonus declaration. The rate of interest given is before deduction of Income Tax except where marked (N)—net.

Valuation.—The valuation returns which are required to be made by the companies to the Department of Trade and Industry indicate liability under existing policies, after making allowance for the amounts to be paid and received. It is assumed that deaths will occur in accordance with a mortality table (various tables are used) and that interest will be earned at a certain rate. If a company assumes that it will earn a high rate of interest in the future the net liability will appear less than if it assumes a low rate, while the liability on account of mortality appears greater by some tables than by others. The position of an office is most satisfactory when a stringent basis of valuation is adopted, because the margin between the calculated and experienced

liability is larger and the surplus available for bonuses is greater. The lower the rate of interest assumed the more stringent is the valuation. The foregoing remarks, however, do not apply in the case of an office which has adopted a Bonus Reserve Valuation.

Types of policy.—Although there are scores of life offices in Britain each offering their own particular products under a wide variety of labels, there are really only four basic types of contract. These are:

1. " Term " assurance (sometimes called " temporary " assurance). With this type of policy the assurer, in return for a regular premium agrees to pay the sum assured if the person assured should die within the term of years stated by the policy.

Such policies take care of the temporary need for protection of the family while the children are growing up, and the family is therefore most vulnerable. The commonest and most popular forms are to cover the mortgage on the family home or to assume a regular tax-free income for the family over so many years should the breadwinner die. This is much the cheapest form of life assurance because the majority of policies invariably do not result in claims.

2. " Whole-life " assurance is one under which the assured undertake to keep the assurance in force provided the premiums are paid for the whole life of the assured. They will then pay the agreed sum whenever death takes place.

This costs a good deal more than term, naturally. All policies end in claims.

3. " Endowment " assurance. This contract really is one which uses a fund for saving to a particular target sum by a particular future date and at the same time secures payment of the sum assured should the saver die before that date arrives. In return for the continued payment of a regular premium over a fixed number of years, the assurer agrees to pay the sum assured at the end of that time, or earlier if the assured person should die. The bulk of an endowment assurance premium is savings; consequently the premium of such a contract is a lot higher than that for a whole life assurance.

4. " Annuities ". Life assurance can be divided broadly speaking into death or survival benefits. Death benefits are paid to a policyholder's dependants of and when he dies. Survival benefits are paid to the policyholder himself either in the form of a cash sum when he reaches a certain age or in the form of a guaranteed annual income for life, which is known as an annuity. Pensions are annuities of a kind and a very large proportion of the pension due to people are being and will be paid by funds run by life offices.

PRINCIPAL LIFE ASSURANCE COMPANIES

Estab-lished	Class	Name of Office	Life and Annuity Funds	Life Premium Income	Considera-tion for Annuities	Rate of Interest % Earned	Interest % assumed at Valuation
			£m	£	£	£	£
1961	P	Abbey Life.................		40,700,000	35,100,000	7·6	3·75
1849	M	Australian Mutual (C)..........	55·9	4,811,894	519,959	7·38	Various
1925	PO	Avon.....................	5·7	1,729,578	157,756	10·09	Various
1961	P	Bedford Life...............	6·9	1,089,840	55,101	8·5	4·25
1866	PIO	Britannic (Ord.)...........	90·8	9,626,000	508,000	8·69	4·00
1920	PO	British National...........	5·4	831,738	154,279	6·76	2·5 to 4·00
1862	MI	City of Glasgow (Ord.)......	3·7	452,191	—	7·47	2·5
1824	M	Clerical Medical...........	166·2	14,078,000	26,936,000	8·52	7·00
1861	PO	Commercial Union..........	1,219·9	115,078,792	72,705,875	8·36	2·5
1871	P	Confederation (C)..........	45·5	7,996,000	469,000	9·25	2·0 to 4·0
1867	MIO	Co-operative..............	531	85,600,000	1,500,000	8·47	4·25
1899	PO	Crusader..................	84	11,686,000	2,370,000	8·91	Various
1904	PO	Eagle Star................	639	56,470,000	16,614,000	8·543	Various
1887	MO	Ecclesiastical.............	6·5	997,346	82,374	9·63	4·50
1762	M	Equitable†................	142·8	8,460,795	9,614,086	7·21	Various
1844	P	Equity & Law..............	253·5	29,456,000	18,918,000	—	8·25
1899	M	FS Assurance..............	18·8	1,013,634	478,666	10·03	Various
1925	M	Federation Mutual†........	1·4	173,501	18,840	8·07	Various
1832	M	Friends Provident..........	401·5	45,498,000	3,160,000	8·12	2·75
1848	P	Gresham..................	58·4	6,910,000	274,000	8·80	Various
1821	PO	Guardian Royal Exchange†......	832·2	94,600,000	·26,300,000	6·63	Various
1965	P	Hambro...................	217·8	40,800,000	37,300,000	—	
1932	PO	Ideal.....................	1·1	121,595	582	9·98	3·00
1897	M	Imperial Life (C)...........	279·6	42,046,581	—	7·16	2·5 and 3·0
1939	PI	Irish Life.................	129·7	26,126,000	8,897,000	7·31	3·50
1836	PO	Legal and General..........	1,497,7	209,496,000	8,914,000	7·69	Various
1838	P	Life Assoc. of Scotland......	48·5	3,293,764	3,639,878	8·85	Various
1843	MI	Liverpool Victoria (Ord.)........	59	6,126,647	—	7·02	3·00
1869	PIO	London and Manchester......	89	9,961,492	488,667	9·49	3·00
1806	M	London Life...............	170·6	22,514,775	2,033,173	7·79	4·75 to 5·25
1852	M	Marine and General.........	41·3	6,468,804	56,429	7·36	3·50 to 5·00
1884	M	Medical Sickness...........	13·1	1,452,207	4,982	7·58	6·00
1886	M	Mutual Life (C)............	558·9	78,112,127	58,224	6·804	3·50 to 4·50
1890	M	Nalgo Association†..........	5·4	570,000	—	8·0	2·5
1935	P	National Employers.........	37·4	14,563,944	185,192	9·54	Various
1910	MO	Natl. Farmers Union.........	57·1	7,233,545	2,746,350	9·17	Various
1869	M	Natl. Mutual of Austr. (C)†.....	56·5	5,089,667	1,304,694	7·19	Various
1830	M	Natl. Mutual Life..........	68·3	5,730,589	4,740,000	8·04	Various
1835	M	Natl. Provident...........	139·5	15,652,000	1,919,000	—	3·0
1808	M	Norwich Union............	793·9	112,346,000	4,285,000	8·12	5·00
1864	PIO	Pearl (Ord.)...............	372·7	36,818,000	6,736,000	8·47	3·00
1782	PO	Phoenix..................	206·5	36,294,000	761,000	—	5·00
1891	MI	Pioneer Mutual (Ord.).........	18·6	1,777,831	43,811	10·24	5·00
1969	P	Property Growth...........	71	13,700,000	1,059,000	9·9	—
1877	P	Prov. Life Assoc...........	71·3	7,669,795	201,154	6·57	2·5 to 9·5
1840	M	Prov. Mutual.............	152·6	11,588,000	19,931,000	8·26	Various
1848	PIO	Prudential (Ord.)..........	1,673·6	249,154,000	10,271,000	8·76	4·5 to 5·0
1864	PIO	Refuge (Ord.).............	140·8	12,798,000	1,235,000	9·28	3·25
1911	MI	Reliance (Ord.)............	6·5	1,237,042	20,570	8·2	4·50
1845	PO	Royal....................	452·3	40,643,000	28,743,000	8·83	3 to 3·75
1850	MI	Royal Liver. (Ord.).........	36·1	4,566,035	—	7·66	3·75
1861	MIO	Royal London (Ord.)........	73·6	11,577,000	29,000	9·72	5·00
1963	P	Save and Prosper...........	178·1	26,979,000	91,393,000	10·5	—
1826	M	Scottish Amicable..........	214·1	34,733,864	238,832	11·27	Various
1831	M	Scottish Equitable.........	137·1	18,525,345	3,359,073	9·6	3·5 to 4·5
1881	M	Scottish Life..............	100·1	15,855,613	936,010	10·18	Various
1883	MO	Scottish Mutual............	114·2	14,177,793	2,076,396	8·21	2·75 to 3·5
1837	M	Scottish Provident.........	158·1	25,001,107	3,207,278	10·94	Various
1815	M	Scottish Widows†..........	506·1	37,049,158	5,947,447	8·17	Various
1825	M	Standard Life.............	948·7	111,427,911	21,358,697	10·20	Various
1710	PO	Sun Alliance..............	277·3	36,988,000	1,719,000	—	Various
1810	P	Sun Life.................	562·2	33,200,000		7·83	Various
1865	M	Sun of Canada (C).........	1,553·5	1,463,740,000	128,140,000	6·94(N)	Various
1908	P	United Friendly...........	28·3	5,155,401	—	7·5	3·00
1804	M	United Kingdom Provident......	202	13,980,684	4,187,129	8·27	Various
1825	P	University................	33·1	1,472,440	2,596,448	8·4	Various
1841	MIO	Wesleyan & General (Ord.)......	42·9	4,433,585	5,500	8·91	2·75
1837	P	Yorkshire General............	264·4	29,005,000	9,035,000	8·61	3·00

† 1973 figures

(C) denotes Commonwealth office

INDUSTRIAL COMPANIES

Estab-lished	Class	Name of Office	Life Funds	Life Premium Income	Rate of interest % Earned	Interest % assumed at Valuation
			£	£		
1866	PO	Britannic..............................	154,932,000	27,610,000	8·69	4·00
1862	M	City of Glasgow......................	8,636,778	1,077,056	7·47	3·00
1939	P	Irish Life............................	37,580,000	5,506,000	8·88	3·50
1843	M	Liverpool Victoria....................	295,603,664	30,930,171	6·98	3·00
1869	PO	London and Manchester...............	75,286,992	9,802,008	9·51	3·00
1864	PO	Pearl................................	352,252,000	53,377,000	8·46	2·50
1891	M	Pioneer Mutual.......................	20,270,565	3,491,400	10·445	4·00
1848	PO	Prudential...........................	791,306,164	111,808,033	8·72	4·25
1864	PO	Refuge...............................	144,018,000	21,726,000	8·99	4·00
1911	MI	Reliance.............................	5,619,762	1,327,599	8·2	4·80
1850	M	Royal Liver..........................	126,475,062	18,595,050	7·66	3·00
1861	MO	Royal London........................	186,694,000	18,194,000	9·82	4·00
1841	MO	Wesleyan and General................	55,875,685	7,432,723	9·04	3·00

LIFE ASSURANCE NEW BUSINESS 1974

Name of Office	No. of policies issued	Net sums assured	Net annual premiums	Net single premiums
		£	£	£
Abbey Life..............................	103,202	391,089,000	11,712,000	41,370,000
Australian Mutual.......................	8,562	37,859,451	708,784	542,227
Avon...................................	3,310	16,697,885	468,756	3,219
Bedford Life............................	2,449	18,877,974	268,914	57,100
Britannic (Ord.)........................	23,027	50,039,000	1,359,000	89,000
British National........................	1,552	11,077,875	220,087	59
City of Glasgow (Ord.).................	1,022	2,680,636	73,990	40,656
Clerical Medical........................	17,221	77,750,588	1,612,761	23,067
Commercial Union......................	129,112	1,470,283,569	16,383,215	2,722,070
Confederation..........................	8,139	36,424,957	951,963	6,263
Co-operative...........................	678,677	543,000,000	13,600,000	15,000
Crusader...............................	16,076	407,000,000	3,663,000	37,000
Eagle Star..............................	25,405	214,369,000	5,113,000	24,826,000
Ecclesiastical	986	4,826,665	87,262	607
Equitable†	33,090	45,355,761	2,078,196	6,041,892
Equity & Law..........................	99,034	805,674,728	11,976,021	7,476,204
FS Assurance	2,242	10,190,154	274,380	474,155
Federation Mutual†	332	1,210,465	18,713	3,788
Friends Provident......................	36,708	393,000,000	7,800,000	3,800,000
Gresham...............................	9,625	57,803,806	798,738	2,520
Guardian Royal Exchange†	120,989	1,264,849,000	20,657,000	23,265,000
Hambro................................	64,000	242,100,000	10,700,000	56,000,000
Ideal..................................	216	1,108,392	42,165	312
Imperial Life...........................	28,138	411,168,803	4,628,205	3,623,504
Irish Life (Ord.).......................	33,053	194,058,000	6,161,000	6.158,000
Legal and General......................	111,712	1,224,000,000	20,980,000	89,888,000
Life Assoc. of Scotland.................	4,710	52,727,674	1,502,294	707,788
Liverpool Victoria (Ord.)..............	19,851	28,846,485	1,005,633	—
London and Manchester (Ord.).................	13,298	38,767,352	1,399,815	296,643
London Life............................	16,360	72,345,286	1,516,181	113,088
Marine and General.....................	5,720	35,727,406	911,957	1,123
Medical Sickness.......................	1,956	23,017,430	152,856	13,881
Mutual Life............................	90,922	668,755,766	14,772,358	1,962,472
Nalgo Association†	1,793	6,459,000	75,000	—
National Employers.....................	15,033	164,520,758	4,434,090	781,878
Natl. Farmers Union....................	6,917	46,522,715	918,519	7,044
Natl. Mutual of Austr.†	8,230	39,868,595	932,496	8,666
Natl. Mutual Life......................	5,422	42,400,313	1,030,193	9,603
Natl. Provident........................	8,505	92,838,000	3,784,000	1,947,000
Norwich Union.........................	106,056	894,630,000	12,495,000	845,000
Pearl (Ord.)...........................	83,599	265,602,000	6,173,000	7,284,000
Phoenix................................	38,580	852,641,000	9,428,000	2,315,000
Pioneer Mutual (Ord.)..................	7,989	21,525,397	320,125	37,407
Property Growth.......................	6,581	16,367,000	841,800	11,896,000
Prov. Life Assoc.......................	11,346	74,258,064	1,529,567	298,737
Prov. Mutual..........................	31,520	419,078,260	7,717,960	4,071,865
Prudential (Ord.).......................	329,424	2,962,834,645	48,069,486	20,965,910

LIFE ASSURANCE NEW BUSINESS 1974—*continued*

Name of Office	No. of policies issued	Net sums assured	Net annual premiums	Net single premiums
		£	£	£
Refuge (Ord.)	19,730	40,205,859	1,363,649	397,039
Reliance (Ord.)	2,955	10,340,307	178,928	345,214
Royal	69,000	595,221,000	10,759,000	15,445,000
Royal Liver (Ord.)	19,250	24,834,456	960,797	26,402
Royal London (Ord.)	26,533	78,147,000	2,160,000	178,000
Save and Prosper	28,880	40,359,000	1,781,000	7,323,000
Scottish Amicable	38,312	355,263,198	9,693,538	2,104,619
Scottish Equitable	25,593	188,564,227	5,465,817	3,380,057
Scottish Life	9,197	187,784,455	3,537,442	941,828
Scottish Mutual	12,422	79,813,981	2,868,163	38,726
Scottish Provident	36,588	256,850,000	3,000,000	101,000
Scottish Widows†	55,823	414,060,972	3,063,988	162,866
Standard Life	74,456	809,407,791	23,146,965	12,211,028
Sun Alliance	51,880	380,063,000	6,386,000	4,085,000
Sun Life	53,548	649,700,000	46,500,000	—
Sun of Canada	110,683	1,313,100,000	17,380,000	12,287,000
United Friendly	20,536	65,144,155	1,084,578	1,098
United Kingdom Provident	14,152	79,550,406	1,752,443	19,746
University	6,195	11,677,351	501,739	2,893,825
Wesleyan General (Ord.)	6,632	19,018,149	546,217	30,023
Yorkshire General	45,233	491,321,967	3,868,967	299,984

† 1973 figures

INDUSTRIAL LIFE NEW BUSINESS 1974

Name of office	Policies issued	Net sums assured	Net annual premiums
		£	£
Britannic	344,040	87,920,000	6,797,000
City of Glasgow	18,677	3,215,786	224,205
Irish Life	54,523	13,813,000	826,000
Liverpool Victoria	413,900	97,500,000	5,173,000
London and Manchester	87,795	32,814,654	2,261,811
Pearl	467,238	170,807,000	10,916,000
Pioneer Mutual	26,845	5,187,766	318,593
Prudential	897,450	379,228,908	22,084,311
Refuge	226,599	67,003,332	—
Reliance	18,425	4,017,957	246,651
Royal Liver	269,306	46,678,111	—
Royal London	158,792	48,667,000	—
Wesleyan and General	69,483	9,678,889	1,255,027

BONUS DECLARATIONS

Office	Last Valuation	Bonus declared on Whole Life Assurances	Bonus declared on Endowment Assurances	Interim Bonus
		£%	£%	£%
Australian Mutual	1974A	Vary with age, plan and duration		4·25
Avon	1974T	4·25	4·25	4·25
Bedford	1974T	2·00	2·00	2·00
Britannic	1974A	3·80	3·80	3·80
British National	1971T	3·00	3·00	3·00
City of Glasgow	1972T	3·00	3·00	3·00
Clerical Medical	1974T	4·50	4·50	4·50
Commercial Union	1972T	4·50	4·50	4·25
Confederation	1974A	Vary with age, plan and duration		
Co-operative	1974A	3·40	3·40	3·40
Crusader	1974A	4·20	4·00	At rate last declared
Eagle Star	1974T	4·00	4·00	4·00
Ecclesiastical	1975A	4·25	4·25	4·25
Equitable	1970T	£5·00 and upwards	£5 plus £2·50 on existing bonus	At rate last declared
Equity and Law	1974A	3·75	3·75	3·75
FS Assurance	1972T	3·70	3·70	3·70
Federation Mutual	1972T	4·00	4·00	4·00
Friends Provident	1973T	4·00	4·00	4·00
Gresham	1974A	3·15	3·15	3·15
Guardian Royal Exchange	1974A	4·75	4·50	4·75
Ideal	1974T	4·00	4·00	4·00

BONUS DECLARATIONS—*contd.*

Office	Last Valuation	Bonus declared on Whole Life Assurances	Bonus declared on Endowment Assurances	Interim Bonus
		£%	£%	£%
Imperial Life.............	1974A		Vary with age, plan and duration	
Irish Life.................	1974A	5·75	5·75	5·75
Legal and General........	1974A	3·60	3·60	3·60
Life Assoc. of Scotland....	1974A	3·75	3·75	3·75
Liverpool Victoria........	1973A	4·00	4·00	4·00
London and Manchester...	1974A	4·00	4·00	4·00
London Life..............	1974A	4·40	4·40	4·40
Marine and General.......	1974A		Vary with age plan and duration	
Medical Sickness.........	1974A	4·60	4·60	4·60
Mutual Life..............	1974A	2·25	2·25	2·25
Nalgo Association........	1971T	5·00	5·00	5·00
National Employers.......	1974A	2·50	2·50	2·50
Natl. Farmers Union......	1973T	4·00	4·00	4·00
Natl. Mutual of Austr.....	1974A	2·925	2·925	2·925
Natl. Mutual Life........	1974A	3·75	3·50	At rate last declared
Natl. Provident..........	1972T	5·00	4·25	At rate last declared
Norwich Union...........	1974A	3·60	3·60	3·60
Pearl....................	1974A		Vary with age, plan and duration	
Phoenix..................	1974A	4·50	4·50	4·50
Pioneer Mutual...........	1974A	4·40	4·40	4·40
Prov. Life Assoc..........	1974A	4·00	4·00	4·00
Prov. Mutual.............	1974T	3·75	3·25	3·50
Prudential...............	1974A	3·50	3·50	3·50
Refuge...................	1974A	4·00	4·00	4·00
Reliance.................	1974T	4·00	3·25	At rate last declared
Royal....................	1974T	4·50	4·50	4·50
Royal Liver..............	1973T	N/A	N/A	N/A
Royal London............	1974T	4·40	4·40	4·40
Scottish Amicable........	1974T	3·80	3·80	3·80
Scottish Equitable........	1974A	4·00	4·00	4·00
Scottish Life.............	1974A	4·00	4·00	4·00
Scottish Mutual..........	1973T	3·00	3·00	3·00
Scottish Provident........	1974T	4·30	4·30	4·30
Scottish Widows..........	1971T	4·25	4·25	4·00
Standard Life............	1974A	3·65	3·65	3·65
Sun Alliance.............	1972T	4·00	4·00	4·00
Sun Life.................	1973T	4·20	4·20	4·20
Sun of Canada...........	1974A		Vary with age, plan and duration	
United Friendly..........	1974A	4·00	4·00	4·00
United Kingdom Provident	1974T	4·00	4·00	4·00
University...............	1972T	4·50	4·00	At rate last declared
Wesleyan & General......	1974A	3·80	3·80	3·80
Yorkshire General........	1973A	4·80	4·80	4·80

NOTE: A—Annual Valuation
      T—Triennial Valuation

DIRECTORY OF INSURANCE COMPANIES

The class of Insurance undertaken is shown in the second column as follows: A—Accident (which includes Motor, Employers' Liability, etc.); F—Fire (including Burglary); L—Life; and M—Marine. A number of offices are now included in a Group—the initials of which appear after the name. The main Groups are as follows—E.S.—Eagle Star; C.U.—Commercial Union; G.R.E.—Guardian Royal Exchange; G.A.—General Accident; N.U.—Norwich Union; R—Royal; S.A.—Sun Alliance & London.

Est'd	Nature of Business	Name of Company	Address of Head and London Offices
1961	L	Abbey Life.................	1–3 St. Paul's Churchyard, E.C.4.
1960	AFLM	Ansvar....................	St. Leonards Rd., Eastbourne.
1951	AFM	Albion	14 Fenchurch Ave., E.C.3.
1824	AFM	Alliance.............S.A.	1 Bartholomew Lane, E.C.2.
1921	L	American Life..............	*Delaware*, U.S.A.: 12–14 Sydenham Rd., Croydon.
1904	AFM	Army, Navy & General. .E.S.	1 Threadneedle St., E.C.2.
1808	ALFM	Atlas...............G.R.E.	Royal Exchange, E.C.3.
1849	L	Australian Mutual Provident..	*Sydney*: A.M.P. Ho., Dingwall Rd., Croydon.
1925	AFL	Avon.....................	1 Church St., *Stratford-upon-Avon*; 16 Finsbury Circus, E.C.2.
1905	AFM	Baptist...................	4 Southampton Row, W.C.1.
1883	AFM	Beacon................S.A.	1 Bartholomew Lane, E.C.2.
1960	L	Bedford Life..............	Fairfax Ho., Fulwood Pl., High Holborn, W.C.1.
1894	AFM	Bedford General...........	Fairfax Ho., Fulwood Pl., High Holborn, W.C.1.
1925	AFM	Black Sea and Baltic.......	106 Fenchurch St., E.C.3.
1959	AFLM	Bradford.................	North Park, Halifax.
1863	M	British & Foreign Marine. .R.	Liverpool & London Chambers, Exchange, *Liverpool* 2: Lime St., E.C.3.
1878	Machinery	British Engine, &c........R.	Longbridge House, *Manchester* 4; 21 Mark Lane, E.C.3.
1854	AFL	British Equitable......G.R.E.	Royal Exchange, E.C.3.
1904	AFM	British General.........C.U.	St. Helen's, 1 Undershaft, E.C.3.
1888	AFM	British Law.............S.A.	1 Bartholomew Lane, E.C.2.
1896	L	British Life.................	Reliance House, *Tunbridge Wells*, Kent; 123–127 Cannon St., E.C.4.
1920	AFL	British Nat. Life............	Framlington Hse., Ireland Yd., E.C.4.
1908	AFM	British Oak..........G.R.E.	Royal Exchange, E.C.3.
1881	A	Builders' Accident..........	31 & 32 Bedford St., Strand, W.C.2.
1805	AFLM	Caledonian...........G.R.E.	Royal Exchange, E.C.3.
1934	AFM	Cambrian.............G.R.E.	Royal Exchange, E.C.3.
1847	AL	Canada Life...............	*Toronto*: 6 Charles II St., S.W.1.
1932	Dog Ins.	Canine Ins. Assoc...........	24–26 Spring St., W.2.
1903	AFM	Car & General........G.R.E.	Royal Exchange, E.C.3.
1885	AFM	Century..................	7 Leadenhall St., E.C.3.
1922	AFMex-motor	Chemists' Mutual..........	321 Chase Rd., Southgate, N.14.
1862	L	City of Glasgow Friendly.....	200 Bath Street, *Glasgow* C.2.
1824	L	Clerical, Medical & Gen......	15 St. James's Square, S.W.1.
1873	L & Pers. Acc.	Colonial Mutual...........	330 Collins St., *Melbourne*, C.1; 24 Ludgate Hill, E.C.4.
1919	AFM	Comrcl. Ins. Co. of Ireland...	5 Donegall Square, S., *Belfast*, N. Ireland [E.C.4.
1861	AFLM	Commercial Union..........	St. Helen's, 1 Undershaft, E.C.3.
1871	L	Confederation.............	*Toronto*: 120 Regent St., W.1.
1891	AF	Congregational............	21–22 Apsley Crescent, *Bradford* 8.
1867	AFLM	Co-operative..............	Miller St., *Manchester*; Parker St., W.C.2.
1905	AFM	Cornhill..................	32 Cornhill, E.C.3.
1900	L	Crown Life................	*Toronto*: NLA Tower, Addiscombe Rd., Croydon.
1899	AFLM	Crusader.................	Woodhatch, *Reigate*, Surrey; Tower Place, E.C.3.
1908	AFM	Dominion.................	92/94 Gracechurch St., E.C.3.
1904	AFLM	Eagle Star................	1 Threadneedle St., E.C.2.
1887	AFL	Ecclesiastical..............	Aldwych House, W.C.2.
1901	AFLM	Economic.................	Lloyd's Building, 19 Leadenhall St., E.C.3.
1823	AFM	Edinburgh.............C.U.	St. Helen's, 1 Undershaft, E.C.3.
1880	AFM	Employers' Liability.....C.U.	St. Helen's, 1 Undershaft, E.C.3.
1762	L	Equitable Life.............	4 Coleman St., E.C.2.
1844	L	Equity & Law.............	20 Lincoln's Inn Fields, W.C.2.
1802	AF	Essex & Suffolk.......G.R.E.	Royal Exchange, E.C.3.
1894	AFM	Excess...................	13 Fenchurch Avenue, E.C.3.
1904	AF	Federated Employers'.......	77 Whitworth St., *Manchester* 1; 34–35 Leadenhall St., E.C.3.
1925	AFL	Federation Mutual..........	29 Linkfield Lane, *Redhill*, Surrey; 6 Holborn Viaduct, E.C.1.
1890	AF	Fine Art & General.....C.U.	St. Helen's, 1 Undershaft, E.C.3.
1832	L	Friends' Prov..............	*Dorking*, Surrey; 7 Leadenhall St., E.C.3.

Est'd.	Nature of Business	Name of Company	Address of Head and London Offices
1899	L	FS Assurance	190 West George St., Glasgow.
1885	AFM	General Accident	General Buildings, *Perth*, Scotland; Becket House, 36–37, Old Jewry, E.C.2.
1898	L	Gresham Life	2–6 Prince of Wales Rd., Bournemouth.
1910	AFM	Gresham Fire & Accident	11 Queen Victoria St., E.C.4.
1840	AFM	Guarantee Society......G.A.	38 Eastcheap, E.C.3.
1821	AFLM	Guardian............G.R.E.	Royal Exchange, E.C.3.
1965	L	Hambro	7 Old Park Lane, W.1.
1908	AFM	Hibernian	Hawkins St., *Dublin*, 2.
1960	L	Hill Samuel	NLA Tower, Addiscombe Rd., Croydon.
1966	AF	Household & General....S.A.	1 Bartholomew Lane, E.C.2.
1932	FL	Ideal	Pitmaston, *Birmingham*, 13.
1896	L	Imperial Life of Canada	*Toronto:* London Road, Guildford, Surrey.
1824	M	Indemnity Marine	4 Fenchurch Avenue, E.C.3.
1935	AFM	Insurance Corpn. of Ireland	33–36 Dame St., *Dublin* 2; 40 Lime St., E.C.3.
1939	L	Irish Life	Mespil Road, *Dublin* 4.
1880	A	Iron Trades Employers'	Iron Trades Ho., 21–24 Grosvenor Pl., S.W.1.
1845	AF	Law Fire.............S.A.	1 Bartholomew Lane, E.C.2.
1806	AFM	Law Union & Rock.....R.	7 Chancery Lane, W.C.2.
1907	AFM	Legal.................R.	1 North John St., *Liverpool*, 2.
1836	AFLM	Legal and General	Temple Court, 11 Queen Victoria St., E.C.4.
1890	AFLM	Licenses & General....G.R.E.	Royal Exchange, E.C.3.
1838	L	Life Assoc. of Scotland	10 George St., *Edinburgh*; 1 Finsbury Sq., E.C.2.
1836	AFM	L'pool & London & Globe.R.	1 North John St., *Liverpool*; 24 Lombard St., E.C.3.
1918	AFM	Liverpool Marine & General.	7 Leadenhall St., E.C.3.
1843	L	Liverpool Victoria Friendly...	Victoria House, Southampton Row, W.C.1.
1890	AFM	Local Government Guarantee G.R.E.	Royal Exchange, E.C.3.
1836	AFM	Lombard Insurance	3 & 4 Lime St., E.C.3.
1720	AFLM	London Assurance.......S.A.	1 Bartholomew Lane, E.C.2.
1869	AFM	London Guar. & Accident...	4 King William St., E.C.4.
1919	AFM	London & Lancashire	Bread St., E.C.4.
1806	L	London Life	81 King William St., E.C.4.
1919	AFLM	London & Edinburgh	Warren Rd., Worthing.
1869	AFL	London & Manchester	50 Finsbury Square, E.C.2.
1860	AFM	London & Provincial Marine. G.A.	4 Fenchurch Avenue, E.C.3.
1862	AFM	London & Scottish......C.U.	St. Helen's, 1 Undershaft, E.C.3.
1887	L	Manufacturers Life	*Toronto:* St. George's Way, Stevenage.
1836	M	Marine................R.	15–18 Lime St., E.C.3.
1852	L	Marine & General	1 St. Swithin's Lane, E.C.4.
1864	M	Maritime.............N.U.	51 Fenchurch St., E.C.3.
1884	L Sickness A	Med., Sickness, Ann. and Life.	7–10 Chandos St., Cavendish Sq., W.1.
1907	Reinsurance	Mercantile & General	Moorfields House, Moorfields, E.C.2.
1871	M	Merchants' Marine......C.U.	4 Fenchurch Ave., E.C.3.
1872	AF	Methodist	51 Spring Gardens, *Manchester*.
1940	AFM	Minster	Minster House, Arthur St., E.C.4.
1906	AFM	Motor Union........G.R.E.	Royal Exchange, E.C.3.
1903	AF	Municipal Mutual	22 Old Queen St., Westminster, S.W.1.
1886	L	Mutual Life & Citizens'	P.O. Box 200 *North Sydney*, N.S.W., 2060 Australia; 1 Lancaster Place, Strand, W.C.2.
1890	AFL	Nalgo Insurance Association..	8 Harewood Row, N.W.1.
1935	L	National Employers' Life.....	Milton Court, *Dorking*, Surrey.
1914	AFM	National Employers' Mutual..	National Employers House, Bury Street, E.C.3.
1910	AFL	National Farmers' Union.....	Church St., *Stratford-upon-Avon;* 25 Knightsbridge, S.W.1.
1863	Fidelity Guar.	Natl. Guaran. & Suretyship C.U.	St. Helens, 1 Undershaft, E.C.3.
1894	AF	National Ins. & Guarantee Cor.	11–13 Holborn Viaduct, E.C.1.
1830	L	National Mutual Life........	5 Bow Churchyard (off Cheapside), E.C.4.
1869	L	National Mutual of Australasia	*Melbourne:* Austral Ho., Basinghall Ave., E.C.2.
1835	L	National Provident...........	48 Gracechurch St., E.C.3.
1854	Plate Glass	National Provincial....G.R.E.	Royal Exchange, E.C.3.
1921	{Naval Officers} {risks, etc. }	Navigators & General....E.S.	1 Threadneedle St., E.C.2.
1924	L	New Ireland	11/12 Dawson St., *Dublin*, C.2.
1809	AFLM	North British & Mercantile C.U.	St. Helen's, 1 Undershaft, E.C.3.
1862	FM	North Pacific.........G.R.E.	*Hong Kong:* Royal Exchange, E.C.3.
1836	AFLM	Northern..............C.U.	St. Helen's, 1 Undershaft, E.C.3.
1797	AFM	Norwich Union Fire.........	Surrey St., *Norwich*; 51–54 Fenchurch St., E.C.3.

Est'd.	Nature of Business	Name of Company	Address of Head and London Offices
1808	L	Norwich Union Life.........	Surrey St., *Norwich;* 51–54 Fenchurch St., E.C.3.
1871	AFM	Ocean Accident.........C.U.	St. Helen's, 1 Undershaft, E.C.3.
1859	M	Ocean Marine..........C.U.	4 Fenchurch Ave., E.C.3.
1931	AFM	Orion.......................	70–72 King William St., E.C.4.
1886	AF	Palatine.................C.U.	St. Helen's, 1 Undershaft, E.C.3.
1864	AFLM	Pearl.......................	High Holborn, W.C.1.
1958	Sickness A	Permanent..................	7–10 Chandos Street, Cavendish Sq., W.1.
1782	AFLM	Phœnix	Phœnix House, King William St., E.C.4.
1891	L	Pioneer Mutual.............	16 Crosby Rd. N., Liverpool.
1920	AFM	Planet Assurance.........S.A.	1 Bartholomew Lane, E.C.2.
1877	L	Prov. Life Assocn. of London.	246 Bishopsgate, E.C.2.
1840	L	Provident Mutual Life.......	25–31 Moorgate, E.C.2.
1903	AFM	Provincial..................	*Kendal:* Provincial Ho., 100 Cannon St., E.C.4.
1848	AFLM	Prudential..................	Holborn Bars, E.C.1.
1886	AFM	Queensland.................	*Sydney:* Trent House, St. Mary Axe, E.C.3.
1849	AF	Railway Passengers......C.U.	St. Helen's, 1 Undershaft, E.C.3.
1864	AFL	Refuge.....................	Oxford St., *Manchester* 1. [Cannon St., E.C.4.
1911	L	Reliance Mutual............	Reliance Ho., *Tunbridge Wells,* Kent; 123–7
1906	AF	Reliance Fire & Accident....	Reliance Ho., *Tunbridge Wells,* Kent; 123–7 Cannon St., E.C.4.
1881	AFM	Reliance Marine......G.R.E.	Royal Exchange, E.C.3.
1823	Reversions	Reversionary Interest Society .	4 Coleman St., E.C.4.
1918	AF	Road Transport & General G.A.	77 Upper Richmond Rd., S.W.15.
1845	AFLM	Royal.......................	1 North John St., *Liverpool* 2; Bow Bells Hse., Bread St., E.C.4.
1720	AFL	Royal Exchange.............	Royal Exchange, E.C.3.
1850	L	Royal Liver Friendly.......	Royal Liver Building, *Liverpool* 3.
1861	AFL	Royal London..............	Royal London House, Finsbury Square, E.C.2.
1887	L	Royal Nat. Pensions (Nurses) .	15 Buckingham St., W.C.2.
1909	AFM	Salvation Army.............	101 Queen Victoria St., E.C.4.
1963	L	Save and Prosper............	4 Great Helens, E.C.3.
1826	L	Scottish Amicable...........	35 St. Vincent Place, *Glasgow,* C.1.; 17 Tokenhouse Yard, E.C.2.
1881	FM	Scottish Boiler...........G.A.	22 Queen St., *Glasgow,* C.1.; 36 Old Jewry, E.C.2.
1831	L	Scottish Equitable..........	28 St. Andrew Sq., *Edinb.;* 13 Cornhill, E.C.3.
1919	AFM	Scottish General.........G.A.	100 West Nile St., *Glasgow,* C.2.
1852	L	Scottish Legal..............	95 Bothwell St., *Glasgow,* C.2.
1881	L	Scottish Life...............	19 St. Andrew Sq., *Edinburgh,* 2; 36 Poultry, E.C.2.
1876	AF	Scottish Metropolitan....C.U.	St. Helen's, 1 Undershaft, E.C.3. [W.C.2.
1883	AL	Scottish Mutual............	109 St. Vincent St., *Glasgow,* C.2.; 6 Bell Yard,
1837	L	Scottish Provident.........	6 St. Andrew Sq., *Edinburgh*; 3 Lombard St., E.C.3.
1824	AFLM	Scottish Union & National N.U.	Surrey St., *Norwich;* 51–54 Fenchurch St., E.C.3.
1815	L	Scottish Widows'............	9 St. Andrew Sq., *Edinburgh* 2; 28 Cornhill, E.C.3.
1875	AFM	Sea....................S.A.	1 Bartholomew Lane, E.C.2.
1904	AFL	Sentinel...................	11–13 Holborn Viaduct, E.C.1.
1968	L	Slater Walker Insurance......	Bream's Buildings, Fetter Lane, E.C.4.
1872	AFM	South British..............	Shortland St., *Auckland,* N.Z.; 26/28 Fenchurch St., E.C.3.
1825	L	Standard Life..............	3 George St., *Edinburgh;* 3 Abchurch Yard, Cannon St., E.C.4.
1891	AFM	State...................G.R.E.	Royal Exchange, E.C.3.
1710	AFM	Sun....................S.A.	1 Bartholomew Lane, E.C.2.
*	AFLM	Sun Alliance & London......	1 Bartholomew Lane, E.C.2.
1810	AFL	Sun Life...................	107 Cheapside, E.C.2.
1865	L	Sun Life of Canada..........	*Montreal:* 2, 3 & 4 Cockspur St., S.W.1.
1936	FL	Teacher's Assurance........	12 Christchurch Rd., *Bournemouth.*
1894	FM	Thistle....................	3 Lombard St., E.C.3.
1916	AF	Timber & General..........	158 Fenchurch St., E.C.3.
1969	L	Trident....................	19 Hanover Sq., W.1.
1869	L	Tunstall & District.........	Station Chambers, Tunstall, *Stoke on Trent.*
1867	M	Ulster Marine...........G.A.	5 Donegall Sq., S., Belfast.
1714	AFM	Union Assurance.......C.U.	St. Helen's, 1 Undershaft, E.C.3.
1835	AFM	Union Ins. Soc. of Canton G.R.E.	*Hong Kong:* Royal Exchange, E.C.3.
1863	M	Union Marine.............	4–5, King William St. E.C.4.
1915	AFM	United British........G.R.E.	Royal Exchange, E.C.3.
1908	AFL	United Friendly...........	42 Southwark Bridge Road, S.E.1.
1840	L	United Kingdom Prov.......	33–36 Gracechurch St., E.C.3.

Est'd.	Nature of Business	Name of Company	Address of Head and London Offices
1912	AFM	United Scottish............	Warrior Sq., Southend, Essex.
1825	L	University.................	4 Coleman St., E.C.2.
1919	Reinsurance	Victory Insurance...........	122 Leadenhall St., E.C.3.
1859	Machinery	Vulcan Boiler and General S.A.	1 Bartholomew Lane, E.C.3.
1875	AFM	Warden.................R.	1 North John St., *Liverpool.*
1911	AF	Welsh Insurance Corpn..C.U.	St. Helen's, 1 Undershaft, E.C.3.
1841	AFL	Wesleyan & General.........	Colmore Circus, Ringway, *Birmingham,* 4; 116 Cannon St., E.C.4.
1886	AF	West of Scotland.......C.U.	26 George St., *Edinburgh* 2; St. Helen's, 1 Undershaft, E.C.3.
1851	AFM	Western Assurance........R.	*Toronto:* Liverpool and London Chambers, Exchange, *Liverpool.*
1912	AFLM	Western Australian.........	I.O.O.F. Building, 224 St. George's Terrace, *Perth,* W. Australia; 107-111 Fleet St., E.C.4.
1717	AF	Westminster Fire........S.A.	1 Bartholomew Lane, E.C.2.
1865	AF	White Cross............C.U.	St. Helen's, 1 Undershaft, E.C.3.
1894	AFM	World Marine & General C.U.	4 & 7 Fenchurch Avenue, E.C.3.
1837	L	Yorkshire General Life...G.A.	Rougier St., *York.*
1872	AF	Zurich....................	*Zurich:* Fairfax Ho., Fulwood Place, W.C.1.

* Sun Alliance & London—Incorporating Funds established 1720, 1824 and 1883.

THE ENGLISH MILE COMPARED WITH OTHER EUROPEAN MEASURES

	English Mile	English Geog. M.	French Kilom.	German Geog. M.	Russian Verst	Austrian Mile	Dutch Ure	Norweg. Mile	Swedish Mile	Danish Mile	Swiss Stunde
English Statute Mile.	1·000	0·868	1·609	0·217	1·508	0·212	0·289	0·142	0·151	0·213	0·335
English Geog. Mile..	1·153	1·000	1·855	0·250	1·738	0·245	0·333	0·164	0·169	0·246	0·386
Kilometre.........	0·621	0·540	1·000	0·135	0·937	0·132	0·180	0·088	0·094	0·133	0·208
German Geog. Mile.	4·610	4·000	7·420	1·000	6·953	0·978	1·333	0·657	0·694	0·985	1·543
Russian Verst......	0·663	0·575	1·067	0·144	1·000	0·141	0·192	0·094	0·100	0·142	0·222
Austrian Mile......	4·714	4·089	7·586	1·022	7·112	1·000	1·363	0·672	0·710	1·006	1·578
Dutch Ure.........	3·458	3·000	5·565	0·750	5·215	0·734	1·000	0·493	0·520	0·738	1·157
Norwegian Mile....	7·021	6·091	11·299	1·523	10·589	1·489	2·035	1·000	1·057	1·499	2·350
Swedish Mile......	6·644	5·764	10·692	1·441	10·019	1·409	1·921	0·948	1·000	1·419	2·224
Danish Mile........	4·682	4·062	7·536	1·016	7·078	0·994	1·354	0·667	0·705	1·000	1·567
Swiss Stunde.......	2·987	2·592	4·808	0·648	4·505	0·634	0·864	0·425	0·449	0·638	1·000

NORTH ATLANTIC TREATY ORGANIZATION

Headquarters: Brussels 1110, Belgium.

The North Atlantic Treaty was signed on April 4, 1949, by the Foreign Ministers of twelve nations. The twelve are Belgium, Canada, Denmark, France, Iceland, Italy, Luxembourg, the Netherlands, Norway, Portugal, the United Kingdom and United States. Greece and Turkey acceded to the Treaty in 1952 and the Federal Republic of Germany in 1955. The North Atlantic Council is the highest authority of the Alliance and is composed of permanent representatives of the fifteen member countries. It meets at ministerial level at least twice per year. The permanent representatives head national delegations of advisers and experts.

Permanent U.K. Representative, His Excellency Sir Edward (Heywood) Peck, G.C.M.G. (1970)
£14,000

The senior military authority in NATO is the Military Committee composed of a Chief-of-Staff of each member country except France. The Military Committee, which is assisted by an international military staff, functions in permanent session with permanent military representatives and is responsible for higher strategic direction throughout the North Atlantic Treaty area.

Secretary-General, J. M. A. H. Luns (*Netherlands*).
Deputy Secretary-General, P. Pansa Cedronio (*Italy*).
Assistant Secretaries-General, Jörg Kastl (*Fed. Republic of Germany*) (*Political Affairs*); D. C. Humphreys (*U.K.*) (*Defence Planning and Policy*); Dr. G. L. Tucker (*U.S.*) (*Defence Support*); Prof. Nimet Özdas (*Turkey*) (*Scientific Affairs*).
Supreme Allied Commander, Europe, Gen. Alexander M. Haig (U.S.).
Supreme Allied Commander, Atlantic, Admiral Isaac C. Kidd (U.S.).
Allied Commander-in-Chief, Channel, Admiral Sir Terence Lewin, K.C.B., M.V.O., D.S.C. (U.K.).
Chairman, Military Committee, Admiral of the Fleet Sir Peter Hill-Norton, G.C.B. (U.K.).

SOUTH-EAST ASIA TREATY ORGANIZATION

Headquarters: Bangkok, Thailand.

A *South-East Asia Collective Defence Treaty* was signed on Sept. 8, 1954, by representatives of Australia, New Zealand, Pakistan, the Philippines, Thailand, France, the United Kingdom and the United States. Pakistan left the organization in November, 1973. France ceased to participate in military activities of SEATO in 1967, and announced in June 1973 that she would make no further financial contribution to SEATO after June 30, 1974, but has not indicated any intention of withdrawing from the SEATO Treaty. The Treaty consists of eleven Articles. The parties undertake mutual defence responsibilities in the area of the Treaty. Other articles deal with mutual economic assistance, including technical assistance, designed to promote economic progress and social well-being; the rights and obligations of the parties under the Charter of the United Nations; accession of further states; and define the area to which the Treaty applies. Member countries are represented on a Council of Ministers which meets annually to review and determine policy. Its meetings are held in a different member nation capital each year. Between Council Meetings, Council Representatives meet at least monthly in Bangkok to supervise the work of the Organization. The Council Representatives are the Ambassadors to Thailand of 6 member countries and a Thai Foreign Affairs Officer of ambassadorial rank. The United States executed the Treaty with the understanding that its recognition of the effect of aggression and armed attack apply only to Communist aggression, but agreed to consult with the other signatories in the event of any other armed attack.

In a declaration of principles, *The Pacific Charter*, the Treaty powers uphold the principle of equal rights and self-determination of peoples. They will earnestly strive by every peaceful means to promote self-government and to secure the independence of all countries whose peoples desire it and are able to undertake its responsibilities. They will continue to co-operate in the economic, social and cultural fields in order to promote higher living standards, economic progress and social well-being in the region. They are determined to prevent or counter by appropriate means any attempt in the Treaty area to subvert their freedom or destroy their sovereignty or territorial integrity.

Secretary-General, Sunthorn Hongladarom.

CENTRAL TREATY ORGANIZATION

Headquarters: Ankara, Turkey.

A mutual security and defence treaty was concluded between Turkey and Iraq at Baghdad on Feb. 24, 1955. Three further states, the United Kingdom, Iran, and Pakistan signed the *Baghdad Pact* later in the same year. The United States, although not a full member of the Council, participates in an observer capacity, is a member of all major committees, and contributes an equal share to the international staff and budget, as well as a large share of economic and military assistance. Iraq formally withdrew from the Pact on March 24, 1959, and the title Central Treaty Organization (C.E.N.T.O.) was adopted on Aug. 21, 1959.

Secretary-General, Nssir Assar (1972).

THE ARCTIC OCEAN

The Arctic Ocean consists of a deep sea over 2,000 fathoms, on the southern margin of which there is a broad continental shelf with numerous islands. Into this deeper sea there is only one broad channel, about 700 miles, between Greenland and Scandinavia. Behring Strait is only 49 miles wide and 27 fathoms deep. The southern boundary of the Arctic Ocean is the Wyville-Thomson and Faeroe-Icelandic submarine ridge, which separates the North Atlantic from the Norwegian and Greenland Seas. The Norwegian Deep lies between Norway and Jan Mayan and Iceland; it exceeds 1,500 fathoms. The Greenland Deep, of similar depth, lies between Spitsbergen and Greenland. These two depressions are separated by a somewhat deeply submerged ridge from the east of Jan Mayen to Bear Island, south of Spitsbergen. A shallow ridge from the north-west of Spitsbergen to Greenland separates the Greenland Sea from the deep North Polar, Basin. This extends from the north of Spitsbergen and Franz Josef Land to the north of the New Siberia Islands and of the North American Arctic Archipelago. Another more shallow depression is Baffin Bay, less than 1,000 fathoms. This is separated from the North Atlantic by a submarine ridge. Barent's Sea, between Spitsbergen, Norway and Novaya Zemlya, and the Kara Sea, between Novaya Zemlya and the Siberian coast, are respectively below 200 and 100 fathoms. The total area of the Arctic Sea is about 5·5 million square miles, of which 2·3 million square miles are probably covered with floating ice.

AGRICULTURE

Agriculture in the national economy

July/June years	Average of 1964/65 –1965/66	1970/1	1971/2	1972/3	1973/4	
Home production as percentage of UK food supplies†	51·2	53·2	53·6	54·6	—	
Home production as percentage of indigenous-type supplies	64·6	66·9	66·8	66·8	—	

(calendar years)	Average of 1964 & 1965	1970	1971	1972	1973	1974 (provisional)
Agriculture's contribution to gross domestic product						
£ million	928	1,126	1,234	1,437	1,688	1,858
percentage	3·1	2·6	2·6	2·6	2·7	—
Agriculture's share of gross fixed capital formation						
£ million	184	250	286	351	441	575
percentage	3·0	2·7	2·8	3·1	3·1	—
Manpower engaged in agriculture ('000)	931	750	716	790	704	678
Percentage of total manpower in all occupations	3·8	3·1	3·0	3·0	2·9	2·8
Agricultural price index (1968/9–1971/2= 100)						
All products—sales		99·4	106·3	112·9	144·7	162·0
Inputs—selected indicators						
Feedingstuffs	84·9	100·0	110·7	108·9	156·6	209·2
Fertilisers (excl. lime)	73·2	90·4	109·8	128·0	143·3	211·0
Fuel	78·4	96·5	106·8	111·1	117·8	180·0
Labour	65·2	97·9	111·3	124·7	145·8	190·1
Machinery	80·8	99·1	108·4	118·1	129·9	156·6
Imports of food, feed & alcoholic beverages						
£ million	1,755	2,079	2,214	2,375	3,174	3,952
Import volume index (1970= 100)	99·0	100·0	100·0	101·8	102·9	97·4
Import price index (1970 = 100)	85·7	100·0	107·1	113·5	151·2	200·9
Exports of food, feed & alcoholic beverages						
£ million	305	484	567	625	838	1,031
Export volume index (1970= 100)	70·3	100·0	109·5	114·6	137·3	143·8
Export price index	89·5	100·0	105·5	113·0	126·2	150·8
Consumers' expenditure on food and alcoholic beverages						(Jan.–Sept. only)
£ million	7,184	9,684	10,665	11,549	13,336	10,947
Percentage of total consumers' expenditure	32·4	30·9	30·6	29·2	29·7	29·7
Retail price index (January 1962= 100)						
Food	109·7	140·1	155·6	169·4	194·9	230·0
Alcoholic beverages	112·6	143·9	152·7	159·0	164·2	182·1
All items	109·6	140·2	153·4	164·3	179·4	208·2

† The value of food moving into manufacture or distribution derived from home agricultural output.

Crop areas and livestock numbers

At June of each year

	Average of 1963–65	1970	1971	1972	1973	1974
A. Crop areas ('000 acres)						
Total area...............	48,602	47,255	47,234	47,045	46,920	46,974
of which:						
Wheat................	2,223	2,495	2,710	2,786	2,831	3,046
Barley................	5,047	5,542	5,654	5,653	5,603	5,471
Oats..................	1,145	929	896	777	695	624
Mixed corn...........	84	196	137	150	126	104
Rye..................	20	11	16	16	13	11
Maize................	—	—	3	5	3	3
Total cereals†.........	8,519	9,174	9,416	9,386	9,271	9,260
Potatoes..............	762	669	634	584	555	532
Sugar beet............	440	463	471	468	480	482
Oilseed rape..........	—	10	13	17	34	61
Hops.................	21	17	18	17	17	16
Vegetables grown in the open................	376	505	452	441	462	480
Orchard fruit..........	210	160	154	146	141	136
Soft fruit.............	50	45	45	45	45	44
Ornamentals..........	34	37	36	38	40	38
Total horticulture......	670	751	690	674	694	704
Total tillage.........	11,548	12,888	12,139	12,021	11,905	11,955
Temporary grass.......	6,824	5,700	5,718	5,825	5,798	5,722
Total arable..........	18,372	17,788	17,857	17,846	17,703	17,677
Permanent grass........	12,292	12,217	12,172	12,132	12,143	12,157
Rough grazing........	17,938	16,537	16,501	16,342	16,320	16,220
Other land............	—	712	704	725	753	920
B. Livestock numbers ('000 head)						
Total cattle and calves......	11,762	12,581	12,804	13,483	14,445	15,227
of which:						
Dairy cows...........	3,192	3,244	3,234	3,325	3,436	3,402
Beef cows............	1,004	1,300	1,378	1,476	1,678	1,889
Heifers in calf..........	767	863	831	954	988	1,049
Total sheep and lambs......	29,637	26,080	25,981	26,877	27,943	28,639
of which:						
Ewes................	11,899	10,544	10,422	10,668	10,921	11,213
Shearlings............	2,516	2,263	2,263	2,438	2,733	2,673
Total pigs...............	7,406	8,088	8,724	8,619	8,979	8,621
of which:						
Sows for breeding......	754	794	862	832	859	791
Gilts in pigs...........	154	159	121	128	156	107
Total poultry............	116,231	143,430	139,016	140,045	144,079	139,957
of which:						
Table fowls (incl. broilers)............	28,649	49,783	49,730	50,933	58,366	56,781
Laying fowls..........	50,772	55,237	53,705	53,831	51,766	50,130
Growing pullets........	26,967	24,599	22,465	21,678	18,808	18,958

† For threshing.

Number of persons engaged in agriculture

At June of each year   'ooo persons

	Average of 1963–65	1970	1971	1972	1973	1974
Workers						
Whole-time:						
Hired: male	}	186	181	175	170	163
female		16	16	15	16	16
Family: male:		53	50	48	45	39
female		14	15	14	15	14
All male	381	239	231	223	215	230
All female	34	30	31	29	31	30
Total	(415)	(269)	(262)	(252)	(246)	(233)
Part-time:						
All male	96	80	78	78	81	78
All female	70	76	78	76	82	80
Total	(167)	(156)	(156)	(154)	(163)	(158)
Salaried managers	—	—	—	6	7	8
Total employed	582	425	418	412	416	398
Farmers, partners and directors						
Whole-time	}	216	230	229	222	214
Part-time		56	68	68	66	66
Total	—	697	716	709	704	678

Estimated average yields of crops and livestock products

June/May years

	Unit	Average of 1963/64 –1965/66	1970/71	1971/72	1972/73	1973/74	1974/75 (forecast)
Crops							
Wheat	tons/acre	1·62	1·67	1·75	1·69	1·74	1·95
Barley	,, ,,	1·46	1·34	1·49	1·61	1·58	1·63
Oats	,, ,,	1·16	1·30	1·50	1·58	1·53	1·54
Potatoes	,, ,,	9·2	11·0	11·5	11·0	12·1	12·6
Sugar	,, ,,	2·3	2·3	2·7	2·2	2·4	1·5
Oilseed rape	cwts./acre	—	15	15	17	18	15
Apples:							
Dessert	tons/acre	4·6	5·2	5·4	3·5	5·0	3·7
Culinary	,, ,,	5·3	6·1	4·8	4·2	5·1	4·4
Pears	,, ,,	3·9	5·1	5·0	3·6	3·2	3·8
Tomatoes	,, ,,	37·7	41·8	42·1	43·7	46·9	48·3
Cauliflowers	,, ,,	7·8	7·6	7·8	8·2	8·4	8·3
Hops	centrals/acre	14·1	15·4	14·6	11·6	13·7	13·6
Livestock products							
Milk	galls/cow	779	847	867	888	864	864
Eggs	no./bird	200	219·5	225·5	232·5	225·5	232

ROADS

On April 1, 1974, the provisional total mileage of public roads in Great Britain, including green lanes, was 213,470 of which 162,215 were in England, 29,990 in Scotland and 21,265 in Wales. *Highway Authorities.*—The powers and responsibilities of highway authorities in England and Wales are set out in the Highways Act 1959-1971. They are concerned mainly with the construction, improvement and maintenance of highways. The Secretaries of State for the Environment and for Wales are the highway authorities for the trunk roads in England and in Wales respectively. (Trunk roads constitute the national system of routes for through traffic and include most motorways.) Under the Local Government Act 1972, from April 1, 1974, the new county councils are the highway authorities for all highways in England (outside Greater London) and Wales, other than trunk roads. However, the new district councils have a right to maintain unclassified urban roads, footpaths and bridleways and may under agency arrangements carry out other highway functions on behalf of the county councils. In Greater London the most important non-trunk roads are metropolitan roads, for which the Greater London Council is highway authority. The Common Council of the City of London and the London borough councils are highway authorities for all other non-trunk roads in their areas.

For Scotland there is separate legislation under which the Secretary of State for Scotland is the highway authority for trunk roads. The highway authorities for non-trunk public roads are the town councils of large burghs for all such roads and the town councils of small burghs for unclassified roads in their respective areas (under the Roads and Bridges (Scotland) Act 1878), and county councils for all other non-trunk public roads (under the Local Government (Scotland) Act 1889). Under the Local Government (Scotland) Bill the highway authorities for all non-trunk public roads would, after May 15, 1975, be the councils of the proposed new regions and island areas who will have general powers of delegation which will enable them, if they wish, to delegate road functions to district councils.

The system of grant-aiding local authority expenditure on highways has recently been revised. From April 1, 1975, the GLC and all county councils in England and Wales became eligible for an annual grant towards their total transport needs. The grant, known as the transport supplementary grant, represents about one-third of Central Government's aid towards all local transport services; the remaining two-thirds is assisted through the rate support grant along with other rate-borne expenditure. For the financial year beginning April 1, 1975, local authorities received a total of £250,000,000 in transport supplementary grants.

Motorways

The network in England and Wales is based on six main routes—London–Yorkshire (M1), London–South Wales (M4), Birmingham–Bristol–Exeter (M5), Birmingham–Carlisle (M6), London–Folkestone (M20) and Lancashire–Yorkshire (M62). Other motorways in use or under construction include M2 Medway Towns, M3 London–Basingstoke, M18 Rotherham–Goole, M40 London–Oxford, M53 Mid-Wirral, M56 North Cheshire, M73 Maryville, (M74)–Mollisburn (A80), M74 Draffen–Stonehouse (A74)–Glasgow, M9 Edinburgh–Stirling and M90 Inverkeithing–Perth.

At the end of March 1973, 996 miles of motorway were open to traffic in England and Wales and 190 miles were under construction, with a further 318 miles in the firm programme. 195 miles of M1 and 121 miles of M4 were in use; furthermore, with the opening of the Gretna By-pass in 1973 there is now a complete dual carriageway link from London to Glasgow, a length of almost 400 miles.

Motor Vehicles.—The number of vehicles in Great Britain with current licences in 1974 totalled 17,258,000; cars 13,639,000; motor cycles, scooters and mopeds 1,042,000; public transport vehicles 107,000; goods vehicles 1,762,000; agricultural tractors 429,000. There were 172,000 vehicles exempt from licensing.

Driving Tests.—The number of driving tests conducted in Great Britain in the year 1974 was 1,621,070, of which 54·4 per cent. resulted in failure.

Expenditure on roads in Great Britain rose from £881,500,000 in 1972-73 to £1,042,500,000 in 1973-74. The expenditure during 1973-74 may be broken down as follows: New Construction and Improvement, £640,800,000 (Trunk roads, £298,000,000; Principal roads, £244,900,000; Other roads, £97,900,000); Maintenance £269,300,000 (Trunk roads, £58,800,000; Principal roads, £56,700,000; Other roads, £153,800,000); Cleansing, Gritting and Snow-Clearing, £47,800,000 Other roads, £37,800,000); Administration £84,600,000 (Non-trunk roads £77,400,000). In addition to the 1973-74 total of expenditure on roads, the cost of road lighting was £55,400,000, and of vehicle parks £36,200,000 (gross).

Expenditure on new construction and improvement of trunk roads in England during 1973-74 was £258,800,000. In Scotland and Wales, the figures were £18,600,000 and £20,600,000 respectively. Grants made to local highway authorities for the improvement of principal roads in the same financial year were: England, £104,600,000; Scotland, £19,300,000; Wales £6,800,000.

Road Casualties

In 1974 there were 84 vehicles for every mile of road or one vehicle for every 23 yards. Nineteen road users were killed and 870 injured on an average day.

Year	Killed	Injured	Year	Killed	Injured
1957	5,550	268,308	1966	7,985	384,472
1958	5,970	293,797	1967	7,319	362,659
1959	6,520	326,933	1968	6,810	342,398
1960	6,970	340,581	1969	7,365	345,529
1961	6,908	342,859	1970	7,499	355,869
1962	6,709	334,987	1971	7,699	344,328
1963	6,922	349,257	1972	7,779	352,013
1964	7,820	377,679	1973	7,406	346,874
1965	7,952	389,985	1974	6,876	317,726

BRITISH AIRWAYS

Financial	1973–74 £m	1974–75 £m
Turnover...	646·9	748·1
Operating Surplus..................................	54·0	0·7
Group Profit before interest and taxation...........	63·2	5·4
Profit (loss) attributable to British Airways........	16·6	(9·4)

Airline Activity (European, Overseas & Regional Divisions)	1973–74	1974–75
All services		
Available tonne kilometres offered (mills)...........	6,077	5,832
Scheduled services		
Available tonne kilometres offered (mills)...........	5,528	5,388
Revenue tonne kilometres sold (mills)...............	3,062	2,997
Passengers carried (thousands).....................	14,361	13,349
Revenue. Passenger kilometres (mills)...............	24,803	24,171
Freight tonne kilometres (mills)....................	746	721

Staff & Productivity	1973–74	1974–75
British Airways total strength......................	59,111	59,407
Airline Activities		
Strength at year end............................	52,749	53,066
Average number of employees....................	53,186	53,591
Available tonne kilometres per employee..........	114,000	109,000
Revenue per employee...........................	£10,657	£12,450
Average number of staff employed per week by British Airways in the U.K...................................	58,199	48,650
Aggregate remuneration payable to the above employees for the year.	£140·2m	£161·5m

Aircraft Fleet

The following types of aircraft were in service with British Airways: *Tristar*, 6; *Boeing 747*, 17; *Boeing 707-336*, 11; *Boeing 707-436*, 18; *Super VC10*, 15; *Standard VC10*, 6; *Trident Three*, 26; *Trident Two*, 15; *Trident One*, 20; *Trident 1E*, 4; *Super 1-11*, 18; *1-11/400*, 7; *Vanguard*, 3; *Merchantman*, 9; *Viscount*, 35; *Skyliner*, 2. On order: *Concorde*, 5; *Tristar*, 9; *Boeing 747*, 1; *HS 748*, 2.

BUCHAN'S WEATHER PERIODS OR RECURRENCES OF WEATHER

Dr. Alexander Buchan, F.R.S., Secretary of the Scottish Meteorological Society, published in 1867 a paper in the Journal of that Society entitled " Interruptions in the regular rise and fall of temperature in the course of the year ". Buchan gave six cold periods and three warm periods, based on his examination of the mean daily temperature as recorded at stations in Scotland covering long periods. The cold periods were February 7–14, April 11–14, May 9–14, June 29–July 4, August 6–11, November 6–13, and the warm periods July 12–15, August 12–15, and December 3–14. This early work aroused considerable interest later. It should be noted, however, that Buchan claimed no more than the existence of tendencies for short spells of relatively cold or warm weather to occur at certain times of the year.

In recent years these smaller fluctuations of weather super-imposed on the normal seasonal changes have been examined from the aspect of tendencies to stormy or anticyclonic spells over the British Isles and have been referred to as " singularities ". Stormy periods are relatively warm in winter and cool in summer. The following tendencies have been given:—Jan. 5–17 stormy; Jan. 18–24 anticyclonic; Jan. 24–Feb. 1 stormy; Feb. 8–16 anticyclonic; Feb. 21–25 cold; Feb. 26–Mar. 9 stormy; Mar. 12–19 anticyclonic; Mar. 24–31 stormy; April 10–15 stormy; April 23–26 unsettled; June 1–21 summer monsoon; July 10–24 warm; Aug. 20–30 stormy; September 1–17 anticyclonic; Sept. 17–24 stormy; Sept. 24–Oct. 4 anticyclonic; Oct. 5–12 stormy; Oct. 16–20 anticyclonic; Oct. 24–Nov. 13 stormy; Nov. 15–21 anticyclonic; Nov. 24–Dec. 14 stormy; Dec. 18–24 anticyclonic; Dec. 25–Jan. 1 stormy.

BRITISH RAILWAYS IN 1974

The British Railways Board was set up, along with our other separate nationalized transport undertakings, by the terms of the Transport Act, 1962. This Act dissolved the British Transport Commission and shared its assets between the new bodies which assumed their responsibilities on January 1, 1963. Under the Act the finances of the railways were reconstructed and previous restrictions were modified to give them greater commercial freedom than they had enjoyed in the past.

The Transport Act of 1968 reduced the railways' commencing debt from £1,562,000,000 to £300,000,000. The Act also enabled the Secretary of State for the Environment to make grants for the maintenance of unremunerative passenger services.

The Railways Act of 1974 introduced a new system of financial support in accordance with EEC regulations and from January 1 1975 the Board's capital debt was reduced to £250,000,000 and their borrowing limit, including commencing debt, was increased to £600,000,000 extendable to £900,000,000.

The power to make grants for unremunerative passenger services is withdrawn. The Secretary of State is authorised to impose general obligations on the Board in respect of passenger services and is empowered to compensate the Board for providing adequate transport services. Aggregate compensation is limited to £900,000,000 extendable to £1,500,000,000, subject to Parliamentary approval.

For the purposes of management and operation the railways are divided into Regions. They cover the following areas:

1. London Midland Region—bounded by a line joining Carlisle, Oldham, Nottingham, Bedford, London, Banbury, Kidderminster, Aberystwyth.

2. Western Region—west of a line joining Yeovil, Westbury, Reading, London and the southern border of the L.M. Region.

3. Southern Region—south of a line joining Dorchester, Salisbury, London and the Thames.

4. Eastern Region—east of a line joining London, Peterborough, Sheffield, Bradford and Carlisle.

5. Scottish Region—north of a line joining Carlisle and Berwick.

Staff.—On Dec. 31, 1974, British Railways employed a total staff of 194,891, compared with 195,205 on Dec. 31, 1973.

Financial Results, 1974.—The balance sheet for 1974 showed a deficit of £157,800,000, compared with a deficit of £51,600,000 for 1973 while the railway working profit (before taking interest charges or revenue from other activities into account) was £96,900,000, compared with £5,094,000 for the previous year.

Railways		£ million 1974
Gross receipts:		
Passenger (including Grants)....	433.2	
Freight (including parcels and mails)......................	280.8	
Miscellaneous.................	11.8	
TOTAL......................		725.8
Working expenses:		
Train services.................	419.8	
Terminal......................	132.5	
Miscellaneous traffic expenses...	10.4	
Track and signalling...........	165.2	
General expenses..............	155.6	
TOTAL......................		883.5
Railway net loss......................		107.0
Net income from Operational Property (Letting), Advertising and Catering....		10.1
OPERATING LOSS..................		96.9

OPERATING STATISTICS

At the end of 1974, British Railways had 29,268 miles of standard gauge lines and sidings in use, representing 11,229 miles of route of which 2,266 miles were electrified. Standard rail on main line has a weight of 110 lbs. per yard. British Railways had 3,971 locomotives (diesel and diesel electric, 3,619 and electric, 352); 3,427 diesel multiple-unit vehicles, 7,156 electric multiple-unit vehicles and 7,154 locomotive-hauled passenger carriages with a capacity of 1,105,834 seats or berths in 1974. Loaded train miles run in passenger service totalled 198,193,000. 732,786,000 passenger journeys were made during the year, including 296,327,000 made by holders of season tickets. The average distance of each passenger journey on ordinary fare was 32.4 miles; and on season ticket, 17.4 miles. Passenger stations in use in 1974 numbered 2,355 and freight stations 435.

Freight.—There were 241,429 freight-vehicles and 5,501 other vehicles in the non-passenger-carrying stock. 86,616,000 tons of coal and coke were carried in 1974, 30,509,000 tons of iron and steel and 49,299,000 tons of other traffic. Loaded train miles run in freight service totalled 51,159,000.

Casualties in Train Accidents
(includes British Railways, London Transport and other railways)

	Average 1969–73	1973
Fatal Accidents........	19	18
Passengers killed......	7	14
Passengers seriously injured..............	18	6
Railwaymen killed....	5	3
Railwaymen seriously injured............	7	11
Other persons killed...	6	1
Other persons seriously injured............	6	5
Passengers carried per passenger killed.....	206,354,000	91,070,000
Passenger miles run per passenger killed.....	3,345,470,000	1,559,000,000

RAILWAY ACCIDENTS IN WHICH 20 PERSONS AND OVER WERE KILLED IN THE UNITED KINGDOM SINCE 1948

Year	Date	Name of Accident	Railway	Number Killed	Cause
1948	Apl. 17	Winsford	L.M. Region	24	Collision.
1952	Oct. 8	Harrow	L.M. Region	112	Collision.
1957	Dec. 4	Lewisham	S. Region	90	Collision in fog.
1967	Nov. 5	Hither Green	S. Region	49	Track failure
1975	Feb. 28	Moorgate	L.T.E.	43	Terminal

FUEL AND POWER

ELECTRICITY PRODUCTION
England and Wales

In the year ended March 31, 1975, the electricity industry sold 195,944 million units to all consumers, an increase of 3·4 per cent. over 1973–74. Average price per unit to consumers was 1.243p compared with 0.941p in 1973–74. At the end of the year there were 19,306,000 consumers, 1·0 per cent. more than at March 31, 1974.

76,193 million units were supplied to industry (an increase of 3·8 per cent.), 79.471 million to domestic users (1.4 per cent. more) and 30,258 million to commercial users (6·9 per cent. more), 21,657 million units were sold on off-peak tariffs, a decrease of 1·2 per cent. over 1973–74.

On March 31, 1975, the Central Electricity Generating Board had 168 power stations (1974, *169*) with a maximum output capacity of 58,523 *MW*, an increase in capacity of 0·9 per cent. over 1974. Additional output capacity in 1974–75 was 1,739 *MW*. C.E.G.B. power stations supplied 210,948 million kWh in 1974–75, 4·6 per cent. more than in 1973–74. Maximum simultaneous demand met during the year was 40,973 *MW* (1973–74, *39,674*).

Lines owned by the Generating Board during the year totalled 13,800 kms. (1937–74, *13,600*). and the number of substations was 190.

The industry employed 172,483 persons at March 31, 1975, 1,259 more than in 1973–74.

The following results are those of the Electricity Council and Area Boards in England and Wales, the figures being rounded off.

Coal Consumption.—Of the 125,137,000 tons consumed at home in 1974–75, industry used 11,337,000 tons, domestic users 14,201,000 tons,

Electricity Industry Finance 1974–75

	£ million	
	1973–74	1974–75
Revenue		
Sales of Electricity.........	1,783·5	2,454·9
Other....................	22·8	20·9
TOTAL................	1,806·3	2,455·1
Expenditure		
Generation and purchases...	982·9	1,541·9
Main transmission and Distribution..................	103·2	133·7
Consumer Service..........	32·8	40·2
Administration, Collection of Accounts, etc...........	104·4	137·2
Rates....................	64·2	95·8
Depreciation..............	328·0	344·3
Other....................	28·1	14·1
TOTAL................	1,643·6	2,327·2
Operating Profit..........	162·7	127·9
Deduct Interest payable......	339·0	385·5
Loss....................	(–) 176·3	(–) 257·6

COAL PRODUCTION (tons)

Year	Saleable Mined Coal	Open Cast Coal	Total
1968–69	153,007,000	6,574,000	160,595,000
1969–70	139,788,000	6,571,000	147,385,000
1970–71	134,343,000	8,331,377	142,447,264
1971–72	109,224,309	10,422,055	120,358,390
1972–73	129,756,905	10,697,683	141,230,661
1973–74	97,122,040	8,906,566	107,146,509
1974–75	114,991,229	9,109,291	125,151,010

power stations 71,465,000 tons, gas works 55,000 tons, coke ovens 20,183,000 tons, colliery consumption 1,288,000 tons and others 6,608,000.

National Coal Board Finance

	£ million	
Income	1972–73†	1973–74†
From Sales (Net).............	1,092·7	913·6
Principal Items:—		
Coal...................	851·9	716·3
Coke...................	60·6	63·7
Gas, Benzole, Tar, etc.....	12·7	19·9
Processed Fuel...........	26·6	30·4
Other Receipts..............	31·1	28·2
NET INCOME.............	1,092·7	1,019·2
Expenditure		
Wages, Salaries, etc........	626·0	630·9
Open-Cast Contractors' payments................	48·9	51·6
Materials, Stores, Power......	282·5	287·0
Other......................	175·6	162·0
TOTAL EXPENDITURE......	1,133·0	1,131·5
PROFIT/*Loss*	40·3	112·3
Less/Plus Interest Payable, etc.	43·0	32·2
SURPLUS or *DEFICIENCY*...	83·7	1,130·7

† April to March.

GAS SUPPLY

	1974–75	1973–74
	(Million Therms)	
Natural gas for supply direct to customers	12,426	10,240
Natural gas for town gas manufacture	808	1,359
Coal and oil based gas made and bought	458	806
Total gas available	13,692	12,405

Consumption of coal for gas making fell from 17·5 million tons in 1965–66 to 0·03 million tons in 1974–75. Total oil used was 2·7 million tons in 1965–66 compared with 5·9 million tons in 1968–69 and 0·8 million tons in 1974–75.

In 1965–66 8·2 per cent of total gas available was based on natural gas but by 1974–75 the proportion based on natural gas had risen to 96·7 per cent.

Gas Industry Finance

	£ million	
	1972–73	1973–74
Gross Revenue		
Sales—Gas..................	740·2	813·3
By-Products.............	4·8	3·2
Appliances.............	71·3	68·8
Other Revenue..............	88·5	94·2
TOTAL REVENUE	904·8	979·5
Gross Expenditure		
Process Materials—Natural Gas	116·5	147·2
Oil........	20·6	28·7
Other.....	12·1	10·5
Payments to employees.......	194·8	220·9
Cost of Appliances...........	49·7	45·1
Depreciation.................	143·0	187·9
Interest.....................	145·4	155·5
Rates.......................	13·1	15·2
Other materials and services...	203·9	209·8
TOTAL EXPENDITURE	899·1	1020·8
SURPLUS or *DEFICIENCY*....	5·7	41·3*

* Recovered from the Government or arising from price restraint.

ADMINISTRATION OF THE NATIONAL HEALTH SERVICE

Since its inception in 1948 the N.H.S. has been administered according to its three main branches—the hospital and specialist services, the general practitioner services and the local health authority services. These have now been unified under the provisions of the National Health Service Reorganization Act 1973 which came into force on April 1, 1974. The services which were brought together are:

(a) the hospital and specialist services previously administered by Regional Hospital Boards, Hospital Management Committees and Boards of Governors of undergraduate Teaching Hospitals;

(b) the family practitioner services previously administered by Executive Councils;

(c) the personal health services (e.g. ambulance services, epidemiological work, family planning, home nursing and midwifery, maternity and child health care, etc.) previously administered by local authorities through their health committees;

(d) the school health service previously administered by local education authorities.

Under the new structure all these services are administered by Regional and Area Health Authorities.

Regional Health Authorities

There are 14 Regional Health Authorities in England based on the present Hospital Regions. The R.H.A. will develop strategic plans and priorities based on a review of the needs identified by the Area Health Authorities and on its judgement of the right balance between individual areas' claims on resources. It is also responsible for identifying, in consultation with the A.H.A.s, services which need a regional approach rather than an area approach and arranging for their provision. The R.H.A. will allocate resources between the A.H.A.s, after having agreed area plans with them, and will monitor their performance. One of the R.H.A.s executive functions will be the design and construction of new buildings and works. The R.H.A. will itself undertake the more important projects on behalf of the A.H.A.

Area Health Authorities

There are 90 Area Health Authorities in England whose boundaries generally match those of the new non-metropolitan counties and metropolitan districts of local government, or of one or more London boroughs. The A.H.A. is the operational health authority, responsible for assessing needs in its area and for planning, organizing and administering area health services to meet them. The day-to-day running of the services for which the A.H.A. is responsible is based on health districts. These will normally contain a district general hospital or a number of hospitals providing the services of a district general hospital and will usually have a population of between 150,000 and 300,000. There are 205 Health districts in England, including 34 single district areas.

Under the new N.H.S. the status of general medical and dental practitioners, opthalmic medical practitioners, opticians and pharmacists as independent contractors remains unchanged. Each A.H.A. is required to set up a Family Practitioners Committee to administer family practitioner services.

Community Health Councils have been established for each health district. The Council's basic job is to represent to the Area Health Authority the interests of the public in the health services in its district. Councils have power to secure information, to visit hospitals and other institutions, and have access to the A.H.A. and in particular to its senior officers administering the district services. The A.H.A. is required to consult the Community Health Council(s) on its plans for health service developments and the full A.H.A. will meet representatives of all its Community Health Councils at least once a year. The Council will publish an annual report and the A.H.A. is required to publish replies recording action taken on the issues raised.

Complaints

One of the most important innovations in the reorganized N.H.S. is the establishment of a Health Service Commissioner to investigate complaints against N.H.S. authorities. The Commissioner began work on October 1, 1973, and since April 1, 1974 his jurisdiction has covered the whole of the unified N.H.S. Further details of the Commissioner's work and the procedure for making complaints can be obtained from the Office of the Health Service Commissioner, Church House, Great Smith Street, London S.W.1.

NAUTICAL MEASURES

Distance is measured in nautical (or sea) miles. The nautical mile is traditionally defined as the length of a minute of arc of a great circle of the earth; but as this length varies in different latitudes (owing to the fact that the earth is not a perfect sphere), 6,080 feet, a " rounded off value " of the mean length, has been adopted in British practice as the standard length of the nautical mile. On this basis 33 nautical miles exactly equal 38 statute miles; the statute (land) mile contains 5,280 feet. A *cable*, as a measure used by seamen, is 600 feet (100 fathoms) approximately one-tenth of a nautical mile. *Soundings at sea* are recorded in fathoms (6 feet).

6 feet= 1 fathom.
100 fathoms= 1 cable length.
10 cables= 1 nautical mile.

Note.—Some other countries, including the United States in 1954, have adopted the nautical mile of 1,852 metres as recommended by the International Hydrographic Bureau in 1929.

Speed is measured in *nautical miles per hour*, called *knots*. A knot is a measure of speed and is not used to express distance. A ship moving at the rate of 30 nautical miles per hour is said to be " doing 30 knots " and as the nautical mile is longer than the land or statute mile this represents a land speed of over 34½ miles per hour.

Knots	m.p.h.	Knots	m.p.h.	Knots	m.p.h.
1	1·1515	15	17·2727	29	33·3939
2	2·3030	16	18·4242	30	34·5454
3	3·4545	17	19·5757	31	35·6969
4	4·6060	18	20·7272	32	36·8484
5	5·7575	19	21·8787	33	38·0000
6	6·9090	20	23·0303	34	39·1515
7	8·0606	21	24·1818	35	40·3030
8	9·2121	22	25·3333	36	41·4545
9	10·3636	23	26·4848	37	42·6060
10	11·5151	24	27·6363	38	43·7575
11	12·6666	25	28·7878	39	44·9090
12	13·8180	26	29·9393	40	46·0606
13	14·9696	27	31·0908	41	47·2121
14	16·1212	28	32·2424	42	48·3636

Net tonnage.—The gross tonnage less certain deductions for crew space, engine room, water ballast and other spaces not used for passengers or cargo.

Gross tonnage.—The total volume of all the enclosed spaces of a vessel, the unit of measurement being a ton of 100 cubic feet.

Friendly Societies—Great Britain
Act 1974

Friendly societies are mutual insurance societies in which the members subscribe for provident benefits, in particular sickness, death, endowment and old age benefits. Those friendly societies that are known as "collecting societies" because they collect members' premiums for life assurance by house-to-house visits of collectors or agents are subject to the provisions of the Industrial Assurance Acts as well as the Friendly Societies Act. The totals in ordinary type in the table below relate to registered friendly societies proper (including both centralized societies and the Orders with their branches); those in italics relate to collecting societies.

End of Year	No. of Societies on Register		Member-ship	Assurances or Policies	Total Funds	
			Thousands		*£000*	
1973.............	5,847	*66*	4,438	*24,949*	383,183	*558,134*
1938.............	19,600	*149*	8,491	*25,738*	151,613	*84,837*
1913.............	25,475	*71*	6,783	*7,481*	51,489	*11,165*

The first column headed "No. of Societies on Register" in the above table includes (for 1973) 584 societies without branches and 30 societies with branches ("Orders"), the remainder being the separately registered branches of the Orders.

Although recent years have seen the growth of societies registered for such specific purposes as the provision of Institutional treatment or assuring annuities and pensions, most friendly societies continue to provide the customary benefits in sickness and at death. During 1972 Friendly Societies proper paid out £5·6 millions in sickness benefit and 2·5 millions in death benefit.

As compared with the previous year the number of societies without branches decreased in 1973 by 32 and the number of branches by 236. Total membership fell to under 4·5 millions.

Many societies still operate mainly on the old system of accumulating funds on a mutual basis. Others, usually termed deposit societies, allocate all or the greater part of their funds annually to the individual credit of the members to be withdrawn by them as the rules provide. Apart from the National Deposit Society's method of a uniform contribution throughout membership there are several systems operated on individual account lines, one of which (known as the "Holloway" principle) is worked by a contribution increasing with each year of attained age after the member reaches age 30 up to age 65.

The latest available figures of membership and funds set out below indicate the relative strength of several leading old established societies, including the three largest Orders which operate through registered districts and branches subject to a central body:—

FRIENDLY Socs.—Name with (in brackets) Year Established	Membership	Total Funds
		£000
National Deposit Friendly Society (1868).................................	331,000	25,301
Hearts of Oak Benefit Society (1842)...................................	331,000	25,229
Independent Order of Odd Fellows, Manchester Unity (1810)..............	271,000	33,999
Ancient Order of Foresters (1834)......................................	231,000	28,035
Independent Order of Rechabites, Salford Unity (1835)..................	102,000	7,663

COLLECTING Socs.—Name and Year Established	No. of Industrial Assurances		Total Funds
	Premium Paying	Free Paid-up	
			£000
Liverpool Victoria Friendly Society (1843).................	8,616,000	4,169,000	283,666
Royal Liver Friendly Society (1850).......................	5,453,000	2,248,000	121,284
Scottish Legal Life Assurance Society (1852)................	1,602,000	1,063,000	30,198

Long before the term "Friendly Society" came into use, the seeds of voluntary mutual insurance had been sown in the ancient religious and trade "Guilds." As is evident from the many extant parchment returns detailing their rules and possessions under a decree of Richard II, Guilds had become widespread in Britain by the 14th century. By then, the purely charitable character of the original Guilds had largely changed with the emergence of numerous small institutions adopting primitive mutual insurance methods of a regular flat rate contribution to insure relief when sick or in old age and a payment to the widow in the event of death.

The present register of Friendly Societies includes several societies which have been in existence for upwards of 200 years, the oldest, operating in Scotland, being the "Incorporation of Carters in Leith" established as long ago as 1555.

The first Act for the encouragement and protection of "Friendly Societies" in this country was not passed until 1793, but various amending Acts were put on the Statute Book during the next century as the result of the recommendations of successive Select Committees (including a Royal Commission in 1871). For example, it was not until the 1829 Act that all registered Friendly Societies were required to keep proper records of individual sickness and mortality amongst their members, which data enabled the construction of standard actuarial tables showing the expected (average) duration or sickness at successive ages, and also (with data from the Census) the corresponding mortality rates.

The rules and other documents of societies deposited with local justices passed into the custody of the Registrar following the Act of 1846 and are of considerable interest to social historians.

Those relating to some societies no longer on the register have been transferred to the Public Record Office for permanent preservation.

The Act of 1896 allows various specific classes other than "Friendly Societies" to be registered thereunder, but tax exemption (irrespective of the extent of interest income) is enjoyed only by registered "Friendly Societies." The Friendly Societies Act 1974, which came into force on April, 1975, consolidates the nine Acts which comprised the Friendly Societies Acts 1896 to 1971 and a few other minor enactments relating to societies to which those Acts applied.

Industrial and Provident Societies—Great Britain
Acts 1965–1968

The familiar "Co-op" societies are amongst the wide variety which are registered under the Industrial and Provident Societies Act 1965. This consolidating Act, which like the Friendly and the Building Societies Act is administered by the Chief Registrar of Friendly Societies, provides for the registration of societies and lays down the broad framework within which they must operate. Internal relations of societies are governed by their registered rules.

Registration under the Act confers upon a society corporate status by its registered name with perpetual succession and a common seal, and limited liability. A society qualifies for registration if it is carrying on an industry, business or trade, and it satisfies the Registrar that either (a) it is a bona fide co-operative society or (b) in view of the fact that its business is being, or is intended to be, conducted for the benefit of the community there are special reasons why it should be registered under the Act rather than as a company under the Companies Act.

During 1974 the number of registered societies increased by 43 to 9,676. The largest single group was the 4,133 housing societies which accounted for most of the new registrations in 1974—255 out of 345. The largest group in terms of turnover was that consisting of the retail, wholesale and productive societies which includes the "co-ops" with sales in 1974 of £1,575 million and the Co-operative Wholesale Society Limited with 1974 sales of £878 million. The principal statistics at the end of 1974 are given in the table below.

	Retail	Wholesale and Productive	Social and Recreational Clubs	General Service	Housing	Agricultural	Fishing	Total
Number of Societies	321	74	3,536	233	4,133	1,295	84	9,676
Number of Members	000's 10,588	000's 42	000's 2,123	000's 405	000's 137	000's 448	000's 9	000's 13,753
Funds of Members	£000's 252,771	£000's 148,844	£000's 41,227	£000's 570,614	£000's 56,202	£000's 52,145	£000's 703	£000's 1,122,505
Total Assets	£000's 589,342	£000's 283,512	£000's 74,829	£000's 680,979	£000's 650,603	£000's 131,915	£000's 1,806	£000's 2,412,987

Building Societies—Great Britain
Act 1962

Building Societies are associations incorporated with limited liability under the Building Societies Act. All Building Societies are required to register their rules and file their accounts with Registry of Friendly Societies. The following particulars showing the growth of Building Societies (as also that of Friendly and Industrial and Provident Societies) are based on the Chief Registrar's Annual Reports.

During 1974 the assets of the building society movement increased from £17,546 million to £20,094 million, a growth rate of 14·5 per cent.

In the first 3 months of 1974 net receipts from investors fell substantially, continuing the trend which had appeared at the end of 1973, when apparently more attractive investment terms were to be found elsewhere. Many societies in fact experienced a net outflow of funds during this period, but later in the year investment receipts showed a notable recovery and the total over the year was £6,381 million—the highest figure ever. Withdrawals were also higher than ever, increasing from £4,536 million in 1973 to £5,216 million in 1974. The ratio of withdrawals to receipts amounted to 82 per cent. compared with 75 per cent. in 1973.

Despite the uneven pattern of investment and the difficult conditions generally, building societies maintained their sound financial position and in the prevailing circumstances this undoubtedly proved an attraction for many investors. In 1974 the general reserves of all societies increased from £616 million to £690 million: a rise of 11·9 per cent. compared with a rise of 11·2 per cent. in 1973. However, with assets rising by 14·5 per cent. and because interest rates were held to levels which gave societies only very slender operating margins throughout 1974, the result was a slight fall in the ratio of reserves to assets; although the drop of 0·08 per cent. from 3·51 per cent. was significantly less than that experienced in 1973.

The relative increase in withdrawals was undoubtedly one of the factors persuading societies to increase their cash and investments which were up by nearly £1,000 million to £3,783 million at the end of 1974, representing an increase from 15·9 per cent. to 18·8 per cent. in the proportion of cash and investments to total assets. Due in part to this increase, and the high level of interest rates obtaining elsewhere, societies were able to show a useful increase in the income received from authorised investments and bank deposits from £185 million in 1973 to £295 million in 1974.

Another factor in the increase in cash and investments in 1974 was the aim of societies, subsequently embodied in an agreement between the Government and the Building Societies Association in April 1975, to accumulate surplus funds for the maintenance of a high and stable level of lending for house purchase in the future should net receipts at any time be inadequate.

Societies advanced £2,945 million on mortgage compared with £3,513 million in 1973 and £3,630 million in 1972. The number of advances also decreased—546,000 compared with 720,000 in 1973. The average amount advanced on a new mortgage was £6,507, 6·2 per cent. more than in 1973.

The number of building societies decreased further during 1974. At the end of the year there were 416 societies on the register, 31 fewer than at the end of 1973.

There were nearly 16 million shareholding accounts in building societies at the end of 1974 (average shareholding £1,137) and over ½ million deposit accounts (average deposit £987). This does not of course mean that 16½ million people have money invested in building societies since many have shares or deposits in more than one society. There were just over 4¼ million borrowers and the average mortgage debt outstanding was £3,758.

Under the Building Societies Acts, the Chief Registrar exercises certain power of control over building societies. Section 11 of the Prevention of Fraud (Investments) Act, 1958, under which the Registrar had prohibited certain societies from inviting investments was repealed by the Building Societies Act, 1960 (but without prejudice to any order currently in force) and the Chief Registrar was empowered to direct that a building society shall not advertise at all or to give directions to a particular society as to the matter included in its advertisements. In addition he may make an order prohibiting a building society from accepting further investments. The Chief Registrar's Report to Parliament for 1974 disclosed that at the end of that year 3 orders under the 1958 Act were still in force while 9 orders under the 1960 and 1962 Acts prohibiting the acceptance of further investment were in force at the end of 1974. Directions controlling advertising were in force in respect of 5 societies at the end of the year.

BUILDING SOCIETIES, GREAT BRITAIN, 1974—with 1973 in Italics.

Class	Number	Share Investors	Advances during Year *	Amount due to Share-holders †	Amount due to Deposi-tors ‡	General Reserve and Balances C/fd.	Mortgage Assets	Total Assets
		000's	£000	£000	£000	£000	£000	£000
Assets over								
£1 m.......	250	15,815	2,936,300	17,978,700	631,400	686,800	15,989,300	20,045,000
Other Societies..	166	41	8,800	42,700	1,400	3,000	40,300	48,500
1974 TOTALS.	416	15,856	2,945,100	18,021,400	632,800	689,800	16,029,600	20,093,500
1973 TOTALS.	*447*	*14,385*	*3,512,700*	*16,021,500*	*596,300*	*616,300*	*14,532,400*	*17,545,500*

* Total Borrowers, 4,250,000   † Total Share Investors, 15,856,000   ‡ Total Depositors, 641,000

SOCIETIES WITH TOTAL ASSETS EXCEEDING £500,000 AT END OF FINANCIAL YEAR 1973

Year Estab-lished	* Name of Society (abbreviated) Head Office	Share Investors	Assets Total £'000
1849D	Abbey National, Abbey House, Baker St., London NW1 6XL.......	2,633,662	2,575,231
1879	Aberavon Mut. P., 2 Forge Road, Port Talbot, Glam................	654	909
1869D	Accrington Savings and Bldg. Soc., 60 Blackburn Road, Accrington, Lancs. BB5 1LD....................................	3,333	3,463
1875	Accrington Victoria, 7 St. James's St., Accrington, Lancs BB5 1NE...	684	913
1873	Advance, Advance Bldgs, Surtees St., Hartlepool..................	391	687
1885	Aid to Thrift, 38 Finsbury Sq., London EC2A 1PT.................	428	670
1866D	Alfreton, 103 High St., Alfreton, Derby DE5 7DP.................	1,943	2,106
1863D	Alliance, Alliance House, Hove Park, Hove, Sussex BN3 7AZ........	342,022	620,534
1866	Anchor, 8 Coronation St., South Shields..........................	734	829
1848D	Anglia, Abington St., Northampton NN1 2BJ.....................	358,682	345,445
1870D	Argyle, Argyle Ho., 105 Seven Sisters Rd., Holloway, London N7 7QH	4,416	7,120
1945	Ashton-Stamford, Booth St. Chambers, Ashton-u-Lyne, Lancs OL6 7LQ	633	1,047
1965	Banner, Banner Cross Hall, Sheffield S11 9PD....................	5	8,128
1853D	Barnsley P., Regent St., Barnsley, Yorks. S70 2EH................	13,457	18,067
1850D	Barnstaple and North Devon, 17 Joy St., Barnstaple, Devon........	684	913
1922D	Barry Mutual, Lombard Bldgs., Barry, Glam...................	2,538	2,676
1953D	Bath Investment and Bldg. Soc., 20 Charles St., Bath, Som. BA1 1HY	1,337	1,945
1870D	Bath Liberal, 1 South Parade, Bath, Som. BA2 4AA..............	7,931	5,704
1863	Bede P., 5 Grange Road West, Jarrow, Co. Durham, NE32 3JA......	2,506	2,346
1881D	Bedford Crown, 117 Midland Rd., Bedford, MK40 1DE............	870	899
1879D	Bedford P., 65 Midland Rd., Bedford...........................	2,467	2,198
1924D	Bedfordshire, Kingsway, Bedford, MK42 9BD....................	7,292	7,272
		69,612	79,852

* P.=Permanent; B.=Benefit. The words "Building Society" are the last words in every society's name.

Year Established	Name of Society (abbreviated) Head Office	Share Investors	Assets Total £'000
1905	Berkhamsted Dt. P., 322 High St., Berkhamsted, Herts..............	636	835
1866D	Beverley, 16 Lairgate, Beverley, Yorks. HU17 8EE................	3,442	2,289
1914D	Bexhill-on-Sea, 2 Devonshire Sq., Bexhill-on-Sea, Sussex TN40 1AE..	1,836	2,724
1853D	Bideford and North Devon, 5 The Quay, Bideford, Devon.........	3,299	5,004
1889D	Birmingham Citizens, 20 Bennetts Hill, Birmingham B2 5QL.......	14,590	21,381
1847D	Birmingham Incorporated, 42-44 Waterloo St., Birmingham B2 5QB	28,165	41,266
1903D	Blackheath, Cranford Ho., 14 Long Lane, Rowley Regis, Warley, Worcs.	8,924	8,497
1957	Blackheath, Kidbrooke and Chailton, National Westminster Bank Chambers, Blackheath Village, London, SE3............	522	526
1873	Blyth and Morpeth Dt. P. B., 3 Stanley St., Blyth, Nbld...........	752	754
1864D	Bolton, 213 Baker St., London NW1 6HY......................	1,968	4,719
1866D	Bournemouth and Christchurch, 162 Old Christchurch Rd., Bournemouth, Hants..	6,296	12,926
1851D	Bradford and Bingley, P.O. Box 2, Bingley, Yorks................	368,989	435,986
1885D	Bradford P., 57-63 Sunbridge Rd., Bradford BD1 2AU............	81,399	131,270
1921D	Bridgwater, 1 King Sq., Bridgwater, Som......................	55,632	64,908
1849D	Brierley Hill and Stourbridge Incorporated, 12 Hagley Rd., Stourbridge, Worcs DY8 1PS..	7,629	8,129
1867D	Brighton and Shoreham, 115 Western Rd., Brighton, Sussex BN1 2AB	568	1,192
1853D	Bristol Econ. Broad St., Bristol BS1 2HE......................	2,477	3,731
1850D	Bristol and West, Broad Quay, Bristol BS99 7AX................	205,097	270,422
1883D	Bromley, 182 High St., Bromley, Kent BR1 1HE................	2,099	2,586
1907D	Buckinghamshire, High St., Chalfont St., Giles, Bucks...........	5,529	5,161
1850D	Burnley, 12 Grimshaw St., Burnley, Lancs.....................	239,094	321,076
1866D	Bury St. Edmunds P. B., 87 Guildhall St., Bury St. Edmunds IP33 1PU	1,951	3,379
1957	Caledonian, 55 Queen St., Edinburgh EH2 3PA................	606	973
1886	Calne and District P.B., 1 Patford St., Calne, Wilts.............	556	563
1850D	Cambridge, 32 St. Andrew's St., Cambridge CB2 3AR...........	15,627	22,081
1865D	Cardiff, Old Vestry Hall, 75 St. Mary St., Cardiff..............	2,365	4,497
1960D	Catholic, 7 Strutton Ground, London SW1P 2HY..............	1,493	1,482
1899	Century, 21-23 Albany St., Edinburgh EH1 3QW..............	1,114	1,224
1862	Chatham, 27 Lord St., Liverpool L2 9SG.....................	551	567
1898D	Chatham Reliance, Reliance House, Manor Rd., Chatham, Kent....	18,964	18,272
1875D	Chelsea, 110/112 King's Rd., London SW3 4TY................	64,535	110,686
1850D	Cheltenham and Gloucester, 37-43 Clarence St., Cheltenham, Glos. GL50 3JR..	192,865	244,634
1845D	Chesham, 12 Market Sq., Chesham, Bucks.....................	4,614	5,227
1888D	Chesham and Dt. Mut. & P., Norfolk House, Station Rd., Chesham, Bucks..	1,600	1,874
1870D	Cheshire and Northwich, Castle St., Macclesfield SK11 6AH......	37,470	38,220
1861D	Cheshunt, 100 Crossbrook St., Waltham Cross, Herts. EN8 8JJ......	18,012	20,562
1859D	Chorley and Dt., 51 St. Thomas's Rd., Chorley, Lancs...........	3,439	4,096
1866	Chorley P.B., 41 Chapel St., Chorley, Lancs..................	656	689
1905D	Citizens Regency, Citizens Hse., Marlborough Pl., Brighton, Sussex BN1 1WW..	13,562	20,786
1946D	City and Metropolitan, 37 Ludgate Hill, London EC4M 7NA.....	8,180	13,763
1862D	City of London, 34 London Wall, London EC2Y 5JD............	14,918	30,689
1931D	Civil Service, 26 Caxton St., London SW1H 0RE..............	7,335	11,285
1894D	Clacton, 72 Station Rd., Clacton-on-Sea, Essex................	832	1,142
1859D	Clay Cross Benefit, 42 Thanet St., Clay Cross, Chesterfield......	1,978	1,582
1912D	Coalville P., 42 High St., Coalville, Leicester LE6 2AG.........	1,661	1,911
1869D	Colchester Eq., 1-3 Pelhams Lane, Colchester CO1 1JT.........	3,587	5,152
1856D	Colchester P., 11 Sir Isaac's Walk, Colchester CO1 1JL.........	2,031	3,623
1866D	Colne, Albert Rd., Colne, Lancs. BB8 0AJ....................	5,013	8,231
1906	Consett Reliance, 44 Medomsley Rd., Consett Co. Durham.......	877	841
1878D	Cotswold, 11 Long St., Wotton-under-Edge, GL12 7ES..........	2,544	2,410
1884D	Coventry Economic, 19/20 High St., Coventry, Warws. CV1 5QN...	122,409	114,444
1848D	Coventry and Warwickshire B., 23 Bayley Lane, Coventry, Warws..	693	827
1872D	Coventry Provident, Provident Hse., 25 Warwick Rd., Coventry CV1 2ER..	19,721	24,440
1906D	Cradley Heath, 194 High St., Cradley Heath, Warley, Worcs........	4,825	5,039
1850D	Cumberland, 38 Fisher St., Carlisle.........................	30,837	33,828
1946D	Darlington, Tubwell Row, Market Pl., Darlington, Co. Durham.....	25,676	25,787
1847D	Deal and Walmer, 7 Victoria Rd., Deal, Kent..................	743	1,153
1865	Denton, 37 Ashton Rd., Denton, Manchester..................	877	1,041
1859D	Derbyshire P.O. Box No. 48, 7 Iron Gate, Derby DE1 3FW.......	86,632	92,508
1923	Dillwyn P., 11 Cradock St., Swansea, Glam. SA1 3EW..........	1,473	2,352
1879	Dorking, Haybarn Hse., 118 South St., Dorking, Surrey..........	863	1,642
1861	Dover Dt., 3 Market Sq., Dover, Kent.......................	729	1,002
1883	Dover and Folkestone, 27-29 Castle St., Dover, Kent...........	611	883
1865	Driffield, 18 Exchange St., Driffield, Yorks..................	733	612
1866	Duchess of Kent, Marcol Hse., 289-293 Regent St., London, W.1....	359	630

Year Established	Name of Society (abbreviated) Head Office	Share Investors	Assets Total £'000
1858D	Dudley, Dudley Hse., Stone St., Dudley, Worcs.	6,221	7,899
1869D	Dunfermline 48–56, East Port, Dunfermline, Fife.	22,664	31,098
1852D	Dunstable, 13A West St., Dunstable, Beds.	3,734	4,491
1956	Eagle, Chancery Hse., Chancery Lane, London, W.C.2.	528	512
1927D	Ealing and Acton, 55 The Mall, Ealing, London, W5 3TG.	2,462	5,010
1857D	Earl Shilton, 22 The Hollow, Earl Shilton, Leicester LE9 7NB.	5,661	5,685
1903D	East Surrey, 54 Station Rd., Redhill, Surrey.	4,894	6,667
1877D	Eastbourne Mut., 147 Terminus Rd., Eastbourne, Sussex.	20,140	34,406
1855D	Eastern Counties, 13 and 15 Queen St., Ipswich, Suffolk IP1 1SP.	32,145	42,568
1870D	Edinburgh, 32 Castle St., Edinburgh EH2 3JB.	4,733	8,464
1880D	Enfield, 47 London Rd., Enfield EN2 6EG.	23,986	28,088
1899D	Essex and Kent P., 1 Orsett Rd., Grays, Essex RM17 5DA.	1,997	2,855
1847D	Essex Eq., 13 Orsett Rd., Grays, Essex RM17 5DH.	3,293	4,255
1876D	Failsworth P., 546 Oldham Rd., Failsworth, Manchester M35 9DA.	1,277	1,311
1862D	Falkirk, Manse Place, Falkirk, Stirlingshire.	2,724	2,182
1860D	Frome Selwood P., 3 Market Pl., Frome, Som.	4,700	5,697
1865D	Furness, 36 Cornwallis St., Barrow-in-Furness, Lancs.	25,458	23,141
1911D	Gainsborough, 26 Lord St., Gainsborough, Lincs. DN21 2DB.	1,390	1,945
1886	General Thrift P., 7 The Parade, Stroud Green Road, London N4 3ED	861	982
1906D	Glantawe P., 47 Mansel St., Swansea, Glam.	923	2,338
1876D	Goldhawk, 15–17 High Rd., Chiswick, London W4 2NG.	14,996	26,081
1899	Govanhill, 160 Hope St., Glasgow G2 2TJ.	942	1,040
1957D	Grainger and Percy, Hood St., Newcastle upon Tyne NE1 6JP.	23,026	30,595
1875	Grantham, 15 Market Place, Grantham, Lincs.	477	724
1880D	Grays, 22 New Rd., Grays, Essex RM17 6PH.	7,490	8,691
1852D	Greenwich, 281 Greenwich High Rd., London, SE10 8NL.	12,655	16,856
1848D	Grimsby, Osborne Chambers, Osborne St., Grimsby, Lincs.	1,004	1,887
1871D	Guardian, Guardian Hse., 120 High Holborn, London WC1V 6RH.	50,567	127,615
1928D	Hadrian, 30 Fowler St., South Shields, Co. Durham.	2,973	3,363
1849	Halesowen, 20 Stourbridge Rd., Halesowen, Worcs.	1,882	2,017
1853D	Halifax, P.O. Box 60, Trinity Rd., Halifax, Yorks.	2,533,893	3,206,249
1866D	Hampshire, 29–31 Guildhall Walk, Portsmouth, Hants. PO1 2RW.	5,377	7,947
1854D	Hanley Econ., 42 Cheapside, Hanley, Stoke-on-Trent, Staffs. ST1 1EX	19,014	16,263
1953D	Harpenden and Dt., 14 Station Rd., Harpenden, Herts.	1,490	1,851
1882D	Harrow, Cunningham Hse., Bessborough Rd., Harrow, Middx. HA1 3DA.	4,262	7,259
1866	Hartlepool and Dt., 17 Scarborough St., Hartlepool, Co. Durham.	534	837
1851D	Hasbury and Cradley, 5 Summer Hill, Halesowen, Worcs.	3,574	3,358
1931	Haslemere, 17 Petworth Rd., Haslemere, Surrey.	664	876
1849D	Hastings and Thanet, 12–14 Wigmore St., London W1H 0DA.	249,842	286,954
1890D	Haywards Heath and Dt., 33 The Broadway, Haywards Heath, Sussex	10,786	12,629
1875D	Hearts of Oak P., 47–49 Oxford St., London, W1R 2BN.	10,579	21,329
1884D	Hemel Hempstead, 43 Marlowes, Hemel Hempstead, Herts.	7,535	9,706
1926D	Hendon, Central Circus, Hendon, London, N.W.4.	5,542	6,471
1888	Herne Bay, 39 William St., Herne Bay CT6 5NS.	2,297	3,974
1888D	Herts and Essex P., 4 Market Sq., Bishop's Stortford, Herts.	2,836	4,369
1874D	Hibernian P., 22 High St., Cardiff, Glam.	1,724	2,099
1860D	Highgate, Northway Hse., High Rd., Whetstone, London N20 9LP.	481	1,198
1853D	Hinckley and Country, 9 Castle St., Hinckley, Leics. LE10 1DF.	12,607	18,795
1865D	Hinchley P., Upper Bond St., Hinckley, Leics.	15,773	18,842
1881D	Holloway, 46 Upper St., London N1 1RH.	4,466	6,771
1855D	Holmesdale B., 43 Church St., Reigate, Surrey RH2 0AE.	6,413	8,438
1856D	Horsham, 30 Carfax, Horsham, Sussex RH12 1EE.	3,519	4,307
1864D	Huddersfield, Britannia Bldgs., Huddersfield, Yorks. HD1 1LG.	120,732	167,946
1868	Hyde, 5 Corporation St., Hyde, Cheshire SK14 1AF.	1,673	2,200
1853D	Ilkeston P., Queen St., Ilkeston, Derby DE7 5HQ.	2,267	2,536
1891D	Inverness, 21–23 Union St., Inverness.	3,976	5,219
1876D	Ipswich and Dt., 8 Northgate St., Ipswich IP1 3DA.	4,187	4,050
1849D	Ipswich and Suffolk, 44 Upper Brook St., Ipswich IP4 1DP.	12,214	11,428
1847	Kent and Canterbury P.B., 3 The Parade, Canterbury, Kent.	472	870
1869	Kettering P.B., 26–28 Headlands, Kettering.	839	1,156
1961	Kidderminster Eq., 30 Church St., Kidderminster.	555	856
1851	Kidderminster P.B., 29 Church St., Kidderminster, Worcs.	1,445	2,025
1864	Kilmarnock, 57 The Foregate, Kilmarnock.	787	1,194
1917	King Edward, 19 Castle St., Liverpool.	125	603
1865D	Kingston, 6 Eden St., Kingston-on-Thames, Surrey.	6,445	9,516
1852D	Lambeth, 118–120 Westminster Bridge Rd., London SE1 7XE.	27,307	46,271
1867D	Lancashire, 127 Union St., Oldham, Lancs.	2,617	3,966
1853D	Leamington Spa, 24 Warwick New Rd., Leamington Spa, Warws.	9,743	13,051
1875D	Leeds and Holbeck, 105 Albion St., Leeds LS1 5AS.	72,796	97,231
1848D	Leeds P., Permanent Hse., The Headrow, Leeds LS 1NS.	880,604	971,391

Year Established	Name of Society (abbreviated) Head Office	Share Investors	Assets Total £'000
1856D	Leek and Westbourne, P.O. Box 20, Newton Hse., Leek, Staffs. ST13 5RG..........	396,593	475,353
1863D	Leek United and Midlands, 50 St. Edward St., Leek, Staffs. ST13 5DH	30,821	32,392
1853D	Leicester P., Oadby, Leics. LE2 4PF.............................	291,437	437,787
1875D	Leicester Temperance, Halford Hse., Charles St., Leicester LE1 9FT...	101,459	146,025
1875	Leigh P., 12a Leigh Road, Leigh, Lancs.............................	682	1,301
1870D	Lewes, 11 High St., Lewes, Sussex..................................	12,953	14,597
1854	Liverpool Charter, 3 Brunswick St., Liverpool L2 0PQ..............	624	599
1877D	Liverpool, 107 Duke St., Liverpool L69 1DA........................	34,237	50,619
1859	London B., 85 Blackfriars Rd., London SE1 8HA....................	1,023	1,712
1863D	London Commercial, Guildford Hse., Gray's Inn Rd., London, W.C.1.	1,789	2,820
1883D	London and Essex, Security Hse., 2 Romford Rd., London, E.15.....	3,974	6,160
1878	London Grosvenor and Middlesex, 5 Old Brompton Rd., SW7 3H7..	904	1,034
1879D	London Investment, 54 Goldhawk Rd., London W12 8HB..........	18,462	27,867
1848	London P., 14 Tufton St., London SW1P 3QZ.......................	1,415	2,718
1867D	Loughborough P., 16 Baxter Gate, Loughborough, Leics LE11 1TW..	4,240	7,290
1877	Louth, Mablethorpe and Sutton P.B., 3 Eastgate, Louth, Lincs. LN11 9NA	834	1,013
1866D	Luton, 24 King St., Luton, Beds...................................	7,412	12,174
1868D	Magnet, North West Hse., Marylebone Rd., London NW1 5PX.....	46,927	71,223
1922D	Manchester, 18–20 Bridge St., Manchester M3 3BU................	2,851	5,547
1956	Mancunian, 22 Dickinson St., Manchester M1 4LF.................	832	1,250
1870D	Mansfield, Regent Hse., Regent St., Mansfield, Notts.............	9,790	13,622
1867	Margam P.B., 18 Station Rd., Port Talbot SA13 1BU...............	365	766
1870D	Market Harborough, Welland Hse., The Sq., Market Harborough, Leics.	14,451	13,437
1860D	Marsden, 6–20 Russell St., Nelson, Lancs. BB9 7NJ..............	25,970	29,341
1874D	Melton Mowbray, 43 Nottingham St., Melton Mowbray, Leics.......	10,418	14,835
1966D	Mercantile, 75 Howard St., North Shields.........................	7,786	9,838
1851D	Mercia, 52 Lower High Street, Wednesbury, Staffs...............	20,451	17,854
1882	Mersey P., 41 North John St., Liverpool L2 6RR.................	420	729
1886D	Metrogas, 709 Old Kent Rd., London SE15 1JJ....................	1,577	1,556
1872D	Middleton, 99 Long St., Middleton, Manchester M24 3UR........	15,824	17,676
1886D	Mid-Glamorgan, 4 Gelliwastad Rd., Pontypridd, Glam...........	1,928	4,290
1933	Midland P., 3 Lower High St., Cradley Heath, Warley, Worcs.....	437	519
1880D	Mid-Sussex, Mid-Sussex Hse., 66 Church Rd., Burgess Hill, Sussex...	2,948	3,128
1883	Mitcham, 173 London Rd., Mitcham, Surrey CR4 2JB.............	1,837	1,105
1869D	Monmouthshire, Friars Chambers, Dock St., Newport, Mon. NP1 1PX	6,566	10,221
1866D	Mornington P., 158 Kentish Town Rd., London NW5 2BT..........	10,571	12,560
1866	Musselburgh, 8 Bridge St., Musselburgh...........................	1,302	716
1896D	National Counties, Waterloo Hse., High St., Epsom, Surrey........	26,562	56,531
1884D	Nationwide, New Oxford Hse., High Holborn, London, WC1 6PW..	1,213,781	1,294,440
1877D	Nelson and Premier, 3 Westoe Village, South Shields, Co. Durham...	2,080	2,996
1866D	New Cross, 470 New Cross Rd., London, S.E.14....................	3,258	5,632
1882D	New Swindon, 36 Regent Circus, Swindon, Wilts..................	1,702	2,775
1856D	Newbury, 17–20 Bartholomew St., Newbury, Berks.................	13,443	18,422
1863D	Newcastle and Gateshead, St. Nicholas Sq., Newcastle upon Tyne NE1 1DX....	3,443	4,186
1861D	Newcastle upon Tyne P., 37–41 Grainger St., Newcastle upon Tyne..	17,765	31,883
1876D	North East Globe, 18 Ridley Place, Newcastle upon Tyne NE1 8JW..	2,439	3,293
1866D	North Kent, North Kent Hse., Windmill St., Gravesend, Kent DA12 1AZ....	13,948	11,825
1886	North London, 407 Holloway Rd., London N7 6HJ.................	579	1,353
1877D	North of England, 57 Fawcett St., Sunderland, Co. Durham SR1 1SQ	15,520	23,500
1899D	North Wilts Eq., 18 and 19 Commercial Rd., Swindon, Wilts......	3,619	5,132
1888D	Northampton and Midlands, 60 Gold St., Northampton...........	14,528	15,753
1850D	Northern Rock, Northern Rock Hse., Gosforth, Newcastle upon Tyne NE3 4PL....	184,005	216,851
1852D	Norwich, St. Andrew's Hse., St. Andrew St., Norwich, Norfolk.....	24,029	42,455
1850D	Nottingham, Friar Lane, Nottingham NG1 6DU....................	31,506	43,152
1935D	Nottingham Oddfellows, Imperial Bldg., Victoria St., Nottingham..	3,605	2,630
1849	Nuneaton and Warwickshire, 9 Queen's Rd., Nuneaton, Warws......	889	975
1909	Oldbury Britannia, Britannia Hse., 19 High St., West Bromwich, Staffs.	1,117	1,136
1848D	Otley, 34 Boroughgate, Otley, Yorks.............................	6,119	8,309
1869D	Over Darwen, 24 Railway Rd., Darwen BB3 2RG..................	2,808	2,657
1860D	Oxford Prov., 154 Cowley Rd., Oxford OX4 1HA.................	2,085	2,280
1879D	Paddington, 125 Westbourne Grove, London W2 4UP.............	2,266	4,395
1877D	Padiham, 34 Burnley Rd., Padiham, Lancs........................	4,110	5,706
1853D	Paisley, 7 Glasgow Rd., Paisley, Renfrew........................	6,078	9,148
1879D	Peckham Mut., Hanover Park Hse., 14/16 Hanover Park, London, S.E.15	5,869	6,805
1855D	Peckham P., 6–8 Queens Rd., London SE15 2PP..................	1,816	2,665
1856D	Peebles, 90 High St., Peebles....................................	832	1,153
1877D	Penrith, 7 King St., Penrith, Cumb..............................	2,747	4,306
1860D	Peterborough, 5 Cathedral Sq., Peterborough....................	21,300	28,508

Year Established	Name of Society (abbreviated) Head Office	Share Investors	Assets Total £'000
1884	Pioneer P., 51 Lincoln's Inn Fields, London WC2A 3LZ.............	504	950
1848D	Planet, Planet Hse., 215 Strand, London, WC2....................	25,673	40,702
1875	Poole, 58 Parkstone Road, Poole, Dorset BH15 2QB..............	443	817
1881D	Portman, 40 Portman Sq., London W1H 9FH....................	48,722	79,818
1896D	Portsmouth, 176 London Rd., North End, Portsmouth PO2 9DL....	9,918	17,877
1860D	Principality, Principality Bldgs., Queen St., Cardiff CF1 4NA.....	46,861	64,186
1941D	Property Owners, 4 Cavendish Place, London W1M 0AQ.........	16,890	39,218
1849D	Provincial, Provincial Hse., Market St., Bradford BD1 1NL........	346,361	554,966
1933D	Prudential Inv., 1 Leopold Place, Edinburgh EH7 5JP............	1,074	1,704
1886D	Queen Victoria Street, Pearl Assurance Hse., 1A Katherine St., Croydon CR0 1NX......................................	1,058	1,963
1846D	Ramsbury, The Square, Ramsbury, Marlborough, Wilts. SN8 2PF...	26,712	28,769
1859D	Redditch and Worcester, 5–9 St. Nicholas St., Worcester.........	36,490	39,670
1883	Rowland Hill P., Victoria Hse., Southampton Row, London WC1B 4DW..	783	1,353
1888D	Rowley Regis, 223 Halesowen Rd., Crawley Heath, Warley, Worcs..	9,095	9,561
1854D	Rugby and Warwick, Temple Bldgs., Rugby, Warws..............	39,769	38,301
1861D	Rugby Prov., 34 North St., Rugby, Warwicks..................	3,140	3,340
1850	Rye B., 12 High St., Rye, Sussex............................	818	778
1849D	Saffron Walden and Dt., Market Place, Saffron Walden, Essex......	6,092	8,834
1867D	St. Andrew's, 26 Ridley Place, Newcastle upon Tyne NE1 8DY....	1,247	1,681
1937D	St. Pancras, 200 Finchley Rd., London NW3 6DA..............	3,519	6,217
1850	St. Philip's B., 121–123 Edmund Street, Birmingham B3 2HZ.....	679	1,261
1852	Sandbach, 5 Middlewich Rd., Sandbach, Chesh.................	1,968	2,893
1875D	Sandy, 6 Bedford Rd., Sandy, Beds..........................	2,814	3,337
1846D	Scarborough, York Hse., York Place, Scarborough, Yorks.........	11,230	15,865
1848D	Scottish, 2 York Place, Edinburgh EH1 3ER...................	4,176	5,891
1935D	Sheffield, 66 Campo Lane, Sheffield, Yorks S1 2EG.............	2,030	3,292
1879D	Shepshed, Bull Ring, Shepshed, Loughborough, Leics. LE12 9QD....	4,078	3,602
1864	Shields and Washington, 15 Beach Rd., South Shields..........	551	639
1875D	Shields Commercial, Barrington St., South Shields, Co. Durham.....	2,159	2,946
1853D	Skipton, 50 High St., Skipton, Yorks........................	60,986	93,185
1874	South Metropolitan, 44 Woodcote Rd., Wallington, Surrey.......	278	532
1859D	South of England, 58 King St., Maidenhead, Berks..............	79,266	116,241
1876	South Shields, Sun P., Sun Bldgs., Beach Rd., Sth. Shields, Durham..	505	889
1902D	South Staffordshire, 5 Princess St., Wolverhampton, Staffs. WV1 1HJ	58,274	47,132
1875D	South West Wales, 17 The Kingsway, Swansea, Glam.............	2,911	5,252
1867D	Stafford and County P., 1 Martin St., Stafford.................	3,967	6,853
1877D	Stafford Railway, 4 Market Sq., Stafford.....................	4,421	5,860
1875D	Standard, 64 Church Way, North Shields, Nbld.................	2,365	2,590
1970	Stanley and N.W. Durham, Cromarty Hse., Front St., Stanley, Co. Durham...	1,470	1,633
1878D	Steyning and Sussex County, Bank Hse., 62 High St., Steyning, Sussex	11,182	17,224
1856	Sterlingshire, 20 Barnton St., Sterling.......................	452	641
1876	Stockport, 20 Market Place, Stockport.......................	416	825
1877	Stockport and County P., Carlyle Hse., 109 Wellington Rd. Sth., Stockport, Chesh.....................................	588	844
1898D	Stockport Mersey, 72–74 Wellington Rd. South, Stockport, Chesh. SK1 3SU..	965	1,680
1852D	Stoke-on-Trent P., 66–68 Liverpool Rd., Stoke-on-Trent, Staffs. ST4 1BQ..	1,238	2,125
1889D	Stourbridge, Lye and Dt. P., Victoria Chambers, 97 High St., Stourbridge, Worcs.......................................	4,389	4,832
1882	Strand and County P., Strand Hse., Portugal St., London, WC2A 2HS	519	590
1850D	Stroud, 7 Russell St., Stroud, Glos..........................	15,227	14,180
1901D	Summers, Shotton Steel Works, Shotton, Deeside, Flint CH5 2NH..	7,284	3,934
1853D	Sunderland and Shields, 51 Fawcett St., Sunderland, Co. Durham SR1 1SA...	34,106	40,065
1872D	Sussex Mutual, Sussex Hse., 126–127 Western Rd., Hove, Sussex BN3 1DR..	14,210	33,879
1887	Swansea Albion and Gower, 60 Mansel St., Swansea, Glam.......	559	905
1868D	Swindon P., 1 Commercial Rd., Swindon, Wilts................	3,156	5,205
1904	Sydenham and Dist. P., 72 Sydenham Rd., Sydenham...........	460	580
1970	Target, Target Hse., 7–9 Breams Bldgs., London, EC4A 1EU......	565	670
1854D	Tamworth P.B., 6 Victoria Rd., Tamworth, Staffs..............	3,140	3,474
1966	Teachers, 12 Christchurch Rd., Bournemouth..................	7,904	12,108
1854D	Temperance P., P.O. Box 18, Worthing, Sussex.................	121,588	217,147
1883D	Tewkesbury and Dt., 142–143 High St., Tewkesbury, Glos. GL20 5JP.	2,211	2,605
1901D	Tipton and Coseley, 57–60 High St., Tipton, Staffs. DY4 8HG.....	8,620	6,768
1866D	Tyldesley, 213–215 Elliott St., Tyldesley, Manchester M29 8EB......	4,389	5,625
1877D	Tyne Commercial, 10 Grange Rd. West, Jarrow, Co. Durham......	3,337	3,907
1855D	Tynemouth, 53–55 Howard St., North Shields, Nbld.............	4,071	3,855

Year Established	Name of Society (abbreviated) Head Office	Share Investors	Assets Total £'000
1887D	Tynemouth Victoria, 23 West Percy St., North Shields, Nbld........	2,721	4,073
1861	United Provinces, Hamilton Hse., 56 Hamilton St., Birkenhead, Cheshire L41 5HZ..................................	491	513
1863D	Universal, 36 Grey St., Newcastle upon Tyne NE1 6BT.............	14,463	17,274
1924D	Vernon, 26 St. Petersgate, Stockport, Chesh......................	3,990	6,508
1919D	Victory, Victory Hse', Burrow St., South Shields, Co. Durham......	548	940
1846D	Wakefield, 57 Westgate, Wakefield, Yorks........................	18,427	18,695
1863D	Walsall Mut., 41-45 Bridge St., Walsall, Staffs....................	21,379	22,843
1847D	Waltham Abbey, 5 Church St., Waltham Abbey, Essex..............	6,407	8,592
1877D	Walthamstow, 869 Forest Rd., Walthamstow, London E17 4BB.....	19,841	29,650
1867	Warrington, 3 Springfield St., Warrington.......................	655	671
1857	Wellington (Somerset) and Dist., 15 High St., Wellington, Somerset..	561	621
1878D	Welsh Economic, Old Bank Chambers, Pontypridd, Glam...........	912	1,750
1949D	Wessex P., 115 Old Christchurch Rd., Bournemouth, Hants BH1 1HB	7,422	15,545
1849D	West Bromwich, 321 High St., West Bromwich, Staffs..............	82,615	85,777
1882D	West Cumbria, Carleton Hse., Gray St., Workington, CA14 2LT....	1,961	2,814
1850D	West London, 246 Upper Richmond Rd. West, East Sheen, London, SW14 8AQ....................................	2,022	2,778
1907	Westbury and Dt. P., The Butts, Westbury, Wilts.................	617	946
1862D	Western Counties, 20 The Quay, Bideford, Devon.................	24,407	28,487
1866D	West Yorkshire, Church St., Dewsbury, Yorks....................	25,237	33,096
1873D	Wigan, 14 Library St., Wigan, Lancs............................	2,607	2,994
1875D	Wimbledon, 22A Wimbledon Bridge, London, S.W.19.............	607	1,041
1849D	Wolverhampton, 37-41 Lichfield St., Wolverhampton, Staffs. WV1 1EL	30,241	51,553
1847D	Woolwich Eq., Equitable Hse., London SE18 6AB.................	719,369	923,909

IMMIGRATION STATISTICS, 1974

These figures relate to people subject to immigration control under the Immigration Act 1971, including certain holders of United Kingdom passports: they do not include people who are patrial under Section 2 of the Act.

Country or territory issuing passport	Admitted	Embarked
Australia.....................	190,650	207,876
Bangladesh....................	9,897	9,805
Barbados.....................	5,489	3,458
Canada.......................	251,022	269,582
Cyprus.......................	19,852	12,190
Ghana........................	13,117	11,368
Gibraltar.....................	1,130	2,660
Guyana.......................	4,603	3,122
Hong Kong....................	17,840	14,733
India.........................	97,181	77,854
Jamaica......................	27,847	27,498
Kenya........................	14,528	9,213
Malaysia......................	30,765	22,922
Malta........................	16,037	15,957
Mauritius.....................	14,516	11,996
New Zealand..................	43,474	52,304
Nigeria.......................	33,035	28,199
Rhodesia.....................	800	106
Sierra Leone..................	3,691	2,836
Singapore.....................	13,338	10,688
Sri Lanka.....................	11,295	6,445
Tanzania.....................	8,285	4,532
Trinidad and Tobago...........	10,556	9,531
West Indies Associated States...	2,347	2,833
Uganda.......................	4,131	1,388
Zambia.......................	4,017	2,717
U.K. passport holders..........	26,116	8,503
All other territories...........	8,952	9,097
TOTAL....................	**884,511**	**839,413**

UNIT TRUSTS

A Unit Trust is a method of investment by which money subscribed in varying amounts by individual investors is pooled in a fund, the investment and management of which is subject to the strict legal provisions of a Trust Deed. The fund is invested in carefully-selected stocks and shares by a management company and the investments so acquired are held by a Trustee (usually a bank or insurance company). The management company and the Trustee, who must be effectively independent of each other, are parties to the Trust Deed which must be authorized by the Department of Trade (or the Ministry of Commerce in Northern Ireland) before any public offer of units for sale may be made.

Units are readily marketable, being bought or sold at the price (based on the value of the underlying securities) ruling at the time the order for sale or repurchase is received by the Management Company. The Department of Trade regulates the charges which Unit Trust managers may make. These charges are taken by way of an initial service charge (which is included in the sale price unit), and a semi-annual management fee levied on the value of the fund and taken out of either income or capital. Over a 20-year life of a Trust, the initial service charge, together with management fees, may not total more than 13¼ per cent. In order to avoid the need for quoting unit prices with awkward fractions of a penny the managers are also entitled to round off the price of a unit by 1·25p or 1 per cent., whichever is the lower.

Through his subscription to the Trust Fund each subscriber acquires a fractional interest in the block of securities in which the fund is invested, while the dividends received from the investments form the income of the trust. The net income is paid to all investors in the Trust Fund in proportion to the size of their holdings. The dividend income is either paid directly to the investor every six months, or can be used by arrangement to purchase further units for his account. In either case any unit-holder who is not liable to tax at the basic rate of tax deducted can claim appropriate relief from the Inland Revenue.

The past performance of unit trusts has generally been better than direct investment in stocks and shares but being an investment in equities they cannot escape stock market trends. A unit trust investment neither guarantees an increasing income nor ensures continual capital appreciation. They are essentially a long-term form of investment.

Savings Schemes

Most management companies operate savings schemes whereby an investor is able to make contributions at intervals which are utilized to purchase units at the current price, the cash balance remaining from any such purchase being carried forward and added to the next contribution. Savings schemes can be for a direct purchase of units or linked with life assurance. The latter have provided one of the most rapid growth sectors of the Unit Trust movement in recent years. The unit linked schemes enable a person to accumulate a sum of money for retirement, etc., with the protection of life assurance cover for the duration of the planned period of saving. At the end of this period, the investor receives all the units acquired or their cash value. If death occurs beforehand, the dependents receive all the units bought up to date, plus a cash sum equivalent to the total remaining contributions necessary to have completed the savings programme. Tax relief is available on these contributions as with other life assurance premiums.

Arrangements for Children

In general, units cannot be registered in the name of a child but they can be registered in the name of a parent or any other adult, and the registered holding can be designated with the initials of the child. Alternatively, money can be settled on a child under one of the various children's gift plans operated and the units held in trust. Income distributions, less income tax, are invested in further units, and additional units may be purchased at any time. When the child reaches 18 or some chosen later age, the units become his property.

Association of Unit Trust Managers

The unit trust industry has been in operation for some forty-five years.

The Association of Unit Trust Managers of Park House, 16, Finsbury Circus, EC2M 7JP, was formed on October 13, 1959, and membership is open to any management company of an authorized unit trust scheme. The Association's main object is to act as a consulting body amongst its members in order to agree strict standards of unit trust practices for the protection of the interest of unit holders and to maintain the good name of the Unit Trust industry.

At December 31, 1974, the Association represented 294 of the 360 trusts in existence (82%); 97 per cent of all unit holdings being in these trusts.

The total value of all funds under management was £1.31 billion, and out of a total of 90 management groups five had funds in excess of £100 million; 14 between £10 million and £100 million and 40 between £1 million and £10 million.

The following details relating to the management groups operating in Great Britain and Northern Ireland have been extracted from the *Unit Trust Year Book* 1975, published by Fundex Ltd. (Addresses correct to June 1, 1975.)

Unit Trusts 1974–1975

(With value of funds managed and number of unit holdings as at December 31, 1974.)

*ABACUS ARBUTHNOT LTD., Barnett House, Fountain Street, Manchester M22 2AP. *Funds Managed* £1·6 million; *Holdings* 7,485.

*ABBEY UNIT TRUST MANAGERS LTD., 41 Bishopsgate, London EC2. *Funds Managed* £17·5 million; *Holdings* 4,878.

*ALLIED HAMBRO GROUP, Hambro House, Rayleigh Rd., Hutton, Brentwood, Essex. *Funds Managed* £102·5 million; *Holdings* 109,796.

*ANSBACHER UNIT MANAGEMENT CO. LTD., 1 Noble Street, Gresham Street, London EC2V 7JH. *Funds Managed* £0·2 million; *Holdings* 1 009.

*ARCHWAY UNIT TRUST MANAGERS LTD., 24 St. Mary Axe, London EC3A 8EN. *Funds Managed* £0·7 million; *Holdings* 416.

*BARCLAYS UNICORN LTD., Unicorn House, 252/6 Romford Road, London E7 96B. *Funds Managed* £139·5 million; *Holdings* 290,788.

BISHOPSGATE PROGRESSIVE UNIT TRUST MANAGEMENT CO. LTD., 9 Bishopsgate, London EC2N 3AD. *Funds Managed* £2·5 million; *Holdings* 1,600.

*BRANDTS LIMITED, 36 Fenchurch St., London EC3P 3AS. *Funds Managed* £1·3 million; *Holdings* 587.

BRIDGE TALISMAN FUND MANAGERS LTD., Plantation House, 5–8 Mincing Lane, London EC3M 3DX. *Funds Managed* £3·1 million; *Holdings* 2,400.

★BRITISH LIFE OFFICE LTD. (THE), Reliance House, Tunbridge Wells, Kent. *Funds Managed £3·7 million; Holdings* 627.

★CABOT UNIT TRUST MANAGEMENT CO. LTD., The Bristol and West Building, Broad Quay, Bristol 1. *Funds Managed £1·0 million; Holdings* 494.

CANADA LIFE UNIT TRUST MANAGERS LTD., 6 Charles II St., London SW1Y 4AD. *Funds Managed £2·3 million; Holdings* 653.

CARLIOL UNIT FUND MANAGERS LTD., " D " Floor, Milburn House, Dean Street, Newcastle upon Tyne NE1 1LU. *Funds Managed £0·4 million; Holdings* 250.

★CHARTERHOUSE JAPHET UNIT MANAGEMENT LTD., 1 Paternoster Row, St. Pauls, London EC4P 4HP. *Funds Managed £2·2 million; Holdings* 2,483.

★CONFEDERATION FUNDS MANAGEMENT LTD., 120 Regent Street, London W1. *Funds Managed £0·7 million; Holdings* 155.

★COSMOPOLITAN FUND MANAGERS LTD., 56 Copthall Avenue, London EC2 7JX. *Funds Managed £0·2 million; Holdings* 998.

COYNE INVESTMENT MANAGEMENT LTD., Berendsey House, 31–33 High Street, Carshalton, Surrey. *Funds Managed £0·2 million; Holdings* 308.

★CRESCENT UNIT TRUST MANAGERS LTD., 4 Melville Crescent, Edinburgh EH3. *Funds Managed £8·3 million; Holdings* 19,575.

DISCRETIONARY UNIT FUND MANAGERS LTD., Finsbury House, 22 Blomfield Street, London EC2M 7AL. *Funds Managed £1·1 million; Holdings* 805.

★DRAYTON UNIT TRUST MANAGERS LTD., Individual House, 43–45 South Street, Eastbourne, Sussex. *Funds Managed £5·2 million; Holdings* 10,608.

★EMBLEM FUND MANAGEMENT CO. LTD. (THE), 20 Copthall Avenue, London EC2. *Funds Managed £0·2 million; Holdings* 207(1973).

★EQUITAS SECURITIES LTD., 41 Bishopsgate, London EC2. *Funds Managed £0·6 million; Holdings* 240.

EQUITY AND LAW UNIT TRUST MANAGERS LTD., Amersham Rd., High Wycombe, Bucks. *Funds Managed £2·4 million; Holdings* 444.

FIRST NATIONAL EQUITIES LTD., First National House, Finsbury Pavement, London EC2P 2JH. *Funds Managed £0·06 million; Holdings* 91.

FOUNDERS COURT MANAGEMENT SERVICES LTD., Founders Court, Lothbury, London EC2R 7HE. *Funds Managed £0·5 million; Holdings* 207.

FRAMLINGTON UNIT MANAGEMENT LTD., Spencer House, 4 South Place, London EC2. *Funds Managed £1·0 million; Holdings* 1,955.

★FRIENDS' PROVIDENT UNIT TRUST MANAGERS LTD., 7 Leadenhall St., London EC3P 3BA. *Funds Managed £0·4 million; Holdings* 693.

★G and A UNIT TRUST MANAGERS LTD., Hambro House, Rayleigh Road, Hutton, Brentwood, Essex. *Funds Managed £1·2 million; Holdings* 7,951.

★GARTMORE FUND MANAGERS LTD., 2 St. Mary Axe, London EC3A 8BP. *Funds Managed £0·46 million; Holdings* 183.

G.T. UNIT MANAGERS LTD., (6th floor), 16 St. Martins-Le-Grand, London EC1. *Funds Managed £0·6 million; Holdings* 686.

★GUARDIAN ROYAL EXCHANGE UNIT MANAGERS LTD., The Royal Exchange, London EC3P 3DN. *Funds Managed £13·9 million; Holdings* 1,968.

HENDERSON GROSS FUND MANAGEMENT LTD., 28 Austin Friars, London EC2. *Funds Managed £2·0 million; Holdings* 52.

★HENDERSON UNIT TRUST MANAGEMENT LTD., 11 Austin Friars, London EC2N 2ED. *Funds Managed £16·3 million; Holdings* 59,996.

★HILL SAMUEL UNIT TRUST MANAGERS LTD., 45 Beech Street, London EC2P 2LX. *Funds Managed £43·1 million; Holdings* 45,625.

★INTEL FUNDS (MANAGEMENT) LTD., 15 Christopher St., London EC2. *Funds Managed £1·9 million; Holdings* 1,372.

IONIAN UNIT TRUST MANAGEMENT LTD., 64 Coleman St., London EC2. *Funds Managed £1·3 million; Holdings* 295.

JASCOT SECURITIES LTD., 21 Young St., Edinburgh EH2 4HU. *Funds Managed £6·1 million; Holdings* 19,293.

★JOHN GOVETT UNIT MANAGEMENT LTD., Winchester House, 77 London Wall, London EC2N 1DH. *Funds Managed £4·6 million; Holdings* 4,950.

★KEY FUND MANAGERS LTD., 25 Milk Street, London EC2V 8JE. *Funds Managed £1·8 million; Holdings* 610.

★KLEINWORT BENSON UNIT MANAGERS LTD., P.O. Box 560, 20 Fenchurch St., London EC3M 3DB. *Funds Managed £0·3 million; Holdings* 35.

★L & C UNIT TRUST MANAGEMENT LTD., The Stock Exchange, London EC2N. *Funds Managed £0·4 million; Holdings* 198.

LAWSON SECURITIES LTD., 63 George Street, Edinburgh EH2 2JG. *Funds Managed £1·2 million; Holdings* 2,509.

LEGAL AND GENERAL—TYNDALL FUND MANAGERS LTD., 18 Canynge Rd., Bristol BS99 7UA. *Funds Managed £1·5 million; Holdings* 751.

★LLOYDS BANK UNIT TRUST MANAGERS LTD., 71 Lombard St., London EC3P 3BS. *Funds Managed £22·4 million; Holdings* 82,126.

LLOYDS LIFE UNIT TRUST MANAGERS LTD., 72–80 Gatehouse Road, Aylesbury, Buckinghamshire. *Funds Managed £0·1 million; Holdings* 6.

★LONDON WALL GROUP OF UNIT TRUSTS LTD., 1 Finsbury Square, London EC2A 1PD. *Funds Managed £9·3 million; Holdings* 30,778.

★M AND G GROUP LTD., Three Quays, Tower Hill, London EC3R 6BQ. *Funds Managed £143·3 million; Holdings* 132,075.

METROPOLITAN EXEMPT FUND MANAGERS LTD., 28 Haymarket, London SW1Y 4SR. *Funds Managed £1·1 million; Holdings* 32.

★MINSTER FUND MANAGERS LTD., Minster House, Arthur St., London EC4R 9BH. *Funds Managed £0·8 million; Holdings* 148.

★MORGAN GRENFELL FUNDS (MANAGEMENT) LTD., 23 Great Winchester Street, London EC2P 2AX. *Funds Managed £3·1 million; Holdings* 2,367.

★MUTUAL UNIT TRUST MANAGERS LTD., 4 Token House Buildings, Kings Arms Yard, London EC2R 7AD. *Funds Managed £5·0 million; Holdings* 17,477.

NATIONAL PROVIDENT INVESTMENT MANAGERS LTD., 48 Gracechurch St., London EC3. *Funds Managed £1·1 million; Holdings* 670.

★NATIONAL WESTMINSTER UNIT TRUST MANAGERS LTD., 41 Lothbury, London EC2. *Funds Managed £29·0 million; Holdings* 66,970.

N.E.L. TRUST MANAGERS LTD., Milton Court Dorking, Surrey. *Funds Managed £3·1 million; Holdings* 1,241.

NEW COURT FUND MANAGERS LTD., New Court, St. Swithin's Lane, London EC4. *Funds Managed £19·1 million; Holdings* 3,771.

★NORWICH GENERAL TRUST LTD., Surrey Street, Norwich NR1 3NJ. *Funds Managed £0·9 million; Holdings* 2.

★OCEANIC UNIT TRUST MANAGERS LTD., 3–5 Norwich Street, Fetter Lane, London EC4P 4DA. *Funds Managed £7·9 million; Holdings* 57,079.

★PEARL MONTAGU TRUST MANAGERS LTD., 114 Old Broad St., London EC2P 2HY. *Funds Managed £1·1 million; Holdings* 3,039.

*PELICAN UNITS ADMINISTRATION LTD., 21 Spring Gardens, Manchester M2 1FB. *Funds Managed* £0·9 million; *Holdings* 257.

*PERPETUAL UNIT TRUST MANAGEMENT LTD., 48–50 Hart Street, Henley-on-Thames, Oxon RG9 2AZ. *Funds Managed* £0·05 million; *Holdings* 22.

PICCADILLY UNIT TRUST MANAGERS LTD., 63 London Wall, London EC2. *Funds Managed* £1·0 million; *Holdings* 2,070.

PORTFOLIO FUND MANAGERS LTD., 10 Charterhouse Square, London EC1M 6JU. *Funds Managed* £2·5 million; *Holdings* 1,403.

PRACTICAL INVESTMENT CO. LTD., Europe House, World Trade Centre, London E1. *Funds Managed* £14·8 million; *Holdings* 4,406.

PROVINCIAL LIFE INVESTMENT CO. LTD., 222 Bishopsgate, London EC2M 4JS. *Funds Managed* £3·9 million; *Holdings* 956.

PRUDENTIAL UNIT TRUST MANAGERS LTD., Holborn Bars, London EC1N 2NH. *Funds Managed* £6·7 million; *Holdings* 2,055.

*QUILTER MANAGEMENT COMPANY LTD., Gerrard House, 31–35 Gresham Street, London EC2V 7LH. *Funds Managed* £0·5 million; *Holdings* 408.

RAPHAEL UNIT TRUST MANAGERS LTD., 10 Throgmorton Avenue, London EC2N 2DP. *Funds Managed* £0·08 million; *Holdings* 49.

*REMIGIUM MANAGEMENT LTD., Woolgate House, Coleman Street, London EC2. *Funds Managed* £0·5 million; *Holdings* n.a.

ROTHSCHILD AND LOWNDES MANAGEMENT LTD., New Court, St. Swithin's Lane, London EC4. *Funds Managed* £7·0 million; *Holdings* 127.

*ROWE & PITMAN MANAGEMENT LTD., Woolgate House, Coleman Street, London EC2. *Funds Managed* £2·15 million; *Holdings* 56.

*SAVE AND PROSPER GROUP LTD., 4 Great St. Helen's, London EC3P 3EP. *Funds Managed* £343·5 million; *Holdings* 372,091.

*SCHLESINGER TRUST MANAGERS LTD., 140 South Street, Dorking, Surrey. *Funds Managed* £4·3 million; *Holdings* 6,301.

*J. HENRY SCHRODER WAGG AND CO. LTD., 120 Cheapside, London EC2V 6DS. *Funds Managed* £24·7 million; *Holdings* 11,470.

*SCOTTISH EQUITABLE FUND MANAGERS LTD., 28 St. Andrew Square, Edinburgh EH2 1YF. *Funds Managed* £0·9 million; *Holdings* 53.

SEBAG UNIT TRUST MANAGERS LTD., P.O. BOX 511,

Bucklesbury House, 3 Queen Victoria Street, London EC4N 8DX. *Funds Managed* £0·6 million; *Holdings* 270.

SECURITY SELECTION LTD., 8 Crescent Minories, London EC3N 2LY. *Funds Managed* £0·1 million; *Holdings* 35.

*SLATER WALKER TRUST MANAGEMENT LTD., 130 St. Paul's Church Yard, London EC4. *Funds Managed* £125·3 million; *Holdings* 299,341.

*STEWART UNIT TRUST MANAGERS LTD., 45 Charlotte Square, Edinburgh EH2 4NX. *Funds Managed* £1·4 million; *Holdings* 1,530.

*STRATTON TRUST MANAGERS LTD., 88 Leadenhall Street, London EC3A 3DT. *Funds Managed* £2·0 million; *Holdings* 763.

SUN ALLIANCE FUND MANAGEMENT LTD., 1 Bartholomew Lane, London EC2. *Funds Managed* £0·9 million; *Holdings* 400.

*TARGET TRUST MANAGERS LTD., Target House, 7/9 Breams Buildings, London EC4 1EU. *Funds Managed* £35·7 million; *Holdings* 82,600.

*TARGET TRUST MANAGERS (SCOTLAND) LTD., 19 Atholl Crescent, Edinburgh EH2 8HO. *Funds Managed* £1·8 million; *Holdings* 3,800.

*TRADES UNION UNIT TRUST MANAGERS LTD., 100 Wood St., London EC2P 2AJ. *Funds Managed* £3·5 million; *Holdings* 457.

*TRANSATLANTIC AND GENERAL SECURITIES CO. LTD., 91–99 New London Road, Chelmsford, Essex. *Funds Managed* £14·3 million; *Holdings* 7,050.

*TRUSTEE SAVINGS BANKS UNIT TRUST MANAGERS LTD., White Bear House, 21 Chantry Way, Andover, Hants. *Funds Managed* £17·0 million; *Holdings* 56,447.

TYNDALL MANAGERS LTD., 18 Canynge Rd., Bristol BS99 7UA. *Funds Managed* £34·5 million; *Holdings* 26,000.

TYNDALL ULSTER MANAGERS LTD., c/o Harris, Marrian & Co. Ltd., 140/142 Gt. Victoria St., Belfast BT2. *Funds Managed* £3·7 million; *Holdings* 263.

*ULSTER BANK UNIT TRUST MANAGERS LTD., P.O. Box 233, Waring St., Belfast BT1 2ER. *Funds Managed* £0·7 million; *Holdings* 2,395.

UNIT TRUST ACCOUNTING & MANAGEMENT LTD., Plantation House, 5–8 Mincing Lane, London EC3M 3DX. *Funds Managed* £0·7 million; *Holdings* 690.

* *Members of the Association of Unit Trust Managers.*

TABLE OF INCOME OR WAGES

Per Year	Per Month	Per Week	Per Day	Per Year	Per Month	Per Week	Per Day	Per Year	Per Month	Per Week	Per Day
£	£	£	£	£	£	£	£	£	£	£	£
0·50	0·04	0·01	—	8·00	0·67	0·15	0·02	18·00	1·50	0·35	0·05
1·00	0·08	0·02	—	8·40	0·70	0·16	0·03	18·90	1·57	0·36	0·05
1·50	0·13	0·03	—	8·50	0·71	0·16	0·03	19·00	1·58	0·37	0·05
2·00	0·17	0·04	—	9·00	0·75	0·17	0·03	20·00	1·67	0·38	0·05
2·10	0·17	0·05	—	9·45	0·79	0·18	0·03	30·00	2·50	0·58	0·08
2·50	0·21	0·05	—	10·00	0·83	0·19	0·03	40·00	3·33	0·77	0·11
3·00	0·25	0·06	—	10·50	0·87	0·20	0·03	50·00	4·17	0·96	0·14
3·15	0·26	0·06	0·01	11·00	0·92	0·21	0·03	60·00	5·00	1·15	0·17
3·50	0·29	0·07	0·01	11·55	0·96	0·23	0·03	70·00	5·83	1·35	0·19
4·00	0·33	0·07	0·01	12·00	1·00	0·23	0·03	80·00	6·67	1·54	0·22
4·20	0·35	0·08	0·01	12·60	1·05	0·24	0·03	90·00	7·50	1·73	0·25
4·50	0·37	0·09	0·01	13·00	1·08	0·25	0·04	100·00	8·33	1·92	0·27
5·00	0·42	0·10	0·01	13·65	1·14	0·26	0·04	200·00	16·67	3·85	0·55
5·25	0·44	0·10	0·01	14·00	1·17	0·27	0·04	300·00	25·00	5·77	0·82
5·50	0·46	0·12	0·01	14·70	1·23	0·28	0·04	400·00	33·33	7·69	1·10
6·00	0·50	0·12	0·02	15·00	1·25	0·29	0·04	500·00	41·67	9·62	1·37
6·30	0·53	0·13	0·02	15·75	1·31	0·30	0·04	600·00	50·00	11·54	1·64
6·50	0·54	0·13	0·02	16·00	1·33	0·31	0·05	700·00	58·33	13·46	1·92
7·00	0·58	0·13	0·02	16·80	1·40	0·32	0·05	800·00	66·67	15·38	2·19
7·35	0·61	0·14	0·02	17·00	1·42	0·33	0·05	900·00	75·00	17·31	2·47
7·50	0·63	0·15	0·02	17·85	1·49	0·34	0·05	1000·00	83·33	19·23	2·74

Legal Notes

IMPORTANT

The Purpose of these notes is to outline some of the more common parts of the law as they may affect the average person, and they are, of course believed to be correct at the time of going to press. The law is constantly developing and changing, however, and it is dangerous for the layman to seek to be his own lawyer— he may not have access to completely up to date books and his case may, because of its special facts, come within an exception to the general rules set out herein.

It is always best to take expert advice, and if you have a Solicitor who has acted for you in the past you should take any legal problems you have to him. If you do not have a Solicitor a friend may be able to recommend one. Failing this your local Citizens' Advice Bureau (whose address can be obtained from the Telephone Directory or from any Post Office or Town Hall) has a list of Solicitors in your area who deal with that particular type of problem which you have. If you are not able to find a Solicitor in any of these ways you should ask for help in doing so from The Law Society, 113 Chancery Lane, London, W.C.2 or 27 Drumsheugh Gardens, Edinburgh.

The Legal Aid and Legal Advice and Assistance schemes (see pages 1178/79) exist to make the help of the trained lawyer available to everyone whatever their means as of right. The best policy is if in doubt go to a Solicitor without delay—timely advice will set your mind at rest but sitting on your rights can mean that you lose them.

Remember also that it is not necessary for a dispute to have arisen before you go to a Solicitor—the Legal Advice and Assistance Scheme enables him to advise you on your rights say under a tenancy agreement, the estate of a deceased person or in connection with matrimonial and consumer matters, and to write letters or take other steps on your behalf. He can also act for you where there is no question of a dispute at all, e.g. in the making of a will.

Your entitlement to take advantage of the Scheme depends on your means (see below) but a Solicitor will be able to tell you whether you are covered by it.

BRITISH NATIONALITY AND CITIZENSHIP OF THE UNITED KINGDOM AND COLONIES

General.—The law as to British Nationality is now to be found mainly in the British Nationality Act 1948, which came into force on Jan. 1, 1949.

The Act introduces a new term, " citizenship." Every person who under the Act is a citizen of the United Kingdom and Colonies, or any citizen (by virtue of legislation in that country) of Canada, Australia, New Zealand, India, Southern Rhodesia, Sri Lanka, Ghana, Malaysia, Cyprus, Nigeria, Sierra Leone, Tanzania, Jamaica, Trinidad and Tobago, Uganda, Kenya, Malawi, Zambia, Malta, Gambia, Guyana, Botswana, Lesotho, Singapore, Barbados, Mauritius, Swaziland, Tonga, Fiji, The Bahamas, Bangladesh and Grenada (hereafter referred to as " the Dominions ") has by virtue of that citizenship the status of a British subject and may be known either as a British subject or as a Commonwealth citizen. Under s. 2 of the Newfoundland (Consequential Provisions) Act 1950, potential citizens of Newfoundland under the British Nationality Act 1948, are deemed to have been potential citizens of Canada.

Nationality *before* Jan. 1, 1949, was determined mainly by the British Nationality and Status of Aliens Acts 1914–1943, though these Acts did not affect the status of any person born *before* Jan. 1, 1915.

Retention of nationality by persons born in or who are citizens of Eire (now by virtue of the Ireland Act 1949, styled the Republic of Ireland).

By the Ireland Act 1949, a person who was born before Dec. 6, 1922, in what is now the Republic of Ireland (Eire) and was a British subject immediately before Jan. 1, 1949, is not deemed to have ceased to be a British subject unless either (i) he was domiciled in the Irish Free State on Dec. 6, 1922, or (ii) was on or after April 10, 1935, and before Jan. 1, 1949, permanently resident there, or (iii) had before Jan. 1, 1949, been registered as a citizen of Eire under the laws of that country.

In addition, by the British Nationality Act 1948, any citizen of Eire who immediately before Jan. 1, 1949, was also a British subject can retain that status by submitting at any time a claim to the Home Secretary on any of the following grounds: (a) he has been in the service of the United Kingdom government; (b) he holds a British passport issued in the United Kingdom or in any colony, protectorate, United Kingdom mandated or trust territory; (c) he has associations by way of desent, residence or otherwise with any such place; or on complying with similar legislation in any of the " Dominions."

Citizenship of the United Kingdom and Colonies

In the majority of cases, a person who is a British subject becomes also a " citizen," either of one of the " Dominions " by virtue of legislation in that country, or of the United Kingdom and Colonies under the 1948 Act. In the latter case, citizenship is acquired by:—

1. *Birth* on or after Jan. 1, 1949, in the United Kingdom and Colonies (which term does not include the " Dominions "), except

(a) children born to non-citizen fathers enjoying diplomatic immunity from suit or legal process;

(b) children born to fathers who are enemy aliens in enemy occupied territory.

2. *Descent*, if the father was a citizen by *birth*. If the father was a citizen by *descent* only, the child acquires citizenship by descent if either:—

(a) the child is or his father was born in a protectorate, protected state, mandated territory or trust territory, or in a foreign country where Her Majesty then had jurisdiction over British subjects; or

(b) the birth (occurring elsewhere than (a)) is registered at a United Kingdom consulate within one year; or

(c) the father is at the time of birth in the service of the Crown under Her Majesty's United Kingdom government; or

(d) the child is born in one of the " Dominions " in which a citizenship law has then taken effect and does not become a citizen thereof by birth.

3. *Registration* by the Home Secretary upon application by:—

(a) a citizen of one of the " Dominions " or of the Republic of Ireland who can show that he has been (a) ordinarily resident in the United Kingdom; or (b) in Crown service under Her Majesty's Government in the United Kingdom; or (c) partly the one and partly the other throughout the period of five years ending with the date of his application, or such shorter period so ending as the Home Secretary may in the special circumstances of any particular case accept; or, in certain circumstances, if he is serving under an international organization of which the United Kingdom government is a member, or is in the employment of a body established in the United Kingdom;

By the provisions of the Immigration Act 1971, registration as of right in these circumstances is restricted to Commonwealth citizens who are " patrial ", i.e. born to or legally adopted by a parent who at the time of the birth or adoption had citizenship of the United Kingdom and Colonies by his birth in the United Kingdom. In the case of non-patrials, there are additional conditions and the Home Secretary has a discretion whether or not to register.

(b) a woman married to a United Kingdom, etc. citizen. (A woman who marries on or after Jan. 1, 1949, does not by virtue of that marriage acquire citizenship.)

A minor child of a citizen can be registered upon application being made by his parent or guardian.

A person in respect of whom a recommendation for deportation or a deportation order is in force under the Commonwealth Immigrants Act 1962, is not entitled to be registered, although the Home Secretary may register such a person.

4. *Naturalization.*—In order to be eligible for a certificate of naturalization an alien must:—

(a) during the eight years preceding his application have resided for not less than five years (of which not less than one year immediately preceding the application *must* have been spent in the United Kingdom) in the United Kingdom or in any colony, protectorate, United Kingdom mandated or trust territory, or have been for five years in the service of the Crown; and

(b) be of good character and have a sufficient knowledge of the English language; and

(c) intend to reside in the United Kingdom or any colony, etc., or to enter or continue in the service of the Crown or in the service of certain organizations.

A British protected person who satisfies (b) and (c) above can apply for naturalization if he can show that he has been (a) ordinarily resident in the United Kingdom; or (b) in Crown service under Her Majesty's Government in the United Kingdom; or (c) partly the one and partly the other throughout the period of five years ending with the date of his application, or such shorter period as the Home Secretary may in particular case accept.

Instructions for the guidance of persons desiring to apply for a Certificate of Naturalization are supplied with the form of application which may be obtained from H.M. Stationery Office.

5. *Incorporation of Territory* when citizenship is granted to such persons as are specified by Order in Council.

6. *Transitional provisions*, which confer citizenship on a person who was a British subject immediately before Jan. 1, 1949, if either:—

(i) (a) he would, if born after that date, have qualified for citizenship by birth; or

(b) he is a person naturalized in the United Kingdom and Colonies; or

(c) he became a British subject by reason of annexation of territory which on Jan. 1, 1949, was included in the United Kingdom and Colonies; or

(ii) at the time of his birth his father was a British subject and possessed any of the above qualifications; or

(iii) he was born within territory comprised on Jan. 1, 1949, in a protectorate, protected state or United Kingdom trust territory; or

(iv) he was not on that date a citizen or potential citizen of one of the " Dominions "; or

(v) being a woman, had before Jan. 1, 1949, been married to a man who becomes, or would but for his death have become, a citizen.

A British subject who is merely a potential citizen of one of the " Dominions " continues as a British subject without citizenship until he becomes a citizen of such " Dominion " or of the Republic of Ireland, or an alien. If none of these has happened at the date when a citizenship law is passed in the country of which he is potentially a citizen, he becomes a citizen by descent of the United Kingdom and Colonies.

A woman who lost British nationality by reason of marriage to an alien regained it on Jan. 1, 1949.

By the Adoption Act 1958 an adopted child becomes a citizen of the United Kingdom and Colonies as from the date of the adoption order if the adopter or, in the case of a joint adoption, the male adopter, is a citizen of the United Kingdom and Colonies.

Citizenship of the United Kingdom and Colonies can be lost—

(i) by declaration in the prescribed manner by a person who is also a citizen of a " Dominion " or of the Republic of Ireland or a national of a foreign country. The Home Secretary can withhold registration of the declaration in time of war. Under the British Nationality Act 1964 a person who has ceased to be a citizen of the United Kingdom and Colonies as a result of a declaration of renunciation is entitled to registration as a citizen of the United Kingdom and Colonies if he can satisfy the Home Secretary on a number of matters;

(ii) where the Home Secretary is satisfied that citizenship by registration or naturalization was obtained by fraud, false representation, etc.;

(iii) by the Home Secretary depriving a *naturalized* person of citizenship is such person has:—

(a) shown himself by act or speech to be disloyal or disaffected towards Her Majesty; or

(b) in time of war, traded with the enemy; or

(c) within five years after becoming naturalized, been sentenced in any country to a term of twelve months' imprisonment; or

(d) continuously resided in foreign countries for seven years, and during that period has neither at any time been in the service of the Crown or of certain international organizations, nor registered annually at a United Kingdom consulate his intention to retain citizenship;

and the Home Secretary is satisfied that it is not conducive to the public good that such person should retain his citizenship;

(iv) where a naturalized person is deprived of citizenship of a " Dominion " or of the Republic of Ireland, the Home Secretary can also deprive him of citizenship of the United Kingdom and Colonies.

(v) Under a series of Acts, 1958–1973, which contain special provisions relating to Ghana, Cyprus, Nigeria, Sierra Leone, Tanzania, Jamaica, Trinidad and Tobago, Uganda, Malaysia, Kenya, Malawi, Zambia, Malta, Gambia, Guyana, Botswana, Lesotho, Barbados, Aden, Perim and Kuria Muria Islands, Mauritius, Swaziland, Fiji, The Bahamas and Bangladesh.

STATUS OF ALIENS.—Property may be held by an alien in the same manner as by a natural-born British subject, but he may not hold public office, exercise the franchise or own a British ship or aircraft. The Republic of Ireland Act 1949 declares that the Republic, though not part of H.M. Dominions, is not a foreign country, and any reference to an Act of Parliament to foreigners, aliens, foreign countries, etc., shall be construed accordingly.

CONSUMER LAW

1. THE SUPPLY OF GOODS

(a) The Sale of Goods Act 1893 as amended by the Supply of Goods (Implied Terms) Act 1973 provides protection to the purchaser of goods, by implying certain terms into every contract for the Sale of Goods. These implied terms are:—

(i) A condition that the seller will pass good title to the buyer (unless the seller agrees to transfer only such title as he or his principal has) and warranties that the goods will be free from undisclosed encumbrances, and that the buyer will enjoy quiet possession of the goods.

(ii) Where there is a sale of goods by description, a condition that the goods will correspond with that description, and where the sale is by sample and description, a condition that the bulk of the goods shall correspond with both sample and description.

(iii) Where the seller sells goods in the course of a business, a condition that the goods will be of merchantable quality, unless before the contract is made, the buyer has examined the goods and ought to have noticed the defect, or the seller has specifically drawn the attention of the buyer to the defect. Merchantable quality means fit for the purpose for which goods of the kind are commonly bought, taking into account any description applied to them, the price and other relevant circumstances.

(iv) A condition that where the seller sells goods in the course of a business, the goods are reasonably fit for any purpose made known to the seller by the buyer, unless the buyer does not rely on the sellers skill and judgment, or it would be unreasonable for him to do so.

(v) Where there is a sale of goods by sample, conditions that the bulk of the goods shall correspond with the sample in quality, that the buyer will have a reasonable opportunity of comparing the bulk with the sample, and that the goods are free from any defect rendering them unmerchantable, which would not be apparent from the sample.

For these purposes, the broad difference between a condition and a warranty is that the remedy for a breach of an implied condition may enable the buyer to reject the goods and recover damages if he has suffered loss whereas the remedy for a breach of warranty will only enable the buyer to recover damages.

It is possible for a seller to exclude some of the above terms from a contract, subject to restrictions imposed by the 1973 Act given below. These restrictions give more protection to a consumer sale than a non-consumer sale. A consumer sale is a sale by a seller in the course of a business where the goods are of a type ordinarily bought for private use or consumption, and are sold to a person who does not buy or hold himself out as buying them in the course of a business. A sale by auction or competitive tender is never a consumer sale.

The 1973 Act prohibits the exclusion of the implied terms given in (ii) to (v) above, in consumer sales. In non-consumer sales, terms purporting to exclude these implied terms, may be relied upon only to the extent that it would be reasonable to allow reliance. The Act provides guidelines for determining whether it would be reasonable to allow reliance. The implied terms in (i) above cannot be excluded in consumer or non-consumer sales.

(b) *Trading Stamps.*—The 1973 Act provides protection for a person taking goods in exchange for trading stamps, and implies warranties as to title, freedom from encumbrances, quiet possession and merchantable quality, similar to those implied by the Sale of Goods Act.

(c) The Trade Descriptions Act 1968 provides that it is a criminal offence for a trader or businessman to apply a false trade description to any goods, or to supply or offer to supply any goods to which a false trade description has been applied. A trade description includes a description as to quantity, size, method, place and date of manufacture, other history, composition, other physical characteristics, fitness for purpose, behaviour or accuracy, testing or approval. Prosecutions are brought by Inspectors of Weights and Measures.

(d) The Fair Trading Act 1973 is also designed to protect the consumer. It provides for the appointment of a Director General of Fair Trading, whose duties include keeping under review commercial activities in the U.K. relating to the supply of goods or services to consumers, and to collect information to discover practices that may adversely affect the economic interests of the consumer. He may refer certain consumer trade practices to the Consumer Protection Advisory Committee, or, of his own initiative take proceedings against firms that are trading unfairly. He may also publish information and advice to consumers. Examples of practices with which he may be concerned include the use of void exclusion clauses, double pricing, false bottoms in bottles, and the size or complexity of print and wording.

Scotland

The Sale of Goods Act, 1893, as amended by the Supply of Goods (Implied Terms) Act 1973, the Trading Stamp Act, 1964, the Trade Description Act, 1968, and the Fair Trading Act, 1973, all apply with some modification to Scotland. For example, it is not necessary in Scotland to distinguish between the words condition and warranty. The remedies of the buyer in both cases are the same, that is, he can either within a reasonable time reject the goods and treat the contract as repudiated, or retain the goods and treat the failure to perform such material part as a breach which may give rise to a claim for compensation or damages.

2. HIRE PURCHASE

England and Wales

At present, protection of the hirer against unscrupulous dealings and against delivery of shoddy goods is given by the Hire-Purchase Act, 1965, which applies to hire-purchase agreements under which the hire-purchase price, *i.e.*, the total sum payable by the hirer to complete the purchase of the goods, does not exceed £2,000. The Act also provides that where the hirer is a body corporate, the Act is not to apply at all.

Before any agreement is made, the owner of the goods must state in writing to the hirer the cash price at which the goods can be purchased, and the agreement must be in writing signed by the hirer himself and by or on behalf of the owner and any guarantor. The agreement must contain (i) the cash price, (ii) the hire-purchase price, (iii) the amount of each instalment, (iv) when each instalment falls due, (v) a list of the goods, and (vi) a notice informing the hirer of his rights to terminate the agreement (*below*), and of the restrictions on the owner's right to recover the goods (*below*). If the agreement is complete as soon as the hirer signs it he must be given a copy there and then; in all other cases he must be given one copy when he signs and another within seven days of the completion of the agreement. There are also Department of Trade and Industry regulations dealing with such matters as the size of the print. In breach of any of these conditions the owner can neither recover the goods from the hirer nor enforce the agreement or any security given, although the Court can dispense with any of the conditions save that as to the signed agreement. The same results ensures (while default continues) if the owner fails without reasonable cause within four days after written request (with a tender of 12½p for expenses) to supply to the hirer a copy of the agreement and a statement of amounts paid, in arrear, and not yet payable. Before the last instalment becomes due, the hirer may by writing determine the agreement, and, although he remains liable for any instalments already due, he will be under no further obligation *under the agreement*. Under the Act, however, he must allow the owner to retake the goods and, if one-half of the hire-purchase price exceeds the total of the sums paid and due he must pay the difference to the owner unless the court considers that a lesser sum is sufficient to compensate the owner. These rights of the hirer cannot be taken away from him, but he can enforce more favourable rights (if any) under the agreement.

An important new provision in the Act gives the hirer the right to cancel the agreement and recover all sums paid if he signed it at a place other than trade premises. This right (which was designed to cover the activities of door-step salesmen) must be exercised within 4 days of receiving the second copy.

Any provision in the agreement giving the owner a right to enter any premises for the purpose of seizing the goods is invalidated by the Act. Further, even though the agreement may have been terminated because the hirer has broken it, or because the owner has exercised a right to terminate it, if one-third of the hire-purchase price has been paid or tendered, the owner cannot recover the goods otherwise than by action in a County Court, in which the Court can ensure that the hirer is fairly treated. If the owner disregards this provision, the hirer cannot recover the goods, but can recover all sums paid under the agreement.

The Trade Descriptions Act, 1968, further protects the consumer by making it a criminal offence for traders falsely to describe or advertise the quantity or price of goods or services; prosecutions are brought by Inspectors of Weights and Measures. The Act provides no civil remedies.

An important new provision is the Supply of Goods (Implied Terms) Act 1973 which applies to agreements made on or after 18th May 1973. Sections 8–12 which apply to all hire-purchase agreements whether governed by the 1965 Act or not provide that clauses purporting to exclude the owner from liability for defects in the goods shall be void in the case of consumer agreements, and in non-consumer agreements are valid only if they are fair and reasonable in the circumstances.

Consumer Credit Act. This Act has received the Royal Assent, but most of its provisions are not yet in force. It provides a new system for the protection of the consumer, of licensing and control of all matters relating to the provision of credit, or the supply of goods on hire or hire-purchase, administered by the Director-General of Fair Trading. The Act takes the place of previous Acts of Parliament relating to moneylenders, pawnbrokers and hire-purchase traders, and the protection provided by the Trade Description Act 1968 and Supply of Goods (Implied Terms) Act 1973 will be retained. The Act extends to the United Kingdom.

Scotland

The Hire Purchase (Scotland) Act 1965 provides a Scots code corresponding to, but not identical with English law. The Supply of Goods (Implied Terms) Act 1973 also applies to Scotland.

The Sale of Goods Act, 1893, as amended by the Supply of Goods (Implied Terms) Act, 1973, the Trading Stamp Act, 1964, the Trade Description Act, 1968, and the Fair Trading Act, 1973, all apply with little modification to Scotland. The Consumer Credit Act (see above) also extends to Scotland, and goes far in assimilating the Scots law on this topic with English law.

3. RECEIPTS

Receipts should be kept for six years from the date of payment, after which period no action can be brought concerning the goods, etc., received.

In Scotland, the law on receipts has been altered by the Prescription and Limitation (Scotland) Act 1973, which for this purpose, however, does not come into force until 25th July, 1976. As from that date an obligation is extinguished after the expiry of a period of five years without a relevant claim having been made by the creditor during that period.

CROWN—PROCEEDINGS AGAINST

Before 1947 proceedings against the Crown were generally possible only by a procedure known as a petition of right, which placed the litigant at a considerable disadvantage and which was not normally available at all in cases of tort (i.e., civil wrongs other than breach of contract). Thus, no proceedings would normally lie against the Government if a subject were injured by the negligent driving of a Government vehicle (although the driver could be sued) or if a Government employee were injured by the defective condition of the Crown premises on which he worked. Now however, by the Crown Proceedings Act 1947, which came into operation on Jan. 1, 1948, the Crown, in its public capacity, is largely placed in the same position as a subject, although some procedural disadvantages remain. Exceptions to the Act include the immunity of the Crown and any member of the armed forces from liability in tort in respect of death of, or personal injury to, another member of the armed forces on duty, provided that the death or injury is certified as attributable to service for purposes of pension.

Scotland.—The Act extends to Scotland and has the effect of bringing the practice of the two countries as closely together as the different legal systems will permit. While formerly actions against the Crown, when permissible, were confined to the Court of Session, proceedings may now be brought in the Sheriff Court.

The Act lays down that arrestment of money in the hands of the Crown or of a Government Department is competent in any case where arrestment in the hands of a subject would have been competent, but an exception is made in respect of National Savings Bank deposits. Section 2 (1) of the Law Reform (Miscellaneous Provisions) (Scotland) Act 1966 removes the privilege whereby the wages of Crown servants, other than serving members of the armed forces, are exempt from arrestment in execution.

DEATHS
REGISTRATION, BURIAL AND CREMATION
REGISTRATION
(For Certificates, *see* under FAMILY LAW–CERTIFI-CATES)

In England and Wales.—When a death takes place, personal information of it must be given to the local Registrar of Births and Deaths, and the register signed in his presence, by one of the following persons: (1) A relative of the deceased present at the death, or in attendance during the last illness. If they fail (2) some other relative of the deceased. In default of any relatives (3) a person present at the death; or, the occupier of the house in which the death happened. If all the above-named fail (4) an inmate of the house. A person (other than a relative) registering the death must be causing the disposal of the body. Relatives present or in attendance are first required to attend to the registration. The registration must be made within five days of the death, or within the same time written notice of the death sent to the Registrar. If the deceased was attended during his last illness by a registered medical practitioner, a certificate of cause of death must be sent by the doctor to the Registrar. The doctor must give to the informant of the death a written notice of the signing of the certificate, which must be delivered to the Registrar. It is essential that a certificate for disposal should be obtained from the Registrar before the funeral and delivered to the clergyman or other person in charge of the churchyard or cemetery. No fee is chargeable for this certificate. If the death is not registered within five days (or fourteen days if written notice of the occurrence of the death is sent to him) the Registrar may require any one of the above-mentioned persons to attend to register at a stated time and place. Failure to comply involves a penalty of ten pounds. The registration of a death is free of charge. After twelve months no death can be registered without the Registrar General's consent.

A body must not be disposed of until (1) either the Registrar has given a certificate to the effect that he has registered or received notice of the death, or (2) until the Coroner has made a disposal order (*Births and Deaths Registration Act* 1926, S. 1).

A person disposing of a body must within ninety-six hours deliver to the Registrar a notification as to the date, place, and means of the disposal of the body (*ib.*, S. 3).

" Still-born " child (*see* under Births (Registration), p. 1169).

Death at Sea.—The master of a British ship must record any death on board and send particulars to the Registrar General of Shipping.

Death Abroad.—Consular Officers are authorized to register deaths of British subjects occurring abroad. Certificates are procurable at the Registrar General's Office, London. If the deceased was of *Scottish* domicile, particulars are sent to the Registrar General for Scotland.

With regard to the registration of deaths of members of the armed forces, and deaths occurring on H.M. ships and aircraft, *see* the Registration of Births, etc. Act 1957.

Deaths (Registration) in Scotland.—New provisions are included in the Registration of Births, Deaths and Marriages (Scotland) Act 1965 which amends and re-enacts provisions in former Acts.

Personal notification within 8 days must be given to the registrar of (*a*) the registration district in which the death took place or (*b*) any registration district in which the deceased was ordinarily resident immediately befor his death, and (*c*) when a body is found and the place of death is not known, either the registration district in which the body was found or any other registration district appropriate by virtue of the preceding paragraph. When a person dies (in or out of Scotland) in a ship, aircraft or land vehicle during a journey and the body is conveyed therein to any place in Scotland the death shall, unless the Registrar General otherwise directs, be deemed to have occurred at that place.

The register must be signed in the presence of the registrar by one of the following: (*a*) any relative of the deceased; (*b*) any person present at the death; (*c*) the deceased's executor or other legal representative; (*d*) the occupier, at the time of the death, of the premises where the death took place; (*e*) if these fail, any other person having knowledge of the particulars to be registered. Failure to comply involves a penalty not exceeding £20.

The medical practitioner who attended the deceased during the last illness must sign a certificate of the cause of death. If there is no such medical practitioner, any medical practitioner who is able to do so, may sign the certificate. At the time of registering the death the registrar shall, without charge, give the informant a certificate of registration, and the person to whom the certificate is given must hand it to the undertaker previous to cremation. A body may, however, be interred before the death is registered, in which case the undertaker must deliver a certificate of burial to the Registrar within three days.

BURIAL

The duty of burial is incumbent on the deceased person's Executors (if any appointed); it is also a recognized obligation of the husband of a woman, and the parent of a child, also of a householder where the body lies. Funeral expenses of a reasonable amount will be repayable out of deceased's estate in priority to any other claims. Directions as to place and mode of burial are frequently contained in the deceased's will or in some memorandum placed with private papers, or may have been communicated verbally to a relative. Consequently steps should immediately be taken to ascertain the deceased's wishes from the above sources. If the wishes are considered objectionable, they are not necessarily enforceable; legal advice should be taken. A person may legally leave directions for the anatomical examination of his body. As to the place of burial—unless closed by Order in Council—the parish churchyard is the normal burying place for parishioners, or any person dying in the Parish, but nowadays this will apply only in villages and the smaller towns. In populous districts cemeteries and crematoria have been established either by the local council, or a private company, and burials will take place there in accordance with the regulations. For an exclusive right to a burial space in the churchyard a faculty is required from the Ecclesiastical Court. Poor persons may be buried at the public expense by the local authority. As to the necessity for obtaining a registrar's certificate or authority from the Coroner for disposal, *see* above.

CREMATION

Under the Cremation Acts, 1902 and 1952, regulations are made by the Home Secretary dealing fully with the cremation of a body, disposal of ashes, etc., and containing numerous essential safeguards.

If Cremation is desired it is advisable for instructions to be left in writing to that effect.

To arrange for Cremation the Executor or near relative should instruct the undertaker to that effect and obtain from him the Statutory Forms required as given in the Cremation Regulations issued in 1930 (Statutory Rules and Orders, 1930, No. 1016), as amended by the Cremation Regulations 1965 (No. 1146).

INTESTACY
ENGLAND AND WALES

As regards deaths on or after July 1, 1972, the position is governed by the Administration of Estates Act, 1925, as amended by the Intestates' Estates Act, 1952, the Family Provision Act, 1966 and Orders made thereunder. The 1952 and 1966 Acts and S.I. 1972/916 increased the benefits of a surviving spouse of an intestate, and the 1952 Act extended the provisions of the Inheritance (Family Provision) Act, 1938 (*see under* " Wills "), to intestacies. These notes deal with the present position, so that if the death occurred before July 1, 1972 reference must be made elsewhere. If the intestate leaves a spouse and issue, the spouse takes (i) the " personal chattels "; (ii) £15,000 with interest at 4 per cent. from death until payment; and (iii) a life interest in half of the rest of the estate. This life interest can be capitalized at the option of the spouse. " Personal chattels " are articles of household use or ornament (including motor-cars), not used for business purposes. The rest of the estate goes to the issue. If the intestate leaves a spouse and no issue, but leaves a parent or brother or sister of the whole blood or issue of such brothers and sisters the spouse takes (i) the " personal chattels "; (ii) £40,000 with interest at 4 per cent. from death until payment, and (iii) half of the rest of the estate absolutely. The other half of the rest of the estate goes to the parents, equally if more than one, or, if none, to the brothers and sisters of the whole blood. If the intestate leaves a spouse, but no issue, no parents and no brothers or sisters of the whole blood or their issue, the spouse takes the whole estate absolutely. If resident therein at the intestate's death, the surviving spouse may generally require the personal representatives to appropriate the interest of the intestate in the matrimonial home in or towards satisfaction of any absolute interest of the spouse, including the capitalized value of a life interest. In certain cases, leave of Court is required. On a partial intestacy any benefit (other than personal chattels specifically bequeathed) received by the surviving spouse under the will must be brought into account against the statutory legacy of £15,000 or £40,000, as the case may be. If there is no surviving spouse, the estate is distributed among those who survive the intestate in the following order (those entitled under earlier numbers taking to the exclusion of

those entitled under later numbers):—(1) children (2) father or mother (equally, if both alive); (3) brothers and sisters of the whole blood; (4) brothers and sisters of the half blood; (5) grandparents (equally, if more than one alive); (6) uncles and aunts of the whole blood; (7) uncles and aunts of the half blood; (8) the Crown.

In cases (1), (3), (4), (6) and (7) the persons entitled lose their interests unless they or their issue not only survive the intestate, but also attain eighteen or marry under that age, their shares going to the persons (if any) within the same group who do attain eighteen or marry. Moreover, in the same cases, succession is not *per capita*, but *per stirpes*, i.e., by stocks or families. Thus, if the intestate leaves one child and two grandchildren, being the children of a child of the intestate, who pre-deceased the intestate, the two grandchildren represent their deceased parent and take between them one-half of the issue's share, the remaining half going to the surviving child. Similarly, nephews and nieces represent a deceased brother, and so on.

When the deceased died partially intestate (*i.e.*, leaving a will which disposed of only part of his property), the above rules apply to the intestate part.

Children must bring into account (hotchpot) any substantial advances received from the intestate during his lifetime before claiming any further share under the intestacy. Special hotchpot provisions apply to partial intestacy.

By the Family Law Reform Act, 1969, the position of an illegitimate child is equated with that of a legitimate child in respect of all deaths occurring on or after January 1, 1970.

For personal application for Letters of Administration—see p. 1168.

SCOTLAND

The Succession (Scotland) Act, 1964, provides that the whole estate of any person dying intestate shall devolve without distinction between heritable and moveable property. By that Act the surviving spouse of an intestate may, as a prior right (in addition to legal rights, *see* below), claim the matrimonial home to a maximum of £30,000, or a choice of one matrimonial home if more than one (or in certain circumstances the value thereof), with its furniture and plenishings not exceeding £8,000 in value, plus the sum of £4,000 if the deceased left issue or, if no issue, the sum of £8,000. These figures may be increased from time to time by order of the Secretary of State.

The Act has been modified by the Law Reform (Miscellaneous Provisions) (Scotland) Act, 1968, which provided that an illegitimate child had exactly the same rights of succession in the estate of his parents as a legitimate child. However, the position still remains that an illegitimate child has no succession rights in the estate of a grandparent even though such would have fallen to his predeceasing parent.

Legal rights, referred to above, are:—

Jus relicti: right of surviving husband to one-half or one-third of deceased's net moveable estate, after satisfaction of prior rights.

Jus relictae: the corresponding right of a surviving wife in her deceased husband's estate.

Legitim: right of surviving children to one-half or one-third of the net moveable estate of deceased parents after satisfaction of prior rights. There are no legal rights in heritage.

In general, the lines of succession are: (1) descendants; (2) collaterals; (3) ascendants and their collaterals, and so on in the ascending scale. The Crown is ultimus haeres. The right of representation, *i.e.*, the right of the issue of a person, who would have succeeded if he had survived the intestate, is open to any line of succession where previously it was limited to apply only when there were next of kin or the issue of predeceasing next of kin. The surviving mother of an intestate now has equal rights of succession with the surviving father, where formerly these were restricted. The intestate's maternal relations, who prior to the Act had no rights of succession, are now on an equal footing with his paternal relations. Where the intestate is survived only by parents, and by brothers and sisters (collaterals) half of the estate is taken by the parents and the other half by the brothers and sisters, those of the whole blood being preferred to those of the half blood; where, however, succession opens to collaterals—(which expression can include the brothers and sisters of an ancestor of the intestate)—of the half blood, they shall rank equally amongst themselves, whether related to the intestate (or his ancestor) through their father or their mother.

WILLS

IMPORTANT NOTE.—*The following notes must be read subject to the provisions of the Inheritance (Family Provision) Act, 1938, which is liable to affect or modify the will of any person (domiciled in England) dying after July 13, 1939.* This Act empowers the Court to order maintenance out of the testator's estate for the benefit of certain " dependants," *i.e.*, a surviving wife or husband; an unmarried (or invalid) daughter; a son under 21 or who is an invalid. Such order can be made if the will does not itself make " reasonable provision " for the maintenance of the dependent who seeks the order. An application must normally be made within six months of probate. A legally adopted child comes within the definition of a " son " or " daughter " under the Act. For further details as to the limits of an order, the Act, as amended by the Family Provision Act, 1966, and the Family Law Reform Act, 1969, s. 18, should be consulted. *When the Inheritance (Provision for Family and Dependants) Bill receives the Royal Assent, it will repeal these Acts and amend the law e.g. to extend the class of claimants.*

Since the object of the Act is to provide *maintenance* for dependents, an application is not likely to be successful where the estate is very small, *e.g.* two or three hundred pounds, although a lump sum may be ordered.

There are similar provisions under the Matrimonial Causes Act, 1965, whereby the court may order provision out of a deceased's estate for the support of a *former* husband or wife where the marriage has been dissolved or annulled.

REASONS FOR MAKING A WILL.—Every person over the age of 18 should make a will. However small the estate the rules of Intestacy (see above) may not reflect a person's wishes as to his property; in any case a will can do more than just deal with property—it can in particular appoint executors, give directions as to the disposal of the body and appoint guardians to take care of children in the event of the parents' death. For the wealthier person an appropriately drawn will can operate to reduce the burden of Estate Duty.

It is considered desirable for a will to be properly drawn up by a Solicitor, and the making of a will is one of the services which he can provide under the Legal Advice and Assistance Scheme (see above).

In no circumstances should one person prepare a Will for another person where the former is to take any benefit under it—this can easily lead to a suggestion of undue influence which may cause the will to be held bad.

Assuming a lawyer is not employed, a person having resolved to make a will must remember

that it is only after a person is dead, and cannot explain his meaning, that his will can be open to dispute. It is the more necessary, therefore, to express what is meant in language of the utmost clearness, avoiding the use of any word or expression that admits of another meaning than the one intended. Avoid the use of " legal terms," such as " heirs " and " issue," when the same thing may be expressed in plain language. If in writing the will a mistake be made, it is better to rewrite the whole. Before a will is executed (*see below*) an alteration *may* be made by striking through the words with a pen, but opposite to such alteration the testator and witnesses should write their names or place their initials. Never scratch out a word with a knife or other instrument, and no alteration *of any kind whatever* must be made after the will is executed. If the testator afterwards wishes to change the disposition of his estate, it is best to make a new will, revoking the old one. The use of *codicils* should be left to the lawyer. *A will should be written in ink and very legibly, on a single sheet of paper.* Although, of course, forms of wills must vary to suit different cases, the following forms may be found useful to those who, in cases of emergency, are called upon to draw up wills, either for themselves or others.

Nothing more complicated should be attempted. The forms should be studied in conjunction with the notes following.

This is the last will and testament of me [*Thomas Smith*] of [*Vine Cottage, Silver Street, Reading, Berks*] which I make this [*thirteenth*] day of [*February, 1973*] and whereby I revoke all previous wills and testamentary dispositions.

1. I hereby appoint [*John Green of —— and Richard Brown of ——*] to be the executor(s) of this my will.

2. I give all my property real and personal to [*my wife Mary or my sons Raymond and David equally* or as the case may be].

Signed by the testator in the presence of us both present at the same time who,

at his request, in his presence	Thomas Smith
and in the presence of each	*Signature of*
other have hereunto set our	*Testator;*
names as witnesses.	

William Jones (*signed*) of Green Gables, South Street, Reading, tailor.

Henry Morgan (*signed*) of 16, North Street, Reading, butcher.

Should it be desired to give legacies and/or gifts of specific property, instead of giving the whole estate to one or more persons, the form above should be used with the substitution for clause 2 of the following clauses:—

2. I give to —— of —— the sum of £—— and to —— of —— the sum of £—— and to —— of —— all my books (*or as the case may require*).

3. All the residue of my property real and personal I give to —— of ——.

TERMS.—Real property includes freehold land and houses; while personal property includes debts due, arrears of rents, money, leasehold property, house furniture, goods, assurance policies, stocks and shares in companies, and the like. The words " my money," apart from the context, will normally only include actual real money. The expression " goods and chattels " should not be used. In giving *particular* property, ordinary language is sufficient, *e.g.*, " my house, Vine Cottage, Silver Street, Reading, Berks." Such specific gifts fail if not owned by the testator at his death.

RESIDUARY LEGATEES.—It is well in all cases where legacies or specific gifts are made, to leave to some person or persons " the residue of my property," although it may be thought that the whole of the property has been disposed of in legacies, etc., already mentioned in the will. *It should be remembered that a will operates on property acquired after it has been made.*

EXECUTION OF A WILL, AND WITNESSES.—The testator should sign his name at the foot or end of the will, in presence of two witnesses, who will immediately afterwards sign their names in his and in each other's presence. A person who has been left any gift or share of residue in the will, or whose wife or husband has been left such a gift, should not be an attesting witness. Their attestation would be good, but they would forfeit the gift. It is better that a person named as executor should not be a witness. Husband and wife may both be witnesses, provided neither is a legatee. If a solicitor be appointed executor, it is lawful to direct that his ordinary fees and charges shall be paid; but in this case he (as an interested party) must not be a witness to the will.

It is desirable that the witnesses should be fully described, as they may possibly be wanted at some future time. If the testator should be too ill to sign, even by a mark, another person may sign the testator's name to the will for him, in his presence and by his direction, and in this case it should be shown that the testator knew the contents of the document. The attestation clause should therefore be worded: " Signed by Thomas Brown, by the direction and in the presence of the testator, Thomas Smith, in the joint presence of us, who thereupon signed our names in his presence and in the presence of each other, the will having been first read over to the testator, who appeared fully to understand the same."

Where there is any suspecion that the Testator is not, by reason of age or infirmity, fully in command of his faculties it is desirable to ask his Doctor to act as a witness (see Testamentary capacity below).

A *blind person* may make a will in Braille. If the testator be blind the will should be read aloud to him in the presence of the witnesses, and the fact mentioned in the attestation clause. A blind person cannot witness a will.

If by inadvertence the testator should have signed his will without the witnesses being present, then the attestation should be:—" The testator acknowledged his signature already made as his signature to his last will and testament, in the joint presence," etc. Any omission in the observance of these details may invalidate the will. *The stringency of the law as to signature and witnessing of a will is only relaxed in favour of soldiers, sailors and airmen in certain circumstances.*

EXECUTORS.—It is usual to appoint two executors, although one is sufficient; any number up to and including four may be appointed. The name and address of each executor should be given in full. An executor may be a legatee. Thus a child of full age or wife to whom the whole or a portion of the estate is left may be appointed sole executor, or one or two executors. The addresses of the executors are not essential; but it is desirable here as elsewhere, to avoid ambiguity or vagueness.

LAPSED LEGACIES.—If a legatee dies in the lifetime of the testator, the legacy generally lapses and falls into the residue. Where a residuary legatee predeceases the testator, his share of the residuary estate will not generally pass to the other residuary legatees, but will pass to the persons entitled on the deceased's intestacy. In all such cases it is desirable to make a new will.

TESTAMENT CAPACITY.—A person under the age of 18 cannot make a will (except for soldiers,

sailors and airmen and then only in exceptional circumstances).

So far as mental capacity is concerned the Testator must be able to understand and appreciate the nature and effect of making a will, the property of which he can dispose and the claims to which he ought to give effect. If a person is not mentally able to make a will provision exists (under the Mental Health Act, 1959 as amended) for the Court to do this for him.

REVOCATION.—A will is revoked by a subsequent will (but if it does not expressly revoke former wills, only so far such subsequent will operates as an implied revocation as by making other provisions inconsistent with the previous will, for this reason a will should always have a clause revoking previous testamentary dispositions), or by burning, tearing or otherwise *destroying* the will with the intention of revoking it. Such destruction must either be by the testator or by some other person in his presence and at his direction. *It is not sufficient to obliterate the will with a pen.* Marriage in every case acts as the revocation of a will, unless, in the case of a will made on or after Jan. 1, 1926, it is expressed to have been made in contemplation of a particular marriage (Law of Property Act, 1925, s. 177); so that after marriage a new will should be made, except in this last case.

PERSONAL APPLICATION FOR PROBATE OR LETTERS OF ADMINISTRATION

Application for probate or for letters of administration may be made *in person* at the Personal Application Dept. of the Principal Registry of the Family Division, a district probate registry or subregistry, or a probate office by the executors or persons entitled to a grant of administration. Applications should bring (1) the will, if any; (2) a certificate of death; (3) particulars of all property and assets left by the deceased; and (4) a list of debts and funeral expenses.

Intending applicants, before attending at a registry or probate office, should write or telephone to the nearest probate registry or sub-registry for the necessary forms. Postal or telephone applications cannot be dealt with at the local probate offices, which are part-time only.

Certain property can be disposed of on death without a grant of probate or administration, or in pursuance of a nomination made by the deceased, provided the amount involved does not exceed £1,500. *See* the Administration of Estates (Small Payments) Act, 1965.

WHERE TO FIND A PROVED WILL

A will proved since 1858 must have been proved either at the Principal Registry at Somerset House, or a District Registry. In the former case the original will itself is carefully preserved at Somerset House, the copy of which probate has been granted is in the hands of the executors who proved the will, and another copy for Parliament is bound up in a folio volume of wills made by testators of that initial and date; the indices to these volumes fill a room of considerable size at Somerset House, where the indices may be examined and a copy of any will read. In the latter case, the original will proved in the District Registry, is kept there, and may be seen or a *copy* obtained, but a copy is sent to and filed at Somerset House, where also it may be seen. A general index of grants, both probates and administrations, is prepared and printed annually in lexicographical form, and may be seen at either the Principal or a District Registry. This index is usually ready by about October of the following year.

SCOTS LAW OF WILLS

A domiciled Scotsman, unlike a domiciled Englishman, cannot in certain circumstances dispose effectively of the entirety of his estate. If he leave a widow and children, the widow is entitled to a one-third share in the whole of the moveable estate (her *jus relictae*), and the children are entitled to another one-third share equally between them (their *legitim*). If he leave a widow but no children —or children but no widow—the *jus relictae* or *legitim* is increased to a one-half share of the estate. The remaining portion is known as the *dead's part*. A surviving husband and children have comparable rights (*jus reliciti* and *legitim*) in the wife's estate. It should be noted that the amount of any claim of *jus reliciti*, *jus relictae* or *legitim* out of an estate shall be calculated by reference to so much of the net moveable estate as remains after the satisfaction of any prior claims under the Succession (Scotland) Act, 1964—*see* Illegitimacy, Scotland and Intestacy, Scotland, *supra*. The *dead's part* is the only portion of which the testator can freely dispose. All burdens falling upon the representatives in moveables are payable out of the whole of the moveables before any division. Burdens in the nature of legacies are payable out of the *dead's part*. Pupils cannot make wills. Formerly a minor could dispose only of moveables but since the passing of the Succession (Scotland) Act, 1964 he has a like capacity to test on heritable property. A will must be in writing and may be typewritten or even in pencil. A will may be either (1) *holograph*, *i.e.* written by the testator himself, in which case no witnesses are necessary; a printed form filled up by the testator is not necessarily *holograph* but may be made effectual when it has clearly been adopted as *holograph*. Words written on erasure or marginal additions or interlineations in *holograph* writings, if proved to be in the handwriting of the maker of the deed, are valid; (2) *tested*, i.e., signed in presence of two witnesses. It is not necessary that these witnesses should sign in presence of one another, or even that they should see the testator signing so long as the testator acknowledges his signature to the witnesses. The Conveyancing and Feudal Reform (Scotland) Act, 1970 whilst altering generally the rules for the description of deeds, specifically (s. 44 (2)) makes no change in the rules applying to wills which must still be signed by the testator on every page. If the testator cannot write, or is blind, his will may be authenticated by a notary and two witnesses. It is better that the will be not witnessed by a beneficiary thereunder, although this circumstance will not invalidate the attestation of the will or (as it would in England) the gift. A parish minister may act as a notary for the purpose of subscribing a will in his own parish. Wills are registered in the Books of the Sheriffdom in which the deceased died domiciled, and in the Books of Council and Session, H.M. General Register House, Edinburgh. The original deed may be inspected on payment of a small fee and a certified official copy may be obtained. A Scottish will is not revoked by the subsequent marriage of the testator. The subsequent birth of a child, no testamentary provision having been made for him, may revoke a will in whole or in part. A will is revoked by a subsequent will, either expressly or by implication; but in so far as the two can be read together both wills have effect. If a subsequent will is revoked, the earlier will is revived.

"Confirmation," the Scottish equivalent of Probate, is obtained in the Sheriff Court of the Region in which the deceased was domiciled at the date of his death or, where he had no fixed domicile or died abroad in the commissariot of Edinburgh. Executors are either "nominate" or "dative." An Executor nominate is one nominated by the deceased in his will or, where such person has predeceased the testator, by the residuary beneficiary. An Executor dative is one appointed by the Court (1) in the case of intestacy or (2) where the deceased had failed to name an executor in his will. In the former case the deceased's next-of-kin are all entitled to be declared executors dative. An inventory of the deceased's estate and a schedule of debts, together with an affidavit, must first be given up. In estates under £1,000 nett and under £3,000 gross confirmation is obtained under a simplified procedure at reduced fees.

Presumption of Survivorship.—The Succession (Scotland) Act, 1964, referred to above provides that where two persons die in circumstances indicating that they died simultaneously or if it is uncertain which was the survivor, the younger will be deemed to have survived the elder unless the elder person left testamentary provision in favour of the younger, whom failing in favour of a third person, the younger person having died intestate (partially or wholly); but if the persons so dying were husband and wife, neither shall be presumed to have survived the other.

EMPLOYMENT

WAGES AND HOLIDAYS

Under the Truck Acts, it is in general forbidden for an employer to pay wages other than in current coin of the realm, and it is illegal for an employer to deduct from the employee's wages sums alleged to be due to the employer. However, the application of these Acts is confined to manual workers, and domestic servants are specifically excluded from their operation. Even in the case of payments to workmen, certain deductions, including rent and the price of food to be consumed on the employers' premises, are not forbidden where the employee's written consent is obtained. Further, under the Payment of Wages Act, 1960, it is permissible for wages to be paid otherwise than in cash at the request of the employee, *e.g.*, by cheque, money order, postal order or into a banking account.

The Equal Pay Act 1970, which extends to Scotland, but does not come into force until December 29, 1975, prevents discrimination, as regards terms and conditions of employment between men and women.

PARTICULARS OF TERMS OF EMPLOYMENT

Under the Contracts of Employment Act 1972, an employer must give each employee within 13 weeks of the beginning of the employment a written statement containing the following particulars of the contract between them:

(1) the date when the employment began;
(2) the rate of remuneration (or how it is calculated);
(3) the intervals at which wages are paid;
(4) the hours of work;
(5) the employee's entitlement to holidays (including public holidays) and holiday pay;
(6) terms relating to sickness, injury and sick pay;
(7) the length of notice which the employee should give and receive in order to terminate the contract.

In addition, the written particulars must identify the person to whom the employee can apply to seek redress of any grievance and what further steps may ensue.

TERMINATION OF EMPLOYMENT

A employee may be dismissed without notice if he is guilty of gross breach of contract, such as disobedience to a lawful order or dishonesty. He is then only entitled to wages accrued due at the date of dismissal.

In other cases, the employee is entitled to reasonable notice which, under the contracts of Employment Act 1972, must not be less than:

(a) 1 week where he has been continuously employed for up to 2 years;

(b) 2 weeks where the employment has lasted up to 5 years;

(c) 4 weeks where it has lasted 10 years;

(d) 6 weeks where it has lasted up to 15 years;

(e) 8 weeks where it has lasted for over 15 years.

An employer who wrongfully dismisses an employee (i.e. with less than the length of notice to which he is entitled) is generally liable to pay wages for the period of proper notice.

An employee who has a fixed term contract has no claim against his employer for wrongful dismissal if his contract is not renewed when it expires. He may, however, have a claim for a redundancy payment or compensation for unfair dismissal. If he is wrongfully dismissed before his contract expires, he is generally entitled to remuneration payable over the full period of the contract.

Unless the employee has been guilty of misconduct, he may be entitled to a redundancy payment or to compensation for unfair dismissal if he has been continuously employed for at least certain periods and the employment has been terminated by the employer (with or without proper notice) or he has a fixed term contract which expires without being renewed.

Under the Redundancy Payments Act 1965, an employee who satisfies the foregoing conditions and is dismissed by reason of redundancy may be entitled to a redundancy payment calculated by reference to his age, pay and length of service.

The Trade Union and Labour Relations Act 1974 enables an employee who is unfairly dismissed to complain to an Industrial Tribunal (generally within 3 months of dismissal). The onus will then be on the employer to prove that the dismissal was due to capability, conduct, redundancy, illegality or some other substantial reason justifying dismissal, and that he acted reasonably in dismissing the employee. If the tribunal finds that the employer did not act reasonably the dismissal will be unfair, in which case the tribunal can

(a) recommend re-engagement or

(b) reward compensation subject to a limit of £5,200 or 104 weeks' wages, whichever is the less.

For an employee to bring himself within the unfair dismissal provisions, he must have been continuously employed for a period not less than 26 weeks.

All complaints of unfair dismissal are referred to a conciliation officer or the Department of Employment and a very high proportion of complaints are disposed of in this way.

OFFICES, SHOPS AND RAILWAY PREMISES

The Offices, Shops and Railway Premises Act, 1963, which extends to Scotland with minor modifications, applies to office premises, shop premises and railway premises being, in each case, premises where persons are employed to work. Shop premises include a building which is not a shop but of which the main use is the carrying on there of a retail trade or business; a building occupied by a wholesaler where goods are kept for sale wholesale (except a warehouse belonging to the owner of a dock, wharf or quay); and a building to which the public can resort for the purpose of having goods repaired. However, the Act does not apply to premises if the only employees are the spouse, parent, grandparent, child, grandchild or brother or sister of the employer, and it does not apply to premises if the period of time worked there during each week does not normally exceed 21 hours.

The following is a very brief summary of the main provisions affecting premises to which the Act applies—

1. The premises and all furniture etc., must be kept clean, and no dirt or refuse must be allowed to accumulate.

2. No overcrowding so as to cause risk of injury to health is permitted.

3. Provisions must be made for maintaining a reasonable temperature in rooms, and a thermometer must be provided on each floor of a building.

4. Provision must be made for securing adequate ventilation.

5. Provision must be made for securing sufficient and suitable lighting.

6. Suitable and sufficient sanitary conveniences and washing facilities (including a supply of clean, running hot and cold or warm water and, in addition, soap and clean towels or other suitable means of cleaning or drying) must be provided at accessible places; and also an adequate supply of wholesome drinking water.

7. Accommodation must be provided for clothing which is not in use.

8. For each sedentary worker there must be provided a seat of a design, construction and dimensions suitable for that worker.

9. Where persons employed to work in shop premises eat meals there, suitable and sufficient facilities for eating them must be provided.

10. All floors, stairs and passages must be of sound construction and properly maintained.

11. Every dangerous part of any machinery must be securely fenced, unless it is in such a position or of such construction as to be as safe as if it were fenced. No person under 18 can clean machinery if he is thereby exposed to risk of injury from a moving part.

12. No person can be required to lift or carry a load so heavy as to be likely to injure him.

13. A first-aid box or cupboard must be provided.

14. Means of escape in case of fire must be provided, as must appropriate fire-fighting equipment.

15. Where an accident occurs which causes death to an employee or disables him from working for more than 3 days, the occupier of the premises must at once send notice of the accident to the appropriate authority.

FAMILY LAW
ADOPTION OF CHILDREN

In England and Wales the adoption of children is regulated mainly by the Adoption of Children Acts, 1926 to 1949, and the Adoption Act, 1958. An order of court is necessary to legalize the adoption. Adoption puts the child adopted practically on the same footing as a child born to the adopter in lawful wedlock, in all matters of custody, education and maintenance; further, it is provided by the Act of 1958 that an adopted child shall be treated as the child of the adopter (and not the child of its natural parents) for the purpose of the devolution of property on an intestacy occurring, or under any disposition made, after the date of the adoption order. Applications are made to the High Court (Family Division), County Court, or Magistrates Court. Orders will not usually be made for a man to be *sole* adopter of a girl, and the applicant must be either:—

(a) Twenty-five years of age or over; or

(b) Twenty-one years of age or over and a relative (as defined in the Act of 1958) of the infant; or

(c) the mother or father of the infant.

Two spouses may jointly adopt an infant, but unless one of them is the mother or father of the infant, condition (a) or (b) above must be satisfied in respect of one of the applicants *and* the other spouse must have attained the age of twenty-one.

Except in relation to an infant who is not a United Kingdom national (where special provisions apply), the consent of the child's parents or guardian is required before an adoption order will be made, but in certain circumstances (e.g., where the parent or guardian has ill-treated or neglected the child) the Court may dispense with this consent. Since the 1949 Act, marriage between the adopter and the adoptee is prohibited, but marriages of that kind, solemnized before the passing of the Act, are not thereby invalidated.

The 1958 Act places restrictions on societies which make arrangements for the adoption of children.

The Adoption Act, 1964, provides for effect to be given to adoption orders made in Northern Ireland, the Isle of Man and the Channel Islands.

The Adoption Act 1968 (which applies to Scotland) enables an adoption order to be made on the application of a person who is either habitually resident in Great Britain or possesses British nationality. The Act also provides for the recognition of certain overseas adoptions.

Scotland.—The Adoption of Children (Scotland) Acts, 1930 to 1949, and the Adoption Act, 1958, cover the law relating to the adoption of children in Scotland, where an Adopted Children Register is maintained. Applications are made to the Court of Session or the Sheriff Court within whose jurisdiction either the applicant or the child resides at the date of application. The Adoption Act, 1958, which is a consolidating Act, also applies, with modifications, to Scotland, and reference is also made to the Adoption Act, 1960 which amends the law with respect to revocation of adoption orders and to the Adoption Act, 1968 (*see* above). The Succession (Scotland) Act, 1964, gives the adopted child the same rights of succession as a child born to the adopter in wedlock, but deprives him of any such rights in the estates of his natural parents.

All adoptions in Great Britain are registered in the Registers of Adopted Children kept by the Registrars General in London and Edinburgh respectively. Certificates from these registers including short certificates which contain no reference to adoptions, can be obtained on conditions similar to those relating to birth certificates, (See below.)

BIRTHS (REGISTRATION)

When a birth takes place, personal information of it must be given to the Registrar of Births and Deaths for the sub-district in which the birth occurred, and the register signed in his presence, by one of the following persons:—

1. The father or mother of the child. If they fail; 2. the occupier of the house in which the birth happened; 3. a person present at the birth; or, 4. the person having charge of the child. The duty of attending to the registration therefore rests firstly on the parents. The mother is responsible for the registration of the birth of an illegitimate child. The registration is required to be made

within 42 days of the birth. Failure to do this, without reasonable cause, involves liability to a penalty of twenty pounds. The registration of a birth is free. In England or Wales, the informant, instead of attending before the registrar of the sub-district where the birth occurred, may make a declaration of the particulars required to be registered in the presence of any registrar. Under the Public Health Act, 1936, notice of every birth must be given by the father, or person in attendance on the mother, to the district medical officer of health by post within 36 hours of the birth. *This is in addition to the registration already mentioned.*

A " Stillbirth " must be registered and a certificate signed by the doctor or midwife who was present at the birth or has examined the body of the child must be produced to the registrar. The certificate must, where possible, state the cause of death and the estimated duration of the pregnancy. A stillbirth may only be registered within 3 months of the birth.

The re-registration of the birth of a person legitimated by the subsequent marriage of the parents is provided for in the Births and Deaths Registration Act, 1953.

Birth at Sea: The master of a British ship must record any birth on board and send particulars to the Registrar General of Shipping.

Birth Abroad: Consular Officers are authorized to register births of British subjects occurring abroad. Certificates are procurable in due course at Registrar General's Office, London.

The registration of births occurring out of the United Kingdom among members of the armed forces, or occurring on board H.M. ships and aircraft, is provided for by the Registration of Births, Deaths and Marriages (Special Provisions) Act, 1957, applicable also to Scotland.

SCOTLAND

New provisions are included in the Registration of Births, Deaths and Marriages (Scotland) Act, 1965, which amends and re-enacts provisions in former Acts. Personal notification within 21 days of any birth, must be given to the registrar of (a) the registration district in which the birth took place, or (b) any registration district in which the mother of the child was ordinarily resident at the time of the birth and (c) in the case of a foundling child, dead or alive, when the place of birth is not known, the registration district in which the child, or the body was found. When a child is born (in or out of Scotland) in a ship, aircraft or land vehicle during a journey and the child is conveyed therein to any place in Scotland, the birth shall, unless the Registrar General otherwise directs, be deemed to have occurred at that place.

The register must be signed in the presence of the registrar by the father or mother of the child, and if they fail, by one of the following: (a) any relative of either parent who has knowledge of the birth; (b) the occupier of the premises in which the child was, to the knowledge of that occupier, born; (c) any person present at the birth; (d) any person having charge of the child. Failure without reasonable cause involves a penalty not exceeding £20.

The name of the father of an illegitimate child may be entered in the register of births at the time of registration if jointly requested by the mother and father, and the latter's name may also be recorded at a later date on declaration by both parents. A free abbreviated certificate of birth will be issued to the informant at the time of registration. Provision is made for the re-registration of the birth of a person made legitimate by the subsequent marriage of the parents or whose birth entry is affected by any matter respecting status or paternity, or has been so made as to imply that he is a foundling.

A still-birth must be registered and a certificate, signed by the doctor or certified midwife present at the birth or who has examined the body of the child, must be produced.

CERTIFICATES
OF BIRTHS, MARRIAGES, OR DEATHS

England and Wales.—Certificates of Births, Deaths, or Marriages can be obtained at the Office of Population Censuses and Surveys, St. Catherine's House, 10, Kingsway, W.C.2 or from the Superintendent Registrar having the legal custody of the register containing the entry of which a certificate is required. Certificates of marriage can also be obtained from the incumbent of the church in which the marriage took place; or from the Nonconformist minister (or other " authorized person ") where the marriage takes place in a registered building (*see, post*, under Marriage).

Where the certificate is issued by the Local Register Office the fee payable for standard Death and Birth certificates is £1.25 at the time of registration, or untill the completed register is handed over to the Superintendent Registrar. Thereafter the fee is £2.50. Where the certificate is issued by the General Register Office the fee is also £2.50. Certificates at lower rates may be issued under certain statutes, and in particular (under the Births and Deaths Registration Act 1953) a short form of birth certificate showing name, sex and date of birth, but not parentage, may be obtained on payment of a fee of £1.25 from the Registrar General (when £2.75 handling charge is also payable) or from the Superintendent Registrar or Registrar.

It is considered desirable when a certificate is required to consult the nearest Register Office who, if told the exact or approximate date and place of registration, will be able to advise on the best way of obtaining it.

English Registers.—Records of births, deaths and marriages registered in England and Wales since 1837 are kept at the Office of Population Censuses and Surveys, St. Catherine's House, 10, Kingsway, W.C.2. *The Society of Genealogists* 37 Harrington Gardens, S.W.7, possess many records of Baptisms, Marriages and Deaths prior to 1837, including copies, in whole or in part of about 4,000 Parish Registers.

Scottish Registers of Births, Deaths and Marriages.— Certificates of births, deaths or marriages registered from 1855 when compulsory registration commenced in Scotland can be obtained personally at the General Register Office, New Register House, Edinburgh, or from the appropriate local Registrar, on payment of the fee of £1 for a full extract entry of birth, death, or marriage, and 50p for a short certificate of birth. When the period searched is over 20 years additional fees are payable. A short certificate of registration of deaths is issued free of charge for National Insurance purposes in certain cases.

There are also available at the General Register Office old parish registers of the date prior to 1855, which were formally kept under the administration of the Established Church of Scotland. An extract of an entry in these registers may be obtained at the fee of £1. A fee of £1.50 per day is payable for a general search of all the Scottish registers.

DIVORCE, SEPARATION AND ANCILLARY MATTERS

Preliminary.—Matrimonial Suits may be conveniently divided into two classes, viz. (1) those in which it is sought to annul the marriage because of some defect; and (2) those in which, the marriage being admitted, it is sought to end the marriage or the duties arising from it. By virtue of the Matrimonial Causes Act, 1967, all matrimonial causes are now commenced in one of the divorce county courts designated by the Lord Chancellor. If they remain undefended, they are tried by a county court judge in one of these courts which has also been designated as a court of trial, or in the Royal Courts of Justice in London. If the suit becomes defended, it must be transferred to the High Court.

(1) *Nullity of Marriage.*—This is now mainly governed as to England and Wales by the Matrimonial Causes Act 1973. A marriage is void *ab initio* if the parties were within the prohibited degrees of affinity, or were not male and female, or if it was bigamous or if one of the parties was under the age of consent, i.e. 16, or in the case of a polygamous marriage entered into outside England and Wales, that either party was at the time of the marriage domiciled in England and Wales. Where the *formalities* of the marriage were defective, the marriage is generally void if *both* parties knew of the defect (*e.g.*, where marriage took place otherwise than in an authorized building). But absence of the consent of parents or guardians (or of the Court or other authority, in lieu thereof) in the case of minors does not invalidate the marriage.

A marriage is voidable (i.e. a decree of nullity may be obtained but until such time the marriage remains valid) on the following grounds—(*a*) incapacity of either party to consummate; (*b*) respondent's wilful refusal to consummate; (*c*) that either party did not validly consent to the marriage, whether in consequence of duress, mistake, unsoundness of mind or otherwise, (*d*) that either party at the time of marriage was a mentally disordered person; (*e*) that at the time of marriage the respondent was suffering from communicable venereal disease; (*f*) that at the time of the marriage the respondent was pregnant by another man. In cases (*e*) and (*f*) the petitioner must have been ignorant of the grounds at the date of the marriage and in (*c*), (*d*), (*e*) and (*f*) proceedings must be instituted within 3 years of the marriage. In all cases the court shall not grant a decree where the petitioner has led the respondent to believe that he would not seek a decree and it would be unjust for it to be granted.

The 1973 Act provides that a decree of nullity in a voidable marriage only annuls the marriage from the date of the decree. The marriage remains valid until the decree, and any children of the marriage are legitimate. Children of a void marriage are illegitimate unless the father was domiciled in England and Wales at the child's birth (or father's death, if earlier) and at the time of conception (or marriage if later) both or either of the parents reasonably believed the marriage was valid.

A spouse's insistence upon the use of contraceptives will not constitute wilful refusal to consummate within (*b*) above, even though there has been no normal intercourse, but it may in certain circumstances constitute unreasonable behaviour for the purpose of divorce (as to which *see* below). Further it has been allowed as a *defence* to a charge of desertion against the aggrieved party.

(2) *Judicial Separation and Divorce.*—The second class of suit includes a suit for judicial separation (which does not dissolve a marriage) and a suit for divorce (which, if successful, dissolves the marriage altogether and leaves the parties at liberty to marry again). Either spouse may petition for judicial separation. It is not necessary to prove that the marriage has broken down irretrievably and

the five facts listed (*a*) to (*e*) under divorce (below) are grounds for judicial separation.

Divorce.—The sole ground on which a divorce is obtainable by either husband or wife is the irretrievable breakdown of the marriage. However, the court is precluded from holding that a marriage has irretrievably broken down unless it is satisfied of one or more of the following facts: (a) that the respondent has committed adultery since the marriage and the petitioner finds it intolerable to live with the respondent; (b) such behaviour by the respondent that the petitioner cannot reasonably be expected to continue co-habitation; (c) desertion by the respondent for 2 years immediately before the petition; (d) 5 years separation immediately before the petition (but only 2 years where the respondent consents to the decree). Matrimonial Causes Act 1973.

The foregoing is subject to a clause prohibiting any petition for divorce (but not for judicial separation) before the lapse of three years from the date of marriage, except in the case of exceptional hardship (upon petitioner) or of exceptional depravity of respondent.

Desertion may be defined as a voluntary withdrawal from cohabitation by one spouse without just cause and against the wishes of the other. Where one spouse is guilty of conduct of a serious nature which forces the other to leave, the party at fault is said to be guilty of constructive desertion.

Provisions designed to encourage reconciliation.—The 1973 Act requires the solicitor for the petitioner to certify whether he has or has not discussed the possibility of a reconciliation and whether or not he has given the petitioner the names and addresses of persons qualified to help effect a reconciliation.

A total period of less than six months during which the parties have resumed living together is to be disregarded in determining whether the prescribed period of desertion or separation has been continuous. Similar provision for effecting a reconciliation exists in relation to the other proofs of break-down, but a petitioner cannot claim that it is intolerable to live with the other party if they have lived together for more than six months after discovery of the respondent's adultery.

Intervention by Queen's Proctor.—At any time during the progress of a suit, and before the decree *nisi* is made absolute, the Queen's Proctor may intervene.

Decree Absolute.—Every decree of dissolution or nullity is in the first instance a decree *nisi*. The marriage subsists until the decree is made absolute, usually six weeks after decree *nisi*. After that date either spouse may marry again; but as to marriage within " Prohibited Degrees " *see* Marriage—Miscellaneous Notes, p. 1175. Under the 1973 Act, a decree *nisi* cannot normally be made absolute until the court is satisfied that arrangements have been made for the welfare of every child of the family who has not attained the age of sixteen which are satisfactory or the best which can be devised in the circumstances or that it is impracticable for the parties before the court to make any such arrangements.

Maintenance, etc.—The court has wide powers to order either party to the marriage to make financial provision (e.g. periodical payments, a lump sum, the transfer of property) for the other party or any child of the family, having regard to the party's means, the recipient's needs and all the important aspects of the case. The husband can be ordered to pay his wife's costs, even if she is unsuccessful in her suit or defence. A guilty co-respondent may be ordered to pay costs.

The court may, where the husband has wilfully neglected to provide reasonable maintenance for the wife or children, order the husband to make provision for them, *even though* no matrimonial suit is pending between the parties to the marriage, and while such an order is in force the court may also deal with custody of and access to the children.

CUSTODY OF CHILDREN ETC.

The Court may make orders in respect of access to and the custody, maintenance and education of children in connection with a suit for divorce, nullity or judicial separation (above) or with an application to the Magistrates (below) whether the suit succeeds or not. In addition, if there is no other matrimonial suit involved a parent may apply for custody under the Guardianship of Minors Acts 1971 and 1973, and any person may apply to the High Court for the child to be made a ward of court.

In all cases the welfare of the child is the first and paramount consideration. The categories of child who may be covered by any particular type of proceedings differ according to the nature of those proceedings and to the nature of the particular relief sought, but it should be borne in mind that in connection with divorce, nullity and judicial separation a child which has been *treated* by the spouses as a child of the family may be included as well as the children of the spouses themselves. In the case of a Magistrates' order the child must be that of at least one of the spouses which has been *accepted* by the other as a child of the family.

Any dispute relating to the above matters should be placed in the hands of a Solicitor without delay (see Legal Aid, etc. below) and in particular it should be borne in mind that where there is financial need (because of, e.g. continuing education or disability) maintenance may be ordered for children even beyond the age of majority.

SEPARATION BY AGREEMENT

Husband and wife may agree, with or without consideration, to separate and live apart, but the agreement, to be valid, must be followed by an immediate separation. It is most desirable to consult a solicitor in every such case.

MAGISTRATES' SEPARATION AND MAINTENANCE ORDERS

When a husband has been guilty of adultery or has been convicted of certain assaults or has deserted his wife, or has been guilty of persistent cruelty to her or to an infant child of the family, or of wilful neglect to maintain her or such a child, or where he is an habitual drunkard or drug addict, or insists on having intercourse while suffering from a venereal disease, or compels her to submit herself to prostitution, the wife may obtain relief from the local magistrates' court. A husband may apply on similar grounds, so far as they are applicable to him. In particular a wife can sometimes be guilty of the offence of wilful neglect to provide reasonable maintenance for her husband or children and an order can be made against her. The court may declare that the complainant is no longer bound to cohabit with the defendant. It may order the husband to pay a weekly sum in its descretion to the wife and may order her to make a similar payment to him if his earning capacity is impaired by age or illness. Provision may be made for legal custody of and access to any child of the family who is under the age of 16 years and for payment by either or both of the spouses of a weekly sum to the person entrusted with legal custody in respect of each child of the family up to the age of 16. If the court thinks the child would still be a dependent although over that age, similar payments may be ordered for support of the child up to the age of 21. The court cannot make an order that the parties need no longer cohabit or that either spouse shall support the other where the complainant has committed adultery during the marriage, unless the defendant has condoned or connived at, or by wilful neglect or misconduct conduced to, that act of adultery. The court has wide powers of revocation, revival and variation of orders already made. The order must be revoked if the parties have resumed cohabitation, and must be revoked, except so far as the order relates to the children, if the complaint is subsequently proved to have committed adultery since the marriage and the defendant has not condoned or connived at or by wilful neglect or misconduct conduced to that act of adultery. Complaints based on desertion or failure to maintain can be made whilst the offence continues. Complaints based on adultery must usually be made within 6 months of the complainant discovering it, all other complaints within 6 months of the offence itself. The Magistrates' Courts Act, 1952, separates the hearing of matrimonial disputes from ordinary court business; specifies the persons allowed to be present; limits newspaper reports, etc., etc.

SCOTLAND
DIVORCE

Actions of divorce can only be raised in the Court of Session which has jurisdiction to entertain such actions only if either of the parties to the marriage in question (a) is domiciled in Scotland on the date when the action is begun; or (b) was habitually resident in Scotland throughout the period of one year ending with that date.

The following are grounds for divorce:—

1. *Adultery.*—A mere confession by the defender is of itself insufficient; there must be proof of the facts. Direct evidence is not required, if facts can be established which give rise to an inevitable inference of adultery. There must be no collusion between the parties, and the pursuer is required to swear to this. It is not collusion, however, for a guilty spouse to give information of an act of adultery already committed. It is a defence to an action of divorce for adultery to plead that the innocent spouse has condoned the misconduct on which the action is founded, but the adultery shall not be held to have been condoned if cohabitation was continued or resumed with a view to effecting a reconciliation, for any one period not exceeding three months; Divorce (Scotland) Act, 1964.

2. *Desertion.*—The defender must have wilfully and without reasonable cause deserted the pursuer and persisted in such desertion for a period of not less than three years, but in calculating the period no account is taken of any one period not exceeding three months during which the parties resumed cohabitation with a view to reconciliation. It must be shown that the desertion was without reasonable cause, and it is a defence to an action on this ground that during that period the pursuer has refused a genuine and reasonable offer by the defender to adhere; Divorce (Scotland) Act, 1964. Refusal by one spouse to have marital relations with the other for any period of three years without any overt act of desertion does not constitute desertion. Here also, collusion is fatal to the success of the action.

3. *Incurable Insanity.*—The defender must, for five years preceding the raising of the action, have been under care and treatment as an insane person. A curator must be appointed to the defender and the curator is then in charge of the case.

4. *Cruelty.*—The degree of cruelty to be estab-

lished depends on the circumstances of each individual case, but the test, generally speaking, is that the conduct complained of must be such as to endanger the health of the pursuer. Cruelty may take the form of habitual drunkenness on the part of one of the spouses. The cruelty need not be intended to hurt the pursuer, thus the fraudulent activity of one spouse involving the other may amount to cruelty. There must be no condonation but, as in the case of an action on the ground of adultery, the Divorce (Scotland) Act 1964 provides a reconciliation period not exceeding three months.

5. *Unnatural Sexual Offences.*—An extract of the criminal conviction is sufficient proof.

Maintenance etc. The position is governed by the Succession (Scotland) Act 1964. The Act gives the Court power to order the guilty spouse to pay either a capital sum or a periodical allowance or both. The latter may be varied by the Court where there is a change in the circumstances of either party after the divorce.

A husband, being liable for his wife's debts, may be ordered to pay her costs, even though he has successfully defended the action. A paramour, if named as a defender, may be required to pay expenses.

Nullity of Marriage.—A declaration of nullity of marriage may be obtained on the ground of any impediment, viz., consanguinity and affinity, subsistence of a previous marriage, non-age of one of the parties, incapacity or insanity of one of the parties, or by the absence of genuine consent.

SEPARATION

A decree of judicial separation may be obtained by one spouse against the other on the grounds of (a) adultery, (b) cruelty and (c) habitual drunkenness. This entitles the parties to live apart, but does not dissolve the marriage. The husband, if the guilty party, is liable for aliment.

CUSTODY OF CHILDREN

In actions for divorce and separation, the Court has a discretion in awarding the custody of the children of the parties. The welfare of the children is the paramount consideration, and the mere fact that a spouse is the guilty party in the action does not of itself deprive him or her of the right to claim custody.

ILLEGITIMACY AND LEGITIMATION
ENGLAND AND WALES

A man may be summoned to petty sessions on the application of the mother of an illegitimate child, or by the Supplementary Benefits Commission where benefit has been paid for the requirements of the child, and the Justices, on his being proved to be the father of the child, may make an order requiring him to pay for its maintenance and education a sum in their discretion. The woman is not bound to give evidence in every case but if she does so it must be *corroborated* in some material particular. The mother has the custody of her illegitimate children. *Prima facie* every child born of a married woman during a marriage is legitimate; and this presumption can only be rebutted by strong, distinct, satisfactory and conclusive evidence. However, under the Family Reform Act, 1969, any presumption of law as to the legitimacy (or illegitimacy) of any person may in civil proceedings be rebutted by evidence showing that it is more probable than not that the person is illegitimate (or legitimate) and in any proceedings where paternity is in question, blood tests may be ordered. If however the husband and wife are separated under an Order of the Court, a child conceived by the wife during such separation is presumed not to be the husband's child.

LEGITIMATION.—By the *Legitimacy Act, 1926,* which came into force on Jan. 1, 1927, where the parents of an illegitimate person marry, or have married, whether before or after that date, the marriage, if the father is at the date thereof domiciled in England or Wales, renders that person, if living, legitimate as from Jan. 1, 1927, or from the date of the marriage, whichever last happens. Under the Act of 1959, marriage legitimates a person even though the father or mother was married to a third person at the time when the illegitimate person was born. It is the duty of the parents to supply to the Registrar-General information for re-registration of the birth of a legitimated child.

Declarations of Legitimacy.—A person claiming that he, his parents, or any remoter ancestor has become legitimated, may petition the High Court or the County Court for the necessary declaration.

Rights and Duties of Legitimated Persons.—A legitimate person, his spouse or issue may take property under an intestacy occurring after the date of legitimation, or under any disposition (*e.g.,* a will) coming into operation after such date, as if he had been legitimate.

He must maintain all persons whom he would be bound to maintain had he been born legitimate, and he is entitled to the benefit of any Act of Parliament which confers rights on legitimate persons to recover damages or compensation. The Act specially provides that nothing therein contained is to render any person capable of succeeding to or transmitting a right to any dignity or title.

Property Rights of Illegitimate Children.—By the Family Law Reform Act, 1969, the rights of an illegitimate child on an intestacy are now broadly equated with those of a legitimate child. Also, in any deposition made after January 1, 1970, any reference to children and other relatives shall, unless the contrary intension appears, be construed as including references to, and to persons related through, illegitimate children.

SCOTLAND

Illegitimate Children (Scotland) Act, 1930.—The mother of an illegitimate child may raise an action of affiliation and aliment against the father, either in the Court of Session or, more usually, in the Sheriff Court. Where in any such action the Court finds that the defender is the father of the child, the Court shall, in awarding in lying expenses, or ailment, have regard to the means of the parties, and the whole circumstances of the case. The Court may, upon application by the mother or by the father of any illegitimate child, or in any action for aliment for an illegitimate child, make such order as it may think fit regarding the custody of such child and the right of access thereto of either parent, having regard to the welfare of the child and to the conduct of the parents and to the wishes as well of the mother as of the father and may on the application of either parent recall or vary such order. The obligation of the mother and of the father of an illegitimate child to provide aliment for such child shall (without prejudice to any obligation attaching at common law) endure until the child attains the age of sixteen.

By Scots Law an illegitimate child is legitimated by and on the date of the subsequent marriage of its parents and there is no objection to there having been an impediment to the marriage of the parents at the time of the child's conception—*see* the Legitimation (Scotland) Act, 1968, which came into operation on June 8, 1968, on which date thousands of existing illegitimate children were regarded as legitimated. By the Registration of Births, Deaths and Marriages (Scotland) Act, 1965, a child so legitimated, who has already been registered as illegitimate, may be re-registered as legitimate. The consent of the father of an illegitimate child to its adoption is not required.

The Law Reform (Miscellaneous Provisions) (Scotland) Act, 1968, gives an illegitimate child full rights of succession (including legitim) in the estate of both parents, while the father and mother share equally in the estate of their illegitimate child. Unless expressly excluded, a reference in a deed executed on or after 25th November, 1968, to a relationship, *e.g.* " issue " or " children " is presumed to include illegitimate children.

MARRIAGE

A.—MARRIAGE ACCORDING TO RITES OF THE CHURCH OF ENGLAND

1. MARRIAGE BY BANNS.—The Marriage Act, 1949, prescribes audible publication according to the rubric, on three Sundays preceding the ceremony during morning service or, if there is no morning service on a Sunday on which the banns are to be published, during evening service. Where the parties reside in different parishes, the banns must be published in both. Under the Act, banns may be published and the marriage solemnized in the parish church, *which is the usual place of worship* of the persons to be married or either of them, although neither of such persons dwells in such parish; but this publication of banns is *in addition* to any other publication required by law and does not apply if the church or the residence of either party is in Wales. The Act provides specially for the case where one of the parties resides in Scotland and the other in England, the publication being then in the parish in England in which one party resides, and, according to the law and custom in Scotland, in the place where the other party resides. After the lapse of three months from the last time of publication, the banns become useless, and the parties must either obtain a licence (*see below*), or submit to the republication of banns.

2. MARRIAGE BY LICENCE.—Marriage licences are of two kinds:—

(i)· *A Common Licence,* dispensing with the necessity for banns, granted by the Archbishops and Bishops through their Surrogates, for marriages in any church or chapel duly licensed for marriages. A Common Licence can be obtained in London by application at the Faculty Office (1 The Sanctuary, Westminster, S.W.1) and (for marriages in London) at the Bishop of London's Diocesan Registry (1 The Sanctuary, S.W.1), by one of the parties about to be married. In the country they may be obtained at the offices of the Bishops' Registrars, but licences obtained at the Bishop's Diocesan Registry only enable the parties to be married in the diocese in which they are issued; those procured at the Faculty Office are available for *all* England and Wales. No instructions, either verbal or in writing, can be received, except from one of the parties. Affidavits are prepared from the personal instructions of one of the parties about to be married, and the licence is delivered to the party upon payment of fees amounting to six pounds. *No previous notice is required and the licence is available as soon as it is issued.* Before a licence can be granted one of the parties must make an affidavit that there is no legal impediment to the intended marriage; and also that one of such parties has had his or her usual place of abode for the space of fifteen days immediately preceding the issuing of the licence within the parish or ecclesiastical district of the church in which the marriage is to be solemnized, *or* the church in which the marriage is to be solemnized is the usual place of worship of the parties or one of them. In the country there may generally be found a parochial clergyman (Surrogate) before whom the affidavit may be taken, and whose office it is to deliver the licence personally to the applicant. (In some dioceses it is necessary for the Surrogate to procure the licence from the Bishop's Registry.) The licence continues in force for three months from its date.

(ii) *A Special Lincence* granted by the Archbishop of Canterbury, under special circumstances, for marriage at any place with or without previous residence in the district, or at any time, etc.; but the reasons assigned must meet with his Grace's approval. Application must be made to the Faculty Office. Fees for licence, etc., £25.

3. MARRIAGE UNDER SUPERINTENDENT REGISTRAR'S CERTIFICATE.—A marriage may be performed in church on the Superintendent Registrar's Certificate (as to which see below) without banns, provided that the incumbent's consent is obtained. One of the parties must be resident within the ecclesiastical parish of the church in which the marriage is to take place unless the church is the usual place of worship of the parties or one of them.

MARRIAGE FEES.—The Church Commissioners settle tables of fees for all parishes. The usual fees are paid although a stranger-clergyman may be invited to perform the service.

B.—MARRIAGE UNDER SUPERINTENDENT REGISTRAR'S CERTIFICATE

The following marriages may be solemnized on the authority of a Superintendent Registrar's Certificate (either with or without a licence):—

(a) A marriage in a registered building (*e.g.*, a nonconformist church registered for the solemnization of marriages therein).

(b) A marriage in a register office.

(c) A marriage according to the usages of the Society of Friends (commonly called Quakers).

(d) A marriage between two persons professing the Jewish religion according to the usages of the Jews.

(e) A marriage according to the rites of the Church of England (*see* above—in this case the marriage can only be *without* licence.

NOTICE.—Notice of the intended marriage must be given as follows:—

(i) Marriage by certificate (*without* licence)—if both parties reside in the same regisration district, they must both have resided there for seven days before the notice can be given. It may then be given by either party. If the parties reside in different registration districts, notice must be given by each to the Superintendent Registrar of the district in which he or she resides, and the preliminary residential qualification of seven days must be fulfilled by each before either notice can be given.

(ii) Marriage by certificate (*with* licence)—One notice only is necessay, whether the parties live in the same or in different registration

districts. Either party may give the notice, which must be given to the Superintendent Registrar of any registration district in which one of the parties has resided for the period of fifteen days immediately preseding the giving of notice, but both parties must be resident in England or Wales on the day notice is given.

The notice (in either case) must be in the prescribed form and must contain particulars as to names, marital status, occupation, residence, length of residence, and the building in which the marriage is to take place. The notice must also contain or have added at the foot thereof a solemn declaration that there is no legal impediment to the marriage, and, in the case of minors, that the consent of the person whose consent to the marriage is required by law (*see below*) has been duly given, and that the residential qualifications (mentioned above) have been complied with. A person making a false declaration renders himself or herself liable to prosecution for perjury. The notice is entered in the marriage notice book.

ISSUE OF CERTIFICATE:

(i) *Without licence.*—The notice (or an exact copy thereof) is affixed in some conspicuous place in the Superintendent Registrar's office for 21 days next after the notice was entered in the marriage notice book. After the lapse of this period the Superintendent Registrar may, provided no impediment is shown, issue his certificate for the marriage which can then take place at any time within three months from the date of the entry of the notice.

(ii) *With licence.*—The notice in this case is not affixed in the office of the Superintendent Registrar. After the lapse of one whole day (other than a Sunday, Christmas Day or Good Friday) from the date of entry of the notice, the Superintendent Registrar may, provided no impediment is shown, issue his certificate and licence for the marriage, which can then take place on any day within three months from the date of entry of the notice.

SOLEMNIZATION OF THE MARRIAGE:

(i) *In a Registered Building.*—The marriage must generally take place at a building within the district of residence of one of the parties, but if the usual place of worship of either is outside the district of his or her residence, it may take place in such usual place of worship. Further, if there is not within the district of residence of one of the parties a registered building within which marriages are solemnized according to the rites and ceremonies which the parties desire to adopt in solemnizing their marriage, it may take place in an appropriate registered building in the nearset district.

The presence of a Registrar of Marriages is not necessary at marriages at registered buildings which have adopted the provisions of section 43 of the Marriage Act, 1949. This section provides for the appointment of an " authorized person " (a person, usually the minister or an official of the building, certified by the trustees or governing body as having been duly authorized for the purpose) who must be present and must register the marriage.

The marriage must be solemnized between the hours of 8 a.m. and 6 p.m. with open doors in the presence of two or more witnesses. The parties must at some time during the ceremony make the following declaration—" I do solemnly declare that I know not of any lawful impediment why I. A. B., may not be joined in matrimony to C. D." Also each of the parties must say to the other: " I call upon these persons here present to witness that I, A. B., do take thee, C. D., to be my lawful wedded wife [or husband]," *or*, if the marriage is solemnized in the presence of an authorized person without the presence of a Registrar, each party may say in lieu thereof: " I, A. B., do take thee, C. D., to be my wedded wife [or husband]."

(ii) *In a Register Office.*—The marriage may be solemnized in the office of the Superintendent Registrar to whom notice of the marriage has been given. The marriage must be solemnized between the hours of 8 a.m. and 6 p.m., with open doors in the presence of the Superintendent Registrar or a Registrar of the registration district of that Superintendent Registrar, and in the presence of two witnesses. The parties must make the following declaration: " I do solemnly declare that I know not of any lawful impediment why I, A. B., may not be joined in matrimony to C. D.," and each party must say to the other: " I call upon these persons here present to witness that I, A. B., do take thee, C. D., to be my lawful wedded wife [or husband]." No religious ceremony may take place in the Register Office, though the parties may, on production of their marriage certificate, go through a subsequent religious ceremony in any church or persuasion of which they are members.

(iii) *Other Cases.*—If both parties are members of the Society of Friends (Quakers), or if, not being in membership, they have been authorized by the Society of Friends to solemnize their marriage in accordance with its usages, they may be married in a Friends' meeting-house. The marriage must be registered by the registering officer of the Society appointed to act for the district in which the meeting house is situated. The presence of a Registrar of Marriages is not necessary.

If both parties are Jews they may marry according to their usages in a synagogue, which has certificate marriage secretary, or private dwelling-house at any hour; the building may be situated within or without the district of residence. The marriage must be registered by the secretary of the synagogue of which the man is a member. The presence of a Registrar of Marriages is not necessary.

FEES OF SUPERINTENDING REGISTRARS

For entering notice of a marriage by certificate (with or without licence) in the marriage notice book.................... £2

For a licence for marriage.................. £8

For a marriage by certificate (with or without licence) in the presence of a Registrar (including cost of certificate).... £3

C.—MARRIAGE UNDER REGISTRAR GENERAL'S LICENCE

The main purpose of the Marriage (Registrar General's Licence) Act, 1970, which came into force on January 1, 1971, is to enable non-Anglicans to be married in unregistered premises where one of the persons to be married is seriously ill, is not expected to recover and cannot be moved to registered premises. A fee of £15 is payable to the Registrar General for the licence, though he has power to remit this in whole or in part to avoid hardship.

MISCELLANEOUS NOTES

Consanguinity and Affinity.—A marriage between persons within the prohibited degrees of consaguinity or affinity is void. Relaxations have, however, been made by various statutes which have now been replaced by the Marriage Act, 1949 (see the 1st Schedule to the Act) and the Marriage (Enabling) Act, 1960. It is now permitted to contract a marriage with:—

Sister, aunt or niece of a former wife (whether living or not). Former wife of brother, uncle or nephew (whether living or not).

No clergyman can be compelled to solemnize any of the foregoing marriages, but he may allow his church to be used for the purpose by another minister.

Minors.—Persons under 18 years of age are generally required to obtain the consent of certain persons (see Marriage Act, 1949, section 3 and 2nd Schedule as amended by the Family Law Reform Act, 1969). Where both parents are living, both must consent, where one is dead, the survivor, or, if there is a guardian appointed by the deceased parent, the guardian and the survivor. No consent is required in the case of an infant's second marriage. In certain exceptional cases consent may be dispensed with, *e.g.*, the insanity of a parent. If consent is refused the Court may, on application being made, consent to the marriage; application can be made for this purpose to the High Court, the County Court, or a Court of Summary Jurisdiction. The Act *prohibits* any marriage where either party is under 16 years of age.

D.—MARRIAGE IN ENGLAND OR WALES WHEN ONE PARTY LIVES IN SCOTLAND OR NORTHERN IRELAND

Notice for a marriage by a Superintendent Registrar's certificate in a register office or registered building may be given in the usual way by the party resident in England. As regards Scotland, the party there, after a residence of fifteen days should either apply to the session clerk to publish banns or give notice of marriage to the registrar; as regards Northern Ireland, the party there, after a residence of seven days, must give notice to the District Registrar of Marriages. Notice cannot be given for such marriages to take place by Certificate *with* licence of the Superintendent Registrar.

Marriage of such parties may take place in a church of the Church of England after the publication of banns, or by Ecclesiastical licence.

MARRIAGES IN SCOTLAND

According to the law of Scotland, marriage is a contract which is completed by the mutual consent of parties.

Impediments to marriage: These render the marriage null and void. (*a*) Age: If either party is under the age of 16. (*b*) Forbidden Degrees: If the parties are within certain degrees of relationship. (*c*) Subsisting previous marriage. (*d*) Impotency of either party. (*e*) Non-residence, *i.e.*, if the legal requirement of prior residence of one or other of the parties in Scotland have not been complied with. (*f*) Insanity of either party.

No consent of parents or guardians is necessary. Marriages may be regular or " irregular."

Regular Marriages.

A regular marriage is one which is celebrated by a Minister of religion or authorized Registrar after due notice by the proclamation of banns or publication by the Registrar, or by a Sheriff's licence. Any Minister of any denomination (including a person officiating at a Quaker wedding) who performs the ceremony is reckoned to be a minister of religion. It must be performed before two witnesses and one of the parties must either have his or her usual residence in the Registration District, or have resided there for at least 15 days before the ceremony or have a parent so residing there. No form, place or hours are prescribed by law. There are no canonical hours as in England. Public proclamation is made by (a) banns, or (b) notice by the Registrar. Banns must be proclaimed in a parish church situated within the registration district of the qualifying address of each party. It is ordered that the proclamation of banns should be made twice, but by immemorial practice proclamation on one Sunday is sufficient. The Clerk of the Kirk Session of the Parish takes in notices of banns and issues certificates of proclamation. The fee for proclamation may not exceed 75p. A certificate of proclamation of banns is only valid for three months.

Under the Marriage Notices (Scotland) Act, 1878, amended by the Marriage (Scotland) Act, 1956, a notice posted up in a conspicuous or accessible place on the board or outer wall of the Registrar's office is equivalent to the proclamation of banns, but a minister of the Church of Scotland is not bound, although he is entitled, to celebrate a marriage not preceded by banns. The statute is limited to persons with qualifying residence in Scotland or having parents so residing. Exhibition is made for 7 consecutive days, during which time any person may appear personally and lodge an objection in writing subscribed by him. If no objections are lodged the Registrar issues a certificate. Such certificate of publication is only valid for three months. Regulation made under the Births, Deaths and Marriages (Scotland) Act, 1965 provide that the cost of publication is 75p, which includes the issue of a certificate by the Registrar (any subsequent extract costs £1). The Naval Marriages Act, 1908, regulates the publication of banns or of notice on board H.M. ships and the granting of certificates by the Officer-Commanding.

Marriage before Registrar: After obtaining a certificate of due publication as above it is competent for the parties to contract the marriage in the office of the authorized Registrar in his presence and in the presence of two witnesses. The fee for the ceremony is £2. Such a marriage is regular and valid in all respects.

Marriage by Licence: In unforeseen and exceptional circumstances—*see* Section 2 of the Marriage (Scotland) Act, 1939—where normal method of publication cannot be carried through, the Sheriff, on application by the parties may grant a licence (valid for ten days) which is otherwise deemed in all respects to be equivalent to a certificate of publication.

Irregular Marriages

Since the passing of the Marriage (Scotland) Act, 1939, only one form of irregular marriage is recognized, *viz.* marriage by co-habitation and habit and repute. If parties live together constantly as husband and wife, and if they are held to be such by the general repute of the neighbourhood, then there may arise a presumption from which marriage can be inferred. Before such marriage can be registered, however, a decree of declarator of marriage must be obtained from the Court of Session.

JURY SERVICE

Every local or parliamentary elector between the ages of eighteen and sixty-five who has resided in the United Kingdom, Channel Islands or Isle of Man for at least five years since he attained the age of thirteen will be qualified to serve on a jury unless he is " ineligible " or " disqualified ".

Ineligible persons include those who have at any time been judges, magistrates and certain senior court officials, those who within the previous ten years have been concerned with the law (such as barristers and solicitors and their clerks, court officers, coroners, police, prison and probation officers); priests of any religion and vowed members of religious communities; and certain sufferers from mental illness.

Disqualified persons are those who have at any time been sentenced by a Court in the United Kingdom, Channel Islands or Isle of Man, to a term of imprisonment exceeding five years, or who have in the previous ten years served any part of a sentence exceeding three months or been sentenced to Borstal.

Some others are excusable as of right. These include members and officers of the Houses of Parliament, full-time serving members of the forces (including Women's forces) and registered and practising members of the medical, dental, nursing, veterinary and pharmaceutical professions and any person who has served on a jury in the two years before he is summoned. In other cases the court may excuse a juror at its discretion (e.g. where the service would be a hardship to the juror).

If a person serves on a jury knowing himself to be disqualified or ineligible he is liable to be fined up to £400 or £100 respectively.

A juror is entitled to subsistence and travelling expenses, compensation for other expenses incurred in consequence of attendance for jury service, loss of earnings and loss of national insurance benefits but certain maximum figures (which are revised from time to time) are laid down.

A verdict of a jury must normally be unanimous but after two hours consideration (or such longer period as the Court thinks reasonable), a majority verdict is acceptable if ten jurors agree to it (or nine if the size of the jury has been reduced to ten, e.g. by illness during the trial).

Jury trial is now very unusual in civil cases but a person charged with any but the least serious crimes is entitled to be tried by a jury. The defendant may object to any juror if he can show that that juror ought not be on the jury (e.g. because he is ineligible or is biased against him) and may object to seven jurors without giving any reason.

JURY SERVICE IN SCOTLAND

It is the duty of the sheriff principal of each sheriffdom, in respect of each sheriff court district in his sheriffdom, to maintain a book, known as the " general jury book ", containing the names and designations of persons within the district who are qualified and liable to serve as jurors. The book, which is compiled from information which every householder is required to provide, is kept open for the inspection by any person, upon payment of a nominal fee, at the sheriff clerk's office for the district. Part II of the Juries Act 1949 (amended by the Juries Act 1954 with regulations following thereon) applies only to Scotland and provides, inter alia, for the payment of travelling expenses and subsistence allowances to jurors and for loss of earnings.

The number of a jury in a civil cause in the Court of Session is twelve and in the Sheriff Court seven. In a criminal trial the number is fifteen, and in inquiries by Sheriff and jury under the Fatal Accidents Inquiry (Scotland) Act 1895 or the Fatal

Accidents and Sudden Deaths Inquiry (Scotland) Act 1906 the number is seven. In Scotland there is no Coroner's Inquest.

QUALIFICATIONS

Every man or woman between the ages of 21 and 60 who is possessed of heritable property of the yearly value of at least £5, or of moveable property of the value of at least £200 Sterling, is qualified to serve on a jury.

Exemptions.—The following persons are exempt from serving on juries: peers, judges of the supreme courts, sheriffs, ministers of religion, parochial schoolmasters, practising lawyers, clerks and other officers of any court of justice, prison offices, university professors, practising physicians, surgeons, registered veterinary surgeons or midwives, registered dentists (if they wish to be exempt), officers in the Army, Navy or Air Force on full pay, officers of the Customs and Excise, messengers at arms, police and other officers of law, commissioners and other officers and employees of the Inland Revenue, lighthouse keepers and their assistants, soldiers of the regular Army or Air Force, officers and men of the Territorial Army and Royal Auxiliary Air Force, factory inspectors and airport police. Officers of the Post Office will not be compelled to serve.

Jurors failing to attend without good cause are liable to a penalty.

LANDLORD AND TENANT
ENGLAND AND WALES

Although basically the relationship between the parties to the lease is governed by the lease itself, the position is complicated by numerous statutory provisions. The few points dealt with may show the desirability of seeking professional assistance in these matters. Important provisions include:—

(1) As to agricultural holdings—the Agricultural Holdings Act, 1948. Among other things, this Act regulates the length of notice necessary to determine an agricultural tenancy, the tenant's right to remove fixtures on the land, his right to compensation for damage done by game, for improvements and for disturbance, and his right to require the consent of the Agricultural Land Tribunal to the operation of a notice to quit.

(2) As to business premises—the Landlord and Tenant Acts, 1927 and 1954, and the Law of Property Act 1969, Pt. I. Part II of the 1954 Act gives security of tenure to the tenant of most business premises, and in effect he can only be ousted on one or more of the seven grounds set out in the Act. In some cases, where the landlord can resume possession, the tenant is entitled to compensation.

(3) As to dwelling houses. The complicated mass of legislation is now mainly embodied in the Rent Acts 1968 and 1974, which does not extend to Scotland or Northern Ireland. If the house is within the Act, a tenant has a personal right to reside there, and he may only be ousted on certain grounds.

Such tenancies may be either controlled or regulated. A controlled tenancy is one which has been in existence since July 6, 1957; had at that time the protection of the Rent Acts and is of a house or part of a house the rateable value of which did not exceed £40 in London or £30 elsewhere on November 7, 1956. A regulated tenancy is one which is not controlled, and which falls within the following limits:—

(a) Rateable value on March 23, 1965 (or when first rated, if later)—not in excess of £400 in Greater London or £200 elsewhere OR

(b) Rateable value on March 22, 1973 (or when first rated, if later)—not in excess of £600 in Greater London or £300 elsewhere. OR

(c) Rateable value on April 1, 1973 (or when first rated, if later)—not in excess of £1500 in Greater London or £750 elsewhere.

The essential difference between controlled tenancies and regulated tenancies is in the maximum rent recoverable. Under controlled tenancies, the maximum rent is ascertained by taking an appropriate multiple of the gross value for rating purposes of the property on November 7, 1956, whereas the maximum rent under a regulated tenancy is the rent agreed between the landlord and tenant, unless a fair rent has been registered, in which case that is the maximum rent recoverable. Application for the registration of a fair rent may be made by either the landlord or tenant, to the Local Rent Officer, and appeal against his decision lies to the Rent Assessment Committee.

S27 of the Housing Finance Act 1972 provides for the conversion of a controlled tenancy into a regulated tenancy on the issue of a certificate by the Local Authority that the house is provided with all standard amenities. The Housing Rents and Subsidies Act 1975 has repealed the former provision for conversion by reference to rateable value on a specific date. This Act also provides for the phasing of rent increases in the private sector.

(4) As to dwelling houses with resident landlords. The Rent Act 1974 gives tenants of furnished dwellings the same security of tenure as those of unfurnished dwellings unless the landlord lives in part of the house. In the latter case, and in the case of a tenancy of an unfurnished dwelling granted by a resident landlord after 13th August 1974, the tenancy may fall within Part VI of the Rent Act 1968, and the tenant may be granted relief from eviction by application to the Rent Tribunal after a notice to quit has been served, but before it has expired. The Rent Tribunal is empowered to delay the operation of the notice to quit by 6 months, and by the end of that period, the tenant may apply for a further delay of 6 months. The landlord or the tenant may also apply to the Rent Tribunal for a reasonable rent to be registered, and once registered, this is the maximum rent recoverable.

(5) The Rent Act 1965 Act also provides that if any person with intent to cause the residential occupier of any premises to give up the occupation thereof does any act calculated to interfere with the peace or comfort of the residential occupier or members of his household, he shall be guilty of an offence. A further provision prevents a landlord enforcing a right to possession against a tenant (who is not already protected by any security of tenure legislation) without a court order, and there are special rules in such cases relating to agricultural employees.

(6) A notice to quit any dwellinghouse must be given at least four weeks before it is to take effect.

(7) Part I of the Landlord and Tenant Act, 1954, applies to most tenancies of houses for over twenty-one years at a ground rent. Where it applies, the contractual tenancy is continued until brought to an end in the manner prescribed by the Act, and in effect the landlord can only get possession on limited grounds.

Further, under the Leasehold Reform Act, 1967, tenants of houses under leases for over twenty-one years at rent less than two-thirds of the rateable value of the house are in most cases given a right to purchase the freehold or to take an extended lease for a term of fifty years, provided the tenant at the time when he seeks to exercise the right has been occupying the house as his residence for the last five years or for periods amounting to five years in the last ten years.

(8) Under the Housing Act, 1961 (which does not extend to Scotland), in a lease of a dwelling-house granted after October 24, 1961, for a term of less than 7 years, there is implied a covenant by the landlord (a) to keep in repair the structure and exterior of the house and (b) to keep in repair and proper working order the installations in the house (i) for the supply of water, gas and electricity, and for sanitation, and (ii) for space heating or heating water.

SCOTLAND

A Lease is a Contract, the relationship of the parties being governed by the terms thereof. As is also the case in England (see the foregoing Section) legislation has played an important part in regulating that relationship. Thus, what at Common Law was an Agreement binding only the parties to the deed, becomes in virtue of Statute 1449 c. 17, a contract binding the landlord's successors, as purchasers or creditors, provided the following four conditions are observed; (1) the lease, if for more than one year, must be in writing, (2) there must be a rent, (3) there must be a term of expiry, and (4) the tenant must have entered into possession.

It would be impracticable in a brief section of these Notes to enter upon a general discussion of this branch of the law and, accordingly, the plan adopted in the preceding Section of quoting a few important Statutes is followed here.

The Agricultural Holdings (Scotland) Act, 1949 (amended by the Agriculture Act, 1958), which is a consolidating Act applicable to Scotland, contains provisions similar to those in the English Act, alluded to in the preceding Section. It cannot here be analysed in detail.

It is of interest to note that the Small Landholders Act, 1911, provided for the setting up of the Land Court which has jurisdiction over a large proportion of agricultural and pastoral land in Scotland.

In Scotland business premises are not controlled by Statute to so great an extent as in England, but the Tenancy of Shops (Scotland) Acts, 1949 and 1964 give a measure of security to tenants of shops. These Acts enable the tenant of a shop who is threatened with eviction to apply to the Sheriff for a renewal of the tenancy. If the landlord has offered to sell the subjects to the tenant at an agreed price the application for a renewal of the tenancy may be dismissed. Reference should be made to Section 1 (3) of the 1949 Act for particulars of other circumstances under which the Sheriff has a discretion to dismiss an application. The Acts apply to premises held by the Crown or Government Departments, either as landlord or tenant.

The Housing (Scotland) Act 1969 and the Rent (Scotland) Act 1971, as amended by the Rent Act 1974, define controlled tenancies and regulated tenancies, both furnished and unfurnished, and lay down the system by which a landlord or tenant may obtain from the Rent Officer registration of a fair rent. The Acts also give to the tenants either of furnished or unfurnished lets a substantial degree of security of tenure. There are, however, certain exceptions; thus, they do not apply to tenancies where the interest belongs to the Crown, or to a local authority, a development corporation or the Housing Corporation of new towns. There must be a true tenancy for the Acts to apply. They do not apply to licensees such as lodgers or persons allowed to occupy houses on a grace and favour basis or to service occupiers. The Acts define the

circumstances under which a landlord may apply for increased rent as a consequence of having carried out improvements to his property and also lay down the system of phasing of such rent increases. On the death of a statutory successor to a tenancy the tenancy may pass for a second time to a member of the family or a relative who has been in residence in the house for a period of at least six months The Acts also lay down the duties and functions of Rent Officers and Rent Assessment Committees with regard to unfurnished accommodation and of Rent Tribunals for furnished accommodation.

LEGAL AID
LEGAL AID IN CIVIL PROCEEDINGS

The Legal Aid Act 1974, is designed to make legal aid and advice more readily available for persons of small and moderate means. The main structure of the service is contained in the Act itself and the Regulations made thereunder, administered by the Law Society.

Legal aid is available for proceedings (including matrimonial causes) in the House of Lords, Court of Appeal, High Court, County Courts, Lands Tribunal, Restrictive Practices Court, before the Commons Commissioners, and civil proceedings in Magistrates' Courts. In any event, an application for legal aid will not be approved if it appears that the applicant would gain only a trivial advantage from the proceedings. Further, proceedings wholly or partly in respect of defamation are excepted from the scheme, as are also relator actions and election petitions.

Where a person is concerned in proceedings only in a representative, fiduciary or official capacity, his personal resources are not to be taken into account in considering eligibility for legal aid. Apart from this, eligibility in civil proceedings depends upon an applicant's " disposable income " and " disposable capital ". Legal aid cannot be granted if the former exceeds £1,580 per annum, and a person may be refused assistance if he has a disposable capital of more than £1,200 and it appears that he can afford to proceed without legal aid. Even so, the applicant *may* be required to contribute up to one third the excess of his disposable income above £500, together with the whole excess of his disposable capital above £250. Disposable income is calculated by making deductions from gross income in respect of certain matters such as dependants, interest on loans, income tax, rates, rent and other matters for which the applicant must or reasonably may provide. Disposable capital is calculated by excluding from gross capital part of the value of the house in which the applicant resides, of furniture and household possessions; allowances are made in respect of dependants. Except in cases where the spouses are living apart, or have a contrary interest, any resources of a person's wife or husband are to be treated as that person's resources. These figures will be assessed by the Department of Health and Social Security, and will be certified to a Local Committee, who will determine whether reasonable grounds exist for the grant of a civil aid certificate. Appeal from refusal of a certificate lies to an Area Committee. A person resident in England or Wales desiring legal aid may apply for a certificate to any Local Committee; if resident elsewhere application should be made to a Local Committee for London. However, if the application is made in respect of proceedings in an *appellate* court and the applicant is resident in England or Wales, application should generally be made to any *Area* Committee—if resident elsewhere, to an *Area* Committee for London. If a certificate is granted, the applicant may select his solicitor, and, if necessary, counsel from a panel. The costs of the assisted person's solicitor and counsel will be paid out of the legal aid fund. The court may order that the costs of a successful unassisted party shall be paid out of the legal aid fund.

LEGAL ADVICE AND ASSISTANCE

The Scheme is governed by the Legal Aid Act 1974.

Under this legal advice and assistance scheme a client may obtain such advice or assistance as is normally provided by a solicitor and if necessary the advice of a barrister may be obtained, but the scheme does not extend to taking any step in any proceedings before any court or tribunal. Where legal aid is available for civil proceedings (see above) or in criminal cases (see below) the scheme covers work done in making application for such legal aid.

A person is eligible for advice or assistance under the scheme provided his disposable capital does not exceed £250 and his disposable income does not exceed £29·00 per week or if he receives Supplementary Benefit or Family Income Supplement. For a married man or person with children or other dependants deductions will be made from gross income and capital and allowances are made in respect of income tax, National Insurance contributions, etc. It is intended that the financial limits shall approximate to those applying for legal aid in civil proceedings (see above). Except when they are separated or have conflicting interests the means of husband and wife will be aggregated for the purpose of determining financial eligibility. If a person's disposable income exceeds £15·00 per week he will be required to pay a contribution as follows:—

Disposable income over—

£15·00 but not over	£16·00 contribution	£1·50
£16·00 ,, ,, ,,	£17·00 ,,	£4·00
£17·00 ,, ,, ,,	£19·00 ,,	£6·50
£19·00 ,, ,, ,,	£21·00 ,,	£9·00
£21·00 ,, ,, ,,	£23·00 ,,	£12·00
£23·00 ,, ,, ,,	£25·00 ,,	£15·00
£25·00 ,, ,, ,,	£27·00 ,,	£18·00
£27·00 ,, ,, ,,	£29·00 ,,	£21·00

Solicitor's costs and expenses, which should not together exceed £25 (V.A.T. exclusive) without leave of the Area Legal Aid Committee, will be paid out of the client's contribution and any monies recovered in respect of costs or damages from another party and the balance will be paid by the Legal Aid Fund.

The Act also extends the scheme to cover the costs of a solicitor who is present within the precincts of a magistrates' court or county court and is requested by the court to advise or represent a person who is in need of help.

LEGAL AID IN CRIMINAL CASES

The Legal Aid Act 1974 Part II provides for legal aid in criminal proceedings. A criminal court (e.g., magistrates' court, Crown Court) has power to order legal aid to be granted where it appears desirable to do so in the interests of justice. The court shall make an order in certain cases, e.g. where a person is committed for trial on a charge of murder. However, the court may not make an order unless it appears to the court that the person's means are such that he requires assistance in meeting the costs of the particular proceedings in question. Application should be made to the appropriate court where proceedings are to take place.

An applicant may be required to make a contribution towards the costs of the action. In order to ascertain the amount of this contribution he will have to produce written evidence of his means. Any assessment of means will be carried out by the Supplementary Benefits Commission, which will report to the court. No contribution will be required from a person who has insufficient means.

Any practising barrister or solicitor may act for a legally aided person in criminal proceedings unless excluded by reason of misconduct. In general where legal aid is given it will normally include representation by both counsel and solicitor. However, in connection with magistrates' courts, representation will be by solicitor alone unless it is a serious offence.

Where any doubt arises about the grant of a legal aid order that doubt is to be resolved in favour of the applicant. The court also has power to amend or revoke a legal aid order. Legal aid may also be granted in connection with appellate proceedings, e.g., on appeal to the Criminal Division of the Court of Appeal under the Criminal Appeal Act, 1968.

SCOTLAND
Civil Proceedings

The Legal Aid (Scotland) Act, 1967 and the Legal Advice and Assistance Act, 1972 form the basis of a scheme to provide legal advice in civil actions in the House of Lords on appeals from the Court of Session, in the Court of Session, the Lands Valuation Appeal Court, the Scottish Land Court, the Sheriff Court, the Restrictive Practices Court and Lands Tribunal for Scotland, except in actions in respect of defamation or verbal injury, breach of promise of marriage, the inducement of one spouse to leave or remain apart from the other, election petitions (under the Representative of the People Act, 1949), and small debt proceedings (i.e. under £50) and proceedings for summary removing, in both of which liability for the debt and the amount thereof are admitted.

As to those to whom legal aid is available, the same considerations as to income and capital apply in Scotland as in England. (*See* the preceding paragraph.) A person believing himself to be eligible may instruct any solicitor of his own choice who is on the official lists, or he may apply for a solicitor to one of the various Legal Aid Committees which are set up to administer the scheme. In a case where litigation is not immediately necessary, the client can seek advice under the Legal Advice and Assistance Act 1972 which is similar to the legal advice and assistance provisions of the Legal Aid Act 1974 (see above). In an instance where litigation is expected, application for a certificate granting legal aid is thereafter made to the appropriate Committee by the applicant's solicitor, who is required to prepare, for the signature of the applicant, a memorandum setting forth the grounds of the proposed action. Investigation into the applicant's financial means is carried out by the Supplementary Benefits Commission after the Committee has considered the memorandum and, on a suitable contribution, if any, by the applicant being approved, a Certificate is granted enabling the applicant to proceed with his action. The Legal Aid (Scotland) Act, 1967 provides for the payment (to a limited extent) out of the legal aid funds of expenses incurred by successful opponents of legally aided litigants.

LEGAL ADVICE

Legal advice, as distinct from legal aid in proceedings, is available to anyone in Scotland on terms similar to those stated in a preceding paragraph dealing with legal advice in England,—the Scottish scheme being administered under the Legal Advice and Assistance Act 1972.

Criminal Proceedings

Legal Aid (Scotland) (Criminal Proceedings) Regulations, 1964, which came into operation in October 1964, provide for the administration of criminal legal aid.

TOWN AND COUNTRY PLANNING

The Town and Country Planning Act 1971 (consolidating earlier Acts) contains very far-reaching provisions affecting the liberty of an owner of land to develop and use it as he will. A person has generally to get planning permission before carrying out any development on his land from the Local Planning Authority. Development charge is not payable in respect of operations begun or uses of land instituted on or after November 18, 1952. By the Land Commission (Dissolution) Act 1971, betterment levy, which was formerly payable on the realization of the development value of land, is not chargeable on any transactions carried out after July 23, 1970. This Act extends to Scotland.

What is Development:—

(a) Carrying out of building, engineering, mining or other operations.

(b) Making a material change in use.

It is expressly provided that if one dwelling-house is converted into two or more dwelling-houses, this involves a material change in use.

Examples of what is not deemed Development:—

(a) Maintaining, improving or altering the interior of a building (except works for making good war damage), provided there is no material change to the exterior, with the exception that since January 1, 1969, any expansion of a building below ground level constitutes development.

(b) Change of use of property within the curtilage of a dwelling-house for a purpose incidental to the use of the dwelling-house as such. (It will, however, be development if building operations are carried out.)

Application can be made to the Local Planning Authority to determine whether or not an operation or change of use constitutes development.

Planning Permission.—Application for such permission is not always necessary, as the Secretary of State may make Development Orders giving general permission for a specified type of development. Thus a General Development Order of 1973 specifies a number of types of development for which no permission is required, e.g., enlargement of a dwelling-house (including erection of a garage), so long as the cubic content of the original dwelling (external measurement) is not exceeded by more than 50 cubic metres or one-tenth, whichever is greater, subject to a maximum of 115 cubic metres.

Appeal against refusal of permission lies to the Secretary of State and from his decision, in limited circumstances, to the High Court. If the result of the appeal is unsatisfactory, an applicant may in certain circumstances require the Council to purchase the land.

Enforcement Notice.—If development is carried out without permission, or in defiance of conditions attached to such permission, the Local Planning Authority may serve an enforcement notice on the owner of the land calling upon him to demolish or alter any building, of to discontinue the use of land, or to comply with the said conditions. If the notice is not complied with, the Local Planning Authority may take appropriate steps to enforce it, recovering their expenses from the owner for the time being of the land. Appeal against an enforcement notice lies to the Secretary of State.

VOTERS' QUALIFICATIONS

The franchise is governed by the Representation of the People Acts, the most important of which are the Act of 1949 (as amended) and the Act of 1969. Those entitled to vote as electors at a parliamentary election in any constituency are all persons resident there on the qualifying date who, at that date are British subjects or citizens of the Republic of Ireland of at least 18 years of age and not subject to any legal incapacity to vote. In addition, a person who is of voting age on the date of the poll at a parliamentary or local government election is entitled to vote, whether or not he is of voting age on the qualifying date. Accordingly, a qualified person will be entitled to be registered in a register of parliamentary electors or a register of local government electors if he will attain voting age within twelve months from the date on which the register is required to be published. Since the Electoral Registers Act of 1949, the registers are prepared once in each year only. Under the Electoral Registers Act, 1953, the Register (of parliamentary and local government electors or, in Northern Ireland, of parliamentary electors) is published not later than February 15 in each year and is for use in the period of 12 months commencing on February 16. The qualifying date referred to is, in England, Wales and Scotland the preceding October 10, and in Northern Ireland the preceding September 15.

The Register is prepared by the Registration Officer in each constituency in Great Britain. It is the registration officer's duty to have a house to house or other official inquiry made as to the persons entitled to be registered and to publish preliminary electors lists showing the persons appearing to him to be entitled to be registered. Any person whose name is omitted may claim registration, and any person on the list may object to the inclusion therein of other persons' names: the registration officer determines the claims and objections which must generally be lodged by December 16 in each year. The procedure is slightly different for Northern Ireland.

Special provision is made for " Service voters " (and persons employed by the British Council in posts outside the United Kingdom), who include wives of Service voters resident with their husbands outside the United Kingdom. Such persons may make a Service declaration in a prescribed form and are then treated as resident at the address specified in the declaration. Service voters may vote by post or by proxy, on making the necessary application to the registration officer.

Certain other persons (e.g., those unable to go in person to the polling station owing to the general nature of their occupation, blindness or other physical incapacity, etc.) may vote by post or in some cases, by proxy as " absent voters". Section 5 of the 1969 Act extends to certain married persons the right to vote by proxy or by post.

The local government franchise now depends solely upon residence in the area, the previous non-resident qualification for owners of property having been abolished by the Representation of the People Act, 1969, with effect from February 16, 1970. There are provisions, similar to those relating to the parliamentary franchise, for the preparation of registers, etc., and in fact the same register is used, as far as possible, with a mark indicating those persons entitled to vote for local government purposes only. The Acts apply generally to Scotalnd where certain matters relating to local government and parliamentary elections are further regulated by Representation of the People (Scotland) Regulations, 1949.

INCOME TAX 1975–76

In his budget statement on April 15, 1975, Mr. Healey, the Chancellor of the Exchequer, announced the following measures affecting income tax:

(a) Increase of 2 percentage points in the rates of income tax on all bands of taxable income (i.e. after deduction of all allowances) except the highest. The new rates on the various bands (excluding investment income surcharge where applicable) are shown below.

Taxable income band £	Old rate	New rate
	(per cent)	
0–4,500	33	35
4,500–5,000	38	40
5,000–6,000	43	45
6,000–7,000	48	50
7,000–8,000	53	55
8,000–10,000	58	60
10,000–12,000	63	65
12,000–15,000	68	70
15,000–20,000	73	75
over 20,000	83	83

(b) Single person's allowance and maximum wife's earned income relief each raised from £625 to £675 and married allowance from £865 to £955.

(c) Additional personal allowance (payable to single parent who is also entitled to child allowance for a child living with him or her) increased from £180 to £280.

(d) Tighter regulations to be introduced for dealing with tax and national insurance abuses in the contruction industry; the pay-as-you-earn system to apply to the pay of office workers and other staff engaged through agencies; benefits enjoyed by an employee where his employer operated a medical insurance scheme to be taxable at all income levels; steps to be taken to prevent avoidance of tax by the issue of vouchers to employees instead of normal pay (although no change in the existing luncheon voucher concession); and measures to be introduced to encourage the more prompt payment of tax.

The tables which follow show the tax payable for 1974–75 and 1975–76 and the corresponding effective rate of tax, *i.e.*, the average rate per cent over the whole income.

The personal allowances and reliefs appropriate to the circumstances shown are taken into account but a taxpayer may be entitled to further reliefs which would reduce the tax payable.

The earned income of a married couple is assumed to be the husband's; where any of the income is earned by the wife, the tax payable will be less than the amount shown.

The income includes family allowances where there is more than one child in the family, even though at some income levels it would be to the taxpayer's advantage not to claim it; " clawback " has also been taken into account at all levels of income.

SINGLE PERSONS—INCOME ALL EARNED

Income	1974–75		1975–76	
	Income tax	Effective rate	Income tax	Effective rate
£	£	Per cent	£	Per cent
700	24·75	3·5	8·75	1·3
800	57·75	7·2	43·75	5·5
900	90·75	10·1	78·75	8·8
1,000	123·75	12·4	113·75	11·4
1,100	156·75	14·3	148·75	13·5
1,200	189·75	15·8	183·75	15·3
1,300	222·75	17·1	218·75	16·8
1,400	255·75	18·3	253·75	18·1
1,500	288·75	19·3	288·75	19·3
1,600	321·75	20·1	323·75	20·2
1,700	354·75	20·9	358·75	21·1
1,800	387·75	21·5	393·75	21·9
1,900	420·75	22·1	428·75	22·6
2,000	453·75	22·7	463·75	23·2
2,500	618·75	24·8	638·75	25·6
3,000	783·75	26·1	813·75	27·1
4,000	1,113·75	27·8	1,163·75	29·1
5,000	1,443·75	28·9	1,513·75	30·3
6,000	1,836·25	30·6	1,921·25	32·0
7,000	2,285·00	32·6	2,387·50	34·1
8,000	2,783·75	34·8	2,903·75	36·3
9,000	3,332·50	37·0	3,470·00	38·6
10,000	3,912·50	39·1	4,070·00	40·7
15,000	7,150·00	47·7	7,402·50	49·4
20,000	10,768·75	53·8	11,118·75	55·6
30,000	19,006·25	63·4	19,364·75	64·5
50,000	35,606·25	71·2	35,964·75	71·9
100,000	77,106·25	77·1	77,464·75	77·5

SINGLE PERSONS—INCOME ALL FROM INVESTMENTS

Income	1974–75		1975–76	
	Income tax	Effective rate	Income tax	Effective rate
£	£	Per cent	£	Per cent
700	24·75	3·5	8·75	1·3
800	57·75	7·2	43·75	5·5
900	90·75	10·1	78·75	8·8
1,000	123·75	12·4	113·75	11·4
1,100	166·75	15·2	158·75	14·4
1,200	209·75	17·5	203·75	17·0
1,300	252·75	19·4	248·75	19·1
1,400	295·75	21·1	293·75	21·1
1,500	338·75	22·6	338·75	22·6
1,600	381·75	23·9	383·75	24·0
1,700	424·75	25·0	428·75	25·2
1,800	467·75	26·0	473·75	26·3
1,900	510·75	26·9	518·75	27·3
2,000	553·75	27·7	563·75	28·2
2,500	793·75	31·8	813·75	32·6
3,000	1,033·75	34·5	1,063·75	35·5
4,000	1,513·75	37·8	1,563·75	39·1
5,000	1,993·75	39·9	2,063·75	41·3
6,000	2,536·25	42·3	2,621·25	43·7
7,000	3,135·00	44·8	3,237·50	46·3
8,000	3,783·75	47·3	3,903·75	48·8
9,000	4,482·50	49·8	4,620·00	51·3
10,000	5,212·50	52·1	5,370·00	53·7
15,000	9,200·00	61·3	9,452·50	63·0
20,000	13,568·75	67·8	13,918·75	69·6
30,000	23,306·25	77·7	23,664·75	78·9
50,000	42,906·25	85·8	43,264·75	86·5
100,000	91,906·25	91·9	92,264·75	92·3

SINGLE PERSON WITH ADDITIONAL PERSONAL ALLOWANCE
ONE CHILD NOT OVER 11—INCOME ALL EARNED

Income	1974–75		1975–76	
	Income tax	Effective rate	Income tax	Effective rate
£	£	Per cent	£	Per cent
1,100	18·15	1·7	—	—
1,200	51·15	4·3	1·75	0·1
1,300	84·15	6·5	36·75	2·8
1,400	117·15	8·4	71·75	5·1
1,500	150·15	10·0	106·75	7·1
1,600	183·15	11·4	141·75	8·9
1,700	216·15	12·7	176·75	10·4
1,800	249·15	13·8	211·75	11·8
1,900	282·15	14·9	246·75	13·0
2,000	315·15	15·8	281·75	14·1
2,500	480·15	16·6	456·75	18·3
3,000	645·15	21·5	631·75	21·1
4,000	975·15	24·4	981·75	24·5
5,000	1,305·15	26·1	1,331·75	26·6
6,000	1,657·90	27·6	1,697·00	28·3
7,000	2,085·65	29·8	2,137·25	30·5
8,000	2,563·40	32·0	2,627·50	32·8
9,000	3,091·15	34·3	3,167·75	35·2
10,000	3,668·90	36·7	3,758·00	37·6
15,000	6,864·40	45·8	7,038·50	46·9
20,000	10,462·15	52·3	10,728·75	53·6
30,000	18,657·65	62·2	18,933·15	63·1
50,000	35,257·65	70·5	35,533·15	71·1
100,000	76,757·65	76·8	77,033·15	77·0

MARRIED COUPLES—INCOME ALL EARNED

| Income | 1974–75 | | 1975–76 | |
	Income tax	Effective rate	Income tax	Effective rate
£	£	Per cent	£	Per cent
900	11·55	1·3	—	—
1,000	44·55	4·5	15·75	1·6
1,100	77·55	7·1	50·75	4·6
1,200	110·55	9·2	85·75	7·1
1,300	143·55	11·0	120·75	9·3
1,400	176·55	12·6	155·75	11·1
1,500	209·55	14·0	190·75	12·7
1,600	242·55	15·2	225·75	14·1
1,700	275·55	16·2	260·75	15·3
1,800	308·55	17·1	295·75	16·4
1,900	341·55	18·0	330·75	17·4
2,000	374·55	18·7	365·75	18·3
2,500	539·55	21·6	540·75	21·6
3,000	704·55	23·5	715·75	23·9
4,000	1,034·55	25·9	1,065·75	26·6
5,000	1,364·55	27·3	1,415·75	28·3
6,000	1,733·05	28·9	1,795·25	29·9
7,000	2,169·80	31·0	2,247·50	32·1
8,000	2,656·55	33·2	2,749·75	34·4
9,000	3,193·30	35·5	3,302·00	36·7
10,000	3,773·30	37·7	3,902·00	39·0
15,000	6,986·80	46·6	7,206·50	48·0
20,000	10,593·55	53·0	10,908·75	54·5
30,000	18,807·05	62·7	19,132·35	63·8
50,000	35,407·05	70·8	35,732·35	71·5
100,000	76,907·05	76·9	77,232·35	77·2

MARRIED COUPLES—INCOME ALL FROM INVESTMENTS

| Income | 1974–75 | | 1975–76 | |
	Income tax	Effective rate	Income tax	Effective rate
£	£	Per cent	£	Per cent
900	11·55	1·3	—	—
1,000	44·55	4·5	15·75	1·6
1,100	87·55	8·0	60·75	5·5
1,200	130·55	10·9	105·75	8·8
1,300	173·55	13·4	150·75	11·6
1,400	216·55	15·5	195·75	14·0
1,500	259·55	17·3	240·75	16·1
1,600	302·55	18·9	285·75	17·9
1,700	345·55	20·3	330·75	19·5
1,800	388·55	21·6	375·75	20·9
1,900	431·55	22·7	420·75	22·1
2,000	474·55	23·7	465·75	23·3
2,500	714·55	28·6	715·75	28·6
3,000	954·55	31·8	965·75	32·2
4,000	1,434·55	35·9	1,465·75	36·6
5,000	1,914·55	38·3	1,965·75	39·3
6,000	2,433·05	40·6	2,495·25	41·6
7,000	3,019·80	43·1	3,097·50	44·3
8,000	3,656·55	45·7	3,749·75	46·9
9,000	4,343·30	48·3	4,452·00	49·5
10,000	5,073·30	50·7	5,202·00	52·0
15,000	9,036·80	60·2	9,256·50	61·7
20,000	13,393·55	67·0	13,708·75	68·5
30,000	23,107·05	77·0	23,432·35	78·1
50,000	42,707·05	85·4	43,032·35	86·1
100,000	91,707·05	91·7	92,032·35	92·0

MARRIED COUPLES, WITH ONE CHILD NOT OVER 11—INCOME ALL EARNED

Income	1974–75		1975–76	
	Income tax	Effective rate	Income tax	Effective rate
£	£	Per cent.	£	Per cent.
1,200	31·35	2·6	1·75	0·1
1,300	64·35	5·0	36·75	2·8
1,400	97·35	7·0	71·75	5·1
1,500	130·35	8·7	106·75	7·1
1,600	163·35	10·2	141·75	8·9
1,700	196·35	11·6	176·75	10·4
1,800	229·35	12·7	211·75	11·8
1,900	262·35	13·8	246·75	13·0
2,000	295·35	14·8	281·75	14·1
2,500	460·35	18·4	456·75	18·3
3,000	625·35	20·8	631·75	21·1
4,000	955·35	23·9	981·75	24·5
5,000	1,285·35	25·7	1,331·75	26·6
6,000	1,635·10	27·3	1,697·00	28·3
7,000	2,059·85	29·4	2,137·25	30·5
8,000	2,534·60	31·7	2,627·50	32·8
9,000	3,059·35	34·0	3,167·75	35·2
10,000	3,634·10	36·3	3,758·00	37·6
15,000	6,823·60	45·5	7,038·50	46·9
20,000	10,418·35	52·1	10,728·75	53·6
30,000	18,607·85	62·0	18,933·15	63·1
50,000	35,207·85	70·4	35,533·15	71·1
100,000	76,707·85	76·7	77,033·15	77·0

MARRIED COUPLES, WITH TWO CHILDREN NOT OVER 11—INCOME ALL EARNED

Income	1974–75		1975–76	
	Income Tax	Effective rate	Income tax	Effective rate
£	£	Per cent.	£	Per cent.
1,300	2·31	0·2	—	
1,400	35·31	2·5	5·95	0·4
1,500	68·31	4·6	40·95	2·7
1,600	101·31	6·3	75·95	4·7
1,700	134·31	7·9	110·95	6·5
1,800	167·31	9·3	145·95	8·1
1,900	200·31	10·5	180·95	9·5
2,000	233·31	11·7	215·95	10·8
2,500	398·31	15·9	390·95	15·6
3,000	563·31	18·8	565·95	18·9
4,000	893·31	22·3	915·95	22·9
5,000	1,223·31	24·5	1,265·95	25·3
6,000	1,563·66	26·1	1,621·80	27·0
7,000	1,979·01	28·3	2,052·65	29·3
8,000	2,444·36	30·6	2,533·50	31·7
9,000	2,959·71	32·9	3,064·35	34·0
10,000	3,525·06	35·3	3,645·20	36·5
15,000	6,695·76	44·6	6,906·90	46·0
20,000	10,281·11	51·4	10,587·75	52·9
30,000	18,451·81	61·5	18,777·11	62·6
50,000	35,051·81	70·1	35,377·11	70·8
100,000	76,551·81	76·6	76,877·11	76·9

INCOME UP TO £60 A WEEK—ALL EARNED

Income	1974–75		1975–76	
	Income tax	Effective rate	Income tax	Effective rate
£	£	Per cent.	£	Per cent.

Single persons

Income	Income tax	Effective rate	Income tax	Effective rate
728 (£14 a week).........	33·99	4·7	18·55	2·5
832 (£16 a week).........	68·31	8·2	54·95	6·6
936 (£18 a week).........	102·63	11·0	91·35	9·8
1,040 (£20 a week).........	136·95	13·2	127·75	12·3
1,144 (£22 a week).........	171·27	15·0	164·15	14·3
1,248 (£24 a week).........	205·59	16·5	200·55	16·1
1,352 (£26 a week).........	239·91	17·7	236·95	17·5
1,456 (£28 a week).........	274·23	18·8	273·35	18·8
1,560 (£30 a week).........	308·55	19·8	309·75	19·9
1,820 (£35 a week).........	394·35	21·7	400·75	22·0
2,080 (£40 a week).........	480·15	23·1	391·75	23·6
2,340 (£45 a week).........	565·95	24·2	582·75	24·9
2,600 (£50 a week).........	651·75	25·1	673·75	25·9
2,860 (£55 a week).........	737·55	25·8	764·75	26·7
3,120 (£60 a week).........	823·35	26·4	855·75	27·4

Married couples

Income	Income tax	Effective rate	Income tax	Effective rate
936 (£18 a week).........	23·43	2·5	—	—
1,040 (£20 a week).........	57·75	5·6	29·75	2·9
1,144 (£22 a week).........	92·07	8·0	66·15	5·8
1,248 (£24 a week).........	126·39	10·1	102·55	8·2
1,352 (£26 a week).........	160·71	11·9	138·95	10·3
1,456 (£28 a week).........	195·03	13·4	175·35	12·0
1,560 (£30 a week).........	229·35	14·7	211·75	13·6
1,820 (£35 a week).........	315·15	17·3	302·75	16·6
2,080 (£40 a week).........	400·95	19·3	393·75	18·9
2,340 (£45 a week).........	486·75	20·8	484·75	20·7
2,600 (£50 a week).........	572·55	22·0	575·75	22·1
2,860 (£55 a week).........	658·35	23·0	666·75	23·3
3,120 (£60 a week).........	744·15	23·9	757·75	24·3

Married couples, with one child not over 11

Income	Income tax	Effective rate	Income tax	Effective rate
1,144 (£22 a week).........	12·87	1·1	—	—
1,248 (£24 a week).........	47·19	3·8	18·55	1·5
1,352 (£26 a week).........	81·51	6·0	54·95	4·1
1,456 (£28 a week).........	115·83	8·0	91·35	6·3
1,560 (£30 a week).........	150·15	9·6	127·75	8·2
1,820 (£35 a week).........	235·95	13·0	218·75	12·0
2,080 (£40 a week).........	321·75	15·5	309·75	14·9
2,340 (£45 a week).........	407·55	17·4	400·75	17·1
2,600 (£50 a week).........	493·35	19·0	491·75	18·9
2,860 (£55 a week).........	579·15	20·3	582·75	20·4
3,120 (£60 a week).........	664·95	21·3	673·75	21·6

Married couples, with two children not over 11

Income	Income tax	Effective rate	Income tax	Effective rate
1,352 (£26 a week).........	19·47	1·4	—	—
1,456 (£28 a week).........	53·79	3·7	25·55	1·8
1,560 (£30 a week).........	88·11	5·6	61·95	4·0
1,820 (£35 a week).........	173·91	9·6	152·95	8·4
2,080 (£40 a week).........	259·71	12·5	243·95	11·7
2,340 (£45 a week).........	345·51	14·8	334·95	14·3
2,600 (£50 a week).........	431·31	16·6	425·95	16·4
2,860 (£55 a week).........	517·11	18·1	516·95	18·1
3,120 (£60 a week).........	602·91	19·3	607·95	19·5

ELDERLY PERSONS—INCOME ALL EARNED

Income	1974–75		1975–76	
	Income tax	Effective rate	Income tax	Effective rate
£	£	Per cent.	£	Per cent.

Single person—aged 65 or over

900	49·50	5·5	—	—
1,000	104·50	10·5	17·50	1·8
1,100	156·75	14·3	52·50	4·8
1,200	189·75	15·8	87·50	7·3
1,300	222·75	17·1	122·50	9·4
1,400	255·75	18·3	157·50	11·3
1,500	288·75	19·3	192·50	12·8
1,600	321·75	20·1	227·50	14·2
1,700	354·75	20·9	262·50	15·4
1,800	387·75	21·5	297·50	16·5
1,900	420·75	22·1	332·50	17·5
2,000	453·75	22·7	367·50	18·4
2,500	618·75	24·8	542·50	21·7
3,000	783·75	26·1	717·50	23·9

Married couple—either of whom is aged 65 or over

1,200	16·50	1·4	—	—
1,300	71·60	5·5	—	—
1,400	125·50	9·0	—	—
1,500	181·50	12·1	26·25	1·8
1,600	236·50	14·8	61·25	3·8
1,700	275·55	16·2	96·25	5·7
1,800	308·55	17·1	131·25	7·3
1,900	341·55	18·0	166·25	8·8
2,000	374·55	18·7	201·25	10·1
2,500	539·55	21·6	376·25	15·1
3,000	704·55	23·5	551·25	18·4

OTHER TAXES AND STAMP DUTIES

The Commissioners as a general rule allow deeds, etc., to be stamped after execution:—

WITHOUT PENALTY, ON PAYMENT OF DUTY ONLY. Deeds and instruments not otherwise excepted, within 30 days of *first* execution.

NOTE.—Where wholly executed *abroad*, the period begins to run from the date of arrival here.

PENALTIES ENFORCEABLE ON STAMPING, IN ADDITION TO DUTY:—

Instruments presented after the proper time (subject to special provisions in some cases) £10

AGREEMENT for Lease, *see* LEASES.

AGREEMENT FOR SALE OF PROPERTY—charged with *ad val.* duty as if in actual conveyance on sale with certain exceptions, *e.g.* agreements for the sale of land, stocks and shares, goods, wares or merchandise, or a ship (*see* s. 59 (1), Stamp Act 1891). If *ad val.* duty is paid on an agreement in accordance with this provision, the subsequent conveyance or transfer is not chargeable with any *ad val.* duty and the Commissioners will upon application either place a denoting stamp on such conveyance or transfer or will transfer the *ad val.* duty thereto. Further, if such an agreement is rescinded, not performed, etc., the Commissioners will return the *ad val.* duty paid.

AGREEMENT, not otherwise charged with duty, under seal or with clause of registration... 50p

APPOINTMENT of a new trustee or in exercise of a power over property, not being by a will; also on retirement of trustee, although no new trustee be appointed............. 50p

ASSIGNMENT:

By way of sale—*see* Conveyance.

By way of gift—*see* Voluntary Disposition.

ASSURANCE—*see* Insurance Policies.

BEARER INSTRUMENT:

Inland bearer instrument, i.e. share warrant, stock certificate to bearer or any other instrument to bearer by which stock can be transferred, issued by a company or body formed or established in U.K. Duty of an amount equal to three times the transfer duty (usually £6% of the market value).

Overseas bearer instrument, *i.e.*, such an instrument issued in G.B. by a company formed out of the U.K. Duty equal to twice the transfer duty (usually £4% of the market value). Even if issued out of G.B. the instrument must be stamped before transfer in G.B. The issue or transfer of a bearer instrument relating to stock expressed in the currency of a territory outside the Scheduled territories is exempt from duty.

BILL OF SALE, Absolute, *see* CONVEYANCE ON SALE.

CAPITAL DUTY.—Where a *chargeable transaction* of a *capital company* takes place after July 31, 1973, duty of £1 is payable on every £100 or fraction of £100 of the actual value of the assets contributed by the members (as opposed to the previous duty of 50p per £100 of the nominal capital), provided the place of effective management of the company is in G.B. or its registered office is in G.B. but the place of its effective management is outside the E.E.C. (Finance Act 1973).

A statement containing prescribed particulars must be delivered to the Commissioners within one month of the transaction unless there is an obligation under the Companies Act 1948 (*e.g.*, on the formation of a limited liability company) or the Limited Partnerships Act 1907 (*e.g.*, on the registration of a limited partnership) to send a statement to the registrar of companies as a result of the transaction.

Capital company includes a company incorporated with limited liability under U.K. law, a limited partnership under the Limited Partnerships Act 1907, a company incorporated according to the law of any other member of the E.E.C. and any other corporation or body of persons whose members have the right to dispose of their shares and whose liability for debts is limited.

Chargeable transaction includes the formation of a capital company, an increase in its capital by the contribution of assets of any kind, the transfer to G.B. of its place of effective management from a country outside the E.E.C. if its registered office is in such a country, and the transfer to G.B. of its registered office from a country outside the E.E.C. if its place of effective management is in such a country.

CAPITAL TRANSFER TAX

A new tax on the transmission of wealth, made by way of gift during a person's lifetime and on death, has been introduced by the Finance Act 1975. It applies retrospectively to March 27, 1974, unless the donor dies before March 13, 1975 (when Estate Duty or modified Estate Duty will apply).

Tax is charged at progressive rates on the cumulative totals of chargeable gifts made during a person's lifetime, with a final cumulation of the value of a person's estate on his death. The rates of tax for lifetime transfers are those shown in Table 1. For transfers on death, or within 3 years of death, the rates applicable are those in Table 2.

TABLE 1

Value transferred		Rate of tax
Lower limit £	Upper limit £	Per cent.
0	15,000	Nil
15,000	20,000	5
20,000	25,000	7½
25,000	30,000	10
30,000	40,000	12½
40,000	50,000	15
50,000	60,000	17½
60,000	80,000	20
80,000	100,000	22½
100,000	120,000	27½
120,000	150,000	35
150,000	200,000	42½
200,000	250,000	50
250,000	300,000	55
300,000	500,000	60
500,000	1,000,000	65
1,000,000	2,000,000	70
2,000,000	—	75

TABLE 2

Value transferred		Rate of tax
Lower limit £	Upper limit £	Per cent.
0	15,000	Nil
15,000	20,000	10
20,000	25,000	15
25,000	30,000	20
30,000	40,000	25
40,000	50,000	30
50,000	60,000	35
60,000	80,000	40
80,000	100,000	45
100,000	120,000	50
120,000	150,000	55
150,000	500,000	60
500,000	1,000,000	65
1,000,000	2,000,000	70
2,000,000	—	75

In calculating the value transferred on lifetime gifts, the amount of tax paid by the donor on the gift must be taken into account. The value transferred on death is the value of the person's estate at his death.

Certain exemptions and reliefs are given, including:

(a) *For lifetime transfers only:*

(i) The first £1,000 of gifts made in each tax year (April 6 to the following April 5) are exempt. Only the balance over £1,000 is taxable. There is provision for the carry forward of this relief for one year only, in so far as it has not been used in the previous year.

(ii) Gifts not exceeding £100 to any one donee in the tax year are exempt. The excess only is taxable. This relief is in addition to the £1,000 relief.

(iii) Gifts which are normal expenditure out of income are exempt, provided the donor is left with sufficient income to maintain his standard of living.

(iv) Gifts in consideration of marriage are exempt up to £5,000 if made by a parent; £2,500 if made by a grandparent or some other lineal ancestor, or by one party to another; and £1,000 in any other case.

(b) *For lifetime transfers and on death:*

(i) Transfers between spouses are exempt to the extent that the gift increases the value of the donee spouse's estate.

(ii) Lifetime gifts to Charities and certain Political Parties are exempt without limit. If made on death or within one year of death, gifts are exempt up to £100,000 only.

(iii) Gifts to listed heritage bodies, including National Gallery, British Museum, and Government Departments, are exempt.

(iv) Gifts of certain types of property, including works of art are exempt if made to a body not established or conducted for profit.

(v) Agricultural relief:
Provided certain conditions are satisfied, on a transfer of Agricultural land, a sum known as the " Multiplied Rental Value " of Agricultural land may be substituted for the Agricultural value of that land. The Multiplied Rental Value for Agricultural land in Great Britain is at present 20 × Rental Value.
To satisfy the conditions, *inter alia*, the transferor must be a working farmer (as defined) and must have occupied the land for the purposes of Agriculture for two years up to the time of the transfer.

(c) *For transfers on death only:*
Conditional exemptions exist for works of art, timber and for death on active service.

Tax must be paid within 6 months of the end of the month in which the chargeable event occurs unless the event is a lifetime transfer, made between April 5 and October 1 in any year, when tax is due at the end of the next following April. In certain circumstances, tax may be payable by instalments.

Interest on unpaid tax runs from the date the tax is due, at 6% p.a. on death and 9% p.a. otherwise.

The transition from Estate Duty
The normal rules for Estate Duty apply for deaths up to November 12, 1974 (*see post*, p. 1189). For deaths after that date and before March 13, 1975, Estate Duty is levied, but at the rates given in Table 2 above, and, *inter alia*, transfers between spouses are totally exempt (and not limited to £15,000). No Capital Transfer Tax is payable on lifetime gifts where death occurs before March 13, 1975.
For deaths after March 12, 1975, Capital Transfer Tax only, applies.

CONTRACT, *see* AGREEMENT.

CONTRACT NOTE for the sale or purchase of any stock or marketable security; where the value of the stock or marketable security—

Exceeds £100 and does not exceed £500...		10p
,, £500 ,, ,, ,, ,, £1,500..		30p
,, £1,500.................		60p

(Special adhesive stamps)

Option Contract Notes are chargeable with half the above rates only, unless the option is a double one.

Contract Note following a duly stamped option contract note chargeable with half the above rates only.

CONTRACT OR GRANT FOR PAYMENT OF A SUPERANNUATION ANNUITY: for every £10 or fractional part of £10.............. 5p

CONVEYANCE OR TRANSFER on sale or by way of gift *inter vivos* of Stock or Marketable Securities: where the purchase money (or in the case of a gift the middle market value on the date of the transaction) does

not exceed £5........................	10p
Exceeding £5 but not exceeding £100, for every £10 or part of £10..........	20p
Exceeding £100 but not exceeding £300, for every £20 or part..........	40p
Exceeding £300 per every £50 or part.....	£1

NOTE.—The rate chargeable in respect of a transfer of commonwealth government stock is 10p for every £20 or part if not exceeding £300 and in every other case 50p for every £100 or part.
" Marketable Security " includes the Registered Bonds and Debentures generally of Companies, Corporations, and Public Bodies.

CONVEYANCE OR TRANSFER ON SALE (in the case of a Voluntary Disposition, *see* below, p. 1194) of any property (*except* stock or marketable securities for which, *see* above), where the Conveyance or Transfer contains a certificate of value certifying that the transaction does not form part of a larger transaction or a series of transactions in respect of which the aggregate amount or

value of the consideration exceeds £15,000.	nil
Exceeds £20,000 (for every £50 or fraction of £50)............................	25p
Exceeds £25,000 (for every £50 or fraction of £50)............................	50p
Exceeds £30,000 (for every £50 or fraction of £50)............................	75p

If the Conveyance or Transfer on Sale does not contain the appropriate statement duty at the full rate of £1 for every £50 or fraction of £50 will be payable whatever the amount of the consideration.

However, if the consideration does not exceed £300, and the instrument does not contain a certificate of value, then: Where the consideration:

Does not exceed £5.................	10p
Exceeds £5 but does not exceed £100, 20p per £10 or part.	
Exceeds £100 but does not exceed £300, 40p per £20 or part.	

If in such a case the instrument is certified at £20,000 it is stamped at 25% of the above rates with a minimum of 5p; if certified at £25,000 it is stamped at 50% of the above rates; if certified at £30,000 it is stamped at 75% of the above rates with a minimum of 10p.

CONVEYANCE OR TRANSFER of any other kind ....fixed duty	50p

Included under this head are Transfers for

nominal consideration within any of the following categories:

(a) Transfers vesting the property in trustees on the appointment of a new trustee of a pre-existing trust, or on the retirement of a trustee.

(b) Transfers, where no beneficial interest in the property passes, (i) to a mere nominee of the transferor; (ii) from a mere nominee of the transferee; (iii) from one nominee to another nominee of the same beneficial owner.

(c) Transfer to a residuary legatee of stock, etc., forming part of the residue divisible under a will.

(d) Transfers to a beneficiary under a will of a specific legacy of stock, etc. (*Note.*—Transfers by executors in discharge, or partial discharge, of a pecuniary legacy (unless made under an express power of appropriation) are chargeable with *ad valorem* duty on the amount of the legacy so discharged.)

(e) Transfers of stock, etc., forming part of an intestate's estate to the person entitled to it.

(f) Transfers to a beneficiary under settlement on a distribution of the trust funds of stock, etc., forming the share or part of the share of those funds to which the beneficiary is entitled in accordance with the terms of the settlement.

(g) Transfers on the occasion of a marriage to trustees of stocks, etc., to be held on the terms of a settlement made in consideration of marriage.

(h) Transfers by the liquidator of a company of stocks, etc., forming part of the assets of the company to the persons who were shareholders, in satisfaction of their rights on a winding-up.

The evidence necessary to establish that a transfer is liable to the fixed duty of 50p should take the form of a certificate setting forth the facts of the transaction. In cases falling within (b) such a certificate should be signed by (1) both transferor and transferee or (2) a member of a Stock Exchange or a solicitor acting for one or other of the parties or (3) an accredited representative of a bank; in the last case when the bank or its official nominee is a party to the transfer, the certificate, instead of setting out the facts, may be to the effect that " the transfer is excepted from Section 74 of the Finance (1909–10) Act 1910." A certificate in other cases should be signed by a solicitor or other person (*e.g.*, a bank acting as trustee or executor) having a full knowledge of the facts.

Registering Officers will in any case in which a Marketing Officer's certificate has not been given require such evidence in order to satisfy themselves that a transfer stamped with the 50p fixed duty is duly stamped.

COVENANT—For original creation and sale of any annuity, *see* CONVEYANCE.

Separate Deed of, made on occasion of sale, but not being an instrument chargeable with *ad valorem* duty as a Conveyance: same duty as a Conveyance on sale, but not to exceed........................... 50p

DEATH DUTIES, *see* ESTATE DUTY.

DECLARATION OF TRUST, not being a Will or Settlement............................. 50p

DEED of any kind not charged under some special head............................. 50p

DEMISE, *see* LEASE.

DUPLICATE OR COUNTERPART
Same duty as original, but not to exceed.. 50p

ESTATE DUTY, *see also* CAPITAL TRANSFER TAX
In the case of every person dying on or after March 22, 1972 and before November 13, 1974 the total duty payable on an estate is found by adding up the amounts of duty payable on various slices of the estate, according to a scale laid down in F.A. 1969, Schedule 17, as amended.

The rates of duty are as follows:
On the first	£15,000—*Nil*	
On the next	£ 5,000—25 per cent.	
On the next	£10,000—30 per cent.	
On the next	£10,000—35 per cent.	
On the next	£10,000—40 per cent.	
On the next	£10,000—45 per cent.	
On the next	£20,000—50 per cent.	
On the next	£20,000—55 per cent.	
On the next	£50,000—60 per cent.	
On the next	£50,000—65 per cent.	
On the next	£300,000—70 per cent.	
On excess over	£500,000—75 per cent.	

The rate of duty for any particular asset is found by dividing the total duty by the aggregate value of the estate.

Property given to or devolving on a deceased's widow or widower up to a limit of £15,000 is exempt from estate duty. (This is in addition to the exemption of the first £15,000 of the estate.) Property given to the British Museum, the National Gallery, the National Trust and other similar institutions is also exempt.

The amount of duty payable in certain circumstances on property passing on two deaths occurring within 5 years of one another is reduced. (Finance Act 1958.)

A reduction of 45 per cent. is applied to the " agricultural value " of agricultural property; and (as respects deaths on and after July 30, 1954) to certain business assets, viz.: " industrial hereditaments " and " machinery or plant " (Finance Act 1954, s. 28).

Gifts to charities not exceeding £50,000 whether by will or in the deceased's lifetime are exempt from estate duty. In the case of gifts to charities during the deceased's life exceeding £50,000, these are liable to estate duty unless made more than twelve months before death. Other gifts are liable for duty, unless made more than seven years before death (although if the donor dies at any time within the fifth year after making the gift, the value of the property the subject of the gift is for estate duty purposes reduced by 15 per cent.; if he dies within the sixth year it is reduced by 30 per cent.; and if he dies within the seventh year it is reduced by 60 per cent.). Gifts made in consideration of marriage by a parent or grandparent to either spouse or by one spouse to the other excepted as to the first £5,000 (or £1,000 if made by any other person). Gifts forming part of deceased's normal expenditure (subject to certain conditions) and gifts not exceeding £100 in value or amount (or in certain circumstances £500) also excepted.

Payment of Estate Duty may, by agreement with the Commissioners, be made wholly or in part, in the form of real or leasehold property comprised in the estate.

Interest at 3 per cent. per annum is also payable on the Estate Duty on personalty from the day after the death up to that of delivery of the affidavit or account.

The Estate Duty on real property, leasehold property, shares in certain companies and a business or interest therein may be paid, if desired, by eight yearly or sixteen half-yearly instalments, and 3 per cent. interest is charged on all unpaid instalments from twelve months after death.

FEES are taken in all Public Departments by means of Stamps: such payments are accounted for to the Exchequer under the heading of Miscellaneous Revenue.

GIFT (*see* VOLUNTARY DISPOSITION, p. 1194).

GUARANTEE:
If under seal............................ 50p

HIRE-PURCHASE AGREEMENTS:
Under seal............................ 50p
(Finance Act 1907, s. 7)
N.B.—If the agreement amounts to a " credit-sale " the position is the same.

INSURANCE POLICIES:
Life:—
Exc. £50 and not exc. £1,000 for every £100 or part of £100............... 5p
Exc. £1,000, for every £1,000 or any fractional part of £1,000 .... 50p
Made after 1 August 1966 for period not exceeding 2 years................. 5p

LEASES:—Lease or tack for any definite term less than a year of any furnished dwelling-house or apartments where the rent for such term exceeds £250, £1; of any lands, tenements, etc., in consideration of any rent, according to the following table:—

Annual rent not exceeding	*Term not exceeding			Term exceeding 100 years
	7 years	35 years	100 years	
£	£ p	£ p	£ p	£ p
5	Nil	0·10	0·60	1·20
10	Nil	0·20	1·20	2·40
15	Nil	0·30	1·80	3·60
20	Nil	0·40	2·40	4·80
25	Nil	0·50	3·00	6·00
50	Nil	1·00	6·00	12·00
75	Nil	1·50	9·00	18·00
100	Nil	2·00	12·00	24·00
150	Nil	3·00	18·00	36·00
200	Nil	4·00	24·00	48·00
250	Nil	5·00	30·00	60·00
Exceeding £250 for every £50 or fraction of £50	0·05	1·00	6·00	12·00

*If the term is indefinite the same duty is payable as if the term did not exceed 7 years. Agreement for lease not exceeding 35 years, same as actual lease.

Where a consideration other than rent is payable and duty is charged on that consideration at conveyance rates, the same graduation applies where the consideration does not exceed £30,000 as under Conveyance or Transfer on Sale (except stock or marketable securities), provided that any rent payable does not exceed £150 a year.

MORTGAGES are exempt.

POWER OF ATTORNEY, etc., for receiving certain prize-money or wages 5p
For the receipt of any money, or bill, or note, not exceeding £20, or of any periodical payments not exceeding £10 annually.............................. 25p

For the receipt of dividends or interest of any stock, if for one payment only..... 5p
Ditto in any other case 25p
Power of attorney of any other kind 50p

PROCURATION, Deed, etc., of.............. 50p

RECEIPTS FOR SALARIES, Wages and Superannuation, and other like allowances are exempt.

REVOCATION of any TRUST of Property not being a Will 50p

TRANSFER OF STOCK, *see* CONVEYANCE.

UNIT TRUST INSTRUMENT—Any trust instrument of a unit trust scheme—For every £100, and also for any fractional part of £100, of the amount or value of the property subject to the trusts created or recorded by the instrument.............. 25p

VOLUNTARY DISPOSITION *inter vivos*:—
On any instrument being a voluntary disposition (*inter vivos*) of any property (except stock or marketable securities, *see ante*, under Conveyance or Transfer) where the value of the property conveyed or transferred does not exceed £15,000.......... nil

Exceeds £15,000 but does not exceed £20,000 for every £50 and fraction of £50 25p

Exceeds £20,000 but does not exceed £25,000, for every £50 and fraction of £50 .... 50p

Exceeds £25,000 but does not exceed £30,000 for every £50 and fraction of £50 ...... 75p

Exceeds £30,000, for every £50 and fraction of £50................................. £1

The instrument must contain similar certificates of value as a Conveyance or Transfer on Sale (*see* p. 1192), with the substitution of the words " property conveyed or transferred " for the word " consideration."

If the value of the property does not exceed £300 the same graduated rates apply as under Conveyance or Transfer on Sale (except Stock or marketable securities).

NATIONAL HEALTH SERVICE
(and Local Authority Personal Social Services)

The National Health Service came into being on July 5, 1948, as a result of the *National Health Service Act* 1946. The Act placed a duty on the Secretary of State for Social Services to promote the establishment in England of a comprehensive Health Service designed to secure improvement in the mental and physical health of the people and the prevention, diagnosis and treatment of illness. The Secretary of State for Wales administers the National Health Service in Wales. There are separate Acts for Scotland and Northern Ireland, where the Health Services are run on very similar lines. The Secretaries of State are responsible to Parliament for seeing that Health Services of all kinds of the highest possible quality are available to all who need them. They are advised by the Personal Social Services Council and the Central Health Services Council (and certain Standing Advisory Committees), appointed after consultation with the various interested bodies.

The National Health Service covers a comprehensive range of hospital, specialist, general practitioner (medical, dental, ophthalmic and pharmaceutical), artificial limb and appliance, and community health services. Everyone normally resident in this country is entitled to use any of these services, there are no contribution conditions and the charges made (except those for amenity beds) are reduced or waived in cases of hardship. In addition the Secretary of State for Social Services is responsible under the Local Authority Social Services Act 1970 for the provision by local authorities of social services for the elderly, the handicapped, the disabled and also for families and children. Most of the cost of running the service is met from the Consolidated Fund—that is, from taxes. Other sources of finance are: (1) the weekly National Health Service contributions (since September 1957), which are estimated to produce about £225 million. (For convenience these are collected with the National Insurance contribution in a single combined weekly contribution); (2) local taxation, excluding Consolidated Fund grant to local authorities personal social services; (3) partial charges to patients for drugs and dressings, spectacles, dentures and dental treatment and amenity beds in hospital. The cost of the Health and Personal Social Services in England and Wales rose from £860 million in 1960–61 to an estimated total of £4,262 million in 1974–75. In Scotland the National Health Service vote totalled £535 million (estimate) in 1974–75 compared with a revised estimate of £390 million in 1973–74.

THE HEALTH SERVICES

Family Doctor Service

In England and Wales the Family Doctor Service is organized by 98 Family Practitioner Committees which also organize the General Dental, Pharmaceutical and Ophthalmic Services for their areas. There is a Family Practitioner Committee for each Area Health Authority; members, who serve voluntarily, are appointed by local doctors, dentists, pharmacists and opticians (15), the Local Authority (4) and the Area Health Authority (11). Any doctor may take part in the Family Doctor Scheme, provided the area in which he wishes to practise has not already an adequate number of doctors, and about 23,000 general practitioners do so. They may at the same time have private fee-paying patients. Family doctors are paid for their Health Service work in accordance with a scheme of remuneration which includes *inter alia* a basic practice allowance, capitation fees, reimbursement of certain practice expenses and payments for " out of hours " work.

Everyone aged 16 or over can choose his doctor (parents or guardians choose for children under 16) and the doctor is also free to accept a person or not as he chooses. A person may change his doctor if he wishes, either at once if he has changed his address or obtained permission of the doctor on whose list he is, or by informing the Family Practitioners Committee (in which case 14 days must elapse before the other doctor can accept him). When people are away from home they can still use the Family Doctor Service if they ask to be treated as " temporary residents ", and in an emergency, if a person's own doctor is not available, any doctor in the service will give treatment and advice.

Patients are treated either in the Doctor's surgery or, when necessary, at home. Doctors may prescribe for their patients all drugs and medicines which are medically necessary for their treatment and also a certain number of surgical appliances (the more elaborate being provided through the hospitals).

Drugs, Medicines and Appliances.—The number of chemists (including drug stores and appliance suppliers) in England, within the National Health Service during 1973 was 10,689.

Dental Service

Dentists, like doctors, may take part in the Service and may also have private patients. About 11,000 of the dentists available for general practice in England have joined the National Health Service. They are responsible to the Family Practitioners Committee in whose areas they provide services.

Patients are free to go to any dentist taking part in the Service and willing to accept them, and cannot register with any particular dentist. Dentists receive payment for items of treatment for individual patients, instead of the capitation fee received by doctors. There is no need for the patient to obtain a recommendation before seeking dental treatment. The dentist is able to carry out at once all normal conservative treatment (*e.g.* fillings), provision of dentures in some cases, emergency treatment and ordinary denture repairs; he seeks prior approval from the Dental Estimates Board before undertaking treatment when it involves the extraction of teeth and the provision of dentures (in some cases); extensive and prolonged treatment of the gums; inlays and crowns (in some cases); special appliances and oral surgery and certain other items.

A dentist may, with the approval of the Dental Estimates Board, charge his patients a prescribed sum for such types of treatment as crowns, inlays or metal dentures where these are not clinically necessary, if the patient wishes to have them. Where a denture supplied under the Service has to be replaced because of loss or damage the whole or part of the cost may be charged to the patient if he has been careless. In May, 1951, charges were introduced for dentures; these were increased in May, 1961, to £2 5s.–£2 15s. for the supply of one denture or up to £5 for a set. In June, 1952, a charge of £1, or the full cost of any treatment if less than £1, was introduced. This charge was increased to £1 10s. from May 1, 1968. From Aug, 11, 1969, the charge for a set of dentures was increased to £6 5s., with proportionate increases for partial dentures. From April 1, 1971, the system of charges was changed so that patients became liable for a proportion of the cost of treatment, including the supply of dentures, if required, up to a maximum charge of £10 for one course of treatment, unless they were exempt from charges or entitled to remission on income grounds. No charge is made for clinical examination of a patient's mouth. Expectant mothers or mothers who have had a child during the preceding twelve months, children under 16, or 16 or over, but still in full-time attendance at school, do not pay charges. Other patients between 16 and 21 years of age pay half the cost for dentures and for alterations and additions to them.

General Ophthalmic Service

General Ophthalmic Services, which are administered by Family Practitioner Committees, form part of the ophthalmic services available under the National Health Service and provide for the testing of sight and supply of glasses to meet more normal needs only. Diagnosis and specialist treatment of eye conditions is available through the Hospital Eye Service as well as the provision of glasses of a special type. Testing of sight may be carried out by any ophthalmic medical practitioner or ophthalmic optician, and glasses supplied by any ophthalmic optician or dispensing optician taking part in the Services. On the first occasion a person wishes to use the Services he must obtain a medical recommendation from his doctor that his sight needs testing. No further recommendation is required subsequently and the Services may be used direct.

Sight testing is free. The charges for lenses broadly cover the cost of the lenses and the opticians' dispensing fee. They range from £1.20 per lens to a maximum of £3.50 per lens. The cost of the frame must also be paid. Children up to the age of 16 or older children attending school full-time may be supplied free of charge with standard lenses in children's standard frames. Additionally, school-children aged 10 years or over may be supplied with standard lenses without charge if any other type of NHS frame is used. The charge for the frame must then be paid.

Hospitals and Specialists

On July 5, 1948, ownership of 2,688 out of 3,040 voluntary and municipal hospitals in England and Wales was vested in the Minister of Health (now Secretary of State for Social Services). The Secretary of State has a duty to provide, to such extent as, he/she considers necessary to meet all reasonable requirements, hospital and other accommodation; medical, dental, nursing and ambulance services; other facilities for the care of expectant and nursing mothers and young children, facilities for the prevention of illness, and the care and after-care of persons suffering from illness and such other services as are required for the diagnosis and treatment of illness. Convalescent treatment may also be provided for those who need it and surgical and medical appliances are supplied in appropriate cases.

Specialists and consultants who take part in the Service (and most of them do so) hold hospital appointments on a whole or part-time basis. Those who have part-time appointments can engage in private practice, including the treatment of their private patients in N.H.S. hospitals.

In a number of hospitals accommodation is available for the treatment of private in-patients who undertake to pay full hospital maintenance costs and (usually) separate medical fees to a specialist as well. The amount of these fees is a matter for agreement between doctor and patient.

Hospital charges for private resident patients are determined annually, on a national basis for classes of hospitals, by the Secretary of State in accordance with the Health Services and Public Health Act 1968. These charges are revised annually from April 1 each year to reflect the average cost for each class of hospital, which it is estimated will be incurred during the current financial year in the treatment of in-patients. They may also include a contribution towards capital costs.

For in-patients paying specialists' fees separately, the hospital daily charges from April 1, 1975 for accommodation and services in each class of hospital are as follows:

Class A. Long stay hospitals (other than hospitals in classes D and E).

Single Room	*Other Accommodation*
£14·80	£13·40

Class B. Psychiatric hospitals (other than hospitals in classes D and E)

Single Room	*Other Accommodation*
£9·30	£8·50

Class C. Acute and other hospitals (other than hospitals in Classes D and E)

Single Room	*Other Accommodation*
£26·28	£24·30

Class D. London Teaching hospitals as at 31/3/75.

Single Room	*Other Accommodation*
£37·10	£33·70

Class E. Provincial teaching hospitals and University hospitals as at 31/3/75.

Single Room	*Other Accommodation*
£31·20	£28·30

Certain hospitals have accommodation in single rooms or small wards which, if not required for patients who need privacy for medical reasons, may be made available to patients who desire it as an amenity. Amenity bed charges are at present £3 per day in single rooms and £1·50 per day in small wards. In such cases the patients are treated in every other respect as National Health patients.

With certain exceptions, hospital out-patients have to pay fixed charges for dentures and glasses. The charge for glasses will be related to the type of lens prescribed; and for dentures to the type of denture provided, subject to a maximum charge of £10.00.

Local Authority Personal Social Services

Local authorities are responsible for the organization, management and administration of the personal social services and each authority has a Director of Social Services and a Social Services Committee responsible for the social services functions placed upon them by the Local Authority Social Services Act 1970. The "personal social services" are broadly speaking as follows: The services for children, including the care of children and young persons received into care, the provision of treatment for young offenders and adoption; family services, including the day care of pre-school children in day nurseries and by child minders, the care of unsupported mothers both in the community and in mother and baby homes, and the home help and meals on wheels services; services for the elderly and physically handicapped, including day centres, luncheon clubs and residential accommodation; services for the mentally ill and mentally handicapped, including day centres, clubs, adult training centres, workshops and residential accommodation.

CRIMINAL STATISTICS
ENGLAND AND WALES

In 1974 the total number of persons found guilty of offences of all kinds was 1,933,649 of whom 374,918 (males, 321,566; females, 53,352) were found guilty of indictable offences, 1,558,631 of non-indictable offences. The most numerous offences in 1973 and 1974 are listed below. In addition 79,335 persons (70,484 under 17 years) were cautioned by the police in 1974 for indictable offences and 24,519 (8,705 juveniles) for non-indictable (other than motoring) offences.

Ages of Offenders.—The 46,790 persons found guilty of indictable offences by the *higher courts* in 1974 included 1,258 persons under 17 years of age, 12,997 persons aged 17 and under 21, and 32,535 persons aged 21 and over. In *magistrates' courts*, of 327,128 persons convicted of indictable offences in 1974, 25,306 were under 14 years of age, 65,315 were aged 14 and under 17, 79,292 persons were aged 17 and under 21 and 157,225 were aged 21 years and over.

Persons Found Guilty of Indictable Offences in 1973

Age Group and Sex		Violence against the person	Sexual offences	Burglary	Robbery	Theft and handling stolen goods	Fraud and Forgery	Criminal damage	Other offences	Total
Under 14	M	593	127	8,901	309	9,691	144	3,128	61	23,054
	F	103	1	364	23	1,722	35	150	14	2,112
14 and under 17	M	4,009	653	19,854	615	28,470	517	6,515	265	56,898
	F	524	7	642	53	4,829	217	368	25	6,665
17 and under 21	M	8,203	1,067	14,981	882	42,736	2,582	10,599	1,362	82,412
	F	435	4	514	36	7,320	943	453	162	9,863
21 and over	M	18,029	5,312	18,352	814	81,352	10,783	13,921	6,739	155,302
	F	1,275	33	507	35	27,941	2,484	1,167	1,016	34,458
All ages	M	30,834	7,159	62,088	2,620	162,249	14,026	34,163	8,427	
	F	2,337	45	2,027	147	41,812	3,679	2,088	1,217	
All persons		33,171	7,204	64,165	2,767	203,061	17,705	36,251	9,644	374,918

Persons Found Guilty

	1973	1974
Motoring	1,191,808	1,226,961
Highways Acts	22,551	22,647
Intoxicating Liquor Laws	105,200	111,047
Revenue Offences*	92,997	95,582
Railway Offences	11,417	13,240
Social Security and National Insurance Acts	12,881	15,000
Disorderly Behaviour	8,851	9,689
Betting or Gaming	1,581	1,741
Assaults	12,054	16,090
Education Acts	2,328	2,602
Drug Offences	11,988	11,883
Offences by Prostitutes	2,976	3,091
Vagrancy Acts	4,659	5,983
Wireless Telegraphy Acts	42,734	34,183
Firearms Act	7,191	7,493
Prevention of Crime Act	6,655	7,389
Other Offences	53,351	60,980
TOTAL	1,591,222	1,645,403

* Mainly failure to take out licences for dogs or motor vehicles.

In 1974, 600 offences were recorded by the police as homicide. Of these, the courts decided that 114 were murder, 258 were manslaughter and 16 in-

fanticide, with 61 decisions pending. In 40 cases there was no suspect, and in 37 cases, the suspect died, committed suicide or was found insane; in 9 cases no further proceedings were brought against the suspect. The remaining 65 cases were no longer recorded as homicide, the courts deciding that 17 were self defence, 21 were accidents and 6 on other grounds, with 21 being decided as lesser offences.

In 1974, 377 persons were indicted for murder, 90 for manslaughter and 14 for infanticide. Of these 4 were not tried, 3 were found unfit to plead, 2 were found not guilty by reason of insanity, 113 were convicted of murder, 266 of manslaughter, 16 of infanticide and 28 of lesser offences; 49 persons were acquitted.

In 1974, 521 persons were committed for trial for homicide; of the 57 not committed for trial, 19 committed suicide or died, 8 were not proceeded against, 16 were discharged, 13 cases were pending and 1 was not committed on other grounds.

In the 114 cases decided by court as murder in 1974, the method of murder was classified as follows: Sharp instrument, 43; blunt instrument, 21, hitting, kicking, etc., 9; strangulation or asphyxiation, 20; shooting, 8; explosion, 12: other methods, 1.

The relationship of the victim to the principal suspect in these 114 cases was: son or daughter, 4; parent, 2; spouse or co-habitant, 22; other relative, 4; lover, etc., 9; other associate, 8; others, 65.

POSTAL REGULATIONS

(Note: Pages 1194–1208 do not contain price increases introduceed by Post Office in autumn, 1975.)
For full conditions, exceptions, etc., *see* Post Office Guide. Associated volumes are London Post Offices and Streets, Postal Address and Index to Postcode Directions, and Post Offices in the United Kingdom.

CHIEF POSTAL SERVICES
LETTERS AND CARDS

Inland (U.K., Channel Islands and Irish Republic):—

Not over	First Class	Second Class
60 g.	7p	5½p
100 g.	9½p	5½p
150 g.	12p	9p
200 g.	14p	10½p
250 g.	16p	12p
300 g.	18p	13½p
350 g.	20p	15p
400 g.	22p	16½p
450 g.	24p	18p
500 g.	26p	19½p
750 g.	36p	26p
1 kg.	46p	Not admissible
Each extra 250 g or part thereof	10p	over 750 g

Overseas:
(a) Surface mail. Not over 1 oz. 5½p; 2 oz. 11p; 4 oz. 15p; 8 oz. 30p; 1 lb. 55p; 2 lb. 90p; 4 lb. 150p.
Not over 20 g. 8p; 50 g. 15p; 100 g. 20p; 250 g. 40p; 500 g. 80p; 1000 g. 135p; 2000 g. 215p.
WEIGHT LIMITS:—Inland, First Class, none. Second Class 750 g. Elsewhere, 2 kg.
SIZE LIMITS: (A) If in roll form:—Inland and elsewhere (35 in. for the greatest dimension); length + twice diameter, 1040 mm. (B) not in roll form:—(i) United Kingdom, Irish Republic; 610 mm × 460 mm × 460 mm. (ii) Overseas, length 600 mm. length + width + depth, 900 m. Envelopes weighing under 60 g. should be oblong in shape, with the longer side at least 1·414 times the shorter side—minimum size 90 mm × 140 mm, maximum 120 mm × 235 mm. Envelopes outside these sizes and weighing under 60 g. will eventually be charged extra. Within the Inland Service envelopes or cards less than 100 mm × 70 mm must not be used. The standard of thickness for cards is 250 micrometres (0·01 in.) with a tolerance to an absolute limit of 230 micrometres (0·009 in.). To all overseas destinations the minimum limits for letters in the form of a roll are 170 mm for the length and twice the diameter combined (at least 100 mm for the greatest dimension), unless provided with a strong address label at least 100 mm in length and 70 mm in width. For letters other than in the form of a roll the minimum limits are one surface 140 mm in length, 90 mm in width, unless provided with a strong address label of 100 mm × 70 mm.

POST CARDS

To all destinations overseas:—6p.
Limit of size for destinations abroad: maximum, 148 mm in length, 105 mm in width; minimum, 140 mm in length, 90 mm in width.

PRINTED PAPERS, BOOKS

Overseas:—
Single packets
Not over 20 g, 6p; not over 50 g, 8p; not over 100 g, 10p; not over 250 g, 16p; not over 500 g, 28p; not over 1000 g, 48p; not over 2000 g, 80p. Normal weight limit 2000 g; but consignments of books or booklets weighing up to 5000 g may be sent as Printed Papers, as follows: not over 3000 g, 120p; not over 4000 g, 160p; not over 5000 g, 200p.
Posted in bulk as Direct Agents Bags.
Direct Agents Bags:—
Full rate: 38p per kg.
    Max rate (bags 30 kg max.) £11·40.
    Min rate bags(up to 23 kg) £8·74.

Reduced rate: 32p per kg.
    Max. rate (bags up to 30 kg max.) £9·60.
    Min. rate (bags up to 23 kg) £7·36.
Exceptionally, newspapers, periodicals, books, pamphlets, maps and musical scores which comply with the conditions shown in the Post Office Guide under Printed Papers at Reduced Rates may be sent abroad by surface mail only at the postage rate of:
Single packets
Not over 100 g, 9p; not over 250 g, 18p; not over 500 g, 30p; not over 1000 g, 54p.
Posted in bulk as Direct Agents Bags.

NEWSPAPERS

Inland (Newspapers " Registered at P.O."):—
Not over: 60 g, 5½p; 100 g, 7½p; 150 g, 9p; 200 g, 10½p; 250 g, 12p; 300 g, 13½p; 350 g, 15p; 400 g, 16½p; 450 g, 18p; 500 g, 19½p; 750 g, 26p.
Publications registered at the P.O. as newspapers will be given First Class service at the newspapers postage rate, but *only* if posted by publishers or their agents, and prominently marked *Newspaper Post.* All other newspapers are transmitted as first or second class letters. Limit of weight 750 g. Limit of size as Letters.
Overseas: See printed papers.

SMALL PACKETS (*See also* p. 1200).

Overseas:
Not exceeding 100 g, 9p; 250 g, 18p; 500 g, 30p; 1 kg, 54p.
LIMITS: Maximum size, as for letters A and B ii. Minimum limits of size as for letters; Weight 1 kg in general but some countries only accept Small Packets weighing up to 500 g.

PARCELS

Should be marked " Parcel Post," and must be handed over the counter; postage must be prepaid by stamps, affixed by the sender.
Posters of over 2,500 parcels *per annum* may sign contracts to which special conditions apply.
The name and address of sender should be inside and (not too prominent) on the outside of every parcel and preferably be to the left of and at right angles to the name and address of the addressee.
A rural postman will accept any packets he can conveniently carry, except overseas letters intended for insurance or any parcels for abroad; but if on foot or cycle not more, without notice, than 10 kg from one person. Maildrivers need not accept between regular stopping points.
Parcels to or from Irish Republic, Channel Is. or I. of Man are liable to customs duty: except in last case, the sender must declare contents when posting. Addressee must pay a clearance fee if any duty be payable. Senders can undertake to pay customs charges of Irish Republic, Channel Islands and some *countries overseas* (a deposit is required).
Inland:—(Limit of size: length, 1·070 m.; length and girth combined, 2 m.):—

U.K. and Irish Republic:—

Not over	Ordinary	Local	
1 kg	37p	30p	Note: The Local Parcel Delivery Area comprises all places which have in their postal address the same post town name as that of the office of posting. For further details consult your local post office.
2 kg	48p	41p	
3 kg	57p	50p	
4 kg	66p	59p	
5 kg	74p	67p	
6 kg	82p	75p	
7 kg	89p	81p	
8 kg	96p	88p	
9 kg	103p	95p	
10 kg	109p	101p	

Air Mail Services

For mode of packing, prohibitions, limits of size, &c., see Post Office Guide

Normal regulations as to make-up and acceptance of various categories of postal packets and parcels apply equally to air mail items. A blue air-mail label, obtainable free from post offices, must be affixed to each air mail item except letters, letter packets and postcards for Europe, for which no special air mail marking is required. Special air-mail rates apply to correspondence for members of H.M. Forces overseas (see leaflet PL(B)3116)

AIR LETTER FORMS, postage 8½ and 9p, may be sent to all countries. Enclosures are not permitted. You may get the special forms at post offices or use privately-manufactured forms which bear a statement that they have been approved by the Post Office, with the approval number. Unapproved forms will be treated as ordinary air mail letters.

PRINTED PAPERS. Small Packets and Newspapers may be sent by air to countries outside Europe at the rates shown in col. 3 below. NEWSPAPERS: Publications registered at the P.O. as newspapers may be sent at the reduced rates indicated in col. 4 below. There is no air mail service to Europe for these items. If the quickest transmission is desired the letter post rate should be paid.

European Countries (and The Azores)

Letters, letter packets and postcards for all European countries, prepaid at the ordinary international postage rates, are in general despatched daily by air or surface transport, whichever offer; earlier delivery. The rates are:—

Letters—Not over 60g, 7p; 100g, 9½p; 150g, 12p; 200g, 14p; 250g, 16p; 300g, 18p; 350g, 20p; 400g, 22p; 450g, 24p; 500g, 26p; 750g, 36p; 1000g, 46p; 1250g, 56p; 1500g, 66p; 1750g, 76p; 2000g, 86p.

Postcards, 7p.

Air mail labels are not necessary.

Air Parcel Post to Europe. Rates are included in the Overseas Parcel Post tables, see pp. 1205–8.

Countries Outside Europe

Rates for letters, postcards and printed papers etc. appear below; for air parcel rates see pp. 1205–8.

COUNTRIES OUTSIDE EUROPE

For air mail services to Europe, see above; Air Parcel Rates, pp. 1205–8.

Destination	Letters First ½ oz. or part thereof	Letters Each ½ oz. after or part thereof	Post Cards	Printed Papers Small Packets, Insured Boxes (Ins. Box: min. 20p) First ½ oz. or part thereof	Printed Papers Small Packets, Insured Boxes (Ins. Box: min. 20p) Each ½ oz. after or part thereof	Newspapers periodicals (on the P.O. Register) First ½ oz. or part thereof	Newspapers periodicals (on the P.O. Register) Each ½ oz. after or part thereof
	p	p	p	p	p	p	p
Abu Dhabi...	8½	7	6½	6	3½	5	2½
Afghanistan..	10	9	7½	6	4½	5	3
Ajman†	8½	7	6½	6	3½	5	2½
Algeria	8½	7	6½	6	3½	5	2½
Antigua	10	9	7½	6	4½	5	3
Argentina	10	9	7½	6	4½	5	3
Ascension†	10	9	7½	6	4½	5	3
Australia†‡	12	11	9	7	5½	6	3½
Bahamas†	10	9	7½	6	4½	5	3
Bahrain (State of)†..	8½	7	6½	6	3½	5	2½
Bangladesh†	10	9	7½	6	4½	5	3
Barbados†	10	9	7½	6	4½	5	3
Belize†	10	9	7½	6	4½	5	3
Bermuda	10	9	7½	6	4½	5	3
Bhutan†	10	9	7½	6	4½	5	3
Bolivia†‡	10	9	7½	6	4½	5	3
Botswana†	10	9	7½	6	4½	5	3
Brazil†	10	9	7½	6	4½	5	3
British Honduras...	See Belize						
British Ind.... Oc. Territy..	No service						
Brunei†	10	9	7½	6	4½	5	3
Burma‡	10	9	7½	6	4½	5	3
Burundi†	10	9	7½	6	4½	5	3
Cameroon†	10	9	7½	6	4½	5	3
Canada†‡	10	9	7½	6	4½	5	3
Caroline Islands†	12	11	9	7	5½	6	3½
Cayman Islands†	10	9	7½	6	4½	5	3
Cent. African Republic†	10	9	7½	6	4½	5	3
Chad†	10	9	7½	6	4½	5	3
Chile‡	10	9	7½	6	4½	5	3
China†	12	11	9	7	5½	6	3½
Christmas Is. (Ind. Oc.)†..	10	9	7½	6	4½	5	3
Cocos(Keeling) Islands	10	9	7½	6	4½	5	3
Colombia†‡	10	9	7½	6	4½	5	3
Comoro Islands†	10	9	7½	6	4½	5	3
Congo(People's Republic)†..	10	9	7½	6	4½	5	3
Costa Rica†	10	9	7½	6	4½	5	3
Cuba†‡	10	9	7½	6	4½	5	3
Dahomey†	10	9	7½	6	4½	5	3
Dominica†	10	9	7½	6	4½	5	3

‡Maximum weight limit for Small Packets: 1 lb.   † No insured box service available for air mail.

Destination	Letters		Post Cards	Printed Papers Small Packets, Insured Boxes (Ins. Box: min. 20p)		Newspapers periodicals (on the P.O. Register)		Destination	Letters		Post Cards	Printed Papers Small Packets, Insured Boxes (Ins. Box: min. 20p)		Newspapers periodicals (on the P.O. Register)	
	First ½ oz. or part thereof	Each ½ oz. after or part thereof		First ½ oz. or part thereof	Each ½ oz. after or part thereof	First ½ oz. or part thereof	Each ½ oz. after or part thereof		First ½ oz. or part thereof	Each ½ oz. after or part thereof		First ½ oz. or part thereof	Each ½ oz. after or part thereof	First ½ oz. or part thereof	Each ½ oz. after or part thereof
	p	p	p	p	p	p	p		p	p	p	p	p	p	p
Dominican Republic†..	10	9	7½	6	4½	5	3	Kenya.......	10	9	7½	6	4½	5	3
Dubai†.......	8½	7	6½	6	3½	5	2½	Khmer Republic†..	10	9	7½	6	4½	5	3
Ecuador†.....	10	9	7½	6	4½	5	3	Korea†........	12	11	9	7	5½	6	3½
Egypt (Arab Republic of)	8½	7	6½	6	3½	5	2½	Kuwait......	8½	7	6½	6	3½	5	2½
El Salvador†..	10	9	7½	6	4½	5	3	Laos†........	10	9	7½	6	4½	5	3
Equatorial Guinea†....	10	9	7½	6	4½	5	3	Lebanon†.....	8½	7	6½	6	3½	5	2½
Ethiopia†....	8½	7	6½	6	3½	5	2½	Lesotho†.....	10	9	7½	6	4½	5	3
Falkland Islds. and Dependencies......	10	9	7½	6	4½	5	3	Liberia†......	10	9	7½	6	4½	5	3
Fiji..........	12	11	9	7	5½	6	3½	Libyan Arab Republic†...	8½	7	6½	6	3½	5	2½
French Guiana†....	10	9	7½	6	4½	5	3	Macao.......	10	9	7½	6	4½	5	3
French Polynesia†..	12	11	9	7	5½	6	3½	Malagasy Republic†..	10	9	7½	6	4½	5	3
French Territory of the Afars and Issas ...	8½	7	6½	6	3½	5	2½	Malawi	10	9	7½	6	4½	5	3
French West Indies†.....	10	9	7½	6	4½	5	3	Malaya.......	10	9	7½	6	4½	5	3
Fujairah†....	8½	7	6½	6	3½	5	2½	Maldives (Rep. of)†..	10	9	7½	6	4½	5	3
Gabon†......	10	9	7½	6	4½	5	3	Mali†........	10	9	7½	6	4½	5	3
Gambia, The†..	10	9	7½	6	4½	5	3	Mariana Islands†....	12	11	9	7	5½	6	3½
Gaza and Khan Yunis†.....	8½	7	6½	6	3½	5	2½	Marshall Islands†....	12	11	9	7	5½	6	3½
Ghana.......	10	9	7½	6	4½	5	3	Mauritania†.	10	9	7½	6	4½	5	3
Gilbert and Ellice Islds†...	12	11	9	7	5½	6	3½	Mauritius.....	10	9	7½	6	4½	5	3
Grenada†.....	10	9	7½	6	4½	5	3	Mexico†......	10	9	7½	6	4½	5	3
Guatemala†...	10	9	7½	6	4½	5	3	Mongolia (People's Republic)†..	12	11	9	7	5½	6	3½
Guinea†......	10	9	7½	6	4½	5	3	Montserrat†...	10	9	7½	6	4½	5	3
Guinea-Bissau† (Formerly Port. Gna...	10	9	7½	6	4½	5	3	Morocco†.....	8½	7	6½	6	3½	5	2½
Guyana......	10	9	7½	6	4½	5	3	Nauru Island†.	12	11	9	7	5½	6	3½
Haiti†.......	10	9	7½	6	4½	5	3	Nepal........	10	9	7½	6	4½	5	3
Honduras (Rep. of)†..	10	9	7½	6	4½	5	3	Netherlands Antilles....	10	9	7½	6	4½	5	3
Hong Kong...	10	9	7½	6	4½	5	3	New Caledonia...	12	11	9	7	5½	6	3½
India.......	10	9	7½	6	4½	5	3	New Hebrides†..	12	11	9	7	5½	6	3½
Indonesia†....	10	9	7½	6	4½	5	3	New Zealand..	12	11	9	7	5½	6	3½
Iran.........	8½	7	6½	6	3½	5	2½	New Zealand Territories†.	12	11	9	7	5½	6	3½
Iraq†........	8½	7	6½	6	3½	5	2½	Nicaragua†...	10	9	7½	6	4½	5	3
Israel†.......	8½	7	6½	6	3½	5	2½	Nigeria.......	10	9	7½	6	4½	5	3
Ivory Coast† .	10	9	7½	6	4½	5	3	Niger Republic†...	10	9	7½	6	4½	5	3
Jamaica†.....	10	9	7½	6	4½	5	3	Norfolk Island†...	12	11	9	7	5½	6	3½
Japan.......	12	11	9	7	5½	6	3½	Oman (Sultanate of)†...	8½	7	6½	6	3½	5	2½
Jordan†......	8½	7	6½	6	3½	5	2½	Pakistan......	10	9	7½	6	4½	5	3
								Panama (Republic of)†.	10	9	7½	6	4½	5	3

† No insured box service available for air mail.

Destination	Letters First ½ oz. or part thereof	Each ½ oz. after or part thereof	Post Cards	Printed Papers Small Packets, Insured Boxes (Ins. Box: min. 20p) First ½ oz. or part thereof	Each ½ oz. after or part thereof	Newspapers periodicals (on the P.O. Register) First ½ oz. or part thereof	Each ½ oz. after or part thereof
	p	p	p	p	p	p	p
Panama Canal Zone†	10	9	7½	6	4½	5	3
Papua New Guinea†	12	11	9	7	5½	6	3½
Paraguay†	10	9	7½	6	4½	5	3
Peru†	10	9	7½	6	4½	5	3
Philippines†	12	11	9	7	5½	6	3½
Pitcairn Island†	12	11	9	7	5½	6	3½
Portuguese East Africa†	10	9	7½	6	4½	5	3
Portuguese Timor†	12	11	9	7	5½	6	3½
Portuguese West Africa†	10	9	7½	6	4½	5	3
Puerto Rico†	10	9	7½	6	4½	5	3
Qatar (State of)†	8½	7	6½	6	3½	5	2½
Ras Al Khaimah†	8½	7	6½	6	3½	5	2½
Reunion†	10	9	7½	6	4½	5	3
Rhodesia†	10	9	7½	6	4½	5	3
Rwanda†	10	9	7½	6	4½	5	3
Sabah†	10	9	7½	6	4½	5	3
St. Helena†	10	9	7½	6	4½	5	3
St. Kitts-Nevis-Anguilla†	10	9	7½	6	4½	5	3
St. Lucia†	10	9	7½	6	4½	5	3
St. Pierre and Miquelon†	10	9	7½	6	4½	5	3
St. Vincent†	10	9	7½	6	4½	5	3
Samoa (U.S.A. Territory)†	12	11	9	7	5½	6	3½
Sarawak†	10	9	7½	6	4½	5	3
Saudi Arabia†	8½	7	6½	6	3½	5	2½
Senegal†	10	9	7½	6	4½	5	3
Seychelles†	10	9	7½	6	4½	5	3
Sharjah†	8½	7	6½	6	3½	5	2½
Sierra Leone†	10	9	7½	6	4½	5	3
Singapore (Rep. of)	10	9	7½	6	4½	5	3
Solomon Islands†	12	11	9	7	5½	6	3½
Somali Dem. Republic	10	9	7½	6	4½	5	3
South Africa (Rep. of)†	10	9	7½	6	4½	5	3
Spanish Territories of North Africa†	8½	7	6½	6	3½	5	2½
Spanish W. Africa†	8½	7	6½	6	3½	5	2½
Sri Lanka (Rep. of)	10	9	7½	6	4½	5	3
Sudan (Dem. Rep. of)†	8½	7	6½	6	3½	5	2½
Surinam	10	9	7½	6	4½	5	3
Swaziland†	10	9	7½	6	4½	5	3
Syrian Arab Rep.	8½	7	6½	6	3½	5	2½
Taiwan (Formosa)	12	11	9	7	5½	6	3½
Tanzania	10	9	7½	6	4½	5	3
Thailand†	10	9	7½	6	4½	5	3
Tibet†	10	9	7½	6	4½	5	3
Togo†	10	9	7½	6	4½	5	3
Tonga (Friendly Islands)†	12	11	9	7	5½	6	3½
Tortola (British Virgin Is.)†	10	9	7½	6	4½	5	3
Trinidad and Tobago†	10	9	7½	6	4½	5	3
Tristan da Cunha†	10	9	7½	6	4½	5	3
Tunisia†	8½	7	6½	6	3½	5	2½
Turks and Caicos Islds†	10	9	7½	6	4½	5	3
Uganda	10	9	7½	6	4½	5	3
Umm al Qaiwain†	8½	7	6½	6	3½	5	2½
U.S.A.†	10	9	7½	6	4½	5	3
Upper Volta†	10	9	7½	6	4½	5	3
Uruguay†	10	9	7½	6	4½	5	3
Venezuela†	10	9	7½	6	4½	5	3
Vietnam†	10	9	7½	6	4½	5	3
Virgin Islds of U.S.A.†	10	9	7½	6	4½	5	3
Wake Island†	12	11	9	7	5½	6	3½
Western Samoa†	12	11	9	7	5½	6	3½
Yemen Arab Republic†	8½	7	6½	6	3½	5	2½
Yemen (People's Dem. Rep. of)	8½	7	6½	6	3½	5	2½
Zaire (Rep. of)†	10	9	7½	6	4½	5	3
Zambia†	10	9	7½	6	4½	5	3

† No insured box service available for air mail.

GENERAL REGULATIONS

EXPORT RESTRICTIONS.—Under Department of Trade and Industry regulations the exportation of some goods by post is prohibited except under Department of Trade licence. Enquiries in the matter should be addressed to the Export Data Branch, Export Services and Promotions Division, Department of Trade and Industry, Export House, 50 Ludgate Hill, London, EC4M 7HU.

PROHIBITED ARTICLES.—Among prohibitions are offensive or dangerous things, packets likely to impede the P.O. sorters, and certain kinds of advertisement.

CERTIFICATE OF POSTING.—For non C.F. parcels the fee is 1p each (maximum 10p). May also be obtained for unregistered letters and unregistered postal packets (fee 1p).

RECORDED DELIVERY (inland, *not to Irish Republic*). Charge: 7p.—This service provides for a record of posting and delivery. Advice of delivery, a further 10p at time of posting, 20p after time of posting. Money and jewellery are not allowed, The service does not apply to parcels, railex or railway letters. Ask at the post office for full details.

UNPAID PACKETS, are charged *double postage* on delivery; UNDERPAID PACKETS, *double the deficiency.*

UNDELIVERED POSTAL PACKETS.—Undelivered postal packets are returned to the sender without charge provided the return address is indicated either on the outside of the envelope or inside. If the sender's address is not available, items not containing property are destroyed; however, if the packet contains something of intrinsic value, it is retained for up to three months pending reclaim before being disposed of. Perishable items within this category are dealt with as requisite. Exceptionally, items in the minimum weight step on which a rebate of postage has been allowed are destroyed unopened unless there is a return address shown on the outside of the cover. In addition, undeliverable second class mail in the minimum weight step, which, upon opening, is found to consist only of newspapers, magazines or commercial advertising material is also destroyed. (These rules are currently under revision: for the up-to-date position, consult the nearest post office.) *British packets undelivered abroad*; instructions for disposal are required if parcel is undeliverable and must be given at the time of posting.

REPLY COUPONS, for the purpose of prepaying replies to letters, are exchangeable abroad for stamps representing the minimum surface mail letter rate from the country concerned to the U.K. International Reply Coupons (valid in most countries) 13p. Sold at chief offices.

POSTE RESTANTE (solely for the convenience of travellers, and for three months only in any one town).—A packet may be addressed as a rule to any Post Office except Town Sub-Offices, and should have the words " Poste Restante " or " to be called for " in the address. If addressed to initials, fictitious names, or Christian name only, it is treated as undeliverable. Applicants must furnish sufficient particulars to ensure delivery to the proper person. Redirection from a Poste Restante is not undertaken for more than 1 month unless longer (up to 3 months) is applied for. Letters at a seaport for an expected ship are kept 2 months; otherwise letters are kept for 2 weeks—or for 1 month if originating from abroad—at the end of which time they are treated as undeliverable, unless bearing a request for return at or before the end of the period.

REDIRECTION.—(1) By agent of addressee: *Packets other than parcels, business reply and Freepost items* may be reposted free not later than the day after delivery (not counting Sundays and public holidays) if unopened and not tampered with, and if original addressee's name is unobscured. *Parcels* may be redirected free of charge within the same time limits, only if the original and the substituted address are both within the same local parcel delivery area (or within the London Postal Area). *Registered packets*, which must be taken to a Post Office, are *re-registered* free only up to day after delivery. (2) By the Post Office: Requests for redirection of *letters*, etc., should be on printed forms, obtainable from any post office, and must be signed by the person to whom the letters are to be addressed. The fees for redirection are as follows:— Redirection for a period not exceeding one month 75p; redirection or renewal for a period not exceeding three months £2; redirection or renewal for a period not exceeding twelve months £5. A fee is payable for each different surname on the application form. Additional postage is generally due on redirected parcels (*see* above). Separate forms must be filled in for the forwarding of *telegrams*.

REGISTRATION, INLAND (First Class letters only).— All packets intended for registration should be marked " Registered " in bottom left-hand corner, and *must be handed to an officer of the Post Office, and a receipt taken.* The packets must be made up in a reasonably strong cover appropriate to their contents. Packets and letters must be fastened with adhesive (if tape is used it must be transparent and each piece must be signed or distinctively marked), or sealed with wax, lead, etc. Minimum fee: 35p, exclusive of postage. Advice of delivery, a further 10p at time of posting, 20p after time of posting. The latest time for registering is usually half an hour before the latest time for posting ordinary packets. Compulsory registration is applied to (*a*) any letter packet apparently meant for registration and wrongly posted (minimum fee less any prepaid excess postage); (*b*) letter packets found open (or undeliverable) and containing any bank or currency note, coin, jewellery, stamps, uncrossed bearer cheques, uncrossed postal orders without payee's name, etc., in each case £2 or more in value. Ask at the post office for full details.

COMPENSATION, INLAND.—Subject to certain prescribed regulations which are set out in the Post Office Guide, the Post Office pays compensation for (i) loss of or damage to registered letters, (ii) though not as a legal right, for loss of or damage to recorded delivery packets, parcels on which a compensation fee has been paid and for unregistered packets conveyed by Express Messenger all the way. The onus of making up properly any packet sent by post and of packing adequately any article or articles enclosed therein lies on the sender, and the Post Office does not accept any responsibility for loss arising from faulty or inadequate packing. No compensation is paid for consequential injury or damage arising in respect of anything sent by post. *Registered letters* (*including items sent to the Irish Republic and the Channel Islands*): The fees for registration are : 35p covering compensation up to £150; 40p, £300; 45p, £500 (maximum). (No legal right to compensation exists in respect of registered letters sent to and from Irish Republic or the Channel Islands.) Compensation Fee (C.F.) parcels, fees: 5p for compensation up to £10; 10p up to £50; 20p up to £100. *Recorded delivery packets:* maximum compensation £2 provided no contents inadmissible. *Unregistered packets* conveyed by Express Messenger all the way: Maximum compensation £5.

Compensation in respect of money of any kind (coin, notes, orders, cheques, stamps, etc.) is only given if the money is sent by *registered letter* post in one of the special envelopes sold officially and, in the case of paper money, if particulars (for identification) are kept; the maximum compensation for coin, which must be packed so as not to move about, will not exceed £5 except in a case where the value of each coin exceeds its face value, *i.e.* numismatic coins. Compensation cannot be paid for loss or damage in the case of any packet containing anything not legally transmissible by post; and for fragile articles only if they have been adequately packed and the cover is conspicuously marked " Fragile, with care ". No compensation is paid for deterioration due to delay of perishable articles, liquids or semi-liquids sent by letter or parcel post to or from Irish Republic, whether registered or not.

REGISTRATION, OVERSEAS (except for parcels and printed paper items posted in bulk), is in force to all countries with the exception of Chagos Islands, British Indian Ocean Territory, Republic of Maldives or North Vietnam. No compensation is payable for the loss of or damage to valuable articles or other items sent in an unregistered letter. Fee 35p. If claimed within a year compensation is paid to the sender for entire loss of registered packets while in the custody of a country in the Universal Postal Union, subject to certain conditions. Compensation is also payable for the partial or complete loss of or damage to the contents of registered items in the service with certain countries (*see* Post Office Guide for list).

INSURANCE, OVERSEAS, may be effected on packets to many countries at the following rates:— 40p for up to £72 cover; 4p for each additional £36 up to 88p for £500. *For H.M. Ships abroad and also members of H.M. Army and Air Force overseas using closed Forces addresses* (*e.g.*, British Forces Post Office followed by a number) only parcels are insurable, up to £100. Packets containing valuable papers, (bank-notes, etc.), documents (press, etc.) and, in some cases, valuable articles such as jewellery, can be insured as letters, or as parcels if the country of origin does not accept durable goods in the letter post.

INSURED BOX POST.—Jewellery and precious articles (*not* letters or paper valuables) may be sent in insured boxes to certain countries. Customs declarations must be filled in.

The Post Office Guide should be consulted for details of the conditions of Insurance.

COMPENSATION up to a maximum of £8·20 may be given for loss or damage in the U.K. to *uninsured* parcels to or from most overseas countries, if certificate of posting is produced.

No compensation will be paid for any loss or damage due to the act of the Queen's Enemies.

CASH ON DELIVERY SERVICE, INLAND (*not* to or from Irish Republic, nor to H.M. Ships).—A sum (Trade Charge) up to £50 can, under certain conditions, be collected from addressee and remitted to sender of a parcel or registered letter posted at a Money Order Office. Fee (extra to normal postage and registration charges): 35p.

CASH ON DELIVERY, OVERSEAS.—Applicable to parcels only, but not all countries, nor to H.M. Naval and Military Forces and R.A.F. serving overseas. A fee of 75p per parcel must be prepaid in addition to the postage. The Trade Charge (amount to be collected) may not exceed £50, but to some countries the limit is lower. Addressee

has also to pay on delivery, besides Customs, if any a further fee (15p in U.K.) not prepayable. If Trade Charge cannot be collected, special rules for undeliverable C.O D. parcels apply.

EXPRESS and SPECIAL SERVICES (INLAND).— In general the express service are limited to the hours of telegraph business, but the times vary according to the service used and local conditions. (1) *All the way*, by P.O. messenger, of packets, conspicuously marked " Express " above the address, handed over the counter. Inclusive charge, 50p per mile, or part of a mile, with 3p on each *separate* packet after the first. Live animals, liquids, and money may be delivered by this service. (2) *After transmission by post*, on *addressee's* application (50p per mile, or part of a mile, and 2½p for every ten or less additional packets). (3) *After transmission by post*, at *sender's* request " Special Delivery " from the ordinary delivery office, if messengers are available (40p.+ postage). This service is restricted to First Class letters and to parcels. Packets must be marked " Special Delivery, " and letters bear a broad blue or black vertical line back and front. A similar line must be drawn completely round a packet or parcel. (4) *Special delivery on Sunday of postal packets* (*except parcels*) *handed in on Saturdays.* Limited inter-city services, for London, Belfast, and certain provincial cities (except that the service is not in operation from Southampton to Belfast) are available *only:* (1) Sundays: reciprocally between certain towns as shown in the Post Office Guide; (2) Good Friday: *to* London only *from* towns in (1). Delivery is made from offices only during periods when they are open for telegraphic business. The handing-in offices in London are:—The London Chief Office, King Edward St., London EC1A 1AA, W. and S.W. District Offices, and Camberwell Green, Clapham Common, Hammersmith, Holloway, Trafalgar Sq., Stratford, and Swiss Cottage (Branch Offices). Packets marked "Express: Sunday Delivery," must be handed in in time to catch *preceeding* night mails (in London 12.45 p.m.–5.0 p.m. for provincial towns). The latest time of posting to Belfast should be ascertained at selected office of posting. Fee is £1 in addition to postage. Not available for parcels. (5) (*Railex.*) Postal packets which cannot be registered are despatched by rail, met, and specially delivered in Great Britain, Northern Ireland (Belfast, Larne and Londonderry only). Inclusive charges irrespective of weight but not exceeding 1 lb., £2, but packets handed in in Northern Ireland for destinations in Great Britain or Northern Ireland may not exceed 2 oz. (6) *A Railway Parcel* is similary accelerated at the cost of a telegram, of railway charges, and of Service (1) at both ends of its journey. It should be marked " Railway Parcel, to be handed to Post Office messenger at .... Station."

RAILWAY LETTERS, &C.—A First Class letter, not liable to registration, may be handed in at the parcel or passenger booking office of a railway station of British Rail and certain other minor railway companies, at any time when the station is open to the public, for conveyance by the next available train. A railway letter may either be addressed to be called for at a station, or to the residence of the addressee in which case it is posted at the station named in the address. The service is available between any two stations in Great Britain and Northern Ireland and from Great Britain and Northern Ireland to the Irish Republic. It is not available at or to stations of the London Transport Executive. Fees (besides postage) are charged by British Rail or the minor railway companies on which railway letters travel. Enquiries about these fees should be made at the station at which railway letters are handed in. For other combinations of rail and express, *see* preceding paragraph, Services (5) and (6).

AIRWAY LETTERS.—On certain internal air routes operated by the British Airways Corporation, First Class letters may be handed in at the airport or town terminal for conveyance by the next available direct air service to be transferred to the post at the distant airport or town terminal or to be called for at the airport or town terminal. Fee (besides postage) 55p, maximum weight 1 lb. The conditions on which this service operates are, in general, similar to those applying to the Railway Letter Service. This service is not available to the Irish Republic, Isle of Man or to any country overseas. Full information can be obtained from any office of British Airways (European Division).

INTERNATIONAL EXPRESS SERVICE.—From the office of delivery by special messenger is available to or from certain countries. In some countries the service is restricted to certain towns. 40p is paid by the sender, the rest, if any, by addressee, according to the local regulations. (*See* P.O. Guide.)

DATAPOST.—This service offers a door-to-door overnight service to most parts of the country on a contract basis. Charges are negotiated with individual customers and reflect the services performed. Head Postmasters will provide full information on request.

This service is also available to the U.S.A., Brazil, Belgium, France, Japan, the Netherlands and Hong Kong.

BUSINESS REPLY AND FREEPOST (Inland, excluding Irish Republic).—These services enable a person or firm to receive replies to advertisements, letters from clients, etc. without prepayment of postage, the addressee paying the postage together with a handling charge of ½p per item delivered. A licence costing £10 p.a. must be obtained to use either service and these are available from Head Postmasters who will also provide any further information required.

POSTAGE FORWARD PARCEL SERVICE.—This service enables a person or firm to receive parcels from clients without prepayment of postage. A special label is used for this service. A licence costing £10 p.a., to use the service must first be obtained from the local Head Postmaster.

ARTICLES FOR THE BLIND (Inland, including Irish Republic). Books, papers, literature and specified articles specially adapted for the use of the blind are admissible subject to certain conditions. A packet should bear on the outside the indication "Articles for the Blind" and the name and address of the sender. Packets must be capable of easy examination in the post. Postage free.

BLIND LITERATURE, OVERSEAS (in other respects treated as Printed Papers):—Papers, periodicals and books, if printed in special type (also plates for embossing blind literature, and voice recordings and special paper intended solely for the use of the blind) subject to certain conditions of posting, marked outside "Literature for the Blind (Cécogrammes)", with name and address of sender. Packets must be capable of easy examination in the post. They may be sent post free by surface route to all parts.

SMALL PACKETS POST (OVERSEAS).—For the transmission of goods (including trade samples) in the same mails as Printed Papers up to 1 kg. Registration is allowed; not insurance. Available to all countries, but to some countries there is a limit of 500 g. A customs declaration is required.

NEWSPAPER POST (INLAND).—For newspapers "registered at the P.O." (p. 1195).

Copies of registered newspapers may be posted by the publishers or their agents in wrappers open at both ends, in unsealed envelopes approved by the Post Office for the purpose or without covers and tied with string which can be removed without cutting. Wrappers and envelopes must be prominently marked NEWSPAPER POST in the top left-hand corner and be easily removable for the purpose of examination. No writing or additional printing is permitted, other than the words "with compliments", name and address of sender, request for return if undeliverable and a reference to a page.

Newspapers posted by the public or supplements to registered newspapers despatched apart from their ordinary publications are transmitted under the conditions governing the First or Second Class Letter Services.

STAMPS, ENVELOPES, POSTCARDS, &c.

£sd stamps are no longer valid for postage.

POSTAGE STAMPS (used also for receipts, telegrams and certain Inland Revenue duties) are sold for the respective values of ½p, 1p, 1½p, 2p, 2½p, 3p, 3½p, 4p, 4½p, 5p, 5½p, 6p, 6½p, 7p, 7½p, 8p, 9p, 10p, 20p, 50p and £1. Books containing 2 at ½p, 2 at 1p 2 at 1½p, 2 at 2p, 10p; 10 at 3½p, 35p. Rolls of 3½p stamps are sold. There are also mixed rolls made up of strips of 2p, ½p, ½p, 1p, 1p.

REGISTERED LETTER ENVELOPES printed with a 42p stamp (35p for registration and 7p for postage) are of three sizes: G, 6⅛″ × 3¾″ 43½p each ; H, 8″ × 4¾″ 44p each; K, 11½″ × 6″ 46p each.

FORCES AIR LETTER FORMS issued against purchase of 4½p stamp.

LETTERCARDS printed with 5½p stamp, 6½p each 7p stamp, 8p each.

POSTCARDS printed with 7p stamp, 7½p each.

ENVELOPES printed with 5½p stamp: A (5¾″ × 3¾″) 6½p each; B(9¼″ × 4¾″) 6½p each. With 7p stamp: A (5¾″ × 3¾″) 8p each; B (9¼″ × 4¾″) 8p each.

AIR LETTER FORMS printed with 8½p or 9p stamp, 8½p or 9p each.

Printed postage stamps cut out of envelopes, postcards, lettercards, air letter forms or newspaper-wrappers may be used as adhesive stamps in payment of postage or telegrams provided they are not imperfect, mutilated or defaced in any way.

MONEY ORDERS

There is no Inland Ordinary Money Order Service. *Overseas Service.* Advice of Payment: 7½p (to certain countries). Payment may be stopped (fee 7½p).

Inland Telegraph Money Orders (and to Irish Republic, Channel Islands and Isle of Man).

Money may be transmitted by this means from most offices which despatch telegrams, and paid at most of those which also deliver telegrams, and at some other offices. On Sundays, Christmas Day, Boxing Day and Good Friday special arrangements apply (*see* Post Office Guide).

The fee is £1·25 per order (maximum value £100) plus cost of official Telegram of Advice, 80p minimum for Inland Orders (including orders to Channel Islands and Isle of Man) and 85p minimum for Irish Republic Orders and where applicable the charge for any private message sent with the order, 5p per word. (All charges for telegrams are subject to Value Added Tax in addition to the charges shown above).

Ordinary Money Orders for Abroad

The fee is £2 per order. Limits of amount of each order vary according to destination but in any case may not exceed £50; validity varies between one and twelve months (*see* Post Office Guide).

Telegraph Money Orders for Abroad

The fee is £2 per order, *plus* cost of official Telegram of Advice (at Letter Telegram rate, if desired, to certain countries).

Application to remit money orders to countries outside the Scheduled Territories (formerly known as the Sterling Area) must be made on a special declaration form upon which the purpose of the remittance must be stated. This form is obtainable at any money order office, where it may be ascertained whether any particular country with which a money order service is in operation is outside the Scheduled Territories.

POSTAL ORDERS

Postal Orders (British pattern) are issued and paid at nearly all post offices in the United Kingdom during the ordinary hours of business on weekdays. They are also issued and/or paid in many countries within the Commonwealth and in a few other countries. Transmission of postal orders to overseas countries is restricted under Exchange Control Regulations and is prohibited to any country outside the British Postal Order Area, except to members of H.M. Forces under special arrangements (particulars of Exchange Control restrictions may be obtained at any post office transacting Postal Order business). British postal orders are paid and issued in the Channel Islands and the Isle of Man, and paid in the Irish Republic. They are printed with a counterfoil, for 5p, then 7½p and every multiple of 2½p up to 25p, then 30p and every multiple of 5p up to £1, then in £1 steps to £10. Adhesive unmarked current British Postage Stamps not exceeding two in number, if affixed in the two spaces provided, may increase the value of the order by not more than 4½p. Fees 5p up to £1, 6p; £2, £3, £4, £5, £6, £7, £8, £9, or £10, 8p. The name of the payee must be inserted. If not presented within six months of the last day of the month of issue, Orders must be sent to the local Head Postmaster, or in London to the District Postmaster to ascertain whether the order may still be paid.

INLAND TELEGRAMS

Telegrams are accepted during counter business hours at any post office at which telegraph business is transacted. They may also be handed with the necessary payment to messengers delivering telegrams or express letters. Telegrams may be tendered by telephone or telex at all times. All charges for telegrams are subject to Value Added Tax in addition to the charges shown below. Rate, 30p per telegram, plus 5p for each word. (To Irish Republic 35p per telegram plus 5p for each word.) Greetings telegrams on appropriately designed forms in decorative envelopes cost the rate of an ordinary telegram plus a surcharge of 40p. Greetings telegrams may be tendered by telephone or handed in in advance for delivery on a specified day. On Mondays to Fridays, if the Greetings telegram is handed in at any time before noon of the day before delivery is required, the surcharge is reduced to 20p. (Greetings service not available to and from Irish Republic.)

Overnight Telegram

An Overnight telegram may be tendered between 8 a.m. and 10.30 p.m. for delivery, normally by first post, the following morning. On days when there is no postal delivery, Overnight telegrams are held until the next postal delivery. The charge is 20p per telegram plus 3p for each word. The Overnight service is not available to the Irish Republic. A redirection charge of 50p per telegram is made if the original and new addresses are in the same delivery area or London Postal District. Overnight telegrams are normally redirected by post free of charge. In all other cases the redirection charge is at the ordinary inland rate. Telegrams, handed in on *Sundays, New Year's Day* and (exc. Scotland) *Good Friday* or *Christmas Day* are charged 45p extra. Replies may be prepaid within the limits of 50p (minimum) and £1·50 (maximum), Irish Republic 65p

(minimum) and £1 (maximum); the reply vouchers may be used in payment or part payment of any Post Office telegram or any telegraph, telex or telephone account rendered by the Post Office, or its value refunded to sender, the addressee or person applying on behalf of the sender of the original telegram, on completion of the declaration on the back of the voucher. Receipt for charges on telegrams accepted at post office counters free on request. Certified copy 45p; application to the local Head Postmaster must be within 3 months of the date of sending. There is no charge for delivery in the United Kingdom. In the Irish Republic delivery is free to addresses within 1 mile of the delivery office; beyond that any necessary charge will be collected on delivery.

TELEGRAPH OFFICE ALWAYS OPEN IN LONDON: — Trafalgar Sq., 24–28 William IV Street, WC2N 4DL.

INTERNATIONAL TELEGRAMS

The per word charges for ordinary or Full Rate telegrams from the United Kingdom to places abroad are shown on pp. 1205–8. Urgent Telegrams may be sent to many countries at double the ordinary per word rates.

For telegrams of a social character the GLT (Commonwealth Social Telegram) service at half the ordinary per word rates is available to Commonwealth countries. The service indicator GLT will be counted as a chargeable word. The minimum charge will be as for 11 words including the indicator GLT.

Letter telegrams to certain countries are admitted at half the ordinary per word rates for messages in plain language of a lengthy though less urgent character for which the minimum charge is as for 22 words including the indicator LT. Full particulars as to which countries this facility is available can be obtained from any Post Office or International Telegraph Office.

In addition to these per word charges, the following fixed charges per telegram apply, irrespective of destination.

Ordinary	30p
Urgent	60p
GLT	20p
LT	20p

Phototelegrams, i.e. pictures, photographs, drawings, plans, printed, typed or written documents may be telegraphed in facsimile to many places in the world. Full particulars of all telegraph charges and services available to any country will be given on enquiry at any Post Office or International Telegraph Office.

RADIOTELEGRAMS

Radiotelegrams for transmission to ships at sea in any part of the world may be handed in at any Postal Telegraph Office or dictated over the telephone. The charge for radiotelegrams is 12p per word (standard rate). Radiotelegrams at the standard rate should be addressed Portishead Radio unless the sender nominates another coast station. The address should contain (1) the name or rank of the addressee, (2) the name of the ship and (3) the name of the coast station in the British Isles if the sender knows that the ship is within range of that station.

The charge for messages to H.M. Ships is 10p a word. The address should contain (1) the name of the addressee and his rank or rating, (2) the word "Warship" (or "Submarine"), (3) the name of the ship (or identifying letters and number) and (4) the word "Admiraltyradio".

In addition to the per word charges quoted a fixed charge of 30p per radiotelegram applies.

Radiotelegrams may also be sent to R.A.F. vessels. Such radiotelegrams should be addressed in the same way as for commercial vessels and in addition should include the words " R.A.F. Vessel " before the name of the ship.

The minimum charge is as for seven words.

RADIOTELEPHONE SERVICE

Radiotelephone services are available between telephone subscribers (but not from coin-box telephones or call offices unless the caller is a holder of a telephone credit card) in Great Britain, Northern Ireland, the Channel Islands and the Isle of Man and suitably equipped ships. The service is generally available at all hours of the day and night, but the periods of communication with a particular ship vary with the ship's position and are dependent on radio conditions.

Calls are normally made through the coast stations, listed below, and callers should ask the local exchange telephone operator for SHIPS' TELEPHONE SERVICE adding, if known, the telephone number and name of the coast station through which the call should be made. If the name of the coast station is not known, the caller will be connected to Portishead Radio. When connected to the coast station operator, the caller should ask for SHIPS' RADIO TELEPHONE CALL giving the name of the ship and the name (or designation) of the person required.

Anglesey Radio.........	0407 83 0541
Bacton Radio (restricted short range VHF services)	Mablethorpe 3447
Clyde Radio (restricted short range VHF services)	Portpatrick 311
Cullercoats Radio........	089 44 31318
Humber Radio...........	Mablethorpe 3447
Ilfracombe Radio........	Ilfracombe 3453
Land's End Radio........	0736 77 493
Niton Radio.............	0983 730495
North Foreland Radio.....	0843 20592
Oban Radio.............	0631 2059
Portishead Radio........	027 878 3291
Portpatrick Radio........	0776 81 311
Stonehaven Radio........	0569 2 2917
Thames Radio (restricted short range VHF services)	0843 20592
Wick Radio.............	Wick 2271
Shetland Radio (restricted short range VHF services)	Wick 2271

Charges vary according to the position of the ship. The rates are (for minimum of 3 minutes) Short range (within 50 miles of VHF station) 63p for 3 minutes. 21p for each additional minute.

Medium range (within 250 miles of U.K.). £1·08 for 3 minutes. 36p for each additional minute.

Long range (dependent on position of ship). £2·70 or £3·15 for 3 minutes, 90p or £1·05 respectively for each additional minute.

The service is available, for calls to and from H.M. Ships, subject to the approval of the Duty Commander M.O.D. Navy, through whom all calls to H.M. Ships should be booked. The charges are the same as those for merchant ships but as H.M. Ships do not normally keep watch for private radiotelephone calls from the shore, no attempt should be made to book a call to one of H.M. Ships unless prior arrangements have been made with the person concerned on the ship. The caller must be able to give the name of the coast station through which the call is to be made, or the approximate position of the ship at the time the call is required.

The holder of a telephone credit card issued in Great Britain, Northern Ireland, the Channel Islands or the Isle of Man may use it to make radiotelephone calls to ships at sea from any telephone in this country (including coin-box telephones and call offices) and have the charges debited to his own account.

INLAND TELEPHONES

The quarterly rental for an exclusive business exchange line is £9·75 and £8·25 for any other exclusive exchange line. For shared service, in which two subscribers share one line but have practically the same facilities as those provided by individual lines, each customer pays £4 per annum less than for exclusive line service. A condition of telephone service is that all new and removing residential customers since January, 1948, are liable to share their lines if called upon to do so. Subscriber trunk dialling (STD) facilities are provided at an increasing number of exchanges. Local and dialled trunk calls from these exchanges are charged in 1·8p units, 2p units from pay on answer coin-box lines. Charges from coin-box lines are Value Added Tax included whereas from ordinary lines Value Added Tax is not included on individual call charges but an 8 per cent. charge is made on customer's total bill to cover Value Added Tax. The length of time per unit depends on the distance of the call, from three minutes for a local call to ten seconds for distances over 56 kilometres. Additional time is allowed during the cheaper rates period.

From other exchanges local calls are charged 1·8p from ordinary lines and 2p from a call office or coin-box line. All trunk calls are obtained via the operator. Operator-controlled trunk calls from any exchange have a three minute minimum charge which varies with the distance but does not exceed 39p (45p to Irish Republic from non-coin-box telephones). Operator-controlled calls made from coin-box lines are charged in 3 minute periods at the coin-box tariff. All trunk calls are cheaper if made after 6 p.m. or at weekends. Personal calls (to specified person) 12p extra, if the person cannot be found nothing further is charged. For fuller information *see* Preface to Telephone Directory, Dialling Instruction Booklet (where appropriate) and Post Office Guide.

TELEX SERVICE

Annual rental of teleprinter, associated equipment and line to Telex exchange is from £380 per annum (depending upon the equipment required). The minimum call charge for International calls via the operator is three minutes for subscriber-dialled calls to some Inter-Continental countries, where the minimum call charge is one minute, and subscriber-dialled calls to the Continent which are charged in 1½p units (*see* Post Office Guide for rates). Automatic equipment allowing messages to be sent at the maximum speed of 400 characters (60–70 words) per minute can be rented in addition. Descriptive booklet available from all Telephone Area Offices; for local address *see* Telephone Directory.

DATA COMMUNICATIONS SERVICES

Data communications services provide for data transmission at speeds ranging from 50–50,000 bits per second (bit/s) over telegraph, speech and wideband circuits. They accommodate a number of additional facilities such as automatic calling and answering, Dataplex and midnight line service. The services can be described briefly as follows:

Datel 100 provides for data transmission over telegraph type circuits either on the public switched telex network or privately rented circuits at speeds up to 110 bit/s. PO terminals at 50 bit/s are provided on telex. On telegraph circuits either PO or privately supplied terminals which have been granted permission for connection may be used.

Datel 200 provides for duplex data transmission over speech type circuits either privately rented or on the public switched telephone network (PSTN) at up to 300 bit/s using PO modems and privately supplied terminal equipment which has been permitted for connection to the network.

Datel 600 provides for duplex data transmission over speech type circuits either privately rented or on the PSTN at up to 1200 bit/s using PO modems and privately supplied terminal equipment which has been permitted for connection to the network.

Datel 2400 provides for synchronous duplex data transmission over speech type private circuits at up to 2400 bit/s using PO modems and privately supplied terminal equipment which has been permitted for connection to the network.

Datel 2400 Dial-Up provides for synchronous duplex data transmission over the PSTN at up to 2400 bit/s using PO modems and privately supplied terminal equipment which has been permitted for connection to the network.

Datel 400 is a telemetry service providing for unidirectional data transmission at $\pm$ 0·5 volts, 300 Hz analogue, or 600 bit/s digital over the PSTN or private circuits. A weather-proof outstation case is available for exposed locations.

Datel 48K provides for data transmission at 40·8K, 48K or 50K bit/s over specially engineered wideband circuits using PO modems and privately supplied terminal equipment which has been permitted for connection to the network.

Data Control Equipment enables terminal to automatically originate and answer calls over the switched network.

Dataplex allows the data from a number of low speed terminals to be sent over a single high speed link, resulting in reduced user costs.

Midnight Line Service provides for unlimited subscriber dialled inland calls between midnight and 6 a.m. for a moderate fixed annual rental.

INTERNATIONAL DATA TRANSMISSION SERVICES

(i) *Datel Services*

In the International context the term Datel has been adopted to refer to data transmission over the public switched telephone (or telex) networks.

Datel 100

This service provides for serial transmission of data at 50 bits per second using the telex network and is available to most European countries.

Datel 200

This service provides full duplex (simultaneous both way) serial transmission of data at speeds up to 200 bits per second using the public telephone network. Service is available to most of Europe, Bahrain, Dubai and the U.S.A. Note: Non European traffic is connected on a manual basis via the international exchange.

Datel 600

This service provides half duplex (bothway, but not simultaneous) serial transmission of data within the speed range of 600 to 1200 bits per second. Telephone networks, although designed for speech transmission are usually capable of carrying data transmissions at 600 bits per second and on some

connections, 1200 bits per second should be obtainable. Service is available to most European countries and Australia, Bahrain and Dubai, Canada, Hong Kong, New Zealand, Singapore and the U.S.A. (Note: Non-European traffic is connected on a manual basis via the international exchange.)

Datel 2400 (expected to be available the latter half of 1976). This service will allow serial transmission of digital data at 2400 bits per second using the public telephone network. A new Post Office modem, which will be obligatory in this service, is expected to be available in the latter half of 1976. Until that time the Post Office is prepared to allow the use of permitted non-Post Office modems by customers with a need for 2400 bits per second data transmission facilities over the international public telephone network subject to the agreement of the foreign administration(s) concerned.

The Post Office can give no guarantee of the rate or quality of data transmission in the case of facilities using non-Post Office modems.

Customers wishing to use non-Post Office modems to establish a facility must obtain permission to proceed from the Post Office.

(ii) *Leased Circuits*

International leased circuits are available for data transmission and are provided in accordance with the Recommendations of the International Telephone & Telegraph Consultative Committee (CCITT). Depending on the modulation method used, higher transmission rates than those offered by the Datel services are usually obtainable over voice bandwidth circuits.

In addition, high speed data transmission, e.g. 48K bits per second, may be achieved over wideband leases (telephone circuits grouped together to give 48KHz bandwidth) or by using special facilities provided via the INTELSAT satellite.

INTERNATIONAL TELEPHONES

The same charges apply for calls originating in any part of Great Britain, Northern Ireland and the Isle of Man. Callers with STD in many parts of this country can dial direct to numbers on many exchanges on the continent and in some other countries. Access to this facility (International Subscriber Dialling—ISD) is progressively being made available to more places in this country, and the number of places abroad to which calls may be dialled is also increasing, callers should consult their dialling instructions booklets for information on how to make calls.

Directly dialled calls are charged in units of time costing 1·8p for many ISD calls, cheap rates apply from 8 p.m. to 6 a.m. nightly, and at any time on Saturdays and Sundays. Where access to ISD is not yet available, callers should ask the local operator for the International Exchange, specifying the country required.

The charges for calls via an operator are based on a three minute minimum. Transferred charge (collect) calls are available with some countries, and British Post Office credit cards can be issued in many countries for calls to the U.K.; charges for such calls incoming to this country may be higher than those for outgoing calls. A personal call service is available. (In many cases with an additional surcharge).

Calls to Ships
For calls to ships at sea, *see* p. 1202.

SUNDAY ARRANGEMENTS
(For Express Services see p. 1199).
On SUNDAY *THROUGHOUT THE U.K.* there is no general delivery of letters and parcels.

Place	Charge Code —(see below)	Place	Charge Code —(see below)	Place	Charge Code —(see below)	Place	Charge Code —(see below)
Afghanistan	K	Faroe Is.	C	Madeira	F	Samoa (U.S.A. Territory)	K
Alaska	I	Fiji	J	Malagasy Rep.	K	Samoa (Western)	K
Albania	F	Finland	C	Malawi	K	San Marino	B
Algeria	F	France	A	Malaysia	J	Sao Tome	K
Andorra	A	French Guiana	K	Maldive Is.	J	Saudi Arabia	K
Angola	K	French Polynesia	K	Mali	K	Senegal	K
Antigua	I	French Territory of the		Malta	F	Seychelles	K
Antilles	I	Afars and Issas	K	Mariana Is.	K	Sierra Leone	K
Argentina	J	Gabon	K	Martinique	I	Singapore	L
Ascension	K	Gambia	K	Mauritania	K	Solomon Is.	K
Australia	L	Germany (Dem. Rep.)	C	Mauritius	K	Somali Dem. Rep.	K
Austria	C	Germany (Federal Rep.)	B	Mexico	K	South Africa	M
Azores	F	Ghana	K	Midway Island	K	South Vietnam	K
Bahamas	I	Gibraltar	C	Monaco	A	Spain	B
Bahrain	K	Gilbert and Ellice Is.	K	Montserrat	I	Spanish Territories of
Barbados	H	Greece	D	Morocco	F	North Africa	C
Belgium	A	Greenland	J	Mozambique	K	Sri Lanka	J
Belize	I	Grenada	I	Nauru Island	K	Sudan	K
Bermuda	I	Guadeloupe	I	Netherlands	A	Surinam	K
Bolivia	K	Guatemala	K	New Caledonia	K	Swaziland	K
Botswana	J	Guinea	K	New Hebrides	K	Sweden	B
Brazil	J	Guinea Bissau	K	New Zealand	J	Switzerland	B
Brunei	K	Guyana	I	Nicaragua	K	Syria	K
Bulgaria	F	Haiti	I	Niger	K	Taiwan	K
Burma	K	Hawaii	H	Nigeria	J	Tanzania	J
Burundi	K	Honduras	K	Niue Island	K	Thailand	J
Cameroon	K	Hong Kong	L	Norfolk Island	K	Tobago	H
Canada	G	Hungary	E	Norway	B	Togo	K
Cape Verde Islands	K	Iceland	E	Oman (except Masirah)	K	Tongo	K
Carriacou	I	India	J	(Masirah only)	J	Tortola	I
Cayman Islands	H	Indonesia	K	Pakistan	K	Trinidad	H
Central African Rep	K	Iran	J	Panama	J	Trucial States	K
Chad	K	Iraq	K	Panama Canal Zone	J	Tunisia	F
Chile	K	Israel	M	Papua New Guinea	K	Turkey	F
Christmas Island	K	Italy	B	Paraguay	K	Turks Island	I
Colombia	J	Ivory Coast	K	Peru	J	Uganda	J
Congo	K	Jamaica	I	Philippines	J	Upper Volta	K
Cook (or Hervey) Is.	K	Japan	K	Poland	C	Uruguay	K
Costa Rica	K	Jordan	K	Portugal	C	U.S.A. (Except Alaska
Cuba	I	Kenya	J	Portuguese Timor	K	and Hawaii)	G
Cyprus	F	Khmer Rep.	K	Principe	K	U.S.S.R.	E
Czechoslovakia	C	Korea (North)	K	Puerto Rico	H	Vatican City	B
Dahomey	K	Korea (South)	K	Qatar	K	Venezuela	J
Denmark	B	Kuwait	J	Reunion	K	Virgin Is. of U.S.A.	H
Dominica	I	Laos	K	Rhodesia	K	Wake Island	K
Dominion Rep.	I	Lebanon	J	Rodriguez Island	K	Yemen (Arab Rep.)	K
Ecuador	K	Lesotho	J	Rumania	E	Yemen (People's Dem.
Egypt	K	Liberia	K	Rwanda	K	Rep.)	K
El Salvador	K	Libya	E	St. Helena	K	Yugoslavia	C
Equatorial Guinea	K	Liechtenstein	B	St. Kitts-Nevis-Anguilla	I	Zaire	K
Ethiopia	K	Luxembourg	A	St. Lucia	I	Zambia	J
Falkland Is.	J	Macao	K	St. Pierre and Miquelon	I		
				St. Vincent	I		

CHARGE CODES

	Calls Dialled Direct		Calls connected by the Operator		
	Full Rate	Cheap Rate	Minimum Charge	Per Additional Minute	Personal Call Surcharge
Charge Code	Seconds for 1·8p	Seconds for 1·8p			
			£	£	£
A	7·20	9·60	0·69	0·23	0·46
B	5·14	8·00	0·87	0·29	0·58
C	—	—	0·87	0·29	0·58
D	4·00	6·00	1·05	0·35	0·70
E	—	—	1·05	0·35	0·70
F	—	—	1·80	0·60	1·20
G	1·60	2·00	2·40	0·80	2·50
H	—	—	2·40	0·80	2·50
I	—	—	4·90	0·80	—
J	—	—	3·15	1·05	2·50
K	—	—	5·65	1·05	
L	1·20	1·20	3·15	1·05	2·50
M	1·20	1·71	3·15	1·05	2·50

For mode of packing, prohibitions, etc., *see* Post office Guide.

Telegrams	DESTINATION	SURFACE MAIL Each parcel not over:				AIR MAIL Each parcel	
		1 kg	3 kg	5 kg	10 kg	Not over ½ kg	Each ½ kg after or part thereof
		£	£	£	£	£	£
16	Abu Dhabi......................	1·60	2·45	3·45	5·40	1·70	0·45
16	Afghanistan (via USSR)..............	1·90	2·60	3·60	5·90	2·30	0·50
16	Ajman★........................	1·60	2·45	3·45	5·40	No service	
9	Albania★.......................	1·70	2·25	3·10	4·80	1·65	0·25
9	Algeria........................	1·55	2·00	2·70	4·10	1·60	0·30
9	Andorra (via France)...............	1·60	2·00	2·55	3·65	2·00	0·15
	Andorra (via Spain)................	1·50	1·90	2·60	3·85	1·75	0·25
11	Antigua........................	1·75	2·30	3·15	4·40	2·00	0·55
16	Argentina.......................	1·85	2·80	3·85	6·25	2·75	0·95
16	Ascension★.....................	1·25	1·65	2·25	3·30	No service	
16	Australia★‡.....................	1·70	2·80	3·95	6·40	2·80	1·35
9	Austria★.......................	1·45	1·90	2·55	3·80	1·50	0·20
9	Azores.........................	1·45	2·05	2·80	4·45	1·60	0·25
11	Bahamas★......................	1·45	2·00	2·75	4·30	1·75	0·60
16	Bahrain (State of)★...............	1·80	2·60	3·65	5·40	2·20	0·40
9	Balearic Isles★..................	1·50	1·90	2·60	3·85	1·75	0·25
16	Bangladesh★....................	1·60	2·50	3·30	5·25	2·00	0·70
11	Barbados.......................	1·55	2·10	2·85	4·40	2·05	0·50
9	Belgium........................	1·45	1·85	2·45	3·60	1·60	0·15
11	Belize.........................	1·45	2·00	2·75	4·30	2·25	0·55
11	Bermuda.......................	1·45	1·95	2·70	4·05	1·85	0·40
16	Bhutan★.......................	1·75	2·60	3·60	5·90	2·45	0·75
16	Bolivia★‡......................	1·75	2·85	4·00	6·65	2·40	0·95
16	Botswana★......................	1·45	2·10	3·05	4·65	} 1·75	} 0·75
	Botswana (Kasana and Kazungula).......	1·55	2·30	3·30	5·20		
16	Brazil★........................	2·20	3·10	4·15	6·45	2·70	0·80
	British Honduras (see Belize)						
	British Indian Ocean Territory★.......	1·40	1·95	2·75	4·20	No service	
16	Brunei.........................	2·00	2·80	3·95	5·90	3·05	0·80
9	Bulgaria........................	1·70	2·25	3·20	5·00	1·75	0·25
16	Burma‡.........................	1·65	2·40	3·30	5·25	2·40	0·75
16	Burundi........................	1·80	2·65	3·65	5·70	1·90	0·75
16	Cameroon.......................	1·65	2·35	3·20	5·00	1·90	0·65
11	Canada★‡......................	1·45	2·10	2·95	4·55	1·75	0·60
9	Canary Isles★...................	1·50	1·95	2·60	3·95	1·75	0·25
16	Cape Verde Isles.................	1·60	2·25	3·10	4·90	1·70	0·55
16	Caroline Islands★................	1·65	2·80	4·35	8·00	2·75	0·90
11	Cayman Isislands★...............	1·70	2·65	3·90	6·45	1·95	0·55
16	Central African Republic............	1·75	2·30	3·45	5·20	2·00	0·65
16	Chad..........................	1·60	2·10	3·10	4·95	1·80	0·65
16	Chile‡.........................	1·75	2·70	3·60	6·25	2·60	0·95
16	China (People's Republic of)★........	1·60	2·40	3·60	5·65	1·95	1·10
16	Christmas Island (Indian Ocean)★......	1·80	2·75	3·95	5·80	2·20	0·85
16	Cocos (Keeling) Islands★...........	1·70	2·80	3·95	6·40	2·80	1·35
16	Colombia★‡.....................	1·80	2·75	3·75	6·15	2·45	0·80
16	Comoro Islands..................	1·90	2·55	3·45	5·35	2·40	0·80
16	Congo (People's Republic of).........	1·50	2·05	2·90	4·50	1·70	0·65
9	Corsica........................	1·60	2·05	2·75	4·05	2·00	0·15
16	Costa Rica★....................	1·60	2·35	3·30	5·30	2·35	0·60
11	Cuba★‡ (Direct).................	1·55	2·00	2·75	4·40	} 2·10	} 0·80
	Cuba (Guantanamo Bay via U.S.A.)......	1·65	2·80	4·35	7·30		
9	Cyprus.........................	1·85	2·50	3·25	5·15	2·05	0·30
9	Czechoslovakia★.................	1·55	2·00	2·75	4·20	1·60	0·20
16	Dahomey.......................	1·75	2·40	3·20	4·95	2·25	0·75
9	Denmark (Direct).................	1·35	1·75	2·30	3·45	} 1·45	} 0·15
	Denmark (via Netherlands)...........	1·45	1·90	2·60	3·95		
11	Dominica.......................	1·35	1·90	2·60	4·05	1·75	0·55
11	Dominican Republic★..............	1·45	1·95	2·65	4·00	1·90	0·60
16	Dubai★........................	1·60	2·45	3·45	5·40	1·85	0·45
16	Ecuador★......................	1·85	2·85	3·95	6·50	2·70	0·70
9	Egypt (Arab Republic of)...........	1·55	2·15	2·90	4·50	1·70	0·30
16	El Salvador★...................	1·85	2·55	3·40	5·50	2·60	0·60
16	Equatorial Guinea★...............	1·50	2·00	2·85	4·30	1·85	0·65
16	Ethiopia★......................	1·75	2·75	3·85	6·35	2·10	0·60
16	Falkland Islands and Dependencies.....	1·55	2·40	3·35	5·45	2·05	0·80
9	Faroe Isles.....................	1·35	1·75	2·30	3·45	1·45	0·15
16	Fiji...........................	1·65	2·45	3·40	5·50	2·50	1·30
9	Finland★.......................	1·50	2·00	2·65	3·95	1·55	0·30
9	France.........................	1·60	2·00	2·55	3·65	2·00	0·15
16	French Guiana...................	1·65	2·20	3·00	4·50	2·25	1·00
16	French Polynesia.................	1·80	2·35	3·25	4·90	3·50	1·35
16	French Territory of the Afars and Issas.....	1·85	2·75	3·75	6·05	2·15	0·55
11	French West Indies...............	1·65	2·15	3·00	4·45	2·15	0·75
16	Fujairah★......................	1·60	2·45	3·45	5·40	No service	

‡Maximum weight limit for small packets: 1 lb.   ★ No insured box service available.

For mode of packing, prohibitions, etc., *see* Post office Guide.

Telegrams	DESTINATION	SURFACE MAIL Each parcel not over:				AIR MAIL Each parcel	
		1 kg	3 kg	5 kg	10 kg	Not over ½ kg	Each ¼ kg after or part thereof
p		£	£	£	£	£	£
16	Gabon	1·60	2·30	3·40	4·85	1·80	0·75
16	Gambia	1·65	2·45	3·20	4·80	2·00	0·40
	Gaza and Khan Yunis	1·65	2·35	3·30	5·10	1·75	0·35
9	Germany, Democratic Republic of	1·50	2·00	2·70	4·05	1·50	0·20
9	Germany, Federal Republic of	1·50	1·90	2·55	3·80	1·50	0·20
16	Ghana	1·65	2·40	3·30	5·15	2·05	0·40
9	Gibraltar	1·35	1·85	2·50	3·70	1·55	0·20
16	Gilbert and Ellice Islands★	1·65	2·80	4·00	6·55	3·00	1·15
9	Greece★ (Direct)	1·55	2·20	2·95	4·60	2·00	0·30
	Greece (via Belgium)	1·70	2·25	3·15	4·90	—	
9	Greenland (by sea to Denmark)	1·35	1·75	2·30	3·45	1·75	0·50
	Greenland (via Netherlands to Denmark)	1·45	1·90	2·60	3·95	—	
11	Grenada	1·50	2·10	3·00	4·40	2·15	0·55
16	Guatemala★	1·65	2·35	3·20	5·05	2·35	0·60
16	Guinea★	1·60	2·10	2·95	4·45	1·85	0·65
	Guinea-Bissau (Formerly Portuguese Guinea)	1·60	2·25	3·15	5·05	1·80	0·50
11	Guyana	1·75	2·35	3·20	4·85	2·35	0·50
11	Haiti★	1·40	1·85	2·60	3·95	2·20	0·60
16	Honduras (Republic of)★	1·55	2·10	2·85	4·40	2·10	0·60
16	Hong Kong	1·40	2·05	2·85	4·50	2·00	0·70
9	Hungary	1·50	1·95	2·70	4·20	1·70	0·20
9	Iceland★	1·55	1·90	2·55	3·75	1·75	0·25
16	India	1·85	2·60	3·45	5·40	2·05	0·60
16	Indonesia★	1·60	2·30	3·15	5·05	2·90	0·85
16	Iran★	1·60	2·20	3·15	4·95	1·75	0·35
16	Iraq★	1·65	2·55	3·45	5·60	1·75	0·45
9	Israel★	1·65	2·35	3·30	5·10	1·75	0·35
9	Italy★	1·50	1·90	2·60	3·85	1·50	0·25
16	Ivory Coast	1·50	2·05	2·90	4·35	1·75	0·70
11	Jamaica★	1·65	2·25	3·05	4·50	2·25	0·50
16	Japan (Direct)	1·75	2·45	3·30	5·15	}2·60	0·75
	Japan (via U.S.S.R.)	2·10	3·10	4·50	7·10		
16	Jordan★	1·55	2·20	2·95	4·65	1·65	0·35
16	Kenya	1·60	2·40	3·35	5·15	1·65	0·50
16	Khmer Republic★	1·60	2·20	3·05	4·70	2·25	1·00
16	Korea★	1·65	2·45	3·45	5·55	2·85	0·75
16	Kuwait	1·60	2·40	3·35	5·40	1·75	0·40
16	Laos★	1·70	2·45	3·40	5·40	2·25	1·05
	Lebanon	1·60	2·40	3·35	5·40	1·60	0·35
16	Lesotho★	1·75	2·45	3·45	5·15	2·20	0·80
16	Liberia★	1·55	2·25	3·10	4·95	2·00	0·80
19	Libyan Arab Republic★	1·60	2·30	3·20	5·10	1·70	0·35
9	Luxembourg	1·35	1·75	2·35	3·50	1·35	0·15
16	Macao	1·60	2·30	3·20	5·25	2·25	0·75
9	Madeira	1·35	1·85	2·50	3·80	1·60	0·25
16	Malagasy Republic	1·65	2·30	3·35	5·15	2·10	0·95
16	Malawi (via Capetown)	1·95	2·80	4·00	6·25	2·15	0·60
16	Malaya	1·40	2·05	2·85	4·30	2·25	0·75
	Maldives (Republic of)★	1·65	2·45	3·50	5·60	2·00	0·75
16	Mali	1·70	2·35	3·35	5·50	1·90	0·55
16	Mariana Islands★	1·65	2·80	4·35	8·00	2·25	1·50
16	Marshall Islands★	1·60	2·65	4·05	7·40	2·75	1·45
9	Malta	1·50	2·05	2·80	4·30	1·80	0·25
16	Mauritania	1·60	2·40	3·35	5·50	1·80	0·75
16	Mauritius	1·45	2·15	2·95	4·70	1·95	0·90
16	Mexico (ex Chetumal)★	1·55	2·10	2·85	4·40	}2·20	0·75
	Mexico (Chetumal only)★	1·70	2·25	3·05	4·60		
	Mongolia (People's Republic)★	No service				No service	
11	Montserrat★	1·40	1·95	2·80	4·15	1·85	0·55
9	Morocco	1·45	1·95	2·70	4·10	1·50	0·25
16	Nauru Islands★	1·60	2·65	3·75	6·25	3·00	1·30
16	Nepal	1·65	2·50	3·45	5·60	1·75	0·60
9	Netherlands	1·45	1·80	2·40	3·50	1·65	0·10
11	Netherlands Antilles	1·45	2·00	2·75	4·35	2·20	0·60
16	New Caledonia	1·90	2·90	4·10	6·85	3·00	1·20
16	New Hebrides★	1·90	2·90	4·10	6·85	3·00	1·10
16	New Zealand	1·70	2·65	3·70	5·95	3·30	1·20
	New Zealand Island Territories	1·70	2·65	3·70	5·95	2·70	1·80
16	Nicaragua★	1·55	2·20	3·05	4·80	2·50	0·65
16	Nigeria	1·70	2·45	3·35	5·05	2·05	0·40
16	Niger Republic	1·75	2·45	3·55	5·80	1·90	0·70
16	Norfolk Island★	1·70	2·80	3·95	6·40	2·50	1·50
9	Norway★	1·65	2·05	2·65	3·80	1·85	0·20
16	Oman (Sultanate of)★	1·60	2·45	3·45	5·40	1·85	0·40
16	Pakistan	1·60	2·50	3·30	5·25	2·05	00·70

★ No insured box service available.

For mode of packing, prohibitions, etc., *see* Post office Guide.

Telegrams	DESTINATION	SURFACE MAIL Each parcel not over:				AIR MAIL Each parcel	
		1 kg	3 kg	5 kg	10 kg	Not over ½ kg	Each ½ kg after or part thereof
p		£	£	£	£	£	£
16	Panama (Republic of)★............	1·55	2·20	3·05	4·75	2·25	0·60
16	Panama Canal Zone★............	1·40	2·25	3·35	5·45	1·95	0·65
16	Papua New Guinea★...........	1·55	2·30	3·20	5·20	2·80	1·75
16	Paraguay★...................	1·75	2·80	4·00	6·65	2·30	0·80
16	Peru★......................	1·95	2·95	4·05	6·45	3·00	0·75
16	Philippines★.................	1·35	2·00	2·75	4·05	2·15	0·80
16	Pitcairn Islands★.............	1·40	2·35	3·40	5·60	2·30	1·45
9	Poland★....................	1·45	1·90	2·55	3·75	1·60	0·20
9	Portugal....................	1·40	1·95	2·65	4·15	1·80	0·25
16	Portuguese East Africa.........	1·70	2·40	3·40	5·25	2·35	0·75
16	Portuguese Timor★............	1·70	2·50	3·50	5·70	2·50	1·30
	Portuguese West Africa.........	1·60	2·25	3·15	5·05	Angola, Principe and São Tomé	
11	Puerto Rico★.................	1·45	2·25	3·35	5·50	1·75	0·70
16	Qatar (State of)★.............	1·55	2·30	3·25	5·15	1·85	0·40
	Ras Al Khaimah★.............	1·60	2·45	3·45	5·40	No service	
16	Reunion....................	1·70	2·25	3·10	4·65	2·20	0·95
16	Rhodesia★..................	1·65	2·40	3·45	5·25	1·75	0·75
9	Rumania★...................	1·65	2·15	2·95	4·65	1·80	0·25
16	Rwanda★...................	1·75	2·55	3·55	5·55	1·80	0·80
16	Sabah......................	1·40	2·05	2·85	4·30	2·25	0·80
16	St. Helena..................	1·40	1·90	2·55	3·90	No service	
16	St. Kitts–Nevis–Anguilla........	1·25	1·85	2·65	4·05	1·55	0·50
11	St. Lucia★..................	1·45	2·00	2·70	3·95	1·95	0·55
11	St. Pierre and Miquelon.........	1·75	2·45	3·40	5·55	1·75	0·60
11	St. Vincent.................	1·50	2·05	2·85	4·15	1·90	0·55
16	Samoa (U.S.A. Territory)★......	1·65	2·80	4·35	8·00	2·70	1·30
16	Sarawak...................	1·40	2·05	2·85	4·30	2·20	0·80
16	Saudi Arabia................	1·55	2·40	3·35	5·45	1·70	0·60
16	Senegal....................	1·55	2·25	3·10	4·95	1·85	0·55
16	Seychelles..................	1·40	1·95	2·75	4·20	1·60	0·60
16	Sharjah★...................	1·60	2·45	3·45	5·40	2·65	0·40
16	Sierra Leone★...............	1·65	2·45	3·40	5·15	2·10	0·45
16	Singapore (Republic of).........	1·40	2·05	2·85	4·35	2·20	0·75
16	Solomon Islands★.............	1·80	3·45	4·30	6·90	2·50	1·50
16	Somali Democratic Republic......	1·75	2·75	3·90	6·50	2·15	0·55
16	South Africa (Republic of)★......	1·35	1·95	2·80	4·10	2·35	0·75
9	Spain★.....................	1·50	1·90	2·60	3·85	1·75	0·25
9	Spanish Territories of North Africa★	1·50	1·90	2·60	3·85	1·60	0·20
	Spanish Sahara★.............	1·55	2·05	2·90	4·45	1·60	0·40
	Spitzbergen★................	1·65	2·05	2·65	3·80	No service	
16	Sri Lanka (Republic of).........	1·55	2·35	3·30	5·10	2·05	0·65
16	Sudan (Democratic Republic of).★..	1·70	2·50	3·45	5·60	2·15	0·45
16	Surinam....................	1·45	2·00	2·75	4·35	2·20	0·75
16	Swaziland★.................	1·40	2·20	3·30	5·10	1·95	0·80
9	Sweden....................	1·60	2·00	2·60	3·80	1·65	0·20
9	Switzerland.................	1·40	1·85	2·45	3·65	1·60	0·10
16	Taiwan (Formosa).............	1·60	2·30	3·25	5·25	2·45	0·85
16	Tanzania...................	1·60	2·40	3·35	5·15	2·15	0·55
16	Thailand★..................	1·70	2·35	3·20	5·10	2·35	0·75
	Tibet★.....................	No service				No service	
16	Togo......................	1·75	2·30	3·30	5·10	2·20	0·70
16	Tonga (Friendly Islands)........	1·90	2·95	4·20	6·80	3·30	1·15
11	Tortola (British Virgin Islands)★...	1·55	2·20	3·10	4·60	2·10	0·55
11	Trinidad and Tobago★..........	1·55	2·10	2·80	4·05	2·00	0·50
16	Tristan da Cunha★............	1·40	2·20	3·25	5·05	2·35	0·75
9	Tunisia....................	1·45	1·90	2·60	4·00	1·45	0·25
9	Turkey (Direc.)..............	1·55	2·25	3·05	4·80	} 2·20	0·30
9	Turkey (via Belgium)..........	1·75	2·40	3·40	5·35		
11	Turks and Caicos Islands★.......	1·65	2·80	4·35	7·30	1·85	0·60
16	Uganda....................	1·60	2·40	3·35	5·15	1·95	0·55
16	Umm Al Qaiwain★............	1·60	2·45	3·45	5·40	No service	
11★	U.S.A.★....................	1·45	2·25	3·35	5·50	1·45	0·80
16	Upper Volta.................	1·60	2·20	3·20	5·25	1·85	0·65
16	Uruguay★...................	1·70	2·75	3·85	6·45	2·45	0·80
9	U.S.S.R. in Europe★...........	1·40	1·90	2·55	3·95	1·95	0·45
	U.S.S.R. in Asia★............	1·70	2·30	3·15	5·05	2·05	0·50
9	Vatican City State★...........	1·40	1·80	2·45	3·70	1·50	0·25
16	Venezuela★..................	1·75	2·35	3·10	4·65	2·65	0·60
16	Vietnam South only★...........	1·60	2·20	3·05	4·70	2·35	1·05
11	Virgin Islands (U.S.A.)★........	1·45	2·30	3·45	5·55	1·55	0·75
16	Wake Island★................	1·60	2·65	4·05	7·40	2·25	1·20
16	Western Samoa..............	1·55	2·35	3·30	5·45	2·70	1·15
16	Yemen Arab Republic★..........	1·70	2·60	3·65	6·00	2·20	0·60

★ No insured box service available.

For mode of packing, prohibitions, etc., *see* Post office Guide.

Telegrams	DESTINATION	SURFACE MAIL Each parcel not over:				AIR MAIL Each parcel	
		1 kg	3 kg	5 kg	10 kg	Not over ½ kg	Each ½ kg after or part thereof
		£	£	£	£	£	£
p 16	Yemen People's Democratic Republic.......	1·65	2·60	3·60	5·95	2·00	0·45
9	Yugoslavia.......................	1·60	2·10	2·85	4·40	1·80	0·25
16	Zaire (Republic of)★......................	1·55	2·35	3·30	5·40	1·90	0·65
16	Zambia★................................	2·10	3·00	4·30	6·70	2·35	0·65

★ No insured box service available.

THE PERIODS OF ENGLISH ARCHITECTURE

Date	*Style*
I. Before 55 B.C................................	Ancient British.
II. 55 B.C. to A.D. 420...........................	Roman Period.
III. A.D. 449 to Norman Conquest (1066)...........	Anglo-Saxon.
IV. 1066–1189 (*i.e.* to end 12th cent.)...............	Norman.
V. 1189–1307 (*i.e.* 13th cent.)......................	Early English (Lancet, or Geometrical).
VI. 1307–1377 (*i.e.* 14th cent.).....................	Decorated (or Curvilinear).
VII. 1377–1485 (*i.e.* 15th cent.).....................	Perpendicular (or Rectilinear).
VIII. 1485–1558 (*i.e.* first half 16th cent.)...............	Tudor
IX. A.D. 1558–1625. Early Renaissance...........	{Elizabeth (A.D. 1558–1603). {Jacobean (A.D. 1603–1625).
X. A.D. 1625–1830. Late Renaissance.............	{Stuart (A.D. 1625–1702). {Queen Anne and Georgian (A.D. 1702–1830).
XI. Modern Architecture {19th cent............... (The Age of Revivals) {	{William IV. (A.D. 1830–1837). {Victoria (A.D. 1837–1901).
XII. Recent Architecture. 20th cent.................	{Edward VII. (A.D. 1901–1910). {George V. (A.D. 1910–1935). {Edward VIII. (A.D. 1936). {George VI. (A.D. 1936–1952).

FUEL AND POWER MEASURES

British Thermal Unit (B.Th.U.) = The amount of heat required to raise 1 lb of water through 1 degree Fahrenheit at or near 39·1 degrees F. 1 B.Th.U. = 1·055 06kJ].

Unit of electricity (kilowatt-hour) = Output of 1,000 watts for one hour. 1 k.w.h. = 3,413 B.Th.U.

Therm = 100,000 B.Th.U. = 29·3 k.w.h. = 105·506 MJ.

Atmosphere = pressure of 14·223 lb. per sq. in. = 1 kilogram per sq. cm.

Petroleum

Barrel = 35 Imperial gallons = 42 U.S. gallons.
Petroleum products are commonly quoted in metric tonnes, the conversion to barrels varying slightly according to the specific gravity of the product, e.g. the metric tonne in the major oil producing states (U.S.A., Venezuela, Persian Gulf, Saudi-Arabia, Iraq, etc.) varies from 7·0 barrels per metric tonne to 7·7 barrels, and in the smaller oil producing states (e.g., Albania) is as low as 6·7 barrels per tonne. Crude petroleum in the United Kingdom, 7·355 barrels per metric tonne (2,205 lbs.); 7·472 barrels per long ton (2,240 lbs.).

A TABLE OF THE NUMBER OF DAYS FROM ANY DAY IN ONE MONTH TO THE SAME IN ANY OTHER MONTH IN ORDINARY YEARS

	Jan.	Feb.	Mar.	April	May	June	July	Aug.	Sept.	Oct.	Nov.	Dec.
January.......	365	31	59	90	120	151	181	212	243	273	304	334
February.....	334	365	28	59	89	120	150	181	212	242	273	303
March........	306	337	365	31	61	92	122	153	184	214	245	275
April.........	275	306	334	365	30	61	91	122	153	183	214	244
May..........	245	276	304	335	365	31	61	92	123	153	184	214
June.........	214	245	273	304	334	365	30	61	92	122	153	183
July.........	184	215	243	274	304	335	365	31	62	92	123	153
August.......	153	184	212	243	273	304	334	365	31	61	92	122
September....	122	153	181	212	242	273	303	334	365	30	61	91
October......	92	123	151	182	212	243	273	304	335	365	31	61
November....	61	92	120	151	181	212	242	273	304	334	365	30
December.....	31	62	90	121	151	182	212	243	274	304	335	365

BRITISH MONETARY UNITS

COIN

GOLD COINS	CUPRO-NICKEL (SILVER)
†Five Pound £5	Crown 5s. (25p)
†Two Pound £2	Florin 2s. (10p)
†Sovereign £1	Shilling 1s. (5p)
†Half-Sovereign 10s.	Sixpence 6d. (2½p)
† Discontinued	*50 New Pence 50p
	*10 New Pence 10p
BRONZE COINS	*5 New Pence 5p

*2 New Pence 2p
*1 New Penny 1p
*½ New Penny ½p
*For further details of decimal coins, *see* p. 1210.

SILVER
Maundy Money‡

Fourpence 4p	Twopence 2p
Threepence 3p	Penny 1p

‡ Gifts of special money distributed by the Sovereign annually on Maundy Thursday to the number of aged poor persons corresponding to the Sovereign's own age.

Gold Coin.—Gold ceased to circulate during the First World War. An Order of April 27, 1966, made it illegal for U.K. residents to continue holding more than 4 gold coins minted after 1837, or to acquire such coins unless they had been licensed as genuine collectors by the Bank of England. This Order was revoked on April 1, 1971, by the Exchange Control (Gold Coins Exemption) Order, 1971, whereby residents of the United Kingdom, Channel Islands and the Isle of Man may freely buy and sell and hold gold coins.

The 1971 order was revoked on April 15, 1975, by the Exchange Control (Gold Coin Exemption) Order 1975. Under this Order Section 1 of the Exchange Control Act 1947 (which prohibits dealings in gold or foreign currency except with Treasury permission) is exempted for gold coins minted in or before 1837. But in relation to gold coins minted after 1837, the Order exempts from Section 1 the following transactions only:

(a) Buying and selling such coins if held in the U.K. and if the seller is resident in the U.K. and is not selling on behalf of a non-resident.

(b) Borrowing and lending such coins if held in the U.K. and if the borrower and lender are resident in the U.K.

Accordingly any other transactions in gold coins minted after 1837 (if prohibited by Section 1) now require Treasury permission.

The English sovereign, however, is still used as currency in certain Middle East countries and to meet foreign demand during the years 1958–1968 the Royal Mint struck some 44·5 million sovereigns.

Silver.—Prior to 1920 our silver coins were struck from standard silver—an alloy of which 925 parts in 1,000 were silver. In 1920 the proportion of silver was reduced to 500 parts. From January 1, 1947 all ' silver ' coins, except Maundy money, have been struck from cupro-nickel—an alloy of copper 75 parts and nickel 25 parts. Maundy coins since 1947 have been struck from standard silver.

Bronze, introduced in 1860 to replace copper, is an alloy of copper 97 parts, zinc 2½ parts and tin ½ part. These proportions are subject to slight variation.

The ' Remedy ' is the amount of variation from standard permitted in weight and fineness of coins when first issued from the Mint.

Legal tender of coin.—Gold, dated 1838 onwards, if not below least current weight, is legal tender to any amount. Since Decimal Day cupro-nickel (silver) coins with values up to and including the 10p have been legal tender up to £5. The 50p coin has been legal tender up to £10 from the date

of its introduction. Bronze coins are legal tender for amounts up to 20p. Farthings ceased to be legal tender on December 31, 1960, the halfpenny on August 1, 1969, the halfcrown on January 1, 1970, and the threepence and penny on August 31, 1971.

THE WORK OF THE ROYAL MINT DURING 1974

During the year under review, the Royal Mint produced some 1197 million coins, almost all of which were struck at Llantrisant. Tower Hill concentrated on the manufacture of sovereigns, coinage blanks, official and commercial medals and the production of embossing seals and revenue dies.

The domestic coinage production was made up as follows:

Sovereign	1,000,000
50p	25,400,000
10p	89,100,000
5p	206,000
1p	271,864,000
½p	341,888,000
U.K. Decimal Proof Coin	1,405,340
U.K. £. s. d. Proof Coin	496,720
Maundy Money	4,456
Overseas Coin	465,890,685
Overseas Proof Coin	251,004

Coinage for overseas governments accounted for nearly 39% of the year's total production: in addition, some 243 million coins for export were struck by sub-contractors working under Royal Mint supervision. Countries and territories to which coins have been supplied include: Afghanistan, Bahamas, Belize, Bermuda, Brunei, Cayman Island, Costa Rica, Cyprus, Dominican Republic, Ecuador, Eire, El Salvador, The Gambia, Guyana, Guernsey, Hong Kong, Iceland, Indonesia, Iraq, Jamaica, Jordan, Kenya, Kuwait, Libya, Malawi, Malta, Mauritius, Morocco, Nicaragua, Oman, Rwanda, Seychelles, Sierra Leone, Sri Lanka, St. Helena, Swaziland, Tanzania, United Arab Emirates, Uganda, Yemen Arab Republic, People's Democratic Republic of Yemen and Zambia.

BANK NOTES

Bank of England notes are currently issued in denominations of £1, £5, £10 and £20 for the amount of the Fiduciary Note Issue, and are legal tender in England and Wales. Only £1 notes are legal tender in Scotland and Northern Ireland.

The last of the old white £5 notes dated up to September 20, 1956, and the £5 notes issued between 1957 and 1963, bearing a portrait of Britannia, ceased to be legal tender on March 14, 1961, and June 27, 1967, respectively. The next series of £5 notes—the first to bear a portrait of the Queen—were first issued in 1963 and ceased to be legal tender on September 1, 1973. The old series of £1 notes issued during the years 1928 to 1960 and the 10s. notes of the same type issued from 1928 to 1961—those without the royal portrait—ceased to be legal tender on May 29 and October 30, 1962, respectively. The 10s. note was replaced by the 50p coin in October 1969, and ceased to be legal tender on November 21, 1970. Bank notes which are no longer legal tender are payable when presented at the Head Office of the Bank of England in London.

The old white notes for £10, £20, £50, £100, £500 and £1,000, which were issued until April 22, 1943, ceased to be legal tender in May 1945. However, on February 28, 1975, the value of these notes still outstanding amounted to some £978,000.

The £10 note—after an interval of 21 years—

was restored on February 21, 1964. This completed the original series bearing portraits of the Queen, plans for which were announced in November 1959.

In 1968 the Bank announced that a new series of Bank notes generally smaller in size than the notes they replace, would be issued in the 1970's. First of the series was a £20 note, which the Bank of England introduced on July 9, 1970. This was followed by the new £5 note introduced on November 11, 1971, and the new £10 note introduced on February 20, 1975. A new £1 note will be introduced in due course to complete the series.

Note circulation is highest at the two peak spending periods of the year—around Christmas and the end of August. On December 18, 1974, it reached a peak of £5,793 million, which was £665 million more than the previous peak of £5,128 million reached on August 28, 1974.

£5 notes continue to enjoy popularity and now represent over 56 per cent of the total value of notes in circulation as against 14 per cent in 1956. On the other hand, the proportion of £1 notes has dropped from 76 per cent to a fraction over 16 per cent. The percentages of £10 notes in circulation has increased steadily since 1965 and now represents over 15 per cent of the total. The proportion of £20 notes in circulation now amounts to under 8 per cent of the total compared with just over 2 per cent in 1971. On February 28, 1975, the values of notes in circulation were:—£20: £397,056,000; £10: £814,600,000; £5: £3,013,773,000; £1: £883,749,000; 10s: £12,983,000.

Partly because of the rapidly growing preference by the public for new notes rather than used ones, the demand for new bank notes has increased greatly in recent years. Between 1957 and 1974 the average life of a £1 note fell from 19 months to 11, and consequently it has been necessary for the Bank of England to print more notes per head of the population than in comparable countries abroad.

To alleviate the high cost of the note replacement, the 50p coin was introduced in October, 1969, in place of the 10s. note. The Bank of England has been conducting a campaign, in conjunction with the commercial banks, to encourage the public to accept more used but clean notes and this has been successful in reducing the public's requirements of new notes.

Other Bank Notes.—Bank Notes are issued by three Scottish banks —Bank of Scotland, Clydesdale Bank Ltd., Royal Bank of Scotland Ltd. Notes of the latter's constituent banks—Royal Bank of Scotland and National Commercial Bank of Scotland Ltd.—are being withdrawn from circulation, as are those of the former British Linen Bank. These banks issue notes for £1, £5, £10, £20 and £100. Scottish notes are not legal tender, but in Scotland they enjoy a status equal to that of the Bank of England note.

Channel Isles and the Isle of Man.—The States of Jersey and Guernsey issue notes for £10, £5 and £1. The Government of the Isle of Man issues notes for £10, £5, £1 and 50 new pence. These are legal tender only in their respective islands.

Although none of the series of notes specified above are legal tender in the United Kingdom they are generally accepted by the banks irrespective of their place of issue. At one time English banks made a small commission charge for handling Scottish and Irish notes but this was abolished some years ago.

Currency Notes.—Under the provision of the Currency and Bank Notes Act 1928, Currency Notes (popularly known as Treasury Notes) of the value of 10s and £1 were replaced by the issue of Bank of England Notes of the same denominations as from November 22, 1928. Although no longer legal tender, Currency Notes are payable on presentation at the Head Office of the Bank of England.

Denomination	Metal	Standard Weight (grams)	Standard Diameter (centimetres)
New halfpenny	bronze	1·78200	1·7145
New penny	bronze	3·56400	2·0320
2 New pence	bronze	7·12800	2·5910
5 New pence	cupro-nickel	5·65518	2·3595
10 New pence	cupro-nickel	11·31036	2·8500
50 New pence	cupro-nickel	13·5	3·0

WIND FORCE MEASURES

The *Beaufort Scale* of wind force has been accepted internationally and is used in communicating weather conditions. Devised originally by Admiral Sir Francis Beaufort in 1805, it now consists of the numbers 0–17, each representing a certain strength or velocity of wind at 10 m. (33 ft.) above ground in the open.

Scale No.	Wind Force	M.p.h.	Knots	Scale No.	Wind Force	M.p.h.	Knots
0	Calm	1	1	9	Strong gale	47–54	41–47
1	Light air	1–3	1–3	10	Whole gale	55–63	48–55
2	Slight breeze	4–7	4–6	11	Storm	64–72	56–63
3	Gentle breeze	8–12	7–10	12	Hurricane	73–82	64–71
4	Moderate breeze	13–18	11–16	13	—	83–92	72–80
5	Fresh breeze	19–24	17–21	14	—	93–103	81–89
6	Strong breeze	25–31	22–27	15	—	104–114	90–99
7	High wind	32–38	28–33	16	—	115–125	100–108
8	Gale	39–46	34–40	17	—	126–136	109–118

BRITISH PASSPORT REGULATIONS

Applications for United Kingdom passports must be made on the forms obtainable at any of the Passport Offices (addresses given below) or at any Main Post Office.

London.—Clive House, 70–78 Petty France, S.W.1.

Liverpool.—India Buildings, Water Street, Liverpool, 2.

Newport, Gwent.—Olympia House, Upper Dock Street.

Peterborough.—Passport Office, 55 Westfield Road, Peterborough.

Glasgow.—1st Floor, Empire House, 131 West Nile Street, Glasgow, C.1.

Hours. The above offices are open Mon.-Fri. 9 a.m. to 4.30 p.m. The Passport Offices are also open for cases of special emergency (*e.g.* death or serious illness) arising outside normal office hours between 4.30 p.m. and 5.30 p.m. (6.00 p.m. in London); Saturdays 10.00–12.00, and in *London* on Sundays and Public Holidays between 10 a.m. and noon (except Christmas Day).

Completed forms of application should be sent to one of the five Passport Offices, with photographs, supporting documents and the fee of £6, in the form of a Cheque or Postal Order which should be crossed and made payable to the Passport Office.

Persons resident in *Northern Ireland* may apply *in person* to the Foreign and Commonwealth Office Passport Agency, 1st Flr., Marlborough House, 30 Victoria Street, Belfast, or *by post* to the Passport Office, Glasgow.

A Passport cannot be issued or renewed by the Foreign and Commonwealth Office on behalf of *a person already abroad*; such person should apply, in a foreign country, to the nearest British Mission or Consulate, or, within the British Commonwealth outside the United Kingdom of Great Britain and N. Ireland, to the nearest British Passport issuing authority.

United Kingdom Passports are granted:—

   (i) To citizens of the United Kingdom and Colonies.

   (ii) To British subjects without citizenship.

   (iii) To British Protected Persons.

Passports are available for *ten years* unless otherwise stated. They are not available *beyond ten years from the original date of issue.* Thereafter, or if at any time the Passport contains no further space for visas, a new Passport must be obtained.

A Passport including particulars of the *holder's spouse* is not available for his/her use when he/she is travelling alone. A spouse's particulars may *only* be added at the time of issue of a passport.

Children who have reached the age of sixteen years require separate Passports. Their applications must be signed by one of their parents.

Passport applications must be countersigned by a Member of Parliament, Justice of the Peace, Minister of Religion, Doctor, Lawyer, Bank Officer, established Civil Servant, Public Official, Police Officer or any person of similar standing who has been personally acquainted with the applicant for at least two years. The applicant's birth certificate and other evidence in support of the statements made in the application must be produced.

In the case of children under the age of 16 requiring a separate passport, an application should be made by one of the parents on form (B).

If the applicant for a Passport be a citizen of the United Kingdom and Colonies by naturalization or registration, the Certificate of Naturalization or registration must be produced with the application.

British Passports are generally available for travel *to all countries.* The possession of a Passport does not, however, exempt the holder from compliance with any *Immigration Regulations* in force in British or foreign countries, or from the necessity of obtaining a *visa* where required.

PHOTOGRAPHS

Duplicate unmounted photographs of applicant (and his wife, if to be included in the Passport) must be sent. These photographs should be printed on *thin* paper and must not be glazed on the reverse side. They should measure not more than 2½ in. by 2 in. (63 mm. by 50 mm.), or less than 2 in. by 1½ in. (50 mm. by 38 mm.), and should be taken full face without a hat.

RENEWAL OF PASSPORTS

Applications for the renewal of United Kingdom passports must be made on Form D.

94-PAGE PASSPORTS

On May 1, 1973, a new type of passport became available. Intended to meet the needs of frequent travellers who fill standard passports well before the ten-year validity has expired, it contains 94 pages, is valid for ten years and costs £12.

British Visitors' Passports

A simplified form of travel document is available for British subjects (Citizens of the United Kingdom and Colonies) wishing to pay short visits (not exceeding three months) to certain foreign countries, *viz.*

ANDORRA; AUSTRIA; BELGIUM; DENMARK†; FINLAND†; FRANCE (incl. CORSICA); GREECE (& THE GREEK ISLANDS); W. GERMANY (incl. West Berlin by air only); ICELAND; ITALY; LIECHTENSTEIN; LUXEMBURG; MONACO; NETHERLANDS; NORWAY†; PORTUGAL (incl. MADEIRA & AZORES); SAN MARINO; SPAIN (incl. BALEARIC & CANARY ISLANDS); SWEDEN†; SWITZERLAND; TURKEY.

†Length of stay restricted to three months in any nine months in Nordic Group Countries (including Finland and Iceland) as a whole. Holders may also pay short visits to Canada, Gibraltar and Malta.

A fee of £3·00 is charged for the issue of a British Visitors' Passport, which is valid for 12 months, cannot be amended and is not renewable; on expiry application should be made for a new passport if required. Particulars of an applicant's spouse and/or children under 16 years can be included at *the time of issue only* at no extra cost. A child of 8 years of age and over is eligible to hold a British Visitors' Passport. Applications for, or including, a person under 18 years of age (unless married or serving in H.M. Forces) must be countersigned by the legal guardian.

British Visitors' Passports are obtainable by application on Form VP (from any Main Post Office). Applicants in England, Scotland and Wales should take the completed form in person to any Main Post Office which will normally issue the passport without further delay; applicants in Northern Ireland to any local office of the Ministry of Health and Social Services. *British Visitors' Passports are not obtainable from the Passport Offices.* Two recent passport photographs will be required of the applicant and of his/her spouse, if to be included; photographs of children are not required. Size of photographs must be 2 in.× 1½ in. (50 mm. by 38 mm.) (*see also* PHOTOGRAPHS above). No visas are required on British Visitors' Passports.

Applicants must also produce for the purpose of identification a N.H.S. Medical Card, birth certificate or retirement pension book.

HALL-MARKS ON GOLD AND SILVER WARES

London (Goldsmiths' Hall) Date Marks
From 1478 to 1976.

	Lombardic, double cusps	1478–9 to 1497–8		Roman letter, small	1736–7 to 1755–6
	Black letter, small......	1498–9 ,, 1517–8		Old English, capitals	1756–7 ,, 1775–6
	Lombardic	1518–9 ,, 1537–8		Roman letter, small...	1776–7 ,, 1795–6
	Roman and other capitals...................	1538–9 ,, 1557–8		Roman letter, capitals	1796–7 ,, 1815–6
	Black letter, small ...	1558–9 , 1577–8		Roman letter, small...	1816–7 ,, 1835–6
	Roman letter, capitals	1578–9 ,, 1597–8		Old English, capitals	1836–7 ,, 1855–6
	Lombardic, external cusps	1598–9 ,, 1617–8			
	Italic letter, small ...	1618–9 ,, 1637–8		Old English, small ...	1856–7 ,, 1875–6
	Court hand	1638–9 ,, 1657–8		Roman letter, capitals [A to M *square* shield N to Z as shown.]	1876–7 ,, 1895–6
	Black letter, capitals	1658–9 ,, 1677–8		Roman letter, small...	1896–7 ,, 1915–6
	Black letter, small ...	1678–9 ,, 1696–7		Black letter, small ...	1916–7 ,, 1935–6
	Court hand	1697 ,, 1715–6 (From March 1697 only.)		Roman letter, capital	1936–7 ,, 1955–6
	Roman letter, capitals	1716–7 ,, 1735–6		Italic letter, small ...	1956–7 ,, 1975–6

Hall-marks are the symbols stamped on gold or silver articles to indicate that they have been chemically tested and that they conform to one of the legal standards. With certain exceptions, all gold or silver articles are required by law to be hall-marked before they are offered for sale. Hall-marking was instituted in 1300 under a statute of Edward I.

Normally a complete modern hall-mark consists of four symbols—the maker's mark, assay office mark, standard mark and date letter. Additional marks have been authorized from time to time.

Maker's Mark.—Instituted in 1363, the maker's mark was originally a device such as a bird or *fleur-de-lys* and now consists invariably of the initials of the Christian and surnames of the maker or of the firm.

Assay Office Mark.—The existing assay offices and their distinguishing marks are:—

LONDON (Goldsmiths' Hall).
A leopard's head (uncrowned from 1300 to 1478–9, when it became crowned until 1821, since when it has been uncrowned). From

1697-1720 this mark was used in London for gold only and not for silver.

BIRMINGHAM......................An anchor
SHEFFIELD............A crown for silver and a York rose for gold
EDINBURGH.........................A castle

Offices formerly existed in other towns, *e.g.* Chester, Glasgow, Newcastle, Exeter, York and Norwich, each having its own distinguishing mark.

Standard Mark.—Instituted in 1544. The current legal standards and their marks are as follows:—

SILVER.—Sterling silver (92.5 per cent. silver) is marked by English assay offices with a *lion passant* and by the Edinburgh Assay Office with a *thistle*. A full-length figure of *Britannia* was impressed on

silver of a higher standard (95.84 per cent. silver) between 1697 and 1720 and this mark is still used occasionally by all British assay offices.

GOLD.—22 carat articles (91.6 per cent. gold) are marked by English offices with a crown followed by the figure 22; by the Edinburgh office with the figure 22 following the standard mark as for sterling silver (*see above*).

18 carat articles (75 per cent. gold) are marked by English assay offices with a crown followed by the figure 18.

All British assay offices mark 14 carat gold (58.5 per cent. gold) with the figures 14.585 and 9 carat gold (37.5 per cent. gold) with the figures 9.375.

Date Letter.—Instituted in 15th Century. The date letter denotes the year in which an article was assayed or hall-marked. Each alphabetical cycle

has a distinctive style of lettering or shape of shield. The date letters are different at the various assay offices and the particular office must be established from the assay office mark before reference is made to tables of date letters. The date letter is changed at the London Office in May each year and at Birmingham and Sheffield in July. Specimen shields and letters used by the London Office in each period from 1438 to date are shown on p. 1212.

OTHER MARKS

Duty Mark.—In 1784 an additional mark of the reigning sovereign's head was introduced to signify that the excise duty had been paid. The mark became obsolete on the abolition of the duty in 1890.

Silver Jubilee and Coronation Marks.—Voluntary marks were authorized to be used at manufacturers' request to commemorate the silver jubilee of King George V and Queen Mary and the

 Coronation of Her Majesty Queen Elizabeth II. The Jubilee Mark was used on silver made in 1933, 1934 and 1935 and the Coronation Mark on gold and

silver with date letter 1952/3 or 1953/4.

Foreign Wares.—Since 1842 foreign wares imported into Great Britain have been required to be hall-marked before sale. The marks consist of the importer's mark, a special assay office mark (*see above*), the decimal figures denoting fineness (together with the carat figure in the case of gold) and the annual date letter. The current assay office marks for foreign wares are as follows:—

LONDON.—The sign of the Constellation Leo.
BIRMINGHAM.—Equilateral triangle.
SHEFFIELD.—The sign of the Constellation Libra.
EDINBURGH.—St. Andrew's Cross.

CLOSE TIMES

Wild Birds.—The *Protection of Wild Birds Act, 1954*, lays down a close season for wild birds (other than Game Birds) from February 1 to August 31 inclusive, each year. Exceptions to these dates are made for—

Capercaillie and (except Scotland) *Woodcock,* Feb. 1—Sept. 30.
Snipe, Feb. 1—Aug. 11.
Wild Duck and Wild Goose (in or over water areas), Feb. 21—Aug. 31.

Birds which may be killed or taken outside the close season (except in Scotland on Sundays, on Christmas Day or in a prescribed area) are the above and coot, curlew (other than stone curlew), bar-tailed godwit, moorhen, plover (golden or grey), common red-shank, certain wild duck (common pochard, gadwall, mallard, pintail, shoveller, teal, tufted duck, wigeon) and certain wild geese (bean, Canada, pink-footed and white-fronted).

Certain wild birds may be killed or taken at any time by authorized persons—cormorant, crow, gull (black-backed or herring), jackdaw, jay, magpie, rook, shag, sparrow, starling, stock-dove and wood pigeon; and, in Scotland only, goosander, red-breasted merganser and rock-dove. The sale of Wild Birds' Eggs is prohibited, except that gulls' eggs may be sold at any time and those of the lapwing (green or black plover) from Jan. 1—

April 14 inclusive.

Game Birds—In each case the dates are inclusive:—

Black Game—Dec. 11 to Aug. 19 (Aug. 31 in Somerset, Devon, and New Forest).
*Grouse—Dec. 11 to Aug. 11.
*Partridge—Feb. 2 to Aug. 31.
*Pheasant—Feb. 2 to Sept. 30.
*Ptarmigan—(Scotland only) Dec. 11 to Aug. 11.

It is also unlawful (in *England* and *Wales*) to kill the game marked * on a Sunday or Christmas Day.

Hunting and Ground Game.—There is no statutory close-time for fox-hunting or rabbit-shooting, nor for hares: but by an Act passed in 1892 the *sale* of hares or leverets in Great Britain is prohibited from March 1 to July 31 inclusive under a penalty of a pound. The First of November is the recognized date for the opening of the *fox-hunting* season, which continues till the following April. *Otter-hunting* lasts from mid-April to mid-September.

Deer.—The Deer Act, 1963, effective from Nov. 1, 1963, imposed the following close times. *Red Deer and Sika Deer:* Stags, May 1–July 31; Hinds, March 1–Oct. 31. *Fallow Deer and Roe Deer:* Buck, May 1–July 31; Doe, March 1–Oct. 31. Under the Act it is an offence to take or wilfully kill deer of any species from one hour after sunset to one hour before sunrise.

WEIGHTS AND MEASURES

The Weights and Measures Act of 1963 enacts the legal measures for Great Britain, basing them upon "United Kingdom primary standards" in the custody of the Standards Department of the Dept. of Trade. The primary standards are the yard, pound, metre and kilogramme. The GALLON, the capacity standard, wet or dry, is based upon the Pound. The Act of 1963 defines the GALLON as the space occupied by 10 pounds weight of distilled water of density 0·998 859 gramme per millilitre weighed in air of density 0·001 217 gramme per millilitre against weights of density 8·136 grammes per millilitre. The METRE and the LITRE have the meanings assigned by order of the Dept. of Trade to reproduce in English the international definition of these measures in force at the time of making of the orders.

New definitions for an *international yard* and *pound* were adopted on Jan. 1, 1959, by the standards laboratories of the United Kingdom, Canada, Australia, New Zealand, South Africa and the United States:
international yard = 0·914 4 metre.   international pound = 0·453 592 37 kilogramme.

The following list shows the definitions of measures set out in the Weights and Measures Act, 1963 and some useful conversions. *See also* Conversion Tables, p. 1218.

Measurement of Length

Imperial Units

Mile=1,760 yards.	1 mil=1/1000 inch.
Furlong=220 yards.	12 inches (*in.*)=1 foot (*ft.*).
Chain=22 yards.	3 feet=1 yard (*yd.*).
YARD=0·914 4 metre.	6 feet=1 fathom.
Foot1=⅓ yard.	22 yards=1 chain=100 links.
Inch"=1/36 yard.	10 chains=1 furlong.
	8 furlongs=1 mile=1,760 yards.

Metric Units

Kilometre=1,000 metres.	10 millimetres (*mm.*)=1 centimetre (*cm.*)=0·393 701 inch.
METRE (*see above*)=1·094 yards.	10 centimetres=1 decimetre (*dm.*)=3·937 011 inches.
Decimetre=1/10 metre.	10 decimetres=1 METRE (*m.*)=1·093 614 yards.
Centimetre=1/000 metre.	10 metres=1 dekametre (*dam.*)=10·936 143 yards.
Millimetre=1/1000 metre.	10 dekametres=1 hectometre (*hm.*)=109·361 43 yards.
	10 hectometres=1 kilometre (*km.*)=0·621 371 mile.

A kilometre is approximately *five-eighths* of a mile, so that 8 kilometres may be regarded as 5 miles.

Measurement of Area

Imperial Units

Square mile=640 acres.	144 sq. inches=1 sq. foot.
Acre=4,840 square yards.	9 sq. feet=1 sq. yard.
Rood=1,210 square yards.	4 roods=1 acre.
SQUARE YARD=a superficial area equal to that of a square	10 square chains=1 acre=4,840 sq. yards.
each side of which measures one yard.	640 acres=1 square mile.
Square foot=1/9 square yard.	
Square inch=1/144 square foot.	

Metric Units

Hectare=100 acres.	1 sq. centimetre=0·155 sq. inch.
Dekare=10 ares.	1 sq. METRE=10·763 9 sq. feet=1·195 99 sq. yds.
Are=100 square metres.	1 are (*a.*)=0·098 8 rood.
SQUARE METRE=a superficial area equal to that of	1 hectare (10,000 sq. metres) (*ha.*)=2·471 05 acres.
a square each side of which measures one metre.	1 sq. kilometre=0·386 102 sq. mile.
Square decimetre=1/100 square metre.	
Square centimetre=1/100 square decimetre.	
Square millimetre=1/100 square centimetre.	

Measurement of Volume

Imperial Units

CUBIC YARD=a volume equal to that of a cube each edge of which	1,728 cubic inches=1 cubic foot.
measures one yard.	27 cubic feet=1 cubic yard.
Cubic foot=1/27 cubic yard.	
Cubic inch=1/1728 cubic foot.	

Metric Units

CUBIC METRE=a volume equal to that of a cube	1 cubic metre (*cbm.* or *m³.*)=35·314 7 cu. ft.=1·307
each edge of which measures one metre.	95 cu. yds.
Cubic decimetre=1/1000 cubic metre.	(1 stere (=1 cu. metre) is used as a unit of measurement of timber.)
Cubic centimetre=1/1000 cubic decimetre.	1 cubic cm. (water)=1 gram; 1,000 cubic cm. (water) or 1 litre=1 kilogram; 1 cubic metre (1,000 litres, 1,000 kilograms)=1 metric ton.

Measurement of Capacity

Imperial Units

GALLON (*see above*).	4 gills=1 pint.
Quart=¼ gallon.	2 pints=1 quart.
Pint=½ quart.	4 quarts=1 GALLON.
Gill=¼ pint.	1 gallon=160 fluid ounces.
Fluid ounce=1/20 pint.	=277·274 cubic inches.

Bushel=8 gallons.	2 gallons=1 peck.	1 hectolitre=2·749 69 bushels.
Peck=2 gallons.	4 pecks=1 bushel.	1 hectolitre per hectare=1·11 bushels per acre.
	8 bushels=1 quarter.	1 quintal=3·674 3 bushels.
	A chaldron is 36 bushels=4½ quarters.	1 quintal per hectare=1·49 bushels per acre.

Measurement of Capacity—*continued*

Fluid drachm=⅛ fluid ounce. | *See* Apothecaries' Weight (*below*).
Minim= 1/60 fluid drachm.

Metric Units

Hectolitre= 100 litres.
LITRE= The volume occupied by the mass of 1 kilogramme of pure water at its temperature of maximum density and under a pressure of one standard atmosphere (14·696 lb. per sq. inch).
Decilitre= 1/10 litre.
Centilitre= 1/100 litre.
Millilitre= 1/1000 litre.

1 centilitre (*cl.*)=0·070 4 gill.
1 LITRE* (1/1,000 cubic metre) (*lit.*)= 1·759 8 pints
= 0·88 Imp. quart= 0·22 Imp. gallon= 61·025 5 cu. inch= 0·035 315 7 cu. ft.
1 hectolitre (*hl.*)= 21·997 5 Imp. gallons= 26·417 1 U.S. gallons= 2·749 Imp. bushels= 2·837 7 U.S. bushels.

Measurement of Mass or Weight

Imperial Units

Ton= 2,240 pounds.
Hundredweight= 112 pounds.
Cental= 100 pounds.
Quarter= 28 pounds.
Stone= 14 pounds.
POUND= 0·453 592 37 kilogram.
Ounce= 1/16 pound.
Dram= 1/16 ounce.
Grain= 1/7,000 pound.

7,000 grains (*gr.*)= 1 pound (*lb.*).
16 drams (*dr.*)= 1 ounce (*oz.*).
16 ounces= 1 POUND (*lb.*).
14 pounds= 1 stone.
28 pounds= 1 quarter (of a *cwt.*).
4 quarters (112 *lb.*)= 1 hundredweight (*cwt.*).
20 hundredweight (2,240 *lb.*)= 1 ton.

20 pennyweights (*dwt.*)= 1 Troy ounce.

Ounce Troy= 480 grains
Pennyweight= 24 grains

For gold and silver the ounce, divided decimally, and *not* into grains, is the sole unit of weight. The Troy ounce is the same as the Apothecaries' ounce= 480 Avoirdupois grains (31·1035 *Grammes*) in weight. A Troy POUND (= 5,760 grains) is legalized in the United States.

Ounce apothecaries'= 480 grains. | *See* Apothecaries' Weight (*below*)
Drachm=⅛ ounce apothecaries.
Scruple=⅓ drachm.

Metric Units

Metric ton= 1,000 kilograms.
Quintal= 100 kilograms.

1 centigram (*cg.*)=0·154 32 grains.
1 decigram (*dg.*)= 1·543 2 grains.
1 gramme (*grm.*)= 15·432 4 grains.
1 dekagram (*dag.*)= 5·643 8 drams.
1 hectogram (*hg.*)= 3·527 4 oz.
1 KILOGRAM (*kg.*)= 32·150 7 oz.   Troy= 35·273 4 oz.   Avoirdupois = 2·204 62 lb. Avoirdupois.
1 myriagram= 22·046 2 lb. Avoirdupois.
1 quintal (*q.*)= 100 kg.= 220·5 lb.   Avoirdupois= 1·968 4 cwt.
1 tonne (*t.*)= 0·984 207 U.K. or long ton= 1·102 31 U.S. or short ton.

Measurement of Electricity

Units of measurement of electricity, the AMPERE (unit of electrical current), the OHM (unit of electrical resistance), the VOLT (unit of difference of electrical potential) and the WATT (unit of electrical power) have the meanings assigned to them respectively by order of the Dept. of Trade, to reproduce in English the international definitions in force at the date of the making of the order.

Kilowatt= 1,000 watts.   Megawatt= 1,000,000 watts.

Apothecaries' Weight

Measures of Weight.

20 grains = 1 scruple (℈1).
3 scruples = 1 drachm (Ʒ1).
8 drachms= 1 ounce.

Measures of Capacity.

60 minims (*min.*) = 1 fluid drachm.
8 fluid drachms = 1 fluid ounce.
5 fluid ounces = 1 gill.
4 gills = 1 pint.
8 pints = 1 GALLON.

The Apothecaries' grain is the Avoirdupois grain, and the Apothecaries' ounce is the Troy ounce, of 480 grains. The Apothecaries' *drachm* is not the same as the Avoirdupois *dram*, and is spelled differently. A fluid ounce of distilled water at a temperature of 62° Fahrenheit is equal in weight to the Avoirdupois ounce (437·5 grains). A fluid *drachm* (54·6875 grains) is equal in weight to TWO Avoirdupois *drams*.

Angular or Circular Measure

60 seconds (″)= 1 minute (′).
60 minutes= 1 degree (°).

90 degrees= 1 right angle or quadrant.
Diameter of circle × 3·141 6= circumference.
Diameter squared × ·7854= area of circle.
Diameter squared × 3·141 6= surface of sphere.
Diameter cubed × ·523= solidity of sphere.
One degree of circumference × 57·3= radius.*
Diameter of cylinder × 3·141 6; product by length or height, gives the surface.
Diameter squared × ·7854; product by length or height, gives solid content.

* Or, one radian (the angle subtended at the centre of a circle by an arc of the circumference equal in length to the radius)= 57·3 degrees, nearly.

Note.—A circle of 7 yards diameter has, in practice, a circumference of 22 yards= 1 chain.

Water Measures

Cubic inch.............. = 252·458 grains.
Gallon (277·274 cu. in.).... = 10 lb. (distilled).
Cubic foot.............. = 62·321 lb.
35·943 cubic ft. (224 gals.).. = 1 ton.
Water for Ships: Tun, 210 gals., Butt 110, Puncheon 72, Barrel 36, Kilderkin 18 gals.

THERMOMETER COMPARISONS

Comparison between Scales of Fahrenheit, Réaumur and Centigrade.

CENT.	FAH'T.	RMR.	CENT.	FAH'T.	RMR.
°	°	°	°	°	°
100B.	212B.	80B.	25	77	20
99	210·2	79·2	24	75·2	19·2
98	208·4	78·4	23	73·4	18·4
97	206·6	77·6	22	71·6	17·6
96	204·8	76·8	21	69·8	16·8
95	203	76	20	68	16
94	201·2	75·2	19	66·2	15·2
93	199·4	74·4	18	64·4	14·4
92	197·6	73·6	17	62·6	13·6
91	195·8	72·8	16	60·8	12·8
90	194	72	15	59	12
89	192·2	71·2	14	57·2	11·2
88	190·4	70·4	13	55·4	10·4
87	188·6	69·6	12	53·6	9·6
86	186·8	68·8	11	51·8	8·8
85	185	68	10	50	8
84	183·2	67·2	9	48·2	7·2
83	181·4	66·4	8	46·4	6·4
82	179·6	65·6	7	44·6	5·6
81	177·8	64·8	6	42·8	4·8
80	176	64	5	41	4
79	174·2	63	4	39·2	3·2
78	172·4	62·4	3	37·4	2·4
77	170·6	61·6	2	35·6	1·6
76	168·8	60·8	1	33·8	0·8
75	167	60	*zero*	32	*zero*
74	165·2	59·2	1	30·2	0·8
73	163·4	58·4	2	28·4	1·6
72	161·6	57·6	3	26·6	2·4
71	159·8	56·8	4	24·8	3·2
70	158	56	5	23	4
69	156·2	55·2	6	21·2	4·8
68	154·4	54·4	7	19·4	5·6
67	152·6	53·6	8	17·6	6·4
66	150·8	52·8	9	15·8	7·2
65	149	52	10	14	8
64	147·2	51·2	11	12·2	8·8
63	145·4	50·4	12	10·4	9·6
62	143·6	49·6	13	8·6	10·4
61	141·8	48·8	14	6·8	11·2
60	140	48	15	5	12
59	138·2	47·2	16	3·2	12·8
58	136·4	46·4	17	1·4	13·6
57	134·6	45·6	18	*0·4*	14·4
56	132·8	44·8	19	2·2	15·2
55	131	44	20	4	16
54	129·2	43·2	21	5·8	16·8
53	127·4	42·4	22	7·6	17·6
52	125·6	41·6	23	9·3	18·4
51	123·8	40·8	24	11·2	19·2
50	122	40	25	13	20
49	120·2	39·2	26	14·8	20·8
48	118·4	38·4	27	16·6	21·6
47	116·6	37·6	28	18·4	22·4
46	114·8	36·8	29	20·2	23·2
45	113	36	30	22	24
44	111·2	35·2	31	23·8	24·8
43	109·4	34·4	32	25·6	25·6
42	107·6	33·6	33	27·4	26·4
41	105·8	32·8	34	29·2	27·2
40	104	32	35	31	28
39	102·2	31·2	36	32·8	28·8
38	100·4	30·4	37	34·6	29·6
37	98·6	29·6	38	36·4	30·4
36	96·8	28·8	39	38·2	31·2
35	95	28	40	40	32
34	93·2	27·2	41	41·8	32·8
33	91·4	26·4	42	43·6	33·6
32	89·6	25·6	43	45·4	34·4
31	87·8	24·8	44	47·2	35·2
30	86	24	45	49	36
29	84·2	23·2	46	50·8	36·8
28	82·4	22·4	47	52·6	37·6
27	80·6	21·6	48	54·4	38·4
26	78·8	20·8	49	56·2	39·2

CONVERSION — Let F = Fahr., ,, C = Cent., ,, R = Réaum.

$\star F = \frac{9C}{5} + 32$ $\quad F = C + R + 32$

$F = \frac{9R}{4} + 32$

$C = 5\frac{(F-32)}{9}$ $\quad R = \frac{4(F-32)}{9}$

NOTE.—The *normal* temperature of the *human body* is 98·4° F., or 37° (36·9°) C., or 29·5° R. *Freezing* point = 32° F. = 0° C. = 0° R.; *Boiling* point = 212° F. = 100° C. = 80° R. "*Absolute*" *Temperature* is Temperature reckoned from "*Absolute Zero*," which is at 273° C. below 0° C., 459·4° below 0° F., and 218·4° below 0° R. and is denoted by the letter "K."

★ Below 32° F. *subtract* 32.

An *Inch of Rain* on the surface of an acre (43,560 sq. feet) = 3,630 cubic feet = 100.992 tons.

Cisterns: A cistern 4 feet by 2½ and 3 deep will hold brimful 186·963 gallons, weighing 16 cwt. 2 qrs. 21·6 lbs. in addition to its own weight.

Million, Billion, etc.

Value in the United Kingdom

Million.............thousand × thousand (10^6)
Billion.............million × million (10^{12})
Trillion.............million × billion (10^{18})
Quadrillion...........million × trillion (10^{24})

Value in U.S.A.

Million.............thousand × thousand (10^6)
Billion.............thousand × million (10^9)
Trillion.............million × million (10^{12})
Quadrillion...........million × billion U.S. (10^{15})

United Kingdom (and other European) usage above follows the decision of the 9th Gen. Conference on Weights and Measures, 1948.

PAPER AND BOOK MEASURES

Writing Paper	*Printing Paper*
480 sheets = 1 ream	516 sheets = 1 ream
24 sheets = 1 quire	2 reams = 1 bundle
20 quires = 1 ream	5 bundles = 1 bale

Sizes of Writing and Drawing Papers

Emperor..................	=	72 × 48	inches
Antiquarian..............	=	53 × 31	,,
Double Elephant..........	=	40 × 26¾	,,
Grand Eagle..............	=	42 × 28¾	,,
Atlas....................	=	34 × 26	,,
Colombier................	=	34½ × 23½	,,
Imperial.................	=	30 × 22	,,
Elephant.................	=	28 × 23	,,
Cartridge................	=	26 × 21	,,
Super Royal..............	=	27 × 19	,,
Royal....................	=	24 × 19	,,
Medium...................	=	22 × 17½	,,
Large Post...............	=	21 × 16½	,,
Copy or Draft............	=	20 × 16	,,
Demy.....................	=	20 × 15½	,,
Post.....................	=	19 × 15¼	,,
Pinched Post.............	=	18½ × 14¾	,,
Foolscap.................	=	17 × 13½	,,
Sheet and ⅓ Foolscap......	=	22 × 13½	,,
Sheet and ½ Foolscap......	=	24½ × 13½	,,
Double Foolscap..........	=	26½ × 16½	,,
Double Post..............	=	30½ × 19	,,
Double Large Post........	=	33 × 21	,,
Double Demy..............	=	31 × 20	,,
Brief....................	=	16½ × 13¼	,,
Pott.....................	=	15 × 12½	,,

Sizes of Printing Papers

Foolscap.................	=	17 × 13½	inches
Double Foolscap..........	=	27 × 17	,,
Crown....................	=	20 × 15	,,
Double Crown.............	=	30 × 20	,,
Quad Crown...............	=	40 × 30	,,
Double Quad Crown........	=	60 × 40	,,
Post.....................	=	19¼ × 15½	,,
Double Post..............	=	31½ × 19½	,,
Double Large Post........	=	33 × 21	,,
Sheet and ½ Post.........	=	23½ × 19½	,,
Demy.....................	=	22½ × 17½	,,
Double Demy..............	=	35 × 22½	,,
Quad Demy................	=	45 × 35	,,
Music Demy...............	=	20 × 15½	,,
Medium...................	=	23 × 18	,,
Royal....................	=	25 × 20	,,
Super Royal..............	=	27½ × 20½	,,
Elephant.................	=	28 × 23	,,
Imperial.................	=	30 × 22	,,

Sizes of Brown Papers

Casing..................	=	46×36	inches
Double Imperial..........	=	45×29	,,
Elephant................	=	34×24	,,
Double Four Pound.......	=	31×21	,,
Imperial Cap............	=	29×22	,,
Haven Cap...............	=	26×21	,,
Bag Cap.................	=	$24 \times 19\frac{1}{2}$	,,
Kent Cap................	=	21×18	,,

Sizes of Bound Books

Demy 16mo.............	=	$5\frac{5}{8} \times 4\frac{3}{8}$	inches
Demy 18mo.............	=	$5\frac{3}{4} \times 3\frac{3}{4}$	,,
Foolscap Octavo (8vo).....	=	$6\frac{3}{4} \times 4\frac{1}{4}$	,,
Crown 8vo..............	=	$7\frac{1}{2} \times 5$	,,
Large Crown 8vo.........	=	$8 \times 5\frac{1}{4}$	,,
Demy 8vo...............	=	$8\frac{3}{8} \times 5\frac{5}{8}$	,,
Medium 8vo.............	=	$9\frac{1}{2} \times 6$	,,
Royal 8vo..............	=	$10 \times 6\frac{1}{4}$	,,
Super Royal 8vo.........	=	$10\frac{1}{4} \times 6\frac{7}{8}$	,,
Imperial 8vo............	=	$11 \times 7\frac{1}{2}$	,,
Foolscap Quarto (4to).....	=	$8\frac{1}{2} \times 6\frac{3}{4}$	,,
Crown 4to..............	=	$10 \times 7\frac{1}{2}$	,,
Demy 4to...............	=	$11\frac{1}{4} \times 8\frac{3}{4}$	,,
Royal 4to..............	=	$12\frac{1}{2} \times 10$	,,
Imperial 4to............	=	15×11	,,
Crown Folio.............	=	15×10	,,
Demy Folio..............	=	$17\frac{1}{2} \times 11\frac{1}{4}$	,,
Royal Folio.............	=	$20 \times 12\frac{1}{2}$	,,
Music..................	=	$14 \times 10\frac{1}{4}$	,,

NOTE.—*Folio* means a sheet folded in half, *quarto* folded into four, and so on; thus, a crown 8vo page is one-eighth the size of a crown sheet. Books are usually bound up in sheets of 16 or 32 pages. *Octavo* books are generally printed 64 pages at a time (32 pages on each side of a sheet of quad); a crown octavo book of 320 pages will therefore require 5 sheets of quad crown, or 10 reams per 1,000 copies, the odd 16 sheets in each ream being allowed as waste. Newspapers (and some books in editions of 50,000 or over) are printed on rotary presses, for which the paper is supplied in continuous reels.

INTERNATIONAL PAPER SIZES

Simplification of the large number of stock paper sizes in use in the United Kingdom has been proceeding since publication of British Standard 730 in 1937. Recommendations made by the International Organization for Standardization were accepted by the United Kingdom in 1959 and it is considered that general adoption of the international or A size will bring great economies to users of paper.

The basis of the international series of paper sizes is a rectangle having an area of one square metre, the sides of which are in the proportion of $1 : \sqrt{2}$. In other words, taking one side as X and the other as Y, the basic size provides the equation—$X : Y = 1 : \sqrt{2}$; and $X \times Y = 1$. It may be noted that the proportions $1 : \sqrt{2}$ have a geometrical relationship, the side and diagonal of any square being in this proportion. As the basic size is one square metre in area, this means that $X = 841$ millimetres and $Y = 1{,}189$ millimetres. The effect of this arrangement is that if the short side is doubled or the longer side is halved, *i.e.*, if the area of the sheet is doubled or halved, the shorter side and the longer side of the new sheet are still in the same proportion $1 : \sqrt{2}$. This feature is particularly useful where photographic enlargement or reduction is used, as the proportions remain the same.

Description of the A series is by capital A followed by a figure. The basic size has the description A0 and the higher the figure following the letter, the greater is the number of sub-divisions and therefore the smaller the sheet. Half A0 is A1 and half A1 is A2. Where larger dimensions are required the A is *preceded* by a figure. Thus 2A means twice the size A0; 4A is four times the size of A0.

It is an essential feature of these series that the dimensions are of the trimmed or finished size.

'A' SERIES OF TRIMMED SIZES

Designation	SIZE	
	mm	inches
A 0	841 × 1189	33·11 × 46·81
A 1	594 × 841	23·39 × 33·11
A 2	420 × 594	16·54 × 23·39
A 3	297 × 420	11·69 × 16·54
A 4	210 × 297	8·27 × 11·69
A 5	148 × 210	5·83 × 8·27
A 6	105 × 148	4·13 × 5·83
A 7	74 × 105	2·91 × 4·13
A 8	52 × 74	2·05 × 2·91
A 9	37 × 52	1·46 × 2·05
A 10	26 × 37	1·02 × 1·46

Subsidiary Series.—A series of B sizes has been devised for use in exceptional circumstances when sizes intermediate between any two adjacent sizes of the A series are needed.

'B' SERIES OF TRIMMED SIZES

Designation	SIZE	
	mm	inches
B 0	1000 × 1414	39·37 × 55·67
B 1	707 × 1000	27·83 × 39·37
B 2	500 × 707	19·68 × 27·83
B 3	353 × 500	13·90 × 19·68
B 4	250 × 353	9·84 × 13·90
B 5	176 × 250	6·93 × 9·84
B 6	125 × 176	4·92 × 6·93
B 7	88 × 125	3·46 × 4·92
B 8	62 × 88	2·44 × 3·46
B 9	44 × 62	1·73 × 2·44
B 10	31 × 44	1·22 × 1·73

In addition there is a series of C sizes which is used much less. A is for magazines and books, B for posters, wall charts and other large items, C for envelopes particularly where it is necessary for an envelope (in C series) to fit into another envelope. The size recommended for business correspondence is A4.

Long Sizes.—Long sizes are obtainable by dividing any appropriate sizes from the two series above into three, four or eight equal parts parallel with the shorter side in such a manner that the proportions mentioned in paragraph 2 (above) are not maintained, the ratio between the longer and the shorter sides being greater than $\sqrt{2} : 1$. In practice long sizes should be produced from the A series only.

CONVERSION TABLES FOR WEIGHTS AND MEASURES

NOTE.—The central figures in heavy type represent either of the two columns beside them, as the case may be. *Examples:*—1 centimetre = 0·394 inch and 1 inch = 2·540 centimetres. 1 metre = 1·094 yards and 1 yard = 0·914 metre. 1 kilometre = 0·621 mile and 1 mile = 1·609 kilometres.

Length			Area			Volume			Weight (Mass.)					
Centimetres		Inches	Square Centimetres		Square Inches	Cubic Centimetres		Cubic Inches	Long Tons		Short Tons	Metric Tonnes		Short Tons
2·540	1	0·394	6·452	1	0·155	16·387	1	0·061	0·893	1	1·120	0·907	1	1·102
5·080	2	0·787	12·903	2	0·310	32·774	2	0·122	1·786	2	2·240	1·814	2	2·205
7·620	3	1·181	19·355	3	0·465	49·161	3	0·183	2·679	3	3·360	2·722	3	3·305
10·160	4	1·575	25·806	4	0·620	65·548	4	0·244	3·571	4	4·480	3·629	4	4·409
12·700	5	1·969	32·258	5	0·775	81·936	5	0·305	4·464	5	5·600	4·536	5	5·512
15·240	6	2·362	38·710	6	0·930	98·323	6	0·366	5·357	6	6·720	5·443	6	6·614
17·780	7	2·756	45·161	7	1·085	114·710	7	0·427	6·250	7	7·840	6·350	7	7·716
20·320	8	3·150	51·613	8	1·240	131·097	8	0·488	7·143	8	8·960	7·257	8	8·818
22·860	9	3·543	58·064	9	1·395	147·484	9	0·549	8·036	9	10·080	8·165	9	9·921
25·400	10	3·937	64·516	10	1·550	163·871	10	0·610	8·929	10	11·200	9·072	10	11·023
50·800	20	7·874	129·032	20	3·100	327·742	20	1·220	17·857	20	22·400	18·144	20	22·046
76·200	30	11·811	193·548	30	4·650	491·613	30	1·831	26·786	30	33·600	27·216	30	33·069
101·600	40	15·748	258·064	40	6·200	655·484	40	2·441	35·714	40	44·800	36·287	40	44·092
127·000	50	19·685	322·580	50	7·750	819·355	50	3·051	44·643	50	56·000	45·359	50	55·116
152·400	60	23·622	387·096	60	9·300	983·226	60	3·661	53·571	60	67·200	54·431	60	66·139
177·800	70	27·559	451·612	70	10·850	1147·097	70	4·272	62·500	70	78·400	63·503	70	77·162
203·200	80	31·496	516·128	80	12·400	1310·968	80	4·882	71·429	80	89·600	72·575	80	88·185
228·600	90	35·433	580·644	90	13·950	1474·839	90	5·492	80·357	90	100·800	81·647	90	99·208
254·000	100	39·370	645·160	100	15·500	1638·710	100	6·102	89·286	100	112·000	90·719	100	110·231

Metres		Yards	Square Metres		Square Yards	Cubic Metres		Cubic Yards	Metric Tonnes		Long Tons	Kilograms		Av. Pounds
0·914	1	1·094	0·836	1	1·196	0·765	1	1·308	1·016	1	0·984	0·454	1	2·205
1·829	2	2·187	1·672	2	2·392	1·529	2	2·616	2·032	2	1·968	0·907	2	4·409
2·743	3	3·281	2·508	3	3·588	2·294	3	3·924	3·048	3	2·953	1·361	3	6·614
3·658	4	4·374	3·345	4	4·784	3·058	4	5·232	4·064	4	3·937	1·814	4	8·819
4·572	5	5·468	4·181	5	5·980	3·823	5	6·540	5·080	5	4·921	2·268	5	11·023
5·486	6	6·562	5·017	6	7·176	4·587	6	7·848	6·096	6	5·905	2·722	6	13·228
6·401	7	7·655	5·853	7	8·372	5·352	7	9·156	7·112	7	6·889	3·175	7	15·432
7·315	8	8·749	6·689	8	9·568	6·116	8	10·464	8·128	8	7·874	3·629	8	17·637
8·230	9	9·843	7·525	9	10·764	6·881	9	11·772	9·144	9	8·858	4·082	9	19·842
9·144	10	10·936	8·361	10	11·960	7·646	10	13·080	10·161	10	9·842	4·536	10	22·046
18·288	20	21·872	16·723	20	23·920	15·291	20	26·159	20·321	20	19·684	9·072	20	44·092
27·432	30	32·808	25·084	30	35·880	22·937	30	39·239	30·481	30	29·526	13·608	30	66·139
36·576	40	43·745	33·445	40	47·840	30·582	40	52·318	40·642	40	39·368	18·144	40	88·185
45·720	50	54·681	41·806	50	59·799	38·228	50	65·398	50·802	50	49·210	22·680	50	110·231
54·864	60	65·617	50·168	60	71·759	45·873	60	78·477	60·963	60	59·052	27·216	60	132·277
64·008	70	76·553	58·529	70	83·719	53·519	70	91·557	71·123	70	68·894	31·752	70	154·324
73·152	80	87·489	66·890	80	95·679	61·164	80	104·636	81·284	80	78·737	36·287	80	176·370
82·296	90	98·425	75·251	90	107·639	68·810	90	117·716	91·444	90	88·579	40·823	90	198·416
91·440	100	109·361	83·613	100	119·599	76·455	100	130·795	101·605	100	98·421	45·359	100	220·464

Kilometres		Miles	Square Kilometres		Square Miles	Litres		Gallons	Bushels U.S.		Bushels U.K.	Hectares		Acres
1·609	1	0·621	2·590	1	0·386	4·546	1	0·220	1·032	1	0·969	0·405	1	2·471
3·219	2	1·243	5·180	2	0·772	9·092	2	0·440	2·064	2	1·938	0·809	2	4·942
4·828	3	1·864	7·770	3	1·158	13·638	3	0·660	3·096	3	2·907	1·214	3	7·413
6·437	4	2·485	10·360	4	1·544	18·184	4	0·880	4·128	4	3·876	1·619	4	9·884
8·047	5	3·107	12·950	5	1·931	22·730	5	1·100	5·160	5	4·845	2·023	5	12·355
9·656	6	3·728	15·540	6	2·317	27·276	6	1·320	6·192	6	5·814	2·428	6	14·826
11·265	7	4·350	18·130	7	2·703	31·822	7	1·540	7·224	7	6·783	2·833	7	17·297
12·875	8	4·971	20·720	8	3·089	36·368	8	1·760	8·256	8	7·752	3·237	8	19·769
14·484	9	5·592	23·310	9	3·475	40·914	9	1·980	9·288	9	8·721	3·642	9	22·240
16·093	10	6·214	25·900	10	3·861	45·460	10	2·200	10·321	10	9·689	4·047	10	24·711
32·187	20	12·427	51·800	20	7·722	90·919	20	4·400	20·641	20	19·379	8·094	20	49·421
48·280	30	18·641	77·700	30	11·583	136·379	30	6·599	30·962	30	29·068	12·140	30	74·132
64·374	40	24·855	103·600	40	15·444	181·839	40	8·799	41·282	40	38·758	16·187	40	98·842
80·467	50	31·069	129·499	50	19·305	227·298	50	10·999	51·603	50	48·447	20·234	50	123·555
96·561	60	37·282	153·399	60	23·166	272·758	60	13·199	61·923	60	58·137	24·281	60	148·263
112·654	70	43·496	181·299	70	27·027	318·217	70	15·398	72·244	70	67·826	28·328	70	172·974
128·748	80	49·710	207·199	80	30·888	363·677	80	17·598	82·564	80	77·516	32·375	80	197·684
144·841	90	55·923	233·099	90	34·749	409·137	90	19·798	92·885	90	87·205	36·422	90	222·395
160·934	100	62·137	258·999	100	38·610	454·596	100	21·998	103·205	100	96·695	40·469	100	247·105

SYMBOLS FOR CORRECTING PROOFS

Supplied by WILLIAM CLOWES & SONS LTD, Beccles, Suffolk, Printers of "WHITAKER"

Letter(s) or word(s) requiring alteration should be struck through IN INK in the text and the substitution should be written in the nearest margin followed by ⁄ (the symbol used to denote that the marginal mark is concluded). Insertions should be indicated by ⋏ or ∧ at the conclusion of the marginal mark *and* at the desired place in the text.

Alteration required	Mark in margin	Mark in text	Alteration required	Mark in margin	Mark in text
Delete (take out)	ℐ or ℐ℩	⁄ or —— Vertical stroke to delete one or two letters; horizontal line to delete more	Take letter(s) or word(s) from beginning of one line to end of preceding line	*back* or *take back*	⌐ ⌐
Delete and close up	ℨ or ℨ℩	Strike out letter(s) not required and add "close up" mark above and below	Begin a new paragraph	n.p.	[before first word of new paragraph
Close up: delete space between letters	⌣	linking letters or words	No new para. here or run on with later matter on previous matter	*run on*	between paras. or other matter
Use ligature (fi, fl, ffl, etc.) or diphthong (æ, œ)	⌣ *enclosing ligature or diphthong required*	⌣ enclosing letters to be altered	Spell out in full the abbreviation, contraction, or figure	*spell out*	Encircle words, etc., or figures concerned
Insert space between letters or words	#⋏	⋏	Insert omitted portion of copy	*out—see copy*	⋏ Attach the relevant copy to the proof, indicating omitted portion
Leave as printed (i.e. a cancellation of previous marking)	*stet*	.... under letter(s) or word(s) crossed out but to be retained	Inserted or substituted letter(s), figure(s), or sign(s) under which this is placed to be superscript (i.e. high alignment) [1]	⁊ *(see footnote)*	⋏ for insertions For substitutions encircle letter(s), figure(s), or sign(s) to be altered
Invert type (of letter(s) upside down)	↻	Encircle letter(s) to be altered	Inserted or substituted letter(s), figure(s), or sign(s) over which this is placed to be subscript (low alignment) [2]	⁊ *(see footnote)*	⋏ for insertions For substitutions encircle letter(s), figure(s), etc., to be altered
"Battered" letter(s) to be replaced by similar but undamaged characters	✕	Encircle letter(s) or word(s) to be replaced and write the correct letter(s) in the margin	Change to lower case	*l.c.*	Encircle letter(s) to be altered
Push down space or "high" letter(s) or word(s)	⊥	Encircle space, letter(s), or word(s) affected	Replace "wrong fount" by letter(s) of correct fount	*w.f.*	Encircle letter(s) or word(s) to be altered
Transpose	*tr.* or *trs.*	⌐⌐ between letters or words, numbered when necessary	Change to capital letters	*caps.*	≡ under letter(s) or word(s) to be altered
Take letter(s) or word(s) from end of one line to beginning of next line	*take over* or *over*	⌐	Change to small capitals	*s.c.*	≡ under letter(s) or word(s) to be altered

⁊ indicates a superior (superscript) figure one   ⁊ indicates an inferior (subscript) figure two

Alteration required	Mark in margin	Mark in text	Alteration required	Mark in margin	Mark in text
Use capital letters for initial letter(s) (as desired) and small capitals for rest of word(s)	*caps* & *s.c.*	under initial letter(s) and under the remainder of the word(s)	Move lines to the left		at right side of group of lines to be moved (indicating approx. position)
Change to bold type	*bold*	Draw wavy line under letter(s) or word(s) to be altered	Move portion of matter so that it is positioned as indicated		at limits of required position
Change to roman type	*rom.*	Encircle letter(s) or word(s) to be altered	Raise lines	*raise*	over lines to be raised
Change to italic type	*italic*	Draw this straight line under letter(s) or word(s) to be altered	Lower lines	*lower*	under lines to be lowered
Letter(s) or word(s) to be underlined	*underline*	under letter(s), word(s), etc., to be underlined	Correct the vertical alignment	‖	‖
			Straighten lines		through lines to be straightened
Equalize space between words	*eq. #*	between words	Insert parentheses (round-shaped brackets)	(/) or (/)	
Reduce space	*less #*	between words	Insert [square] brackets	[/] or [/]	
Space to be inserted between lines or paragraphs	#>	*Amount of space should be indicated*	Insert hyphen	/-/	
To be placed in centre of line, etc.	*centre*	Position to be indicated by	Insert en (=half-em) rule (*see above*)	*en*	
Indent one en (approx. space occupied by n of type in use)	*en*	indicating approximate position	Insert one-em rule (*see above*)	*em*	
Indent one em (approx. space occupied by M of type in use)	*em*	Ditto	Insert two-em rule (*see above*)	*2-em*	
Indent two ems (approx. space occupied by MM of type in use)		Ditto	Insert apostrophe		
Move to the left		Ditto	Insert single quotation marks		
Move to the right		Ditto	Insert double quotation marks		
Move lines to the right		at left side of group of lines to be moved (indicating approx. position)	Insert ellipsis	•••	
			Insert leader (*visual guide to alignment in contents pages, etc.*)	••• •• •	(*three, two, or one dot*)
			Insert shilling stroke (oblique)	(/)	

Punctuation

THE WORLD